To the Reader.

This Figure, that thou here seest put,
    It was for gentle Shakespeare cut;
Wherein the Grauer had a strife
    with Nature, to out-doo the life:
O, could he but haue drawne his wit
    As well in brasse, as he hath hit
His face; the Print would then surpasse
    All, that was euer writ in brasse.
But, since he cannot, Reader, looke
    Not on his Picture, but his Booke.

                                B. I.

THE

Complete

WORKS

OF

Shakespeare

EDITED

BY

HARDIN CRAIG

SCOTT, FORESMAN

AND COMPANY

LIBRARY OF CONGRESS CATALOG CARD NUMBER 61–13714

COPYRIGHT © 1961 BY SCOTT, FORESMAN AND COMPANY, GLENVIEW, ILLINOIS 60025

PREVIOUS COPYRIGHT 1951 BY SCOTT, FORESMAN AND COMPANY

PRINTED IN THE UNITED STATES OF AMERICA

ALL RIGHTS RESERVED

REGIONAL OFFICES OF SCOTT, FORESMAN AND COMPANY ARE LOCATED IN

ATLANTA, DALLAS, GLENVIEW, PALO ALTO AND OAKLAND, N.J.

PREFACE

In order fully to understand and appreciate Shakespeare, it is necessary to see him as a whole. It is not enough to read individual passages, scenes, and plays as independent units; they should be studied in their relation to the development of Shakespeare's powers as a dramatist, to the drama itself, and to Renaissance literature. The student who would know Shakespeare needs to know the temper of the Elizabethan age. As the student comes to understand better the meaning that Shakespeare had in his own day he will at the same time, the editor believes, develop a richer appreciation of the qualities of Shakespeare's genius that have given his work meaning in all ages.

The aim of this complete edition of Shakespeare has been, as far as was possible in one volume, to provide the reader or student with the information he normally needs in order to understand and appreciate Shakespeare. The editor has tried to present the most important background materials and at the same time to digest and make available to the student the most authoritative critical and textual work offered by Shakespeare scholars. By and large, the general objective of this complete edition of Shakespeare's works is the same as that of the editor's *Shakespeare: A Historical and Critical Study with Annotated Texts of Twenty-one Plays*, published by Scott, Foresman and Company in 1931. This, however, is a new edition throughout and carries over from the older book only those materials in the introductions and notes that the editor regards as still valid, still representative of the best information and judgment he could bring to bear upon the subject.

The plays and poems are arranged in the order in which most scholars believe they were written.

The text used is that of the widely known Globe, edited by William George Clark and William Aldis Wright (first printed in 1864) on the basis of the so-called Cambridge Shakespeare by these same editors (7 volumes, 1863-1866). The Globe was the first reliable edition of Shakespeare in convenient form and on modern lines. It appeared at a time when it was available for use in the large number of Shakespearean reference works that were published toward the end of the nineteenth century—dictionaries, concordances, studies of meter and words, comparative considerations of text, and so on. The result was that the Globe Shakespeare with the Cambridge line numbering attained a wide currency. Later conservative editions of Shakespeare, such as those of W. J. Craig, W. A. Neilson, and G. L. Kittredge, do not differ greatly from the Globe in their handling of the text—its punctuation, format, line numbering, and the placing of such things as act and scene divisions, names of speakers, stage directions, entrances and exits.

The Globe text is a good one, conservative and sensible, and it has been faithfully followed in this edition. However, more recent scholarship has shown a number of readings in which the Globe is clearly in error. It sometimes, as in the case of *King Lear* and *Richard III*, gives preference to what have since been proved inferior texts. In this edition, the Globe readings have been replaced in cases where the editor thought they were wrong. In order not to destroy the value for purposes of reference of the Globe text, all such changes have been carefully recorded in the notes. The dagger (†) placed by the Globe editors in front of lines which they considered corrupt has been retained, since that symbol still serves the reader as a warning and has come to be a ready and easy way of locating cruxes in the text.

Because almost all references to Shakespeare follow the line numbers in the Globe edition, care has been taken to reproduce these numbers in the present text. Uninterrupted lines of verse will, of course, have the same numbers in any edition, but in prose passages, owing to differences in column width and type used, the actual number of lines in a given passage does not always correspond exactly with that in the Globe or any other edition. This merely means that the reader must make some allowance for these differences when he is counting lines of prose to locate a particular word or sentence.

In the footnotes to the plays and poems, annotated words and passages are designated by the numbers of the lines in which they occur; and for every change of act and scene, a new paragraph is begun in the footnotes. The notes for facing pages are arranged in even blocks below the text.

For instruction in Shakespeare's language there is provided in the General Introduction (pp. 59-64) an account of "Shakespeare's English." There is also a glossary of the most frequently used Shakespearean words and meanings. This avoids tiresome repetition in the notes. Such words and meanings are, however, introduced into the notes and defined there in at least their first two occurrences in the plays and poems.

An attempt to supply a key to the wide range of information in this volume has been made in the index. Although limiting itself strictly to introductions and notes, the index records the names of plays and characters, with comments both general and specific; the names of persons, places, and literary works which are discussed or cited; and, under general headings, references to drama, literature, manners and customs, current beliefs, learned opinions, and the ideals of the age. Bibliographies are listed in the index, but not the books, articles, and authors which are included in these bibliographies.

In order to save space one great group of names has been omitted from the index: the names of commentators and critics who are referred to in the footnotes of the plays. In this edition the greatest care has been exercised to give exact credit to every commentator whose words or ideas have been followed. This has ordinarily been done by putting the surname of the authority in parentheses after the citation. For example, (Malone) after a statement or definition means that the authority for that note is the eighteenth-century scholar Edmund Malone. A list of these editors, textual critics, and commentators appears on the page immediately preceding the index. In addition, the names of some forty-five general editors of Shakespeare are recorded in the section of the General Introduction called "Editions, Editors, and Actors of Shakespeare" (pp. 54-55). These names do not occur in the index unless these editors are specifically mentioned in the introductory materials in connection with some opinion or achievement.

The illustrations reproduced in the book have been chosen for their suggestive portrayal of the life and spirit, the beliefs and practices of the Renaissance. They have been gathered from many sources, and it is hoped that they will introduce an element of variety into the illustration of Shakespeare texts.

The editor was fortunate in having in the early stages of this work the painstaking and scholarly assistance of Dr. Sina Spiker, now of the University of Wisconsin Press. He wishes to express his gratitude to her. He wishes also to thank Miss Josephine Pearce of the English Department of the University of Missouri for her assistance in the latest stages of his editorial work. Professor Carroll Camden of the Rice Institute was kind enough to supply a number of valuable notes, particularly on *Othello*, *King Lear*, and *Macbeth*. Professor Madeleine Doran of the University of Wisconsin read all of the introductions and editorial material in this edition while they were in galley proof. The editor feels that his book was improved by her criticisms and suggestions. Finally, the editor wishes to express on his own behalf and on that of the publishers, gratitude to Miss Dorothy Bowen and other members of the staff of the Henry E. Huntington Library and to Dr. James G. McManaway and Dr. Giles E. Dawson of the Folger Library for assistance in collecting materials to be used for illustration.

HARDIN CRAIG

Columbia, Missouri

TABLE OF CONTENTS

ILLUSTRATIONS

The illustrative materials throughout this book have been carefully selected from a variety of sixteenth- and seventeenth-century sources. Whenever possible, the reader has been given the original source for each picture. A large majority of the illustrative material was made available through the cooperation of the Folger Shakespeare Library in Washington, D.C., and the Henry E. Huntington Library in San Marino, California. In each case, the name of the library in whose collection the picture appears has been indicated in parentheses after the original source.

The endsheet maps have been specially prepared for this book. We are grateful to Marchette Chute for the use of her map of London in developing our own. The design preceding the title page is reproduced from the First Folio, 1623. (Folger)

THE COMPLETE WORKS OF SHAKESPEARE

GENERAL INTRODUCTION

Shakespeare as an English Dramatist

Life in Shakespeare's England

No generation can tell very clearly what features of its life are old and what are relatively new. For example, many of our institutions such as the church, the state, the municipality, the school, the university, and the law court go back to the Middle Ages. Others are as new as the twentieth century. At times of rapid social change, as in the sixteenth and early seventeenth centuries, the old and the new are not blended harmoniously. They jarred each other in Shakespeare's time. He was a representative of the new age of the Renaissance, but the forms and ideals of the Middle Ages, which were close to him in time, stand in his works side by side with those of the Renaissance. His works show such medieval characteristics as a rigid demarcation of social classes, a reverence for authority and precedent, a firm adherence to marriage and family ties, and a reliance on formal studies, such as logic and rhetoric. The motives of crusaders, preaching friars, alchemists, burgesses, and highwaymen were easy for him to grasp.

And yet Shakespeare's point of view was modern; he tended to face forward. In his own great art, that of the drama, he was an innovator. He found it crude and chaotic, and he left it orderly and splendid. When we speak of the development of the Elizabethan drama, we are speaking, whether we realize it or not, about the development of Shakespeare. It is the fascinating story of his progress that we wish to tell in this book.

England had not undergone any very great social or, indeed, physical changes since the Middle Ages. London itself showed the greatest alterations, since it was growing rapidly under the influence of unprecedented prosperity. Throughout the rest of England, the things which the Middle Ages had

created remained for the most part undisturbed. But the older order was passing away, without, however, any uniform progress or any very clear idea as to what was happening. Religious, political, and social revolutions were gathering head, so that after the triumph of Puritanism under Oliver Cromwell, England was never the same in its religion, its social ethics, or its politics. Even in the reign of Queen Elizabeth social classes were shifting rapidly, and many ancient social barriers were breaking down.

The Renaissance affected all departments of life, including art, letters, philosophy, science; but while one group or nation was proceeding along one particular path of change, it might be, and often was, fiercely conservative with reference to other matters, and the great mass of beliefs and principles of which civilized life was made up continued to be medieval. The Renaissance produced great scientists like Galileo, Copernicus, Bacon, and Harvey, but left recognition of their value to succeeding, less gifted ages. More than a century elapsed before Shakespeare's transcendent greatness was recognized.

Englishmen had begun to study in Italy during the fifteenth century, and in the early sixteenth century— in England as in other countries—there appeared in connection with the revival of learning, a group of scholars called humanists. They were the forerunners of the Renaissance in literature and the arts, who fostered the study of Greek and exemplified its importance by editions, translations, and imitations of some of the literary treasures of the ancient world. Poets of the early Tudor period received a new impulse that later expressed itself in the great sonnet cycles of Sidney, Spenser, and Shakespeare. We shall later see how the humanistic movement exercised its influence on Renaissance drama. The great Queen Elizabeth was reared in the tradition of the humanists and became in herself typical of the transitional age in which she reigned. She clung steadfastly to medieval ideas of order and stability, and yet in matters personal and artistic she was completely the child of the new age.

ENGLAND AND ITS NEIGHBORS

The reign of Queen Elizabeth (1558-1603) saw the end of the ancient English ambition for a continental empire or even for a port on the French coast. The continental possessions of the English crown were all gone, and the statement in the royal title that Elizabeth was queen of France as well as of England and Ireland had become a mere reminiscence. Elizabeth gained and held Havre for a little time but had to abandon it; the English were then confined to their island home.

But England was gaining strength. In 1588, in the defeat of the Spanish Armada, the English achieved an easy victory over the greatest power the modern world had seen, and found in it a becoming source of pride. Besides this, the English were enjoying the prospect of added power in the anticipated annexation of Scotland. Although this country was an independent kingdom, both peoples were looking forward with more or less expectancy to a union of the crowns under Elizabeth's second cousin, James VI of Scotland. The kingdoms were drawing closer together, and the Scotch were beginning, as schoolmasters and traders, their peaceful invasion of England. The common people of Scotland were now being educated, and were adapting themselves, for the profit of both countries, to the ways of English life. On the other hand, Ireland, loosely held and turbulent, was subjected at the end of the queen's long reign to the most terrible of its conquests. But the main issue in foreign politics and the main source of political unrest during the queen's reign arose from the fact that England stood as the champion of Protestantism against the power of Catholic Spain.

THE KINGDOM

England was a land in which its people might well take pride. Yet what a different aspect from that of modern England it must have presented! There were probably not more than five million people in the England ruled over by Elizabeth, not so many as there are now in London, or in the state of Ohio. By and large, England was a rural land. Much of the kingdom was still wooded, though the timber was being destroyed to burn lime, smelt iron, and build ships. The greatest contrast to modern days would appear in the survey of a county like York or Lancaster. There were then in the landscape no heaps of slag and cinders as there are now, no blackened, scanty vegetation; it was a region of great trees, green fields, and clear streams, like modern Shropshire or rural regions in the Midlands.

The chief industry of the country was agriculture. It had been in a bad way for two generations when Elizabeth came to the throne, but was destined to improve during her reign. The growing of crops,

however, was giving way more and more to cattle raising, which, compared to the old-fashioned agriculture, was a capitalized industry. Moreover, the seizure of common lands and the eviction of tenants from cultivated areas in order to increase pasturage were still, as they had been for generations past, sources of discontent and agrarian misery. It may be said in very general terms that England in the reign of Queen Elizabeth, like the United States during the last sixty years, was transforming itself at the cost of the tillers of the soil into a commercial and, to some extent, an industrial nation. Manufacture was at first slack or inconsiderable, commerce was undeveloped and crude in its methods, and social and economic legislation was of the poorest. But all of these conditions improved during the queen's reign. The English began to weave woolen cloth; the north country began to shake off its ancient backwardness and turbulence and to make beginnings in the great career of manufacture which has made it one of the greatest productive regions of the world.

Thus during the first thirty years of Elizabeth's reign the country, though still liable to outbreaks of lawlessness and rebellion, passed gradually from poverty, civil broil, and social injustice into a condition of fair stability, domestic prosperity, and national unity. The opportunity for this development came out of the peace with the Continent of Europe which Elizabeth, in spite of many temptations, insisted on maintaining. But these things were gradual growths to be recognized only by the eye of history.

LONDON

Sixteenth-century London was at once more attractive and less attractive than twentieth-century London (before bombing). It was full of trees and gardens; meadows and cultivated lands came in some places down to its very walls. The way in which it bordered clear streams and green fields might be imagined from a distant view of some uncommercial provincial city of modern times, like Lincoln, York, or Hereford. Most American cities are too smoky even to suggest it. But London had its ugly side, too. Something like the narrowness and filth of the crooked streets of old London, used as places of trade, social intercourse, and congregation, may be found in southern Europe or the Near East.

London was a walled city, or rather, a city just overflowing its walls. The fortification along the river Thames had disappeared but the wall was intact along the east, north, and west of the city. The course of the walls is still easily traced in the midst of the modern city, for the old names of streets and gateways have been very largely retained. The ancient city was in the form of an irregular parallelogram on the north bank of the Thames, about a mile long east and west, and about a half mile wide north and south. If you begin with the Tower of London and follow the street called Minories northwesterly to Aldgate, then still more westerly along the streets

From John Speed, "The Theatre of the Empire," London, 1611. (Folger)

Camomile, Wormwood, and London Wall, you come to the Church of St. Giles, Cripplegate, roughly the northwest corner of the city wall. From St. Giles, Cripplegate, you can go south along Noble Street, west close to the site of Aldersgate, southwest between St. Bartholomew's Church and Christ's Hospital to Newgate, and thence to Ludgate Circus and the river. This area is roughly that known as the City, which now probably occupies not more than one fortieth of the modern metropolis.

There were in Shakespeare's time perhaps one hundred thousand people within the walls, and as many more in the suburbs. London was for its time a marvel of rapid metropolitan growth. Southwark across the river, where in those days stood Southwark Cathedral and other ancient monuments, was the largest of the suburbs; but the city had also extended westward along the Strand and the river toward Westminster, which was the capital of the kingdom, and northwestward to Clerkenwell. Houses were being built outside the wall in every direction, though Islington was still in the fields, and Camdentown, Hampstead, and Highgate were remote villages. From its central hill, old St. Paul's, even without its spire, dominated the irregular and closely packed city with its many churches. All told, it was a fine city, though in the reign of Henry VIII it had lost some of its glory with the ruin and pillage of monastic establishments, which had been rich and magnificent institutions. From the point of view of social and economic importance, however, London was, in comparison with the rest of the kingdom, relatively greater even than London is today.

TRAVEL

Travel was still extremely painful and slow because of the unimproved condition of the roads. It was also dangerous on account of highway robbers, although English inns seem to have been good, certainly much better than the inns of the Continent. Travel on horseback was the most common method, and, one may believe, the most comfortable, for coachbuilding was a new and imperfect art. Coaches of state, some of which we see in prints and pictures, were lumbering affairs, no doubt handsome enough in processions, but springless, unwieldy, and hard to transport. Carts and wagons were used for carrying merchandise, but that too went most quickly, safely, and easily on the packsaddle. Under such difficulties, no metropolitan area as great as London could possibly have subsisted from the interior; the river with its foreign commerce built London into a great city.

COMMERCE

The most important foreign trade which England had when Elizabeth came to the throne was with Antwerp, Bruges, and other Belgian cities. When the Spanish king Philip II made his onslaught on his Protestant subjects in the Low Countries, Elizabeth's government held off from openly aiding them for a long time because a war with Spain would have broken down English commerce with Belgium; but through his short-sighted policy of punishing religious obduracy King Philip managed to undo himself. In 1576 eight thousand citizens of Antwerp were put to the sword; and in 1585 when the duke of Parma besieged the city and captured it, Antwerp, the commercial metropolis of northern Europe, was totally ruined. One third of its merchants are said to have settled in London, bringing with them their expert knowledge of commerce. Two things are notable: England was becoming the home of the refugee; and, as the export trade of Flanders died away, London became the greatest market in the world.

English ships took over the Mediterranean trade, formerly carried on mainly by the Venetians, and also the trade of the Baltic, which formerly the free cities of the Hanseatic League had borne. Bristol thrived on commerce with Ireland and subsequently on trade with the Western Hemisphere. Boston and Hull increased their business with Scandinavian ports. Archangel was discovered, and a new trade sprang up with Russia. Fisheries were developed in the North Sea, in the waters north of Ireland, and off the banks of Newfoundland. The greatness of Elizabeth and her ministers is seen in the fact that they encouraged this commerce. Nearly all other kings and rulers whom Europe had seen until that time had regarded commerce with jealousy and preyed on it themselves like pirates. Elizabeth and her ministers, however, were so surprisingly intelligent and advanced in their views that they made definite efforts to foster both foreign and domestic trade.

THE POOR LAWS

The obvious and important result of this new prosperity under Queen Elizabeth was a decrease in unemployment, but there was room for vast improvement. The country had, particularly since the suppression of the monasteries (1536-1539), been more or less flooded with unemployed, both those of the vagabond class and the helpless poor. The reign of Elizabeth brought about a betterment of conditions in the lightening of the burden of their support. In 1572 an act of Parliament was passed which made the mayors, magistrates, and county officials responsible for the care of their local poor and for the enforcement of stern measures against vagabonds. Under this act vagabonds were arrested and sent back to their own

Whipping vagabonds at the cart's tail.
From the Bodleian Library copy of Harman's "Caueat."

parishes and there compelled to work. This localization of responsibility laid the basis for what has been known historically as the poor rate, or the local tax levied for the support of the poor, and for that sinister institution, the workhouse. The provisions of the act of 1572 were continued for centuries. We, from our more extensive knowledge, think of them as inadequate and liable to abuse. But, for their day, they were serviceable and progressive. This law, together

with some improvement in agriculture and manufacture and much improvement in commerce, reduced unemployment and made prosperity general.

AN AGE OF OPPORTUNITY

Another result of this prosperity was a social readjustment which is sometimes spoken of as the passing of feudalism, but which might be better described as a condition in which society needed more men. England became what we should call an important world power with extended interests and a new dignity and efficiency; London became a world market and later a cultural center; and, as a result of these things, opportunity came more abundantly to the ordinary man.

Such an opening up of opportunity, more perhaps than any other one thing, had brought about the Italian Renaissance. In the Italy of the fourteenth and fifteenth centuries there had been many little states and dukedoms, rather prosperous, but mutually jealous, the power shifting from leader to leader, each attended by a new flock of men. Any man who could use a sword had an opportunity to use it, and any man who could contribute by his purse, his pen, his brush, or his chisel to the glory of his princely master's little court was in demand. In the England of Elizabeth there was also a chance for new men, which arose from a sort of shuffling in the ranks of society. This new freedom enabled Shakespeare and other literary men to rise to power and importance, although he and certain of the conservative thinkers of the age inveighed against it because they saw in it something inimical to the good old times. Many of Elizabeth's favorites were men whose families were of no social importance. It was an age of self-made men. No American ought to have difficulty in understanding a situation in which young men had a chance to make their fortunes and to rise in the social scale.

THE BEGGAR ON HORSEBACK

Not only did the lovers of the old order see, as they always do in every social change, the disagreeable spectacle of the beggar on horseback; but, since the rise of all sorts and conditions of men was marked and advertised by the display of luxury, they saw also degeneracy and social decay. The Puritan saw an alarming increase of worldliness and sin. Immersed as they were in the changing order, writers were unable to comprehend the greatness of the time; and never was satire more active and more bitter, and social pessimism more genuine.

It cannot be said, however, that Shakespeare voices the reaction more potently than he does the spirit of progress. Perhaps it is fair to see something of social conscience in his depiction of the wickedness of city life in *Measure for Measure*, or in his casual pictures of upstart courtiers and the paintings and patchings of court ladies; but in general, one turns to Shakespeare's contemporaries for the recognition of

The "Black Art"—picking locks.
Illustration from Greene's "A Notable Discovery of Coosenage," 1591.

social evils in the large. Shakespeare, being a man from the country, knew mainly three classes, the nobleman, the artisan, and the farmer. He does not distress himself about the aggressions of the new commercial magnate, or the impertinent ways of the city madam, his wife. It is Jonson, Chapman, and Beaumont and Fletcher who do this.

THE RISE IN THE SCALE OF LIVING

Most of the best thinkers of the day saw ominous things in the increase of wealth and the improvement of the scale of living. Harrison, a brilliant man but a thoroughgoing reactionary, in his *Description of England* saw disaster in the fine new Elizabethan dwelling houses, built of oak, with locked doors, glazed windows, and many chimneys. These things made men delicate, he thought, and he attributed the increase in rheums and catarrhs to the fact that householders no longer breathed in their own healthful smoke, but sent it up the new chimneys.

In similar vein, conservative thinkers regarded the longbow as the mainstay of the kingdom in war, although, in point of fact, guns and artillery had long before superseded it. In the armory at the Tower of London there is a corselet shot through with a bullet at Bosworth Field. It illustrates what had happened to the knightly style of warfare, though Elizabethan aristocrats, with their countless jousts and tourneys, refused to recognize it. The French rapier with a new style of fence had superseded the sword and buckler. Although this change was disgusting to Mercutio and many a stout gallant of the old order,

the rapier, because of its thrusting style of fence, was a much more dangerous weapon than the old broadsword with its "swashing blow."

Satirists and reactionaries saw the country beset with "flaming youth" and dangerous modernism. The introduction of Italian manners had been cried out against for two generations; but still the young men resorted to Italy and came back, as it was thought, godless in their manner of life and corrupted in the purity of their religion. French clothes were also an abomination. Never had Englishmen worn such wealth on their backs. There is a familiar story of a country nobleman who came to court in the reign of Henry VIII dressed rudely in country apparel, but with a hundred stout followers in his train. The king reproved him for his lack of propriety in his dress; he returned later in silk and velvet. When the king asked him about his hundred retainers, he threw down his cloak and his feathered hat and declared that he had put his retainers on his back. Plain gentlemen, citizens, and even yeomen dressed better than had the earls and barons of an earlier time.

Nothing so offended the strictness of the Puritans as to behold this vanity in dress; since Adam's fall was symbolized by his adoption of raiment in place of innocent nudity, fine clothes seemed to advertise man's submergence in sin and to flout God's will. Not only was raiment fine in Elizabeth's day, a thing which was of itself bad enough in the minds of Puritans, but clothes were slashed, trimmed, and ornamented as never before. Rouge and false hair became common, along with the great and growing pleated collar known as the ruff, its expansive stiffness made possible by the discovery of starch. Breeches were first narrow and then wide, for Dame Fashion had never been so busy in changing styles. Other causes for consternation and disgust were the new habit of "tobacco drinking," the use of many new sorts of wines to the point of drunkenness, and the general chameleonlike behavior of the Englishman, who, according to the texts of a hundred satires, derived his goods and his fashions from every quarter. "What say you, then, to Falconbridge, the young baron of England?" asks Nerissa of Portia, who in her reply declares, "How oddly he is suited! I think he bought his doublet in Italy, his round hose in France, his bonnet in Germany, and his behavior everywhere" (*The Merchant of Venice*, I, ii, 71, 79-82).

The contrasts between rich and poor were, of course, very great. Along with the youth seeking his fortune were innumerable masterless men—mercenary soldiers who had been engaged in continental wars, decayed servingmen, knaves in buckram, and the pitifully poor, whose condition was made worse than of old by the greedy quest for wealth, the desertion of the country by ancient landholders, the enclosure of common lands, and the enormous increase in rents. The era was one of inflation; and although men were richer, there was something factitious in their prosperity.

Life in
Shakespeare's
England

5

Perhaps the most hated man among those who preyed on society was the usurer or dealer in money, for no point was clearer in Elizabethan morals than the belief that interest-taking was a sin. Interest-taking is made the chief mark of discrimination between Shylock the Jew and Antonio the Christian in *The Merchant of Venice*. Lord Burghley recognized the danger of having power in the hands of those who control money. He wanted usurers and smugglers to desist from their ill-gotten gains because of the evil results to the kingdom. To achieve this he used an almost modern style of propaganda in seeking to develop public morals and public conscience. He sought to prevent high prices by a similar moral suasion, and to foster industry by an appeal to patriotism.

ELIZABETHAN HOUSES

As England grew rich with its national and usually international peace, its wise and thrifty government, and its prosperous trade, the old-fashioned thatched and wattled houses of the peasantry, like the narrow cottage of Chaucer's poor widow in *The Nun's Priest's Tale*, gave place to houses of brick and stone. Chimneys were built for fireplaces, so that the smoke no longer wandered about the house searching for the hole in the roof by which to escape. Pewter, or even silver dishes, took the place of the wooden spoon and trencher. Beds and even pillows became common. Carpets were replacing rushes as covering for the floors; wainscoting, tapestries or hangings, and pictures appeared on the walls; and, most wonderful of all, glass began to be used extensively for windows.

Let those who "viewed with alarm" say what they might, domestic comfort established itself in England. In witness of this fact there still stand, with their gardens and terraces, a good many of the lofty Tudor mansions. The battlement, the moat, the fortified gate, the narrow window for archery or firearms, were no longer necessary in a land at peace; nor was it any longer imperative for the peasant to bring his cows, his pigs, and his poultry into his house at night in order to protect them from thieves. The row of splendid houses of the Elizabethan nobility along the bank of the Thames in London was swept away by the fire of 1666, as were the really fine houses of city merchants, bankers, and traders. However, a little bit of the old city was left by the fire along the eastern wall, in Holborn, and in the vicinity of Smithfield. Before the destruction of World War II, a few of the old city houses and one of the old churches still stood, and there were many sixteenth-century houses in provincial cities such as Chester and Coventry. They were often large and imposing structures, three or four stories in height, usually framed of strong oak with the walls filled in with brick and plaster. The frontage on the street in old London was usually narrow, but there were trees and gardens at the rear.

With these finer houses, too, came features of privacy which we are accustomed to associate with culture. Most of the life of the household of the medieval magnate had gone on in the great hall, which was often kitchen, dining hall, and sitting room for the whole body of family and retainers, the men drinking there in the evenings and sleeping there at night. In the new houses there were withdrawing rooms into which, even if dinner were taken in the hall, the family and the chief guests were able to retire for privacy.

The Elizabethans did their building and improvements well. Not only do we still admire their houses, but from their oriel windows and bits of their stained glass, from the broad staircases by which they approached their newly invented second stories, from their jewels and their costumes, we can see that they were children of the Renaissance indulging a characteristic love of beauty. Graphic and plastic arts did not thrive as in Italy, or even as in France and the Low Countries, but literature, drama, and architecture became flourishing arts in the English Renaissance.

THE QUEEN

The most dominant, versatile, and beneficent figure of the reign of Queen Elizabeth was the queen herself. Her character and her brains, her tastes and opinions, produced greater results than any other single force. On one side of her nature she was a masculine woman possessed of some of the finest of masculine qualities. Her judgment was sound, her policy simple and firm, and her courage strong. She wished England to prosper, and therefore worked to keep it out of foreign wars and domestic disturbances. To an important degree she was successful, but there were many occasions for both kinds of discord. Reformation and Counter Reformation were fighting it out all over Europe, and England sided strongly with the Protestant cause. Within the kingdom religious quarrels were fierce and incessant, and the matter of the succession to the crown was unsure. Elizabeth's subjects had many invitations to rebel against her in behalf of one or another claimant to power.

She was not in general a theorist in governmental matters, but she had a few simple principles which were in line with the best political thinking of the Renaissance. She avoided partisanship, believed strongly in social gradation, in the supremacy of wise princes, and in governmental economy. She was imperious to a degree, headstrong in fact; but, when it came to the final issue, reason rose above passion, and she was able to take advice. Whatever her vanities of ostentation and display, or her mad quest for pleasure, she understood that business is business. It may even be said that she took to heart the most widely current maxim of the Renaissance, that self-knowledge is the *summum bonum*. She therefore indulged her vanities in her court and acted the statesman in her council. She could deny herself her dearest wish if, after having tried in vain to bully her

*From Edmund Spenser,
"The Shepheardes
Calender," 1586.
(Folger)*

advisers into agreement with her, she found that they still stood out against her proposal.

TUDOR ABSOLUTISM

The crown had been the dominant force in English government since the time of Edward IV, and the last strongholds of baronical authority had been broken down under Henry VIII. There had been occasional revivals of oligarchical power among the greater nobles, such as that of Somerset in the reign of Edward VI; but, for the most part, the only rival of the crown was the authority of the House of Commons of Parliament. The Commons had been strengthened by the growth in wealth of the commercial classes and by a league with rural magnates. They were making themselves felt under Elizabeth and were to become the controlling element under her successors. No doubt one reason for Elizabeth's rigid economy in government was her desire to be independent of the Commons. As it was, she had conceded a good deal to the Parliament for the sake of harmony. She had convened Parliament several times to obtain grants to cover the expenses of her wars, and they had shown a disposition to demand redress of grievances and a desire to get power into their hands. But she had managed affairs so well that the burden of taxes was light and there was little reason to ask questions about the expenditures of the crown, whereas her successor, King James I, exhausted his exchequer, and Parliament secured its hold through the power of the purse.

Elizabeth had little partisanship, but used men of all parties, played rivals off against each other, and made the best of her counselors; and therein lay probably her greatest ability. If one follows the history of her relations with her great minister, William Cecil, Baron of Burghley, one learns the story. Burghley was a Protestant and a partisan, not free from self-seeking, but, as a whole, honest and reliable.

She knew she could get the truth from him even when it was against herself; and when she had failed to make him abandon his position on any question, she knew that it was a statesman's opinion with which she had to reckon, and, in the end, she usually heeded him. He, too, desired the prosperity and peace of England, though for religious and political reasons he would often enough have been glad to go to war. Here, however, the queen controlled him and insisted on maintaining peace. Elizabeth had other able ministers like Walsingham and Sir Nicholas Bacon, father of the famous Lord Chancellor, and their counsel, too, she respected.

Out of the queen's opinions and her relation to Parliament and the people, and out of the political doctrines of France and Italy transplanted into England, there grew the characteristic political views which Shakespeare expresses. For example, people believed deeply in the glory and inviolability of sovereignty; they recognized the greatness of honest courtiers and the wickedness of flatterers; and, above all, they felt the glory and greatness of the commonwealth.

THE VIRGIN QUEEN

The queen, being unmarried, made a cult of her virginity. Her vanity and her ridiculous affectation of youth and beauty, her greed of flattery and adulation, caused her to adopt favorite after favorite, often for no better reason than his charm of person and manner. Of these the most famous is Robert Dudley the Earl of Leicester, whom at one time the queen may have been tempted to marry. Later in her reign, when Burghley was dead and the queen was older and more foolish, the ill-starred earl of Essex was a prime favorite. This was the time when Shakespeare may have come to court, and one has a feeling that there may have been a basis for Aubrey's statement about Shakespeare: "If he was invited to

COACH and SEDAN,

Pleaſantly Diſputing for Place and Precedence;

The *Breyers-Cart* being Moderator.

Spectatum admiſſi, riſum teneatis amici?

Title page of a book printed in London, 1636. (Folger)

court, he was in pain." He may have resented the overthrow of Essex and Southampton, for he wrote no commendatory verses when the queen died.

THE AMUSEMENTS OF ELIZABETH

We have our picture of Good Queen Bess cuffing a disobedient lady-in-waiting, reproving a statesman, laughing at coarse jests and making them herself, witnessing the cruel sport of bearbaiting, delivering addresses in Latin or Greek, riding with great ceremony in her litter surrounded by lords and ladies, entering London, her great sword of state borne before her, or "going a progress" through the counties of England. She loved to travel about her kingdom visiting provincial cities and the country-seats of noblemen; and these things pleased her particularly well when, like an invading army, she could live off the country.

The queen enjoyed plays and pageants and supported with some liberality the Office of the Revels under the Lord Chamberlain, in whose records we first find Shakespeare's name after his departure from Stratford. The Master of the Revels from 1578 to 1610, Edmund Tilney, called the players together before Christmas and selected from their repertory those plays which were to be presented before Her Majesty, and for their service the actors received a reward generally amounting to £10. Many of Shakespeare's plays were so performed, and he may have had to do with other dramatic activity at court.

The masque, a form of drama combined with music and pageantry and introduced from the Continent, was the rival of the play. Under King James, probably because his greater generosity provided its producers with more money, it was to

grow, with Ben Jonson and the architect Inigo Jones, into something much more gorgeous than the drama. The masque was, however, well established at the time when Shakespeare wrote *Love's Labour's Lost, A Midsummer-Night's Dream,* and *Much Ado about Nothing.* Other plays have features from the masque, and no doubt most of his comedies dared to be more poetical, more dainty, and more grotesque because of his knowledge of this form of entertainment.

POLITICS, EDUCATION, THE STATE

Shakespeare was not interested in politics in the narrow sense in which we usually use the word, but in the broad Aristotelian sense of social welfare he was certainly not indifferent to political considerations. Like Plutarch and the chroniclers, he saw politics and history as always embodied in the persons of kings and leaders. From his historical plays it is clear that with Shakespeare the character of the government lies in the character of the prince. Anarchy and disunion were all too well known, and the questions at issue were not so much about ideals and general principles as about conditions arising out of the simple theory that, with a wise prince and an honest court, a country might secure prosperity at home and peace and safety abroad. The flatterer, a selfish man placed near the prince and often responsible for his actions, was thus the worst enemy of the state and of the people.

The educational theory of the day was also simple and perfectly understood. It moved in the same direction, calling for the liberal education of princes and rulers of the state in morals, intellect, and personality. The vulgar herd below made no difference; there must be virtue and power at the top to hold the bottom in order. Such were Shakespeare's views, and in this respect he aligns himself with the greatest thinkers of his time, particularly conservatives like Hooker. Rank and grade in society were necessary and beneficent in a grand system of coordination and subordination extending from inanimate nature to heaven itself, through the degrees of vegetable and animal kingdoms, mankind, spirits, angels, archangels, dominions, principalities, powers, up to the godhead. It was the law of nature that each order should know and observe its sphere and its limitations, for it was by ambition that the angels in heaven fell. Likewise, on earth there were grades in society which bore the sanction of God in every degree from beggar to king. On the contented discharge of function in each rank rested the condition of social order; witness the speech of Ulysses in *Troilus and Cressida:*

> Degree being vizarded,
> The unworthiest shows as fairly in the mask.
> The heavens themselves, the planets and this centre
> Observe degree, priority and place,
> Insisture, course, proportion, season, form,
> Office and custom, in all line of order;
> And therefore is the glorious planet Sol
> In noble eminence enthroned and sphered

Amidst the other; whose medicinable eye
Corrects the ill aspects of planets evil,
And posts, like the commandment of a king,
Sans check to good and bad: but when the planets
In evil mixture to disorder wander,
What plagues and what portents! what mutiny!
What raging of the sea! shaking of earth!
Commotion in the winds! frights, changes, horrors,
Divert and crack, rend and deracinate
The unity and married calm of states
Quite from their fixture! O, when degree is shaked,
Which is the ladder to all high designs,
The enterprise is sick! How could communities,
Degrees in schools and brotherhoods in cities,
Peaceful commerce from dividable shores,
The primogenitive and due of birth,
Prerogative of age, crowns, sceptres, laurels,
But by degree, stand in authentic place?
Take but degree away, untune that string,
And, hark, what discord follows! each thing meets
In mere oppugnancy: the bounded waters
Should lift their bosoms higher than the shores
And make a sop of all this solid globe:
Strength should be lord of imbecility,
And the rude son should strike his father dead:
Force should be right; or rather, right and wrong,
Between whose endless jar justice resides,
Should lose their names, and so should justice too.
Then every thing includes itself in power,
Power into will, will into appetite;
And appetite, an universal wolf,
So doubly seconded with will and power,
Must make perforce an universal prey,
And last eat up himself.   (I, iii, 83-124)

This is the approved mode of Renaissance thought about politics. Machiavelli's *Prince* lays down with cold-blooded calculation the rules by which a sovereign may govern securely and successfully. This book is not a document of oppression and tyranny, although lovers of human liberty have long considered it so. It is a calm discussion of the methods by which the conditions of social order recommended by Shakespeare's Ulysses and by Richard Hooker may be maintained. From the end of the speech of Ulysses it will be seen that tyrannical absolutism is the last thing to be thought of. What Shakespeare puts into the mouth of the Greek statesman is not the blind obedience taught by modern totalitarianism but a rational order for which all citizens from top to bottom are responsible.

Shakespeare was on the side of the royal government; and, although he does not often expound the doctrines of Tudor absolutism, they are everywhere implicit in his treatment of society. They are in his delineations of kings and, particularly, in his descriptions of mobs like those in *2 Henry VI*, *Julius Caesar*, and *Coriolanus*. The reasons why this is not more apparent to the casual reader are that Shakespeare apparently was not anxious to expound this or any doctrine except dramatically, and that there is in Shakespeare always a quality of breadth and fairness. His common men have in them a dash of humanity and nobility, as his kings are made to have a kinship with common men; and both kings and common men have intelligible motives, as do even his worst villains. In his pictures of society there is always a coloring of elemental justice. But Shakespeare certainly entertained no views except those described above, and it is absurd to hunt in his works for nineteenth-century theories of social justice or to blame him for not expressing views possible only to later generations.

THE RELIGIOUS QUESTION

After Elizabeth came to the throne there was a bitter reaction against the Catholics. Those Protestants who had fled abroad to avoid persecution under Queen Mary brought back with them continental ideas of theology and a new and stiffer type of Protestantism. The Church of England assumed a middle position between this extreme Protestantism and Catholicism; this was the position of Burghley and of Queen Elizabeth. By the middle of her reign extreme Protestantism, commonly called Puritanism, was expressing itself either in Presbyterianism or Inde-

A tavern scene.
From Philip Stubbes'
"Anatomy of Abuses,"
1583. (Folger)

pendency, and the time came when it offered a violent attack on the middle position held by the Church of England. Shakespeare hardly shows himself aware of this powerful and pregnant force. His allusions to the Puritans are few and indefinite, but they have been thought to be scornful. His position on religious matters was probably that of the queen. He is equally noncommittal as regards the Church of Rome, although he shows a sympathetic understanding of the institutions of the Catholic church in *Hamlet*, *King John*, and elsewhere.

THE MORAL QUESTION

There was a great change in the temper of the public in moral matters in the early years of King James' reign. Elizabethan gaiety gave place to satire and moral reflection, and grave men were thinking critically, though not always fruitfully, about the state of the church and the state of society. Human life was seen by such thinkers more and more against a background of responsibility to God, iniquity in man, and uncertainty of fate. This may be the temper which we see reflected in the tragedies of Shakespeare as well as in the bitter carelessness of his later contemporaries, their sensuality, and their adoption of the point of view of a class instead of the point of view of humanity at large. The later dramatists belonged to the court.

There was something innocent in the frank love of finery, sport, and show in Elizabeth Tudor; for she loved books and art as well as clothes and jewels, and she labored to make herself a mistress of languages and learning. Possibly her love affairs were silly rather than wicked. Certainly in her court, decency usually prevailed, whereas in the court of King James I there was sordid intrigue. It is a very fortunate circumstance that Shakespeare was old enough to have felt hopefully with Marlowe and Spenser rather than young enough to have felt cynically with Fletcher and Ford.

We have seen that Shakespeare's England—still largely rural and medieval, but coming into possession of material wealth in the midst of a long peace—was much better governed and unified than it had ever been, and socially so constituted that the individual, of whatever rank and station, had a reasonable opportunity for recognition.

RENAISSANCE LEARNING

Renaissance learning was largely a development and amplification of medieval learning. It retained the old science, not only of the earlier Middle Ages, but all the additions that were made to it by the thirteenth and later centuries from their study of classical antiquity. For the men of the Renaissance the material universe was still geocentric. Even the circumnavigation of the globe seemed to fit in with that conception. Around about the earth there still moved as hollow spheres the seven planets, the fixed stars, and the *primum mobile*. Beyond this spherical universe

was Chaos organized at the top into the Empyrean, or dwelling place of God, and at the bottom into Hell, where dwelt the fallen angels with their chieftain Lucifer. The Renaissance, as we have seen, still believed in an order of beings made up, in ascending series and perfect subordination of powers and privileges, of inanimate objects, plants, animals, man (further divided into common men, nobles, and kings),

A demon's flight from the body of a possessed woman.
From Pierre Boaistuau, "Histoires prodigieuses," 1575. (Huntington)

the nine orders of the angels, and God himself. The doctrine of providence was still largely astrological, for the Renaissance thought that God communicated His will to man through the mysteriously varied regularity of the movements of heavenly bodies.

As to man himself, he was regarded as a microcosm, made up of the four elements—earth, air, fire, and water—his nature being determined by the proportion in him of the four qualities of hot, dry, cold, and moist. As a microcosm he corresponded in his parts to the outside world, or the macrocosm. This embraced the doctrine of planetary and elemental correspondences; namely, that the temperament, fortunes, and physique of the human being are dependent upon the mixture within him of the four elements and on the influence of the stars and planets, which have in them corresponding parts. All things in heaven and earth had been created, according to this belief, to fit into proper places in a perfectly constructed system.

This means that the man of science did not expect to find any new principle, but merely to fit things into their pre-established places. The science of the time was bad, not so much because things were crowded into the wrong pigeonholes, as because the pigeonholes themselves were often unwarranted restrictions of the freedom and variety of nature. Compared to modern thought of the abstract kind, Renaissance thought was superficial and vague, often made up merely of comparison or the enunciation of old postulates under new forms. It was prone, therefore, to quackery and the too ready acceptance of analogy. It was not, however, lacking in variety and was so active in the observation of likeness and unlikeness that it lent itself readily to the uses of poetry.

BASAL KNOWLEDGE

The following brief list may indicate the material of Elizabethan thought: (1) matter pertaining particularly to the Renaissance, such as the proverb or dictum, and the habit of aphoristic thought, the belief in culture, in the freedom of the will, and in the adaptability of the individual; (2) matter from the classics, such as the intimate interest in mythology, ancient history and story, eloquence, and the sort of philosophic reflection which one associates with Cicero; (3) matters of current fashion, including the theme of the good old times versus modernity, clothes, fashions, and courtly life; (4) matters of domestic life, such as the management of the household, woman's sphere, the relations of parent and child, husband and wife, master and servant, courtship and betrothal, clownage, conviviality; (5) magic, the ways of the occult world, folklore, superstition, ghosts, witches, demons, signs, omens, old wives' tales, and childbed superstitions; (6) a body of popular natural history (which, erroneous as it was, no doubt helped men at least to understand themselves) about the ape, the cat, the bat, the hare, the hedgehog, the rat, the cock, the basilisk, the toad, the bee, and the spider, as well as a knowledge of various herbs and stones and their properties.

The lives of ordinary men must, of course, have been steeped in such lore as was in common circulation. In fact, we have abundant testimony from the age of Queen Elizabeth that such was the case. Reginald Scot, whose book, *The Discovery of Witchcraft*, was published in 1584, gives the following description of the superstitious terrors against which he protested; for Scot was a skeptic with reference to witchcraft and superstition, in which, however, King James I devoutly believed:

In our childhood our mothers' maids have so terrified us with an ugly devil having horns on his head, fire in his mouth, and a tail in his breech, eyes like a bason, fangs like a dog, claws like a bear, a skin like a nigger, and a voice roaring like a lion, whereby we start and are afraid when we hear one cry Boo: and they have so frayed us with bull-beggars, spirits, witches, urchins, elves, hags, fairies, satyrs, pans, fauns, sylens, Kit with the canstick, tritons, centaurs, dwarfs, giants, imps, calcars, conjurors, nymphs, changelings, incubus, Robin Goodfellow, the spoorne, the mare, the man in the oak, the hell wain, the firedrake, the puckle, Tom Thumb, hobgoblin, Tom Tumbler, boneless, and such other bugs, that we are afraid of our own shadows: in so much that some never fear the devil, but in a dark night; and then a polled sheep is a perilous beast, and many times is taken for our father's soul, specially in a churchyard, where a right hardy man heretofore scant durst pass by night, but his hair would stand upright. (Pp. 152-153)

In an age when superstitions of the kinds just described were so common, when there was so much ignorance and so much misinformation, how could the minds of men have been free?

And yet they were relatively free. Man had acquired a new measure of freedom and responsibility. The Reformation had put his salvation into his own hands and made him responsible for it. The invention of printing, the cheapness of the printed book, and the extension of the ability to read had given him the wherewithal to learn. The spirit of the Englishman of the Renaissance rose with a noble aspiration, and he put out his hand to reach, not only the newly realized joys of salvation, but also the newly revealed promises of science. But the age of authority was by no means over, and the sciences, supported by the prestige of antiquity, had enormous authority back of their alluring promises. What were the things offered by learning to this, the first generation of modern times equipped to enjoy them?

WHAT LEARNING HAD TO OFFER

The main source of learning was, of course, the curriculum of schools and colleges, and this curriculum the Renaissance took over almost unchanged from the Middle Ages. It was made up of the Seven Liberal Arts: grammar, rhetoric, and logic, called the trivium and corresponding roughly to our work for a bachelor's degree; and arithmetic, geometry, astronomy, and music, called the quadrivium and corresponding roughly to the work for a master's degree. Since the thirteenth century there had been added to it what were known as the Three Philosophies, namely, natural philosophy, ethics, and metaphysics (made up mainly of psychology). This addition, consisting largely of the works of Aristotle, introduced into Europe from the Arabs, had served to enrich the curriculum of liberal studies and had been in the schools long enough to have made its way into the minds of educated persons, whether university bred or not. The Seven Liberal Arts went back to Aristotle and the Greeks by the long road of the Middle Ages; the Three Philosophies were a more recent importation from the same source. To be sure, by the end of the sixteenth century the curricula of schools and colleges had been expanded in various practical ways—by the study of history, of modern languages, of geography and cosmology, optics, mensuration, and of other subjects, and the Huguenot scholar Petrus Ramus had rendered both logic and rhetoric more practical.

Aristotelian logic offered, and still offers, much. It claims to be able to discover truth and detect error. Elizabethan writers on the subject said that they could unlock the Scriptures, avoid the snares of the papacy, and reward their students with salvation. Dudley Fenner wrote a book of logic in which he taught how to solve all the problems of domestic life by means of logic, and Abraham Fraunce showed how it might straighten out all the wrinkles and kinks of the law. Aristotelian ethics is also a practical subject. It had been made more so when it came to Elizabethan England in the works of Italian Aristotelians. It was, and is, a science of behavior. There is no categorical imperative in it; no hortatory quality; no positivism; no Christian piety. It tells men how to live successfully and tells them to be good in order to be successful. It flatters man by supposing that there is no limit to the possibility of his attainment. Politics is but a continuation of ethics both in Aristotle and in the Renaissance. It teaches how to rule a state, how to gain power and hold it, how to educate a governor and a statesman, and how to conduct wars and negotiate the treaties which interrupt them. Its ideal is efficiency. Alchemy, astrology, and magic were practical as well as learned arts, and they had their claims and their followers.

The subjects mentioned in the preceding catalog were old sciences that were for the first time advertised and rendered easily accessible. There were some sciences, however, which underwent important adaptations and, therefore, exercised special influences. Psychology, derived also from the writings of Aristotle, had always had implications of importance in man's life on earth. The psychology of Aristotle and his followers offers a shrewd and, for the most part, a satisfactory explanation of what takes place in the mental constitution of man. Its erroneous anatomy and physiology are largely compensated for by careful observation in the realm of human consciousness.

The ancients themselves, Chaucer, and other later writers had made free use of psychology in their determination of motive and in their description of the passions of the mind. In the last quarter of the sixteenth century there arose a far wider realization of the possibilities of psychology and a far greater faith in what it might accomplish. Timothy Bright and Robert Burton applied it to the diagnosis and cure of insanity. John Huarte offered it as a method by which men might be classified for trades and professions, through a determination of the proportions in them of the qualities of hot, cold, moist, and dry. Besides these there was a great group of writers, partly scientific and partly popular, who saw in psychological phenomena, often called "humors," a means of explaining and depicting the emotional life

of man. The subject passed from the scientist to the literary man, just as we have seen pragmatism and psychoanalysis pass in our own day. Shakespeare and nearly all the dramatists became psychologists and, according to their ability and genius, made use of psychology in their plays.

Among the influential doctrines of the age, the current belief about the nature and power of speech should not be forgotten. Speech was the characteristic which distinguished man from the lower animals and was very immediately the expression of the human soul. It followed that truth, if exactly expressed, had to be accepted. Therefore, eloquence was, in the minds of Renaissance thinkers, an irresistible force. Shakespeare's poetry rises to meet every issue of persuasion or comprehension.

The new learning which came from Greece and Rome through France and Italy was, and is, serviceable to those who wish to know the world. It was conspicuous in the exorbitance of claims that, in the nature of things, could never be realized; but the act of faith, the belief in learning, brought the Elizabethan further in creative and imaginative insight than any modern age has ever been brought in the same length of time. It seems that learning offered a great intellectual bargain counter, and the men of the English Renaissance were foolish enough, or wise enough, to invest.

We have thus passed in rapid review what Elizabethan men knew and believed and what they tried to learn. The things which we ordinarily associate with them, however, are not these things, although they are fundamental to correct understanding. We normally and correctly enough think of the Elizabethan age as a time when there were many poets, many soldiers, and many explorers; as a time when the race was reaching out in every direction in response to its love of power and beauty. Perhaps never has the spirit of a race and an age been so active and so bold. It was also an age of versatility. Sir Philip Sidney was a gallant soldier; he was also a poet, a novelist, a critic, and no mean thinker about the affairs of state. Raleigh, the soldier, warrior, and courtier, was a world in himself, being also a skillful poet and spending his long years in prison in the writing of a learned history. Bacon was capable of almost anything practical, scientific, or literary. There was no man who showed quite the diversity of splendid talent which appeared in Leonardo da Vinci at the height of the Italian Renaissance, but the tendency to a full participation in all the available activities of life was present and widespread. Shakespeare we know only as a poet and dramatist, but his vast comprehension of the variety of life and its zest makes his the most significant voice of the age.

SHAKESPEARE AND THE RENAISSANCE

Shakespeare's known occupations, which were numerous, all show influences peculiar to his time. He was, besides being a citizen and businessman in the town of Stratford, a poet, a playwright, an actor, a part owner of a theater, and no doubt, therefore, a theatrical manager. As a poet he was affected by the now obsolete system of patronage, according to which poets wrote in the hope of favor and gain to be derived from persons of wealth and influence, to whom they dedicated their works. As an actor, he was a member of a sort of trade guild and was affected by the rules and customs of his association. As a playwright, his immediate activity in the writing of plays was controlled by the demands of the company of actors who hired his services and, consequently, by the dictates of fashion in the theater and the rivalry of other companies of players; and as a dramatic artist he was affected by the situation then present in the development of the drama. During the period of about twenty years (1590-1610) in which he was active, drama passed from a crude amalgam of folk play, didactic interlude, and classical comedy and tragedy to the new form of romantic drama of which Shakespeare's own plays are the best examples.

It is to some extent an accident of the times that Shakespeare secured the great representative audience that he seems to have had. During the period of his activity the propriety of stage plays was being more and more called in question by religious persons— for religious and moral scruples bore heavily on the theater—and before Shakespeare ceased writing, the religious element of the community had definitely consigned the stage to the powers of evil and had withdrawn itself from the theater. Had the Puritans remained in the audience and won the battle against the more worldly-minded elements of society, they might have made of the drama a religious institution. We might, in that case, have had something as noble as the religious tragedies of Racine; but it would not have been the Elizabethan drama. Fortunately for Shakespeare and for us, the Puritans could not dominate the stage. It was protected by the favor of Queen Elizabeth and King James I and of the nobility, all of whom were turning away from Puritanism. But during most of Shakespeare's career as a dramatist, ordinary Londoners were still in the theater making their wishes and interests felt, so that Shakespeare, not perhaps of his own desire, wrote for all classes of society. At a later time, that of Shakespeare's immediate successors, dramatists wrote mainly to please the courtly classes.

This man from a country town did not, however, write mainly about country matters; he made up his plays and poems from the newly imported culture of France and Italy, coloring it and making it real by his closeness to ordinary English life. We must think of Shakespeare's work, therefore, as part of the literary tradition and book culture of the Renaissance. If we would know Shakespeare, we must attend to this great basic fact. He does not yield his full message to those who approach him from the point of view of the uneducated. Most of the important things which Shakespeare has to tell us about life are,

except for the special touch of his genius, merely the best that his age was able to discover about life. This expression of the culture of his age is a large part of what we mean by Shakespeare. Many of the ideas to which he gave artistic expression and embodiment are commonplaces in the learning of the age; it remained for him to make them vital and applicable.

SHAKESPEARE THROUGH THE AGES

Even when we have studied Shakespeare's life, his relation to his age, and his own artistic development, we are not yet finished. The great significance of Shakespeare is that in spite of the many differences between his age and ours, some perhaps trivial and some of far-reaching importance, he gives us in his plays life patterns that are continuous in the history of the human race. Shakespeare has, therefore, been a favorite topic in the world's thought for more than two hundred years, and because he has been so often read and played, so often interpreted and misinterpreted, he is not the same poet he would be had he lain obscure for three centuries to be rediscovered by the scholarship of our own day.

Even in such a case his importance would have been quickly recognized, so that he would have been studied in somewhat the same way in which Chaucer has been studied during the last eighty or ninety years. But Shakespeare has been with us so long that his phrases and allusions, like "yeoman's service," "caviare to the general," and "a Daniel come to judgment," have become parts of our ordinary speech. Situations in his plots are part of our folklore, and his characters exist in the popular mind almost independent of the dramas in which they appear. He has in a very real sense created his own world public. One does not approach Shakespeare as one approaches authors less well known, authors to whom the track has been opened mainly by historical scholars. The road to Shakespeare is a well-traveled highway. Every modern person who has any pretense to culture knows something about Shakespeare and considers himself in some sense an authority in the interpretation of such characters as Hamlet and Shylock, and usually has a firmly rooted opinion that Shakespeare was a self-made man with a proclivity for deer stealing. To ask a person if he knows anything about Shakespeare is to ask him if he belongs to a respectable family and has had any care in his upbringing. No author ingrained in popular thought as Shakespeare is, no author whose words are proverbs for daily use, can be properly studied without some attention to such questions as how he got into print and how his fame grew and thrived through the centuries.

The materials gathered together in the following pages are intended to furnish grounds for a liberal and just comprehension of this greatest of all authors, and, in some measure, as a corrective of popular error.

BESANT, SIR WALTER. *London.* 1903-1909. Made up of works on various periods.

BURCKHARDT, JACOB. *The Civilization of the Renaissance in Italy.* New ed. London, 1929.

BURR, GEORGE L. "Anent the Middle Ages," *American Historical Review,* XVIII, 710-726. Consideration of the limits of the Middle Ages and the Renaissance, with references.

BYRNE, MURIEL ST. CLARE. *Elizabethan Life in Town and Country.* Rev. ed. London, 1934.

Cambridge Medieval History. Vol. V, *et passim.*

Cambridge Modern History. Vol. I, chs. i, ii, vi, vii, xiii, xiv, xv, xvi, xix; Vol. III, chs. ii (French Humanism and Montaigne), ix, x (Last Years of Elizabeth), xi (The Elizabethan Age of English Literature), xix (The End of the Italian Renaissance).

CHAMBERS, SIR EDMUND K. *The Elizabethan Stage.* 4 vols. Oxford, 1923.

CHAMBERS, R. W. *Thomas More.* New York, 1935.

CHEW, S. C. *The Crescent and the Rose: Islam and England during the Renaissance.* New York, 1937.

CHEYNEY, EDWARD P. *A History of England from the Defeat of the Spanish Armada to the Death of Elizabeth.* London, 1914, 1926.

CHUTE, MARCHETTE. *Shakespeare of London.* New York, 1949.

CRAIG, HARDIN. *The Enchanted Glass.* New York, 1936.

CREIGHTON, M. *The Age of Elizabeth.* New York, 1892.

CREIZENACH, W. *The English Drama in the Age of Shakespeare* (translation of Band IV, *Geschichte des neueren Dramas*). London, 1916.

DAVIS, H. W. C. *Mediaeval England;* New edition of Barnard's *Companion to English History.* Oxford, 1924.

EINSTEIN, LEWIS. *The Italian Renaissance in England.* New York, 1913.

HARBAGE, ALFRED. *Shakespeare's Audience.* New York, 1941.

HARRISON, G. B. *An Elizabethan Journal.* London, 1929, supplements; *Shakespeare at Work.* Ann Arbor, 1958.

HARRISON, WILLIAM. *Description of Britaine and England.* 1577 (in Holinshed's *Chronicle;* a number of reprints).

HADYN, HIRAM. *The Counter-Renaissance.* New York, 1950.

HUIZINGA, J. *The Waning of the Middle Ages.* London, 1924.

INNES, ARTHUR D. *England Under the Tudors.* London, 1905.

JUDGES, E. V. (ed.). *The Elizabethan Underworld.* London, 1930.

JUSSERAND, J. J. *A Literary History of the English People.* 2 vols. in 3. New York, 1895-1909; *English Wayfaring Life in the Middle Ages.* Third ed. London, 1890.

KNAPPEN, M. M. *Tudor Puritanism.* Chicago, 1939.

KNIGHTS, L. C. *Drama and Society in the Age of Jonson.* London, 1937.

LEE, SIR SIDNEY. *The French Renaissance in England.* New York, 1910; *Great Englishmen of the Sixteenth Century.* New York, 1904; *Stratford-on-Avon from the Earliest Times to the Death of Shakespeare.* London, 1907.

MADDEN, D. H. *The Diary of Master William Silence: A Study of Shakespeare and of Elizabethan Sport.* Second ed. London, 1927.

MUIR, KENNETH. *Shakespeare's Sources.* Vol. I. London, 1957. (In progress)

NICHOLS, J. *The Progresses and Processions of Queen Elizabeth.* New ed. London, 1823; *The Progresses, Processions, and Festivities of King James I.* London, 1828.

READ, CONYERS. *Mr. Secretary Walsingham and the Policy of Queen Elizabeth.* Cambridge, 1925; *The Tudors: Personalities and Politics in Sixteenth Century England.* New York, 1936.

SEEBOHM, FREDERIC. *The Oxford Reformers.* London, 1867. Many later editions.

SELLERY, G. C. *The Renaissance.* Madison, 1950.

Shakespeare's England: An Account of the Life and Manners of His Age. 2 vols. Oxford, 1916.

STEPHENSON, H. T. *Shakespeare's London.* New York, 1905; *The Elizabethan People.* New York, 1910.

STOW, JOHN. *Survey of London.* Ed. C. L. Kingsford. Oxford, 1908.

STRACHEY, LYTTON. *Elizabeth and Essex.* London, 1928.

STRUTT, J. *Sports and Pastimes of the People of England.* New ed. London, 1903.

SYMONDS, JOHN ADDINGTON. *Renaissance in Italy.* 8 vols. New York, 1887-1888; 1921-1923.

TAYLOR, HENRY OSBORN. *The Mediaeval Mind.* 2 vols. New York, 1919; *Thought and Expression in the Sixteenth Century.* New York, 1920.

TRAILL, H. D. *Social England.* Vol II: *From the Accession of Edward I to the Death of Henry VII;* Vol. III: *From the Accession of Henry VIII to the Death of Elizabeth.* New York, 1894.

TREVELYAN, G. M. *English Social History.* London, 1942. Now being reissued as *Illustrated Social History.* Vol. I: *Chaucer's England and the Early Tudors.* Vol. II: *The Age of Shakespeare and the Stuart Period.* London, 1949.

WEBB, SIDNEY AND BEATRICE. *English Poor Law History.* Part I. London, 1927.

WHEATLEY, H. B., *London, Past and Present.* London, 1891.

WILSON, J. DOVER. *Life in Shakespeare's England.* Cambridge, 1911.

Bibliographies will be found in *Cambridge Modern History, Cambridge History of English Literature, Shakespeare's England, Cambridge Bibliography of English Literature,* and *A Shakespeare Bibliography* (EBISCH and SCHÜCKING, Oxford, 1931; Supplement, Oxford, 1937).

The Drama Before Shakespeare

At some time between 1585 and 1592 William Shakespeare left Stratford-on-Avon and established himself, apparently in a position of relative importance, in the theater in London. The theater was even then an important institution and was of such complexity that it is necessary for us to inquire into its origin and growth in order to understand the opportunity that it offered Shakespeare and the power, both personal and literary, that it enabled him to achieve. We must consider the origin of the Elizabethan drama as an artistic form, the gradual provision of an adequate physical equipment for the theater and the stage, and the assemblage and organization of the personnel, under proper leadership, into licensed companies of players with effective business management.

MYSTERY PLAYS

From very early times, certainly from the beginning of the fourteenth century, until Shakespeare's own day, there had existed in England what we should call a community drama acted mainly by amateurs.

The most important variety of it had been made up of mystery plays presented usually by craft guilds and telling in varying forms, but with conventional patterns, the story of the Bible, or rather the story of man's creation, fall, redemption, and ultimate judgment as depicted in the church services of the liturgical year. This drama had begun in the ninth century with certain musical variations of the ritual called tropes, which in the course of a century and a half developed into dramatic "offices," special services presenting, still in song, scenes of the Resurrection and the Nativity in the services of Easter and Christmas.

By 1300 these beginnings had grown with the addition of scene after scene into two great dramas, had been transferred—we do not know exactly how— from the hands of the clergy to the hands of the laity, and had been translated gradually from Latin into the modern languages. One of these treated the Passion and the Resurrection, and probably the patriarchs of the Old Testament; and the other, the Messianic prophets, the Nativity, and probably the Last Judgment.

Other church festivals had also developed dramatic offices, or, as they are called, liturgical dramas, dealing with special subjects such as the Conversion of St. Paul, the Life of St. Mary Magdalene, and the Miracles of the Blessed Virgin Mary. The festival of Corpus Christi was established in honor of the Sacrament by the church in 1264 and was carried into

Family worship.
From John Day's "The Whole Psalms in foure partes," *1563. (Folger)*

complete observance in Europe by about 1320. Somewhere in Europe, possibly in England itself, there was invented a significant device for the celebration of the new festival. The Easter and the Christmas group of plays, and possibly plays from other festivals, were combined into a gigantic continuous story, the Corpus Christi play, and were acted on Corpus Christi Day. Its most important subjects were the Creation, the Fall of Man and his Expulsion from Paradise, Cain and Abel, Noah and the Flood, Abraham and Isaac, Moses, the Prophets, the Annunciation, the Visit of the Shepherds and the Magi, the Flight into Egypt

with the Slaughter of the Innocents, Christ before the Doctors, the Entry into Jerusalem, the Betrayal, the Capture, the Trial, the Crucifixion, the Burial with the Setting of the Watch, the Resurrection with the Harrowing of Hell, the Appearances to the Disciples, the Ascension, Pentecost, the Assumption of the Blessed Virgin Mary, the Coming of Antichrist, and Doomsday.

THE CORPUS CHRISTI PLAY

The festival of Corpus Christi seems from the beginning to have called for a procession, and the play was in most places made processional; that is, each scene or group of scenes was put on a movable stage, called a pageant, and was hauled through the streets of the city on Corpus Christi Day. These pageants with their actors stopped at open places in the city where a crowd might assemble, and acted their scenes, one after another in the order demanded by the story as a whole. Any given audience remained stationary.

This practical device brought with it a significant change in staging. Previously, the aggregated play had been performed on a stage of multiple places, where Rome and Jerusalem, Heaven and Hell, Calvary and the Temple, were ranged about the same open space and conventionally understood to be separated by various distances. By mounting only the one or two settings required for a particular scene on a float and conveying it from station to station, the individual mystery play no doubt achieved a superior degree of unity.

The processional play was not universal, however, even in England. In places like Wakefield, where the streets were very narrow, or Lincoln, where they were very steep, the older multiple-place stage was probably retained. In the market place at Wakefield and in the cathedral close at Lincoln, the pageants were ranged in order about the open space and the spectators themselves moved on from scene to scene. They certainly had the multiple-place stage in London and in the south of England, and it was the regular form of the mystery-play stage on the Continent.

Each subject or group of subjects in the Corpus Christi play was assigned to a particular company of artisans or to certain associated companies, who had their own playbook and pageant, and even pageant-house in which to store the pageant. For example, at Coventry the shearmen and tailors for a long time acted the scenes of the Nativity, the Shepherds, the Visit of the Magi, the Flight into Egypt, and the Slaughter of the Innocents. The weavers acted the story of the Presentation of Jesus in the Temple and the Disputation of Jesus with the Jewish Doctors. The texts of both of these plays are preserved. In the former, the *Shearmen and Taylors Pageant*, Herod is a comic character who acts what Bottom in *A Midsummer-Night's Dream* calls "a part to tear a cat in." At the point where the Magi, warned by an angel to depart into their own country by another way, escape Herod's clutches, a quaint stage direction in the play says, "Here Erode ragis in the pagond and in the strete also," a detail which indicates what Hamlet means when he says, "it out-herods Herod." The scenes dealing with the infancy of Jesus, though very crude, are full of sweetness and reverence. The rich mercers' company of Coventry, able to supply clothes and hangings galore, acted the magnificent pageant of the Assumption of the Blessed Virgin Mary. In some other places we find the goldsmiths' company presenting the play of the Magi or "The Three Kings of Cologne," apparently because they were able to supply the necessary crowns and jewels. At Coventry the drapers' company presented the play of the Last Judgment and each year made provision for three "worlds" to be burnt. They had also an earthquake "with a barrel for the same." Among their characters were God, two demons, three white souls, three black souls, two spirits, four angels, three patriarchs, two worms of conscience, a prologue, two "clarks" for singing (one to sing bass), and a Pharisee. Unfortunately the text of this pageant, as well as that of the mercers, has been lost.

The annual Corpus Christi play was a source of municipal pride at Coventry and elsewhere, and of profit also, since it drew crowds of spectators. Royal persons and great noblemen frequently attended. It is recorded, for example, that King Richard III, being at Kenilworth in 1484, came to Coventry at Corpus Christi-tide to see the pageants, rejoicing perhaps in the Slaughter of the Innocents. There were possibly as many as twenty full-scope plays, mostly of the Corpus Christi type, in the kingdom, though the complete texts of only four have been preserved. We have the cycles from York and Chester and two others: the Towneley cycle, almost certainly acted at Wakefield, and *Ludus Coventriae*, possibly acted at Lincoln. There are two pageants, fragments of the full Corpus Christi play, from Coventry, one each from Norwich and Newcastle-on-Tyne, and several other single scenes from places not located.

There is also preserved, in the now extinct Celtic language of Cornwall, an example of another type of religious drama, a great passion play of the form common on the Continent. The passion play, which seems also to have been the type acted at London and in the south of England, centers in the theme of man's redemption and does not contain the scenes dealing with the Nativity. The Cornish cycle includes Old Testament subjects, a circumstance not unusual in the continental passion plays.

MIRACLES AND MORALITIES

The miracle play, also widely current in England, shows a different variety of religious drama, although mystery plays and miracle plays shade off gradually into each other and are not different in origin. Miracle plays, as distinguished from mystery plays, are those which tell the stories of the lives and miracles of saints and martyrs. English records are preserved in considerable numbers of plays on St. Katharine, St.

Laurence, St. Nicholas, and other saints; but the texts of only two or three have been preserved, and they are not representative. To know what went on dramatically in honor of the saints one must study the plays preserved in French. One finds there a variety of saints' plays as well as the great *Miracles de Nôtre Dame*.

Besides these, there was a great group of dramatized allegories of varying lengths, known as moralities. A number of them, such as *The Castle of Perseverance*, *Mankind*, and *Everyman*, are still in existence. Moralities were less offensive to the taste of the Reformation than were mystery and miracle plays, so that they had a better chance to survive. There was, finally, in the late Middle Ages, much miscellaneous dramatic activity, often so casual and ephemeral as to escape record. This included Robin Hood plays, of which examples have been preserved, farces, and other forms of the drama, which have mainly been lost to posterity.

This popular drama, existing for many centuries and carried out over wide areas, must have affected very greatly the moral and religious instruction of the common people. It must have given them a command of a form of literary culture and trained them in dramatic ways of thinking. The plays were so dear to the popular heart that they yielded slowly to the influences of the Reformation and the Renaissance. They had bred a sort of dramatizing habit which expressed itself in the heterogeneous drama of the first nine decades of the sixteenth century, in which we see the old forms of mystery play, morality, and farce undergoing transformation through the influence of tragedy and comedy reintroduced by the Renaissance from Greece and Rome. The old drama in its native sincerity, humor, and realism—all popular qualities—laid an excellent foundation for the Elizabethan drama.

SHAKESPEARE'S KNOWLEDGE OF THE OLD DRAMA

That Shakespeare knew the mystery and morality plays in their old forms is evident from his references, always containing a suggestion of ridicule, to various episodes and characters in them. Herod, who was a blood-and-thunder tyrant in the mystery plays, and Termagant, who figured in a similar role in the play of St. Nicholas, appear together in Hamlet's advice to the players (*Hamlet*, III, ii, 14-16). Shakespeare compares Falstaff (*1 Henry IV*, II, iv, 498) to the Manningtree ox, a reference which seems to show knowledge of the Manningtree fair, if not of the Manningtree morals, and it is Falstaff himself who remarks contemptuously of Justice Shallow, "And now is this Vice's dagger become a squire" (*2 Henry IV*, III, ii, 343). The Vice, the principal clownish character in the moralities, was armed with a dagger of lath. The language of "that reverend vice, that grey iniquity, that father ruffian, that vanity in years" as well as "that old white-bearded Satan" (*1 Henry IV*, II, iv, 500-509) certainly recalls the morality plays. Again Falstaff is reported to have likened a flea on

Bardolph's nose to a black soul burning in hell-fire (*Henry v*, II, iii, 42-44), which may well be an allusion to the play of the Last Judgment.

Shakespeare had opportunity to see the old plays, for the Corpus Christi play was performed annually at Coventry, only fourteen miles from Stratford, until he was sixteen years old. It is no extravagant guess that he joined the throng of those who attended the play at the chief city in Warwickshire. In some places in England the Corpus Christi play continued to be performed until after the beginning of the seventeenth century in spite of the fact that such plays were obviously "blasted with antiquity." Shakespeare was a child of his time and therefore looked with amusement, if not contempt, on these old-fashioned folk practices. He and his colleagues in the theater were absorbed in the new art of the Renaissance. His picture of the play of "Pyramus and Thisbe" presented by the "rude mechanicals" in *A Midsummer-Night's Dream* furnishes an indication of his point of view. The grotesqueness of the old technique is revealed by the delicacy of Ovid's tragic little tale.

EARLY TUDOR DRAMA

If Shakespeare began his work as a playwright about 1590, the Tudor drama had come well into line with the standards of the Renaissance before he began, and several great Elizabethan dramatists had already made their appearance. However, these things had not occurred very long before his time. Sixteenth-century drama is in general a drama of transition and experiment. With the exception of certain definite imitations, or translations of imitations, of ancient comedy and tragedy, sixteenth-century drama from the reign of Henry VII to the last twenty years of Elizabeth's reign (that is, approximately from 1485 to 1585) consists of what were and are rather puzzlingly called interludes. These are plays made up in varying proportions of native elements from the

moralities, from the dialogue or *débat*, from the farce, and even from the mystery and miracle plays, more or less imperfectly reshaped according to the models of classical or romantic tragedy and comedy.

Other countries in Europe were undergoing, or had undergone, somewhat the same process of transformation in their drama, and a new drama had sprung up in imitation of classical comedy and tragedy. The English copied this and at the same time translated and imitated the classics themselves. Since both the originals and the new continental drama were equally available, it is not always easy to tell whether we have to do with direct imitations of the works of Plautus and Terence, the Latin comedy writers, and Seneca, the writer of Latin tragedy, or with continental adaptations and imitations of these authors. In any case, it was the inferior Latin drama which was imitated and not the superior drama of Greece. In spite of these influences, however, Elizabethan drama was not destined to follow closely in the path of the classics. Perfection of form, conventionality, and restraint—qualities which we call classical—did not commend themselves to the enterprising, ebullient, and sentimental Elizabethans. In building their drama, freedom of fancy in conception and treatment, variety, adventure, and vigor if not extravagance of sentiment pleased them better, and we call their drama romantic.

In the shaping of the English drama of the Renaissance the amateur element is relatively large. Schools and colleges, their masters and graduates, felt most strongly the new influence coming in from the Continent and were the first to write and act the new drama. The Tudors themselves were proponents of Renaissance culture, and royal entertainment was a chief occasion for the composition and production of drama. *Ralph Roister Doister*, written by Nicholas Udall, headmaster of Eton College and later of Westminster School, is a scholastic play imitative of Terence and intended probably to please the royal

Pipes and ale.
From Philip Stubbes'
"Anatomy of Abuses,"
1583. (Folger)

taste. *Gammer Gurton's Needle* originated at Cambridge at about the same time. *Gorboduc, or Ferrex and Porrex*, written by Thomas Sackville and Thomas Norton, two young law students of the Inner Temple, and acted before Queen Elizabeth on January 18, 1562, is Senecan and voices the Senecan craze of Italy and all Europe. Seneca, the most romantic of the ancients, satisfied the taste of the Renaissance, since he was, in spite of his classical manner, cosmopolitan, sententious, passionate, and sensational.

Such plays as the three just mentioned, and there were many of them, were written by educated men largely for royal and noble entertainment and were acted in royal palaces, the houses of noblemen, the dining halls of colleges, and, when they got into the hands of professional actors, in the courtyards of inns. The staging was thus to some extent impromptu. Schoolboys had been acting plays for perhaps a century before Queen Elizabeth was crowned. The Children of the Royal Chapel are known to have presented plays as early as 1506. The boys of St. Paul's School acted before King Henry VIII in 1528. Boys of other schools also gave theatrical performances. The Children of the Royal Chapel and the Children of Paul's were later organized into professional companies and have a long dramatic history. Schoolmasters and choirmasters became the first professional playwrights. Early Tudor drama and the contemporaneous continental drama are colored by their scholastic origins. For example, there is a collection of Latin plays called *Dramata Sacra*, published at Basle in 1547, which exercised great influence in England.

The great diversity of the early Tudor drama may be more easily illustrated than defined. The influence of the Continent is present in the school plays, which show the process of adapting native themes to Latin models, a process which had gone on more rapidly on the Continent than in England. Some plays on biblical subjects, like *Godly Queen Hester*, *Jacob and Esau*, and *King Darius*, were certainly derived from the scholastic drama of the Continent rather than from an English dramatic impulse, as is also true of certain plays on heroic subjects such as *Apius and Virginia*, *Damon and Pithias*, and *Calisto and Meliboea*. At the same time there were native survivals of medieval techniques. Bishop John Bale wrote *Kynge Johan* and many dramas on religious themes quite according to the old technique of the mystery plays. *Kynge Johan* is not a history play; it is, rather, the mystery play of *Antichrist* rewritten to serve as a controversial document against Catholicism. The play was so named because tradition had misrepresented King John as an antagonist of the pope. John Skelton's *Magnificence* is merely a morality play. Lewis Wager's *Life and Repentance of Mary Magdalene* is a most interesting combination of mystery and morality. John Heywood, several of whose plays are French farces, wrote some which are merely dialogues. The mawkish and ridiculous *Cambises* by Thomas Preston, "a la-

mentable tragedie mixed full of pleasant mirth," is poetically and dramatically as crude as the mystery play of Noah.

As Tudor drama developed, it preferred to draw its themes from ancient writers, like Ovid, and from the Bible or from allegory. Italy supplied a number of bright comedies after the Roman model. *The Supposes*, translated from the Italian poet Ariosto by George Gascoigne, supplied the minor plot for both *The Taming of a Shrew* and *The Taming of the Shrew*; *Bugbears* is a jolly play translated from Grazzini's *La spiritata;* and there are others directly out of the Italian.

The Tudor interlude is therefore indefinable. It is merely a name applied to a disconnected and varied body of survivals, borrowings, and sporadic beginnings. The only group of dramatists which had any cohesion is made up of Henry Medwall, John Rastell, and John Heywood; and even this cohesion was due not so much to similarity of dramatic work as to association with the circle of Sir Thomas More. Medwall was the author of a morality called *Nature*, which is not without poetic interest, and a romantic drama, *Fulgens and Lucrece*. Both of his plays were printed by John Rastell, with whom he was associated, like More, in the service of Cardinal Morton. Rastell, who married More's sister, certainly was the author of the moral interlude of the *Four Elements* and probably of *Gentleness and Nobility*. John Heywood, son-in-law of John Rastell, was the most important and versatile dramatist of the group. All his plays except *Witty and Witless*, which has been preserved in manuscript, were printed by John Rastell or his son William Rastell. Heywood's plays form a really delightful group of significant variety. There are among them three small comic interludes, scarcely more than dialogues in form: *The Play of Love*, *The Play of the Wether*, and *Witty and Witless*. In the second of these a gentleman, a merchant, a forest ranger, a water-miller, a wind-miller, a gentlewoman, a launderer, and a small boy ("the least that can play"), all in turn petition Jupiter to send them the kind of weather that each would like to have. Of course they do not agree, so that Jupiter has to send what he pleases. There are also three farces—*The Pardoner and the Friar; John, Tib, and Sir John;* and *The Four PP*—which are of a more robust nature, so that the latest commentator thinks they were done under the manly influence of Sir Thomas More.

The really significant contribution made by the Heywood group is Medwall's *Fulgens and Lucrece*, which foreshadows the sentiment and humor characteristic of Lyly, Peele, and Shakespeare. It has been suggested also that Medwall adapted and compiled *Calisto and Meliboea* on the basis of the Spanish comedy *Celestina;* if so, he was likewise carrying on the traditions of the romantic drama. The dramatization of romantic story with little discrimination between comedy and tragedy is the central feature of Elizabethan drama. This fact was demonstrated by the late C. R. Baskervill,[1] who discovered fifteenth- and earlier sixteenth-century records of the dramatization of such stories in considerable numbers. The early and continued existence and the ultimate triumph of romantic drama on the English stage change our conception of the subject. The Tudor interlude, made up so largely of Plautus, Terence, and Seneca, consists in an attempt, not ultimately successful, to remake English native drama along classical lines. Although the romantic drama prevailed in the end, the attempt to reshape it was not without influence and is so interesting in and for itself as to be universally regarded as the history of the pre-Shakespearean drama. In point of fact, the central stem or core of the art form was vigorous throughout and finally gave us Shakespeare and most of his contemporaries.

EARLY COMEDY

Among the really important achievements of the sixteenth century are two comedies already casually mentioned, *Ralph Roister Doister* and *Gammer Gurton's Needle*. Both show the influence of Latin comedy, and both arose from the practice in the sixteenth century of schoolmasters presenting the comedies of Plautus and Terence, or comedies imitated from them, on stages in their schools with their scholars as actors. *Ralph Roister Doister* is the work of Nicholas Udall, and was acted probably by the boys of Westminster School between 1552 and 1554. It is perhaps the first play in English in which there is a clearly constructed plot, a rapid dialogue, and a set of characters so conceived as to furnish a dramatic clash. To be sure, the characters are to some degree modeled on Plautus and Terence, but they are sufficiently adapted to their English situation to bring the comedy through satisfactorily. It is still amusing to see on the stage. Roister Doister is a conceited braggart who pays court to a virtuous lady, Dame Custance, not for herself but for her thousand pounds. He cannot imagine being refused by her. Her refusal, when it comes, is couched in a letter which the ingenuity of his rascally servant Matthew Merrygreek construes, by changing the punctuation of clauses, into an acceptance. Roister Doister advances upon his lady-love but is routed in warlike fashion by the lady and her maids.

Gammer Gurton's Needle was shown by the late distinguished scholar, Henry Bradley, to be the work of William Stevenson, fellow of Christ's College, Cambridge, and to date probably from almost exactly the same time as *Ralph Roister Doister*. It is a secular comedy in English, the only one of its kind preserved, and has about it a roaring farcical quality which suggests the English village of the sixteenth century in

all its naturalness. It is much slighter in plot than *Roister Doister;* it is, in fact, a farce and not a comedy, but it was done by a man who knew the movement of Latin comedy, and is, as a piece of literature, far superior to Udall's piece. A needle in the sixteenth century was, we may believe, a precious possession. Gammer Gurton loses her needle while mending her servant's breeches. A lively search is instituted for its recovery. She suspects various people in turn of stealing it. She carries on for five acts; in the fifth and last act Hodge, her servant, painfully finds the needle in the seat of his breeches when he receives a blow. The play contains a song, a feature which was to become characteristic of English comedy:

> I cannot eat but little meat;
> My stomach is not good;
> But sure I think that I could drink
> With him that wear'th an hood.
> Drink is my life; although my wife
> Some time do chide and scold,
> Yet spare I not to ply the pot
> Of jolly good ale and old.
>
> *Back and side go bare, go bare;*
> *Both hand and foot grow cold;*
> *But, belly, send thee good ale enough,*
> *Whether it be new or old.*

EARLY TRAGEDY

In the establishment of comedy on the English stage, even in its characteristic romantic form, there was no battle of the critics in behalf of classical principles. Plautus and Terence contributed their share of technique, in the matter of comic devices and scenes, in plot, and in the matter of characterization. They were the ultimate models of Jonson and his school in the comedy of manners; but, because comedy was a freer dramatic *genre* than tragedy, the comic dramatists, liberally and without reproach, added their sentiment to the Romans' wit. But there was an essential clash between classical tragedy and the native sort, and it was necessary to invent a new kind of tragedy, or at least to shape into more ordered form romantic stories of tragic import. The most important of the differences between classical and romantic (or Elizabethan) tragedy arises from the fact that the latter chose to tell a complete story while the former contented itself merely with the climax. This is, of course, only roughly true, but it may be said to hold by and large that the classical mode concerned itself mainly with what an Elizabethan tragedy would have embodied in the fifth act. The rest of the story, so far as it needed to be known, was presented in the form of narrative. It follows that, in classical tragedy, narrative interest is subordinated to dramatic or lyrical interest.

Most of the plots of the tragedy of the Greeks and Romans were entirely familiar to the audiences for whom they were written; the stories were already well known in literature and in mythology, which to Greeks and Romans was religion. A tragedy was thus

[1]"Some Evidence for Early Romantic Plays in England," *Modern Philology*, XIV (1916), 229-251, 467-521; also "Conventional Features of Medwall's *Fulgens and Lucrece*," ibid., XXIV (1927), 419-442. See also *Fulgens and Lucrece: A Fifteenth-Century Secular Play by Henry Medwall*, F. S. Boas and A. W. Reed, ed. (Oxford, 1926), Introduction.

exploitation of a great event. Oratory, poetry, music, and philosophic comment, the latter usually from the mouths of a chorus, all united to produce a single great effect. Unity was thus the most striking quality of classical tragedy, and, when the tragedy was revived and restudied in the Renaissance, was regarded as all-important. Unity, which had been more or less an inevitable characteristic of classical tragedy, was understood by the dramatic critics of the Renaissance to mean not only unity of action, but unity of time and place, and even unity of sentiment, so that the element of comedy was theoretically excluded from tragedy because it was thought to destroy the perfection of tragic tone. These are the views, not of the ancients themselves, but of Renaissance commentators on Aristotle; and these commentators failed to understand that the three unities, as they conceived them, cannot be preserved if a sweep of epic material is presented, and that there is a different and a broader type of unity possible even when complete narratives are treated.

SIR PHILIP SIDNEY: DRAMATIC CRITIC

There is a possibility that romantic tragedy would never have developed in England to so high a point or been accepted as the standard form of tragedy but for two things: in the first place, very few Elizabethan dramatists knew how to write classical tragedy; and, in the second, the Elizabethan audience, with a taste for native English drama, demanded new, varied, sensational plots accompanied with clownage and vaudeville in the shape of songs and special features. Such drama was condemned by well-informed persons for following popular taste rather than classical models, but to make it comply with classical rules would have meant changing its nature. In France, where in Shakespeare's time the drama came into the control of the court and the learned classes, tragedy developed according to classical rules into the drama of Corneille and Racine; but in England, fortunately for the world, Shakespeare and his fellows made a virtue of their necessities and created, no doubt against their better judgment, the new form of romantic tragedy. Neither they nor their critics knew exactly what the issues were. The most famous classical reformer was Sir Philip Sidney. He has given us his views in a very charming book called *The Defence of Poesie*, written in 1581 or slightly later. One can see from the following passage how he looked at the English drama of his day:

Our tragedies and comedies not without cause cried out against, observing rules neither of honest civility nor of skilful poetry, excepting Gorboduc—again I say of those that I have seen. Which not withstanding as it is full of stately speeches and well-sounding phrases, climbing to the height of Seneca's style, and as full of notable morality, which it doth most delightfully teach, and so obtain the very end of poesy; yet in truth it is very defectious in the circumstances, which grieves me, because it might not remain as an exact model of all tragedies.

For it is faulty both in place and time, the two necessary companions of all corporal actions. For where the stage should always represent but one place, and the uttermost time presupposed in it should be, both by Aristotle's precept and common reason, but one day; there is both many days and many places inartificially imagined.

But if it be so in Gorboduc, how much more in all the rest? where you shall have Asia of the one side and Afric of the other, and so many other under-kingdoms, that the player, when he cometh in, must ever begin with telling where he is, or else the tale will not be conceived. Now ye shall have three ladies walk to gather flowers, and then we must believe the stage to be a garden. By and by we hear news of shipwreck in the same place, and then we are to blame if we accept it not for a rock. Upon the back of that comes out a hideous monster with fire and smoke, and then the miserable beholders are bound to take it for a cave. While in the meantime two armies fly in, represented with four swords and bucklers, and then what hard heart will not receive it for a pitched field?

Now of time they are much more liberal. For ordinary it is that two young princes fall in love; after many traverses she is got with child, delivered of a fair boy; he is lost, groweth a man, falleth in love, and is ready to get another child,—and all this in two hours space; which how absurd it is in sense even sense may imagine, and art hath taught, and all ancient examples justified, and at this day the ordinary players in Italy will not err in. . . .

Later he tells us that English plays are "neither right tragedies nor right comedies," but that they mingle clowns and kings with "neither decency nor discretion."

This merrily written criticism presents an excellent picture of the conditions prevailing upon the English stage when Sidney wrote, and, as criticism from a strictly classical point of view, it is perfectly just. But after all, it is just as easy for an audience to imagine the lapse of a period of twenty years with its concomitant changes as to imagine the lapse of a period of two hours. And if an audience is willing so far to grant any author "that willing suspension of disbelief for the moment which constitutes poetic faith," as Coleridge puts it, that they will believe one scene in the theater is in Asia instead of London, they will be equally willing to believe in the same way that another scene following it is in Africa. Human emotion, moreover, is sufficiently mobile to switch itself quickly from a serious to a comic theme and back again. In human emotion the comic, the pathetic, the grotesque, and the tragic often blend and reinforce each other in the most inexplicable ways, so that Shakespeare and his fellows seem to have had nature as well as native bias on their side. No doubt the steady and monotonous pressure of an emotion born of fear, as in classical French tragedy, will finally break through the deadness which it generates and triumph over its victim; but certainly there is another and a quicker road to emotional intensification. The effect of alternately making and breaking the line of suspense, whether by a frustrated hope of escape or by mere diversion, usually results, not in annoyance or in loss of interest, but in heightened or heightening feeling.

In other words, recurrence is more poignant than continued strain.

EARLY SENECAN TRAGEDY

The tragedy of *Gorboduc*, praised by Sidney, is an interesting work in the history of the English drama. The play was written in the Senecan manner, the first three acts by Thomas Norton and the last two

An Elizabethan hanging.
Illustration from a ballad in the Pepysian Collection.

by Thomas Sackville, for performance before the queen at Whitehall in 1562. For the first time in English tragedy, it employs blank verse, a dignified and yet flexible measure. *Gorboduc* is also a forerunner of the chronicle play, since it deals with the mythical history of Britain as told by Geoffrey of Monmouth in *Historia Regum Britanniae*. The authors wished to impress upon the queen the necessity of immediate marriage, so that England might be saved from the disorder and confusion arising from a condition in which there were rival claimants for the crown. Not only, therefore, is *Gorboduc* a forerunner of *Tamburlaine*, the first great English tragedy, in the use of blank verse and in the maintenance of a serious tragic tone; but in its use of the chronicles and its pursuance of a patriotic purpose, it is also a forerunner of the history play. In 1587 eight gentlemen of Gray's Inn, led by Thomas Hughes and including Francis Bacon, presented before the queen a drama similar in form to *Gorboduc*, namely, *The Misfortunes of Arthur*. It violates the unities, as does *Gorboduc*, but it differs from *Gorboduc* in borrowing from Seneca not only chorus, messengers, and machinery, but ideas, sentiments, and words. *The Misfortunes of Arthur* again resorts to the chronicle history of Britain, which became one of the chief sources of the subject matter of English tragedy.

Another principal source of tragic themes was the Italian short story, which, because it was also impassioned and serious, offered to writers of tragedy many themes. *Gismond of Salerne* dramatizes a well-known Italian tale, and, like *Gorboduc* and *The Misfortunes of Arthur*, is Senecan in form and nature. It was acted before the queen in 1568. In the same magazine of narrative, Shakespeare was later to find his sources for *Romeo and Juliet* and *Othello* and for such tragi-comedies as *The Merchant of Venice* and *Measure for Measure*.

JOHN LYLY'S INFLUENCE

In facing the problem of understanding just what Elizabethan drama was and how it became what it was, we are forced to recognize that the classification of drama into comedy and tragedy by the ancients does not tell the whole story. Even when we add the history or chronicle play to these two divisions of drama, we have at best a rough classification which leaves out a great deal and implies that these three forms were sharply discriminated. In point of fact Elizabethan drama is, generally speaking, a blend of many elements. Nearly all Elizabethan tragedies have in them comic scenes and by-plots; most comedies have in them serious issues, which might conceivably result in disaster; and history plays are often, to all intents and purposes, capable of being classified as comedies or as tragedies. It seems well, therefore, to consider the varied works of a number of dramatists whose practice was successful on the stage and who influenced Shakespeare and his immediate contemporaries. Of these, John Lyly is one of the most important.

John Lyly (1554?-1606), an Oxford man who also studied at Cambridge, acquired fame by a single stroke—by the publication in 1579 of the famous and influential book *Euphues, the Anatomy of Wit*. One of the curiosities of literature, it stands as the most sensational and brilliant effort in the struggle of English prose to acquire a conscious artistic manner. The style, as far as the author could achieve such a thing, is made up wholly of devices. He makes use of antithesis, personification, rhetorical question, metaphor and simile, and above all of balance reinforced by alliteration. *Euphues, the Anatomy of Wit* and its sequel, *Euphues and his England*, which came out in 1580, were ardently followed by dozens of writers, including Robert Greene and Thomas Lodge, and seem to have set a new fashion of smart speech in the court of Queen Elizabeth. "Euphuism" itself had a vast influence on the style of the drama and other literature both in poetry and in prose.

Euphues and its sequel are made up of the slight adventures and the interminable discussions and letters of a seeker after true education and culture. They borrow facts, illustrations, and ideas from Plutarch, Pliny, Guevera, and many other writers, and may be said to embody the materials of Renaissance culture in the form of a handbook for the courtier, the lover, the traveler, and the statesman. They served to make the favorite ideas of the Renaissance current among ordinary educated men and women, and the expression of them conscious and adequate. The material of Shakespeare's thought and of the thought of his time was disseminated by this means, and a greater sensitiveness to style became apparent; the writing of prose was no longer a matter of muddling through without a standard, but was revealed as an individual thing which each writer might achieve for himself in his own way. As for the actual fad of euphuistic speech, Shakespeare joins with those who ridiculed it; but, none the less, there are qualities in *Love's Labour's Lost*, *A Midsummer-Night's Dream*, *As You Like It*, and elsewhere which could not have been as they are but for Lyly.

Lyly also influenced drama directly, since he was the author of at least eight comedies. They were written to suit the taste of the court and were possibly all acted before the queen by the children of the Chapel Royal or of St. Paul's School. These comedies are sufficiently Plautine to indicate that the characteristic features of Latin comedy had by this time (1580-1590) become naturalized on the English stage. *Mother Bombie*, like Shakespeare's *The Comedy of Errors*, is a fairly close adaptation of Latin comedy. The stock figures of Latin comedy, such as the pedant, the rascally servant, the duped parent, the parasite, and the aged lover, are there; but usually in the comic parts of all Lyly's plays he reminds us not so much of the Latin comedy as of the earlier English rough clownage. T. W. Baldwin argues that Lyly owes his five-act structure to the influence of Terence.

However much Lyly may recall classical Latin comedy, he is most important as the inventor of a gay and fanciful type of comedy which found its high point in such plays as Shakespeare's *A Midsummer-Night's Dream* and *As You Like It*. Lyly's *Sapho and Phao*, *Endymion*, and *Midas* have romantic plots derived from Ovidian mythology, made more delightful to Elizabeth's court by the embodiment of topical allegory. Three others, *Gallathea*, *Love's Metamorphosis*, and *The Woman in the Moon*, are pastoral comedies— that is, comedies whose characters are shepherds and shepherdesses after the tradition of the ancient Arcadia. *Gallathea* has the realistic sort of pastoralism. The scene is laid in Lincolnshire, just as one suspects that the scene of *As You Like It* is laid in Warwickshire. Two maidens are disguised as boys, and a good deal of the mythology, like that in *A Midsummer-Night's Dream*, is manufactured for the occasion.

The Woman in the Moon is written in verse; all the rest of Lyly's plays are in prose, which is, of course, euphuistic. But here the euphuism is turned to a purpose; it brightens the plays. The style is suited to dialogue and gives it a pungency and even a naturalness as dramatic conversation which the drama had hitherto lacked. It has been thought that Lyly learned something about the true sound of dialogue from the *Colloquies* of Erasmus, a much used schoolbook for

Title page of the 1615 edition of Kyd's "Spanish Tragedie." (Folger)

Latin classes; and it is also possible that he may have learned a great deal of the new comic method he followed from the *Dialogues* of Lucian, which he knew. In any case, Lyly's followers in the drama learned much from him about the writing of dialogue.

GEORGE PEELE, FORERUNNER

Another author who contributed to the romantic and poetical tone of Shakespearean comedy was George Peele (1558?-1597), whose *Arraignment of Paris*, written about 1581 in varied and brilliant blank verse, is one of the most delightful things of its time. Peele follows Virgil, as Lyly followed Ovid, and connects himself with the spirit of Spenser's *Shepheardes Calender*. He shows knowledge of the famous French group of poets headed by Clement Marot and known as the Pleiades. Fortunately Shakespeare, as the immediate follower of Lyly and Peele, and subjected to the same influences as they, began his work early enough to catch the fine imaginative fervor of the poets and dramatists of the decade from 1580 to 1590.

ROBERT GREENE, FORERUNNER

Another of the striking figures of this decade is Robert Greene (1558-1592), a man whose dissolute and yet romantic impatience with the ways of the world became his own destruction. His undoubted talent and immense energy expressed themselves in a dozen love stories in euphuistic prose, largely based on the Greek novel. This novel comes not from the great times of the Greek drama and Greek philosophy, but mainly from the second, third, and fourth centuries A.D., when the Greeks had been long under Roman rule and were scattered round the shores of the Mediterranean. The Greeks were the merchants, traders, sailors, and schoolmasters of the Roman Empire, and this earliest form of the prose romance reflects the adventurous life which they lived. Such romances, as written by Heliodorus, Achilles Tatius, and others, are made up of a succession of strange and often improbable adventures, chance meetings, piracies, children exposed in infancy and restored grown and beautiful to their parents, families separated and reunited, indistinguishable twins, and many of the plot devices rendered familiar to us in the literature of the Renaissance; for the Renaissance, in its thirst for antiquity, did not distinguish between this kind of sensationalism and the real classics.

From the Greek novel, and also no doubt from his own experience in life, Greene got the new conception of woman which the world has learned from Shakespeare. The society depicted by the Greek novel gave women great liberty, and like them Greene's heroines are independent, witty, resourceful, and boylike, though at the same time feminine. Greene's dramas are almost the first modern productions in which woman is in any degree represented as assuming her station as the friend and companion of man.

The Greek novel itself had a large element of the pastoral, and here again we find a parallel in Greene. His plays, particularly *James IV* and *Friar Bacon and Friar Bungay*, give us that blend of the pastoral and the romantic which the world has enjoyed in *As You Like It* and *Love's Labour's Lost*. Greene must be regarded as the first great master of plot in the English drama.

Toward the wretched end of his life Greene wrote many pamphlets, some about London roguery, some about his own hard usage at the hands of the world. In one of the latter, *A Groatsworth of Wit Bought with a Million of Repentance* (1592), he gave us our first personal reference to Shakespeare, a circumstance which must engage our attention later. It should be pointed out that it was not only Shakespeare who felt the influence of Greene, but Munday, Dekker, and most of the popular dramatists of the next decade.

THOMAS KYD, FORERUNNER

While romantic comedy was being shaped and developed in the hands of Lyly, Peele, and Greene, the Senecan tradition was finding its proponents on the popular stage, which had chosen just the parts of Senecan tragedy that were suited to its purpose. This appears from a large number of crude native dramas which display the Senecan element of intensity and sensationalism while they still retain clownage and disorderly action. It remained for the genius of Thomas Kyd (1558-1594) to seize upon the essentials of Senecan action and adapt them to conditions on the English stage. His *The Spanish Tragedy* (1583-1584?), a stirring melodrama in blank verse and the pattern of subsequent revenge plays, was acted perhaps a thousand times during the next fifteen years. Kyd caught the unabashed brutality and horror of Senecan story and revealed it openly. Instead of having the action reported as taking place off the stage, he presented it. For tales of Greek mythology he substituted a modern story of love, conspiracy, murder, and political intrigue. He retained the Senecan ghost, the revenge motive, the spirit of stoicism, and a modified form of the chorus. He tells the tale of the revenge of Hieronimo, whose son, Horatio, had been seized and hanged in the garden of his father's house by Balthazar, his rival in love, and Lorenzo, his enemy in politics. Hieronimo feigns insanity and waits for his revenge. Ultimately, in a masque which he had written for the entertainment of the court, Hieronimo plays a part and in deadly earnest stabs his enemies, who likewise were actors in the tragic masque. Probably Kyd is also the author of the first dramatic version of the story of Hamlet, an important circumstance to be treated later.

CHRISTOPHER MARLOWE

Kyd's work gave rise to a series of revenge plays not only in his own time, but later, in 1600 and the years following, when the revenge tragedy again became fashionable. Moreover, Kyd seems to have had a shaping influence on Greene and on Christopher Marlowe (1564-1593). *The Spanish Tragedy* probably preceded by three or four years Marlowe's *Tamburlaine*, which is conjecturally dated 1587. In blank-verse style Kyd was, therefore, the forerunner of Marlowe, whose *Jew of Malta* (c. 1589) in its extravagance and sensational intrigue seems to follow *The Spanish Tragedy*.

From the title page of Joseph Swetnam's
"The Schoole of the Noble and Worthy Science of Defence," *1617.*

Gambling in a brothel
during the time
of Elizabeth.
From Philip Stubbes'
"Anatomy of Abuses,"
1583. (Folger)

Nevertheless, however much Kyd may have contributed in matters of style and form, the fact remains that Marlowe became the leader in the great romantic type of Elizabethan tragedy. He is the one who shaped the *genre* subsequently perfected by Shakespeare. This he achieved by giving the English drama a hero more striking even than Hieronimo and by centering dramatic interest in personality and character; for the aspiring spirit of the Renaissance finds expression in Marlowe's heroes. Tamburlaine has a thirst for world conquest; Dr. Faustus would go to the utmost bounds of knowledge and the power which knowledge gives; and Barabas in *The Jew of Malta* sets no limit to his longing for wealth. Back of Marlowe lies the hero worship of the times, which had expressed itself in a taste for ballads and romances and in plays from medieval romance, a veritable worship of deeds. There is little idea of structure or tragic conflict in *Tamburlaine*. It was enough for the Elizabethan playgoer to behold the Scythian warrior proceeding from conquest to conquest and to hear him "threatening the world with high astounding terms." The plot is merely a series of episodes.

The same is true of *Dr. Faustus* (*c.* 1588), so far as the theme itself would permit merely successive action; but Faustus sells his soul to the common enemy of mankind, and, when the day of payment comes, the situation of Faustus becomes tragic. In the last scene of the play, therefore, Marlowe reaches the first high point in the structural progress of English tragedy in the concrete representation of the struggle of a human soul. The play is thus a series of episodes enveloped by a tragic theme. In *The Jew of Malta* Marlowe treats a melodramatic plot, but makes no use of the tragic principle of the conflict of characters. Whether he makes use of this principle in *Edward II* (*c.* 1592) is a matter of doubt. In that play Marlowe does not center the interest in the psychology of one character only, as in the earlier plays, but introduces a succession of characters in opposition to his hero. The protagonist or leading figure of tragedy Marlowe had reinvented, and he needed only to embody his adversative forces in one character to have the antagonist also.

It is doubtful whether the principle of the interplay of two characters, one upon another, was hit upon by anybody before Shakespeare. In *Richard II* Shakespeare has, in the person of the king, a great central figure whom he exploits after the Marlowan fashion; but, possibly because his plot was so much like that which Marlowe had used in *Edward II*, he placed over against King Richard the contrasting figure of Bolingbroke and thus discovered that principle which he was later to use in Othello and Iago and in whole groups of contrasting characters as they appear in *Julius Caesar*, *King Lear*, and other plays. *Richard III* and *Henry V* are dramas of Marlowan technique, that is, in the prominence given a central eloquent figure, and so even is *Hamlet*, though, of course, the epic quality which comes from Marlowe is much slighter in *Hamlet* than in the others.

Even if Marlowe himself never consciously employed the principle of dramatic conflict, he gave to English tragedy its realization of character and still more its dignity and seriousness. Marlowe, educated at Cambridge, was a good scholar and a born poet. He gave to the English drama the aspiration of the Renaissance. Shakespeare was to be followed by a group of realists and satirists, but fortunately—let it be said again—he was early enough in his appearance to catch the enthusiasm for beauty which Spenser and Marlowe had. Not the least among Marlowe's gifts to English drama is a new and more flexible blank-verse style. In this matter he was conscious of what he was doing. In the following familiar lines which constitute the prologue to *Tamburlaine the Great*, Part I, it will be seen that Marlowe does not treat each blank-verse line as a separate unit, but runs the sense on from line to line and produces what might be described as a blank-verse paragraph, a thing most necessary to drama if it was to represent widely varying emotions, thoughts, and characters:

> From jigging veins of rhyming mother wits,
> And such conceits as clownage keeps in pay,
> We'll lead you to the stately tent of war,
> Where you shall hear the Scythian Tamburlaine
> Threat'ning the world with high astounding terms,
> And scourging kingdoms with his conquering sword.
> View but his picture in this tragic glass,
> And then applaud his fortunes as you please.

This is not only the pronunciamento of tragic seriousness; it is also, in spite of its elevated style, one of the first examples in English tragedy of vigorous, natural, straightforward expression. Tamburlaine in his utterances is a typical Renaissance poet on the themes of both love and war; and the following lines, almost as familiar to students of the English drama as those just quoted, will express the insatiable quality of Marlowe's aspiration:

> If all the pens that ever poets held
> Had fed the feeling of their masters' thoughts,
> And every sweetness that inspir'd their hearts,
> Their minds, and muses on admired themes;
> If all the heavenly quintessence they still
> From their immortal flowers of poesy,
> Wherein, as in a mirror, we perceive
> The highest reaches of a human wit;
> If these had made one poem's period,
> And all combin'd in beauty's worthiness,
> Yet should there hover in their restless heads
> One thought, one grace, one wonder, at the least,
> Which into words no virtue can digest.
> —*Tamburlaine*, Pt. I, V, ii, 98-110

One feels that but for Marlowe Shakespeare might not have talked so bravely about "the young-eyed cherubins" or the "lights that do mislead the morn."

ELEMENTS OF TRAGEDY AND COMEDY IN SHAKESPEARE

Shakespearean tragedy is thus to be described roughly as a combination of Marlowe and Kyd: poetry, character, and style from Marlowe; motive, plot, and tragic intensity from Kyd. It was for Shakespeare himself in some of his great plays, such as *Richard II*, *Julius Caesar*, *Othello*, and *King Lear*, to make tragic action spring from tragic motive. One cannot say that Shakespeare was conscious of the thing he was doing. He was "holding the mirror up to nature" and showing "virtue her own feature, scorn her own image, and the very age and body of the time his form and pressure." He achieved the perfect union of action and character in the first instance possibly because it resided in certain stories which he chose to tell, such as that of Hamlet or of Richard II. Great art does not need to be conscious of its ways. All that one can say of Shakespeare and Aristotelian tragedy is that sometimes, when Shakespeare is telling a story of universal human significance, he does exemplify Aristotelian principles. Greene and many others sought to imitate Marlowe in tragedy

with but indifferent success. Shakespeare was Marlowe's only successful imitator, and he bettered Marlowe by humanizing him and rendering more natural those very qualities for which he was indebted to him.

Likewise the elements of Shakespearean comedy are in part derivative from Lyly, Peele, and Greene. The contributions of Lyly and Peele were those of style, setting, and movement. Greene, primarily a writer of romance, an adapter of the Greek novel, furnished the element of love and adventure which makes so many Elizabethan plays delightful merely as stories; and, although there are not many women in comedy and tragedy who illustrate the type, one acknowledges that it was Greene who put upon the stage the witty, independent-minded woman, usually in boy's clothes, who gives point and naturalness to love intrigue whether in serious drama or in comedy. Not only did Shakespeare, who was a far greater genius than any of them, combine the elements of the comedies of these men and better the instruction, but, as his career went on, he realized on a broad scale the possibilities of the comic point of view in the representation of human life and character. Atmosphere in his comedies reinforces plot, and plot gives rise to character. Even the simple episodic clownage of his predecessors becomes organic in his hands and contributes to the total artistic effect he chooses to produce.

All in all, we find Shakespeare falling heir to a form which through three centuries of religious drama had become endeared to the tastes of the popular mind, and which had, in the early sixteenth-century interlude, undergone a process of development at the hands of conscious creators. This traditional pattern, improved by the skill of the later dramatists and infused with new spirit by his immediate predecessors, offered to Shakespeare an instrument which under his touch became a transcendent artistic medium for the depiction of human emotions and experiences. Shakespeare became not only the greatest of romantic dramatists, but the greatest of dramatists.

REFERENCES

ADAMS, J. Q. *Shakespearean Playhouses*. Boston, 1917.
BALDWIN, T. W. *William Shakspere's Five-Act Structure*. Urbana, 1947.
BENTLEY, G. E. *The Jacobean and Caroline Stage*. 6 vols. Oxford, 1941-1956.
BOAS, F. S. *Shakspere and his Predecessors*. London and New York, 1896; *An Introduction to Tudor Drama*. Oxford, 1933; *University Drama in the Tudor Age*. Oxford, 1914.
BOND, R. W. *Early Plays from the Italian*. Oxford, 1911.
BROOKE, C. F. TUCKER. *The Tudor Drama*. Boston, 1912.
CHAMBERS, SIR E. K. *The Mediaeval Stage*. 2 vols. Oxford, 1903; *The Elizabethan Stage*. 4 vols. Oxford, 1923.
CRAIG, HARDIN. *English Religious Drama of the Middle Ages*. Oxford, 1955.
CREIZENACH, W. *The English Drama in the Age of Shakespeare*. London, 1916. This is translated from the fourth

volume of the writer's comprehensive and important *Geschichte des neueren Dramas*, 1893-1916.

CUNLIFFE, J. W. *Early English Classical Tragedies.* Oxford, 1912.

GARDINER, H. C. *Mysteries' End: ... Last Days of the Medieval Religious Stage.* New Haven, 1946.

GREG, W. W. *A List of English Plays written before 1643 and printed before 1700.* Bibliographical Society, 1900; *A list of Masques, Pageants, etc..* Bibliographical Society, 1902; *A Bibliography of English Printed Drama to the Restoration.* Vol. I. London, 1939, in progress; *Pastoral Poetry and Pastoral Drama.* London, 1906.

LEA, KATHLEEN M. *Italian Popular Comedy.* 2 vols. Oxford, 1934.

LUCAS, F. L. *Seneca and Elizabethan Tragedy.* Cambridge, 1922.

PARROTT, THOMAS M., and R. H. BALL. *A Short View of Elizabethan Drama.* New York, 1943.

REED, A. W. *Early Tudor Drama.* London, 1926.

SCHELLING, F. E. *Elizabethan Drama.* 2 vols. Boston, 1908; *The English Chronicle Play,* New York, 1902; *English Literature during the Lifetime of Shakespeare.* New York, 1910. Other works by the same important author.

STOPES, MRS. C. C. *The Life of Henry, Third Earl of Southampton.* Cambridge, 1922. Other works by the same author.

STRATMAN, C. J. *Bibliography of Medieval Drama.* Berkeley and Los Angeles, 1954.

Texts of the plays will be found in the following works:

ADAMS, J. Q. *Chief Pre-Shakespearean Dramas.* Boston, 1924.

BRANDL, ALOIS. *Quellen des weltlichen Dramas in England vor Shakespeare.* Strassburg, 1898.

DODSLEY, ROBERT. *A Collection of Old English Plays,* edited by W. C. Hazlitt, 1874-1876.

GAYLEY, C. M. *Representative English Comedies.* 3 vols. New York, 1903-1914.

Malone Society Reprints. 1906 ff.

MANLY, J. M. *Specimens of the Pre-Shakespearean Drama.* 2 vols. Boston, 1897.

Materialien zur Kunde des älteren englischen Dramas. Louvain, edited by W. Bang, 1902-1915; 1926 ff.

Mermaid Series. *The Best Plays of the Old Dramatists.*

POLLARD, A. W. *English Miracle Plays, Moralities and Interludes.* Seventh ed. London, 1923.

Student's Facsimile Edition. *Old English Plays,* 1909-1914, edited by J. S. Farmer.

Tudor Facsimile Texts. Edited by J. S. Farmer, 1909-1913.

WHITE, H. O. *Plagiarism and Imitation during the English Renaissance.* Cambridge, Mass., 1935.

Most of the remains of the mystery and morality plays have been edited for the Early English Text Society: The Towneley plays, the Chester plays, *Ludus Coventriae* or Hegge plays, and the two fragments of the true Coventry plays, the non-cycle plays, the Digby plays, and the Macro morals. The York plays were edited for the Clarendon Press by Miss Lucy Toulmin Smith in 1884, and the ancient Cornish cycle was published with a translation by E. Norris in 1859.

Mention should also be made of the modern collected editions of Shakespeare's early contemporaries; as J. Churton Collins' *Greene,* F. S. Boas' *Kyd,* R. W. Bond's *Lyly,* R. H. Case's *Marlowe,* R. B. McKerrow's *Nashe,* A. H. Bullen's *Peele.*

London Theaters and Dramatic Companies

Throughout Shakespeare's life the propriety of acting any plays at all was a matter of bitter controversy. Indeed, when one considers the power and earnestness of the opposition, one is surprised that there could come into being such a wealth of dramatic excellence, and that Shakespeare's plays should reflect so little the bitterness of the controversy waged in his time.

RELIGIOUS AND MORAL OPPOSITION TO THE THEATER

The Puritans objected to the plays because they thought them immoral. The Puritan city of London was naturally the headquarters of this opposition. By an order of the Common Council of London, dated

From the title page of "The famous game of Chess-play," 1614.

December 6, 1574, the players were driven out of the city. The order cites the reasons. The players, it was charged, had been acting in the innyards of the city, which in consequence were haunted by great multitudes of people, especially youths. These gatherings had been the occasions of frays and quarrels, "evil practices of incontinency in great inns"; the players published "uncomely and immodest speeches and doings," withdrew the queen's subjects from divine service on Sundays and holidays, wasted the money of "poor and fond persons," gave opportunity to pickpockets, uttered "busy and seditious matters," and injured and maimed people by engines, by the falling of their scaffolds, and by weapons and powder used in plays. The order goes on to state the Common Council's fear that if the plays, which had been forbidden on account of the plague, should be resumed, God's wrath would manifest itself by an increase of the infection. Therefore, no innkeeper, tavernkeeper, or other person, might cause or suffer to be openly played "any play, interlude, comedy, tragedy, matter, or show" which had not been first licensed by the mayor and the court of aldermen.

The mayor and aldermen did not always state their case plainly, because Queen Elizabeth was a patron of the players, and because the players had friends and patrons in the Privy Council and among the nobility; sometimes, however, they did so quite boldly. One sees the case against plays stated syllogistically in the following words of Thomas White, a preacher at Paul's Cross in 1577:

Looke but vppon the common playes of London, and see the multitude that flocketh to them and followeth them: beholde the sumptuous Theater houses, a continuall monument of London prodigalitie and folly. But I vnderstande they are now forbidden bycause of the plague. I like the pollicye well if it hold still, for a disease is but bodged or patched vp that is not cured in the cause, and the cause of plagues is sinne, if you looke to it well: and the cause of sinne are playes: therfore the cause of plagues are playes.[1]

Moved, no doubt, by the prohibition of the Common Council, James Burbage, with a company of actors under the patronage of the earl of Leicester, leased a site in Shoreditch, a London suburb in Middlesex, beyond the immediate jurisdiction of the official enemies in the Common Council, whose authority extended only to the city limits. By 1576 he had completed the Theatre. In general, this building was patterned after the innyard, being open to the sky and having galleries round about like the porches and balconies of the innyard, with a stage at one side and dressing rooms back of it. Because he expected that the same building would be used for bearbaiting and bullbaiting, Burbage made it circular in form. The Theatre thus became the model for the public playhouses such as the Curtain, the Swan, and the Globe which were constructed later.

Burbage had in this manner availed himself of that immunity from the enforcement of law which arises from indirect jurisdiction. The city fathers could not suppress plays nor control them with perfect success if they were performed in Middlesex or on the famous Bankside across the Thames in Surrey. In order to get at them in these suburban regions it was necessary to petition the queen's Privy Council to give orders to the magistrates and officers of the law in these counties. The queen's Privy Council, although always on the most polite terms with the Lord Mayor and his brethren of the city and always open to the argument that the assemblage of crowds caused the spread of the plague, were to a much less degree in sympathy with the moral scruples of the city. There were, moreover, current arguments for the plays, derived from the works of scholars, poets, and playwrights; namely, that there was precedent in antiquity for dramatic spectacles; that by drawing a true picture of both the bad and the good in life, plays enabled men to choose the good; that the people should have wholesome amusement; and that plays provided livelihood for loyal subjects of the queen.

[1] From A Sermon preached at Paules Cross . . . in the time of the Plague. (1578).

Of these arguments the Privy Council made little use, resting the case for plays on what was no doubt an unanswerable argument—that, since the players were to appear before Her Majesty, the players needed practice in order to prepare themselves to please the royal taste. There was a good deal of politic fencing over the whole matter, and, so far as orders, complaints, and denunciations were concerned, the Puritan opposition had much the better of it. The preachers thundered against plays. Pamphleteers denounced all matters pertaining to the stage: Stephen Gosson in The Schoole of Abuse, Containing a pleasaunt invectiue against Poets, Pipers, plaiers, Iesters and such like Caterpillars of a Commonwealth (1579) and other works; Philip Stubbes in The Anatomie of Abuses (1583); and finally and most furiously of all, William Prynne in Histrio-Mastix: the Players Scourge or Actors Tragedy (1633). Gosson spoke of plays as "the inventions of the devil, the offerings of idolatry, the pomp of worldlings, the blossoms of vanity, the root of apostacy, food of iniquity, riot and adultery." "Detest them," he warns. "Players are masters of vice, teachers of wantonness, spurs to impurity, the sons of idleness."

Since such extreme bitterness is hardly warranted by what we know of the Elizabethan drama or the men who created it, we look for an explanation of the Puritan opposition in the not unexpected quarter of political and religious partisanship. Though the subject matter of plays had become somewhat less biblical and their connection with any branch of the church was broken, they were associated from their origin with the old religion; therefore, to have the people cling to them was, in the minds of Puritan leaders, to have them cling to idolatry and adopt the fashions of the Catholic Continent. Because of their banishment from the city and from the favor of the more godly classes of people, plays and players were thrown into bad company. Shoreditch and the Bankside were low and vicious regions. Plays were patronized by the idle and the ungodly. Fortunately they were also patronized by the queen, the highest nobility, and by many cultivated and intelligent persons. In spite, however, of the strength and viru-

London Theaters and Dramatic Companies

27

A judicial complaint.
From Philip Stubbes' "Anatomy of Abuses," 1583. (Folger)

lence of the opposition, the theater flourished. One does not know just how it managed to do so.

THE PUBLIC THEATERS

A year or more after Burbage built the Theatre, the Curtain was put up near it by Philip Henslowe, or possibly by Henry Laneman, or Lanman. About ten years later Henslowe built the Rose, the first playhouse on the Bankside. The Swan was built there in 1594. In 1599 Richard and Cuthbert Burbage, sons of James Burbage, the former being the great actor of Shakespeare's heroes, tore down the Theatre because of trouble about the lease of the land and rebuilt it as the Globe on the Bankside. This Globe was the theater that burned June 29, 1613, from cannon wadding which set fire to the roof after the discharge of ordnance during the acting of a play called *All is True*, thought to be identical with Shakespeare's *Henry VIII*. The Globe was rebuilt, probably in octagonal form. In 1614 Henslowe built the Fortune, specifications for which have been preserved at Dulwich College with the other invaluable papers of the old theater manager. This college, it may be said in passing, was founded by the munificence of the great actor Edward Alleyn, who had married Henslowe's stepdaughter.

Henslowe's Fortune Theatre was apparently a countermove to the activities of the Burbage group, who constituted a joint stock company for the support of the king's company, whereas Henslowe operated as theater proprietor. He managed the Lord Admiral's men and secured, we may be sure, a large part of the profits of their activities. The contract for building the Fortune was let to the same contractor who had built the new Globe, and, since it was specified that it should be like the Globe in all its main features, except that it was to be square instead of octagonal, we may gain from these specifications an idea of the Globe. This circumstance is not altered by I. A. Shapiro's argument that the new as well as the old Globe was round and not octagonal. There is also preserved a drawing of the Swan, a Bankside theater, which accompanies a description of the playhouse by Johannes De Witt, who visited London in 1596. The drawing, which was discovered in the University Library at Utrecht, is the work of one Van Buchell and may be based on drawings by De Witt himself. Besides these there are two or three little pictures of the Elizabethan public stage on the title pages of published plays, the most important being that on the title page of William Alabaster's *Roxana* (1632).

THE PUBLIC STAGE

From these documents and pictures and from scattered references to the theaters, as well as from extended studies of stage directions and scenic conditions in plays themselves, it has come about that we have a fairly clear idea of the public stage. Its features are these: a pit, usually circular and open to the sky; surrounding this, galleries in three tiers, where were

the most expensive seats; a rectangular stage, longer than it was broad, sometimes on trestles, so that it could be removed if the house was also customarily used for bearbaiting and bullbaiting. Part of the stage was covered by a sort of wooden awning, which might constitute "the heavens." At the back of the stage was a partition wall with at least two doors opening out of the actors' dressing rooms. Between these two doors a

Title page from William Alabaster's "Roxana," 1632. (Folger)

third opening, probably wide and curtained off, led to the rear-stage, a recess ordinarily used for interior scenes, such as bedchambers, grottoes, caves, and tombs. An arras, or curtain, was stretched along the back wall, just how far from it one cannot tell. Over the inner-room behind the stage was a gallery used for city walls, upper windows, and all sorts of high places. Above this, in turn, arose a turret from the top of which a flag was hung out when a play was about to begin, and from which, for further advertisement, a trumpeter blew three blasts to announce the opening of the performance.

There still are unanswered questions about the staging of Elizabethan plays. For example, though some of the seats most prized by the spectators were those in the gallery behind the stage, it is hard to perceive how such persons could have seen and heard while the recess was in use or while action was going on under the canopy. One does, however, get an excellent idea of the general conditions and, particularly, of how the Elizabethan public stage got along with the same scenic conditions as those of the miracles and morality plays, namely, actors on a central platform and the audience around them on every side. From such a situation we can understand the close intimacy between the actor and the audience, some of whom possibly sat on the stage, and the consequent opportunities as well as difficulties which were before the dramatist.[2]

This public stage of the London theaters represents a development, through intermediate adaptations for innyard performances, from the early pageants of the religious drama. When the players of Tudor interludes resorted to innyards to act their plays in towns and cities, they carried with them two general features from the medieval stage: a stage of three dimensions, like the individual pageants of the Corpus Christi plays, and a central multiple stage like that shown in the famous drawings of *The Castle of Perseverance*, in which the play was performed in a central area with the spectators seated or standing around it, or like that on which the passion play at Valenciennes was acted in 1547.[3] This stage, presenting two or more separate places, was originally an out-of-doors stage with a central playing "place" and various *loca* or *sedes* for particular minor actions. In other words, features from both the pageant stage and the multiple stage were used in the interlude as acted in innyards. The innyard stage was later adopted by James Burbage for use in the Theatre.

THE COURT STAGE

Meanwhile, another type of stage, for which some, at least, of Shakespeare's plays were written to be performed, found favor in London. This was the so-called court stage, one designed for indoor performance and set up in a hall or, in later times, in a roofed-in theater. Indirectly it was a development from the ancient classical theater, at least as regards a fixed structural background, which suggested, if it did not enforce, unity of place. This type of stage came to England from Italy, where there had been preserved, or rather regained, some knowledge of the ancient stage. Such changes of scene as the Italian drama

allowed were provided for by the introduction of properties or possibly by labels over the fixed structures at the rear. These fixed structures provided background, essentially a classical element.

The problem in which the European stage was engaged for centuries was not, however, continuity of scenes, but change of scenes. France and most of the Continent had, during the Renaissance, accepted the medieval solution of the difficulty by adopting a multiple stage, like that of *The Castle of Perseverance*, in which the audience was asked to believe for the purpose of the drama that a series of independent structures within a few feet of each other represented places as far apart as Rome and Jerusalem, or Heaven and Hell. This stage, as naïve as the games of children, had been used in all European countries in the Middle Ages, and was apparently accepted without difficulty. There are cases in the Corpus Christi play where two or more quite distant places were conceived of as being located on different parts of the same pageant wagon. Sidney and others who knew the classical drama felt deeply the absurdity of this convention, but the convention maintained its hold; scenes representing more than one place appear in Tudor drama and even in Shakespeare more than once. An instance occurs in the fifth act of *Richard III*, where the tents of the rival commanders, Richard and Richmond, are conventionally located on opposite sides of the same narrow stage. Although the convention is usually not so apparent as here, the principle continued in the wide use of the unlocated scene, which was simply a "general" scene descended from the *platea*, or unlocated middle area, of the medieval stage. The stage managers, however, brought up trees through the trap, let down thrones or gallowses, and carried in tables, chairs, or even beds, and thus by suggestion, gave a location to the general scene. On the public stage, scenes were continuous and the division into acts merely provided pauses in the performance.

Such changes of scene as could be provided for by changes in the background were possible only on the court stage. We know certainly that for the court stage, "houses" made of lath and canvas were erected, analogous to the *case* of the Italian stages. Certain features of the public stage had, however, been borrowed from the court stage, such as the two side doors with a central aperture and the rear tapestry, or arras, sometimes painted in perspective with attempts at foreshortening to represent the houses of a city street. All such fixation of background indicates continental influence. Oxford, Cambridge, and London had many direct connections with Italy by which such influences could become effective. Italian plays were translated and Italian players visited England. There may also have been slighter Italian influences from France, into which Italian elements had made their way.

The court stage, then, brought with it certain features of another set of theatrical conditions dif-

---

[2]On the many perplexities connected with both the public and the court stages, see F. E. Schelling, *Elizabethan Drama*, Vol. II, ch. iv, and the references there given; also G. P. Baker, *The Development of Shakespeare as a Dramatist*, pp. 75-76, *et passim;* Chambers, *Elizabethan Stage*, Vol. IV; G. F. Reynolds, *The Staging of Elizabethan Plays, passim.*

[3]Brander Matthews, *A Study of the Drama* (1910); and Gustave Cohen, *Le Théâtre en France au Moyen Âge* (Paris, 1928), Vol. I, plate xl.

ferent from those of the native traditional stage. However, it did not bring them very perfectly into England. This deficiency is due, no doubt, to two factors. In the first place, the hall or court drama in its most primitive form was probably acted simply on the floor of a hall with the more noble guests looking down on it from a raised dais, the inferior guests moving aside to give it room. The convenient custom of placing actors on the platform or dais must quickly have established itself. It was so in the early Black-friars and, of course, in the halls of schools and colleges. On the other hand, the public theaters, like the Globe, had pretty thoroughly established scenic conventions before the roofed-in theaters like Black-friars were very much used. English tradition, as we have seen, followed the statuesque type of stage which was to be looked at from all sides like a group of statuary. The continental stage was more picture-like and was to be looked at from the front only.

It must not be thought that the continental stage succeeded widely in England or played a large part in Shakespeare's staging; but it was known, ad-vocated, and had a certain influence both on the form of the stage and on the drama. When Polonius speaks of "scene individable, or poem unlimited," he is recognizing the continuity of action in one place, which was admired in Shakespeare's time, and which Shakespeare himself respects up to a certain point in most of his comedies. The great matter, to be sure, is that all of these theatrical conditions affected Shake-speare; for no dramatist, whether Shakespeare, Sophocles, or Molière, can be entirely independent of stage conditions, and no dramatist can be properly appreciated unless one understands what parts and qualities of his work are there because of the neces-sities which conditioned him in the telling of his dramatic story. Influences of the continental stage were, of course, felt in the staging of the Jacobean masque and were increasingly important in drama itself as the seventeenth century went on.

LONDON COURT THEATERS

The important court theaters of Shakespeare's London were two in the precinct, or "liberty," of Blackfriars, an early one in Whitefriars about which little is known, a later one there, and a theater at Paul's, the exact location and nature of which is not known. In the thirteenth century, the mother house in the Dominican friars, or Blackfriars, was established on the sloping ground between St. Paul's Cathedral and the river. It was a great institution, which ultimately covered about five acres of ground. It stood on the very border of the city, and, after the custom of the time, was made a liberty; that is to say, it had its own local government and was removed from the immediate jurisdiction of the city of London. After the suppression of the friary and the confiscation of its lands, the jealousy existing between the Privy Council, representing the crown, and the

THE NOBLE ARTE OF
VENERIE OR HVNTING.

VVherein is handled and set out the Vertues, Nature, and Pro-perties of fiuetene sundrie Chaces together, with the order and maner how to Hunte and kill euery one of them.

Translated and collected for the pleafure of all Noblemen and Gen-tlemen, out of the best approued Authors, which haue written any thing concerning the same: And reduced into such order and proper termes as are vsed here, in this noble Realme of England.

Title page from a book by George Gascoigne, 1575. (Folger)

mayor and aldermen, representing the city and probably also the rights of property holders, pre-vented the district of the Blackfriars from losing its political independence of the municipality. It was still a liberty and, therefore, offered a fair chance for the encroachments of play-lovers upon those who regarded theaters as sinful abominations. Also Black-friars no doubt gathered into its precincts many persons whose activities were slightly beyond the pale of the law; but there were also aristocratic residents in the region who demanded protection, and the crown had certain rights still in its control.

From 1576 to 1584 the Children of the Queen's Chapel, one of the two most important companies of boy actors, had used a hall in the precinct of Black-friars in which to act their plays. Here were acted some, at least, of Lyly's plays and also Peele's *Arraign-ment of Paris*. In 1596 James Burbage purchased property in this precinct and seems to have spent a good deal of money in its adaptation for use as an indoor theater. He probably appreciated its advan-tages over Cripplegate or the Bankside, particularly for use in winter. But the aristocratic residents of the Blackfriars by petition to the Privy Council pre-vented him from making use of his theater. Plays within the city proper had only recently been finally and successfully prohibited, and the petitioners no doubt objected to their intrusion into Blackfriars on the grounds that they and their crowds were a nuisance.

Burbage's new indoor theater may have lain idle from the time of its preparation until 1600; but, in any case, in that year it became the scene of many plays. It was let by lease to a group of men for the use of the Children of the Chapel, who in 1604 became the Children of the Queen's Revels. These theater managers brought into their service a number of new dramatists, Jonson, Marston, Chapman, and later Webster; the vogue of the plays acted by the Children of the Chapel was so great as to damage the patronage of the established companies and to compel them to go on the road. Out of this rivalry between the children and the adult actors arose that "War of the Theaters" alluded to in *Hamlet* (II, ii). In 1608 the Burbage interests secured the evacuation of the lease, so that the theater in Blackfriars became the winter playhouse of Shakespeare's company from that time forward.

SYSTEM OF PATRONAGE

In 1572 common players of interludes, along with minstrels, bearwards, and fencers, were included within the hard terms of the act for the punishment of vagabonds, provided that such common players were not enrolled as the servants of a baron of the realm or of some honorable person of greater degree. The result was the system of patronage of theatrical companies in Elizabethan and Jacobean times, according to which players became the "servants" of some nobleman or of some member of the royal family.

There were in existence before Shakespeare came to London more than a dozen of these companies, some of them long antedating the passage of the act of 1572. In the provincial records of the visits of players to various towns and cities it is sometimes difficult, however, to tell whether we have to do with actors or with acrobats, since other public performers, as well as players, were similarly organized. At any rate, we may say that there were in London about the time that Shakespeare arrived there companies of players under the patronage of the queen, the earl of Worcester, the earl of Leicester, the earl of Oxford, the earl of Sussex, the Lord Admiral, and Charles Lord Howard of Effingham. The companies were gradually to be very greatly reduced in number, so that there were usually only three adult companies acting in London during Shakespeare's prime. In addition to these were the children's companies, privately controlled, acting intermittently, but at times very successfully. The most important of these were the Children of the Chapel and Queen's Revels and the Children of Paul's; but there were also boy players of Windsor, Eton College, The Merchant Taylors, Westminster, and other schools.

SHAKESPEARE AND THE LORD
CHAMBERLAIN'S COMPANY

In the first mention of Shakespeare as an actor and in all subsequent notices of him in that capacity, he is associated with the group of men originally under the patronage of the earl of Leicester. It is probable, then, that he joined that group when he first came to London and remained with them throughout his career. This supposition is strengthened by the consideration that, if he served an apprenticeship as an actor, which along with his fellow actors he may have done, there would have been no reason for mentioning him until he became a full-fledged member of a company. His obscurity during the period from about 1585 to 1592 would thus be accounted for. The first mention of Shakespeare indicates that he was a member of a company in 1594, and, if one subtracts the seven years' apprenticeship period from about 1592, one accounts for the "seven dark years." If he began his work as a playwright before his apprenticeship was over, as he may well have done, his career would be normal and intelligible. It has been ordinarily thought that the earl of Leicester's men formed the nucleus of a company which was reconstructed under the patronage of Lord Strange about 1590-1591 and that was known after September 25, 1593, as Lord Derby's men. In 1594 this in turn probably became the new company of the Lord Chamberlain of which Shakespeare was a member when he was first mentioned.

But the matter is somewhat complicated. In 1594 the theatrical companies had for four or five years been greatly disturbed in their membership, so that there is much likelihood that the Lord Chamberlain's company of 1594 was made up of various elements. Shakespeare's apprenticeship, if he served one, may, therefore, have been in some other company besides that successively under the patronage of the earl of Leicester, Lord Strange, and the earl of Derby, supposing that this nucleus was in a true sense continuous. The important features of the alignment of 1594 are these: A company with Edward Alleyn as its principal actor and the Lord Admiral as its patron reconstructed itself to act in Henslowe's theaters; and a company with Richard Burbage as its principal actor and the Lord Chamberlain and later King James as its patrons reconstituted itself as an independent stock company to act at the Theatre, the Globe, and the Blackfriars. Thus were the two great rival companies formed—the first mentioned was already illuminated through the activities of its great tragedian, Edward Alleyn, acting in the plays of Marlowe and Greene, and was henceforth to be served by the dramatists Dekker, Chettle, Drayton, Munday, and Middleton; and the second, then less popular, was subsequently to become far the more important through the activities of the great tragic actor, Richard Burbage, and through the plays of Shakespeare, Jonson, and Beaumont and Fletcher. This latter company had, besides Burbage, for whom Shakespeare wrote his great tragic parts, John Heminge, or Heminges, Augustine Phillips, Will Kemp, Henry Condell, and a number of other competent actors.

SHAKESPEARE PROBABLY NOT A MEMBER OF LORD PEMBROKE'S COMPANY

We owe to J. Q. Adams and other recent writers on Shakespeare the interesting and, on some grounds, plausible argument that Shakespeare was first associated with Lord Pembroke's company. This theory is based on the belief that two of his plays, *Titus Andronicus* and *1 Henry VI*, as well as several other plays which he subsequently rewrote, were originally in the repertory of Lord Pembroke's company.

The following piece of stage history also bears on this question. It happens that for Lord Strange's company we have for the year 1592 particularly full records. During this year it was acting in one of the theaters—the Rose or Newington Butts—owned and operated by Philip Henslowe, who left behind him his famous *Diary*, found in the papers of his son-in-law, Edward Alleyn, at Dulwich College. This diary is a sort of journal or account book in which Henslowe entered sums of money taken in at the plays and amounts paid for various manuscripts or lent on account to various actors and dramatists. Of the plays of Shakespeare which are believed to have been written before 1594, not one is certainly mentioned by Henslowe as acted by Lord Strange's players during their engagement with Henslowe in 1592; nor does Shakespeare's name appear in two different lists which have been elsewhere preserved of the members of Lord Strange's company. Henslowe, however, does mention a play of "harey the vj," which has sometimes been thought to indicate a connection with Shakespeare, and a play of "Tittus and Vespacia," thought without sufficient reason to be *Titus Andronicus*. Also, three plays associated with Shakespeare's name, *Titus Andronicus*, *The Taming of a Shrew*, and a *Hamlet* (probably an early play on the same subject as Shakespeare's masterpiece) were, according to the *Diary*, acted in Henslowe's theater during the brief period in 1594 in which the Lord Chamberlain's company was acting in conjunction with the Lord Admiral's men. All three were probably old plays, and although they were new to Henslowe's theater he does not mark them, according to his cus-

tom, as "ne." They had not appeared when Lord Strange's men were acting with Henslowe in 1592. Shakespeare may have brought them in from elsewhere into the newly formed Lord Chamberlain's company, but it is a matter of doubt.

FURTHER DETAIL ABOUT THE PEMBROKE PLAYS

Although publishers were eager enough to issue them, plays did not ordinarily get into print unless the company found it no longer profitable to act them, or unless the owners disposed of them to the printers in some unusual circumstances. It happens that several plays which had evidently belonged to Lord Pembroke's company were printed in 1594, some of which are plays connected with Shakespeare's name. The company, which had started out prosperously about 1590 with Marlowe as chief dramatist and the earl of Pembroke as generous patron, fell into adversity. All plays in London were, at the end of June 1592, stopped by order of the Privy Council because of riots among London apprentices. Before the theaters could open again the plague made its appearance, and plays were again interdicted for a period of nearly two years, except for a little while in December and January, 1592-1593. We know from a letter from Henslowe to his son-in-law Alleyn, dated September 28, 1593, that the earl of Pembroke's company, which like other companies had taken to the road, failed in their tour of the provinces and were obliged to pawn their property:

As for my Lord Pembroke's [men], which you desire to know where they be, they are all at home, and have been these five or six weeks, for they cannot save their charges with travel, as I hear, and were fain to pawn their apparel.

We hear no more of that company. Its players found new connections, and its repertory of plays was apparently sold. The Lord Chamberlain's men seem to have obtained some of them, for they are later played by this company; and the printers procured, probably in part at least by purchase from members of the disbanding company, also a number of plays, including *The First Part of the Contention betwixt the Two Famous Houses of York and Lancaster* and *The*

A contemporary view of London Bridge, by John Norden. (Folger)

True Tragedy of Richard Duke of York,[4] plays on the same subjects as *2* and *3 Henry VI*, respectively. It is stated on the title page of *The Taming of a Shrew* (1594) and of *Titus Andronicus* (1594) that these plays had been acted by Lord Pembroke's men, the latter being said also to have been acted by the servants of the earl of Derby, the earl of Sussex, and the Lord Chamberlain. The ownership of *Titus Andronicus* was probably in dispute, a circumstance which may account for its publication. There were thus published as acted by Lord Pembroke's men, poor versions of certain plays with which Shakespeare is thought to have had some connection; but the more important plays which he had by this time written, such as *Love's Labour's Lost*, *The Two Gentlemen of Verona*, *Romeo and Juliet*, and *Richard III*, were neither printed nor mentioned. They may have been taken over by the Lord Chamberlain's men (if Shakespeare joined that company first in 1594), or may have continued in their possession (if he had already been associated with that company). Shakespeare's plays were thus pretty well protected from the publishers, and several of even the earliest ones did not see the light in printed form until the issue of the First Folio in 1623.

Adams does not contend that Shakespeare, if he belonged to Lord Pembroke's unfortunate company, went on the road with them; but rather that he stayed behind and occupied himself as a poet, writing, in the romantic manner then fashionable, *Venus and Adonis* and *The Rape of Lucrece*, and possibly the *Sonnets*, or some considerable part of them. The case then for Shakespeare's membership in Lord Pembroke's company or Lord Strange's company is by no means clear, and some scholars have seen evidence for his affiliation with the queen's players or those of the earl of Sussex.

REFERENCES

ADAMS, JOHN C. *The Globe Playhouse*. Cambridge, Mass., 1942.

ADAMS, J. Q. *Shakespearean Playhouses*. Boston, 1917.

ALBRIGHT, VICTOR. *The Shakespearian Stage*. New Edition. New York, 1926.

BALDWIN, T. W. *The Organization and Personnel of the Shakespearean Company*. Princeton, 1927; article "Posting Henslowe's Accounts," *Journal of English and Germanic Philology*, XXVI (1927), 42-90.

CAMPBELL, LILY B. *Scenes and Machines on the English Stage during the Renaissance*. Cambridge, 1923.

CHAMBERS, SIR E. K. *The Elizabethan Stage*, Bks. III and IV.

FEUILLERAT, A. *Documents relating to the Office of the Revels in the Time of Queen Elizabeth* (Materialien xxi), 1908. Other publications by the same author.

FLEAY, F. G. *A Chronicle History of the London Stage, 1559-1642*. London, 1890.

GRAVES, T. S. *The Court and the London Theaters during the Reign of Elizabeth*. Chicago, 1913; also, "Notes on Puritanism and the Stage," *Studies in Philology*, XVII (1921), 141-169, and other magazine articles by the same author.

Henslowe's Diary. Edited by W. W. Greg, London, 1904-1908; *The Henslowe Papers*, by the same editor, London, 1907.

HILLEBRAND, H. N. *The Child Actors*. Urbana, 1926.

HODGES, C. W. *The Globe Restored*. London, 1953.

LAWRENCE, W. J. *The Elizabethan Playhouse and Other Studies*. Stratford-upon-Avon, 1912, 1913; *The Physical Conditions of the Elizabethan Public Playhouse*. Cambridge, 1927.

MATTHEWS, BRANDER. *A Study of Drama*. Boston, 1910.

MURRAY, J. T., *English Dramatic Companies, 1558-1642*. 2 vols. London, 1910.

NICOLL, ALLARDYCE. *The English Theatre: A Short History*. London, 1936; *The Development of the Theatre*. 3rd ed. New York, 1946.

ORDISH, T. F. *Early London Theatres*. London, 1894.

POEL, W. *Shakespeare in the Theater*. London, 1913.

REYNOLDS, G. F. "Some Principles of Elizabethan Staging," *Modern Philology*, II, 581-614; III, 609-907; *The Staging of Elizabethan Plays at the Red Bull Theater, 1605-1625*. New York, 1940.

SCHELLING, F. E. *Elizabethan Drama*, as above.

SHAPIRO, I. A. "The Bankside Theatres: Early Engravings," *Shakespeare Survey* I (Cambridge, 1949), pp. 25-37; "An Original Drawing of the Globe Theatre," *Shakespeare Survey* II (1949), pp. 21-23.

SHARPE, ROBERT. *The Real War of the Theaters*. Boston, 1935.

THOMPSON, E. N. S. *The Controversy between the Puritans and the Stage*. New Haven, 1903.

THORNDIKE, A. H. *Shakespeare's Theater*. New York, 1916.

WALLACE, C. W. *The Children at Blackfriars*. Lincoln, Nebr., 1908.

The Order of Shakespeare's Plays: His Dramatic Development

The plays of Shakespeare in the first collected edition (the First Folio, published in 1623) are arranged in three groups—Comedies, Histories, and Tragedies, with no recognition of the order of their composition. The first comedy is *The Tempest*, which is known to be one of the very latest plays; the second is *The Two Gentlemen of Verona*, one of the very earliest. The Histories are arranged in order of the English kings whose reigns they treat, although it is obvious that Shakespeare did not write them in this order. There is no discoverable order in the arrangement of the tragedies. If we are to understand Shakespeare, we must view him as a whole, or, as we say, come to a knowledge of his development. Since this cannot be done if his work is studied as a conglomerate of isolated plays, we must see what scholars have discovered about the order in which Shakespeare wrote his plays and the methods which they have followed in their investigations.

---

[4]P. Alexander, *Shakespeare's "Henry VI" and "Richard III"* (Cambridge, 1929). These plays were long thought of as early versions of *2* and *3 Henry VI* and were usually attributed to Marlowe. It has lately been argued convincingly that these plays are too faulty to be attributed to any competent playwright and that they must have come into existence by being written down mainly from memory by actors who had played parts in *2* and *3 Henry VI*; and that the plays are, therefore, to be regarded as "reported" versions of Shakespeare's play.

EXTERNAL EVIDENCE

Eighteen of the thirty-six plays in the First Folio had been previously published singly at various dates in quarto form. The remaining eighteen were published for the first time in the First Folio. *Pericles* was not included in the First Folio, but existed only as a quarto until its inclusion in the Third Folio of 1663-1664. All the quarto editions, except *Romeo and Juliet* and *Love's Labour's Lost*, appear in the Register of the Stationers' Company of London; and two, *As You Like It* (1600) and *Antony and Cleopatra* (1608), which were not printed in quarto, are entered there, this step having been taken, possibly, to forestall publication by printers who had no right to them. The date of entry of a play in the register indicates that by that time the play was at least in existence. The quarto editions have also certain information on their title pages regarding date, author, and publisher, and sometimes tell what theatrical company had acted the play.

Since we know something of the history of the companies, it not infrequently happens that we can infer something as to the date of the play from that knowledge. References to the performance of certain plays have been found in diaries, journals, and accounts; there are also quotations from plays and allusions to them in various literary works. There are a few complimentary references to Shakespeare as a dramatist and poet which allude to his plays, such as John Weever's sonnet *Ad Gulielmum Shakespeare* (1599), which refers to "Richard" and "Romeo." The most important of these references is an enumeration, in a book called *Palladis Tamia, or Wit's Treasury*, by Francis Meres, of plays Shakespeare had written by 1598, the date at which the book was published. The enumeration was probably not intended to be complete.

> As the soule of *Euphorbus* was thought to liue in *Pythagoras:* so the sweete wittie soule of *Ouid* liues in mellifluous & hony-tongued *Shakespeare*, witnes his *Venus and Adonis*, his *Lucrece*, his sugred Sonnets among his priuate friends, &c.
> As *Plautus* and *Seneca* are accounted the best for Comedy and Tragedy among the Latines: so *Shakespeare* among yͤ English is the most excellent in both kinds for the stage; for Comedy, witnes his *Gentlemen of Verona*, his *Errors*, his *Loue labors lost*, his *Loue labours wonne*, his *Midsummers night dreame*, & his *Merchant of Venice:* for Tragedy his *Richard the 2.*, *Richard the 3.*, *Henry the 4.*, *King John*, *Titus Andronicus* and his *Romeo and Iuliet*.
> As *Epius Stolo* said, that the Muses would speake with *Plautus* tongue, if they would speak Latin: so I say that the Muses would speake with *Shakespeares* fine filed phrase, if they would speake English. . . .
> And as *Horace* saith of his; *Exegi monumentum ære perennius; Regalique; situ pyramidum altius; Quod non imber edax; Non Aquilo impotens possit diruere; aut innumerabilis annorum feries &c fuga temporum:* so say I seuerally of sir *Philip Sidneys, Spencers, Daniels, Draytons, Shakespeares*, and *Warners workes*.

Such references as this one, which shows that certain plays had been written by 1598, are usually described as external evidence for the dating of the plays.

EVIDENCE PARTLY INTERNAL AND PARTLY EXTERNAL

So also there are in a few instances within the plays allusions to contemporary events of known dates. For instance, the prologue to the fifth act of *Henry V* alludes to the earl of Essex as being in command of the queen's army in Ireland in his campaign in the spring of 1599 against Tyrone's rebellion. The expedition turned out disastrously, and the allusion would not have been appropriate except during a few months. It is sometimes thought also that the Nurse's allusion to the earthquake eleven years before as a means of fixing Juliet's age in *Romeo and Juliet* (I, iii, 22-34) shows that the play was first written in 1591, since there was a famous earthquake in England in 1580. Likewise, when the Porter in *Macbeth* (II, iii, 4-5) speaks of the "farmer, that hanged himself on the expectation of plenty," it is thought that he alludes to the plentiful harvest and the consequent low price of grain in the year 1606.

Evidence of this kind, although abundant, is often uncertain, since in most cases the allusions are by their very nature vague or capable of more than one interpretation; this is in spite of the fact that the Elizabethan drama has a constant habit of alluding to contemporary events and of making the time of its plays correspond to the current calendar. For example, the allusion to the earthquake of 1580 in *Romeo and Juliet* is a bare possibility, whereas that to France "armed and reverted making war against her heir" in *The Comedy of Errors* is much more definite, and that to Essex as "the general of our gracious empress" in *Henry V* is a practical certainty.

EVIDENCE WHOLLY INTERNAL

It is possible to say from evidence of the kinds just described that certain plays are undoubtedly early, middle, or late in Shakespeare's career; and, by a consideration of the qualities of style which appear in them, to see that Shakespeare's manner of writing underwent certain known and predictable variations during the course of his work as a dramatist. By putting down, so to speak, certain plays as fixed points of departure one can arrange plays of like style together and make a list which is approximately sequential for the whole body of his work. Having determined such an order, one is able to make freer use of vague and casual allusions, to see how Shakespeare reflected the varying tastes of his time, and, above all, to observe his development as a dramatist. From this synoptic view comes a unified conception of Shakespeare and the ability to achieve an understanding of his progressively developing attitude and style.

We are not concerned, however, with a development of style in Shakespeare only, but in other dramatists as well, his associates and contemporaries.

Elizabeth Regina.

From "A Booke of Christian Prayers," 1590. (Metropolitan Museum)

English poetry was undergoing, particularly in the drama, a great growth in the direction of freedom and skill. Shakespeare and other dramatic poets were learning how to express themselves on the stage. Various forms of expression had been tried out in the drama before the Elizabethan mixture of blank verse and prose was hit upon. The writers of older chronicle plays and interludes had used native accentual measures, such as doggerel, preserved for us in such nursery rhymes as:

There was a man in our town, and he was wondrous wise;
He jumped into a bramble bush and scratched out both
    his eyes.

Lyly and Gascoigne had used prose; but Marlowe had established blank verse and taught it to his fellows. Shakespeare naturally began where the literary skill of the day then was, namely, with Marlowan blank verse, and we can see in him and others a progressive growth in the direction of freedom from the more awkward and constraining forms in the style employed on the stage when he began. In general, dramatic verse became better suited to dialogue.

DIFFICULTIES IN THE PROBLEM

One is to understand, of course, that there was a whole body of characteristic changes in subject mat-

ter as well as in style; but it has been found possible to isolate and tabulate particular changes in style as distinguished from subject matter and other features. Since these changes in style are unconscious responses on Shakespeare's part to his own needs and to the fashion of the times, they form an independent record of his progress. If they are used cautiously, they are a means for the approximate dating of his plays. Such evidence is spoken of as wholly internal.

The matter would be relatively simple if we could be sure that Shakespeare wrote each play at one time and in the form in which it has come down to us and had not revised his work at later times, or had not re-written other men's work and left much of it standing, or in early work had not anticipated a late style, or in late work recurred to an earlier style, or, finally, had not during his career had various collaborators in his undertakings. Unfortunately, we know that all of these puzzling things happened. Moreover, when we get beyond the consideration of the unconscious record and have to resort to our sympathetic interpretation of how Shakespeare would have felt at a certain time, how the circumstances of his private life might have been affecting him, or what the activities of other playwrights might have caused him to say or to refrain from saying, we are on very shaky ground. Although in this favorite exercise of amateur critics we may satisfy ourselves and make matters plausible to others, so great is the difference of taste, knowledge, and temperament among critics that we cannot claim to be dealing with facts. Nevertheless, if we take time to examine the element of style, we shall see that a great deal of our knowledge of Shakespeare is based upon it.

MIXTURE OF PROSE AND BLANK VERSE

Shakespeare's use of prose is slight in certain early plays, such as *Richard III*, produced under the influence of Marlowe. However, from the earliest times, in plays not of a Marlowan character, prose is freely employed for the speeches of clowns, servants, and rustics. Marlowe himself in *Dr. Faustus* and elsewhere had used it in this way. Later in his career, however, Shakespeare extended the use of prose to matter which we should call high comedy, as in *Much Ado about Nothing* and *The Merry Wives of Windsor*, and used it even in speeches of sententious importance or great formal dignity, as in the oration of Brutus in *Julius Caesar* (III, ii, 13-52). Very little can be told as to the date of a play merely by the amount of prose it contains; it is at best only an indication. Similarly, the amount of blank verse is not definitive. The plays written under the influence of Marlowe early in Shakespeare's career tend, with the exception of *Richard II*, to have a disproportionate amount of blank verse; but the general principle is valid: from the beginning of Shakespeare's work and throughout his career much of the serious business of the plot and most passages of dignity and poetic beauty appear in blank verse. There is, of course, a greater general use of prose in comedy from about 1597 to the time of *The Tempest*.

RHYME

The amount of rhyme is more significant. In early plays, such as *A Midsummer-Night's Dream* and *Romeo and Juliet*, there is a great deal of rhyme, and in the latest plays there is practically none. The commonest form of rhyme is the pentameter measure rhymed in couplets; as when Phebe, quoting Marlowe's *Hero and Leander*, says in *As You Like It* (III, v, 81-82),

> Dead shepherd, now I find thy saw of might,
> 'Who ever loved that loved not at first sight?'

But Shakespeare in his rhyming sometimes goes even further than the couplet. *Romeo and Juliet* and *Love's Labour's Lost* each contain a number of complete sonnets, as well as rhymed sequences made up of a quatrain followed by a couplet, and a good deal of alternate rhyme. Doggerel appears in some of the early plays.

One quite formal use of the rhymed couplet, which should be noted here, interrupts the calculation as to the significance of the amount of rhyme: there was, of course, no dropping of a curtain at the close of a scene in the Elizabethan theater. The actors simply left the stage at the end of a scene, carrying with them sick, wounded, or slain persons, or other impedimenta, so that the stage might be left empty. In order to mark strongly the cue for the first actor in the succeeding scene, so it is thought, the dramatist composed a couplet to mark the close of the scene. Thus Hamlet leaves the stage at the end of the fifth scene of the first act crying,

> The time is out of joint: O cursed spite,
> That ever I was born to set it right!

The chief thing to remember about the use of rhyme is that it is always consciously employed. Shakespeare tends to use it for sentiment and the conversation of lovers and to mark other passages of lighter tone. When so used, a large quantity is indicative of an early date.

QUALITY OF THE BLANK VERSE

The way in which Shakespeare composed blank verse in his early plays and in his later ones forms the basis of a more significant test than the mere amount of blank verse or of rhyme. There is in Shakespeare's blank verse a gradual movement in the direction of freedom from formality, which is progressive and therefore safely calculable. Blank verse is five-foot iambic measure without rhyme, and if composed with perfect regularity, it is monotonous. If every line is made to contain five feet and each foot two syllables, the second accented and the first unaccented, we say that the verse is regular. If there is a pause, however slight, in the sense, and consequently also in the rhythm, at the end of the line, we say the verse is end-stopped. The single verse and not a group of verses is then the unit of composition.

Blank verse before Marlowe's time was written very much in this formal manner, and what Marlowe did for it, and therefore for dramatic style, was to provide for continuity of thought. His verses, although prevailingly end-stopped, are so constructed that they flow into each other. In other words, they have the same effect as run-on lines. Marlowe also varied the measure by breaking up the regularity in the forms of the individual feet within the line, sometimes substituting for the regular iambic, a trochaic foot. But the shifting of the medial pause, or caesura, was the chief means of rendering the verse sufficiently flexible to be used in dialogue. Compared to Shakespeare in his later works, Marlowe is relatively stiff in manner.

*A professor
with his students.
From Philip Stubbes'
"Anatomy of Abuses,"
1583. (Folger)*

St. Paul's Cathedral.
From John Speed's "Theatre of the Empire," 1611. (Folger)

It may be said of Shakespeare, however, that in certain passages of his early works he out-Marlowes Marlowe in the rigidity of his style. Later, along with other dramatists, he varied his style with the greatest freedom. Fletcher carried this license so far that, if his lines are written as prose, one would have difficulty in rearranging them as verse. The relation in numbers of run-on lines to end-stopped lines at any one time in Shakespeare's career forms a convenient test for placing his plays roughly in the order in which he wrote them. If, for example, a play has many run-on lines, the pauses occurring not at the ends of lines but within them, it would be judged late in date of composition.

The following passage from Clarence's description of his dream in *Richard III* (I, iv, 21-33) may be taken as an example of Shakespeare's earlier manner. Note that there is a pause at the end of every line except the ninth:

> Lord, Lord! methought, what pain it was to drown!
> What dreadful noise of waters in mine ears!
> What ugly sights of death within mine eyes!
> Methought I saw a thousand fearful wrecks;
> Ten thousand men that fishes gnaw'd upon;
> Wedges of gold, great anchors, heaps of pearl,
> Inestimable stones, unvalued jewels,
> All scatter'd in the bottom of the sea:

> Some lay in dead men's skulls; and, in those holes
> Where eyes did once inhabit, there were crept,
> As 'twere in scorn of eyes, reflecting gems,
> Which woo'd the slimy bottom of the deep,
> And mock'd the dead bones that lay scatter'd by.

As an example of the latest manner, consider Prospero's description of his magic in *The Tempest* (V, i, 33-50) where only the first, fifth, eighth, and tenth lines are end-stopped:

> Ye elves of hills, brooks, standing lakes and groves,
> And ye that on the sands with printless foot
> Do chase the ebbing Neptune and do fly him
> When he comes back; you demi-puppets that
> By moonshine do the green sour ringlets make,
> Whereof the ewe not bites, and you whose pastime
> Is to make midnight mushrooms, that rejoice
> To hear the solemn curfew; by whose aid,
> Weak masters though ye be, I have bedimm'd
> The noontide sun, call'd forth the mutinous winds,
> And 'twixt the green sea and the azured vault
> Set roaring war: to the dread rattling thunder
> Have I given fire and rifted Jove's stout oak
> With his own bolt; the strong-based promontory
> Have I made shake and by the spurs pluck'd up
> The pine and cedar: graves at my command
> Have waked their sleepers, oped, and let 'em forth
> By my so potent art.

It should be noted that the two passages given for illustration are both set speeches and in them, formal features are conspicuous. They therefore serve well for comparison. But in dialogue, argument, and sustained thought, there is perceptible in Marlowe and his contemporaries, as well as in the earliest plays of Shakespeare, a tendency toward complication of syntax and freedom from verse restraint.

THE SPEECH-ENDING TEST

A phenomenon somewhat akin to the principle of the end-stopped and run-on lines is the growing habit of dividing a line between two speakers, or even among several speakers. These speech endings which break lines increase steadily from *The Comedy of Errors*, where there are almost none, to *The Winter's Tale*, where eighty-seven per cent of the speeches end in this fashion. The speech-ending test would be one of the very best but for the fact that, in cases where the play has been cut for acting or otherwise tampered with, the way in which the speeches end has been modified after the play was first written.

FEMININE ENDINGS

Another variation in the way in which blank verse is written is in the kind of foot which stands at the end of the line. In the early type of dramatic blank verse the lines were usually end-stopped, the last syllable was accented, and the line closed abruptly; thus the line is emphasized as the unit of composition. In the passage from *Richard III* quoted above, it will be noticed that every line except possibly the seventh ends in an accented syllable. As a means of breaking away from

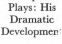

The Order of Shakespeare's Plays: His Dramatic Development

37

NAME OF PLAY	NO. OF LINES	PROSE	BLANK VERSE	5-FOOT RHYMES	RUN-ON LINES %	DOUBLE ENDINGS	SPEECH ENDING %	NO. LIGHT WEAK END.	PROBABLE DATES[1]
L. L. L........	2789	1086	579	1028	18.4	9	10.0	3	1588w,[2] 1594-1595,[3] (1597)
Com. Er......	1778	240	1150	380	12.9	137	0.6	0	1589w,[2] 1592-1593,[3] 1593
Two Gent.....	2294	409	1510	116	12.4	203	5.8	0	1590s,[2] 1594-1595[3]
Tit. And......	2523	43	2338	144	9.5	154	2.5	5	1592s,[2] 1593-1594[3]
1 Hen. VI......	2677	0	2379	314	10.4	140	0.5	4	1591w,[2] 1591-1592[3]
2 Hen. VI......	3162	448	2562	122	11.4	255	1.1	3	1591w,[2] 1590-1591[3]
3 Hen. VI......	2904	0	2749	155	9.5	346	0.9	3	1591w,[2] 1591-1592[3]
Rich. III......	3619	55(?)	3374	170	13.1	570	2.9	4	1593w,[2] 1592-1593[3]
R. & J........	3052	405	2111	486	14.2	118	14.9	7	1591s,[2] 1594-1595[3]
Tam. Shrew....	2649	516	1971	169	8.1	260	3.6	14(?)	1594w,[2] 1593-1594[3]
Mids. Dream...	2174	441	878	731	13.2	29	17.3	1	1594s,[2] 1595-1596[3]
K. John......	2570	0	2403	150	17.7	54	12.7	7	1595s,[2] 1596-1597[3]
Rich. II........	2756	0	2107	537	19.9	148	7.3	4	1595w,[2] 1595-1596[3]
Mer. Ven......	2660	673	1896	93	21.5	297	22.2	7	1597s,[2] 1596-1597[3]
1 Hen. IV......	3176	1464	1622	84	22.8	60	14.2	7	1596s,[2] 1597-1598[3]
2 Hen. IV......	3446	1860	1417	74	21.4	203	16.8	1	1596w,[2] 1597-1598[3]
Much Ado.....	2826	2106	643	40	19.3	129	20.7	2	1598w,[2] 1598-1599[3]
Hen. V........	3380	1531	1678	101	21.8	291	18.3	2	1599s,[2] 1598-1599[3]
Merry Wives...	3018	2703	227	69	20.1	32	20.5	1	(1592)w,[2] 1597-1601[3]
J. C..........	2478	165	2241	34	19.3	369	20.3	10	1599w,[2] 1599-1600[3]
A. Y. L. I.....	2857	1681	925	71	17.1	211	21.6	2	1600s,[2] 1599-1600[3]
12th Night.....	2690	1741	763	120	14.7	152	36.3	4	1600w,[2] 1599-1600[3]
T. & C........	3496	1186	2025	196	27.4	441	31.3	6	1601s,[2] 1601-1602[3]
All's Well......	2966	1453	1234	280	28.4	223	74.4	13	(1589)s,[2] 1602-1603,[3] 1607s[2]
Hamlet........	3931	1208	2490	81	23.1	508	51.6	8	(1593)s,[2] 1600-1601,[3] 1603s[2]
Meas. Meas....	2821	1134	1574	73	23.0	338	51.4	7	1604w,[2] 1604-1605[3]
Othello........	3316	541	2672	86	19.5	646	41.4	2	1604s,[2] 1604-1605[3]
K. Lear.......	3334	903	2238	74	29.3	567	60.9	6	1605w,[2] 1605-1606[3]
Macbeth.......	2108	158	1588	118	36.6	399	77.2	23	1606s,[2] 1605-1606[3]
A. & C........	3063	255	2761	42	43.3	613	77.5	99	1606w,[2] 1606-1607[3]
Tim. of Ath....	2373	596	1560	184	32.5	257	62.8	30	1605s,[2] 1607-1608[3]
Coriolanus.....	3410	829	2521	42	45.9	708	79.0	104	1608s,[2] 1607-1608[3]
Pericles	2389	418	1436	225	18.2	120	71.0	82	1607s,[2] 1608-1609[3]
Cymbeline.....	3339	638	2585	107	46.0	726	85.0	130	1610w,[2] 1609-1610[3]
Wint. Tale.....	3075	844	1825	0	37.5	639	87.6	100	1611s,[2] 1610-1611[3]
Tempest.......	2064	458	1458	2	41.5	476	84.5	67	1611w,[2] 1611-1612[3]
Henry VIII.....	2822	67(?)	2613	16	46.3	1195	72.4	82	1612w,[2] 1612-1613[3]

[1]When there is a wide divergence of opinion among critics, two dates, separated by commas, are given. Dates in parentheses indicate early versions or late revisions.
[2]T. W. Baldwin, *Organization and Personnel of the Shakespearean Company* (Princeton, 1927), pp. 229-283 *et passim*. Summer and winter are indicated by "s" and "w."
[3] Chambers, *loc. cit.*, I, 270-271 *et passim*.

this regular and monotonous partition of the sense, Shakespeare introduces more and more frequently words of two syllables at the ends of lines, thus making the line consist of eleven instead of ten syllables. There are, even in the blank verse of *Richard III* and other early plays of Shakespeare, a good many more double-endings than in that of Marlowe.

By those who discovered this stylistic peculiarity it was thought that the effect on the ear was sweeter and less abrupt, and they said that these lines having an extra syllable at the end had "feminine" endings, whereas those which ended in an accented syllable were said to have "masculine" endings. The relative number of masculine and feminine endings forms another test of the time of composition, since feminine endings increase as Shakespeare's development progresses. A similar tendency also causes the introduction, more and more, of extra syllables before the pauses within the lines.

LIGHT AND WEAK ENDINGS

One other among the various tests is of major importance. Early in his career Shakespeare almost never ended lines with conjunctions, prepositions, auxiliary verbs, possessive pronouns, and other lightly stressed words. After 1600, however, he used such endings with increasing freedom. There are more than a hundred such lines each in *Coriolanus* and *Cymbeline*. In *The Comedy of Errors* and *The Two Gentlemen of Verona* there are none at all. We have, therefore, the light- and weak-ending test. A line ending in an unstressed word, such as a pronoun or an auxiliary verb, is said to have a light ending. A weak ending carries the process still further and seems to forbid any vocal stress at all. Prepositions and conjunctions, such as *in, to, and, if, or*, produce this effect.

In order to show the results of all these tests, I have constructed a table based in general on F. G. Fleay (as interpreted and corrected by Dr. F. J. Furnivall) and on G. König. It is printed on page 38. The latest counting of lines is by Sir Edmund Chambers,[1] whose estimates differ slightly from those in the table.

DOWDEN'S GROUPING OF SHAKESPEARE'S PLAYS

The late Edward Dowden, guided by the evidence described and by his sympathetic interpretation of Shakespeare's mind and art, made groupings of Shakespeare's plays which show the varying quality of his dramatic life, and suggest somewhat fancifully the phases of experience through which he was passing.

The first period (1590-1594) Dowden called "In the Workshop." By this he meant Shakespeare's period of pupilage, during which he was doing his first original plays and rewriting old ones, either alone or with some other, possibly more experienced, dramatist to assist him. Here belong the Henry VI plays, *Love's Labour's Lost, The Comedy of Errors, The Two Gentlemen of Verona*, and that crude and terrible play *Titus Andronicus*. We may suppose that the period closes with the two youthful masterpieces *Richard III* and *A Midsummer-Night's Dream*. There was probably in this period also an early version of *Romeo and Juliet*.

The second period (1595-1601) Dowden called "In the World," for Shakespeare, having by that time learned his art, was rising on the tide of success as a dramatist. We may be pretty sure that *Richard II* and *The Merchant of Venice* belong at the very beginning of this period and that there was also a draft of the Henry IV plays very early in it. The final versions of these plays and *Henry V*, together with the brilliant romantic comedies, *Much Ado about Nothing, As You Like It*, and *Twelfth Night*, are the characteristic plays of the period.

Dowden's third period, called "De Profundis," or "Out of the Depths," in which tragic or gloomy subjects engage Shakespeare's pen, occupied the years 1602-1608. He then wrote his great tragedies, beginning, let us say, with *Hamlet*. Included in this group are *Othello, King Lear*, and *Macbeth*, and the "bitter" comedies *All's Well that Ends Well* and *Measure for Measure*.

Finally Dowden provided a fourth period (1608-1612), "On the Heights," so called because the plays composed during the period reveal a quiet serenity and conscious reconciliation to life as "somehow good." The characteristic plays of the period are *Cymbeline, The Tempest*, and *The Winter's Tale*, which are rather reflective romances than comedies.

Many writers, like George Brandes and Frank Harris, have seen in this succession of moods an immediate reflection of the stages of experience through which Shakespeare was passing in his life and have brought into connection with the plays various events of his life. It has, however, been shown that Shakespeare followed the fashion of the stage and that other dramatists were writing plays of the successive styles and kinds that he wrote; it has also been shown that Shakespeare was influenced by current movements of literary thought. If this is true, we may say that the more Shakespeare was reflecting current fashions, the less chance there is that he was expressing independently his personal feelings about life. We would not say that his art is less sincere, but would be disposed to call in question the overly romantic interpretations of certain critics. It is nevertheless convenient, as well as customary, to divide his plays into four groups: first, those which were probably written by the beginning of 1595 when Shakespeare first emerged as a member of the Lord Chamberlain's company; second, those written between this date and 1600, except that certain comedies written soon after 1600 agree in spirit with the second group; third, those written between 1600 and 1608; fourth, the latest plays, those written after 1608.

REFERENCES

BAYFIELD, M. A. *A Study of Shakespeare's Versification.* Cambridge, 1920.

CHAMBERS, SIR E. K. *William Shakespeare.* 2 vols. Oxford, 1930. Appendix H, with bibliographical note.

DOWDEN, EDWARD. *Introduction to Shakspere.* New York and London, 1893; *Shakspere, his Mind and Art.* New York and London, 1874; *A Shakspere Primer.* New York, 1877.

FLEAY, F. G. *Shakspere Manual.* London, 1878.

FURNIVALL, F. J. *The Leopold Shakespeare.* London, 1876. The preface contains an explanation of the system of testing and dating plays.

FURNIVALL, F. J., and JOHN MUNRO. *Shakespeare, Life and Work.* London, 1908.

KÖNIG, G. "Der Vers in Shaksperes Dramen," *Quellen und Forschungen*, Vol. LXI, 1888. Contains the most extensive presentation of the numerical results of verse tests.

LAMBERT, D. H. *Shakespeare Documents.* London, 1904.

MUNRO, JOHN, editor. *The Shakespeare Allusion Book: A Collection of Allusions to Shakespeare from 1591 to 1700.* 2 vols. London and New York, 1909. Reissue by SIR EDMUND CHAMBERS, London, 1932.

New Shakespeare Society. *Publications*, 1874. Contains Fleay's original tests, Furnivall's discussion, and Ingram on weak endings; *Publications*, 1877-1879. Con-

[1] E. K. Chambers, *William Shakespeare* (Oxford, 1930), II, 397-408.

tains F. S. Pulling's work on the speech-ending test; this work is summarized in Fleay's *Shakspere Manual*.

SAINTSBURY, GEORGE. *A History of English Prosody from the Twelfth Century to the Present Day*. London, 1906-1910. Vol. II.

VAN DAM, B. A. P., and C. STOFFEL. *William Shakespeare, Prosody and Text*. Leyden, 1900.

WELLS, HENRY W. *Elizabethan and Jacobean Playwrights*. New York, 1939.

Nearly all modern editions of Shakespeare contain discussions of the dating of his plays.

Shakespeare Criticism: How to Read Shakespeare

The critics of the seventeenth century appreciated Shakespeare's genius although they found him crude and faulty when compared to the French classical dramatists, whom they regarded as a standard; but since they were actually closer to Shakespeare in point of time and consequent ease of comprehension, and were not theory-ridden, they had certain advantages over later critics in understanding Shakespeare, but not often in appreciating him. Dryden in his essay *Of Dramatick Poesie* (1668) writes eloquently of Shakespeare as the man of all the moderns who "had the largest and most comprehensive soul," and yet he is careful to point out Shakespeare's irregularities and inconsistencies. Thomas Rymer in *A Short View of Tragedy* (1693) states the case of late seventeenth-century England against Shakespeare, saying he was barbarous, irrational, and overexuberant; and, though there was no lack of defenders, that is the gist of the dramatic criticism of the age.

Yet it was practically always admitted that Shakespeare was possessed of a transcendent genius. It may even be said that such adaptations as Nahum Tate's version of *King Lear* (which has a happy ending), Dryden's version of *Antony and Cleopatra*, entitled *All for Love*, and Colley Cibber's version of *Richard III* (still on the stage) are evidences that the proponents of French classicism usually admired Shakespeare's genius. They were not disposed to err on the side of Shakespeare worship;[1] nor, indeed, were the critics of the eighteenth century. Dr. Samuel Johnson, an editor of Shakespeare, was in most respects an admirable Shakespeare critic. He had no metaphysical theory of Shakespeare's genius but looked at Shakespeare directly and sensibly. It was he who first paid serious attention to the conditions under which Shakespeare did his work.[2] Late in the eighteenth century, the great Shakespeare scholar Edmund Malone (1741-1812) and his contemporaries did Shakespeare the honor to study him and his age profoundly. They gave us our principal body of Elizabethan material for the study of Shakespeare.

[1]See *The Tempest, The Mock Tempest,* and *King Lear*, ed. Montague Summers (1922); George C. D. Odell, *Shakespeare from Betterton to Irving* (1920); Hazelton Spencer, *Shakespeare Improved* (Cambridge, 1928).
[2]Karl Young, "Samuel Johnson on Shakespeare: One Aspect," *University of Wisconsin Studies in Language and Literature*, No. 18.

The macrocosm and microcosm.
From Robert Fludd's "Utriusque Cosmi Historia," 1555. (*Huntington*)

SHAKESPEARE AND THE ROMANTIC GENERATION

A powerful impulse came to the study and appreciation of Shakespeare with the generation who lived during the epoch of the French Revolution. A new Shakespeare criticism was part of that revival of art and letters which we ordinarily call the Romantic Movement. The thinkers of that day were interested in a wider variety of ideas about life than were the pseudo-classicists. They found in Shakespeare such a marvelously significant and consistent picture of life that they came to think of him as endowed with the insight of a seer and the power of a poet, as greater and more significant than life itself. Each of his plays became a microcosm capable of yielding to the student, if he came with love and admiration in his heart, finer truth than science could yield. Science, they argued, bounds itself by fact; poetry has no such limits, but is a mode of revelation of the philosophy of life, presenting in concrete and constructive form what life means and what life might be. Shakespeare, the poet, was thus metamorphosed into a philosopher and teacher, so that his works became a hunting ground where one might find the greatest thoughts about existence.

This his admirers did in the strength of the conviction that his had been a vision of life at its fullest, purest, and most significant stage. Since Coleridge's day the world has belonged to Shakespeare. The approach of Coleridge and his contemporaries to

Shakespeare is still the prevailing one, as witnessed by our textbooks, which are made from this idealistic, if not mystical, point of view. Coleridge himself was a follower of Schlegel, and in Coleridge's wake came the critics we know best—Lamb, Hazlitt, De Quincey, Carlyle, Emerson, and Swinburne; the greater Germans—Gervinus, Kreyssig, Elze. Later appeared Edward Dowden, a great interpreter of Shakespeare, F. J. Furnivall, a scholar and promoter of scholarship, Stopford A. Brooke, the vigorous romantic critic George Brandes, A. C. Bradley, and many other editors of Shakespeare and critics of his work.

THE NEW POINT OF VIEW

Shakespeare, like every artist, has a right to be seen and understood as he desired to be seen and understood. There has sprung up, mainly in the twentieth century, a group of critics whose methods are more strictly historical and whose attitude toward the perfections of Shakespeare's work is more skeptical. They are as willing to recognize the limits placed upon Shakespeare by the time in which he lived, the conditions in which he practiced his art, and even the flaws in his workmanship, as were the critics of the seventeenth and eighteenth centuries. They consequently regard with distrust the great body of panegyrical criticism of the nineteenth century. Their object, in the words reported from the eminent American Shakespeare scholar G. L. Kittredge, is to ascertain what Shakespeare said and what he meant when he said it.[3]

THE CONDITIONS UNDER WHICH SHAKESPEARE WORKED

Although the Shakespearean drama was not acted under such conditions as now prevail in dramatic production, it is at least so far one and the same with modern drama that it can be freely enacted on the modern stage and seen by the modern spectator with great enjoyment and fair comprehension. But it cannot be seen exactly as it was seen by the Elizabethan Londoners for whom it was written. Perhaps no art, literary or pictorial, can be brought back exactly as it was originally produced and enjoyed. Matthew Arnold points out in his lectures "On Translating Homer," that we cannot know exactly the effect of a classic on the age for which it was written; we can only approximate such knowledge. All art of a bygone age necessarily has this limitation.

Everyone would admit, however, that the more nearly we can see as Shakespeare meant us to see, the more adequate will be our vision and the keener our enjoyment. Neither the Elizabethan writer nor the Elizabethan audience had a body of ideas like ours, knew what we know or in the way we know it, wanted the same things from life that we want, or thought of drama or life as we think of them. Much water, so to speak, has flowed under the bridge since Bacon and Bruno were making their tentative beginnings in the scientific thought which has transformed the world. All the magnification of the individual man and his immediate relation to God which came from Puritanism; all the democracy or republicanism which came from Algernon Sidney, John Locke, and J. J. Rousseau; all that was done in the way of untying men's minds by the idealism of Berkeley and Kant, by the rationalism of Hume and his followers, and by Hegelianism, transcendentalism, pessimism, socialism, Nietzscheism; all the social teachings of the nineteenth century, the doctrine of organic evolution, the development of experimental science and of public education, the extension of European civilization over the world—these things and a thousand more are influences in the enlightened mind of today which were unknown to the Englishman of the sixteenth century. Since Shakespeare did not and could not think and talk in terms of such ideas, he should not be made to do so.

SHAKESPEARE ON THE STAGE

No doubt, however, if we know the meaning of the Elizabethan language used, the rudiments of the culture of Elizabethan times, the fashions and opinions then current, and something of the dramatic practices of the day, we may proceed to the enjoyment of Shakespeare's drama without hindrance. Human nature remains the same from age to age.

Indeed, any misreading of Shakespeare is more likely to come because we do not see his plays on the stage very frequently; or because when we do, they are acted on a very different stage from Shakespeare's and are frequently deformed by false critical interpretations. In the physical conditions of dramatic art, there are two factors, a stage and an audience, and both of these have changed since Shakespeare's time; the audience, multifariously; the stage, definitely and specifically. Writers on the stage have called the modern stage two-dimensional and have likened it to a picture; they have called the Elizabethan stage three-dimensional, and have likened it to a pageant, or a procession, or an athletic contest. In the modern theater we sit like privileged spies and behold what we are asked to accept as a section of actual life. Since we are not supposed to be present, we do not wish to be talked to in asides and soliloquy, because such practices spoil the illusion. In the Elizabethan theater the actors were literally surrounded by the audience, some of whom actually sat on the stage, and it was the allowed convention

---

[3]See G. L. Kittredge, *Shakespeare* (Cambridge, 1916); L. L. Schücking, *Character Problems in Shakespeare's Plays* (1922); Barrett Wendell, *William Shakespeare* (1894); *The Works of William Shakespeare*, ed. R. Bridges (Stratford, 1907), X, 321-324; C. M. Lewis, *The Genesis of "Hamlet"* (1907); John Corbin, *The Elizabethan "Hamlet"* (1895); J. M. Robertson, *The Problem of "Hamlet"* (1919), and other works by the same author; G. B. Shaw, *Dramatic Opinions and Other Essays* (1907), and various introductions and prefaces; E. E. Stoll, *Shakespeare Studies* (1927), and various articles in learned journals. The historical point of view is not wanting in A. C. Bradley's work, though his chief adherence is to philosophical considerations. See for a general statement of the position, Karl Young's review of Schücking, *Philological Quarterly*, I, 228-234, and "Shakespeare Skeptics," *North American Review*, CCXV, 382-393; also L. Abercrombie, *A Plea for the Liberty of Interpreting* (Oxford, 1930).

of that drama that the actors might talk to the audience much more intimately than they may now talk, and make them comprehend the story by actual explanation. The Elizabethan audience was too much a fact to be disregarded, and the dramatist made terms with it just because it was at hand. But there was a further reason for direct contact—

Piece out our imperfections with your thoughts,

cries Shakespeare in the prologue to *Henry V;* and he elsewhere shows us that he realizes his difficulties. He must have the cooperation of his audience if his play, on such a stage and relatively without realistic costume or scenery, is to be understood. In *A Midsummer-Night's Dream* (V, i, 213-217) Theseus replies to Hippolyta's statement that the interlude of "Pyramus and Thisbe" is the silliest stuff she ever heard, with these words:

The best in this kind are but shadows; and the worst are no worse, if imagination amend them.

And she retorts,

It must be your imagination then, and not theirs.

They thus express the principle at the basis of all artistic appreciation, which Coleridge described as "that willing suspension of disbelief for the moment which constitutes poetic faith."

ELIZABETHAN DRAMATIC ART WAS CONVENTIONAL

Elizabethan dramatic art was certainly more conventional than most modern dramatic art. That is, it followed a mode of representing plays which was customary, accepted, and unrealistic. As acted on our stage, Shakespeare's plays are made more naturalistic than they were on the Elizabethan stage. They are less declamatory and more conversational now. Our actors are usually costumed according to the time and place of the plot and do not appear merely in the ruff, the doublet, and the trunk hose of the Tudor stage, although there have been a few experiments in the coat, waistcoat, and trousers of our own day. Women's parts are played by women; on Shakespeare's stage they were played by boys. On our stage, scenes are set with care and appropriateness; the stage is not bare, and it has a curtain. Actors take time to characterize by gesture and movement to a greater degree than they did at the time the plays were written. The prologue to *Romeo and Juliet* speaks of the play as "the two hours' traffic of our stage," thus indicating the approximate length of an Elizabethan play. The performance of a full text of a Shakespearean play acted with the slower modern methods may become a horror from sheer length.

Unfortunately most of us do not like to see Shakespeare done in the old way. It might be better if we did. The fashions and conventions of our own theater are difficult to see objectively, simply because

we are so used to them, and in a presentation of Shakespeare they may come between us and his mind. In the judgment of contemporary art it is difficult not to mistake mere novelty for originality. In the art of a past age, however, fashions and conventions betray themselves to us very quickly. Not infrequently, even when the art is good, we find ourselves repelled by its antique fashion. It is the essence of literary education to learn to look beyond these unaccustomed and sometimes absurd features to the mind of the artist, and if possible to see the work of earlier writers like Shakespeare, Chaucer, and Dante so sympathetically that the limits of their technique and their knowledge are accepted and endorsed as they were accepted and endorsed by the keenest and most appreciative of their contemporaries.

SHAKESPEARE NOT DEVOID OF NATURALISM

Some careful study of nature is necessary in every great school of art. That Shakespeare sought naturalism we know from the character of his works and from Hamlet's words on the art of playing—"whose end, both at the first and now, was and is, to hold, as 'twere, the mirror up to nature; to show virtue her own feature, scorn her own image, and the very age and body of the time his form and pressure" (*Hamlet,* III, ii, 18-39). A swing from conventionality to naturalism can be traced from Shakespeare's early plays to his late ones, and can be followed with equal certainty in the works of his contemporaries. He himself, from his consistent character, achieved balance between the objective and the subjective spirit, or, as we say, between naturalism and conventionality. But this belief in his naturalism can be easily exaggerated. He did not go the whole way in ridding himself of obvious conventionalities, such as the use of the aside and the soliloquy; for, after all, he could not change the habits of his

The hydra.
As pictured in Gesner's "Historia Animalium," 1587. (Huntington)

A seventeenth-century concept of the heavens and the elements. From "A Prospect of the Most Famous Parts of the World." Written by John Speed, 1631. (Folger)

audience or the form of his stage and theater. If we understand that Shakespeare's mind flourished in an earlier time than ours in the history of thought, and that his task—the telling of a story by histrionic and theatrical means—was primarily an artist's task, recognized by him in some such terms as those quoted above, we shall be better able to avoid the habit of reading into his plays things that he never meant to say. We shall also be able to find a method of approach which will lead to a fuller, more genuine enjoyment of his work.

THE MATERIAL OF SHAKESPEARE'S IDEAS

In considering the cultural and psychological background of Shakespeare and his audience we have to do not only with tastes and temperaments in the age of Elizabeth, but with the actual fund of ideas of that age. Shakespeare's stock of ideas was relatively small, most of them coming from Aristotle and the Renaissance; and he utters his great simple truths, exalted commonplaces, and aphoristic wisdoms without calling them very consciously into question. He presents the insoluble problems of life, but he does not do so speculatively. It is fate or the stars which are to blame. Our trap is his suggestiveness. As a poet he calls up modern concepts and terms in our minds—instincts, sensations, motor impulses, emotions and thoughts; these we sublimate, carrying his suggestions further than he could have carried them, into the higher region of ideals and rational actions. There is little gain and much confusion in making this greatest of poets into an elucidator or even an illustrator of philosophic enigmas, many of which he never dreamed of. By taking him on his own terms we may often reinforce his greatness by

perceiving his anticipations of the thought of a more advanced age.

Still, if we exaggerate the differences between Shakespeare's age and ours, we make a greater mistake than if we minimize them; for the essentials of social and domestic life remain, in most of their important aspects, relatively unchanged. In so far as the conduct of life is determined by elemental biological fact and by fundamental social institutions, Shakespeare deals with it for our world as for his own. Parental and filial love, courtship and marriage, youth and age, riches and poverty, sickness and health, peace and war; the social interrelations which spring out of these conditions; most matters of law and civil polity; the qualities which come from the practice of trades and professions; the fundamental types of human character; the behavior of individual men arising from their instincts, emotions, and affections; man's essential relation to generation, death, God, and the hereafter—these things remain, so that Shakespeare's favorite world is the one in which we spend most of our lives. There is usually only a difference of emphasis to be known and noted. For example, Shakespeare had exalted ideals of loyalty and hospitality, so that when Macbeth murders Duncan, he is killing his king and his guest. Well may Macbeth speak of the "deep damnation of his taking off," for it is as horrible a sin as Shakespeare could imagine for his hero to commit.

COLLECTIVE TREATMENT OF SHAKESPEARE'S SOURCES

The belief that Shakespeare was a careless worker, putting his plays hastily together largely out of other people's ideas, is erroneous. His genius was, no doubt, happy and rapid, but there is no positive evidence that he slighted his work or regarded it as a perfunctory means of making his livelihood. In most instances of apparent carelessness there are indications that the work was tampered with after it left his hand. The evidence points rather to a studious person who was conscientious about his art.

In order to understand this matter and to form a fair opinion on so important a question, it is necessary that we should consider his relation to his sources. The discovery of a Shakespearean source is an interesting fact in and for itself and because it tells us what materials the great poet made to serve his turn; but, after all, the knowledge that Shakespeare used such and such a work is of little importance compared to the knowledge of how he used it. Did he follow it slavishly? If so, was it worth following? How did he change it? What did it teach him or suggest to him? Did he content himself with one source only? Did he respect a serious historical source? These are a few of the really important questions about Shakespeare's sources. In point of fact, Shakespeare invented very few incidents. Almost every episode in every play has somewhere a source or a suggestion.

The unicorn.
From Gesner's "Historia Animalium," 1603. (Huntington)

The books Shakespeare knew were of two sorts: those he used in the making of plays and those he encountered apparently as a general reader and student. Of the former class the most striking are the old plays which we have reason to believe he used. The number of these plays is surprising, and in order to understand how Shakespeare, a great original genius, could have used so much second-hand material, we have to recall to our minds the fact that stories were more or less common property and that their interest did not depend upon their novelty. We must likewise ask about the way in which Shakespeare used his borrowed plots. Only a general idea can be given here, since the specific cases are considered in the introductions to various plays further on in this volume.

Among the comedies we have one play, George Whetstone's *Promos and Cassandra*, which Shakespeare certainly rewrote as *Measure for Measure*. *The Taming of a Shrew* is not the original for Shakespeare's *The Taming of the Shrew*, but we have George Gascoigne's *The Supposes*, which is ultimately the source of Shakespeare's minor plot, and we have reason to believe that there was an old "shrew" play, now lost, back of the major plot. For *The Comedy of Errors* we have Plautus' *Menaechmi* and his *Amphitruo*. There was, it is thought, an intermediary play (now lost) between Shakespeare and Plautus, possibly the *Historie of Error*, acted at Hampton Court by the Children of Paul's on New Year's Day 1577. It is believed on various grounds that earlier plays, now lost, existed on the subjects treated in *The Two Gentlemen of Verona, The Merchant of Venice, Much Ado about Nothing, The Merry Wives of Windsor,* and *Troilus and Cressida.* Not much then can be told from Shakespeare's comedies about his methods of work, though it is noteworthy that he did a thorough job on Whet-

stone's play, rewriting it completely and modifying it in such a manner as to change its significance as a whole, and that he knew Plautus at first hand and that he made direct use of *The Supposes*.

It is in the history plays that one really sees how Shakespeare went to work. Probably every historical subject he treated, including *Henry VIII*, had been put on the stage before he used it. This may not be true in the case of *2* and *3 Henry VI*, though many Shakespeare scholars still believe that it was. There was certainly an old play, now lost, on the same subject as *1 Henry VI*; at least two plays on Richard III; probably several dramatic treatments of Richard II; and there is extant a play on King John. For *1* and *2 Henry IV* and *Henry V* we have in *The Famous Victories of Henry V* a badly garbled version of Shakespeare's source. From *The Famous Victories*, or more probably from the play which it so inadequately represents, Shakespeare drew only scenes and suggestions for the comic and the biographic parts of his play. For the historical events of the three plays he went to the best book of English history of his time, namely, Raphael Holinshed's *Chronicles of England, Scotland, and Ireland*, which he used in the second edition of 1587. This he did for all the historical plays. For *Richard II* and *1* and *2 Henry IV*, he used also Samuel Daniel's *History of the Civil Wars*, a compendious historical poem published in 1595. So many details in the history plays of Shakespeare seem to be drawn from Hall's *Chronicles* and from Stow's *Annals* that one is almost forced to conclude that Shakespeare also knew these sources. In *Henry VIII* we find not only Holinshed but John Foxe's *Acts and Monuments*. For *King John* there exists a full and meritorious dramatic source, *The Troublesome Raigne of John King of England*, published in two parts in 1591. Here it must be admitted that Shakespeare followed very closely his anonymous source, which in turn, however, had followed Holinshed with fidelity and dramatic skill. Shakespeare does little violence anywhere to historical truth as he knew it. Richard III, as Shakespeare presents him, is the Richard III of Tudor history, as pictured originally by Sir Thomas More and by Polydore Vergil. Shakespeare's version is far more "historical" than is *The True Tragedy of Richard III*, from which he is wrongly supposed to have borrowed.

In the tragedies again we have not much to go upon. Old plays on the subjects treated in *Titus Andronicus* and *Romeo and Juliet* probably existed. His handling of the former we cannot pass judgment upon, for we have no source; but the latter is written directly from Arthur Brooke's poem *Romeus and Juliet*, with such changes and artistic developments as we might expect. There were no doubt many plays on Julius Caesar; but Shakespeare's play is a masterly and respectful dramatization of the best available source—Plutarch's lives of Caesar, Brutus, and Antonius, with possible hints from Appian's *Chronicle of the Roman Wars*. About *Hamlet* we can tell little. There was an old play on the subject, possibly by Thomas Kyd, which is now lost. Other earlier sources are remote.

It is *King Lear* from which we get our great lesson. There Shakespeare had an old play to work on, *The True Chronicle History of King Leir and his three daughters*, published in 1605. Shakespeare drew some features of his major plot from this play, but he cannot be said to have rewritten it; for before he composed his play he actually read up on his story in practically every known version: Holinshed's *Chronicles*, *The Mirror for Magistrates*, Spenser's *The Faerie Queene*, William Warner's *Albion's England*, and even Geoffrey of Monmouth's *Historia Regum Britonum*. His minor plot, which carried with it the tragic theme, he drew from Sidney's *Arcadia*.

Here then at least is a clear case, clearer even than that of *Richard II*, where Shakespeare, having before him a literary task, underwent the labor and study of a literary man in order to accomplish his results. With reference to his sources, Shakespeare seems to have followed a very simple plan. If the sources were good, he followed them closely; if they were not, he did not. Some of his later plays show this very clearly. *Antony and Cleopatra* and *Coriolanus* are based closely on Plutarch; the parallels are often striking. *Othello*, one of Shakespeare's finest pieces of workmanship, is based on a very crude tale in Giraldi Cinthio's *Hecatommithi*. From it he borrows nothing but the thread of the narrative. *The Winter's Tale* is likewise quite remote from its source in Greene's *Pandosto*.

Shakespeare's working library seems then to have been made up of Holinshed and the other chroniclers, Plutarch, old plays, and collections of stories, most of these from the Italian. He enriched the themes he derived from these sources from his general reading. This was made up of Ovid, Virgil, and other Latin authors such as Terence; of English poets and prose writers, such as Chaucer, Gower, Spenser, Marlowe, Sidney, Daniel, Drayton, Lyly, Greene, and Lodge; of Arthurian romances, popular songs and ballads, proverbs, and fables; of Montaigne, whom he seems to have known well; and of the Bible (and the Prayer Book), of which his knowledge was extensive. He was acquainted with Rabelais, Ronsard, the Greek romances, Hakluyt and other voyagers, with a good many current pamphlets, and apparently with popular works on psychology, demonology, and ethics. Probably his reading in classical criticism was slight or none at all. We do not, therefore, expect to find in him a high degree of theoretical dramatic art, though he was the greatest of all dramatists.

HIS PURPOSE WAS TO TELL A STORY

Shakespeare's purpose as a writer of plays was really very simple. It was to tell a story on the stage in accordance with the practice of the best Elizabethan dramatists; and this practice paid scant respect to Aristotle and to theories of dramatic construction. It was as a storyteller that he used his scenes and characters. Hence, it is a mistake to think of the scenes as actual events and of the characters as actual people tied to history or to consistency as by the events of a life—these things were symbols and dramatic puppets employed with the object of narration. Again, as a storyteller, Shakespeare was certainly not indifferent to the moral of his tales; but he did not, any more than other great storytellers, tell the tale for the sake of the moral. He did not fail, of course, to bring in "wise saws and modern instances," which he no doubt, as well as his audience, greatly enjoyed, even though "some necessary question of the play be then to be considered." Technically, also, he is conditioned, not only by the theater in which he worked and the kind of drama he had learned to write, but, apparently, by his personal situation. In a few instances he shows signs of haste or carelessness, omitting or slurring over steps in a story; sometimes he writes with a rapidity and compression almost impossible to follow.

DRAMATIC SITUATION AND CONVENTION

Many of the artistic conventions according to which Shakespeare worked arose out of the Elizabethan stage. Among these was his practice of using characters in certain situations, like the soliloquy, as his mouthpieces. We must accept at face value what characters say seriously, especially in soliloquies, about themselves and their motives, and what other characters say seriously about them in dialogue. These seem to have been Shakespeare's usual ways of imparting to the audience his own conceptions of his plots and characters. We should, therefore, usually accept as valid explicitly stated motives. We are told, for example, that Hamlet is not mad but that he "puts an antic disposition on"; that Shylock hates Antonio not out of gratuitous malice, but because Antonio is a Christian and because "in low simplicity he lends out money gratis and brings down the rate of usance here with us in Venice"; and that Iago's grudge is in part at least a soldier's grudge, because in his case the principle of "old gradation" has been violated.

For further conventions somewhat (but not entirely) peculiar to the Elizabethan stage we may acknowledge that Shakespeare often mixes up his time schemes, because on his stage the inconsistency would not be noticed. In the treatment of episodes, characters may run away with his imagination, violate consistency, and thus strain the old readymade plot by putting into it utterance which is too vigorous, original, or poetic for the situation. Shakespeare may drag in bits of historical or fictional action which are not in harmony with his treatment of the plot, because presumably they please him or are parts of his source. He is certainly not averse to

Night watch with dog.
From the title page of "The Belman of London," 1608. (Folger)

sententious and poetical speeches which are un-dramatic and for which the clue in character or plot is of doubtful appropriateness; as when Falstaff soliloquizes on honor, Mercutio describes Queen Mab, or Romeo, having heard of Juliet's death, stops in his suicidal purpose to speculate on gold, "worse poison to men's souls . . . than these poor compounds that thou mayst not sell."

SHAKESPEAREAN EXUBERANCE

All of this repeats from another point of view an age-old criticism of Shakespeare; namely, that he is an exuberant artist, that he is not restrained and classical. But this exuberance has been his chief source of power; we merely cite the facts in order to control, in the interest of a true and vivid appreciation of Shakespeare, idle and unintelligent speculation on the interpretation of Shakespearean characters and plots. We should learn to surrender ourselves so completely and so intelligently to Shake-speare's artistic appeal that we, like the audiences for whom he wrote, can enjoy his art in spite of its conventions. In doing this we shall not need com-mentators who insist forever on doing the work over in needless paraphrases of plot and endless discussions of characters. We should put ourselves, if we can, into a sufficiently receptive mood to enjoy Shakespeare's appeal to simple emotions, though in so doing it may be necessary for us to suspend our demand for naturalism and philosophy. We should recognize that what we have is a story, told usually marvelously well, with the somewhat crude device of the Eliza-bethan stage; and that it is a story which, however replete with originality, was usually already familiar to the audience for which it was written.

REFERENCES

Seventeenth and Eighteenth Centuries

BABCOCK, R. W. *The Genesis of Shakespeare Idolatry, 1766-1799.* Chapel Hill, 1931.

BENTLEY, G. E. *Shakespeare and Jonson: Their Reputations in the Seventeenth Century Compared.* 2 vols. Chicago, 1945.

DRYDEN, JOHN. *Essays,* edited by W. P. Ker. Oxford, 1900.

FARMER, RICHARD. *Essay on the Learning of Shakespeare.* London, 1767.

JOHNSON, SAMUEL. Preface to an edition of Shakespeare and current criticism within the edition, 1765.

LOUNSBURY, T. R. *Shakespearian Wars.* New Haven, 1901.

MORGANN, MAURICE. *Essay on the Dramatic Character of Sir John Falstaff.* London, 1777.

MUNRO, JOHN. *Shakespeare Allusion-Book.* London, 1909.

SMITH, D. NICHOL, editor. *Eighteenth Century Essays on Shakespeare.* Glasgow, 1903; *Shakespeare in the Eighteenth Century.* Oxford, 1928; *Shakespearean Criticism.* World's Classics, 1916.

SPENCER, HAZELTON. *Shakespeare Improved.* Cambridge, 1928.

SPINGARN, J. E., editor. *Critical Essays of the Seventeenth Century.* Oxford, 1908.

WARNER, B. E. *Famous Introductions to Shakespeare's Plays.* New York, 1906.

WESTFALL, A. VAN R. *American Shakespearean Criticism, 1607-1865.* New York, 1939.

Extensive quotations from the literary criticism of Shakespeare will be found in Furness' Variorum editions of the plays and in Moulton's *Library of Literary Criticism.*

Nineteenth Century

BOAS, F. S. *Shakspere and His Predecessors.* New York, 1910.

BRANDES, GEORGE. *William Shakespeare.* Engl. trans., New York, 1924.

BROOKE, S. A. *On Ten Plays of Shakespeare* and *On Ten More Plays of Shakespeare.* London, 1905, 1913.

COLERIDGE, S. T. *Notes and Lectures upon Shakespeare* (many reprints). T. M. RAYSOR. *Coleridge's Shakespeare Criticism.* 2 vols. Cambridge (Mass.), 1931.

DOWDEN, EDWARD. *Shakspere, His Mind and Art.* London, 1875.

ELZE, KARL. *William Shakespeare.* Engl. trans., London, 1888.

EMERSON, R. W. "Shakespeare the Poet," in *Representative Men.*

HAZLITT, WILLIAM. *Characters of Shakespeare's Plays* (many reprints).

HUDSON, H. N. *Shakespeare, His Life, Art and Characters.* New edition. London, 1895.

JAMESON, ANNA. *Characteristics of Women.* Boston, 1898; reprinted as *Shakespeare's Women.*

LAMB, CHARLES. "On the Tragedies of Shakespeare," in *Miscellaneous Essays.*

MARTIN, LADY (HELEN FAUCIT). *On Some of Shakespeare's Female Characters.* Edinburgh, 1887.

MOULTON, R. G. *Shakespeare as a Dramatic Artist.* Oxford, 1906; *The Moral System of Shakespeare.* New York, 1903; reissued under the title *Shakespeare as a Dramatic Thinker.*

SCHLEGEL, A. W. VON. *Lectures on Dramatic Art and Literature.* Engl. trans., second edition, London, 1902.

SWINBURNE, A. C. *A Study of Shakespeare.* London, 1895.

WENDELL, BARRETT. *William Shakespeare.* New York, 1894.

WHITE, R. G. *Studies in Shakespeare,* Boston, 1885.

Twentieth Century

BAKER, GEORGE P. *The Development of Shakespeare as a Dramatist.* New York, 1907.

BALDWIN, T. W. *William Shakspere's Small Latine and Lesse Greeke.* Urbana, 1944.

BRADLEY, A. C. *Shakespearian Tragedy.* London, 1904; *Oxford Lectures on Poetry.* London, 1908.

CAMPBELL, LILY B. *Shakespeare's Tragic Heroes, Slaves of Passion.* Cambridge, 1930.

CHAMBERS, SIR EDMUND K. *William Shakespeare.* 2 vols. Oxford, 1930.

CHARLTON, H. B. *Shakespearian Comedy.* London, 1938.

CRAIG, HARDIN. *An Interpretation of Shakespeare.* New York, 1948.

FAIRCHILD, A. H. R. *Shakespeare and the Arts of Design.* Columbia, Mo., 1937.

FARNHAM, WILLARD. *The Medieval Heritage of Elizabethan Tragedy.* Berkeley, 1936.

GRANVILLE-BARKER, H. *Prefaces to Shakespeare.* Four series. London, 1927, 1929, 1936; 2 vols. Princeton, 1946-1947.

KITTREDGE, G. L. *Shakspere: An Address.* Cambridge (Mass.), 1916.

LAWRENCE, W. W. *Shakespeare's Problem Comedies.* New York, 1931.

LEE, SIR SIDNEY. *Shakespeare and the Modern Stage.* New York, 1906.

MACCALLUM, M. W. *Shakespeare's Roman Plays and their Background.* London, 1910.

MACKAIL, J. W. *The Approach to Shakespeare.* Oxford, 1930.

MATTHEWS, BRANDER. *Shakespeare as a Playwright.* New York, 1913.

MAXWELL, RUTH ANDERSON. *Elizabethan Psychology and Shakespeare's Plays.* Iowa City, 1927.

PARROTT, T. M. *Shakespearean Comedy.* New York, 1949.

RIBNER, IRVING. *The English History Play in the Age of Shakespeare.* Princeton, 1957.

RALLI, AUGUSTUS. *A History of Shakespeare Criticism.* 2 vols. London, 1932.

SCHELLING, F. E. *Elizabethan Drama.* Boston, 1908. Invaluable in its presentation of Shakespeare in his relation to Elizabethan drama as a whole.

SCHÜCKING, L. L. *Character Problems in Shakespeare's Plays.* New York, 1922.

SPENCER, HAZELTON. *The Art and Life of William Shakespeare.* New York, 1940.

SPENCER, THEODORE. *Shakespeare and the Nature of Man.* New York, 1945.

STOLL, E. E. *Shakespeare Studies,* New York, 1927; *Art and Artifice in Shakespeare: A Study in Dramatic Contrast and Illusion.* Cambridge, 1933; also other later works.

TILLYARD, E. M. W. *Shakespeare's History Plays.* New York, 1946.

VAN DOREN, MARK. *Shakespeare.* New York, 1939.

WHITAKER, VIRGIL. *Shakespeare's Use of Learning.* San Marino, Calif., 1953.

Drama as a Fine Art

BAKER, GEORGE P. *Dramatic Technique.* Boston, 1919.

BUTCHER, SAMUEL H. *Aristotle's Theory of Poetry and Fine Art.* Second edition. London, 1898.

COOPER, LANE. Amplified edition of Aristotle's *Poetics.* Boston, 1913; *Aristotelian Theory of Comedy.* New York, 1922.

FREYTAG, G. *Technique of the Drama.* Engl. trans., Chicago, 1895.

MATTHEWS, BRANDER. *A Study of the Drama.* Boston, 1910.

WOODBRIDGE, ELISABETH. *The Drama, Its Law and Technique.* Boston, 1900.

Editions, Editors, and Actors of Shakespeare— Shakespeare Through the Ages

During the period of Shakespeare's dramatic activity, eighteen of his plays were printed separately in quarto editions.[1] A nineteenth, *Othello*, appeared in quarto in 1622. In 1623, seven years after Shakespeare's death, John Heminges and Henry Condell, two of his fellow actors, collected for publication the texts of thirty-six plays, which were printed in a single folio volume—the First Folio—bearing a title page as follows:

MR. WILLIAM / SHAKESPEARES / COMEDIES, / HISTORIES, & / TRAGEDIES. / Published according to the True Originall Copies. / [Droeshout engraving here] / *LONDON* / Printed by Isaac Iaggard and Ed. Blount. 1623.

THE FIRST FOLIO

The book contains an epistle dedicatory to the earl of Pembroke and the earl of Montgomery, Shakespeare's patrons, and an address *To the Great Variety of Readers*, both signed by John Heminges and Henry Condell; also Ben Jonson's famous ode *To the memory of my beloued, The AVTHOR Mr. William Shakespeare: And what he hath left us*, and other commendatory verses signed variously by Hugh Holland, L. Digges, and I [ames] M [abbe]. Another important document in the book is a list of "The Names of the Principall Actors in all these Playes."

The plays in the volume are grouped as comedies, histories, and tragedies. Each new group begins with separate pagination—a circumstance which may indicate that the publishers had originally planned to make it a three-volume work. *Troilus and Cressida* is omitted from the table of contents, but is inserted with incomplete and erroneous pagination between the histories and the tragedies. *Pericles*, which had appeared in quarto in 1609 with Shakespeare's name on its title page, is omitted altogether.

The introductory material to the First Folio supplies us with considerable information. Ben Jonson's prophetic ode with its high evaluation of Shakespeare's talents offers an estimate by his most rigorous contemporary critic. Jonson hails him as:

Soule of the Age!
The applause! delight! the wonder of our Stage!
My *Shakespeare*, rise; I will not lodge thee by
Chaucer, or *Spenser*, or bid *Beaumont* lye
A little further, to make thee a roome:
Thou art a Moniment, without a tombe,
And art aliue still, while thy Booke doth liue,
And we haue wit to read, and praise to giue.

[1] A sheet of the printing paper used by the Elizabethans was about the size of a sheet of modern foolscap. If the sheet was folded once, it provided space for four large pages, and a book made up of such sheets was called a folio. If the sheet was folded twice, it afforded space for eight smaller pages, and the book was called a quarto.

That I not mixe thee so, my braine excuses;
　　I meane with great, but disproportion'd *Muses:*
For, if I thought my iudgement were of yeeres,
　　I should commit thee surely with thy peeres
And tell, how farre thou didst our *Lily* out-shine,
　　Or sporting *Kid*, or *Marlowes* mighty line.
And though thou hadst small *Latine*, and lesse *Greeke*,
　　From thence to honour thee, I would not seeke
For names; but call forth thund'ring *Æschilus*,
　　Euripides, and *Sophocles* to vs,
Paccuuius, *Accius*, him of *Cordoua* dead,
　　To life againe, to heare thy Buskin tread,
And shake a Stage: Or, when thy Sockes were on,
　　Leaue thee alone, for the comparison
Of all, that insolent *Greece*, or haughtie *Rome*
　　Sent forth, or since did from their ashes come.
Triumph, my *Britaine*, thou hast one to showe,
　　To whom all Scenes of *Europe* homage owe.
He was not of an age, but for all time!

　　. 　. 　. 　. 　. 　. 　. 　. 　. 　.

Nature her selfe was proud of his designes,
　　And ioy'd to weare the dressing of his lines!
Which were so richly spun, and wouen so fit,
　　As, since, she will vouchsafe no other Wit.

　　. 　. 　. 　. 　. 　. 　. 　. 　. 　.

Yet must I not giue Nature all: Thy Art,
　　My gentle *Shakespeare*, must enioy a part.
For though the *Poets* matter, Nature be,
　　His art doth giue the fashion. 　. 　. 　.
. 　. 　. 　. 　. 　. 　. 　. 　. Looke how the fathers face
　　Liues in his issue, euen so, the race
Of *Shakespeares* minde, and manners brightly shines,
　　In his well torned, and true-filed lines:
In each of which, he seemes to shake a Lance,
　　As brandish't at the eyes of Ignorance.
Sweet Swan of *Auon!* what a sight it were
　　To see thee in our waters yet appeare,
And make those flights vpon the bankes of *Thames*,
　　That so did take *Eliza*, and our *Iames!*
But stay, I see thee in the *Hemisphere*
　　Aduanc'd, and made a Constellation there!
Shine forth, thou Starre of *Poets*. . . .

Heminges and Condell in the epistle dedicatory
seem to assume the responsibility for the publication
of the Folio, claiming that their act is purely a labor
of love:

We haue but collected them [the plays], and done an
office to the dead, to procure his Orphanes, Guardians;
vvithout ambition either of selfe-profit, or fame: onely to
keepe the memory of so worthy a Friend, & Fellow aliue,
as was our Shakespeare. . . .

In the advertisement *To the Great Variety of Readers*,
they repeat this claim; they also make assertions
which, at the hands of editors and critics, have been
made to yield a number of inferences concerning the
nature of the original materials used in making up
the printed text of the Folio:

It had bene a thing, we confesse, worthie to haue bene
wished, that the Author himselfe had liu'd to haue set
forth, and ouerseen his owne writings; But since it hath
bin ordain'd otherwise, and he by death departed from
that right, we pray you do not envie his Friends, the
office of their care, and paine, to haue collected & pub-

lish'd them; and so to haue publish'd them, as where
(before) you were abus'd with diuerse stolne, and surreptitious copies, maimed, and deformed by the frauds
and stealthes of iniurious impostors, that expos'd them:
euen those, are now offer'd to your view cur'd, and perfect of their limbes; and all the rest, absolute in their
numbers, as he conceiued them. Who, as he was a happie
imitator of Nature, was a most gentle expresser of it. His
mind and hand went together: And what he thought, he
vttered with that easinesse, that wee haue scarse receiued
from him a blot in his papers. But it is not our prouince,
who onely gather his works, and giue them you, to praise
him. It is yours that reade him.

Teacher with students.
From J. Stanbridge's "Vocabula," c. 1503. (Folger)

In view of the fact that the quarto texts in the
majority of instances differ in varying degrees from
those of the Folio, the Shakespeare student often has
two versions of a play to consider. For many years
after the appearance of the First Folio, the editors
and critics accorded the greater authenticity to it,
basing their ascriptions of superiority on the circumstances of its publication and on the claims made
by Heminges and Condell in the prefatory matter.
In its various addresses to the reader, in its commendatory verses by Shakespeare's fellow poets, and
in the very sanction of the two senior members of the
dramatic company which held Shakespeare's plays
in its possession, the Folio has strong claims to authenticity. The title page of the book announces that
the plays are "Published according to the True
Originall Copies," as does the page containing the

list of actors, where it is stated that the book contains "all his comedies, histories, and tragedies: truely set forth, according to their first originall."

THE COPY FOR THE FOLIO

Although it is more or less generally agreed that the use of superlatives in these addresses is conventional eulogy, much significance is to be attached to some of the statements there made. Heminges and Condell, regretting that Shakespeare did not live to "haue set forth, and ouerseen his owne writings," make no professions of having done it for him. They have merely "collected them, and done an office to the dead"; that is, they have brought together and turned over to the printer copies of the plays which they had at hand. Furthermore, the reference to the unblotted pages would imply that these copies were in Shakespeare's own autograph. This, however, is questioned. J. Dover Wilson contends,[2] perhaps mistakenly, that eight Folio plays were printed from existing quartos: *Titus Andronicus, Much Ado about Nothing, Love's Labour's Lost, A Midsummer-Night's Dream, The Merchant of Venice, Richard II, 1 Henry IV,* and *Romeo and Juliet.* At least two of the plays, *The Two Gentlemen of Verona* and *The Merry Wives of Windsor,* he thinks, have been assembled "by piecing together the players' parts and arranging them in scenes with the aid of the 'plot.'" By "plot" is meant a skeleton of the play used in staging it and containing, scene by scene, the names of the characters and the actors in order of their entrance. A considerable number of the plays in the Folio, Wilson shows, were printed directly from the prompt books of the Globe Theatre. Others had almost certainly been copied by a scrivener before they were sent to the publishers.

THE GOOD AND THE BAD QUARTOS

Most conspicuous among the assertions of Heminge and Condell is that concerning the "diuerse stolne, and surreptitious copies, maimed, and deformed by the frauds and stealthes of iniurious impostors." For a long time this statement was regarded by many as a condemnation of the quartos that had previously appeared. However, the fact that the quartos frequently offer as good texts as the Folio, occasionally even better, and that Shakespeare's fellows perhaps used some of them in preparing the Folio copy, caused a group of recent scholars to subject all the quartos to bibliographical examination. A. W. Pollard, a pioneer in this type of investigation,[3] offers as a result a new classification of Shakespeare texts wherein the quartos fall into two distinct groups which he designates as "good" and "bad." In arriving at this grouping, Pollard selects as good texts those quartos that he thought had been used as copy for the Folio, and, secondly, those which

have been generally agreed upon by Shakespeare editors as being good texts. There are fourteen:

Titus Andronicus................1594
Richard II.....................1597
Richard III....................1597
Love's Labour's Lost............1598
1 Henry IV....................1598
Romeo and Juliet...............1599
The Merchant of Venice.........1600
Much Ado about Nothing.........1600
2 Henry IV....................1600
A Midsummer-Night's Dream......1600
Hamlet...................1604-1605
King Lear....................1608
Troilus and Cressida..........1609
Othello.......................1622

Of these fourteen "good" quartos, twelve, Pollard notes, were regularly entered in the Stationers' Register to the printers or publishers whose names appear on the title pages. The two exceptions are *Love's Labour's Lost* and *Romeo and Juliet.* A very poor version of the latter play had been published in 1597, in allusion to which the good quarto of 1599 bore on its title page the statement, "*Newly corrected, augmented, and amended.*" Since this good copy was a second edition, license for its publication was not required. The title page of *Love's Labour's Lost* indicates that it too may possibly have superseded a quarto (now lost), and that license was not required

From Thomas Hill's
"The Gardeners Labyrinth," *1652. (Huntington)*

for its reissue. Finding the absence of an entry in the Stationers' Register in the case of these two good quartos explainable by their possibly being second editions, Mr. Pollard proposes, as another characteristic of the "good quarto," its authorized publication.

The converse of this situation is true in regard to the "bad" quartos. The texts which he places in this group are:

Romeo and Juliet...............1597
Henry V......................1600
The Merry Wives of Windsor......1602
Hamlet.......................1603
Pericles......................1609

[2] J. Dover Wilson, "The Task of Heminge and Condell," *Studies in he First Folio,* pp. 55-77.
[3] See A. W. Pollard, *Shakespeare's Folios and Quartos* (1909) and *Shakespeare's Fight with the Pirates* (Cambridge, 1920).

Of these quartos *Romeo and Juliet* and *Henry V* were printed without license from the Stationers' Company, and *Hamlet* and *Pericles* were entered to other firms than those publishing them. *The Merry Wives of Windsor* presents the anomaly of having been transferred to a second publisher on the very day of its license. John Busby, the man to whom it was entered, and the printer, Thomas Creed, were also responsible for the bad version of *Henry V* in 1600—another circumstance which gives the quarto of *The Merry Wives of Windsor* a questionable reputation. The actual publisher, Arthur Johnson, Pollard remarks, was probably cautious enough to insist on Busby's entering the book before he would buy it for publication. At any rate, all five of these quartos have suspicious records with respect to the regulations of the book trade. To this group should also be added *The First Part of the Contention betwixt the two famous Houses of York and Lancaster* (1594) and *The True Tragedy of Richard Duke of York* (1595) as imperfect versions of *2* and *3 Henry VI* respectively. The former was entered in the Stationers' Register; the latter was not. Perhaps in addition should be listed *The Taming of a Shrew*, which is a degenerate version, not of *The Taming of the Shrew*, but of a lost shrew play on which Shakespeare's play is also based. *Pericles* is not a "bad" quarto at all but is Shakespeare's revision of a lost play on the same subject.

These "bad" quartos, in addition to their not being regularly authorized for publication, present inferior texts; that is, they are abbreviated and badly garbled in comparison with the texts of corresponding plays in the Folio. This condition has been thought to be due to their having been copied by stenography during a performance, or to a dishonest actor's patching up of a version from his own player's part and what he could remember of the parts of others. These thefts may have been, and probably were, committed in order to get a version for acting rather than for printing; and such stolen texts may later have fallen into the hands of the printers. The piracy explanation is in accord with Heminges and Condell's allusion to the "stolne and surreptitious copies." In most cases, however, these "bad" quartos are merely stage versions that have undergone degeneration in the process of being acted on the road.

The final discrimination between good and bad texts must rest on the relation they bear to the manuscripts as the author prepared them. In whatever way the bad texts came into existence, there is every indication that they are some distance removed from the author's original. For some plays the Folio is the only authoritative source of text; for others, good quartos claim superiority to the Folio. However, in a few cases, such as *Richard III*, there is occasion for indecision between a quarto and the Folio, since each presents a text independent of the other, and both are in themselves good. The "goodness" of the quarto of *Richard III* and of the 1608 quarto of *King Lear* has also been called into question. Neither exception

is perhaps well taken, since the quarto of *Richard III* offers a differing version but a very good one, and the *King Lear* quarto is apparently printed from Shakespeare's original manuscript.

THE PLAYWRIGHT AND HIS PLAY

Such is the complex situation with regard to Shakespeare's printed texts. How Shakespeare got into print is a problem which owes its complexity to the fact that the poet was in no way concerned with the printing of his plays; he did not even prepare his manuscripts with any expectation of their appearing in printed form. Shakespeare wrote, apparently, with one idea in mind—that of producing plays which

A sheet of music for five-part singing.
From "Teares or Lamentations of a Sorrowfull Soule."
Written by W. Leighton, 1614. (Folger)

would act well on the stage, attract large numbers of spectators, and swell the receipts of the Globe Theatre. The somewhat hostile reception in 1616 of the folio collection of Ben Jonson's plays indicates a lack of regard on the part of the Elizabethan public for stage plays as serious literary productions.

The relation of the playwright to his play and to its actors explains one aspect of the problem. Playwriting was an occupation of the hour, an activity in which men engaged to supply an immediate demand. A dramatist was usually attached by contract to a specific company for which he was under bond to furnish a stipulated number of plays. He did not work out his play independently of the players. In fact, it was his duty to produce a piece which would provide parts for the several actors of the company. Shakespeare's skill in adapting roles to actors is attested in the new type of clown which he introduced into his plays about 1599, when, by a change in the Lord Chamberlain's company, Robert Armin took Will Kemp's place as chief comic actor. For Kemp he had written clownish parts like Bottom and Dogberry; for the more courtly Armin he provided Touchstone and Feste.

The poet may have chosen his own theme for a play, he may have been given a piece to revise, or he may have been instructed to write a new play to rival a popular one in another theater. At any rate, the company bought the completed play outright; and with the exception, possibly, of realizing a "benefit" for its first performances, or in case he were also an actor, of assuming one of its roles, or of subjecting it later to revision, the dramatist was severed by the sale from all connections with his drama. If the play made its appearance in print, the text for it had to be acquired by the publisher through the company owning it or some version of it.

THE PRINTING OF PLAYS

It was not to the interests of a dramatic company to have its plays printed. A popular play, available to the public only through a stage performance by its owners, was one of the greatest assets of a company. The agreement among sharers in the Whitefriars Theatre in 1608 attests the higher value which was placed on an unprinted play. Among other terms, they agree:

That no man of the said company shall at any time hereafter put into print, or cause to be put in print, any manner of play-book now in use, or that hereafter shall be sold unto them, upon the penalty and forfeiture of forty pounds sterling, or the loss of his place and share of all things amongst them.[4]

Nevertheless, many stage plays were printed. The Stationers' Register shows that between 1590 and 1600 over 150 plays were authorized for publication. As J. Q. Adams observes,[5] it is difficult to believe that such a large number would have been so authorized without the consent of the owners. Adams points out possible reasons for which acting companies may have released manuscripts for printing. In the first place, when a company disbanded, play manuscripts, along with their other mutual property, were divided among the shareholders, who, to realize some profit, might sell them either to other acting companies or to publishers. In the second place, some misfortune might necessitate the sale of play manuscripts. It is significant that at times when the theaters were closed for long periods on account of the plague, or were threatened by Puritan agitation, the number of plays licensed for printing increased greatly. Again, the publication of a play might follow upon some unusual circumstance. It is thought that *1 Henry IV* was printed soon after its composition and while it was still creating a great sensation, in order to pla-

cate the Cobham family, who had taken offense at the use of their ancestral name Oldcastle for the fat knight whom Shakespeare subsequently rechristened Falstaff. Finally, the company might give an author permission to have a play or a collection of plays printed. Instances of this are found in the publication of Heywood's *The Rape of Lucrece* and Ben Jonson's folio collection of 1616. Indeed, Shakespeare's First Folio itself is an instance in which the owners authorized the publication of plays.

When acting companies permitted the printing of their plays, the publisher who bought the book from the company would take the manuscript to the warden of the Stationers' Company, to whom he paid sixpence for having it entered on the Register of the company. The Stationers' Company was an association of London printers and publishers incorporated in 1557 for the control of the book trade.

Minting coins.
From Holinshed's "Chronicles," 1577. (Folger)

Pollard observes that the presence in London of more printers than there was work for contributed to the prevalence of piracy of books. An unscrupulous printer, if he were in hard straits financially, would be willing to pay a few pence for a bad copy. A means of piracy which is frequently used in explanation of a bad text is that of the shorthand reporter. That such men sat in the theater and took down plays by stenography is known. Thomas Heywood alludes to such a method when he makes the complaint that some of his plays had, without his knowledge or direction, "come into the Printers hands, and therefore so corrupt and mangled, (coppied only by the eare) that I have been as vnable to know them, as ashamed to challenge them. . . ."[6] Recent scholarship has also attempted to explain some of the bad texts by means of the theory of the dishonest actor. Some one of the cast, most likely not a shareholder of the company but a hired man, would, they think, put together a garbled text, piecing it out from memory with the aid of his own lines and cues. Something of this sort must have been alluded to by Heminges and Condell when they decried the "stolne, and surreptitious copies, maimed, and deformed by iniurious imposters." Either method, it is obvious, would produce a bad text.

Since so many of the poorer quartos bear evidence of having been acted on the stage, one must believe that they were made up in the first instance to be acted, and, at a later time, fell into the hands of the printers. Too great stress has perhaps been put on the eagerness of dramatic companies to protect their plays from printers, since there were many plays and some of them no doubt were regarded as of little value. The cost of copying a play would be prohibitive, and it may be that, when an extra manuscript existed, it was disposed of to printers almost casually.[7]

PLAYS "TO BE STAYED"

Some of the plays are entered in the Stationers' Register with special provisions which have been regarded as means of precaution against piracy. *The Merchant of Venice* was licensed on July 22, 1598, to James Roberts, "Prouided, that yt bee not prynted by the said James Robertes or anye other whatsoeuer without lycence first had from the Right honorable the lord Chamberlen." *Troilus and Cressida* was entered to Roberts in 1603 "to print when he hath gotten sufficient aucthority for yt." Evidently sufficient authority was not forthcoming, for in 1609 this play was printed after a second entry "by *G. Eld* for *R. Bonian* and *H. Walley.*" *Henry V, As You Like It,* and *Much Ado about Nothing* are named "to be staied" on a flyleaf of *Register C* on August 4, 1600, in a list of "My lord chamberlens mens plaies Entred." In commenting on this note Pollard says, "As there is no book-seller's name to the staying entries, it is clear that they were made directly at the instance of 'my lord chamberlens men.'"[8] Such notes and entries, Pollard thinks, indicate precaution on the part of the company to safeguard its property.

The known facts and inferences with regard to original Shakespeare texts may be summed up as follows: in 1623, thirty-six of the plays were authoritatively published in the First Folio. Prior to this date nineteen had appeared in quarto—twelve of these present texts undoubtedly authentic; three have every indication of illegitimate origin; two exist in both good and bad quartos; *The Contention* and *The True Tragedy,* distorted versions of *2* and *3 Henry VI,* are also to be regarded as "bad" quartos. Repeated editions of some of the quartos evince Shakespeare's popularity. *Richard III* and *1 Henry IV* were each

printed five times during Shakespeare's lifetime. Several other plays went through three or four editions before the printing of the Folio in 1623.

THE COLLECTION OF 1619

In 1619 an attempt was made to publish a collection of Shakespeare's plays. Thomas Pavier, a stationer of questionable standing in the brotherhood, undertook the project. He had the copyright to *Henry V*[9] and to four other plays which had some connection with Shakespeare's name. These plays are *A Yorkshire Tragedy,* printed in 1608 for Pavier with Shakespeare's name on the title page; *The Whole Contention between the Famous Houses of Lancaster and York,* already published separately as *The Contention* and *The True Tragedy;* and *Sir John Oldcastle,* which is related in subject to the Henry IV plays. With these five plays as a nucleus, he appropriated five other plays to which he had no right: *The Merchant of Venice, A Midsummer-Night's Dream, The Merry Wives of Windsor, King Lear,* and *Pericles.* It appears that his design was to publish these ten plays in a single quarto volume which William Jaggard was to print for him. For some reason Pavier abandoned his original plan, but, in order that he might not suffer too great financial loss, he broke the volume up into separate quartos. Why he abandoned his scheme is a matter for conjecture. It may be that some of the rightful owners of the good quartos got wind of the venture and threatened to prosecute him. His unscrupulousness is thought to appear in his placing on some of the title pages fictitious dates, and on all of them curtailed and abbreviated imprints;[10] however, there may have been no fraudulent intent, since he may have intended to place a correctly dated title page in front of the collected volume. But Pavier's publication gives us certain quartos with the same dates as the first editions, something which puzzled the scholars; however, Pavier's quartos are only reprints. They are distinguished from the true first editions by the differing imprints and by various new errors in the printing.

THE FOLIO COPYRIGHTS

This abandoned attempt at a collected edition of Shakespeare may have furnished the suggestion for publishing the 1623 Folio. At any rate, the Folio followed hard upon the Pavier venture. Since William Jaggard was the printer in both enterprises, one is tempted to infer that he was the promoter of this second project. But if he did conceive the idea, he could not consummate it alone. In the first place, he possessed copyrights of only those plays which had been licensed to James Roberts, whose printing business he had acquired in 1608. The copyrights of

[7]R. B. McKerrow, "The Elizabethan Printers and Dramatic Manuscripts," *The Library,* N. S., XII (1931), 253-275.
[8]*Shakespeare's Folios and Quartos* (1909), p. 35.

[9]This play was assigned to Pavier, by whom it is not stated, on August 14, 1600, ten days after a staying entry.
[10]For a full discussion see A. W. Pollard, *Shakespeare's Folios and Quartos* (1909), ch. iv; W. J. Neidig, "The Shakespeare Quartos of 1619," *Modern Philology,* VII (1910), 145 ff.

the other quartos were distributed principally between William Aspley and John Smethwick. Matters were facilitated by bringing these men in as joint publishers. Edward Blount, who held the right to *Antony and Cleopatra* and to *Pericles*, also became a member of the partnership. By such a coalition the group had control of all the licensed quartos except *Troilus and Cressida*, which belonged to Henry Walley, *Richard II*, *Richard III*, and *1 Henry IV*, all belonging to Matthew Law, and the two other plays, *Henry V* and *The Merry Wives of Windsor*, belonging to Thomas Pavier and Arthur Johnson respectively. What negotiation took place between the Folio editors and these men is not known. The fact that *Troilus and Cressida* is inserted between the histories and the tragedies with incorrect pagination, and is omitted from the catalog of plays at the head of the volume, has suggested that Walley for a long time refused to allow the inclusion of this play. Its inclusion was finally achieved. There remained then the eighteen plays as yet unprinted in any form to be supplied by the King's men. This copy, one may believe, was not always in easily usable condition. For more than twenty years many of the manuscripts had been used as prompt books. In at least two cases, as has been mentioned, it is possible that texts for the Folio were made up from players' parts with the aid of the "plot." Heminges and Condell were, however, able to produce respectable texts of *2* and *3 Henry VI*, *Henry V*, and *The Merry Wives of Windsor*, which had been circulating for twenty years or more in only maimed and deformed state. On November 8, 1623, the entry for the First Folio was made in the Stationers' Register.

M^r. Blounte: Isaak Jaggard. Entred for their Copie vnder the hands of Mr. Doctor Worrall and Mr. Cole, Warden, M^r. William Shakspeers Comedyes, Histories and Tragedyes, soe manie of the said Copies as are not formerly entred to other men. vizt, Comedyes. The Tempest. The two gentlemen of Verona. Measure for Measure. The Comedy of Errors. As you Like it. All's well that ends well. Twelft Night. The winters tale. Histories. The thirde parte of Henry the sixt. Henry the eight. Coriolanus. Timon of Athens. Julius Caesar. Tragedies. Mackbeth. Anthonie and Cleopatra. Cymbeline.

It is impossible to know how many copies of the book were printed. Sir Sidney Lee has estimated that there were about 750, although that number is probably too small. About 150 copies are now extant. The book sold in 1623 for twenty shillings. In 1922 the Burdett-Coutts copy was sold in London for 8600 pounds.

THE LATER FOLIOS

After nine years, the first edition of the First Folio being exhausted, a second was printed. In 1663 a third appeared. A second issue of the third edition came out in 1664 in which were included seven pseudo-Shakespearean plays not previously printed in folio: *Pericles*, *The London Prodigal*, *The History of Thomas Lord Cromwell*, *Sir John Oldcastle*, *The Puritan Widow*, *A Yorkshire Tragedy*, and *Locrine*. All of these have been rejected from the canon except *Pericles*, and its claim is sometimes questioned. These seven plays were also included in the Fourth Folio of 1685. Each of the three folios subsequent to the first is a reprint of the one next preceding it, each adding new errors and frequently unwarranted corrections.

*The Globe Theatre,
as reproduced by
Irwin Smith.*

The formal editing of Shakespeare began in 1709 with Nicholas Rowe's seven-volume work, containing the plays as they are in the Fourth Folio. He made some corrections, some emendations, marked the exits and entrances of characters, divided the plays into acts and scenes where this had not been already done, and placed a list of *dramatis personae* at the beginning of each play. His edition was reissued in 1714.

Alexander Pope next undertook the editing of Shakespeare. His edition, comprising six volumes, appeared in 1725. He excluded from his work the spurious plays which had been added to the Third Folio. His text is based substantially on that of Rowe, but he added to each scene the place of action and made some changes in scene-division. Pope sometimes rewrote the text of Shakespeare, regularizing the blank verse, filling in passages with his own composition, and rejecting some passages which he considered spurious.

The next editor was Lewis Theobald, a man of unusual critical skill, who made many brilliant conjectural emendations. He was the first to consult the original quartos and the First Folio. His text,

first appearing in 1733, was reissued in 1740, 1752, 1772, and 1773. There followed successively editions by Sir Thomas Hanmer in 1744, by Bishop Warburton in 1747, by Dr. Samuel Johnson in 1765 (who made a beginning in the historical point of view in Shakespeare criticism), by Edward Capell in 1768, and by George Steevens in 1773 (a revision of the edition of Dr. Johnson).

In 1790 Edmund Malone produced his ten-volume edition. He reintroduced *Pericles*, which had been excluded since the time of Pope. Malone was a man of great intellectual vigor and a careful scholar. Not content to work on Shakespeare's text in isolation, he read widely in the Elizabethan drama and collected numerous letters and documents of the time. He made use of Henslowe's *Diary*, the Stationers' Register, and the records of the Master of Revels. Malone began work on the first Variorum edition of Shakespeare, an edition recording all textual variants. This was completed in 1821 by James Boswell, the son of Johnson's biographer. Malone's work marks the close of the first period of Shakespeare scholarship. It is a period characterized by objective treatment, with no search for subtleties. Texts were usually determined by a selection of readings that seemed to editors to make the best sense, and there was little discrimination among versions; whereas, at the present time, an editor determines the history of older texts and gives precedence to those versions that best reproduce what Shakespeare wrote. The first edition to follow a modern method was the Cambridge (listed below) by Clark and Wright and the Globe, which is Wright's reissue in one volume of the Cambridge. These editions gave the world a standard text of Shakespeare that is still excellent and in wide use.

The nineteenth century produced many editions of Shakespeare, and the work of editing still goes on. The following editions are the more important. They are listed here in order to make intelligible many references in the notes to the plays and poems. William Harness (1825, 8 vols.), S. W. Singer (1826, 1856, 10 vols.), J. Payne Collier (1841-1844, 8 vols.), Charles Knight (1838-1842, 8 vols.), Alexander Dyce (1857, 9 vols.), Howard Staunton (1868-1870, 3 vols.), Nikolaus Delius (1854-1861, 7 vols.), H. N. Hudson (1851-1856, 11 vols.), J. O. Halliwell [-Phillipps] (1853-1861, 15 vols.), William George Clark and Aldis Wright (Cambridge, 1863-1866, 9 vols.; Globe, 1864, 1 vol.), Richard Grant White (1857-1865, 12 vols.), W. J. Rolfe (1871-1896, 40 vols.), Appleton Morgan (Bankside, 1888 ff.), F. A. Marshall and others (The Henry Irving Shakespeare, 1888-1890, 8 vols.), C. H. Herford (Eversley, 1899, 10 vols.), F. J. Furnivall (Leopold with Delius' text, 1874, 1 vol.), Sir Israel Gollancz (Temple, 1894-1895, 40 vols.), W. J. Craig (Oxford, 1894, 1 vol.), Helen Porter and Charlotte Clarke (First Folio, 1903-1914, 40 vols.), W. A. Neilson (1906, 1 vol.; new edition, 1942), G. L. Kittredge (Boston, 1936, 1 vol.).

Shakespeare as an English Dramatist

54

A gentleman.
From Philip Stubbes' "Anatomy of Abuses," 1583. (Folger)

*An instrument
of clownage.
(Huntington)*

give the background of his life and work; such as the British Museum, the Bodleian Library at Oxford, the Folger Shakespeare Library in Washington, D.C., and the Henry E. Huntington Library in San Marino, California. Other important collections are: the Birmingham (England) Public Library, the Boston Public Library (Barton Collection), Cambridge University Library (Sandars Collection), the Dyce Collection at the Victoria and Albert Museum in London, Edinburgh University Library (Drummond and Halliwell Collections), Harvard University Library (White Collection), John Carter Brown Library, Providence, Rhode Island, the Pierpont Morgan Library in New York, the Shakespeare Birthplace Library and the Shakespeare Memorial Libraries in Stratford-on-Avon, and the library of Trinity College, Cambridge (Capell Collection). Besides these there are many smaller collections and much material is in private hands.

Besides these there are the recently completed annotated editions, one play to the volume, under the editorship of various scholars: Tudor (W. A. Neilson and A. H. Thorndike, general editors), Arden (W. J. Craig, general editor), and Yale (W. L. Cross, Tucker Brooke, and W. H. Durham, general editors). The new Variorum Edition, under the editorship of H. H. Furness, later of H. H. Furness, Jr., now of a committee of the Modern Language Association of America, is still in progress; rather more than half the total number of Shakespeare's plays have appeared.

A facsimile of the First Folio with an introduction by Sir Sidney Lee was published by the Oxford University Press in 1902, and facsimiles of all four Folios by Methuen, 1904-1910. Most of the early quartos were reproduced by a photo-lithographic by J. W. Griggs under the supervision of F. J. Furnivall, 1883-1888, in 43 volumes, but are not wholly trustworthy. A good many of the quartos have appeared in new accurate facsimiles done in collotype reproduction. The Huntington Library has issued both the 1603 and the 1604-1605 quartos of *Hamlet;* the Folger Shakespeare Library, *Titus Andronicus* of 1594; and the Shakespeare Association (London), *King Lear* of 1608, *The Merchant of Venice* of 1600, *The Merry Wives of Windsor* of 1602, *Hamlet* of 1604-1605, *Pericles* of 1609, and *Romeo and Juliet* of 1599, with others in progress. Facsimiles of a number of First Folio texts of separate plays have been issued under the editorship of J. Dover Wilson. A good deal of the work of nineteenth-century English scholars is included in the publications of the Shakespeare Society (1841-1853) and of the New Shakespeare Society (1874-1894), though Shakespeare material is scattered over a wide range.

Of the utmost interest and value to students of Shakespeare are the great collections of early editions of Shakespeare's works and books and documents that

SHAKESPEARE ON THE CONTINENT

In the later years of Queen Elizabeth and in the time of King James, English players traveled widely in Scotland, Ireland, France, and the countries of northern Europe. They carried with them their plays, and in Germany particularly the English drama took root. The players had their patrons and their imitators on German soil. The days of the wanderings of the English actors extended from about 1586 until at least the time of the outbreak of the Thirty Years' War in 1618.

A number of their play lists are in existence, and most of the plays can be recognized as those of the London stage. A few of the plays themselves have been preserved—translated into German, adapted to German tastes, and often rendered almost unrecognizable. There is no one of them of which it can be certainly said that it is based on a play of Shakespeare, although there are six or more which are somehow related to his plays. We seem in every case to have to do with pre-Shakespearean versions rather than with Shakespeare, a condition to be explained by the circumstance that the greater number of the English dramas imported by the players into Germany were carried there in the early nineties of the sixteenth century.

A volume of *Englische Comedien und Tragedien* (1620) contains among others *Julio und Hyppolita,* related to *The Two Gentlemen of Verona,* and *Titus Andronicus,* related to Shakespeare's play of the same name. Jacob Ayrer of Nuremberg wrote about 1595, apparently under English influence, *Die schöne Sidea,* and *Die schöne Phoenicia,* related in theme to *The Tempest* and *Much Ado about Nothing,* respectively. There is a German *Romeo and Juliet* from a seventeenth-century Vienna manuscript; and the best known of all is *Der bestraffte Brudermord,* a play on the subject of *Hamlet,* derived from a manuscript now lost which bore the date 1710. There are also a few other puzzling relations between Shakespeare and the plays of this first period of English influence in Germany.[11]

The Continent yielded slowly to Shakespeare's influence. After Lessing's *Hamburgische Dramaturgie* (1767), however, there began in Germany a profound interest in Shakespeare, which has increased rather than diminished in force as time has gone on. Germany has produced a great group of Shakespeare scholars. Goethe was much interested in Shakespeare, and Schiller was his imitator. Among the important German names in Shakespeare scholarship are A. W. von Schlegel and Ludwig Tieck, who together produced a famous translation of Shakespeare, which has itself taken rank as a classic; others are: Hermann Ulrici, G. G. Gervinus, Friedrich Kreyssig, Karl Elze, Nikolaus Delius, Bernhard ten Brink (a Hollander, most of whose work was in German), Wilhelm Creizenach, Wolfgang Keller, and L. L. Schücking. The Germans have been, until recently, effective students of staging, and indeed always have given Shakespeare the advantage of frequent presentation on the stage. Much of the work of German Shakespeareans is contained in the *Shakespeare-Jahrbuch.*

In France though Shakespeare met with long opposition, he won the favor of Victor Hugo, and has been frequently seen on the French stage, and now has a relatively large following. In Italy, likewise, Shakespeare was little known before the nineteenth century, but there too he has been acted with great success and has attracted the attention of many scholars. In recent years Shakespeare has been eagerly studied in Slavic countries, in Japan, and in India.

STAGE HISTORY

It may be that the seventeenth and eighteenth centuries were inferior to the nineteenth in high appreciation of Shakespeare's genius and in their methods of studying his plays; but in another respect they were not inferior. They acted Shakespeare so well that the foundations of his posthumous reputation were laid by his career on the stage. The results of the work of scholars and critics are slow in coming, their appeal being to readers; interpretation by actors is, on the other hand, immediately addressed to the audience, who have been deliberately prepared in their emotions both to understand and to feel.

The actors for whom Shakespeare wrote his plays were evidently a great group. This appears in the case of Richard Burbage, for whom he created the parts of Richard III, Romeo, Brutus, Hamlet, Othello, Lear, Macbeth, Antony, Coriolanus, and Prospero; in actors like Thomas Pope, for whom he may have written the part of Falstaff; John Heminges, who may have played the parts of Polonius and Kent; Will Kemp, who played Dogberry and may have played Bottom; Robert Armin, for whom Shakespeare wrote the parts of Touchstone, Feste, and the

Fool in *King Lear;* and, finally, the boy actor, possibly Robert Goffe, who played Portia and Juliet, and the one, possibly John Edmans, to whom was given the task of playing Lady Macbeth and Cleopatra. Burbage's immediate successor in the principal roles was Joseph Taylor, who is known to have played the part of Iago and who played leading roles in the dramas of Beaumont and Fletcher and of Massinger.

When the theaters were reopened after the Restoration of Charles II, Shakespeare was frequently acted. At this time there appeared, in Thomas Betterton

RICHARD TARLETON
one of the first Actors in
SHAKESPEARS PLAYS.

(Huntington)

(1635?-1710), a great Shakespearean actor. Betterton made some investigations as to Shakespeare's life, learned what he could about the stage tradition of the earlier age, and acted a large number of Shakespeare roles, principally Hamlet, Othello, Brutus, Coriolanus, and Macbeth. He encouraged the appearance of women in women's parts on the stage, instead of boys in these parts as had been the Elizabethan and Jacobean custom; his wife, who was first known on the stage as Mrs. Saunderson, played Ophelia to his Hamlet and Lady Macbeth to his Macbeth. Another actor of the time was Barton Booth (1681-1733), a man of great ability and charming disposition. The

[11]A. Cohn, *Shakespeare in Germany* (1865); W. Creizenach, *Schauspiele der englischen Komödianten* (Berlin, 1903); E. K. Chambers, *The Elizabethan Stage,* I, 342-347; II, 272-292.

Irishman Robert Wilks (1635?-1732) was on the stage in time to be Betterton's rival. He was an actor of very great versatility and appeared in many plays. Charles Macklin (1697?-1797), also Irish, carried on the Betterton tradition. He is illustrious because it was he who perceived the deeper human qualities in the character of Shylock, a part which had been played as a sort of comic villain until Macklin made of him a figure of dignity and pathos.

The great David Garrick (1717-1779) made his appearance on the stage in 1741 and for thirty-five years was a completely dominant figure. Garrick is the originator of the modern school of acting. Before his time acting was highly conventionalized and certainly declamatory. Garrick "held a mirror up to nature," and the consequent variety of passion and mood and versatility in impersonation gave the English stage its preëminence for a hundred years. He was a scholarly, intelligent man who saw that Shakespeare was better than his adapters, and, although he did do a good deal of violence to Shakespeare in the texts he played, his claim that he had restored the true Shakespeare to the stage is probably by and large valid.

Mrs. Clive, Mrs. Cibber, and Mrs. Pritchard played leading women's parts in Garrick's performances. He had won his reputation with the part of Richard III and acted that play as part of the repertory of his farewell appearance in 1776; with him on that occasion Sarah Siddons (1755-1831), the greatest of English tragic actresses, played the part of Lady Anne. Her career really began in 1782 and lasted until her retirement in 1812. She belonged to the famous stage family of the Kembles. Her brother Charles Kemble was a talented actor, and her elder brother John Philip Kemble (1757-1825) succeeded Garrick in the leadership of the English stage. John Philip Kemble was a man of such taste, learning, and power that his influence was long felt.

A few years before Kemble's death a new star of the first magnitude appeared. Edmund Kean (1787-1833), who is regarded as the greatest genius who has ever appeared on the English stage, played in London for the first time on February 26, 1814, at Drury Lane Theater in the part of Shylock. He was the greatest of Richards, Hamlets, and Othellos, and his King Lear has set the pattern for all subsequent impersonations and has probably never been equaled. His wonderful career came to an end in 1833. After Kean, William Charles Macready (1793-1873) was the leading Shakespearean actor in England for more than forty years. Associated with him were Mrs. Warner and Helen Faucit (Lady Martin).

One of the most important ventures in the acting of Shakespeare during the nineteenth century was a series of excellent revivals of nearly all the plays under the leadership of Samuel Phelps (1804-1878) at Sadler's Wells Theater from 1844 to 1862. Nothing quite so extensive and so successful has been done in England since. Sir Henry Irving (1838-1905), an actor of great distinction, played in many roles and was noteworthy for the perfection of his staging and costumes. From 1878 until 1901 he was assisted by Dame Ellen Terry. The most important actor of Shakespeare since Sir Henry Irving is Sir Johnston Forbes-Robertson (1853-1937).

Meantime in America there had sprung up a vigorous interest in the dramatic presentation of Shakespeare. Contemporary with Kean and Macready were Junius Brutus Booth (1796-1852) and Edwin Forrest (1806-1892). Then came John Edward McCullough (1837-1885), a follower of Forrest in the more rhetorical style of acting. Edwin Booth (1833-1893) was the greatest of American actors of Shakespeare. Refined in his methods and not wanting in culture and scholarship, he was a highly gifted actor, and his fame was worldwide. Associated with him for a time in the acting of Shakespeare was Lawrence Barrett (1831-1891). Since Booth's time we have had the very excellent work of E. H. Sothern, who has carried on the Booth tradition. Great American Shakespeare actresses have been Charlotte Cushman (1816-1876), Mary Anderson (1859-1940), Ada Rehan (1860-1916), and Julia Marlowe (1866-1950).

About the beginning of the present century there began a movement to do away with the elaborate costuming and scenery which had characterized the playing of Shakespeare in the nineteenth century; people became interested in the production of Shakespeare's plays on the bare stage of the Elizabethans. A part of the change was a greater simplicity and sincerity in the acting itself. This so-called Elizabethan stage movement was led by William Poel, F. R. Benson, Ben Greet, and some others.

The development indicated may perhaps be connected with a notable revival of interest in Shakespeare which has characterized the present century. Shakespeare has been studied in schools and colleges as never before, and it is perhaps fair to claim two things for the most recent Shakespeare revival—a revival still in progress: (1) superiority in intelligence including deeper and truer knowledge of Shakespeare, his life and times, and (2) extension of Shakespeare's appeal. There has been much acting of Shakespeare by numerous well-trained professionals and by many excellent amateurs, so that Shakespeare has had stage presentation on a scale perhaps never before equaled. The activities, influencing the whole world, of the Stratford repertory company and the stock company at the "Old Vic" in London have been distinguished by the genuineness of their appeal to the public. Noteworthy was the experiment at the world's fairs of Chicago and San Diego of a strictly popular "Globe" theater. Ordinary people attended in a casual and genuine fashion, even as on the Bankside of Shakespeare's days, and liked the plays not because they were classics, but because they appealed to the public taste. In this current Shakespeare revival have appeared actors of great power and charm.

Possibly the two Englishmen John Gielgud and Maurice Evans have been the most important individuals, but this distinction is slightly invidious, since the nature of the movement itself has brought about this altogether desirable condition—that there have appeared, not single stars, but numerous excellent Shakespearean actors.

On the moving-picture screen a number of Shakespeare's plays have appeared, but it cannot be said that the problem of adapting Shakespeare to that medium has been solved. From the nature of the performance much of the language and poetry of Shakespeare has to be sacrificed, and the extreme stress on setting, to which the screen lends itself so remarkably, has the effect, however beautiful and impressive, of distorting or changing Shakespeare. Shakespeare becomes too much a feast of the eye and too little a feast of the mind. Still, the form is young, and some of the performances, such as those of *Romeo and Juliet* and *A Midsummer-Night's Dream*, have been very striking. Certainly Sir Laurence Olivier's presentations of *Henry V* and *Hamlet* have set a standard of the highest dramatic excellence.

The four eminent actors of Shakespeare in Germany in the nineteenth century, as given by Sir Sidney Lee, were Friedrich Ulrich Ludwig Schroeder (1744-1816), Ludwig Devrient (1784-1832), his nephew Gustav Emil Devrient (1803-1872), and Ludwig Barnay (1842-1924). In recent years work of the greatest distinction was done by Max Reinhardt (1873-1943). From 1893 to 1903 he was an actor at Salzburg and at Berlin. After 1903 he produced at the Deutsches Theater and his own theaters in Berlin practically all of Shakespeare, as well as of Molière, Goethe, Ibsen, and other important dramatists. His method of staging, which employed the principle of artistic suggestion in form and color rather than accurate historical detail, has been followed all over the world. His performance of *A Midsummer-Night's Dream* surprised and delighted America by its beauty and its sheer elaborateness. Shakespeare seems to lend himself to every sort of dramatic presentation, from the bare boards to the utmost appeal of pageantry. In England the new staging methods have been used in the work of Edward Gordon Craig, Harley Granville-Barker, and Sir Barry Jackson. France has produced a few eminent Shakespeare actors including Mme. Bernhardt, and Italy has had Mmes. Ristori, Salvini, and Rossi.

A scorpion.
From Gesner's "Historia Animalium," 1587. (Huntington)

REFERENCES

ADAMS, J. Q. *A Life of William Shakespeare,* Chapters xxvii, xxviii, xxix, xxx. Boston, 1923.

ALBRIGHT, EVELYN MAY. *Dramatic Publication in England, 1580-1640.* New York, 1927.

ALEXANDER, PETER. *Shakespeare's "Henry VI" and "Richard III."* Cambridge, 1929.

Aspects of Shakespeare. Being British Academy Lectures. Oxford, 1933.

BALDWIN, T. W. *Organization and Personnel of the Shakespearean Company.* Princeton, 1927.

BARTLETT, HENRIETTA C. *Mr. William Shakespeare: Original and Early Editions of His Quartos and Folios, His Source Books, etc.* New Haven, 1923.

CHAMBERS, SIR EDMUND K. *William Shakespeare. A Study of Facts and Problems.* 2 vols. Oxford, 1930; *A Short Life of William Shakespeare.* Abridged by CHARLES WILLIAMS from SIR EDMUND CHAMBERS' *William Shakespeare. A Study of Facts and Problems.* Oxford, 1933; *The Disintegration of Shakespeare.* Annual Shakespeare Lecture of the British Academy. Oxford, 1924.

CRAIG, HARDIN. *A New Look at Shakespeare's Quartos.* Stanford, 1961.

FARNHAM, WILLARD. *The Medieval Heritage of Elizabethan Tragedy.* Berkeley, 1936.

GREG, SIR WALTER. *Two Elizabethan Stage Abridgements:* . . . . Oxford, 1923; *Principles of Emendation in Shakespeare.* Annual Shakespeare Lecture, British Academy. Oxford, 1928; *The Editorial Problem in Shakespeare.* Oxford, 1942; *The Shakespeare First Folio.* Oxford, 1955.

HARRISON, G. B. and HARLEY GRANVILLE-BARKER. *A Companion to Shakespeare Studies.* Cambridge, 1934.

HART, ALFRED. *Shakespeare and the Homilies.* Melbourne, 1934; *Stolne and Surreptitious Copies: A Comparative Study of Shakespeare's Bad Quartos.* Melbourne, 1942.

HERFORD, C. H. *A Sketch of Recent Shakespeare Investigation.* London, 1923.

LEE, SIR SIDNEY. Introduction to the Oxford Facsimile of the First Folio, 1902.

LINTHICUM, M. CHANNING. *Costume in the Drama of Shakespeare and his Contemporaries.* Oxford, 1936.

MCKERROW, RONALD B. *An Introduction to Bibliography.* Oxford, 1927; "The Elizabethan Printer and Dramatic Manuscripts," in *The Library,* Four Ser., XII (1931), 253-275; *Prolegomena for the Oxford Shakespeare.* Oxford, 1939.

NEIDIG, W. J. "The Shakespeare Quartos of 1619," in *Modern Philology,* VIII (1910), 145 ff.

PLOMER, H. R. "The Printers of Shakespeare's Plays and Poems," in *The Library,* new series, VII (1916), 149 ff.

POLLARD, A. W. *Foundations of Shakespeare's Text.* London, 1923; *Shakespeare's Fight with the Pirates.* Cambridge, 1920; *Shakespeare's Folios and Quartos.* London, 1909; Edition of *The Tragedy of King Richard II.* Introduction. London, 1916.

POLLARD, A. W., and H. C. BARTLETT. *A Census of Shakespeare's Plays in Quarto, 1594-1709.* New Haven and London, 1916.

POLLARD, A. W. and OTHERS. *Shakespeare's Hand in the Play of "Sir Thomas More."* Cambridge, 1923.

POLLARD, A. W., and J. DOVER WILSON. "The 'Stolne and Surreptitious' Copies," articles in the *Times Literary Supplement,* Jan. 9, 1919, p. 18; Jan. 16, 1919, p. 20; Mar. 13, 1919, p. 134; Aug. 7, 1919, p. 420; Aug. 14, 1919, p. 434.

RHODES, RAYMOND CROMPTON. *Shakespeare's First Folio: A*

Study. Oxford, 1923; "Shakespeare's Prompt Books," in the *Times Literary Supplement*, July 21, 1921, p. 467; July 28, 1921, p. 482.

SIMPSON, PERCY. "The Bibliographical Study of Shakespeare," Oxford Bibliographical Society, *Proceedings and Papers*, I, 19-53.

Studies in the First Folio (1623-1923), written for the Shakespeare Association. Oxford, 1924.

THOMPSON, SIR E. MAUNDE. *Shakespeare's Handwriting: A Study.* Oxford, 1916; also "Handwriting," in *Shakespeare's England*, Oxford, 1917. I, 284-310.

WILSON, J. DOVER. Textual introduction to *The Tempest.* Cambridge, 1921. *The Manuscript of Shakespeare's "Hamlet" and the Problems of Its Transmission.* 2 vols. Cambridge, 1934.

For further bibliography of textual studies of particular plays, of the stenographic theory of the origin of the bad quartos, and of other special problems of the transmission of Shakespeare's text, consult Ebisch and Schücking, *A Shakespeare Bibliography* (1931) and *Supplement* (1936); *Cambridge Bibliography of English Literature*, I, 539-608; Chambers, *William Shakespeare, passim;* Hazelton Spencer, *op. cit.*, bibliography for "Textual Matters" and for each play; Greg, *The Editorial Problem in Shakespeare, passim;* and current annual bibliographies.

Bibliographies of Shakespeare on the Continent will be found in *The Cambridge History of English Literature*, V, 456-472; Ebisch and Schücking, *A Shakespeare Bibliography*, pp. 129-130; and in *Cambridge Bibliography of English Literature*, I, 599-608. See also the following books on the subject:

BÖHTLINGK, A. R. A. *Goethe und Shakespeare.* Leipzig, 1909.

CROCE, BENEDETTO. *Ariosto, Shakespeare and Corneille.* New York, 1922.

GENÉE, R. *Geschichte der Shakespeareschen Dramen in Deutschland.* Leipzig, 1870.

GUNDOLF, FRIEDRICH. *Shakespeare und der deutsche Geist.* Berlin, 1922.

HAINES, C. M. *Shakespeare in France.* London, 1928.

HUGO, VICTOR. *William Shakespeare.* Paris, 1864.

JUSSERAND, J. J. *Shakespeare in France under the ancien régime.* London, 1899.

KREYSSIG, F. *Vorlesungen über Shakespeare.* 2 vols. Berlin, 1877.

LEE, SIR SIDNEY. "Shakespeare in France," in *Shakespeare and the Modern Stage.* London, 1907.

LOUNSBURY, T. R. *Shakespeare and Voltaire.* New York, 1902.

PASCAL, R. (ed.) *Shakespeare Criticism in Germany, 1740-1815.* Cambridge, 1937.

STENDHAL [MARIE HENRI BEYLE]. *Racine et Shakespeare.* Paris, 1925.

TEN BRINK, BERNHARD. *Shakespeare.* Strassburg, 1893.

TOLSTOI, L. N. *Tolstoi on Shakespeare.* London and New York, 1907.

The lives and memoirs of actors and dramatic critics offer important information on the stage history of Shakespeare's plays; for example, those of Betterton, Booth, Cibber, Forbes-Robertson, Garrick, Irving, Kean, Kemble, Macready, Macklin, Phelps, Winter. See also the following list of books:

BAKER, HENRY BARTON. *Our Old Actors.* 2 vols. London, 1878.

BROWN, J. S. *A History of the New York Stage, 1732-1901.* 3 vols. New York, 1903.

CONKLIN, PAUL S. *A History of Hamlet Criticism, 1601-1821.* New York, 1947.

DORAN, JOHN. *Annals of the English Stage from Thomas Betterton to Edmund Kean.* Edited and revised by Robert W. Lowe. London, 1888.

FITZGERALD, PERCY. *A New History of the English Stage.* 2 vols. London, 1882.

GENEST, J. *Some Account of the English Stage, from the Restoration in 1660 to 1830.* 10 vols. Bath, 1832.

LEE, SIR SIDNEY. *Life of William Shakespeare.* London. 1925, pp. 342-371.

MURRAY, JOHN TUCKER. *English Dramatic Companies, 1558-1642.* 2 vols. London, 1910.

ODELL, G. C. D. *Shakespeare from Betterton to Irving.* New York, 1920; *Annals of the New York Stage.* 4 vols. New York, 1927-1928.

SCOTT, CLEMENT. *The Drama of Yesterday and Today.* 2 vols. London, 1899.

SEILHAMER, G. O. *A History of the American Theater.* Philadelphia, 1891.

SPENCER, HAZELTON. *The Art and Life of William Shakespeare.* New York, 1940.

Shakespeare's English

We could probably understand the spoken English of Shakespeare's time; but the speaker, even when his words were just the ones we would use, would seem to us to be speaking a strange dialect. This is because spoken English, mainly in the pronunciation of vowel sounds, has undergone many striking changes. Some authorities have claimed that the original pronunciation adds something to the melody of Shakespeare's verse and to the vividness of his speech, so that the experiment of learning it may be worth trying. One can, however, indicate only approximately what the pronunciation was, because local dialects seem then to have been far more commonly used by educated persons than they are now and because several of the commonest vowel sounds were in a state of transition and are, therefore, difficult to fix definitely.

We know that Sir Walter Raleigh spoke his native Devonshire dialect, and it may be that Shakespeare's oral utterance was colored by the Warwickshire dialect. A few Warwickshire words and expressions occur in his plays. The London dialect had become even more dominant than it was in Chaucer's time, but because of a wider national intercourse London speech had taken in a large admixture of northern, eastern, and southern forms.

PRONUNCIATION

Consonants were in general pronounced as they are now. There were, however, a few differences. The *k* and *g* were pronounced in such words as *knife* and *gnaw*, and *l* was sounded in *should, would, folk*, etc. The *-tion* and *-sion* endings were usually pronounced as two syllables and were not yet given the sounds of *sh* and *zh*. The letter *r* was clearly pronounced, but was probably losing its trilled quality.

The short vowels *a*, *e*, and *i* were pronounced as at present, although short *a* was in transition from *a* in *Colorado* (*o* in *folly*) to *a* in *that*. Short *o* was probably more distinctly an *o*-sound than it is with us; that is, it was like the *o* in *folk* rather than the *o* in *hot*. A greater number of the short *u*'s had the genuine *u*-sound, rather than the lax vowel we now hear in many words; that is, *brush* rhymed exactly with *push*, and *dull* with *pull*. Long *a* in words like *state* was an open sound like the *a* in *hat* prolonged and diphthongized. Open and close long *e* were discriminated; that is, *seam* and *seem* were not sounded alike, the former being somewhat like *same* only more open (*a* in *hat* prolonged), and the latter pretty much as it is now. Long *i* was in a transitional state and was variously uttered. Bradley[1] expresses the opinion that it usually had the sound of *i* in *pin* followed by the consonantal *y*. Long open *o* (like the *oa* in *broad*) still had its proper sound, so that a word like *old* was pronounced *auld*. Long close *o* had probably completed its change from the long *o*-sound to the *oo*-sound. Long *u* was approximately short *i* followed by *w*, so that *tiwn* and *riwl* represent the pronunciation of *tune* and *rule*. The change which gave us our pronunciation of *blue*, *rue*, and *jury* did not occur until the eighteenth century. Perhaps *ai* and *ay* were usually pronounced like our long *i;* that is, *day* was like our word *die*. The diphthong *oi* (*oy*) may be represented by *ooi*. The sound of *ou* and *ow* varied, as it still does, according to descent. When the sound came from Old English long *u* or French *ou*, it was like *oo* in *boot;* when it came from Old English *ag*, *ah*, *aw*, or *ow* with a long vowel, it was sounded like *au* in *autumn;* for example, *house* was pronounced *hoos*, and *soul*, *know*, and *own*, as *saul*, *knaw*, and *awn*, respectively.

A matter of more practical importance than phonetic changes is that of differences in Shakespeare's English and ours in the accentuation of syllables. There are many cases of variable stress in Shakespeare, in which he seems to have been at liberty to accent the word in two different ways; in other cases words were customarily accented on a different syllable from that in current speech. For example, the following accentuations are either usual or frequent: *aspect'*, *charac'ter*, *com'mendable*, *com'plete*, *con'ceal'd*, *con'fessor*, *consort'* (n.), *contract'* (n.), *de'testable*, *dis'tinct*, *envy'*, *for'lorn*, *hu'mane*, *instinct'*, *ob'scure*, *persev'er*, *pi'oner*, *ple'beians*, *portents'*, *pur'sue*, *record'* (n.), *reven'ue*, *se'cure*, *sinis'ter*, *welcome'*.

Not only are *-tion* and *-sion* regularly pronounced as two syllables, but the same situation causes other words in which *e* or *i* stand before vowels to be uttered in Shakespeare's language with one more syllable than in ours; for example, *oce-an*, *courti-er*, *marri-age*. We may even have *cre-ature*, *tre-asure*, and *venge-ance*. Nasals and liquids are frequently pronounced as if an extra vowel were introduced between them and a preceding letter. We accordingly have *wrest(e)ler*,

Eng(e)land, *assemb(e)ly*, and *ent(e)rance*, as well as *de-ar*, *you(e)r*, and *mo-re*. Final *-er* often has a greater syllabic importance than it ever has in later poetry, as in the line: "And thére / upón, / gíve me / your daúgh / tér" (*Henry v*, V, ii, 375). Final *-(e)s* in the genitive singular and the plural of nouns not ending in an *s*- sound may constitute a separate syllable; for example, "To show his teeth as white as wha-*le's* bone" (*Love's Labour's Lost*, V, ii, 332).

An idea of the spelling and of the pronunciation of the Shakespearean language may be gained from the following passage (*King Lear*, IV, vi, 11–24), which is reproduced, first, in the text of the First Folio and, secondly, in Vietor's transcription of the English of the First Folio in the International Phonetic Alphabet as he employed it. The transcribed passage has the punctuation of the Globe text.[2]

How fearefull
And dizie 'tis to cast ones eyes so low,
The Crowes and Choughes, that wing the midway ayre
Shew scarce so grosse as Beetles. Halfe way downe
Hangs one that gathers Sampire: dreadfull Trade:
Me thinkes he seemes no bigger then his head.
The Fishermen, that walke vpon the beach
Appeare like Mise: and yond tall Anchoring Barke,
Diminish'd to her Cocke: her Cocke, a Buoy
Almost too small for sight. The murmering Surge,
That on th'vnnumbered idle Pebble chafes
Cannot be heard so high. Ile looke no more,
Least my braine turne, and the deficient sight
Topple downe headlong.

huw feːrful
ænd dizi tiz, tu kæst oːnz ijz soː loː!
ðe krouz ænd tʃufs ðæt wiŋ ðe midwæi æir
ʃoːskærs so groːs æz biːt,lz : haːf wæi duwn
hænz oːn ðæt gæðerz sæmpijr, dre(ː)dful træːd!
mi θinks hi siːmz no biger ðen hiz hed:
ðe fiʃermen, ðæt waːk upon ðe beːtʃ
æpeːr lijk mijs; ænd jond taːl ænk(o)riŋ bærk,
diminiʃt tu her kok : her kok, æ bwoi
aːlmoːst tu smaːl for sijt : ðe murm(u)riŋ surdʒ,
ðæt on ðunnumbred ijd,l peb,l, tʃaeːfs,
kænot bi hærd so hij. ijl luːk no moːr;
le(ː)st mij bræin turn, ænd ðe defisient sijt
top,l duwn hedloŋ.

There thus arises in the reading and scansion of Shakespeare a problem as to how many syllables the poet intended a given word to have, for as compared to current English a Shakespearean word (a) may have an additional syllable or (b) may have one

<hr>

[2] Key: The symbol is given first, then the key-word in Modern English. Explanations are in parentheses. æ:, *name* (*a* in *hat* prolonged); æ, *hat*; æi, *day* (*a* in *hat* followed by *e* in *be*); a:, *saw*; e:, *there*; e, *get*; eu, *few* (*e* in *get* followed by *oo* in *too*); i:, *be*; i, *bit*; ij, *by* (slightly prolonged in pronunciation); iu, *mute*; o, *folk*; o:, *saw* (slightly less open); oi, *boy* (first element of the sound slightly closer to long *o*); ou, *own* (slightly closer to *ow* in *gown*); u:, *too*; u, *full*; uw, *too* (*oo* followed by *w*); ŋ, *sing*; ð, *the*; θ, *thin*; ʃ, *shall*; ʒ, *urge*.

Shakespeare as an English Dramatist

60

[1] Henry Bradley, article on "Shakespeare's English" in *Shakespeare's England* (1904), II, 543.

Kemps nine daies vvonder.
Performed in a daunce from
London to Norwich.

*Containing the pleafure, paines and kinde entertainment
of William Kemp betweene London and that Citty
in his late Morrice.*

Wherein is fomewhat fet downe worth note ; to reprooue
the flaunders fpred of him : many things merry,
nothing hurtfull.

Written by himfelfe to fatisfie his friends.

LONDON
Printed by *E. A.* for *Nicholas Ling*, and are to be
folde at his fhop at the weft doore of Saint
Paules Church 1600.

Title page of "Kemps nine daies vvonder," *1600. (Folger)*

fewer syllables, or (c) two adjoining syllables in different words may coalesce. The difficulty is that such differences may or may not appear in the spelling of words. The following lines and words will illustrate these situations.

(a) I do wander every where,
   Swifter than the moon'ş sphere.
          (*A Midsummer-Night's Dream*, II, i, 6-7)
   O me! You juggĺer! You canker-blossom.
          (*A Midsummer-Night's Dream*, III, ii, 282)
   After the prompter: for our entïrance.
                    (*Romeo and Juliet*, I, iv, 8)
   Mislike me not for my complexïon.
                    (*The Merchant of Venice*, II, i, 1)

The words *caṗtain, monstŕous, esperancë, this* (*this is*), *Georgë* (*Richard III*, V, v, 9), *valiant, villain, jealous,* have extra syllables in pronunciation.

(b) Good mother, do not marry me to yond fool.
          (*The Merry Wives of Windsor*, III, iv, 87)

The words *lineal, journeying, carrion, celestial, herald, royal, malice, absolute, perjury, madame, needle, taken, gentleman, unpeople, forward, gather, innocent, violet, Africa, eagle, listen, venomous,* have usually one fewer syllables than in current English.

(c) Why should I joy in any abortive birth?
                    (*Love's Labour's Lost*, I, i, 104)
   He was paid for that.   (*Cymbeline*, IV, ii, 246)
   The lover, all as frantic.
             (*A Midsummer-Night's Dream*, V, i, 10)
   Romans, do me right. (*Titus Andronicus*, I, i, 203)

Differences in accentuation and lengthening of words, of course, have great importance in the reading and scanning of Shakespeare's verse, as also do the various ways by which words are shortened. Shortening of words by elision or by slurring is, of course, very common in Shakespeare, but in this matter the modern practice forms a good guide. Syllables ending in vowels are not infrequently elided before words beginning with a vowel, as in "How cáme / *we ashóre*" (*The Tempest*, I, ii, 158) and "too hárd / a knót / for mé / *to untie*" (*Twelfth Night*, II, ii, 42). Syncopation, or the omission of a syllable, often occurs in words with *r*, as "I wár-*rant* / it wíll" (*Hamlet*, I, ii, 243); and in final -*er*, -*el*, and -*le*, as "Trável you / far ón" (*The Taming of the Shrew*, IV, ii, 73) and "I am / a gént*le* / mán of / a cóm / paný" (*Henry v*, IV, i, 39). The following words and other similar ones may be treated as monosyllabic in Shakespeare's verse: *whether, ever, hither, other, father, evil, having.* Almost any unaccented syllable of a polysyllabic word (especially if it contains an *i*) may be softened and ignored; this syncopation is frequent in polysyllabic words and proper names; as "Thoughts spécu / latíve" (*Macbeth*, V, iv, 19) and "Did sláy / this Fórt*inbras;* / who, bý / a seál'd / compáct" (*Hamlet*, I, i, 86). Other occasions for slurring, as listed by Abbott in his *Shakespearian Grammar*, are light vowels preceded by heavy vowels, as *po*wer, *dy*ing, etc.; plurals and possessives of nouns ending in an *s*-sound, final -*ed* following *d* or *t*, as "you háve/ excéed*ed* / all prómise" (*As You Like It*, I, ii, 256); and the -*est* of superlatives (pronounced -*st*) after dentals and liquids, as "the stérn'st / good-níght" (*Macbeth*, II, ii, 4) and "thy éld'st / son's són" (*King John*, II, i, 177).

GRAMMAR

Shakespeare's grammar presents but few differences in forms from the grammar of current modern English. The -*eth* ending in the third person singular of the present tense, indicative mood, was very commonly used, especially in serious prose. Shakespeare frequently uses the older form, especially *hath, doth,* and *saith,* but seems to prefer the form in -*s* or -*es*. There are also a few cases in which he seems to use the old northern plural in -*s* or -*es* in the third person of the present indicative; as ". . . at those springs On chaliced flowers that *lies*" (*Cymbeline*, II, iii, 24-25). He does not always agree with modern usage in the forms of the past tenses and the perfect participles of the verbs that he employs. He retains some lost forms of the strong verbs, sometimes confuses the past tense with the perfect participle, or vice versa, and treats some verbs as weak (or regular) which are now strong (or irregular). For example, he uses *arose* for *arisen, swam* for *swum, foughten* for *fought, gave* for *given, took* for *taken, sprung* for *sprang, writ* for *wrote*. He has *blowed* for *blew, weaved* for *wove, shaked* for *shaken*. Forms like *degenerate* for *degenerated* and *exhaust* for *exhausted* are especially common. There are a few cases of the archaic *y-* with the past participle, as in *yclad*. The regular form of the possessive case of the neuter personal pronoun *it* was *his*. This is Shake-

Shakespeare's
English

61

speare's usual form; but he has also a possessive form *it*, and in the First Folio, published seven years after Shakespeare's death, there are several occurrences of the new form *its*. Shakespeare uses the old form *moe* as the plural of *many*, and the form *enow* as the plural of *enough*. *Near* and *next* are employed, along with *nearer* and *nearest*, as the comparative and superlative of *nigh*. These are the most obvious of the formal differences between Shakespeare's grammar and our own.

A hornbook, c. 1550. (Folger)

The functional differences are more considerable. Elizabethan language exercised an extraordinary freedom, even for English, in the use of one part of speech for another. Shakespeare uses verbs, adjectives, adverbs, and pronouns as nouns. He makes verbs out of nouns and adjectives, and, of course, uses nouns as adjectives, for this is a distinguishing characteristic of English speech; but he uses also adverbs, verbs, and prepositional phrases as adjectives. Almost any adjective may be freely used as an adverb. He makes active words, both adjectives and adverbs, discharge a passive function; as "the sightless [invisible] couriers of the air" (*Macbeth*, I, vii, 23) and "this aspect of mine Hath fear'd the valiant," i.e., caused the valiant to be afraid (*The Merchant of Venice*, II, i, 8-9). There is a wider use in Shakespeare

of the infinitive as a verbal noun or as a gerundive participle than in our language; as "This to be true, I do engage my life" (*As You Like It*, V, iv, 171-172), "My operant powers their functions leave to do" (*Hamlet*, III, ii, 184), "Nor do I now make moan to be abridged" (*The Merchant of Venice*, I, i, 126), and "you might have saved me my pains, to have taken [by having taken] it away yourself" (*Twelfth Night*, II, ii, 6). The functions of prepositions in Elizabethan English were so various that one can only refer the student to the notes to the text or to a dictionary.

In certain other features, however, Shakespeare's language is as restricted and conventional as ours is at formal levels, or even more so. *Shall* is regularly used in Shakespeare to express something inevitable in future time, and is, therefore, the usual future tense for all persons. *Will*, which originally expressed intention, determination, or willingness, was, however, beginning to encroach on *shall* for the expression of futurity in the second and third persons; but in its use there is usually a consciousness of its original meaning. *Should* and *would* had their original senses of obligation and volition, respectively, and had other peculiarities, then as now, of considerable difficulty. The subjunctive mood was not only vital in Shakespeare but was used carefully. It expressed condition, doubt, concession, and command. It was used to express wish or desire and in dependent clauses to express indefiniteness, purpose, or sometimes simple futurity. Note the following examples:

But if my father *had* not scanted me . . .
Yourself, renowned prince, then *stood* as fair.
　　　　　　　(*The Merchant of Venice*, II, i, 17, 20)
　　　　　　　　　　　Live a thousand years,
I *shall* not find myself so apt to die.
　　　　　　　(*Julius Caesar*, III, i, 159-160)
Lest your retirement *do amaze* your friends.
　　　　　　　(*1 Henry IV*, V, iv, 6)
'Twere best he speak no harm of Brutus here.
　　　　　　　(*Julius Caesar*, III, ii, 73)
Melt Egypt into Nile! and kindly creatures
Turn all to serpents! (*Antony and Cleopatra*, II, v, 78-79)
　　　　　　　　　　　Yet were it true
To say this boy *were* like me.
　　　　　　　(*The Winter's Tale*, I, ii, 134-135)
And may direct his course as *please* himself.
　　　　　　　(*Richard III*, II, ii, 129)

The following minor features of Shakespeare's grammar deserve notice: he often omits the relative pronoun; often uses the nominative case of the pronoun for the accusative case, and vice versa; uses *him, her, me,* and *them* as true reflexives to mean *himself, herself, myself,* and *themselves;* employs double negatives and double comparatives and superlatives; shows a consciousness in the use of *thee* and *thou* of their application to intimates and inferiors and of their insulting quality when addressed to strangers (e.g., "If thou thouest him some thrice, it shall not be amiss," *Twelfth Night*, III, ii, 48); employs *which* to refer to both persons and things; and does not discriminate closely between *ye*, nominative, and *you*, objective. Finally, he makes frequent use of the dative constructions, i.e., the objective forms of the pronouns, *me*, *thee*, *you*, *him*, *her*, etc., without prepositions where the meaning is "by me," "for me," "with me," "to me," "of me," etc. For example:

I am appointed *him* [by him] to murder you.
(*The Winter's Tale*, I, ii, 412)
She looks *us* [to us] like
A thing made more of malice than of duty.
(*Cymbeline*, III, v, 32-33)

Particular mention should be made of the ethical dative, a construction in which the pronoun is used to indicate the person interested in the statement. In *King John* (III, iv, 146) we have "John lays *you* plots," i.e., "plots which you may profit by." In the following, *me* means "to my detriment" or "to my disadvantage":

See how this river comes *me* cranking in,
And cuts *me*, from the best of all my land,
A huge half moon.   (*1 Henry IV*, III, i, 98-100)

"Whip *me* such honest knaves" (*Othello*, I, i, 49) means "In my judgment such knaves should be whipped." In Quickly's description of Mistress Page, the dative *you* is equivalent to "mark you," "take notice":

. . . a civil modest wife, and one, I tell you, that will not miss *you* morning nor evening prayer, as any is in Windsor. (*The Merry Wives of Windsor*, II, ii, 100-103)

Of the forms and figures of rhetoric there are in Shakespeare, as in other poets, innumerable instances. He is very fond, for example, of using the abstract for the concrete, as in the words addressed by Surrey to Cardinal Wolsey, "Thou scarlet sin" (*Henry VIII*, III, ii, 255). Transpositions are numerous, as are inversions, ellipses, and broken or confused constructions, as in the following examples:

That thing you speak of,
I took it for a man = absolute construction.
(*King Lear*, IV, vi, 77-78)
Souls and bodies hath he divorced three = transposition of adjective.   (*Twelfth Night*, III, iv, 260)
A happy gentleman in blood and lineaments = transposition of adjectival phrase.   (*Richard II*, III, i, 9)
Your state of fortune and your due of birth = transposition of pronoun.   (*Richard III*, III, vii, 120)
She calls me proud, and [says] that she could not love me = ellipsis.   (*As You Like It*, IV, iii, 16)
Returning were as tedious as [to] go o'er = ellipsis.
(*Macbeth*, III, iv, 138)
They call him Doricles; and boasts himself
To have a worthy feeding = ellipsis of nominative.
(*The Winter's Tale*, IV, iv, 168-169)
Of all men else I have avoided thee = confusion of two constructions.   (*Macbeth*, V, viii, 4)
The venom of such looks, we fairly hope,
Have lost their quality = confusion of number arising from proximity.   (*Henry V*, V, ii, 18-19)
Rather proclaim it, Westmoreland, through my host,
That he which hath no stomach to this fight,

Let him depart = construction changed by change of thought.   (*Henry V*, IV, iii, 34-36)
For always I am Cæsar = inversion of adverb.
(*Julius Caesar*, I, ii, 212)

THE SHAKESPEAREAN VOCABULARY

With reference to words and their meanings the spirit of the Renaissance manifested itself in England in very great hospitality to foreign importations. Large numbers of words were taken directly from Latin. In fact there was an inundation of classicism, for it was a fashion among writers to pillage the Latin language. Many of the words so introduced were naturalized and served to enrich the language, its power to express thought, and its rhythmical capabilities; many were discarded. The principal borrowings were in the realm of learning and culture, and they were usually employed with distinct recollection of their Latin sense. Sometimes such words have not replaced native words of the same meaning, so that we have such pairs of synonyms as *acknowledge* and *confess;* just as Shakespeare had *wonder* and *admiration*. It follows that even a slight knowledge of Latin is a great advantage in the correct understanding of Elizabethan writers, since many Latin borrowings have taken on since the sixteenth century a different shade of meaning from that in which they were borrowed. The Latin sense of *aggravate* still struggles for recognition; but *apparent* no longer means primarily *visible* or *evident*, and *intention* does not convey the idea of *intentness*.

Latin words were often taken over in their Latin forms, as *objectum* and *subjectum*, *statua* and *aristo-cratia*, and later were made to conform to English spelling and accentuation, though a few, such as *decorum*, still have a Latin form. French continued to be drawn upon and sometimes caused a new Latin borrowing to be adopted in a French form; just as, on the other hand, such words as *adventure* were supplied with a *d* to make them conform to Latin spelling. Note that this principle is illustrated in the pedantry of Holofernes when he objects (*Love's Labour's Lost*, V, i, 25) to "det" as the pronunciation of "debt." Spanish, Italian, and Dutch were made to supply many terms. Spanish gave words having to do with commerce, religion, and the New World; such as *mosquito*, *alligator*, *ambuscado*, and *grandee*. From Italian came terms of art, learning, and dueling: *bandetto*, *portico*, *canto*, *stoccato*. The Dutch contributed many nautical and oriental words.

These foreign borrowings were a part of what might be called the linguistic ambition of the age, a desire for forcible expression. Language was in a plastic state, so that it had an unparalleled freedom in both vocabulary and form; and with this came a consequent confusion, since there were in Elizabethan times few efforts at grammatical precision. Such efforts were made by the age of Dryden and the Royal Society, who felt that English was too vague and irregular for use as a means of scientific expression. Indeed the task of rendering the language more precise has been the object of the learned part of the population ever since the sixteenth century, and yet it must be acknowledged that English could never have been as great a language as it is without its Renaissance expansion and its subsequent absorption with Shakespeare and the English Bible. It gained, for example, an increased facility in the making of compounds. Shakespeare, with his *cloud-capp'd towers* and his *home-keeping wits*, was a genius at this. Likewise from Shakespeare's time came the English power in the use of prefixes, such as *dis-*, *re-*, *en-*, and of suffixes, such as *-ful*, *-less*, *-ness*, *-hood*.

Obsolete words, however, and words employed by Shakespeare in entirely different meanings give the student little trouble. The difficulty arises from the innumerable cases in which the student is able to get without effort an idea fairly close to Shakespeare's meaning, so that he constantly understands Shakespeare imperfectly. He is thus liable to miss the exact shade of meaning and consequently the tone of Shakespeare's feeling. In Othello's account to the Venetian senators of the circumstances of his courtship of Desdemona (*Othello*, I, iii, 158-166) he says:

My story being done,
She gave me for my pains a world of sighs: . . .
She wish'd she had not heard it, yet she wish'd
That heaven had made her such a man; she thank'd me,
And bade me, if I had a friend that lov'd her,
I should but teach him how to tell my story,
And that would woo her. Upon this *hint* I spake.

The word *hint* means *occasion* or *opportunity;* it does not mean *invitation* or *suggestion by covert allusion.* To understand the word in the contemporary sense changes subtly the meaning of the passage.

The real secret of Shakespeare's language is to learn the attitude toward speech accepted by him and his contemporaries. Speech was traditionally and piously regarded as God's final and consummate gift to man, and speech in the thought of the Elizabethans was ultimately powerful. Truth, if truly uttered, was bound to prevail. To have heard truth and to have rejected it was an unnatural thing. It showed that Satan had entered the obdurate heart and caused it to reject God's truth. Christians were bound to preach the Word, and, when the Word had been uttered clearly and rejected, the heretic or culprit should be destroyed. Hence, the struggle to excel in utterance, the practice, the sincerity, and the eloquence.

REFERENCES

ABBOTT, E. A. *A Shakespearian Grammar.* London, 1869; often reprinted.

ATKINS, J. W. H. "The Language from Chaucer to Shakespeare," in *Cambridge History of English Literature,* III, 499-530; accompanied by a bibliography of sixteenth-century English language.

BARTLETT, JOHN. *Concordance to Shakespeare.* New edition. London, 1922.

BAUGH, ALBERT C. *A History of the English Language,* New York, 1935. Chapter viii.

BRADLEY, HENRY. "Shakespeare's English," in *Shakespeare's England,* II, 539-574; *The Making of English,* London, 1904.

CUNLIFFE, R. J. *New Shakespearean Dictionary.* London, 1910.

FRANZ, W. *Shakespeare-Grammatik.* Second edition. Heidelberg, 1909.

GORDON, GEORGE. *Shakespeare's English.* Oxford, 1928.

JESPERSEN, OTTO. *Growth and Structure of the English Language.* Third Edition. Leipzig, 1919.

KÖKERITZ, HELGE. *Shakespeare's Names: A Pronouncing Dictionary.* New Haven, 1959.

ONIONS, C. T. *A Shakespeare Glossary.* Oxford, 1911, 1919.

NARES, ROBERT. *A Glossary to Shakespeare and His Contemporaries.* New ed. by J. O. Halliwell and Thomas Wright. 2 vols. London, 1901.

A New English Dictionary. Oxford, 1888-1928.

SCHMIDT, ALEXANDER. *Shakespeare-Lexicon.* Third edition. Berlin, 1902.

VIETOR, W. *A Shakespeare Phonology.* Marburg, 1906.

WYLD, H. C. *Short History of English.* London, 1914.

ZACHRISSEN, R. E. *Pronunciation of English Vowels,* 1400-1700. Göteborg, 1913.

A Note on Doubtful and Lost Plays

The latest editor of the Shakespeare *Apocrypha* enumerates forty-two plays, other than those included in the First Folio, which at one time or another have been ascribed to Shakespeare.[1] Thirty-six plays, some of them attributed in whole or in part to other authors, have the sanction of having been included by Heminges and Condell in the folio edition of *Shakespeare's Comedies, Histories and Tragedies* in 1623. The effect of recent intensive study of the First Folio has been to increase the respect of scholars for the work of Shakespeare's two fellow actors and to make disagreement with them more cautious. The canon now stands pretty much as the contents of the First Folio. To the thirty-six therein contained *Pericles* has been added. Some scholars believe that Shakespeare collaborated with John Fletcher in the authorship of *The Two Noble Kinsmen*, but the matter is extremely doubtful. Recently a noteworthy attempt has been made to establish Shakespeare's authorship of certain scenes in *Sir Thomas More*. Beyond this there is nothing established or accepted with reference to any of the vast group of doubtful plays. If the list be reduced by the rejection of utterly baseless attributions, there remains a body of about a dozen plays which without absurdity may be thought of as possibly somehow touched by Shakespeare's hand.

The Two Noble Kinsmen

In 1634 was entered in the Stationers' Register by John Watterson "A Tragi Comedy called the two

[1] *The Shakespeare Apocrypha,* C. F. Tucker Brooke, ed. (Oxford, 1908, 1918). See bibliography of the subject of doubtful plays in *Cambridge Bibliography of English Literature,* I, 576-580.

noble kinsmen by John Fletcher and William Shakespeare." The same year appeared: "*The Two Noble Kinsmen: Presented at the Black-friers by the Kings Maiesties servants, with great applause: Written by the memorable Worthies of their time; Mr. John Fletcher, and Mr. William Shakespeare, Gent.* Tho. Cotes for John Watterson." *The Two Noble Kinsmen* is to be dated pretty certainly in 1613.[2]

In spite of the testimony of the title page of the 1634 quarto, critical opinion has been much divided on the question of whether or not Shakespeare had any hand in the composition of *The Two Noble Kinsmen;* about Fletcher's hand there is no doubt. It is obvious at a glance that the play was written by two authors of very different styles; one of these styles seems to be Fletcher's and the other compares in some respects with Shakespeare's in his latest period. The only objection to Shakespeare's part authorship is that the parts of the play attributed to him fall far short of the quality of *Cymbeline, The Winter's Tale,* and *The Tempest.* On the other hand, it is hard to find any other author who could equal some of the poetry in those parts. C. H. Herford has advanced the hypothesis that the Shakespearean parts are late poetical fragments pieced together by Fletcher, and, some critics add, Massinger. The subject of the authorship of the play has engaged a great deal of attention, and opinions are still very much divided.[3]

The Two Noble Kinsmen is based immediately on Chaucer's *The Knight's Tale,* recounting in dramatic form and in close detail the story of the rivalry of the two Theban cousins, Palamon and Arcite, for the hand of the fair Emilia—their imprisonment, their infatuation with the lady, their quarrel, their escapes from prison, their duel in the lists, the victory and death of Arcite, and the union of Palamon and Emilia.

A play called *Palaemon and Arcyte* by Richard Edwards was performed before Queen Elizabeth at Oxford in 1566, and a "Palamon and Arsett" is mentioned in Henslowe's *Diary* in 1594; but neither play could have affected *The Two Noble Kinsmen* very greatly since, as announced in its prologue, it is a new play and since it follows Chaucer with great fidelity. At the time of the Restoration, *The Two Noble Kinsmen,* having been altered by D'Avenant, was produced (1664) under the name of *The Rivals* (published in 1668). Since then the stage history of the play is a complete blank. It has perhaps been performed on rare occasions on the public stage in Germany and possibly by amateurs in England and America.

ADDITIONS TO THE THIRD FOLIO

A number of the doubtful plays were published with Shakespeare's name or initials on their title pages, in some cases while he was living and in other cases after his death. A group of seven of these was included in the second printing of the Third Folio of 1664: *Pericles Prince of Tyre, The London Prodigal, The History of Thomas Lord Cromwell, Sir John Oldcastle Lord Cobham, The Puritan or the Widow of Watling Street, The Yorkshire Tragedy, The Tragedy of Locrine.*

Of this group *Pericles* has been accepted since the time of Malone as in large part the work of Shakespeare.

The London Prodigal was published in 1605 by Nathaniel Butter (who published *King Lear*), "As it was plaied by the Kings Maiesties seruants. By William Shakespeare." It is a very good comedy of London life, full of humors and manners, but unlike anything known to have been written by Shakespeare.

Thomas Lord Cromwell was printed for William Jones in 1602, "As it hath beene sundrie times publikely Acted by the Right Honorable the Lord Chamberlaine his Seruants. Written by W. S." It is a poverty-stricken specimen of the biographical history play. There seem to be no grounds for attributing it to Shakespeare, since even the initials "W. S." may have been intended to designate some other author.

Sir John Oldcastle, ascribed to Shakespeare in a quarto of 1600, is known from Henslowe's *Diary* to have been written for the Lord Admiral's company by Drayton, Hathway, Munday, and Wilson.

The Puritan, a fair comedy of manners, was printed by G. Eld in 1607, as "Acted by the Children of Paules. Written by W. S." Brooke points out certain resemblances between this play and *Eastward Hoe!* and suggests tentatively that Marston had a hand in it. There seems no reason to connect it with Shakespeare.

A Yorkshire Tragedy is on better ground. Shakespeare's name appears both in the entry in the Stationers' Register and on the title page of the quarto of 1608. In the latter place it is also stated that it was "Acted by his Maiesties Players at the Globe." So far as the use of Shakespeare's name is concerned, however, it may well have been due to the desire of the notorious piratical publisher, Thomas Pavier, to make dishonest gain. *A Yorkshire Tragedy* is a murder play, hasty and formless, but of great intensity. The Calverly murder, which it dramatizes, had occurred in 1605, and Shakespeare's company had no doubt taken immediate advantage of the sensation to prepare and present the play. It is hard to think that Shakespeare at such a time in his career could have been employed on such a job; but, since there are prose passages in the play of profound psychological knowledge and insight and of breathless intensity, many critics have thought that they at least show the touch of his hand.

Locrine is a tragedy of an early stiff type, like *Gorboduc* and *The Misfortunes of Arthur;* and, since it resembles the works of Robert Greene, *Selimus* (?) and *Alphonsus, King of Aragon,* Brooke argues strongly that it is Greene's work and earlier than either of those

A Note on
Doubtful and
Lost Plays

65

---

[2]E. K. Chambers, *The Elizabethan Stage,* III, 226-227; *William Shakespeare,* I, 528-532.
[3]See edition of the play by Harold Littlehale, New Shakespeare Society (1876, 1881); and Chambers, as in the preceding note.

mentioned. It was printed by Thomas Creed in 1595 as "Newly set foorth, overseene and corrected, By W. S." This may mean exactly what it says, and the "W. S." may again indicate some other author than Shakespeare.

THE CHARLES II GROUP

In the library of King Charles II was a volume in which three quartos were bound together and given on the outside the title "Shakespeare, Vol. I." The volume contained *Fair Em*, *Mucedorus*, and *The Merry Devil of Edmonton*. All had been printed anonymously, all were popular favorites, and the binding together and labeling may have been due to the belief that Shakespeare had written all of the most popular plays of the preceding generation, or to any other ignorant belief.

Fair Em was printed first without date (as acted by Lord Strange's servants) and later, in 1631, for John Wright. It is a crude comedy, rather pleasant, and gives a truly middle-class picture of royal and noble life. It has been attributed to Robert Greene, because it is thought to resemble *The Pinner of Wakefield*, which, in turn, is thought to resemble *Friar Bacon and Friar Bungay*. *Fair Em* was probably written around 1590.

Mucedorus was one of the most popular plays of the age. It appeared in at least seventeen quarto editions, the third of which (1610) states that it is "Amplified with new additions, as it was acted before the Kings Maiestie at White-hall on Shrove-Sunday night. By his Highness Seruants usually playing at the Globe." The first edition was in 1598. It is mere impertinence to attribute the original play to Shakespeare; but, since the "new additions" referred to on the title page of the third quarto are superior to the rest of the play, they have sometimes been regarded as Shakespeare's. Robert Greene has again been regarded without sufficient warrant as original author.

The text of *The Merry Devil of Edmonton*, a better play than either of the others, looks as if the play had been worn by much acting and many alterations. The suspected Revels Accounts of Peter Cunningham connect it with Shakespeare's company, as does the title page of the first quarto, printed for Arthur Johnson in 1608. The play was again entered in the Stationers' Register to Humphrey Moseley, the bookseller, in 1653, this time with Shakespeare's name as author. *The Merry Devil of Edmonton* was a popular play and was early connected with Shakespeare's name. There is no other probability of its being his play, and but little of his having revised it; but it would do him no discredit.

OTHER ATTRIBUTIONS

The remaining plays worthy of consideration find their connection with Shakespeare on various grounds. A play whose case is like that of *The Two Noble Kinsmen*, but by no means so good, is *The Birth of Merlin*. The first edition was published by Francis Kirkman in 1662. It is said on the title page to have been "Written by William Shakespear and William Rowley." Kirkman, an unreliable person, also attributed the tragi-comedy of *The Birth of Merlin* to Shakespeare and Rowley in his catalogues. The play seems to date from the reign of King James. Recent critics, though willing to let Rowley suffer, have denied vigorously that Shakespeare could have had any share in the authorship of so poor and so loosely constructed a play.

Arden of Feversham, the first of the murder plays and splendidly written, was published without attribution of authorship by Edward White in 1592. Edward Jacob, a citizen of Feversham, printed the play in 1770 and attributed it to Shakespeare. His grounds for doing so were inadequate, nor have any valid grounds been found since. It is absurd to argue against the possibility, since the authorship would be

A witch raising a storm. From Olaus Magnus, "Historia de Gentibus Septentrionalibus," 1555. (Huntington)

as appropriate and becoming in Shakespeare as in Kyd or another. The story is of a murder done at Feversham in 1551, the account of which is embodied in Holinshed. There is no evidence so far discovered which connects it with Shakespeare or any other dramatist; although E. H. C. Oliphant put forward the unsupported but attractive suggestion that the play is the joint work of Marlowe and Kyd.

Edward III is another anonymous play selected for Shakespeare because of its merit. It was first printed by Cuthbert Burby in 1596 and first attributed to Shakespeare in a bookseller's leaflet in 1654. The Shakespeare scholar, Edward Capell, edited it in 1760 and argued that it was by Shakespeare. The arguments consist mainly in appreciative criticism of the play and of the discovery that it quotes one line from the 94th sonnet: "Lilies that fester smell far worse than weeds." A number of high authorities in the nineteenth century felt sure of Shakespeare's hand at least in the first episode.

Sir Thomas More

There exists in Harleian Ms. 7368 at the British Museum a play labeled "The Booke of Sir Thomas Moore." It was first edited for the Shakespeare Society by Alexander Dyce in 1844. In 1871 the Shakespeare scholars Richard Simpson and James Spedding put forward the idea that certain scenes in this play were not only the work of Shakespeare but were written in his own hand. Simpson rested his case mainly on literary evidence and the "Shakespearian flavor."

The play is a biographical chronicle made up of three main episodes, or groups of scenes. The first of these describes the anti-alien riots of the "ill Mayday" of 1517 and introduces Sir Thomas More, sheriff of London, in the act of pacifying the anti-alien rioters by his oratory. Since the subject was one of immediate bearing on a current issue in the London of about 1595, it was only to be expected that the authorities would not suffer it to be performed. The play shows evidence, therefore, of having been heavily cut by the censor, Edward Tilney, who bade the players leave the insurrection out completely. The result of his censorship is the disappearance of two long passages. The play seems to have been originally written by Anthony Munday, and perhaps in anticipation of the objections of the censor another hand was employed to rewrite these scenes of the mob in a style not calculated to give offense. There are three such sheets, a total of 147 lines. They are gay, vigorous, and wise. The rioters talk in a genuinely comic way, like the mob in *Julius Caesar*, or Cade's followers in *2 Henry VI*. Then More appears, addresses them good-naturedly, pointing out the blessings of peace and order and the godlike position of the king. In 1916 Sir E. Maunde Thompson, the paleographer, reasserted Shakespeare's authorship of these three sheets dealing with the "ill May-day" mob. He attempted to prove by comparison with the handwriting of the six unquestioned signatures of Shakespeare that these sheets were indeed written in Shakespeare's hand. Since that time there has been a controversy pro and con. The play is dated by various critics from 1592 to 1601.[4]

LOST PLAYS

A drama called *The History of Cardenio* was entered in the Stationers' Register, but apparently never printed, by Humphrey Moseley on September 9, 1653, as "by Mr. Fletcher and Shakespeare." A play *Cardenno* or *Cardenna* was twice acted before the king by Shakespeare's company in 1613, it being probably the same play as *The History of Cardenio*. There is, moreover, a puzzling later history. The theme is an episode in Cervantes' *Don Quixote* (Part I, chs. xxiii-xxxvii). In 1728 Lewis Theobald, the editor of Shakespeare, published *The Double Falsehood, or the Distrest Lovers*, a play on the story of Cardenio. This was described by Theobald as "written originally by W. Shakespeare, and now revised and adapted to the stage by Mr. Theobald." Theobald claimed to have in his possession three manuscripts of the original; but none of them is now known, and many critics have suspected Theobald of having written *The Double Falsehood* himself and palmed it off as originally the work of Shakespeare. Theobald was, however, a reputable man, and his play strongly suggests Fletcher if not Shakespeare.

At the same time that Moseley entered *The History of Cardenio* in the Stationers' Register, he also entered *The Merry Devil of Edmonton*, which he ascribed to Shakespeare, and "*Henry ye first, & Hen: the 2d* by Shakespeare, & Davenport." On June 29, 1660, he entered "*The History of King Stephen; Duke Humphrey, a Tragedy; Iphis & Iantha or a marriage without a man*, a "Comedy" [all four inclosed in brackets]: by Will. Shakespeare."

Among the manuscript plays burned by Warburton's cook were "*Henry ye 1st* by Will. Shakespear & Rob. Davenport, *Duke Humphrey* [by] Will. Shakespear," and "A Play by Will. Shakespear."[5] John Warburton (1682-1759), antiquary and book collector, got into his possession a body of manuscripts of rare Elizabethan and Jacobean plays most of which were, he said, through his own "carelessness and the ignorance" of Betsy Baker, his servant, "unluckily burnd or put under pye bottoms."

How great was the world's loss in the plays mentioned by Moseley and Warburton we do not know. An obvious and tantalizing speculation is that Shakespeare may have written more history plays treating the early period to which *King John* belongs, perhaps a cycle of them.

A Note on
Doubtful and
Lost Plays

67

[4]Sir E. Maunde Thompson, *Shakespeare's Handwriting* (1916); A. W. Pollard and others, *Shakespeare's Hand in the Play of Sir Thomas More* (Cambridge, 1923); Sir E. K. Chambers, *The Elizabethan Stage*, IV, 32-34; Sir Sidney Lee, *Life of William Shakespeare*, Preface to latest edition; S. A. Tannenbaum, *The Booke of Sir Thomas Moore* (1927).
[5]W. W. Greg, "The Bakings of Betsy," *The Library*, 3rd ser., II, 225 ff.

Houses of York and Lancaster

EDWARD III 1312-1377

EDWARD 1330-1376 the Black Prince

RICHARD II 1367-1400 *King Richard II*

LIONEL 1338-1368 Duke of Clarence

PHILIPPA *m.* Edmund Mortimer 1351-1381

ROGER MORTIMER 1374-1398 Earl of March

*EDMUND *m.* the daughter of Owen Glendower *1 King Henry IV*

**ELIZABETH *m.* Sir Henry Percy (Hotspur) *1 King Henry IV*

ANNE MORTIMER *m.* Richard Earl of Cambridge

RICHARD PLANTAGENET (see York line)

EDMUND MORTIMER 1391-1425 Earl of March *1 King Henry VI*

HENRY 1387-1422 of Monmouth, later Henry V *1, 2 King Henry IV King Henry V*

HENRY VI 1421-1471 *1, 2, 3 King Henry VI*

EDWARD 1453-1471 Prince of Wales (killed at Tewkesbury) *3 King Henry VI*

Blanche of Lancaster *m.* JOHN 1340-1399 *m.* Catherine Swynford of Gaunt *King Richard II*

HENRY BOLINGBROKE 1367-1413 Duke of Hereford, later Henry IV *King Richard II, 1, 2 King Henry IV*

THOMAS 1388-1421 Duke of Clarence *2 King Henry IV*

JOHN 1389-1445 of Lancaster, later Duke of Bedford *1, 2 King Henry IV King Henry V 1 King Henry VI*

HUMPHREY 1390-1447 Duke of Gloucester *2 King Henry IV, King Henry V, 1, 2 King Henry VI*

JOHN BEAUFORT *c.* 1375-1410 Duke of Somerset

HENRY BEAUFORT *d.* 1447 Bishop of Winchester, later Cardinal *1, 2 King Henry VI*

THOMAS BEAUFORT *d.* 1427 Duke of Exeter *King Henry V 1 King Henry VI*

JOHN BEAUFORT *d.* 1444 Duke of Somerset *1 King Henry VI*

JOHN BEAUFORT *d.* 1444 Duke of Somerset *1 King Henry VI*

MARGARET *m.* Edmund Tudor 1430-1456 Earl of Richmond

HENRY TUDOR 1457-1509 *m.* Elizabeth of York Earl of Richmond, later Henry VII *3 King Henry VI King Richard III*

EDMUND BEAUFORT *d.* 1455 Duke of Somerset (killed at St. Albans) *2 King Henry VI*

EDMUND BEAUFORT Duke of Somerset (executed by Edward IV) *3 Henry VI*

HENRY BEAUFORT 1436-1464 Duke of Somerset (executed by Edward IV) *3 King Henry VI*

EDMUND 1341-1402 Duke of York *King Richard II*

EDWARD 1373-1415 Duke of Aumerle, later Duke of York *King Richard II, King Henry V*

RICHARD 1375-1415 *m.* Anne Mortimer Earl of Cambridge (executed by Henry V) *King Henry V*

RICHARD PLANTAGENET 1411-1460 Earl of Cambridge, later Duke of York (killed at Wakefield) *1, 2, 3 King Henry VI*

EDWARD 1442-1483 Earl of March, later Edward IV *2, 3 King Henry VI King Richard III*

EDMUND 1443-1460 Earl of Rutland (killed at Wakefield) *3 King Henry VI*

GEORGE 1449-1478 Duke of Clarence (murdered in the Tower) *3 King Henry VI King Richard III*

RICHARD 1452-1485 Duke of Gloucester, later Richard III (killed at Bosworth) *2, 3 King Henry VI King Richard III*

ELIZABETH *b.* 1465 *m.* Henry VII

EDWARD V 1470-1483 (murdered in the Tower) *King Richard III*

RICHARD *d.* 1483 (murdered in the Tower) *King Richard III*

THOMAS 1355-1397 of Woodstock (murdered at Calais)

*In *1 King Henry IV* this character is apparently confused with his nephew, the Earl of March. Glendower's son-in-law is an obscure character historically; it is thought he died a prisoner. This obscurity may account for the dramatic treatment of the Earl of March in *1 King Henry VI*, II, v. **In *1 King Henry IV* she is erroneously called "Kate."

SHAKESPEARE'S LIFE AND WORK

The Early Period, 1564-1594

It is important, before we attempt to give a connected account of Shakespeare's life and work, to indicate how and where we gather the facts about him. There are two sources for the biography of Shakespeare—documents and traditions. Formal written records are impersonal, often official, and may usually be relied upon implicitly. No motive for falsification existed in the making of the legal and commercial records that concerned Shakespeare. Such records, because they often give us only the insignificant and routine features of his life, remain dead and dry. Tradition, on the other hand, is likely to be fanciful, even false, arising as it does, for the most part, from posterity's craving for personal detail and anecdote.

DOCUMENTS

Manuscripts of some of Shakespeare's plays and many documents containing personal information about him must have perished in the great fire of London in 1666. However, the records of Stratford, where he spent his first and his last years, still remain and give us about what we should expect. Dates for his birth and death are determined from the baptismal and burial registers of Stratford-on-Avon. The *Episcopal Register* of the Diocese of Worcester records the issue of his marriage license and of the marriage bond. At Somerset House in London, a British government building which contains a depository of legal documents, is to be found his will, dated March 25, 1616. Other records, as those of the land that he bought and sold, the lawsuits to which he was a party, and the tax returns which listed his property for taxation, indicate his financial resources and his activities as a man of the world. From these purely official documents one can usually learn where Shakespeare happened to be living at a particular time of his life, and often something about his activities at such times.

The accumulation of these documentary details about Shakespeare has been carried on with unparalleled zeal. Our own generation, even after more than two centuries of Shakespeare research, has made very considerable additions to the formal records of Shakespeare's life. Such formal records often lead to important inferences. For example, in 1910 C. W. Wallace published[1] his discovery, in the Public Record Office in London, of papers pertaining to a suit in Chancery in the year 1612, in which Shakespeare was called as a witness. Shakespeare's deposition in the case is signed with his own hand. Thus, there was added a sixth authentic signature to those previously known. Shakespeare's testimony in this lawsuit shows that he had been, possibly for some years after 1602, a lodger in the house of a Huguenot wigmaker named Mountjoy, at the corner of Muggle and Silver streets, London. One infers from this document that, whether Shakespeare knew French or not, he was for a long time in contact with French-speaking people.

Of Shakespeare's correspondence only one short letter is known to exist; in it a Stratford neighbor, Richard Quyny, asked Shakespeare for the loan of thirty pounds. Shakespeare is mentioned, however, in several letters, mainly in connection with his activities as a citizen of Stratford. Notes on his plays and one or two personal anecdotes about him appear in diaries of the time. Because he acted with his company at court, the accounts of the Revels office, a sort of royal department of court amusements, often contain his name. Also, being one of the principal members of his company, he is several times mentioned among those to whom payment is made.

First publications of Shakespeare's works furnish a great deal of information about him. The famous

[1]C. W. Wallace, "Shakespeare and His London Associates," in *University Studies* (Lincoln, Nebraska), Vol. X, No. 4.

First Folio of 1623 was edited by his fellow actors, John Heminges and Henry Condell, whose names are signed to a dedicatory epistle and to an epistle "To the great Variety of Readers." The book contains, besides other laudatory verses, a poetic eulogy of Shakespeare by his celebrated contemporary Ben Jonson. The title pages and dedicatory epistles of the two poems *Venus and Adonis* (1593) and *The Rape of Lucrece* (1594), the title pages of various plays issued singly before the collected edition of 1623, and the entries of plays in the register of the Stationers' Company of London furnish information as to Shakespeare's claims to courtly patronage, his association with printers and dramatic companies, and approximate dates of composition of some of his works.

The practice of quoting Shakespeare and alluding to his work apparently began as soon as his plays appeared on the stage and there is a wealth of such material. Some of it is contemporary, some late; sometimes it is definite, sometimes vague and uncertain. Where the quotations are unmistakable, they constitute a valuable kind of information. Outstanding among contemporary allusions is the estimate of Francis Meres, who published in 1598 an odd and formal little book on contemporary literature and art called *Palladis Tamia, or Wit's Treasury*, which gave an early and enthusiastic recognition of Shakespeare's greatness as a poet and dramatist.[2]

TRADITIONS

Matters of this kind are matters of fact, all too scanty and bare, though very considerable in amount— more considerable than about any other Elizabethan playwright except Ben Jonson. But posterity has craved personal details about Shakespeare as it always does about its heroes, and has made an attempt to collect them. Thus has arisen the body of what are called traditions. Such traditions, usually late in getting recorded, are often inconsistent with each other and with the knowledge we have from more definite sources; hence, one faces always the question of their validity. They are important because they may be true and because even our own day clings to them. However much scholars may do to discredit them, they continue to crop up. One has simply to record them and do one's best to discriminate amongst them.

The seventeenth century, from which come the best of the traditions, was not indifferent to Shakespeare, though we sometimes think that it was. It issued and consumed four full editions of his plays besides numerous reprints of single plays and of the poems. This century was also interested in Shakespeare's life and made numerous characteristic efforts to accumulate information about him. Fuller wrote a useless little life in his *Worthies* (1662). John Aubrey includes Shakespeare in his *Lives of Eminent Men* (compiled between 1669 and 1696, but not published until

1813), where he records matters derived from the actor and theater manager, William Beeston, whose father had almost certainly been an associate of Shakespeare's. The Reverend John Ward, vicar of Stratford, the Reverend William Fulman, and the Reverend Richard Davies, and some others collected local traditions and examined some records. All of these accounts, except Aubrey's, were gathered up and used by the first modern editor of Shakespeare, Nicholas Rowe, who prefixed a life of the dramatist to his edition of the plays in 1709.

Not only was the science of biography in a bad state in the seventeenth century, but these investigators were too late in beginning. Too many generations had passed since Shakespeare lived, and the fire of London of 1666 had done its work. Most of the more important personal mementos of the poet had perished, and his family was practically extinct. But there were traditions about Shakespeare floating about unrecorded even as late as the time of the great Shakespeare editors, Dr. Samuel Johnson and Edmund Malone, in the second half of the eighteenth century.

A tradition is not necessarily negligible because it is late, but its lateness is at least an occasion of suspicion. Take, for example, two well-known traditions, the first of which seems improbable because it does not fit into what we know from other sources; the other probable because, though less well descended, it does. The *Lives of the Poets* (1753), attributed to Theophilus Cibber, states that Shakespeare's first employment in the theater after he came to London was as a holder of horses for the gentlemen who rode to the playhouse to see the plays; and further that Shakespeare organized the boys of the neighborhood into a company of horseholders known as "Will's Boys." This is on the basis of a tradition claimed to be handed down through William D'Avenant and Betterton, the Restoration theatrical manager and Shakespearean actor. It is a well-descended tradition, but it simply does not fit in with anything we know about the conditions of entry into the craft of acting.

The other tradition comes through William Oldys, who, writing about 1750-1760, says that one of Shakespeare's younger brothers, "who lived to a good old age, even some years, as I compute, after the Restoration of King Charles the Second," came, on more than one occasion, to London to see his brother act in plays. When he was asked at a later time what parts his brother played, "he was so stricken in years, and possibly his memory so weakened with infirmities, which might make him the easier pass for a man of weak intellects, that he could give them but little light into their inquiries; and all that could be recollected from him of his brother Will in that station was the faint, general, and almost lost ideas he had of having once seen him act a part in one of his own comedies, wherein, being to personate a decrepit old man, he wore a long beard, and appeared so weak and drooping and unable to walk, that he was forced to be supported and carried by another person to a table,

---

[2] Quoted on p. 34 above.

at which he was seated among some company who were eating, and one of them sung a song." Shakespeare, who died in 1616, outlived all of his brothers, and the tradition on its face is a bad one. Yet, it bears the mark of being an authentic recollection, and its reference to the part of Adam in *As You Like It* is unmistakable. Little was to be gained by the fabrication of such a tradition, and we know that Shakespeare acted just such parts in plays.

We cannot be content with a bare documentary record of a person so interesting as Shakespeare. Nor do we find it necessary to agree with a particular school of critics who insist that Shakespeare was so completely objective and stood so apart from his work that, even if we knew all about his life, it would have no significance in the interpretation of his work. On the other hand, one cannot give credence to a body of ignorant and inconsistent traditions. Neither can we agree with the practice of critics like Harris and Brandes, who manufacture a biography for Shakespeare out of the characters and situations of his plays. The scholarship of recent years has brought great gain in our ability to see the real Shakespeare, and we can but believe that with the further application of thought to the materials we now have, and with the possible discovery of other materials, greater progress will be made.

STRATFORD-ON-AVON

Some members of the group of critics who have in recent years sought to rob Shakespeare of the authorship of the plays in favor of Francis or of Anthony Bacon, the earl of Rutland, the earl of Southampton, the earl of Derby, the earl of Oxford, Sir Walter Raleigh, the earl of Devonshire, or others, have formed the habit of referring scornfully to William Shakespeare as "the man of Stratford." In this there is at least a recognition of the fact that Shakespeare from birth to death is very solidly connected with the town of Stratford-on-Avon. Some excellent critics also insist that Shakespeare, in spite of his mastery of Renaissance lore, was to the end a local genius, never losing the point of view of his native town. If so, it must be that we have exemplified in him Thoreau's doctrine that, if one knows his own neighborhood, one knows the world.

At any rate, it is worth while to consider the Stratford of Shakespeare's day. It was a little market town of 1500 people, with narrow, crooked streets, and timbered houses roofed with thatch—picturesque but unsanitary. It had something to boast of in the way of beauty and antiquity, particularly the river Avon, sluggish but clear-watered. This was spanned by the noble bridge of fourteen arches, which had been built in 1496 by Sir Hugh Clopton, Lord Mayor of London. Beside the Avon stood Trinity Church, built on the site of a Saxon monastery. The chapel of the Guild of the Holy Trinity, dating from the thirteenth century, and an old King Edward VI grammar school, no very pretentious affair, complete the list of the monuments of Shakespeare's day and of the present time. Strat-

ford had maintained a grammar school at least since 1424 and probably long before that. It was a town without the domination of clergy, aristocracy, or great wealth, where simple, honest people plied their trades and occupied their own positions of honor in the local society.

WARWICKSHIRE

Warwickshire, in which Stratford lies, is a midland county just south of the center of England and almost as far inland as one can get in that country. On the north side is Staffordshire, on the south Gloucestershire and Oxfordshire, on the east Leicestershire and Northampton, and on the west Worcestershire. It is

The wheel of fortune.
From Barclay's "Ship of Fools," 1509. *(Folger)*

an agricultural region broken by the rich valleys of the Avon, the Stour, and the Thames. The northern part of the county was once occupied by the Forest of Arden, but even in Shakespeare's day almost the whole county was under cultivation. In his time the famous industrial city of Birmingham was inconspicuous. Coventry, which is now a manufacturing center, was a neat, clean, progressive borough devoted to varied industries of the old-fashioned sort and noted for its active community life.

Warwick, the county seat, where the great Warwick Castle still stands, and Kenilworth, whose royal castle was destroyed by Oliver Cromwell, are on the road between Stratford and Coventry, the total distance between these places being about fourteen miles. Warwickshire, in the reign of Queen Elizabeth, was a rich county in which the standard of living was relatively high. Families and towns were more or less independent and self-supporting units, and agriculture was the basal occupation. Familiarity with the abundant fifteenth- and sixteenth-century records of Coventry convinces one that the ordinary people of Warwickshire were not only fundamentally sound and honest, but fundamentally open-minded and aspiring.

THE SHAKESPEARES

The family which bore the name of Shakespeare was well distributed throughout England, but was especially numerous in Warwickshire. A name "Saquespee" in various spellings, is found in Normandy at an early date. It means, according to J. Q. Adams, "to draw out the sword quickly." That name, in the form "Sakspee," with many variants, is found in England; also the name "Saksper," varying gradually to the form "Shakespeare." It may have been wrought into that form by the obvious military meaning of "one who shakes the spear." We have a substantial beginning of the line with Richard Shakespeare, who was in all probability Shakespeare's grandfather, a farmer living in the village of Snitterfield four miles from Stratford. He was a tenant on the property of Robert Arden of Wilmcote, a wealthy man with the social status of gentleman. Richard Shakespeare died about 1561 possessed of an estate valued at the very respectable sum of £38 17s.

JOHN SHAKESPEARE

No doubt the prosperity of Richard laid the basis for the fortunes of John, the poet's father. John Shakespeare, who is the first of the family to become in any way conspicuous, was a man about whom it is possible to know a good deal. He made a great step forward in the world by his marriage with Mary Arden, daughter of his father's landlord. She became the mother of William Shakespeare. John Shakespeare had some property of his own and through his wife acquired a good deal more. He moved from Snitterfield to Stratford at some date before 1552. He rose to great local importance in Stratford and bought several houses, among them in 1564, the one on Henley Street familiar to all the world as Shakespeare's birthplace. This house, though changed in various and unknown ways during the years which have intervened since Shakespeare's birth, still stands. It is of considerable size, having four rooms on the ground floor, and must, therefore, have been an important business house in the Stratford of those days. The business that John Shakespeare carried on seems to have been that of a glover. The records also indicate that he was a tanner and a dealer in wool, grain, malt, and other farm produce.

The long story, beginning in 1552, of John Shakespeare's success and misfortunes in Stratford is attested by many borough records. He held various city offices. He was ale taster (inspector of bread and malt), burgess (petty constable), affeeror (assessor of fines), city chamberlain (treasurer), and bailiff of the town— which was a position of very considerable honor. These are his successes. When William was fourteen

years old, John Shakespeare's misfortunes began. He got into debt, lost the fine farms of Asbies and Snitterfield, inherited by his wife from her father, was involved, as time went on, in much litigation, was finally dismissed from membership in the town council, and in 1586 was declared a bankrupt.

About 1576, in the midst of his prosperity, John Shakespeare had applied to the Herald's office for the right to bear arms. This would give him the right to have a coat-of-arms and to sign himself as a person belonging to the class of gentleman. This application was later to be renewed and carried through by his famous son. Through all of John Shakespeare's troubles and lawsuits, he seems from the evidence to have been respected and spared by his fellow townsmen. The impression he leaves is that of a hopeful, aspiring, unsuccessful man, more sinned against than sinning.

In 1904, a note in the Memoranda of Archdeacon Plume of Rochester, written about 1656, came to light, which gives us our only bit of personal detail about John Shakespeare. It means that the old man thought well of his own wit and was willing to match it at any time against that of his famous son in the current game of wit-combat:

> He [Shakespeare] was a glover's son. Sir John Mennes saw once his old father in his shop—a merry cheekt old man that said, "Will was a good honest fellow, but he [himself] darest have crackt a jest with him at any time."

This, although a probable enough tradition, is as regards Sir John Mennes historically impossible, since John Shakespeare died in 1601 and Mennes was born in 1599.

The family of Shakespeare's mother was of the best, and his father, in spite of his troubles, was a citizen oi importance. John Shakespeare made his mark instead of writing his name, but so did other men of the time who we know could read and write. His offices, particularly that of chamberlain, and the various public functions he discharged, indicate that he must have had some education.

SHAKESPEARE IN SCHOOL

It is strange that one should have to argue that such a man as John Shakespeare in such a community as Stratford did actually send his son to school. However, as there are no records of the grammar school covering the period of Shakespeare's school years, such is the case. There are several principal reasons for believing that Shakespeare went to school. First, because, as the son of a member of the town council, he would have been entitled to attend the grammar school without charge. In any case, the family during his boyhood was abundantly able to have had him attend.

Secondly, Shakespeare shows in his works familiarity with the studies of just such a school as the King Edward VI Grammar School of Stratford. On this point F. J. Furnivall quotes J. H. Lupton, the editor of Colet, as follows:

I think you would be safe in concluding that at such a school as Stratford, about 1570, there would be taught— (1) an 'A B C book,' for which a pupil teacher, or 'A-B-C-darius,' is sometimes mentioned as having a salary; (2) a catechism in English and Latin, probably Nowell's; (3) the authorized Latin grammar, i.e., Lilly's, put out with a proclamation adapted to each king's reign; (4) some easy Latin construing book, such as Erasmus's *Colloquies*, Corderius's *Colloquies*, or Baptista Mantuanus [an Italian poet of the Renaissance who wrote Latin eclogues; quoted by Shakespeare in *Love's Labour's Lost*]; and the familiar 'Cato,' or *Disticha de Moribus*, which is often prescribed in Statutes.

Furnivall adds: "From these easier Latin books the students proceeded to construe such Latin authors as Seneca, Terence, Plautus, Cicero, Ovid, and Vergil." Instruction in Greek, he says, was more rare, "but the quickest scholars were often given lessons in it."

Thirdly, it was the period of the Renaissance, when all the world was eagerly interested in education, and, since we must recognize in Shakespeare a true child of the Renaissance, the probabilities of his having been properly schooled are still further increased. The conception of Shakespeare as an educated man, by the standards of his time, is of importance, since from it one gets a truer idea of the nature of his works; namely, that they are not the output of untutored genius, but works whose texture is the culture of his time. Shakespeare did not build his plays out of what he saw in the streets of Stratford and London; their substance is primarily the literary culture of the Renaissance.

SHAKESPEARE AND PSEUDO-
SHAKESPEARE

It has already appeared that what is known of Shakespeare's life is considerable. It is made up all the way through of just the sort of information that one would expect. It hangs together and refers to one man and one career. We know more about Shakespeare's life than we know about the lives of any dramatist of the time except Ben Jonson and possibly George Chapman, both of whom were more famous in their day than was Shakespeare. It will be seen further that Shakespeare was known to his contemporaries as a dramatist and poet of ability and as a man of position and character. He is so referred to by John Webster, Michael Drayton, William Camden, and many others—particularly by Ben Jonson. The record, although lacking in the personal details we should like to have, is so adequate and so abundant and the man revealed is so noble an Elizabethan Englishman, such an honor to his race and such a gift to the world, that one wonders at the concerted, perverse, and unreasonable attempt that has been made to rob him of his glory. Perhaps humanity still has in it the quality that caused the Athenians to ostracize Aristides because they were tired of hearing him called "the Just." But it is possible in the history of thought to throw some light on the origin of the anti-Shakespearean movement.

Certain people observed that, compared with modern authors, the records of Shakespeare's life were relatively bare. They forgot that, owing to the wholesale destruction of written records in the fire of London in 1666, life records of all writers in the period are also scanty and imperfect. They knew he was brought up in the country and supposed he was the child of humble parents. There were no records of his schooling preserved, and they concluded that he was uneducated. Those who admired him made a theory to fit his supposed case and said he had dispensed with learning, that he "warbled his native woodnotes wild." Over against this theory is the fact that his plays are full of erudition and could not have been written by any but an educated man. This caused the skeptics to conclude that no man born in low station and without early educational advantages could possibly rise to heights of culture and greatness. One might pause to call this conclusion in question and cite the cases of Abraham Lincoln and of Mark Twain (himself a Baconian) in refutation. Not believing that a man such as they thought Shakespeare was could have written the dramas, they looked about for a substitute, a man of known culture, to whom they might attribute the authorship of Shakespeare's plays. Bacon, one of the greatest of men, was the first candidate. He was a man whose culture, interests, and mental quality were obviously divergent from those of the author of the dramas, and there was little to support the claim. J. M. Robertson in *The Baconian Heresy* (1913) destroyed what shadowy validity there was in the Bacon case, and the claims put forward for the earl of Oxford and others have no tangible support. The issue lives on in the popular mind largely because of the misunderstood principle that where there is smoke there is sure to be fire. In this case there is nothing but smoke and smoke makers.

But suppose we should turn the question about and, instead of offering counterarguments, deny and disprove the original propositions, and that is what has to be done. It has been shown that William Shakespeare belonged to a good stock and, especially on his mother's side, to a good family, and that his works show incontestable evidence that they were written by a man who had been educated in just such a school as the Stratford grammar school. He refers to the books studied in such schools and shows familiarity with the classics read in them. Many scholars have worked on this subject, but we owe at this time a particular debt of gratitude to T. W. Baldwin, who in two works, *William Shakespere's Petty School* (1943) and *William Shakespere's Small Latine and Lesse Greeke* (1944), has put the question of Shakespeare's education in the Stratford schools beyond peradventure. A good Elizabethan grammar school would be, in spite of its differences, as adequate educationally as any four-year college. One might add to Baldwin's argument a reverse proposition to the effect that Shakespeare did not, as did

Marlowe, Greene, and Spenser, attend a university. We are thus furnished with the groundwork of Renaissance culture revealed in Shakespeare's plays.

SHAKESPEARE'S MARRIAGE

When Shakespeare was eighteen years old, at the time when his father was in the depths of financial distress, he married. The bishop's register of Worcester, the central city of the diocese, shows for November 28, 1582, the issue of a bishop's license for the marriage of William Shakespeare and Anne Hathaway. She has been identified with all reasonable probability as Agnes (or Anne) Hathaway, daughter of the then recently deceased Richard Hathaway of the hamlet of Shottery, a short distance from Stratford. The custom of asking the banns on three separate Sundays or holy days was regularly suspended during the period of about two months from Advent Sunday to the Octave of Epiphany, and the method of securing a license through the bishop enabled persons to be married without asking the banns and thus losing the time of the prohibited period.

A Basilisk.
From Conrad Gesner's "Historia Animalium," 1587. (Huntington)

One does not know where the young couple were married. It would naturally have been in the parish of which the bride was a resident. It has been suggested with some probability that it was at Temple Grafton, where Anne Hathaway had relatives. In any case, Shakespeare and his wife became resident in Stratford, where on May 26, 1583, Susanna, their daughter, was baptized. It should be pointed out that the parties to this marriage may have been betrothed and that a betrothal had the validity of a marriage. On February 2, 1585, Shakespeare's only other children, the twins Hamnet and Judith, were baptized in Stratford Church. The twins seem to have been named after Shakespeare's friends and neighbors, Hamnet Sadler, a baker of Stratford, and his wife, Judith.

With this entry of the baptism of his children, the connection with the records of Stratford and vicinity for William Shakespeare in the period of his youth and obscurity comes to an end. We are then faced with a great blank of seven or nine years which history has failed to fill and which conjecture has filled entirely too full.

In 1592, Shakespeare is apparently alluded to by the poet Robert Greene as an actor and dramatist of growing importance. The next year his poem *Venus and Adonis* is entered for publication in the Stationers' Register and published in London. In 1595 his name appears, for the first time, in the accounts of the Treasurer of the Royal Chamber as a member of the Lord Chamberlain's company of players, who had been summoned to present two comedies before Queen Elizabeth at Greenwich in the Christmas season of 1594.

SHAKESPEARE POSSIBLY TAUGHT SCHOOL

The fascinating question of what Shakespeare did during the dark years may yet be answered. In the meantime, one can only record traditions and guesses. One of the oldest and one of the most probable and authentic accounts has received the support of J. Q. Adams in his life of Shakespeare and is not ruled out by Sir Sidney Lee. It comes from John Aubrey. In collecting information about actors and dramatists for his "Minutes of Lives" he resorted to William Beeston, whom Dryden characterized as "the chronicle of the stage." Aubrey seems also to have had a high opinion of Beeston's knowledge, for he noted on his manuscript, "W. Shakespeare—quære (i.e., inquire of) Mr. Beeston, who knows most of him." Then, apparently in refutation of Ben Jonson's famous charge that Shakespeare knew "small Latin and less Greek," Aubrey says,

Though, as Ben Jonson says of him, that he had but little Latin and less Greek, he understood Latin pretty well, for he had been in his younger years a schoolmaster in the country.

On the margin opposite this Aubrey writes "from Mr. Beeston." William Beeston had been a theatrical manager all his life. He was the son of an actor and theater manager who was unquestionably associated with Shakespeare during his career in London.

The idea of Shakespeare's having taught school is not unattractive and explains much. School teaching would, in some measure, have taken the place of a university in his education and would go far in accounting for his technical knowledge of schoolbooks and schoolmasters in plays, such as *Love's Labour's Lost* and *The Comedy of Errors*. It would also account for his familiarity with Ovid appearing in *Titus Andronicus, Venus and Adonis*, and *The Rape of Lucrece*. Also, it would change the conception of his early relation to the theater, putting it more in line with that of other dramatists of the time. It would show him, like Marlowe and Greene, coming up to London in order to fulfill his ambition as a poet and to try his fortune in the newly fashionable profession of playwright. All in all, however, it seems more probable that Shakespeare served an apprenticeship as an actor.

POSSIBLE APPRENTICESHIP

In other traditions, the idea has prevailed of Shakespeare as an unlettered genius and self-made man, a notion always fascinating to the popular mind. One of these traditions was picked up by John Dowdall when traveling through Warwickshire in 1693, from an old parish clerk who was showing him about the town of Stratford. Shakespeare, he was told, was bound apprentice to a butcher, but ran from his master to London, where he was received into the playhouse as a "serviture." Part of this Aubrey also records, namely, that "when he [Shakespeare] was a boy he exercised his father's trade," which Aubrey thought was that of butcher; and "when he killed a calf, he would doe it in a high style and make a speech." There is no other evidence that Shakespeare was a runaway apprentice. He was of age in 1585 and would have been free to go where he pleased. The allusion to "killing a calf" throws doubt on the whole thing. Canon Raine explained, half a century ago, that the words are an allusion to an ancient rural amusement which consisted in representing, behind a curtain, the slaughter of a calf, a sort of semi-dramatic game in which we may believe simple visitors at country fairs took great delight. From some casual recollection of Shakespeare's participation in this forgotten game, probably when he was a boy, may have come, absurdly enough, the tradition that he was a butcher's apprentice. "Killing a calf in a high style": butcher's apprentice—and the tradition is complete.[3]

DEERSTEALING ALSO A DOUBTFUL TRADITION

Another tradition, that of the deerstealing, has some plausibility about it and has been widely accepted. It appears as one of the gossipy interpolations made, after 1688 and before 1709, by the Reverend Richard Davies in the manuscripts of the Reverend William Fulman, who in his collections of antiquarian detail made notes on Shakespeare and Stratford.

In 1709 the tradition was seized upon and augmented by Nicholas Rowe. Shakespeare introduced Justice Shallow into 2 Henry IV as a butt for Falstaff's humor. Shallow was a popular character, and Shakespeare introduced him again into The Merry Wives of Windsor. He is a caricature of the rural magistrate and country squire. In the opening scene of the latter play there is a vulgar pun, a very old and easy joke,

on Justice Shallow's coat of arms, which Shakespeare imagines as consisting of a dozen white luces. The luce is a fish frequently employed as a heraldic device. Parson Evans, desiring to flatter Shallow and misled by the similarity of sounds between the words "luce" and "louse," says,

The dozen white louses do become an old coat [of arms] well; it agrees well, passant; it is a familiar beast to man, and signifies love. (I, i, 19-21)

When Falstaff enters in the same scene, Justice Shallow thus accuses him: "Knight, you have beaten my men, killed my deer, and broke open my lodge." And the Justice is disposed to make a "star-chamber matter" of it.

It happens that a family of gentry named Lucy, who lived at Charlecote Hall near Stratford, had by an easy pun on their own name adopted three white luces as a device; and that in the end of the seventeenth century, though not in Shakespeare's youth, they owned a deer park. These local circumstances seem to have been used to explain the puns and allusions in the play, and these in turn to support a tradition arising out of such an explanation. Rowe gives the following flamboyant version:

He had, by a misfortune common enough to young fellows, fallen into ill company, and amongst them, some that made a frequent practice of deer-stealing engaged him more than once in robbing a park that belonged to Sir Thomas Lucy of Charlecote, near Stratford. For this he was prosecuted by that gentleman, as he thought, somewhat too severely; and in order to revenge that ill usage he made a ballad upon him. And though this, probably the first essay of his poetry, be lost, yet it is said to have been so very bitter that it redoubled the prosecution against him to that degree that he was obliged to leave his business and family in Warwickshire for some time, and shelter himself in London.[4]

The ballad, however, is preserved and turns out to be manifestly a late production.

SHAKESPEARE'S SOCIAL POSITION

That Shakespeare must have spent some time in Gloucestershire is argued by D. H. Madden,[5] since he betrays in more than one of his plays an intimate knowledge of that county and its people. One asks how he obtained this knowledge and still more how it is that even his earliest plays show so perfect a familiarity with the ways of good society; particularly, since social behavior is a kind of knowledge which must be acquired by social contacts. Too much stress has been put upon Shakespeare's lowly origin. His family was of good position and, on the mother's side, well connected. There were gentlefolk in the neighborhood of Stratford with whom, when he retired to his native town, he is known to have had social relations. It is certainly no very wild conjecture to sup-

---

[3]See review of Joseph Quincy Adams, A Life of William Shakespeare, by John M. Manly, New Republic, September 26, 1923.

[4]For a different interpretation, see below, p. 500.
[5]D. H. Madden, The Diary of Master William Silence (1897), pp. 372-374.

pose that such associations were also open to Shakespeare in his youth, before he betook himself to London.

SHAKESPEARE'S ARRIVAL IN LONDON

Betake himself to London he did, whether for refuge, as Rowe puts it, or not. Conjecture has busied itself with the way in which he made his start in the theatrical world. In 1790 Malone made the unsupported statement that "his first office in the theatre was that as prompter's attendant," which Sir Sidney Lee explains as "call boy." There is, of course, no reason to think that Shakespeare, a young man from the country, would not have had to begin at the bottom. His intimate knowledge of stagecraft fits in well with the idea that he may have had experience in the prompter's end of the business. In any case, as a young man of education and probably an aspiring poet, he would have come very early into the society of his fellows. In all probability, he had at least one prosperous acquaintance in London, namely, Richard Field, formerly of Stratford and the son of an associate of Shakespeare's father. Field was a printer, and in 1593 and 1594 published for Shakespeare, in very good style, his two poems, *Venus and Adonis* and *The Rape of Lucrece*.

"THE ONELY SHAKE-SCENE IN A COUNTREY"

There comes into consideration at this time one of the best known but most puzzling references to Shakespeare in his whole life story, the first allusion to him after the Stratford days. It is the attack of an enemy, one who was himself disappointed, ruined, and dying in poverty. Robert Greene, in a pamphlet entitled *A Groatsworth of Wit Bought with a Million of Repentance*, attacks the players who have deserted him and advises three other dramatists to quit writing plays, since, if they continue to do so, they too will suffer a like fate to his. The pamphlet was written in the summer before Greene's death on the third of September, 1592. He attacks particularly a fourth playwright, a man of the baser sort, who has, he thinks, superseded him in the favor of the actors. This is apparently Shakespeare.

The three dramatists he addresses are his fellow University Wits, Christopher Marlowe, Thomas Nashe, and George Peele. "Gentlemen, his Quondam acquaintance, that spend their wits in making Plaies, R. G. wisheth a better exercise, and to preuent his extremities":

... Base minded men al three of you, if by my miserie ye be not warnd: for vnto none of you (like mee) sought those burres to cleaue: those Puppets (I meane) that spake from our mouths, those Anticks garnisht in our colours. Is it not strange that I, to whom they al haue beene beholding: is it not like that you, to whome they all haue beene beholding, shall (were yee in that case that I am now) bee both at once of them forsaken? Yes trust them not: for there is an vpstart Crow, beautified

with our feathers, that with his Tygers hart wrapt in a Players hyde, supposes he is as well able to bombast out a blanke verse as the best of you: and beeing an absolute *Iohannes fac totum*, is in his owne conceit the onely Shakescene in a countrey.

The "burres" are the actors who have forsaken him in his poverty for the rival playwright, "Shake-scene," or we must believe, Shakespeare. He is also properly enough described as a "Johannes Factotum," or Jack-at-all-trades—actor, playwright, poet, and probably engaged in various ways about the management of the theater. To make the reference still more unmistakable, there is the burlesque line, "Tygers hart wrapt in a Players hyde," modeled after, "O tiger's heart wrapt in a woman's hide!" which occurs in *3 Henry VI* (I, iv, 137). A possible implication is that this highly rhetorical line is one of the "fine feathers" with which Shakespeare has "beautified" himself, though it is almost certainly merely a selected example of bombast.

CHETTLE'S APOLOGY

There is evidence that Shakespeare or his friends were with good reason offended at this attack. So, apparently, was Marlowe, since Greene states in his address that he had once been an atheist as Marlowe was, but now saw the folly and wickedness of atheism. As to reparations, Greene was dead and beyond reach. However, Nashe, who was a bitter satirist, was suspected of having had a hand in the affair. Nashe denied this vigorously, and Henry Chettle, also a dramatist, was brought into the matter. Chettle, in his *Kind-Harts Dreame*, denied any responsibility except that which arose from his having prepared Greene's manuscript for the press:

... I had onely in the copy this share: it was il written, as sometime *Greenes* hand was none of the best; licensd it must be, ere it could bee printed, which could neuer be if it might not be read. To be breife, *I* writ it ouer; and as neare as *I* could, followed the copy; onely in that letter *I* put something out, but in the whole booke not a worde in; for I protest it was all *Greenes*, not mine nor Maister *Nashes*, as some vniustly haue affirmed.

With reference to Marlowe, whose reputation as an atheist was then at its height, he says:

With neither of them that take offence was *I* acquainted, and with one of them [Marlowe] *I* care not if *I* neuer be.

He then goes on more particularly about Shakespeare:

The other, whome at that time I did not so much spare, as since I wish I had, for that as *I* haue moderated the heate of liuing writers, and might haue vsde my owne discretion (especially in such a case) the Author beeing dead, that *I* did not, *I* am as sory as if the originall fault had beene my fault, because my selfe haue seene his demeanor no lesse ciuill, than he exelent in the qualitie he professes: Besides, diuers of worship haue reported his vprightnes of dealing, which argues his honesty, and his facetious grace in writting, that approoues his Art.

About this handsome apology one notes that Shakespeare, hitherto unknown to Chettle, has made a characteristic impression of personal civility upon him. Also that Shakespeare is excellent in the "qualitie" he professes, that is, excellent as an actor. Shakespeare is also not without the favor of persons of importance, some of whom have borne witness to his uprightness in dealing. By "divers of worship" Chettle does not mean actors or theatrical people, but persons of gentle blood. This first rather rancorous allusion to Shakespeare serves then to bring out the fact that in 1592 Shakespeare was regarded as a man of pleasant demeanor, honest reputation, and acknowledged skill as an actor and writer; and that he was a popular dramatist of imitative tendencies.

DRAMATIC APPRENTICESHIP

By the end of the year 1594, when after the long plague the theatrical companies were again permitted to act before London audiences, we find Shakespeare a member of the Lord Chamberlain's company. He had, it is believed on various grounds, written eleven plays—comedies: *Love's Labour's Lost, The Comedy of Errors, The Two Gentlemen of Verona, The Taming of the Shrew,* and *A Midsummer-Night's Dream;* histories: *1, 2,* and *3 Henry VI,* and *Richard III;* tragedies: *Titus Andronicus* and *Romeo and Juliet.* Many critics, to be sure, deny him the authorship of *Titus Andronicus* and any but a small part in the Henry VI plays. However, nobody questions the facts that they are early plays and that in the general principles of grouping they belong here. Almost every one of the plays shows evidence of having been revised at a later time, so that we have before us the difficult task of dating plays from what seem to be their earliest parts. Among these plays certain ones, *Love's Labour's Lost, The Comedy of Errors, The Two Gentlemen of Verona,* the Henry VI plays, *Titus Andronicus,* and perhaps *The Taming of the Shrew,* belong to the earliest period. *A Midsummer-Night's Dream, Romeo and Juliet,* and *Richard III* might be associated with *King John* and *Richard II* to form an early, but not the earliest, group of Shakespeare's plays.

It is possible that we do not possess all of the plays that Shakespeare wrote during the period of his apprenticeship, and no play can be accurately dated. A play, not otherwise known, called *Love's Labour's Won,* is mentioned by Francis Meres in *Palladis Tamia.* It is natural to believe from its title that such a play was a companion piece to *Love's Labour's Lost* and was, therefore, written at about the same time. These two plays may be his earliest dramatic efforts; if so, they may go back to 1588 or 1589.

Shakespeare's early development is hard to follow, since he seems to have revised so many of his early plays, presumably for stage revivals, that one and the same play shows both earlier and later styles. Also he, a learner making rapid progress in the skill of his art, was subjected to outside influences which can be only partly determined. One of these, we may be

sure, was the dramatic style of the plays he revamped and of the plays contemporary dramatists were writing for his company and for the rival companies. If one could define these influences and form an idea of the kinds of plays acceptable on the stage during his early period, one could better understand the group of plays written by the year 1594.

Fortunately we are not without material for doing this, since Henslowe's *Diary* records the daily performances of plays by the Lord Strange's men from the 19th of February to the 22nd of June 1592. Many of their plays unfortunately are lost, but enough of them are preserved to indicate the taste of the time. They had Marlowe's *Jew of Malta,* Greene's *Orlando Furioso* and *Friar Bacon and Friar Bungay,* Lodge's *A Looking Glass for London,* Kyd's *The Spanish Tragedy,* the anonymous cutpurse comedy *A Knack to Know a Knave,* possibly Peele's *Battle of Alcazar,* and an early form of Shakespeare's *1 Henry VI.* There is, thus, a tragedy with a villain hero, a heroic play, a play of a necromancer, a moral satire, a revenge tragedy, a comedy of London life, and two history plays, the one English, the other foreign in theme. There are other plays, now lost, whose titles are suggestive of rough clownage and of wide romantic sweep.

Probably few plays were written during the period when plays were forbidden because of the long plague of 1592-1594. When the Lord Chamberlain's men and the Lord Admiral's men acted together under Henslowe's management at the suburban theater of Newington Butts from June 3 to 13, 1594, their repertories seem to have consisted largely of old plays. In this brief period, before we lose sight of them, the Lord Chamberlain's men are thought to have acted *Titus Andronicus, Hamlet* (probably the pre-Shakespearean play), *The Taming of a Shrew,* and a lost play called *Hester and Ahasuerus.*

The Lord Admiral's men probably moved at once to the Rose on the Bankside, across the river Thames from the city of London, where they continued to play under Henslowe's management until 1603. During the years 1594-1597 Henslowe kept in his *Diary* a careful record of their plays and of the sums of money taken. This circumstance enables us to know a great deal more about the repertory of Shakespeare's rival company than we can ever know about his own. When the Lord Admiral's men began again in 1594, they had five of Marlowe's plays. They seem also to have had Peele's *Edward I,* Kyd's *The Spanish Tragedy,* and a Henry V play. They may also have had plays by both Greene and Peele (Henslowe's illiteracy makes it hard to determine), although some of the principal dramas of these two authors had probably ceased to be acted.

We do not know the repertory of the Lord Chamberlain's company as a whole as we do that of the Lord Admiral's. We know enough of it, however, to be sure that in 1594, both companies were acting the same sort of thing that had been on the boards in 1592. We have, therefore, grounds for assuming that, in spite of the loss of many plays (some of which may have been very potent), the chief influences upon Shakespeare during his early period were those of Marlowe, Greene, Peele, and Kyd. As an actor in Lord Strange's company he would have been familiar with their plays.

He learned a great deal from Lyly, but how this came about is more puzzling. Lyly wrote mainly for the boys' company at St. Paul's, and, when their acting was suspended about 1591, a number of his plays were printed. One concludes, therefore, that Shakespeare, although he may have seen Lyly's plays on the stage, is more likely to have read them in print than to have acted in them. In any case, Shakespeare's trend as a dramatist was determined by the powerful group who from about 1581 to 1591 created the Elizabethan drama. As will appear in the following account of the plays of Shakespeare's early period, there are from the first many original features which are not to be accounted for on any theory of imitation.

THE EARLY PLAYS

We see Shakespeare, then, writing tragedy with the revenge motive and all the attendant horrors of murder and cruelty, comedy with the Plautine theme of mistaken identity, and chronicle plays of a strongly patriotic nature. In these forms and with these underlying purposes he follows the great group of his early contemporaries in whose curiosity, energy, and aspirations he fully participates. From the influence of Lyly, Greene, and Peele he had begun in *Love's Labour's Lost*, *The Two Gentlemen of Verona*, and *A Midsummer-Night's Dream* his production of romantic comedy, the comedy of love and friendship, in which form he was to excel, producing later such plays as *The Merchant of Venice*, *As You Like It*, and *Twelfth Night*. What were, one asks, the powers that were specifically his in the writing of these early plays?

The most striking of his powers was that of construction. He was careful about it, ingenious, and detailed even to the point of formalism. Back of *The Comedy of Errors* lie two skillfully plotted plays of the great master Plautus. Shakespeare combines them, betters them, renders them more intricate but not less clear. In *Love's Labour's Lost*, he selects a theme from the more fashionable culture of the day, arranges four lovers over against their four ladyloves, and carries his formal plot to a triumphant denouement. This element of careful balance is obvious also in *The Two Gentlemen of Verona*. *A Midsummer-Night's Dream* is a still more brilliant piece of plotting, there being four parallel or contrasting themes woven together, each displaying its own special order of existence: Theseus and Hippolyta of the blood royal, mature and regulative; the four young lovers from the court, most ingeniously shifted about in their attachments until a proper relation is achieved; the fairy king and queen, Oberon and Titania, themselves quite humanly at cross purposes and manipu-

lating human affairs with a combination of magic and chance; and, finally, Bottom and his associates burlesquing serious love interest in their play of Pyramus and Thisbe. *Titus Andronicus* is also a play of careful construction, and we may believe that the story of *Romeo and Juliet* was chosen, in part at least, because in that case Shakespeare found already shaped to his hand a perfectly articulated plot.

The greatest manifestation, however, of his early eminence in architectonic ability is to be seen in the history plays. The many events, the many various characters, and the long expanse of time of the Wars

Illustration from William Turner's "Herbal," 1568. (Huntington)

of the Roses are condensed and unified. Richard III is made, quite according to the best historical authority, to bear the final and supreme burden of tragic guilt and to embody the rancors of a century. One of the best evidences for Shakespeare's authorship of *1, 2,* and *3 Henry VI* is the way in which they lead up, through the characters of Suffolk, York, Margaret, Henry VI, and Gloucester, to the play of *Richard III*, and the extent to which they are mindful of the historic past in the dethronement of Richard II, and of the principle of loyalty to king and country.

Something has already been said about Shakespeare's early style. It is a style which bears the impress of youth, but of youth burning with enthusiasm and gifted with wonderful powers. He had been trained according to the prevailing sixteenth-century rhetorical pattern and had acquired its liveliness and its eloquence, but he still retained some of its artificiality. His characters, although the most individual thitherto created in Elizabethan drama, are still sometimes too close to mere types and do not always as yet speak words appropriate to them and to them only. We have too many puns, conceits, and ingenious stylistic devices, such as oxymoron, stichomythia, clownish quibbling, and far-fetched allusions. The plays are examples of mental and verbal agility, but from the point of view of construction as well as that of pure poetry, they are great plays. They are great also as embodiments of Renaissance spirit with no social problems, as yet, to mar their expression of faith in human destiny.

REFERENCES

ADAMS, J. Q. *A Life of William Shakespeare*. Boston, 1923.

ALEXANDER, PETER. *Shakespeare's Life and Art*. London, 1939.

BALDWIN, T. W. *The Organization and Personnel of the Shakespearean Company*. Princeton, 1927.

BARTON, SIR D. P. *Links between Shakespeare and the Law*. London, 1929.

BROOKE, C. F. TUCKER. *The Tudor Drama*. Boston, 1912; *Shakespeare of Stratford*. New Haven, 1926.

CHAMBERS, SIR E. K. *William Shakespeare*. Oxford, 1930; *The Elizabethan Stage*. Oxford, 1923.

EBISCH, WALTHER, and L. L. SCHÜCKING. *A Shakespeare Bibliography*. Oxford, 1931; *Supplement*, 1937.

FRIPP, EDGAR I., and RICHARD SAVAGE. *Minutes and Accounts of the Corporation of Stratford-upon-Avon and other Records*. London, 1924, 1926; *Shakespeare, Man and Artist*. 2 vols. London, 1938.

FURNIVALL, F. J., and JOHN MUNRO. *Shakespeare Life and Work*. London, 1908.

GRAY, J. W. *Shakespeare's Marriage*. London, 1905.

HALLIWELL-PHILLIPS, J. O. *Outlines of the Life of Shakespeare*. Eleventh ed., London, 1907; the greatest collection of Shakespeare documents.

HARRISON, G. B. *Shakespeare at Work, 1592-1603*. London, 1933.

HOLZKNECHT, KARL J. *The Backgrounds of Shakespeare's Plays*. New York, 1950.

HOTSON, LESLIE. *Shakespeare versus Shallow*. London, 1931; *I, William Shakespeare, do Appoint Thomas Russell, Esquire*. London, 1937; *Shakespeare's Sonnets Dated and Other Essays*. London, 1949.

LAMBERT, D. H. *Shakespeare Documents*. London, 1904.

LEE, SIR SIDNEY. *A Life of William Shakespeare*. Fourth edition of the revised version, rewritten and enlarged. London, 1925.

NEILSON, WILLIAM ALLAN, and ASHLEY H. THORNDIKE. *Facts about Shakespeare*. New York, 1913.

NICOLL, ALLARDYCE. *British Drama*. London and New York, 1925.

RALEIGH, SIR WALTER. *Shakespeare* (English Men of Letters). New York, 1907.

ROLFE, W. J. *Life of Shakespeare*. Boston, 1904; *Shakespeare the Boy*. New York, 1896.

Shakespeare's England. Oxford, 1916.

SPENCER, HAZELTON. *The Art and Life of William Shakespeare*. New York, 1940.

STOPES, MRS C. C. *Shakespeare's Family*. London, 1901; *Shakespeare's Warwickshire Contemporaries*. Stratford-upon-Avon, 1907; *Shakespeare's Environment*. London, 1914. Other works by the same author.

WALLACE, C. W. "New Shakespeare Discoveries," *Harper's Magazine*, March 1910.

Additional references will be found in the General Introduction, pages 39-40, 46-47. The articles on Shakespeare in the ninth and the eleventh editions of the *Encyclopaedia Britannica* are also worth the student's attention.

On the general problem of academic culture in Shakespeare see the editor's *The Enchanted Glass*. New York, 1936. See also WILLARD FARNHAM, *The Medieval Heritage of Elizabethan Tragedy*. Berkeley, Calif., 1936. On Shakespeare's book learning in school and out the following are important sources of information:

ANDERS, H. R. D. *Shakespeare's Books*. Berlin, 1904.

BALDWIN, T. W. *William Shakespere's Petty School*. Urbana, 1943; *William Shakespere's Small Latine and Lesse Greeke*. 2 vols. Urbana, 1944; also various other works.

BAYNES, T. S. "What Shakespeare Learned at School," in *Shakespeare Studies*. London, 1894.

BOSWELL-STONE, W. G. *Shakespeare's Holinshed*. London, 1907.

COLLINS, J. C. "Shakespeare as a Classical Scholar," in *Studies in Shakespeare*. Westminster, 1904.

CUNLIFFE, JOHN W. *The Influence of Seneca on Elizabethan Tragedy*. New York, 1925. For a statement of the Senecan problem in Shakespeare and for further references see the editor's "The Shackling of Accidents: A Study of Elizabethan Tragedy." *Philological Quarterly*, XIX (1940), 1-19.

FARMER, R. *Essay on the Learning of Shakespeare*. Cambridge, 1767. This important work is not usually readily accessible.

GOLLANCZ, SIR ISRAEL. *The Shakespeare Classics*. A series begun in 1907 which has reprinted the chief sources of Shakespeare's plays.

HAZLITT, W. C. *Shakespeare's Library*. 6 vols. London, 1875.

NICOLL, JOSEPHINE and ALLARDYCE. *Holinshed's Chronicle as Used in Shakespeare's Plays*. Everyman's Library, 1927.

SKEAT, W. W. *Shakespeare's Plutarch*. London, 1875; also in *The Shakespeare Classics*, there edited by C. F. Tucker Brooke.

Further bibliographical materials will be found in F. E. SCHELLING's *Elizabethan Drama*, Boston, 1908, in Rolfe's and Lee's lives of Shakespeare, in Ebisch and Schücking, *A Shakespeare Bibliography* and *Supplement* for the years 1930-1935 (Oxford, 1937), and in the voluminous *Shakespeare Bibliography* by W. Jaggard, Stratford-upon-Avon, 1911; also in many editions of the works of Shakespeare and of separate plays. Furness' Variorum edition of Shakespeare reprints many sources of plays and many citations from Shakespeare criticism. Sir E. K. Chambers' *William Shakespeare* furnishes extensive bibliography, both general and special, and reprints practically the whole body of Shakespeare documents. In this connection also it will be advisable for the advanced student to consult the considerable number of annual bibliographies, such as that of the Modern Humanities Research Association, the *Shakespeare-Jahrbuch*, *The Shakespeare Association Bulletin*, *Studies in Philology* (April numbers), *The Year's Work in English Studies*, and the recently established *Shakespeare Survey*.

EARLY COMEDIES

THE
Comedy of Errors

The first known edition of *The Comedy of Errors* is that of the First Folio in 1623. There are, however, a number of indications that the play was in existence at an early date. Mention is made of a performance of the play on Holy Innocents' Day, December 28, 1594. At this time the members of Gray's Inn, one of the four ancient societies of lawyers and law students in London, were celebrating an annual revel which had begun, according to custom, with the election of a Lord of Misrule on December 20. They had invited the members of the Inner Temple to be present with them on the night of the twenty-eighth, on which occasion they had arranged with Shakespeare's company for the performance of a play. So many outside guests had been asked, however, that when the Templars arrived, there were no seats for them, and such a hubbub ensued that the play could not proceed. Offended at this, the members of the Inner Temple left, after which the play was performed. The *Gesta Grayorum*, a chronicle history of Gray's Inn by Henry Helmes (?), gives a facetious account of the night, describing the performance of the play in the following terms:

. . . . . after such sports, a Comedy of Errors (like to Plautus his *Menechmus*) was played by the players. So that the night was begun and continued to the end in nothing but confusion and errors; whereupon it was ever afterwards called *The Night of Errors*.

INDICATIONS OF REVISIONS

Certain features, moreover, within the play itself suggest that it was not at the date of this performance a new production. (1) There is an allusion to France in Act III, scene ii, by Dromio of Syracuse as "armed and reverted, making war against her heir," which seems to refer to the fact that between August 1589 and July 1593, Henry of Navarre, later Henry IV of France, was at war with the Catholic League and had indeed been heir to the French crown and at war with France since 1585. In the same scene (line 140) Dromio represents Spain in the same vulgar fashion as sending "whole armadoes of caracks to be ballast at her nose," which seems to allude to the Invincible Armada and to indicate some reasonable nearness to its overthrow in 1588. (2) In no other play does Shakespeare show so much artificiality of style, as evidenced by an abundance of doggerel verses, speeches balanced between characters, alternate rhymes, puns and conceits—all indicative of an early period. The play has little prose, few run-on lines, and proportionally still fewer light and weak endings. (3) The plot construction of *The Comedy of Errors* is bookish and obviously "careful." Almost nowhere else does Shakespeare take such pains in the elaboration of a plot and the knitting together of certain sources and structural ideas. This feature is, of course, characteristic of Shakespeare's workmanship in all of his greater plays; but in later plays, such as *Twelfth Night*, *Hamlet*, and *King Lear*, his structural manipulations are concealed by his increased skill. (4) Finally, the text as it appears in the Folio shows evidence of the revision of the play in a later style.

What were the features of this revision? In the first two acts the Antipholi appear as "Antipholus Erotes" and "Antipholus Sereptus," as if these names had been their earlier designations and had been carelessly left standing at the time of the revision. So old-fashioned are the fourteen-syllable doggerel verses of the Dromios that some critics have thought they come bodily from an early play on which Shakespeare originally worked. A *Historie of Error*, now lost, was acted before the queen at Hampton Court by the children of St. Paul's School on New Year's night, 1577. Nothing is known about this play, but the title is so suggestive that many critics have believed it to be Shakespeare's original source. However, the only similarity between the two plays is the likeness of the names. It is, however, possible to see that Shakespeare revised his own work, perhaps on the occasion when the play was revived for presentation at Gray's Inn.[1]

SOURCES

In the light of his use of known sources, about to be mentioned, one must admit that Shakespeare worked from the first with a good deal of originality. He would certainly have known the *Menaechmi* and the *Amphitruo*, the most popular of the plays of Plautus. On the *Menaechmi* rests the plot of the indistinguishable twins, and on the *Amphitruo* the incident of the exclusion of Antipholus of Ephesus and his servant from his own house. It was probably also the construction of the *Amphitruo* which caused Shakespeare to begin his play on a basis of error, whereas the *Menaechmi* begins on a basis of truth. That Shakespeare, even supposing there was in existence an old play on the same theme, went directly to Plautus is fairly evident.

Also, the chances are that he used the Latin version

[1]See the edition of the play by Sir Arthur Quiller-Couch and John Dover Wilson in the New Cambridge Shakespeare (Cambridge University Press, 1922); Allison Gaw, "The Evolution of *The Comedy of Errors*," *PMLA*, XLI, 620-666; T. W. Baldwin, Introduction to *The Comedy of Errors* (1928), pp. xvi-xix; *William Shakespeare's Five-Act Structure* (Urbana, 1947), pp. 619-718 *et passim*.

and not an English translation. Although a translation of Plautus was published in 1595 and may previously have been circulated in manuscript, there are few cases in which Shakespeare's words resemble those of the translator. Moreover, Shakespeare uses names from the original which do not appear in the translation.

SHAKESPEARE AND PLAUTUS

Shakespeare has enveloped the two plots from Plautus with a romantic story of the separation and ultimate reunion of the members of one family. This theme was familiar in Greek romance, an example of which lived throughout the ages in the old story of Apollonius of Tyre. Shakespeare has preserved a good deal of the spirit of Roman comedy, and, working with the technique of that dramatic form, has given us something which in sheer confusions is superior to his original. It might be thought that in giving us two Dromios to Plautus' one he has violated probability. However, it is as easy to believe in two sets of identical twins as in one, particularly since the whole comedy is played in an atmosphere of conventionality and make-believe, and since it preserves a Plautine atmosphere of the witch-haunted Ephesus.

One must admit that but for the example of Plautus, a master in the management of intricate plot, Shakespeare could not have succeeded as he did. Since Plautine comedy had been on the English stage for many years, it was easier for the youthful Shakespeare to achieve mastery in that form than in the form of romantic comedy in which he was later to excel all dramatists ancient and modern. In this play itself, however, Shakespeare's most significant advance toward his own greatness was in his use of romantic material, for he thus adapted his Latin comedy to a public which craved variety of a deeper interest as well as a greater emotional appeal.

The Antipholi of Shakespeare correspond to the Menaechmi of Plautus; Dromio of Syracuse to Messenio; Adriana to Mulier; the Courtesan to Erotium; Pinch to Medicus. Plautus' parasite is discarded, probably because the type was unknown to Shakespeare's age and country. Another Dromio (of Ephesus), exactly like Dromio of Syracuse, is added. Plautus' cook and handmaiden are omitted as unimportant, and the role of the Courtesan is greatly reduced; perhaps Shakespeare found Roman libertinism out of place in Elizabethan London. In this play may be seen Shakespeare's characteristic quality of moral stability, as well as his justice and tenderness of heart.

Although the plot remains superficially the same in *The Comedy of Errors* as in the *Menaechmi*, Shakespeare's changes are significant. Senex, the father of Mulier, who acts as her adviser, is replaced by Luciana, the charming sister of Adriana. Luciana becomes the counselor of her sister, serves as a ladylove for the unattached Antipholus of Syracuse, and prefigures the dutiful and obedient wife in contrast to her sister Adriana, who is a shrew. Adriana, who is losing the affection of her husband by her virago-like behavior, is thus made to see the error of her way. Shakespeare supplies outright Solinus, Aegeon, Aemilia, Luce, and the two merchants, new characters who produce a great change in the atmosphere of the play. The main plot goes on in its dry, unmoral, somewhat rascally and licentious fashion, but the romantic minor plot of Aegeon and Aemilia deepens the seriousness of the whole story.

Shakespeare loved to play with edged tools. Somebody's life, or somebody's happiness must be at stake even in his comedies. Shakespearean comedy is not, therefore, pure comedy at all. It lacks the independent,

The Comedy of Errors

81

From Robert Greene's "A Quip for an Upstart Courtier," 1592.

carefree coolness of Plautus, Molière, and Sheridan, or even of Shakespeare's contemporary, Ben Jonson. After the introduction of the good Aegeon with his moving appeal to the magistrate to spare his life—an episode possibly resting on very moving personal observation[2]—we never get him out of our minds, and, in the midst of the fun and confusion, we continue to wonder if he will be saved. The love affair between Luciana and Antipholus of Syracuse is a characteristic feature of romantic comedy. It interrupts and modifies the comedy of errors, which with its wit and satire on Roman types was enough to satisfy Plautus, but not Shakespeare. Even the crudeness of the conventional comedy of women, Adriana representing the shrew and Luciana the obedient wife, is humanized by the fact that Aemilia the abbess advises her newly found daughter-in-law in a natural and affectionate way. Shakespeare's people are real people whose destinies matter. Finally, the element of surprise is made more emotionally gratifying by the completed family reunion in the fifth act.

In spite of these changes the comedy is still Plautine: the masters beat the wrong slaves; the wife scolds the wrong husband; one master is arrested for lunacy, the other for dishonesty; the servants quibble and lie in truly Plautine fashion. In the end all persons are by one means or another assembled in front of the priory, and everything is explained. No doubt from this exercise Shakespeare learned the device, brilliantly employed in such plays as *Twelfth Night* and *Cymbeline*, of keeping certain persons apart while the story was running and bringing them together for inevitable explanations when the fifth act had been reached. Comedies of mistaken identity were already numerous on the London stage and continued long afterwards to be popular, as witnessed by Shakespeare's employment of that kind of plot again in his *Twelfth Night*.

STAGE HISTORY

The only recorded performance of *The Comedy of Errors* for more than one hundred and fifty years after the one described in the *Gesta Grayorum*, was before King James 1 at Whitehall on Innocents' Night, 1604. An adaptation of the play called *'Tis all a Mistake* was played at Covent Garden in 1734. After that it was acted for the next hundred years, probably always in altered versions, with considerable frequency. Thomas Hull's adaptation of the comedy held the boards until 1855, when Samuel Phelps presented Shakespeare's version at Sadler's Wells. Since then it has been staged in public theaters only a few times. It has gone well as a farce, and its greatest successes have arisen from a happy casting of the Dromios. *The Comedy of Errors* was notably successful when played in abbreviated form in the "Globe" Theaters at the expositions in Chicago and San Diego, and a musical comedy, *The Boys from Syracuse*, based on Shakespeare's play, was popular in 1938.

[2]See T. W. Baldwin, *Shakespeare Adapts a Hanging* (Princeton, 1931).

THE
Comedy of Errors

DRAMATIS PERSONAE

SOLINUS, duke of Ephesus.
ÆGEON, a merchant of Syracuse.
ANTIPHOLUS of Ephesus, } twin brothers, and
ANTIPHOLUS of Syracuse, } sons to Ægeon and Æmilia.
DROMIO of Ephesus, } twin brothers, and attendants on the two Antipholuses.
DROMIO of Syracuse, }
BALTHAZAR, a merchant.
ANGELO, a goldsmith.
First Merchant, friend to Antipholus of Syracuse.
Second Merchant, to whom Angelo is a debtor.
PINCH, a schoolmaster.

ÆMILIA, wife to Ægeon, an abbess at Ephesus.
ADRIANA, wife to Antipholus of Ephesus.
LUCIANA, her sister.
LUCE, servant to Adriana.
A Courtezan.

Gaoler, Officers, and other Attendants.

SCENE: *Ephesus.*

ACT I.

SCENE I. *A hall in the* DUKE's *palace.*

Enter DUKE, ÆGEON, Gaoler, Officers, *and other* Attendants.

Æge. Proceed, Solinus, to procure my fall
And by the doom of death end woes and all.
Duke. Merchant of Syracusa, plead no more;
I am not partial to infringe our laws:
The enmity and discord which of late
Sprung from the rancorous outrage of your duke
To merchants, our well-dealing countrymen,
Who wanting guilders to redeem their lives
Have seal'd his rigorous statutes with their bloods,
Excludes all pity from our threatening looks. 10
For, since the mortal and intestine jars
'Twixt thy seditious countrymen and us,
It hath in solemn synods been decreed,
Both by the Syracusians and ourselves,
To admit no traffic to our adverse towns:
Nay, more,
If any born at Ephesus be seen
At any Syracusian marts and fairs;
Again: if any Syracusian born
Come to the bay of Ephesus, he dies, 20
His goods confiscate to the duke's dispose,
Unless a thousand marks be levied,
To quit the penalty and to ransom him.
Thy substance, valued at the highest rate,

Cannot amount unto a hundred marks;
Therefore by law thou art condemn'd to die.
    Æge. Yet this my comfort: when your words are
        done,
My woes end likewise with the evening sun.
    Duke. Well, Syracusian, say in brief the cause
Why thou departed'st from thy native home   30
And for what cause thou camest to Ephesus.
    Æge. A heavier task could not have been imposed
Than I to speak my griefs unspeakable:
Yet, that the world may witness that my end
Was wrought by nature, not by vile offence,
I'll utter what my sorrow gives me leave.
In Syracusa was I born, and wed
Unto a woman, happy but for me,
And by me, had not our hap been bad.
With her I lived in joy; our wealth increased   40
By prosperous voyages I often made
To Epidamnum; till my factor's death
And the great care of goods at random left
Drew me from kind embracements of my spouse:
From whom my absence was not six months old
Before herself, almost at fainting under
The pleasing punishment that women bear,
Had made provision for her following me
And soon and safe arrived where I was.
There had she not been long but she became   50
A joyful mother of two goodly sons;
And, which was strange, the one so like the other
As could not be distinguish'd but by names.
That very hour and in the self-same inn
A meaner woman was delivered
Of such a burden, male twins, both alike:
Those, for their parents were exceeding poor,
I bought and brought up to attend my sons.
My wife, not meanly proud of two such boys,
Made daily motions for our home return: 60
Unwilling I agreed; alas! too soon
We came aboard.
A league from Epidamnum had we sail'd,
Before the always wind-obeying deep
Gave any tragic instance of our harm:
But longer did we not retain much hope;
For what obscured light the heavens did grant
Did but convey unto our fearful minds
A doubtful warrant of immediate death;
Which though myself would gladly have embraced, 70
Yet the incessant weepings of my wife,
Weeping before for what she saw must come,
And piteous plainings of the pretty babes,
That mourn'd for fashion, ignorant what to fear,
Forced me to seek delays for them and me.

And this it was, for other means was none:
The sailors sought for safety by our boat,
And left the ship, then sinking-ripe, to us:
My wife, more careful for the latter-born,
Had fasten'd him unto a small spare mast,   80
Such as seafaring men provide for storms;
To him one of the other twins was bound,
Whilst I had been like heedful of the other:
The children thus disposed, my wife and I,
Fixing our eyes on whom our care was fix'd,
Fasten'd ourselves at either end the mast;
And floating straight, obedient to the stream,
Was carried towards Corinth, as we thought.
At length the sun, gazing upon the earth,
Dispersed those vapours that offended us;   90
And, by the benefit of his wished light,
The seas wax'd calm, and we discovered
Two ships from far making amain to us,
Of Corinth that, of Epidaurus this:
But ere they came,—O, let me say no more!
Gather the sequel by that went before.
    Duke. Nay, forward, old man; do not break off so;
For we may pity, though not pardon thee.
    Æge. O, had the gods done so, I had not now
Worthily term'd them merciless to us!   100
For, ere the ships could meet by twice five leagues,
We were encounter'd by a mighty rock;
Which being violently borne upon,
Our helpful ship was splitted in the midst;
So that, in this unjust divorce of us,
Fortune had left to both of us alike
What to delight in, what to sorrow for.
Her part, poor soul! seeming as burdened
With lesser weight but not with lesser woe,
Was carried with more speed before the wind;   110
And in our sight they three were taken up
By fishermen of Corinth, as we thought.
At length, another ship had seized on us;
And, knowing whom it was their hap to save,
Gave healthful welcome to their shipwreck'd guests;
And would have reft the fishers of their prey,
Had not their bark been very slow of sail;
And therefore homeward did they bend their course.
Thus have you heard me sever'd from my bliss,
That by misfortunes was my life prolong'd,   120
To tell sad stories of my own mishaps.
    Duke. And, for the sake of them thou sorrowest for,
Do me the favour to dilate at full
What hath befall'n of them and thee till now.
    Æge. My youngest boy, and yet my eldest care,
At eighteen years became inquisitive
After his brother: and importuned me

ACT I. SCENE I. *Stage Direction: **A hall in the Duke's palace.*** The New
Cambridge editors (*The Works of Shakespeare,* edited by Sir Arthur
Quiller-Couch and John Dover Wilson, Cambridge University Press,
in progress) limit the settings of the entire play to two. Considering the
play as preserved to have been prepared for acting on the dais of a hall
with three rear doors, they suggest two localities: (*a*) an open space before the house of Antipholus with a priory on one side and a street exit
on the other; and (*b*) the Mart with Courtesan's house in the center and
street exits on each side, one of them leading to the bay. The setting for
the first scene is (*a*). 2. **doom,** judgment. 4. **partial,** sufficiently disposed to favor you. 8. **guilders,** money; the guilder was a Dutch
silver coin worth about 1s. 8d. English; also a gold coin used in the
Netherlands, and parts of Germany. 9. **seal'd,** ratified; see glossary.
11. **mortal,** deadly; see glossary. **intestine.** The usual meaning is
"civil" or "internal"; used with *mortal* it emphasizes the idea of
"deadly civil war." **jars,** quarrels; see glossary. 21. **confiscate,**
confiscated; accent on second syllable. **dispose,** disposal; see glossary.

22. **marks.** A mark was the sum of 13s. 4d. 23. **quit,** pay or clear off;
see glossary. 24. **rate,** estimate; see glossary. 35. **nature,** i.e., by
natural affection, which prompted him to seek his son at Ephesus.
42. **factor's,** agent's. 44. **kind,** affectionate; see glossary. 53. **As,**
that they; see glossary. 55. **meaner,** i.e., of lower rank; see *mean* in
glossary. 59. **meanly,** in a slight degree. 60. **motions,** proposals. 65.
instance, proof, sign; see glossary. 69. **doubtful,** i.e., almost certain;
see glossary. 73. **plainings,** wailings. 78. **sinking-ripe,** ready to sink.
79. **careful,** attentive; see glossary. **latter-born.** Cf. line 125, from
which we learn that the younger of the twins was saved with the father.
84. **disposed,** stowed; see glossary. 93. **amain,** with might and main.
94. **Epidaurus,** a town in Argolis on the Saronic Gulf. 96. **that,** that
which. 104. **helpful.** Rowe's conjecture *helpless* is unnecessary; the
word may refer to the masts after the wreck (ll. 80-86) or to the general
quality of the ship while she held together. 105. **unjust,** unjustified;
see glossary. 115. **healthful,** implying, perhaps, *recovery* from the sufferings of shipwreck (Cuningham). 123. **dilate,** relate.

That his attendant—so his case was like,
Reft of his brother, but retain'd his name—
Might bear him company in the quest of him: 130
Whom whilst I labour'd of a love to see,
I hazarded the loss of whom I loved.
Five summers have I spent in furthest Greece,
Roaming clean through the bounds of Asia,
And, coasting homeward, came to Ephesus;
Hopeless to find, yet loath to leave unsought
Or that or any place that harbours men.
But here must end the story of my life;
And happy were I in my timely death,
Could all my travels warrant me they live.   140
    Duke. Hapless Ægeon, whom the fates have mark'd
To bear the extremity of dire mishap!
Now, trust me, were it not against our laws,
Against my crown, my oath, my dignity,
Which princes, would they, may not disannul,
My soul should sue as advocate for thee.
But, though thou art adjudged to the death
And passed sentence may not be recall'd
But to our honour's great disparagement,
Yet I will favour thee in what I can.   150
Therefore, merchant, I'll limit thee this day
To seek thy life by beneficial help:
Try all the friends thou hast in Ephesus;
Beg thou, or borrow, to make up the sum,
And live; if no, then thou art doom'd to die.
Gaoler, take him to thy custody.
    Gaol. I will, my lord.
    Æge. Hopeless and helpless doth Ægeon wend,
But to procrastinate his lifeless end.   [*Exeunt.*

84

SCENE II. *The Mart.*

Enter ANTIPHOLUS of Syracuse, DROMIO of Syracuse,
  and First Merchant.

    First Mer. Therefore give out you are of
      Epidamnum,
Lest that your goods too soon be confiscate.
This very day a Syracusian merchant
Is apprehended for arrival here;
And not being able to buy out his life
According to the statute of the town
Dies ere the weary sun set in the west.
There is your money that I had to keep.
    Ant. S. Go bear it to the Centaur, where we host,
And stay there, Dromio, till I come to thee.   10
Within this hour it will be dinner-time:
Till that, I'll view the manners of the town,
Peruse the traders, gaze upon the buildings,
And then return and sleep within mine inn,
For with long travel I am stiff and weary.
Get thee away.
    Dro. S. Many a man would take you at your word,

And go indeed, having so good a mean.   [*Exit.*
    Ant. S. A trusty villain, sir, that very oft,
When I am dull with care and melancholy,   20
Lightens my humour with his merry jests.
What, will you walk with me about the town,
And then go to my inn and dine with me?
    First Mer. I am invited, sir, to certain merchants,
Of whom I hope to make much benefit;
I crave your pardon. Soon at five o'clock,
Please you, I'll meet with you upon the mart
And afterward consort you till bed-time:
My present business calls me from you now.
    Ant. S. Farewell till then: I will go lose myself   30
And wander up and down to view the city.
    First Mer. Sir, I commend you to your own content.
                            [*Exit.*
    Ant. S. He that commends me to mine own content
Commends me to the thing I cannot get.
I to the world am like a drop of water
That in the ocean seeks another drop,
Who, falling there to find his fellow forth,
Unseen, inquisitive, confounds himself:
So I, to find a mother and a brother,
In quest of them, unhappy, lose myself.   40

Enter DROMIO *of Ephesus.*

Here comes the almanac of my true date.
What now? how chance thou art return'd so soon?
    Dro. E. Return'd so soon! rather approach'd too
      late:
The capon burns, the pig falls from the spit,
The clock hath strucken twelve upon the bell;
My mistress made it one upon my cheek:
She is so hot because the meat is cold;
The meat is cold because you come not home;
You come not home because you have no stomach;
You have no stomach having broke your fast;   50
But we that know what 'tis to fast and pray
Are penitent for your default to-day.
    Ant. S. Stop in your wind, sir: tell me this, I pray:
Where have you left the money that I gave you?
    Dro. E. O,—sixpence, that I had o' Wednesday
      last
To pay the saddler for my mistress' crupper?
The saddler had it, sir; I kept it not.
    Ant. S. I am not in a sportive humour now:
Tell me, and dally not, where is the money?
We being strangers here, how darest thou trust   60
So great a charge from thine own custody?
    Dro. E. I pray you, jest, sir, as you sit at dinner:
I from my mistress come to you in post;
If I return, I shall be post indeed,
For she will score your fault upon my pate.
Methinks your maw, like mine, should be your clock
And strike you home without a messenger.
    Ant. S. Come, Dromio, come, these jests are out of
      season;

---

128. **so his case was like.** In *Menaechmi* of Plautus one twin takes the
name of his stolen brother Menaechmus; in a similar way in this play
Shakespeare has taken it for granted that the twin slave has taken the
name of his lost brother Dromio (cf. l. 53). 131. **of,** i.e., out of,
impelled by; see glossary. 134. **clean,** entirely. 137. **Or . . . or,**
either . . . or; see glossary. 139. **timely,** early, speedy. 140. **travels,**
"travails" as well as *travels.* **warrant,** assure. 145. **disannul,** annul.
147. **the death,** i.e., death by judicial sentence. 152. **life.** F: *helpe,*
possibly for *helthe* meaning "welfare."
    SCENE II. 8. **keep,** guard, care for; see glossary. 9. **host,** lodge,
put up. 13. **Peruse,** observe. 18. **mean,** opportunity, money; see

glossary. 19. **villain,** used good-humoredly, or as a term of endearment. 21. **humour,** mood, disposition, vagary; see glossary. 26.
Soon at, about. 28. **consort,** attend. 29. **present,** immediate; see glossary. 37. **fellow,** companion; see glossary. **forth,** out. 38. **confounds,**
mingles indistinguishably; see glossary. 40. *Stage Direction:* **Enter
Dromio of Ephesus.** Shakespeare's technique resembles that of *Amphitruo* rather than that of *Menaechmi,* which he definitely follows in his plot.
Menaechmi begins with a true situation which is followed by a false
situation; *Amphitruo,* like *The Comedy of Errors,* begins with a false
situation to be followed by a true situation. The confusion is, therefore,
more bewildering and interesting because of this method. 41. **al-**

Reserve them till a merrier hour than this.
Where is the gold I gave in charge to thee? 70
    Dro. E. To me, sir? why, you gave no gold to me.
    Ant. S. Come on, sir knave, have done your
        foolishness
And tell me how thou hast disposed thy charge.
    Dro. E. My charge was but to fetch you from the
        mart
Home to your house, the Phœnix, sir, to dinner:
My mistress and her sister stays for you.
    Ant. S. Now, as I am a Christian, answer me
In what safe place you have bestow'd my money,
Or I shall break that merry sconce of yours
That stands on tricks when I am undisposed: 80
Where is the thousand marks thou hadst of me?
    Dro. E. I have some marks of yours upon my pate,
Some of my mistress' marks upon my shoulders,
But not a thousand marks between you both.
If I should pay your worship those again,
Perchance you will not bear them patiently.
    Ant. S. Thy mistress' marks? what mistress, slave,
        hast thou?
    Dro. E. Your worship's wife, my mistress at the
        Phœnix,
She that doth fast till you come home to dinner
And prays that you will hie you home to dinner. 90
    Ant. S. What, wilt thou flout me thus unto my face,
Being forbid? There, take you that, sir knave.
    Dro. E. What mean you, sir? for God's sake, hold
        your hands!
Nay, an you will not, sir, I'll take my heels. [*Exit.*
    Ant. S. Upon my life, by some device or other
The villain is o'er-raught of all my money.
They say this town is full of cozenage,
As, nimble jugglers that deceive the eye,
Dark-working sorcerers that change the mind,
Soul-killing witches that deform the body, 100
Disguised cheaters, prating mountebanks,
And many such-like liberties of sin:
If it prove so, I will be gone the sooner.
I'll to the Centaur, to go seek this slave:
I greatly fear my money is not safe. [*Exit.*

ACT II.

SCENE I. *The house of* ANTIPHOLUS *of Ephesus.*

Enter ADRIANA *and* LUCIANA.

    Adr. Neither my husband nor the slave return'd,
That in such haste I sent to seek his master!
Sure, Luciana, it is two o'clock.
    Luc. Perhaps some merchant hath invited him
And from the mart he 's somewhere gone to dinner.
Good sister, let us dine and never fret:
A man is master of his liberty:
Time is their master, and when they see time

They'll go or come: if so, be patient, sister.
    Adr. Why should their liberty than ours be more? 10
    Luc. Because their business still lies out o' door.
    Adr. Look, when I serve him so, he takes it ill.
    Luc. O, know he is the bridle of your will.
    Adr. There 's none but asses will be bridled so.
    Luc. Why, headstrong liberty is lash'd with woe.
There 's nothing situate under heaven's eye
But hath his bound, in earth, in sea, in sky:
The beasts, the fishes and the winged fowls
Are their males' subjects and at their controls:
Men, more divine, the masters of all these, 20
Lords of the wide world and wild watery seas,
Indued with intellectual sense and souls,
Of more pre-eminence than fish and fowls,
Are masters to their females, and their lords:
Then let your will attend on their accords.
    Adr. This servitude makes you to keep unwed.
    Luc. Not this, but troubles of the marriage-bed.
    Adr. But, were you wedded, you would bear some
        sway.
    Luc. Ere I learn love, I'll practise to obey.
    Adr. How if your husband start some other where? 30
    Luc. Till he come home again, I would forbear.
    Adr. Patience unmoved! no marvel though she
        pause;
They can be meek that have no other cause.
A wretched soul, bruised with adversity,
We bid be quiet when we hear it cry;
But were we burden'd with like weight of pain,
As much or more we should ourselves complain:
So thou, that hast no unkind mate to grieve thee,
With urging helpless patience wouldst relieve me;
But, if thou live to see like right bereft, 40
This fool-begg'd patience in thee will be left.
    Luc. Well, I will marry one day, but to try.
Here comes your man; now is your husband nigh.

Enter DROMIO *of Ephesus.*

    Adr. Say, is your tardy master now at hand?
    Dro. E. Nay, he 's at two hands with me, and that
my two ears can witness.
    Adr. Say, didst thou speak with him? know'st thou
        his mind?
    Dro. E. Ay, ay, he told his mind upon mine ear:
Beshrew his hand, I scarce could understand it.
    Luc. Spake he so doubtfully, thou couldst not feel his
meaning? 51
    Dro. E. Nay, he struck so plainly, I could too well feel
his blows; and withal so doubtfully that I could scarce
understand them.
    Adr. But say, I prithee, is he coming home?
It seems he hath great care to please his wife.
    Dro. E. Why, mistress, sure my master is horn-mad.
    Adr. Horn-mad, thou villain!
    Dro. E.   I mean not cuckold-mad;
But, sure, he is stark mad.

When I desired him to come home to dinner, 60
He ask'd me for a thousand marks in gold:
' 'Tis dinner-time,' quoth I; 'My gold!' quoth he:
'Your meat doth burn,' quoth I; 'My gold!' quoth he:
'Will you come home?' quoth I; 'My gold!' quoth he,
'Where is the thousand marks I gave thee, villain?'
'The pig,' quoth I, 'is burn'd;' 'My gold!' quoth he:
'My mistress, sir,' quoth I; 'Hang up thy mistress!
I know not thy mistress; out on thy mistress!'
   Luc. Quoth who?
   Dro. E. Quoth my master: 70
'I know,' quoth he, 'no house, no wife, no mistress.'
So that my errand, due unto my tongue,
I thank him, I bare home upon my shoulders;
For, in conclusion, he did beat me there.
   Adr. Go back again, thou slave, and fetch him
     home.
   Dro. E. Go back again, and be new beaten home?
For God's sake, send some other messenger.
   Adr. Back, slave, or I will break thy pate across.
   Dro. E. And he will bless that cross with other
     beating:
Between you I shall have a holy head. 80
   Adr. Hence, prating peasant! fetch thy master
     home.
   Dro. E. Am I so round with you as you with me,
That like a football you do spurn me thus?
You spurn me hence, and he will spurn me hither:
If I last in this service, you must case me in leather.
                             [Exit.
   Luc. Fie, how impatience loureth in your face!
   Adr. His company must do his minions grace,
Whilst I at home starve for a merry look.
Hath homely age the alluring beauty took
From my poor cheek? then he hath wasted it: 90
Are my discourses dull? barren my wit?
If voluble and sharp discourse be marr'd,
Unkindness blunts it more than marble hard:
Do their gay vestments his affections bait?
That 's not my fault; he 's master of my state:
What ruins are in me that can be found,
By him not ruin'd? then is he the ground
Of my defeatures. My decayed fair
A sunny look of his would soon repair:
But, too unruly deer, he breaks the pale 100
And feeds from home; poor I am but his stale.
   Luc. Self-harming jealousy! fie, beat it hence!
   Adr. Unfeeling fools can with such wrongs dispense.
I know his eye doth homage otherwhere;
Or else what lets it but he would be here?
Sister, you know he promised me a chain;
Would that alone, alone he would detain,
So he would keep fair quarter with his bed!
I see the jewel best enamelled
Will lose his beauty; yet the gold bides still, 110
That others touch, and often touching will
†Wear gold: and no man that hath a name,

By falsehood and corruption doth it shame.
Since that my beauty cannot please his eye,
I'll weep what 's left away, and weeping die.
   Luc. How many fond fools serve mad jealousy!
                                [Exeunt.

SCENE II. *A public place.*

Enter ANTIPHOLUS *of Syracuse.*

   Ant. S. The gold I gave to Dromio is laid up
Safe at the Centaur; and the heedful slave
Is wander'd forth, in care to seek me out
By computation and mine host's report.
I could not speak with Dromio since at first
I sent him from the mart. See, here he comes.

Enter DROMIO *of Syracuse.*

How now, sir! is your merry humour alter'd?
As you love strokes, so jest with me again.
You know no Centaur? you received no gold?
Your mistress sent to have me home to dinner? 10
My house was at the Phœnix? Wast thou mad,
That thus so madly thou didst answer me?
   Dro. S. What answer, sir? when spake I such a word?
   Ant. S. Even now, even here, not half an hour since.
   Dro. S. I did not see you since you sent me hence,
Home to the Centaur, with the gold you gave me.
   Ant. S. Villain, thou didst deny the gold's receipt
And told'st me of a mistress and a dinner;
For which, I hope, thou felt'st I was displeased.
   Dro. S. I am glad to see you in this merry vein: 20
What means this jest? I pray you, master, tell me.
   Ant. S. Yea, dost thou jeer and flout me in the teeth?
Think'st thou I jest? Hold, take thou that, and that.
                        [Beating him.
   Dro. S. Hold, sir, for God's sake! now your jest is
     earnest:
Upon what bargain do you give it me?
   Ant. S. Because that I familiarly sometimes
Do use you for my fool and chat with you,
Your sauciness will jest upon my love
And make a common of my serious hours.
When the sun shines let foolish gnats make sport, 30
But creep in crannies when he hides his beams.
If you will jest with me, know my aspect
And fashion your demeanour to my looks,
Or I will beat this method in your sconce.
   Dro. S. Sconce call you it? so you would leave bat-
tering, I had rather have it a head: an you use these
blows long, I must get a sconce for my head and
insconce it too; or else I shall seek my wit in my
shoulders. But, I pray, sir, why am I beaten? 40
   Ant. S. Dost thou not know?
   Dro. S. Nothing, sir, but that I am beaten.
   Ant. S. Shall I tell you why?

---

72. **due unto my tongue,** i.e., instead of committing to me a message that I might deliver (with my tongue), he gave me one to bear home on my shoulders (i.e., a beating). 79. **bless,** consecrate; also, beat. 80. **holy,** with quibble on the sense "full of holes." 82. **round,** spherical, with pun on the sense of "plain-spoken"; see glossary. 86. **loureth,** frowns. 87. **minions,** favorites, darlings; see glossary. **grace,** honor; see glossary. 91. **discourses,** conversations; see glossary. 94. **affections,** passions; see glossary. **bait,** entice. 95. **state,** outward display, i.e., clothes; see glossary. 97. **ground,** cause. 98. **defeatures,** disfigurements. **decayed,** departed, perished; see glossary. **fair,** beauty; see glossary. 101. **stale.** She is stale to him, he dear (*deer*) to her; a *stale* is a lover made into a dupe, or a laughingstock. 103. **dispense,**

pardon, condone by dispensation. 105. **lets,** hinders; see glossary. 107. **detain,** withhold. 108. **keep fair quarter,** be on good terms. 109-113. **I see . . . shame.** This is a difficult passage, possibly corrupt. Herford explains: "The best enameled jewel tarnishes, but the gold setting keeps its luster; however, it may be worn by the touch. Similarly, a man of assured reputation can commit domestic infidelity without blasting it." 112. **Wear,** so Theobald; F: *Where.* 116. **fond,** doting; see glossary.
SCENE II. *Stage Direction: A public place.* New Cambridge: *The Mart of Ephesus.* 22. **in the teeth,** to my face. 24. **earnest,** money paid as an installment to secure a bargain, with quibble on the meaning "serious"; see glossary. 28. **jest upon,** trifle with. 29. **common,** pub-

Dro. S. Ay, sir, and wherefore; for they say every why
hath a wherefore.

Ant. S. Why, first,—for flouting me; and then,
    wherefore,—
For urging it the second time to me.

Dro. S. Was there ever any man thus beaten out of
    season,
When in the why and the wherefore is neither rhyme
    nor reason?
Well, sir, I thank you.   50

Ant. S. Thank me, sir! for what?

Dro. S. Marry, sir, for this something that you gave
me for nothing.

Ant. S. I'll make you amends next, to give you
nothing for something. But say, sir, is it dinner-time?

Dro. S. No, sir: I think the meat wants that I have.

Ant. S. In good time, sir; what's that?

Dro. S. Basting.

Ant. S. Well, sir, then 'twill be dry.   60

Dro. S. If it be, sir, I pray you, eat none of it.

Ant. S. Your reason?

Dro. S. Lest it make you choleric and purchase me
another dry basting.

Ant. S. Well, sir, learn to jest in good time: there's a
time for all things.

Dro. S. I durst have denied that, before you were so
choleric.

Ant. S. By what rule, sir?

Dro. S. Marry, sir, by a rule as plain as the plain
bald pate of father Time himself.   71

Ant. S. Let's hear it.

Dro. S. There's no time for a man to recover his
hair that grows bald by nature.

Ant. S. May he not do it by fine and recovery?

Dro. S. Yes, to pay a fine for a periwig and recover
the lost hair of another man.

Ant. S. Why is Time such a niggard of hair, being,
as it is, so plentiful an excrement?   79

Dro. S. Because it is a blessing that he bestows on
beasts; and what he hath scanted men in hair he hath
given them in wit.

Ant. S. Why, but there's many a man hath more
hair than wit.

Dro. S. Not a man of those but he hath the wit to
lose his hair.

Ant. S. Why, thou didst conclude hairy men plain
dealers without wit.

Dro. S. The plainer dealer, the sooner lost: yet he
loseth it in a kind of jollity.   90

Ant. S. For what reason?

Dro. S. For two; and sound ones too.

Ant. S. Nay, not sound, I pray you.

Dro. S. Sure ones then.

Ant. S. Nay, not sure, in a thing falsing.

Dro. S. Certain ones then.

Ant. S. Name them.

Dro. S. The one, to save the money that he spends in
tiring; the other that at dinner they should not drop
in his porridge.   100

Ant. S. You would all this time have proved there is
no time for all things.

Dro. S. Marry, and did, sir; namely, no time to
recover hair lost by nature.

Ant. S. But your reason was not substantial, why
there is no time to recover.

Dro. S. Thus I mend it: Time himself is bald and
therefore to the world's end will have bald followers.

Ant. S. I knew 'twould be a bald conclusion: But,
soft! who wafts us yonder?   111

Enter ADRIANA *and* LUCIANA.

Adr. Ay, ay, Antipholus, look strange and frown:
Some other mistress hath thy sweet aspects;
I am not Adriana nor thy wife.
The time was once when thou unurged wouldst vow
That never words were music to thine ear,
That never object pleasing in thine eye,
That never touch well welcome to thy hand,
That never meat sweet-savour'd in thy taste,
Unless I spake, or look'd, or touch'd, or carved to
    thee.   120
How comes it now, my husband, O, how comes it,
That thou art thus estranged from thyself?
Thyself I call it, being strange to me,
That, undividable, incorporate,
Am better than thy dear self's better part.
Ah, do not tear away thyself from me!
For know, my love, as easy mayst thou fall
A drop of water in the breaking gulf
And take unmingled thence that drop again,
Without addition or diminishing,   130
As take from me thyself and not me too.
How dearly would it touch thee to the quick,
Shouldst thou but hear I were licentious
And that this body, consecrate to thee,
By ruffian lust should be contaminate!
Wouldst thou not spit at me and spurn at me
And hurl the name of husband in my face
And tear the stain'd skin off my harlot-brow
And from my false hand cut the wedding-ring
And break it with a deep-divorcing vow?   140
I know thou canst; and therefore see thou do it.
I am possess'd with an adulterate blot;
My blood is mingled with the crime of lust:
For if we two be one and thou play false,
I do digest the poison of thy flesh,
Being strumpeted by thy contagion.
Keep then fair league and truce with thy true bed;
I live unstain'd, thou undishonoured.

Ant. S. Plead you to me, fair dame? I know you not:
In Ephesus I am but two hours old,   150
As strange unto your town as to your talk;
Who, every word by all my wit being scann'd,
Want wit in all one word to understand.

lic playground. 32. **aspect,** look, expression; also, favor or disfavor
of a heavenly body. 34. **sconce,** head; fort (l. 35); helmet (l. 38).
37. **use,** make a practice of; see glossary. 38. **insconce,** to shelter
behind or within a *sconce,* or fortification. 39. **seek . . . shoulders,**
run away, show my back (Cuningham); but Dromio probably means
that his head will be beaten into his shoulders. 57. **wants,** lacks; see
glossary. **that,** what. 58. **In good time,** indeed. 63. **choleric.** Hot or
dry food would produce or aggravate the choleric humor. 64. **dry
basting,** hard beating. 70. **Marry,** an oath by the Virgin Mary; see
glossary. 75. **fine and recovery,** legal procedure; Schmidt: "finery and
recovery." 79. **excrement,** outgrowth (of hair). 84. **more . . . wit,** a
proverbial phrase. 85-86. **he . . . hair,** a reference to the diseases in
which loss of hair was a symptom. 90. **jollity.** This word and *sound*
and *falsing* (ll. 93, 95) continue the reference to disease. 95. **falsing,**
deceptive. 99. **tiring,** dressing the hair. 103. **no time,** so F₂; F: *in no
time;* Capell: *e'en no time.* 110. **bald,** senseless. 111. **wafts,** beckons.
112. **strange,** estranged, unfriendly; see glossary. 125. **better part,**
i.e., soul, spirit. 127. **fall,** i.e., let fall; see glossary. 145. **digest,**
assimilate; see glossary. 146. **strumpeted,** made a strumpet. 148. **unstain'd.** The F reading *distain'd* Dyce interpreted as "I, as a wife, receive
the *stain* of your present conduct, while you, as a husband, suffer no
loss of honour."

Luc. Fie, brother! how the world is changed with
    you!
When were you wont to use my sister thus?
She sent for you by Dromio home to dinner.
    Ant. S. By Dromio?
    Dro. S. By me?
    Adr. By thee; and this thou didst return from him,
That he did buffet thee and in his blows   160
Denied my house for his, me for his wife.
    Ant. S. Did you converse, sir, with this gentle-
    woman?
What is the course and drift of your compact?
    Dro. S. I, sir? I never saw her till this time.
    Ant. S. Villain, thou liest; for even her very words
Didst thou deliver to me on the mart.
    Dro. S. I never spake with her in all my life.
    Ant. S. How can she thus then call us by our names?
Unless it be by inspiration.
    Adr. How ill agrees it with your gravity   170
To counterfeit thus grossly with your slave,
Abetting him to thwart me in my mood!
Be it my wrong you are from me exempt,
But wrong not that wrong with a more contempt.
Come, I will fasten on this sleeve of thine:
Thou art an elm, my husband, I a vine,
Whose weakness married to thy stronger state
Makes me with thy strength to communicate:
If aught possess thee from me, it is dross,
Usurping ivy, brier, or idle moss;   180
Who, all for want of pruning, with intrusion
Infect thy sap and live on thy confusion.
    Ant. S. To me she speaks; she moves me for her
    theme:
What, was I married to her in my dream?
Or sleep I now and think I hear all this?
What error drives our eyes and ears amiss?
Until I know this sure uncertainty,
I'll entertain the offer'd fallacy.
    Luc. Dromio, go bid the servants spread for dinner.
    Dro. S. O, for my beads! I cross me for a sinner.   190
This is the fairy land: O spite of spites!
We talk with goblins, owls and sprites:
If we obey them not, this will ensue,
They'll suck our breath or pinch us black and blue.
    Luc. Why pratest thou to thyself and answer'st not?
Dromio, thou drone, thou snail, thou slug, thou sot!
    Dro. S. I am transformed, master, am I not?
    Ant. S. I think thou art in mind, and so am I.
    Dro. S. Nay, master, both in mind and in my shape.
    Ant. S. Thou hast thine own form.
    Dro. S.   No, I am an ape.   200
    Luc. If thou art changed to aught, 'tis to an ass.
    Dro. S. 'Tis true; she rides me and I long for grass.
'Tis so, I am an ass; else it could never be
But I should know her as well as she knows me.
    Adr. Come, come, no longer will I be a fool,
To put the finger in the eye and weep,
Whilst man and master laugh my woes to scorn.

Come, sir, to dinner. Dromio, keep the gate.
Husband, I'll dine above with you to-day
And shrive you of a thousand idle pranks.   210
Sirrah, if any ask you for your master,
Say he dines forth and let no creature enter.
Come, sister. Dromio, play the porter well.
    Ant. S. Am I in earth, in heaven, or in hell?
Sleeping or waking? mad or well-advised?
Known unto these, and to myself disguised!
I'll say as they say and persever so
And in this mist at all adventures go.
    Dro. S. Master, shall I be porter at the gate?
    Adr. Ay; and let none enter, lest I break your pate.
    Luc. Come, come, Antipholus, we dine too late.   221
                                        [*Exeunt.*

ACT III.

SCENE I. *Before the house of* ANTIPHOLUS *of* Ephesus.

Enter ANTIPHOLUS *of* Ephesus, DROMIO *of* Ephesus,
    ANGELO, *and* BALTHAZAR.

    Ant. E. Good Signior Angelo, you must excuse us
    all;
My wife is shrewish when I keep not hours:
Say that I linger'd with you at your shop
To see the making of her carcanet
And that to-morrow you will bring it home.
But here 's a villain that would face me down
He met me on the mart and that I beat him
And charged him with a thousand marks in gold
And that I did deny my wife and house.   9
Thou drunkard, thou, what didst thou mean by this?
    Dro. E. Say what you will, sir, but I know what I
    know;
That you beat me at the mart, I have your hand to
    show:
If the skin were parchment and the blows you gave
    were ink,
Your own handwriting would tell you what I think.
    Ant. E. I think thou art an ass.
    Dro. E.   Marry, so it doth appear
By the wrongs I suffer and the blows I bear.
I should kick, being kick'd; and, being at that pass,
You would keep from my heels and beware of an ass.
    Ant. E. You 're sad, Signior Balthazar: pray God
    our cheer
May answer my good will and your good welcome
    here.   20
    Bal. I hold your dainties cheap, sir, and your
    welcome dear.
    Ant. E. O, Signior Balthazar, either at flesh or fish,
A table full of welcome makes scarce one dainty dish.
    Bal. Good meat, sir, is common; that every churl
    affords.
    Ant. E. And welcome more common; for that 's
    nothing but words.

163. **compact,** plot. 172. **mood,** anger, displeasure. 173. **exempt,**
separated. 180. **idle,** unprofitable. 182. **confusion,** overthrow, ruin;
see glossary. 183. **moves,** appeals to; see glossary. **theme,** subject,
i. e., trouble. 186. **error.** Cf. I, ii, 97, *this town is full of cozenage;*
Antipholus and Dromio continue in their belief in the witchery of
Ephesus. 188. **entertain,** accept; see glossary. **fallacy,** delusive notion,
error. 190. **beads,** rosary. 194. **suck . . . breath.** This piece of folklore was perhaps connected with the old idea that the breath of man
was his soul. 196. **sot,** fool. 209. **dine above.** This indicates that the
balcony is used in the next scene. 210. **shrive,** to hear a person's confession and give him absolution. 211. **Sirrah,** customary form of ad-

dress to servants; see glossary. 212. **forth,** out. 215. **well-advised,** in
my right mind.
ACT III. SCENE I. 4. **carcanet,** necklace of jewels. 6. **face me down,**
maintain to my face that. 8. **with,** i.e., with possession of. 9. **deny,**
disown; see glossary. 11 ff. Note the appearance of doggerel at this
point and in the following lines. Balthazar appears here only; Luce is
elsewhere known as Nell; the conversation of the Dromios is possibly
from the old play taken over as it stood. 12. **hand,** quibble on "handwriting." 19. **sad,** serious; see glossary. 20. **answer,** agree with;
see glossary. 24. **churl,** one of mean station. 28. **cates,** dainties.
31. **Gillian, Ginn,** Juliana, Jenny (?) 32. **Mome,** dolt, blockhead. **malt-**

Bal. Small cheer and great welcome makes a
　　merry feast.
Ant. E. Ay to a niggardly host and more sparing
　　guest:
But though my cates be mean, take them in good part;
Better cheer may you have, but not with better heart.
But, soft! my door is lock'd. Go bid them let us in.　30
Dro. E. Maud, Bridget, Marian, Cicely, Gillian,
　　Ginn!
Dro. S. [*Within*] Mome, malt-horse, capon, cox-
　　comb, idiot, patch!
Either get thee from the door or sit down at the hatch.
Dost thou conjure for wenches, that thou call'st for
　　such store,
When one is one too many? Go get thee from the door.
Dro. E. What patch is made our porter? My master
　　stays in the street.
Dro. S. [*Within*] Let him walk from whence he
　　came, lest he catch cold on 's feet.
Ant. E. Who talks within there? ho, open the door!
Dro. S. [*Within*] Right, sir; I'll tell you when, an
　　you'll tell me wherefore.
Ant. E. Wherefore? for my dinner: I have not dined
　　to-day.　40
Dro. S. [*Within*] Nor to-day here you must not;
　　come again when you may.
Ant. E. What art thou that keepest me out from the
　　house I owe?
Dro. S. [*Within*] The porter for this time, sir, and
　　my name is Dromio.
Dro. E. O villain! thou hast stolen both mine
　　office and my name.
The one ne'er got me credit, the other mickle blame.
If thou hadst been Dromio to-day in my place,
Thou wouldst have changed thy face for a name or
　　thy name for an ass.
Luce. [*Within*] What a coil is there, Dromio? who
　　are those at the gate?
Dro. E. Let my master in, Luce.
Luce.　　　　　　　[*Within*] Faith, no; he comes too
　　late;
And so tell your master.
Dro. E.　　　　　　O Lord, I must laugh!　50
Have at you with a proverb—Shall I set in my staff?
Luce. [*Within*] Have at you with another; that 's—
When? can you tell?
Dro. S. [*Within*] If thy name be call'd Luce,—Luce,
　　thou hast answer'd him well.
Ant. E. Do you hear, you minion? you'll let us in, I
　　hope?
Luce. [*Within*] I thought to have ask'd you.
Dro. S.　　　　　　[*Within*] And you said no.
Dro. E. So, come, help: well struck! there was blow
　　for blow.
Ant. E. Thou baggage, let me in.
Luce.　　　　　　　　[*Within*] Can you tell for whose
　　sake?
Dro. E. Master, knock the door hard.

Luce.　　　　　　　　[*Within*] Let him knock till it
　　ache.
Ant. E. You'll cry for this, minion, if I beat the door
　　down.
Luce. [*Within*] What needs all that, and a pair of
　　stocks in the town?　60
Adr. [*Within*] Who is that at the door that keeps all
　　this noise?
Dro. S. [*Within*] By my troth, your town is troubled
　　with unruly boys.
Ant. E. Are you there, wife? you might have come
　　before.
Adr. [*Within*] Your wife, sir knave! go get you from
　　the door.
Dro. E. If you went in pain, master, this 'knave'
　　would go sore.
Ang. Here is neither cheer, sir, nor welcome: we
　　would fain have either.
Bal. In debating which was best, we shall part with
　　neither.
Dro. E. They stand at the door, master; bid them
　　welcome hither.
Ant. E. There is something in the wind, that we
　　cannot get in.
Dro. E. You would say so, master, if your garments
　　were thin.　70
Your cake there is warm within; you stand here in the
　　cold:
It would make a man mad as a buck, to be so bought
　　and sold.
Ant. E. Go fetch me something: I'll break ope the
　　gate.
Dro. S. [*Within*] Break any breaking here, and I'll
　　break your knave's pate.
Dro. E. A man may break a word with you, sir, and
　　words are but wind,
Ay, and break it in your face, so he break it not
　　behind.
Dro. S. [*Within*] It seems thou want'st breaking:
　　out upon thee, hind!
Dro. E. Here 's too much 'out upon thee!' I pray
　　thee, let me in.
Dro. S. [*Within*] Ay, when fowls have no feathers
　　and fish have no fin.
Ant. E. Well, I'll break in: go borrow me a crow.　80
Dro. E. A crow without feather? Master, mean you
　　so?
For a fish without a fin, there 's a fowl without a
　　feather:
If a crow help us in, sirrah, we'll pluck a crow
　　together.
Ant. E. Go get thee gone; fetch me an iron crow.
Bal. Have patience, sir; O, let it not be so!
Herein you war against your reputation
And draw within the compass of suspect
The unviolated honour of your wife.
Once this,—your long experience of her wisdom,
Her sober virtue, years and modesty,　90

Plead on her part some cause to you unknown;
And doubt not, sir, but she will well excuse
Why at this time the doors are made against you.
Be ruled by me: depart in patience,
And let us to the Tiger all to dinner,
And about evening come yourself alone
To know the reason of this strange restraint.
If by strong hand you offer to break in
Now in the stirring passage of the day,
A vulgar comment will be made of it,   100
And that supposed by the common rout
Against your yet ungalled estimation
That may with foul intrusion enter in
And dwell upon your grave when you are dead;
For slander lives upon succession,
For ever housed where it gets possession.
    Ant. E. You have prevail'd: I will depart in quiet,
And, in despite of mirth, mean to be merry.
I know a wench of excellent discourse,
Pretty and witty, wild and yet, too, gentle: 110
There will we dine. This woman that I mean,
My wife—but, I protest, without desert—
Hath oftentimes upbraided me withal:
To her will we to dinner. [*To Ang.*] Get you home
And fetch the chain; by this I know 'tis made:
Bring it, I pray you, to the Porpentine;
For there 's the house: that chain will I bestow—
Be it for nothing but to spite my wife—
Upon mine hostess there: good sir, make haste.
Since mine own doors refuse to entertain me,   120
I'll knock elsewhere, to see if they'll disdain me.
    Ang. I'll meet you at that place some hour hence.
    Ant. E. Do so. This jest shall cost me some expense.
                                                  [*Exeunt.*

SCENE II. *The same.*

Enter LUCIANA *and* ANTIPHOLUS of Syracuse.

    Luc. And may it be that you have quite forgot
A husband's office? shall, Antipholus,
Even in the spring of love, thy love-springs rot?
    Shall love, in building, grow so ruinous?
If you did wed my sister for her wealth,
    Then for her wealth's sake use her with more
        kindness:
Or if you like elsewhere, do it by stealth;
    Muffle your false love with some show of blindness:
Let not my sister read it in your eye;
    Be not thy tongue thy own shame's orator;   10
Look sweet, speak fair, become disloyalty;
    Apparel vice like virtue's harbinger:
Bear a fair presence, though your heart be tainted;
    Teach sin the carriage of a holy saint;
Be secret-false: what need she be acquainted?
    What simple thief brags of his own attaint?
'Tis double wrong, to truant with your bed
    And let her read it in thy looks at board:

Shame hath a bastard fame, well managed;
    Ill deeds are doubled with an evil word.   20
Alas, poor women! make us but believe,
    Being compact of credit, that you love us;
Though others have the arm, show us the sleeve;
    We in your motion turn and you may move us.
Then, gentle brother, get you in again;
    Comfort my sister, cheer her, call her wife:
'Tis holy sport to be a little vain,
    When the sweet breath of flattery conquers strife.
    Ant. S. Sweet mistress,—what your name is else, I
        know not,
Nor by what wonder you do hit of mine,—   30
Less in your knowledge and your grace you show not
    Than our earth's wonder, more than earth divine.
Teach me, dear creature, how to think and speak;
    Lay open to my earthy-gross conceit,
Smother'd in errors, feeble, shallow, weak,
    The folded meaning of your words' deceit.
Against my soul's pure truth why labour you
    To make it wander in an unknown field?
Are you a god? would you create me new?
    Transform me then, and to your power I'll yield.   40
But if that I am I, then well I know
    Your weeping sister is no wife of mine,
Nor to her bed no homage do I owe:
    Far more, far more to you do I decline.
O, train me not, sweet mermaid, with thy note,
    To drown me in thy sister's flood of tears:
Sing, siren, for thyself and I will dote:
    Spread o'er the silver waves thy golden hairs,
And as a bed I'll take them and there lie,
    And in that glorious supposition think   50
He gains by death that hath such means to die:
    Let Love, being light, be drowned if she sink!
    Luc. What, are you mad, that you do reason so?
    Ant. S. Not mad, but mated; how, I do not know.
    Luc. It is a fault that springeth from your eye.
    Ant. S. For gazing on your beams, fair sun, being by.
    Luc. Gaze where you should, and that will clear
        your sight.
    Ant. S. As good to wink, sweet love, as look on night.
    Luc. Why call you me love? call my sister so.
    Ant. S. Thy sister's sister.
    Luc.   That 's my sister.
    Ant. S.   No;   60
It is thyself, mine own self's better part,
Mine eye's clear eye, my dear heart's dearer heart,
My food, my fortune and my sweet hope's aim,
My sole earth's heaven and my heaven's claim.
    Luc. All this my sister is, or else should be.
    Ant. S. Call thyself sister, sweet, for I am thee.
Thee will I love and with thee lead my life:
Thou hast no husband yet nor I no wife.
Give me thy hand.
    Luc.   O, soft, sir! hold you still:
I'll fetch my sister, to get her good will.   [*Exit.* 70

Enter DROMIO of Syracuse.

92. **excuse,** justify; see glossary. 93. **made,** fastened. 98. **offer,** venture; see glossary. 99. **passage,** people passing by. 100. **vulgar,** public. 102. **ungalled,** uninjured. 105. **slander . . . succession,** i.e., one slander grows out of another. 108. **in . . . mirth,** in despite of mirth, which has abandoned me. Theobald suggested *wrath* for *mirth.* 112. **desert,** my deserving it. 115. **this,** this time. 116. **Porpentine,** name of an inn; the word means "porcupine."
    SCENE II. 1. **may,** can; see glossary. 3. **love-springs,** tender "shoots" of love. 11. **fair,** courteously; see glossary. **become dis-**

loyalty, carry falseness gracefully. 14. **carriage,** demeanor, behavior. 16. **attaint,** stain, dishonor; or possibly, conviction of crime. 18. **board,** table. 19. **fame,** reputation; see glossary. 22. **compact of credit,** made up of credulity. 27. **vain,** false. 30. **hit of,** hit upon, guess. 32. **earth's wonder.** Douce sees in this a reference to Queen Elizabeth. 34. **conceit,** wit, mental faculty; see glossary. 36. **folded,** concealed. 44. **decline,** incline, lean toward. 45. **train,** entice, allure; see glossary. 52. **light,** buoyant, with quibble on the sense of "wanton." The idea is that *Love* cannot possibly sink. 53. **reason,**

Ant. S. Why, how now, Dromio! where runn'st thou so fast?

Dro. S. Do you know me, sir? am I Dromio? am I your man? am I myself?

Ant. S. Thou art Dromio, thou art my man, thou art thyself.

Dro. S. I am an ass, I am a woman's man and besides myself.

Ant. S. What woman's man? and how besides thyself? 80

Dro. S. Marry, sir, besides myself, I am due to a woman; one that claims me, one that haunts me, one that will have me.

Ant. S. What claim lays she to thee?

Dro. S. Marry, sir, such claim as you would lay to your horse; and she would have me as a beast: not that, I being a beast, she would have me; but that she, being a very beastly creature, lays claim to me.

Ant. S. What is she? 90

Dro. S. A very reverent body; ay, such a one as a man may not speak of without he say 'Sir-reverence.' I have but lean luck in the match, and yet is she a wondrous fat marriage.

Ant. S. How dost thou mean a fat marriage?

Dro. S. Marry, sir, she 's the kitchen wench and all grease; and I know not what use to put her to but to make a lamp of her and run from her by her own light. I warrant, her rags and the tallow in them will burn a Poland winter: if she lives till doomsday, she'll burn a week longer than the whole world.

Ant. S. What complexion is she of?

Dro. S. Swart, like my shoe, but her face nothing like so clean kept: for why, she sweats; a man may go over shoes in the grime of it.

Ant. S. That 's a fault that water will mend.

Dro. S. No, sir, 'tis in grain; Noah's flood could not do it.

Ant. S. What 's her name? 110

Dro. S. Nell, sir; but her name and three quarters, that 's an ell and three quarters, will not measure her from hip to hip.

Ant. S. Then she bears some breadth?

Dro. S. No longer from head to foot than from hip to hip; she is spherical, like a globe; I could find out countries in her.

Ant. S. In what part of her body stands Ireland?

Dro. S. Marry, sir, in her buttocks: I found it out by the bogs. 121

Ant. S. Where Scotland?

Dro. S. I found it by the barrenness; hard in the palm of the hand.

Ant. S. Where France?

Dro. S. In her forehead; armed and reverted, making war against her heir.

Ant. S. Where England?

Dro. S. I looked for the chalky cliffs, but I could find no whiteness in them; but I guess it stood in her chin, by the salt rheum that ran between France and it.

Ant. S. Where Spain?

Dro. S. Faith, I saw it not; but I felt it hot in her breath.

Ant. S. Where America, the Indies?

Dro. S. Oh, sir, upon her nose, all o'er embellished with rubies, carbuncles, sapphires, declining their rich aspect to the hot breath of Spain; who sent whole armadoes of caracks to be ballast at her nose. 141

Ant. S. Where stood Belgia, the Netherlands?

Dro. S. Oh, sir, I did not look so low. To conclude, this drudge, or diviner, laid claim to me; called me Dromio; swore I was assured to her; told me what privy marks I had about me, as, the mark of my shoulder, the mole in my neck, the great wart on my left arm, that I amazed ran from her as a witch:

And, I think, if my breast had not been made of faith
 and my heart of steel, 150
She had transform'd me to a curtal dog and made me
 turn i' the wheel.

Ant. S. Go hie thee presently, post to the road:
An if the wind blow any way from shore,
I will not harbour in this town to-night:
If any bark put forth, come to the mart,
Where I will walk till thou return to me.
If every one knows us and we know none,
'Tis time, I think, to trudge, pack and be gone.

Dro. S. As from a bear a man would run for life,
So fly I from her that would be my wife. [*Exit.* 160

Ant. S. There 's none but witches do inhabit here;
And therefore 'tis high time that I were hence.
She that doth call me husband, even my soul
Doth for a wife abhor. But her fair sister,
Possess'd with such a gentle sovereign grace,
Of such enchanting presence and discourse,
Hath almost made me traitor to myself:
But, lest myself be guilty to self-wrong,
I'll stop mine ears against the mermaid's song.

Enter ANGELO *with the chain.*

Ang. Master Antipholus,—
Ant. S.   Ay, that 's my name. 170
Ang. I know it well, sir: lo, here is the chain.
I thought to have ta'en you at the Porpentine:
The chain unfinish'd made me stay thus long.

Ant. S. What is your will that I shall do with this?

Ang. What please yourself, sir: I have made it for
 you.

Ant. S. Made it for me, sir! I bespoke it not.

Ang. Not once, nor twice, but twenty times you
 have.
Go home with it and please your wife withal;
And soon at supper-time I'll visit you
And then receive my money for the chain. 180

Ant. S. I pray you, sir, receive the money now,
For fear you ne'er see chain nor money more.

Ang. You are a merry man, sir: fare you well. [*Exit.*

Ant. S. What I should think of this, I cannot tell:
But this I think, there 's no man is so vain
That would refuse so fair an offer'd chain.
I see a man here needs not live by shifts,

---

talk. 54. **mated,** amazed, confounded, with quibble on the sense of "matched with a wife." 56. **being by,** i.e., being near you. 58. **wink,** close the eyes in sleep; see glossary. 64. **My . . . claim,** i.e., my heaven on earth and my claim on heaven hereafter. 93. **'Sir-reverence,'** i.e., save your reverence, an expression used in apology for the remark that follows it. **lean,** poor, meager. 104. **Swart,** swarthy, dark. 108. **in grain,** indelible, ineradicable. 123. **barrenness.** New Cambridge editors print *barren-nesses*, indicating a pun on *ness*, a promontory. 126. **armed and reverted.** See Introduction for explanation of reference

to the French war. 130. **them,** i.e., her teeth. 140. **armadoes of caracks,** fleets of galleons. 141. **ballast,** loaded, freighted. 144. **diviner,** sorceress. 145. **assured,** affianced. 151. **curtal dog,** dog with docked tail, of no service in the chase. **turn . . . wheel.** Dogs, by running in a wheel, turned the spit. 152. **presently,** at once; see glossary. **post,** hasten; see glossary. **road,** harbor, roadstead. 158. **pack,** depart; see glossary. 165. **Possess'd with,** having possession of; see *possess* in glossary. 168. **to,** of. 187. **shifts,** stratagems, tricks; see glossary.

When in the streets he meets such golden gifts.
I'll to the mart and there for Dromio stay:
If any ship put out, then straight away.   [*Exit.* 190

ACT IV.

Enter Second Merchant, ANGELO, *and an* Officer.

Sec. Mer. You know since Pentecost the sum is due,
And since I have not much importuned you;
Nor now I had not, but that I am bound
To Persia and want guilders for my voyage:
Therefore make present satisfaction,
Or I'll attach you by this officer.
  Ang. Even just the sum that I do owe to you
Is growing to me by Antipholus,
And in the instant that I met with you
He had of me a chain: at five o'clock   10
I shall receive the money for the same.
Pleaseth you walk with me down to his house,
I will discharge my bond and thank you too.

Enter ANTIPHOLUS of Ephesus *and* DROMIO of
  Ephesus *from the courtezan's.*

Off. That labour may you save: see where he comes.
  Ant. E. While I go to the goldsmith's house, go thou
And buy a rope's end: that will I bestow
Among my wife and her confederates,
For locking me out of my doors by day.
But, soft! I see the goldsmith. Get thee gone;
Buy thou a rope and bring it home to me.   20
  Dro. E. I buy a thousand pound a year: I buy a
    rope.   [*Exit.*
  Ant. E. A man is well holp up that trusts to you:
I promised your presence and the chain;
But neither chain nor goldsmith came to me.
Belike you thought our love would last too long,
If it were chain'd together, and therefore came not.
  Ang. Saving your merry humour, here's the note
How much your chain weighs to the utmost carat,
The fineness of the gold and chargeful fashion,
Which doth amount to three odd ducats more   30
Than I stand debted to this gentleman:
I pray you, see him presently discharged,
For he is bound to sea and stays but for it.
  Ant. E. I am not furnish'd with the present money;
Besides, I have some business in the town.
Good signior, take the stranger to my house
And with you take the chain and bid my wife
Disburse the sum on the receipt thereof:
Perchance I will be there as soon as you.
  Ang. Then you will bring the chain to her yourself?
  Ant. E. No; bear it with you, lest I come not time
    enough.   41
  Ang. Well, sir, I will. Have you the chain about
    you?

Ant. E. An if I have not, sir, I hope you have;
Or else you may return without your money.
  Ang. Nay, come, I pray you, sir, give me the chain:
Both wind and tide stays for this gentleman,
And I, to blame, have held him here too long.
  Ant. E. Good Lord! you use this dalliance to excuse
Your breach of promise to the Porpentine.
I should have chid you for not bringing it,   50
But, like a shrew, you first begin to brawl.
  Sec. Mer. The hour steals on; I pray you, sir,
    dispatch.
  Ang. You hear how he importunes me;—the chain!
  Ant. E. Why, give it to my wife and fetch your
    money.
  Ang. Come, come, you know I gave it you even now.
Either send the chain or send me by some token.
  Ant. E. Fie, now you run this humour out of breath,
Come, where's the chain? I pray you, let me see it.
  Sec. Mer. My business cannot brook this dalliance.
Good sir, say whether you'll answer me or no: 60
If not, I'll leave him to the officer.
  Ant. E. I answer you! what should I answer you?
  Ang. The money that you owe me for the chain.
  Ant. E. I owe you none till I receive the chain.
  Ang. You know I gave it you half an hour since.
  Ant. E. You gave me none: you wrong me much to
    say so.
  Ang. You wrong me more, sir, in denying it:
Consider how it stands upon my credit.
  Sec. Mer. Well, officer, arrest him at my suit.
  Off. I do; and charge you in the duke's name to
    obey me.   70
  Ang. This touches me in reputation.
Either consent to pay this sum for me
Or I attach you by this officer.
  Ant. E. Consent to pay thee that I never had!
Arrest me, foolish fellow, if thou darest.
  Ang. Here is thy fee; arrest him, officer.
I would not spare my brother in this case,
If he should scorn me so apparently.
  Off. I do arrest you, sir: you hear the suit.
  Ant. E. I do obey thee till I give thee bail.   80
But, sirrah, you shall buy this sport as dear
As all the metal in your shop will answer.
  Ang. Sir, sir, I shall have law in Ephesus,
To your notorious shame; I doubt it not.

Enter DROMIO of Syracuse, *from the bay.*

Dro. S. Master, there is a bark of Epidamnum
That stays but till her owner comes aboard
And then, sir, she bears away. Our fraughtage, sir,
I have convey'd aboard and I have bought
The oil, the balsamum and aqua-vitæ.
The ship is in her trim: the merry wind   90
Blows fair from land: they stay for nought at all
But for their owner, master, and yourself.
  Ant. E. How now! a madman! Why, thou peevish
    sheep,

---

190. **straight,** immediately; see glossary.
ACT IV. SCENE I. *Stage Direction: A public place.* New Cambridge:
Place in the Mart. 6. **attach,** arrest, seize; see glossary. 8. **growing,**
due, accruing. 16. **bestow,** employ. 21. **buy a thousand pound a
year,** doubtfully explained as "a thousand pounds (blows) a year";
possibly, "I'll buy a rope as gladly as I would buy," etc. 22. **holp,**
helped; see glossary. 29. **chargeful,** expensive. 31. **debted,** indebted.
56. **send . . . token,** i.e., send me with some sign authorizing me to receive payment. 59. **brook,** endure; see glossary. 68. **stands upon,**
concerns. 87. **fraughtage,** freight. 89. **balsamum, aqua-vitæ,** balm,

ardent spirits. 90. **in her trim,** rigged and ready to sail. 93. **peevish,**
silly, senseless; see glossary. **sheep,** a pun; pronounced much like "ship."
95. **waftage,** conveyance by ship. 98. **rope's end,** a hangman's noose.
101. **list,** listen to; see glossary. 110. **Dowsabel,** used ironically for
Nell; from *douce et belle.*
SCENE II. 2. **austerely,** i.e., not being affected by his pleas. 6.
meteors, changes of color and expression. 7ff. Note the use of stichomythia, dialogue in which each speech consists of a single line; much
used in classical drama. 8. **spite,** grief. 14. **honest,** honorable; see
glossary. 20. **shapeless,** misshapen. 22. **Stigmatical,** crooked, or

What ship of Epidamnum stays for me?
  Dro. S. A ship you sent me to, to hire waftage.
  Ant. E. Thou drunken slave, I sent thee for a rope
And told thee to what purpose and what end.
  Dro. S. You sent me for a rope's end as soon:
You sent me to the bay, sir, for a bark.
  Ant. E. I will debate this matter at more leisure   100
And teach your ears to list me with more heed.
To Adriana, villain, hie thee straight:
Give her this key, and tell her, in the desk
That's cover'd o'er with Turkish tapestry
There is a purse of ducats; let her send it:
Tell her I am arrested in the street
And that shall bail me: hie thee, slave, be gone!
On, officer, to prison till it come.
      [*Exeunt Sec. Merchant, Angelo, Officer, and Ant. E.*
  Dro. S. To Adriana! that is where we dined,
Where Dowsabel did claim me for her husband: 110
She is too big, I hope, for me to compass.
Thither I must, although against my will,
For servants must their masters' minds fulfil.   [*Exit.*

SCENE II. *The house of* ANTIPHOLUS *of Ephesus.*

Enter ADRIANA *and* LUCIANA.

  Adr. Ah, Luciana, did he tempt thee so?
Mightst thou perceive austerely in his eye
That he did plead in earnest? yea or no?
Look'd he or red or pale, or sad or merrily?
What observation madest thou in this case
Of his heart's meteors tilting in his face?
  Luc. First he denied you had in him no right.
  Adr. He meant he did me none; the more my spite.
  Luc. Then swore he that he was a stranger here.
  Adr. And true he swore, though yet forsworn he
    were.   10
  Luc. Then pleaded I for you.
  Adr.   And what said he?
  Luc. That love I begg'd for you he begg'd of me.
  Adr. With what persuasion did he tempt thy love?
  Luc. With words that in an honest suit might move.
First he did praise my beauty, then my speech.
  Adr. Didst speak him fair?
  Luc.   Have patience, I beseech.
  Adr. I cannot, nor I will not, hold me still;
My tongue, though not my heart, shall have his will.
He is deformed, crooked, old and sere,
Ill-faced, worse bodied, shapeless everywhere;   20
Vicious, ungentle, foolish, blunt, unkind,
Stigmatical in making, worse in mind.
  Luc. Who would be jealous then of such a one?
No evil lost is wail'd when it is gone.
  Adr. Ah, but I think him better than I say,
And yet would herein others' eyes were worse.
Far from her nest the lapwing cries away:
My heart prays for him, though my tongue do curse.

Enter DROMIO *of Syracuse.*

  Dro. S. Here! go; the desk, the purse! sweet, now,
    make haste.
  Luc. How hast thou lost thy breath?
  Dro. S.   By running fast.   30
  Adr. Where is thy master, Dromio? is he well?
  Dro. S. No, he's in Tartar limbo, worse than hell.
†A devil in an everlasting garment hath him;
One whose hard heart is button'd up with steel;
A fiend, a fury, pitiless and rough;
A wolf, nay, worse, a fellow all in buff;
A back-friend, a shoulder-clapper, one that
    countermands
The passages of alleys, creeks and narrow lands;
A hound that runs counter and yet draws dry-foot
    well;
One that before the judgement carries poor souls to
    hell.   40
  Adr. Why, man, what is the matter?
  Dro. S. I do not know the matter: he is 'rested on
    the case.
  Adr. What, is he arrested? Tell me at whose suit.
  Dro. S. I know not at whose suit he is arrested well;
But he's in a suit of buff which 'rested him, that can I
    tell.
Will you send him, mistress, redemption, the money
    in his desk?
  Adr. Go fetch it, sister. [*Exit Luciana.*] This I wonder at,
That he, unknown to me, should be in debt.
Tell me, was he arrested on a band?
  Dro. S. Not on a band, but on a stronger thing;   50
A chain, a chain! Do you not hear it ring?
  Adr. What, the chain?
  Dro. S. No, no, the bell: 'tis time that I were gone:
It was two ere I left him, and now the clock strikes
    one.
  Adr. The hours come back! that did I never hear.
  Dro. S. O, yes; if any hour meet a sergeant, a' turns
    back for very fear.
  Adr. As if Time were in debt! how fondly dost thou
    reason!
  Dro. S. Time is a very bankrupt and owes more than
    he's worth to season.
Nay, he's a thief too: have you not heard men say,
That Time comes stealing on by night and day?   60
If Time be in debt and theft, and a sergeant in the
    way,
Hath he not reason to turn back an hour in a day?

Re-enter LUCIANA *with a purse.*

  Adr. Go, Dromio; there's the money, bear it
    straight,
And bring thy master home immediately.
Come, sister: I am press'd down with conceit—
Conceit, my comfort and my injury.   [*Exeunt.*

SCENE III. *A public place.*

Enter ANTIPHOLUS *of Syracuse.*

---

branded with deformity. **making,** form. 32. **Tartar limbo,** Tartar or Mohammedan hell, worse than Christian hell. 33. **everlasting garment,** leather used as the attire of police officers; reference to *buff* (l. 36). 37. **back-friend,** a false friend; the police officer who comes up behind and claps one on the back. **countermands,** prohibits, forbids. 38. **creeks,** narrow or winding passages. **narrow lands,** possible reference to strips into which agricultural lands were anciently divided (New Cambridge). 39. **runs counter,** follows a trail in a direction opposite to that which the game has taken, with quibble on *counter,* a prison. **draws dry-foot,** follows game by mere scent of the foot. 40.

judgement, quibble on "day of judgment" and "legal decision." **hell,** debtor's prison. 42. **case,** form of procedure, "action on the case," with quibble on *case* meaning "the container of *matter.*" 46. **mistress, redemption.** New Cambridge editors read *Mistress Redemption,* with F4, as suggestive of morality plays alluded to in *judgement,* etc., above. 49. **band,** bond; also, manacle, leash for a dog; see glossary. 56. **a',** he (it); see glossary. 58. **season,** opportunity.
  SCENE III. *Stage Direction:* **A public place.** New Cambridge: *The Mart.*

Ant. S. There 's not a man I meet but doth salute me
As if I were their well-acquainted friend;
And every one doth call me by my name.
Some tender money to me; some invite me;
Some other give me thanks for kindnesses;
Some offer me commodities to buy:
Even now a tailor call'd me in his shop
And show'd me silks that he had bought for me
And therewithal took measure of my body.
Sure, these are but imaginary wiles   10
And Lapland sorcerers inhabit here.

Enter DROMIO *of Syracuse.*

Dro. S. Master, here 's the gold you sent me for.
What, have you got the picture of old Adam new-
apparelled?
Ant. S. What gold is this? what Adam dost thou
mean?
Dro. S. Not that Adam that kept the Paradise, but
that Adam that keeps the prison: he that goes in the
calf's skin that was killed for the Prodigal; he that
came behind you, sir, like an evil angel, and bid you
forsake your liberty.   20
Ant. S. I understand thee not.
Dro. S. No? why, 'tis a plain case: he that went, like
a bass-viol, in a case of leather; the man, sir, that,
when gentlemen are tired, gives them a sob and 'rests
them; he, sir, that takes pity on decayed men and
gives them suits of durance; he that sets up his rest to
do more exploits with his mace than a morris-pike.   28
Ant. S. What, thou meanest an officer?
Dro. S. Ay, sir, the sergeant of the band; he that
brings any man to answer it that breaks his band; one
that thinks a man always going to bed and says 'God
give you good rest!'
Ant. S. Well, sir, there rest in your foolery. Is there
any ship puts forth to-night? may we be gone?
Dro. S. Why, sir, I brought you word an hour since
that the bark Expedition put forth to-night; and then
were you hindered by the sergeant, to tarry for the
hoy Delay. Here are the angels that you sent for to
deliver you.   41
Ant. S. The fellow is distract, and so am I;
And here we wander in illusions:
Some blessed power deliver us from hence!

Enter a Courtezan.

Cour. Well met, well met, Master Antipholus.
I see, sir, you have found the goldsmith now:
Is that the chain you promised me to-day?
Ant. S. Satan, avoid! I charge thee, tempt me not.
Dro. S. Master, is this Mistress Satan?
Ant. S. It is the devil.   50
Dro. S. Nay, she is worse, she is the devil's dam; and
here she comes in the habit of a light wench: and
thereof comes that the wenches say 'God damn me;'
that 's as much to say 'God make me a light wench.'
It is written, they appear to men like angels of light:
light is an effect of fire, and fire will burn; ergo, light

wenches will burn. Come not near her.
Cour. Your man and you are marvellous merry, sir.
Will you go with me? We'll mend our dinner here?   60
Dro. S. Master, if you do, expect spoon-meat; or
bespeak a long spoon.
Ant. S. Why, Dromio?
Dro. S. Marry, he must have a long spoon that must
eat with the devil.
Ant. S. Avoid then, fiend! what tell'st thou me of
supping?
Thou art, as you are all, a sorceress:
I conjure thee to leave me and be gone.
Cour. Give me the ring of mine you had at dinner,
Or, for my diamond, the chain you promised,   70
And I'll be gone, sir, and not trouble you.
Dro. S. Some devils ask but the parings of one's nail,
A rush, a hair, a drop of blood, a pin,
A nut, a cherry-stone;
But she, more covetous, would have a chain.
Master, be wise: and if you give it her,
The devil will shake her chain and fright us with it.
Cour. I pray you, sir, my ring, or else the chain:
I hope you do not mean to cheat me so.
Ant. S. Avaunt, thou witch! Come, Dromio, let us go.
Dro. S. 'Fly pride,' says the peacock: mistress, that
you know.   [*Exeunt Ant. S. and Dro. S.*   81
Cour. Now, out of doubt Antipholus is mad,
Else would he never so demean himself.
A ring he hath of mine worth forty ducats,
And for the same he promised me a chain:
Both one and other he denies me now.
The reason that I gather he is mad,
Besides this present instance of his rage,
Is a mad tale he told to-day at dinner,
Of his own doors being shut against his entrance.   90
Belike his wife, acquainted with his fits,
On purpose shut the doors against his way.
My way is now to hie home to his house,
And tell his wife that, being lunatic,
He rush'd into my house and took perforce
My ring away. This course I fittest choose;
For forty ducats is too much to lose.   [*Exit.*

SCENE IV. *A street.*

Enter ANTIPHOLUS *of Ephesus and the* Officer.

Ant. E. Fear me not, man; I will not break away:
I'll give thee, ere I leave thee, so much money,
To warrant thee, as I am 'rested for.
My wife is in a wayward mood to-day,
And will not lightly trust the messenger.
That I should be attach'd in Ephesus,
I tell you, 'twill sound harshly in her ears.

Enter DROMIO *of Ephesus with a rope's-end.*

Here comes my man; I think he brings the money.
How now, sir! have you that I sent you for?
Dro. E. Here 's that, I warrant you, will pay them
all.   10

11. **Lapland sorcerers.** Lapland was said to surpass all nations in the practice of witchcraft and sorcery. 14. **old Adam.** This is taken to mean, "Have you got rid of the picture of old Adam, namely, the sergeant dressed in buff, as Adam was dressed in skins" (Genesis 3:21). 18-19. **calf's . . . Prodigal.** Cf. Luke 15:23. 25. **sob,** breathing space. 27. **durance,** a kind of long-wearing cloth like buff, as well as prison. **sets . . . rest,** stakes his all; metaphor from the game of primero. 28. **mace,** staff of office carried by a sergeant. **morris-pike,** Moorish pike. 40. **hoy,** a small coasting vessel. 41. **angels,** gold coins worth

about 10s.; good angels this time, sent by Mistress Redemption (New Cambridge). 42. **distract,** distracted. 49. **Mistress Satan,** yet another character in Dromio's miracle play (New Cambridge). 52. **habit,** demeanor, manner; see glossary. 53. **light,** wanton. 56. **angels of light.** Cf. II Corinthians 11:14. 58. **will burn,** i.e., are diseased. 60. **mend,** supplement, supply the deficiencies. 61. **spoon-meat,** food for infants, hence, delicacies; but the sense is obscure. 72-77. **Some . . . it.** F prints this as prose, which fact, with the broken line at 74, suggests revision or abridgment (New Cambridge). 81. '**Fly . . . peacock.**

Ant. E. But where 's the money?

Dro. E. Why, sir, I gave the money for the rope.

Ant. E. Five hundred ducats, villain, for a rope?

Dro. E. I'll serve you, sir, five hundred at the rate.

Ant. E. To what end did I bid thee hie thee home?

Dro. E. To a rope's-end, sir; and to that end am I returned.

Ant. E. And to that end, sir, I will welcome you.
[*Beating him.*

Off. Good sir, be patient.

Dro. E. Nay, 'tis for me to be patient; I am in adversity. 21

Off. Good now, hold thy tongue.

Dro. E. Nay, rather persuade him to hold his hands.

Ant. E. Thou whoreson, senseless villain!

Dro. E. I would I were senseless, sir, that I might not feel your blows.

Ant. E. Thou art sensible in nothing but blows, and so is an ass. 29

Dro. E. I am an ass, indeed; you may prove it by my long ears. I have served him from the hour of my nativity to this instant, and have nothing at his hands for my service but blows. When I am cold, he heats me with beating; when I am warm, he cools me with beating: I am waked with it when I sleep; raised with it when I sit; driven out of doors with it when I go from home; welcomed home with it when I return: nay, I bear it on my shoulders, as a beggar wont her brat; and, I think, when he hath lamed me, I shall beg with it from door to door.

Ant. E. Come, go along; my wife is coming yonder.

Enter ADRIANA, LUCIANA, *the* COURTEZAN, *and* PINCH.

Dro. E. Mistress, 'respice finem,' respect your end; or rather, †the prophecy like the parrot, 'beware the rope's end.' 46

Ant. E. Wilt thou still talk? [*Beating him.*

Cour. How say you now? is not your husband mad?

Adr. His incivility confirms no less.
Good Doctor Pinch, you are a conjurer; 50
Establish him in his true sense again,
And I will please you what you will demand.

Luc. Alas, how fiery and how sharp he looks!

Cour. Mark how he trembles in his ecstasy!

Pinch. Give me your hand and let me feel your pulse.

Ant. E. There is my hand, and let it feel your ear.
[*Striking him.*

Pinch. I charge thee, Satan, housed within this man,
To yield possession to my holy prayers
And to thy state of darkness hie thee straight:
I conjure thee by all the saints in heaven! 60

Ant. E. Peace, doting wizard, peace! I am not mad.

Adr. O, that thou wert not, poor distressed soul!

Ant. E. You minion, you, are these your customers?
Did this companion with the saffron face
Revel and feast it at my house to-day,
Whilst upon me the guilty doors were shut
And I denied to enter in my house?

Adr. O husband, God doth know you dined at home;
Where would you had remain'd until this time,
Free from these slanders and this open shame! 70

Ant. E. Dined at home! Thou villain, what sayest thou?

Dro. E. Sir, sooth to say, you did not dine at home.

Ant. E. Were not my doors lock'd up and I shut out?

Dro. E. Perdie, your doors were lock'd and you shut out.

Ant. E. And did not she herself revile me there?

Dro. E. Sans fable, she herself reviled you there.

Ant. E. Did not her kitchen-maid rail, taunt and scorn me?

Dro. E. Certes, she did; the kitchen-vestal scorn'd you.

Ant. E. And did not I in rage depart from thence?

Dro. E. In verity you did; my bones bear witness, 80
That since have felt the vigour of his rage.

Adr. Is 't good to soothe him in these contraries?

Pinch. It is no shame: the fellow finds his vein
And yielding to him humours well his frenzy.

Ant. E. Thou hast suborn'd the goldsmith to arrest me.

Adr. Alas, I sent you money to redeem you,
By Dromio here, who came in haste for it.

Dro. E. Money by me! heart and good-will you might;
But surely, master, not a rag of money.

Ant. E. Went'st not thou to her for a purse of ducats? 90

Adr. He came to me and I deliver'd it.

Luc. And I am witness with her that she did.

Dro. E. God and the rope-maker bear me witness
That I was sent for nothing but a rope!

Pinch. Mistress, both man and master is possess'd;
I know it by their pale and deadly looks:
They must be bound and laid in some dark room.

Ant. E. Say, wherefore didst thou lock me forth to-day?
And why dost thou deny the bag of gold?

Adr. I did not, gentle husband, lock thee forth. 100

Dro. E. And, gentle master, I received no gold;
But I confess, sir, that we were lock'd out.

Adr. Dissembling villain, thou speak'st false in both.

Ant. E. Dissembling harlot, thou art false in all
And art confederate with a damned pack
To make a loathsome abject scorn of me:
But with these nails I'll pluck out these false eyes
That would behold in me this shameful sport.

Enter three or four, and offer to bind him. He strives.

Adr. O, bind him, bind him! let him not come near me.

Pinch. More company! The fiend is strong within him. 110

Luc. Ay me, poor man, how pale and wan he looks!

Ant. E. What, will you murder me? Thou gaoler, thou,

The Comedy of Errors
ACT IV : SC IV

95

The accusation of dishonesty coming from this woman, whom Dromio takes to be dishonest, seems to him as out of place as a warning against pride given by the peacock. 83. **demean,** conduct. 88. **rage,** madness; see glossary. 95. **perforce,** forcibly; see glossary.
SCENE IV. 22. **Good now,** pray thee. 28. **sensible,** sensitive; see glossary. 40. **wont,** i.e., is wont to carry. 44. **'respice finem.'** *Respice funem,* "consider the hangman's rope," was a jesting variant of this expression. 46. **'beware the rope's end,'** i.e., beware the halter; possibly a phrase taught by sailors to parrots. 50. **conjurer.** Being able to speak Latin, Pinch could conjure spirits. 52. **please,** pay. **demand,** request; see glossary. 54. **ecstasy,** madness; see glossary. 63. **customers,** guests (in a bad sense). 64. **companion,** fellow; see glossary. **saffron,** yellow. 74. **Perdie,** oath from *par Dieu.* 76. **Sans,** without; see glossary. 78. **kitchen-vestal,** her charge being like that of the vestal virgins, to keep the fire burning (Johnson). 82. **soothe,** encourage, humor. 89. **rag,** scrap. 96. **deadly,** death-like. 97. **bound . . . room,** the regular treatment for lunacy in Shakespeare's day.

I am thy prisoner: wilt thou suffer them
To make a rescue?
   Off.   Masters, let him go:
He is my prisoner, and you shall not have him.
   Pinch. Go bind this man, for he is frantic too.
                  [They offer to bind Dro. E.
   Adr. What wilt thou do, thou peevish officer?
Hast thou delight to see a wretched man
Do outrage and displeasure to himself?
   Off. He is my prisoner: if I let him go,   120
The debt he owes will be required of me.
   Adr. I will discharge thee ere I go from thee:
Bear me forthwith unto his creditor
And, knowing how the debt grows, I will pay it.
Good master doctor, see him safe convey'd
Home to my house. O most unhappy day!
   Ant. E. O most unhappy strumpet!
   Dro. E. Master, I am here enter'd in bond for you.
   Ant. E. Out on thee, villain! wherefore dost thou
     mad me?
   Dro. E. Will you be bound for nothing? be mad,
good master: cry 'The devil!'   131
   Luc. God help, poor souls, how idly do they talk!
   Adr. Go bear him hence. Sister, go you with me.
             [Exeunt all but Adriana, Luciana,
                      Officer and Courtezan.
Say now, whose suit is he arrested at?
   Off. One Angelo, a goldsmith: do you know him?
   Adr. I know the man. What is the sum he owes?
   Off. Two hundred ducats.
   Adr.   Say, how grows it due?
   Off. Due for a chain your husband had of him.
   Adr. He did bespeak a chain for me, but had it not.
   Cour. When as your husband all in rage to-day   140
Came to my house and took away my ring—
The ring I saw upon his finger now—
Straight after did I meet him with a chain.
   Adr. It may be so, but I did never see it.
Come, gaoler, bring me where the goldsmith is:
I long to know the truth hereof at large.

   Enter ANTIPHOLUS *of Syracuse with his rapier drawn,*
     and DROMIO *of Syracuse.*

   Luc. God, for thy mercy! they are loose again.
   Adr. And come with naked swords.
Let 's call more help to have them bound again.
   Off. Away! they'll kill us.   150
             [Exeunt all but Ant. S. and Dro. S.
   Ant. S. I see these witches are afraid of swords.
   Dro. S. She that would be your wife now ran from
     you.
   Ant. S. Come to the Centaur; fetch our stuff from
     thence:
I long that we were safe and sound aboard.
   Dro. S. Faith, stay here this night; they will surely
do us no harm: you saw they speak us fair, give us
gold: methinks they are such a gentle nation that, but
for the mountain of mad flesh that claims marriage of
me, I could find in my heart to stay here still and turn
witch.   160
   Ant. S. I will not stay to-night for all the town;

Therefore away, to get our stuff aboard.   *[Exeunt.*

ACT V.

SCENE I. *A street before a Priory.*

Enter Second Merchant *and* ANGELO.

   Ang. I am sorry, sir, that I have hinder'd you;
But, I protest, he had the chain of me,
Though most dishonestly he doth deny it.
   Sec. Mer. How is the man esteem'd here in the city?
   Ang. Of very reverend reputation, sir,
Of credit infinite, highly beloved,
Second to none that lives here in the city:
His word might bear my wealth at any time.
   Sec. Mer. Speak softly: yonder, as I think, he walks.

   Enter ANTIPHOLUS *of Syracuse and* DROMIO *of*
     Syracuse.

   Ang. 'Tis so; and that self chain about his neck   10
Which he forswore most monstrously to have.
Good sir, draw near to me, I'll speak to him.
Signior Antipholus, I wonder much
That you would put me to this shame and trouble;
And, not without some scandal to yourself,
With circumstance and oaths so to deny
This chain which now you wear so openly:
Beside the charge, the shame, imprisonment,
You have done wrong to this my honest friend,
Who, but for staying on our controversy,   20
Had hoisted sail and put to sea to-day:
This chain you had of me; can you deny it?
   Ant. S. I think I had; I never did deny it.
   Sec. Mer. Yes, that you did, sir, and forswore it too.
   Ant. S. Who heard me to deny it or forswear it?
   Sec. Mer. These ears of mine, thou know'st, did hear
     thee.
Fie on thee, wretch! 'tis pity that thou livest
To walk where any honest men resort.
   Ant. S. Thou art a villain to impeach me thus:
I'll prove mine honour and mine honesty   30
Against thee presently, if thou darest stand.
   Sec. Mer. I dare, and do defy thee for a villain.
                      [They draw.

   Enter ADRIANA, LUCIANA, *the* Courtezan, *and others.*

   Adr. Hold, hurt him not, for God's sake! he is mad.
Some get within him, take his sword away:
Bind Dromio too, and bear them to my house.
   Dro. S. Run, master, run; for God's sake, take a
     house!
This is some priory. In, or we are spoil'd!
     [Exeunt Ant. S. and Dro. S. to the Priory.

   Enter the Lady Abbess.

   Abb. Be quiet, people. Wherefore throng you
     hither?
   Adr. To fetch my poor distracted husband hence.
Let us come in, that we may bind him fast   40
And bear him home for his recovery.

126, 127. **unhappy**, fatal; miserable; see glossary. 139. **bespeak**,
order. 140. **When as**, when. 146. **at large**, in full, in detail; see *large*
in glossary. 150. *Stage Direction:* **Exeunt all**, etc. F prints *Runne all
out* after line 149, and *Exeunt omnes as fast as may be, frighted*, after
line 150. *Exeunt omnes* was the original stage direction, the rest being
written in the margin of the manuscript (New Cambridge). 153.

stuff, goods, baggage.
ACT V. SCENE I. *Stage Direction:* **A street before a Priory.** New
Cambridge: *The square before the house of Antipholus.* 8. **bear**, carry
off. 11. **forswore**, repudiated on oath or with strong words. 12. **to
me.** Hudson conjectures *with me.* 16. **circumstance**, details, particulars; see glossary. 32. **defy**, challenge; see glossary. 34. **within him**,

Ang. I knew he was not in his perfect wits.

Sec. Mer. I am sorry now that I did draw on him.

Abb. How long hath this possession held the man?

Adr. This week he hath been heavy, sour, sad,
And much different from the man he was;
But till this afternoon his passion
Ne'er brake into extremity of rage.

Abb. Hath he not lost much wealth by wreck of sea?
Buried some dear friend? Hath not else his eye   50
Stray'd his affection in unlawful love?
A sin prevailing much in youthful men,
Who give their eyes the liberty of gazing.
Which of these sorrows is he subject to?

Adr. To none of these, except it be the last;
Namely, some love that drew him oft from home.

Abb. You should for that have reprehended him.

Adr. Why, so I did.

Abb.   Ay, but not rough enough.

Adr. As roughly as my modesty would let me.

Abb. Haply, in private.

Adr.   And in assemblies too.   60

Abb. Ay, but not enough.

Adr. It was the copy of our conference:
In bed he slept not for my urging it;
At board he fed not for my urging it;
Alone, it was the subject of my theme;
In company I often glanced it;
Still did I tell him it was vile and bad.

Abb. And thereof came it that the man was mad:
The venom clamours of a jealous woman
Poisons more deadly than a mad dog's tooth.   70
It seems his sleeps were hinder'd by thy railing,
And thereof comes it that his head is light.
Thou say'st his meat was sauced with thy upbraidings:
Unquiet meals make ill digestions;
Thereof the raging fire of fever bred;
And what's a fever but a fit of madness?
Thou say'st his sports were hinder'd by thy brawls:
Sweet recreation barr'd, what doth ensue
But moody and dull melancholy,
Kinsman to grim and comfortless despair,   80
And at her heels a huge infectious troop
Of pale distemperatures and foes to life?
In food, in sport and life-preserving rest
To be disturb'd, would mad or man or beast:
The consequence is then thy jealous fits
Have scared thy husband from the use of wits.

Luc. She never reprehended him but mildly,
When he demean'd himself rough, rude and wildly.
Why bear you these rebukes and answer not?

Adr. She did betray me to my own reproof.   90
Good people, enter and lay hold on him.

Abb. No, not a creature enters in my house.

Adr. Then let your servants bring my husband forth.

Abb. Neither: he took this place for sanctuary,
And it shall privilege him from your hands
Till I have brought him to his wits again,
Or lose my labour in assaying it.

Adr. I will attend my husband, be his nurse,
Diet his sickness, for it is my office,
And will have no attorney but myself;   100

And therefore let me have him home with me.

Abb. Be patient; for I will not let him stir
Till I have used the approved means I have,
With wholesome syrups, drugs and holy prayers,
To make of him a formal man again:
It is a branch and parcel of mine oath,
A charitable duty of my order.
Therefore depart and leave him here with me.

Adr. I will not hence and leave my husband here:
And ill it doth beseem your holiness   110
To separate the husband and the wife.

Abb. Be quiet and depart: thou shalt not have him.
                                         [*Exit.*

Luc. Complain unto the duke of this indignity.

Adr. Come, go: I will fall prostrate at his feet
And never rise until my tears and prayers
Have won his grace to come in person hither
And take perforce my husband from the abbess.

Sec. Mer. By this, I think, the dial points at five:
Anon, I'm sure, the duke himself in person
Comes this way to the melancholy vale,   120
The place of death and sorry execution,
Behind the ditches of the abbey here.

Ang. Upon what cause?

Sec. Mer. To see a reverend Syracusian merchant,
Who put unluckily into this bay
Against the laws and statutes of this town,
Beheaded publicly for his offence.

Ang. See where they come: we will behold his
death.

Luc. Kneel to the duke before he pass the abbey.

Enter DUKE, *attended;* ÆGEON *bareheaded; with the*
Headsman *and other* Officers.

Duke. Yet once again proclaim it publicly,   130
If any friend will pay the sum for him,
He shall not die; so much we tender him.

Adr. Justice, most sacred duke, against the abbess!

Duke. She is a virtuous and a reverend lady:
It cannot be that she hath done thee wrong.

Adr. May it please your grace, Antipholus my
husband,
Whom I made lord of me and all I had,
At your important letters,—this ill day
A most outrageous fit of madness took him;
That desperately he hurried through the street,—   140
With him his bondman, all as mad as he,—
Doing displeasure to the citizens
By rushing in their houses, bearing thence
Rings, jewels, any thing his rage did like.
Once did I get him bound and sent him home,
Whilst to take order for the wrongs I went
That here and there his fury had committed.
Anon, I wot not by what strong escape,
He broke from those that had the guard of him;
And with his mad attendant and himself,   150
Each one with ireful passion, with drawn swords,
Met us again and madly bent on us
Chased us away, till raising of more aid
We came again to bind them. Then they fled
Into this abbey, whither we pursued them:

*The
Comedy of
Errors*
ACT V : SC I

97

And here the abbess shuts the gates on us
And will not suffer us to fetch him out,
Nor send him forth that we may bear him hence.
Therefore, most gracious duke, with thy command
Let him be brought forth and borne hence for help. 160
    Duke. Long since thy husband served me in my
        wars,
And I to thee engaged a prince's word,
When thou didst make him master of thy bed,
To do him all the grace and good I could.
Go, some of you, knock at the abbey-gate
And bid the lady abbess come to me.
I will determine this before I stir.

    Enter a Servant.

    Serv. O mistress, mistress, shift and save yourself!
My master and his man are both broke loose,
Beaten the maids a-row and bound the doctor, 170
Whose beard they have singed off with brands of fire;
And ever, as it blazed, they threw on him
Great pails of puddled mire to quench the hair:
My master preaches patience to him and the while
His man with scissors nicks him like a fool,
And sure, unless you send some present help,
Between them they will kill the conjurer.
    Adr. Peace, fool! thy master and his man are here.
And that is false thou dost report to us.
    Serv. Mistress, upon my life, I tell you true; 180
I have not breathed almost since I did see it.
He cries for you and vows, if he can take you,
To scorch your face and to disfigure you.   [*Cry within.*
Hark, hark! I hear him, mistress: fly, be gone!
    Duke. Come, stand by me; fear nothing. Guard
        with halberds!
    Adr. Ay me, it is my husband! Witness you,
That he is borne about invisible:
Even now we housed him in the abbey here;
And now he 's there, past thought of human reason.

    Enter ANTIPHOLUS *of Ephesus and* DROMIO *of*
        Ephesus.

    Ant. E. Justice, most gracious duke, O, grant me
        justice!   190
Even for the service that long since I did thee,
When I bestrid thee in the wars and took
Deep scars to save thy life; even for the blood
That then I lost for thee, now grant me justice.
    Æge. Unless the fear of death doth make me dote,
I see my son Antipholus and Dromio.
    Ant. E. Justice, sweet prince, against that woman
        there!
She whom thou gavest to me to be my wife,
That hath abused and dishonour'd me
Even in the strength and height of injury!   200
Beyond imagination is the wrong
That she this day hath shameless thrown on me.
    Duke. Discover how, and thou shalt find me just.
    Ant. E. This day, great duke, she shut the doors
        upon me,
While she with harlots feasted in my house.
    Duke. A grievous fault! Say, woman, didst thou so?

    Adr. No, my good lord: myself, he and my sister
To-day did dine together. So befall my soul
As this is false he burdens me withal!
    Luc. Ne'er may I look on day, nor sleep on night, 210
But she tells to your highness simple truth!
    Ang. O perjured woman! They are both forsworn:
In this the madman justly chargeth them.
    Ant. E. My liege, I am advised what I say,
Neither disturbed with the effect of wine,
Nor heady-rash, provoked with raging ire,
Albeit my wrongs might make one wiser mad.
This woman lock'd me out this day from dinner:
That goldsmith there, were he not pack'd with her,
Could witness it, for he was with me then;   220
Who parted with me to go fetch a chain,
Promising to bring it to the Porpentine,
Where Balthazar and I did dine together.
Our dinner done, and he not coming thither,
I went to seek him: in the street I met him
And in his company that gentleman.
There did this perjured goldsmith swear me down
That I this day of him received the chain,
Which, God he knows, I saw not: for the which
He did arrest me with an officer.   230
I did obey, and sent my peasant home
For certain ducats: he with none return'd.
Then fairly I bespoke the officer
To go in person with me to my house.
By the way we met
My wife, her sister, and a rabble more
Of vile confederates. Along with them
They brought one Pinch, a hungry lean-faced
        villain,
A mere anatomy, a mountebank,
A threadbare juggler and a fortune-teller,
A needy, hollow-eyed, sharp-looking wretch,   240
A living-dead man: this pernicious slave,
Forsooth, took on him as a conjurer,
And, gazing in mine eyes, feeling my pulse,
And with no face, as 'twere, outfacing me,
Cries out, I was possess'd. Then all together
They fell upon me, bound me, bore me thence
And in a dark and dankish vault at home
There left me and my man, both bound together;
Till, gnawing with my teeth my bonds in sunder,
I gain'd my freedom and immediately   250
Ran hither to your grace; whom I beseech
To give me ample satisfaction
For these deep shames and great indignities.
    Ang. My lord, in truth, thus far I witness with him,
That he dined not at home, but was lock'd out.
    Duke. But had he such a chain of thee or no?
    Ang. He had, my lord: and when he ran in here,
These people saw the chain about his neck.
    Sec. Mer. Besides, I will be sworn these ears of
        mine
Heard you confess you had the chain of him   260
After you first forswore it on the mart:
And thereupon I drew my sword on you;
And then you fled into this abbey here,
From whence, I think, you are come by miracle.

162. **engaged,** pledged; see glossary. 170. **a-row,** one after another.
175. **nicks him like a fool.** Fools or professional jesters were accustomed
to cut their hair in fantastic shapes. 192. **bestrid,** stood over to defend
him when fallen in battle. 199. **abused,** maltreated; see glossary.
203. **Discover,** reveal; see glossary. 205. **harlots,** probably, vagabonds,
rascals. 209. **burdens,** charges. **withal,** with; see glossary. 214. **am
advised,** know very well. 219. **pack'd with,** in conspiracy with; see
pack in glossary. 231. **peasant,** servant. 233. **fairly,** civilly; see
glossary. 238. **mere,** absolute, pure; see glossary. **anatomy,** skeleton.
mountebank, quack, charlatan. 242. **took . . . as,** pretended to be.
269. **impeach,** charge, accusation. 270. **Circe's cup,** the poisoned cup,
a draft of which turned men into beasts. 272. **coldly,** calmly.

Ant. E. I never came within these abbey-walls,
Nor ever didst thou draw thy sword on me:
I never saw the chain, so help me Heaven!
And this is false you burden me withal.
  Duke. Why, what an intricate impeach is this!
I think you all have drunk of Circe's cup.   270
If here you housed him, here he would have been;
If he were mad, he would not plead so coldly:
You say he dined at home; the goldsmith here
Denies that saying. Sirrah, what say you?
  Dro. E. Sir, he dined with her there, at the
    Porpentine.
  Cour. He did, and from my finger snatch'd that
    ring.
  Ant. E. 'Tis true, my liege; this ring I had of her.
  Duke. Saw'st thou him enter at the abbey here?
  Cour. As sure, my liege, as I do see your grace.
  Duke. Why, this is strange. Go call the abbess
    hither.   280
I think you are all mated or stark mad.
                    [*Exit one to the Abbess.*
  Æge. Most mighty duke, vouchsafe me speak a
    word:
Haply I see a friend will save my life
And pay the sum that may deliver me.
  Duke. Speak freely, Syracusian, what thou wilt.
  Æge. Is not your name, sir, call'd Antipholus?
And is not that your bondman, Dromio?
  Dro. E. Within this hour I was his bondman, sir,
But he, I thank him, gnaw'd in two my cords:
Now am I Dromio and his man unbound.   290
  Æge. I am sure you both of you remember me.
  Dro. E. Ourselves we do remember, sir, by you;
For lately we were bound, as you are now.
You are not Pinch's patient, are you, sir?
  Æge. Why look you strange on me? you know me
    well.
  Ant. E. I never saw you in my life till now.
  Æge. O, grief hath changed me since you saw me
    last.
And careful hours with time's deformed hand
Have written strange defeatures in my face:
But tell me yet, dost thou not know my voice?   300
  Ant. E. Neither.
  Æge. Dromio, nor thou?
  Dro. E.   No, trust me, sir, nor I.
  Æge. I am sure thou dost.
  Dro. E. Ay, sir, but I am sure I do not; and whatso-
ever a man denies, you are now bound to believe him.
  Æge. Not know my voice! O time's extremity,
Hast thou so crack'd and splitted my poor tongue
In seven short years, that here my only son
Knows not my feeble key of untuned cares?   310
Though now this grained face of mine be hid
In sap-consuming winter's drizzled snow
And all the conduits of my blood froze up,
Yet hath my night of life some memory,
My wasting lamps some fading glimmer left,
My dull deaf ears a little use to hear:
All these old witnesses—I cannot err—
Tell me thou art my son Antipholus.

  Ant. E. I never saw my father in my life.
  Æge. But seven years since, in Syracusa, boy,   320
Thou know'st we parted: but perhaps, my son,
Thou shamest to acknowledge me in misery.
  Ant. E. The duke and all that know me in the city
Can witness with me that it is not so:
I ne'er saw Syracusa in my life.
  Duke. I tell thee, Syracusian, twenty years
Have I been patron to Antipholus,
During which time he ne'er saw Syracusa:
I see thy age and dangers make thee dote.

    Re-enter Abbess, *with* ANTIPHOLUS *of Syracuse
        and* DROMIO *of Syracuse.*

  Abb. Most mighty duke, behold a man much
    wrong'd.   [*All gather to see them.*   330
  Adr. I see two husbands, or mine eyes deceive me.
  Duke. One of these men is Genius to the other;
And so of these, which is the natural man,
And which the spirit? who deciphers them?
  Dro. S. I, sir, am Dromio: command him away.
  Dro. E. I, sir, am Dromio: pray, let me stay.
  Ant. S. Ægeon art thou not? or else his ghost?
  Dro. S. O, my old master! who hath bound him
    here?
  Abb. Whoever bound him, I will loose his bonds
And gain a husband by his liberty.   340
Speak, old Ægeon, if thou be'st the man
That hadst a wife once call'd Æmilia
That bore thee at a burden two fair sons:
O, if thou be'st the same Ægeon, speak,
And speak unto the same Æmilia!
  Duke. Why, here begins his morning story right:
These two Antipholuses, these two so like,
And these two Dromios, one in semblance,—
Besides her urging of her wreck at sea,—
These are the parents to these children,   350
Which accidentally are met together.
  Æge. If I dream not, thou art Æmilia:
If thou art she, tell me where is that son
That floated with thee on the fatal raft?
  Abb. By men of Epidamnum he and I
And the twin Dromio all were taken up;
But by and by rude fishermen of Corinth
By force took Dromio and my son from them
And me they left with those of Epidamnum.
What then became of them I cannot tell;   360
I to this fortune that you see me in.
  Duke. Antipholus, thou camest from Corinth first?
  Ant. S. No, sir, not I; I came from Syracuse.
  Duke. Stay, stand apart; I know not which is which.
  Ant. E. I came from Corinth, my most gracious
    lord,—
  Dro. E. And I with him.
  Ant. E. Brought to this town by that most famous
    warrior,
Duke Menaphon, your most renowned uncle.
  Adr. Which of you two did dine with me to-day?
  Ant. S. I, gentle mistress.
  Adr.   And are not you my husband?   370
  Ant. E. No; I say nay to that.

---

294. Pinch's patient. Dromio refers to the binding, evidently the feature of Pinch's treatment which most impressed him. **298. deformed,** deforming. **307. Not know my voice.** Genuine feeling comes out in the speech of Aegeon, a feature of this play which aligns it with Shakespeare's romantic comedies. **310. my . . . cares,** the whole tone of my voice which is altered by sorrow. **311. grained,** lined, furrowed.

315. lamps, eyes. **332. Genius,** attendant spirit. **333.** So F; Globe places period after *these.* **343. burden,** birth. **348. semblance,** trisyllabic; likewise *children* in line 350. **356-361.** Globe follows Capell and places these lines after line 345. Text follows F.

Ant. S. And so do I; yet did she call me so:
And this fair gentlewoman, her sister here,
Did call me brother. [*To Luc.*] What I told you then,
I hope I shall have leisure to make good;
If this be not a dream I see and hear.
    Ang. That is the chain, sir, which you had of me.
    Ant. S. I think it be, sir; I deny it not.
    Ant. E. And you, sir, for this chain arrested me.
    Ang. I think I did, sir; I deny it not.   380
    Adr. I sent you money, sir, to be your bail,
By Dromio; but I think he brought it not.
    Dro. E. No, none by me.
    Ant. S. This purse of ducats I received from you
And Dromio my man did bring them me.
I see we still did meet each other's man,
And I was ta'en for him, and he for me,
And thereupon these ERRORS are arose.
    Ant. E. These ducats pawn I for my father here.
    Duke. It shall not need; thy father hath his life.   390
    Cour. Sir, I must have that diamond from you.
    Ant. E. There, take it; and much thanks for my
        good cheer.
    Abb. Renowned duke, vouchsafe to take the pains
To go with us into the abbey here
And hear at large discoursed all our fortunes:
And all that are assembled in this place,
That by this sympathized one day's error
Have suffer'd wrong, go keep us company,
And we shall make full satisfaction.
Thirty-three years have I but gone in travail   400
Of you, my sons; and till this present hour
My heavy burthen ne'er delivered.
The duke, my husband and my children both,
And you the calendars of their nativity,
Go to a gossips' feast, and go with me;
After so long grief, such festivity!
    Duke. With all my heart, I'll gossip at this feast.
              [*Exeunt all but Ant. S., Ant. E.,*
                      Dro. S., and Dro. E.
    Dro. S. Master, shall I fetch your stuff from
        shipboard?
    Ant. E. Dromio, what stuff of mine hast thou
        embark'd?
    Dro. S. Your goods that lay at host, sir, in the
        Centaur.   410
    Ant. S. He speaks to me. I am your master, Dromio:
Come, go with us; we'll look to that anon:
Embrace thy brother there; rejoice with him.
              [*Exeunt Ant. S. and Ant. E.*
    Dro. S. There is a fat friend at your master's house,
That kitchen'd me for you to-day at dinner:
She now shall be my sister, not my wife.
    Dro. E. Methinks you are my glass, and not my
        brother:
I see by you I am a sweet-faced youth.
Will you walk in to see their gossiping?
    Dro. S. Not I, sir; you are my elder.   420
    Dro. E. That 's a question: how shall we try it?
    Dro. S. We'll draw cuts for the senior: till then lead
        thou first.
    Dro. E. Nay, then, thus:

397. **sympathized,** i.e., from which all have suffered.   404. **calendars
. . . nativity,** the Dromios.   405. **gossips' feast.** A gossip is the god-
parent to one's child.   407. **gossip,** i.e., be a gossip, in the sense of
boon companion, familiar acquaintance.   410. **lay at host,** were put
up.   415. **kitchen'd,** entertained in the kitchen.   419. **gossiping,**
merrymaking.

We came into the world like brother and brother;
And now let 's go hand in hand, not one before
    another.   [*Exeunt.*

Love's Labour's Lost

Love's *Labour's Lost* was issued in 1598 in quarto
form with the following title page:

A PLEASANT Conceited Comedie CALLED, Loues
labors lost. As it vvas presented before her Highnes this
last Christmas. Newly corrected and augmented *By W.
Shakespere.* Imprinted at London by *W. W.* for *Cutbert
Burby.* 1598.

Noteworthy here is the information that the play
was acted before Queen Elizabeth at Christmas, 1597;
and, in addition to this, that the text in hand purports
to supplant an unauthorized and probably incorrect
version of the play. A parallel inference from a similar
statement on the title page of the quarto of *Romeo and
Juliet* printed in 1599 that the play was "newly corrected, augmented, and amended," is substantiated
by the existence of a bad quarto of that play printed in
1597. No early and imperfect version of *Love's Labour's
Lost* has been preserved. However, the probability of
there having been, to use the words of the Folio
editors, "a stolen and surreptitious copy," is increased
by the fact that the play was never entered in the
Stationers' Register. If the play had already been
published, even from a dishonestly acquired copy and
without the consent of the Stationers' Company, it
would not have been necessary to relicense it in order
to issue another text. The text itself, moreover, shows
evidence of revision in at least two places: Biron's
speech in Act IV, scene iii, lines 289-365, shows parts
of the old version and the new standing side by side.
Lines 296-304, for example, are repeated in expanded
form in lines 318-351. Again in Act V, scene ii,
Rosaline's speech in lines 828-832 is apparently the
first draft of her speech in lines 851-864. There is also
a certain amount of confusion in the play in the
assignment of speeches, which can often be explained
on the assumption that the speech in question was
part of the revised version and was wrongly labeled
by the printer when he set up the copy. Cuthbert
Burby was apparently a friend of the players and
would not have stolen their play, which fact, taken
with the appearance of Shakespeare's name on the
title page and the excellence of the text, points to this
quarto as an authorized version. The text of the play
in the First Folio was printed from a playhouse copy,
itself a transcript of the manuscript behind the quarto.

THE DATE

In 1598 *Love's Labour's Lost* is mentioned by Francis Meres in *Palladis Tamia* and is alluded to by Robert Tofte in *Alba*. It must have been an old work by 1598, since it shows, even in what is evidently a

revised state, all the characteristics of Shakespeare's earliest style. The play abounds in rhyme, both in couplets and quatrains, in doggerel verse, and in blank verse which is largely end-stopped and free from light and weak endings. Numerous sonnets are also introduced into the text. In these qualities it is on a par with *The Comedy of Errors*, so that no one can tell on purely internal evidence which is the older of these two plays. *Love's Labour's Lost*, like *The Comedy of Errors*, teems with puns and conceits and is artificial and highly elaborate in plot. The characters are balanced off one against another—a princess and three ladies in waiting are wooed with mechanical ardor by a prince and three attendant lords.

It has been suggested that the play was written in the first instance to be performed before the queen, and that the performance of 1597 was, therefore, a revival. T. W. Baldwin dates the play in the winter of 1588. J. Q. Adams thinks it was one of the two plays presented before Her Majesty by Lord Pembroke's men in the Christmas season of 1592. J. D. Wilson holds, on the basis of what he regards as allusions to Gabriel Harvey's *Pierce's Supererogation* and to Chapman's *Shadow of Night*, both published late in 1593, that Shakespeare's first revision of the play was in preparation for some performance at Christmas, 1593.[1]

TOPICAL ALLUSIONS IN THE PLAY

Love's Labour's Lost is one of the few plays of Shakespeare's for which no definite source is known; it

introduces, nevertheless, in larger quantity than elsewhere references which seem to bear upon contemporary matters. Henry of Navarre was the popular figure of the day. The names Biron and Longaville belonged to two of his followers; Dumain seems also to have been a French nobleman of Henry's time. Some critics have seen in the play a reminiscence of a meeting between Ferdinand of Navarre and a French princess, an event from the earlier history of Navarre, at which meeting about 1425 certain territory was ceded by Navarre to France. Others have seen a poetical treatment of one of the progresses of Queen Elizabeth in which she was entertained with plays and masques. Armado and his page, Moth, are thought to burlesque, respectively, a certain "fantastical Spaniard," resident at the court of the queen, and a French ambassador, De la Mothe, long popular in England. The disguising of the lovers as Russians seems to travesty a well-known incident of the year 1584, when Russian ambassadors came to England to seek among the nobility for a wife for the czar, an event which was both flattering and amusing to the queen. Tubal Holofernes, tutor of Gargantua in Rabelais, seems to supply the name for the schoolmaster and also, of course, some of his pedantry, although pedants were stock characters in sixteenth-century comedy in England, France, and Italy.

The French scholar Abel Lefranc, in his unsuccessful attempt to prove that the earl of Derby was the author of Shakespeare's plays, discovered an important parallel to the events narrated in *Love's Labour's Lost*. Catherine de' Medici and her daughter Marguerite, subsequently the wife of Henry of Navarre, made an expedition to the court of Navarre at Nérac in 1578 in order to effect a settlement of the question of sovereignty of Aquitaine and the matter of the payment of one hundred thousand crowns to Navarre by the king of France. The diplomatic matters being quickly turned over to specialists, the king and his court devoted themselves to festivities for the entertainment of their royal guests.

It has been suggested that *Love's Labour's Lost* was devised at the instigation of Southampton for the entertainment of Queen Elizabeth on the occasion of her visit to Tichfield Park in 1591, since the plot seems to suit his desire at that time of postponing his marriage with Lady Elizabeth Vere.[2]

THE PLAY

The serious interest of *Love's Labour's Lost*, in so far as it has a serious interest, is to be found in its exploitation of the theme of love. It exalts true love as the sonneteers exalted it and depicts it as a divine emotion. The main plot shows that love may not and should not be put aside and neglected or treated

[1] *Love's Labour's Lost*, New Cambridge edition, 1923, pp. 125-130. For the supposed connection of *Love's Labour's Lost* with the Nashe-Harvey quarrel see also Rupert Taylor, *The Date of Love's Labour's Lost* (1932). On the supposed connection of the play with the School of Night, see Arthur Acheson, *Shakespeare and the Rival Poet* (1903), pp. xxviii-xxxii; Florence A. Yates, *A Study of Love's Labour's Lost* (Cambridge, 1936).

[2] See O. J. Campbell, "*Love's Labour's Lost* Restudied," in *Studies in Shakespeare, Milton, and Donne*, by Members of the English Department of the University of Michigan (Ann Arbor, 1925); and Austin K. Gray, "The Secret of *Love's Labour's Lost* and the Earl of Southampton," *PMLA*, XXXIX, 581-611; Abel Lefranc, *Sous le masque de William Shakespeare* (Paris, 1919), II, 87-100.

frivolously. The minor plot shows that sensual love is to be condemned. This same conception of love appears in *The Merchant of Venice, Twelfth Night,* and other later plays.

Of all Shakespeare's plays *Love's Labour's Lost* is closest to John Lyly, the creator of the social comedy of the court. One sees in the play the Renaissance fashion of establishing academies for the pursuit of learning and the training of courtiers, the gossip of the court itself, and the language of euphuism. All are so employed that it is difficult to say how far Shakespeare means to ridicule these things and how far he was working delightedly in an atmosphere and style whose extravagance he really enjoyed. Men and women never grow tired of having it demonstrated to them that they cannot live without each other. *Love's Labour's Lost* goes further and says something which Tudor England found much to its liking; namely, that there is no true learning without true love. This play, featuring an ideal commonwealth of learning from which all women were to be excluded, recalls a vast array of courtly circles, learned coteries in Italy, France, and England, for the discussion of such Renaissance topics as the relation of men and women, education true and false, and the value of courtly culture. It is no wonder the play was popular at court.[3]

The minor plot is filled with stock characters from the comedy of the time, particularly from French comedy and the Italian *commedia dell' arte* (a form of drama played extemporaneously from an outline of the plot), such as the pedant, the braggart, the hedge-priest, the fool, the boy, and the stupid constable.[4] Biron is the most highly individualized character of the play; a scourger of the follies of others, his own folly is hardest of all to eradicate. This type was to appear later in Jaques in *As You Like It.*

STAGE HISTORY

Love's Labour's Lost is said on the title page of the 1598 quarto to have been "presented before her Highnes this last Christmas," which probably means the Christmas of 1597. It was also presented before King James in 1604 and probably performed with fair frequency at the Globe and the Blackfriars. It was not heard of on the stage again until 1839, when it was presented by Charles James Mathews at Covent Garden. *Love's Labour's Lost* was acted by Phelps in 1857 and has been acted several times at the Shakespeare Memorial Theater at Stratford and at the Royal Victoria Hall ("Old Vic") in London. It has also been elaborately presented on the public stage at least twice in America. It has not been a popular play but has been received with pleasure on the few occasions on which it has been presented.

Love's Labour's Lost

DRAMATIS PERSONAE

FERDINAND, king of Navarre.
BIRON,
LONGAVILLE, } lords attending on the King.
DUMAIN,
BOYET, } lords attending on the Princess of
MERCADE, } France.
DON ADRIANO DE ARMADO, a fantastical Spaniard.
SIR NATHANIEL, a curate.
HOLOFERNES, a schoolmaster.
DULL, a constable.
COSTARD, a clown.
MOTH, page to Armado.
A Forester.

The PRINCESS of France.
ROSALINE,
MARIA, } ladies attending on the Princess.
KATHARINE,
JAQUENETTA, a country wench.

Lords, Attendants, &c.

SCENE: *Navarre.*

ACT I.

SCENE I. *The king of Navarre's park.*

Enter FERDINAND, *king of* NAVARRE, BIRON, LONGAVILLE, *and* DUMAIN.

King. Let fame, that all hunt after in their lives,
Live register'd upon our brazen tombs
And then grace us in the disgrace of death;
When, spite of cormorant devouring Time,
The endeavour of this present breath may buy
That honour which shall bate his scythe's keen edge
And make us heirs of all eternity.
Therefore, brave conquerors,—for so you are,
That war against your own affections
And the huge army of the world's desires,— 10
Our late edict shall strongly stand in force:
Navarre shall be the wonder of the world;
Our court shall be a little Academe,
Still and contemplative in living art.
You three, Biron, Dumain, and Longaville,
Have sworn for three years' term to live with me
My fellow-scholars and to keep those statutes
That are recorded in this schedule here:
Your oaths are pass'd; and now subscribe your names,
That his own hand may strike his honour down 20
That violates the smallest branch herein:
If you are arm'd to do as sworn to do,
Subscribe to your deep oaths, and keep it too.
Long. I am resolved; 'tis but a three years' fast:

The mind shall banquet, though the body pine:
Fat paunches have lean pates, and dainty bits
Make rich the ribs, but bankrupt quite the wits.
 Dum. My loving lord, Dumain is mortified:
The grosser manner of these world's delights
He throws upon the gross world's baser slaves: 30
To love, to wealth, to pomp, I pine and die;
With all these living in philosophy.
 Biron. I can but say their protestation over;
So much, dear liege, I have already sworn,
That is, to live and study here three years.
But there are other strict observances;
As, not to see a woman in that term,
Which I hope well is not enrolled there;
And one day in a week to touch no food
And but one meal on every day beside, 40
The which I hope is not enrolled there;
And then, to sleep but three hours in the night,
And not be seen to wink of all the day—
When I was wont to think no harm all night
And make a dark night too of half the day—
Which I hope well is not enrolled there:
O, these are barren tasks, too hard to keep,
Not to see ladies, study, fast, not sleep!
 King. Your oath is pass'd to pass away from these.
 Biron. Let me say no, my liege, an if you please: 50
I only swore to study with your grace
And stay here in your court for three years' space.
 Long. You swore to that, Biron, and to the rest.
 Biron. By yea and nay, sir, then I swore in jest.
What is the end of study? let me know.
 King. Why, that to know, which else we should not
  know.
 Biron. Things hid and barr'd, you mean, from
  common sense?
 King. Ay, that is study's god-like recompense.
 Biron. Come on, then; I will swear to study so,
To know the thing I am forbid to know: 60
As thus,—to study where I well may dine,
 When I to feast expressly am forbid;
Or study where to meet some mistress fine,
 When mistresses from common sense are hid;
Or, having sworn too hard a keeping oath,
Study to break it and not break my troth.
If study's gain be thus and this be so,
Study knows that which yet it doth not know:
Swear me to this, and I will ne'er say no.

 King. These be the stops that hinder study quite 70
And train our intellects to vain delight.
 Biron. Why, all delights are vain; but that most
  vain,
Which with pain purchased doth inherit pain:
As, painfully to pore upon a book
 To seek the light of truth; while truth the while
Doth falsely blind the eyesight of his look:
 Light seeking light doth light of light beguile:
So, ere you find where light in darkness lies,
Your light grows dark by losing of your eyes.
Study me how to please the eye indeed 80
 By fixing it upon a fairer eye,
Who dazzling so, that eye shall be his heed
 And give him light that it was blinded by.
Study is like the heaven's glorious sun
 That will not be deep-search'd with saucy looks:
Small have continual plodders ever won
 Save base authority from others' books.
These earthly godfathers of heaven's lights
 That give a name to every fixed star
Have no more profit of their shining nights 90
 Than those that walk and wot not what they are.
Too much to know is to know nought but fame;
And every godfather can give a name.
 King. How well he's read, to reason against reading!
 Dum. Proceeded well, to stop all good proceeding!
 Long. He weeds the corn and still lets grow the
  weeding.
 Biron. The spring is near when green geese are
  a-breeding.
 Dum. How follows that?
 Biron.   Fit in his place and time.
 Dum. In reason nothing.
 Biron.   Something then in rhyme.
 King. Biron is like an envious sneaping frost 100
  That bites the first-born infants of the spring.
 Biron. Well, say I am; why should proud summer
  boast
  Before the birds have any cause to sing?
Why should I joy in any abortive birth?
At Christmas I no more desire a rose
Than wish a snow in May's new-fangled shows;
But like of each thing that in season grows.
So you, to study now it is too late,
Climb o'er the house to unlock the little gate.
 King. Well, sit you out: go home, Biron: adieu. 110

ACT I. SCENE I. 2. **brazen**, brass. 3. **grace**, honor; see glossary. **disgrace**, disfigurement. 4. **cormorant**, ravenous, rapacious. 6. **bate**, abate, blunt; see glossary. 9. **affections**, emotions, feelings; see glossary. 13. **Academe**, academy, from the name of the grove near Athens where Plato and his followers gathered. 14. **living art**, that art of which we shall give a living proof (Furness, who finds an antithesis between *still* and *living*); the phrase is a probable adaptation of *ars vitae* or *ars vivendi* (the art of life, the art of living), phrases familiar to Renaissance men through their study of the Stoic philosophers. 15. **Biron**, accent on second syllable; in IV, iii, 232 it is made to rhyme with *moon*. 18. **schedule**, slip of paper or scroll containing writing. 19. **pass'd**, pledged; see glossary. 28. **mortified**, deprived of feeling. Dumain's extravagant oath suggests almost its literal sense; cf. l. 31. 29. **manner**, kind, sort. 32. **With . . . philosophy**, i.e., the pleasure afforded by these I find in philosophy. 43. **wink**, close the eyes; see glossary. **of all the day**, during the day; see *of* in glossary; cf. *Hamlet*, I, v, 60, *of the afternoon*; also the expression still current, "of a sudden." 44-45. **no . . . day**, no harm to sleep all night and half the day. 47. **barren**, dull, pointless. 50. **an if**, if; see glossary. 54. **By yea and nay**, an oath biblical in its connotation. Biron assumes mock seriousness, an attitude by which the Puritans were often ridiculed. 57. **barr'd**, excluded. **common sense**, common observation or knowledge; see *sense* in glossary. 65. **too . . . oath**, an oath too hard to keep. 70. **stops**, obstacles. 71. **train**, allure, entice; see glossary. 73. **pain**, labor, effort, with quibble on the meaning "suffering"; see glossary. **purchased**, acquired; see glossary. 74. **As**, that is;

see glossary. 76. **falsely**, treacherously; see glossary. **his**, its; see glossary; the antecedent is *eyesight*. **look**, power to see; see glossary. 77. **light**, multiple quibble on the meanings "the eye," "knowledge," and "vision" or "power to see"; i.e., the eye (*light*) by study (*seeking light*) beguiles or deprives itself of power to see (*light*). 80. **me**, probably, for me, by my advice; i.e., I would have you study thus. The pronoun is what is known as the ethical dative, an old construction that survives today in but a very few phrases. Cf. Abbott, 220, where the English dative is explained and amply illustrated; cf. also the General Introduction, the section on Shakespeare's English. 82. **Who**. The antecedent is *eye* (l. 81). **dazzling**, becoming dazzled. **heed**, guard, means of safety. 85. **deep-search'd**, scrutinized. 86. **Small**, used substantively, little. 88. **earthly godfathers**, alluding to the custom in baptism of having the godparents pronounce the name of the child. 91. **wot**, know; see glossary. 92. **fame**, reputation; see glossary. 95. **Proceeded**, the academic sense of taking a university degree. 97. **green geese**, grass-fed geese; those marketed in autumn were "stubble-fed"; green-goose fair, a season of merriment, was held on Whitmonday. 99. **reason . . . rhyme**. Cf. the saying, "neither rhyme nor reason." 100. **envious**, malignant, malicious; see glossary. **sneaping**, biting. 101. **infants . . . spring**, flower buds. 106. **shows**, so QF; Globe: *mirth*. 107. **like of**, approve of. 108-109. **So . . . gate**, i.e., you are beginning at the wrong end —doing now what you should have done as boys. 110. **sit you out**, a term from card playing.

Biron. No, my good lord; I have sworn to stay with
  you:
And though I have for barbarism spoke more
  Than for that angel knowledge you can say,
Yet confident I'll keep what I have swore
  And bide the penance of each three years' day.
Give me the paper; let me read the same;
And to the strict'st decrees I'll write my name.
  King. How well this yielding rescues thee from
  shame!
  Biron [*reads*]. 'Item, That no woman shall come
within a mile of my court:' Hath this been pro-
claimed?   121
  Long. Four days ago.
  Biron. Let 's see the penalty. [*Reads*] 'On pain of
losing her tongue.' Who devised this penalty?
  Long. Marry, that did I.
  Biron. Sweet lord, and why?
  Long. To fright them hence with that dread
  penalty.
  Biron. A dangerous law against gentility!
  [*Reads*] 'Item, If any man be seen to talk with a
woman within the term of three years, he shall endure
such public shame as the rest of the court can possibly
devise.'
This article, my liege, yourself must break;
  For well you know here comes in embassy
The French king's daughter with yourself to speak—
  A maid of grace and complete majesty—
About surrender up of Aquitaine
  To her decrepit, sick and bedrid father:
Therefore this article is made in vain,   140
  Or vainly comes the admired princess hither.
  King. What say you, lords? why, this was quite
  forgot.
  Biron. So study evermore is overshot:
While it doth study to have what it would
It doth forget to do the thing it should,
And when it hath the thing it hunteth most,
'Tis won as towns with fire, so won, so lost.
  King. We must of force dispense with this decree;
She must lie here on mere necessity.
  Biron. Necessity will make us all forsworn   150
  Three thousand times within this three years'
  space;
For every man with his affects is born,
  Not by might master'd but by special grace:
If I break faith, this word shall speak for me;
I am forsworn on 'mere necessity.'
So to the laws at large I write my name: [*Subscribes.*
  And he that breaks them in the least degree
Stands in attainder of eternal shame:
  Suggestions are to other as to me;
But I believe, although I seem so loath,   160
I am the last that will last keep his oath.
But is there no quick recreation granted?

King. Ay, that there is. Our court, you know,
  is haunted
With a refined traveller of Spain;
A man in all the world's new fashion planted,
  That hath a mint of phrases in his brain;
One who the music of his own vain tongue
  Doth ravish like enchanting harmony;
A man of complements, whom right and wrong
  Have chose as umpire of their mutiny: 170
This child of fancy that Armado hight
  For interim to our studies shall relate
In high-born words the worth of many a knight
  From tawny Spain lost in the world's debate.
How you delight, my lords, I know not, I;
But, I protest, I love to hear him lie
And I will use him for my minstrelsy.
  Biron. Armado is a most illustrious wight,
A man of fire-new words, fashion's own knight.
  Long. Costard the swain and he shall be our sport;
And so to study, three years is but short.   181

Enter DULL *with a letter, and* COSTARD.

  Dull. Which is the duke's own person?
  Biron. This, fellow: what wouldst?
  Dull. I myself reprehend his own person, for I am
his grace's farborough: but I would see his own person
in flesh and blood.
  Biron. This is he.
  Dull. Signior Arme-Arme-commends you. There 's
villany abroad: this letter will tell you more.   190
  Cost. Sir, the contempts thereof are as touching me.
  King. A letter from the magnificent Armado.
  Biron. How low soever the matter, I hope in God for
high words.
  Long. A high hope for a low heaven: God grant us
patience!
  Biron. To hear? or forbear hearing?
  Long. To hear meekly, sir, and to laugh moderately;
or to forbear both.   200
  Biron. Well, sir, be it as the style shall give us cause
to climb in the merriness.
  Cost. The matter is to me, sir, as concerning
Jaquenetta. The manner of it is, I was taken with the
manner.
  Biron. In what manner?
  Cost. In manner and form following, sir; all those
three: I was seen with her in the manor-house, sitting
with her upon the form, and taken following her into
the park; which, put together, is in manner and
form following. Now, sir, for the manner,—it is the
manner of a man to speak to a woman: for the form,
—in some form.
  Biron. For the following, sir?
  Cost. As it shall follow in my correction and God
defend the right!
  King. Will you hear this letter with attention?

112. **barbarism,** ignorance; opposed to *knowledge* (l. 113). 114. **confident,** used adverbially. 115. **bide,** endure. **each . . . day,** every
day of the three years. 126. **Marry,** a mild interjection equivalent
to "Indeed!"; originally an oath by the Virgin Mary; see glossary.
135. **in embassy,** as an ambassador. 137. **complete,** fully endowed; see
glossary. 141. **admired,** exciting wonder; see glossary. 148. **of force,**
necessarily. 149. **lie,** reside; see glossary. 152. **affects,** natural
tendencies. 153. **grace,** divine favor; see glossary. 155. **mere,** absolute, pure; see glossary. 156. **at large,** as a whole, in general; see
large in glossary. 158. **attainder,** dishonoring accusation. 159. **Suggestions,** temptations; see glossary. 162. **quick,** lively; see glossary.
163. **haunted,** frequented, visited. 167. **who,** so QF; Globe: *whom.*
Who in the objective position is frequent in Shakespeare; see Abbott,
274. 169. **complements,** those accomplishments which go to complete

a gentleman; cf. Armado's words below (I, ii, 46-47), *the varnish of a
complete man.* 170. **mutiny,** discord. 171. **child of fancy,** fantastic
or grotesque creature; see *fancy* in glossary. 172. **interim,** interlude.
174. **tawny,** probably a reference to the complexion of the people. 175.
How you delight, what delights you, how you are delighted. 180.
Costard. The name means a large apple; the term is frequently applied
humorously or derisively to the head; cf. III, i, 71. **swain,** young man in
love; especially a rustic. 183. **fellow,** customary form of address to a
servant; see glossary. 184. **reprehend,** represent. We have in this play
Shakespeare's first employment of the comic device of malapropism,
which he brought to such perfection in characterizing the constable of
Much Ado about Nothing. 185. **farborough,** so Q; Dull means *thar-
borough* (the Globe reading), a common variant of "thirdborough," a
petty officer. 193. **magnificent,** boastful. 198. **hearing,** so QF; Globe,

Biron. As we would hear an oracle.

Cost. Such is the simplicity of man to hearken after the flesh. 220

King [*reads*]. 'Great deputy, the welkin's vicegerent and sole dominator of Navarre, my soul's earth's god, and body's fostering patron.'

Cost. Not a word of Costard yet.

King [*reads*]. 'So it is,'—

Cost. It may be so: but if he say it is so, he is, in telling true, but so.

King. Peace!

Cost. Be to me and every man that dares not fight!

King. No words! 231

Cost. Of other men's secrets, I beseech you.

King [*reads*]. 'So it is, besieged with sable-coloured melancholy, I did commend the black-oppressing humour to the most wholesome physic of thy health-giving air; and, as I am a gentleman, betook myself to walk. The time when. About the sixth hour; when beasts most graze, birds best peck, and men sit down to that nourishment which is called supper: so much for the time when. Now for the ground which; which, I mean, I walked upon: it is ycleped thy park. Then for the place where; where, I mean, I did encounter that obscene and most preposterous event, that draweth from my snow-white pen the ebon-coloured ink, which here thou viewest, beholdest, surveyest, or seest: but to the place where; it standeth north-north-east and by east from the west corner of thy curious-knotted garden: there did I see that low-spirited swain, that base minnow of thy mirth,'— 251

Cost. Me?

King [*reads*]. 'that unlettered small-knowing soul,'—

Cost. Me?

King [*reads*]. 'that shallow vassal,'—

Cost. Still me?

King [*reads*]. 'which, as I remember. hight Costard,'—

Cost. O, me! 260

King [*reads*]. 'sorted and consorted, contrary to thy established proclaimed edict and continent canon, which with,—O, with—but with this I passion to say wherewith,'—

Cost. With a wench.

King [*reads*]. 'with a child of our grandmother Eve, a female; or, for thy more sweet understanding, a woman. Him I, as my ever-esteemed duty pricks me on, have sent to thee, to receive the meed of punishment, by thy sweet grace's officer, Anthony Dull; a man of good repute, carriage, bearing, and estimation.' 272

Dull. Me, an 't shall please you; I am Anthony Dull.

King [*reads*]. 'For Jaquenetta,—so is the weaker vessel called which I apprehended with the aforesaid swain,—I keep her as a vessel of thy law's fury; and shall, at the least of thy sweet notice, bring her to

trial. Thine, in all compliments of devoted and heart-burning heat of duty.   DON ADRIANO DE ARMADO.'

Biron. This is not so well as I looked for, but the best that ever I heard.

King. Ay, the best for the worst. But, sirrah, what say you to this?

Cost. Sir, I confess the wench.

King. Did you hear the proclamation?

Cost. I do confess much of the hearing it, but little of the marking of it.

King. It was proclaimed a year's imprisonment, to be taken with a wench. 290

Cost. I was taken with none, sir: I was taken with a damsel.

King. Well, it was proclaimed 'damsel.'

Cost. This was no damsel neither, sir; she was a virgin.

King. It is so varied too; for it was proclaimed 'virgin.'

Cost. If it were, I deny her virginity: I was taken with a maid.

King. This maid will not serve your turn, sir. 300

Cost. This maid will serve my turn, sir.

King. Sir, I will pronounce your sentence: you shall fast a week with bran and water.

Cost. I had rather pray a month with mutton and porridge.

King. And Don Armado shall be your keeper.
My Lord Biron, see him deliver'd o'er:
And go we, lords, to put in practice that
Which each to other hath so strongly sworn.
    [*Exeunt King, Longaville, and Dumain.*

Biron. I'll lay my head to any good man's hat, 310
These oaths and laws will prove an idle scorn.
Sirrah, come on.

Cost. I suffer for the truth, sir; for true it is, I was taken with Jaquenetta, and Jaquenetta is a true girl; and therefore welcome the sour cup of prosperity! Affliction may one day smile again; and till then, sit thee down, sorrow!   [*Exeunt.*

SCENE II. *The same.*

Enter ARMADO *and* MOTH.

Arm. Boy, what sign is it when a man of great spirit grows melancholy?

Moth. A great sign, sir, that he will look sad.

Arm. Why, sadness is one and the self-same thing, dear imp.

Moth. No, no; O Lord, sir, no.

Arm. How canst thou part sadness and melancholy, my tender juvenal?

Moth. By a familiar demonstration of the working, my tough senior. 10

Arm. Why tough senior? why tough senior?

following Capell and others: *laughing*. 201. **style,** quibble on "stile," which gives point to *climb* (l. 202). 205. **with the manner,** with the stolen goods; an Anglo-French law term *mainoure* (from *manœuvre*). 209. **form,** bench or long seat. 215. **correction,** punishment. 221. **welkin's,** sky's, heaven's; see glossary. 227. **but so,** indifferent; cf. the modern phrase "so, so." 234-235. **black-oppressing humour,** i.e., black choler or melancholy; see *humour* in glossary. 235. **physic,** medicine, medical treatment; see glossary. 242. **ycleped,** called (archaic); an affectation on Armado's part. 244. **obscene,** disgusting. 245. **snow-white pen,** i.e., the white goose quill. 249. **curious-knotted,** delicately or intricately designed; see *curious* in glossary. 251. **minnow,** contemptible little person. 256. **vassal,** base slave. 261. **sorted and consorted,** associated. 262-263. **continent canon,** restraint enforced by law; note the affectation of legal language. 264. **passion,**

grieve; see glossary. 283. **sirrah,** ordinary form of address to inferiors; see glossary. 287, 288. **hearing, marking.** This may be an echo of the collect for the second Sunday in Advent: "hear, read, mark, learn, and inwardly digest." 300. **serve your turn,** answer your purpose; see *serve* in glossary. 304. **mutton,** possible glance at the meaning "prostitute." 310. **lay,** wager. **good man's,** probably should be read *goodman's,* i.e., citizen's, husband's.

SCENE II. 5. **imp,** child. 8. **juvenal,** youth, with possible reference here to the classical satirist, Juvenal. Those who find treatment in this play of the Harvey-Nashe quarrel think this an allusion to Nashe's satirical vein. 9. **familiar,** plain, easily understood; see glossary.

Moth. Why tender juvenal? why tender juvenal?

Arm. I spoke it, tender juvenal, as a congruent epitheton appertaining to thy young days, which we may nominate tender.

Moth. And I, tough senior, as an appertinent title to your old time, which we may name tough.

Arm. Pretty and apt. 19

Moth. How mean you, sir? I pretty, and my saying apt? or I apt, and my saying pretty?

Arm. Thou pretty, because little.

Moth. Little pretty, because little. Wherefore apt?

Arm. And therefore apt, because quick.

Moth. Speak you this in my praise, master?

Arm. In thy condign praise.

Moth. I will praise an eel with the same praise.

Arm. What, that an eel is ingenious?

Moth. That an eel is quick. 30

Arm. I do say thou art quick in answers: thou heatest my blood.

Moth. I am answered, sir.

Arm. I love not to be crossed.

Moth. [*Aside*] He speaks the mere contrary; crosses love not him.

Arm. I have promised to study three years with the duke.

Moth. You may do it in an hour, sir.

Arm. Impossible. 40

Moth. How many is one thrice told?

Arm. I am ill at reckoning; it fitteth the spirit of a tapster.

Moth. You are a gentleman and a gamester, sir.

Arm. I confess both: they are both the varnish of a complete man.

Moth. Then, I am sure, you know how much the gross sum of deuce-ace amounts to.

Arm. It doth amount to one more than two. 50

Moth. Which the base vulgar do call three.

Arm. True.

Moth. Why, sir, is this such a piece of study? Now here is three studied, ere ye'll thrice wink: and how easy it is to put 'years' to the word 'three,' and study three years in two words, the dancing horse will tell you.

Arm. A most fine figure!

Moth. To prove you a cipher. 59

Arm. I will hereupon confess I am in love: and as it is base for a soldier to love, so am I in love with a base wench. If drawing my sword against the humour of affection would deliver me from the reprobate thought of it, I would take Desire prisoner, and ransom him to any French courtier for a new-devised courtesy. I think scorn to sigh: methinks I should outswear Cupid. Comfort me, boy: what great men have been in love?

Moth. Hercules, master. 69

Arm. Most sweet Hercules! More authority, dear boy, name more; and, sweet my child, let them be men of good repute and carriage.

Moth. Samson, master: he was a man of good carriage, great carriage, for he carried the town-gates on his back like a porter: and he was in love.

Arm. O well-knit Samson! strong-jointed Samson! I do excel thee in my rapier as much as thou didst me in carrying gates. I am in love too. Who was Samson's love, my dear Moth? 80

Moth. A woman, master.

Arm. Of what complexion?

Moth. Of all the four, or the three, or the two, or one of the four.

Arm. Tell me precisely of what complexion.

Moth. Of the sea-water green, sir.

Arm. Is that one of the four complexions? 85

Moth. As I have read, sir; and the best of them too.

Arm. Green indeed is the colour of lovers; but to have a love of that colour, methinks Samson had small reason for it. He surely affected her for her wit.

Moth. It was so, sir; for she had a green wit.

Arm. My love is most immaculate white and red.

Moth. Most maculate thoughts, master, are masked under such colours.

Arm. Define, define, well-educated infant.

Moth. My father's wit and my mother's tongue, assist me! 101

Arm. Sweet invocation of a child; most pretty and pathetical!

Moth. If she be made of white and red,
　　　Her faults will ne'er be known,
　　For blushing cheeks by faults are bred
　　　And fears by pale white shown:
　　Then if she fear, or be to blame,
　　　By this you shall not know,
　　For still her cheeks possess the same 110
　　　Which native she doth owe.

A dangerous rhyme, master, against the reason of white and red.

Arm. Is there not a ballad, boy, of the King and the Beggar?

Moth. The world was very guilty of such a ballad some three ages since: but I think now 'tis not to be found; or, if it were, it would neither serve for the writing nor the tune. 119

Arm. I will have that subject newly writ o'er, that I may example my digression by some mighty precedent. Boy, I do love that country girl that I took in the park with the rational hind Costard: she deserves well.

Moth. [*Aside*] To be whipped; and yet a better love than my master.

Arm. Sing, boy; my spirit grows heavy in love.

Moth. And that's great marvel, loving a light wench.

Arm. I say, sing. 130
Moth. Forbear till this company be past.

Enter DULL, COSTARD, *and* JAQUENETTA.

Dull. Sir, the duke's pleasure is, that you keep Costard safe: and you must suffer him to take no delight nor no penance; but a' must fast three days a week. For this damsel, I must keep her at the park: she is allowed for the day-woman. Fare you well.

Arm. I do betray myself with blushing. Maid!
Jaq. Man?
Arm. I will visit thee at the lodge. 140
Jaq. That 's hereby.
Arm. I know where it is situate.
Jaq. Lord, how wise you are!
Arm. I will tell thee wonders.
Jaq. With that face?
Arm. I love thee.
Jaq. So I heard you say.
Arm. And so, farewell.
Jaq. Fair weather after you!
Dull. Come, Jaquenetta, away! 150
[*Exeunt Dull and Jaquenetta.*
Arm. Villain, thou shalt fast for thy offences ere thou be pardoned.
Cost. Well, sir, I hope, when I do it, I shall do it on a full stomach.
Arm. Thou shalt be heavily punished.
Cost. I am more bound to you than your fellows, for they are but lightly rewarded.
Arm. Take away this villain; shut him up.
Moth. Come, you transgressing slave; away!
Cost. Let me not be pent up, sir: I will fast, being loose. 161
Moth. No, sir; that were fast and loose: thou shalt to prison.
Cost. Well, if ever I do see the merry days of desolation that I have seen, some shall see.
Moth. What shall some see?
Cost. Nay, nothing, Master Moth, but what they look upon. It is not for prisoners to be too silent in their words; and therefore I will say nothing: I thank God I have as little patience as another man; and therefore I can be quiet. [*Exeunt Moth and Costard.*
Arm. I do affect the very ground, which is base, where her shoe, which is baser, guided by her foot, which is basest, doth tread. I shall be forsworn, which is a great argument of falsehood, if I love. And how can that be true love which is falsely attempted? Love is a familiar; Love is a devil: there is no evil angel but Love. Yet was Samson so tempted, and he had an excellent strength; yet was Solomon so seduced, and he had a very good wit. Cupid's butt-shaft is too hard for Hercules' club; and therefore too much odds for a Spaniard's rapier. The first and

second cause will not serve my turn; the passado he respects not, the duello he regards not: his disgrace is to be called boy; but his glory is to subdue men. Adieu, valour! rust, rapier! be still, drum! for your manager is in love; yea, he loveth. Assist me, some extemporal god of rhyme, for I am sure I shall turn sonnet. Devise, wit; write, pen; for I am for whole volumes in folio. [*Exit.*

ACT II.

SCENE I. *The same.*

Enter the Princess of France, ROSALINE, MARIA, KATHARINE, BOYET, Lords, *and other* Attendants.

Boyet. Now, madam, summon up your dearest
  spirits:
Consider who the king your father sends,
To whom he sends, and what 's his embassy:
Yourself, held precious in the world's esteem,
To parley with the sole inheritor
Of all perfections that a man may owe,
Matchless Navarre; the plea of no less weight
Than Aquitaine, a dowry for a queen.
Be now as prodigal of all dear grace
As Nature was in making graces dear 10
When she did starve the general world beside
And prodigally gave them all to you.
  Prin. Good Lord Boyet, my beauty, though but
  mean,
Needs not the painted flourish of your praise:
Beauty is bought by judgement of the eye,
Not utter'd by base sale of chapmen's tongues:
I am less proud to hear you tell my worth
Than you much willing to be counted wise
In spending your wit in the praise of mine.
But now to task the tasker: good Boyet, 20
You are not ignorant, all-telling fame
Doth noise abroad, Navarre hath made a vow,
Till painful study shall outwear three years,
No woman may approach his silent court:
Therefore to 's seemeth it a needful course,
Before we enter his forbidden gates,
To know his pleasure; and in that behalf,
Bold of your worthiness, we single you
As our best-moving fair solicitor.
Tell him, the daughter of the King of France, 30
On serious business, craving quick dispatch,
Importunes personal conference with his grace:
Haste, signify so much; while we attend,
Like humble-visaged suitors, his high will.
  Boyet. Proud of employment, willingly I go.
  Prin. All pride is willing pride, and yours is so.
[*Exit Boyet.*

---

full stomach, probably a quibble on the idea of "full-stomached," meaning "with good courage"; see *stomach* in glossary. It may be a slur at the Puritans. 157. lightly, i.e., only slightly. 162. fast and loose, a cheating or gambling trick executed with a stick and a cord or belt. The phrase was very early applied metaphorically to matters of conduct with the meaning "inconstant, tricky, slippery." Shakespeare so used it in *King John*, III, i, 242. 177. familiar, attendant spirit; see glossary. 181. butt-shaft, unbarbed arrow used in archery practice; applied to Cupid's darts because, although they hit hard, they were easily extracted. 183-184. first . . . cause. Cf. *The Booke of Honor and Armes* (1590): " . . . the causes of a quarrell wherevpon it behoueth to vse the triall of Armes, may be reduced into two. . . . Wherefore whensoeuer one man doth accuse another of such a crime as meriteth death, in that case the Combat ought to be graunted. The second cause of Combat is Honor, because among persons of reputation, Honor is

preferred before life." (*Modern Language Review*, II, 76-77.) 184. passado, forward thrust with the sword, one foot being advanced at the same time. 185. respects, heeds; see glossary. duello, established code of duelists. 189. extemporal, impromptu.
ACT II. SCENE I. 1. dearest, best. 9, 10. dear, quibble on the meanings "beloved," "cherished," and "bearing a high price"; see glossary. 13. mean, average, moderate; see glossary. 15. Beauty . . . eye, i.e., the buyer's judgment, not the merchant's advertising, is the determinant. 16. chapmen's, merchants'; sometimes taken to be an allusion to the poet Chapman. 20. task, lay a task upon. 25. to 's, to us. 28. Bold of, as a consequence of. 29. best-moving, most eloquent. fair, just; see glossary.

Who are the votaries, my loving lords,
That are vow-fellows with this virtuous duke?
    First Lord. Lord Longaville is one.
    Prin.   Know you the man?
    Mar. I know him, madam: at a marriage-feast,   40
Between Lord Perigort and the beauteous heir
Of Jaques Falconbridge, solemnized
In Normandy, saw I this Longaville:
A man of sovereign parts he is esteem'd;
Well fitted in arts, glorious in arms:
Nothing becomes him ill that he would well.
The only soil of his fair virtue's gloss,
If virtue's gloss will stain with any soil,
Is a sharp wit match'd with too blunt a will;
Whose edge hath power to cut, whose will still wills   50
It should none spare that come within his power.
    Prin. Some merry mocking lord, belike; is't so?
    Mar. They say so most that most his humours
        know.
    Prin. Such short-lived wits do wither as they grow.
Who are the rest?
    Kath. The young Dumain; a well-accomplished
        youth,
Of all that virtue love for virtue loved:
Most power to do most harm, least knowing ill;
For he hath wit to make an ill shape good,
And shape to win grace though he had no wit.   60
I saw him at the Duke Alençon's once;
And much too little of that good I saw
Is my report to his great worthiness.
    Ros. Another of these students at that time
Was there with him, if I have heard a truth.
Biron they call him; but a merrier man,
Within the limit of becoming mirth,
I never spent an hour's talk withal:
His eye begets occasion for his wit;
For every object that the one doth catch   70
The other turns to a mirth-moving jest,
Which his fair tongue, conceit's expositor,
Delivers in such apt and gracious words
That aged ears play truant at his tales
And younger hearings are quite ravished;
So sweet and voluble is his discourse.
    Prin. God bless my ladies! are they all in love,
That every one her own hath garnished
With such bedecking ornaments of praise?
    First Lord. Here comes Boyet.

Re-enter BOYET.

    Prin.   Now, what admittance, lord?   80
    Boyet. Navarre had notice of your fair approach;
And he and his competitors in oath
Were all address'd to meet you, gentle lady,
Before I came. Marry, thus much I have learnt:
He rather means to lodge you in the field,
Like one that comes here to besiege his court,
Than seek a dispensation for his oath,
To let you enter his unpeopled house.

Here comes Navarre.

    Enter KING, LONGAVILLE, DUMAIN, BIRON, *and*
        Attendants.

    King. Fair princess, welcome to the court of
        Navarre.   90
    Prin. 'Fair' I give you back again; and 'welcome'
I have not yet: the roof of this court is too high to
be yours; and welcome to the wide fields too base to
be mine.
    King. You shall be welcome, madam, to my court.
    Prin. I will be welcome, then: conduct me thither.
    King. Hear me, dear lady; I have sworn an oath.
    Prin. Our Lady help my lord! he'll be forsworn.
    King. Not for the world, fair madam, by my will.
    Prin. Why, will shall break it; will and nothing else.
    King. Your ladyship is ignorant what it is.   101
    Prin. Were my lord so, his ignorance were wise,
Where now his knowledge must prove ignorance.
I hear your grace hath sworn out house-keeping:
'Tis deadly sin to keep that oath, my lord,
And sin to break it.
But pardon me, I am too sudden-bold:
To teach a teacher ill beseemeth me.
Vouchsafe to read the purpose of my coming,
And suddenly resolve me in my suit.   110
    King. Madam, I will, if suddenly I may.
    Prin. You will the sooner, that I were away;
For you'll prove perjured if you make me stay.
    Biron. Did not I dance with you in Brabant once?
    Ros. Did not I dance with you in Brabant once?
    Biron. I know you did.
    Ros. How needless was it then to ask the question!
    Biron. You must not be so quick.
    Ros. 'Tis 'long of you that spur me with such
        questions.
    Biron. Your wit's too hot, it speeds too fast, 'twill
        tire.   120
    Ros. Not till it leave the rider in the mire.
    Biron. What time o' day?
    Ros. The hour that fools should ask.
    Biron. Now fair befall your mask!
    Ros. Fair fall the face it covers!
    Biron. And send you many lovers!
    Ros. Amen, so you be none.
    Biron. Nay, then will I be gone.
    King. Madam, your father here doth intimate
The payment of a hundred thousand crowns;   130
Being but the one half of an entire sum
Disbursed by my father in his wars.
But say that he or we, as neither have,
Received that sum, yet there remains unpaid
A hundred thousand more; in surety of the which,
One part of Aquitaine is bound to us,
Although not valued to the money's worth.
If then the king your father will restore
But that one half which is unsatisfied,
We will give up our right in Aquitaine,   140

37. **votaries,** those who have taken vows. 44. **sovereign parts,** excellent qualities. 46. **would well,** wants to do well. 47. **virtue's gloss,** appearance of general excellence; see *virtue* and *gloss* in glossary. 49. **too blunt a will,** i.e., too insensitive to the feelings of others. 56-60. **The . . . wit.** Dumain, a highly accomplished young nobleman, esteemed for his virtue by all who love virtue; one who, by his talent and graceful person has the utmost power of doing the greatest harm by the ill employment of those qualities, is nevertheless ignorant of evil (Halliwell). 72. **conceit's expositor,** interpreter of fanciful ideas: see *conceit* in glossary. 76. **discourse,** art of conversing; see glossary. 82. **competitors,** associates. 88. **unpeopled,** so F; Q: *unpeeled,*

which probably represents an Elizabethan pronunciation. 104. **sworn out,** renounced. **house-keeping,** hospitality. 107. **sudden-bold,** rashly bold. 110. **resolve,** answer; see glossary. 119. **'long of,** on account of; see glossary. 124. **fair befall,** an optative expression frequent in Elizabethan literature, equivalent to "Good luck!" 125. **fall,** befall; see glossary. 129-149. **your . . . is.** Cf. I, i, 138-139. The French king offers to discharge but half his debt to Navarre, for which Aquitaine has been the surety. The king of Navarre objects, insisting that Aquitaine, weakened as it is, is insufficient security for the 100,000 crowns that would still be owing. He holds out for payment in full. 147. **depart withal,** part with; see *depart* and *withal* in glossary. 149.

And hold fair friendship with his majesty.
But that, it seems, he little purposeth,
For here he doth demand to have repaid
A hundred thousand crowns; and not demands,
On payment of a hundred thousand crowns,
To have his title live in Aquitaine;
Which we much rather had depart withal
And have the money by our father lent
Than Aquitaine so gelded as it is.
Dear princess, were not his requests so far   150
From reason's yielding, your fair self should make
A yielding 'gainst some reason in my breast
And go well satisfied to France again.
     Prin. You do the king my father too much wrong
And wrong the reputation of your name,
In so unseeming to confess receipt
Of that which hath so faithfully been paid.
     King. I do protest I never heard of it;
And if you prove it, I'll repay it back
Or yield up Aquitaine.
     Prin.   We arrest your word.   160
Boyet, you can produce acquittances
For such a sum from special officers
Of Charles his father.
     King.   Satisfy me so.
     Boyet. So please your grace, the packet is not come
Where that and other specialties are bound:
To-morrow you shall have a sight of them.
     King. It shall suffice me: at which interview
All liberal reason I will yield unto.
Meantime receive such welcome at my hand
As honour without breach of honour may   170
Make tender of to thy true worthiness:
You may not come, fair princess, within my gates;
But here without you shall be so received
As you shall deem yourself lodged in my heart,
Though so denied fair harbour in my house.
Your own good thoughts excuse me, and farewell:
To-morrow shall we visit you again.
     Prin. Sweet health and fair desires consort your
     grace!
     King. Thy own wish wish I thee in every place!
                                        [*Exit.*
     Biron. Lady, I will commend you to mine own
     heart.   180
     Ros. Pray you, do my commendations; I would be
glad to see it.
     Biron. I would you heard it groan.
     Ros. Is the fool sick?
     Biron. Sick at the heart.
     Ros. Alack, let it blood.
     Biron. Would that do it good?
     Ros. My physic says 'ay.'
     Biron. Will you prick 't with your eye?
     Ros. No point, with my knife.   190
     Biron. Now, God save thy life!
     Ros. And yours from long living!
     Biron. I cannot stay thanksgiving.   [*Retiring.*

     Dum. Sir, I pray you, a word: what lady is that
     same?
     Boyet. The heir of Alençon, Katharine her name.
     Dum. A gallant lady. Monsieur, fare you well. [*Exit.*
     Long. I beseech you a word: what is she in the
     white?
     Boyet. A woman sometimes, an you saw her in the
     light.
     Long. Perchance light in the light. I desire her
     name.
     Boyet. She hath but one for herself; to desire that
     were a shame.   200
     Long. Pray you, sir, whose daughter?
     Boyet. Her mother's, I have heard.
     Long. God's blessing on your beard!
     Boyet. Good sir, be not offended.
She is an heir of Falconbridge.
     Long. Nay, my choler is ended.
She is a most sweet lady.
     Boyet. Not unlike, sir, that may be.   [*Exit Long.*
     Biron. What 's her name in the cap?
     Boyet. Rosaline, by good hap.   210
     Biron. Is she wedded or no?
     Boyet. To her will, sir, or so.
     Biron. You are welcome, sir: adieu.
     Boyet. Farewell to me, sir, and welcome to you.
                                        [*Exit Biron.*
     Mar. That last is Biron, the merry mad-cap lord:
Not a word with him but a jest.
     Boyet.   And every jest but a word.
     Prin. It was well done of you to take him at his
     word.
     Boyet. I was as willing to grapple as he was to
     board.
     Mar. Two hot sheeps, marry.
     Boyet.   And wherefore not ships?
No sheep, sweet lamb, unless we feed on your lips.   220
     Mar. You sheep, and I pasture: shall that finish
     the jest?
     Boyet. So you grant pasture for me.
                                        [*Offering to kiss her.*
     Mar.   Not so, gentle beast:
My lips are no common, though several they be.
     Boyet. Belonging to whom?
     Mar.   To my fortunes and me.
     Prin. Good wits will be jangling; but, gentles, agree:
This civil war of wits were much better used
On Navarre and his book-men; for here 'tis abused.
     Boyet. If my observation, which very seldom lies,
By the heart's still rhetoric disclosed with eyes,
Deceive me not now, Navarre is infected.   230
     Prin. With what?
     Boyet. With that which we lovers entitle affected.
     Prin. Your reason?
     Boyet. Why, all his behaviours did make their
     retire
To the court of his eye, peeping thorough desire:
His heart, like an agate, with your print impress'd,

gelded, weakened. 156. **unseeming,** i.e., apparently unwilling.
160. **arrest,** take as security. 165. **specialties,** special contracts for
payment of money. 168. **liberal,** becoming a gentleman; see glossary.
172. **within,** so Q; Globe, following F: *in.* 178. **consort,** attend,
accompany. 181. **do my commendations,** convey my greetings (i.e., to
your heart). 186. **let it blood,** bleed it; a reference to the medical
practice of drawing blood. 190. **No point,** not at all; with quibble;
cf. V, ii, 277. 193. **stay thanksgiving,** i.e., wait for thanks to be said;
an allusion to the long grace before meals; see *stay* in glossary. 199.
light in the light, wanton when her conduct is known (brought to
light). 203. **God's . . . beard.** The Yale editors think this a recognition of Boyet's years, with which his remarks are not in keeping. Hart
points out that any reference to one's beard was dangerous or unmannerly. 214. **welcome to you,** you are welcome to go. 218.
grapple, board, tactics of sea warfare. 219. **sheeps, ships.** Cf. *Two
Gentlemen of Verona,* I, i, 72, 73, note. 223. **common,** common land.
several, private enclosed land, with quibble on the meaning, "more
than one"; see glossary. 227. **abused,** misapplied; see glossary.
229. **still,** silent, mute; see glossary. 234. **retire,** retirement. 235.
thorough, through; see glossary. 236. **agate,** an allusion to small
figures cut in agate.

Proud with his form, in his eye pride express'd:
His tongue, all impatient to speak and not see,
Did stumble with haste in his eyesight to be;
All senses to that sense did make their repair, 240
To feel only looking on fairest of fair:
Methought all his senses were lock'd in his eye,
As jewels in crystal for some prince to buy;
Who, tendering their own worth from where they
    were glass'd,
Did point you to buy them, along as you pass'd:
His face's own margent did quote such amazes
That all eyes saw his eyes enchanted with gazes.
I'll give you Aquitaine and all that is his,
An you give him for my sake but one loving kiss.
    Prin. Come to our pavilion: Boyet is disposed. 250
    Boyet. But to speak that in words which his eye hath
        disclosed.
I only have made a mouth of his eye,
By adding a tongue which I know will not lie.
    Ros. Thou art an old love-monger and speakest
        skilfully.
    Mar. He is Cupid's grandfather and learns news of
        him.
    Ros. Then was Venus like her mother, for her father
        is but grim.
    Boyet. Do you hear, my mad wenches?
    Mar.   No.
    Boyet.   What then, do you see?
    Ros. Ay, our way to be gone.
    Boyet.   You are too hard for me.
                                              [*Exeunt.*

ACT III.

SCENE I. *The same.*

Enter ARMADO *and* MOTH.

Arm. Warble, child; make passionate my sense of
hearing.
    Moth. Concolinel.   [*Singing.*
    Arm. Sweet air! Go, tenderness of years; take this
key, give enlargement to the swain, bring him festi-
nately hither: I must employ him in a letter to my
love.
    Moth. Master, will you win your love with a French
brawl?
    Arm. How meanest thou? brawling in French? 10
    Moth. No, my complete master: but to jig off a tune
at the tongue's end, canary to it with your feet,
humour it with turning up your eye-lids, sigh a note
and sing a note, sometime through the throat, as if
you swallowed love with singing love, sometime
through the nose, as if you snuffed up love by smelling
love; with your hat penthouse-like o'er the shop of
your eyes; with your arms crossed on your thin-belly
doublet like a rabbit on a spit; or your hands in your
pocket like a man after the old painting; and keep not
too long in one tune, but a snip and away. These are

complements, these are humours; these betray nice
wenches, that would be betrayed without these; and
make them men of note—do you note? men—that
most are affected to these.
    Arm. How hast thou purchased this experience?
    Moth. By my pen of observation.
    Arm. But O,—but O,—
    Moth. 'The hobby-horse is forgot.' 30
    Arm. Callest thou my love 'hobby-horse'?
    Moth. No, master; the hobby-horse is but a colt,
and your love perhaps a hackney. But have you forgot
your love?
    Arm. Almost I had.
    Moth. Negligent student! learn her by heart.
    Arm. By heart and in heart, boy.
    Moth. And out of heart, master: all those three I will
prove.
    Arm. What wilt thou prove? 40
    Moth. A man, if I live; and this, by, in, and without,
upon the instant: by heart you love her, because your
heart cannot come by her; in heart you love her,
because your heart is in love with her; and out of
heart you love her, being out of heart that you cannot
enjoy her.
    Arm. I am all these three.
    Moth. And three times as much more, and yet
nothing at all.
    Arm. Fetch hither the swain: he must carry me a
letter. 51
    Moth. A message well sympathized; a horse to be
ambassador for an ass.
    Arm. Ha, ha! what sayest thou?
    Moth. Marry, sir, you must send the ass upon the
horse, for he is very slow-gaited. But I go.
    Arm. The way is but short: away!
    Moth. As swift as lead, sir.
    Arm. The meaning, pretty ingenious?
Is not lead a metal heavy, dull, and slow? 60
    Moth. Minimè, honest master; or rather, master,
no.
    Arm. I say lead is slow.
    Moth.   You are too swift, sir, to say so:
Is that lead slow which is fired from a gun?
    Arm. Sweet smoke of rhetoric!
He reputes me a cannon; and the bullet, that's he:
I shoot thee at the swain.
    Moth.   Thump then and I flee. [*Exit.*
    Arm. A most acute juvenal; volable and free of
        grace!
By thy favour, sweet welkin, I must sigh in thy face:
Most rude melancholy, valour gives thee place.
My herald is return'd. 70

Re-enter MOTH *with* COSTARD.

    Moth. A wonder, master! here's a costard broken in
a shin.
    Arm. Some enigma, some riddle: come, thy l'envoy;
begin.

Cost. No egma, no riddle, no l'envoy; no salve †in the mail, sir: O, sir, plantain, a plain plantain! no l'envoy, no l'envoy; no salve, sir, but a plantain!

Arm. By virtue, thou enforcest laughter; thy silly thought my spleen; the heaving of my lungs provokes me to ridiculous smiling. O, pardon me, my stars! Doth the inconsiderate take salve for l'envoy, and the word l'envoy for a salve? 80

Moth. Do the wise think them other? is not l'envoy a salve?

Arm. No, page: it is an epilogue or discourse, to make plain
Some obscure precedence that hath tofore been sain.
I will example it:
　　The fox, the ape and the humble-bee,
　　Were still at odds, being but three.
There 's the moral. Now the l'envoy.

Moth. I will add the l'envoy. Say the moral again.

Arm. The fox, the ape, the humble-bee, 90
　　Were still at odds, being but three.

Moth. Until the goose came out of door,
　　And stay'd the odds by adding four.
Now will I begin your moral, and do you follow with my l'envoy.
　　The fox, the ape and the humble-bee,
　　Were still at odds, being but three.

Arm. Until the goose came out of door,
　　Staying the odds by adding four.

Moth. A good l'envoy, ending in the goose: would you desire more? 101

Cost. The boy hath sold him a bargain, a goose, that 's flat.
Sir, your pennyworth is good, an your goose be fat.
To sell a bargain well is as cunning as fast and loose:
Let me see; a fat l'envoy; ay, that 's a fat goose.

Arm. Come hither, come hither. How did this argument begin?

Moth. By saying that a costard was broken in a shin.
Then call'd you for the l'envoy.

Cost. True, and I for a plantain: thus came your argument in;
Then the boy's fat l'envoy, the goose that you bought;
And he ended the market. 111

Arm. But tell me; how was there a costard broken in a shin.

Moth. I will tell you sensibly.

Cost. Thou hast no feeling of it, Moth: I will speak that l'envoy:
　　I Costard, running out, that was safely within,
　　Fell over the threshold, and broke my shin.

Arm. We will talk no more of this matter.

Cost. Till there be more matter in the shin. 120

Arm. Sirrah Costard, I will enfranchise thee.

Cost. O, marry me to one Frances: I smell some l'envoy, some goose, in this.

Arm. By my sweet soul, I mean setting thee at liberty, enfreedoming thy person: thou wert immured, restrained, captivated, bound.

Cost. True, true; and now you will be my purgation and let me loose.

Arm. I give thee thy liberty, set thee from durance; and, in lieu thereof, impose on thee nothing but this: bear this significant [*giving a letter*] to the country maid Jaquenetta: there is remuneration; for the best ward of mine honour is rewarding my dependents. Moth, follow. [*Exit.*

Moth. Like the sequel, I. Signior Costard, adieu.

Cost. My sweet ounce of man's flesh! my incony Jew! [*Exit Moth.*
Now will I look to his remuneration. Remuneration! O, that 's the Latin word for three farthings: three farthings—remuneration. 'What 's the price of this inkle?'—'One penny.'—'No, I'll give you a remuneration:' why, it carries it. Remuneration! why, it is a fairer name than French crown. I will never buy and sell out of this word.

Enter BIRON.

Biron. O, my good knave Costard! exceedingly well met.

Cost. Pray you, sir, how much carnation ribbon may a man buy for a remuneration?

Biron. What is a remuneration?

Cost. Marry, sir, halfpenny farthing.

Biron. Why, then, three-farthing worth of silk. 150

Cost. I thank your worship: God be wi' you!

Biron. Stay, slave; I must employ thee:
As thou wilt win my favour, good my knave,
Do one thing for me that I shall entreat.

Cost. When would you have it done, sir?

Biron. This afternoon.

Cost. Well, I will do it, sir: fare you well.

Biron. Thou knowest not what it is.

Cost. I shall know, sir, when I have done it.

Biron. Why, villain, thou must know first. 160

Cost. I will come to your worship to-morrow morning.

Biron. It must be done this afternoon.
Hark, slave, it is but this:
The princess comes to hunt here in the park,
And in her train there is a gentle lady;
When tongues speak sweetly, then they name her name,
And Rosaline they call her: ask for her;
And to her white hand see thou do commend
This seal'd-up counsel. There 's thy guerdon; go. 170
　　　　　　　　[*Giving him a shilling.*

Cost. Gardon, O sweet gardon! better than remuneration, a 'leven-pence farthing better: most sweet gardon! I will do it, sir, in print. Gardon! Remuneration! [*Exit.*

Biron. And I, forsooth, in love! I, that have been love's whip;
A very beadle to a humorous sigh;
A critic, nay, a night-watch constable;
A domineering pedant o'er the boy;

Than whom no mortal so magnificent! 180
This wimpled, whining, purblind, wayward boy;
This senior-junior, giant-dwarf, Dan Cupid;
Regent of love-rhymes, lord of folded arms,
The anointed sovereign of sighs and groans,
Liege of all loiterers and malcontents,
Dread prince of plackets, king of codpieces,
Sole imperator and great general
Of trotting 'paritors:—O my little heart!—
And I to be a corporal of his field,
And wear his colours like a tumbler's hoop! 190
What? I love! I sue! I seek a wife!
A woman, that is like a German clock,
Still a-repairing, ever out of frame,
And never going aright, being a watch,
But being watch'd that it may still go right!
Nay, to be perjured, which is worst of all;
And, among three, to love the worst of all;
A whitely wanton with a velvet brow,
With two pitch-balls stuck in her face for eyes;
Ay, and, by heaven, one that will do the deed 200
Though Argus were her eunuch and her guard:
And I to sigh for her! to watch for her!
To pray for her! Go to; it is a plague
That Cupid will impose for my neglect
Of his almighty dreadful little might.
Well, I will love, write, sigh, pray, sue, groan:
Some men must love my lady and some Joan. [Exit.

ACT IV.

SCENE I. *The same.*

Enter the Princess, *and her train, a* Forester, BOYET,
ROSALINE, MARIA, *and* KATHARINE.

Prin. Was that the king, that spurr'd his horse so
hard
Against the steep uprising of the hill?
Boyet. I know not; but I think it was not he.
Prin. Whoe'er a' was, a' show'd a mounting mind.
Well, lords, to-day we shall have our dispatch:
On Saturday we will return to France.
Then, forester, my friend, where is the bush
That we must stand and play the murderer in?
For. Hereby, upon the edge of yonder coppice;
A stand where you may make the fairest shoot. 10
Prin. I thank my beauty, I am fair that shoot,
And thereupon thou speak'st the fairest shoot.
For. Pardon me, madam, for I meant not so.
Prin. What, what? first praise me and again say no?
O short-lived pride! Not fair? alack for woe!
For. Yes, madam, fair.
Prin.   Nay, never paint me now:
Where fair is not, praise cannot mend the brow.

Here, good my glass, take this for telling true:
Fair payment for foul words is more than due.
For. Nothing but fair is that which you inherit. 20
Prin. See, see, my beauty will be saved by merit!
O heresy in fair, fit for these days!
A giving hand, though foul, shall have fair praise.
But come, the bow: now mercy goes to kill,
And shooting well is then accounted ill.
Thus will I save my credit in the shoot:
Not wounding, pity would not let me do 't;
If wounding, then it was to show my skill,
That more for praise than purpose meant to kill.
And out of question so it is sometimes, 30
Glory grows guilty of detested crimes,
When, for fame's sake, for praise, an outward part,
We bend to that the working of the heart;
As I for praise alone now seek to spill
The poor deer's blood, that my heart means no ill.
Boyet. Do not curst wives hold that self-sovereignty
Only for praise sake, when they strive to be
Lords o'er their lords?
Prin. Only for praise: and praise we may afford
To any lady that subdues a lord. 40
Boyet. Here comes a member of the commonwealth.

Enter COSTARD.

Cost. God dig-you-den all! Pray you, which is the
head lady?
Prin. Thou shalt know her, fellow, by the rest that
have no heads.
Cost. Which is the greatest lady, the highest?
Prin. The thickest and the tallest.
Cost. The thickest and the tallest! it is so; truth is
truth.
An your waist, mistress, were as slender as my wit,
One o' these maids' girdles for your waist should be
fit. 50
Are not you the chief woman? you are the thickest
here.
Prin. What 's your will, sir? what 's your will?
Cost. I have a letter from Monsieur Biron to one
Lady Rosaline.
Prin. O, thy letter, thy letter! he 's a good friend of
mine:
Stand aside, good bearer. Boyet, you can carve;
Break up this capon.
Boyet.   I am bound to serve.
This letter is mistook, it importeth none here;
It is writ to Jaquenetta.
Prin.   We will read it, I swear.
Break the neck of the wax, and every one give ear. 59
Boyet [*reads*]. 'By heaven, that thou art fair, is most
infallible; true, that thou art beauteous; truth itself,
that thou art lovely. More fairer than fair, beautiful

181. **wimpled,** blindfold. 188. **'paritors,** apparitors, summoners of
ecclesiastical courts. 189. **corporal of his field,** a superior officer
of the army in the 16th and 17th centuries, who acted as assistant
to the sergeant major (*NED*); cf. IV, iii, 86, note. 191. **What?** So
QF; Globe: *What, I!* 193. **Still,** always; see glossary. **a-repairing,**
needing repair. 198. **whitely,** pale, sallow; so New Cambridge
editors, following Q: *whitley;* F: *whitly;* Globe: *wightly,* i.e., nimble.
201. **Argus,** a fabulous monster with a hundred eyes, some of which were
always awake; he was charmed to sleep and slain by Hermes. 202.
watch, lose sleep; see glossary. 206. **sue, groan.** QF: *shue, groan;*
Globe: *sue and groan.* 207. **my lady . . . Joan,** a common antithesis
made familiar through the proverb, "Joan's as good as my lady." Joan
was a name proverbial for servant girls; cf. *King John,* I, i, 184.

ACT IV. SCENE I. 10. **stand,** flat-roofed building erected for the
purpose of giving the hunter a better aim. 16. **paint,** flatter. 18.
good my glass. The princess' speech embodies a Renaissance commonplace concerning the relation between the ruler and his courtiers. Most

to be abhorred was the flatterer, and most valued was the honest counselor who appraised his sovereign truthfully. The princess amuses herself
with these ideas, much to the Forester's discomfort. The figure of the
honest counselor as a mirror wherein the prince saw himself as he was
is frequent. 20. **inherit,** have in possession. 36. **curst,** shrewish;
see glossary. 41. **member of the commonwealth,** possibly one of the
common folk; perhaps a derisive reference to Navarre's newly ordered
court. 42. **God dig-you-den,** God give you good even. 47. **thickest,
tallest,** probably a humorous allusion to the stature of the boy who
played the part. 56. **Break . . . capon.** Like the French *poulet, capon*
designates figuratively a love letter. *Break up* is a technical phrase in
carving; cf. *break the neck of the wax,* l. 59. 66-67. **king . . . Zenelophon,**
another reference to the king and the beggar; cf. I, ii, 114-115. 69.
annothanize, explain, interpret; probably for "anatomize." 77. **catastrophe,** technical dramatic term, the conclusion of a drama or that
which brings about the conclusion. 86. **tittles,** points or dots; specifically applied to the dots commonly printed at the end of the alphabet

than beauteous, truer than truth itself, have commiseration on thy heroical vassal! The magnanimous and most illustrate king Cophetua set eye upon the pernicious and indubitate beggar Zenelophon; and he it was that might rightly say, Veni, vidi, vici; which to annothanize in the vulgar,—O base and obscure vulgar!—videlicet, He came, saw, and overcame: he came, one; saw, two; overcame, three. Who came? the king: why did he come? to see: why did he see? to overcome: to whom came he? to the beggar: what saw he? the beggar: who overcame he? the beggar. The conclusion is victory: on whose side? the king's. The captive is enriched: on whose side? the beggar's. The catastrophe is a nuptial: on whose side? the king's: no, on both in one, or one in both. I am the king; for so stands the comparison: thou the beggar; for so witnesseth thy lowliness. Shall I command thy love? I may: shall I enforce thy love? I could: shall I entreat thy love? I will. What shalt thou exchange for rags? robes; for tittles? titles; for thyself? me. Thus, expecting thy reply, I profane my lips on thy foot, my eyes on thy picture, and my heart on thy every part. Thine, in the dearest design of industry,

          Don Adriano de Armado.'
Thus dost thou hear the Nemean lion roar   90
   'Gainst thee, thou lamb, that standest as his prey.
Submissive fall his princely feet before,
   And he from forage will incline to play:
But if thou strive, poor soul, what art thou then?
Food for his rage, repasture for his den.
   Prin. What plume of feathers is he that indited this letter?
What vane? what weathercock? did you ever hear better?
   Boyet. I am much deceived but I remember the style.
   Prin. Else your memory is bad, going o'er it erewhile.
   Boyet. This Armado is a Spaniard, that keeps here in court;   100
A phantasime, a Monarcho, and one that makes sport
To the prince and his bookmates.
   Prin.   Thou fellow, a word:
Who gave thee this letter?
   Cost.   I told you; my lord.
   Prin. To whom shouldst thou give it?
   Cost.   From my lord to my lady.
   Prin. From which lord to which lady?
   Cost. From my lord Biron, a good master of mine,
To a lady of France that he call'd Rosaline.
   Prin. Thou hast mistaken his letter. Come, lords, away.
[*To Ros.*] Here, sweet, put up this: 'twill be thine
   another day.   [*Exeunt Princess and train.*

   Boyet. Who is the suitor? who is the suitor?
   Ros.   Shall I teach you to know?   110
   Boyet. Ay, my continent of beauty.
   Ros.   Why, she that bears the bow.
Finely put off!
   Boyet. My lady goes to kill horns; but, if thou marry,
Hang me by the neck, if horns that year miscarry.
Finely put on!
   Ros. Well, then, I am the shooter.
   Boyet.   And who is your deer?
   Ros. If we choose by the horns, yourself come not near.
Finely put on, indeed!
   Mar. You still wrangle with her, Boyet, and she strikes at the brow.
   Boyet. But she herself is hit lower: have I hit her now?   120
   Ros. Shall I come upon thee with an old saying, that was a man when King Pepin of France was a little boy, as touching the hit it?
   Boyet. So I may answer thee with one as old, that was a woman when Queen Guinover of Britain was a little wench, as touching the hit it.
   Ros.   Thou canst not hit it, hit it, hit it,
       Thou canst not hit it, my good man.
   Boyet. An I cannot, cannot, cannot,
       An I cannot, another can.   130
                [*Exeunt Ros. and Kath.*
   Cost. By my troth, most pleasant: how both did fit it!
   Mar. A mark marvellous well shot, for they both did hit it.
   Boyet. A mark! O, mark but that mark! A mark, says my lady!
Let the mark have a prick in 't, to mete at, if it may be.
   Mar. Wide o' the bow hand! i' faith, your hand is out.
   Cost. Indeed, a' must shoot nearer, or he'll ne'er hit the clout.
   Boyet. An if my hand be out, then belike your hand is in.
   Cost. Then will she get the upshoot by cleaving the pin.
   Mar. Come, come, you talk greasily; your lips grow foul.
   Cost. She 's too hard for you at pricks, sir: challenge her to bowl.   140
   Boyet. I fear too much rubbing. Good night, my good owl.   [*Exeunt Boyet and Maria.*
   Cost. By my soul, a swain! a most simple clown!
Lord, Lord, how the ladies and I have put him down!
O' my troth, most sweet jests! most incony vulgar wit!
When it comes so smoothly off, so obscenely, as it were, so fit.
Armado o' th' one side,—O, a most dainty man!

in horn books. 87. **profane**, desecrate, pollute; a frequent complimentary closing in letters to ladies was, "I kiss your hand." 89. **industry**, zeal; i.e., in her service; hence, gallantry. 90-95. **Thus ... den.** These lines represent the sonnet which Armado was devising above (I, ii, 190). 90. **Nemean lion.** One of Hercules' labors was to strangle the lion which infested the region of Nemea. 93. **forage**, raging, ravening; i.e., foraging. 95. **repasture**, food. 96. **What plume of feathers**, what kind of bird. 101. **phantasime**, fantastic creature. **Monarcho**, title assumed by an insane Italian who fancied himself the emperor of the world; hence applied to one who is the object of ridicule for his absurd pretensions (Onions). 110. **suitor**, a play on *shooter*, line 116, archer; the pronunciation was probably identical. The pun, a frequent one, gains point from Cupid's being an archer. 111. **continent**, summary, sum; see glossary. 119. **strikes ... brow**, takes good aim; i.e., strikes at the brow, antler. 120. **hit lower**, i.e., in the heart. 121. **come upon thee.** Rosaline continues the metaphor from hunting and marksmanship, which is the basis for much of the word-play of this passage. 122. **King Pepin**, a French king of the ninth century; Rosaline refers to the staleness of the saying. 123. **hit it**, catch or round to be sung dancing. 125-126. **Queen Guinover ... wench.** The name was not a respectable one because of this queen's liaison with Lancelot; there is a probable quibble in *wench* on the meanings "a young girl" and "a prostitute." 127-130. **Thou ... can**, words of the "hit it" mentioned above. Chappell gives the tune in his *Popular Music of the Olden Time.* 134. **prick**, spot in the center of the target, the bull's eye. **mete at**, measure with the eye; i.e., aim at. 135. **Wide ... hand**, wide of the mark on the left side; i.e., too far to the left. **out**, aimed the wrong way; see glossary. 136. **clout**, cloth marking the center of the target. 139. **greasily**, grossly. 141. **rubbing**, encountering obstacles; a bowling term; see glossary. 145. **obscenely**, another of Costard's malapropisms. 146. **dainty**, refined, elegant; see glossary.

To see him walk before a lady and to bear her fan!
To see him kiss his hand! and how most sweetly a'
    will swear!
And his page o' t'other side, that handful of wit!
Ah, heavens, it is a most pathetical nit!   150
Sola, sola!   [*Shout within.*
                      [*Exit Costard, running.*

SCENE II. *The same.*

Enter HOLOFERNES, SIR NATHANIEL, *and* DULL.

Nath. Very reverend sport, truly; and done in the testimony of a good conscience.

Hol. The deer was, as you know, sanguis, in blood; ripe as the pomewater, who now hangeth like a jewel in the ear of caelo, the sky, the welkin, the heaven; and anon falleth like a crab on the face of terra, the soil, the land, the earth.

Nath. Truly, Master Holofernes, the epithets are sweetly varied, like a scholar at the least: but, sir, I assure ye, it was a buck of the first head.   10

Hol. Sir Nathaniel, haud credo.

Dull. 'Twas not a haud credo; 'twas a pricket.

Hol. Most barbarous intimation! yet a kind of insinuation, as it were, in via, in way, of explication; facere, as it were, replication, or rather, ostentare, to show, as it were, his inclination, after his undressed, unpolished, uneducated, unpruned, untrained, or rather, unlettered, or ratherest, unconfirmed fashion, to insert again my haud credo for a deer.   20

Dull. I said the deer was not a haud credo; 'twas a pricket.

Hol. Twice-sod simplicity, bis coctus!
O thou monster Ignorance, how deformed dost thou
    look!

Nath. Sir, he hath never fed of the dainties that are
    bred in a book;
he hath not eat paper, as it were; he hath not drunk
ink: his intellect is not replenished; he is only an
animal, only sensible in the duller parts:
And such barren plants are set before us, that we
    thankful should be,
Which we of taste and feeling are, for those parts that
    do fructify in us more than he.   30
For as it would ill become me to be vain, indiscreet,
    or a fool,
So were there a patch set on learning, to see him in a
    school:
But omne bene, say I; being of an old father's mind,
Many can brook the weather that love not the wind.

Dull. You two are book-men: can you tell me by
    your wit

What was a month old at Cain's birth, that's not five
    weeks old as yet?

Hol. Dictynna, goodman Dull; Dictynna, goodman
    Dull.

Dull. What is Dictynna?

Nath. A title to Phœbe, to Luna, to the moon.

Hol. The moon was a month old when Adam was
    no more,   40
And raught not to five weeks when he came to five-
    score.
The allusion holds in the exchange.

Dull. 'Tis true indeed; the collusion holds in the
    exchange.

Hol. God comfort thy capacity! I say, the allusion holds in the exchange.

Dull. And I say, the pollution holds in the exchange; for the moon is never but a month old: and I say beside that, 'twas a pricket that the princess killed.   49

Hol. Sir Nathaniel, will you hear an extemporal epitaph on the death of the deer? And, to humour the ignorant, call I the deer the princess killed a pricket.

Nath. Perge, good Master Holofernes, perge; so it shall please you to abrogate scurrility.

Hol. I will something affect the letter, for it argues facility.
The preyful princess pierced and prick'd a pretty
    pleasing pricket;
Some say a sore; but not a sore, till now made sore
    with shooting.
The dogs did yell; put L to sore, then sorel jumps from
    thicket;   60
    Or pricket sore, or else sorel; the people fall
    a-hooting.
If sore be sore, then L to sore makes fifty sores one
    sorel.
Of one sore I an hundred make by adding but one
    more L.

Nath. A rare talent!

Dull. [*Aside*] If a talent be a claw, look how he claws him with a talent.

Hol. This is a gift that I have, simple, simple; a foolish extravagant spirit, full of forms, figures, shapes, objects, ideas, apprehensions, motions, revolutions: these are begot in the ventricle of memory, nourished in the womb of pia mater, and delivered upon the mellowing of occasion. But the gift is good in those in whom it is acute, and I am thankful for it.

Nath. Sir, I praise the Lord for you: and so may my parishioners; for their sons are well tutored by you, and their daughters profit very greatly under you: you are a good member of the commonwealth.   79

Hol. Mehercle, if their sons be ingenuous, they shall want no instruction; if their daughters be capable, I

150. **nit,** egg of a small insect; hence, anything very small, often contemptuously applied.
    Scene II. 4. **pomewater,** a kind of apple, large and juicy. 11. **haud credo,** I cannot believe it. 12. **pricket,** buck in its second year, or, as Nathaniel has already said, *a buck of the first head.* 23. **Twice-sod,** sodden. **bis coctus,** twice cooked, insipid. 28. **sensible,** capable of perception; see glossary. 32. **patch,** fool, dolt; i.e., setting a fool to learn. 33. **omne bene,** all well. **mind,** opinion; see glossary. 34. **Many . . . wind,** apparently a current but unidentified proverb. **brook,** endure; see glossary. 37, 39. **Dictynna, Phœbe, Luna,** classical names for the moon. The first is uncommon and is appropriate to the pedant. It occurs in Golding's Ovid, a book which Shakespeare knew. 41. **raught,** attained; an old past tense of "reach." 42. **allusion,** likening, application; or perhaps, jest—an obsolete meaning. **exchange,** change; the riddle usually appeared with Adam instead of Cain. 54. **Perge,** proceed. 56. **something,** somewhat; see

glossary. **affect the letter,** use alliteration. 59. **sore,** a buck in its fourth year. 60. **sorel,** a buck in its third year. 66. **claws,** flatters. 69. **motions,** impulses; see glossary. 71. **pia mater,** the brain. 80. **Mehercle,** a mild oath; probably a corruption of "By Hercules." 81. **want,** lack; see glossary. 82. **capable,** intelligent; see glossary. 82-83. **vir . . . loquitur,** he is a wise man who speaks little. 85, 86, 89. **pers-on, pierced,** Piercing. The pronunciation of the root syllables was probably identical. These are sometimes taken as allusions to Nashe's *Pierce Penniless, His Supplication to the Devil,* a fantastic satire in which the author, in the character of Pierce, comments on the vices of the times; also to Harvey's answer, *Pierce's Supererogation.* In the latter Pierce is referred to as "the hogges-head of witt"; cf. l. 89. 89-90. **lustre of conceit,** gleam of the intelligence. 95-97. **Fauste . . . Mantuan,** "Faustus, while the cattle chew their cud in the cool shade. . . ." This is the first line of the first eclogue of the Renaissance poet, Mantuan. It was no doubt familiar to every schoolboy. QF have *Facile* for *Fauste,* which was cor-

*Love's
Labour's Lost*
ACT IV : SC I

114

will put it to them: but vir sapit qui pauca loquitur; a soul feminine saluteth us.

Enter JAQUENETTA *and* COSTARD.

Jaq. God give you good morrow, master Parson.

Hol. Master Parson, *quasi* pers-on. An if one should be pierced, which is the one?

Cost. Marry, master schoolmaster, he that is likest to a hogshead.

Hol. Piercing a hogshead! a good lustre of conceit in a turf of earth; fire enough for a flint, pearl enough for a swine: 'tis pretty; it is well. 91

Jaq. Good master Parson, be so good as read me this letter: it was given me by Costard, and sent me from Don Armado: I beseech you, read it.

Hol. Fauste, precor gelida quando pecus omne sub umbra Ruminat,—and so forth. Ah, good old Mantuan! I may speak of thee as the traveller doth of Venice;

Venetia, Venetia,
Chi non ti vede non ti pretia. 100

Old Mantuan, old Mantuan! who understandeth thee not, loves thee not. Ut, re, sol, la, mi, fa. Under pardon, sir, what are the contents? or rather, as Horace says in his—What, my soul, verses?

Nath. Ay, sir, and very learned.

Hol. Let me hear a staff, a stanze, a verse; lege, domine.

Nath. [*reads*]

If love make me forsworn, how shall I swear to love?
Ah, never faith could hold, if not to beauty vow'd!
Though to myself forsworn, to thee I'll faithful prove;
Those thoughts to me were oaks, to thee like osiers bow'd. 112
Study his bias leaves and makes his book thine eyes,
Where all those pleasures live that art would comprehend:
If knowledge be the mark, to know thee shall suffice;
Well learned is that tongue that well can thee commend,
All ignorant that soul that sees thee without wonder;
Which is to me some praise that I thy parts admire:
Thy eye Jove's lightning bears, thy voice his dreadful thunder,
Which, not to anger bent, is music and sweet fire. 120
Celestial as thou art, O, pardon love this wrong,
That sings heaven's praise with such an earthly tongue.

Hol. You find not the apostraphas, and so miss the accent: let me supervise the canzonet. Here are only numbers ratified; but, for the elegancy, facility, and golden cadence of poesy, caret. Ovidius Naso was the man: and why, indeed, Naso, but for smelling out the odoriferous flowers of fancy, the jerks of invention?

Imitari is nothing: so doth the hound his master, the ape his keeper, the tired horse his rider. But, damosella virgin, was this directed to you?

Jaq. Ay, sir, from one Monsieur Biron, one of the strange queen's lords.

Hol. I will overglance the superscript: 'To the snow-white hand of the most beauteous Lady Rosaline.' I will look again on the intellect of the letter, for the nomination of the party writing to the person written unto: 'Your ladyship's in all desired employment, BIRON.' Sir Nathaniel, this Biron is one of the votaries with the king; and here he hath framed a letter to a sequent of the stranger queen's, which accidentally, or by the way of progression, hath miscarried. Trip and go, my sweet; deliver this paper into the royal hand of the king: it may concern much. Stay not thy compliment; I forgive thy duty: adieu.

Jaq. Good Costard, go with me. Sir, God save your life! 150

Cost. Have with thee, my girl. [*Exeunt Cost. and Jaq.*

Nath. Sir, you have done this in the fear of God, very religiously; and, as a certain father saith,—

Hol. Sir, tell not me of the father; I do fear colourable colours. But to return to the verses: did they please you, Sir Nathaniel?

Nath. Marvellous well for the pen.

Hol. I do dine to-day at the father's of a certain pupil of mine; where, if, before repast, it shall please you to gratify the table with a grace, I will, on my privilege I have with the parents of the foresaid child or pupil, undertake your ben venuto; where I will prove those verses to be very unlearned, neither savouring of poetry, wit, nor invention: I beseech your society.

Nath. And thank you too; for society, saith the text, is the happiness of life.

Hol. And, certes, the text most infallibly concludes it. [*To Dull*] Sir, I do invite you too; you shall not say me nay: pauca verba. Away! the gentles are at their game, and we will to our recreation. [*Exeunt.*

SCENE III. *The same.*

Enter BIRON, *with a paper.*

Biron. The king he is hunting the deer; I am coursing myself: they have pitched a toil; I am toiling in a pitch,—pitch that defiles: defile! a foul word. Well, set thee down, sorrow! for so they say the fool said, and so say I, and I the fool: well proved, wit! By the Lord, this love is as mad as Ajax: it kills sheep; it kills me, I a sheep: well proved again o' my side! I will not love: if I do, hang me; i' faith, I will not. O,

rected by Theobald. The correction is adopted by most editors, although some (notably the New Cambridge) retain the misquotation, thus impugning the pedant's Latin. 99-100. **Venetia . . . pretia**. Venice, Venice, who sees thee not esteems thee not. 102. **Ut . . . fa.** If Holofernes intends here to sing the hexachord, he displays his ignorance. 108. **lege, domine**, read, Master. 109-122. **If . . . tongue.** These lines were printed in *The Passionate Pilgrim* (1599), a collection of poems by various authors but attributed to Shakespeare. Two others of the volume are from this play, that read by Longaville (IV, iii, 60-73) and that by Dumain (IV, iii, 101-120). 113. **bias**, inclination or bent; i.e., the student leaves his special study; see glossary. 123. **apostrophas**, apostrophes, feigned addresses to an absent person or thing, or to an abstract idea. 124. **supervise**, glance over, peruse. 125. **only numbers ratified**, i.e., merely language made metrical, or perhaps merely conventional verse. The author of the "extemporal epitaph on the death of the deer" is criticizing Biron's lines for their lack of genuine poetic feeling. 127. **caret**, it is wanting. **Naso**, from Latin *nasus*, nose. 129. **invention**, the creative faculty; see glossary. **Imitari**, to imitate. 134. **strange**, foreign; see glossary. 135. **superscript**, address. 137. **intellect**, meaning, import; hence, contents. 142. **sequent**, follower, attendant. 143-144. **by . . . progression**, in process of delivery. 151. **Have with thee**, I'll go with you; see glossary. 156. **colourable colours**, plausible pretexts; probably a quibbling allusion to the "colors" of rhetoric; see glossary. 164. **ben venuto**, welcome. 171. **pauca verba**, few words. 172. **gentles**, gentle folk.

SCENE III. 2. **coursing**, pursuing. **pitched a toil**, set a snare. 3. **toiling . . . pitch**, generally taken as a quibbling reference to Rosaline's eyes, which he has earlier (III, i, 199) called *two pitch-balls*. 7. **mad as Ajax**, an allusion to the fable of Ajax, who, maddened by his failure in a contest for Achilles' armor, attacked a flock of sheep, supposing them to be a hostile army.

but her eye,—by this light, but for her eye, I would not love her; yes, for her two eyes. Well, I do nothing in the world but lie, and lie in my throat. By heaven, I do love: and it hath taught me to rhyme and to be melancholy; and here is part of my rhyme, and here my melancholy. Well, she hath one o' my sonnets already: the clown bore it, the fool sent it, and the lady hath it: sweet clown, sweeter fool, sweetest lady! By the world, I would not care a pin, if the other three were in. Here comes one with a paper: God give him grace to groan! [Stands aside. 21

Enter the King, *with a paper.*

King. Ay me!
Biron. [*Aside*] Shot, by heaven! Proceed, sweet Cupid: thou hast thumped him with thy bird-bolt under the left pap. In faith, secrets!
King [*reads*].
So sweet a kiss the golden sun gives not
To those fresh morning drops upon the rose,
As thy eye-beams, when their fresh rays have smote
    The night of dew that on my cheeks down flows:
Nor shines the silver moon one half so bright   30
    Through the transparent bosom of the deep,
As doth thy face through tears of mine give light;
    Thou shinest in every tear that I do weep:
No drop but as a coach doth carry thee;
    So ridest thou triumphing in my woe.
Do but behold the tears that swell in me,
    And they thy glory through my grief will show:
But do not love thyself; then thou wilt keep
My tears for glasses, and still make me weep.
O queen of queens! how far dost thou excel,   40
No thought can think, nor tongue of mortal tell.
How shall she know my griefs? I'll drop the paper:
Sweet leaves, shade folly. Who is he comes here?
                                [*Steps aside.*
What, Longaville! and reading! listen, ear.
    Biron. Now, in thy likeness, one more fool appear!

Enter Longaville, *with a paper.*

Long. Ay me, I am forsworn!
Biron. Why, he comes in like a perjure, wearing papers.
King. In love, I hope: sweet fellowship in shame!
Biron. One drunkard loves another of the name.   50
Long. Am I the first that have been perjured so?
Biron. I could put thee in comfort. Not by two that
    I know:
Thou makest the triumviry, the corner-cap of society,
The shape of Love's Tyburn that hangs up simplicity.
Long. I fear these stubborn lines lack power to
    move.
O sweet Maria, empress of my love!
These numbers will I tear, and write in prose.
Biron. O, rhymes are guards on wanton Cupid's
    hose:
Disfigure not his slop.
Long.   This same shall go.   [*Reads.*

Did not the heavenly rhetoric of thine eye,   60
    'Gainst whom the world cannot hold argument,
Persuade my heart to this false perjury?
Vows for thee broke deserve not punishment.
A woman I forswore; but I will prove,
    Thou being a goddess, I forswore not thee:
My vow was earthly, thou a heavenly love;
    Thy grace being gain'd cures all disgrace in me.
Vows are but breath, and breath a vapour is:
    Then thou, fair sun, which on my earth dost shine,
Exhalest this vapour-vow; in thee it is: 70
    If broken then, it is no fault of mine:
If by me broke, what fool is not so wise
To lose an oath to win a paradise?
Biron. This is the liver-vein, which makes flesh a
    deity,
A green goose a goddess: pure, pure idolatry.
God amend us, God amend! we are much out o' the
    way.
Long. By whom shall I send this?—Company! stay.
                                [*Steps aside.*
Biron. All hid, all hid; an old infant play.
Like a demigod here sit I in the sky,
And wretched fools' secrets heedfully o'er-eye.   80
More sacks to the mill! O heavens, I have my wish!

Enter Dumain, *with a paper.*

Dumain transform'd! four woodcocks in a dish!
Dum. O most divine Kate!
Biron. O most profane coxcomb!
Dum. By heaven, the wonder in a mortal eye!
Biron. By earth, she is not, corporal, there you lie.
Dum. Her amber hair for foul hath amber quoted.
Biron. An amber-colour'd raven was well noted.
Dum. As upright as the cedar.
Biron.   Stoop, I say;
Her shoulder is with child.
Dum.   As fair as day.   90
Biron. Ay, as some days; but then no sun must
    shine.
Dum. O that I had my wish!
Long.   And I had mine!
King. And I mine too, good Lord!
Biron. Amen, so I had mine: is not that a good
    word?
Dum. I would forget her; but a fever she
Reigns in my blood and will remember'd be.
Biron. A fever in your blood! why, then incision
Would let her out in saucers: sweet misprision!
Dum. Once more I'll read the ode that I have writ.
Biron. Once more I'll mark how love can vary wit.
Dum. [*reads*]
    On a day—alack the day!—   101
    Love, whose month is ever May,
    Spied a blossom passing fair
    Playing in the wanton air:
    Through the velvet leaves the wind,
    All unseen, can passage find;
    That the lover, sick to death,

47. **perjure,** perjurer.   48. **wearing papers,** an allusion to the custom of attaching to a felon's breast a description of his offense; there is a glance here at the poem Longaville is carrying.   54. **Tyburn,** a reference to the triangular gallows at Tyburn hill.   58. **guards,** bands on a garment.   59. **slop,** loose, baggy breeches; QF: *shop,* taken by some editors as an older pronunciation and spelling of "shape." 60-73. **Did . . . paradise.** Cf. IV, ii, 109-122, note.   74. **liver-vein,** the vein or style of a lover, since the liver was assumed to be the seat of the passion.   75. **green goose.** Cf. I, i, 97, note.   81. **More . . . mill,** a proverbial expression, "there's more to come."   82. **woodcocks,** birds

typifying stupidity.   85. **mortal,** human; see glossary.   86. **she . . . corporal.** Several explanations have been offered. Theobald emended to *she is but corporal,* a reading adopted by several editors. The New Cambridge editors define *corporal* as "champion," adding that in the sixteenth century there were four "corporals of the field" in every regiment. Note that in III, i, 189, Biron refers to himself as corporal of Cupid's field.   87. **quoted,** taken on.   89. **Stoop,** usually taken as the antithesis of *upright* in the preceding speech. Biron means that Dumain's language is too lofty.   90. **shoulder . . . child,** i.e., describing her posture. which is not as Dumain has said, *upright as the cedar.*   94. **is**

Wish himself the heaven's breath.
Air, quoth he, thy cheeks may blow;
Air, would I might triumph so!   110
But, alack, my hand is sworn
Ne'er to pluck thee from thy thorn;
Vow, alack, for youth unmeet,
Youth so apt to pluck a sweet!
Do not call it sin in me,
That I am forsworn for thee;
Thou for whom Jove would swear
Juno but an Ethiope were;
And deny himself for Jove,
Turning mortal for thy love.   120
This will I send and something else more plain,
That shall express my true love's fasting pain.
O, would the king, Biron, and Longaville,
Were lovers too! Ill, to example ill,
Would from my forehead wipe a perjured note;
For none offend where all alike do dote.
    Long. [*advancing*]. Dumain, thy love is far from
        charity,
That in love's grief desirest society:
You may look pale, but I should blush, I know,
To be o'erheard and taken napping so.   130
    King [*advancing*]. Come, sir, you blush; as his your
        case is such;
You chide at him, offending twice as much;
You do not love Maria; Longaville
Did never sonnet for her sake compile,
Nor never lay his wreathed arms athwart
His loving bosom to keep down his heart.
I have been closely shrouded in this bush
And mark'd you both and for you both did blush:
I heard your guilty rhymes, observed your fashion,
Saw sighs reek from you, noted well your passion: 140
Ay me! says one; O Jove! the other cries;
One, her hairs were gold, crystal the other's eyes:
[*To Long.*] You would for paradise break faith and
        troth;
[*To Dum.*] And Jove, for your love, would infringe
        an oath.
What will Biron say when that he shall hear
Faith so infringed, which such zeal did swear?
How will he scorn! how will he spend his wit!
How will he triumph, leap and laugh at it!
For all the wealth that ever I did see,
I would not have him know so much by me.   150
    Biron. Now step I forth to whip hypocrisy. [*Advancing.*
Ah, good my liege, I pray thee, pardon me!
Good heart, what grace hast thou, thus to reprove
These worms for loving, that art most in love?
Your eyes do make no coaches; in your tears
There is no certain princess that appears;
You'll not be perjured, 'tis a hateful thing;
Tush, none but minstrels like of sonneting!
But are you not ashamed? nay, are you not,
All three of you, to be thus much o'ershot?   160
You found his mote; the king your mote did see;
But I a beam do find in each of three.

O, what a scene of foolery have I seen,
Of sighs, of groans, of sorrow and of teen!
O me, with what strict patience have I sat,
To see a king transformed to a gnat!
To see great Hercules whipping a gig,
And profound Solomon to tune a jig,
And Nestor play at push-pin with the boys,
And critic Timon laugh at idle toys!   170
Where lies thy grief, O, tell me, good Dumain?
And, gentle Longaville, where lies thy pain?
And where my liege's? all about the breast:
A caudle, ho!
    King.   Too bitter is thy jest.
Are we betray'd thus to thy over-view?
    Biron. Not you to me, but I betray'd by you:
I, that am honest; I, that hold it sin
To break the vow I am engaged in;
I am betray'd, by keeping company
†With men like men of inconstancy.   180
When shall you see me write a thing in rhyme?
Or groan for love? or spend a minute's time
In pruning me? When shall you hear that I
Will praise a hand, a foot, a face, an eye,
A gait, a state, a brow, a breast, a waist,
A leg, a limb?
    King.   Soft! whither away so fast?
A true man or a thief that gallops so?
    Biron. I post from love: good lover, let me go.

Enter JAQUENETTA *and* COSTARD.

    Jaq. God bless the king!
    King.   What present hast thou there?
    Cost. Some certain treason.
    King.   What makes treason here?   190
    Cost. Nay, it makes nothing, sir.
    King.   If it mar nothing neither,
The treason and you go in peace away together.
    Jaq. I beseech your grace, let this letter be read:
Our parson misdoubts it; 'twas treason, he said.
    King. Biron, read it over.   [*Giving him the paper.*
Where hadst thou it?
    Jaq. Of Costard.
    King. Where hadst thou it?
    Cost. Of Dun Adramadio, Dun Adramadio.
                                [*Biron tears the letter.*
    King. How now! what is in you? why dost thou
        tear it?   200
    Biron. A toy, my liege, a toy: your grace needs not
        fear it.
    Long. It did move him to passion, and therefore
        let 's hear it.
    Dum. It is Biron's writing, and here is his name.
                                [*Gathering up the pieces.*
    Biron. [*To Costard*] Ah, you whoreson loggerhead!
        you were born to do me shame.
Guilty, my lord, guilty! I confess, I confess.
    King. What?
    Biron. That you three fools lack'd me fool to make
        up the mess:

. . . **word?** Is that not kind of me? (Hart). 97. **incision**, letting blood.
98. **saucers**, saucerfuls. **misprision**, mistake. 101-120. **On . . . love.**
Cf. IV, ii, 109-122, note. 124. **example ill**, furnish a bad example.
135-136. **wreathed . . . bosom**, a conventional pose of the lover. 140.
passion, amorous disposition. 145. **when that**, when. 155. **coaches**,
an allusion to the king's sonnet, where this conceit is employed (l.34).
160. **o'ershot**, wide of the mark; i.e., in error. 164. **teen**, affliction,
grief. 169. **Nestor**, a Greek chieftain in the Trojan War. The reference here is to his extreme old age and to his reputation for sagacity.
170. **Timon**, a citizen of Athens in the fifth century B.C., notorious

for his misanthropy. He is the central figure of Shakespeare's play,
Timon of Athens. **toys**, trifles; see glossary. 174. **caudle**, warm drink
given to sick people. 178. **engaged in**, sworn to; see *engage* in glossary.
180. **men like men**, a corrupt phrase for which there are many conjectures: *men-like men; men like you, men; moon-like men*; etc. 183. **pruning**, preening; i.e., trimming, dressing up. 188. **post**, hasten; see
glossary. 190. **makes treason**, has treason to do; see *make* in glossary.
194. **misdoubts**, suspects; see glossary.

He, he, and you, and you, my liege, and I,
Are pick-purses in love, and we deserve to die.
O, dismiss this audience, and I shall tell you more. 210
   Dum. Now the number is even.
   Biron.   True, true; we are four.
Will these turtles be gone?
   King.   Hence, sirs; away!
   Cost. Walk aside the true folk, and let the traitors
      stay.   [*Exeunt Costard and Jaquenetta.*
   Biron. Sweet lords, sweet lovers, O, let us embrace!
As true we are as flesh and blood can be:
The sea will ebb and flow, heaven show his face;
Young blood doth not obey an old decree:
We cannot cross the cause why we were born;
Therefore of all hands must we be forsworn.
   King. What, did these rent lines show some love of
      thine?   220
   Biron. Did they, quoth you? Who sees the heavenly
      Rosaline,
That, like a rude and savage man of Ind,
    At the first opening of the gorgeous east,
Bows not his vassal head and strucken blind
    Kisses the base ground with obedient breast?
What peremptory eagle-sighted eye
    Dares look upon the heaven of her brow,
That is not blinded by her majesty?
   King. What zeal, what fury hath inspired thee
      now?
My love, her mistress, is a gracious moon;   230
    She an attending star, scarce seen a light.
   Biron. My eyes are then no eyes, nor I Biron:
    O, but for my love, day would turn to night!
Of all complexions the cull'd sovereignty
    Do meet, as at a fair, in her fair cheek,
Where several worthies make one dignity,
    Where nothing wants that want itself doth seek.
Lend me the flourish of all gentle tongues,—
    Fie, painted rhetoric! O, she needs it not:
To things of sale a seller's praise belongs,   240
    She passes praise; then praise too short doth blot.
A wither'd hermit, five-score winters worn,
    Might shake off fifty, looking in her eye:
Beauty doth varnish age, as if new-born,
    And gives the crutch the cradle's infancy:
O, 'tis the sun that maketh all things shine.
   King. By heaven, thy love is black as ebony.
   Biron. Is ebony like her? O wood divine!
A wife of such wood were felicity.
O, who can give an oath? where is a book?   250
    That I may swear beauty doth beauty lack,
If that she learn not of her eye to look:
    No face is fair that is not full so black.
   King. O paradox! Black is the badge of hell,
    The hue of dungeons and the suit of night;
And beauty's crest becomes the heavens well.
   Biron. Devils soonest tempt, resembling spirits of
    light.

O, if in black my lady's brows be deck'd,
    It mourns that painting and usurping hair
Should ravish doters with a false aspect;   260
    And therefore is she born to make black fair.
Her favour turns the fashion of the days,
    For native blood is counted painting now;
And therefore red, that would avoid dispraise,
    Paints itself black, to imitate her brow.
   Dum. To look like her are chimney-sweepers black.
   Long. And since her time are colliers counted bright.
   King. And Ethiopes of their sweet complexion
    crack.
   Dum. Dark needs no candles now, for dark is light.
   Biron. Your mistresses dare never come in rain,   270
For fear their colours should be wash'd away.
   King. 'Twere good, yours did; for, sir, to tell you
    plain,
I'll find a fairer face not wash'd to-day.
   Biron. I'll prove her fair, or talk till doomsday here.
   King. No devil will fright thee then so much as she.
   Dum. I never knew man hold vile stuff so dear.
   Long. Look, here 's thy love: my foot and her face
    see.
   Biron. O, if the streets were paved with thine eyes,
Her feet were much too dainty for such tread!
   Dum. O vile! then, as she goes, what upward lies   280
The street should see as she walk'd overhead.
   King. But what of this? are we not all in love?
   Biron. Nothing so sure; and thereby all forsworn.
   King. Then leave this chat; and, good Biron, now
    prove
Our loving lawful, and our faith not torn.
   Dum. Ay, marry, there; some flattery for this evil.
   Long. O, some authority how to proceed;
Some tricks, some quillets, how to cheat the devil.
   Dum. Some salve for perjury.
   Biron.   'Tis more than need.
Have at you, then, affection's men at arms.   290
Consider what you first did swear unto,
To fast, to study, and to see no woman;
Flat treason 'gainst the kingly state of youth.
Say, can you fast? your stomachs are too young;
And abstinence engenders maladies.
And where that you have vow'd to study, lords,
In that each of you have forsworn his book,
Can you still dream and pore and thereon look?
For when would you, my lord, or you, or you,
Have found the ground of study's excellence   300
Without the beauty of a woman's face?
[From women's eyes this doctrine I derive;
They are the ground, the books, the academes
From whence doth spring the true Promethean fire.]
Why, universal plodding prisons up
The nimble spirits in the arteries,
As motion and long-during action tires
The sinewy vigour of the traveller.
Now, for not looking on a woman's face,

Love's
Labour's Lost
ACT IV : SC III

118

222. **Ind,** usually written "Inde," a very common name in the sixteenth century for India. 231. **scarce ... light,** a light scarcely to be
seen. 234. **cull'd,** chosen; i.e., the others are culls. 236. **worthies,**
excellencies. 241. **praise ... blot,** inadequate praise detracts. 255.
suit, QF: *Schoole*. Many emendations have been proposed: *scowl, stole,*
soul, soil, scroll, shroud, seal, etc. Those disposed to retain the original
reading think it may have a contemporary reference to an actual
group of poets or scholars known as the School of Night. 256. **beauty's**
crest, i.e., brightness. 262. **favour,** countenance; see glossary. 288.
quillets, verbal niceties, subtle distinctions; see glossary. 290. **Have**

at you, I come at you, i.e., listen to me; see glossary. 293. **state,** majesty; see glossary. 302-304. These lines seem out of place and repeti-
tive; regarded as evidence of revision. 304. **Promethean fire,** divine
fire, from the legend that Prometheus stole fire from heaven and gave
it to mankind; cf. *Othello*, V, ii, 12. 305. **prisons,** so Theobald; Globe,
following QF: *poisons*. 324. **entirely,** without intermission. 329.
elements, atmospheric agencies; see glossary. 336. **head of theft,**
i.e., ears of a thief. 354. **aught,** anything. 370. **glozes,** pretenses.
375. **attach,** seize; see glossary. 383. **Allons!** Let's be going! 384.
measure, proportion; see glossary. 385. **Light,** frivolous, merry; also

You have in that forsworn the use of eyes 310
And study too, the causer of your vow;
For where is any author in the world
Teaches such beauty as a woman's eye?
Learning is but an adjunct to ourself
And where we are our learning likewise is:
Then when ourselves we see in ladies' eyes,
Do we not likewise see our learning there?
O, we have made a vow to study, lords,
And in that vow we have forsworn our books.
For when would you, my liege, or you, or you, 320
In leaden contemplation have found out
Such fiery numbers as the prompting eyes
Of beauty's tutors have enrich'd you with?
Other slow arts entirely keep the brain;
And therefore, finding barren practisers,
Scarce show a harvest of their heavy toil:
But love, first learned in a lady's eyes,
Lives not alone immured in the brain;
But, with the motion of all elements,
Courses as swift as thought in every power, 330
And gives to every power a double power,
Above their functions and their offices.
It adds a precious seeing to the eye;
A lover's eyes will gaze an eagle blind;
A lover's ear will hear the lowest sound,
When the suspicious head of theft is stopp'd:
Love's feeling is more soft and sensible
Than are the tender horns of cockled snails;
Love's tongue proves dainty Bacchus gross in taste:
For valour, is not Love a Hercules, 340
Still climbing trees in the Hesperides?
Subtle as Sphinx; as sweet and musical
As bright Apollo's lute, strung with his hair;
And when Love speaks, the voice of all the gods
Make heaven drowsy with the harmony.
Never durst poet touch a pen to write
Until his ink were temper'd with Love's sighs;
O, then his lines would ravish savage ears
And plant in tyrants mild humility.
From women's eyes this doctrine I derive: 350
They sparkle still the right Promethean fire;
They are the books, the arts, the academes,
That show, contain and nourish all the world:
Else none at all in aught proves excellent.
Then fools you were these women to forswear,
Or keeping what is sworn, you will prove fools.
For wisdom's sake, a word that all men love,
Or for love's sake, a word that loves all men,
Or for men's sake, the authors of these women,
Or women's sake, by whom we men are men, 360
Let us once lose our oaths to find ourselves,
Or else we lose ourselves to keep our oaths.
It is religion to be thus forsworn,
For charity itself fulfils the law,
And who can sever love from charity?
  King. Saint Cupid, then! and, soldiers, to the field!

  Biron. Advance your standards, and upon them, lords;
Pell-mell, down with them! but be first advised,
In conflict that you get the sun of them.
  Long. Now to plain-dealing; lay these glozes by: 370
Shall we resolve to woo these girls of France?
  King. And win them too: therefore let us devise
Some entertainment for them in their tents.
  Biron. First, from the park let us conduct them thither;
Then homeward every man attach the hand
Of his fair mistress: in the afternoon
We will with some strange pastime solace them,
Such as the shortness of the time can shape;
For revels, dances, masks and merry hours
Forerun fair Love, strewing her way with flowers. 380
  King. Away, away! no time shall be omitted
That will betime, and may by us be fitted.
  Biron. Allons! allons! Sow'd cockle reap'd no corn;
And justice always whirls in equal measure:
Light wenches may prove plagues to men forsworn;
If so, our copper buys no better treasure.   [*Exeunt.*

ACT V.

SCENE I. *The same.*

Enter HOLOFERNES, SIR NATHANIEL, *and* DULL.

  Hol. Satis quid sufficit.
  Nath. I praise God for you, sir: your reasons at dinner have been sharp and sententious: pleasant without scurrility, witty without affection, audacious without impudency, learned without opinion, and strange without heresy. I did converse this quondam day with a companion of the king's, who is intituled, nominated, or called, Don Adriano de Armado. 9
  Hol. Novi hominem tanquam te: his humour is lofty, his discourse peremptory, his tongue filed, his eye ambitious, his gait majestical, and his general behaviour vain, ridiculous, and thrasonical. He is too picked, too spruce, too affected, too odd, as it were, too peregrinate, as I may call it.
  Nath. A most singular and choice epithet. 17
          [*Draws out his table-book.*
  Hol. He draweth out the thread of his verbosity finer than the staple of his argument. I abhor such fanatical phantasimes, such insociable and point-devise companions; such rackers of orthography, as to speak dout, fine, when he should say doubt; det, when he should pronounce debt,—d, e, b, t, not d, e, t: he clepeth a calf, cauf; half, hauf; neighbour vocatur nebour; neigh abbreviated ne. This is abhominable,—which he would call abbominable: it insinuateth †me of insanie: ne intelligis, domine? to make frantic, lunatic.
  Nath. Laus Deo, bene intelligo. 30

wanton, with quibble.
  ACT V. SCENE I. 1. **quid,** so QF; Globe, following Rowe and others in correcting the pedant's faulty Latin: *quod.* The phrase is the equivalent of the proverb, "Enough is as good as a feast." 6. **opinion,** self-conceit, arrogance; see glossary. 7. **this quondam,** the other. 10. **Novi . . . te,** I know the man as well as I know you. 11. **peremptory,** positive, overbearing. 12. **filed,** polished. 14. **thrasonical,** boastful. 15. **peregrinate,** having the manner of one who has traveled. 17. *Stage Direction: table-book,* notebook. 21. **point-devise,** extremely precise. **companions,** fellows (used contemptuously); see glossary.

21-22. **rackers of orthography.** Holofernes' tirade represents a conscious attempt of Renaissance educators to conform the English spelling and pronunciation of certain borrowed words more nearly to their Latin originals. 22. **fine,** mincingly. 26. **abhominable.** Here Holofernes' pedantry has run aground; the word is derived from the Latin *ab + omen* (a foreboding) and not from *ab + homine.* 28. **ne,** so QF; Globe: *anne.* **ne . . . domine?** Do you understand, Master? 30. **Laus . . . intelligo,** praise God, I understand well.

Hol. Bon, bon, fort bon! Priscian a little scratched, 'twill serve.

Nath. Videsne quis venit?

Hol. Video, et gaudeo.

Enter ARMADO, MOTH, *and* COSTARD.

Arm. Chirrah! [*To Moth.*

Hol. Quare chirrah, not sirrah?

Arm. Men of peace, well encountered.

Hol. Most military sir, salutation.

Moth. [*Aside to Costard*] They have been at a great feast of languages, and stolen the scraps. 40

Cost. O, they have lived long on the alms-basket of words. I marvel thy master hath not eaten thee for a word; for thou art not so long by the head as honorificabilitudinitatibus: thou art easier swallowed than a flap-dragon.

Moth. Peace! the peal begins.

Arm. [*To Hol.*] Monsieur, are you not lettered?

Moth. Yes, yes; he teaches boys the horn-book. What is a, b, spelt backward, with the horn on his head? 51

Hol. Ba, pueritia, with a horn added.

Moth. Ba, most silly sheep with a horn. You hear his learning.

Hol. Quis, quis, thou consonant?

Moth. The third of the five vowels, if you repeat them; or the fifth, if I.

Hol. I will repeat them,—a, e, i,—

Moth. The sheep: the other two concludes it,— o, u. 60

Arm. Now, by the salt wave of the Mediterraneum, a sweet touch, a quick venue of wit! snip, snap, quick and home! it rejoiceth my intellect: true wit!

Moth. Offered by a child to an old man; which is wit-old.

Hol. What is the figure? what is the figure?

Moth. Horns.

Hol. Thou disputest like an infant: go, whip thy gig. 70

Moth. Lend me your horn to make one, and I will whip about your infamy circum circa,—a gig of a cuckold's horn.

Cost. An I had but one penny in the world, thou shouldst have it to buy gingerbread: hold, there is the very remuneration I had of thy master, thou halfpenny purse of wit, thou pigeon-egg of discretion. O, an the heavens were so pleased that thou wert but my bastard, what a joyful father wouldst thou make me! Go to; thou hast it ad dunghill, at the fingers' ends, as they say.

Hol. O, I smell false Latin; dunghill for unguem.

Arm. Arts-man, preambulate, we will be singuled from the barbarous. Do you not educate youth

at the charge-house on the top of the mountain?

Hol. Or mons, the hill.

Arm. At your sweet pleasure, for the mountain.

Hol. I do, sans question. 91

Arm. Sir, it is the king's most sweet pleasure and affection to congratulate the princess at her pavilion in the posteriors of this day, which the rude multitude call the afternoon.

Hol. The posterior of the day, most generous sir, is liable, congruent and measurable for the afternoon: the word is well culled, chose, sweet and apt, I do assure you, sir, I do assure. 99

Arm. Sir, the king is a noble gentleman, and my familiar, I do assure ye, very good friend: for what is inward between us, let it pass. I do beseech thee, remember thy courtesy; I beseech thee, apparel thy head: and among other importunate and most serious designs, and of great import indeed, too, but let that pass: for I must tell thee, it will please his grace, by the world, sometime to lean upon my poor shoulder, and with his royal finger, thus, dally with my excrement, with my mustachio; but, sweet heart, let that pass. By the world, I recount no fable: some certain special honours it pleaseth his greatness to impart to Armado, a soldier, a man of travel, that hath seen the world; but let that pass. The very all of all is,—but, sweet heart, I do implore secrecy,—that the king would have me present the princess, sweet chuck, with some delightful ostentation, or show, or pageant, or antique, or firework. Now, understanding that the curate and your sweet self are good at such eruptions and sudden breaking out of mirth, as it were, I have acquainted you withal, to the end to crave your assistance. 123

Hol. Sir, you shall present before her the Nine Worthies. Sir, as concerning some entertainment of time, some show in the posterior of this day, to be rendered by our assistants, at the king's command, and this most gallant, illustrate, and learned gentleman, before the princess; I say none so fit as to present the Nine Worthies. 130

Nath. Where will you find men worthy enough to present them?

Hol. †Joshua, yourself; myself and this gallant gentleman, Judas Maccabæus; this swain, because of his great limb or joint, shall pass Pompey the Great; the page, Hercules,—

Arm. Pardon, sir; error: he is not quantity enough for that Worthy's thumb: he is not so big as the end of his club. 139

Hol. Shall I have audience? he shall present Hercules in minority: his enter and exit shall be strangling a snake; and I will have an apology for that purpose.

Moth. An excellent device! so, if any of the audience hiss, you may cry 'Well done, Hercules! now thou

---

31. **Bon . . . Priscian.** QF: *Bome boon for boon prescian.* There are several suggested emendations. Theobald's *Bone? bone for bene* calls for emending *bene* to *bone* in the preceding speech. This reading has been favored by some editors. **Priscian,** a grammarian; Holofernes means, "Your Latin is a little faulty." 33. **Videsne quis venit?** Do you see who comes? 34. **Video, et gaudeo,** I see and I rejoice. This trivial Latin dialogue is after the manner of schoolboys' exercises. 36. **Quare,** why. 44. **honorificabilitudinitatibus,** reputably the longest known word. It is an inflected form of a genuine medieval Latin word, meaning something like "honorableness." 45. **flap-dragon,** the raisin or plum in burning brandy to be snapped with the mouth in the game of snapdragon. 52. **pueritia,** boyhood. 55. **Quis,** who. 62. **venue,** a thrust in fencing. 63. **home,** effectually, to the quick; see glossary. 66. **wit-old,** mentally feeble, with quibble on "wittol," a cuckold. 69. **disputest, reasonest;** see glossary. 72. **circum circa,** round and round; Theobald's emendation of QF *vnum cita,*

which has not been satisfactorily explained. Perhaps Furness is right in assuming that it is a fragment of schoolboy nonsense rhyme. 84. **unguem.** *Ad unguem* (to a nicety, perfectly) were the last words of a proverbial expression used of a lesson well learned; probably recited to schoolboys by their masters. It is not unlikely that we have in *ad dunghill* a schoolboys' perversion of the phrase. 85. **singuled,** singled out. 87. **charge-house,** a reference not identified. Hart suggests that it may mean a school where children were taught at the expense of the parish, or merely a school for their charge or care. 91. **sans,** without; see glossary. 105. **importunate,** so Q_2Ff; Globe: *important,* following Capell's rendering of Q_1: *important.* 109. **excrement,** outgrowth (of hair). 117. **chuck,** i.e., chick, a term of endearment. 118. **pageant,** spectacular entertainment; see glossary. 124. **Nine Worthies,** a conventional subject familiar to Shakespeare's audience in poems, pageants, and tapestries. The nine were three pagans, Hector of Troy, Alexander the Great, and Julius Caesar; three Jews, Joshua, David, and

crushest the snake!' that is the way to make an offence
gracious, though few have the grace to do it.

Arm. For the rest of the Worthies?—

Hol. I will play three myself. 150

Moth. Thrice-worthy gentleman!

Arm. Shall I tell you a thing?

Hol. We attend.

Arm. We will have, if this fadge not, an antique. I
beseech you, follow.

Hol. Via, goodman Dull! thou hast spoken no word
all this while.

Dull. Nor understood none neither, sir.

Hol. Allons! we will employ thee.

Dull. I'll make one in a dance, or so; or I will play
On the tabor to the Worthies, and let them dance the
  hay. 161

Hol. Most dull, honest Dull! To our sport, away!

[*Exeunt.*

SCENE II. *The same.*

Enter the Princess, KATHARINE, ROSALINE, *and*
MARIA.

Prin. Sweet hearts, we shall be rich ere we depart,
If fairings come thus plentifully in:
A lady wall'd about with diamonds!
Look you what I have from the loving king.

Ros. Madame, came nothing else along with that?

Prin. Nothing but this! yes, as much love in rhyme
As would be cramm'd up in a sheet of paper,
Writ o' both sides the leaf, margent and all,
That he was fain to seal on Cupid's name.

Ros. That was the way to make his godhead wax, 10
For he hath been five thousand years a boy.

Kath. Ay, and a shrewd unhappy gallows too.

Ros. You'll ne'er be friends with him; a' kill'd your
  sister.

Kath. He made her melancholy, sad, and heavy;
And so she died: had she been light, like you,
Of such a merry, nimble, stirring spirit,
She might ha' been a grandam ere she died:
And so may you; for a light heart lives long.

Ros. What's your dark meaning, mouse, of this light
  word?

Kath. A light condition in a beauty dark. 20

Ros. We need more light to find your meaning out.

Kath. You'll mar the light by taking it in snuff;
Therefore I'll darkly end the argument.

Ros. Look, what you do, you do it still i' the dark.

Kath. So do not you, for you are a light wench.

Ros. Indeed I weigh not you, and therefore light.

Kath. You weigh me not? O, that's you care not for
  me.

Ros. Great reason; for 'past cure is still past care.'

Prin. Well bandied both; a set of wit well play'd.
But, Rosaline, you have a favour too: 30
Who sent it? and what is it?

Ros. I would you knew:
An if my face were but as fair as yours,
My favour were as great; be witness this.
Nay, I have verses too, I thank Biron:
The numbers true; and, were the numbering too,
I were the fairest goddess on the ground:
I am compared to twenty thousand fairs.
O, he hath drawn my picture in his letter!

Prin. Any thing like?

Ros. Much in the letters; nothing in the praise. 40

Prin. Beauteous as ink; a good conclusion.

Kath. Fair as a text B in a copy-book.

Ros. 'Ware pencils, ho! let me not die your debtor,
My red dominical, my golden letter:
O that your face were not so full of O's!

Kath. A pox of that jest! and I beshrew all shrows.

Prin. But, Katharine, what was sent to you from fair
  Dumain?

Kath. Madam, this glove.

Prin. Did he not send you twain?

Kath. Yes, madam, and moreover
Some thousand verses of a faithful lover, 50
A huge translation of hypocrisy,
Vilely compiled, profound simplicity.

Mar. This and these pearls to me sent Longaville:
The letter is too long by half a mile.

Prin. I think no less. Dost thou not wish in heart
The chain were longer and the letter short?

Mar. Ay, or I would these hands might never part.

Prin. We are wise girls to mock our lovers so.

Ros. They are worse fools to purchase mocking so.
That same Biron I'll torture ere I go: 60
O that I knew he were but in by the week!
How I would make him fawn and beg and seek
And wait the season and observe the times
And spend his prodigal wits in bootless rhymes
And shape his service wholly to my hests
And make him proud to make me proud that jests!
†So perttaunt-like would I o'ersway his state
That he should be my fool and I his fate.

Prin. None are so surely caught, when they are
  catch'd,
As wit turn'd fool: folly, in wisdom hatch'd, 70
Hath wisdom's warrant and the help of school
And wit's own grace to grace a learned fool.

Ros. The blood of youth burns not with such excess
As gravity's revolt to wantonness.

Mar. Folly in fools bears not so strong a note
As foolery in the wise, when wit doth dote;
Since all the power thereof it doth apply

Judas Maccabaeus; and three Christians, Arthur, Charlemagne, and
Godfrey of Bouillon. Shakespeare does not adhere to this list but introduces Pompey and Hercules. 130. **present,** represent; see glossary.
142. **strangling a snake.** According to legend, Hercules as an infant displayed his great strength by strangling two serpents sent by the envious
Juno to destroy him in his cradle. 154. **fadge,** fit, be suitable. 156.
Via, an interjection of encouragement, used by commanders to their
troops and by riders to their horses. 161. **the hay,** a country dance.
  SCENE II. 2. **fairings,** complimentary gifts. 10. **wax,** increase,
with quibble on the noun. 12. **shrewd,** bad; see glossary. **unhappy,**
ill-fated; see glossary. **gallows,** one deserving to be hanged. 19.
mouse, term of endearment. 20. **condition,** disposition, temperament;
see glossary. 22. **taking . . . snuff,** taking offense, with quibble on
snuff, a burning candlewick. 44. **dominical,** from the Latin *dies domin-
ica* (Lord's day). It is customary in ecclesiastical calendars (see, for
example, the *Book of Common Prayer*) to designate the day in January
on which the first Sunday falls by one of the first seven letters of the
alphabet—*A* when it falls on New Year's Day, *B* when it falls on the
second, etc., up to *G*. This is called the dominical letter for the year.
It was often printed in red and gold on church calendars to denote
Sundays. Here it refers quibblingly to Katharine's fair complexion.
46. **beshrew,** curse, blame; see glossary. **shrows,** shrews. 57. **Ay . . .
part.** This speech is probably accompanied by some stage business
with the chain that Maria is handling. 61. **in . . . week,** caught,
trapped; contemporary uses of the phrase indicate that it may imply
conditions of servitude or imprisonment. (See Furness Variorum.) 67.
perttaunt-like, so Q; of the many emendations suggested, *planet-like*
(New Cambridge) is the most convincing; Hanmer's *portent-like* deserves
consideration.

To prove, by wit, worth in simplicity.
Prin. Here comes Boyet, and mirth is in his face.

Enter BOYET.

Boyet. O, I am stabb'd with laughter! Where 's her
    grace? 80
Prin. Thy news, Boyet?
Boyet.   Prepare, madam, prepare!
Arm, wenches, arm! encounters mounted are
Against your peace: Love doth approach disguised,
Armed in arguments; you'll be surprised:
Muster your wits; stand in your own defence;
Or hide your heads like cowards, and fly hence.
    Prin. Saint Denis to Saint Cupid! What are they
That charge their breath against us? say, scout, say.
    Boyet. Under the cool shade of a sycamore
I thought to close mine eyes some half an hour; 90
When, lo! to interrupt my purposed rest,
Toward that shade I might behold addrest
The king and his companions: warily
I stole into a neighbour thicket by,
And overheard what you shall overhear;
That, by and by, disguised they will be here.
Their herald is a pretty knavish page,
That well by heart hath conn'd his embassage:
Action and accent did they teach him there;
'Thus must thou speak,' and 'thus thy body bear:' 100
And ever and anon they made a doubt
Presence majestical would put him out;
'For,' quoth the king, 'an angel shalt thou see;
Yet fear not thou, but speak audaciously.'
The boy replied, 'An angel is not evil;
I should have fear'd her had she been a devil.'
With that, all laugh'd and clapp'd him on the
    shoulder,
Making the bold wag by their praises bolder:
One rubb'd his elbow thus, and fleer'd and swore
A better speech was never spoke before; 110
Another, with his finger and his thumb,
Cried, 'Via! we will do 't, come what will come;'
The third he caper'd, and cried, 'All goes well;'
The fourth turn'd on the toe, and down he fell.
With that, they all did tumble on the ground,
With such a zealous laughter, so profound,
That in this spleen ridiculous appears,
To check their folly, passion's solemn tears.
    Prin. But what, but what, come they to visit us?
    Boyet. They do, they do; and are apparell'd thus, 120
Like Muscovites or Russians, as I guess.
Their purpose is to parle, to court and dance;
And every one his love-feat will advance
Unto his several mistress, which they'll know
By favours several which they did bestow.
    Prin. And will they so? the gallants shall be task'd;
For, ladies, we will every one be mask'd;
And not a man of them shall have the grace,
Despite of suit, to see a lady's face.
Hold, Rosaline, this favour thou shalt wear, 130
And then the king will court thee for his dear;
Hold, take thou this, my sweet, and give me thine,

So shall Biron take me for Rosaline.
And change you favours too; so shall your loves
Woo contrary, deceived by these removes.
    Ros. Come on, then; wear the favours most in sight.
    Kath. But in this changing what is your intent?
    Prin. The effect of my intent is to cross theirs:
They do it but in mockery-merriment;
And mock for mock is only my intent. 140
Their several counsels they unbosom shall
To loves mistook, and so be mock'd withal
Upon the next occasion that we meet,
With visages display'd, to talk and greet.
    Ros. But shall we dance, if they desire us to 't?
    Prin. No, to the death, we will not move a foot;
Nor to their penn'd speech render we no grace,
But while 'tis spoke each turn away her face.
    Boyet. Why, that contempt will kill the speaker's
    heart,
And quite divorce his memory from his part. 150
    Prin. Therefore I do it; and I make no doubt
The rest will ne'er come in, if he be out.
There 's no such sport as sport by sport o'erthrown,
To make theirs ours and ours none but our own:
So shall we stay, mocking intended game,
And they, well mock'd, depart away with shame.
                  [*Trumpets sound within.*
    Boyet. The trumpet sounds: be mask'd; the maskers
    come.   [*The Ladies mask.*

Enter Blackamoors with music; MOTH; *the* King, BIRON,
LONGAVILLE, *and* DUMAIN, *in Russian habits, and
masked.*

    Moth. All hail, the richest beauties on the earth!—
    Boyet. Beauties no richer than rich taffeta.
    Moth. A holy parcel of the fairest dames 160
           [*The Ladies turn their backs to him.*
That ever turn'd their—backs—to mortal views!
    Biron. [*Aside to Moth*] Their eyes, villain, their eyes.
    Moth. That ever turn'd their eyes to mortal views!—
Out—
    Boyet. True; out indeed.
    Moth. Out of your favours, heavenly spirits,
    vouchsafe
Not to behold—
    Biron. [*Aside to Moth*] Once to behold, rogue.
    Moth. Once to behold with your sun-beamed eyes,
——with your sun-beamed eyes—
    Boyet. They will not answer to that epithet; 170
You were best call it 'daughter-beamed eyes.'
    Moth. They do not mark me, and that brings me
    out.
    Biron. Is this your perfectness? be gone, you rogue!
                        [*Exit Moth.*
    Ros. What would these strangers? know their minds,
    Boyet:
If they do speak our language, 'tis our will
That some plain man recount their purposes:
Know what they would.
    Boyet. What would you with the princess?
    Biron. Nothing but peace and gentle visitation.

82. **encounters,** encounterers. **mounted,** raised; the figure implied
is of an artillery attack; cf. *charge,* l. 88. 87. **Saint Denis,** patron saint
of France. 92. **might,** could; see *may* in glossary. **addrest,** directed.
95. **overhear,** hear over again. 98. **embassage,** message. 101. **made
a doubt,** were apprehensive; see *doubt* in glossary. 117. **spleen ridiculous,** foolish impulse. 121. **Muscovites or Russians,** costumes not
uncommon in court masquerades. 122. **parle,** parley; see glossary.
126. **task'd,** tried, tested. 129. **suit,** petition, entreaty. 135. **removes,**

removals, changes; see glossary. 136. **most in sight,** conspicuously.
139. **mockery-merriment,** so Q; Globe, following F: *mocking merriment.* 141. **counsels,** private intentions, secret purposes. 144. **greet,**
be amicably together (Schmidt). 152. **if . . . out,** if he be confused
or annoyed. 159. **taffeta,** i.e., their masks of taffeta. 160. **parcel,**
small party or company. 174. **What would,** etc. Rosaline, masked as
the princess, presides over the occasion. 184. **measured,** traversed,
with quibble; see glossary. 200. **accompt,** reckoning. 206. **eyne,** eyes;

Ros. What would they, say they? 180
Boyet. Nothing but peace and gentle visitation.
Ros. Why, that they have; and bid them so be gone.
Boyet. She says, you have it, and you may be gone.
King. Say to her, we have measured many miles
To tread a measure with her on this grass.
Boyet. They say, that they have measured many a
mile
To tread a measure with you on this grass.
Ros. It is not so. Ask them how many inches
Is in one mile: if they have measured many,
The measure then of one is easily told. 190
Boyet. If to come hither you have measured miles,
And many miles, the princess bids you tell
How many inches doth fill up one mile.
Biron. Tell her, we measure them by weary steps.
Boyet. She hears herself.
Ros. How many weary steps,
Of many weary miles you have o'ergone,
Are number'd in the travel of one mile?
Biron. We number nothing that we spend for you:
Our duty is so rich, so infinite,
That we may do it still without accompt. 200
Vouchsafe to show the sunshine of your face,
That we, like savages, may worship it.
Ros. My face is but a moon, and clouded too.
King. Blessed are clouds, to do as such clouds do!
Vouchsafe, bright moon, and these thy stars, to shine,
Those clouds removed, upon our watery eyne.
Ros. O vain petitioner! beg a greater matter;
Thou now request'st but moonshine in the water.
King. Then, in our measure do but vouchsafe one
change.
Thou bid'st me beg: this begging is not strange. 210
Ros. Play, music, then! Nay, you must do it soon.
[*Music plays.*
Not yet! no dance! Thus change I like the moon.
King. Will you not dance? How come you thus
estranged?
Ros. You took the moon at full, but now she's
changed.
King. Yet still she is the moon, and I the man.
The music plays; vouchsafe some motion to it.
Ros. Our ears vouchsafe it.
King. But your legs should do it.
Ros. Since you are strangers and come here by
chance,
We'll not be nice: take hands. We will not dance.
King. Why take we hands, then?
Ros. Only to part friends: 220
Curtsy, sweet hearts; and so the measure ends.
King. More measure of this measure; be not nice.
Ros. We can afford no more at such a price.
King. Prize you yourselves: what buys your
company?
Ros. Your absence only.
King. That can never be.
Ros. Then cannot we be bought: and so, adieu;
Twice to your visor, and half once to you.
King. If you deny to dance, let's hold more chat.

Ros. In private, then.
King. I am best pleased with that.
[*They converse apart.*
Biron. White-handed mistress, one sweet word with
thee. 230
Prin. Honey, and milk, and sugar; there is three.
Biron. Nay then, two treys, and if you grow so nice,
Metheglin, wort, and malmsey: well run, dice!
There's half-a-dozen sweets.
Prin. Seventh sweet, adieu:
Since you can cog, I'll play no more with you.
Biron. One word in secret.
Prin. Let it not be sweet.
Biron. Thou grievest my gall.
Prin. Gall! bitter.
Biron. Therefore meet. [*They converse apart.*
Dum. Will you vouchsafe with me to change a word?
Mar. Name it.
Dum. Fair lady,—
Mar. Say you so? Fair lord,—
Take that for your fair lady.
Dum. Please it you, 240
As much in private, and I'll bid adieu.
[*They converse apart.*
Kath. What, was your vizard made without a
tongue?
Long. I know the reason, lady, why you ask.
Kath. O for your reason! quickly, sir; I long.
Long. You have a double tongue within your mask,
And would afford my speechless vizard half.
Kath. Veal, quoth the Dutchman. Is not 'veal' a
calf?
Long. A calf, fair lady!
Kath. No, a fair lord calf.
Long. Let's part the word.
Kath. No, I'll not be your half:
Take all, and wean it; it may prove an ox. 250
Long. Look, how you butt yourself in these sharp
mocks!
Will you give horns, chaste lady? do not so.
Kath. Then die a calf, before your horns do grow.
Long. One word in private with you, ere I die.
Kath. Bleat softly then; the butcher hears you cry.
[*They converse apart.*
Boyet. The tongues of mocking wenches are as keen
As is the razor's edge invisible,
Cutting a smaller hair than may be seen,
Above the sense of sense; so sensible
Seemeth their conference; their conceits have wings
Fleeter than arrows, bullets, wind, thought, swifter
things. 261
Ros. Not one word more, my maids; break off, break
off.
Biron. By heaven, all dry-beaten with pure scoff!
King. Farewell, mad wenches; you have simple wits.
Prin. Twenty adieus, my frozen Muscovits.
[*Exeunt King, Lords, and Blackamoors.*
Are these the breed of wits so wonder'd at?
Boyet. Tapers they are, with your sweet breaths
puff'd out.

archaic plural. **208. moonshine in the water,** proverbial expression
for a waste of time. **209. change,** round in dancing (Schmidt). **227.
Twice . . . you.** Rosaline means her courtesy is not given to the king,
for whom she has none to spare; but to the mask which is identical
with Biron's (Hart). **228. deny,** refuse; see glossary. **233. Metheglin,**
a spiced drink made from herbs and honey. **wort,** sweet unfermented
beer. **malmsey,** a strong sweet wine. **235. cog,** cheat; see glossary.
247. Veal, quibble on the Dutch pronunciation of "well" and the meaning "calf" (Schmidt); also, possibly, "dunce"; the Cambridge editors
took *Dutchman* to mean German and *veal* to be equivalent to German *viel,*
i.e., much. The word is introduced irrelevantly for the sake of the subsequent word-play. **259. Above . . . sense,** quibble on the meanings
"mental" and "physical perception"; see *sense* in glossary. **263. dry-
beaten,** beaten soundly without blood drawn. **264. simple,** common,
not distinguished by any excellence.

Ros. Well-liking wits they have; gross, gross; fat, fat.
Prin. O poverty in wit, kingly-poor flout!
Will they not, think you, hang themselves to-night? 270
  Or ever, but in vizards, show their faces?
This pert Biron was out of countenance quite.
Ros. O, they were all in lamentable cases!
The king was weeping-ripe for a good word.
Prin. Biron did swear himself out of all suit.
Mar. Dumain was at my service, and his sword:
No point, quoth I; my servant straight was mute.
Kath. Lord Longaville said, I came o'er his heart;
And trow you what he call'd me?
Prin.   Qualm, perhaps.
Kath. Yes, in good faith.
Prin.   Go, sickness as thou art! 280
Ros. Well, better wits have worn plain statute-caps.
But will you hear? the king is my love sworn.
Prin. And quick Biron hath plighted faith to me.
Kath. And Longaville was for my service born.
Mar. Dumain is mine, as sure as bark on tree.
Boyet. Madam, and pretty mistresses, give ear:
Immediately they will again be here
In their own shapes; for it can never be
They will digest this harsh indignity.
Prin. Will they return?
Boyet.   They will, they will, God knows,
And leap for joy, though they are lame with blows: 291
Therefore change favours; and, when they repair,
Blow like sweet roses in this summer air.
Prin. How blow? how blow? speak to be understood.
Boyet. Fair ladies mask'd are roses in their bud;
Dismask'd, their damask sweet commixture shown,
Are angels vailing clouds, or roses blown.
Prin. Avaunt, perplexity! What shall we do,
If they return in their own shapes to woo?
Ros. Good madam, if by me you 'll be advised, 300
Let 's mock them still, as well known as disguised:
Let us complain to them what fools were here,
Disguised like Muscovites, in shapeless gear;
And wonder what they were and to what end
Their shallow shows and prologue vilely penn'd
And their rough carriage so ridiculous,
Should be presented at our tent to us.
Boyet. Ladies, withdraw: the gallants are at hand.
Prin. Whip to our tents, as roes run o'er land.

  [*Exeunt Princess, Rosaline, Katharine, and Maria.*

Re-enter the King, BIRON, LONGAVILLE, *and*
DUMAIN, *in their proper habits.*

King. Fair sir, God save you! Where 's the princess?
Boyet. Gone to her tent. Please it your majesty 311
Command me any service to her thither?
King. That she vouchsafe me audience for one word.
Boyet. I will; and so will she, I know, my lord. [*Exit.*
Biron. This fellow pecks up wit as pigeons pease,
And utters it again when God doth please:
He is wit's pedler, and retails his wares
At wakes and wassails, meetings, markets, fairs;
And we that sell by gross, the Lord doth know,

Have not the grace to grace it with such show. 320
This gallant pins the wenches on his sleeve;
Had he been Adam, he had tempted Eve;
A' can carve too, and lisp: why, this is he
That kiss'd his hand away in courtesy;
This is the ape of form, monsieur the nice,
That, when he plays at tables, chides the dice
In honourable terms: nay, he can sing
A mean most meanly; and in ushering
Mend him who can: the ladies call him sweet;
The stairs, as he treads on them, kiss his feet: 330
This is the flower that smiles on every one,
To show his teeth as white as whale's bone;
And consciences, that will not die in debt,
Pay him the due of honey-tongued Boyet.
King. A blister on his sweet tongue, with my heart,
That put Armado's page out of his part!
Biron. See where it comes! Behaviour, what wert thou
Till this madman show'd thee? and what art thou now?

Re-enter the Princess, *ushered by* BOYET; ROSALINE,
MARIA, *and* KATHARINE.

King. All hail, sweet madam, and fair time of day!
Prin. 'Fair' in 'all hail' is foul, as I conceive. 340
King. Construe my speeches better, if you may.
Prin. Then wish me better; I will give you leave.
King. We came to visit you, and purpose now
To lead you to our court; vouchsafe it then.
Prin. This field shall hold me; and so hold your vow:
Nor God, nor I, delights in perjured men.
King. Rebuke me not for that which you provoke:
The virtue of your eye must break my oath.
Prin. You nickname virtue: vice you should have spoke;
For virtue's office never breaks men's troth. 350
Now by my maiden honour, yet as pure
  As the unsullied lily, I protest,
A world of torments though I should endure,
  I would not yield to be your house's guest;
So much I hate a breaking cause to be
Of heavenly oaths, vow'd with integrity.
King. O, you have lived in desolation here,
Unseen, unvisited, much to our shame.
Prin. Not so, my lord; it is not so, I swear;
We have had pastimes here and pleasant game: 360
A mess of Russians left us but of late.
King. How, madam! Russians!
Prin.   Ay, in truth, my lord:
Trim gallants, full of courtship and of state.
Ros. Madam, speak true. It is not so, my lord:
My lady, to the manner of the days,
In courtesy gives undeserving praise.
We four indeed confronted were with four
In Russian habit: here they stay'd an hour,
And talk'd apace; and in that hour, my lord,
They did not bless us with one happy word. 370
I dare not call them fools; but this I think,

268. **Well-liking,** in good condition, plump. 269. **kingly-poor flout,** poor mockery of a king (Schmidt); the New Cambridge editors see here a reversal of *Well-liking* in Rosaline's speech (l. 268): king-ly-poor, not well-ly-king. 274. **weeping-ripe,** ready to weep. 277. **No point,** quibble on the meaning "sword's point" and the French negative *ne point* (not at all); cf. II, i, 190. **straight,** immediately; see glossary. 279. **trow you,** would you believe; see glossary. **Qualm,** pronounced as "calm," with quibble; *came* in the preceding line probably approximated the same pronunciation. 281. **statute-caps,** woolen caps ordered

by act of Parliament (1571) to be worn "upon the Saboth and Holy Daye," by "all and every person and persons above Thage of syxe yeres," except women and certain officials (Onions). Hart thinks the *plain statute-caps* were those worn by London apprentices. 289. **digest,** put up with; see glossary. 292. **repair,** return. 297. **vailing,** letting fall, lowering; see glossary. The line has caused some perplexity because *vailing* (French *avaler*) has been confused with "veiling." Johnson paraphrased: Ladies unmasked are like angels vailing clouds, or letting those clouds which obscured their brightness sink from before them.

When they are thirsty, fools would fain have drink.

Biron. This jest is dry to me. Fair gentle sweet,
Your wits makes wise things foolish: when we greet,
With eyes best seeing, heaven's fiery eye,
By light we lose light: your capacity
Is of that nature that to your huge store
Wise things seem foolish and rich things but poor.

Ros. This proves you wise and rich, for in my eye,—

Biron. I am a fool, and full of poverty.   380

Ros. But that you take what doth to you belong,
It were a fault to snatch words from my tongue.

Biron. O, I am yours, and all that I possess!

Ros. All the fool mine?

Biron.   I cannot give you less.

Ros. Which of the vizards was it that you wore?

Biron. Where? when? what vizard? why demand you
    this?

Ros. There, then, that vizard; that superfluous case
That hid the worse and show'd the better face.

King. We were descried; they'll mock us now
    downright.

Dum. Let us confess and turn it to a jest.   390

Prin. Amazed, my lord? why looks your highness
    sad?

Ros. Help, hold his brows! he'll swoon! Why look
    you pale?
Sea-sick, I think, coming from Muscovy.

Biron. Thus pour the stars down plagues for perjury.
Can any face of brass hold longer out?
Here stand I: lady, dart thy skill at me;
    Bruise me with scorn, confound me with a flout;
Thrust thy sharp wit quite through my ignorance;
    Cut me to pieces with thy keen conceit;
And I will wish thee never more to dance,   400
    Nor never more in Russian habit wait.
O, never will I trust to speeches penn'd,
    Nor to the motion of a schoolboy's tongue,
Nor never come in vizard to my friend,
    Nor woo in rhyme, like a blind harper's song!
Taffeta phrases, silken terms precise,
    Three-piled hyperboles, spruce affectation,
Figures pedantical; these summer-flies
    Have blown me full of maggot ostentation:
I do forswear them; and I here protest,   410
    By this white glove,—how white the hand, God
        knows!—
Henceforth my wooing mind shall be express'd
    In russet yeas and honest kersey noes:
And, to begin, wench,—so God help me, la!—
My love to thee is sound, sans crack or flaw.

Ros. Sans sans, I pray you.

Biron.   Yet I have a trick
Of the old rage: bear with me, I am sick;
I'll leave it by degrees. Soft, let us see:
Write, 'Lord have mercy on us' on those three;
They are infected; in their hearts it lies;   420
They have the plague, and caught it of your eyes;
These lords are visited; you are not free,
For the Lord's tokens on you do I see.

Prin. No, they are free that gave these tokens to us.

Biron. Our states are forfeit: seek not to undo us.

Ros. It is not so; for how can this be true,
That you stand forfeit, being those that sue?

Biron. Peace! for I will not have to do with you.

Ros. Nor shall not, if I do as I intend.

Biron. Speak for yourselves; my wit is at an end.   430

King. Teach us, sweet madam, for our rude
    transgression
Some fair excuse.

Prin.   The fairest is confession.
Were not you here but even now disguised?

King. Madam, I was.

Prin.   And were you well advised?

King. I was, fair madam.

Prin.   When you then were here,
What did you whisper in your lady's ear?

King. That more than all the world I did respect
    her.

Prin. When she shall challenge this, you will reject
    her.

King. Upon mine honour, no.

Prin.   Peace, peace! forbear:
Your oath once broke, you force not to forswear.   440

King. Despise me, when I break this oath of mine.

Prin. I will: and therefore keep it. Rosaline,
What did the Russian whisper in your ear?

Ros. Madam, he swore that he did hold me dear
As precious eyesight, and did value me
Above this world; adding thereto moreover
That he would wed me, or else die my lover.

Prin. God give thee joy of him! the noble lord
Most honourably doth uphold his word.

King. What mean you, madam? by my life, my
    troth,   450
I never swore this lady such an oath.

Ros. By heaven, you did; and to confirm it plain,
You gave me this: but take it, sir, again.

King. My faith and this the princess I did give:
I knew her by this jewel on her sleeve.

Prin. Pardon me, sir, this jewel did she wear;
And Lord Biron, I thank him, is my dear.
What, will you have me, or your pearl again?

Biron. Neither of either; I remit both twain.
I see the trick on 't: here was a consent,   460
Knowing aforehand of our merriment,
To dash it like a Christmas comedy:
Some carry-tale, some please-man, some slight zany,
Some mumble-news, some trencher-knight, some
    Dick,
That smiles his cheek in years and knows the trick
To make my lady laugh when she 's disposed,
Told our intents before; which once disclosed,
The ladies did change favours: and then we,
Following the signs, woo'd but the sign of she.
Now, to our perjury to add more terror,   470
We are again forsworn, in will and error.
Much upon this it is: and might not you   [*To Boyet.*
Forestall our sport, to make us thus untrue?

---

303. **shapeless,** unshapely, ugly. **gear,** apparel; see glossary. 309. **Whip,** move quickly. 315. **pease,** plural of "pea." 319. **by gross,** by wholesale. 323. **carve,** show courtesy and affability. 328. **mean,** tenor; see glossary. **meanly,** moderately well. **ushering,** introducing, as a forerunner or harbinger. 329. **Mend,** improve on. 337. **it,** contemptuous reference to Boyet. 349. **nickname,** mention by mistake. 368. **habit,** costume; see glossary. 374. **wits,** so QF; Globe: *wit.* **greet,** regard, look on. 386. **demand,** inquire; see glossary. 389. **were,** so Q; Globe: *are.* **descried,** spied upon, discovered. 395. **face**

of brass, self-confidence. 397. **confound,** destroy; see glossary. 400. **wish,** entreat. 405. **blind harper's,** a proverbial expression. 409. **blown,** filled with eggs, made foul. 413. **russet,** simple, homespun. **kersey,** plain, homely. 416. **Sans sans,** without *sans;* i.e., without affection of foreign phrases; see glossary. 417. **rage,** vehement pain; see glossary. 425. **undo,** ruin; see glossary. 434. **well advised,** in one's right mind. 440. **force,** attach force or importance to, think of the consequences; hence, hesitate. 464. **trencher-knight,** serving man at table. **Dick.** Cf. the current expression, "Tom, Dick and Harry."

Do not you know my lady's foot by the squier,
  And laugh upon the apple of her eye?
And stand between her back, sir, and the fire,
  Holding a trencher, jesting merrily?
You put our page out: go, you are allow'd;
Die when you will, a smock shall be your shroud.
You leer upon me, do you? there 's an eye   480
Wounds like a leaden sword.
  Boyet.   Full merrily
Hath this brave manage, this career, been run.
  Biron. Lo, he is tilting straight! Peace! I have
    done.

Enter COSTARD.

Welcome, pure wit! thou partest a fair fray.
  Cost. O Lord, sir, they would know
Whether the three Worthies shall come in or no.
  Biron. What, are there but three?
  Cost.   No, sir; but it is vara fine,
For every one pursents three.
  Biron.   And three times thrice is nine.
  Cost. Not so, sir; under correction, sir; I hope it is
    not so.
You cannot beg us, sir, I can assure you, sir; we know
    what we know: 490
I hope, sir, three times thrice, sir,—
  Biron. Is not nine.
  Cost. Under correction, sir, we know whereuntil it
doth amount.
  Biron. By Jove, I always took three threes for nine.
  Cost. O Lord, sir, it were pity you should get your
living by reckoning, sir.
  Biron. How much is it?   499
  Cost. O Lord, sir, the parties themselves, the actors,
sir, will show whereuntil it doth amount: for mine own
part, I am, as they say, but to parfect one man in one
poor man, Pompion the Great, sir.
  Biron. Art thou one of the Worthies?
  Cost. It pleased them to think me worthy of Pom-
pion the Great: for mine own part, I know not the
degree of the Worthy, but I am to stand for him.
  Biron. Go, bid them prepare.   510
  Cost. We will turn it finely off, sir; we will take some
    care.   [*Exit.*
  King. Biron, they will shame us: let them not
    approach.
  Biron. We are shame-proof, my lord: and 'tis some
    policy
To have one show worse than the king's and his
    company.
  King. I say they shall not come.
  Prin. Nay, my good lord, let me o'errule you now:
That sport best pleases that doth least know how:
†Where zeal strives to content, and the contents
Dies in the zeal of that which it presents:

Their form confounded makes most form in mirth,   520
When great things labouring perish in their birth.
  Biron. A right description of our sport, my lord.

Enter ARMADO.

  Arm. Anointed, I implore so much expense of thy
royal sweet breath as will utter a brace of words.
                [*Converses apart with the King, and*
                            delivers him a paper.
  Prin. Doth this man serve God?
  Biron. Why ask you?
  Prin. A' speaks not like a man of God his making. 529
  Arm. That is all one, my fair, sweet, honey mon-
arch; for, I protest, the schoolmaster is exceeding
fantastical; too too vain, too too vain: but we will put
it, as they say, to fortuna della guerra. I wish you the
peace of mind, most royal couplement!   [*Exit.*
  King. Here is like to be a good presence of Worthies.
He presents Hector of Troy; the swain, Pompey the
Great; the parish curate, Alexander; Armado's page,
Hercules; the pedant, Judas Maccabæus: 540
And if these four Worthies in their first show thrive,
These four will change habits, and present the other
    five.
  Biron. There is five in the first show.
  King. You are deceived; 'tis not so.
  Biron. The pedant, the braggart, the hedge-priest,
the fool and the boy:—
†Abate throw at novum, and the whole world again
Cannot pick out five such, take each one in his vein.
  King. The ship is under sail, and here she comes
    amain.

Enter COSTARD. *for Pompey.*

  Cost. I Pompey am,—
  Boyet.   You lie, you are not he.   550
  Cost. I Pompey am,—
  Boyet.   With libbard's head on knee.
  Biron. Well said, old mocker: I must needs be
    friends with thee.
  Cost. I Pompey am, Pompey surnamed the Big,—
  Dum. The Great.
  Cost. It is, 'Great', sir:—
                     Pompey surnamed the Great;
That oft in field with targe and shield, did make my
    foe to sweat:
And travelling along this coast. I here am come by
    chance,
And lay my arms before the legs of this sweet lass of
    France.
If your ladyship would say, 'Thanks, Pompey,' I had
    done.
  Prin. Great thanks, great Pompey.   560
  Cost. 'Tis not so much worth; but I hope I was
perfect: I made a little fault in 'Great.'

474. **squier,** foot rule. 477. **trencher,** wooden dish or plate; see
glossary. 479. **smock,** woman's undergarment; see glossary; here a
sign of effeminacy. 481. **leaden sword,** mock weapon (used figuratively). 482. **brave,** fine; see glossary. **manage,** short gallop at full
speed; see glossary. 487. **vara,** dialect pronunciation of "very." 503.
parfect, Costard's malapropism for, probably, "perform" or "present."
513. **policy,** trick; see glossary. 518-519. **Where . . . presents.** The
lines have been variously explained, depending on the interpretation
of *contents:* where the unintelligent zeal of the actors strives to content the audience, and the gist (*contents*) of the entertainment is destroyed by this very zeal in performance (Yale); where zeal strives
to give contentment, and the contentment (*contents*) dies in the zeal
for that sport which zeal presents (Furness). Most explanations incline toward one or the other of these two paraphrases. 528. **A',** so Q;

Globe, following F: *He.* **God his,** so Q; Globe, following F: *God's.*
533-534. **fortuna della guerra,** the fortune of war. 533. **della,** Globe:
de la. 535. **couplement,** couple. 536. **presence,** assembly. 545.
hedge-priest, illiterate, rural priest. 547. **Abate,** leave out of count; see
glossary. **novum,** the game *novum quinque,* so called from the principal
throws of the dice—nine and five. The line is obscure and several
emendations have been suggested. Malone's *Abate a throw,* etc., has
been most generally adopted. The Yale editors paraphrase: Except for a
rare throw at dice. A quibble is observable here on the notion of Nine
Worthies being presented by five players. 551. **libbard's,** leopard's; an
allusion to the ornaments occasionally worn on knees or elbows of garments. 568-569. **Your . . . knight.** These remarks refer to reputed
physical peculiarities of Alexander—a wry neck, which would make his
features stand not *right* but obliquely, and a sweet breath and a bodily

Biron. My hat to a halfpenny, Pompey proves the best Worthy.

Enter Sir Nathaniel, *for Alexander.*

Nath. When in the world I lived, I was the world's
 commander;
By east, west, north, and south, I spread my con-
 quering might:
My scutcheon plain declares that I am Alisander,—
 Boyet. Your nose says, no, you are not; for it stands
  too right.
 Biron. Your nose smells 'no' in this, most tender-
  smelling knight.
 Prin. The conqueror is dismay'd. Proceed, good
  Alexander. 570
 Nath. When in the world I lived, I was the world's
  commander,—
 Boyet. Most true, 'tis right; you were so, Alisander.
 Biron. Pompey the Great,—
 Cost. Your servant, and Costard.
 Biron. Take away the conqueror, take away Alisander.
 Cost. [*To Sir Nath.*] O, sir, you have overthrown
Alisander the conqueror! You will be scraped out of
the painted cloth for this: your lion, that holds his
poll-axe sitting on a close-stool, will be given to Ajax:
he will be the ninth Worthy. A conqueror, and afeard
to speak! run away for shame, Alisander. [*Nath.
retires.*] There, an 't shall please you; a foolish mild
man; an honest man, look you, and soon dashed. He
is a marvellous good neighbour, faith, and a very good
bowler: but, for Alisander,—alas, you see how 'tis,—a
little o'erparted. But there are Worthies a-coming will
speak their mind in some other sort. 590
 Prin. Stand aside, good Pompey.

Enter Holofernes, *for Judas; and* Moth *for Hercules.*

Hol. Great Hercules is presented by this imp,
 Whose club kill'd Cerberus, that three-headed
  canis;
And when he was a babe, a child, a shrimp,
 Thus did he strangle serpents in his manus.
Quoniam he seemeth in minority,
Ergo I come with this apology.
Keep some state in thy exit, and vanish. [*Moth retires.*
 Judas I am,—
 Dum. A Judas! 600
 Hol. Not Iscariot, sir.
 Judas I am, ycliped Maccabæus.
 Dum. Judas Maccabæus clipt is plain Judas.
 Biron. A kissing traitor. How art thou proved Judas?
 Hol. Judas I am,—
 Dum. The more shame for you, Judas.
 Hol. What mean you, sir?
 Boyet. To make Judas hang himself.
 Hol. Begin, sir; you are my elder.

Biron. Well followed: Judas was hanged on an elder.
Hol. I will not be put out of countenance. 611
Biron. Because thou hast no face.
Hol. What is this?
Boyet. A cittern-head.
Dum. The head of a bodkin.
Biron. A Death's face in a ring.
Long. The face of an old Roman coin, scarce seen.
Boyet. The pommel of Cæsar's falchion.
Dum. The carved-bone face on a flask.
Biron. Saint George's half-cheek in a brooch. 620
Dum. Ay, and in a brooch of lead.
Biron. Ay, and worn in the cap of a tooth-drawer.
And now forward; for we have put thee in
 countenance.
Hol. You have put me out of countenance.
Biron. False; we have given thee faces.
Hol. But you have out-faced them all.
Biron. An thou wert a lion, we would do so.
Boyet. Therefore, as he is an ass, let him go.
And so adieu, sweet Jude! nay, why dost thou stay?
Dum. For the latter end of his name. 630
Biron. For the ass to the Jude; give it him:—Jud-as,
 away!
Hol. This is not generous, not gentle, not humble.
Boyet. A light for Monsieur Judas! it grows dark,
 he may stumble. [*Hol. retires.*
Prin. Alas, poor Maccabæus, how hath he been
 baited!

Enter Armado, *for Hector.*

Biron. Hide thy head, Achilles: here comes Hector
in arms.
Dum. Though my mocks come home by me, I will
now be merry.
King. Hector was but a Troyan in respect of this. 640
Boyet. But is this Hector?
King. I think Hector was not so clean-timbered.
Long. His leg is too big for Hector's.
Dum. More calf, certain.
Boyet. No; he is best indued in the small.
Biron. This cannot be Hector.
Dum. He 's a god or a painter; for he makes faces.
Arm. The armipotent Mars, of lances the almighty,
Gave Hector a gift,— 651
Dum. A gilt nutmeg.
Biron. A lemon.
Long. Stuck with cloves.
Dum. No, cloven.
Arm. Peace!—
The armipotent Mars, of lances the almighty,
 Gave Hector a gift, the heir of Ilion;
A man so breathed, that certain he would fight; yea
 From morn till night, out of his pavilion. 660
I am that flower,—

odor of "marvellous good savour." The details would be familiar to Shakespeare from North's Plutarch. 579. **scraped . . . cloth,** an allusion to the frequent representation of the Nine Worthies painted on an arras or tapestry. 579-581. **your lion . . . close-stool.** Theobald found in Gerard Leigh's *Accidens of Armorie* (1591) a description of the armorial emblems of the Nine Worthies, where Alexander's is described as "a lion or [gold] seiante [sitting] in a chayer, holding a battle-ax." 581. **Ajax,** quibble on "a jakes," a latrine. This unsavory pun is not infrequent. 588. **o'erparted,** having a part too difficult. 591. **Stand . . . Pompey.** After this line the early texts have a stage direction: Q: *Exit Curat;* F₁: *Exit Cu.;* F₂₋₄: *Exit Clo.* Costard probably left the stage at this point. His absence during the remainder of the entertainment motivates his conduct later at line 678. 593. **Cerberus,** three-headed dog at the entrance to Hades, the capturing of which was

one of Hercules' twelve labors. **canis,** dog. 595. **manus,** hands. 596. **Quoniam,** since. 613. **What is this.** Holofernes points to his face, provoking the quips which follow. 614. **cittern,** cithern, guitar. The head was usually grotesquely carved. 615. **bodkin,** long, jeweled pin for a lady's hair. 618. **falchion,** curved sword. 620. **half-cheek,** profile. **brooch,** any jeweled ornament. 640. **Troyan,** Trojan; term of contempt. 642. **clean-timbered,** clean-limbed. 647. **indued,** endowed. **small,** part of the leg below the calf. 649. **a god or a painter,** a proverbial expression. 650. **armipotent,** powerful in arms; an epithet commonly applied to Mars. 652. **gilt,** an old cookery term—glazed with egg yolk, saffron, etc. There are several contemporary references to gilded nutmegs. The gilding may have been a preservative. 659. **so breathed,** i.e., in good condition, valiant. 660. **pavilion,** tent or camp, whither the combatant retired when not engaged in a fight.

Dum.   That mint.
Long.   That columbine.
Arm. Sweet Lord Longaville, rein thy tongue.
Long. I must rather give it the rein, for it runs against Hector.
Dum. Ay, and Hector 's a greyhound.
Arm. The sweet war-man is dead and rotten; sweet chucks, beat not the bones of the buried: when he breathed, he was a man. But I will forward with my device. [*To the Princess*] Sweet royalty, bestow on me the sense of hearing.   670
Prin. Speak, brave Hector: we are much delighted.
Arm. I do adore thy sweet grace's slipper.
Boyet. [*Aside to Dum.*] Loves her by the foot.
Dum. [*Aside to Boyet*] He may not by the yard.
Arm. This Hector far surmounted Hannibal,—
Cost. The party is gone, fellow Hector, she is gone; she is two months on her way.
Arm. What meanest thou?   680
Cost. Faith, unless you play the honest Troyan, the poor wench is cast away: she 's quick; the child brags in her belly already: 'tis yours.
Arm. Dost thou infamonize me among potentates? thou shalt die.
Cost. Then shall Hector be whipped for Jaquenetta that is quick by him and hanged for Pompey that is dead by him.
Dum. Most rare Pompey!
Boyet. Renowned Pompey!   690
Biron. Greater than great, great, great, great Pompey! Pompey the Huge!
Dum. Hector trembles.
Biron. Pompey is moved. More Ates, more Ates! stir them on! stir them on!
Dum. Hector will challenge him.
Biron. Ay, if a' have no more man's blood in 's belly than will sup a flea.
Arm. By the north pole, I do challenge thee.   699
Cost. I will not fight with a pole, like a northern man: I'll slash; I'll do it by the sword. I bepray you, let me borrow my arms again.
Dum. Room for the incensed Worthies!
Cost. I'll do it in my shirt.
Dum. Most resolute Pompey!
Moth. Master, let me take you a button-hole lower. Do you not see Pompey is uncasing for the combat? What mean you? You will lose your reputation.
Arm. Gentlemen and soldiers, pardon me; I will not combat in my shirt.   711
Dum. You may not deny it: Pompey hath made the challenge.
Arm. Sweet bloods, I both may and will.
Biron. What reason have you for 't?
Arm. The naked truth of it is, I have no shirt; I go woolward for penance.
Boyet. True, and it was enjoined him in Rome for want of linen: since when, I'll be sworn, he wore none

but a dishclout of Jaquenetta's, and that a' wears next his heart for a favour.

Enter MERCADE.

Mer. God save you, madam!
Prin. Welcome, Mercade;
But that thou interrupt'st our merriment.
Mer. I am sorry, madam; for the news I bring
Is heavy in my tongue. The king your father—
Prin. Dead, for my life!
Mer. Even so; my tale is told.   730
Biron. Worthies, away! the scene begins to cloud.
Arm. For mine own part, I breathe free breath. I have seen the day of wrong through the little hole of discretion, and I will right myself like a soldier.
                                        [*Exeunt Worthies.*
King. How fares your majesty?
Prin. Boyet, prepare; I will away to-night.
King. Madam, not so; I do beseech you, stay.
Prin. Prepare, I say. I thank you, gracious lords,
For all your fair endeavours; and entreat,   740
Out of a new-sad soul, that you vouchsafe
In your rich wisdom to excuse or hide
The liberal opposition of our spirits,
If over-boldly we have borne ourselves
In the converse of breath: your gentleness
Was guilty of it. Farewell, worthy lord!
A heavy heart bears not a humble tongue:
Excuse me so, coming too short of thanks
For my great suit so easily obtain'd.
King. The extreme parts of time extremely forms 750
All causes to the purpose of his speed,
And often at his very loose decides
That which long process could not arbitrate:
And though the mourning brow of progeny
Forbid the smiling courtesy of love
The holy suit which fain it would convince,
Yet, since love's argument was first on foot,
Let not the cloud of sorrow justle it
From what it purposed; since, to wail friends lost
Is not by much so wholesome-profitable   760
As to rejoice at friends but newly found.
Prin. I understand you not: my griefs are double.
Biron. Honest plain words best pierce the ear of
          grief;
And by these badges understand the king.
For your fair sakes have we neglected time,
Play'd foul play with our oaths: your beauty, ladies,
Hath much deform'd us, fashioning our humours
Even to the opposed end of our intents:
And what in us hath seem'd ridiculous,—
As love is full of unbefitting strains,   770
All wanton as a child, skipping and vain,
Form'd by the eye and therefore, like the eye,
Full of strange shapes, of habits and of forms,
Varying in subjects as the eye doth roll
To every varied object in his glance:

---

670. QF have a stage direction here: *Berowne steppes forth.* The stage business at this point probably had something to do with Costard's conduct immediately below.   678. **The . . . gone.** QF print these words as part of Armado's speech, as do the New Cambridge editors, who think they have something to do with the stage direction just noted.   694. **Ates,** incitements to mischief. Ate was the goddess of mischief.   706-707. **Master . . . lower,** help remove your doublet, with a quibble on the proverbial "take down a hole"; i.e., humiliate.   717. **woolward,** with woolen clothing next to the skin; i.e., instead of linen or silk, suggesting the hair shirt of the penitent.   743. **liberal opposition,** deliberate antagonism.   745. **converse of breath,** conversation.   747. **humble,** civil, complimentary; so QF; Globe, following Theobald: *nimble.*

750-753. **The . . . arbitrate,** i.e., much is accomplished in the last minutes after a long period of dallying. The observation is not an uncommon one although the expression here is obscure. The difficulty of the passage is due in part to lack of agreement between the grammatical subject *parts,* its verbs *forms* and *decides,* and its pronoun *he.* The actual subject is *time.* Capell so paraphrases it: Time in his extreme parts, or drawing to his extreme, etc. Such grammatical usage is not un-Shakespearean. The word *loose* (l. 752) is an archery term, the discharge of an arrow; *at his very loose,* at the last moment. The New Cambridge editors, finding the passage corrupt, would emend *parts* to *pulse* (sixteenth-century spelling, *pouls*).   776-777. **Which . . . if,** an instance of a Latinism common in Renaissance English in which the relative

Which parti-coated presence of loose love
Put on by us, if, in your heavenly eyes,
Have misbecomed our oaths and gravities,
Those heavenly eyes, that look into these faults,
Suggested us to make. Therefore, ladies, 780
Our love being yours, the error that love makes
Is likewise yours: we to ourselves prove false,
By being once false for ever to be true
To those that make us both,—fair ladies, you:
And even that falsehood, in itself a sin,
Thus purifies itself and turns to grace.
   Prin. We have received your letters full of love;
Your favours, the ambassadors of love;
And, in our maiden council, rated them
At courtship, pleasant jest and courtesy 790
As bombast and as lining to the time:
But more devout than this in our respects
Have we not been; and therefore met your loves
In their own fashion, like a merriment.
   Dum. Our letters, madam, show'd much more than
   jest.
   Long. So did our looks.
   Ros.   We did not quote them so.
   King. Now, at the latest minute of the hour,
Grant us your loves.
   Prin.   A time, methinks, too short
To make a world-without-end bargain in.
No, no, my lord, your grace is perjured much, 800
Full of dear guiltiness; and therefore this:
If for my love, as there is no such cause,
You will do aught, this shall you do for me:
Your oath I will not trust; but go with speed
To some forlorn and naked hermitage,
Remote from all the pleasures of the world;
There stay until the twelve celestial signs
Have brought about the annual reckoning.
If this austere insociable life
Change not your offer made in heat of blood; 810
If frosts and fasts, hard lodging and thin weeds
Nip not the gaudy blossoms of your love,
But that it bear this trial and last love;
Then, at the expiration of the year,
Come challenge me, challenge me by these deserts,
And, by this virgin palm now kissing thine,
I will be thine; and till that instant shut
My woeful self up in a mourning house,
Raining the tears of lamentation
For the remembrance of my father's death. 820
If this thou do deny, let our hands part,
Neither intitled in the other's heart.
   King. If this, or more than this, I would deny,
   To flatter up these powers of mine with rest,
The sudden hand of death close up mine eye!
   Hence ever then my heart is in thy breast.
   [*Biron.* And what to me, my love? and what to me?
   Ros. You must be purged too, your sins are rack'd,
You are attaint with faults and perjury:

Therefore if you my favour mean to get, 830
A twelvemonth shall you spend, and never rest,
But seek the weary beds of people sick.]
   Dum. But what to me, my love? but what to me?
A wife?
   Kath. A beard, fair health, and honesty;
With three-fold love I wish you all these three.
   Dum. O, shall I say, I thank you, gentle wife?
   Kath. Not so, my lord; a twelvemonth and a day
I'll mark no words that smooth-faced wooers say:
Come when the king doth to my lady come;
Then, if I have much love, I'll give you some. 840
   Dum. I'll serve thee true and faithfully till then.
   Kath. Yet swear not, lest ye be forsworn again.
   Long. What says Maria?
   Mar.   At the twelvemonth's end
I'll change my black gown for a faithful friend.
   Long. I'll stay with patience; but the time is long.
   Mar. The liker you; few taller are so young.
   Biron. Studies my lady? mistress, look on me;
Behold the window of my heart, mine eye,
What humble suit attends thy answer there:
Impose some service on me for thy love. 850
   Ros. Oft have I heard of you, my Lord Biron,
Before I saw you; and the world's large tongue
Proclaims you for a man replete with mocks,
Full of comparisons and wounding flouts,
Which you on all estates will execute
That lie within the mercy of your wit.
To weed this wormwood from your fruitful brain,
And therewithal to win me, if you please,
Without the which I am not to be won,
You shall this twelvemonth term from day to day 860
Visit the speechless sick and still converse
With groaning wretches; and your task shall be,
With all the fierce endeavour of your wit
To enforce the pained impotent to smile.
   Biron. To move wild laughter in the throat of death?
It cannot be; it is impossible:
Mirth cannot move a soul in agony.
   Ros. Why, that's the way to choke a gibing spirit,
Whose influence is begot of that loose grace
Which shallow laughing hearers give to fools: 870
A jest's prosperity lies in the ear
Of him that hears it, never in the tongue
Of him that makes it: then, if sickly ears,
Deaf'd with the clamours of their own dear groans,
Will hear your idle scorns, continue then,
And I will have you and that fault withal;
But if they will not, throw away that spirit,
And I shall find you empty of that fault,
Right joyful of your reformation.
   Biron. A twelvemonth! well; befall what will befall,
I'll jest a twelvemonth in an hospital. 881
   Prin. [*To the King*] Ay, sweet my lord; and so I take
   my leave.
   King. No, madam; we will bring you on your way.

serves the double function of coordinating conjunction and substantive, equivalent here to "and if this presence," etc., after the Latin construction *qui si* (Abbott, 418). 776. **parti-coated**, dressed like a fool, in motley. **loose**, unrestrained. 780. **Suggested**, tempted; see glossary. 789. **rated**, computed, estimated; see glossary. 791. **bombast**, a loosely made fabric used for padding or stuffing garments. 792. **respects**, considerations; see glossary. 796. **quote**, take mental note of. 807. **twelve celestial signs**, signs of the zodiac. 811. **thin weeds**, probably garments, although Hart suggests a reference to fasting, i.e., unnourishing herbs and roots; see *weed* in glossary. 816. **palm . . . thine**, an image frequent in referring to clasping of hands, particularly those of lovers; cf. *Romeo and Juliet*, I, v, 102. 826. **ever**,

so Ff; Q: *herrite*; the New Cambridge editors, following a suggestion of A. W. Pollard (*Library*, Series iii, VII, 370), emend to *hermit*. 827-832. Regarded as evidence of imperfect cancellation; see Introduction. 828. **rack'd**, extended "to the top of their bent" (Malone); Rowe's emendation *rank* is adopted by many editors. Steevens noted the appropriateness of this emendation, citing *Hamlet*, III, iii, 36. See, however, *rack* and *rank* in glossary. 854. **comparisons**, i.e., witty, sarcastic comparisons. 855. **all estates**, all classes of people. 861. **converse**, associate with; see glossary. 869. **influence**, an astronomical metaphor; see glossary.

Biron. Our wooing doth not end like an old play;
Jack hath not Jill: these ladies' courtesy
Might well have made our sport a comedy.
  King. Come, sir, it wants a twelvemonth and a day,
And then 'twill end.
  Biron.   That 's too long for a play.

Re-enter ARMADO.

  Arm. Sweet majesty, vouchsafe me,—
  Prin. Was not that Hector?
  Dum. The worthy knight of Troy.   890
  Arm. I will kiss thy royal finger, and take leave. I
am a votary; I have vowed to Jaquenetta to hold the
plough for her sweet love three years. But, most
esteemed greatness, will you hear the dialogue that
the two learned men have compiled in praise of the
owl and the cuckoo? it should have followed in the end
of our show.
  King. Call them forth quickly; we will do so.
  Arm. Holla! approach.   900

Re-enter HOLOFERNES, NATHANIEL, MOTH,
COSTARD, *and others.*

This side is Hiems, Winter, this Ver, the Spring; the
one maintained by the owl, the other by the cuckoo.
Ver, begin.

THE SONG.

SPRING.

When daisies pied and violets blue
    And lady-smocks all silver-white
And cuckoo-buds of yellow hue
    Do paint the meadows with delight,
The cuckoo then, on every tree,
Mocks married men; for thus sings he,
          Cuckoo;   910
Cuckoo, cuckoo: O word of fear,
Unpleasing to a married ear!

When shepherds pipe on oaten straws
    And merry larks are ploughmen's clocks,
When turtles tread, and rooks, and daws,
    And maidens bleach their summer smocks,
The cuckoo then, on every tree,
Mocks married men; for thus sings he,
          Cuckoo;
Cuckoo, cuckoo: O word of fear,   920
Unpleasing to a married ear!

WINTER.

When icicles hang by the wall
    And Dick the shepherd blows his nail
And Tom bears logs into the hall
    And milk comes frozen home in pail,
When blood is nipp'd and ways be foul,
Then nightly sings the staring owl,
          Tu-whit;
Tu-who, a merry note,
While greasy Joan doth keel the pot.   930

893. **hold the plough,** become a farmer, a rustic. 905. **lady-smocks,**
cuckoo flowers, the *cardamine pratensis;* probably for "our Lady's
smock." 906. **cuckoo-buds of yellow,** a flower not positively identified; perhaps cowslip or crowfoot. 912. **Unpleasing,** i.e., because
the cuckoo suggests cuckoldry; the latter word is derived from the
former, from the popular notion that the cuckoo laid its eggs in other
birds' nests. 930. **keel,** skim.

When all aloud the wind doth blow
    And coughing drowns the parson's saw
And birds sit brooding in the snow
    And Marian's nose looks red and raw,
When roasted crabs hiss in the bowl,
Then nightly sings the staring owl,
          Tu-whit;
Tu-who, a merry note,
While greasy Joan doth keel the pot.   939
  Arm. The words of Mercury are harsh after the
songs of Apollo. You that way: we this way.   [*Exeunt.*

932. **saw,** maxim, moral observation. 935. **crabs,** crab apples.
940. **words of Mercury.** The reference is to Mercury as the god of
eloquence in antithesis to Apollo as the god of music.

THE

Two Gentlemen of Verona

The *Two Gentlemen of Verona* was first published in
the First Folio in 1623. It is not mentioned in any
way prior to that date except in the list of Shakespeare's comedies given by Francis Meres in *Palladis
Tamia* in 1598. It has been assigned on internal
evidence to the very earliest period, since it has the
same stylistic qualities which distinguish *The Comedy
of Errors* and *Love's Labour's Lost.*

PUBLICATION

The text of *The Two Gentlemen of Verona* in the First
Folio is a peculiar one. Because it is, the editors of
the New Cambridge Shakespeare have suggested that
the copy for the printers was made up in an unusual
fashion. In the acting of an Elizabethan play there
were three necessary documents: (1) a copy for the
use of the prompter, frequently the author's manuscript, which bore on it the certification of license by
the Master of the Revels; (2) the players' parts
written out with cues for the use of actors; and (3) a
single sheet called the plot or plat, which was hung
up behind the scenes so that it might be consulted by
the actors while the play was in progress. The
prompter's copy contained entrances, exits, and stage
directions, all at their appropriate places in the text.
The separate parts contained no such information,
but were probably from the point of view of intelligi-
bility very accurate, since they presented the lines as
spoken. The plat contained nothing but scene
divisions and the names of actors who were to play
in the different scenes, the beginning of scenes being
indicated by horizontal lines drawn across the sheet
and beneath them the names of the actors in the
order in which they were to appear in the scene. [1]

[1] See facsimile reproductions of these documents in W. W. Greg's
Dramatic Documents from Elizabethan Playhouses (Oxford, 1931), Vol. II.

Since the 1623 folio text of *The Two Gentlemen of Verona* contains almost no stage directions, entrances, or exits, and since the names of actors are grouped together at the beginnings of scenes and not distributed throughout at the places where they enter, it is argued that, in this case, we do not have a prompter's copy. The hypothesis suggested is that, when the editors of the First Folio came to prepare the manuscript of this play for the printers, the prompt copy could not be found. Therefore, they sent the players' parts and the plat to a copyist who made up the play anew from these documents. It followed that he produced an intelligible text, but a text without stage directions. This is an ingenious and plausible hypothesis, but the peculiarities of the text may be due merely to the play's having been printed from a scrivener's manuscript. The plays of the Latin dramatists and those of Ben Jonson grouped characters at the beginning of scenes as is done in the folio version of *The Two Gentlemen of Verona*. The New Cambridge editors also advance the theory that the play has been shortened for some special stage presentation by the cutting out of about six hundred lines. As compared to the normal length of an Elizabethan play, about 3000 lines, *The Two Gentlemen of Verona* has but 2380, a fact which would indicate abridgment.[2] These editors also find indications of abridgment in the curtailment of scenes and speeches, the disruption of the time scheme of the play, confusion of names of places, and dramatic inferiority in several different parts, particularly in the last scene. In order to account for these inferiorities in the last scene, the editors assign a good many passages to an adapter, always a doubtful procedure.[3]

SOURCES

At the basis of the plot[4] lies the story of a lover Proteus, who, having left his faithful sweetheart Julia behind him in Verona, falls in love with Silvia, the sweetheart of his best friend. This act, which is a violation of the proper canons of friendship as well as of love, furnishes a typical Renaissance theme. It appears in all forms of amatory literature, serving always to give occasion for the courtly discriminations in which the Renaissance delighted. The fact that this theme is employed in *The Two Gentlemen of Verona*, with its numerous discussions of love and friendship, duty and honor, throws the play at once into the commonest current of Renaissance literature. In plot *The Two Gentlemen of Verona* is a typical Italian comedy, for dozens of Italian comedies parallel the play either in the principal situation of friendship

versus love or in the minor devices by which it is carried out.[5] Nothing is so common as to have the heroine disguise herself as a page. An Italian dramatist could not plausibly present a respectable girl as walk-

VERONE

ing abroad (since the stage was a general scene in the open) unless she were disguised. The only other device was to have her speak from a balcony. A like degree of conventionality belongs to the attack by robbers, the rescue, and other events, but particularly to the mixture of sincere emotion and mere ingenuity in the discussion of love, sometimes called Petrarchism, which permeated European literature during the Renaissance. Nothing can be more absurd than to imagine that Shakespeare constructed this plot with the free hand of a modern author. His originality consisted in infusing into a plot, already developed in detail, actual forms of life and authentic emotion.

It has long been thought that this particular version of a favorite Renaissance plot came from a pastoral romance, *Diana Enamorada*, by the Portuguese Jorge de Montemayor (1520-1561), in which Felismena is wooed by Don Felix, a courtship which resembles that of Julia by Proteus in the matter of the delivery of the letter by the lady's maid. The father of Don Felix disapproves of the match with Felismena and sends Don Felix away to court. Felismena, like Julia, disguises herself as a page and follows Don Felix. The host of the inn where Felismena stops takes her to a place to hear music. There she overhears a passionate serenade addressed by her false lover to the lady Celia, just as Julia listens to Proteus at the window of Silvia. Felismena enters the service of her false lover as a page and bears messages and gifts to Celia. Here the resemblance between Montemayor's story and *The Two Gentlemen of Verona* ceases. Celia falls in love with the disguised Felismena, as Olivia in *Twelfth Night* falls in love with the disguised Viola, and, finding her passion unreturned, dies of a broken heart. Felix dis-

---

[2]Alfred Hart argues from extensive data, that Elizabethan plays on the stage could not have been more than about 2500 lines in length because of the lack of time for acting. See *Shakespeare and the Homilies* (Melbourne, 1934), pp. 77-153.

[3]See Sir Arthur Quiller-Couch and John Dover Wilson, edition of *The Two Gentlemen of Verona*, in the New Cambridge Shakespeare, pp. xii-xvi, 72-82.

[4]T. P. Harrison, Jr., "Concerning *Two Gentlemen of Verona* and Montemayor's *Diana*," *MLN*, XLI, 251-252.

[5]O. J. Campbell, "*The Two Gentlemen of Verona* and Italian Comedy," *Studies in Shakespeare, Milton and Donne* (1925), pp. 47-63.

appears. Felismena becomes a shepherdess. One day, by her skill in archery, she rescues a knight beset by three foemen. This rescued knight turns out to be Don Felix; the two lovers recognize each other and are united.

Montemayor's novel may well have served as a primary source for Shakespeare's play. It was translated into French in 1578 and may have existed in English, at least in manuscript form. However, we are prevented from concluding that Shakespeare did use it by the interposition of another old play. A comedy, now lost, called *Felix and Philiomena* (certainly an error for *Philismena*) is known from the records of the Office of the Revels to have been acted before Queen Elizabeth on January 3, 1584.

Another recently discovered source[6] seems to supply the parts of the plot which have been engrafted on the *Diana* passage in order to complete the story of *The Two Gentlemen of Verona*. It is the tale of Claribel and Floradine, the fifth of five tales in *A Courtlie Controversie of Cupids Cautels*, translated by Henry Wotton in 1578 from Jacques d'Yver's *Le printemps d'Yver* (1572). By adding the story of a sworn friend false in love and thus providing lovers for both women to Montemayor's partly tragic tale of the forsaken mistress, Shakespeare gave his play a happy ending. He also secured an opportunity to exploit the theme of the rivalry of friendship and love, a theme already rendered popular in England by Lyly's *Euphues*. Such a union of plots is evident, whether original with Shakespeare or not, and at least some of the inconsistencies of the play may be attributed to this major structural revision.

Such plots as that of Montemayor existed not merely for dramatization, but for the sake of their sentimental material. There are many parallels in thought and sentiment between *The Two Gentlemen of Verona* and Sidney's *Arcadia*, Lyly's *Euphues*, the Elizabethan sonnet sequences, and numerous contemporary works all over Europe. The greatest critical crux of the play arises out of Renaissance sentiment. Valentine, the faithful hero, forgives his false friend Proteus, from whose ravishing clutches he has just rescued Silvia. And, when Proteus has repented and asked forgiveness, Valentine makes a fine speech and offers to renounce Silvia in favor of Proteus. For the modern critic this is simply too much; he cannot believe that Shakespeare would ever have put down in black and white such a ridiculous and unendurable piece of false sentiment. It is in vain to say that the theme called for just such artificial heroics. Therefore, all editors, including the New Cambridge editors, have devoted themselves unnecessarily to proving that Shakespeare could not have been responsible for this particular conclusion to the comedy.

[6]Dorothy F. Atkinson, "Source of *The Two Gentlemen of Verona*," *Studies in Philology*, XL (1944), 223-234; see also an important article on the sources of *The Two Gentlemen of Verone*, by Ralph M. Sargent, "Sir Thomas Elyot and the Integrity of *The Two Gentlemen of Verona*," *PMLA*, LXV (1950), 1166-1180.

Shakespeare did not invent the type of comedy represented in *The Two Gentlemen of Verona*. It existed in all of its important features long before his day. What then is the significance of this play? Shakespeare took a slender and conventional dramatic form and attempted, with but mediocre success, to engraft upon it a body of material in which he and his audiences were interested. Part of this is stock-in-trade Petrarchism; part of it is perhaps English life in an English atmosphere. The smallest part of all, and yet the most precious, is in those few cases where Shakespeare has rendered certain of his characters individual.

The most original thing Shakespeare did in this play was to center the interest of his story in the disguised woman, a thing which had never been so definitely done before in England or in Italy. There is a new consistency in Julia's character. Shakespeare has indicated to us how she felt as a woman in man's clothes and how she took her helplessness. It is often said that Julia is an early sketch of Viola and Imogen, and it is true that the psychology of a woman in Julia's situation is presented more excellently in these later characters; but the dramatic discovery had already been made in Julia. Similarly, the presentation of Silvia may have suggested to Shakespeare the self-contained, humorous, and efficient women he was later to give us in Portia and Rosalind. The two women in *The Two Gentlemen of Verona* are at least conceived of in the Shakespearean way.

Launce and Speed, themselves no doubt from Italian comedy, are forerunners of a long line of funny servingmen, the one a dull-witted rustic, the other a quick-witted rogue. The poetry of the play is also often memorable; as, for example,

> O, how this spring of love resembleth
> The uncertain glory of an April day!

STAGE HISTORY

The *Two Gentlemen of Verona* has not been a popular or successful stage play. It appeared in altered versions three or four times in the eighteenth century and in the repertory of the Kembles. It was revived in the nineteenth century on special occasions which brought about the staging of the less well-known Shakespearean plays: by Phelps and Macready; at the Shakespeare Festival of 1890; and at the Court Theater in London in 1904. Whenever it has been staged, its runs have been very short.

The Two Gentlemen of Verona is, however, a better play on the stage than it has the reputation of being. It is a very artificial play and must not be taken too seriously. The performance at Stratford-upon-Avon in 1938 was so young and so gay that the spectator soon ceased to regard the fallings in and out of love of the young people in this comedy with any greater seriousness than one usually attributes to the love affairs of boys and girls in high school.

THE

Two Gentlemen of Verona

DRAMATIS PERSONAE

DUKE OF MILAN, Father to Silvia.
VALENTINE,⎱ the two Gentlemen.
PROTEUS, ⎰
ANTONIO, Father to Proteus.
THURIO, a foolish rival to Valentine.
EGLAMOUR, Agent for Silvia in her escape.
HOST, where Julia lodges.
OUTLAWS, with Valentine.
SPEED, a clownish servant to Valentine.
LAUNCE, the like to Proteus.
PANTHINO, Servant to Antonio.

JULIA, beloved of Proteus.
SILVIA, beloved of Valentine.
LUCETTA, waiting-woman to Julia.

Servants, Musicians.

SCENE, *Verona; Milan; the frontiers of Mantua.*

ACT I.

SCENE I. *Verona. An open place.*

Enter VALENTINE *and* PROTEUS.

Val. Cease to persuade, my loving Proteus:
Home-keeping youth have ever homely wits.
Were 't not affection chains thy tender days
To the sweet glances of thy honour'd love,
I rather would entreat thy company
To see the wonders of the world abroad
Than, living dully sluggardized at home,
Wear out thy youth with shapeless idleness.
But since thou lovest, love still and thrive therein,
Even as I would when I to love begin. 10
   Pro. Wilt thou be gone? Sweet Valentine, adieu!
Think on thy Proteus, when thou haply seest
Some rare note-worthy object in thy travel:
Wish me partaker in thy happiness
When thou dost meet good hap; and in thy danger,
If ever danger do environ thee,
Commend thy grievance to my holy prayers,
For I will be thy beadsman, Valentine.
   Val. And on a love-book pray for my success?
   Pro. Upon some book I love I'll pray for thee. 20
   Val. That 's on some shallow story of deep love:
How young Leander cross'd the Hellespont.
   Pro. That 's a deep story of a deeper love;
For he was more than over shoes in love.
   Val. 'Tis true; for you are over boots in love,
And yet you never swum the Hellespont.
   Pro. Over the boots? nay, give me not the boots.
   Val. No, I will not, for it boots thee not.
   Pro.   What?

   Val. To be in love, where scorn is bought with
    groans;
Coy looks with heart-sore sighs; one fading moment's
    mirth 30
With twenty watchful, weary, tedious nights:
If haply won, perhaps a hapless gain;
If lost, why then a grievous labour won;
However, but a folly bought with wit,
Or else a wit by folly vanquished.
   Pro. So, by your circumstance, you call me fool.
   Val. So, by your circumstance, I fear you'll prove.
   Pro. 'Tis love you cavil at: I am not Love.
   Val. Love is your master, for he masters you:
And he that is so yoked by a fool, 40
Methinks, should not be chronicled for wise.
   Pro. Yet writers say, as in the sweetest bud
The eating canker dwells, so eating love
Inhabits in the finest wits of all.
   Val. And writers say, as the most forward bud
Is eaten by the canker ere it blow,
Even so by love the young and tender wit
Is turn'd to folly, blasting in the bud,
Losing his verdure even in the prime
And all the fair effects of future hopes. 50
But wherefore waste I time to counsel thee
That art a votary to fond desire?
Once more adieu! my father at the road
Expects my coming, there to see me shipp'd.
   Pro. And thither will I bring thee, Valentine.
   Val. Sweet Proteus, no; now let us take our leave.
To Milan let me hear from thee by letters
Of thy success in love and what news else
Betideth here in absence of thy friend;
And I likewise will visit thee with mine. 60
   Pro. All happiness bechance to thee in Milan!
   Val. As much to you at home! and so, farewell. [*Exit.*
   Pro. He after honour hunts, I after love:
He leaves his friends to dignify them more;
I leave myself, my friends and all, for love.
Thou, Julia, thou hast metamorphosed me,
Made me neglect my studies, lose my time,
War with good counsel, set the world at nought;
Made wit with musing weak, heart sick with thought.

Enter SPEED.

   Speed. Sir Proteus, save you! Saw you my master? 70
   Pro. But now he parted hence, to embark for Milan.

ACT I. SCENE I.   3. **affection,** passion, love; see glossary. 9. **still,** always, constantly; see glossary. 18. **beadsman,** one engaged to pray for others. 19. **on a love-book,** i.e., instead of a prayer book. 20 ff. The puns and conceits throughout this and following dialogues are characteristic of Shakespeare's early style. As Shakespeare matures, such passages, when they occur, are more and more closely integrated into the substance of scene or character and have less the effect of a mere *tour de force.* Here the style sets the artificial tone which permeates the play. 27. **give me not the boots,** don't fool with me; don't be so flippant. 28. **boots,** avails, profits; see glossary. 29-30. **To . . . mirth,** typical Renaissance chatter in discussions of love. These are conventional details frequently attributed to lovers. Cf. ll. 65-69 and II, i, 17-33, below. 36, 37. **circumstance,** in the first instance, "detailed discourse," or "circumlocution"; in the second, "condition," or "state of affairs"; see glossary. 42-50. **Yet . . . hopes.** This passage offers an early instance of what is to become a characteristic of Shakespeare's felicitous style; that is, the repetition of phrases and images with infinite variety in treatment and substance. The best known example is *As You Like It,* II, vii, 113-226. 52. **fond,** foolish; see glossary. 57. **To Milan.** Today one does not travel from Verona to Milan by ship. In the sixteenth century this may have been the easier route. 58. **success,** outcome; see glossary. 64. **dignify,** i.e., by leaving them for self-improvement he will add luster to them. 71. **parted,** departed; see glossary.

Speed. Twenty to one then he is shipp'd already,
And I have play'd the sheep in losing him.
Pro. Indeed, a sheep doth very often stray,
An if the shepherd be a while away.
Speed. You conclude that my master is a shepherd
then and I a sheep?
Pro. I do.
Speed. Why then, my horns are his horns, whether
I wake or sleep. 80
Pro. A silly answer and fitting well a sheep.
Speed. This proves me still a sheep.
Pro. True; and thy master a shepherd.
Speed. Nay, that I can deny by a circumstance.
Pro. It shall go hard but I'll prove it by another.
Speed. The shepherd seeks the sheep, and not the
sheep the shepherd; but I seek my master, and my
master seeks not me: therefore I am no sheep. 91
Pro. The sheep for fodder follow the shepherd; the
shepherd for food follows not the sheep: thou for
wages followest thy master; thy master for wages fol-
lows not thee: therefore thou art a sheep.
Speed. Such another proof will make me cry 'baa.'
Pro. But, dost thou hear? gavest thou my letter to
Julia? 100
Speed. Ay, sir: I, a lost mutton, gave your letter to
her, a laced mutton, and she, a laced mutton, gave
me, a lost mutton, nothing for my labour.
Pro. Here's too small a pasture for such store of
muttons.
Speed. If the ground be overcharged, you were best
stick her.
Pro. Nay: in that you are astray, 'twere best pound
you. 110
Speed. Nay, sir, less than a pound shall serve me for
carrying your letter.
Pro. You mistake; I mean the pound,—a pinfold.
Speed. From a pound to a pin? fold it over and
over,
'Tis threefold too little for carrying a letter to your
lover.
Pro. But what said she?
Speed. [*First nodding*] Ay.
Pro. Nod—Ay—why, that's noddy. 119
Speed. You mistook, sir; I say, she did nod: and you
ask me if she did nod; and I say, 'Ay.'
Pro. And that set together is noddy.
Speed. Now you have taken the pains to set it to-
gether, take it for your pains.
Pro. No, no; you shall have it for bearing the letter.
Speed. Well, I perceive I must be fain to bear with
you.
Pro. Why, sir, how do you bear with me?
Speed. Marry, sir, the letter, very orderly; having
nothing but the word 'noddy' for my pains. 131
Pro. Beshrew me, but you have a quick wit.
Speed. And yet it cannot overtake your slow purse.

Pro. Come, come, open the matter in brief: what
said she?
Speed. Open your purse, that the money and the
matter may be both at once delivered.
Pro. Well, sir, here is for your pains. What said she?
Speed. Truly, sir, I think you'll hardly win her. 141
Pro. Why, couldst thou perceive so much from her?
Speed. Sir, I could perceive nothing at all from her;
no, not so much as a ducat for delivering your letter:
and being so hard to me that brought your mind, I
fear she'll prove as hard to you in telling your mind.
Give her no token but stones; for she's as hard as steel.
Pro. What said she? nothing? 150
Speed. No, not so much as 'Take this for thy pains.'
To testify your bounty, I thank you, you have testerned
me; in requital whereof, henceforth carry your letters
yourself: and so, sir, I'll commend you to my master.
Pro. Go, go, be gone, to save your ship from wreck,
Which cannot perish having thee aboard,
Being destined to a drier death on shore. [*Exit Speed.*
I must go send some better messenger:
I fear my Julia would not deign my lines, 160
Receiving them from such a worthless post. [*Exit.*

SCENE II. *The same. Garden of* JULIA'S *house.*

Enter JULIA *and* LUCETTA.

Jul. But say, Lucetta, now we are alone,
Wouldst thou then counsel me to fall in love?
Luc. Ay, madam, so you stumble not unheedfully.
Jul. Of all the fair resort of gentlemen
That every day with parle encounter me,
In thy opinion which is worthiest love?
Luc. Please you repeat their names, I'll show my
mind
According to my shallow simple skill.
Jul. What think'st thou of the fair Sir Eglamour?
Luc. As of a knight well-spoken, neat and fine; 10
But, were I you, he never should be mine.
Jul. What think'st thou of the rich Mercatio?
Luc. Well of his wealth; but of himself, so so.
Jul. What think'st thou of the gentle Proteus?
Luc. Lord, Lord! to see what folly reigns in us!
Jul. How now! what means this passion at his
name?
Luc. Pardon, dear madam: 'tis a passing shame
That I, unworthy body as I am,
Should censure thus on lovely gentlemen.
Jul. Why not on Proteus, as of all the rest? 20
Luc. Then thus: of many good I think him best.
Jul. Your reason?
Luc. I have no other but a woman's reason; I think
him so because I think him so.
Jul. And wouldst thou have me cast my love on him?
Luc. Ay, if you thought your love not cast away.

72, 73. **shipp'd, sheep.** Elizabethan pronunciation doubtless made
the pun obvious. 75. **An if,** though, even if; see glossary. 101, 102.
lost, laced. As with *shipp'd, sheep*, above, the Elizabethan pronunciation of the two words was similar. 102. **laced mutton,** a courtesan.
119. **noddy,** a simpleton. The New Cambridge editors suggest a
quibble with "nothing." 130. **Marry,** mild oath, equivalent to "Indeed!" See glossary. 132. **Beshrew,** curse; see glossary. 141. **hardly,**
with difficulty; see glossary. 145. **ducat,** silver coin worth about 3s.
6d. 147. **mind,** desires, intentions; see glossary. 153. **testerned,**
given (me) a testern, a sixpence. 157-158. **Which . . . shore,** an
allusion to the proverb, "He that is born to be hanged shall never be
drowned." Cf. *The Tempest*, I, i, 31-32. 161. **post,** messenger; see
glossary.

SCENE II. 4. **resort,** persons resorting to, or visiting (often by
way of courtship). 5. **parle,** talk; see glossary. 7. **repeat their names.**
Shakespeare uses this expository device with more point and greater
effectiveness in *The Merchant of Venice*, where Portia has Nerissa recount
the names of her suitors as a means of informing the audience. 9. **Sir
Eglamour,** not to be identified with Silvia's friend of the same name.
The New Cambridge editors suggest that in an earlier version of the
play they were the same person. 16. **passion,** passionate outburst; see
glossary. 17. **passing,** surpassing; see glossary. 19. **censure,** pass
sentence; see glossary. 25-32. **And wouldst . . . their love.** This artificial style of speaking, in which the dialogue alternates line by line
between two characters, is called stichomythia. It is a device from
classical drama that Shakespeare employed occasionally in his

Jul. Why he, of all the rest, hath never moved me.
Luc. Yet he, of all the rest, I think, best loves ye.
Jul. His little speaking shows his love but small.
Luc. Fire that 's closest kept burns most of all. 30
Jul. They do not love that do not show their love.
Luc. O, they love least that let men know their love.
Jul. I would I knew his mind.
Luc. Peruse this paper, madam.
Jul. 'To Julia.' Say, from whom?
Luc. That the contents will show.
Jul. Say, say, who gave it thee?
Luc. Sir Valentine's page; and sent, I think, from
  Proteus.
He would have given it you; but I, being in the way,
Did in your name receive it: pardon the fault, I pray.
Jul. Now, by my modesty, a goodly broker! 41
Dare you presume to harbour wanton lines?
To whisper and conspire against my youth?
Now, trust me, 'tis an office of great worth
And you an officer fit for the place.
There, take the paper: see it be return'd;
Or else return no more into my sight.
Luc. To plead for love deserves more fee than hate.
Jul. Will ye be gone?
Luc.   That you may ruminate. [*Exit.*
Jul. And yet I would I had o'erlooked the letter: 50
It were a shame to call her back again
And pray her to a fault for which I chid her.
What 'fool is she, that knows I am a maid,
And would not force the letter to my view!
Since maids, in modesty, say 'no' to that
Which they would have the profferer construe 'ay.'
Fie, fie, how wayward is this foolish love
That, like a testy babe, will scratch the nurse
And presently all humbled kiss the rod!
How churlishly I chid Lucetta hence, 60
When willingly I would have had her here!
How angerly I taught my brow to frown,
When inward joy enforced my heart to smile!
My penance is to call Lucetta back
And ask remission for my folly past.
What ho! Lucetta!

Re-enter LUCETTA.

Luc.   What would your ladyship?
Jul. Is 't near dinner-time?
Luc.   I would it were,
That you might kill your stomach on your meat
And not upon your maid.
Jul. What is 't that you took up so gingerly? 70
Luc. Nothing.
Jul. Why didst thou stoop, then?
Luc. To take a paper up that I let fall.
Jul. And is that paper nothing?
Luc. Nothing concerning me.
Jul. Then let it lie for those that it concerns.

Luc. Madam, it will not lie where it concerns,
Unless it have a false interpreter.
Jul. Some love of yours hath writ to you in rhyme.
Luc. That I might sing it, madam, to a tune. 80
Give me a note: your ladyship can set.
Jul. As little by such toys as may be possible.
Best sing it to the tune of 'Light o' love.'
Luc. It is too heavy for so light a tune.
Jul. Heavy! belike it hath some burden then?
Luc. Ay, and melodious were it, would you sing it.
Jul. And why not you?
Luc.   I cannot reach so high.
Jul. Let 's see your song. How now, minion!
Luc. Keep tune there still, so you will sing it out:
And yet methinks I do not like this tune. 90
Jul. You do not?
Luc.   No, madam; it is too sharp.
Jul. You, minion, are too saucy.
Luc. Nay, now you are too flat
And mar the concord with too harsh a descant:
There wanteth but a mean to fill your song.
Jul. The mean is drown'd with your unruly bass.
Luc. Indeed, I bid the base for Proteus.
Jul. This babble shall not henceforth trouble me.
Here is a coil with protestation! [*Tears the letter.*
Go get you gone, and let the papers lie: 100
You would be fingering them, to anger me.
Luc. She makes it strange; but she would be best
  pleased
To be so anger'd with another letter. [*Exit.*
Jul. Nay, would I were so anger'd with the same!
O hateful hands, to tear such loving words!
Injurious wasps, to feed on such sweet honey
And kill the bees that yield it with your stings!
I'll kiss each several paper for amends.
Look, here is writ 'kind Julia.' Unkind Julia!
As in revenge of thy ingratitude, 110
I throw thy name against the bruising stones,
Trampling contemptuously on thy disdain.
And here is writ 'love-wounded Proteus.'
Poor wounded name! my bosom as a bed
Shall lodge thee till thy wound be throughly heal'd;
And thus I search it with a sovereign kiss.
But twice or thrice was 'Proteus' written down.
Be calm, good wind, blow not a word away
Till I have found each letter in the letter,
Except mine own name: that some whirlwind bear 120
Unto a ragged fearful-hanging rock
And throw it thence into the raging sea!
Lo, here in one line is his name twice writ,
'Poor forlorn Proteus, passionate Proteus,
To the sweet Julia:' that I'll tear away.
And yet I will not, sith so prettily
He couples it to his complaining names.
Thus will I fold them one upon another:
Now kiss, embrace, contend, do what you will.

earlier plays. **27. moved,** made a proposal to, appealed or applied to; see glossary. **41. broker,** agent, intermediary (particularly in love affairs). **53. What 'fool,** so F; Globe: *What a fool.* **68. stomach,** a quibble on the meanings "appetite" and "angry temper"; see glossary. **meat,** pronounced more nearly like "mate," punning on *maid* in the next line. **80-97. That . . . Proteus.** The quibbles on musical terms here are obvious enough in themselves; but their rapid succession, probably accompanied by gestures and stage business, makes the passage difficult to follow in reading. **81. note,** a quibbling reference to Proteus' letter. **set,** i.e., set to music, with quibble on "writing a letter." **82. toys,** trifles; see glossary. **83. 'Light o' love,'** an air well known at the time. Cf. *Much Ado about Nothing*, III, iv, 44, where it is mentioned **as** here with a quibble on *burden*. **85. burden,** bass accompaniment

to a melody. **87. reach so high.** Proteus' rank is too high for Lucetta to aspire to. **88. minion,** saucy woman; see glossary. **89. tune,** temper, mood. **91, 93. sharp, flat.** The New Cambridge editors suggest a pinch and a slap as accompanying stage business. **94. descant,** improvised harmony accompanying a melody. **95. mean,** tenor part; a reference to Proteus; see glossary. **97. bid the base,** a challenge in the game of prisoner's base. **99. coil,** noise, disturbance; see glossary. **protestation,** solemn declaration or promise. **102. makes it strange,** pretends indifference or ignorance; see *strange* in glossary. **108. several,** separate; see glossary. **109. Unkind,** unnatural, cruel; see glossary. **116. search,** probe, as a wound. **126. sith,** since; see glossary.

Re-enter LUCETTA.

Luc. Madam,　　　　　　　　　　　　　　　　130
Dinner is ready, and your father stays.
　Jul. Well, let us go.
　Luc. What, shall these papers lie like telltales here?
　Jul. If you respect them, best to take them up.
　Luc. Nay, I was taken up for laying them down:
Yet here they shall not lie, for catching cold.
　Jul. I see you have a month's mind to them.
　Luc. Ay, madam, you may say what sights you see;
I see things too, although you judge I wink.
　Jul. Come, come; will 't please you go?　　[*Exeunt.* 140

SCENE III. *The same.* ANTONIO'S *house.*

Enter ANTONIO *and* PANTHINO.

　Ant. Tell me, Panthino, what sad talk was that
Wherewith my brother held you in the cloister?
　Pan. 'Twas of his nephew Proteus, your son.
　Ant. Why, what of him?
　Pan.　　　　　　　　He wonder'd that your lordship
Would suffer him to spend his youth at home,
While other men, of slender reputation,
Put forth their sons to seek preferment out:
Some to the wars, to try their fortune there;
Some to discover islands far away;
Some to the studious universities.　　　　　　10
For any or for all these exercises
He said that Proteus your son was meet,
And did request me to importune you
To let him spend his time no more at home,
Which would be great impeachment to his age,
In having known no travel in his youth.
　Ant. Nor need'st thou much importune me to that
Whereon this month I have been hammering.
I have consider'd well his loss of time
And how he cannot be a perfect man,　　　　20
Not being tried and tutor'd in the world:
Experience is by industry achieved
And perfected by the swift course of time.
Then tell me, whither were I best to send him?
　Pan. I think your lordship is not ignorant
How his companion, youthful Valentine,
Attends the emperor in his royal court.
　Ant. I know it well.
　Pan. 'Twere good, I think, your lordship sent him
　　thither:
There shall he practise tilts and tournaments,　　30
Hear sweet discourse, converse with noblemen,
And be in eye of every exercise
Worthy his youth and nobleness of birth.
　Ant. I like thy counsel; well hast thou advised:
And that thou mayst perceive how well I like it
The execution of it shall make known.
Even with the speediest expedition
I will dispatch him to the emperor's court.

Pan. To-morrow, may it please you, Don Alphonso
With other gentlemen of good esteem　　　　40
Are journeying to salute the emperor
And to commend their service to his will.
　Ant. Good company; with them shall Proteus go:
And, in good time! now will we break with him.

Enter PROTEUS.

　Pro. Sweet love! sweet lines! sweet life!
Here is her hand, the agent of her heart;
Here is her oath for love, her honour's pawn.
O, that our fathers would applaud our loves,
To seal our happiness with their consents!
O heavenly Julia!　　　　　　　　　　　50
　Ant. How now! what letter are you reading there?
　Pro. May 't please your lordship, 'tis a word or two
Of commendations sent from Valentine,
Deliver'd by a friend that came from him.
　Ant. Lend me the letter; let me see what news.
　Pro. There is no news, my lord, but that he writes
How happily he lives, how well beloved
And daily graced by the emperor;
Wishing me with him, partner of his fortune.
　Ant. And how stand you affected to his wish?　　60
　Pro. As one relying on your lordship's will
And not depending on his friendly wish.
　Ant. My will is something sorted with his wish.
Muse not that I thus suddenly proceed;
For what I will, I will, and there an end.
I am resolved that thou shalt spend some time
With Valentinus in the emperor's court:
What maintenance he from his friends receives,
Like exhibition thou shalt have from me.
To-morrow be in readiness to go:　　　　　70
Excuse it not, for I am peremptory.
　Pro. My lord, I cannot be so soon provided:
Please you, deliberate a day or two.
　Ant. Look, what thou want'st shall be sent after
　　thee:
No more of stay! to-morrow thou must go.
Come on, Panthino: you shall be employ'd
To hasten on his expedition.　　[*Exeunt Ant. and Pan.*
　Pro. Thus have I shunn'd the fire for fear of burning,
And drench'd me in the sea, where I am drown'd.
I fear'd to show my father Julia's letter,　　　80
Lest he should take exceptions to my love;
And with the vantage of mine own excuse
Hath he excepted most against my love.
O, how this spring of love resembleth
　The uncertain glory of an April day,
Which now shows all the beauty of the sun,
　And by and by a cloud takes all away!

Re-enter PANTHINO.

　Pan. Sir Proteus, your father calls for you:
　He is in haste; therefore, I pray you, go.
　Pro. Why, this it is: my heart accords thereto,　　90
　And yet a thousand times it answers 'no.' [*Exeunt.*

---

131. **stays,** waits; see glossary; cf. note to II, ii, 13, below.　134. **re-spect,** prize, esteem; see glossary.　137. **month's mind,** inclination, liking.　139. **wink,** have the eyes closed; see glossary.
　SCENE III.　1. **sad,** serious; see glossary.　4-16. **He . . . youth.** These lines reflect some Renaissance customs in the education of young gentlemen; cf. ll. 30-32, below.　6. **slender reputation,** i.e., men of lower station than yourself.　7. **Put . . . sons,** send their sons away from home. **out,** abroad; see glossary.　15. **impeachment . . . age,** detriment or cause for reproach to him in his mature years.　18. **hammer-**

ing, beating (an idea) into shape; cf. *Richard II*, V, v, 5.　27. **emperor,** i.e., the duke of Milan, not the ruler of the Holy Roman Empire.　30. **practise,** perform, take part in; see glossary.　31. **discourse,** conversation; see glossary. **converse,** associate with; see glossary.　44. **break with,** reveal, disclose (it to him).　49. **seal,** conclude, ratify; see glossary.　58. **graced,** favored; see glossary.　60. **affected,** disposed, inclined; see glossary.　63. **something,** somewhat; see glossary. **sorted,** adapted, made to agree.　69. **exhibition,** allowance of money.　71. **Excuse,** decline, offer no excuses; see glossary.　82. **vantage,** ad-

ACT II.

SCENE I. *Milan. The* DUKE'S *palace.*

Enter VALENTINE *and* SPEED.

Speed. Sir, your glove.
Val. Not mine; my gloves are on.
Speed. Why, then, this may be yours, for this is but
one.
Val. Ha! let me see: ay, give it me, it's mine:
Sweet ornament that decks a thing divine!
Ah, Silvia, Silvia!
Speed. Madam Silvia! Madam Silvia!
Val. How now, sirrah?
Speed. She is not within hearing, sir.
Val. Why, sir, who bade you call her?
Speed. Your worship, sir; or else I mistook.   10
Val. Well, you'll still be too forward.
Speed. And yet I was last chidden for being too slow.
Val. Go to, sir: tell me, do you know Madam Silvia?
Speed. She that your worship loves?
Val. Why, how know you that I am in love?
Speed. Marry, by these special marks: first, you have
learned, like Sir Proteus, to wreathe your arms, like a
malecontent; to relish a love-song, like a robin-red-
breast; to walk alone, like one that had the pestilence;
to sigh, like a schoolboy that had lost his A B C; to
weep, like a young wench that had buried her
grandam; to fast, like one that takes diet; to watch,
like one that fears robbing; to speak puling, like a
beggar at Hallowmas. You were wont, when you
laughed, to crow like a cock; when you walked, to
walk like one of the lions; when you fasted, it was
presently after dinner; when you looked sadly, it was
for want of money: and now you are metamorphosed
with a mistress, that, when I look on you, I can hardly
think you my master.   33
Val. Are all these things perceived in me?
Speed. They are all perceived without ye.
Val. Without me? they cannot.
Speed. Without you? nay, that's certain, for, without
you were so simple, none else would: but you are so
without these follies, that these follies are within you
and shine through you like the water in an urinal, that
not an eye that sees you but is a physician to comment
on your malady.
Val. But tell me, dost thou know my lady Silvia?
Speed. She that you gaze on so as she sits at supper?
Val. Hast thou observed that? even she, I mean.
Speed. Why, sir, I know her not.   50
Val. Dost thou know her by my gazing on her, and
yet knowest her not?
Speed. Is she not hard-favoured, sir?
Val. Not so fair, boy, as well-favoured.
Speed. Sir, I know that well enough.
Val. What dost thou know?
Speed. That she is not so fair as, of you, well favoured.
Val. I mean that her beauty is exquisite, but her
favour infinite.   60

Speed. That's because the one is painted and the
other out of all count.
Val. How painted? and how out of count?
Speed. Marry, sir, so painted, to make her fair, that
no man counts of her beauty.
Val. How esteemest thou me? I account of her
beauty.
Speed. You never saw her since she was deformed.   70
Val. How long hath she been deformed?
Speed. Ever since you loved her.
Val. I have loved her ever since I saw her; and still
I see her beautiful.
Speed. If you love her, you cannot see her.
Val. Why?
Speed. Because Love is blind. O, that you had mine
eyes; or your own eyes had the lights they were wont
to have when you chid at Sir Proteus for going
ungartered!
Val. What should I see then?   80
Speed. Your own present folly and her passing de-
formity: for he, being in love, could not see to garter
his hose, and you, being in love, cannot see to put on
your hose.
Val. Belike, boy, then, you are in love; for last
morning you could not see to wipe my shoes.
Speed. True, sir; I was in love with my bed: I thank
you, you swinged me for my love, which makes me
the bolder to chide you for yours.
Val. In conclusion, I stand affected to her.
Speed. I would you were set, so your affection would
cease.
Val. Last night she enjoined me to write some lines
to one she loves.
Speed. And have you?
Val. I have.
Speed. Are they not lamely writ?
Val. No, boy, but as well as I can do them. Peace!
here she comes.   99
Speed. [*Aside*] O excellent motion! O exceeding pup-
pet! Now will he interpret to her.

Enter SILVIA.

Val. Madam and mistress, a thousand good-
morrows.
Speed. [*Aside*] O, give ye good even! here's a million
of manners.
Sil. Sir Valentine and servant, to you two thousand.
Speed. [*Aside*] He should give her interest, and she
gives it him.
Val. As you enjoin'd me, I have writ your letter   110
Unto the secret nameless friend of yours;
Which I was much unwilling to proceed in
But for my duty to your ladyship.
Sil. I thank you, gentle servant: 'tis very clerkly
done.
Val. Now trust me, madam, it came hardly off;
For being ignorant to whom it goes
I writ at random, very doubtfully.
Sil. Perchance you think too much of so much pains?

---

vantage; i.e., by my excuse I have given him the advantage whereby he
makes my love to suffer most; see glossary.
ACT II. SCENE I. 14. **Go to,** an expression of remonstrance; see
glossary. 19. **wreathe . . . malecontent,** allusion to the posture of an
unhappy malcontent. 23. **A B C,** ABC book, primer. 25. **watch,** lie
awake, sit up at night; see glossary. 26-27. **a beggar at Hallowmas,** a
reference to a custom of begging alms on All Saints' Day. 30. **presently,** immediately; see glossary. 60. **favour,** charm, attraction; see
glossary. 62. **out . . . count,** incalculable. 65. **counts,** makes account

of. 70. **deformed,** i.e., the lover's distorted vision alters his lady's true
appearance. 91. **set,** seated, as opposed to *stand* in the preceding line,
with a quibble on the meaning "concluded." 100, 101. **motion, puppet, interpret.** In a puppet show (called *motion*), the voice speaking for
the puppet is said to *interpret. Motion* and *puppet* refer to Silvia, probably splendidly dressed. 106. **servant,** a term of gallantry, denoting
a man devoted to serving a lady. 113. **duty,** obedience, submission;
see glossary. 114. **clerkly,** in a scholarly manner.

Val. No, madam; so it stead you, I will write,
Please you command, a thousand times as much;   120
And yet—
    Sil. A pretty period! Well, I guess the sequel;
And yet I will not name it; and yet I care not;
And yet take this again; and yet I thank you,
Meaning henceforth to trouble you no more.
    Speed. [*Aside*] And yet you will; and yet another
        'yet.'
    Val. What means your ladyship? do you not like it?
    Sil. Yes, yes: the lines are very quaintly writ;
But since unwillingly, take them again.
Nay, take them.   130
    Val. Madam, they are for you.
    Sil. Ay, ay: you writ them, sir, at my request;
But I will none of them; they are for you;
I would have had them writ more movingly.
    Val. Please you, I'll write your ladyship another.
    Sil. And when it's writ, for my sake read it over,
And if it please you, so; if not, why, so.
    Val. If it please me, madam, what then?
    Sil. Why, if it please you, take it for your labour:
And so, good morrow, servant.   [*Exit.* 140
    Speed. O jest unseen, inscrutable, invisible,
As a nose on a man's face, or a weathercock on a
        steeple!
My master sues to her, and she hath taught her suitor,
He being her pupil, to become her tutor.
O excellent device! was there ever heard a better,
That my master, being scribe, to himself should write
        the letter?
    Val. How now, sir? what are you reasoning with
yourself?
    Speed. Nay, I was rhyming: 'tis you that have the
reason.   150
    Val. To do what?
    Speed. To be a spokesman from Madam Silvia.
    Val. To whom?
    Speed. To yourself: why, she wooes you by a figure.
    Val. What figure?
    Speed. By a letter, I should say.
    Val. Why, she hath not writ to me?
    Speed. What need she, when she hath made you
write to yourself? Why, do you not perceive the jest? 160
    Val. No, believe me.
    Speed. No believing you, indeed, sir. But did you
perceive her earnest?
    Val. She gave me none, except an angry word.
    Speed. Why, she hath given you a letter.
    Val. That's the letter I writ to her friend.
    Speed. And that letter hath she delivered, and there
an end.
    Val. I would it were no worse.
    Speed. I'll warrant you, 'tis as well: 170
For often have you writ to her, and she, in modesty,
Or else for want of idle time, could not again reply;
Or fearing else some messenger that might her mind
        discover,
Herself hath taught her love himself to write unto her
        lover.
All this I speak in print, for in print I found it.

Why muse you, sir? 'tis dinner-time.
    Val. I have dined.
    Speed. Ay, but hearken, sir; though the chameleon
Love can feed on the air, I am one that am nourished
by my victuals and would fain have meat. O, be not
like your mistress; be moved, be moved.   [*Exeunt.*

SCENE II. *Verona.* JULIA'S *house.*

Enter PROTEUS *and* JULIA.

    Pro. Have patience, gentle Julia.
    Jul. I must, where is no remedy.
    Pro. When possibly I can, I will return.
    Jul. If you turn not, you will return the sooner.
Keep this remembrance for thy Julia's sake.
                    [*Giving a ring.*
    Pro. Why, then, we'll make exchange; here, take
        you this.
    Jul. And seal the bargain with a holy kiss.
    Pro. Here is my hand for my true constancy;
And when that hour o'erslips me in the day
Wherein I sigh not, Julia, for thy sake,   10
The next ensuing hour some foul mischance
Torment me for my love's forgetfulness!
My father stays my coming; answer not;
The tide is now: nay, not thy tide of tears;
That tide will stay me longer than I should.
Julia, farewell!   [*Exit Julia.*
                What, gone without a word?
Ay, so true love should do: it cannot speak;
For truth hath better deeds than words to grace it.

Enter PANTHINO.

    Pan. Sir Proteus, you are stay'd for.
    Pro. Go: I come, I come.   20
Alas! this parting strikes poor lovers dumb.   [*Exeunt.*

SCENE III. *The same. A street.*

Enter LAUNCE, *leading a dog.*

    Launce. Nay, 'twill be this hour ere I have done
weeping; all the kind of the Launces have this very
fault. I have received my proportion, like the prodigious son, and am going with Sir Proteus to the
Imperial's court. I think Crab my dog be the sourest-
natured dog that lives: my mother weeping, my father
wailing, my sister crying, our maid howling, our cat
wringing her hands, and all our house in a great
perplexity, yet did not this cruel-hearted cur shed one
tear: he is a stone, a very pebblestone, and has no
more pity in him than a dog: a Jew would have wept
to have seen our parting; why, my grandam, having
no eyes, look you, wept herself blind at my parting.
Nay, I'll show you the manner of it. This shoe is my
father: no, this left shoe is my father: no, no, this left
shoe is my mother: nay, that cannot be so neither:
yes, it is so, it is so, it hath the worser sole. This shoe,

119. **stead,** help; be of use to; see glossary.   154. **figure,** device,
ruse, perhaps with a quibble on the rhetorical sense.   163. **earnest,**
quibble between "seriousness" and "money paid as an installment to
secure a bargain"; see glossary.   175. **speak in print,** i.e., he has
memorized the verse.
    SCENE II.   2. **where,** where there; an instance of a type of ellipsis
frequent in Elizabethan English in which the conjunctive serves a double

function.   13. **stays,** waits for; so likewise *stay'd for* (l. 19 below),
where modern usage employs the active, "they wait for you"; see
glossary.
    SCENE III.   2. **kind,** kindred, race; see glossary.   3. **proportion,**
portion, allotment; see glossary.   30-31. **a wood woman.** F: *a would-
woman.* The emendation is Theobald's and is accepted by all modern
editors; *wood* meaning "mad," with quibble on "wooden shoe." The New

with the hole in it, is my mother, and this my father; a vengeance on 't! there 'tis: now, sir, this staff is my sister, for, look you, she is as white as a lily and as small as a wand: this hat is Nan, our maid: I am the dog: no, the dog is himself, and I am the dog—Oh! the dog is me, and I am myself; ay, so, so. Now come I to my father; Father, your blessing: now should not the shoe speak a word for weeping: now should I kiss my father; well, he weeps on. Now come I to my mother: O, that she could speak now like a wood woman! Well, I kiss her; why, there 'tis; here 's my mother's breath up and down. Now come I to my sister; mark the moan she makes. Now the dog all this while sheds not a tear nor speaks a word; but see how I lay the dust with my tears.

Enter PANTHINO.

Pan. Launce, away, away, aboard! thy master is shipped and thou art to post after with oars. What 's the matter? why weepest thou, man? Away, ass! you'll lose the tide, if you tarry any longer. 40

Launce. It is no matter if the tied were lost; for it is the unkindest tied that ever any man tied.

Pan. What 's the unkindest tide?

Launce. Why, he that 's tied here, Crab, my dog.

Pan. Tut, man, I mean thou 'lt lose the flood, and, in losing the flood, lose thy voyage, and, in losing thy voyage, lose thy master, and, in losing thy master, lose thy service, and, in losing thy service,—Why dost thou stop my mouth? 51

Launce. For fear thou shouldst lose thy tongue.

Pan. Where should I lose my tongue?

Launce. In thy tale.

Pan. In my tail!

Launce. Lose the tide, and the voyage, and the master, and the service, and the tied! Why, man, if the river were dry, I am able to fill it with my tears; if the wind were down, I could drive the boat with my sighs. 60

Pan. Come, come away, man; I was sent to call thee.

Launce. Sir, call me what thou darest.

Pan. Wilt thou go?

Launce. Well, I will go. [*Exeunt.*

SCENE IV. *Milan. The* DUKE'S *palace.*

Enter SILVIA, VALENTINE, THURIO, *and* SPEED.

Sil. Servant!

Val. Mistress?

Speed. Master, Sir Thurio frowns on you.

Val. Ay, boy, it 's for love.

Speed. Not of you.

Val. Of my mistress, then.

Speed. 'Twere good you knocked him. [*Exit.*

Sil. Servant, you are sad.

Val. Indeed, madam, I seem so.

Thu. Seem you that you are not? 10

Val. Haply I do.

Thu. So do counterfeits.

Val. So do you.

Thu. What seem I that I am not?

Val. Wise.

Thu. What instance of the contrary?

Val. Your folly.

Thu. And how quote you my folly?

Val. I quote it in your jerkin.

Thu. My jerkin is a doublet. 20

Val. Well, then, I'll double your folly.

Thu. How?

Sil. What, angry, Sir Thurio! do you change colour?

Val. Give him leave, madam; he is a kind of chameleon.

Thu. That hath more mind to feed on your blood than live in your air.

Val. You have said, sir.

Thu. Ay, sir, and done too, for this time. 30

Val. I know it well, sir; you always end ere you begin.

Sil. A fine volley of words, gentlemen, and quickly shot off.

Val. 'Tis indeed, madam; we thank the giver.

Sil. Who is that, servant?

Val. Yourself, sweet lady; for you gave the fire. Sir Thurio borrows his wit from your ladyship's looks, and spends what he borrows kindly in your company.

Thu. Sir, if you spend word for word with me, I shall make your wit bankrupt.

Val. I know it well, sir; you have an exchequer of words, and, I think, no other treasure to give your followers, for it appears, by their bare liveries, that they live by your bare words.

Sil. No more, gentlemen, no more: here comes my father.

Enter DUKE.

Duke. Now, daughter Silvia, you are hard beset.
Sir Valentine, your father 's in good health: 50
What say you to a letter from your friends
Of much good news?

Val. My lord, I will be thankful
To any happy messenger from thence.

Duke. Know ye Don Antonio, your countryman?

Val. Ay, my good lord, I know the gentleman
To be of worth and worthy estimation
And not without desert so well reputed.

Duke. Hath he not a son?

Val. Ay, my good lord; a son that well deserves
The honour and regard of such a father. 60

Duke. You know him well?

Val. I know him as myself; for from our infancy
We have conversed and spent our hours together:
And though myself have been an idle truant,
Omitting the sweet benefit of time
To clothe mine age with angel-like perfection,
Yet hath Sir Proteus, for that 's his name,
Made use and fair advantage of his days;
His years but young, but his experience old;
His head unmellow'd, but his judgement ripe; 70
And, in a word, for far behind his worth

Cambridge editors see a possible misreading by the compositor of *a nould* (i.e., an old) *woman,* and suggest another possibility, *a wold-woman,* i.e., a country woman. 37. **post,** hasten; see glossary. 55. **my,** so Hanmer; Globe, following F: *thy.*

SCENE IV. 16. **instance,** proof; see glossary. 18. **quote,** notice, observe. 19. **jerkin,** close-fitting jacket, frequently of leather. 20. **doublet,** close-fitting garment with or without sleeves; possible quibble

on the sense of "duplicity." 38-40. **Sir Thurio . . . company,** i.e., what he borrows from you he naturally (*kindly*) spends in your company. 49. **hard,** much. The New Cambridge editors suspect a cut here because of the abruptness of the remark.

Comes all the praises that I now bestow,
He is complete in feature and in mind
With all good grace to grace a gentleman.
   Duke. Beshrew me, sir, but if he make this good,
He is as worthy for an empress' love
As meet to be an emperor's counsellor.
Well, sir, this gentleman is come to me,
With commendation from great potentates;
And here he means to spend his time awhile: 80
I think 'tis no unwelcome news to you.
   Val. Should I have wish'd a thing, it had been he.
   Duke. Welcome him then according to his worth.
Silvia, I speak to you, and you, Sir Thurio;
For Valentine, I need not cite him to it:
I will send him hither to you presently.   [*Exit.*
   Val. This is the gentleman I told your ladyship
Had come along with me, but that his mistress
Did hold his eyes lock'd in her crystal looks.
   Sil. Belike that now she hath enfranchised them   90
Upon some other pawn for fealty.
   Val. Nay, sure, I think she holds them prisoners
     still.
   Sil. Nay, then he should be blind; and, being blind,
How could he see his way to seek out you?
   Val. Why, lady, Love hath twenty pair of eyes.
   Thu. They say that Love hath not an eye at all.
   Val. To see such lovers, Thurio, as yourself:
Upon a homely object Love can wink.
   Sil. Have done, have done; here comes the
     gentleman.   [*Exit Thurio.*

Enter PROTEUS.

   Val. Welcome, dear Proteus! Mistress, I beseech
     you,   100
Confirm his welcome with some special favour.
   Sil. His worth is warrant for his welcome hither,
If this be he you oft have wish'd to hear from.
   Val. Mistress, it is: sweet lady, entertain him
To be my fellow-servant to your ladyship.
   Sil. Too low a mistress for so high a servant.
   Pro. Not so, sweet lady: but too mean a servant
To have a look of such a worthy mistress.
   Val. Leave off discourse of disability:
Sweet lady, entertain him for your servant.   110
   Pro. My duty will I boast of; nothing else.
   Sil. And duty never yet did want his meed:
Servant, you are welcome to a worthless mistress.
   Pro. I'll die on him that says so but yourself.
   Sil. That you are welcome?
   Pro.   That you are worthless.

Re-enter THURIO.

   Thu. Madam, my lord your father would speak with
     you.
   Sil. I wait upon his pleasure. Come, Sir Thurio,
Go with me. Once more, new servant, welcome:
I'll leave you to confer of home affairs;
When you have done, we look to hear from you.   120
   Pro. We'll both attend upon your ladyship.
             [*Exeunt Silvia and Thurio.*
   Val. Now, tell me how do all from whence you
     came?

   Pro. Your friends are well and have them much
     commended.
   Val. And how do yours?
   Pro.   I left them all in health.
   Val. How does your lady? and how thrives your
     love?
   Pro. My tales of love were wont to weary you;
I know you joy not in a love-discourse.
   Val. Ay, Proteus, but that life is alter'd now:
I have done penance for contemning Love,
Whose high imperious thoughts have punish'd me   130
With bitter fasts, with penitential groans,
With nightly tears and daily heart-sore sighs;
For in revenge of my contempt of love,
Love hath chased sleep from my enthralled eyes
And made them watchers of mine own heart's sorrow.
O gentle Proteus, Love's a mighty lord
And hath so humbled me as I confess
There is no woe to his correction
Nor to his service no such joy on earth.
Now no discourse, except it be of love;   140
Now can I break my fast, dine, sup and sleep,
Upon the very naked name of love.
   Pro. Enough; I read your fortune in your eye.
Was this the idol that you worship so?
   Val. Even she; and is she not a heavenly saint?
   Pro. No; but she is an earthly paragon.
   Val. Call her divine.
   Pro.   I will not flatter her.
   Val. O, flatter me; for love delights in praises.
   Pro. When I was sick, you gave me bitter pills,
And I must minister the like to you.   150
   Val. Then speak the truth by her; if not divine,
Yet let her be a principality,
Sovereign to all the creatures on the earth.
   Pro. Except my mistress.
   Val.   Sweet, except not any;
Except thou wilt except against my love.
   Pro. Have I not reason to prefer mine own?
   Val. And I will help thee to prefer her too:
She shall be dignified with this high honour—
To bear my lady's train, lest the base earth
Should from her vesture chance to steal a kiss   160
And, of so great a favour growing proud,
Disdain to root the summer-swelling flower
And make rough winter everlastingly.
   Pro. Why, Valentine, what braggardism is this?
   Val. Pardon me, Proteus: all I can is nothing
To her whose worth makes other worthies nothing;
She is alone.
   Pro.   Then let her alone.
   Val. Not for the world: why, man, she is mine own,
And I as rich in having such a jewel
As twenty seas, if all their sand were pearl,   170
The water nectar and the rocks pure gold.
Forgive me that I do not dream on thee,
Because thou see'st me dote upon my love.
My foolish rival, that her father likes
Only for his possessions are so huge,
Is gone with her along, and I must after,
For love, thou know'st, is full of jealousy.
   Pro. But she loves you?

73. **complete,** perfect; see glossary. **feature,** shape or form of body; see glossary. 90. **Belike that,** perhaps. 104. **entertain,** take into one's service; see glossary. 112. **want,** lack, be without; see glossary. **his,** its; see glossary. 135. **watchers of,** those who stay awake with; cf. *watch,* II, i, 25. 137. **as,** that; see glossary. 156, 157. **prefer,** in

the first instance, the modern sense; in the second, "advance." 165. **can,** know; see glossary. 196. **Is . . . praise.** This line has not been emended satisfactorily. It is possible that the text has been tampered with at this point in order to shorten the soliloquy. 198. **reasonless,** without justification, wrongly. 207. **advice,** deliberation, reflection;

Val. Ay, and we are betroth'd: nay, more, our
    marriage-hour,
With all the cunning manner of our flight,   180
Determined of; how I must climb her window,
The ladder made of cords, and all the means
Plotted and 'greed on for my happiness.
Good Proteus, go with me to my chamber,
In these affairs to aid me with thy counsel.
    Pro. Go on before; I shall inquire you forth:
I must unto the road, to disembark
Some necessaries that I needs must use,
And then I'll presently attend you.
    Val. Will you make haste?   190
    Pro. I will.   [*Exit Valentine.*
Even as one heat another heat expels,
Or as one nail by strength drives out another,
So the remembrance of my former love
Is by a newer object quite forgotten.
†Is it mine, or Valentine's praise,
Her true perfection, or my false transgression,
That makes me reasonless to reason thus?
She is fair; and so is Julia that I love—
That I did love, for now my love is thaw'd;   200
Which, like a waxen image 'gainst a fire,
Bears no impression of the thing it was.
Methinks my zeal to Valentine is cold,
And that I love him not as I was wont.
O, but I love his lady too too much,
And that's the reason I love him so little.
How shall I dote on her with more advice,
That thus without advice begin to love her!
'Tis but her picture I have yet beheld,
And that hath dazzled my reason's light;   210
But when I look on her perfections,
There is no reason but I shall be blind.
If I can check my erring love, I will:
If not, to compass her I'll use my skill.   [*Exit.*

SCENE V. *The same. A street.*

Enter SPEED *and* LAUNCE *severally.*

Speed. Launce! by mine honesty, welcome to Milan!
Launce. Forswear not thyself, sweet youth, for I am
not welcome. I reckon this always, that a man is never
undone till he be hanged, nor never welcome to a
place till some certain shot be paid and the hostess say
'Welcome!'
Speed. Come on, you madcap, I'll to the alehouse
with you presently; where, for one shot of five pence,
thou shalt have five thousand welcomes. But, sirrah,
how did thy master part with Madam Julia?
Launce. Marry, after they closed in earnest, they
parted very fairly in jest.
Speed. But shall she marry him?
Launce. No.
Speed. How then? shall he marry her?
Launce. No, neither.
Speed. What, are they broken?
Launce. No, they are both as whole as a fish.   20
Speed. Why, then, how stands the matter with them?

Launce. Marry, thus; when it stands well with him,
it stands well with her.
Speed. What an ass art thou! I understand thee not.
Launce. What a block art thou, that thou canst not!
My staff understands me.
Speed. What thou sayest?
Launce. Ay, and what I do too: look thee, I'll but
lean, and my staff understands me.   31
Speed. It stands under thee, indeed.
Launce. Why, stand-under and under-stand is all
one.
Speed. But tell me true, will 't be a match?
Launce. Ask my dog: if he say ay, it will; if he say no,
it will; if he shake his tail and say nothing, it will.
Speed. The conclusion is then that it will.
Launce. Thou shalt never get such a secret from me
but by a parable.   41
Speed. 'Tis well that I get it so. But, Launce, how
sayest thou, that my master is become a notable
lover?
Launce. I never knew him otherwise.
Speed. Than how?
Launce. A notable lubber, as thou reportest him to
be.
Speed. Why, thou whoreson ass, thou mistakest me.
Launce. Why, fool, I meant not thee; I meant thy
master.
Speed. I tell thee, my master is become a hot lover.
Launce. Why, I tell thee, I care not though he burn
himself in love. If thou wilt, go with me to the ale-
house; if not, thou art an Hebrew, a Jew, and not
worth the name of a Christian.
Speed. Why?   59
Launce. Because thou hast not so much charity in
thee as to go to the ale with a Christian. Wilt thou go?
Speed. At thy service.   [*Exeunt.*

SCENE VI. *The same. The* DUKE'S *palace.*

Enter PROTEUS.

Pro. To leave my Julia, shall I be forsworn;
To love fair Silvia, shall I be forsworn;
To wrong my friend, I shall be much forsworn;
And even that power which gave me first my oath
Provokes me to this threefold perjury.
Love bade me swear and Love bids me forswear.
O sweet-suggesting Love, if thou hast sinn'd,
Teach me, thy tempted subject, to excuse it!
At first I did adore a twinkling star,
But now I worship a celestial sun.   10
Unheedful vows may heedfully be broken,
And he wants wit that wants resolved will
To learn his wit to exchange the bad for better.
Fie, fie, unreverend tongue! to call her bad,
Whose sovereignty so oft thou hast preferr'd
With twenty thousand soul-confirming oaths.
I cannot leave to love, and yet I do;
But there I leave to love where I should love.
Julia I lose and Valentine I lose:
If I keep them, I needs must lose myself;   20

see glossary. 213. **check,** restrain; see glossary.
    SCENE V. 2. **Milan.** F: *Padua.* Other errors in place names occur at
III, i, 81 and V, iv, 129. 5. **undone,** ruined; see glossary. 7. **shot,**
fee; tavern reckoning. 11. **sirrah,** ordinary form of address to inferiors; see glossary. 13. **closed,** came to terms. 14. **fairly,** kindly,
gently; see glossary. 41. **parable,** enigmatical talk. 61. **ale,** church
ale or festival.
    SCENE VI. 7. **sweet-suggesting,** sweetly seductive. 13. **learn,** teach;
see glossary. 15. **preferr'd,** introduced, recommended. 17. **leave to
love,** cease loving.

If I lose them, thus find I by their loss
For Valentine myself, for Julia Silvia.
I to myself am dearer than a friend,
For love is still most precious in itself;
And Silvia—witness Heaven, that made her fair!—
Shows Julia but a swarthy Ethiope.
I will forget that Julia is alive,
Remembering that my love to her is dead;
And Valentine I'll hold an enemy,
Aiming at Silvia as a sweeter friend. 30
I cannot now prove constant to myself,
Without some treachery used to Valentine.
This night he meaneth with a corded ladder
To climb celestial Silvia's chamber-window,
Myself in counsel, his competitor.
Now presently I'll give her father notice
Of their disguising and pretended flight;
Who, all enraged, will banish Valentine;
For Thurio, he intends, shall wed his daughter;
But, Valentine being gone, I'll quickly cross 40
By some sly trick blunt Thurio's dull proceeding.
Love, lend me wings to make my purpose swift,
As thou hast lent me wit to plot this drift!   [*Exit.*

SCENE VII. *Verona.* JULIA's *house.*

Enter JULIA *and* LUCETTA.

Jul. Counsel, Lucetta; gentle girl, assist me;
And even in kind love I do conjure thee,
Who art the table wherein all my thoughts
Are visibly character'd and engraved,
To lesson me and tell me some good mean
How, with my honour, I may undertake
A journey to my loving Proteus.
     Luc. Alas, the way is wearisome and long!
     Jul. A true-devoted pilgrim is not weary
To measure kingdoms with his feeble steps; 10
Much less shall she that hath Love's wings to fly,
And when the flight is made to one so dear,
Of such divine perfection, as Sir Proteus.
     Luc. Better forbear till Proteus make return.
     Jul. O, know'st thou not his looks are my soul's
          food?
Pity the dearth that I have pined in,
By longing for that food so long a time.
Didst thou but know the inly touch of love,
Thou wouldst as soon go kindle fire with snow
As seek to quench the fire of love with words. 20
     Luc. I do not seek to quench your love's hot fire,
But qualify the fire's extreme rage,
Lest it should burn above the bounds of reason.
     Jul. The more thou damm'st it up, the more it
          burns.
The current that with gentle murmur glides,
Thou know'st, being stopp'd, impatiently doth rage;
But when his fair course is not hindered,
He makes sweet music with the enamell'd stones,
Giving a gentle kiss to every sedge

He overtaketh in his pilgrimage, 30
And so by many winding nooks he strays
With willing sport to the wild ocean.
Then let me go and hinder not my course:
I'll be as patient as a gentle stream
And make a pastime of each weary step,
Till the last step have brought me to my love;
And there I'll rest, as after much turmoil
A blessed soul doth in Elysium.
     Luc. But in what habit will you go along?
     Jul. Not like a woman; for I would prevent 40
The loose encounters of lascivious men:
Gentle Lucetta, fit me with such weeds
As may beseem some well-reputed page.
     Luc. Why, then, your ladyship must cut your hair.
     Jul. No, girl; I'll knit it up in silken strings
With twenty odd-conceited true-love knots.
To be fantastic may become a youth
Of greater time than I shall show to be.
     Luc. What fashion, madam, shall I make your
          breeches?
     Jul. That fits as well as 'Tell me, good my lord, 50
What compass will you wear your farthingale?'
Why even what fashion thou best likest, Lucetta.
     Luc. You must needs have them with a codpiece,
          madam.
     Jul. Out, out, Lucetta! that will be ill-favour'd.
     Luc. A round hose, madam, now 's not worth a pin,
Unless you have a codpiece to stick pins on.
     Jul. Lucetta, as thou lovest me, let me have
What thou thinkest meet and is most mannerly.
But tell me, wench, how will the world repute me
For undertaking so unstaid a journey? 60
I fear me, it will make me scandalized.
     Luc. If you think so, then stay at home and go not.
     Jul. Nay, that I will not.
     Luc. Then never dream on infamy, but go.
If Proteus like your journey when you come,
No matter who 's displeased when you are gone:
I fear me, he will scarce be pleased withal.
     Jul. That is the least, Lucetta, of my fear:
A thousand oaths, an ocean of his tears
And instances of infinite of love 70
Warrant me welcome to my Proteus.
     Luc. All these are servants to deceitful men.
     Jul. Base men, that use them to so base effect!
But truer stars did govern Proteus' birth;
His words are bonds, his oaths are oracles,
His love sincere, his thoughts immaculate,
His tears pure messengers sent from his heart,
His heart as far from fraud as heaven from earth.
     Luc. Pray heaven he prove so, when you come to
          him!
     Jul. Now, as thou lovest me, do him not that wrong
To bear a hard opinion of his truth: 81
Only deserve my love by loving him;
And presently go with me to my chamber,
To take a note of what I stand in need of,
To furnish me upon my longing journey.
All that is mine I leave at thy dispose,

35. **competitor**, associate, partner.   43. **drift**, scheme, plot.
     SCENE VII.   3. **table**, tablet; see glossary.   4. **character'd**, engraved,
inscribed; see glossary.   10. **measure**, traverse; see glossary.   18.
inly, inward.   22. **qualify**, control, regulate.   40. **prevent**, forestall; see glossary.   42. **weeds**, garments; see glossary.   46. **odd-conceited**, strangely devised.   48. **of greater time,** of greater years, older.
51. **compass**, circumference; i.e., its fullness or width around the bottom. **farthingale**, hooped petticoat.   53. **codpiece**, a bagged append-

age to the front of close-fitting hose or breeches worn by men from
the fifteenth to the seventeenth century, often conspicuous and ornamented.   54. **Out,** an expression of reproach or indignation; see glossary.   60. **unstaid**, unbecoming.   67. **withal**, with it; see glossary.
70. **infinite**, infinity.   85. **furnish**, fit out; see glossary. **longing**,
prompted by longing.   86. **dispose**, disposal; see glossary.
     ACT III. SCENE I.   1. **give us leave,** a polite form of dismissal.   4.
discover, reveal; see glossary.   5. **The law of friendship.** Violation

My goods, my lands, my reputation;
Only, in lieu thereof, dispatch me hence.
Come, answer not, but to it presently!
I am impatient of my tarriance.   [*Exeunt.* 90

ACT III.

SCENE I. *Milan. The* DUKE's *palace.*

Enter DUKE, THURIO, *and* PROTEUS.

Duke. Sir Thurio, give us leave, I pray, awhile;
We have some secrets to confer about.   [*Exit Thu.*
Now, tell me, Proteus, what 's your will with me?
  Pro. My gracious lord, that which I would discover
The law of friendship bids me to conceal;
But when I call to mind your gracious favours
Done to me, undeserving as I am,
My duty pricks me on to utter that
Which else no worldly good should draw from me.
Know, worthy prince, Sir Valentine, my friend,   10
This night intends to steal away your daughter:
Myself am one made privy to the plot.
I know you have determined to bestow her
On Thurio, whom your gentle daughter hates;
And should she thus be stol'n away from you,
It would be much vexation to your age.
Thus, for my duty's sake, I rather chose
To cross my friend in his intended drift
Than, by concealing it, heap on your head
A pack of sorrows which would press you down,   20
Being unprevented, to your timeless grave.
  Duke. Proteus, I thank thee for thine honest care;
Which to requite, command me while I live.
This love of theirs myself have often seen,
Haply when they have judged me fast asleep,
And oftentimes have purposed to forbid
Sir Valentine her company and my court:
But fearing lest my jealous aim might err
And so unworthily disgrace the man,
A rashness that I ever yet have shunn'd,   30
I gave him gentle looks, thereby to find
That which thyself hast now disclosed to me.
And, that thou mayst perceive my fear of this,
Knowing that tender youth is soon suggested,
I nightly lodge her in an upper tower,
The key whereof myself have ever kept;
And thence she cannot be convey'd away.
  Pro. Know, noble lord, they have devised a mean
How he her chamber-window will ascend
And with a corded ladder fetch her down;   40
For which the youthful lover now is gone
And this way comes he with it presently;
Where, if it please you, you may intercept him.
But, good my lord, do it so cunningly
That my discovery be not aimed at;
For love of you, not hate unto my friend,
Hath made me publisher of this pretence.

Duke. Upon mine honour, he shall never know
That I had any light from thee of this.
  Pro. Adieu, my lord; Sir Valentine is coming.   [*Exit.*

Enter VALENTINE.

  Duke. Sir Valentine, whither away so fast?   51
  Val. Please it your grace, there is a messenger
That stays to bear my letters to my friends,
And I am going to deliver them.
  Duke. Be they of much import?
  Val. The tenour of them doth but signify
My health and happy being at your court.
  Duke. Nay then, no matter; stay with me awhile;
I am to break with thee of some affairs
That touch me near, wherein thou must be secret.   60
'Tis not unknown to thee that I have sought
To match my friend Sir Thurio to my daughter.
  Val. I know it well, my lord; and, sure, the match
Were rich and honourable; besides, the gentleman
Is full of virtue, bounty, worth and qualities
Beseeming such a wife as your fair daughter:
Cannot your grace win her to fancy him?
  Duke. No, trust me; she is peevish, sullen, froward,
Proud, disobedient, stubborn, lacking duty,
Neither regarding that she is my child   70
Nor fearing me as if I were her father;
And, may I say to thee, this pride of hers,
Upon advice, hath drawn my love from her;
And, where I thought the remnant of mine age
Should have been cherish'd by her child-like duty,
I now am full resolved to take a wife
And turn her out to who will take her in:
Then let her beauty be her wedding-dower;
For me and my possessions she esteems not.
  Val. What would your grace have me to do in this?
  Duke. †There is a lady in Verona here   81
Whom I affect; but she is nice and coy
And nought esteems my aged eloquence:
Now therefore would I have thee to my tutor—
For long agone I have forgot to court;
Besides, the fashion of the time is changed—
How and which way I may bestow myself
To be regarded in her sun-bright eye.
  Val. Win her with gifts, if she respect not words:
Dumb jewels often in their silent kind   90
More than quick words do move a woman's mind.
  Duke. But she did scorn a present that I sent her.
  Val. A woman sometimes scorns what best contents
    her.
Send her another; never give her o'er;
For scorn at first makes after-love the more.
If she do frown, 'tis not in hate of you,
But rather to beget more love in you:
If she do chide, 'tis not to have you gone;
For why, the fools are mad, if left alone.
Take no repulse, whatever she doth say;   100
For 'get you gone,' she doth not mean 'away!'
Flatter and praise, commend, extol their graces;
Though ne'er so black, say they have angels' faces.
That man that hath a tongue, I say, is no man,

---

of this law—a well-formalized code in the Renaissance period—is Proteus' crime. See Introduction for a discussion of the importance of this code to an understanding of the play. 22. **honest,** decent, proper; see glossary. 28. **aim,** conjecture, guess. 34. **suggested,** tempted; see glossary. 45. **aimed at,** guessed. 64. **Were,** would be; subjunctive. 65. **virtue,** good accomplishments; see glossary. **qualities,** gifts, attainments; see glossary. 68. **peevish,** obstinate; see glossary. 81. **Verona,** so F; an obvious error, due to possible revision. The fact

that *Verona* makes the line metrical whereas "Milan" does not, indicates that the former may have been the reading in the original. A similar error occurs at V, iv, 129; cf. II, v, 1, note. 82. **affect,** am fond of; see glossary. **nice,** shy; see glossary. 87. **bestow,** behave, conduct. 90. **kind,** manner, fashion; see glossary. 93-101. **A woman . . . 'away.'** This is the courtship code observed earlier in the play (I, ii) by Julia when she received Proteus' letter. 99. **For why,** because; see glossary.

If with his tongue he cannot win a woman.

Duke. But she I mean is promised by her friends
Unto a youthful gentleman of worth,
And kept severely from resort of men,
That no man hath access by day to her.

Val. Why, then, I would resort to her by night. 110

Duke. Ay, but the doors be lock'd and keys kept safe,
That no man hath recourse to her by night.

Val. What lets but one may enter at her window?

Duke. Her chamber is aloft, far from the ground,
And built so shelving that one cannot climb it
Without apparent hazard of his life.

Val. Why then, a ladder quaintly made of cords,
To cast up, with a pair of anchoring hooks,
Would serve to scale another Hero's tower,
So bold Leander would adventure it. 120

Duke. Now, as thou art a gentleman of blood,
Advise me where I may have such a ladder.

Val. When would you use it? pray, sir, tell me that.

Duke. This very night; for Love is like a child,
That longs for every thing that he can come by.

Val. By seven o'clock I'll get you such a ladder.

Duke. But, hark thee; I will go to her alone:
How shall I best convey the ladder thither?

Val. It will be light, my lord, that you may bear it
Under a cloak that is of any length. 130

Duke. A cloak as long as thine will serve the turn?

Val. Ay, my good lord.

Duke. Then let me see thy cloak:
I'll get me one of such another length.

Val. Why, any cloak will serve the turn, my lord.

Duke. How shall I fashion me to wear a cloak?
I pray thee, let me feel thy cloak upon me.
What letter is this same? What 's here? 'To Silvia'!
And here an engine fit for my proceeding.
I'll be so bold to break the seal for once. [*Reads.*
'My thoughts do harbour with my Silvia nightly, 140
    And slaves they are to me that send them flying:
O, could their master come and go as lightly,
    Himself would lodge where senseless they are lying!
My herald thoughts in thy pure bosom rest them;
    While I, their king, that hither them importune,
Do curse the grace that with such grace hath bless'd
        them,
    Because myself do want my servants' fortune:
I curse myself, for they are sent by me,
    That they should harbour where their lord would be.'
What 's here? 150
    'Silvia, this night I will enfranchise thee.'
'Tis so; and here 's the ladder for the purpose.
Why, Phaethon,—for thou art Merops' son,—
Wilt thou aspire to guide the heavenly car
And with thy daring folly burn the world?
Wilt thou reach stars, because they shine on thee?
Go, base intruder! overweening slave!
Bestow thy fawning smiles on equal mates,
And think my patience, more than thy desert,
Is privilege for thy departure hence: 160
Thank me for this more than for all the favours

Which all too much I have bestow'd on thee.
But if thou linger in my territories
Longer than swiftest expedition
Will give thee time to leave our royal court,
By heaven! my wrath shall far exceed the love
I ever bore my daughter or thyself.
Be gone! I will not hear thy vain excuse;
But, as thou lovest thy life, make speed from hence.
[*Exit.*

Val. And why not death rather than living torment?
To die is to be banish'd from myself; 171
And Silvia is myself: banish'd from her
Is self from self: a deadly banishment!
What light is light, if Silvia be not seen?
What joy is joy, if Silvia be not by?
Unless it be to think that she is by
And feed upon the shadow of perfection.
Except I be by Silvia in the night,
There is no music in the nightingale;
Unless I look on Silvia in the day, 180
There is no day for me to look upon;
She is my essence, and I leave to be,
If I be not by her fair influence
Foster'd, illumined, cherish'd, kept alive.
I fly not death, to fly his deadly doom:
Tarry I here, I but attend on death:
But, fly I hence, I fly away from life.

Enter PROTEUS *and* LAUNCE.

Pro. Run, boy, run, run, and seek him out.

Launce. Soho, soho!

Pro. What seest thou? 190

Launce. Him we go to find: there 's not a hair on 's
head but 'tis a Valentine.

Pro. Valentine?

Val. No.

Pro. Who then? his spirit?

Val. Neither.

Pro. What then?

Val. Nothing.

Launce. Can nothing speak? Master, shall I strike?

Pro. Who wouldst thou strike? 200

Launce. Nothing.

Pro. Villain, forbear.

Launce. Why, sir, I'll strike nothing: I pray you,—

Pro. Sirrah, I say, forbear. Friend Valentine, a word.

Val. My ears are stopt and cannot hear good news,
So much of bad already hath possess'd them.

Pro. Then in dumb silence will I bury mine,
For they are harsh, untuneable and bad.

Val. Is Silvia dead?

Pro. No, Valentine. 210

Val. No Valentine, indeed, for sacred Silvia.
Hath she forsworn me?

Pro. No, Valentine.

Val. No Valentine, if Silvia have forsworn me.
What is your news?

Launce. Sir, there is a proclamation that you are
vanished.

113. **lets,** hinders; see glossary. 116. **apparent,** plain, evident;
see glossary. 119-120. **Hero's . . . Leander,** a reference to the story
of Hero and Leander, two lovers who lived on the opposite shores
of the Hellespont. See I, i, 22 ff. 131. **serve the turn,** answer the
purpose; see *serve* in glossary. 138. **engine,** mechanical contrivance;
see glossary. 143. **lying,** dwelling; see *lie* in glossary. 146. **grace
. . . grace,** good fortune . . . charm, favor; see glossary. 151. **enfranchise,** release from confinement. 153. **Phaethon, Merops'.** Phaethon
was the son of Phoebus and Clymene, lawful wife of Merops. A possible
play on "ropes" has been suggested. Another suggestion is that the

duke wishes to plague Valentine with the taunt of inferior birth.
The story of Phaethon's attempt to drive the chariot of the sun was
familiar to Shakespeare from his acquaintance with Golding's Ovid.
157. **overweening,** arrogant, presumptuous. 177. **shadow,** image; see
glossary. 182. **leave to be,** die, cease to be. 183. **influence,** metaphorical reference to an ethereal fluid supposed to flow from the stars and
to have power over the destinies of men; see glossary. 185. **I . . .
doom.** I shall not escape death by flying from it, for if I do, I shall
die at once. 189. **Soho,** hunting cry used when a hare is descried. 192.
Valentine, token of true love; cf. l. 211 below. 216, 217. **you, thou.**

Pro. That thou art banished—O, that 's the news!—
From hence, from Silvia and from me thy friend.

Val. O, I have fed upon this woe already,
And now excess of it will make me surfeit. 220
Doth Silvia know that I am banished?

Pro. Ay, ay; and she hath offer'd to the doom—
Which, unreversed, stands in effectual force—
A sea of melting pearl, which some call tears:
Those at her father's churlish feet she tender'd;
With them, upon her knees, her humble self;
Wringing her hands, whose whiteness so became
  them
As if but now they waxed pale for woe:
But neither bended knees, pure hands held up,
Sad sighs, deep groans, nor silver-shedding tears, 230
Could penetrate her uncompassionate sire;
But Valentine, if he be ta'en, must die.
Besides, her intercession chafed him so,
When she for thy repeal was suppliant,
That to close prison he commanded her,
With many bitter threats of biding there.

Val. No more; unless the next word that thou
  speak'st
Have some malignant power upon my life:
If so, I pray thee, breathe it in mine ear,
As ending anthem of my endless dolour. 240

Pro. Cease to lament for that thou canst not help,
And study help for that which thou lament'st.
Time is the nurse and breeder of all good.
Here if thou stay, thou canst not see thy love;
Besides, thy staying will abridge thy life.
Hope is a lover's staff; walk hence with that
And manage it against despairing thoughts.
Thy letters may be here, though thou art hence;
Which, being writ to me, shall be deliver'd
Even in the milk-white bosom of thy love. 250
The time now serves not to expostulate:
Come, I'll convey thee through the city-gate;
And, ere I part with thee, confer at large
Of all that may concern thy love-affairs.
As thou lovest Silvia, though not for thyself,
Regard thy danger, and along with me!

Val. I pray thee, Launce, an if thou seest my boy,
Bid him make haste and meet me at the North-gate.

Pro. Go, sirrah, find him out. Come, Valentine.

Val. O my dear Silvia! Hapless Valentine! 260
                              [*Exeunt Val. and Pro.*

Launce. I am but a fool, look you; and yet I have the
wit to think my master is a kind of a knave: but
that 's all one, if he be but one knave. He lives not now
that knows me to be in love; yet I am in love; but a
team of horse shall not pluck that from me; nor who
'tis I love; and yet 'tis a woman; but what woman, I
will not tell myself; and yet 'tis a milkmaid; yet 'tis
not a maid, for she hath had gossips; yet 'tis a maid,
for she is her master's maid, and serves for wages. She
hath more qualities than a water-spaniel; which is
much in a bare Christian. [*Pulling out a paper.*] Here
is the cate-log of her condition. 'Imprimis: She can

fetch and carry.' Why, a horse can do no more: nay,
a horse cannot fetch, but only carry; therefore is she
better than a jade. 'Item: She can milk;' look you, a
sweet virtue in a maid with clean hands.

Enter SPEED.

Speed. How now, Signior Launce! what news with
your mastership? 280

Launce. With my master's ship? why, it is at sea.

Speed. Well, your old vice still; mistake the word.
What news, then, in your paper?

Launce. The blackest news that ever thou heardest.

Speed. Why, man, how black?

Launce. Why, as black as ink.

Speed. Let me read them. 290

Launce. Fie on thee, jolt-head! thou canst not read.

Speed. Thou liest; I can.

Launce. I will try thee. Tell me this: who begot thee?

Speed. Marry, the son of my grandfather.

Launce. O illiterate loiterer! it was the son of thy
grandmother: this proves that thou canst not read.

Speed. Come, fool, come; try me in thy paper.

Launce. There; and Saint Nicholas be thy speed!

Speed. [*Reads*] 'Imprimis: She can milk.' 302

Launce. Ay, that she can.

Speed. 'Item: She brews good ale.'

Launce. And thereof comes the proverb: 'Blessing of
your heart, you brew good ale.'

Speed. 'Item: She can sew.'

Launce. That 's as much as to say, Can she so?

Speed. 'Item: She can knit.' 310

Launce. What need a man care for a stock with a
wench, when she can knit him a stock?

Speed. 'Item: She can wash and scour.'

Launce. A special virtue; for then she need not be
washed and scoured.

Speed. 'Item: She can spin.'

Launce. Then may I set the world on wheels, when
she can spin for her living.

Speed. 'Item: She hath many nameless virtues.' 320

Launce. That 's as much as to say, bastard virtues;
that, indeed, know not their fathers and therefore have
no names.

Speed. 'Here follow her vices.'

Launce. Close at the heels of her virtues.

Speed. 'Item: She is not to be kissed fasting, in respect of her breath.'

Launce. Well, that fault may be mended with a
breakfast. Read on.

Speed. 'Item: She hath a sweet mouth.' 330

Launce. That makes amends for her sour breath.

Speed. 'Item: She doth talk in her sleep.'

Launce. It 's no matter for that, so she sleep not in her
talk.

Speed. 'Item: She is slow in words.'

Launce. O villain, that set this down among her
vices! To be slow in words is a woman's only virtue: I
pray thee, out with 't, and place it for her chief virtue.

Speed. 'Item: She is proud.' 341

The
Two Gentlemen
of Verona
ACT III : SC I

145

Observe that Launce addresses Valentine as *you*, the polite form of pronoun used in addressing one's superiors, whereas Proteus uses the
familiar *thou* because of both their social equality and their intimacy.
This distinction is commonly maintained by Shakespeare and his
contemporaries. **222. doom,** verdict, sentence. **234. repeal,** recall
from exile. **235. close,** enclosed; see glossary. **236. biding,** per-
manently dwelling. **242. study,** be intent upon, devise. **247. manage,** wield, handle (as a weapon). **253. confer at large,** discuss at
length; see *large* in glossary. **269. gossips,** godparents to a child of
hers. **273. cate-log.** Although this is an early spelling of "catalog,"

most editors retain the old form, believing a mispronunciation is
intended. The New Cambridge editors think that it is no more than
a common Shakespearean spelling which editors have mistaken for
a joke. **condition,** qualities; see glossary. **277. jade,** ill-conditioned
horse; also a term of contempt for a woman. **290. jolt-head,** blockhead. **300. Saint Nicholas,** the patron saint of scholars. **301. speed,**
protection; see glossary. **311. stock,** dowry. **312. stock,** stocking.
317. set . . . wheels, take life easy. **330. sweet mouth,** sweet tooth, with
a wanton sense.

Launce. Out with that too; it was Eve's legacy, and cannot be ta'en from her.

Speed. 'Item: She hath no teeth.'

Launce. I care not for that neither, because I love crusts.

Speed. 'Item: She is curst.'

Launce. Well, the best is, she hath no teeth to bite.

Speed. 'Item: She will often praise her liquor.' 351

Launce. If her liquor be good, she shall: if she will not, I will; for good things should be praised.

Speed. 'Item: She is too liberal.'

Launce. Of her tongue she cannot, for that's writ down she is slow of; of her purse she shall not, for that I'll keep shut: now, of another thing she may, and that cannot I help. Well, proceed. 360

Speed. 'Item: She hath more hair than wit, and more faults than hairs, and more wealth than faults.'

Launce. Stop there; I'll have her: she was mine, and not mine, twice or thrice in that last article. Rehearse that once more.

Speed. 'Item: She hath more hair than wit,'—

Launce. More hair than wit? It may be: I'll prove it. The cover of the salt hides the salt, and therefore it is more than the salt; the hair that covers the wit is more than the wit, for the greater hides the less. What's next?

Speed. 'And more faults than hairs,'—

Launce. That's monstrous: O, that that were out!

Speed. 'And more wealth than faults.'

Launce. Why, that word makes the faults gracious. Well, I'll have her: and if it be a match, as nothing is impossible,—

Speed. What then? 380

Launce. Why, then will I tell thee—that thy master stays for thee at the North-gate.

Speed. For me?

Launce. For thee! ay, who art thou? he hath stayed for a better man than thee.

Speed. And must I go to him?

Launce. Thou must run to him, for thou hast stayed so long that going will scarce serve the turn. 389

Speed. Why didst not tell me sooner? pox of your love-letters! [*Exit.*

Launce. Now will he be swinged for reading my letter; an unmannerly slave, that will thrust himself into secrets! I'll after, to rejoice in the boy's correction.
[*Exit.*

SCENE II. *The same. The* DUKE's *palace.*

Enter DUKE *and* THURIO.

Duke. Sir Thurio, fear not but that she will love you,
Now Valentine is banish'd from her sight.

Thu. Since his exile she hath despised me most,
Forsworn my company and rail'd at me,
That I am desperate of obtaining her.

Duke. This weak impress of love is as a figure
Trenched in ice, which with an hour's heat
Dissolves to water and doth lose his form.

A little time will melt her frozen thoughts
And worthless Valentine shall be forgot. 10

Enter PROTEUS.

How now, Sir Proteus! Is your countryman
According to our proclamation gone?

Pro. Gone, my good lord.

Duke. My daughter takes his going grievously.

Pro. A little time, my lord, will kill that grief.

Duke. So I believe; but Thurio thinks not so.
Proteus, the good conceit I hold of thee—
For thou hast shown some sign of good desert—
Makes me the better to confer with thee.

Pro. Longer than I prove loyal to your grace 20
Let me not live to look upon your grace.

Duke. Thou know'st how willingly I would effect
The match between Sir Thurio and my daughter.

Pro. I do, my lord.

Duke. And also, I think, thou art not ignorant
How she opposes her against my will.

Pro. She did, my lord, when Valentine was here.

Duke. Ay, and perversely she persevers so.
What might we do to make the girl forget
The love of Valentine and love Sir Thurio? 30

Pro. The best way is to slander Valentine
With falsehood, cowardice and poor descent,
Three things that women highly hold in hate.

Duke. Ay, but she'll think that it is spoke in hate.

Pro. Ay, if his enemy deliver it:
Therefore it must with circumstance be spoken
By one whom she esteemeth as his friend.

Duke. Then you must undertake to slander him.

Pro. And that, my lord, I shall be loath to do:
'Tis an ill office for a gentleman, 40
Especially against his very friend.

Duke. Where your good word cannot advantage him,
Your slander never can endamage him;
Therefore the office is indifferent,
Being entreated to it by your friend.

Pro. You have prevail'd, my lord: if I can do it
By aught that I can speak in his dispraise,
She shall not long continue love to him.
But say this weed her love from Valentine,
It follows not that she will love Sir Thurio. 50

Thu. Therefore, as you unwind her love from him,
Lest it should ravel and be good to none,
You must provide to bottom it on me;
Which must be done by praising me as much
As you in worth dispraise Sir Valentine.

Duke. And, Proteus, we dare trust you in this kind,
Because we know, on Valentine's report,
You are already Love's firm votary
And cannot soon revolt and change your mind.
Upon this warrant shall you have access 60
Where you with Silvia may confer at large;
For she is lumpish, heavy, melancholy,
And, for your friend's sake, will be glad of you;
Where you may temper her by your persuasion
To hate young Valentine and love my friend.

Pro. As much as I can do, I will effect:

---

347. **curst,** perverse, shrewish; see glossary. 392. **swinged,** thrashed. SCENE II. 3. **Since his exile.** This would indicate that some days have elapsed since Valentine's departure. It is evident, however, from lines 11-12 that this is not so. Later in the play (IV, i, 21) Valentine says he has been away from Verona sixteen months, an unduly long period for the requirements of the plot. The New Cambridge editors believe the discrepancies to be due to revision and abridgment. 5. **That,**

so that. 6. **impress of love,** impression made by love. 17. **conceit,** opinion, estimate; see glossary. 19. **the better,** the rather; i.e., more willingly. 26. **opposes her,** contends. 42. **advantage,** profit; see glossary. 44. **indifferent,** neither good nor bad. 49. **weed.** *Wean* (Rowe) and *wend* (New Cambridge) have been suggested as emendations. 53. **bottom,** wind, as a skein of thread; a weaver's term. 62. **lumpish,** dull. 68. **lime,** birdlime, a sticky substance smeared on twigs

But you, Sir Thurio, are not sharp enough;
You must lay lime to tangle her desires
By wailful sonnets, whose composed rhymes
Should be full-fraught with serviceable vows. 70
   Duke. Ay,
Much is the force of heaven-bred poesy.
   Pro. Say that upon the altar of her beauty
You sacrifice your tears, your sighs, your heart:
Write till your ink be dry, and with your tears
Moist it again, and frame some feeling line
That may discover such integrity:
For Orpheus' lute was strung with poets' sinews,
Whose golden touch could soften steel and stones,
Make tigers tame and huge leviathans 80
Forsake unsounded deeps to dance on sands.
After your dire-lamenting elegies,
Visit by night your lady's chamber-window
With some sweet consort; to their instruments
Tune a deploring dump: the night's dead silence
Will well become such sweet-complaining grievance.
This, or else nothing, will inherit her.
   Duke. This discipline shows thou hast been in love.
   Thu. And thy advice this night I'll put in practice.
Therefore, sweet Proteus, my direction-giver, 90
Let us into the city presently
To sort some gentlemen well skill'd in music.
I have a sonnet that will serve the turn
To give the onset to thy good advice.
   Duke. About it, gentlemen!
   Pro. We'll wait upon your grace till after supper,
And afterward determine our proceedings.
   Duke. Even now about it! I will pardon you. [*Exeunt.*

ACT IV.

SCENE I. *The frontiers of Mantua. A forest.*

Enter certain Outlaws.

First Out. Fellows, stand fast; I see a passenger.
   Sec. Out. If there be ten, shrink not, but down with
'em.

Enter VALENTINE *and* SPEED.

   Third Out. Stand, sir, and throw us that you have
     about ye:
If not, we'll make you sit and rifle you.
   Speed. Sir, we are undone; these are the villains
That all the travellers do fear so much.
   Val. My friends,—
   First Out. That 's not so, sir: we are your enemies.
   Sec. Out. Peace! we'll hear him.
   Third Out. Ay, by my beard, will we, for he 's a
     proper man. 10
   Val. Then know that I have little wealth to lose:
A man I am cross'd with adversity;
My riches are these poor habiliments,
Of which if you should here disfurnish me,
You take the sum and substance that I have.
   Sec. Out. Whither travel you?
   Val. To Verona.

   First Out. Whence came you?
   Val. From Milan.
   Third Out. Have you long sojourned there? 20
   Val. Some sixteen months, and longer might have
     stay'd,
If crooked fortune had not thwarted me.
   First Out. What, were you banish'd thence?
   Val. I was.
   Sec. Out. For what offence?
   Val. For that which now torments me to rehearse:
I kill'd a man, whose death I much repent;
But yet I slew him manfully in fight,
Without false vantage or base treachery.
   First Out. Why, ne'er repent it, if it were done so. 30
But were you banish'd for so small a fault?
   Val. I was, and held me glad of such a doom.
   Sec. Out. Have you the tongues?
   Val. My youthful travel therein made me happy,
Or else I often had been miserable.
   Third Out. By the bare scalp of Robin Hood's fat
     friar,
This fellow were a king for our wild faction!
   First Out. We'll have him. Sirs, a word.
   Speed. Master, be one of them; it 's an honourable
kind of thievery. 40
   Val. Peace, villain!
   Sec. Out. Tell us this: have you any thing to take to?
   Val. Nothing but my fortune.
   Third Out. Know, then, that some of us are
     gentlemen,
Such as the fury of ungovern'd youth
Thrust from the company of awful men:
Myself was from Verona banished
For practising to steal away a lady,
An heir, and near allied unto the duke.
   Sec. Out. And I from Mantua, for a gentleman, 50
Who, in my mood, I stabb'd unto the heart.
   First Out. And I for such like petty crimes as these.
But to the purpose—for we cite our faults,
That they may hold excused our lawless lives;
And partly, seeing you are beautified
With goodly shape and by your own report
A linguist and a man of such perfection
As we do in our quality much want—
   Sec. Out. Indeed, because you are a banish'd man,
Therefore, above the rest, we parley to you: 60
Are you content to be our general?
To make a virtue of necessity
And live, as we do, in this wilderness?
   Third Out. What say'st thou? wilt thou be of our
     consort?
Say ay, and be the captain of us all:
We'll do thee homage and be ruled by thee,
Love thee as our commander and our king.
   First Out. But if thou scorn our courtesy, thou diest.
   Sec. Out. Thou shalt not live to brag what we have
     offer'd.
   Val. I take your offer and will live with you, 70
Provided that you do no outrages
On silly women or poor passengers.
   Third Out. No, we detest such vile base practices.

of trees to ensnare small birds. 84. **consort,** a company of musicians;
so F; Globe: *concert.* 85. **dump,** mournful melody or song. 87. **in-**
herit, put you in possession of. 92. **sort,** choose. 94. **onset,** beginning.
ACT IV. SCENE I. 10. **proper,** good-looking; see glossary. 14. **dis-**
furnish, deprive. 21. **sixteen months.** Cf. III, ii, 3, note. 22.
crooked, perverse, malignant. 27. **I kill'd a man.** There is no obvious
motive for Valentine's giving a false reason for his banishment. 33.

the **tongues,** foreign languages. 37. **faction,** class, set (of persons);
see glossary. 46. **awful,** commanding reverential fear or profound respect; see glossary. 51. **mood,** anger, displeasure. 64. **consort,** fellowship, company. 72. **silly,** helpless, defenseless.

Come, go with us, we'll bring thee to our crews,
And show thee all the treasure we have got;
Which, with ourselves, all rest at thy dispose. [*Exeunt.*

SCENE II. *Milan. Outside the* DUKE's *palace, under*
SILVIA's *chamber.*

Enter PROTEUS.

Pro. Already have I been false to Valentine
And now I must be as unjust to Thurio.
Under the colour of commending him,
I have access my own love to prefer:
But Silvia is too fair, too true, too holy,
To be corrupted with my worthless gifts.
When I protest true loyalty to her,
She twits me with my falsehood to my friend;
When to her beauty I commend my vows,
She bids me think how I have been forsworn   10
In breaking faith with Julia whom I loved:
And notwithstanding all her sudden quips,
The least whereof would quell a lover's hope,
Yet, spaniel-like, the more she spurns my love,
The more it grows and fawneth on her still.
But here comes Thurio: now must we to her window,
And give some evening music to her ear.

Enter THURIO *and* Musicians.

Thu. How now, Sir Proteus, are you crept before
us?
Pro. Ay, gentle Thurio: for you know that love
Will creep in service where it cannot go.   20
Thu. Ay, but I hope, sir, that you love not here.
Pro. Sir, but I do; or else I would be hence.
Thu. Who? Silvia?
Pro.   Ay, Silvia; for your sake.
Thu. I thank you for your own. Now, gentlemen,
Let's tune, and to it lustily awhile.

Enter, at a distance, Host, *and* JULIA *in boy's clothes.*

Host. Now, my young guest, methinks you're ally-
cholly: I pray you, why is it?   28
Jul. Marry, mine host, because I cannot be merry.
Host. Come, we'll have you merry: I'll bring you
where you shall hear music and see the gentleman that
you asked for.
Jul. But shall I hear him speak?
Host. Ay, that you shall.
Jul. That will be music.   [*Music plays.*
Host. Hark, hark!
Jul. Is he among these?
Host. Ay: but, peace! let's hear 'em.

SONG.

Who is Silvia? what is she,
    That all our swains commend her?   40
Holy, fair and wise is she;
    The heaven such grace did lend her,
That she might admired be.

Is she kind as she is fair?
    For beauty lives with kindness.
Love doth to her eyes repair,

To help him of his blindness,
And, being help'd, inhabits there.

Then to Silvia let us sing,
    That Silvia is excelling;   50
She excels each mortal thing
    Upon the dull earth dwelling:
To her let us garlands bring.

Host. How now! are you sadder than you were be-
fore? How do you, man? the music likes you not.
Jul. You mistake; the musician likes me not.
Host. Why, my pretty youth?
Jul. He plays false, father.
Host. How? out of tune on the strings?   60
Jul. Not so; but yet so false that he grieves my very
heart-strings.
Host. You have a quick ear.
Jul. Ay, I would I were deaf; it makes me have a
slow heart.
Host. I perceive you delight not in music.
Jul. Not a whit, when it jars so.
Host. Hark, what fine change is in the music!
Jul. Ay, that change is the spite.
Host. You would have them always play but one
thing?   71
Jul. I would always have one play but one thing.
But, host, doth this Sir Proteus that we talk on
Often resort unto this gentlewoman?
Host. I tell you what Launce, his man, told me: he
loved her out of all nick.
Jul. Where is Launce?
Host. Gone to seek his dog; which tomorrow, by his
master's command, he must carry for a present to his
lady.   80
Jul. Peace! stand aside: the company parts.
Pro. Sir Thurio, fear not you: I will so plead
That you shall say my cunning drift excels.
Thu. Where meet we?
Pro.   At Saint Gregory's well.
Thu.   Farewell.
                         [*Exeunt Thu. and Musicians.*

Enter SILVIA *above.*

Pro. Madam, good even to your ladyship.
Sil. I thank you for your music, gentlemen.
Who is that that spake?
Pro. One, lady, if you knew his pure heart's truth,
You would quickly learn to know him by his voice.
Sil. Sir Proteus, as I take it.   90
Pro. Sir Proteus, gentle lady, and your servant.
Sil. What's your will?
Pro.   That I may compass yours.
Sil. You have your wish; my will is even this:
That presently you hie you home to bed.
Thou subtle, perjured, false, disloyal man!
Think'st thou I am so shallow, so conceitless,
To be seduced by thy flattery,
That hast deceived so many with thy vows?
Return, return, and make thy love amends.
For me, by this pale queen of night I swear,   100
I am so far from granting thy request
That I despise thee for thy wrongful suit,

---

74. **crews,** bands.
SCENE II. 2. **unjust,** dishonest; see glossary. 3. **colour,** pretext;
see glossary. 12. **quips,** sharp, sarcastic remarks. 18. **crept,** moved
unnoticed. 20. **creep,** move slowly, as if disabled. **go,** walk at an
ordinary pace. 27. **allycholly,** mallycholly, an old form of *melancholy.*

43. **admired,** wondered at; see glossary. 56. **likes,** pleases, with quibble on the modern sense in the following speech; see glossary. 67.
jars, is discordant; see glossary. 68. **change,** modulation, a musical
term. In the next speech Julia quibbles on it with reference to Proteus' inconstancy. 76. **out of all nick,** beyond all reckoning. 83.

And by and by intend to chide myself
Even for this time I spend in talking to thee.
    Pro. I grant, sweet love, that I did love a lady;
But she is dead.
    Jul. [*Aside*] 'Twere false, if I should speak it;
For I am sure she is not buried.
    Sil. Say that she be; yet Valentine thy friend
Survives; to whom, thyself art witness,   110
I am betroth'd: and art thou not ashamed
To wrong him with thy importunacy?
    Pro. I likewise hear that Valentine is dead.
    Sil. And so suppose am I; for in his grave
Assure thyself my love is buried.
    Pro. Sweet lady, let me rake it from the earth.
    Sil. Go to thy lady's grave and call hers thence,
Or, at the least, in hers sepulchre thine.
    Jul. [*Aside*] He heard not that.
    Pro. Madam, if your heart be so obdurate,   120
Vouchsafe me yet your picture for my love,
The picture that is hanging in your chamber;
To that I'll speak, to that I'll sigh and weep:
For since the substance of your perfect self
Is else devoted, I am but a shadow;
And to your shadow will I make true love.
    Jul. [*Aside*] If 'twere a substance, you would, sure,
      deceive it,
And make it but a shadow, as I am.
    Sil. I am very loath to be your idol, sir;
But since your falsehood shall become you well   130
To worship shadows and adore false shapes,
Send to me in the morning and I'll send it:
And so, good rest.
    Pro.   As wretches have o'ernight
That wait for execution in the morn.
                    [*Exeunt Pro. and Sil. severally.*
    Jul. Host, will you go?
    Host. By my halidom, I was fast asleep.
    Jul. Pray you, where lies Sir Proteus?
    Host. Marry, at my house. Trust me, I think 'tis
almost day.
    Jul. Not so; but it hath been the longest night   140
That e'er I watch'd and the most heaviest.   [*Exeunt.*

SCENE III. *The same.*

Enter EGLAMOUR.

    Egl. This is the hour that Madam Silvia
Entreated me to call and know her mind:
There 's some great matter she 'ld employ me in.
Madam, madam!

Enter SILVIA *above.*

    Sil.   Who calls?
    Egl.   Your servant and your
      friend;
One that attends your ladyship's command.
    Sil. Sir Eglamour, a thousand times good morrow.
    Egl. As many, worthy lady, to yourself:
According to your ladyship's impose,
I am thus early come to know what service
It is your pleasure to command me in.   10

    Sil. O Eglamour, thou art a gentleman—
Think not I flatter, for I swear I do not—
Valiant, wise, remorseful, well accomplish'd:
Thou art not ignorant what dear good will
I bear unto the banish'd Valentine,
Nor how my father would enforce me marry
Vain Thurio, whom my very soul abhors.
Thyself hast loved; and I have heard thee say
No grief did ever come so near thy heart
As when thy lady and thy true love died,   20
Upon whose grave thou vow'dst pure chastity.
Sir Eglamour, I would to Valentine,
To Mantua, where I hear he makes abode;
And, for the ways are dangerous to pass,
I do desire thy worthy company,
Upon whose faith and honour I repose.
Urge not my father's anger, Eglamour,
But think upon my grief, a lady's grief,
And on the justice of my flying hence,
To keep me from a most unholy match,   30
Which heaven and fortune still rewards with plagues.
I do desire thee, even from a heart
As full of sorrows as the sea of sands,
To bear me company and go with me:
If not, to hide what I have said to thee,
That I may venture to depart alone.
    Egl. Madam, I pity much your grievances;
Which since I know they virtuously are placed,
I give consent to go along with you,
Recking as little what betideth me   40
As much I wish all good befortune you.
When will you go?
    Sil.   This evening coming.
    Egl. Where shall I meet you?
    Sil.   At Friar Patrick's cell,
Where I intend holy confession.
    Egl. I will not fail your ladyship. Good morrow,
gentle lady.
    Sil. Good morrow, kind Sir Eglamour.
                    [*Exeunt severally.*

SCENE IV. *The same.*

Enter LAUNCE, *with his Dog.*

    Launce. When a man's servant shall play the cur
with him, look you, it goes hard: one that I brought
up of a puppy; one that I saved from drowning, when
three or four of his blind brothers and sisters went to
it. I have taught him, even as one would say precisely,
'thus I would teach a dog.' I was sent to deliver him
as a present to Mistress Silvia from my master; and I
came no sooner into the dining-chamber but he steps
me to her trencher and steals her capon's leg: O, 'tis
a foul thing when a cur cannot keep himself in all
companies! I would have, as one should say, one that
takes upon him to be a dog indeed, to be, as it were, a
dog at all things. If I had not had more wit than he,
to take a fault upon me that he did, I think verily he
had been hanged for 't; sure as I live, he had suffered
for 't: you shall judge. He thrusts me himself into the
company of three or four gentlemanlike dogs, under

---

drift, scheme. 96. **conceitless,** witless. 112. **importunacy,** importunity. 130. **become,** befit. 136. **By my halidom,** originally an oath on
the holy relics; subsequently a weak asseveration. 141. **heaviest,** most
grievous.
    SCENE III. 8. **impose,** injunction. 13. **remorseful,** compassionate.

37. **grievances,** trouble, distress. 40. **Recking,** caring for, heeding.
    SCENE IV. 3. **of,** from; see glossary. 9. **steps me,** i.e., to my in-
jury, to my detriment; the ethical dative; cf. *thrusts me,* l. 18. 10.
trencher, wooden dish or plate; see glossary. 11. **keep,** restrain; see
glossary.

the duke's table: he had not been there—bless the mark!—a pissing while, but all the chamber smelt him. 'Out with the dog!' says one: 'What cur is that?' says another: 'Whip him out' says the third: 'Hang him up' says the duke. I, having been acquainted with the smell before, knew it was Crab, and goes me to the fellow that whips the dogs: 'Friend,' quoth I, 'you mean to whip the dog?' 'Ay, marry, do I,' quoth he. 'You do him the more wrong,' quoth I; ''twas I did the thing you wot of.' He makes me no more ado, but whips me out of the chamber. How many masters would do this for his servant? Nay, I'll be sworn, I have sat in the stocks for puddings he hath stolen, otherwise he had been executed; I have stood on the pillory for geese he hath killed, otherwise he had suffered for 't. Thou thinkest not of this now. Nay, I remember the trick you served me when I took my leave of Madam Silvia: did not I bid thee still mark me and do as I do? when didst thou see me heave up my leg and make water against a gentlewoman's farthingale? didst thou ever see me do such a trick?

Enter PROTEUS *and* JULIA.

Pro. Sebastian is thy name? I like thee well
And will employ thee in some service presently.
   Jul. In what you please: I'll do what I can.
   Pro. I hope thou wilt. [*To Launce*] How now, you
     whoreson peasant!
Where have you been these two days loitering?
   Launce. Marry, sir, I carried Mistress Silvia the dog 50
you bade me.
   Pro. And what says she to my little jewel?
   Launce. Marry, she says your dog was a cur, and tells you currish thanks is good enough for such a present.
   Pro. But she received my dog?
   Launce. No, indeed, did she not: here have I brought him back again.
   Pro. What, didst thou offer her this from me? 58
   Launce. Ay, sir; the other squirrel was stolen from me by the hangman boys in the market-place: and then I offered her mine own, who is a dog as big as ten of yours, and therefore the gift the greater.
   Pro. Go get thee hence, and find my dog again,
Or ne'er return again into my sight.
Away, I say! stay'st thou to vex me here? [*Exit Launce.*
A slave, that still an end turns me to shame!
Sebastian, I have entertained thee,
Partly that I have need of such a youth
That can with some discretion do my business, 70
For 'tis no trusting to yond foolish lout,
But chiefly for thy face and thy behaviour,
Which, if my augury deceive me not,
Witness good bringing up, fortune and truth:
Therefore know thou, for this I entertain thee.
Go presently and take this ring with thee,
Deliver it to Madam Silvia:
She loved me well deliver'd it to me.
   Jul. It seems you loved not her, to leave her token.
She is dead, belike?
   Pro.   Not so; I think she lives. 80

Jul. Alas!
   Pro. Why dost thou cry 'alas'?
   Jul.   I cannot choose
But pity her.
   Pro.   Wherefore shouldst thou pity her?
   Jul. Because methinks that she loved you as well
As you do love your lady Silvia:
She dreams on him that has forgot her love;
You dote on her that cares not for your love.
'Tis pity love should be so contrary;
And thinking on it makes me cry 'alas!'
   Pro. Well, give her that ring and therewithal 90
This letter. That's her chamber. Tell my lady
I claim the promise for her heavenly picture.
Your message done, hie home unto my chamber,
Where thou shalt find me, sad and solitary. [*Exit.*
   Jul. How many women would do such a message?
Alas, poor Proteus! thou hast entertain'd
A fox to be the shepherd of thy lambs.
Alas, poor fool! why do I pity him
That with his very heart despiseth me?
Because he loves her, he despiseth me; 100
Because I love him, I must pity him.
This ring I gave him when he parted from me,
To bind him to remember my good will;
And now am I, unhappy messenger,
To plead for that which I would not obtain,
To carry that which I would have refused,
To praise his faith which I would have dispraised.
I am my master's true-confirmed love;
But cannot be true servant to my master,
Unless I prove false traitor to myself. 110
Yet will I woo for him, but yet so coldly
As, heaven it knows, I would not have him speed.

Enter SILVIA, *attended.*

Gentlewoman, good day! I pray you, be my mean
To bring me where to speak with Madam Silvia.
   Sil. What would you with her, if that I be she?
   Jul. If you be she, I do entreat your patience
To hear me speak the message I am sent on.
   Sil. From whom?
   Jul. From my master, Sir Proteus, madam.
   Sil. O, he sends you for a picture. 120
   Jul. Ay, madam.
   Sil. Ursula, bring my picture there.
Go give your master this: tell him from me,
One Julia, that his changing thoughts forget,
Would better fit his chamber than this shadow.
   Jul. Madam, please you peruse this letter.—
Pardon me, madam; I have unadvised
Deliver'd you a paper that I should not:
This is the letter to your ladyship.
   Sil. I pray thee, let me look on that again. 130
   Jul. It may not be; good madam, pardon me.
   Sil. There, hold!
I will not look upon your master's lines:
I know they are stuff'd with protestations
And full of new-found oaths; which he will break
As easily as I do tear his paper.
   Jul. Madam, he sends your ladyship this ring.

30. **wot of,** know about; see glossary. 59. **squirrel,** a contemptuous reference to the little dog which Proteus asked him to deliver to Silvia. 60. **hangman,** i.e., fit for the hangman. 90. **therewithal,** in addition to that, at the same time. 98. **fool,** term of pity and endearment; see glossary. 112. **speed,** succeed; see glossary. 115. **if that,** if. 126-129. **Madam . . . ladyship.** This reference to a letter in Julia's possession is without motive. It suggests that the play has been

revised or abridged. 159. **starved,** caused to die; see glossary. 161. **black,** of a dark complexion. 164. **pageants of delight,** delightful entertainments; see *pageants* in glossary. 170. **agood,** in earnest. 172. **Ariadne,** daughter of Minos, king of Crete. She fell in love with one of her father's captives, Theseus, an Athenian hero. When he was shut up in the labyrinth, she gave him a clue of thread by which he was able to find his way among the intricate passages. He escaped, carried her

Sil. The more shame for him that he sends it me;
For I have heard him say a thousand times
His Julia gave it him at his departure. 140
Though his false finger have profaned the ring,
Mine shall not do his Julia so much wrong.
  Jul. She thanks you.
  Sil. What say'st thou?
  Jul. I thank you, madam, that you tender her.
Poor gentlewoman! my master wrongs her much.
  Sil. Dost thou know her?
  Jul. Almost as well as I do know myself:
To think upon her woes I do protest
That I have wept a hundred several times. 150
  Sil. Belike she thinks that Proteus hath forsook her.
  Jul. I think she doth; and that 's her cause of
  sorrow.
  Sil. Is she not passing fair?
  Jul. She hath been fairer, madam, than she is:
When she did think my master loved her well,
She, in my judgement, was as fair as you;
But since she did neglect her looking-glass
And threw her sun-expelling mask away,
The air hath starved the roses in her cheeks
And pinch'd the lily-tincture of her face, 160
That now she is become as black as I.
  Sil. How tall was she?
  Jul. About my stature; for at Pentecost,
When all our pageants of delight were play'd,
Our youth got me to play the woman's part,
And I was trimm'd in Madam Julia's gown,
Which served me as fit, by all men's judgements,
As if the garment had been made for me:
Therefore I know she is about my height.
And at that time I made her weep agood, 170
For I did play a lamentable part:
Madam, 'twas Ariadne passioning
For Theseus' perjury and unjust flight;
Which I so lively acted with my tears
That my poor mistress, moved therewithal,
Wept bitterly; and would I might be dead
If I in thought felt not her very sorrow!
  Sil. She is beholding to thee, gentle youth.
Alas, poor lady, desolate and left!
I weep myself to think upon thy words. 180
Here, youth, there is my purse; I give thee this
For thy sweet mistress' sake, because thou lovest her.
Farewell.   [*Exit Silvia, with attendants.*
  Jul. And she shall thank you for 't, if e'er you know
  her.
A virtuous gentlewoman, mild and beautiful!
I hope my master's suit will be but cold,
Since she respects my mistress' love so much.
Alas, how love can trifle with itself!
Here is her picture: let me see; I think,
If I had such a tire, this face of mine 190
Were full as lovely as is this of hers:
And yet the painter flatter'd her a little,
Unless I flatter with myself too much.
Her hair is auburn, mine is perfect yellow:
If that be all the difference in his love,
I'll get me such a colour'd periwig.

Her eyes are grey as glass, and so are mine:
Ay, but her forehead 's low, and mine 's as high.
What should it be that he respects in her
But I can make respective in myself, 200
If this fond Love were not a blinded god?
Come, shadow, come, and take this shadow up,
For 'tis thy rival. O thou senseless form,
Thou shalt be worshipp'd, kiss'd, loved and adored!
And, were there sense in his idolatry,
My substance should be statue in thy stead.
I'll use thee kindly for thy mistress' sake,
That used me so; or else, by Jove I vow,
I should have scratch'd out your unseeing eyes,
To make my master out of love with thee!   [*Exit.*

ACT V.

SCENE I. *Milan. An abbey.*

Enter EGLAMOUR.

  Egl. The sun begins to gild the western sky;
And now it is about the very hour
That Silvia, at Friar Patrick's cell, should meet me.
She will not fail, for lovers break not hours,
Unless it be to come before their time;
So much they spur their expedition.
See where she comes.

Enter SILVIA.

              Lady, a happy evening!
  Sil. Amen, amen! Go on, good Eglamour,
Out at the postern by the abbey-wall:
I fear I am attended by some spies. 10
  Egl. Fear not: the forest is not three leagues off;
If we recover that, we are sure enough.   [*Exeunt.*

SCENE II. *The same. The* DUKE's *palace.*

Enter THURIO, PROTEUS, *and* JULIA.

  Thu. Sir Proteus, what says Silvia to my suit?
  Pro. O, sir, I find her milder than she was;
And yet she takes exceptions at your person.
  Thu. What, that my leg is too long?
  Pro. No; that it is too little.
  Thu. I'll wear a boot, to make it somewhat rounder.
  Jul. [*Aside*] But love will not be spurr'd to what it
  loathes.
  Thu. What says she to my face?
  Pro. She says it is a fair one.
  Thu. Nay then, the wanton lies; my face is black. 10
  Pro. But pearls are fair; and the old saying is,
Black men are pearls in beauteous ladies' eyes.
  Jul. [*Aside*] 'Tis true; such pearls as put out ladies'
  eyes;
For I had rather wink than look on them.
  Thu. How likes she my discourse?
  Pro. Ill, when you talk of war.
  Thu. But well, when I discourse of love and peace?

The
Two Gentlemen
of Verona
ACT V : SC II

151

away, and married her. Later, when he forsook her, she hanged herself.
passioning, sorrowing, grieving. 178. **beholding,** indebted. 190. **tire,**
headdress, attire. 194. **auburn,** whitish, flaxen. **perfect yellow,** the
color of Queen Elizabeth's hair; hence the fashionable color. 202.
Come . . . up, i.e., the shadow of myself takes up this shadow of my
rival—Silvia's picture; see *shadow* in glossary. **take up,** i.e., in the
hostile sense of accepting a challenge. 205. **sense,** rational meaning;

see glossary.
  ACT V. SCENE I. 9. **postern,** small back or side door. 12. **recover,**
get to, reach, arrive at.
  SCENE II. 3. **takes exceptions at,** disapproves, finds fault with.
7. **spurr'd,** incited; a quibble on *boot* (i.e., riding boot) in the preceding line.

Jul. [*Aside*] But better, indeed, when you hold your
    peace.
Thu. What says she to my valour?
Pro. O, sir, she makes no doubt of that. 20
Jul. [*Aside*] She needs not, when she knows it
    cowardice.
Thu. What says she to my birth?
Pro. That you are well derived.
Jul. [*Aside*] True; from a gentleman to a fool.
Thu. Considers she my possessions?
Pro. O, ay; and pities them.
Thu. Wherefore?
Jul. [*Aside*] That such an ass should owe them.
Pro. That they are out by lease.
Jul. Here comes the duke. 30

Enter DUKE.

Duke. How now, Sir Proteus! how now, Thurio!
Which of you saw Sir Eglamour of late?
Thu. Not I.
Pro.   Nor I.
Duke.   Saw you my daughter?
Pro.   Neither.
Duke. Why then,
She 's fled unto that peasant Valentine;
And Eglamour is in her company.
'Tis true; for Friar Laurence met them both,
As he in penance wander'd through the forest;
Him he knew well, and guess'd that it was she,
But, being mask'd, he was not sure of it; 40
Besides, she did intend confession
At Patrick's cell this even; and there she was not;
These likelihoods confirm her flight from hence.
Therefore, I pray you, stand not to discourse,
But mount you presently and meet with me
Upon the rising of the mountain-foot
That leads toward Mantua, whither they are fled:
Dispatch, sweet gentlemen, and follow me. [*Exit.*
Thu. Why, this it is to be a peevish girl,
That flies her fortune when it follows her. 50
I'll after, more to be revenged on Eglamour
Than for the love of reckless Silvia. [*Exit.*
Pro. And I will follow, more for Silvia's love
Than hate of Eglamour that goes with her. [*Exit.*
Jul. And I will follow, more to cross that love
Than hate for Silvia that is gone for love. [*Exit.*

SCENE III. *The frontiers of Mantua. The forest.*

Enter Outlaws *with* SILVIA.

First Out. Come, come,
Be patient; we must bring you to our captain.
Sil. A thousand more mischances than this one
Have learn'd me how to brook this patiently.
Sec. Out. Come, bring her away.
First Out. Where is the gentleman that was with her?
Third Out. Being nimble-footed, he hath outrun us,
But Moyses and Valerius follow him.

Go thou with her to the west end of the wood;
There is our captain: we'll follow him that 's fled; 10
The thicket is beset; he cannot 'scape.
First Out. Come, I must bring you to our captain's
    cave:
Fear not; he bears an honourable mind,
And will not use a woman lawlessly.
Sil. O Valentine, this I endure for thee! [*Exeunt.*

SCENE IV. *Another part of the forest.*

Enter VALENTINE.

Val. How use doth breed a habit in a man!
This shadowy desert, unfrequented woods,
I better brook than flourishing peopled towns:
Here can I sit alone, unseen of any,
And to the nightingale's complaining notes
Tune my distresses and record my woes.
O thou that dost inhabit in my breast,
Leave not the mansion so long tenantless,
Lest, growing ruinous, the building fall
And leave no memory of what it was! 10
Repair me with thy presence, Silvia;
Thou gentle nymph, cherish thy forlorn swain!
What halloing and what stir is this to-day?
These are my mates, that make their wills their law,
Have some unhappy passenger in chase.
They love me well; yet I have much to do
To keep them from uncivil outrages.
Withdraw thee, Valentine: who 's this comes here?

Enter PROTEUS, SILVIA, *and* JULIA.

Pro. Madam, this service I have done for you,
Though you respect not aught your servant doth, 20
To hazard life and rescue you from him
That would have forced your honour and your love;
Vouchsafe me, for my meed, but one fair look;
A smaller boon than this I cannot beg
And less than this, I am sure, you cannot give.
Val. [*Aside*] How like a dream is this I see and hear!
Love, lend me patience to forbear awhile.
Sil. O miserable, unhappy that I am!
Pro. Unhappy were you, madam, ere I came;
But by my coming I have made you happy. 30
Sil. By thy approach thou makest me most unhappy
Jul. [*Aside*] And me, when he approacheth to your
    presence.
Sil. Had I been seized by a hungry lion,
I would have been a breakfast to the beast,
Rather than have false Proteus rescue me.
O, Heaven be judge how I love Valentine,
Whose life 's as tender to me as my soul!
And full as much, for more there cannot be,
I do detest false perjured Proteus.
Therefore be gone; solicit me no more. 40
Pro. What dangerous action, stood it next to death,
Would I not undergo for one calm look!
O, 'tis the curse in love, and still approved,
When women cannot love where they 're beloved!

23. **derived,** descended, which gives point for the modern reader
to Julia's aside; see glossary. 26. **pities,** despises. 28. **owe,** own;
see glossary.
    SCENE III. 4. **brook,** endure; tolerate; see glossary.
    SCENE IV. 1. **use,** custom; see glossary. **habit,** demeanor, bearing,
manner; see glossary. 9. **growing ruinous,** brought to ruin. 12. **cherish,** treat with kindness. 23. **Vouchsafe,** etc. Silvia is wearing a
mask. 42. **undergo,** undertake; see glossary. 61. **fashion,** kind, sort.

62. **common,** as opposed to extraordinary. 73. **confounds,** ruins; see
glossary. 77. **commit,** sin. 82-83. **And . . . thee.** This passage has
provoked much critical comment. Bond finds the lines to be intentionally ambiguous in order to motivate Julia's swooning, paraphrasing it
as, "All the love that I felt in Silvia's case I extend to thee." 86-90.
Why, boy . . . done. These lines present a crux of some difficulty.
A number of editors attempt to make blank verse of them. In F they appear as prose. Julia's words here contradict preceding action and dia-

Sil. When Proteus cannot love where he 's beloved.
Read over Julia's heart, thy first best love,
For whose dear sake thou didst then rend thy faith
Into a thousand oaths; and all those oaths
Descended into perjury, to love me.
Thou hast no faith left now, unless thou 'dst two;　50
And that 's far worse than none; better have none
Than plural faith which is too much by one:
Thou counterfeit to thy true friend!
　　Pro.　　　　　　In love
Who respects friend?
　　Sil.　　　　　　　All men but Proteus.
　　Pro. Nay, if the gentle spirit of moving words
Can no way change you to a milder form,
I'll woo you like a soldier, at arms' end,
And love you 'gainst the nature of love,—force ye.
　　Sil. O heaven!
　　Pro.　　　　　I'll force thee yield to my desire.
　　Val. Ruffian, let go that rude uncivil touch,　60
Thou friend of an ill fashion!
　　Pro.　　　　　　Valentine!
　　Val. Thou common friend, that 's without faith or
　　love,
For such is a friend now; treacherous man!
Thou hast beguiled my hopes; nought but mine eye
Could have persuaded me: now I dare not say
I have one friend alive; thou wouldst disprove me.
Who should be trusted, when one's own right hand
Is perjured to the bosom? Proteus,
I am sorry I must never trust thee more,
But count the world a stranger for thy sake.　70
The private wound is deepest: O time most accurst,
'Mongst all foes that a friend should be the worst!
　　Pro. My shame and guilt confounds me.
Forgive me, Valentine: if hearty sorrow
Be a sufficient ransom for offence,
I tender 't here; I do as truly suffer
As e'er I did commit.
　　Val.　　　　　Then I am paid;
And once again I do receive thee honest.
Who by repentance is not satisfied
Is nor of heaven nor earth, for these are pleased.　80
By penitence the Eternal's wrath 's appeased:
And, that my love may appear plain and free,
All that was mine in Silvia I give thee.
　　Jul. O me unhappy!　　　　　　[*Swoons.*
　　Pro. Look to the boy.
　　Val. Why, boy! why, wag! how now! what 's the
matter? Look up; speak.
　　Jul. O good sir, my master charged me to deliver a
ring to Madam Silvia, which, out of my neglect, was
never done.　90
　　Pro. Where is that ring, boy?
　　Jul.　　　　　Here 'tis; this is it.
　　Pro. How! let me see:
Why, this is the ring I gave to Julia.
　　Jul. O, cry you mercy, sir, I have mistook: This is
the ring you sent to Silvia.
　　Pro. But how camest thou by this ring? At my
　　depart

I gave this unto Julia.
　　Jul. And Julia herself did give it me;
And Julia herself hath brought it hither.
　　Pro. How! Julia!　　　　　　　　100
　　Jul. Behold her that gave aim to all thy oaths,
And entertain'd 'em deeply in her heart.
How oft hast thou with perjury cleft the root!
O Proteus, let this habit make thee blush!
Be thou ashamed that I have took upon me
Such an immodest raiment, if shame live
In a disguise of love:
It is the lesser blot, modesty finds,
Women to change their shapes than men their minds.
　　Pro. Than men their minds! 'tis true. O heaven!
　　were man　　110
But constant, he were perfect. That one error
Fills him with faults; makes him run through all the
　　sins:
Inconstancy falls off ere it begins.
What is in Silvia's face, but I may spy
More fresh in Julia's with a constant eye?
　　Val. Come, come, a hand from either:
Let me be blest to make this happy close;
'Twere pity two such friends should be long foes.
　　Pro. Bear witness, Heaven, I have my wish for ever.
　　Jul. And I mine.　　　　　　　　120

Enter Outlaws, *with* DUKE *and* THURIO.

　　Outlaws. A prize, a prize, a prize!
　　Val. Forbear, forbear, I say! it is my lord the duke.
Your grace is welcome to a man disgraced,
Banished Valentine.
　　Duke.　　　　　Sir Valentine!
　　Thu. Yonder is Silvia; and Silvia 's mine.
　　Val. Thurio, give back, or else embrace thy death;
Come not within the measure of my wrath;
Do not name Silvia thine; if once again,
†Verona shall not hold thee. Here she stands:
Take but possession of her with a touch:　130
I dare thee but to breathe upon my love.
　　Thu. Sir Valentine, I care not for her, I:
I hold him but a fool that will endanger
His body for a girl that loves him not:
I claim her not, and therefore she is thine.
　　Duke. The more degenerate and base art thou,
To make such means for her as thou hast done
And leave her on such slight conditions.
Now, by the honour of my ancestry,
I do applaud thy spirit, Valentine,　140
And think thee worthy of an empress' love:
Know then, I here forget all former griefs,
Cancel all grudge, repeal thee home again,
Plead a new state in thy unrival'd merit,
To which I thus subscribe: Sir Valentine,
Thou art a gentleman and well derived;
Take thou thy Silvia, for thou hast deserved her.
　　Val. I thank your grace; the gift hath made me
　　happy.
I now beseech you, for your daughter's sake,
To grant one boon that I shall ask of you.　150

logue; cf. IV, iv, 139-142. These observations, taken with Silvia's inexplicable silence from this point on, support the hypothesis for revision and abridgment. 86. **wag,** boy. The New Cambridge editors think it unlikely that Valentine would use such familiar address to a page he had not seen before. 94. **cry you mercy,** beg your pardon; see glossary. 101. **aim,** direction. 104. **this habit,** i.e., her page's costume. 113. **falls off,** withdraws from allegiance. 115. **constant,** steady, loyal. 117. **close,** conclusion. 129. **Verona,** for *Milan*; cf. III,

i, 81, note. 144. **a new state,** a new standing for myself (Neilson). Bond suggests emending to *a new statute,* i.e., a new order of things; as an alternative he conjectures *Plant* for *Plead,* i.e., establish a new order, alluding to Valentine's union with Silvia. Steevens placed a period after the preceding line and made *Plead* an imperative, i.e., "Put in a plea for reinstatement."

Duke. I grant it, for thine own, whate'er it be.
Val. These banish'd men that I have kept withal
Are men endued with worthy qualities:
Forgive them what they have committed here
And let them be recall'd from their exile:
They are reformed, civil, full of good
And fit for great employment, worthy lord.
Duke. Thou hast prevail'd; I pardon them and thee:
Dispose of them as thou know'st their deserts.
Come, let us go: we will include all jars   160
With triumphs, mirth and rare solemnity.
Val. And, as we walk along, I dare be bold
With our discourse to make your grace to smile.
What think you of this page, my lord?
Duke. I think the boy hath grace in him; he blushes.
Val. I warrant you, my lord, more grace than boy.
Duke. What mean you by that saying?
Val. Please you, I'll tell you as we pass along,
That you will wonder what hath fortuned.
Come, Proteus; 'tis your penance but to hear   170
The story of your loves discovered:
That done, our day of marriage shall be yours;
One feast, one house, one mutual happiness.   [*Exeunt.*

160. **include,** conclude.

THE
Taming of the Shrew

The *Taming of the Shrew* is a well-known and successful play on the stage. It is made up of three very distinct parts and has back of its main plot, a source of more than usual value; namely, a shrew play. *The Taming of a Shrew*, a play which had apparently belonged to the repertory of the Lord Pembroke's company, is usually regarded as that source, but certainly is not. It is probably, as ten Brink thought, a play derived from a common original with Shakespeare's play, or, according to a more recent idea, a version of Shakespeare's play taken down from oral delivery and carefully revamped.[1] The original shrew play, if there was one, is lost. It seems fairly clear, however, that *The Taming of the Shrew* is not derived from *The Taming of a Shrew*, since the two plays supplement each other. Shakespeare's play preserves the original chronology[2] and is much closer to the source of the minor plot than is *The Taming of a Shrew*. On the other hand, the latter play preserves a relatively full form of the Induction, whereas Christopher Sly disappears from Shakespeare's play after the first act. The plot of *The Taming of a Shrew* is in other respects more formal and complete; as, for

example, by the inclusion of a third sister to be married off to the character corresponding to Hortensio. There are few verbal similarities. On the whole it seems probable that Shakespeare rewrote a play now lost of which *The Taming of a Shrew* is a degenerate version and that he did away with the continued use of the Induction and altered other formal features of the play.[3]

PUBLICATION

The *Taming of a Shrew* was published in 1594, 1596, and 1607; *The Taming of the Shrew* in the First Folio in 1623. There is in both plays, first of all, an Induction in which a drunken tinker is picked up at an alehouse by a noble lord returned with his train from hunting, put into the best bed in the inn, clothed and waited on as if he were a great nobleman, and ultimately persuaded that he is such indeed. This is the theme of an oriental tale which appears in the *Arabian Nights* as "The Sleeper Awakened," and has various other versions in English and other languages. To entertain his supposed lordship a band of strolling players, like those in *Hamlet*, present a comedy which has two neatly joined plots. The one, native, popular, and farcical, tells about the taming of a shrew. This part of the plot is kept alive in a popular ballad, still current, called *A Merry Geste of a Shrewd and Curst Wife lapped in Morrelles Skin*, which is known to have been in existence before 1575. In the ballad the wife-tamer beats his wife and wraps her up in a horse's skin, newly removed and salted. The main plot of *The Taming of the Shrew* has kept a farcical quality in line with this crude source. The minor plot, one of the best examples in English of the Italian comedy of intrigue, tells how a youth changes places with his servant in order to woo his lady and ultimately wins his father's consent to his marriage by a combination of cleverness and pure accident. This plot is based on the fourth and fifth acts of Gascoigne's *The Supposes*, a translation of Ariosto's *Gli Suppositi*. Shakespeare has gone directly to Gascoigne and followed his source very closely.

DATE

There seems no way of telling when Shakespeare did this work. The play is not mentioned by Meres in 1598, although some critics have identified it with *Love's Labour's Won* in Meres' list. A still larger body of critics, as we shall see, have thought that *Love's Labour's Won* is an early version of *All's Well that Ends Well*. *The Taming of the Shrew* seems to be an early play and must, therefore, have been in existence by 1598. Meres' omission of it has always seemed easily accounted for on the ground that he is making a formal list of examples and not enumerating all of Shakespeare's comedies. It is more likely that the confusion of the two shrew plays, which seems to have existed in people's minds until the

[1]Peter Alexander, "The Taming of a Shrew," Literary Supplement, *The Times*, Sept. 16, 1926, p. 614.
[2]R. A. Houk, "The Evolution of *The Taming of the Shrew*," *PMLA*, LVII (1942), 1009-1038, and "The Strata in *The Taming of the Shrew*," *Studies in Philology*, XXXIX, 291-302.

[3]See article by the present writer, "The Shrew and a Shrew," *Elizabethan Studies in Honor of George F. Reynolds* (Boulder, 1945), pp. 150-154.

publication of the First Folio, prevented Meres from knowing that Shakespeare had made a version of his own.

Stylistic qualities tell one very little about the age of the play. And, because critics have seen in the minor plot such stylistic differences from the major plot, they have almost universally assigned it to some other hand than Shakespeare's. But the line between the plots is not easy to draw. If Shakespeare had a collaborator in *The Taming of the Shrew*, he must have worked very closely with his associate, since the union of the plots is an almost perfect piece of joinery, and the differences in style are by no means so striking as they are said to be. Shakespeare's revision of the old play is thoroughgoing and drastic in the major plot of Katharina and Petruchio, and he has worked over the minor plot with great care, introducing new elements into the Gremio-Hortensio-Lucentio-Tranio plot.[4] If in writing the minor plot Shakespeare was adapting *The Supposes* to his purpose, one would expect a certain degree of irregularity and inferiority in his style as compared to the major plot, in which his free-running dramatic impulse was untrammeled. Because this is true, one may believe, on the whole, that Shakespeare wrote the whole play, and, as to date, 1593[5] is perhaps as good a guess as another.[6]

THE PLAY

Christopher Sly, the Warwickshire tinker, who has been carried into the inn and treated as a nobleman, is hard to convince:

Am not I Christopher Sly, old Sly's son of Burton-heath, by birth a pedlar, by education a card-maker, by transmutation a bear-herd, and now by present profession a tinker?

The fat alewife of Wincot can identify him because he owes her money. But under the influence of music and painting and the beautiful lady, whom they have made for him out of a page, he is convinced that he is a lord and signalizes his conviction by beginning to speak blank verse. After the first scene of the play he does not speak again except to make the memorable statement,

'Tis a very excellent piece of work, madam lady: would 'twere done!

Perhaps Shakespeare forgot him, or, as J. Q. Adams suggests, he may have entrusted the task of putting Sly back on the alehouse steps to the clowns to be done *ex tempore*.

The Jovial Tinker from Philip Stubbes, "Anatomy of the Abuses," 1583.

The scene of the play, thus introduced, is at Padua and at a country house nearby. One Baptista Minola has two daughters, Bianca, the younger, whom Lucentio, old Gremio, and Hortensio, all wish to wed, because of her sweetness; and Kate, an elder daughter, whom nobody wishes to wed, because she is a frightful shrew. Baptista does not want Kate left on his hands, and will not let Bianca marry until Kate is out of the way. This domestic situation is made with marvelous constructive skill to provide the wife-tamer of the old tale with a wife to tame. Petruchio, a soldier of fortune and a man of the world, who says frankly that he is looking for a rich wife, engages to marry Kate, to whose temper, he declares, he has not the least objection. The plot of the taming absorbs the interest of the play and is one of the liveliest pieces of comedy in Shakespeare.

There is method in Petruchio's madness from the start. He wishes to make Kate see herself as others see her, and for her benefit he transforms himself into an image of unreasonable conduct. She is immediately thrown into confusion by the novelty of having him (or anybody) side with her. He disregards her rude refusal of his offer of marriage, swears to her father that they are on the most affectionate terms and are to be married at once. She is so swept off her feet by her unruly lover and so hostile to her father and her sister that she lets the marriage proceed. Petruchio behaves atrociously at the wedding and, sword in hand, carries Kate off to his country place without letting her attend the marriage feast. All this he does on the pretense that he is defending her. He carries his pretended championship of her cause throughout the adventures and misadventures in the country. Back of the major plot lies the conception of the crude old story that a wild young woman must be tamed by physical reduction like a wild young falcon; but

The Taming of the Shrew

155

---

[4]See Florence Huber Ashton, "The Revision of the Folio Text of *The Taming of the Shrew*," *Philological Quarterly*, VI, 151-160.

[5]A play which Henslowe called "the tamynge of A shrowe" was acted for him on June 11, 1594, while the Admiral's and the Chamberlain's men were playing together or alternately at his theater at Newington Butts. See *Henslowe's Diary*, ed. W. W. Greg (1904-1908), II, 164. This was probably Shakespeare's play rather than *The Taming of a Shrew*, since the latter is said on its title page to have been acted by the earl of Pembroke's servants. On their disbanding, it presumably passed into the hands of the printers.

[6]On the question of the date and authorship of *The Taming of the Shrew* see F. S. Boas' edition of *The Taming of a Shrew* (The Shakespeare Classics, 1908); Chambers, *The Elizabethan Stage*, III, 472-473, IV, 48-49, and *William Shakespeare*, I, 322-328; H. Dugdale Sykes, *The Authorship of "The Taming of a Shrew"* (Shakespeare Association, 1920); A. H. Tolman, "Shakespeare's Part in *The Taming of the Shrew*," in *Views about "Hamlet"* (1906); E. P. Kuhl, "The Authorship of *The Taming of the Shrew*," *PMLA*, XL, 551-618; articles by R. A. Houk cited in note 2 above; G. I. Duthie, "*The Taming of a Shrew* and *The Taming of the Shrew*," *Review of English Studies*, XIX (1948), 337-356.

in Petruchio the older motive of the subjection of woman is replaced by action of a far more subtle character. When on the way back to Padua he makes her agree that the sun is the moon (IV, v, 2-22), something happens in Kate's mind. She seems to see the joke. She sees that procedure against his utterly unreasonable conduct, and by analogy her own, is impossible. She indicates her conversion by making a very good joke, her first:

> Then God be bless'd, it is the blessed sun:
> But sun it is not, when you say it is not;
> And the moon changes even as your mind.

The minor plot proceeds with its Italianate intrigue. Lucentio gets rid of his rivals by the aid of a clever servant Tranio and, to provide a show of parental sanction, puts a pedant in place of his father, as in *The Supposes*; but, as in that play, he is forgiven when the real father arrives. Hortensio consoles himself with a widow. In a final scene Lucentio and Hortensio twit Petruchio with the shrewishness of Kate. He bets them a hundred crowns apiece that Kate will prove herself more obedient than their wives, and wins his bet. The play closes with a long and somewhat conventional discourse by Katharina on the duty of obeying husbands.

STAGE HISTORY

The disposition of the seventeenth and eighteenth centuries to lay violent hands on the texts of Shakespeare manifests itself in no case more completely than in their handling of *The Taming of the Shrew*. The Restoration actor John Lacy produced in 1667 an abominable version called *Sauny the Scot*, in which the character of chief interest is Grumio transformed into a supposedly funny Scotch servant. The Induction is gone and also the poetry of the play. For Petruchio's humors are substituted grotesque banalities. However, Lacy's farce was long popular. Garrick, though saving much of Shakespeare's text, cut the Induction and the minor plot and produced *Catharine and Petruchio* (1754), which stayed on the stage until almost the end of the nineteenth century.

The true version was presented by Benjamin Webster in 1837 and by Samuel Phelps at Sadler's Wells in 1856. The modern popularity of Shakespeare's play begins with Augustin Daly's revival in 1887, on which occasion John Drew and Ada Rehan appeared in the chief roles. In England the Benson company and others have played *The Taming of the Shrew* successfully, and in this country, among others, E. H. Sothern and Julia Marlowe.

More recently Margaret Anglin played Kate, Maurice Evans, Petruchio. The play, although not a farce, as it is sometimes said to be, lends itself to farcical presentation. The performance by Alfred Lunt and Lynn Fontanne was done with the utmost extravagance and was uproariously applauded. This shows how Shakespeare lends himself to almost every variety of interpretation.

THE
Taming of the Shrew

DRAMATIS PERSONAE

A Lord.
CHRISTOPHER SLY, a tinker.
Hostess, Page, Players, Huntsmen, and Servants.
} Persons in the Induction.

BAPTISTA, a rich gentleman of Padua.
VINCENTIO, an old gentleman of Pisa.
LUCENTIO, son to Vincentio, in love with Bianca.
PETRUCHIO, a gentleman of Verona, a suitor to Katharina.
GREMIO,
HORTENSIO,
} suitors to Bianca.
TRANIO,
BIONDELLO,
} servants to Lucentio.
GRUMIO,
CURTIS,
} servants to Petruchio.
A Pedant.

KATHARINA, the shrew,
BIANCA,
Widow.
} daughters to Baptista.

Tailor, Haberdasher, and Servants attending on Baptista and Petruchio.

SCENE: *Padua, and Petruchio's country house.*

INDUCTION.

SCENE I. *Before an alehouse on a heath.*

Enter HOSTESS *and* SLY.

Sly. I'll pheeze you, in faith.

Host. A pair of stocks, you rogue!

Sly. Ye are a baggage: the Slys are no rogues; look in the chronicles; we came in with Richard Conqueror. Therefore paucas pallabris; let the world slide: sessa!

Host. You will not pay for the glasses you have burst?

Sly. No, not a denier. Go by, Jeronimy: go to thy cold bed, and warm thee.   10

Host. I know my remedy; I must go fetch the third-borough.   [*Exit.*

Sly. Third, or fourth, or fifth borough, I'll answer him by law: I'll not budge an inch, boy: let him come, and kindly.   [*Falls asleep.*

Horns winded. Enter a Lord *from hunting, with his train.*

Lord. Huntsman, I charge thee, tender well my
    hounds:
†Brach Merriman, the poor cur is emboss'd;
And couple Clowder with the deep-mouth'd brach.
Saw'st thou not, boy, how Silver made it good

At the hedge-corner, in the coldest fault? 20
I would not lose the dog for twenty pound.
  First Hun. Why, Belman is as good as he, my lord;
He cried upon it at the merest loss
And twice to-day pick'd out the dullest scent:
Trust me, I take him for e better dog.
  Lord. Thou art a fool: if Echo were as fleet,
I would esteem him worth a dozen such.
But sup them well and look unto them all:
To-morrow I intend to hunt again.
  First Hun. I will, my lord. 30
  Lord. What's here? one dead, or drunk? See, doth
    he breathe?
  Sec. Hun. He breathes, my lord. Were he not warm'd
    with ale,
This were a bed but cold to sleep so soundly.
  Lord. O monstrous beast! how like a swine he lies!
Grim death, how foul and loathsome is thine image!
Sirs, I will practise on this drunken man.
What think you, if he were convey'd to bed,
Wrapp'd in sweet clothes, rings put upon his fingers,
A most delicious banquet by his bed,
And brave attendants near him when he wakes, 40
Would not the beggar then forget himself?
  First Hun. Believe me, lord, I think he cannot
    choose.
  Sec. Hun. It would seem strange unto him when he
    waked.
  Lord. Even as a flattering dream or worthless fancy.
Then take him up and manage well the jest:
Carry him gently to my fairest chamber
And hang it round with all my wanton pictures:
Balm his foul head in warm distilled waters
And burn sweet wood to make the lodging sweet:
Procure me music ready when he wakes, 50
To make a dulcet and a heavenly sound;
And if he chance to speak, be ready straight
And with a low submissive reverence
Say 'What is it your honour will command?'
Let one attend him with a silver basin
Full of rose-water and bestrew'd with flowers;
Another bear the ewer, the third a diaper,
And say 'Will 't please your lordship cool your hands?'
Some one be ready with a costly suit
And ask him what apparel he will wear; 60
Another tell him of his hounds and horse,
And that his lady mourns at his disease:
Persuade him that he hath been lunatic;
†And when he says he is, say that he dreams,
For he is nothing but a mighty lord.
This do and do it kindly, gentle sirs:
It will be pastime passing excellent,
If it be husbanded with modesty.

  First Hun. My lord, I warrant you we will play our
    part,
As he shall think by our true diligence 70
He is no less than what we say he is.
  Lord. Take him up gently and to bed with him;
And each one to his office when he wakes.
      [*Some bear out Sly. A trumpet sounds.*
Sirrah, go see what trumpet 'tis that sounds:
      [*Exit Servingman.*
Belike, some noble gentleman that means,
Travelling some journey, to repose him here.

      Re-enter Servingman.

How now! who is it?
  Serv.   An 't please your honour, players
That offer service to your lordship.
  Lord. Bid them come near.

      Enter Players.

            Now, fellows, you are welcome.
  Players. We thank your honour. 80
  Lord. Do you intend to stay with me tonight?
  A Player. So please your lordship to accept our duty.
  Lord. With all my heart. This fellow I remember,
Since once he play'd a farmer's eldest son:
'Twas where you woo'd the gentlewoman so well:
I have forgot your name; but, sure, that part
Was aptly fitted and naturally perform'd.
  A Player. I think 'twas Soto that your honour
    means.
  Lord. 'Tis very true: thou didst it excellent.
Well, you are come to me in happy time; 90
The rather for I have some sport in hand
Wherein your cunning can assist me much.
There is a lord will hear you play to-night:
But I am doubtful of your modesties;
Lest over-eyeing of his odd behaviour,—
For yet his honour never heard a play—
You break into some merry passion
And so offend him; for I tell you, sirs,
If you should smile he grows impatient.
  A Player. Fear not, my lord: we can contain
    ourselves, 100
Were he the veriest antic in the world.
  Lord. Go, sirrah, take them to the buttery,
And give them friendly welcome every one:
Let them want nothing that my house affords.
      [*Exit one with the Players.*
Sirrah, go you to Barthol'mew my page,
And see him dress'd in all suits like a lady:
That done, conduct him to the drunkard's chamber;
And call him 'madam,' do him obeisance.
Tell him from me, as he will win my love,

INDUCTION. SCENE I. **1. pheeze,** beat; possibly an echo of the
Hostess' threat (Bond). **5. paucas pallabris,** a blunder for Spanish
pocas palabras, few words. **6. sessa,** an interjection of doubtful import
(Onions); Spanish *cessa* (Theobald); French *cessez* (Halliwell), i.e.,
be quiet; German *sa sa* (Schmidt), a term of applause or encouragement; an exhortation to swift running (Bond, citing *King Lear,* III, iv,
104; III, vi, 77). **9. denier,** French coin, the twelfth of a *sou.* **Go by,
Jeronimy,** a phrase from Kyd's *Spanish Tragedy.* **12. third-borough,**
constable. **16. tender,** treat with tenderness. **17. Brach,** female of
the hound kind, here used as an epithet to Merriman; so F; the New
Cambridge editors emend to *Broach* (early spelling probably *Broch*),
explaining as "bleed," a probable veterinarian remedy in the sixteenth
century for an *emboss'd* hound. Other conjectures and emendations:
Trash, Leech, Bathe, Brace. Gollancz proposed that *Brach* be taken to
mean "mate, couple," hardly agreeable to the context. **emboss'd,**
foaming at the mouth from exhaustion. **18. brach,** kind of hound that
hunts by scent, especially a female hound. **20. fault,** loss of scent.

23. cried upon it, bayed, gave mouth. **merest loss,** i.e., no scent or
trace at all; see *mere* in glossary. **35. image,** likeness; see glossary.
36. practise on, play a joke on; see glossary. **40. brave,** finely arrayed,
showy; see glossary. **44. fancy,** flight of imagination; see glossary.
50. me, the ethical dative. **57. diaper,** towel. **64. And . . . is,** i.e.,
and when he says what he really is. **67. passing,** surpassingly; see
glossary. **82. duty,** expression of respect; see glossary. **88. Soto,**
a character in Fletcher's *Woman Pleased* (1620). The New Cambridge
editors point out the alternatives that this reference is a late non-
Shakespearean insertion or that the Fletcher play is based on an
earlier production which belonged to the Shakespearean company.
The latter they find to be the more probable. **94. doubtful,** apprehensive; see glossary. **your modesties,** i.e., lest the players stare
rudely at Sly. **97. merry passion,** outburst of laughter; see *passion* in
glossary. **101. antic,** buffoon. **104. want,** lack; see glossary. **106. in
all suits,** in every detail.

He bear himself with honourable action, 110
Such as he hath observed in noble ladies
Unto their lords, by them accomplished:
Such duty to the drunkard let him do
With soft low tongue and lowly courtesy,
And say 'What is 't your honour will command,
Wherein your lady and your humble wife
May show her duty and make known her love?'
And then with kind embracements, tempting kisses,
And with declining head into his bosom,
Bid him shed tears, as being overjoy'd 120
To see her noble lord restored to health,
Who for this seven years hath esteemed him
No better than a poor and loathsome beggar:
And if the boy have not a woman's gift
To rain a shower of commanded tears,
An onion will do well for such a shift,
Which in a napkin being close convey'd
Shall in despite enforce a watery eye.
See this dispatch'd with all the haste thou canst:
Anon I'll give thee more instructions. 130

[*Exit a Servingman.*

I know the boy will well usurp the grace,
Voice, gait and action of a gentlewoman:
I long to hear him call the drunkard husband,
And how my men will stay themselves from laughter
When they do homage to this simple peasant.
I'll in to counsel them; haply my presence
May well abate the over-merry spleen
Which otherwise would grow into extremes. [*Exeunt.*

SCENE II. *A bedchamber in the* Lord's *house.*

Enter aloft SLY, *with* Attendants; *some with apparel,
others with basin and ewer and other appurtenances;
and* Lord.

Sly. For God's sake, a pot of small ale.
First Serv. Will 't please your lordship drink a cup of
sack?
Sec. Serv. Will 't please your honour taste of these
conserves?
Third Serv. What raiment will your honour wear
to-day?
Sly. I am Christophero Sly; call not me 'honour' nor
'lordship:' I ne'er drank sack in my life; and if you
give me any conserves, give me conserves of beef: ne'er
ask me what raiment I'll wear; for I have no more
doublets than backs, no more stockings than legs, nor
no more shoes than feet; nay, sometime more feet than
shoes, or such shoes as my toes look through the over-
leather.
Lord. Heaven cease this idle humour in your
honour!
O, that a mighty man of such descent, 15
Of such possessions and so high esteem,

Should be infused with so foul a spirit!
Sly. What, would you make me mad? Am not I
Christopher Sly, old Sly's son of Burton-heath, by
birth a pedlar, by education a card-maker, by transmutation a bear-herd, and now by present profession
a tinker? Ask Marian Hacket, the fat ale-wife of Win-
cot, if she know me not: if she say I am not fourteen
pence on the score for sheer ale, score me up for the
lyingest knave in Christendom. What! I am not be-
straught: here 's—
Third Serv. O, this it is that makes your lady mourn!
Sec. Serv. O, this is it that makes your servants droop!
Lord. Hence comes it that your kindred shuns your
house, 30
As beaten hence by your strange lunacy.
O noble lord, bethink thee of thy birth,
Call home thy ancient thoughts from banishment
And banish hence these abject lowly dreams.
Look how thy servants do attend on thee,
Each in his office ready at thy beck.
Wilt thou have music? hark! Apollo plays [*Music.*
And twenty caged nightingales do sing:
Or wilt thou sleep? we'll have thee to a couch
Softer and sweeter than the lustful bed 40
On purpose trimm'd up for Semiramis.
Say thou wilt walk; we will bestrew the ground:
Or wilt thou ride? thy horses shall be trapp'd,
Their harness studded all with gold and pearl.
Dost thou love hawking? thou hast hawks will soar
Above the morning lark: or wilt thou hunt?
Thy hounds shall make the welkin answer them
And fetch shrill echoes from the hollow earth.
First Serv. Say thou wilt course; thy greyhounds are
as swift
As breathed stags, ay, fleeter than the roe. 50
Sec. Serv. Dost thou love pictures? we will fetch thee
straight
Adonis painted by a running brook,
And Cytherea all in sedges hid,
Which seem to move and wanton with her breath,
Even as the waving sedges play with wind.
Lord. We'll show thee Io as she was a maid,
And how she was beguiled and surprised,
As lively painted as the deed was done.
Third Serv. Or Daphne roaming through a thorny
wood,
Scratching her legs that one shall swear she bleeds, 60
And at that sight shall sad Apollo weep,
So workmanly the blood and tears are drawn.
Lord. Thou art a lord and nothing but a lord:
Thou hast a lady far more beautiful
Than any woman in this waning age.
First Serv. And till the tears that she hath shed for
thee
Like envious floods o'er-run her lovely face,
She was the fairest creature in the world;

And yet she is inferior to none.

Sly. Am I a lord? and have I such a lady? 70
Or do I dream? or have I dream'd till now?
I do not sleep: I see, I hear, I speak;
I smell sweet savours and I feel soft things:
Upon my life, I am a lord indeed
And not a tinker nor Christophero Sly.
Well, bring our lady hither to our sight;
And once again, a pot o' the smallest ale.

Sec. Serv. Will 't please your mightiness to wash your
    hands?
O, how we joy to see your wit restored!
O, that once more you knew but what you are! 80
These fifteen years you have been in a dream;
Or when you waked, so waked as if you slept.

Sly. These fifteen years! by my fay, a goodly nap.
But did I never speak of all that time?

First Serv. O, yes, my lord, but very idle words:
For though you lay here in this goodly chamber,
Yet would you say ye were beaten out of door;
And rail upon the hostess of the house;
And say you would present her at the leet,
Because she brought stone jugs and no seal'd quarts: 90
Sometimes you would call out for Cicely Hacket.

Sly. Ay, the woman's maid of the house.

Third Serv. Why, sir, you know no house nor no such
    maid,
Nor no such men as you have reckon'd up,
As Stephen Sly and old John Naps of Greece
And Peter Turph and Henry Pimpernell
And twenty more such names and men as these
Which never were nor no man ever saw.

Sly. Now Lord be thanked for my good amends!

All. Amen. 100

Sly. I thank thee: thou shalt not lose by it.

Enter the Page *as a lady, with attendants.*

Page. How fares my noble lord?

Sly. Marry, I fare well; for here is cheer enough.
Where is my wife?

Page. Here, noble lord: what is thy will with her?

Sly. Are you my wife and will not call me husband?
My men should call me 'lord:' I am your goodman.

Page. My husband and my lord, my lord and
    husband;
I am your wife in all obedience.

Sly. I know it well. What must I call her? 110

Lord. Madam.

Sly. Al'ce madam, or Joan madam?

Lord. 'Madam,' and nothing else: so lords call
    ladies.

Sly. Madam wife, they say that I have dream'd
And slept above some fifteen year or more.

Page. Ay, and the time seems thirty unto me,
Being all this time abandon'd from your bed.

Sly. 'Tis much. Servants, leave me and her alone.

Madam, undress you and come now to bed.

Page. Thrice-noble lord, let me entreat of you 120
To pardon me yet for a night or two,
Or, if not so, until the sun be set:
For your physicians have expressly charged,
In peril to incur your former malady,
That I should yet absent me from your bed:
I hope this reason stands for my excuse.

Sly. Ay, it stands so that I may hardly tarry so long.
But I would be loath to fall into my dreams again: I
will therefore tarry in despite of the flesh and the
blood. 130

Enter a MESSENGER.

Mess. Your honour's players, hearing your amend-
    ment,
Are come to play a pleasant comedy;
For so your doctors hold it very meet,
Seeing too much sadness hath congeal'd your blood,
And melancholy is the nurse of frenzy:
Therefore they thought it good you hear a play
And frame your mind to mirth and merriment,
Which bars a thousand harms and lengthens life.

Sly. Marry, I will, let them play it. Is not a comonty
a Christmas gambold or a tumbling-trick? 141

Page. No, my good lord; it is more pleasing stuff.

Sly. What, household stuff?

Page. It is a kind of history.

Sly. Well, we'll see 't. Come, madam wife, sit by my
side and let the world slip: we shall ne'er be younger.
    Flourish.

ACT I.

SCENE 1. *Padua. A public place.*

Enter LUCENTIO *and his man* TRANIO.

Luc. Tranio, since for the great desire I had
To see fair Padua, nursery of arts,
I am arrived for fruitful Lombardy,
The pleasant garden of great Italy;
And by my father's love and leave am arm'd
With his good will and thy good company,
My trusty servant, well approved in all,
Here let us breathe and haply institute
A course of learning and ingenious studies.
Pisa renown'd for grave citizens 10
Gave me my being and my father first,
A merchant of great traffic through the world,
Vincentio, come of the Bentivolii.
Vincentio's son brought up in Florence
It shall become to serve all hopes conceived,
To deck his fortune with his virtuous deeds:
And therefore, Tranio, for the time I study,
Virtue and that part of philosophy

accustomed to violent exercise. 53. **Cytherea,** one of the names for
Venus, goddess of love. 56. **Io,** one of Jupiter's paramours. Juno in
a jealous rage changed her into a heifer. 59. **Daphne,** a wood nymph
beloved by Apollo. When he pursued her, Diana changed her into a
laurel tree in order to preserve her from assault. 67. **envious,** spiteful; see glossary. 83. **fay,** faith. 89. **leet,** special court of record
which the lords of certain manors were empowered to hold yearly or
half-yearly. 90. **seal'd quarts,** officially stamped as of that capacity.
Malone noted that sale of liquors in sealed or unsealed measures was
matter for inquiry in a leet (Kitchen's *Courts*, 1663). 95. **Stephen Sly
and old John Naps of Greece.** There was a genuine Stephen Sly who
was in the dramatist's day a self-assertive citizen of Stratford; and
'Greece,' whence 'old John Naps' derived his cognomen, is an obvious

misreading of Greet, a hamlet by Winchmere in Gloucestershire, not
far removed from Shakespeare's native town (Sir Sidney Lee, *Life*,
1904, 167). 127. **may,** can; see glossary. 140-141. **comonty,
gambold,** Sly's blunders for "comedy" and "gambol."
ACT I. SCENE I. 2. **Padua . . . arts,** one of the most renowned of
universities during Shakespeare's time. 2, 3. **Padua, Lombardy.**
Shakespeare's geography here is inaccurate. From subsequent mentions
in the play (e.g., I. 42) it is evident that he thought of Padua as a sea-
port. It is in the province of Venetia, a few miles inland from Venice.
3. **for,** at (Perry); for a stay (Bond). 7. **well . . . all,** i.e., he has
proved himself trustworthy in all things. 8. **institute,** begin. 9. **ingenious,** pertaining to the wits, intellectual. 15. **all hopes conceived,**
i.e., the hopes entertained for me by my friends.

Will I apply that treats of happiness
By virtue specially to be achieved.   20
Tell me thy mind; for I have Pisa left
And am to Padua come, as he that leaves
A shallow plash to plunge him in the deep
And with satiety seeks to quench his thirst.
    Tra. Mi perdonato, gentle master mine,
I am in all affected as yourself;
Glad that you thus continue your resolve
To suck the sweets of sweet philosophy.
Only, good master, while we do admire
This virtue and this moral discipline,   30
Let 's be no stoics nor no stocks, I pray;
Or so devote to Aristotle's checks
As Ovid be an outcast quite abjured:
Balk logic with acquaintance that you have
And practise rhetoric in your common talk;
Music and poesy use to quicken you;
The mathematics and the metaphysics,
Fall to them as you find your stomach serves you;
No profit grows where is no pleasure ta'en:
In brief, sir, study what you most affect.   40
    Luc. Gramercies, Tranio, well dost thou advise.
If, Biondello, thou wert come ashore,
We could at once put us in readiness,
And take a lodging fit to entertain
Such friends as time in Padua shall beget.
But stay a while: what company is this?
    Tra. Master, some show to welcome us to town.

Enter BAPTISTA, KATHARINA, BIANCA, GREMIO, *and*
    HORTENSIO. LUCENTIO *and* TRANIO *stand by.*

    Bap. Gentlemen, importune me no farther,
For how I firmly am resolved you know;
That is, not to bestow my youngest daughter   50
Before I have a husband for the elder:
If either of you both love Katharina,
Because I know you well and love you well,
Leave shall you have to court her at your pleasure.
    Gre. [*Aside*] To cart her rather: she 's too rough for
      me.
There, there, Hortensio, will you any wife?
    Kath. I pray you, sir, is it your will
To make a stale of me amongst these mates?
    Hor. Mates, maid! how mean you that? no mates for
      you,
Unless you were of gentler, milder mould.   60
    Kath. I' faith, sir, you shall never need to fear:
I wis it is not half way to her heart;
But if it were, doubt not her care should be
To comb your noddle with a three-legg'd stool
And paint your face and use you like a fool.
    Hor. From all such devils, good Lord deliver us!
    Gre. And me too, good Lord!
    Tra. Hush, master! here 's some good pastime
      toward:
That wench is stark mad or wonderful froward.
    Luc. But in the other's silence do I see   70

Maid's mild behaviour and sobriety.
Peace, Tranio!
    Tra. Well said, master; mum! and gaze your fill.
    Bap. Gentlemen, that I may soon make good
What I have said, Bianca, get you in:
And let it not displease thee, good Bianca,
For I will love thee ne'er the less, my girl.
    Kath. A pretty peat! it is best
Put finger in the eye, an she knew why.
    Bian. Sister, content you in my discontent.   80
Sir, to your pleasure humbly I subscribe:
My books and instruments shall be my company,
On them to look and practise by myself.
    Luc. Hark, Tranio! thou may'st hear Minerva speak.
    Hor. Signior Baptista, will you be so strange?
Sorry am I that our good will effects
Bianca's grief.
    Gre.   Why will you mew her up,
Signior Baptista, for this fiend of hell,
And make her bear the penance of her tongue?
    Bap. Gentlemen, content ye; I am resolved: 90
Go in, Bianca: [*Exit Bianca.*
And for I know she taketh most delight
In music, instruments and poetry,
Schoolmasters will I keep within my house,
Fit to instruct her youth. If you, Hortensio,
Or Signior Gremio, you, know any such,
Prefer them hither; for to cunning men
I will be very kind, and liberal
To mine own children in good bringing up:
And so farewell. Katharina, you may stay;   100
For I have more to commune with Bianca.   [*Exit.*
    Kath. Why, and I trust I may go too, may I not?
What, shall I be appointed hours; as though, belike,
I knew not what to take, and what to leave, ha? [*Exit.*
    Gre. You may go to the devil's dam: your gifts are
so good, here 's none will hold you. Their love is not so
great, Hortensio, but we may blow our nails together,
and fast it fairly out: our cake 's dough on both sides.
Farewell: yet, for the love I bear my sweet Bianca, if I
can by any means light on a fit man to teach her that
wherein she delights, I will wish him to her father.
    Hor. So will I, Signior Gremio: but a word, I pray.
Though the nature of our quarrel yet never brooked
parle, know now, upon advice, it toucheth us both,
that we may yet again have access to our fair mistress
and be happy rivals in Bianca's love, to labour and
effect one thing specially.   121
    Gre. What 's that, I pray?
    Hor. Marry, sir, to get a husband for her sister.
    Gre. A husband! a devil.
    Hor. I say, a husband.
    Gre. I say, a devil. Thinkest thou, Hortensio, though
her father be very rich, any man is so very a fool to be
married to hell?   129
    Hor. Tush, Gremio, though it pass your patience
and mine to endure her loud alarums, why, man,
there be good fellows in the world, an a man could

---

23. **plash,** pool. 25. **Mi perdonato,** pardon me. 26. **affected,** disposed; see glossary. 31. **stocks,** blockheads. 32. **devote,** devoted. **checks,** restraints; see glossary. Blackstone's suggestion that this is an error for "ethics" has much to recommend it. 33. **Ovid,** a Latin love poet. The antithesis is between serious study, as typified by Aristotle, and preoccupation with lighter entertainment, as typified by Ovid. 34. **Balk logic,** chop logic, bandy words (Onions). 38. **stomach,** inclination, disposition; see glossary. 40. **what . . . affect,** what pleases you most; see *affect* in glossary. 55. **cart,** carry in a cart through the streets by way of punishment or public exposure. 58. **stale,** laughing-

stock, with play on the meaning "harlot." **mates,** rude fellows. 68. **toward,** about to take place; see glossary. 78. **peat,** darling, pet. 87. **mew her up,** coop her up; see *mew* in glossary. 108. **Their,** so F. The antecedent has been variously explained: women in general; Baptista and Bianca (for her suitors); Katharina and Bianca (for each other); Baptista and Bianca (for each other). The New Cambridge editors adopt the reading of the 1631 Q: *There loue,* punctuating *Therelove,* etc. 109. **blow . . . together,** equivalent to the modern expression "twirl our thumbs." **fairly,** handsomely (used contemptuously); see glossary. 117. **brooked,** endured, tolerated; see glossary. **parle,** con-light on them, would take her with all faults, and money enough.

Gre. I cannot tell; but I had as lief take her dowry with this condition, to be whipped at the high cross every morning.

Hor. Faith, as you say, there's small choice in rotten apples. But come; since this bar in law makes us friends, it shall be so far forth friendly maintained till by helping Baptista's eldest daughter to a husband we set his youngest free for a husband, and then have to 't afresh. Sweet Bianca! Happy man be his dole! He that runs fastest gets the ring. How say you, Signior Gremio?

Gre. I am agreed; and would I had given him the best horse in Padua to begin his wooing that would thoroughly woo her, wed her and bed her and rid the house of her! Come on.   [*Exeunt Gremio and Hortensio.*

Tra. I pray, sir, tell me, is it possible   151
That love should of a sudden take such hold?

Luc. O Tranio, till I found it to be true,
I never thought it possible or likely;
But see, while idly I stood looking on,
I found the effect of love in idleness:
And now in plainness do confess to thee,
That art to me as secret and as dear
As Anna to the queen of Carthage was,
Tranio, I burn, I pine, I perish, Tranio,   160
If I achieve not this young modest girl.
Counsel me, Tranio, for I know thou canst;
Assist me, Tranio, for I know thou wilt.

Tra. Master, it is no time to chide you now;
Affection is not rated from the heart:
If love have touch'd you, nought remains but so,
'Redime te captum quam queas minimo.'

Luc. Gramercies, lad, go forward; this contents:
The rest will comfort, for thy counsel's sound.

Tra. Master, you look'd so longly on the maid,   170
Perhaps you mark'd not what 's the pith of all.

Luc. O yes, I saw sweet beauty in her face,
Such as the daughter of Agenor had,
That made great Jove to humble him to her hand,
When with his knees he kiss'd the Cretan strand.

Tra. Saw you no more? mark'd you not how her sister
Began to scold and raise up such a storm
That mortal ears might hardly endure the din?

Luc. Tranio, I saw her coral lips to move
And with her breath she did perfume the air: 180
Sacred and sweet was all I saw in her.

Tra. Nay, then, 'tis time to stir him from his trance.
I pray, awake, sir: if you love the maid,
Bend thoughts and wits to achieve her. Thus it stands:
Her elder sister is so curst and shrewd
That till the father rid his hands of her,
Master, your love must live a maid at home;
And therefore has he closely mew'd her up,
Because she will not be annoy'd with suitors.

Luc. Ah, Tranio, what a cruel father 's he!   190

But art thou not advised, he took some care
To get her cunning schoolmasters to instruct her?

Tra. Ay, marry, am I, sir; and now 'tis plotted.

Luc. I have it, Tranio.

Tra.   Master, for my hand,
Both our inventions meet and jump in one.

Luc. Tell me thine first.

Tra.   You will be schoolmaster
And undertake the teaching of the maid:
That 's your device.

Luc.   It is: may it be done?

Tra. Not possible; for who shall bear your part,
And be in Padua here Vincentio's son,   200
Keep house and ply his book, welcome his friends,
Visit his countrymen and banquet them?

Luc. Basta; content thee, for I have it full.
We have not yet been seen in any house,
Nor can we be distinguish'd by our faces
For man or master; then it follows thus;
Thou shalt be master, Tranio, in my stead,
Keep house and port and servants, as I should:
I will some other be, some Florentine,
Some Neapolitan, or meaner man of Pisa.   210
'Tis hatch'd and shall be so: Tranio, at once
Uncase thee; take my colour'd hat and cloak:
When Biondello comes, he waits on thee;
But I will charm him first to keep his tongue.

Tra. So had you need.
In brief, sir, sith it your pleasure is,
And I am tied to be obedient;
For so your father charged me at our parting,
'Be serviceable to my son,' quoth he,
Although I think 'twas in another sense;   220
I am content to be Lucentio,
Because so well I love Lucentio.

Luc. Tranio, be so, because Lucentio loves.
And let me be a slave, to achieve that maid
Whose sudden sight hath thrall'd my wounded eye.
Here comes the rogue.

Enter BIONDELLO.

         Sirrah, where have you been?

Bion. Where have I been! Nay, how now! where are you? Master, has my fellow Tranio stolen your clothes? Or you stolen his? or both? pray, what 's the news?   230

Luc. Sirrah, come hither: 'tis no time to jest,
And therefore frame your manners to the time.
Your fellow Tranio here, to save my life,
Puts my apparel and my countenance on,
And I for my escape have put on his;
For in a quarrel since I came ashore
I kill'd a man and fear I was descried:
Wait you on him, I charge you, as becomes,
While I make way from hence to save my life:
You understand me?

Bion.   I, sir! ne'er a whit.   240

Luc. And not a jot of Tranio in your mouth:
Tranio is changed into Lucentio.

---

ference; see glossary. **advice,** reflection; see glossary. 137. **high cross,** cross set on a pedestal in a market place or center of a town. 144. **dole,** portion in life, destiny; i.e., may it be his dole to be called "Happy man!" (Onions). 145. **the ring,** an allusion to the sport of riding at the ring, with quibble on "wedding ring." 156. **love in idleness,** the flower heartsease, pansy, to which was attributed magical power in love. 159. **Anna . . . Carthage.** Anna was the confidante of her sister, Dido, queen of Carthage. 165. **rated,** driven away by chiding; see glossary. 167. **'Redime . . . minimo,'** buy yourself out of bondage for as little as you can. 173. **daughter of Agenor,** Europa; the story is

related in Ovid's *Metamorphoses.* 185. **curst,** shrewish; see glossary. **shrewd,** ill-natured; see glossary. 192. **cunning,** skillful. 195. **inventions,** plans; see glossary. **jump,** tally, agree; see glossary. 203. **Basta,** enough. 208. **port,** state, social station; see glossary. 210. **meaner,** of a lower social class; see *mean* in glossary. 216. **sith,** since; see glossary. 225. **Whose sudden sight,** i.e., the sudden sight of whom. 226. **Sirrah,** ordinary form of addressing servants; see glossary.

Bion. The better for him: would I were so too!

Tra. So could I, faith, boy, to have the next wish after,
That Lucentio indeed had Baptista's youngest daughter.
But, sirrah, not for my sake, but your master's, I advise
You use your manners discreetly in all kind of companies:
When I am alone, why, then I am Tranio;
But in all places else your master Lucentio. 249

Luc. Tranio, let's go: one thing more rests, that thyself execute, to make one among these wooers: if thou ask me why, sufficeth, my reasons are both good and weighty. [*Exeunt.*

The presenters above speak.

First Serv. My lord, you nod; you do not mind the play.

Sly. Yes, by Saint Anne, do I. A good matter, surely: comes there any more of it?

Page. My lord, 'tis but begun.

Sly. 'Tis a very excellent piece of work, madam lady: would 'twere done! [*They sit and mark.* 259

SCENE II. *Padua. Before* HORTENSIO'S *house.*

Enter PETRUCHIO *and his man* GRUMIO.

Pet. Verona, for a while I take my leave,
To see my friends in Padua, but of all
My best beloved and approved friend,
Hortensio; and I trow this is his house.
Here, sirrah Grumio; knock, I say.

Gru. Knock, sir! whom should I knock? is there any man has rebused your worship?

Pet. Villain, I say, knock me here soundly.

Gru. Knock you here, sir! why, sir, what am I, sir, that I should knock you here, sir? 10

Pet. Villain, I say, knock me at this gate
And rap me well, or I'll knock your knave's pate.

Gru. My master is grown quarrelsome. I should knock you first,
And then I know after who comes by the worst.

Pet. Will it not be?
Faith, sirrah, an you'll not knock, I'll ring it;
I'll try how you can sol, fa, and sing it.
[*He wrings him by the ears.*

Gru. Help, masters, help! my master is mad.

Pet. Now, knock when I bid you, sirrah villain! 19

Enter HORTENSIO.

Hor. How now! what's the matter? My old friend Grumio! and my good friend Petruchio! How do you all at Verona?

Pet. Signior Hortensio, come you to part the fray?
'Con tutto il cuore, ben trovato,' may I say.

Hor. 'Alla nostra casa ben venuto, molto honorato signor mio Petruchio.'

Rise, Grumio, rise: we will compound this quarrel. 27

Gru. Nay, 'tis no matter, sir, what he 'leges in Latin. If this be not a lawful cause for me to leave his service, look you, sir, he bid me knock him and rap him soundly, sir: well, was it fit for a servant to use his master so, being perhaps, for aught I see, two and thirty, a pip out?
Whom would to God I had well knock'd at first,
Then had not Grumio come by the worst.

Pet. A senseless villain! Good Hortensio,
I bade the rascal knock upon your gate
And could not get him for my heart to do it. 38

Gru. Knock at the gate! O heavens! Spake you not these words plain, 'Sirrah, knock me here, rap me here, knock me well, and knock me soundly'? And come you now with, 'knocking at the gate'?

Pet. Sirrah, be gone, or talk not, I advise you.

Hor. Petruchio, patience; I am Grumio's pledge:
Why, this's a heavy chance 'twixt him and you,
Your ancient, trusty, pleasant servant Grumio.
And tell me now, sweet friend, what happy gale
Blows you to Padua here from old Verona?

Pet. Such wind as scatters young men through the world 50
To seek their fortunes farther than at home
Where small experience grows. But in a few,
Signior Hortensio, thus it stands with me:
Antonio, my father, is deceased;
And I have thrust myself into this maze,
Haply to wive and thrive as best I may:
Crowns in my purse I have and goods at home,
And so am come abroad to see the world.

Hor. Petruchio, shall I then come roundly to thee
And wish thee to a shrewd ill-favour'd wife? 60
Thou 'ldst thank me but a little for my counsel:
And yet I'll promise thee she shall be rich
And very rich: but thou 'rt too much my friend,
And I'll not wish thee to her.

Pet. Signior Hortensio, 'twixt such friends as we
Few words suffice; and therefore, if thou know
One rich enough to be Petruchio's wife,
As wealth is burden of my wooing dance,
Be she as foul as was Florentius' love,
As old as Sibyl and as curst and shrewd 70
As Socrates' Xanthippe, or a worse,
She moves me not, or not removes, at least,
Affection's edge in me, were she as rough
As are the swelling Adriatic seas:
I come to wive it wealthily in Padua;
If wealthily, then happily in Padua.

Gru. Nay, look you, sir, he tells you flatly what his mind is: why, give him gold enough and marry him to a puppet or an aglet-baby; or an old trot with ne'er a tooth in her head, though she have as many diseases as two and fifty horses: why, nothing comes amiss, so money comes withal.

Hor. Petruchio, since we are stepp'd thus far in,
I will continue that I broach'd in jest.

I can, Petruchio, help thee to a wife
With wealth enough and young and beauteous,
Brought up as best becomes a gentlewoman:
Her only fault, and that is faults enough,
Is that she is intolerable curst
And shrewd and froward, so beyond all measure   90
That, were my state far worser than it is,
I would not wed her for a mine of gold.

    Pet. Hortensio, peace! thou know'st not gold's
        effect?
Tell me her father's name and 'tis enough;
For I will board her, though she chide as loud
As thunder when the clouds in autumn crack.

    Hor. Her father is Baptista Minola,
An affable and courteous gentleman:
Her name is Katharina Minola,
Renown'd in Padua for her scolding tongue.   100

    Pet. I know her father, though I know not her;
And he knew my deceased father well.
I will not sleep, Hortensio, till I see her;
And therefore let me be thus bold with you
To give you over at this first encounter,
Unless you will accompany me thither.

    Gru. I pray you, sir, let him go while the humour
lasts. O' my word, an she knew him as well as I do,
she would think scolding would do little good upon
him: she may perhaps call him half a score knaves or
so: why, that's nothing; an he begin once, he'll rail in
his rope-tricks. I'll tell you what, sir, an she stand
him but a little, he will throw a figure in her face and
so disfigure her with it that she shall have no more eyes
to see withal than a cat. You know him not, sir.

    Hor. Tarry, Petruchio, I must go with thee,
For in Baptista's keep my treasure is:
He hath the jewel of my life in hold,
His youngest daughter, beautiful Bianca,   120
And her withholds from me and other more,
Suitors to her and rivals in my love,
Supposing it a thing impossible,
For those defects I have before rehearsed,
That ever Katharina will be woo'd;
Therefore this order hath Baptista ta'en,
That none shall have access unto Bianca
Till Katharine the curst have got a husband.

    Gru. Katharine the curst!
A title for a maid of all titles the worst.   130

    Hor. Now shall my friend Petruchio do me grace,
And offer me disguised in sober robes
To old Baptista as a schoolmaster
Well seen in music, to instruct Bianca;
That so I may, by this device, at least
Have leave and leisure to make love to her
And unsuspected court her by herself.

    Gru. Here's no knavery! See, to beguile the old
folks, how the young folks lay their heads together! 140

    Enter GREMIO, *and* LUCENTIO *disguised.*

Master, master, look about you: who goes there, ha?

    Hor. Peace, Grumio! it is the rival of my love.
Petruchio, stand by a while.

    Gru. A proper stripling and an amorous!

    Gre. O, very well; I have perused the note.
Hark you, sir; I'll have them very fairly bound:
All books of love, see that at any hand;
And see you read no other lectures to her:
You understand me: over and beside
Signior Baptista's liberality,   150
I'll mend it with a largess. Take your paper too,
And let me have them very well perfumed:
For she is sweeter than perfume itself
To whom they go to. What will you read to her?

    Luc. Whate'er I read to her, I'll plead for you
As for my patron, stand you so assured,
As firmly as yourself were still in place:
Yea, and perhaps with more successful words
Than you, unless you were a scholar, sir.

    Gre. O this learning, what a thing it is!   160

    Gru. O this woodcock, what an ass it is!

    Pet. Peace, sirrah!

    Hor. Grumio, mum! God save you, Signior Gremio.

    Gre. And you are well met, Signior Hortensio.
Trow you whither I am going? To Baptista Minola.
I promised to inquire carefully
About a schoolmaster for the fair Bianca:
And by good fortune I have lighted well
On this young man, for learning and behaviour
Fit for her turn, well read in poetry   170
And other books, good ones, I warrant ye.

    Hor. 'Tis well; and I have met a gentleman
Hath promised me to help me to another,
A fine musician to instruct our mistress;
So shall I no whit be behind in duty
To fair Bianca, so beloved of me.

    Gre. Beloved of me; and that my deeds shall prove.

    Gru. And that his bags shall prove.

    Hor. Gremio, 'tis now no time to vent our love:
Listen to me, and if you speak me fair,   180
I'll tell you news indifferent good for either.
Here is a gentleman whom by chance I met,
Upon agreement from us to his liking,
Will undertake to woo curst Katharine,
Yea, and to marry her, if her dowry please.

    Gre. So said, so done, is well.
Hortensio, have you told him all her faults?

    Pet. I know she is an irksome brawling scold:
If that be all, masters, I hear no harm.

    Gre. No, say'st me so, friend? What countryman? 190

    Pet. Born in Verona, old Antonio's son:
My father dead, my fortune lives for me;
And I do hope good days and long to see.

    Gre. O sir, such a life, with such a wife, were strange!
But if you have a stomach, to't i' God's name:
You shall have me assisting you in all.
But will you woo this wild-cat?

    Pet.   Will I live?

    Gru. Will he woo her? ay, or I'll hang her.

---

70. **Sibyl,** prophetess of Cumae to whom Apollo gave as many years
of life as she held grains of sand in her hand. 71. **Xanthippe,** the
philosopher's notoriously shrewish wife. 78. **mind,** intention; see
glossary. 79. **aglet-baby,** small figure carved on the tag of a lace.
80. **trot,** old woman. 82. **withal,** with it; see glossary. 95. **board,**
accost. 105. **give you over,** desert you. 112. **rope-tricks,** variously
explained: Grumio's blunder for "rhetoric," borne out by his use of
figure below; tricks deserving a halter—i.e., hanging (Perry); Bond
recalls the nurse in *Romeo and Juliet* (II, iv, 154) characterizing Mercutio's remarks as *ropery,* and suspects similar coarse allusions here.

113. **stand,** withstand. 114. **figure,** figure of speech. 131. **do me
grace,** do me a favor; see *grace* in glossary. 134. **Well seen,** well skilled.
144. **proper,** handsome (used facetiously); see glossary. Grumio is alluding to the old Gremio, not to Lucentio. 147. **at any hand,** in any case.
151. **largess,** free gift of money. 161. **woodcock,** a bird easily caught;
frequently used to indicate a simpleton. 180. **fair,** civilly, courteously;
see glossary. 181. **indifferent,** equally. 183. **Upon . . . liking,** on
terms agreeable to him. A few lines below (215-216) we learn that
Bianca's suitors will *bear his charge of wooing.*

Pet. Why came I hither but to that intent?
Think you a little din can daunt mine ears? 200
Have I not in my time heard lions roar?
Have I not heard the sea puff'd up with winds
Rage like an angry boar chafed with sweat?
Have I not heard great ordnance in the field,
And heaven's artillery thunder in the skies?
Have I not in a pitched battle heard
Loud 'larums, neighing steeds, and trumpets' clang?
And do you tell me of a woman's tongue,
That gives not half so great a blow to hear
As will a chestnut in a farmer's fire? 210
Tush, tush! fear boys with bugs.
   Gru.   For he fears none.
   Gre. Hortensio, hark:
This gentleman is happily arrived,
My mind presumes, for his own good and ours.
   Hor. I promised we would be contributors
And bear his charge of wooing, whatsoe'er.
   Gre. And so we will, provided that he win her.
   Gru. I would I were as sure of a good dinner.

Enter TRANIO *brave, and* BIONDELLO.

   Tra. Gentlemen, God save you. If I may be bold,
Tell me, I beseech you, which is the readiest way 220
To the house of Signior Baptista Minola?
   Bion. He that has the two fair daughters: is 't he
you mean?
   Tra. Even he, Biondello.
   Gre. Hark you, sir; you mean not her to—
   Tra. Perhaps, him and her, sir: what have you to
do?
   Pet. Not her that chides, sir, at any hand, I pray.
   Tra. I love no chiders, sir. Biondello, let 's away.
   Luc. Well begun, Tranio.
   Hor.   Sir, a word ere you go;
Are you a suitor to the maid you talk of, yea or no? 230
   Tra. And if I be, sir, is it any offence?
   Gre. No; if without more words you will get you
      hence.
   Tra. Why, sir, I pray, are not the streets as free
For me as for you?
   Gre.   But so is not she.
   Tra. For what reason, I beseech you?
   Gre.   For this reason, if you'll know,
That she 's the choice love of Signior Gremio.
   Hor. That she 's the chosen of Signior Hortensio.
   Tra. Softly, my masters! if you be gentlemen,
Do me this right; hear me with patience.
Baptista is a noble gentleman, 240
To whom my father is not all unknown;
And were his daughter fairer than she is,
She may more suitors have and me for one.
Fair Leda's daughter had a thousand wooers;
Then well one more may fair Bianca have:
And so she shall; Lucentio shall make one,
Though Paris came in hope to speed alone.
   Gre. What! this gentleman will out-talk us all.
   Luc. Sir, give him head: I know he'll prove a jade.
   Pet. Hortensio, to what end are all these words? 250
   Hor. Sir, let me be so bold as ask you,

Did you yet ever see Baptista's daughter?
   Tra. No, sir; but hear I do that he hath two,
The one as famous for a scolding tongue
As is the other for beauteous modesty.
   Pet. Sir, sir, the first 's for me; let her go by.
   Gre. Yea, leave that labour to great Hercules;
And let it be more than Alcides' twelve.
   Pet. Sir, understand you this of me in sooth:
The youngest daughter whom you hearken for 260
Her father keeps from all access of suitors,
And will not promise her to any man
Until the elder sister first be wed:
The younger then is free and not before.
   Tra. If it be so, sir, that you are the man
Must stead us all and me amongst the rest,
And if you break the ice and do this feat,
Achieve the elder, set the younger free
For our access, whose hap shall be to have her
Will not so graceless be to be ingrate. 270
   Hor. Sir, you say well and well you do conceive;
And since you do profess to be a suitor,
You must, as we do, gratify this gentleman,
To whom we all rest generally beholding.
   Tra. Sir, I shall not be slack: in sign whereof,
Please ye we may contrive this afternoon,
And quaff carouses to our mistress' health,
And do as adversaries do in law,
Strive mightily, but eat and drink as friends.
   Gru. Bion. O excellent motion! Fellows, let 's be
      gone. 280
   Hor. The motion 's good indeed and be it so,
Petruchio, I shall be your ben venuto.   [*Exeunt.*

ACT II.

SCENE I. *Padua. A room in* BAPTISTA'S *house.*

Enter KATHARINA *and* BIANCA.

   Bian. Good sister, wrong me not, nor wrong your-
      self,
To make a bondmaid and a slave of me;
That I disdain: but for these other gawds,
Unbind my hands, I'll pull them off myself,
Yea, all my raiment, to my petticoat;
Or what you will command me will I do,
So well I know my duty to my elders.
   Kath. Of all thy suitors, here I charge thee, tell
Whom thou lovest best: see thou dissemble not.
   Bian. Believe me, sister, of all the men alive 10
I never yet beheld that special face
Which I could fancy more than any other.
   Kath. Minion, thou liest. Is 't not Hortensio?
   Bian. If you affect him, sister, here I swear
I'll plead for you myself, but you shall have him.
   Kath. O then, belike, you fancy riches more:
You will have Gremio to keep you fair.
   Bian. Is it for him you do envy me so?
Nay then you jest, and now I well perceive
You have but jested with me all this while: 20
I prithee, sister Kate, untie my hands.

204. **ordnance,** cannon. 211. **fear . . . bugs,** frighten children with
bugbears; see *fear* in glossary. 244. **Fair Leda's daughter,** Helen of
Troy. 247. **speed,** succeed; see glossary. 249. **prove a jade,** tire like
an ill-conditioned horse. 258. **Alcides',** son of Alcaeus, i.e., Hercules,
who, noted for the achievement of the twelve great labors, is the only
one capable of conquering Katharina. 270. **graceless,** rude, with

play on the meaning "ungrateful." **ingrate,** ungrateful; cf. *gratify*
(l. 273). 273. **gratify,** requite. 276. **contrive,** spend, pass (time); see
glossary. 280. **motion,** suggestion, proposal; see glossary. 282. **ben
venuto,** welcome; Hortensio is host to Petruchio.
   ACT II. SCENE I. 3. **gawds,** ornaments, articles of jewelry. 13.
Minion, saucy woman; see glossary. 17. **fair,** resplendent with finery;

Kath. If that be jest, then all the rest was so.
[*Strikes her.*

Enter BAPTISTA.

Bap. Why, how now, dame! whence grows this
insolence?
Bianca, stand aside. Poor girl! she weeps.
Go ply thy needle; meddle not with her.
For shame, thou hilding of a devilish spirit,
Why dost thou wrong her that did ne'er wrong thee?
When did she cross thee with a bitter word?
Kath. Her silence flouts me, and I'll be revenged.
[*Flies after Bianca.*
Bap. What, in my sight? Bianca, get thee in. 30
[*Exit Bianca.*
Kath. What, will you not suffer me? Nay, now I see
She is your treasure, she must have a husband;
I must dance bare-foot on her wedding day
And for your love to her lead apes in hell.
Talk not to me: I will go sit and weep
Till I can find occasion of revenge. [*Exit.*
Bap. Was ever gentleman thus grieved as I?
But who comes here?

Enter GREMIO, LUCENTIO *in the habit of a mean man;*
PETRUCHIO, *with* HORTENSIO *as a musician; and*
TRANIO, *with* BIONDELLO *bearing a lute and books.*

Gre. Good morrow, neighbour Baptista.
Bap. Good morrow, neighbour Gremio. God save
you, gentlemen! 41
Pet. And you, good sir! Pray, have you not a
daughter
Call'd Katharina, fair and virtuous?
Bap. I have a daughter, sir, called Katharina.
Gre. You are too blunt: go to it orderly.
Pet. You wrong me, Signior Gremio: give me leave.
I am a gentleman of Verona, sir,
That, hearing of her beauty and her wit,
Her affability and bashful modesty,
Her wondrous qualities and mild behaviour, 50
Am bold to show myself a forward guest
Within your house, to make mine eye the witness
Of that report which I so oft have heard.
And, for an entrance to my entertainment,
I do present you with a man of mine,
[*Presenting Hortensio.*
Cunning in music and the mathematics,
To instruct her fully in those sciences,
Whereof I know she is not ignorant:
Accept of him, or else you do me wrong:
His name is Licio, born in Mantua. 60
Bap. You 're welcome, sir; and he, for your good
sake.
But for my daughter Katharine, this I know,
She is not for your turn, the more my grief.
Pet. I see you do not mean to part with her,
Or else you like not of my company.
Bap. Mistake me not; I speak but as I find.
Whence are you, sir? what may I call your name?
Pet. Petruchio is my name; Antonio's son,
A man well known throughout all Italy.

Bap. I know him well: you are welcome for his sake.
Gre. Saving your tale, Petruchio, I pray, 71
Let us, that are poor petitioners, speak too:
Baccare! you are marvellous forward.
Pet. O, pardon me, Signior Gremio; I would fain be
doing.
Gre. I doubt it not, sir; but you will curse your
wooing.
Neighbour, this is a gift very grateful, I am sure of it.
To express the like kindness, myself, that have been
more kindly beholding to you than any, freely give
unto you this young scholar [*presenting Lucentio*], that
hath been long studying at Rheims; as cunning in
Greek, Latin, and other languages, as the other in
music and mathematics: his name is Cambio; pray,
accept his service.
Bap. A thousand thanks, Signior Gremio. Welcome,
good Cambio. [*To Tranio*] But, gentle sir, methinks
you walk like a stranger: may I be so bold to know the
cause of your coming?
Tra. Pardon me, sir, the boldness is mine own,
That, being a stranger in this city here, 90
Do make myself a suitor to your daughter,
Unto Bianca, fair and virtuous.
Nor is your firm resolve unknown to me,
In the preferment of the eldest sister.
This liberty is all that I request,
That, upon knowledge of my parentage,
I may have welcome 'mongst the rest that woo
And free access and favour as the rest:
And, toward the education of your daughters,
I here bestow a simple instrument, 100
And this small packet of Greek and Latin books:
If you accept them, then their worth is great.
Bap. Lucentio is your name; of whence, I pray?
Tra. Of Pisa, sir; son to Vincentio.
Bap. A mighty man of Pisa; by report
I know him well: you are very welcome, sir.
Take you the lute, and you the set of books;
You shall go see your pupils presently.
Holla, within!

Enter a Servant.
Sirrah, lead these gentlemen
To my daughters; and tell them both, 110
These are their tutors: bid them use them well.
[*Exit Servant, with Lucentio and Hortensio,
Biondello following.*
We will go walk a little in the orchard,
And then to dinner. You are passing welcome,
And so I pray you all to think yourselves.
Pet. Signior Baptista, my business asketh haste.
And every day I cannot come to woo.
You knew my father well, and in him me,
Left solely heir to all his lands and goods,
Which I have better'd rather than decreased:
Then tell me, if I get your daughter's love, 120
What dowry shall I have with her to wife?
Bap. After my death the one half of my lands,
And in possession twenty thousand crowns.
Pet. And, for that dowry, I'll assure her of

Her widowhood, be it that she survive me,
In all my lands and leases whatsoever:
Let specialties be therefore drawn between us,
That covenants may be kept on either hand.
   Bap. Ay, when the special thing is well obtain'd,
That is, her love; for that is all in all. 130
   Pet. Why, that is nothing; for I tell you, father,
I am as peremptory as she proud-minded;
And where two raging fires meet together
They do consume the thing that feeds their fury:
Though little fire grows great with little wind,
Yet extreme gusts will blow out fire and all:
So I to her and so she yields to me;
For I am rough and woo not like a babe.
   Bap. Well mayst thou woo, and happy be thy speed!
But be thou arm'd for some unhappy words. 140
   Pet. Ay, to the proof; as mountains are for winds,
That shake not, though they blow perpetually.

       Re-enter HORTENSIO, *with his head broke.*

   Bap. How now, my friend! why dost thou look so
     pale?
   Hor. For fear, I promise you, if I look pale.
   Bap. What, will my daughter prove a good
     musician?
   Hor. I think she'll sooner prove a soldier:
Iron may hold with her, but never lutes.
   Bap. Why, then thou canst not break her to the
     lute?
   Hor. Why, no; for she hath broke the lute to me.
I did but tell her she mistook her frets, 150
And bow'd her hand to teach her fingering;
When, with a most impatient devilish spirit,
'Frets, call you these?' quoth she; 'I'll fume with
     them:'
And, with that word, she struck me on the head,
And through the instrument my pate made way;
And there I stood amazed for a while,
As on a pillory, looking through the lute;
While she did call me rascal fiddler
And twangling Jack; with twenty such vile terms,
As had she studied to misuse me so. 160
   Pet. Now, by the world, it is a lusty wench;
I love her ten times more than e'er I did:
O, how I long to have some chat with her!
   Bap. Well, go with me and be not so discomfited:
Proceed in practice with my younger daughter;
She 's apt to learn and thankful for good turns.
Signior Petruchio, will you go with us,
Or shall I send my daughter Kate to you?
   Pet. I pray you do. [*Exeunt all but Petruchio.*] I will
     attend her here,
And woo her with some spirit when she comes. 170
Say that she rail; why then I'll tell her plain
She sings as sweetly as a nightingale:
Say that she frown; I'll say she looks as clear
As morning roses newly wash'd with dew:

Say she be mute and will not speak a word;
Then I'll commend her volubility,
And say she uttereth piercing eloquence:
If she do bid me pack, I'll give her thanks,
As though she bid me stay by her a week:
If she deny to wed, I'll crave the day 180
When I shall ask the banns and when be married.
But here she comes; and now, Petruchio, speak.

    Enter KATHARINA.

Good morrow, Kate; for that 's your name, I hear.
   Kath. Well have you heard, but something hard of
     hearing:
They call me Katharine that do talk of me.
   Pet. You lie, in faith; for you are call'd plain Kate,
And bonny Kate and sometimes Kate the curst;
But Kate, the prettiest Kate in Christendom,
Kate of Kate Hall, my super-dainty Kate,
For dainties are all Kates, and therefore, Kate, 190
Take this of me, Kate of my consolation;
Hearing thy mildness praised in every town,
Thy virtues spoke of, and thy beauty sounded,
Yet not so deeply as to thee belongs,
Myself am moved to woo thee for my wife.
   Kath. Moved! in good time: let him that moved you
     hither
Remove you hence: I knew you at the first
You were a moveable.
   Pet.   Why, what 's a moveable?
   Kath. A join'd-stool.
   Pet.   Thou hast hit it: come, sit on me.
   Kath. Asses are made to bear, and so are you. 200
   Pet. Women are made to bear, and so are you.
   Kath. No such jade as you, if me you mean.
   Pet. Alas! good Kate, I will not burden thee;
For, knowing thee to be but young and light—
   Kath. Too light for such a swain as you to catch;
And yet as heavy as my weight should be.
   Pet. Should be! should—buzz!
   Kath.   Well ta'en, and like a buzzard.
   Pet. O slow-wing'd turtle! shall a buzzard take thee?
   Kath. Ay, for a turtle, as he takes a buzzard.
   Pet. Come, come, you wasp; i' faith, you are too
     angry. 210
   Kath. If I be waspish, best beware my sting.
   Pet. My remedy is then, to pluck it out.
   Kath. Ay, if the fool could find it where it lies.
   Pet. Who knows not where a wasp does wear his
sting? In his tail.
   Kath. In his tongue.
   Pet. Whose tongue?
   Kath. Yours, if you talk of tails: and so farewell.
   Pet. What, with my tongue in your tail? nay, come
     again,
Good Kate; I am a gentleman.
   Kath.   That I'll try. [*She strikes him.* 220
   Pet. I swear I'll cuff you, if you strike again.

125. **widowhood,** i.e., as long as she remains a widow. 127. **specialties,** terms of contract. 140. **unhappy,** evil; see glossary. 141. **to
the proof,** i.e., in armor, proof against her shrewishness; see *proof* in
glossary. 147. **hold with,** hold out against. 150. **frets,** metal or
ivory ridges across the finger boards of stringed instruments, such as
the lute, to indicate where the string is to be shortened for raising the
tone. 153. **Frets . . . fume,** an echo of the alliterative pair, fume and
fret. 165. **practice,** exercises for instruction; see glossary. 178. **pack,**
be gone; see glossary. 180. **deny,** refuse; see glossary. 184. **heard,
hard,** pronounced nearly alike. **something,** somewhat; see glossary.
189. **Kate Hall,** taken by the New Cambridge editors to allude to
"a dining-house at Katharine Hall," a place where Elizabeth stopped

on a progress through the south of England in 1591; also taken by
some to allude to St. Catherine's Hall at Cambridge. 190. **all Kates,**
quibble on "cates," confections. 191. **of,** from; see glossary. 196.
in good time, a common ejaculation, most frequently used to express
acquiescence, but also occasionally indignation or scorn, as here.
205. **swain,** young man in love, usually indicating a rustic. 206. **And
. . . be.** The New Cambridge editors take this as an allusion to catch-
weights in horse racing, i.e., the weight of a contestant as he happens
or chooses to be, instead of as fixed by rule. 207. **Should . . . buzz.**
There are several puns here to give the passage point. Petruchio
implies a double understanding of Katharina's lightness (l. 205); *buzz*
implies a pun on *be* and is itself a quibble on the verb and the inter-

Kath. So may you lose your arms:
If you strike me, you are no gentleman;
And if no gentleman, why then no arms.
    Pet. A herald, Kate? O, put me in thy books!
    Kath. What is your crest? a coxcomb?
    Pet. A combless cock, so Kate will be my hen.
    Kath. No cock of mine; you crow too like a craven.
    Pet. Nay, come, Kate, come; you must not look so
      sour.
    Kath. It is my fashion, when I see a crab.   230
    Pet. Why, here 's no crab; and therefore look not
      sour.
    Kath. There is, there is.
    Pet. Then show it me.
    Kath. Had I a glass, I would.
    Pet. What, you mean my face?
    Kath. Well aim'd of such a young one.
    Pet. Now, by Saint George, I am too young for you.
    Kath. Yet you are wither'd.
    Pet. 'Tis with cares.   240
    Kath. I care not.
    Pet. Nay, hear you, Kate: in sooth you scape not so.
    Kath. I chafe you, if I tarry: let me go.
    Pet. No, not a whit: I find you passing gentle.
'Twas told me you were rough and coy and sullen,
And now I find report a very liar;
For thou art pleasant, gamesome, passing courteous,
But slow in speech, yet sweet as spring-time flowers:
Thou canst not frown, thou canst not look askance,
Nor bite the lip, as angry wenches will,   250
Nor hast thou pleasure to be cross in talk,
But thou with mildness entertain'st thy wooers,
With gentle conference, soft and affable.
Why does the world report that Kate doth limp?
O slanderous world! Kate like the hazel-twig
Is straight and slender and as brown in hue
As hazel nuts and sweeter than the kernels.
O, let me see thee walk: thou dost not halt.
    Kath. Go, fool, and whom thou keep'st command.
    Pet. Did ever Dian so become a grove   260
As Kate this chamber with her princely gait?
O, be thou Dian, and let her be Kate;
And then let Kate be chaste and Dian sportful!
    Kath. Where did you study all this goodly speech?
    Pet. It is extempore, from my mother-wit.
    Kath. A witty mother! witless else her son.
    Pet. Am I not wise?
    Kath. Yes; keep you warm.
    Pet. Marry, so I mean, sweet Katharine, in thy bed:
And therefore, setting all this chat aside,   270
Thus in plain terms: your father hath consented
That you shall be my wife; your dowry 'greed on;
And, will you, nill you, I will marry you.
Now, Kate, I am a husband for your turn;
For, by this light, whereby I see thy beauty,
Thy beauty, that doth make me like thee well,
Thou must be married to no man but me;

For I am he am born to tame you, Kate,
And bring you from a wild Kate to a Kate
Conformable as other household Kates.   280
Here comes your father: never make denial;
I must and will have Katharine to my wife.

    Re-enter BAPTISTA, GREMIO, *and* TRANIO.

    Bap. Now, Signior Petruchio, how speed you with
      my daughter?
    Pet. How but well, sir? how but well?
It were impossible I should speed amiss.
    Bap. Why, how now, daughter Katharine! in your
      dumps?
    Kath. Call you me daughter? now, I promise you,
You have show'd a tender fatherly regard,
To wish me wed to one half lunatic;
A mad-cap ruffian and a swearing Jack,   290
That thinks with oaths to face the matter out.
    Pet. Father, 'tis thus: yourself and all the world,
That talk'd of her, have talk'd amiss of her:
If she be curst, it is for policy,
For she 's not froward, but modest as the dove;
She is not hot, but temperate as the morn;
For patience she will prove a second Grissel,
And Roman Lucrece for her chastity:
And to conclude, we have 'greed so well together,
That upon Sunday is the wedding-day.   300
    Kath. I'll see thee hang'd on Sunday first.
    Gre. Hark, Petruchio; she says she'll see thee
      hang'd first.
    Tra. Is this your speeding? nay, then, good night
      our part!
    Pet. Be patient, gentlemen; I choose her for myself:
If she and I be pleased, what 's that to you?
'Tis bargain'd 'twixt us twain, being alone,
That she shall still be curst in company.
I tell you, 'tis incredible to believe
How much she loves me: O, the kindest Kate!
She hung about my neck; and kiss on kiss   310
She vied so fast, protesting oath on oath,
That in a twink she won me to her love.
O, you are novices! 'tis a world to see,
How tame, when men and women are alone,
A meacock wretch can make the curstest shrew.
Give me thy hand, Kate: I will unto Venice,
To buy apparel 'gainst the wedding-day.
Provide the feast, father, and bid the guests;
I will be sure my Katharine shall be fine.
    Bap. I know not what to say: but give me your
      hands;   320
God send you joy, Petruchio! 'tis a match.
    Gre. Tra. Amen, say we: we will be witnesses.
    Pet. Father, and wife, and gentlemen, adieu;
I will to Venice; Sunday comes apace:
We will have rings and things and fine array;
And kiss me, Kate, we will be married o' Sunday.
    [*Exeunt Petruchio and Katharina severally.*

jection. 207, 208, 209. **buzzard,** an inferior kind of hawk, useless in falconry; also a type of stupidity. Most editors regard Katharina's remarks as quibbling on these two meanings. Onions suggests a third quibble on the meaning "a buzzing insect," which offers a play on *wasp* (l. 210). 208. **turtle,** turtle dove. 224. **no arms,** no coat of arms. 225. **thy books,** the official records of the college of heralds, with quibble on the phrase "to be in a person's books," i.e., to be in good standing with a person. 228. **craven,** a cock that is not "game" (Onions). 230. **crab,** crab apple. 238. **too young,** too strong (New Cambridge); perhaps, too nimble-witted. 245. **coy,** disdainful. 259. **whom thou keep'st,** i.e., those whom you employ—your servants; see *keep* in glossary. 260. **Dian,** goddess of the hunt and of chastity.

263. **sportful,** amorous. 267-268. **wise . . . warm,** an allusion to the proverbial phrase "enough wit to keep oneself warm." 273. **nill,** will not. 279. **wild Kate,** a quibble on "wildcat." Theobald saw a similar pun in *household Kates* in the next line. 294. **policy,** cunning, i.e., she has some motive for assuming this pose; see glossary. 297. **second Grissel,** an allusion to the story of Patient Griselda, the epitome of wifely patience and devotion. The story was told by Chaucer in *The Clerk's Tale* and earlier by Boccaccio and Petrarch. 298. **Roman Lucrece,** an allusion to the story of Lucretia, a Roman lady who took her own life after her chastity had been violated by the Tarquin prince, Sextus. Shakespeare told the story in *The Rape of Lucrece.* 315. **meacock,** effeminate, cowardly.

Gre. Was ever match clapp'd up so suddenly?
Bap. Faith, gentlemen, now I play a merchant's
    part,
And venture madly on a desperate mart.
   Tra. 'Twas a commodity lay fretting by you: 330
'Twill bring you gain, or perish on the seas.
  Bap. The gain I seek is, quiet in the match.
  Gre. No doubt but he hath got a quiet catch.
But now, Baptista, to your younger daughter:
Now is the day we long have looked for:
I am your neighbour, and was suitor first.
   Tra. And I am one that love Bianca more
Than words can witness, or your thoughts can guess.
  Gre. Youngling, thou canst not love so dear as I.
  Tra. Greybeard, thy love doth freeze.
  Gre.   But thine doth fry.   340
Skipper, stand back: 'tis age that nourisheth.
   Tra. But youth in ladies' eyes that flourisheth.
  Bap. Content you, gentlemen: I will compound this
    strife:
'Tis deeds must win the prize; and he of both
That can assure my daughter greatest dower
Shall have my Bianca's love.
Say, Signior Gremio, what can you assure her?
  Gre. First, as you know, my house within the city
Is richly furnished with plate and gold;
Basins and ewers to lave her dainty hands;   350
My hangings all of Tyrian tapestry;
In ivory coffers I have stuff'd my crowns;
In cypress chests my arras counterpoints,
Costly apparel, tents, and canopies,
Fine linen, Turkey cushions boss'd with pearl,
Valance of Venice gold in needlework,
Pewter and brass and all things that belong
To house or housekeeping: then, at my farm
I have a hundred milch-kine to the pail,
Sixscore fat oxen standing in my stalls,   360
And all things answerable to this portion.
Myself am struck in years, I must confess;
And if I die to-morrow, this is hers,
If whilst I live she will be only mine.
   Tra. That 'only' came well in. Sir, list to me:
I am my father's heir and only son:
If I may have your daughter to my wife,
I'll leave her houses three or four as good,
Within rich Pisa walls, as any one
Old Signior Gremio has in Padua;   370
Besides two thousand ducats by the year
Of fruitful land, all which shall be her jointure.
What, have I pinch'd you, Signior Gremio?
  Gre. Two thousand ducats by the year of land!
My land amounts not to so much in all:
That she shall have; besides an argosy
That now is lying in Marseilles' road.
What, have I choked you with an argosy?
   Tra. Gremio, 'tis known my father hath no less
Than three great argosies; besides two galliases,   380
And twelve tight galleys: these I will assure her,
And twice as much, whate'er thou offer'st next.

  Gre. Nay, I have offer'd all, I have no more;
And she can have no more than all I have:
If you like me, she shall have me and mine.
   Tra. Why, then the maid is mine from all the world,
By your firm promise: Gremio is out-vied.
  Bap. I must confess your offer is the best;
And, let your father make her the assurance,
She is your own; else, you must pardon me,   390
If you should die before him, where 's her dower?
   Tra. That 's but a cavil: he is old, I young.
  Gre. And may not young men die, as well as old?
  Bap. Well, gentlemen,
I am thus resolved: on Sunday next you know
My daughter Katharine is to be married:
Now, on the Sunday following, shall Bianca
Be bride to you, if you make this assurance;
If not, to Signior Gremio:
And so, I take my leave, and thank you both.   400
  Gre. Adieu, good neighbour.   [*Exit Baptista.*
           Now I fear thee not:
Sirrah young gamester, your father were a fool
To give thee all, and in his waning age
Set foot under thy table: tut, a toy!
An old Italian fox is not so kind, my boy.   [*Exit.*
   Tra. A vengeance on your crafty wither'd hide!
Yet I have faced it with a card of ten.
'Tis in my head to do my master good:
I see no reason but supposed Lucentio
Must get a father, call'd 'supposed Vincentio;'   410
And that 's a wonder: fathers commonly
Do get their children; but in this case of wooing,
A child shall get a sire, if I fail not of my cunning. [*Exit.*

ACT III.

SCENE I. *Padua.* BAPTISTA'S *house.*

Enter LUCENTIO, HORTENSIO, *and* BIANCA.

  Luc. Fiddler, forbear; you grow too forward, sir:
Have you so soon forgot the entertainment
Her sister Katharine welcomed you withal?
  Hor. But, wrangling pedant, this is
The patroness of heavenly harmony:
Then give me leave to have prerogative;
And when in music we have spent an hour,
Your lecture shall have leisure for as much.
  Luc. Preposterous ass, that never read so far
To know the cause why music was ordain'd!   10
Was it not to refresh the mind of man
After his studies or his usual pain?
Then give me leave to read philosophy,
And while I pause, serve in your harmony.
  Hor. Sirrah, I will not bear these braves of thine.
  Bian. Why, gentlemen, you do me double wrong,
To strive for that which resteth in my choice:
I am no breeching scholar in the schools;
I'll not be tied to hours nor 'pointed times,
But learn my lessons as I please myself.   20

330. **lay.** The subject is "which," understood. **fretting,** said of goods such as cloth destroyed by moth or grain infested by weevil, with quibble on the more obvious meaning. 341. **Skipper,** flighty fellow. 344. **he of both,** i.e., the one of you two. 353. **arras,** tapestried. **counterpoints,** counterpanes. 355. **boss'd,** embossed. 359. **milch-kine . . . pail,** cows whose milk is not going to their calves (New Cambridge). 376. **That she shall have,** i.e., all of my land. **argosy,** merchant vessel of the largest size. 380. **galliases,** heavy, low-built vessels. 381. **tight,** not leaking, sound. 402. **were,** subjunctive,

which implies Gremio's disbelief of the pretended Lucentio's resources. 404. **toy,** trifle; see glossary. 407. **faced . . . ten,** brazened it out with only a ten-spot of cards.
ACT III. SCENE I. 6. **prerogative,** precedence. 9. **Preposterous,** used here in its literal sense of inverting the natural order of things (Herford). 14. **serve in,** i.e., as if music were an after-dinner trifle (New Cambridge). 18. **breeching scholar,** schoolboy liable to be whipped. 24. **in tune,** used here and in the next line with quibble on the meaning "in good temper" (New Cambridge). 28-29. **'Hic . . .**

And, to cut off all strife, here sit we down:
Take you your instrument, play you the whiles;
His lecture will be done ere you have tuned.
   Hor. You'll leave his lecture when I am in tune?
   Luc. That will be never: tune your instrument.
   Bian. Where left we last?
   Luc. Here, madam:
     'Hic ibat Simois; hic est Sigeia tellus;
      Hic steterat Priami regia celsa senis.'
   Bian. Construe them. 30
   Luc. 'Hic ibat,' as I told you before, 'Simois,' I am
Lucentio, hic est,' son unto Vincentio of Pisa, 'Sigeia
tellus,' disguised thus to get your love; 'Hic steterat,'
and that Lucentio that comes a-wooing, 'Priami,'
is my man Tranio, 'regia,' bearing my port, 'celsa
senis,' that we might beguile the old pantaloon.
   Hor. Madam, my instrument 's in tune.
   Bian. Let 's hear. O fie! the treble jars.
   Luc. Spit in the hole, man, and tune again. 40
   Bian. Now let me see if I can construe it:
'Hic ibat Simois,' I know you not, 'hic est Sigeia
tellus,' I trust you not; 'Hic steterat Priami,' take
heed he hear us not, 'regia,' presume not, 'celsa senis,'
despair not.
   Hor. Madam, 'tis now in tune.
   Luc.   All but the base.
   Hor. The base is right; 'tis the base knave that jars.
   [*Aside*] How fiery and forward our pedant is!
Now, for my life, the knave doth court my love:
Pedascule, I'll watch you better yet. 50
   Bian. In time I may believe, yet I mistrust.
   Luc. Mistrust it not; for, sure, Æacides
Was Ajax, call'd so from his grandfather.
   Bian. I must believe my master; else, I promise you,
I should be arguing still upon that doubt:
But let it rest. Now, Licio, to you:
Good masters, take it not unkindly, pray,
That I have been thus pleasant with you both.
   Hor. You may go walk, and give me leave a while:
My lessons make no music in three parts. 60
   Luc. Are you so formal, sir? well, I must wait,
[*Aside*] And watch withal; for, but I be deceived,
Our fine musician groweth amorous.
   Hor. Madam, before you touch the instrument,
To learn the order of my fingering,
I must begin with rudiments of art;
To teach you gamut in a briefer sort,
More pleasant, pithy and effectual,
Than hath been taught by any of my trade:
And there it is in writing, fairly drawn. 70
   Bian. Why, I am past my gamut long ago.
   Hor. Yet read the gamut of Hortensio.
   Bian. [*Reads*] " 'Gamut' I am, the ground of all
     accord,
     'A re,' to plead Hortensio's passion;
    'B mi,' Bianca, take him for thy lord,
     'C fa ut,' that loves with all affection:
    'D sol re,' one clef, two notes have I:
     'E la mi,' show pity, or I die."

Call you this gamut? tut, I like it not:
Old fashions please me best; I am not so nice, 80
To change true rules for old inventions.

   Enter a Servant.

   Serv. Mistress, your father prays you leave your
     books
And help to dress your sister's chamber up:
You know to-morrow is the wedding-day.
   Bian. Farewell, sweet masters both; I must be gone.
               [*Exeunt Bianca and Servant.*
   Luc. Faith, mistress, then I have no cause to stay.
                     [*Exit.*
   Hor. But I have cause to pry into this pedant:
Methinks he looks as though he were in love:
Yet if thy thoughts, Bianca, be so humble
To cast thy wandering eyes on every stale, 90
Seize thee that list: if once I find thee ranging,
Hortensio will be quit with thee by changing.   [*Exit.*

SCENE II. *Padua. Before* BAPTISTA'S *house.*

Enter BAPTISTA, GREMIO, TRANIO, KATHARINA,
  BIANCA, LUCENTIO, *and* others, attendants.

   Bap. [*To Tranio*] Signior Lucentio, this is the
     'pointed day
That Katharine and Petruchio should be married,
And yet we hear not of our son-in-law.
What will be said? what mockery will it be,
To want the bridegroom when the priest attends
To speak the ceremonial rites of marriage!
What says Lucentio to this shame of ours?
   Kath. No shame but mine: I must, forsooth, be
     forced
To give my hand opposed against my heart
Unto a mad-brain rudesby full of spleen; 10
Who woo'd in haste and means to wed at leisure.
I told you, I, he was a frantic fool,
Hiding his bitter jests in blunt behaviour:
And, to be noted for a merry man,
He'll woo a thousand, 'point the day of marriage,
Make feasts, invite friends, and proclaim the banns;
Yet never means to wed where he hath woo'd.
Now must the world point at poor Katharine,
And say, 'Lo, there is mad Petruchio's wife,
If it would please him come and marry her!' 20
   Tra. Patience, good Katharine, and Baptista too.
Upon my life, Petruchio means but well,
Whatever fortune stays him from his word:
Though he be blunt, I know him passing wise;
Though he be merry, yet withal he 's honest.
   Kath. Would Katharine had never seen him
     though! [*Exit weeping, followed by Bianca and others.*
   Bap. Go, girl; I cannot blame thee now to weep;
For such an injury would vex a very saint,
Much more a shrew of thy impatient humour.

   Enter BIONDELLO.

---

senis,' here flowed the river Simois, here is the Sigeian land; here stood
the lofty palace of old Priam (Ovid, *Heroides*, I, 33). **37. old pantaloon,**
enfeebled old man, old fool; at Gremio's first entrance (I, i, 47) the
stage direction in F is *Enter . . . Gremio a Pantelowne.* The pantaloon was
a stock character in Italian comedy. **39. jars,** is discordant; see glossary. **40. Spit in the hole,** i.e., to make the peg stick. **50. Pedascule,**
a word contemptuously coined by Hortensio, the vocative of *pedasculus,*
little pedant. **52-53. Æacides . . . grandfather,** a pointless remark to
mislead Hortensio. **67. gamut,** the scale, from the alphabet name

(*gamma*) of the first note plus *ut,* its syllable name, now commonly
called *do.* The *gamut* of Hortensio begins on G instead of on C, the first
note of the natural scale. **80. nice,** fastidious, particular; see glossary.
91. thee, frequently used for the nominative with imperatives; see
Abbott, 212. **list,** desire, with probable quibble on "strip of cloth"
(a contemptuous reference to Lucentio in the disguise of a pedant);
see glossary. **ranging,** inconstant; see glossary. **92. quit,** quits; see
glossary. **by changing,** i.e., by loving another.
   SCENE II. **10. rudesby,** unmannerly fellow.

Bion. Master, master! news, old news, and such news as you never heard of! 31

Bap. Is it new and old too? how may that be?

Bion. Why, is it not news, to hear of Petruchio's coming?

Bap. Is he come?

Bion. Why, no, sir.

Bap. What then?

Bion. He is coming.

Bap. When will he be here?

Bion. When he stands where I am and sees you there. 41

Tra. But say, what to thine old news?

Bion. Why, Petruchio is coming in a new hat and an old jerkin, a pair of old breeches thrice turned, a pair of boots that have been candle-cases, one buckled, another laced, an old rusty sword ta'en out of the town-armoury, with a broken hilt, and chapeless; with two broken points: his horse hipped with an old mothy saddle and stirrups of no kindred; besides, possessed with the glanders and like to mose in the chine; troubled with the lampass, infected with the fashions, full of windgalls, sped with spavins, rayed with the yellows, past cure of the fives, stark spoiled with the staggers, begnawn with the bots, swayed in the back and shoulder-shotten; near-legged before and with a half-cheeked bit and a head-stall of sheep's leather which, being restrained to keep him from stumbling, hath been often burst and now repaired with knots; one girth six times pieced and a woman's crupper of velure, which hath two letters for her name fairly set down in studs, and here and there pieced with packthread. 64

Bap. Who comes with him?

Bion. O, sir, his lackey, for all the world caparisoned like the horse; with a linen stock on one leg and a kersey boot-hose on the other, gartered with a red and blue list; an old hat and 'the humour of forty fancies' pricked in 't for a feather: a monster, a very monster in apparel, and not like a Christian footboy or a gentleman's lackey. 73

Tra. 'Tis some odd humour pricks him to this fashion;

Yet oftentimes he goes but mean-apparell'd.

Bap. I am glad he 's come, howsoe'er he comes.

Bion. Why, sir, he comes not.

Bap. Didst thou not say he comes?

Bion. Who? that Petruchio came?

Bap. Ay, that Petruchio came. 80

Bion. No, sir; I say his horse comes, with him on his back.

Bap. Why, that 's all one.

Bion. Nay, by Saint Jamy,
I hold you a penny,
A horse and a man
Is more than one,
And yet not many.

Enter PETRUCHIO *and* GRUMIO.

Pet. Come, where be these gallants? who 's at home?

Bap. You are welcome, sir.

Pet. And yet I come not well. 90

Bap. And yet you halt not.

Tra. Not so well apparell'd
As I wish you were.

Pet. Were it better, I should rush in thus.
But where is Kate? where is my lovely bride?
How does my father? Gentles, methinks you frown:
And wherefore gaze this goodly company,
As if they saw some wondrous monument,
Some comet or unusual prodigy?

Bap. Why, sir, you know this is your wedding-day:
First were we sad, fearing you would not come; 100
Now sadder, that you come so unprovided.
Fie, doff this habit, shame to your estate,
An eye-sore to our solemn festival!

Tra. And tell us, what occasion of import
Hath all so long detain'd you from your wife,
And sent you hither so unlike yourself?

Pet. Tedious it were to tell, and harsh to hear:
Sufficeth, I am come to keep my word,
Though in some part enforced to digress;
Which, at more leisure, I will so excuse 110
As you shall well be satisfied withal.
But where is Kate? I stay too long from her:
The morning wears, 'tis time we were at church.

Tra. See not your bride in these unreverent robes:
Go to my chamber; put on clothes of mine.

Pet. Not I, believe me: thus I'll visit her.

Bap. But thus, I trust, you will not marry her.

Pet. Good sooth, even thus; therefore ha' done with words:
To me she 's married, not unto my clothes:
Could I repair what she will wear in me, 120
As I can change these poor accoutrements,
'Twere well for Kate and better for myself.
But what a fool am I to chat with you,
When I should bid good morrow to my bride,
And seal the title with a lovely kiss!

[*Exeunt Petruchio and Grumio.*

Tra. He hath some meaning in his mad attire:
We will persuade him, be it possible,
To put on better ere he go to church.

Bap. I'll after him, and see the event of this.

[*Exeunt Baptista, Gremio, and attendants.*

Tra. But to her love concerneth us to add 130
Her father's liking: which to bring to pass,
As I before imparted to your worship,
I am to get a man,—whate'er he be,
It skills not much, we'll fit him to our turn,—
And he shall be Vincentio of Pisa;
And make assurance here in Padua
Of greater sums than I have promised.
So shall you quietly enjoy your hope,
And marry sweet Bianca with consent.

45. **candle-cases,** i.e., discarded and used to contain candle ends. 48. **chapeless,** without the chape, the metal plate or mounting of a scabbard, especially that which covers the point. 49. **points,** tagged laces for attaching hose to doublet. **hipped,** lamed in the hip. Bond notes that almost all the diseases here named are described in Gervase Markham's *How to chuse, ride, trayne, and dyet, both Hunting Horses and Running Horses. . . . Also a Discourse of Horsemanship,* probably first published in 1593. 51. **mose . . . chine,** suffer from glanders; *mose,* not found elsewhere, is taken by the New Cambridge editors to be a misprint for *pose,* a form of glanders; mourn of the chine, i.e., backbone, is, however, a common expression for the nasal discharge of horses with glanders. 52. **lampass.** Bond quotes Markham: ". . . a thicke

spongie fleshe growing ouer a Horses vpper teeth, hindering the coniunction of his Chappes in such sorte that he can hardlye eate." 53. **fashions,** a corruption of "farcin," a disease closely allied to glanders. **windgalls,** a soft tumor or swelling generally found on the fetlock joint, so called from having been supposed to contain air. **spavins,** a disease of the hock, marked by a small bony enlargement inside the leg. 54. **yellows,** jaundice. **fives,** avives, a glandular disease. 56. **bots,** a disease from parasitic worms. **shoulder-shotten,** sprained in the shoulder. 57. **near-legged before,** with forelegs close together, knock-kneed. **half-cheeked bit,** one to which the bridle is attached halfway up the cheek or sidepiece so as not to give sufficient control over the horse. 58. **head-stall,** part of the bridle over the head. **sheep's**

Luc. Were it not that my fellow-schoolmaster 140
Doth watch Bianca's steps so narrowly,
'Twere good, methinks, to steal our marriage;
Which once perform'd, let all the world say no,
I'll keep mine own, despite of all the world.
   Tra. That by degrees we mean to look into,
And watch our vantage in this business:
We'll over-reach the greybeard, Gremio,
The narrow-prying father, Minola,
The quaint musician, amorous Licio;
All for my master's sake, Lucentio. 150

       Re-enter GREMIO.

Signior Gremio, came you from the church?
   Gre. As willingly as e'er I came from school.
   Tra. And is the bride and bridegroom coming
     home?
   Gre. A bridegroom say you? 'tis a groom indeed,
A grumbling groom, and that the girl shall find.
   Tra. Curster than she? why, 'tis impossible.
   Gre. Why, he 's a devil, a devil, a very fiend.
   Tra. Why, she 's a devil, a devil, the devil's dam.
   Gre. Tut, she 's a lamb, a dove, a fool to him!
I'll tell you, Sir Lucentio: when the priest 160
Should ask, if Katharine should be his wife,
'Ay, by gogs-wouns,' quoth he; and swore so loud,
That, all-amazed, the priest let fall the book;
And, as he stoop'd again to take it up,
This mad-brain'd bridegroom took him such a cuff
That down fell priest and book and book and priest:
'Now take them up,' quoth he, 'if any list.'
   Tra. What said the wench when he rose again?
   Gre. Trembled and shook; for why, he stamp'd and
     swore,
As if the vicar meant to cozen him. 170
But after many ceremonies done,
He calls for wine: 'A health!' quoth he, as if
He had been aboard, carousing to his mates
After a storm; quaff'd off the muscadel
And threw the sops all in the sexton's face;
Having no other reason
But that his beard grew thin and hungerly
And seem'd to ask him sops as he was drinking.
This done, he took the bride about the neck
And kiss'd her lips with such a clamorous smack 180
That at the parting all the church did echo:
And I seeing this came thence for very shame;
And after me, I know, the rout is coming.
Such a mad marriage never was before:
Hark, hark! I hear the minstrels play.   [*Music.*

   Re-enter PETRUCHIO, KATHARINA, BIANCA,
   BAPTISTA, HORTENSIO, GRUMIO, *and Train.*

   Pet. Gentlemen and friends, I thank you for your
     pains:
I know you think to dine with me to-day,
And have prepared great store of wedding cheer;

But so it is, my haste doth call me hence,
And therefore here I mean to take my leave. 190
   Bap. Is 't possible you will away to-night?
   Pet. I must away to-day, before night come:
Make it no wonder; if you knew my business,
You would entreat me rather go than stay.
And, honest company, I thank you all,
That have beheld me give away myself
To this most patient, sweet and virtuous wife:
Dine with my father, drink a health to me;
For I must hence; and farewell to you all.
   Tra. Let us entreat you stay till after dinner. 200
   Pet. It may not be.
   Gre.   Let me entreat you.
   Pet. It cannot be.
   Kath.   Let me entreat you.
   Pet. I am content.
   Kath.   Are you content to stay?
   Pet. I am content you shall entreat me stay;
But yet not stay, entreat me how you can.
   Kath. Now, if you love me, stay.
   Pet.   Grumio, my horse.
   Gru. Ay, sir, they be ready: the oats have eaten the
horses.
   Kath. Nay, then,
Do what thou canst, I will not go to-day; 210
No, nor to-morrow, not till I please myself.
The door is open, sir; there lies your way;
You may be jogging whiles your boots are green;
For me, I'll not be gone till I please myself:
'Tis like you'll prove a jolly surly groom,
That take it on you at the first so roundly.
   Pet. O Kate, content thee; prithee, be not angry.
   Kath. I will be angry: what hast thou to do?
Father, be quiet: he shall stay my leisure.
   Gre. Ay, marry, sir, now it begins to work. 220
   Kath. Gentlemen, forward to the bridal dinner:
I see a woman may be made a fool,
If she had not a spirit to resist.
   Pet. They shall go forward, Kate, at thy command.
Obey the bride, you that attend on her;
Go to the feast, revel and domineer,
Carouse full measure to her maidenhead,
Be mad and merry, or go hang yourselves:
But for my bonny Kate, she must with me.
Nay, look not big, nor stamp, nor stare, nor fret; 230
I will be master of what is mine own:
She is my goods, my chattels; she is my house,
My household stuff, my field, my barn,
My horse, my ox, my ass, my any thing;
And here she stands, touch her whoever dare;
I'll bring mine action on the proudest he
That stops my way in Padua. Grumio,
Draw forth thy weapon, we are beset with thieves;
Rescue thy mistress, if thou be a man.
Fear not, sweet wench, they shall not touch thee,
     Kate: 240

leather. Pigskin was used for strongest harness; hence of inferior quality. 59. **restrained,** drawn back. 61. **crupper,** leather loop passing under the horse's tail and fastened to the saddle. 62. **velure,** velvet, used sometimes on horses ridden by ladies. 67. **stock,** stocking. 68. **kersey boot-hose,** overstocking of coarse material. 70. **'the humour . . . fancies,'** probably the title of a pamphlet book of songs or ballads. 101. **unprovided,** ill-equipped. 102. **estate,** position, station, as in the modern phrase, "man's estate." 125. **seal,** confirm, ratify; see glossary. 129. **event,** outcome; see glossary. 134. **skills not,** makes no difference. 146. **vantage,** opportunity, advantage; see glossary. 154. **a groom indeed,** i.e., a serving man. 159. **fool,** term of endearment and pity; see glossary. 162. **gogs-wouns,** God's wounds, a common oath. 165. **took,** struck; see *take* in glossary. 169. **for why,** because; see glossary. 170. **cozen,** cheat, i.e., by not performing the ceremony with all regularity. 173. **aboard,** i.e., aboard ship. 175. **sops,** pieces of cake soaked in wine. 183. **rout,** wedding party. 193. **Make,** consider; see glossary. 195. **honest,** kind; see glossary. 213. **whiles . . . green,** i.e., new; proverbial for "getting an early start," with a sarcastic allusion to his unseemly attire. 215. **jolly,** arrogant. 226. **domineer,** feast riotously. 230. **look not big,** addressed to the onlookers, ignoring—as were his tactics—Katharina's conduct. **big,** haughty, pompous. 234. **ox . . . any thing.** This catalog of a man's possessions is from the Tenth Commandment.

I'll buckler thee against a million.

[*Exeunt Petruchio, Katharina, and Grumio.*

Bap. Nay, let them go, a couple of quiet ones.

Gre. Went they not quickly, I should die with
laughing.

Tra. Of all mad matches never was the like.

Luc. Mistress, what's your opinion of your sister?

Bian. That, being mad herself, she's madly mated.

Gre. I warrant him, Petruchio is Kated.

Bap. Neighbours and friends, though bride and
bridegroom wants
For to supply the places at the table,
You know there wants no junkets at the feast.   250
Lucentio, you shall supply the bridegroom's place;
And let Bianca take her sister's room.

Tra. Shall sweet Bianca practise how to bride it?

Bap. She shall, Lucentio. Come, gentlemen, let's go.

[*Exeunt.*

ACT IV.

<small>SCENE I. PETRUCHIO'S *country house.*</small>

Enter GRUMIO.

Gru. Fie, fie on all tired jades, on all mad masters,
and all foul ways! Was ever man so beaten? was ever
man so rayed? was ever man so weary? I am sent before to make a fire, and they are coming after to warm
them. Now, were not I a little pot and soon hot, my
very lips might freeze to my teeth, my tongue to the
roof of my mouth, my heart in my belly, ere I should
come by a fire to thaw me: but I, with blowing the
fire, shall warm myself; for, considering the weather,
a taller man than I will take cold. Holla, ho! Curtis.   11

Enter CURTIS.

Curt. Who is that calls so coldly?

Gru. A piece of ice: if thou doubt it, thou mayst
slide from my shoulder to my heel with no greater a
run but my head and my neck. A fire, good Curtis.

Curt. Is my master and his wife coming, Grumio?

Gru. O, ay, Curtis, ay: and therefore fire, fire; cast
on no water.   21

Curt. Is she so hot a shrew as she's reported?

Gru. She was, good Curtis, before this frost: but,
thou knowest, winter tames man, woman and beast;
for it hath tamed my old master and my new mistress
and myself, fellow Curtis.

Curt. Away, you three-inch fool! I am no beast.   28

Gru. Am I but three inches? why, thy horn is a foot;
and so long am I at the least. But wilt thou make a fire,
or shall I complain on thee to our mistress, whose
hand, she being now at hand, thou shalt soon feel, to
thy cold comfort, for being slow in thy hot office?

Curt. I prithee, good Grumio, tell me, how goes the
world?   36

Gru. A cold world, Curtis, in every office but thine;
and therefore fire: do thy duty, and have thy duty;
for my master and mistress are almost frozen to death.

Curt. There's fire ready; and therefore, good Grumio, the news.

Gru. Why, 'Jack boy! ho! boy!' and as much news
as will thaw.

Curt. Come, you are so full of cony-catching!   45

Gru. Why, therefore fire; for I have caught extreme
cold. Where's the cook? is supper ready, the house
trimmed, rushes strewed, cobwebs swept; the serving-
men in their new fustian, their white stockings, and
every officer his wedding-garment on? Be the jacks
fair within, the jills fair without, the carpets laid, and
every thing in order?

Curt. All ready; and therefore, I pray thee, news.

Gru. First, know, my horse is tired; my master and
mistress fallen out.

Curt. How?

Gru. Out of their saddles into the dirt; and thereby
hangs a tale.   60

Curt. Let's ha't, good Grumio.

Gru. Lend thine ear.

Curt. Here.

Gru. There.   [*Strikes him.*

Curt. This is to feel a tale, not to hear a tale.

Gru. And therefore 'tis called a sensible tale: and
this cuff was but to knock at your ear, and beseech
listening. Now I begin: Imprimis, we came down a
foul hill, my master riding behind my mistress,—   70

Curt. Both of one horse?

Gru. What's that to thee?

Curt. Why, a horse.

Gru. Tell thou the tale: but hadst thou not crossed
me, thou shouldst have heard how her horse fell and
she under her horse; thou shouldst have heard in how
miry a place, how she was bemoiled, how he left her
with the horse upon her, how he beat me because her
horse stumbled, how she waded through the dirt to
pluck him off me, how he swore, how she prayed, that
never prayed before, how I cried, how the horses ran
away, how her bridle was burst, how I lost my crupper, with many things of worthy memory, which now
shall die in oblivion and thou return unexperienced
to thy grave.   86

Curt. By this reckoning he is more shrew than
she.

Gru. Ay; and that thou and the proudest of you all
shall find when he comes home. But what talk I of
this? Call forth Nathaniel, Joseph, Nicholas, Philip,
Walter, Sugarsop and the rest: let their heads be
sleekly combed, their blue coats brushed and their
garters of an indifferent knit; let them curtsy with their
left legs and not presume to touch a hair of my
master's horse-tail till they kiss their hands. Are they
all ready?

Curt. They are.

Gru. Call them forth.

Curt. Do you hear, ho? you must meet my master to
countenance my mistress.   101

Gru. Why, she hath a face of her own.

Curt. Who knows not that?

Gru. Thou, it seems, that calls for company to
countenance her.

Curt. I call them forth to credit her.

Gru. Why, she comes to borrow nothing of them.

*The Taming
of the Shrew*
ACT III : SC II

172

<small>241. **buckler**, shield, defend. 250. **junkets**, sweetmeats.

ACT IV. SCENE I. 3. **rayed**, dirtied, fouled. 6. **a little . . . hot**, a
proverbial expression; Grumio refers to his small stature. 11. **taller**,
finer, better; see glossary. 27. **three-inch fool**, another reference to
Grumio's size. 27-28. **I am no beast.** Grumio has paralleled himself
with *beast* (l. 25) and has then called Curtis *fellow*. 43. '**Jack . . . boy,**'</small>

<small>the first line of a song. 45. **cony-catching**, cheating. 48. **rushes
strewed.** Floors were strewn with green rushes on ceremonial occasions.
49. **fustian**, coarse cloth of cotton and flax. 51, 52. **jacks, jills,** drinking
measures of one-half and one-fourth pints (used quibblingly). 66.
sensible, capable of sensation, with quibble on the current meaning;
see glossary. 68. **Imprimis**, in the first place. 77. **bemoiled**, befouled</small>

Enter four or five Serving-men.

Nath. Welcome home, Grumio!
Phil. How now, Grumio!
Jos. What, Grumio! 110
Nich. Fellow Grumio!
Nath. How now, old lad?
Gru. Welcome, you;—how now, you;—what, you;
—fellow, you;—and thus much for greeting. Now,
my spruce companions, is all ready, and all things
neat?
Nath. All things is ready. How near is our master? 119
Gru. E'en at hand, alighted by this; and therefore be
not—Cock's passion, silence! I hear my master.

Enter PETRUCHIO *and* KATHARINA.

Pet. Where be these knaves? What, no man at door
To hold my stirrup nor to take my horse!
Where is Nathaniel, Gregory, Philip?
All Serv. Here, here, sir; here, sir.
Pet. Here, sir! here, sir! here, sir! here, sir!
You logger-headed and unpolish'd grooms!
What, no attendance? no regard? no duty?
Where is the foolish knave I sent before? 130
Gru. Here, sir; as foolish as I was before.
Pet. You peasant swain! you whoreson malt-horse
　　drudge!
Did I not bid thee meet me in the park,
And bring along these rascal knaves with thee?
Gru. Nathaniel's coat, sir, was not fully made,
And Gabriel's pumps were all unpink'd i' the heel;
There was no link to colour Peter's hat,
And Walter's dagger was not come from sheathing:
There were none fine but Adam, Ralph, and Gregory;
The rest were ragged, old, and beggarly; 140
Yet, as they are, here are they come to meet you.
Pet. Go, rascals, go, and fetch my supper in.
　　　　　　　　　　　　[*Exeunt Servants.*
[*Singing*] Where is the life that late I led—
Where are those—Sit down, Kate, and welcome.—
Soud, soud, soud, soud!

Re-enter Servants *with supper.*

Why, when, I say? Nay, good sweet Kate, be merry.
Off with my boots, you rogues! you villains, when?
[*Sings*] It was the friar of orders grey,
　　As he forth walked on his way:—
Out, you rogue! you pluck my foot awry: 150
Take that, and mend the plucking off the other.
　　　　　　　　　　　　[*Strikes him.*
Be merry, Kate. Some water, here; what, ho!
Where's my spaniel Troilus? Sirrah, get you hence,
And bid my cousin Ferdinand come hither:
One, Kate, that you must kiss, and be acquainted
　　with.
Where are my slippers? Shall I have some water?

Enter one with water.

Come, Kate, and wash, and welcome heartily.
You whoreson villain! will you let it fall? [*Strikes him.*
Kath. Patience, I pray you; 'twas a fault unwilling.
Pet. A whoreson beetle-headed, flap-ear'd knave! 160

Come, Kate, sit down; I know you have a stomach.
Will you give thanks, sweet Kate; or else shall I?
What's this? mutton?
　　First Serv.　　　　　　Ay.
　　Pet.　　　　　　Who brought it?
　　Peter.　　　　　　　I.
Pet. 'Tis burnt; and so is all the meat.
What dogs are these! Where is the rascal cook?
How durst you, villains, bring it from the dresser,
And serve it thus to me that love it not?
There, take it to you, trenchers, cups, and all:
　　　　　　[*Throws the meat, &c. about the stage.*
You heedless joltheads and unmanner'd slaves!
What, do you grumble? I'll be with you straight. 170
Kath. I pray you, husband, be not so disquiet:
The meat was well, if you were so contented.
Pet. I tell thee, Kate, 'twas burnt and dried away;
And I expressly am forbid to touch it,
For it engenders choler, planteth anger;
And better 'twere that both of us did fast,
Since, of ourselves, ourselves are choleric,
Than feed it with such over-roasted flesh.
Be patient; to-morrow 't shall be mended,
And, for this night, we'll fast for company: 180
Come, I will bring thee to thy bridal chamber. [*Exeunt.*

Re-enter Servants *severally.*

Nath. Peter, didst ever see the like?
Peter. He kills her in her own humour.

Re-enter CURTIS.

Gru. Where is he?
Curt. In her chamber, making a sermon of con-
tinency to her;
And rails, and swears, and rates, that she, poor soul,
Knows not which way to stand, to look, to speak,
And sits as one new-risen from a dream.
Away, away! for he is coming hither. [*Exeunt.* 190

Re-enter PETRUCHIO.

Pet. Thus have I politicly begun my reign,
And 'tis my hope to end successfully.
My falcon now is sharp and passing empty;
And till she stoop she must not be full-gorged,
For then she never looks upon her lure.
Another way I have to man my haggard,
To make her come and know her keeper's call,
That is, to watch her, as we watch these kites
That bate and beat and will not be obedient.
She eat no meat to-day, nor none shall eat; 200
Last night she slept not, nor to-night she shall not;
As with the meat, some undeserved fault
I'll find about the making of the bed;
And here I'll fling the pillow, there the bolster,
This way the coverlet, another way the sheets:
Ay, and amid this hurly I intend
That all is done in reverend care of her;
And in conclusion she shall watch all night:
And if she chance to nod I'll rail and brawl
And with the clamour keep her still awake. 210
This is a way to kill a wife with kindness;

The Taming of the Shrew
ACT IV : SC I

173

with mire. **121. Cock's,** a perversion of "God's"; used in oaths.
136. unpink'd, not scalloped. **137. link,** torch, material from which
was used as blackening. **145. Soud,** a nonsense syllable sung as a
refrain. **150. Out,** exclamation of anger or reproach; see glossary.
168. trenchers, wooden dishes or plates; see glossary. **169. joltheads,**
blockheads. **170. with you,** i.e., even with you (Hart). **straight,**
immediately; see glossary. **178. feed it,** partake of food. **196. man,**
tame, accustom to the presence of men; a term of falconry. **haggard,**
wild female hawk; hence, an intractable woman. **198. watch her,**
keep her watching, i.e., awake; see glossary. **199. bate,** beat the
wings impatiently and flutter away from the hand or perch. **beat,** flap
the wings; the pronunciation of *bate* and *beat* was somewhat alike.

And thus I'll curb her mad and headstrong humour.
He that knows better how to tame a shrew,
Now let him speak: 'tis charity to show.   [*Exit.*

SCENE II. *Padua. Before* BAPTISTA'S *house.*

Enter TRANIO *and* HORTENSIO.

Tra. Is 't possible, friend Licio, that Mistress
        Bianca
Doth fancy any other but Lucentio?
I tell you, sir, she bears me fair in hand.
Hor. Sir, to satisfy you in what I have said,
Stand by and mark the manner of his teaching.

Enter BIANCA *and* LUCENTIO.

Luc. Now, mistress, profit you in what you read?
Bian. What, master, read you? first resolve me that.
Luc. I read that I profess, the Art to Love.
Bian. And may you prove, sir, master of your art!
Luc. While you, sweet dear, prove mistress of my
        heart!   10
Hor. Quick proceeders, marry! Now, tell me, I pray,
You that durst swear that your mistress Bianca
Loved none in the world so well as Lucentio.
Tra. O despiteful love! unconstant womankind!
I tell thee, Licio, this is wonderful.
Hor. Mistake no more: I am not Licio,
Nor a musician, as I seem to be;
But one that scorn to live in this disguise,
For such a one as leaves a gentleman,
And makes a god of such a cullion: 20
Know, sir, that I am call'd Hortensio.
Tra. Signior Hortensio, I have often heard
Of your entire affection to Bianca;
And since mine eyes are witness of her lightness,
I will with you, if you be so contented,
Forswear Bianca and her love for ever.
Hor. See, how they kiss and court! Signior Lucentio,
Here is my hand, and here I firmly vow
Never to woo her more, but do forswear her,
As one unworthy all the former favours   30
That I have fondly flatter'd her withal.
Tra. And here I take the like unfeigned oath,
Never to marry with her though she would entreat:
Fie on her! see, how beastly she doth court him!
Hor. Would all the world but he had quite
        forsworn!
For me, that I may surely keep mine oath,
I will be married to a wealthy widow,
Ere three days pass, which hath as long loved me
As I have loved this proud disdainful haggard.
And so farewell, Signior Lucentio.   40
Kindness in women, not their beauteous looks,
Shall win my love: and so I take my leave,
In resolution as I swore before.   [*Exit.*
Tra. Mistress Bianca, bless you with such grace
As 'longeth to a lover's blessed case!
Nay, I have ta'en you napping, gentle love,
And have forsworn you with Hortensio.
Bian. Tranio, you jest: but have you both forsworn
        me?
Tra. Mistress, we have.

Luc.   Then we are rid of Licio.
Tra. I' faith, he'll have a lusty widow now,   50
That shall be woo'd and wedded in a day.
Bian. God give him joy!
Tra. Ay, and he'll tame her.
Bian.   He says so, Tranio.
Tra. Faith, he is gone unto the taming-school.
Bian. The taming-school! what, is there such a
        place?
Tra. Ay, mistress, and Petruchio is the master;
That teacheth tricks eleven and twenty long,
To tame a shrew and charm her chattering tongue.

Enter BIONDELLO.

Bion. O master, master, I have watch'd so long
That I am dog-weary: but at last I spied   60
†An ancient angel coming down the hill,
Will serve the turn.
Tra.   What is he, Biondello?
Bion. Master, a mercatante, or a pedant,
I know not what; but formal in apparel,
In gait and countenance surely like a father.
Luc. And what of him, Tranio?
Tra. If he be credulous and trust my tale,
I'll make him glad to seem Vincentio,
And give assurance to Baptista Minola,
As if he were the right Vincentio.   70
Take in your love, and then let me alone.
                      [*Exeunt Lucentio and Bianca.*

Enter a Pedant.

Ped. God save you, sir!
Tra.   And you, sir! you are welcome.
Travel you far on, or are you at the farthest?
Ped. Sir, at the farthest for a week or two:
But then up farther, and as far as Rome;
And so to Tripoli, if God lend me life.
Tra. What countryman, I pray?
Ped.   Of Mantua.
Tra. Of Mantua, sir? marry, God forbid!
And come to Padua, careless of your life?
Ped. My life, sir! how, I pray? for that goes hard. 80
Tra. 'Tis death for any one in Mantua
To come to Padua. Know you not the cause?
Your ships are stay'd at Venice, and the duke,
For private quarrel 'twixt your duke and him,
Hath publish'd and proclaim'd it openly:
'Tis marvel, but that you are but newly come,
You might have heard it else proclaim'd about.
Ped. Alas! sir, it is worse for me than so;
For I have bills for money by exchange
From Florence and must here deliver them.   90
Tra. Well, sir, to do you courtesy,
This will I do, and this I will advise you:
First, tell me, have you ever been at Pisa?
Ped. Ay, sir, in Pisa have I often been,
Pisa renowned for grave citizens.
Tra. Among them know you one Vincentio?
Ped. I know him not, but I have heard of him;
A merchant of incomparable wealth.
Tra. He is my father, sir; and, sooth to say,
In countenance somewhat doth resemble you.   100
Bion. [*Aside*] As much as an apple doth an oyster,
        and all one.

SCENE II. **7. resolve,** answer; see glossary. **8. Art to Love,** Ovid's
Ars amandi. **11. proceeders,** candidates for degrees, suggested by the
phrase *master of your art* (l. 9), with quibble on the ordinary sense.
20. cullion, base creature. **50. lusty,** merry, pleasant. **57. eleven**

and twenty, an allusion to the card game, one-and-thirty; cf. note to
I, ii, 33. **61. ancient angel,** generally explained as a fellow of the
good old stamp, i.e., the stamp of the archangel on the coin as distinguished from the debased coinage of the day. **62. serve the turn.**

Tra. To save your life in this extremity,
This favour will I do you for his sake;
And think it not the worst of all your fortunes
That you are like to Sir Vincentio.
His name and credit shall you undertake,
And in my house you shall be friendly lodged:
Look that you take upon you as you should;
You understand me, sir: so shall you stay
Till you have done your business in the city: 110
If this be courtesy, sir, accept of it.
    Ped. O sir, I do; and will repute you ever
The patron of my life and liberty.
    Tra. Then go with me to make the matter good.
This, by the way, I let you understand;
My father is here look'd for every day,
To pass assurance of a dower in marriage
'Twixt me and one Baptista's daughter here:
In all these circumstances I'll instruct you:
Go with me to clothe you as becomes you.   [*Exeunt.* 120

SCENE III. *A room in* PETRUCHIO'S *house.*

Enter KATHARINA *and* GRUMIO.

    Gru. No, no, forsooth; I dare not for my life.
    Kath. The more my wrong, the more his spite
        appears:
What, did he marry me to famish me?
Beggars, that come unto my father's door
Upon entreaty have a present alms;
If not, elsewhere they meet with charity:
But I, who never knew how to entreat,
Nor never needed that I should entreat,
Am starved for meat, giddy for lack of sleep,
With oaths kept waking and with brawling fed: 10
And that which spites me more than all these wants,
He does it under name of perfect love;
As who should say, if I should sleep or eat,
'Twere deadly sickness or else present death.
I prithee go and get me some repast;
I care not what, so it be wholesome food.
    Gru. What say you to a neat's foot?
    Kath. 'Tis passing good: I prithee let me have it.
    Gru. I fear it is too choleric a meat.
How say you to a fat tripe finely broil'd?   20
    Kath. I like it well: good Grumio, fetch it me.
    Gru. I cannot tell; I fear 'tis choleric.
What say you to a piece of beef and mustard?
    Kath. A dish that I do love to feed upon.
    Gru. Ay, but the mustard is too hot a little.
    Kath. Why then, the beef, and let the mustard rest.
    Gru. Nay then, I will not: you shall have the
        mustard,
Or else you get no beef of Grumio.
    Kath. Then both, or one, or any thing thou wilt.
    Gru. Why then, the mustard without the beef.   30
    Kath. Go, get thee gone, thou false deluding slave,
                                    [*Beats him.*
That feed'st me with the very name of meat:
Sorrow on thee and all the pack of you,
That triumph thus upon my misery!
Go, get thee gone, I say.

Enter PETRUCHIO *and* HORTENSIO *with meat.*

    Pet. How fares my Kate? What, sweeting, all
        amort?
    Hor. Mistress, what cheer?
    Kath.   Faith, as cold as can be.
    Pet. Pluck up thy spirits; look cheerfully upon me.
Here, love; thou see'st how diligent I am
To dress thy meat myself and bring it thee: 40
I am sure, sweet Kate, this kindness merits thanks.
What, not a word? Nay, then thou lovest it not;
And all my pains is sorted to no proof.
Here, take away this dish.
    Kath.   I pray you, let it stand.
    Pet. The poorest service is repaid with thanks;
And so shall mine, before you touch the meat.
    Kath. I thank you, sir.
    Hor. Signior Petruchio, fie! you are to blame.
Come, Mistress Kate, I'll bear you company.
    Pet. [*Aside*] Eat it up all, Hortensio, if thou lovest
        me.   50
Much good do it unto thy gentle heart!
Kate, eat apace: and now, my honey love,
Will we return unto thy father's house
And revel it as bravely as the best,
With silken coats and caps and golden rings,
With ruffs and cuffs and fardingales and things;
With scarfs and fans and double change of bravery,
With amber bracelets, beads and all this knavery.
What, hast thou dined? The tailor stays thy leisure,
To deck thy body with his ruffling treasure.   60

Enter Tailor.

Come, tailor, let us see these ornaments:
Lay forth the gown.

Enter Haberdasher.
            What news with you, sir?
    Hab. Here is the cap your worship did bespeak.
    Pet. Why, this was moulded on a porringer;
A velvet dish: fie, fie! 'tis lewd and filthy:
Why, 'tis a cockle or a walnut-shell,
A knack, a toy, a trick, a baby's cap:
Away with it! let me have a bigger.
    Kath. I'll have no bigger: this doth fit the time,
And gentlewomen wear such caps as these.   70
    Pet. When you are gentle, you shall have one too,
And not till then.
    Hor.   [*Aside*] That will not be in haste.
    Kath. Why, sir, I trust I may have leave to speak;
And speak I will; I am no child, no babe:
Your betters have endured me say my mind,
And if you cannot, best you stop your ears.
My tongue will tell the anger of my heart,
Or else my heart concealing it will break,
And rather than it shall, I will be free
Even to the uttermost, as I please, in words.   80
    Pet. Why, thou say'st true; it is a paltry cap,
A custard-coffin, a bauble, a silken pie:
I love thee well, in that thou likest it not.
    Kath. Love me or love me not, I like the cap;
And it I will have, or I will have none.
                                [*Exit Haberdasher.*
    Pet. Thy gown? why, ay: come, tailor, let us see 't.

---

answer the purpose; see *serve* in glossary. 63. **mercatante,** merchant.
119. **circumstances,** details; see glossary.
    SCENE III. 5. **present,** immediate, prompt; see glossary. 17. **neat,**
any cattle of the ox kind. 36. **all amort,** dejected, dispirited. 43. **sorted**

to no proof, proved to be to no purpose (Schmidt). 54. **bravely,**
splendidly dressed. 56. **fardingales,** hooped petticoats. 64. **porringer,**
porridge bowl. 66. **cockle,** scallop shell. 82. **custard-coffin,** crust
over a custard, with quibble on "costard" meaning "head."

O mercy, God! what masquing stuff is here?
What 's this? a sleeve? 'tis like a demi-cannon:
What, up and down, carved like an apple-tart?
Here 's snip and nip and cut and slish and slash,   90
Like to a censer in a barber's shop:
Why, what, i' devil's name, tailor, call'st thou this?
   Hor. [*Aside*] I see she 's like to have neither cap nor
     gown.
   Tai. You bid me make it orderly and well,
According to the fashion and the time.
   Pet. Marry, and did; but if you be remember'd,
I did not bid you mar it to the time.
Go, hop me over every kennel home,
For you shall hop without my custom, sir:
I'll none of it: hence! make your best of it.   100
   Kath. I never saw a better-fashion'd gown,
More quaint, more pleasing, nor more commendable:
Belike you mean to make a puppet of me.
   Pet. Why, true; he means to make a puppet of thee.
   Tai. She says your worship means to make a puppet
of her.
   Pet. O monstrous arrogance! Thou liest, thou
thread, thou thimble,
Thou yard, three-quarters, half-yard, quarter, nail!
Thou flea, thou nit, thou winter-cricket thou!   110
Braved in mine own house with a skein of thread?
Away, thou rag, thou quantity, thou remnant;
Or I shall so be-mete thee with thy yard
As thou shalt think on prating whilst thou livest!
I tell thee, I, that thou hast marr'd her gown.
   Tai. Your worship is deceived; the gown is made
Just as my master had direction:
Grumio gave order how it should be done.
   Gru. I gave him no order; I gave him the stuff.
   Tai. But how did you desire it should be made?   120
   Gru. Marry, sir, with needle and thread.
   Tai. But did you not request to have it cut?
   Gru. Thou hast faced many things.
   Tai. I have.
   Gru. Face not me: thou hast braved many men;
brave not me; I will neither be faced nor braved. I
say unto thee, I bid thy master cut out the gown; but
I did not bid him cut it to pieces: ergo, thou liest.
   Tai. Why, here is the note of the fashion to testify. 131
   Pet. Read it.
   Gru. The note lies in 's throat, if he say I said so.
   Tai. [*Reads*] 'Imprimis, a loose-bodied gown:'
   Gru. Master, if ever I said loose-bodied gown, sew
me in the skirts of it, and beat me to death with a
bottom of brown thread: I said a gown.
   Pet. Proceed.
   Tai. [*Reads*] 'With a small compassed cape:'   140
   Gru. I confess the cape.
   Tai. [*Reads*] 'With a trunk sleeve:'
   Gru. I confess two sleeves.
   Tai. [*Reads*] 'The sleeves curiously cut.'
   Pet. Ay, there 's the villany.
   Gru. Error i' the bill, sir; error i' the bill. I com-
manded the sleeves should be cut out and sewed up
again; and that I'll prove upon thee, though thy little
finger be armed in a thimble.

   Tai. This is true that I say: an I had thee in place
where, thou shouldst know it.   151
   Gru. I am for thee straight: take thou the bill, give
me thy mete-yard, and spare not me.
   Hor. God-a-mercy, Grumio! then he shall have no
odds.
   Pet. Well, sir, in brief, the gown is not for me.
   Gru. You are i' the right, sir: 'tis for my mistress.
   Pet. Go, take it up unto thy master's use.
   Gru. Villain, not for thy life: take up my mistress'
gown for thy master's use!   161
   Pet. Why, sir, what 's your conceit in that?
   Gru. O, sir, the conceit is deeper than you think for:
Take up my mistress' gown to his master's use!
O, fie, fie, fie!
   Pet. [*Aside*] Hortensio, say thou wilt see the tailor
     paid.
Go take it hence; be gone, and say no more.
   Hor. Tailor, I'll pay thee for thy gown to-morrow:
Take no unkindness of his hasty words:
Away! I say; commend me to thy master. [*Exit Tailor.*
   Pet. Well, come, my Kate; we will unto your
     father's   171
Even in these honest mean habiliments:
Our purses shall be proud, our garments poor;
For 'tis the mind that makes the body rich;
And as the sun breaks through the darkest clouds,
So honour peereth in the meanest habit.
What is the jay more precious than the lark,
Because his feathers are more beautiful?
Or is the adder better than the eel,
Because his painted skin contents the eye?   180
O, no, good Kate; neither art thou the worse
For this poor furniture and mean array,
If thou account'st it shame, lay it on me;
And therefore frolic: we will hence forthwith,
To feast and sport us at thy father's house.
Go, call my men, and let us straight to him;
And bring our horses unto Long-lane end;
There will we mount, and thither walk on foot.
Let 's see; I think 'tis now some seven o'clock,
And well we may come there by dinner-time.   190
   Kath. I dare assure you, sir, 'tis almost two;
And 'twill be supper-time ere you come there.
   Pet. It shall be seven ere I go to horse:
Look, what I speak, or do, or think to do,
You are still crossing it. Sirs, let 't alone:
I will not go to-day; and ere I do,
It shall be what o'clock I say it is.
   Hor. [*Aside*] Why, so this gallant will command the
     sun.   [*Exeunt.*

SCENE IV. *Padua. Before* BAPTISTA'S *house.*

Enter TRANIO, *and the* Pedant *dressed like* VINCENTIO.

   Tra. Sir, this is the house: please it you that I call?
   Ped. Ay, what else? and but I be deceived
Signior Baptista may remember me,
Near twenty years ago, in Genoa,
Where we were lodgers at the Pegasus.

Tra. 'Tis well; and hold your own, in any case,
With such austerity as 'longeth to a father.
Ped. I warrant you.

Enter BIONDELLO.

But, sir, here comes your boy;
'Twere good he were school'd.
Tra. Fear you not him. Sirrah Biondello,   10
Now do your duty throughly, I advise you:
Imagine 'twere the right Vincentio.
Bion. Tut, fear not me.
Tra. But hast thou done thy errand to Baptista?
Bion. I told him that your father was at Venice,
And that you look'd for him this day in Padua.
Tra. Thou 'rt a tall fellow: hold thee that to drink.
Here comes Baptista: set your countenance, sir.

Enter BAPTISTA *and* LUCENTIO.

Signior Baptista, you are happily met.   19
[*To the Pedant*] Sir, this is the gentleman I told you of:
I pray you, stand good father to me now,
Give me Bianca for my patrimony.
Ped. Soft, son!
Sir, by your leave: having come to Padua
To gather in some debts, my son Lucentio
Made me acquainted with a weighty cause
Of love between your daughter and himself:
And, for the good report I hear of you
And for the love he beareth to your daughter
And she to him, to stay him not too long,   30
I am content, in a good father's care,
To have him match'd; and if you please to like
No worse than I, upon some agreement
Me shall you find ready and willing
With one consent to have her so bestow'd;
For curious I cannot be with you,
Signior Baptista, of whom I hear so well.
Bap. Sir, pardon me in what I have to say:
Your plainness and your shortness please me well.
Right true it is, your son Lucentio here   40
Doth love my daughter and she loveth him,
Or both dissemble deeply their affections:
And therefore, if you say no more than this,
That like a father you will deal with him
And pass my daughter a sufficient dower,
The match is made, and all is done:
Your son shall have my daughter with consent.
Tra. I thank you, sir. Where then do you know best
We be affied and such assurance ta'en
As shall with either part's agreement stand?   50
Bap. Not in my house, Lucentio; for, you know,
Pitchers have ears, and I have many servants:
Besides, old Gremio is hearkening still;
And happily we might be interrupted.
Tra. Then at my lodging, an it like you:
There doth my father lie; and there, this night,
We'll pass the business privately and well.
Send for your daughter by your servant here;
My boy shall fetch the scrivener presently.
The worst is this, that, at so slender warning,   60
You are like to have a thin and slender pittance.

Bap. It likes me well. Cambio, hie you home,
And bid Bianca make her ready straight;
And, if you will, tell what hath happened,
Lucentio's father is arrived in Padua,
And how she 's like to be Lucentio's wife.
Bion. I pray the gods she may with all my heart!
Tra. Dally not with the gods, but get thee gone.
                             [*Exit Bion.*
Signior Baptista, shall I lead the way?
Welcome! one mess is like to be your cheer: 70
Come, sir; we will better it in Pisa.
Bap. I follow you. [*Exeunt Tranio, Pedant, and Baptista.*

Re-enter BIONDELLO.

Bion. Cambio!
Luc. What sayest thou, Biondello?
Bion. You saw my master wink and laugh upon you?
Luc. Biondello, what of that?
Bion. Faith, nothing; but has left me here behind, to
expound the meaning or moral of his signs and tokens.
Luc. I pray thee, moralize them.   81
Bion. Then thus. Baptista is safe, talking with the
deceiving father of a deceitful son.
Luc. And what of him?
Bion. His daughter is to be brought by you to the
supper.
Luc. And then?
Bion. The old priest of Saint Luke's church is at your
command at all hours.
Luc. And what of all this?   90
Bion. I cannot tell; expect they are busied about a
counterfeit assurance: take you assurance of her, 'cum
privilegio ad imprimendum solum:' to the church;
take the priest, clerk, and some sufficient honest witnesses:
If this be not that you look for, I have no more to say,
But bid Bianca farewell for ever and a day.
Luc. Hearest thou, Biondello?
Bion. I cannot tarry: I knew a wench married in an
afternoon as she went to the garden for parsley to stuff
a rabbit; and so may you, sir: and so, adieu, sir. My
master hath appointed me to go to Saint Luke's, to bid
the priest be ready to come against you come with
your appendix.   [*Exit.* 104
Luc. I may, and will, if she be so contented:
She will be pleased; then wherefore should I doubt?
Hap what hap may, I'll roundly go about her:
It shall go hard if Cambio go without her.   [*Exit.*

SCENE V. *A public road.*

Enter PETRUCHIO, KATHARINA, HORTENSIO, *and*
Servants.

Pet. Come on, i' God's name; once more toward our
father's.
Good Lord, how bright and goodly shines the moon!
Kath. The moon! the sun: it is not moonlight now.
Pet. I say it is the moon that shines so bright.
Kath. I know it is the sun that shines so bright.
Pet. Now, by my mother's son, and that 's myself,

"godfather." 36. **curious**, particular; see glossary. 49. **affied**, betrothed. 53. **hearkening still**, continually listening; see *still* in glossary.
54. **happily**, haply; see glossary. 55. **like**, please; see glossary. 56. **lie**,
lodge; see glossary. 59. **scrivener**, notary, one to draw up contracts.
62. **Cambio**, so F; Globe: *Biondello.* 66. **like**, likely. 70. **mess**, dish,
course of food. **cheer**, welcome, entertainment. 92. **assurance**, be-

trothal. 93. **'cum . . . solum,'** with exclusive copyright, here jokingly
applied to the actual marriage; the phrase appeared often on the
title pages of books. 104. **appendix, i.e.,** your bride.

It shall be moon, or star, or what I list,
Or ere I journey to your father's house.
Go on, and fetch our horses back again.
Evermore cross'd and cross'd; nothing but cross'd! 10
   Hor. Say as he says, or we shall never go.
   Kath. Forward, I pray, since we have come so far,
And be it moon, or sun, or what you please:
An if you please to call it a rush-candle,
Henceforth I vow it shall be so for me.
   Pet. I say it is the moon.
   Kath.   I know it is the moon.
   Pet. Nay, then you lie: it is the blessed sun.
   Kath. Then, God be bless'd, it is the blessed sun:
But sun it is not, when you say it is not;
And the moon changes even as your mind. 20
What you will have it named, even that it is;
And so it shall be so for Katharine.
   Hor. Petruchio, go thy ways; the field is won.
   Pet. Well, forward, forward! thus the bowl should
      run,
And not unluckily against the bias.
But, soft! company is coming here.

   Enter VINCENTIO.

[*To Vincentio*] Good morrow, gentle mistress: where
      away?
Tell me, sweet Kate, and tell me truly too,
Hast thou beheld a fresher gentlewoman?
Such war of white and red within her cheeks! 30
What stars do spangle heaven with such beauty,
As those two eyes become that heavenly face?
Fair lovely maid, once more good day to thee.
Sweet Kate, embrace her for her beauty's sake.
   Hor. A' will make the man mad, to make a woman
of him.
   Kath. Young budding virgin, fair and fresh and
      sweet,
Whither away, or where is thy abode?
Happy the parents of so fair a child;
Happier the man, whom favourable stars 40
Allot thee for his lovely bed-fellow!
   Pet. Why, how now, Kate! I hope thou art not mad:
This is a man, old, wrinkled, faded, wither'd,
And not a maiden, as thou say'st he is.
   Kath. Pardon, old father, my mistaking eyes,
That have been so bedazzled with the sun
That everything I look on seemeth green:
Now I perceive thou art a reverend father;
Pardon, I pray thee, for my mad mistaking.
   Pet. Do, good old grandsire; and withal make
      known 50
Which way thou travellest: if along with us,
We shall be joyful of thy company.
   Vin. Fair sir, and you my merry mistress,
That with your strange encounter much amazed me,
My name is call'd Vincentio; my dwelling Pisa;
And bound I am to Padua; there to visit
A son of mine, which long I have not seen.
   Pet. What is his name?
   Vin.   Lucentio, gentle sir.
   Pet. Happily met; the happier for thy son.

And now by law, as well as reverend age, 60
I may entitle thee my loving father:
The sister to my wife, this gentlewoman,
Thy son by this hath married. Wonder not,
Nor be not grieved: she is of good esteem,
Her dowry wealthy, and of worthy birth;
Beside, so qualified as may beseem
The spouse of any noble gentleman.
Let me embrace with old Vincentio,
And wander we to see thy honest son,
Who will of thy arrival be full joyous. 70
   Vin. But is this true? or is it else your pleasure,
Like pleasant travellers, to break a jest
Upon the company you overtake?
   Hor. I do assure thee, father, so it is.
   Pet. Come, go along, and see the truth hereof;
For our first merriment hath made thee jealous.
                   [*Exeunt all but Hortensio.*
   Hor. Well, Petruchio, this has put me in heart.
Have to my widow! and if she be froward,
Then hast thou taught Hortensio to be untoward.
                            [*Exit.*

ACT V.

SCENE I. *Padua. Before* LUCENTIO'S *house.*

GREMIO *discovered. Enter behind* BIONDELLO, LUCENTIO,
   and BIANCA.

   Bion. Softly and swiftly, sir; for the priest is ready.
   Luc. I fly, Biondello: but they may chance to need
thee at home; therefore leave us.
   Bion. Nay, faith, I'll see the church o' your back;
and then come back to my master's as soon as I can.
           [*Exeunt Lucentio, Bianca, and Biondello.*
   Gre. I marvel Cambio comes not all this while.

   Enter PETRUCHIO, KATHARINA, VINCENTIO, GRUMIO,
   with Attendants.

   Pet. Sir, here's the door, this is Lucentio's house:
My father's bears more toward the marketplace; 10
Thither must I, and here I leave you, sir.
   Vin. You shall not choose but drink before you go:
I think I shall command your welcome here,
And, by all likelihood, some cheer is toward. [*Knocks.*
   Gre. They're busy within; you were best knock
louder.

   Pedant *looks out of the window.*

   Ped. What's he that knocks as he would beat down
the gate?
   Vin. Is Signior Lucentio within, sir?
   Ped. He's within, sir, but not to be spoken withal. 21
   Vin. What if a man bring him a hundred pound or
two, to make merry withal?
   Ped. Keep your hundred pounds to yourself: he shall
need none, so long as I live.
   Pet. Nay, I told you your son was well beloved in
Padua. Do you hear, sir? To leave frivolous circum-

SCENE V. 8. **Or ere,** before; see *or* in glossary. 12. **Forward, I
pray,** etc. In the resolving of this merry and complicated plot, nothing
is so artistically pleasing as the resolution of the strife between Petruchio
and Katharina, where we see the shrew emerge as a witty, sanguine
person, none the less spirited for all her taming. The turn in her
character occurs when she is able to see and to make a joke. 14. **rush-**

candle, a rush dipped into tallow; hence a very feeble light. 25.
against the bias, contrary to the normal tendency; see *bias* in glossary.
35. **A',** he; see glossary. 47. **green,** young and fresh. 76. **jealous,**
suspicious. 79. **untoward,** unmannerly.
ACT V. SCENE I. *Stage Direction:* **Gremio *discovered;*** F: *Gremio is out
before.* The New Cambridge editors give the scene and directions as

stances, I pray you, tell Signior Lucentio that his father is come from Pisa and is here at the door to speak with him. 30

Ped. Thou liest: his father is come from Padua and here looking out at the window.

Vin. Art thou his father?

Ped. Ay, sir; so his mother says, if I may believe her.

Pet. [*To Vincentio*] Why, how now, gentleman! why, this is flat knavery, to take upon you another man's name.

Ped. Lay hands on the villain: I believe a' means to cozen somebody in this city under my countenance. 41

Re-enter BIONDELLO.

Bion. I have seen them in the church together: God send 'em good shipping! But who is here? mine old master Vincentio! now we are undone and brought to nothing.

Vin. [*Seeing Biondello*] Come hither, crack-hemp.

Bion. I hope I may choose, sir.

Vin. Come hither, you rogue. What, have you forgot me? 50

Bion. Forgot you! no, sir: I could not forget you, for I never saw you before in all my life.

Vin. What, you notorious villain, didst thou never see thy master's father, Vincentio?

Bion. What, my old worshipful old master? yes, marry, sir: see where he looks out of the window.

Vin. Is 't so, indeed? [*Beats Biondello.*

Bion. Help, help, help! here 's a madman will murder me. [*Exit.* 61

Ped. Help, son! help, Signior Baptista!
[*Exit from above.*

Pet. Prithee, Kate, let 's stand aside and see the end of this controversy. [*They retire.*

Re-enter Pedant *below;* TRANIO, BAPTISTA, *and* Servants.

Tra. Sir, what are you that offer to beat my servant?

Vin. What am I, sir! nay, what are you, sir? O immortal gods! O fine villain! A silken doublet! a velvet hose! a scarlet cloak! and a copatain hat! O, I am undone! I am undone! while I play the good husband at home, my son and my servant spend all at the university.

Tra. How now! what 's the matter?

Bap. What, is the man lunatic?

Tra. Sir, you seem a sober ancient gentleman by your habit, but your words show you a madman. Why, sir, what 'cerns it you if I wear pearl and gold? I thank my good father, I am able to maintain it. 79

Vin. Thy father! O villain! he is a sailmaker in Bergamo.

Bap. You mistake, sir, you mistake, sir. Pray, what do you think is his name?

Vin. His name! as if I knew not his name: I have brought him up ever since he was three years old, and his name is Tranio.

Ped. Away, away, mad ass! his name is Lucentio; and he is mine only son, and heir to the lands of me, Signior Vincentio. 89

Vin. Lucentio! O, he hath murdered his master! Lay hold on him, I charge you, in the duke's name. O, my son, my son! Tell me, thou villain, where is my son Lucentio?

Tra. Call forth an officer.

Enter one with an Officer.

Carry this mad knave to the gaol. Father Baptista, I charge you see that he be forthcoming.

Vin. Carry me to the gaol!

Gre. Stay, officer: he shall not go to prison.

Bap. Talk not, Signior Gremio: I say he shall go to prison. 100

Gre. Take heed, Signior Baptista, lest you be cony-catched in this business: I dare swear this is the right Vincentio.

Ped. Swear, if thou darest.

Gre. Nay, I dare not swear it.

Tra. Then thou wert best say that I am not Lucentio.

Gre. Yes, I know thee to be Signior Lucentio.

Bap. Away with the dotard! to the gaol with him! 110

Vin. Thus strangers may be haled and abused: O monstrous villain!

Re-enter BIONDELLO, *with* LUCENTIO *and* BIANCA.

Bion. O! we are spoiled and—yonder he is: deny him, forswear him, or else we are all undone.

Luc. [*Kneeling*] Pardon, sweet father.

Vin. Lives my sweet son?
[*Exeunt Biondello, Tranio, and Pedant, as fast as may be.*

Bian. Pardon, dear father.

Bap. How hast thou offended? Where is Lucentio?

Luc. Here 's Lucentio, Right son to the right Vincentio; That have by marriage made thy daughter mine, While counterfeit supposes blear'd thine eyne. 120

Gre. Here 's packing, with a witness, to deceive us all!

Vin. Where is that damned villain Tranio, That faced and braved me in this matter so?

Bap. Why, tell me, is not this my Cambio?

Bian. Cambio is changed into Lucentio.

Luc. Love wrought these miracles. Bianca's love Made me exchange my state with Tranio, While he did bear my countenance in the town; And happily I have arrived at the last 130 Unto the wished haven of my bliss. What Tranio did, myself enforced him to; Then pardon him, sweet father, for my sake.

Vin. I'll slit the villain's nose, that would have sent me to the gaol.

Bap. But do you hear, sir? have you married my daughter without asking my good will?

Vin. Fear not, Baptista; we will content you, go to: but I will in, to be revenged for this villany. [*Exit.*140

Bap. And I, to sound the depth of this knavery. [*Exit.*

Luc. Look not pale, Bianca; thy father will not frown. [*Exeunt Lucentio and Bianca.*

Gre. My cake is dough; but I'll in among the rest,

follows: *The square in Padua. Gremio seated under the trees, nodding; the door of Baptista's house opens softly; Biondello, Lucentio (in his proper habit) and Bianca (muffled) steal forth.* 43. **good shipping,** bon voyage. 44. **undone,** ruined; see glossary. 46. **crack-hemp,** gallows bird. 48. **I hope . . . sir,** allow me, sir; spoken to a disagreeable person who bars one's path (New Cambridge). 69. **copatain hat,** high, sugar-loaf hat. 71. **good husband,** good provider, manager. 111. **abused,** maltreated; see glossary. 120. **supposes,** substitutions; an allusion to Gascoigne's *Supposes,* an adaptation of *I Suppositi* by Ariosto, from which Shakespeare took the Lucentio-Bianca plot of intrigue. Hart notes that *supposes* was the name for a social pastime familiar to the age. 128. **state,** station; see glossary.

Out of hope of all, but my share of the feast.　　[*Exit.*
　Kath. Husband, let 's follow, to see the end of this
　　ado.
　Pet. First kiss me, Kate, and we will.
　Kath. What, in the midst of the street?
　Pet. What, art thou ashamed of me?　　　　　　150
　Kath. No, sir, God forbid; but ashamed to kiss.
　Pet. Why, then let 's home again. Come, sirrah,
　　let 's away.
　Kath. Nay, I will give thee a kiss: now pray thee,
　　love, stay.
　Pet. Is not this well? Come, my sweet Kate:
Better once than never, for never too late.　　[*Exeunt.*

SCENE II. *Padua.* LUCENTIO's *house.*

Enter BAPTISTA, VINCENTIO, GREMIO, *the Pedant,*
LUCENTIO, BIANCA, PETRUCHIO, KATHARINA,
HORTENSIO, *and* WIDOW, TRANIO, BIONDELLO,
and GRUMIO: *the Serving-men with Tranio
bringing in a banquet.*

　Luc. At last, though long, our jarring notes agree:
And time it is, when raging war is done,
To smile at scapes and perils overblown.
My fair Bianca, bid my father welcome,
While I with self-same kindness welcome thine.
Brother Petruchio, sister Katharina,
And thou, Hortensio, with thy loving widow,
Feast with the best, and welcome to my house:
My banquet is to close our stomachs up,
After our great good cheer. Pray you, sit down;　　10
For now we sit to chat as well as eat.
　Pet. Nothing but sit and sit, and eat and eat!
　Bap. Padua affords this kindness, son Petruchio.
　Pet. Padua affords nothing but what is kind.
　Hor. For both our sakes, I would that word were
　　true.
　Pet. Now, for my life, Hortensio fears his widow.
　Wid. Then never trust me, if I be afeard.
　Pet. You are very sensible, and yet you miss my
　　sense:
I mean, Hortensio is afeard of you.
　Wid. He that is giddy thinks the world turns round.
　Pet. Roundly replied.
　Kath.　　　　　Mistress, how mean you that?　21
　Wid. Thus I conceive by him.
　Pet. Conceives by me! How likes Hortensio that?
　Hor. My widow says, thus she conceives her tale.
　Pet. Very well mended. Kiss him for that, good
　　widow.
　Kath. 'He that is giddy thinks the world turns
　　round:'
I pray you, tell me what you meant by that.
　Wid. Your husband, being troubled with a shrew,
Measures my husband's sorrow by his woe:
And now you know my meaning.　　　　　　　30
　Kath. A very mean meaning.
　Wid.　　　　　　Right, I mean you.
　Kath. And I am mean indeed, respecting you.
　Pet. To her, Kate!

　Hor. To her, widow!
　Pet. A hundred marks, my Kate does put her down.
　Hor. That 's my office.
　Pet. Spoke like an officer: ha' to thee, lad!
　　　　　　　　　　　　　　[*Drinks to Hortensio.*
　Bap. How likes Gremio these quick-witted folks?
　Gre. Believe me, sir, they butt together well.
　Bian. Head, and butt! an hasty-witted body　　40
Would say your head and butt were head and horn.
　Vin. Ay, mistress bride, hath that awaken'd you?
　Bian. Ay, but not frighted me; therefore I'll sleep
　　again.
　Pet. Nay, that you shall not: since you have begun,
Have at you for a bitter jest or two!
　Bian. Am I your bird? I mean to shift my bush;
And then pursue me as you draw your bow.
You are welcome all.
　　　　　　[*Exeunt Bianca, Katharina, and Widow.*
　Pet. She hath prevented me. Here, Signior Tranio,
This bird you aim'd at, though you hit her not;　　50
Therefore a health to all that shot and miss'd.
　Tra. O, sir, Lucentio slipp'd me like his greyhound,
Which runs himself and catches for his master.
　Pet. A good swift simile, but something currish.
　Tra. 'Tis well, sir, that you hunted for yourself:
'Tis thought your deer does hold you at a bay.
　Bap. O ho, Petruchio! Tranio hits you now.
　Luc. I thank thee for that gird, good Tranio.
　Hor. Confess, confess, hath he not hit you here?
　Pet. A' has a little gall'd me, I confess;　　　　60
And, as the jest did glance away from me,
'Tis ten to one it maim'd you two outright.
　Bap. Now, in good sadness, son Petruchio,
I think thou hast the veriest shrew of all.
　Pet. Well, I say no: and therefore for assurance
Let 's each one send unto his wife;
And he whose wife is most obedient
To come at first when he doth send for her,
Shall win the wager which we will propose.
　Hor. Content. What is the wager?
　Luc.　　　　　　Twenty crowns.　　　　　　70
　Pet. Twenty crowns!
I'll venture so much of my hawk or hound,
But twenty times so much upon my wife.
　Luc. A hundred then.
　Hor.　　　　　Content.
　Pet.　　　　　　　A match! 'tis done.
　Hor. Who shall begin?
　Luc.　　　　　　That will I.
Go, Biondello, bid your mistress come to me.
　Bion. I go.　　　　　　　　　　　　　　[*Exit.*
　Bap. Son, I'll be your half, Bianca comes.
　Luc. I'll have no halves; I'll bear it all myself.

Re-enter BIONDELLO.

How now! what news?
　Bion.　　　　　　Sir, my mistress sends you word
That she is busy and she cannot come.　　　　　　81
　Pet. How! she is busy and she cannot come!
Is that an answer?
　Gre.　　　　　Ay, and a kind one too:
Pray God, sir, your wife send you not a worse.

SCENE II.　9. **banquet,** dessert.　**stomachs,** used with quibble on the
meaning "quarrels."　17. **afeard,** suspicious.　29. **Measures,** judges;
see glossary.　32. **mean,** used quibblingly; see glossary.　**respecting,**
compared to.　45. **Have at,** I shall come at; see glossary.　58. **gird,**

sharp, biting jest.　63. **sadness,** seriousness; see glossary.　99. **holidame,**
halidom; cf. *The Two Gentlemen of Verona,* IV, ii, 136, note.　104.
Swinge, thrash.　**me,** the ethical dative.　109. **awful rule,** i.e., authority respected; see *awful* in glossary.　140. **Confounds,** ruins; see

Pet. I hope, better.

Hor. Sirrah Biondello, go and entreat my wife
To come to me forthwith.   [*Exit Bion.*

Pet.   O, ho! entreat her!
Nay, then she must needs come.

Hor.   I am afraid, sir,
Do what you can, yours will not be entreated.

Re-enter BIONDELLO.

Now, where 's my wife?   90

Bion. She says you have some goodly jest in hand:
She will not come; she bids you come to her.

Pet. Worse and worse; she will not come! O vile,
Intolerable, not to be endured!
Sirrah Grumio, go to your mistress;
Say, I command her come to me.   [*Exit Grumio.*

Hor. I know her answer.

Pet.   What?

Hor.   She will not.

Pet. The fouler fortune mine, and there an end.

Bap. Now, by my holidame, here comes Katharina!

Re-enter KATHARINA.

Kath. What is your will, sir, that you send for me? 100

Pet. Where is your sister, and Hortensio's wife?

Kath. They sit conferring by the parlour fire.

Pet. Go, fetch them hither: if they deny to come,
Swinge me them soundly forth unto their husbands:
Away, I say, and bring them hither straight.
           [*Exit Katharina.*

Luc. Here is a wonder, if you talk of a wonder.

Hor. And so it is: I wonder what it bodes.

Pet. Marry, peace it bodes, and love and quiet life,
And awful rule and right supremacy;
And, to be short, what not, that 's sweet and happy? 110

Bap. Now, fair befal thee, good Petruchio!
The wager thou hast won; and I will add
Unto their losses twenty thousand crowns;
Another dowry to another daughter,
For she is changed, as she had never been.

Pet. Nay, I will win my wager better yet
And show more sign of her obedience,
Her new-built virtue and obedience.
See where she comes and brings your froward wives
As prisoners to her womanly persuasion.   120

Re-enter KATHARINA, *with* BIANCA *and* Widow.

Katharine, that cap of yours becomes you not:
Off with that bauble, throw it under-foot.

Wid. Lord, let me never have a cause to sigh,
Till I be brought to such a silly pass!

Bian. Fie! what a foolish duty call you this?

Luc. I would your duty were as foolish too:
The wisdom of your duty, fair Bianca,
Hath cost me an hundred crowns since suppertime.

Bian. The more fool you, for laying on my duty.

Pet. Katharine, I charge thee, tell these headstrong
    women   130
What duty they do owe their lords and husbands.

Wid. Come, come, you 're mocking: we will have
    no telling.

Pet. Come on, I say; and first begin with her.

Wid. She shall not.

Pet. I say she shall: and first begin with her.

Kath. Fie, fie! unknit that threatening unkind
    brow,
And dart not scornful glances from those eyes,
To wound thy lord, thy king, thy governor:
It blots thy beauty as frosts do bite the meads,
Confounds thy fame as whirlwinds shake fair buds, 140
And in no sense is meet or amiable.
A woman moved is like a fountain troubled,
Muddy, ill-seeming, thick, bereft of beauty;
And while it is so, none so dry or thirsty
Will deign to sip or touch one drop of it.
Thy husband is thy lord, thy life, thy keeper,
Thy head, thy sovereign; one that cares for thee,
And for thy maintenance commits his body
To painful labour both by sea and land,
To watch the night in storms, the day in cold,   150
Whilst thou liest warm at home, secure and safe;
And craves no other tribute at thy hands
But love, fair looks and true obedience;
Too little payment for so great a debt.
Such duty as the subject owes the prince
Even such a woman oweth to her husband;
And when she is froward, peevish, sullen, sour,
And not obedient to his honest will,
What is she but a foul contending rebel
And graceless traitor to her loving lord?   160
I am ashamed that women are so simple
To offer war where they should kneel for peace,
Or seek for rule, supremacy and sway,
When they are bound to serve, love and obey.
Why are our bodies soft and weak and smooth,
Unapt to toil and trouble in the world,
But that our soft conditions and our hearts
Should well agree with our external parts?
Come, come, you froward and unable worms!
My mind hath been as big as one of yours,   170
My heart as great, my reason haply more,
To bandy word for word and frown for frown;
But now I see our lances are but straws,
Our strength as weak, our weakness past compare,
That seeming to be most which we indeed least are.
Then vail your stomachs, for it is no boot,
And place your hands below your husband's foot:
In token of which duty, if he please,
My hand is ready; may it do him ease.

Pet. Why, there 's a wench! Come on, and kiss me,
    Kate.   180

Luc. Well, go thy ways, old lad; for thou shalt ha 't.

Vin. 'Tis a good hearing when children are toward.

Luc. But a harsh hearing when women are froward.

Pet. Come, Kate, we'll to bed.
We three are married, but you two are sped.
[*To Luc.*] 'Twas I won the wager, though you hit the
    white;
And, being a winner, God give you good night!
         [*Exeunt Petruchio and Katharina.*

Hor. Now, go thy ways; thou hast tamed a curst
    shrew.

Luc. 'Tis a wonder, by your leave, she will be tamed
    so.   [*Exeunt.*

glossary. **fame,** reputation; see glossary. 142. **moved,** angry; see glossary. 157. **peevish,** obstinate; see glossary. 167. **conditions,** qualities; see glossary. 176. **vail,** lower; see glossary. **boot,** profit, advantage; see glossary. 179. **do . . . ease,** give pleasure or assistance;

see *ease* in glossary. 186. **white,** the center of the target, with quibble on the name of Bianca, which in Italian means "white."

A
Midsummer-Night's Dream

A *Midsummer-Night's Dream* is first mentioned by Francis Meres in 1598 as one of Shakespeare's excellent comedies. It is dated by pretty general agreement in the winter of 1594-1595. It was entered in the Stationers' Register on October 8, 1600, and issued that year as a quarto:

A Midsommer nights dreame. As it hath beene sundry times pub*lickely acted, by the Right honourable,* the Lord Chamberlaine his *seruants. Written by William Shakespeare.* Imprinted at London, for *Thomas Fisher,* and are to be soulde at his shoppe, at the Signe of the White Hart, in *Fleete-streete.* 1600.

PUBLICATION

There exists also another quarto bearing the same date and the statement, "Printed by James Roberts." Critics were for a long time undecided as to which of these was the earlier. The recent investigations of W. J. Neidig, A. W. Pollard, and W. W. Greg have, however, made it clear that Thomas Pavier, the publisher who was about to issue a collection of Shakespeare's plays in 1619 together with others attributed to Shakespeare, was somehow stopped in his venture and gave to this quarto, and others printed in 1619, fictitious dates. His text is a very good reproduction of the first quarto and may have been consulted by the folio printers, although the detailed stage directions and the text itself indicate that the folio was set from a playhouse manuscript.[1]

OCCASION

Because of the appropriateness of the play to a wedding festival it has long been thought that it must have been prepared for the occasion of some wedding in courtly circles. The marriage of the earl of Derby to Elizabeth Vere, daughter of the earl of Oxford, on January 26, 1595, and that of Thomas, son of Lord Berkeley, to Elizabeth, daughter of Sir George Carey, on February 19, 1596, have both been suggested, as well as that of the third earl of Bedford to Lucy Harrington, on December 12, 1594.[2]

The passage (II, i, 148 ff.) known as "Oberon's Vision" seems meant to recall to the queen herself some occasion of festival and pageantry. A very probable event of this kind is the famous entertainment of the queen by her favorite Leicester at Kenilworth in 1575. Shakespeare may easily have had personal recollections of it. Scott seems to have this play in mind as he writes *Kenilworth.* Many scholars have also given assent to the suggestion.

An American scholar has more recently advanced an attractive theory; namely, that the play is a reminiscence, not of the festivities at Kenilworth in 1575, but of those at Elvetham held in 1591 by Edward Seymour, earl of Hertford.[3] The resemblances between the play and the description of the pageant at Elvetham are closer than those to the Kenilworth pageant, for a contemporary pamphlet shows a picture of a "promontory" at the north, the queen herself "throned by the west," and a mermaid on the deck of a ship (which may have been described figuratively as a "dolphin").

In 1560, the earl of Hertford had secretly married Lady Catherine Grey, who was descended from the duchess of Suffolk, a sister of Henry VIII, by whose will any legitimate child of hers stood next in succession to the throne. A son was born to the earl of Hertford and his countess. On her discovery of the marriage Queen Elizabeth, out of fear and jealousy, had the marriage declared illegal and the child illegitimate, and so the status had continued. Another son was born, and in 1568 Lady Catherine died of the harsh treatment she had received. Hertford's one ambition, of course, throughout the rest of his life, was to have his sons and heirs rendered legitimate, and the entertainment at Elvetham was part of his long and repeated effort to win the favor of the queen. This situation may have offered an occasion for the play. Since Hertford had continued to protest the findings of the court with reference to his marriage, matters were brought to a head in 1595 when his protests came to the attention of the queen. He was put in the Tower in jeopardy of his life.

Possibly in anticipation of this event, so it is conjectured, Shakespeare, known to certain noblemen intimate with Hertford, was induced to prepare a play of more than courtly grace for the palate of the queen. That this was in 1594-1595 is borne out by the familiar reference in "the lion among ladies" (III, i, 30 ff.) to the baptismal ceremony of the infant Prince Henry at Sterling, August 30, 1594, where a Moor, for reasons of prudence, was substituted for a lion to draw the baptismal car; also by the weather passage (II, i, 82 ff.) which has long been taken to refer to the bad season extending from the spring of 1594 to the summer of 1595. According to this interpretation the votaress of Titania (that is, of Elizabeth as the virgin queen), who had died, represents Lady Catherine Grey; and her child, the "changeling boy," becomes the son whose legitimacy Queen Elizabeth had im-

[1]W. J. Neidig, "The Shakespeare Quartos of 1619," *Modern Philology,* VII, 145; A. W. Pollard, *Shakespeare Folios and Quartos* (1909) and *Shakespeare's Fight with the Pirates* (Cambridge, 1920).

[2]Sir Sidney Lee, *A Life of William Shakespeare,* pp. 165-166; E. K. Chambers, *The Elizabethan Stage,* II, 194; Sir Israel Gollancz, "The Occasion of *A Midsummer Night's Dream,"* in *A Book of Homage to Shakespere* (Oxford, 1916). See also John W. Draper, "The Date of *A Midsummer Nights Dreame,"* *Modern Language Notes,* LIII (1938), 266-268.

[3]Edith Rickert, "Political Propaganda and Satire in *A Midsummer Night's Dream,"* *Modern Philology,* XXI, 53-87, 133-154. The reference to Elvetham instead of Kenilworth is also accepted by Chambers, *The Elizabethan Stage,* I, 122-124.

pugned. But since the queen had been in her way gracious to this boy, he is a member of her train. He belongs, however, properly to the train of Oberon. Oberon stands in various works of the time for Henry VIII, whose will had designated this child as his next heir. It should be said that the interpretation just given has been vigorously opposed and almost universally rejected, but, nevertheless, it is at least sufficiently plausible to be worth repeating.

PLOTS AND SOURCES

Whatever revisions may have been made, the fact remains that no play composed of such various elements achieves a more satisfactory blending into one than does *A Midsummer-Night's Dream*. No less than four plots are in progress throughout this play, each intersecting or tangent to the others at some point. Shakespeare derives plot materials from such diversified sources as classical myth and legend, native English fairy lore, and his own intimate knowledge of amateur theatricals. A somewhat detailed consideration of the treatment of these various factors will illustrate Shakespeare's skill in plot manipulation.

THESEUS-HIPPOLYTA PLOT

The Theseus-Hippolyta story with which the play opens announces the theme of love and marriage. We have in the approaching nuptials of the duke and his Amazon bride the closing episode of their romance. Shakespeare had learned of Theseus from North's translation of Plutarch's *Lives of the Noble Grecians and Romans*. To him and his age Theseus was as historical as Julius Caesar. Shakespeare knew also the gracious, authoritative, and noble Theseus from Chaucer's *Knight's Tale*. The season of the pre-nuptial festivities of Theseus and Hippolyta becomes here, as in *The Knight's Tale* and *The Two Noble Kinsmen*, the temporal setting for the various plots of the play proper.

THE PLOT OF THE LOVERS

The major plot, an Italianate story whose immediate source is not known, is also an affair of a proposed marriage. It interrupts, early in the scene, the tranquil anticipations of the royal lovers with the discordant cry that "the course of true love never did run smooth." The theme here of the willful and disobedient daughter who would choose her own husband is a familiar one. Shakespeare probably did not deny the conventional right of fathers to arrange their daughters' marriages, yet he and his audiences, like all persons and all audiences, sympathized with true love. This major plot is in itself highly intricate. Before the play opened and before Demetrius deserted Helena, the situation was this:

> Demetrius loved Helena
> Lysander loved Hermia.

When the play opens, however, matters stand as follows:

> Demetrius loves Hermia
> Lysander loves Hermia
> Helena is forsaken.

Demetrius' affections must be shunted back; but by magic and mistake the faithful Lysander is tampered with and we have:

> Demetrius loves Hermia
> Lysander loves Helena.

This is confusion worse confounded. Two more changes are necessary to swing the whole circle. First, it is brought about that:

> Demetrius loves Helena
> Lysander loves Helena
> Hermia is forsaken.

Then comes the final corrective change which reproduces the first situation. In Puck's words,

> Jack shall have Jill;
> Nought shall go ill;
> The man shall have his mare again and all shall be well.

THE FAIRY PLOT

The transformations in the love plot are wrought by fairy magic. The materials used here were familiar to both Shakespeare and his audience. There were fairies on the stage in John Lyly's *Endymion*, for example, before *A Midsummer-Night's Dream*. Oberon, the fairy king, appears as prologue in Greene's *James IV*, a play which Shakespeare knew well. Oberon has been identified with Alberich, king of the elves and guardian of the treasure of the Nibelungs. He also appears as a character in the romance *Huon of Bordeaux*, translated by Lord Berners and read by thousands of people in Shakespeare's time. The lore of fairies blended with that of nymphs, satyrs, and mermaids in the pageantry of the day. Although the fairies form an organic part of the plot structure in that they maneuver the events of the love story, they are at the same time engaged in difficulties of their own. Their story, independent in itself—sufficiently so that it has been allegorically construed—finds a point of contact not only with the main plot, but also with the ludicrous activities of the "rude mechanicals."

THE "RUDE MECHANICALS"

In the Pyramus and Thisbe episode, Shakespeare is making fun of the rustic drama, a form which was at one time strictly religious. Now, in the hands of the artisans, it was branching out to the treatment of delicate romantic stories with the stiffness of technique which, in the traditional plays, had been in some sense venerable. This group, a sort of artisans' dramatic club, having heard of the royal desire for theatrical entertainments, meets at the home of the carpenter Peter Quince, their stage manager, to plan something worthy of the occasion. They have decided upon *The most lamentable comedy, and most cruel death of Pyramus and Thisby*, a pitiful tale in Ovid, and the worst of all possible choices. This consideration does not deter Peter Quince and his crew. Others, their betters, had presented on the public stage, plays with names almost as absurd, as, for example, Preston's "lamentable tragedy, mixed full of pleasant mirth, containing the life of Cambises, king of Persia." Much is

Mumming

to be learned from the rustic actors about the formal membership of a dramatic troupe, the nature of the current rustic drama, and the trials of a stage manager, about which last Shakespeare may have had special knowledge. Bottom expects to be cast in one of two parts, a lover or a tyrant. He prefers the role of tyrant; in fact he recites a few lines in "Ercles' vein." Hercules became with Seneca's play, *Hercules Furens*, in ancient times and in its revival in the Renaissance, a character famous for ranting on the stage. Flute is reluctant to play women's parts, because he has a beard coming; he would prefer to be a "wandering knight." One also learns about the use of masks and beards and other properties and something about the trials of rehearsal where amateur actors already showed a disposition to recite their parts, cues and all. The presentation of Lion, Moonshine, and Wall gives Shakespeare opportunity to display the literalness of the rustic mind, which insisted upon casting as actors' parts even the scenery and the stage setting.[4]

The different groups of characters in the play are discriminated by the style which appears in their lines. The rustics, of course, speak in prose. The story of the young lovers is written largely in rhyme, a sign of Shakespeare's early period. Rhyme in this case is particularly appropriate, since it prevents us from taking the lovers' scenes too seriously. The kingly actions of Theseus come out in blank verse. The fairies speak in a bright meter of their own, always rhymed, usually in lyrical lines of four trochaic feet each, although sometimes Oberon, as a royal person, shifts to five-foot unrhymed iambics.

THE TYING TOGETHER OF THE PLOTS

All of these varying interests have a meeting place in the Theseus episode, which, as has been said,

provides the outer shell for the plot proper. Hermia's fate is to be decided on Theseus' and Hippolyta's wedding day. The fairies have come hither "from the farthest steep of India" to give joy and prosperity to the nuptials, and the "hempen homespuns" will furnish merriment for the occasion. In the progress of events, however, the fairy magic controls the fortunes of the young lovers, and the rustic weaver, Bottom, becomes the punishment of Titania. Finally, when all has been righted, the young lovers join the celebrations of Theseus and Hippolyta, the rude mechanicals entertain them with a lamentable love comedy, and the fairies, having reconciled their differences, call down good fortune on the newly wedded pairs.

STAGE HISTORY

A *Midsummer-Night's Dream* evidently continued to be acted until the closing of the theaters in 1642, possibly sometimes in the form of a "droll," or clown play. Such a piece, called *The Merry Conceited Humors of Bottom the Weaver*, was published in 1661. The comedy as Shakespeare wrote it was revived when plays began again after the Restoration of Charles II, but was soon subjected to revision and alteration and practically lost to the stage. *A Midsummer-Night's Dream* was specially liable to be revamped, Garrick himself probably having done violence to the play in *The Fairies* (published in 1755). The play has always been popular, and false versions continued to hold the stage until well into the nineteenth century, when Charles Mathews (1840) and Samuel Phelps (1853) restored the original version. Phelps was famous as Bottom the Weaver.

Since the restoration of the true version *A Midsummer-Night's Dream* has been one of the most popular of Shakespeare's plays with amateurs and stock companies. When it has been put on by the greater stage managers in the greater metropolitan centers it has had the most elaborate of presentations. Such were those of Augustin Daly in 1888, of F. R. Benson in 1889, of Beerbohm Tree in 1900, and of Granville-Barker in 1914. All of these, however,

Morris dancers

were outdone by Max Reinhardt in 1935. In his production he made use of all that modern lighting, costume, and scenery could do to make of the play a romantic spectacle, in which it almost passed over from the realm of spoken drama into that of opera, ballet, and pantomime.

[4]For possible resemblances in style between the Pyramus and Thisbe play and Thomas Moffett's *The Silkworms and their Flies* (1599) see Margaret L. Farrand, "An Additional Source for *A Midsummer-Night's Dream*," *Studies in Philology*, XXVII (1930), 233-243, and Douglas Bush, "The Tedious Brief Scene of Pyramus and Thisbe," *Modern Language Notes*, XLVI (1931), 144-147.

A
Midsummer-Night's Dream

DRAMATIS PERSONAE

THESEUS, Duke of Athens.
EGEUS, father to Hermia.
LYSANDER,
DEMETRIUS, } in love with Hermia.
PHILOSTRATE, master of the revels to Theseus.

QUINCE, a carpenter.
SNUG, a joiner.
BOTTOM, a weaver.
FLUTE, a bellows-mender.
SNOUT, a tinker.
STARVELING, a tailor.

HIPPOLYTA, queen of the Amazons, betrothed
    to Theseus.
HERMIA, daughter to Egeus, in love with
    Lysander.
HELENA, in love with Demetrius.

OBERON, king of the fairies.
TITANIA, queen of the fairies.
PUCK, or Robin Goodfellow.
PEASEBLOSSOM,
COBWEB,
MOTH, } fairies.
MUSTARDSEED,
Other fairies attending their King and Queen.

Attendants on Theseus and Hippolyta.

SCENE: *Athens, and a wood near it.*

ACT I.

SCENE I. *Athens. The palace of* THESEUS.

Enter THESEUS, HIPPOLYTA, PHILOSTRATE, *and*
    Attendants.

The. Now, fair Hippolyta, our nuptial hour
Draws on apace; four happy days bring in
Another moon: but, O, methinks, how slow
This old moon wanes! she lingers my desires,
Like to a step-dame or a dowager
Long withering out a young man's revenue.
    Hip. Four days will quickly steep themselves in
        night;
Four nights will quickly dream away the time;
And then the moon, like to a silver bow
New-bent in heaven, shall behold the night   10
Of our solemnities.
    The.   Go, Philostrate,

Stir up the Athenian youth to merriments;
Awake the pert and nimble spirit of mirth:
Turn melancholy forth to funerals;
The pale companion is not for our pomp.
                            [*Exit Philostrate.*
Hippolyta, I woo'd thee with my sword,
And won thy love, doing thee injuries;
But I will wed thee in another key,
With pomp, with triumph and with revelling.

    Enter EGEUS, HERMIA, LYSANDER, *and* DEMETRIUS.

    Ege. Happy be Theseus, our renowned duke!   20
    The. Thanks, good Egeus: what's the news with
        thee?
    Ege. Full of vexation come I, with complaint
Against my child, my daughter Hermia.
Stand forth, Demetrius. My noble lord,
This man hath my consent to marry her.
Stand forth, Lysander: and, my gracious duke,
This man hath bewitch'd the bosom of my child:
Thou, thou, Lysander, thou hast given her rhymes
And interchanged love-tokens with my child:
Thou hast by moonlight at her window sung   30
With feigning voice verses of feigning love,
And stolen the impression of her fantasy
With bracelets of thy hair, rings, gawds, conceits,
Knacks, trifles, nosegays, sweetmeats, messengers
Of strong prevailment in unharden'd youth:
With cunning hast thou filch'd my daughter's heart,
Turn'd her obedience, which is due to me,
To stubborn harshness: and, my gracious duke,
Be it so she will not here before your grace
Consent to marry with Demetrius,   40
I beg the ancient privilege of Athens,
As she is mine, I may dispose of her:
Which shall be either to this gentleman
Or to her death, according to our law
Immediately provided in that case.
    The. What say you, Hermia? be advised, fair maid:
To you your father should be as a god;
One that composed your beauties, yea, and one
To whom you are but as a form in wax
By him imprinted and within his power   50
To leave the figure or disfigure it.
Demetrius is a worthy gentleman.
    Her. So is Lysander.
    The.   In himself he is;
But in this kind, wanting your father's voice,
The other must be held the worthier.
    Her. I would my father look'd but with my eyes.
    The. Rather your eyes must with his judgement
        look.
    Her. I do entreat your grace to pardon me.
I know not by what power I am made bold,
Nor how it may concern my modesty,   60
In such a presence here to plead my thoughts;
But I beseech your grace that I may know
The worst that may befall me in this case,

ACT I. SCENE I. **5. step-dame,** stepmother. **dowager,** widow with a jointure or dower. **13. pert,** lively, brisk. **19. triumph,** public festivity. **27. bosom,** here thought of as the seat of the passions. **32. And . . . fantasy,** made her fall in love with you (imprinting your image on her fancy) by dishonest means; see *fantasy* in glossary. **33. gawds,** playthings. **34. Knacks,** knickknacks. **35. strong prevailment,** superior influence. **45. Immediately,** expressly. **51. disfigure,** obliterate. **54. kind,** respect; see glossary. **voice,** authority, approval. **60. concern,** befit.

If I refuse to wed Demetrius.

   The. Either to die the death or to abjure
For ever the society of men.
Therefore, fair Hermia, question your desires;
Know of your youth, examine well your blood,
Whether, if you yield not to your father's choice,
You can endure the livery of a nun,   70
For aye to be in shady cloister mew'd,
To live a barren sister all your life,
Chanting faint hymns to the cold fruitless moon.
Thrice-blessed they that master so their blood,
To undergo such maiden pilgrimage;
But earthlier happy is the rose distill'd,
Than that which withering on the virgin thorn
Grows, lives and dies in single blessedness.

   Her. So will I grow, so live, so die, my lord,
Ere I will yield my virgin patent up   80
Unto his lordship, whose unwished yoke
My soul consents not to give sovereignty.

   The. Take time to pause; and, by the next new
      moon—
The sealing-day betwixt my love and me,
For everlasting bond of fellowship—
Upon that day either prepare to die
For disobedience to your father's will,
Or else to wed Demetrius, as he would;
Or on Diana's altar to protest
For aye austerity and single life.   90

   Dem. Relent, sweet Hermia: and, Lysander, yield
Thy crazed title to my certain right.

   Lys. You have her father's love, Demetrius;
Let me have Hermia's: do you marry him.

   Ege. Scornful Lysander! true, he hath my love,
And what is mine my love shall render him.
And she is mine, and all my right of her
I do estate unto Demetrius.

   Lys. I am, my lord, as well derived as he,
As well possess'd; my love is more than his;   100
My fortunes every way as fairly rank'd,
If not with vantage, as Demetrius';
And, which is more than all these boasts can be,
I am beloved of beauteous Hermia;
Why should not I then prosecute my right?
Demetrius, I'll avouch it to his head,
Made love to Nedar's daughter, Helena,
And won her soul; and she, sweet lady, dotes,
Devoutly dotes, dotes in idolatry,
Upon this spotted and inconstant man.   110

   The. I must confess that I have heard so much,
And with Demetrius thought to have spoke thereof;
But, being over-full of self-affairs,
My mind did lose it. But, Demetrius, come;
And come, Egeus; you shall go with me,
I have some private schooling for you both.
For you, fair Hermia, look you arm yourself
To fit your fancies to your father's will;
Or else the law of Athens yields you up—
Which by no means we may extenuate—   120

To death, or to a vow of single life.
Come, my Hippolyta: what cheer, my love?
Demetrius and Egeus, go along:
I must employ you in some business
Against our nuptial and confer with you
Of something nearly that concerns yourselves.

   Ege. With duty and desire we follow you.
      [*Exeunt all but Lysander and Hermia*

   Lys. How now, my love! why is your cheek so pale?
How chance the roses there do fade so fast?

   Her. Belike for want of rain, which I could well   130
Beteem them from the tempest of my eyes.

   Lys. Ay me! for aught that I could ever read,
Could ever hear by tale or history,
The course of true love never did run smooth;
But, either it was different in blood,—

   Her. O cross! too high to be enthrall'd to low.

   Lys. Or else misgraffed in respect of years,—

   Her. O spite! too old to be engaged to young.

   Lys. Or else it stood upon the choice of friends,—

   Her. O hell! to choose love by another's eyes.   140

   Lys. Or, if there were a sympathy in choice,
War, death, or sickness did lay siege to it,
Making it momentany as a sound,
Swift as a shadow, short as any dream;
Brief as the lightning in the collied night,
That, in a spleen, unfolds both heaven and earth,
And ere a man hath power to say 'Behold!'
The jaws of darkness do devour it up:
So quick bright things come to confusion.

   Her. If then true lovers have been ever cross'd,   150
It stands as an edict in destiny:
Then let us teach our trial patience,
Because it is a customary cross,
As due to love as thoughts and dreams and sighs,
Wishes and tears, poor fancy's followers.

   Lys. A good persuasion: therefore, hear me,
      Hermia.
I have a widow aunt, a dowager
Of great revenue, and she hath no child:
From Athens is her house remote seven leagues;
And she respects me as her only son.   160
There, gentle Hermia, may I marry thee;
And to that place the sharp Athenian law
Cannot pursue us. If thou lovest me then,
Steal forth thy father's house to-morrow night;
And in the wood, a league without the town,
Where I did meet thee once with Helena,
To do observance to a morn of May,
There will I stay for thee.

   Her.   My good Lysander!
I swear to thee, by Cupid's strongest bow,
By his best arrow with the golden head,   170
By the simplicity of Venus' doves,
By that which knitteth souls and prospers loves,
And by that fire which burn'd the Carthage queen,
When the false Troyan under sail was seen,
By all the vows that ever men have broke,

69. **Whether,** one syllable, like "where." 71. **mew'd,** shut in (as used of a hawk); see glossary. 74. **blood,** supposed source of passions; see glossary. 76. **earthlier happy,** happier as respects this world. 80. **patent,** privilege. 89. **protest,** vow. 92. **crazed,** unsound. 98. **estate unto,** settle or bestow upon. 99. **derived,** descended, i.e., as well born; see glossary. 100. **As well possess'd,** possessed of as much wealth; see **possess** in glossary. 101. **fairly,** handsomely; see glossary. 102. **vantage,** superiority; see glossary. 106. **avouch . . . head,** declare it to his face. 117. **look,** take care; see glossary. 118. **fancies,** likings, tastes; see glossary. 120. **extenuate,** mitigate. 125. **Against,** by the

time of. 126. **nearly that,** that closely. 127. **duty,** reverence; see glossary. 130. **Belike,** very likely. 131. **Beteem,** grant. 137. **misgraffed,** badly matched. 143. **momentany,** lasting but a moment. 145. **collied,** blackened, darkened. 146. **spleen,** violent passion; see glossary. **unfolds,** discloses; see glossary. 149. **quick,** living; see glossary. **confusion,** ruin, destruction; see glossary. 155. **fancy's,** amorous passion's; see glossary. 160. **respects,** regards, considers; see glossary. 167. **do . . . May,** perform the ceremonies of May Day. 171-251. **By the simplicity,** etc. The style here shifts to the rhymed couplet. While Theseus was on the scene and the business was serious,

In number more than ever women spoke,
In that same place thou hast appointed me,
To-morrow truly will I meet with thee.
   Lys. Keep promise, love. Look, here comes Helena.

   Enter HELENA.

   Her. God speed fair Helena! whither away?   180
   Hel. Call you me fair? that fair again unsay.
Demetrius loves your fair: O happy fair!
Your eyes are lode-stars; and your tongue 's sweet air
More tuneable than lark to shepherd's ear,
When wheat is green, when hawthorn buds appear.
Sickness is catching: O, were favour so,
Yours would I catch, fair Hermia, ere I go;
My ear should catch your voice, my eye your eye,
My tongue should catch your tongue's sweet melody.
Were the world mine, Demetrius being bated,   190
The rest I 'ld give to be to you translated.
O, teach me how you look, and with what art
You sway the motion of Demetrius' heart.
   Her. I frown upon him, yet he loves me still.
   Hel. O that your frowns would teach my smiles such
    skill!
   Her. I give him curses, yet he gives me love.
   Hel. O that my prayers could such affection move!
   Her. The more I hate, the more he follows me.
   Hel. The more I love, the more he hateth me.
   Her. His folly, Helena, is no fault of mine.   200
   Hel. None, but your beauty: would that fault were
    mine!
   Her. Take comfort: he no more shall see my face;
Lysander and myself will fly this place.
Before the time I did Lysander see,
Seem'd Athens as a paradise to me:
O, then, what graces in my love do dwell,
That he hath turn'd a heaven unto a hell!
   Lys. Helen, to you our minds we will unfold:
To-morrow night, when Phœbe doth behold
Her silver visage in the watery glass,   210
Decking with liquid pearl the bladed grass,
A time that lovers' flights doth still conceal,
Through Athens' gates have we devised to steal.
   Her. And in the wood, where often you and I
Upon faint primrose-beds were wont to lie,
Emptying our bosoms of their counsel sweet,
There my Lysander and myself shall meet;
And thence from Athens turn away our eyes,
To seek new friends and stranger companies.
Farewell, sweet playfellow: pray thou for us;   220
And good luck grant thee thy Demetrius!
Keep word, Lysander: we must starve our sight
From lovers' food till morrow deep midnight.
   Lys. I will, my Hermia.   [*Exit Herm*.
      Helena, adieu:
As you on him, Demetrius dote on you!   [*Exit*.
   Hel. How happy some o'er other some can be!
Through Athens I am thought as fair as she.
But what of that? Demetrius thinks not so;

He will not know what all but he do know:
And as he errs, doting on Hermia's eyes,   230
So I, admiring of his qualities:
Things base and vile, holding no quantity,
Love can transpose to form and dignity:
Love looks not with the eyes, but with the mind;
And therefore is wing'd Cupid painted blind:
Nor hath Love's mind of any judgement taste;
Wings and no eyes figure unheedy haste:
And therefore is Love said to be a child,
Because in choice he is so oft beguiled.
As waggish boys in game themselves forswear,   240
So the boy Love is perjured every where:
For ere Demetrius look'd on Hermia's eyne,
He hail'd down oaths that he was only mine;
And when this hail some heat from Hermia felt,
So he dissolved, and showers of oaths did melt.
I will go tell him of fair Hermia's flight:
Then to the wood will he to-morrow night
Pursue her; and for this intelligence
If I have thanks, it is a dear expense:
But herein mean I to enrich my pain,   250
To have his sight thither and back again.   [*Exit*.

      SCENE II. *Athens*. QUINCE'S *house*.

   Enter QUINCE, SNUG, BOTTOM, FLUTE, SNOUT, *and*
    STARVELING.

   Quin. Is all our company here?
   Bot. You were best to call them generally, man by
man, according to the scrip.
   Quin. Here is the scroll of every man's name, which
is thought fit, through all Athens, to play in our interlude before the duke and the duchess, on his wedding-
day at night.
   Bot. First, good Peter Quince, say what the play
treats on, then read the names of the actors, and so
grow to a point.   10
   Quin. Marry, our play is, The most lamentable
comedy, and most cruel death of Pyramus and
Thisby.
   Bot. A very good piece of work, I assure you, and a
merry. Now, good Peter Quince, call forth your actors
by the scroll. Masters, spread yourselves.
   Quin. Answer as I call you. Nick Bottom, the
weaver.
   Bot. Ready. Name what part I am for, and proceed.
   Quin. You, Nick Bottom, are set down for Pyramus.
   Bot. What is Pyramus? a lover, or a tyrant?   24
   Quin. A lover, that kills himself most gallant for
love.
   Bot. That will ask some tears in the true perform-
ing of it: if I do it, let the audience look to their eyes;
I will move storms, I will condole in some measure.
To the rest: yet my chief humour is for a tyrant: I

---

the play was in blank verse. The transition indicates the lighter import
of the conversation of the lovers. 173, 174. **Carthage queen, false
Troyan.** According to Virgil (*Aeneid* iv.) Dido, queen of Carthage,
slew herself after desertion by the Trojan hero Aeneas. 182. **fair,**
beauty; see glossary. 183. **lode-stars,** stars of guidance. 184. **tuneable,** tuneful. 186. **favour,** appearance; see glossary. 190. **bated,**
excepted; see glossary. 193. **motion,** impulse; see glossary. 194-201.
I . . . mine. Each character speaks one line of the dialogue. This
artificiality of style is called stichomythia; it is characteristic of classical
drama. 197. **affection,** passion; see glossary. **move,** arouse; see

glossary. 209. **Phœbe,** Diana, the moon. 215. **faint,** pale. 231.
admiring of, wondering at; see glossary. 237. **figure,** are a symbol of.
242. **eyne,** eyes; old form of plural. 249. **a dear expense,** a thing which
will be costly to me; see *dear* in glossary.
   SCENE II. 2. **generally,** Bottom's blunder for "severally." 3. **scrip,**
writing, written list. 10. **grow to,** come to. 11. **Marry,** a mild oath;
see glossary. 29. **condole,** grieve; here in some blundering sense.
30. **humour,** inclination, whim; see glossary.

could play Ercles rarely, or a part to tear a cat in,
to make all split.

> The raging rocks
> And shivering shocks
> Shall break the locks
> Of prison gates;
> And Phibbus' car
> Shall shine from far
> And make and mar
> The foolish Fates. 40

This was lofty! Now name the rest of the players.
This is Ercles' vein, a tyrant's vein; a lover is more
condoling.

Quin. Francis Flute, the bellows-mender.

Flu. Here, Peter Quince.

Quin. Flute, you must take Thisby on you.

Flu. What is Thisby? a wandering knight?

Quin. It is the lady that Pyramus must love.

Flu. Nay, faith, let not me play a woman; I have a
beard coming. 50

Quin. That's all one: you shall play it in a mask,
and you may speak as small as you will.

Bot. An I may hide my face, let me play Thisby
too, I'll speak in a monstrous little voice, 'Thisne,
Thisne;' 'Ah Pyramus, my lover dear! thy Thisby
dear, and lady dear!'

Quin. No, no; you must play Pyramus: and, Flute,
you Thisby.

Bot. Well, proceed.

Quin. Robin Starveling, the tailor. 60

Star. Here, Peter Quince.

Quin. Robin Starveling, you must play Thisby's
mother. Tom Snout, the tinker.

Snout. Here, Peter Quince.

Quin. You, Pyramus' father: myself, Thisby's father.
Snug, the joiner; you, the lion's part: and, I hope,
here is a play fitted.

Snug. Have you the lion's part written? pray you,
if it be, give it me, for I am slow of study.

Quin. You may do it extempore, for it is nothing but
roaring. 71

Bot. Let me play the lion too: I will roar, that I
will do any man's heart good to hear me; I will roar,
that I will make the duke say 'Let him roar again,
let him roar again.'

Quin. An you should do it too terribly, you would
fright the duchess and the ladies, that they would
shriek; and that were enough to hang us all.

All. That would hang us, every mother's son. 80

Bot. I grant you, friends, if that you should fright
the ladies out of their wits, they would have no more
discretion but to hang us: but I will aggravate my
voice so that I will roar you as gently as any sucking
dove; I will roar you an 'twere any nightingale.

Quin. You can play no part but Pyramus; for
Pyramus is a sweet-faced man; a proper man, as one

shall see in a summer's day; a most lovely gentleman-
like man: therefore you must needs play Pyramus. 91

Bot. Well, I will undertake it. What beard were I
best to play it in?

Quin. Why, what you will.

Bot. I will discharge it in either your straw-colour
beard, your orange-tawny beard, your purple-in-
grain beard, or your French-crown-colour beard,
your perfect yellow. 98

Quin. Some of your French crowns have no hair at
all, and then you will play barefaced. But, masters,
here are your parts: and I am to entreat you, request
you and desire you, to con them by to-morrow night;
and meet me in the palace wood, a mile without the
town, by moonlight; there will we rehearse, for if we
meet in the city, we shall be dogged with company,
and our devices known. In the meantime I will
draw a bill of properties, such as our play wants. I
pray you, fail me not. 109

Bot. We will meet; and there we may rehearse most
obscenely and courageously. Take pains; be perfect:
adieu.

Quin. At the duke's oak we meet.

Bot. Enough; hold or cut bow-strings. [*Exeunt.*

ACT II.

SCENE I. *A wood near Athens.*

Enter, from opposite sides, a Fairy, *and* PUCK.

Puck. How now, spirit! whither wander you?

Fai. Over hill, over dale,
> Thorough bush, thorough brier,
> Over park, over pale,
> Thorough flood, thorough fire,
> I do wander every where,
> Swifter than the moon's sphere;
> And I serve the fairy queen,
> To dew her orbs upon the green.
> The cowslips tall her pensioners be: 10
> In their gold coats spots you see;
> Those be rubies, fairy favours,
> In those freckles live their savours:
I must go seek some dewdrops here
And hang a pearl in every cowslip's ear.
Farewell, thou lob of spirits; I'll be gone:
Our queen and all her elves come here anon.

Puck. The king doth keep his revels here to-night:
Take heed the queen come not within his sight;
For Oberon is passing fell and wrath, 20
Because that she as her attendant hath
A lovely boy, stolen from an Indian king;
She never had so sweet a changeling;
And jealous Oberon would have the child
Knight of his train, to trace the forests wild;

31. **Ercles,** Hercules, a popular character in Tudor drama. From Seneca's *Hercules Furens* had come the tradition of ranting in this part, as in the case of Herod in the mystery plays. **tear a cat,** proverbial for "rant." 32. **make all split,** proverbial for "cause a commotion." 37. **Phibbus',** Phoebus'. 47. **wandering knight,** knight-errant. 54. **An,** if; see glossary. 84. **aggravate,** Bottom's blunder for "diminish." 88. **proper,** handsome; see glossary. 95. **discharge,** perform. 97. **purple-in-grain,** very deep red. **French-crown-colour,** color of a French crown; a gold coin. 103. **con,** learn by heart. 107. **devices,** things devised for dramatic presentation. 111. **obscenely,** Bottom's blunder for "obscurely" (?) 114. **hold . . . bow-strings,** an archer's expression not definitely explained, but easy to understand; Chambers suggests, "keep your promises, or give up the play."

ACT II. SCENE I. 3. **thorough,** through; see glossary. 9. **orbs,** fairy rings. 10. **pensioners,** bodyguards of the sovereign; possible allusion to Queen Elizabeth's fifty gentlemen pensioners. 13. **savours,** sweet smells. 16. **lob,** country bumpkin. 17. **anon,** at once; see glossary. 20. **passing fell,** exceedingly angry; see *passing* in glossary. **wrath,** wrathful. 23. **changeling,** child left by fairies in exchange for one stolen; here, the stolen child. 26. **perforce,** forcibly; see glossary. 30. **square,** quarrel. 33. **shrewd,** mischievous; see glossary. 34. **Robin Goodfellow,** a mischievous household spirit of very ancient folklore; Shakespeare associates him with fairies. 35. **villagery,** villages or villagers collectively. 36. **quern,** handmill. 38. **sometime,** at times; see glossary. **barm,** yeast. 47. **gossip's bowl,** drink of gossiping women. 48. **crab,** crab apple. 50. **dewlap,** loose skin on neck.

But she perforce withholds the loved boy,
Crowns him with flowers and makes him all her joy:
And now they never meet in grove or green,
By fountain clear, or spangled starlight sheen,
But they do square, that all their elves for fear   30
Creep into acorn-cups and hide them there.

   Fai. Either I mistake your shape and making quite,
Or else you are that shrewd and knavish sprite
Call'd Robin Goodfellow: are not you he
That frights the maidens of the villagery;
Skim milk, and sometimes labour in the quern
And bootless make the breathless housewife churn;
And sometime make the drink to bear no barm;
Mislead night-wanderers, laughing at their harm?
Those that Hobgoblin call you and sweet Puck,   40
You do their work, and they shall have good luck:
Are you not he?

   Puck.   Thou speak'st aright;
I am that merry wanderer of the night.
I jest to Oberon and make him smile
When I a fat and bean-fed horse beguile,
Neighing in likeness of a filly foal:
And sometime lurk I in a gossip's bowl,
In very likeness of a roasted crab,
And when she drinks, against her lips I bob
And on her wither'd dewlap pour the ale.   50
The wisest aunt, telling the saddest tale,
Sometime for three-foot stool mistaketh me;
Then slip I from her bum, down topples she,
And 'tailor' cries, and falls into a cough,
And then the whole quire hold their hips and laugh,
And waxen in their mirth and neeze and swear
A merrier hour was never wasted there.
But, room, fairy! here comes Oberon.

   Fai. And here my mistress. Would that he were
     gone!

   Enter, from one side, OBERON, *with his train; from the
    other,* TITANIA, *with hers.*

   Obe. Ill met by moonlight, proud Titania.   60
   Tita. What, jealous Oberon! Fairies, skip hence:
I have forsworn his bed and company.

   Obe. Tarry, rash wanton: am not I thy lord?
   Tita. Then I must be thy lady: but I know
When thou hast stolen away from fairy land,
And in the shape of Corin sat all day,
Playing on pipes of corn and versing love
To amorous Phillida. Why art thou here,
Come from the farthest steep of India?
But that, forsooth, the bouncing Amazon,   70
Your buskin'd mistress and your warrior love,
To Theseus must be wedded, and you come
To give their bed joy and prosperity.

   Obe. How canst thou thus for shame, Titania,
Glance at my credit with Hippolyta,
Knowing I know thy love to Theseus?

Didst thou not lead him through the glimmering
    night
From Perigenia, whom he ravished?
And make him with fair Ægle break his faith,
With Ariadne and Antiopa?   80
   Tita. These are the forgeries of jealousy:
And never, since the middle summer's spring,
Met we on hill, in dale, forest or mead,
By paved fountain or by rushy brook,
Or in the beached margent of the sea,
To dance our ringlets to the whistling wind,
But with thy brawls thou hast disturb'd our sport.
Therefore the winds, piping to us in vain,
As in revenge, have suck'd up from the sea
Contagious fogs; which falling in the land   90
Have every pelting river made so proud
That they have overborne their continents:
The ox hath therefore stretch'd his yoke in vain,
The ploughman lost his sweat, and the green corn
Hath rotted ere his youth attain'd a beard;
The fold stands empty in the drowned field,
And crows are fatted with the murrion flock;
The nine men's morris is fill'd up with mud,
And the quaint mazes in the wanton green
For lack of tread are undistinguishable: 100
The human mortals want their winter here;
No night is now with hymn or carol blest:
Therefore the moon, the governess of floods,
Pale in her anger, washes all the air,
That rheumatic diseases do abound:
And thorough this distemperature we see
The seasons alter: hoary-headed frosts
Fall in the fresh lap of the crimson rose,
And on old Hiems' thin and icy crown
An odorous chaplet of sweet summer buds   110
Is, as in mockery, set: the spring, the summer,
The childing autumn, angry winter, change
Their wonted liveries, and the mazed world,
By their increase, now knows not which is which:
And this same progeny of evils comes
From our debate, from our dissension;
We are their parents and original.

   Obe. Do you amend it then; it lies in you:
Why should Titania cross her Oberon?
I do but beg a little changeling boy,   120
To be my henchman.

   Tita.   Set your heart at rest:
The fairy land buys not the child of me.
His mother was a votaress of my order:
And, in the spiced Indian air, by night,
Full often hath she gossip'd by my side,
And sat with me on Neptune's yellow sands,
Marking the embarked traders on the flood,
When we have laugh'd to see the sails conceive
And grow big-bellied with the wanton wind;
Which she, with pretty and with swimming gait   130

51. **aunt,** old woman.   54. **'tailor' cries,** allusion obscure; *NED* suggests that *tailor* (corruption of *tailard*), means "one with a tail."   56. **neeze,** sneeze. 66, 68. **Corin, Phillida,** names of pastoral lovers. 67. **pipes of corn,** tubular wind instruments made of straw. 69. **steep,** mountain range; so F; Globe, following Q_1: *steppe*. 71. **buskin'd,** shod with half boots. 75. **Glance at,** hit at, reflect upon. 78. **Perigenia,** Perigouna (Grant White), daughter of the robber Sinnis; a story from Plutarch. 79. **Ægle,** a nymph beloved by Theseus, for whom he deserted Ariadne; QF: *Eagles,* corrected by Rowe; form should be *Aegles* as in Plutarch's *Life of Theseus,* from which Shakespeare took the names in this passage. 80. **Ariadne,** daughter of Minos, king of Crete; by her aid Theseus slew the Minotaur and escaped from the labyrinth. **Antiopa,** queen of the Amazons and wife of Theseus, elsewhere called

Hippolyta. 82. **middle summer's spring,** beginning of midsummer. 85. **in,** on. **margent,** edge, border. 86. **ringlets.** See *orbs* above, line 9. 91. **pelting,** paltry. 92. **continents,** i.e., banks that contain them; see glossary. 97. **murrion,** murrain (plague); here, diseased. 98. **nine men's morris,** rustic game played on a board or on squares laid out on the village green with nine pebbles or pegs. 99. **quaint,** ingeniously wrought; see glossary. **mazes,** figures marked out on the village green for sports. **wanton,** luxuriant or sportive. 101. **want,** lack; see glossary. 106. **distemperature,** ill humor; also, bad weather. 109. **Hiems'.** Hiems is the god of winter. 112. **childing,** fruitful. 113. **mazed,** bewildered. 117. **original,** origin. 121. **henchman,** attendant, page.

Following,—her womb then rich with my young
    squire,—
Would imitate, and sail upon the land,
To fetch me trifles, and return again,
As from a voyage, rich with merchandise.
But she, being mortal, of that boy did die;
And for her sake do I rear up her boy,
And for her sake I will not part with him.
    Obe. How long within this wood intend you stay?
    Tita. Perchance till after Theseus' wedding-day.
If you will patiently dance in our round   140
And see our moonlight revels, go with us;
If not, shun me, and I will spare your haunts.
    Obe. Give me that boy, and I will go with thee.
    Tita. Not for thy fairy kingdom. Fairies, away!
We shall chide downright, if I longer stay.
                    [*Exit Titania with her train.*
    Obe. Well, go thy way: thou shalt not from this
    grove
Till I torment thee for this injury.
My gentle Puck, come hither. Thou rememberest
Since once I sat upon a promontory,
And heard a mermaid on a dolphin's back   150
Uttering such dulcet and harmonious breath
That the rude sea grew civil at her song
And certain stars shot madly from their spheres,
To hear the sea-maid's music.
    Puck   I remember.
    Obe. That very time I saw, but thou couldst not,
Flying between the cold moon and the earth,
Cupid all arm'd: a certain aim he took
At a fair vestal throned by the west,
And loosed his love-shaft smartly from his bow,
As it should pierce a hundred thousand hearts;   160
But I might see young Cupid's fiery shaft
Quench'd in the chaste beams of the watery moon,
And the imperial votaress passed on,
In maiden meditation, fancy-free.
Yet mark'd I where the bolt of Cupid fell:
It fell upon a little western flower,
Before milk-white, now purple with love's wound,
And maidens call it love-in-idleness.
Fetch me that flower; the herb I shew'd thee once:
The juice of it on sleeping eye-lids laid   170
Will make or man or woman madly dote
Upon the next live creature that it sees.
Fetch me this herb; and be thou here again
Ere the leviathan can swim a league.
    Puck. I'll put a girdle round about the earth
In forty minutes.   [*Exit.*
    Obe.   Having once this juice,
I'll watch Titania when she is asleep,
And drop the liquor of it in her eyes.
The next thing then she waking looks upon,
Be it on lion, bear, or wolf, or bull,   180
On meddling monkey, or on busy ape,
She shall pursue it with the soul of love:
And ere I take this charm from off her sight,
As I can take it with another herb,
I'll make her render up her page to me.
But who comes here? I am invisible;

And I will overhear their conference.

Enter DEMETRIUS, HELENA *following him.*

    Dem. I love thee not, therefore pursue me not.
Where is Lysander and fair Hermia?
The one I'll slay, the other slayeth me.   190
Thou told'st me they were stolen unto this wood;
And here am I, and wode within this wood,
Because I cannot meet my Hermia.
Hence, get thee gone, and follow me no more.
    Hel. You draw me, you hard-hearted adamant;
But yet you draw not iron, for my heart
Is true as steel: leave you your power to draw,
And I shall have no power to follow you.
    Dem. Do I entice you? do I speak you fair?
Or, rather, do I not in plainest truth   200
Tell you, I do not, nor I cannot love you?
    Hel. And even for that do I love you the more.
I am your spaniel; and, Demetrius,
The more you beat me, I will fawn on you:
Use me but as your spaniel, spurn me, strike me,
Neglect me, lose me; only give me leave,
Unworthy as I am, to follow you.
What worser place can I beg in your love,—
And yet a place of high respect with me,—
Than to be used as you use your dog?   210
    Dem. Tempt not too much the hatred of my spirit,
For I am sick when I do look on thee.
    Hel. And I am sick when I look not on you.
    Dem. You do impeach your modesty too much,
To leave the city and commit yourself
Into the hands of one that loves you not;
To trust the opportunity of night
And the ill counsel of a desert place
With the rich worth of your virginity.
    Hel. Your virtue is my privilege: for that   220
It is not night when I do see your face,
Therefore I think I am not in the night;
Nor doth this wood lack worlds of company,
For you in my respect are all the world:
Then how can it be said I am alone,
When all the world is here to look on me?
    Dem. I'll run from thee and hide me in the brakes,
And leave thee to the mercy of wild beasts.
    Hel. The wildest hath not such a heart as you.
Run when you will, the story shall be changed: 230
Apollo flies, and Daphne holds the chase;
The dove pursues the griffin; the mild hind
Makes speed to catch the tiger; bootless speed,
When cowardice pursues and valour flies.
    Dem. I will not stay thy questions; let me go:
Or, if thou follow me, do not believe
But I shall do thee mischief in the wood.
    Hel. Ay, in the temple, in the town, the field,
You do me mischief. Fie, Demetrius!
Your wrongs do set a scandal on my sex: 240
We cannot fight for love, as men may do;
We should be woo'd and were not made to woo.
                    [*Exit Dem.*
I'll follow thee and make a heaven of hell,
To die upon the hand I love so well.   [*Exit.*

148-168. **Thou . . . love-in-idleness.** This famous passage contains an
allusion to Queen Elizabeth and probably to some entertainment in
her honor at Kenilworth in 1575, or more probably at Elvetham in
1591; see Introduction. 151. **breath,** voice, notes. 157. **all,** fully.
161. **might,** could; see glossary. 168. **love-in-idleness,** pansy, heartsease. 176. **forty,** used indefinitely. 192. **wode,** mad; usual form,
wood. 195. **adamant,** very hard stone; here lodestone. 197. **leave,**
give up. 199. **fair,** courteously; see glossary. 220. **virtue,** goodness,
sense of honor; see glossary. **privilege,** safeguard. **for that,** because;
see glossary. 224. **in my respect,** as far as I am concerned; see *respect*
in glossary. 231. **Apollo . . . chase,** allusion to the story of Apollo's
pursuit of Daphne; here Daphne *holds the chase,* or pursues, instead of
Apollo. 232. **griffin,** a fabulous monster with the head of an eagle and
the body of a lion. **hind,** female of the red deer. 235. **stay,** wait for;

Obe. Fare thee well, nymph: ere he do leave this
    grove,
Thou shalt fly him and he shall seek thy love.

           Re-enter PUCK.

Hast thou the flower there? Welcome, wanderer.
    Puck. Ay, there it is.
    Obe.   I pray thee, give it me.
I know a bank where the wild thyme blows,
Where oxlips and the nodding violet grows,   250
†Quite over-canopied with luscious woodbine,
With sweet musk-roses and with eglantine:
There sleeps Titania sometime of the night,
Lull'd in these flowers with dances and delight;
And there the snake throws her enamell'd skin,
Weed wide enough to wrap a fairy in:
And with the juice of this I'll streak her eyes,
And make her full of hateful fantasies.
Take thou some of it, and seek through this grove:
A sweet Athenian lady is in love   260
With a disdainful youth: anoint his eyes;
But do it when the next thing he espies
May be the lady: thou shalt know the man
By the Athenian garments he hath on.
Effect it with some care that he may prove
More fond on her than she upon her love:
And look thou meet me ere the first cock crow.
    Puck. Fear not, my lord, your servant shall do so.
                        [*Exeunt.*

    SCENE II. *Another part of the wood.*

Enter TITANIA, *with her train.*

    Tita. Come, now a roundel and a fairy song;
Then, for the third part of a minute, hence;
Some to kill cankers in the musk-rose buds,
Some war with rere-mice for their leathern wings,
To make my small elves coats, and some keep back
The clamorous owl that nightly hoots and wonders
At our quaint spirits. Sing me now asleep;
Then to your offices and let me rest.

          The Fairies sing.

You spotted snakes with double tongue,
    Thorny hedgehogs, be not seen;   10
Newts and blind-worms, do no wrong,
    Come not near our fairy queen.
      Philomel, with melody
      Sing in our sweet lullaby;
Lulla, lulla, lullaby, lulla, lulla, lullaby:
      Never harm,
      Nor spell nor charm,
    Come our lovely lady nigh;
    So, good night, with lullaby.
Weaving spiders, come not here;   20

    Hence, you long-legg'd spinners, hence!
    Beetles black, approach not near;
      Worm nor snail, do no offence.
      Philomel, with melody, &c.

A Fairy. Hence, away! now all is well:
    One aloof stand sentinel.
          [*Exeunt Fairies. Titania sleeps.*

Enter OBERON, *and squeezes the flower on Titania's
    eyelids.*

    Obe. What thou seest when thou dost wake,
    Do it for thy true-love take,
    Love and languish for his sake:
    Be it ounce, or cat, or bear,   30
    Pard, or boar with bristled hair,
    In thy eye that shall appear
    When thou wakest, it is thy dear:
    Wake when some vile thing is near.   [*Exit.*

Enter LYSANDER *and* HERMIA.

    Lys. Fair love, you faint with wandering in the wood;
    And to speak troth, I have forgot our way:
We'll rest us, Hermia, if you think it good,
    And tarry for the comfort of the day.
    Her. Be it so, Lysander: find you out a bed;
For I upon this bank will rest my head.   40
    Lys. One turf shall serve as pillow for us both;
One heart, one bed, two bosoms and one troth.
    Her. Nay, good Lysander; for my sake, my dear,
Lie further off yet, do not lie so near.
    Lys. O, take the sense, sweet, of my innocence!
Love takes the meaning in love's conference.
I mean, that my heart unto yours is knit
So that but one heart we can make of it;
Two bosoms interchained with an oath;
So then two bosoms and a single troth.   50
Then by your side no bed-room me deny;
For lying so, Hermia, I do not lie.
    Her. Lysander riddles very prettily:
Now much beshrew my manners and my pride,
If Hermia meant to say Lysander lied.
But, gentle friend, for love and courtesy
Lie further off; in human modesty,
Such separation as may well be said
Becomes a virtuous bachelor and a maid,
So far be distant; and, good night, sweet friend: 60
Thy love ne'er alter till thy sweet life end!
    Lys. Amen, amen, to that fair prayer, say I;
And then end life when I end loyalty!
Here is my bed: sleep give thee all his rest!
    Her. With half that wish the wisher's eyes be press'd!
                        [*They sleep.*

Enter PUCK.

    Puck. Through the forest have I gone,
    But Athenian found I none,
    On whose eyes I might approve
    This flower's force in stirring love.
    Night and silence.—Who is here?   70
    Weeds of Athens he doth wear:
    This is he, my master said,
    Despised the Athenian maid;
    And here the maiden, sleeping sound,
    On the dank and dirty ground.
    Pretty soul! she durst not lie

Near this lack-love, this kill-courtesy.
Churl, upon thy eyes I throw
All the power this charm doth owe.
When thou wakest, let love forbid 80
Sleep his seat on thy eyelid:
So awake when I am gone;
For I must now to Oberon. [Exit.

Enter DEMETRIUS *and* HELENA, *running.*

Hel. Stay, though thou kill me, sweet Demetrius.
Dem. I charge thee, hence, and do not haunt me
thus.
Hel. O, wilt thou darkling leave me? do not so.
Dem. Stay, on thy peril: I alone will go. [Exit.
Hel. O, I am out of breath in this fond chase!
The more my prayer, the lesser is my grace.
Happy is Hermia, wheresoe'er she lies; 90
For she hath blessed and attractive eyes.
How came her eyes so bright? Not with salt tears:
If so, my eyes are oftener wash'd than hers.
No, no, I am as ugly as a bear;
For beasts that meet me run away for fear:
Therefore no marvel though Demetrius
Do, as a monster, fly my presence thus.
What wicked and dissembling glass of mine
Made me compare with Hermia's sphery eyne?
But who is here? Lysander! on the ground! 100
Dead? or asleep? I see no blood, no wound.
Lysander, if you live, good sir, awake.
Lys. [*Awaking*] And run through fire I will for
thy sweet sake.
Transparent Helena! Nature shows art,
That through thy bosom makes me see thy heart.
Where is Demetrius? O, how fit a word
Is that vile name to perish on my sword!
Hel. Do not say so, Lysander; say not so.
What though he love your Hermia? Lord, what
though?
Yet Hermia still loves you: then be content. 110
Lys. Content with Hermia! No; I do repent
The tedious minutes I with her have spent.
Not Hermia but Helena I love:
Who will not change a raven for a dove?
The will of man is by his reason sway'd;
And reason says you are the worthier maid.
Things growing are not ripe until their season:
So I, being young, till now ripe not to reason;
And touching now the point of human skill,
Reason becomes the marshal to my will 120
And leads me to your eyes, where I o'erlook
Love's stories written in love's richest book.
Hel. Wherefore was I to this keen mockery born?
When at your hands did I deserve this scorn?
Is 't not enough, is 't not enough, young man,
That I did never, no, nor never can,
Deserve a sweet look from Demetrius' eye,
But you must flout my insufficiency?
Good troth, you do me wrong, good sooth, you do,
In such disdainful manner me to woo. 130
But fare you well: perforce I must confess

I thought you lord of more true gentleness.
O, that a lady, of one man refused,
Should of another therefore be abused! [Exit.
Lys. She sees not Hermia. Hermia, sleep thou there:
And never mayst thou come Lysander near!
For as a surfeit of the sweetest things
The deepest loathing to the stomach brings,
Or as the heresies that men do leave
Are hated most of those they did deceive, 140
So thou, my surfeit and my heresy,
Of all be hated, but the most of me!
And, all my powers, address your love and might
To honour Helen and to be her knight! [Exit.
Her. [*Awaking*] Help me, Lysander, help me! do thy
best
To pluck this crawling serpent from my breast!
Ay me, for pity! what a dream was here!
Lysander, look how I do quake with fear:
Methought a serpent eat my heart away,
And you sat smiling at his cruel prey. 150
Lysander! what, removed? Lysander! lord!
What, out of hearing? gone? no sound, no word?
Alack, where are you? speak, an if you hear;
Speak, of all loves! I swoon almost with fear.
No? then I well perceive you are not nigh:
Either death or you I'll find immediately. [Exit.

ACT III.

SCENE I. *The wood. Titania lying asleep.*

Enter QUINCE, SNUG, BOTTOM, FLUTE, SNOUT, *and*
STARVELING.

Bot. Are we all met?
Quin. Pat, pat; and here 's a marvellous convenient
place for our rehearsal. This green plot shall be our
stage, this hawthorn-brake our tiring-house; and we
will do it in action as we will do it before the duke.
Bot. Peter Quince,—
Quin. What sayest thou, bully Bottom?
Bot. There are things in this comedy of Pyramus
and Thisby that will never please. First, Pyramus
must draw a sword to kill himself; which the ladies
cannot abide. How answer you that? 13
Snout. By 'r lakin, a parlous fear.
Star. I believe we must leave the killing out, when
all is done.
Bot. Not a whit: I have a device to make all well.
Write me a prologue; and let the prologue seem to
say, we will do no harm with our swords and that
Pyramus is not killed indeed; and, for the more better
assurance, tell them that I Pyramus am not Pyramus,
but Bottom the weaver: this will put them out of fear.
Quin. Well, we will have such a prologue; and it
shall be written in eight and six. 25
Bot. No, make it two more; let it be written in eight
and eight.
Snout. Will not the ladies be afeard of the lion?
Star. I fear it, I promise you.

79. **owe**, own; see glossary. 86. **darkling**, in the dark. 89. **grace**,
favor I obtain; see glossary. 90. **lies**, dwells; see glossary. 99. **sphery
eyne**, starlike eyes. 103. **run through fire**, proverbial for any hard
task. 118. **ripe**, usually understood as a verb in this passage meaning "grow ripe." 133. **of**, by; see glossary. 134. **abused**, maltreated;
see glossary. 150. **prey**, act of preying upon. 154. **of all loves**, for
all love's sake.
ACT III. SCENE I. 5. **tiring-house**, dressing room. 8. **bully**, term

of companionship. 14. **By 'r lakin**, by our ladykin, i.e., the Virgin
Mary. **parlous**, perilous. 25. **eight and six**, alternate lines of eight
and six syllables, ballad measure. 32. **lion among ladies.** Malone
called attention to a pamphlet (*Somers' Tracts*, ii, 179) which tells
how at the christening of Prince Henry, eldest son of King James I,
then James VI of Scotland, a "blackmoor" instead of a lion drew the
triumphal chariot, since the lion's presence might have "brought some
fear to the nearest." This circumstance has been used in the interpre-

Bot. Masters, you ought to consider with yourselves: to bring in—God shield us!—a lion among ladies, is a most dreadful thing; for there is not a more fearful wild-fowl than your lion living; and we ought to look to 't.

Snout. Therefore another prologue must tell he is not a lion. 36

Bot. Nay, you must name his name, and half his face must be seen through the lion's neck: and he himself must speak through, saying thus, or to the same defect,—'Ladies,'—or 'Fair ladies,—I would wish you,'—or 'I would request you,'—or 'I would entreat you,—not to fear, not to tremble: my life for yours. If you think I come hither as a lion, it were pity of my life: no, I am no such thing; I am a man as other men are;' and there indeed let him name his name, and tell them plainly he is Snug the joiner.

Quin. Well, it shall be so. But there is two hard things; that is, to bring the moonlight into a chamber; for, you know, Pyramus and Thisby meet by moonlight. 51

Snout. Doth the moon shine that night we play our play?

Bot. A calendar, a calendar! look in the almanac; find out moonshine, find out moonshine.

Quin. Yes, it doth shine that night.

Bot. Why, then may you leave a casement of the great chamber window, where we play, open, and the moon may shine in at the casement. 59

Quin. Ay; or else one must come in with a bush of thorns and a lanthorn, and say he comes to disfigure, or to present, the person of Moonshine. Then, there is another thing: we must have a wall in the great chamber; for Pyramus and Thisby, says the story, did talk through the chink of a wall.

Snout. You can never bring in a wall. What say you, Bottom? 68

Bot. Some man or other must present Wall: and let him have some plaster, or some loam, or some rough-cast about him, to signify wall; and let him hold his fingers thus, and through that cranny shall Pyramus and Thisby whisper.

Quin. If that may be, then all is well. Come, sit down, every mother's son, and rehearse your parts. Pyramus, you begin: when you have spoken your speech, enter into that brake: and so every one according to his cue.

Enter PUCK *behind.*

Puck. What hempen home-spuns have we
    swaggering here,
So near the cradle of the fairy queen? 80
What, a play toward! I'll be an auditor;
An actor too perhaps, if I see cause.

Quin. Speak, Pyramus. Thisby, stand forth.

Bot. Thisby, the flowers of odious savours sweet,—

Quin. Odours, odours.

Bot. —— odours savours sweet:
So hath thy breath, my dearest Thisby dear.
But hark, a voice! stay thou but here awhile,

And by and by I will to thee appear.   [*Exit.*

Puck. A stranger Pyramus than e'er played here. 90
                                 [*Exit.*

Flu. Must I speak now?

Quin. Ay, marry, must you; for you must understand he goes but to see a noise that he heard, and is to come again.

Flu. Most radiant Pyramus, most lily-white of hue,
  Of colour like the red rose on triumphant brier,
Most brisky juvenal and eke most lovely Jew,
  As true as truest horse that yet would never tire. 98
I'll meet thee, Pyramus, at Ninny's tomb.

Quin. 'Ninus' tomb,' man: why, you must not speak that yet; that you answer to Pyramus: you speak all your part at once, cues and all. Pyramus enter: your cue is past; it is, 'never tire.'

Flu. O,—As true as truest horse, that yet would
    never tire.

Re-enter PUCK, *and* BOTTOM *with an ass's head.*

Bot. If I were fair, Thisby, I were only thine.

Quin. O monstrous! O strange! we are haunted. Pray, masters! fly, masters! Help!
    [*Exeunt Quince, Snug, Flute, Snout, and Starveling.*

Puck. I'll follow you, I'll lead you about a round,
  Through bog, through bush, through brake,
    through brier: 110
Sometime a horse I'll be, sometime a hound,
  A hog, a headless bear, sometime a fire;
And neigh, and bark, and grunt, and roar, and burn,
Like horse, hound, hog, bear, fire, at every turn. [*Exit.*

Bot. Why do they run away? this is a knavery of them to make me afeard.

Re-enter SNOUT.

Snout. O Bottom, thou art changed! what do I see on thee?

Bot. What do you see? you see an ass-head of your own, do you?   [*Exit Snout.*

Re-enter QUINCE.

Quin. Bless thee, Bottom! bless thee! thou art translated.   [*Exit.* 122

Bot. I see their knavery: this is to make an ass of me; to fright me, if they could. But I will not stir from this place, do what they can: I will walk up and down here, and I will sing, that they shall hear I am not afraid.   [*Sings.*
    The ousel cock so black of hue,
      With orange-tawny bill,
    The throstle with his note so true,   130
      The wren with little quill,—

Tita. [*Awaking*] What angel wakes me from my
    flowery bed?

Bot. [*Sings*]
    The finch, the sparrow and the lark,
      The plain-song cuckoo gray,
    Whose note full many a man doth mark,
      And dares not answer nay;—
for, indeed, who would set his wit to so foolish a bird?

tation of the allegory; see Introduction. 33. **fearful,** fear-inspiring; see glossary. 40. **defect,** Bottom's blunder for "effect." 44. **pity of my life,** sad thing for me. 62. **disfigure,** blunder for "prefigure." **present,** represent; see glossary. 71. **rough-cast,** coarse plaster for the outside of buildings. 81. **toward,** about to take place; see glossary. 97. **brisky juvenal,** brisk juvenile or youth. **Jew,** probably an absurd repetition of the first syllable of *juvenal.* 100. **'Ninus,'** mythical founder of Babylon, at which place the scene of the story of Pyramus

and Thisbe is laid. 106. *Stage Direction:* **Re-enter . . . head.** F has *Enter Pyramus with the Asse head,* a form of statement which indicates one particular stage property. 122. **translated,** transformed. 128. **ousel,** blackbird. 134. **plain-song,** melody without variations; here used as an adjective.

who would give a bird the lie, though he cry 'cuckoo'
never so?

Tita. I pray thee, gentle mortal, sing again: 140
Mine ear is much enamour'd of thy note;
So is mine eye enthralled to thy shape;
And thy fair virtue's force perforce doth move me
On the first view to say, to swear, I love thee.

Bot. Methinks, mistress, you should have little
reason for that: and yet, to say the truth, reason and
love keep little company together now-a-days; the
more the pity that some honest neighbours will not
make them friends. Nay, I can gleek upon occasion. 150

Tita. Thou art as wise as thou art beautiful.

Bot. Not so, neither: but if I had wit enough to get
out of this wood, I have enough to serve mine own
turn.

Tita. Out of this wood do not desire to go:
Thou shalt remain here, whether thou wilt or no.
I am a spirit of no common rate:
The summer still doth tend upon my state;
And I do love thee: therefore, go with me;
I'll give thee fairies to attend on thee,   160
And they shall fetch thee jewels from the deep,
And sing while thou on pressed flowers dost sleep:
And I will purge thy mortal grossness so
That thou shalt like an airy spirit go.
Peaseblossom! Cobweb! Moth! and Mustardseed!

Enter PEASEBLOSSOM, COBWEB, MOTH, *and*
    MUSTARDSEED.

Peas. Ready.
Cob.   And I.
Moth.   And I.
Mus.   And I.
All.   Where shall we go?
Tita. Be kind and courteous to this gentleman;
Hop in his walks and gambol in his eyes;
Feed him with apricocks and dewberries,
With purple grapes, green figs, and mulberries;   170
The honey-bags steal from the humble-bees,
And for night-tapers crop their waxen thighs
And light them at the fiery glow-worm's eyes,
To have my love to bed and to arise;
And pluck the wings from painted butterflies
To fan the moonbeams from his sleeping eyes:
Nod to him, elves, and do him courtesies.

Peas. Hail, mortal!
Cob. Hail!
Moth. Hail!   180
Mus. Hail!

Bot. I cry your worships mercy, heartily: I beseech
your worship's name.

Cob. Cobweb.

Bot. I shall desire you of more acquaintance, good
Master Cobweb: if I cut my finger, I shall make bold
with you. Your name, honest gentleman?

Peas. Peaseblossom.   189

Bot. I pray you, commend me to Mistress Squash,
your mother, and to Master Peascod, your father.
Good Master Peaseblossom, I shall desire you of more
acquaintance too. Your name, I beseech you, sir?

Mus. Mustardseed.

Bot. Good Master Mustardseed, I know your
patience well: that same cowardly, giant-like ox-beef
hath devoured many a gentleman of your house: I
promise you your kindred hath made my eyes water
ere now. I desire your more acquaintance, good
Master Mustardseed.   201

Tita. Come wait upon him; lead him to my bower.
The moon methinks looks with a watery eye;
And when she weeps, weeps every little flower,
Lamenting some enforced chastity.
Tie up my love's tongue, bring him silently. [*Exeunt.*

SCENE II. *Another part of the wood.*

Enter OBERON.

Obe. I wonder if Titania be awaked;
Then, what it was that next came in her eye,
Which she must dote on in extremity.

Enter PUCK.

Here comes my messenger.
                  How now, mad spirit!
What night-rule now about this haunted grove?

Puck. My mistress with a monster is in love.
Near to her close and consecrated bower,
While she was in her dull and sleeping hour,
A crew of patches, rude mechanicals,
That work for bread upon Athenian stalls,   10
Were met together to rehearse a play
Intended for great Theseus' nuptial-day.
The shallowest thick-skin of that barren sort,
Who Pyramus presented, in their sport
Forsook his scene and enter'd in a brake:
When I did him at this advantage take,
An ass's nole I fixed on his head:
Anon his Thisbe must be answered,
And forth my mimic comes. When they him spy,
As wild geese that the creeping fowler eye,   20
Or russet-pated choughs, many in sort,
Rising and cawing at the gun's report,
Sever themselves and madly sweep the sky,
So, at his sight, away his fellows fly;
And, at our stamp, here o'er and o'er one falls;
He murder cries and help from Athens calls.
Their sense thus weak, lost with their fears thus strong,
Made senseless things begin to do them wrong;
For briers and thorns at their apparel snatch;
Some sleeves, some hats, from yielders all things catch.
I led them on in this distracted fear,   31
And left sweet Pyramus translated there:
When in that moment, so it came to pass,
Titania waked and straightway loved an ass.

Obe. This falls out better than I could devise.
But hast thou yet latch'd the Athenian's eyes
With the love-juice, as I did bid thee do?

Puck. I took him sleeping,—that is finish'd too,—
And the Athenian woman by his side;
That, when he waked, of force she must be eyed.   40

Enter HERMIA *and* DEMETRIUS.

Obe. Stand close : this is the same Athenian.
Puck. This is the woman, but not this the man.
Dem. O, why rebuke you him that loves you so?
Lay breath so bitter on your bitter foe.
Her. Now I but chide ; but I should use thee worse,
For thou, I fear, hast given me cause to curse.
If thou hast slain Lysander in his sleep,
Being o'er shoes in blood, plunge in the deep,
And kill me too.
The sun was not so true unto the day   50
As he to me : would he have stolen away
From sleeping Hermia? I'll believe as soon
This whole earth may be bored and that the moon
May through the centre creep and so displease
Her brother's noontide with the Antipodes.
It cannot be but thou hast murder'd him;
So should a murderer look, so dead, so grim.
Dem. So should the murder'd look, and so should I,
Pierced through the heart with your stern cruelty:
Yet you, the murderer, look as bright, as clear,   60
As yonder Venus in her glimmering sphere.
Her. What 's this to my Lysander? where is he?
Ah, good Demetrius, wilt thou give him me?
Dem. I had rather give his carcass to my hounds.
Her. Out, dog! out, cur! thou drivest me past the
    bounds
Of maiden's patience. Hast thou slain him, then?
Henceforth be never number'd among men!
O, once tell true, tell true, even for my sake!
Durst thou have look'd upon him being awake,
And hast thou kill'd him sleeping? O brave touch!   70
Could not a worm, an adder, do so much?
An adder did it; for with doubler tongue
Than thine, thou serpent, never adder stung.
Dem. You spend your passion on a misprised mood :
I am not guilty of Lysander's blood;
Nor is he dead, for aught that I can tell.
Her. I pray thee, tell me then that he is well.
Dem. An if I could, what should I get therefore?
Her. A privilege never to see me more.
And from thy hated presence part I so: 80
See me no more, whether he be dead or no.   [*Exit.*
Dem. There is no following her in this fierce vein:
Here therefore for a while I will remain.
So sorrow's heaviness doth heavier grow
For debt that bankrupt sleep doth sorrow owe;
Which now in some slight measure it will pay,
If for his tender here I make some stay.
                              [*Lies down and sleeps.*
Obe. What hast thou done? thou hast mistaken quite
And laid the love-juice on some true-love's sight:
Of thy misprision must perforce ensue   90
Some true love turn'd and not a false turn'd true.
Puck. Then fate o'er-rules, that, one man holding
    troth,
A million fail, confounding oath on oath.
Obe. About the wood go swifter than the wind,
And Helena of Athens look thou find:
All fancy-sick she is and pale of cheer,

With sighs of love, that costs the fresh blood dear:
By some illusion see thou bring her here:
I'll charm his eyes against she do appear.
Puck. I go, I go ; look how I go,   100
Swifter than arrow from the Tartar's bow.   [*Exit.*
Obe.   Flower of this purple dye,
              Hit with Cupid's archery,
              Sink in apple of his eye.
              When his love he doth espy,
              Let her shine as gloriously
              As the Venus of the sky.
              When thou wakest, if she be by,
              Beg of her for remedy.

                    Re-enter PUCK.

Puck.   Captain of our fairy band,   110
              Helena is here at hand;
              And the youth, mistook by me,
              Pleading for a lover's fee.
              Shall we their fond pageant see?
              Lord, what fools these mortals be!
Obe. Stand aside: the noise they make
              Will cause Demetrius to awake.
Puck. Then will two at once woo one;
              That must needs be sport alone;
              And those things do best please me   120
              That befal preposterously.

Enter LYSANDER *and* HELENA.

Lys. Why should you think that I should woo in
    scorn?
Scorn and derision never come in tears:
Look, when I vow, I weep; and vows so born,
  In their nativity all truth appears.
How can these things in me seem scorn to you,
Bearing the badge of faith, to prove them true?
Hel. You do advance your cunning more and more.
  When truth kills truth, O devilish-holy fray!
These vows are Hermia's: will you give her o'er?   130
  Weigh oath with oath, and you will nothing weigh:
Your vows to her and me, put in two scales,
Will even weigh, and both as light as tales.
Lys. I had no judgement when to her I swore.
Hel. Nor none, in my mind, now you give her o'er.
Lys. Demetrius loves her, and he loves not you.
Dem. [*Awaking*] O Helen, goddess, nymph,
    perfect, divine!
To what, my love, shall I compare thine eyne?
Crystal is muddy. O, how ripe in show
Thy lips, those kissing cherries, tempting grow!   140
That pure congealed white, high Taurus' snow,
Fann'd with the eastern wind, turns to a crow
When thou hold'st up thy hand: O, let me kiss
This princess of pure white, this seal of bliss!
Hel. O spite! O hell! I see you all are bent
To set against me for your merriment:
If you were civil and knew courtesy,
You would not do me thus much injury.
Can you not hate me, as I know you do,
But you must join in souls to mock me too?   150
If you were men, as men you are in show,

serpent. 74. **passion,** violent feelings; see glossary. **misprised,** mistaken. 86-87. **Which . . . stay,** i.e., if he waits until sleep "tenders" itself, he will derive some consolation for his sorrow. 90. **misprision,** mistake. 93. **confounding . . . oath,** i.e., invalidating one oath with another; see *confound* in glossary. 96. **fancy-sick,** lovesick. **cheer,** face. 97. **sighs . . . blood,** allusion to the physiological theory that each sigh cost the heart a drop of blood. 101. **Tartar's bow.** Tartars

were famed for their skill with the bow. 114. **fond pageant,** foolish exhibition; see *fond* and *pageant* in glossary. 121. **preposterously,** in inverted order. 124-125. **vows . . . appears,** i.e., vows so born appear in their nativity to be wholly true. 135. **mind,** opinion; see glossary. 141. **Taurus',** a lofty mountain range in Asia Minor. 144. **seal,** pledge, covenant.

You would not use a gentle lady so;
To vow, and swear, and superpraise my parts,
When I am sure you hate me with your hearts.
You both are rivals, and love Hermia;
And now both rivals, to mock Helena:
A trim exploit, a manly enterprise,
To conjure tears up in a poor maid's eyes
With your derision! none of noble sort
Would so offend a virgin and extort   160
A poor soul's patience, all to make you sport.
    Lys. You are unkind, Demetrius; be not so;
For you love Hermia; this you know I know:
And here, with all good will, with all my heart,
In Hermia's love I yield you up my part;
And yours of Helena to me bequeath,
Whom I do love and will do till my death.
    Hel. Never did mockers waste more idle breath.
    Dem. Lysander, keep thy Hermia; I will none:
If e'er I loved her, all that love is gone.   170
My heart to her but as guest-wise sojourn'd,
And now to Helen is it home return'd,
There to remain.
    Lys.   Helen, it is not so.
    Dem. Disparage not the faith thou dost not know,
Lest, to thy peril, thou aby it dear.
Look, where thy love comes; yonder is thy dear.

Re-enter HERMIA.

    Her. Dark night, that from the eye his function
            takes,
The ear more quick of apprehension makes;
Wherein it doth impair the seeing sense,
It pays the hearing double recompense.   180
Thou art not by mine eye, Lysander, found;
Mine ear, I thank it, brought me to thy sound.
But why unkindly didst thou leave me so?
    Lys. Why should he stay, whom love doth press
            to go?
    Her. What love could press Lysander from my side?
    Lys. Lysander's love, that would not let him bide,
Fair Helena, who more engilds the night
Than all yon fiery oes and eyes of light.
Why seek'st thou me? could not this make thee know,
The hate I bear thee made me leave thee so?   190
    Her. You speak not as you think: it cannot be.
    Hel. Lo, she is one of this confederacy!
Now I perceive they have conjoin'd all three
To fashion this false sport, in spite of me.
Injurious Hermia! most ungrateful maid!
Have you conspired, have you with these contrived
To bait me with this foul derision?
Is all the counsel that we two have shared,
The sisters' vows, the hours that we have spent,
When we have chid the hasty-footed time   200
For parting us,—O, is it all forgot?
All school-days' friendship, childhood innocence?
We, Hermia, like two artificial gods,
Have with our needles created both one flower,
Both on one sampler, sitting on one cushion,
Both warbling of one song, both in one key,
As if our hands, our sides, voices and minds,

Had been incorporate. So we grew together,
Like to a double cherry, seeming parted,
But yet an union in partition;   210
Two lovely berries moulded on one stem;
So, with two seeming bodies, but one heart;
Two of the first, like coats in heraldry,
Due but to one and crowned with one crest.
And will you rent our ancient love asunder,
To join with men in scorning your poor friend?
It is not friendly, 'tis not maidenly:
Our sex, as well as I, may chide you for it,
Though I alone do feel the injury.
    Her. I am amazed at your passionate words.   220
I scorn you not: it seems that you scorn me.
    Hel. Have you not set Lysander, as in scorn,
To follow me and praise my eyes and face?
And made your other love, Demetrius,
Who even but now did spurn me with his foot,
To call me goddess, nymph, divine and rare,
Precious, celestial? Wherefore speaks he this
To her he hates? and wherefore doth Lysander
Deny your love, so rich within his soul,
And tender me, forsooth, affection,   230
But by your setting on, by your consent?
What though I be not so in grace as you,
So hung upon with love, so fortunate,
But miserable most, to love unloved?
This you should pity rather than despise.
    Her. I understand not what you mean by this.
    Hel. Ay, do, persever, counterfeit sad looks,
Make mouths upon me when I turn my back;
Wink each at other; hold the sweet jest up:
This sport, well carried, shall be chronicled.   240
If you have any pity, grace, or manners,
You would not make me such an argument.
But fare ye well: 'tis partly my own fault;
Which death or absence soon shall remedy.
    Lys. Stay, gentle Helena; hear my excuse:
My love, my life, my soul, fair Helena!
    Hel. O excellent!
    Her.   Sweet, do not scorn her so.
    Dem. If she cannot entreat, I can compel.
    Lys. Thou canst compel no more than she entreat:
Thy threats have no more strength than her weak
            prayers.   250
Helen, I love thee; by my life, I do:
I swear by that which I will lose for thee,
To prove him false that says I love thee not.
    Dem. I say I love thee more than he can do.
    Lys. If thou say so, withdraw, and prove it too.
    Dem. Quick, come!
    Her.   Lysander, whereto tends all this?
    Lys. Away, you Ethiope!
    Dem.   †No, no; he'll . . .
Seem to break loose; take on as you would follow,
But yet come not: you are a tame man, go!
    Lys. Hang off, thou cat, thou burr! vile thing, let
            loose,   260
Or I will shake thee from me like a serpent!
    Her. Why are you grown so rude? what change is
            this?

153. **superpraise,** overpraise. **parts,** qualities. 157. **trim,** pretty;
used ironically. 169. **will none,** i.e., of her. 175. **aby,** pay for. 177.
his, its; see glossary. 188. **oes,** general word for "circles" and "orbs."
195. **Injurious,** insulting. 196. **contrived,** plotted; see glossary.
203. **artificial,** skilled in art. 208. **incorporate,** united in one body.
213. **Two of the first,** i.e., two bodies, referred to like colors in the
description of a coat-of-arms. "The first" is the color first mentioned.

237. **persever,** persevere; accented on the second syllable. **sad,**
grave, serious; see glossary. 238. **Make mouths upon,** make faces
at. 240. **carried,** managed; see glossary. 242. **argument,** subject
for a story; see glossary. 257. **No, no; he'll.** Q: *No, no: heele.* F: *No,
Sir;* text apparently corrupt. We may understand that Demetrius
first addresses Helena and breaks off, then turns to chide Lysander.
260. **Hang off,** let go. 272. **what news?** What is the matter? 274.

Sweet love,—

Lys.   Thy love! out, tawny Tartar, out!
Out, loathed medicine! hated potion, hence!

Her. Do you not jest?

Hel.   Yes, sooth; and so do you.

Lys. Demetrius, I will keep my word with thee.

Dem. I would I had your bond, for I perceive
A weak bond holds you: I'll not trust your word.

Lys. What, should I hurt her, strike her, kill her
     dead?
Although I hate her, I'll not harm her so.   270

Her. What, can you do me greater harm than hate?
Hate me! wherefore? O me! what news, my love!
Am not I Hermia? are not you Lysander?
I am as fair now as I was erewhile.
Since night you loved me; yet since night you left me:
Why, then you left me—O, the gods forbid!—
In earnest, shall I say?

Lys.   Ay, by my life;
And never did desire to see thee more.
Therefore be out of hope, of question, of doubt;
Be certain, nothing truer; 'tis no jest   280
That I do hate thee and love Helena.

Her. O me! you juggler! you cankerblossom!
You thief of love! what, have you come by night
And stolen my love's heart from him?

Hel.   Fine, i' faith!
Have you no modesty, no maiden shame,
No touch of bashfulness? What, will you tear
Impatient answers from my gentle tongue?
Fie, fie! you counterfeit, you puppet, you!

Her. Puppet? why so? ay, that way goes the game.
Now I perceive that she hath made compare   290
Between our statures; she hath urged her height;
And with her personage, her tall personage,
Her height, forsooth, she hath prevail'd with him.
And are you grown so high in his esteem,
Because I am so dwarfish and so low?
How low am I, thou painted maypole? speak;
How low am I? I am not yet so low
But that my nails can reach unto thine eyes.

Hel. I pray you, though you mock me, gentlemen,
Let her not hurt me: I was never curst;   300
I have no gift at all in shrewishness;
I am a right maid for my cowardice:
Let her not strike me. You perhaps may think,
Because she is something lower than myself,
That I can match her.

Her.   Lower! hark, again.

Hel. Good Hermia, do not be so bitter with me.
I evermore did love you, Hermia,
Did ever keep your counsels, never wrong'd you;
Save that, in love unto Demetrius,
I told him of your stealth unto this wood.   310
He follow'd you; for love I follow'd him;
But he hath chid me hence and threaten'd me
To strike me, spurn me, nay, to kill me too:
And now, so you will let me quiet go,
To Athens will I bear my folly back
And follow you no further: let me go:
You see how simple and how fond I am.

Her. Why, get you gone: who is 't that hinders you?

Hel. A foolish heart, that I leave here behind.

Her. What, with Lysander?

Hel.   With Demetrius.   320

Lys. Be not afraid; she shall not harm thee, Helena.

Dem. No, sir, she shall not, though you take her part.

Hel. O, when she 's angry, she is keen and shrewd!
She was a vixen when she went to school;
And though she be but little, she is fierce.

Her. 'Little' again! nothing but 'low' and 'little'!
Why will you suffer her to flout me thus?
Let me come to her.

Lys.   Get you gone, you dwarf;
You minimus, of hindering knot-grass made;
You bead, you acorn.

Dem.   You are too officious   330
In her behalf that scorns your services.
Let her alone: speak not of Helena;
Take not her part; for, if thou dost intend
Never so little show of love to her,
Thou shalt aby it.

Lys.   Now she holds me not;
Now follow, if thou darest, to try whose right,
Of thine or mine, is most in Helena.

Dem. Follow! nay, I'll go with thee, cheek by jole.

     [*Exeunt Lysander and Demetrius.*

Her. You, mistress, all this coil is 'long of you:
Nay, go not back.

Hel.   I will not trust you, I,   340
Nor longer stay in your curst company.
Your hands than mine are quicker for a fray,
My legs are longer though, to run away.   [*Exit.*

Her. I am amazed, and know not what to say. [*Exit.*

Obe. This is thy negligence: still thou mistakest,
Or else committ'st thy knaveries wilfully.

Puck. Believe me, king of shadows, I mistook.
Did not you tell me I should know the man
By the Athenian garments he had on?
And so far blameless proves my enterprise,   350
That I have 'nointed an Athenian's eyes;
And so far am I glad it so did sort
As this their jangling I esteem a sport.

Obe. Thou see'st these lovers seek a place to fight:
Hie therefore, Robin, overcast the night;
The starry welkin cover thou anon
With drooping fog as black as Acheron,
And lead these testy rivals so astray
As one come not within another's way.
Like to Lysander sometime frame thy tongue,   360
Then stir Demetrius up with bitter wrong;
And sometime rail thou like Demetrius;
And from each other look thou lead them thus,
Till o'er their brows death-counterfeiting sleep
With leaden legs and batty wings doth creep:
Then crush this herb into Lysander's eye;
Whose liquor hath this virtuous property,
To take from thence all error with his might,
And make his eyeballs roll with wonted sight.
When they next wake, all this derision   370
Shall seem a dream and fruitless vision,
And back to Athens shall the lovers wend,

---

erewhile, just now. 288. **puppet.** This word, *Ethiope* (l. 257), and
dwarfish (l. 295) indicate that Hermia is short and dark. 300. **curst,**
shrewish; see glossary. 302. **right,** true. 304. **something,** somewhat;
see glossary. 310. **stealth,** stealing away. 329. **minimus,** diminutive
creature. **knot-grass,** a weed (*polygonum aviculare*), an infusion of which
was thought to stunt the growth. 333. **intend,** offer, or incline to.
338. **cheek by jole,** cheek by jowl, side by side. 339. **coil,** turmoil; see

glossary. **'long of you,** on account of you; see glossary. 347. **king
of shadows.** Note the suggestion in this and other passages of a larger
aspect of Oberon's power. 352. **sort,** turn out. 356. **welkin,** sky;
see glossary. 357. **Acheron,** river of hell, which Shakespeare seems
to have thought of as a pit or lake. 359. **As,** so that; see glossary.
370. **derision,** four syllables.

With league whose date till death shall never end.
Whiles I in this affair do thee employ,
I'll to my queen and beg her Indian boy;
And then I will her charmed eye release
From monster's view, and all things shall be peace.
    Puck. My fairy lord, this must be done with haste,
For night's swift dragons cut the clouds full fast,
And yonder shines Aurora's harbinger;   380
At whose approach, ghosts, wandering here and there,
Troop home to churchyards: damned spirits all,
That in crossways and floods have burial,
Already to their wormy beds are gone;
For fear lest day should look their shames upon,
They wilfully themselves exile from light
And must for aye consort with black-brow'd night.
    Obe. But we are spirits of another sort:
I with the morning's love have oft made sport,
And, like a forester, the groves may tread,   390
Even till the eastern gate, all fiery-red,
Opening on Neptune with fair blessed beams,
Turns into yellow gold his salt green streams.
But, notwithstanding, haste; make no delay:
We may effect this business yet ere day.   [*Exit.*
    Puck. Up and down, up and down,
        I will lead them up and down:
        I am fear'd in field and town:
        Goblin, lead them up and down.
Here comes one.   400

A Midsummer-Night's Dream
ACT III : SC II

198

Re-enter LYSANDER.

Lys. Where art thou, proud Demetrius? speak thou
    now.
    Puck. Here, villain; drawn and ready. Where art
    thou?
    Lys. I will be with thee straight.
    Puck.   Follow me, then,
To plainer ground. [*Exit Lysander, as following the voice.*

Re-enter DEMETRIUS.

Dem.   Lysander! speak again:
Thou runaway, thou coward, art thou fled?
Speak! In some bush? Where dost thou hide thy head?
    Puck. Thou coward, art thou bragging to the stars,
Telling the bushes that thou look'st for wars,
And wilt not come? Come, recreant; come, thou child,
I'll whip thee with a rod: he is defiled   410
That draws a sword on thee.
    Dem.   Yea, art thou there?
    Puck. Follow my voice: we'll try no manhood here.
                                                [*Exeunt.*

Re-enter LYSANDER.

Lys. He goes before me and still dares me on:
When I come where he calls, then he is gone.
The villain is much lighter-heel'd than I:
I follow'd fast, but faster he did fly;
That fallen am I in dark uneven way,
And here will rest me. [*Lies down.*] Come, thou gentle
    day!
For if but once thou show me thy grey light,

I'll find Demetrius and revenge this spite.   [*Sleeps.* 420

Re-enter PUCK and DEMETRIUS.

    Puck. Ho, ho, ho! Coward, why comest thou not?
    Dem. Abide me, if thou darest; for well I wot
Thou runn'st before me, shifting every place,
And darest not stand, nor look me in the face.
Where art thou now?
    Puck.   Come hither: I am here.
    Dem. Nay, then, thou mock'st me. Thou shalt buy
    this dear,
If ever I thy face by daylight see:
Now, go thy way. Faintness constraineth me
To measure out my length on this cold bed.
By day's approach look to be visited.   430
                            [*Lies down and sleeps.*

Re-enter HELENA.

    Hel. O weary night, O long and tedious night,
Abate thy hours! Shine comforts from the east,
That I may back to Athens by daylight,
From these that my poor company detest:
And sleep, that sometimes shuts up sorrow's eye,
Steal me awhile from mine own company.
                            [*Lies down and sleeps.*
    Puck. Yet but three? Come one more;
        Two of both kinds makes up four.
        Here she comes, curst and sad:
        Cupid is a knavish lad,   440
        Thus to make poor females mad.

Re-enter HERMIA.

    Her. Never so weary, never so in woe,
Bedabbled with the dew and torn with briers,
I can no further crawl, no further go;
    My legs can keep no pace with my desires.
Here will I rest me till the break of day.
Heavens shield Lysander, if they mean a fray!
                            [*Lies down and sleeps.*
    Puck.   On the ground
                    Sleep sound:
                    I'll apply   450
                    To your eye,
        Gentle lover, remedy.
            [*Squeezing the juice on Lysander's eyes.*
                    When thou wakest,
                    Thou takest
                    True delight
                    In the sight
        Of thy former lady's eye:
        And the country proverb known,
        That every man should take his own,
        In your waking shall be shown: 460
                Jack shall have Jill;
                Nought shall go ill;
The man shall have his mare again, and all shall be
    well.   [*Exit.*

---

373. **date,** term of existence; see glossary.   379. **dragons,** supposed by Shakespeare to be yoked to the car of the goddess of night.   380. **Aurora's harbinger,** the morning star.   383. **crossways . . . burial.** Those who had committed suicide were buried at crossways, with a stake driven through them; those drowned, i.e., buried in floods or great waters, would be condemned to wander disconsolate for want of burial rites.   389. **morning's love,** Cephalus, a beautiful youth beloved

by Diana; sometimes taken to refer to the goddess herself.   402. **drawn,** with drawn sword.   403. **straight,** immediately; see glossary.   409. **recreant,** cowardly wretch; see glossary.   422. **wot,** know; see glossary. 432. **Abate,** lessen; see glossary.
ACT IV. SCENE I.   2. **coy,** caress.   20. **neaf,** fist.   21. **leave your courtesy,** put on your hat.   25. **Cavalery,** cavalero, gentleman; form of address.   31. **tongs . . . bones,** instruments for rustic music, the

ACT IV.

SCENE I. *The same.* LYSANDER, DEMETRIUS, HELENA, *and* HERMIA *lying asleep.*

Enter TITANIA *and* BOTTOM; PEASEBLOSSOM, COBWEB, MOTH, MUSTARDSEED, *and other Fairies attending;* OBERON *behind unseen.*

Tita. Come, sit thee down upon this flowery bed,
While I thy amiable cheeks do coy,
And stick musk-roses in thy sleek smooth head,
And kiss thy fair large ears, my gentle joy.
Bot. Where 's Peaseblossom?
Peas. Ready.
Bot. Scratch my head, Peaseblossom.
Where 's Mounsieur Cobweb?
Cob. Ready.   9
Bot. Mounsieur Cobweb, good mounsieur, get you your weapons in your hand, and kill me a red-hipped humble-bee on the top of a thistle; and, good mounsieur, bring me the honey-bag. Do not fret yourself too much in the action, mounsieur; and, good mounsieur, have a care the honey-bag break not; I would be loath to have you overflown with a honey-bag, signior. Where 's Mounsieur Mustardseed?
Mus. Ready.   19
Bot. Give me your neaf, Mounsieur Mustardseed. Pray you, leave your courtesy, good mounsieur.
Mus. What 's your will?
Bot. Nothing, good mounsieur, but to help Cavalery Cobweb to scratch. I must to the barber's, mounsieur; for methinks I am marvellous hairy about the face; and I am such a tender ass, if my hair do but tickle me, I must scratch.
Tita. What, wilt thou hear some music, my sweet love?   29
Bot. I have a reasonable good ear in music. Let 's have the tongs and the bones.
Tita. Or say, sweet love, what thou desirest to eat.
Bot. Truly, a peck of provender: I could munch your good dry oats. Methinks I have a great desire to a bottle of hay: good hay, sweet hay, hath no fellow.
Tita. I have a venturous fairy that shall seek
The squirrel's hoard, and fetch thee new nuts.
Bot. I had rather have a handful or two of dried peas. But, I pray you, let none of your people stir me: I have an exposition of sleep come upon me.   42
Tita. Sleep thou, and I will wind thee in my arms.
Fairies, be gone, and be all ways away. [*Exeunt fairies.*
So doth the woodbine the sweet honeysuckle
Gentle entwist; the female ivy so
Enrings the barky fingers of the elm.
O, how I love thee! how I dote on thee!   [*They sleep.*

Enter PUCK.

Obe. [*Advancing*] Welcome, good Robin. See'st
thou this sweet sight?
Her dotage now I do begin to pity: 50
For, meeting her of late behind the wood,
Seeking sweet favours for this hateful fool,
I did upbraid her and fall out with her;
For she his hairy temples then had rounded

With coronet of fresh and fragrant flowers;
And that same dew, which sometime on the buds
Was wont to swell like round and orient pearls,
Stood now within the pretty flowerets' eyes
Like tears that did their own disgrace bewail.
When I had at my pleasure taunted her   60
And she in mild terms begg'd my patience,
I then did ask of her her changeling child;
Which straight she gave me, and her fairy sent
To bear him to my bower in fairy land.
And now I have the boy, I will undo
This hateful imperfection of her eyes:
And, gentle Puck, take this transformed scalp
From off the head of this Athenian swain;
That, he awaking when the other do,
May all to Athens back again repair   70
And think no more of this night's accidents
But as the fierce vexation of a dream.
But first I will release the fairy queen.
    Be as thou wast wont to be;
    See as thou wast wont to see:
    Dian's bud o'er Cupid's flower
    Hath such force and blessed power.
Now, my Titania; wake you, my sweet queen.
Tita. My Oberon! what visions have I seen!
Methought I was enamour'd of an ass.   80
Obe. There lies your love.
Tita.   How came these things to pass?
O, how mine eyes do loathe his visage now!
Obe. Silence awhile. Robin, take off this head.
Titania, music call; and strike more dead
Than common sleep of all these five the sense.
Tita. Music, ho! music, such as charmeth sleep!
          [*Music, still.*
Puck. Now, when thou wakest, with thine own fool's
eyes peep.
Obe. Sound, music! Come, my queen, take hands
with me,
And rock the ground whereon these sleepers be.   90
Now thou and I are new in amity
And will to-morrow midnight solemnly
Dance in Duke Theseus' house triumphantly
And bless it to all fair prosperity:
There shall the pairs of faithful lovers be
Wedded, with Theseus, all in jollity.
Puck. Fairy king, attend, and mark:
    I do hear the morning lark.
Obe. Then, my queen, in silence sad,
    Trip we after night's shade: 100
    We the globe can compass soon,
    Swifter than the wandering moon.
Tita. Come, my lord, and in our flight
    Tell me how it came this night
    That I sleeping here was found
    With these mortals on the ground.   [*Exeunt.*
          [*Horns winded within.*

Enter THESEUS, HIPPOLYTA, EGEUS, *and train.*

The. Go, one of you, find out the forester;
For now our observation is perform'd;
And since we have the vaward of the day,

---

former described as an instrument played like the triangle; the latter are bones held between the fingers and used as clappers. 35. **bottle,** bundle (of hay). 36. **fellow,** equal; see glossary. 42. **exposition,** Bottom's word for "disposition." 44. **all ways,** in all directions. 52. **favours,** i.e., nosegays of flowers. 57. **orient pearls,** i.e., the most beautiful of all pearls, those coming from the Orient. 69. **other,** others. 76. **Dian's bud,** sometimes defined as *agnus castus* or chaste-tree, which

could preserve chastity; perhaps simply invented by Shakespeare to correspond to Cupid's flower. 85. **these five,** i.e., the four lovers and Bottom. 100. **night's,** dissyllable. 108. **observation,** i.e., *observance to a morn of May* (I, i, 167). 109. **vaward,** vanguard.

My love shall hear the music of my hounds. 110
Uncouple in the western valley; let them go:
Dispatch, I say, and find the forester. [*Exit an Attendant.*
We will, fair queen, up to the mountain's top
And mark the musical confusion
Of hounds and echo in conjunction.

Hip. I was with Hercules and Cadmus once,
When in a wood of Crete they bay'd the bear
With hounds of Sparta: never did I hear
Such gallant chiding; for, besides the groves,
The skies, the fountains, every region near 120
Seem'd all one mutual cry: I never heard
So musical a discord, such sweet thunder.

The. My hounds are bred out of the Spartan kind,
So flew'd, so sanded, and their heads are hung
With ears that sweep away the morning dew;
Crook-knee'd, and dew-lapp'd like Thessalian bulls;
Slow in pursuit, but match'd in mouth like bells,
Each under each. A cry more tuneable
Was never holla'd to, nor cheer'd with horn,
In Crete, in Sparta, nor in Thessaly: 130
Judge when you hear. But, soft! what nymphs are
    these?

Ege. My lord, this is my daughter here asleep;
And this, Lysander; this Demetrius is;
This Helena, old Nedar's Helena:
I wonder of their being here together.

The. No doubt they rose up early to observe
The rite of May, and, hearing our intent,
Came here in grace of our solemnity.
But speak, Egeus; is not this the day
That Hermia should give answer of her choice? 140

Ege. It is, my lord.

The. Go, bid the huntsmen wake them with their
    horns.

      [*Horns and shout within. Lys., Dem.,*
      Hel., and Her., wake and start up.

Good morrow, friends. Saint Valentine is past:
Begin these wood-birds but to couple now?

Lys. Pardon, my lord.

The.   I pray you all, stand up.
I know you two are rival enemies:
How comes this gentle concord in the world,
That hatred is so far from jealousy,
To sleep by hate, and fear no enmity?

Lys. My lord, I shall reply amazedly, 150
Half sleep, half waking: but as yet, I swear,
I cannot truly say how I came here;
But, as I think,—for truly would I speak,
And now I do bethink me, so it is,—
I came with Hermia hither: our intent
Was to be gone from Athens, where we might,
Without the peril of the Athenian law.

Ege. Enough, enough, my lord; you have enough:
I beg the law, the law, upon his head.
They would have stolen away; they would, Demetrius,
Thereby to have defeated you and me, 161
You of your wife and me of my consent,
Of my consent that she should be your wife.

Dem. My lord, fair Helen told me of their stealth,
Of this their purpose hither to this wood;
And I in fury hither follow'd them,
Fair Helena in fancy following me.
But, my good lord, I wot not by what power,—
But by some power it is,—my love to Hermia,
Melted as the snow, seems to me now 170
As the remembrance of an idle gawd
Which in my childhood I did dote upon;
And all the faith, the virtue of my heart,
The object and the pleasure of mine eye,
Is only Helena. To her, my lord,
Was I betroth'd ere I saw Hermia:
But, like in sickness, did I loathe this food;
But, as in health, come to my natural taste,
Now I do wish it, love it, long for it,
And will for evermore be true to it. 180

The. Fair lovers, you are fortunately met:
Of this discourse we more will hear anon.
Egeus, I will overbear your will;
For in the temple, by and by, with us
These couples shall eternally be knit:
And for the morning now is something worn,
Our purposed hunting shall be set aside.
Away with us to Athens; three and three,
We'll hold a feast in great solemnity.
Come, Hippolyta. 190
    [*Exeunt Theseus, Hippolyta, Egeus, and train.*

Dem. These things seem small and undistinguish-
    able,
Like far-off mountains turned into clouds.

Her. Methinks I see these things with parted eye,
When every thing seems double.

Hel.   So methinks:
And I have found Demetrius like a jewel,
Mine own, and not mine own.

Dem.   Are you sure
That we are awake? It seems to me
That yet we sleep, we dream. Do not you think
The duke was here, and bid us follow him?

Her. Yea; and my father.

Hel.   And Hippolyta. 200

Lys. And he did bid us follow to the temple.

Dem. Why, then, we are awake: let 's follow him;
And by the way let us recount our dreams. [*Exeunt.*

Bot. [*Awaking*] When my cue comes, call me, and
I will answer: my next is, 'Most fair Pyramus.' Heigh-
ho! Peter Quince! Flute, the bellows-mender! Snout,
the tinker! Starveling! God 's my life, stolen hence,
and left me asleep! I have had a most rare vision. I
have had a dream, past the wit of man to say what
dream it was: man is but an ass, if he go about to
expound this dream. Methought I was—there is no
man can tell what. Methought I was,—and methought I had,—but man is but a patched fool, if he
will offer to say what methought I had. The eye of
man hath not heard, the ear of man hath not seen,
man's hand is not able to taste, his tongue to conceive, nor his heart to report, what my dream was. I

116-122. **I was . . . thunder.** This reminiscence, which brings such
unlikely huntsmen into the field together, is probably of Shakespeare's
invention. Hounds of Crete and of Sparta were alike celebrated, the
Spartan the more famous. The whole passage is, of course, made up of
the talk of English huntsmen. 124. **flew'd,** with large overhanging
jaws. **sanded,** of sandy color. 127. **mouth,** voice (of hounds). 128.
Each under each, with differing notes. **cry,** pack of hounds. 138.
solemnity, i.e., solemnization of their marriage. 143. **Saint Valentine.**
Birds were supposed to choose their mates on St. Valentine's Day.

156. **where,** wherever. 157. **Without,** outside of, beyond. 158.
Enough, i.e., evidence to convict him. 161. **defeated,** ruined, thwarted;
see glossary. 212. **go about,** attempt. 216. **patched,** wearing motley,
i.e., a dress of various colors. **offer,** venture; see glossary.
    SCENE II. 4. **transported,** carried off, or possibly, transformed.
20. **sixpence a day,** i.e., as a royal pension. 26. **hearts,** good fellows.
27. **courageous,** used blunderingly. 29. **discourse,** relate; see glossary. 38. **presently,** immediately; see glossary. 40. **preferred,** selected
for consideration.

will get Peter Quince to write a ballad of this dream: it shall be called Bottom's Dream, because it hath no bottom; and I will sing it in the latter end of a play, before the duke: peradventure, to make it the more gracious, †I shall sing it at her death. [*Exit.*

SCENE II. *Athens.* QUINCE'S *house.*

Enter QUINCE, FLUTE, SNOUT, *and* STARVELING.

Quin. Have you sent to Bottom's house? is he come home yet?
Star. He cannot be heard of. Out of doubt he is transported.
Flu. If he come not, then the play is marred: it goes not forward, doth it?
Quin. It is not possible: you have not a man in all Athens able to discharge Pyramus but he.
Flu. No, he hath simply the best wit of any handicraft man in Athens. 10
Quin. Yea, and the best person too; and he is a very paramour for a sweet voice.
Flu. You must say 'paragon:' a paramour is, God bless us, a thing of naught.

Enter SNUG.

Snug. Masters, the duke is coming from the temple, and there is two or three lords and ladies more married: if our sport had gone forward, we had all been made men. 18
Flu. O sweet bully Bottom! Thus hath he lost sixpence a day during his life; he could not have 'scaped sixpence a day: an the duke had not given him sixpence a day for playing Pyramus, I'll be hanged; he would have deserved it: sixpence a day in Pyramus, or nothing.

Enter BOTTOM.

Bot. Where are these lads? where are these hearts? 26
Quin. Bottom! O most courageous day! O most happy hour!
Bot. Masters, I am to discourse wonders: but ask me not what; for if I tell you, I am no true Athenian. I will tell you every thing, right as it fell out.
Quin. Let us hear, sweet Bottom. 33
Bot. Not a word of me. All that I will tell you is, that the duke hath dined. Get your apparel together, good strings to your beards, new ribbons to your pumps; meet presently at the palace; every man look o'er his part; for the short and the long is, our play is preferred. In any case, let Thisby have clean linen; and let not him that plays the lion pare his nails, for they shall hang out for the lion's claws. And, most dear actors, eat no onions nor garlic, for we are to utter sweet breath; and I do not doubt but to hear them say, it is a sweet comedy. No more words: away! go, away! [*Exeunt.*

ACT V.

SCENE I. *Athens. The palace of* THESEUS.

Enter THESEUS, HIPPOLYTA, PHILOSTRATE, Lords, *and* Attendants.

Hip. 'Tis strange, my Theseus, that these lovers speak of.
The. More strange than true: I never may believe
These antique fables, nor these fairy toys.
Lovers and madmen have such seething brains,
Such shaping fantasies, that apprehend
More than cool reason ever comprehends.
The lunatic, the lover and the poet
Are of imagination all compact:
One sees more devils than vast hell can hold,
That is, the madman: the lover, all as frantic,   10
Sees Helen's beauty in a brow of Egypt:
The poet's eye, in a fine frenzy rolling,
Doth glance from heaven to earth, from earth to heaven;
And as imagination bodies forth
The forms of things unknown, the poet's pen
Turns them to shapes and gives to airy nothing
A local habitation and a name.
Such tricks hath strong imagination,
That, if it would but apprehend some joy,
It comprehends some bringer of that joy;   20
Or in the night, imagining some fear,
How easy is a bush supposed a bear!
Hip. But all the story of the night told over,
And all their minds transfigured so together,
More witnesseth than fancy's images
And grows to something of great constancy;
But, howsoever, strange and admirable.
The. Here come the lovers, full of joy and mirth.

Enter LYSANDER, DEMETRIUS, HERMIA, *and* HELENA.

Joy, gentle friends! joy and fresh days of love
Accompany your hearts!
Lys.   More than to us   30
Wait in your royal walks, your board, your bed!
The. Come now; what masques, what dances shall we have,
To wear away this long age of three hours
Between our after-supper and bed-time?
Where is our usual manager of mirth?
What revels are in hand? Is there no play,
To ease the anguish of a torturing hour?
Call Philostrate.
Phil.   Here, mighty Theseus.
The. Say, what abridgement have you for this evening?
What masque? what music? How shall we beguile   40
The lazy time, if not with some delight?
Phil. There is a brief how many sports are ripe:
Make choice of which your highness will see first.
                     [*Giving a paper.*

ACT V. SCENE I. 2. **may**, can; see glossary. 3. **antique**, strange, grotesque. **toys**, trifles; see glossary. 4-22. **Lovers . . . bear.** These lines furnish a probable illustration of the discoveries of the bibliographical students of Shakespeare. If lines 4-6, 9-11, and 18-22 are read consecutively without paying attention to the lines omitted, it will be found that they make complete sense, and that they refer only to the madman and the lover. The other lines, which refer to the poet, are found in the earliest printed texts of the play to be slightly deranged in verse form. It is inferred that Shakespeare's first draft introduced only

the figures of the lover and the madman, and that he subsequently expanded them in his happiest vein with the lines referring to the poet, writing the new lines on the margin. The printers, working from the original playbook, were unable to get them exactly correct in the alignment of the verse. 8. **compact**, formed, composed. 11. **Helen's**, i.e., Helen of Troy, pattern of beauty. **brow of Egypt**, i. e., the face of a gypsy. 21. **fear**, object of fear; see glossary. 25. **images**, creations of the imagination; see glossary. 26. **constancy**, certainty. 39. **abridgement**, pastime. 42. **brief**, short written statement.

The. [*Reads*] 'The battle with the Centaurs, to be
  sung
By an Athenian eunuch to the harp.'
We'll none of that: that have I told my love,
In glory of my kinsman Hercules.
[*Reads*] 'The riot of the tipsy Bacchanals,
Tearing the Thracian singer in their rage.'
That is an old device; and it was play'd   50
When I from Thebes came last a conqueror.
[*Reads*] 'The thrice three Muses mourning for the
  death
Of Learning, late deceased in beggary.'
That is some satire, keen and critical,
Not sorting with a nuptial ceremony.
[*Reads*] 'A tedious brief scene of young Pyramus
And his love Thisbe; very tragical mirth.'
Merry and tragical! tedious and brief!
That is, hot ice and wondrous strange snow.
How shall we find the concord of this discord?   60
  Phil. A play there is, my lord, some ten words long,
Which is as brief as I have known a play;
But by ten words, my lord, it is too long,
Which makes it tedious; for in all the play
There is not one word apt, one player fitted:
And tragical, my noble lord, it is;
For Pyramus therein doth kill himself.
Which, when I saw rehearsed, I must confess,
Made mine eyes water; but more merry tears
The passion of loud laughter never shed.   70
  The. What are they that do play it?
  Phil. Hard-handed men that work in Athens here,
Which never labour'd in their minds till now,
And now have toil'd their unbreathed memories
With this same play, against your nuptial.
  The. And we will hear it.
  Phil.   No, my noble lord;
It is not for you: I have heard it over,
And it is nothing, nothing in the world;
Unless you can find sport in their intents,
Extremely stretch'd and conn'd with cruel pain,   80
To do you service.
  The.   I will hear that play;
For never anything can be amiss,
When simpleness and duty tender it.
Go, bring them in: and take your places, ladies.
                                [*Exit Philostrate.*
  Hip. I love not to see wretchedness o'er-charged
And duty in his service perishing.
  The. Why, gentle sweet, you shall see no such thing.
  Hip. He says they can do nothing in this kind.
  The. The kinder we, to give them thanks for nothing.
Our sport shall be to take what they mistake: 90
And what poor duty cannot do, noble respect
†Takes it in might, not merit.
Where I have come, great clerks have purposed
To greet me with premeditated welcomes;
Where I have seen them shiver and look pale,
Make periods in the midst of sentences,

Throttle their practised accent in their fears
And in conclusion dumbly have broke off,
Not paying me a welcome. Trust me, sweet,
Out of this silence yet I pick'd a welcome;   100
And in the modesty of fearful duty
I read as much as from the rattling tongue
Of saucy and audacious eloquence.
Love, therefore, and tongue-tied simplicity
In least speak most, to my capacity.

        Re-enter PHILOSTRATE.

  Phil. So please your grace, the Prologue is address'd.
  The. Let him approach.   [*Flourish of trumpets.*

Enter QUINCE *for the* Prologue.

  Pro. If we offend, it is with our good will.
That you should think, we come not to offend,
But with good will. To show our simple skill,   110
That is the true beginning of our end.
Consider then we come but in despite.
We do not come as minding to content you,
Our true intent is. All for your delight
We are not here. That you should here repent you,
The actors are at hand and by their show
You shall know all that you are like to know.
  The. This fellow doth not stand upon points.   118
  Lys. He hath rid his prologue like a rough colt; he
knows not the stop. A good moral, my lord: it is not
enough to speak, but to speak true.
  Hip. Indeed he hath played on his prologue like a
child on a recorder; a sound, but not in government.
  The. His speech was like a tangled chain; nothing
impaired, but all disordered. Who is next?

Enter PYRAMUS *and* THISBE, WALL, MOONSHINE, *and*
        LION.

  Pro. Gentles, perchance you wonder at this show;
But wonder on, till truth make all things plain.
This man is Pyramus, if you would know;   130
  This beauteous lady Thisby is certain.
This man, with lime and rough-cast, doth present
  Wall, that vile Wall which did these lovers sunder;
And through Wall's chink, poor souls, they are
    content
  To whisper. At the which let no man wonder.
This man, with lanthorn, dog, and bush of thorn,
  Presenteth Moonshine; for, if you will know,
By moonshine did these lovers think no scorn
  To meet at Ninus' tomb, there, there to woo.
This grisly beast, which Lion hight by name,   140
The trusty Thisby, coming first by night,
Did scare away, or rather did affright;
And, as she fled, her mantle she did fall,
  Which Lion vile with bloody mouth did stain.
Anon comes Pyramus, sweet youth and tall,
  And finds his trusty Thisby's mantle slain:
Whereat, with blade, with bloody blameful blade,
  He bravely broach'd his boiling bloody breast;

---

44. **battle with the Centaurs,** probably refers to the battle of the
Centaurs and the Lapithae, as narrated in Ovid, *Metamorphoses*, Bk. xii.
47. **kinsman.** Plutarch's *Life of Theseus* states that Hercules and Theseus
were near kinsmen. 48-49. **tipsy . . . singer.** This was the story of the
death of Orpheus, as told in *Metamorphoses*, Bk. xi. 52-53. '**The . . .
beggary.'** These two lines were long thought to have some reference
to Spenser's *Teares of the Muses* (1591) and were connected by Knight
with the death in poverty of the learned poet, Robert Greene. The
editors of the New Cambridge Shakespeare see in the lines following,
which describe the piece as a satire, a mild retaliation on Shakespeare's
part for Greene's attack on Shakespeare as "an upstart crow"; see

Shakespeare's Life and Work, Early Period.   55. **Not sorting with,** not
befitting. 74. **unbreathed,** unexercised. 80. **stretch'd,** strained. 92.
Takes . . . merit, values it for the effort made rather than for the excellence achieved (?). 93. **clerks,** learned men. 96. **periods,** full stops.
100. **I pick'd a welcome.** In the kindly speech of Theseus we are
probably to see a tribute to the graciousness of Queen Elizabeth.
Attempts have been made to see in the passage a reference to a particular occasion. 105. **to my capacity,** as far as I am able to understand. 106. **Prologue,** speaker of the Prologue. **address'd,** ready.
108-117. **If . . . to know.** The humor of the passage is in the blunders of
its punctuation. There is a similar piece in *Ralph Roister Doister*, which is

And Thisby, tarrying in mulberry shade,
His dagger drew, and died. For all the rest, 150
Let Lion, Moonshine, Wall, and lovers twain
At large discourse, while here they do remain.

[*Exeunt Prologue, Pyramus, Thisbe, Lion, and*
Moonshine.

The. I wonder if the lion be to speak.

Dem. No wonder, my lord: one lion may, when many asses do.

Wall. In this same interlude it doth befall
That I, one Snout by name, present a wall;
And such a wall, as I would have you think,
That had in it a crannied hole or chink,
Through which the lovers, Pyramus and Thisby, 160
Did whisper often very secretly.
This loam, this rough-cast and this stone doth show
That I am that same wall; the truth is so:
And this the cranny is, right and sinister,
Through which the fearful lovers are to whisper.

The. Would you desire lime and hair to speak better?

Dem. It is the wittiest partition that ever I heard discourse, my lord.

Re-enter PYRAMUS.

The. Pyramus draws near the wall: silence! 170

Pyr. O grim-look'd night! O night with hue so black!
O night, which ever art when day is not!
O night, O night! alack, alack, alack,
I fear my Thisby's promise is forgot!
And thou, O wall, O sweet, O lovely wall,
That stand'st between her father's ground and mine!
Thou wall, O wall, O sweet and lovely wall,
Show me thy chink, to blink through with mine eyne! [*Wall holds up his fingers.*
Thanks, courteous wall: Jove shield thee well for this!
But what see I? No Thisby do I see. 180
O wicked wall, through whom I see no bliss!
Cursed be thy stones for thus deceiving me!

The. The wall, methinks, being sensible, should curse again.

Pyr. No, in truth, sir, he should not. 'Deceiving me' is Thisby's cue: she is to enter now, and I am to spy her through the wall. You shall see, it will fall pat as I told you. Yonder she comes.

Re-enter THISBE.

This. O wall, full often hast thou heard my moans, 190
For parting my fair Pyramus and me!
My cherry lips have often kiss'd thy stones,
Thy stones with lime and hair knit up in thee.

Pyr. I see a voice: now will I to the chink,
To spy an I can hear my Thisby's face.
Thisby!

This. My love thou art, my love I think.

Pyr. Think what thou wilt, I am thy lover's grace;

And, like Limander, am I trusty still.

This. And I like Helen, till the Fates me kill.

Pyr. Not Shafalus to Procrus was so true. 200

This. As Shafalus to Procrus, I to you.

Pyr. O, kiss me through the hole of this vile wall!

This. I kiss the wall's hole, not your lips at all.

Pyr. Wilt thou at Ninny's tomb meet me straightway?

This. 'Tide life, 'tide death, I come without delay.

[*Exeunt Pyramus and Thisbe.*

Wall. Thus have I, Wall, my part discharged so;
And, being done, thus Wall away doth go. [*Exit.*

The. Now is the mural down between the two neighbours.

Dem. No remedy, my lord, when walls are so wilful to hear without warning. 211

Hip. This is the silliest stuff that ever I heard.

The. The best in this kind are but shadows; and the worst are no worse, if imagination amend them.

Hip. It must be your imagination then, and not theirs.

The. If we imagine no worse of them than they of themselves, they may pass for excellent men. Here come two noble beasts in, a man and a lion. 221

Re-enter LION *and* MOONSHINE.

Lion. You, ladies, you, whose gentle hearts do fear
The smallest monstrous mouse that creeps on floor,
May now perchance both quake and tremble here,
When lion rough in wildest rage doth roar.
Then know that I, one Snug the joiner, am
A lion-fell, nor else no lion's dam;
For, if I should as lion come in strife
Into this place, 'twere pity on my life. 229

The. A very gentle beast, and of a good conscience.

Dem. The very best at a beast, my lord, that e'er I saw.

Lys. This lion is a very fox for his valour.

The. True; and a goose for his discretion.

Dem. Not so, my lord; for his valour cannot carry his discretion; and the fox carries the goose.

The. His discretion, I am sure, cannot carry his valour; for the goose carries not the fox. It is well: leave it to his discretion, and let us listen to the moon.

Moon. This lanthorn doth the horned moon present;—

Dem. He should have worn the horns on his head.

The. He is no crescent, and his horns are invisible within the circumference.

Moon. This lanthorn doth the horned moon present;
Myself the man i' the moon do seem to be.

The. This is the greatest error of all the rest: the man should be put into the lanthorn. How is it else the man i' the moon? 252

Dem. He dares not come there for the candle; for, you see, it is already in snuff.

Hip. I am aweary of this moon: would he would change!

quoted in Wilson's *Arte of Rhetoric*, which Shakespeare probably knew. **113. minding,** intending; see glossary. **118. not stand upon points,** quibbling upon the two meanings (1) "to be overscrupulous" and (2) "to mind his stops in reading." **123. recorder,** a wind instrument like a flute or flageolet. **124. government,** control. **140. hight,** is called. **143. fall,** let fall; see glossary. **145. tall,** fine; see glossary. **148. broach'd,** stabbed; used rantingly. **152. At large,** in full; see *large* in glossary. **164. sinister,** left. **168. partition,** wall, and section of a learned book. **171. grim-look'd,** grim-looking. **183. sensible,** capable of feeling; see glossary. **198-199. Limander . . . Helen,** blunders for "Leander" and "Hero." **201. Shafalus to Procrus,** blunder for

"Cephalus" to "Procris," also famous lovers. **205. 'Tide life, 'tide death,** whether life or death betide. **213. shadows,** likenesses, representations; see glossary. **214. if imagination amend them.** The idea in this passage is fundamental in art and recurs so frequently in Shakespeare as to be a recognizable article of his faith. **227. lion-fell,** lion's skin; QF: *lion fell,* i.e., fierce lion. **244. horns on his head,** the customary jest about the horns of the cuckold. **253. for,** because of. **254. in snuff,** pun on the meanings "to be offended" and "to be in need of snuffing."

The. It appears, by his small light of discretion, that he is in the wane; but yet, in courtesy, in all reason, we must stay the time.

Lys. Proceed, Moon. 260

Moon. All that I have to say, is, to tell you that the lanthorn is the moon; I, the man in the moon; this thorn-bush, my thorn-bush; and this dog, my dog.

Dem. Why, all these should be in the lanthorn; for all these are in the moon. But, silence! here comes Thisbe.

Re-enter THISBE.

This. This is old Ninny's tomb. Where is my love?

Lion. [*Roaring*] Oh—— [*Thisbe runs off.*

Dem. Well roared, Lion. 270

The. Well run, Thisbe.

Hip. Well shone, Moon. Truly, the moon shines with a good grace.

[*The Lion shakes Thisbe's mantle, and exit.*

The. Well moused, Lion.

Lys. And so the lion vanished.

Dem. And then came Pyramus.

Re-enter PYRAMUS.

Pyr. Sweet Moon, I thank thee for thy sunny
   beams;
I thank thee, Moon, for shining now so bright;
For, by thy gracious, golden, glittering gleams,
I trust to take of truest Thisby sight. 280
   But stay, O spite!
   But mark, poor knight,
What dreadful dole is here!
   Eyes, do you see?
   How can it be?
O dainty duck! O dear!
   Thy mantle good,
   What, stain'd with blood!
Approach, ye Furies fell!
   O Fates, come, come, 290
   Cut thread and thrum;
   Quail, crush, conclude, and quell!

The. This passion, and the death of a dear friend, would go near to make a man look sad.

Hip. Beshrew my heart, but I pity the man.

Pyr. O wherefore, Nature, didst thou lions frame?
Since lion vile hath here deflower'd my dear:
Which is—no, no—which was the fairest dame
That lived, that loved, that liked, that look'd with
   cheer.
   Come, tears, confound; 300
   Out, sword, and wound
The pap of Pyramus;
   Ay, that left pap,
   Where heart doth hop: [*Stabs himself.*
Thus die I, thus, thus, thus.
   Now am I dead,
   Now am I fled;
   My soul is in the sky:
Tongue, lose thy light;

Moon, take thy flight: [*Exit Moonshine.* 310
   Now die, die, die, die, die. [*Dies.*

Dem. No die, but an ace, for him; for he is but one.

Lys. Less than an ace, man; for he is dead; he is nothing.

The. With the help of a surgeon he might yet recover, and prove an ass.

Hip. How chance Moonshine is gone before Thisbe comes back and finds her lover?

The. She will find him by starlight. Here she comes; and her passion ends the play. 321

Re-enter THISBE.

Hip. Methinks she should not use a long one for such a Pyramus: I hope she will be brief.

Dem. A mote will turn the balance, which Pyramus, which Thisbe, is the better; he for a man, God warrant us; she for a woman, God bless us.

Lys. She hath spied him already with those sweet eyes.

Dem. And thus she means, videlicet:— 330

This. Asleep, my love?
   What, dead, my dove?
O Pyramus, arise!
   Speak, speak. Quite dumb?
   Dead, dead? A tomb
Must cover thy sweet eyes.
   These lily lips,
   This cherry nose,
These yellow cowslip cheeks,
   Are gone, are gone: 340
   Lovers, make moan:
His eyes were green as leeks.
   O Sisters Three,
   Come, come to me,
With hands as pale as milk;
   Lay them in gore,
   Since you have shore
With shears his thread of silk.
   Tongue, not a word:
   Come, trusty sword; 350
Come, blade, my breast imbrue: [*Stabs herself.*
   And, farewell, friends;
   Thus Thisby ends:
   Adieu, adieu, adieu. [*Dies.*

The. Moonshine and Lion are left to bury the dead.

Dem. Ay, and Wall too.

Bot. [*Starting up*] No, I assure you; the wall is down that parted their fathers. Will it please you to see the epilogue, or to hear a Bergomask dance between two of our company? 360

The. No epilogue, I pray you; for your play needs no excuse. Never excuse; for when the players are all dead, there need none to be blamed. Marry, if he that writ it had played Pyramus and hanged himself in Thisbe's garter, it would have been a fine tragedy: and so it is, truly; and very notably discharged. But, come, your Bergomask; let your epilogue alone.

[*A dance.*

A Midsummer-Night's Dream
ACT V : SC I

204

283. **dole,** grief. 291. **thread and thrum,** the warp in weaving and the loose end of the warp; Bottom was a weaver. 292. **Quail,** overpower. **quell,** kill, destroy. 299. **cheer,** face. 312. **ace,** the side of the die containing the single pip, or spot. 330. **means,** moans, laments. 343. **Sisters Three,** the Fates. 347. **shore,** shorn. 351. **imbrue,** stain with blood. 360. **Bergomask dance,** dance named from Bergamo, a province in the state of Venice, noted for the rusticity of its manners. The New Cambridge edition points out that this rustic dance is the antimasque, or grotesque contrasting measure, to the dance of the

fairies that is to follow. 363. **excuse,** seek to extenuate (a fault); see glossary. 370. **told,** counted; see *tell* in glossary. 374. **palpablegross,** palpably gross, obviously crude. 381. **fordone,** exhausted. 391. **triple Hecate's.** Hecate ruled in three capacities: as Luna or Cynthia in heaven, as Diana on earth, and as Proserpina in hell. 394. **frolic,** merry. 397. **sweep the dust behind the door,** i.e., where it would not show. Robin Goodfellow was a household spirit and helped good housemaids and punished lazy ones. 398-407. **Through . . . place.** The editors of the New Cambridge Shakespeare find

The iron tongue of midnight hath told twelve: 370
Lovers, to bed; 'tis almost fairy time.
I fear we shall out-sleep the coming morn
As much as we this night have overwatch'd.
This palpable-gross play hath well beguiled
The heavy gait of night. Sweet friends, to bed.
A fortnight hold we this solemnity,
In nightly revels and new jollity. [Exeunt.

  Enter PUCK.

  Puck. Now the hungry lion roars,
  And the wolf behowls the moon;
Whilst the heavy ploughman snores, 380
  All with weary task fordone.
Now the wasted brands do glow,
  Whilst the screech-owl, screeching loud,
Puts the wretch that lies in woe
  In remembrance of a shroud.
Now it is the time of night
  That the graves all gaping wide,
Every one lets forth his sprite,
  In the church-way paths to glide:
And we fairies, that do run 390
  By the triple Hecate's team,
From the presence of the sun,
  Following darkness like a dream,
Now are frolic: not a mouse
Shall disturb this hallow'd house:
I am sent with broom before,
To sweep the dust behind the door.

  Enter OBERON and TITANIA with their train.

  Obe. Through the house give glimmering light,
  By the dead and drowsy fire:
  Every elf and fairy sprite 400
  Hop as light as bird from brier;
  And this ditty, after me,
  Sing, and dance it trippingly.
  Tita. First, rehearse your song by rote,
  To each word a warbling note:
  Hand in hand, with fairy grace,
  Will we sing, and bless this place. [Song and dance.
  Obe. Now, until the break of day,
  Through this house each fairy stray.
  To the best bride-bed will we, 410
  Which by us shall blessed be;
  And the issue there create
  Ever shall be fortunate.
  So shall all the couples three
  Ever true in loving be;
  And the blots of Nature's hand
  Shall not in their issue stand;
  Never mole, hare lip, nor scar,
  Nor mark prodigious, such as are
  Despised in nativity, 420
  Shall upon their children be.
  With this field-dew consecrate,
  Every fairy take his gait;
  And each several chamber bless,

in this passage evidence that the play was written for performance in the great chamber of some private house on the occasion of the celebration of a marriage. Theseus and the court leave the stage; the lights are extinguished, all but one; the fairies enter, kindle their torches at the remaining flame, place them on their heads and exhibit their dance; then depart as if to bless the bridal chamber. 412. **create,** created. 419. **prodigious,** monstrous, unnatural. 422. **consecrate,** consecrated. 424. **several,** separate; see glossary.

Through this palace, with sweet peace;
And the owner of it blest
Ever shall in safety rest.
Trip away; make no stay;
Meet me all by break of day.
            [Exeunt Oberon, Titania, and train.
  Puck. If we shadows have offended, 430
  Think but this, and all is mended,
  That you have but slumber'd here
  While these visions did appear.
  And this weak and idle theme,
  No more yielding but a dream,
  Gentles, do not reprehend:
  If you pardon, we will mend:
  And, as I am an honest Puck,
  If we have unearned luck
  Now to 'scape the serpent's tongue, 440
  We will make amends ere long;
  Else the Puck a liar call:
  So, good night unto you all.
  Give me your hands, if we be friends,
  And Robin shall restore amends. [Exit.

432. **That . . . here,** i.e., that it is a "midsummer-night's dream." 440. **serpent's tongue,** hissing. 444. **Give . . . hands,** applaud by clapping.

EARLY HISTORY

PLAYS

THE

Henry the Sixth Plays

For a long time the accepted opinion with reference to the three plays known as *1, 2,* and *3 Henry VI* was that we have in them the hand of Shakespeare as a reviser of the work of other men. Some critics have been disposed to deny to Shakespeare any hand at all in these plays because of the supposed inferiority of the workmanship. But when proper allowance is made for the fact that as a beginner Shakespeare did not completely know his art either as poet or dramatist, that his work throughout his career is not of uniform and perfect excellence, and that, when all faults have been admitted, the Henry VI plays remain as dramas of great vividness and power, this wholesale rejection loses its propriety. It has also been pointed out that these plays are not mentioned by Francis Meres in his list in *Palladis Tamia*, but Meres sets six comedies over against six tragedies and probably did not intend to enumerate all of the plays which Shakespeare had written by 1598. He merely gave formal examples to prove Shakespeare's double superiority in both tragedy and comedy. A principal reason for thinking the Henry VI plays are Shakespeare's work is that they were included by his colleagues, Heminges and Condell, in the First Folio and must have been known in the repertory of the theater as Shakespeare's plays. Almost all critics have found in them evidences of Shakespeare's work, and *Henry V* and *Richard III*, which respectively precede and follow them in historical sequence, both show many evidences of the knitting together of all the plays as one great historical group.[1]

1 Henry VI

It is probable that Shakespeare wrote *2* and *3 Henry VI* in 1591-1592 or earlier, and *1 Henry VI* at an early date soon after he had written *2* and *3 Henry VI*. In the case of *1 Henry VI*, we have a slightly different type of problem from that presented by its sequels. The only early text of the play is that of the Folio, something which makes determination of a date difficult. A play of "Harry the Sixth" makes its appearance in Henslowe's *Diary* in the spring of 1592 as acted by Lord Strange's men at the Rose Theater. This may have been a version of the story which Shakespeare had not yet touched, although there is only very general evidence to prove that Shakespeare had not written it. It seemed probable to J. Q. Adams in his *Life of Shakespeare* (pp. 214-215) that the later parts of the story of King Henry VI which are treated in *2* and *3 Henry VI* were written or revamped by Shakespeare for Lord Pembroke's company in order to form a counterattraction to this very play which Henslowe calls "harey vi" then enjoying enormous popularity at the Rose as acted by Lord Strange's men. As an indication of this popularity we have not only Henslowe's entries of numerous performances and good returns, but we have independent testimony from Jonson and from Shakespeare himself. The folio play of *1 Henry VI*, whether or not it is

"harey vi," tells from a strongly patriotic point of view the story of the warfare, betrayal, and heroic death of the English general Talbot, who was fighting in France to save that kingdom from reconquest by the French king and Joan of Arc. The play in its oldest form is sometimes thought to have been the work of George Peele; at any rate, Peele's friend Thomas Nashe in *Pierce Penniless* (1592) has this to say:

How it would haue ioyed brave Talbot (the terror of the French) to thinke that after he had lyne two hundred yeares in his Tombe, hee should triumphe again on the Stage, and haue his bones newe embalmed with the teares of ten thousand spectators at least (at seuerall times), who, in the Tragedian that represents his person, imagine that they behold him fresh bleeding.

Tucker Brooke finds some indications that *1 Henry VI* may have been revived about 1599 in order to take advantage of the interest in the theme reawakened by the popularity of *Henry V* and thinks that the reference to Henry VI in the Epilogue of *Henry V* is a hint of such a revival. He also finds indications of a revision at that time in the publication of Talbot's epitaph in Richard Crompton's *Mansion of Magnanimitie* (1599), for Shakespeare (IV, vii, 63-71) follows it almost word for word.[2] The truth of the matter is that Shakespeare's plays were for a long time stock plays in the repertory of the theater and were likely to be revised and revived at almost any time up to 1623. Early and late work is inextricably mixed in many plays, and probably this is true in *1 Henry VI*. Some confirmation of the general theory of a rewriting of *1 Henry VI* by Shakespeare for the purpose of making the play into a first member of a Henry VI trilogy is found by C. F. Denny, who tries to determine objectively what parts of the play come most directly from Holinshed's *Chronicle* and to determine the scope of the latest revision.[3]

AUTHORSHIP OF 1 Henry VI

As to authorship, there has been a long debate. Almost nobody now believes that Shakespeare was the author of the original play. On the other hand, few people now believe that he had no share in revising it. The original "Harry the Sixth" has been attributed to Marlowe, Greene, and Peele severally or with collaboration among them. Peele's claim seems the best because of the frequent parallels between the play as we have it and the known work of Peele. Also, the spirit of rampant patriotism, or chauvinism, which must have characterized the original version and which is not absent from the present play, is characteristic of Peele. Shakespeare's revision is most clearly seen in those parts of the play which make it fit into a series with *2* and *3 Henry VI* and *Richard III*.

[1]Adams, *Life of Shakespeare*, passim; Boswell-Stone, *Shakespeare's Holinshed*; C. F. Tucker Brooke, *The Authorship of the Second and Third Parts of "King Henry the Sixth"* (New Haven, 1912); the same author's edition of all three parts in the Yale Shakespeare; Fleay, *Life and Works of Shakespeare*; Charles T. Prouty, *The Contention and Shakespeare's 2 Henry VI: A Comparative Study* (New Haven, 1954); Chambers, *William Shakespeare*, I, 277-293; Halliwell-Phillipps, *The First Sketches of the Second and Third Parts of "King Henry the Sixth"* (Shakespeare Society, 1843); J. B. Henneman, "The Episodes in *1 Henry VI*," *PMLA*, XV, 290-320; Sir A. W. Ward, *Collected Papers*, III, 231-291 (Cambridge, 1921); Madeleine Doran, "Henry VI," *Parts II and III: Their Relation to the "Contention" and the "True Tragedy"* (Iowa City, 1928); Peter Alexander, *Shakespeare's "Henry VI" and "Richard III"* (Cambridge, 1929); Allison Gaw, *The Origin and Development of "1 Henry VI" in relation to Shakespeare, Marlowe, Peele, and Greene* (Los Angeles, 1926); Lucille King, "The Use of Hall's *Chronicles* in the Folio and Quarto Texts of *Henry VI*," *Philological Quarterly*, XIII (1934), 321-332, and "Text Sources of the Folio and Quarto *Henry VI*," *PMLA* (1936), LI, 702-718.

[2]Josephine A. Pearce, "An Earlier Talbot Epitaph," *Modern Language Notes*, LIX (1944), 327-329, finds the Talbot epitaph in the dedication to *An Armor of Proofe*, a poem by Roger Cotton published in 1596.

[3]"The Sources of *1 Henry VI* as an Indication of Revision," *Philological Quarterly*, XVI (1937), 225-248.

The play has been analyzed according to two leading parts, the Talbot or French portion, and the Henry VI or English portion.[4] The action, however, is presented episodically by means of five independent character groups. (1) The English court, which is the least integral, serves as background for (2) and (4) below. The only action arising from within the group itself is the Gloucester-Winchester rivalry, which is, however, wholly independent of the other themes or groups in the play. Although it flares out violently

in two scenes (I, iii; III, i), it never takes on plot characteristics; i.e., there are no complications or consequences. It disappears from the play with the latter of these two scenes, with the exception of two brief mentions—V, i, 28-33, where Exeter alludes to the cardinal's pride, and V, iv, 56-63, in a short soliloquy by the cardinal. This, with other unresolved actions in this play, reappears with greater plot motivation in 2 Henry VI. (2) The Talbot theme has points of contact with all the others except the Suffolk-Margaret episode. Talbot's fortunes in France—his defeat and capture—are reported to the court (I, i); he has audience with the king and is made earl of Shrewsbury (III, iv, 1-27); he is present at the coronation, where he removes Fastolfe's garter and where, after the reading of Burgundy's letter, he is dispatched "to give him chastisement." This chastisement of Burgundy is a promise of action not later realized. Talbot is the play's protagonist in opposition to La Pucelle through the first three acts. She defeats him at Orleans (I, v); he recaptures Orleans (II, i); he drives her from Rouen (III, ii). The York-Somerset quarrel prevents these lords from coming to his assistance. The Talbot story, moreover, is the only one of the five that has anything like completed dramatic structure; it has an "exposition," a complicating action, and a catastrophe. (3) The York-Somerset rivalry has the points of contact with Talbot,

[4] J. B. Henneman, "Episodes in Shakespeare's 1 Henry VI," PMLA (1900), XV, 290-320.

just noted; with the court, where York is made successively duke of York and regent of France, and where the king hears the "braving" of Vernon and Basset (III, i, 148-200; IV, i, 78-194); and with the La Pucelle theme in her capture (V, iii) and her trial (V, iv). Except for the quarrel, Somerset does not figure in the action at all. York, however, offers a consistent and unified subject. He heads a faction (II, iv); his background and motives are made explicit (II, v); he becomes duke of York (III, i, 148 ff.) and is made regent of France (IV, i, 78); he becomes the dominant figure in France after Talbot's death—captures La Pucelle (V, iii, 30-44), presides at her trial (V, iv, 1-93), and is the principal figure in peace negotiations (V, iv, 94-175). His is a rising action the consequences of which do not appear until later in the trilogy. (4) The function structurally of the fourth group, the French soldiers and La Pucelle, is that of antagonist. They serve as such mainly with respect to Talbot. The English-French military scenes alternate through the first three acts with almost perfect regularity. This balanced presentation stops abruptly with the desertion of Burgundy. After this event La Pucelle drops out of the Talbot plot and reappears as the victim of York. La Pucelle has no point of contact with the English court group. She is not once mentioned by them. The French courtiers meet for peace negotiations with the English—not with the court group, which had discussed a possible peace, but with York. Winchester's appearance in this scene seems to be a somewhat artificial attempt to bring these lines of action together. (5) The Suffolk-Margaret scenes, the fifth action group, are intruded into the play obviously as a preparation for 2 Henry VI. They serve no dramatic purpose within the plot. This mingling of several themes accounts for obvious difficulties: confusion of dates, chronological disorders, repetitions of events, obscurities of reference, and peculiarities and contradictions in character conception.

Critics recognize Shakespeare's hand most clearly in the Temple Garden scene (II, iv), in the scene of the death of Mortimer (II, v), in some of the Talbot scenes (IV, ii-vii), and in the episode of the wooing of Margaret by Suffolk (V, iii). Bearing this in mind we might apply to these five themes of the play, Henneman's definition of Shakespeare's purpose in revising 1 Henry VI:

To work up or rewrite the Talbot portions of the Chronicles, probably, though not necessarily, already crystallized into an old play on the triumph of 'brave Talbot' over the French, which possessed the hated Joan of Arc scenes and all; to intensify the figure and character of Talbot; to work over or add scenes like those touching Talbot's death; to connect him with the deplorable struggles of the nobles; to invent, by a happy poetical thought, the origin of the factions of the Red and White Roses in the Temple Garden; to sound at once the note of weakness in the king continued in the succeeding Parts, and thus convert the old Talbot material effectually into a Henry VI. drama; and to close with the wooing of Margaret as specific introduction to Part II.,—something like this seems the task that the dramatist set himself to perform.[5]

It will be seen from this analysis that Shakespeare must have concerned himself with all of the five principal themes of the play—with the court, the York-Somerset rivalry, and the Suffolk-Margaret episodes primarily, but also with the defeat and death of Talbot; least of all, perhaps, with the earlier activities of La Pucelle.

2 AND 3 Henry VI

To the second and third members of the Henry VI trilogy there exist parallel versions as follows:

THE First part of the Contention betwixt the two famous Houses of Yorke and Lancaster, with the death of the good Duke Humphrey: And the banishment and death of the Duke of *Suffolke*, and the Tragicall end of the proud Cardinall of *VVinchester*, vvith the notable Rebellion of *Iacke Cade: And the Duke of Yorkes first claime vnto the Crowne*. LONDON. Printed by Thomas Creed, for Thomas Millington, and are to be sold at his shop *vnder* Saint Peters Church in Cornwall. 1594.

and its sequel:

The true Tragedie of Richard *Duke of Yorke*, and the death of good King Henrie the Sixt, *with the whole contention betweene* the two Houses Lancaster and Yorke, as it was sundrie times acted by the Right Honourable the Earle of Pembrooke his seruants. Printed at London by P.S. for Thomas Milling*ton, and are to be sold at his* shoppe under Saint Peters Church in Cornwal. 1595.

Two theories are offered to account for the existence of double versions of the two plays in question. According to one of these theories the folio texts of *2* and *3 Henry VI* are regarded as Shakespeare's revisions of the two chronicle plays whose elaborate title pages have just been quoted, they themselves being the works of other dramatists, Marlowe and Greene or Peele. According to the other, which is now preferred, *The Contention* and *The True Tragedy* are versions of *2* and *3 Henry VI* supplied to the printers by actors who had debased them to some degree, probably by acting them on the road.[6]

Greene's attack on Shakespeare in *A Groatsworth of Wit* as "an upstart crow beautified with our feathers," and, particularly, the allusion to the "tyger's heart wrapped in a player's hyde," which parodies a line occurring both in *The True Tragedy* and in *3 Henry VI*, furnishes a date (June 1592) at which both parts of the play were in existence.

[5]*Ibid.*, p. 297.
[6]P. Alexander, "*II Henry VI* and the Copy for '*The Contention*' (1594)," Literary Supplement of the *Times*, Oct. 9, 1924, pp. 629-630, and "*III Henry VI* and *Richard Duke of York*," *ibid.*, Nov. 13, 1924, p. 730; see also Pollard, "The Quartos of '*The Contention*' and *Richard Duke of York*," *ibid.*, Nov. 27, 1924, p. 797; and the fuller treatments of the same theme by Miss Doran, Alexander and Prouty listed in note 1 above. In a 1619 collection of plays of Shakespeare or associated with Shakespeare these two quartos appear combined into one as *The Whole Contention betweene the two Famous Houses, Lancaster and Yorke*

2 Henry VI

If *2 Henry VI* is earlier than Marlowe's *Edward II*, which it may be, it is possible to see in it a new departure in the writing of history plays. Instead of attempting to elevate one figure to supreme importance, as Marlowe had done in his tragedies, this play presents a whole group with almost equal

emphasis and does so with perfect ease and with great success—King Henry VI himself involved with Suffolk and Margaret, Gloucester and Winchester, Somerset and York, Salisbury and Warwick, Clifford and Richard Crookback. These figures are moreover presented according to dramatic design, not episodically. That design is derived from history, so that the play, in spite of various necessary telescopings, is faithful to history as it was known and understood. This faithfulness to fact in the dramatization of history is a Shakespearean characteristic. An early date for *2 Henry VI* is also indicated by its careful workmanship in the Senecan style.[7]

It has been seen that *1 Henry VI* had prepared the way for, or had been so thoroughly revised as to embody, all of the main themes of *2 Henry VI*. This play has to do with York's struggle for the crown; but, since Humphrey Duke of Gloucester was the principal obstacle to York's ambition, the first three acts are taken up with the overthrow of the Good Duke Humphrey. The story as such has remarkable unity and appeal, and this is not surprising when it is remembered that the story of Humphrey of Gloucester had an independent existence in narrative and dramatic literature. Duke Humphrey, the king's uncle, his best friend, long his protector, has opposed the king's marriage to Margaret of Anjou and is in consequence hated by her and by her lover Suffolk; also by the bishop of Winchester, his lifelong enemy, and by Plantagenet, now duke of York. He thus becomes the object of general attack. Through the folly of his duchess he is overthrown, and in the third act, since the king is too weak to protect him, he is murdered. Concomitant with this action is the destruction of Suffolk. He is banished in the third act and early in the fourth he is killed by pirates into whose hands he

[7]See the present writer's "Shakespeare and the History Play," *Joseph Quincy Adams Memorial Studies* (Washington, D.C., 1948), pp. 55-64.

has fallen. Winchester also dies in the third act, so that the play breaks in the middle. It is only fair to say that up to the end of the third act it is extremely well constructed.

Between the time that the way is cleared for the realization of York's ambitions and his return from Ireland, the gap in the action is filled by matter very interesting in the whole picture of Shakespeare's dramatic development—a realistic account of the rebellion of the famous Jack Cade. It is humorous, vivid, and, although a comic episode, is characteristically connected with the main action. Before York goes to Ireland, ostensibly to fight against rebels but really to create for himself an army, he stirs up the peasant revolt. The treatment of this revolt gives an early indication as to what Shakespeare thought of political activities by the lower classes. When Cade rules England, "seven halfpenny loaves shall be sold for a penny; the three-hooped pot shall have ten hoops"; and he will make it a felony to drink small beer. Lord Say is beheaded because he has "most traitorously corrupted the youth of this realm in erecting a grammar school"; besides he has been known to talk of "a noun and a verb, and such abominable words as no Christian ear can endure to hear." The Clerk of Chatham is hanged because he can write his name. And yet there is a bold, manly quality, in spite of ignorance and degradation, in Cade's death in the last scene of Act IV. Shakespeare never forgets that he has to do with human beings.

The main line of action—York's struggle for the crown—is resumed in the last act. He returns from Ireland, defeats the king at the Battle of St. Alban's, and the play ends in a Yorkist triumph. All three of the Henry VI plays are shaped to that end, and in all three we see developed in Henry VI himself a character of almost paradoxical quality. Henry is an incompetent ruler, a calamity to his party and his country, and yet Shakespeare has been true to the tradition that he was a saint on earth. In him piety itself suffices. He is devoid of evil, without desire for revenge, and is unafraid of the present or the future. His is the one fine and self-sufficient soul in the whole group.

3 Henry VI

The last play of the Henry VI trilogy shows a growth in stylistic and possibly poetic power, although it is by no means so good a play as the second member. It marches up to a climax in the destinies of York, and in its closing scene anticipates the sequel, Richard III, where begins the downward movement in the drama of the York family. Although 3 Henry VI is more episodic than is 2 Henry VI, it is not without at least two important structural features—one connected with Margaret and the other with Richard of Gloucester. Margaret's power appears in the first act. After the Battle of St. Alban's, York proceeds to London and at a parliament at Westminster seats himself on the throne. In the wrangle that ensues

Henry VI weakly agrees that, if he may rule quietly during his life, York and his heirs shall be his successors to the crown, thus disinheriting his own son. Queen Margaret, known as the "she-wolf of France," flies to battle in defense of her son's rights, beats the Yorkists at Wakefield, and gloats over the murder of York. She thus becomes and continues to be the chief protagonist of the play.

The Battle of Wakefield ends the first act, with Lancaster in the ascendancy. The second act also marks a stage in the construction of the play; for York's three sons, Edward, later King Edward IV, George Duke of Clarence, and Richard Duke of Gloucester, rally their forces and, with the help of Warwick the kingmaker, win the fierce Battle of Towton. Henry escapes to Scotland, and Margaret and the young prince to France. The Yorkists are in their turn triumphant at the end of the second act; but base personal motive interferes with their prosperity. The third act has to do with Edward IV's rejection of Bona, the French king's sister-in-law, in favor of Lady Grey and the consequent alienation of Warwick. It is also well unified. The fourth act presents Warwick reseating King Henry VI on his throne, only to have the king surprised and captured by Edward IV, who has escaped from captivity and returned with troops from Flanders. The fourth act is crowded, but as a battle piece it is rather fine. The same matter runs on into the fifth act, and, as exciting warfare on the stage, is equaled by Shakespeare perhaps only in Henry V. The fifth act begins before the city of Coventry, where the "false, fleeting, perjured Clarence" of Richard III deserts Warwick for Edward. At the famous Battle of Barnet, which Bulwer-Lytton makes the climax of his The Last of the Barons, Warwick is defeated and slain. The fifth act is also too crowded for clarity. Queen Margaret, having returned from France, gives battle to the Yorkists at Tewkesbury, but is also overthrown. Then enter again the personal features of these plays, the killings and gloatings. Prince Edward, the hopeful young Lancastrian heir, is murdered by the Yorkist brothers, and Richard Crookback posts off to London. In a scene in the Tower Richard prowls like a wolf around the weak and saintly king and then murders him in cold blood.

It is in connection with these personal motives and actions that we find what might be thought of as a second general feature of 3 Henry VI. It is seen in a rather sudden development in the character of Richard Duke of Gloucester. Although he had been thought of as a somewhat sinister force in all of his appearances in 2 and 3 Henry VI, he had fought loyally for his family and had even betrayed normal human emotions. It is not until the end of the second scene of the third act that he speaks with his own voice. Richard of Gloucester, later King Richard III, was a well-known historical character. His History by Sir Thomas More, Saint, thought to have been largely derived from Cardinal Morton, had been embodied in the chronicles. It presents at a high level of literary genius the remorseless villain, fratricide and infanticide, that we know from Shakespeare's *Richard III*.

In a soliloquy at the end of the second scene of the third act Richard suddenly becomes himself. It is as if Shakespeare, foreseeing his own composition of a play about Richard of Gloucester, or at least foreseeing his intended use of Richard as the murderer of King Henry VI, had read, or reread, More's *History*. From that moment Richard becomes, in the third and fourth acts of *3 Henry VI*, a great driving force in the destruction of the House of Lancaster. Richard is frequently called a Machiavellian villain, and there is no doubt that Shakespeare thought of him in connection with villains so described (*3 Henry VI*, III, ii, 193), but Richard III is not a typical Machiavel. He is too personal both in his ambitions and in his villainy. He has less of the general love of evil that characterizes Marlowe's Barabas and more of the particularized criminality that characterizes Edmund and Macbeth. Shakespeare thought of him as a historical character and, as will be seen in the reading of *Richard III*, endowed him with a conscience.

STAGE HISTORY

Evidence has been given to the effect that a play on King Henry VI celebrating the bravery of the English general Talbot was a popular play at the time when Shakespeare was probably beginning his career as a dramatist. And further that *1 Henry VI* was probably revived about 1599 in connection with the interest aroused by Shakespeare's *Henry V* in the history of the House of Lancaster. J. H. Merivale constructed a play called *Richard, Duke of York*, to be acted by Edmund Kean in 1817, out of *2 Henry VI* with slight additions from *1* and *3 Henry VI*, and Charles Kemble made an abridgment of all three parts, which was, however, probably never acted. *1 Henry VI* was revived in 1738 and was staged in recent times by Benson at the Stratford Memorial Theater in May 1906, at which time the entire series from *Richard II* to *Richard III* was presented. Beyond this the play has almost no stage history.

John Crowne wrote Restoration versions of both *2* and *3 Henry VI* for the Bettertons at the Duke of York's Theater. Ambrose Philips wrote a play called *Humfrey Duke of Gloucester* which is based on *2 Henry VI* and is also the main source of the play, *Richard, Duke of York*, written by Merivale for Kean. The third part underwent adaptation by Crowne and contributed to Merivale's play, to Charles Kemble's condensation, and to Colley Cibber's stage version of *Richard III*. Like the other parts of the series it appeared in Benson's revival at Stratford in 1906.

The thrid and last battell was fought nere unto the towne of high Barnet upon the 14. of Aprill being Easter daye, by the Earles of Warwick, and Oxford, and Marques Montacule against King Ed. 4. whoe led with him king H. 6. his prisoner unto that feild, and obtayned that daye the victorye against his enemyes. There were slaine in this bloody Battel Richard Nevill the Stout Earle of Warwick with his brother the Marques and the Earle of Oxford put to flight, & the Duke of Excester sore wounded, and leeft in the feild for dead. On King Edwards part were slaine, the Lords Cromwell, Boucher, and Barnes. And on Both parts the nomber of tenn thousand men. Anno 1471.

THE FIRST PART OF

King Henry the Sixth

DRAMATIS PERSONAE

KING HENRY the Sixth.
DUKE OF GLOUCESTER, uncle to the King, and
  Protector.
DUKE OF BEDFORD, uncle to the King, and
  Regent of France.
THOMAS BEAUFORT, Duke of Exeter, great-uncle
  to the King.
HENRY BEAUFORT, great-uncle to the King,
  Bishop of Winchester, and afterwards
  Cardinal.
JOHN BEAUFORT, Earl, afterwards Duke, of
  Somerset.
RICHARD PLANTAGENET, son of Richard late
  Earl of Cambridge, afterwards Duke of York.
EARL OF WARWICK.
EARL OF SALISBURY.
EARL OF SUFFOLK.
LORD TALBOT, afterwards Earl of Shrewsbury.
JOHN TALBOT, his son.
EDMUND MORTIMER, Earl of March.
SIR JOHN FASTOLFE.
SIR WILLIAM LUCY.
SIR WILLIAM GLANSDALE.
SIR THOMAS GARGRAVE.
Mayor of London.
WOODVILE, Lieutenant of the Tower.
VERNON, of the White-Rose or York faction.
BASSET, of the Red-Rose or Lancaster faction.
A Lawyer. Mortimer's Keepers.

CHARLES, Dauphin, and afterwards King, of
  France.
REIGNIER, Duke of Anjou, and titular King of
  Naples.
DUKE OF BURGUNDY.
DUKE OF ALENÇON.
BASTARD OF ORLEANS.
Governor of Paris.
Master-Gunner of Orleans, and his Son.
General of the French forces in Bourdeaux.
A French Sergeant. A Porter.
An old Shepherd, father to Joan la Pucelle.

MARGARET, daughter to Reignier, afterwards
  married to King Henry.
COUNTESS OF AUVERGNE.
JOAN LA PUCELLE, commonly called Joan of
  Arc.

Lords, Warders of the Tower, Heralds, Officers,
  Soldiers, Messengers, and Attendants.

Fiends appearing to La Pucelle.

SCENE: *Partly in England, and partly in France.*

ACT I.

SCENE I. *Westminster Abbey.*

Dead March. Enter the Funeral of KING HENRY the
  Fifth, *attended on by the* DUKE OF BEDFORD, *Regent
  of France; the* DUKE OF GLOUCESTER, *Protector; the*
  DUKE OF EXETER, *the* EARL OF WARWICK, *the*
  BISHOP OF WINCHESTER, Heralds, *&c.*

Bed. Hung be the heavens with black, yield day to
    night!
Comets, importing change of times and states,
Brandish your crystal tresses in the sky,
And with them scourge the bad revolting stars
That have consented unto Henry's death!
King Henry the Fifth, too famous to live long!
England ne'er lost a king of so much worth.
  Glou. England ne'er had a king until his time.
Virtue he had, deserving to command:
His brandish'd sword did blind men with his beams: 10
His arms spread wider than a dragon's wings;
His sparkling eyes, replete with wrathful fire,
More dazzled and drove back his enemies
Than mid-day sun fierce bent against their faces.
What should I say? his deeds exceed all speech:
He ne'er lift up his hand but conquered.
  Exe. We mourn in black: why mourn we not in
    blood?
Henry is dead and never shall revive:
Upon a wooden coffin we attend,
And death's dishonourable victory   20
We with our stately presence glorify,
Like captives bound to a triumphant car.
What! shall we curse the planets of mishap
That plotted thus our glory's overthrow?
Or shall we think the subtle-witted French
Conjurers and sorcerers, that afraid of him
By magic verses have contrived his end?
  Win. He was a king bless'd of the King of kings.
Unto the French the dreadful judgement-day
So dreadful will not be as was his sight.   30
The battles of the Lord of hosts he fought:
The church's prayers made him so prosperous.
  Glou. The church! where is it? Had not churchmen
    pray'd,
His thread of life had not so soon decay'd:
None do you like but an effeminate prince,
Whom, like a school-boy, you may over-awe.
  Win. Gloucester, whate'er we like, thou art
    protector
And lookest to command the prince and realm.
Thy wife is proud; she holdeth thee in awe,
More than God or religious churchmen may.   40
  Glou. Name not religion, for thou lovest the flesh,

ACT I. SCENE I. 1. **Hung . . . black,** a metaphor from the theatrical
practice of draping the stage in black when a tragedy was to be performed. (*Shakespeare's England*, II, 280.) 2. **Comets.** That comets boded
evil to princes and to the state was a widespread popular belief; cf.
King John, III, iv, 153-159; *Julius Caesar*, II, ii, 30-31. 3. **crystal,**
bright, shining; the epithet was frequently applied to astral phenomena.
8. **England ne'er had a king,** etc. This speech and others in the scene
reflect the traditional opinion of King Henry v, who was a national
hero of the English for centuries. 9. **Virtue,** excellence in culture; see
glossary. 10. **his,** its; see glossary. 16. **lift,** lifted; see Abbott, 342.
19. **wooden,** probably a quibble on the meanings "dull, dead, as the
sound of wood when struck" and "senseless." 21. **our stately presence,**
the stately funeral procession. 27. **contrived,** plotted; see glossary.
34. **decay'd,** been destroyed; see glossary. 39. **Thy wife is proud,** a
reference to Gloucester's ambitious wife, Elinor, whose inordinate
desire for greatness is depicted in *2 Henry VI*.

And ne'er throughout the year to church thou go'st
Except it be to pray against thy foes.
 Bed. Cease, cease these jars and rest your minds in
  peace:
Let 's to the altar: heralds, wait on us:
Instead of gold, we'll offer up our arms;
Since arms avail not now that Henry 's dead.
Posterity, await for wretched years,
When at their mothers' moist eyes babes shall suck,
Our isle be made a nourish of salt tears,   50
And none but women left to wail the dead.
Henry the Fifth, thy ghost I invocate:
Prosper this realm, keep it from civil broils,
Combat with adverse planets in the heavens!
A far more glorious star thy soul will make
Than Julius Cæsar or bright——

 Enter a Messenger.

 Mess. My honourable lords, health to you all!
Sad tidings bring I to you out of France,
Of loss, of slaughter and discomfiture:
Guienne, Champagne, Rheims, Orleans,   60
Paris, Guysors, Poictiers, are all quite lost.
 Bed. What say'st thou, man, before dead Henry's
  corse?
Speak softly, or the loss of those great towns
Will make him burst his lead and rise from death.
 Glou. Is Paris lost? is Rouen yielded up?
If Henry were recall'd to life again,
These news would cause him once more yield the
  ghost.
 Exe. How were they lost? what treachery was used?
 Mess. No treachery; but want of men and money.
Amongst the soldiers this is muttered,   70
That here you maintain several factions,
And whilst a field should be dispatch'd and fought,
You are disputing of your generals:
One would have lingering wars with little cost;
Another would fly swift, but wanteth wings;
A third thinks, without expense at all,
By guileful fair words peace may be obtain'd
Awake, awake, English nobility!
Let not sloth dim your honours new-begot:
Cropp'd are the flower-de-luces in your arms;   80
Of England's coat one half is cut away.
 Exe. Were our tears wanting to this funeral,
These tidings would call forth their flowing tides.
 Bed. Me they concern; Regent I am of France.
Give me my steeled coat. I'll fight for France.
Away with these disgraceful wailing robes!
Wounds will I lend the French instead of eyes,
To weep their intermissive miseries.

 Enter to them another Messenger.

 Mess. Lords, view these letters full of bad mischance.

France is revolted from the English quite,   90
Except some petty towns of no import:
The Dauphin Charles is crowned king in Rheims;
The Bastard of Orleans with him is join'd;
Reignier, Duke of Anjou, doth take his part;
The Duke of Alençon flieth to his side.
 Exe. The Dauphin crowned king! all fly to him!
O, whither shall we fly from this reproach?
 Glou. We will not fly, but to our enemies' throats.
Bedford, if thou be slack, I'll fight it out.
 Bed. Gloucester, why doubt'st thou of my
  forwardness?   100
An army have I muster'd in my thoughts,
Wherewith already France is overrun.

 Enter another Messenger.

 Mess. My gracious lords, to add to your laments,
Wherewith you now bedew King Henry's hearse,
I must inform you of a dismal fight
Betwixt the stout Lord Talbot and the French.
 Win. What! wherein Talbot overcame? is 't so?
 Mess. O, no; wherein Lord Talbot was o'erthrown:
The circumstance I'll tell you more at large.
The tenth of August last this dreadful lord,   110
Retiring from the siege of Orleans,
Having full scarce six thousand in his troop,
By three and twenty thousand of the French
Was round encompassed and set upon.
No leisure had he to enrank his men;
He wanted pikes to set before his archers;
Instead whereof sharp stakes pluck'd out of hedges
They pitched in the ground confusedly,
To keep the horsemen off from breaking in.
More than three hours the fight continued;   120
Where valiant Talbot above human thought
Enacted wonders with his sword and lance:
Hundreds he sent to hell, and none durst stand him;
Here, there, and every where, enraged he flew:
The French exclaim'd, the devil was in arms;
All the whole army stood agazed on him:
His soldiers spying his undaunted spirit
A Talbot! a Talbot! cried out amain
And rush'd into the bowels of the battle.
Here had the conquest fully been seal'd up,   130
If Sir John Fastolfe had not play'd the coward:
He, being in the vaward, placed behind
With purpose to relieve and follow them,
Cowardly fled, not having struck one stroke.
Hence grew the general wreck and massacre;
Enclosed were they with their enemies:
A base Walloon, to win the Dauphin's grace,
Thrust Talbot with a spear into the back,
Whom all France with their chief assembled strength
Durst not presume to look once in the face.   140
 Bed. Is Talbot slain? then I will slay myself,

44. **jars,** discords; usually applied to music; see glossary. 50. **nourish,** nurse; early spelling "nourice." 54. **adverse planets,** an allusion to the supposed influence exerted on human and terrestrial affairs by celestial bodies. 64. **lead,** leaden coffin. 71. **factions,** groups, sets of persons; see glossary. 73. **of,** about; see Abbott, 174. 80. **flower-de-luces,** the *fleurs-de-lis,* or iris, national emblem of France. According to the Treaty of Troyes, 1420, the crown of France was ceded to England but was nominally to belong to the French king, Charles vi, as long as he lived. Henry v's title was designated "King of England and Heir of France." At his death this title passed to Henry vi; but within two months after this took place, Charles vi died and his son Charles vii was proclaimed king. The loss of the French crown would deprive the English king of the right to display the *fleur-de-lis* in his coat of arms. 82. **wanting,** lacking; see glossary. 87-88. **Wounds**

. . . **weep,** i.e., he will make them shed blood instead of weep tears. 88. **intermissive,** intermittent; having a short intermission (Warburton and others). 105. **dismal,** ill-boding, sinister. 109. **circumstance,** particulars; see glossary. **at large,** in full detail; see *large* in glossary. 116. **pikes,** ironbound stakes sharpened at the ends and set in the ground in front of archers as protection against cavalry charges. 125. **exclaim'd,** protested; see glossary. 126. **agazed,** astounded. 128. **amain,** with full force. 130. **seal'd up,** completed; see *seal* in glossary. 131. **Sir John Fastolfe,** a historical character mentioned in the chronicles, not to be confused with Sir John Falstaff of *1* and *2 Henry IV.* 132. **vaward,** vanguard. 137. **Walloon,** an inhabitant of that province, now a part of southern Belgium. 146. **Lord Scales, Lord Hungerford,** English lords who participated in the wars in France. Both are mentioned in Holinshed. 154. **Saint George's feast,** the

For living idly here in pomp and ease,
Whilst such a worthy leader, wanting aid,
Unto his dastard foemen is betray'd.

Mess. O no, he lives; but is took prisoner,
And Lord Scales with him and Lord Hungerford:
Most of the rest slaughter'd or took likewise.

Bed. His ransom there is none but I shall pay:
I'll hale the Dauphin headlong from his throne:
His crown shall be the ransom of my friend;   150
Four of their lords I'll change for one of ours.
Farewell, my masters; to my task will I;
Bonfires in France forthwith I am to make,
To keep our great Saint George's feast withal:
Ten thousand soldiers with me I will take,
Whose bloody deeds shall make all Europe quake.

Mess. So you had need; for Orleans is besieged;
The English army is grown weak and faint:
The Earl of Salisbury craveth supply,
And hardly keeps his men from mutiny,   160
Since they, so few, watch such a multitude.

Exe. Remember, lords, your oaths to Henry sworn,
Either to quell the Dauphin utterly,
Or bring him in obedience to your yoke.

Bed. I do remember it; and here take my leave,
To go about my preparation.   [*Exit.*

Glou. I'll to the Tower with all the haste I can,
To view the artillery and munition;
And then I will proclaim young Henry king.   [*Exit.*

Exe. To Eltham will I, where the young king is,   170
Being ordain'd his special governor,
And for his safety there I'll best devise.   [*Exit.*

Win. Each hath his place and function to attend:
I am left out; for me nothing remains.
But long I will not be Jack out of office:
The king from Eltham I intend to steal
And sit at chiefest stern of public weal.   [*Exeunt.*

SCENE II. *France. Before Orleans.*

Sound a flourish. Enter CHARLES, ALENÇON, *and*
REIGNIER, *marching with drum and Soldiers.*

Char. Mars his true moving, even as in the heavens
So in the earth, to this day is not known:
Late did he shine upon the English side;
Now we are victors; upon us he smiles.
What towns of any moment but we have?
At pleasure here we lie near Orleans;
Otherwhiles the famish'd English, like pale ghosts,
Faintly besiege us one hour in a month.

Alen. They want their porridge and their fat bull-
     beeves:
Either they must be dieted like mules   10
And have their provender tied to their mouths

Or piteous they will look, like drowned mice.

Reig. Let 's raise the siege: why live we idly here?
Talbot is taken, whom we wont to fear:
Remaineth none but mad-brain'd Salisbury;
And he may well in fretting spend his gall,
Nor men nor money hath he to make war.

Char. Sound, sound alarum! we will rush on them.
Now for the honour of the forlorn French!
Him I forgive my death that killeth me   20
When he sees me go back one foot or fly.   [*Exeunt.*

*Here alarum; they are beaten back by the English with
     great loss. Re-enter* CHARLES, ALENÇON, *and*
     REIGNIER.

Char. Who ever saw the like? what men have I!
Dogs! cowards! dastards! I would ne'er have fled,
But that they left me 'midst my enemies.

Reig. Salisbury is a desperate homicide;
He fighteth as one weary of his life.
The other lords, like lions wanting food,
Do rush upon us as their hungry prey.

Alen. Froissart, a countryman of ours, records,
England all Olivers and Rowlands bred   30
During the time Edward the Third did reign.
More truly now may this be verified;
For none but Samsons and Goliases
It sendeth forth to skirmish. One to ten!
Lean raw-boned rascals! who would e'er suppose
They had such courage and audacity?

Char. Let 's leave this town; for they are hare-brain'd
     slaves,
And hunger will enforce them to be more eager:
Of old I know them; rather with their teeth
The walls they'll tear down than forsake the siege.   40

Reig. I think, by some odd gimmors or device
Their arms are set like clocks, still to strike on;
Else ne'er could they hold out so as they do.
By my consent, we'll even let them alone.

Alen. Be it so.

Enter the BASTARD *of Orleans.*

Bast. Where 's the Prince Dauphin? I have news for
     him.

Char. Bastard of Orleans, thrice welcome to us.

Bast. Methinks your looks are sad, your cheer
     appall'd?
Hath the late overthrow wrought this offence?
Be not dismay'd, for succour is at hand: 50
A holy maid hither with me I bring,
Which by a vision sent to her from heaven
Ordained is to raise this tedious siege
And drive the English forth the bounds of France.
The spirit of deep prophecy she hath,
Exceeding the nine sibyls of old Rome:
What 's past and what 's to come she can descry.

1 Henry VI
ACT I : SC II

213

---

twenty-third of April. St. George was the patron saint of England. To celebrate his day in a foreign land would be a boastful, chauvinistic action.   167. **the Tower.** The Tower of London, ancient palace-fortress, later a prison for persons of eminence, was begun by William the Conqueror and enlarged at different times by his successors.   175. **Jack out of office,** an unimportant fellow with nothing to do.   177. **at chiefest stern,** in a position of supreme control.

SCENE II. *Stage Direction:* **flourish,** fanfare of trumpets; see glossary.   1. **Mars . . . moving.** The ordinary man during Shakespeare's time seems to have had some knowledge of the astronomers' perplexity regarding the eccentricity of the orbit of Mars; cf. *All's Well that Ends Well,* I, i, 206-210. (*Shakespeare's England,* I, 448-449.)   9. **fat bull-beeves,** food supposed to confer courage (Hart).   16. **spend,** expend, waste.   **gall,** bitterness of spirit.   28. **hungry prey,** hungry for prey;

a transferred epithet.   29. **Froissart,** a fourteenth-century French chronicler who wrote of recent and contemporary events of Flanders, France, Spain, and England.   30. **Olivers and Rowlands,** paladins in the Charlemagne legends, the most famous of the twelve for their daring exploits.   33. **Samsons, Goliases,** Biblical characters typifying great physical strength.   35. **rascals,** young, lean, or inferior deer of a herd.   41. **gimmors,** gimmals, joints or connecting parts for transmitting motion.   48. **appall'd,** made pale.   56. **nine . . . Rome,** inspired women of the ancient world, not of Rome.   The phrase here is probably due to a confusion with the sibyl who came to Tarquin with nine prophetic books.   57. **descry,** discover, discern.

Speak, shall I call her in? Believe my words,
For they are certain and unfallible.
    Char. Go, call her in. [*Exit Bastard.*] But first, to try
        her skill,   60
Reignier, stand thou as Dauphin in my place:
Question her proudly; let thy looks be stern:
By this means shall we sound what skill she hath.

Re-enter the BASTARD *of Orleans, with*
JOAN LA PUCELLE.

    Reig. Fair maid, is 't thou wilt do these wondrous
        feats?
    Puc. Reignier, is 't thou that thinkest to beguile me?
Where is the Dauphin? Come, come from behind;
I know thee well, though never seen before.
Be not amazed, there 's nothing hid from me:
In private will I talk with thee apart.
Stand back, you lords, and give us leave awhile.   70
    Reig. She takes upon her bravely at first dash.
    Puc. Dauphin, I am by birth a shepherd's daughter,
My wit untrain'd in any kind of art.
Heaven and our Lady gracious hath it pleased
To shine on my contemptible estate:
Lo, whilst I waited on my tender lambs,
And to sun's parching heat display'd my cheeks,
God's mother deigned to appear to me
And in a vision full of majesty
Will'd me to leave my base vocation   80
And free my country from calamity:
Her aid she promised and assured success:
In complete glory she reveal'd herself;
And, whereas I was black and swart before,
With those clear rays which she infused on me
That beauty am I bless'd with which you see.
Ask me what question thou canst possible,
And I will answer unpremeditated:
My courage try by combat, if thou darest,
And thou shalt find that I exceed my sex.   90
Resolve on this, thou shalt be fortunate,
If thou receive me for thy warlike mate.
    Char. Thou hast astonish'd me with thy high terms:
Only this proof I'll of thy valour make,
In single combat thou shalt buckle with me,
And if thou vanquishest, thy words are true;
Otherwise I renounce all confidence.
    Puc. I am prepared: here is my keen-edged sword,
Deck'd with five flower-de-luces on each side;
The which at Touraine, in Saint Katharine's
        churchyard,   100
Out of a great deal of old iron I chose forth.
    Char. Then come, o' God's name; I fear no woman.
    Puc. And while I live, I'll ne'er fly from a man.
        [*Here they fight, and Joan La Pucelle overcomes.*
    Char. Stay, stay thy hands! thou art an Amazon
And fightest with the sword of Deborah.

    Puc. Christ's mother helps me, else I were too weak.
    Char. Whoe'er helps thee, 'tis thou that must help
        me:
Impatiently I burn with thy desire;
My heart and hands thou hast at once subdued.
Excellent Pucelle, if thy name be so,   110
Let me thy servant and not sovereign be:
'Tis the French Dauphin sueth to thee thus.
    Puc. I must not yield to any rites of love,
For my profession 's sacred from above:
When I have chased all thy foes from hence,
Then will I think upon a recompense.
    Char. Meantime look gracious on thy prostrate
        thrall.
    Reig. My lord, methinks, is very long in talk.
    Alen. Doubtless he shrives this woman to her
        smock;
Else ne'er could he so long protract his speech.   120
    Reig. Shall we disturb him, since he keeps no mean?
    Alen. He may mean more than we poor men do
        know:
These women are shrewd tempters with their tongues.
    Reig. My lord, where are you? what devise you on?
Shall we give over Orleans, or no?
    Puc. Why, no, I say, distrustful recreants!
Fight till the last gasp; I will be your guard.
    Char. What she says I'll confirm; we'll fight it out.
    Puc. Assign'd am I to be the English scourge.
This night the siege assuredly I'll raise: 130
Expect Saint Martin's summer, halcyon days,
Since I have entered into these wars.
Glory is like a circle in the water,
Which never ceaseth to enlarge itself
Till by broad spreading it disperse to nought.
With Henry's death the English circle ends;
Dispersed are the glories it included.
Now am I like that proud insulting ship
Which Cæsar and his fortune bare at once.
    Char. Was Mahomet inspired with a dove?   140
Thou with an eagle art inspired then.
Helen, the mother of great Constantine,
Nor yet Saint Philip's daughters, were like thee.
Bright star of Venus, fall'n down on the earth,
How may I reverently worship thee enough?
    Alen. Leave off delays, and let us raise the siege.
    Reig. Woman, do what thou canst to save our
        honours;
Drive them from Orleans and be immortalized.
    Char. Presently we'll try: come, let 's away about it:
No prophet will I trust, if she prove false.   [*Exeunt.* 150

SCENE III. *London. Before the Tower.*

Enter the DUKE OF GLOUCESTER, *with his* Serving-men
in blue coats.

Glou. I am come to survey the Tower this day:
Since Henry's death, I fear, there is conveyance.
Where be these warders, that they wait not here?
Open the gates; 'tis Gloucester that calls.
  First Warder. [*Within*] Who 's there that knocks so
    imperiously?
  First Serv. It is the noble Duke of Gloucester.
  Second Warder. [*Within*] Whoe'er he be, you may not
    be let in.
  First Serv. Villains, answer you so the lord protector?
  First Warder. [*Within*] The Lord protect him! so we
    answer him:
We do no otherwise than we are will'd.   10
  Glou. Who willed you? or whose will stands but
    mine?
There 's none protector of the realm but I.
Break up the gates, I'll be your warrantize:
Shall I be flouted thus by dunghill grooms?
    [*Gloucester's men rush at the Tower Gates, and Woodvile*
                        the Lieutenant speaks within.
  Woodv. What noise is this? what traitors have we
    here?
  Glou. Lieutenant, is it you whose voice I hear?
Open the gates; here 's Gloucester that would enter.
  Woodv. Have patience, noble duke; I may not open;
The Cardinal of Winchester forbids:
From him I have express commandment   20
That thou nor none of thine shall be let in.
  Glou. Faint-hearted Woodvile, prizest him 'fore me?
Arrogant Winchester, that haughty prelate,
Whom Henry, our late sovereign, ne'er could brook?
Thou art no friend to God or to the king:
Open the gates, or I'll shut thee out shortly.
  Serving-men. Open the gates unto the lord protector,
Or we'll burst them open, if that you come not
    quickly.

Enter to the Protector at the Tower Gates WINCHESTER
and his men in tawny coats.

  Win. How now, ambitious Humphrey! what means
    this?
  Glou. Peel'd priest, dost thou command me to be
    shut out?   30
  Win. I do, thou most usurping proditor,
And not protector, of the king or realm.
  Glou. Stand back, thou manifest conspirator,
Thou that contrivedst to murder our dead lord;
Thou that givest whores indulgences to sin:
I'll canvass thee in thy broad cardinal's hat,
If thou proceed in this thy insolence.
  Win. Nay, stand thou back; I will not budge a foot:
This be Damascus, be thou cursed Cain,
To slay thy brother Abel, if thou wilt.   40
  Glou. I will not slay thee, but I'll drive thee back:
Thy scarlet robes as a child's bearing-cloth

I'll use to carry thee out of this place.
  Win. Do what thou darest; I beard thee to thy face.
  Glou. What! am I dared and bearded to my face?
Draw, men, for all this privileged place;
Blue coats to tawny coats. Priest, beware your beard;
I mean to tug it and to cuff you soundly:
Under my feet I stamp thy cardinal's hat:
In spite of pope or dignities of church,   50
Here by the cheeks I'll drag thee up and down.
  Win. Gloucester, thou wilt answer this before the
    pope.
  Glou. Winchester goose, I cry, a rope! a rope!
Now beat them hence; why do you let them stay?
Thee I'll chase hence, thou wolf in sheep's array.
Out, tawny coats! out, scarlet hypocrite!

Here Gloucester's men beat out the Cardinal's men, and
  enter in the hurly-burly the Mayor of London *and his*
  Officers.

  May. Fie, lords! that you, being supreme
    magistrates,
Thus contumeliously should break the peace!
  Glou. Peace, mayor! thou know'st little of my
    wrongs:
Here 's Beaufort, that regards nor God nor king,   60
Hath here distrain'd the Tower to his use.
  Win. Here 's Gloucester, a foe to citizens,
One that still motions war and never peace,
O'ercharging your free purses with large fines,
That seeks to overthrow religion,
Because he is protector of the realm,
And would have armour here out of the Tower,
To crown himself king and suppress the prince.
  Glou. I will not answer thee with words, but blows.
                        [*Here they skirmish again.*
  May. Nought rests for me in this tumultuous strife 70
But to make open proclamation:
Come, officer; as loud as e'er thou canst
Cry.
  Off. All manner of men assembled here in arms this
day against God's peace and the king's, we charge and
command you, in his highness' name, to repair to your
several dwelling-places; and not to wear, handle, or
use any sword, weapon, or dagger, henceforward, upon
pain of death.
  Glou. Cardinal, I'll be no breaker of the law: 80
But we shall meet, and break our minds at large.
  Win. Gloucester, we will meet; to thy cost, be sure:
Thy heart-blood I will have for this day's work.
  May. I'll call for clubs, if you will not away.
This cardinal's more haughty than the devil.
  Glou. Mayor, farewell: thou dost but what thou
    mayst.
  Win. Abominable Gloucester, guard thy head;

instigation, the Council refused to recognize him as such, conferring on him instead the title Lord Protector, with powers granted "by consent of the Council." In the fourth year of Henry VI's reign, Gloucester presented to the Parliament articles of accusation against the bishop, the first of which was that Gloucester had been refused admission to the Tower "by the Commaundement of my saied Lord of Winchester." 2. **conveyance**, trickery. 10. **will'd**, commanded. 13. **warrantize**, guarantee. 24. **brook**, endure; see glossary. 26. **I'll . . . shortly**, i.e., he will take possession shortly and shut Woodvile out. 30. **Peel'd**, shaven, tonsured. 31. **proditor**, traitor. 34. **Thou . . . lord.** Gloucester, in his bill of particulars against Winchester, charged that the latter had suborned someone to hide in Henry V's bedchamber and to slay the king in his bed. 36. **canvass**, deal with severely; a metaphor from tossing someone in a canvas or blanket as sport or punishment. 39. **Damascus**, a city reputed to have been built on the site of Cain's

quarrel with Abel. 40. **thy brother.** Winchester was Gloucester's uncle; see the Genealogical Table. 42. **bearing-cloth**, christening robe. 44. **beard**, openly defy. 46. **privileged place.** The Tower, as a royal residence, was one of the precincts where drawing of weapons was forbidden by the law of arms; cf. II, iv, 86, note. 47. **Blue coats,** customarily worn by serving men. **tawny coats,** worn by attendants on a church dignitary. 52. **answer**, render an account of; see glossary. 56. **out, scarlet**, referring to the cardinal's red cassock. An exclamation of reproach; see *out* in glossary. 58. **contumeliously**, arrogantly, contemptuously. 61. **distrain'd**, confiscated. 63. **still**, always, continuously; see glossary. **motions**, proposes. 64. **O'ercharging . . . purses,** an instance of transferred epithet: freely o'ercharging their purses, i.e., generously filling. 79. **pain**, punishment; see glossary. 81. **break our minds,** reveal our purposes; see *mind* in glossary.

For I intend to have it ere long.
[*Exeunt, severally, Gloucester and Winchester with
their Serving-men.*
May. See the coast clear'd, and then we will depart.
Good God, these nobles should such stomachs bear! 90
I myself fight not once in forty year. [*Exeunt.*

SCENE IV. *Orleans.*

Enter, on the walls, a Master Gunner *and his* Boy.

M. Gun. Sirrah, thou know'st how Orleans is
besieged,
And how the English have the suburbs won.
Boy. Father, I know; and oft have shot at them,
Howe'er unfortunate I miss'd my aim.
M. Gun. But now thou shalt not. Be thou ruled by
me:
Chief master-gunner am I of this town;
Something I must do to procure me grace.
The prince's espials have informed me
How the English, in the suburbs close intrench'd,
Wont through a secret grate of iron bars 10
In yonder tower to overpeer the city
And thence discover how with most advantage
They may vex us with shot or with assault.
To intercept this inconvenience,
A piece of ordnance 'gainst it I have placed;
And even these three days have I watch'd,
If I could see them.
Now do thou watch, for I can stay no longer.
If thou spy'st any, run and bring me word;
And thou shalt find me at the governor's. [*Exit.* 20
Boy. Father, I warrant you; take you no care;
I'll never trouble you, if I may spy them. [*Exit.*

Enter, on the turrets, the LORDS SALISBURY *and* TALBOT,
SIR WILLIAM GLANSDALE, SIR THOMAS GARGRAVE,
and others.

Sal. Talbot, my life, my joy, again return'd!
How wert thou handled being prisoner?
Or by what means got'st thou to be released?
Discourse, I prithee, on this turret's top.
Tal. The Duke of Bedford had a prisoner
Call'd the brave Lord Ponton de Santrailles;
For him was I exchanged and ransomed.
But with a baser man of arms by far 30
Once in contempt they would have barter'd me:
Which I disdaining scorn'd and craved death
Rather than I would be so vile-esteem'd.
In fine, redeem'd I was as I desired.
But, O! the treacherous Fastolfe wounds my heart,
Whom with my bare fists I would execute,
If I now had him brought into my power.
Sal. Yet tell'st thou not how thou wert entertain'd.
Tal. With scoffs and scorns and contumelious
taunts.
In open market-place produced they me, 40
To be a public spectacle to all:
Here, said they, is the terror of the French,

The scarecrow that affrights our children so.
Then broke I from the officers that led me,
And with my nails digg'd stones out of the ground,
To hurl at the beholders of my shame:
My grisly countenance made others fly;
None durst come near for fear of sudden death.
In iron walls they deem'd me not secure;
So great fear of my name 'mongst them was spread 50
That they supposed I could rend bars of steel
And spurn in pieces posts of adamant:
Wherefore a guard of chosen shot I had
That walk'd about me every minute while;
And if I did but stir out of my bed,
Ready they were to shoot me to the heart.

Enter the Boy *with a linstock.*

Sal. I grieve to hear what torments you endured,
But we will be revenged sufficiently.
Now it is supper-time in Orleans:
Here, through this grate, I count each one 60
And view the Frenchmen how they fortify:
Let us look in; the sight will much delight thee.
Sir Thomas Gargrave, and Sir William Glansdale,
Let me have your express opinions
Where is best place to make our battery next.
Gar. I think, at the north gate; for there stand lords.
Glan. And I, here, at the bulwark of the bridge.
Tal. For aught I see, this city must be famish'd,
Or with light skirmishes enfeebled.
[*Here they shoot. Salisbury and Gargrave fall.*
Sal. O Lord, have mercy on us, wretched sinners! 70
Gar. O Lord, have mercy on me, woful man!
Tal. What chance is this that suddenly hath cross'd
us?
Speak, Salisbury; at least, if thou canst speak:
How farest thou, mirror of all martial men?
One of thy eyes and thy cheek's side struck off!
Accursed tower! accursed fatal hand
That hath contrived this woful tragedy!
In thirteen battles Salisbury o'ercame;
Henry the Fifth he first train'd to the wars;
Whilst any trump did sound, or drum struck up, 80
His sword did ne'er leave striking in the field.
Yet livest thou, Salisbury? though thy speech doth fail,
One eye thou hast, to look to heaven for grace:
The sun with one eye vieweth all the world.
Heaven, be thou gracious to none alive,
If Salisbury wants mercy at thy hands!
Bear hence his body; I will help to bury it.
Sir Thomas Gargrave, hast thou any life?
Speak unto Talbot; nay, look up to him.
Salisbury, cheer thy spirit with this comfort; 90
Thou shalt not die whiles—
He beckons with his hand and smiles on me,
As who should say 'When I am dead and gone,
Remember to avenge me on the French.'
Plantagenet, I will; and like thee, Nero,
Play on the lute, beholding the towns burn:

ACT I : SC III

1 Henry VI
ACT I : SC III

216

---

90. **stomachs,** angry tempers; see glossary.
SCENE IV. 1. **Sirrah,** customary form of address to an inferior; see glossary. 7. **do . . . grace,** reflect credit on; see glossary. 8. **espials,** spies. 14. **inconvenience,** mischief. 26. **Discourse,** tell it; see glossary. 34. **In fine,** finally; see *fine* in glossary. 47. **grisly,** grim, horrible. 52. **spurn,** kick. 53. **chosen shot,** excellent marksmanship. 56. *Stage Direction:* **linstock,** staff about three feet long having a forked head to hold a lighted match for firing cannon. 69. *Stage Direction:* **Here they shoot,** i.e., the French. 71. **woful,** causing grief, calam-

itous. 95. **Plantagenet,** an unexplained error on the part of the dramatist. The earl of Salisbury was Thomas Montacute; cf. II, iv, 36, note. 100. **head,** an armed force; see glossary. 107. **puzzel,** drab, slut. **dolphin.** The English spelling is retained here for the sake of the pun; this is the usual spelling in F. 110. **me,** the ethical dative.
SCENE V. 12. **high-minded,** arrogant. 14. **go victual,** proceed to supply with provisions. 21. **like Hannibal,** i.e., by stratagem rather than by force of arms. 22. **lists,** pleases; see glossary. 30. **treacherous,**

Wretched shall France be only in my name.
        [*Here an alarum, and it thunders and lightens.*
What stir is this? what tumult 's in the heavens?
Whence cometh this alarum and the noise?

Enter a Messenger.

Mess. My lord, my lord, the French have gather'd
        head: 100
The Dauphin, with one Joan la Pucelle join'd,
A holy prophetess new risen up,
Is come with a great power to raise the siege.
        [*Here Salisbury lifteth himself up and groans.*
Tal. Hear, hear how dying Salisbury doth groan!
It irks his heart he cannot be revenged.
Frenchmen, I'll be a Salisbury to you:
Pucelle or puzzel, dolphin or dogfish,
Your hearts I'll stamp out with my horse's heels,
And make a quagmire of your mingled brains.
Convey me Salisbury into his tent,   110
And then we'll try what these dastard Frenchmen
        dare.   [*Alarum. Exeunt.*

SCENE V. *The same.*

Here an alarum again: and TALBOT *pursueth the*
DAUPHIN, *and driveth him: then enter* JOAN LA
PUCELLE, *driving Englishmen before her, and exit
after them: then re-enter* TALBOT.

Tal. Where is my strength, my valour, and my
        force?
Our English troops retire, I cannot stay them;
A woman clad in armour chaseth them.

Re-enter LA PUCELLE.

Here, here she comes, I'll have a bout with thee;
Devil or devil's dam, I'll conjure thee:
Blood will I draw on thee, thou art a witch,
And straightway give thy soul to him thou servest.
        Puc. Come, come, 'tis only I that must disgrace thee.
                            [*Here they fight.*
Tal. Heavens, can you suffer hell so to prevail?
My breast I'll burst with straining of my courage   10
And from my shoulders crack my arms asunder,
But I will chastise this high-minded strumpet.
                            [*They fight again.*
Puc. Talbot, farewell; thy hour is not yet come:
I must go victual Orleans forthwith.
        [*A short alarum: then enter the town with soldiers.*
O'ertake me, if thou canst; I scorn thy strength.
Go, go, cheer up thy hungry-starved men;
Help Salisbury to make his testament:
This day is ours, as many more shall be.   [*Exit.*
Tal. My thoughts are whirled like a potter's wheel;
I know not where I am, nor what I do: 20
A witch, by fear, not force, like Hannibal,
Drives back our troops and conquers as she lists:
So bees with smoke and doves with noisome stench
Are from their hives and houses driven away.
They call'd us for our fierceness English dogs;

Now, like to whelps, we crying run away.
                            [*A short alarum.*
Hark, countrymen! either renew the fight,
Or tear the lions out of England's coat;
Renounce your soil, give sheep in lions' stead:
Sheep run not half so treacherous from the wolf,   30
Or horse or oxen from the leopard,
As you fly from your oft-subdued slaves.
                    [*Alarum. Here another skirmish.*
It will not be: retire into your trenches:
You all consented unto Salisbury's death,
For none would strike a stroke in his revenge.
Pucelle is enter'd into Orleans,
In spite of us or aught that we could do.
O, would I were to die with Salisbury!
The shame hereof will make me hide my head.
            [*Exit Talbot. Alarum; retreat; flourish.*

SCENE VI. *The same.*

Enter, on the walls, LA PUCELLE, CHARLES, REIGNIER,
ALENÇON, *and Soldiers.*

Puc. Advance our waving colours on the walls;
Rescued is Orleans from the English:
Thus Joan la Pucelle hath perform'd her word.
Char. Divinest creature, Astræa's daughter,
How shall I honour thee for this success?
Thy promises are like Adonis' gardens
That one day bloom'd and fruitful were the next.
France, triumph in thy glorious prophetess!
Recover'd is the town of Orleans:
More blessed hap did ne'er befall our state.   10
Reig. Why ring not out the bells aloud throughout
        the town?
Dauphin, command the citizens make bonfires
And feast and banquet in the open streets,
To celebrate the joy that God hath given us.
Alen. All France will be replete with mirth and joy,
When they shall hear how we have play'd the men.
Char. 'Tis Joan, not we, by whom the day is won;
For which I will divide my crown with her,
And all the priests and friars in my realm
Shall in procession sing her endless praise.   20
A statelier pyramis to her I'll rear
Than Rhodope's or Memphis' ever was:
In memory of her when she is dead,
Her ashes, in an urn more precious
Than the rich-jewel'd coffer of Darius,
Transported shall be at high festivals
Before the kings and queens of France.
No longer on Saint Denis will we cry,
But Joan la Pucelle shall be France's saint.
Come in, and let us banquet royally,   30
After this golden day of victory.   [*Flourish. Exeunt.*

ACT II.

SCENE I. *Before Orleans.*

Enter a Sergeant *of a band, with two* Sentinels.

---

cowardly.
    SCENE VI.   1. **Advance,** lift up.   4. **Astræa's daughter,** daughter of
Justice.   6. **Adonis' gardens.** Tucker Brooke's note: "What these were
in classic literature has been acrimoniously disputed, but a beautiful
and extended description, which perhaps inspired the present line, is
given by Spenser, *Faerie Queen,* III, iv."   16. **play'd the men,** proved
or represented in general men.   21. **pyramis,** pyramid.   22. **Rhodope's.**
Rhodope was a Greek courtesan who became the wife of the king of
Egypt. A legend was current that she built the third pyramid.

Memphis'. Memphis is an ancient city of Egypt near which stand the
pyramids of Rameses II.   25. **Darius,** king of Persia, conquered by
Alexander the Great. The latter, according to legend, used Darius'
rich-jewel'd coffer to carry about the poems of Homer. The passage has
a parallel in Puttenham's *Art of English Poesie.*   28. **Saint Denis,**
patron saint of France.

Serg. Sirs, take your places and be vigilant:
If any noise or soldier you perceive
Near to the walls, by some apparent sign
Let us have knowledge at the court of guard.
  First Sent. Sergeant, you shall. [*Exit Sergeant.*] Thus
    are poor servitors,
When others sleep upon their quiet beds,
Constrain'd to watch in darkness, rain and cold.

Enter TALBOT, BEDFORD, BURGUNDY, *and forces, with
  scaling-ladders, their drums beating a dead march.*

  Tal. Lord Regent, and redoubted Burgundy,
By whose approach the regions of Artois,
Wallon and Picardy are friends to us,   10
This happy night the Frenchmen are secure,
Having all day caroused and banqueted:
Embrace we then this opportunity
As fitting best to quittance their deceit
Contrived by art and baleful sorcery.
  Bed. Coward of France! how much he wrongs his
    fame,
Despairing of his own arm's fortitude,
To join with witches and the help of hell!
  Bur. Traitors have never other company.
But what's that Pucelle whom they term so pure?   20
  Tal. A maid, they say.
  Bed.   A maid! and be so martial!
  Bur. Pray God she prove not masculine ere long,
If underneath the standard of the French
She carry armour as she hath begun.
  Tal. Well, let them practise and converse with
    spirits:
God is our fortress, in whose conquering name
Let us resolve to scale their flinty bulwarks.
  Bed. Ascend, brave Talbot; we will follow thee.
  Tal. Not all together: better far, I guess,
That we do make our entrance several ways;   30
That, if it chance that one of us do fail,
The other yet may rise against their force.
  Bed. Agreed: I'll to yond corner.
  Bur.   And I to this.
  Tal. And here will Talbot mount, or make his
    grave.
Now, Salisbury, for thee, and for the right
Of English Henry, shall this night appear
How much in duty I am bound to both.
  Sent. Arm! arm! the enemy doth make assault!
    [*Cry: 'St. George,' 'A Talbot.'*

*The French leap over the walls in their shirts. Enter,
  several ways, the* BASTARD *of Orleans,* ALENÇON,
  and REIGNIER, *half ready, and half unready.*

  Alen. How now, my lords! what, all unready so?
  Bast. Unready! ay, and glad we 'scaped so well.   40
  Reig. 'Twas time, I trow, to wake and leave our beds,
Hearing alarums at our chamber-doors.
  Alen. Of all exploits since first I follow'd arms,
Ne'er heard I of a warlike enterprise
More venturous or desperate than this.

Bast. I think this Talbot be a fiend of hell.
Reig. If not of hell, the heavens, sure, favour him.
Alen. Here cometh Charles: I marvel how he sped.
Bast. Tut, holy Joan was his defensive guard.

Enter CHARLES *and* LA PUCELLE.

  Char. Is this thy cunning, thou deceitful dame?   50
Didst thou at first, to flatter us withal,
Make us partakers of a little gain,
That now our loss might be ten times so much?
  Puc. Wherefore is Charles impatient with his friend?
At all times will you have my power alike?
Sleeping or waking must I still prevail,
Or will you blame and lay the fault on me?
Improvident soldiers! had your watch been good,
This sudden mischief never could have fall'n.
  Char. Duke of Alençon, this was your default,   60
That, being captain of the watch to-night,
Did look no better to that weighty charge.
  Alen. Had all your quarters been as safely kept
As that whereof I had the government,
We had not been thus shamefully surprised.
  Bast. Mine was secure.
  Reig.   And so was mine, my lord.
  Char. And, for myself, most part of all this night,
Within her quarter and mine own precinct
I was employ'd in passing to and fro,
About relieving of the sentinels: 70
Then how or which way should they first break in?
  Puc. Question, my lords, no further of the case,
How or which way: 'tis sure they found some place
But weakly guarded, where the breach was made.
And now there rests no other shift but this;
To gather our soldiers, scatter'd and dispersed,
And lay new platforms to endamage them.

Alarum. Enter an English Soldier, *crying 'A Talbot! a
  Talbot!' They fly, leaving their clothes behind.*

  Sold. I'll be so bold to take what they have left.
The cry of Talbot serves me for a sword;
For I have loaden me with many spoils,   80
Using no other weapon but his name.   [*Exit.*

SCENE II. *Orleans. Within the town.*

Enter TALBOT, BEDFORD, BURGUNDY, *a* Captain,
  and others.

  Bed. The day begins to break, and night is fled,
Whose pitchy mantle over-veil'd the earth.
Here sound retreat, and cease our hot pursuit.
                              [*Retreat sounded.*
  Tal. Bring forth the body of old Salisbury,
And here advance it in the market-place,
The middle centre of this cursed town.
Now have I paid my vow unto his soul;
For every drop of blood was drawn from him
There hath at least five Frenchmen died tonight.
And that hereafter ages may behold   10

ACT II. SCENE I. 3. **apparent,** plain; see glossary. 7. *Stage Direction:*
Burgundy. The presence of the duke of Burgundy among the English
is explained by the fact that the duchy of Burgundy, which included the
provinces of Artois, Wallon, and Picardy, was under the English crown
in accordance with terms of the Treaty of Troyes (cf. I, i, 80, note);
its allegiance was further secured by the Treaty of Amiens, 1423, negotiated by the duke of Bedford. *a dead march,* i.e., for Salisbury;
cf. II, ii, 4. 14. **quittance,** requite. 16. **fame,** reputation; see glossary. 25. **practice,** scheme, plot; see glossary. **converse,** hold intercourse; see glossary. 30. **several ways,** i.e., by different ways;
see *several* in glossary. 37. **duty,** obedience; see glossary. 38.
Stage Direction: The French . . . shirts. The details of the hasty
flight of the French, i.e., *in their shirts,* are recorded in Holinshed's
account of the battle of Le Mans, where Talbot had a leading part.
Historically Talbot was not present at Orleans. 39. **unready,** not
fully clothed. 41. **trow,** believe; see glossary. 48. **sped,** fared; see
glossary. 68. **her,** i.e., Joan's. 75. **shift,** strategy; see glossary.
77. **platforms,** plans.
  SCENE II. 8. **was,** which was; the omission of the relative is common;
cf. Abbott, 244. 19. **muse,** wonder; see glossary. 20. **virtuous**

What ruin happen'd in revenge of him,
Within their chiefest temple I'll erect
A tomb, wherein his corpse shall be interr'd:
Upon the which, that every one may read,
Shall be engraved the sack of Orleans,
The treacherous manner of his mournful death
And what a terror he had been to France.
But, lords, in all our bloody massacre,
I muse we met not with the Dauphin's grace,
His new-come champion, virtuous Joan of Arc,   20
Nor any of his false confederates.
    Bed. 'Tis thought, Lord Talbot, when the fight
      began,
Roused on the sudden from their drowsy beds,
They did amongst the troops of armed men
Leap o'er the walls for refuge in the field.
    Bur. Myself, as far as I could well discern
For smoke and dusky vapours of the night,
Am sure I scared the Dauphin and his trull,
When arm in arm they both came swiftly running,
Like to a pair of loving turtle-doves   30
That could not live asunder day or night.
After that things are set in order here,
We'll follow them with all the power we have.

    Enter a Messenger.

    Mess. All hail, my lords! Which of this princely
      train
Call ye the warlike Talbot, for his acts
So much applauded through the realm of France?
    Tal. Here is the Talbot: who would speak with him?
    Mess. The virtuous lady, Countess of Auvergne,
With modesty admiring thy renown,
By me entreats, great lord, thou wouldst vouchsafe   40
To visit her poor castle where she lies,
That she may boast she hath beheld the man
Whose glory fills the world with loud report.
    Bur. Is it even so? Nay, then, I see our wars
Will turn unto a peaceful comic sport,
When ladies crave to be encounter'd with.
You may not, my lord, despise her gentle suit.
    Tal. Ne'er trust me then; for when a world of men
Could not prevail with all their oratory,
Yet hath a woman's kindness over-ruled: 50
And therefore tell her I return great thanks,
And in submission will attend on her.
Will not your honours bear me company?
    Bed. No, truly; it is more than manners will:
And I have heard it said, unbidden guests
Are often welcomest when they are gone.
    Tal. Well then, alone, since there 's no remedy,
I mean to prove this lady's courtesy.
Come hither, captain. [*Whispers.*] You perceive my
      mind?   59
    Capt. I do, my lord, and mean accordingly. [*Exeunt.*

    SCENE III. *Auvergne. The* COUNTESS's *castle.*

    Enter the COUNTESS *and her* Porter.

    Count. Porter, remember what I gave in charge;
And when you have done so, bring the keys to me.
    Port. Madam, I will.   [*Exit.*
    Count. The plot is laid: if all things fall out right,
I shall as famous be by this exploit
As Scythian Tomyris by Cyrus' death.
Great is the rumour of this dreadful knight,
And his achievements of no less account:
Fain would mine eyes be witness with mine ears,
To give their censure of these rare reports.   10

    Enter Messenger *and* TALBOT.

    Mess. Madam,
According as your ladyship desired,
By message craved, so is Lord Talbot come.
    Count. And he is welcome. What! is this the man?
    Mess. Madam, it is.
    Count.   Is this the scourge of France?
Is this the Talbot, so much fear'd abroad
That with his name the mothers still their babes?
I see report is fabulous and false:
I thought I should have seen some Hercules,
A second Hector, for his grim aspect,   20
And large proportion of his strong-knit limbs.
Alas, this is a child, a silly dwarf!
It cannot be this weak and writhled shrimp
Should strike such terror to his enemies.
    Tal. Madam, I have been bold to trouble you;
But since your ladyship is not at leisure,
I'll sort some other time to visit you.
    Count. What means he now? Go ask him whither he
      goes.
    Mess. Stay, my Lord Talbot; for my lady craves
To know the cause of your abrupt departure.   30
    Tal. Marry, for that she 's in a wrong belief,
I go to certify her Talbot 's here.

    Re-enter Porter *with keys.*

    Count. If thou be he, then art thou prisoner.
    Tal. Prisoner! to whom?
    Count.   To me, blood-thirsty lord;
And for that cause I train'd thee to my house.
Long time thy shadow hath been thrall to me,
For in my gallery thy picture hangs:
But now the substance shall endure the like,
And I will chain these legs and arms of thine,
That hast by tyranny these many years   40
Wasted our country, slain our citizens
And sent our sons and husbands captivate.
    Tal. Ha, ha, ha!
    Count. Laughest thou, wretch? thy mirth shall turn
      to moan.
    Tal. I laugh to see your ladyship so fond
To think that you have aught but Talbot's shadow
Whereon to practise your severity.
    Count. Why, art not thou the man?
    Tal.   I am indeed.
    Count. Then have I substance too.
    Tal. No, no, I am but shadow of myself: 50

Joan of Arc, spoken contemptuously. 28. **trull,** strumpet; contemptuous reference to Joan of Arc. 39. **admiring,** wondering at; see glossary. 41. **lies,** dwells; see glossary. 45. **comic,** ludicrous, merry; used in antithesis to "tragic"—as war is tragic. 58. **prove,** put to test; see glossary.
    SCENE III. 6. **Scythian Tomyris,** tribal queen of the Messagetae, who slew Cyrus the Great when he invaded her territory. The epithet *Scythian* is used to suggest her savagery. 10. **censure,** critical opinion; see glossary. 19, 20. **Hercules, Hector,** types of great physical strength. 21. **proportion,** size; see glossary. 22. **child, dwarf.** These

words may be merely contemptuous and not actually descriptive of Talbot's size; but cf. line 52, where Talbot appears to acquiesce in references to his small stature. Tucker Brooke, taking this as a description of Talbot, argues against it from historical evidence. 23. **writhled,** wrinkled. Talbot was eighty years old when he was killed in battle (1453). 31. **Marry,** mild interjection; see glossary. **for that,** because; see glossary. 35. **train'd,** lured, enticed; see glossary. 36. **shadow,** image, likeness; see glossary. **thrall,** enslaved. 37. **thy picture.** The countess may mean that she was practicing witchcraft on his image. 45. **fond,** foolish; see glossary.

You are deceived, my substance is not here;
For what you see is but the smallest part
And least proportion of humanity:
I tell you, madam, were the whole frame here,
It is of such a spacious lofty pitch,
Your roof were not sufficient to contain 't.
   Count. This is a riddling merchant for the nonce;
He will be here, and yet he is not here:
How can these contrarieties agree?
     Tal. That will I show you presently.   60
       [Winds his horn. Drums strike up: a peal of ordnance.
                                      Enter Soldiers.
How say you, madam? are you now persuaded
That Talbot is but shadow of himself?
These are his substance, sinews, arms and strength,
With which he yoketh your rebellious necks,
Razeth your cities and subverts your towns
And in a moment makes them desolate.
   Count. Victorious Talbot! pardon my abuse:
I find thou art no less than fame hath bruited
And more than may be gather'd by thy shape.
Let my presumption not provoke thy wrath;   70
For I am sorry that with reverence
I did not entertain thee as thou art.
   Tal. Be not dismay'd, fair lady; nor misconstrue
The mind of Talbot, as you did mistake
The outward composition of his body.
What you have done hath not offended me;
Nor other satisfaction do I crave,
But only, with your patience, that we may
Taste of your wine and see what cates you have;
For soldiers' stomachs always serve them well.   80
   Count. With all my heart, and think me honoured
To feast so great a warrior in my house.   *[Exeunt.*

SCENE IV. *London. The Temple-garden.*

Enter the EARLS OF SOMERSET, SUFFOLK, *and* WAR-
  WICK; RICHARD PLANTAGENET, VERNON, *and*
  another Lawyer.

   Plan. Great lords and gentlemen, what means this
     silence?
Dare no man answer in a case of truth?
   Suf. Within the Temple-hall we were too loud;
The garden here is more convenient.
   Plan. Then say at once if I maintain'd the truth;
Or else was wrangling Somerset in the error?
   Suf. Faith, I have been a truant in the law,
And never yet could frame my will to it;
And therefore frame the law unto my will.
   Som. Judge you, my Lord of Warwick, then,
     between us.   10

War. Between two hawks, which flies the higher
     pitch;
Between two dogs, which hath the deeper mouth;
Between two blades, which bears the better temper:
Between two horses, which doth bear him best;
Between two girls, which hath the merriest eye;
I have perhaps some shallow spirit of judgement;
But in these nice sharp quillets of the law,
Good faith, I am no wiser than a daw.
   Plan. Tut, tut, here is a mannerly forbearance:
The truth appears so naked on my side   20
That any purblind eye may find it out.
   Som. And on my side it is so well apparell'd,
So clear, so shining and so evident
That it will glimmer through a blind man's eye.
   Plan. Since you are tongue-tied and so loath to
     speak,
In dumb significants proclaim your thoughts:
Let him that is a true-born gentleman
And stands upon the honour of his birth,
If he suppose that I have pleaded truth,
From off this brier pluck a white rose with me.   30
   Som. Let him that is no coward nor no flatterer,
But dare maintain the party of the truth,
Pluck a red rose from off this thorn with me.
   War. I love no colours, and without all colour
Of base insinuating flattery
I pluck this white rose with Plantagenet.
   Suf. I pluck this red rose with young Somerset
And say withal I think he held the right.
   Ver. Stay, lords and gentlemen, and pluck no more,
Till you conclude that he upon whose side   40
The fewest roses are cropp'd from the tree
Shall yield the other in the right opinion.
   Som. Good Master Vernon, it is well objected:
If I have fewest, I subscribe in silence.
   Plan. And I.
   Ver. Then for the truth and plainness of the case,
I pluck this pale and maiden blossom here,
Giving my verdict on the white rose side.
   Som. Prick not your finger as you pluck it off,
Lest bleeding you do paint the white rose red   50
And fall on my side so, against your will.
   Ver. If I, my lord, for my opinion bleed,
Opinion shall be surgeon to my hurt
And keep me on the side where still I am.
   Som. Well, well, come on: who else?
   Law. Unless my study and my books be false,
The argument you held was wrong in you;
                            [To Somerset.
In sign whereof I pluck a white rose too.
   Plan. Now, Somerset, where is your argument?
   Som. Here in my scabbard, meditating that   60
Shall dye your white rose in a bloody red.

---

55. **pitch,** height; see glossary. 56. **roof,** house; an instance of me-
tonymy. 57. **riddling merchant,** dealer in riddles. 67. **abuse,** error;
see glossary. 68. **bruited,** reported, rumored. 79. **cates,** delicacies,
dainty confections.
  SCENE IV. *Stage Direction: Temple-garden.* The Temple was a district of London which took its name from the Knights Templars, who
owned it during the twelfth and thirteenth centuries. It was leased to
law students and converted into Inns of Court (the Inner Temple and
the Middle Temple) in the fourteenth century. This scene placed in the
garden has no basis in history. 12. **mouth,** voice. 16. **shallow . . .
judgement,** superficial ability to judge. 17. **quillets,** verbal niceties,
subtle distinctions; see glossary. 18. **daw,** jackdaw; a type of foolishness. 21. **purblind,** dimsighted. 26. **significants,** tokens, signs. 30.
white rose, badge of the house of York. 32. **party,** part, side; cf. l. 123;
see glossary. 33. **red rose,** badge of the house of Lancaster. 34.
colours, colour, pretexts, appearance; see glossary. 36. **Plantagenet.**
This was the nickname of Geoffrey of Anjou, father of Henry II, founder

of the dynasty. None of Geoffrey's descendants assumed the name until
Richard Duke of York adopted it in order to proclaim his superior right
to the crown. The name first appears in the rolls of Parliament for 1460.
53. **Opinion,** public opinion, i.e., my reputation; see glossary. 57.
argument, reason; see glossary. 60. **that,** that which. 70. **his,** its; the
antecedent is *rose* (l. 69). 76. **peevish,** sullen; see glossary. 79. **I'll . . .
throat,** he will throw the lies or slanders back into the throat from
which they proceeded. 80. **William de la Pole,** the name of the duke
of Suffolk. 81. **grace,** do honor to; see glossary. **yeoman,** a small
freeholder, to be contrasted with a landed gentleman; cf. *crestless
yeoman* (l. 85). 83. **His . . . Clarence.** Lionel was Richard's maternal
great-great-grandfather; Edmund Duke of York was his paternal grandfather, whose estates and title Richard inherited from his father's
brother, Edward (see the Genealogical Table). His blood was "corrupted" because of his father's treason. Warwick appears here to be
urging Richard's *ancient gentry* because of his maternal inheritance. It
was through the maternal line that his claim to the throne was ad-

Plan. Meantime your cheeks do counterfeit our
    roses;
For pale they look with fear, as witnessing
The truth on our side.
    Som.   No, Plantagenet,
'Tis not for fear but anger that thy cheeks
Blush for pure shame to counterfeit our roses,
And yet thy tongue will not confess thy error.
    Plan. Hath not thy rose a canker, Somerset?
    Som. Hath not thy rose a thorn, Plantagenet?
    Plan. Ay, sharp and piercing, to maintain his
    truth;   70
Whiles thy consuming canker eats his falsehood.
    Som. Well, I'll find friends to wear my bleeding
    roses,
That shall maintain what I have said is true,
Where false Plantagenet dare not be seen.
    Plan. Now, by this maiden blossom in my hand,
I scorn thee and thy fashion, peevish boy.
    Suf. Turn not thy scorns this way, Plantagenet.
    Plan. Proud Pole, I will, and scorn both him and
    thee.
    Suf. I'll turn my part thereof into thy throat.
    Som. Away, away, good William de la Pole!   80
We grace the yeoman by conversing with him.
    War. Now, by God's will, thou wrong'st him,
    Somerset;
His grandfather was Lionel Duke of Clarence,
Third son to the third Edward King of England;
Spring crestless yeomen from so deep a root?
    Plan. He bears him on the place's privilege,
Or durst not, for his craven heart, say thus.
    Som. By him that made me, I'll maintain my words
On any plot of ground in Christendom.
Was not thy father, Richard Earl of Cambridge,   90
For treason executed in our late king's days?
And, by his treason, stand'st not thou attainted,
Corrupted, and exempt from ancient gentry?
His trespass yet lives guilty in thy blood;
And, till thou be restored, thou art a yeoman.
    Plan. My father was attached, not attainted,
Condemn'd to die for treason, but no traitor;
And that I'll prove on better men than Somerset,
Were growing time once ripen'd to my will.
For your partaker Pole and you yourself,   100
I'll note you in my book of memory,
To scourge you for this apprehension:
Look to it well and say you are well warn'd.
    Som. Ah, thou shalt find us ready for thee still;
And know us by these colours for thy foes,
For these my friends in spite of thee shall wear.
    Plan. And, by my soul, this pale and angry rose,
As cognizance of my blood-drinking hate,
Will I for ever and my faction wear,

Until it wither with me to my grave   110
Or flourish to the height of my degree.
    Suf. Go forward and be choked with thy ambition!
And so farewell until I meet thee next.   [*Exit*.
    Som. Have with thee, Pole. Farewell, ambitious
    Richard.   [*Exit*.
    Plan. How I am braved and must perforce endure
    it!
    War. This blot that they object against your house
Shall be wiped out in the next parliament
Call'd for the truce of Winchester and Gloucester;
And if thou be not then created York,
I will not live to be accounted Warwick.   120
Meantime, in signal of my love to thee,
Against proud Somerset and William Pole,
Will I upon thy party wear this rose:
And here I prophesy: this brawl to-day,
Grown to this faction in the Temple-garden,
Shall send between the red rose and the white
A thousand souls to death and deadly night.
    Plan. Good Master Vernon, I am bound to you,
That you on my behalf would pluck a flower.
    Ver. In your behalf still will I wear the same.   130
    Law. And so will I.
    Plan. Thanks, gentle sir.
Come, let us four to dinner: I dare say
This quarrel will drink blood another day.   [*Exeunt*.

SCENE V. *The Tower of London.*
Enter MORTIMER, *brought in a chair, and* Gaolers.
    Mor. Kind keepers of my weak decaying age,
Let dying Mortimer here rest himself.
Even like a man new haled from the rack,
So fare my limbs with long imprisonment;
And these grey locks, the pursuivants of death,
Nestor-like aged in an age of care,
Argue the end of Edmund Mortimer.
These eyes, like lamps whose wasting oil is spent,
Wax dim, as drawing to their exigent;
Weak shoulders, overborne with burthening grief,   10
And pitiless arms, like to a wither'd vine
That droops his sapless branches to the ground:
Yet are these feet, whose strengthless stay is numb,
Unable to support this lump of clay,
Swift-winged with desire to get a grave,
As witting I no other comfort have.
But tell me, keeper, will my nephew come?
    First Gaol. Richard Plantagenet, my lord, will come:
We sent unto the Temple, unto his chamber;
And answer was return'd that he will come.   20
    Mor. Enough: my soul shall then be satisfied.
Poor gentleman! his wrong doth equal mine.
Since Henry Monmouth first began to reign,

Before whose glory I was great in arms,
This loathsome sequestration have I had;
And even since then hath Richard been obscured,
Deprived of honour and inheritance.
But now the arbitrator of despairs,
Just death, kind umpire of men's miseries,
With sweet enlargement doth dismiss me hence: 30
I would his troubles likewise were expired,
That so he might recover what was lost.

Enter RICHARD PLANTAGENET.

First Gaol. My lord, your loving nephew now is come.
Mor. Richard Plantagenet, my friend, is he come?
Plan. Ay, noble uncle, thus ignobly used,
Your nephew, late despised Richard, comes.
Mor. Direct mine arms I may embrace his neck,
And in his bosom spend my latter gasp:
O, tell me when my lips do touch his cheeks,
That I may kindly give one fainting kiss. 40
And now declare, sweet stem from York's great stock,
Why didst thou say, of late thou wert despised?
Plan. First, lean thine aged back against mine arm;
And, in that ease, I'll tell thee my disease.
This day, in argument upon a case,
Some words there grew 'twixt Somerset and me;
Among which terms he used his lavish tongue
And did upbraid me with my father's death:
Which obloquy set bars before my tongue,
Else with the like I had requited him. 50
Therefore, good uncle, for my father's sake,
In honour of a true Plantagenet
And for alliance sake, declare the cause
My father, Earl of Cambridge, lost his head.
Mor. That cause, fair nephew, that imprison'd me
And hath detain'd me all my flowering youth
Within a loathsome dungeon, there to pine,
Was cursed instrument of his decease.
Plan. Discover more at large what cause that was,
For I am ignorant and cannot guess. 60
Mor. I will, if that my fading breath permit
And death approach not ere my tale be done.
Henry the Fourth, grandfather to this king,
Deposed his nephew Richard, Edward's son,
The first-begotten and the lawful heir
Of Edward king, the third of that descent:
During whose reign the Percies of the north,
Finding his usurpation most unjust,
Endeavour'd my advancement to the throne:
The reason moved these warlike lords to this 70
Was, for that—young King Richard thus removed,
Leaving no heir begotten of his body—
I was the next by birth and parentage;
For by my mother I derived am
From Lionel Duke of Clarence, the third son
To King Edward the Third; whereas he
From John of Gaunt doth bring his pedigree,
Being but fourth of that heroic line.
But mark: as in this haughty great attempt

They laboured to plant the rightful heir, 80
I lost my liberty and they their lives.
Long after this, when Henry the Fifth,
Succeeding his father Bolingbroke, did reign,
Thy father, Earl of Cambridge, then derived
From famous Edmund Langley, Duke of York,
Marrying my sister that thy mother was,
Again in pity of my hard distress
Levied an army, weening to redeem
And have install'd me in the diadem:
But, as the rest, so fell that noble earl 90
And was beheaded. Thus the Mortimers,
In whom the title rested, were suppress'd.
Plan. Of which, my lord, your honour is the last.
Mor. True; and thou seest that I no issue have
And that my fainting words do warrant death:
Thou art my heir; the rest I wish thee gather:
But yet be wary in thy studious care.
Plan. Thy grave admonishments prevail with me:
But yet, methinks, my father's execution
Was nothing less than bloody tyranny. 100
Mor. With silence, nephew, be thou politic:
Strong-fixed is the house of Lancaster
And like a mountain, not to be removed.
But now thy uncle is removing hence;
As princes do their courts, when they are cloy'd
With long continuance in a settled place.
Plan. O, uncle, would some part of my young years
Might but redeem the passage of your age!
Mor. Thou dost then wrong me, as that slaughterer
  doth
Which giveth many wounds when one will kill. 110
Mourn not, except thou sorrow for my good;
Only give order for my funeral:
And so farewell, and fair be all thy hopes
And prosperous be thy life in peace and war! [*Dies.*
Plan. And peace, no war, befall thy parting soul!
In prison hast thou spent a pilgrimage
And like a hermit overpass'd thy days.
Well, I will lock his counsel in my breast;
And what I do imagine let that rest.
Keepers, convey him hence, and I myself 120
Will see his burial better than his life.
  [*Exeunt Gaolers, bearing out the body of Mortimer.*
Here dies the dusky torch of Mortimer,
Choked with ambition of the meaner sort:
And for those wrongs, those bitter injuries,
Which Somerset hath offer'd to my house,
I doubt not but with honour to redress;
And therefore haste I to the parliament,
Either to be restored to my blood,
Or make my ill the advantage of my good. [*Exit.*

ACT III.

SCENE I. *London. The Parliament-house.*

Flourish. Enter KING, EXETER, GLOUCESTER, WAR-

WICK, SOMERSET, *and* SUFFOLK; *the* BISHOP OF
WINCHESTER, RICHARD PLANTAGENET, *and
others.* GLOUCESTER *offers to put up a bill;* WIN-
CHESTER *snatches it, and tears it.*

Win. Comest thou with deep premeditated lines,
With written pamphlets studiously devised,
Humphrey of Gloucester? If thou canst accuse,
Or aught intend'st to lay unto my charge,
Do it without invention, suddenly;
As I with sudden and extemporal speech
Purpose to answer what thou canst object.
  Glou. Presumptuous priest! this place commands my
        patience,
Or thou shouldst find thou hast dishonour'd me.
Think not, although in writing I preferr'd   10
The manner of thy vile outrageous crimes,
That therefore I have forged, or am not able
Verbatim to rehearse the method of my pen:
No, prelate; such is thy audacious wickedness,
Thy lewd, pestiferous and dissentious pranks,
As very infants prattle of thy pride.
Thou art a most pernicious usurer,
Froward by nature, enemy to peace;
Lascivious, wanton, more than well beseems
A man of thy profession and degree;   20
And for thy treachery, what 's more manifest?
In that thou laid'st a trap to take my life,
As well at London bridge as at the Tower.
Beside, I fear me, if thy thoughts were sifted,
The king, thy sovereign, is not quite exempt
From envious malice of thy swelling heart.
  Win. Gloucester, I do defy thee. Lords, vouchsafe
To give me hearing what I shall reply.
If I were covetous, ambitious or perverse,
As he will have me, how am I so poor?   30
Or how haps it I seek not to advance
Or raise myself, but keep my wonted calling?
And for dissension, who preferreth peace
More than I do?—except I be provoked.
No, my good lords, it is not that offends;
It is not that that hath incensed the duke:
It is, because no one should sway but he;
No one but he should be about the king;
And that engenders thunder in his breast
And makes him roar these accusations forth.   40
But he shall know I am as good—
  Glou.   As good!
Thou bastard of my grandfather!
  Win. Ay, lordly sir; for what are you, I pray,
But one imperious in another's throne?
  Glou. Am I not protector, saucy priest?
  Win. And am not I a prelate of the church?
  Glou. Yes, as an outlaw in a castle keeps
And useth it to patronage his theft.
  Win. Unreverent Gloster!
  Glou.   Thou art reverent
Touching thy spiritual function, not thy life.   50

Win. Rome shall remedy this.
War.   Roam thither, then.
Som. My lord, it were your duty to forbear.
War. Ay, see the bishop be not overborne.
Som. Methinks my lord should be religious
And know the office that belongs to such.
  War. Methinks his lordship should be humbler;
It fitteth not a prelate so to plead.
  Som. Yes, when his holy state is touch'd so near.
  War. State holy or unhallow'd, what of that?
Is not his grace protector to the king?   60
  Plan. [*Aside*] Plantagenet, I see, must hold his
        tongue,
Lest it be said 'Speak, sirrah, when you should;
Must your bold verdict enter talk with lords?'
Else would I have a fling at Winchester.
  King. Uncles of Gloucester and of Winchester,
The special watchmen of our English weal,
I would prevail, if prayers might prevail,
To join your hearts in love and amity.
O, what a scandal is it to our crown,
That two such noble peers as ye should jar!   70
Believe me, lords, my tender years can tell
Civil dissension is a viperous worm
That gnaws the bowels of the commonwealth.
[*A noise within,* 'Down with the tawny-coats!'
What tumult 's this?
  War.   An uproar, I dare warrant,
Begun through malice of the bishop's men.
        [*A noise again,* 'Stones! stones!'

Enter Mayor.

  May. O, my good lords, and virtuous Henry,
Pity the city of London, pity us!
The bishop and the Duke of Gloucester's men,
Forbidden late to carry any weapon,
Have fill'd their pockets full of pebble stones   80
And banding themselves in contrary parts
Do pelt so fast at one another's pate
That many have their giddy brains knock'd out:
Our windows are broke down in every street
And we for fear compell'd to shut our shops.

Enter Serving-men, *in skirmish, with bloody pates.*

  King. We charge you, on allegiance to ourself,
To hold your slaughtering hands and keep the peace.
Pray, uncle Gloucester, mitigate this strife.
  First Serv. Nay, if we be forbidden stones, we'll fall
to it with our teeth.   90
  Sec. Serv. Do what ye dare, we are as resolute.
        [*Skirmish again.*
  Glou. You of my household, leave this peevish broil
And set this unaccustom'd fight aside.
  Third Serv. My lord, we know your grace to be a man
Just and upright; and, for your royal birth,
Inferior to none but to his majesty:
And ere that we will suffer such a prince,
So kind a father of the commonweal,

1 Henry VI
ACT III : SC I

223

---

tents. 23. at London bridge. Gloucester's articles of accusation
against Winchester presented to the Parliament stated that the latter
had "set men of armes and archers, at thende of London bridge next
Southwerke," to prevent Gloucester's going to Eltham to interfere with
the bishop's plans regarding the young king. 26. envious, wicked; see
glossary. swelling, inflated with pride. 30. how am I so poor. As a
matter of fact, Winchester was extremely rich. 42. Thou bastard.
Winchester—son of John of Gaunt and Catherine Swynford—was, with
his two brothers and one sister, legitimatized by act of Parliament in
Richard II's reign. 47. keeps, dwells; see glossary. 53. overborne,
subdued. 58. state, degree, rank; see glossary. touch'd so near, so

closely concerned. 70. jar, quarrel; see glossary. 71. my tender
years. The king was actually five years old at the time of this episode.
73. Stage Direction: tawny-coats. Cf. I, iii, 47, note. 78-85. The . . .
shops. Boswell-Stone finds an account to parallel this scene in Fabyan's
Chronicle: "Proclamacyons were made, that men shulde leue theyr
Swerdes & other wepeyns in theyr Innys, the people toke great battes
& stauys in theyr neckes, and so folowed theyr lordes and maisters vnto
the Parliament. And whan that wepyn was Inhybyted theym, then they
toke stonys & plummettes of lede, & trussyed them secretely in theyr
sleuys & bosomys." 96. Inferior . . . majesty. The serving-man
alludes to the close kinship of Gloucester with the young king.

To be disgraced by an inkhorn mate,
We and our wives and children all will fight   100
And have our bodies slaughter'd by thy foes.
    First Serv. Ay, and the very parings of our nails
Shall pitch a field when we are dead.   [*Begin again.*
    Glou.   Stay, stay, I say!
And if you love me, as you say you do,
Let me persuade you to forbear awhile.
    King. O, how this discord doth afflict my soul!
Can you, my Lord of Winchester, behold
My sighs and tears and will not once relent?
Who should be pitiful, if you be not?
Or who should study to prefer a peace,   110
If holy churchmen take delight in broils?
    War. Yield, my lord protector; yield, Winchester;
Except you mean with obstinate repulse
To slay your sovereign and destroy the realm.
You see what mischief and what murder too
Hath been enacted through your enmity;
Then be at peace, except ye thirst for blood.
    Win. He shall submit, or I will never yield.
    Glou. Compassion on the king commands me stoop;
Or I would see his heart out, ere the priest   120
Should ever get that privilege of me.
    War. Behold, my Lord of Winchester, the duke
Hath banish'd moody discontented fury,
As by his smoothed brows it doth appear:
Why look you still so stern and tragical?
    Glou. Here, Winchester, I offer thee my hand.
    King. Fie, uncle Beaufort! I have heard you preach
That malice was a great and grievous sin;
And will not you maintain the thing you teach,
But prove a chief offender in the same?   130
    War. Sweet king! the bishop hath a kindly gird.
For shame, my Lord of Winchester, relent!
What, shall a child instruct you what to do?
    Win. Well, Duke of Gloucester, I will yield to thee;
Love for thy love and hand for hand I give.
    Glou. [*Aside*] Ay, but, I fear me, with a hollow
        heart.—
See here, my friends and loving countrymen,
This token serveth for a flag of truce
Betwixt ourselves and all our followers:
So help me God, as I dissemble not!   140
    Win. [*Aside*] So help me God, as I intend it not!
    King. O loving uncle, kind Duke of Gloucester,
How joyful am I made by this contract!
Away, my masters! trouble us no more;
But join in friendship, as your lords have done.
    First Serv. Content: I'll to the surgeon's.
    Sec. Serv.   And so will I.
    Third Serv. And I will see what physic the tavern
affords.   [*Exeunt Serving-men, Mayor, &c.*
    War. Accept this scroll, most gracious sovereign,
Which in the right of Richard Plantagenet   150
We do exhibit to your majesty.
    Glou. Well urged, my Lord of Warwick: for, sweet
        prince,
An if your grace mark every circumstance,

You have great reason to do Richard right;
Especially for those occasions
At Eltham Place I told your majesty.
    King. And those occasions, uncle, were of force:
Therefore, my loving lords, our pleasure is
That Richard be restored to his blood.
    War. Let Richard be restored to his blood;   160
So shall his father's wrongs be recompensed.
    Win. As will the rest, so willeth Winchester.
    King. If Richard will be true, not that alone
But all the whole inheritance I give
That doth belong unto the house of York,
From whence you spring by lineal descent.
    Plan. Thy humble servant vows obedience
And humble service till the point of death.
    King. Stoop then and set your knee against my foot;
And, in reguerdon of that duty done,   170
I gird thee with the valiant sword of York:
Rise, Richard, like a true Plantagenet,
And rise created princely Duke of York.
    Plan. And so thrive Richard as thy foes may fall!
And as my duty springs, so perish they
That grudge one thought against your majesty!
    All. Welcome, high prince, the mighty Duke of
        York!
    Som. [*Aside*] Perish, base prince, ignoble Duke of
        York!
    Glou. Now will it best avail your majesty
To cross the seas and to be crown'd in France: 180
The presence of a king engenders love
Amongst his subjects and his loyal friends,
As it disanimates his enemies.
    King. When Gloucester says the word, King Henry
        goes;
For friendly counsel cuts off many foes.
    Glou. Your ships already are in readiness.
            [*Sennet. Flourish. Exeunt all but Exeter.*
    Exe. Ay, we may march in England or in France,
Not seeing what is likely to ensue.
This late dissension grown betwixt the peers
Burns under feigned ashes of forged love   190
And will at last break out into a flame:
As fester'd members rot but by degree,
Till bones and flesh and sinews fall away,
So will this base and envious discord breed.
And now I fear that fatal prophecy
Which in the time of Henry named the Fifth
Was in the mouth of every sucking babe;
That Henry born at Monmouth should win all
And Henry born at Windsor lose all:
Which is so plain that Exeter doth wish   200
His days may finish ere that hapless time.   [*Exit.*

SCENE II. *France. Before Rouen.*

Enter LA PUCELLE *disguised, with four* Soldiers *with
    sacks upon their backs.*

    Puc. These are the city gates, the gates of Rouen,

---

99. **inkhorn mate,** scribbler.   102-103. **the . . . dead,** i.e., our zest for Gloucester's cause is such that we shall prepare for battle barehanded even after we are dead; typical extravagant boasting of servants.   131. **kindly,** appropriate; see glossary.   **gird,** rebuke.   147. **physic,** remedy; see glossary.   153. **An if,** if; see glossary.   155. **occasions,** reasons. 170. **reguerdon,** reward.   183. **disanimates,** discourages.   186. *Stage Direction:* **Sennet,** set of notes played on a trumpet as a signal for the approach and departure of processions; see glossary.   195. **fatal prophecy.** Cf. Holinshed: "This yeare, at Windsore, on the daie of

saint Nicholas, in December, the queene was deliuered of a sonne named Henrie. . . . The king, being certified hereof, as he laie at seige before Meaux, gaue God thanks. . . . But, when he heard reported the place of his natiuitie, were it that he [was] warned by some prophesie, or had some foreknowledge, or else iudged himselfe of his sonnes fortune, he said vnto the lord Fitz Hugh, his trustie chamberleine, these words: 'My lord, I *Henrie, borne at Monmouth*, shall small time reigne, & much get; *and Henrie, borne at Windsore*, shall long reigne, and *all loose:* but, as God will, so be it.'"

Through which our policy must make a breach:
Take heed, be wary how you place your words;
Talk like the vulgar sort of market men
That come to gather money for their corn.
If we have entrance, as I hope we shall,
And that we find the slothful watch but weak,
I'll by a sign give notice to our friends,
That Charles the Dauphin may encounter them.

First Sol. Our sacks shall be a mean to sack the city, 10
And we be lords and rulers over Rouen;
Therefore we'll knock.   [*Knocks.*

Watch. [*Within*] Qui est là?

Puc. Paysans, pauvres gens de France;
Poor market folks that come to sell their corn.

Watch. Enter, go in; the market bell is rung.

Puc. Now, Rouen, I'll shake thy bulwarks to the
ground.   [*Exeunt.*

Enter CHARLES, *the* BASTARD *of Orleans,* ALENÇON,
REIGNIER, *and forces.*

Char. Saint Denis bless this happy stratagem!
And once again we'll sleep secure in Rouen.

Bast. Here enter'd Pucelle and her practisants; 20
Now she is there, how will she specify
Where is the best and safest passage in?

Reig. By thrusting out a torch from yonder tower;
Which, once discern'd, shows that her meaning is,
No way to that, for weakness, which she enter'd.

Enter LA PUCELLE *on the top, thrusting out a torch
burning.*

Puc. Behold, this is the happy wedding torch
That joineth Rouen unto her countrymen,
But burning fatal to the Talbotites!   [*Exit.*

Bast. See, noble Charles, the beacon of our friend;
The burning torch in yonder turret stands.   30

Char. Now shine it like a comet of revenge,
A prophet to the fall of all our foes!

Reig. Defer no time, delays have dangerous ends;
Enter, and cry 'The Dauphin!' presently,
And then do execution on the watch. [*Alarum. Exeunt.*

An alarum. Enter TALBOT *in an excursion.*

Tal. France, thou shalt rue this treason with thy
tears,
If Talbot but survive thy treachery.
Pucelle, that witch, that damned sorceress,
Hath wrought this hellish mischief unawares,
That hardly we escaped the pride of France.   [*Exit.* 40

An alarum: excursions. BEDFORD, *brought in sick in a
chair. Enter* TALBOT *and* BURGUNDY *without: within*
LA PUCELLE, CHARLES, BASTARD, ALENÇON, *and*
REIGNIER, *on the walls.*

Puc. Good morrow, gallants! want ye corn for
bread?
I think the Duke of Burgundy will fast
Before he'll buy again at such a rate:
'Twas full of darnel; do you like the taste?

Bur. Scoff on, vile fiend and shameless courtezan!
I trust ere long to choke thee with thine own
And make thee curse the harvest of that corn.

Char. Your grace may starve perhaps before that
time.

Bed. O, let no words, but deeds, revenge this
treason!

Puc. What will you do, good grey-beard? break a
lance,   50
And run a tilt at death within a chair?

Tal. Foul fiend of France, and hag of all despite,
Encompass'd with thy lustful paramours!
Becomes it thee to taunt his valiant age
And twit with cowardice a man half dead?
Damsel, I'll have a bout with you again,
Or else let Talbot perish with this shame.

Puc. Are ye so hot, sir? yet, Pucelle, hold thy peace;
If Talbot do but thunder, rain will follow.
[*The English whisper together in council.*
God speed the parliament! who shall be the speaker?

Tal. Dare ye come forth and meet us in the field? 61

Puc. Belike your lordship takes us then for fools,
To try if that our own be ours or no.

Tal. I speak not to that railing Hecate,
But unto thee, Alençon, and the rest;
Will ye, like soldiers, come and fight it out?

Alen. Signior, no.

Tal. Signior, hang! base muleters of France!
Like peasant foot-boys do they keep the walls
And dare not take up arms like gentlemen.   70

Puc. Away, captains! let's get us from the walls;
For Talbot means no goodness by his looks.
God be wi' you, my lord! we came but to tell you
That we are here.   [*Exeunt from the walls.*

Tal. And there will we be too, ere it be long,
Or else reproach be Talbot's greatest fame!
Vow, Burgundy, by honour of thy house,
Prick'd on by public wrongs sustain'd in France,
Either to get the town again or die:
And I, as sure as English Henry lives   80
And as his father here was conqueror,
As sure as in this late-betrayed town
Great Cœur-de-lion's heart was buried,
So sure I swear to get the town or die.

Bur. My vows are equal partners with thy vows.

Tal. But, ere we go, regard this dying prince,
The valiant Duke of Bedford. Come, my lord,
We will bestow you in some better place,
Fitter for sickness and for crazy age.

Bed. Lord Talbot, do not so dishonour me: 90
Here will I sit before the walls of Rouen
And will be partner of your weal or woe.

Bur. Courageous Bedford, let us now persuade you.

Bed. Not to be gone from hence; for once I read
That stout Pendragon in his litter sick
Came to the field and vanquished his foes:
Methinks I should revive the soldiers' hearts,
Because I ever found them as myself.

Tal. Undaunted spirit in a dying breast!

SCENE II. 2. **policy,** stratagem; see glossary. 10. **a mean,** means; see glossary. 16. **market bell,** bell rung to announce the opening of a market. 20. **practisants,** plotters, conspirators. 25. **No . . . enter'd,** i.e., it is not comparable in weakness to that by which she entered. 35. *Stage Direction:* **excursion,** stage battle or skirmish; see glossary. 40. *Stage Direction:* **Bedford . . . sick.** There are two historical errors in this scene: Bedford outlived Joan of Arc three years; moreover, at his death he was still comparatively young. 44. **darnel,** injurious weed. 64. **Hecate,** goddess of night and of magic. 68. **muleters,** mule drivers (contemptuously). 83. **Great . . . heart.** According to Holinshed, Richard Coeur-de-Lion (king of England 1189-1199) had willed that "his heart be conueied vnto Rouen, and there buried; in testimonie of the loue which he had eur borne vnto that citie. . . ." 95. **Pendragon,** an allusion to the legend—attributed to the Welsh chieftain, Uther Pendragon, by Geoffrey of Monmouth, but to his brother by Holinshed —that "euen sicke as he was, [he] caused himselfe to be caried forth *in a litter;* with whose presence his people were so incouraged, that in-countring with the Saxons, they wan the victorie. . . ."

Then be it so: heavens keep old Bedford safe! 100
And now no more ado, brave Burgundy,
But gather we our forces out of hand
And set upon our boasting enemy.
[*Exeunt all but Bedford and Attendants.*

An alarum: excursions. Enter Sir John Fastolfe *and a*
Captain.

Cap. Whither away, Sir John Fastolfe, in such haste?
Fast. Whither away! to save myself by flight:
We are like to have the overthrow again.
Cap. What! will you fly, and leave Lord Talbot?
Fast. Ay,
All the Talbots in the world, to save my life. [*Exit.*
Cap. Cowardly knight! ill fortune follow thee! [*Exit.*

Retreat: excursions. La Pucelle, Alençon, *and*
Charles *fly.*

Bed. Now, quiet soul, depart when heaven please, 110
For I have seen our enemies' overthrow.
What is the trust or strength of foolish man?
They that of late were daring with their scoffs
Are glad and fain by flight to save themselves.
[*Bedford dies, and is carried in by two in his chair.*

An alarum. Re-enter Talbot, Burgundy,
and the rest.

Tal. Lost, and recover'd in a day again!
This is a double honour, Burgundy:
Yet heavens have glory for this victory!
Bur. Warlike and martial Talbot, Burgundy
Enshrines thee in his heart and there erects
Thy noble deeds as valour's monuments. 120
Tal. Thanks, gentle duke. But where is Pucelle
    now?
I think her old familiar is asleep:
Now where 's the Bastard's braves, and Charles his
    gleeks?
What, all amort? Rouen hangs her head for grief
That such a valiant company are fled.
Now will we take some order in the town,
Placing therein some expert officers,
And then depart to Paris to the king,
For there young Henry with his nobles lie.
Bur. What wills Lord Talbot pleaseth Burgundy. 130
Tal. But yet, before we go, let 's not forget
The noble Duke of Bedford late deceased,
But see his exequies fulfill'd in Rouen:
A braver soldier never couched lance,
A gentler heart did never sway in court;
But kings and mightiest potentates must die,
For that 's the end of human misery. [*Exeunt.*

SCENE III. *The plains near Rouen.*

Enter Charles, *the* Bastard *of Orleans,* Alençon,
La Pucelle, *and forces.*

Puc. Dismay not, princes, at this accident,
Nor grieve that Rouen is so recovered:
Care is no cure, but rather corrosive,

For things that are not to be remedied.
Let frantic Talbot triumph for a while
And like a peacock sweep along his tail;
We'll pull his plumes and take away his train,
If Dauphin and the rest will be but ruled.
Char. We have been guided by thee hitherto
And of thy cunning had no diffidence: 10
One sudden foil shall never breed distrust.
Bast. Search out thy wit for secret policies,
And we will make thee famous through the world.
Alen. We'll set thy statue in some holy place,
And have thee reverenced like a blessed saint:
Employ thee then, sweet virgin, for our good.
Puc. Then thus it must be; this doth Joan devise:
By fair persuasions mix'd with sugar'd words
We will entice the Duke of Burgundy
To leave the Talbot and to follow us. 20
Char. Ay, marry, sweeting, if we could do that,
France were no place for Henry's warriors;
Nor should that nation boast it so with us,
But be extirped from our provinces.
Alen. For ever should they be expulsed from France
And not have title of an earldom here.
Puc. Your honours shall perceive how I will work
To bring this matter to the wished end.
[*Drum sounds afar off.*
Hark! by the sound of drum you may perceive
Their powers are marching unto Paris-ward. 30

*Here sound an English march. Enter, and pass over at a
distance,* Talbot *and his forces.*

There goes the Talbot, with his colours spread,
And all the troops of English after him.

French march. Enter the Duke of Burgundy *and forces.*

Now in the rearward comes the duke and his:
Fortune in favour makes him lag behind.
Summon a parley; we will talk with him.
[*Trumpets sound a parley.*
Char. A parley with the Duke of Burgundy!
Bur. Who craves a parley with the Burgundy?
Puc. The princely Charles of France, thy
    countryman.
Bur. What say'st thou, Charles? for I am marching
    hence.
Char. Speak, Pucelle, and enchant him with thy
    words. 40
Puc. Brave Burgundy, undoubted hope of France!
Stay, let thy humble handmaid speak to thee.
Bur. Speak on; but be not over-tedious.
Puc. Look on thy country, look on fertile France,
And see the cities and the towns defaced
By wasting ruin of the cruel foe.
As looks the mother on her lowly babe
When death doth close his tender dying eyes,
See, see the pining malady of France;
Behold the wounds, the most unnatural wounds, 50
Which thou thyself hast given her woful breast.
O, turn thy edged sword another way;
Strike those that hurt, and hurt not those that help.
One drop of blood drawn from thy country's bosom

---

122. **familiar,** demon; see glossary. 123. **gleeks,** gibes, jests. 124. **all amort,** sick to death, dispirited. 133. **exequies,** funeral rites. 135. **sway in court,** exercise power and influence in court.
SCENE III. 10. **diffidence,** distrust, suspicion. 11. **foil,** repulse, defeat. 24. **extirped,** rooted out. 34. **in favour,** benevolently, i.e., in our favor; see *favour* in glossary. 41. **undoubted,** fearless. 60.

exclaims on, denounces, accuses. 85. **Done . . . again.** This aside, spoken out of character, is addressed to the prejudice of the English audience, for whom the inconstancy of the French was a common subject of satire. It was suggested by Warburton that this might allude to the conversion of Henry of Navarre to Catholicism in 1593. 91. **prejudice,** i.e., devise his overthrow.

Should grieve thee more than streams of foreign gore:
Return thee therefore with a flood of tears,
And wash away thy country's stained spots.
　Bur. Either she hath bewitch'd me with her words,
Or nature makes me suddenly relent.
　Puc. Besides, all French and France exclaims on
　　　thee,　　　　　　　　　　　　　　　　60
Doubting thy birth and lawful progeny.
Who join'st thou with but with a lordly nation
That will not trust thee but for profit's sake?
When Talbot hath set footing once in France
And fashion'd thee that instrument of ill,
Who then but English Henry will be lord
And thou be thrust out like a fugitive?
Call we to mind, and mark but this for proof,
Was not the Duke of Orleans thy foe?
And was he not in England prisoner?　　　70
But when they heard he was thine enemy,
They set him free without his ransom paid,
In spite of Burgundy and all his friends.
See, then, thou fight'st against thy countrymen
And join'st with them will be thy slaughter-men.
Come, come, return; return, thou wandering lord;
Charles and the rest will take thee in their arms.
　Bur. I am vanquished; these haughty words of hers
Have batter'd me like roaring cannon-shot,
And made me almost yield upon my knees.　80
Forgive me, country, and sweet countrymen,
And, lords, accept this hearty kind embrace:
My forces and my power of men are yours:
So farewell, Talbot; I'll no longer trust thee.
　Puc. [*Aside*] Done like a Frenchman: turn, and turn
　　again!
　Char. Welcome, brave duke! thy friendship makes
　　us fresh.
　Bast. And doth beget new courage in our breasts.
　Alen. Pucelle hath bravely play'd her part in this,
And doth deserve a coronet of gold.　　　89
　Char. Now let us on, my lords, and join our powers,
And seek how we may prejudice the foe.　　*[Exeunt.*

───────────

SCENE IV. *Paris. The palace.*

Enter the KING, GLOUCESTER, BISHOP OF WINCHESTER,
YORK, SUFFOLK, SOMERSET, WARWICK, EXETER:
VERNON, BASSET, *and others. To them with his*
Soldiers, TALBOT.

　Tal. My gracious prince, and honourable peers,
Hearing of your arrival in this realm,
I have awhile given truce unto my wars,
To do my duty to my sovereign:
In sign whereof, this arm, that hath reclaim'd
To your obedience fifty fortresses,
Twelve cities and seven walled towns of strength,
Beside five hundred prisoners of esteem,
Lets fall his sword before your highness' feet,
And with submissive loyalty of heart　　　10
Ascribes the glory of his conquest got
First to my God and next unto your grace.　*[Kneels.*
　King. Is this the Lord Talbot, uncle Gloucester,

That hath so long been resident in France?
　Glou. Yes, if it please your majesty, my liege.
　King. Welcome, brave captain and victorious lord!
When I was young, as yet I am not old,
I do remember how my father said
A stouter champion never handled sword.
Long since we were resolved of your truth,　20
Your faithful service and your toil in war;
Yet never have you tasted our reward,
Or been reguerdon'd with so much as thanks,
Because till now we never saw your face:
Therefore, stand up; and, for these good deserts,
We here create you Earl of Shrewsbury;
And in our coronation take your place.
　　[*Sennet. Flourish. Exeunt all but Vernon and Basset.*
　Ver. Now, sir, to you, that were so hot at sea,
Disgracing of these colours that I wear
In honour of my noble Lord of York:　　　30
Darest thou maintain the former words thou spakest?
　Bas. Yes, sir; as well as you dare patronage
The envious barking of your saucy tongue
Against my lord the Duke of Somerset.
　Ver. Sirrah, thy lord I honour as he is.
　Bas. Why, what is he? as good a man as York.
　Ver. Hark ye; not so: in witness, take ye that.
　　　　　　　　　　　　　　　　　[*Strikes him.*
　Bas. Villain, thou know'st the law of arms is such
That whoso draws a sword, 'tis present death,
Or else this blow should broach thy dearest blood.　40
But I'll unto his majesty, and crave
I may have liberty to venge this wrong;
When thou shalt see I'll meet thee to thy cost.
　Ver. Well, miscreant, I'll be there as soon as you;
And, after, meet you sooner than you would.　[*Exeunt.*

───────────

ACT IV.

SCENE I. *Paris. A hall of state.*

Enter the KING, GLOUCESTER, BISHOP OF WINCHESTER,
YORK, SUFFOLK, SOMERSET, WARWICK, TALBOT,
EXETER, *the* Governor of Paris, *and others.*

　Glou. Lord bishop, set the crown upon his head.
　Win. God save King Henry, of that name the sixth!
　Glou. Now, governor of Paris, take your oath,
That you elect no other king but him;
Esteem none friends but such as are his friends,
And none your foes but such as shall pretend
Malicious practices against his state:
This shall ye do, so help you righteous God!

Enter SIR JOHN FASTOLFE.

　Fast. My gracious sovereign, as I rode from Calais,
To haste unto your coronation,　　　　　10
A letter was deliver'd to my hands,
Writ to your grace from the Duke of Burgundy.
　Tal. Shame to the Duke of Burgundy and thee!
I vow'd, base knight, when I did meet thee next,
To tear the garter from thy craven's leg, [*Plucking it off.*
Which I have done, because unworthily

───────────

SCENE IV. 18. **I . . . said.** Henry VI was an infant of nine months
at his father's death. 20. **resolved,** convinced; see glossary. 28. **so
hot at sea.** The details of this quarrel are recited below, IV, i, 89-97.
38. **the law of arms.** Cf. I, iii, 46, note. 39. **present,** instant; see
glossary. 40. **broach,** tap, draw. **dearest,** i.e., life blood; see glossary.

ACT IV. SCENE I. 4. **elect,** acknowledge. 6. **pretend,** purpose,
intend. 7. **practices,** stratagems; see glossary. 15. **garter,** badge of
the Knights of the Garter, a ribbon of blue velvet edged and buckled
with gold, worn below the left knee.

Thou wast installed in that high degree.
Pardon me, princely Henry, and the rest:
This dastard, at the battle of Patay,
When but in all I was six thousand strong   20
And that the French were almost ten to one,
Before we met or that a stroke was given,
Like to a trusty squire did run away:
In which assault we lost twelve hundred men;
Myself and divers gentlemen beside
Were there surprised and taken prisoners.
Then judge, great lords, if I have done amiss;
Or whether that such cowards ought to wear
This ornament of knighthood, yea or no.
   Glou. To say the truth, this fact was infamous   30
And ill beseeming any common man,
Much more a knight, a captain and a leader.
   Tal. When first this order was ordain'd, my lords,
Knights of the garter were of noble birth,
Valiant and virtuous, full of haughty courage,
Such as were grown to credit by the wars;
Not fearing death, nor shrinking for distress,
But always resolute in most extremes.
He then that is not furnish'd in this sort
Doth but usurp the sacred name of knight,   40
Profaning this most honourable order,
And should, if I were worthy to be judge,
Be quite degraded, like a hedge-born swain
That doth presume to boast of gentle blood.
   King. Stain to thy countrymen, thou hear'st thy
     doom!
Be packing, therefore, thou that wast a knight:
Henceforth we banish thee, on pain of death.
                         [*Exit Fastolfe.*
And now, my lord protector, view the letter
Sent from our uncle Duke of Burgundy.
   Glou. What means his grace, that he hath changed
     his style?   50
No more but, plain and bluntly, 'To the king!'
Hath he forgot he is his sovereign?
Or doth this churlish superscription
Pretend some alteration in good will?
What 's here? [*Reads*] 'I have, upon especial cause,
Moved with compassion of my country's wreck,
Together with the pitiful complaints
Of such as your oppression feeds upon,
Forsaken your pernicious faction
And join'd with Charles, the rightful King of France.'
O monstrous treachery! can this be so,   61
That in alliance, amity and oaths,
There should be found such false dissembling guile?
   King. What! doth my uncle Burgundy revolt?
   Glou. He doth, my lord, and is become your foe.
   King. Is that the worst this letter doth contain?
   Glou. It is the worst, and all, my lord, he writes.
   King. Why, then, Lord Talbot there shall talk with
     him
And give him chastisement for this abuse.
How say you, my lord? are you not content?   70
   Tal. Content, my liege! yes, but that I am
     prevented,

I should have begg'd I might have been employ'd.
   King. Then gather strength and march unto him
     straight:
Let him perceive how ill we brook his treason
And what offence it is to flout his friends.
   Tal. I go, my lord, in heart desiring still
You may behold confusion of your foes.   [*Exit.*

   Enter VERNON *and* BASSET.

   Ver. Grant me the combat, gracious sovereign.
   Bas. And me, my lord, grant me the combat too.
   York. This is my servant: hear him, noble prince.   80
   Som. And this is mine: sweet Henry, favour him.
   King. Be patient, lords; and give them leave to
     speak.
Say, gentlemen, what makes you thus exclaim?
And wherefore crave you combat? or with whom?
   Ver. With him, my lord; for he hath done me
     wrong.
   Bas. And I with him; for he hath done me wrong.
   King. What is that wrong whereof you both
     complain?
First let me know, and then I'll answer you.
   Bas. Crossing the sea from England into France,
This fellow here, with envious carping tongue,   90
Upbraided me about the rose I wear;
Saying, the sanguine colour of the leaves
Did represent my master's blushing cheeks,
When stubbornly he did repugn the truth
About a certain question in the law
Argued betwixt the Duke of York and him;
With other vile and ignominious terms:
In confutation of which rude reproach
And in defence of my lord's worthiness,
I crave the benefit of law of arms.   100
   Ver. And that is my petition, noble lord:
For though he seem with forged quaint conceit
To set a gloss upon his bold intent,
Yet know, my lord, I was provoked by him;
And he first took exceptions at this badge,
Pronouncing that the paleness of this flower
Bewray'd the faintness of my master's heart.
   York. Will not this malice, Somerset, be left?
   Som. Your private grudge, my Lord of York, will
     out,
Though ne'er so cunningly you smother it.   110
   King. Good Lord, what madness rules in brainsick
     men,
When for so slight and frivolous a cause
Such factious emulations shall arise!
Good cousins both, of York and Somerset,
Quiet yourselves, I pray, and be at peace.
   York. Let this dissension first be tried by fight,
And then your highness shall command a peace.
   Som. The quarrel toucheth none but us alone;
Betwixt ourselves let us decide it then.
   York. There is my pledge; accept it, Somerset.   120
   Ver. Nay, let it rest where it began at first.
   Bas. Confirm it so, mine honourable lord.
   Glou. Confirm it so! Confounded be your strife!

1 Henry VI
ACT IV : SC I

228

23. **trusty squire,** used contemptuously. 30. **fact,** deed; see glossary.
35. **haughty,** exalted. 39. **furnish'd,** endowed; see glossary. 43.
hedge-born, lowly born; cf. *2 Henry VI*, IV, ii, 55. 46. **packing,**
departing; see glossary. 54. **Pretend,** import. 64. **my uncle,** a
reference to the alliance of the Lancastrian and Burgundian houses by
the marriage of the duke of Bedford, the king's uncle, to Anne, sister
of the duke of Burgundy. 71. **prevented,** forestalled, anticipated; see
glossary. 73. **straight,** immediately; see glossary. 77. **confusion,**
destruction; see glossary. 78. **the combat,** permission to fight; cf. I,
iii, 46, note. 90. **fellow,** an insulting form of reference or address; see
glossary. 94. **repugn,** oppose, resist. 100. **benefit . . . arms,** right
to protect one's honor in a duel. 102. **quaint,** carefully elaborated;
see glossary. **conceit,** device, fanciful design; see glossary. 103.
gloss, speciously fair appearance; see glossary. 107. **Bewray'd,** revealed. 113. **emulations,** contentions between rivals. 114. **cousins,**
any relatives not of one's immediate family; see glossary. 123. **Con-**

And perish ye, with your audacious prate!
Presumptuous vassals, are you not ashamed
With this immodest clamorous outrage
To trouble and disturb the king and us?
And you, my lords, methinks you do not well
To bear with their perverse objections;
Much less to take occasion from their mouths   130
To raise a mutiny betwixt yourselves:
Let me persuade you take a better course.
   Exe. It grieves his highness: good my lords, be
    friends.
   King. Come hither, you that would be combatants:
Henceforth I charge you, as you love our favour,
Quite to forget this quarrel and the cause.
And you, my lords, remember where we are;
In France, amongst a fickle wavering nation:
If they perceive dissension in our looks
And that within ourselves we disagree,   140
How will their grudging stomachs be provoked
To wilful disobedience, and rebel!
Beside, what infamy will there arise,
When foreign princes shall be certified
That for a toy, a thing of no regard,
King Henry's peers and chief nobility
Destroy'd themselves, and lost the realm of France!
O, think upon the conquest of my father,
My tender years, and let us not forego
That for a trifle that was bought with blood!   150
Let me be umpire in this doubtful strife.
I see no reason, if I wear this rose, [*Putting on a red rose.*
That any one should therefore be suspicious
I more incline to Somerset than York:
Both are my kinsmen, and I love them both:
As well they may upbraid me with my crown,
Because, forsooth, the king of Scots is crown'd.
But your discretions better can persuade
Than I am able to instruct or teach:
And therefore, as we hither came in peace,   160
So let us still continue peace and love.
Cousin of York, we institute your grace
To be our regent in these parts of France:
And, good my Lord of Somerset, unite
Your troops of horsemen with his bands of foot;
And, like true subjects, sons of your progenitors,
Go cheerfully together and digest
Your angry choler on your enemies.
Ourself, my lord protector and the rest
After some respite will return to Calais;   170
From thence to England; where I hope ere long
To be presented, by your victories,
With Charles, Alençon and that traitorous rout.
   [*Flourish. Exeunt all but York, Warwick, Exeter
                 and Vernon.*
   War. My Lord of York, I promise you, the king
Prettily, methought, did play the orator.
   York. And so he did; but yet I like it not,
In that he wears the badge of Somerset.
   War. Tush, that was but his fancy, blame him not;
I dare presume, sweet prince, he thought no harm.
   York. An if I wist he did,—but let it rest;   180

Other affairs must now be managed.
               [*Exeunt all but Exeter.*
   Exe. Well didst thou, Richard, to suppress thy
    voice;
For, had the passions of thy heart burst out,
I fear we should have seen decipher'd there
More rancorous spite, more furious raging broils,
Than yet can be imagined or supposed.
But howsoe'er, no simple man that sees
This jarring discord of nobility,
This shouldering of each other in the court,
This factious bandying of their favourites,   190
But that it doth presage some ill event.
'Tis much when sceptres are in children's hands;
But more when envy breeds unkind division;
There comes the ruin, there begins confusion.   [*Exit.*

SCENE II. *Before Bourdeaux.*

Enter TALBOT, *with trump and drum.*

   Tal. Go to the gates of Bourdeaux, trumpeter;
Summon their general unto the wall.

Trumpet sounds. Enter General *and others, aloft.*

English John Talbot, captains, calls you forth,
Servant in arms to Harry King of England;
And thus he would: Open your city gates;
Be humble to us; call my sovereign yours,
And do him homage as obedient subjects;
And I'll withdraw me and my bloody power:
But, if you frown upon this proffer'd peace,
You tempt the fury of my three attendants,   10
Lean famine, quartering steel, and climbing fire;
Who in a moment even with the earth
Shall lay your stately and air-braving towers,
If you forsake the offer of their love.
   Gen. Thou ominous and fearful owl of death,
Our nation's terror and their bloody scourge!
The period of thy tyranny approacheth.
On us thou canst not enter but by death;
For, I protest, we are well fortified
And strong enough to issue out and fight: 20
If thou retire, the Dauphin, well appointed,
Stands with the snares of war to tangle thee:
On either hand thee there are squadrons pitch'd,
To wall thee from the liberty of flight;
And no way canst thou turn thee for redress,
But death doth front thee with apparent spoil
And pale destruction meets thee in the face.
Ten thousand French have ta'en the sacrament
To rive their dangerous artillery
Upon no Christian soul but English Talbot.   30
Lo, there thou stand'st, a breathing valiant man,
Of an invincible unconquer'd spirit!
This is the latest glory of thy praise
That I, thy enemy, due thee withal;
For ere the glass, that now begins to run,
Finish the process of his sandy hour,
These eyes, that see thee now well coloured,

---

founded, spent, wasted; see glossary. 129. **objections,** charges,
accusations. 144. **certified,** made certain. 145. **toy,** trifle; see glossary. 167. **digest,** disperse, dissipate; see glossary. 191. **event,** outcome; see glossary. 193. **unkind,** unnatural; see glossary.
   SCENE II. 10. **my three attendants.** Cf. Hall's *Chronicle,* Seventh
Year of Henry v: "The Goddess of warre . . . hath these three hand-
maydes, euer of necessitie to attend vpon her, that is, blood, fyre and
famine"; cf. *Henry V,* Prologue, 7. 15. **fearful,** exciting fear; see

glossary. **owl of death.** The call of the owl was regarded as a prognostication of death; cf. *Macbeth,* II, ii, 3-4. 17. **period,** termination. 21.
appointed, equipped. 23. **thee,** i.e., of thee; dative of reference; see
Abbott, 220. 26. **spoil,** destruction; see glossary. 28. **ta'en the
sacrament,** i.e., taken the most solemn oaths. 29. **rive,** burst. 34.
due, endue, invest. 37. **well coloured,** in health.

Shall see thee wither'd, bloody, pale and dead.
               [Drum afar off.
Hark! hark! the Dauphin's drum, a warning bell,
Sings heavy music to thy timorous soul;   40
And mine shall ring thy dire departure out.
           [Exeunt General, &c.
 Tal. He fables not; I hear the enemy:
Out, some light horsemen, and peruse their wings.
O, negligent and heedless discipline!
How are we park'd and bounded in a pale,
A little herd of England's timorous deer,
Mazed with a yelping kennel of French curs!
If we be English deer, be then in blood;
Not rascal-like, to fall down with a pinch,
But rather, moody-mad and desperate stags, 50
Turn on the bloody hounds with heads of steel
And make the cowards stand aloof at bay:
Sell every man his life as dear as mine,
And they shall find dear deer of us, my friends.
God and Saint George, Talbot and England's right,
Prosper our colours in this dangerous fight! *[Exeunt.*

SCENE III. *Plains in Gascony.*

Enter a Messenger *that meets* YORK. *Enter* YORK *with trumpet and many* Soldiers.

 York. Are not the speedy scouts return'd again,
That dogg'd the mighty army of the Dauphin?
 Mess. They are return'd, my lord, and give it out
That he is march'd to Bourdeaux with his power,
To fight with Talbot: as he march'd along,
By your espials were discovered
Two mightier troops than that the Dauphin led,
Which join'd with him and made their march for
  Bourdeaux.
 York. A plague upon that villain Somerset,
That thus delays my promised supply   10
Of horsemen, that were levied for this siege!
Renowned Talbot doth expect my aid,
And I am lowted by a traitor villain
And cannot help the noble chevalier:
God comfort him in this necessity!
If he miscarry, farewell wars in France.

 Enter SIR WILLIAM LUCY.

 Lucy. Thou princely leader of our English strength,
Never so needful on the earth of France,
Spur to the rescue of the noble Talbot,
Who now is girdled with a waist of iron   20
And hemm'd about with grim destruction:
To Bourdeaux, warlike duke! to Bourdeaux, York!
Else, farewell Talbot, France, and England's honour.
 York. O God, that Somerset, who in proud heart
Doth stop my cornets, were in Talbot's place!
So should we save a valiant gentleman
By forfeiting a traitor and a coward.
Mad ire and wrathful fury makes me weep,
That thus we die, while remiss traitors sleep.
 Lucy. O, send some succour to the distress'd lord! 30
 York. He dies, we lose; I break my warlike word;
We mourn, France smiles; we lose, they daily get;

All 'long of this vile traitor Somerset.
 Lucy. Then God take mercy on brave Talbot's soul;
And on his son young John, who two hours since
I met in travel toward his warlike father!
This seven years did not Talbot see his son;
And now they meet where both their lives are done.
 York. Alas, what joy shall noble Talbot have
To bid his young son welcome to his grave? 40
Away! vexation almost stops my breath,
That sunder'd friends greet in the hour of death.
Lucy, farewell: no more my fortune can,
But curse the cause I cannot aid the man.
Maine, Blois, Poictiers, and Tours, are won away,
'Long all of Somerset and his delay.
         [Exit, with his soldiers.
 Lucy. Thus, while the vulture of sedition
Feeds in the bosom of such great commanders,
Sleeping neglection doth betray to loss
The conquest of our scarce cold conqueror, 50
That ever living man of memory,
Henry the Fifth: whiles they each other cross,
Lives, honours, lands and all hurry to loss. *[Exit.*

SCENE IV. *Other plains in Gascony.*

Enter SOMERSET, *with his army; a* Captain *of* TALBOT'S *with him.*

 Som. It is too late; I cannot send them now:
This expedition was by York and Talbot
Too rashly plotted: all our general force
Might with a sally of the very town
Be buckled with: the over-daring Talbot
Hath sullied all his gloss of former honour
By this unheedful, desperate, wild adventure:
York set him on to fight and die in shame,
That, Talbot dead, great York might bear the name.
 Cap. Here is Sir William Lucy, who with me 10
Set from our o'ermatch'd forces forth for aid.

 Enter SIR WILLIAM LUCY.

 Som. How now, Sir William! whither were you sent?
 Lucy. Whither, my lord? from bought and sold Lord
  Talbot,
Who, ring'd about with bold adversity,
Cries out for noble York and Somerset,
To beat assailing death from his weak legions:
And whiles the honourable captain there
Drops bloody sweat from his war-wearied limbs,
And, in advantage lingering, looks for rescue,
You, his false hopes, the trust of England's honour, 20
Keep off aloof with worthless emulation.
Let not your private discord keep away
The levied succours that should lend him aid,
While he, renowned noble gentleman,
Yields up his life unto a world of odds:
Orleans the Bastard, Charles, Burgundy,
Alençon, Reignier, compass him about,
And Talbot perisheth by your default.
 Som. York set him on; York should have sent him aid.
 Lucy. And York as fast upon your grace exclaims; 30
Swearing that you withhold his levied host,

---

43. **peruse,** survey, inspect. 49. **rascal-like.** Cf. I, ii, 35, note. 55.
Saint George. Cf. I, i, 154, note.
 SCENE III. 13. **lowted,** variant of *louted,* i.e., stooped, humbled.
25. **cornets,** cavalry units, so called from their long, horn-shaped standards. 33. **'long of,** on account of; see glossary.

 SCENE IV. 4. **the very town,** i.e., the mere garrison, unsupported by
the relieving armies (Tucker Brooke). 5. **Be buckled with,** be joined
in combat. 19. **in advantage lingering,** protracting his resistance by
the advantage of a strong post (Johnson); making the most of every desperate chance (Tucker Brooke).

Collected for this expedition.

Som. York lies; he might have sent and had the
horse;
I owe him little duty, and less love;
And take foul scorn to fawn on him by sending.
Lucy. The fraud of England, not the force of France,
Hath now entrapp'd the noble-minded Talbot:
Never to England shall he bear his life;
But dies, betray'd to fortune by your strife.
Som. Come, go; I will dispatch the horsemen
straight: 40
Within six hours they will be at his aid.
Lucy. Too late comes rescue: he is ta'en or slain;
For fly he could not, if he would have fled;
And fly would Talbot never, though he might.
Som. If he be dead, brave Talbot, then adieu!
Lucy. His fame lives in the world, his shame in you.
[*Exeunt.*

SCENE V. *The English camp near Bourdeaux.*

Enter TALBOT *and* JOHN *his son.*

Tal. O young John Talbot! I did send for thee
To tutor thee in stratagems of war,
That Talbot's name might be in thee revived
When sapless age and weak unable limbs
Should bring thy father to his drooping chair.
But, O malignant and ill-boding stars!
Now thou art come unto a feast of death,
A terrible and unavoided danger:
Therefore, dear boy, mount on my swiftest horse;
And I'll direct thee how thou shalt escape 10
By sudden flight: come, dally not, be gone.
John. Is my name Talbot? and am I your son?
And shall I fly? O, if you love my mother,
Dishonour not her honourable name,
To make a bastard and a slave of me!
The world will say, he is not Talbot's blood,
That basely fled when noble Talbot stood.
Tal. Fly, to revenge my death, if I be slain.
John. He that flies so will ne'er return again.
Tal. If we both stay, we both are sure to die. 20
John. Then let me stay; and, father, do you fly:
Your loss is great, so your regard should be;
My worth unknown, no loss is known in me.
Upon my death the French can little boast;
In yours they will, in you all hopes are lost.
Flight cannot stain the honour you have won;
But mine it will, that no exploit have done:
You fled for vantage, every one will swear;
But, if I bow, they'll say it was for fear.
There is no hope that ever I will stay, 30
If the first hour I shrink and run away.
Here on my knee I beg mortality,
Rather than life preserved with infamy.
Tal. Shall all thy mother's hopes lie in one tomb?
John. Ay, rather than I'll shame my mother's
womb.
Tal. Upon my blessing, I command thee go.
John. To fight I will, but not to fly the foe.
Tal. Part of thy father may be saved in thee.

John. No part of him but will be shame in me.
Tal. Thou never hadst renown, nor canst not lose it.
John. Yes, your renowned name: shall flight abuse
it? 41
Tal. Thy father's charge shall clear thee from that
stain.
John. You cannot witness for me, being slain.
If death be so apparent, then both fly.
Tal. And leave my followers here to fight and die?
My age was never tainted with such shame.
John. And shall my youth be guilty of such blame?
No more can I be sever'd from your side,
Than can yourself yourself in twain divide:
Stay, go, do what you will, the like do I; 50
For live I will not, if my father die.
Tal. Then here I take my leave of thee, fair son,
Born to eclipse thy life this afternoon.
Come, side by side together live and die;
And soul with soul from France to heaven fly. [*Exeunt.*

SCENE VI. *A field of battle.*

Alarum: excursions, wherein TALBOT's Son *is hemmed
about, and* TALBOT *rescues him.*

Tal. Saint George and victory! fight, soldiers, fight:
The regent hath with Talbot broke his word
And left us to the rage of France his sword.
Where is John Talbot? Pause, and take thy breath;
I gave thee life and rescued thee from death.
John. O, twice my father, twice am I thy son!
The life thou gavest me first was lost and done,
Till with thy warlike sword, despite of fate,
To my determined time thou gavest new date.
Tal. When from the Dauphin's crest thy sword
struck fire, 10
It warm'd thy father's heart with proud desire
Of bold-faced victory. Then leaden age,
Quicken'd with youthful spleen and warlike rage,
Beat down Alençon, Orleans, Burgundy,
And from the pride of Gallia rescued thee.
The ireful bastard Orleans, that drew blood
From thee, my boy, and had the maidenhood
Of thy first fight, I soon encountered,
And interchanging blows I quickly shed
Some of his bastard blood; and in disgrace 20
Bespoke him thus; 'Contaminated, base
And misbegotten blood I spill of thine,
Mean and right poor, for that pure blood of mine
Which thou didst force from Talbot, my brave boy:'
Here, purposing the Bastard to destroy
Came in strong rescue. Speak, thy father's care,
Art thou not weary, John? how dost thou fare?
Wilt thou yet leave the battle, boy, and fly,
Now thou art seal'd the son of chivalry?
Fly, to revenge my death when I am dead: 30
The help of one stands me in little stead.
O, too much folly is it, well I wot,
To hazard all our lives in one small boat!
If I to-day die not with Frenchmen's rage,
To-morrow I shall die with mickle age:
By me they nothing gain an if I stay;

SCENE V. 22. **regard,** heed for yourself. 28. **vantage,** advantage,
i.e., for some military strategy; see glossary.
SCENE VI. 2. **The regent,** the duke of York; cf. IV. i, 162-163.
3. **France his,** France's. 9. **date,** termination, i.e., postponed my hour
of death; see glossary. 13. **spleen,** impetuosity; see glossary. 15.

Gallia, France. 25. **purposing,** as I purposed. 32. **wot,** know; see
glossary. 35. **mickle age,** great old age.

'Tis but the shortening of my life one day:
In thee thy mother dies, our household's name,
My death's revenge, thy youth, and England's fame:
All these and more we hazard by thy stay; 40
All these are saved if thou wilt fly away.
    John. The sword of Orleans hath not made me
        smart;
These words of yours draw life-blood from my heart:
On that advantage, bought with such a shame,
To save a paltry life and slay bright fame,
Before young Talbot from old Talbot fly,
The coward horse that bears me fall and die!
And like me to the peasant boys of France,
To be shame's scorn and subject of mischance!
Surely, by all the glory you have won, 50
An if I fly, I am not Talbot's son:
Then talk no more of flight, it is no boot;
If son to Talbot, die at Talbot's foot.
    Tal. Then follow thou thy desperate sire of Crete,
Thou Icarus; thy life to me is sweet:
If thou wilt fight, fight by thy father's side;
And, commendable proved, let 's die in pride. [*Exeunt.*

SCENE VII. *Another part of the field.*

Alarum: excursions. Enter old TALBOT *led by a* Servant.

    Tal. Where is my other life? mine own is gone;
O, where 's young Talbot? where is valiant John?
Triumphant death, smear'd with captivity,
Young Talbot's valour makes me smile at thee:
When he perceived me shrink and on my knee,
His bloody sword he brandish'd over me,
And, like a hungry lion, did commence
Rough deeds of rage and stern impatience;
But when my angry guardant stood alone,
Tendering my ruin and assail'd of none, 10
Dizzy-eyed fury and great rage of heart
Suddenly made him from my side to start
Into the clustering battle of the French;
And in that sea of blood my boy did drench
His over-mounting spirit, and there died,
My Icarus, my blossom, in his pride.
    Serv. O my dear lord, lo, where your son is borne!

Enter Soldiers, *with the body of young* TALBOT.

    Tal. Thou antic death, which laugh'st us here to
        scorn,
Anon, from thy insulting tyranny,
Coupled in bonds of perpetuity, 20
Two Talbots, winged through the lither sky,
In thy despite shall 'scape mortality.
O thou, whose wounds become hard-favour'd death,
Speak to thy father ere thou yield thy breath!
Brave death by speaking, whether he will or no;
Imagine him a Frenchman and thy foe.
Poor boy! he smiles, methinks, as who should say,
Had death been French, then death had died to-day.

Come, come and lay him in his father's arms:
My spirit can no longer bear these harms. 30
Soldiers, adieu! I have what I would have,
Now my old arms are young John Talbot's grave. [*Dies.*

Enter CHARLES, ALENÇON, BURGUNDY, BASTARD,
    LA PUCELLE, *and forces.*

    Char. Had York and Somerset brought rescue in,
We should have found a bloody day of this.
    Bast. How the young whelp of Talbot's,
        raging-wood,
Did flesh his puny sword in Frenchmen's blood!
    Puc. Once I encounter'd him, and thus I said:
'Thou maiden youth, be vanquish'd by a maid:'
But, with a proud majestical high scorn,
He answer'd thus: 'Young Talbot was not born 40
To be the pillage of a giglot wench:'
So, rushing in the bowels of the French,
He left me proudly, as unworthy fight.
    Bur. Doubtless he would have made a noble knight:
See, where he lies inhearsed in the arms
Of the most bloody nurser of his harms.
    Bast. Hew them to pieces, hack their bones asunder,
Whose life was England's glory, Gallia's wonder.
    Char. O, no, forbear! for that which we have fled
During the life, let us not wrong it dead. 50

Enter SIR WILLIAM LUCY, *attended;* Herald *of the*
    French *preceding.*

    Lucy. Herald, conduct me to the Dauphin's tent,
To know who hath obtain'd the glory of the day.
    Char. On what submissive message art thou sent?
    Lucy. Submission, Dauphin! 'tis a mere French
        word;
We English warriors wot not what it means.
I come to know what prisoners thou hast ta'en
And to survey the bodies of the dead.
    Char. For prisoners ask'st thou? hell our prison is.
But tell me whom thou seek'st.
    Lucy. But where 's the great Alcides of the field, 60
Valiant Lord Talbot, Earl of Shrewsbury,
Created, for his rare success in arms,
Great Earl of Washford, Waterford and Valence;
Lord Talbot of Goodrig and Urchinfield,
Lord Strange of Blackmere, Lord Verdun of Alton,
Lord Cromwell of Wingfield, Lord Furnival of
        Sheffield,
The thrice-victorious Lord of Falconbridge;
Knight of the noble order of Saint George,
Worthy Saint Michael and the Golden Fleece;
Great marshal to Henry the Sixth 70
Of all his wars within the realm of France?
    Puc. Here is a silly stately style indeed!
The Turk, that two and fifty kingdoms hath,
Writes not so tedious a style as this.
Him that thou magnifiest with all these titles
Stinking and fly-blown lies here at our feet.
    Lucy. Is Talbot slain, the Frenchmen's only scourge,

48. **like me,** liken me. 52. **boot,** profit; see glossary. 55. **Thou Icarus,** an allusion to the story of Daedalus, sire of Crete, and his son Icarus, who escaped from the Labyrinth by means of wings that the father's ingenuity had devised. As they flew across the sea, Icarus mounted too high, the sun's heat melted the wax by which his wings were attached, and he fell into the sea (hence, called the Icarian Sea) and was lost.
    SCENE VII. 3. **smear'd,** disgraced. 9. **guardant,** guardian. 10. **Tendering,** being concerned for. 13. **battle,** army; see glossary. 18. **Thou antic death,** one of the personifications of death suggested, probably, by the grotesque pictorial representations of the Middle Ages

and early Renaissance, such as the Dance of Death; cf. *Richard II*, III, ii, 162. 19. **Anon,** soon; see glossary. 21. **lither,** yielding. 23. **become . . . death,** make death, otherwise hideous, beautiful. 35. **raging-wood,** furiously mad. 36. **flesh,** use for the first time in battle; see glossary. 41. **giglot,** lewd, wanton. 54. **mere,** pure, absolute; see glossary. 60. **Alcides,** Hercules, son of Alcaeus. 61-67. **Valiant . . . Falconbridge.** These titles of Lord Talbot are in the epitaph fixed on his tomb in Rouen. They appear first to have been reproduced in print in Cotton's *An Armor of Proofe* (1596), where occurs the form *Washford,* more commonly Wexford. These observations suggest that Shakespeare may have revised the play after 1596. 73. **The Turk,**

Your kingdom's terror and black Nemesis?
O, were mine eye-balls into bullets turn'd,
That I in rage might shoot them at your faces! 80
O, that I could but call these dead to life!
It were enough to fright the realm of France:
Were but his picture left amongst you here,
It would amaze the proudest of you all.
Give me their bodies, that I may bear them hence
And give them burial as beseems their worth.
   Puc. I think this upstart is old Talbot's ghost,
He speaks with such a proud commanding spirit.
For God's sake, let him have 'em; to keep them here,
They would but stink, and putrefy the air. 90
   Char. Go, take their bodies hence.
   Lucy. I'll bear them hence; but from their ashes
     shall be rear'd
A phœnix that shall make all France afeard.
   Char. So we be rid of them, do with 'em what thou
     wilt.
And now to Paris, in this conquering vein
All will be ours, now bloody Talbot 's slain.   *[Exeunt.*

ACT V.

SCENE I. *London. The palace.*

Sennet. Enter KING, GLOUCESTER, *and* EXETER.

   King. Have you perused the letters from the pope,
The emperor and the Earl of Armagnac?
   Glou. I have, my lord: and their intent is this:
They humbly sue unto your excellence
To have a godly peace concluded of
Between the realms of England and of France.
   King. How doth your grace affect their motion?
   Glou. Well, my good lord; and as the only means
To stop effusion of our Christian blood
And stablish quietness on every side. 10
   King. Ay, marry, uncle; for I always thought
It was both impious and unnatural
That such immanity and bloody strife
Should reign among professors of one faith.
   Glou. Beside, my lord, the sooner to effect
And surer bind this knot of amity,
The Earl of Armagnac, near knit to Charles,
A man of great authority in France,
Proffers his only daughter to your grace
In marriage, with a large and sumptuous dowry. 20
   King. Marriage, uncle! alas, my years are young!
And fitter is my study and my books
Than wanton dalliance with a paramour.
Yet call the ambassadors; and, as you please,
So let them have their answers every one:
I shall be well content with any choice
Tends to God's glory and my country's weal.

Enter WINCHESTER *in Cardinal's habit, a* Legate *and
   two* Ambassadors.

   Exe. What! is my Lord of Winchester install'd,
And call'd unto a cardinal's degree?
Then I perceive that will be verified 30
Henry the Fifth did sometime prophesy,
'If once he come to be a cardinal,
He'll make his cap co-equal with the crown.'
   King. My lords ambassadors, your several suits
Have been consider'd and debated on.
Your purpose is both good and reasonable;
And therefore are we certainly resolved
To draw conditions of a friendly peace;
Which by my Lord of Winchester we mean
Shall be transported presently to France. 40
   Glou. And for the proffer of my lord your master,
I have inform'd his highness so at large
As liking of the lady's virtuous gifts,
Her beauty and the value of her dower,
He doth intend she shall be England's queen.
   King. In argument and proof of which contract,
Bear her this jewel, pledge of my affection.
And so, my lord protector, see them guarded
And safely brought to Dover; where inshipp'd
Commit them to the fortune of the sea. 50
       [Exeunt all but Winchester and Legate.
   Win. Stay, my lord legate: you shall first receive
The sum of money which I promised
Should be deliver'd to his holiness
For clothing me in these grave ornaments.
   Leg. I will attend upon your lordship's leisure.
   Win. [*Aside*] Now Winchester will not submit, I
     trow,
Or be inferior to the proudest peer.
Humphrey of Gloucester, thou shalt well perceive
That, neither in birth or for authority,
The bishop will be overborne by thee: 60
I'll either make thee stoop and bend thy knee,
Or sack this country with a mutiny.   *[Exeunt.*

SCENE II. *France. Plains in Anjou.*

Enter CHARLES, BURGUNDY, ALENÇON, BASTARD,
   REIGNIER, LA PUCELLE, *and forces.*

   Char. These news, my lords, may cheer our drooping
     spirits:
'Tis said the stout Parisians do revolt
And turn again unto the warlike French.
   Alen. Then march to Paris, royal Charles of France,
And keep not back your powers in dalliance.
   Puc. Peace be amongst them, if they turn to us;
Else, ruin combat with their palaces!

Enter Scout.

   Scout. Success unto our valiant general,
And happiness to his accomplices! 9
   Char. What tidings send our scouts? I prithee, speak.
   Scout. The English army, that divided was
Into two parties, is now conjoin'd in one

ACT V : SC II

233

used as equivalent of *Islam.* **two and fifty kingdoms,** an instance of
hyperbole. 93. **phœnix,** fabulous bird, the only one of its kind, which
every five hundred years built itself a funeral pile and died upon it;
from the ashes a new phoenix arose.
   ACT V. SCENE I. 1-2. **pope . . . Armagnac.** During the year 1434
efforts were made by the emperor and other potentates to effect a peace.
The marriage proposal of the king to the earl of Armagnac's daughter,
however, was made nine years later. 7. **affect,** incline toward; see
glossary. **motion,** proposal; see glossary. 9. **effusion,** shedding (of
blood); cf. Hall's *Chronicle:* ". . . all christendom lamented . . . the
effusion of so muche Christen bloud." 13. **immanity,** atrocious

savagery. 17. **knit,** i.e., by ties of kinship. 27. **Tends,** which tends.
31-33. **Henry . . . crown.** The prophecy is recorded in Hall and
Holinshed, Fifth Year of Henry VI: "whiche degree, kyng Henry the
fifth knowyng the haute corage, and the ambicious mynde of the man,
prohibited hym on his allegeaunce once, either to sue for or to take,
meanyng that cardinalles Hattes should not presume to be egall with
Princes." 31. **sometime,** at one time; see glossary. 41. **my lord your
master,** addressed to the ambassadors. 49. **inshipp'd,** embarked.
   SCENE II. 7. **Else . . . palaces!** Otherwise, let ruin destroy their
palaces!

And means to give you battle presently.

 Char. Somewhat too sudden, sirs, the warning is;
But we will presently provide for them.

 Bur. I trust the ghost of Talbot is not there:
Now he is gone, my lord, you need not fear.

 Puc. Of all base passions, fear is most accursed.
Command the conquest, Charles, it shall be thine,
Let Henry fret and all the world repine.   20

 Char. Then on, my lords; and France be fortunate!
              [*Exeunt.*

SCENE III. *Before Angiers.*

Alarum. Excursions. Enter LA PUCELLE.

 Puc. The regent conquers, and the Frenchmen fly.
Now help, ye charming spells and periapts;
And ye choice spirits that admonish me
And give me signs of future accidents.   [*Thunder.*
You speedy helpers, that are substitutes
Under the lordly monarch of the north,
Appear and aid me in this enterprise.

Enter Fiends.

This speedy and quick appearance argues proof
Of your accustom'd diligence to me.
Now, ye familiar spirits, that are cull'd   10
Out of the powerful regions under earth,
Help me this once, that France may get the field.
        [*They walk, and speak not.*
O, hold me not with silence over-long!
Where I was wont to feed you with my blood,
I'll lop a member off and give it you
In earnest of a further benefit,
So you do condescend to help me now.
         [*They hang their heads.*
No hope to have redress? My body shall
Pay recompense, if you will grant my suit.
         [*They shake their heads.*
Cannot my body nor blood-sacrifice   20
Entreat you to your wonted furtherance?
Then take my soul, my body, soul and all,
Before that England give the French the foil.
           [*They depart.*
See, they forsake me! Now the time is come
That France must vail her lofty-plumed crest
And let her head fall into England's lap.
My ancient incantations are too weak,
And hell too strong for me to buckle with:
Now, France, thy glory droopeth to the dust. [*Exit.*

Excursions. Re-enter LA PUCELLE *fighting hand to
hand with* YORK: LA PUCELLE *is taken. The
French fly.*

 York. Damsel of France, I think I have you fast: 30
Unchain your spirits now with spelling charms
And try if they can gain your liberty.
A goodly prize, fit for the devil's grace!
See, how the ugly witch doth bend her brows,
As if with Circe she would change my shape!

 Puc. Changed to a worser shape thou canst not **be.**

 York. O, Charles the Dauphin is a proper man;
No shape but his can please your dainty eye.

 Puc. A plaguing mischief light on Charles and thee!
And may ye both be suddenly surprised   40
By bloody hands, in sleeping on your beds!

 York. Fell banning hag, enchantress, hold thy
  tongue!

 Puc. I prithee, give me leave to curse awhile.

 York. Curse, miscreant, when thou comest to the
  stake.   [*Exeunt.*

Alarum. Enter SUFFOLK, *with* MARGARET *in his hand.*

 Suf. Be what thou wilt, thou art my prisoner.
           [*Gazes on her.*
O fairest beauty, do not fear nor fly!
For I will touch thee but with reverent hands;
I kiss these fingers for eternal peace,
And lay them gently on thy tender side.
Who art thou? say, that I may honour thee.   50

 Mar. Margaret my name, and daughter to a king,
The King of Naples, whosoe'er thou art.

 Suf. An earl I am, and Suffolk am I call'd.
Be not offended, nature's miracle,
Thou art allotted to be ta'en by me:
So doth the swan her downy cygnets save,
Keeping them prisoner underneath her wings.
Yet, if this servile usage once offend,
Go and be free again as Suffolk's friend. [*She is going.*
O, stay! I have no power to let her pass;   60
My hand would free her, but my heart says no.
As plays the sun upon the glassy streams,
Twinkling another counterfeited beam,
So seems this gorgeous beauty to mine eyes.
Fain would I woo her, yet I dare not speak:
I'll call for pen and ink, and write my mind.
Fie, de la Pole! disable not thyself;
Hast not a tongue? is she not here?
Wilt thou be daunted at a woman's sight?
Ay, beauty's princely majesty is such,   70
Confounds the tongue and makes the senses rough.

 Mar. Say, Earl of Suffolk—if thy name be so—
What ransom must I pay before I pass?
For I perceive I am thy prisoner.

 Suf. How canst thou tell she will deny thy suit,
Before thou make a trial of her love?

 Mar. Why speak'st thou not? what ransom must I
  pay?

 Suf. She 's beautiful and therefore to be woo'd;
She is a woman, therefore to be won.

 Mar. Wilt thou accept of ransom? yea, or no.   80

 Suf. Fond man, remember that thou hast a wife;
Then how can Margaret be thy paramour?

 Mar. I were best to leave him, for he will not hear.

 Suf. There all is marr'd; there lies a cooling card.

 Mar. He talks at random; sure, the man is mad.

 Suf. And yet a dispensation may be had.

 Mar. And yet I would that you would answer me.

 Suf. I'll win this Lady Margaret. For whom?
Why, for my king: tush, that 's a wooden thing!

 Mar. He talks of wood: it is some carpenter.   90

---

15. **provide for,** get ready for.
SCENE III. 1. **The regent,** i.e., the duke of York. 2. **periapts,**
amulets. 3. **admonish,** advise. 4. **accidents,** occurrences. 6. **north.**
Evil spirits were frequently associated with the north. 14. **feed . . .
blood,** a reference to the belief that witches fed their "familiars"
with their own blood. 16. **earnest,** partial payment; see glossary.

25. **vail,** lower; see glossary. 31. **spirits,** i.e., the demons—"familiars"
—attending on Joan; cf. l. 10. **spelling charms,** charms that cast a
spell. 35. **Circe,** sorceress celebrated for her power to change men
into swine. 37. **proper,** handsome; see glossary. 38. **dainty, particular;** see glossary. 42. **Fell,** fierce, cruel. **banning, cursing.**
44. **miscreant,** base villain. 63. **Twinkling,** causing to twinkle. **75.**

Suf. Yet so my fancy may be satisfied,
And peace established between these realms.
But there remains a scruple in that too;
For though her father be the King of Naples,
Duke of Anjou and Maine, yet is he poor,
And our nobility will scorn the match.
    Mar. Hear ye, captain, are you not at leisure?
    Suf. It shall be so, disdain they ne'er so much:
Henry is youthful and will quickly yield.
Madam, I have a secret to reveal.   100
    Mar. What though I be enthrall'd? he seems a
    knight,
And will not any way dishonour me.
    Suf. Lady, vouchsafe to listen what I say.
    Mar. Perhaps I shall be rescued by the French;
And then I need not crave his courtesy.
    Suf. Sweet madam, give me hearing in a cause—
    Mar. Tush, women have been captivate ere now.
    Suf. Lady, wherefore talk you so?
    Mar. I cry you mercy, 'tis but Quid for Quo.
    Suf. Say, gentle princess, would you not suppose   110
Your bondage happy, to be made a queen?
    Mar. To be a queen in bondage is more vile
Than is a slave in base servility;
For princes should be free.
    Suf.   And so shall you,
If happy England's royal king be free.
    Mar. Why, what concerns his freedom unto me?
    Suf. I'll undertake to make thee Henry's queen,
To put a golden sceptre in thy hand
And set a precious crown upon thy head,
If thou wilt condescend to be my—
    Mar.   What?   120
    Suf. His love.
    Mar. I am unworthy to be Henry's wife.
    Suf. No, gentle madam; I unworthy am
To woo so fair a dame to be his wife
And have no portion in the choice myself.
How say you, madam, are ye so content?
    Mar. An if my father please, I am content.
    Suf. Then call our captains and our colours forth.
And, madam, at your father's castle walls
We'll crave a parley, to confer with him.   130

    A parley sounded. Enter REIGNIER *on the walls.*

See, Reignier, see, thy daughter prisoner!
    Reig. To whom?
    Suf.   To me.
    Reig.   Suffolk, what remedy?
I am a soldier and unapt to weep
Or to exclaim on fortune's fickleness.
    Suf. Yes, there is remedy enough, my lord:
Consent, and for thy honour give consent,
Thy daughter shall be wedded to my king;
Whom I with pain have woo'd and won thereto;
And this her easy-held imprisonment
Hath gain'd thy daughter princely liberty.   140
    Reig. Speaks Suffolk as he thinks?
    Suf.   Fair Margaret knows
That Suffolk doth not flatter, face, or feign.
    Reig. Upon thy princely warrant, I descend

To give thee answer of thy just demand.
                    [*Exit from the walls.*
    Suf. And here I will expect thy coming.

    Trumpets sound. Enter REIGNIER, *below.*

    Reig. Welcome, brave earl, into our territories:
Command in Anjou what your honour pleases.
    Suf. Thanks, Reignier, happy for so sweet a child,
Fit to be made companion with a king:
What answer makes your grace unto my suit?   150
    Reig. Since thou dost deign to woo her little worth
To be the princely bride of such a lord;
Upon condition I may quietly
Enjoy mine own, the country Maine and Anjou,
Free from oppression or the stroke of war,
My daughter shall be Henry's, if he please.
    Suf. That is her ransom; I deliver her;
And those two counties I will undertake
Your grace shall well and quietly enjoy.
    Reig. And I again, in Henry's royal name,   160
As deputy unto that gracious king,
Give thee her hand, for sign of plighted faith.
    Suf. Reignier of France, I give thee kingly thanks,
Because this is in traffic of a king.
[*Aside*] And yet, methinks, I could be well content
To be mine own attorney in this case.
I'll over then to England with this news,
And make this marriage to be solemnized.
So farewell, Reignier: set this diamond safe
In golden palaces, as it becomes.   170
    Reig. I do embrace thee, as I would embrace
The Christian prince, King Henry, were he here.
    Mar. Farewell, my lord: good wishes, praise and
    prayers
Shall Suffolk ever have of Margaret.   [*Going.*
    Suf. Farewell, sweet madam: but hark you,
    Margaret;
No princely commendations to my king?
    Mar. Such commendations as becomes a maid,
A virgin and his servant, say to him.
    Suf. Words sweetly placed and modestly directed.
But, madam, I must trouble you again;   180
No loving token to his majesty?
    Mar. Yes, my good lord, a pure unspotted heart,
Never yet taint with love, I send the king.
    Suf. And this withal.   [*Kisses her.*
    Mar. That for thyself: I will not so presume
To send such peevish tokens to a king.
              [*Exeunt Reignier and Margaret.*
    Suf. O, wert thou for myself! But, Suffolk, stay;
Thou mayst not wander in that labyrinth;
There Minotaurs and ugly treasons lurk.
Solicit Henry with her wondrous praise: 190
Bethink thee on her virtues that surmount,
And natural graces that extinguish art;
Repeat their semblance often on the seas,
That, when thou comest to kneel at Henry's feet,
Thou mayst bereave him of his wits with wonder.
                              [*Exit.*

---

deny, refuse; see glossary.   84. **cooling card,** apparently a term of some
lost card game; figuratively, something that cools one's ardor (Onions);
card played by an adversary which dashes one's hope (Tucker Brooke).
89. **wooden thing,** awkward business (Steevens); expressionless, insensible thing, referring to the king (Hart). 109. **cry you mercy,** beg
your pardon; see glossary. **Quid for Quo,** tit for tat. 142. **face,**
show a false face. 164. **traffic,** business. 188. **labyrinth,** a structure
built by Daedalus consisting of intricate passageways where the
Minotaur—a monster born from the union of the Cretan king's wife
with a bull—was confined.

SCENE IV. *Camp of the* DUKE OF YORK *in Anjou.*

Enter YORK, WARWICK, *and others.*

York. Bring forth that sorceress condemn'd to burn.

Enter LA PUCELLE, *guarded, and a* Shepherd.

Shep. Ah, Joan, this kills thy father's heart outright!
Have I sought every country far and near,
And, now it is my chance to find thee out,
Must I behold thy timeless cruel death?
Ah, Joan, sweet daughter Joan, I'll die with thee!
Puc. Decrepit miser! base ignoble wretch!
I am descended of a gentler blood:
Thou art no father nor no friend of mine.
Shep. Out, out! My lords, an please you, 'tis not so; 10
I did beget her, all the parish knows:
Her mother liveth yet, can testify
She was the first fruit of my bachelorship.
War. Graceless! wilt thou deny thy parentage?
York. This argues what her kind of life hath been,
Wicked and vile; and so her death concludes.
Shep. Fie, Joan, that thou wilt be so obstacle!
God knows thou art a collop of my flesh;
And for thy sake have I shed many a tear:
Deny me not, I prithee, gentle Joan. 20
Puc. Peasant, avaunt! You have suborn'd this man,
Of purpose to obscure my noble birth.
Shep. 'Tis true, I gave a noble to the priest
The morn that I was wedded to her mother.
Kneel down and take my blessing, good my girl.
Wilt thou not stoop? Now cursed be the time
Of thy nativity! I would the milk
Thy mother gave thee when thou suck'dst her breast,
Had been a little ratsbane for thy sake!
Or else, when thou didst keep my lambs a-field, 30
I wish some ravenous wolf had eaten thee!
Dost thou deny thy father, cursed drab?
O, burn her, burn her! hanging is too good. [*Exit.*
York. Take her away; for she hath lived too long,
To fill the world with vicious qualities.
Puc. First, let me tell you whom you have
condemn'd:
Not me begotten of a shepherd swain,
But issued from the progeny of kings;
Virtuous and holy; chosen from above,
By inspiration of celestial grace, 40
To work exceeding miracles on earth.
I never had to do with wicked spirits:
But you, that are polluted with your lusts,
Stain'd with the guiltless blood of innocents,
Corrupt and tainted with a thousand vices,
Because you want the grace that others have,
You judge it straight a thing impossible
To compass wonders but by help of devils.
No, misconceived! Joan of Arc hath been
A virgin from her tender infancy, 50
Chaste and immaculate in very thought;
Whose maiden blood, thus rigorously effused,
Will cry for vengeance at the gates of heaven.
York. Ay, ay: away with her to execution!
War. And hark ye, sirs; because she is a maid,

Spare for no faggots, let there be enow:
Place barrels of pitch upon the fatal stake,
That so her torture may be shortened.
Puc. Will nothing turn your unrelenting hearts?
Then, Joan, discover thine infirmity, 60
That warranteth by law to be thy privilege.
I am with child, ye bloody homicides:
Murder not then the fruit within my womb,
Although ye hale me to a violent death.
York. Now heaven forfend! the holy maid with child!
War. The greatest miracle that e'er ye wrought:
Is all your strict preciseness come to this?
York. She and the Dauphin have been juggling:
I did imagine what would be her refuge.
War. Well, go to; we'll have no bastards live; 70
Especially since Charles must father it.
Puc. You are deceived; my child is none of his:
It was Alençon that enjoy'd my love.
York. Alençon! that notorious Machiavel!
It dies, an if it had a thousand lives.
Puc. O, give me leave, I have deluded you:
'Twas neither Charles nor yet the duke I named,
But Reignier, king of Naples, that prevail'd.
War. A married man! that 's most intolerable.
York. Why, here 's a girl! I think she knows not well,
There were so many, whom she may accuse. 81
War. It 's sign she hath been liberal and free.
York. And yet, forsooth, she is a virgin pure.
Strumpet, thy words condemn thy brat and thee:
Use no entreaty, for it is in vain.
Puc. Then lead me hence; with whom I leave my
curse:
May never glorious sun reflex his beams
Upon the country where you make abode;
But darkness and the gloomy shade of death
Environ you, till mischief and despair 90
Drive you to break your necks or hang yourselves!
[*Exit, guarded.*
York. Break thou in pieces and consume to ashes,
Thou foul accursed minister of hell!

Enter CARDINAL BEAUFORT, Bishop of Winchester,
attended.

Car. Lord regent, I do greet your excellence
With letters of commission from the king.
For know, my lords, the states of Christendom,
Moved with remorse of these outrageous broils,
Have earnestly implored a general peace
Betwixt our nation and the aspiring French;
And here at hand the Dauphin and his train 100
Approacheth, to confer about some matter.
York. Is all our travail turn'd to this effect?
After the slaughter of so many peers,
So many captains, gentlemen and soldiers,
That in this quarrel have been overthrown
And sold their bodies for their country's benefit,
Shall we at last conclude effeminate peace?
Have we not lost most part of all the towns,
By treason, falsehood and by treachery,
Our great progenitors had conquered? 110
O, Warwick, Warwick! I foresee with grief

SCENE IV. 4. **find thee out,** discover you. 5. **timeless,** premature. 17. **obstacle,** stubborn. 18. **collop,** slice of meat; figuratively applied to offspring. 23. **noble,** coin worth 6s. 8d. 29. **ratsbane,** rat poison. 35. **qualities,** arts, tricks (Schmidt); see glossary. 49. **misconceived,** having a wrong idea. 65. **forfend,** forbid; see glossary. 74. **Machiavel,** an allusion to the Elizabethan conception of Niccolò Machiavelli,

an Italian political philosopher who advocated the practice of expediency regardless of the ethics involved. To the Elizabethan he symbolized crafty and ruthless ambition. 82. **liberal,** unrestrained, licentious; see glossary. 86. **whom.** The antecedent is in the understood subject of the imperative verb *lead.* 96. **states of Christendom.** Cf. Hall's *Chronicle,* Twenty-second Year of Henry VI: ". . . all the

The utter loss of all the realm of France.
War. Be patient, York: if we conclude a peace,
It shall be with such strict and severe covenants
As little shall the Frenchmen gain thereby.

Enter CHARLES, ALENÇON, BASTARD, REIGNIER,
and others.

Char. Since, lords of England, it is thus agreed
That peaceful truce shall be proclaim'd in France,
We come to be informed by yourselves
What the conditions of that league must be.   119
York. Speak, Winchester; for boiling choler chokes
The hollow passage of my poison'd voice,
By sight of these our baleful enemies.
Car. Charles, and the rest, it is enacted thus:
That, in regard King Henry gives consent,
Of mere compassion and of lenity,
To ease your country of distressful war,
And suffer you to breathe in fruitful peace,
You shall become true liegemen to his crown:
And, Charles, upon condition thou wilt swear
To pay him tribute, and submit thyself,   130
Thou shalt be placed as viceroy under him,
And still enjoy thy regal dignity.
Alen. Must he be then as shadow of himself?
Adorn his temples with a coronet,
And yet, in substance and authority,
Retain but privilege of a private man?
This proffer is absurd and reasonless.
Char. 'Tis known already that I am possess'd
With more than half the Gallian territories,
And therein reverenced for their lawful king: 140
Shall I, for lucre of the rest unvanquish'd,
Detract so much from that prerogative,
As to be call'd but viceroy of the whole?
No, lord ambassador, I'll rather keep
That which I have than, coveting for more,
Be cast from possibility of all.
York. Insulting Charles! hast thou by secret means
Used intercession to obtain a league,
And, now the matter grows to compromise,
Stand'st thou aloof upon comparison?   150
Either accept the title thou usurp'st,
Of benefit proceeding from our king
And not of any challenge of desert,
Or we will plague thee with incessant wars.
Reig. My lord, you do not well in obstinacy
To cavil in the course of this contract:
If once it be neglected, ten to one
We shall not find like opportunity.
Alen. To say the truth, it is your policy
To save your subjects from such massacre   160
And ruthless slaughters as are daily seen
By our proceeding in hostility;
And therefore take this compact of a truce,
Although you break it when your pleasure serves.
War. How say'st thou, Charles? shall our condition
      stand?
Char. It shall;
Only reserved, you claim no interest
In any of our towns of garrison.

York. Then swear allegiance to his majesty,
As thou art knight, never to disobey   170
Nor be rebellious to the crown of England,
Thou, nor thy nobles, to the crown of England.
So, now dismiss your army when ye please;
Hang up your ensigns, let your drums be still,
For here we entertain a solemn peace.   [*Exeunt.*

SCENE V. *London. The palace.*

Enter SUFFOLK *in conference with the* KING, GLOUCES-
TER *and* EXETER.

King. Your wondrous rare description, noble earl,
Of beauteous Margaret hath astonish'd me:
Her virtues graced with external gifts
Do breed love's settled passions in my heart:
And like as rigour of tempestuous gusts
Provokes the mightiest hulk against the tide,
So am I driven by breath of her renown
Either to suffer shipwreck or arrive
Where I may have fruition of her love.
Suf. Tush, my good lord, this superficial tale   10
Is but a preface of her worthy praise;
The chief perfections of that lovely dame,
Had I sufficient skill to utter them,
Would make a volume of enticing lines,
Able to ravish any dull conceit:
And, which is more, she is not so divine,
So full-replete with choice of all delights,
But with as humble lowliness of mind
She is content to be at your command;
Command, I mean, of virtuous chaste intents,   20
To love and honour Henry as her lord.
King. And otherwise will Henry ne'er presume.
Therefore, my lord protector, give consent
That Margaret may be England's royal queen.
Glou. So should I give consent to flatter sin.
You know, my lord, your highness is betroth'd
Unto another lady of esteem:
How shall we then dispense with that contract,
And not deface your honour with reproach?
Suf. As doth a ruler with unlawful oaths;   30
Or one that, at a triumph having vow'd
To try his strength, forsaketh yet the lists
By reason of his adversary's odds:
A poor earl's daughter is unequal odds,
And therefore may be broke without offence.
Glou. Why, what, I pray, is Margaret more than
      that?
Her father is no better than an earl,
Although in glorious titles he excel.
Suf. Yes, my lord, her father is a king,
The King of Naples and Jerusalem;   40
And of such great authority in France
As his alliance will confirm our peace
And keep the Frenchmen in allegiance.
Glou. And so the Earl of Armagnac may do,
Because he is near kinsman unto Charles.
Exe. Beside, his wealth doth warrant a liberal dower,
Where Reignier sooner will receive than give.

---

princes of Christendom, so muche labored and trauailed, by their orators and Ambassadors, that the frostie hartes of bothe the parties wer somewhat mollified, and their indurate stomackes greatly asswaged." 97. **remorse of,** compassion on account of; see glossary. 114. **covenants,** clauses or articles of a contract. 120. **choler,** red bile, humor dominant in angry tempers; see *humour* in glossary. 150.

comparison, quibbling rhetoric (Tucker Brooke); satirical or scoffing similes (Onions). 156. **cavil,** raise frivolous or fault-finding objections. 165. **condition,** treaty, contract; see glossary. 168. **towns of garrison,** fortified towns.
SCENE V. 4. **settled,** fixed, rooted. 31. **triumph,** tournament. 35. **broke,** i.e., negotiations may be broken off.

Suf. A dower, my lords! disgrace not so your king,
That he should be so abject, base and poor,
To choose for wealth and not for perfect love. 50
Henry is able to enrich his queen
And not to seek a queen to make him rich:
So worthless peasants bargain for their wives,
As market-men for oxen, sheep, or horse.
Marriage is a matter of more worth
Than to be dealt in by attorneyship;
Not whom we will, but whom his grace affects,
Must be companion of his nuptial bed:
And therefore, lords, since he affects her most,
It most of all these reasons bindeth us, 60
In our opinions she should be preferr'd.
For what is wedlock forced but a hell,
An age of discord and continual strife?
Whereas the contrary bringeth bliss,
And is a pattern of celestial peace.
Whom should we match with Henry, being a king,
But Margaret, that is daughter to a king?
Her peerless feature, joined with her birth,
Approves her fit for none but for a king:
Her valiant courage and undaunted spirit, 70
More than in women commonly is seen,
Will answer our hope in issue of a king;
For Henry, son unto a conqueror,
Is likely to beget more conquerors,
If with a lady of so high resolve
As is fair Margaret he be link'd in love.
Then yield, my lords; and here conclude with me
That Margaret shall be queen, and none but she.

King. Whether it be through force of your report,
My noble Lord of Suffolk, or for that 80
My tender youth was never yet attaint
With any passion of inflaming love,
I cannot tell; but this I am assured,
I feel such sharp dissension in my breast,
Such fierce alarums both of hope and fear,
As I am sick with working of my thoughts.
Take, therefore, shipping; post, my lord, to France;
Agree to any covenants, and procure
That Lady Margaret do vouchsafe to come
To cross the seas to England and be crown'd 90
King Henry's faithful and anointed queen:
For your expenses and sufficient charge,
Among the people gather up a tenth.
Be gone, I say; for, till you do return,
I rest perplexed with a thousand cares.
And you, good uncle, banish all offence:
If you do censure me by what you were,
Not what you are, I know it will excuse
This sudden execution of my will.
And so, conduct me where, from company, 100
I may revolve and ruminate my grief.   [*Exit.*
    Glou. Ay, grief, I fear me, both at first and last.
                        [*Exeunt Gloucester and Exeter.*
    Suf. Thus Suffolk hath prevail'd; and thus he goes,
As did the youthful Paris once to Greece,
With hope to find the like event in love,
But prosper better than the Trojan did.
Margaret shall now be queen, and rule the king;
But I will rule both her, the king and realm.   [*Exit.*

56. **by attorneyship,** by an attorney, by proxy. 68. **feature,** figure; see glossary. 81. **attaint.** infected. 87. **post,** hasten; see glossary. 93. **gather up a tenth,** levy a tax of ten per cent. 95. **rest,** remain. 97. **censure,** judge; see glossary. 100. **from company,** i.e., alone.

In this Countie at three severall tymes, three mortall and bloody Battells of Englands ciuill discentions have bene fought. The first whereof chaunced the 23 of Maye Anno 1455. in the towne of St. Albons by Richard Duke of Yorke, with his assotiats, the Earls of Warwick, and Salesbury and Lords of saw conbridg, and Cobham, against King H. 6. In whos defence Edmund Duke of Somerset, Henry Earl of Northumberland, and Iohn Lord Clifford with 5000 more lost their lives, the king himselfe was wounded in the neck with an arrowe, the Duke of Buckingham and Lorde Sudley in their faces. Humfrey Earle Stafford in his right hand, and the Earle Dorset almost slaine. On the Dukes part only 600. were slaine. The king by them was brought to London, and a reconciliation made by their aduancments unto dignityes and Offices

The second Battell was likewise fought in the towne of S. Albons by Queene Margaret, against the Duke of Norfolke, and Suffolke, the Earls of Warwick, and Arundell, that by force kept with them the king her husband, with whome by constrayt he held, and on their syde fought untill the feild was lost and the Lords fled, when with great ioye he was received by his Queene and younge sone Prince Edward this Battell fell the 17. of February being Shrouestuesday Anno 1461.

THE SECOND PART OF

King Henry the Sixth

DRAMATIS PERSONAE

KING HENRY the Sixth.
HUMPHREY, Duke of Gloucester, his uncle.
CARDINAL BEAUFORT, Bishop of Winchester,
　great-uncle to the King.
RICHARD PLANTAGENET, Duke of York.
EDWARD and RICHARD, his sons.
DUKE OF SOMERSET.
DUKE OF SUFFOLK.
DUKE OF BUCKINGHAM.
LORD CLIFFORD.
YOUNG CLIFFORD, his son.
EARL OF SALISBURY.
EARL OF WARWICK.
LORD SCALES.
LORD SAY.
SIR HUMPHREY STAFFORD, and WILLIAM
　STAFFORD, his brother.
SIR JOHN STANLEY.
VAUX.
MATTHEW GOFFE.
A Sea-captain, Master, and Master's-Mate, and
　WALTER WHITMORE.
Two Gentlemen, prisoners with Suffolk.
JOHN HUME and JOHN SOUTHWELL, priests.
BOLINGBROKE, a conjurer.
THOMAS HORNER, an armourer. PETER, his
　man.
Clerk of Chatham. Mayor of Saint Alban's.
SIMPCOX, an impostor.
ALEXANDER IDEN, a Kentish gentleman.
JACK CADE, a rebel.
GEORGE BEVIS, JOHN HOLLAND, DICK the
　butcher, SMITH the weaver, MICHAEL,
　&c., followers of Cade.
Two Murderers.

MARGARET, Queen to King Henry.
ELEANOR, Duchess of Gloucester.
MARGARET JOURDAIN, a witch.
Wife to Simpcox.

Lords, Ladies, and Attendants, Petitioners,
　Aldermen, a Herald, a Beadle, Sheriff, and
　Officers, Citizens, 'Prentices, Falconers,
　Guards, Soldiers, Messengers, &c.

A Spirit.

SCENE: *England.*

ACT I.

SCENE I. *London. The palace.*

Flourish of trumpets: then hautboys. Enter the KING,
HUMPHREY, Duke of GLOUCESTER, SALISBURY,

WARWICK, *and* CARDINAL BEAUFORT, *on the one
side; the* QUEEN, SUFFOLK, YORK, SOMERSET, *and*
BUCKINGHAM, *on the other.*

　Suf. As by your high imperial majesty
I had in charge at my depart for France,
As procurator to your excellence,
To marry Princess Margaret for your grace,
So, in the famous ancient city Tours,
In presence of the Kings of France and Sicil,
The Dukes of Orleans, Calaber, Bretagne and
　Alençon,
Seven earls, twelve barons and twenty reverend
　bishops,
I have perform'd my task and was espoused:
And humbly now upon my bended knee,　　　10
In sight of England and her lordly peers,
Deliver up my title in the queen
To your most gracious hands, that are the substance
Of that great shadow I did represent;
The happiest gift that ever marquess gave,
The fairest queen that ever king received.
　King. Suffolk, arise. Welcome, Queen Margaret:
I can express no kinder sign of love
Than this kind kiss. O Lord, that lends me life,
Lend me a heart replete with thankfulness!　　20
For thou hast given me in this beauteous face
A world of earthly blessings to my soul,
If sympathy of love unite our thoughts.
　Queen. Great King of England and my gracious
　lord,
The mutual conference that my mind hath had,
By day, by night, waking and in my dreams,
In courtly company or at my beads,
With you, mine alder-liefest sovereign,
Makes me the bolder to salute my king
With ruder terms, such as my wit affords　　30
And over-joy of heart doth minister.
　King. Her sight did ravish; but her grace in
　speech,
Her words y-clad with wisdom's majesty,
Makes me from wondering fall to weeping joys;
Such is the fulness of my heart's content.
Lords, with one cheerful voice welcome my love.
　All [*kneeling*]. Long live Queen Margaret, England's
　happiness!
　Queen. We thank you all.　　　　　[*Flourish.*
　Suf. My lord protector, so it please your grace,
Here are the articles of contracted peace　　40
Between our sovereign and the French king Charles,
For eighteen months concluded by consent.
　Glou. [*Reads*] 'Imprimis, It is agreed between the
French king Charles, and William de la Pole, Mar-

ACT I. SCENE I. *Stage Direction:* **hautboys,** double-reed wind instruments, oboes.　2. **I . . . France.** Cf. *1 Henry VI*, V, iii, and V, v, where Suffolk negotiates with the duke Reignier for the marriage of his daughter to the English king. **depart,** departure.　3. **procurator,** agent, proxy. The language of the play here follows Hall and Holinshed: "The marquesse of Suffolke, as procurator to king Henrie, espoused the said ladie in the church of saint Martins. At the which mariage were present the father and mother of the bride: the French king himselfe, which was vncle to the husband; and the French queene also, which was aunt to the wife. There were also the dukes of Orleance, of Calabre, of Alanson, and of Britaine, seauen earles, twelue barons, twentie bishops, besides knights and gentlemen." 6. **Sicil,** Sicily, of which Margaret's father was titular king.　14. **shadow,** image, i.e., of royalty; see glossary.　18. **kinder,** more natural; see *kind* in glossary.　28. **alder-liefest,** most loved.　30. **ruder,** not properly respectful.　33. **y-clad,** clothed. 43. **Imprimis,** in the first place.

quess of Suffolk, ambassador for Henry King of
England, that the said Henry shall espouse the Lady
Margaret, daughter unto Reignier King of Naples,
Sicilia and Jerusalem, and crown her Queen of Eng-
land ere the thirtieth of May next ensuing. Item, that
the duchy of Anjou and the county of Maine shall be
released and delivered to the king her father'— 52
[*Lets the paper fall.*

King. Uncle, how now!
Glou.   Pardon me, gracious lord;
Some sudden qualm hath struck me at the heart
And dimm'd mine eyes, that I can read no further.
King. Uncle of Winchester, I pray, read on.
Car. [*Reads*] 'Item, It is further agreed between
them, that the duchies of Anjou and Maine shall be
released and delivered over to the king her father, and
she sent over of the King of England's own proper cost
and charges, without having any dowry.' 62
King. They please us well. Lord marquess, kneel
down:
We here create thee the first duke of Suffolk,
And gird thee with the sword. Cousin of York,
We here discharge your grace from being regent
I' the parts of France, till term of eighteen months
Be full expired. Thanks, uncle Winchester,
Gloucester, York, Buckingham, Somerset,
Salisbury, and Warwick; 70
We thank you all for this great favour done,
In entertainment to my princely queen.
Come, let us in, and with all speed provide
To see her coronation be perform'd.
[*Exeunt King, Queen, and Suffolk.*

Glou. Brave peers of England, pillars of the state,
To you Duke Humphrey must unload his grief,
Your grief, the common grief of all the land.
What! did my brother Henry spend his youth,
His valour, coin and people, in the wars?
Did he so often lodge in open field, 80
In winter's cold and summer's parching heat,
To conquer France, his true inheritance?
And did my brother Bedford toil his wits,
To keep by policy what Henry got?
Have you yourselves, Somerset, Buckingham,
Brave York, Salisbury, and victorious Warwick,
Received deep scars in France and Normandy?
Or hath mine uncle Beaufort and myself,
With all the learned council of the realm,
Studied so long, sat in the council-house 90
Early and late, debating to and fro
How France and Frenchmen might be kept in awe,
And had his highness in his infancy
Crowned in Paris in despite of foes?
And shall these labours and these honours die?
Shall Henry's conquest, Bedford's vigilance,
Your deeds of war and all our counsel die?
O peers of England, shameful is this league!

Fatal this marriage, cancelling your fame,
Blotting your names from books of memory, 100
Razing the characters of your renown,
Defacing monuments of conquer'd France,
Undoing all, as all had never been!
Car. Nephew, what means this passionate discourse,
This peroration with such circumstance?
For France, 'tis ours; and we will keep it still.
Glou. Ay, uncle, we will keep it, if we can;
But now it is impossible we should:
Suffolk, the new-made duke that rules the roast,
Hath given the duchy of Anjou and Maine 110
Unto the poor King Reignier, whose large style
Agrees not with the leanness of his purse.
Sal. Now, by the death of Him that died for all,
These counties were the keys of Normandy.
But wherefore weeps Warwick, my valiant son?
War. For grief that they are past recovery:
For, were there hope to conquer them again,
My sword should shed hot blood, mine eyes no tears.
Anjou and Maine! myself did win them both;
Those provinces these arms of mine did conquer: 120
And are the cities, that I got with wounds,
Deliver'd up again with peaceful words?
Mort Dieu!
York. For Suffolk's duke, may he be suffocate,
That dims the honour of this warlike isle!
France should have torn and rent my very heart,
Before I would have yielded to this league.
I never read but England's kings have had
Large sums of gold and dowries with their wives;
And our King Henry gives away his own, 130
To match with her that brings no vantages.
Glou. A proper jest, and never heard before,
That Suffolk should demand a whole fifteenth
For costs and charges in transporting her!
She should have stay'd in France and starved in
France,
Before—
Car. My Lord of Gloucester, now ye grow too hot:
It was the pleasure of my lord the king.
Glou. My Lord of Winchester, I know your mind;
'Tis not my speeches that you do mislike, 140
But 'tis my presence that doth trouble ye.
Rancour will out: proud prelate, in thy face
I see thy fury: if I longer stay,
We shall begin our ancient bickerings.
Lordings, farewell; and say, when I am gone,
I prophesied France will be lost ere long. [*Exit.*
Car. So, there goes our protector in a rage.
'Tis known to you he is mine enemy,
Nay, more, an enemy unto you all,
And no great friend, I fear me, to the king. 150
Consider, lords, he is the next of blood,
And heir apparent to the English crown:
Had Henry got an empire by his marriage,

And all the wealthy kingdoms of the west,
There 's reason he should be displeased at it.
Look to it, lords; let not his smoothing words
Bewitch your hearts; be wise and circumspect.
What though the common people favour him,
Calling him 'Humphrey, the good Duke of
    Gloucester,'
Clapping their hands, and crying with loud voice, 160
'Jesu maintain your royal excellence!'
With 'God preserve the good Duke Humphrey!'
I fear me, lords, for all this flattering gloss,
He will be found a dangerous protector.
   Buck. Why should he, then, protect our sovereign,
He being of age to govern of himself?
Cousin of Somerset, join you with me,
And all together, with the Duke of Suffolk,
We 'll quickly hoise Duke Humphrey from his seat.
   Car. This weighty business will not brook delay; 170
I 'll to the Duke of Suffolk presently.   [*Exit.*
   Som. Cousin of Buckingham, though Humphrey's
    pride
And greatness of his place be grief to us,
Yet let us watch the haughty cardinal:
His insolence is more intolerable
Than all the princes in the land beside:
If Gloucester be displaced, he 'll be protector.
   Buck. Or thou or I, Somerset, will be protector,
Despite Duke Humphrey or the cardinal.
         [*Exeunt Buckingham and Somerset.*
   Sal. Pride went before, ambition follows him.   180
While these do labour for their own preferment,
Behoves it us to labour for the realm.
I never saw but Humphrey Duke of Gloucester
Did bear him like a noble gentleman.
Oft have I seen the haughty cardinal,
More like a soldier than a man o' the church,
As stout and proud as he were lord of all,
Swear like a ruffian and demean himself
Unlike the ruler of a commonweal.
Warwick, my son, the comfort of my age,   190
Thy deeds, thy plainness and thy housekeeping,
Hath won the greatest favour of the commons,
Excepting none but good Duke Humphrey:
And, brother York, thy acts in Ireland,
In bringing them to civil discipline,
Thy late exploits done in the heart of France,
When thou wert regent for our sovereign,
Have made thee fear'd and honour'd of the people:
Join we together, for the public good,
In what we can, to bridle and suppress   200
The pride of Suffolk and the cardinal,
With Somerset's and Buckingham's ambition;
And, as we may, cherish Duke Humphrey's deeds,
While they do tend the profit of the land.
   War. So God help Warwick, as he loves the land,
And common profit of his country!

   York. [*Aside*] And so says York, for he hath greatest
    cause.
   Sal. Then let 's make haste away, and look unto the
    main.
   War. Unto the main! O father, Maine is lost;
That Maine which by main force Warwick did win, 210
And would have kept so long as breath did last!
Main chance, father, you meant; but I meant Maine,
Which I will win from France, or else be slain.
         [*Exeunt Warwick and Salisbury.*
   York. Anjou and Maine are given to the French;
Paris is lost; the state of Normandy
Stands on a tickle point, now they are gone:
Suffolk concluded on the articles,
The peers agreed, and Henry was well pleased
To change two dukedoms for a duke's fair daughter.
I cannot blame them all: what is 't to them?   220
'Tis thine they give away, and not their own.
Pirates may make cheap pennyworths of their pillage
And purchase friends and give to courtezans,
Still revelling like lords till all be gone;
While as the silly owner of the goods
Weeps over them and wrings his hapless hands
And shakes his head and trembling stands aloof,
While all is shared and all is borne away,
Ready to starve and dare not touch his own:
So York must sit and fret and bite his tongue,   230
While his own lands are bargain'd for and sold.
Methinks the realms of England, France and Ireland
Bear that proportion to my flesh and blood
As did the fatal brand Althæa burn'd
Unto the prince's heart of Calydon.
Anjou and Maine both given unto the French!
Cold news for me, for I had hope of France,
Even as I have of fertile England's soil.
A day will come when York shall claim his own;
And therefore I will take the Nevils' parts   240
And make a show of love to proud Duke Humphrey,
And, when I spy advantage, claim the crown,
For that 's the golden mark I seek to hit:
Nor shall proud Lancaster usurp my right,
Nor hold the sceptre in his childish fist,
Nor wear the diadem upon his head,
Whose church-like humours fits not for a crown.
Then, York, be still awhile, till time do serve:
Watch thou and wake when others be asleep,
To pry into the secrets of the state;   250
Till Henry, surfeiting in joys of love,
With his new bride and England's dear-bought
    queen,
And Humphrey with the peers be fall'n at jars:
Then will I raise aloft the milk-white rose,
With whose sweet smell the air shall be perfumed;
And in my standard bear the arms of York,
To grapple with the house of Lancaster;
And, force perforce, I 'll make him yield the crown,

2 Henry VI

ACT I : SC I

241

---

ence to New World possessions. **159. good . . . Gloucester.** Gloucester's popularity is recorded in the chronicles, where he is represented as "an vpright and politike gouernour." **163. gloss,** specious appearance; see glossary. **169. hoise,** remove. **170. brook,** endure; see glossary. **172. Cousin,** any relative not of one's immediate family; see glossary. **180. Pride,** i.e., Winchester. **ambition,** i.e., Buckingham and Somerset. **191. housekeeping,** hospitality. **208. the main,** important business. **216. tickle,** easily shifted, insecure. **222. cheap pennyworths,** bargains. **234. Althæa,** mother of Meleager, at whose birth the three Fates were present and bestowed gifts—courage, strength, and duration of life only as long as a brand, at the time burning on the fire, remained

unconsumed. When the three had departed, the infant's mother snatched the brand, extinguished it, and put it in safe keeping. Years later, when Meleager quarreled with Althaea's brothers and slew them, she resentfully threw the fatal brand into the fire, and as it was reduced to ashes Meleager died. **240. the Nevils'.** York's wife was Cecille Nevil, sister to the earl of Salisbury and aunt to the earl of Warwick. **242. advantage,** opportunity; see glossary. **247. humours,** temperament, cast of mind; see glossary. **248. do serve,** is favorable; see *serve* in glossary. **253. jars,** discords (as in music); see glossary. **258. force perforce,** by violent compulsion; see *perforce* in glossary.

Whose bookish rule hath pull'd fair England down.
[*Exit.*

SCENE II. *The* DUKE OF GLOUCESTER'S *house.*

Enter DUKE HUMPHREY *and his wife* ELEANOR.

Duch. Why droops my lord, like overripen'd corn,
Hanging the head at Ceres' plenteous load?
Why doth the great Duke Humphrey knit his brows,
As frowning at the favours of the world?
Why are thine eyes fix'd to the sullen earth,
Gazing on that which seems to dim thy sight?
What seest thou there? King Henry's diadem,
Enchased with all the honours of the world?
If so, gaze on, and grovel on thy face,
Until thy head be circled with the same.   10
Put forth thy hand, reach at the glorious gold.
What, is 't too short? I'll lengthen it with mine;
And, having both together heaved it up,
We'll both together lift our heads to heaven,
And never more abase our sight so low
As to vouchsafe one glance unto the ground.
Glou. O Nell, sweet Nell, if thou dost love thy lord,
Banish the canker of ambitious thoughts.
And may that thought, when I imagine ill
Against my king and nephew, virtuous Henry,   20
Be my last breathing in this mortal world!
My troublous dream this night doth make me sad.
Duch. What dream'd my lord? tell me, and I'll
      requite it
With sweet rehearsal of my morning's dream.
Glou. Methought this staff, mine office-badge in
      court,
Was broke in twain; by whom I have forgot,
But, as I think, it was by the cardinal;
And on the pieces of the broken wand
Were placed the heads of Edmund Duke of Somerset,
And William de la Pole, first duke of Suffolk.   30
This was my dream: what it doth bode, God knows.
Duch. Tut, this was nothing but an argument
That he that breaks a stick of Gloucester's grove
Shall lose his head for his presumption.
But list to me, my Humphrey, my sweet duke:
Methought I sat in seat of majesty
In the cathedral church of Westminster,
And in that chair where kings and queens are
      crown'd;
Where Henry and dame Margaret kneel'd to me
And on my head did set the diadem.   40
Glou. Nay, Eleanor, then must I chide outright:
Presumptuous dame, ill-nurtured Eleanor,
Art thou not second woman in the realm,
And the protector's wife, beloved of him?
Hast thou not worldly pleasure at command,
Above the reach or compass of thy thought?
And wilt thou still be hammering treachery,
To tumble down thy husband and thyself
From top of honour to disgrace's feet?

Away from me, and let me hear no more!   50
Duch. What, what, my lord! are you so choleric
With Eleanor, for telling but her dream?
Next time I'll keep my dreams unto myself,
And not be check'd.
Glou. Nay, be not angry; I am pleased again.

Enter Messenger.

Mess. My lord protector, 'tis his highness' pleasure
You do prepare to ride unto Saint Alban's,
Where as the king and queen do mean to hawk.
Glou. I go. Come, Nell, thou wilt ride with us?
Duch. Yes, my good lord, I'll follow presently.   60
[*Exeunt Gloucester and Messenger.*
Follow I must; I cannot go before,
While Gloucester bears this base and humble mind.
Were I a man, a duke, and next of blood,
I would remove these tedious stumbling-blocks
And smooth my way upon their headless necks;
And, being a woman, I will not be slack
To play my part in Fortune's pageant.
Where are you there? Sir John! nay, fear not, man,
We are alone; here 's none but thee and I.

Enter HUME.

Hume. Jesus preserve your royal majesty!   70
Duch. What say'st thou? majesty! I am but grace.
Hume. But, by the grace of God, and Hume's advice,
Your grace's title shall be multiplied.
Duch. What say'st thou, man? hast thou as yet
      conferr'd
With Margery Jourdain, the cunning witch,
With Roger Bolingbroke, the conjurer?
And will they undertake to do me good?
Hume. This they have promised, to show your
      highness
A spirit raised from depth of under-ground,
That shall make answer to such questions   80
As by your grace shall be propounded him.
Duch. It is enough; I'll think upon the questions:
When from Saint Alban's we do make return,
We'll see these things effected to the full.
Here, Hume, take this reward; make merry, man,
With thy confederates in this weighty cause.   [*Exit.*
Hume. Hume must make merry with the duchess'
      gold;
Marry, and shall. But, how now, Sir John Hume!
Seal up your lips, and give no words but mum:
The business asketh silent secrecy.   90
Dame Eleanor gives gold to bring the witch:
Gold cannot come amiss, were she a devil.
Yet have I gold flies from another coast;
I dare not say, from the rich cardinal
And from the great and new-made Duke of Suffolk,
Yet I do find it so; for, to be plain,
They, knowing Dame Eleanor's aspiring humour,
Have hired me to undermine the duchess
And buz these conjurations in her brain.
They say 'A crafty knave does need no broker;'   100
Yet am I Suffolk and the cardinal's broker.

---

259. **bookish rule,** i.e., in accordance with a formal ethical code.
SCENE II. 2. **Ceres',** goddess of the harvest. 8. **Enchased,** adorned
as with gems. 21. **mortal,** i.e., pertaining to human affairs; see glossary. 32. **argument,** reason, excuse; see glossary. 42. **Presumptuous
dame.** Cf. Winchester's words, *1 Henry VI,* I, i, 39-40. 47. **hammering,**
devising. 67. **pageant,** spectacular entertainment; see glossary. 71.
I am but grace. "Your grace" is the appropriate address to a duchess.

88. **Marry,** mild interjection; see glossary. 93. **flies,** i.e., that flies.
106. **attainture,** disgrace.
SCENE III. 3-4. **in the quill,** simultaneously (Hart); in a body
(Onions); possibly, "in writing." 7. **a',** he; see glossary. 11. **fellow,**
contemptuous or condescending form of address; see glossary. 24. **enclosing the commons,** the action of a lord of a manor in enclosing or
converting into private property lands formerly undivided and used by

Hume, if you take not heed, you shall go near
To call them both a pair of crafty knaves.
Well, so it stands; and thus, I fear, at last
Hume's knavery will be the duchess' wreck,
And her attainture will be Humphrey's fall:
Sort how it will, I shall have gold for all.   [*Exit.*

SCENE III. *The palace.*

Enter three or four Petitioners, PETER, *the Armourer's
man, being one.*

First Petit. My masters, let's stand close: my lord
protector will come this way by and by, and then we
may deliver our supplications in the quill.

Sec. Petit. Marry, the Lord protect him, for he's a
good man! Jesu bless him!

Enter SUFFOLK *and* QUEEN.

Peter. Here a' comes, methinks, and the queen with
him. I'll be the first, sure.

Sec. Petit. Come back, fool; this is the Duke of
Suffolk, and not my lord protector.   10

Suf. How now, fellow! wouldst any thing with me?

First Petit. I pray, my lord, pardon me; I took ye for
my lord protector.

Queen. [*Reading*] 'To my Lord Protector!' Are your
supplications to his lordship? Let me see them: what is
thine?

First Petit. Mine is, an 't please your grace, against
John Goodman, my lord cardinal's man, for keeping
my house, and lands, and wife and all, from me.   21

Suf. Thy wife too! that's some wrong, indeed.
What's yours? What's here! [*Reads*] 'Against the Duke
of Suffolk, for enclosing the commons of Melford.'
How now, sir knave!

Sec. Petit. Alas, sir, I am but a poor petitioner of our
whole township.

Peter. [*Giving his petition*] Against my master,
Thomas Horner, for saying that the Duke of York was
rightful heir to the crown.   30

Queen. What say'st thou? did the Duke of York say
he was rightful heir to the crown?

Peter. That my master was? no, forsooth: my master
said that he was, and that the king was an usurper.

Suf. Who is there? [*Enter Servant.*] Take this fellow in,
and send for his master with a pursuivant presently:
we'll hear more of your matter before the king.
          [*Exit Servant with Peter.*

Queen. And as for you, that love to be protected   40
Under the wings of our protector's grace,
Begin your suits anew, and sue to him.
          [*Tears the supplications.*
Away, base cullions! Suffolk, let them go.

All. Come, let's be gone.   [*Exeunt.*

Queen. My Lord of Suffolk, say, is this the guise,
Is this the fashion in the court of England?
Is this the government of Britain's isle,
And this the royalty of Albion's king?

What, shall King Henry be a pupil still
Under the surly Gloucester's governance?   50
Am I a queen in title and in style,
And must be made a subject to a duke?
I tell thee, Pole, when in the city Tours
Thou ran'st a tilt in honour of my love
And stolest away the ladies' hearts of France,
I thought King Henry had resembled thee
In courage, courtship and proportion:
But all his mind is bent to holiness,
To number Ave-Maries on his beads;
His champions are the prophets and apostles,   60
His weapons holy saws of sacred writ,
His study is his tilt-yard, and his loves
Are brazen images of canonized saints.
I would the college of the cardinals
Would choose him pope and carry him to Rome,
And set the triple crown upon his head:
That were a state fit for his holiness.

Suf. Madam, be patient: as I was cause
Your highness came to England, so will I
In England work your grace's full content.   70

Queen. Beside the haughty protector, have we
          Beaufort
The imperious churchman, Somerset, Buckingham,
And grumbling York; and not the least of these
But can do more in England than the king.

Suf. And he of these that can do most of all
Cannot do more in England than the Nevils:
Salisbury and Warwick are no simple peers.

Queen. Not all these lords do vex me half so much
As that proud dame, the lord protector's wife.
She sweeps it through the court with troops of
          ladies,   80
More like an empress than Duke Humphrey's wife:
Strangers in court do take her for the queen:
She bears a duke's revenues on her back,
And in her heart she scorns our poverty:
Shall I not live to be avenged on her?
Contemptuous base-born callet as she is,
She vaunted 'mongst her minions t'other day,
The very train of her worst wearing gown
Was better worth than all my father's lands,
Till Suffolk gave two dukedoms for his daughter.   90

Suf. Madam, myself have limed a bush for her,
And placed a quire of such enticing birds,
That she will light to listen to the lays,
And never mount to trouble you again.
So, let her rest: and, madam, list to me;
For I am bold to counsel you in this.
Although we fancy not the cardinal,
Yet must we join with him and with the lords,
Till we have brought Duke Humphrey in disgrace.
As for the Duke of York, this late complaint   100
Will make but little for his benefit.
So, one by one, we'll weed them all at last,
And you yourself shall steer the happy helm.

Sound a sennet. Enter the KING, DUKE HUMPHREY *of*
          Gloucester, CARDINAL BEAUFORT, BUCKINGHAM,

---

the community as a whole. 37. **pursuivant.** messenger. 43. **cullions,**
base fellows. 48. **Albion's king,** Albion is a poetic name for England.
57. **courtship,** court manners. **proportion,** carriage, build; see
glossary. 58-61. **to holiness . . . writ.** The pious and idealistic character of the king is touched upon in *1 Henry VI,* III, i, and IV, i.
76. **the Nevils.** Cf. I, i, 240, note. This mention prepares for the
important role played by Warwick later in the Henry VI cycle. 86.

callet, lewd woman. 87. **minions,** followers, with quibble on the
meaning "saucy women"; see glossary. 91. **limed a bush,** set a trap;
a metaphor from the practice of catching birds by liming twigs of
trees. 93. **lays,** songs. 103. *Stage Direction:* **sennet,** set of notes played
on a trumpet as a signal for the approach or departure of processions;
see glossary.

YORK, SOMERSET, SALISBURY, WARWICK, *and the*
DUCHESS OF GLOUCESTER.

King. For my part, noble lords, I care not which;
Or Somerset or York, all 's one to me.

York. If York have ill demean'd himself in France,
Then let him be denay'd the regentship.

Som. If Somerset be unworthy of the place,
Let York be regent; I will yield to him.

War. Whether your grace be worthy, yea or no, 110
Dispute not that: York is the worthier.

Car. Ambitious Warwick, let thy betters speak.

War. The cardinal 's not my better in the field.

Buck. All in this presence are thy betters, Warwick.

War. Warwick may live to be the best of all.

Sal. Peace, son! and show some reason, Buckingham,
Why Somerset should be preferr'd in this.

Queen. Because the king, forsooth, will have it so.

Glou. Madam, the king is old enough himself
To give his censure: these are no women's matters. 120

Queen. If he be old enough, what needs your grace
To be protector of his excellence?

Glou. Madam, I am protector of the realm;
And, at his pleasure, will resign my place.

Suf. Resign it then and leave thine insolence.
Since thou wert king—as who is king but thou?—
The commonwealth hath daily run to wreck;
The Dauphin hath prevail'd beyond the seas;
And all the peers and nobles of the realm
Have been as bondmen to thy sovereignty. 130

Car. The commons hast thou rack'd; the clergy's
bags
Are lank and lean with thy extortions.

Som. Thy sumptuous buildings and thy wife's attire
Have cost a mass of public treasury.

Buck. Thy cruelty in execution
Upon offenders hath exceeded law
And left thee to the mercy of the law.

Queen. Thy sale of offices and towns in France,
If they were known, as the suspect is great,
Would make thee quickly hop without thy head. 140
[*Exit Gloucester. The Queen drops her fan.*
Give me my fan: what, minion! can ye not?
[*She gives the Duchess a box on the ear.*
I cry you mercy, madam; was it you?

Duch. Was 't I! yea, I it was, proud Frenchwoman:
Could I come near your beauty with my nails,
I 'ld set my ten commandments in your face.

King. Sweet aunt, be quiet; 'twas against her will.

Duch. Against her will! good king, look to 't in time;
She'll hamper thee, and dandle thee like a baby:
Though in this place most master wear no breeches,
She shall not strike Dame Eleanor unrevenged. [*Exit.*

Buck. Lord cardinal, I will follow Eleanor, 151
And listen after Humphrey, how he proceeds:
She 's tickled now; her fume needs no spurs,
She'll gallop far enough to her destruction. [*Exit.*

Re-enter GLOUCESTER.

Glou. Now, lords, my choler being over-blown

With walking once about the quadrangle,
I come to talk of commonwealth affairs.
As for your spiteful false objections,
Prove them, and I lie open to the law:
But God in mercy so deal with my soul, 160
As I in duty love my king and country!
But, to the matter that we have in hand:
I say, my sovereign, York is meetest man
To be your regent in the realm of France.

Suf. Before we make election, give me leave
To show some reason, of no little force,
That York is most unmeet of any man.

York. I'll tell thee, Suffolk, why I am unmeet:
First, for I cannot flatter thee in pride;
Next, if I be appointed for the place, 170
My Lord of Somerset will keep me here,
Without discharge, money, or furniture,
Till France be won into the Dauphin's hands:
Last time, I danced attendance on his will
Till Paris was besieged, famish'd, and lost.

War. That can I witness; and a fouler fact
Did never traitor in the land commit.

Suf. Peace, headstrong Warwick!

War. Image of pride, why should I hold my peace?

Enter HORNER, *the Armourer, and his man* PETER,
guarded.

Suf. Because here is a man accused of treason: 180
Pray God the Duke of York excuse himself!

York. Doth any one accuse York for a traitor?

King. What mean'st thou, Suffolk; tell me, what are
these?

Suf. Please it your majesty, this is the man
That doth accuse his master of high treason:
His words were these: that Richard Duke of York
Was rightful heir unto the English crown
And that your majesty was an usurper.

King. Say, man, were these thy words? 189

Hor. An 't shall please your majesty, I never said nor
thought any such matter: God is my witness, I am
falsely accused by the villain.

Pet. By these ten bones, my lords, he did speak them
to me in the garret one night, as we were scouring my
Lord of York's armour.

York. Base dunghill villain and mechanical,
I'll have thy head for this thy traitor's speech.
I do beseech your royal majesty,
Let him have all the rigour of the law. 199

Hor. Alas, my lord, hang me, if ever I spake the
words. My accuser is my 'prentice; and when I did
correct him for his fault the other day, he did vow
upon his knees he would be even with me: I have good
witness of this; therefore I beseech your majesty, do
not cast away an honest man for a villain's accusation.

King. Uncle, what shall we say to this in law?

Glou. This doom, my lord, if I may judge:
Let Somerset be regent o'er the French,
Because in York this breeds suspicion: 210
And let these have a day appointed them

---

105. **Or . . . or,** whether . . . or; see glossary. 107. **denay'd,** denied. 120. **censure,** opinion; see glossary. 131. **rack'd,** strained beyond the capacity to endure; see glossary. 135-136. **Thy . . . law.** The charge is recorded in the chronicles that Gloucester "had caused men adjudged to die, to be put to other execution than the law of the land assigned." Gloucester's enemies repeat the charge in III, i, 58-59. 139. **suspect,** suspicion. 142. **cry you mercy,** beg your pardon; see glossary. 145. **my ten commandments,** i.e., marks of her ten fingers. 148. **dandle,** rock on the knee, fondle. 153. **tickled,** vexed, irritated. 161. **duty,**

reverence; see glossary. 163. **meetest,** answering the purpose best, fittest. 172. **discharge,** formal license to proceed (Tucker Brooke). 176. **fact,** deed; see glossary. 181. **excuse,** vindicate; see glossary. 192. **falsely,** treacherously; see glossary. 193. **bones,** fingers. 196. **mechanical,** common workman. 211. **these,** i.e., Peter and Horner. 212. **single combat,** fight between two, duel. 214-216. **Then be . . . the French.** These two lines, omitted from the Globe text, are not in F; they are supplied from the quarto of *The Contention.* 222. **Sirrah,** customary form of address to servants; see glossary.

For single combat in convenient place,
For he hath witness of his servant's malice:
This is the law, and this Duke Humphrey's doom.
  King. Then be it so. My lord of Somerset,
We make your grace lord regent o'er the French.
  Som. I humbly thank your royal majesty.
  Hor. And I accept the combat willingly.
  Pet. Alas, my lord, I cannot fight; for God's sake,
pity my case. The spite of man prevaileth against me.
O Lord, have mercy upon me! I shall never be able to
fight a blow. O Lord, my heart!   221
  Glou. Sirrah, or you must fight, or else be hang'd.
  King. Away with them to prison; and the day of
combat shall be the last of the next month. Come,
Somerset, we'll see thee sent away.   [*Flourish. Exeunt.*

SCENE IV. GLOUCESTER'S *garden.*

Enter MARGERY JOURDAIN, HUME, SOUTHWELL,
and BOLINGBROKE.

  Hume. Come, my masters; the duchess, I tell you,
expects performance of your promises.
  Boling. Master Hume, we are therefore provided:
will her ladyship behold and hear our exorcisms?
  Hume. Ay, what else? fear you not her courage.
  Boling. I have heard her reported to be a woman of
an invincible spirit: but it shall be convenient, Master
Hume, that you be by her aloft, while we be busy
below; and so, I pray you, go, in God's name, and
leave us. [*Exit Hume.*] Mother Jourdain, be you
prostrate and grovel on the earth; John Southwell,
read you; and let us to our work.

Enter Duchess *aloft,* HUME *following.*

  Duch. Well said, my masters; and welcome all. To
this gear the sooner the better.
  Boling. Patience, good lady; wizards know their
          times:
Deep night, dark night, the silent of the night,
The time of night when Troy was set on fire;   20
The time when screech-owls cry and ban-dogs howl
And spirits walk and ghosts break up their graves,
That time best fits the work we have in hand.
Madam, sit you and fear not: whom we raise,
We will make fast within a hallow'd verge.
     [*Here they do the ceremonies belonging, and make
        the circle; Bolingbroke or Southwell reads,* Conjuro
        te, *&c. It thunders and lightens terribly; then
                                the Spirit riseth.*
  Spir. Adsum.
  M. Jourd. Asmath,
By the eternal God, whose name and power
Thou tremblest at, answer that I shall ask;
For, till thou speak, thou shalt not pass from hence. 30
  Spir. Ask what thou wilt. That I had said and done!
  Boling. 'First of the king: what shall of him become?'
                           [*Reading out of a paper.*

  Spir. The duke yet lives that Henry shall depose;
But him outlive, and die a violent death.
     [*As the Spirit speaks, Southwell writes the answer.*
  Boling. 'What fates await the Duke of Suffolk?'
  Spir. By water shall he die, and take his end.
  Boling. 'What shall befall the Duke of Somerset?'
  Spir. Let him shun castles;
Safer shall he be upon the sandy plains
Than where castles mounted stand.   40
Have done, for more I hardly can endure.
  Boling. Descend to darkness and the burning lake!
False fiend, avoid!   [*Thunder and lightning. Exit Spirit.*

Enter the DUKE OF YORK *and the* DUKE OF BUCKING-
HAM *with their* Guard *and break in.*

  York. Lay hands upon these traitors and their trash.
Beldam, I think we watch'd you at an inch.
What, madam, are you there? the king and
          commonweal
Are deeply indebted for this piece of pains:
My lord protector will, I doubt it not,
See you well guerdon'd for these good deserts.
  Duch. Not half so bad as thine to England's king, 50
Injurious duke, that threatest where's no cause.
  Buck. True, madam, none at all: what call you this?
Away with them! let them be clapp'd up close,
And kept asunder. You, madam, shall with us.
Stafford, take her to thee.
       [*Exeunt above Duchess and Hume, guarded.*
We'll see your trinkets here all forthcoming.
All, away!   [*Exeunt guard with Jourdain, Southwell, &c.*
  York. Lord Buckingham, methinks, you watch'd her
          well:
A pretty plot, well chosen to build upon!
Now, pray, my lord, let's see the devil's writ.   60
What have we here?   [*Reads.*
'The duke yet lives, that Henry shall depose;
But him outlive, and die a violent death.'
Why, this is just
'Aio te, Æacida, Romanos vincere posse.'
Well, to the rest:
'Tell me what fate awaits the Duke of Suffolk?
By water shall he die, and take his end.
What shall betide the Duke of Somerset?
Let him shun castles;   70
Safer shall he be upon the sandy plains
Than where castles mounted stand.'
Come, come, my lords;
These oracles are hardly attain'd,
And hardly understood.
The king is now in progress towards Saint Alban's,
With him the husband of this lovely lady:
Thither go these news, as fast as horse can carry them:
A sorry breakfast for my lord protector.
  Buck. Your grace shall give me leave, my Lord of
          York,   80
To be the post, in hope of his reward.
  York. At your pleasure, my good lord. Who's
          within there, ho!

SCENE IV. 5. **exorcisms,** conjurations, calling up spirits. 6. **fear,**
doubt; see glossary. 17. **gear,** business; see glossary. 21. **ban-dogs,**
watchdogs. 25. **hallow'd verge,** magic circle. *Stage Direction:* **the**
ceremonies belonging, i.e., the "hocus-pocus" necessary to conjure
spirits, such as drawing a magic circle and reciting a formula. 26.
Adsum, I am here. 27. **Asmath,** probably "Asmenoth, guider of the
North" in Greene's *Friar Bacon* (Hart); cf. *1 Henry VI,* V, iii, 6. 33-34.
The . . . death. The first line of the prophecy, as is characteristic of
such utterances, is capable of a double construction. The second line

is fulfilled in *3 Henry VI* in the death of York. 45. **watch'd . . . inch,**
caught you right in the act. 47. **piece of pains,** example of trouble
undergone (used ironically). 56. **trinkets,** trifles, rubbish. 65.
'Aio . . . posse,' ambiguous answer given by the Delphic oracle to
Pyrrhus, quoted from Ennius by Cicero (*De divinatione* II, lvi): "I say
that thou, Aeacides, canst conquer the Romans, or that the Romans
can conquer thee." 74. **hardly,** with difficulty; see glossary. 76.
progress, state journey made by a sovereign. 81. **post,** messenger;
see glossary.

Enter a Servingman.

Invite my Lords of Salisbury and Warwick
To sup with me to-morrow night. Away!   [*Exeunt.*

ACT II.

SCENE I. *Saint Alban's.*

Enter the KING, QUEEN, GLOUCESTER, CARDINAL,
and SUFFOLK, *with* Falconers *halloing.*

Queen. Believe me, lords, for flying at the brook,
I saw not better sport these seven years' day:
Yet, by your leave, the wind was very high;
And, ten to one, old Joan had not gone out.
   King. But what a point, my lord, your falcon made,
And what a pitch she flew above the rest!
To see how God in all his creatures works!
Yea, man and birds are fain of climbing high.
   Suf. No marvel, an it like your majesty,
My lord protector's hawks do tower so well;   10
They know their master loves to be aloft
And bears his thoughts above his falcon's pitch.
   Glou. My lord, 'tis but a base ignoble mind
That mounts no higher than a bird can soar.
   Car. I thought as much; he would be above the
     clouds.
   Glou. Ay, my lord cardinal? how think you by that?
Were it not good your grace could fly to heaven?
   King. The treasury of everlasting joy.
   Car. Thy heaven is on earth; thine eyes and
     thoughts
Beat on a crown, the treasure of thy heart;   20
Pernicious protector, dangerous peer,
That smooth'st it so with king and commonweal!
   Glou. What, cardinal, is your priesthood grown
     peremptory?
Tantæne animis cœlestibus iræ?
Churchmen so hot? good uncle, hide such malice;
With such holiness can you do it?
   Suf. No malice, sir; no more than well becomes
So good a quarrel and so bad a peer.
   Glou. As who, my lord?
   Suf.   Why, as you, my lord,
An 't like your lordly lord-protectorship.   30
   Glou. Why, Suffolk, England knows thine insolence.
   Queen. And thy ambition, Gloucester.
   King. I prithee, peace, good queen,
And whet not on these furious peers;
For blessed are the peacemakers on earth.
   Car. Let me be blessed for the peace I make,
Against this proud protector, with my sword!
   Glou. [*Aside to Car.*] Faith, holy uncle, would 'twere
     come to that!
   Car. [*Aside to Glou.*] Marry, when thou darest.
   Glou. [*Aside to Car.*] Make up no factious numbers
     for the matter;   40
In thine own person answer thy abuse.

   Car. [*Aside to Glou.*] Ay, where thou darest not peep:
     an if thou darest,
This evening, on the east side of the grove.
   King. How now, my lords!
   Car.   Believe me, cousin Gloucester,
Had not your man put up the fowl so suddenly,
We had had more sport. [*Aside to Glou.*] Come with thy
     two-hand sword.
   Glou. True, uncle.
   Car. [*Aside to Glou.*] Are ye advised? the east side of
     the grove?
   Glou. [*Aside to Car.*] Cardinal, I am with you.
   King.   Why, how now, uncle Glouces-
     ter!
   Glou. Talking of hawking; nothing else, my lord.   50
[*Aside to Car.*] Now, by God's mother, priest, I'll
     shave your crown for this,
Or all my fence shall fail.
   Car. [*Aside to Glou.*] Medice, teipsum—
Protector, see to 't well, protect yourself.
   King. The winds grow high; so do your stomachs,
     lords.
How irksome is this music to my heart!
When such strings jar, what hope of harmony?
I pray, my lords, let me compound this strife.

Enter a Townsman *of Saint Alban's, crying* 'A miracle!'

   Glou. What means this noise?
Fellow, what miracle dost thou proclaim?   60
   Towns. A miracle! a miracle!
   Suf. Come to the king and tell him what miracle.
   Towns. Forsooth, a blind man at Saint Alban's
     shrine,
Within this half-hour, hath received his sight;
A man that ne'er saw in his life before.
   King. Now, God be praised, that to believing souls
Gives light in darkness, comfort in despair!

Enter the Mayor *of Saint Alban's and his brethren,
bearing* SIMPCOX, *between two in a chair,* SIMPCOX'S
Wife *following.*

   Car. Here comes the townsmen on procession,
To present your highness with the man.
   King. Great is his comfort in this earthly vale,   70
Although by his sight his sin be multiplied.
   Glou. Stand by, my masters: bring him near the
     king;
His highness' pleasure is to talk with him.
   King. Good fellow, tell us here the circumstance,
That we for thee may glorify the Lord.
What, hast thou been long blind and now restored?
   Simp. Born blind, an 't please your grace.
   Wife. Ay, indeed, was he.
   Suf. What woman is this?
   Wife. His wife, an 't like your worship.   80
   Glou. Hadst thou been his mother, thou couldst
     have better told.
   King. Where wert thou born?
   Simp. At Berwick in the north, an 't like your grace.

ACT II. SCENE I. 1. **flying . . . brook,** hawking for waterfowl. 2. **these . . . day,** in seven years' time. 4. **old Joan,** name of a hawk. **had not,** would not have. 5. **point,** advantageous position from which the hawk attacks the bird. 6. **pitch,** height to which a hawk soars before descending on its prey; see glossary. 8. **of,** as regards; cf. the modern expression "desirous of"; see glossary. 9. **an,** if; see glossary. **like,** please; see glossary. 22. **smooth'st,** flatterest, humorest. 24. **Tantæne . . . iræ?** Is there such resentment in the minds of the

gods? (Virgil, *Aeneid* I, 13.) 41. **abuse,** offense, insult; see glossary. 47. **Are ye advised?** Do you understand? 52. **fence,** defense. 53. **Medice, teipsum,** physician, heal thyself. 55. **stomachs,** tempers; see glossary. 58. **compound,** settle; see glossary. *Stage Direction:* **Enter a Townsman,** etc. This scene serves dramatically to illustrate Gloucester's perspicacity and his efficiency as an administrator. 63. **Saint Alban's shrine.** St. Alban, the first Christian martyr in Britain, was executed under the edicts of Diocletian in the third century for sheltering a

King. Poor soul, God's goodness hath been great to
thee:
Let never day nor night unhallow'd pass,
But still remember what the Lord hath done.
  Queen. Tell me, good fellow, camest thou here by
chance,
Or of devotion, to this holy shrine?
  Simp. God knows, of pure devotion; being call'd
A hundred times and oftener, in my sleep,   90
By good Saint Alban; who said, 'Simpcox, come,
Come, offer at my shrine, and I will help thee.'
  Wife. Most true, forsooth; and many time and oft
Myself have heard a voice to call him so.
  Car. What, art thou lame?
  Simp.   Ay, God Almighty help me!
  Suf. How camest thou so?
  Simp.   A fall off of a tree.
  Wife. A plum-tree, master.
  Glou.   How long hast thou been blind?
  Simp. O, born so, master.
  Glou.   What, and wouldst climb a tree?
  Simp. But that in all my life, when I was a youth.
  Wife. Too true; and bought his climbing very dear.
  Glou. Mass, thou lovedst plums well, that wouldst
venture so.   101
  Simp. Alas, good master, my wife desired some
damsons,
And made me climb, with danger of my life.
  Glou. A subtle knave! but yet it shall not serve.
Let me see thine eyes: wink now: now open them:
In my opinion yet thou see'st not well.
  Simp. Yes, master, clear as day, I thank God and
Saint Alban.
  Glou. Say'st thou me so? What colour is this cloak of?
  Simp. Red, master; red as blood.   110
  Glou. Why, that's well said. What colour is my
gown of?
  Simp. Black, forsooth: coal-black as jet.
  King. Why, then, thou know'st what colour jet is of?
  Suf. And yet, I think, jet did he never see.
  Glou. But cloaks and gowns, before this day, a many.
  Wife. Never, before this day, in all his life.
  Glou. Tell me, sirrah, what's my name?
  Simp. Alas, master, I know not.
  Glou. What's his name?
  Simp. I know not.   120
  Glou. Nor his?
  Simp. No, indeed, master.
  Glou. What's thine own name?
  Simp. Saunder Simpcox, an if it please you, master.
  Glou. Then, Saunder, sit there, the lyingest knave in
Christendom. If thou hadst been born blind, thou
mightst as well have known all our names as thus to
name the several colours we do wear. Sight may dis-
tinguish of colours, but suddenly to nominate them
all, it is impossible. My lords, Saint Alban here hath
done a miracle; and would ye not think his cunning
to be great, that could restore this cripple to his legs
again?
  Simp. O master, that you could!

  Glou. My masters of Saint Alban's, have you not
beadles in your town, and things called whips?
  May. Yes, my lord, if it please your grace.
  Glou. Then send for one presently.   139
  May. Sirrah, go fetch the beadle hither straight.
                            [*Exit an Attendant.*
  Glou. Now fetch me a stool hither by and by. Now,
sirrah, if you mean to save yourself from whipping,
leap me over this stool and run away.
  Simp. Alas, master, I am not able to stand alone:
You go about to torture me in vain.

Enter a Beadle *with whips.*

  Glou. Well, sir, we must have you find your legs.
Sirrah beadle, whip him till he leap over that same
stool.
  Bead. I will, my lord. Come on, sirrah; off with
your doublet quickly.   151
  Simp. Alas, master, what shall I do? I am not able to
stand.
    [*After the Beadle hath hit him once, he leaps over the
      stool and runs away; and they follow and cry, 'A
                                            miracle!'*
  King. O God, seest Thou this, and bearest so long?
  Queen. It made me laugh to see the villain run.
  Glou. Follow the knave; and take this drab away.
  Wife. Alas, sir, we did it for pure need.
  Glou. Let them be whipped through every market-
town, till they come to Berwick, from whence they
came.   [*Exeunt Wife, Beadle, Mayor, &c.*   160
  Car. Duke Humphrey has done a miracle to-day.
  Suf. True; made the lame to leap and fly away.
  Glou. But you have done more miracles than I;
You made in a day, my lord, whole towns to fly.

Enter BUCKINGHAM.

  King. What tidings with our cousin Buckingham?
  Buck. Such as my heart doth tremble to unfold.
A sort of naughty persons, lewdly bent,
Under the countenance and confederacy
Of Lady Eleanor, the protector's wife,
The ringleader and head of all this rout,   170
Have practised dangerously against your state,
Dealing with witches and with conjurers:
Whom we have apprehended in the fact;
Raising up wicked spirits from under ground,
Demanding of King Henry's life and death,
And other of your highness' privy-council;
As more at large your grace shall understand.
  Car. [*Aside to Glou.*] And so, my lord protector, by
this means
Your lady is forthcoming yet at London.
This news, I think, hath turn'd your weapon's edge;
'Tis like, my lord, you will not keep your hour.   181
  Glou. Ambitious churchman, leave to afflict my
heart:
Sorrow and grief have vanquish'd all my powers;
And, vanquish'd as I am, I yield to thee,
Or to the meanest groom.
  King. O God, what mischiefs work the wicked ones,

2 *Henry VI*
ACT II : SC I

247

Christian priest. He was put to death on a hill overlooking the ancient
city of Verulam, the ruins of which are across the river Ver from
the modern city of St. Albans. 68. **comes.** The present tense, third
person plural verb in *s* is not uncommon in Shakespeare; see Abbott,
333. 71. **his sin be multiplied,** i.e., he may now be guilty of the sins
of seeing; a probable allusion to this category of sins in the confes-
sional rubric. 91. **Simpcox,** a diminutive of *Simon.* 101. **Mass,**
by the Mass (oath). 105. **wink,** close the eyes; see glossary. 130.

nominate, call by name. 137. **beadles,** inferior parish officers who
might punish petty offenses. 141. **straight,** immediately; see glossary.
142. **by and by,** at once, presently. 144. **me,** the ethical dative. 166.
unfold, disclose; see glossary. 167. **sort,** lot. **naughty,** wicked; see
glossary. 175. **Demanding,** inquiring about. 179. **forthcoming,**
ready to appear (in court). 182. **leave to afflict,** cease afflicting.
185. **meanest,** of lowest degree; see glossary.

Heaping confusion on their own heads thereby!
    Queen. Gloucester, see here the tainture of thy nest,
And look thyself be faultless, thou wert best.
    Glou. Madam, for myself, to heaven I do appeal,   190
How I have loved my king and commonweal:
And, for my wife, I know not how it stands;
Sorry I am to hear what I have heard:
Noble she is, but if she have forgot
Honour and virtue and conversed with such
As, like to pitch, defile nobility,
I banish her my bed and company
And give her as a prey to law and shame,
That hath dishonour'd Gloucester's honest name.
    King. Well, for this night we will repose us here: 200
To-morrow toward London back again,
To look into this business thoroughly
And call these foul offenders to their answers
And poise the cause in justice' equal scales,
Whose beam stands sure, whose rightful cause
    prevails.   *[Flourish. Exeunt.*

SCENE II. *London. The* DUKE OF YORK'S *garden.*

Enter YORK, SALISBURY, *and* WARWICK.

    York. Now, my good Lords of Salisbury and
    Warwick,
Our simple supper ended, give me leave
In this close walk to satisfy myself,
In craving your opinion of my title,
Which is infallible, to England's crown.
    Sal. My lord, I long to hear it at full.
    War. Sweet York, begin: and if thy claim be good,
The Nevils are thy subjects to command.
    York. Then thus:
Edward the Third, my lords, had seven sons: 10
The first, Edward the Black Prince, Prince of Wales;
The second, William of Hatfield, and the third,
Lionel Duke of Clarence; next to whom
Was John of Gaunt, the Duke of Lancaster;
The fifth was Edmund Langley, Duke of York;
The sixth was Thomas of Woodstock, Duke of
    Gloucester;
William of Windsor was the seventh and last.
Edward the Black Prince died before his father
And left behind him Richard, his only son,
Who after Edward the Third's death reign'd as
    king;   20
Till Henry Bolingbroke, Duke of Lancaster,
The eldest son and heir of John of Gaunt,
Crown'd by the name of Henry the Fourth,
Seized on the realm, deposed the rightful king,
Sent his poor queen to France, from whence she came,
And him to Pomfret; where, as all you know,
Harmless Richard was murder'd traitorously.
    War. Father, the duke hath told the truth;
Thus got the house of Lancaster the crown.
    York. Which now they hold by force and not by
    right;   30
For Richard, the first son's heir, being dead,

The issue of the next son should have reign'd.
    Sal. But William of Hatfield died without an heir.
    York. The third son, Duke of Clarence, from whose
    line
I claim the crown, had issue, Philippe, a daughter,
Who married Edmund Mortimer, Earl of March:
Edmund had issue, Roger Earl of March;
Roger had issue, Edmund, Anne and Eleanor.
    Sal. This Edmund, in the reign of Bolingbroke,
As I have read, laid claim unto the crown;   40
And, but for Owen Glendower, had been king,
Who kept him in captivity till he died.
But to the rest.
    York.   His eldest sister, Anne,
My mother, being heir unto the crown,
Married Richard Earl of Cambridge; who was son
To Edmund Langley, Edward the Third's fifth son.
By her I claim the kingdom: she was heir
To Roger Earl of March, who was the son
Of Edmund Mortimer, who married Philippe,
Sole daughter unto Lionel Duke of Clarence: 50
So, if the issue of the elder son
Succeed before the younger, I am king.
    War. What plain proceeding is more plain than
    this?
Henry doth claim the crown from John of Gaunt,
The fourth son; York claims it from the third,
Till Lionel's issue fails, his should not reign:
It fails not yet, but flourishes in thee
And in thy sons, fair slips of such a stock.
Then, father Salisbury, kneel we together;
And in this private plot be we the first   60
That shall salute our rightful sovereign
With honour of his birthright to the crown.
    Both. Long live our sovereign Richard, England's
    king!
    York. We thank you, lords. But I am not your king
Till I be crown'd and that my sword be stain'd
With heart-blood of the house of Lancaster;
And that 's not suddenly to be perform'd,
But with advice and silent secrecy.
Do you as I do in these dangerous days:
Wink at the Duke of Suffolk's insolence,   70
At Beaufort's pride, at Somerset's ambition,
At Buckingham and all the crew of them,
Till they have snared the shepherd of the flock,
That virtuous prince, the good Duke Humphrey:
'Tis that they seek, and they in seeking that
Shall find their deaths, if York can prophesy.
    Sal. My lord, break we off; we know your mind at
    full.
    War. My heart assures me that the Earl of Warwick
Shall one day make the Duke of York a king.
    York. And, Nevil, this I do assure myself: 80
Richard shall live to make the Earl of Warwick
The greatest man in England but the king.   *[Exeunt.*

SCENE III. *A hall of justice.*

Sound trumpets. Enter the KING, *the* QUEEN, GLOUCES-

187. **confusion,** destruction; see glossary. 188. **tainture,** defilement.
189. **look,** take care; see glossary. 195. **conversed,** had to do with;
see glossary.   SCENE II. 42. **till he died.** This historical error is repeated from
the chronicles; cf. *1 Henry VI,* II, v, 1. 56. **fails,** dies out; see glossary.
62. **birthright,** right by primogeniture.

SCENE III. 4. **by God's book,** a reference to the commandments in
the Bible against witches (Exodus 22:18) and enchantments (Leviticus
19:26). 13. **With . . . Stanley.** Stanley was appointed the duchess'
custodian. 21. **would,** would have; *would* here has the force of Old
English "willan," to wish. 23. **staff.** Cf. I, ii, 25, where Gloucester
calls his staff *mine office-badge in court.* 41. **shrewd,** grievous, severe;

TER, YORK, SUFFOLK, *and* SALISBURY; *the*
DUCHESS OF GLOUCESTER, MARGERY JOURDAIN,
SOUTHWELL, HUME, *and* BOLINGBROKE, *under
guard.*

King. Stand forth, Dame Eleanor Cobham,
  Gloucester's wife:
In sight of God and us, your guilt is great:
Receive the sentence of the law for sins
Such as by God's book are adjudged to death.
You four, from hence to prison back again;
From thence unto the place of execution:
The witch in Smithfield shall be burn'd to ashes,
And you three shall be strangled on the gallows.
You, madam, for you are more nobly born,
Despoiled of your honour in your life,   10
Shall, after three days' open penance done,
Live in your country here in banishment,
With Sir John Stanley, in the Isle of Man.
  Duch. Welcome is banishment; welcome were my
  death.
  Glou. Eleanor, the law, thou see'st, hath judged thee:
I cannot justify whom the law condemns.
          [Exeunt Duchess and other prisoners, guarded.
Mine eyes are full of tears, my heart of grief.
Ah, Humphrey, this dishonour in thine age
Will bring thy head with sorrow to the ground!
I beseech your majesty, give me leave to go;   20
Sorrow would solace and mine age would ease.
  King. Stay, Humphrey Duke of Gloucester:
  ere thou go,
Give up thy staff: Henry will to himself
Protector be; and God shall be my hope,
My stay, my guide and lantern to my feet:
And go in peace, Humphrey, no less beloved
Than when thou wert protector to thy king.
  Queen. I see no reason why a king of years
Should be to be protected like a child.
God and King Henry govern England's realm.   30
Give up your staff, sir, and the king his realm.
  Glou. My staff? here, noble Henry, is my staff:
As willingly do I the same resign
As e'er thy father Henry made it mine;
And even as willingly at thy feet I leave it
As others would ambitiously receive it.
Farewell, good king: when I am dead and gone,
May honourable peace attend thy throne!   *[Exit.*
  Queen. Why, now is Henry king, and Margaret
  queen;
And Humphrey Duke of Gloucester scarce himself, 40
That bears so shrewd a maim; two pulls at once;
His lady banish'd, and a limb lopp'd off.
This staff of honour raught, there let it stand
Where it best fits to be, in Henry's hand.
  Suf. Thus droops this lofty pine and hangs his sprays;
Thus Eleanor's pride dies in her youngest days.
  York. Lords, let him go. Please it your majesty,
This is the day appointed for the combat;
And ready are the appellant and defendant,
The armourer and his man, to enter the lists,   50
So please your highness to behold the fight.

Queen. Ay, good my lord; for purposely therefore
Left I the court, to see this quarrel tried.
  King. O' God's name, see the lists and all things fit:
Here let them end it; and God defend the right!
  York. I never saw a fellow worse bested,
Or more afraid to fight, than is the appellant,
The servant of this armourer, my lords.

  Enter at one door, HORNER, *the Armourer, and his*
    Neighbours, *drinking to him so much that he is drunk;*
    and he enters with a drum before him and his staff with
    a sand-bag fastened to it; and at the other door PETER,
    his man, with a drum and sand-bag, and 'Prentices
    drinking to him.

  First Neigh. Here, neighbour Horner, I drink to
you in a cup of sack: and fear not, neighbour, you
shall do well enough.   61
  Sec. Neigh. And here, neighbour, here's a cup of
charneco.
  Third Neigh. And here's a pot of good double beer,
neighbour: drink, and fear not your man.
  Hor. Let it come, i' faith, and I'll pledge you all;
and a fig for Peter!
  First 'Pren. Here, Peter, I drink to thee: and be not
afraid.
  Sec. 'Pren. Be merry, Peter, and fear not thy master:
fight for credit of the 'prentices.   71
  Peter. I thank you all: drink, and pray for me, I
pray you; for I think I have taken my last draught in
this world. Here, Robin, an if I die, I give thee my
apron: and, Will, thou shalt have my hammer: and
here, Tom, take all the money that I have. O Lord
bless me! I pray God! for I am never able to deal with
my master, he hath learnt so much fence already.
  Sal. Come, leave your drinking, and fall to blows.
Sirrah, what 's thy name?   81
  Peter. Peter, forsooth.
  Sal. Peter! what more?
  Peter. Thump.
  Sal. Thump! then see thou thump thy master well.
  Hor. Masters, I am come hither, as it were, upon
my man's instigation, to prove him a knave and my-
self an honest man: and touching the Duke of York,
I will take my death, I never meant him any ill, nor
the king, nor the queen: and therefore, Peter, have at
thee with a downright blow!
  York. Dispatch: this knave's tongue begins to
double.   94
Sound, trumpets, alarum to the combatants!
     [Alarum. They fight, and Peter strikes him down.
  Hor. Hold, Peter, hold! I confess, I confess treason.
                    [Dies.
  York. Take away his weapon. Fellow, thank God,
and the good wine in thy master's way.
  Peter. O God, have I overcome mine enemy in this
presence? O Peter, thou hast prevailed in right!   102
  King. Go, take hence that traitor from our sight;
For by his death we do perceive his guilt:
And God in justice hath reveal'd to us
The truth and innocence of this poor fellow,
Which he had thought to have murder'd wrongfully.

---

see glossary. **maim,** mutilation. **pulls,** pluckings (of feathers); i.e.,
has suffered two mutilations. 43. **raught,** attained, seized. 46. **her
youngest days.** *Her* may refer to Eleanor's ambition or pride (Hart);
or it may refer to Eleanor, *youngest* meaning "last." 49. **appellant,**
challenger. 56. **bested,** i.e., bestead, situated. 60. **sack,** generic term
for Spanish and Canary wines; see glossary. 63. **charneco,** a kind of

wine. 79. **fence,** skill in fencing. 90. **take my death,** i.e., take an
oath on my death. 92. **have at,** let me at; see glossary. 94. **double,**
thicken, as an intoxicated person's.

Come, fellow, follow us for thy reward.
                    [*Sound a flourish.   Exeunt.*

SCENE IV. *A street.*

Enter GLOUCESTER *and his Servingmen, in mourning
    cloaks.*

Glou. Thus sometimes hath the brightest day a
        cloud;
And after summer evermore succeeds
Barren winter, with his wrathful nipping cold:
So cares and joys abound, as seasons fleet.
Sirs, what's o'clock?
    Serv.   Ten, my lord.
    Glou. Ten is the hour that was appointed me
To watch the coming of my punish'd duchess:
Uneath may she endure the flinty streets,
To tread them with her tender-feeling feet.
Sweet Nell, ill can thy noble mind abrook   10
The abject people gazing on thy face,
With envious looks, laughing at thy shame,
That erst did follow thy proud chariot-wheels
When thou didst ride in triumph through the streets.
But, soft! I think she comes; and I'll prepare
My tear-stain'd eyes to see her miseries.

Enter the DUCHESS OF GLOUCESTER *in a white sheet,
    and a taper burning in her hand; with* SIR JOHN
    STANLEY, *the* Sheriff *and* Officers.

Serv. So please your grace, we'll take her from the
        sheriff.
Glou. No, stir not, for your lives; let her pass by.
Duch. Come you, my lord, to see my open shame?
Now thou dost penance too. Look how they gaze!   20
See how the giddy multitude do point,
And nod their heads, and throw their eyes on thee!
Ah, Gloucester, hide thee from their hateful looks,
And, in thy closet pent up, rue my shame,
And ban thine enemies, both mine and thine!
    Glou. Be patient, gentle Nell; forget this grief.
    Duch. Ah, Gloucester, teach me to forget myself!
For whilst I think I am thy married wife
And thou a prince, protector of this land,
Methinks I should not thus be led along,   30
Mail'd up in shame, with papers on my back,
And follow'd with a rabble that rejoice
To see my tears and hear my deep-fet groans.
The ruthless flint doth cut my tender feet,
And when I start, the envious people laugh
And bid me be advised how I tread.
Ah, Humphrey, can I bear this shameful yoke?
Trow'st thou that e'er I'll look upon the world,
Or count them happy that enjoy the sun?
No; dark shall be my light and night my day;   40
To think upon my pomp shall be my hell.
Sometime I'll say, I am Duke Humphrey's wife,
And he a prince and ruler of the land:
Yet so he ruled and such a prince he was
As he stood by whilst I, his forlorn duchess,

Was made a wonder and a pointing-stock
To every idle rascal follower.
But be thou mild and blush not at my shame,
Nor stir at nothing till the axe of death
Hang over thee, as, sure, it shortly will;   50
For Suffolk, he that can do all in all
With her that hateth thee and hates us all,
And York and impious Beaufort, that false priest,
Have all limed bushes to betray thy wings,
And, fly thou how thou canst, they'll tangle thee:
But fear not thou, until thy foot be snared,
Nor never seek prevention of thy foes.
    Glou. Ah, Nell, forbear! thou aimest all awry;
I must offend before I be attainted;
And had I twenty times so many foes,   60
And each of them had twenty times their power,
All these could not procure me any scathe,
So long as I am loyal, true and crimeless.
Wouldst have me rescue thee from this reproach?
Why, yet thy scandal were not wiped away,
But I in danger for the breach of law.
Thy greatest help is quiet, gentle Nell:
I pray thee, sort thy heart to patience;
These few days' wonder will be quickly worn.

Enter a Herald.

Her. I summon your grace to his majesty's
        parliament,   70
Holden at Bury the first of this next month.
    Glou. And my consent ne'er ask'd herein before!
This is close dealing. Well, I will be there. [*Exit Herald.*
My Nell, I take my leave: and, master sheriff,
Let not her penance exceed the king's commission.
    Sher. An 't please your grace, here my commission
        stays,
And Sir John Stanley is appointed now
To take her with him to the Isle of Man.
    Glou. Must you, Sir John, protect my lady here?
    Stan. So am I given in charge, may 't please your
        grace.   80
    Glou. Entreat her not the worse in that I pray
You use her well: the world may laugh again;
And I may live to do you kindness if
You do it her: and so, Sir John, farewell!
    Duch. What, gone, my lord, and bid me not farewell!
    Glou. Witness my tears, I cannot stay to speak.
                [*Exeunt Gloucester and Servingmen.*
    Duch. Art thou gone too? all comfort go with thee!
For none abides with me: my joy is death;
Death, at whose name I oft have been afear'd,
Because I wish'd this world's eternity.   90
Stanley, I prithee, go, and take me hence;
I care not whither, for I beg no favour,
Only convey me where thou art commanded.
    Stan. Why, madam, that is to the Isle of Man;
There to be used according to your state.
    Duch. That 's bad enough, for I am but reproach:
And shall I then be used reproachfully?
    Stan. Like to a duchess, and Duke Humphrey's lady;
According to that state you shall be used.

SCENE IV. 8. **Uneath**, with difficulty. 10. **abrook**, endure. 11.
abject, lowly born. 12. **envious**, full of malice; see glossary. 31.
Mail'd up, enveloped. She refers to the white sheet, the garment she
was required to wear while doing public penance. **papers on my back**,
i.e., a schedule pinned to her back containing a description of the sin
for which she is doing the penance. 33. **deep-fet**, fetched from the
depths. 35. **start**, startle, wince. 38. **Trow'st**, believest; see glossary.

57. **prevention**, forestalling. 62. **scathe**, injury. 69. **wonder**, surprise,
astonishment. 73. **close**, secret; see glossary. 76. **stays**, stops; see
glossary. 96. **I . . . reproach**, I am the embodiment of reproach or
disgrace. 100. **better than I fare**, may you fare better than I. 101.
conduct, conductor.

ACT III. SCENE I. 1. **muse**, wonder; see glossary. 2. **wont**, custom,
habit. 9. **since**, when. 12. **admired**, wondered at; see glossary.

Duch. Sheriff, farewell, and better than I fare, 100
Although thou hast been conduct of my shame.
  Sher. It is my office; and, madam, pardon me.
  Duch. Ay, ay, farewell; thy office is discharged.
Come, Stanley, shall we go?
  Stan. Madam, your penance done, throw off this
        sheet,
And go we to attire you for our journey.
  Duch. My shame will not be shifted with my sheet:
No, it will hang upon my richest robes
And show itself, attire me how I can.
Go, lead the way; I long to see my prison. [*Exeunt.* 110

ACT III.

SCENE I. *The Abbey at Bury St. Edmund's.*

Sound a sennet. Enter the KING, *the* QUEEN, CARDINAL
BEAUFORT, SUFFOLK, YORK, BUCKINGHAM, SALIS-
BURY *and* WARWICK *to the Parliament.*

  King. I muse my Lord of Gloucester is not come:
'Tis not his wont to be the hindmost man,
Whate'er occasion keeps him from us now.
  Queen. Can you not see? or will ye not observe
The strangeness of his alter'd countenance?
With what a majesty he bears himself,
How insolent of late he is become,
How proud, how peremptory, and unlike himself?
We know the time since he was mild and affable,
And if we did but glance a far-off look, 10
Immediately he was upon his knee,
That all the court admired him for submission:
But meet him now, and, be it in the morn,
When every one will give the time of day,
He knits his brow and shows an angry eye
And passeth by with stiff unbowed knee,
Disdaining duty that to us belongs.
Small curs are not regarded when they grin;
But great men tremble when the lion roars;
And Humphrey is no little man in England. 20
First note that he is near you in descent,
And should you fall, he is the next will mount.
Me seemeth then it is no policy,
Respecting what a rancorous mind he bears
And his advantage following your decease,
That he should come about your royal person
Or be admitted to your highness' council.
By flattery hath he won the commons' hearts,
And when he please to make commotion,
'Tis to be fear'd they all will follow him. 30
Now 'tis the spring, and weeds are shallow-rooted;
Suffer them now, and they'll o'ergrow the garden
And choke the herbs for want of husbandry.
The reverent care I bear unto my lord
Made me collect these dangers in the duke.
If it be fond, call it a woman's fear;
Which fear if better reasons can supplant,
I will subscribe and say I wrong'd the duke.
My Lord of Suffolk, Buckingham, and York,

Reprove my allegation, if you can; 40
Or else conclude my words effectual.
  Suf. Well hath your highness seen into this duke;
And, had I first been put to speak my mind,
I think I should have told your grace's tale.
The duchess by his subornation,
Upon my life, began her devilish practices:
Or, if he were not privy to those faults,
Yet, by reputing of his high descent,
As next the king he was successive heir,
And such high vaunts of his nobility, 50
Did instigate the bedlam brain-sick duchess
By wicked means to frame our sovereign's fall.
Smooth runs the water where the brook is deep;
And in his simple show he harbours treason.
The fox barks not when he would steal the lamb.
No, no, my sovereign; Gloucester is a man
Unsounded yet and full of deep deceit.
  Car. Did he not, contrary to form of law,
Devise strange deaths for small offences done?
  York. And did he not, in his protectorship, 60
Levy great sums of money through the realm
For soldiers' pay in France, and never sent it?
By means whereof the towns each day revolted.
  Buck. Tut, these are petty faults to faults unknown,
Which time will bring to light in smooth Duke
        Humphrey.
  King. My lords, at once: the care you have of us,
To mow down thorns that would annoy our foot,
Is worthy praise: but, shall I speak my conscience,
Our kinsman Gloucester is as innocent
From meaning treason to our royal person 70
As is the sucking lamb or harmless dove:
The duke is virtuous, mild and too well given
To dream on evil or to work my downfall.
  Queen. Ah, what 's more dangerous than this fond
        affiance!
Seems he a dove? his feathers are but borrow'd,
For he 's disposed as the hateful raven:
Is he a lamb? his skin is surely lent him,
For he 's inclined as is the ravenous wolf.
Who cannot steal a shape that means deceit?
Take heed, my lord; the welfare of us all 80
Hangs on the cutting short that fraudful man.

Enter SOMERSET.

  Som. All health unto my gracious sovereign!
  King. Welcome, Lord Somerset. What news from
        France?
  Som. That all your interest in those territories
Is utterly bereft you; all is lost.
  King. Cold news, Lord Somerset: but God's will be
        done!
  York. [*Aside*] Cold news for me; for I had hope of
        France
As firmly as I hope for fertile England.
Thus are my blossoms blasted in the bud
And caterpillars eat my leaves away; 90
But I will remedy this gear ere long,
Or sell my title for a glorious grave.

---

18. **grin,** bare their teeth. 23. **Me seemeth,** it seems to me. 24.
Respecting, considering; see glossary. 28. **By . . . hearts.** Holinshed
records that Gloucester was "verie louing to the poore commons, and so
beloued of them again." The queen's words here underline Suffolk's
contempt for the Commons, expressed at several points in the play. 33.
husbandry, care of the soil. 35. **collect,** gather, infer. 36. **fond,**
foolish; see glossary. 40. **Reprove,** correct, prove (me) wrong. 46.

practices, intrigues; see glossary. 59. **Devise . . . done.** Cf. I, iii,
135-136, note. 66. **at once,** all of you, or, without more ado (Tucker
Brooke); possibly, once for all. 74. **affiance,** trust. 79. **steal . . .
deceit,** deceitfully assume an attitude. 83. **news from France.** Somerset presumably is just returned from exercising his office as regent of
France, to which he was appointed in I, iii.

Enter GLOUCESTER.

Glou. All happiness unto my lord the king!
Pardon, my liege, that I have stay'd so long.
  Suf. Nay, Gloucester, know that thou art come too
    soon,
Unless thou wert more loyal than thou art:
I do arrest thee of high treason here.
  Glou. Well, Suffolk, thou shalt not see me blush
Nor change my countenance for this arrest:
A heart unspotted is not easily daunted.   100
The purest spring is not so free from mud
As I am clear from treason to my sovereign:
Who can accuse me? wherein am I guilty?
  York. 'Tis thought, my lord, that you took bribes of
    France,
And, being protector, stay'd the soldiers' pay;
By means whereof his highness hath lost France.
  Glou. Is it but thought so? what are they that think it?
I never robb'd the soldiers of their pay,
Nor ever had one penny bribe from France.
So help me God, as I have watch'd the night,   110
Ay, night by night, in studying good for England,
That doit that e'er I wrested from the king,
Or any groat I hoarded to my use,
Be brought against me at my trial-day!
No; many a pound of mine own proper store,
Because I would not tax the needy commons,
Have I dispursed to the garrisons,
And never ask'd for restitution.
  Car. It serves you well, my lord, to say so much.
  Glou. I say no more than truth, so help me God!   120
  York. In your protectorship you did devise
Strange tortures for offenders never heard of,
That England was defamed by tyranny.
  Glou. Why, 'tis well known that, whiles I was
    protector,
Pity was all the fault that was in me;
For I should melt at an offender's tears,
And lowly words were ransom for their fault.
Unless it were a bloody murderer,
Or foul felonious thief that fleeced poor passengers,
I never gave them condign punishment;   130
Murder indeed, that bloody sin, I tortured
Above the felon or what trespass else.
  Suf. My lord, these faults are easy, quickly answer'd:
But mightier crimes are laid unto your charge,
Whereof you cannot easily purge yourself.
I do arrest you in his highness' name;
And here commit you to my lord cardinal
To keep, until your further time of trial.
  King. My Lord of Gloucester, 'tis my special hope
That you will clear yourself from all suspect: 140
My conscience tells me you are innocent.
  Glou. Ah, gracious lord, these days are dangerous:
Virtue is choked with foul ambition
And charity chased hence by rancour's hand;
Foul subornation is predominant
And equity exiled your highness' land.
I know their complot is to have my life,
And if my death might make this island happy
And prove the period of their tyranny,

I would expend it with all willingness: 150
But mine is made the prologue to their play;
For thousands more, that yet suspect no peril,
Will not conclude their plotted tragedy.
Beaufort's red sparkling eyes blab his heart's malice,
And Suffolk's cloudy brow his stormy hate;
Sharp Buckingham unburthens with his tongue
The envious load that lies upon his heart;
And dogged York, that reaches at the moon,
Whose overweening arm I have pluck'd back,
By false accuse doth level at my life: 160
And you, my sovereign lady, with the rest,
Causeless have laid disgraces on my head
And with your best endeavour have stirr'd up
My liefest liege to be mine enemy:
Ay, all of you have laid your heads together—
Myself had notice of your conventicles—
And all to make away my guiltless life.
I shall not want false witness to condemn me,
Nor store of treasons to augment my guilt;
The ancient proverb will be well effected: 170
'A staff is quickly found to beat a dog.'
  Car. My liege, his railing is intolerable:
If those that care to keep your royal person
From treason's secret knife and traitors' rage
Be thus upbraided, chid and rated at,
And the offender granted scope of speech,
'Twill make them cool in zeal unto your grace.
  Suf. Hath he not twit our sovereign lady here
With ignominious words, though clerkly couch'd,
As if she had suborned some to swear   180
False allegations to o'erthrow his state?
  Queen. But I can give the loser leave to chide.
  Glou. Far truer spoke than meant: I lose, indeed;
Beshrew the winners, for they play'd me false!
And well such losers may have leave to speak.
  Buck. He'll wrest the sense and hold us here all day:
Lord cardinal, he is your prisoner.
  Car. Sirs, take away the duke, and guard him sure.
  Glou. Ah! thus King Henry throws away his crutch
Before his legs be firm to bear his body.   190
Thus is the shepherd beaten from thy side
And wolves are gnarling who shall gnaw thee first.
Ah, that my fear were false! ah, that it were!
For, good King Henry, thy decay I fear. [*Exit, guarded.*
  King. My lords, what to your wisdoms seemeth best,
Do or undo, as if ourself were here.
  Queen. What, will your highness leave the
    parliament?
  King. Ay, Margaret; my heart is drown'd with grief,
Whose flood begins to flow within mine eyes,
My body round engirt with misery,   200
For what's more miserable than discontent?
Ah, uncle Humphrey! in thy face I see
The map of honour, truth and loyalty:
And yet, good Humphrey, is the hour to come
That e'er I proved thee false or fear'd thy faith.
What louring star now envies thy estate,
That these great lords and Margaret our queen
Do seek subversion of thy harmless life?
Thou never didst them wrong nor no man wrong;

112. **doit,** small Dutch coin, one-half an English farthing; see glossary. 113. **groat,** coin equal to four pence; see glossary. 130. **condign,** worthily deserved. 132. **Above . . . else,** beyond any other kind of felony or misdemeanor (Tucker Brooke). 145. **predominant,** in the ascendant, ruling; an astronomical metaphor. 146. **exiled,** exiled from. 147. **complot,** plot, conspiracy. 160. **accuse,** accusation.

level, aim; see glossary. 164. **liefest,** dearest. 166. **notice,** pronounced as one syllable, like "notes." **conventicles,** private or secret meetings. 168. **want,** lack; see glossary. 175. **rated,** scolded; see glossary. 176. **scope,** freedom; see glossary. 179. **clerkly,** learnedly. 184. **Beshrew,** curse; see glossary. 194. **decay,** downfall; see glossary. 206. **louring,** frowning, looking sullen or ominous. 229. **slough,** skin. 236. **colour,**

And as the butcher takes away the calf 210
And binds the wretch and beats it when it strays,
Bearing it to the bloody slaughter-house,
Even so remorseless have they borne him hence;
And as the dam runs lowing up and down,
Looking the way her harmless young one went,
And can do nought but wail her darling's loss,
Even so myself bewails good Gloucester's case
With sad unhelpful tears, and with dimm'd eyes
Look after him and cannot do him good,
So mighty are his vowed enemies. 220
His fortunes I will weep and 'twixt each groan
Say 'Who's a traitor? Gloucester he is none.'
[Exeunt all but Queen, Cardinal Beaufort, Suffolk, and
                    York; Somerset remains apart.
Queen. Free lords, cold snow melts with the sun's
    hot beams.
Henry my lord is cold in great affairs,
Too full of foolish pity, and Gloucester's show
Beguiles him as the mournful crocodile
With sorrow snares relenting passengers,
Or as the snake roll'd in a flowering bank,
With shining checker'd slough, doth sting a child
That for the beauty thinks it excellent. 230
Believe me, lords, were none more wise than I—
And yet herein I judge mine own wit good—
This Gloucester should be quickly rid the world,
To rid us from the fear we have of him.
Car. That he should die is worthy policy;
But yet we want a colour for his death:
'Tis meet he be condemn'd by course of law.
Suf. But, in my mind, that were no policy:
The king will labour still to save his life,
The commons haply rise, to save his life; 240
And yet we have but trivial argument,
More than mistrust, that shows him worthy death.
York. So that, by this, you would not have him die.
Suf. Ah, York, no man alive so fain as I!
York. 'Tis York that hath more reason for his death.
But, my lord cardinal, and you, my Lord of Suffolk,
Say as you think, and speak it from your souls,
Were 't not all one, an empty eagle were set
To guard the chicken from a hungry kite,
As place Duke Humphrey for the king's protector? 250
Queen. So the poor chicken should be sure of death.
Suf. Madam, 'tis true; and were 't not madness,
    then,
To make the fox surveyor of the fold?
Who being accused a crafty murderer,
His guilt should be but idly posted over,
Because his purpose is not executed.
No; let him die, in that he is a fox,
By nature proved an enemy to the flock,
Before his chaps be stain'd with crimson blood,
As Humphrey, proved by reasons, to my liege. 260
And do not stand on quillets how to slay him:
Be it by gins, by snares, by subtlety,
Sleeping or waking, 'tis no matter how,
So he be dead; for that is good deceit
Which mates him first that first intends deceit.
Queen. Thrice-noble Suffolk, 'tis resolutely spoke.

Suf. Not resolute, except so much were done;
For things are often spoke and seldom meant:
But that my heart accordeth with my tongue,
Seeing the deed is meritorious, 270
And to preserve my sovereign from his foe,
Say but the word, and I will be his priest.
Car. But I would have him dead, my Lord of
    Suffolk,
Ere you can take due orders for a priest:
Say you consent and censure well the deed,
And I'll provide his executioner,
I tender so the safety of my liege.
Suf. Here is my hand, the deed is worthy doing.
Queen. And so say I.
York. And I: and now we three have spoke it, 280
It skills not greatly who impugns our doom.

Enter a Post.

Post. Great lords, from Ireland am I come amain,
To signify that rebels there are up
And put the Englishmen unto the sword:
Send succours, lords, and stop the rage betime,
Before the wound do grow uncurable;
For, being green, there is great hope of help.
Car. A breach that craves a quick expedient stop!
What counsel give you in this weighty cause?
York. That Somerset be sent as regent thither: 290
'Tis meet that lucky ruler be employ'd;
Witness the fortune he hath had in France.
Som. If York, with all his far-fet policy,
Had been the regent there instead of me,
He never would have stay'd in France so long.
York. No, not to lose it all, as thou hast done:
I rather would have lost my life betimes
Than bring a burthen of dishonour home
By staying there so long till all were lost.
Show me one scar character'd on thy skin: 300
Men's flesh preserved so whole do seldom win.
Queen. Nay, then, this spark will prove a raging fire,
If wind and fuel be brought to feed it with:
No more, good York; sweet Somerset, be still:
Thy fortune, York, hadst thou been regent there,
Might happily have proved far worse than his.
York. What, worse than nought? nay, then, a
    shame take all!
Som. And, in the number, thee that wishest shame!
Car. My Lord of York, try what your fortune is.
The uncivil kerns of Ireland are in arms 310
And temper clay with blood of Englishmen:
To Ireland will you lead a band of men,
Collected choicely, from each county some,
And try your hap against the Irishmen?
York. I will, my lord, so please his majesty.
Suf. Why, our authority is his consent,
And what we do establish he confirms:
Then, noble York, take thou this task in hand.
York. I am content: provide me soldiers, lords,
Whiles I take order for mine own affairs. 320
Suf. A charge, Lord York, that I will see perform'd.
But now return we to the false Duke Humphrey.
Car. No more of him; for I will deal with him

pretext; see glossary. 244. **fain,** glad, pleased. 249. **kite,** bird of prey, hawk. 255. **posted over,** ignored, hastened over; see *post* in glossary. 258. **proved,** shown by experience to be; see glossary. 261. **quillets,** subtle distinctions; see glossary. 262. **gins,** traps, devices for catching game. 265. **mates,** stupefies, confounds. 272. **be his priest,** i.e., perform the last rites for him. 275. **censure well,** pass a favorable judg-

ment on; see *censure* in glossary. 277. **tender,** am concerned for, care for. 281. **skills not,** makes no (great) difference. **doom,** decision. 282. **amain,** with full speed. 285. **betime,** early. 293. **far-fet,** far-fetched. 300. **character'd,** written; see glossary. 306. **happily,** perhaps; see glossary. 310. **uncivil,** disorderly. **kerns,** light-armed Irish soldiers. 311. **temper clay,** moisten the soil.

That henceforth he shall trouble us no more.
And so break off; the day is almost spent:
Lord Suffolk, you and I must talk of that event.
 York. My Lord of Suffolk, within fourteen days
At Bristol I expect my soldiers;
For there I'll ship them all for Ireland.
 Suf. I'll see it truly done, my Lord of York. 330
          [Exeunt all but York.
 York. Now, York, or never, steel thy fearful thoughts,
And change misdoubt to resolution:
Be that thou hopest to be, or what thou art
Resign to death; it is not worth the enjoying:
Let pale-faced fear keep with the mean-born man,
And find no harbour in a royal heart.
Faster than spring-time showers comes thought on
  thought,
And not a thought but thinks on dignity.
My brain more busy than the labouring spider
Weaves tedious snares to trap mine enemies. 340
Well, nobles, well, 'tis politicly done,
To send me packing with an host of men:
I fear me you but warm the starved snake,
Who, cherish'd in your breasts, will sting your hearts.
'Twas men I lack'd and you will give them me:
I take it kindly; yet be well assured
You put sharp weapons in a madman's hands.
Whiles I in Ireland nourish a mighty band,
I will stir up in England some black storm
Shall blow ten thousand souls to heaven or hell; 350
And this fell tempest shall not cease to rage
Until the golden circuit on my head,
Like to the glorious sun's transparent beams,
Do calm the fury of this mad-bred flaw.
And, for a minister of my intent,
I have seduced a headstrong Kentishman,
John Cade of Ashford,
To make commotion, as full well he can,
Under the title of John Mortimer.
In Ireland have I seen this stubborn Cade 360
Oppose himself against a troop of kerns,
And fought so long, till that his thighs with darts
Were almost like a sharp-quill'd porpentine;
And, in the end being rescued, I have seen
Him caper upright like a wild Morisco,
Shaking the bloody darts as he his bells.
Full often, like a shag-hair'd crafty kern,
Hath he conversed with the enemy,
And undiscover'd come to me again
And given me notice of their villanies. 370
This devil here shall be my substitute;
For that John Mortimer, which now is dead,
In face, in gait, in speech, he doth resemble:
By this I shall perceive the commons' mind,
How they affect the house and claim of York.
Say he be taken, rack'd and tortured,
I know no pain they can inflict upon him
Will make him say I moved him to those arms.
Say that he thrive, as 'tis great like he will,
Why, then from Ireland come I with my strength 380
And reap the harvest which that rascal sow'd;
For Humphrey being dead, as he shall be,

And Henry put apart, the next for me.   *[Exit.*

SCENE II. *Bury St. Edmund's. A room of state.*

Enter certain Murderers, *hastily.*

 First Mur. Run to my Lord of Suffolk; let him know
We have dispatch'd the duke, as he commanded.
 Sec. Mur. O that it were to do! What have we done?
Didst ever hear a man so penitent?

Enter SUFFOLK.

 First Mur. Here comes my lord.
 Suf. Now, sirs, have you dispatch'd this thing?
 First Mur. Ay, my good lord, he 's dead.
 Suf. Why, that 's well said. Go, get you to my house;
I will reward you for this venturous deed.
The king and all the peers are here at hand. 10
Have you laid fair the bed? Is all things well,
According as I gave directions?
 First Mur. 'Tis, my good lord.
 Suf. Away! be gone.   *[Exeunt Murderers.*

 Sound trumpets. Enter the KING, *the* QUEEN, CARDINAL
  BEAUFORT, SOMERSET, *with Attendants.*

 King. Go, call our uncle to our presence straight;
Say we intend to try his grace to-day,
If he be guilty, as 'tis published.
 Suf. I'll call him presently, my noble lord. *[Exit.*
 King. Lords, take your places; and, I pray you all,
Proceed no straiter 'gainst our uncle Gloucester 20
Than from true evidence of good esteem
He be approved in practice culpable.
 Queen. God forbid any malice should prevail,
That faultless may condemn a nobleman!
Pray God he may acquit him of suspicion!
 King. I thank thee, Meg; these words content me
  much.

Re-enter SUFFOLK.

How now! why look'st thou pale? why tremblest thou?
Where is our uncle? what 's the matter, Suffolk?
 Suf. Dead in his bed, my lord; Gloucester is dead.
 Queen. Marry, God forfend! 30
 Car. God's secret judgement: I did dream to-night
The duke was dumb and could not speak a word.
         [The King swoons.
 Queen. How fares my lord? Help, lords! the king is
  dead.
 Som. Rear up his body; wring him by the nose.
 Queen. Run, go, help, help! O Henry, ope thine eyes!
 Suf. He doth revive again: madam, be patient.
 King. O heavenly God!
 Queen.   How fares my gracious lord?
 Suf. Comfort, my sovereign! gracious Henry,
  comfort!
 King. What, doth my Lord of Suffolk comfort me?
Came he right now to sing a raven's note, 40
Whose dismal tune bereft my vital powers;
And thinks he that the chirping of a wren,
By crying comfort from a hollow breast,

Can chase away the first-conceived sound?
Hide not thy poison with such sugar'd words;
Lay not thy hands on me; forbear, I say;
Their touch affrights me as a serpent's sting.
Thou baleful messenger, out of my sight!
Upon thy eye-balls murderous tyranny
Sits in grim majesty, to fright the world.   50
Look not upon me, for thine eyes are wounding:
Yet do not go away: come, basilisk,
And kill the innocent gazer with thy sight;
For in the shade of death I shall find joy;
In life but double death, now Gloucester 's dead.
    Queen. Why do you rate my Lord of Suffolk thus?
Although the duke was enemy to him,
Yet he most Christian-like laments his death:
And for myself, foe as he was to me,
Might liquid tears or heart-offending groans   60
Or blood-consuming sighs recall his life,
I would be blind with weeping, sick with groans,
Look pale as primrose with blood-drinking sighs,
And all to have the noble duke alive.
What know I how the world may deem of me?
For it is known we were but hollow friends:
It may be judged I made the duke away;
So shall my name with slander's tongue be wounded,
And princes' courts be fill'd with my reproach.
This get I by his death: ay me, unhappy!   70
To be a queen, and crown'd with infamy!
    King. Ah, woe is me for Gloucester, wretched man!
    Queen. Be woe for me, more wretched than he is.
What, dost thou turn away and hide thy face?
I am no loathsome leper; look on me.
What! art thou, like the adder, waxen deaf?
Be poisonous too and kill thy forlorn queen.
Is all thy comfort shut in Gloucester's tomb?
Why, then, dame Margaret was ne'er thy joy.
Erect his statua and worship it,   80
And make my image but an alehouse sign.
Was I for this nigh wreck'd upon the sea
And twice by awkward wind from England's bank
Drove back again unto my native clime?
What boded this, but well forewarning wind
Did seem to say 'Seek not a scorpion's nest,
Nor set no footing on this unkind shore'?
What did I then, but cursed the gentle gusts
And he that loosed them forth their brazen caves;
And bid them blow towards England's blessed shore,
Or turn our stern upon a dreadful rock?   91
Yet Æolus would not be a murderer,
But left that hateful office unto thee:
The pretty-vaulting sea refused to drown me,
Knowing that thou wouldst have me drown'd on
        shore,
With tears as salt as sea, through thy unkindness:
The splitting rocks cower'd in the sinking sands
And would not dash me with their ragged sides,
Because thy flinty heart, more hard than they,
Might in thy palace perish Margaret.   100
As far as I could ken thy chalky cliffs,
When from thy shore the tempest beat us back,
I stood upon the hatches in the storm,

And when the dusky sky began to rob
My earnest-gaping sight of thy land's view,
I took a costly jewel from my neck,
A heart it was, bound in with diamonds,
And threw it towards thy land: the sea received it,
And so I wish'd thy body might my heart:
And even with this I lost fair England's view   110
And bid mine eyes be packing with my heart
And call'd them blind and dusky spectacles,
For losing ken of Albion's wished coast.
How often have I tempted Suffolk's tongue,
The agent of thy foul inconstancy,
To sit and witch me, as Ascanius did
When he to madding Dido would unfold
His father's acts commenced in burning Troy!
Am I not witch'd like her? or thou not false like him?
Ay me, I can no more! die, Margaret!   120
For Henry weeps that thou dost live so long.

    Noise within. Enter WARWICK, SALISBURY, *and many*
        Commons.

    War. It is reported, mighty sovereign,
That good Duke Humphrey traitorously is murder'd
By Suffolk and the Cardinal Beaufort's means.
The commons, like an angry hive of bees
That want their leader, scatter up and down
And care not who they sting in his revenge.
Myself have calm'd their spleenful mutiny,
Until they hear the order of his death.
    King. That he is dead, good Warwick, 'tis too true;
But how he died God knows, not Henry: 131
Enter his chamber, view his breathless corpse,
And comment then upon his sudden death.
    War. That shall I do, my liege. Stay, Salisbury,
With the rude multitude till I return.   [*Exit.*
    King. O Thou that judgest all things, stay my
        thoughts,
My thoughts, that labour to persuade my soul
Some violent hands were laid on Humphrey's life!
If my suspect be false, forgive me, God,
For judgement only doth belong to Thee.   140
Fain would I go to chafe his paly lips
With twenty thousand kisses and to drain
Upon his face an ocean of salt tears,
To tell my love unto his dumb deaf trunk
And with my fingers feel his hand unfeeling:
But all in vain are these mean obsequies;
And to survey his dead and earthy image,
What were it but to make my sorrow greater?

    Re-enter WARWICK, *and others, bearing* GLOUCESTER'S
        body on a bed.

    War. Come hither, gracious sovereign, view this
        body.
    King. That is to see how deep my grave is made;   150
For with his soul fled all my worldly solace,
For seeing him I see my life in death.
    War. As surely as my soul intends to live
With that dread King that took our state upon him
To free us from his father's wrathful curse,
I do believe that violent hands were laid

---

presaged death. 52. **basilisk,** fabulous reptile, said to kill by its look;
see glossary. 61, 63. **blood-consuming, blood-drinking.** It was commonly believed that a sigh cost the heart a drop of blood. 76. **like
the adder.** Cf. Psalms 58:4-5: ". . . the deaf adder that stoppeth her
ear, which hearkeneth not to the voice of charmers." References to the
deafness of the adder are common in Renaissance books. **waxen,**
grown. 89. **he,** for "him"; see Abbott, 206-207; the antecedent is

Æolus, god of the winds (l. 92). 101. **ken,** sight. 112. **spectacles,**
organs of sight. 116. **Ascanius,** young son of Aeneas. During Aeneas'
narration of his adventures and misfortunes in the court of Queen Dido,
Venus, Aeneas' mother, sent Cupid to assume Ascanius' form in order
to inflict the queen with love for Aeneas. 141. **chafe,** warm.

Upon the life of this thrice-famed duke.
Suf. A dreadful oath, sworn with a solemn tongue!
What instance gives Lord Warwick for his vow?
War. See how the blood is settled in his face. 160
Oft have I seen a timely-parted ghost,
Of ashy semblance, meagre, pale and bloodless,
Being all descended to the labouring heart;
Who, in the conflict that it holds with death,
Attracts the same for aidance 'gainst the enemy;
Which with the heart there cools and ne'er returneth
To blush and beautify the cheek again.
But see, his face is black and full of blood,
His eye-balls further out than when he lived,
Staring full ghastly like a strangled man; 170
His hair uprear'd, his nostrils stretched with
struggling;
His hands abroad display'd, as one that grasp'd
And tugg'd for life and was by strength subdued:
Look, on the sheets his hair, you see, is sticking;
His well-proportion'd beard made rough and rugged,
Like to the summer's corn by tempest lodged.
It cannot be but he was murder'd here;
The least of all these signs were probable.
Suf. Why, Warwick, who should do the duke to
death?
Myself and Beaufort had him in protection; 180
And we, I hope, sir, are no murderers.
War. But both of you were vow'd Duke Humphrey's
foes,
And you, forsooth, had the good duke to keep:
'Tis like you would not feast him like a friend;
And 'tis well seen he found an enemy.
Queen. Then you, belike, suspect these noblemen
As guilty of Duke Humphrey's timeless death.
War. Who finds the heifer dead and bleeding fresh
And sees fast by a butcher with an axe,
But will suspect 'twas he that made the slaughter? 190
Who finds the partridge in the puttock's nest,
But may imagine how the bird was dead,
Although the kite soar with unbloodied beak?
Even so suspicious is this tragedy.
Queen. Are you the butcher, Suffolk? Where's your
knife?
Is Beaufort term'd a kite? Where are his talons?
Suf. I wear no knife to slaughter sleeping men;
But here's a vengeful sword, rusted with ease,
That shall be scoured in his rancorous heart
That slanders me with murder's crimson badge. 200
Say, if thou darest, proud Lord of Warwickshire,
That I am faulty in Duke Humphrey's death.
    [*Exeunt Cardinal, Somerset, and others.*
War. What dares not Warwick, if false Suffolk dare
him?
Queen. He dares not calm his contumelious spirit
Nor cease to be an arrogant controller,
Though Suffolk dare him twenty thousand times.
War. Madam, be still; with reverence may I say;
For every word you speak in his behalf
Is slander to your royal dignity.
Suf. Blunt-witted lord, ignoble in demeanour! 210
If ever lady wrong'd her lord so much,

Thy mother took into her blameful bed
Some stern untutor'd churl, and noble stock
Was graft with crab-tree slip; whose fruit thou art
And never of the Nevils' noble race.
War. But that the guilt of murder bucklers thee
And I should rob the deathsman of his fee,
Quitting thee thereby of ten thousand shames,
And that my sovereign's presence makes me mild,
I would, false murderous coward, on thy knee 220
Make thee beg pardon for thy passed speech
And say it was thy mother that thou meant'st,
That thou thyself wast born in bastardy;
And after all this fearful homage done,
Give thee thy hire and send thy soul to hell,
Pernicious blood-sucker of sleeping men!
Suf. Thou shalt be waking while I shed thy blood,
If from this presence thou darest go with me.
War. Away even now, or I will drag thee hence:
Unworthy though thou art, I'll cope with thee 230
And do some service to Duke Humphrey's ghost.
    [*Exeunt Suffolk and Warwick.*
King. What stronger breastplate than a heart
untainted!
Thrice is he arm'd that hath his quarrel just,
And he but naked, though lock'd up in steel,
Whose conscience with injustice is corrupted.
    [*A noise within.*
Queen. What noise is this?

Re-enter SUFFOLK *and* WARWICK, *with their weapons
drawn.*

King. Why, how now, lords! your wrathful weapons
drawn
Here in our presence! dare you be so bold?
Why, what tumultuous clamour have we here?
Suf. The traitorous Warwick with the men of Bury
Set all upon me, mighty sovereign. 241
Sal. [*To the Commons, entering*] Sirs, stand apart; the
king shall know your mind.
Dread lord, the commons send you word by me,
Unless Lord Suffolk straight be done to death,
Or banished fair England's territories,
They will by violence tear him from your palace
And torture him with grievous lingering death.
They say, by him the good Duke Humphrey died;
They say, in him they fear your highness' death;
And mere instinct of love and loyalty, 250
Free from a stubborn opposite intent,
As being thought to contradict your liking,
Makes them thus forward in his banishment.
They say, in care of your most royal person,
That if your highness should intend to sleep
And charge that no man should disturb your rest
In pain of your dislike or pain of death,
Yet, notwithstanding such a strait edict,
Were there a serpent seen, with forked tongue,
That slily glided towards your majesty, 260
It were but necessary you were waked,
Lest, being suffer'd in that harmful slumber,
The mortal worm might make the sleep eternal;
And therefore do they cry, though you forbid,

That they will guard you, whether you will or no,
From such fell serpents as false Suffolk is,
With whose envenomed and fatal sting,
Your loving uncle, twenty times his worth,
They say, is shamefully bereft of life.
    Commons. [*Within*] An answer from the king, my
      Lord of Salisbury!   270
    Suf. 'Tis like the commons, rude unpolish'd hinds,
Could send such message to their sovereign:
But you, my lord, were glad to be employ'd,
To show how quaint an orator you are:
But all the honour Salisbury hath won
Is, that he was the lord ambassador
Sent from a sort of tinkers to the king.
    Commons. [*Within*] An answer from the king, or we
      will all break in!
    King. Go, Salisbury, and tell them all from me,
I thank them for their tender loving care;   280
And had I not been cited so by them,
Yet did I purpose as they do entreat;
For, sure, my thoughts do hourly prophesy
Mischance unto my state by Suffolk's means:
And therefore, by His majesty I swear,
Whose far unworthy deputy I am,
He shall not breathe infection in this air
But three days longer, on the pain of death.
                          [*Exit Salisbury.*
    Queen. O Henry, let me plead for gentle Suffolk!
    King. Ungentle queen, to call him gentle Suffolk! 290
No more, I say: if thou dost plead for him,
Thou wilt but add increase unto my wrath.
Had I but said, I would have kept my word,
But when I swear, it is irrevocable.
If, after three days' space, thou here be'st found
On any ground that I am ruler of,
The world shall not be ransom for thy life.
Come, Warwick, come, good Warwick, go with me;
I have great matters to impart to thee.
             [*Exeunt all but Queen and Suffolk.*
    Queen. Mischance and sorrow go along with you! 300
Heart's discontent and sour affliction
Be playfellows to keep you company!
There 's two of you; the devil make a third!
And threefold vengeance tend upon your steps!
    Suf. Cease, gentle queen, these execrations
And let thy Suffolk take his heavy leave.
    Queen. Fie, coward woman and soft-hearted wretch!
Hast thou not spirit to curse thine enemy?
    Suf. A plague upon them! wherefore should I curse
      them?
Would curses kill, as doth the mandrake's groan,   310
I would invent as bitter-searching terms,
As curst, as harsh and horrible to hear,
Deliver'd strongly through my fixed teeth,
With full as many signs of deadly hate,
As lean-faced Envy in her loathsome cave:
My tongue should stumble in mine earnest words;
Mine eyes should sparkle like the beaten flint;
Mine hair be fix'd on end, as one distract;
Ay, every joint should seem to curse and ban:
And even now my burthen'd heart would break,   320

Should I not curse them. Poison be their drink!
Gall, worse than gall, the daintiest that they taste!
Their sweetest shade a grove of cypress trees!
Their chiefest prospect murdering basilisks!
Their softest touch as smart as lizards' stings!
Their music frightful as the serpent's hiss,
And boding screech-owls make the concert full!
All the foul terrors in dark-seated hell—
    Queen. Enough, sweet Suffolk; thou torment'st
      thyself;
And these dread curses, like the sun 'gainst glass,   330
Or like an overcharged gun, recoil,
And turn the force of them upon thyself.
    Suf. You bade me ban, and will you bid me leave?
Now, by the ground that I am banish'd from,
Well could I curse away a winter's night,
Though standing naked on a mountain top,
Where biting cold would never let grass grow,
And think it but a minute spent in sport.
    Queen. O, let me entreat thee cease. Give me thy
      hand,
That I may dew it with my mournful tears;   340
Nor let the rain of heaven wet this place,
To wash away my woful monuments.
O, could this kiss be printed in thy hand,
That thou mightst think upon these by the seal,
Through whom a thousand sighs are breathed for
    thee!
So, get thee gone, that I may know my grief;
'Tis but surmised whiles thou art standing by,
As one that surfeits thinking on a want.
I will repeal thee, or, be well assured,
Adventure to be banished myself: 350
And banished I am, if but from thee.
Go; speak not to me; even now be gone.
O, go not yet! Even thus two friends condemn'd
Embrace and kiss and take ten thousand leaves,
Loather a hundred times to part than die.
Yet now farewell; and farewell life with thee!
    Suf. Thus is poor Suffolk ten times banished;
Once by the king, and three times thrice by thee.
'Tis not the land I care for, wert thou thence;
A wilderness is populous enough,   360
So Suffolk had thy heavenly company:
For where thou art, there is the world itself,
With every several pleasure in the world,
And where thou art not, desolation.
I can no more: live thou to joy thy life;
Myself no joy in nought but that thou livest.

Enter Vaux.

    Queen. Whither goes Vaux so fast? what news, I
      prithee?
    Vaux. To signify unto his majesty
That Cardinal Beaufort is at point of death;
For suddenly a grievous sickness took him,   370
That makes him gasp and stare and catch the air,
Blaspheming God and cursing men on earth.
Sometime he talks as if Duke Humphrey's ghost
Were by his side; sometime he calls the king
And whispers to his pillow as to him

---

faced Envy, a conventional description of this one of the **seven** deadly sins. Spenser depicts Envy riding on a ravenous wolf. (*Faerie Queene*, I, iv.) Hart points out as the probable immediate source of this passage the following lines from Golding's Ovid:
    She goes me straight to Envies house, a foule and irksome cave,
    Replete with blacke and lothly filth. . . .
    There saw she Envie . . .

    Hir body leane as any Rake. . . .
319. **ban,** curse. 323. **cypress trees,** symbols of grief. 327. **concert,** company of musicians. 342. **monuments,** i.e., traces of her tears. 349. **repeal,** recall from banishment. 350. **Adventure,** risk. 373. **Sometime,** from time to time; see glossary.

The secrets of his overcharged soul:
And I am sent to tell his majesty
That even now he cries aloud for him.
　　Queen. Go tell this heavy message to the king.
　　　　　　　　　　　　　　　　　　　　[*Exit Vaux.*
Ay me! what is this world! what news are these! 　. 380
But wherefore grieve I at an hour's poor loss,
Omitting Suffolk's exile, my soul's treasure?
Why only, Suffolk, mourn I not for thee,
And with the southern clouds contend in tears,
Theirs for the earth's increase, mine for my sorrows?
Now get thee hence: the king, thou know'st, is coming;
If thou be found by me, thou art but dead.
　　Suf. If I depart from thee, I cannot live;
And in thy sight to die, what were it else
But like a pleasant slumber in thy lap? 　　　　390
Here could I breathe my soul into the air,
As mild and gentle as the cradle-babe
Dying with mother's dug between its lips:
Where, from thy sight, I should be raging mad
And cry out for thee to close up mine eyes,
To have thee with thy lips to stop my mouth;
So shouldst thou either turn my flying soul,
Or I should breathe it so into thy body,
And then it lived in sweet Elysium.
To die by thee were but to die in jest; 　　　　400
From thee to die were torture more than death:
O, let me stay, befall what may befall!
　　Queen. Away! though parting be a fretful corrosive,
It is applied to a deathful wound.
To France, sweet Suffolk: let me hear from thee;
For wheresoe'er thou art in this world's globe,
I'll have an Iris that shall find thee out.
　　Suf. I go.
　　Queen. 　　　　　　　　And take my heart with thee.
　　Suf. A jewel, lock'd into the wofull'st cask
That ever did contain a thing of worth. 　　　410
Even as a splitted bark, so sunder we:
This way fall I to death.
　　Queen. 　　　　　　This way for me.
　　　　　　　　　　　　　　　　　[*Exeunt severally.*

SCENE III. *A bedchamber.*

Enter the KING, SALISBURY, WARWICK, *to the*
　　CARDINAL *in bed.*

　　King. How fares my lord? speak, Beaufort, to thy
　　　　sovereign.
　　Car. If thou be'st death, I'll give thee England's
　　　　treasure,
Enough to purchase such another island,
So thou wilt let me live, and feel no pain.
　　King. Ah, what a sign it is of evil life,
Where death's approach is seen so terrible!
　　War. Beaufort, it is thy sovereign speaks to thee.
　　Car. Bring me unto my trial when you will.

Died he not in his bed? where should he die?
Can I make men live, whether they will or no? 　　10
O, torture me no more! I will confess.
Alive again? then show me where he is:
I'll give a thousand pound to look upon him.
He hath no eyes, the dust hath blinded them.
Comb down his hair; look, look! it stands upright,
Like lime-twigs set to catch my winged soul.
Give me some drink; and bid the apothecary
Bring the strong poison that I bought of him.
　　King. O thou eternal Mover of the heavens,
Look with a gentle eye upon this wretch! 　　　20
O, beat away the busy meddling fiend
That lays strong siege unto this wretch's soul
And from his bosom purge this black despair!
　　War. See, how the pangs of death do make him grin!
　　Sal. Disturb him not; let him pass peaceably.
　　King. Peace to his soul, if God's good pleasure be!
Lord cardinal, if thou think'st on heaven's bliss,
Hold up thy hand, make signal of thy hope.
He dies, and makes no sign. O God, forgive him!
　　War. So bad a death argues a monstrous life. 　30
　　King. Forbear to judge, for we are sinners all.
Close up his eyes and draw the curtain close;
And let us all to meditation. 　　　　　　[*Exeunt.*

ACT IV.

SCENE I. *The coast of Kent.*

Alarum. Fight at sea. Ordnance goes off. Enter a Captain,
a Master, *a* Master's-Mate, WALTER WHITMORE,
and others; with them SUFFOLK, *and others, prisoners.*

　　Cap. The gaudy, blabbing and remorseful day
Is crept into the bosom of the sea;
And now loud-howling wolves arouse the jades
That drag the tragic melancholy night;
Who, with their drowsy, slow and flagging wings,
Clip dead men's graves and from their misty jaws
Breathe foul contagious darkness in the air.
Therefore bring forth the soldiers of our prize;
For, whilst our pinnace anchors in the Downs,
Here shall they make their ransom on the sand, 　　10
Or with their blood stain this discolour'd shore.
Master, this prisoner freely give I thee;
And thou that art his mate, make boot of this;
The other, Walter Whitmore, is thy share.
　　First Gent. What is my ransom, master? let me know.
　　Mast. A thousand crowns, or else lay down your
　　　　head.
　　Mate. And so much shall you give, or off goes yours.
　　Cap. What, think you much to pay two thousand
　　　　crowns,
And bear the name and port of gentlemen?
Cut both the villains' throats; for die you shall: 　　2?
The lives of those which we have lost in fight

Be counterpoised with such a petty sum!
First Gent. I'll give it, sir; and therefore spare my
    life.
Sec. Gent. And so will I and write home for it straight.
Whit. I lost mine eye in laying the prize aboard,
And therefore to revenge it, shalt thou die;   [*To Suf.*
And so should these, if I might have my will.
Cap. Be not so rash; take ransom, let him live.
Suf. Look on my George; I am a gentleman;
Rate me at what thou wilt, thou shalt be paid.   30
Whit. And so am I; my name is Walter Whitmore.
How now! why start'st thou? what, doth death
    affright?
Suf. Thy name affrights me, in whose sound is death.
A cunning man did calculate my birth
And told me that by water I should die:
Yet let not this make thee be bloody-minded;
Thy name is Gaultier, being rightly sounded.
Whit. Gaultier or Walter, which it is, I care not:
Never did base dishonour blur our name,
But with our sword we wiped away the blot;   40
Therefore, when merchant-like I sell revenge,
Broke be my sword, my arms torn and defaced,
And I proclaim'd a coward through the world!
Suf. Stay, Whitmore; for thy prisoner is a prince,
The Duke of Suffolk, William de la Pole.
Whit. The Duke of Suffolk muffled up in rags!
Suf. Ay, but these rags are no part of the duke:
Jove sometime went disguised, and why not I?
Cap. But Jove was never slain, as thou shalt be.
Suf. Obscure and lowly swain, King Henry's blood,
The honourable blood of Lancaster,   51
Must not be shed by such a jaded groom.
Hast thou not kiss'd thy hand and held my stirrup?
Bare-headed plodded by my foot-cloth mule
And thought thee happy when I shook my head?
How often hast thou waited at my cup,
Fed from my trencher, kneel'd down at the board,
When I have feasted with Queen Margaret?
Remember it and let it make thee crest-fall'n,
Ay, and allay this thy abortive pride;   60
How in our voiding lobby hast thou stood
And duly waited for my coming forth?
This hand of mine hath writ in thy behalf
And therefore shall it charm thy riotous tongue.
Whit. Speak, captain, shall I stab the forlorn swain?
Cap. First let my words stab him, as he hath me.
Suf. Base slave, thy words are blunt and so art thou.
Cap. Convey him hence and on our longboat's side
Strike off his head.
Suf.   Thou darest not, for thy own.
Cap. Yes, Pole.
Suf.   Pole!
Cap.   Pool! Sir Pool! lord!   70
Ay, kennel, puddle, sink; whose filth and dirt
Troubles the silver spring where England drinks.
Now will I dam up this thy yawning mouth

For swallowing the treasure of the realm:
Thy lips that kiss'd the queen shall sweep the ground;
And thou that smiledst at good Duke Humphrey's
    death
Against the senseless winds shalt grin in vain,
Who in contempt shall hiss at thee again:
And wedded be thou to the hags of hell,
For daring to affy a mighty lord   80
Unto the daughter of a worthless king,
Having neither subject, wealth, nor diadem.
By devilish policy art thou grown great
And, like ambitious Sylla, overgorged
With gobbets of thy mother's bleeding heart.
By thee Anjou and Maine were sold to France,
The false revolting Normans thorough thee
Disdain to call us lord, and Picardy
Hath slain their governors, surprised our forts
And sent the ragged soldiers wounded home.   90
The princely Warwick, and the Nevils all,
Whose dreadful swords were never drawn in vain,
As hating thee, are rising up in arms:
And now the house of York, thrust from the crown
By shameful murder of a guiltless king
And lofty proud encroaching tyranny,
Burns with revenging fire; whose hopeful colours
Advance our half-faced sun, striving to shine,
Under the which is writ 'Invitis nubibus.'
The commons here in Kent are up in arms: 100
And, to conclude, reproach and beggary
Is crept into the palace of our king,
And all by thee. Away! convey him hence.
Suf. O that I were a god, to shoot forth thunder
Upon these paltry, servile, abject drudges!
Small things make base men proud: this villain here,
Being captain of a pinnace, threatens more
Than Bargulus the strong Illyrian pirate.
Drones suck not eagles' blood but rob beehives:
It is impossible that I should die   110
By such a lowly vassal as thyself.
Thy words move rage and not remorse in me:
I go of message from the queen to France;
I charge thee waft me safely cross the Channel.
Cap. Walter,—
Whit. Come, Suffolk, I must waft thee to thy death.
Suf. Gelidus timor occupat artus, it is thee I fear.
Whit. Thou shalt have cause to fear before I leave
    thee.
What, are ye daunted now? now will ye stoop?
First Gent. My gracious lord, entreat him, speak him
    fair.   120
Suf. Suffolk's imperial tongue is stern and rough,
Used to command, untaught to plead for favour.
Far be it we should honour such as these
With humble suit: no, rather let my head
Stoop to the block than these knees bow to any
Save to the God of heaven and to my king;
And sooner dance upon a bloody pole

head lieng there on the sands. Which corps, being there found by a chapleine of his, was conueied to Wingfield college in Suffolke, and there buried." 29. **George,** the gold or jeweled figure of St. George, worn as the insignium of the Order of the Knights of the Garter. 33. **Thy name,** i.e., Walter, pronounced like "water"; cf. line 37 below, where Suffolk tries desperately to avert the prophecy referred to in lines 34-35 (cf. I, iv, 35-36) by urging the French form of the name— Gaultier. 54. **foot-cloth,** large, richly ornamented cloth laid over the back of a horse, hanging down to the ground on each side. 57. **trencher,** wooden dish or plate; see glossary. 61. **voiding lobby,** ante-room. 70. **Pole, Pool,** words pronounced somewhat alike in Elizabethan speech. 71. **kennel,** gutter, sink, cesspool. 80. **affy,** betroth. 84.

ambitious Sylla, i.e., Sulla, Roman dictator of the first century B.C., now chiefly remembered for his ruthless destruction of his political enemies. 85. **gobbets,** pieces of raw flesh. 87. **thorough,** through; see glossary. 95. **shameful . . . king,** i.e., Richard II. 98. **Advance,** raise (Onions); display (Tucker Brooke). **half-faced sun.** This may possibly allude to the banner of Edward III, which according to Camden (*Remains*) was "the rays of the sun dispersing themselues out of a cloud." Cf. *3 Henry VI*, II, i, 39-40, where Edward IV adopted the sun as an emblem. 99. **'Invitus nubibus,'** in spite of the clouds. 108. **Bargulus,** an allusion to Cicero's *De officiis*, where this famous pirate is mentioned. 112. **remorse,** pity; see glossary. 117. **Gelidus . . . artus,** cold fear takes hold of the limbs. 120. **fair,** courteously; see glossary.

Than stand uncover'd to the vulgar groom.
True nobility is exempt from fear:
More can I bear than you dare execute. 130
    Cap. Hale him away, and let him talk no more.
    Suf. Come, soldiers, show what cruelty ye can,
That this my death may never be forgot!
Great men oft die by vile bezonians:
A Roman sworder and banditto slave
Murder'd sweet Tully; Brutus' bastard hand
Stabb'd Julius Cæsar; savage islanders
Pompey the Great; and Suffolk dies by pirates.
                    [*Exeunt Whitmore and others with Suffolk.*
    Cap. And as for these whose ransom we have set,
It is our pleasure one of them depart: 140
Therefore come you with us and let him go.
                    [*Exeunt all but the First Gentleman.*

                Re-enter WHITMORE *with* SUFFOLK's *body.*
    Whit. There let his head and lifeless body lie,
Until the queen his mistress bury it.   [*Exit.*
    First Gent. O barbarous and bloody spectacle!
His body will I bear unto the king:
If he revenge it not, yet will his friends;
So will the queen, that living held him dear.
                    [*Exit with the body.*

────────────

                SCENE II. *Blackheath.*

            Enter GEORGE BEVIS *and* JOHN HOLLAND.

    Bevis. Come, and get thee a sword, though made of
a lath: they have been up these two days.
    Holl. They have the more need to sleep now, then.
    Bevis. I tell thee, Jack Cade the clothier means to
dress the commonwealth, and turn it, and set a new
nap upon it.
    Holl. So he had need, for 'tis threadbare. Well, I say
it was never merry world in England since gentlemen
came up. 10
    Bevis. O miserable age! virtue is not regarded in
handicrafts-men.
    Holl. The nobility think scorn to go in leather
aprons.
    Bevis. Nay, more, the king's council are no good
workmen.
    Holl. True; and yet it is said, labour in thy vocation;
which is as much to say as, let the magistrates be
labouring men; and therefore should we be magistrates. 20
    Bevis. Thou hast hit it; for there 's no better sign of a
brave mind than a hard hand.
    Holl. I see them! I see them! There 's Best's son, the
tanner of Wingham,—
    Bevis. He shall have the skins of our enemies, to
make dog's-leather of.
    Holl. And Dick the Butcher,—
    Bevis. Then is sin struck down like an ox, and
iniquity's throat cut like a calf.
    Holl. And Smith the weaver,— 30
    Bevis. Argo, their thread of life is spun.

    Holl. Come, come, let 's fall in with them.

    Drum. Enter CADE, DICK *Butcher*, SMITH *the Weaver,
        and a Sawyer, with infinite numbers.*

    Cade. We John Cade, so termed of our supposed
father,—
    Dick. [*Aside*] Or rather, of stealing a cade of
herrings.
    Cade. For our enemies shall fall before us, inspired
with the spirit of putting down kings and princes,—
Command silence.
    Dick. Silence!
    Cade. My father was a Mortimer,— 40
    Dick. [*Aside*] He was an honest man, and a good
bricklayer.
    Cade. My mother a Plantagenet,—
    Dick. [*Aside*] I knew her well; she was a midwife.
    Cade. My wife descended of the Lacies,—
    Dick. [*Aside*] She was, indeed, a pedler's daughter,
and sold many laces. 49
    Smith. [*Aside*] But now of late, not able to travel
with her furred pack, she washes bucks here at home.
    Cade. Therefore am I of an honourable house.
    Dick. [*Aside*] Ay, by my faith, the field is honour-
able; and there was he born, under a hedge, for his
father had never a house but the cage.
    Cade. Valiant I am.
    Smith. [*Aside*] A' must needs; for beggary is valiant.
    Cade. I am able to endure much. 60
    Dick. [*Aside*] No question of that; for I have seen
him whipped three market-days together.
    Cade. I fear neither sword nor fire.
    Smith. [*Aside*] He need not fear the sword; for his
coat is of proof.
    Dick. [*Aside*] But methinks he should stand in fear of
fire, being burnt i' the hand for stealing of sheep. 68
    Cade. Be brave, then; for your captain is brave, and
vows reformation. There shall be in England seven
halfpenny loaves sold for a penny: the three-hooped
pot shall have ten hoops; and I will make it felony to
drink small beer: all the realm shall be in common;
and in Cheapside shall my palfry go to grass: and
when I am king, as king I will be,—
    All. God save your majesty!
    Cade. I thank you, good people: there shall be no
money; all shall eat and drink on my score; and I will
apparel them all in one livery, that they may agree
like brothers and worship me their lord. 83
    Dick. The first thing we do, let 's kill all the lawyers.
    Cade. Nay, that I mean to do. Is not this a lamen-
table thing, that of the skin of an innocent lamb should
be made parchment? that parchment, being scribbled
o'er, should undo a man? Some say the bee stings: but
I say, 'tis the bee's wax; for I did but seal once to a
thing, and I was never mine own man since. How
now! who 's there? 91

    Enter some, bringing forward the Clerk of Chatham.

    Smith. The clerk of Chatham: he can write and read
and cast accompt.

Cade. O monstrous!

Smith. We took him setting of boys' copies.

Cade. Here's a villain!

Smith. Has a book in his pocket with red letters in 't.

Cade. Nay, then, he is a conjurer.

Dick. Nay, he can make obligations, and write court-hand. 101

Cade. I am sorry for 't: the man is a proper man, of mine honour; unless I find him guilty, he shall not die. Come hither, sirrah, I must examine thee: what is thy name?

Clerk. Emmanuel.

Dick. They use to write it on the top of letters: 'twill go hard with you.

Cade. Let me alone. Dost thou use to write thy name? or hast thou a mark to thyself, like an honest plain-dealing man? 111

Clerk. Sir, I thank God, I have been so well brought up that I can write my name.

All. He hath confessed: away with him! he's a villain and a traitor.

Cade. Away with him, I say! hang him with his pen and ink-horn about his neck. [*Exit one with the Clerk.*

Enter MICHAEL.

Mich. Where's our general?

Cade. Here I am, thou particular fellow. 119

Mich. Fly, fly, fly! Sir Humphrey Stafford and his brother are hard by, with the king's forces.

Cade. Stand, villain, stand, or I'll fell thee down. He shall be encountered with a man as good as himself: he is but a knight, is a'?

Mich. No.

Cade. To equal him, I will make myself a knight presently. [*Kneels*] Rise up Sir John Mortimer. [*Rises*] Now have at him!

Enter SIR HUMPHREY STAFFORD *and his* Brother, *with drum and soldiers.*

Staf. Rebellious hinds, the filth and scum of Kent, 130
Mark'd for the gallows, lay your weapons down;
Home to your cottages, forsake this groom:
The king is merciful, if you revolt.

Bro. But angry, wrathful, and inclined to blood,
If you go forward; therefore yield, or die.

Cade. As for these silken-coated slaves, I pass not:
It is to you, good people, that I speak,
Over whom, in time to come, I hope to reign;
For I am rightful heir unto the crown.

Staf. Villain, thy father was a plasterer; 140
And thou thyself a shearman, art thou not?

Cade. And Adam was a gardener.

Bro. And what of that?

Cade. Marry, this: Edmund Mortimer, Earl of March,
Married the Duke of Clarence' daughter, did he not?

Staf. Ay, sir.

Cade. By her he had two children at one birth.

Bro. That's false.

Cade. Ay, there's the question; but I say, 'tis true:

The elder of them, being put to nurse,
Was by a beggar-woman stolen away;
And, ignorant of his birth and parentage,
Became a bricklayer when he came to age:
His son am I; deny it, if you can.

Dick. Nay, 'tis too true; therefore he shall be king.

Smith. Sir, he made a chimney in my father's house, and the bricks are alive at this day to testify it; therefore deny it not.

Staf. And will you credit this base drudge's words,
That speaks he knows not what? 160

All. Ay, marry, will we; therefore get ye gone.

Bro. Jack Cade, the Duke of York hath taught you this.

Cade. [*Aside*] He lies, for I invented it myself.
Go to, sirrah, tell the king from me, that, for his father's sake, Henry the Fifth, in whose time boys went to span-counter for French crowns, I am content he shall reign; but I'll be protector over him.

Dick. And furthermore, we'll have the Lord Say's head for selling the dukedom of Maine.

Cade. And good reason; for thereby is England mained, and fain to go with a staff, but that my puissance holds it up. Fellow kings, I tell you that that Lord Say hath gelded the commonwealth, and made it an eunuch: and more than that, he can speak French; and therefore he is a traitor.

Staf. O gross and miserable ignorance! 178

Cade. Nay, answer, if you can: the Frenchmen are our enemies; go to, then, I ask but this: can he that speaks with the tongue of an enemy be a good counsellor, or no?

All. No, no; and therefore we'll have his head.

Bro. Well, seeing gentle words will not prevail,
Assail them with the army of the king.

Staf. Herald, away; and throughout every town
Proclaim them traitors that are up with Cade;
That those which fly before the battle ends
May, even in their wives' and children's sight,
Be hang'd up for example at their doors: 190
And you that be the king's friends, follow me.
[*Exeunt the two Staffords, and soldiers.*

Cade. And you that love the commons, follow me.
Now show yourselves men; 'tis for liberty.
We will not leave one lord, one gentleman:
Spare none but such as go in clouted shoon;
For they are thrifty honest men and such
As would, but that they dare not, take our parts.

Dick. They are all in order and march toward us.

Cade. But then are we in order when we are most out of order. Come, march forward. [*Exeunt.* 200

SCENE III. *Another part of Blackheath.*

Alarums to the fight, wherein both the STAFFORDS *are slain. Enter* CADE *and the rest.*

Cade. Where's Dick, the butcher of Ashford?

Dick. Here, sir.

Cade. They fell before thee like sheep and oxen, and

account. 88. **undo,** ruin; see glossary. 95. **setting . . . copies,** writing out words, etc., as models to be reproduced by boys. 101. **court-hand,** professional hand, used in preparing legal documents. 106. **Emmanuel,** i.e., God with us, used frequently as heading for letters and documents. 119. **particular,** opposed to *general* (l. 118). 166. **span-counter,** a boys' game in which one throws a counter or piece of money that the other wins if he can throw another that hits it or falls within

a span of it. 169-170. **Lord Say,** etc. As treasurer of England, this peer was implicated in the dealings negotiated by Suffolk that resulted in the loss of Anjou and Maine. He, among others, was accused by the irate Commons as one of the agents of the negotiations. 172. **mained,** old form of "maimed." 195. **clouted,** patched (?). **shoon,** shoes.

thou behavedst thyself as if thou hadst been in thine own slaughter-house: therefore thus will I reward thee, the Lent shall be as long again as it is; and thou shalt have a license to kill for a hundred lacking one.

Dick. I desire no more. 10

Cade. And, to speak truth, thou deservest no less. This monument of the victory will I bear [*putting on Sir Humphrey's brigandine*]; and the bodies shall be dragged at my horse heels till I do come to London, where we will have the mayor's sword borne before us.

Dick. If we mean to thrive and do good, break open the gaols and let out the prisoners.

Cade. Fear not that, I warrant thee. Come, let's march towards London. [*Exeunt.* 20

SCENE IV. *London. The palace.*

Enter the KING *with a supplication, and the* QUEEN *with Suffolk's head, the* DUKE OF BUCKINGHAM *and the* LORD SAY.

Queen. Oft have I heard that grief softens the mind
And makes it fearful and degenerate;
Think therefore on revenge and cease to weep.
But who can cease to weep and look on this?
Here may his head lie on my throbbing breast:
But where's the body that I should embrace?

Buck. What answer makes your grace to the rebels' supplication?

King. I'll send some holy bishop to entreat;
For God forbid so many simple souls 10
Should perish by the sword! And I myself,
Rather than bloody war shall cut them short,
Will parley with Jack Cade their general:
But stay, I'll read it over once again.

Queen. Ah, barbarous villains! hath this lovely face
Ruled, like a wandering planet, over me,
And could it not enforce them to relent,
That were unworthy to behold the same?

King. Lord Say, Jack Cade hath sworn to have thy head.

Say. Ay, but I hope your highness shall have his. 20

King. How now, madam!
Still lamenting and mourning for Suffolk's death?
I fear me, love, if that I had been dead,
Thou wouldest not have mourn'd so much for me.

Queen. No, my love, I should not mourn, but die for thee.

Enter a Messenger.

King. How now! what news? why comest thou in such haste?

Mess. The rebels are in Southwark; fly, my lord!
Jack Cade proclaims himself Lord Mortimer,
Descended from the Duke of Clarence' house,
And calls your grace usurper openly 30
And vows to crown himself in Westminster.
His army is a ragged multitude
Of hinds and peasants, rude and merciless:
Sir Humphrey Stafford and his brother's death
Hath given them heart and courage to proceed:

All scholars, lawyers, courtiers, gentlemen,
They call false caterpillars and intend their death.

King. O graceless men! they know not what they do.

Buck. My gracious lord, retire to Killingworth,
Until a power be raised to put them down. 40

Queen. Ah, were the Duke of Suffolk now alive,
These Kentish rebels would be soon appeased!

King. Lord Say, the traitors hate thee;
Therefore away with us to Killingworth.

Say. So might your grace's person be in danger.
The sight of me is odious in their eyes;
And therefore in this city will I stay
And live alone as secret as I may.

Enter another Messenger.

Mess. Jack Cade hath gotten London bridge:
The citizens fly and forsake their houses: 50
The rascal people, thirsting after prey,
Join with the traitor, and they jointly swear
To spoil the city and your royal court.

Buck. Then linger not, my lord; away, take horse.

King. Come, Margaret; God, our hope, will succour us.

Queen. My hope is gone, now Suffolk is deceased.

King. Farewell, my lord: trust not the Kentish rebels.

Buck. Trust nobody, for fear you be betray'd.

Say. The trust I have is in mine innocence,
And therefore am I bold and resolute. [*Exeunt.* 60

SCENE V. *London. The Tower.*

Enter LORD SCALES *upon the Tower, walking. Then enter two or three* Citizens *below.*

Scales. How now! is Jack Cade slain?

First Cit. No, my lord, nor likely to be slain; for they have won the bridge, killing all those that withstand them: the lord mayor craves aid of your honour from the Tower to defend the city from the rebels.

Scales. Such aid as I can spare you shall command;
But I am troubled here with them myself;
The rebels have assay'd to win the Tower.
But get you to Smithfield and gather head, 10
And thither I will send you Matthew Goffe;
Fight for your king, your country and your lives;
And so, farewell, for I must hence again. [*Exeunt.*

SCENE VI. *London. Cannon Street.*

Enter JACK CADE *and the rest, and strikes his staff on London-stone.*

Cade. Now is Mortimer lord of this city. And here, sitting upon London-stone, I charge and command that, of the city's cost, the pissing-conduit run nothing but claret wine this first year of our reign. And now henceforward it shall be treason for any that calls me other than Lord Mortimer.

Enter a Soldier, *running.*

Sold. Jack Cade! Jack Cade!

SCENE III. **7-9. the Lent . . . lacking one.** The eating of flesh during Lent was forbidden in Elizabeth's reign, and killing of beasts at that time was permitted only by special license to provide for invalids (supposedly) unable to dispense with flesh. A license to kill for ninety-nine a week during a doubled Lent would thus constitute a valuable monopoly. *For* in line 9 may mean "at the rate of," allowing Dick to slaughter ninety-nine beasts a week (Tucker Brooke).

SCENE V. **9. assay'd,** attempted; see glossary. **10. head,** an armed force; see glossary.
SCENE VI. **2. London-stone,** according to Camden, the central milestone of the town. (*Shakespeare's England*, II, 165.) **4. pissing-conduit,** popular name of a conduit near the Royal Exchange. (*Ibid.*, note.)
SCENE VII. **2. the Savoy.** This palace, residence of the duke of Lancaster, was destroyed during Wat Tyler's rebellion in 1381. **23.**

Cade. Knock him down there.   [*They kill him.* 9

Smith. If this fellow be wise, he'll never call ye Jack Cade more: I think he hath a very fair warning.

Dick. My lord, there's an army gathered together in Smithfield.

Cade. Come, then, let's go fight with them: but first, go and set London bridge on fire; and, if you can, burn down the Tower too. Come, let's away. [*Exeunt.*

SCENE VII. *London. Smithfield.*

Alarums. MATTHEW GOFFE *is slain, and all the rest. Then enter* JACK CADE, *with his company.*

Cade. So, sirs: now go some and pull down the Savoy; others to the inns of court; down with them all.

Dick. I have a suit unto your lordship.

Cade. Be it a lordship, thou shalt have it for that word.

Dick. Only that the laws of England may come out of your mouth.

Holl. [*Aside*] Mass, 'twill be sore law, then; for he was thrust in the mouth with a spear, and 'tis not whole yet. 11

Smith. [*Aside*] Nay, John, it will be stinking law; for his breath stinks with eating toasted cheese.

Cade. I have thought upon it, it shall be so. Away, burn all the records of the realm: my mouth shall be the parliament of England.

Holl. [*Aside*] Then we are like to have biting statutes, unless his teeth be pulled out.

Cade. And henceforward all things shall be in common. 21

Enter a Messenger.

Mess. My lord, a prize, a prize! here's the Lord Say, which sold the towns in France; he that made us pay one and twenty fifteens, and one shilling to the pound, the last subsidy.

Enter GEORGE BEVIS, *with the* LORD SAY.

Cade. Well, he shall be beheaded for it ten times. Ah, thou say, thou serge, nay, thou buckram lord! now art thou within point-blank of our jurisdiction regal. What canst thou answer to my majesty for giving up of Normandy unto Mounsieur Basimecu, the dauphin of France? Be it known unto thee by these presence, even the presence of Lord Mortimer, that I am the besom that must sweep the court clean of such filth as thou art. Thou hast most traitorously corrupted the youth of the realm in erecting a grammar school: and whereas, before, our forefathers had no other books but the score and the tally, thou hast caused printing to be used, and, contrary to the king, his crown and dignity, thou hast built a paper-mill. It will be proved to thy face that thou hast men about thee that usually talk of a noun and a verb, and such abominable words as no Christian ear can endure to hear. Thou hast appointed justices of peace, to call poor men before them about matters they were not able to answer. Moreover, thou hast put them in prison; and because

they could not read, thou hast hanged them; when, indeed, only for that cause they have been most worthy to live. Thou dost ride in a foot-cloth, dost thou not? 51

Say. What of that?

Cade. Marry, thou oughtest not to let thy horse wear a cloak, when honester men than thou go in their hose and doublets.

Dick. And work in their shirt too; as myself, for example, that am a butcher.

Say. You men of Kent,—

Dick. What say you of Kent? 60

Say. Nothing but this; 'tis 'bona terra, mala gens.'

Cade. Away with him, away with him! he speaks Latin.

Say. Hear me but speak, and bear me where you will.

Kent, in the Commentaries Cæsar writ,
Is term'd the civil'st place of all this isle:
Sweet is the country, because full of riches;
The people liberal, valiant, active, wealthy;
Which makes me hope you are not void of pity.
I sold not Maine, I lost not Normandy, 70
Yet, to recover them, would lose my life.
Justice with favour have I always done;
Prayers and tears have moved me, gifts could never.
When have I aught exacted at your hands,
But to maintain the king, the realm and you?
Large gifts have I bestow'd on learned clerks,
Because my book preferr'd me to the king,
And seeing ignorance is the curse of God,
Knowledge the wing wherewith we fly to heaven,
Unless you be possess'd with devilish spirits, 80
You cannot but forbear to murder me:
This tongue hath parley'd unto foreign kings
For your behoof,—

Cade. Tut, when struck'st thou one blow in the field?

Say. Great men have reaching hands: oft have I struck
Those that I never saw and struck them dead.

Geo. O monstrous coward! what, to come behind folks?

Say. These cheeks are pale for watching for your good. 90

Cade. Give him a box o' the ear and that will make 'em red again.

Say. Long sitting to determine poor men's causes Hath made me full of sickness and diseases.

Cade. Ye shall have a hempen caudle then and the help of hatchet.

Dick. Why dost thou quiver, man?

Say. The palsy, and not fear, provokes me.

Cade. Nay, he nods at us, as who should say, I'll be even with you: I'll see if his head will stand steadier on a pole, or no. Take him away, and behead him. 102

Say. Tell me wherein have I offended most?
Have I affected wealth or honour? speak.
Are my chests fill'd up with extorted gold?
Is my apparel sumptuous to behold?
Whom have I injured, that ye seek my death?
These hands are free from guiltless blood-shedding,

Lord Say. Cf. IV, ii, 169-170, note. **24. one . . . fifteens,** probably a reference to the matter that had been discussed more conservatively by the courtiers; cf. I, i, 131-134. **27, 28. say, serge, buckram,** kinds of cloth. **31. Mounsieur Basimecu,** contemptuous term for a Frenchman. **34. besom,** broom. **39. printing,** an anachronism; the first printing press was set up in England twenty-seven years after Cade's rebellion. **61. 'bona . . . gens,'** good land, bad people. **68. liberal,** refined, having the characteristics of gentlemen; see glossary. **95. caudle,** warm gruel mixed with wine or ale, sweetened and spiced, given to sick people. The implication of the word *hempen* is that his remedy will be hanging.

This breast from harbouring foul deceitful thoughts.
O, let me live! 110

Cade. [*Aside*] I feel remorse in myself with his words; but I'll bridle it: he shall die, an it be for pleading so well for his life. Away with him! he has a familiar under his tongue; he speaks not o' God's name. Go, take him away, I say, and strike off his head presently; and then break into his son-in-law's house, Sir James Cromer, and strike off his head, and bring them both upon two poles hither.

All. It shall be done. 120

Say. Ah, countrymen! if when you make your
        prayers,
God should be so obdurate as yourselves,
How would it fare with your departed souls?
And therefore yet relent, and save my life.

Cade. Away with him! and do as I command ye.
        [*Exeunt some with Lord Say.*
The proudest peer in the realm shall not wear a head on his shoulders, unless he pay me tribute; there shall not a maid be married, but she shall pay to me her maidenhead ere they have it: men shall hold of me in capite; and we charge and command that their wives be as free as heart can wish or tongue can tell. 133

Dick. My lord, when shall we go to Cheapside and take up commodities upon our bills?

Cade. Marry, presently.

All. O, brave!

Re-enter one with the heads.

Cade. But is not this braver? Let them kiss one another, for they loved well when they were alive. Now part them again, lest they consult about the giving up of some more towns in France. Soldiers, defer the spoil of the city until night: for with these borne before us, instead of maces, will we ride through the streets; and at every corner have them kiss. Away!
        [*Exeunt.*

SCENE VIII. *Southwark.*

Alarum and retreat. Enter CADE *and all his rabblement.*

Cade. Up Fish Street! down Saint Magnus' Corner! kill and knock down! throw them into Thames! [*Sound a parley.*] What noise is this I hear? Dare any be so bold to sound retreat or parley, when I command them kill?

Enter BUCKINGHAM *and old* CLIFFORD, *attended.*

Buck. Ay, here they be that dare and will disturb
        thee:
Know, Cade, we come ambassadors from the king
Unto the commons whom thou hast misled;
And here pronounce free pardon to them all
That will forsake thee and go home in peace. 10

Clif. What say ye, countrymen? will ye relent,
And yield to mercy whilst 'tis offer'd you;
Or let a rebel lead you to your deaths?
Who loves the king and will embrace his pardon,
Fling up his cap, and say 'God save his majesty!'
Who hateth him and honours not his father,

Henry the Fifth, that made all France to quake,
Shake he his weapon at us and pass by.

All. God save the king! God save the king! 19

Cade. What, Buckingham and Clifford, are ye so brave? And you, base peasants, do ye believe him? will you needs be hanged with your pardons about your necks? Hath my sword therefore broke through London gates, that you should leave me at the White Hart in Southwark? I thought ye would never have given out these arms till you had recovered your ancient freedom: but you are all recreants and dastards, and delight to live in slavery to the nobility. Let them break your backs with burthens, take your houses over your heads, ravish your wives and daughters before your faces: for me, I will make shift for one; and so, God's curse light upon you all!

All. We'll follow Cade, we'll follow Cade!

Clif. Is Cade the son of Henry the Fifth,
That thus you do exclaim you'll go with him?
Will he conduct you through the heart of France,
And make the meanest of you earls and dukes?
Alas, he hath no home, no place to fly to; 40
Nor knows he how to live but by the spoil,
Unless by robbing of your friends and us.
Were 't not a shame, that whilst you live at jar,
The fearful French, whom you late vanquished,
Should make a start o'er seas and vanquish you?
Methinks already in this civil broil
I see them lording it in London streets,
Crying 'Villiago!' unto all they meet.
Better ten thousand base-born Cades miscarry
Than you should stoop unto a Frenchman's mercy. 50
To France, to France, and get what you have lost;
Spare England, for it is your native coast:
Henry hath money, you are strong and manly;
God on our side, doubt not of victory.

All. A Clifford! a Clifford! we'll follow the king and Clifford.

Cade. Was ever feather so lightly blown to and fro as this multitude? The name of Henry the Fifth hales them to an hundred mischiefs and makes them leave me desolate. I see them lay their heads together to surprise me. My sword make way for me, for here is no staying. In despite of the devils and hell, have through the very middest of you! and heavens and honour be witness that no want of resolution in me, but only my followers' base and ignominious treasons, makes me betake me to my heels. [*Exit.*

Buck. What, is he fled? Go some, and follow him;
And he that brings his head unto the king
Shall have a thousand crowns for his reward. 70
        [*Exeunt some of them.*
Follow me, soldiers: we'll devise a mean
To reconcile you all unto the king. [*Exeunt.*

SCENE IX. *Kenilworth Castle.*

Sound trumpets. Enter KING, QUEEN, *and* SOMERSET, *on the terrace.*

King. Was ever king that joy'd an earthly throne,
And could command no more content than I?

114. **familiar,** familiar spirit; see glossary; cf. *1 Henry VI*, V, iii, 10. 131. **in capite,** legal term: as a tenant in chief, directly from the crown. 135. **bills,** military weapons having wooden handles and a blade or ax-shaped head, with quibble here on the meaning "credit." 137. **brave,** fine; see glossary. 142. **spoil,** plundering; see glossary. 144.

maces, staves of office carried by sergeants.
SCENE VIII. 9. **free,** generous; see glossary. 28. **recreants,** cowardly wretches; see glossary. 32-33. **make shift,** manage; see *shift* in glossary. 48. **'Villiago,'** villain. 64. **have through . . . you,** may I go through the very midst of you. 71. **mean,** means, method; see

No sooner was I crept out of my cradle
But I was made a king, at nine months old.
Was never subject long'd to be a king
As I do long and wish to be a subject.

Enter BUCKINGHAM *and old* CLIFFORD.

Buck. Health and glad tidings to your majesty!
King. Why, Buckingham, is the traitor Cade
  surprised?
Or is he but retired to make him strong?

Enter, below, multitudes, with halters about their necks.

Clif. He is fled, my lord, and all his powers do yield;
And humbly thus, with halters on their necks,   11
Expect your highness' doom, of life or death.
King. Then, heaven, set ope thy everlasting gates,
To entertain my vows of thanks and praise!
Soldiers, this day have you redeem'd your lives
And show'd how well you love your prince and
  country:
Continue still in this so good a mind,
And Henry, though he be infortunate,
Assure yourselves, will never be unkind:
And so, with thanks and pardon to you all,   20
I do dismiss you to your several countries.
All. God save the king! God save the king!

Enter a Messenger.

Mess. Please it your grace to be advertised
The Duke of York is newly come from Ireland,
And with a puissant and a mighty power
Of gallowglasses and stout kerns
Is marching hitherward in proud array,
And still proclaimeth, as he comes along,
His arms are only to remove from thee
The Duke of Somerset, whom he terms a traitor.   30
King. Thus stands my state, 'twixt Cade and York
  distress'd;
Like to a ship that, having 'scaped a tempest,
Is straightway calm'd and boarded with a pirate:
But now is Cade driven back, his men dispersed;
And now is York in arms to second him.
I pray thee, Buckingham, go and meet him,
And ask him what 's the reason of these arms.
Tell him I'll send Duke Edmund to the Tower;
And, Somerset, we will commit thee thither,
Until his army be dismiss'd from him.   40
Som. My lord,
I'll yield myself to prison willingly,
Or unto death, to do my country good.
King. In any case, be not too rough in terms;
For he is fierce and cannot brook hard language.
Buck. I will, my lord; and doubt not so to deal
As all things shall redound unto your good.
King. Come, wife, let 's in, and learn to govern
  better;
For yet may England curse my wretched reign.
                            [*Flourish. Exeunt.*

SCENE X. *Kent. Iden's garden.*

Enter CADE.

Cade. Fie on ambition! fie on myself, that have a
sword, and yet am ready to famish! These five days
have I hid me in these woods and durst not peep out,
for all the country is laid for me; but now am I so
hungry that if I might have a lease of my life for a
thousand years I could stay no longer. Wherefore, on
a brick wall have I climbed into this garden, to see if
I can eat grass, or pick a sallet another while, which
is not amiss to cool a man's stomach this hot weather.
And I think this word 'sallet' was born to do me
good: for many a time, but for a sallet, my brain-pan
had been cleft with a brown bill; and many a time,
when I have been dry and bravely marching, it
hath served me instead of a quart pot to drink in;
and now the word 'sallet' must serve me to feed on.

Enter IDEN.

Iden. Lord, who would live turmoiled in the court,
And may enjoy such quiet walks as these?
This small inheritance my father left me   20
Contenteth me, and worth a monarchy.
I seek not to wax great by others' waning,
Or gather wealth, I care not, with what envy:
Sufficeth that I have maintains my state
And sends the poor well pleased from my gate.
Cade. Here 's the lord of the soil come to seize me
for a stray, for entering his fee-simple without leave.
Ah, villain, thou wilt betray me, and get a thousand
crowns of the king by carrying my head to him: but
I'll make thee eat iron like an ostrich, and swallow
my sword like a great pin, ere thou and I part.   32
Iden. Why, rude companion, whatsoe'er thou be,
I know thee not; why, then, should I betray thee?
Is 't not enough to break into my garden,
And, like a thief, to come to rob my grounds,
Climbing my walls in spite of me the owner,
But thou wilt brave me with these saucy terms?
Cade. Brave thee! ay, by the best blood that ever
was broached, and beard thee too. Look on me well:
I have eat no meat these five days; yet, come thou and
thy five men, and if I do not leave you all as dead as
a doornail, I pray God I may never eat grass more. 44
Iden. Nay, it shall ne'er be said, while England
  stands,
That Alexander Iden, an esquire of Kent,
Took odds to combat a poor famish'd man.
Oppose thy steadfast-gazing eyes to mine,
See if thou canst outface me with thy looks:
Set limb to limb, and thou art far the lesser;   50
Thy hand is but a finger to my fist,
Thy leg a stick compared with this truncheon;
My foot shall fight with all the strength thou hast;
And if mine arm be heaved in the air,
Thy grave is digg'd already in the earth.
As for words, whose greatness answers words,
Let this my sword report what speech forbears.
Cade. By my valour, the most complete champion
that ever I heard! Steel, if thou turn the edge, or cut
not out the burly-boned clown in chines of beef ere
thou sleep in thy sheath, I beseech God on my knees
thou mayst be turned to hobnails.
                            [*Here they fight. Cade falls.*

O, I am slain! famine and no other hath slain me:
let ten thousand devils come against me, and give me
but the ten meals I have lost, and I 'ld defy them all.
Wither, garden; and be henceforth a burying-place
to all that do dwell in this house, because the unconquered soul of Cade is fled.   70

Iden. Is 't Cade that I have slain, that monstrous
traitor?
Sword, I will hallow thee for this thy deed,
And hang thee o'er my tomb when I am dead:
Ne'er shall this blood be wiped from thy point;
But thou shalt wear it as a herald's coat,
To emblaze the honour that thy master got.

Cade. Iden, farewell, and be proud of thy victory.
Tell Kent from me, she hath lost her best man, and
exhort all the world to be cowards; for I, that never
feared any, am vanquished by famine, not by valour.
[*Dies.*

Iden. How much thou wrong'st me, heaven be my
judge.   82
Die, damned wretch, the curse of her that bare thee;
And as I thrust thy body in with my sword,
So wish I, I might thrust thy soul to hell.
Hence will I drag thee headlong by the heels
Unto a dunghill which shall be thy grave,
And there cut off thy most ungracious head;
Which I will bear in triumph to the king,
Leaving thy trunk for crows to feed upon.   [*Exit.* 90

ACT V.

SCENE I. *Fields between Dartford and Blackheath.*

Enter YORK, *and his army of Irish, with drum and colours.*

York. From Ireland thus comes York to claim his
right,
And pluck the crown from feeble Henry's head:
Ring, bells, aloud; burn, bonfires, clear and bright,
To entertain great England's lawful king.
Ah! sancta majestas, who would not buy thee dear?
Let them obey that know not how to rule;
This hand was made to handle nought but gold.
I cannot give due action to my words,
Except a sword or sceptre balance it:
A sceptre shall it have, have I a soul,   10
On which I'll toss the flower-de-luce of France.

Enter BUCKINGHAM.

Whom have we here? Buckingham, to disturb me?
The king hath sent him, sure: I must dissemble.

Buck. York, if thou meanest well, I greet thee well.

York. Humphrey of Buckingham, I accept thy
greeting.
Art thou a messenger, or come of pleasure?

Buck. A messenger from Henry, our dread liege,
To know the reason of these arms in peace;
Or why thou, being a subject as I am,
Against thy oath and true allegiance sworn,   20
Should raise so great a power without his leave,

Or dare to bring thy force so near the court.

York. [*Aside*] Scarce can I speak, my choler is so
great:
O, I could hew up rocks and fight with flint,
I am so angry at these abject terms;
And now, like Ajax Telamonius,
On sheep or oxen could I spend my fury.
I am far better born than is the king,
More like a king, more kingly in my thoughts:
But I must make fair weather yet a while,   30
Till Henry be more weak and I more strong.—
Buckingham, I prithee, pardon me,
That I have given no answer all this while;
My mind was troubled with deep melancholy.
The cause why I have brought this army hither
Is to remove proud Somerset from the king,
Seditious to his grace and to the state.

Buck. That is too much presumption on thy part:
But if thy arms be to no other end,
The king hath yielded unto thy demand: 40
The Duke of Somerset is in the Tower.

York. Upon thine honour, is he prisoner?

Buck. Upon mine honour, he is prisoner.

York. Then, Buckingham, I do dismiss my powers.
Soldiers, I thank you all; disperse yourselves;
Meet me to-morrow in Saint George's field,
You shall have pay and every thing you wish.
And let my sovereign, virtuous Henry,
Command my eldest son, nay, all my sons,
As pledges of my fealty and love;   50
I'll send them all as willing as I live:
Lands, goods, horse, armour, any thing I have,
Is his to use, so Somerset may die.

Buck. York, I commend this kind submission:
We twain will go into his highness' tent.

Enter KING *and* Attendants.

King. Buckingham, doth York intend no harm to us,
That thus he marcheth with thee arm in arm?

York. In all submission and humility
York doth present himself unto your highness.

King. Then what intends these forces thou dost
bring?   60

York. To heave the traitor Somerset from hence,
And fight against that monstrous rebel Cade,
Who since I heard to be discomfited.

Enter IDEN, *with* CADE's *head.*

Iden. If one so rude and of so mean condition
May pass into the presence of a king,
Lo, I present your grace a traitor's head,
The head of Cade, whom I in combat slew.

King. The head of Cade! Great God, how just art
Thou!
O, let me view his visage, being dead,
That living wrought me such exceeding trouble.   70
Tell me, my friend, art thou the man that slew him?

Iden. I was, an 't like your majesty.

King. How art thou call'd? and what is thy degree?

Iden. Alexander Iden, that 's my name;
A poor esquire of Kent, that loves his king.

ACT V. SCENE I.   4. **England's lawful king.** York's claims are rehearsed by the dying Mortimer in *1 Henry VI*, II, v, 63-97, and again
by York himself in *2 Henry VI*, II, ii, 9-52.   5. **sancta majestas,** sacred
majesty.   10. **have I a soul,** i.e., as I have a soul.   11. **toss,** carry
aloft on the point of a pike.   13. **dissemble,** assume a false appearance.
25. **abject,** servile.   26. **Ajax Telamonius,** Ajax, son of Telamon, one

of the Greek heroes of the Trojan War. When the weapons of Achilles
were allotted to Ulysses, Ajax in his fury slaughtered a flock of sheep.
64. **condition,** rank; see glossary.   100. **Achilles' spear.** Telephus,
wounded by Achilles' spear, learned from an oracle that he could be
cured only by the wounder. He was eventually cured by an application
of rust from the point of the spear.   117. **Neapolitan.** The queen's

Buck. So please it you, my lord, 'twere not amiss
He were created knight for his good service.
    King. Iden, kneel down. [*He kneels.*] Rise up a
        knight.
We give thee for reward a thousand marks,
And will that thou henceforth attend on us.   80
    Iden. May Iden live to merit such a bounty,
And never live but true unto his liege!   [*Rises.*

Enter QUEEN *and* SOMERSET.

    King. See, Buckingham, Somerset comes with the
        queen:
Go, bid her hide him quickly from the duke.
    Queen. For thousand Yorks he shall not hide his
        head,
But boldly stand and front him to his face.
    York. How now! is Somerset at liberty?
Then, York, unloose thy long-imprison'd thoughts,
And let thy tongue be equal with thy heart.
Shall I endure the sight of Somerset?   90
False king! why hast thou broken faith with me,
Knowing how hardly I can brook abuse?
King did I call thee? no, thou art not king,
Not fit to govern and rule multitudes,
Which darest not, no, nor canst not rule a traitor.
That head of thine doth not become a crown;
Thy hand is made to grasp a palmer's staff,
And not to grace an awful princely sceptre.
That gold must round engirt these brows of mine,
Whose smile and frown, like to Achilles' spear, 100
Is able with the change to kill and cure.
Here is a hand to hold a sceptre up
And with the same to act controlling laws.
Give place: by heaven, thou shalt rule no more
O'er him whom heaven created for thy ruler.
    Som. O monstrous traitor! I arrest thee, York,
Of capital treason 'gainst the king and crown:
Obey, audacious traitor; kneel for grace.
    York. Wouldst have me kneel? first let me ask of
        these,
If they can brook I bow a knee to man.   110
Sirrah, call in my sons to be my bail: [*Exit Attendant.*
I know, ere they will have me go to ward,
They'll pawn their swords for my enfranchisement.
    Queen. Call hither Clifford; bid him come amain,
To say if that the bastard boys of York
Shall be the surety for their traitor father.
                                      [*Exit Buckingham.*
    York. O blood-bespotted Neapolitan,
Outcast of Naples, England's bloody scourge!
The sons of York, thy betters in their birth,
Shall be their father's bail; and bane to those 120
That for my surety will refuse the boys!

Enter EDWARD *and* RICHARD.

See where they come: I'll warrant they'll make it
    good.

Enter old CLIFFORD *and his* Son.

    Queen. And here comes Clifford to deny their bail.

Clif. Health and all happiness to my lord the king!
                                            [*Kneels.*
    York. I thank thee, Clifford: say, what news with
        thee?
Nay, do not fright us with an angry look:
We are thy sovereign, Clifford, kneel again;
For thy mistaking so, we pardon thee.
    Clif. This is my king, York, I do not mistake;
But thou mistakest me much to think I do: 130
To Bedlam with him! is the man grown mad?
    King. Ay, Clifford; a bedlam and ambitious
        humour
Makes him oppose himself against his king.
    Clif. He is a traitor; let him to the Tower,
And chop away that factious pate of his.
    Queen. He is arrested, but will not obey;
His sons, he says, shall give their words for him.
    York. Will you not, sons?
    Edw. Ay, noble father, if our words will serve. 139
    Rich. And if words will not, then our weapons shall.
    Clif. Why, what a brood of traitors have we here!
    York. Look in a glass, and call thy image so:
I am thy king, and thou a false-heart traitor.
Call hither to the stake my two brave bears,
That with the very shaking of their chains
They may astonish these fell-lurking curs:
Bid Salisbury and Warwick come to me.

Enter the EARLS OF WARWICK *and* SALISBURY.

    Clif. Are these thy bears? we'll bait thy bears to
        death,
And manacle the bear-ward in their chains,
If thou darest bring them to the baiting place.   150
    Rich. Oft have I seen a hot o'erweening cur
Run back and bite, because he was withheld;
Who, being suffer'd with the bear's fell paw,
Hath clapp'd his tail between his legs and cried:
And such a piece of service will you do,
If you oppose yourselves to match Lord Warwick.
    Clif. Hence, heap of wrath, foul indigested lump,
As crooked in thy manners as thy shape!
    York. Nay, we shall heat you thoroughly anon.
    Clif. Take heed, lest by your heat you burn
        yourselves.   160
    King. Why, Warwick, hath thy knee forgot to bow?
Old Salisbury, shame to thy silver hair,
Thou mad misleader of thy brain-sick son!
What, wilt thou on thy death-bed play the ruffian,
And seek for sorrow with thy spectacles?
O, where is faith? O, where is loyalty?
If it be banish'd from the frosty head,
Where shall it find a harbour in the earth?
Wilt thou go dig a grave to find out war,
And shame thine honourable age with blood?   170
Why art thou old, and want'st experience?
Or wherefore dost abuse it, if thou hast it?
For shame! in duty bend thy knee to me
That bows unto the grave with mickle age.
    Sal. My lord, I have consider'd with myself
The title of this most renowned duke;
And in my conscience do repute his grace

father was titular king of Naples. 123. **deny,** refuse; see glossary.
131. **Bedlam,** hospital of St. Mary of Bethlehem in London, used as an
asylum for the mentally deranged. The common noun in the next line
means an inmate of Bedlam, or an insane person. 144. **brave bears.**
Cf. lines 202-203 below, where Warwick describes the badge of his
house. The passage here is a metaphor from the popular Elizabethan
sport of bearbaiting. 153. **being suffer'd,** having been injured. 157.
indigested, ill-formed. 158. **As . . . shape.** Young Richard, later King
Richard III, was a hunchback. References to his deformity grow more
and more pointed as this cycle of plays proceeds. 159. **anon,** soon; see
glossary. 172. **abuse,** put to a bad use; see glossary.

The rightful heir to England's royal seat.

King. Hast thou not sworn allegiance unto me?

Sal. I have.   180

King. Canst thou dispense with heaven for such an
oath?

Sal. It is great sin to swear unto a sin,
But greater sin to keep a sinful oath.
Who can be bound by any solemn vow
To do a murderous deed, to rob a man,
To force a spotless virgin's chastity,
To reave the orphan of his patrimony,
To wring the widow from her custom'd right,
And have no other reason for this wrong
But that he was bound by a solemn oath?   190

Queen. A subtle traitor needs no sophister.

King. Call Buckingham, and bid him arm himself.

York. Call Buckingham, and all the friends thou
hast,
I am resolved for death or dignity.

Clif. The first I warrant thee, if dreams prove true.

War. You were best to go to bed and dream again,
To keep thee from the tempest of the field.

Clif. I am resolved to bear a greater storm
Than any thou canst conjure up to-day;
And that I'll write upon thy burgonet,   200
Might I but know thee by thy household badge.

War. Now, by my father's badge, old Nevil's crest,
The rampant bear chain'd to the ragged staff,
This day I'll wear aloft my burgonet,
As on a mountain top the cedar shows
That keeps his leaves in spite of any storm,
Even to affright thee with the view thereof.

Clif. And from thy burgonet I'll rend thy bear
And tread it under foot with all contempt,
Despite the bear-ward that protects the bear.   210

Y. Clif. And so to arms, victorious father,
To quell the rebels and their complices.

Rich. Fie! charity, for shame! speak not in spite,
For you shall sup with Jesu Christ to-night.

Y. Clif. Foul stigmatic, that 's more than thou canst
tell.

Rich. If not in heaven, you'll surely sup in hell.
                                                          [*Exeunt severally.*

SCENE II. *Saint Alban's.*

Alarums to the battle. Enter WARWICK.

War. Clifford of Cumberland, 'tis Warwick calls:
And if thou dost not hide thee from the bear,
Now, when the angry trumpet sounds alarum
And dead men's cries do fill the empty air,
Clifford, I say, come forth and fight with me:
Proud northern lord, Clifford of Cumberland,
Warwick is hoarse with calling thee to arms.

Enter YORK.

How now, my noble lord! what, all afoot?

York. The deadly-handed Clifford slew my steed,
But match to match I have encounter'd him   10
And made a prey for carrion kites and crows

Even of the bonny beast he loved so well.

Enter old CLIFFORD.

War. Of one or both of us the time is come.

York. Hold, Warwick, seek thee out some other
chase,
For I myself must hunt this deer to death.

War. Then, nobly, York; 'tis for a crown thou
fight'st.
As I intend, Clifford, to thrive to-day,
It grieves my soul to leave thee unassail'd.   [*Exit.*

Clif. What seest thou in me, York? why dost thou
pause?

York. With thy brave bearing should I be in love,   20
But that thou art so fast mine enemy.

Clif. Nor should thy prowess want praise and
esteem,
But that 'tis shown ignobly and in treason.

York. So let it help me now against thy sword
As I in justice and true right express it.

Clif. My soul and body on the action both!

York. A dreadful lay! Address thee instantly.
                          [*They fight, and Clifford falls.*

Clif. La fin couronne les œuvres.   [*Dies.*

York. Thus war hath given thee peace, for thou art
still.
Peace with his soul, heaven, if it be thy will!   [*Exit.* 30

Enter young CLIFFORD.

Y. Clif. Shame and confusion! all is on the rout;
Fear frames disorder, and disorder wounds
Where it should guard. O war, thou son of hell,
Whom angry heavens do make their minister,
Throw in the frozen bosoms of our part
Hot coals of vengeance! Let no soldier fly.
He that is truly dedicate to war
Hath no self-love, nor he that loves himself
Hath not essentially but by circumstance
The name of valour. [*Seeing his dead father*] O, let the
vile world end,   40
And the premised flames of the last day
Knit earth and heaven together!
Now let the general trumpet blow his blast,
Particularities and petty sounds
To cease! Wast thou ordain'd, dear father,
To lose thy youth in peace, and to achieve
The silver livery of advised age,
And, in thy reverence and thy chair-days, thus
To die in ruffian battle? Even at this sight
My heart is turn'd to stone: and while 'tis mine,   50
It shall be stony. York not our old men spares;
No more will I their babes: tears virginal
Shall be to me even as the dew to fire,
And beauty that the tyrant oft reclaims
Shall to my flaming wrath be oil and flax.
Henceforth I will not have to do with pity:
Meet I an infant of the house of York,
Into as many gobbets will I cut it
As wild Medea young Absyrtus did:
In cruelty will I seek out my fame.   60
Come, thou new ruin of old Clifford's house:

182-190. **It is great sin,** etc. A parallel to this kind of casuistry occurs in *King John,* III, i, 268-273. 191. **sophister,** cunning or caviling disputer (Cotgrave). 200. **burgonet,** light casque or steel cap. 215. **stigmatic,** one branded by nature with deformity.
SCENE II. 21. **fast,** completely. 26. **action,** outcome of action. 27. **lay,** wager, oath. **Address thee,** prepare yourself. 28. **La fin . . . œuvres,** the end crowns the work. 32. **frames,** causes. 35. **part.**

party, faction; see *party* in glossary. 39. **not . . . circumstance,** not by any virtue of his own, but accidentally. 41. **premised,** foreordained. 44. **Particularities,** individual affairs. 48. **chair-days,** old age, days of inactivity. 54. **reclaims,** reduces to obedience. 59. **Medea,** daughter of Aeëtes, king of Colchis, who helped Jason recover the Golden Fleece. She fled with him and, to delay her father's pursuit, killed her brother Absyrtus and left his dismembered body in the father's path.

As did Æneas old Anchises bear,
So bear I thee upon my manly shoulders;
But then Æneas bare a living load,
Nothing so heavy as these woes of mine.
                    [*Exit, bearing off his father.*

Enter RICHARD *and* SOMERSET *to fight.* SOMERSET *is
    killed.*

Rich. So, lie thou there;
For underneath an alehouse' paltry sign,
The Castle in Saint Alban's, Somerset
Hath made the wizard famous in his death.
Sword, hold thy temper; heart, be wrathful still: 70
Priests pray for enemies, but princes kill.   [*Exit.*

Fight: excursions. Enter KING, QUEEN, *and others.*

Queen. Away, my lord! you are slow; for shame,
    away!
King. Can we outrun the heavens? good Margaret,
    stay.
Queen. What are you made of? you'll nor fight nor
    fly:
Now is it manhood, wisdom and defence,
To give the enemy way, and to secure us
By what we can, which can no more but fly.
                    [*Alarum afar off.*
If you be ta'en, we then should see the bottom
Of all our fortunes: but if we haply scape,
As well we may, if not through your neglect,   80
We shall to London get, where you are loved
And where this breach now in our fortunes made
May readily be stopp'd.

        Re-enter young CLIFFORD.

Y. Clif. But that my heart 's on future mischief set,
I would speak blasphemy ere bid you fly:
But fly you must; uncurable discomfit
Reigns in the hearts of all our present parts.
Away, for your relief! and we will live
To see their day and them our fortune give:
Away, my lord, away!   [*Exeunt.* 90

SCENE III. *Fields near St. Alban's.*

Alarum. Retreat. Enter YORK, RICHARD, WARWICK,
    and Soldiers, with drum and colours.

York. Of Salisbury, who can report of him,
That winter lion, who in rage forgets
Aged contusions and all brush of time,
And, like a gallant in the brow of youth,
Repairs him with occasion? This happy day
Is not itself, nor have we won one foot,
If Salisbury be lost.
Rich.   My noble father,
Three times to-day I holp him to his horse,
Three times bestrid him; thrice I led him off,
Persuaded him from any further act: 10
But still, where danger was, still there I met him;
And like rich hangings in a homely house,
So was his will in his old feeble body.
But, noble as he is, look where he comes.

Enter SALISBURY.

Sal. Now, by my sword, well hast thou fought
    to-day;
By the mass, so did we all. I thank you, Richard:
God knows how long it is I have to live;
And it hath pleased him that three times to-day
You have defended me from imminent death.
Well, lords, we have not got that which we have: 20
'Tis not enough our foes are this time fled,
Being opposites of such repairing nature.
York. I know our safety is to follow them;
For, as I hear, the king is fled to London,
To call a present court of parliament.
Let us pursue him ere the writs go forth.
What says Lord Warwick? shall we after them?
War. After them! nay, before them, if we can.
Now, by my faith, lords, 'twas a glorious day:
Saint Alban's battle won by famous York   30
Shall be eternized in all age to come.
Sound drums and trumpets, and to London all:
And more such days as these to us befall!   [*Exeunt.*

---

62. **Æneas, Anchises.** Aeneas, fleeing from Troy, carried his aged
father on his shoulders; cf. *Julius Caesar*, I, ii, 112-114. 64. **bare,**
bore; archaic past tense. 65. **Nothing,** not at all; see glossary.
67-69. **underneath . . . death.** Cf. I, iv, 38-40. 87. **our present parts,**
those now adhering to our party.

SCENE III. 5. **Repairs . . . occasion,** i.e., occasion stimulates him so
that his strength is renewed. 8. **holp,** helped; see glossary. 22.
opposites, adversaries. **repairing,** that recover easily. 25. **present,**
instant; see glossary. 26. **the writs,** official summons issued by the
king to members of Parliament.

At Tewkesburye was fought the last battell betwene King Edward .4. and K. Henry
6. wherin prince Edward ÿ generall was slaine. and Quene Margaret ÿ maintayner
of these quarels taken prisoner. ther died also in ÿ battayll Tho: E. of Deuonshire. Iohn Mar:
Dorset. ÿ L. Wenlake. & Edmund D. of Somerset ther taken & beheaded. This was fought. 1471.

THE THIRD PART OF

King Henry the Sixth

DRAMATIS PERSONAE

KING HENRY the Sixth.
EDWARD, PRINCE OF WALES, his son.
LEWIS XI. KING OF FRANCE.
DUKE OF SOMERSET.
DUKE OF EXETER.
EARL OF OXFORD.
EARL OF NORTHUMBERLAND.
EARL OF WESTMORELAND.
LORD CLIFFORD.
RICHARD PLANTAGENET, Duke of York.
EDWARD, Earl of March, afterwards
  King Edward IV.,
EDMUND, Earl of Rutland,   his
GEORGE, afterwards Duke of Clarence,   sons.
RICHARD, afterwards Duke of Gloucester,
DUKE OF NORFOLK.
MARQUESS OF MONTAGUE.
EARL OF WARWICK.
EARL OF PEMBROKE.
LORD HASTINGS.
LORD STAFFORD.
SIR JOHN MORTIMER,   uncles to the Duke
SIR HUGH MORTIMER,   of York.
HENRY, Earl of Richmond, a youth.
LORD RIVERS, brother to Lady Grey.
SIR WILLIAM STANLEY.
SIR JOHN MONTGOMERY.
SIR JOHN SOMERVILLE.
Tutor to Rutland. Mayor of York.
Lieutenant of the Tower. A Nobleman.
Two Keepers. A Huntsman.
A Son that has killed his father.
A Father that has killed his son.

QUEEN MARGARET.
LADY GREY, afterwards Queen to Edward IV.
BONA, sister to the French Queen.

Soldiers, Attendants, Messengers, Watchmen,
  &c.

SCENE: *England and France.*

ACT I.

SCENE I. *London. The Parliament-house.*

Alarum. Enter the DUKE OF YORK, EDWARD, RICHARD,
NORFOLK, MONTAGUE, WARWICK, *and soldiers.*

War. I wonder how the king escaped our hands.
York. While we pursued the horsemen of the north,
He slily stole away and left his men:
Whereat the great Lord of Northumberland,
Whose warlike ears could never brook retreat,

Cheer'd up the drooping army; and himself,
Lord Clifford and Lord Stafford, all abreast,
Charged our main battle's front, and breaking in
Were by the swords of common soldiers slain.
    Edw. Lord Stafford's father, Duke of Buckingham, 10
Is either slain or wounded dangerously;
I cleft his beaver with a downright blow:
That this is true, father, behold his blood.
    Mont. And, brother, here 's the Earl of Wiltshire's
      blood,
Whom I encounter'd as the battles join'd.
    Rich. Speak thou for me and tell them what I did.
          [*Throwing down the Duke of Somerset's head.*
    York. Richard hath best deserved of all my sons.
But is your grace dead, my Lord of Somerset?
    Norf. Such hope have all the line of John of Gaunt!
    Rich. Thus do I hope to shake King Henry's head. 20
    War. And so do I. Victorious Prince of York,
Before I see thee seated in that throne
Which now the house of Lancaster usurps,
I vow by heaven these eyes shall never close.
This is the palace of the fearful king,
And this the regal seat: possess it, York;
For this is thine and not King Henry's heirs'.
    York. Assist me, then, sweet Warwick, and I will;
For hither we have broken in by force.
    Norf. We'll all assist you; he that flies shall die.   30
    York. Thanks, gentle Norfolk: stay by me, my lords;
And, soldiers, stay and lodge by me this night.
                       [*They go up.*
    War. And when the king comes, offer him no
      violence,
Unless he seek to thrust you out perforce.
    York. The queen this day here holds her parliament,
But little thinks we shall be of her council:
By words or blows here let us win our right.
    Rich. Arm'd as we are, let 's stay within this house.
    War. The bloody parliament shall this be call'd,
Unless Plantagenet, Duke of York, be king,   40
And bashful Henry deposed, whose cowardice
Hath made us by-words to our enemies.
    York. Then leave me not, my lords; be resolute;
I mean to take possession of my right.
    War. Neither the king, nor he that loves him best,
The proudest he that holds up Lancaster,
Dares stir a wing, if Warwick shake his bells.
I'll plant Plantagenet, root him up who dares:
Resolve thee, Richard; claim the English crown.

    Flourish. Enter KING HENRY, CLIFFORD, NORTHUM-
BERLAND, WESTMORELAND, EXETER, *and the rest.*

    K. Hen. My lords, look where the sturdy rebel sits, 50
Even in the chair of state: belike he means,
Back'd by the power of Warwick, that false peer,
To aspire unto the crown and reign as king.
Earl of Northumberland, he slew thy father,
And thine, Lord Clifford; and you both have vow'd
      revenge

ACT I. SCENE I. 4, 7. **Lord of Northumberland, Lord Clifford, Lord
Stafford.** There are some historical discrepancies here. Northumberland, Stafford, and Clifford (i.e., the Young Clifford of *2 Henry VI*)
were killed at the Battle of Towton on Palm Sunday, 1461; but that
battle is presented dramatically below (II, iii-vi; Clifford dies in scene
vi). York's account here appears to be of the Battle of St. Albans,
where Old Clifford was killed. As to the two Staffords, the one mentioned here (l. 7) was Sir Harry, a Lancastrian sympathizer and son
of the duke of Buckingham. The Lord Stafford of this play is Sir
Humphrey, a York partisan who was raised to the peerage by Edward
IV after the attainder of Sir Harry Stafford for opposition to the Yorkists.

Or him, his sons, his favourites and his friends.
North. If I be not, heavens be revenged on me!
Clif. The hope thereof makes Clifford mourn in
steel.
West. What, shall we suffer this? let 's pluck him
down:
My heart for anger burns; I cannot brook it.   60
K. Hen. Be patient, gentle Earl of Westmoreland.
Clif. Patience is for poltroons, such as he:
He durst not sit there, had your father lived.
My gracious lord, here in the parliament
Let us assail the family of York.
North. Well hast thou spoken, cousin: be it so.
K. Hen. Ah, know you not the city favours them,
And they have troops of soldiers at their beck?
Exe. But when the duke is slain, they'll quickly fly.
K. Hen. Far be the thought of this from Henry's
heart,   70
To make a shambles of the parliament-house!
Cousin of Exeter, frowns, words and threats
Shall be the war that Henry means to use.
Thou factious Duke of York, descend my throne,
And kneel for grace and mercy at my feet;
I am thy sovereign.
York.   I am thine.
Exe. For shame, come down: he made thee Duke of
York.
York. 'Twas my inheritance, as the earldom was.
Exe. Thy father was a traitor to the crown.
War. Exeter, thou art a traitor to the crown   80
In following this usurping Henry.
Clif. Whom should he follow but his natural king?
War. True, Clifford; and that 's Richard Duke of
York.
K. Hen. And shall I stand, and thou sit in my throne?
York. It must and shall be so: content thyself.
War. Be Duke of Lancaster; let him be king.
West. He is both king and Duke of Lancaster;
And that the Lord of Westmoreland shall maintain.
War. And Warwick shall disprove it. You forget
That we are those which chased you from the field   90
And slew your fathers, and with colours spread
March'd through the city to the palace gates.
North. Yes, Warwick, I remember it to my grief;
And, by his soul, thou and thy house shall rue it.
West. Plantagenet, of thee and these thy sons,
Thy kinsmen and thy friends, I'll have more lives
Than drops of blood were in my father's veins.
Clif. Urge it no more; lest that, instead of words,
I send thee, Warwick, such a messenger
As shall revenge his death before I stir.   100
War. Poor Clifford! how I scorn his worthless
threats!
York. Will you we show our title to the crown?
If not, our swords shall plead it in the field.
K. Hen. What title hast thou, traitor, to the crown?
Thy father was, as thou art, Duke of York;
Thy grandfather, Roger Mortimer, Earl of March:

I am the son of Henry the Fifth,
Who made the Dauphin and the French to stoop
And seized upon their towns and provinces.
War. Talk not of France, sith thou hast lost it all.   110
K. Hen. The lord protector lost it, and not I:
When I was crown'd I was but nine months old.
Rich. You are old enough now, and yet, methinks,
you lose.
Father, tear the crown from the usurper's head.
Edw. Sweet father, do so; set it on your head.
Mont. Good brother, as thou lovest and honourest
arms,
Let 's fight it out and not stand cavilling thus.
Rich. Sound drums and trumpets, and the king will
fly.
York. Sons, peace!
K. Hen. Peace, thou! and give King Henry leave to
speak.   120
War. Plantagenet shall speak first: hear him, lords;
And be you silent and attentive too,
For he that interrupts him shall not live.
K. Hen. Think'st thou that I will leave my kingly
throne,
Wherein my grandsire and my father sat?
No: first shall war unpeople this my realm;
Ay, and their colours, often borne in France,
And now in England to our heart's great sorrow,
Shall be my winding-sheet. Why faint you, lords?
My title 's good, and better far than his.   130
War. Prove it, Henry, and thou shalt be king.
K. Hen. Henry the Fourth by conquest got the
crown.
York. 'Twas by rebellion against his king.
K. Hen. [*Aside*] I know not what to say; my title 's
weak.—
Tell me, may not a king adopt an heir?
York. What then?
K. Hen. An if he may, then am I lawful king;
For Richard, in the view of many lords,
Resign'd the crown to Henry the Fourth,
Whose heir my father was, and I am his.   140
York. He rose against him, being his sovereign,
And made him to resign his crown perforce.
War. Suppose, my lords, he did it unconstrain'd,
Think you 'twere prejudicial to his crown?
Exe. No; for he could not so resign his crown
But that the next heir should succeed and reign.
K. Hen. Art thou against us, Duke of Exeter?
Exe. His is the right, and therefore pardon me.
York. Why whisper you, my lords, and answer not?
Exe. My conscience tells me he is lawful king.   150
K. Hen. [*Aside*] All will revolt from me, and turn to
him.
North. Plantagenet, for all the claim thou lay'st,
Think not that Henry shall be so deposed.
War. Deposed he shall be, in despite of all.
North. Thou art deceived: 'tis not thy southern
power,

5. **brook,** endure; see glossary.   **retreat,** i.e., the call sounding retreat.
8. **battle's,** army's; see glossary.   12. **beaver,** face guard of a helmet.
14. **And, brother.** Montague was brother to Warwick. His father (Salisbury of *2 Henry VI*) was brother-in-law of York; cf. I, i, 209, note.
18. **But . . . Somerset?** Is it really true that Somerset is dead?   19. **all
. . . Gaunt.** Somerset was the grandson of John of Gaunt and Catherine
Swynford. This malediction falls, of course, on King Henry VI, great-grandson of Gaunt.   34. **perforce,** forcibly; see glossary.   40. **be,**
become.   41. **bashful,** easily cowed.   45-46. **he . . . Lancaster,** any
of the Lancastrian party.   47. **shake his bells,** a metaphor from
falconry; bells were sometimes fastened to the legs of the hawk.   49.

Resolve thee, be resolved, resolute; see glossary.   62. **poltroons,** arrant
cowards.   66. **cousin,** any relative not of one's immediate family; see
glossary.   77-78. **he . . . was.** Cf. *1 Henry VI,* III, i, 163-173, where the
king restored to Richard the whole inheritance of the house of York,
which included the earldom of March.   79. **Thy . . . traitor.** Cf. *Henry
V,* II, ii; *1 Henry VI,* II, iv, 90-94; II, v, 84-91.   105. **Thy . . . York,**
a historical inaccuracy; Richard's father was never duke of York; cf.
1 Henry VI, II, iv, 83, note.   110. **sith,** since; see glossary.   129.
winding-sheet, sheet in which a corpse was wrapped.

Of Essex, Norfolk, Suffolk, nor of Kent,
Which makes thee thus presumptuous and proud,
Can set the duke up in despite of me.
    Clif. King Henry, be thy title right or wrong,
Lord Clifford vows to fight in thy defence: 160
May that ground gape and swallow me alive,
Where I shall kneel to him that slew my father!
    K. Hen. O Clifford, how thy words revive my heart!
    York. Henry of Lancaster, resign thy crown.
What mutter you, or what conspire you, lords?
    War. Do right unto this princely Duke of York,
Or I will fill the house with armed men,
And over the chair of state, where now he sits,
Write up his title with usurping blood.
    [*He stamps with his foot, and the Soldiers show themselves.*
    K. Hen. My Lord of Warwick, hear me but one
        word: 170
Let me for this my life-time reign as king.
    York. Confirm the crown to me and to mine heirs,
And thou shalt reign in quiet while thou livest.
    King. I am content: Richard Plantagenet,
Enjoy the kingdom after my decease.
    Clif. What wrong is this unto the prince your son!
    War. What good is this to England and himself!
    West. Base, fearful and despairing Henry!
    Clif. How hast thou injured both thyself and us!
    West. I cannot stay to hear these articles. 180
    North. Nor I.
    Clif. Come, cousin, let us tell the queen these news.
    West. Farewell, faint-hearted and degenerate king,
In whose cold blood no spark of honour bides.
    North. Be thou a prey unto the house of York,
And die in bands for this unmanly deed!
    Clif. In dreadful war mayst thou be overcome,
Or live in peace abandon'd and despised!
    [*Exeunt North., Clif., and West.*
    War. Turn this way, Henry, and regard them not.
    Exe. They seek revenge and therefore will not yield.
    K. Hen. Ah, Exeter!
    War.   Why should you sigh, my lord?
    K. Hen. Not for myself, Lord Warwick, but my son,
Whom I unnaturally shall disinherit.
But be it as it may: I here entail
The crown to thee and to thine heirs for ever;
Conditionally, that here thou take an oath
To cease this civil war, and, whilst I live,
To honour me as thy king and sovereign,
And neither by treason nor hostility
To seek to put me down and reign thyself. 200
    York. This oath I willingly take and will perform.
    War. Long live King Henry! Plantagenet, embrace
        him.
    K. Hen. And long live thou and these thy forward
        sons!
    York. Now York and Lancaster are reconciled.
    Exe. Accursed be he that seeks to make them foes!
    [*Sennet. Here they come down.*
    York. Farewell, my gracious lord; I'll to my castle.
    War. And I'll keep London with my soldiers.
    Norf. And I to Norfolk with my followers.

    Mont. And I unto the sea from whence I came.
    [*Exeunt York and his Sons, Warwick, Norfolk,
        Montague, their Soldiers, and Attendants.*
    K. Hen. And I, with grief and sorrow, to the court. 210

Enter QUEEN MARGARET *and the* PRINCE OF WALES.

    Exe. Here comes the queen, whose looks bewray her
        anger:
I'll steal away.
    K. Hen.   Exeter, so will I.
    Q. Mar. Nay, go not from me; I will follow thee.
    K. Hen. Be patient, gentle queen, and I will stay.
    Q. Mar. Who can be patient in such extremes?
Ah, wretched man! would I had died a maid,
And never seen thee, never borne thee son,
Seeing thou hast proved so unnatural a father!
Hath he deserved to lose his birthright thus?
Hadst thou but loved him half so well as I, 220
Or felt that pain which I did for him once,
Or nourish'd him as I did with my blood,
Thou wouldst have left thy dearest heart-blood there,
Rather than have made that savage duke thine heir
And disinherited thine only son.
    Prince. Father, you cannot disinherit me:
If you be king, why should not I succeed?
    K. Hen. Pardon me, Margaret; pardon me, sweet
        son:
The Earl of Warwick and the duke enforced me.
    Q. Mar. Enforced thee! art thou king, and wilt be
        forced? 230
I shame to hear thee speak. Ah, timorous wretch!
Thou hast undone thyself, thy son and me;
And given unto the house of York such head
As thou shalt reign but by their sufferance.
To entail him and his heirs unto the crown,
What is it, but to make thy sepulchre
And creep into it far before thy time?
Warwick is chancellor and the lord of Calais;
Stern Falconbridge commands the narrow seas;
The duke is made protector of the realm; 240
And yet shalt thou be safe? such safety finds
The trembling lamb environed with wolves.
Had I been there, which am a silly woman,
The soldiers should have toss'd me on their pikes
Before I would have granted to that act.
But thou preferr'st thy life before thine honour:
And seeing thou dost, I here divorce myself
Both from thy table, Henry, and thy bed,
Until that act of parliament be repeal'd
Whereby my son is disinherited. 250
The northern lords that have forsworn thy colours
Will follow mine, if once they see them spread;
And spread they shall be, to thy foul disgrace
And utter ruin of the house of York.
Thus do I leave thee. Come, son, let's away;
Our army is ready; come, we'll after them.
    K. Hen. Stay, gentle Margaret, and hear me speak.
    Q. Mar. Thou hast spoke too much already: get thee
        gone.
    K. Hen. Gentle son Edward, thou wilt stay with me?

---

186. **bands,** fetters, bonds; see glossary. 193. **unnaturally,** contrary to nature. 203. **forward,** ardent, zealous. 205. *Stage Direction:* **Sennet,** series of notes sounded on a trumpet to announce the approach of a procession; see glossary. 209. **unto the sea.** Cf. l. 239. Tucker Brooke points out a possible amalgamation of the roles of Montague and Faulconbridge. The latter was York's brother-in-law (cf. I, i, 14),

who during this period controlled Calais and the Strait of Dover. Montague did not come from or return to the sea, as this speech represents him as doing. Mention of Faulconbridge, moreover, does not occur anywhere else in the play. 215. **patient,** pronounced as trisyllabic. 232. **undone,** ruined; see glossary. 233. **head,** headway. 243. **silly,** helpless. 245. **granted,** yielded. 269. **Tire,** prey upon.

Q. Mar. Ay, to be murder'd by his enemies.   260
Prince. When I return with victory from the field
I'll see your grace: till then I'll follow her.
Q. Mar. Come, son, away; we may not linger thus.
          [*Exeunt Queen Margaret and the Prince.*
K. Hen. Poor queen! how love to me and to her son
Hath made her break out into terms of rage!
Revenged may she be on that hateful duke,
Whose haughty spirit, winged with desire,
Will cost my crown, and like an empty eagle
Tire on the flesh of me and of my son!
The loss of those three lords torments my heart: 270
I'll write unto them and entreat them fair.
Come, cousin, you shall be the messenger.
Exe. And I, I hope, shall reconcile them all. [*Exeunt.*

SCENE II. *Sandal Castle.*

Enter RICHARD, EDWARD, *and* MONTAGUE.

Rich. Brother, though I be youngest, give me leave.
Edw. No, I can better play the orator.
Mont. But I have reasons strong and forcible.

Enter the DUKE OF YORK.

York. Why, how now, sons and brother! at a strife?
What is your quarrel? how began it first?
Edw. No quarrel, but a slight contention.
York. About what?
Rich. About that which concerns your grace and us;
The crown of England, father, which is yours.
York. Mine, boy? not till King Henry be dead.   10
Rich. Your right depends not on his life or death.
Edw. Now you are heir, therefore enjoy it now:
By giving the house of Lancaster leave to breathe,
It will outrun you, father, in the end.
York. I took an oath that he should quietly reign.
Edw. But for a kingdom any oath may be broken:
I would break a thousand oaths to reign one year.
Rich. No; God forbid your grace should be forsworn.
York. I shall be, if I claim by open war.
Rich. I'll prove the contrary, if you'll hear me speak.
York. Thou canst not, son; it is impossible.   21
Rich. An oath is of no moment, being not took
Before a true and lawful magistrate,
That hath authority over him that swears:
Henry had none, but did usurp the place;
Then, seeing 'twas he that made you to depose,
Your oath, my lord, is vain and frivolous.
Therefore, to arms! And, father, do but think
How sweet a thing it is to wear a crown;
Within whose circuit is Elysium   30
And all that poets feign of bliss and joy.
Why do we linger thus? I cannot rest
Until the white rose that I wear be dyed
Even in the lukewarm blood of Henry's heart.
York. Richard, enough; I will be king, or die.
Brother, thou shalt to London presently,
And whet on Warwick to this enterprise.
Thou, Richard, shalt to the Duke of Norfolk,

And tell him privily of our intent.
You, Edward, shall unto my Lord Cobham,   40
With whom the Kentishmen will willingly rise:
In them I trust; for they are soldiers,
Witty, courteous, liberal, full of spirit.
While you are thus employ'd, what resteth more,
But that I seek occasion how to rise,
And yet the king not privy to my drift,
Nor any of the house of Lancaster?

Enter a Messenger.

But, stay: what news? Why comest thou in such post?
Mess. The queen with all the northern earls and
          lords
Intend here to besiege you in your castle: 50
She is hard by with twenty thousand men;
And therefore fortify your hold, my lord.
York. Ay, with my sword. What! think'st thou that
          we fear them?
Edward and Richard, you shall stay with me;
My brother Montague shall post to London:
Let noble Warwick, Cobham, and the rest,
Whom we have left protectors of the king,
With powerful policy strengthen themselves,
And trust not simple Henry nor his oaths.
Mont. Brother, I go; I'll win them, fear it not: 60
And thus most humbly I do take my leave.   [*Exit.*

Enter SIR JOHN MORTIMER *and* SIR HUGH MORTIMER.

York. Sir John and Sir Hugh Mortimer, mine uncles,
You are come to Sandal in a happy hour;
The army of the queen mean to besiege us.
Sir John. She shall not need; we'll meet her in the
          field.
York. What, with five thousand men?
Rich. Ay, with five hundred, father, for a need:
A woman 's general; what should we fear?
          [*A march afar off.*
Edw. I hear their drums: let 's set our men in order,
And issue forth and bid them battle straight.   70
York. Five men to twenty! though the odds be great,
I doubt not, uncle, of our victory.
Many a battle have I won in France,
When as the enemy hath been ten to one:
Why should I not now have the like success?
          [*Alarum. Exeunt.*

SCENE III. *Field of battle betwixt Sandal Castle
and Wakefield.*

Alarums. Enter RUTLAND *and his* Tutor.

Rut. Ah, whither shall I fly to 'scape their hands?
Ah, tutor, look where bloody Clifford comes!

Enter CLIFFORD *and* Soldiers.

Clif. Chaplain, away! thy priesthood saves thy life.
As for the brat of this accursed duke,
Whose father slew my father, he shall die.
Tut. And I, my lord, will bear him company.

271. **fair,** civilly, kindly; see glossary.
    SCENE II. 4. **brother.** Cf. I, i, 14; I, i, 209, stage direction. 22.
moment, significance. 26. **depose,** take an oath. 30. **Elysium,**
according to Greek mythology, the abode of good souls, a realm of
complete happiness. The passage suggests Marlowe's *Tamburlaine.*
36. **presently,** immediately; see glossary. 43. **liberal,** possessed of

qualities of gentlemen; see glossary. 48. **stay,** stop, wait; see glossary.
post, haste; see glossary. 52. **hold,** stronghold. 58. **powerful policy,**
power gained by craft; see *policy* in glossary. 70. **straight,** immediately; see glossary.

Clif. Soldiers, away with him!

Tut. Ah, Clifford, murder not this innocent child,
Lest thou be hated both of God and man!

[Exit, dragged off by Soldiers.

Clif. How now! is he dead already? or is it fear   10
That makes him close his eyes? I'll open them.

Rut. So looks the pent-up lion o'er the wretch
That trembles under his devouring paws;
And so he walks, insulting o'er his prey,
And so he comes, to rend his limbs asunder.
Ah, gentle Clifford, kill me with thy sword,
And not with such a cruel threatening look.
Sweet Clifford, hear me speak before I die.
I am too mean a subject for thy wrath:
Be thou revenged on men, and let me live.   20

Clif. In vain thou speak'st, poor boy; my father's
        blood
Hath stopp'd the passage where thy words should
        enter.

Rut. Then let my father's blood open it again:
He is a man, and, Clifford, cope with him.

Clif. Had I thy brethren here, their lives and thine
Were not revenge sufficient for me;
No, if I digg'd up thy forefathers' graves
And hung their rotten coffins up in chains,
It could not slake mine ire, nor ease my heart.
The sight of any of the house of York   30
Is as a fury to torment my soul;
And till I root out their accursed line
And leave not one alive, I live in hell.
Therefore—   *[Lifting his hand.*

Rut. O, let me pray before I take my death!
To thee I pray; sweet Clifford, pity me!

Clif. Such pity as my rapier's point affords.

Rut. I never did thee harm: why wilt thou slay me?

Clif. Thy father hath.

Rut.   But 'twas ere I was born.
Thou hast one son; for his sake pity me,   40
Lest in revenge thereof, sith God is just,
He be as miserably slain as I.
Ah, let me live in prison all my days;
And when I give occasion of offence,
Then let me die, for now thou hast no cause.

Clif. No cause!
Thy father slew my father; therefore, die.   *[Stabs him.*

Rut. Di faciant laudis summa sit ista tuæ!   *[Dies.*

Clif. Plantagenet! I come, Plantagenet!
And this thy son's blood cleaving to my blade   50
Shall rust upon my weapon, till thy blood,
Congeal'd with this, do make me wipe off both.   *[Exit.*

SCENE IV. *Another part of the field.*

Alarum. Enter RICHARD, Duke of York.

York. The army of the queen hath got the field:
My uncles both are slain in rescuing me;
And all my followers to the eager foe
Turn back and fly, like ships before the wind

Or lambs pursued by hunger-starved wolves.
My sons, God knows what hath bechanced them:
But this I know, they have demean'd themselves
Like men born to renown by life or death.
Three times did Richard make a lane to me,
And thrice cried 'Courage, father! fight it out!'   10
And full as oft came Edward to my side,
With purple falchion, painted to the hilt
In blood of those that had encounter'd him:
And when the hardiest warriors did retire,
Richard cried, 'Charge! and give no foot of ground!'
And cried 'A crown, or else a glorious tomb!
A sceptre, or an earthly sepulchre!'
With this, we charged again: but, out, alas!
We bodged again; as I have seen a swan
With bootless labour swim against the tide   20
And spend her strength with over-matching waves.

[A short alarum within.

Ah, hark! the fatal followers do pursue;
And I am faint and cannot fly their fury:
And were I strong, I would not shun their fury:
The sands are number'd that make up my life;
Here must I stay, and here my life must end.

Enter QUEEN MARGARET, CLIFFORD, NORTHUM-
BERLAND, *the* young Prince, *and* Soldiers.

Come, bloody Clifford, rough Northumberland,
I dare your quenchless fury to more rage:
I am your butt, and I abide your shot.

North. Yield to our mercy, proud Plantagenet.   30

Clif. Ay, to such mercy as his ruthless arm,
With downright payment, show'd unto my father.
Now Phaëthon hath tumbled from his car,
And made an evening at the noontide prick.

York. My ashes, as the phœnix, may bring forth
A bird that will revenge upon you all:
And in that hope I throw mine eyes to heaven,
Scorning whate'er you can afflict me with.
Why come you not? what! multitudes, and fear?

Clif. So cowards fight when they can fly no further;
So doves do peck the falcon's piercing talons;   41
So desperate thieves, all hopeless of their lives,
Breathe out invectives 'gainst the officers.

York. O Clifford, but bethink thee once again,
And in thy thought o'er-run my former time;
And, if thou canst for blushing, view this face,
And bite thy tongue, that slanders him with
        cowardice
Whose frown hath made thee faint and fly ere this!

Clif. I will not bandy with thee word for word,
But buckle with thee blows, twice two for one.   50

Q. Mar. Hold, valiant Clifford! for a thousand
        causes
I would prolong awhile the traitor's life.
Wrath makes him deaf: speak thou, Northumberland.

North. Hold, Clifford! do not honour him so much
To prick thy finger, though to wound his heart:
What valour were it, when a cur doth grin,
For one to thrust his hand between his teeth,
When he might spurn him with his foot away?
It is war's prize to take all vantages;

SCENE III.   14. **insulting**, gloating.   19. **mean**, of low degree; see glossary.   24. **cope with**, encounter; see glossary.   29. **slake**, relieve, assuage.   48. **Di . . . tuæ!** The gods grant that this may be the height of thy glory!
SCENE IV.   12. **falchion**, sword somewhat curved, with the edge on the convex side.   18. **out**, an expression of reproach; see glossary.   19. **bodged**, gave way.   29. **butt**, target; archery term.   33. **Phaëthon**, son of Phoebus. Prompted by pride, he begged his father to allow him to drive the chariot of the sun. Incapable of handling the fiery horses, he soon wandered from the proper course and came so near to the earth that it was threatened with destruction. Zeus hurled a thunderbolt at him to stop his disastrous course.   34. **noontide prick**, exact point of noon on a sundial.   35. **as the phœnix**. Cf. note to *1 Henry VI*, IV, vii, 93.   50. **buckle**, join in close combat.   60. **impeach**, act

And ten to one is no impeach of valour. 60
[*They lay hands on York, who struggles.*
Clif. Ay, ay, so strives the woodcock with the gin.
North. So doth the cony struggle in the net.
York. So triumph thieves upon their conquer'd
    booty;
So true men yield, with robbers so o'ermatch'd.
    North. What would your grace have done unto him
    now?
    Q. Mar. Brave warriors, Clifford and
    Northumberland,
Come, make him stand upon this molehill here,
That raught at mountains with outstretched arms,
Yet parted but the shadow with his hand.
What! was it you that would be England's king? 70
Was 't you that revell'd in our parliament,
And made a preachment of your high descent?
Where are your mess of sons to back you now?
The wanton Edward, and the lusty George?
And where 's that valiant crook-back prodigy,
Dicky your boy, that with his grumbling voice
Was wont to cheer his dad in mutinies?
Or, with the rest, where is your darling Rutland?
Look, York! I stain'd this napkin with the blood
That valiant Clifford, with his rapier's point, 80
Made issue from the bosom of the boy;
And if thine eyes can water for his death,
I give thee this to dry thy cheeks withal.
Alas, poor York! but that I hate thee deadly,
I should lament thy miserable state.
I prithee, grieve, to make me merry, York.
What, hath thy fiery heart so parch'd thine entrails
That not a tear can fall for Rutland's death?
Why art thou patient, man? thou shouldst be mad;
And I, to make thee mad, do mock thee thus. 90
Stamp, rave, and fret, that I may sing and dance.
Thou wouldst be fee'd, I see, to make me sport:
York cannot speak, unless he wear a crown.
A crown for York! and, lords, bow low to him:
Hold you his hands, whilst I do set it on.
[*Putting a paper crown on his head.*
Ay, marry, sir, now looks he like a king!
Ay, this is he that took King Henry's chair,
And this is he was his adopted heir.
But how is it that great Plantagenet
Is crown'd so soon, and broke his solemn oath? 100
As I bethink me, you should not be king
Till our King Henry had shook hands with death.
And will you pale your head in Henry's glory,
And rob his temples of the diadem,
Now in his life, against your holy oath?
O, 'tis a fault too too unpardonable!
Off with the crown; and, with the crown, his head;
And, whilst we breathe, take time to do him dead.
    Clif. That is my office, for my father's sake.
    Q. Mar. Nay, stay; let 's hear the orisons he makes.
    York. She-wolf of France, but worse than wolves of
    France, 111
Whose tongue more poisons than the adder's tooth!
How ill-beseeming is it in thy sex
To triumph, like an Amazonian trull,

Upon their woes whom fortune captivates!
But that thy face is, visard-like, unchanging,
Made impudent with use of evil deeds,
I would assay, proud queen, to make thee blush.
To tell thee whence thou camest, of whom derived,
Were shame enough to shame thee, wert thou not
    shameless. 120
Thy father bears the type of King of Naples,
Of both the Sicils and Jerusalem,
Yet not so wealthy as an English yeoman.
Hath that poor monarch taught thee to insult?
It needs not, nor it boots thee not, proud queen,
Unless the adage must be verified,
That beggars mounted run their horse to death.
'Tis beauty that doth oft make women proud;
But, God he knows, thy share thereof is small:
'Tis virtue that doth make them most admired; 130
The contrary doth make thee wonder'd at:
'Tis government that makes them seem divine;
The want thereof makes thee abominable:
Thou art as opposite to every good
As the Antipodes are unto us,
Or as the south to the septentrion.
O tiger's heart wrapt in a woman's hide!
How couldst thou drain the life-blood of the child,
To bid the father wipe his eyes withal,
And yet be seen to bear a woman's face? 140
Women are soft, mild, pitiful and flexible;
Thou stern, obdurate, flinty, rough, remorseless.
Bid'st thou me rage? why, now thou hast thy wish:
Wouldst have me weep? why, now thou hast thy will:
For raging wind blows up incessant showers,
And when the rage allays, the rain begins.
These tears are my sweet Rutland's obsequies:
And every drop cries vengeance for his death,
'Gainst thee, fell Clifford, and thee, false
    Frenchwoman.
    North. Beshrew me, but his passion moves me so 150
That hardly can I check my eyes from tears.
    York. That face of his the hungry cannibals
Would not have touch'd, would not have stain'd
    with blood:
But you are more inhuman, more inexorable,
O, ten times more, than tigers of Hyrcania.
See, ruthless queen, a hapless father's tears:
This cloth thou dip'dst in blood of my sweet boy,
And I with tears do wash the blood away.
Keep thou the napkin, and go boast of this:
And if thou tell'st the heavy story right, 160
Upon my soul, the hearers will shed tears;
Yea even my foes will shed fast-falling tears,
And say 'Alas, it was a piteous deed!'
There, take the crown, and, with the crown, my
    curse;
And in thy need such comfort come to thee
As now I reap at thy too cruel hand!
Hard-hearted Clifford, take me from the world:
My soul to heaven, my blood upon your heads!
    North. Had he been slaughter-man to all my kin,
I should not for my life but weep with him, 170
To see how inly sorrow gripes his soul.

of calling in question. 61. **woodcock,** stupid bird; type of stupidity. 62. **cony,** rabbit. 68. **raught,** reached. 77. **cheer,** incite. 79. **napkin,** handkerchief; see glossary. 110. **orisons,** prayers. 114. **trull,** prostitute. 117. **with use of,** accustomed to; see *use* in glossary. 118. **assay,** attempt; see glossary. 125. **boots,** profits; see glossary. 135. **Antipodes,** parts of the globe diametrically opposite. 136. **septentrion,** north. 137. **O . . . hide.** This line has been made famous by Greene's

application of it in the often-quoted allusion to Shakespeare—"the only Shake-scene of a country": "O Tyger's heart wrapt in a Players hide." 141. **pitiful,** capable of pity. 150. **passion,** grief; see glossary. 151. **check,** keep; see glossary. 155. **Hyrcania,** region of the ancient Persian empire, reputed to abound in wild beasts. 171. **inly,** inwardly.

Q. Mar. What, weeping-ripe, my Lord
    Northumberland?
Think but upon the wrong he did us all,
And that will quickly dry thy melting tears.
    Clif. Here 's for my oath, here 's for my father's
    death.   *[Stabbing him.*
    Q. Mar. And here 's to right our gentlehearted
    king.   *[Stabbing him.*
    York. Open Thy gate of mercy, gracious God!
My soul flies through these wounds to seek out Thee.
                        [Dies.
    Q. Mar. Off with his head, and set it on York gates;
So York may overlook the town of York.   180
                  [Flourish. Exeunt.

ACT II.

SCENE I. *A plain near Mortimer's Cross in Herefordshire.*

A march. Enter EDWARD, RICHARD, *and their power.*

    Edw. I wonder how our princely father 'scaped,
Or whether he be 'scaped away or no
From Clifford's and Northumberland's pursuit:
Had he been ta'en, we should have heard the news;
Had he been slain, we should have heard the news;
Or had he 'scaped, methinks we should have heard
The happy tidings of his good escape.
How fares my brother? why is he so sad?
    Rich. I cannot joy, until I be resolved
Where our right valiant father is become.   10
I saw him in the battle range about;
And watch'd him how he singled Clifford forth.
Methought he bore him in the thickest troop
As doth a lion in a herd of neat;
Or as a bear, encompass'd round with dogs,
Who having pinch'd a few and made them cry,
The rest stand all aloof, and bark at him.
So fared our father with his enemies;
So fled his enemies my warlike father:
Methinks, 'tis prize enough to be his son.   20
See how the morning opes her golden gates,
And takes her farewell of the glorious sun!
How well resembles it the prime of youth,
Trimm'd like a younker prancing to his love!
    Edw. Dazzle mine eyes, or do I see three suns?
    Rich. Three glorious suns, each one a perfect sun;
Not separated with the racking clouds,
But sever'd in a pale clear-shining sky.
See, see! they join, embrace, and seem to kiss,
As if they vow'd some league inviolable: 30
Now are they but one lamp, one light, one sun.
In this the heaven figures some event.
    Edw. 'Tis wondrous strange, the like yet never
    heard of.
I think it cites us, brother, to the field,

That we, the sons of brave Plantagenet,
Each one already blazing by our meeds,
Should notwithstanding join our lights together
And over-shine the earth as this the world.
Whate'er it bodes, henceforward will I bear
Upon my target three fair-shining suns.   40
    Rich. Nay, bear three daughters: by your leave I
    speak it,
You love the breeder better than the male.

Enter a Messenger.

But what art thou, whose heavy looks foretell
Some dreadful story hanging on thy tongue?
    Mess. Ah, one that was a wofui looker-on
When as the noble Duke of York was slain,
Your princely father and my loving lord!
    Edw. O, speak no more, for I have heard too much.
    Rich. Say how he died, for I will hear it all.
    Mess. Environed he was with many foes,   50
And stood against them, as the hope of Troy
Against the Greeks that would have enter'd Troy.
But Hercules himself must yield to odds;
And many strokes, though with a little axe,
Hew down and fell the hardest-timber'd oak.
By many hands your father was subdued;
But only slaughter'd by the ireful arm
Of unrelenting Clifford and the queen,
Who crown'd the gracious duke in high despite,
Laugh'd in his face; and when with grief he wept,   60
The ruthless queen gave him to dry his cheeks
A napkin steeped in the harmless blood
Of sweet young Rutland, by rough Clifford slain:
And after many scorns, many foul taunts,
They took his head, and on the gates of York
They set the same; and there it doth remain,
The saddest spectacle that e'er I view'd.
    Edw. Sweet Duke of York, our prop to lean upon,
Now thou art gone, we have no staff, no stay.
O Clifford, boisterous Clifford! thou hast slain   70
The flower of Europe for his chivalry;
And treacherously hast thou vanquish'd him,
For hand to hand he would have vanquish'd thee.
Now my soul's palace is become a prison:
Ah, would she break from hence, that this my body
Might in the ground be closed up in rest!
For never henceforth shall I joy again,
Never, O never, shall I see more joy!
    Rich. I cannot weep; for all my body's moisture
Scarce serves to quench my furnace-burning heart: 80
Nor can my tongue unload my heart's great burthen;
For selfsame wind that I should speak withal
Is kindling coals that fires all my breast,
And burns me up with flames that tears would
    quench.
To weep is to make less the depth of grief:
Tears then for babes; blows and revenge for me!
Richard, I bear thy name; I'll venge thy death,

---

178. **My . . . wounds.** The soul was believed to issue from the body through an aperture, as the mouth (with the last breath) or a wound (with the outflow of blood).
ACT II. SCENE I. 9. **resolved,** informed; see glossary. 10. **Where . . . become,** what is become of. 14. **neat,** cattle. 16. **pinch'd,** bit. 19. **fled his enemies,** his enemies fled from. 24. **younker,** youngling. 25. **three suns.** Holinshed records that Edward "met with his enemies in a faire plaine neere to Mortimers crosse, not far from Hereford east, on Candlemasse daie in the morning. At which time the sun (as some write) appeared to the earle of March like three sunnes, and suddenlie ioined altogither in one. Upon which sight he took such courage, that

he, fiercelie setting on his enemies, put them to flight: and for this cause men imagined that he gaue the sunne in his full brightness for his badge or cognisance." 27. **racking,** driving. 32. **figures,** prefigures. 34. **cites,** impels, incites. 36. **meeds,** worth, deserts. 40. **target,** shield; see glossary. 49. **I will hear it all.** The character of Richard begins to reveal itself as a hard, relentless personality as his position in the play becomes more prominent. He is later (III, ii, 124-195) to emerge as a thoroughgoing Machiavel, a character which he maintains throughout this play and its sequel, *Richard III*. 51. **hope of Troy,** Hector. 59. **despite,** scorn. 68-69. **Sweet . . . stay.** Tucker Brooke calls attention to the similarity of these lines to a passage in Marlowe's

Or die renowned by attempting it.

Edw. His name that valiant duke hath left with
thee;
His dukedom and his chair with me is left. 90

Rich. Nay, if thou be that princely eagle's bird,
Show thy descent by gazing 'gainst the sun:
For chair and dukedom, throne and kingdom say;
Either that is thine, or else thou wert not his.

March. Enter WARWICK, MARQUESS OF MONTAGUE,
and their army.

War. How now, fair lords! What fare? what news
abroad?
Rich. Great Lord of Warwick, if we should recount
Our baleful news, and at each word's deliverance
Stab poniards in our flesh till all were told,
The words would add more anguish than the wounds.
O valiant lord, the Duke of York is slain! 100

Edw. O Warwick, Warwick! that Plantagenet,
Which held thee dearly as his soul's redemption,
Is by the stern Lord Clifford done to death.

War. Ten days ago I drown'd these news in tears;
And now, to add more measure to your woes,
I come to tell you things sith then befall'n.
After the bloody fray at Wakefield fought,
Where your brave father breathed his latest gasp,
Tidings, as swiftly as the posts could run,
Were brought me of your loss and his depart. 110
I, then in London, keeper of the king,
Muster'd my soldiers, gather'd flocks of friends,
And very well appointed, as I thought,
March'd toward Saint Alban's to intercept the queen,
Bearing the king in my behalf along;
For by my scouts I was advertised
That she was coming with a full intent
To dash our late decree in parliament
Touching King Henry's oath and your succession.
Short tale to make, we at Saint Alban's met, 120
Our battles join'd, and both sides fiercely fought:
But whether 'twas the coldness of the king,
Who look'd full gently on his warlike queen,
That robb'd my soldiers of their heated spleen;
Or whether 'twas report of her success;
Or more than common fear of Clifford's rigour,
Who thunders to his captives blood and death,
I cannot judge: but, to conclude with truth,
Their weapons like to lightning came and went;
Our soldiers', like the night-owl's lazy flight, 130
Or like an idle thresher with a flail,
Fell gently down, as if they struck their friends.
I cheer'd them up with justice of our cause,
With promise of high pay and great rewards:
But all in vain; they had no heart to fight,
And we in them no hope to win the day;
So that we fled; the king unto the queen;
Lord George your brother, Norfolk and myself,
In haste, post-haste, are come to join with you;

For in the marches here we heard you were, 140
Making another head to fight again.

Edw. Where is the Duke of Norfolk, gentle
Warwick?
And when came George from Burgundy to England?
War. Some six miles off the duke is with the
soldiers;
And for your brother, he was lately sent
From your kind aunt, Duchess of Burgundy,
With aid of soldiers to this needful war.

Rich. 'Twas odds, belike, when valiant Warwick
fled:
Oft have I heard his praises in pursuit,
But ne'er till now his scandal of retire. 150

War. Nor now my scandal, Richard, dost thou
hear;
For thou shalt know this strong right hand of mine
Can pluck the diadem from faint Henry's head,
And wring the awful sceptre from his fist,
Were he as famous and as bold in war
As he is famed for mildness, peace, and prayer.

Rich. I know it well, Lord Warwick; blame me not:
'Tis love I bear thy glories makes me speak.
But in this troublous time what's to be done?
Shall we go throw away our coats of steel, 160
And wrap our bodies in black mourning gowns,
Numbering our Ave-Maries with our beads?
Or shall we on the helmets of our foes
Tell our devotion with revengeful arms?
If for the last, say ay, and to it, lords.

War. Why, therefore Warwick came to seek you
out;
And therefore comes my brother Montague.
Attend me, lords. The proud insulting queen,
With Clifford and the haught Northumberland,
And of their feather many moe proud birds, 170
Have wrought the easy-melting king like wax.
He swore consent to your succession,
His oath enrolled in the parliament;
And now to London all the crew are gone,
To frustrate both his oath and what beside
May make against the house of Lancaster.
Their power, I think, is thirty thousand strong:
Now, if the help of Norfolk and myself,
With all the friends that thou, brave Earl of March,
Amongst the loving Welshmen canst procure, 180
Will but amount to five and twenty thousand,
Why, Via! to London will we march amain,
And once again bestride our foaming steeds,
And once again cry 'Charge upon our foes!'
But never once again turn back and fly.

Rich. Ay, now methinks I hear great Warwick
speak:
Ne'er may he live to see a sunshine day,
That cries 'Retire,' if Warwick bid him stay.

Edw. Lord Warwick, on thy shoulder will I lean;
And when thou fail'st—as God forbid the hour!— 190

Massacre at Paris: "Sweet Duke of Guise, our prop to leane vpon, Now thou art dead, heere is no stay for vs." 72. **treacherously,** sometimes the equivalent of "cowardly," which it seems to be here. 79-84. **I . . . quench.** This passage is not a conceit but a literal description of the effects of anger, which, according to Elizabethan psychologists, "maketh the blood to boil in our hearts" and "puts the whole body into a fire and fever." (Charron, *Of Wisdom,* Bk. I, Ch. XXV.) 90. **his chair,** the throne. 92. **gazing . . . sun.** Hart quotes from Holland's Pliny: ". . . the Aegle . . . to prove and trie her yong birds, useth to force them for to look directly upon the sunne. . . ." 95. **What fare?** How do our fortunes fare? 98. **poniards,** daggers. 110. **depart,** departure, i.e.,

death; see glossary. 115. **in my behalf,** in my army, on my side. 116. **advertised,** informed. 124. **heated spleen,** courage roused to a high pitch; see *spleen* in glossary. 138. **Lord George,** third son of York, next younger than Edmund Earl of Rutland; subsequently duke of Clarence. 140. **the marches,** the borders of Wales. 141. **head,** armed force; see glossary. 148. **'Twas odds,** i.e., the odds were against you. 164. **Tell,** count, continuing the figure from line 162; see glossary. 167. **my brother Montague.** Cf. I, i, 209, note. 169. **haught,** haughty. 170. **moe,** more; see glossary. 176. **make,** be effective; see glossary. 179. **brave Earl of March,** addressed to Edward, who at his father's death inherited this with other titles. 182. **amain,** with full force or speed.

Must Edward fall, which peril heaven forfend!
War. No longer Earl of March, but Duke of York:
The next degree is England's royal throne;
For King of England shalt thou be proclaim'd
In every borough as we pass along;
And he that throws not up his cap for joy
Shall for the fault make forfeit of his head.
King Edward, valiant Richard, Montague,
Stay we no longer, dreaming of renown,
But sound the trumpets, and about our task. 200
Rich. Then, Clifford, were thy heart as hard as
steel,
As thou hast shown it flinty by thy deeds,
I come to pierce it, or to give thee mine.
Edw. Then strike up drums: God and Saint George
for us!

Enter a Messenger.

War. How now! what news?
Mess. The Duke of Norfolk sends you word by me,
The queen is coming with a puissant host;
And craves your company for speedy counsel.
War. Why then it sorts, brave warriors, let 's away.
[*Exeunt.*

SCENE II. *Before York.*

Flourish. Enter KING HENRY, QUEEN MARGARET,
the PRINCE OF WALES, CLIFFORD, *and* NORTH-
UMBERLAND, *with drum and trumpets.*

Q. Mar. Welcome, my lord, to this brave town of
York.
Yonder 's the head of that arch-enemy
That sought to be encompass'd with your crown:
Doth not the object cheer your heart, my lord?
K. Hen. Ay, as the rocks cheer them that fear their
wreck:
To see this sight, it irks my very soul.
Withhold revenge, dear God! 'tis not my fault,
Nor wittingly have I infringed my vow.
Clif. My gracious liege, this too much lenity
And harmful pity must be laid aside. 10
To whom do lions cast their gentle looks?
Not to the beast that would usurp their den.
Whose hand is that the forest bear doth lick?
Not his that spoils her young before her face.
Who 'scapes the lurking serpent's mortal sting?
Not he that sets his foot upon her back.
The smallest worm will turn being trodden on,
And doves will peck in safeguard of their brood.
Ambitious York did level at thy crown,
Thou smiling while he knit his angry brows: 20
He, but a duke, would have his son a king,
And raise his issue, like a loving sire;
Thou, being a king, blest with a goodly son,
Didst yield consent to disinherit him,
Which argued thee a most unloving father.
Unreasonable creatures feed their young;
And though man's face be fearful to their eyes,
Yet, in protection of their tender ones,

Who hath not seen them, even with those wings
Which sometime they have used with fearful flight, 30
Make war with him that climb'd unto their nest,
Offering their own lives in their young's defence?
For shame, my liege, make them your precedent!
Were it not pity that this goodly boy
Should lose his birthright by his father's fault,
And long hereafter say unto his child,
'What my great-grandfather and grandsire got
My careless father fondly gave away'?
Ah, what a shame were this! Look on the boy;
And let his manly face, which promiseth 40
Successful fortune, steel thy melting heart
To hold thine own and leave thine own with him.
K. Hen. Full well hath Clifford play'd the orator,
Inferring arguments of mighty force.
But, Clifford, tell me, didst thou never hear
That things ill-got had ever bad success?
And happy always was it for that son
Whose father for his hoarding went to hell?
I'll leave my son my virtuous deeds behind;
And would my father had left me no more! 50
For all the rest is held at such a rate
As brings a thousand-fold more care to keep
Than in possession any jot of pleasure.
Ah, cousin York! would thy best friends did know
How it doth grieve me that thy head is here!
Q. Mar. My lord, cheer up your spirits: our foes
are nigh,
And this soft courage makes your followers faint.
You promised knighthood to our forward son:
Unsheathe your sword, and dub him presently.
Edward, kneel down. 60
K. Hen. Edward Plantagenet, arise a knight;
And learn this lesson, draw thy sword in right.
Prince. My gracious father, by your kingly leave,
I'll draw it as apparent to the crown,
And in that quarrel use it to the death.
Clif. Why, that is spoken like a toward prince.

Enter a Messenger.

Mess. Royal commanders, be in readiness:
For with a band of thirty thousand men
Comes Warwick, backing of the Duke of York;
And in the towns, as they do march along, 70
Proclaims him king, and many fly to him:
Darraign your battle, for they are at hand.
Clif. I would your highness would depart the field:
The queen hath best success when you are absent.
Q. Mar. Ay, good my lord, and leave us to our
fortune.
K. Hen. Why, that 's my fortune too; therefore I'll
stay.
North. Be it with resolution then to fight.
Prince. My royal father, cheer these noble lords
And hearten those that fight in your defence:
Unsheathe your sword, good father; cry 'Saint
George!' 80

March. Enter EDWARD, GEORGE, RICHARD,
WARWICK, NORFOLK, MONTAGUE, *and* Soldiers.

191. **forfend,** forbid; see glossary. 209. **sorts,** is fitting.
 SCENE II. 1. **brave,** fine; see glossary. 19. **level,** aim; see glossary.
22. **raise,** raise in dignity; i.e., advance his son to the crown. 30.
sometime, from time to time; see glossary. 44. **Inferring,** alleging,
adducing. 46-48. **things . . . hell.** Hart finds several parallels to the
two proverbs given here. The first appears in several forms, one of
which is in Spenser's *Mother Hubbard's Tale:* "Ill might it prosper

that ill gotten was." The second is found in one of Latimer's sermons:
"Happy is the child whose father goeth to the devil." The king states
the first here declaratively and the second he poses as a question.
46. **success,** outcome; see glossary. 51. **rate,** estimate; see glossary.
66. **toward,** ready, bold; see glossary. 72. **Darraign,** set in battle
array. 81. **grace,** mercy, pardon; see glossary. 83. **bide,** wait for.
mortal, fatal; see glossary. 84. **rate,** chide, berate; see glossary.

Edw. Now, perjured Henry! wilt thou kneel for
    grace,
And set thy diadem upon my head;
Or bide the mortal fortune of the field?
    Q. Mar. Go, rate thy minions, proud insulting boy!
Becomes it thee to be thus bold in terms
Before thy sovereign and thy lawful king?
    Edw. I am his king, and he should bow his knee;
I was adopted heir by his consent:
Since when, his oath is broke; for, as I hear,
You, that are king, though he do wear the crown,   90
Have caused him, by new act of parliament,
To blot me out, and put his own son in.
    Clif. And reason too:
Who should succeed the father but the son?
    Rich. Are you there, butcher? O, I cannot speak!
    Clif. Ay, crook-back, here I stand to answer thee,
Or any he the proudest of thy sort.
    Rich. 'Twas you that kill'd young Rutland, was it
    not?
    Clif. Ay, and old York, and yet not satisfied.
    Rich. For God's sake, lords, give signal to the fight.
    War. What say'st thou, Henry, wilt thou yield the
    crown?   101
    Q. Mar. Why, how now, long-tongued Warwick!
    dare you speak?
When you and I met at Saint Alban's last,
Your legs did better service than your hands.
    War. Then 'twas my turn to fly, and now 'tis thine.
    Clif. You said so much before, and yet you fled.
    War. 'Twas not your valour, Clifford, drove me
    thence.
    North. No, nor your manhood that durst make you
    stay.
    Rich. Northumberland, I hold thee reverently.
Break off the parley; for scarce I can refrain   110
The execution of my big-swoln heart
Upon that Clifford, that cruel child-killer.
    Clif. I slew thy father, call'st thou him a child?
    Rich. Ay, like a dastard and a treacherous coward,
As thou didst kill our tender brother Rutland;
But ere sunset I'll make thee curse the deed.
    K. Hen. Have done with words, my lords, and hear
    me speak.
    Q. Mar. Defy them then, or else hold close thy lips.
    K. Hen. I prithee, give no limits to my tongue:
I am a king, and privileged to speak.   120
    Clif. My liege, the wound that bred this meeting
    here
Cannot be cured by words; therefore be still.
    Rich. Then, executioner, unsheathe thy sword:
By him that made us all, I am resolved
That Clifford's manhood lies upon his tongue.
    Edw. Say, Henry, shall I have my right, or no?
A thousand men have broke their fasts to-day,
That ne'er shall dine unless thou yield the crown.
    War. If thou deny, their blood upon thy head;
For York in justice puts his armour on.   130
    Prince. If that be right which Warwick says is right,
There is no wrong, but every thing is right.
    Rich. Whoever got thee, there thy mother stands;

For, well I wot, thou hast thy mother's tongue.
    Q. Mar. But thou art neither like thy sire nor dam;
But like a foul mis-shapen stigmatic,
Mark'd by the destinies to be avoided,
As venom toads, or lizards' dreadful stings.
    Rich. Iron of Naples hid with English gilt,
Whose father bears the title of a king,—   140
As if a channel should be call'd the sea,—
Shamest thou not, knowing whence thou art
    extraught,
To let thy tongue detect thy base-born heart?
    Edw. A wisp of straw were worth a thousand
    crowns,
To make this shameless callet know herself.
Helen of Greece was fairer far than thou,
Although thy husband may be Menelaus;
And ne'er was Agamemnon's brother wrong'd
By that false woman, as this king by thee.
His father revell'd in the heart of France,   150
And tamed the king, and made the dauphin stoop;
And had he match'd according to his state,
He might have kept that glory to this day;
But when he took a beggar to his bed,
And graced thy poor sire with his bridal-day,
Even then that sunshine brew'd a shower for him,
That wash'd his father's fortunes forth of France,
And heap'd sedition on his crown at home.
For what hath broach'd this tumult but thy pride?
Hadst thou been meek, our title still had slept;   160
And we, in pity of the gentle king,
Had slipp'd our claim until another age.
    Geo. But when we saw our sunshine made thy
    spring,
And that thy summer bred us no increase,
We set the axe to thy usurping root;
And though the edge hath something hit ourselves,
Yet, know thou, since we have begun to strike,
We'll never leave till we have hewn thee down,
Or bathed thy growing with our heated bloods.
    Edw. And, in this resolution, I defy thee;   170
Not willing any longer conference,
Since thou deniest the gentle king to speak.
Sound trumpets! let our bloody colours wave!
And either victory, or else a grave.
    Q. Mar. Stay, Edward.
    Edw. No, wrangling woman, we'll no longer stay:
These words will cost ten thousand lives this day.
                           [*Exeunt.*

SCENE III. *A field of battle between Towton
and Saxton, in Yorkshire.*

Alarum. Excursions. Enter WARWICK.

War. Forspent with toil, as runners with a race,
I lay me down a little while to breathe;
For strokes received, and many blows repaid,
Have robb'd my strong-knit sinews of their strength,
And spite of spite needs must I rest awhile.

Enter EDWARD, *running.*

---

minions, followers; see glossary. 97. **any he**, any man. 111. **execution**, i.e., giving practical effect to his passion. **big-swoln**, i.e., overcharged with anger. 127. **A . . . to-day**, i.e., have had breakfast.
129. **deny**, refuse; see glossary. 133. **got**, begot; see *get* in glossary.
134. **wot**, know; see glossary. 136. **stigmatic**. Cf. *2 Henry VI*, V, i, 215.
139. **of Naples**. The queen's father was titular king of Naples. 142.
extraught, descended. 143. **detect**, expose. 145. **callet**, lewd woman,
strumpet. 147. **Menelaus**, Helen of Troy's husband and brother of
Agamemnon. 152. **match'd . . . state**, married someone equal to him
in social position; see *state* in glossary. 155. **graced**, honored; see
glossary. 159. **broach'd**, introduced.
SCENE III. 5. **spite of spite**, in spite of vexation.

Edw. Smile, gentle heaven! or strike, ungentle
    death!
For this world frowns, and Edward's sun is clouded.
    War. How now, my lord! what hap? what hope of
    good?

Enter GEORGE.

    Geo. Our hap is loss, our hope but sad despair;
Our ranks are broke, and ruin follows us: 10
What counsel give you? whither shall we fly?
    Edw. Bootless is flight, they follow us with wings;
And weak we are and cannot shun pursuit.

Enter RICHARD.

    Rich. Ah, Warwick, why hast thou withdrawn
    thyself?
Thy brother's blood the thirsty earth hath drunk,
Broach'd with the steely point of Clifford's lance;
And in the very pangs of death he cried,
Like to a dismal clangor heard from far,
'Warwick, revenge! brother, revenge my death!'
So, underneath the belly of their steeds,   20
That stain'd their fetlocks in his smoking blood,
The noble gentleman gave up the ghost.
    War. Then let the earth be drunken with our
    blood:
I'll kill my horse, because I will not fly.
Why stand we like soft-hearted women here,
Wailing our losses, whiles the foe doth rage;
And look upon, as if the tragedy
Were play'd in jest by counterfeiting actors?
Here on my knee I vow to God above,
I'll never pause again, never stand still,   30
Till either death hath closed these eyes of mine
Or fortune given me measure of revenge.
    Edw. O Warwick, I do bend my knee with thine;
And in this vow do chain my soul to thine!
And, ere my knee rise from the earth's cold face,
I throw my hands, mine eyes, my heart to thee,
Thou setter up and plucker down of kings,
Beseeching thee, if with thy will it stands
That to my foes this body must be prey,
Yet that thy brazen gates of heaven may ope,   40
And give sweet passage to my sinful soul!
Now, lords, take leave until we meet again,
Where'er it be, in heaven or in earth.
    Rich. Brother, give me thy hand; and, gentle
    Warwick,
Let me embrace thee in my weary arms:
I, that did never weep, now melt with woe
That winter should cut off our spring-time so.
    War. Away, away! Once more, sweet lords,
    farewell.
    Geo. Yet let us all together to our troops,
And give them leave to fly that will not stay;   50
And call them pillars that will stand to us;
And, if we thrive, promise them such rewards
As victors wear at the Olympian games:
This may plant courage in their quailing breasts;
For yet is hope of life and victory.

Forslow no longer, make we hence amain.   [*Exeunt.*

SCENE IV. *Another part of the field.*

Excursions. Enter RICHARD *and* CLIFFORD.

    Rich. Now, Clifford, I have singled thee alone:
Suppose this arm is for the Duke of York,
And this for Rutland; both bound to revenge,
Wert thou environ'd with a brazen wall.
    Clif. Now, Richard, I am with thee here alone:
This is the hand that stabb'd thy father York;
And this the hand that slew thy brother Rutland;
And here 's the heart that triumphs in their death
And cheers these hands that slew thy sire and brother
To execute the like upon thyself;   10
And so, have at thee!
            [*They fight. Warwick comes; Clifford flies.*
    Rich. Nay, Warwick, single out some other chase;
For I myself will hunt this wolf to death   [*Exeunt.*

SCENE V. *Another part of the field.*

Alarum. Enter KING HENRY *alone.*

    King. This battle fares like to the morning's war,
When dying clouds contend with growing light,
What time the shepherd, blowing of his nails,
Can neither call it perfect day nor night.
Now sways it this way, like a mighty sea
Forced by the tide to combat with the wind;
Now sways it that way, like the selfsame sea
Forced to retire by fury of the wind:
Sometime the flood prevails, and then the wind;
Now one the better, then another best;   10
Both tugging to be victors, breast to breast,
Yet neither conqueror nor conquered:
So is the equal poise of this fell war.
Here on this molehill will I sit me down.
To whom God will, there be the victory!
For Margaret my queen, and Clifford too,
Have chid me from the battle; swearing both
They prosper best of all when I am thence.
Would I were dead! if God's good will were so;
For what is in this world but grief and woe?   20
O God! methinks it were a happy life,
To be no better than a homely swain;
To sit upon a hill, as I do now,
To carve out dials quaintly, point by point,
Thereby to see the minutes how they run,
How many make the hour full complete;
How many hours bring about the day;
How many days will finish up the year;
How many years a mortal man may live.
When this is known, then to divide the times: 30
So many hours must I tend my flock;
So many hours must I take my rest;
So many hours must I contemplate;
So many hours must I sport myself;

7. **Edward's sun.** The metaphor contains a reference to Edward's emblem; cf. II, i, 25.   15-32. **Thy . . . revenge.** Warwick's brother, the Bastard of Salisbury, is not among the *Dramatis Personae.* Holinshed gives a graphic account of Warwick's conduct on hearing of his death: "When the earle of Warwike was informed hereof, like a man desperat, he mounted on his hacknie, and hasted puffing and blowing to king Edward, saieng: 'Sir, I praie God haue mercie of their soules, which in the beginning of your enterprise haue lost their liues! And bicause I

see no succors of the world but in God, I remit the vengeance to him our creator and redeemer.' With that he alighted downe, and slue his horse with his sword, saieng: 'Let him flee that will, for suerlie I will tarrie with him that will tarrie with me': and kissed the crosse of his sword as it were for a vow to the promise." 37. **Thou . . . kings.** Its position—and Warwick's nickname of "kingmaker"—tempt one to think that this line might be addressed to Warwick, although the lines immediately following indicate that it is addressed to heaven. Margaret

So many days my ewes have been with young;
So many weeks ere the poor fools will ean;
So many years ere I shall shear the fleece:
So minutes, hours, days, months, and years,
Pass'd over to the end they were created,
Would bring white hairs unto a quiet grave.   40
Ah, what a life were this! how sweet! how lovely!
Gives not the hawthorn-bush a sweeter shade
To shepherds looking on their silly sheep,
Than doth a rich embroider'd canopy
To kings that fear their subjects' treachery?
O, yes, it doth; a thousand-fold it doth.
And to conclude, the shepherd's homely curds,
His cold thin drink out of his leather bottle,
His wonted sleep under a fresh tree's shade,
All which secure and sweetly he enjoys,   50
Is far beyond a prince's delicates,
His viands sparkling in a golden cup,
His body couched in a curious bed,
When care, mistrust, and treason waits on him.

Alarum. Enter a Son *that has killed his father, dragging
in the dead body.*

Son. Ill blows the wind that profits nobody.
This man, whom hand to hand I slew in fight,
May be possessed with some store of crowns;
And I, that haply take them from him now,
May yet ere night yield both my life and them
To some man else, as this dead man doth me.   60
Who's this? O God! it is my father's face,
Whom in this conflict I unwares have kill'd.
O heavy times, begetting such events!
From London by the king was I press'd forth;
My father, being the Earl of Warwick's man,
Came on the part of York, press'd by his master;
And I, who at his hands received my life,
Have by my hands of life bereaved him.
Pardon me, God, I knew not what I did!
And pardon, father, for I knew not thee!   70
My tears shall wipe away these bloody marks;
And no more words till they have flow'd their fill.
     K. Hen. O piteous spectacle! O bloody times!
Whiles lions war and battle for their dens,
Poor harmless lambs abide their enmity.
Weep, wretched man, I'll aid thee tear for tear;
And let our hearts and eyes, like civil war,
Be blind with tears, and break o'ercharged with grief.

Enter a Father *that has killed his son, bringing in the body.*

Fath. Thou that so stoutly hast resisted me,
Give me thy gold, if thou hast any gold;   80
For I have bought it with an hundred blows.
But let me see: is this our foeman's face?
Ah, no, no, no, it is mine only son!
Ah, boy, if any life be left in thee,
Throw up thine eye! see, see what showers arise,
Blown with the windy tempest of my heart,
Upon thy wounds, that kill mine eye and heart!
O, pity, God, this miserable age!

What stratagems, how fell, how butcherly,
Erroneous, mutinous and unnatural,   90
This deadly quarrel daily doth beget!
O boy, thy father gave thee life too soon,
And hath bereft thee of thy life too late!
     K. Hen. Woe above woe! grief more than common
          grief!
O that my death would stay these ruthful deeds!
O, pity, pity, gentle heaven, pity!
The red rose and the white are on his face,
The fatal colours of our striving houses:
The one his purple blood right well resembles;
The other his pale cheeks, methinks, presenteth: 100
Wither one rose, and let the other flourish;
If you contend, a thousand lives must wither.
     Son. How will my mother for a father's death
Take on with me and ne'er be satisfied!
     Fath. How will my wife for slaughter of my son
Shed seas of tears and ne'er be satisfied!
     K. Hen. How will the country for these woful
          chances
Misthink the king and not be satisfied!
     Son. Was ever son so rued a father's death?
     Fath. Was ever father so bemoan'd his son?   110
     K. Hen. Was ever king so grieved for subjects' woe?
Much is your sorrow; mine ten times so much.
     Son. I'll bear thee hence, where I may weep my fill.
          [*Exit with the body.*
     Fath. These arms of mine shall be thy winding-
          sheet;
My heart, sweet boy, shall be thy sepulchre,
For from my heart thine image ne'er shall go;
My sighing breast shall be thy funeral bell;
And so obsequious will thy father be,
†Even for the loss of thee, having no more,
As Priam was for all his valiant sons.   120
I'll bear thee hence; and let them fight that will,
For I have murdered where I should not kill.
          [*Exit with the body.*
     K. Hen. Sad-hearted men, much overgone with
          care,
Here sits a king more woful than you are.

Alarums: excursions. Enter QUEEN MARGARET, *the*
PRINCE, *and* EXETER.

     Prince. Fly, father, fly! for all your friends are fled,
And Warwick rages like a chafed bull:
Away! for death doth hold us in pursuit.
     Q. Mar. Mount you, my lord; towards Berwick
          post amain:
Edward and Richard, like a brace of greyhounds
Having the fearful flying hare in sight,   130
With fiery eyes sparkling for very wrath,
And bloody steel grasp'd in their ireful hands,
Are at our backs; and therefore hence amain.
     Exe. Away! for vengeance comes along with them:
Nay, stay not to expostulate, make speed;
Or else come after: I'll away before.
     K. Hen. Nay, take me with thee, good sweet Exeter:
Not that I fear to stay, but love to go

speaks a similar line to Warwick, III, iii, 157.   56. **Forslow**, delay.
     SCENE IV.   11. **have at**, let me at; see glossary.   12. **chase**, hunting
ground.
     SCENE V.   3. **blowing . . . nails**, i.e., his hands are cold; cf. *Love's
Labour's Lost*, V, ii, 923.   13. **poise**, weight.   14. **molehill**. Hart finds
in this an allusion to the old saw "king of a molehill." The saying has
application to the duke of York's death scene (I, iv).   26-34. **hour,
hours**, pronounced throughout this passage as dissyllabic.   36. **fools**,
a term of pity; see glossary.   **ean**, bring forth (lambs).   53. **curious**,
skillfully and daintily made; see glossary.   57. **possessed**, in possession
of; see glossary.   64. **press'd forth**, impressed into military service.
90. **Erroneous**, criminal.   100. **presenteth**, representeth; see glossary.
108. **Misthink**, think ill of.   118. **obsequious**, dutiful in manifesting
regard for the dead.   123. **overgone**, overcome.   126. **chafed**, enraged.
135. **expostulate**, discuss.

Whither the queen intends. Forward; away! [*Exeunt.*

SCENE VI. *Another part of the field.*

A loud alarum. Enter CLIFFORD, *wounded.*

Clif. Here burns my candle out; ay, here it dies,
Which, whiles it lasted, gave King Henry light.
O Lancaster, I fear thy overthrow
More than my body's parting with my soul!
My love and fear glued many friends to thee;
And, now I fall, thy tough commixture melts.
Impairing Henry, strengthening misproud York,
The common people swarm like summer flies;
And whither fly the gnats but to the sun?
And who shines now but Henry's enemies? 10
O Phœbus, hadst thou never given consent
That Phaëthon should check thy fiery steeds,
Thy burning car never had scorch'd the earth!
And, Henry, hadst thou sway'd as kings should do,
Or as thy father and his father did,
Giving no ground unto the house of York,
They never then had sprung like summer flies;
I and ten thousand in this luckless realm
Had left no mourning widows for our death;
And thou this day hadst kept thy chair in peace. 20
For what doth cherish weeds but gentle air?
And what makes robbers bold but too much lenity?
Bootless are plaints, and cureless are my wounds;
No way to fly, nor strength to hold out flight:
The foe is merciless, and will not pity;
For at their hands I have deserved no pity.
The air hath got into my deadly wounds,
And much effuse of blood doth make me faint.
Come, York and Richard, Warwick and the rest;
I stabb'd your fathers' bosoms, split my breast. 30
[*He faints.*

Alarum and retreat. Enter EDWARD, GEORGE,
RICHARD, MONTAGUE, WARWICK, *and* Soldiers.

Edw. Now breathe we, lords: good fortune bids us
pause,
And smooth the frowns of war with peaceful looks.
Some troops pursue the bloody-minded queen,
That led calm Henry, though he were a king,
As doth a sail, fill'd with a fretting gust,
Command an argosy to stem the waves.
But think you, lords, that Clifford fled with them?
War. No, 'tis impossible he should escape;
For, though before his face I speak the words,
Your brother Richard mark'd him for the grave: 40
And wheresoe'er he is, he 's surely dead.
[*Clifford groans, and dies.*
Edw. Whose soul is that which takes her heavy leave?
Rich. A deadly groan, like life and death's
departing.
Edw. See who it is: and, now the battle 's ended,
If friend or foe, let him be gently used.
Rich. Revoke that doom of mercy, for 'tis Clifford;
Who not contented that he lopp'd the branch
In hewing Rutland when his leaves put forth,

But set his murdering knife unto the root
From whence that tender spray did sweetly spring, 50
I mean our princely father, Duke of York.
War. From off the gates of York fetch down the
head,
Your father's head, which Clifford placed there;
Instead whereof let this supply the room:
Measure for measure must be answered.
Edw. Bring forth that fatal screech-owl to our house,
That nothing sung but death to us and ours:
Now death shall stop his dismal threatening sound,
And his ill-boding tongue no more shall speak.
War. I think his understanding is bereft. 60
Speak, Clifford, dost thou know who speaks to thee?
Dark cloudy death o'ershades his beams of life,
And he nor sees nor hears us what we say.
Rich. O, would he did! and so perhaps he doth:
'Tis but his policy to counterfeit,
Because he would avoid such bitter taunts
Which in the time of death he gave our father.
Geo. If so thou think'st, vex him with eager words.
Rich. Clifford, ask mercy and obtain no grace.
Edw. Clifford, repent in bootless penitence. 70
War. Clifford, devise excuses for thy faults.
Geo. While we devise fell tortures for thy faults.
Rich. Thou didst love York, and I am son to York.
Edw. Thou pitied'st Rutland; I will pity thee.
Geo. Where 's Captain Margaret, to fence you now?
War. They mock thee, Clifford: swear as thou wast
wont.
Rich. What, not an oath? nay, then the world goes
hard
When Clifford cannot spare his friends an oath.
I know by that he 's dead; and, by my soul,
If this right hand would buy two hours' life, 80
That I in all despite might rail at him,
This hand should chop it off, and with the issuing
blood
Stifle the villain whose unstanched thirst
York and young Rutland could not satisfy.
War. Ay, but he 's dead: off with the traitor's head,
And rear it in the place your father's stands.
And now to London with triumphant march,
There to be crowned England's royal king:
From whence shall Warwick cut the sea to France,
And ask the Lady Bona for thy queen: 90
So shalt thou sinew both these lands together;
And, having France thy friend, thou shalt not dread
The scatter'd foe that hopes to rise again;
For though they cannot greatly sting to hurt,
Yet look to have them buzz to offend thine ears.
First will I see the coronation;
And then to Brittany I'll cross the sea,
To effect this marriage, so it please my lord.
Edw. Even as thou wilt, sweet Warwick, let it be;
For in thy shoulder do I build my seat, 100
And never will I undertake the thing
Wherein thy counsel and consent is wanting.
Richard, I will create thee Duke of Gloucester,
And George, of Clarence: Warwick, as ourself,
Shall do and undo as him pleaseth best.

SCENE VI. 5. **My love and fear,** fear and love of me. 6. **com-mixture,** compound. 9. **the sun,** probable quibble on Edward's emblem. 11, 12. **Phœbus, Phaëthon.** Cf. I, iv, 33, note. 14. **sway'd,** reigned. 24. **hold out,** sustain. 28. **effuse,** effusion. 34. **though he were,** a contrary-to-fact subjunctive. 36. **argosy,** merchant vessel of the largest size. 39. **his,** i.e., Richard's. 55. **answered,** accounted for; see glossary. 56. **fatal screech-owl.** The owl was superstitiously regarded as a prognosticator of death; cf. *Macbeth,* II, ii, 3. 75. **fence,** defend. 90. **Lady Bona,** sister to the queen of France. 107. **Gloucester's . . . ominous.** Two dukes of Gloucester had met with violent deaths. Thomas, youngest son of Edward III, was murdered at Calais in 1397; and Humphrey (as dramatized in *2 Henry VI*) was murdered in

Rich. Let me be Duke of Clarence, George of
    Gloucester;
For Gloucester's dukedom is too ominous.
  War. Tut, that 's a foolish observation:
Richard, be Duke of Gloucester. Now to London,
To see these honours in possession.   [*Exeunt.* 110

ACT III.

SCENE I. *A forest in the north of England.*

Enter two Keepers, *with cross-bows in their hands.*

First Keep. Under this thick-grown brake we'll
    shroud ourselves;
For through this laund anon the deer will come;
And in this covert will we make our stand,
Culling the principal of all the deer.
  Sec. Keep. I'll stay above the hill, so both may shoot.
  First Keep. That cannot be; the noise of thy
    cross-bow
Will scare the herd, and so my shoot is lost.
Here stand we both, and aim we at the best:
And, for the time shall not seem tedious,
I'll tell thee what befel me on a day   10
In this self-place where now we mean to stand.
  Sec. Keep. Here comes a man; let 's stay till he be
    past.

Enter KING HENRY, *disguised, with a prayer-book.*

  K. Hen. From Scotland am I stol'n, even of pure
    love,
To greet mine own land with my wishful sight.
No, Harry, Harry, 'tis no land of thine;
Thy place is fill'd, thy sceptre wrung from thee,
Thy balm wash'd off wherewith thou wast anointed:
No bending knee will call thee Cæsar now,
No humble suitors press to speak for right,
No, not a man comes for redress of thee;   20
For how can I help them, and not myself?
  First Keep. Ay, here 's a deer whose skin 's a keeper's
    fee:
This is the quondam king; let 's seize upon him.
  K. Hen. Let me embrace thee, sour adversity,
For wise men say it is the wisest course.
  Sec. Keep. Why linger we? let us lay hands upon
    him.
  First Keep. Forbear awhile; we'll hear a little more.
  K. Hen. My queen and son are gone to France for
    aid;
And, as I hear, the great commanding Warwick
Is thither gone, to crave the French king's sister   30
To wife for Edward: if this news be true,
Poor queen and son, your labour is but lost;
For Warwick is a subtle orator,
And Lewis a prince soon won with moving words.
By this account then Margaret may win him;
For she 's a woman to be pitied much:
Her sighs will make a battery in his breast;
Her tears will pierce into a marble heart;
The tiger will be mild whiles she doth mourn;

And Nero will be tainted with remorse,   40
To hear and see her plaints, her brinish tears.
Ay, but she 's come to beg, Warwick, to give;
She, on his left side, craving aid for Henry,
He, on his right, asking a wife for Edward.
She weeps, and says her Henry is deposed;
He smiles, and says his Edward is install'd;
That she, poor wretch, for grief can speak no more;
Whiles Warwick tells his title, smooths the wrong,
Inferreth arguments of mighty strength,
And in conclusion wins the king from her,   50
With promise of his sister, and what else,
To strengthen and support King Edward's place.
O Margaret, thus 'twill be; and thou, poor soul,
Art then forsaken, as thou went'st forlorn!
  Sec. Keep. Say, what art thou that talk'st of kings
    and queens?
  K. Hen. More than I seem, and less than I was born
    to:
A man at least, for less I should not be;
And men may talk of kings, and why not I?
  Sec. Keep. Ay, but thou talk'st as if thou wert a
    king.
  K. Hen. Why, so I am, in mind; and that 's enough.
  Sec. Keep. But, if thou be a king, where is thy
    crown?   61
  K. Hen. My crown is in my heart, not on my head;
Not deck'd with diamonds and Indian stones,
Nor to be seen: my crown is called content:
A crown it is that seldom kings enjoy.
  Sec. Keep. Well, if you be a king crown'd with
    content,
Your crown content and you must be contented
To go along with us; for, as we think,
You are the king King Edward hath deposed;
And we his subjects sworn in all allegiance   70
Will apprehend you as his enemy.
  K. Hen. But did you never swear, and break an
    oath?
  Sec. Keep. No, never such an oath; nor will not now.
  K. Hen. Where did you dwell when I was King of
    England?
  Sec. Keep. Here in this country, where we now
    remain.
  K. Hen. I was anointed king at nine months old;
My father and my grandfather were kings,
And you were sworn true subjects unto me:
And tell me, then, have you not broke your oaths?
  First Keep. No;   80
For we were subjects but while you were king.
  K. Hen. Why, am I dead? do I not breathe a man?
Ah, simple men, you know not what you swear!
Look, as I blow this feather from my face,
And as the air blows it to me again,
Obeying with my wind when I do blow,
And yielding to another when it blows,
Commanded always by the greater gust;
Such is the lightness of you common men.
But do not break your oaths; for of that sin   90
My mild entreaty shall not make you guilty.
Go where you will, the king shall be commanded;

3 Henry VI
ACT III : SC I

283

---

the Tower in 1447. The former's death figures as a motive in the political intrigues depicted in *Richard II*; cf. *Richard II*, I, i, 100, note.   110.
To . . . possession, to possess ourselves of these honors.

ACT III. SCENE I.   1. **brake,** thicket.   2. **laund,** glade.   **anon,** soon;
see glossary.   9. **for,** so that.   11. **self-place,** selfsame place.   23.
quondam, one-time.   37. **battery,** wound, bruise.   40. **tainted,** used

metaphorically to imply something entirely contrary to one's nature;
i.e., remorse is a foreign quality in a tyrant and corresponds to a corruption in an otherwise good nature; it is like "some stain of soldier" in
Parolles (*All's Well that Ends Well*, I, i, 122).   **remorse,** pity; see
glossary.   71. **apprehend,** arrest.

And be you kings, command, and I'll obey.
  First Keep. We are true subjects to the king, King
    Edward.
  K. Hen. So would you be again to Henry,
If he were seated as King Edward is.
  First Keep. We charge you, in God's name, and the
    king's,
To go with us unto the officers.
  K. Hen. In God's name, lead; your king's name be
    obey'd:
And what God will, that let your king perform;   100
And what he will, I humbly yield unto.   [*Exeunt*.

———————————

SCENE II. *London. The palace.*

Enter KING EDWARD, GLOUCESTER, CLARENCE, *and*
  LADY GREY.

  K. Edw. Brother of Gloucester, at Saint Alban's
    field
This lady's husband, Sir Richard Grey, was slain,
His lands then seized on by the conqueror:
Her suit is now to repossess those lands;
Which we in justice cannot well deny,
Because in quarrel of the house of York
The worthy gentleman did lose his life.
  Glou. Your highness shall do well to grant her suit;
It were dishonour to deny it her.
  K. Edw. It were no less; but yet I'll make a pause. 10
  Glou. [*Aside to Clar*.] Yea, is it so?
I see the lady hath a thing to grant,
Before the king will grant her humble suit.
  Clar. [*Aside to Glou*.] He knows the game: how true
    he keeps the wind!
  Glou. [*Aside to Clar*.] Silence!
  K. Edw. Widow, we will consider of your suit;
And come some other time to know our mind.
  L. Grey. Right gracious lord, I cannot brook delay:
May it please your highness to resolve me now;
And what your pleasure is, shall satisfy me.   20
  Glou. [*Aside to Clar*.] Ay, widow? then I'll warrant
    you all your lands,
An if what pleases him shall pleasure you.
Fight closer, or, good faith, you'll catch a blow.
  Clar. [*Aside to Glou*.] I fear her not, unless she chance
    to fall.
  Glou. [*Aside to Clar*.] God forbid that! for he'll take
    vantages.
  K. Edw. How many children hast thou, widow? tell
    me.
  Clar. [*Aside to Glou*.] I think he means to beg a child
    of her.
  Glou. [*Aside to Clar*.] Nay, whip me then: he'll
    rather give her two.
  L. Grey. Three, my most gracious lord.
  Glou. [*Aside to Clar*.] You shall have four, if you'll
    be ruled by him.   30
  K. Edw. 'Twere pity they should lose their father's
    lands.
  L. Grey. Be pitiful, dread lord, and grant it then.
  K. Edw. Lords, give us leave: I'll try this widow's
    wit.

3 Henry VI
ACT III : SC I

284

  Glou. [*Aside to Clar*.] Ay, good leave have you; for
    you will have leave,
Till youth take leave and leave you to the crutch.
                    [*Glou. and Clar. retire*
  K. Edw. Now tell me, madam, do you love your
    children?
  L. Grey. Ay, full as dearly as I love myself.
  K. Edw. And would you not do much to do them
    good?
  L. Grey. To do them good, I would sustain some
    harm.
  K. Edw. Then get your husband's lands, to do them
    good.   40
  L. Grey. Therefore I came unto your majesty.
  K. Edw. I'll tell you how these lands are to be got.
  L. Grey. So shall you bind me to your highness'
    service.
  K. Edw. What service wilt thou do me, if I give
    them?
  L. Grey. What you command, that rests in me to do.
  K. Edw. But you will take exceptions to my boon.
  L. Grey. No, gracious lord, except I cannot do it.
  K. Edw. Ay, but thou canst do what I mean to ask.
  L. Grey. Why, then I will do what your grace
    commands.
  Glou. [*Aside to Clar*.] He plies her hard; and much
    rain wears the marble.   50
  Clar. [*Aside to Glou*.] As red as fire! nay, then her
    wax must melt.
  L. Grey. Why stops my lord? shall I not hear my
    task?
  K. Edw. An easy task; 'tis but to love a king.
  L. Grey. That's soon perform'd, because I am a
    subject.
  K. Edw. Why, then, thy husband's lands I freely
    give thee.
  L. Grey. I take my leave with many thousand
    thanks.
  Glou. [*Aside to Clar*.] The match is made; she seals it
    with a curtsy.
  K. Edw. But stay thee, 'tis the fruits of love I mean.
  L. Grey. The fruits of love I mean, my loving liege.
  K. Edw. Ay, but, I fear me, in another sense.   60
What love, think'st thou, I sue so much to get?
  L. Grey. My love till death, my humble thanks, my
    prayers;
That love which virtue begs and virtue grants.
  K. Edw. No, by my troth, I did not mean such love.
  L. Grey. Why, then you mean not as I thought you
    did.
  K. Edw. But now you partly may perceive my mind.
  L. Grey. My mind will never grant what I perceive
Your highness aims at, if I aim aright.
  K. Edw. To tell thee plain, I aim to lie with thee.
  L. Grey. To tell you plain, I had rather lie in prison.
  K. Edw. Why, then thou shalt not have thy
    husband's lands.   71
  L. Grey. Why, then mine honesty shall be my
    dower;
For by that loss I will not purchase them.
  K. Edw. Therein thou wrong'st thy children
    mightily.

L. Grey. Herein your highness wrongs both them
   and me.
But, mighty lord, this merry inclination
Accords not with the sadness of my suit:
Please you dismiss me, either with 'ay' or 'no.'
   K. Edw. Ay, if thou wilt say 'ay' to my request;
No, if thou dost say 'no' to my demand.   80
   L. Grey. Then, no, my lord. My suit is at an end.
   Glou. [*Aside to Clar.*] The widow likes him not, she
   knits her brows.
   Clar. [*Aside to Glou.*] He is the bluntest wooer in
   Christendom.
   K. Edw. [*Aside*] Her looks do argue her replete with
   modesty;
Her words do show her wit incomparable;
All her perfections challenge sovereignty:
One way or other, she is for a king;
And she shall be my love, or else my queen.—
Say that King Edward take thee for his queen?
   L. Grey. 'Tis better said than done, my gracious
   lord: 90
I am a subject fit to jest withal,
But far unfit to be a sovereign.
   K. Edw. Sweet widow, by my state I swear to thee
I speak no more than what my soul intends;
And that is, to enjoy thee for my love.
   L. Grey. And that is more than I will yield unto:
I know I am too mean to be your queen,
And yet too good to be your concubine.
   K. Edw. You cavil, widow: I did mean, my queen.
   L. Grey. 'Twill grieve your grace my sons should call
   you father.   100
   K. Edw. No more than when my daughters call thee
   mother.
Thou art a widow, and thou hast some children;
And, by God's mother, I, being but a bachelor,
Have other some: why, 'tis a happy thing
To be the father unto many sons.
Answer no more, for thou shalt be my queen.
   Glou. [*Aside to Clar.*] The ghostly father now hath
   done his shrift.
   Clar. [*Aside to Glou.*] When he was made a shriver,
   'twas for shift.
   K. Edw. Brothers, you muse what chat we two have
   had.   109
   Glou. The widow likes it not, for she looks very sad.
   K. Edw. You 'ld think it strange if I should marry
   her.
   Clar. To whom, my lord?
   K. Edw.   Why, Clarence, to myself.
   Glou. That would be ten days' wonder at the least.
   Clar. That 's a day longer than a wonder lasts.
   Glou. By so much is the wonder in extremes.
   K. Edw. Well, jest on, brothers: I can tell you both
Her suit is granted for her husband's lands.

   Enter a Nobleman.

   Nob. My gracious lord, Henry your foe is taken,
And brought your prisoner to your palace gate.
   K. Edw. See that he be convey'd unto the Tower: 120
And go we, brothers, to the man that took him,
To question of his apprehension.

Widow, go you along. Lords, use her honourably.
           [*Exeunt all but Gloucester.*
   Glou. Ay, Edward will use women honourably.
Would he were wasted, marrow, bones and all,
That from his loins no hopeful branch may spring,
To cross me from the golden time I look for!
And yet, between my soul's desire and me—
The lustful Edward's title buried—
Is Clarence, Henry, and his son young Edward,   130
And all the unlook'd for issue of their bodies,
To take their rooms, ere I can place myself:
A cold premeditation for my purpose!
Why, then, I do but dream on sovereignty;
Like one that stands upon a promontory,
And spies a far-off shore where he would tread,
Wishing his foot were equal with his eye,
And chides the sea that sunders him from thence,
Saying, he'll lade it dry to have his way:
So do I wish the crown, being so far off;   140
And so I chide the means that keeps me from it;
And so I say, I'll cut the causes off,
Flattering me with impossibilities.
My eye 's too quick, my heart o'erweens too much,
Unless my hand and strength could equal them.
Well, say there is no kingdom then for Richard;
What other pleasure can the world afford?
I'll make my heaven in a lady's lap,
And deck my body in gay ornaments,
And witch sweet ladies with my words and looks.   150
O miserable thought! and more unlikely
Than to accomplish twenty golden crowns!
Why, love forswore me in my mother's womb:
And, for I should not deal in her soft laws,
She did corrupt frail nature with some bribe,
To shrink mine arm up like a wither'd shrub;
To make an envious mountain on my back,
Where sits deformity to mock my body;
To shape my legs of an unequal size;
To disproportion me in every part,   160
Like to a chaos, or an unlick'd bear-whelp
That carries no impression like the dam.
And am I then a man to be beloved?
O monstrous fault, to harbour such a thought!
Then, since this earth affords no joy to me,
But to command, to check, to o'erbear such
As are of better person than myself,
I'll make my heaven to dream upon the crown,
And, whiles I live, to account this world but hell,
Until my mis-shaped trunk that bears this head   170
Be round impaled with a glorious crown.
And yet I know not how to get the crown,
For many lives stand between me and home:
And I,—like one lost in a thorny wood,
That rends the thorns and is rent with the thorns,
Seeking a way and straying from the way;
Not knowing how to find the open air,
But toiling desperately to find it out,—
Torment myself to catch the English crown:
And from that torment I will free myself,   180
Or hew my way out with a bloody axe.
Why, I can smile, and murder whiles I smile,
And cry 'Content' to that which grieves my heart,

3 Henry VI
ACT III : SC II

285

here anticipates the Machiavellian king in *Richard III*. Cf. II, i, 49,
note. 132. **rooms,** places. 133. **cold premeditation,** hopeless outlook.
139. **lade,** empty (by bailing). 143. **me,** myself. 144. **o'erweens too
much,** is overambitious. 157. **envious,** spiteful; see glossary. 161.
unlick'd bear-whelp. It was a popular notion that bears licked their
newly born cubs into a proper shape. 171. **impaled,** enclosed;
specifically, encircled with a crown; cf. III, iii, 189.

And wet my cheeks with artificial tears,
And frame my face to all occasions.
I'll drown more sailors than the mermaid shall;
I'll slay more gazers than the basilisk;
I'll play the orator as well as Nestor,
Deceive more slily than Ulysses could,
And, like a Sinon, take another Troy.   190
I can add colours to the chameleon,
Change shapes with Proteus for advantages,
And set the murderous Machiavel to school.
Can I do this, and cannot get a crown?
Tut, were it farther off, I'll pluck it down.   [Exit.

SCENE III. *France. The* KING'S *palace.*

Flourish. Enter LEWIS *the French King, his sister* BONA,
his Admiral, called BOURBON: PRINCE EDWARD,
QUEEN MARGARET, *and the* EARL OF OXFORD.
LEWIS *sits, and riseth up again.*

K. Lew. Fair Queen of England, worthy Margaret,
Sit down with us: it ill befits thy state
And birth, that thou shouldst stand while Lewis doth
    sit.
Q. Mar. No, mighty King of France: now Margaret
Must strike her sail and learn awhile to serve
Where kings command. I was, I must confess,
Great Albion's queen in former golden days:
But now mischance hath trod my title down,
And with dishonour laid me on the ground;
Where I must take like seat unto my fortune,   10
And to my humble seat conform myself.
K. Lew. Why, say, fair queen, whence springs this
    deep despair?
Q. Mar. From such a cause as fills mine eyes with
    tears
And stops my tongue, while heart is drown'd in cares.
K. Lew. Whate'er it be, be thou still like thyself,
And sit thee by our side: [*Seats her by him*] yield not thy
    neck
To fortune's yoke, but let thy dauntless mind
Still ride in triumph over all mischance.
Be plain, Queen Margaret, and tell thy grief;
It shall be eased, if France can yield relief.   20
Q. Mar. Those gracious words revive my drooping
    thoughts
And give my tongue-tied sorrows leave to speak.
Now, therefore, be it known to noble Lewis,
That Henry, sole possessor of my love,
Is of a king become a banish'd man,
And forced to live in Scotland a forlorn;
While proud ambitious Edward Duke of York
Usurps the regal title and the seat
Of England's true-anointed lawful king.
This is the cause that I, poor Margaret,   30
With this my son, Prince Edward, Henry's heir,
Am come to crave thy just and lawful aid;
And if thou fail us, all our hope is done:
Scotland hath will to help, but cannot help;

Our people and our peers are both misled,
Our treasure seized, our soldiers put to flight,
And, as thou seest, ourselves in heavy plight.
K. Lew. Renowned queen, with patience calm the
    storm,
While we bethink a means to break it off.
Q. Mar. The more we stay, the stronger grows our
    foe.   40
K. Lew. The more I stay, the more I'll succour thee.
Q. Mar. O, but impatience waiteth on true sorrow.
And see where comes the breeder of my sorrow!

Enter WARWICK.

K. Lew. What 's he approacheth boldly to our
    presence?
Q. Mar. Our Earl of Warwick, Edward's greatest
    friend.
K. Lew. Welcome, brave Warwick! What brings
    thee to France?   [*He descends. She ariseth.*
Q. Mar. Ay, now begins a second storm to rise;
For this is he that moves both wind and tide.
War. From worthy Edward, King of Albion,
My lord and sovereign, and thy vowed friend,   50
I come, in kindness and unfeigned love,
First, to do greetings to thy royal person;
And then to crave a league of amity;
And lastly, to confirm that amity
With nuptial knot, if thou vouchsafe to grant
That virtuous Lady Bona, thy fair sister,
To England's king in lawful marriage.
Q. Mar. [*Aside*] If that go forward, Henry's hope is
    done.
War. [*To Bona*] And, gracious madam, in our king's
    behalf,
I am commanded, with your leave and favour,   60
Humbly to kiss your hand and with my tongue
To tell the passion of my sovereign's heart;
Where fame, late entering at his heedful ears,
Hath placed thy beauty's image and thy virtue.
Q. Mar. King Lewis and Lady Bona, hear me speak,
Before you answer Warwick. His demand
Springs not from Edward's well-meant honest love,
But from deceit bred by necessity;
For how can tyrants safely govern home,
Unless abroad they purchase great alliance?   70
To prove him tyrant this reason may suffice,
That Henry liveth still; but were he dead,
Yet here Prince Edward stands, King Henry's son.
Look, therefore, Lewis, that by this league and
    marriage
Thou draw not on thy danger and dishonour;
For though usurpers sway the rule awhile,
Yet heavens are just, and time suppresseth wrongs.
War. Injurious Margaret!
Prince.   And why not queen?
War. Because thy father Henry did usurp;
And thou no more art prince than she is queen.   80
Oxf. Then Warwick disannuls great John of Gaunt,
Which did subdue the greatest part of Spain;
And, after John of Gaunt, Henry the Fourth,
Whose wisdom was a mirror to the wisest;

3 Henry VI
ACT III : SC II

286

---

186. **drown . . . shall.** Mermaids allegedly had the power to lure sailors to destruction by their singing or weeping. 187. **basilisk,** fabulous reptile said to kill by its look; see glossary. 188. **Nestor,** one of the Greek leaders in the siege of Troy, famous among other things for his eloquence. 189. **Ulysses.** The epithet "crafty" is frequently applied to Ulysses in the Homeric poems. 190. **Sinon,** Greek soldier who allowed himself to be taken prisoner by the Trojans, pretending that

the Greeks had misused him. He persuaded Priam to bring the wooden horse within the city walls and at night released the soldiers hidden within it. 192. **Proteus,** old man of the sea, able to assume different shapes. **for advantages,** as it suits my convenience; see *advantage* in glossary. 193. **set the . . . school,** teach Machiavelli how to be ruthless; cf. *1 Henry VI*, V, iv, 74, note.
SCENE III. 7. **Albion's,** England's. 25. **of,** instead of; see glossary.

And, after that wise prince, Henry the Fifth,
Who by his prowess conquered all France:
From these our Henry lineally descends.
    War. Oxford, how haps it, in this smooth discourse,
You told not how Henry the Sixth hath lost
All that which Henry the Fifth had gotten?   90
Methinks these peers of France should smile at that.
But for the rest, you tell a pedigree
Of threescore and two years; a silly time
To make prescription for a kingdom's worth.
    Oxf. Why, Warwick, canst thou speak against thy
      liege,
Whom thou obeyed'st thirty and six years,
And not bewray thy treason with a blush?
    War. Can Oxford, that did ever fence the right,
Now buckler falsehood with a pedigree?
For shame! leave Henry, and call Edward king.   100
    Oxf. Call him my king by whose injurious doom
My elder brother, the Lord Aubrey Vere,
Was done to death? and more than so, my father,
Even in the downfall of his mellow'd years,
When nature brought him to the door of death?
No, Warwick, no; while life upholds this arm,
This arm upholds the house of Lancaster.
    War. And I the house of York.
    K. Lew. Queen Margaret, Prince Edward, and
      Oxford,
Vouchsafe, at our request, to stand aside,   110
While I use further conference with Warwick.
                    [They stand aloof.
    Q. Mar. Heavens grant that Warwick's words
      bewitch him not!
    K. Lew. Now, Warwick, tell me, even upon thy
      conscience,
Is Edward your true king? for I were loath
To link with him that were not lawful chosen.
    War. Thereon I pawn my credit and mine honour.
    K. Lew. But is he gracious in the people's eye?
    War. The more that Henry was unfortunate.
    K. Lew. Then further, all dissembling set aside,
Tell me for truth the measure of his love   120
Unto our sister Bona.
    War.   Such it seems
As may beseem a monarch like himself.
Myself have often heard him say and swear
That this his love was an eternal plant,
Whereof the root was fix'd in virtue's ground,
The leaves and fruit maintain'd with beauty's sun,
Exempt from envy, but not from disdain,
Unless the Lady Bona quit his pain.
    K. Lew. Now, sister, let us hear your firm resolve.
    Bona. Your grant, or your denial, shall be mine: 130
[To War.] Yet I confess that often ere this day,
When I have heard your king's desert recounted,
Mine ear hath tempted judgement to desire.
    K. Lew. Then, Warwick, thus: our sister shall be
      Edward's;
And now forthwith shall articles be drawn
Touching the jointure that your king must make,
Which with her dowry shall be counterpoised.
Draw near, Queen Margaret, and be a witness

That Bona shall be wife to the English king.
    Prince. To Edward, but not to the English king.   140
    Q. Mar. Deceitful Warwick! it was thy device
By this alliance to make void my suit:
Before thy coming Lewis was Henry's friend.
    K. Lew. And still is friend to him and Margaret:
But if your title to the crown be weak,
As may appear by Edward's good success,
Then 'tis but reason that I be released
From giving aid which late I promised.
Yet shall you have all kindness at my hand
That your estate requires and mine can yield.   150
    War. Henry now lives in Scotland at his ease,
Where having nothing, nothing can he lose.
And as for you yourself, our quondam queen,
You have a father able to maintain you;
And better 'twere you troubled him than France.
    Q. Mar. Peace, impudent and shameless Warwick,
      peace,
Proud setter up and puller down of kings!
I will not hence, till, with my talk and tears,
Both full of truth, I make King Lewis behold
Thy sly conveyance and thy lord's false love;   160
For both of you are birds of selfsame feather.
                    [Post blows a horn within.
    K. Lew. Warwick, this is some post to us or thee.

    Enter a Post.

    Post. *[To War*.] My lord ambassador, these letters
      are for you,
Sent from your brother, Marquess Montague:
[To Lewis] These from our king unto your majesty:
[To Margaret] And, madam, these for you; from
      whom I know not.   *[They all read their letters*.
    Oxf. I like it well that our fair queen and mistress
Smiles at her news, while Warwick frowns at his.
    Prince. Nay, mark how Lewis stamps, as he were
      nettled:
I hope all 's for the best.   170
    K. Lew. Warwick, what are thy news? and yours,
      fair queen?
    Q. Mar. Mine, such as fill my heart with unhoped
      joys.
    War. Mine, full of sorrow and heart's discontent.
    K. Lew. What! has your king married the Lady
      Grey?
And now, to soothe your forgery and his,
Sends me a paper to persuade me patience?
Is this the alliance that he seeks with France?
Dare he presume to scorn us in this manner?
    Q. Mar. I told your majesty as much before: 179
This proveth Edward's love and Warwick's honesty.
    War. King Lewis, I here protest, in sight of
      heaven,
And by the hope I have of heavenly bliss,
That I am clear from this misdeed of Edward's,
No more my king, for he dishonours me,
But most himself, if he could see his shame.
Did I forget that by the house of York
My father came untimely to his death?
Did I let pass the abuse done to my niece?

26. **forlorn**, outcast. 41. **The . . . thee**, the longer preparation I make, the greater help I can give. 44. **he**, he who. 63. **fame**, report; see glossary. 81. **disannuls**, takes no account of. 93. **threescore and two**, i.e., from 1399, the date of Henry IV's accession, to 1461, that of Edward's. 94. **prescription**, claim founded upon long use. 97. **bewray**, reveal, betray. 127. **envy**, ill will, malice; see glossary. 128. **quit**, requite; see glossary. 133. **tempted . . . desire**, indulged in wishful thinking. 157. **Proud . . . kings**. Cf. II, iii, 37. 160. **conveyance**, underhand dealing. 175. **forgery**, deceit. 188. **abuse . . . niece**. Cf. a passage in Holinshed relating "that king Edward did attempt a thing once in the earles house, which was much against the earles honestie; (whether he would haue defloured his daughter or his neece, the certeintie was not for both their honours openlie reuealed;) for suerlie, such a thing was attempted by king Edward. . . ."

Did I impale him with the regal crown?
Did I put Henry from his native right? 190
And am I guerdon'd at the last with shame?
Shame on himself! for my desert is honour:
And to repair my honour lost for him,
I here renounce him and return to Henry.
My noble queen, let former grudges pass,
And henceforth I am thy true servitor:
I will revenge his wrong to Lady Bona
And replant Henry in his former state.
   Q. Mar. Warwick, these words have turn'd my hate
     to love;
And I forgive and quite forget old faults, 200
And joy that thou becomest King Henry's friend.
   War. So much his friend, ay, his unfeigned friend,
That, if King Lewis vouchsafe to furnish us
With some few bands of chosen soldiers,
I'll undertake to land them on our coast
And force the tyrant from his seat by war.
'Tis not his new-made bride shall succour him:
And as for Clarence, as my letters tell me,
He's very likely now to fall from him,
For matching more for wanton lust than honour, 210
Or than for strength and safety of our country.
   Bona. Dear brother, how shall Bona be revenged
But by thy help to this distressed queen?
   Q. Mar. Renowned prince, how shall poor Henry
     live,
Unless thou rescue him from foul despair?
   Bona. My quarrel and this English queen's are one.
   War. And mine, fair lady Bona, joins with yours.
   K. Lew. And mine with hers, and thine, and
     Margaret's.
Therefore at last I firmly am resolved
You shall have aid. 220
   Q. Mar. Let me give humble thanks for all at once.
   K. Lew. Then, England's messenger, return in post,
And tell false Edward, thy supposed king,
That Lewis of France is sending over masquers
To revel it with him and his new bride:
Thou seest what's past, go fear thy king withal.
   Bona. Tell him, in hope he'll prove a widower
     shortly,
I'll wear the willow garland for his sake.
   Q. Mar. Tell him, my mourning weeds are laid
     aside,
And I am ready to put armour on. 230
   War. Tell him from me that he hath done me
     wrong,
And therefore I'll uncrown him ere 't be long.
There's thy reward: be gone.   [*Exit Post*
   K. Lew.   But, Warwick,
Thou and Oxford, with five thousand men,
Shall cross the seas, and bid false Edward battle;
And, as occasion serves, this noble queen
And prince shall follow with a fresh supply.
Yet, ere thou go, but answer me one doubt,
What pledge have we of thy firm loyalty?
   War. This shall assure my constant loyalty, 240
That if our queen and this young prince agree,
I'll join mine eldest daughter and my joy
To him forthwith in holy wedlock bands.
   Q. Mar. Yes, I agree, and thank you for your motion.

Son Edward, she is fair and virtuous,
Therefore delay not, give thy hand to Warwick;
And, with thy hand, thy faith irrevocable,
That only Warwick's daughter shall be thine.
   Prince. Yes, I accept her, for she well deserves it;
And here, to pledge my vow, I give my hand. 250
         [*He gives his hand to Warwick.*
   K. Lew. Why stay we now? These soldiers shall be
     levied,
And thou, Lord Bourbon, our high admiral,
Shalt waft them over with our royal fleet.
I long till Edward fall by war's mischance,
For mocking marriage with a dame of France.
         [*Exeunt all but Warwick.*
   War. I came from Edward as ambassador,
But I return his sworn and mortal foe:
Matter of marriage was the charge he gave me,
But dreadful war shall answer his demand.
Had he none else to make a stale but me? 260
Then none but I shall turn his jest to sorrow.
I was the chief that raised him to the crown,
And I'll be chief to bring him down again:
Not that I pity Henry's misery,
But seek revenge on Edward's mockery.   [*Exit.*

ACT IV.

SCENE I. *London. The palace.*

Enter GLOUCESTER, CLARENCE, SOMERSET, *and*
MONTAGUE.

   Glou. Now tell me, brother Clarence, what think
     you
Of this new marriage with the Lady Grey?
Hath not our brother made a worthy choice?
   Clar. Alas, you know, 'tis far from hence to France;
How could he stay till Warwick made return?
   Som. My lords, forbear this talk; here comes the king.
   Glou. And his well-chosen bride.
   Clar. I mind to tell him plainly what I think.

Flourish. Enter KING EDWARD, *attended;* LADY GREY,
   as Queen; PEMBROKE, STAFFORD, HASTINGS, *and*
   others.

   K. Edw. Now, brother of Clarence, how like you our
     choice,
That you stand pensive, as half malcontent? 10
   Clar. As well as Lewis of France, or the Earl of
     Warwick,
Which are so weak of courage and in judgement
That they'll take no offence at our abuse.
   K. Edw. Suppose they take offence without a cause,
They are but Lewis and Warwick: I am Edward,
Your king and Warwick's, and must have my will.
   Glou. And shall have your will, because our king:
Yet hasty marriage seldom proveth well.
   K. Edw. Yea, brother Richard, are you offended too?
   Glou. Not I: 20
No, God forbid that I should wish them sever'd
Whom God hath join'd together; ay, and 'twere pity
To sunder them that yoke so well together.

191. **guerdon'd,** rewarded. 226. **fear,** frighten; see glossary. 228.
willow garland, contemptuous reference to the willow as the symbol of
a forsaken lover. 229. **weeds,** garments; see glossary. 242. **eldest
daughter,** a historical inaccuracy. Prince Edward married a younger

daughter of Warwick; the eldest was already the wife of the duke of
Clarence. 244. **motion,** proposal; see glossary. 260. **stale,** tool,
laughingstock. 262. **chief,** principal person.
  ACT IV. SCENE I. 8. **I mind,** I have it in mind. 10. **malcontent,**

K. Edw. Setting your scorns and your mislike aside,
Tell me some reason why the Lady Grey
Should not become my wife and England's queen.
And you too, Somerset and Montague,
Speak freely what you think.

Clar. Then this is mine opinion: that King Lewis
Becomes your enemy, for mocking him   30
About the marriage of the Lady Bona.

Glou. And Warwick, doing what you gave in charge,
Is now dishonoured by this new marriage.

K. Edw. What if both Lewis and Warwick be
     appeased
By such invention as I can devise?

Mont. Yet, to have join'd with France in such
     alliance
Would more have strengthen'd this our commonwealth
'Gainst foreign storms than any home-bred marriage.

Hast. Why, knows not Montague that of itself
England is safe, if true within itself?   40

Mont. But the safer when 'tis back'd with France.

Hast. 'Tis better using France than trusting France:
Let us be back'd with God and with the seas
Which He hath given for fence impregnable,
And with their helps only defend ourselves;
In them and in ourselves our safety lies.

Clar. For this one speech Lord Hastings well
     deserves
To have the heir of the Lord Hungerford.

K. Edw. Ay, what of that? it was my will and grant;
And for this once my will shall stand for law.   50

Glou. And yet methinks your grace hath not done
     well,
To give the heir and daughter of Lord Scales
Unto the brother of your loving bride;
She better would have fitted me or Clarence:
But in your bride you bury brotherhood.

Clar. Or else you would not have bestow'd the heir
Of the Lord Bonville on your new wife's son,
And leave your brothers to go speed elsewhere.

K. Edw. Alas, poor Clarence! is it for a wife
That thou art malcontent? I will provide thee.   60

Clar. In choosing for yourself, you show'd your
     judgement,
Which being shallow, you shall give me leave
To play the broker in mine own behalf;
And to that end I shortly mind to leave you.

K. Edw. Leave me, or tarry, Edward will be king,
And not be tied unto his brother's will.

Q. Eliz. My lords, before it pleased his majesty
To raise my state to title of a queen,
Do me but right, and you must all confess
That I was not ignoble of descent;   70
And meaner than myself have had like fortune.
But as this title honours me and mine,
So your dislike, to whom I would be pleasing,
Doth cloud my joys with danger and with sorrow.

K. Edw. My love, forbear to fawn upon their frowns:
What danger or what sorrow can befall thee,
So long as Edward is thy constant friend,
And their true sovereign, whom they must obey?
Nay, whom they shall obey, and love thee too,
Unless they seek for hatred at my hands;   80
Which if they do, yet will I keep thee safe,

And they shall feel the vengeance of my wrath.

Glou. I hear, yet say not much, but think the more.
                                        [*Aside.*

Enter a Post.

K. Edw. Now, messenger, what letters or what news
From France?

Post. My sovereign liege, no letters; and few words,
But such as I, without your special pardon,
Dare not relate.

K. Edw. Go to, we pardon thee: therefore, in brief,
Tell me their words as near as thou canst guess them. 90
What answer makes King Lewis unto our letters?

Post. At my depart, these were his very words:
'Go tell false Edward, thy supposed king,
That Lewis of France is sending over masquers
To revel it with him and his new bride.'

K. Edw. Is Lewis so brave? belike he thinks me
     Henry.
But what said Lady Bona to my marriage?

Post. These were her words, utter'd with mild
     disdain:
'Tell him, I hope he'll prove a widower shortly,
I'll wear the willow garland for his sake.'   100

K. Edw. I blame not her, she could say little less;
She had the wrong. But what said Henry's queen?
For I have heard that she was there in place.

Post. 'Tell him,' quoth she, 'my mourning weeds are
     done,
And I am ready to put armour on.'

K. Edw. Belike she minds to play the Amazon.
But what said Warwick to these injuries?

Post. He, more incensed against your majesty
Than all the rest, discharged me with these words:
'Tell him from me that he hath done me wrong,   110
And therefore I'll uncrown him ere 't be long.'

K. Edw. Ha! durst the traitor breathe out so proud
     words?
Well, I will arm me, being thus forewarn'd:
They shall have wars and pay for their presumption.
But say, is Warwick friends with Margaret?

Post. Ay, gracious sovereign; they are so link'd in
     friendship,
That young Prince Edward marries Warwick's
     daughter.

Clar. Belike the elder; Clarence will have the
     younger.
Now, brother king, farewell, and sit you fast,
For I will hence to Warwick's other daughter;   120
That, though I want a kingdom, yet in marriage
I may not prove inferior to yourself.
You that love me and Warwick, follow me.
               [*Exit Clarence, and Somerset follows*

Glou. [*Aside*] Not I:
My thoughts aim at a further matter; I
Stay not for the love of Edward, but the crown.

K. Edw. Clarence and Somerset both gone to
     Warwick!
Yet am I arm'd against the worst can happen;
And haste is needful in this desperate case.
Pembroke and Stafford, you in our behalf   130
Go levy men, and make prepare for war;
They are already, or quickly will be landed:

discontented; a cant term of the age suggesting a melancholy affection.
35. **invention,** scheme, plan; see glossary. 48. **To . . . Hungerford.**
The reference is to the marriage of Lord Hastings to the daughter of
Lord Hungerford. 58. **speed,** be successful; see glossary. 73. **dislike,**
displeasure. 90. **guess,** remember, i.e., reproduce from memory.
118. **the elder.** Cf. III, iii, 242, note. 128. **worst can,** worst that can.
131. **prepare,** preparation.

Myself in person will straight follow you.
                              [*Exeunt Pembroke and Stafford.*
But, ere I go, Hastings and Montague,
Resolve my doubt. You twain, of all the rest,
Are near to Warwick by blood and by alliance:
Tell me if you love Warwick more than me?
If it be so, then both depart to him;
I rather wish you foes than hollow friends:
But if you mind to hold your true obedience,   140
Give me assurance with some friendly vow,
That I may never have you in suspect.
  Mont. So God help Montague as he proves true!
  Hast. And Hastings as he favours Edward's cause!
  K. Edw. Now, brother Richard, will you stand by us?
  Glou. Ay, in despite of all that shall withstand you.
  K. Edw. Why, so! then am I sure of victory.
Now therefore let us hence; and lose no hour,
Till we meet Warwick with his foreign power. [*Exeunt.*

SCENE II. *A plain in Warwickshire.*

Enter WARWICK *and* OXFORD, *with French soldiers.*

  War. Trust me, my lord, all hitherto goes well;
The common people by numbers swarm to us.

Enter CLARENCE *and* SOMERSET.

But see where Somerset and Clarence comes!
Speak suddenly, my lords, are we all friends?
  Clar. Fear not that, my lord.
  War. Then, gentle Clarence, welcome unto
                              Warwick;
And welcome, Somerset: I hold it cowardice
To rest mistrustful where a noble heart
Hath pawn'd an open hand in sign of love;
Else might I think that Clarence, Edward's brother, 10
Were but a feigned friend to our proceedings:
But welcome, sweet Clarence; my daughter shall be
                              thine.
And now what rests but, in night's coverture,
Thy brother being carelessly encamp'd,
His soldiers lurking in the towns about,
And but attended by a simple guard,
We may surprise and take him at our pleasure?
Our scouts have found the adventure very easy:
That as Ulysses and stout Diomede
With sleight and manhood stole to Rhesus' tents,   20
And brought from thence the Thracian fatal steeds,
So we, well cover'd with the night's black mantle,
At unawares may beat down Edward's guard
And seize himself; I say not, slaughter him,
For I intend but only to surprise him.
You that will follow me to this attempt,
Applaud the name of Henry with your leader.
                              [*They all cry, 'Henry!'*
Why, then, let's on our way in silent sort:
For Warwick and his friends, God and Saint George!
                              [*Exeunt.*

SCENE III. *Edward's camp, near Warwick.*

Enter three Watchmen, *to guard the* KING'S *tent.*

First Watch. Come on, my masters, each man take
      his stand:
The king by this is set him down to sleep.
  Second Watch. What, will he not to bed?
  First Watch. Why, no; for he hath made a solemn
      vow
Never to lie and take his natural rest
Till Warwick or himself be quite suppress'd.
  Second Watch. To-morrow then belike shall be the
      day,
If Warwick be so near as men report.
  Third Watch. But say, I pray, what nobleman is that
That with the king here resteth in his tent?   10
  First Watch. 'Tis the Lord Hastings, the king's
      chiefest friend.
  Third Watch. O, is it so? But why commands the king
That his chief followers lodge in towns about him,
While he himself keeps in the cold field?
  Second Watch. 'Tis the more honour, because more
      dangerous.
  Third Watch. Ay, but give me worship and quietness;
I like it better than a dangerous honour.
If Warwick knew in what estate he stands,
'Tis to be doubted he would waken him.
  First Watch. Unless our halberds did shut up his
      passage.   20
  Second Watch. Ay, wherefore else guard we his royal
      tent,
But to defend his person from night-foes?

Enter WARWICK, CLARENCE, OXFORD, SOMERSET,
      and French soldiers, silent all.

  War. This is his tent; and see where stand his guard.
Courage, my masters! honour now or never!
But follow me, and Edward shall be ours.
  First Watch. Who goes there?
  Second Watch. Stay, or thou diest!
      [*Warwick and the rest cry all, 'Warwick! Warwick!'*
      and set upon the Guard, who fly, crying, 'Arm! arm!'
                Warwick and the rest following them.

The drum playing and trumpet sounding, re-enter
WARWICK, SOMERSET, *and the rest, bringing the*
KING *out in his gown, sitting in a chair.* RICHARD
      and HASTINGS *fly over the stage.*

  Som. What are they that fly there?
  War. Richard and Hastings: let them go; here is
The duke.
  K. Edw. The duke! Why, Warwick, when we parted,
Thou call'dst me king.
  War.   Ay, but the case is alter'd: 31
When you disgraced me in my embassade,
Then I degraded you from being king,
And come now to create you Duke of York.
Alas! how should you govern any kingdom,
That know not how to use ambassadors,
Nor how to be contented with one wife,
Nor how to use your brothers brotherly,
Nor how to study for the people's welfare,
Nor how to shroud yourself from enemies?   40
  K. Edw. Yea, brother of Clarence, art thou here too?
Nay, then I see that Edward needs must down.

Yet, Warwick, in despite of all mischance,
Of thee thyself and all thy complices,
Edward will always bear himself as king:
Though fortune's malice overthrow my state,
My mind exceeds the compass of her wheel.
   War. Then, for his mind, be Edward England's
     king: [*Takes off his crown.*
But Henry now shall wear the English crown,
And be true king indeed, thou but the shadow.   50
My lord of Somerset, at my request,
See that forthwith Duke Edward be convey'd
Unto my brother, Archbishop of York.
When I have fought with Pembroke and his fellows,
I'll follow you, and tell what answer
Lewis and the Lady Bona send to him.
Now, for a while farewell, good Duke of York.
                [*They lead him out forcibly.*
   K. Edw. What fates impose, that men must needs
     abide;
It boots not to resist both wind and tide. [*Exit, guarded.*
   Oxf. What now remains, my lords, for us to do   60
But march to London with our soldiers?
   War. Ay, that's the first thing that we have to do;
To free King Henry from imprisonment
And see him seated in the regal throne.   [*Exeunt.*

SCENE IV. *London. The palace.*

Enter QUEEN ELIZABETH *and* RIVERS.

   Riv. Madam, what makes you in this sudden change?
   Q. Eliz. Why, brother Rivers, are you yet to learn
What late misfortune is befall'n King Edward?
   Riv. What! loss of some pitch'd battle against
     Warwick?
   Q. Eliz. No, but the loss of his own royal person.
   Riv. Then is my sovereign slain?
   Q. Eliz. Ay, almost slain, for he is taken prisoner,
Either betray'd by falsehood of his guard
Or by his foe surprised at unawares:
And, as I further have to understand,   10
Is new committed to the Bishop of York,
Fell Warwick's brother and by that our foe.
   Riv. These news I must confess are full of grief;
Yet, gracious madam, bear it as you may:
Warwick may lose, that now hath won the day.
   Q. Eliz. Till then fair hope must hinder life's decay.
And I the rather wean me from despair
For love of Edward's offspring in my womb:
This is it that makes me bridle passion
And bear with mildness my misfortune's cross;   20
Ay, ay, for this I draw in many a tear
And stop the rising of blood-sucking sighs,
Lest with my sighs or tears I blast or drown
King Edward's fruit, true heir to the English crown.
   Riv. But, madam, where is Warwick then become?
   Q. Eliz. I am inform'd that he comes towards
     London,
To set the crown once more on Henry's head:
Guess thou the rest; King Edward's friends must
     down,
But, to prevent the tyrant's violence,—

For trust not him that hath once broken faith,—   30
I'll hence forthwith unto the sanctuary,
To save at least the heir of Edward's right:
There shall I rest secure from force and fraud.
Come, therefore, let us fly while we may fly:
If Warwick take us we are sure to die.   [*Exeunt.*

SCENE V. *A park near Middleham Castle in Yorkshire.*

Enter GLOUCESTER, LORD HASTINGS, *and* SIR WILLIAM
   STANLEY.

   Glou. Now, my Lord Hastings and Sir William
     Stanley,
Leave off to wonder why I drew you hither,
Into this chiefest thicket of the park.
Thus stands the case: you know our king, my brother,
Is prisoner to the bishop here, at whose hands
He hath good usage and great liberty,
And, often but attended with weak guard,
Comes hunting this way to disport himself.
I have advertised him by secret means
That if about this hour he make this way   10
Under the colour of his usual game,
He shall here find his friends with horse and men
To set him free from his captivity.

Enter KING EDWARD *and a Huntsman with him.*

   Hunt. This way, my lord; for this way lies the game.
   K. Edw. Nay, this way, man: see where the
     huntsmen stand.
Now, brother of Gloucester, Lord Hastings, and the
     rest,
Stand you thus close, to steal the bishop's deer?
   Glou. Brother, the time and case requireth haste:
Your horse stands ready at the park-corner.
   K. Edw. But whither shall we then?
   Hast.   To Lynn, my lord,   20
And ship from thence to Flanders.
   Glou. Well guess'd, believe me; for that was my
     meaning.
   K. Edw. Stanley, I will requite thy forwardness.
   Glou. But wherefore stay we? 'tis no time to talk.
   K. Edw. Huntsman, what say'st thou? wilt thou go
     along?
   Hunt. Better do so than tarry and be hang'd.
   Glou. Come then, away; let's ha' no more ado.
   K. Edw. Bishop, farewell: shield thee from
     Warwick's frown;
And pray that I may repossess the crown.   [*Exeunt.*

SCENE VI. *London. The Tower.*

Flourish. Enter KING HENRY, CLARENCE, WARWICK,
   SOMERSET, *young* RICHMOND, OXFORD, MONTAGUE,
   and Lieutenant of the Tower.

   K. Hen. Master lieutenant, now that God and
     friends
Have shaken Edward from the regal seat,
And turn'd my captive state to liberty,

---

long handles.   **32. embassade,** mission as an ambassador.   **48. for his
mind,** i.e., in his own thoughts.   **54. fellows,** companions; see glossary.
    SCENE IV.   **22. blood-sucking sighs.** Cf. *2 Henry VI*, III, ii, 61, 63,
note.   **28. must down,** will inevitably be put down.   **29. prevent,**
forestall; see glossary.

SCENE V.   **2. Leave off,** cease.   **11. colour,** pretext; see glossary.
17. close, concealed; see glossary.   **23. forwardness,** zeal.

My fear to hope, my sorrows unto joys,
At our enlargement what are thy due fees?
   Lieu. Subjects may challenge nothing of their
    sovereigns;
But if an humble prayer may prevail,
I then crave pardon of your majesty.
   K. Hen. For what, lieutenant? for well using me?
Nay, be thou sure I'll well requite thy kindness,   10
For that it made my imprisonment a pleasure;
Ay, such a pleasure as incaged birds
Conceive when after many moody thoughts
At last by notes of household harmony
They quite forget their loss of liberty.
But, Warwick, after God, thou set'st me free,
And chiefly therefore I thank God and thee;
He was the author, thou the instrument.
Therefore, that I may conquer fortune's spite
By living low, where fortune cannot hurt me,   20
And that the people of this blessed land
May not be punish'd with my thwarting stars,
Warwick, although my head still wear the crown,
I here resign my government to thee,
For thou art fortunate in all thy deeds.
   War. Your grace hath still been famed for virtuous;
And now may seem as wise as virtuous,
By spying and avoiding fortune's malice,
For few men rightly temper with the stars:
Yet in this one thing let me blame your grace,   30
For choosing me when Clarence is in place.
   Clar. No, Warwick, thou art worthy of the sway,
To whom the heavens in thy nativity
Adjudged an olive branch and laurel crown,
As likely to be blest in peace and war;
And therefore I yield thee my free consent.
   War. And I choose Clarence only for protector.
   K. Hen. Warwick and Clarence, give me both your
    hands:
Now join your hands, and with your hands your
    hearts,
That no dissension hinder government: 40
I make you both protectors of this land,
While I myself will lead a private life
And in devotion spend my latter days,
To sin's rebuke and my Creator's praise.
   War. What answers Clarence to his sovereign's
    will?
   Clar. That he consents, if Warwick yield consent;
For on thy fortune I repose myself.
   War. Why, then, though loath, yet must I be
    content:
We'll yoke together, like a double shadow
To Henry's body, and supply his place;   50
I mean, in bearing weight of government,
While he enjoys the honour and his ease.
And, Clarence, now then it is more than needful
Forthwith that Edward be pronounced a traitor,
And all his lands and goods be confiscate.
   Clar. What else? and that succession be determined.
   War. Ay, therein Clarence shall not want his part.
   K. Hen. But, with the first of all your chief affairs,
Let me entreat, for I command no more,

That Margaret your queen and my son Edward   60
Be sent for, to return from France with speed;
For, till I see them here, by doubtful fear
My joy of liberty is half eclipsed.
   Clar. It shall be done, my sovereign, with all speed.
   K. Hen. My Lord of Somerset, what youth is that,
Of whom you seem to have so tender care?
   Som. My liege, it is young Henry, earl of Richmond.
   K. Hen. Come hither, England's hope. [*Lays his hand
    on his head*] If secret powers
Suggest but truth to my divining thoughts,
This pretty lad will prove our country's bliss.   70
His looks are full of peaceful majesty,
His head by nature framed to wear a crown,
His hand to wield a sceptre, and himself
Likely in time to bless a regal throne.
Make much of him, my lords, for this is he
Must help you more than you are hurt by me.

   Enter a Post.

   War. What news, my friend?
   Post. That Edward is escaped from your brother,
And fled, as he hears since, to Burgundy.
   War. Unsavoury news! but how made he escape?   80
   Post. He was convey'd by Richard Duke of
    Gloucester
And the Lord Hastings, who attended him
In secret ambush on the forest side
And from the bishop's huntsmen rescued him;
For hunting was his daily exercise.
   War. My brother was too careless of his charge.
But let us hence, my sovereign, to provide
A salve for any sore that may betide.
    [*Exeunt all but Somerset, Richmond, and Oxford.*
   Som. My lord, I like not of this flight of Edward's;
For doubtless Burgundy will yield him help,   90
And we shall have more wars before 't be long.
As Henry's late presaging prophecy
Did glad my heart with hope of this young Richmond,
So doth my heart misgive me, in these conflicts
What may befall him, to his harm and ours:
Therefore, Lord Oxford, to prevent the worst,
Forthwith we'll send him hence to Brittany,
Till storms be past of civil enmity.
   Oxf. Ay, for if Edward repossess the crown,
'Tis like that Richmond with the rest shall down.   100
   Som. It shall be so; he shall to Brittany.
Come, therefore, let 's about it speedily.   [*Exeunt.*

SCENE VII. *Before York.*

Flourish. Enter KING EDWARD, GLOUCESTER,
HASTINGS, *and* Soldiers.

   K. Edw. Now, brother Richard, Lord Hastings,
    and the rest,
Yet thus far fortune maketh us amends,
And says that once more I shall interchange
My waned state for Henry's regal crown.
Well have we pass'd and now repass'd the seas
And brought desired help from Burgundy:

SCENE VI.   5. **enlargement,** freedom from captivity or imprisonment.
6. **challenge,** claim as a right.   22. **thwarting,** crossing; cf. *Romeo and
Juliet,* Prologue, 6.   29. **temper with,** blend or accord with.   34. **olive
branch,** symbol of peace. **laurel crown,** symbol of honor.   36. **free,**
generous; see glossary.   57. **Clarence . . . part.** Holinshed makes
explicit this veiled reference to Clarence's nearness to the crown. If

Edward and his heirs were set aside—as an attainder for treason would
entail—and if Henry's line should die out, Clarence would be in a
position to claim the kingship. This possibility was glanced at by
Gloucester earlier in the play (III, ii, 130). **want,** lack; see glossary.
67. **Henry, earl of Richmond,** Henry Tudor, great-great-grandson of
John of Gaunt and Catherine Swynford through his mother, Margaret

What then remains, we being thus arrived
From Ravenspurgh haven before the gates of York,
But that we enter, as into our dukedom?
 Glou. The gates made fast! Brother, I like not this; 10
For many men that stumble at the threshold
Are well foretold that danger lurks within.
 K. Edw. Tush, man, abodements must not now
  affright us:
By fair or foul means we must enter in,
For hither will our friends repair to us.
 Hast. My liege, I'll knock once more to summon
  them.

 Enter, on the walls, the Mayor of York, *and his Brethren.*

 May. My lords, we were forewarned of your
  coming,
And shut the gates for safety of ourselves;
For now we owe allegiance unto Henry.
 K. Edw. But, master mayor, if Henry be your king,20
Yet Edward at the least is Duke of York.
 May. True, my good lord; I know you for no less.
 K. Edw. Why, and I challenge nothing but my
  dukedom,
As being well content with that alone.
 Glou. [*Aside*] But when the fox hath once got in his
  nose,
He'll soon find means to make the body follow.
 Hast. Why, master mayor, why stand you in a
  doubt?
Open the gates; we are King Henry's friends.
 May. Ay, say you so? the gates shall then be open'd.
            [*They descend.*
 Glou. A wise stout captain, and soon persuaded! 30
 Hast. The good old man would fain that all were
  well,
So 'twere not 'long of him; but being enter'd,
I doubt not, I, but we shall soon persuade
Both him and all his brothers unto reason.

 Enter the Mayor *and two* Aldermen, *below.*

 K. Edw. So, master mayor: these gates must not be
  shut
But in the night or in the time of war.
What! fear not, man, but yield me up the keys;
            [*Takes his keys.*
For Edward will defend the town and thee,
And all those friends that deign to follow me.

 March. Enter MONTGOMERY, *with drum and soldiers.*

 Glou. Brother, this is Sir John Montgomery, 40
Our trusty friend, unless I be deceived.
 K. Edw. Welcome, Sir John! But why come you in
  arms?
 Mont. To help King Edward in his time of storm,
As every loyal subject ought to do.
 K. Edw. Thanks, good Montgomery; but we now
  forget
Our title to the crown and only claim
Our dukedom till God please to send the rest.
 Mont. Then fare you well, for I will hence again:
I came to serve a king and not a duke.

Drummer, strike up, and let us march away. 50
         [*The drum begins to march.*
 K. Edw. Nay, stay, Sir John, awhile, and we'll
  debate
By what safe means the crown may be recover'd.
 Mont. What talk you of debating? in few words,
If you'll not here proclaim yourself our king,
I'll leave you to your fortune and be gone
To keep them back that come to succour you:
Why shall we fight, if you pretend no title?
 Glou. Why, brother, wherefore stand you on nice
  points?
 K. Edw. When we grow stronger, then we'll make
  our claim:
Till then, 'tis wisdom to conceal our meaning. 60
 Hast. Away with scrupulous wit! now arms must
  rule.
 Glou. And fearless minds climb soonest unto
  crowns.
Brother, we will proclaim you out of hand;
The bruit thereof will bring you many friends.
 K. Edw. Then be it as you will; for 'tis my right,
And Henry but usurps the diadem.
 Mont. Ay, now my sovereign speaketh like himself;
And now will I be Edward's champion.
 Hast. Sound trumpet; Edward shall be here
  proclaim'd:
Come, fellow-soldier, make thou proclamation. 70
            [*Flourish.*
 Sold. Edward the Fourth, by the grace of God, king
of England and France, and lord of Ireland, &c.
 Mont. And whosoe'er gainsays King Edward's
  right,
By this I challenge him to single fight.
         [*Throws down his gauntlet.*
 All. Long live Edward the Fourth!
 K. Edw. Thanks, brave Montgomery; and thanks
  unto you all:
If fortune serve me, I'll requite this kindness.
Now, for this night, let 's harbour here in York;
And when the morning sun shall raise his car 80
Above the border of this horizon,
We'll forward towards Warwick and his mates;
For well I wot that Henry is no soldier.
Ah, froward Clarence! how evil it beseems thee,
To flatter Henry and forsake thy brother!
Yet, as we may, we'll meet both thee and Warwick
Come on, brave soldiers: doubt not of the day,
And, that once gotten, doubt not of large pay. [*Exeunt.*

   SCENE VIII. *London. The palace.*

 Flourish. Enter KING HENRY, WARWICK, MONTAGUE,
  CLARENCE, EXETER, *and* OXFORD.

 War. What counsel, lords? Edward from Belgia,
With hasty Germans and blunt Hollanders,
Hath pass'd in safety through the narrow seas,
And with his troops doth march amain to London;
And many giddy people flock to him.
 K. Hen. Let 's levy men, and beat him back again.

Beaufort. He became King Henry VII in 1485. This intruded allusion is
a direct compliment to Queen Elizabeth, granddaughter of King Henry
VII; it is adapted from a similar compliment in Holinshed. Somerset is
Henry Tudor's cousin. **79. he.** The antecedent is *brother.*
 SCENE VII. **9. as,** as if; see glossary. **13. abodements,** omens. **51.
debate,** discuss; see glossary. **58. stand . . . points?** Are you over-

scrupulous? **61. scrupulous,** cautious, crafty. **63. out of hand,** at
once. **64. bruit,** rumor. **78. serve,** be favorable; see glossary. **80.
his car,** i.e., Phoebus' chariot. **87. the day,** the day's outcome.
 SCENE VIII. **1. Belgia,** Flanders; cf. IV, v, 21.

Clar. A little fire is quickly trodden out;
Which, being suffer'd, rivers cannot quench.

War. In Warwickshire I have true-hearted friends,
Not mutinous in peace, yet bold in war;   10
Those will I muster up: and thou, son Clarence,
Shalt stir up in Suffolk, Norfolk and in Kent,
The knights and gentlemen to come with thee:
Thou, brother Montague, in Buckingham,
Northampton and in Leicestershire, shalt find
Men well inclined to hear what thou command'st:
And thou, brave Oxford, wondrous well beloved,
In Oxfordshire shalt muster up thy friends.
My sovereign, with the loving citizens,
Like to his island girt in with the ocean,   20
Or modest Dian circled with her nymphs,
Shall rest in London till we come to him.
Fair lords, take leave and stand not to reply.
Farewell, my sovereign.
    K. Hen. Farewell, my Hector, and my Troy's true
       hope.
    Clar. In sign of truth, I kiss your highness' hand.
    K. Hen. Well-minded Clarence, be thou fortunate!
    Mont. Comfort, my lord; and so I take my leave.
    Oxf. And thus I seal my truth, and bid adieu.
    K. Hen. Sweet Oxford, and my loving Montague, 30
And all at once, once more a happy farewell.
    War. Farewell, sweet lords: let 's meet at Coventry.
           [Exeunt all but King Henry and Exeter.
    K. Hen. Here at the palace will I rest awhile.
Cousin of Exeter, what thinks your lordship?
Methinks the power that Edward hath in field
Should not be able to encounter mine.
    Exe. The doubt is that he will seduce the rest.
    K. Hen. That 's not my fear; my meed hath got me
       fame:
I have not stopp'd mine ears to their demands,
Nor posted off their suits with slow delays;   40
My pity hath been balm to heal their wounds,
My mildness hath allay'd their swelling griefs,
My mercy dried their water-flowing tears;
I have not been desirous of their wealth,
Nor much oppress'd them with great subsidies,
Nor forward of revenge, though they much err'd:
Then why should they love Edward more than me?
No, Exeter, these graces challenge grace:
And when the lion fawns upon the lamb,
The lamb will never cease to follow him.   50
        [Shout within, 'A Lancaster! A Lancaster!'
    Exe. Hark, hark, my lord! what shouts are these?

Enter KING EDWARD, GLOUCESTER, *and soldiers.*

    K. Edw. Seize on the shame-faced Henry, bear him
       hence;
And once again proclaim us king of England.
You are the fount that makes small brooks to flow:
Now stops thy spring; my sea shall suck them dry,
And swell so much the higher by their ebb.
Hence with him to the Tower; let him not speak.
           [Exeunt some with King Henry.
And, lords, towards Coventry bend we our course,
Where peremptory Warwick now remains:

The sun shines hot; and, if we use delay,   60
Cold biting winter mars our hoped-for hay.
    Glou. Away betimes, before his forces join,
And take the great-grown traitor unawares:
Brave warriors, march amain towards Coventry.
                  [Exeunt.

ACT V.

SCENE I. *Coventry.*

Enter WARWICK, *the* Mayor of Coventry, *two*
  Messengers, *and others upon the walls.*

    War. Where is the post that came from valiant
      Oxford?
How far hence is thy lord, mine honest fellow?
    First Mess. By this at Dunsmore, marching
      hitherward.
    War. How far off is our brother Montague?
Where is the post that came from Montague?
    Second Mess. By this at Daintry, with a puissant
      troop.

Enter SIR JOHN SOMERVILLE.

    War. Say, Somerville, what says my loving son?
And, by thy guess, how nigh is Clarence now?
    Som. At Southam I did leave him with his forces,
And do expect him here some two hours hence.   10
                   [Drum heard.
    War. Then Clarence is at hand; I hear his drum.
    Som. It is not his, my lord; here Southam lies:
The drum your honour hears marcheth from
    Warwick.
    War. Who should that be? belike, unlook'd-for
      friends.
    Som. They are at hand, and you shall quickly
      know.

March: flourish. Enter KING EDWARD, GLOUCESTER,
  and soldiers.

    K. Edw. Go, trumpet, to the walls, and sound a
      parle.
    Glou. See how the surly Warwick mans the wall!
    War. O unbid spite! is sportful Edward come?
Where slept our scouts, or how are they seduced,
That we could hear no news of his repair?   20
    K. Edw. Now, Warwick, wilt thou ope the city
      gates,
Speak gentle words and humbly bend thy knee,
Call Edward king and at his hands beg mercy?
And he shall pardon thee these outrages.
    War. Nay, rather, wilt thou draw thy forces hence,
Confess who set thee up and pluck'd thee down,
Call Warwick patron and be penitent?
And thou shalt still remain the Duke of York.
    Glou. I thought, at least, he would have said the
      king;
Or did he make the jest against his will?   30
    War. Is not a dukedom, sir, a goodly gift?
    Glou. Ay, by my faith, for a poor earl to give:

---

21. **modest Dian,** chaste Diana; a probable reference to Queen Elizabeth; see *modest* in glossary. 23. **stand,** wait. 37. **doubt,** danger,
risk; see glossary. 38. **meed,** merits. 40. **posted off,** put off. 59.
peremptory, overbearing.
    ACT V. SCENE I. 16. **parle,** bugle call for a parley; see glossary.

18. **unbid,** unwelcome. **spite,** vexatious circumstance. 20. **repair,**
recovery. 26. **set . . . down.** Cf. II, iii, 37; III, iii, 157. 36. **Atlas,**
an allusion to the mythological character who carried the world on
his shoulders. 52. **bear . . . sail,** be so humble, abject. 65. **rouse,**
cause (an animal) to rise from his lair. 73. **Two of thy name,** Edmund,

I'll do thee service for so good a gift.

War. 'Twas I that gave the kingdom to thy brother.

K. Edw. Why then 'tis mine, if but by Warwick's
gift.

War. Thou art no Atlas for so great a weight:
And, weakling, Warwick takes his gift again;
And Henry is my king, Warwick his subject.

K. Edw. But Warwick's king is Edward's prisoner:
And, gallant Warwick, do but answer this: 40
What is the body when the head is off?

Glou. Alas, that Warwick had no more forecast,
But, whiles he thought to steal the single ten,
The king was slily finger'd from the deck!
You left poor Henry at the Bishop's palace,
And, ten to one, you'll meet him in the Tower.

K. Edw. 'Tis even so; yet you are Warwick still.

Glou. Come, Warwick, take the time; kneel down,
kneel down:
Nay, when? strike now, or else the iron cools.

War. I had rather chop this hand off at a blow, 50
And with the other fling it at thy face,
Than bear so low a sail, to strike to thee.

K. Edw. Sail how thou canst, have wind and tide
thy friend.
This hand, fast wound about thy coal-black hair,
Shall, whiles thy head is warm and new cut off,
Write in the dust this sentence with thy blood,
'Wind-changing Warwick now can change no more.'

Enter OXFORD, *with drum and colours.*

War. O cheerful colours! see where Oxford comes!

Oxf. Oxford, Oxford, for Lancaster!
[*He and his forces enter the city.*

Glou. The gates are open, let us enter too. 60

K. Edw. So other foes may set upon our backs.
Stand we in good array; for they no doubt
Will issue out again and bid us battle:
If not, the city being but of small defence,
We'll quickly rouse the traitors in the same.

War. O, welcome, Oxford! for we want thy help.

Enter MONTAGUE, *with drum and colours.*

Mont. Montague, Montague, for Lancaster!
[*He and his forces enter the city.*

Glou. Thou and thy brother both shall buy this
treason
Even with the dearest blood your bodies bear.

K. Edw. The harder match'd, the greater victory: 70
My mind presageth happy gain and conquest.

Enter SOMERSET, *with drum and colours.*

Som. Somerset, Somerset, for Lancaster!
[*He and his forces enter the city.*

Glou. Two of thy name, both Dukes of Somerset,
Have sold their lives unto the house of York;
And thou shalt be the third, if this sword hold.

Enter CLARENCE, *with drum and colours.*

War. And lo, where George of Clarence sweeps
along,
Of force enough to bid his brother battle;

With whom an upright zeal to right prevails
More than the nature of a brother's love!
Come, Clarence, come; thou wilt, if Warwick call. 80

Clar. Father of Warwick, know you what this
means? [*Taking his red rose out of his hat.*
Look here, I throw my infamy at thee:
I will not ruinate my father's house,
Who gave his blood to lime the stones together,
And set up Lancaster. Why, trow'st thou, Warwick,
That Clarence is so harsh, so blunt, unnatural,
To bend the fatal instruments of war
Against his brother and his lawful king?
Perhaps thou wilt object my holy oath:
To keep that oath were more impiety 90
Than Jephthah's, when he sacrificed his daughter.
I am so sorry for my trespass made
That, to deserve well at my brother's hands,
I here proclaim myself thy mortal foe,
With resolution, wheresoe'er I meet thee—
As I will meet thee, if thou stir abroad—
To plague thee for thy foul misleading me.
And so, proud-hearted Warwick, I defy thee,
And to my brother turn my blushing cheeks.
Pardon me, Edward, I will make amends: 100
And, Richard, do not frown upon my faults,
For I will henceforth be no more unconstant.

K. Edw. Now welcome more, and ten times more
beloved,
Than if thou never hadst deserved our hate.

Glou. Welcome, good Clarence; this is brother-like.

War. O passing traitor, perjured and unjust!

K. Edw. What, Warwick, wilt thou leave the town
and fight?
Or shall we beat the stones about thine ears?

War. Alas, I am not coop'd here for defence!
I will away towards Barnet presently, 110
And bid thee battle, Edward, if thou darest.

K. Edw. Yes, Warwick, Edward dares, and leads
the way.
Lords, to the field; Saint George and victory!
[*Exeunt King Edward and his company. March.
Warwick and his company follow.*

———————————

SCENE II. *A field of battle near Barnet.*

Alarum and excursions. Enter KING EDWARD, *bringing
forth* WARWICK *wounded.*

K. Edw. So, lie thou there: die thou, and die our
fear;
For Warwick was a bug that fear'd us all.
Now, Montague, sit fast; I seek for thee,
That Warwick's bones may keep thine company. [*Exit.*

War. Ah, who is nigh? come to me, friend or foe,
And tell me who is victor, York or Warwick?
Why ask I that? my mangled body shows,
My blood, my want of strength, my sick heart shows,
That I must yield my body to the earth
And, by my fall, the conquest to my foe. 10
Thus yields the cedar to the axe's edge,
Whose arms gave shelter to the princely eagle,

killed at St. Albans in 1455, and his son Henry (not a character in this play), beheaded in 1464 for his Lancastrian sympathies. The duke addressed here is Henry's brother Edmund. They were Beauforts, descendants of John of Gaunt (see Genealogical Table). 84. **lime,** cement. 85. **trow'st,** believest; see glossary. 89. **object,** urge (i.e., in

the sense "remind me of"). 91. **Jephthah's.** Cf. Judges 11 : 30 ff. for the account of Jephthah's vow to sacrifice, if victorious, the first living creature that came to meet him on his return. His daughter was the victim. 106. **unjust,** unfaithful, false; see glossary.
SCENE II. 2. **bug,** bogey.

Under whose shade the ramping lion slept,
Whose top-branch overpeer'd Jove's spreading tree
And kept low shrubs from winter's powerful wind.
These eyes, that now are dimm'd with death's black
    veil,
Have been as piercing as the mid-day sun,
To search the secret treasons of the world:
The wrinkles in my brows, now fill'd with blood,
Were liken'd oft to kingly sepulchres;   20
For who lived king, but I could dig his grave?
And who durst smile when Warwick bent his brow?
Lo, now my glory smear'd in dust and blood!
My parks, my walks, my manors that I had,
Even now forsake me, and of all my lands
Is nothing left me but my body's length.
Why, what is pomp, rule, reign, but earth and dust?
And, live we how we can, yet die we must.

Enter OXFORD *and* SOMERSET.

Som. Ah, Warwick, Warwick! wert thou as we are,
We might recover all our loss again: 30
The queen from France hath brought a puissant
    power:
Even now we heard the news: ah, couldst thou fly!
War. Why, then I would not fly. Ah, Montague,
If thou be there, sweet brother, take my hand,
And with thy lips keep in my soul awhile!
Thou lovest me not; for, brother, if thou didst,
Thy tears would wash this cold congealed blood
That glues my lips and will not let me speak.
Come quickly, Montague, or I am dead.
Som. Ah, Warwick! Montague hath breathed his
    last;   40
And to the latest gasp cried out for Warwick
And said 'Commend me to my valiant brother.'
And more he would have said, and more he spoke,
Which sounded like a clamour in a vault,
That mought not be distinguish'd; but at last
I well might hear, deliver'd with a groan,
'O, farewell, Warwick!'
War. Sweet rest his soul! Fly, lords, and save
    yourselves;
For Warwick bids you all farewell, to meet in heaven.
        [*Dies.*
Oxf. Away, away, to meet the queen's great power!
    [*Here they bear away his body. Exeunt.*

SCENE III. *Another part of the field.*

Flourish. Enter KING EDWARD *in triumph; with*
    GLOUCESTER, CLARENCE, *and the rest.*

K. Edw. Thus far our fortune keeps an upward
    course,
And we are graced with wreaths of victory.
But, in the midst of this bright-shining day,
I spy a black, suspicious, threatening cloud,
That will encounter with our glorious sun,
Ere he attain his easeful western bed:
I mean, my lords, those powers that the queen
Hath raised in Gallia have arrived our coast
And, as we hear, march on to fight with us.

Clar. A little gale will soon disperse that cloud   10
And blow it to the source from whence it came:
The very beams will dry those vapours up,
For every cloud engenders not a storm.
Glou. The queen is valued thirty thousand strong,
And Somerset, with Oxford, fled to her:
If she have time to breathe, be well assured
Her faction will be full as strong as ours.
K. Edw. We are advertised by our loving friends
That they do hold their course toward Tewksbury:
We, having now the best at Barnet field,   20
Will thither straight, for willingness rids way;
And, as we march, our strength will be augmented
In every county as we go along.
Strike up the drum; cry 'Courage!' and away. [*Exeunt.*

SCENE IV. *Plains near Tewksbury.*

March. Enter QUEEN MARGARET, PRINCE EDWARD,
    SOMERSET, OXFORD, *and soldiers.*

Q. Mar. Great lords, wise men ne'er sit and wail
    their loss,
But cheerly seek how to redress their harms.
What though the mast be now blown overboard,
The cable broke, the holding-anchor lost,
And half our sailors swallow'd in the flood?
Yet lives our pilot still. Is 't meet that he
Should leave the helm and like a fearful lad
With tearful eyes add water to the sea
And give more strength to that which hath too much,
Whiles, in his moan, the ship splits on the rock,   10
Which industry and courage might have saved?
Ah, what a shame! ah, what a fault were this!
Say Warwick was our anchor; what of that?
And Montague our topmast; what of him?
Our slaughter'd friends the tackles; what of these?
Why, is not Oxford here another anchor?
And Somerset another goodly mast?
The friends of France our shrouds and tacklings?
And, though unskilful, why not Ned and I
For once allow'd the skilful pilot's charge?   20
We will not from the helm to sit and weep,
But keep our course, though the rough wind say no,
From shelves and rocks that threaten us with wreck.
As good to chide the waves as speak them fair.
And what is Edward but a ruthless sea?
What Clarence but a quicksand of deceit?
And Richard but a ragged fatal rock?
All these the enemies to our poor bark.
Say you can swim; alas, 'tis but a while!
Tread on the sand; why, there you quickly sink: 30
Bestride the rock; the tide will wash you off,
Or else you famish; that 's a threefold death.
This speak I, lords, to let you understand,
If case some one of you would fly from us,
That there 's no hoped-for mercy with the brothers
More than with ruthless waves, with sands and rocks.
Why, courage then! what cannot be avoided
'Twere childish weakness to lament or fear.
Prince. Methinks a woman of this valiant spirit
Should, if a coward heard her speak these words,   40

14-15. **Whose . . . wind.** Two independent references are merged here: the oak, sacred to Jove, and the fable of the oak and the briar, related in Spenser's *Shepheardes Calender.* 25-26. **of all . . . length,** a variant of the "earth upon earth" motif; cf. *Richard II*, III, iii, 153-154; *1 Henry IV*, V, iv, 89-92. 35. **with thy lips,** with a kiss; a reference to the belief

that the soul left the body through the open mouth.
    SCENE III. 8. **arrived,** reached; used transitively. 16. **time to breathe,** opportunity to muster her strength. 21. **rids way,** makes rapid progress.
    SCENE IV. 1-2. **Great . . . harms.** Cf. *Richard II*, III, ii, 178-179.

Infuse his breast with magnanimity
And make him, naked, foil a man at arms.
I speak not this as doubting any here;
For did I but suspect a fearful man,
He should have leave to go away betimes,
Lest in our need he might infect another
And make him of like spirit to himself.
If any such be here—as God forbid!—
Let him depart before we need his help.

Oxf. Women and children of so high a courage, 50
And warriors faint! why, 'twere perpetual shame.
O brave young prince! thy famous grandfather
Doth live again in thee: long mayst thou live
To bear his image and renew his glories!

Som. And he that will not fight for such a hope,
Go home to bed, and like the owl by day,
If he arise, be mock'd and wonder'd at.

Q. Mar. Thanks, gentle Somerset; sweet Oxford,
thanks.

Prince. And take his thanks that yet hath nothing
else.

Enter a Messenger.

Mess. Prepare you, lords, for Edward is at hand, 60
Ready to fight; therefore be resolute.

Oxf. I thought no less: it is his policy
To haste thus fast, to find us unprovided.

Som. But he 's deceived; we are in readiness.

Q. Mar. This cheers my heart, to see your
forwardness.

Oxf. Here pitch our battle; hence we will not
budge.

Flourish and march. Enter KING EDWARD, GLOUCESTER,
CLARENCE, *and soldiers.*

K. Edw. Brave followers, yonder stands the thorny
wood,
Which, by the heavens' assistance and your strength,
Must by the roots be hewn up yet ere night.
I need not add more fuel to your fire, 70
For well I wot ye blaze to burn them out:
Give signal to the fight, and to it, lords!

Q. Mar. Lords, knights, and gentlemen, what I
should say
My tears gainsay; for every word I speak,
Ye see, I drink the water of mine eyes.
Therefore, no more but this: Henry, your sovereign,
Is prisoner to the foe; his state usurp'd,
His realm a slaughter-house, his subjects slain,
His statutes cancell'd and his treasure spent;
And yonder is the wolf that makes this spoil. 80
You fight in justice: then, in God's name, lords,
Be valiant and give signal to the fight.
[*Alarum: Retreat: Excursions. Exeunt.*

SCENE V. *Another part of the field.*

Flourish. Enter KING EDWARD, GLOUCESTER,
CLARENCE, *and soldiers; with* QUEEN MARGARET,
OXFORD, *and* SOMERSET, *prisoners.*

K. Edw. Now here a period of tumultuous broils.

Away with Oxford to Hames Castle straight:
For Somerset, off with his guilty head.
Go, bear them hence; I will not hear them speak.

Oxf. For my part, I'll not trouble thee with words.

Som. Nor I, but stoop with patience to my fortune.
[*Exeunt Oxford and Somerset, guarded.*

Q. Mar. So part we sadly in this troublous world,
To meet with joy in sweet Jerusalem.

K. Edw. Is proclamation made, that who finds
Edward
Shall have a high reward, and he his life? 10

Glou. It is: and lo, where youthful Edward comes!

Enter soldiers, with PRINCE EDWARD.

K. Edw. Bring forth the gallant, let us hear him
speak.
What! can so young a thorn begin to prick?
Edward, what satisfaction canst thou make
For bearing arms, for stirring up my subjects,
And all the trouble thou hast turn'd me to?

Prince. Speak like a subject, proud ambitious York!
Suppose that I am now my father's mouth;
Resign thy chair, and where I stand kneel thou,
Whilst I propose the selfsame words to thee, 20
Which, traitor, thou wouldst have me answer to.

Q. Mar. Ah, that thy father had been so resolved!

Glou. That you might still have worn the petticoat,
And ne'er have stol'n the breech from Lancaster.

Prince. Let Æsop fable in a winter's night;
His currish riddles sort not with this place.

Glou. By heaven, brat, I'll plague ye for that word.

Q. Mar. Ay, thou wast born to be a plague to men.

Glou. For God's sake, take away this captive scold.

Prince. Nay, take away this scolding crook-back
rather. 30

K. Edw. Peace, wilful boy, or I will charm your
tongue.

Clar. Untutor'd lad, thou art too malapert.

Prince. I know my duty; you are all undutiful:
Lascivious Edward, and thou perjured George,
And thou mis-shapen Dick, I tell ye all
I am your better, traitors as ye are:
And thou usurp'st my father's right and mine.

K. Edw. Take that, thou likeness of this railer here.
[*Stabs him.*

Glou. Sprawl'st thou? take that, to end thy agony.
[*Stabs him.*

Clar. And there 's for twitting me with perjury. 40
[*Stabs him.*

Q. Mar. O, kill me too!

Glou. Marry, and shall. [*Offers to kill her.*

K. Edw. Hold, Richard, hold; for we have done too
much.

Glou. Why should she live, to fill the world with
words?

K. Edw. What, doth she swoon? use means for her
recovery.

Glou. Clarence, excuse me to the king my brother;
I'll hence to London on a serious matter:
Ere ye come there, be sure to hear some news.

Clar. What? what?

Glou. The Tower, the Tower. [*Exit.* 50

3 Henry VI
ACT V : SC V

297

---

9. **give . . . much.** Cf. *As You Like It*, II, i, 48-49. 23. **shelves,** sandbanks. 63. **unprovided,** unprepared. 80. **spoil,** destruction; see glossary.
SCENE V. 1. **period,** termination. 25. **Æsop,** an allusion to Gloucester's deformity. Aesop was reputed to have been similarly deformed.

26. **sort not,** are not appropriate to. 32. **malapert,** saucy. 38. **this railer here,** i.e., Queen Margaret.

Q. Mar. O Ned, sweet Ned! speak to thy mother, boy!
Canst thou not speak? O traitors! murderers!
They that stabb'd Cæsar shed no blood at all,
Did not offend, nor were not worthy blame,
If this foul deed were by to equal it:
He was a man; this, in respect, a child:
And men ne'er spend their fury on a child.
What's worse than murderer, that I may name it?
No, no, my heart will burst, an if I speak:
And I will speak, that so my heart may burst. 60
Butchers and villains! bloody cannibals!
How sweet a plant have you untimely cropp'd!
You have no children, butchers! if you had,
The thought of them would have stirr'd up remorse:
But if you ever chance to have a child,
Look in his youth to have him so cut off
As, deathsmen, you have rid this sweet young prince!
   K. Edw. Away with her; go, bear her hence perforce.
   Q. Mar. Nay, never bear me hence, dispatch me here;
Here sheathe thy sword, I'll pardon thee my death: 70
What, wilt thou not? then, Clarence, do it thou.
   Clar. By heaven, I will not do thee so much ease.
   Q. Mar. Good Clarence, do; sweet Clarence, do thou it.
   Clar. Didst thou not hear me swear I would not do it?
   Q. Mar. Ay, but thou usest to forswear thyself:
'Twas sin before, but now 'tis charity.
What, wilt thou not? Where is that devil's butcher,
Hard-favour'd Richard? Richard, where art thou?
Thou art not here: murder is thy alms-deed;
Petitioners for blood thou ne'er put'st back. 80
   K. Edw. Away, I say; I charge ye, bear her hence.
   Q. Mar. So come to you and yours, as to this prince!
                  [Exit, led out forcibly.
   K. Edw. Where's Richard gone?
   Clar. To London, all in post; and, as I guess,
To make a bloody supper in the Tower.
   K. Edw. He's sudden, if a thing comes in his head,
Now march we hence: discharge the common sort
With pay and thanks, and let's away to London
And see our gentle queen how well she fares:
By this, I hope, she hath a son for me.   *[Exeunt.* 90

SCENE VI. *London. The Tower.*

Enter KING HENRY *and* GLOUCESTER, *with the* Lieutenant, *on the walls.*

   Glou. Good day, my lord. What, at your book so hard?
   K. Hen. Ay, my good lord:—my lord, I should say rather;
'Tis sin to flatter; 'good' was little better:
'Good Gloucester' and 'good devil' were alike,
And both preposterous; therefore, not 'good lord.'
   Glou. Sirrah, leave us to ourselves: we must confer.
                  [Exit Lieutenant.

   K. Hen. So flies the reckless shepherd from the wolf;
So first the harmless sheep doth yield his fleece
And next his throat unto the butcher's knife.
What scene of death hath Roscius now to act? 10
   Glou. Suspicion always haunts the guilty mind;
The thief doth fear each bush an officer.
   K. Hen. The bird that hath been limed in a bush,
With trembling wings misdoubteth every bush;
And I, the hapless male to one sweet bird,
Have now the fatal object in my eye
Where my poor young was limed, was caught and kill'd.
   Glou. Why, what a peevish fool was that of Crete,
That taught his son the office of a fowl!
And yet, for all his wings, the fool was drown'd. 20
   K. Hen. I, Dædalus; my poor boy, Icarus;
Thy father, Minos, that denied our course;
The sun that sear'd the wings of my sweet boy
Thy brother Edward, and thyself the sea
Whose envious gulf did swallow up his life.
Ah, kill me with thy weapon, not with words!
My breast can better brook thy dagger's point
Than can my ears that tragic history.
But wherefore dost thou come? is't for my life?
   Glou. Think'st thou I am an executioner? 30
   K. Hen. A persecutor, I am sure, thou art:
If murdering innocents be executing,
Why, then thou art an executioner.
   Glou. Thy son I kill'd for his presumption.
   K. Hen. Hadst thou been kill'd when first thou didst presume,
Thou hadst not lived to kill a son of mine.
And thus I prophesy, that many a thousand,
Which now mistrust no parcel of my fear,
And many an old man's sigh and many a widow's,
And many an orphan's water-standing eye— 40
Men for their sons, wives for their husbands,
And orphans for their parents' timeless death—
Shall rue the hour that ever thou wast born.
The owl shriek'd at thy birth,—an evil sign;
The night-crow cried, aboding luckless time;
Dogs howl'd, and hideous tempest shook down trees;
The raven rook'd her on the chimney's top,
And chattering pies in dismal discords sung.
Thy mother felt more than a mother's pain,
And yet brought forth less than a mother's hope, 50
To wit, an indigested and deformed lump,
Not like the fruit of such a goodly tree.
Teeth hadst thou in thy head when thou wast born,
To signify thou camest to bite the world:
And, if the rest be true which I have heard,
Thou camest—
   Glou. I'll hear no more: die, prophet, in thy speech:
                  [Stabs him.
For this, amongst the rest, was I ordain'd.
   K. Hen. Ay, and for much more slaughter after this.
O, God forgive my sins, and pardon thee!   *[Dies.* 60
   Glou. What, will the aspiring blood of Lancaster
Sink in the ground? I thought it would have mounted.
See how my sword weeps for the poor king's death!
O, may such purple tears be alway shed
From those that wish the downfall of our house!

---

56. **respect,** comparison. 63. **You . . . butchers.** This is not historically true; both Edward and Clarence were fathers of families. The speech is hardly comparable to Macduff's "He has no children" (*Macbeth,* IV, iii, 216); the following lines indicate that Margaret is speaking literally.

SCENE VI. 5. **preposterous,** contrary to the natural order of things. 6. **Sirrah,** customary form of address to inferiors; see glossary. 10. **Roscius,** celebrated Roman actor. 14. **misdoubteth,** is mistrustful of; see glossary. 18. **peevish,** silly; see glossary. 21. **Dædalus,** Icarus. Cf. *1 Henry VI,* IV, vi, 55, note. 38. **mistrust no parcel,** suspect no

If any spark of life be yet remaining,
Down, down to hell; and say I sent thee thither:
[Stabs him again.
I, that have neither pity, love, nor fear.
Indeed, 'tis true that Henry told me of;
For I have often heard my mother say   70
I came into the world with my legs forward:
Had I not reason, think ye, to make haste,
And seek their ruin that usurp'd our right?
The midwife wonder'd and the women cried
'O, Jesus bless us, he is born with teeth!'
And so I was; which plainly signified
That I should snarl and bite and play the dog.
Then, since the heavens have shaped my body so,
Let hell make crook'd my mind to answer it.
I have no brother, I am like no brother;   80
And this word 'love,' which greybeards call divine,
Be resident in men like one another
And not in me: I am myself alone.
Clarence, beware; thou keep'st me from the light:
But I will sort a pitchy day for thee;
For I will buz abroad such prophecies
That Edward shall be fearful of his life,
And then, to purge his fear, I'll be thy death.
King Henry and the prince his son are gone:
Clarence, thy turn is next, and then the rest,   90
Counting myself but bad till I be best.
I'll throw thy body in another room
And triumph, Henry, in thy day of doom.
[Exit, with the body.

SCENE VII. *London. The palace.*

Flourish. Enter KING EDWARD, QUEEN ELIZABETH,
CLARENCE, GLOUCESTER, HASTINGS, *a* Nurse *with
the young Prince, and* Attendants.

K. Edw. Once more we sit in England's royal
    throne,
Re-purchased with the blood of enemies.
What valiant foemen, like to autumn's corn,
Have we mow'd down in tops of all their pride!
Three Dukes of Somerset, threefold renown'd
For hardy and undoubted champions;
Two Cliffords, as the father and the son,
And two Northumberlands; two braver men
Ne'er spurr'd their coursers at the trumpet's sound;
With them, the two brave bears, Warwick and
    Montague,   10
That in their chains fetter'd the kingly lion
And made the forest tremble when they roar'd.
Thus have we swept suspicion from our seat
And made our footstool of security.
Come hither, Bess, and let me kiss my boy.
Young Ned, for thee, thine uncles and myself
Have in our armours watch'd the winter's night,
Went all afoot in summer's scalding heat,
That thou mightst repossess the crown in peace;
And of our labours thou shalt reap the gain.   20
    Glou. [Aside] I'll blast his harvest, if your head were
        laid;
For yet I am not look'd on in the world.

This shoulder was ordain'd so thick to heave;
And heave it shall some weight, or break my back:
Work thou the way,—and thou shalt execute.
    K. Edw. Clarence and Gloucester, love my lovely
        queen;
And kiss your princely nephew, brothers both.
    Clar. The duty that I owe unto your majesty
I seal upon the lips of this sweet babe.
    Q. Eliz. Thanks, noble Clarence; worthy brother,
        thanks.   30
    Glou. And, that I love the tree from whence thou
        sprang'st,
Witness the loving kiss I give the fruit.
[Aside] To say the truth, so Judas kiss'd his master,
And cried 'all hail!' when as he meant all harm.
    K. Edw. Now am I seated as my soul delights,
Having my country's peace and brothers' loves.
    Clar. What will your grace have done with
        Margaret?
Reignier, her father, to the king of France
Hath pawn'd the Sicils and Jerusalem,
And hither have they sent it for her ransom.   40
    K. Edw. Away with her, and waft her hence to
        France,
And now what rests but that we spend the time
With stately triumphs, mirthful comic shows,
Such as befits the pleasure of the court?
Sound drums and trumpets! farewell sour annoy!
For here, I hope, begins our lasting joy.   [Exeunt.

THE TRAGEDY OF
King Richard the Third

The first edition of *Richard III* was issued in
quarto form in 1597 with the following descriptive
title page:

THE TRAGEDY OF King Richard the third. Containing, His treacherous Plots against his brother
Clarence: the pittiefull murther of his innocent nephewes:
his tyrannicall vsurpation: with the whole course of
his detested life, and most deserued death. As it hath
beene lately Acted by the Right honourable the Lord
Chamberlaine his seruants. AT LONDON. Printed by
Valentine Sims, for Andrew Wise, dwelling in Paules
Church-yard, at the Signe of the Angell. 1597.

This is apparently an authentic version printed from
a prompter's copy. Possibly it had been sold to the
printer along with *Richard II* in order to prevent the
sort of piracy the players had suffered in the corrupt
and unlicensed edition of *Romeo and Juliet,* and
possibly *Love's Labour's Lost,* issued that year. The
same version of the play was reissued in 1598, 1602,

1605, 1612, 1622, 1629, 1634, all in quarto and all ultimately derived from the first quarto. The numerous printings of the play indicate its popularity.

When the editors of the First Folio came to select their text for the collected edition, however, they chose to print an independent version, certainly authentic, containing a good many variations and expansions. We have, therefore, as had Heminges and Condell, a choice between two versions, both good. The folio version, which is longer and more ornate in style than the quarto, was certainly set up from the playhouse copy. Some parts, such as the rejection of Buckingham in the second scene of the fourth act, appear only in the quarto.[1]

DATE

In 1599 John Weever's *Epigrams* was published. According to him, however, it was written two or three years earlier. In his epigram *Ad Gulielmum Shakespeare* he refers to:

Romea, Richard, more whose names I know not.

But the strongest evidence of an early date is strictly internal. The high percentage of end-stopped lines in the blank verse, the scarcity of rhyme and prose, and the Senecan quality of the play both as to style and tone indicate the period when Marlowe was dominant in tragedy. Richard's soliloquies are like the choruses of Senecan tragedy, and also like that form are the abundant use of dramatic irony and the thread of nemesis, or the working out of fate, which run through the play. We have also ghosts, murders, and bloodshed, and a declamatory quality, all of which are unmistakable features of the tragedy of Marlowe and of his contemporary Kyd.[2] The very immediate connection both in style and in subject with the Henry VI plays is another indication of early date. On the basis of internal evidence *Richard III* is assigned to 1593 or 1594. It is perhaps earlier.

RICHARD AND THE CHRONICLERS

The house of York went down in defeat before Henry Tudor, the proponent of the house of Lancaster, who became Henry VII. There were, however, doubtful features in the claim of Henry VII, since his legitimate descent from John of Gaunt admitted of question, and since a son and daughter of the duke of Clarence still lived. It was thought also that one at least of the sons of Edward IV might have escaped being put to death; hence, the importance in the eyes of Henry VII that his claim should be supported in every possible way.

Out of the struggle for the crown during the Wars of the Roses had come the conception of Richard III as the evil genius of his own house and a monster in shape of man. Polydore Vergil in *Historia Angliæ* (1534) had so presented him. Polydore Vergil was an Italian and was, therefore, familiar with the Renaissance conception of absolute villainy. His making of Richard III the scapegoat for the crimes of his family and of his time was no doubt gratifying to Henry VII, who considered himself Lancastrian. By making Richard a villain and a usurper beyond the pale of human sympathy Henry VII's own claim was the more completely vindicated. Sir Thomas More, Lord Chancellor under Henry VIII, also wrote in the same unfair manner *The History of King Richard III*, which was adopted by the chroniclers Hall, Grafton (publisher of Hall), and Holinshed himself, so that the belief that Richard was a human fiend became universal. Richard was bad enough, and although he may not have been the chief instrument in the murder of Clarence, no doubt committed most of the terrible crimes imputed to him, and some others besides.[3] The things which probably most misrepresent him, however, are endowing him with superhuman subtlety and hypocrisy and putting him with his self-confessed accursedness before us as a living force. These features are literary and not historical. Shakespeare used his sources with a considerable degree of freedom.[4]

In *3 Henry VI* Richard Duke of Gloucester is a fearful menace to all good and is the ultimate doom of the house of York. *Richard III*, the final play of the series, further develops this idea, and, going back through both Hall and Holinshed,[5] to Polydore Vergil and Sir Thomas More, it seizes upon another conception which does much to humanize and render terrible the picture of Richard's villainy; namely, the attribution to Richard of a conscience. Vergil invented Richard's horrible dream in which his victims return to reproach him for his crimes, and, in true Renaissance spirit, traced out in his career the idea of fate or nemesis.

Richard III AS A TRAGEDY

We have, therefore, not only the antique conception of tragedy as the story of one who stood high in the world's eyes and fell from his great estate, but also the conception, probably somewhat unconsciously developed on Shakespeare's part, of the working out of inscrutable providence. This conception is at once true to Aristotle and to the best knowledge and taste. The play also takes lessons from the English followers of Seneca, and proceeds through dreams, portents, superstitions, inspired and

[1]David Lyall Patrick, *The Textual History of "Richard III"* (Stanford University, 1936).
[2]J. W. Cunliffe, *The Influence of Seneca on Elizabethan Tragedy* (1893) and introduction to *Early Classical Tragedies* (Oxford, 1912); Rudolf Fischer, *Zur Kunstentwicklung der englischen Tragödie* (Strassburg, 1893); F. L. Lucas, *Seneca and Elizabethan Tragedy* (Cambridge, 1927); Henry W. Wells, "Senecan Influence on Elizabethan Tragedy," *Shakespeare Association Bulletin*. XIX, 71-84.

[3]G. B. Churchill, *Richard III up to Shakespeare* (Berlin, 1900).
[4]See R. A. Law, "*Richard the Third:* A Study in Shakespeare's Composition," *PMLA*, LX (1945), 689-696.
[5]See Edleen Begg, "Shakespeare's Debt to Holinshed in *Richard III*," *Studies in Philology*, XXXII (1935), 189-196.

inescapable curses, bloodshed, broken oaths, and revenge. These darker forces express themselves very largely through the words of the dethroned queen, Margaret. On the other hand, not only do we get a sense of the certainty of the downfall of the wicked, but of their torments in this world. Our general sense of human insecurity is wrought upon by beholding an unnatural war on kindred, innocent bystanders, weak women, and defenseless children. A great national struggle over the subordination of public welfare to the ambitions of wicked men ends in the triumph of virtue. The righteous Henry Earl of Richmond is seated on the English throne, bringing with him a promise of peace and security for the kingdom. Henry VII, a selfish, rather mean ruler, hardly deserves to be presented as an unstained hero and leader, like Fortinbras in *Hamlet* and Malcolm in *Macbeth;* but in the light of beneficent Tudor rule and greatness, it was a proper compliment to Queen Elizabeth, his granddaughter, so to present him.

Richard III is written in blank verse of a Marlowan type, and, like Marlowe's *Tamburlaine*, it has very little prose in it; that is to say, very little comicality, for the expression of which it was customary to employ prose. Shakespeare probably meant the play to be somber. It has very little rhyme. Kyd had used a good deal of rhyme largely for the expression of sententious wisdom and for variety in the effects of speeches, but Marlowe had been opposed to the use of rhyme, so that in the use of blank verse, the play is Marlowan. *Richard III* has in it also a great deal of artificiality in the form of repetitions, balanced utterances, and stichomythia, a device borrowed from Senecan tragedy in which the characters engaged in dialogue each utter a single complete line. The effects of these rhetorical peculiarities, frequently employed in the women's parts in the expression of grief and other passions, are far from the naturalness of style in the great tragedies that Shakespeare was yet to write.

RICHARD AS A STAGE VILLAIN

Remembering then the effect that was to be produced, we may consider the manner in which it was done. Shakespeare takes up the story at the moment of complete Yorkist triumph. The kingdom is at peace. The king, Edward IV, is provided with a gallant young prince as his heir. His brother, Clarence, is trustworthy; his brothers-in-law are powerful nobles and devoted to his throne; most of the noblemen of his court are loyal and brave, though split by factions; he himself, as his death approaches, is moved by a desire to provide for the future by making peace among all jarring elements. Against this established virtue stands Richard, a deformed and malignant hunchback, hated by all the world. He is an example of the single dominant character about whom Marlowe had learned to unify his plays. The unnatural conventions of the Marlowan drama

had made it proper for the villain hero to avow his villainy and explain it. Such was thought to be Machiavellian policy, for the great Florentine statesman had come to stand in the popular mind for open, complete, and unscrupulous malignity.[6]

Perhaps the bareness of the stage and the crudity of the dramatic technique had made it almost necessary for the drama to proceed by soliloquy and open confession in order that the plot might be understood. The actor thus dominated the audience face to face and front to front. The villainy, from that of Marlowe's Barabas in *The Jew of Malta* on, is cynical as well as malignant. It is also opportunist; that is, it does not plot long ahead of the current time, but plots step by step and stands ready to profit by whatever may occur. This opportunism is in Marlowe, and is a feature which Shakespeare learned and later employed in Iago, his greatest scoundrel.

THE HISTORY OF THE PLAY

Richard III has lived as a popular play on the stage ever since its composition. It is evident, however, that it is the character of Richard, rather than Shakespeare's play as a whole, that has had the power to maintain itself from age to age without the prestige of artistic and learned approval. *Richard III* was evidently first made popular by the acting of Shakespeare's companion, Richard Burbage, and no other play is more frequently alluded to in the literature of the time. It disappeared with the closing of the theaters in 1642, but Richard III himself was presented in several dramas of the Restoration with something approaching the force of Shakespeare's conception.

In the year 1700 the play was rewritten by the actor and dramatist Colley Cibber. Cibber begins his play with the scene of the murder of King Henry VI from *3 Henry VI*, shortens the play by dropping many scenes, omits the parts of Margaret and Clarence, invents a scene in which the fiendlike Richard chuckles with malign satisfaction as he overhears the murderers at their work of killing the little princes, and makes of the play the picture of a single dominant villain. Some familiar quotations, often thought to be from Shakespeare, such as, "So much for Buckingham," and "Richard's himself again," are really from Cibber. In this version have appeared the greatest actors of England and America—Garrick, Kean, Kemble, Edwin Forrest, and the Booths. Edwin Booth and Sir Henry Irving went back to Shakespeare's text, from which by abridgment they made their versions. But it can hardly be said that Cibber's version has ever been superseded. The fine breadth and careful articulation, therefore, of Shakespeare's work have often been lost except to students.

[6]E. S. Meyer, *Machiavelli and the Elizabethan Drama* (Weimar, 1897); C. V. Boyer, *The Villain as Hero in Elizabethan Tragedy* (1914).

THE TRAGEDY OF

King Richard the Third

DRAMATIS PERSONAE

KING EDWARD the Fourth.
EDWARD, Prince of Wales,
    afterwards King Edward V., } sons to the King.
RICHARD, Duke of York,
GEORGE, Duke of Clarence,
RICHARD, Duke of Gloucester, } brothers to the King.
    afterwards King Richard III.,
A young son of Clarence.
HENRY, Earl of Richmond, afterwards King
    Henry VII.
CARDINAL BOURCHIER, Archbishop of
    Canterbury.
THOMAS ROTHERHAM, Archbishop of York.
JOHN MORTON, Bishop of Ely.
DUKE OF BUCKINGHAM.
DUKE OF NORFOLK.
EARL OF SURREY, his son.
EARL RIVERS, brother to Elizabeth.
MARQUIS OF DORSET and LORD GREY, sons to
    Elizabeth.
EARL OF OXFORD.
LORD HASTINGS.
LORD STANLEY, called also EARL OF DERBY.
LORD LOVEL.
SIR THOMAS VAUGHAN.
SIR RICHARD RATCLIFF.
SIR WILLIAM CATESBY.
SIR JAMES TYRREL.
SIR JAMES BLOUNT.
SIR WALTER HERBERT.
SIR ROBERT BRAKENBURY, Lieutenant of the
    Tower.
CHRISTOPHER URSWICK, a priest. Another
    Priest.
TRESSEL and BERKELEY, gentlemen attending
    on the Lady Anne.
Lord Mayor of London. Sheriff of Wiltshire.

ELIZABETH, queen to King Edward IV.
MARGARET, widow of King Henry VI.
DUCHESS OF YORK, mother to King
    Edward IV.
LADY ANNE, widow of Edward Prince of Wales,
    son to King Henry VI.; afterwards married
    to Richard.
A young daughter of Clarence (MARGARET
    PLANTAGENET).

Ghosts of those murdered by Richard III.,
    Lords and other Attendants; a Pursuivant,
    Scrivener, Citizens, Murderers, Messengers,
    Soldiers, &c.

SCENE: *England.*

ACT I.

SCENE I. *London. A street.*

Enter RICHARD, DUKE OF GLOUCESTER, *solus.*

Glou. Now is the winter of our discontent
Made glorious summer by this sun of York;
And all the clouds that lour'd upon our house
In the deep bosom of the ocean buried.
Now are our brows bound with victorious wreaths;
Our bruised arms hung up for monuments;
Our stern alarums changed to merry meetings,
Our dreadful marches to delightful measures.
Grim-visaged war hath smooth'd his wrinkled front;
And now, instead of mounting barbed steeds   10
To fright the souls of fearful adversaries,
He capers nimbly in a lady's chamber
To the lascivious pleasing of a lute.
But I, that am not shaped for sportive tricks,
Nor made to court an amorous looking-glass;
I, that am rudely stamp'd, and want love's majesty
To strut before a wanton ambling nymph;
I, that am curtail'd of this fair proportion,
Cheated of feature by dissembling nature,
Deform'd, unfinish'd, sent before my time   20
Into this breathing world, scarce half made up,
And that so lamely and unfashionable
That dogs bark at me as I halt by them;
Why, I, in this weak piping time of peace,
Have no delight to pass away the time,
Unless to spy my shadow in the sun
And descant on mine own deformity:
And therefore, since I cannot prove a lover,
To entertain these fair well-spoken days,
I am determined to prove a villain   30
And hate the idle pleasures of these days.
Plots have I laid, inductions dangerous,
By drunken prophecies, libels and dreams,
To set my brother Clarence and the king
In deadly hate the one against the other:
And if King Edward be as true and just
As I am subtle, false and treacherous,
This day should Clarence closely be mew'd up,
About a prophecy, which says that G
Of Edward's heirs the murderer shall be.   40
Dive, thoughts, down to my soul: here Clarence
    comes.

Enter CLARENCE, *guarded, and* BRAKENBURY.

Brother, good day: what means this armed guard
That waits upon your grace?

ACT I. SCENE I. 2. **sun of York.** Edward IV assumed a sun as his badge in memory of the three suns which appeared to him before the Battle of Mortimer's Cross in 1461 (*3 Henry VI*, II, i, 26-40). As used here there is a play on the words "son" and "sun," probably reflected in the readings of Ff: *son,* and Qq: *sonne.* 3. **lour'd,** frowned, looked sullen or ominous. 6. **monuments,** probably memorial trophies. 8. **measures,** stately dances; see glossary. 9. **front,** forehead; see glossary. 10. **barbed,** properly, "barded," i.e., armored. 14. **sportive,** amorous. 16. **want,** lack; see glossary. 17. **ambling,** walking affectedly, i.e., wantonly. 18-23. **I . . . them.** From Sir Thomas More's life of Richard III comes the information that Richard was small of stature, ill-shapen in limbs, crookbacked, left shoulder higher than the right, ugly in visage. According to the theory of Plato, beauty of person should go with beauty of soul, an idea which is reflected in this passage and elsewhere in the play. 18. **proportion,** shape; see glossary. 19. **feature,** shapeliness; see glossary. **dissembling,** fraudulent, false. 22. **unfashionable,** without comeliness. 24. **piping time,** i.e., a time when

Clar. His majesty,
Tendering my person's safety, hath appointed
This conduct to convey me to the Tower.
  Glou. Upon what cause?
  Clar. Because my name is George.
  Glou. Alack, my lord, that fault is none of yours;
He should, for that, commit your godfathers:
O, belike his majesty hath some intent
That you shall be new-christen'd in the Tower. 50
But what 's the matter, Clarence? may I know?
  Clar. Yea, Richard, when I know; for I protest
As yet I do not: but, as I can learn,
He hearkens after prophecies and dreams;
And from the cross-row plucks the letter G,
And says a wizard told him that by G
His issue disinherited should be;
And, for my name of George begins with G,
It follows in his thought that I am he.
These, as I learn, and such like toys as these 60
Have moved his highness to commit me now.
  Glou. Why, this it is, when men are ruled by women:
'Tis not the king that sends you to the Tower;
My Lady Grey his wife, Clarence, 'tis she
That tempers him to this extremity.
Was it not she and that good man of worship,
Anthony Woodville, her brother there,
That made him send Lord Hastings to the Tower,
From whence this present day he is deliver'd?
We are not safe, Clarence; we are not safe. 70
  Clar. By heaven, I think there 's no man is secure
But the queen's kindred and night-walking heralds
That trudge betwixt the king and Mistress Shore.
Heard ye not what an humble suppliant
Lord Hastings was to her for his delivery?
  Glou. Humbly complaining to her deity
Got my lord chamberlain his liberty.
I'll tell you what; I think it is our way,
If we will keep in favour with the king,
To be her men and wear her livery: 80
The jealous o'erworn widow and herself,
Since that our brother dubb'd them gentlewomen,
Are mighty gossips in this monarchy.
  Brak. I beseech your graces both to pardon me;
His majesty hath straitly given in charge
That no man shall have private conference,
Of what degree soever, with his brother.
  Glou. Even so; an 't please your worship,
  Brakenbury,
You may partake of any thing we say:
We speak no treason, man: we say the king 90
Is wise and virtuous, and his noble queen
Well struck in years, fair, and not jealous;
We say that Shore's wife hath a pretty foot,

A cherry lip, a bonny eye, a passing pleasing tongue;
And that the queen's kindred are made gentlefolks:
How say you, sir? can you deny all this?
  Brak. With this, my lord, myself have nought to do.
  Glou. Naught to do with Mistress Shore! I tell thee,
    fellow,
He that doth naught with her, excepting one,
Were best he do it secretly, alone. 100
  Brak. What one, my lord?
  Glou. Her husband, knave: wouldst thou betray me?
  Brak. I beseech your grace to pardon me, and
    withal
Forbear your conference with the noble duke.
  Clar. We know thy charge, Brakenbury, and will
    obey.
  Glou. We are the queen's abjects, and must obey.
Brother, farewell: I will unto the king;
And whatsoever you will employ me in,
Were it to call King Edward's widow sister,
I will perform it to enfranchise you. 110
Meantime, this deep disgrace in brotherhood
Touches me deeper than you can imagine.
  Clar. I know it pleaseth neither of us well.
  Glou. Well, your imprisonment shall not be long;
I will deliver you, or else lie for you:
Meantime, have patience.
  Clar. I must perforce. Farewell.
    [*Exeunt Clarence, Brakenbury, and Guard.*
  Glou. Go, tread the path that thou shalt ne'er
    return,
Simple, plain Clarence! I do love thee so,
That I will shortly send thy soul to heaven,
If heaven will take the present at our hands. 120
But who comes here? the new-deliver'd Hastings?

Enter LORD HASTINGS.

  Hast. Good time of day unto my gracious lord!
  Glou. As much unto my good lord chamberlain!
Well are you welcome to the open air.
How hath your lordship brook'd imprisonment?
  Hast. With patience, noble lord, as prisoners must:
But I shall live, my lord, to give them thanks
That were the cause of my imprisonment.
  Glou. No doubt, no doubt; and so shall Clarence
    too;
For they that were your enemies are his, 130
And have prevail'd as much on him as you.
  Hast. More pity that the eagle should be mew'd,
While kites and buzzards prey at liberty.
  Glou. What news abroad?
  Hast. No news so bad abroad as this at home;
The king is sickly, weak and melancholy,
And his physicians fear him mightily.

---

the music heard is that of pipes and not fifes and drums. 27. **descant,** make varied comments on. 29. **entertain,** pass away pleasurably; see glossary. 30. **I . . . villain.** This frank announcement is characteristic of the Machiavellian villain of Marlowe and other early dramatists and is to be connected with the idea that Richard is born outside the pale of normal humanity, so that his trend is toward evil as that of normal men is toward good. 32. **inductions,** preparations, beginnings. 33. **drunken,** outrageously impossible and irresponsible. **libels,** defamatory bills or pamphlets. 38. **mew'd up,** confined; see glossary 39. **prophecy . . . G.** The prophecy is mentioned in Holinshed; the quibble is that *G* stands for Gloucester and not George, given name of the duke of Clarence. 48. **commit your godfathers,** an example of Richard's cynical humor. 54. **hearkens,** inquires. 55. **cross-row,** Christ-cross-row, or alphabet, so called from the cross printed before the alphabet in the hornbook. 60. **toys,** trifles; see glossary. 61. **moved,** prompted; see glossary. **commit,** arrest. 64. **My Lady Grey,** a disrespectful reference to the queen, whose maiden name was Eliza-

beth Woodville and who, when the king married her, was the widow of Sir John Grey. 65. **tempers,** changes the normal mixture of the humors in him. 67. **Woodville,** three syllables; originally, Wydeville. 73. **Mistress Shore.** Jane Shore, the king's mistress, was the daughter of a Cheapside merchant and the wife of a goldsmith in Lombard Street. 77. **chamberlain,** i.e., Hastings. 81. **jealous o'erworn widow,** i.e., the queen. **herself,** i.e., Jane Shore. 82. **gentlewomen,** a sneer at the queen's family, which was gentle but not noble until after her marriage with the king; Jane Shore was, of course, neither gentle nor noble. 83. **gossips,** companions (conveying the idea of vulgar familiarity). 98. **Naught.** Richard quibbles on the meanings "nothing" and "wickedness"; see glossary. 106. **abjects,** abjectly servile subjects. 109. **King Edward's widow,** i.e., the widow whom he has made queen. 115. **lie,** quibble on "lying in prison" and "telling lies"; see glossary. 116. **perforce,** necessarily; see glossary. 125. **brook'd,** endured; see glossary. 127. **give them thanks,** ironical for "pay them off." 133. **kites,** birds of prey, hawks. **buzzards,** common species of hawk.

Glou. Now, by Saint Paul, this news is bad indeed.
O, he hath kept an evil diet long,
And overmuch consumed his royal person: 140
'Tis very grievous to be thought upon.
What, is he in his bed?
    Hast. He is.
    Glou. Go you before, and I will follow you.
                                              [*Exit Hastings.*
He cannot live, I hope; and must not die
Till George be pack'd with post-horse up to heaven.
I'll in, to urge his hatred more to Clarence,
With lies well steel'd with weighty arguments;
And, if I fail not in my deep intent,
Clarence hath not another day to live: 150
Which done, God take King Edward to his mercy,
And leave the world for me to bustle in!
For then I'll marry Warwick's youngest daughter.
What though I kill'd her husband and her father?
The readiest way to make the wench amends
Is to become her husband and her father:
The which will I; not all so much for love
As for another secret close intent,
By marrying her which I must reach unto.
But yet I run before my horse to market: 160
Clarence still breathes; Edward still lives and reigns:
When they are gone, then must I count my gains.
                                                     [*Exit.*

SCENE II. *The same. Another street.*

Enter the corpse of KING HENRY *the Sixth, Gentlemen
with halberds to guard it;* LADY ANNE *being the
mourner.*

    Anne. Set down, set down your honourable load,
If honour may be shrouded in a hearse,
Whilst I awhile obsequiously lament
The untimely fall of virtuous Lancaster.
Poor key-cold figure of a holy king!
Pale ashes of the house of Lancaster!
Thou bloodless remnant of that royal blood!
Be it lawful that I invocate thy ghost,
To hear the lamentations of poor Anne,
Wife to thy Edward, to thy slaughter'd son,   10
Stabb'd by the selfsame hand that made these
        wounds!
Lo, in these windows that let forth thy life,
I pour the helpless balm of my poor eyes.
Cursed be the hand that made these fatal holes!
Cursed be the heart that had the heart to do it!
Cursed the blood that let this blood from hence!
More direful hap betide that hated wretch,
That makes us wretched by the death of thee,
Than I can wish to adders, spiders, toads,
Or any creeping venom'd thing that lives!   20
If ever he have child, abortive be it,
Prodigious, and untimely brought to light,
Whose ugly and unnatural aspect
May fright the hopeful mother at the view;

And that be heir to his unhappiness!
If ever he have wife, let her be made
As miserable by the death of him
As I am made by my poor lord and thee!
Come, now towards Chertsey with your holy load,
Taken from Paul's to be interred there;   30
And still, as you are weary of the weight,
Rest you, whiles I lament King Henry's corse.

    Enter GLOUCESTER.

    Glou. Stay, you that bear the corse, and set it
        down.
    Anne. What black magician conjures up this fiend,
To stop devoted charitable deeds?
    Glou. Villains, set down the corse; or, by Saint Paul,
I'll make a corse of him that disobeys.
    Gent. My lord, stand back, and let the coffin pass.
    Glou. Unmanner'd dog! stand thou, when I
        command!
Advance thy halberd higher than my breast,   40
Or, by Saint Paul, I'll strike thee to my foot,
And spurn upon thee, beggar, for thy boldness.
    Anne. What, do you tremble? are you all afraid?
Alas, I blame you not; for you are mortal,
And mortal eyes cannot endure the devil.
Avaunt, thou dreadful minister of hell!
Thou hadst but power over his mortal body,
His soul thou canst not have; therefore, be gone.
    Glou. Sweet saint, for charity, be not so curst.
    Anne. Foul devil, for God's sake, hence, and trouble
        us not;   50
For thou hast made the happy earth thy hell,
Fill'd it with cursing cries and deep exclaims.
If thou delight to view thy heinous deeds,
Behold this pattern of thy butcheries.
O, gentlemen, see, see! dead Henry's wounds
Open their congeal'd mouths and bleed afresh!
Blush, blush, thou lump of foul deformity;
For 'tis thy presence that exhales this blood
From cold and empty veins, where no blood dwells;
Thy deed, inhuman and unnatural,   60
Provokes this deluge most unnatural.
O God, which this blood madest, revenge his death!
O earth, which this blood drink'st, revenge his death!
Either heaven with lightning strike the murderer
        dead,
Or earth, gape open wide and eat him quick,
As thou dost swallow up this good king's blood,
Which his hell-govern'd arm hath butchered!
    Glou. Lady, you know no rules of charity,
Which renders good for bad, blessings for curses.
    Anne. Villain, thou know'st no law of God nor man:
No beast so fierce but knows some touch of pity.   71
    Glou. But I know none, and therefore am no beast.
    Anne. O wonderful, when devils tell the truth!
    Glou. More wonderful, when angels are so angry.
Vouchsafe, divine perfection of a woman,
Of these supposed evils, to give me leave,
By circumstance, but to acquit myself.
    Anne. Vouchsafe, defused infection of a man,

---

146. **with post-horse,** by post horses, i.e., by swiftest possible means.
148. **arguments,** causes; see glossary. 153. **Warwick's youngest
daughter.** Lady Anne, regarded by Shakespeare (following the chronicle) as widow of Edward Prince of Wales, son of King Henry VI, was,
in fact, only his betrothed.
    SCENE II. *Stage Direction:* **halberds,** battle-axes, long-handled
weapons. 3. **obsequiously,** as befits the funeral, mournfully. 5. **key-**

cold, extremely cold; used proverbially. 8. **invocate,** invoke. 13.
helpless, useless, unavailing. 17. **hap,** fortune. 22. **Prodigious,**
monstrous, unnatural. 25. **that,** i.e., that creature. **unhappiness,**
prodigious nature. 29. **Chertsey,** a town in Surrey, where King
Henry's body was buried. 30. **Paul's,** St. Paul's Church in London.
31. **still,** as often as; see glossary. 33. **Stay,** stop; see glossary. 34.
black magician, one leagued with the devil. 35. **devoted,** pious, holy.

For these known evils, but to give me leave,
By circumstance, to curse thy cursed self.   80
   Glou. Fairer than tongue can name thee, let me
     have
Some patient leisure to excuse myself.
   Anne. Fouler than heart can think thee, thou canst
     make
No excuse current, but to hang thyself.
   Glou. By such despair, I should accuse myself.
   Anne. And, by despairing, shouldst thou stand
     excused;
For doing worthy vengeance on thyself,
Which didst unworthy slaughter upon others.
   Glou. Say that I slew them not?
   Anne.   Why, then they are not dead:
But dead they are, and, devilish slave, by thee.   90
   Glou. I did not kill your husband.
   Anne.   Why, then he is alive.
   Glou. Nay, he is dead; and slain by Edward's hand.
   Anne. In thy foul throat thou liest: Queen
     Margaret saw
Thy murderous falchion smoking in his blood;
The which thou once didst bend against her breast,
But that thy brothers beat aside the point.
   Glou. I was provoked by her slanderous tongue,
Which laid their guilt upon my guiltless shoulders.
   Anne. Thou wast provoked by thy bloody mind,
Which never dreamt on aught but butcheries: 100
Didst thou not kill this king?
   Glou.   I grant ye.
   Anne. Dost grant me, hedgehog? then, God grant
     me too
Thou mayst be damned for that wicked deed!
O, he was gentle, mild, and virtuous!
   Glou. The fitter for the King of heaven, that hath
     him.
   Anne. He is in heaven, where thou shalt never come.
   Glou. Let him thank me, that holp to send him
     thither;
For he was fitter for that place than earth.
   Anne. And thou unfit for any place but hell.
   Glou. Yes, one place else, if you will hear me name it.
   Anne. Some dungeon.
   Glou.   Your bed-chamber.   111
   Anne. Ill rest betide the chamber where thou liest!
   Glou. So will it, madam, till I lie with you.
   Anne. I hope so.
   Glou.   I know so. But, gentle Lady Anne,
To leave this keen encounter of our wits,
And fall somewhat into a slower method,
Is not the causer of the timeless deaths
Of these Plantagenets, Henry and Edward,
As blameful as the executioner?
   Anne. Thou art the cause, and most accursed effect.
   Glou. Your beauty was the cause of that effect;   121
Your beauty, which did haunt me in my sleep
To undertake the death of all the world,
So I might live one hour in your sweet bosom.
   Anne. If I thought that, I tell thee, homicide,
These nails should rend that beauty from my cheeks.

   Glou. These eyes could never endure sweet beauty's
     wreck;
You should not blemish it, if I stood by:
As all the world is cheered by the sun,
So I by that; it is my day, my life.   130
   Anne. Black night o'ershade thy day, and death thy
     life!
   Glou. Curse not thyself, fair creature; thou art both.
   Anne. I would I were, to be revenged on thee.
   Glou. It is a quarrel most unnatural,
To be revenged on him that loveth you.
   Anne. It is a quarrel just and reasonable,
To be revenged on him that slew my husband.
   Glou. He that bereft thee, lady, of thy husband,
Did it to help thee to a better husband.
   Anne. His better doth not breathe upon the earth.   140
   Glou. He lives that loves thee better than he could.
   Anne. Name him.
   Glou.   Plantagenet.
   Anne.   Why, that was he.
   Glou. The selfsame name, but one of better nature.
   Anne. Where is he?
   Glou.   Here. [*She spitteth at him.*] Why
     dost thou spit at me?
   Anne. Would it were mortal poison, for thy sake!
   Glou. Never came poison from so sweet a place.
   Anne. Never hung poison on a fouler toad.
Out of my sight! thou dost infect my eyes.
   Glou. Thine eyes, sweet lady, have infected mine.   150
   Anne. Would they were basilisks, to strike thee
     dead!
   Glou. I would they were, that I might die at once;
For now they kill me with a living death.
Those eyes of thine from mine have drawn salt tears,
Shamed their aspect with store of childish drops:
These eyes, which never shed remorseful tear,
No, when my father York and Edward wept,
To hear the piteous moan that Rutland made
When black-faced Clifford shook his sword at him;
Nor when thy warlike father, like a child,   160
Told the sad story of my father's death,
And twenty times made pause to sob and weep,
That all the standers-by had wet their cheeks,
Like trees bedash'd with rain: in that sad time
My manly eyes did scorn an humble tear;
And what these sorrows could not thence exhale,
Thy beauty hath, and made them blind with weeping.
I never sued to friend nor enemy;
My tongue could never learn sweet smoothing
     words;
But, now thy beauty is proposed my fee,   170
My proud heart sues and prompts my tongue to speak.
                [*She looks scornfully at him.*
Teach not thy lips such scorn, for they were made
For kissing, lady, not for such contempt.
If thy revengeful heart cannot forgive,
Lo, here I lend thee this sharp-pointed sword;
Which if thou please to hide in this true bosom,
And let the soul forth that adoreth thee,
I lay it naked to the deadly stroke,

---

49. **curst**, spiteful, shrewish; see glossary. 52. **exclaims**, exclamations.
54. **pattern**, example. 58. **thy presence**, an allusion to the legend that
dead bodies bleed in the presence of their murderers. 65. **quick**, alive;
see glossary. 76. **evils**. Some editors follow the F reading, *crimes*,
which preserves the parallelism of lines 75-77 and 78-80. 77. **circumstance**, detailed argument; see glossary. 78. **defused**, disordered,
shapeless. 82. **patient**, tranquil. **excuse myself**, maintain my innocence; see *excuse* in glossary. 84. **current**, genuine. 94. **falchion**,
a curved sword. 95. **bend**, direct, aim. 102. **hedgehog**, a double
allusion to Richard's hump and to his heraldic emblem, a boar. 107.
holp, helped; see glossary. 117. **timeless**, untimely. 120. **effect**,
agent. 151. **basilisks**, fabulous reptiles said to kill by their looks; see
glossary. 158. **Rutland**, second son of Richard Duke of York. 163.
That, so that. 169. **smoothing**, flattering.

And humbly beg the death upon my knee.
                  [*He lays his breast open: she offers at it with his sword.*
Nay, do not pause; for I did kill King Henry,   180
But 'twas thy beauty that provoked me.
Nay, now dispatch; 'twas I that stabb'd young
         Edward,
But 'twas thy heavenly face that set me on.
                           [*Here she lets fall the sword.*
Take up the sword again, or take up me.
     Anne. Arise, dissembler: though I wish thy death,
I will not be the executioner.
     Glou. Then bid me kill myself, and I will do it.
     Anne. I have already.
     Glou.   Tush, that was in thy rage:
Speak it again, and, even with the word,
That hand, which, for thy love, did kill thy love,   190
Shall, for thy love, kill a far truer love;
To both their deaths thou shalt be accessary.
     Anne. I would I knew thy heart.
     Glou. 'Tis figured in my tongue.
     Anne. I fear me both are false.
     Glou. Then never man was true.
     Anne. Well, well, put up your sword.
     Glou. Say, then, my peace is made.
     Anne. That shall you know hereafter.
     Glou. But shall I live in hope?   200
     Anne. All men, I hope, live so.
     Glou. Vouchsafe to wear this ring.
     Anne. To take is not to give.
     Glou. Look, how this ring encompasseth thy finger,
Even so thy breast encloseth my poor heart;
Wear both of them, for both of them are thine.
And if thy poor devoted suppliant may
But beg one favour at thy gracious hand,
Thou dost confirm his happiness for ever.
     Anne. What is it?   210
     Glou. That it would please thee leave these sad
         designs
To him that hath more cause to be a mourner,
And presently repair to Crosby Place;
Where, after I have solemnly interr'd
At Chertsey monastery this noble king,
And wet his grave with my repentant tears,
I will with all expedient duty see you:
For divers unknown reasons, I beseech you,
Grant me this boon.
     Anne. With all my heart; and much it joys me too,
To see you are become so penitent.   221
Tressel and Berkeley, go along with me.
     Glou. Bid me farewell.
     Anne.   'Tis more than you deserve;
But since you teach me how to flatter you,
Imagine I have said farewell already.
                  [*Exeunt Lady Anne, Tressel, and Berkeley.*
     Glou. Sirs, take up the corse.
     Gent.   Towards Chertsey, noble lord?
     Glou. No, to White-Friars; there attend my coming.
                           [*Exeunt all but Gloucester.*
Was ever woman in this humour woo'd?

Was ever woman in this humour won?
I'll have her; but I will not keep her long.   230
What! I, that kill'd her husband and his father,
To take her in her heart's extremest hate,
With curses in her mouth, tears in her eyes,
The bleeding witness of her hatred by;
Having God, her conscience, and these bars against
         me,
And I nothing to back my suit at all,
But the plain devil and dissembling looks,
And yet to win her, all the world to nothing!
Ha!
Hath she forgot already that brave prince,   240
Edward, her lord, whom I, some three months since,
Stabb'd in my angry mood at Tewksbury?
A sweeter and a lovelier gentleman,
Framed in the prodigality of nature,
Young, valiant, wise, and, no doubt, right royal,
The spacious world cannot again afford:
And will she yet debase her eyes on me,
That cropp'd the golden prime of this sweet prince,
And made her widow to a woful bed?
On me, whose all not equals Edward's moiety?   250
On me, that halt and am unshapen thus?
My dukedom to a beggarly denier,
I do mistake my person all this while:
Upon my life, she finds, although I cannot,
Myself to be a marvellous proper man.
I'll be at charges for a looking-glass,
And entertain some score or two of tailors,
To study fashions to adorn my body:
Since I am crept in favour with myself,
I will maintain it with some little cost.   260
But first I'll turn yon fellow in his grave;
And then return lamenting to my love.
Shine out, fair sun, till I have bought a glass,
That I may see my shadow as I pass.   [*Exit.*

SCENE III. *The palace.*

Enter QUEEN ELIZABETH, LORD RIVERS, *and* LORD
     GREY.

     Riv. Have patience, madam: there 's no doubt his
         majesty
Will soon recover his accustom'd health.
     Grey. In that you brook it ill, it makes him worse:
Therefore, for God's sake, entertain good comfort,
And cheer his grace with quick and merry words.
     Q. Eliz. If he were dead, what would betide of me?
     Riv. No other harm but loss of such a lord.
     Q. Eliz. The loss of such a lord includes all harm.
     Grey. The heavens have bless'd you with a goodly
         son,
To be your comforter when he is gone.   10
     Q. Eliz. Oh, he is young, and his minority
Is put unto the trust of Richard Gloucester,
A man that loves not me, nor none of you.

---

179. **the death,** i.e., death after judicial sentence. 194. **figured,**
portrayed. 213. **presently,** at once; see glossary. **Crosby Place,**
built by Sir John Crosby in 1456 and fronted on Bishop's-gate Street
Within. Richard, when Lord Protector, was lodged in this house. 217.
expedient, expeditious. 227. **White-Friars,** the Carmelite priory in
ancient London; the chronicles, however, state that the body was taken
to Blackfriars. 228-229. **Was . . . won.** Similar passages are found in
Titus Andronicus, II, i, 82-83, and *1 Henry VI*, V, iii, 77-78. 234. **her**

hatred, i.e., Henry's wounds are a witness to the justice of Anne's
hatred. 244. **the . . . nature,** i.e., nature's most prodigal mood. 245.
right royal. This compliment to the young prince is to be understood,
not as characteristic justice in Richard, but as a conventional means of
informing the audience through soliloquy. 250. **moiety,** part of
(Edward's virtues); see glossary. 252. **denier,** small copper coin, the
twelfth part of a sou. 255. **proper,** handsome; see glossary. 261.
in, into.

Riv. Is it concluded he shall be protector?

Q. Eliz. It is determined, not concluded yet:
But so it must be, if the king miscarry.

Enter BUCKINGHAM *and* DERBY.

Grey. Here come the lords of Buckingham and
    Derby.

Buck. Good time of day unto your royal grace!

Der. God make your majesty joyful as you have
    been!

Q. Eliz. The Countess Richmond, good my Lord of
    Derby,   20
To your good prayers will scarcely say amen.
Yet, Derby, notwithstanding she 's your wife,
And loves not me, be you, good lord, assured
I hate not you for her proud arrogance.

Der. I do beseech you, either not believe
The envious slanders of her false accusers;
Or, if she be accused in true report,
Bear with her weakness, which, I think, proceeds
From wayward sickness, and no grounded malice.

Riv. Saw you the king to-day, my Lord of Derby? 30

Der. But now the Duke of Buckingham and I
Are come from visiting his majesty.

Q. Eliz. What likelihood of his amendment, lords?

Buck. Madam, good hope; his grace speaks
    cheerfully.

Q. Eliz. God grant him health! Did you confer with
    him?

Buck. Madam, we did: he desires to make
    atonement
Betwixt the Duke of Gloucester and your brothers,
And betwixt them and my lord chamberlain;
And sent to warn them to his royal presence.

Q. Eliz. Would all were well! but that will never be:
I fear our happiness is at the highest.   41

Enter GLOUCESTER, HASTINGS, *and* DORSET.

Glou. They do me wrong, and I will not endure it:
Who are they that complain unto the king,
That I, forsooth, am stern and love them not?
By holy Paul, they love his grace but lightly
That fill his ears with such dissentious rumours.
Because I cannot flatter and speak fair,
Smile in men's faces, smooth, deceive and cog,
Duck with French nods and apish courtesy,
I must be held a rancorous enemy.   50
Cannot a plain man live and think no harm,
But thus his simple truth must be abused
By silken, sly, insinuating Jacks?

Riv. To whom in all this presence speaks your grace?

Glou. To thee, that hast nor honesty nor grace.
When have I injured thee? when done thee wrong?
Or thee? or thee? or any of your faction?
A plague upon you all! His royal person,—
Whom God preserve better than you would wish!—
Cannot be quiet scarce a breathing-while,   60
But you must trouble him with lewd complaints.

Q. Eliz. Brother of Gloucester, you mistake
    the matter.

The king, of his own royal disposition,
And not provoked by any suitor else;
Aiming, belike, at your interior hatred,
Which in your outward actions shows itself
Against my kindred, brothers, and myself,
Makes him to send; that thereby he may gather
The ground of your ill-will, and so remove it.

Glou. I cannot tell: the world is grown so bad,   70
That wrens make prey where eagles dare not perch:
Since every Jack became a gentleman,
There 's many a gentle person made a Jack.

Q. Eliz. Come, come, we know your meaning,
    brother Gloucester;
You envy my advancement and my friends':
God grant we never may have need of you!

Glou. Meantime, God grants that we have need of
    you:
Our brother is imprison'd by your means,
Myself disgraced, and the nobility
Held in contempt; whilst many fair promotions   80
Are daily given to ennoble those
That scarce, some two days since, were worth a noble.

Q. Eliz. By Him that raised me to this careful
    height
From that contented hap which I enjoy'd,
I never did incense his majesty
Against the Duke of Clarence, but have been
An earnest advocate to plead for him.
My lord, you do me shameful injury,
Falsely to draw me in these vile suspects.

Glou. You may deny that you were not the cause   90
Of my Lord Hastings' late imprisonment.

Riv. She may, my lord, for—

Glou. She may, Lord Rivers! why, who knows not
    so?
She may do more, sir, than denying that:
She may help you to many fair preferments;
And then deny her aiding hand therein,
And lay those honours on your high deserts.
What may she not? She may, yea, marry, may she,—

Riv. What, marry, may she?

Glou. What, marry, may she! marry with a king,   100
A bachelor, a handsome stripling too:
I wis your grandam had a worser match.

Q. Eliz. My Lord of Gloucester, I have too long
    borne
Your blunt upbraidings and your bitter scoffs:
By heaven, I will acquaint his majesty
With those gross taunts I often have endured.
I had rather be a country servant-maid
Than a great queen, with this condition,
To be thus taunted, scorn'd, and baited at:

Enter QUEEN MARGARET, *behind.*

Small joy have I in being England's queen.   110

Q. Mar. And lessen'd be that small, God, I beseech
    thee!
Thy honour, state and seat is due to me.

Glou. What! threat you me with telling of the king?

SCENE III. 6. **betide of,** become of. 15. **determined . . . concluded,** i.e., decided though not performed. 16. **miscarry,** perish. 20. **Countess Richmond,** Margaret Beaufort (1443-1509), who married successively Edmund Tudor Earl of Richmond, Lord Henry Stafford, and Thomas Lord Stanley (here called also earl of Derby). She was not friendly to Queen Elizabeth's faction. 26. **envious,** malicious; see glossary. 47. **fair,** courteously; see glossary. 48. **cog,** cheat; see glossary. 53. **Jacks,** lowbred persons. 57. **faction,** party; see glossary. 60.

breathing-while, moment of rest. 61. **lewd,** vile, base. 63. **disposition,** inclination. 72. **Jack,** peasant, with play on the meaning "base fellow" in the next line. 77. **need of you,** are in trouble on account of you. 82. **noble,** a coin, with quibble on the sense of "ennoblement." 89. **Falsely,** treacherously; see glossary. **suspects,** suspicions. 100. **marry with.** In all preceding cases the word *marry* has been used as an oath meaning "by the Virgin Mary"; see glossary. 112. **state,** degree; see glossary. **seat,** throne.

Tell him, and spare not: look, what I have said
I will avouch in presence of the king:
I dare adventure to be sent to the Tower.
'Tis time to speak; my pains are quite forgot.
    Q. Mar. Out, devil! I remember them too well:
Thou slewest my husband Henry in the Tower,
And Edward, my poor son, at Tewksbury.   120
    Glou. Ere you were queen, yea, or your husband
        king,
I was a pack-horse in his great affairs;
A weeder-out of his proud adversaries,
A liberal rewarder of his friends:
To royalise his blood I spilt mine own.
    Q. Mar. Yea, and much better blood than his or
        thine.
    Glou. In all which time you and your husband Grey
Were factious for the house of Lancaster;
And, Rivers, so were you. Was not your husband
In Margaret's battle at Saint Alban's slain?   130
Let me put in your minds, if you forget,
What you have been ere now, and what you are;
Withal, what I have been, and what I am.
    Q. Mar. A murderous villain, and so still thou art.
    Glou. Poor Clarence did forsake his father,
        Warwick;
Yea, and forswore himself,—which Jesu pardon!—
    Q. Mar. Which God revenge!
    Glou. To fight on Edward's party for the crown;
And for his meed, poor lord, he is mew'd up.
I would to God my heart were flint, like Edward's;   140
Or Edward's soft and pitiful, like mine:
I am too childish-foolish for this world.
    Q. Mar. Hie thee to hell for shame, and leave the
        world,
Thou cacodemon! there thy kingdom is.
    Riv. My Lord of Gloucester, in those busy days
Which here you urge to prove us enemies,
We follow'd then our lord, our lawful king:
So should we you, if you should be our king.
    Glou. If I should be! I had rather be a pedlar:
Far be it from my heart, the thought of it!   150
    Q. Eliz. As little joy, my lord, as you suppose
You should enjoy, were you this country's king,
As little joy may you suppose in me,
That I enjoy, being the queen thereof.
    Q. Mar. A little joy enjoys the queen thereof;
For I am she, and altogether joyless.
I can no longer hold me patient.   [_Advancing._
Hear me, you wrangling pirates, that fall out
In sharing that which you have pill'd from me!
Which of you trembles not that looks on me?   160
If not, that, I being queen, you bow like subjects,
Yet that, by you deposed, you quake like rebels?
O gentle villain, do not turn away!
    Glou. Foul wrinkled witch, what makest thou in my
        sight?
    Q. Mar. But repetition of what thou hast marr'd;
That will I make before I let thee go.

    Glou. Wert thou not banished on pain of death?
    Q. Mar. I was; but I do find more pain in
        banishment
Than death can yield me here by my abode.
A husband and a son thou owest to me;   170
And thou a kingdom; all of you allegiance:
The sorrow that I have, by right is yours,
And all the pleasures you usurp are mine.
    Glou. The curse my noble father laid on thee,
When thou didst crown his warlike brows with paper
And with thy scorns drew'st rivers from his eyes,
And then, to dry them, gavest the duke a clout
Steep'd in the faultless blood of pretty Rutland,—
His curses, then from bitterness of soul
Denounced against thee, are all fall'n upon thee;   180
And God, not we, hath plagued thy bloody deed.
    Q. Eliz. So just is God, to right the innocent.
    Hast. O, 'twas the foulest deed to slay that babe,
And the most merciless that e'er was heard of!
    Riv. Tyrants themselves wept when it was reported.
    Dor. No man but prophesied revenge for it.
    Buck. Northumberland, then present, wept to see it.
    Q. Mar. What! were you snarling all before I came,
Ready to catch each other by the throat,
And turn you all your hatred now on me?   190
Did York's dread curse prevail so much with heaven
That Henry's death, my lovely Edward's death,
Their kingdom's loss, my woful banishment,
Could all but answer for that peevish brat?
Can curses pierce the clouds and enter heaven?
Why, then, give way, dull clouds, to my quick curses!
If not by war, by surfeit die your king,
As ours by murder, to make him a king!
Edward thy son, which now is Prince of Wales,
For Edward my son, which was Prince of Wales,   200
Die in his youth by like untimely violence!
Thyself a queen, for me that was a queen,
Outlive thy glory, like my wretched self!
Long mayst thou live to wail thy children's loss;
And see another, as I see thee now,
Deck'd in thy rights, as thou art stall'd in mine!
Long die thy happy days before thy death;
And, after many lengthen'd hours of grief,
Die neither mother, wife, nor England's queen!
Rivers and Dorset, you were standers by,   210
And so wast thou, Lord Hastings, when my son
Was stabb'd with bloody daggers: God, I pray him,
That none of you may live your natural age,
But by some unlook'd accident cut off!
    Glou. Have done thy charm, thou hateful wither'd
        hag!
    Q. Mar. And leave out thee? stay, dog, for thou
        shalt hear me.
If heaven have any grievous plague in store
Exceeding those that I can wish upon thee,
O, let them keep it till thy sins be ripe,
And then hurl down their indignation   220
On thee, the troubler of the poor world's peace!

_Richard
the Third_
ACT I : SC III

308

---

116. **adventure to be,** risk being.   118. **Out,** exclamation of anger; see
glossary.   121-122. **Ere . . . affairs.** Edward IV became king in 1460
when Richard was eight years old.   130. **Margaret's battle,** probably,
the Battle of Bernard's Heath fought at St. Alban's in 1461.   138.
party, side; see glossary.   144. **cacodemon,** evil spirit.   159. **pill'd,**
robbed, pillaged.   160-162. **Which . . . rebels?** If you do not tremble
before me, bowing in awe because I am your queen, you quake as rebels
who have deposed me?   164. **makest,** dost; see glossary.   165. **But . . .
marr'd.** I merely rehearse your crimes.   167. **banished.** Margaret was
banished in 1464, returned to England in 1471, and after the Battle of
Tewksbury was confined in the Tower until 1476 when she returned

to France, dying there in 1482, one year before the historical time of this
scene.   170. **thou,** Richard.   171. **thou,** i.e., Elizabeth.   174. **curse.**
Cf. _3 Henry VI,_ I, iv, 164-166.   177. **clout,** cloth.   187 **Northumberland,**
Sir Henry Percy, third earl of Northumberland, killed at Towton in
1461. Cf. _3 Henry VI,_ I, iv, 150-151, 169-174.   194. **answer,** atone for;
see glossary.   **peevish,** silly; see glossary.   196. **quick,** sharp, piercing;
see glossary.   197. **surfeit,** luxurious living.   206. **stall'd,** installed.
214. **cut off,** elliptic, but coordinate with the preceding line, i.e.,
live until you are cut off.   222. **begnaw,** gnaw, corrode (intensive).
228. **elvish-mark'd,** marked by elves at birth. **rooting hog,** an
allusion to Richard's badge, the wild boar. In 1484 William Colyng-

The worm of conscience still begnaw thy soul!
Thy friends suspect for traitors while thou livest,
And take deep traitors for thy dearest friends!
No sleep close up that deadly eye of thine,
Unless it be whilst some tormenting dream
Affrights thee with a hell of ugly devils!
Thou elvish-mark'd, abortive, rooting hog!
Thou that wast seal'd in thy nativity
The slave of nature and the son of hell!   230
Thou slander of thy mother's heavy womb!
Thou loathed issue of thy father's loins!
Thou rag of honour! thou detested—
   Glou. Margaret.
   Q. Mar.   Richard!
   Glou.   Ha!
   Q. Mar.   I call thee not.
   Glou. I cry thee mercy then, for I had thought
That thou hadst call'd me all these bitter names.
   Q. Mar. Why, so I did; but look'd for no reply.
O, let me make the period to my curse!
   Glou. 'Tis done by me, and ends in 'Margaret.'
   Q. Eliz. Thus have you breathed your curse against
     yourself.   240
   Q. Mar. Poor painted queen, vain flourish of my
     fortune!
Why strew'st thou sugar on that bottled spider,
Whose deadly web ensnareth thee about?
Fool, fool! thou whet'st a knife to kill thyself.
The time will come when thou shalt wish for me
To help thee curse that poisonous bunch-back'd toad.
   Hast. False-boding woman, end thy frantic curse,
Lest to thy harm thou move our patience.
   Q. Mar. Foul shame upon you! you have all moved
     mine.
   Riv. Were you well served, you would be taught
     your duty.   250
   Q. Mar. To serve me well, you all should do me
     duty,
Teach me to be your queen, and you my subjects:
O, serve me well, and teach yourselves that duty!
   Dor. Dispute not with her; she is lunatic.
   Q. Mar. Peace, master marquess, you are malapert:
Your fire-new stamp of honour is scarce current.
O, that your young nobility could judge
What 'twere to lose it, and be miserable!
They that stand high have many blasts to shake them;
And if they fall, they dash themselves to pieces.   260
   Glou. Good counsel, marry: learn it, learn it,
     marquess.
   Dor. It toucheth you, my lord, as much as me.
   Glou. Yea, and much more: but I was born so high,
Our aery buildeth in the cedar's top,
And dallies with the wind and scorns the sun.
   Q. Mar. And turns the sun to shade; alas! alas!
Witness my son, now in the shade of death;
Whose bright out-shining beams thy cloudy wrath
Hath in eternal darkness folded up.
Your aery buildeth in our aery's nest.   270

O God, that seest it, do not suffer it;
As it was won with blood, lost be it so!
   Buck. Have done! for shame, if not for charity.
   Q. Mar. Urge neither charity nor shame to me:
Uncharitably with me have you dealt,
And shamefully by you my hopes are butcher'd.
My charity is outrage, life my shame;
And in that shame still live my sorrow's rage!
   Buck. Have done, have done.
   Q. Mar. O princely Buckingham, I'll kiss thy hand,
In sign of league and amity with thee: 281
Now fair befal thee and thy noble house!
Thy garments are not spotted with our blood,
Nor thou within the compass of my curse.
   Buck. Nor no one here; for curses never pass
The lips of those that breathe them in the air.
   Q. Mar. I'll not believe but they ascend the sky,
And there awake God's gentle-sleeping peace.
O Buckingham, take heed of yonder dog!
Look, when he fawns, he bites; and when he bites,   290
His venom tooth will rankle to the death:
Have not to do with him, beware of him;
Sin, death, and hell have set their marks on him,
And all their ministers attend on him.
   Glou. What doth she say, my Lord of Buckingham?
   Buck. Nothing that I respect, my gracious lord.
   Q. Mar. What, dost thou scorn me for my gentle
     counsel?
And soothe the devil that I warn thee from?
O, but remember this another day,
When he shall split thy very heart with sorrow,   300
And say poor Margaret was a prophetess!
Live each of you the subjects to his hate,
And he to yours, and all of you to God's!   [*Exit.*
   Hast. My hair doth stand on end to hear her curses.
   Riv. And so doth mine: I muse why she 's at liberty.
   Glou. I cannot blame her: by God's holy mother,
She hath had too much wrong; and I repent
My part thereof that I have done to her.
   Q. Eliz. I never did her any, to my knowledge.
   Glou. But you have all the vantage of her wrong.   310
I was too hot to do somebody good,
That is too cold in thinking of it now.
Marry, as for Clarence, he is well repaid;
He is frank'd up to fatting for his pains:
God pardon them that are the cause of it!
   Riv. A virtuous and a Christian-like conclusion,
To pray for them that have done scathe to us.
   Glou. So do I ever: [*Aside*] being well advised.
For had I cursed now, I had cursed myself.

   Enter CATESBY.

   Cates. Madam, his majesty doth call for you;   320
And for your grace; and you, my noble lords.
   Q. Eliz. Catesby, we come. Lords, will you go with
     us?
   Riv. Madam, we will attend your grace.
               [*Exeunt all but Gloucester.*

borne, a Wiltshire gentleman, was executed for publishing the lines:
"The Cat, the Rat, and Louell our dog | Rull all England vnder an
hog." 229. **seal'd,** stamped; see glossary. 230. **slave of nature,** i.e.,
by the malignancy of nature. 235. **cry thee mercy,** beg thy pardon;
see glossary. 238. **period,** conclusion. 239. **by me,** i.e., in line 234
where he completes Margaret's sentence. 241. **painted,** counterfeit; see
glossary. **vain . . . fortune,** i.e., mere ornament of a position which is
mine by right. 242. **bottled,** bottle-shaped, swollen. 250. **well
served,** i.e., if you had what you have deserved. Margaret takes the
word in its other sense in line 253. **duty,** i.e., submission to authority;
see glossary. 255. **malapert,** impudent. 256. **fire-new,** newly coined.

current, put into circulation. 264. **aery,** brood of an eagle. 277.
My . . . outrage, i.e., instead of charity I receive outrage. 285-286.
curses . . . air. Probably, curses have no effect except on those who
utter them. 291. **venom,** envenomed. **rankle,** cause a festering
wound. 296. **respect,** heed; see glossary. 298. **soothe,** flatter. 310.
vantage, advantage; see glossary. 311. **hot,** eager. 312. **cold,** ungrateful. 314. **frank'd up,** shut up in a frank, or sty. **to fatting,** to
be fattened. 317. **scathe,** harm. 319. **cursed myself,** i.e., Richard
himself is the *cause* mentioned in line 315.

Glou. I do the wrong, and first begin to brawl.
The secret mischiefs that I set abroach
I lay unto the grievous charge of others.
Clarence, whom I, indeed, have laid in darkness,
I do beweep to many simple gulls;
Namely, to Hastings, Derby, Buckingham;
And say it is the queen and her allies   330
That stir the king against the duke my brother.
Now, they believe it; and withal whet me
To be revenged on Rivers, Vaughan, Grey:
But then I sigh; and, with a piece of scripture,
Tell them that God bids us do good for evil:
And thus I clothe my naked villany
With old odd ends stolen out of holy writ;
And seem a saint, when most I play the devil.

Enter two Murderers.

But, soft! here come my executioners.
How now, my hardy, stout resolved mates!   340
Are you now going to dispatch this deed?
    First Mur. We are, my lord; and come to have the
        warrant,
That we may be admitted where he is.
    Glou. Well thought upon; I have it here about me.
                                    [*Gives the warrant.*
When you have done, repair to Crosby Place.
But, sirs, be sudden in the execution,
Withal obdurate, do not hear him plead;
For Clarence is well-spoken, and perhaps
May move your hearts to pity, if you mark him.
    First Mur. Tush!   350
Fear not, my lord, we will not stand to prate;
Talkers are no good doers: be assured
We come to use our hands and not our tongues.
    Glou. Your eyes drop millstones, when fools' eyes
        drop tears:
I like you, lads; about your business straight;
Go, go, dispatch.
    First Mur. We will, my noble lord.   [*Exeunt.*

SCENE IV. *London. The Tower.*

Enter CLARENCE *and* BRAKENBURY.

    Brak. Why looks your grace so heavily to-day?
    Clar. O, I have pass'd a miserable night,
So full of ugly sights, of ghastly dreams,
That, as I am a Christian faithful man,
I would not spend another such a night,
Though 'twere to buy a world of happy days,
So full of dismal terror was the time!
    Brak. What was your dream? I long to hear you tell
        it.
    Clar. Methoughts that I had broken from the
        Tower,
And was embark'd to cross to Burgundy;   10
And, in my company, my brother Gloucester;
Who from my cabin tempted me to walk
Upon the hatches: thence we look'd toward England,
And cited up a thousand fearful times,
During the wars of York and Lancaster

That had befall'n us. As we paced along
Upon the giddy footing of the hatches,
Methought that Gloucester stumbled; and, in falling,
Struck me, that thought to stay him, overboard,
Into the tumbling billows of the main.   20
Lord, Lord! methought, what pain it was to drown!
What dreadful noise of waters in mine ears!
What ugly sights of death within mine eyes!
Methought I saw a thousand fearful wrecks;
Ten thousand men that fishes gnaw'd upon;
Wedges of gold, great anchors, heaps of pearl,
Inestimable stones, unvalued jewels,
All scatter'd in the bottom of the sea:
Some lay in dead men's skulls; and, in those holes
Where eyes did once inhabit, there were crept,   30
As 'twere in scorn of eyes, reflecting gems,
Which woo'd the slimy bottom of the deep,
And mock'd the dead bones that lay scatter'd by.
    Brak. Had you such leisure in the time of death
To gaze upon the secrets of the deep?
    Clar. Methought I had; and often did I strive
To yield the ghost: but still the envious flood
Kept in my soul, and would not let it forth
To seek the empty, vast and wandering air;
But smother'd it within my panting bulk,   40
Which almost burst to belch it in the sea.
    Brak. Awaked you not with this sore agony?
    Clar. O, no, my dream was lengthen'd after life;
O, then began the tempest to my soul,
Who pass'd, methought, the melancholy flood,
With that grim ferryman which poets write of,
Unto the kingdom of perpetual night.
The first that there did greet my stranger soul,
Was my great father-in-law, renowned Warwick;
Who cried aloud, 'What scourge for perjury   50
Can this dark monarchy afford false Clarence?'
And so he vanish'd: then came wandering by
A shadow like an angel, with bright hair
Dabbled in blood; and he squeak'd out aloud,
'Clarence is come; false, fleeting, perjured Clarence,
That stabb'd me in the field by Tewksbury;
Seize on him, Furies, take him to your torments!'
With that, methoughts, a legion of foul fiends
Environ'd me about, and howled in mine ears
Such hideous cries, that with the very noise   60
I trembling waked, and for a season after
Could not believe but that I was in hell,
Such terrible impression made the dream.
    Brak. No marvel, my lord, though it affrighted you;
I promise you, I am afraid to hear you tell it.
    Clar. O Brakenbury, I have done those things,
Which now bear evidence against my soul,
For Edward's sake; and see how he requites me!
O God! if my deep prayers cannot appease thee,
But thou wilt be avenged on my misdeeds,   70
Yet execute thy wrath in me alone,
O, spare my guiltless wife and my poor children!
I pray thee, gentle keeper, stay by me;
My soul is heavy, and I fain would sleep.
    Brak. I will, my lord: God give your grace good
        rest!   [*Clarence sleeps.*

325. **set abroach,** begin, set on foot.   355. **straight,** immediately; see
glossary.
    SCENE IV.   10. **Burgundy,** i.e., the Netherlands. Clarence when a
child had been under the Burgundian protection at Utrecht.   14.
fearful, exciting fear; see glossary.   39. **vast.** Malone suggests that this
word is a substantive.   40. **bulk,** body.   45. **melancholy flood,** i.e.,

the river Styx.   46. **ferryman,** i.e., Charon, who ferried souls to Hades,
the kingdom of perpetual night (l. 47).   49. **father-in-law.** Clarence's
wife, Isabel Neville, was the elder daughter of the earl of Warwick.
50. **scourge for perjury.** Cf. *3 Henry VI,* V, i, 106.   53. **shadow,** i.e.,
ghost of Edward Prince of Wales, son of Henry VI; see glossary.   55.
fleeting, fickle, deceitful.   56. **stabb'd me.** Cf. *3 Henry VI,* V, v, 40.

Sorrow breaks seasons and reposing hours,
Makes the night morning, and the noon-tide night.
Princes have but their titles for their glories,
An outward honour for an inward toil;
And, for unfelt imagination, 80
They often feel a world of restless cares:
So that, betwixt their titles and low names,
There's nothing differs but the outward fame.

Enter the two Murderers.

First Murd. Ho! who's here?
Brak. In God's name what are you, and how came
you hither?
First Murd. I would speak with Clarence, and I came
hither on my legs.
Brak. Yea, are you so brief?
Sec. Murd. O sir, it is better to be brief than tedious.
Show him our commission; talk no more.
                              [*Brakenbury reads it.*
Brak. I am, in this, commanded to deliver
The noble Duke of Clarence to your hands:
I will not reason what is meant hereby,
Because I will be guiltless of the meaning.
Here are the keys, there sits the duke asleep:
I'll to the king; and signify to him
That thus I have resign'd my charge to you.
First Murd. Do so, it is a point of wisdom: fare you
well.   [*Exit Brakenbury.* 100
Sec. Murd. What, shall we stab him as he sleeps?
First Murd. No; then he will say 'twas done cow-
ardly, when he wakes.
Sec. Murd. When he wakes! why, fool, he shall never
wake till the judgement-day.
First Murd. Why, then he will say we stabbed him
sleeping.
Sec. Murd. The urging of that word 'judgement'
hath bred a kind of remorse in me. 110
First Murd. What, art thou afraid?
Sec. Murd. Not to kill him, having a warrant for it;
but to be damned for killing him, from which no
warrant can defend us.
First Murd. I thought thou hadst been resolute.
Sec. Murd. So I am, to let him live.
First Murd. Back to the Duke of Gloucester, tell him
so. 119
Sec. Murd. I pray thee, stay a while: I hope my holy
humour will change; 'twas wont to hold me but while
one would tell twenty.
First Murd. How dost thou feel thyself now?
Sec. Murd. 'Faith, some certain dregs of conscience
are yet within me.
First Murd. Remember our reward, when the deed
is done.
Sec. Murd. 'Zounds, he dies: I had forgot the
reward.
First Murd. Where is thy conscience now?
Sec. Murd. In the Duke of Gloucester's purse. 131
First Murd. So when he opens his purse to give us
our reward, thy conscience flies out.
Sec. Murd. Let it go; there's few or none will enter-
tain it.

First Murd. How if it come to thee again?
Sec. Murd. I'll not meddle with it: it is a dangerous
thing: it makes a man a coward: a man cannot steal,
but it accuseth him; he cannot swear, but it checks
him; he cannot lie with his neighbour's wife, but it
detects him: 'tis a blushing shamefast spirit that
mutinies in a man's bosom; it fills one full of obstacles:
it made me once restore a purse of gold that I found;
it beggars any man that keeps it: it is turned out of all
towns and cities for a dangerous thing; and every
man that means to live well endeavours to trust to
himself and to live without it.
First Murd. 'Zounds, it is even now at my elbow,
persuading me not to kill the duke. 150
Sec. Murd. Take the devil in thy mind, and believe
him not: he would insinuate with thee but to make
thee sigh.
First Murd. Tut, I am strong-framed, he cannot
prevail with me, I warrant thee.
Sec. Murd. Spoke like a tall fellow that respects his
reputation. Come, shall we to this gear?
First Murd. Take him over the costard with the hilts
of thy sword, and then we will chop him in the
malmsey-butt in the next room. 161
Sec. Murd. O excellent device! make a sop of him.
First Murd. Hark! he stirs: shall I strike?
Sec. Murd. No, first let's reason with him.
Clar. Where art thou, keeper? give me a cup of wine.
Sec. Murd. You shall have wine enough, my lord,
anon.
Clar. In God's name, what art thou?
Sec. Murd. A man, as you are. 170
Clar. But not, as I am, royal.
Sec. Murd. Nor you, as we are, loyal.
Clar. Thy voice is thunder, but thy looks are
humble.
Sec. Murd. My voice is now the king's, my looks
mine own.
Clar. How darkly and how deadly dost thou speak!
Your eyes do menace me: why look you pale?
Who sent you hither? Wherefore do you come?
Both. To, to, to—
Clar. To murder me?
Both. Ay, ay.
Clar. You scarcely have the hearts to tell me so, 180
And therefore cannot have the hearts to do it.
Wherein, my friends, have I offended you?
First Murd. Offended us you have not, but the king.
Clar. I shall be reconciled to him again.
Sec. Murd. Never, my lord; therefore prepare to die.
Clar. Are you call'd forth from out a world of men
To slay the innocent? What is my offence?
Where are the evidence that do accuse me?
What lawful quest have given their verdict up
Unto the frowning judge? or who pronounced 190
The bitter sentence of poor Clarence' death?
Before I be convict by course of law,
To threaten me with death is most unlawful.
I charge you, as you hope to have redemption
By Christ's dear blood shed for our grievous sins,
That you depart and lay no hands on me:

80. **unfelt,** unrealized. 83. **fame,** reputation; see glossary. 122. **tell,**
count; see glossary. 135. **entertain it,** follow the dictates of conscience. 140. **checks,** reproves; see glossary. 142. **shamefast,** bashful.
152. **him,** conscience, which he identifies with the devil. 156. **tall,**
fine; see glossary. 158. **gear,** business; see glossary. 159. **costard,**
head; literally, a kind of large apple. 161. **malmsey-butt,** wine

barrel. 162. **sop,** bread dipped in wine. 168. **anon,** soon; see glossary. 175. **darkly,** frowningly. 189. **quest,** inquest; possibly, jury.
192. **convict,** convicted.

The deed you undertake is damnable.
　First Murd. What we will do, we do upon command.
　Sec. Murd. And he that hath commanded is the king.
　Clar. Erroneous vassal! the great King of kings　200
Hath in the tables of his law commanded
That thou shalt do no murder: and wilt thou, then,
Spurn at his edict and fulfil a man's?
Take heed; for he holds vengeance in his hands,
To hurl upon their heads that break his law.
　Sec. Murd. And that same vengeance doth he hurl
　　on thee,
For false forswearing and for murder too:
Thou didst receive the holy sacrament,
To fight in quarrel of the house of Lancaster.
　First Murd. And, like a traitor to the name of God,210
Didst break that vow; and with thy treacherous blade
Unrip'dst the bowels of thy sovereign's son.
　Sec. Murd. Whom thou wert sworn to cherish and
　　defend.
　First Murd. How canst thou urge God's dreadful
　　law to us,
When thou hast broke it in so dear degree?
　Clar. Alas! for whose sake did I that ill deed?
For Edward, for my brother, for his sake:
Why, sirs,
He sends ye not to murder me for this;
For in this sin he is as deep as I.　220
If God will be revenged for this deed,
O, know you yet, he doth it publicly:
Take not the quarrel from his powerful arm;
He needs no indirect nor lawless course
To cut off those that have offended him.
　First Murd. Who made thee, then, a bloody minister,
When gallant-springing brave Plantagenet,
That princely novice, was struck dead by thee?
　Clar. My brother's love, the devil, and my rage.
　First Murd. Thy brother's love, our duty, and thy
　　fault,　230
Provoke us hither now to slaughter thee.
　Clar. Oh, if you love my brother, hate not me;
I am his brother, and I love him well.
If you be hired for meed, go back again,
And I will send you to my brother Gloucester,
Who shall reward you better for my life
Than Edward will for tidings of my death.
　Sec. Murd. You are deceived, your brother
　　Gloucester hates you.
　Clar. O, no, he loves me, and he holds me dear:
Go you to him from me.
　Both.　　　　　　Ay, so we will.　240
　Clar. Tell him, when that our princely father York
Bless'd his three sons with his victorious arm,
And charged us from his soul to love each other,
He little thought of this divided friendship:
Bid Gloucester think of this, and he will weep.
　First Murd. Ay, millstones; as he lesson'd us to weep.
　Clar. O, do not slander him, for he is kind.
　First Murd. Right,
As snow in harvest. Thou deceivest thyself:
'Tis he that sent us hither now to slaughter thee.　250
　Clar. It cannot be; for when I parted with him,

He hugg'd me in his arms, and swore, with sobs,
That he would labour my delivery.
　Sec. Murd. Why, so he doth, now he delivers thee
From this world's thraldom to the joys of heaven.
　First Murd. Make peace with God, for you must die,
　　my lord.
　Clar. Hast thou that holy feeling in thy soul,
To counsel me to make my peace with God,
And art thou yet to thy own soul so blind,
That thou wilt war with God by murdering me?　260
Ah, sirs, consider, he that set you on
To do this deed will hate you for the deed.
　Sec. Murd. What shall we do?
　Clar.　　　　　　Relent, and save your souls.
　First Murd. Relent! 'tis cowardly and womanish:
　Clar. Not to relent is beastly, savage, devilish.
Which of you, if you were a prince's son,
Being pent from liberty, as I am now,
If two such murderers as yourselves came to you,
Would not entreat for life?
My friend, I spy some pity in thy looks;　270
O, if thine eye be not a flatterer,
Come thou on my side, and entreat for me,
As you would beg, were you in my distress:
A begging prince what beggar pities not?
　Sec. Murd. Look behind you, my lord.
　First Murd. Take that, and that: if all this will not
　　do,　　　　　　　　　　　*[Stabs him.*
I'll drown you in the malmsey-butt within.
　　　　　　　　　　　　　[Exit, with the body.
　Sec. Murd. A bloody deed, and desperately
　　dispatch'd!
How fain, like Pilate, would I wash my hands
Of this most grievous guilty murder done!　280

　　　　　　Re-enter First Murderer.

　First Murd. How now! what mean'st thou, that thou
　　help'st me not?
By heavens, the duke shall know how slack thou art!
　Sec. Murd. I would he knew that I had saved his
　　brother!
Take thou the fee, and tell him what I say;
For I repent me that the duke is slain.　　　*[Exit.*
　First Murd. So do not I: go, coward as thou art.
Now must I hide his body in some hole,
Until the duke take order for his burial:
And when I have my meed, I must away;
For this will out, and here I must not stay.　*[Exit.* 290

ACT II.

SCENE I. *London. The palace.*

Flourish. Enter KING EDWARD *sick*, QUEEN ELIZABETH,
　DORSET, RIVERS, HASTINGS, BUCKINGHAM, GREY,
　and others.

　K. Edw. Why, so: now have I done a good day's
　　work:
You peers, continue this united league:
I every day expect an embassage

200. **Erroneous,** mistaken. 201. **tables,** tablets; see glossary. 215.
dear, grievous; see glossary. 227. **gallant-springing,** blooming, in the
springtime of life. 228. **novice,** youth. 247. **kind,** affectionate; see
glossary. 249. **snow in harvest.** Cf. Proverbs 26:1. 253. **labour my
delivery,** i.e., work to procure my freedom. 267. **pent from,** shut up
from. 277. **malmsey-butt.** Shakespeare here follows Holinshed. Up

to this point, the scene has no historical basis.
　ACT II. SCENE I. 5. **part,** depart; see glossary. 8. **Dissemble . . .
hatred,** i.e., do not conceal it merely. 12. **dally,** trifle. 14. **Confound,**
undo, i.e., by exposing; see glossary. 15. **Either . . . end,** i.e., each
of you to die at the hands of the other. 20. **factious,** i.e., guilty of
factious conduct. 37. **most,** am most. 50. **of,** out of; see glossary.

From my Redeemer to redeem me hence;
And now in peace my soul shall part to heaven,
Since I have set my friends at peace on earth.
Rivers and Hastings, take each other's hand;
Dissemble not your hatred, swear your love.
    Riv. By heaven, my heart is purged from grudging
        hate;
And with my hand I seal my true heart's love.   10
    Hast. So thrive I, as I truly swear the like!
    K. Edw. Take heed you dally not before your king;
Lest he that is the supreme King of kings
Confound your hidden falsehood, and award
Either of you to be the other's end.
    Hast. So prosper I, as I swear perfect love!
    Riv. And I, as I love Hastings with my heart!
    K. Edw. Madam, yourself are not exempt in this,
Nor your son Dorset, Buckingham, nor you;
You have been factious one against the other.   20
Wife, love Lord Hastings, let him kiss your hand;
And what you do, do it unfeignedly.
    Q.Eliz. Here, Hastings; I will never more remember
Our former hatred, so thrive I and mine!
    K. Edw. Dorset, embrace him; Hastings, love lord
        marquess.
    Dor. This interchange of love, I here protest,
Upon my part shall be unviolable.
    Hast. And so swear I, my lord.   [*They embrace.*
    K. Edw. Now, princely Buckingham, seal thou this
        league
With thy embracements to my wife's allies,   30
And make me happy in your unity.
    Buck. Whenever Buckingham doth turn his hate
On you or yours [*to the Queen*], but with all duteous
        love
Doth cherish you and yours, God punish me
With hate in those where I expect most love!
When I have most need to employ a friend,
And most assured that he is a friend,
Deep, hollow, treacherous, and full of guile,
Be he unto me! this do I beg of God,   39
When I am cold in zeal to you or yours. [*They embrace.*
    K. Edw. A pleasing cordial, princely Buckingham,
Is this thy vow unto my sickly heart.
There wanteth now our brother Gloucester here,
To make the perfect period of this peace.
    Buck. And, in good time, here comes the noble
        duke.

Enter GLOUCESTER.

    Glou. Good morrow to my sovereign king and queen;
And, princely peers, a happy time of day!
    K. Edw. Happy, indeed, as we have spent the day.
Brother, we have done deeds of charity;
Made peace of enmity, fair love of hate,   50
Between these swelling wrong-incensed peers.
    Glou. A blessed labour, my most sovereign liege:
Amongst this princely heap, if any here,
By false intelligence, or wrong surmise,
Hold me a foe;
If I unwittingly, or in my rage,
Have aught committed that is hardly borne

By any in this presence, I desire
To reconcile me to his friendly peace:
'Tis death to me to be at enmity;   60
I hate it, and desire all good men's love.
First, madam, I entreat true peace of you,
Which I will purchase with my duteous service;
Of you, my noble cousin Buckingham,
If ever any grudge were lodged between us;
Of you, Lord Rivers, and, Lord Grey, of you;
That all without desert have frown'd on me;
Dukes, earls, lords, gentlemen; indeed, of all.
I do not know that Englishman alive
With whom my soul is any jot at odds   70
More than the infant that is born to-night:
I thank my God for my humility.
    Q. Eliz. A holy day shall this be kept hereafter:
I would to God all strifes were well compounded.
My sovereign liege, I do beseech your majesty
To take our brother Clarence to your grace.
    Glou. Why, madam, have I offer'd love for this,
To be so flouted in this royal presence?
Who knows not that the noble duke is dead?
                                    [*They all start.*
You do him injury to scorn his corse.   80
    Riv. Who knows not he is dead! who knows he is?
    Q. Eliz. All-seeing heaven, what a world is this!
    Buck. Look I so pale, Lord Dorset, as the rest?
    Dor. Ay, my good lord; and no one in this presence
But his red colour hath forsook his cheeks.
    K. Edw. Is Clarence dead? the order was reversed.
    Glou. But he, poor soul, by your first order died,
And that a winged Mercury did bear;
Some tardy cripple bore the countermand,
That came too lag to see him buried.   90
God grant that some, less noble and less loyal,
Nearer in bloody thoughts, but not in blood,
Deserve not worse than wretched Clarence did,
And yet go current from suspicion!

Enter DERBY.

    Der. A boon, my sovereign, for my service done!
    K. Edw. I pray thee, peace: my soul is full of sorrow.
    Der. I will not rise, unless your highness grant.
    K. Edw. Then speak at once what is it thou
        demand'st.
    Der. The forfeit, sovereign, of my servant's life;
Who slew to-day a riotous gentleman   100
Lately attendant on the Duke of Norfolk.
    K. Edw. Have I a tongue to doom my brother's
        death,
And shall the same give pardon to a slave?
My brother slew no man; his fault was thought,
And yet his punishment was cruel death.
Who sued to me for him? who, in my rage,
Kneel'd at my feet, and bade me be advised?
Who spake of brotherhood? who spake of love?
Who told me how the poor soul did forsake
The mighty Warwick, and did fight for me?   110
Who told me, in the field by Tewksbury,
When Oxford had me down, he rescued me,
And said, 'Dear brother, live, and be a king'?

---

51. **swelling**, i.e., with anger or rivalry. 53. **heap**, assembly. 54. **false intelligence**, being misinformed. 57. **hardly borne**, taken amiss; see *hardly* in glossary. 63. **purchase**, obtain; see glossary. 66. **Lord Rivers**. There is a difficult crux in this passage. After line 67 F adds *Of you Lord Wooduill and Lord Scales of you*. Woodville was Lord **Rivers** and, also, Lord Scales by right of his wife. Thus in F one person is given three names. 67. **without desert**, i.e., on my part. 74. **compounded**, settled; see glossary. 90. **lag**, late. 94. **current . . . suspicion**, free and not attacked by suspicion. 98. **demand'st**, requestest; see glossary. 99. **forfeit**, i.e., the remission of the forfeit. 107. **advised**, cautious. 112. **Oxford**. Cf. *3 Henry VI*, V, v, 2.

Who told me, when we both lay in the field
Frozen almost to death, how he did lap me
Even in his own garments, and gave himself,
All thin and naked, to the numb cold night?
All this from my remembrance brutish wrath
Sinfully pluck'd, and not a man of you
Had so much grace to put it in my mind.   120
But when your carters or your waiting-vassals
Have done a drunken slaughter, and defaced
The precious image of our dear Redeemer,
You straight are on your knees for pardon, pardon;
And I, unjustly too, must grant it you:
But for my brother not a man would speak,
Nor I, ungracious, speak unto myself
For him, poor soul. The proudest of you all
Have been beholding to him in his life;
Yet none of you would once plead for his life.   130
O God, I fear thy justice will take hold
On me, and you, and mine, and yours for this!
Come, Hastings, help me to my closet. Oh, poor
    Clarence!   [*Exeunt some with King and Queen.*
    Glou. This is the fruit of rashness! Mark'd you not
How that the guilty kindred of the queen
Look'd pale when they did hear of Clarence' death?
O, they did urge it still unto the king!
God will revenge it. But come, let us in,
To comfort Edward with our company.
    Buck. We wait upon your grace.   [*Exeunt.* 140

SCENE II. *The palace.*

Enter the DUCHESS OF YORK, *with the two children of*
CLARENCE.

    Boy. Tell me, good grandam, is our father dead?
    Duch. No, boy.
    Boy. Why do you wring your hands, and beat your
        breast,
And cry 'O Clarence, my unhappy son!'
    Girl. Why do you look on us, and shake your head,
And call us wretches, orphans, castaways,
If that our noble father be alive?
    Duch. My pretty cousins, you mistake me much;
I do lament the sickness of the king,
As loath to lose him, not your father's death;   10
It were lost sorrow to wail one that 's lost.
    Boy. Then, grandam, you conclude that he is dead.
The king my uncle is to blame for this:
God will revenge it; whom I will importune
With daily prayers all to that effect.
    Girl. And so will I.
    Duch. Peace, children, peace! the king doth love
        you well:
Incapable and shallow innocents,
You cannot guess who caused your father's death.
    Boy. Grandam, we can; for my good uncle
        Gloucester   20
Told me, the king, provoked by the queen,
Devised impeachments to imprison him:
And when my uncle told me so, he wept,

And hugg'd me in his arm, and kindly kiss'd my
    cheek;
Bade me rely on him as on my father,
And he would love me dearly as his child.
    Duch. Oh, that deceit should steal such gentle
        shapes,
And with a virtuous vizard hide foul guile!
He is my son; yea, and therein my shame;
Yet from my dugs he drew not this deceit.   30
    Boy. Think you my uncle did dissemble, grandam?
    Duch. Ay, boy.
    Boy. I cannot think it. Hark! what noise is this?

Enter QUEEN ELIZABETH, *with her hair about her ears;*
    RIVERS *and* DORSET *after her.*

    Q. Eliz. Oh, who shall hinder me to wail and weep,
To chide my fortune, and torment myself?
I'll join with black despair against my soul,
And to myself become an enemy.
    Duch. What means this scene of rude impatience?
    Q. Eliz. To make an act of tragic violence:
Edward, my lord, your son, our king, is dead.   40
Why grow the branches now the root is wither'd?
Why wither not the leaves the sap being gone?
If you will live, lament; if die, be brief,
That our swift-winged souls may catch the king's;
Or, like obedient subjects, follow him
To his new kingdom of perpetual rest.
    Duch. Ah, so much interest have I in thy sorrow
As I had title in thy noble husband!
I have bewept a worthy husband's death,
And lived by looking on his images: 50
But now two mirrors of his princely semblance
Are crack'd in pieces by malignant death,
And I for comfort have but one false glass,
Which grieves me when I see my shame in him.
Thou art a widow; yet thou art a mother,
And hast the comfort of thy children left thee:
But death hath snatch'd my husband from mine arms,
And pluck'd two crutches from my feeble limbs,
Edward and Clarence. O, what cause have I,
Thine being but a moiety of my grief,   60
To overgo thy plaints and drown thy cries!
    Boy. Good aunt, you wept not for our father's
        death;
How can we aid you with our kindred tears?
    Girl. Our fatherless distress was left unmoan'd;
Your widow-dolour likewise be unwept!
    Q. Eliz. Give me no help in lamentation;
I am not barren to bring forth complaints:
All springs reduce their currents to mine eyes,
That I, being govern'd by the watery moon,
May send forth plenteous tears to drown the world!   70
Oh for my husband, for my dear lord Edward!
    Chil. Oh for our father, for our dear lord Clarence!
    Duch. Alas for both, both mine, Edward and
        Clarence!
    Q. Eliz. What stay had I but Edward? and he 's
        gone.
    Chil. What stay had we but Clarence? and he 's
        gone.

SCENE II. 8. **cousins**, relations; here, grandchildren; see glossary.
18. **Incapable**, unable to understand. 22. **impeachments**, accusations.
28. **vizard**, mask. 39. **make**, make up, complete; see glossary. 40.
Edward . . . dead. Clarence's death (February 1478) and Edward IV's
death (April 1483) are treated as if they had occurred near together.
50. **images**, likenesses; here, children; see glossary. 53. **false glass**,

i.e., Richard. 65. **widow-dolour**, widow's grief. 67. **barren to**, unable to. 68. **reduce**, bring back. 94. **opposite with**, in opposition to.
112. **cloudy**, clouded with grief. 117-119. **The . . . kept**, i.e., the
differences caused by the inveterate bitterness of the rancor in your
hearts toward each other have recently been healed, and this peace
between you must be preserved. 118. **splinter'd**, splinted, bound up

Duch. What stays had I but they? and they are
  gone.
Q. Eliz. Was never widow had so dear a loss!
Chil. Were never orphans had so dear a loss!
Duch. Was never mother had so dear a loss!
Alas, I am the mother of these moans!   80
Their woes are parcell'd, mine are general.
She for an Edward weeps, and so do I;
I for a Clarence weep, so doth not she:
These babes for Clarence weep, and so do I;
I for an Edward weep, so do not they:
Alas, you three, on me, threefold distress'd,
Pour all your tears! I am your sorrow's nurse,
And I will pamper it with lamentations.
  Dor. Comfort, dear mother; God is much displeased
That you take with unthankfulness his doing: 90
In common worldly things, 'tis call'd ungrateful,
With dull unwillingness to repay a debt
Which with a bounteous hand was kindly lent;
Much more to be thus opposite with heaven,
For it requires the royal debt it lent you.
  Riv. Madam, bethink you, like a careful mother,
Of the young prince your son: send straight for him;
Let him be crown'd; in him your comfort lives:
Drown desperate sorrow in dead Edward's grave,
And plant your joys in living Edward's throne.   100

Enter GLOUCESTER, BUCKINGHAM, DERBY, HASTINGS,
  and RATCLIFF.

  Glou. Madam, have comfort: all of us have cause
To wail the dimming of our shining star;
But none can cure their harms by wailing them.
Madam, my mother, I do cry you mercy;
I did not see your grace: humbly on my knee
I crave your blessing.
  Duch. God bless thee; and put meekness in thy
    mind,
Love, charity, obedience, and true duty!
  Glou. [*Aside*] Amen; and make me die a good old
    man!
That is the butt-end of a mother's blessing: 110
I marvel why her grace did leave it out.
  Buck. You cloudy princes and heart-sorrowing
    peers,
That bear this mutual heavy load of moan,
Now cheer each other in each other's love:
Though we have spent our harvest of this king,
We are to reap the harvest of his son.
The broken rancour of your high-swoln hearts,
But lately splinter'd, knit, and join'd together,
Must gently be preserved, cherish'd, and kept:
Me seemeth good, that, with some little train,   120
Forthwith from Ludlow the young prince be fetch'd
Hither to London, to be crown'd our king.
  Riv. Why with some little train, my Lord of
    Buckingham?
  Buck. Marry, my lord, lest, by a multitude,
The new-heal'd wound of malice should break out;
Which would be so much the more dangerous,
By how much the estate is green and yet ungovern'd:
Where every horse bears his commanding rein,

And may direct his course as please himself,
As well the fear of harm, as harm apparent,   130
In my opinion, ought to be prevented.
  Glou. I hope the king made peace with all of us;
And the compact is firm and true in me.
  Riv. And so in me; and so, I think, in all:
Yet, since it is but green, it should be put
To no apparent likelihood of breach,
Which haply by much company might be urged:
Therefore I say with noble Buckingham,
That it is meet so few should fetch the prince.
  Hast. And so say I.   140
  Glou. Then be it so; and go we to determine
Who they shall be that straight shall post to Ludlow.
Madam, and you, my mother, will you go
To give your censures in this weighty business?
  Q. Eliz.⎫
  Duch. ⎬With all our hearts.
        [*Exeunt all but Buckingham and Gloucester.*
  Buck. My lord, whoever journeys to the prince,
For God's sake, let not us two be behind;
For, by the way, I'll sort occasion,
As index to the story we late talk'd of,
To part the queen's proud kindred from the king.   150
  Glou. My other self, my counsel's consistory,
My oracle, my prophet! My dear cousin,
I, like a child, will go by thy direction.
Towards Ludlow then, for we'll not stay behind.
                                    [*Exeunt.*

SCENE III. *London. A street.*

Enter two Citizens, *meeting.*

  First Cit. Neighbour, well met: whither away so
    fast?
  Sec. Cit. I promise you, I scarcely know myself:
Hear you the news abroad?
  First Cit.   Ay, that the king is dead.
  Sec. Cit. Bad news, by 'r lady; seldom comes the
    better:
I fear, I fear 'twill prove a troublous world.

Enter another Citizen.

  Third Cit. Neighbours, God speed!
  First Cit.   Give you good morrow, sir.
  Third Cit. Doth this news hold of good King
    Edward's death?
  Sec. Cit. Ay, sir, it is too true; God help the while!
  Third Cit. Then, masters, look to see a troublous
    world.
  First Cit. No, no; by God's good grace his son shall
    reign.   10
  Third Cit. Woe to that land that's govern'd by a
    child!
  Sec. Cit. In him there is a hope of government,
That in his nonage council under him,
And in his full and ripen'd years himself,
No doubt, shall then and till then govern well.
  First Cit. So stood the state when Henry the Sixth
Was crown'd in Paris but at nine months old.

---

with splints. 121. **Ludlow,** the royal castle at Ludlow in Wales. 127.
estate, state, government. **green,** i.e., newly established. 130. **apparent,** evident; see glossary. 137. **urged,** encouraged. 144. **censures,**
judgments; see glossary. 148. **sort occasion,** contrive opportunity.
151. **consistory,** council chamber.
  SCENE III. 4. **by 'r lady,** by our Lady (oath by the Virgin Mary).

11. **Woe . . . child.** Cf. Ecclesiastes 10:16. 13. **nonage,** minority.
17. **nine months.** Henry VI, proclaimed king of France, October 1422,
was then about a year old. He was not crowned in Paris until December
1430.

Third Cit. Stood the state so? No, no, good friends,
    God wot;
For then this land was famously enrich'd
With politic grave counsel; then the king   20
Had virtuous uncles to protect his grace.
    First Cit. Why, so hath this, both by the father and
    mother.
    Third Cit. Better it were they all came by the father,
Or by the father there were none at all;
For emulation now, who shall be nearest,
Will touch us all too near, if God prevent not.
O, full of danger is the Duke of Gloucester!
And the queen's sons and brothers haught and proud:
And were they to be ruled, and not to rule,
This sickly land might solace as before.   30
    First Cit. Come, come, we fear the worst; all shall
    be well.
    Third Cit. When clouds appear, wise men put on
    their cloaks;
When great leaves fall, the winter is at hand;
When the sun sets, who doth not look for night?
Untimely storms make men expect a dearth.
All may be well; but, if God sort it so,
'Tis more than we deserve, or I expect.
    Sec. Cit. Truly, the souls of men are full of dread:
Ye cannot reason almost with a man
That looks not heavily and full of fear.   40
    Third Cit. Before the times of change, still is it so:
By a divine instinct men's minds mistrust
Ensuing dangers; as, by proof, we see
The waters swell before a boisterous storm.
But leave it all to God. Whither away?
    Sec. Cit. Marry, we were sent for to the justices.
    Third Cit. And so was I: I'll bear you company.
                                        [*Exeunt.*

SCENE IV. *London. The palace.*

Enter the ARCHBISHOP OF YORK, *the young* DUKE OF
    YORK, QUEEN ELIZABETH, *and the* DUCHESS OF
    YORK.

    Arch. Last night, I hear, they lay at Northampton;
At Stony-Stratford will they be to-night:
To-morrow, or next day, they will be here.
    Duch. I long with all my heart to see the prince:
I hope he is much grown since last I saw him.
    Q. Eliz. But I hear, no; they say my son of York
Hath almost overta'en him in his growth.
    York. Ay, mother; but I would not have it so.
    Duch. Why, my young cousin, it is good to grow.
    York. Grandam, one night, as we did sit at supper, 10
My uncle Rivers talk'd how I did grow
More than my brother: 'Ay,' quoth my uncle
    Gloucester,
'Small herbs have grace, great weeds do grow apace:'
And since, methinks, I would not grow so fast,
Because sweet flowers are slow and weeds make haste.

    Duch. Good faith, good faith, the saying did not
    hold
In him that did object the same to thee:
He was the wretched'st thing when he was young,
So long a-growing and so leisurely,
That, if this rule were true, he should be gracious. 20
    Arch. Why, madam, so, no doubt, he is.
    Duch. I hope he is; but yet let mothers doubt.
    York. Now, by my troth, if I had been remember'd,
I could have given my uncle's grace a flout,
To touch his growth nearer than he touch'd mine.
    Duch. How, my pretty York? I pray thee, let me
    hear it.
    York. Marry, they say my uncle grew so fast
That he could gnaw a crust at two hours old:
'Twas full two years ere I could get a tooth.
Grandam, this would have been a biting jest.   30
    Duch. I pray thee, pretty York, who told thee this?
    York. Grandam, his nurse.
    Duch. His nurse! why, she was dead ere thou wert
    born.
    York. If 'twere not she, I cannot tell who told me.
    Q. Eliz. A parlous boy: go to, you are too shrewd.
    Arch. Good madam, be not angry with the child.
    Q. Eliz. Pitchers have ears.

Enter a Messenger.

    Arch. Here comes a messenger. What news?
    Mess. Such news, my lord, as grieves me to unfold.
    Q. Eliz. How fares the prince?
    Mess.   Well, madam, and in health.   40
    Duch. What is thy news then?
    Mess. Lord Rivers and Lord Grey are sent to
    Pomfret,
With them Sir Thomas Vaughan, prisoners.
    Duch. Who hath committed them?
    Mess.   The mighty dukes
Gloucester and Buckingham.
    Arch.   For what offence?
    Mess. The sum of all I can, I have disclosed;
Why or for what these nobles were committed
Is all unknown to me, my gracious lady.
    Q. Eliz. Ay me, I see the downfall of our house!
The tiger now hath seized the gentle hind;   50
Insulting tyranny begins to jet
Upon the innocent and aweless throne:
Welcome, destruction, death, and massacre!
I see, as in a map, the end of all.
    Duch. Accursed and unquiet wrangling days,
How many of you have mine eyes beheld!
My husband lost his life to get the crown;
And often up and down my sons were toss'd,
For me to joy and weep their gain and loss:
And being seated, and domestic broils   60
Clean over-blown, themselves, the conquerors,
Make war upon themselves; blood against blood,
Self against self: O, preposterous
And frantic outrage, end thy damned spleen;
Or let me die, to look on death no more!

18. **wot,** knows; see glossary.   30. **solace,** be happy, have comfort.
40. **heavily,** sad.   43. **proof,** experience; see glossary.
    SCENE IV.   *Stage Direction: **Enter the**Archbishop of York. The arch-
bishop of York was Thomas Rotherham; the Cardinal of III, i, was
Thomas Bourchier, made archbishop of Canterbury in 1454. The Qq
stage direction, *Enter Cardinal,* indicates perhaps that one actor took
both parts.   1-3. **Last . . . here.** Stony-Stratford is nearer London; the
prince was taken back to Northampton after the arrest of Rivers, Grey,
and Vaughan. The F reading (which interchanges these two place

names) is in accordance with the facts, but it is dramatically impossible,
for if the archbishop is to have news of Richard's movements he must
know also of his actions. That he does not know is clear from his conduct
in this scene.   24. **flout,** dig, insult.   28. **That . . . old.** The legend is
mentioned by More; cf. also *3 Henry VI,* V, vi, 53-54.   35 **parlous,** terrible (exaggerated epithet).   **go to,** expression of impatience; see glossary.   **shrewd,** malicious; see glossary.   37. **Pitchers have ears.**
Proverb: "Little pitchers have large ears."   39. **unfold,** reveal; see
glossary.   45. ***Arch.,*** so F; Globe: *Q. Eliz.*   50. **hind,** (loe.   51. **jet,**

Q. Eliz. Come, come, my boy; we will to sanctuary.
Madam, farewell.
 Duch.   I'll go along with you.
 Q. Eliz. You have no cause.
 Arch.   My gracious lady, go;
And thither bear your treasure and your goods.
For my part, I'll resign unto your grace   70
The seal I keep: and so betide to me
As well I tender you and all of yours!
Come, I'll conduct you to the sanctuary. [*Exeunt.*

ACT III.

SCENE I. *London. A street.*

The trumpets sound. Enter the young PRINCE, *the Dukes of* GLOUCESTER *and* BUCKINGHAM, CARDINAL BOURCHIER, CATESBY, *and others.*

 Buck. Welcome, sweet prince, to London, to your
  chamber.
 Glou. Welcome, dear cousin, my thoughts'
  sovereign:
The weary way hath made you melancholy.
 Prince. No, uncle; but our crosses on the way
Have made it tedious, wearisome, and heavy:
I want more uncles here to welcome me.
 Glou. Sweet prince, the untainted virtue of your
  years
Hath not yet dived into the world's deceit:
Nor more can you distinguish of a man
Than of his outward show; which, God he knows, 10
Seldom or never jumpeth with the heart.
Those uncles which you want were dangerous;
Your grace attended to their sugar'd words,
But look'd not on the poison of their hearts:
God keep you from them, and from such false friends!
 Prince. God keep me from false friends! but they
  were none.
 Glou. My lord, the mayor of London comes to greet
  you.

Enter the Lord Mayor, *and his train.*

 May. God bless your grace with health and happy
  days!
 Prince. I thank you, good my lord; and thank you
  all.
I thought my mother, and my brother York, 20
Would long ere this have met us on the way:
Fie, what a slug is Hastings, that he comes not
To tell us whether they will come or no!

Enter LORD HASTINGS.

 Buck. And, in good time, here comes the sweating
  lord.
 Prince. Welcome, my lord: what, will our mother
  come?
 Hast. On what occasion, God he knows, not I,
The queen your mother, and your brother York,

Have taken sanctuary: the tender prince
Would fain have come with me to meet your grace,
But by his mother was perforce withheld. 30
 Buck. Fie, what an indirect and peevish course
Is this of hers! Lord cardinal, will your grace
Persuade the queen to send the Duke of York
Unto his princely brother presently?
If she deny, Lord Hastings, go with him,
And from her jealous arms pluck him perforce.
 Card. My Lord of Buckingham, if my weak oratory
Can from his mother win the Duke of York,
Anon expect him here; but if she be obdurate
To mild entreaties, God in heaven forbid 40
We should infringe the holy privilege
Of blessed sanctuary! not for all this land
Would I be guilty of so deep a sin.
 Buck. You are too senseless-obstinate, my lord,
Too ceremonious and traditional:
Weigh it but with the grossness of this age,
You break not sanctuary in seizing him.
The benefit thereof is always granted
To those whose dealings have deserved the place,
And those who have the wit to claim the place: 50
This prince hath neither claim'd it nor deserved it;
And therefore, in mine opinion, cannot have it:
Then, taking him from thence that is not there,
You break no privilege nor charter there.
Oft have I heard of sanctuary men;
But sanctuary children ne'er till now.
 Card. My lord, you shall o'er-rule my mind for
  once.
Come on, Lord Hastings, will you go with me?
 Hast. I go, my lord.
 Prince. Good lords, make all the speedy haste you
  may. [*Exeunt Cardinal and Hastings.* 60
Say, uncle Gloucester, if our brother come,
Where shall we sojourn till our coronation?
 Glou. Where it seems best unto your royal self.
If I may counsel you, some day or two
Your highness shall repose you at the Tower:
Then where you please, and shall be thought most fit
For your best health and recreation.
 Prince. I do not like the Tower, of any place.
Did Julius Cæsar build that place, my lord?
 Buck. He did, my gracious lord, begin that place; 70
Which, since, succeeding ages have re-edified.
 Prince. Is it upon record, or else reported
Successively from age to age, he built it?
 Buck. Upon record, my gracious lord.
 Prince. But say, my lord, it were not register'd,
Methinks the truth should live from age to age,
As 'twere retail'd to all posterity,
Even to the general all-ending day.
 Glou. [*Aside*] So wise so young, they say, do never
  live long.
 Prince. What say you, uncle? 80
 Glou. I say, without characters, fame lives long,
[*Aside*] Thus, like the formal vice, Iniquity,
I moralize two meanings in one word.

swagger, walk pompously. 52. **aweless,** i.e., because of the youth of the king. 64. **spleen,** anger; see glossary. 66. **sanctuary.** Queen Elizabeth lodged in the building which served as a legal refuge for criminals and persons in danger of their lives. 71. **seal,** i.e., the Great Seal. 71-72. **so . . . you,** may my fortunes be measured by the care I take of yours.
 ACT III. SCENE I. 1. **chamber,** i.e., London, anciently called the *camera regis,* or king's chamber. 11. **jumpeth,** agrees; see glossary. 22. **slug,** sluggard; it also means "impediment to progress." 26. **On what occasion,** for what reason. 35. **deny,** refuse; see glossary. 44.

senseless-obstinate, unreasonably obstinate. 46. **Weigh . . . age,** i.e., take into consideration the laxness with which this age regards the right of sanctuary. 65. **Tower.** In the fifteenth century the Tower of London was a royal palace. 68. **of any place,** I dislike it most of all places. 71. **re-edified,** rebuilt. 77. **retail'd,** handed down from one to another. 81. **without characters,** lack of written records, with quibble on the sense, "having no moral character"; these are the *two meanings* referred to in line 83; see *characters* in glossary. 82. **vice,** conventional comic villain of the morality plays.

Prince. That Julius Cæsar was a famous man;
With what his valour did enrich his wit,
His wit set down to make his valour live:
Death makes no conquest of this conqueror;
For now he lives in fame, though not in life.
I'll tell you what, my cousin Buckingham,—
  Buck. What, my gracious lord? 90
  Prince. An if I live until I be a man,
I'll win our ancient right in France again,
Or die a soldier, as I lived a king.
  Glou. [*Aside*] Short summers lightly have a forward
    spring.

Enter young YORK, HASTINGS, *and the* CARDINAL.

  Buck. Now, in good time, here comes the Duke of
    York.
  Prince. Richard of York! how fares our loving
    brother?
  York. Well, my dread lord; so must I call you now.
  Prince. Ay, brother, to our grief, as it is yours:
Too late he died that might have kept that title,
Which by his death hath lost much majesty. 100
  Glou. How fares our cousin, noble Lord of York?
  York. I thank you, gentle uncle. O, my lord,
You said that idle weeds are fast in growth:
The prince my brother hath outgrown me far.
  Glou. He hath, my lord.
  York.   And therefore is he idle?
  Glou. O, my fair cousin, I must not say so.
  York. Then he is more beholding to you than I.
  Glou. He may command me as my sovereign;
But you have power in me as in a kinsman.
  York. I pray you, uncle, give me this dagger. 110
  Glou. My dagger, little cousin? with all my heart.
  Prince. A beggar, brother?
  York. Of my kind uncle, that I know will give;
And being but a toy, which is no grief to give.
  Glou. A greater gift than that I'll give my cousin.
  York. A greater gift! O, that 's the sword to it.
  Glou. Ay, gentle cousin, were it light enough.
  York. O, then, I see, you will part but with light
    gifts;
In weightier things you'll say a beggar nay.
  Glou. It is too heavy for your grace to wear. 120
  York. I weigh it lightly, were it heavier.
  Glou. What, would you have my weapon, little
    lord?
  York. I would, that I might thank you as you call
    me.
  Glou. How?
  York. Little.
  Prince. My Lord of York will still be cross in talk:
Uncle, your grace knows how to bear with him.
  York. You mean, to bear me, not to bear with me:
Uncle, my brother mocks both you and me;
Because that I am little, like an ape, 130
He thinks that you should bear me on your shoulders.
  Buck. With what a sharp-provided wit he reasons!
To mitigate the scorn he gives his uncle,

He prettily and aptly taunts himself:
So cunning and so young is wonderful.
  Glou. My lord, will 't please you pass along?
Myself and my good cousin Buckingham
Will to your mother, to entreat of her
To meet you at the Tower and welcome you.
  York. What, will you go unto the Tower, my lord?
  Prince. My lord protector needs will have it so. 141
  York. I shall not sleep in quiet at the Tower.
  Glou. Why, what should you fear?
  York. Marry, my uncle Clarence' angry ghost:
My grandam told me he was murder'd there.
  Prince. I fear no uncles dead.
  Glou. Nor none that live, I hope.
  Prince. An if they live, I hope I need not fear.
But come, my lord; and with a heavy heart,
Thinking on them, go I unto the Tower. 150
    [*A Sennet. Exeunt all but Gloucester, Buckingham
                                  and Catesby.*

  Buck. Think you, my lord, this little prating York
Was not incensed by his subtle mother
To taunt and scorn you thus opprobriously?
  Glou. No doubt, no doubt: O, 'tis a parlous boy;
Bold, quick, ingenious, forward, capable:
He is all the mother's, from the top to toe.
  Buck. Well, let them rest. Come hither, Catesby.
Thou art sworn as deeply to effect what we intend
As closely to conceal what we impart:
Thou know'st our reasons urged upon the way; 160
What think'st thou? is it not an easy matter
To make William Lord Hastings of our mind,
For the instalment of this noble duke
In the seat royal of this famous isle?
  Cate. He for his father's sake so loves the prince,
That he will not be won to aught against him.
  Buck. What think'st thou, then, of Stanley? what
    will he?
  Cate. He will do all in all as Hastings doth.
  Buck. Well, then, no more but this: go, gentle
    Catesby,
And, as it were far off, sound thou Lord Hastings, 170
How he doth stand affected to our purpose;
And summon him to-morrow to the Tower,
To sit about the coronation.
If thou dost find him tractable to us,
Encourage him, and show him all our reasons:
If he be leaden, icy-cold, unwilling,
Be thou so too; and so break off your talk,
And give us notice of his inclination:
For we to-morrow hold divided councils,
Wherein thyself shalt highly be employ'd. 180
  Glou. Commend me to Lord William: tell him,
    Catesby,
His ancient knot of dangerous adversaries
To-morrow are let blood at Pomfret-castle;
And bid my friend, for joy of this good news,
Give Mistress Shore one gentle kiss the more.
  Buck. Good Catesby, go, effect this business soundly.
  Cate. My good lords both, with all the heed I may.

85. **what,** that with which.   94. **lightly,** commonly, often.   99. **Too
. . . died,** i.e., the loss is fresh in our memories.   109. **in me,** with me.
121. **were it heavier,** i.e., I should still consider it a trifling gift.   128-
131. **bear . . . shoulders.** At fairs the bear commonly carried an
ape on his back. The speech is doubtless an allusion to Richard's
hump.   133. **scorn,** taunt, insult.   148. **fear,** i.e., fear for the uncles
Richard has had arrested.   150. *Stage Direction:* **Sennet,** series of
notes played on a trumpet to announce the approach or departure
of processions; see glossary.   152. **incensed,** instigated.   155. **capable,**

intelligent; see glossary.   160. **the way,** the journey to London.   162.
mind, opinion; see glossary.   165. **his father's sake.** Hastings was
particularly intimate with Edward IV.   170. **far off,** i.e., with great
tact.   171. **affected,** disposed; see glossary.   173. **sit,** sit in council.
179. **divided councils.** Richard would be plotting to seize the crown,
while Hastings and others friendly to the prince were arranging for
his coronation.   180. **highly,** i.e., on important errands.   183. **let
blood,** i.e., are executed.   185. **Mistress Shore.** Jane Shore had become
the mistress of Hastings after the death of Edward IV.   187. **may,** can;

Glou. Shall we hear from you, Catesby, ere we
  sleep?
Cate. You shall, my lord.
Glou. At Crosby Place, there shall you find us both.
                                        [*Exit Catesby.*
Buck. Now, my lord, what shall we do, if we
  perceive   191
Lord Hastings will not yield to our complots?
Glou. Chop off his head, man; somewhat we will do:
And, look, when I am king, claim thou of me
The earldom of Hereford, and the moveables
Whereof the king my brother stood possess'd.
Buck. I'll claim that promise at your grace's hands.
Glou. And look to have it yielded with all willingness.
Come, let us sup betimes, that afterwards
We may digest our complots in some form. [*Exeunt.* 200

SCENE II. *Before Lord Hastings' house.*

Enter a Messenger.

Mess. What, ho! my lord!
Hast. [*Within*] Who knocks at the door?
Mess. A messenger from the Lord Stanley.

Enter LORD HASTINGS.

Hast. What is 't o'clock?
Mess. Upon the stroke of four.
Hast. Cannot thy master sleep these tedious nights?
Mess. So it should seem by that I have to say.
First, he commends him to your noble lordship.
Hast. And then?
Mess. And then he sends you word   10
He dreamt to-night the boar had razed his helm:
Besides, he says there are two councils held;
And that may be determined at the one
Which may make you and him to rue at the other.
Therefore he sends to know your lordship's pleasure,
If presently you will take horse with him,
And with all speed post with him toward the north,
To shun the danger that his soul divines.
Hast. Go, fellow, go, return unto thy lord;
Bid him not fear the separated councils: 20
His honour and myself are at the one,
And at the other is my servant Catesby;
Where nothing can proceed that toucheth us
Whereof I shall not have intelligence.
Tell him his fears are shallow, wanting instance:
And for his dreams, I wonder he is so fond
To trust the mockery of unquiet slumbers:
To fly the boar before the boar pursues,
Were to incense the boar to follow us
And make pursuit where he did mean no chase.   30
Go, bid thy master rise and come to me;
And we will both together to the Tower,
Where, he shall see, the boar will use us kindly.
Mess. My gracious lord, I'll tell him what you say.
                                        [*Exit.*

Enter CATESBY.

Cate. Many good morrows to my noble lord!
Hast. Good morrow, Catesby; you are early
  stirring:
What news, what news, in this our tottering state?
Cate. It is a reeling world, indeed, my lord;
And I believe 'twill never stand upright
Till Richard wear the garland of the realm.   40
Hast. How! wear the garland! dost thou mean the
  crown?
Cate. Ay, my good lord.
Hast. I'll have this crown of mine cut from my
  shoulders
Ere I will see the crown so foul misplaced.
But canst thou guess that he doth aim at it?
Cate. Ay, on my life; and hopes to find you forward
Upon his party for the gain thereof:
And thereupon he sends you this good news,
That this same very day your enemies,
The kindred of the queen, must die at Pomfret.   50
Hast. Indeed, I am no mourner for that news,
Because they have been still mine enemies:
But, that I'll give my voice on Richard's side,
To bar my master's heirs in true descent,
God knows I will not do it, to the death.
Cate. God keep your lordship in that gracious mind!
Hast. But I shall laugh at this a twelve-month
  hence,
That they who brought me in my master's hate,
I live to look upon their tragedy.
I tell thee, Catesby,—   60
Cate. What, my lord?
Hast. Ere a fortnight make me elder,
I'll send some packing that yet think not on it.
Cate. 'Tis a vile thing to die, my gracious lord,
When men are unprepared and look not for it.
Hast. O monstrous, monstrous! and so falls it out
With Rivers, Vaughan, Grey: and so 'twill do
With some men else, who think themselves as safe
As thou and I; who, as thou know'st, are dear
To princely Richard and to Buckingham.   70
Cate. The princes both make high account of you;
[*Aside*] For they account his head upon the bridge.
Hast. I know they do; and I have well deserved it.

Enter LORD STANLEY.

Come on, come on; where is your boar-spear, man?
Fear you the boar, and go so unprovided?
Stan. My lord, good morrow; good morrow,
  Catesby:
You may jest on, but, by the holy rood,
I do not like these several councils, I.
Hast. My lord,
I hold my life as dear as you do yours;   80
And never in my life, I do protest,
Was it more precious to me than 'tis now:
Think you, but that I know our state secure,
I would be so triumphant as I am?
Stan. The lords at Pomfret, when they rode from
  London,

---

see glossary. **192. complots,** conspiracies. **195. earldom of Hereford.**
This is an important promise. Buckingham claimed this earldom by
right of his descent from Thomas of Woodstock. The offer is therefore
peculiarly tempting to Buckingham. **200. digest,** arrange, perfect;
see glossary.
  SCENE II. **11. boar,** Richard. **razed,** cut, slashed. **19. fellow,**
form of address to inferiors; see glossary. **25. instance,** proof, evidence; see glossary. **26. fond,** foolish; see glossary. **33. kindly,**
gently, courteously; see glossary. The sense "according to his nature"

is not intended by Hastings, but is present as dramatic irony. **47.
Upon his party,** on his side. **55. to the death,** though I lose my life.
71. high account, great estimation; the quibble on *high* appears in the
next line. **72. the bridge,** London Bridge, on a tower of which the
heads of traitors were exposed. **77. holy rood,** the cross of Christ.
78. several, separate; see glossary. **85. London.** Ludlow seems to have
been intended.

Were jocund, and supposed their state was sure,
And they indeed had no cause to mistrust;
But yet, you see, how soon the day o'ercast.
This sudden stab of rancour I misdoubt:
Pray God, I say, I prove a needless coward! 90
What, shall we toward the Tower? the day is spent.
    Hast. Come, come, have with you. Wot you what,
        my lord?
To-day the lords you talk of are beheaded.
    Stan. They, for their truth, might better wear their
        heads
Than some that have accused them wear their hats.
But come, my lord, let us away.

    Enter a Pursuivant.
    Hast. Go on before; I'll talk with this good fellow.
        [*Exeunt Stanley and Catesby.*
How now, sirrah! how goes the world with thee?
    Purs. The better that your lordship please to ask.
    Hast. I tell thee, man, 'tis better with me now 100
Than when I met thee last where now we meet:
Then was I going prisoner to the Tower,
By the suggestion of the queen's allies;
But now, I tell thee—keep it to thyself—
This day those enemies are put to death,
And I in better state than e'er I was.
    Purs. God hold it, to your honour's good content!
    Hast. Gramercy, fellow: there, drink that for me.
        [*Throws him his purse.*
    Purs. God save your lordship! [*Exit.*

    Enter a Priest.
    Priest. Well met, my lord; I am glad to see your
        honour. 110
    Hast. I thank thee, good Sir John, with all my heart.
I am in your debt for your last exercise;
Come the next Sabbath, and I will content you.
        [*He whispers in his ear.*

    Enter BUCKINGHAM.
    Buck. What, talking with a priest, lord chamberlain?
Your friends at Pomfret, they do need the priest;
Your honour hath no shriving work in hand.
    Hast. Good faith, and when I met this holy man,
Those men you talk of came into my mind.
What, go you toward the Tower?
    Buck. I do, my lord; but long I shall not stay: 120
I shall return before your lordship thence.
    Hast. 'Tis like enough, for I stay dinner there.
    Buck. [*Aside*] And supper too, although thou
        know'st it not.
Come, will you go?
    Hast. I'll wait upon your lordship. [*Exeunt.*

SCENE III. *Pomfret Castle.*

Enter SIR RICHARD RATCLIFF, *with halberds, carrying*
RIVERS, GREY, *and* VAUGHAN *to death.*

    Rat. Come, bring forth the prisoners.
    Riv. Sir Richard Ratcliff, let me tell thee this:

To-day shalt thou behold a subject die
For truth, for duty, and for loyalty.
    Grey. God keep the prince from all the pack of you!
A knot you are of damned blood-suckers.
    Vaug. You live that shall cry woe for this hereafter.
    Rat. Dispatch; the limit of your lives is out.
    Riv. O Pomfret, Pomfret! O thou bloody prison,
Fatal and ominous to noble peers! 10
Within the guilty closure of thy walls
Richard the second here was hack'd to death;
And, for more slander to thy dismal seat,
We give thee up our guiltless blood to drink.
    Grey. Now Margaret's curse is fall'n upon our
        heads,
For standing by when Richard stabb'd her son.
    Riv. Then cursed she Hastings, then cursed she
        Buckingham,
Then cursed she Richard. O, remember, God,
To hear her prayers for them, as now for us!
And for my sister and her princely sons, 20
Be satisfied, dear God, with our true blood,
Which, as thou know'st, unjustly must be spilt.
    Rat. Make haste; the hour of death is expiate.
    Riv. Come, Grey, come, Vaughan, let us all
        embrace:
And take our leave, until we meet in heaven. [*Exeunt.*

SCENE IV. *The Tower of London.*

Enter BUCKINGHAM, DERBY, HASTINGS, *the* BISHOP OF
ELY, RATCLIFF, LOVEL, *with others, and take their
seats at a table.*

    Hast. My lords, at once: the cause why we are met
Is, to determine of the coronation.
In God's name, speak: when is the royal day?
    Buck. Are all things fitting for that royal time?
    Der. It is, and wants but nomination.
    Ely. To-morrow, then, I judge a happy day.
    Buck. Who knows the lord protector's mind herein?
Who is most inward with the noble duke?
    Ely. Your grace, we think, should soonest know his
        mind.
    Buck. Who, I, my lord! we know each other's faces, 10
But for our hearts, he knows no more of mine,
Than I of yours;
Nor I no more of his, than you of mine.
Lord Hastings, you and he are near in love.
    Hast. I thank his grace, I know he loves me well;
But, for his purpose in the coronation,
I have not sounded him, nor he deliver'd
His gracious pleasure any way therein:
But you, my noble lords, may name the time;
And in the duke's behalf I'll give my voice, 20
Which, I presume, he'll take in gentle part.

    Enter GLOUCESTER.
    Ely. Now in good time, here comes the duke himself.
    Glou. My noble lords and cousins all, good morrow.
I have been long a sleeper; but, I hope,
My absence doth neglect no great designs,

92. **have with you,** come along; see glossary. 95. **wear their hats,**
i.e., hold their offices. 96. *Stage Direction:* **Pursuivant.** According to
More the pursuivant's name was also Hastings. A *pursuivant* is an
attendant upon a herald. 98. **sirrah,** form of address to servants; see
glossary. 103. **suggestion,** instigation. 107. **hold it,** continue it.
112. **exercise,** sermon or religious service. 116. **shriving work,** confession and absolution.
    SCENE III. 8. **out,** at an end; see glossary. 23. **expiate,** termi-
nated.
    SCENE IV. 2. **determine of,** decide upon. 8. **inward with,** i.e.,
acquainted with the mind of, intimate. 25. **designs,** projects, enterprises. 34. **strawberries,** apparently intended for the dinner after the

Which by my presence might have been concluded.

Buck. Had not you come upon your cue, my lord,
William Lord Hastings had pronounced your part,—
I mean, your voice,—for crowning of the king.

Glou. Than my Lord Hastings no man might be
bolder; 30
His lordship knows me well, and loves me well.

Hast. I thank your grace.

Glou. My lord of Ely!

Ely. My lord?

Glou. When I was last in Holborn,
I saw good strawberries in your garden there:
I do beseech you send for some of them.

Ely. Marry, and will, my lord, with all my heart.
[*Exit.*

Glou. Cousin of Buckingham, a word with you.
[*Drawing him aside.*
Catesby hath sounded Hastings in our business,
And finds the testy gentleman so hot,
As he will lose his head ere give consent 40
His master's son, as worshipful he terms it,
Shall lose the royalty of England's throne.

Buck. Withdraw you hence, my lord, I'll follow you.
[*Exit Gloucester, Buckingham following.*

Der. We have not yet set down this day of triumph.
To-morrow, in mine opinion, is too sudden;
For I myself am not so well provided
As else I would be, were the day prolong'd.

Re-enter BISHOP OF ELY.

Ely. Where is my lord protector? I have sent for
these strawberries.

Hast. His grace looks cheerfully and smooth to-day;
There 's some conceit or other likes him well, 51
When he doth bid good morrow with such a spirit.
I think there 's never a man in Christendom
That can less hide his love or hate than he;
For by his face straight shall you know his heart.

Der. What of his heart perceive you in his face
By any likelihood he show'd to-day?

Hast. Marry, that with no man here he is offended;
For, were he, he had shown it in his looks.

Der. I pray God he be not, I say. 60

Re-enter GLOUCESTER *and* BUCKINGHAM.

Glou. I pray you all, tell me what they deserve
That do conspire my death with devilish plots
Of damned witchcraft, and that have prevail'd
Upon my body with their hellish charms?

Hast. The tender love I bear your grace, my lord,
Makes me most forward in this noble presence
To doom the offenders, whatsoever they be:
I say, my lord, they have deserved death.

Glou. Then be your eyes the witness of this ill:
See how I am bewitch'd; behold mine arm 70
Is, like a blasted sapling, wither'd up:
And this is Edward's wife, that monstrous witch,
Consorted with that harlot strumpet Shore,
That by their witchcraft thus have marked me.

Hast. If they have done this thing, my gracious
lord,—

Glou. If! thou protector of this damned strumpet,
Tellest thou me of 'ifs'? Thou art a traitor:
Off with his head! Now, by Saint Paul I swear,
I will not dine until I see the same.
Lovel and Ratcliff, look that it be done: 80
The rest, that love me, rise and follow me.
[*Exeunt all but Hastings, Ratcliff, and Lovel.*

Hast. Woe, woe for England! not a whit for me;
For I, too fond, might have prevented this.
Stanley did dream the boar did raze his helm;
But I disdain'd it, and did scorn to fly:
Three times to-day my foot-cloth horse did stumble,
And startled, when he look'd upon the Tower,
As loath to bear me to the slaughter-house.
O, now I want the priest that spake to me:
I now repent I told the pursuivant, 90
As 'twere triumphing at mine enemies,
How they at Pomfret bloodily were butcher'd,
And I myself secure in grace and favour.
O Margaret, Margaret, now thy heavy curse
Is lighted on poor Hastings' wretched head!

Rat. Dispatch, my lord; the duke would be at
dinner:
Make a short shrift; he longs to see your head.

Hast. O momentary grace of mortal men,
Which we more hunt for than the grace of God!
Who builds his hopes in air of your good looks, 100
Lives like a drunken sailor on a mast,
Ready, with every nod, to tumble down
Into the fatal bowels of the deep.

Lov. Come, come, dispatch; 'tis bootless to exclaim.

Hast. O bloody Richard! miserable England!
I prophesy the fearfull'st time to thee
That ever wretched age hath look'd upon.
Come, lead me to the block; bear him my head:
They smile at me that shortly shall be dead. [*Exeunt.*

SCENE V. *The Tower-walls.*

Enter GLOUCESTER *and* BUCKINGHAM, *in rotten armour,
marvellous ill-favoured.*

Glou. Come, cousin, canst thou quake, and change
thy colour,
Murder thy breath in middle of a word,
And then begin again, and stop again,
As if thou wert distraught and mad with terror?

Buck. Tut, I can counterfeit the deep tragedian;
Speak and look back, and pry on every side,
Tremble and start at wagging of a straw,
Intending deep suspicion: ghastly looks
Are at my service, like enforced smiles;
And both are ready in their offices, 10
At any time, to grace my stratagems.
But what, is Catesby gone?

Glou. He is; and, see, he brings the mayor along.

Enter the Mayor *and* CATESBY.

Buck. Lord mayor,—

Glou. Look to the drawbridge there!

Buck. Hark! a drum.

meeting of the council. Richard is engaged in disarming suspicion.
47. **prolong'd,** postponed. 50. **smooth,** mild, bland. 51. **conceit,**
idea, fancy; see glossary. **likes,** pleases; see glossary. 80. **look,** see
to it; see glossary. 83. **prevented,** anticipated; see glossary. 86.
foot-cloth, a large, richly ornamented cloth laid over the back of a
horse, and hanging down to the ground on each side. **stumble.** The

stumbling of one's horse was an omen of misfortune. 100. **air,** outward
appearance, manner. 104. **exclaim,** protest; see glossary.
SCENE V. *Stage Direction:* **rotten,** rusty. 8. **Intending,** pretending.
10. **offices,** uses, functions.

Glou. Catesby, o'erlook the walls.
Buck. Lord mayor, the reason we have sent—
Glou. Look back, defend thee, here are enemies.
Buck. God and our innocency defend and guard us!
Glou. Be patient, they are friends, Ratcliff and
  Lovel.   21

Enter LOVEL *and* RATCLIFF, *with* HASTINGS' *head.*

Lov. Here is the head of that ignoble traitor,
The dangerous and unsuspected Hastings.
  Glou. So dear I loved the man, that I must weep.
I took him for the plainest harmless creature
That breathed upon this earth a Christian;
Made him my book, wherein my soul recorded
The history of all her secret thoughts:
So smooth he daub'd his vice with show of virtue,
That, his apparent open guilt omitted,   30
I mean, his conversation with Shore's wife,
He lived from all attainder of suspect.
  Buck. Well, well, he was the covert'st shelter'd
    traitor
That ever lived.
Would you imagine, or almost believe,
Were 't not that, by great preservation,
We live to tell it you, the subtle traitor
This day had plotted, in the council-house
To murder me and my good Lord of Gloucester?
  May. What, had he so?   40
  Glou. What, think you we are Turks or infidels?
Or that we would, against the form of law,
Proceed thus rashly to the villain's death,
But that the extreme peril of the case,
The peace of England and our persons' safety,
Enforced us to this execution?
  May. Now, fair befall you! he deserved his death;
And you my good lords, both have well proceeded,
To warn false traitors from the like attempts.
I never look'd for better at his hands,   50
After he once fell in with Mistress Shore.
  Glou. Yet had not we determined he should die,
Until your lordship came to see his death;
Which now the loving haste of these our friends,
Somewhat against our meaning, have prevented:
Because, my lord, we would have had you heard
The traitor speak, and timorously confess
The manner and the purpose of his treason;
That you might well have signified the same
Unto the citizens, who haply may   60
Misconstrue us in him and wail his death.
  May. But, my good lord, your grace's word shall
    serve,
As well as I had seen and heard him speak:
And doubt you not, right noble princes both,
But I'll acquaint our duteous citizens
With all your just proceedings in this cause.
  Glou. And to that end we wish'd your lordship here,
To avoid the carping censures of the world.
  Buck. But since you come too late of our intents,
Yet witness what you hear we did intend: 70

And so, my good lord mayor, we bid farewell.
                                        [*Exit Mayor.*
  Glou. Go, after, after, cousin Buckingham.
The mayor towards Guildhall hies him in all post:
There, at your meet'st advantage of the time,
Infer the bastardy of Edward's children:
Tell them how Edward put to death a citizen,
Only for saying he would make his son
Heir to the crown; meaning indeed his house,
Which, by the sign thereof, was termed so.
Moreover, urge his hateful luxury,   80
And bestial appetite in change of lust;
Which stretched to their servants, daughters, wives,
Even where his lustful eye or savage heart,
Without control, listed to make his prey.
Nay, for a need, thus far come near my person:
Tell them, when that my mother went with child
Of that unsatiate Edward, noble York
My princely father then had wars in France;
And, by just computation of the time,
Found that the issue was not his begot;   90
Which well appeared in his lineaments,
Being nothing like the noble duke my father:
But touch this sparingly, as 'twere far off;
Because you know, my lord, my mother lives.
  Buck. Fear not, my lord, I'll play the orator
As if the golden fee for which I plead
Were for myself: and so, my lord, adieu.
  Glou. If you thrive well, bring them to Baynard's
    Castle;
Where you shall find me well accompanied
With reverend fathers and well-learned bishops.   100
  Buck. I go; and towards three or four o'clock
Look for the news that the Guildhall affords.   [*Exit.*
  Glou. Go, Lovel, with all speed to Doctor Shaw;
[*To Cate.*] Go thou to Friar Penker; bid them both
Meet me within this hour at Baynard's Castle.
                            [*Exeunt all but Gloucester.*
Now will I in, to take some privy order,
To draw the brats of Clarence out of sight;
And to give notice, that no manner of person
At any time have recourse unto the princes.   [*Exit.*

SCENE VI. *The same. A street.*

Enter a Scrivener, *with a paper in his hand.*

  Scriv. This is the indictment of the good Lord
    Hastings;
Which in a set hand fairly is engross'd,
That it may be this day read o'er in Paul's.
And mark how well the sequel hangs together:
Eleven hours I spent to write it over,
For yesternight by Catesby was it brought me;
The precedent was full as long a-doing:
And yet within these five hours lived Lord Hastings,
Untainted, unexamined, free, at liberty.
Here 's a good world the while! Why who 's so gross, 10
That seeth not this palpable device?

*Richard
the Third*
ACT III : SC V

322

---

30. **omitted,** i.e., aside from that. 31. **conversation,** association; see glossary. 35. **almost,** even. 55. **have,** has. 73. **post,** haste; see glossary. 74. **meet'st advantage,** most suitable opportunity; see *advantage* in glossary. 75. **Infer,** allege, adduce. **bastardy.** It was said that Edward was contracted to one Elizabeth Lucy before his marriage to Lady Grey, the mother of his children. 76. **a citizen,** a grocer of Cheapside named Walker (or, according to Hall, Burdet). 80. **luxury,** lechery. 81. **in change of,** instead of (possibly, as being worse than). 84.

listed, desired; see glossary. 98. **Baynard's Castle,** on the north bank of the Thames, between Paul's-wharf and Blackfriars. It was founded by Baynard, a nobleman of the time of the Conquest, and belonged to Richard's father, duke of York. 103, 104. **Doctor Shaw, Friar Penker.** These men delivered sermons in Richard's favor. More describes them as "John Shaa clerke brother to the Maier, and freer Penker prouincial of the Augustine freers, both doctors of diuinite, both gret prechars, both of more learning then vertue, of more fame then learning."

Yet who's so blind, but says he sees it not?
Bad is the world; and all will come to nought,
When such bad dealing must be seen in thought. [*Exit.*

SCENE VII. *Baynard's Castle.*

Enter GLOUCESTER *and* BUCKINGHAM, *at several doors.*

Glou. How now, my lord, what say the citizens?
Buck. Now, by the holy mother of our Lord,
The citizens are mum and speak not a word.
Glou. Touch'd you the bastardy of Edward's
 children?
Buck. I did; with his contract with Lady Lucy,
And his contract by deputy in France;
The insatiate greediness of his desires,
And his enforcement of the city wives;
His tyranny for trifles; his own bastardy,
As being got, your father then in France,   10
And his resemblance, being not like the duke:
Withal I did infer your lineaments,
Being the right idea of your father,
Both in your form and nobleness of mind:
Laid open all your victories in Scotland,
Your discipline in war, wisdom in peace,
Your bounty, virtue, fair humility;
Indeed, left nothing fitting for the purpose
Untouch'd, or slightly handled, in discourse:
And when mine oratory grew to an end,   20
I bid them that did love their country's good
Cry 'God save Richard, England's royal king!'
Glou. Ah! and did they so?
Buck. No, so God help me, they spake not a word;
But, like dumb statuas or breathing stones,
Gazed each on other, and look'd deadly pale.
Which when I saw, I reprehended them;
And ask'd the mayor what meant this wilful silence:
His answer was, the people were not wont
To be spoke to but by the recorder.   30
Then he was urged to tell my tale again,
'Thus saith the duke, thus hath the duke inferr'd;'
But nothing spake in warrant from himself.
When he had done, some followers of mine own,
At the lower end of the hall, hurl'd up their caps,
And some ten voices cried 'God save King Richard!'
And thus I took the vantage of those few,
'Thanks, gentle citizens and friends,' quoth I;
'This general applause and loving shout
Argues your wisdoms and your love to Richard:' 40
And even here brake off, and came away.
Glou. What tongueless blocks were they! would they
 not speak?
Buck. No, by my troth, my lord.
Glou. Will not the mayor then and his brethren
 come?
Buck. The mayor is here at hand: intend some fear;
Be not you spoke with, but by mighty suit:
And look you get a prayer-book in your hand,
And stand betwixt two churchmen, good my lord;

For on that ground I'll build a holy descant:
And be not easily won to our request: 50
Play the maid's part, still answer nay, and take it.
Glou. I go; and if you plead as well for them
As I can say nay to thee for myself,
No doubt we'll bring it to a happy issue.
Buck. Go, go, up to the leads; the lord mayor knocks.
                       [*Exit Gloucester.*

Enter the Mayor *and* Citizens.

Welcome, my lord: I dance attendance here;
I think the duke will not be spoke withal.

Enter CATESBY.

Here comes his servant: how now, Catesby,
What says he?
Cate. My lord, he doth entreat your grace
To visit him to-morrow or next day: 60
He is within, with two right reverend fathers,
Divinely bent to meditation;
And in no worldly suit would he be moved,
To draw him from his holy exercise.
Buck. Return, good Catesby, to thy lord again;
Tell him, myself, the mayor and citizens,
In deep designs and matters of great moment,
No less importing than our general good,
Are come to have some conference with his grace.
Cate. I'll tell him what you say, my lord. [*Exit.* 70
Buck. Ah, ha, my lord, this prince is not an Edward!
He is not lolling on a lewd day-bed,
But on his knees at meditation;
Not dallying with a brace of courtezans,
But meditating with two deep divines;
Not sleeping, to engross his idle body,
But praying, to enrich his watchful soul:
Happy were England, would this gracious prince
Take on himself the sovereignty thereof:
But, sure, I fear, we shall ne'er win him to it. 80
May. Marry, God forbid his grace should say us
 nay!
Buck. I fear he will.

Re-enter CATESBY.

How now, Catesby, what says your lord?
Cate.   My lord,
He wonders to what end you have assembled
Such troops of citizens to speak with him,
His grace not being warn'd thereof before:
My lord, he fears you mean no good to him.
Buck. Sorry I am my noble cousin should
Suspect me, that I mean no good to him:
By heaven, I come in perfect love to him;   90
And so once more return and tell his grace.
                       [*Exit Catesby.*
When holy and devout religious men
Are at their beads, 'tis hard to draw them thence,
So sweet is zealous contemplation.

Enter GLOUCESTER *aloft, between two* Bishops. CATESBY
returns.

SCENE VI. 2. **fairly,** handsomely; see glossary. 4. **sequel,** what
follows. 9. **Untainted,** unaccused. 10. **gross,** dull. 12. **blind,** i.e.,
to the danger of speaking.
SCENE VII. 6. **deputy.** Cf. *3 Henry VI,* III, iii, 49 ff., where Warwick,
as deputy, contracts with Louis VI of France for the marriage of King
Edward to Lady Bona, sister of the French queen. 9. **tyranny for
trifles,** cruelty on account of trifling matters. 10. **got,** begot; see glossary. 13. **right idea,** exact image. 15. **victories in Scotland.** Richard

had commanded the English forces in the Scottish expedition of 1482.
17. **bounty,** liberality. 19. **discourse,** relating, i.e., by speech; see glossary. 30. **recorder,** keeper of the city rolls; at this time Thomas
Fitzwilliam. 33. **in . . . himself,** on his own responsibility. 49.
descant, argument. 53. **thee,** i.e., Buckingham, as spokesman for the
citizens. 54. **it,** i.e., the plan to make Richard king. 55. **leads,** roof.
72. **lolling,** so Pope; QqF: *lulling.* 76. **engross,** fatten. 94. *Stage
Direction:* **aloft,** i.e., on the gallery above the stage.

May. See, where he stands between two clergymen!
   Buck. Two props of virtue for a Christian prince,
To stay him from the fall of vanity:
And, see, a book of prayer in his hand,
True ornaments to know a holy man.
Famous Plantagenet, most gracious prince,   100
Lend favourable ears to our request;
And pardon us the interruption
Of thy devotion and right Christian zeal.
   Glou. My lord, there needs no such apology:
I rather do beseech you pardon me,
Who, earnest in the service of my God,
Neglect the visitation of my friends.
But, leaving this, what is your grace's pleasure?
   Buck. Even that, I hope, which pleaseth God above,
And all good men of this ungovern'd isle.   110
   Glou. I do suspect I have done some offence
That seems disgracious in the city's eyes,
And that you come to reprehend my ignorance.
   Buck. You have, my lord: would it might please
      your grace,
At our entreaties, to amend that fault!
   Glou. Else wherefore breathe I in a Christian land?
   Buck. Then know, it is your fault that you resign
The supreme seat, the throne majestical,
The scepter'd office of your ancestors,
Your state of fortune and your due of birth,   120
The lineal glory of your royal house,
To the corruption of a blemish'd stock:
Whilst, in the mildness of your sleepy thoughts,
Which here we waken to our country's good,
This noble isle doth want her proper limbs;
Her face defaced with scars of infamy,
Her royal stock graft with ignoble plants,
And almost shoulder'd in the swallowing gulf
Of blind forgetfulness and dark oblivion.
Which to recure, we heartily solicit   130
Your gracious self to take on you the charge
And kingly government of this your land,
Not as protector, steward, substitute,
Or lowly factor for another's gain;
But as successively from blood to blood,
Your right of birth, your empery, your own.
For this, consorted with the citizens,
Your very worshipful and loving friends,
And by their vehement instigation,
In this just suit come I to move your grace.   140
   Glou. I know not whether to depart in silence,
Or bitterly to speak in your reproof,
Best fitteth my degree or your condition:
If not to answer, you might haply think
Tongue-tied ambition, not replying, yielded
To bear the golden yoke of sovereignty,
Which fondly you would here impose on me;
If to reprove you for this suit of yours,
So season'd with your faithful love to me,
Then, on the other side, I check'd my friends.   150
Therefore, to speak, and to avoid the first,

And then, in speaking, not to incur the last,
Definitely thus I answer you.
Your love deserves my thanks; but my desert
Unmeritable shuns your high request.
First, if all obstacles were cut away,
And that my path were even to the crown,
As my ripe revenue and due by birth;
Yet so much is my poverty of spirit,
So mighty and so many my defects,   160
As I had rather hide me from my greatness,
Being a bark to brook no mighty sea,
Than in my greatness covet to be hid,
And in the vapour of my glory smother'd.
But, God be thanked, there 's no need of me,
And much I need to help you, if need were;
The royal tree hath left us royal fruit,
Which, mellow'd by the stealing hours of time,
Will well become the seat of majesty,
And make, no doubt, us happy by his reign.   170
On him I lay what you would lay on me,
The right and fortune of his happy stars;
Which God defend that I should wring from him!
   Buck. My lord, this argues conscience in your grace;
But the respects thereof are nice and trivial,
All circumstances well considered.
You say that Edward is your brother's son:
So say we too, but not by Edward's wife;
For first he was contract to Lady Lucy—
Your mother lives a witness to that vow—   180
And afterward by substitute betroth'd
To Bona, sister to the King of France.
These both put by, a poor petitioner,
A care-crazed mother of a many children,
A beauty-waning and distressed widow,
Even in the afternoon of her best days,
Made prize and purchase of his lustful eye,
Seduced the pitch and height of all his thoughts
To base declension and loathed bigamy:
By her, in his unlawful bed, he got   190
This Edward, whom our manners term the prince.
More bitterly could I expostulate,
Save that, for reverence to some alive,
I give a sparing limit to my tongue.
Then, good my lord, take to your royal self
This proffer'd benefit of dignity;
If not to bless us and the land withal,
Yet to draw forth your noble ancestry
From the corruption of abusing times,
Unto a lineal true-derived course.   200
   May. Do, good my lord, your citizens entreat you.
   Buck. Refuse not, mighty lord, this proffer'd love.
   Cate. O, make them joyful, grant their lawful suit!
   Glou. Alas, why would you heap these cares on me?
I am unfit for state and majesty:
I do beseech you, take it not amiss;
I cannot nor I will not yield to you.
   Buck. If you refuse it,—as, in love and zeal,
Loath to depose the child, your brother's son;

97. **stay**, sustain; see glossary. **the . . . vanity**, i.e., falling into the sin of vanity. 99. **ornaments**, i.e., the bishops as well as the prayer book. 112. **disgracious**, unbecoming. 116. **Else**, if not, otherwise. 128. **shoulder'd**, jostled; or it may mean "immersed up to the shoulders." Johnson conjectured *smouldered*, smothered; anonymous conjecture: *foundered*. 130. **recure**, restore, make whole. 134. **factor**, agent. 136. **empery**, empire. 137. **consorted**, associated, leagued. 143. **degree**, rank. **condition**, social status; see glossary. 155. **Unmeritable**, undeserving. 157. **even**, smooth; see glossary. 158. **ripe revenue**, a possession ready to be inherited. 161. **my greatness**, my claim to the

throne. 163. in **my greatness**, i.e., as king. **covet**, desire. 164. **vapour of my glory**, effluence of my kingship. 166. **need**, ought; perhaps, as Johnson suggested, lack the ability requisite. 175. **respects thereof**, considerations by which you support your argument. **nice**, insignificant; see glossary. 179-182. **For . . . France**. In the petition of 1484, ratified by Parliament at Richard's accession, it was stated that before his marriage to Elizabeth, Edward IV was engaged by trothplight to Lady Eleanor Butler, daughter of the earl of Shrewsbury. A later tradition which Shakespeare followed held that Richard's mother, in her opposition to Edward's intention of marrying Lady Grey, which

As well we know your tenderness of heart 210
And gentle, kind, effeminate remorse,
Which we have noted in you to your kin,
And egally indeed to all estates,—
Yet whether you accept our suit or no,
Your brother's son shall never reign our king;
But we will plant some other in the throne,
To the disgrace and downfall of your house:
And in this resolution here we leave you.—
Come, citizens: 'zounds! I'll entreat no more.
   Glou. O, do not swear, my lord of Buckingham. 220
                 [Exit Buckingham with the Citizens.
   Cate. Call them again, my lord, and accept their
   suit.
   Another. Do, good my lord, lest all the land do rue it.
   Glou. Would you enforce me to a world of care?
Well, call them again. I am not made of stones,
But penetrable to your kind entreats,
Albeit against my conscience and my soul.

     Re-enter BUCKINGHAM *and the rest.*

Cousin of Buckingham, and you sage, grave men,
Since you will buckle fortune on my back,
To bear her burthen, whether I will or no,
I must have patience to endure the load: 230
But if black scandal or foul-faced reproach
Attend the sequel of your imposition,
Your mere enforcement shall acquittance me
From all the impure blots and stains thereof;
For God he knows, and you may partly see,
How far I am from the desire thereof.
   May. God bless your grace! we see it, and will say it.
   Glou. In saying so, you shall but say the truth.
   Buck. Then I salute you with this kingly title:
Long live Richard, England's royal king! 240
   May. and Cit. Amen.
   Buck. To-morrow will it please you to be crown'd?
   Glou. Even when you please, since you will have
   it so.
   Buck. To-morrow, then, we will attend your grace:
And so most joyfully we take our leave.
   Glou. Come, let us to our holy task again.
Farewell, good cousin; farewell, gentle friends. *[Exeunt.*

ACT IV.

SCENE I. *Before the Tower.*

Enter, on one side, QUEEN ELIZABETH, DUCHESS OF
   YORK, *and* MARQUESS OF DORSET; *on the other,*
   ANNE, DUCHESS OF GLOUCESTER, *leading* LADY
   MARGARET PLANTAGENET, CLARENCE'S *young*
   Daughter.

   Duch. Who meets us here? my niece Plantagenet
Led in the hand of her kind aunt of Gloucester?
Now, for my life, she 's wandering to the Tower,
On pure heart's love to greet the tender princes.

Daughter, well met.
   Anne.   God give your graces both
A happy and a joyful time of day!
   Q. Eliz. As much to you, good sister! Whither
   away?
   Anne. No farther than the Tower; and, as I guess,
Upon the like devotion as yourselves,
To gratulate the gentle princes there. 10
   Q. Eliz. Kind sister, thanks: we'll enter all together.

     Enter BRAKENBURY.

And, in good time, here the lieutenant comes.
Master lieutenant, pray you, by your leave,
How doth the prince, and my young son of York?
   Brak. Right well, dear madam. By your patience,
I may not suffer you to visit them;
The king hath straitly charged the contrary.
   Q. Eliz. The king! why, who 's that?
   Brak. I cry you mercy: I mean the lord protector.
   Q. Eliz. The Lord protect him from that kingly
   title! 20
Hath he set bounds betwixt their love and me?
I am their mother; who should keep me from them?
   Duch. I am their father's mother; I will see them.
   Anne. Their aunt I am in law, in love their mother:
Then bring me to their sights; I'll bear thy blame
And take thy office from thee, on my peril.
   Brak. No, madam, no; I may not leave it so:
I am bound by oath, and therefore pardon me. *[Exit.*

     Enter LORD STANLEY.

   Stan. Let me but meet you, ladies, one hour hence,
And I'll salute your grace of York as mother, 30
And reverend looker on, of two fair queens.
[*To Anne*] Come, madam, you must straight to
   Westminster,
There to be crowned Richard's royal queen.
   Q. Eliz. O, cut my lace in sunder, that my pent
   heart
May have some scope to beat, or else I swoon
With this dead-killing news!
   Anne. Despiteful tidings! O unpleasing news!
   Dor. Be of good cheer: mother, how fares your
   grace?
   Q. Eliz. O Dorset, speak not to me, get thee hence!
Death and destruction dog thee at the heels; 40
Thy mother's name is ominous to children.
If thou wilt outstrip death, go cross the seas,
And live with Richmond, from the reach of hell:
Go, hie thee, hie thee from this slaughter-house,
Lest thou increase the number of the dead;
And make me die the thrall of Margaret's curse,
Nor mother, wife, nor England's counted queen.
   Stan. Full of wise care is this your counsel, madam.
Take all the swift advantage of the hours;
You shall have letters from me to my son 50
To meet you on the way, and welcome you.
Be not ta'en tardy by unwise delay.

---

was interfering with the negotiations for his marriage to Bona of Savoy,
asserted that Lady Elizabeth Lucy was already Edward's trothplight
wife. Cf. III, v, 75, and vii, 6. **187. purchase,** booty; see glossary.
188. pitch, height; see glossary. **189. declension,** falling away from a
high standard. **192. expostulate,** discourse, discuss. **193-194. reverence . . . tongue.** The allusion is to the pretended illegitimacy of
Edward and Clarence. By *some alive* he means their mother, the duchess
of York; cf. III, v, 93-94, where Richard says *my mother lives.* **213.
egally,** equally, evenly. **232. your imposition,** the duty which you
lay upon me. **243. please,** so Malone; Qq: *will.*

ACT IV. SCENE I. **1. niece,** here, granddaughter. **9. like devotion,**
same devout errand. **10. gratulate,** greet, salute. **21. bounds,**
barriers. **31. reverend looker on,** one who esteems reverently. **two
fair queens,** Elizabeth and Anne. **34. pent heart.** According to Elizabethan psychology, the passion of sorrow would cause a rush of spirits
to the heart, thus making it swell. **43. with Richmond,** i.e., Henry
Tudor, earl of Richmond, at this time in Brittany. **47. counted,**
accepted. **50. son,** Richmond, whose mother Stanley had married.

Duch. O ill-dispersing wind of misery!
O my accursed womb, the bed of death!
A cockatrice hast thou hatch'd to the world,
Whose unavoided eye is murderous.
   Stan. Come, madam, come; I in all haste was sent.
   Anne. And I in all unwillingness will go.
I would to God that the inclusive verge
Of golden metal that must round my brow   60
Were red-hot steel, to sear me to the brain!
Anointed let me be with deadly venom,
And die, ere men can say, God save the queen!
   Q. Eliz. Go, go, poor soul, I envy not thy glory;
To feed my humour, wish thyself no harm.
   Anne. No! why? When he that is my husband now
Came to me, as I follow'd Henry's corse,
When scarce the blood was well wash'd from his
    hands
Which issued from my other angel husband
And that dead saint which then I weeping follow'd; 70
O, when, I say, I look'd on Richard's face,
This was my wish: 'Be thou,' quoth I, 'accursed,
For making me, so young, so old a widow!
And, when thou wed'st, let sorrow haunt thy bed;
And be thy wife—if any be so mad—
As miserable by the life of thee
As thou hast made me by my dear lord's death!'
Lo, ere I can repeat this curse again,
Even in so short a space, my woman's heart
Grossly grew captive to his honey words   80
And proved the subject of my own soul's curse,
Which ever since hath kept my eyes from rest;
For never yet one hour in his bed
Have I enjoy'd the golden dew of sleep,
But have been waked by his timorous dreams.
Besides, he hates me for my father Warwick;
And will, no doubt, shortly be rid of me.
   Q. Eliz. Poor heart, adieu! I pity thy complaining.
   Anne. No more than from my soul I mourn for
    yours.
   Q. Eliz. Farewell, thou woful welcomer of glory! 90
   Anne. Adieu, poor soul, that takest thy leave of it!
   Duch. [*To Dorset*] Go thou to Richmond, and good
    fortune guide thee!
[*To Anne*] Go thou to Richard, and good angels
    guard thee!
[*To Queen Eliz.*] Go thou to sanctuary, and good
    thoughts possess thee!
I to my grave, where peace and rest lie with me!
Eighty odd years of sorrow have I seen,
And each hour's joy wreck'd with a week of teen.
   Q. Eliz. Stay, yet look back with me unto the
    Tower.
Pity, you ancient stones, those tender babes
Whom envy hath immured within your walls!   100
Rough cradle for such little pretty ones!
Rude ragged nurse, old sullen playfellow
For tender princes, use my babies well!
So foolish sorrow bids your stones farewell.   [*Exeunt.*

SCENE II. *London. The palace.*

Sennet. Enter RICHARD, *in pomp, crowned;* BUCKING-
   HAM, CATESBY, *a* Page, *and others.*

   K. Rich. Stand all apart. Cousin of Buckingham!
   Buck. My gracious sovereign?
   K. Rich. Give me thy hand. [*Here he ascendeth his
   throne.*] Thus high, by thy advice
And thy assistance, is King Richard seated:
But shall we wear these honours for a day?
Or shall they last, and we rejoice in them?
   Buck. Still live they and for ever may they last!
   K. Rich. O Buckingham, now do I play the touch,
To try if thou be current gold indeed:
Young Edward lives: think now what I would say. 10
   Buck. Say on, my loving lord.
   K. Rich. Why, Buckingham, I say, I would be king.
   Buck. Why, so you are, my thrice renowned liege.
   K. Rich. Ha! am I king? 'tis so: but Edward lives.
   Buck. True, noble prince.
   K. Rich.   O bitter consequence,
That Edward still should live! 'True, noble prince!'
Cousin, thou wert not wont to be so dull:
Shall I be plain? I wish the bastards dead;
And I would have it suddenly perform'd.
What sayest thou? speak suddenly; be brief.   20
   Buck. Your grace may do your pleasure.
   K. Rich. Tut, tut, thou art all ice, thy kindness
    freezeth:
Say, have I thy consent that they shall die?
   Buck. Give me some breath, some little pause, my
    lord,
Before I positively speak herein:
I will resolve your grace immediately.   [*Exit.*
   Cate. [*Aside to a stander by*] The king is angry: see, he
    bites the lip.
   K. Rich. I will converse with iron-witted fools
And unrespective boys: none are for me
That look into me with considerate eyes: 30
High-reaching Buckingham grows circumspect.
Boy!
   Page. My lord?
   K. Rich. Know'st thou not any whom corrupting
    gold
Would tempt unto a close exploit of death?
   Page. My lord, I know a discontented gentleman,
Whose humble means match not his haughty mind:
Gold were as good as twenty orators,
And will, no doubt, tempt him to any thing.
   K. Rich. What is his name?
   Page.   His name, my lord, is Tyrrel. 40
   K. Rich. I partly know the man: go, call him hither.
                          [*Exit Page.*
The deep-revolving witty Buckingham
No more shall be the neighbour to my counsel:
Hath he so long held out with me untired,
And stops he now for breath?

Enter STANLEY.

       How now! what news with you?

Stan. My lord, I hear the Marquis Dorset 's fled
To Richmond, in those parts beyond the sea
Where he abides.   [*Stands apart.*
  K. Rich. Catesby!
  Cate. My lord?   50
  K. Rich. Rumour it abroad
That Anne, my wife, is sick and like to die:
I will take order for her keeping close.
Inquire me out some mean-born gentleman,
Whom I will marry straight to Clarence' daughter:
The boy is foolish, and I fear not him.
Look, how thou dream'st! I say again, give out
That Anne my wife is sick and like to die:
About it; for it stands me much upon,
To stop all hopes whose growth may damage me.   60
                                    [*Exit Catesby.*
I must be married to my brother's daughter,
Or else my kingdom stands on brittle glass.
Murder her brothers, and then marry her!
Uncertain way of gain! But I am in
So far in blood that sin will pluck on sin:
Tear-falling pity dwells not in this eye.

          Re-enter Page, *with* TYRREL.

Is thy name Tyrrel?
  Tyr. James Tyrrel, and your most obedient subject.
  K. Rich. Art thou, indeed?
  Tyr.   Prove me, my gracious sovereign.
  K. Rich. Darest thou resolve to kill a friend of mine?
  Tyr. Ay, my lord;   71
But I had rather kill two enemies.
  K. Rich. Why, there thou hast it: two deep enemies,
Foes to my rest and my sweet sleep's disturbers
Are they that I would have thee deal upon:
Tyrrel, I mean those bastards in the Tower.
  Tyr. Let me have open means to come to them,
And soon I'll rid you from the fear of them.
  K. Rich. Thou sing'st sweet music. Hark, come
      hither, Tyrrel:
Go, by this token: rise, and lend thine ear: [*Whispers.*
There is no more but so: say it is done,   81
And I will love thee, and prefer thee too.
  Tyr. 'Tis done, my gracious lord.
  K. Rich. Shall we hear from thee, Tyrrel, ere we
      sleep?
  Tyr. Ye shall, my lord.   [*Exit.*

          Re-enter BUCKINGHAM.

  Buck. My lord, I have consider'd in my mind
The late demand that you did sound me in.
  K. Rich. Well, let that pass. Dorset is fled to Rich-
      mond.
  Buck. I hear that news, my lord.
  K. Rich. Stanley, he is your wife's son: well, look
      to it.   90
  Buck. My lord, I claim your gift, my due by promise,
For which your honour and your faith is pawn'd;
The earldom of Hereford and the moveables
The which you promised I should possess.
  K. Rich. Stanley, look to your wife: if she convey

Letters to Richmond, you shall answer it.
  Buck. What says your highness to my just demand?
  K. Rich. As I remember, Henry the Sixth
Did prophesy that Richmond should be king,
When Richmond was a little peevish boy.   100
A king, perhaps, perhaps,—
  Buck. My lord!
  K. Rich. How chance the prophet could not at that
      time
Have told me, I being by, that I should kill him?
  Buck. My lord, your promise for the earldom,—
  K. Rich. Richmond! When last I was at Exeter,
The mayor in courtesy show'd me the castle,
And call'd it Rougemont: at which name I started,
Because a bard of Ireland told me once,
I should not live long after I saw Richmond.   110
  Buck. My lord!
  K. Rich. Ay, what 's o'clock?
  Buck. I am thus bold to put your grace in mind
Of what you promised me.
  K. Rich.   Well, but what 's o'clock?
  Buck. Upon the stroke of ten.
  K. Rich.   Well, let it strike.
  Buck. Why let it strike?
  K. Rich. Because that, like a Jack, thou keep'st the
      stroke
Betwixt thy begging and my meditation.
I am not in the giving vein to-day.
  Buck. Why, then resolve me whether you will or no.
  K. Rich. Tut, tut,   121
Thou troublest me; I am not in the vein.
                        [*Exeunt all but Buckingham.*
  Buck. Is it even so? rewards he my true service
With such deep contempt? made I him king for this?
O, let me think on Hastings, and be gone
To Brecknock, while my fearful head is on!   [*Exit.*

          SCENE III. *The same.*

Enter TYRREL.

  Tyr. The tyrannous and bloody deed is done,
The most arch act of piteous massacre
That ever yet this land was guilty of.
Dighton and Forrest, whom I did suborn
To do this ruthless piece of butchery,
Although they were flesh'd villains, bloody dogs,
Melting with tenderness and kind compassion
Wept like two children in their deaths' sad stories.
'Lo, thus,' quoth Dighton, 'lay those tender babes:'
'Thus, thus,' quoth Forrest, 'girdling one another 10
Within their innocent alabaster arms:
Their lips were four red roses on a stalk,
Which in their summer beauty kiss'd each other.
A book of prayers on their pillow lay;
Which once,' quoth Forrest, 'almost changed my
      mind;
But O! the devil'— there the villain stopp'd;
Whilst Dighton thus told on: 'We smothered
The most replenished sweet work of nature,

me. 61. **brother's daughter,** i.e., Elizabeth of York, daughter to
Edward IV, who became the queen of Henry VII. 64-66. **But . . . eye.**
Cf. *Macbeth,* III, iv, 136-138. 65. **pluck on,** draw on. 69. **Prove,** test;
see glossary. 75. **deal upon,** set to work upon. 82. **prefer,** promote,
advance. 90. **he,** i.e., Richmond. 96. **it,** i.e., for it. 117. **Jack,** the
figure of a man which strikes the bell on the outside of a clock. 117-
118. **thou . . . meditation,** i.e., regularly or mechanically as the striking

of a clock you interrupt my meditation with your begging. 126.
Brecknock, Brecknock Castle in Wales on Buckingham's estate.
SCENE III. 2. **arch act,** i.e., chief or notorious act. 4. **Dighton and
Forrest.** John Dighton, Tyrrel's horsekeeper, and Miles Forrest,
one of the four appointed by Tyrrel to take charge of the princes.
6. **flesh'd,** trained, hardened; see glossary. 18. **replenished,** complete,
perfect.

That from the prime creation e'er she framed.'
Thus both are gone with conscience and remorse; 20
They could not speak; and so I left them both,
To bring this tidings to the bloody king.
And here he comes.

Enter KING RICHARD.

               All hail, my sovereign liege!
K. Rich. Kind Tyrrel, am I happy in thy news?
Tyr. If to have done the thing you gave in charge
Beget your happiness, be happy then,
For it is done, my lord.
   K. Rich.   But didst thou see them dead?
Tyr. I did, my lord.
   K. Rich.   And buried, gentle Tyrrel?
Tyr. The chaplain of the Tower hath buried them;
But how or in what place I do not know.   30
   K. Rich. Come to me, Tyrrel, soon at after supper,
And thou shalt tell the process of their death.
Meantime, but think how I may do thee good,
And be inheritor of thy desire.
Farewell till soon.   *[Exit Tyrrel.*
The son of Clarence have I pent up close;
His daughter meanly have I match'd in marriage;
The sons of Edward sleep in Abraham's bosom,
And Anne my wife hath bid the world good night.
Now, for I know the Breton Richmond aims   40
At young Elizabeth, my brother's daughter,
And, by that knot, looks proudly o'er the crown,
To her I go, a jolly thriving wooer.

Enter CATESBY.

Cate. My lord!
K. Rich. Good news or bad, that thou comest in so
   bluntly?
Cate. Bad news, my lord: Ely is fled to Richmond;
And Buckingham, back'd with the hardy Welshmen,
Is in the field, and still his power increaseth.
   K. Rich. Ely with Richmond troubles me more near
Than Buckingham and his rash-levied army.   50
Come, I have heard that fearful commenting
Is leaden servitor to dull delay;
Delay leads impotent and snail-paced beggary:
Then fiery expedition be my wing,
Jove's Mercury, and herald for a king!
Come, muster men: my counsel is my shield;
We must be brief when traitors brave the field. *[Exeunt.*

SCENE IV. *Before the palace.*

Enter QUEEN MARGARET.

Q. Mar. So, now prosperity begins to mellow
And drop into the rotten mouth of death.
Here in these confines slily have I lurk'd,
To watch the waning of mine adversaries.

A dire induction am I witness to,
And will to France, hoping the consequence
Will prove as bitter, black, and tragical.
Withdraw thee, wretched Margaret: who comes here?

Enter QUEEN ELIZABETH *and the* DUCHESS OF YORK.

   Q. Eliz. Ah, my young princes! ah, my tender babes!
My unblown flowers, new-appearing sweets!   10
If yet your gentle souls fly in the air
And be not fix'd in doom perpetual,
Hover about me with your airy wings
And hear your mother's lamentation!
   Q. Mar. Hover about her; say, that right for right
Hath dimm'd your infant morn to aged night.
   Duch. So many miseries have crazed my voice,
That my woe-wearied tongue is mute and dumb;
Edward Plantagenet, why art thou dead?
   Q. Mar. Plantagenet doth quit Plantagenet.   20
Edward for Edward pays a dying debt.
   Q. Eliz. Wilt thou, O God, fly from such gentle
   lambs,
And throw them in the entrails of the wolf?
When didst thou sleep when such a deed was done?
   Q. Mar. When holy Harry died, and my sweet son.
   Duch. Blind sight, dead life, poor mortal living
   ghost,
Woe's scene, world's shame, grave's due by life
   usurp'd,
Brief abstract and record of tedious days,
Rest thy unrest on England's lawful earth,
                        [Sitting down.
Unlawfully made drunk with innocents' blood!   30
   Q. Eliz. O, that thou wouldst as well afford a grave
As thou canst yield a melancholy seat!
Then would I hide my bones, not rest them here.
O, who hath any cause to mourn but I?
                     [Sitting down by her.
   Q. Mar. If ancient sorrow be most reverend,
Give mine the benefit of seniory,
And let my woes frown on the upper hand.
If sorrow can admit society,   *[Sitting down with them.*
Tell o'er your woes again by viewing mine:
I had an Edward, till a Richard kill'd him;
I had a Harry, till a Richard kill'd him: 40
Thou hadst an Edward, till a Richard kill'd him;
Thou hadst a Richard, till a Richard kill'd him.
   Duch. I had a Richard too, and thou didst kill him;
I had a Rutland too, thou holp'st to kill him.
   Q. Mar. Thou hadst a Clarence too, and Richard
   kill'd him.
From forth the kennel of thy womb hath crept
A hell-hound that doth hunt us all to death:
That dog, that had his teeth before his eyes,
To worry lambs and lap their gentle blood,   50
That foul defacer of God's handiwork,
That excellent grand tyrant of the earth,

19. **prime,** first. 20. **gone with,** completely overcome by. 25. **gave
in charge,** ordered, commanded. 30. **I . . . know.** More records that
Tyrrel ordered the murderers to bury the bodies "at the staire foot,
meetlie deepe in the ground vnder a great heape of stone." In 1674,
during some repairs at the White Tower, there was unearthed a
wooden chest containing bones which were pronounced those of two
boys of 13 and 11 years. By the order of Charles II they were removed to
Westminster Abbey. 31. **soon,** toward evening. **at after supper,** i.e.,
dessert after supper. 32. **process,** story; see glossary. 36. **The . . .
close.** Richard kept Clarence's son prisoner at Sheriff Hutton Castle in
Yorkshire. 37. **His . . . marriage.** Margaret Plantagenet was about
twelve years old when Richard died. Shakespeare has apparently confused her with Lady Cicely, her first cousin, whom Richard, according
to Holinshed, intended to marry to "a man found in a cloud, and of an

unknown linage and familie." 38. **Abraham's bosom.** See Luke 16:22.
41. **my brother's,** Edward's. 42. **by that knot,** by virtue of that
alliance. 46. **Ely,** John Morton, bishop of Ely, who had been kept
prisoner at Brecknock Castle. 51-52. **fearful . . . delay,** timorous
thought and cautious disquisition are dull attendants on delay (Johnson). 54-55. **fiery . . . king.** Fiery expedition is to be Richard's herald,
as Mercury was Jove's herald. 57. **brave,** challenge; see glossary.
   SCENE IV. 5. **induction,** first step. 6. **the consequence,** what follows,
the sequel. 10. **unblown,** unopened. 15. **right for right,** a just
punishment for an offense against justice (Wright). 16. **dimm'd . . .
night,** i.e., brought your recently acquired glory to eternal ruin. 20.
Plantagenet, Plantagenet, Edward IV; Edward, son of Henry VI and
Margaret, former prince of Wales, killed by the Yorkists at Tewksbury.
quit, requite, pay for; see glossary. 25. **Harry,** i.e., Henry VI. 26-27.

'That reigns in galled eyes of weeping souls,
Thy womb let loose, to chase us to our graves.
O upright, just, and true-disposing God,
How do I thank thee, that this carnal cur
Preys on the issue of his mother's body,
And makes her pew-fellow with others' moan!
    Duch. O Harry's wife, triumph not in my woes!
God witness with me, I have wept for thine.   60
    Q. Mar. Bear with me; I am hungry for revenge,
And now I cloy me with beholding it.
Thy Edward he is dead, that stabb'd my Edward;
Thy other Edward dead, to quit my Edward;
Young York he is but boot, because both they
Match not the high perfection of my loss:
Thy Clarence he is dead that kill'd my Edward;
And the beholders of this tragic play,
The adulterate Hastings, Rivers, Vaughan, Grey,
Untimely smother'd in their dusky graves.   70
Richard yet lives, hell's black intelligencer,
Only reserved their factor, to buy souls
And send them thither: but at hand, at hand,
Ensues his piteous and unpitied end:
Earth gapes, hell burns, fiends roar, saints pray,
To have him suddenly convey'd away.
Cancel his bond of life, dear God, I pray,
That I may live to say, The dog is dead!
    Q. Eliz. O, thou didst prophesy the time would
      come
That I should wish for thee to help me curse   80
That bottled spider, that foul bunch-back'd toad!
    Q. Mar. I call'd thee then vain flourish of my
      fortune;
I call'd thee then poor shadow, painted queen;
The presentation of but what I was;
The flattering index of a direful pageant;
One heaved a-high, to be hurl'd down below;
A mother only mock'd with two sweet babes;
A dream of what thou wert, a breath, a bubble,
A sign of dignity, a garish flag,
To be the aim of every dangerous shot;   90
A queen in jest, only to fill the scene.
Where is thy husband now? where be thy brothers?
Where are thy children? wherein dost thou joy?
Who sues to thee and cries 'God save the queen'?
Where be the bending peers that flatter'd thee?
Where be the thronging troops that follow'd thee?
Decline all this, and see what now thou art:
For happy wife, a most distressed widow;
For joyful mother, one that wails the name;
For queen, a very caitiff crown'd with care;   100
For one being sued to, one that humbly sues;
For one that scorn'd at me, now scorn'd of me;
For one being fear'd of all, now fearing one;
For one commanding all, obey'd of none.
Thus hath the course of justice wheel'd about,
And left thee but a very prey to time;

Having no more but thought of what thou wert,
To torture thee the more, being what thou art.
Thou didst usurp my place, and dost thou not
Usurp the just proportion of my sorrow?   110
Now thy proud neck bears half my burthen'd yoke;
From which even here I slip my weary neck,
And leave the burthen of it all on thee.
Farewell, York's wife, and queen of sad mischance:
These English woes will make me smile in France.
    Q. Eliz. O thou well skill'd in curses, stay awhile,
And teach me how to curse mine enemies!
    Q. Mar. Forbear to sleep the nights, and fast the
      days;
Compare dead happiness with living woe;
Think that thy babes were fairer than they were,   120
And he that slew them fouler than he is:
Bettering thy loss makes the bad causer worse:
Revolving this will teach thee how to curse.
    Q. Eliz. My words are dull; O, quicken them with
      thine!
    Q. Mar. Thy woes will make them sharp, and pierce
      like mine.   [*Exit.*
    Duch. Why should calamity be full of words?
    Q. Eliz. Windy attorneys to their client woes,
Airy succeeders of intestate joys,
Poor breathing orators of miseries!
Let them have scope: though what they do impart 130
Help not at all, yet do they ease the heart.
    Duch. If so, then be not tongue-tied: go with me,
And in the breath of bitter words let 's smother
My damned son, which thy two sweet sons smother'd.
I hear his drum: be copious in exclaims.

Enter KING RICHARD, *marching, with drums and
    trumpets.*

    K. Rich. Who intercepts my expedition?
    Duch. O, she that might have intercepted thee,
By strangling thee in her accursed womb,
From all the slaughters, wretch, that thou hast done!
    Q. Eliz. Hidest thou that forehead with a golden
      crown,   140
Where should be graven, if that right were right,
The slaughter of the prince that owed that crown,
And the dire death of my two sons and brothers?
Tell me, thou villain slave, where are my children?
    Duch. Thou toad, thou toad, where is thy brother
      Clarence?
And little Ned Plantagenet, his son?
    Q. Eliz. Where is kind Hastings, Rivers, Vaughan,
      Grey?
    K. Rich. A flourish, trumpets! strike alarum, drums!
Let not the heavens hear these tell-tale women
Rail on the Lord's anointed: strike, I say!   150
                  [*Flourish. Alarums.*
Either be patient, and entreat me fair,
Or with the clamorous report of war

Blind . . . usurp'd. By these paradoxes the mother of Edward IV
describes herself and expresses her sense of the disordered state of the
land. 36. **seniory,** superiority of claim, priority. 37. **on . . . hand,** i.e.,
in the place of precedence. 40. **Edward,** her son, former prince of
Wales; cf. l. 20, note. 41. **Harry,** her husband. 42. **Edward,** i.e.,
Edward IV. 43. **Richard,** the young duke of York, son of Edward IV and
Elizabeth Woodville. 44. **Richard,** duke of York, her husband and
father of Richard III, killed by Margaret's army at the Battle of Wakefield in 1460. 45. **Rutland,** Edmund, son of the duke of York, also
killed at Wakefield. 49. **teeth,** an allusion to the legend that Richard
was born with teeth. 53. **galled,** sore with weeping. 56. **carnal,** flesh-
eating. 58. **pew-fellow,** intimate associate. 63. **Thy Edward,** Edward
IV. **my Edward,** son of Henry VI. 64. **other Edward,** Edward V. 65.
Young York, Richard, duke of York, the younger of the princes mur-

dered in the Tower. **but boot,** merely that which is "thrown in"; see
boot in glossary. 69. **adulterate,** adulterous. 71. **intelligencer,** agent,
go-between. 72. **factor,** agent (of the powers of hell). 85. **index,** argument, preface, prologue. **pageant,** spectacular entertainment; see glossary. 89. **sign,** mere sign. 97. **Decline,** go through from beginning to
end. 100. **caitiff,** wretch, slave (term of reproach). 102. **scorn'd at,**
taunted. **scorn'd of,** taunted by. 110. **Usurp,** here used for "deserve." 122. **Bettering,** exaggerating. 127. **their client,** so Hanmer;
F: *their Clients.* 128. **intestate,** apparently used in the sense "bequeathing nothing," the general notion being that words are of no consequence. 129. **breathing,** speaking. 135. **exclaims,** exclamations.
141. **right were right,** justice were done. 142. **owed,** owned; see glossary. 146. **Ned Plantagenet.** Cf. note, IV, iii, 36. 148. **alarum,** the
cry or signal "allarme" (to arms). 149. **tell-tale,** tattling, gabbling.

Thus will I drown your exclamations.
Duch. Art thou my son?
K. Rich. Ay, I thank God, my father, and yourself.
Duch. Then patiently hear my impatience.
K. Rich. Madam, I have a touch of your condition,
Which cannot brook the accent of reproof.
Duch. O, let me speak!
K. Rich.　　　　Do then; but I'll not hear.
Duch. I will be mild and gentle in my speech.　　160
K. Rich. And brief, good mother; for I am in haste.
Duch. Art thou so hasty? I have stay'd for thee,
God knows, in anguish, pain and agony.
K. Rich. And came I not at last to comfort you?
Duch. No, by the holy rood, thou know'st it well,
Thou camest on earth to make the earth my hell.
A grievous burthen was thy birth to me;
Tetchy and wayward was thy infancy;
Thy school-days frightful, desperate, wild, and furious,
Thy prime of manhood daring, bold, and venturous,
Thy age confirm'd, proud, subtle, bloody, treacherous,
More mild, but yet more harmful, kind in hatred:　172
What comfortable hour canst thou name,
That ever graced me in thy company?
K. Rich. Faith, none, but Humphrey Hour, that
　　call'd your grace
To breakfast once forth of my company.
If I be so disgracious in your sight,
Let me march on, and not offend your grace.
Strike up the drum.
Duch.　　　　I prithee, hear me speak.
K. Rich. You speak too bitterly.
Duch.　　　　Hear me a word;　　180
For I shall never speak to thee again.
K. Rich. So.
Duch. Either thou wilt die, by God's just ordinance,
Ere from this war thou turn a conqueror,
Or I with grief and extreme age shall perish
And never look upon thy face again.
Therefore take with thee my most heavy curse;
Which, in the day of battle, tire thee more
Than all the complete armour that thou wear'st!
My prayers on the adverse party fight;　　190
And there the little souls of Edward's children
Whisper the spirits of thine enemies
And promise them success and victory.
Bloody thou art, bloody will be thy end;
Shame serves thy life and doth thy death attend. [*Exit.*
Q. Eliz. Though far more cause, yet much less
　　spirit to curse
Abides in me; I say amen to all.
K. Rich. Stay, madam; I must speak a word with
　　you.
Q. Eliz. I have no moe sons of the royal blood
For thee to murder: for my daughters, Richard,　200
They shall be praying nuns, not weeping queens;
And therefore level not to hit their lives.
K. Rich. You have a daughter call'd Elizabeth,
Virtuous and fair, royal and gracious.
Q. Eliz. And must she die for this? O, let her live,
And I'll corrupt her manners, stain her beauty;

Slander myself as false to Edward's bed;
Throw over her the veil of infamy:
So she may live unscarr'd of bleeding slaughter,
I will confess she was not Edward's daughter.　　210
K. Rich. Wrong not her birth, she is of royal blood.
Q. Eliz. To save her life, I'll say she is not so.
K. Rich. Her life is only safest in her birth.
Q. Eliz. And only in that safety died her brothers.
K. Rich. Lo, at their births good stars were opposite.
Q. Eliz. No, to their lives bad friends were contrary.
K. Rich. All unavoided is the doom of destiny.
Q. Eliz. True, when avoided grace makes destiny:
My babes were destined to a fairer death,
If grace had bless'd thee with a fairer life.　　220
K. Rich. You speak as if that I had slain my cousins.
Q. Eliz. Cousins, indeed; and by their uncle cozen'd
Of comfort, kingdom, kindred, freedom, life.
Whose hand soever lanced their tender hearts,
Thy head, all indirectly, gave direction:
No doubt the murderous knife was dull and blunt
Till it was whetted on thy stone-hard heart,
To revel in the entrails of my lambs.
But that still use of grief makes wild grief tame,
My tongue should to thy ears not name my boys　230
Till that my nails were anchor'd in thine eyes;
And I, in such a desperate bay of death,
Like a poor bark, of sails and tackling reft,
Rush all to pieces on thy rocky bosom.
K. Rich. Madam, so thrive I in my enterprise
And dangerous success of bloody wars,
As I intend more good to you and yours
Than ever you or yours were by me wrong'd!
Q. Eliz. What good is cover'd with the face of
　　heaven,
To be discover'd, that can do me good?　　240
K. Rich. The advancement of your children, gentle
　　lady.
Q. Eliz. Up to some scaffold, there to lose their
　　heads?
K. Rich. No, to the dignity and height of honour,
The high imperial type of this earth's glory.
Q. Eliz. Flatter my sorrows with report of it;
Tell me what state, what dignity, what honour,
Canst thou demise to any child of mine?
K. Rich. Even all I have; yea, and myself and all,
Will I withal endow a child of thine;
So in the Lethe of thy angry soul　　250
Thou drown the sad remembrance of those wrongs
Which thou supposest I have done to thee.
Q. Eliz. Be brief, lest that the process of thy kindness
Last longer telling than thy kindness' date.
K. Rich. Then know, that from my soul I love thy
　　daughter.
Q. Eliz. My daughter's mother thinks it with her
　　soul.
K. Rich. What do you think?
Q. Eliz. That thou dost love my daughter from thy
　　soul:
So from thy soul's love didst thou love her brothers;
And from my heart's love I do thank thee for it.　260

*Richard
the Third*
ACT IV : SC IV

330

157. touch . . . condition, a dash of your disposition.　**162. stay'd for,**
waited the coming of; see *stay* in glossary.　**168. Tetchy,** fretful,
peevish.　**170. prime of,** first.　**171. age confirm'd,** riper manhood.
172. kind in hatred, concealing hatred under pretense of kindness.　**174.
graced,** honored, favored; see glossary.　**175. Humphrey Hour.** To
"dine with Duke Humphrey" was to go hungry. The passage is obscure
but seems to mean that Richard's comfortable hour came when his
mother did not appear for breakfast.　**188. tire.** This and the coordinate

verbs *fight* (l. 190), *Whisper* (l. 192), and *promise* (l. 193) are optative
subjunctives.　195. **serves,** accompanies.　199. **moe;** see glossary.　202. **level,** aim; see glossary.　206. **manners,** morals.　214. **only
in,** by reason of.　215. **opposite,** hostile, antagonistic.　216. **contrary,**
opposed.　217. **unavoided,** unavoidable.　218. **avoided grace,** i.e.,
Richard, in whom grace is void or lacking.　222. **cozen'd,** cheated; obvious pun.　229. **still,** constant; see glossary. **use,** habit; see glossary.
232. **bay,** a body of water in which the *poor bark* is floundering, and also a

K. Rich. Be not so hasty to confound my meaning:
I mean, that with my soul I love thy daughter,
And mean to make her queen of England.
    Q. Eliz. Say then, who dost thou mean shall be her
      king?
    K. Rich. Even he that makes her queen : who should
      be else?
    Q. Eliz. What, thou?
    K. Rich. I, even I : what think you of it, madam?
    Q. Eliz. How canst thou woo her?
    K. Rich.   That would I learn of you,
As one that are best acquainted with her humour.
    Q. Eliz. And wilt thou learn of me?
    K. Rich.   Madam, with all my heart. 270
    Q. Eliz. Send to her, by the man that slew her
      brothers,
A pair of bleeding hearts ; thereon engrave
Edward and York ; then haply she will weep :
Therefore present to her,—as sometime Margaret
Did to thy father, steep'd in Rutland's blood,—
A handkerchief ; which, say to her, did drain
The purple sap from her sweet brother's body.
And bid her dry her weeping eyes therewith.
If this inducement force her not to love,
Send her a story of thy noble acts ;   280
Tell her thou madest away her uncle Clarence,
Her uncle Rivers ; yea, and, for her sake,
Madest quick conveyance with her good aunt Anne.
    K. Rich. Come, come, you mock me ; this is not the
      way
To win your daughter.
    Q. Eliz.   There is no other way ;
Unless thou couldst put on some other shape,
And not be Richard that hath done all this.
    K. Rich. Say that I did all this for love of her.
    Q. Eliz. Nay, then indeed she cannot choose but
      hate thee,
Having bought love with such a bloody spoil.   290
    K. Rich. Look, what is done cannot be now
      amended :
Men shall deal unadvisedly sometimes,
Which after hours give leisure to repent.
If I did take the kingdom from your sons,
To make amends, I'll give it to your daughter.
If I have kill'd the issue of your womb,
To quicken your increase, I will beget
Mine issue of your blood upon your daughter :
A grandam's name is little less in love
Than is the doting title of a mother ;   300
They are as children but one step below,
Even of your mettle, of your very blood ;
Of all one pain, save for a night of groans
Endured of her, for whom you bid like sorrow.
Your children were vexation to your youth,
But mine shall be a comfort to your age.
The loss you have is but a son being king,
And by that loss your daughter is made queen.
I cannot make you what amends I would,
Therefore accept such kindness as I can.   310
Dorset your son, that with a fearful soul

Leads discontented steps in foreign soil,
This fair alliance quickly shall call home
To high promotions and great dignity :
The king, that calls your beauteous daughter wife,
Familiarly shall call thy Dorset brother ;
Again shall you be mother to a king,
And all the ruins of distressful times
Repair'd with double riches of content.
What! we have many goodly days to see :   320
The liquid drops of tears that you have shed
Shall come again, transform'd to orient pearl,
Advantaging their loan with interest
Of ten times double gain of happiness.
Go, then, my mother, to thy daughter go ;
Make bold her bashful years with your experience ;
Prepare her ears to hear a wooer's tale ;
Put in her tender heart the aspiring flame
Of golden sovereignty ; acquaint the princess
With the sweet silent hours of marriage joys :   330
And when this arm of mine hath chastised
The petty rebel, dull-brain'd Buckingham,
Bound with triumphant garlands will I come
And lead thy daughter to a conqueror's bed ;
To whom I will retail my conquest won,
And she shall be sole victress, Cæsar's Cæsar.
    Q. Eliz. What were I best to say? her father's
      brother
Would be her lord? or shall I say, her uncle?
Or, he that slew her brothers and her uncles?
Under what title shall I woo for thee,   340
That God, the law, my honour and her love,
Can make seem pleasing to her tender years?
    K. Rich. Infer fair England's peace by this alliance.
    Q. Eliz. Which she shall purchase with still lasting
      war.
    K. Rich. Say that the king, which may command,
      entreats.
    Q. Eliz. That at her hands which the king's King
      forbids.
    K. Rich. Say, she shall be a high and mighty queen.
    Q. Eliz. To wail the title, as her mother doth.
    K. Rich. Say, I will love her everlastingly.
    Q. Eliz. But how long shall that title 'ever' last?   350
    K. Rich. Sweetly in force unto her fair life's end.
    Q. Eliz. But how long fairly shall her sweet life last?
    K. Rich. So long as heaven and nature lengthens it.
    Q. Eliz. So long as hell and Richard likes of it.
    K. Rich. Say, I, her sovereign, am her subject love.
    Q. Eliz. But she, your subject, loathes such
      sovereignty.
    K. Rich. Be eloquent in my behalf to her.
    Q. Eliz. An honest tale speeds best being plainly
      told.
    K. Rich. Then in plain terms tell her my loving tale.
    Q. Eliz. Plain and not honest is too harsh a style.   360
    K. Rich. Your reasons are too shallow and too quick.
    Q. Eliz. O no, my reasons are too deep and dead ;
Too deep and dead, poor infants, in their grave.
    K. Rich. Harp not on that string, madam ; that is
      past.

reference to the position of a hunted animal who has turned to face the
hounds. 236. **success,** sequel, result ; see glossary. 247. **demise,** convey, transmit, lease. 249. **withal,** with this ; see glossary. 250. **Lethe,**
the river Lethe, the waters of which produce forgetfulness. 254. **date,**
term of existence ; see glossary. 259. **from,** used sarcastically in the
sense "apart from." 270. **wilt thou,** i.e., do you really wish to. 274.
Therefore, for that reason. **sometime,** once ; see glossary. 283. **conveyance,** removal. 293. **Which,** i.e., from which dealing. 297.

quicken, make pregnant. 302. **mettle,** temper, disposition. 304. **bid,**
endured. 307. **son being king,** Edward, who was Edward v. 311-312.
Dorset . . . soil. Dorset did not join Richmond abroad until after the
failure of Buckingham's revolt. 322. **orient,** bright, shining. 323.
Advantaging, augmenting ; see glossary. 343. **Infer,** possibly, bring
about ; or adduce (as a reason). 351. **in force,** i.e., my love will continue. 358. **speeds,** succeeds ; see glossary. 360. **too . . . style,** i.e., a
discordant combination. 361. **reasons,** observations, remarks.

Q. Eliz. Harp on it still shall I till heartstrings
   break.
K. Rich. Now, by my George, my garter, and my
   crown,—
Q. Eliz. Profaned, dishonour'd, and the third
   usurp'd.
K. Rich. I swear—
Q. Eliz.   By nothing; for this is no oath:
The George, profaned, hath lost his holy honour;
The garter, blemish'd, pawn'd his knightly virtue;   370
The crown, usurp'd, disgraced his kingly glory.
If something thou wilt swear to be believed,
Swear then by something that thou hast not wrong'd.
K. Rich. Now, by the world—
Q. Eliz.   'Tis full of thy foul wrongs.
K. Rich. My father's death—
Q. Eliz.   Thy life hath that dishonour'd.
K. Rich. Then, by myself—
Q. Eliz.   Thyself thyself misusest.
K. Rich. Why then, by God—
Q. Eliz.   God's wrong is most of all.
If thou hadst fear'd to break an oath by Him,
The unity the king thy brother made
Had not been broken, nor my brother slain: 380
If thou hadst fear'd to break an oath by Him,
The imperial metal, circling now thy brow,
Had graced the tender temples of my child,
And both the princes had been breathing here,
Which now, two tender playfellows for dust,
Thy broken faith hath made a prey for worms.
What canst thou swear by now?
K. Rich.   The time to come.
Q. Eliz. That thou hast wronged in the time
   o'erpast;
For I myself have many tears to wash
Hereafter time, for time past wrong'd by thee.   390
The children live, whose parents thou hast
   slaughter'd,
Ungovern'd youth, to wail it in their age;
The parents live, whose children thou hast butcher'd,
Old wither'd plants, to wail it with their age.
Swear not by time to come; for that thou hast
Misused ere used, by time misused o'erpast.
  K. Rich. As I intend to prosper and repent,
So thrive I in my dangerous attempt
Of hostile arms! myself myself confound!
Heaven and fortune bar me happy hours!   400
Day, yield me not thy light; nor, night, thy rest!
Be opposite all planets of good luck
To my proceedings, if, with pure heart's love,
Immaculate devotion, holy thoughts,
I tender not thy beauteous princely daughter!
In her consists my happiness and thine;
Without her, follows to this land and me,
To thee, herself, and many a Christian soul,
Death, desolation, ruin and decay:
It cannot be avoided but by this;   410
It will not be avoided but by this.
Therefore, good mother,—I must call you so—

Be the attorney of my love to her:
Plead what I will be, not what I have been;
Not my deserts, but what I will deserve:
Urge the necessity and state of times,
And be not peevish-fond in great designs.
  Q. Eliz. Shall I be tempted of the devil thus?
  K. Rich. Ay, if the devil tempt thee to do good.
  Q. Eliz. Shall I forget myself to be myself?   420
  K. Rich. Ay, if yourself's remembrance wrong
   yourself.
  Q. Eliz. But thou didst kill my children.
  K. Rich. But in your daughter's womb I bury
   them:
Where in that nest of spicery they shall breed
Selves of themselves, to your recomforture.
  Q. Eliz. Shall I go win my daughter to thy will?
  K. Rich. And be a happy mother by the deed.
  Q. Eliz. I go. Write to me very shortly,
And you shall understand from me her mind.
  K. Rich. Bear her my true love's kiss; and so,
   farewell.   [*Exit Queen Elizabeth.* 430
Relenting fool, and shallow, changing woman!

Enter RATCLIFF; CATESBY *following.*

How now! what news?
  Rat. My gracious sovereign, on the western coast
Rideth a puissant navy; to the shore
Throng many doubtful hollow-hearted friends,
Unarm'd, and unresolved to beat them back:
'Tis thought that Richmond is their admiral;
And there they hull, expecting but the aid
Of Buckingham to welcome them ashore.
  K. Rich. Some light-foot friend post to the Duke of
   Norfolk: 440
Ratcliff, thyself, or Catesby; where is he?
  Cate. Here, my lord.
  K. Rich. Fly to the duke: [*To Ratcliff*] Post thou to
   Salisbury:
When thou comest thither,—[*To Catesby*] Dull,
   unmindful villain,
Why stand'st thou still, and go'st not to the duke?
  Cate. First, mighty sovereign, let me know your
   mind,
What from your grace I shall deliver to him.
  K. Rich. O, true, good Catesby: bid him levy
   straight
The greatest strength and power he can make,
And meet me presently at Salisbury.   450
  Cate. I go.   [*Exit.*
  Rat. What is 't your highness' pleasure I shall do
At Salisbury?
  K. Rich. Why, what wouldst thou do there before I
   go?
  Rat. Your highness told me I should post before.
  K. Rich. My mind is changed, sir, my mind is
   changed.

Enter LORD STANLEY.

How now, what news with you?

---

366. **George . . . garter.** The George, a badge showing St. George
slaying the dragon, was not added to the insignia of the Order of the
Garter until the reign of Henry VII or Henry VIII.   390. **Hereafter,**
after this.   392. **Ungovern'd,** i.e., without a father's guidance or rule.
397-398. **As . . . I,** i.e., I swear that as I hope to thrive and intend
to repent.   399. **myself . . . confound,** may I destroy myself.   405.
tender, have a tender regard for.   406. **consists,** resides, inheres.
417. **peevish-fond,** childishly foolish; see *peevish* and *fond* in glossary.
420. **myself . . . myself,** i.e., that person wronged by Richard.   421.

wrong yourself, i.e., interfere with what is to your advantage.   424.
nest of spicery, a reference to the fabled phoenix which rose anew
from the nest of spices, its funeral pyre.   425. **recomforture,** comfort,
consolation.   438. **hull,** drift with the sails furled.   440. **light-foot,**
swift-footed.   446-447. **First . . . him.** Note this first evidence of
confusion in Richard's mind.   450. **at Salisbury,** where Richard
would be in a position to prevent the junction of Buckingham and
Richmond.   465. **White-liver'd,** cowardly.   **runagate,** renegade.
473. **great York's,** i.e., Richard, duke of York, father of Edward IV.

Stan. None good, my lord, to please you with the
    hearing;
Nor none so bad, but it may well be told.
    K. Rich. Hoyday, a riddle! neither good nor bad! 460
Why dost thou run so many mile about,
When thou mayst tell thy tale a nearer way?
Once more, what news?
    Stan.   Richmond is on the seas.
    K. Rich. There let him sink, and be the seas on him!
White-liver'd runagate, what doth he there?
    Stan. I know not, mighty sovereign, but by guess.
    K. Rich. Well, sir, as you guess, as you guess?
    Stan. Stirr'd up by Dorset, Buckingham, and Ely,
He makes for England, there to claim the crown.
    K. Rich. Is the chair empty? is the sword unsway'd?
Is the king dead? the empire unpossess'd?   471
What heir of York is there alive but we?
And who is England's king but great York's heir?
Then, tell me, what doth he upon the sea?
    Stan. Unless for that, my liege, I cannot guess.
    K. Rich. Unless for that he comes to be your liege,
You cannot guess wherefore the Welshman comes.
Thou wilt revolt, and fly to him, I fear.
    Stan. No, mighty liege; therefore mistrust me not.
    K. Rich. Where is thy power, then, to beat him back?
Where are thy tenants and thy followers?   481
Are they not now upon the western shore,
Safe-conducting the rebels from their ships?
    Stan. No, my good lord, my friends are in the north.
    K. Rich. Cold friends to Richard: what do they in
    the north,
When they should serve their sovereign in the west?
    Stan. They have not been commanded, mighty
    sovereign:
Please it your majesty to give me leave,
I'll muster up my friends, and meet your grace
Where and what time your majesty shall please.   490
    K. Rich. Ay, ay, thou wouldst be gone to join with
    Richmond:
I will not trust you, sir.
    Stan.   Most mighty sovereign,
You have no cause to hold my friendship doubtful:
I never was nor never will be false.
    K. Rich. Well,
Go muster men; but, hear you, leave behind
Your son, George Stanley: look your faith be firm,
Or else his head's assurance is but frail.
    Stan. So deal with him as I prove true to you.   [*Exit.*

Enter a Messenger.

    Mess. My gracious sovereign, now in Devonshire, 500
As I by friends am well advertised,
Sir Edward Courtney, and the haughty prelate
Bishop of Exeter, his brother there,
With many moe confederates, are in arms.

Enter another Messenger.

    Sec. Mess. My liege, in Kent the Guildfords are
    in arms;

And every hour more competitors
Flock to their aid, and still their power increaseth.

Enter another Messenger.

    Third Mess. My lord, the army of the Duke of
    Buckingham—
    K. Rich. Out on you, owls! nothing but songs of
    death?   [*He striketh him.*
Take that, until thou bring me better news.   510
    Third Mess. The news I have to tell your majesty
Is, that by sudden floods and fall of waters,
Buckingham's army is dispersed and scatter'd;
And he himself wander'd away alone,
No man knows whither.
    K. Rich.   I cry thee mercy:
There is my purse to cure that blow of thine.
Hath any well-advised friend proclaim'd
Reward to him that brings the traitor in?
    Third Mess. Such proclamation hath been made,
    my liege.

Enter another Messenger.

    Fourth Mess. Sir Thomas Lovel and Lord Marquis
    Dorset,   520
'Tis said, my liege, in Yorkshire are in arms.
Yet this good comfort bring I to your grace,
The Breton navy is dispersed by tempest:
Richmond, in Dorsetshire, sent out a boat
Unto the shore, to ask those on the banks
If they were his assistants, yea or no;
Who answer'd him, they came from Buckingham
Upon his party: he, mistrusting them,
Hoised sail and made away for Brittany.
    K. Rich. March on, march on, since we are up in
    arms;   530
If not to fight with foreign enemies,
Yet to beat down these rebels here at home.

Re-enter CATESBY.

    Cate. My liege, the Duke of Buckingham is taken;
That is the best news: that the Earl of Richmond
Is with a mighty power landed at Milford,
Is colder tidings, yet they must be told.
    K. Rich. Away towards Salisbury! while we reason
    here,
A royal battle might be won and lost:
Some one take order Buckingham be brought
To Salisbury; the rest march on with me.   540
                              [*Flourish. Exeunt.*

SCENE V. *Lord Derby's house.*

Enter DERBY *and* SIR CHRISTOPHER URSWICK.

    Der. Sir Christopher, tell Richmond this from me:
That in the sty of this most bloody boar
My son George Stanley is frank'd up in hold:
If I revolt, off goes young George's head;

475. **that,** i.e., to claim the crown.   477. **Welshman.** Richmond was the grandson of Owen Tudor, a Welshman of Anglesea, who had married Catharine of France, widow of Henry v. Richmond's claim was descent through the Beauforts from John of Gaunt and Catharine Swynford.   479. **therefore,** on that account.   501. **advertised,** informed.   502. **Sir Edward Courtney,** i.e., of Haccombe, created earl of Devon on the accession of Henry vii. He was only distantly related to Peter Courtenay, bishop of Exeter.   505. **Guildfords,** a family led by Sir Richard Guildford of Hempstead in Kent.   506. **competitors,** confederates.   509. **owls.** It was thought that the cry of the owl portended death.   529. **Hoised,** hoisted.   535. **Milford,** Milford Haven on the coast of Wales in the county of Pembroke. A gap of two years is bridged here. Richmond's first fruitless expedition was in October 1483; his landing at Milford was in August 1485.   536. **colder,** more chilling, dampening.   538. **royal battle,** battle on which a kingdom depends.   SCENE V. *Stage Direction:* **Sir Christopher Urswick,** a priest, confessor to the countess of Richmond, Henry vii's mother.   3. **hold,** custody, prison.

The fear of that withholds my present aid.
But, tell me, where is princely Richmond now?
   Chris. At Pembroke, or at Ha'rford-west, in Wales.
   Der. What men of name resort to him?
   Chris. Sir Walter Herbert, a renowned soldier;
Sir Gilbert Talbot, Sir William Stanley;   10
Oxford, redoubted Pembroke, Sir James Blunt,
And Rice ap Thomas, with a valiant crew;
And many moe of noble fame and worth:
And towards London they do bend their course,
If by the way they be not fought withal.
   Der. Return unto thy lord; commend me to him:
Tell him the queen hath heartily consented
He shall espouse Elizabeth her daughter.
These letters will resolve him of my mind.
Farewell.   *[Exeunt.* 20

ACT V.

SCENE I. *Salisbury. An open place.*

Enter the Sheriff, *and* BUCKINGHAM, *with halberds, led
to execution.*

   Buck. Will not King Richard let me speak with
     him?
   Sher. No, my good lord; therefore be patient.
   Buck. Hastings, and Edward's children, Rivers,
     Grey,
Holy King Henry, and thy fair son Edward,
Vaughan, and all that have miscarried
By underhand corrupted foul injustice,
If that your moody discontented souls
Do through the clouds behold this present hour,
Even for revenge mock my destruction!
This is All-Souls' day, fellows, is it not?   10
   Sher. It is, my lord.
   Buck. Why, then All-Souls' day is my body's
     doomsday.
This is the day that, in King Edward's time,
I wish'd might fall on me, when I was found
False to his children or his wife's allies;
This is the day wherein I wish'd to fall
By the false faith of him I trusted most;
This, this All-Souls' day to my fearful soul
Is the determined respite of my wrongs:
That high All-Seer that I dallied with   20
Hath turn'd my feigned prayer on my head
And given in earnest what I begg'd in jest.
Thus doth he force the swords of wicked men
To turn their own points on their masters' bosoms:
Now Margaret's curse is fallen upon my head;
'When he,' quoth she, 'shall split thy heart with
     sorrow,
Remember Margaret was a prophetess.'
Come, sirs, convey me to the block of shame;
Wrong hath but wrong, and blame the due of blame.
                         [Exeunt.

SCENE II. *The camp near Tamworth.*

Enter RICHMOND, OXFORD, BLUNT, HERBERT, *and
others, with drum and colours.*

   Richm. Fellows in arms, and my most loving friends,
Bruised underneath the yoke of tyranny,
Thus far into the bowels of the land
Have we march'd on without impediment;
And here receive we from our father Stanley
Lines of fair comfort and encouragement.
The wretched, bloody, and usurping boar,
That spoil'd your summer fields and fruitful vines,
Swills your warm blood like wash, and makes his
     trough
In your embowell'd bosoms, this foul swine   10
Lies now even in the centre of this isle,
Near to the town of Leicester, as we learn:
From Tamworth thither is but one day's march.
In God's name, cheerly on, courageous friends,
To reap the harvest of perpetual peace
By this one bloody trial of sharp war.
   Oxf. Every man's conscience is a thousand swords,
To fight against that bloody homicide.
   Herb. I doubt not but his friends will fly to us.
   Blunt. He hath no friends but who are friends for
     fear,   20
Which in his greatest need will shrink from him.
   Richm. All for our vantage. Then, in God's name,
     march:
True hope is swift, and flies with swallow's wings;
Kings it makes gods, and meaner creatures kings.
                       [Exeunt.

SCENE III. *Bosworth Field.*

Enter KING RICHARD *in arms, with* NORFOLK, *the* EARL
OF SURREY, *and others.*

   K. Rich. Here pitch our tents, even here in Bosworth
     field.
My Lord of Surrey, why look you so sad?
   Sur. My heart is ten times lighter than my looks.
   K. Rich. My Lord of Norfolk,—
   Nor.   Here, most gracious liege.
   K. Rich. Norfolk, we must have knocks; ha! must
     we not?
   Nor. We must both give and take, my gracious lord.
   K. Rich. Up with my tent there! here will I lie
     to-night;
But where to-morrow? Well, all 's one for that.
Who hath descried the number of the foe?
   Nor. Six or seven thousand is their utmost power.   10
   K. Rich. Why, our battalion trebles that account:
Besides, the king's name is a tower of strength,
Which they upon the adverse party want.
Up with my tent there! Valiant gentlemen,
Let us survey the vantage of the field;
Call for some men of sound direction:

---

5. **present,** prompt; see glossary. 7. **Ha'rford-west,** Haverfordwest,
near Milford Haven. 8. **name,** honorable repute. 9. **Sir Walter
Herbert,** a Welshman of old family and considerable influence. 10. **Sir
Gilbert Talbot,** uncle to the young earl of Shrewsbury. **Sir William
Stanley,** brother to Thomas, Lord Stanley. 11. **Oxford,** John de Vere,
earl of Oxford. **redoubted,** valiant, formidable. **Pembroke,** Jasper
Tudor, earl of Pembroke, uncle to Richmond. **Sir James Blunt,** son
of Sir Walter Blunt, Baron Mountjoy; he was lieutenant of Hammes
Castle, 1476, where he was custodian of the earl of Oxford. 12. **Rice
ap Thomas,** an influential Welsh knight. 19. **resolve him of,** inform

him concerning.
ACT V. SCENE I. 4. **thy,** i.e., Henry's. 5. **miscarried,** perished.
10. **All-Souls' day,** *Festa Animarum,* November 2, in commemoration
of the dead, who on this day may communicate with the living. 13 **l
day.** Cf. II, i, 32 ff. 19. **determined . . . wrongs,** the time to which
the punishment of my evil practices was respited (Johnson following
Hanmer). 22. **earnest,** money paid as an instalment to secure a bargain; see glossary. 26. **'When he' . . . sorrow.** Cf. I, iii, 300-301.
SCENE II. 5. **Stanley,** Sir William Stanley. 9. **wash,** hog's wash,
swill. 10. **embowell'd,** disemboweled. 20. **for fear,** i.e., because they

Let 's want no discipline, make no delay;
For, lords, to-morrow is a busy day.   [*Exeunt.*

Enter, on the other side of the field, RICHMOND, SIR
    WILLIAM BRANDON, OXFORD, *and others. Some of the*
    Soldiers *pitch Richmond's tent.*

Richm. The weary sun hath made a golden set,
And, by the bright track of his fiery car,   20
Gives signal of a goodly day to-morrow.
Sir William Brandon, you shall bear my standard.
Give me some ink and paper in my tent:
I'll draw the form and model of our battle,
Limit each leader to his several charge,
And part in just proportion our small strength.
My Lord of Oxford, you, Sir William Brandon,
And you, Sir Walter Herbert, stay with me.
The Earl of Pembroke keeps his regiment:
Good Captain Blunt, bear my good-night to him,   30
And by the second hour in the morning
Desire the earl to see me in my tent:
Yet one thing more, good Blunt, before thou go'st,
Where is Lord Stanley quarter'd, dost thou know?
Blunt. Unless I have mista'en his colours much,
Which well I am assured I have not done,
His regiment lies half a mile at least
South from the mighty power of the king.
Richm. If without peril it be possible,
Good Captain Blunt, bear my good-night to him,   40
And give him from me this most needful scroll.
Blunt. Upon my life, my lord, I'll undertake it;
And so, God give you quiet rest to-night!
Richm. Good night, good Captain Blunt. Come,
    gentlemen,
Let us consult upon to-morrow's business:
In to our tent; the air is raw and cold.
                              [*They withdraw into the tent.*

Enter, to his tent, KING RICHARD, NORFOLK,
    RATCLIFF, CATESBY, *and others.*

K. Rich. What is 't o'clock?
Cate.   It 's supper-time, my lord;
It 's nine o'clock.
K. Rich.   I will not sup to-night.
Give me some ink and paper.
What, is my beaver easier than it was?   50
And all my armour laid into my tent?
Cate. It is, my liege; and all things are in readiness.
K. Rich. Good Norfolk, hie thee to thy charge;
Use careful watch, choose trusty sentinels.
Nor. I go, my lord.
K. Rich. Stir with the lark to-morrow, gentle
    Norfolk.
Nor. I warrant you, my lord.   [*Exit.*
K. Rich. Catesby!
Cate. My lord?
K. Rich.   Send out a pursuivant at arms
To Stanley's regiment; bid him bring his power   60
Before sunrising, lest his son George fall

Into the blind cave of eternal night.   [*Exit Catesby.*
Fill me a bowl of wine. Give me a watch.
Saddle white Surrey for the field to-morrow.
Look that my staves be sound, and not too heavy.
Ratcliff!
Rat. My lord?
K. Rich. Saw'st thou the melancholy Lord
    Northumberland?
Rat. Thomas the Earl of Surrey, and himself,
Much about cock-shut time, from troop to troop   70
Went through the army, cheering up the soldiers.
K. Rich. So, I am satisfied. Give me a bowl of wine:
I have not that alacrity of spirit,
Nor cheer of mind, that I was wont to have.
Set it down. Is ink and paper ready?
Rat. It is, my lord.
K. Rich.   Bid my guard watch; leave
    me.
Ratcliff, about the mid of night come to my tent
And help to arm me. Leave me, I say.
                              [*Exeunt Ratcliff and the other Attendants.*

Enter DERBY *to* RICHMOND *in his tent, Lords and others*
    attending.

Der. Fortune and victory sit on thy helm!
Richm. All comfort that the dark night can afford   80
Be to thy person, noble father-in-law!
Tell me, how fares our loving mother?
Der. I, by attorney, bless thee from thy mother,
Who prays continually for Richmond's good:
So much for that. The silent hours steal on,
And flaky darkness breaks within the east.
In brief,—for so the season bids us be,—
Prepare thy battle early in the morning,
And put thy fortune to the arbitrement
Of bloody strokes and mortal-staring war.   90
I, as I may—that which I would I cannot,—
With best advantage will deceive the time,
And aid thee in this doubtful shock of arms:
But on thy side I may not be too forward,
Lest, being seen, thy brother, tender George,
Be executed in his father's sight.
Farewell: the leisure and the fearful time
Cuts off the ceremonious vows of love
And ample interchange of sweet discourse,
Which so long sunder'd friends should dwell upon: 100
God give us leisure for these rites of love!
Once more, adieu: be valiant, and speed well!
Richm. Good lords, conduct him to his regiment:
I'll strive, with troubled thoughts, to take a nap,
Lest leaden slumber peise me down to-morrow,
When I should mount with wings of victory:
Once more, good night, kind lords and gentlemen.
                              [*Exeunt all but Richmond.*
O Thou, whose captain I account myself,
Look on my forces with a gracious eye;
Put in their hands thy bruising irons of wrath,   110
That they may crush down with a heavy fall

fear him.   24. **meaner,** of lower degree; see glossary.
    SCENE III.   8. **all 's . . . that,** be that as it may.   11. **battalion,** army.
16. **sound direction,** true judgment, sound military skill.   20. **fiery
car,** a reference to the car of Phoebus.   24. **model,** pattern; see glossary.
29. **keeps,** i.e., is with; see glossary.   50. **beaver,** helmet.   **easier,**
more loosely fitting.   57. **warrant,** promise.   59. **pursuivant at arms,**
one of the junior officers attendant on the heralds.   63. **watch,** watch
light, a candle marked into equal divisions to show time; or perhaps,
sentinel.   64. **white Surrey.** The name seems to be Shakespeare's
invention. Hall says that Richard was mounted on a "great white

courser."   65. **staves,** the staves or handles of his lances.   70. **cock-
shut time,** evening twilight; possibly, the time at which poultry are
shut up.   81. **father-in-law.** Stanley was stepfather to Richmond.   86.
flaky, broken into flakes of cloud.   87. **season,** time of day.   90.
mortal-staring, fatal-visaged.   91. **that . . . cannot,** i.e., sleep.   92.
With best advantage, to the best purpose.   94. **be too forward,** appear
too openly.   95. **tender,** young, of tender years. In point of fact
George Stanley was a mature man.   97. **leisure,** i.e., lack of leisure.
105. **peise,** weigh.   110. **bruising irons,** maces, weapons.

The usurping helmets of our adversaries!
Make us thy ministers of chastisement,
That we may praise thee in the victory!
To thee I do commend my watchful soul,
Ere I let fall the windows of mine eyes:
Sleeping and waking, O, defend me still!　　　[*Sleeps.*

Enter the Ghost of PRINCE EDWARD, *son to* HENRY *the
Sixth.*

Ghost. [*To Richard*] Let me sit heavy on thy soul
　　to-morrow!
Think, how thou stab'dst me in my prime of youth
At Tewksbury: despair, therefore, and die!　　　120
[*To Richmond*] Be cheerful, Richmond; for the
　　wronged souls
Of butcher'd princes fight in thy behalf:
King Henry's issue, Richmond, comforts thee.

Enter the Ghost of HENRY *the Sixth.*

Ghost. [*To Richard*] When I was mortal, my
　　anointed body
By thee was punched full of deadly holes:
Think on the Tower and me: despair, and die!
Harry the Sixth bids thee despair and die!
[*To Richmond*] Virtuous and holy, be thou conqueror!
Harry, that prophesied thou shouldst be king,
Doth comfort thee in thy sleep: live, and flourish!　　130

Enter the Ghost of CLARENCE.

Ghost. [*To Richard*] Let me sit heavy on thy soul
　　to-morrow!
I, that was wash'd to death with fulsome wine,
Poor Clarence, by thy guile betrayed to death!
To-morrow in the battle think on me,
And fall thy edgeless sword: despair, and die!—
[*To Richmond*] Thou offspring of the house of
　　Lancaster,
The wronged heirs of York do pray for thee:
Good angels guard thy battle! live, and flourish!

Enter the Ghosts of RIVERS, GREY, *and* VAUGHAN.

Ghost of R. [*To Richard*] Let me sit heavy on thy soul
　　to-morrow,
Rivers, that died at Pomfret! despair, and die!　　140
Ghost of G. [*To Richard*] Think upon Grey, and let
　　thy soul despair!
Ghost of V. [*To Richard*] Think upon Vaughan, and,
　　with guilty fear,
Let fall thy lance: despair, and die!
All. [*To Richmond*] Awake, and think our wrongs in
　　Richard's bosom
Will conquer him! awake, and win the day!

Enter the Ghost of HASTINGS.

Ghost. [*To Richard*] Bloody and guilty, guiltily
　　awake,
And in a bloody battle end thy days!
Think on Lord Hastings: despair, and die!
[*To Richmond*] Quiet untroubled soul, awake, awake!
Arm, fight, and conquer, for fair England's sake!　　150

Enter the Ghosts of the two young Princes.

Ghosts. [*To Richard*] Dream on thy cousins
　　smother'd in the Tower:

Let us be lead within thy bosom, Richard,
And weigh thee down to ruin, shame, and death!
Thy nephews' souls bid thee despair and die!
[*To Richmond*] Sleep, Richmond, sleep in peace, and
　　wake in joy;
Good angels guard thee from the boar's annoy!
Live, and beget a happy race of kings!
Edward's unhappy sons do bid thee flourish.

Enter the Ghost of LADY ANNE.

Ghost. [*To Richard*] Richard, thy wife, that wretched
　　Anne thy wife,
That never slept a quiet hour with thee,　　160
Now fills thy sleep with perturbations:
To-morrow in the battle think on me,
And fall thy edgeless sword: despair, and die!
[*To Richmond*] Thou quiet soul, sleep thou a quiet
　　sleep;
Dream of success and happy victory!
Thy adversary's wife doth pray for thee.

Enter the Ghost of BUCKINGHAM.

Ghost. [*To Richard*] The first was I that help'd thee
　　to the crown;
The last was I that felt thy tyranny:
O, in the battle think on Buckingham,
And die in terror of thy guiltiness!　　170
Dream on, dream on, of bloody deeds and death:
Fainting, despair; despairing, yield thy breath!
[*To Richmond*] I died for hope ere I could lend thee
　　aid:
But cheer thy heart, and be thou not dismay'd:
God and good angels fight on Richmond's side;
And Richard falls in height of all his pride.
　　　[*The Ghosts vanish. King Richard starts out of his dream.*
K. Rich. Give me another horse: bind up my
　　wounds.
Have mercy, Jesu!—Soft! I did but dream.
O coward conscience, how dost thou afflict me!
The lights burn blue. It is now dead midnight.　　180
Cold fearful drops stand on my trembling flesh.
What do I fear? myself? there 's none else by:
Richard loves Richard; that is, I am I.
Is there a murderer here? No. Yes, I am:
Then fly. What, from myself? Great reason why:
Lest I revenge. What, myself upon myself?
Alack, I love myself. Wherefore? for any good
That I myself have done unto myself?
O, no! alas, I rather hate myself
For hateful deeds committed by myself!　　190
I am a villain: yet I lie, I am not.
Fool, of thyself speak well: fool, do not flatter.
My conscience hath a thousand several tongues,
And every tongue brings in a several tale,
And every tale condemns me for a villain.
Perjury, perjury, in the high'st degree;
Murder, stern murder, in the direst degree;
All several sins, all used in each degree,
Throng to the bar, crying all, Guilty! guilty!
I shall despair. There is no creature loves me;　　200
And if I die, no soul shall pity me:
Nay, wherefore should they, since that I myself

---

119. **prime,** early time. 123. **issue,** son. 126. **Tower,** where Henry
VI was supposed to have been murdered. 132. **wash'd to death,** i.e.,
drowned in the butt of malmsey. **fulsome,** cloying. 135. **fall,** may
it fall. **edgeless,** futile. 156. **the boar's annoy,** i.e., Richard's attack.
173. **for hope,** i.e., for want of hope; Steevens conjectured *for holpe,*

deserted, unhelped. 180. **lights burn blue,** superstitiously regarded
as evidence of the presence of ghosts. 193. **several,** different; see
glossary. 198. **used,** committed; see glossary. 199. **bar,** i.e., bar of
justice. 218. **substance,** bodies; used in contrast to *shadows* (l. 216).
219. **in proof,** in armor which is proof against weapons. 231. **cried**

Find in myself no pity to myself?
Methought the souls of all that I had murder'd
Came to my tent; and every one did threat
To-morrow's vengeance on the head of Richard.

Enter RATCLIFF.

Rat. My lord!
K. Rich. 'Zounds! who is there?
Rat. Ratcliff, my lord; 'tis I. The early village-cock
Hath twice done salutation to the morn;   210
Your friends are up, and buckle on their armour.
    K. Rich. O Ratcliff, I have dream'd a fearful dream!
What thinkest thou, will our friends prove all true?
    Rat. No doubt, my lord.
    K. Rich.   O Ratcliff, I fear, I fear,—
    Rat. Nay, good my lord, be not afraid of shadows.
    K. Rich. By the apostle Paul, shadows to-night
Have struck more terror to the soul of Richard
Than can the substance of ten thousand soldiers
Armed in proof, and led by shallow Richmond.
It is not yet near day. Come, go with me;   220
Under our tents I'll play the eaves-dropper,
To see if any mean to shrink from me.   [*Exeunt.*

Enter the Lords *to* RICHMOND, *sitting in his tent.*

Lords. Good morrow, Richmond!
Richm. Cry mercy, lords and watchful gentlemen,
That you have ta'en a tardy sluggard here.
    Lords. How have you slept, my lord?
    Richm. The sweetest sleep, and fairest-boding
        dreams
That ever enter'd in a drowsy head,
Have I since your departure had, my lords.
Methought their souls, whose bodies Richard
        murder'd,   230
Came to my tent, and cried on victory:
I promise you, my soul is very jocund
In the remembrance of so fair a dream.
How far into the morning is it, lords?
    Lords. Upon the stroke of four.
    Richm. Why, then 'tis time to arm and give direction.

His oration to his soldiers.

More than I have said, loving countrymen,
The leisure and enforcement of the time
Forbids to dwell upon: yet remember this,
God and our good cause fight upon our side;   240
The prayers of holy saints and wronged souls,
Like high-rear'd bulwarks, stand before our faces;
Richard except, those whom we fight against
Had rather have us win than him they follow:
For what is he they follow? truly, gentlemen,
A bloody tyrant and a homicide;
One raised in blood, and one in blood establish'd;
One that made means to come by what he hath,
And slaughter'd those that were the means to help
        him;
A base foul stone, made precious by the foil   250
Of England's chair, where he is falsely set;
One that hath ever been God's enemy:
Then, if you fight against God's enemy,
God will in justice ward you as his soldiers;

If you do sweat to put a tyrant down,
You sleep in peace, the tyrant being slain;
If you do fight against your country's foes,
Your country's fat shall pay your pains the hire;
If you do fight in safeguard of your wives,
Your wives shall welcome home the conquerors;   260
If you do free your children from the sword,
Your children's children quit it in your age.
Then, in the name of God and all these rights,
Advance your standards, draw your willing swords.
For me, the ransom of my bold attempt
Shall be this cold corpse on the earth's cold face;
But if I thrive, the gain of my attempt
The least of you shall share his part thereof.
Sound drums and trumpets boldly and cheerfully;
God and Saint George! Richmond and victory!   270
                                        [*Exeunt.*

Re-enter KING RICHARD, RATCLIFF, *Attendants
        and Forces.*

K. Rich. What said Northumberland as touching
        Richmond?
Rat. That he was never trained up in arms.
K. Rich. He said the truth: and what said Surrey
        then?
Rat. He smiled and said 'The better for our purpose.'
K. Rich. He was in the right; and so indeed it is.
                                        [*Clock striketh.*
Tell the clock there. Give me a calendar.
Who saw the sun to-day?
    Rat.   Not I, my lord.
    K. Rich. Then he disdains to shine; for by the book
He should have braved the east an hour ago:
A black day will it be to somebody.   280
Ratcliff!
    Rat. My lord?
    K. Rich.   The sun will not be seen to-day;
The sky doth frown and lour upon our army.
I would these dewy tears were from the ground.
Not shine to-day! Why, what is that to me
More than to Richmond? for the selfsame heaven
That frowns on me looks sadly upon him.

Enter NORFOLK.

Nor. Arm, arm, my lord; the foe vaunts in the field.
K. Rich. Come, bustle, bustle; caparison my horse.
Call up Lord Stanley, bid him bring his power: 290
I will lead forth my soldiers to the plain,
And thus my battle shall be ordered:
My foreward shall be drawn out all in length,
Consisting equally of horse and foot;
Our archers shall be placed in the midst:
John Duke of Norfolk, Thomas Earl of Surrey,
Shall have the leading of this foot and horse.
They thus directed, we will follow
In the main battle, whose puissance on either side
Shall be well winged with our chiefest horse.   300
This, and Saint George to boot! What think'st thou,
        Norfolk?
    Nor. A good direction, warlike sovereign.
This found I on my tent this morning.
                                        [*He sheweth him a paper.*

on, uttered the cry of. 236. **direction,** orders. 238. **leisure,** i.e., lack
of leisure. **enforcement,** exigency. 247. **raised . . . establish'd,** i.e.,
in the kingship. 250. **foil,** a thin leaf of metal placed under a gem to
set it off to advantage. 254. **ward,** protect. 258. **fat,** prosperity,
wealth. 265. **ransom, etc.** If he fails, there will be no question of
ransom, but of death. 272. **up in,** i.e., to. 278. **book,** i.e., the
calendar. 279. **braved,** made splendid; see glossary. 288. **vaunts,**
boasts. 289. **caparison,** put on the trappings. 293. **foreward,** vanguard. 299. **main battle,** main body of troops. 301. **to boot,** i.e., to
give us aid in addition.

K. Rich. [*Reads*] 'Jockey of Norfolk, be not too bold,
For Dickon thy master is bought and sold.'
A thing devised by the enemy.
Go, gentlemen, every man unto his charge:
Let not our babbling dreams affright our souls:
Conscience is but a word that cowards use,
Devised at first to keep the strong in awe: 310
Our strong arms be our conscience, swords our law.
March on, join bravely, let us to 't pell-mell;
If not to heaven, then hand in hand to hell.

His oration to his Army.

What shall I say more than I have inferr'd?
Remember whom you are to cope withal;
A sort of vagabonds, rascals, and runaways,
A scum of Bretons, and base lackey peasants,
Whom their o'er-cloyed country vomits forth
To desperate ventures and assured destruction.
You sleeping safe, they bring to you unrest;   320
You having lands, and blest with beauteous wives,
They would restrain the one, distain the other.
And who doth lead them but a paltry fellow,
Long kept in Bretagne at our mother's cost?
A milk-sop, one that never in his life
Felt so much cold as over shoes in snow?
Let 's whip these stragglers o'er the seas again;
Lash hence these overweening rags of France,
These famish'd beggars, weary of their lives;
Who, but for dreaming on this fond exploit,   330
For want of means, poor rats, had hang'd themselves:
If we be conquer'd, let men conquer us,
And not these bastard Bretons; whom our fathers
Have in their own land beaten, bobb'd, and thump'd,
And in record, left them the heirs of shame.
Shall these enjoy our lands? lie with our wives?
Ravish our daughters? [*Drum afar off.*] Hark! I hear
    their drum.
Fight, gentlemen of England! fight, bold yeomen!
Draw, archers, draw your arrows to the head!
Spur your proud horses hard, and ride in blood;   340
Amaze the welkin with your broken staves!

Enter a Messenger.

What says Lord Stanley? will he bring his power?
Mess. My lord, he doth deny to come.
K. Rich. Off with his son George's head!
Nor. My lord, the enemy is past the marsh:
After the battle let George Stanley die.
    K. Rich. A thousand hearts are great within my
        bosom:
Advance our standards, set upon our foes;
Our ancient word of courage, fair Saint George,
Inspire us with the spleen of fiery dragons!   350
Upon them! Victory sits on our helms.   [*Exeunt.*

SCENE IV. *Another part of the field.*

Alarum: excursions. Enter NORFOLK *and forces fighting;
to him* CATESBY.

Cate. Rescue, my Lord of Norfolk, rescue, rescue!
The king enacts more wonders than a man,
Daring an opposite to every danger:
His horse is slain, and all on foot he fights,
Seeking for Richmond in the throat of death.
Rescue, fair lord, or else the day is lost!

Alarums. Enter KING RICHARD.

K. Rich. A horse! a horse! my kingdom for a horse!
Cate. Withdraw, my lord; I'll help you to a horse.
K. Rich. Slave, I have set my life upon a cast,
And I will stand the hazard of the die: 10
I think there be six Richmonds in the field;
Five have I slain to-day instead of him.
A horse! a horse! my kingdom for a horse!   [*Exeunt.*

SCENE V. *Another part of the field.*

Alarum. Enter RICHARD *and* RICHMOND; *they fight.*
RICHARD *is slain. Retreat and flourish. Re-enter*
RICHMOND, DERBY *bearing the crown, with divers
other Lords.*

Richm. God and your arms be praised, victorious
    friends;
The day is ours, the bloody dog is dead.
    Der. Courageous Richmond, well hast thou acquit
        thee.
Lo, here, this long-usurped royalty
From the dead temples of this bloody wretch
Have I pluck'd off, to grace thy brows withal:
Wear it, enjoy it, and make much of it.
    Richm. Great God of heaven, say Amen to all!
But, tell me, is young George Stanley living?
    Der. He is, my lord, and safe in Leicester town;   10
Whither, if it please you, we may now withdraw us.
    Richm. What men of name are slain on either side?
    Der. John Duke of Norfolk, Walter Lord Ferrers,
Sir Robert Brakenbury, and Sir William Brandon.
    Richm. Inter their bodies as becomes their births:
Proclaim a pardon to the soldiers fled
That in submission will return to us:
And then, as we have ta'en the sacrament,
We will unite the white rose and the red:
Smile heaven upon this fair conjunction,   20
That long have frown'd upon their enmity!
What traitor hears me, and says not amen?
England hath long been mad, and scarr'd herself;
The brother blindly shed the brother's blood,
The father rashly slaughter'd his own son,
The son, compell'd, been butcher to the sire:
All this divided York and Lancaster,
Divided in their dire division,
O, now, let Richmond and Elizabeth,
The true succeeders of each royal house,   30
By God's fair ordinance conjoin together!
And let their heirs, God, if thy will be so,
Enrich the time to come with smooth-faced peace,

304-305. 'Jockey . . . sold.' The rhyme occurs in the chronicles. 304.
Jockey, familiar form of "Jack." 305. Dickon, i.e., Dick, Richard.
bought and sold, betrayed for a bribe. 308. babbling, foolish. 314.
inferr'd, stated. 317. lackey, a running footman; here, servile. 322.
restrain, keep back, withhold.   distain, defile, sully. 324. our mother's.
Richmond's mother was not Richard's. This error occurs in the second
edition of Holinshed's *Chronicles.* The first edition reads "brothers,"
the reference being to the fact that Richmond had been supported at
the court of the duke of Bretagne at the cost of the duke of Burgundy,
Richard's brother-in-law. 326. as over shoes, i.e., as one being
over his shoe-tops. 331. want of means, poverty. 334. bobb'd,

banged. 335. record, history. 341. Amaze . . . staves, i.e., fright
the skies with the shining of your lances (Johnson); see *welkin* in
glossary.
    SCENE IV.   2. than a man, than seems possible for a human being.
3. Daring . . . danger, boldly facing every danger of battle. 10.
hazard . . . die, i.e., the turn of the die.
    SCENE V.   18. as . . . sacrament, as I am sworn to do. 19. white
. . . red, house of York and house of Lancaster, i.e., by his marriage
to Elizabeth, daughter of Edward IV. 28. division, estrangement.
33. smooth-faced, calm-visaged.

With smiling plenty and fair prosperous days!
Abate the edge of traitors, gracious Lord,
That would reduce these bloody days again,
And make poor England weep in streams of blood!
Let them not live to taste this land's increase
That would with treason wound this fair land's
peace!
Now civil wounds are stopp'd, peace lives again: 40
That she may long live here, God say amen! [Exeunt.

35. **Abate the edge**, i.e., render their opposition ineffective. 38.
increase, i.e., new prosperity.

THE LIFE AND DEATH OF
King John

Among the "tragedies" mentioned by Francis
Meres in *Palladis Tamia* is *King John*, which must,
therefore, have been written before 1598. The only
known early publication of the play is that of the
First Folio in 1623. One is consequently left to determine the date of the play mainly by internal evidence.
Since it represents stylistically about the same stage of
development as *Richard II*, some critics place it just
before that play and some just after it, that is, about
1595. It may thus stand midway between the early
group of four plays dealing with the Wars of the Roses
and the later group of four plays dealing with the
earlier history of the Lancastrian usurpation.

THE SOURCE

King John rests immediately upon an earlier play
called *The Troublesome Raigne of John King of England*,
in two parts, published in 1591, again in 1611 as
written by "W. Sh.," and in 1622 as written by "W.
Shakespeare." It was thus mistaken for Shakespeare's
play, or palmed off as such, and the editors of the
First Folio did not enter *King John* in the Stationers'
Register as a new play, but regarded the entry of the
older form as sufficient. *King John* and *The Troublesome
Raigne*, however, differ very greatly. Shakespeare
has condensed the two parts into one, has rewritten it
throughout line for line, changed the emphasis, and
developed the characters. The older playwright compressed Holinshed's chronicle, invented the main
features of the plot, and gave to the whole a strongly
Protestant coloring with a good deal of that exaggerated patriotism which is known as chauvinism. It
is full of defamation of the French and glorification of
the English, and has exploited the tradition that
King John was the first of the English kings to assert
national independence against the papacy. This had
already given his name, hardly more, to the Protestant
morality play on the Antichrist theme known as
Kynge Johan (1540?) by Bishop John Bale.

KING JOHN IN HISTORY

King John could not, even from Holinshed, be
made into a hero, Protestant or otherwise, so that
we are prepared for the reduction of the title role
at Shakespeare's hands. The conception of the character, however, is left confused and imperfect. If
the story of King John were truly told for the stage,
his part would be that of a king who, like Richard
III, murdered, or sought to murder, his nephew and
rightful sovereign, and who, like Richard II and
Henry VI, lost the realms in France. He is, therefore,
a poor peg on which to hang patriotism. It is hard to
see just how far Shakespeare went beyond the old
play for his materials, but he probably read Holinshed
for himself and, in this way, came to his somewhat
truer realization of the significance of the facts recorded. Scenes of the despoiling of the monasteries,
which appear in *The Troublesome Raigne*, do not appear
in Shakespeare, and it has been thought that Shakespeare omitted them; but it is at least as possible that
Shakespeare wrote something of the sort that was
later excised from his play.

A CHRONICLE PLAY

Elizabethan art was not insistent upon unity, and
for that reason the Elizabethans possibly got more
enjoyment from the history or chronicle play as such
than we do. The canvas in *King John* is broad; the
characters, interests, and events are many. Such
unity as the play has is a unity of setting, idea, and
spirit, none of which is definitely centered in a figure
or event. England, perhaps, is the greatest hero of the
piece. There seems no better way to bring out the
essential nature of the chronicle play than a review of
events.

THE STORY

The French king and the count of Lymoges (confused with the duke of Austria) demand the English
crown for Arthur, son of Geoffrey Duke of Bretagne,
an elder brother of King John. Arthur's claim is good,
but John has possession. John, spurred on by his
shrewish mother, Elinor, proceeds to France to fight
for his claim. Before he sets out there arrives at his
court the most striking character of the play, Philip,
the Bastard Faulconbridge, son of Richard Coeur-
de-Lion. He is a blunt and daring spirit who renounces his claim to the name and estate of Faulconbridge, preferring to be regarded as the base son
of a great king rather than the proper son of a base
man. Faulconbridge follows the court, fights for England in the field, and becomes King John's mainstay.

The armies meet before Angiers, but the governor
of the city will not admit either party until he learns
which is the real king. The armies fight a drawn
battle and again assemble before the town. Faulconbridge wishes them to join forces, reduce the town,
and then fight it out; but the canny governor makes
peace between the parties by suggesting a marriage

between Blanch of Spain, King John's niece, and Lewis, the dauphin of France. John gives away vast provinces and a large dower, and in return his enemies abandon the claims of Arthur. The grief of Constance, the mother of Arthur, at her son's displacement is passionate and eloquent. Shakespeare, apparently

cessful in battle, has to make peace when his reinforcements and supplies are lost by disaster at sea. The ending is mixed, politic, and tame, but it follows the chronicle. John, being ill with a fever, takes refuge in a monastery at Swinstead, where he is poisoned by a monk acting as his taster, who dies himself for the sake

Raro antecedentem Scelestum:

Campian

F. Parsons et Campian F.H. fecit

Rebellion the effect of Monasteries.

From "A Thankfull Remembrance . . . ," *1630, symbolic of the long-standing struggle between various English monarchs and the Church.*

King John

340

seeing through her sentimentality, shows us that she loves mainly herself and her will in the person of her son. Pandulph, the pope's legate, enters as the peace is consummated and excommunicates John for despoiling the monasteries and refusing to permit Stephen Langton, the pope's appointee, to become archbishop of Canterbury. The French and English armies fight, the English win, and Arthur is captured. Constance goes wild with grief and subsequently dies.

Arthur is turned over by King John to Hubert, whom the king bribes to blind and then murder him. The entrance of Hubert and the executioners to carry out their black purpose opens one of Shakespeare's most moving scenes of pure humanity. Arthur so begs for his eyesight that Hubert spares him, but tells the king that Arthur is dead. John's nobles revolt at his horrid butchery. Hubert then confesses that he has spared Arthur, and John sends after the nobles to placate them; but, meanwhile, Arthur in a desperate attempt to escape from prison has leaped down from the wall and slain himself. The nobles, still believing John guilty of Arthur's death, join the dauphin, who, urged on by Pandulph, is now making rapid headway in a conquest of England. John basely surrenders his crown to Pandulph in token of submission, and Pandulph orders the dauphin to withdraw. The dauphin refuses; the English nobles return to their allegiance to John when they learn that the dauphin intends to put them to death after he has employed them to overthrow John. The dauphin, though suc-

of destroying the king.

This event is not intelligible in Shakespeare, who has omitted scenes from *The Troublesome Raigne* in which monasteries are sacked and the ecclesiastics satirized. Such scenes if once present in Shakespeare's play have been cut out. A scene in the old play shows John surrendering in despair his crown to Pandulph, consoled only by the thought that at a later time the cause against the pope will be fought and won.

The result of these omissions from Shakespeare's *King John* is to remove from the play its extreme anti-Romanism and part at least of its evil abuse of France. Pandulph becomes a truly impressive ecclesiastical statesman. In Shakespeare's hands Arthur and Constance become deeply humanized, and Faulconbridge a simple, honest, humorous, English patriot, who, in the midst of crookedness and intrigue, holds fast to love of country, honest service, and bravery in warfare. He speaks at the end of the play:

This England never did, nor never shall,
Lie at the proud foot of a conqueror,
But when it first did help to wound itself.
Now these her princes are come home again,
Come the three corners of the world in arms,
And we shall shock them. Nought shall make us rue,
If England to itself do rest but true.

Thus, we have a long and complicated story—a story already dramatized on a high level. We see Shakespeare rewriting it in detail, very thoughtfully and well; but not with one clear purpose. One can say that it is Shakespeare's most typical chronicle play, the depiction without interpretation of varied events on a wide canvas. This is perhaps true, but at best it merely offers a substitute for thinking, or following Shakespeare's thought. The play on close study proves to be significant in what it says, though strangely noncommittal. King John, an unattractive character, a usurping king, and a murderer, at least by intention, becomes in the play, particularly when seen on the stage, a symbol of government and a rallying point for patriotism. Faulconbridge, a bastard with the antisocial qualities believed to belong to illegitimacy, finds that nature crescent within him makes him love his country and be loyal to his king. Again, the wise and dexterous Pandulph presents the figure of loyalty to the pope, almost in medieval terms. Small flashes of realism come out of the play. Elinor, because John is her favorite child and because she hates her daughter-in-law, throws justice to the winds. The canvas turns out to be a rich one; the unity of the play rests mainly in the synthesis of an inconsistent theme. The people live. It is not too much to say that *King John* is a great play.

STAGE HISTORY

King John has not been a popular play, though its stage history is eminently respectable. It has in it at least three good male parts, King John, Pandulph, and Faulconbridge, and one female part, that of Constance, of unusual tragic appeal. It is a far better play on the stage than it is in the closet, a situation not unusual in Elizabethan drama. There is no evidence that the play had any unusual vogue in its own day or was honored by revival during the Restoration. It all but escaped the almost inevitable adaptation of the late seventeenth and eighteenth centuries and might have done so completely had not Colley Cibber seen in it an opportunity for anti-Catholic propaganda. In 1736 he made a version called *Papal Tyranny in the Reign of King John*. Soon after this, Shakespeare's play was put on by Garrick, and since his time most of the greater Shakespearean actors and actresses have appeared in it: Macklin, Quin (who played King John in Cibber's version), the Kembles and their sister Sarah Siddons (with whom Constance was a favorite role), and Edmund Kean and his son Charles. Ellen Terry, then ten years old, played the part of Arthur in Charles Kean's last revival of *King John* in 1858 and was magnificently great in the part of Constance toward the end of the nineteenth century in a revival in which Sir Henry Irving played the part of Pandulph.

Opportunities for seeing *King John* on the stage in recent years have not been numerous. A quarter of a century ago, it was to be seen in the repertory of R. B. Mantell, and in 1925 and later years Randle Ayrton, an English actor, played the part of King John and revealed by his acting the surprising theatrical appeal of the part. *King John* was played at the Shakespeare Memorial Theatre at Stratford-upon-Avon in 1948.

THE LIFE AND DEATH OF

King John

DRAMATIS PERSONAE

KING JOHN.
PRINCE HENRY, son to the king.
ARTHUR, Duke of Bretagne, nephew to the king.
The Earl of PEMBROKE.
The Earl of ESSEX.
The Earl of SALISBURY.
The Lord BIGOT.
HUBERT DE BURGH.
ROBERT FAULCONBRIDGE, son to Sir Robert
    Faulconbridge.
PHILIP the BASTARD, his half-brother.
JAMES GURNEY, servant to Lady Faulconbridge.
PETER of Pomfret, a prophet.

PHILIP, King of France.
LEWIS, the Dauphin.
LYMOGES, Duke of AUSTRIA.
CARDINAL PANDULPH, the Pope's legate.
MELUN, a French Lord.
CHATILLON, ambassador from France to King
    John.

QUEEN ELINOR, mother to King John.
CONSTANCE, mother to Arthur.
BLANCH of Spain, niece to King John.
LADY FAULCONBRIDGE.

Lords, Citizens of Angiers, Sheriff, Heralds,
    Officers, Soldiers, Messengers, and other
    Attendants.

SCENE: *Partly in England, and partly in France.*

ACT I.

SCENE I. KING JOHN'S *palace.*

Enter KING JOHN, QUEEN ELINOR, PEMBROKE,
ESSEX, SALISBURY, *and others, with* CHATILLON.

K. John. Now, say, Chatillon, what would France
    with us?
Chat. Thus, after greeting, speaks the King of France
In my behaviour to the majesty,
The borrow'd majesty, of England here.
  Eli. A strange beginning: 'borrow'd majesty!'
  K. John. Silence, good mother; hear the embassy.
  Chat. Philip of France, in right and true behalf
Of thy deceased brother Geffrey's son,
Arthur Plantagenet, lays most lawful claim
To this fair island and the territories,   10
To Ireland, Poictiers, Anjou, Touraine, Maine,
Desiring thee to lay aside the sword
Which sways usurpingly these several titles,
And put the same into young Arthur's hand,
Thy nephew and right royal sovereign.

K. John. What follows if we disallow of this?

Chat. The proud control of fierce and bloody war,
To enforce these rights so forcibly withheld.

K. John. Here have we war for war and blood for
    blood,
Controlment for controlment: so answer France.   20

Chat. Then take my king's defiance from my mouth,
The farthest limit of my embassy.

K. John. Bear mine to him, and so depart in peace:
Be thou as lightning in the eyes of France;
For ere thou canst report I will be there,
The thunder of my cannon shall be heard:
So hence! Be thou the trumpet of our wrath
And sullen presage of your own decay.
An honourable conduct let him have:
Pembroke, look to 't. Farewell, Chatillon.   30
              [Exeunt Chatillon and Pembroke.

Eli. What now, my son! have I not ever said
How that ambitious Constance would not cease
Till she had kindled France and all the world,
Upon the right and party of her son?
This might have been prevented and made whole
With very easy arguments of love,
Which now the manage of two kingdoms must
With fearful bloody issue arbitrate.

K. John. Our strong possession and our right for us.

Eli. Your strong possession much more than your
    right,   40
Or else it must go wrong with you and me:
So much my conscience whispers in your ear,
Which none but heaven and you and I shall hear.

Enter a Sheriff.

Essex. My liege, here is the strangest controversy
Come from the country to be judged by you
That e'er I heard: shall I produce the men?

K. John. Let them approach.
Our abbeys and our priories shall pay
This expedition's charge.

Enter ROBERT FAULCONBRIDGE, *and* PHILIP *his bastard
brother.*

                What men are you?

Bast. Your faithful subject I, a gentleman   50
Born in Northamptonshire and eldest son,
As I suppose, to Robert Faulconbridge,
A soldier, by the honour-giving hand
Of Cœur-de-lion knighted in the field.

K. John. What art thou?

Rob. The son and heir to that same Faulconbridge.

K. John. Is that the elder, and art thou the heir?
You came not of one mother then, it seems.

Bast. Most certain of one mother, mighty king;

That is well known; and, as I think, one father: 60
But for the certain knowledge of that truth
I put you o'er to heaven and to my mother:
Of that I doubt, as all men's children may.

Eli. Out on thee, rude man! thou dost shame thy
    mother
And wound her honour with this diffidence.

Bast. I, madam? no, I have no reason for it;
That is my brother's plea and none of mine;
The which if he can prove, a' pops me out
At least from fair five hundred pound a year:
Heaven guard my mother's honour and my land!   70

K. John. A good blunt fellow. Why, being younger
    born,
Doth he lay claim to thine inheritance?

Bast. I know not why, except to get the land.
But once he slander'd me with bastardy:
But whether I be as true begot or no,
That still I lay upon my mother's head;
But that I am as well begot, my liege,—
Fair fall the bones that took the pains for me!—
Compare our faces and be judge yourself.
If old sir Robert did beget us both   80
And were our father and this son like him,
O old sir Robert, father, on my knee
I give heaven thanks I was not like to thee!

K. John. Why, what a madcap hath heaven lent us
    here!

Eli. He hath a trick of Cœur-de-lion's face;
The accent of his tongue affecteth him.
Do you not read some tokens of my son
In the large composition of this man?

K. John. Mine eye hath well examined his parts
And finds them perfect Richard. Sirrah, speak,   90
What doth move you to claim your brother's land?

Bast. Because he hath a half-face, like my father.
With half that face would he have all my land:
A half-faced groat five hundred pound a year!

Rob. My gracious liege, when that my father lived,
Your brother did employ my father much,—

Bast. Well, sir, by this you cannot get my land:
Your tale must be how he employ'd my mother.

Rob. And once dispatch'd him in an embassy
To Germany, there with the emperor   100
To treat of high affairs touching that time.
The advantage of his absence took the king
And in the mean time sojourn'd at my father's;
Where how he did prevail I shame to speak,
But truth is truth: large lengths of seas and shores
Between my father and my mother lay,
As I have heard my father speak himself,
When this same lusty gentleman was got.
Upon his death-bed he by will bequeath'd

King John
ACT I : SC I

342

His lands to me, and took it on his death 110
That this my mother's son was none of his;
And if he were, he came into the world
Full fourteen weeks before the course of time.
Then, good my liege, let me have what is mine,
My father's land, as was my father's will.

    K. John. Sirrah, your brother is legitimate;
Your father's wife did after wedlock bear him,
And if she did play false, the fault was hers;
Which fault lies on the hazards of all husbands
That marry wives. Tell me, how if my brother, 120
Who, as you say, took pains to get this son,
Had of your father claim'd this son for his?
In sooth, good friend, your father might have kept
This calf bred from his cow from all the world;
In sooth he might; then, if he were my brother's,
My brother might not claim him; nor your father,
Being none of his, refuse him: this concludes;
My mother's son did get your father's heir;
Your father's heir must have your father's land.

    Rob. Shall then my father's will be of no force 130
To dispossess that child which is not his?

    Bast. Of no more force to dispossess me, sir,
Than was his will to get me, as I think.

    Eli. Whether hadst thou rather be a Faulconbridge
And like thy brother, to enjoy thy land,
Or the reputed son of Cœur-de-lion,
Lord of thy presence and no land beside?

    Bast. Madam, an if my brother had my shape,
And I had his, sir Robert's his, like him;
And if my legs were two such riding-rods, 140
My arms such eel-skins stuff'd, my face so thin
That in mine ear I durst not stick a rose
Lest men should say 'Look, where three-farthings
    goes!'
And, to his shape, were heir to all this land,
Would I might never stir from off this place,
I would give it every foot to have this face;
I would not be sir Nob in any case.

    Eli. I like thee well: wilt thou forsake thy fortune,
Bequeath thy land to him and follow me?
I am a soldier and now bound to France. 150

    Bast. Brother, take you my land, I'll take my chance.
Your face hath got five hundred pound a year,
Yet sell your face for five pence and 'tis dear.
Madam, I'll follow you unto the death.

    Eli. Nay, I would have you go before me thither.

    Bast. Our country manners give our betters way.

    K. John. What is thy name?

    Bast. Philip, my liege, so is my name begun;
Philip, good old sir Robert's wife's eldest son.

    K. John. From henceforth bear his name whose form
    thou bear'st: 160

Kneel thou down Philip, but rise more great,
Arise sir Richard and Plantagenet.

    Bast. Brother by the mother's side, give me your
    hand:
My father gave me honour, yours gave land.
Now blessed be the hour, by night or day,
When I was got, sir Robert was away!

    Eli. The very spirit of Plantagenet!
I am thy grandam, Richard; call me so.

    Bast. Madam, by chance but not by truth; what
    though?
Something about, a little from the right, 170
    In at the window, or else o'er the hatch:
Who dares not stir by day must walk by night,
    And have is have, however men do catch:
Near or far off, well won is still well shot,
And I am I, howe'er I was begot.

    K. John. Go, Faulconbridge: now hast thou thy
    desire:
A landless knight makes thee a landed squire.
Come, madam, and come, Richard, we must speed
For France, for France, for it is more than need.

    Bast. Brother, adieu: good fortune come to thee! 180
For thou wast got i' the way of honesty.
                  [Exeunt all but Bastard.
A foot of honour better than I was;
But many a many foot of land the worse.
Well, now can I make any Joan a lady.
'Good den, sir Richard!'—'God-a-mercy, fellow!'—
And if his name be George, I'll call him Peter;
For new-made honour doth forget men's names;
'Tis too respective and too sociable
For your conversion. Now your traveller,
He and his toothpick at my worship's mess, 190
And when my knightly stomach is sufficed,
Why then I suck my teeth and catechize
My picked man of countries: 'My dear sir,'
Thus, leaning on mine elbow, I begin,
'I shall beseech you'—that is question now;
And then comes answer like an Absey book:
'O sir,' says answer, 'at your best command;
At your employment; at your service, sir:'
'No, sir,' says question, 'I, sweet sir, at yours:'
And so, ere answer knows what question would, 200
Saving in dialogue of compliment,
And talking of the Alps and Apennines,
The Pyrenean and the river Po,
It draws toward supper in conclusion so.
But this is worshipful society
And fits the mounting spirit like myself,
For he is but a bastard to the time
That doth not smack of observation;
And so am I, whether I smack or no;

i.e., of your identity as the son of Coeur-de-Lion, implying that such noble origin gives dignity which compensates for loss of lands. 138. **an if**; see glossary. 140. **riding-rods**, switches. 142. **stick a rose.** The queen's likeness on the three-farthing coin was distinguished from that on the three half-pence by a rose behind her head. The Bastard's taunt is based on the thinness of the coin. 147. **Nob.** Two explanations have been offered: diminutive of *Robert*, which might imply a taunt at his brother's size or at his juniority; and head, particularly the head of a stick, with reference again to Faulconbridge's slenderness. 169. **not by truth**, not honorably. 170. **Something about**, somewhat roundabout, clandestinely; see *something* in glossary. **a little . . . right**, away from the right. The New Cambridge editors see a suggestion of the "bar sinister," a term of heraldry. A bar is a set of horizontal stripes crossing the shield. It is sometimes said that illegitimacy was designated by a bar on the left (the sinister) field of the escutcheon. 171. **hatch**, lower half door. 184. **Joan**, frequently used to designate any girl, usually of the lower class; cf. *Love's Labour's Lost*,

III, i, 207. 185-199. **'Good den . . . at yours.'** The Bastard amuses himself with an imaginary dialogue in *worshipful society*, where he represents himself with his *new-made honour* as a parvenu. Throughout he ridicules the artificial refinements of courtly circles. 185. **Good den**, good-even. **'God-a-mercy**, God have mercy. **fellow**, a condescending form of address; see glossary. 188. **respective**, considerate, careful, with reference to good breeding. 189. **conversion**, change of status, referring to his *new-made honour*. **traveller**, man of the world. 190. **toothpick**, significant of his refined manners, or foppishness. 192. **I suck my teeth**, i.e., in contrast to the toothpick of the *traveller*. 193. **picked**, refined. 196. **Absey**, A B C. 201. **dialogue of compliment**, polite but inane conversation. 204. **toward . . . conclusion.** The after-dinner conversation lasts until supper time. 207-208. **a bastard . . . observation**, i.e., not a true son of the times unless he observes the niceties of polite society.

And not alone in habit and device, 210
Exterior form, outward accoutrement,
But from the inward motion to deliver
Sweet, sweet, sweet poison for the age's tooth:
Which, though I will not practise to deceive,
Yet, to avoid deceit, I mean to learn;
For it shall strew the footsteps of my rising.
But who comes in such haste in riding-robes?
What woman-post is this? hath she no husband
That will take pains to blow a horn before her?

Enter LADY FAULCONBRIDGE *and* JAMES GURNEY.

O me! it is my mother. How now, good lady! 220
What brings you here to court so hastily?
  Lady F. Where is that slave, thy brother? where is he,
That holds in chase mine honour up and down?
  Bast. My brother Robert? old sir Robert's son?
Colbrand the giant, that same mighty man?
Is it sir Robert's son that you seek so?
  Lady F. Sir Robert's son! Ay, thou unreverend boy,
Sir Robert's son: why scorn'st thou at sir Robert?
He is sir Robert's son, and so art thou.
  Bast. James Gurney, wilt thou give us leave awhile?
  Gur. Good leave, good Philip.
  Bast.   Philip! sparrow: James, 231
There's toys abroad: anon I'll tell thee more.
                                    [*Exit Gurney.*
Madam, I was not old sir Robert's son:
Sir Robert might have eat his part in me
Upon Good-Friday and ne'er broke his fast:
Sir Robert could do well: marry, to confess,
Could he get me? Sir Robert could not do it:
We know his handiwork: therefore, good mother,
To whom am I beholding for these limbs?
Sir Robert never holp to make this leg. 240
  Lady F. Hast thou conspired with thy brother too,
That for thine own gain shouldst defend mine honour?
What means this scorn, thou most untoward knave?
  Bast. Knight, knight, good mother, Basilisco-like.
What! I am dubb'd! I have it on my shoulder.
But, mother, I am not sir Robert's son;
I have disclaim'd sir Robert and my land;
Legitimation, name and all is gone:
Then, good my mother, let me know my father;
Some proper man, I hope: who was it, mother? 250
  Lady F. Hast thou denied thyself a Faulconbridge?
  Bast. As faithfully as I deny the devil.
  Lady F. King Richard Cœur-de-lion was thy
father:
By long and vehement suit I was seduced
To make room for him in my husband's bed:
Heaven lay not my transgression to my charge!
Thou art the issue of my dear offence,
Which was so strongly urged past my defence.
  Bast. Now, by this light, were I to get again,

Madam, I would not wish a better father. 260
Some sins do bear their privilege on earth,
And so doth yours; your fault was not your folly:
Needs must you lay your heart at his dispose,
Subjected tribute to commanding love,
Against whose fury and unmatched force
The aweless lion could not wage the fight,
Nor keep his princely heart from Richard's hand.
He that perforce robs lions of their hearts
May easily win a woman's. Ay, my mother,
With all my heart I thank thee for my father! 270
Who lives and dares but say thou didst not well
When I was got, I'll send his soul to hell.
Come, lady, I will show thee to my kin;
  And they shall say, when Richard me begot,
If thou hadst said him nay, it had been sin:
  Who says it was, he lies; I say 'twas not.   [*Exeunt.*

ACT II.

SCENE I. *France. Before Angiers.*

Enter AUSTRIA *and forces, drums, etc. on one side: on the
other* KING PHILIP *of France and his power;* LEWIS,
ARTHUR, CONSTANCE *and attendants.*

  K. Phi. Before Angiers well met, brave Austria.
Arthur, that great forerunner of thy blood,
Richard, that robb'd the lion of his heart
And fought the holy wars in Palestine,
By this brave duke came early to his grave:
And for amends to his posterity,
At our importance hither is he come,
To spread his colours, boy, in thy behalf,
And to rebuke the usurpation
Of thy unnatural uncle, English John: 10
Embrace him, love him, give him welcome hither.
  Arth. God shall forgive you Cœur-de-lion's death
The rather that you give his offspring life,
Shadowing their right under your wings of war:
I give you welcome with a powerless hand,
But with a heart full of unstained love:
Welcome before the gates of Angiers, duke.
  K. Phi. A noble boy! Who would not do thee right?
  Aust. Upon thy cheek lay I this zealous kiss,
As seal to this indenture of my love, 20
That to my home I will no more return,
Till Angiers and the right thou hast in France,
Together with that pale, that white-faced shore,
Whose foot spurns back the ocean's roaring tides
And coops from other lands her islanders,
Even till that England, hedged in with the main,
That water-walled bulwark, still secure
And confident from foreign purposes,
Even till that utmost corner of the west

Salute thee for her king: till then, fair boy, 30
Will I not think of home, but follow arms.
    Const. O, take his mother's thanks, a widow's
        thanks,
Till your strong hand shall help to give him strength
To make a more requital to your love!
    Aust. The peace of heaven is theirs that lift their
        swords
In such a just and charitable war.
    K. Phi. Well then, to work: our cannon shall be bent
Against the brows of this resisting town.
Call for our chiefest men of discipline,
To cull the plots of best advantages: 40
We'll lay before this town our royal bones,
Wade to the market-place in Frenchmen's blood,
But we will make it subject to this boy.
    Const. Stay for an answer to your embassy,
Lest unadvised you stain your swords with blood:
My Lord Chatillon may from England bring
That right in peace which here we urge in war,
And then we shall repent each drop of blood
That hot rash haste so indirectly shed.

    Enter CHATILLON.

    K. Phi. A wonder, lady! lo, upon thy wish, 50
Our messenger Chatillon is arrived!
What England says, say briefly, gentle lord;
We coldly pause for thee; Chatillon, speak.
    Chat. Then turn your forces from this paltry siege
And stir them up against a mightier task.
England, impatient of your just demands,
Hath put himself in arms: the adverse winds,
Whose leisure I have stay'd, have given him time
To land his legions all as soon as I;
His marches are expedient to this town, 60
His forces strong, his soldiers confident.
With him along is come the mother-queen,
An Ate, stirring him to blood and strife;
With her her niece, the Lady Blanch of Spain;
With them a bastard of the king's deceased;
And all the unsettled humours of the land,
Rash, inconsiderate, fiery voluntaries,
With ladies' faces and fierce dragons' spleens,
Have sold their fortunes at their native homes,
Bearing their birthrights proudly on their backs, 70
To make a hazard of new fortunes here:
In brief, a braver choice of dauntless spirits
Than now the English bottoms have waft o'er
Did never float upon the swelling tide,
To do offence and scath in Christendom. [*Drum beats.*
The interruption of their churlish drums
Cuts off more circumstance: they are at hand,
To parley or to fight; therefore prepare.
    K. Phi. How much unlook'd for is this expedition!
    Aust. By how much unexpected, by so much 80

We must awake endeavour for defence;
For courage mounteth with occasion:
Let them be welcome then; we are prepared.

    Enter KING JOHN, ELINOR, BLANCH, *the* Bastard,
        Lords, *and forces.*

    K. John. Peace be to France, if France in peace
        permit
Our just and lineal entrance to our own;
If not, bleed France, and peace ascend to heaven,
Whiles we, God's wrathful agent, do correct
Their proud contempt that beats His peace to heaven.
    K. Phi. Peace be to England, if that war return
From France to England, there to live in peace. 90
England we love; and for that England's sake
With burden of our armour here we sweat.
This toil of ours should be a work of thine;
But thou from loving England art so far,
That thou hast under-wrought his lawful king,
Cut off the sequence of posterity,
Out-faced infant state and done a rape
Upon the maiden virtue of the crown.
Look here upon thy brother Geffrey's face;
These eyes, these brows, were moulded out of his: 100
This little abstract doth contain that large
Which died in Geffrey, and the hand of time
Shall draw this brief into as huge a volume.
That Geffrey was thy elder brother born,
And this his son; England was Geffrey's right
And this is Geffrey's: in the name of God
How comes it then that thou art call'd a king,
When living blood doth in these temples beat,
Which owe the crown that thou o'ermasterest?
    K. John. From whom hast thou this great
        commission, France, 110
To draw my answer from thy articles?
    K. Phi. From that supernal judge, that stirs good
        thoughts
In any breast of strong authority,
To look into the blots and stains of right:
That judge hath made me guardian to this boy:
Under whose warrant I impeach thy wrong
And by whose help I mean to chastise it.
    K. John. Alack, thou dost usurp authority.
    K. Phi. Excuse; it is to beat usurping down.
    Eli. Who is it thou dost call usurper, France? 120
    Const. Let me make answer; thy usurping son.
    Eli. Out, insolent! thy bastard shall be king,
That thou mayst be a queen, and check the world!
    Const. My bed was ever to thy son as true
As thine was to thy husband; and this boy
Liker in feature to his father Geffrey
Than thou and John in manners; being as like
As rain to water, or devil to his dam.
My boy a bastard! By my soul, I think

2. **forerunner.** Arthur was not a descendant of Richard—if that is what is intended by this word—but a nephew; cf. l. 6. 5. **By . . . duke,** a confusion of the duke of Austria with Viscount Limoges, before whose castle Richard was mortally wounded. The roles of the two were combined in *The Troublesome Raigne* as they are in this play. 7. **importance,** importunity. 23. **pale . . . shore,** the chalk cliffs at Dover. 39. **men of discipline,** men trained in military strategy. 40. **To . . . advantages,** to select positions which are most favorable for attack (Wright). 44. **Stay,** wait; see glossary. 45. **unadvised,** unwisely. 49. **indirectly,** wrongly. 53. **coldly,** calmly. 60. **expedient,** speedy. 63. **Ate,** goddess of vengeance. 65. **of . . . deceased,** of the deceased king's. 66. **unsettled humours,** i.e., disgruntled individuals; see *humour* in glossary. 67. **voluntaries,** volunteers. 68. **ladies' faces,** beardless young men. **fierce dragons' spleens,** i.e., utmost fierceness; see *spleen* in glossary. 72. **choice,** picked company. 73. **bottoms,** keels

or hulls of ships. 77. **circumstance,** ceremony; see glossary. 85. **lineal,** by right of birth. 89. **if that,** if. 95. **under-wrought,** undermined. 96. **sequence of posterity,** lawful succession. 97. **Out-faced,** browbeat, intimidated. **infant state,** majesty of a boy-king (New Cambridge). 101. **little abstract,** miniature copy; cf. *Hamlet*, II, ii, 548. 109. **owe,** own; see glossary. 111. **articles,** clauses or stipulations of a legal document. John challenges Philip's presumption in thus chiding him. 114. **of right,** on justice. 116. **impeach,** accuse. 122. **Out,** exclamation of anger; see glossary. 123. **check,** control; see glossary. 124-128. **My . . . dam.** I am every bit as true as you were, and my Arthur far less likely to be a bastard than your son John (although he is as like you as the devil is to his dam) or for the matter of that than your son Geoffrey himself (New Cambridge). 126. **feature,** form or shape of body; see glossary.

His father never was so true begot: 130
It cannot be, an if thou wert his mother.
   Eli. There 's a good mother, boy, that blots thy
     father.
   Const. There 's a good grandam, boy, that would
     blot thee.
   Aust. Peace!
   Bast.   Hear the crier.
   Aust.   What the devil art thou?
   Bast. One that will play the devil, sir, with you,
An a' may catch your hide and you alone:
You are the hare of whom the proverb goes,
Whose valour plucks dead lions by the beard:
I'll smoke your skin-coat, an I catch you right;
Sirrah, look to 't; i' faith, I will, i' faith. 140
   Blanch. O, well did he become that lion's robe
That did disrobe the lion of that robe!
   Bast. It lies as sightly on the back of him
As great Alcides' shows upon an ass:
But, ass, I'll take that burthen from your back,
Or lay on that shall make your shoulders crack.
   Aust. What cracker is this same that deafs our ears
With this abundance of superfluous breath?
   K. Phi. Lewis, determine what we shall do straight.
   Lew. Women and fools, break off your conference.
King John, this is the very sum of all; 151
England and Ireland, Anjou, Touraine, Maine,
In right of Arthur do I claim of thee:
Wilt thou resign them and lay down thy arms?
   K. John. My life as soon: I do defy thee, France.
Arthur of Bretagne, yield thee to my hand;
And out of my dear love I'll give thee more
Than e'er the coward hand of France can win:
Submit thee, boy.
   Eli.   Come to thy grandam, child.
   Const. Do, child, go to it grandam, child; 160
Give grandam kingdom, and it grandam will
Give it a plum, a cherry, and a fig:
There 's a good grandam.
   Arth.   Good my mother, peace!
I would that I were low laid in my grave:
I am not worth this coil that 's made for me.
   Eli. His mother shames him so, poor boy, he weeps.
   Const. Now shame upon you, whether she does or no!
His grandam's wrongs, and not his mother's shames,
Draws those heaven-moving pearls from his poor eyes,
Which heaven shall take in nature of a fee; 170
Ay, with these crystal beads heaven shall be bribed
To do him justice and revenge on you.
   Eli. Thou monstrous slanderer of heaven and earth!
   Const. Thou monstrous injurer of heaven and earth!
Call not me slanderer; thou and thine usurp
The dominations, royalties and rights
Of this oppressed boy: this is thy eld'st son's son,
Infortunate in nothing but in thee:
Thy sins are visited in this poor child;
The canon of the law is laid on him, 180
Being but the second generation
Removed from thy sin-conceiving womb.
   K. John. Bedlam, have done.

   Const.   I have but this to say,
That he is not only plagued for her sin,
But God hath made her sin and her the plague
On this removed issue, plagued for her
And with her plague; her sin his injury,
Her injury the beadle to her sin,
All punish'd in the person of this child,
And all for her; a plague upon her! 190
   Eli. Thou unadvised scold, I can produce
A will that bars the title of thy son.
   Const. Ay, who doubts that? a will! a wicked will;
A woman's will; a canker'd grandam's will!
   K. Phi. Peace, lady! pause, or be more temperate:
It ill beseems this presence to cry aim
To these ill-tuned repetitions.
Some trumpet summon hither to the walls
These men of Angiers: let us hear them speak
Whose title they admit, Arthur's or John's. 200

Trumpet sounds. Enter certain Citizens *upon the walls.*

   First Cit. Who is it that hath warn'd us to the walls?
   K. Phi. 'Tis France, for England.
   K. John.   England, for itself.
You men of Angiers, and my loving subjects,—
   K. Phi. You loving men of Angiers, Arthur's
     subjects,
Our trumpet call'd you to this gentle parle—
   K. John. For our advantage; therefore hear us first.
These flags of France, that are advanced here
Before the eye and prospect of your town,
Have hither march'd to your endamagement:
The cannons have their bowels full of wrath, 210
And ready mounted are they to spit forth
Their iron indignation 'gainst your walls:
All preparation for a bloody siege
And merciless proceeding by these French
Confronts your city's eyes, your winking gates;
And but for our approach those sleeping stones,
That as a waist doth girdle you about,
By the compulsion of their ordinance
By this time from their fixed beds of lime
Had been dishabited, and wide havoc made 220
For bloody power to rush upon your peace.
But on the sight of us your lawful king,
Who painfully with much expedient march
Have brought a countercheck before your gates,
To save unscratch'd your city's threatened cheeks,
Behold, the French amazed vouchsafe a parle;
And now, instead of bullets wrapp'd in fire,
To make a shaking fever in your walls,
They shoot but calm words folded up in smoke,
To make a faithless error in your ears: 230
Which trust accordingly, kind citizens,
And let us in, your king, whose labour'd spirits,
Forwearied in this action of swift speed,
Crave harbourage within your city walls.
   K. Phi. When I have said, make answer to us both.
Lo, in this right hand, whose protection
Is most divinely vow'd upon the right
Of him it holds, stands young Plantagenet,

Son to the elder brother of this man,
And king o'er him and all that he enjoys: 240
For this down-trodden equity, we tread
In warlike march these greens before your town,
Being no further enemy to you
Than the constraint of hospitable zeal
In the relief of this oppressed child
Religiously provokes. Be pleased then
To pay that duty which you truly owe
To him that owes it, namely this young prince:
And then our arms, like to a muzzled bear,
Save in aspect, hath all offence seal'd up; 250
Our cannons' malice vainly shall be spent
Against the invulnerable clouds of heaven;
And with a blessed and unvex'd retire,
With unhack'd swords and helmets all unbruised,
We will bear home that lusty blood again
Which here we came to spout against your town,
And leave your children, wives and you in peace.
But if you fondly pass our proffer'd offer,
'Tis not the roundure of your old-faced walls
Can hide you from our messengers of war, 260
Though all these English and their discipline
Were harbour'd in their rude circumference.
Then tell us, shall your city call us lord,
In that behalf which we have challenged it?
Or shall we give the signal to our rage
And stalk in blood to our possession?
   First Cit. In brief, we are the king of England's
     subjects:
For him, and in his right, we hold this town.
   K. John. Acknowledge then the king, and let me in.
   First Cit. That can we not; but he that proves the
     king, 270
To him will we prove loyal: till that time
Have we ramm'd up our gates against the world.
   K. John. Doth not the crown of England prove the
     king?
And if not that, I bring you witnesses,
Twice fifteen thousand hearts of England's breed,—
   Bast. Bastards, and else.
   K. John. To verify our title with their lives.
   K. Phi. As many and as well-born bloods as those,—
   Bast. Some bastards too.
   K. Phi. Stand in his face to contradict his claim. 280
   First Cit. Till you compound whose right is
     worthiest,
We for the worthiest hold the right from both.
   K. John. Then God forgive the sin of all those souls
That to their everlasting residence,
Before the dew of evening fall, shall fleet,
In dreadful trial of our kingdom's king!
   K. Phi. Amen, amen! Mount, chevaliers to arms!
   Bast. Saint George, that swinged the dragon, and
     e'er since
Sits on his horse back at mine hostess' door,
Teach us some fence! [*To Aust.*] Sirrah, were I at
     home, 290
At your den, sirrah, with your lioness,
I would set an ox-head to your lion's hide,

And make a monster of you.
   Aust.   Peace! no more.
   Bast. O, tremble, for you hear the lion roar.
   K. John. Up higher to the plain; where we'll set
     forth
In best appointment all our regiments.
   Bast. Speed then, to take advantage of the field.
   K. Phi. It shall be so; and at the other hill
Command the rest to stand. God and our right!
                        [*Exeunt.*

Here after excursions, enter the Herald of France, *with
   trumpets, to the gates.*

   F. Her. You men of Angiers, open wide your gates,
And let young Arthur, Duke of Bretagne, in, 301
Who by the hand of France this day hath made
Much work for tears in many an English mother,
Whose sons lie scattered on the bleeding ground;
Many a widow's husband grovelling lies,
Coldly embracing the discolour'd earth;
And victory, with little loss, doth play
Upon the dancing banners of the French,
Who are at hand, triumphantly display'd,
To enter conquerors and to proclaim 310
Arthur of Bretagne England's king and yours.

Enter English Herald, *with trumpet.*

   E. Her. Rejoice, you men of Angiers, ring your bells;
King John, your king and England's, doth approach,
Commander of this hot malicious day:
Their armours, that march'd hence so silver-bright,
Hither return all gilt with Frenchmen's blood;
There stuck no plume in any English crest
That is removed by a staff of France;
Our colours do return in those same hands
That did display them when we first march'd forth; 320
And, like a jolly troop of huntsmen, come
Our lusty English, all with purpled hands,
Dyed in the dying slaughter of their foes:
Open your gates and give the victors way.
   First Cit. Heralds, from off our towers we might
     behold,
From first to last, the onset and retire
Of both your armies; whose equality
By our best eyes cannot be censured:
Blood hath bought blood and blows have answer'd
     blows;
Strength match'd with strength, and power
     confronted power: 330
Both are alike; and both alike we like.
One must prove greatest: while they weigh so even,
We hold our town for neither, yet for both.

Re-enter the two KINGS, *with their powers, severally.*

   K. John. France, hast thou yet more blood to cast
     away?
Say, shall the current of our right run on?
Whose passage, vex'd with thy impediment,
Shall leave his native channel and o'erswell
With course disturb'd even thy confining shores,

Unless thou let his silver water keep
A peaceful progress to the ocean. 340
    K. Phi. England, thou hast not saved one drop of
      blood,
In this hot trial, more than we of France;
Rather, lost more. And by this hand I swear,
That sways the earth this climate overlooks,
Before we will lay down our just-borne arms,
We'll put thee down, 'gainst whom these arms we
    bear,
Or add a royal number to the dead,
Gracing the scroll that tells of this war's loss
With slaughter coupled to the name of kings.
    Bast. Ha, majesty! how high thy glory towers, 350
When the rich blood of kings is set on fire!
O, now doth Death line his dead chaps with steel;
The swords of soldiers are his teeth, his fangs;
And now he feasts, mousing the flesh of men,
In undetermined differences of kings.
Why stand these royal fronts amazed thus?
Cry, 'havoc!' kings; back to the stained field,
You equal potents, fiery kindled spirits!
Then let confusion of one part confirm 359
The other's peace; till then, blows, blood and death!
    K. John. Whose party do the townsmen yet admit?
    K. Phi. Speak, citizens, for England; who 's your
      king?
    First Cit. The king of England, when we know the
      king.
    K. Phi. Know him in us, that here hold up his right.
    K. John. In us, that are our own great deputy,
And bear possession of our person here,
Lord of our presence, Angiers, and of you.
    First Cit. A greater power than we denies all this;
And till it be undoubted, we do lock
Our former scruple in our strong-barr'd gates; 370
King'd of our fears, until our fears, resolved,
Be by some certain king purged and deposed.
    Bast. By heaven, these scroyles of Angiers flout you,
      kings,
And stand securely on their battlements,
As in a theatre, whence they gape and point
At your industrious scenes and acts of death.
Your royal presences be ruled by me:
Do like the mutines of Jerusalem,
Be friends awhile and both conjointly bend
Your sharpest deeds of malice on this town: 380
By east and west let France and England mount
Their battering cannon charged to the mouths,
Till their soul-fearing clamours have brawl'd down
The flinty ribs of this contemptuous city:
I 'ld play incessantly upon these jades,
Even till unfenced desolation
Leave them as naked as the vulgar air.
That done, dissever your united strengths,
And part your mingled colours once again;
Turn face to face and bloody point to point; 390
Then, in a moment, Fortune shall cull forth

King John
ACT II : SC I

348

Out of one side her happy minion,
To whom in favour she shall give the day,
And kiss him with a glorious victory.
How like you this wild counsel, mighty states?
Smacks it not something of the policy?
    K. John. Now, by the sky that hangs above our
      heads,
I like it well. France, shall we knit our powers
And lay this Angiers even with the ground;
Then after fight who shall be king of it? 400
    Bast. An if thou hast the mettle of a king,
Being wrong'd as we are by this peevish town,
Turn thou the mouth of thy artillery,
As we will ours, against these saucy walls;
And when that we have dash'd them to the ground,
Why then defy each other, and pell-mell
Make work upon ourselves, for heaven or hell.
    K. Phi. Let it be so. Say, where will you assault?
    K. John. We from the west will send destruction
Into this city's bosom. 410
    Aust. I from the north.
    K. Phi.   Our thunder from the south
Shall rain their drift of bullets on this town.
    Bast. O prudent discipline! From north to south:
Austria and France shoot in each other's mouth:
I'll stir them to it. Come, away, away!
    First Cit. Hear us, great kings: vouchsafe awhile to
      stay,
And I shall show you peace and fair-faced league;
Win you this city without stroke or wound;
Rescue those breathing lives to die in beds,
That here come sacrifices for the field: 420
Persever not, but hear me, mighty kings.
    K. John. Speak on with favour; we are bent to hear.
    First Cit. That daughter there of Spain, the Lady
      Blanch,
Is niece to England: look upon the years
Of Lewis the Dauphin and that lovely maid:
If lusty love should go in quest of beauty,
Where should he find it fairer than in Blanch?
If zealous love should go in search of virtue,
Where should he find it purer than in Blanch?
If love ambitious sought a match of birth, 430
Whose veins bound richer blood than Lady Blanch?
Such as she is, in beauty, virtue, birth,
Is the young Dauphin every way complete:
If not complete of, say he is not she;
And she again wants nothing, to name want,
If want it be not that she is not he:
He is the half part of a blessed man,
Left to be finished by such as she;
And she a fair divided excellence,
Whose fulness of perfection lies in him. 440
O, two such silver currents, when they join,
Do glorify the banks that bound them in;
And two such shores to two such streams made one,
Two such controlling bounds shall you be, kings,
To these two princes, if you marry them.

---

344. **climate,** region. 347. **a royal number,** i.e., King Philip himself.
352. **chaps,** chops. 354. **mousing,** tearing. 355. **undetermined . . .
kings,** i.e., making no difference between the flesh of kings and that
of common men (New Cambridge). The phrase touches on an often
recurring theme in Shakespeare and in other Elizabethan literature—
that all are equal in death. 356. **royal fronts,** faces of kings; see *front*
in glossary. 358. **potents,** potentates. 359. **confusion,** destruction,
overthrow; see glossary. **part,** faction, party. 369. **it.** The antecedent is the idea expressed in line 359, the *confusion of one part.* **undoubted,** unquestioned. 371. **King'd of,** ruled by. **resolved,** dis-

solved, dissipated; see glossary. 373. **scroyles,** scoundrels. 378.
mutines, mutineers. **Jerusalem.** During the siege of Jerusalem by
Titus, two rival Jewish factions united to resist the Romans. 383. **soul-
fearing,** inspiring fear in the soul. 385. **jades,** ill-conditioned horses
(used contemptuously). 392. **minion,** favorite; see glossary. 395.
mighty states, kings, i.e., persons of state. 396. **the policy,** the art of
politics (Moore-Smith, who cites *The Taming of the Shrew*, I, i, 37:
the mathematics, the metaphysics). 402. **peevish,** stubborn; see glossary.
406. **defy,** challenge to combat; see glossary. 421. **Persever,** accented
on the second syllable. 422. **favour,** permission; see glossary. 433.

This union shall do more than battery can
To our fast-closed gates; for at this match,
With swifter spleen than powder can enforce,
The mouth of passage shall we fling wide ope,
And give you entrance: but without this match,   450
The sea enraged is not half so deaf,
Lions more confident, mountains and rocks
More free from motion, no, not Death himself
In mortal fury half so peremptory,
As we to keep this city.
    Bast.   Here 's a stay
That shakes the rotten carcass of old Death
Out of his rags! Here 's a large mouth, indeed,
That spits forth death and mountains, rocks and seas,
Talks as familiarly of roaring lions
As maids of thirteen do of puppy-dogs!   460
What cannoneer begot this lusty blood?
He speaks plain cannon fire, and smoke and bounce;
He gives the bastinado with his tongue:
Our ears are cudgell'd; not a word of his
But buffets better than a fist of France:
Zounds! I was never so bethump'd with words
Since I first call'd my brother's father dad.
    Eli. Son, list to this conjunction, make this match;
Give with our niece a dowry large enough:
For by this knot thou shalt so surely tie   470
Thy now unsured assurance to the crown,
That yon green boy shall have no sun to ripe
The bloom that promiseth a mighty fruit.
I see a yielding in the looks of France;
Mark, how they whisper: urge them while their souls
Are capable of this ambition,
Lest zeal, now melted by the windy breath
Of soft petitions, pity and remorse,
Cool and congeal again to what it was.
    First Cit. Why answer not the double majesties   480
This friendly treaty of our threaten'd town?
    K. Phi. Speak England first, that hath been forward first
To speak unto this city: what say you?
    K. John. If that the Dauphin there, thy princely son,
Can in this book of beauty read 'I love,'
Her dowry shall weigh equal with a queen:
For Anjou and fair Touraine, Maine, Poictiers,
And all that we upon this side the sea,
Except this city now by us besieged,
Find liable to our crown and dignity,   490
Shall gild her bridal bed and make her rich
In titles, honours and promotions,
As she in beauty, education, blood,
Holds hand with any princess of the world.
    K. Phi. What say'st thou, boy? look in the lady's face.
    Lew. I do, my lord; and in her eye I find
A wonder, or a wondrous miracle,
The shadow of myself form'd in her eye;
Which, being but the shadow of your son,
Becomes a sun and makes your son a shadow: 500

I do protest I never loved myself
Till now infixed I beheld myself
Drawn in the flattering table of her eye.
                    [*Whispers with Blanch.*
    Bast. Drawn in the flattering table of her eye!
Hang'd in the frowning wrinkle of her brow!
And quarter'd in her heart! he doth espy
    Himself love's traitor: this is pity now,
That, hang'd and drawn and quarter'd, there should be
In such a love so vile a lout as he.
    Blanch. My uncle's will in this respect is mine: 510
If he see aught in you that makes him like,
That any thing he sees, which moves his liking,
I can with ease translate it to my will;
Or if you will, to speak more properly,
I will enforce it easily to my love.
Further I will not flatter you, my lord,
That all I see in you is worthy love,
Than this; that nothing do I see in you,
Though churlish thoughts themselves should be your judge,
That I can find should merit any hate.   520
    K. John. What say these young ones? What say you, my niece?
    Blanch. That she is bound in honour still to do
What you in wisdom still vouchsafe to say.
    K. John. Speak then, prince Dauphin; can you love this lady?
    Lew. Nay, ask me if I can refrain from love;
For I do love her most unfeignedly.
    K. John. Then do I give Volquessen, Touraine, Maine,
Poictiers and Anjou, these five provinces,
With her to thee; and this addition more,
Full thirty thousand marks of English coin.   530
Philip of France, if thou be pleased withal,
Command thy son and daughter to join hands.
    K. Phi. It likes us well; young princes, close your hands.
    Aust. And your lips too; for I am well assured
That I did so when I was first assured.
    K. Phi. Now, citizens of Angiers, ope your gates,
Let in that amity which you have made;
For at Saint Mary's chapel presently
The rites of marriage shall be solemnized.
Is not the Lady Constance in this troop?   540
I know she is not, for this match made up
Her presence would have interrupted much:
Where is she and her son? tell me, who knows.
    Lew. She is sad and passionate at your highness' tent.
    K. Phi. And, by my faith, this league that we have made
Will give her sadness very little cure.
Brother of England, how may we content
This widow lady? In her right we came;
Which we, God knows, have turn'd another way,

complete, accomplished; see glossary. **434-440. If . . . him.** The idea here appears to be that the two young people lack only each other to be perfect in themselves. **434. complete of,** generally regarded as corrupt; *complete, oh,* and *complete so* have been offered as emendations. The New Cambridge editors suggest *complete all* (spelled *al*) which would mean "complete in every way"; but see Abbott, 171. **435. wants,** lacks; see glossary. **455. stay,** hindrance, obstacle. **462. bounce,** i.e., the noise of the cannon. **463. bastinado,** beating with a stick. **476. capable of,** susceptible to; see glossary. **477. zeal,** i.e., the French king's zeal in Arthur's behalf. The metaphor is one of melting and hardening wax (New Cambridge). **478. remorse,** compassion; see glossary. **490. liable,** subject or subservient to. **498. shadow,** image, reflection; see glossary. **503. table,** tablet; see glossary. **519. churlish,** sparing of praise. **527-528. Then . . . provinces.** The lines are identical with a corresponding passage in *The Troublesome Raigne.* **527. Volquessen,** the ancient country of the Velocasses, whose capital was Rouen (Wright). **531. withal,** with these; see glossary. **533. likes,** pleases; see glossary. **535. assured,** betrothed. **538. presently,** at once; see glossary.

To our own vantage.

K. John. We will heal up all; 550
For we'll create young Arthur Duke of Bretagne
And Earl of Richmond; and this rich fair town
We make him lord of. Call the Lady Constance;
Some speedy messenger bid her repair
To our solemnity: I trust we shall,
If not fill up the measure of her will,
Yet in some measure satisfy her so
That we shall stop her exclamation.
Go we, as well as haste will suffer us,
To this unlook'd for, unprepared pomp. 560
[Exeunt all but the Bastard.

Bast. Mad world! mad kings! mad composition!
John, to stop Arthur's title in the whole,
Hath willingly departed with a part,
And France, whose armour conscience buckled on,
Whom zeal and charity brought to the field
As God's own soldier, rounded in the ear
With that same purpose-changer, that sly devil,
That broker, that still breaks the pate of faith,
That daily break-vow, he that wins of all,
Of kings, of beggars, old men, young men, maids, 570
Who, having no external thing to lose
But the word 'maid,' cheats the poor maid of that,
That smooth-faced gentleman, tickling Commodity,
Commodity, the bias of the world,
The world, who of itself is peised well,
Made to run even upon even ground,
Till this advantage, this vile-drawing bias,
This sway of motion, this Commodity,
Makes it take head from all indifferency,
From all direction, purpose, course, intent: 580
And this same bias, this Commodity,
This bawd, this broker, this all-changing word,
Clapp'd on the outward eye of fickle France,
Hath drawn him from his own determined aid,
From a resolved and honourable war,
To a most base and vile-concluded peace.
And why rail I on this Commodity?
But for because he hath not woo'd me yet:
Not that I have the power to clutch my hand,
When his fair angels would salute my palm; 590
But for my hand, as unattempted yet,
Like a poor beggar, raileth on the rich.
Well, whiles I am a beggar, I will rail
And say there is no sin but to be rich;
And being rich, my virtue then shall be
To say there is no vice but beggary.
Since kings break faith upon commodity,
Gain, be my lord, for I will worship thee. _[Exit._

ACT III.

SCENE I. _The French_ KING'S _pavilion._

Enter CONSTANCE, ARTHUR, _and_ SALISBURY.

Const. Gone to be married! gone to swear a peace!

False blood to false blood join'd! gone to be friends!
Shall Lewis have Blanch, and Blanch those provinces?
It is not so; thou hast misspoke, misheard;
Be well advised, tell o'er thy tale again:
It cannot be; thou dost but say 'tis so:
I trust I may not trust thee; for thy word
Is but the vain breath of a common man:
Believe me, I do not believe thee, man;
I have a king's oath to the contrary. 10
Thou shalt be punish'd for thus frighting me,
For I am sick and capable of fears,
Oppress'd with wrongs and therefore full of fears,
A widow, husbandless, subject to fears,
A woman, naturally born to fears;
And though thou now confess thou didst but jest,
With my vex'd spirits I cannot take a truce,
But they will quake and tremble all this day.
What dost thou mean by shaking of thy head?
Why dost thou look so sadly on my son? 20
What means that hand upon that breast of thine?
Why holds thine eye that lamentable rheum,
Like a proud river peering o'er his bounds?
Be these sad signs confirmers of thy words?
Then speak again; not all thy former tale,
But this one word, whether thy tale be true.

Sal. As true as I believe you think them false
That give you cause to prove my saying true.

Const. O, if thou teach me to believe this sorrow,
Teach thou this sorrow how to make me die, 30
And let belief and life encounter so
As doth the fury of two desperate men
Which in the very meeting fall and die.
Lewis marry Blanch! O boy, then where art thou?
France friend with England, what becomes of me?
Fellow, be gone: I cannot brook thy sight:
This news hath made thee a most ugly man.

Sal. What other harm have I, good lady, done,
But spoke the harm that is by others done?

Const. Which harm within itself so heinous is 40
As it makes harmful all that speak of it.

Arth. I do beseech you, madam, be content.

Const. If thou, that bid'st me be content, wert grim,
Ugly and slanderous to thy mother's womb,
Full of unpleasing blots and sightless stains,
Lame, foolish, crooked, swart, prodigious,
Patch'd with foul moles and eye-offending marks,
I would not care, I then would be content,
For then I should not love thee, no, nor thou
Become thy great birth nor deserve a crown. 50
But thou art fair, and at thy birth, dear boy,
Nature and Fortune join'd to make thee great:
Of Nature's gifts thou mayst with lilies boast
And with the half-blown rose. But Fortune, O,
She is corrupted, changed and won from thee;
She adulterates hourly with thine uncle John,
And with her golden hand hath pluck'd on France
To tread down fair respect of sovereignty,
And made his majesty the bawd to theirs.

---

550. **vantage,** advantage; see glossary. 563. **departed with,** given up; see glossary. 566. **rounded,** whispered. 567. **purpose-changer,** turncoat, timeserver. 574. **bias,** swaying influence; see glossary. 575. **peised,** poised, in equilibrium.

ACT III. SCENE I. 22. **lamentable rheum,** tears. 28. **prove,** find out by experience; see glossary. 36. **brook,** endure; see glossary. 45. **sightless,** unsightly. 65. **under-bear,** endure. 69-74: **For . . . it.** Several conjectures and explanations have been offered to elucidate this passage; most favored is Hanmer's _stout_ for _stoop_ (l. 69). Malone finds the difficulty in a too sudden "bounding" from one idea to another.

The New Cambridge editors suggest the image of grief as a crown too heavy to be borne. The obscurity is due less to the inconsistency of the image than to the order of its presentation. The metaphor has two aspects: Constance conceives of her grief as a master before whom she must stoop in acknowledgment of his power; at the same time she identifies herself as the supporter or medium of that grief. The two images are not consecutive but parallel. In the second aspect of the figure she conceives of her grief—and of herself as the embodiment of that grief—as a person of state to whom kings must come; and only the earth itself is firm enough to serve as a throne to sustain her. 82, 83.

France is a bawd to Fortune and King John, 60
That strumpet Fortune, that usurping John!
Tell me, thou fellow, is not France forsworn?
Envenom him with words, or get thee gone
And leave those woes alone which I alone
Am bound to under-bear.
   Sal.   Pardon me, madam,
I may not go without you to the kings.
   Const. Thou mayst, thou shalt; I will not go with
      thee:
I will instruct my sorrows to be proud;
For grief is proud and makes his owner stoop.
To me and to the state of my great grief 70
Let kings assemble; for my grief 's so great
That no supporter but the huge firm earth
Can hold it up: here I and sorrows sit;
Here is my throne, bid kings come bow to it.
                  [Seats herself on the ground.

Enter KING JOHN, KING PHILIP, LEWIS, BLANCH,
  ELINOR, *the* BASTARD, AUSTRIA, *and* Attendants.

   K. Phi. 'Tis true, fair daughter; and this blessed day
Ever in France shall be kept festival:
To solemnize this day the glorious sun
Stays in his course and plays the alchemist,
Turning with splendour of his precious eye
The meagre cloddy earth to glittering gold: 80
The yearly course that brings this day about
Shall never see it but a holiday.
   Const. A wicked day, and not a holy day!   *[Rising.*
What hath this day deserved? what hath it done,
That it in golden letters should be set
Among the high tides in the calendar?
Nay, rather turn this day out of the week,
This day of shame, oppression, perjury.
Or, if it must stand still, let wives with child
Pray that their burthens may not fall this day, 90
Lest that their hopes prodigiously be cross'd:
But on this day let seamen fear no wreck;
No bargains break that are not this day made:
This day, all things begun come to ill end,
Yea, faith itself to hollow falsehood change!
   K. Phi. By heaven, lady, you shall have no cause
To curse the fair proceedings of this day:
Have I not pawn'd to you my majesty?
   Const. You have beguiled me with a counterfeit
Resembling majesty, which, being touch'd and tried,
Proves valueless: you are forsworn, forsworn; 101
You came in arms to spill mine enemies' blood,
But now in arms you strengthen it with yours:
The grappling vigour and rough frown of war
Is cold in amity and painted peace,
And our oppression hath made up this league.
Arm, arm, you heavens, against these perjured kings!
A widow cries; be husband to me, heavens!
Let not the hours of this ungodly day
Wear out the day in peace; but, ere sunset, 110
Set armed discord 'twixt these perjured kings!

Hear me, O, hear me!
   Aust.   Lady Constance, peace!
   Const. War! war! no peace! peace is to me a war.
O Lymoges! O Austria! thou dost shame
That bloody spoil: thou slave, thou wretch, thou
      coward!
Thou little valiant, great in villany!
Thou ever strong upon the stronger side!
Thou Fortune's champion that dost never fight
But when her humorous ladyship is by
To teach thee safety! thou art perjured too, 120
And soothest up greatness. What a fool art thou,
A ramping fool, to brag and stamp and swear
Upon my party! Thou cold-blooded slave,
Hast thou not spoke like thunder on my side,
Been sworn my soldier, bidding me depend
Upon thy stars, thy fortune and thy strength,
And dost thou now fall over to my foes?
Thou wear a lion's hide! doff it for shame,
And hang a calf's-skin on those recreant limbs. 129
   Aust. O, that a man should speak those words to me!
   Bast. And hang a calf's-skin on those recreant limbs.
   Aust. Thou darest not say so, villain, for thy life.
   Bast. And hang a calf's-skin on those recreant limbs.
   K. John. We like not this; thou dost forget thyself.

Enter PANDULPH.

   K. Phi. Here comes the holy legate of the pope.
   Pand. Hail, you anointed deputies of heaven!
To thee, King John, my holy errand is.
I Pandulph, of fair Milan cardinal,
And from Pope Innocent the legate here,
Do in his name religiously demand 140
Why thou against the church, our holy mother,
So wilfully dost spurn; and force perforce
Keep Stephen Langton, chosen archbishop
Of Canterbury, from that holy see?
This, in our foresaid holy father's name,
Pope Innocent, I do demand of thee.
   K. John. What earthy name to interrogatories
Can task the free breath of a sacred king?
Thou canst not, cardinal, devise a name
So slight, unworthy and ridiculous, 150
To charge me to an answer, as the pope.
Tell him this tale; and from the mouth of England
Add thus much more, that no Italian priest
Shall tithe or toll in our dominions;
But as we, under heaven, are supreme head,
So under Him that great supremacy,
Where we do reign, we will alone uphold,
Without the assistance of a mortal hand:
So tell the pope, all reverence set apart
To him and his usurp'd authority. 160
   K. Phi. Brother of England, you blaspheme in this.
   K. John. Though you and all the kings of
      Christendom
Are led so grossly by this meddling priest,
Dreading the curse that money may buy out;

And by the merit of vile gold, dross, dust,
Purchase corrupted pardon of a man,
Who in that sale sells pardon from himself,
Though you and all the rest so grossly led
This juggling witchcraft with revenue cherish,
Yet I alone, alone do me oppose   170
Against the pope and count his friends my foes.
    Pand. Then, by the lawful power that I have,
Thou shalt stand cursed and excommunicate:
And blessed shall he be that doth revolt
From his allegiance to an heretic;
And meritorious shall that hand be call'd,
Canonized and worshipp'd as a saint,
That takes away by any secret course
Thy hateful life.
    Const.   O, lawful let it be
That I have room with Rome to curse awhile!   180
Good father cardinal, cry thou amen
To my keen curses; for without my wrong
There is no tongue hath power to curse him right.
    Pand. There 's law and warrant, lady, for my curse.
    Const. And for mine too: when law can do no right,
Let it be lawful that law bar no wrong:
Law cannot give my child his kingdom here,
For he that holds his kingdom holds the law;
Therefore, since law itself is perfect wrong,
How can the law forbid my tongue to curse?   190
    Pand. Philip of France, on peril of a curse,
Let go the hand of that arch-heretic;
And raise the power of France upon his head,
Unless he do submit himself to Rome.
    Eli. Look'st thou pale, France? do not let go thy
    hand.
    Const. Look to that, devil; lest that France repent,
And by disjoining hands, hell lose a soul.
    Aust. King Philip, listen to the cardinal.
    Bast. And hang a calf's-skin on his recreant limbs.
    Aust. Well, ruffian, I must pocket up these wrongs,
Because—
    Bast.   Your breeches best may carry
    them.   201
    K. John. Philip, what say'st thou to the cardinal?
    Const. What should he say, but as the cardinal?
    Lew. Bethink you, father; for the difference
Is purchase of a heavy curse from Rome,
Or the light loss of England for a friend:
Forego the easier.
    Blanch.   That 's the curse of Rome.
    Const. O Lewis, stand fast! the devil tempts thee
    here
In likeness of a new untrimmed bride.
    Blanch. The Lady Constance speaks not from her
    faith,   210
But from her need.
    Const.   O, if thou grant my need,
Which only lives but by the death of faith,
That need must needs infer this principle,
That faith would live again by death of need.
O then, tread down my need, and faith mounts up;

Keep my need up, and faith is trodden down!
    K. John. The king is moved, and answers not to this.
    Const. O, be removed from him, and answer well!
    Aust. Do so, King Philip; hang no more in doubt.
    Bast. Hang nothing but a calf's-skin, most sweet
    lout.   220
    K. Phi. I am perplex'd, and know not what to say.
    Pand. What canst thou say but will perplex thee
    more,
If thou stand excommunicate and cursed?
    K. Phi. Good reverend father, make my person
    yours,
And tell me how you would bestow yourself.
This royal hand and mine are newly knit,
And the conjunction of our inward souls
Married in league, coupled and link'd together
With all religious strength of sacred vows;
The latest breath that gave the sound of words   230
Was deep-sworn faith, peace, amity, true love
Between our kingdoms and our royal selves,
And even before this truce, but new before,
No longer than we well could wash our hands
To clap this royal bargain up of peace,
Heaven knows, they were besmear'd and overstain'd
With slaughter's pencil, where revenge did paint
The fearful difference of incensed kings:
And shall these hands, so lately purged of blood,
So newly join'd in love, so strong in both,   240
Unyoke this seizure and this kind regreet?
Play fast and loose with faith? so jest with heaven,
Make such unconstant children of ourselves,
As now again to snatch our palm from palm,
Unswear faith sworn, and on the marriage-bed
Of smiling peace to march a bloody host,
And make a riot on the gentle brow
Of true sincerity? O, holy sir,
My reverend father, let it not be so!
Out of your grace, devise, ordain, impose   250
Some gentle order; and then we shall be blest
To do your pleasure and continue friends.
    Pand. All form is formless, order orderless,
Save what is opposite to England's love.
Therefore to arms! be champion of our church,
Or let the church, our mother, breathe her curse,
A mother's curse, on her revolting son.
France, thou mayst hold a serpent by the tongue,
A chafed lion by the mortal paw,
A fasting tiger safer by the tooth,   260
Than keep in peace that hand which thou dost hold.
    K. Phi. I may disjoin my hand, but not my faith.
    Pand. So makest thou faith an enemy to faith;
And like a civil war set'st oath to oath,
Thy tongue against thy tongue. O, let thy vow
First made to heaven, first be to heaven perform'd,
That is, to be the champion of our church!
What since thou sworest is sworn against thyself
And may not be performed by thyself,
For that which thou hast sworn to do amiss   270
Is not amiss when it is truly done,

167. **from himself,** i.e., not from God (New Cambridge). 180. **room, Rome,** an obvious pun; cf. *Julius Caesar*, I, ii, 156. 200. **pocket up,** submit to. 205. **purchase,** acquisition; see glossary. 209. **new untrimmed,** a phrase variously explained: newly divested of her bridal trimmings (John); with her hair hanging loose after the fashion of brides (Onions); *new and trimmed, new untamed, new betrimmed, new up-trimmed, new-intervened* are some of the suggested corrections. Constance may mean that the marriage had been arranged and performed with such dispatch that the bride was not adorned (trimmed) in the usual

manner. 224. **make . . . yours,** put yourself in my place. 228. **Married, coupled, link'd.** The auxiliary verb *are* (l. 226) is understood with these verbs. 233. **new before,** recently. 235. **clap . . . up,** conclude with a handshake. 237. **pencil,** brush. 238. **difference,** dissension; see glossary. 240. **in both,** i.e., blood and love. 241. **Unyoke this seizure,** disjoin this handclasp. **regreet,** greeting. 242. **Play . . . loose.** Cf. *Love's Labour's Lost*, I, ii, 162, note. 265-266. **thy vow . . . heaven,** i.e., his coronation vow to defend the church. 268-273. **What . . . it.** What you have sworn since then is sworn against yourself and cannot be per-

And being not done, where doing tends to ill,
The truth is then most done not doing it:
The better act of purposes mistook
Is to mistake again; though indirect,
Yet indirection thereby grows direct,
And falsehood falsehood cures, as fire cools fire
Within the scorched veins of one new-burn'd.
It is religion that doth make vows kept;
But thou hast sworn against religion, 280
By what thou swear'st against the thing thou swear'st,
And makest an oath the surety for thy truth
Against an oath: †the truth thou art unsure
To swear, swears only not to be forsworn;
Else what a mockery should it be to swear!
But thou dost swear only to be forsworn;
And most forsworn, to keep what thou dost swear.
Therefore thy later vows against thy first
Is in thyself rebellion to thyself;
And better conquest never canst thou make 290
Than arm thy constant and thy nobler parts
Against these giddy loose suggestions:
Upon which better part our prayers come in,
If thou vouchsafe them. But if not, then know
The peril of our curses light on thee
So heavy as thou shalt not shake them off,
But in despair die under their black weight.
    Aust. Rebellion, flat rebellion!
    Bast.   Will 't not be?
Will not a calf's-skin stop that mouth of thine?
    Lew. Father, to arms!
    Blanch.   Upon thy wedding-day? 300
Against the blood that thou hast married?
What, shall our feast be kept with slaughter'd men?
Shall braying trumpets and loud churlish drums,
Clamours of hell, be measures to our pomp?
O husband, hear me! ay, alack, how new
Is husband in my mouth! even for that name,
Which till this time my tongue did ne'er pronounce,
Upon my knee I beg, go not to arms
Against mine uncle.
    Const.   O, upon my knee,
Made hard with kneeling, I do pray to thee, 310
Thou virtuous Dauphin, alter not the doom
Forethought by heaven!
    Blanch. Now shall I see thy love: what motive may
Be stronger with thee than the name of wife?
    Const. That which upholdeth him that thee upholds,
His honour: O, thine honour, Lewis, thine honour!
    Lew. I muse your majesty doth seem so cold,
When such profound respects do pull you on.
    Pand. I will denounce a curse upon his head.
    K. Phi. Thou shalt not need. England, I will fall
      from thee. 320
    Const. O fair return of banish'd majesty!
    Eli. O foul revolt of French inconstancy!
    K. John. France, thou shalt rue this hour within this
      hour.
    Bast. Old Time the clock-setter, that bald sexton
      Time,

Is it as he will? well then, France shall rue.
    Blanch. The sun 's o'ercast with blood: fair day,
      adieu!
Which is the side that I must go withal?
I am with both: each army hath a hand;
And in their rage, I having hold of both,
They whirl asunder and dismember me. 330
Husband, I cannot pray that thou mayst win;
Uncle, I needs must pray that thou mayst lose;
Father, I may not wish the fortune thine;
Grandam, I will not wish thy wishes thrive:
Whoever wins, on that side shall I lose;
Assured loss before the match be play'd.
    Lew. Lady, with me, with me thy fortune lies.
    Blanch. There where my fortune lives, there my life
      dies.
    K. John. Cousin, go draw our puissance together.
                      [*Exit Bastard.*
France, I am burn'd up with inflaming wrath; 340
A rage whose heat hath this condition,
That nothing can allay, nothing but blood,
The blood, and dearest-valued blood, of France.
    K. Phi. Thy rage shall burn thee up, and thou shalt
      turn
To ashes, ere our blood shall quench that fire:
Look to thyself, thou art in jeopardy.
    K. John. No more than he that threats. To arms
      let 's hie!   [*Exeunt.*

SCENE II. *The same. Plains near Angiers.*

Alarums, excursions. Enter the BASTARD, *with* AUSTRIA'S
  head.

    Bast. Now, by my life, this day grows wondrous hot;
Some airy devil hovers in the sky
And pours down mischief. Austria's head lie there,
While Philip breathes.

Enter KING JOHN, ARTHUR, *and* HUBERT.
    K. John. Hubert, keep this boy. Philip, make up:
My mother is assailed in our tent,
And ta'en, I fear.
    Bast.   My lord, I rescued her;
Her highness is in safety, fear you not:
But on, my liege; for very little pains
Will bring this labour to an happy end.   [*Exeunt.* 10

SCENE III. *The same.*

Alarums, excursions, retreat. Enter KING JOHN, ELINOR,
ARTHUR, *the* BASTARD, HUBERT, *and* Lords.

    K. John. [*To Elinor*] So shall it be; your grace shall
      stay behind
So strongly guarded. [*To Arthur*] Cousin, look not sad:
Thy grandam loves thee; and thy uncle will
As dear be to thee as thy father was.

Arth. O, this will make my mother die with grief!

K. John. [*To the Bastard*] Cousin, away for England!
    haste before:
And, ere our coming, see thou shake the bags
Of hoarding abbots; imprisoned angels
Set at liberty: the fat ribs of peace
Must by the hungry now be fed upon: 10
Use our commission in his utmost force.

    Bast. Bell, book, and candle shall not drive me
    back,
When gold and silver becks me to come on.
I leave your highness. Grandam, I will pray,
If ever I remember to be holy,
For your fair safety; so, I kiss your hand.

    Eli. Farewell, gentle cousin.

    K. John.   Coz, farewell. [*Exit Bastard.*

    Eli. Come hither, little kinsman; hark, a word.

    K. John. Come hither, Hubert. O my gentle Hubert,
We owe thee much! within this wall of flesh   20
There is a soul counts thee her creditor
And with advantage means to pay thy love:
And, my good friend, thy voluntary oath
Lives in this bosom, dearly cherished.
Give me thy hand. I had a thing to say,
But I will fit it with some better time.
By heaven, Hubert, I am almost ashamed
To say what good respect I have of thee.

    Hub. I am much bounden to your majesty.

    K. John. Good friend, thou hast no cause to say so
    yet,   30
But thou shalt have; and creep time ne'er so slow,
Yet it shall come for me to do thee good.
I had a thing to say, but let it go:
The sun is in the heaven, and the proud day,
Attended with the pleasures of the world,
Is all too wanton and too full of gawds
To give me audience: if the midnight bell
Did, with his iron tongue and brazen mouth,
Sound on into the drowsy race of night;
If this same were a churchyard where we stand,   40
And thou possessed with a thousand wrongs,
Or if that surly spirit, melancholy,
Had baked thy blood and made it heavy-thick,
Which else runs tickling up and down the veins,
Making that idiot, laughter, keep men's eyes
And strain their cheeks to idle merriment—
A passion hateful to my purposes;
Or if that thou couldst see me without eyes,
Hear me without thine ears, and make reply
Without a tongue, using conceit alone,   50
Without eyes, ears and harmful sound of words;
Then, in despite of brooded watchful day,
I would into thy bosom pour my thoughts:
But, ah, I will not! yet I love thee well;
And, by my troth, I think thou lovest me well.

    Hub. So well, that what you bid me undertake,
Though that my death were adjunct to my act,
By heaven, I would do it.

    K. John.   Do not I know thou wouldst?
Good Hubert, Hubert, Hubert, throw thine eye

On yon young boy: I'll tell thee what, my friend,   60
He is a very serpent in my way;
And wheresoe'er this foot of mine doth tread,
He lies before me: dost thou understand me?
Thou art his keeper.

    Hub.   And I'll keep him so,
That he shall not offend your majesty.

    K. John.   Death.

    Hub. My lord?

    K. John.   A grave.

    Hub.   He shall not live.

    K. John.   Enough.
I could be merry now. Hubert, I love thee;
Well, I'll not say what I intend for thee:
Remember. Madam, fare you well:
I'll send those powers o'er to your majesty.   70

    Eli. My blessing go with thee!

    K. John.   For England, cousin, go:
Hubert shall be your man, attend on you
With all true duty. On toward Calais, ho!   [*Exeunt.*

SCENE IV. *The same. The French* KING'S *tent.*

Enter KING PHILIP, LEWIS, PANDULPH, *and*
    Attendants.

    K. Phi. So, by a roaring tempest on the flood,
A whole armado of convicted sail
Is scatter'd and disjoin'd from fellowship.

    Pand. Courage and comfort! all shall yet go well.

    K. Phi. What can go well, when we have run so ill?
Are we not beaten? Is not Angiers lost?
Arthur ta'en prisoner? divers dear friends slain?
And bloody England into England gone,
O'erbearing interruption, spite of France?

    Lew. What he hath won, that hath he fortified: 10
So hot a speed with such advice disposed,
Such temperate order in so fierce a cause,
Doth want example: who hath read or heard
Of any kindred action like to this?

    K. Phi. Well could I bear that England had this
    praise,
So we could find some pattern of our shame.

Enter CONSTANCE.

Look, who comes here! a grave unto a soul;
Holding the eternal spirit, against her will,
In the vile prison of afflicted breath.
I prithee, lady, go away with me.   20

    Const. Lo, now! now see the issue of your peace.

    K. Phi. Patience, good lady! comfort, gentle
    Constance!

    Const. No, I defy all counsel, all redress,
But that which ends all counsel, true redress,
Death, death; O amiable lovely death!
Thou odoriferous stench! sound rottenness!
Arise forth from the couch of lasting night,
Thou hate and terror to prosperity,
And I will kiss thy detestable bones
And put my eyeballs in thy vaulty brows   30

And ring these fingers with thy household worms
And stop this gap of breath with fulsome dust
And be a carrion monster like thyself:
Come, grin on me, and I will think thou smilest
And buss thee as thy wife. Misery's love,
O, come to me!
    K. Phi.   O fair affliction, peace!
    Const. No, no, I will not, having breath to cry:
O, that my tongue were in the thunder's mouth!
Then with a passion would I shake the world;
And rouse from sleep that fell anatomy   40
Which cannot hear a lady's feeble voice,
Which scorns a modern invocation.
    Pand. Lady, you utter madness, and not sorrow.
    Const. Thou art not holy to belie me so;
I am not mad: this hair I tear is mine;
My name is Constance; I was Geffrey's wife;
Young Arthur is my son, and he is lost:
I am not mad: I would to heaven I were!
For then, 'tis like I should forget myself:
O, if I could, what grief should I forget!   50
Preach some philosophy to make me mad,
And thou shalt be canonized, cardinal;
For being not mad but sensible of grief,
My reasonable part produces reason
How I may be deliver'd of these woes,
And teaches me to kill or hang myself:
If I were mad, I should forget my son,
Or madly think a babe of clouts were he:
I am not mad; too well, too well I feel
The different plague of each calamity.   60
    K. Phi. Bind up those tresses. O, what love I note
In the fair multitude of those her hairs!
Where but by chance a silver drop hath fallen,
Even to that drop ten thousand wiry friends
Do glue themselves in sociable grief,
Like true, inseparable, faithful loves,
Sticking together in calamity.
    Const. To England, if you will.
    K. Phi.   Bind up your hairs.
    Const. Yes, that I will; and wherefore will I do it?
I tore them from their bonds and cried aloud   70
'O that these hands could so redeem my son,
As they have given these hairs their liberty!'
But now I envy at their liberty,
And will again commit them to their bonds,
Because my poor child is a prisoner.
And, father cardinal, I have heard you say
That we shall see and know our friends in heaven:
If that be true, I shall see my boy again;
For since the birth of Cain, the first male child,
To him that did but yesterday suspire,   80
There was not such a gracious creature born.
But now will canker sorrow eat my bud
And chase the native beauty from his cheek
And he will look as hollow as a ghost,
As dim and meagre as an ague's fit,
And so he'll die; and, rising so again,
When I shall meet him in the court of heaven
I shall not know him: therefore never, never

Must I behold my pretty Arthur more.
    Pand. You hold too heinous a respect of grief.   90
    Const. He talks to me that never had a son.
    K. Phi. You are as fond of grief as of your child.
    Const. Grief fills the room up of my absent child,
Lies in his bed, walks up and down with me,
Puts on his pretty looks, repeats his words,
Remembers me of all his gracious parts,
Stuffs out his vacant garments with his form;
Then, have I reason to be fond of grief?
Fare you well: had you such a loss as I,
I could give better comfort than you do.   100
I will not keep this form upon my head,
When there is such disorder in my wit.
O Lord! my boy, my Arthur, my fair son!
My life, my joy, my food, my all the world!
My widow-comfort, and my sorrows' cure!   [*Exit.*
    K. Phi. I fear some outrage, and I'll follow her. [*Exit.*
    Lew. There's nothing in this world can make me joy:
Life is as tedious as a twice-told tale
Vexing the dull ear of a drowsy man;
And bitter shame hath spoil'd the sweet world's taste,
That it yields nought but shame and bitterness.   111
    Pand. Before the curing of a strong disease,
Even in the instant of repair and health,
The fit is strongest; evils that take leave,
On their departure most of all show evil:
What have you lost by losing of this day?
    Lew. All days of glory, joy and happiness.
    Pand. If you had won it, certainly you had.
No, no; when Fortune means to men most good,
She looks upon them with a threatening eye.   120
'Tis strange to think how much King John hath lost
In this which he accounts so clearly won:
Are not you grieved that Arthur is his prisoner?
    Lew. As heartily as he is glad he hath him.
    Pand. Your mind is all as youthful as your blood.
Now hear me speak with a prophetic spirit;
For even the breath of what I mean to speak
Shall blow each dust, each straw, each little rub,
Out of the path which shall directly lead
Thy foot to England's throne; and therefore mark. 130
John hath seized Arthur; and it cannot be
That, whiles warm life plays in that infant's veins,
The misplaced John should entertain an hour,
One minute, nay, one quiet breath of rest.
A sceptre snatch'd with an unruly hand
Must be as boisterously maintain'd as gain'd;
And he that stands upon a slippery place
Makes nice of no vile hold to stay him up:
That John may stand, then Arthur needs must fall;
So be it, for it cannot be but so.   140
    Lew. But what shall I gain by young Arthur's fall?
    Pand. You, in the right of Lady Blanch your wife,
May then make all the claim that Arthur did.
    Lew. And lose it, life and all, as Arthur did.
    Pand. How green you are and fresh in this old world!
John lays you plots; the times conspire with you;
For he that steeps his safety in true blood
Shall find but bloody safety and untrue.

place; see glossary. **53. sensible of,** capable of feeling; see glossary.
58. babe of clouts, rag doll. **68. To England.** Many ingenious
attempts have been made to explain the connection of this speech with
the context, to which it has no apparent relation; the most generally
accepted is that it is Constance's answer to Philip's invitation at line
20. The New Cambridge editors regard the difficulty as evidence of
text revision (cf. their Introduction, xlix-l). **96. Remembers,** reminds.
101. keep . . . head. Some stage business accompanies the line. Most

editors introduce a stage direction here, indicating that she tears off
her headdress or loosens her hair. **128. rub,** obstacle; see glossary.
138. Makes nice of, is scrupulous about; see *makes* and *nice* in glossary.
146. lays you plots, i.e., plots by which you will profit. **147. true
blood,** blood of a true prince.

This act so evilly born shall cool the hearts
Of all his people and freeze up their zeal, 150
That none so small advantage shall step forth
To check his reign, but they will cherish it;
No natural exhalation in the sky,
No scope of nature, no distemper'd day,
No common wind, no customed event,
But they will pluck away his natural cause
And call them meteors, prodigies and signs,
Abortives, presages and tongues of heaven,
Plainly denouncing vengeance upon John.
　Lew. May be he will not touch young Arthur's life,
But hold himself safe in his prisonment. 161
　Pand. O, sir, when he shall hear of your approach,
If that young Arthur be not gone already,
Even at that news he dies; and then the hearts
Of all his people shall revolt from him
And kiss the lips of unacquainted change
And pick strong matter of revolt and wrath
Out of the bloody fingers' ends of John.
Methinks I see this hurly all on foot:
And, O, what better matter breeds for you 170
Than I have named! The bastard Faulconbridge
Is now in England, ransacking the church,
Offending charity: if but a dozen French
Were there in arms, they would be as a call
To train ten thousand English to their side,
Or as a little snow, tumbled about,
Anon becomes a mountain. O noble Dauphin,
Go with me to the king: 'tis wonderful
What may be wrought out of their discontent,
Now that their souls are topfull of offence. 180
For England go: I will whet on the king.
　Lew. Strong reasons make strong actions: let us go:
If you say ay, the king will not say no. 　　*[Exeunt.*

ACT IV.

SCENE I. *A room in a castle.*

Enter HUBERT *and* Executioners.

　Hub. Heat me these irons hot; and look thou stand
Within the arras: when I strike my foot
Upon the bosom of the ground, rush forth,
And bind the boy which you shall find with me
Fast to the chair: be heedful: hence, and watch.
　First Exec. I hope your warrant will bear out the
　　deed.
　Hub. Uncleanly scruples! fear not you: look to 't.
　　　　　　　　　　[Exeunt Executioners.
Young lad, come forth; I have to say with you.

Enter ARTHUR.

　Arth. Good morrow, Hubert.
　Hub. 　　　　　Good morrow, little prince.
　Arth. As little prince, having so great a title 10
To be more prince, as may be. You are sad.
　Hub. Indeed, I have been merrier.
　Arth. 　　　　　Mercy on me!
Methinks no body should be sad but I:

Yet, I remember, when I was in France,
Young gentlemen would be as sad as night,
Only for wantonness. By my christendom,
So I were out of prison and kept sheep,
I should be as merry as the day is long;
And so I would be here, but that I doubt
My uncle practises more harm to me: 20
He is afraid of me and I of him:
Is it my fault that I was Geffrey's son?
No, indeed, is 't not; and I would to heaven
I were your son, so you would love me, Hubert.
　Hub. [*Aside*] If I talk to him, with his innocent prate
He will awake my mercy which lies dead:
Therefore I will be sudden and dispatch.
　Arth. Are you sick, Hubert? you look pale to-day:
In sooth, I would you were a little sick,
That I might sit all night and watch with you: 30
I warrant I love you more than you do me.
　Hub. [*Aside*] His words do take possession of my
　　bosom.
Read here, young Arthur. 　　　*[Showing a paper.*
　　　　　　[*Aside*] How now, foolish rheum!
Turning dispiteous torture out of door!
I must be brief, lest resolution drop
Out at mine eyes in tender womanish tears.
Can you not read it? is it not fair writ?
　Arth. Too fairly, Hubert, for so foul effect:
Must you with hot irons burn out both mine eyes?
　Hub. Young boy, I must.
　Arth. 　　　　　And will you?
　Hub. 　　　　　　　　And I will. 40
　Arth. Have you the heart? When your head did but
　　ache,
I knit my handkercher about your brows,
The best I had, a princess wrought it me,
And I did never ask it you again;
And with my hand at midnight held your head,
And like the watchful minutes to the hour,
Still and anon cheer'd up the heavy time,
Saying, 'What lack you?' and 'Where lies your grief?'
Or 'What good love may I perform for you?'
Many a poor man's son would have lien still 50
And ne'er have spoke a loving word to you;
But you at your sick service had a prince.
Nay, you may think my love was crafty love
And call it cunning: do, an if you will:
If heaven be pleased that you must use me ill,
Why then you must. Will you put out mine eyes?
These eyes that never did nor never shall
So much as frown on you.
　Hub. 　　　　　I have sworn to do it;
And with hot irons must I burn them out.
　Arth. Ah, none but in this iron age would do it! 60
The iron of itself, though heat red-hot,
Approaching near these eyes, would drink my tears
And quench his fiery indignation
Even in the matter of mine innocence;
Nay, after that, consume away in rust,
But for containing fire to harm mine eye.
Are you more stubborn-hard than hammer'd iron?
An if an angel should have come to me

151. **none . . . forth,** no benefit will be too small. 153-157. **exhalation
. . . meteors.** Such phenomena were regarded as omens of disaster
to princes and states; cf. *Julius Caesar*, II, ii, 30-31; *1 Henry VI*, I, i, 2.
158. **Abortives,** untimely or monstrous births. 166. **kiss . . . change,**
i.e., welcome any change. 169. **hurly,** commotion. 173. **Offending
charity,** violating the instruments of charity. 174. **call,** decoy. 175.
train, attract; see glossary.

ACT IV. SCENE I. 1. **look,** take care; see glossary. 7. **Uncleanly,**
improper. 10-11. **having . . . prince,** i.e., entitled to be greater.
16. **wantonness,** playful or frolicsome behavior. **By my christendom,**
as I am a Christian. 19. **doubt,** fear; see glossary. 20. **practises,**
plots; see glossary. 34. **dispiteous,** pitiless. 37. **fair,** handsomely; see
glossary. 52. **your sick service,** service when you were sick. 64.
matter . . . innocence, substance which betokens my innocence—the

And told me Hubert should put out mine eyes,
I would not have believed him,—no tongue but
    Hubert's. 70
Hub. Come forth. [*Stamps*.

    Re-enter Executioners, *with a cord, irons, &c.*

Do as I bid you do.
    Arth. O, save me, Hubert, save me! my eyes are out
Even with the fierce looks of these bloody men.
    Hub. Give me the iron, I say, and bind him here.
    Arth. Alas, what need you be so boisterous-rough?
I will not struggle, I will stand stone-still.
For heaven sake, Hubert, let me not be bound!
Nay, hear me, Hubert, drive these men away,
And I will sit as quiet as a lamb; 80
I will not stir, nor wince, nor speak a word,
Nor look upon the iron angerly:
Thrust but these men away, and I'll forgive you,
Whatever torment you do put me to.
    Hub. Go, stand within; let me alone with him.
    First Exec. I am best pleased to be from such a deed.
              [*Exeunt Executioners*.
    Arth. Alas, I then have chid away my friend!
He hath a stern look, but a gentle heart:
Let him come back, that his compassion may
Give life to yours.
    Hub.   Come, boy, prepare yourself. 90
    Arth. Is there no remedy?
    Hub.   None, but to lose your eyes.
    Arth. O heaven, that there were but a mote in yours,
A grain, a dust, a gnat, a wandering hair,
Any annoyance in that precious sense!
Then feeling what small things are boisterous there,
Your vile intent must needs seem horrible.
    Hub. Is this your promise? go to, hold your tongue.
    Arth. Hubert, the utterance of a brace of tongues
Must needs want pleading for a pair of eyes:
Let me not hold my tongue, let me not, Hubert; 100
Or, Hubert, if you will, cut out my tongue,
So I may keep mine eyes: O, spare mine eyes,
Though to no use but still to look on you!
Lo, by my troth, the instrument is cold
And would not harm me.
    Hub.   I can heat it, boy.
    Arth. No, in good sooth; the fire is dead with grief,
Being create for comfort, to be used
In undeserved extremes: see else yourself;
There is no malice in this burning coal;
The breath of heaven hath blown his spirit out 110
And strew'd repentant ashes on his head.
    Hub. But with my breath I can revive it, boy.
    Arth. An if you do, you will but make it blush
And glow with shame of your proceedings, Hubert:
Nay, it perchance will sparkle in your eyes;
And like a dog that is compell'd to fight,
Snatch at his master that doth tarre him on.
All things that you should use to do me wrong
Deny their office: only you do lack
That mercy which fierce fire and iron extends, 120
Creatures of note for mercy-lacking uses.
    Hub. Well, see to live; I will not touch thine eye

For all the treasure that thine uncle owes:
Yet am I sworn and I did purpose, boy,
With this same very iron to burn them out.
    Arth. O, now you look like Hubert! all this while
You were disguised.
    Hub.   Peace; no more. Adieu.
Your uncle must not know but you are dead;
I'll fill these dogged spies with false reports:
And, pretty child, sleep doubtless and secure, 130
That Hubert, for the wealth of all the world,
Will not offend thee.
    Arth.   O heaven! I thank you, Hubert.
    Hub. Silence; no more: go closely in with me:
Much danger do I undergo for thee.   [*Exeunt*.

SCENE II. KING JOHN'S *palace*.

Enter KING JOHN, PEMBROKE, SALISBURY, *and other*
    Lords.

    K. John. Here once again we sit, once again
    crown'd,
And looked upon, I hope, with cheerful eyes.
    Pem. This 'once again,' but that your highness
    pleased,
Was once superfluous: you were crown'd before,
And that high royalty was ne'er pluck'd off,
The faiths of men ne'er stained with revolt;
Fresh expectation troubled not the land
With any long'd-for change or better state.
    Sal. Therefore, to be possess'd with double pomp,
To guard a title that was rich before, 10
To gild refined gold, to paint the lily,
To throw a perfume on the violet,
To smooth the ice, or add another hue
Unto the rainbow, or with taper-light
To seek the beauteous eye of heaven to garnish,
Is wasteful and ridiculous excess.
    Pem. But that your royal pleasure must be done,
This act is as an ancient tale new told,
And in the last repeating troublesome,
Being urged at a time unseasonable. 20
    Sal. In this the antique and well noted face
Of plain old form is much disfigured;
And, like a shifted wind unto a sail,
It makes the course of thoughts to fetch about,
Startles and frights consideration,
Makes sound opinion sick and truth suspected,
For putting on so new a fashion'd robe.
    Pem. When workmen strive to do better than well,
They do confound their skill in covetousness;
And oftentimes excusing of a fault 30
Doth make the fault the worse by the excuse,
As patches set upon a little breach
Discredit more in hiding of the fault
Than did the fault before it was so patch'd.
    Sal. To this effect, before you were new crown'd,
We breathed our counsel: but it pleased your highness
To overbear it, and we are all well pleased,
Since all and every part of what we would
Doth make a stand at what your highness will.

King John
ACT IV : SC II

357

K. John. Some reasons of this double coronation 40
I have possess'd you with and think them strong;
And more, more strong, then lesser is my fear,
I shall indue you with: meantime but ask
What you would have reform'd that is not well,
And well shall you perceive how willingly
I will both hear and grant you your requests.

Pem. Then I, as one that am the tongue of these
To sound the purposes of all their hearts,
Both for myself and them, but, chief of all,
Your safety, for the which myself and them 50
Bend their best studies, heartily request
The enfranchisement of Arthur; whose restraint
Doth move the murmuring lips of discontent
To break into this dangerous argument,—
If what in rest you have in right you hold,
Why then your fears, which, as they say, attend
The steps of wrong, should move you to mew up
Your tender kinsman and to choke his days
With barbarous ignorance and deny his youth
The rich advantage of good exercise? 60
That the time's enemies may not have this
To grace occasions, let it be our suit
That you have bid us ask his liberty;
Which for our goods we do no further ask
Than whereupon our weal, on you depending,
Counts it your weal he have his liberty.

Enter HUBERT.

K. John. Let it be so: I do commit his youth
To your direction. Hubert, what news with you?
[*Taking him apart.*

Pem. This is the man should do the bloody deed;
He show'd his warrant to a friend of mine: 70
The image of a wicked heinous fault
Lives in his eye; that close aspect of his
Does show the mood of a much troubled breast;
And I do fearfully believe 'tis done,
What we so fear'd he had a charge to do.

Sal. The colour of the king doth come and go
Between his purpose and his conscience,
Like heralds 'twixt two dreadful battles set:
His passion is so ripe, it needs must break.

Pem. And when it breaks, I fear will issue thence 80
The foul corruption of a sweet child's death.

K. John. We cannot hold mortality's strong hand:
Good lords, although my will to give is living,
The suit which you demand is gone and dead:
He tells us Arthur is deceased to-night.

Sal. Indeed we fear'd his sickness was past cure.

Pem. Indeed we heard how near his death he was
Before the child himself felt he was sick:
This must be answer'd either here or hence.

K. John. Why do you bend such solemn brows on
me? 90
Think you I bear the shears of destiny?
Have I commandment on the pulse of life?

Sal. It is apparent foul play; and 'tis shame
That greatness should so grossly offer it:
So thrive it in your game! and so, farewell.

Pem. Stay yet, Lord Salisbury; I'll go with thee,

And find the inheritance of this poor child,
His little kingdom of a forced grave.
That blood which owed the breadth of all this isle,
Three foot of it doth hold: bad world the while! 100
This must not be thus borne: this will break out
To all our sorrows, and ere long I doubt. [*Exeunt Lords.*

K. John. They burn in indignation. I repent:
There is no sure foundation set on blood,
No certain life achieved by others' death.

Enter a Messenger.

A fearful eye thou hast: where is that blood
That I have seen inhabit in those cheeks?
So foul a sky clears not without a storm:
Pour down thy weather: how goes all in France?

Mess. From France to England. Never such a
power 110
For any foreign preparation
Was levied in the body of a land.
The copy of your speed is learn'd by them;
For when you should be told they do prepare,
The tidings comes that they are all arrived.

K. John. O, where hath our intelligence been drunk?
Where hath it slept? Where is my mother's care,
That such an army could be drawn in France,
And she not hear of it?

Mess.　　　　　　My liege, her ear
Is stopp'd with dust; the first of April died 120
Your noble mother: and, as I hear, my lord,
The Lady Constance in a frenzy died
Three days before: but this from rumour's tongue
I idly heard; if true or false I know not.

K. John. Withhold thy speed, dreadful occasion!
O, make a league with me, till I have pleased
My discontented peers! What! mother dead!
How wildly then walks my estate in France!
Under whose conduct came those powers of France
That thou for truth givest out are landed here? 130

Mess. Under the Dauphin.

K. John.　　　　　　Thou hast made me giddy
With these ill tidings.

Enter the BASTARD *and* PETER *of Pomfret.*

　　　　　Now, what says the world
To your proceedings? do not seek to stuff
My head with more ill news, for it is full.

Bast. But if you be afeard to hear the worst,
Then let the worst unheard fall on your head.

K. John. Bear with me, cousin; for I was amazed
Under the tide: but now I breathe again
Aloft the flood, and can give audience
To any tongue, speak it of what it will. 140

Bast. How I have sped among the clergymen,
The sums I have collected shall express.
But as I travell'd hither through the land,
I find the people strangely fantasied;
Possess'd with rumours, full of idle dreams,
Not knowing what they fear, but full of fear:
And here 's a prophet, that I brought with me
From forth the streets of Pomfret, whom I found
With many hundreds treading on his heels;

42. **And more**, i.e., more reasons. 43. **indue**, furnish. 55. **in rest**, in security. 57. **mew up**, imprison; see glossary. 61. **the time's enemies**, enemies of the present state of affairs. 64. **goods**, i.e., our good, equivalent to *weal* in the next line. 72. **close**, uncommunicative, secret; see glossary. 78. **battles**, armies; see glossary. 84. **demand**, request; see glossary. 89. **answer'd**, atoned for; see glossary. 93. **apparent**, evident; see glossary. 94. **offer**, dare; see glossary. 95. **So**,

i.e., *grossly*, with reference to the preceding line; probably a quibble on the meaning "flagrantly" (l. 94) and the implied meaning "stupidly, clumsily" in this line. 97-100. **inheritance . . . hold.** The contrast between the greatness of kingdoms and the smallness of the graves of kings was a Renaissance commonplace; cf. *Richard II*, III, iii, 153-154. 109. **weather**, storm, tempest. 113. **copy**, example; see glossary. 116. **our intelligence**, our spies. 125. **occasion**, course of

To whom he sung, in rude harsh-sounding rhymes, 150
That, ere the next Ascension-day at noon,
Your highness should deliver up your crown.
    K. John. Thou idle dreamer, wherefore didst
       thou so?
    Peter. Foreknowing that the truth will fall out so.
    K. John. Hubert, away with him; imprison him;
And on that day at noon, whereon he says
I shall yield up my crown, let him be hang'd.
Deliver him to safety; and return,
For I must use thee.   [*Exit Hubert with Peter.*
           O my gentle cousin,
Hear'st thou the news abroad, who are arrived? 160
    Bast. The French, my lord; men's mouths are full
       of it:
Besides, I met Lord Bigot and Lord Salisbury,
With eyes as red as new-enkindled fire,
And others more, going to seek the grave
Of Arthur, whom they say is kill'd to-night
On your suggestion.
    K. John.   Gentle kinsman, go,
And thrust thyself into their companies:
I have a way to win their loves again;
Bring them before me.
    Bast.   I will seek them out.
    K. John. Nay, but make haste; the better foot
       before.   170
O, let me have no subject enemies,
When adverse foreigners affright my towns
With dreadful pomp of stout invasion!
Be Mercury, set feathers to thy heels,
And fly like thought from them to me again.
    Bast. The spirit of the time shall teach me speed.
                [*Exit.*
    K. John. Spoke like a sprightful noble gentleman.
Go after him; for he perhaps shall need
Some messenger betwixt me and the peers;
And be thou he.
    Mess.   With all my heart, my liege. 180
                [*Exit.*
    K. John. My mother dead!

       Re-enter HUBERT.

    Hub. My lord, they say five moons were seen
       to-night;
Four fixed, and the fifth did whirl about
The other four in wondrous motion.
    K. John. Five moons!
    Hub.   Old men and beldams in the
       streets
Do prophesy upon it dangerously:
Young Arthur's death is common in their mouths:
And when they talk of him, they shake their heads
And whisper one another in the ear;
And he that speaks doth gripe the hearer's wrist, 190
Whilst he that hears makes fearful action,
With wrinkled brows, with nods, with rolling eyes.
I saw a smith stand with his hammer, thus,
The whilst his iron did on the anvil cool,
With open mouth swallowing a tailor's news;
Who, with his shears and measure in his hand,

Standing on slippers, which his nimble haste
Had falsely thrust upon contrary feet,
Told of a many thousand warlike French
That were embattailed and rank'd in Kent: 200
Another lean unwash'd artificer
Cuts off his tale and talks of Arthur's death.
    K. John. Why seek'st thou to possess me with these
       fears?
Why urgest thou so oft young Arthur's death?
Thy hand hath murder'd him: I had a mighty
       cause
To wish him dead, but thou hadst none to kill him.
    Hub. No had, my lord! why, did you not provoke
       me?
    K. John. It is the curse of kings to be attended
By slaves that take their humours for a warrant
To break within the bloody house of life,   210
And on the winking of authority
To understand a law, to know the meaning
Of dangerous majesty, when perchance it frowns
More upon humour than advised respect.
    Hub. Here is your hand and seal for what I did.
    K. John. O, when the last account 'twixt heaven
       and earth
Is to be made, then shall this hand and seal
Witness against us to damnation!
How oft the sight of means to do ill deeds
Make deeds ill done! Hadst not thou been by,   220
A fellow by the hand of nature mark'd,
Quoted and sign'd to do a deed of shame,
This murder had not come into my mind:
But taking note of thy abhorr'd aspect,
Finding thee fit for bloody villany,
Apt, liable to be employ'd in danger,
I faintly broke with thee of Arthur's death;
And thou, to be endeared to a king,
Made it no conscience to destroy a prince.
    Hub. My lord,—   230
    K. John. Hadst thou but shook thy head or made a
       pause
When I spake darkly what I purposed,
Or turn'd an eye of doubt upon my face,
As bid me tell my tale in express words,
Deep shame had struck me dumb, made me break off,
And those thy fears might have wrought fears in me:
But thou didst understand me by my signs
And didst in signs again parley with sin;
Yea, without stop, didst let thy heart consent,
And consequently thy rude hand to act   240
The deed, which both our tongues held vile to name.
Out of my sight, and never see me more!
My nobles leave me; and my state is braved,
Even at my gates, with ranks of foreign powers:
Nay, in the body of this fleshly land,
This kingdom, this confine of blood and breath,
Hostility and civil tumult reigns
Between my conscience and my cousin's death.
    Hub. Arm you against your other enemies,
I'll make a peace between your soul and you.   250
Young Arthur is alive: this hand of mine
Is yet a maiden and an innocent hand,

events (Onions); hour of trial (John). **137. amazed,** bewildered.
144. fantasied, full of strange fancies; see glossary. **158. safety,**
safe keeping. **174. set feathers,** an allusion to Mercury's winged
sandals. **177. sprightful,** spirited. **185. beldams,** old women. **198.**
falsely, improperly, wrongly; see glossary. **200. embattailed,** drawn
up in battle array. **207. No had,** had I not. **210. bloody . . . life,**
the body animated by life blood; possibly, the body become bloody.

211. winking of authority, facial expression of a king. **215. your**
hand and seal, the *warrant* referred to in line 70. **227. broke with,** i.e.,
broached the subject. **243. my state is braved,** my power is challenged.
245-246. body . . . breath. The figure is the common one of the microcosm, in which man is conceived as the epitome of the universe. **246.**
confine, territorial limit.

Not painted with the crimson spots of blood.
Within this bosom never enter'd yet
The dreadful motion of a murderous thought;
And you have slander'd nature in my form,
Which, howsoever rude exteriorly,
Is yet the cover of a fairer mind
Than to be butcher of an innocent child.
　　K. John. Doth Arthur live? O, haste thee to the
　　　　peers,　　　　　　　　　　　　　　　　　260
Throw this report on their incensed rage,
And make them tame to their obedience!
Forgive the comment that my passion made
Upon thy feature; for my rage was blind,
And foul imaginary eyes of blood
Presented thee more hideous than thou art.
O, answer not, but to my closet bring
The angry lords with all expedient haste.
I conjure thee but slowly; run more fast.　　[*Exeunt.*

　　SCENE III. *Before the castle.*

Enter ARTHUR, *on the walls.*

　　Arth. The wall is high, and yet will I leap down:
Good ground, be pitiful and hurt me not!
There 's few or none do know me: if they did,
This ship-boy's semblance hath disguised me quite.
I am afraid; and yet I'll venture it.
If I get down, and do not break my limbs,
I'll find a thousand shifts to get away:
As good to die and go, as die and stay.　　[*Leaps down.*
O me! my uncle's spirit is in these stones:
Heaven take my soul, and England keep my bones! 10
　　　　　　　　　　　　　　　　　　　　　　[*Dies.*

Enter PEMBROKE, SALISBURY, *and* BIGOT.

　　Sal. Lords, I will meet him at Saint Edmundsbury:
It is our safety, and we must embrace
This gentle offer of the perilous time.
　　Pem. Who brought that letter from the cardinal?
　　Sal. The Count Melun, a noble lord of France;
Whose private with me of the Dauphin's love
Is much more general than these lines import.
　　Big. To-morrow morning let us meet him then.
　　Sal. Or rather then set forward; for 'twill be
Two long days' journey, lords, or ere we meet.　　20

Enter the BASTARD.

　　Bast. Once more to-day well met, distemper'd
　　　　lords!
The king by me requests your presence straight.
　　Sal. The king hath dispossess'd himself of us:
We will not line his thin bestained cloak
With our pure honours, nor attend the foot
That leaves the print of blood where'er it walks.
Return and tell him so: we know the worst.
　　Bast. Whate'er you think, good words, I think, were
　　　　best.
　　Sal. Our griefs, and not our manners, reason now.
　　Bast. But there is little reason in your grief;　　30

Therefore 'twere reason you had manners now.
　　Pem. Sir, sir, impatience hath his privilege.
　　Bast. 'Tis true, to hurt his master, no man else.
　　Sal. This is the prison. What is he lies here?
　　　　　　　　　　　　　　　　　　　　　[*Seeing Arthur.*
　　Pem. O death, made proud with pure and princely
　　　　beauty!
The earth had not a hole to hide this deed.
　　Sal. Murder, as hating what himself hath done,
Doth lay it open to urge on revenge.
　　Big. Or, when he doom'd this beauty to a grave,
Found it too precious-princely for a grave.　　40
　　Sal. Sir Richard, what think you? have you beheld,
Or have you read or heard? or could you think?
Or do you almost think, although you see,
That you do see? could thought, without this object,
Form such another? This is the very top,
The height, the crest, or crest unto the crest,
Of murder's arms: this is the bloodiest shame,
The wildest savagery, the vilest stroke,
That ever wall-eyed wrath or staring rage
Presented to the tears of soft remorse.　　50
　　Pem. All murders past do stand excused in this;
And this, so sole and so unmatchable,
Shall give a holiness, a purity,
To the yet unbegotten sin of times;
And prove a deadly bloodshed but a jest,
Exampled by this heinous spectacle.
　　Bast. It is a damned and a bloody work;
The graceless action of a heavy hand,
If that it be the work of any hand.
　　Sal. If that it be the work of any hand!　　60
We had a kind of light what would ensue:
It is the shameful work of Hubert's hand;
The practice and the purpose of the king:
From whose obedience I forbid my soul,
Kneeling before this ruin of sweet life,
And breathing to his breathless excellence
The incense of a vow, a holy vow,
Never to taste the pleasures of the world,
Never to be infected with delight,
Nor conversant with ease and idleness,　　70
Till I have set a glory to this hand,
By giving it the worship of revenge.
　　Pem. ⎱
　　Big. ⎰ Our souls religiously confirm thy words.

Enter HUBERT.

　　Hub. Lords, I am hot with haste in seeking you:
Arthur doth live; the king hath sent for you.
　　Sal. O, he is bold and blushes not at death.
Avaunt, thou hateful villain, get thee gone!
　　Hub. I am no villain.
　　Sal.　　　　　　　Must I rob the law?
　　　　　　　　　　　　　　　　　[*Drawing his sword.*
　　Bast. Your sword is bright, sir; put it up again.
　　Sal. Not till I sheathe it in a murderer's skin.　　80
　　Hub. Stand back, Lord Salisbury, stand back, I say;
By heaven, I think my sword 's as sharp as yours:
I would not have you, lord, forget yourself,

255. **motion**, impulse, prompting; see glossary. 269. **conjure**, beseech, influence (used quibblingly perhaps).
　SCENE III. 7. **shifts**, stratagems; see glossary. 16. **private with me**, private communication to me (generally accepted); the New Cambridge editors suggest as emendation *private warrant.* 20. **or ere**, before; see *or* in glossary. 38. **lay . . . open**, display, expose. 49. **wall-eyed**, having defective eyes which appear to glare fiercely. 54. **times**, i.e., future times. 63. **practice**, plot, treachery; see glossary. 70. **ease**,

inactivity, leisure; see glossary. 71. **glory**, halo (Schmidt). **this hand**, i.e., his own hand, which is raised in taking the vow. 79. **bright**, unused (said contemptuously); cf. *Othello*, I, ii, 59. 84. **tempt**, risk. 90. **prove me so**, i.e., make me a murderer by tempting me to kill you. 94. **gall**, wound. 98. **betime**, promptly. 99. **toasting-iron**, sword (used contemptuously). 101. **renowned Faulconbridge**. Salisbury in this scornful belittlement of the Bastard taunts him with illegitimacy and refuses to recognize his newly received knighthood. 106. **date**,

Nor tempt the danger of my true defence;
Lest I, by marking of your rage, forget
Your worth, your greatness and nobility.
 Big. Out, dunghill! darest thou brave a nobleman?
 Hub. Not for my life: but yet I dare defend
My innocent life against an emperor.
 Sal. Thou art a murderer.
 Hub.   Do not prove me so;   90
Yet I am none: whose tongue soe'er speaks false,
Not truly speaks; who speaks not truly, lies.
 Pem. Cut him to pieces.
 Bast.   Keep the peace, I say.
 Sal. Stand by, or I shall gall you, Faulconbridge.
 Bast. Thou wert better gall the devil, Salisbury:
If thou but frown on me, or stir thy foot,
Or teach thy hasty spleen to do me shame,
I'll strike thee dead. Put up thy sword betime;
Or I'll so maul you and your toasting-iron,
That you shall think the devil is come from hell.   100
 Big. What wilt thou do, renowned Faulconbridge?
Second a villain and a murderer?
 Hub. Lord Bigot, I am none.
 Big.   Who kill'd this prince?
 Hub. 'Tis not an hour since I left him well:
I honour'd him, I loved him, and will weep
My date of life out for his sweet life's loss.
 Sal. Trust not those cunning waters of his eyes,
For villany is not without such rheum;
And he, long traded in it, makes it seem
Like rivers of remorse and innocency.   110
Away with me, all you whose souls abhor
The uncleanly savours of a slaughter-house;
For I am stifled with this smell of sin.
 Big. Away toward Bury, to the Dauphin there!
 Pem. There tell the king he may inquire us out.
          [*Exeunt Lords*.
 Bast. Here's a good world! Knew you of this fair
          work?
Beyond the infinite and boundless reach
Of mercy, if thou didst this deed of death,
Art thou damn'd, Hubert.
 Hub.   Do but hear me, sir.
 Bast. Ha! I'll tell thee what;   120
Thou 'rt damn'd as black—nay, nothing is so black;
Thou art more deep damn'd than Prince Lucifer:
There is not yet so ugly a fiend of hell
As thou shalt be, if thou didst kill this child.
 Hub. Upon my soul—
 Bast.   If thou didst but consent
To this most cruel act, do but despair;
And if thou want'st a cord, the smallest thread
That ever spider twisted from her womb
Will serve to strangle thee; a rush will be a beam
To hang thee on; or wouldst thou drown thyself,   130
Put but a little water in a spoon,
And it shall be as all the ocean,
Enough to stifle such a villain up.
I do suspect thee very grievously.
 Hub. If I in act, consent, or sin of thought,
Be guilty of the stealing that sweet breath

Which was embounded in this beauteous clay,
Let hell want pains enough to torture me.
I left him well.
 Bast.   Go, bear him in thine arms.
I am amazed, methinks, and lose my way   140
Among the thorns and dangers of this world.
How easy dost thou take all England up!
From forth this morsel of dead royalty,
The life, the right and truth of all this realm
Is fled to heaven; and England now is left
To tug and scamble and to part by the teeth
The unowed interest of proud-swelling state.
Now for the bare-pick'd bone of majesty
Doth dogged war bristle his angry crest
And snarleth in the gentle eyes of peace: 150
Now powers from home and discontents at home
Meet in one line; and vast confusion waits,
As doth a raven on a sick-fall'n beast,
The imminent decay of wrested pomp.
Now happy he whose cloak and cincture can
Hold out this tempest. Bear away that child
And follow me with speed: I'll to the king:
A thousand businesses are brief in hand,
And heaven itself doth frown upon the land.   [*Exeunt*.

<hr>

ACT V.

SCENE I. KING JOHN's *palace*.

Enter KING JOHN, PANDULPH, *and* Attendants.

 K. John. Thus have I yielded up into your hand
The circle of my glory.   [*Giving the crown*.
 Pand.   Take again
From this my hand, as holding of the pope
Your sovereign greatness and authority.
 K. John. Now keep your holy word: go meet the
          French,
And from his holiness use all your power
To stop their marches 'fore we are inflamed.
Our discontented counties do revolt;
Our people quarrel with obedience,
Swearing allegiance and the love of soul   10
To stranger blood, to foreign royalty.
This inundation of mistemper'd humour
Rests by you only to be qualified:
Then pause not; for the present time 's so sick,
That present medicine must be minister'd,
Or overthrow incurable ensues.
 Pand. It was my breath that blew this tempest up,
Upon your stubborn usage of the pope;
But since you are a gentle convertite,
My tongue shall hush again this storm of war   20
And make fair weather in your blustering land.
On this Ascension-day, remember well,
Upon your oath of service to the pope,
Go I to make the French lay down their arms.   [*Exit*.
 K. John. Is this Ascension-day? Did not the prophet
Say that before Ascension-day at noon
My crown I should get off? Even so I have:

duration; see glossary. 122. **Prince Lucifer,** Satan, prince of the rebel
angels who were expelled from heaven. 146. **scamble,** scramble,
acquire by undignified means. 151. **from home,** i.e., foreign. 152.
waits, waits for. 154. **wrested pomp,** usurped majesty. Ivor John notes
that *Usurpyd Power* was one of the characters in Bale's *Kyng Johan*. 155.
cincture, girdle. 158. **are brief in hand,** demand immediate action.
ACT V. SCENE I. 3. **as . . . pope.** John, in receiving his crown
back, acknowledges the supremacy of the pope as the highest prince in

Christendom. **holding,** property held in possession. 8. **counties,**
shires; possibly nobles. 10. **love of soul,** most sincere love. 12-13.
inundation . . . qualified, excess of one humor is to be reduced to its
right proportion (*qualified*). 15. **present,** prompt; see glossary. 19.
convertite, convert.

I did suppose it should be on constraint;
But, heaven be thank'd, it is but voluntary.

Enter the BASTARD.

Bast. All Kent hath yielded; nothing there holds out
But Dover castle: London hath received,   31
Like a kind host, the Dauphin and his powers:
Your nobles will not hear you, but are gone
To offer service to your enemy,
And wild amazement hurries up and down
The little number of your doubtful friends.

K. John. Would not my lords return to me again,
After they heard young Arthur was alive?

Bast. They found him dead and cast into the streets,
An empty casket, where the jewel of life   40
By some damn'd hand was robb'd and ta'en away.

K. John. That villain Hubert told me he did live.

Bast. So, on my soul, he did, for aught he knew.
But wherefore do you droop? why look you sad?
Be great in act, as you have been in thought;
Let not the world see fear and sad distrust
Govern the motion of a kingly eye:
Be stirring as the time; be fire with fire;
Threaten the threatener and outface the brow
Of bragging horror: so shall inferior eyes,   50
That borrow their behaviours from the great,
Grow great by your example and put on
The dauntless spirit of resolution.
Away, and glister like the god of war,
When he intendeth to become the field:
Show boldness and aspiring confidence.
What, shall they seek the lion in his den,
And fright him there? and make him tremble there?
O, let it not be said: forage, and run
To meet displeasure farther from the doors,   60
And grapple with him ere he come so nigh.

K. John. The legate of the pope hath been with me,
And I have made a happy peace with him;
And he hath promised to dismiss the powers
Led by the Dauphin.

Bast.   O inglorious league!
Shall we, upon the footing of our land,
Send fair-play orders and make compromise,
Insinuation, parley and base truce
To arms invasive? shall a beardless boy,
A cocker'd silken wanton, brave our fields,   70
And flesh his spirit in a warlike soil,
Mocking the air with colours idly spread,
And find no check? Let us, my liege, to arms:
Perchance the cardinal cannot make your peace;
Or if he do, let it at least be said
They saw we had a purpose of defence.

K. John. Have thou the ordering of this present
    time.

Bast. Away, then, with good courage! yet, I know,
Our party may well meet a prouder foe.   [*Exeunt.*

SCENE II. *The* DAUPHIN'S *camp at St. Edmundsbury.*

Enter, in arms, LEWIS, SALISBURY, MELUN,
PEMBROKE, BIGOT, *and* Soldiers.

Lew. My Lord Melun, let this be copied out,
And keep it safe for our remembrance:
Return the precedent to these lords again;
That, having our fair order written down,
Both they and we, perusing o'er these notes,
May know wherefore we took the sacrament
And keep our faiths firm and inviolable.

Sal. Upon our sides it never shall be broken.
And, noble Dauphin, albeit we swear
A voluntary zeal and an unurged faith   10
To your proceedings; yet believe me, prince,
I am not glad that such a sore of time
Should seek a plaster by contemn'd revolt,
And heal the inveterate canker of one wound
By making many. O, it grieves my soul,
That I must draw this metal from my side
To be a widow-maker! O, and there
Where honourable rescue and defence
Cries out upon the name of Salisbury!
But such is the infection of the time,   20
That, for the health and physic of our right,
We cannot deal but with the very hand
Of stern injustice and confused wrong.
And is 't not pity, O my grieved friends,
That we, the sons and children of this isle,
Were born to see so sad an hour as this;
Wherein we step after a stranger march
Upon her gentle bosom, and fill up
Her enemies' ranks,—I must withdraw and weep
Upon the spot of this enforced cause,—   30
To grace the gentry of a land remote,
And follow unacquainted colours here?
What, here? O nation, that thou couldst remove!
That Neptune's arms, who clippeth thee about,
Would bear thee from the knowledge of thyself,
And grapple thee unto a pagan shore;
Where these two Christian armies might combine
The blood of malice in a vein of league,
And not to spend it so unneighbourly!

Lew. A noble temper dost thou show in this;   40
And great affections wrestling in thy bosom
Doth make an earthquake of nobility.
O, what a noble combat hast thou fought
Between compulsion and a brave respect!
Let me wipe off this honourable dew,
That silverly doth progress on thy cheeks:
My heart hath melted at a lady's tears,
Being an ordinary inundation;
But this effusion of such manly drops,
This shower, blown up by tempest of the soul,   50
Startles mine eyes, and makes me more amazed
Than had I seen the vaulty top of heaven
Figured quite o'er with burning meteors.
Lift up thy brow, renowned Salisbury,
And with a great heart heave away this storm;
Commend these waters to those baby eyes
That never saw the giant world enraged;

---

36. **doubtful,** not to be relied on. 55. **become,** grace, adorn. 68. **Insinuation,** act of currying favor, self-ingratiation. 70. **cocker'd . . . wanton,** spoiled child. 71. **flesh,** initiate in or inure to bloodshed (Onions); make savage by a foretaste of flesh (John); see glossary. 73. **check,** restraint; see glossary.
SCENE II. 1. **this,** the agreement with the English lords; cf. lines 30-34 of the preceding scene. 3. **precedent,** original document. 19. **Cries out upon,** denounces; possibly invokes with outcries. 21. **physic,**

remedy; see glossary. 30. **spot,** stain, blot. **enforced cause,** i.e., cause into which I am forced. 31. **grace,** honor; see glossary. 32. **unacquainted colours,** i.e., the banners of a foreign power. 34. **clippeth,** embraces; see glossary. 44. **compulsion,** compelling circumstances. 52. **had I seen,** if I had seen; an instance of the subjunctive used conditionally; see Abbott, 361. 64. **an angel spake.** There are several explanations: that the remark is prompted by the entrance of the papal legate with the *warrant from the hand of heaven* (Malone); that it refers

Nor met with fortune other than at feasts,
Full of warm blood, of mirth, of gossiping.
Come, come; for thou shalt thrust thy hand as
  deep   60
Into the purse of rich prosperity
As Lewis himself: so, nobles, shall you all,
That knit your sinews to the strength of mine.
And even there, methinks, an angel spake:

Enter PANDULPH.

Look, where the holy legate comes apace,
To give us warrant from the hand of heaven,
And on our actions set the name of right
With holy breath.
 Pand.   Hail, noble prince of France!
The next is this, King John hath reconciled
Himself to Rome; his spirit is come in, 70
That so stood out against the holy church,
The great metropolis and see of Rome:
Therefore thy threatening colours now wind up;
And tame the savage spirit of wild war,
That, like a lion foster'd up at hand,
It may lie gently at the foot of peace,
And be no further harmful than in show.
 Lew. Your grace shall pardon me, I will not back:
I am too high-born to be propertied,
To be a secondary at control, 80
Or useful serving-man and instrument,
To any sovereign state throughout the world.
Your breath first kindled the dead coal of wars
Between this chastised kingdom and myself,
And brought in matter that should feed this fire;
And now 'tis far too huge to be blown out
With that same weak wind which enkindled it.
You taught me how to know the face of right,
Acquainted me with interest to this land,
Yea, thrust this enterprise into my heart; 90
And come ye now to tell me John hath made
His peace with Rome? What is that peace to me?
I, by the honour of my marriage-bed,
After young Arthur, claim this land for mine;
And, now it is half-conquer'd, must I back
Because that John hath made his peace with Rome?
Am I Rome's slave? What penny hath Rome borne,
What men provided, what munition sent,
To underprop this action? Is 't not I
That undergo this charge? who else but I, 100
And such as to my claim are liable,
Sweat in this business and maintain this war?
Have I not heard these islanders shout out
'Vive le roi!' as I have bank'd their towns?
Have I not here the best cards for the game,
To win this easy match play'd for a crown?
And shall I now give o'er the yielded set?
No, no, on my soul, it never shall be said.
 Pand. You look but on the outside of this work.
 Lew. Outside or inside, I will not return 110
Till my attempt so much be glorified
As to my ample hope was promised
Before I drew this gallant head of war,

And cull'd these fiery spirits from the world,
To outlook conquest and to win renown
Even in the jaws of danger and of death.
        [*Trumpet sounds.*
What lusty trumpet thus doth summon us?

Enter the BASTARD, *attended.*

 Bast. According to the fair play of the world,
Let me have audience; I am sent to speak:
My holy lord of Milan, from the king 120
I come, to learn how you have dealt for him;
And, as you answer, I do know the scope
And warrant limited unto my tongue.
 Pand. The Dauphin is too wilful-opposite,
And will not temporize with my entreaties;
He flatly says he'll not lay down his arms.
 Bast. By all the blood that ever fury breathed,
The youth says well. Now hear our English king;
For thus his royalty doth speak in me.
He is prepared, and reason too he should: 130
This apish and unmannerly approach,
This harness'd masque and unadvised revel,
This unhair'd sauciness and boyish troops,
The king doth smile at; and is well prepared
To whip this dwarfish war, these pigmy arms,
From out the circle of his territories.
That hand which had the strength, even at your door,
To cudgel you and make you take the hatch,
To dive like buckets in concealed wells,
To crouch in litter of your stable planks, 140
To lie like pawns lock'd up in chests and trunks,
To hug with swine, to seek sweet safety out
In vaults and prisons, and to thrill and shake
Even at the crying of your nation's crow,
Thinking his voice an armed Englishman;
Shall that victorious hand be feebled here,
That in your chambers gave you chastisement?
No: know the gallant monarch is in arms
And like an eagle o'er his aery towers,
To souse annoyance that comes near his nest. 150
And you degenerate, you ingrate revolts,
You bloody Neroes, ripping up the womb
Of your dear mother England, blush for shame;
For your own ladies and pale-visaged maids
Like Amazons come tripping after drums,
Their thimbles into armed gauntlets change,
Their needles to lances, and their gentle hearts
To fierce and bloody inclination.
 Lew. There end thy brave, and turn thy face in
  peace;
We grant thou canst outscold us: fare thee well; 160
We hold our time too precious to be spent
With such a brabbler.
 Pand.   Give me leave to speak.
 Bast. No, I will speak.
 Lew.   We will attend to neither.
Strike up the drums; and let the tongue of war
Plead for our interest and our being here.
 Bast. Indeed, your drums, being beaten, will cry
  out;

to a trumpet fanfare announcing the legate's arrival (Cowden Clarke, adopted by the New Cambridge editors, who introduce the stage direction, *a trumpet sounds*). The pun on *angel*, a coin (cf. III, iii, 8), is suggested by the words *purse* and *nobles* (gold coins) above. The Cambridge editors regarded the line as an "aside" contemptuously alluding to the dauphin's mercenary allies. 79. **propertied,** made a tool of. 89. **interest,** title, right. 101. **liable,** subject. 104. **bank'd,** coasted, skirted. 107. **give o'er,** abandon. **the yielded set,** the game already

won; a figure from tennis or cards. 115. **outlook,** stare down. 125. **temporize,** come to an agreement. 132. **harness'd,** i.e., in armor. 133. **unhair'd,** beardless. 138. **take the hatch,** leap over the lower half door; i.e., make a hasty and undignified retreat. 141. **pawns,** things in pawn. 150. **souse,** to swoop down upon (as a bird of prey). 151. **revolts,** rebels. 159. **thy brave,** your boasting.

And so shall you, being beaten: do but start
An echo with the clamour of thy drum,
And even at hand a drum is ready braced
That shall reverberate all as loud as thine;   170
Sound but another, and another shall
As loud as thine rattle the welkin's ear
And mock the deep-mouth'd thunder: for at hand,
Not trusting to this halting legate here,
Whom he hath used rather for sport than need,
Is warlike John; and in his forehead sits
A bare-ribb'd death, whose office is this day
To feast upon whole thousands of the French.   178
   Lew. Strike up your drums, to find this danger out.
   Bast. And thou shalt find it, Dauphin, do not doubt.
                               [*Exeunt.*

SCENE III. *The field of battle.*

Alarums. Enter KING JOHN *and* HUBERT.

   K. John. How goes the day with us? O, tell me,
    Hubert.
   Hub. Badly, I fear. How fares your majesty?
   K. John. This fever, that hath troubled me so long,
Lies heavy on me; O, my heart is sick!

Enter a Messenger.

   Mess. My lord, your valiant kinsman, Faulcon-
    bridge,
Desires your majesty to leave the field
And send him word by me which way you go.
   K. John. Tell him, toward Swinstead, to the abbey
    there.
   Mess. Be of good comfort; for the great supply
That was expected by the Dauphin here,   10
Are wreck'd three nights ago on Goodwin Sands.
This news was brought to Richard but even now:
The French fight coldly, and retire themselves.
   K. John. Ay me! this tyrant fever burns me up,
And will not let me welcome this good news.
Set on toward Swinstead: to my litter straight;
Weakness possesseth me, and I am faint.   [*Exeunt.*

SCENE IV. *Another part of the field.*

Enter SALISBURY, PEMBROKE, *and* BIGOT.

   Sal. I did not think the king so stored with friends.
   Pem. Up once again; put spirit in the French:
If they miscarry, we miscarry too.
   Sal. That misbegotten devil, Faulconbridge,
In spite of spite, alone upholds the day.
   Pem. They say King John sore sick hath left the
    field.

Enter MELUN, *wounded.*

   Mel. Lead me to the revolts of England here.
   Sal. When we were happy we had other names.
   Pem. It is the Count Melun.
   Sal.   Wounded to death.

   Mel. Fly, noble English, you are bought and sold;   10
Unthread the rude eye of rebellion
And welcome home again discarded faith.
Seek out King John and fall before his feet;
For if the French be lords of this loud day,
He means to recompense the pains you take
By cutting off your heads: thus hath he sworn
And I with him, and many moe with me,
Upon the altar at Saint Edmundsbury;
Even on that altar where we swore to you
Dear amity and everlasting love.   20
   Sal. May this be possible? may this be true?
   Mel. Have I not hideous death within my view,
Retaining but a quantity of life,
Which bleeds away, even as a form of wax
Resolveth from his figure 'gainst the fire?
What in the world should make me now deceive,
Since I must lose the use of all deceit?
Why should I then be false, since it is true
That I must die here and live hence by truth?
I say again, if Lewis do win the day,   30
He is forsworn, if e'er those eyes of yours
Behold another day break in the east:
But even this night, whose black contagious breath
Already smokes about the burning crest
Of the old, feeble and day-wearied sun,
Even this ill night, your breathing shall expire,
Paying the fine of rated treachery
Even with a treacherous fine of all your lives,
If Lewis by your assistance win the day.
Commend me to one Hubert with your king: 40
The love of him, and this respect besides,
For that my grandsire was an Englishman,
Awakes my conscience to confess all this.
In lieu whereof, I pray you, bear me hence
From forth the noise and rumour of the field,
Where I may think the remnant of my thoughts
In peace, and part this body and my soul
With contemplation and devout desires.
   Sal. We do believe thee: and beshrew my soul
But I do love the favour and the form   50
Of this most fair occasion, by the which
We will untread the steps of damned flight,
And like a bated and retired flood,
Leaving our rankness and irregular course,
Stoop low within those bounds we have o'erlook'd
And calmly run on in obedience
Even to our ocean, to our great King John.
My arm shall give thee help to bear thee hence;
For I do see the cruel pangs of death
Right in thine eye. Away, my friends! New flight;   60
And happy newness, that intends old right.
                   [*Exeunt, leading off Melun.*

SCENE V. *The French camp.*

Enter LEWIS *and his train.*

   Lew. The sun of heaven methought was loath to set,
But stay'd and made the western welkin blush,

---

169. **ready braced,** i.e., tightened, ready to be struck.   172. **welkin's,** heaven's, sky's; see glossary.
   SCENE IV.   11. **Unthread the rude eye,** i.e., withdraw from the hazardous undertaking in which they were engaged.   15. **He,** the French king.   17. **moe,** more; see glossary.   24-25. **as . . . fire.** An alleged practice of necromancers was to make and then abuse a waxen effigy of an enemy, who was believed to suffer in accordance with the treatment given the wax representation. As the waxen figure melted away before a

fire, the enemy, it was believed, would die. The passage is a metaphor; Melun does not necessarily mean that he is a victim of witchcraft.   37. **rated,** assessed, exposed; with quibble (New Cambridge); see glossary. 38. **fine,** end; see glossary.   54. **rankness,** fullness to overflowing.
   SCENE V.   3. **measure,** traverse; see glossary.   7. **clearly,** completely. 14. **shrewd,** of evil import; see glossary.   20. **quarter,** watch.
   SCENE VI.   12. **Unkind remembrance.** Hubert chides his own faulty memory; see *unkind* in glossary.   16. **sans,** without; see glossary.   28.

When English measure backward their own ground
In faint retire. O, bravely came we off,
When with a volley of our needless shot,
After such bloody toil, we bid good night;
And wound our tattering colours clearly up,
Last in the field, and almost lords of it!

Enter a Messenger.

Mess. Where is my prince, the Dauphin?
Lew.   Here: what news?   9
Mess. The Count Melun is slain; the English lords
By his persuasion are again fall'n off,
And your supply, which you have wish'd so long,
Are cast away and sunk on Goodwin Sands.
Lew. Ah, foul shrewd news! beshrew thy very heart!
I did not think to be so sad to-night
As this hath made me. Who was he that said
King John did fly an hour or two before
The stumbling night did part our weary powers?
Mess. Whoever spoke it, it is true, my lord.
Lew. Well; keep good quarter and good care
      to-night: 20
The day shall not be up so soon as I,
To try the fair adventure of to-morrow.   [*Exeunt.*

SCENE VI. *An open place in the neighbourhood of
Swinstead Abbey.*

Enter the BASTARD *and* HUBERT, *severally.*

Hub. Who's there? speak, ho! speak quickly, or I
      shoot.
Bast. A friend. What art thou?
Hub.   Of the part of England.
Bast. Whither dost thou go?
Hub. What's that to thee? why may not I demand
Of thine affairs, as well as thou of mine?
Bast. Hubert, I think?
Hub.   Thou hast a perfect thought:
I will upon all hazards well believe
Thou art my friend, that know'st my tongue so well.
Who art thou?
Bast.   Who thou wilt: and if thou
      please,
Thou mayst befriend me so much as to think   10
I come one way of the Plantagenets.
Hub. Unkind remembrance! thou and eyeless night
Have done me shame: brave soldier, pardon me,
That any accent breaking from thy tongue
Should 'scape the true acquaintance of mine ear.
Bast. Come, come; sans compliment, what news
      abroad?
Hub. Why, here walk I in the black brow of night,
To find you out.
Bast.   Brief, then; and what's the
      news?
Hub. O, my sweet sir, news fitting to the night,
Black, fearful, comfortless and horrible.   20
Bast. Show me the very wound of this ill news:
I am no woman, I'll not swoon at it.

Hub. The king, I fear, is poison'd by a monk:
I left him almost speechless; and broke out
To acquaint you with this evil, that you might
The better arm you to the sudden time,
Than if you had at leisure known of this.
Bast. How did he take it? who did taste to him?
Hub. A monk, I tell you; a resolved villain,
Whose bowels suddenly burst out: the king   30
Yet speaks and peradventure may recover.
Bast. Who didst thou leave to tend his majesty?
Hub. Why, know you not? the lords are all come
      back,
And brought Prince Henry in their company;
At whose request the king hath pardon'd them,
And they are all about his majesty.
Bast. Withhold thine indignation, mighty heaven,
And tempt us not to bear above our power!
I'll tell thee, Hubert, half my power this night,
Passing these flats, are taken by the tide;   40
These Lincoln Washes have devoured them;
Myself, well mounted, hardly have escaped.
Away before: conduct me to the king;
I doubt he will be dead or ere I come.   [*Exeunt.*

SCENE VII. *The orchard in Swinstead Abbey.*

Enter Prince HENRY, SALISBURY, *and* BIGOT.

P. Hen. It is too late: the life of all his blood
Is touch'd corruptibly, and his pure brain,
Which some suppose the soul's frail dwelling-house,
Doth by the idle comments that it makes
Foretell the ending of mortality.

Enter PEMBROKE.

Pem. His highness yet doth speak, and holds belief
That, being brought into the open air,
It would allay the burning quality
Of that fell poison which assaileth him.
P. Hen. Let him be brought into the orchard here. 10
Doth he still rage?   [*Exit Bigot.*
Pem.   He is more patient
Than when you left him; even now he sung.
P. Hen. O vanity of sickness! fierce extremes
In their continuance will not feel themselves.
Death, having prey'd upon the outward parts,
Leaves them invisible, and his siege is now
Against the mind, the which he pricks and wounds
With many legions of strange fantasies,
Which, in their throng and press to that last hold,
Confound themselves. 'Tis strange that death should
      sing.   20
I am the cygnet to this pale faint swan,
Who chants a doleful hymn to his own death,
And from the organ-pipe of frailty sings
His soul and body to their lasting rest.
Sal. Be of good comfort, prince; for you are born
To set a form upon that indigest
Which he hath left so shapeless and so rude.

---

who did taste to him, a reference to the practice of having a "taster"
eat a portion of everything the king was to eat in order to protect him
from poisoning (cf. *Richard II*, V, v, 99). The monk who did so here,
took the poison knowingly—as a *resolved villain*—to insure the king's
death. 38. tempt . . . power, don't try us beyond our power of
endurance. 40. Passing, traversing; see glossary.
      SCENE VII. 16. invisible. *Insensible, invincible, ill-visited* have been
offered as emendations. The New Cambridge editors suggest *invasible*

(modifying *outward parts*), i.e., easy of access. Most editors concur in
Malone's explanation of *invisible* as an adverb. 18. fantasies, fancies,
creatures of the imagination; cf. IV, ii, 144; see glossary. 21. cygnet,
the young swan. It was a popular belief that the swan sang just before
it died. 26. indigest, shapeless mass.

Enter Attendants, *and* Bigot, *carrying* King John *in a chair.*

K. John. Ay, marry, now my soul hath elbow-room;
It would not out at windows nor at doors.
There is so hot a summer in my bosom, 30
That all my bowels crumble up to dust:
I am a scribbled form, drawn with a pen
Upon a parchment, and against this fire
Do I shrink up.
  P. Hen.　　　　　　How fares your majesty?
  K. John. Poison'd,—ill fare—dead, forsook, cast off:
And none of you will bid the winter come
To thrust his icy fingers in my maw,
Nor let my kingdom's rivers take their course
Through my burn'd bosom, nor entreat the north
To make his bleak winds kiss my parched lips 40
And comfort me with cold. I do not ask you much,
I beg cold comfort; and you are so strait
And so ingrateful, you deny me that.
  P. Hen. O that there were some virtue in my tears,
That might relieve you!
  K. John.　　　　　　The salt in them is hot.
Within me is a hell; and there the poison
Is as a fiend confined to tyrannize
On unreprievable condemned blood.

Enter the Bastard.

  Bast. O, I am scalded with my violent motion,
And spleen of speed to see your majesty! 50
  K. John. O cousin, thou art come to set mine eye:
The tackle of my heart is crack'd and burn'd,
And all the shrouds wherewith my life should sail
Are turned to one thread, one little hair:
My heart hath one poor string to stay it by,
Which holds but till thy news be uttered;
And then all this thou seest is but a clod
And module of confounded royalty.
  Bast. The Dauphin is preparing hitherward,
Where heaven He knows how we shall answer him; 60
For in a night the best part of my power,
As I upon advantage did remove,
Were in the Washes all unwarily
Devoured by the unexpected flood.　　　*[The king dies.*
  Sal. You breathe these dead news in as dead an ear.
My liege! my lord! but now a king, now thus.
  P. Hen. Even so must I run on, and even so stop.
What surety of the world, what hope, what stay,
When this was now a king, and now is clay?
  Bast. Art thou gone so? I do but stay behind 70
To do the office for thee of revenge,
And then my soul shall wait on thee to heaven,
As it on earth hath been thy servant still.
Now, now, you stars that move in your right spheres,
Where be your powers? show now your mended
　　　faiths,
And instantly return with me again,
To push destruction and perpetual shame
Out of the weak door of our fainting land.
Straight let us seek, or straight we shall be sought;
The Dauphin rages at our very heels. 80
  Sal. It seems you know not, then, so much as we:
The Cardinal Pandulph is within at rest,
Who half an hour since came from the Dauphin,

32. **scribbled form,** badly drawn portrait.　42. **strait,** niggardly.　51. **set mine eye,** close my eyes in death.　58. **module,** counterfeit, mere image.　80. **rages,** pursues furiously; see glossary.

And brings from him such offers of our peace
As we with honour and respect may take,
With purpose presently to leave this war.
  Bast. He will the rather do it when he sees
Ourselves well sinewed to our defence.
  Sal. Nay, it is in a manner done already;
For many carriages he hath dispatch'd 90
To the sea-side, and put his cause and quarrel
To the disposing of the cardinal:
With whom yourself, myself and other lords,
If you think meet, this afternoon will post
To consummate this business happily.
  Bast. Let it be so: and you, my noble prince,
With other princes that may best be spared,
Shall wait upon your father's funeral.
  P. Hen. At Worcester must his body be interr'd;
For so he will'd it.
  Bast.　　　　　　Thither shall it then: 100
And happily may your sweet self put on
The lineal state and glory of the land!
To whom, with all submission, on my knee
I do bequeath my faithful services
And true subjection everlastingly.
  Sal. And the like tender of our love we make,
To rest without a spot for evermore.
  P. Hen. I have a kind soul that would give you
　　　thanks
And knows not how to do it but with tears.
  Bast. O, let us pay the time but needful woe, 110
Since it hath been beforehand with our griefs.
This England never did, nor never shall,
Lie at the proud foot of a conqueror,
But when it first did help to wound itself.
Now these her princes are come home again,
Come the three corners of the world in arms,
And we shall shock them. Nought shall make us rue,
If England to itself do rest but true.　　　*[Exeunt.*

94. **post,** hasten; see glossary.　102. **lineal state,** the crown by right of succession.　116. **three . . . world,** England being the fourth (New Cambridge).

EARLY TRAGEDIES

Titus Andronicus

There has been a disposition on the part of critics to deny to Shakespeare the authorship of *Titus Andronicus* because of its exaggerated expression of passion and its repulsive subject matter. Everyone agrees that, if it is Shakespeare's play, it is certainly his first essay in tragedy, written when he was unskilled and inexperienced; or, rather, written before his naturally gentle tastes had had time to assert themselves.[1] Nobody doubts the power of the play, which beats even the writers of the tragedy of blood and revenge at their own game.

The style too would have been, it is said, more "Shakespearean" had Shakespeare written the play. The style does, however, assume in places a very penetrating and impressive quality. Indeed, it may be said that the level of the style is high, though the style is not of a free or original quality. Shakespeare's work is not inspired, but labored and at times inferior, probably because of the fact that he was writing formally in the Senecan manner and, at the same time, imitating Marlowe. In *Titus Andronicus* he was also taking a leaf from Marlowe's book, for thence come such characterizations as Aaron and Tamora, as do the wildness and scope of event. But in *Titus Andronicus* Shakespeare has a still more insistent model, that of the man who was most Senecan of Elizabethan dramatists, Thomas Kyd. We have only one original play which we are absolutely certain is by Kyd—that is, *The Spanish Tragedy*, a revenge play of the utmost influence on the history of the drama. Titus Andronicus himself is modeled after the hero of Kyd's play, Hieronimo, whose madness, tricks, delays, and passion for vengeance are repeated in Titus.

THE HISTORY OF THE PLAY

Almost no early play of Shakespeare's has a clearer title, on the basis of external evidence, to be considered genuine. A play entitled *A Noble Roman Historye of Tytus Andronicus* was entered for publication in the Stationers' Register on January 23, 1594. In 1905 a copy of a first edition, hitherto unknown, was discovered at Malmö in Sweden. It has this title page:

The Most Lamentable Romaine Tragedie of Titus Andronicus: As it was Plaide by the Right Honourable the Earle of Darbie, Earle of Pembrooke, and Earle of Sussex their Seruants. London. Printed by Iohn Danter, and are to be sold by Edward White & Thomas Millington, at the little North doore of Paules at the signe of the Gunne. 1594.[2]

A second quarto edition appeared in 1600, adding the Lord Chamberlain's company to those who had acted the play, and a third quarto, printed from the second, in 1611. The text in the First Folio is printed from the playhouse copy and adds a new scene, the second of the third act. This circumstance indicates that the Folio editors had at their disposal some text of their own, independent of the printed versions. There is nothing to indicate that the new scene is by another than the original author. The play evidently belonged to the repertory of Shakespeare's company since Heminges and Condell regarded it as Shakespeare's work. Francis Meres in his list of 1598 mentions *Titus Andronicus* as one of Shakespeare's tragedies. Ravenscroft reported (1687) a stage tradition that the play was by a "private author" but had been touched up by Shakespeare.

SOURCE

In 1936 in his Edition of the first quarto the late J. Q. Adams announced the discovery of a source for *Titus Andronicus* in a unique chapbook in the Folger Shakespeare Library, *The History of Titus Andronicus, The Renowned Roman General.* . . . Newly translated from the *Italian* Copy printed at Rome. London: Printed and Sold by C. Dicey in *Bow* Church-Yard, and at his wholesale Warehouse in *Northampton*. To this he assigned a date between 1736 and 1764 and gave reason to believe that this book had been passed down from printer to printer from 1594, when it was entered in the Stationers' Register to John Danter as "The Noble Roman Historye of Tytus Andronicus" with "the ballad thereof."[3] If this is true, all copies of earlier editions have been lost.

According to the chapbook, Titus Andronicus was "Governor of the Province of Achaia" in Greece. He went into the field to rescue Rome from besieging Goths, relieved the city, beat the enemy, and captured the queen of the Goths. After this the war continued for ten years, and Titus lost twenty-two of his twenty-five sons. The unnamed Roman emperor, weary of the conflict, ended it by a treaty according to which he was to take the Gothic queen Attava to wife, and in case he should die without issue the queen's sons should succeed to the empire. The story then begins to run in some measure parallel to that of Shakespeare's play. The preliminary matters occupy more than two of the six short chapters of the little book.

This eighteenth-century chapbook no doubt preserves the original source of Shakespeare's play, but there is evidence that certain treatments of the subject intervened between the story in the chapbook and *Titus Andronicus*. Something about these can be ascertained from existing plays on the subject and from records of such plays. On April 11, 1591, Henslowe enters in his *Diary* a new play which he calls "Titus and Vespacia" as acted by Lord Strange's men, which with varying spellings he carries through the rest of the recorded engagements until January

[1]H. Dugdale Sykes, *Sidelights on Shakespeare* (1920); J. M. Robertson, *The Authorship of "Titus Andronicus": An Introduction to the Study of the Canon of Shakespeare* (1924); E. K. Chambers, *William Shakespeare*, I, 312-322; H. T. Price, "The Authorship of *Titus Andronicus*," *Journal of English and Germanic Philology*, XLII (1943), 55-81. See also J. Dover Wilson's edition of *Titus Andronicus* (Cambridge, 1948), particularly pp. xxv-l, in which he contends that the play is mainly the work of George Peele.

[2]See *Shakespeare's Titus Andronicus*. The First Quarto of 1594. Reproduced in facsimile from the unique copy in the Folger Shakespeare Library with an introduction by J. Q. Adams (1936). Adams' collation of Q_1 and Q_2 establishes the fact that the latter was printed directly from the former. It is evident, as Adams demonstrates, that the copy of Q_1 from which Q_2 was taken was damaged in places to the extent of making necessary some extensive emendations.

[3]One entry in Stationers' Register seems to have served Danter's turn for printing both the story and the ballad and the play by Shakespeare. As to the ballad, it seems to be based immediately on the story, although one slight touch in it may be an echo of the figures of Revenge, Rape, and Murder of the second scene of the fifth act of *Titus Andronicus*.

29, 1593. That this may have been a play on the same theme as *Titus Andronicus* is indicated by one piece of confirmatory evidence: in a German version called *Tito Andronico*, published in 1620, Lucius, the son of Titus, is called by the name Vespasian. And, in any case, the German play offers a dramatic treatment of the story of Titus Andronicus less highly developed than that in Shakespeare's play. It belongs to a group of plays carried by English players to Germany mainly in the early 1590's and subsequently translated into German. It is clear that to the original of this German play Shakespeare owes many features of his tragedy. The first of these is the selection of a starting point, which in *Tito Andronico* as in *Titus Andronicus* is the return to Rome of the victorious Titus, bringing with him the queen of the Goths and her sons as prisoners. Besides this German version there is a Dutch play (1641) called *Aran en Titus* by Jan Vos, as there is also the program of a play on Titus Andronicus acted probably at Linz in 1699. H. De W. Fuller, who made a comparative study of all four of these dramatic versions of the story of Titus Andronicus,[4] contends on very good grounds that *Tito Andronico*, on the one hand, and *Aran en Titus* with the very similar Linz program, on the other, preserve earlier forms of the story than that of *Titus Andronicus*. With reference to *Tito Andronico* there can be no doubt that this is true. Again Henslowe records as "ne" (by which he indicated revisions as well as new plays) a play under the illiterate title "titus and ondronicus" as acted by the earl of Sussex's servants. Later still he records what is apparently the same play as acted by the Lord Admiral's and the Lord Chamberlain's men at Newington Butts on June 5, 1594. Fuller is convinced that we have to do with two lost English plays, the one represented by *Tito Andronico*, the other by *Aran en Titus*, which together formed the immediate source of Shakespeare's tragedy.

THE PLAY

The interesting thing is to see, if we can, what Shakespeare did with the crude story he chose to dramatize. To begin with, he adjusted, amplified, and rearranged the plot in such a way as to give it the structure and motivation of a drama of revenge, such as Kyd's *Spanish Tragedy*. Shakespeare gathers together all the basal revenge motives, invents new ones, and places them in the first act. He invents the rivalry of Saturninus and Bassianus for the throne and makes it a tragic error on the part of Titus to award it to Saturninus; also the rivalry of the two sons of the emperor for the hand of Lavinia and out

of this, somewhat inconsistently, he manages to create in Saturninus a desire for vengeance. He invents the killing by Titus of his son Mutius, a second tragic blunder, and, principally, he invents the sacrifice of Alarbus, son of Tamora, at the tomb of the slain sons of Titus, and thus implants in Tamora an un-

Woodcut from the Folger Library copy of "Titus Andronicus."

quenchable thirst for revenge. All these are in the first act. The working out of them in the action brings Titus to the low point in his tragic career (III, i). Bassianus has been murdered, Lavinia ravished and mutilated, two of Titus' three remaining sons falsely accused and put to death, and he himself tricked into the sacrifice of his hand. At that point the tables are turned, and the vengeance of Titus begins. The point is marked by the departure into banishment of Lucius resolved to raise an army of Goths and overthrow Saturninus.

To Shakespeare then is due the motivation and symmetry in *Titus Andronicus* as a tragedy of revenge, not in the second movement so much, as in the first part and in the play as a whole. What is more obvious perhaps than these structural changes, but not more important, are the rich special features with which Shakespeare has embellished the play in the later acts. He invented or developed from mere suggestions the great Hieronimo-like plea of Titus before the Roman tribunes (III, i, 1 ff.), the charming and naturalistic role of the young Lucius, with the family dinner at which the "black ill-favour'd fly" is killed (III, ii, 66), the famous use of Ovid's tale of Philomela (IV, i, 30-82), the presentation on the stage of Titus shooting arrows, labeled *Ad Jovem*, *Ad Apollonem*, and *Ad Martem*, at the sky to the accompaniment of his great, mad words (IV, ii, 42 ff.), the peculiar development of the scene of Aaron with his cub, present also in *Tito Andronico* (II, v, 20 ff.), and, particularly striking, Titus' disclosure of his cannibalistic plan to Tamora's sons before he kills them, since it was part of the revenge code that the victim should know his avenger.

As to the form which Shakespeare was realizing in *Titus Andronicus*, it is sometimes described as Senecan,

[4]H. De W. Fuller, "The Sources of *Titus Andronicus*," *PMLA*, XVI,

but that epithet needs some qualification. The immediate influence of Ovid is strong in the play and that of Virgil is also apparent. In a most pitiful scene Lavinia reveals the guilt of the sons of Tamora, partly by directing attention to the story of Philomela in Ovid's *Metamorphoses* and, partly, by writing an Ovidian word in the sand with a staff held between the stumps of her arms. Since the stories of both Lucrece and Virginia are paralleled in that of Lavinia and since the influence of Seneca is also present, *Titus Andronicus* has been thought to draw upon Shakespeare's reading of ancient authors in school, and this, in general, is perhaps true. G. L. Kittredge gives as literary sources or influences Seneca's *Thyestes* and *Troades*, Ovid's *Metamorphoses*, and the Roman legends of Coriolanus and Virginius. *Troades* supplies the theme of the sacrifice at the tomb of the Andronici and *Thyestes* the banquet of human flesh. Indeed, there are at least three unmistakable borrowings from Seneca in the text of the play. The story of Coriolanus suggests the victorious return of Lucius from banishment and that of Virginius the slaying of Lavinia by Titus. R. A. Law finds in *Titus Andronicus* parallels to the later books of the *Aeneid* and to Plutarch's life of Scipio Africanus.[5]

Some of these classical themes are found in the chapbook source, but most of them are ornamental and belong to the composition of the play and are therefore Shakespeare's. Shakespeare's manipulation of the plot is not, however, so much a matter of the influence of Seneca himself as of the influence of the revenge tragedy, ultimately derived from him, in France and Italy in various plays and in England in such tragedies as *Gorboduc*, *The Misfortunes of Arthur*, *The Spanish Tragedy*, *Locrine*, and *Selimus*. This form of romantic or Senecan tragedy differed in many ways from the plays of Seneca himself.

STAGE HISTORY

Titus Andronicus was popular in its own day, and the play, or some version of it, was recorded fifteen times in Henslowe's *Diary*. The Elizabethans were apparently not squeamish. Ben Jonson, looking back at its vogue, speaks scornfully in *Bartholomew Fair* (1614) of those "who swear *Ieronimo* and *Andronicus* are the best plays yet." A recently discovered illustration in pen and ink drawing of a scene in *Titus Andronicus* has been much discussed. It is attributed to Henry Peacham and seems to be an indication of the contemporary importance of the play. Ravenscroft made a Restoration version of *Titus Andronicus*, acted in 1678, and it was revived at Drury Lane Theatre in 1717. The only performance recorded in the nineteenth century was that of Ira Aldridge in London and Dublin in 1852-1856. It is said that Aldridge's company were reluctant to appear in it. *Titus Andronicus* was staged at the "Old Vic" in 1923, but more or less as a curiosity.

[5]R. A. Law, "The Roman Background of *Titus Andronicus*," *Studies in Philology*, XL (1943), 145-153.

Titus Andronicus

DRAMATIS PERSONAE

SATURNINUS, son to the late Emperor of Rome, and afterwards declared Emperor.
BASSIANUS, brother to Saturninus; in love with Lavinia.
TITUS ANDRONICUS, a noble Roman, general against the Goths.
MARCUS ANDRONICUS, tribune of the people, and brother to Titus.
LUCIUS,
QUINTUS,
MARTIUS, } sons to Titus Andronicus.
MUTIUS,
YOUNG LUCIUS, a boy, son to Lucius.
PUBLIUS, son to Marcus the Tribune.
SEMPRONIUS,
CAIUS, } kinsmen to Titus.
VALENTINE,
ÆMILIUS, a noble Roman.
ALARBUS,
DEMETRIUS, } sons to Tamora.
CHIRON,
AARON, a Moor, beloved by Tamora.
A Captain, Tribune, Messenger, and Clown; Romans.
Goths and Romans.

TAMORA, Queen of the Goths.
LAVINIA, daughter to Titus Andronicus.
A Nurse.

Senators, Tribunes, Officers, Soldiers, and Attendants.

SCENE: *Rome, and the country near it.*

ACT I.

SCENE I. *Rome. Before the Capitol.*

The Tomb of the ANDRONICI *appearing; the* Tribunes *and* Senators *aloft. Enter, below, from one side,* SATURNINUS *and his* Followers; *and, from the other side,* BASSIANUS *and his* Followers; *with drum and colours.*

Sat. Noble patricians, patrons of my right,
Defend the justice of my cause with arms,
And, countrymen, my loving followers,
Plead my successive title with your swords:
I am his first-born son, that was the last
That ware the imperial diadem of Rome;
Then let my father's honours live in me,
Nor wrong mine age with this indignity.
  Bas. Romans, friends, followers, favourers of my right,
If ever Bassianus, Cæsar's son,
Were gracious in the eyes of royal Rome,

10

Keep then this passage to the Capitol
And suffer not dishonour to approach
The imperial seat, to virtue consecrate,
To justice, continence and nobility;
But let desert in pure election shine,
And, Romans, fight for freedom in your choice.

Enter MARCUS ANDRONICUS, *aloft, with the crown.*

Marc. Princes, that strive by factions and by friends
Ambitiously for rule and empery,
Know that the people of Rome, for whom we stand   20
A special party, have, by common voice,
In election for the Roman empery,
Chosen Andronicus, surnamed Pius
For many good and great deserts to Rome:
A nobler man, a braver warrior,
Lives not this day within the city walls:
He by the senate is accited home
From weary wars against the barbarous Goths;
That, with his sons, a terror to our foes,
Hath yoked a nation strong, train'd up in arms.   30
Ten years are spent since first he undertook
This cause of Rome and chastised with arms
Our enemies' pride: five times he hath return'd
Bleeding to Rome, bearing his valiant sons
In coffins from the field; and at this day
To the monument of the Andronici,
Done sacrifice of expiation,
And slain the noblest prisoner of the Goths.
And now at last, laden with honour's spoils,
Returns the good Andronicus to Rome,
Renowned Titus, flourishing in arms.
Let us entreat, by honour of his name,
Whom worthily you would have now succeed,   40
And in the Capitol and senate's right,
Whom you pretend to honour and adore,
That you withdraw you and abate your strength;
Dismiss your followers and, as suitors should,
Plead your deserts in peace and humbleness.
Sat. How fair the tribune speaks to calm my
   thoughts!
Bas. Marcus Andronicus, so I do affy
In thy uprightness and integrity,
And so I love and honour thee and thine,
Thy noble brother Titus and his sons,   50
And her to whom my thoughts are humbled all,
Gracious Lavinia, Rome's rich ornament,
That I will here dismiss my loving friends,
And to my fortunes and the people's favour
Commit my cause in balance to be weigh'd.
   [*Exeunt the Followers of Bassianus.*
Sat. Friends, that have been thus forward in my
   right,
I thank you all and here dismiss you all,
And to the love and favour of my country
Commit myself, my person and the cause.
   [*Exeunt the Followers of Saturninus.*
Rome, be as just and gracious unto me   60
As I am confident and kind to thee.
Open the gates, and let me in.

Bas. Tribunes, and me, a poor competitor.
   [*Flourish. Saturninus and Bassianus go up
      into the Capitol.*

Enter a Captain.

Cap. Romans, make way: the good Andronicus,
Patron of virtue, Rome's best champion,
Successful in the battles that he fights,
With honour and with fortune is return'd
From where he circumscribed with his sword,
And brought to yoke, the enemies of Rome.

Drums and trumpets sounded. Enter MARTIUS *and*
   MUTIUS; *after them, two* Men *bearing a coffin covered
   with black; then* LUCIUS *and* QUINTUS. *After them,*
   TITUS ANDRONICUS; *and then* TAMORA, *with*
   ALARBUS, DEMETRIUS, CHIRON, AARON, *and other*
   Goths, *prisoners;* Soldiers *and* People *following.*
   The Bearers *set down the coffin, and* TITUS *speaks.*

Tit. Hail, Rome, victorious in thy mourning weeds!
Lo, as the bark, that hath discharged her fraught,   71
Returns with precious lading to the bay
From whence at first she weigh'd her anchorage,
Cometh Andronicus, bound with laurel boughs,
To re-salute his country with his tears,
Tears of true joy for his return to Rome.
Thou great defender of this Capitol,
Stand gracious to the rites that we intend!
Romans, of five and twenty valiant sons,
Half of the number that King Priam had,   80
Behold the poor remains, alive and dead!
These that survive let Rome reward with love;
These that I bring unto their latest home,
With burial amongst their ancestors:
Here Goths have given me leave to sheathe my sword.
Titus, unkind and careless of thine own,
Why suffer'st thou thy sons, unburied yet,
To hover on the dreadful shore of Styx?
Make way to lay them by their brethren.
   [*The tomb is opened.*
There greet in silence, as the dead are wont,   90
And sleep in peace, slain in your country's wars!
O sacred receptacle of my joys,
Sweet cell of virtue and nobility,
How many sons hast thou of mine in store,
That thou wilt never render to me more!
Luc. Give us the proudest prisoner of the Goths,
That we may hew his limbs, and on a pile
Ad manes fratrum sacrifice his flesh,
Before this earthy prison of their bones;
That so the shadows be not unappeased,   100
Nor we disturb'd with prodigies on earth.
Tit. I give him you, the noblest that survives,
The eldest son of this distressed queen.
Tam. Stay, Roman brethren! Gracious conqueror,
Victorious Titus, rue the tears I shed,
A mother's tears in passion for her son:
And if thy sons were ever dear to thee,
O, think my son to be as dear to me!
Sufficeth not that we are brought to Rome,

ACT I. SCENE I.   4. **successive title,** title to the succession.   6. **ware,**
so Q₁; Globe (orig. ed.), *wore.*   8. **age,** seniority.   12. **Keep,** defend;
see glossary.   14. **consecrate,** consecrated.   16. **pure election,** free
choice; i.e., of the Roman citizens.   18. **factions,** parties, groups;
see glossary.   20-23. **for . . . Andronicus,** i.e., we are a faction that
has chosen Andronicus as our candidate.   27. **accited,** summoned.
30. **yoked,** subdued.   35 ff. **and at . . . the Goths.** These lines, not
in Q₂₋₃F and consequently not in Globe, are introduced from the
quarto of 1594, hereafter referred to as Q₁.   **the Andronici,** Q₁: *that*

Andronici.   42. **pretend,** assert, profess.   43. **abate,** diminish, reduce;
see glossary.   46. **fair,** courteously, gently; see glossary.   47. **affy,** trust.
61. **confident,** without suspicion.   68. **circumscribed,** restrained, put
limits on.   70. **weeds,** garments; see glossary.   71. **fraught,** freight,
cargo.   80. **King Priam,** king of Troy at the time of its fall; he had
fifty sons.   86. **unkind,** unnatural; see glossary.   90. **greet in silence,**
i.e., greet each other.   94. **sons . . . mine,** so Q₁; Globe, following
Q₃F: *sons of mine hast thou.*   98. **Ad manes fratrum,** to the departed
spirits of the brothers.   106. **passion,** violent grief; see glossary.   122,

To beautify thy triumphs and return, 110
Captive to thee and to thy Roman yoke,
But must my sons be slaughter'd in the streets,
For valiant doings in their country's cause?
O, if to fight for king and commonweal
Were piety in thine, it is in these.
Andronicus, stain not thy tomb with blood:
Wilt thou draw near the nature of the gods?
Draw near them then in being merciful:
Sweet mercy is nobility's true badge:
Thrice noble Titus, spare my first-born son. 120
   Tit. Patient yourself, madam, and pardon me.
These are their brethren, whom you Goths beheld
Alive and dead, and for their brethren slain
Religiously they ask a sacrifice:
To this your son is mark'd, and die he must,
To appease their groaning shadows that are gone.
   Luc. Away with him! and make a fire straight;
And with our swords, upon a pile of wood,
Let 's hew his limbs till they be clean consumed.
        [*Exeunt Lucius, Quintus, Martius, and Mutius,*
                         with Alarbus.
   Tam. O cruel, irreligious piety! 130
   Chi. Was never Scythia half so barbarous.
   Dem. Oppose not Scythia to ambitious Rome.
Alarbus goes to rest; and we survive
To tremble under Titus' threatening look.
Then, madam, stand resolved, but hope withal
The self-same gods that arm'd the Queen of Troy
With opportunity of sharp revenge
Upon the Thracian tyrant in his tent,
May favour Tamora, the Queen of Goths—
When Goths were Goths and Tamora was queen— 140
To quit the bloody wrongs upon her foes.

   Re-enter Lucius, Quintus, Martius, *and* Mutius,
        with their swords bloody.

   Luc. See, lord and father, how we have perform'd
Our Roman rites: Alarbus' limbs are lopp'd,
And entrails feed the sacrificing fire,
Whose smoke, like incense, doth perfume the sky.
Remaineth nought, but to inter our brethren,
And with loud 'larums welcome them to Rome.
   Tit. Let it be so; and let Andronicus
Make this his latest farewell to their souls.
     [*Trumpets sounded, and the coffin laid in the tomb.*
In peace and honour rest you here, my sons; 150
Rome's readiest champions, repose you here in rest,
Secure from worldly chances and mishaps!
Here lurks no treason, here no envy swells,
Here grow no damned grudges; here are no storms,
No noise, but silence and eternal sleep:
In peace and honour rest you here, my sons!

   Enter Lavinia.

   Lav. In peace and honour live Lord Titus long;
My noble lord and father, live in fame!
Lo, at this tomb my tributary tears
I render, for my brethren's obsequies; 160
And at thy feet I kneel, with tears of joy,

Shed on this earth, for thy return to Rome:
O, bless me here with thy victorious hand,
Whose fortunes Rome's best citizens applaud!
   Tit. Kind Rome, that hast thus lovingly reserved
The cordial of mine age to glad my heart!
Lavinia, live; outlive thy father's days,
And fame's eternal date, for virtue's praise!

   Enter, below, Marcus Andronicus *and* Tribunes;
     re-enter Saturninus *and* Bassianus, *attended.*

   Mar. Long live Lord Titus, my beloved brother,
Gracious triumpher in the eyes of Rome! 170
   Tit. Thanks, gentle tribune, noble brother Marcus.
   Marc. And welcome, nephews, from successful
     wars,
You that survive, and you that sleep in fame!
Fair lords, your fortunes are alike in all,
That in your country's service drew your swords:
But safer triumph is this funeral pomp,
That hath aspired to Solon's happiness
And triumphs over chance in honour's bed.
Titus Andronicus, the people of Rome,
Whose friend in justice thou hast ever been, 180
Send thee by me, their tribune and their trust,
This palliament of white and spotless hue;
And name thee in election for the empire,
With these our late-deceased emperor's sons:
Be candidatus then, and put it on,
And help to set a head on headless Rome.
   Tit. A better head her glorious body fits
Than his that shakes for age and feebleness:
What should I don this robe, and trouble you?
Be chosen with proclamations to-day, 190
To-morrow yield up rule, resign my life,
And set abroad new business for you all?
Rome, I have been thy soldier forty years,
And led my country's strength successfully,
And buried one and twenty valiant sons,
Knighted in field, slain manfully in arms,
In right and service of their noble country:
Give me a staff of honour for mine age,
But not a sceptre to control the world:
Upright he held it, lords, that held it last. 200
   Marc. Titus, thou shalt obtain and ask the empery.
   Sat. Proud and ambitious tribune, canst thou tell?
   Tit. Patience, Prince Saturninus.
   Sat.   Romans, do me right:
Patricians, draw your swords, and sheathe them not
Till Saturninus be Rome's emperor.
Andronicus, would thou wert shipp'd to hell,
Rather than rob me of the people's hearts!
   Luc. Proud Saturnine, interrupter of the good
That noble-minded Titus means to thee!
   Tit. Content thee, prince; I will restore to thee 210
The people's hearts, and wean them from themselves.
   Bas. Andronicus, I do not flatter thee,
But honour thee, and will do till I die:
My faction if thou strengthen with thy friends,
I will most thankful be; and thanks to men
Of noble minds is honourable meed.

123, 124. **These, their, their, they.** The reference in each case is to the sons of Titus. 131. **never,** so Q₁; Globe, following Q₃F: *ever,* making the line a question. **Scythia,** the district north of the Black Sea; its people were notorious for their savagery. 134. **look,** so Qq; Globe, following F: *looks.* 135. **withal,** together with this, at the same time; see glossary. 136. **Queen of Troy,** Hecuba, wife of Priam, who after the fall of Troy was carried to Greece as a slave; here she found occasion to avenge the deaths of her children by killing the king of Thrace, Polymnestor. 160. **obsequies,** acts performed in honor of

the dead. 162. **this earth,** so Q₁; Globe, following Q₃F: *the earth.* 166. **cordial,** restorative; or perhaps merely comfort, pleasure. 168. **date,** duration; see glossary. 177. **Solon's happiness,** the happiness defined by Solon: that no man may be called happy until after his death. 182. **palliament,** white gown of a candidate. 185. **candidatus,** candidate; properly, one clothed in white. 211. **wean . . . themselves,** i.e., wean them over from their predisposition to favor me. 216. **meed,** recompense, reward.

Tit. People of Rome, and people's tribunes here,
I ask your voices and your suffrages:
Will you bestow them friendly on Andronicus?
   Tribunes. To gratify the good Andronicus,   220
And gratulate his safe return to Rome,
The people will accept whom he admits.
   Tit. Tribunes, I thank you: and this suit I make,
That you create your emperor's eldest son,
Lord Saturnine; whose virtues will, I hope,
Reflect on Rome as Titan's rays on earth,
And ripen justice in this commonweal:
Then, if you will elect by my advice,
Crown him, and say 'Long live our emperor!'
   Marc. With voices and applause of every sort,   230
Patricians and plebeians, we create
Lord Saturninus Rome's great emperor,
And say 'Long live our Emperor Saturnine!'
              [*A long flourish till they come down.*
   Sat. Titus Andronicus, for thy favours done
To us in our election this day,
I give thee thanks in part of thy deserts,
And will with deeds requite thy gentleness:
And, for an onset, Titus, to advance
Thy name and honourable family,
Lavinia will I make my empress,   240
Rome's royal mistress, mistress of my heart,
And in the sacred Pantheon her espouse:
Tell me, Andronicus, doth this motion please thee?
   Tit. It doth, my worthy lord; and in this match
I hold me highly honour'd of your grace:
And here in sight of Rome to Saturnine,
King and commander of our commonweal,
The wide world's emperor, do I consecrate
My sword, my chariot and my prisoners;   250
Presents well worthy Rome's imperious lord:
Receive them then, the tribute that I owe,
Mine honour's ensigns humbled at thy feet.
   Sat. Thanks, noble Titus, father of my life!
How proud I am of thee and of thy gifts
Rome shall record, and when I do forget
The least of these unspeakable deserts,
Romans, forget your fealty to me.
   Tit. [*To Tamora*] Now, madam, are you prisoner
    to an emperor;
To him that, for your honour and your state,
Will use you nobly and your followers.   260
   Sat. A goodly lady, trust me; of the hue
That I would choose, were I to choose anew.
Clear up, fair queen, that cloudy countenance:
Though change of war hath wrought this change of
    cheer,
Thou comest not to be made a scorn in Rome:
Princely shall be thy usage every way.
Rest on my word, and let not discontent
Daunt all your hopes: madam, he comforts you
Can make you greater than the Queen of Goths.
Lavinia, you are not displeased with this?   270
   Lav. Not I, my lord; sith true nobility
Warrants these words in princely courtesy.
   Sat. Thanks, sweet Lavinia. Romans, let us go:
Ransomless here we set our prisoners free:
Proclaim our honours, lords, with trump and drum.
       [*Flourish. Saturninus courts Tamora in dumb show.*

Bas. Lord Titus, by your leave, this maid is mine.
                    [*Seizing Lavinia.*
   Tit. How, sir! are you in earnest then, my lord?
   Bas. Ay, noble Titus; and resolved withal
To do myself this reason and this right.
   Marc. 'Suum cuique' is our Roman justice: 280
This prince in justice seizeth but his own.
   Luc. And that he will, and shall, if Lucius live.
   Tit. Traitors, avaunt! Where is the emperor's
    guard?
Treason, my lord! Lavinia is surprised!
   Sat. Surprised! by whom?
   Bas.   By him that justly may
Bear his betroth'd from all the world away.
      [*Exeunt Bassianus and Marcus with Lavinia.*
   Mut. Brothers, help to convey her hence away,
And with my sword I'll keep this door safe.
          [*Exeunt Lucius, Quintus, and Martius.*
   Tit. Follow, my lord, and I'll soon bring her back.
   Mut. My lord, you pass not here.
   Tit.   What, villain boy!   290
Barr'st me my way in Rome?   [*Stabbing Mutius.*
   Mut.   Help, Lucius, help!   [*Dies.*
   [*During the fray, Saturninus, Tamora, Demetrius,
   Chiron and Aaron go out and re-enter, above.*

         Re-enter LUCIUS.

   Luc. My lord, you are unjust, and, more than so,
In wrongful quarrel you have slain your son.
   Tit. Nor thou, nor he, are any sons of mine;
My sons would never so dishonour me:
Traitor, restore Lavinia to the emperor.
   Luc. Dead, if you will; but not to be his wife,
That is another's lawful promised love.   [*Exit.*
   Sat. No, Titus, no; the emperor needs her not,
Nor her, nor thee, nor any of thy stock: 300
I'll trust, by leisure, him that mocks me once;
Thee never, nor thy traitorous haughty sons,
Confederates all thus to dishonour me.
Was none in Rome to make a stale,
But Saturnine? Full well, Andronicus,
Agree these deeds with that proud brag of thine,
That said'st I begg'd the empire at thy hands.
   Tit. O monstrous! what reproachful words are
    these?
   Sat. But go thy ways; go, give that changing piece
To him that flourish'd for her with his sword: 310
A valiant son-in-law thou shalt enjoy;
One fit to bandy with thy lawless sons,
To ruffle in the commonwealth of Rome.
   Tit. These words are razors to my wounded heart.
   Sat. And therefore, lovely Tamora, queen of Goths,
That like the stately Phœbe 'mongst her nymphs
Dost overshine the gallant'st dames of Rome,
If thou be pleased with this my sudden choice,
Behold, I choose thee, Tamora, for my bride,
And will create thee empress of Rome.   320
Speak, Queen of Goths, dost thou applaud my choice?
And here I swear by all the Roman gods,
Sith priest and holy water are so near
And tapers burn so bright and every thing
In readiness for Hymenæus stand,
I will not re-salute the streets of Rome,

221. **gratulate,** salute, greet. 243. **motion,** proposal; see glossary.
245. **of,** by; see glossary. 250. **imperious,** so Q_1; Globe, following
Q_3F: *imperial.* 264. **change,** so Q_1; Globe, following $Q_{2-3}F_1$: *chance.*
cheer, countenance, appearance. 268-269. **he . . . Goths,** i.e., he who
can; the relative is frequently omitted. See Abbott, 244. 271. **sith,**

since; see glossary. 280. **'Suum cuique,'** to every man his own. 284.
surprised, assaulted, or perhaps taken. 301. **by leisure,** barely, not at
all. 304. **Was none,** so QqF_1; Globe, following F_{2-4}: *Was there none else.*
stale, tool, laughingstock. 309. **piece,** applied to a woman or girl; here
contemptuously. 313. **ruffle,** cause disturbance. 316. **Phœbe,** one of

Or climb my palace, till from forth this place
I lead espoused my bride along with me.

Tam. And here, in sight of heaven, to Rome I
swear,
If Saturnine advance the Queen of Goths, 330
She will a handmaid be to his desires,
A loving nurse, a mother to his youth.

Sat. Ascend, fair queen, Pantheon. Lords,
accompany
Your noble emperor and his lovely bride,
Sent by the heavens for Prince Saturnine,
Whose wisdom hath her fortune conquered:
There shall we consummate our spousal rites.

[*Exeunt all but Titus.*

Tit. I am not bid to wait upon this bride.
Titus, when wert thou wont to walk alone,
Dishonour'd thus, and challenged of wrongs? 340

Re-enter MARCUS, LUCIUS, QUINTUS, *and* MARTIUS.

Marc. O Titus, see, O, see what thou hast done!
In a bad quarrel slain a virtuous son.

Tit. No, foolish tribune, no; no son of mine,
Nor thou, nor these, confederates in the deed
That hath dishonour'd all our family;
Unworthy brother, and unworthy sons!

Luc. But let us give him burial, as becomes;
Give Mutius burial with our brethren.

Tit. Traitors, away! he rests not in this tomb:
This monument five hundred years hath stood, 350
Which I have sumptuously re-edified:
Here none but soldiers and Rome's servitors
Repose in fame; none basely slain in brawls:
Bury him where you can; he comes not here.

Marc. My lord, this is impiety in you:
My nephew Mutius' deeds do plead for him;
He must be buried with his brethren.

Quin.
Mart. } And shall, or him we will accompany.

Tit. 'And shall!' what villain was it spake that
word?

Quin. He that would vouch it in any place but here.

Tit. What, would you bury him in my despite? 361

Marc. No, noble Titus, but entreat of thee
To pardon Mutius and to bury him.

Tit. Marcus, even thou hast struck upon my crest,
And, with these boys, mine honour thou hast
wounded:
My foes I do repute you every one;
So, trouble me no more, but get you gone.

Mart. He is not with himself; let us withdraw.

Quin. Not I, till Mutius' bones be buried.

[*Marcus and the Sons of Titus kneel.*

Marc. Brother, for in that name doth nature
plead,— 370

Quin. Father, and in that name doth nature
speak,—

Tit. Speak thou no more, if all the rest will speed.

Marc. Renowned Titus, more than half my soul,—

Luc. Dear father, soul and substance of us all,—

Marc. Suffer thy brother Marcus to inter
His noble nephew here in virtue's nest,
That died in honour and Lavinia's cause.
Thou art a Roman; be not barbarous:

The Greeks upon advice did bury Ajax
That slew himself; and wise Laertes' son 380
Did graciously plead for his funerals:
Let not young Mutius, then, that was thy joy,
Be barr'd his entrance here.

Tit.   Rise, Marcus, rise.
The dismall'st day is this that e'er I saw,
To be dishonour'd by my sons in Rome!
Well, bury him, and bury me the next.

[*Mutius is put into the tomb.*

Luc. There lie thy bones, sweet Mutius, with thy
friends,
Till we with trophies do adorn thy tomb.

All. [*Kneeling*] No man shed tears for noble Mutius;
He lives in fame that died in virtue's cause. 390

Marc. My lord, to step out of these dreary dumps,
How comes it that the subtle Queen of Goths
Is of a sudden thus advanced in Rome?

Tit. I know not, Marcus; but I know it is:
Whether by device or no, the heavens can tell:
Is she not then beholding to the man
That brought her for this high good turn so far?
Yes, and will nobly him remunerate.

Flourish. Re-enter, from one side, SATURNINUS *attended,*
TAMORA, DEMETRIUS, CHIRON, *and* AARON; *from the*
other, BASSIANUS, LAVINIA, *and others.*

Sat. So, Bassianus, you have play'd your prize:
God give you joy, sir, of your gallant bride! 400

Bas. And you of yours, my lord! I say no more,
Nor wish no less; and so, I take my leave.

Sat. Traitor, if Rome have law or we have power,
Thou and thy faction shall repent this rape.

Bas. Rape, call you it, my lord, to seize my own,
My true-betrothed love and now my wife?
But let the laws of Rome determine all;
Meanwhile I am possess'd of that is mine.

Sat. 'Tis good, sir: you are very short with us;
But, if we live, we'll be as sharp with you. 410

Bas. My lord, what I have done, as best I may,
Answer I must and shall do with my life.
Only thus much I give your grace to know:
By all the duties that I owe to Rome,
This noble gentleman, Lord Titus here,
Is in opinion and in honour wrong'd;
That in the rescue of Lavinia
With his own hand did slay his youngest son,
In zeal to you and highly moved to wrath
To be controll'd in that he frankly gave: 420
Receive him, then, to favour, Saturnine,
That hath express'd himself in all his deeds
A father and a friend to thee and Rome.

Tit. Prince Bassianus, leave to plead my deeds:
'Tis thou and those that have dishonour'd me.
Rome and the righteous heavens be my judge,
How I have loved and honour'd Saturnine!

Tam. My worthy lord, if ever Tamora
Were gracious in those princely eyes of thine,
Then hear me speak indifferently for all; 430
And at my suit, sweet, pardon what is past.

Sat. What, madam! be dishonour'd openly,
And basely put it up without revenge?

Tam. Not so, my lord; the gods of Rome forfend

the names of the moon goddess. 325. **Hymenæus**, god of marriage.
340. **challenged**, accused. 366. **repute**, think of, consider. 372. **speed**,
succeed; see glossary. 379. **Ajax**, one of the heroes of the Trojan War.
Enraged because the arms of Achilles were allotted to Ulysses, he
stabbed himself. 380. **Laertes' son**, Ulysses. 391. **dreary dumps**,
mournful songs. 399. **play'd your prize**, won as in a contest. 408.
that, that which. 416. **opinion**, reputation; see glossary. 424. **leave to**
plead, cease pleading. 434. **forfend**, avert, forbid; see glossary.

I should be author to dishonour you!
But on mine honour dare I undertake
For good Lord Titus' innocence in all;
Whose fury not dissembled speaks his griefs:
Then, at my suit, look graciously on him;
Lose not so noble a friend on vain suppose, 440
Nor with sour looks afflict his gentle heart.
[Aside to Sat.] My lord, be ruled by me, be won at last;
Dissemble all your griefs and discontents:
You are but newly planted in your throne;
Lest, then, the people, and patricians too,
Upon a just survey, take Titus' part,
And so supplant you for ingratitude,
Which Rome reputes to be a heinous sin,
Yield at entreats; and then let me alone:
I'll find a day to massacre them all 450
And raze their faction and their family,
The cruel father and his traitorous sons,
To whom I sued for my dear son's life,
And make them know what 'tis to let a queen
Kneel in the streets and beg for grace in vain.

Come, come, sweet emperor; come, Andronicus;
Take up this good old man, and cheer the heart
That dies in tempest of thy angry frown.
    Sat. Rise, Titus, rise; my empress hath prevail'd.
    Tit. I thank your majesty, and her, my lord: 460
These words, these looks, infuse new life in me.
    Tam. Titus, I am incorporate in Rome,
A Roman now adopted happily,
And must advise the emperor for his good.
This day all quarrels die, Andronicus;
And let it be mine honour, good my lord,
That I have reconciled your friends and you.
For you, Prince Bassianus, I have pass'd
My word and promise to the emperor,
That you will be more mild and tractable. 470
And fear not, lords, and you, Lavinia;
By my advice, all humbled on your knees,
You shall ask pardon of his majesty.
    Luc. We do, and vow to heaven and to his highness,
That what we did was mildly as we might,
Tendering our sister's honour and our own.
    Marc. That, on mine honour, here I do protest.
    Sat. Away, and talk not; trouble us no more.
    Tam. Nay, nay, sweet emperor, we must all be
        friends:
The tribune and his nephews kneel for grace; 480
I will not be denied: sweet heart, look back.
    Sat. Marcus, for thy sake and thy brother's here,
And at my lovely Tamora's entreats,
I do remit these young men's heinous faults:
Stand up.
Lavinia, though you left me like a churl,
I found a friend, and sure as death I swore
I would not part a bachelor from the priest.
Come, if the emperor's court can feast two brides,
You are my guest, Lavinia, and your friends. 490
This day shall be a love-day, Tamora.

    Tit. To-morrow, an it please your majesty
To hunt the panther and the hart with me,
With horn and hound we'll give your grace bonjour.
    Sat. Be it so, Titus, and gramercy too.

[*Flourish. Exeunt.*

ACT II.

SCENE I. *Rome. Before the palace.*

Enter AARON.

    Aar. Now climbeth Tamora Olympus' top,
Safe out of fortune's shot; and sits aloft,
Secure of thunder's crack or lightning flash;
Advanced above pale envy's threatening reach.
As when the golden sun salutes the morn,
And, having gilt the ocean with his beams,
Gallops the zodiac in his glistering coach,
And overlooks the highest-peering hills;
So Tamora:
Upon her wit doth earthly honour wait, 10
And virtue stoops and trembles at her frown.
Then, Aaron, arm thy heart, and fit thy thoughts,
To mount aloft with thy imperial mistress,
And mount her pitch, whom thou in triumph long
Hast prisoner held, fetter'd in amorous chains
And faster bound to Aaron's charming eyes
Than is Prometheus tied to Caucasus.
Away with slavish weeds and servile thoughts!
I will be bright, and shine in pearl and gold,
To wait upon this new-made empress. 20
To wait, said I? to wanton with this queen,
This goddess, this Semiramis, this nymph,
This siren, that will charm Rome's Saturnine,
And see his shipwreck and his commonweal's.
Holloa! what storm is this?

Enter DEMETRIUS *and* CHIRON, *braving.*

    Dem. Chiron, thy years wants wit, thy wits wants
        edge,
And manners, to intrude where I am graced;
And may, for aught thou know'st, affected be.
    Chi. Demetrius, thou dost over-ween in all;
And so in this, to bear me down with braves. 30
'Tis not the difference of a year or two
Makes me less gracious or thee more fortunate:
I am as able and as fit as thou
To serve, and to deserve my mistress' grace;
And that my sword upon thee shall approve,
And plead my passions for Lavinia's love.
    Aar. [*Aside*] Clubs, clubs! these lovers will not keep
        the peace.
    Dem. Why, boy, although our mother, unadvised,
Gave you a dancing-rapier by your side,
Are you so desperate grown, to threat your friends? 40
Go to; have your lath glued within your sheath
Till you know better how to handle it.
    Chi. Meanwhile, sir, with the little skill I have,

Full well shalt thou perceive how much I dare.
  Dem. Ay, boy, grow ye so brave?   [*They draw*
  Aar.   [*Coming forward*] Why, how
    now, lords!
So near the emperor's palace dare you draw,
And maintain such a quarrel openly?
Full well I wot the ground of all this grudge:
I would not for a million of gold
'The cause were known to them it most concerns;   50
Nor would your noble mother for much more
Be so dishonour'd in the court of Rome.
For shame, put up.
  Dem.   Not I, till I have sheathed
My rapier in his bosom and withal
Thrust these reproachful speeches down his throat
That he hath breathed in my dishonour here.
  Chi. For that I am prepared and full resolved.
Foul-spoken coward, that thunder'st with thy tongue,
And with thy weapon nothing darest perform!
  Aar. Away, I say!   60
Now, by the gods that warlike Goths adore,
This petty brabble will undo us all.
Why, lords, and think you not how dangerous
It is to jet upon a prince's right?
What, is Lavinia then become so loose,
Or Bassianus so degenerate,
That for her love such quarrels may be broach'd
Without controlment, justice, or revenge?
Young lords, beware! an should the empress know
This discord's ground, the music would not please.   70
  Chi. I care not, I, knew she and all the world:
I love Lavinia more than all the world.
  Dem. Youngling, learn thou to make some meaner
    choice:
Lavinia is thine elder brother's hope.
  Aar. Why, are ye mad? or know ye not, in Rome
How furious and impatient they be,
And cannot brook competitors in love?
I tell you, lords, you do but plot your deaths
By this device.
  Chi.   Aaron, a thousand deaths
Would I propose to achieve her whom I love.   80
  Aar. To achieve her! how?
  Dem.   Why makest thou it so strange?
She is a woman, therefore may be woo'd;
She is a woman, therefore may be won;
She is Lavinia, therefore must be loved.
What, man! more water glideth by the mill
Than wots the miller of; and easy it is
Of a cut loaf to steal a shive, we know:
Though Bassianus be the emperor's brother,
Better than he have worn Vulcan's badge.
  Aar. [*Aside*] Ay, and as good as Saturninus may.   90
  Dem. Then why should he despair that knows to
    court it
With words, fair looks and liberality?
What, hast not thou full often struck a doe,
And borne her cleanly by the keeper's nose?
  Aar. Why, then, it seems, some certain snatch or so

Would serve your turns.
  Chi.   Ay, so the turn were served.
  Dem. Aaron, thou hast hit it.
  Aar.   Would you had hit it too!
Then should not we be tired with this ado.
Why, hark ye, hark ye! and are you such fools
To square for this? would it offend you, then,   100
That both should speed?
  Chi. Faith, not me.
  Dem.   Nor me, so I were one.
  Aar. For shame, be friends, and join for that you
    jar:
'Tis policy and stratagem must do
That you affect; and so must you resolve,
That what you cannot as you would achieve,
You must perforce accomplish as you may.
Take this of me: Lucrece was not more chaste
Than this Lavinia, Bassianus' love.
A speedier course than lingering languishment   110
Must we pursue, and I have found the path.
My lords, a solemn hunting is in hand;
There will the lovely Roman ladies troop:
The forest walks are wide and spacious;
And many unfrequented plots there are
Fitted by kind for rape and villany:
Single you thither then this dainty doe,
And strike her home by force, if not by words:
This way, or not at all, stand you in hope.
Come, come, our empress, with her sacred wit   120
To villany and vengeance consecrate,
Will we acquaint with all that we intend;
And she shall file our engines with advice,
That will not suffer you to square yourselves,
But to your wishes' height advance you both.
The emperor's court is like the house of Fame,
The palace full of tongues, of eyes, and ears:
The woods are ruthless, dreadful, deaf, and dull;
There speak, and strike, brave boys, and take your
    turns;
There serve your lust, shadow'd from heaven's eye,   130
And revel in Lavinia's treasury.
  Chi. Thy counsel, lad, smells of no cowardice.
  Dem. Sit fas aut nefas, till I find the stream
To cool this heat, a charm to calm these fits,
Per Styga, per manes vehor.   [*Exeunt.*

SCENE II. *A forest near Rome. Horns and cry of hounds heard.*

Enter TITUS ANDRONICUS, *with* Hunters, &c.,
MARCUS, LUCIUS, QUINTUS, *and* MARTIUS.

  Tit. The hunt is up, the morn is bright and grey,
The fields are fragrant and the woods are green:
Uncouple here and let us make a bay
And wake the emperor and his lovely bride
And rouse the prince and ring a hunter's peal,
That all the court may echo with the noise.
Sons, let it be your charge, as it is ours,
To attend the emperor's person carefully:

restraint. **70. discord's ground,** cause for discord. **73. meaner,** of
lower degree; see glossary. **77. brook,** endure; see glossary. **80.**
propose, look forward to, be ready to meet. **87. shive,** slice. **89.**
Vulcan's badge, cuckold's horns, alluding to the public shame to which
Venus, his wife, was exposed in her intrigue with Mars. **95. snatch,**
sudden or swift catch. **96. serve your turns,** answer your purposes;
see glossary. **103. join,** conspire. **jar,** quarrel; see glossary. **104.**
policy, contrivance, craft; see glossary. **107. perforce,** necessarily;
see glossary. **110. languishment,** long courtship. **113. troop,** march.
116. by kind, by nature; see *kind* in glossary; cf. the description (IV, i,
52-59) where this spot is said to be *by nature made for murders and for rapes.*

118. home, effectually, thoroughly; see glossary. **123. file,** rub
smooth, polish; here perhaps, perfect. **engines,** devices, plots; see
glossary. **126. house of Fame,** an allusion to *Chaucer's Hous of Fame.*
130. lust, so Qq; Globe, following F: *lusts.* **133. Sit fas aut nefas,** be it
right or wrong. **135. Per Styga, per manes vehor,** I am carried
across the Styx through the realm of the shades.
  SCENE II. **1. grey,** cold, sunless light of early morning; the phrase
is equivalent to "bright and early." **3. Uncouple,** unleash the hounds.
make a bay, keep up a deep, prolonged barking.

I have been troubled in my sleep this night,
But dawning day new comfort hath inspired. 10

A cry of hounds, and horns winded in a peal. Enter
SATURNINUS, TAMORA, BASSIANUS, LAVINIA,
DEMETRIUS, CHIRON, *and* Attendants.

Many good morrows to your majesty;
Madam, to you as many and as good:
I promised your grace a hunter's peal.
   Sat. And you have rung it lustily, my lords;
Somewhat too early for new-married ladies.
   Bas. Lavinia, how say you?
   Lav.   I say, no;
I have been broad awake two hours and more.
   Sat. Come on, then; horse and chariots let us have,
And to our sport. [*To Tamora*] Madam, now shall ye
   see
Our Roman hunting.
   Marc.   I have dogs, my lord, 20
Will rouse the proudest panther in the chase,
And climb the highest promontory top.
   Tit. And I have horse will follow where the game
Makes way, and run like swallows o'er the plain.
   Dem. Chiron, we hunt not, we, with horse nor
   hound,
But hope to pluck a dainty doe to ground.   [*Exeunt.*

SCENE III. *A lonely part of the forest.*

Enter AARON, *with a bag of gold.*

   Aar. He that had wit would think that I had none,
To bury so much gold under a tree,
And never after to inherit it.
Let him that thinks of me so abjectly
Know that this gold must coin a stratagem,
Which, cunningly effected, will beget
A very excellent piece of villany:
And so repose, sweet gold, for their unrest
                   [*Hides the gold.*
That have their alms out of the empress' chest.

Enter TAMORA.

   Tam. My lovely Aaron, wherefore look'st thou sad,
When every thing doth make a gleeful boast? 11
The birds chant melody on every bush,
The snake lies rolled in the cheerful sun,
The green leaves quiver with the cooling wind
And make a chequer'd shadow on the ground:
Under their sweet shade, Aaron, let us sit,
And, whilst the babbling echo mocks the hounds,
Replying shrilly to the well-tuned horns,
As if a double hunt were heard at once,
Let us sit down and mark their yellowing noise; 20
And, after conflict such as was supposed
The wandering prince and Dido once enjoy'd,
When with a happy storm they were surprised
And curtain'd with a counsel-keeping cave,
We may, each wreathed in the other's arms,
Our pastimes done, possess a golden slumber;

Whiles hounds and horns and sweet melodious birds
Be unto us as is a nurse's song
Of lullaby to bring her babe asleep.
   Aar. Madam, though Venus govern your desires, 30
Saturn is dominator over mine:
What signifies my deadly-standing eye,
My silence and my cloudy melancholy,
My fleece of woolly hair that now uncurls
Even as an adder when she doth unroll
To do some fatal execution?
No, madam, these are no venereal signs:
Vengeance is in my heart, death in my hand,
Blood and revenge are hammering in my head.
Hark, Tamora, the empress of my soul, 40
Which never hopes more heaven than rests in thee,
This is the day of doom for Bassianus:
His Philomel must lose her tongue to-day,
Thy sons make pillage of her chastity
And wash their hands in Bassianus' blood.
Seest thou this letter? take it up, I pray thee,
And give the king this fatal-plotted scroll.
Now question me no more; we are espied;
Here comes a parcel of our hopeful booty,
Which dreads not yet their lives' destruction. 50
   Tam. Ah, my sweet Moor, sweeter to me than life!
   Aar. No more, great empress; Bassianus comes:
Be cross with him; and I'll go fetch thy sons
To back thy quarrels, whatsoe'er they be.   [*Exit.*

Enter BASSIANUS *and* LAVINIA.

   Bas. Who have we here? Rome's royal empress,
Unfurnish'd of her well-beseeming troop?
Or is it Dian, habited like her,
Who hath abandoned her holy groves
To see the general hunting in this forest?
   Tam. Saucy controller of our private steps! 60
Had I the power that some say Dian had,
Thy temples should be planted presently
With horns, as was Actæon's; and the hounds
Should drive upon thy new-transformed limbs,
Unmannerly intruder as thou art!
   Lav. Under your patience, gentle empress,
'Tis thought you have a goodly gift in horning;
And to be doubted that your Moor and you
Are singled forth to try experiments:
Jove shield your husband from his hounds to-day! 70
'Tis pity they should take him for a stag.
   Bas. Believe me, queen, your swarthy Cimmerian
Doth make your honour of his body's hue,
Spotted, detested, and abominable.
Why are you sequester'd from all your train,
Dismounted from your snow-white goodly steed,
And wander'd hither to an obscure plot,
Accompanied but with a barbarous Moor,
If foul desire had not conducted you?
   Lav. And, being intercepted in your sport, 80
Great reason that my noble lord be rated
For sauciness. I pray you, let us hence,
And let her joy her raven-colour'd love;
This valley fits the purpose passing well.

---

9. **troubled . . . sleep.** The ominousness of bad dreams is a commonplace in Elizabethan tragedy. 14. **lords,** so QqFf; Globe, following
Dyce: *lord.*
  SCENE III. 4. **abjectly,** basely. 5. **coin,** fabricate; here, to further
Aaron's plot. 13. **rolled,** coiled. 20. **yellowing,** (so Qq), baying; a
rarely used word, now obsolete (*NED* gives three instances of its
occurrence, including this one); Globe, following F: *yelping.* 24.
counsel-keeping, secret-keeping. 31. **Saturn . . . mine.** Aaron describes
himself in terms of current astrology, according to which the planet

Saturn exercised a malign influence over those whom it dominated.
32. **deadly-standing,** fixed with a deathly stare. 37. **venereal,** erotic.
43. **Philomel,** an allusion to the story in Ovid's *Metamorphoses* of Philomela, raped by her brother-in-law, Tereus (cf. II, iv, 26 below); he cut
out her tongue so that she could not disclose his villainy. She succeeded in
weaving the account of her misfortune in a tapestry. 47. **fatal-plotted,**
designed to prove fatal. 49. **parcel,** small party or company. 57.
Dian, Diana, huntress and goddess of chastity; here used sarcastically.
62. **presently,** immediately; see glossary. 63. **Actæon's,** an allusion

Bas. The king my brother shall have notice of this.
Lav. Ay, for these slips have made him noted long:
Good king, to be so mightily abused!
Tam. Why have I patience to endure all this?

Enter DEMETRIUS *and* CHIRON.

Dem. How now, dear sovereign, and our gracious
    mother!
Why doth your highness look so pale and wan?   90
Tam. Have I not reason, think you, to look pale?
These two have 'ticed me hither to this place:
A barren detested vale, you see it is;
The trees, though summer, yet forlorn and lean,
O'ercome with moss and baleful mistletoe:
Here never shines the sun; here nothing breeds,
Unless the nightly owl or fatal raven:
And when they show'd me this abhorred pit,
They told me, here, at dead time of the night,
A thousand fiends, a thousand hissing snakes,   100
Ten thousand swelling toads, as many urchins,
Would make such fearful and confused cries
As any mortal body hearing it
Should straight fall mad, or else die suddenly.
No sooner had they told this hellish tale,
But straight they told me they would bind me here
Unto the body of a dismal yew,
And leave me to this miserable death:
And then they call'd me foul adulteress,
Lascivious Goth, and all the bitterest terms   110
That ever ear did hear to such effect:
And, had you not by wondrous fortune come,
This vengeance on me had they executed.
Revenge it, as you love your mother's life,
Or be ye not henceforth call'd my children.
Dem. This is a witness that I am thy son.
                                [*Stabs Bassianus.*
Chi. And this for me, struck home to show my
    strength.   [*Also stabs Bassianus, who dies.*
Lav. Ay, come, Semiramis, nay, barbarous Tamora,
For no name fits thy nature but thy own!   119
Tam. Give me thy poniard; you shall know, my boys,
Your mother's hand shall right your mother's wrong.
Dem. Stay, madam; here is more belongs to her;
First thrash the corn, then after burn the straw:
This minion stood upon her chastity,
Upon her nuptial vow, her loyalty,
†And with that painted hope braves your mightiness:
And shall she carry this unto her grave?
Chi. An if she do, I would I were an eunuch.
Drag hence her husband to some secret hole,
And make his dead trunk pillow to our lust.   130
Tam. But when ye have the honey ye desire,
Let not this wasp outlive, us both to sting.
Chi. I warrant you, madam, we will make that sure.
Come, mistress, now perforce we will enjoy
That nice-preserved honesty of yours.
Lav. O Tamora! thou bear'st a woman's face,—
Tam. I will not hear her speak; away with her!
Lav. Sweet lords, entreat her hear me but a word.
Dem. Listen, fair madam: let it be your glory

To see her tears; but be your heart to them   140
As unrelenting flint to drops of rain.
Lav. When did the tiger's young ones teach the
    dam?
O, do not learn her wrath; she taught it thee;
The milk thou suck'dst from her did turn to marble;
Even at thy teat thou hadst thy tyranny.
Yet every mother breeds not sons alike:
[*To Chiron*] Do thou entreat her show a woman's pity.
Chi. What, wouldst thou have me prove myself a
    bastard?
Lav. 'Tis true; the raven doth not hatch a lark:
Yet have I heard,—O, could I find it now!—   150
The lion moved with pity did endure
To have his princely paws pared all away:
Some say that ravens foster forlorn children,
The whilst their own birds famish in their nests:
O, be to me, though thy hard heart say no,
Nothing so kind, but something pitiful!
Tam. I know not what it means; away with her!
Lav. O, let me teach thee! for my father's sake,
That gave thee life, when well he might have slain
    thee,
Be not obdurate, open thy deaf ears.   160
Tam. Hadst thou in person ne'er offended me,
Even for his sake am I pitiless.
Remember, boys, I pour'd forth tears in vain,
To save your brother from the sacrifice;
But fierce Andronicus would not relent:
Therefore, away with her, and use her as you will,
The worse to her, the better loved of me.
Lav. O Tamora, be call'd a gentle queen,
And with thine own hands kill me in this place!
For 'tis not life that I have begg'd so long;   170
Poor I was slain when Bassianus died.
Tam. What begg'st thou, then? fond woman, let me
    go.
Lav. 'Tis present death I beg; and one thing more
That womanhood denies my tongue to tell:
O, keep me from their worse than killing lust,
And tumble me into some loathsome pit,
Where never man's eye may behold my body:
Do this, and be a charitable murderer.
Tam. So should I rob my sweet sons of their fee:
No, let them satisfy their lust on thee.   180
Dem. Away! for thou hast stay'd us here too long.
Lav. No grace? no womanhood? Ah, beastly
    creature!
The blot and enemy to our general name!
Confusion fall—
Chi. Nay, then I'll stop your mouth. Bring thou her
    husband:
This is the hole where Aaron bid us hide him.
    [*Demetrius throws the body of Bassianus into the pit; then
        exeunt Demetrius and Chiron, dragging off Lavinia.*
Tam. Farewell, my sons: see that you make her sure.
Ne'er let my heart know merry cheer indeed,
Till all the Andronici be made away.
Now will I hence to seek my lovely Moor,   190
And let my spleenful sons this trull deflour.   [*Exit.*

to the story of Actaeon, who was changed into a stag by Diana as
punishment for watching her and her nymphs at their bath. 68.
doubted, suspected, feared; see glossary. 72. **swarthy,** Qq: *swartie;*
Globe, following F: *swarth.* **Cimmerian,** an allusion to the Cimmerii
in the *Odyssey,* a race who lived in perpetual darkness; the reference is
to Aaron's black complexion. 81. **rated,** chidden; see glossary. 85.
notice, so QqFf; Globe, following Pope: *note;* the pronunciation is
"notes." 86. **noted,** stigmatized. The line suggests an unaccountable
passing of time. 87. **abused,** deceived; see glossary. 92. **'ticed,** enticed.

101. **urchins,** hedgehogs. 103. **mortal,** human; see glossary. 110.
Goth, a quibble; the word was pronounced somewhat like "goat,"
which is the allegorical symbol of lechery. 124. **minion,** favorite (used
contemptuously); see glossary. 126. **painted,** specious, unreal; see
glossary. 143. **learn,** teach; see glossary. 147. **woman's,** so Q₁; Globe,
following Q₂-₃F: *woman.* 153. **forlorn,** wretched in appearance,
meager. 156. **Nothing,** not at all; see glossary. **something,** somewhat;
see glossary. 172. **fond,** foolish; see glossary. 173. **present,** immediate;
see glossary. 174. **denies,** refuses permission; see glossary.

Re-enter AARON, *with* QUINTUS *and* MARTIUS.

Aar. Come on, my lords, the better foot before:
Straight will I bring you to the loathsome pit
Where I espied the panther fast asleep.
Quin. My sight is very dull, whate'er it bodes.
Mart. And mine, I promise you; were 't not for
    shame,
Well could I leave our sport to sleep awhile.
                                 [Falls into the pit.
Quin. What, art thou fall'n? What subtle hole is this,
Whose mouth is cover'd with rude-growing briers,
Upon whose leaves are drops of new-shed blood   200
As fresh as morning dew distill'd on flowers?
A very fatal place it seems to me.
Speak, brother, hast thou hurt thee with the fall?
Mart. O brother, with the dismall'st object hurt
That ever eye with sight made heart lament!
Aar. [*Aside*] Now will I fetch the king to find them
    here,
That he thereby may give a likely guess
How these were they that made away his brother.[*Exit.*
Mart. Why dost not comfort me, and help me out
From this unhallowed and blood-stained hole?   210
Quin. I am surprised with an uncouth fear:
A chilling sweat o'er-runs my trembling joints:
My heart suspects more than mine eye can see.
Mart. To prove thou hast a true-divining heart,
Aaron and thou look down into this den,
And see a fearful sight of blood and death.
Quin. Aaron is gone; and my compassionate heart
Will not permit mine eyes once to behold
The thing whereat it trembles by surmise:
O, tell me who it is; for ne'er till now   220
Was I a child to fear I know not what.
Mart. Lord Bassianus lies embrewed here,
All on a heap, like to a slaughter'd lamb,
In this detested, dark, blood-drinking pit.
Quin. If it be dark, how dost thou know 'tis he?
Mart. Upon his bloody finger he doth wear
A precious ring, that lightens all this hole,
Which, like a taper in some monument,
Doth shine upon the dead man's earthy cheeks,
And shows the ragged entrails of this pit: 230
So pale did shine the moon on Pyramus
When he by night lay bathed in maiden blood.
O brother, help me with thy fainting hand—
If fear hath made thee faint, as me it hath—
Out of this fell devouring receptacle,
As hateful as Cocytus' misty mouth.
Quin. Reach me thy hand, that I may help thee out;
Or, wanting strength to do thee so much good,
I may be pluck'd into the swallowing womb
Of this deep pit, poor Bassianus' grave.   240
I have no strength to pluck thee to the brink.
Mart. Nor I no strength to climb without thy help.
Quin. Thy hand once more; I will not loose again,
Till thou art here aloft, or I below:
Thou canst not come to me: I come to thee.   [*Falls in.*

Enter SATURNINUS *with* AARON.

Sat. Along with me: I'll see what hole is here,

And what he is that now is leap'd into it.
Say, who art thou that lately didst descend
Into this gaping hollow of the earth?
Mart. The unhappy sons of old Andronicus;   250
Brought hither in a most unlucky hour,
To find thy brother Bassianus dead.
Sat. My brother dead! I know thou dost but jest:
He and his lady both are at the lodge
Upon the north side of this pleasant chase;
'Tis not an hour since I left him there.
Mart. We know not where you left them all alive;
But, out, alas! here have we found him dead.

Re-enter TAMORA, *with* Attendants; TITUS
    ANDRONICUS, *and* LUCIUS.

Tam. Where is my lord the king?
Sat. Here, Tamora, though grieved with killing
    grief.   260
Tam. Where is thy brother Bassianus?
Sat. Now to the bottom dost thou search my wound:
Poor Bassianus here lies murdered.
Tam. Then all too late I bring this fatal writ,
The complot of this timeless tragedy;
And wonder greatly that man's face can fold
In pleasing smiles such murderous tyranny.
                   [She giveth Saturnine a letter.
Sat. [*Reads*] 'An if we miss to meet him handsomely—
Sweet huntsman, Bassianus 'tis we mean—
Do thou so much as dig the grave for him: 270
Thou know'st our meaning. Look for thy reward
Among the nettles at the elder-tree
Which overshades the mouth of that same pit
Where we decreed to bury Bassianus.
Do this, and purchase us thy lasting friends.'
O Tamora! was ever heard the like?
This is the pit, and this the elder-tree.
Look, sirs, if you can find the huntsman out
That should have murder'd Bassianus here.
Aar. My gracious lord, here is the bag of gold.   280
Sat. [*To Titus*] Two of thy whelps, fell curs of
    bloody kind,
Have here bereft my brother of his life.
Sirs, drag them from the pit unto the prison:
There let them bide until we have devised
Some never-heard-of torturing pain for them.
Tam. What, are they in this pit? O wondrous thing!
How easily murder is discovered!
Tit. High emperor, upon my feeble knee
I beg this boon, with tears not lightly shed,
That this fell fault of my accursed sons,   290
Accursed, if the fault be proved in them,—
Sat. If it be proved! you see it is apparent.
Who found this letter? Tamora, was it you?
Tam. Andronicus himself did take it up.
Tit. I did, my lord: yet let me be their bail:
For, by my father's reverend tomb, I vow
They shall be ready at your highness' will
To answer their suspicion with their lives.
Sat. Thou shalt not bail them: see thou follow me.
Some bring the murder'd body, some the murderers:
Let them not speak a word; the guilt is plain;   301
For, by my soul, were there worse end than death,

---

193. **Straight,** immediately; see glossary. 217. **compassionate,** piteous, lamenting. 220. **who,** so Q_{1-2}; Globe, following Q_3F_1: *how.* 222. **embrewed here,** stained with blood. This is the Q_2 correction of Q_1: *bereaud in blood.* The unique copy of Q_1 has a marginal correction here in contemporary handwriting: "heere reau'd of lyfe." 227. **A precious ring,** presumably the carbuncle, which was believed to emit light.

this, so Q_{1-2}; Globe, following Q_3F_1: *the.* 230. **this,** so Qq; Globe, following F_1: *the.* 231. **Pyramus.** Cf. the story of Pyramus and Thisbe dramatized by the "rude mechanicals" in *A Midsummer-Night's Dream,* I, ii; III, i; and V, i, 127-369. 236. **Cocytus,** one of the rivers of Hades —the river of lamentations. 250. **sons,** so Q_1; Globe, following $Q_{2-3}F_1$: *son.* 257. **them,** so Qq; Globe, following F_1: *him.* 292. **apparent,** evi-

That end upon them should be executed.
  Tam. Andronicus, I will entreat the king:
Fear not thy sons; they shall do well enough.
  Tit. Come, Lucius, come; stay not to talk with
    them.   [*Exeunt.*

SCENE IV. *Another part of the forest.*

Enter DEMETRIUS *and* CHIRON *with* LAVINIA, *ravished;
  her hands cut off, and her tongue cut out.*

  Dem. So, now go tell, an if thy tongue can speak,
Who 'twas that cut thy tongue and ravish'd thee.
  Chi. Write down thy mind, bewray thy meaning so,
An if thy stumps will let thee play the scribe.
  Dem. See, how with signs and tokens she can scrowl.
  Chi. Go home, call for sweet water, wash thy hands.
  Dem. She hath no tongue to call, nor hands to wash;
And so let 's leave her to her silent walks.
  Chi. An 'twere my cause, I should go hang myself.
  Dem. If thou hadst hands to help thee knit the cord.
                        [*Exeunt Demetrius and Chiron.*

Enter MARCUS.

  Mar. Who is this? my niece, that flies away so fast! 11
Cousin, a word; where is your husband?
If I do dream, would all my wealth would wake me!
If I do wake, some planet strike me down,
That I may slumber in eternal sleep!
Speak, gentle niece, what stern ungentle hands
Hath lopp'd and hew'd and made thy body bare
Of her two branches, those sweet ornaments,
Whose circling shadows kings have sought to sleep in,
And might not gain so great a happiness   20
As have thy love? Why dost not speak to me?
Alas, a crimson river of warm blood,
Like to a bubbling fountain stirr'd with wind,
Doth rise and fall between thy rosed lips,
Coming and going with thy honey breath.
But, sure, some Tereus hath deflowered thee,
And, lest thou shouldst detect him, cut thy tongue.
Ah, now thou turn'st away thy face for shame!
And, notwithstanding all this loss of blood,
As from a conduit with three issuing spouts,   30
Yet do thy cheeks look red as Titan's face
Blushing to be encounter'd with a cloud.
Shall I speak for thee? shall I say 'tis so?
O, that I knew thy heart; and knew the beast,
That I might rail at him, to ease my mind!
Sorrow concealed, like an oven stopp'd,
Doth burn the heart to cinders where it is.
Fair Philomela, she but lost her tongue,
And in a tedious sampler sew'd her mind:
But, lovely niece, that mean is cut from thee;   40
A craftier Tereus, cousin, hast thou met,
And he hath cut those pretty fingers off,
That could have better sew'd than Philomel.
O, had the monster seen those lily hands
Tremble, like aspen-leaves, upon a lute,
And make the silken strings delight to kiss them,
He would not then have touch'd them for his life!
Or, had he heard the heavenly harmony

Which that sweet tongue hath made,
He would have dropp'd his knife, and fell asleep   50
As Cerberus at the Thracian poet's feet.
Come, let us go, and make thy father blind;
For such a sight will blind a father's eye:
One hour's storm will drown the fragrant meads;
What will whole months of tears thy father's eyes?
Do not draw back, for we will mourn with thee:
O, could our mourning ease thy misery!   [*Exeunt.*

ACT III.

SCENE I. *Rome. A street.*

Enter Judges, Senators *and* Tribunes, *with* MARTIUS
  and QUINTUS, *bound, passing on to the place of
  execution;* TITUS *going before, pleading.*

  Tit. Hear me, grave fathers! noble tribunes, stay!
For pity of mine age, whose youth was spent
In dangerous wars, whilst you securely slept;
For all my blood in Rome's great quarrel shed;
For all the frosty nights that I have watch'd;
And for these bitter tears, which now you see
Filling the aged wrinkles in my cheeks;
Be pitiful to my condemned sons,
Whose souls is not corrupted as 'tis thought.
For two and twenty sons I never wept,   10
Because they died in honour's lofty bed.
        [*Lieth down; the Judges, &c. pass by him, and Exeunt.*
For these, tribunes, in the dust I write
My heart's deep languor and my soul's sad tears:
Let my tears stanch the earth's dry appetite;
My sons' sweet blood will make it shame and blush.
O earth, I will befriend thee more with rain,
That shall distil from these two ancient urns,
Than youthful April shall with all his showers:
In summer's drought I'll drop upon thee still;
In winter with warm tears I'll melt the snow,   20
And keep eternal spring-time on thy face,
So thou refuse to drink my dear sons' blood.

Enter LUCIUS, *with his sword drawn.*

O reverend tribunes! O gentle, aged men!
Unbind my sons, reverse the doom of death;
And let me say, that never wept before,
My tears are now prevailing orators.
  Luc. O noble father, you lament in vain:
The tribunes hear you not; no man is by;
And you recount your sorrows to a stone.
  Tit. Ah, Lucius, for thy brothers let me plead.   30
Grave tribunes, once more I entreat of you,—
  Luc. My gracious lord, no tribune hears you speak.
  Tit. Why, 'tis no matter, man: if they did hear,
They would not mark me, or if they did mark,
They would not pity me, yet plead I must;
†And bootless unto them. . . . .
Therefore I tell my sorrows to the stones;
Who, though they cannot answer my distress,
Yet in some sort they are better than the tribunes,
For that they will not intercept my tale: 40
When I do weep, they humbly at my feet

---

dent; see glossary.   298. **their suspicion,** i.e., suspicion they are under.
  SCENE IV.   3. **bewray,** reveal.   5. **scrowl,** scrawl, with play on
"scroll."   9. **cause,** so QqF₁; Globe, following Pope: *case.*   12. **Cousin,**
kinswoman; see glossary.   17. **Hath,** so QqF₁; Globe, following F₂₋₄:
Have.   26. **Tereus.** Cf. II, iii, 43, note.   27. **detect,** expose.   40. **mean,**
means, agency; see glossary.   51. **Thracian poet's,** Orpheus'.

ACT III. SCENE I.   4. **my blood,** i.e., blood of my sons.   9. **is,** so
QqF₁; Globe, following F₂₋₄: *are.*   12. **these,** so QqF; Globe, following
F₂₋₄: *these, these.*   40. **For that,** because; see glossary.

Receive my tears and seem to weep with me;
And, were they but attired in grave weeds,
Rome could afford no tribunes like to these.
A stone is soft as wax,—tribunes more hard than
    stones;
A stone is silent, and offendeth not,
And tribunes with their tongues doom men to death.
                                                      [*Rises.*
But wherefore stand'st thou with thy weapon drawn?
    Luc. To rescue my two brothers from their death:
For which attempt the judges have pronounced   50
My everlasting doom of banishment.
    Tit. O happy man! they have befriended thee.
Why, foolish Lucius, dost thou not perceive
That Rome is but a wilderness of tigers?
Tigers must prey, and Rome affords no prey
But me and mine: how happy art thou, then,
From these devourers to be banished!
But who comes with our brother Marcus here?

        Enter MARCUS *and* LAVINIA.

    Marc. Titus, prepare thy aged eyes to weep;
Or, if not so, thy noble heart to break: 60
I bring consuming sorrow to thine age.
    Tit. Will it consume me? let me see it, then.
    Marc. This was thy daughter.
    Tit.   Why, Marcus, so she is.
    Luc. Ay me, this object kills me!
    Tit. Faint-hearted boy, arise, and look upon her.
Speak, Lavinia, what accursed hand
Hath made thee handless in thy father's sight?
What fool hath added water to the sea,
Or brought a faggot to bright-burning Troy?
My grief was at the height before thou camest,   70
And now, like Nilus, it disdaineth bounds.
Give me a sword, I'll chop off my hands too;
For they have fought for Rome, and all in vain;
And they have nursed this woe, in feeding life;
In bootless prayer have they been held up,
And they have served me to effectless use:
Now all the service I require of them
Is that the one will help to cut the other.
'Tis well, Lavinia, that thou hast no hands;
For hands, to do Rome service, is but vain.   80
    Luc. Speak, gentle sister, who hath martyr'd thee?
    Marc. O, that delightful engine of her thoughts,
That blabb'd them with such pleasing eloquence,
Is torn from forth that pretty hollow cage,
Where, like a sweet melodious bird, it sung
Sweet varied notes, enchanting every ear!
    Luc. O, say thou for her, who hath done this deed?
    Marc. O, thus I found her, straying in the park,
Seeking to hide herself, as doth the deer
That hath received some unrecuring wound.   90
    Tit. It was my deer; and he that wounded her
Hath hurt me more than had he kill'd me dead:
For now I stand as one upon a rock
Environ'd with a wilderness of sea,
Who marks the waxing tide grow wave by wave,
Expecting ever when some envious surge
Will in his brinish bowels swallow him.
This way to death my wretched sons are gone;

Here stands my other son, a banish'd man,
And here my brother, weeping at my woes: 100
But that which gives my soul the greatest spurn,
Is dear Lavinia, dearer than my soul.
Had I but seen thy picture in this plight,
It would have madded me: what shall I do
Now I behold thy lively body so?
Thou hast no hands, to wipe away thy tears,
Nor tongue, to tell me who hath martyr'd thee:
Thy husband he is dead; and for his death
Thy brothers are condemn'd, and dead by this.
Look, Marcus! ah, son Lucius, look on her!   110
When I did name her brothers, then fresh tears
Stood on her cheeks, as doth the honey-dew
Upon a gather'd lily almost wither'd.
    Marc. Perchance she weeps because they kill'd her
        husband;
Perchance because she knows them innocent.
    Tit. If they did kill thy husband, then be joyful,
Because the law hath ta'en revenge on them.
No, no, they would not do so foul a deed;
Witness the sorrow that their sister makes.
Gentle Lavinia, let me kiss thy lips;   120
Or make some sign how I may do thee ease:
Shall thy good uncle, and thy brother Lucius,
And thou, and I, sit round about some fountain,
Looking all downwards, to behold our cheeks
How they are stain'd, as meadows, yet not dry,
With miry slime left on them by a flood?
And in the fountain shall we gaze so long
Till the fresh taste be taken from that clearness,
And made a brine-pit with our bitter tears?
Or shall we cut away our hands, like thine?   130
Or shall we bite our tongues, and in dumb shows
Pass the remainder of our hateful days?
What shall we do? let us, that have our tongues,
Plot some device of further misery,
To make us wonder'd at in time to come.
    Luc. Sweet father, cease your tears; for, at your grief,
See how my wretched sister sobs and weeps.
    Marc. Patience, dear niece. Good Titus, dry thine
        eyes.
    Tit. Ah, Marcus, Marcus! brother, well I wot
Thy napkin cannot drink a tear of mine,   140
For thou, poor man, hast drown'd it with thine own.
    Luc. Ah, my Lavinia, I will wipe thy cheeks.
    Tit. Mark, Marcus, mark! I understand her signs:
Had she a tongue to speak, now would she say
That to her brother which I said to thee:
His napkin, with his true tears all bewet,
Can do no service on her sorrowful cheeks.
O, what a sympathy of woe is this,
As far from help as Limbo is from bliss!

        Enter AARON.

    Aar. Titus Andronicus, my lord the emperor   150
Sends thee this word,—that, if thou love thy sons,
Let Marcus, Lucius, or thyself, old Titus,
Or any one of you, chop off your hand,
And send it to the king: he for the same
Will send thee hither both thy sons alive;
And that shall be the ransom for their fault.

44. **tribunes,** so Q$_1$; Globe, following Q$_{2-3}$F$_1$: *tribune.* 80. **is,** so QqF$_1$;
Globe, following Rowe: *are.* 90. **unrecuring,** incurable. 96. **envious,**
spiteful; see glossary. 104. **madded,** maddened. 121. **ease,** comfort;
see glossary. 140. **napkin,** handkerchief; see glossary. 148. **sympathy,**
agreement, conformity. 149. **Limbo,** region bordering Hell, where
were confined the souls of those barred from heaven through no fault

of their own, such as good men who lived before the Christian era.
179. **meet,** fit, ready. 203-206. **O . . . face.** This is the conventional
pose of the Machiavellian villain, who frankly analyzes his character
and motives in "asides" to the audience. His villainy is without other
motive than a desire to express a character absolutely evil. The convention was made popular on the Elizabethan stage by Marlowe's

Tit. O gracious emperor! O gentle Aaron!
Did ever raven sing so like a lark,
That gives sweet tidings of the sun's uprise?
With all my heart, I'll send the emperor   160
My hand:
Good Aaron, wilt thou help to chop it off?
   Luc. Stay, father! for that noble hand of thine,
That hath thrown down so many enemies,
Shall not be sent: my hand will serve the turn:
My youth can better spare my blood than you;
And therefore mine shall save my brothers' lives.
   Marc. Which of your hands hath not defended Rome,
And rear'd aloft the bloody battle-axe,
Writing destruction on the enemy's castle?   170
O, none of both but are of high desert:
My hand hath been but idle; let it serve
To ransom my two nephews from their death;
Then have I kept it to a worthy end.
   Aar. Nay, come, agree whose hand shall go along,
For fear they die before their pardon come.
   Marc. My hand shall go.
   Luc.   By heaven, it shall not go!
   Tit. Sirs, strive no more: such wither'd herbs as
      these
Are meet for plucking up, and therefore mine.
   Luc. Sweet father, if I shall be thought thy son,   180
Let me redeem my brothers both from death.
   Marc. And, for our father's sake and mother's care,
Now let me show a brother's love to thee.
   Tit. Agree between you; I will spare my hand.
   Luc. Then I'll go fetch an axe.
   Marc. But I will use the axe.
                              [*Exeunt Lucius and Marcus.*
   Tit. Come hither, Aaron; I'll deceive them both:
Lend me thy hand, and I will give thee mine.
   Aar. [*Aside*] If that be call'd deceit, I will be honest,
And never, whilst I live, deceive men so: 190
But I'll deceive you in another sort,
And that you'll say, ere half an hour pass.
                              [*Cuts off Titus's hand.*

Re-enter LUCIUS *and* MARCUS.

   Tit. Now stay your strife: what shall be is
      dispatch'd.
Good Aaron, give his majesty my hand:
Tell him it was a hand that warded him
From thousand dangers; bid him bury it;
More hath it merited; that let it have.
As for my sons, say I account of them
As jewels purchased at an easy price;
And yet dear too, because I bought mine own.   200
   Aar. I go, Andronicus: and for thy hand
Look by and by to have thy sons with thee.
[*Aside*] Their heads, I mean. O, how this villany
Doth fat me with the very thoughts of it!
Let fools do good, and fair men call for grace,
Aaron will have his soul black like his face.   [*Exit.*
   Tit. O, here I lift this one hand up to heaven,
And bow this feeble ruin to the earth:
If any power pities wretched tears,
To that I call! [*To Lav.*] What, wouldst thou kneel
      with me?   210

Do, then, dear heart; for heaven shall hear our
      prayers;
Or with our sighs we'll breathe the welkin dim,
And stain the sun with fog, as sometime clouds
When they do hug him in their melting bosoms.
   Marc. O brother, speak with possibilities,
And do not break into these deep extremes.
   Tit. Is not my sorrow deep, having no bottom?
Then be my passions bottomless with them.
   Marc. But yet let reason govern thy lament.
   Tit. If there were reason for these miseries,   220
Then into limits could I bind my woes:
When heaven doth weep, doth not the earth o'erflow?
If the winds rage, doth not the sea wax mad,
Threatening the welkin with his big-swoln face?
And wilt thou have a reason for this coil?
I am the sea; hark, how her sighs do blow!
She is the weeping welkin, I the earth:
Then must my sea be moved with her sighs;
Then must my earth with her continual tears
Become a deluge, overflow'd and drown'd;   230
For why my bowels cannot hide her woes,
But like a drunkard must I vomit them.
Then give me leave, for losers will have leave
To ease their stomachs with their bitter tongues.

Enter a Messenger, *with two heads and a hand.*

   Mess. Worthy Andronicus, ill art thou repaid
For that good hand thou sent'st the emperor.
Here are the heads of thy two noble sons;
And here's thy hand, in scorn to thee sent back;
Thy griefs their sports, thy resolution mock'd;
That woe is me to think upon thy woes   240
More than remembrance of my father's death.   [*Exit.*
   Marc. Now let hot Ætna cool in Sicily,
And be my heart an ever-burning hell!
These miseries are more than may be borne.
To weep with them that weep doth ease some deal;
But sorrow flouted at is double death.
   Luc. Ah, that this sight should make so deep a
      wound,
And yet detested life not shrink thereat!
That ever death should let life bear his name,
Where life hath no more interest but to breathe!   250
                              [*Lavinia kisses Titus.*
   Marc. Alas, poor heart, that kiss is comfortless
As frozen water to a starved snake.
   Tit. When will this fearful slumber have an end?
   Marc. Now, farewell, flattery: die, Andronicus;
Thou dost not slumber: see, thy two sons' heads,
Thy warlike hand, thy mangled daughter here;
Thy other banish'd son, with this dear sight
Struck pale and bloodless; and thy brother, I,
Even like a stony image, cold and numb.
Ah, now no more will I control thy griefs: 260
Rend off thy silver hair, thy other hand
Gnawing with thy teeth; and be this dismal sight
The closing up of our most wretched eyes:
Now is a time to storm; why art thou still?
   Tit. Ha, ha, ha!
   Marc. Why dost thou laugh? it fits not with this
      hour.

Barabas in *The Jew of Malta*. Shakespeare employed it in several characters—Richard III, Edmund in *King Lear*, and Iago in *Othello*, in the
last of which it is treated with consummate art. 210. **wouldst**, so Q₁;
Globe, following Ff: *wilt*. 212. **welkin**, sky, heavens; see glossary.
213. **sometime**, from time to time; see glossary. 215. **speak with
possibilities**, speak of things possible. 225. **coil**, noise, fuss; see glossary.

231. **For why**, because. 234. **stomachs**, resentful feelings; see glossary.
239. **resolution**, resolute conduct. 242. Ætna, volcanic mountain on
the island of Sicily. 245. **some deal**, somewhat, a little. 252. **starved**,
benumbed with cold; see glossary. 253. **fearful**, fear-inspiring,
dreadful; see glossary. 254. **flattery**, gratifying deception. 257. **dear**,
grievous; see glossary.

Tit. Why, I have not another tear to shed:
Besides, this sorrow is an enemy,
And would usurp upon my watery eyes,
And make them blind with tributary tears: 270
Then which way shall I find Revenge's cave?
For these two heads do seem to speak to me,
And threat me I shall never come to bliss
Till all these mischiefs be return'd again
Even in their throats that hath committed them.
Come, let me see what task I have to do.
You heavy people, circle me about,
That I may turn me to each one of you,
And swear unto my soul to right your wrongs.
The vow is made. Come, brother, take a head; 280
And in this hand the other will I bear.
Lavinia, thou shalt be employ'd: these arms!
Bear thou my hand, sweet wench, between thy teeth.
As for thee, boy, go get thee from my sight;
Thou art an exile, and thou must not stay:
Hie to the Goths, and raise an army there:
And, if you love me, as I think you do,
Let 's kiss and part, for we have much to do.
                    [*Exeunt Titus, Marcus, and Lavinia.*
    Luc. Farewell, Andronicus, my noble father,
The wofull'st man that ever lived in Rome: 290
Farewell, proud Rome; till Lucius come again,
He leaves his pledges dearer than his life:
Farewell, Lavinia, my noble sister;
O, would thou wert as thou tofore hast been!
But now nor Lucius nor Lavinia lives
But in oblivion and hateful griefs.
If Lucius live, he will requite your wrongs;
And make proud Saturnine and his empress
Beg at the gates, like Tarquin and his queen.
Now will I to the Goths, and raise a power, 300
To be revenged on Rome and Saturnine. [*Exit.*

SCENE II. *A room in Titus's house. A banquet set out.*

Enter TITUS, MARCUS, LAVINIA, *and young* LUCIUS, *a*
    Boy.

    Tit. So, so; now sit: and look you eat no more
Than will preserve just so much strength in us
As will revenge these bitter woes of ours.
Marcus, unknit that sorrow-wreathen knot:
Thy niece and I, poor creatures, want our hands,
And cannot passionate our tenfold grief
With folded arms. This poor right hand of mine
Is left to tyrannize upon my breast;
Who, when my heart, all mad with misery,
Beats in this hollow prison of my flesh, 10
Then thus I thump it down.
    [*To Lavinia*] Thou map of woe, that thus dost talk in
        signs!
When thy poor heart beats with outrageous beating,
Thou canst not strike it thus to make it still.
Wound it with sighing, girl, kill it with groans;
Or get some little knife between thy teeth,
And just against thy heart make thou a hole;
That all the tears that thy poor eyes let fall

May run into that sink, and soaking in
Drown the lamenting fool in sea-salt tears. 20
    Marc. Fie, brother, fie! teach her not thus to lay
Such violent hands upon her tender life.
    Tit. How now! has sorrow made thee dote already?
Why, Marcus, no man should be mad but I.
What violent hands can she lay on her life?
Ah, wherefore dost thou urge the name of hands;
To bid Æneas tell the tale twice o'er,
How Troy was burnt and he made miserable?
O, handle not the theme, to talk of hands,
Lest we remember still that we have none. 30
Fie, fie, how franticly I square my talk,
As if we should forget we had no hands,
If Marcus did not name the word of hands!
Come, let 's fall to; and, gentle girl, eat this:
Here is no drink! Hark, Marcus, what she says;
I can interpret all her martyr'd signs;
She says she drinks no other drink but tears,
Brew'd with her sorrow, mesh'd upon her cheeks:
Speechless complainer, I will learn thy thought;
In thy dumb action will I be as perfect 40
As begging hermits in their holy prayers:
Thou shalt not sigh, nor hold thy stumps to heaven,
Nor wink, nor nod, nor kneel, nor make a sign,
But I of these will wrest an alphabet
And by still practice learn to know thy meaning.
    Boy. Good grandsire, leave these bitter deep
        laments:
Make my aunt merry with some pleasing tale.
    Marc. Alas, the tender boy, in passion moved,
Doth weep to see his grandsire's heaviness.
    Tit. Peace, tender sapling; thou art made of tears, 50
And tears will quickly melt thy life away.
                    [*Marcus strikes the dish with a knife.*
What dost thou strike at, Marcus, with thy knife?
    Marc. At that that I have kill'd, my lord; a fly.
    Tit. Out on thee, murderer! thou kill'st my heart;
Mine eyes are cloy'd with view of tyranny:
A deed of death done on the innocent
Becomes not Titus' brother: get thee gone;
I see thou art not for my company.
    Marc. Alas, my lord, I have but kill'd a fly.
    Tit. But how, if that fly had a father and mother? 60
How would he hang his slender gilded wings,
And buzz lamenting doings in the air!
Poor harmless fly,
That, with his pretty buzzing melody,
Came here to make us merry! and thou hast kill'd
        him.
    Marc. Pardon me, sir; it was a black ill-favour'd fly,
Like to the empress' Moor; therefore I kill'd him.
    Tit. O, O, O,
Then pardon me for reprehending thee,
For thou hast done a charitable deed. 70
Give me thy knife, I will insult on him;
Flattering myself, as if it were the Moor
Come hither purposely to poison me.—
There 's for thyself, and that 's for Tamora.
Ah, sirrah!
Yet, I think, we are not brought so low,

But that between us we can kill a fly
That comes in likeness of a coal-black Moor.
  Marc. Alas, poor man! grief has so wrought on him,
He takes false shadows for true substances.   80
  Tit. Come, take away. Lavinia, go with me:
I'll to thy closet; and go read with thee
Sad stories chanced in the times of old.
Come, boy, and go with me: thy sight is young,
And thou shalt read when mine begin to dazzle.
                        [*Exeunt.*

ACT IV.

SCENE I. *Rome. Titus's garden.*

Enter young LUCIUS, *and* LAVINIA *running after him,
and the boy flies from her, with books under his arm.
Then enter* TITUS *and* MARCUS.

  Young Luc. Help, grandsire, help! my aunt Lavinia
Follows me every where, I know not why:
Good uncle Marcus, see how swift she comes.
Alas, sweet aunt, I know not what you mean.
  Marc. Stand by me, Lucius; do not fear thine aunt.
  Tit. She loves thee, boy, too well to do thee harm.
  Young Luc. Ay, when my father was in Rome she did.
  Marc. What means my niece Lavinia by these signs?
  Tit. Fear her not, Lucius: somewhat doth she mean:
See, Lucius, see how much she makes of thee: 10
Somewhither would she have thee go with her.
Ah, boy, Cornelia never with more care
Read to her sons than she hath read to thee
Sweet poetry and Tully's Orator.
  Marc. Canst thou not guess wherefore she plies thee
    thus?
  Young Luc. My lord, I know not, I, nor can I guess,
Unless some fit or frenzy do possess her:
For I have heard my grandsire say full oft,
Extremity of griefs would make men mad;
And I have read that Hecuba of Troy   20
Ran mad for sorrow: that made me to fear;
Although, my lord, I know my noble aunt
Loves me as dear as e'er my mother did,
And would not, but in fury, fright my youth:
Which made me down to throw my books, and fly,—
Causeless, perhaps. But pardon me, sweet aunt:
And, madam, if my uncle Marcus go,
I will most willingly attend your ladyship.
  Marc. Lucius, I will.
       [*Lavinia turns over with her stumps the books which
                     Lucius has let fall.*
  Tit. How now, Lavinia! Marcus, what means this? 30
Some book there is that she desires to see.
Which is it, girl, of these? Open them, boy.
But thou art deeper read, and better skill'd:
Come, and take choice of all my library,
And so beguile thy sorrow, till the heavens
Reveal the damn'd contriver of this deed.
Why lifts she up her arms in sequence thus?
  Marc. I think she means that there was more than
    one

Confederate in the fact: ay, more there was;
Or else to heaven she heaves them for revenge.   40
  Tit. Lucius, what book is that she tosseth so?
  Young Luc. Grandsire, 'tis Ovid's Metamorphoses;
My mother gave it me.
  Marc.   For love of her that's gone,
Perhaps she cull'd it from among the rest.
  Tit. Soft! so busily she turns the leaves!
Help her. What would she find? Lavinia, shall I read?
This is the tragic tale of Philomel,
And treats of Tereus' treason and his rape;
And rape, I fear, was root of thine annoy.
  Marc. See, brother, see; note how she quotes the
    leaves.   50
  Tit. Lavinia, wert thou thus surprised, sweet girl,
Ravish'd and wrong'd, as Philomela was,
Forced in the ruthless, vast, and gloomy woods?
See, see!
Ay, such a place there is, where we did hunt—
O, had we never, never hunted there!—
Pattern'd by that the poet here describes,
By nature made for murders and for rapes.
  Marc. O, why should nature build so foul a den,
Unless the gods delight in tragedies?   60
  Tit. Give signs, sweet girl, for here are none but
    friends,
What Roman lord it was durst do the deed:
Or slunk not Saturnine, as Tarquin erst,
That left the camp to sin in Lucrece' bed?
  Marc. Sit down, sweet niece: brother, sit down by
    me.
Apollo, Pallas, Jove, or Mercury,
Inspire me, that I may this treason find!
My lord, look here: look here, Lavinia:
This sandy plot is plain; guide, if thou canst,
This after me, when I have writ my name   70
Without the help of any hand at all.
      [*He writes his name with his staff, and guides it with
                           feet and mouth.*
Cursed be that heart that forced us to this shift!
Write thou, good niece; and here display, at last,
What God will have discover'd for revenge:
Heaven guide thy pen to print thy sorrows plain,
That we may know the traitors and the truth!
      [*She takes the staff in her mouth, and guides it with her
                       stumps, and writes.*
  Tit. O, do ye read, my lord, what she hath writ?
'Stuprum. Chiron. Demetrius.'
  Marc. What, what! the lustful sons of Tamora
Performers of this heinous, bloody deed?   80
  Tit. Magni Dominator poli,
Tam lentus audis scelera? tam lentus vides?
  Marc. O, calm thee, gentle lord; although I know
There is enough written upon this earth
To stir a mutiny in the mildest thoughts
And arm the minds of infants to exclaims.
My lord, kneel down with me; Lavinia, kneel;
And kneel, sweet boy, the Roman Hector's hope;
And swear with me, as, with the woful fere
And father of that chaste dishonour'd dame,   90
Lord Junius Brutus sware for Lucrece' rape,

---

82. **closet,** private apartment. 85. **dazzle,** become dazzled.
ACT IV. SCENE I. 12. **Cornelia,** the mother of the Gracchi, the two most famous tribunes in Roman history. 14. **Tully's Orator,** Cicero's treatise on rhetoric, *De Oratore.* 24. **fury,** insane madness. 37. **in sequence,** one after the other. 40. **heaves,** lifts. 45. **so,** so QqFf; Globe, following Rowe: *see how.* 46. **Help her,** so QqFf; Globe, following a conjecture of Dyce: *Helping her,* printed as a stage direction. 47, 48. **Philomel, Tereus'.** Cf. II, iii, 43, note. 50. **quotes,** examines,

observes. 74. **discover'd,** revealed, uncovered; see glossary. 78. **Stuprum,** violation, rape. 81-82. **Magni . . . vides?** Ruler of the mighty heavens, art thou so slow to see and hear the crimes that are committed? 86. **exclaims,** exclamations. 88. **the Roman Hector's,** i.e., Andronicus', whose warlike deeds are held comparable to the Trojan hero's. 89. **fere,** spouse.

That we will prosecute by good advice
Mortal revenge upon these traitorous Goths,
And see their blood, or die with this reproach.
   Tit. 'Tis sure enough, an you knew how.
But if you hunt these bear-whelps, then beware:
The dam will wake; and, if she wind you once,
She's with the lion deeply still in league,
And lulls him whilst she playeth on her back,
And when he sleeps will she do what she list.   100
You are a young huntsman, Marcus; let it alone;
And, come, I will go get a leaf of brass,
And with a gad of steel will write these words,
And lay it by: the angry northern wind
Will blow these sands, like Sibyl's leaves, abroad,
And where's our lesson, then? Boy, what say you?
   Young Luc. I say, my lord, that if I were a man,
Their mother's bed-chamber should not be safe
For these bad bondmen to the yoke of Rome.
   Marc. Ay, that's my boy! thy father hath full oft   110
For his ungrateful country done the like.
   Young Luc. And, uncle, so will I, an if I live.
   Tit. Come, go with me into mine armoury;
Lucius, I'll fit thee; and withal, my boy,
Shalt carry from me to the empress' sons
Presents that I intend to send them both:
Come, come; thou'lt do thy message, wilt thou not?
   Young Luc. Ay, with my dagger in their bosoms,
     grandsire.
   Tit. No, boy, not so; I'll teach thee another course.
Lavinia, come. Marcus, look to my house: 120
Lucius and I'll go brave it at the court;
Ay, marry, will we, sir; and we'll be waited on.
            [Exeunt Titus, Lavinia, and Young Lucius.
   Marc. O heavens, can you hear a good man groan,
And not relent, or not compassion him?
Marcus, attend him in his ecstasy,
That hath more scars of sorrow in his heart
Than foemen's marks upon his batter'd shield;
But yet so just that he will not revenge.
Revenge, ye heavens, for old Andronicus!   *[Exit.*

    SCENE II. *The same. A room in the palace.*

  Enter, from one side, AARON, DEMETRIUS, *and* CHIRON;
    from the other side, young LUCIUS, *and an* Attendant,
    with a bundle of weapons, and verses writ upon them.

   Chi. Demetrius, here's the son of Lucius;
He hath some message to deliver us.
   Aar. Ay, some mad message from his mad grand-
    father.
   Young Luc. My lords, with all the humbleness I
    may,
I greet your honours from Andronicus.
[*Aside*] And pray the Roman gods confound you
    both!
   Dem. Gramercy, lovely Lucius: what's the news?
   Young Luc. [*Aside*] That you are both decipher'd,
    that's the news,
For villains mark'd with rape.—May it please you,
My grandsire, well advised, hath sent by me   10

The goodliest weapons of his armoury
To gratify your honourable youth,
The hope of Rome; for so he bade me say;
And so I do, and with his gifts present
Your lordships, that, whenever you have need,
You may be armed and appointed well:
And so I leave you both: [*Aside*] like bloody villains.
           [Exeunt young Lucius and Attendant.
   Dem. What's here? A scroll; and written round
    about?
Let's see:
[*Reads*] 'Integer vitæ, scelerisque purus,   20
    Non eget Mauri jaculis, nec arcu.'
   Chi. O, 'tis a verse in Horace; I know it well:
I read it in the grammar long ago.
   Aar. Ay, just; a verse in Horace; right, you have it.
[*Aside*] Now, what a thing it is to be an ass!
Here's no sound jest! the old man hath found their
    guilt;
And sends them weapons wrapp'd about with lines,
That wound, beyond their feeling, to the quick.
But were our witty empress well afoot,
She would applaud Andronicus' conceit: 30
But let her rest in her unrest awhile.

And now, young lords, was't not a happy star
Led us to Rome, strangers, and more than so,
Captives, to be advanced to this height?
It did me good, before the palace gate
To brave the tribune in his brother's hearing.
   Dem. But me more good, to see so great a lord
Basely insinuate and send us gifts.
   Aar. Had he not reason, Lord Demetrius?
Did you not use his daughter very friendly?   40
   Dem. I would we had a thousand Roman dames
At such a bay, by turn to serve our lust.
   Chi. A charitable wish and full of love.
   Aar. Here lacks but your mother for to say amen.
   Chi. And that would she for twenty thousand more.
   Dem. Come, let us go; and pray to all the gods
For our beloved mother in her pains.
   Aar. [*Aside*] Pray to the devils; the gods have given
    us over.   *[Trumpets sound within.*
   Dem. Why do the emperor's trumpets flourish thus?
   Chi. Belike, for joy the emperor hath a son.   50
   Dem. Soft! who comes here?

  Enter a Nurse, *with a blackamoor* Child *in her arms.*

   Nur.   Good morrow, lords:
O, tell me, did you see Aaron the Moor?
   Aar. Well, more or less, or ne'er a whit at all,
Here Aaron is; and what with Aaron now?
   Nur. O gentle Aaron, we are all undone!
Now help, or woe betide thee evermore!
   Aar. Why, what a caterwauling dost thou keep!
What dost thou wrap and fumble in thine arms?
   Nur. O, that which I would hide from heaven's eye,
Our empress' shame, and stately Rome's disgrace!   60
She is deliver'd, lords; she is deliver'd.
   Aar. To whom?
   Nur.   I mean, she is brought a-bed.

---

92. **advice,** deliberation; see glossary. 94. **reproach,** disgrace, infamy.
97. **wind,** scent. 100. **list,** choose; see glossary. 105. **Sibyl's leaves.**
The Cumaean Sibyl, an inspired woman, wrote her prophecies on
leaves which she placed at the entrance to her cave. Those wishing
to consult them had to do so before they were scattered by the wind.
106. **our,** so Q_1; Globe, following Q_3F: *your.* 121. **brave it,** put
on a bold front. 122. **marry,** mild interjection equivalent to "Indeed!"; originally an oath by the Virgin Mary; see glossary. **we'll**

. . . on, i.e., demand attention. 125. **ecstasy,** state of being beside
oneself; see glossary.
    SCENE II. 4. **may,** can; see glossary. 6. **confound,** destroy; see
glossary. 20-21. '**Integer . . . arcu.**' The opening lines of perhaps the
best known of the Odes of Horace (I, 22): "He who is spotless in life
and free of crime needs not the Moorish bow and arrow." 30. **conceit,**
design; see glossary. 38. **insinuate,** i.e., to ingratiate himself with us
by sending gifts. 68. **breeders,** used of female animals. 72. **blowse,**

Aar. Well, God give her good rest! What hath he
    sent her?
Nur. A devil.
Aar. Why, then she is the devil's dam; a joyful issue.
Nur. A joyless, dismal, black, and sorrowful issue:
Here is the babe, as loathsome as a toad
Amongst the fairest breeders of our clime:
The empress sends it thee, thy stamp, thy seal,
And bids thee christen it with thy dagger's point. 70
Aar. 'Zounds, ye whore! is black so base a hue?
Sweet blowse, you are a beauteous blossom, sure.
    Dem. Villain, what hast thou done?
    Aar. That which thou canst not undo.
    Chi. Thou hast undone our mother.
    Aar. Villain, I have done thy mother.
    Dem. And therein, hellish dog, thou hast undone
    her.
Woe to her chance, and damn'd her loathed choice!
Accursed the offspring of so foul a fiend!
    Chi. It shall not live. 80
    Aar. It shall not die.
    Nur. Aaron, it must; the mother wills it so.
    Aar. What, must it, nurse? then let no man but I
Do execution on my flesh and blood.
    Dem. I'll broach the tadpole on my rapier's point:
Nurse, give it me; my sword shall soon dispatch it.
    Aar. Sooner this sword shall plough thy bowels up.
        [*Takes the Child from the Nurse, and draws.*
Stay, murderous villains! will you kill your brother?
Now, by the burning tapers of the sky,
That shone so brightly when this boy was got, 90
He dies upon my scimitar's sharp point
That touches this my first-born son and heir!
I tell you, younglings, not Enceladus,
With all his threatening band of Typhon's brood,
Nor great Alcides, nor the god of war,
Shall seize this prey out of his father's hands.
What, what, ye sanguine, shallow-hearted boys!
Ye white-limed walls! ye alehouse painted signs!
Coal-black is better than another hue,
In that it scorns to bear another hue; 100
For all the water in the ocean
Can never turn the swan's black legs to white,
Although she lave them hourly in the flood.
Tell the empress from me, I am of age
To keep mine own, excuse it how she can.
    Dem. Wilt thou betray thy noble mistress thus?
    Aar. My mistress is my mistress; this myself,
The vigour and the picture of my youth:
This before all the world do I prefer;
This maugre all the world will I keep safe, 110
Or some of you shall smoke for it in Rome.
    Dem. By this our mother is for ever shamed.
    Chi. Rome will despise her for this foul escape.
    Nur. The emperor, in his rage, will doom her death.
    Chi. I blush to think upon this ignomy.
    Aar. Why, there's the privilege your beauty bears.
Fie, treacherous hue, that will betray with blushing
The close enacts and counsels of the heart!
Here's a young lad framed of another leer:
Look, how the black slave smiles upon the father, 120

As who should say 'Old lad, I am thine own.'
He is your brother, lords, sensibly fed
Of that self-blood that first gave life to you,
And from that womb where you imprison'd were
He is enfranchised and come to light:
Nay, he is your brother by the surer side,
Although my seal be stamped in his face.
    Nur. Aaron, what shall I say unto the empress?
    Dem. Advise thee, Aaron, what is to be done,
And we will all subscribe to thy advice: 130
Save thou the child, so we may all be safe.
    Aar. Then sit we down, and let us all consult.
My son and I will have the wind of you:
Keep there: now talk at pleasure of your safety.
                                    [*They sit.*
    Dem. How many women saw this child of his?
    Aar. Why, so, brave lords! when we join in league,
I am a lamb: but if you brave the Moor,
The chafed boar, the mountain lioness,
The ocean swells not so as Aaron storms.
But say, again, how many saw the child? 140
    Nur. Cornelia the midwife and myself;
And no one else but the deliver'd empress.
    Aar. The empress, the midwife, and yourself:
Two may keep counsel when the third's away:
Go to the empress, tell her this I said. [*He kills the nurse.*
Weke, weke! so cries a pig prepared to the spit.
    Dem. What mean'st thou, Aaron? wherefore didst
    thou this?
    Aar. O Lord, sir, 'tis a deed of policy:
Shall she live to betray this guilt of ours,
A long-tongued babbling gossip? no, lords, no: 150
And now be it known to you my full intent.
Not far, one Muli lives, my countryman;
His wife but yesternight was brought to bed;
His child is like to her, fair as you are:
Go pack with him, and give the mother gold,
And tell them both the circumstance of all,
And how by this their child shall be advanced,
And be received for the emperor's heir,
And substituted in the place of mine,
To calm this tempest whirling in the court; 160
And let the emperor dandle him for his own.
Hark ye, lords; you see I have given her physic,
                            [*Pointing to the nurse.*
And you must needs bestow her funeral;
The fields are near, and you are gallant grooms:
This done, see that you take no longer days,
But send the midwife presently to me.
The midwife and the nurse well made away,
Then let the ladies tattle what they please.
    Chi. Aaron, I see thou wilt not trust the air
With secrets.
    Dem.   For this care of Tamora, 170
Herself and hers are highly bound to thee.
        [*Exeunt Dem. and Chi. bearing off the Nurse's body.*
    Aar. Now to the Goths, as swift as swallow flies;
There to dispose this treasure in mine arms,
And secretly to greet the empress' friends.
Come on, you thick-lipp'd slave, I'll bear you hence;
For it is you that puts us to our shifts:

*Titus
Andronicus*
ACT IV : SC II

3**85**

---

ruddy-faced fat wench (Onions). 77. **undone her,** so Q_{1-2}; Globe,
following Q_3F: *undone.* 90. **got,** begotten; see *get* in glossary. 91.
scimitar's. The scimitar was apparently a sword with a sharp point.
93. **Enceladus,** one of the Titans, sons of the giant Typhon (cf. l. 94,
Typhon's brood), all of whom waged war against the gods on Olympus.
95. **Alcides,** i.e., Hercules. 97. **sanguine,** an allusion to the red and
white complexions of the Goths. 110. **maugre,** in spite of. 111.
smoke, suffer, have a "warm" time. 113. **escape,** outrageous transgres-

sion; so used in *Othello,* I, iii, 197. 118. **close,** secret; see glossary. **enacts,** purposes. 119. **leer,** countenance, complexion. 155. **pack,**
conspire; see glossary. 156. **circumstance of all,** all the particulars;
see *circumstance* in glossary. 162. **you,** so Q_{1-2}; Globe, following Q_3F:
ye. **physic,** medicine; see glossary. 173. **dispose,** make use of; see
glossary. 176. **shifts,** stratagems, tricks; see glossary.

I'll make you feed on berries and on roots,
And †feed on curds and whey, and suck the goat,
And cabin in a cave, and bring you up
To be a warrior, and command a camp. [*Exit.* 180

SCENE III. *The same. A public place.*

Enter TITUS, *bearing arrows with letters at the ends of
them; with him,* MARCUS, *young* LUCIUS, PUBLIUS,
SEMPRONIUS, CAIUS, *and other* Gentlemen, *with
bows.*

Tit. Come, Marcus; come, kinsmen; this is the way.
Sir boy, let me see your archery;
Look ye draw home enough, and 'tis there straight.
Terras Astræa reliquit:
Be you remember'd, Marcus, she 's gone, she 's fled.
Sirs, take you to your tools. You, cousins, shall
Go sound the ocean, and cast your nets;
Happily you may catch her in the sea;
Yet there 's as little justice as at land:
No; Publius and Sempronius, you must do it; 10
'Tis you must dig with mattock and with spade,
And pierce the inmost centre of the earth:
Then, when you come to Pluto's region,
I pray you, deliver him this petition;
Tell him, it is for justice and for aid,
And that it comes from old Andronicus,
Shaken with sorrows in ungrateful Rome.
Ah, Rome! Well, well; I made thee miserable
What time I threw the people's suffrages
On him that thus doth tyrannize o'er me. 20
Go, get you gone; and pray be careful all,
And leave you not a man-of-war unsearch'd:
This wicked emperor may have shipp'd her hence;
And, kinsmen, then we may go pipe for justice.
Marc. O Publius, is not this a heavy case,
To see thy noble uncle thus distract?
Pub. Therefore, my lord, it highly us concerns
By day and night to attend him carefully,
And feed his humour kindly as we may,
Till time beget some careful remedy. 30
Marc. Kinsmen, his sorrows are past remedy.
Join with the Goths; and with revengeful war
Take wreak on Rome for this ingratitude,
And vengeance on the traitor Saturnine.
Tit. Publius, how now! how now, my masters!
What, have you met with her?
Pub. No, my good lord; but Pluto sends you word,
If you will have Revenge from hell, you shall:
Marry, for Justice, she is so employ'd,
He thinks, with Jove in heaven, or somewhere else, 40
So that perforce you must needs stay a time.
Tit. He doth me wrong to feed me with delays.
I'll dive into the burning lake below,
And pull her out of Acheron by the heels.
Marcus, we are but shrubs, no cedars we,
No big-boned men framed of the Cyclops' size;
But metal, Marcus, steel to the very back,
Yet wrung with wrongs more than our backs can bear:
And, sith there 's no justice in earth nor hell,
We will solicit heaven and move the gods 50
To send down Justice for to wreak our wrongs.

Come, to this gear. You are a good archer, Marcus;
[*He gives them the arrows.*
'Ad Jovem,' that 's for you: here, 'Ad Apollinem:'
'Ad Martem,' that 's for myself:
Here, boy, to Pallas: here, to Mercury:
To Saturn, Caius, not to Saturnine;
You were as good to shoot against the wind.
To it, boy! Marcus, loose when I bid.
Of my word, I have written to effect;
There 's not a god left unsolicited. 60
Marc. Kinsmen, shoot all your shafts into the court:
We will afflict the emperor in his pride.
Tit. Now, masters, draw. [*They shoot.*] O, well
said, Lucius!
Good boy, in Virgo's lap; give it Pallas.
Marc. My lord, I aim a mile beyond the moon;
Your letter is with Jupiter by this.
Tit. Ha, ha!
Publius, Publius, what hast thou done?
See, see, thou hast shot off one of Taurus' horns.
Marc. This was the sport, my lord: when Publius
shot, 70
The Bull, being gall'd, gave Aries such a knock
That down fell both the Ram's horns in the court;
And who should find them but the empress' villain?
She laugh'd, and told the Moor he should not choose
But give them to his master for a present.
Tit. Why, there it goes: God give his lordship joy!

Enter a Clown, *with a basket, and two pigeons in it.*

News, news from heaven! Marcus, the post is come.
Sirrah, what tidings? have you any letters?
Shall I have justice? what says Jupiter? 79
Clo. O, the gibbet-maker! he says that he hath
taken them down again, for the man must not be
hanged till the next week.
Tit. But what says Jupiter, I ask thee?
Clo. Alas, sir, I know not Jupiter, I never drank
with him in all my life.
Tit. Why, villain, art not thou the carrier?
Clo. Ay, of my pigeons, sir; nothing else.
Tit. Why, didst thou not come from heaven? 88
Clo. From heaven! alas, sir, I never came there:
God forbid I should be so bold to press to heaven in
my young days. Why, I am going with my pigeons to
the tribunal plebs, to take up a matter of brawl be-
twixt my uncle and one of the emperial's men.
Marc. Why, sir, that is as fit as can be to serve for
your oration; and let him deliver the pigeons to the
emperor from you.
Tit. Tell me, can you deliver an oration to the
emperor with a grace? 99
Clo. Nay, truly, sir, I could never say grace in all
my life.
Tit. Sirrah, come hither: make no more ado,
But give your pigeons to the emperor:
By me thou shalt have justice at his hands.
Hold, hold; meanwhile here 's money for thy charges.
Give me pen and ink. Sirrah, can you with a grace
deliver up a supplication?
Clo. Ay, sir.
Tit. Then here is a supplication for you. And when
you come to him, at the first approach you must kneel,

SCENE III. 2. **boy, let,** so QqF; Globe; following F$_{2-4}$: *boy, now let.*
4. **Terras Astræa reliquit,** Astrea has abandoned the earth; a passage
from Ovid's *Metamorphoses;* cf. *1 Henry VI,* I, vi, 4. 8. **Happily,** perhaps; see glossary. 24. **pipe,** look in vain. 26. **distract,** crazed,
desperate. 29. **humour,** mood, whim; see glossary. 47. **metal,** i.e.,
in contrast to the idea contained in *big-boned,* line 46. 52. **gear,**
business; see glossary. 53, 54. **'Ad Jovem,' 'Ad Apollinem:,' 'Ad
Martem,'** to Jove, to Apollo, to Mars. 58. **loose,** let fly, discharge.
64. **in Virgo's lap,** the constellation, the Virgin. 69, 71. **Taurus,
Aries,** the Bull, the Ram; signs of the zodiac. 77. **post,** messenger; see
glossary. 107. **deliver up,** so Q$_1$; Globe, following Q$_{2-3}$Ff: *deliver.*
SCENE IV. 4. **egal,** equal. 8. **even,** conformable; see glossary. 11.

then kiss his foot, then deliver up your pigeons, and
then look for your reward. I'll be at hand, sir; see you
do it bravely.   113

   Clo. I warrant you, sir, let me alone.

   Tit. Sirrah, hast thou a knife? come, let me see it.
Here, Marcus, fold it in the oration;
For thou hast made it like an humble suppliant.
And when thou hast given it the emperor,
Knock at my door, and tell me what he says.

   Clo. God be with you, sir; I will.   120

   Tit. Come, Marcus, let us go. Publius, follow me.
                                          [*Exeunt.*

SCENE IV. *The same. Before the palace.*

Enter SATURNINUS, TAMORA, DEMETRIUS, CHIRON,
   Lords, *and others;* SATURNINUS *with the arrows in his*
   hand that TITUS *shot.*

   Sat. Why, lords, what wrongs are these! was ever
      seen
An emperor in Rome thus overborne,
Troubled, confronted thus; and, for the extent
Of egal justice, used in such contempt?
My lords, you know, as know the mightful gods,
However these disturbers of our peace
Buz in the people's ears, there nought hath pass'd,
But even with law, against the wilful sons
Of old Andronicus. And what an if
His sorrows have so overwhelm'd his wits,   10
Shall we be thus afflicted in his wreaks,
His fits, his frenzy, and his bitterness?
And now he writes to heaven for his redress:
See, here 's to Jove, and this to Mercury;
This to Apollo; this to the god of war;
Sweet scrolls to fly about the streets of Rome!
What 's this but libelling against the senate,
And blazoning our injustice every where?
A goodly humour, is it not, my lords?
As who would say, in Rome no justice were.   20
But if I live, his feigned ecstasies
Shall be no shelter to these outrages:
But he and his shall know that justice lives
In Saturninus' health, whom, if she sleep,
He'll so awake as she in fury shall
Cut off the proud'st conspirator that lives.

   Tam. My gracious lord, my lovely Saturnine,
Lord of my life, commander of my thoughts,
Calm thee, and bear the faults of Titus' age,
The effects of sorrow for his valiant sons,   30
Whose loss hath pierced him deep and scarr'd his
      heart;
And rather comfort his distressed plight
Than prosecute the meanest or the best
For these contempts. [*Aside*] Why, thus it shall
      become
High-witted Tamora to gloze with all:
But, Titus, I have touch'd thee to the quick,
Thy life-blood out; if Aaron now be wise,
Then is all safe, the anchor in the port.

   Enter Clown.

How now, good fellow! wouldst thou speak with us?

   Clo. Yea, forsooth, an your mistressship be emperial.

   Tam. Empress I am, but yonder sits the emperor.   41

   Clo. 'Tis he. God and Saint Stephen give you good
den: I have brought you a letter and a couple of
pigeons here.   [*Saturninus reads the letter.*

   Sat. Go, take him away, and hang him presently.

   Clo. How much money must I have?

   Tam. Come, sirrah, you must be hanged.

   Clo. Hanged! by 'r lady, then I have brought up a
neck to a fair end.   [*Exit, guarded.*

   Sat. Despiteful and intolerable wrongs!   50
Shall I endure this monstrous villany?
I know from whence this same device proceeds:
May this be borne?—as if his traitorous sons,
That died by law for murder of our brother,
Have by my means been butcher'd wrongfully!
Go, drag the villain hither by the hair;
Nor age nor honour shall shape privilege:
For this proud mock I'll be thy slaughter-man;
Sly frantic wretch, that holp'st to make me great,
In hope thyself should govern Rome and me.   60

   Enter ÆMILIUS.

What news with thee, Æmilius?

   Æmil. Arm, arm, my lords;—Rome never had
      more cause.
The Goths have gather'd head; and with a power
Of high-resolved men, bent to the spoil,
They hither march amain, under conduct
Of Lucius, son to old Andronicus;
Who threats, in course of this revenge, to do
As much as ever Coriolanus did.

   Sat. Is warlike Lucius general of the Goths?
These tidings nip me, and I hang the head   70
As flowers with frost or grass beat down with storms:
Ay, now begins our sorrows to approach:
'Tis he the common people love so much;
Myself hath often over-heard them say,
When I have walked like a private man,
That Lucius' banishment was wrongfully,
And they have wish'd that Lucius were their emperor.

   Tam. Why should you fear? is not your city strong?

   Sat. Ay, but the citizens favour Lucius,
And will revolt from me to succour him.   80

   Tam. King, be thy thoughts imperious, like thy
      name.
Is the sun dimm'd, that gnats do fly in it?
The eagle suffers little birds to sing,
And is not careful what they mean thereby,
Knowing that with the shadow of his wings
He can at pleasure stint their melody:
Even so mayst thou the giddy men of Rome.
Then cheer thy spirit: for know, thou emperor,
I will enchant the old Andronicus
With words more sweet, and yet more dangerous,   90
Than baits to fish, or honey-stalks to sheep,
When as the one is wounded with the bait,
The other rotted with delicious feed.

   Sat. But he will not entreat his son for us.

   Tam. If Tamora entreat him, then he will:
For I can smooth and fill his aged ears
With golden promises; that, were his heart
Almost impregnable, his old ears deaf,

Yet should both ear and heart obey my tongue.
[*To Æmilius*] Go thou before, to be our ambassador:
Say that the emperor requests a parley   101
Of warlike Lucius, and appoint the meeting
Even at his father's house, the old Andronicus.
  Sat. Æmilius, do this message honourably:
And if he stand in hostage for his safety,
Bid him demand what pledge will please him best.
  Æmil. Your bidding shall I do effectually.   [*Exit.*
  Tam. Now will I to that old Andronicus,
And temper him with all the art I have,
To pluck proud Lucius from the warlike Goths.   110
And now, sweet emperor, be blithe again,
And bury all thy fear in my devices.
  Sat. Then go successantly, and plead to him. [*Exeunt.*

ACT V.

Enter LUCIUS *with an army of* Goths, *with drum and colours.*

  Luc. Approved warriors, and my faithful friends,
I have received letters from great Rome,
Which signify what hate they bear their emperor
And how desirous of our sight they are.
Therefore, great lords, be, as your titles witness,
Imperious and impatient of your wrongs,
And wherein Rome hath done you any scath,
Let him make treble satisfaction.
  First Goth. Brave slip, sprung from the great
          Andronicus,
Whose name was once our terror, now our comfort; 10
Whose high exploits and honourable deeds
Ingrateful Rome requites with foul contempt,
Be bold in us: we'll follow where thou lead'st,
Like stinging bees in hottest summer's day
Led by their master to the flowered fields,
And be avenged on cursed Tamora.
  All the Goths. And as he saith, so say we all with him.
  Luc. I humbly thank him, and I thank you all.
But who comes here, led by a lusty Goth?

Enter a Goth, *leading* AARON *with his Child in his arms.*

  Sec. Goth. Renowned Lucius, from our troops I
          stray'd   20
To gaze upon a ruinous monastery;
And, as I earnestly did fix mine eye
Upon the wasted building, suddenly
I heard a child cry underneath a wall.
I made unto the noise; when soon I heard
The crying babe controll'd with this discourse:
'Peace, tawny slave, half me and half thy dam!
Did not thy hue bewray whose brat thou art,
Had nature lent thee but thy mother's look,
Villain, thou mightst have been an emperor: 30
But where the bull and cow are both milk-white,
They never do beget a coal-black calf.
Peace, villain, peace!'—even thus he rates the babe,—
'For I must bear thee to a trusty Goth;
Who, when he knows thou art the empress' babe,
Will hold thee dearly for thy mother's sake.'
With this, my weapon drawn, I rush'd upon him,

Surprised him suddenly, and brought him hither,
To use as you think needful of the man.
  Luc. O worthy Goth, this is the incarnate devil   40
That robb'd Andronicus of his good hand;
This is the pearl that pleased your empress' eye,
And here's the base fruit of his burning lust.
Say, wall-eyed slave, whither wouldst thou convey
This growing image of thy fiend-like face?
Why dost not speak? what, deaf? not a word?
A halter, soldiers! hang him on this tree,
And by his side his fruit of bastardy.
  Aar. Touch not the boy; he is of royal blood.
  Luc. Too like the sire for ever being good.   50
First hang the child, that he may see it sprawl;
A sight to vex the father's soul withal.
Get me a ladder.
          [*A ladder brought, which Aaron is made to ascend.*
  Aar.   Lucius, save the child,
And bear it from me to the empress.
If thou do this, I'll show thee wondrous things,
That highly may advantage thee to hear:
If thou wilt not, befall what may befall,
I'll speak no more but 'Vengeance rot you all!'
  Luc. Say on: an if it please me which thou speak'st,
Thy child shall live, and I will see it nourish'd.   60
  Aar. An if it please thee! why, assure thee, Lucius,
'Twill vex thy soul to hear what I shall speak;
For I must talk of murders, rapes and massacres,
Acts of black night, abominable deeds,
Complots of mischief, treason, villanies
Ruthful to hear, yet piteously perform'd:
And this shall all be buried by my death,
Unless thou swear to me my child shall live.
  Luc. Tell on thy mind; I say thy child shall live.
  Aar. Swear that he shall, and then I will begin.   70
  Luc. Who should I swear by? thou believest no god:
That granted, how canst thou believe an oath?
  Aar. What if I do not? as, indeed, I do not;
Yet, for I know thou art religious
And hast a thing within thee called conscience,
With twenty popish tricks and ceremonies,
Which I have seen thee careful to observe,
Therefore I urge thy oath; for that I know
An idiot holds his bauble for a god
And keeps the oath which by that god he swears,   80
To that I'll urge him: therefore thou shalt vow
By that same god, what god soe'er it be,
That thou adorest and hast in reverence,
To save my boy, to nourish and bring him up;
Or else I will discover nought to thee.
  Luc. Even by my god I swear to thee I will.
  Aar. First know thou, I begot him on the empress.
  Luc. O most insatiate and luxurious woman!
  Aar. Tut, Lucius, this was but a deed of charity
To that which thou shalt hear of me anon.   90
'Twas her two sons that murder'd Bassianus;
They cut thy sister's tongue and ravish'd her
And cut her hands and trimm'd her as thou saw'st.
  Luc. O detestable villain! call'st thou that trimming?
  Aar. Why, she was wash'd and cut and trimm'd,
          and 'twas
Trim sport for them that had the doing of it.
  Luc. O barbarous, beastly villains, like thyself!
  Aar. Indeed, I was their tutor to instruct them:

100. **to be**, so Qq; Globe, following Capell: *be.*   105. **in**, so QqF$_{1-3}$;
Globe, following F$_4$: *on.*   106. **demand**, request; see glossary.   113.
successantly, successfully.
     ACT V. SCENE I.   1. **Approved**, put to proof, tried.   7. **scath**, injury.

13. **in us**, i.e., because we support you.   21. **ruinous**, decayed.   44.
wall-eyed, glaring, having the iris of the eye discolored.   45. **image**,
likeness; see glossary.   56. **advantage**, be of benefit to; see glossary.
65. **Complots**, conspiracies.   66. **piteously**, in a way to excite pity.

That codding spirit had they from their mother,
As sure a card as ever won the set; 100
That bloody mind, I think, they learn'd of me,
As true a dog as ever fought at head.
Well, let my deeds be witness of my worth.
I train'd thy brethren to that guileful hole
Where the dead corpse of Bassianus lay:
I wrote the letter that thy father found
And hid the gold within the letter mention'd,
Confederate with the queen and her two sons:
And what not done, that thou hast cause to rue,
Wherein I had no stroke of mischief in it? 110
I play'd the cheater for thy father's hand,
And, when I had it, drew myself apart
And almost broke my heart with extreme laughter:
I pry'd me through the crevice of a wall
When, for his hand, he had his two sons' heads;
Beheld his tears, and laugh'd so heartily,
That both mine eyes were rainy like to his:
And when I told the empress of this sport,
She swooned almost at my pleasing tale,
And for my tidings gave me twenty kisses. 120
    First Goth. What, canst thou say all this, and never
      blush?
    Aar. Ay, like a black dog, as the saying is.
    Luc. Art thou not sorry for these heinous deeds?
    Aar. Ay, that I had not done a thousand more.
Even now I curse the day—and yet, I think,
Few come within the compass of my curse—
Wherein I did not some notorious ill,
As kill a man, or else devise his death,
Ravish a maid, or plot the way to do it,
Accuse some innocent and forswear myself, 130
Set deadly enmity between two friends,
†Make poor men's cattle break their necks;
Set fire on barns and hay-stacks in the night,
And bid the owners quench them with their tears.
Oft have I digg'd up dead men from their graves,
And set them upright at their dear friends' door,
Even when their sorrows almost was forgot;
And on their skins, as on the bark of trees,
Have with my knife carved in Roman letters,
'Let not your sorrow die, though I am dead.' 140
Tut, I have done a thousand dreadful things
As willingly as one would kill a fly,
And nothing grieves me heartily indeed
But that I cannot do ten thousand more.
    Luc. Bring down the devil; for he must not die
So sweet a death as hanging presently.
    Aar. If there be devils, would I were a devil,
To live and burn in everlasting fire,
So I might have your company in hell,
But to torment you with my bitter tongue! 150
    Luc. Sirs, stop his mouth, and let him speak no
      more.

Enter a Goth.

    Third Goth. My lord, there is a messenger from
      Rome
Desires to be admitted to your presence.
    Luc. Let him come near.

Enter ÆMILIUS.

Welcome, Æmilius: what's the news from Rome?

    Æmil. Lord Lucius, and you princes of the Goths,
The Roman emperor greets you all by me;
And, for he understands you are in arms,
He craves a parley at your father's house,
Willing you to demand your hostages, 160
And they shall be immediately deliver'd.
    First Goth. What says our general?
    Luc. Æmilius, let the emperor give his pledges
Unto my father and my uncle Marcus,
And we will come. March away.   [*Exeunt.*

SCENE II. *Rome. Before Titus's house.*

Enter TAMORA, DEMETRIUS, *and* CHIRON, *disguised.*

    Tam. Thus, in this strange and sad habiliment,
I will encounter with Andronicus,
And say I am Revenge, sent from below
To join with him and right his heinous wrongs.
Knock at his study, where, they say, he keeps,
To ruminate strange plots of dire revenge;
Tell him Revenge is come to join with him,
And work confusion on his enemies.   [*They knock.*

Enter TITUS, *above.*

    Tit. Who doth molest my contemplation?
Is it your trick to make me ope the door, 10
That so my sad decrees may fly away,
And all my study be to no effect?
You are deceived: for what I mean to do
See here in bloody lines I have set down;
And what is written shall be executed.
    Tam. Titus, I am come to talk with thee.
    Tit. No, not a word; how can I grace my talk,
Wanting a hand to give it action?
Thou hast the odds of me; therefore no more.
    Tam. If thou didst know me, thou wouldest talk
      with me. 20
    Tit. I am not mad; I know thee well enough:
Witness this wretched stump, witness these crimson
    lines;
Witness these trenches made by grief and care;
Witness the tiring day and heavy night;
Witness all sorrow, that I know thee well
For our proud empress, mighty Tamora:
Is not thy coming for my other hand?
    Tam. Know, thou sad man, I am not Tamora;
She is thy enemy, and I thy friend:
I am Revenge: sent from the infernal kingdom, 30
To ease the gnawing vulture of thy mind,
By working wreakful vengeance on thy foes.
Come down, and welcome me to this world's light;
Confer with me of murder and of death:
There's not a hollow cave or lurking-place,
No vast obscurity or misty vale,
Where bloody murder or detested rape
Can couch for fear, but I will find them out;
And in their ears tell them my dreadful name,
Revenge, which makes the foul offender quake. 40
    Tit. Art thou Revenge? and art thou sent to me,
To be a torment to mine enemies?
    Tam. I am; therefore come down, and welcome me.
    Tit. Do me some service, ere I come to thee.

99. **codding**, lustful. 104. **train'd**, lured; see glossary. 136. **door**, so Q₁; Globe, following Q₂F₁: *doors.* 137. **was**, so QqFf; Globe, following Malone: *were.*
    SCENE II. 18. **to give it action**, i.e., to gesticulate; a term in actors' parlance; cf. *Hamlet*, III, ii, 19.

Lo, by thy side where Rape and Murder stands;
Now give some surance that thou art Revenge,
Stab them, or tear them on thy chariot-wheels;
And then I'll come and be thy waggoner,
And whirl along with thee about the globe.
Provide thee two proper palfreys, black as jet, 50
To hale thy vengeful waggon swift away,
And find out murderers in their guilty caves:
And when thy car is loaden with their heads,
I will dismount, and by the waggon-wheel
Trot, like a servile footman, all day long,
Even from Hyperion's rising in the east
Until his very downfall in the sea:
And day by day I'll do this heavy task,
So thou destroy Rapine and Murder there.
    Tam. These are my ministers, and come with me. 60
    Tit. Are these thy ministers? what are they call'd?
    Tam. Rapine and Murder; therefore called so,
Cause they take vengeance of such kind of men.
    Tit. Good Lord, how like the empress' sons they
        are!
And you, the empress! but we worldly men
Have miserable, mad, mistaking eyes.
O sweet Revenge, now do I come to thee;
And, if one arm's embracement will content thee,
I will embrace thee in it by and by.   [*Exit above.*
    Tam. This closing with him fits his lunacy: 70
Whate'er I forge to feed his brain-sick humours,
Do you uphold and maintain in your speeches,
For now he firmly takes me for Revenge;
And, being credulous in this mad thought,
I'll make him send for Lucius his son;
And, whilst I at a banquet hold him sure,
I'll find some cunning practice out of hand,
To scatter and disperse the giddy Goths,
Or, at the least, make them his enemies.
See, here he comes, and I must ply my theme. 80

    Enter TITUS *below.*

    Tit. Long have I been forlorn, and all for thee:
Welcome, dread Fury, to my woful house:
Rapine and Murder, you are welcome too.
How like the empress and her sons you are!
Well are you fitted, had you but a Moor:
Could not all hell afford you such a devil?
For well I wot the empress never wags
But in her company there is a Moor;
And, would you represent our queen aright,
It were convenient you had such a devil: 90
But welcome, as you are. What shall we do?
    Tam. What wouldst thou have us do, Andronicus?
    Dem. Show me a murderer, I'll deal with him.
    Chi. Show me a villain that hath done a rape,
And I am sent to be revenged on him.
    Tam. Show me a thousand that hath done thee
        wrong,
And I will be revenged on them all.
    Tit. Look round about the wicked streets of Rome;
And when thou find'st a man that's like thyself,
Good Murder, stab him; he's a murderer. 100
Go thou with him; and when it is thy hap
To find another that is like to thee,
Good Rapine, stab him; he's a ravisher.
Go thou with them; and in the emperor's court

There is a queen, attended by a Moor;
Well mayst thou know her by thy own proportion,
For up and down she doth resemble thee:
I pray thee, do on them some violent death;
They have been violent to me and mine.
    Tam. Well hast thou lesson'd us; this shall we do. 110
But would it please thee, good Andronicus,
To send for Lucius, thy thrice-valiant son,
Who leads towards Rome a band of warlike Goths,
And bid him come and banquet at thy house;
When he is here, even at thy solemn feast,
I will bring in the empress and her sons,
The emperor himself and all thy foes;
And at thy mercy shall they stoop and kneel,
And on them shalt thou ease thy angry heart.
What says Andronicus to this device? 120
    Tit. Marcus, my brother! 'tis sad Titus calls.

    Enter MARCUS.

Go, gentle Marcus, to thy nephew Lucius;
Thou shalt inquire him out among the Goths:
Bid him repair to me, and bring with him
Some of the chiefest princes of the Goths;
Bid him encamp his soldiers where they are:
Tell him the emperor and the empress too
Feast at my house, and he shall feast with them.
This do thou for my love; and so let him,
As he regards his aged father's life. 130
    Marc. This will I do, and soon return again.   [*Exit.*
    Tam. Now will I hence about thy business,
And take my ministers along with me.
    Tit. Nay, nay, let Rape and Murder stay with me;
Or else I'll call my brother back again,
And cleave to no revenge but Lucius.
    Tam. [*Aside to her sons*] What say you, boys? will
        you abide with him,
Whiles I go tell my lord the emperor
How I have govern'd our determined jest?
Yield to his humour, smooth and speak him fair, 140
And tarry with him till I turn again.
    Tit. [*Aside*] I know them all, though they suppose
        me mad,
And will o'erreach them in their own devices:
A pair of cursed hell-hounds and their dam!
    Dem. Madam, depart at pleasure; leave us here.
    Tam. Farewell, Andronicus: Revenge now goes
To lay a complot to betray thy foes.
    Tit. I know thou dost; and, sweet Revenge,
        farewell.   [*Exit Tamora.*
    Chi. Tell us, old man, how shall we be employ'd?
    Tit. Tut, I have work enough for you to do. 150
Publius, come hither, Caius, and Valentine!

    Enter PUBLIUS *and others.*

    Pub. What is your will?
    Tit. Know you these two?
    Pub. The empress' sons, I take them, Chiron and
Demetrius.
    Tit. Fie, Publius, fie! thou art too much deceived;
The one is Murder, Rape is the other's name;
And therefore bind them, gentle Publius.
Caius and Valentine, lay hands on them.
Oft have you heard me wish for such an hour, 160
And now I find it; therefore bind them sure,

50. **proper,** excellent; see glossary. 56. **Hyperion,** one of the Titans; father of the sun; frequently used for the sun itself. 71. **humours,** so Q_1; Globe, following $Q_{2-3}F$: *fits*. 76. **hold him sure,** keep him harmless. 77. **practice,** conspiracy; see glossary. 96. **hath,** so Q_1; Globe, following

$Q_{2-3}F$: *have*. 106. **proportion,** form, appearance; see glossary. 137. **abide,** so Q_1; Globe, following $Q_{2-3}F$: *bide*. 189. **coffin,** pie crust. 196. **worse than Progne,** an allusion to Progne's revenge on Tereus for raping her sister (cf. II, iii, 43, note); she killed her son Itys and served

And stop their mouths, if they begin to cry.   [*Exit.*
            [*Publius, &c. lay hold on Chiron and Demetrius.*
Chi. Villains, forbear! we are the empress' sons.
Pub. And therefore do we what we are commanded.
Stop close their mouths, let them not speak a word.
Is he sure bound? look that you bind them fast.

        Re-enter TITUS, *with* LAVINIA; *he bearing a knife,*
                and she a basin.

Tit. Come, come, Lavinia; look, thy foes are bound.
Sirs, stop their mouths, let them not speak to me;
But let them hear what fearful words I utter.
O villains, Chiron and Demetrius!   170
Here stands the spring whom you have stain'd with
        mud,
This goodly summer with your winter mix'd.
You kill'd her husband, and for that vile fault
Two of her brothers were condemn'd to death,
My hand cut off and made a merry jest;
Both her sweet hands, her tongue, and that more dear
Than hands or tongue, her spotless chastity,
Inhuman traitors, you constrain'd and forced.
What would you say, if I should let you speak?
Villains, for shame you could not beg for grace.   180
Hark, wretches! how I mean to martyr you.
This one hand yet is left to cut your throats,
Whilst that Lavinia 'tween her stumps doth hold
The basin that receives your guilty blood.
You know your mother means to feast with me,
And calls herself Revenge, and thinks me mad:
Hark, villains! I will grind your bones to dust
And with your blood and it I'll make a paste,
And of the paste a coffin I will rear
And make two pasties of your shameful heads,   190
And bid that strumpet, your unhallow'd dam,
Like to the earth swallow her own increase.
This is the feast that I have bid her to,
And this the banquet she shall surfeit on;
For worse than Philomel you used my daughter,
And worse than Progne I will be revenged:
And now prepare your throats. Lavinia, come,
                            [*He cuts their throats.*
Receive the blood: and when that they are dead,
Let me go grind their bones to powder small
And with this hateful liquor temper it;   200
And in that paste let their vile heads be baked.
Come, come, be every one officious
To make this banquet; which I wish may prove
More stern and bloody than the Centaurs' feast.
So, now bring them in, for I'll play the cook,
And see them ready 'gainst their mother comes.
                    [*Exeunt, bearing the dead bodies.*

SCENE III. *Court of Titus's house. A banquet set out.*

Enter LUCIUS, MARCUS, *and* Goths, *with* AARON
        prisoner.

Luc. Uncle Marcus, since it is my father's mind
That I repair to Rome, I am content.
First Goth. And ours with thine, befall what fortune
        will.
Luc. Good uncle, take you in this barbarous Moor,
This ravenous tiger, this accursed devil;

Let him receive no sustenance, fetter him,
Till he be brought unto the empress' face,
For testimony of her foul proceedings:
And see the ambush of our friends be strong;
I fear the emperor means no good to us.   10
Aar. Some devil whisper curses in mine ear,
And prompt me, that my tongue may utter forth
The venomous malice of my swelling heart!
Luc. Away, inhuman dog! unhallow'd slave!
Sirs, help our uncle to convey him in.
            [*Exeunt Goths, with Aaron. Flourish within.*
The trumpets show the emperor is at hand.

    Enter SATURNINUS *and* TAMORA, *with* ÆMILIUS,
            Tribunes, Senators, *and others.*

Sat. What, hath the firmament more suns than one?
Luc. What boots it thee to call thyself a sun?
Marc. Rome's emperor, and nephew, break the
        parle;
These quarrels must be quietly debated.   20
The feast is ready, which the careful Titus
Hath ordain'd to an honourable end,
For peace, for love, for league, and good to Rome:
Please you, therefore, draw nigh, and take your
        places.
Sat. Marcus, we will.
            [*Hautboys sound. The Company sit down at table.*

    Enter TITUS *dressed like a Cook,* LAVINIA *veiled, young*
        LUCIUS, *and others.* TITUS *places the dishes on the table.*

Tit. Welcome, my gracious lord; welcome, dread
        queen;
Welcome, ye warlike Goths; welcome, Lucius;
And welcome, all: although the cheer be poor,
'Twill fill your stomachs; please you eat of it.
Sat. Why art thou thus attired, Andronicus?   30
Tit. Because I would be sure to have all well,
To entertain your highness and your empress.
Tam. We are beholding to you, good Andronicus.
Tit. An if your highness knew my heart, you were.
My lord the emperor, resolve me this:
Was it well done of rash Virginius
To slay his daughter with his own right hand,
Because she was enforced, stain'd, and deflower'd?
Sat. It was, Andronicus.
Tit. Your reason, mighty lord?   40
Sat. Because the girl should not survive her shame,
And by her presence still renew his sorrows.
Tit. A reason mighty, strong, and effectual;
A pattern, precedent, and lively warrant,
For me, most wretched, to perform the like.
Die, die, Lavinia, and thy shame with thee;
                            [*Kills Lavinia.*
And, with thy shame, thy father's sorrow die!
Sat. What hast thou done, unnatural and unkind?
Tit. Kill'd her, for whom my tears have made me
        blind.
I am as woful as Virginius was,   50
And have a thousand times more cause than he
To do this outrage: and it now is done.
Sat. What, was she ravish'd? tell who did the deed.
Tit. Will 't please you eat? will 't please your
        highness feed?
Tam. Why hast thou slain thine only daughter thus?

---

his flesh to Tereus, his father.   204. **Centaurs' feast,** refers to a wedding
feast at which the Centaurs (fabulous creatures, half men and half
horses), drunk with wine, offered violence to the women present.
SCENE III.   17. **more suns than one.** Lucius has assumed an imperial

manner, which offends Saturninus. 18. **boots,** profits, avails; see glossary. 19. **break the parle,** i.e., cease quarreling; see *parle* in glossary.
20. **debated,** fought; see glossary. 25. *Stage Direction: Hautboys,*
oboes. 35. **resolve,** answer; see glossary.

Tit. Not I; 'twas Chiron and Demetrius:
They ravish'd her, and cut away her tongue;
And they, 'twas they, that did her all this wrong.
   Sat. Go fetch them hither to us presently.
   Tit. Why, there they are both, baked in this pie; 60
Whereof their mother daintily hath fed,
Eating the flesh that she herself hath bred.
'Tis true, 'tis true; witness my knife's sharp point.
                          [Kills Tamora.
   Sat. Die, frantic wretch, for this accursed deed!
                           [Kills Titus.
   Luc. Can the son's eye behold his father bleed?
There 's meed for meed, death for a deadly deed!
   [Kills Saturninus. A great tumult. Lucius, Marcus, and
               others go up into the balcony.
   Marc. You sad-faced men, people and sons of
     Rome,
By uproars sever'd, as a flight of fowl
Scatter'd by winds and high tempestuous gusts,
O, let me teach you how to knit again   70
This scatter'd corn into one mutual sheaf,
These broken limbs again into one body;
Lest Rome herself be bane unto herself,
And she whom mighty kingdoms court'sy to,
Like a forlorn and desperate castaway,
Do shameful execution on herself.
But if my frosty signs and chaps of age,
Grave witnesses of true experience,
Cannot induce you to attend my words,
   [*To Lucius*] Speak, Rome's dear friend, as erst our
     ancestor,   80
When with his solemn tongue he did discourse
To love-sick Dido's sad attending ear
The story of that baleful burning night
When subtle Greeks surprised King Priam's Troy,
Tell us what Sinon hath bewitch'd our ears,
Or who hath brought the fatal engine in
That gives our Troy, our Rome, the civil wound.
My heart is not compact of flint nor steel;
Nor can I utter all our bitter grief,
But floods of tears will drown my oratory,   90
And break my utterance, even in the time
When it should move ye to attend me most,
And force you to commiseration.
Here 's Rome's young captain, let him tell the tale;
While I stand by and weep to hear him speak.
   Luc. Then, gracious auditory, be it known to you,
That Chiron and the damn'd Demetrius
Were they that murdered our emperor's brother;
And they it were that ravished our sister:
For their fell faults our brothers were beheaded; 100
Our father's tears despised, and basely cozen'd
Of that true hand that fought Rome's quarrel out,
And sent her enemies unto the grave.
Lastly, myself unkindly banished,
The gates shut on me, and turn'd weeping out,
To beg relief among Rome's enemies;
Who drown'd their enmity in my true tears,
And oped their arms to embrace me as a friend.
I am the turned forth, be it known to you,

Titus
Andronicus
ACT V : SC III

392

That have preserved her welfare in my blood;   110
And from her bosom took the enemy's point,
Sheathing the steel in my adventurous body.
Alas, you know I am no vaunter, I;
My scars can witness, dumb although they are,
That my report is just and full of truth.
But, soft! methinks I do digress too much,
Citing my worthless praise: O, pardon me;
For when no friends are by, men praise themselves.
   Marc. Now is my turn to speak. Behold this child:
     [Pointing to the Child in the arms of an Attendant.
Of this was Tamora delivered;   120
The issue of an irreligious Moor,
Chief architect and plotter of these woes:
The villain is alive in Titus' house,
†And as he is, to witness this is true.
Now judge what cause had Titus to revenge
These wrongs, unspeakable, past patience,
Or more than any living man could bear.
Now you have heard the truth, what say you,
     Romans?
Have we done aught amiss,—show us wherein,
And, from the place where you behold us pleading, 130
The poor remainder of Andronici
Will, hand in hand, all headlong hurl ourselves,
And on the ragged stones beat forth our souls,
And make a mutual closure of our house.
Speak, Romans, speak; and if you say we shall,
Lo, hand in hand, Lucius and I will fall.
   Æmil. Come, come, thou reverend man of Rome,
And bring our emperor gently in thy hand,
Lucius our emperor; for well I know
The common voice do cry it shall be so.   140
   All. Lucius, all hail, Rome's royal emperor!
   Marc. Go, go into old Titus' sorrowful house,
                       [To Attendants.
And hither hale that misbelieving Moor,
To be adjudged some direful slaughtering death,
As punishment for his most wicked life.
                     [Exeunt Attendants.

LUCIUS, MARCUS, *and the others descend.*

   All. Lucius, all hail, Rome's gracious governor!
   Luc. Thanks, gentle Romans: may I govern so,
To heal Rome's harms, and wipe away her woe!
But, gentle people, give me aim awhile,
For nature puts me to a heavy task: 150
Stand all aloof: but, uncle, draw you near,
To shed obsequious tears upon this trunk.
O, take this warm kiss on thy pale cold lips,
                     [Kissing Titus.
These sorrowful drops upon thy blood-stain'd face,
The last true duties of thy noble son!
   Marc. Tear for tear, and loving kiss for kiss,
Thy brother Marcus tenders on thy lips:
O, were the sum of these that I should pay
Countless and infinite, yet would I pay them!
   Luc. Come hither, boy; come, come, and learn of us
To melt in showers: thy grandsire loved thee well: 161
Many a time he danced thee on his knee,

60. **this,** so Q_1; Globe, following $Q_{2-3}F$: *that.* 68. **uproars,** so QqF_1; Globe, following F_{2-4}: *uproar.* **as,** so Q_{1-2}; Globe, following Q_3F: *like.* 71. **corn,** small grain. 77. **chaps,** wrinkles. 88. **compact,** composed of. 92. **ye,** so Q_1; Globe, following $Q_{2-3}F$: *you.* 93. **And force you to,** so Q_1; Globe, following Q_2: *Lending your kind.* 94. **Here 's Rome's young,** so Q_1; Globe, following Q_2: *Here is a.* 95. **While I stand by,** so Q_1; Globe, following Q_2: *Your hearts will throb.* 96. **gracious,** so Q_1; Globe, following Q_2: *noble.* 97. **Chiron and the damn'd,** so Q_1; Globe, following Q_2: *cursed Chiron and.* 101. **cozen'd,** cheated. 130. **pleading,** so Q_1; Globe, following Q_2: *now.* 132. **hurl ourselves,** so Q_1; Globe,

following Q_2: *cast us down.* 133. **souls,** so Q_1; Globe, following Q_2: *brains.* 134. **closure,** conclusion, death. 164. **story,** so Q_1; Globe, following $Q_{2-3}F_1$: *matter.* 165-171. **And bid . . . of them.** These lines are found only in Q_1; Q_2 and all subsequent texts based on it, including the Globe, have the following (see Introduction):

   Meet and agreeing with thine infancy;
   In that respect, then, like a loving child,
   Shed yet some small drops from thy tender spring,
   Because kind nature doth require it so:
   Friends should associate friends in grief and woe:

Sung thee asleep, his loving breast thy pillow;
Many a story hath he told to thee,
And bid thee bear his pretty tales in mind,
And talk of them when he was dead and gone.
   Marc. How many thousand times hath these poor
     lips,
When they were living, warmed themselves on thine?
Oh now, sweet boy, give them their latest kiss.
Bid them farewell; commit him to the grave;   170
Do them that kindness and take leave of them.
   Young Luc. O grandsire, grandsire! even with all my
     heart
Would I were dead, so you did live again!
O Lord, I cannot speak to him for weeping;
My tears will choke me, if I ope my mouth.

      Re-enter Attendants *with* AARON.

   Æmie. You sad Andronici, have done with woes:
Give sentence on this execrable wretch,
That hath been breeder of these dire events.
   Luc. Set him breast-deep in earth, and famish him;
There let him stand, and rave, and cry for food: 180
If any one relieves or pities him,
For the offence he dies. This is our doom:
Some stay to see him fasten'd in the earth.
   Aar. O, why should wrath be mute, and fury dumb?
I am no baby, I, that with base prayers
I should repent the evils I have done:
Ten thousand worse than ever yet I did
Would I perform, if I might have my will:
If one good deed in all my life I did,
I do repent it from my very soul.   190
   Luc. Some loving friends convey the emperor
     hence,
And give him burial in his father's grave:
My father and Lavinia shall forthwith
Be closed in our household's monument.
As for that heinous tiger, Tamora,
No funeral rite, nor man in mourning weeds,
No mournful bell shall ring her burial;
But throw her forth to beasts and birds of prey:
Her life was beastly and devoid of pity;
And, being dead, let birds on her take pity.   [*Exeunt.*

    Bid him farewell; commit him to the grave;
    Do him that kindness, and take leave of him.
182. doom, decision, judgment. **199. beastly**, so Qq; Globe, following
F_1: *beast-like.* **200.** The Q_1 text closes the play with this line. Q_2,
and all subsequent texts, including the Globe, add the following four
lines:
    See justice done on Aaron, that damn'd Moor,
    By whom our heavy haps had their beginning:
    Then, afterwards, to order well the state,
    That like events may ne'er it ruinate.

Romeo and Juliet

In 1597 a corrupt edition in quarto of *Romeo and
Juliet* appeared with the following title page:

AN EXCELLENT conceited Tragedie *OF* Romeo and
Iuliet, As it hath been often (with great applause) plaid
publiquely, by the right Honourable the L. of *Hunsdon*
his Seruants. LONDON, Printed by Iohn Danter. 1597.

John Danter was an outlaw publisher, and the "great

applause" referred to was probably the cause of his
unlicensed venture.[1]

   Two years later, as if out of mortification at having
so bad a version in circulation, or possibly to prevent
its reissue, a second quarto was published:

THE MOST EXcellent and lamentable Tragedie, of
Romeo and *Juliet. Newly corrected, augmented, and amended:*
As it hath bene sundry times publiquely acted, by the
right Honourable the Lord Chamberlaine his Seruants.
LONDON. Printed by Thomas Creede, for Cuthbert
Burby, and are to be sold at his shop neare the Exchange.
1599.

The version thus issued as "corrected, augmented,
and amended" is in the main the same version as the
earlier one, but is fuller and more correct.

   We have in these two publications the reflection of
a situation more than once repeated in the printing
of Shakespeare's plays. Something similar seems to
have happened, as we have seen, in the case of *Love's
Labour's Lost.* It is highly probable that the text of
Q_1 was made, not for the sake of publication, but for
the sake of being acted in the provinces, with a
diminished company. This stage version, degenerated
in ways not fully understood, was later sold to Danter.
That in issuing the second, "good" quarto of *Romeo
and Juliet,* the printers used a playhouse copy, can be
seen from the fact that we have at one place for the
entry of the clown, not "Enter Peter," but "Enter
Will Kempe." Will Kemp was one of the actors in
Shakespeare's company. The same fact seems also
reflected in other stage directions of the second quarto,
which are often just those brief hortatory notes a stage
manager might make to direct the performance; such
as "Whistle, Boy," "Knock," and "Play, Music."
There are evidences of manuscript revisions in III,
iii, 33-41; V, iii, 102-120, and other places, all of
which indicate that the quarto of 1599 must have
been printed from Shakespeare's own manuscript.

   A third quarto of *Romeo and Juliet* came out in 1609,
and there were later quartos, all based on the second
quarto. The text in the First Folio was set up from
a playhouse manuscript, not from a quarto.

THE DATE OF THE PLAY

The many allusions to the play in the years following 1597 indicate that it enjoyed great popularity.
For certain reasons, however, it is impossible to conclude that the play was written so late as that. Its
close kinship with the sonnets, which were probably
being written in 1593-1596, and to *Venus and Adonis*
(1593) and *The Rape of Lucrece* (1594), its lyrical
quality, its youthful zest, and the stiffness of much of
its blank verse are certainly indications of an early
date. Yet one need not, for these reasons, put it far
in advance of *A Midsummer-Night's Dream,* or even
The Merchant of Venice. The title page of the first

[1]See Harry R. Hoppe, *The Bad Quarto of Romeo and Juliet: A Bibliographical and Textual Study* (Ithaca, 1948).

quarto refers to Shakespeare's company as "Lord Hunsdon's servants," by which name they were designated from July 22, 1596, to April 17, 1597. Weever refers to the play in his *Epigrams*, believed to have been written by 1596 and possibly before 1595. Finally, the Nurse reckons Juliet's age by an earthquake eleven years before. The Nurse is probably not to be taken too seriously as a chronologer; but, if she were taken literally, her words would refer to a famous earthquake in England in 1580 and would point to 1591 as the date of composition. If there is any virtue in the dating of Shakespeare's plays by internal evidence, as we feel that there is, we must conclude that at least a part of the play was written early in Shakespeare's career. A great deal of rhyme appears in *Romeo and Juliet*, in couplets, quatrains, sestets, and even in sonnets. There are also a number of set lyrical pieces in blank verse (I, iv, 53 ff.; III, ii, 1 ff.); and here, more markedly than in his mature work, Shakespeare revels in puns and conceits, wit combats, and passages of elaborate social courtesy.

THE SOURCES OF THE PLAY

In spite of these artificial and conventional features, however, there is something new to Shakespeare and to English drama in *Romeo and Juliet*. It is a tragedy, not Senecan or Marlowan, although there are certain tricks of the older form still retained, such as its declamatory speeches and poetical reminiscences of classical mythology. *Romeo and Juliet* is, nevertheless, more original and independent than much of the work Shakespeare was yet to do. The mystery is in part explained by the story of the play, which comes from the Italian *novella*, a form influential on Shakespeare's genius. These novels, or short stories, had been known in Italy for more than two hundred and fifty years, and had been very popular since the middle of the fourteenth century, when Boccaccio wrote the *Decameron*. Many of them had been translated into French and from French into English. They were made up of materials from history, tradition, romance, fable, popular anecdote and narrative, and in some instances perhaps from invention.

Among them is a story of more than usually broad appeal. It tells of a woman who, in order to escape a hated marriage about to be forced upon her, took a sleeping potion. This is earliest found in the *Ephesiaca*, a Greek romance of about the fifth century A.D., attributed to Xenophon of Ephesus. The story appears also in a collection of *Novellini* in 1476 by Masuccio of Salerno. In this version Mariotto of Siena marries Gianozza privately by the good offices of a friar and is shortly afterwards compelled to flee the country for killing a fellow citizen in a street fight. He has an interview with his wife before he departs, and, after he is gone, she has a marriage urged upon her by her friends. She takes into her confidence the friar, who gives her a soporific powder by which she may be thrown into a trance. She swallows the

powder, is laid away in a tomb, and on her awakening is rescued, thus escaping the marriage. Before Mariotto, who has fled to Alexandria, receives a letter from the friar explaining the plot, the word reaches him that she is dead. Gianozza awakes and sets out to seek her husband at Alexandria. Mariotto, having returned to shed tears at his wife's grave, is arrested and put to death. Gianozza retires to a convent and soon dies.

This is essentially Shakespeare's story; but it was yet to receive full localization and final form at the hands of Luigi da Porto, or, as some think, at the hands of his patron, the famous Cardinal Bembo. Luigi's work, called *Istoria novellamente ritrovata di due nobili amanti*, was published at Venice about 1530. The scene is laid in Verona. The story grows out of a feud between the two noble families of Montecchi and Capelli; the lovers are called Romeo and Giulietta. It passed into the famous *Novelle* of Bandello (1554); thence into the French translation of Boaistuau (1559); thence, in 1562, into an English poetical version by Arthur Brooke, *The Tragicall History of Romeus and Juliet*, a poem very well written in old-fashioned rhyming couplets of twelve and fourteen syllables alternately. Brooke followed Boaistuau very closely, and it cannot be shown that Shakespeare had any other source than Brooke. Brooke, however, introduces another possibility as to Shakespeare's source, for he says in his preface,

Though I saw the same argument lately set forth on the stage with more commendation, then I can looke for: (being there much better set forth then I have or can dooe) yet the same matter penned as it is, may serve to lyke good effect.

This brings up the ever present possibility that Shakespeare was working over an old play. We have every reason to think, however, in the light of his known practice and of the detailed resemblances, that he read Brooke and other sources in addition to the old play.[2] The story of Romeo and Juliet appears also in Painter's *Palace of Pleasure*, although it is not thought that Shakespeare made use of that source.[3]

THE TECHNIQUE OF THE PLAY

The general technique of tragedy at the time went hardly further than the Senecan forms of Kyd and the Marlowan type of heroic play built about a single colossal figure. For the rest, it was merely the telling of a story on the stage in the best way one could. Therefore, it follows that the best chance of success would lie in having a good story to tell. Although the love story of Romeo and Juliet did not lend itself to either Kyd's or Marlowe's pattern, it was an extremely good story, set in the very heart of Italian domestic

[2]Dr. H. De W. Fuller (*Modern Philology*, IV, 75) has argued that the Dutch play *Romeo en Juliette* rests, not upon Shakespeare's, but upon a lost play, probably that referred to by Brooke.
[3]See John Munro's introduction to *Brooke's Romeus and Juliet* (1938).

and civil life. It must not be forgotten that Shakespeare followed his truly artistic source with great fidelity. Much, though by no means all, of the greatness of his masterpiece lies in this fact.

HOW SHAKESPEARE TELLS THE STORY

Shakespeare's part in the story is, of course, his management of it, his realization of the interplay of human character and motive, his sense of the scene and background of the action, and, more than all, the poetic beauty of his style. The household of the Capulets is made over into an Elizabethan household with enough, however, of the original to preserve the comradeship of the Italian servant and master. The young gentlemen of the story become Elizabethans with tastes and occupations of current fashion. Note, for example, Mercutio's prejudice against new forms of swordplay, and also the wit combats in which he, Benvolio, and Romeo engage.

In Shakespeare's version the story is begun by the henchmen of the jarring houses in a quarrel in the street, which catches the attention of the audience and reveals the atmosphere of the feud. In the same sensational fashion, Shakespeare introduces the furious Tybalt into the merry scene of the Capulets' ball. Shakespeare's is the visit of the County Paris to the tomb of Juliet. The part of Mercutio is greatly amplified in Shakespeare, and the Nurse of the original is transformed according to an earlier dramatic model, the *balia* of Italian comedy, into a garrulous serving woman. These are Shakespeare's principal additions to the story; he also permeates it with his spirit.

STAGE HISTORY

The stage history of *Romeo and Juliet* is long and illustrious. Apparently popular in its own day, it was revived immediately after the reopening of the theaters in 1660. Betterton played Romeo and Mrs. Saunderson, Juliet. Before long, however, the Shakespearean version was displaced by Thomas Otway's famous adaptation *The History and Fall of Caius Marius*. It was in this degenerate form that Mrs. Barry and Mrs. Bracegirdle won applause. Garrick played the Shakespearean play (with modifications) with Mrs. Bellamy as Juliet at Drury Lane. It was at the time of Garrick's triumph that occurred the famous rivalry between him and the Irish actor Spranger Barry, who was also playing Romeo, with Mrs. Cibber as Juliet, at Covent Garden. "Had I been Juliet to Garrick's Romeo," said a lady who had witnessed both performances, "so ardent and impassioned was he, I should have expected that he would *come up* to me in the balcony; but had I been Juliet to Barry's Romeo, so tender, so eloquent, and so seductive was he, I should certainly have *gone down* to him." Since the return of Shakespeare's play to the stage it has been popular all over the world, and the greatest actors and actresses have played in it.

Romeo and Juliet

DRAMATIS PERSONAE

ESCALUS, prince of Verona.
PARIS, a young nobleman, kinsman to the prince.
MONTAGUE,⎱ heads of two houses at variance
CAPULET, ⎰ with each other.
An old man, cousin to Capulet.
ROMEO, son to Montague.
MERCUTIO, kinsman to the prince, and friend to Romeo.
BENVOLIO, nephew to Montague, and friend to Romeo.
TYBALT, nephew to Lady Capulet.
FRIAR LAURENCE,⎱ Franciscans.
FRIAR JOHN, ⎰
BALTHASAR, servant to Romeo.
SAMPSON,⎱ servants to Capulet.
GREGORY,⎰
PETER, servant to Juliet's nurse.
ABRAHAM, servant to Montague.
An Apothecary.
Three Musicians.
Page to Paris; another Page; an Officer.

LADY MONTAGUE, wife to Montague.
LADY CAPULET, wife to Capulet.
JULIET, daughter to Capulet.
Nurse to Juliet.

Citizens of Verona; several Men and Women, relations to both houses; Maskers, Guards, Watchmen, and Attendants.

Chorus.

SCENE: *Verona: Mantua.*

PROLOGUE.

Two households, both alike in dignity,
  In fair Verona, where we lay our scene,
From ancient grudge break to new mutiny,
  Where civil blood makes civil hands unclean.
From forth the fatal loins of these two foes
  A pair of star-cross'd lovers take their life;
Whose misadventured piteous overthrows
  Do with their death bury their parents' strife.
The fearful passage of their death-mark'd love,
  And the continuance of their parents' rage   10
Which, but their children's end, nought could remove,
  Is now the two hours' traffic of our stage;
The which if you with patient ears attend,
What here shall miss, our toil shall strive to mend.

ACT I.

SCENE I. *Verona. A public place.*

Enter Sampson *and* Gregory, *of the house of Capulet,
armed with swords and bucklers.*

Sam. Gregory, o' my word, we'll not carry coals.

Gre. No, for then we should be colliers.

Sam. I mean, an we be in choler, we'll draw.

Gre. Ay, while you live, draw your neck out o' the
collar.

Sam. I strike quickly, being moved.

Gre. But thou art not quickly moved to strike.

Sam. A dog of the house of Montague moves me. 10

Gre. To move is to stir; and to be valiant is to stand:
therefore, if thou art moved, thou runn'st away.

Sam. A dog of that house shall move me to stand:
I will take the wall of any man or maid of Montague's.

Gre. That shows thee a weak slave; for the weakest
goes to the wall.

Sam. True; and therefore women, being the weaker
vessels, are ever thrust to the wall: therefore I will
push Montague's men from the wall, and thrust his
maids to the wall.

Gre. The quarrel is between our masters and us their
men.

Sam. 'Tis all one, I will show myself a tyrant: when
I have fought with the men, I will be cruel with the
maids, and cut off their heads.

Gre. The heads of the maids? 29

Sam. Ay, the heads of the maids, or their maidenheads; take it in what sense thou wilt.

Gre. They must take it in sense that feel it.

Sam. Me they shall feel while I am able to stand:
and 'tis known I am a pretty piece of flesh.

Gre. 'Tis well thou art not fish; if thou hadst, thou
hadst been poor John. Draw thy tool; here comes two
of the house of the Montagues.

Sam. My naked weapon is out: quarrel, I will back
thee. 40

Gre. How! turn thy back and run?

Sam. Fear me not.

Gre. No, marry; I fear thee!

Sam. Let us take the law of our sides; let them
begin.

Gre. I will frown as I pass by, and let them take it as
they list.

Sam. Nay, as they dare. I will bite my thumb at
them; which is a disgrace to them, if they bear it. 50

Enter Abraham *and* Balthasar.

Abr. Do you bite your thumb at us, sir?

Sam. I do bite my thumb, sir.

Abr. Do you bite your thumb at us, sir?

Sam. [*Aside to Gre.*] Is the law of our side, if I say ay?

Gre. No.

Sam. No, sir, I do not bite my thumb at you, sir, but
I bite my thumb, sir.

Gre. Do you quarrel, sir?

Abr. Quarrel, sir! no, sir. 60

Sam. If you do, sir, I am for you: I serve as good a
man as you.

Abr. No better.

Sam. Well, sir.

Gre. Say 'better:' here comes one of my master's
kinsmen.

Sam. Yes, better, sir.

Abr. You lie.

Sam. Draw, if you be men. Gregory, remember thy
swashing blow.   [*They fight.* 70

Enter Benvolio.

Ben. Part, fools!
Put up your swords; you know not what you do.
                              [*Beats down their swords.*

Enter Tybalt.

Tyb. What, art thou drawn among these heartless
    hinds?
Turn thee, Benvolio, look upon thy death.

Ben. I do but keep the peace: put up thy sword,
Or manage it to part these men with me.

Tyb. What, drawn, and talk of peace! I hate the
    word,
As I hate hell, all Montagues, and thee:
Have at thee, coward!   [*They fight.*

Enter several of both houses, who join the fray; then enter
    Citizens, *with clubs.*

First Cit. Clubs, bills, and partisans! strike! beat
    them down!   80
Down with the Capulets! down with the Montagues!

Enter Capulet *in his gown, and* Lady Capulet.

Cap. What noise is this? Give me my long sword, ho!

La. Cap. A crutch, a crutch! why call you for a
    sword?

Cap. My sword, I say! Old Montague is come,
And flourishes his blade in spite of me.

Enter Montague *and* Lady Montague.

Mon. Thou villain Capulet,—Hold me not, let me
    go.

La. Mon. Thou shalt not stir a foot to seek a foe.

Enter Prince, *with* Attendants.

Prin. Rebellious subjects, enemies to peace,
Profaners of this neighbour-stained steel,—
Will they not hear? What, ho! you men, you beasts, 90
That quench the fire of your pernicious rage
With purple fountains issuing from your veins,
On pain of torture, from those bloody hands
Throw your mistemper'd weapons to the ground,
And hear the sentence of your moved prince.
Three civil brawls, bred of an airy word,
By thee, old Capulet, and Montague,
Have thrice disturb'd the quiet of our streets,
And made Verona's ancient citizens
Cast by their grave beseeming ornaments,   100
To wield old partisans, in hands as old,
Canker'd with peace, to part your canker'd hate:

If ever you disturb our streets again,
Your lives shall pay the forfeit of the peace.
For this time, all the rest depart away:
You, Capulet, shall go along with me:
And, Montague, come you this afternoon,
To know our further pleasure in this case,
To old Free-town, our common judgement-place.
Once more, on pain of death, all men depart.   110
      [*Exeunt all but Montague, Lady Montague,
                                    and Benvolio.*

Mon. Who set this ancient quarrel new abroach?
Speak, nephew, were you by when it began?
  Ben. Here were the servants of your adversary,
And yours, close fighting ere I did approach:
I drew to part them: in the instant came
The fiery Tybalt, with his sword prepared,
Which, as he breathed defiance to my ears,
He swung about his head and cut the winds,
Who nothing hurt withal hiss'd him in scorn:
While we were interchanging thrusts and blows,   120
Came more and more and fought on part and part,
Till the prince came, who parted either part.
  La. Mon. O, where is Romeo? saw you him to-day?
Right glad I am he was not at this fray.
  Ben. Madam, an hour before the worshipp'd sun
Peer'd forth the golden window of the east,
A troubled mind drave me to walk abroad;
Where, underneath the grove of sycamore
That westward rooteth from the city's side,
So early walking did I see your son: 130
Towards him I made, but he was ware of me
And stole into the covert of the wood:
I, measuring his affections by my own,
That most are busied when they 're most alone,
Pursued my humour not pursuing his,
And gladly shunn'd who gladly fled from me.
  Mon. Many a morning hath he there been seen,
With tears augmenting the fresh morning's dew,
Adding to clouds more clouds with his deep sighs;
But all so soon as the all-cheering sun   140
Should in the furthest east begin to draw
The shady curtains from Aurora's bed,
Away from light steals home my heavy son,
And private in his chamber pens himself,
Shuts up his windows, locks fair daylight out
And makes himself an artificial night:
Black and portentous must this humour prove,
Unless good counsel may the cause remove.
  Ben. My noble uncle, do you know the cause?
  Mon. I neither know it nor can learn of him.   150
  Ben. Have you importuned him by any means?
  Mon. Both by myself and many other friends:
But he, his own affections' counsellor,
Is to himself—I will not say how true—
But to himself so secret and so close,
So far from sounding and discovery,
As is the bud bit with an envious worm,
Ere he can spread his sweet leaves to the air,

Or dedicate his beauty to the sun.
Could we but learn from whence his sorrows grow,   160
We would as willingly give cure as know.

  Enter ROMEO.

  Ben. See, where he comes: so please you, step aside;
I'll know his grievance, or be much denied.
  Mon. I would thou wert so happy by thy stay,
To hear true shrift. Come, madam, let 's away.
                          [*Exeunt Montague and Lady.*
  Ben. Good morrow, cousin.
  Rom.   Is the day so young?
  Ben. But new struck nine.
  Rom.   Ay me! sad hours seem long.
Was that my father that went hence so fast?
  Ben. It was. What sadness lengthens Romeo's hours?
  Rom. Not having that, which, having, makes them
    short.   170
  Ben. In love?
  Rom. Out—
  Ben. Of love?
  Rom. Out of her favour, where I am in love.
  Ben. Alas, that love, so gentle in his view,
Should be so tyrannous and rough in proof!
  Rom. Alas, that love, whose view is muffled still,
Should, without eyes, see pathways to his will!
Where shall we dine? O me! What fray was here?
Yet tell me not, for I have heard it all.   180
Here 's much to do with hate, but more with love.
Why, then, O brawling love! O loving hate!
O any thing, of nothing first create!
O heavy lightness! serious vanity!
Mis-shapen chaos of well-seeming forms!
Feather of lead, bright smoke, cold fire, sick health!
Still-waking sleep, that is not what it is!
This love feel I, that feel no love in this.
Dost thou not laugh?
  Ben.   No, coz, I rather weep.   189
  Rom. Good heart, at what?
  Ben.   At thy good heart's oppression.
  Rom. Why, such is love's transgression.
Griefs of mine own lie heavy in my breast,
Which thou wilt propagate, to have it prest
With more of thine: this love that thou hast shown
Doth add more grief to too much of mine own.
Love is a smoke raised with the fume of sighs;
Being purged, a fire sparkling in lovers' eyes;
Being vex'd, a sea nourish'd with lovers' tears:
What is it else? a madness most discreet,
A choking gall and a preserving sweet.   200
Farewell, my coz.
  Ben.   Soft! I will go along;
An if you leave me so, you do me wrong.
  Rom. Tut, I have lost myself; I am not here;
This is not Romeo, he 's some other where.
  Ben. Tell me in sadness, who is that you love.
  Rom. What, shall I groan and tell thee?
  Ben.   Groan! why, no:

thee, defend thyself; see glossary. 80. **Clubs, bills, and partisans,** a
rallying cry of London apprentices. *Bills* and *partisans* were long-
handled spears with cutting blades. 83. **crutch,** i.e., a crutch would
befit him better than a sword. 102. **Canker'd . . . canker'd,** corroded
. . . malignant. 109. **Free-town,** Villa Franca in Brooke's poem
Romeus and Juliet. 111. **set . . . abroach,** reopened. 119. **nothing,** not
at all; see glossary. **withal,** with this; see glossary. 133. **affections,**
wishes, inclination; see glossary. 135. **humour,** mood, whim; see
glossary. 143. **heavy,** sad. 151. **means,** agency; see *mean* in glossary.
155. **close,** secret, private; see glossary. 157. **envious,** malicious; see
glossary. 159. **sun,** so Theobald; Qq: *same.* 163. **denied,** refused;

see *deny* in glossary. 165. **shrift,** confession. 166. **morrow,** morning.
cousin, any relative not belonging to one's immediate family; see glossary. 168. **Was . . . fast.** This line is matter of fact, not sentimental
like Romeo's other utterances. See also line 179. 174. **favour,** good
will, liking; see glossary. 176. **proof,** experience; see glossary. 181-
188. **Here 's . . . this.** These lines, abounding in paradoxical phrases
called oxymoron, such as *loving hate, cold fire,* are characteristic of artificial love poetry. They indicate Romeo's sentimentality. 193.
propagate, increase.

But sadly tell me who.
  Rom. Bid a sick man in sadness make his will:
Ah, word ill urged to one that is so ill!
In sadness, cousin, I do love a woman. 210
  Ben. I aim'd so near, when I supposed you loved.
  Rom. A right good mark-man! And she's fair I love.
  Ben. A right fair mark, fair coz, is soonest hit.
  Rom. Well, in that hit you miss: she'll not be hit
With Cupid's arrow; she hath Dian's wit;
And, in strong proof of chastity well arm'd,
From love's weak childish bow she lives unharm'd.
She will not stay the siege of loving terms,
Nor bide the encounter of assailing eyes,
Nor ope her lap to saint-seducing gold: 220
O, she is rich in beauty, only poor,
That when she dies with beauty dies her store.
  Ben. Then she hath sworn that she will still live
      chaste?
  Rom. She hath, and in that sparing makes huge
      waste,
For beauty starved with her severity
Cuts beauty off from all posterity.
She is too fair, too wise, wisely too fair,
To merit bliss by making me despair:
She hath forsworn to love, and in that vow
Do I live dead that live to tell it now. 230
  Ben. Be ruled by me, forget to think of her.
  Rom. O, teach me how I should forget to think.
  Ben. By giving liberty unto thine eyes;
Examine other beauties.
  Rom.   'Tis the way
To call hers exquisite, in question more:
These happy masks that kiss fair ladies' brows
Being black put us in mind they hide the fair;
He that is strucken blind cannot forget
The precious treasure of his eyesight lost:
Show me a mistress that is passing fair, 240
What doth her beauty serve, but as a note
Where I may read who pass'd that passing fair?
Farewell: thou canst not teach me to forget.
  Ben. I'll pay that doctrine, or else die in debt.
                                    [*Exeunt.*

SCENE II. *A street.*

Enter CAPULET, PARIS, *and* Servant.

  Cap. But Montague is bound as well as I,
In penalty alike; and 'tis not hard, I think,
For men so old as we to keep the peace.
  Par. Of honourable reckoning are you both;
And pity 'tis you lived at odds so long.
But now, my lord, what say you to my suit?
  Cap. But saying o'er what I have said before:
My child is yet a stranger in the world;
She hath not seen the change of fourteen years;
Let two more summers wither in their pride, 10
Ere we may think her ripe to be a bride.
  Par. Younger than she are happy mothers made.

Romeo
and Juliet
ACT I : SC I

398

  Cap. And too soon marr'd are those so early made.
The earth hath swallow'd all my hopes but she,
She is the hopeful lady of my earth:
But woo her, gentle Paris, get her heart,
My will to her consent is but a part;
An she agree, within her scope of choice
Lies my consent and fair according voice.
This night I hold an old accustom'd feast,
Whereto I have invited many a guest,
Such as I love; and you, among the store,
One more, most welcome, makes my number more.
At my poor house look to behold this night
Earth-treading stars that make dark heaven light:
Such comfort as do lusty young men feel
When well-apparell'd April on the heel
Of limping winter treads, even such delight
Among fresh female buds shall you this night
Inherit at my house; hear all, all see, 30
And like her most whose merit most shall be:
†Which on more view, of many mine being one
May stand in number, though in reckoning none.
Come, go with me. [*To Serv., giving a paper.*] Go,
      sirrah, trudge about
Through fair Verona; find those persons out
Whose names are written there, and to them say,
My house and welcome on their pleasure stay. 37
                    [*Exeunt Capulet and Paris.*

  Serv. Find them out whose names are written here!
It is written, that the shoemaker should meddle with
his yard, and the tailor with his last, the fisher with his
pencil, and the painter with his nets; but I am sent to
find those persons whose names are here writ, and can
never find what names the writing person hath here
writ. I must to the learned.—In good time. 45

Enter BENVOLIO *and* ROMEO.

  Ben. Tut, man, one fire burns out another's
      burning,
One pain is lessen'd by another's anguish;
Turn giddy, and be holp by backward turning;
One desperate grief cures with another's languish:
Take thou some new infection to thy eye, 50
And the rank poison of the old will die.
  Rom. Your plaintain-leaf is excellent for that.
  Ben. For what, I pray thee?
  Rom.   For your broken shin.
  Ben. Why, Romeo, art thou mad?
  Rom. Not mad, but bound more than a madman is;
Shut up in prison, kept without my food,
Whipp'd and tormented and—God-den, good fellow.
  Serv. God gi' god-den. I pray, sir, can you read?
  Rom. Ay, mine own fortune in my misery. 60
  Serv. Perhaps you have learned it without book: but,
I pray, can you read any thing you see?
  Rom. Ay, if I know the letters and the language.
  Serv. Ye say honestly: rest you merry!
  Rom. Stay, fellow; I can read.   [*Reads.*
'Signior Martino and his wife and daughters;
County Anselme and his beauteous sisters; the lady

208. **sadness**, seriousness; see glossary. 212. **fair**, beautiful; see glossary. 213. **fair**, clear, distinct; see glossary. 218. **stay**, withstand; see glossary. 222. **store.** She will die without children and therefore her beauty will die with her. 225. **starved**, allowed to die; see glossary. 235. **in question more**, into greater consideration. 240. **passing**, surpassingly; see glossary. 244. **pay that doctrine**, give that instruction.
SCENE II. 4. **reckoning**, estimation, repute. 8. **stranger in the world.** Capulet's reluctance is largely a matter of manners. 17. **My**

. . . part. This is also a conventional statement, since Capulet has no idea of letting Juliet have her way. 18. **An**, if; see glossary. **scope**, limit; see glossary. 29. **female**, so Q_1; Q_2 and F read *fennel*, which can be justified by the circumstance that fennel was thought to have the power of awakening passion. 32-33. **Which . . . none.** Capulet may mean that his daughter will lose her identity by being swallowed up in a number of others. He is punning on the saying, "one is no number." The Arden editor places a comma after *of* and dashes after *many* and *one*. He explains *reckoning* to mean "estimation" (as in line 4,

widow of Vitruvio; Signior Placentio and his lovely
nieces; Mercutio and his brother Valentine; mine
uncle Capulet, his wife, and daughters; my fair niece
Rosaline; Livia; Signior Valentio and his cousin
Tybalt; Lucio and the lively Helena.'   74
A fair assembly: whither should they come?
   Serv. Up.
   Rom. Whither?
   Serv. To supper; to our house.
   Rom. Whose house?
   Serv. My master's.   80
   Rom. Indeed, I should have asked you that before.
   Serv. Now I'll tell you without asking: my master is
the great rich Capulet; and if you be not of the house
of Montagues, I pray, come and crush a cup of wine.
Rest you merry!   [*Exit.*
   Ben. At this same ancient feast of Capulet's
Sups the fair Rosaline whom thou so lovest,
With all the admired beauties of Verona:
Go thither; and, with unattainted eye,   90
Compare her face with some that I shall show,
And I will make thee think thy swan a crow.
   Rom. When the devout religion of mine eye
   Maintains such falsehood, then turn tears to fires;
And these, who often drown'd could never die,
   Transparent heretics, be burnt for liars!
One fairer than my love! the all-seeing sun
Ne'er saw her match since first the world begun.
   Ben. Tut, you saw her fair, none else being by,
Herself poised with herself in either eye: 100
But in that crystal scales let there be weigh'd
Your lady's love against some other maid
That I will show you shining at this feast,
And she shall scant show well that now shows best.
   Rom. I'll go along, no such sight to be shown,
But to rejoice in splendour of mine own.   [*Exeunt.*

    SCENE III. *A room in Capulet's house.*

Enter LADY CAPULET *and* Nurse.

   La. Cap. Nurse, where 's my daughter? call her forth
    to me.
   Nurse. Now, by my maidenhead, at twelve year old,
I bade her come. What, lamb! what, ladybird!
God forbid! Where 's this girl? What, Juliet!

Enter JULIET.

   Jul. How now! who calls?
   Nurse.   Your mother.
   Jul.   Madam, I am here.
What is your will?
   La. Cap. This is the matter:—Nurse, give leave
    awhile,
We must talk in secret:—nurse, come back again;
I have remember'd me, thou 's hear our counsel.
Thou know'st my daughter 's of a pretty age.   10
   Nurse. Faith, I can tell her age unto an hour.
   La. Cap. She 's not fourteen.

   Nurse.   I'll lay fourteen of my teeth,—
And yet, to my teen be it spoken, I have but four,—
She is not fourteen. How long is it now
To Lammas-tide?
   La. Cap.   A fortnight and odd days.
   Nurse. Even or odd, of all days in the year,
Come Lammas-eve at night shall she be fourteen.
Susan and she—God rest all Christian souls!—
Were of an age: well, Susan is with God;
She was too good for me: but, as I said,   20
On Lammas-eve at night shall she be fourteen;
That shall she, marry; I remember it well.
'Tis since the earthquake now eleven years;
And she was wean'd,—I never shall forget it,—
Of all the days of the year, upon that day:
For I had then laid wormwood to my dug,
Sitting in the sun under the dove-house wall;
My lord and you were then at Mantua:—
Nay, I do bear a brain:—but, as I said,
When it did taste the wormwood on the nipple   30
Of my dug and felt it bitter, pretty fool,
To see it tetchy and fall out with the dug!
'Shake' quoth the dove-house: 'twas no need, I trow,
To bid me trudge:
And since that time it is eleven years;
For then she could stand alone; nay, by the rood,
She could have run and waddled all about;
For even the day before, she broke her brow:
And then my husband—God be with his soul!
A' was a merry man—took up the child: 40
'Yea,' quoth he, 'dost thou fall upon thy face?
Thou wilt fall backward when thou hast more wit;
Wilt thou not, Jule?' and, by my holidame,
The pretty wretch left crying and said 'Ay.'
To see, now, how a jest shall come about!
I warrant, an I should live a thousand years,
I never should forget it: 'Wilt thou not, Jule?' quoth
    he;
And, pretty fool, it stinted and said 'Ay.'
   La. Cap. Enough of this; I pray thee, hold thy
    peace.   49
   Nurse. Yes, madam: yet I cannot choose but laugh,
To think it should leave crying and say 'Ay.'
And yet, I warrant, it had upon it brow
A bump as big as a young cockerel's stone;
A parlous knock; and it cried bitterly:
'Yea,' quoth my husband, 'fall'st upon thy face?
Thou wilt fall backward when thou comest to age;
Wilt thou not, Jule?' it stinted and said 'Ay.'
   Jul. And stint thou too, I pray thee, nurse, say I.
   Nurse. Peace, I have done. God mark thee to his
    grace!
Thou wast the prettiest babe that e'er I nursed: 60
An I might live to see thee married once,
I have my wish.
   La. Cap. Marry, that 'marry' is the very theme
I came to talk of. Tell me, daughter Juliet,
How stands your disposition to be married?
   Jul. It is an honour that I dream not of.

above), with word play, i.e., "counting heads." 34. **sirrah,** customary
form of address to servants; see glossary. 48. **holp,** helped; see glossary. 51. **rank,** corrupt; see glossary. 57. **God-den,** good evening.
fellow, usual term for a servant; see glossary. 86. **crush a cup of wine,**
drink a cup of wine. Cf. "crack a bottle." 87. **ancient,** customary.
89. **admired,** wondered at; see glossary. 90. **unattainted,** impartial.
95. **these,** i.e., these eyes.
   SCENE III. 7. **give leave,** leave us. 9. **thou 's,** thou shalt. 13.
teen, sorrow. 15. **Lammas-tide,** August 1. 23. **'Tis . . . years.** It

has been thought that Shakespeare was alluding in this line to a
famous earthquake in 1580 and was, therefore, writing in 1591. 29.
bear a brain. The nurse prides herself on her memory. 31. **fool,**
term of endearment; see glossary. 32. **tetchy,** fretful. 33. **trow,** believe; see glossary. 40. **A',** he; see glossary. 43. **holidame,** same as
"halidom," a relic or holy thing. 48. **stinted,** ceased. 52. **it,** so
QqF; Globe: *its.*

Nurse. An honour! were not I thine only nurse,
I would say thou hadst suck'd wisdom from thy teat.
   La. Cap. Well, think of marriage now; younger than
you,
Here in Verona, ladies of esteem,   70
Are made already mothers: by my count,
I was your mother much upon these years
That you are now a maid. Thus then in brief:
The valiant Paris seeks you for his love.
   Nurse. A man, young lady! lady, such a man
As all the world—why, he 's a man of wax.
   La. Cap. Verona's summer hath not such a flower.
   Nurse. Nay, he 's a flower; in faith, a very flower.
   La. Cap. What say you? can you love the gentleman?
This night you shall behold him at our feast;   80
Read o'er the volume of young Paris' face
And find delight writ there with beauty's pen;
Examine every married lineament
And see how one another lends content,
And what obscured in this fair volume lies
Find written in the margent of his eyes.
This precious book of love, this unbound lover,
To beautify him, only lacks a cover:
The fish lives in the sea, and 'tis much pride
For fair without the fair within to hide: 90
That book in many's eyes doth share the glory,
That in gold clasps locks in the golden story;
So shall you share all that he doth possess,
By having him, making yourself no less.
   Nurse. No less! nay, bigger; women grow by men.
   La. Cap. Speak briefly, can you like of Paris' love?
   Jul. I'll look to like, if looking liking move:
But no more deep will I endart mine eye
Than your consent gives strength to make it fly.   99

   Enter a Servant.

   Serv. Madam, the guests are come, supper served up,
you called, my young lady asked for, the nurse cursed
in the pantry, and every thing in extremity. I must
hence to wait; I beseech you, follow straight.
   La. Cap. We follow thee. [*Exit Servant.*] Juliet, the
   county stays.   105
   Nurse. Go, girl, seek happy nights to happy days.
                                [*Exeunt.*

<hr>

SCENE IV. *A street.*

Enter ROMEO, MERCUTIO, BENVOLIO, *with five or six*
Maskers, Torch-bearers, *and others.*

   Rom. What, shall this speech be spoke for our
excuse?
Or shall we on without apology?
   Ben. The date is out of such prolixity:
We'll have no Cupid hoodwink'd with a scarf,
Bearing a Tartar's painted bow of lath,
Scaring the ladies like a crow-keeper;

Nor no without-book prologue, faintly spoke
After the prompter, for our entrance:
But let them measure us by what they will;
We'll measure them a measure, and be gone.   10
   Rom. Give me a torch: I am not for this ambling;
Being but heavy, I will bear the light.
   Mer. Nay, gentle Romeo, we must have you dance.
   Rom. Not I, believe me: you have dancing shoes
With nimble soles: I have a soul of lead
So stakes me to the ground I cannot move.
   Mer. You are a lover; borrow Cupid's wings,
And soar with them above a common bound.
   Rom. I am too sore enpierced with his shaft
To soar with his light feathers, and so bound,   20
I cannot bound a pitch above dull woe:
Under love's heavy burden do I sink.
   Mer. And, to sink in it, should you burden love;
Too great oppression for a tender thing.
   Rom. Is love a tender thing? it is too rough,
Too rude, too boisterous, and it pricks like thorn.
   Mer. If love be rough with you, be rough with love;
Prick love for pricking, and you beat love down.
Give me a case to put my visage in:
A visor for a visor! what care I   30
What curious eye doth quote deformities?
Here are the beetle brows shall blush for me.
   Ben. Come, knock and enter; and no sooner in,
But every man betake him to his legs.
   Rom. A torch for me: let wantons light of heart
Tickle the senseless rushes with their heels,
For I am proverb'd with a grandsire phrase;
I'll be a candle-holder, and look on.
The game was ne'er so fair, and I am done.
   Mer. Tut, dun 's the mouse, the constable's own
   word: 40
If thou art dun, we'll draw thee from the mire
Of this sir-reverence love, wherein thou stick'st
Up to the ears. Come, we burn daylight, ho!
   Rom. Nay, that 's not so.
   Mer.   I mean, sir, in delay
We waste our lights in vain, like lamps by day.
Take our good meaning, for our judgement sits
Five times in that ere once in our five wits.
   Rom. And we mean well in going to this mask;
But 'tis no wit to go.
   Mer.   Why, may one ask?
   Rom. I dream'd a dream to-night.
   Mer.   And so did I.   50
   Rom. Well, what was yours?
   Mer.   That dreamers often lie.
   Rom. In bed asleep, while they do dream things
   true.
   Mer. O, then, I see Queen Mab hath been with
   you.
She is the fairies' midwife, and she comes
In shape no bigger than an agate-stone
On the fore-finger of an alderman,

<hr>

76. **a man of wax,** such as one would picture in wax, i.e., handsome.
83. **married,** harmonized into mutual helpfulness (Hudson). 86.
margent, commentary or marginal gloss. 89. **fish lives in the sea.**
The figure of speech is of the binding of a book; since fishskins were
used to cover books, this "unbound lover" is yet to be made complete.
97-99. **I'll . . . fly.** Juliet's attitude is one of proper obedience. 105.
county, count.
   SCENE IV. 1. **speech.** The older fashion was for maskers to be preceded by a messenger with a set speech, but *the date is out* for *such
prolixity; see date* and *out* in glossary. 4. **hoodwink'd,** blindfolded.
5. **Tartar's painted bow.** Tartar's bows are said to have resembled the

old Roman bow with which Cupid was pictured. 6. **crow-keeper,**
scarecrow. 10. **measure . . . measure,** perform a dance; see glossary.
11. **ambling,** walking affectedly; used contemptuously of dancing.
21. **pitch,** height; see glossary. 30. **visor,** a mask, for an ugly masklike
face. 31. **quote,** take notice of. 36. **rushes.** Rushes were used for
floor coverings. 38. **candle-holder,** an allusion to the proverb "A good
candle-holder (i.e., a mere onlooker) is a good gamester." 40. **dun 's
the mouse,** a common phrase usually taken to mean "keep still." *Dun*
(l. 41) alludes to a Christmas game, "Dun is in the mire," in which a
heavy log was lifted by the players. 42. **sir-reverence,** corruption of
"save-reverence" (*salve-reverentia*), an apology for something improper.

Drawn with a team of little atomies
Athwart men's noses as they lie asleep;
Her waggon-spokes made of long spinners' legs,
The cover of the wings of grasshoppers,   60
The traces of the smallest spider's web,
The collars of the moonshine's watery beams,
Her whip of cricket's bone, the lash of film,
Her waggoner a small grey-coated gnat,
Not half so big as a round little worm
Prick'd from the lazy finger of a maid;
Her chariot is an empty hazel-nut
Made by the joiner squirrel or old grub,
Time out o' mind the fairies' coachmakers.
And in this state she gallops night by night   70
Through lovers' brains, and then they dream of love;
O'er courtiers' knees, that dream on court'sies
      straight,
O'er lawyers' fingers, who straight dream on fees,
O'er ladies' lips, who straight on kisses dream,
Which oft the angry Mab with blisters plagues,
Because their breaths with sweetmeats tainted are:
Sometime she gallops o'er a courtier's nose,
And then dreams he of smelling out a suit;
And sometime comes she with a tithe-pig's tail
Tickling a parson's nose as a' lies asleep,   80
Then dreams he of another benefice:
Sometime she driveth o'er a soldier's neck,
And then dreams he of cutting foreign throats,
Of breaches, ambuscadoes, Spanish blades,
Of healths five-fathom deep; and then anon
Drums in his ear, at which he starts and wakes,
And being thus frighted swears a prayer or two
And sleeps again. This is that very Mab
That plats the manes of horses in the night,
And bakes the elf-locks in foul sluttish hairs,   90
Which once untangled much misfortune bodes:
This is the hag, when maids lie on their backs,
That presses them and learns them first to bear,
Making them women of good carriage:
This is she—
    Rom.   Peace, peace, Mercutio, peace!
Thou talk'st of nothing.
    Mer.   True, I talk of dreams,
Which are the children of an idle brain,
Begot of nothing but vain fantasy,
Which is as thin of substance as the air
And more inconstant than the wind, who wooes   100
Even now the frozen bosom of the north,
And, being anger'd, puffs away from thence,
Turning his face to the dew-dropping south.
    Ben. This wind, you talk of, blows us from
      ourselves;
Supper is done, and we shall come too late.
    Rom. I fear, too early: for my mind misgives
Some consequence yet hanging in the stars
Shall bitterly begin his fearful date
With this night's revels and expire the term

Of a despised life closed in my breast   110
By some vile forfeit of untimely death.
But He, that hath the steerage of my course,
Direct my sail! On, lusty gentlemen.
    Ben. Strike, drum.   [*Exeunt.*

SCENE V. *A hall in Capulet's house.*

Musicians *waiting. Enter* Servingmen, *with napkins.*

First Serv. Where's Potpan, that he helps not to take
away? He shift a trencher? he scrape a trencher!
Sec. Serv. When good manners shall lie all in one or
two men's hands and they unwashed too, 'tis a foul
thing.
First Serv. Away with the joint-stools, remove the
court-cupboard, look to the plate. Good thou, save me
a piece of marchpane; and, as thou lovest me, let the
porter let in Susan Grindstone and Nell. Antony, and
Potpan!   11
Sec. Serv. Ay, boy, ready.
First Serv. You are looked for and called for, asked
for and sought for, in the great chamber.
Sec. Serv. We cannot be here and there too. Cheerly,
boys; be brisk awhile, and the longer liver take all.

Enter CAPULET, *with* JULIET *and others of his house,*
      meeting the Guests *and* Maskers.

Cap. Welcome, gentlemen! ladies that have their
      toes
Unplagued with corns will have a bout with you.
Ah ha, my mistresses! which of you all   20
Will now deny to dance? she that makes dainty,
She, I'll swear, hath corns; am I come near ye now?
Welcome, gentlemen! I have seen the day
That I have worn a visor and could tell
A whispering tale in a fair lady's ear,
Such as would please: 'tis gone, 'tis gone, 'tis gone:
You are welcome, gentlemen! Come, musicians,
      play.
A hall, a hall! give room! and foot it, girls.
                         [*Music plays, and they dance.*
More light, you knaves; and turn the tables up,
And quench the fire, the room is grown too hot.   30
Ah, sirrah, this unlook'd-for sport comes well.
Nay, sit, nay, sit, good cousin Capulet;
For you and I are past our dancing days:
How long is 't now since last yourself and I
Were in a mask?
    Sec. Cap.   By 'r lady, thirty years.
    Cap. What, man! 'tis not so much, 'tis not so much:
'Tis since the nuptial of Lucentio,
Come pentecost as quickly as it will,
Some five and twenty years; and then we mask'd.
    Sec. Cap. 'Tis more, 'tis more: his son is elder, sir;   40
His son is thirty.
    Cap.   Will you tell me that?

---

47. **five wits,** the five faculties, usually given as common wit, imagination, fantasy, judgment, and reason. 53. **Queen Mab,** a name of Celtic origin for the fairy queen. Mercutio's famous speech interested the audience, no doubt, but has little connection with plot or character. 57. **atomies,** tiny creatures. 63. **film,** gossamer thread. 64. **waggoner,** coachman. 65. **worm.** This alludes to an ancient and no doubt useful superstition that "worms breed in the fingers of the idle." 70. **state,** pomp, dignity; see glossary. 73. **straight,** immediately; see glossary. 77. **Sometime,** from time to time, sometimes; see glossary. 78. **suit,** a request or plea at court. 79. **tithe-pig's tail.** This alludes to the tenth pig given the parson as a church tax. 85. **anon,** by and by; see

glossary. 89. **plats the manes of horses,** an allusion to the familiar superstition of "witches stirrups," tangles in the manes of horses. 93. **learns,** teaches; see glossary. 98. **vain,** empty, foolish. **fantasy,** imagination; see glossary. 108. **date,** time; see glossary. 109. **expire,** (transitive), bring to an end.
    SCENE V. 2. **trencher,** wooden dish or plate; see glossary. 7. **joint-stools,** stools, properly those made by a joiner. 8. **court-cupboard,** sideboard. 9. **marchpane,** cake made from sugar and almonds. 21. **makes dainty,** hesitates from affectation to dance; see *dainty* in glossary. 29. **turn the tables up.** Tables were probably made of hinged leaves and placed on trestles. They were put aside for dancing.

His son was but a ward two years ago.
    Rom. [*To a Servingman*] What lady is that, which
        doth enrich the hand
Of yonder knight?
    Serv. I know not, sir.
    Rom. O, she doth teach the torches to burn bright!
It seems she hangs upon the cheek of night
Like a rich jewel in an Ethiope's ear;
Beauty too rich for use, for earth too dear!
So shows a snowy dove trooping with crows,   50
As yonder lady o'er her fellows shows.
The measure done, I'll watch her place of stand,
And, touching hers, make blessed my rude hand.
Did my heart love till now? forswear it, sight!
For I ne'er saw true beauty till this night.
    Tyb. This, by his voice, should be a Montague.
Fetch me my rapier, boy. What dares the slave
Come hither, cover'd with an antic face,
To fleer and scorn at our solemnity?
Now, by the stock and honour of my kin,   60
To strike him dead I hold it not a sin.
    Cap. Why, how now, kinsman! wherefore storm
        you so?
    Tyb. Uncle, this is a Montague, our foe,
A villain that is hither come in spite,
To scorn at our solemnity this night.
    Cap. Young Romeo is it?
    Tyb.   'Tis he, that villain Romeo.
    Cap. Content thee, gentle coz, let him alone;
He bears him like a portly gentleman;
And, to say truth, Verona brags of him
To be a virtuous and well govern'd youth: 70
I would not for the wealth of all the town
Here in my house do him disparagement:
Therefore be patient, take no note of him:
It is my will, the which if thou respect,
Show a fair presence and put off these frowns,
An ill-beseeming semblance for a feast.

    Tyb. It fits, when such a villain is a guest:
I'll not endure him.
    Cap.   He shall be endured:
What, goodman boy! I say, he shall: go to;
Am I the master here, or you? go to.   80
You'll not endure him! God shall mend my soul!
You'll make a mutiny among my guests!
You will set cock-a-hoop! you'll be the man!
    Tyb. Why, uncle, 'tis a shame.
    Cap.   Go to, go to;
You are a saucy boy: is 't so, indeed?
This trick may chance to scathe you, I know what:
You must contrary me! marry, 'tis time.
Well said, my hearts! You are a princox; go:
Be quiet, or—More light, more light! For shame!
I'll make you quiet. What, cheerly, my hearts!   90
    Tyb. Patience perforce with wilful choler meeting
Makes my flesh tremble in their different greeting.
I will withdraw: but this intrusion shall
Now seeming sweet convert to bitter gall.   [*Exit.*

    Rom. [*To Juliet*] If I profane with my unworthiest
        hand
This holy shrine, the gentle fine is this:
My lips, two blushing pilgrims, ready stand
To smooth that rough touch with a tender kiss.
    Jul. Good pilgrim, you do wrong your hand too
        much,
Which mannerly devotion shows in this;   100
For saints have hands that pilgrims' hands do touch,
And palm to palm is holy palmers' kiss.
    Rom. Have not saints lips, and holy palmers too?
    Jul. Ay, pilgrim, lips that they must use in prayer.
    Rom. O, then, dear saint, let lips do what hands do;
They pray, grant thou, lest faith turn to despair.
    Jul. Saints do not move, though grant for prayers'
        sake.
    Rom. Then move not, while my prayer's effect I
        take.
Thus from my lips, by yours, my sin is purged.   109
    Jul. Then have my lips the sin that they have took.
    Rom. Sin from my lips? O trespass sweetly urged!
Give me my sin again.
    Jul.   You kiss by the book.
    Nurse. Madam, your mother craves a word with
        you.
    Rom. What is her mother?
    Nurse.   Marry, bachelor,
Her mother is the lady of the house,
And a good lady, and a wise and virtuous:
I nursed her daughter, that you talk'd withal;
I tell you, he that can lay hold of her
Shall have the chinks.
    Rom.   Is she a Capulet?
O dear account! my life is my foe's debt.   120
    Ben. Away, be gone; the sport is at the best.
    Rom. Ay, so I fear; the more is my unrest.
    Cap. Nay, gentlemen, prepare not to be gone;
We have a trifling foolish banquet towards.
Is it e'en so? why, then, I thank you all;
I thank you, honest gentlemen; good night.
More torches here! Come on then, let 's to bed.
Ah, sirrah, by my fay, it waxes late:
I'll to my rest.   [*Exeunt all but Juliet and Nurse.*
    Jul. Come hither, nurse. What is yond gentleman?
    Nurse. The son and heir of old Tiberio.   131
    Jul. What 's he that now is going out of door?
    Nurse. Marry, that, I think, be young Petrucio.
    Jul. What 's he that follows there, that would not
        dance?
    Nurse. I know not.
    Jul. Go, ask his name: if he be married,
My grave is like to be my wedding bed.
    Nurse. His name is Romeo, and a Montague;
The only son of your great enemy.
    Jul. My only love sprung from my only hate!   140
Too early seen unknown, and known too late!
Prodigious birth of love it is to me,
That I must love a loathed enemy.

42. **ward,** a minor under guardianship. 46-55. **O . . . night.** Romeo's
love is love at first sight, a type of love provided for in Elizabethan
psychological doctrine and, no doubt, in life. 49. **dear,** precious; see
glossary. 57. **Fetch me my rapier.** This speech of Tybalt's is in immediate contrast to the happy sentiment of Romeo's speech. 58.
antic, fantastic. 59. **fleer,** to look mockingly. 68. **portly,** an excellent
bearing. 74. **respect,** regard; see glossary. 79. **goodman boy,** a be-
littling ironical epithet. Capulet has a spirit more reconcilable than
that of Tybalt. **go to,** expression of impatience; see glossary. 83.
cock-a-hoop, complete disorder. 91. **Patience perforce,** patience upon
compulsion; see *perforce* in glossary; *patience* is a general word for

self-control. 94. **convert,** change (to). 95-108. **If . . . take.** These
lines are in the form of a sonnet. They afford an example of Shakespeare's early exuberance in poetic style. 99. **pilgrim.** Romeo was
masquerading as a pilgrim or palmer. 112. **by the book,** according
to rule. 119. **chinks,** money. 120. **my foe's debt,** due to my foe, at
his mercy. 124. **foolish,** insignificant. **banquet,** dessert. **towards,**
in preparation; see glossary. 128. **fay,** faith.
    ACT II. PROLOGUE. 10. **use to swear,** are in the habit of swearing;
see *use* in glossary. 13. **passion,** feeling of love; see glossary.
    SCENE I. 2. **dull earth,** Romeo himself. **thy centre,** Juliet. The
figure of speech is that of man as a microcosm or little world. 6. **con-**

Nurse. What 's this? what 's this?
Jul.   A rhyme I learn'd even now
Of one I danced withal.   [*One calls within* 'Juliet.'
Nurse.   Anon, anon!
Come, let 's away; the strangers all are gone.   [*Exeunt.*

ACT II.

PROLOGUE.

Enter Chorus.

Chor. Now old desire doth in his death-bed lie,
    And young affection gapes to be his heir;
That fair for which love groan'd for and would die,
    With tender Juliet match'd, is now not fair.
Now Romeo is beloved and loves again,
    Alike bewitched by the charm of looks,
But to his foe supposed he must complain,
    And she steal love's sweet bait from fearful hooks:
Being held a foe, he may not have access
    To breathe such vows as lovers use to swear;   10
And she as much in love, her means much less
    To meet her new-beloved any where:
But passion lends them power, time means, to meet,
Tempering extremities with extreme sweet.   [*Exit.*

SCENE I. *A lane by the wall of Capulet's orchard.*

Enter ROMEO.

Rom. Can I go forward when my heart is here?
Turn back, dull earth, and find thy centre out.
        [*He climbs the wall, and leaps down within it.*

Enter BENVOLIO *and* MERCUTIO.

Ben. Romeo! my cousin Romeo!
Mer.   He is wise;
And, on my life, hath stol'n him home to bed.
Ben. He ran this way, and leap'd this orchard wall:
Call, good Mercutio.
Mer.   Nay, I'll conjure too.
Romeo! humours! madman! passion! lover!
Appear thou in the likeness of a sigh:
Speak but one rhyme, and I am satisfied;
Cry but 'Ay me!' pronounce but 'love' and 'dove;'   10
Speak to my gossip Venus one fair word,
One nick-name for her purblind son and heir,
Young Adam Cupid, he that shot so trim,
When King Cophetua loved the beggar-maid!
He heareth not, he stirreth not, he moveth not;
The ape is dead, and I must conjure him.
I conjure thee by Rosaline's bright eyes,
By her high forehead and her scarlet lip,
By her fine foot, straight leg and quivering thigh
And the demesnes that there adjacent lie,   20
That in thy likeness thou appear to us!
    Ben. An if he hear thee, thou wilt anger him.

Mer. This cannot anger him: 'twould anger him
To raise a spirit in his mistress' circle
Of some strange nature, letting it there stand
Till she had laid it and conjured it down;
That were some spite: my invocation
Is fair and honest, and in his mistress' name
I conjure only but to raise up him.
    Ben. Come, he hath hid himself among these trees,   30
To be consorted with the humorous night:
Blind is his love and best befits the dark.
    Mer. If love be blind, love cannot hit the mark.
Now will he sit under a medlar tree,
And wish his mistress were that kind of fruit
As maids call medlars, when they laugh alone.
O, Romeo, that she were, O, that she were
An open et cætera, thou a poperin pear!
Romeo, good night: I'll to my truckle-bed;
This field-bed is too cold for me to sleep: 40
Come, shall we go?
    Ben.   Go, then; for 'tis in vain
To seek him here that means not to be found.   [*Exeunt.*

SCENE II. *Capulet's orchard.*

Enter ROMEO.

Rom. He jests at scars that never felt a wound.
            [*Juliet appears above at a window.*
But, soft! what light through yonder window breaks?
It is the east, and Juliet is the sun.
Arise, fair sun, and kill the envious moon,
Who is already sick and pale with grief,
That thou her maid art far more fair than she:
Be not her maid, since she is envious;
Her vestal livery is but sick and green
And none but fools do wear it; cast it off.
It is my lady, O, it is my love!   10
O, that she knew she were!
She speaks, yet she says nothing: what of that?
Her eye discourses; I will answer it.
I am too bold, 'tis not to me she speaks:
Two of the fairest stars in all the heaven,
Having some business, do entreat her eyes
To twinkle in their spheres till they return.
What if her eyes were there, they in her head?
The brightness of her cheek would shame those stars,
As daylight doth a lamp; her eyes in heaven   20
Would through the airy region stream so bright
That birds would sing and think it were not night.
See, how she leans her cheek upon her hand!
O, that I were a glove upon that hand,
That I might touch that cheek!
    Jul.   Ay me!
    Rom.   She speaks:
O, speak again, bright angel! for thou art
As glorious to this night, being o'er my head,
As is a winged messenger of heaven
Unto the white-upturned wondering eyes

jure, utter incantation. 12. **purblind,** completely blind. 13. **Adam,**
Upton's conjecture; Qq and F: *Abraham.* It is thought that *Adam* may
refer to Adam Bell, a famous archer in the old ballads; *Abraham* is a
form of "abram" or "auburn," which would refer to Cupid's flaxen
hair. 14. **King Cophetua,** reference to the ballad *King Cophetua and the
Beggar Maid.* 16. **ape,** used as a term of endearment. 20. **demesnes,**
regions. 22. **An if,** if; see glossary. 25. **strange,** belonging to another
person; see glossary. 27. **spite,** injury. 28. **honest,** chaste; see glossary. 31. **consorted,** associated. **humorous,** moist; also, influenced
by humor or mood. 34. **medlar,** the fruit of the *Mespilus germanica,*
edible only when partly decayed. 38. **poperin,** variety of pear;

derived from the Flemish town *Poperinghe* in Flanders. 39. **truckle-
bed,** a bed on casters to be shoved under a standing bed. 40. **field-
bed,** large bed; here, the ground.
    SCENE II. There is no break in the action. Romeo must have been
standing on the front stage behind some obstruction to represent the
garden wall. He speaks at once, then turns to observe Juliet. 13.
discourses, speaks; see glossary. 17. **spheres,** transparent concentric
shells supposed to carry the heavenly bodies with them in their revolution around the earth.

Of mortals that fall back to gaze on him   30
When he bestrides the lazy-pacing clouds
And sails upon the bosom of the air.
    Jul. O Romeo, Romeo! wherefore art thou Romeo?
Deny thy father and refuse thy name;
Or, if thou wilt not, be but sworn my love,
And I'll no longer be a Capulet.
    Rom. [*Aside*] Shall I hear more, or shall I speak at
        this?
    Jul. 'Tis but thy name that is my enemy;
Thou art thyself, though not a Montague.
What 's Montague? it is nor hand, nor foot,   40
Nor arm, nor face, nor any other part
Belonging to a man. O, be some other name!
What 's in a name? that which we call a rose
By any other name would smell as sweet;
So Romeo would, were he not Romeo call'd,
Retain that dear perfection which he owes
Without that title. Romeo, doff thy name,
And for that name which is no part of thee
Take all myself.
    Rom.   I take thee at thy word:
Call me but love, and I'll be new baptized;   50
Henceforth I never will be Romeo.
    Jul. What man art thou that thus bescreen'd in
        night
So stumblest on my counsel?
    Rom.   By a name
I know not how to tell thee who I am:
My name, dear saint, is hateful to myself,
Because it is an enemy to thee;
Had I it written, I would tear the word.
    Jul. My ears have not yet drunk a hundred words
Of that tongue's utterance, yet I know the sound:
Art thou not Romeo and a Montague?   60
    Rom. Neither, fair saint, if either thee dislike.
    Jul. How camest thou hither, tell me, and
        wherefore?
The orchard walls are high and hard to climb,
And the place death, considering who thou art,
If any of my kinsmen find thee here.
    Rom. With love's light wings did I o'erperch these
        walls;
For stony limits cannot hold love out,
And what love can do that dares love attempt;
Therefore thy kinsmen are no let to me.
    Jul. If they do see thee, they will murder thee.   70
    Rom. Alack, there lies more peril in thine eye
Than twenty of their swords: look thou but sweet,
And I am proof against their enmity.
    Jul. I would not for the world they saw thee here.
    Rom. I have night's cloak to hide me from their
        sight;
And but thou love me, let them find me here:
My life were better ended by their hate,
Than death prorogued, wanting of thy love.
    Jul. By whose direction found'st thou out this
        place?
    Rom. By love, who first did prompt me to inquire; 80
He lent me counsel and I lent him eyes.
I am no pilot; yet, wert thou as far
As that vast shore wash'd with the farthest sea,

I would adventure for such merchandise.
    Jul. Thou know'st the mask of night is on my face,
Else would a maiden blush bepaint my cheek
For that which thou hast heard me speak tonight.
Fain would I dwell on form, fain, fain deny
What I have spoke: but farewell compliment!
Dost thou love me? I know thou wilt say 'Ay,'   90
And I will take thy word: yet, if thou swear'st,
Thou mayst prove false; at lovers' perjuries,
They say, Jove laughs. O gentle Romeo,
If thou dost love, pronounce it faithfully:
Or if thou think'st I am too quickly won,
I'll frown and be perverse and say thee nay,
So thou wilt woo; but else, not for the world.
In truth, fair Montague, I am too fond,
And therefore thou mayst think my 'haviour light:
But trust me, gentleman, I'll prove more true   100
Than those that have more cunning to be strange.
I should have been more strange, I must confess,
But that thou overheard'st, ere I was ware,
My true love's passion; therefore pardon me,
And not impute this yielding to light love,
Which the dark night hath so discovered.
    Rom. Lady, by yonder blessed moon I swear
That tips with silver all these fruit-tree tops—
    Jul. O, swear not by the moon, the inconstant
        moon,
That monthly changes in her circled orb,   110
Lest that thy love prove likewise variable.
    Rom. What shall I swear by?
    Jul.   Do not swear at all;
Or, if thou wilt, swear by thy gracious self,
Which is the god of my idolatry,
And I'll believe thee.
    Rom.   If my heart's dear love—
    Jul. Well, do not swear: although I joy in thee,
I have no joy of this contract to-night:
It is too rash, too unadvised, too sudden;
Too like the lightning, which doth cease to be
Ere one can say 'It lightens.' Sweet, good night!   120
This bud of love, by summer's ripening breath,
May prove a beauteous flower when next we meet.
Good night, good night! as sweet repose and rest
Come to thy heart as that within my breast!
    Rom. O, wilt thou leave me so unsatisfied?
    Jul. What satisfaction canst thou have to-night?
    Rom. The exchange of thy love's faithful vow for
        mine.
    Jul. I gave thee mine before thou didst request it:
And yet I would it were to give again.
    Rom. Wouldst thou withdraw it? for what purpose,
        love?   130
    Jul. But to be frank, and give it thee again.
And yet I wish but for the thing I have:
My bounty is as boundless as the sea,
My love as deep; the more I give to thee,
The more I have, for both are infinite.
                                    [*Nurse calls within.*
I hear some noise within; dear love, adieu!
Anon, good nurse! Sweet Montague, be true.
Stay but a little, I will come again.   [*Exit, above.*
    Rom. O blessed, blessed night! I am afeard,

30. **mortals,** human beings; see *mortal* in glossary.   46. **owes,** owns; see
glossary.   53. **counsel,** secret thought.   61. **dislike,** displease.   66.
o'er-perch, fly over and perch beyond.   78. **prorogued,** postponed.
wanting, lacking; see *want* in glossary.   89. **compliment,** punctilious-
ness, ceremony.   98. **fond,** foolish; see glossary.   101. **strange,** re-

served; see glossary.   106. **discovered,** revealed; see *discover* in glossary
110. **orb,** equivalent to *sphere;* see above, line 17.   131. **frank,** liberal,
bounteous.   143. **bent,** purpose; from the idea of the tension of a bow.
145. **procure,** cause.   151. **By and by,** immediately.   160. **tassel-
gentle,** tercel-gentle, the male of the goshawk.   173. **still,** always; see

Being in night, all this is but a dream, 140
Too flattering-sweet to be substantial.

Re-enter JULIET, *above.*

Jul. Three words, dear Romeo, and good night
   indeed.
If that thy bent of love be honourable,
Thy purpose marriage, send me word to-morrow,
By one that I'll procure to come to thee,
Where and what time thou wilt perform the rite;
And all my fortunes at thy foot I'll lay
And follow thee my lord throughout the world.
   Nurse. [*Within*] Madam!
   Jul. I come, anon.—But if thou mean'st not well, 150
I do beseech thee—
   Nurse.   [*Within*] Madam!
   Jul.   By and by, I come:—
To cease thy suit, and leave me to my grief:
To-morrow will I send.
   Rom.   So thrive my soul—
   Jul. A thousand times good night!   [*Exit, above.*
   Rom. A thousand times the worse, to want thy light.
Love goes toward love, as schoolboys from their
   books,
But love from love, toward school with heavy looks.
                         [*Retiring.*

Re-enter JULIET, *above.*

   Jul. Hist! Romeo, hist! O, for a falconer's voice,
To lure this tassel-gentle back again! 160
Bondage is hoarse, and may not speak aloud;
Else would I tear the cave where Echo lies,
And make her airy tongue more hoarse than mine,
With repetition of my Romeo's name.
   Rom. It is my soul that calls upon my name:
How silver-sweet sound lovers' tongues by night,
Like softest music to attending ears!
   Jul. Romeo!
   Rom.   My dear?
   Jul.   At what o'clock to-morrow
Shall I send to thee?
   Rom.   At the hour of nine.
   Jul. I will not fail: 'tis twenty years till then. 170
I have forgot why I did call thee back.
   Rom. Let me stand here till thou remember it.
   Jul. I shall forget, to have thee still stand there,
Remembering how I love thy company.
   Rom. And I'll still stay, to have thee still forget,
Forgetting any other home but this.
   Jul. 'Tis almost morning; I would have thee gone:
And yet no further than a wanton's bird;
Who lets it hop a little from her hand,
Like a poor prisoner in his twisted gyves, 180
And with a silk thread plucks it back again,
So loving-jealous of his liberty.
   Rom. I would I were thy bird.
   Jul.   Sweet, so would I:
Yet I should kill thee with much cherishing.
Good night, good night! parting is such sweet sorrow,
That I shall say good night till it be morrow.
                    [*Exit, above.*
   Rom. Sleep dwell upon thine eyes, peace in thy
   breast!

Would I were sleep and peace, so sweet to rest!
Hence will I to my ghostly father's cell,
His help to crave, and my dear hap to tell.   [*Exit.* 190

SCENE III. *Friar Laurence's cell.*

Enter FRIAR LAURENCE, *with a basket.*

   Fri. L. The grey-eyed morn smiles on the frowning
   night,
Chequering the eastern clouds with streaks of light,
And flecked darkness like a drunkard reels
From forth day's path and Titan's fiery wheels:
Now, ere the sun advance his burning eye,
The day to cheer and night's dank dew to dry,
I must up-fill this osier cage of ours
With baleful weeds and precious-juiced flowers.
The earth that's nature's mother is her tomb;
What is her burying grave that is her womb, 10
And from her womb children of divers kind
We sucking on her natural bosom find,
Many for many virtues excellent,
None but for some and yet all different.
O, mickle is the powerful grace that lies
In herbs, plants, stones, and their true qualities:
For nought so vile that on the earth doth live
But to the earth some special good doth give,
Nor aught so good but strain'd from that fair use
Revolts from true birth, stumbling on abuse: 20
Virtue itself turns vice, being misapplied;
And vice sometimes by action dignified.
Within the infant rind of this small flower
Poison hath residence and medicine power:
For this, being smelt, with that part cheers each part;
Being tasted, slays all senses with the heart.
Two such opposed kings encamp them still
In man as well as herbs, grace and rude will;
And where the worser is predominant,
Full soon the canker death eats up that plant. 30

Enter ROMEO.

   Rom. Good morrow, father.
   Fri. L.   Benedicite!
What early tongue so sweet saluteth me?
Young son, it argues a distemper'd head
So soon to bid good morrow to thy bed:
Care keeps his watch in every old man's eye,
And where care lodges, sleep will never lie;
But where unbruised youth with unstuff'd brain
Doth couch his limbs, there golden sleep doth reign:
Therefore thy earliness doth me assure
Thou art up-roused by some distemperature; 40
Or if not so, then here I hit it right,
Our Romeo hath not been in bed to-night.
   Rom. That last is true; the sweeter rest was mine.
   Fri. L. God pardon sin! wast thou with Rosaline?
   Rom. With Rosaline, my ghostly father? no;
I have forgot that name, and that name's woe.
   Fri. L. That's my good son: but where hast thou
   been, then?
   Rom. I'll tell thee, ere thou ask it me again.
I have been feasting with mine enemy,

glossary. 180. **gyves,** fetters. 189. **ghostly,** spiritual. 190. **dear hap,**
good fortune.
  SCENE III. 3. **flecked,** dappled. 4. **Titan's.** Helios, the sun god,
was a descendant of the race of Titans. 7. **osier cage,** willow basket.
15. **mickle,** great. **grace,** beneficent virtue; see glossary. 16. **quali-**

ties, properties; see glossary. 30. **canker,** cankerworm. 33. **distemper'd,** ill; a reference to a state of the humors in the body; see
glossary. 34. **morrow,** morning. 37. **unstuff'd,** not overcharged;
another reference to the state of the humors.

Where on a sudden one hath wounded me, 50
That 's by me wounded: both our remedies
Within thy help and holy physic lies:
I bear no hatred, blessed man, for, lo,
My intercession likewise steads my foe.
  Fri. L. Be plain, good son, and homely in thy drift;
Riddling confession finds but riddling shrift.
  Rom. Then plainly know my heart's dear love is set
On the fair daughter of rich Capulet:
As mine on hers, so hers is set on mine;
And all combined, save what thou must combine 60
By holy marriage: when and where and how
We met, we woo'd and made exchange of vow,
I'll tell thee as we pass; but this I pray,
That thou consent to marry us to-day.
  Fri. L. Holy Saint Francis, what a change is here!
Is Rosaline, whom thou didst love so dear,
So soon forsaken? young men's love then lies
Not truly in their hearts, but in their eyes.
Jesu Maria, what a deal of brine
Hath wash'd thy sallow cheeks for Rosaline! 70
How much salt water thrown away in waste,
To season love, that of it doth not taste!
The sun not yet thy sighs from heaven clears,
Thy old groans ring yet in my ancient ears;
Lo, here upon thy cheek the stain doth sit
Of an old tear that is not wash'd off yet:
If e'er thou wast thyself and these woes thine,
Thou and these woes were all for Rosaline:
And art thou changed? pronounce this sentence then,
Women may fall, when there's no strength in men. 80
  Rom. Thou chid'st me oft for loving Rosaline.
  Fri. L. For doting, not for loving, pupil mine.
  Rom. And bad'st me bury love.
  Fri. L.   Not in a grave,
To lay one in, another out to have.
  Rom. I pray thee, chide not: she whom I love now
Doth grace for grace and love for love allow;
The other did not so.
  Fri. L.   O, she knew well
Thy love did read by rote and could not spell.
But come, young waverer, come, go with me,
In one respect I'll thy assistant be; 90
For this alliance may so happy prove,
To turn your households' rancour to pure love.
  Rom. O, let us hence; I stand on sudden haste.
  Fri. L. Wisely and slow; they stumble that run fast.
                                             [*Exeunt.*

SCENE IV. *A street.*

Enter BENVOLIO *and* MERCUTIO.

  Mer. Where the devil should this Romeo be?
Came he not home to-night?
  Ben. Not to his father's; I spoke with his man.

*Romeo
and Juliet
ACT II : SC III*

406

  Mer. Ah, that same pale hard-hearted wench, that
    Rosaline,
Torments him so, that he will sure run mad.
  Ben. Tybalt, the kinsman of old Capulet,
Hath sent a letter to his father's house.
  Mer. A challenge, on my life.
  Ben. Romeo will answer it.
  Mer. Any man that can write may answer a letter. 10
  Ben. Nay, he will answer the letter's master, how he
dares, being dared.
  Mer. Alas, poor Romeo! he is already dead; stabbed
with a white wench's black eye; shot thorough the ear
with a love-song; the very pin of his heart cleft with
the blind bow-boy's butt-shaft: and is he a man to encounter Tybalt? 17
  Ben. Why, what is Tybalt?
  Mer. More than prince of cats, I can tell you. O, he
is the courageous captain of complements. He fights as
you sing prick-song, keeps time, distance, and proportion; rests me his minim rest, one, two, and the third
in your bosom: the very butcher of a silk button, a
duellist, a duellist; a gentleman of the very first house,
of the first and second cause: ah, the immortal passado! the punto reverso! the hai! 27
  Ben. The what?
  Mer. The pox of such antic, lisping, affecting fan-
tasticoes; these new tuners of accents! 'By Jesu, a very
good blade! a very tall man! a very good whore!' Why,
is not this a lamentable thing, grandsire, that we
should be thus afflicted with these strange flies, these
fashion-mongers, these perdona-mi's, who stand so
much on the new form, that they cannot sit at ease on
the old bench? O, their bones, their bones! 37

Enter ROMEO.

  Ben. Here comes Romeo, here comes Romeo.
  Mer. Without his roe, like a dried herring: O flesh,
flesh, how art thou fishified! Now is he for the numbers that Petrarch flowed in: Laura to his lady was
but a kitchen-wench; marry, she had a better love to
be-rhyme her; Dido a dowdy; Cleopatra a gipsy;
Helen and Hero hildings and harlots; Thisbe a grey
eye or so, but not to the purpose. Signior Romeo, bon
jour! there's a French salutation to your French slop.
You gave us the counterfeit fairly last night.
  Rom. Good morrow to you both. What counterfeit
did I give you? 50
  Mer. The slip, sir, the slip; can you not conceive?
  Rom. Pardon, good Mercutio, my business was
great; and in such a case as mine a man may strain
courtesy.
  Mer. That's as much as to say, such a case as yours
constrains a man to bow in the hams.
  Rom. Meaning, to court'sy.
  Mer. Thou hast most kindly hit it.
  Rom. A most courteous exposition. 60
  Mer. Nay, I am the very pink of courtesy.

Rom. Pink for flower.

Mer. Right.

Rom. Why, then is my pump well flowered.

Mer. Well said: follow me this jest now till thou hast worn out thy pump, that when the single sole of it is worn, the jest may remain after the wearing sole singular.

Rom. O single-soled jest, solely singular for the singleness! 70

Mer. Come between us, good Benvolio; my wits faint.

Rom. Switch and spurs, switch and spurs; or I'll cry a match.

Mer. Nay, if thy wits run the wild-goose chase, I have done, for thou hast more of the wild-goose in one of thy wits than, I am sure, I have in my whole five: was I with you there for the goose?

Rom. Thou wast never with me for any thing when thou wast not there for the goose.

Mer. I will bite thee by the ear for that jest.

Rom. Nay, good goose, bite not. 82

Mer. Thy wit is a very bitter sweeting; it is a most sharp sauce.

Rom. And is it not well served in to a sweet goose?

Mer. O, here 's a wit of cheveril, that stretches from an inch narrow to an ell broad!

Rom. I stretch it out for that word 'broad;' which added to the goose, proves thee far and wide a broad goose. 91

Mer. Why, is not this better now than groaning for love? now art thou sociable, now art thou Romeo; now art thou what thou art, by art as well as by nature: for this drivelling love is like a great natural, that runs lolling up and down to hide his bauble in a hole.

Ben. Stop there, stop there.

Mer. Thou desirest me to stop in my tale against the hair. 100

Ben. Thou wouldst else have made thy tale large.

Mer. O, thou art deceived; I would have made it short: for I was come to the whole depth of my tale; and meant, indeed, to occupy the argument no longer.

Rom. Here 's goodly gear!

Enter Nurse *and* PETER.

Mer. A sail, a sail!

Ben. Two, two; a shirt and a smock.

Nurse. Peter! 110

Peter. Anon!

Nurse. My fan, Peter.

Mer. Good Peter, to hide her face; for her fan 's the fairer face.

Nurse. God ye good morrow, gentlemen.

Mer. God ye good den, fair gentlewoman.

Nurse. Is it good den?

Mer. 'Tis no less, I tell you, for the bawdy hand of the dial is now upon the prick of noon.

Nurse. Out upon you! what a man are you! 120

Rom. One, gentlewoman, that God hath made for himself to mar.

Nurse. By my troth, it is well said; 'for himself to mar,' quoth a'? Gentlemen, can any of you tell me where I may find the young Romeo?

Rom. I can tell you; but young Romeo will be older when you have found him than he was when you sought him: I am the youngest of that name, for fault of a worse.

Nurse. You say well. 130

Mer. Yea, is the worst well? very well took, i' faith; wisely, wisely.

Nurse. If you be he, sir, I desire some confidence with you.

Ben. She will indite him to some supper.

Mer. A bawd, a bawd, a bawd! So ho!

Rom. What hast thou found?

Mer. No hare, sir; unless a hare, sir, in a lenten pie, that is something stale and hoar ere it be spent. [*Sings.*

An old hare hoar, 141
And an old hare hoar,
Is very good meat in lent:
But a hare that is hoar
Is too much for a score,
When it hoars ere it be spent.

Romeo, will you come to your father's? we'll to dinner, thither.

Rom. I will follow you.

Mer. Farewell, ancient lady; farewell, [*singing*] 'lady, lady, lady.' [*Exeunt Mercutio and Benvolio.* 151

Nurse. Marry, farewell! I pray you, sir, what saucy merchant was this, that was so full of his ropery?

Rom. A gentleman, nurse, that loves to hear himself talk, and will speak more in a minute than he will stand to in a month. 157

Nurse. An a' speak any thing against me, I'll take him down, an a' were lustier than he is, and twenty such Jacks; and if I cannot, I'll find those that shall. Scurvy knave! I am none of his flirt-gills; I am none of his skains-mates. And thou must stand by too, and suffer every knave to use me at his pleasure?

Peter. I saw no man use you at his pleasure; if I had, my weapon should quickly have been out, I warrant you: I dare draw as soon as another man, if I see occasion in a good quarrel, and the law on my side. 169

Nurse. Now, afore God, I am so vexed, that every part about me quivers. Scurvy knave! Pray you, sir, a word: and as I told you, my young lady bade me inquire you out; what she bade me say, I will keep to myself: but first let me tell ye, if ye should lead her into a fool's paradise, as they say, it were a very gross kind of behaviour, as they say: for the gentlewoman is young; and, therefore, if you should deal double with her, truly it were an ill thing to be offered to any gentlewoman, and very weak dealing. 181

feit coins were called "slips." 56. **case**, mask. 59. **kindly**, naturally; see glossary. 64. **is my pump well flowered.** The pump is pinked or perforated in ornamental figures. 69. **single-soled**, thin; contemptible, with pun on "soul." 70. **singleness**, feebleness. 74. **cry a match**, claim a victory. 75. **wild-goose chase**, a horse race in which the leading rider might force his competitors to follow him wherever he went. 83. **sweeting**, probably a pun on an apple called the "sweeting." 87. **cheveril**, kid leather. 91. **broad goose**, possibly means that Mercutio is known far and wide as a goose. 96. **natural**, idiot. 100. **against the hair**, against the grain. 107. **gear**, general word meaning "substance" or "stuff"; see glossary. 109. **a shirt . . . smock**, a man and a woman; see *smock* in glossary. 119. **prick**, point on the dial of a clock.

120. **Out upon you**, expression of indignation; see *out* in glossary. 134. **confidence**, the nurse's mistake for "conference." 135. **indite**, Benvolio's malapropism for "invite." 138. **hare**, used as a slang word for "courtesan." 144. **hoar**, moldy. 151. **'lady, lady, lady,'** refrain from the ballad *Chaste Susanna.* 153. **merchant**, fellow. 154. **ropery**, the nurse's mistake for "roguery." 160. **Jacks**, used as a term of disparagement. 162. **flirt-gills**, loose women. 163. **skains-mates**, not well understood; sometimes connected with "skein" (of thread) or with "skain," a dagger.

Rom. Nurse, commend me to thy lady and mistress.
I protest unto thee—
Nurse. Good heart, and, i' faith, I will tell her as much: Lord, Lord, she will be a joyful woman.
Rom. What wilt thou tell her, nurse? thou dost not mark me.
Nurse. I will tell her, sir, that you do protest; which, as I take it, is a gentlemanlike offer.
Rom. Bid her devise   191
Some means to come to shrift this afternoon;
And there she shall at Friar Laurence' cell
Be shrived and married. Here is for thy pains.
Nurse. No, truly, sir; not a penny.
Rom. Go to; I say you shall.
Nurse. This afternoon, sir? well, she shall be there.
Rom. And stay, good nurse, behind the abbey wall:
Within this hour my man shall be with thee,   200
And bring thee cords made like a tackled stair;
Which to the high top-gallant of my joy
Must be my convoy in the secret night.
Farewell; be trusty, and I'll quit thy pains:
Farewell; commend me to thy mistress.
Nurse. Now God in heaven bless thee! Hark you, sir.
Rom. What say'st thou, my dear nurse?
Nurse. Is your man secret? Did you ne'er hear say,
Two may keep counsel, putting one away?
Rom. I warrant thee, my man 's as true as steel.   210
Nurse. Well, sir; my mistress is the sweetest lady—
Lord, Lord! when 'twas a little prating thing:—O, there is a nobleman in town, one Paris, that would fain lay knife aboard; but she, good soul, had as lief see a toad, a very toad, as see him. I anger her sometimes and tell her that Paris is the properer man; but, I'll warrant you, when I say so, she looks as pale as any clout in the versal world. Doth not rosemary and Romeo begin both with a letter?   220
Rom. Ay, nurse; what of that? both with an R.
Nurse. Ah, mocker! that 's the dog's name; R is for the—No; I know it begins with some other letter:— and she hath the prettiest sententious of it, of you and rosemary, that it would do you good to hear it.
Rom. Commend me to thy lady.
Nurse. Ay, a thousand times. [*Exit Romeo.*] Peter! 230
Pet. Anon!
Nurse. Peter, take my fan, and go before, and apace.
                                                          [*Exeunt.*

SCENE V. *Capulet's orchard.*

Enter JULIET.

Jul. The clock struck nine when I did send the nurse;
In half an hour she promised to return.
Perchance she cannot meet him: that 's not so.
O, she is lame! love's heralds should be thoughts,
Which ten times faster glide than the sun's beams,
Driving back shadows over louring hills:
Therefore do nimble-pinion'd doves draw love,
And therefore hath the wind-swift Cupid wings.
Now is the sun upon the highmost hill

Of this day's journey, and from nine till twelve   10
Is three long hours, yet she is not come.
Had she affections and warm youthful blood,
She would be as swift in motion as a ball;
My words would bandy her to my sweet love,
And his to me:
†But old folks, many feign as they were dead;
Unwieldy, slow, heavy and pale as lead.
O God, she comes!

Enter Nurse *and* PETER.

                        O honey nurse, what news?
Hast thou met with him? Send thy man away.
Nurse. Peter, stay at the gate.   [*Exit Peter.* 20
Jul. Now, good sweet nurse,—O Lord, why look'st thou sad?
Though news be sad, yet tell them merrily;
If good, thou shamest the music of sweet news
By playing it to me with so sour a face.
Nurse. I am a-weary, give me leave awhile:
Fie, how my bones ache! what a jaunce have I had!
Jul. I would thou hadst my bones, and I thy news.
Nay, come, I pray thee, speak; good, good nurse, speak.
Nurse. Jesu, what haste? can you not stay awhile?
Do you not see that I am out of breath?   30
Jul. How art thou out of breath, when thou hast breath
To say to me that thou art out of breath?
The excuse that thou dost make in this delay
Is longer than the tale thou dost excuse.
Is thy news good, or bad? answer to that;
Say either, and I'll stay the circumstance:
Let me be satisfied, is 't good or bad?
Nurse. Well, you have made a simple choice; you know not how to choose a man: Romeo! no, not he; though his face be better than any man's, yet his leg excels all men's; and for a hand, and a foot, and a body, though they be not to be talked on, yet they are past compare: he is not the flower of courtesy, but, I'll warrant him, as gentle as a lamb. Go thy ways, wench; serve God. What, have you dined at home?   46
Jul. No, no: but all this did I know before.
What says he of our marriage? what of that?
Nurse. Lord, how my head aches! what a head have I!
It beats as it would fall in twenty pieces.   50
My back o' t' other side,—O my back, my back!
Beshrew your heart for sending me about,
To catch my death with jaunting up and down!
Jul. I' faith, I am sorry that thou art not well.
Sweet, sweet, sweet nurse, tell me, what says my love?
Nurse. Your love says, like an honest gentleman, and a courteous, and a kind, and a handsome, and, I warrant, a virtuous,—Where is your mother?
Jul. Where is my mother! why, she is within;   60
Where should she be? How oddly thou repliest!
'Your love says, like an honest gentleman,
Where is your mother?'
Nurse.   O God's lady dear!
Are you so hot? marry, come up, I trow;

---

183. **protest,** vow. 188. **mark,** attend to. 201. **tackled stair,** rope ladder. 202. **top-gallant,** summit. 203. **convoy,** a thing that conducts. 204. **quit,** reward, requite; see glossary. 208. **secret,** trustworthy. 217. **properer,** handsomer; see glossary. 219. **clout,** rag; a proverbial expression. **versal,** universal. 220. **a,** the same. 223. **the dog's name.** The letter *R* was thought to resemble the dog's growl. 226.

sententious. The nurse probably means "sentences," pithy sayings.
   SCENE V. 7. **love,** Venus, whose chariot was drawn by doves. 14. **bandy,** toss to and fro. 16. **many,** Johnson: marry. 25. **give me leave,** let me alone. 26. **jaunce,** so Q_2; Globe: *jaunt.* 36. **stay the circumstance,** await details; see *circumstance* in glossary. 52. **Beshrew,** common objurgation meaning "ill-luck"; see glossary. 64. **come up,**

Is this the poultice for my aching bones?
Henceforward do your messages yourself.
 Jul. Here 's such a coil! come, what says Romeo?
 Nurse. Have you got leave to go to shrift to-day?
 Jul. I have.
 Nurse. Then hie you hence to Friar Laurence' cell;
There stays a husband to make you a wife: 71
Now comes the wanton blood up in your cheeks,
They'll be in scarlet straight at any news.
Hie you to church; I must another way,
To fetch a ladder, by the which your love
Must climb a bird's nest soon when it is dark:
I am the drudge and toil in your delight,
But you shall bear the burden soon at night.
Go; I'll to dinner; hie you to the cell.
 Jul. Hie to high fortune! Honest nurse, farewell.   80
             [*Exeunt.*

SCENE VI. *Friar Laurence's cell.*

Enter FRIAR LAURENCE *and* ROMEO.

 Fri. L. So smile the heavens upon this holy act,
That after hours with sorrow chide us not!
 Rom. Amen, amen! but come what sorrow can,
It cannot countervail the exchange of joy
That one short minute gives me in her sight:
Do thou but close our hands with holy words,
Then love-devouring death do what he dare;
It is enough I may but call her mine.
 Fri. L. These violent delights have violent ends
And in their triumph die, like fire and powder,   10
Which as they kiss consume: the sweetest honey
Is loathsome in his own deliciousness
And in the taste confounds the appetite:
Therefore love moderately; long love doth so;
Too swift arrives as tardy as too slow.

Enter JULIET.

Here comes the lady: O, so light a foot
Will ne'er wear out the everlasting flint:
A lover may bestride the gossamer
That idles in the wanton summer air,
And yet not fall; so light is vanity.   20
 Jul. Good even to my ghostly confessor.
 Fri. L. Romeo shall thank thee, daughter, for us
  both.
 Jul. As much to him, else is his thanks too much.
 Rom. Ah, Juliet, if the measure of thy joy
Be heap'd like mine and that thy skill be more
To blazon it, then sweeten with thy breath
This neighbour air, and let rich music's tongue
Unfold the imagined happiness that both
Receive in either by this dear encounter.
 Jul. Conceit, more rich in matter than in words,   30
Brags of his substance, not of ornament:
They are but beggars that can count their worth;
But my true love is grown to such excess
I cannot sum up sum of half my wealth.
 Fri. L. Come, come with me, and we will make
  short work;

For, by your leaves, you shall not stay alone
Till holy church incorporate two in one.   [*Exeunt.*

ACT III.

SCENE I. *A public place.*

Enter MERCUTIO, BENVOLIO, Page, *and* Servants.

 Ben. I pray thee, good Mercutio, let 's retire:
The day is hot, the Capulets abroad,
And, if we meet, we shall not scape a brawl;
For now, these hot days, is the mad blood stirring.
 Mer. Thou art like one of those fellows that when he
enters the confines of a tavern claps me his sword upon
the table and says 'God send me no need of thee!' and
by the operation of the second cup draws it on the
drawer, when indeed there is no need.   10
 Ben. Am I like such a fellow?
 Mer. Come, come, thou art as hot a Jack in thy
mood as any in Italy, and as soon moved to be moody,
and as soon moody to be moved.
 Ben. And what to?
 Mer. Nay, an there were two such, we should have
none shortly, for one would kill the other. Thou! why,
thou wilt quarrel with a man that hath a hair more, or
a hair less, in his beard, than thou hast: thou wilt
quarrel with a man for cracking nuts, having no other
reason but because thou hast hazel eyes: what eye but
such an eye would spy out such a quarrel? Thy head
is as full of quarrels as an egg is full of meat, and yet
thy head hath been beaten as addle as an egg for
quarrelling: thou hast quarrelled with a man for
coughing in the street, because he hath wakened thy
dog that hath lain asleep in the sun: didst thou not fall
out with a tailor for wearing his new doublet before
Easter? with another, for tying his new shoes with old
riband? and yet thou wilt tutor me from quarrelling! 33
 Ben. An I were so apt to quarrel as thou art, any
man should buy the fee-simple of my life for an hour
and a quarter.
 Mer. The fee simple! O simple!
 Ben. By my head, here come the Capulets.
 Mer. By my heel, I care not.

Enter TYBALT *and others.*

 Tyb. Follow me close, for I will speak to them.   40
Gentlemen, good den: a word with one of you.
 Mer. And but one word with one of us? couple it
with something; make it a word and a blow.
 Tyb. You shall find me apt enough to that, sir, an
you will give me occasion.
 Mer. Could you not take some occasion without
giving?
 Tyb. Mercutio, thou consort'st with Romeo,—
 Mer. Consort! what, dost thou make us minstrels?
an thou make minstrels of us, look to hear nothing but
discords: here 's my fiddlestick; here 's that shall make
you dance. 'Zounds, consort!   52
 Ben. We talk here in the public haunt of men:
Either withdraw unto some private place,

---

expressive of impatience like "go to."   67. **coil,** turmoil, bustle; see
glossary.
 SCENE VI.   4. **countervail,** equal.   9. **These violent delights,** etc.,
expresses a premonition of evil.   13. **confounds,** destroys; see glossary.
18. **gossamer,** spider's thread.   26. **blazon,** heraldic term meaning
"to describe" or "to set forth."   28. **Unfold,** make known; see glossary.

30. **Conceit,** imagination, thought; see glossary.
 ACT III. SCENE I.   2. **The day is hot.** This offers a little touch of
Italian atmosphere.   14. **moody,** angry.   47. **consort'st.** *To consort*
meant "to accompany" and also "to attend or wait upon."   52.
'Zounds, a modified form of the oath, "by God's wounds."

And reason coldly of your grievances,
Or else depart; here all eyes gaze on us.
 Mer. Men's eyes were made to look, and let them
  gaze;
I will not budge for no man's pleasure, I.

 Enter ROMEO.

 Tyb. Well, peace be with you, sir: here comes my
  man.
 Mer. But I'll be hang'd, sir, if he wear your livery: 60
Marry, go before to field, he'll be your follower;
Your worship in that sense may call him 'man.'
 Tyb. Romeo, the hate I bear thee can afford
No better term than this,—thou art a villain.
 Rom. Tybalt, the reason that I have to love thee
Doth much excuse the appertaining rage
To such a greeting: villain am I none;
Therefore farewell; I see thou know'st me not.
 Tyb. Boy, this shall not excuse the injuries
That thou hast done me; therefore turn and draw. 70
 Rom. I do protest, I never injured thee,
But love thee better than thou canst devise,
Till thou shalt know the reason of my love:
And so, good Capulet,—which name I tender
As dearly as my own,—be satisfied.
 Mer. O calm, dishonourable, vile submission!
Alla stoccata carries it away.   [*Draws.*
Tybalt, you rat-catcher, will you walk?
 Tyb. What wouldst thou have with me?   79
 Mer. Good king of cats, nothing but one of your
nine lives; that I mean to make bold withal, and, as
you shall use me hereafter, dry-beat the rest of the
eight. Will you pluck your sword out of his pilcher by
the ears? make haste, lest mine be about your ears ere
it be out.
 Tyb. I am for you.   [*Drawing.*
 Rom. Gentle Mercutio, put thy rapier up.
 Mer. Come, sir, your passado.   [*They fight.*
 Rom. Draw, Benvolio; beat down their weapons.
Gentlemen, for shame, forbear this outrage!   90
Tybalt, Mercutio, the prince expressly hath
Forbidden bandying in Verona streets:
Hold, Tybalt! good Mercutio!
  [*Tybalt under Romeo's arm stabs Mercutio, and flies*
             with his followers.
 Mer.   I am hurt.
A plague o' both your houses! I am sped.
Is he gone, and hath nothing?
 Ben.   What, art thou hurt?
 Mer. Ay, ay, a scratch, a scratch; marry, 'tis enough.
Where is my page? Go, villain, fetch a surgeon.
            [*Exit Page.*
 Rom. Courage, man; the hurt cannot be much.   98
 Mer. No, 'tis not so deep as a well, nor so wide as a
church-door; but 'tis enough, 'twill serve: ask for me
to-morrow, and you shall find me a grave man. I am
peppered, I warrant, for this world. A plague o' both
your houses! 'Zounds, a dog, a rat, a mouse, a cat, to
scratch a man to death! a braggart, a rogue, a villain,
that fights by the book of arithmetic! Why the devil

came you between us? I was hurt under your arm.
 Rom. I thought all for the best.
 Mer. Help me into some house, Benvolio,   110
Or I shall faint. A plague o' both your houses!
They have made worms' meat of me: I have it,
And soundly too: your houses!
     [*Exeunt Mercutio and Benvolio.*
 Rom. This gentleman, the prince's near ally,
My very friend, hath got his mortal hurt
In my behalf; my reputation stain'd
With Tybalt's slander,—Tybalt, that an hour
Hath been my kinsman! O sweet Juliet,
Thy beauty hath made me effeminate
And in my temper soften'd valour's steel!   120

 Re-enter BENVOLIO.

 Ben. O Romeo, Romeo, brave Mercutio's dead!
That gallant spirit hath aspired the clouds,
Which too untimely here did scorn the earth.
 Rom. This day's black fate on moe days doth depend;
This but begins the woe others must end.
 Ben. Here comes the furious Tybalt back again.
 Rom. Alive, in triumph! and Mercutio slain!
Away to heaven, respective lenity,
And fire-eyed fury be my conduct now!

 Re-enter TYBALT.

Now, Tybalt, take the villain back again,   130
That late thou gavest me; for Mercutio's soul
Is but a little way above our heads,
Staying for thine to keep him company:
Either thou, or I, or both, must go with him.
 Tyb. Thou, wretched boy, that didst consort him
  here,
Shalt with him hence.
 Rom.   This shall determine that.
       [*They fight; Tybalt falls.*
 Ben. Romeo, away, be gone!
The citizens are up, and Tybalt slain.
Stand not amazed: the prince will doom thee death,
If thou art taken: hence, be gone, away!   140
 Rom. O, I am fortune's fool!
 Ben.   Why dost thou stay? [*Exit Romeo.*

 Enter Citizens, &c.

 First Cit. Which way ran he that kill'd Mercutio?
Tybalt, that murderer, which way ran he?
 Ben. There lies that Tybalt.
 First Cit.   Up, sir, go with me;
I charge thee in the prince's name, obey.

 Enter PRINCE, *attended;* MONTAGUE, CAPULET, *their*
  Wives, *and others.*

 Prin. Where are the vile beginners of this fray?
 Ben. O noble prince, I can discover all
The unlucky manage of this fatal brawl:
There lies the man, slain by young Romeo,
That slew thy kinsman, brave Mercutio.   150
 La. Cap. Tybalt, my cousin! O my brother's child!
O prince! O cousin! husband! O, the blood is spilt

61. **field,** field of encounter. 77. **Alla stoccata,** Italian, "with the
thrust"; i.e., the fencing master wins the victory. 78. **rat-catcher,** an
allusion to Tybalt as king of cats (see II, iv, 19). 81. **make bold,** make
free with. 83. **dry-beat,** beat soundly. 84. **pilcher,** scabbard. 88.
passado, forward thrust; used derisively. 94. **sped,** done for. 102.
grave man. Mercutio thus makes puns with his last breath. 106. **by
the book of arithmetic,** merely by theory. Back of the whole scene lies
a current controversy between the old broadsword style of fencing and

the new French style of rapier fencing. 114. **ally,** kinsman. 115.
very, true. 124. **moe,** more; so Q₂F; Globe: *more.* 128. **respective lenity,**
considerate gentleness. 129. **conduct,** guide. 139. **doom,** adjudge.
141. **fortune's fool.** At this crucial moment in the play Romeo again
alludes to destiny. 148. **manage,** management; see glossary. 158.
fair, civilly; see glossary. 159. **nice,** trivial; see glossary. 162. **take
truce,** make peace. **unruly spleen,** ungovernable rage; see *spleen* in
glossary. 163. **tilts,** strikes. 169. **Retorts,** throws back upon his

Of my dear kinsman! Prince, as thou art true,
For blood of ours, shed blood of Montague.
O cousin, cousin!
    Prin. Benvolio, who began this bloody fray?
    Ben. Tybalt, here slain, whom Romeo's hand did
      slay;
Romeo that spoke him fair, bade him bethink
How nice the quarrel was, and urged withal
Your high displeasure: all this uttered   160
With gentle breath, calm look, knees humbly bow'd,
Could not take truce with the unruly spleen
Of Tybalt deaf to peace, but that he tilts
With piercing steel at bold Mercutio's breast,
Who, all as hot, turns deadly point to point,
And, with a martial scorn, with one hand beats
Cold death aside, and with the other sends
It back to Tybalt, whose dexterity
Retorts it: Romeo he cries aloud,
'Hold, friends! friends, part!' and, swifter than his
      tongue,   170
His agile arm beats down their fatal points,
And 'twixt them rushes; underneath whose arm
An envious thrust from Tybalt hit the life
Of stout Mercutio, and then Tybalt fled;
But by and by comes back to Romeo,
Who had but newly entertain'd revenge,
And to 't they go like lightning, for, ere I
Could draw to part them, was stout Tybalt slain,
And, as he fell, did Romeo turn and fly.
This is the truth, or let Benvolio die.   180
    La. Cap. He is a kinsman to the Montague;
Affection makes him false; he speaks not true:
Some twenty of them fought in this black strife,
And all those twenty could but kill one life.
I beg for justice, which thou, prince, must give;
Romeo slew Tybalt, Romeo must not live.
    Prin. Romeo slew him, he slew Mercutio;
Who now the price of his dear blood doth owe?
    Mon. Not Romeo, prince, he was Mercutio's friend;
His fault concludes but what the law should end,   190
The life of Tybalt.
    Prin.   And for that offence
Immediately we do exile him hence:
I have an interest in your hate's proceeding,
My blood for your rude brawls doth lie a-bleeding;
But I'll amerce you with so strong a fine
That you shall all repent the loss of mine:
I will be deaf to pleading and excuses;
Nor tears nor prayers shall purchase out abuses:
Therefore use none: let Romeo hence in haste,
Else, when he 's found, that hour is his last.   200
Bear hence this body and attend our will:
Mercy but murders, pardoning those that kill. [*Exeunt.*

    SCENE II. *Capulet's orchard.*

Enter JULIET.

    Jul. Gallop apace, you fiery-footed steeds,
Towards Phœbus' lodging: such a waggoner

As Phæthon would whip you to the west,
And bring in cloudy night immediately.
Spread thy close curtain, love-performing night,
That runaways' eyes may wink, and Romeo
Leap to these arms, untalk'd of and unseen.
Lovers can see to do their amorous rites
By their own beauties; or, if love be blind,
It best agrees with night. Come, civil night,   10
Thou sober-suited matron, all in black,
And learn me how to lose a winning match,
Play'd for a pair of stainless maidenhoods:
Hood my unmann'd blood, bating in my cheeks,
With thy black mantle; till strange love, grown bold,
Think true love acted simple modesty.
Come, night; come, Romeo; come, thou day in night;
For thou wilt lie upon the wings of night
Whiter than new snow on a raven's back.
Come, gentle night, come, loving, black-brow'd night,
Give me my Romeo; and, when he shall die,   21
Take him and cut him out in little stars,
And he will make the face of heaven so fine
That all the world will be in love with night
And pay no worship to the garish sun.
O, I have bought the mansion of a love,
But not possess'd it, and, though I am sold,
Not yet enjoy'd: so tedious is this day
As is the night before some festival
To an impatient child that hath new robes   30
And may not wear them. O, here comes my nurse,
And she brings news; and every tongue that speaks
But Romeo's name speaks heavenly eloquence.

    Enter Nurse, *with cords.*

Now, nurse, what news? What hast thou there? the
    cords
That Romeo bid thee fetch?
    Nurse.   Ay, ay, the cords.
        [*Throws them down.*
    Jul. Ay me! what news? why dost thou wring thy
      hands?
    Nurse. Ay, well-a-day! he 's dead, he 's dead, he 's
      dead!
We are undone, lady, we are undone!
Alack the day! he 's gone, he 's kill'd, he 's dead!
    Jul. Can heaven be so envious?
    Nurse.   Romeo can,   40
Though heaven cannot: O Romeo, Romeo!
Who ever would have thought it? Romeo!
    Jul. What devil art thou, that dost torment me thus?
This torture should be roar'd in dismal hell.
Hath Romeo slain himself? say thou but 'I,'
And that bare vowel 'I' shall poison more
Than the death-darting eye of cockatrice:
I am not I, if there be such an I;
Or those eyes shut, that make thee answer 'I.'
If he be slain, say 'I'; or if not, no: 50
Brief sounds determine of my weal or woe.
    Nurse. I saw the wound, I saw it with mine eyes,—
God save the mark!—here on his manly breast:
A piteous corse, a bloody piteous corse;

Romeo and Juliet
ACT III : SC II

adversary. 176. **entertain'd,** harbored thoughts of; see glossary. 195. **amerce,** punish by fine. 198. **purchase out,** redeem, exempt from penalty; see *purchase* in glossary. **abuses,** misdeeds; see glossary.

SCENE II. 3. **Phæthon,** son of Helios, who was allowed to assume the reins of the sun for a day; not being able to restrain the steeds, he had to be slain by the thunderbolt of Jupiter in order that the universe might not be destroyed. 6. **runaways' eyes,** a famous crux of which there is no satisfactory explanation. The allusion to Phaethon (l. 3)

may here be repeated. **wink,** shut; see glossary. 10. **civil,** well-ordered. 14. **Hood,** cover; term in falcony. The hawk's eyes were covered so that it would not bate or beat the wings. **unmann'd,** another term in falconry meaning "untamed." 38. **undone,** ruined; see glossary. 45. **'I,'** ay, yes. 47. **cockatrice,** basilisk, a fabulous serpent which could kill by its look. 53. **God save the mark,** God forbid; a familiar oath originally intended to avert ill omen.

Pale, pale as ashes, all bedaub'd in blood,
All in gore-blood; I swounded at the sight.
   Jul. O, break, my heart! poor bankrupt, break at
     once!
To prison, eyes, ne'er look on liberty!
Vile earth, to earth resign; end motion here;
And thou and Romeo press one heavy bier!   60
   Nurse. O Tybalt, Tybalt, the best friend I had!
O courteous Tybalt! honest gentleman!
That ever I should live to see thee dead!
   Jul. What storm is this that blows so contrary?
Is Romeo slaughter'd, and is Tybalt dead?
My dear-loved cousin, and my dearer lord?
Then, dreadful trumpet, sound the general doom!
For who is living, if those two are gone?
   Nurse. Tybalt is gone, and Romeo banished;
Romeo that kill'd him, he is banished.   70
   Jul. O God! did Romeo's hand shed Tybalt's blood?
   Nurse. It did, it did; alas the day, it did!
   Jul. O serpent heart, hid with a flowering face!
Did ever dragon keep so fair a cave?
Beautiful tyrant! fiend angelical!
Dove-feather'd raven! wolvish-ravening lamb!
Despised substance of divinest show!
Just opposite to what thou justly seem'st,
A damned saint, an honourable villain!
O nature, what hadst thou to do in hell,   80
When thou didst bower the spirit of a fiend
In mortal paradise of such sweet flesh?
Was ever book containing such vile matter
So fairly bound? O, that deceit should dwell
In such a gorgeous palace!
   Nurse.   There's no trust,
No faith, no honesty in men; all perjured,
All forsworn, all naught, all dissemblers.
Ah, where's my man? give me some aqua vitæ:
These griefs, these woes, these sorrows make me old.
Shame come to Romeo!
   Jul.   Blister'd be thy tongue   90
For such a wish! he was not born to shame:
Upon his brow shame is ashamed to sit;
For 'tis a throne where honour may be crown'd
Sole monarch of the universal earth.
O, what a beast was I to chide at him!
   Nurse. Will you speak well of him that kill'd your
     cousin?
   Jul. Shall I speak ill of him that is my husband?
Ah, poor my lord, what tongue shall smooth thy name,
When I, thy three-hours wife, have mangled it?
But, wherefore, villain, didst thou kill my cousin?   100
That villain cousin would have kill'd my husband:
Back, foolish tears, back to your native spring;
Your tributary drops belong to woe,
Which you, mistaking, offer up to joy.
My husband lives, that Tybalt would have slain;
And Tybalt's dead, that would have slain my husband:
All this is comfort; wherefore weep I then?
Some word there was, worser than Tybalt's death,
That murder'd me: I would forget it fain;
But, O, it presses to my memory,   110
Like damned guilty deeds to sinners' minds:
'Tybalt is dead, and Romeo—banished;'
That 'banished,' that one word 'banished,'

Hath slain ten thousand Tybalts. Tybalt's death
Was woe enough, if it had ended there:
Or, if sour woe delights in fellowship
And needly will be rank'd with other griefs,
Why follow'd not, when she said 'Tybalt's dead,'
Thy father, or thy mother, nay, or both,
Which modern lamentation might have moved?   120
But with a rearward following Tybalt's death,
'Romeo is banished,' to speak that word,
Is father, mother, Tybalt, Romeo, Juliet,
All slain, all dead. 'Romeo is banished!'
There is no end, no limit, measure, bound,
In that word's death; no words can that woe sound.
Where is my father, and my mother, nurse?
   Nurse. Weeping and wailing over Tybalt's corse:
Will you go to them? I will bring you thither.
   Jul. Wash they his wounds with tears: mine shall be
     spent,   130
When theirs are dry, for Romeo's banishment.
Take up those cords: poor ropes, you are beguiled,
Both you and I; for Romeo is exiled:
He made you for a highway to my bed;
But I, a maid, die maiden-widowed.
Come, cords, come, nurse; I'll to my wedding-bed;
And death, not Romeo, take my maidenhead!
   Nurse. Hie to your chamber: I'll find Romeo
To comfort you: I wot well where he is.
Hark ye, your Romeo will be here at night: 140
I'll to him; he is hid at Laurence' cell.
   Jul. O, find him! give this ring to my true knight,
And bid him come to take his last farewell.   [*Exeunt.*

SCENE III. *Friar Laurence's cell.*

Enter FRIAR LAURENCE.

   Fri. L. Romeo, come forth; come forth, thou fearful
     man:
Affliction is enamour'd of thy parts,
And thou art wedded to calamity.

Enter ROMEO.

   Rom. Father, what news? what is the prince's doom?
What sorrow craves acquaintance at my hand,
That I yet know not?
   Fri. L.   Too familiar
Is my dear son with such sour company:
I bring thee tidings of the prince's doom.
   Rom. What less than dooms-day is the prince's
     doom?
   Fri. L. A gentler judgement vanish'd from his lips,   10
Not body's death, but body's banishment.
   Rom. Ha, banishment! be merciful, say 'death;'
For exile hath more terror in his look,
Much more than death: do not say 'banishment.'
   Fri. L. Hence from Verona art thou banished:
Be patient, for the world is broad and wide.
   Rom. There is no world without Verona walls,
But purgatory, torture, hell itself.
Hence-banished is banish'd from the world,
And world's exile is death: then banished,   20
Is death mis-term'd; calling death banishment,

56. **gore-blood,** clotted blood. 59. **motion,** power of movement; see
glossary. 81. **bower,** give lodging to. 87. **naught,** worthless; see glossary. 117. **needly,** of necessity. 120. **modern,** ordinary; see glossary.

121. **rearward,** rear guard. 139. **wot,** know; see glossary.
SCENE III. 10. **vanish'd,** issued. 26. **rush'd,** thrust (aside). 33.

Thou cutt'st my head off with a golden axe,
And smilest upon the stroke that murders me.
   Fri. L. O deadly sin! O rude unthankfulness!
Thy fault our law calls death; but the kind prince,
Taking thy part, hath rush'd aside the law,
And turn'd that black word death to banishment:
This is dear mercy, and thou seest it not.
   Rom. 'Tis torture, and not mercy: heaven is here,
Where Juliet lives; and every cat and dog   30
And little mouse, every unworthy thing,
Live here in heaven and may look on her;
But Romeo may not: more validity,
More honourable state, more courtship lives
In carrion-flies than Romeo: they may seize
On the white wonder of dear Juliet's hand
And steal immortal blessing from her lips,
Who, even in pure and vestal modesty,
Still blush, as thinking their own kisses sin;
But Romeo may not; he is banished: 40
Flies may do this, but I from this must fly:
They are free men, but I am banished.
And say'st thou yet that exile is not death?
Hadst thou no poison mix'd, no sharp-ground knife,
No sudden mean of death, though ne'er so mean,
But 'banished' to kill me?—'banished'?
O friar, the damned use that word in hell;
Howlings attend it: how hast thou the heart,
Being a divine, a ghostly confessor,
A sin-absolver, and my friend profess'd,   50
To mangle me with that word 'banished'?
   Fri. L. Thou fond mad man, hear me but speak a
     word.
   Rom. O, thou wilt speak again of banishment.
   Fri. L. I'll give thee armour to keep off that word;
Adversity's sweet milk, philosophy,
To comfort thee, though thou art banished.
   Rom. Yet 'banished'? Hang up philosophy!
Unless philosophy can make a Juliet,
Displant a town, reverse a prince's doom,
It helps not, it prevails not: talk no more.   60
   Fri. L. O, then I see that madmen have no ears.
   Rom. How should they, when that wise men have no
     eyes?
   Fri. L. Let me dispute with thee of thy estate.
   Rom. Thou canst not speak of that thou dost not feel:
Wert thou as young as I, Juliet thy love,
An hour but married, Tybalt murdered,
Doting like me and like me banished,
Then mightst thou speak, then mightst thou tear thy
     hair,
And fall upon the ground, as I do now,
Taking the measure of an unmade grave.   70
                          [Knocking within.
   Fri. L. Arise; one knocks; good Romeo, hide thyself.
   Rom. Not I; unless the breath of heart-sick groans,
Mist-like, infold me from the search of eyes. *[Knocking.*
   Fri. L. Hark, how they knock! Who's there?
   Romeo, arise;
Thou wilt be taken. Stay awhile! Stand up; *[Knocking.*
Run to my study. By and by! God's will,
What simpleness is this! I come, I come!   *[Knocking.*
Who knocks so hard? whence come you? what's your
     will?

Nurse. [*Within*] Let me come in, and you shall know
     my errand;
I come from Lady Juliet.
   Fri. L.   Welcome, then.   80

Enter Nurse.

   Nurse. O holy friar, O, tell me, holy friar,
Where is my lady's lord, where's Romeo?
   Fri. L. There on the ground, with his own tears
     made drunk.
   Nurse. O, he is even in my mistress' case,
Just in her case! O woful sympathy!
Piteous predicament! Even so lies she,
Blubbering and weeping, weeping and blubbering.
Stand up, stand up; stand, an you be a man:
For Juliet's sake, for her sake, rise and stand;
Why should you fall into so deep an O?   90
   Rom. Nurse!
   Nurse. Ah sir! ah sir! Well, death's the end of all.
   Rom. Spakest thou of Juliet? how is it with her?
Doth she not think me an old murderer,
Now I have stain'd the childhood of our joy
With blood removed but little from her own?
Where is she? and how doth she? and what says
My conceal'd lady to our cancell'd love?
   Nurse. O, she says nothing, sir, but weeps and weeps;
And now falls on her bed; and then starts up,   100
And Tybalt calls; and then on Romeo cries,
And then down falls again.
   Rom.   As if that name,
Shot from the deadly level of a gun,
Did murder her; as that name's cursed hand
Murder'd her kinsman. O, tell me, friar, tell me,
In what vile part of this anatomy
Doth my name lodge? tell me that I may sack
The hateful mansion.   *[Drawing his sword.*
   Fri. L.   Hold thy desperate hand:
Art thou a man? thy form cries out thou art:
Thy tears are womanish; thy wild acts denote   110
The unreasonable fury of a beast:
Unseemly woman in a seeming man!
Or ill-beseeming beast in seeming both!
Thou hast amazed me: by my holy order,
I thought thy disposition better temper'd.
Hast thou slain Tybalt? wilt thou slay thyself?
And slay thy lady too that lives in thee,
By doing damned hate upon thyself?
Why rail'st thou on thy birth, the heaven, and earth?
Since birth, and heaven, and earth, all three do meet
In thee at once; which thou at once wouldst lose.   121
Fie, fie, thou shamest thy shape, thy love, thy wit;
Which, like a usurer, abound'st in all,
And usest none in that true use indeed
Which should bedeck thy shape, thy love, thy wit:
Thy noble shape is but a form of wax,
Digressing from the valour of a man;
Thy dear love sworn but hollow perjury,
Killing that love which thou hast vow'd to cherish;
Thy wit, that ornament to shape and love,   130
Mis-shapen in the conduct of them both,
Like powder in a skilless soldier's flask,
Is set a-fire by thine own ignorance,
And thou dismember'd with thine own defence.

---

validity, value. 34. **courtship,** both courtliness and wooing. 45. **mean
. . . mean,** means . . . base; see glossary. 63. **dispute,** reason; see

glossary. **estate,** situation. 94. **old,** (colloquial), real, actual. 103.
level, aim; see glossary. 107. **sack,** destroy.

What, rouse thee, man! thy Juliet is alive,
For whose dear sake thou wast but lately dead;
There art thou happy: Tybalt would kill thee,
But thou slew'st Tybalt; there art thou happy too:
The law that threaten'd death becomes thy friend
And turns it to exile; there art thou happy: 140
A pack of blessings lights upon thy back;
Happiness courts thee in her best array;
But, like a misbehaved and sullen wench,
Thou pout'st upon thy fortune and thy love:
Take heed, take heed, for such die miserable.
Go, get thee to thy love, as was decreed,
Ascend her chamber, hence and comfort her:
But look thou stay not till the watch be set,
For then thou canst not pass to Mantua;
Where thou shalt live, till we can find a time 150
To blaze your marriage, reconcile your friends,
Beg pardon of the prince, and call thee back
With twenty hundred thousand times more joy
Than thou went'st forth in lamentation.
Go before, nurse: commend me to thy lady;
And bid her hasten all the house to bed,
Which heavy sorrow makes them apt unto:
Romeo is coming.
    Nurse. O Lord, I could have stay'd here all the night
To hear good counsel: O, what learning is! 160
My lord, I'll tell my lady you will come.
    Rom. Do so, and bid my sweet prepare to chide.
    Nurse. Here, sir, a ring she bid me give you, sir:
Hie you, make haste, for it grows very late.   [*Exit.*
    Rom. How well my comfort is revived by this!
    Fri. L. Go hence; good night; and here stands all
        your state:
Either be gone before the watch be set,
Or by the break of day disguised from hence:
Sojourn in Mantua; I'll find out your man,
And he shall signify from time to time 170
Every good hap to you that chances here:
Give me thy hand; 'tis late: farewell; good night.
    Rom. But that a joy past joy calls out on me,
It were a grief, so brief to part with thee:
Farewell.   [*Exeunt.*

<hr>

SCENE IV. *A room in Capulet's house.*

Enter CAPULET, LADY CAPULET, *and* PARIS.

    Cap. Things have fall'n out, sir, so unluckily,
That we have had no time to move our daughter:
Look you, she loved her kinsman Tybalt dearly,
And so did I:—Well, we were born to die.
'Tis very late, she'll not come down to-night:
I promise you, but for your company,
I would have been a-bed an hour ago.
    Par. These times of woe afford no time to woo.
Madam, good night: commend me to your daughter.
    La. Cap. I will, and know her mind early to-morrow;
To-night she is mew'd up to her heaviness. 11
    Cap. Sir Paris, I will make a desperate tender
Of my child's love: I think she will be ruled
In all respects by me; nay, more, I doubt it not.
Wife, go you to her ere you go to bed;

Acquaint her here of my son Paris' love;
And bid her, mark you me, on Wednesday next—
But, soft! what day is this?
    Par.   Monday, my lord.
    Cap. Monday! ha, ha! Well, Wednesday is too soon,
O' Thursday let it be: o' Thursday, tell her, 20
She shall be married to this noble earl.
Will you be ready? do you like this haste?
We'll keep no great ado,—a friend or two;
For, hark you, Tybalt being slain so late,
It may be thought we held him carelessly,
Being our kinsman, if we revel much:
Therefore we'll have some half a dozen friends,
And there an end. But what say you to Thursday?
    Par. My lord, I would that Thursday were
        to-morrow.
    Cap. Well, get you gone: o' Thursday be it, then. 30
Go you to Juliet ere you go to bed,
Prepare her, wife, against this wedding-day.
Farewell, my lord. Light to my chamber, ho!
Afore me! it is so very very late,
That we may call it early by and by.
Good night.   [*Exeunt.*

<hr>

SCENE V. *Capulet's orchard.*

Enter ROMEO *and* JULIET *above, at the window.*

    Jul. Wilt thou be gone? it is not yet near day:
It was the nightingale, and not the lark,
That pierced the fearful hollow of thine ear;
Nightly she sings on yond pomegranate-tree:
Believe me, love, it was the nightingale.
    Rom. It was the lark, the herald of the morn,
No nightingale: look, love, what envious streaks
Do lace the severing clouds in yonder east:
Night's candles are burnt out, and jocund day
Stands tiptoe on the misty mountain tops. 10
I must be gone and live, or stay and die.
    Jul. Yond light is not day-light, I know it, I:
It is some meteor that the sun exhales,
To be to thee this night a torch-bearer,
And light thee on thy way to Mantua:
Therefore stay yet; thou need'st not to be gone.
    Rom. Let me be ta'en, let me be put to death;
I am content, so thou wilt have it so.
I'll say yon grey is not the morning's eye,
'Tis but the pale reflex of Cynthia's brow; 20
Nor that is not the lark, whose notes do beat
The vaulty heaven so high above our heads:
I have more care to stay than will to go:
Come, death, and welcome! Juliet wills it so.
How is 't, my soul? let 's talk; it is not day.
    Jul. It is, it is: hie hence, be gone, away!
It is the lark that sings so out of tune,
Straining harsh discords and unpleasing sharps.
Some say the lark makes sweet division;
This doth not so, for she divideth us: 30
Some say the lark and loathed toad change eyes;
O, now I would they had changed voices too!
Since arm from arm that voice doth us affray,

<hr>

151. **blaze**, publish, divulge. 157. **apt**, ready, inclined. 166. **here stands all your state,** your fortune depends on what follows.
    SCENE IV. 11. **mew'd**, cooped; see glossary. 12. **desperate tender,** rash offer. 25. **held**, regarded. 34. **Afore me,** by my life.
    SCENE V. 8. **lace**, stripe. 20. **Cynthia's,** the moon's. 28. **sharps,**

high notes. 29. **division,** melody. 31. **change eyes**, an allusion to a popular saying that the toad and the lark had changed eyes, since the lark has ugly eyes and the toad beautiful ones. 34. **hunt's-up,** a song or tune to awaken huntsmen. 57. **fails,** errs; see glossary. 59. **Dry sorrow.** The heat of the body in sorrow and despair was thought to

Hunting thee hence with hunt's-up to the day.
O, now be gone; more light and light it grows.
   Rom. More light and light; more dark and dark our
     woes!

Enter Nurse, *to the chamber.*

Nurse. Madam!
Jul. Nurse?
Nurse. Your lady mother is coming to your
    chamber:
The day is broke; be wary, look about.   [*Exit.* 40
   Jul. Then, window, let day in, and let life out.
   Rom. Farewell, farewell! one kiss, and I'll descend.
                       [*He goeth down.*
   Jul. Art thou gone so? love, lord, ay, husband,
    friend!
I must hear from thee every day in the hour,
For in a minute there are many days:
O, by this count I shall be much in years
Ere I again behold my Romeo!
   Rom. Farewell!
I will omit no opportunity
That may convey my greetings, love, to thee.   50
   Jul. O, think'st thou we shall ever meet again?
   Rom. I doubt it not; and all these woes shall serve
For sweet discourses in our time to come.
   Jul. O God, I have an ill-divining soul!
Methinks I see thee, now thou art below,
As one dead in the bottom of a tomb:
Either my eyesight fails, or thou look'st pale.
   Rom. And trust me, love, in my eye so do you:
Dry sorrow drinks our blood. Adieu, adieu!   [*Exit.*
   Jul. O fortune, fortune! all men call thee fickle: 60
If thou art fickle, what dost thou with him
That is renown'd for faith? Be fickle, fortune;
For then, I hope, thou wilt not keep him long,
But send him back.
   La. Cap. [*Within*] Ho, daughter! are you up?
   Jul. Who is't that calls? is it my lady mother?
Is she not down so late, or up so early?
What unaccustom'd cause procures her hither?

Enter LADY CAPULET.

   La. Cap. Why, how now, Juliet!
   Jul.   Madam, I am not well.   69
   La. Cap. Evermore weeping for your cousin's death?
What, wilt thou wash him from his grave with tears?
An if thou couldst, thou couldst not make him live;
Therefore, have done: some grief shows much of love;
But much of grief shows still some want of wit.
   Jul. Yet let me weep for such a feeling loss.
   La. Cap. So shall you feel the loss, but not the friend
Which you weep for.
   Jul.   Feeling so the loss,
I cannot choose but ever weep the friend.
   La. Cap. Well, girl, thou weep'st not so much for his
    death,
As that the villain lives which slaughter'd him.   80
   Jul. What villain, madam?
   La. Cap.   That same villain, Romeo.
   Jul. [*Aside*] Villain and he be many miles asunder.—
God pardon him! I do, with all my heart;

And yet no man like he doth grieve my heart.
   La. Cap. That is, because the traitor murderer lives.
   Jul. Ay, madam, from the reach of these my hands:
Would none but I might venge my cousin's death!
   La. Cap. We will have vengeance for it, fear thou
    not:
Then weep no more. I'll send to one in Mantua,
Where that same banish'd runagate doth live,   90
Shall give him such an unaccustom'd dram,
That he shall soon keep Tybalt company:
And then, I hope, thou wilt be satisfied.
   Jul. Indeed, I never shall be satisfied
With Romeo, till I behold him—dead—
Is my poor heart so for a kinsman vex'd—
Madam, if you could find out but a man
To bear a poison, I would temper it;
That Romeo should, upon receipt thereof,
Soon sleep in quiet. O, how my heart abhors   100
To hear him named, and cannot come to him,
To wreak the love I bore my cousin
Upon his body that hath slaughter'd him!
   La. Cap. Find thou the means, and I'll find such a
    man.
But now I'll tell thee joyful tidings, girl.
   Jul. And joy comes well in such a needy time:
What are they, I beseech your ladyship?
   La. Cap. Well, well, thou hast a careful father, child;
One who, to put thee from thy heaviness,
Hath sorted out a sudden day of joy,   110
That thou expect'st not nor I look'd not for.
   Jul. Madam, in happy time, what day is that?
   La. Cap. Marry, my child, early next Thursday
    morn,
The gallant, young and noble gentleman,
The County Paris, at Saint Peter's Church,
Shall happily make thee there a joyful bride.
   Jul. Now, by Saint Peter's Church and Peter too,
He shall not make me there a joyful bride.
I wonder at this haste; that I must wed
Ere he, that should be husband, comes to woo.   120
I pray you, tell my lord and father, madam,
I will not marry yet; and, when I do, I swear,
It shall be Romeo, whom you know I hate,
Rather than Paris. These are news indeed!
   La. Cap. Here comes your father; tell him so
    yourself,
And see how he will take it at your hands.

Enter CAPULET *and* Nurse.

   Cap. When the sun sets, the air doth drizzle dew;
But for the sunset of my brother's son
It rains downright.
How now! a conduit, girl? what, still in tears?   130
Evermore showering? In one little body
Thou counterfeit'st a bark, a sea, a wind;
For still thy eyes, which I may call the sea,
Do ebb and flow with tears; the bark thy body is,
Sailing in this salt flood; the winds, thy sighs;
Who, raging with thy tears, and they with them,
Without a sudden calm, will overset
Thy tempest-tossed body. How now, wife!
Have you deliver'd to her our decree?

*Romeo
and Juliet*
ACT III : SC V

4¹5

descend into the bowels and dry up the blood. 67. **down,** in bed.
68. **procures,** induces to come. 84. **like,** so much as. 95. **dead.** This
word is placed between the clauses so that it can be understood with
either what precedes or what follows it. 98. **temper,** used equivocally,
meaning "to mix" or "to alloy." 108. **careful,** provident; see glossary.

112. **in happy time,** a vague expression like "by the way." 130.
conduit, water pipe.

La. Cap. Ay, sir; but she will none, she gives you
   thanks.   140
I would the fool were married to her grave!
   Cap. Soft! take me with you, take me with you, wife.
How! will she none? doth she not give us thanks?
Is she not proud? doth she not count her blest,
Unworthy as she is, that we have wrought
So worthy a gentleman to be her bridegroom?
   Jul. Not proud, you have; but thankful, that you
   have:
Proud can I never be of what I hate;
But thankful even for hate, that is meant love.
   Cap. How now, how now, chop-logic! What is this?
'Proud,' and 'I thank you,' and 'I thank you not;'   151
And yet 'not proud:' mistress minion, you,
Thank me no thankings, nor proud me no prouds,
But fettle your fine joints 'gainst Thursday next,
To go with Paris to Saint Peter's Church,
Or I will drag thee on a hurdle thither.
Out, you green-sickness carrion! out, you baggage!
You tallow-face!
   La. Cap.   Fie, fie! what, are you mad?
   Jul. Good father, I beseech you on my knees,
Hear me with patience but to speak a word.   160
   Cap. Hang thee, young baggage! disobedient
   wretch!
I tell thee what: get thee to church o' Thursday,
Or never after look me in the face:
Speak not, reply not, do not answer me;
My fingers itch. Wife, we scarce thought us blest
That God had lent us but this only child;
But now I see this one is one too much,
And that we have a curse in having her:
Out on her, hilding!
   Nurse.   God in heaven bless her!
You are to blame, my lord, to rate her so.   170
   Cap. And why, my lady wisdom? hold your tongue,
Good prudence; smatter with your gossips, go.
   Nurse. I speak no treason.
   Cap.   O, God ye god-den.
   Nurse. May not one speak?
   Cap.   Peace, you mumbling fool!
Utter your gravity o'er a gossip's bowl;
For here we need it not.
   La. Cap.   You are too hot.
   Cap. † God's bread! it makes me mad:
†Day, night, hour, tide, time, work, play,
Alone, in company, still my care hath been
To have her match'd: and having now provided   180
A gentleman of noble parentage,
Of fair demesnes, youthful, and nobly train'd,
Stuff'd, as they say, with honourable parts,
Proportion'd as one's thought would wish a man;
And then to have a wretched puling fool,
A whining mammet, in her fortune's tender,
To answer 'I'll not wed; I cannot love,
I am too young; I pray you, pardon me.'
But, an you will not wed, I'll pardon you:
Graze where you will, you shall not house with me: 190
Look to 't, think on 't, I do not use to jest.
Thursday is near; lay hand on heart, advise:
An you be mine, I'll give you to my friend;

An you be not, hang, beg, starve, die in the streets,
For, by my soul, I'll ne'er acknowledge thee,
Nor what is mine shall never do thee good:
Trust to 't, bethink you; I'll not be forsworn.   *[Exit.*
   Jul. Is there no pity sitting in the clouds,
That sees into the bottom of my grief?
O, sweet my mother, cast me not away!   200
Delay this marriage for a month, a week;
Or, if you do not, make the bridal bed
In that dim monument where Tybalt lies.
   La. Cap. Talk not to me, for I'll not speak a word:
Do as thou wilt, for I have done with thee.   *[Exit.*
   Jul. O God!—O nurse, how shall this be prevented?
My husband is on earth, my faith in heaven;
How shall that faith return again to earth,
Unless that husband send it me from heaven
By leaving earth? comfort me, counsel me.   210
Alack, alack, that heaven should practise stratagems
Upon so soft a subject as myself!
What say'st thou? hast thou not a word of joy?
Some comfort, nurse.
   Nurse.   Faith, here it is.
Romeo is banish'd; and all the world to nothing,
That he dares ne'er come back to challenge you;
Or, if he do, it needs must be by stealth.
Then, since the case so stands as now it doth,
I think it best you married with the county.
O, he 's a lovely gentleman!   220
Romeo 's a dishclout to him: an eagle, madam,
Hath not so green, so quick, so fair an eye
As Paris hath. Beshrew my very heart,
I think you are happy in this second match,
For it excels your first: or if it did not,
Your first is dead; or 'twere as good he were,
As living here and you no use of him.
   Jul. Speakest thou from thy heart?
   Nurse.   And from my soul too;
Or else beshrew them both.
   Jul.   Amen!
   Nurse.   What?
   Jul. Well, thou hast comforted me marvellous
   much.   230
Go in; and tell my lady I am gone,
Having displeased my father, to Laurence' cell,
To make confession and to be absolved.
   Nurse. Marry, I will; and this is wisely done.   *[Exit.*
   Jul. Ancient damnation! O most wicked fiend!
Is it more sin to wish me thus forsworn,
Or to dispraise my lord with that same tongue
Which she hath praised him with above compare
So many thousand times? Go, counsellor;
Thou and my bosom henceforth shall be twain.   240
I'll to the friar, to know his remedy:
If all else fail, myself have power to die.   *[Exit.*

ACT IV.

SCENE I. *Friar Laurence's cell.*

Enter FRIAR LAURENCE *and* PARIS.

Fri. L. On Thursday, sir? the time is very short.

---

140. **will none**, refuses it. 142. **take me with you**, let me understand
you. 145. **wrought**, procured. 150. **chop-logic**, a shallow and
sophistical arguer. 152. **minion**, favored person; see glossary. 154.
fettle, make ready. 156. **hurdle**, a conveyance for criminals. 157.
green-sickness, an anemic ailment of young women; it suggests Juliet's

paleness. 170. **rate**, berate, scold; see glossary. 172. **smatter**, chatter.
175. **gravity**, wisdom; used contemptuously. 177. **God's bread**, an
oath by the sacrament. 186. **mammet**, doll. **fortune's tender**, offer
of good fortune. 207. **my faith in heaven.** Juliet refers to her marriage
vows. 211. **practise**, scheme, contrive; see glossary. **stratagems,**

Par. My father Capulet will have it so;
And I am nothing slow to slack his haste.
 Fri. L. You say you do not know the lady's mind:
Uneven is the course, I like it not.
 Par. Immoderately she weeps for Tybalt's death,
And therefore have I little talk'd of love;
For Venus smiles not in a house of tears.
Now, sir, her father counts it dangerous
That she doth give her sorrow so much sway,   10
And in his wisdom hastes our marriage,
To stop the inundation of her tears;
Which, too much minded by herself alone,
May be put from her by society:
Now do you know the reason of this haste.
 Fri. L. [*Aside*] I would I knew not why it should be
  slow'd.
Look, sir, here comes the lady towards my cell.

Enter JULIET.

 Par. Happily met, my lady and my wife!
 Jul. That may be, sir, when I may be a wife.
 Par. That may be must be, love, on Thursday next.
 Jul. What must be shall be.
 Fri. L.   That's a certain text.   21
 Par. Come you to make confession to this father?
 Jul. To answer that, I should confess to you.
 Par. Do not deny to him that you love me.
 Jul. I will confess to you that I love him.
 Par. So will ye, I am sure, that you love me.
 Jul. If I do so, it will be of more price,
Being spoke behind your back, than to your face.
 Par. Poor soul, thy face is much abused with tears.
 Jul. The tears have got small victory by that;   30
For it was bad enough before their spite.
 Par. Thou wrong'st it, more than tears, with that
  report.
 Jul. That is no slander, sir, which is a truth;
And what I spake, I spake it to my face.
 Par. Thy face is mine, and thou hast slander'd it.
 Jul. It may be so, for it is not mine own.
Are you at leisure, holy father, now;
Or shall I come to you at evening mass?
 Fri. L. My leisure serves me, pensive daughter, now.
My lord, we must entreat the time alone.   40
 Par. God shield I should disturb devotion!
Juliet, on Thursday early will I rouse ye:
Till then, adieu; and keep this holy kiss.   [*Exit.*
 Jul. O, shut the door! and when thou hast done so,
Come weep with me; past hope, past cure, past help!
 Fri. L. Ah, Juliet, I already know thy grief;
It strains me past the compass of my wits:
I hear thou must, and nothing may prorogue it,
On Thursday next be married to this county.
 Jul. Tell me not, friar, that thou hear'st of this,   50
Unless thou tell me how I may prevent it:
If, in thy wisdom, thou canst give no help,
Do thou but call my resolution wise,
And with this knife I'll help it presently.
God join'd my heart and Romeo's, thou our hands;
And ere this hand, by thee to Romeo seal'd,
Shall be the label to another deed,
Or my true heart with treacherous revolt

Turn to another, this shall slay them both:
Therefore, out of thy long-experienced time,   60
Give me some present counsel, or, behold,
'Twixt my extremes and me this bloody knife
Shall play the umpire, arbitrating that
Which the commission of thy years and art
Could to no issue of true honour bring.
Be not so long to speak; I long to die,
If what thou speak'st speak not of remedy.
 Fri. L. Hold, daughter: I do spy a kind of hope,
Which craves as desperate an execution
As that is desperate which we would prevent.   70
If, rather than to marry County Paris,
Thou hast the strength of will to slay thyself,
Then is it likely thou wilt undertake
A thing like death to chide away this shame,
That copest with death himself to scape from it;
And, if thou darest, I'll give thee remedy.
 Jul. O, bid me leap, rather than marry Paris,
From off the battlements of yonder tower;
Or walk in thievish ways; or bid me lurk
Where serpents are; chain me with roaring bears;   80
Or shut me nightly in a charnel-house,
O'er-cover'd quite with dead men's rattling bones,
With reeky shanks and yellow chapless skulls;
Or bid me go into a new-made grave
And hide me with a dead man in his shroud;
Things that, to hear them told, have made me
  tremble;
And I will do it without fear or doubt,
To live an unstain'd wife to my sweet love.
 Fri. L. Hold, then; go home, be merry, give consent
To marry Paris: Wednesday is to-morrow: 90
To-morrow night look that thou lie alone;
Let not thy nurse lie with thee in thy chamber:
Take thou this vial, being then in bed,
And this distilled liquor drink thou off;
When presently through all thy veins shall run
A cold and drowsy humour, for no pulse
Shall keep his native progress, but surcease:
No warmth, no breath, shall testify thou livest;
The roses in thy lips and cheeks shall fade
To paly ashes, thy eyes' windows fall,   100
Like death, when he shuts up the day of life;
Each part, deprived of supple government,
Shall, stiff and stark and cold, appear like death:
And in this borrow'd likeness of shrunk death
Thou shalt continue two and forty hours,
And then awake as from a pleasant sleep.
Now, when the bridegroom in the morning comes
To rouse thee from thy bed, there art thou dead:
Then, as the manner of our country is,
In thy best robes uncover'd on the bier   110
Thou shalt be borne to that same ancient vault
Where all the kindred of the Capulets lie.
In the mean time, against thou shalt awake,
Shall Romeo by my letters know our drift,
And hither shall he come: and he and I
Will watch thy waking, and that very night
Shall Romeo bear thee hence to Mantua.
And this shall free thee from this present shame;
If no inconstant toy, nor womanish fear,

---

dreadful deeds. 222. **green.** Green was an admired color for eyes.
quick, lively; see glossary.
 ACT IV. SCENE I. 5. **Uneven,** not straightforward. 13. **minded,** perceived, noticed; see glossary. 40. **entreat,** ask to have. 41. **shield,**
prevent (that). 54. **presently,** at once; see glossary. 57. **label,** a

strip attached to a deed to carry the seal. 61. **present,** instant; see
glossary. 62. **extremes,** extreme difficulties. 64. **commission,** authority. 75. **copest,** encounterest; see glossary. 83. **reeky,** mal-
odorous. **chapless,** without the lower jaw. 97. **surcease,** cessation.
119. **toy,** idle fancy; see glossary.

Abate thy valour in the acting it. 120
Jul. Give me, give me! O, tell not me of fear!
Fri. L. Hold; get you gone, be strong and prosperous
In this resolve: I'll send a friar with speed
To Mantua, with my letters to thy lord.
Jul. Love give me strength! and strength shall help
afford.
Farewell, dear father! [*Exeunt.*

SCENE II. *Hall in Capulet's house.*

Enter CAPULET, LADY CAPULET, Nurse, *and two*
Servingmen.

Cap. So many guests invite as here are writ.
[*Exit First Servant.*
Sirrah, go hire me twenty cunning cooks.
Sec. Serv. You shall have none ill, sir; for I'll try if
they can lick their fingers.
Cap. How canst thou try them so?
Sec. Serv. Marry, sir, 'tis an ill cook that cannot lick
his own fingers: therefore he that cannot lick his
fingers goes not with me.
Cap. Go, be gone. [*Exit Sec. Servant.*
We shall be much unfurnish'd for this time. 10
What, is my daughter gone to Friar Laurence?
Nurse. Ay, forsooth.
Cap. Well, he may chance to do some good on her:
A peevish self-will'd harlotry it is.
Nurse. See where she comes from shrift with merry
look.

Enter JULIET.

Cap. How now, my headstrong! where have you
been gadding?
Jul. Where I have learn'd me to repent the sin
Of disobedient opposition
To you and your behests, and am enjoin'd
By holy Laurence to fall prostrate here, 20
And beg your pardon: pardon, I beseech you!
Henceforward I am ever ruled by you.
Cap. Send for the county; go tell him of this:
I'll have this knot knit up to-morrow morning.
Jul. I met the youthful lord at Laurence' cell;
And gave him what becomed love I might,
Not stepping o'er the bounds of modesty.
Cap. Why, I am glad on 't; this is well: stand up:
This is as 't should be. Let me see the county;
Ay, marry, go, I say, and fetch him hither. 30
Now, afore God! this reverend holy friar,
All our whole city is much bound to him.
Jul. Nurse, will you go with me into my closet,
To help me sort such needful ornaments
As you think fit to furnish me to-morrow?
La. Cap. No, not till Thursday; there is time enough.
Cap. Go, nurse, go with her: we'll to church
to-morrow. [*Exeunt Juliet and Nurse.*
La. Cap. We shall be short in our provision:
'Tis now near night.
Cap. Tush, I will stir about,
And all things shall be well, I warrant thee, wife: 40

Go thou to Juliet, help to deck up her;
I'll not to bed to-night; let me alone;
I'll play the housewife for this once. What, ho!
They are all forth. Well, I will walk myself
To County Paris, to prepare him up
Against to-morrow: my heart is wondrous light,
Since this same wayward girl is so reclaim'd. [*Exeunt.*

SCENE III. *Juliet's chamber.*

Enter JULIET *and* Nurse.

Jul. Ay, those attires are best: but, gentle nurse,
I pray thee, leave me to myself to-night;
For I have need of many orisons
To move the heavens to smile upon my state,
Which, well thou know'st, is cross and full of sin.

Enter LADY CAPULET.

La. Cap. What, are you busy, ho? need you my
help?
Jul. No, madam; we have cull'd such necessaries
As are behoveful for our state to-morrow:
So please you, let me now be left alone,
And let the nurse this night sit up with you; 10
For, I am sure, you have your hands full all,
In this so sudden business.
La. Cap. Good night:
Get thee to bed, and rest; for thou hast need.
[*Exeunt Lady Capulet and Nurse.*
Jul. Farewell! God knows when we shall meet
again.
I have a faint cold fear thrills through my veins,
That almost freezes up the heat of life:
I'll call them back again to comfort me:
Nurse! What should she do here?
My dismal scene I needs must act alone.
Come, vial. 20
What if this mixture do not work at all?
Shall I be married then to-morrow morning?
No, no: this shall forbid it: lie thou there.
[*Laying down her dagger.*
What if it be a poison, which the friar
Subtly hath minister'd to have me dead,
Lest in this marriage he should be dishonour'd,
Because he married me before to Romeo?
I fear it is: and yet, methinks, it should not,
For he hath still been tried a holy man.
How if, when I am laid into the tomb, 30
I wake before the time that Romeo
Come to redeem me? there 's a fearful point!
Shall I not, then, be stifled in the vault,
To whose foul mouth no healthsome air breathes in,
And there die strangled ere my Romeo comes?
Or, if I live, is it not very like,
The horrible conceit of death and night,
Together with the terror of the place,—
As in a vault, an ancient receptacle,
Where, for these many hundred years, the bones 40
Of all my buried ancestors are pack'd:
Where bloody Tybalt, yet but green in earth,

120. **Abate,** diminish; see glossary.
SCENE II. 14. **peevish,** silly; see glossary. **harlotry,** hussy. 26. **becomed,** befitting. 33. **closet,** private room. 35. **furnish,** fit out; see glossary.
SCENE III. 3. **orisons,** prayers. 5. **cross,** contrary. 8. **behoveful,** needful. 25. **minister'd,** administered (something healing or the

reverse). 29. **tried,** proved. After this line, Q_1: *I will not entertain so bad a thought.* 39. **As,** namely; see glossary. 47. **mandrakes'.** Mandragora or mandrake was a narcotic plant, the root of which resembled the human form; it was fabled to utter a shriek when torn from the ground. 50. **fears,** objects of fear; see glossary. 53. **rage,** madness; see glossary.

Lies festering in his shroud; where, as they say,
At some hours in the night spirits resort;—
Alack, alack, is it not like that I,
So early waking, what with loathsome smells,
And shrieks like mandrakes' torn out of the earth,
That living mortals, hearing them, run mad:—
O, if I wake, shall I not be distraught,
Environed with all these hideous fears?   50
And madly play with my forefathers' joints?
And pluck the mangled Tybalt from his shroud?
And, in this rage, with some great kinsman's bone,
As with a club, dash out my desperate brains?
O, look! methinks I see my cousin's ghost
Seeking out Romeo, that did spit his body
Upon a rapier's point: stay, Tybalt, stay!
Romeo, I come! this do I drink to thee.
     [*She falls upon her bed, within the curtains.*

SCENE IV. *Hall in Capulet's house.*

Enter LADY CAPULET *and* Nurse.

La. Cap. Hold, take these keys, and fetch more
    spices, nurse.
Nurse. They call for dates and quinces in the pastry.

Enter CAPULET.

Cap. Come, stir, stir, stir! the second cock hath
    crow'd,
The curfew-bell hath rung, 'tis three o'clock:
Look to the baked meats, good Angelica:
Spare not for cost.
Nurse.   Go, you cot-quean, go,
Get you to bed; faith, you'll be sick to-morrow
For this night's watching.
Cap. No, not a whit: what! I have watch'd ere now
All night for lesser cause, and ne'er been sick.   10
La. Cap. Ay, you have been a mouse-hunt in your
    time;
But I will watch you from such watching now.
            [*Exeunt Lady Capulet and Nurse.*
Cap. A jealous-hood, a jealous-hood!

Enter three or four Servingmen, *with spits, logs, and*
    baskets.
           Now, fellow,
What 's there?
First Serv. Things for the cook, sir; but I know not
    what.
Cap. Make haste, make haste. [*Exit First Serv.*] Sirrah,
    fetch drier logs:
Call Peter, he will show thee where they are.
Sec. Serv. I have a head, sir, that will find out logs,
And never trouble Peter for the matter.   [*Exit.*
Cap. Mass, and well said; a merry whoreson, ha!
Thou shalt be logger-head. Good faith, 'tis day: 20
The county will be here with music straight,
For so he said he would: I hear him near.
               [*Music within.*
Nurse! Wife! What, ho! What, nurse, I say!

Re-enter Nurse.

Go waken Juliet, go and trim her up;
I'll go and chat with Paris: hie, make haste,
Make haste; the bridegroom he is come already:
Make haste, I say.   [*Exeunt.*

SCENE V. *Juliet's chamber.*

Enter Nurse.

Nurse. Mistress! what, mistress! Juliet! fast, I
    warrant her, she:
Why, lamb! why, lady! fie, you slug-a-bed!
Why, love, I say! madam! sweet-heart! why, bride!
What, not a word? you take your pennyworths now;
Sleep for a week; for the next night, I warrant,
The County Paris hath set up his rest,
That you shall rest but little. God forgive me,
Marry, and amen, how sound is she asleep!
I must needs wake her. Madam, madam, madam!
Ay, let the county take you in your bed;   10
He'll fright you up, i' faith. Will it not be?
           [*Undraws the curtains.*
What, dress'd! and in your clothes! and down again!
I must needs wake you: Lady! lady! lady!
Alas, alas! Help, help! my lady 's dead!
O, well-a-day, that ever I was born!
Some aqua vitæ, ho! My lord! my lady!

Enter LADY CAPULET.

La. Cap. What noise is here?
Nurse.   O lamentable day!
La. Cap. What is the matter?
Nurse.   Look, look! O heavy day!
La. Cap. O me, O me! My child, my only life,
Revive, look up, or I will die with thee!   20
Help, help! Call help.

Enter CAPULET.

Cap. For shame, bring Juliet forth; her lord is come.
Nurse. She 's dead, deceased, she 's dead; alack the
    day!
La. Cap. Alack the day, she 's dead, she 's dead,
    she 's dead!
Cap. Ha! let me see her: out, alas! she 's cold;
Her blood is settled, and her joints are stiff;
Life and these lips have long been separated:
Death lies on her like an untimely frost
Upon the sweetest flower of all the field.
Nurse. O lamentable day!
La. Cap.   O woful time!   30
Cap. Death, that hath ta'en her hence to make me
    wail,
Ties up my tongue, and will not let me speak.

Enter FRIAR LAURENCE *and* PARIS, *with* Musicians.

Fri. L. Come, is the bride ready to go to church?
Cap. Ready to go, but never to return.
O son! the night before thy wedding-day
Hath Death lain with thy wife. There she lies,
Flower as she was, deflowered by him.
Death is my son-in-law, Death is my heir;

*Romeo
and Juliet*
ACT IV : SC V

419

SCENE IV.   2. **pastry,** room in which pastry was made.   4. **curfew-bell,** apparently rung at other times than at curfew.   5. **baked meats,** pies, pastry.   6. **cot-quean,** a man who acts the housewife.   8. **watching,** waking; see glossary.   11. **mouse-hunt,** hunter of women.   13. **jealous-hood,** jealousy.   19. **Mass,** by the Mass.   20. **logger-head,** blockhead.

SCENE V.   1. **fast,** fast asleep.   4. **pennyworths,** little bits.   6. **set up his rest,** a phrase from the game of primero meaning to complete your hand and wager on it; hence, to be resolved.   26. **settled,** probably congealed.

My daughter he hath wedded: I will die,
And leave him all; life, living, all is Death's.   40
    Par. Have I thought long to see this morning's face,
And doth it give me such a sight as this?
    La. Cap. Accursed, unhappy, wretched, hateful day!
Most miserable hour that e'er time saw
In lasting labour of his pilgrimage!
But one, poor one, one poor and loving child,
But one thing to rejoice and solace in,
And cruel death hath catch'd it from my sight!
    Nurse. O woe! O woful, woful, woful day!
Most lamentable day, most woful day,   50
That ever, ever, I did yet behold!
O day! O day! O day! O hateful day!
Never was seen so black a day as this:
O woful day, O woful day!
    Par. Beguiled, divorced, wronged, spited, slain!
Most detestable death, by thee beguiled,
By cruel cruel thee quite overthrown!
O love! O life! not life, but love in death!
    Cap. Despised, distressed, hated, martyr'd, kill'd!
Uncomfortable time, why camest thou now   60
To murder, murder our solemnity?
O child! O child! my soul, and not my child!
Dead art thou! Alack! my child is dead;
And with my child my joys are buried.
    Fri. L. Peace, ho, for shame! confusion's cure lives
        not
In these confusions. Heaven and yourself
Had part in this fair maid; now heaven hath all,
And all the better is it for the maid:
Your part in her you could not keep from death,
But heaven keeps his part in eternal life.   70
The most you sought was her promotion;
For 'twas your heaven she should be advanced:
And weep ye now, seeing she is advanced
Above the clouds, as high as heaven itself?
O, in this love, you love your child so ill,
That you run mad, seeing that she is well:
She 's not well married that lives married long;
But she 's best married that dies married young.
Dry up your tears, and stick your rosemary
On this fair corse; and, as the custom is,   80
In all her best array bear her to church:
For though fond nature bids us all lament,
Yet nature's tears are reason's merriment.
    Cap. All things that we ordained festival,
Turn from their office to black funeral;
Our instruments to melancholy bells,
Our wedding cheer to a sad burial feast,
Our solemn hymns to sullen dirges change,
Our bridal flowers serve for a buried corse,
And all things change them to the contrary.   90
    Fri. L. Sir, go you in; and, madam, go with him;
And go, Sir Paris; every one prepare
To follow this fair corse unto her grave:
The heavens do lour upon you for some ill;
Move them no more by crossing their high will.
            [*Exeunt Capulet, Lady Capulet, Paris, and Friar.*

    First Mus. Faith, we may put up our pipes, and be
gone.
    Nurse. Honest good fellows, ah, put up, put up;
For, well you know, this is a pitiful case.   [*Exit.*
    First Mus. Ay, by my troth, the case may be
amended.   101

Enter PETER.

    Pet. Musicians, O, musicians, 'Heart's ease, Heart's
ease:' O, an you will have me live, play 'Heart's ease.'
    First Mus. Why 'Heart's ease'?
    Pet. O, musicians, because my heart itself plays 'My
heart is full of woe:' O, play me some merry dump, to
comfort me.   108
    First Mus. Not a dump we; 'tis no time to play now.
    Pet. You will not, then?
    First Mus. No.
    Pet. I will then give it you soundly.
    First Mus. What will you give us?
    Pet. No money, on my faith, but the gleek; I will
give you the minstrel.
    First Mus. Then will I give you the serving-creature.
    Pet. Then will I lay the serving-creature's dagger on
your pate. I will carry no crotchets: I'll re you, I'll fa
you; do you note me?   121
    First Mus. An you re us and fa us, you note us.
    Sec. Mus. Pray you, put up your dagger, and put out
your wit.
    Pet. Then have at you with my wit! I will dry-beat
you with an iron wit, and put up my iron dagger.
Answer me like men:
    'When griping grief the heart doth wound,
        And doleful dumps the mind oppress,
    Then music with her silver sound'—   130
why 'silver sound'? why 'music with her silver sound'?
What say you, Simon Catling?
    First Mus. Marry, sir, because silver hath a sweet
sound.
    Pet. Pretty! What say you, Hugh Rebeck?
    Sec. Mus. I say 'silver sound,' because musicians
sound for silver.
    Pet. Pretty too! What say you, James Soundpost?
    Third Mus. Faith, I know not what to say.   140
    Pet. O, I cry you mercy; you are the singer: I will
say for you. It is 'music with her silver sound,' because
musicians have no gold for sounding:
    'Then music with her silver sound
        With speedy help doth lend redress.'   [*Exit.*
    First Mus. What a pestilent knave is this same!
    Sec. Mus. Hang him, Jack! Come, we'll in here;
tarry for the mourners, and stay dinner.   [*Exeunt.*

ACT V.

SCENE I. *Mantua. A street.*

Enter ROMEO.

Rom. If I may trust the flattering truth of sleep,

---

41. **thought long,** looked forward to. 43. **unhappy,** fatal; see glossary. 61. **solemnity,** festivity. 65. **confusion's,** destruction's; see glossary. 79. **rosemary,** symbol of immortality and enduring love; therefore used at both funerals and weddings. 83. **Yet . . . merriment.** Nature is here used as the opposite of reason. 101. **amended,** bettered. *Stage Direction: Enter* Peter. Q₂ has *Enter Will Kemp*. This well-known comic actor was a member of Shakespeare's company and evidently played this part. His name was written in probably by the prompter; hence one argues that Q₂ was set up from a playhouse copy. 102.

'**Heart's ease,**' popular tune, as also '*My heart is full of woe,*' line 107. 108. **dump,** mournful tune. 115. **gleek,** jest, gibe. 120. **carry,** endure; see glossary. **crotchets,** meaning both "quarter notes" and "whims." 122. **note,** set to music; used punningly. 124. **put out,** exert. 128-130. '**When . . . sound.**' This is a part of a song by Richard Edwards preserved in the *Paradise of Daintie Devices* (1576). 132. **Catling.** A catling was a small lutestring made of catgut. 135. **Rebeck.** A rebeck was a fiddle with three strings. 139. **Soundpost.** A soundpost is the pillar or peg which supports the body of a stringed

My dreams presage some joyful news at hand:
My bosom's lord sits lightly in his throne;
And all this day an unaccustom'd spirit
Lifts me above the ground with cheerful thoughts.
I dreamt my lady came and found me dead—
Strange dream, that gives a dead man leave to
    think!—
And breathed such life with kisses in my lips,
That I revived, and was an emperor.
Ah me! how sweet is love itself possess'd, 10
When but love's shadows are so rich in joy!

Enter BALTHASAR, *booted.*

News from Verona!—How now, Balthasar!
Dost thou not bring me letters from the friar?
How doth my lady? Is my father well?
How fares my Juliet? that I ask again;
For nothing can be ill, if she be well.
    Bal. Then she is well, and nothing can be ill:
Her body sleeps in Capels' monument,
And her immortal part with angels lives.
I saw her laid low in her kindred's vault, 20
And presently took post to tell it you:
O, pardon me for bringing these ill news,
Since you did leave it for my office, sir.
    Rom. Is it even so? then I defy you, stars!
Thou know'st my lodging: get me ink and paper,
And hire post-horses; I will hence to-night.
    Bal. I do beseech you, sir, have patience:
Your looks are pale and wild, and do import
Some misadventure.
    Rom.   Tush, thou art deceived:
Leave me, and do the thing I bid thee do. 30
Hast thou no letters to me from the friar?
    Bal. No, my good lord.
    Rom.   No matter: get thee gone,
And hire those horses; I'll be with thee straight.
                                    [*Exit Balthasar.*
Well, Juliet, I will lie with thee to-night.
Let's see for means: O mischief, thou art swift
To enter in the thoughts of desperate men!
I do remember an apothecary,—
And hereabouts he dwells,—which late I noted
In tatter'd weeds, with overwhelming brows,
Culling of simples; meagre were his looks, 40
Sharp misery had worn him to the bones:
And in his needy shop a tortoise hung,
An alligator stuff'd, and other skins
Of ill-shaped fishes; and about his shelves
A beggarly account of empty boxes,
Green earthen pots, bladders and musty seeds,
Remnants of packthread and old cakes of roses,
Were thinly scatter'd, to make up a show.
Noting this penury, to myself I said
'An if a man did need a poison now, 50
Whose sale is present death in Mantua,
Here lives a caitiff wretch would sell it him.'
O, this same thought did but forerun my need;
And this same needy man must sell it me.

As I remember, this should be the house.
Being holiday, the beggar's shop is shut.
What, ho! apothecary!

Enter Apothecary.
    Ap.   Who calls so loud?
    Rom. Come hither, man. I see that thou art poor:
Hold, there is forty ducats: let me have
A dram of poison, such soon-speeding gear 60
As will disperse itself through all the veins
That the life-weary taker may fall dead
And that the trunk may be discharged of breath
As violently as hasty powder fired
Doth hurry from the fatal cannon's womb.
    Ap. Such mortal drugs I have; but Mantua's law
Is death to any he that utters them.
    Rom. Art thou so bare and full of wretchedness,
And fear'st to die? famine is in thy cheeks,
Need and oppression starveth in thine eyes, 70
Contempt and beggary hangs upon thy back;
The world is not thy friend nor the world's law;
The world affords no law to make thee rich;
Then be not poor, but break it, and take this.
    Ap. My poverty, but not my will, consents.
    Rom. I pay thy poverty, and not thy will.
    Ap. Put this in any liquid thing you will,
And drink it off; and, if you had the strength
Of twenty men, it would dispatch you straight.
    Rom. There is thy gold, worse poison to men's souls,
Doing more murders in this loathsome world, 81
Than these poor compounds that thou mayst not sell.
I sell thee poison; thou hast sold me none.
Farewell: buy food, and get thyself in flesh.
Come, cordial and not poison, go with me
To Juliet's grave; for there must I use thee. [*Exeunt.*

SCENE II. *Friar Laurence's cell.*

Enter FRIAR JOHN.

Fri. J. Holy Franciscan friar! brother, ho!

Enter FRIAR LAURENCE.
    Fri. L. This same should be the voice of Friar John.
Welcome from Mantua: what says Romeo?
Or, if his mind be writ, give me his letter.
    Fri. J. Going to find a bare-foot brother out,
One of our order, to associate me,
Here in this city visiting the sick,
And finding him, the searchers of the town,
Suspecting that we both were in a house
Where the infectious pestilence did reign, 10
Seal'd up the doors, and would not let us forth;
So that my speed to Mantua there was stay'd.
    Fri. L. Who bare my letter, then, to Romeo?
    Fri. J. I could not send it,—here it is again,—
Nor get a messenger to bring it thee,
So fearful were they of infection.
    Fri. L. Unhappy fortune! by my brotherhood,

---

instrument. 141. **cry you mercy,** beg your pardon; see glossary.
143. **sounding,** playing music.
    ACT V. SCENE I. 1. **flattering,** illusive. 2. **presage some joyful
news.** The premonition here is ironical. 3. **bosom's lord,** heart. 11.
shadows, phantoms; see glossary. 21. **took post,** started with post
horses. 24. **then I defy you, stars.** The fatalism of this utterance is
in keeping with the other references to destiny in the play. 39. **weeds,**
clothes; see glossary. **overwhelming,** overhanging. 40. **simples,**
medicinal herbs. 45. **beggarly account,** poor array. 47. **cakes of roses,**

rose petals caked to be used as perfume. 52. **caitiff,** poor. 59. **ducats,**
coins, usually gold, of varying value. 63. **trunk,** body. 67. **utters,**
issues, gives out. 80-86. **There . . . thee,** a passage of general reflection but slightly connected with the action and having no special
appropriateness to Romeo.
    SCENE II. 4. **mind,** thoughts, message; see glossary. 6. **associate,**
accompany. 8. **searchers,** officers of the pestilence.

The letter was not nice but full of charge
Of dear import, and the neglecting it
May do much danger. Friar John, go hence;　20
Get me an iron crow, and bring it straight
Unto my cell.
　　Fri. J. Brother, I'll go and bring it thee.　　　*[Exit.*
　　Fri. L. Now must I to the monument alone;
Within this three hours will fair Juliet wake:
She will beshrew me much that Romeo
Hath had no notice of these accidents;
But I will write again to Mantua,
And keep her at my cell till Romeo come;　29
Poor living corse, closed in a dead man's tomb!　*[Exit.*

———

SCENE III. *A churchyard; in it a tomb belonging to the*
Capulets.

Enter PARIS, *and his* Page *bearing flowers and a torch.*

　　Par. Give me thy torch, boy: hence, and stand
　　　aloof:
Yet put it out, for I would not be seen.
Under yond yew-trees lay thee all along,
Holding thine ear close to the hollow ground;
So shall no foot upon the churchyard tread,
Being loose, unfirm, with digging up of graves,
But thou shalt hear it: whistle then to me,
As signal that thou hear'st something approach.
Give me those flowers. Do as I bid thee, go.
　　Page. [*Aside*] I am almost afraid to stand alone　10
Here in the churchyard; yet I will adventure.　*[Retires.*
　　Par. Sweet flower, with flowers thy bridal bed I
　　　strew,—
O woe! thy canopy is dust and stones;—
Which with sweet water nightly I will dew,
　Or, wanting that, with tears distill'd by moans:
The obsequies that I for thee will keep
Nightly shall be to strew thy grave and weep.
　　　　　　　　　　　　　[The Page whistles.
The boy gives warning something doth approach.
What cursed foot wanders this way to-night,
To cross my obsequies and true love's rite?　20
What, with a torch! muffle me, night, awhile.　*[Retires.*

Enter ROMEO *and* BALTHASAR, *with a torch,*
mattock, &c.

　　Rom. Give me that mattock and the wrenching iron.
Hold, take this letter; early in the morning
See thou deliver it to my lord and father.
Give me the light: upon thy life, I charge thee,
Whate'er thou hear'st or seest, stand all aloof,
And do not interrupt me in my course.
Why I descend into this bed of death,
Is partly to behold my lady's face;
But chiefly to take thence from her dead finger　30
A precious ring, a ring that I must use
In dear employment: therefore hence, be gone:
But if thou, jealous, dost return to pry
In what I further shall intend to do,
By heaven, I will tear thee joint by joint
And strew this hungry churchyard with thy limbs:
The time and my intents are savage-wild,
More fierce and more inexorable far

Than empty tigers or the roaring sea.
　　Bal. I will be gone, sir, and not trouble you.　40
　　Rom. So shalt thou show me friendship. Take thou
　　　that:
Live, and be prosperous: and farewell, good fellow.
　　Bal. [*Aside*] For all this same, I'll hide me
　　　hereabout:
His looks I fear, and his intents I doubt.　　　*[Retires.*
　　Rom. Thou detestable maw, thou womb of death,
Gorged with the dearest morsel of the earth,
Thus I enforce thy rotten jaws to open,
And, in despite, I'll cram thee with more food!
　　　　　　　　　　　　　[Opens the tomb.
　　Par. This is that banish'd haughty Montague,
That murder'd my love's cousin, with which grief,　50
It is supposed, the fair creature died;
And here is come to do some villanous shame
To the dead bodies: I will apprehend him.
　　　　　　　　　　　　　[Comes forward.
Stop thy unhallow'd toil, vile Montague!
Can vengeance be pursued further than death?
Condemned villain, I do apprehend thee:
Obey, and go with me; for thou must die.
　　Rom. I must indeed; and therefore came I hither.
Good gentle youth, tempt not a desperate man;
Fly hence, and leave me: think upon these gone;　60
Let them affright thee. I beseech thee, youth,
Put not another sin upon my head,
By urging me to fury: O, be gone!
By heaven, I love thee better than myself;
For I come hither arm'd against myself:
Stay not, be gone; live, and hereafter say,
A madman's mercy bade thee run away.
　　Par. I do defy thy conjurations,
And apprehend thee for a felon here.　　　　69
　　Rom. Wilt thou provoke me? then have at thee, boy!
　　　　　　　　　　　　　[They fight.
　　Page. O Lord, they fight! I will go call the watch.
　　　　　　　　　　　　　[Exit.
　　Par. O, I am slain! [*Falls.*] If thou be merciful,
Open the tomb, lay me with Juliet.　　　　*[Dies.*
　　Rom. In faith, I will. Let me peruse this face.
Mercutio's kinsman, noble County Paris!
What said my man, when my betossed soul
Did not attend him as we rode? I think
He told me Paris should have married Juliet:
Said he not so? or did I dream it so?
Or am I mad, hearing him talk of Juliet,　　80
To think it was so? O, give me thy hand,
One writ with me in sour misfortune's book!
I'll bury thee in a triumphant grave;
A grave? O, no! a lantern, slaughter'd youth,
For here lies Juliet, and her beauty makes
This vault a feasting presence full of light.
Death, lie thou there, by a dead man interr'd.
　　　　　　　　　　　　　[Laying Paris in the tomb.
How oft when men are at the point of death
Have they been merry! which their keepers call
A lightning before death: O, how may I　　90
Call this a lightning? O my love! my wife!
Death, that hath suck'd the honey of thy breath,
Hath had no power yet upon thy beauty:
Thou art not conquer'd; beauty's ensign yet

18. **charge,** importance.　21. **iron crow,** crowbar.
SCENE III.　3. **all along,** at full length.　16. **obsequies,** dutiful acts
performed in memory of the dead.　21. **muffle,** hide.　33. **jealous,**
suspicious.　44. **doubt,** suspect; see glossary.　45-48. **Thou . . . food.**

The words of these lines seem to echo the wrenching of the door.　66.
conjurations, solemn appeals, which seem perhaps like incantations.
74. **peruse,** scrutinize.　84. **lantern,** a turret full of windows.　86.
presence, presence chamber.　90. **lightning,** a shedding of light; also,

Is crimson in thy lips and in thy cheeks,
And death's pale flag is not advanced there.
Tybalt, liest thou there in thy bloody sheet?
O, what more favour can I do to thee,
Than with that hand that cut thy youth in twain
To sunder his that was thine enemy? 100
Forgive me, cousin! Ah, dear Juliet,
Why art thou yet so fair? shall I believe
That unsubstantial death is amorous,
And that the lean abhorred monster keeps
Thee here in dark to be his paramour?
For fear of that, I still will stay with thee;
And never from this palace of dim night
Depart again: here, here will I remain
With worms that are thy chamber-maids; O, here
Will I set up my everlasting rest, 110
And shake the yoke of inauspicious stars
From this world-wearied flesh. Eyes, look your last!
Arms, take your last embrace! and, lips, O you
The doors of breath, seal with a righteous kiss
A dateless bargain to engrossing death!
Come, bitter conduct, come, unsavoury guide!
Thou desperate pilot, now at once run on
The dashing rocks thy sea-sick weary bark!
Here's to my love! [*Drinks.*] O true apothecary!
Thy drugs are quick. Thus with a kiss I die. [*Dies.* 120

Enter, at the other end of the churchyard, FRIAR
   LAURENCE, *with a lantern, crow, and spade.*

Fri. L. Saint Francis be my speed! how oft to-night
Have my old feet stumbled at graves! Who's there?
Bal. Here's one, a friend, and one that knows you
   well.
Fri. L. Bliss be upon you! Tell me, good my friend,
What torch is yond, that vainly lends his light
To grubs and eyeless skulls? as I discern,
It burneth in the Capels' monument.
Bal. It doth so, holy sir; and there's my master,
One that you love.
Fri. L.   Who is it?
Bal.   Romeo.
Fri. L. How long hath he been there?
Bal.   Full half an hour. 130
Fri. L. Go with me to the vault.
Bal.   I dare not, sir:
My master knows not but I am gone hence;
And fearfully did menace me with death,
If I did stay to look on his intents.
Fri. L. Stay, then; I'll go alone. Fear comes upon
   me:
O, much I fear some ill unlucky thing.
Bal. As I did sleep under this yew-tree here,
I dreamt my master and another fought,
And that my master slew him.
Fri. L.   Romeo!   [*Advances.*
Alack, alack, what blood is this, which stains 140
The stony entrance of this sepulchre?
What mean these masterless and gory swords
To lie discolour'd by this place of peace?
                         [*Enters the tomb.*
Romeo! O, pale! Who else? what, Paris too?
And steep'd in blood? Ah, what an unkind hour
Is guilty of this lamentable chance!

The lady stirs.   [*Juliet wakes.*
   Jul. O comfortable friar! where is my lord?
I do remember well where I should be,
And there I am. Where is my Romeo? [*Noise within.* 150
   Fri. L. I hear some noise. Lady, come from that nest
Of death, contagion, and unnatural sleep:
A greater power than we can contradict
Hath thwarted our intents. Come, come away.
Thy husband in thy bosom there lies dead;
And Paris too. Come, I'll dispose of thee
Among a sisterhood of holy nuns:
Stay not to question, for the watch is coming;
Come, go, good Juliet [*Noise again*], I dare no longer
   stay.
   Jul. Go, get thee hence, for I will not away. 160
                         [*Exit Fri. L.*
What's here? a cup, closed in my true love's hand?
Poison, I see, hath been his timeless end:
O churl! drunk all, and left no friendly drop
To help me after? I will kiss thy lips;
Haply some poison yet doth hang on them,
To make me die with a restorative.   [*Kisses him.*
Thy lips are warm.
   First Watch. [*Within*] Lead, boy: which way?
   Jul. Yea, noise? then I'll be brief. O happy dagger!
                         [*Snatching Romeo's dagger.*
This is thy sheath [*Stabs herself*]; there rust, and let me
   die.   [*Falls on Romeo's body, and dies.* 170

Enter Watch, *with the* Page *of* PARIS.

Page. This is the place; there, where the torch doth
   burn.
   First Watch. The ground is bloody; search about the
   churchyard:
Go, some of you, whoe'er you find attach.
Pitiful sight! here lies the county slain;
And Juliet bleeding, warm, and newly dead,
Who here hath lain these two days buried.
Go, tell the prince: run to the Capulets:
Raise up the Montagues: some others search:
We see the ground whereon these woes do lie;
But the true ground of all these piteous woes 180
We cannot without circumstance descry.

   Re-enter some of the Watch, *with* BALTHASAR.
   Sec. Watch. Here's Romeo's man; we found him in
      the churchyard.
   First Watch. Hold him in safety, till the prince come
      hither.

   Re-enter others of the Watch, *with* FRIAR LAURENCE.
   Third Watch. Here is a friar, that trembles, sighs,
      and weeps:
We took this mattock and this spade from him,
As he was coming from this churchyard side.
   First Watch. A great suspicion: stay the friar too.

   Enter the PRINCE *and* Attendants.
   Prince. What misadventure is so early up,
That calls our person from our morning's rest?

   Enter CAPULET, LADY CAPULET, *and others.*
   Cap. What should it be, that they so shriek abroad?
   La. Cap. The people in the street cry Romeo, 191

*Romeo
and Juliet*
ACT V : SC III

423

a revival of the spirits. **110. set up my everlasting rest.** See IV, v, 6.
The meaning is, "make my final determination," with allusion also to
the idea of repose. **115. dateless,** everlasting. **engrossing,** monopo-
lizing. **121. speed,** protector and assistant; **see glossary. 122.**

stumbled at graves, a bad omen. **137. yew-,** so Pope; Q₃F: *yong*.
162. timeless, everlasting, or untimely. **165. Haply,** perhaps. **173.**
attach, arrest; see glossary.

Some Juliet, and some Paris; and all run,
With open outcry, toward our monument.
 Prince. What fear is this which startles in our ears?
 First Watch. Sovereign, here lies the County Paris
  slain;
And Romeo dead; and Juliet, dead before,
Warm and new kill'd.
 Prince. Search, seek, and know how this foul murder
  comes.
 First Watch. Here is a friar, and slaughter'd Romeo's
  man;
With instruments upon them, fit to open   200
These dead men's tombs.
 Cap. O heavens! O wife, look how our daughter
  bleeds!
This dagger hath mista'en,—for, lo, his house
Is empty on the back of Montague,—
And it mis-sheathed in my daughter's bosom!
 La. Cap. O me! this sight of death is as a bell,
That warns my old age to a sepulchre.

 Enter MONTAGUE *and others.*

 Prince. Come, Montague; for thou art early up,
To see thy son and heir more early down.
 Mon. Alas, my liege, my wife is dead tonight;   210
Grief of my son's exile hath stopp'd her breath:
What further woe conspires against mine age?
 Prince. Look, and thou shalt see.
 Mon. O thou untaught! what manners is in this,
To press before thy father to a grave?
 Prince. Seal up the mouth of outrage for a while,
Till we can clear these ambiguities,
And know their spring, their head, their true descent;
And then will I be general of your woes,
And lead you even to death: meantime forbear,   220
And let mischance be slave to patience.
Bring forth the parties of suspicion.
 Fri. L. I am the greatest, able to do least,
Yet most suspected, as the time and place
Doth make against me, of this direful murder:
And here I stand, both to impeach and purge
Myself condemned and myself excused.
 Prince. Then say at once what thou dost know in
  this.
 Fri. L. I will be brief, for my short date of breath
Is not so long as is a tedious tale.   230
Romeo, there dead, was husband to that Juliet;
And she, there dead, that Romeo's faithful wife:
I married them; and their stol'n marriage-day
Was Tybalt's dooms-day, whose untimely death
Banish'd the new-made bridegroom from this city,
For whom, and not for Tybalt, Juliet pined.
You, to remove that siege of grief from her,
Betroth'd and would have married her perforce
To County Paris: then comes she to me,
And, with wild looks, bid me devise some mean   240
To rid her from this second marriage,
Or in my cell there would she kill herself.
Then gave I her, so tutor'd by my art,
A sleeping potion; which so took effect
As I intended, for it wrought on her
The form of death: meantime I writ to Romeo,
That he should hither come as this dire night,
To help to take her from her borrow'd grave,

Being the time the potion's force should cease.
But he which bore my letter, Friar John,   250
Was stay'd by accident, and yesternight
Return'd my letter back. Then all alone
At the prefixed hour of her waking,
Came I to take her from her kindred's vault;
Meaning to keep her closely at my cell,
Till I conveniently could send to Romeo:
But when I came, some minute ere the time
Of her awaking, here untimely lay
The noble Paris and true Romeo dead.
She wakes; and I entreated her come forth,   260
And bear this work of heaven with patience:
But then a noise did scare me from the tomb;
And she, too desperate, would not go with me,
But, as it seems, did violence on herself.
All this I know; and to the marriage
Her nurse is privy: and, if aught in this
Miscarried by my fault, let my old life
Be sacrificed, some hour before his time,
Unto the rigour of severest law.
 Prince. We still have known thee for a holy man.   270
Where 's Romeo's man? what can he say in this?
 Bal. I brought my master news of Juliet's death;
And then in post he came from Mantua
To this same place, to this same monument.
This letter he early bid me give his father,
And threaten'd me with death, going in the vault,
If I departed not and left him there.
 Prince. Give me the letter; I will look on it.
Where is the county's page, that raised the watch?
Sirrah, what made your master in this place?   280
 Page. He came with flowers to strew his lady's grave;
And bid me stand aloof, and so I did:
Anon comes one with light to ope the tomb;
And by and by my master drew on him;
And then I ran away to call the watch.
 Prince. This letter doth make good the friar's words,
Their course of love, the tidings of her death:
And here he writes that he did buy a poison
Of a poor 'pothecary, and therewithal
Came to this vault to die, and lie with Juliet.   290
Where be these enemies? Capulet! Montague!
See, what a scourge is laid upon your hate,
That heaven finds means to kill your joys with love.
And I for winking at your discords too
Have lost a brace of kinsmen: all are punish'd.
 Cap. O brother Montague, give me thy hand:
This is my daughter's jointure, for no more
Can I demand.
 Mon.   But I can give thee more:
For I will raise her statue in pure gold;
That while Verona by that name is known,   300
There shall no figure at such rate be set
As that of true and faithful Juliet.
 Cap. As rich shall Romeo's by his lady's lie;
Poor sacrifices of our enmity!
 Prince. A glooming peace this morning with it
  brings;
 The sun, for sorrow, will not show his head:
Go hence, to have more talk of these sad things;
 Some shall be pardon'd, and some punished:
For never was a story of more woe
Than this of Juliet and her Romeo.   [*Exeunt.* 310

---

203. **house,** scabbard. 216. **outrage,** outcry. 226. **purge,** purify, cleanse. 247. **as this,** this very. 253. **prefixed,** agreed upon pre-

viously. 255. **closely,** secretly. 273. **post,** haste; see glossary. 297. **jointure,** marriage portion. 301. **rate,** value; see glossary.

POEMS

Venus and Adonis

It will be remembered that the invaluable Francis Meres says in *Palladis Tamia* (1598),

As the soul of Euphorbus was thought to live in Pythagoras: so the sweet witty soul of Ovid lives in mellifluous and honey-tongued Shakespeare, witness his Venus and Adonis, his Lucrece, his sugared Sonnets among his private friends, &c.

In saying this he is offering testimony that Shakespeare's reputation among his contemporaries arose quite as much from the poems as from the plays. This part of his work was no doubt more highly regarded by Shakespeare himself and by his contemporaries than were the plays, since plays were thought of as ephemeral if not mercenary. Most of the playwrights of the age, including Shakespeare, were singularly indifferent to the honor of successful dramatic composition, although John Webster, Thomas Heywood, and especially Ben Jonson show pride in dramatic works. The indifference is perfectly clear in Shakespeare's case. We have only the slightest evidence that he took literary pride in his plays or thought of them as a basis on which his fame might be built. He was sensitive enough to the issues which arose, such as the offense given Lord Cobham over his portrait of Sir John Oldcastle, and had a workmanlike knowledge of how the thing ought to be done, as witnessed by his advice to the Players in *Hamlet;* but there are no boastful prologues from Shakespeare and no personal utterances about his dramas. On the contrary, there is evidence in the *Sonnets* that he regarded his connection with the theater as of doubtful respectability; whereas in the circumstances of the publication of *Venus and Adonis* and *Lucrece* and in the words of the *Sonnets* there is a definite bid for fame.[1]

---

[1]For *Venus and Adonis, The Rape of Lucrece,* and the minor poems see *Shakespeare: The Poems.* A New Variorum Edition, Hyder Edward Rollins, ed. (Philadelphia, 1938).

DATE

It has been said that the public playhouses of London and the suburbs were closed on account of plague, except for two brief periods, from June 1592 to May 1594. We know from Greene's attack on Shakespeare in *A Groatsworth of Wit* (1592) and from Chettle's apology to Shakespeare in *Kind-Harts Dreame* (December 1592) that Shakespeare was an actor and playwright of importance before the closing of the theaters. He would thus have had enforced leisure during the period when his services as a playwright were not required. There is reason to think that he used some portion of this leisure in the composition of poems in the hope that he might by their means gain the favor of a nobleman, who, as a patron of letters, would be of material assistance to him. Under the system of royal and noble patronage such was the hope of many poets and the good fortune of not a few. During the period Shakespeare may also have written and rewritten plays, for a good many of his works group themselves about the years 1594-1595, just after the theaters had reopened.

In any case, we have the publication in 1593 from the press of Richard Field, a native of Stratford and at the time a successful London printer, of *Venus and Adonis*, carefully and correctly printed, and sold "at the signe of the white Greyhound," the bookshop of a respectable bookseller named John Harrison. The poem is dedicated to the third earl of Southampton, then in his twentieth year and recognized at court as a most brilliant and promising youth. In the dedication, printed below, Shakespeare calls the poem "the first heire of my inuention," by which he probably means, disregarding his plays, that it is his first publication or composition as a poet. The epistle is formal and diffident to such a degree that it seems to imply that the dedication was made without Southampton's definite permission. *Venus and Adonis* is composed in a popular and relatively simple six-line iambic stanza rhyming *ababcc*.

SOURCES

In this poem Shakespeare is writing as a courtly poet and following the latest vogue in fashionable literature. Marlowe, who died in 1593, had written a gorgeously worded amatory poem on an Ovidian theme, *Hero and Leander*, left unfinished at his death. It was published in 1598, and supplied the same year with a continuation from the hand of George Chapman. This poem Shakespeare must have known in manuscript; for though some critics have thought that *Venus and Adonis* is the earlier poem, the fact is probably the other way. If so, Shakespeare may have drawn a suggestion for his poem from the following lines from Marlowe:

At Sestos Hero dwelt; Hero the fair,
Whom young Apollo courted for her hair,
And offer'd as a dower his burning throne,
Where she should sit for men to gaze upon.

The outside of her garments were of lawn,
The lining purple silk, with gilt stars drawn;
Her wide sleeves green, and bordered with a grove,
Where Venus in her naked glory strove
To please the careless and disdainful eyes
Of proud Adonis, that before her lies.

In 1589 Thomas Lodge's *Glaucus and Scilla* had appeared under the title *Scillaes Metamorphosis*. Shakespeare drew more than a suggestion from this poem. In it an amorous nymph courts an indifferent swain much as Venus courts Adonis in Shakespeare's poem.[2] The situations are the same, and there are a number of parallels in expression. Both poems are written in sestinas; that is, in five-foot iambic verses grouped in stanzas of six lines each, rhyming *ababcc*.

The suggestion of the amatory Venus and the reluctant Adonis which characterizes Shakespeare's treatment of the theme might have come even better from Henry Chettle's "Sheepheard's Song of Venus and Adonis," provided that the poem antedates *Venus and Adonis*, as there is a fair reason to think that it does.

There were a good many poems of the same genre, including Drayton's *Endimion and Phoebe* and Daniel's *Complaint of Rosamond* (1592), in England, and many on the continent of Europe. Shakespeare made use of the *Metamorphoses* of Ovid for his main theme and for several minor parts. It has also been suggested that the story of the wooing of Adonis has been deepened in its passion by use of another tale in the same poem, that of Salmacis and Hermaphroditus.

COLERIDGE AND *Venus and Adonis*

Venus and Adonis is, as Shakespeare professed it to be, the poem of a beginner. So great is the poem in its promise that none but a Shakespeare could have realized it in his maturity. Coleridge saw this, and in his brief section on "Shakespeare, a Poet Generally" in *Notes and Lectures upon Shakespeare* he selects *Venus and Adonis* to show that Shakespeare possessed "the chief, if not every requisite of a poet—deep feeling and exquisite sense of beauty, both as exhibited to the eye in the combinations of form and to the ear in sweet and appropriate melody; that these feelings were under the command of his own will; that in his very first productions he projected his mind out of his own particular being, and felt, and made others feel, on subjects no way connected with himself, except by force of contemplation and that sublime faculty by which a great mind becomes that on which it meditates." "To this," he says later, "must be added that affectionate love of nature and natural objects, without which no man could have observed so steadily, or painted so truly and passionately, the very minutest beauties of the external world." He then quotes lines 679-708 from *Venus and Adonis*. Coleridge says further, "In this beautiful poem there is an endless activity of thought in all the possible associations of thought with thought, thought with feeling, or with words, of feelings with feelings, and of words with words," quoting this stanza, the first in the poem:

Even as the sun with purple-colour'd face
Had ta'en his last leave of the weeping morn,
Rose-cheek'd Adonis hied him to the chase;
Hunting he loved, but love he laugh'd to scorn;
Sick-thoughted Venus makes amain unto him,
And like a bold-faced suitor 'gins to woo him.

THE RENAISSANCE IDEAL OF LOVE

Perhaps the key to *Venus and Adonis* may be found in the Renaissance doctrine that poetry is imitation and that from this imitation men may learn virtuous action. Love governed by reason was a good, and, according to the Aristotelian doctrine of the golden mean, it was as bad to be excessively abstemious as to be excessively indulgent. Ignorance was not to be tolerated, for only true knowledge could enable man to lead a virtuous life. Temperance, not abnegation, was the perfect virtue in love as in all else. Venus is a goddess and teaches youth, all youth through Adonis, the beauty in love and life. Adonis says in the poem that he is too young to have experienced love. He knows no kind of love but lust, which is misdirected and unrestrained love. Venus expresses the Platonic idea that love is a desire to unite with the beautiful and to bring forth what is beautiful, an idea that pervaded the Renaissance. Adonis is a young man insensible to the caresses of transcendent beauty. He strives to draw a line between the purer and the grosser part of love, prescribing bounds to each. He will have none of love, whereas in his own world he indulges in the excessive gratification of his enjoyment of sports. Shakespeare did not mean to recommend continence as a virtue or to reject it in favor of licentiousness, although perhaps many readers in his age and since have thought that he did. If one regards Venus as a goddess sent to tempt "the fairest of Nature's flowers" whom all mortal women have failed to move, she symbolizes the potentialities of the completely virtuous life. If Adonis had learned the lesson of love, he might have lived his life to its end. He regards the passions as the potential enemy of the rational soul; he has not learned that love, a natural impulse, is essentially good and can lead to virtue as well as to vice. He cannot see Venus as an approach to celestial beauty; and, because she cannot persuade him that she is Love not lust, he goes to his death. Beauty dies with Adonis; he has failed to learn the lesson of youth. Just before Venus, weary of the world of mortals, flies away to Paphos, she prophesies the sorrow and heartache that will henceforth be attendant on earthly love.

It is possible to read the poem, not as an exposition or glorification of sensual love, but as an interpretation of the Renaissance ideal of love on the level of the good that love can bring to the human soul.

[2]Carleton Brown, Introduction to *Venus and Adonis, The Rape of Lucrece and Other Poems* (1913), pp. x-xii.

Venus and Adonis

'Vilia miretur vulgus; mihi flavus Apollo
Pocula Castalia plena ministret aqua.'

TO THE

RIGHT HONOURABLE
HENRY WRIOTHESLY,

EARL OF SOUTHAMPTON,
AND BARON OF TICHFIELD.

RIGHT HONOURABLE

I KNOW not how I shall offend in dedicating
my unpolished lines to your lordship, nor how
the world will censure me for choosing so
strong a prop to support so weak a burden:
only if your honour seem but pleased, I
account myself highly praised, and vow to
take advantage of all idle hours, till I have
honoured you with some graver labour. But
if the first heir of my invention prove deformed, I shall be sorry it had so noble a godfather, and never after ear so barren a land, for
fear it yield me still so bad a harvest. I leave it to
your honourable survey, and your honour to
your heart's content; which I wish may always
answer your own wish and the world's hopeful
expectation.

Your honour's in all duty,

WILLIAM SHAKESPEARE.

Even as the sun with purple-colour'd face
Had ta'en his last leave of the weeping morn,
Rose-cheek'd Adonis hied him to the chase;
Hunting he loved, but love he laugh'd to scorn;
 Sick-thoughted Venus makes amain unto him,
 And like a bold-faced suitor 'gins to woo him.

'Thrice-fairer than myself,' thus she began,
'The field's chief flower, sweet above compare,
Stain to all nymphs, more lovely than a man,
More white and red than doves or roses are;   10
 Nature that made thee, with herself at strife,
 Saith that the world hath ending with thy life.

'Vouchsafe, thou wonder, to alight thy steed,
And rein his proud head to the saddle-bow;
If thou wilt deign this favour, for thy meed
A thousand honey secrets shalt thou know:
 Here come and sit, where never serpent hisses,
 And being set, I'll smother thee with kisses;

'And yet not cloy thy lips with loathed satiety,
But rather famish them amid their plenty,   20
Making them red and pale with fresh variety,
Ten kisses short as one, one long as twenty:
 A summer's day will seem an hour but short,
 Being wasted in such time-beguiling sport.'

With this she seizeth on his sweating palm,
The precedent of pith and livelihood,
And trembling in her passion, calls it balm,
Earth's sovereign salve to do a goddess good:
 Being so enraged, desire doth lend her force
 Courageously to pluck him from his horse.   30

Over one arm the lusty courser's rein,
Under her other was the tender boy,
Who blush'd and pouted in a dull disdain,
With leaden appetite, unapt to toy;
 She red and hot as coals of glowing fire,
 He red for shame, but frosty in desire.

The studded bridle on a ragged bough
Nimbly she fastens:—O, how quick is love!—
The steed is stalled up, and even now
To tie the rider she begins to prove: 40
 Backward she push'd him, as she would be thrust,
 And govern'd him in strength, though not in lust.

So soon was she along as he was down,
Each leaning on their elbows and their hips:
Now doth she stroke his cheek, now doth he frown,
And 'gins to chide, but soon she stops his lips;
 And kissing speaks, with lustful language broken,
 'If thou wilt chide, thy lips shall never open.'

He burns with bashful shame: she with her tears
Doth quench the maiden burning of his cheeks: 50
Then with her windy sighs and golden hairs
To fan and blow them dry again she seeks:
 He saith she is immodest, blames her 'miss;
 What follows more she murders with a kiss.

Even as an empty eagle, sharp by fast,
Tires with her beak on feathers, flesh and bone,
Shaking her wings, devouring all in haste,
Till either gorge be stuff'd or prey be gone;
 Even so she kissed his brow, his cheek, his chin,
 And where she ends she doth anew begin.   60

Forced to content, but never to obey,
Panting he lies and breatheth in her face;
She feedeth on the steam as on a prey,
And calls it heavenly moisture, air of grace;
 Wishing her cheeks were gardens full of flowers,
 So they were dew'd with such distilling showers.

*Venus
and Adonis*

427

MOTTO: **Vilia miretur,** etc. Let the base vulgar admire trash; to me
golden-haired Apollo shall serve goblets filled from the Castalian
spring (Ovid's *Amores*).
DEDICATION: **Henry Wriothesly, Earl of Southampton,** a popular
and brilliant young gentleman of nineteen years, already prominent at
court. Subsequent dedications by Shakespeare and others indicate that
he was a genuinely devoted patron of literature throughout his life.
7. **praised,** appraised. 10. **the first . . . invention.** This phrase has been
variously interpreted to mean Shakespeare's first written work, his
first printed work, his first "invented" work (recognizing that the plots
of his plays were unoriginal), his first work independent of collaborators,
his first "literary" work (recognizing plays to be unliterary in the
Elizabethan sense). The last is the most probable interpretation.
12. **ear,** plough, till.
THE POEM. 1. **purple-colour'd,** i.e., red. 5. **Sick-thoughted,**
oppressed with desire. **makes amain,** hastens. 9. **Stain to,** eclipsing.
11-12. **Nature . . . life,** nature strove to surpass herself in making her
masterpiece, Adonis, and if he dies will cease to work (Pooler). 25-26.
sweating . . . livelihood. Cf. *Othello,* III, iv, 36-43. 29. **enraged,**
ardent. 34. **toy,** dally amorously; see glossary. 39. **stalled,** fastened,
secured. 53. **'miss,** amiss, offense. 55. **by fast,** as a result of
fasting. 56. **Tires,** tears, feeds upon ravenously. 61. **content,**
acquiesce.

Look, how a bird lies tangled in a net,
So fasten'd in her arms Adonis lies;
Pure shame and awed resistance made him fret,
Which bred more beauty in his angry eyes: 70
    Rain added to a river that is rank
    Perforce will force it overflow the bank.

Still she entreats, and prettily entreats,
For to a pretty ear she tunes her tale;
Still is he sullen, still he lours and frets,
'Twixt crimson shame and anger ashy-pale:
    Being red, she loves him best; and being white,
    Her best is better'd with a more delight.

Look how he can, she cannot choose but love;
And by her fair immortal hand she swears,   80
From his soft bosom never to remove,
Till he take truce with her contending tears,
    Which long have rain'd, making her cheeks all wet;
    And one sweet kiss shall pay this countless debt.

Upon this promise did he raise his chin,
Like a dive-dapper peering through a wave,
Who, being look'd on, ducks as quickly in;
So offers he to give what she did crave;
    But when her lips were ready for his pay,
    He winks, and turns his lips another way.   90

Never did passenger in summer's heat
More thirst for drink than she for this good turn.
Her help she sees, but help she cannot get;
She bathes in water, yet her fire must burn:
    'O, pity,' 'gan she cry, 'flint-hearted boy!
    'Tis but a kiss I beg; why art thou coy?

'I have been woo'd, as I entreat thee now,
Even by the stern and direful god of war,
Whose sinewy neck in battle ne'er did bow,
Who conquers where he comes in every jar;   100
    Yet hath he been my captive and my slave,
    And begg'd for that which thou unask'd shalt have.

'Over my altars hath he hung his lance,
His batter'd shield, his uncontrolled crest,
And for my sake hath learn'd to sport and dance,
To toy, to wanton, dally, smile and jest,
    Scorning his churlish drum and ensign red,
    Making my arms his field, his tent my bed.

'Thus he that overruled I oversway'd,
Leading him prisoner in a red-rose chain: 110
Strong-tempered steel his stronger strength obey'd,
Yet was he servile to my coy disdain.
    O, be not proud, nor brag not of thy might,
    For mastering her that foil'd the god of fight!

'Touch but my lips with those fair lips of thine,—
Though mine be not so fair, yet are they red—
The kiss shall be thine own as well as mine.
What seest thou in the ground? hold up thy head:
    Look in mine eye-balls, there thy beauty lies;
    Then why not lips on lips, since eyes in eyes?   120

'Art thou ashamed to kiss? then wink again,
And I will wink; so shall the day seem night;
Love keeps his revels where there are but twain;
Be bold to play, our sport is not in sight:
    These blue-vein'd violets whereon we lean
    Never can blab, nor know not what we mean.

'The tender spring upon thy tempting lip
Shows thee unripe; yet mayst thou well be tasted:
Make use of time, let not advantage slip;
Beauty within itself should not be wasted: 130
    Fair flowers that are not gather'd in their prime
    Rot and consume themselves in little time.

'Were I hard-favour'd, foul, or wrinkled-old,
Ill-nurtured, crooked, churlish, harsh in voice,
O'erworn, despised, rheumatic and cold,
Thick-sighted, barren, lean and lacking juice,
    Then mightst thou pause, for then I were not for
        thee;
    But having no defects, why dost abhor me?

'Thou canst not see one wrinkle in my brow;
Mine eyes are gray and bright and quick in turning;
My beauty as the spring doth yearly grow,   141
My flesh is soft and plump, my marrow burning;
    My smooth moist hand, were it with thy hand felt,
    Would in thy palm dissolve, or seem to melt.

'Bid me discourse, I will enchant thine ear,
Or, like a fairy, trip upon the green,
Or, like a nymph, with long dishevell'd hair,
Dance on the sands, and yet no footing seen:
    Love is a spirit all compact of fire,
    Not gross to sink, but light, and will aspire.   150

'Witness this primrose bank whereon I lie;
These forceless flowers like sturdy trees support me;
Two strengthless doves will draw me through the sky,
From morn till night, even where I list to sport me:
    Is love so light, sweet boy, and may it be
    That thou shouldst think it heavy unto thee?

'Is thine own heart to thine own face affected?
Can thy right hand seize love upon thy left?
Then woo thyself, be of thyself rejected,
Steal thine own freedom and complain on theft.   160
    Narcissus so himself himself forsook,
    And died to kiss his shadow in the brook.

'Torches are made to light, jewels to wear,
Dainties to taste, fresh beauty for the use,
Herbs for their smell, and sappy plants to bear;
Things growing to themselves are growth's abuse:
    Seeds spring from seeds and beauty breedeth
        beauty;
    Thou wast begot; to get it is thy duty.

'Upon the earth's increase why shouldst thou feed,
Unless the earth with thy increase be fed?   170
By law of nature thou art bound to breed,

69. **awed resistance,** resistance which arises from modest timidity (Delius). 86. **dive-dapper,** the dabchick, a common English water bird. 90. **winks,** to shut the eyes or to have them closed (most editors); Lee and W. J. Craig thought the word akin etymologically to "wince"; see glossary. 91. **passenger,** wayfarer. 104. **uncontrolled,** unconquered, i.e., never bowed in acknowledgment to a superior. 131-

132. **Fair . . . time,** a conventional idea in the love poetry of the Renaissance, found in the verse of the Pléiades and other poets; perhaps the best known expression of it in English is Robert Herrick's "Gather ye rosebuds while ye may." 136. **Thick-sighted,** dim-eyed. 148. **footing,** footprints. 150. **aspire,** rise. 161. **Narcissus . . . forsook,** allusion to the story of the beautiful youth who fell in love with his

That thine may live when thou thyself art dead;
  And so, in spite of death, thou dost survive,
  In that thy likeness still is left alive.'

By this the love-sick queen began to sweat,
For where they lay the shadow had forsook them,
And Titan, tired in the mid-day heat,
With burning eye did hotly overlook them;
  Wishing Adonis had his team to guide,
  So he were like him and by Venus' side.   180

And now Adonis, with a lazy spright,
And with a heavy, dark, disliking eye,
His louring brows o'erwhelming his fair sight,
Like misty vapours when they blot the sky,
  Souring his cheeks cries 'Fie, no more of love!
  The sun doth burn my face; I must remove.'

'Ay me,' quoth Venus, 'young, and so unkind?
What bare excuses makest thou to be gone!
I'll sigh celestial breath, whose gentle wind
Shall cool the heat of this descending sun: 190
  I'll make a shadow for thee of my hairs;
  If they burn too, I'll quench them with my tears.

'The sun that shines from heaven shines but warm,
And, lo, I lie between that sun and thee:
The heat I have from thence doth little harm,
Thine eye darts forth the fire that burneth me;
  And were I not immortal, life were done
  Between this heavenly and earthly sun.

'Art thou obdurate, flinty, hard as steel,
Nay, more than flint, for stone at rain relenteth?   200
Art thou a woman's son, and canst not feel
What 'tis to love? how want of love tormenteth?
  O, had thy mother borne so hard a mind,
  She had not brought forth thee, but died unkind.

'What am I, that thou shouldst contemn me this?
Or what great danger dwells upon my suit?
What were thy lips the worse for one poor kiss?
Speak, fair; but speak fair words, or else be mute:
  Give me one kiss, I'll give it thee again,
  And one for interest, if thou wilt have twain.   210

'Fie, lifeless picture, cold and senseless stone,
Well-painted idol, image dull and dead,
Statue contenting but the eye alone,
Thing like a man, but of no woman bred!
  Thou art no man, though of a man's complexion,
  For men will kiss even by their own direction.'

This said, impatience chokes her pleading tongue,
And swelling passion doth provoke a pause;
Red cheeks and fiery eyes blaze forth her wrong;
Being judge in love, she cannot right her cause: 220
  And now she weeps, and now she fain would speak,
  And now her sobs do her intendments break.

Sometimes she shakes her head and then his hand,

Now gazeth she on him, now on the ground;
Sometimes her arms infold him like a band:
She would, he will not in her arms be bound;
  And when from thence he struggles to be gone,
  She locks her lily fingers one in one.

'Fondling,' she saith, 'since I have hemm'd thee here
Within the circuit of this ivory pale,   230
I'll be a park, and thou shalt be my deer;
Feed where thou wilt, on mountain or in dale:
  Graze on my lips; and if those hills be dry,
  Stray lower, where the pleasant fountains lie.

'Within this limit is relief enough,
Sweet bottom-grass and high delightful plain,
Round rising hillocks, brakes obscure and rough,
To shelter thee from tempest and from rain:
  Then be my deer, since I am such a park;   239
  No dog shall rouse thee, though a thousand bark.'

At this Adonis smiles as in disdain,
That in each cheek appears a pretty dimple:
Love made those hollows, if himself were slain,
He might be buried in a tomb so simple;
  Foreknowing well, if there he came to lie,
  Why, there Love lived and there he could not die.

These lovely caves, these round enchanting pits,
Open'd their mouths to swallow Venus' liking.
Being mad before, how doth she now for wits?
Struck dead at first, what needs a second striking?   250
  Poor queen of love, in thine own law forlorn,
  To love a cheek that smiles at thee in scorn!

Now which way shall she turn? what shall she say?
Her words are done, her woes the more increasing;
The time is spent, her object will away,
And from her twining arms doth urge releasing.
  'Pity,' she cries, 'some favour, some remorse!'
  Away he springs and hasteth to his horse.

But, lo, from forth a copse that neighbours by,
A breeding jennet, lusty, young and proud,   260
Adonis' trampling courser doth espy,
And forth she rushes, snorts and neighs aloud:
  The strong-neck'd steed, being tied unto a tree,
  Breaketh his rein, and to her straight goes he.

Imperiously he leaps, he neighs, he bounds,
And now his woven girths he breaks asunder;
The bearing earth with his hard hoof he wounds,
Whose hollow womb resounds like heaven's thunder;
  The iron bit he crusheth 'tween his teeth,
  Controlling what he was controlled with.   270

His ears up-prick'd; his braided hanging mane
Upon his compass'd crest now stand on end;
His nostrils drink the air, and forth again,
As from a furnace, vapours doth he send:
  His eye, which scornfully glisters like fire,
  Shows his hot courage and his high desire.

Venus
and Adonis

429

---

reflection and, for standing over a pool admiring himself, was punished
by being changed into a flower. 163-174. **Torches . . . alive.** The first
seventeen of Shakespeare's sonnets are based on this notion of beauty's
responsibility for perpetuating itself. 177. **tired,** attired. 183. **o'erwhelming,** overhanging, so as to cover. **sight,** eyes. 185. **Souring,**
looking sullen. 188. **bare,** shamelessly inadequate (Pooler). 205.

contemn, refuse scornfully. 219. **blaze,** metaphorical, her eyes appear
to burn. 222. **intendments,** intention to speak. 236. **bottom-grass,**
grass growing in low valleys. 240. **rouse,** to cause to stir from his
lair. 243. **if,** so that if. 260. **jennet,** small Spanish horse. 272.
compass'd, arched by clipping (Pooler).

Sometime he trots, as if he told the steps,
With gentle majesty and modest pride;
Anon he rears upright, curvets and leaps,
As who should say 'Lo, thus my strength is tried,   280
    And this I do to captivate the eye
    Of the fair breeder that is standing by.'

What recketh he his rider's angry stir,
His flattering 'Holla,' or his 'Stand, I say'?
What cares he now for curb or pricking spur?
For rich caparisons or trapping gay?
    He sees his love, and nothing else he sees,
    For nothing else with his proud sight agrees.

Look, when a painter would surpass the life,
In limning out a well-proportion'd steed,   290
His art with nature's workmanship at strife,
As if the dead the living should exceed;
    So did this horse excel a common one
    In shape, in courage, colour, pace and bone.

Round-hoof'd, short-jointed, fetlocks shag and long,
Broad breast, full eye, small head and nostril wide,
High crest, short ears, straight legs and passing strong,
Thin mane, thick tail, broad buttock, tender hide:
    Look, what a horse should have he did not lack,
    Save a proud rider on so proud a back.   300

Sometime he scuds far off and there he stares;
Anon he starts at stirring of a feather;
To bid the wind a base he now prepares,
And whether he run or fly they know not whether;
    For through his mane and tail the high wind sings,
    Fanning the hairs, who wave like feather'd wings.

He looks upon his love and neighs unto her;
She answers him as if she knew his mind:
Being proud, as females are, to see him woo her,
She puts on outward strangeness, seems unkind,   310
    Spurns at his love and scorns the heat he feels,
    Beating his kind embracements with her heels.

Then, like a melancholy malcontent,
He vails his tail that, like a falling plume,
Cool shadow to his melting buttock lent:
He stamps and bites the poor flies in his fume.
    His love, perceiving how he is enraged,
    Grew kinder, and his fury was assuaged.

His testy master goeth about to take him;
When, lo, the unback'd breeder, full of fear,   320
Jealous of catching, swiftly doth forsake him,
With her the horse, and left Adonis there:
    As they were mad, unto the wood they hie them,
    Out-stripping crows that strive to over-fly them.

All swoln with chafing, down Adonis sits,
Banning his boisterous and unruly beast:
And now the happy season once more fits,
That love-sick Love by pleading may be blest;
    For lovers say, the heart hath treble wrong
    When it is barr'd the aidance of the tongue.   330

An oven that is stopp'd, or river stay'd,
Burneth more hotly, swelleth with more rage:
So of concealed sorrow may be said;
Free vent of words love's fire doth assuage;
    But when the heart's attorney once is mute,
    The client breaks, as desperate in his suit.

He sees her coming, and begins to glow,
Even as a dying coal revives with wind,
And with his bonnet hides his angry brow;
Looks on the dull earth with disturbed mind,   340
    Taking no notice that she is so nigh,
    For all askance he holds her in his eye.

O, what a sight it was, wistly to view
How she came stealing to the wayward boy!
To note the fighting conflict of her hue,
How white and red each other did destroy!
    But now her cheek was pale, and by and by
    It flash'd forth fire, as lightning from the sky.

Now was she just before him as he sat,
And like a lowly lover down she kneels;   350
With one fair hand she heaveth up his hat,
Her other tender hand his fair cheek feels:
    His tenderer cheek receives her soft hand's print,
    As apt as new-fall'n snow takes any dint.

O, what a war of looks was then between them!
Her eyes petitioners to his eyes suing;
His eyes saw her eyes as they had not seen them;
Her eyes woo'd still, his eyes disdain'd the wooing:
    And all this dumb play had his acts made plain
    With tears, which, chorus-like, her eyes did rain.   360

Full gently now she takes him by the hand,
A lily prison'd in a gaol of snow,
Or ivory in an alabaster band;
So white a friend engirts so white a foe:
    This beauteous combat, wilful and unwilling,
    Show'd like two silver doves that sit a-billing.

Once more the engine of her thoughts began:
'O fairest mover on this mortal round,
Would thou wert as I am, and I a man,
My heart all whole as thine, thy heart my wound;   370
    For one sweet look thy help I would assure thee,
    Though nothing but my body's bane would cure
        thee.'

'Give me my hand,' saith he, 'why dost thou feel it?'
'Give me my heart,' saith she, 'and thou shalt have it;
O, give it me, lest thy hard heart do steel it,
And being steel'd, soft sighs can never grave it:
    Then love's deep groans I never shall regard,
    Because Adonis' heart hath made mine hard.'

'For shame,' he cries, 'let go, and let me go;
My day's delight is past, my horse is gone,   380
And 'tis your fault I am bereft him so:
I pray you hence, and leave me here alone;
    For all my mind, my thought, my busy care,
    Is how to get my palfrey from the mare.'

277. told, numbered; see glossary. 303. bid the wind a base, challenge the wind, metaphor from the boys' game of prisoner's base. 304. whether, which of two. 310. strangeness, seeming coyness. 319. goeth about, makes an effort. 326. Banning, cursing. 335. heart's

attorney, i.e., the tongue. 343. wistly, earnestly (Rolfe); attentively (Schmidt); steadily (Pooler); intently (*NED*); possibly knowingly. 367. engine of her thoughts, i.e., her tongue; cf. *Titus Andronicus*, III, i, 82-83. 370. thy heart my wound, thy heart wounded as mine is

Thus she replies: 'Thy palfrey, as he should,
Welcomes the warm approach of sweet desire:
Affection is a coal that must be cool'd;
Else, suffer'd, it will set the heart on fire:
  The sea hath bounds, but deep desire hath none;
  Therefore no marvel though thy horse be gone.   390

'How like a jade he stood, tied to the tree,
Servilely master'd with a leathern rein!
But when he saw his love, his youth's fair fee,
He held such petty bondage in disdain;
  Throwing the base thong from his bending crest,
  Enfranchising his mouth, his back, his breast.

'Who sees his true-love in her naked bed,
Teaching the sheets a whiter hue than white,
But, when his glutton eye so full hath fed,
His other agents aim at like delight?   400
  Who is so faint, that dares not be so bold
  To touch the fire, the weather being cold?

'Let me excuse thy courser, gentle boy;
And learn of him, I heartily beseech thee,
To take advantage on presented joy;
Though I were dumb, yet his proceedings teach thee:
  O, learn to love; the lesson is but plain,
  And once made perfect, never lost again.'

'I know not love,' quoth he, 'nor will not know it,
Unless it be a boar, and then I chase it;   410
'Tis much to borrow, and I will not owe it;
My love to love is love but to disgrace it;
  For I have heard it is a life in death,
  That laughs and weeps, and all but with a breath.

'Who wears a garment shapeless and unfinish'd?
Who plucks the bud before one leaf put forth?
If springing things be any jot diminish'd,
They wither in their prime, prove nothing worth:
  The colt that's back'd and burden'd being young
  Loseth his pride and never waxeth strong.   420

'You hurt my hand with wringing; let us part,
And leave this idle theme, this bootless chat:
Remove your siege from my unyielding heart;
To love's alarms it will not ope the gate:
  Dismiss your vows, your feigned tears, your flattery;
  For where a heart is hard they make no battery.'

'What! canst thou talk?' quoth she, 'hast thou a
  tongue?
O, would thou hadst not, or I had no hearing!
Thy mermaid's voice hath done me double wrong;
I had my load before, now press'd with bearing: 430
  Melodious discord, heavenly tune harsh-sounding,
  Ear's deep-sweet music, and heart's deep-sore
    wounding.

'Had I no eyes but ears, my ears would love
That inward beauty and invisible;
Or were I deaf, thy outward parts would move
Each part in me that were but sensible:
  Though neither eyes nor ears, to hear nor see,
  Yet should I be in love by touching thee.

'Say, that the sense of feeling were bereft me,
And that I could not see, nor hear, nor touch,   440
And nothing but the very smell were left me,
Yet would my love to thee be still as much;
  For from the stillitory of thy face excelling
  Comes breath perfumed that breedeth love by
    smelling.

'But, O, what banquet wert thou to the taste,
Being nurse and feeder of the other four!
Would they not wish the feast might ever last,
And bid Suspicion double-lock the door,
  Lest Jealousy, that sour unwelcome guest,
  Should, by his stealing in, disturb the feast?'   450

Once more the ruby-colour'd portal open'd,
Which to his speech did honey passage yield;
Like a red morn, that ever yet betoken'd
Wreck to the seaman, tempest to the field,
  Sorrow to shepherds, woe unto the birds,
  Gusts and foul flaws to herdmen and to herds.

This ill presage advisedly she marketh:
Even as the wind is hush'd before it raineth,
Or as the wolf doth grin before he barketh,
Or as the berry breaks before it staineth,   460
  Or like the deadly bullet of a gun,
  His meaning struck her ere his words begun.

And at his look she flatly falleth down,
For looks kill love and love by looks reviveth;
A smile recures the wounding of a frown;
But blessed bankrupt, that by love so thriveth!
  The silly boy, believing she is dead,
  Claps her pale cheek, till clapping makes it red;

And all amazed brake off his late intent,
For sharply he did think to reprehend her,   470
Which cunning love did wittily prevent:
Fair fall the wit that can so well defend her!
  For on the grass she lies as she were slain,
  Till his breath breatheth life in her again.

He wrings her nose, he strikes her on the cheeks,
He bends her fingers, holds her pulses hard,
He chafes her lips; a thousand ways he seeks
To mend the hurt that his unkindness marr'd:
  He kisses her; and she, by her good will,
  Will never rise, so he will kiss her still.   480

The night of sorrow now is turn'd to day:
Her two blue windows faintly she up-heaveth,
Like the fair sun, when in his fresh array
He cheers the morn and all the earth relieveth;
  And as the bright sun glorifies the sky,
  So is her face illumined with her eye;

Whose beams upon his hairless face are fix'd,
As if from thence they borrow'd all their shine.
Were never four such lamps together mix'd,
Had not his clouded with his brow's repine;   490
  But hers, which through the crystal tears gave light,
  Shone like the moon in water seen by night.

(Malone); or, possessed of my wound. 372. **bane,** ruin. 376. **grave,**
engrave. 387. **coal . . . cool'd.** The pronunciation was sufficiently
alike to make the word play obvious. 393. **fair fee,** due reward
(Rollins). 412. **My . . . it,** my inclination toward love is only a desire

to render it contemptible (Malone). 430. **press'd,** oppressed; the load
was his indifference, the last straw of his refusal (Pooler). 443.
stillitory, alembic, still. 465. **recures,** restores. 475. **wrings her nose.**
Cf. *2 Henry VI,* III, ii, 34. 490. **repine,** dissatisfaction.

'O, where am I?' quoth she, 'in earth or heaven,
Or in the ocean drench'd, or in the fire?
What hour is this? or morn or weary even?
Do I delight to die, or life desire?
    But now I lived, and life was death's annoy;
    But now I died, and death was lively joy.

'O, thou didst kill me: kill me once again:
Thy eyes' shrewd tutor, that hard heart of thine,   500
Hath taught them scornful tricks and such disdain
That they have murder'd this poor heart of mine;
    And these mine eyes, true leaders to their queen,
    But for thy piteous lips no more had seen.

'Long may they kiss each other, for this cure!
O, never let their crimson liveries wear!
And as they last, their verdure still endure,
To drive infection from the dangerous year!
    That the star-gazers, having writ on death,
    May say, the plague is banish'd by thy breath.   510

'Pure lips, sweet seals in my soft lips imprinted,
What bargains may I make, still to be sealing?
To sell myself I can be well contented,
So thou wilt buy and pay and use good dealing;
    Which purchase if thou make, for fear of slips
    Set thy seal-manual on my wax-red lips.

'A thousand kisses buys my heart from me;
And pay them at thy leisure, one by one.
What is ten hundred touches unto thee?
Are they not quickly told and quickly gone?   520
    Say, for non-payment that the debt should double,
    Is twenty hundred kisses such a trouble?'

'Fair queen,' quoth he, 'if any love you owe me,
Measure my strangeness with my unripe years:
Before I know myself, seek not to know me;
No fisher but the ungrown fry forbears:
    The mellow plum doth fall, the green sticks fast,
    Or being early pluck'd is sour to taste.

'Look, the world's comforter, with weary gait,
His day's hot task hath ended in the west;   530
The owl, night's herald, shrieks, " 'Tis very late;"
The sheep are gone to fold, birds to their nest,
    And coal-black clouds that shadow heaven's light
    Do summon us to part and bid good night.

'Now let me say "Good night," and so say you;
If you will say so, you shall have a kiss.'
'Good night,' quoth she, and, ere he says 'Adieu,'
The honey fee of parting tender'd is:
    Her arms do lend his neck a sweet embrace;
    Incorporate then they seem; face grows to face.   540

Till, breathless, he disjoin'd, and backward drew
The heavenly moisture, that sweet coral mouth,
Whose precious taste her thirsty lips well knew,
Whereon they surfeit, yet complain on drouth:
    He with her plenty press'd, she faint with dearth,
    Their lips together glued, fall to the earth.

Now quick desire hath caught the yielding prey,
And glutton-like she feeds, yet never filleth;
Her lips are conquerors, his lips obey,
Paying what ransom the insulter willeth;   550
    Whose vulture thought doth pitch the price so high,
    That she will draw his lips' rich treasure dry:

And having felt the sweetness of the spoil,
With blindfold fury she begins to forage;
Her face doth reek and smoke, her blood doth boil,
And careless lust stirs up a desperate courage;
    Planting oblivion, beating reason back,
    Forgetting shame's pure blush and honour's wrack.

Hot, faint, and weary, with her hard embracing,   559
Like a wild bird being tamed with too much handling,
Or as the fleet-foot roe that 's tired with chasing,
Or like the froward infant still'd with dandling,
    He now obeys, and now no more resisteth,
    While she takes all she can, not all she listeth.

What wax so frozen but dissolves with tempering,
And yields at last to very light impression?
Things out of hope are compass'd oft with venturing,
Chiefly in love, whose leave exceeds commission:
    Affection faints not like a pale-faced coward,   569
    But then woos best when most his choice is froward.

When he did frown, O, had she then gave over,
Such nectar from his lips she had not suck'd.
Foul words and frowns must not repel a lover;
What though the rose have prickles, yet 'tis pluck'd:
    Were beauty under twenty locks kept fast,
    Yet love breaks through and picks them all at last.

For pity now she can no more detain him;
The poor fool prays her that he may depart:
She is resolved no longer to restrain him;
Bids him farewell, and look well to her heart,   580
    The which, by Cupid's bow she doth protest,
    He carries thence incaged in his breast.

'Sweet boy,' she says, 'this night I'll waste in sorrow,
For my sick heart commands mine eyes to watch.
Tell me, Love's master, shall we meet to-morrow?
Say, shall we? shall we? wilt thou make the match?'
    He tells her, no; to-morrow he intends
    To hunt the boar with certain of his friends.

'The boar!' quoth she; whereat a sudden pale,
Like lawn being spread upon the blushing rose,   590
Usurps her cheek; she trembles at his tale,
And on his neck her yoking arms she throws:
    She sinketh down, still hanging by his neck,
    He on her belly falls, she on her back.

Now is she in the very lists of love,
Her champion mounted for the hot encounter:
All is imaginary she doth prove,
He will not manage her, although he mount her;
    That worse than Tantalus' is her annoy,
    To clip Elysium and to lack her joy.   600

507-508. **verdure . . . year,** may allude to the belief in the wholesome effects of plants in the presence of the sick. 508-510. **infection . . . plague,** a probable allusion to the epidemic of bubonic plague raging in London during 1592-1593. 512. **still to be sealing,** i.e., to continue kissing. 515. **slips,** counterfeit money (Steevens); errors (Feuillerat); probably a quibble on these two meanings. 526. **No . . . forebears,** every fisherman spares the ungrown fry. 540. **Incorporate,** united in one body. 557. **Planting oblivion,** causing forgetfulness of all that he ought to remember (Pooler). 568. **exceeds commission,** goes beyond due warrant (Lee). 599. **Tantalus,** a son of Zeus who was punished by perpetual hunger and thirst with food and drink always in sight. 601. **birds . . . grapes,** allusion to Zeuxis, a Greek painter of the fifth

Even as poor birds, deceived with painted grapes,
Do surfeit by the eye and pine the maw,
Even so she languisheth in her mishaps,
As those poor birds that helpless berries saw.
  The warm effects which she in him finds missing
  She seeks to kindle with continual kissing.

But all in vain; good queen, it will not be:
She hath assay'd as much as may be proved;
Her pleading hath deserved a greater fee;
She 's Love, she loves, and yet she is not loved.   610
  'Fie, fie,' he says, 'you crush me; let me go;
  You have no reason to withhold me so.'

'Thou hadst been gone,' quoth she, 'sweet boy, ere
    this,
But that thou told'st me thou wouldst hunt the boar.
O, be advised! thou know'st not what it is
With javelin's point a churlish swine to gore,
  Whose tushes never sheathed he whetteth still,
  Like to a mortal butcher bent to kill.

'On his bow-back he hath a battle set
Of bristly pikes, that ever threat his foes;   620
His eyes, like glow-worms, shine when he doth fret;
His snout digs sepulchres where'er he goes;
  Being moved, he strikes whate'er is in his way,
  And whom he strikes his crooked tushes slay.

'His brawny sides, with hairy bristles arm'd,
Are better proof than thy spear's point can enter;
His short thick neck cannot be easily harm'd;
Being ireful, on the lion he will venture:
  The thorny brambles and embracing bushes,
  As fearful of him, part, through whom he rushes.   630

'Alas, he nought esteems that face of thine,
To which Love's eyes pay tributary gazes;
Nor thy soft hands, sweet lips and crystal eyne,
Whose full perfection all the world amazes;
  But having thee at vantage,—wondrous dread!—
  Would root these beauties as he roots the mead.

'O, let him keep his loathsome cabin still;
Beauty hath nought to do with such foul fiends:
Come not within his danger by thy will;
They that thrive well take counsel of their friends.   640
  When thou didst name the boar, not to dissemble,
  I fear'd thy fortune, and my joints did tremble.

'Didst thou not mark my face? was it not white?
Saw'st thou not signs of fear lurk in mine eye?
Grew I not faint? and fell I not downright?
Within my bosom, whereon thou dost lie,
  My boding heart pants, beats, and takes no rest,
  But, like an earthquake, shakes thee on my breast.

'For where Love reigns, disturbing Jealousy
Doth call himself Affection's sentinel;   650
Gives false alarms, suggesteth mutiny,
And in a peaceful hour doth cry "Kill, kill!"

Distempering gentle Love in his desire,
  As air and water do abate the fire.

'This sour informer, this bate-breeding spy,
This canker that eats up Love's tender spring,
This carry-tale, dissentious Jealousy,
That sometime true news, sometime false doth bring,
  Knocks at my heart and whispers in mine ear
  That if I love thee, I thy death should fear: 660

'And more than so, presenteth to mine eye
The picture of an angry-chafing boar,
Under whose sharp fangs on his back doth lie
An image like thyself, all stain'd with gore;
  Whose blood upon the fresh flowers being shed
  Doth make them droop with grief and hang the
    head.

'What should I do, seeing thee so indeed,
That tremble at the imagination?
The thought of it doth make my faint heart bleed,
And fear doth teach it divination: 670
  I prophesy thy death, my living sorrow,
  If thou encounter with the boar to-morrow.

'But if thou needs wilt hunt, be ruled by me;
Uncouple at the timorous flying hare,
Or at the fox which lives by subtlety,
Or at the roe which no encounter dare:
  Pursue these fearful creatures o'er the downs,
  And on thy well-breath'd horse keep with thy
    hounds.

'And when thou hast on foot the purblind hare,
Mark the poor wretch, to overshoot his troubles   680
How he outruns the wind and with what care
He cranks and crosses with a thousand doubles:
  The many musets through the which he goes
  Are like a labyrinth to amaze his foes.

'Sometime he runs among a flock of sheep,
To make the cunning hounds mistake their smell,
And sometime where earth-delving conies keep,
To stop the loud pursuers in their yell,
  And sometime sorteth with a herd of deer:
  Danger deviseth shifts; wit waits on fear: 690

'For there his smell with others being mingled,
The hot scent-snuffing hounds are driven to doubt,
Ceasing their clamorous cry till they have singled
With much ado the cold fault cleanly out;
  Then do they spend their mouths: Echo replies,
  As if another chase were in the skies.

'By this, poor Wat, far off upon a hill,
Stands on his hinder legs with listening ear,
To hearken if his foes pursue him still:
Anon their loud alarums he doth hear;   700
  And now his grief may be compared well
  To one sore sick that hears the passing-bell.

*Venus
and Adonis*

433

century B.C., so skillful an artist that birds were said to peck at his
picture of a bunch of grapes.   602. **pine the maw,** starve the stomach.
617. **tushes,** tusks.   639. **Come . . . will,** don't willfully expose yourself to the danger it can inflict.   655. **bate-breeding,** breeding strife.
656. **spring,** young shoot of a plant.   678. **well-breath'd,** sound in
wind.   682. **cranks,** winding paths.   683. **musets,** gaps in hedge or

fence.   687. **conies,** rabbits.   689. **sorteth,** mingles.   694. **cold fault,**
cold or lost scent.   697. **Wat,** a common name applied to the hare,
similar to *Tom* for a cat.   702. **passing-bell,** bell rung in the parish
church whenever a member of the parish died.

'Then shalt thou see the dew-bedabbled wretch
Turn, and return, indenting with the way;
Each envious brier his weary legs doth scratch,
Each shadow makes him stop, each murmur stay:
    For misery is trodden on by many,
    And being low never relieved by any.

'Lie quietly, and hear a little more;
Nay, do not struggle, for thou shalt not rise: 710
To make thee hate the hunting of the boar,
Unlike myself thou hear'st me moralize,
    Applying this to that, and so to so;
    For love can comment upon every woe.

'Where did I leave?' 'No matter where;' quoth he,
'Leave me, and then the story aptly ends:
The night is spent.' 'Why, what of that?' quoth she.
'I am,' quoth he, 'expected of my friends;
    And now 'tis dark, and going I shall fall.'
    'In night,' quoth she, 'desire sees best of all.   720

'But if thou fall, O, then imagine this,
The earth, in love with thee, thy footing trips,
And all is but to rob thee of a kiss.
Rich preys make true men thieves; so do thy lips
    Make modest Dian cloudy and forlorn,
    Lest she should steal a kiss and die forsworn.

'Now of this dark night I perceive the reason:
Cynthia for shame obscures her silver shine,
Till forging Nature be condemn'd of treason,
For stealing moulds from heaven that were divine;   730
    Wherein she framed thee in high heaven's despite,
    To shame the sun by day and her by night.

'And therefore hath she bribed the Destinies
To cross the curious workmanship of nature,
To mingle beauty with infirmities,
And pure perfection with impure defeature,
    Making it subject to the tyranny
    Of mad mischances and much misery;

'As burning fevers, agues pale and faint,
Life-poisoning pestilence and frenzies wood,   740
The marrow-eating sickness, whose attaint
Disorder breeds by heating of the blood:
    Surfeits, imposthumes, grief, and damn'd despair,
    Swear Nature's death for framing thee so fair.

'And not the least of all these maladies
But in one minute's fight brings beauty under:
Both favour, savour, hue and qualities,
Whereat the impartial gazer late did wonder,
    Are on the sudden wasted, thaw'd and done,
    As mountain-snow melts with the midday sun.   750

'Therefore, despite of fruitless chastity,
Love-lacking vestals and self-loving nuns,
That on the earth would breed a scarcity
And barren dearth of daughters and of sons,
    Be prodigal: the lamp that burns by night
    Dries up his oil to lend the world his light.

'What is thy body but a swallowing grave,
Seeming to bury that posterity
Which by the rights of time thou needs must have,
If thou destroy them not in dark obscurity?   760
    If so, the world will hold thee in disdain,
    Sith in thy pride so fair a hope is slain.

'So in thyself thyself art made away;
A mischief worse than civil home-bred strife,
Or theirs whose desperate hands themselves do slay,
Or butcher-sire that reaves his son of life.
    Foul-cankering rust the hidden treasure frets,
    But gold that 's put to use more gold begets.'

'Nay, then,' quoth Adon, 'you will fall again
Into your idle over-handled theme: 770
The kiss I gave you is bestow'd in vain,
And all in vain you strive against the stream;
    For, by this black-faced night, desire's foul nurse,
    Your treatise makes me like you worse and worse.

'If love have lent you twenty thousand tongues,
And every tongue more moving than your own,
Bewitching like the wanton mermaid's songs,
Yet from mine ear the tempting tune is blown;
    For know, my heart stands armed in mine ear,
    And will not let a false sound enter there;   780

'Lest the deceiving harmony should run
Into the quiet closure of my breast;
And then my little heart were quite undone,
In his bedchamber to be barr'd of rest.
    No, lady, no; my heart longs not to groan,
    But soundly sleeps, while now it sleeps alone.

'What have you urged that I cannot reprove?
The path is smooth that leadeth on to danger:
I hate not love, but your device in love,
That lends embracements unto every stranger.   790
    You do it for increase: O strange excuse,
    When reason is the bawd to lust's abuse!

'Call it not love, for Love to heaven is fled,
Since sweating Lust on earth usurp'd his name;
Under whose simple semblance he hath fed
Upon fresh beauty, blotting it with blame;
    Which the hot tyrant stains and soon bereaves,
    As caterpillars do the tender leaves.

'Love comforteth like sunshine after rain,
But Lust's effect is tempest after sun;   800
Love's gentle spring doth always fresh remain,
Lust's winter comes ere summer half be done;
    Love surfeits not, Lust like a glutton dies;
    Love is all truth, Lust full of forged lies.

'More I could tell, but more I dare not say;
The text is old, the orator too green.
Therefore, in sadness, now I will away;
My face is full of shame, my heart of teen:
    Mine ears, that to your wanton talk attended,
    Do burn themselves for having so offended.'   810

704. **indenting,** moving in a zigzag line. 729. **forging,** counterfeiting. 736. **defeature,** disfigurement. 740. **wood,** mad. 743. **imposthumes,** abscesses. 748. **impartial,** indifferent. 769. **you will fall,** not an expression of futurity but of volition; i.e., you are determined to fall (Brown). 774. **treatise,** discourse. 779-784. **my . . . rest,** an applica- tion of the psychological notion of the Elizabethans that the senses were the doors through which the soul was assailed by the several passions. (See Anderson, *Elizabethan Psychology,* pp. 119-120.) 787. **reprove,** refute. 789. **device,** manner of thinking, cast of mind (Schmidt). 808. **teen,** affliction, grief. 813. **laund,** glade. 838. **wise . . . witty,**

With this, he breaketh from the sweet embrace
Of those fair arms which bound him to her breast,
And homeward through the dark laund runs apace;
Leaves Love upon her back deeply distress'd.
  Look, how a bright star shooteth from the sky,
  So glides he in the night from Venus' eye;

Which after him she darts, as one on shore
Gazing upon a late-embarked friend,
Till the wild waves will have him seen no more,
Whose ridges with the meeting clouds contend:　820
  So did the merciless and pitchy night
  Fold in the object that did feed her sight.

Whereat amazed, as one that unaware
Hath dropp'd a precious jewel in the flood,
Or stonish'd as night-wanderers often are,
Their light blown out in some mistrustful wood,
  Even so confounded in the dark she lay,
  Having lost the fair discovery of her way.

And now she beats her heart, whereat it groans,
That all the neighbour caves, as seeming troubled,　830
Make verbal repetition of her moans;
Passion on passion deeply is redoubled:
  'Ay me!' she cries, and twenty times 'Woe, woe!'
  And twenty echoes twenty times cry so.

She marking them begins a wailing note
And sings extemporally a woeful ditty;
How love makes young men thrall and old men dote;
How love is wise in folly, foolish-witty:
  Her heavy anthem still concludes in woe,
  And still the choir of echoes answer so.　840

Her song was tedious and outwore the night,
For lovers' hours are long, though seeming short:
If pleased themselves, others, they think, delight
In such-like circumstance, with such-like sport:
  Their copious stories oftentimes begun
  End without audience and are never done.

For who hath she to spend the night withal
But idle sounds resembling parasites,
Like shrill-tongued tapsters answering every call,
Soothing the humour of fantastic wits?　850
  She says ''Tis so:' they answer all ''Tis so;'
  And would say after her, if she said 'No.'

Lo, here the gentle lark, weary of rest,
From his moist cabinet mounts up on high,
And wakes the morning, from whose silver breast
The sun ariseth in his majesty;
  Who doth the world so gloriously behold
  That cedar-tops and hills seem burnish'd gold.

Venus salutes him with this fair good-morrow:
'O thou clear god, and patron of all light,　860
From whom each lamp and shining star doth borrow
The beauteous influence that makes him bright,
  There lives a son that suck'd an earthly mother,
  May lend thee light, as thou dost lend to other.'

This said, she hasteth to a myrtle grove,
Musing the morning is so much o'erworn,
And yet she hears no tidings of her love:
She hearkens for his hounds and for his horn:
  Anon she hears them chant it lustily,
  And all in haste she coasteth to the cry.　870

And as she runs, the bushes in the way
Some catch her by the neck, some kiss her face,
Some twine about her thigh to make her stay:
She wildly breaketh from their strict embrace,
  Like a milch doe, whose swelling dugs do ache,
  Hasting to feed her fawn hid in some brake.

By this, she hears the hounds are at a bay;
Whereat she starts, like one that spies an adder
Wreathed up in fatal folds just in his way,　879
The fear whereof doth make him shake and shudder;
  Even so the timorous yelping of the hounds
  Appals her senses and her spirit confounds.

For now she knows it is no gentle chase,
But the blunt boar, rough bear, or lion proud,
Because the cry remaineth in one place,
Where fearfully the dogs exclaim aloud:
  Finding their enemy to be so curst,
  They all strain courtesy who shall cope him first.

This dismal cry rings sadly in her ear,
Through which it enters to surprise her heart;　890
Who, overcome by doubt and bloodless fear,
With cold-pale weakness numbs each feeling part:
  Like soldiers, when their captain once doth yield,
  They basely fly and dare not stay the field.

Thus stands she in a trembling ecstasy;
Till, cheering up her senses all dismay'd,
She tells them 'tis a causeless fantasy,
And childish error, that they are afraid;
  Bids them leave quaking, bids them fear no more:—
  And with that word she spied the hunted boar,　900

Whose frothy mouth, bepainted all with red,
Like milk and blood being mingled both together,
A second fear through all her sinews spread,
Which madly hurries her she knows not whither:
  This way she runs, and now she will no further,
  But back retires to rate the boar for murther.

A thousand spleens bear her a thousand ways;
She treads the path that she untreads again;
Her more than haste is mated with delays,
Like the proceedings of a drunken brain,　910
  Full of respects, yet nought at all respecting;
  In hand with all things, nought at all effecting.

Here kennell'd in a brake she finds a hound,
And asks the weary caitiff for his master,
And there another licking of his wound,
'Gainst venom'd sores the only sovereign plaster;
  And here she meets another sadly scowling,
  To whom she speaks, and he replies with howling.

probably a quibbling phrase: love applies its wit to doing foolish
things and is foolish in doing sensible things.　849. **tapsters.** Steevens
notes the episode with the tapster in *1 Henry IV*, II, iv.　854. **cabinet,**
dwelling.　870. **coasteth,** makes progress against obstacles (Onions).
888. **strain courtesy,** be punctiliously polite, stand upon ceremony.

The phrase was not infrequently applied to hounds in the chase (see
Rollins, Variorum).　909. **mated,** confounded, checked (Malone).
911. **nought at all respecting,** i.e., heedless.

When he hath ceased his ill-resounding noise,
Another flap-mouth'd mourner, black and grim,   920
Against the welkin volleys out his voice;
Another and another answer him,
    Clapping their proud tails to the ground below,
    Shaking their scratch'd ears, bleeding as they go.

Look, how the world's poor people are amazed
At apparitions, signs and prodigies,
Whereon with fearful eyes they long have gazed,
Infusing them with dreadful prophecies;
    So she at these sad signs draws up her breath
    And sighing it again, exclaims on Death.   930

'Hard-favour'd tyrant, ugly, meagre, lean,
Hateful divorce of love,'—thus chides she Death,—
'Grim-grinning ghost, earth's worm, what dost thou
    mean
To stifle beauty and to steal his breath,
    Who when he lived, his breath and beauty set
    Gloss on the rose, smell to the violet?

'If he be dead,—O no, it cannot be,
Seeing his beauty, thou shouldst strike at it:—
O yes, it may; thou hast no eyes to see,
But hatefully at random dost thou hit.   940
    Thy mark is feeble age, but thy false dart
    Mistakes that aim and cleaves an infant's heart.

*Venus
and Adonis*

436

'Hadst thou but bid beware, then he had spoke,
And, hearing him, thy power had lost his power.
The Destinies will curse thee for this stroke;
They bid thee crop a weed, thou pluck'st a flower:
    Love's golden arrow at him should have fled,
    And not Death's ebon dart, to strike him dead.

'Dost thou drink tears, that thou provokest such
    weeping?
What may a heavy groan advantage thee?   950
Why hast thou cast into eternal sleeping
Those eyes that taught all other eyes to see?
    Now Nature cares not for thy mortal vigour,
    Since her best work is ruin'd with thy rigour.'

Here overcome, as one full of despair,
She vail'd her eyelids, who, like sluices, stopt
The crystal tide that from her two cheeks fair
In the sweet channel of her bosom dropt;
    But through the flood-gates breaks the silver rain,
    And with his strong course opens them again.   960

O, how her eyes and tears did lend and borrow!
Her eyes seen in the tears, tears in her eye;
Both crystals, where they view'd each other's sorrow,
Sorrow that friendly sighs sought still to dry;
    But like a stormy day, now wind, now rain,
    Sighs dry her cheeks, tears make them wet again.

Variable passions throng her constant woe,
As striving who should best become her grief;
All entertain'd, each passion labours so,
That every present sorrow seemeth chief,   970
    But none is best: then join they all together,
    Like many clouds consulting for foul weather.

By this, far off she hears some huntsman hollo;
A nurse's song ne'er pleased her babe so well:
The dire imagination she did follow
This sound of hope doth labour to expel;
    For now reviving joy bids her rejoice,
    And flatters her it is Adonis' voice.

Whereat her tears began to turn their tide,
Being prison'd in her eye like pearls in glass;   980
Yet sometimes falls an orient drop beside,
Which her cheek melts, as scorning it should pass,
    To wash the foul face of the sluttish ground,
    Who is but drunken when she seemeth drown'd.

O hard-believing love, how strange it seems
Not to believe, and yet too credulous!
Thy weal and woe are both of them extremes;
Despair and hope makes thee ridiculous:
    The one doth flatter thee in thoughts unlikely,
    In likely thoughts the other kills thee quickly.   990

Now she unweaves the web that she hath wrought;
Adonis lives, and Death is not to blame;
It was not she that call'd him all-to naught:
Now she adds honours to his hateful name;
    She clepes him king of graves and grave for kings,
    Imperious supreme of all mortal things.

'No, no,' quoth she, 'sweet Death, I did but jest;
Yet pardon me I felt a kind of fear
When as I met the boar, that bloody beast,
Which knows no pity, but is still severe;   1000
    Then, gentle shadow,—truth I must confess,—
    I rail'd on thee, fearing my love's decease.

''Tis not my fault: the boar provoked my tongue;
Be wreak'd on him, invisible commander;
'Tis he, foul creature, that hath done thee wrong;
I did but act, he 's author of thy slander:
    Grief hath two tongues, and never woman yet
    Could rule them both without ten women's wit.'

Thus hoping that Adonis is alive,
Her rash suspect she doth extenuate;   1010
And that his beauty may the better thrive,
With Death she humbly doth insinuate;
    Tells him of trophies, statues, tombs, and stories
    His victories, his triumphs and his glories.

'O Jove,' quoth she, 'how much a fool was I
To be of such a weak and silly mind
To wail his death who lives and must not die
Till mutual overthrow of mortal kind!
    For he being dead, with him is beauty slain,
    And, beauty dead, black chaos comes again.   1020

'Fie, fie, fond love, thou art so full of fear
As one with treasure laden, hemm'd with thieves;
Trifles, unwitnessed with eye or ear,
Thy coward heart with false bethinking grieves.'
    Even at this word she hears a merry horn,
    Whereat she leaps that was but late forlorn.

---

920. **flap-mouth'd,** having broad, hanging lips. 933. **earth's worm.** Death was always associated with the idea of worms. 953. **mortal vigour,** death-dealing power. 967. **throng,** oppress. 993. **all-to,** en-tirely; so explained by Dyce, who introduced the hyphen; Q: *all to naught;* Kittredge explains *all* as adverbial and defines the idiom *call to naught* as "upbraid as villainous." 995. **clepes,** names. 1010.

As falcon to the lure, away she flies;
The grass stoops not, she treads on it so light;
And in her haste unfortunately spies
The foul boar's conquest on her fair delight;   1030
  Which seen, her eyes, as murder'd with the view,
  Like stars ashamed of day, themselves withdrew;

Or, as the snail, whose tender horns being hit,
Shrinks backward in his shelly cave with pain,
And there, all smother'd up, in shade doth sit,
Long after fearing to creep forth again;
  So, at his bloody view, her eyes are fled
  Into the deep dark cabins of her head:

Where they resign their office and their light
To the disposing of her troubled brain;   1040
Who bids them still consort with ugly night,
And never wound the heart with looks again;
  Who, like a king perplexed in his throne,
  By their suggestion gives a deadly groan,

Whereat each tributary subject quakes;
As when the wind, imprison'd in the ground,
Struggling for passage, earth's foundation shakes,
Which with cold terror doth men's minds confound.
  This mutiny each part doth so surprise   1049
  That from their dark beds once more leap her eyes;

And, being open'd, threw unwilling light
Upon the wide wound that the boar had trench'd
In his soft flank; whose wonted lily white
With purple tears, that his wound wept, was drench'd:
  No flower was nigh, no grass, herb, leaf, or weed,
  But stole his blood and seem'd with him to bleed.

This solemn sympathy poor Venus noteth;
Over one shoulder doth she hang her head;
Dumbly she passions, franticly she doteth;
She thinks he could not die, he is not dead: 1060
  Her voice is stopt, her joints forget to bow;
  Her eyes are mad that they have wept till now.

Upon his hurt she looks so steadfastly,
That her sight dazzling makes the wound seem three;
And then she reprehends her mangling eye,
That makes more gashes where no breach should be:
  His face seems twain, each several limb is doubled;
  For oft the eye mistakes, the brain being troubled.

'My tongue cannot express my grief for one,
And yet,' quoth she, 'behold two Adons dead!   1070
My sighs are blown away, my salt tears gone,
Mine eyes are turn'd to fire, my heart to lead:
  Heavy heart's lead, melt at mine eyes' red fire!
  So shall I die by drops of hot desire.

'Alas, poor world, what treasure hast thou lost!
What face remains alive that 's worth the viewing?
Whose tongue is music now? what canst thou boast
Of things long since, or any thing ensuing?
  The flowers are sweet, their colours fresh and trim;
  But true-sweet beauty lived and died with him.   1080

'Bonnet nor veil henceforth no creature wear!
Nor sun nor wind will ever strive to kiss you:
Having no fair to lose, you need not fear;
The sun doth scorn you and the wind doth hiss you:
  But when Adonis lived, sun and sharp air
  Lurk'd like two thieves, to rob him of his fair:

'And therefore would he put his bonnet on,
Under whose brim the gaudy sun would peep;
The wind would blow it off and, being gone,
Play with his locks: then would Adonis weep;   1090
  And straight, in pity of his tender years,
  They both would strive who first should dry his
    tears.

'To see his face the lion walk'd along
Behind some hedge, because he would not fear him;
To recreate himself when he hath sung,
The tiger would be tame and gently hear him;
  If he had spoke, the wolf would leave his prey
  And never fright the silly lamb that day.

'When he beheld his shadow in the brook,
The fishes spread on it their golden gills;   1100
When he was by, the birds such pleasure took,
That some would sing, some other in their bills
  Would bring him mulberries and ripe-red cherries;
  He fed them with his sight, they him with berries.

'But this foul, grim, and urchin-snouted boar,
Whose downward eye still looketh for a grave,
Ne'er saw the beauteous livery that he wore;
Witness the entertainment that he gave:
  If he did see his face, why then I know
  He thought to kiss him, and hath kill'd him so.   1110

''Tis true, 'tis true; thus was Adonis slain:
He ran upon the boar with his sharp spear,
Who did not whet his teeth at him again,
But by a kiss thought to persuade him there;
  And nuzzling in his flank, the loving swine
  Sheathed unaware the tusk in his soft groin.

'Had I been tooth'd like him, I must confess,
With kissing him I should have kill'd him first;
But he is dead, and never did he bless
My youth with his; the more am I accurst.'   1120
  With this, she falleth in the place she stood,
  And stains her face with his congealed blood.

She looks upon his lips, and they are pale;
She takes him by the hand, and that is cold;
She whispers in his ears a heavy tale,
As if they heard the woeful words she told;
  She lifts the coffer-lids that close his eyes,
  Where, lo, two lamps, burnt out, in darkness lies;

Two glasses, where herself herself beheld
A thousand times, and now no more reflect;   1130
Their virtue lost, wherein they late excell'd,
And every beauty robb'd of his effect:
  'Wonder of time,' quoth she, 'this is my spite,
  That, thou being dead, the day should yet be light.

suspect, suspicion. 1012. **insinuate,** ingratiate herself. 1046. **wind
. . . ground,** the common explanation of earthquakes; cf. *1 Henry IV*,
III, i, 30. 1054. **purple tears,** drops of blood; cf. l. 1. 1105. **urchin-**

snouted, having a snout like a hedgehog.

'Since thou art dead, lo, here I prophesy:
Sorrow on love hereafter shall attend:
It shall be waited on with jealousy,
Find sweet beginning, but unsavoury end,
　Ne'er settled equally, but high or low,
　That all love's pleasure shall not match his woe. 1140

'It shall be fickle, false and full of fraud,
Bud and be blasted in a breathing-while;
The bottom poison, and the top o'erstraw'd
With sweets that shall the truest sight beguile:
　The strongest body shall it make most weak,
　Strike the wise dumb and teach the fool to speak.

'It shall be sparing and too full of riot,
Teaching decrepit age to tread the measures;
The staring ruffian shall it keep in quiet,　1149
Pluck down the rich, enrich the poor with treasures;
　It shall be raging-mad and silly-mild,
　Make the young old, the old become a child.

'It shall suspect where is no cause of fear;
It shall not fear where it should most mistrust;
It shall be merciful and too severe,
And most deceiving when it seems most just;
　Perverse it shall be where it shows most toward,
　Put fear to valour, courage to the coward.

'It shall be cause of war and dire events,
And set dissension 'twixt the son and sire;　1160
Subject and servile to all discontents,
As dry combustious matter is to fire:
　Sith in his prime Death doth my love destroy,
　They that love best their loves shall not enjoy.'

By this, the boy that by her side lay kill'd
Was melted like a vapour from her sight,
And in his blood that on the ground lay spill'd,
A purple flower sprung up, chequer'd with white,
　Resembling well his pale cheeks and the blood　1169
　Which in round drops upon their whiteness stood.

She bows her head, the new-sprung flower to smell,
Comparing it to her Adonis' breath,
And says, within her bosom it shall dwell,
Since he himself is reft from her by death:
　She crops the stalk, and in the breach appears
　Green dropping sap, which she compares to tears.

'Poor flower,' quoth she, 'this was thy father's guise—
Sweet issue of a more sweet-smelling sire—
For every little grief to wet his eyes:
To grow unto himself was his desire,　1180
　And so 'tis thine; but know, it is as good
　To wither in my breast as in his blood.

'Here was thy father's bed, here in my breast;
Thou art the next of blood, and 'tis thy right:
Lo, in this hollow cradle take thy rest,
My throbbing heart shall rock thee day and night:
　There shall not be one minute in an hour
　Wherein I will not kiss my sweet love's flower.'

Thus weary of the world, away she hies,
And yokes her silver doves; by whose swift aid　1190
Their mistress mounted through the empty skies
In her light chariot quickly is convey'd;
　Holding their course to Paphos, where their queen
　Means to immure herself and not be seen.

1142. **breathing-while,** short time.　1143. **o'erstraw'd,** strewn over.
1149. **staring,** looking savage.　1193. **Paphos,** a city in Cypress　where stood a temple to Venus.

From E. Spenser,
"The Shepheardes
Calender," *1586.*

THE
Rape of Lucrece

Venus and Adonis was very popular, running through five editions subsequent to the first by 1602. It was, however, criticized for its supposed exploitation of sensuality; at least we may judge so from a number of references. Gabriel Harvey, for example, noted on the margin of his copy of Speght's Chaucer at some time between 1598 and 1601:

The younger sort takes much delight in Shakespeare's Venus and Adonis; but his Lucrece and his tragedy of Hamlet, Prince of Denmark, have it in them to please the wiser sort.

SOURCES AND PUBLICATION

It may have been in response to this censure that Shakespeare set himself immediately to the writing of Lucrece, or it may have been in fulfillment of his promise to Southampton to honor him with "some graver labour." The poem is professedly written in celebration of the virtue of chastity and treats the story of the ravishment of the Roman Lucretia by the tyrant Tarquin. For his material he went to Ovid in the Fasti, Book II, lines 721-852, and to the Roman History of Livy, Book I, chapters 57-59. He may also have known the story as told by Chaucer in The Legend of Good Women and perhaps he was acquainted with other versions of the tale, which was extremely popular during the Renaissance. The poem was issued in 1594, like Venus and Adonis, from the press of Richard Field; but in this case the name of John Harrison appears as publisher. It is likewise addressed to the earl of Southampton but in a very different tone and couched in language so intimate as to show without question that his attempt to gain not only the nobleman's favor but his friendship had been successful. There is no longer any doubt that his gifts will be received as the gifts of a devoted friend. The substantial fact of these two dedications to the earl of Southampton stands out in the midst of a world of conjecture with regard to the identity of Shakespeare's patrons. On this dedication in cordial terms and on that of Venus and Adonis, which is much more diffident in its approach, has been based, quite naturally, the opinion that Henry Wriothesley, third earl of Southampton, was Shakespeare's patron and that we have in these two epistles information as to the beginning and the growth of an unusual intimacy between them. This intimacy, it is widely believed, finds expression in the Sonnets. In spite of some uncertainty and much difference of opinion, the student may at least hold fast to the facts revealed in the dedications.

Lucrece is a finished and elegant poem written in rhyme royal, a seven-line five-foot iambic stanza rhyming ababbcc. Rhyme royal had been employed by Chaucer, Sackville, and Spenser, and was a long-established English verse form, having greater dignity and sweetness than the six-line stanza of Venus and Adonis. More immediately, Shakespeare borrowed the stanza form and certain important ideas of his poem from Daniel's Complaint of Rosamond, which treats with equal seriousness, though from a different point of view, the theme of chastity.

Lucrece is at once greater and less than Venus and Adonis. It is superior in care and elaboration of workmanship and in perfection of thought, but it lacks the naturalness and the brilliancy of the earlier poem. In spite of greater praises it was less popular and passed through only three editions subsequent to the first during the poet's life. Venus and Adonis is frankly amatory though saved by Shakespeare's coolness and objectivity from the excesses of the form to which it belonged. Lucrece is a formal vindication of chastity, carefully and sincerely wrought, but unrelieved and too long. Both poems are full of episodes and digressions, proceeding by images, conceits, and pictures. They are in this sense hardly to be regarded as narrative poems at all.

But of the two, Venus and Adonis is the more sustained and the better proportioned effort. We would say that it is the more dramatic poem of the two. We must, however, believe that Shakespeare's purpose in the later poem differed from that of the earlier one. It is, in fact, plain that he set out to be moral, and when a Renaissance writer, even Shakespeare, undertook to be moral, he became moralistic or sententious. We know, and Shakespeare showed in practice, that the most potent moral lessons are those which arise out of the representation of the concrete. Thus we say that the first seven hundred lines, up to the commission of Tarquin's crime, are excellent in their depiction of event and in their study of motives in the mind of Tarquin. However, the next thousand lines, in spite of Shakespeare's attempts to beautify them, are monotonous, if not tiresome. The theme they present is static, and yet the woeful plight of poor Lucrece may be the raison d'être of the poem.

This situation gave Shakespeare his chance to write as a Renaissance moral writer. His rhetorical presentations are eloquent and wise, but they are less effective, more remote than similar passages in his dramatic work. In the earlier part of the poem are disquisitions on covetousness (ll. 134-154) and on the duty of sovereigns (ll. 610-637) which, connected as they are with Tarquin's storm-tossed mind, seem more organic than the finer things later in the poem, such as the description of the temple of the soul (ll. 719-728), the description of the covetous man (ll. 854-861), the apostrophes to Opportunity, Time, and Night, and the great pictures of Troy.

The Rape of Lucrece

439

THE

Rape of Lucrece

TO THE

RIGHT HONOURABLE
HENRY WRIOTHESLY,

EARL OF SOUTHAMPTON,
AND BARON OF TICHFIELD.

THE love I dedicate to your lordship is without end; whereof this pamphlet, without beginning, is but a superfluous moiety. The warrant I have of your honourable disposition, not the worth of my untutored lines, makes it assured of acceptance. What I have done is yours; what I have to do is yours; being part in all I have, devoted yours. Were my worth greater, my duty would show greater; meantime, as it is, it is bound to your lordship, to whom I wish long life, still lengthened with all happiness.

Your lordship's in all duty,

WILLIAM SHAKESPEARE.

THE ARGUMENT

LUCIUS TARQUINIUS, for his excessive pride surnamed Superbus, after he had caused his own father-in-law Servius Tullius to be cruelly murdered, and, contrary to the Roman laws and customs, not requiring or staying for the people's suffrages, had possessed himself of the kingdom, went, accompanied with his sons and other noblemen of Rome, to besiege Ardea. During which siege the principal men of the army meeting one evening at the tent of Sextus Tarquinius, the king's son, in their discourses after supper every one commended the virtues of his own wife; among whom Collatinus extolled the incomparable chastity of his wife Lucretia. In that pleasant humour they all posted to Rome; and intending, by their secret and sudden arrival, to make trial of that which every one had before avouched, only Collatinus finds his wife, though it were late in the night, spinning amongst her maids: the other ladies were all found dancing and revelling, or in several disports. Whereupon the noblemen yielded Collatinus the victory, and his wife the fame. At that time Sextus Tarquinius being inflamed with Lucrece' beauty, yet smothering his passions for the present, departed with the rest back to the camp; from whence he shortly after privily withdrew himself, and was, according to his estate, royally entertained and lodged by Lucrece at Collatium. The same night he treacherously stealeth into her chamber, violently ravished her, and early in the morning speedeth away. Lucrece, in this lamentable

plight, hastily dispatcheth messengers, one to Rome for her father, another to the camp for Collatine. They came, the one accompanied with Junius Brutus, the other with Publius Valerius; and finding Lucrece attired in mourning habit, demanded the cause of her sorrow. She, first taking an oath of them for her revenge, revealed the actor, and whole manner of his dealing, and withal suddenly stabbed herself. Which done, with one consent they all vowed to root out the whole hated family of the Tarquins; and bearing the dead body to Rome, Brutus acquainted the people with the doer and manner of the vile deed, with a bitter invective against the tyranny of the king: wherewith the people were so moved, that with one consent and a general acclamation the Tarquins were all exiled, and the state government changed from kings to consuls.

FROM the besieged Ardea all in post,
Borne by the trustless wings of false desire,
Lust-breathed Tarquin leaves the Roman host,
And to Collatium bears the lightless fire
Which, in pale embers hid, lurks to aspire
    And girdle with embracing flames the waist
    Of Collatine's fair love, Lucrece the chaste.

Haply that name of 'chaste' unhappily set
This bateless edge on his keen appetite;
When Collatine unwisely did not let   10
To praise the clear unmatched red and white
Which triumph'd in that sky of his delight,
    Where mortal stars, as bright as heaven's beauties,
    With pure aspects did him peculiar duties.

For he the night before, in Tarquin's tent,
Unlock'd the treasure of his happy state;
What priceless wealth the heavens had him lent
In the possession of his beauteous mate;
Reckoning his fortune at such high-proud rate,
    That kings might be espoused to more fame,   20
    But king nor peer to such a peerless dame.

O happiness enjoy'd but of a few!
And, if possess'd, as soon decay'd and done
As is the morning's silver melting dew
Against the golden splendour of the sun!
An expired date, cancell'd ere well begun:
    Honour and beauty, in the owner's arms,
    Are weakly fortress'd from a world of harms.

Beauty itself doth of itself persuade
The eyes of men without an orator;   30
What needeth then apologies be made,

DEDICATION. 2. **pamphlet,** used by Shakespeare, probably in a self-derogatory sense, as something too slight to be called a book. *Pamphlet* was used in the sixteenth century to designate a work of small bulk. **without beginning,** taken by most commentators to mean that Shakespeare takes the reader *in medias res.* 3 **The warrant I have.** Nicholas Rowe in 1709 recorded on William Davenant's authority that Southampton at one time gave Shakespeare "a thousand Pounds to enable him to go through with a Purchase which he heard he had a mind to." Most commentators are inclined to regard the amount as an exaggeration; most of them acknowledge that this dedication expresses gratitude for favors already received.

THE ARGUMENT. 5. **requiring,** requesting. 22. **disports,** pastimes. 23. **fame,** honorable title. 37. **Junius Brutus.** This is the Brutus

To set forth that which is so singular?
Or why is Collatine the publisher
  Of that rich jewel he should keep unknown
  From thievish ears, because it is his own?

Perchance his boast of Lucrece' sovereignty
Suggested this proud issue of a king;
For by our ears our hearts oft tainted be:
Perchance that envy of so rich a thing,
Braving compare, disdainfully did sting   40
  His high-pitch'd thoughts, that meaner men should
        vaunt
  That golden hap which their superiors want.

But some untimely thought did instigate
His all too timeless speed, if none of those:
His honour, his affairs, his friends, his state,
Neglected all, with swift intent he goes
To quench the coal which in his liver glows.
  O rash false heat, wrapp'd in repentant cold,
  Thy hasty spring still blasts, and ne'er grows old!

When at Collatium this false lord arrived,   50
Well was he welcomed by the Roman dame,
Within whose face beauty and virtue strived
Which of them both should underprop her fame:
When virtue bragg'd, beauty would blush for shame;
  When beauty boasted blushes, in despite
  Virtue would stain that o'er with silver white.

But beauty, in that white intituled,
From Venus' doves doth challenge that fair field:
Then virtue claims from beauty beauty's red,
Which virtue gave the golden age to gild   60
Their silver cheeks, and call'd it then their shield;
  Teaching them thus to use it in the fight,
  When shame assail'd, the red should fence the white.

This heraldry in Lucrece' face was seen,
Argued by beauty's red and virtue's white:
Of either's colour was the other queen,
Proving from world's minority their right:
Yet their ambition makes them still to fight;
  The sovereignty of either being so great,
  That oft they interchange each other's seat.   70

Their silent war of lilies and of roses,
Which Tarquin view'd in her fair face's field,
In their pure ranks his traitor eye encloses;
Where, lest between them both it should be kill'd,
The coward captive vanquished doth yield
  To those two armies that would let him go,
  Rather than triumph in so false a foe.

Now thinks he that her husband's shallow tongue,—
The niggard prodigal that praised her so,—

In that high task hath done her beauty wrong,   80
Which far exceeds his barren skill to show:
Therefore that praise which Collatine doth owe
  Enchanted Tarquin answers with surmise,
  In silent wonder of still-gazing eyes.

This earthly saint, adored by this devil,
Little suspecteth the false worshipper;
For unstain'd thoughts do seldom dream on evil;
Birds never limed no secret bushes fear:
So guiltless she securely gives good cheer
  And reverend welcome to her princely guest,   90
  Whose inward ill no outward harm express'd:

For that he colour'd with his high estate,
Hiding base sin in plaits of majesty;
That nothing in him seem'd inordinate,
Save sometime too much wonder of his eye,
Which, having all, all could not satisfy;
  But, poorly rich, so wanteth in his store,
  That, cloy'd with much, he pineth still for more.

But she, that never coped with stranger eyes,
Could pick no meaning from their parling looks,   100
Nor read the subtle-shining secrecies
Writ in the glassy margents of such books:
She touch'd no unknown baits, nor fear'd no hooks;
  Nor could she moralize his wanton sight,
  More than his eyes were open'd to the light.

He stories to her ears her husband's fame,
Won in the fields of fruitful Italy;
And decks with praises Collatine's high name,
Made glorious by his manly chivalry
With bruised arms and wreaths of victory: 110
  Her joy with heaved-up hand she doth express,
  And, wordless, so greets heaven for his success.

Far from the purpose of his coming hither,
He makes excuses for his being there:
No cloudy show of stormy blustering weather
Doth yet in his fair welkin once appear;
Till sable Night, mother of Dread and Fear,
  Upon the world dim darkness doth display,
  And in her vaulty prison stows the Day.

For then is Tarquin brought unto his bed,   120
Intending weariness with heavy spright;
For, after supper, long he questioned
With modest Lucrece, and wore out the night:
Now leaden slumber with life's strength doth fight;
  And every one to rest themselves betake,
  Save thieves, and cares, and troubled minds, that
        wake.

As one of which doth Tarquin lie revolving

---

referred to by Cassius in *Julius Caesar*, I, ii, 159-160.
  THE POEM. 1. **Ardea,** a city twenty-four miles south of Rome. 3. **Lust-breathed,** excited by lust. 4. **Collatium,** a city about ten miles east of Rome. **lightless,** smouldering. 5. **aspire,** rise; i.e., break into flames. 8. **Haply,** perchance. **unhappily,** unfavorably. Q_{1-4} print these words as *Hap'ly* and *vnhap'ly*, which makes the word play more obvious. 9. **bateless,** not to be blunted. 10. **let,** forbear. 13. **mortal,** human; i.e., her eyes; see glossary. 19. **high-proud.** *High* signifies an intensive, very highly, as often in Shakespeare. 24. **silver melting,** so Q; Globe hyphenates, following Malone. 38. **For . . . be.** The relation between the five senses—particularly sight and hearing—and the passions is stressed several times in this poem; cf. ll. 369, 558-559, 1324-1325; and cf. *Venus and Adonis*, 779-784, note. 40. **Braving compare,** challenging comparison. 42. **hap,** fortune. 44. **all too timeless,** so Q; Globe hyphenates, following Malone. **timeless,** unseemly, unseasonable. 47. **liver,** regarded as the seat of the passions. 57. **intituled,** designated, blazoned; the metaphor is derived from heraldry. 58. **challenge,** claim. **field,** the surface of the shield, where the armorial device is displayed. 63. **fence,** defend. 67. **world's minority,** the golden age; i.e., their right is as old as the doves of Venus and the first blush (Pooler). 83. **surmise,** thought, reflection. 90. **reverend,** i.e., because he is the king's son. 93. **plaits of majesty,** the cunning folds or concealments of dignified demeanor (Lee). 100. **parling,** speaking, conferring. 102. **glassy . . . books,** refers to the custom of printing comments in book margins; cf. *Romeo and Juliet*, I, iii, 86. 104. **moralize.** interpret. 121. **Intending,** pretending.

The sundry dangers of his will's obtaining;
Yet ever to obtain his will resolving,
Though weak-built hopes persuade him to abstaining:
Despair to gain doth traffic oft for gaining;   131
    And when great treasure is the meed proposed,
    Though death be adjunct, there's no death
        supposed.

Those that much covet are with gain so fond,
For what they have not, that which they possess
They scatter and unloose it from their bond,
And so, by hoping more, they have but less;
Or, gaining more, the profit of excess
    Is but to surfeit, and such griefs sustain,
    That they prove bankrupt in this poor-rich gain.   140

The aim of all is but to nurse the life
With honour, wealth, and ease, in waning age;
And in this aim there is such thwarting strife,
That one for all, or all for one we gage;
As life for honour in fell battle's rage;
    Honour for wealth; and oft that wealth doth cost
    The death of all, and all together lost.

So that in venturing ill we leave to be
The things we are for that which we expect;
And this ambitious foul infirmity,   150
In having much, torments us with defect
Of that we have: so then we do neglect
    The thing we have; and, all for want of wit,
    Make something nothing by augmenting it.

Such hazard now must doting Tarquin make,
Pawning his honour to obtain his lust;
And for himself himself he must forsake:
Then where is truth, if there be no self-trust?
When shall he think to find a stranger just,
    When he himself himself confounds, betrays   160
    To slanderous tongues and wretched hateful days?

Now stole upon the time the dead of night,
When heavy sleep had closed up mortal eyes:
No comfortable star did lend his light,
No noise but owls' and wolves' death-boding cries;
Now serves the season that they may surprise
    The silly lambs: pure thoughts are dead and still,
    While lust and murder wake to stain and kill.

And now this lustful lord leap'd from his bed,
Throwing his mantle rudely o'er his arm;   170
Is madly toss'd between desire and dread;
Th' one sweetly flatters, th' other feareth harm;
But honest fear, bewitch'd with lust's foul charm
    Doth too too oft betake him to retire,
    Beaten away by brain-sick rude desire.

His falchion on a flint he softly smiteth,
That from the cold stone sparks of fire do fly;
Whereat a waxen torch forthwith he lighteth,
Which must be lode-star to his lustful eye;

And to the flame thus speaks advisedly,   180
    'As from this cold flint I enforced this fire,
    So Lucrece must I force to my desire.'

Here pale with fear he doth premeditate
The dangers of his loathsome enterprise,
And in his inward mind he doth debate
What following sorrow may on this arise:
Then looking scornfully, he doth despise
    His naked armour of still-slaughter'd lust,
    And justly thus controls his thoughts unjust:

'Fair torch, burn out thy light, and lend it not   190
To darken her whose light excelleth thine:
And die, unhallow'd thoughts, before you blot
With your uncleanness that which is divine;
Offer pure incense to so pure a shrine:
    Let fair humanity abhor the deed
    That spots and stains love's modest snow-white
        weed.

'O shame to knighthood and to shining arms!
O foul dishonour to my household's grave!
O impious act, including all foul harms!
A martial man to be soft fancy's slave!   200
True valour still a true respect should have;
    Then my digression is so vile, so base,
    That it will live engraven in my face.

'Yea, though I die, the scandal will survive,
And be an eye-sore in my golden coat;
Some loathsome dash the herald will contrive,
To cipher me how fondly I did dote;
That my posterity, shamed with the note,
    Shall curse my bones, and hold it for no sin
    To wish that I their father had not been.   210

'What win I, if I gain the thing I seek?
A dream, a breath, a froth of fleeting joy.
Who buys a minute's mirth to wail a week?
Or sells eternity to get a toy?
For one sweet grape who will the vine destroy?
    Or what fond beggar, but to touch the crown,
    Would with the sceptre straight be strucken down?

'If Collatinus dream of my intent,
Will he not wake, and in a desperate rage
Post hither, this vile purpose to prevent?   220
This siege that hath engirt his marriage,
This blur to youth, this sorrow to the sage,
    This dying virtue, this surviving shame,
    Whose crime will bear an ever-during blame?

'O, what excuse can my invention make,
When thou shalt charge me with so black a deed?
Will not my tongue be mute, my frail joints shake,
Mine eyes forego their light, my false heart bleed?
The guilt being great, the fear doth still exceed;
    And extreme fear can neither fight nor fly,   230
    But coward-like with trembling terror die.

131. **Despair to gain,** hopelessness of gain. **traffic,** engage in commerce. 136. **bond,** possession. 138. **profit of excess,** advantage of having more than enough. 139. **such griefs sustain,** i.e., to sustain such griefs as accompany surfeit. 144. **gage,** pledge; Pooler suggests "risk." 148. **leave to be,** cease being. 150. **infirmity,** i.e., covetousness. 151. **defect,** deficiency. 155. **doting.** The word suggests the complete overthrow of the understanding by the passions; it carries also the metaphor of the covetous man completely foolish in his ventures. 164. **comfort-**able, cheering, benevolent. 167. **silly,** helpless, defenseless. 188. **naked . . . lust,** i.e., he attacks his lust (despising its armor), always being slaughtered, never killed. 205. **golden coat,** i.e., coat of arms. 206. **loathsome dash,** a glance at the bar sinister. 207. **cipher,** disclose, decipher. 221. **marriage,** state of union (Schmidt); abstract for concrete: his wife (Brown). 244. **saw,** saying, proverb. 245. **painted cloth,** wall hanging in which moral tales and maxims were sometimes depicted; cf. ll. 1366-1456, below, where such a painted cloth is

'Had Collatinus kill'd my son or sire,
Or lain in ambush to betray my life,
Or were he not my dear friend, this desire
Might have excuse to work upon his wife,
  As in revenge or quittal of such strife:
  But as he is my kinsman, my dear friend,
  The shame and fault finds no excuse nor end.

'Shameful it is; ay, if the fact be known:
Hateful it is; there is no hate in loving: 240
I'll beg her love; but she is not her own:
The worst is but denial and reproving:
My will is strong, past reason's weak removing.
  Who fears a sentence or an old man's saw
  Shall by a painted cloth be kept in awe.'

Thus, graceless, holds he disputation
'Tween frozen conscience and hot-burning will,
And with good thoughts makes dispensation,
Urging the worser sense for vantage still;
Which in a moment doth confound and kill   250
  All pure effects, and doth so far proceed,
  That what is vile shows like a virtuous deed.

Quoth he, 'She took me kindly by the hand,
And gazed for tidings in my eager eyes,
Fearing some hard news from the warlike band,
Where her beloved Collatinus lies.
O, how her fear did make her colour rise!
  First red as roses that on lawn we lay,
  Then white as lawn, the roses took away.

'And how her hand, in my hand being lock'd,   260
Forced it to tremble with her loyal fear!
Which struck her sad, and then it faster rock'd,
Until her husband's welfare she did hear;
Whereat she smiled with so sweet a cheer,
  That had Narcissus seen her as she stood,
  Self-love had never drown'd him in the flood.

'Why hunt I then for colour or excuses?
All orators are dumb when beauty pleadeth;
Poor wretches have remorse in poor abuses;
Love thrives not in the heart that shadows dreadeth:
Affection is my captain, and he leadeth;   271
  And when his gaudy banner is display'd,
  The coward fights and will not be dismay'd.

'Then, childish fear, avaunt! debating, die!
Respect and reason, wait on wrinkled age!
My heart shall never countermand mine eye:
Sad pause and deep regard beseem the sage;
My part is youth, and beats these from the stage:
  Desire my pilot is, beauty my prize;
  Then who fears sinking where such treasure lies?' 280

As corn o'ergrown by weeds, so heedful fear
Is almost choked by unresisted lust.
Away he steals with open listening ear,
Full of foul hope and full of fond mistrust;

Both which, as servitors to the unjust,
  So cross him with their opposite persuasion,
  That now he vows a league, and now invasion.

Within his thought her heavenly image sits,
And in the self-same seat sits Collatine:
That eye which looks on her confounds his wits;   290
That eye which him beholds, as more divine,
Unto a view so false will not incline;
  But with a pure appeal seeks to the heart,
  Which once corrupted takes the worser part;

And therein heartens up his servile powers,
Who, flatter'd by their leader's jocund show,
Stuff up his lust, as minutes fill up hours;
And as their captain, so their pride doth grow,
Paying more slavish tribute than they owe.
  By reprobate desire thus madly led,   300
  The Roman lord marcheth to Lucrece' bed.

The locks between her chamber and his will,
Each one by him enforced retires his ward;
But, as they open, they all rate his ill,
Which drives the creeping thief to some regard:
The threshold grates the door to have him heard;
  Night-wandering weasels shriek to see him there;
  They fright him, yet he still pursues his fear.

As each unwilling portal yields him way,
Through little vents and crannies of the place   310
The wind wars with his torch to make him stay,
And blows the smoke of it into his face,
Extinguishing his conduct in this case;
  But his hot heart, which fond desire doth scorch,
  Puffs forth another wind that fires the torch:

And being lighted, by the light he spies
Lucretia's glove, wherein her needle sticks:
He takes it from the rushes where it lies,
And griping it, the needle his finger pricks;
As who should say 'This glove to wanton tricks   320
  Is not inured; return again in haste;
  Thou see'st our mistress' ornaments are chaste.'

But all these poor forbiddings could not stay him;
He in the worst sense construes their denial:
The doors, the wind, the glove, that did delay him,
He takes for accidental things of trial;
Or as those bars which stop the hourly dial,
  Who with a lingering stay his course doth let,
  Till every minute pays the hour his debt.

'So, so,' quoth he, 'these lets attend the time,   330
Like little frosts that sometime threat the spring,
To add a more rejoicing to the prime,
And give the sneaped birds more cause to sing.
Pain pays the income of each precious thing;
  Huge rocks, high winds, strong pirates, shelves and
      sands,
  The merchant fears, ere rich at home he lands.'

described.   248. **makes dispensation** [*with*], sets aside.   269. **have . . .
abuses,** feel remorse for paltry sins.   292. **a view so false.** The eye which
beholds Collatine (in imagination) has a degree of loyalty and will not
be so false as to look toward Lucrece, as the other eye has done; i.e.,
he cannot think of Collatine and Lucrece at the same time.   295.
servile powers, base passions. The image is the common one of the
faculties as an army: the heart as captain of the sensible soul commands
all the affections to serve his lust; cf. l. 426, below.   303. **retires,**
draws back. **ward,** lock, bolt.   305. **regard,** thoughtful consideration.   308. **fear,** i.e., the cause of his fear, his peril (Lee).   313.
conduct, conductor, i.e., his torch.   318. **rushes,** floor covering.
330. **lets,** hindrances, obstacles. **attend the time,** are incidental to
the occasion.   333. **sneaped,** nipped, or pinched with cold.

Now is he come unto the chamber door,
That shuts him from the heaven of his thought,
Which with a yielding latch, and with no more,
Hath barr'd him from the blessed thing he sought. 340
So from himself impiety hath wrought,
    That for his prey to pray he doth begin,
    As if the heavens should countenance his sin.

But in the midst of his unfruitful prayer,
Having solicited th' eternal power
That his foul thoughts might compass his fair fair,
And they would stand auspicious to the hour,
Even there he starts: quoth he, 'I must deflower:
    The powers to whom I pray abhor this fact,
    How can they then assist me in the act? 350

'Then Love and Fortune be my gods, my guide!
My will is back'd with resolution:
Thoughts are but dreams till their effects be tried;
The blackest sin is clear'd with absolution;
Against love's fire fear's frost hath dissolution.
    The eye of heaven is out, and misty night
    Covers the shame that follows sweet delight.'

This said, his guilty hand pluck'd up the latch,
And with his knee the door he opens wide.
The dove sleeps fast that this night-owl will catch: 360
Thus treason works ere traitors be espied.
Who sees the lurking serpent steps aside;
    But she, sound sleeping, fearing no such thing,
    Lies at the mercy of his mortal sting.

Into the chamber wickedly he stalks,
And gazeth on her yet unstained bed.
The curtains being close, about he walks,
Rolling his greedy eyeballs in his head:
By their high treason is his heart misled;
    Which gives the watch-word to his hand full soon 370
    To draw the cloud that hides the silver moon.

Look, as the fair and fiery-pointed sun,
Rushing from forth a cloud, bereaves our sight;
Even so, the curtain drawn, his eyes begun
To wink, being blinded with a greater light:
Whether it is that she reflects so bright,
    That dazzleth them, or else some shame supposed;
    But blind they are, and keep themselves enclosed.

O, had they in that darksome prison died!
Then had they seen the period of their ill; 380
Then Collatine again, by Lucrece' side,
In his clear bed might have reposed still:
But they must ope, this blessed league to kill;
    And holy-thoughted Lucrece to their sight
    Must sell her joy, her life, her world's delight.

Her lily hand her rosy cheek lies under,
Cozening the pillow of a lawful kiss;
Who, therefore angry, seems to part in sunder,
Swelling on either side to want his bliss;
Between whose hills her head entombed is: 390
    Where, like a virtuous monument, she lies,
    To be admired of lewd unhallow'd eyes.

Without the bed her other fair hand was,
On the green coverlet; whose perfect white
Show'd like an April daisy on the grass,
With pearly sweat, resembling dew of night.
Her eyes, like marigolds, had sheathed their light,
    And canopied in darkness sweetly lay,
    Till they might open to adorn the day.

Her hair, like golden threads, play'd with her breath;
O modest wantons! wanton modesty! 401
Showing life's triumph in the map of death,
And death's dim look in life's mortality:
Each in her sleep themselves so beautify,
    As if between them twain there were no strife,
    But that life lived in death, and death in life.

Her breasts, like ivory globes circled with blue,
A pair of maiden worlds unconquered,
Save of their lord no bearing yoke they knew,
And him by oath they truly honoured. 410
These worlds in Tarquin new ambition bred;
    Who, like a foul usurper, went about
    From this fair throne to heave the owner out.

What could he see but mightily he noted?
What did he note but strongly he desired?
What he beheld, on that he firmly doted,
And in his will his wilful eye he tired.
With more than admiration he admired
    Her azure veins, her alabaster skin,
    Her coral lips, her snow-white dimpled chin. 420

As the grim lion fawneth o'er his prey,
Sharp hunger by the conquest satisfied,
So o'er this sleeping soul doth Tarquin stay,
His rage of lust by gazing qualified;
Slack'd, not suppress'd; for standing by her side,
    His eye, which late this mutiny restrains,
    Unto a greater uproar tempts his veins:

And they, like straggling slaves for pillage fighting,
Obdurate vassals fell exploits effecting,
In bloody death and ravishment delighting, 430
Nor children's tears nor mothers' groans respecting,
Swell in their pride, the onset still expecting:
    Anon his beating heart, alarum striking,
    Gives the hot charge and bids them do their liking.

His drumming heart cheers up his burning eye,
His eye commends the leading to his hand;
His hand, as proud of such a dignity,
Smoking with pride, march'd on to make his stand
On her bare breast, the heart of all her land;
    Whose ranks of blue veins, as his hand did scale, 440
    Left their round turrets destitute and pale.

They, mustering to the quiet cabinet
Where their dear governess and lady lies,
Do tell her she is dreadfully beset,
And fright her with confusion of their cries:
She, much amazed, breaks ope her lock'd-up eyes,
    Who, peeping forth this tumult to behold,
    Are by his flaming torch dimm'd and controll'd.

402. **map of death,** i.e., sleep. 417. **tired,** a falconry term: glutted, fed upon ravenously. 418. **more than admiration,** lustful anticipation. 424. **qualified,** softened, abated. 453. **taking,** state of agitation. 459. **antics,** phantoms (Herford); odd and fantastic appearances (Schmidt).

471. **heartless,** spiritless, wanting courage. 507. **Coucheth,** causes (one) to couch, i.e., to remain concealed. 523. **obloquy,** reproach, disgrace. 529. **For lawful policy,** modifies *done* (l. 528). 530. **simple,** ingredient. 531. **compound,** compounded drug. 537. **slavish wipe,**

Imagine her as one in dead of night
From forth dull sleep by dreadful fancy waking, 450
That thinks she hath beheld some ghastly sprite,
Whose grim aspect sets every joint a-shaking:
What terror 'tis! but she, in worser taking,
    From sleep disturbed, heedfully doth view
    The sight which makes supposed terror true.

Wrapp'd and confounded in a thousand fears,
Like to a new-kill'd bird she trembling lies;
She dares not look; yet, winking, there appears
Quick-shifting antics, ugly in her eyes:
Such shadows are the weak brain's forgeries; 460
    Who, angry that the eyes fly from their lights,
    In darkness daunts them with more dreadful sights.

His hand, that yet remains upon her breast,—
Rude ram, to batter such an ivory wall!—
May feel her heart—poor citizen!—distress'd,
Wounding itself to death, rise up and fall,
Beating her bulk, that his hand shakes withal.
    This moves in him more rage and lesser pity,
    To make the breach and enter this sweet city.

First, like a trumpet, doth his tongue begin 470
To sound a parley to his heartless foe;
Who o'er the white sheet peers her whiter chin,
The reason of this rash alarm to know,
Which he by dumb demeanour seeks to show;
    But she with vehement prayers urgeth still
    Under what colour he commits this ill.

Thus he replies: 'The colour in thy face,
That even for anger makes the lily pale,
And the red rose blush at her own disgrace,
Shall plead for me and tell my loving tale: 480
Under that colour am I come to scale
    Thy never-conquer'd fort: the fault is thine,
    For those thine eyes betray thee unto mine.

'Thus I forestall thee, if thou mean to chide:
Thy beauty hath ensnared thee to this night,
Where thou with patience must my will abide;
My will that marks thee for my earth's delight,
Which I to conquer sought with all my might;
    But as reproof and reason beat it dead,
    By thy bright beauty was it newly bred. 490

'I see what crosses my attempt will bring;
I know what thorns the growing rose defends;
I think the honey guarded with a sting;
All this beforehand counsel comprehends:
But will is deaf and hears no heedful friends;
    Only he hath an eye to gaze on beauty,
    And dotes on what he looks, 'gainst law or duty.

'I have debated, even in my soul,
What wrong, what shame, what sorrow I shall breed;
But nothing can affection's course control, 500
Or stop the headlong fury of his speed.
I know repentant tears ensue the deed,
    Reproach, disdain, and deadly enmity;
    Yet strive I to embrace mine infamy.'

This said, he shakes aloft his Roman blade,
Which, like a falcon towering in the skies,
Coucheth the fowl below with his wings' shade,
Whose crooked beak threats if he mount he dies:
So under his insulting falchion lies
    Harmless Lucretia, marking what he tells 510
    With trembling fear, as fowl hear falcon's bells.

'Lucrece,' quoth he, 'this night I must enjoy thee:
If thou deny, then force must work my way,
For in thy bed I purpose to destroy thee:
That done, some worthless slave of thine I'll slay,
To kill thine honour with thy life's decay,
    And in thy dead arms do I mean to place him,
    Swearing I slew him, seeing thee embrace him.

'So thy surviving husband shall remain
The scornful mark of every open eye; 520
Thy kinsmen hang their heads at this disdain,
Thy issue blurr'd with nameless bastardy:
And thou, the author of their obloquy,
    Shalt have thy trespass cited up in rhymes,
    And sung by children in succeeding times.

'But if thou yield, I rest thy secret friend:
The fault unknown is as a thought unacted;
A little harm done to a great good end
For lawful policy remains enacted.
The poisonous simple sometimes is compacted 530
    In a pure compound; being so applied,
    His venom in effect is purified.

'Then, for thy husband and thy children's sake,
Tender my suit: bequeath not to their lot
The shame that from them no device can take,
The blemish that will never be forgot;
Worse than a slavish wipe or birth-hour's blot:
    For marks descried in men's nativity
    Are nature's faults, not their own infamy.'

Here with a cockatrice' dead-killing eye 540
He rouseth up himself and makes a pause;
While she, the picture of pure piety,
Like a white hind under the gripe's sharp claws,
Pleads, in a wilderness where are no laws,
    To the rough beast that knows no gentle right,
    Nor aught obeys but his foul appetite.

But when a black-faced cloud the world doth threat,
In his dim mist the aspiring mountains hiding,
From earth's dark womb some gentle gust doth get,
Which blows these pitchy vapours from their biding,
Hindering their present fall by this dividing; 551
    So his unhallow'd haste her words delays,
    And moody Pluto winks while Orpheus plays.

Yet, foul night-waking cat, he doth but dally,
While in his hold-fast foot the weak mouse panteth:
Her sad behaviour feeds his vulture folly,
A swallowing gulf that even in plenty wanteth:
His ear her prayers admits, but his heart granteth
    No penetrable entrance to her plaining: 559
    Tears harden lust, though marble wear with raining.

The Rape of Lucrece

445

brand with which slaves were marked. **birth-hour's blot,** probably
another reference to the bar sinister. 540. **cockatrice,** the basilisk, said
to be hatched by a serpent from a cock's egg and said to kill by its
breath and look. 543. **gripe's,** vulture's. 556. **folly,** lewdness

(Onions); depravity (Malone); cf. note on *doting*, l. 155.

Her pity-pleading eyes are sadly fixed
In the remorseless wrinkles of his face;
Her modest eloquence with sighs is mixed,
Which to her oratory adds more grace.
She puts the period often from his place;
    And midst the sentence so her accent breaks,
    That twice she doth begin ere once she speaks.

She conjures him by high almighty Jove,
By knighthood, gentry, and sweet friendship's oath,
By her untimely tears, her husband's love,   570
By holy human law, and common troth,
By heaven and earth, and all the power of both,
    That to his borrow'd bed he make retire,
    And stoop to honour, not to foul desire.

Quoth she, 'Reward not hospitality
With such black payment as thou hast pretended;
Mud not the fountain that gave drink to thee;
Mar not the thing that cannot be amended;
End thy ill aim before thy shoot be ended;
    He is no woodman that doth bend his bow   580
    To strike a poor unseasonable doe.

'My husband is thy friend; for his sake spare me:
Thyself art mighty; for thine own sake leave me:
Myself a weakling; do not then ensnare me:
Thou look'st not like deceit; do not deceive me.
My sighs, like whirlwinds, labour hence to heave
        thee:
    If ever man were moved with woman's moans,
    Be moved with my tears, my sighs, my groans:

'All which together, like a troubled ocean,
Beat at thy rocky and wreck-threatening heart,   590
To soften it with their continual motion;
For stones dissolved to water do convert.
O, if no harder than a stone thou art,
    Melt at my tears, and be compassionate!
    Soft pity enters at an iron gate.

'In Tarquin's likeness I did entertain thee:
Hast thou put on his shape to do him shame?
To all the host of heaven I complain me,
Thou wrong'st his honour, wound'st his princely
        name.
Thou art not what thou seem'st; and if the same,   600
    Thou seem'st not what thou art, a god, a king;
    For kings like gods should govern every thing.

'How will thy shame be seeded in thine age,
When thus thy vices bud before thy spring!
If in thy hope thou darest do such outrage,
What darest thou not when once thou art a king?
O, be remember'd, no outrageous thing
    From vassal actors can be wiped away;
    Then kings' misdeeds cannot be hid in clay.

'This deed will make thee only loved for fear;   610
But happy monarchs still are fear'd for love:
With foul offenders thou perforce must bear,
When they in thee the like offences prove:
If but for fear of this, thy will remove;

For princes are the glass, the school, the book,
Where subjects' eyes do learn, do read, do look.

'And wilt thou be the school where Lust shall learn?
Must he in thee read lectures of such shame?
Wilt thou be glass wherein it shall discern
Authority for sin, warrant for blame,   620
To privilege dishonour in thy name?
    Thou back'st reproach against long-living laud,
    And makest fair reputation but a bawd.

'Hast thou command? by him that gave it thee,
From a pure heart command thy rebel will:
Draw not thy sword to guard iniquity,
For it was lent thee all that brood to kill.
Thy princely office how canst thou fulfil,
    When, pattern'd by thy fault, foul sin may say,
    He learn'd to sin, and thou didst teach the way?   630

'Think but how vile a spectacle it were,
To view thy present trespass in another.
Men's faults do seldom to themselves appear;
Their own transgressions partially they smother:
This guilt would seem death-worthy in thy brother.
    O, how are they wrapp'd in with infamies
    That from their own misdeeds askance their eyes!

'To thee, to thee, my heaved-up hands appeal,
Not to seducing lust, thy rash relier:
I sue for exiled majesty's repeal;   640
Let him return, and flattering thoughts retire:
His true respect will prison false desire,
    And wipe the dim mist from thy doting eyne,
    That thou shalt see thy state and pity mine.'

'Have done,' quoth he: 'my uncontrolled tide
Turns not, but swells the higher by this let.
Small lights are soon blown out, huge fires abide,
And with the wind in greater fury fret:
The petty streams that pay a daily debt
    To their salt sovereign, with their fresh falls' haste   650
    Add to his flow, but alter not his taste.'

'Thou art,' quoth she, 'a sea, a sovereign king;
And, lo, there falls into thy boundless flood
Black lust, dishonour, shame, misgoverning,
Who seek to stain the ocean of thy blood.
If all these petty ills shall change thy good,
    Thy sea within a puddle's womb is hearsed,
    And not the puddle in thy sea dispersed.

'So shall these slaves be king, and thou their slave;
Thou nobly base, they basely dignified;   660
Thou their fair life, and they thy fouler grave:
Thou loathed in their shame, they in thy pride:
The lesser thing should not the greater hide;
    The cedar stoops not to the base shrub's foot,
    But low shrubs wither at the cedar's root.

'So let thy thoughts, low vassals to thy state'—
'No more,' quoth he; 'by heaven, I will not hear thee:
Yield to my love; if not, enforced hate,
Instead of love's coy touch, shall rudely tear thee;
That done, despitefully I mean to bear thee   670

Unto the base bed of some rascal groom,
To be thy partner in this shameful doom.'

This said, he sets his foot upon the light,
For light and lust are deadly enemies:
Shame folded up in blind concealing night,
When most unseen, then most doth tyrannize.
The wolf hath seized his prey, the poor lamb cries;
    Till with her own white fleece her voice controll'd
    Entombs her outcry in her lips' sweet fold:

For with the nightly linen that she wears   680
He pens her piteous clamours in her head;
Cooling his hot face in the chastest tears
That ever modest eyes with sorrow shed.
O, that prone lust should stain so pure a bed!
    The spots whereof could weeping purify,
    Her tears should drop on them perpetually.

But she hath lost a dearer thing than life,
And he hath won what he would lose again:
This forced league doth force a further strife;
This momentary joy breeds months of pain;   690
This hot desire converts to cold disdain:
    Pure Chastity is rifled of her store,
    And Lust, the thief, far poorer than before.

Look, as the full-fed hound or gorged hawk,
Unapt for tender smell or speedy flight,
Make slow pursuit, or altogether balk
The prey wherein by nature they delight;
So surfeit-taking Tarquin fares this night:
    His taste delicious, in digestion souring,
    Devours his will, that lived by foul devouring.   700

O, deeper sin than bottomless conceit
Can comprehend in still imagination!
Drunken Desire must vomit his receipt,
Ere he can see his own abomination.
While Lust is in his pride, no exclamation
    Can curb his heat or rein his rash desire,
    Till like a jade Self-will himself doth tire.

And then with lank and lean discolour'd cheek,
With heavy eye, knit brow, and strengthless pace,
Feebly Desire, all recreant, poor, and meek,   710
Like to a bankrupt beggar wails his case:
The flesh being proud, Desire doth fight with Grace,
    For there it revels; and when that decays,
    The guilty rebel for remission prays.

So fares it with this faultful lord of Rome,
Who this accomplishment so hotly chased;
For now against himself he sounds this doom,
That through the length of times he stands disgraced:
Besides, his soul's fair temple is defaced;
    To whose weak ruins muster troops of cares,   720
    To ask the spotted princess how she fares.

She says, her subjects with foul insurrection
Have batter'd down her consecrated wall,
And by their mortal fault brought in subjection
Her immortality, and made her thrall

To living death and pain perpetual:
    Which in her prescience she controlled still,
    But her foresight could not forestall their will.

Even in this thought through the dark night he
        stealeth,
A captive victor that hath lost in gain;   730
Bearing away the wound that nothing healeth,
The scar that will, despite of cure, remain;
Leaving his spoil perplex'd in greater pain.
    She bears the load of lust he left behind,
    And he the burthen of a guilty mind.

He like a thievish dog creeps sadly thence;
She like a wearied lamb lies panting there;
He scowls and hates himself for his offence;
She, desperate, with her nails her flesh doth tear;
He faintly flies, sweating with guilty fear;   740
    She stays, exclaiming on the direful night;
    He runs, and chides his vanish'd, loathed delight.

He thence departs a heavy convertite;
She there remains a hopeless castaway;
He in his speed looks for the morning light;
She prays she never may behold the day,
'For day,' quoth she, 'night's scapes doth open lay,
    And my true eyes have never practised how
    To cloak offences with a cunning brow.

'They think not but that every eye can see   750
The same disgrace which they themselves behold;
And therefore would they still in darkness be,
To have their unseen sin remain untold;
For they their guilt with weeping will unfold,
    And grave, like water that doth eat in steel,
    Upon my cheeks what helpless shame I feel.'

Here she exclaims against repose and rest,
And bids her eyes hereafter still be blind.
She wakes her heart by beating on her breast,
And bids it leap from thence, where it may find   760
Some purer chest to close so pure a mind.
    Frantic with grief thus breathes she forth her spite
    Against the unseen secrecy of night:

'O comfort-killing Night, image of hell!
Dim register and notary of shame!
Black stage for tragedies and murders fell!
Vast sin-concealing chaos! nurse of blame!
Blind muffled bawd! dark harbour for defame!
    Grim cave of death! whispering conspirator
    With close-tongued treason and the ravisher!   770

'O hateful, vaporous, and foggy Night!
Since thou art guilty of my cureless crime,
Muster thy mists to meet the eastern light,
Make war against proportion'd course of time;
Or if thou wilt permit the sun to climb
    His wonted height, yet ere he go to bed,
    Knit poisonous clouds about his golden head.

'With rotten damps ravish the morning air;
Let their exhaled unwholesome breaths make sick

The Rape of Lucrece

447

i.e., they are inscribed in marble or bronze. 621. **privilege,** license, authorize. 640. **repeal,** restoration; i.e., your *majesty* is exiled. 657. **hearsed,** buried, coffined. 743. **heavy,** sad. **convertite,** convert.

768. **defame,** infamy. 774. **proportion'd,** i.e., regulated interchange of day and night.

The life of purity, the supreme fair, 780
Ere he arrive his weary noon-tide prick;
And let thy misty vapours march so thick,
  That in their smoky ranks his smother'd light
  May set at noon and make perpetual night.

'Were Tarquin Night, as he is but Night's child,
The silver-shining queen he would distain;
Her twinkling handmaids too, by him defiled,
Through Night's black bosom should not peep again:
So should I have co-partners in my pain;
  And fellowship in woe doth woe assuage, 790
  As palmers' chat makes short their pilgrimage.

'Where now I have no one to blush with me,
To cross their arms and hang their heads with mine,
To mask their brows and hide their infamy;
But I alone alone must sit and pine,
Seasoning the earth with showers of silver brine,
  Mingling my talk with tears, my grief with groans,
  Poor wasting monuments of lasting moans.

'O Night, thou furnace of foul-reeking smoke,
Let not the jealous Day behold that face 800
Which underneath thy black all-hiding cloak
Immodestly lies martyr'd with disgrace!
Keep still possession of thy gloomy place,
  That all the faults which in thy reign are made
  May likewise be sepulchred in thy shade!

'Make me not object to the tell-tale Day!
The light will show, character'd in my brow,
The story of sweet chastity's decay,
The impious breach of holy wedlock vow:
Yea, the illiterate, that know not how 810
  To cipher what is writ in learned books,
  Will quote my loathsome trespass in my looks.

'The nurse, to still her child, will tell my story,
And fright her crying babe with Tarquin's name;
The orator, to deck his oratory,
Will couple my reproach to Tarquin's shame;
Feast-finding minstrels, tuning my defame,
  Will tie the hearers to attend each line,
  How Tarquin wronged me, I Collatine.

'Let my good name, that senseless reputation, 820
For Collatine's dear love be kept unspotted:
If that be made a theme for disputation,
The branches of another root are rotted,
And undeserved reproach to him allotted
  That is as clear from this attaint of mine
  As I, ere this, was pure to Collatine.

'O unseen shame! invisible disgrace!
O unfelt sore! crest-wounding, private scar!
Reproach is stamp'd in Collatinus' face,
And Tarquin's eye may read the mot afar, 830
How he in peace is wounded, not in war.
  Alas, how many bear such shameful blows,
  Which not themselves, but he that gives them
    knows!

'If, Collatine, thine honour lay in me,
From me by strong assault it is bereft.
My honey lost, and I, a drone-like bee,
Have no perfection of my summer left,
But robb'd and ransack'd by injurious theft:
  In thy weak hive a wandering wasp hath crept,
  And suck'd the honey which thy chaste bee kept. 840

'Yet am I guilty of thy honour's wrack;
Yet for thy honour did I entertain him;
Coming from thee, I could not put him back,
For it had been dishonour to disdain him:
Besides, of weariness he did complain him,
  And talk'd of virtue: O unlook'd-for evil,
  When virtue is profaned in such a devil!

'Why should the worm intrude the maiden bud?
Or hateful cuckoos hatch in sparrows' nests?
Or toads infect fair founts with venom mud? 850
Or tyrant folly lurk in gentle breasts?
Or kings be breakers of their own behests?
  But no perfection is so absolute,
  That some impurity doth not pollute.

'The aged man that coffers-up his gold
Is plagued with cramps and gouts and painful fits;
And scarce hath eyes his treasure to behold,
But like still-pining Tantalus he sits,
And useless barns the harvest of his wits;
  Having no other pleasure of his gain 860
  But torment that it cannot cure his pain.

'So then he hath it when he cannot use it,
And leaves it to be master'd by his young;
Who in their pride do presently abuse it:
Their father was too weak, and they too strong,
To hold their cursed-blessed fortune long.
  The sweets we wish for turn to loathed sours
  Even in the moment that we call them ours.

'Unruly blasts wait on the tender spring;
Unwholesome weeds take root with precious flowers;
The adder hisses where the sweet birds sing; 871
What virtue breeds iniquity devours:
We have no good that we can say is ours,
  But ill-annexed Opportunity
  Or kills his life or else his quality.

'O Opportunity, thy guilt is great!
'Tis thou that executest the traitor's treason:
Thou set'st the wolf where he the lamb may get;
Whoever plots the sin, thou 'point'st the season;
'Tis thou that spurn'st at right, at law, at reason; 880
  And in thy shady cell, where none may spy him,
  Sits Sin, to seize the souls that wander by him.

'Thou makest the vestal violate her oath;
Thou blow'st the fire when temperance is thaw'd;
Thou smother'st honesty, thou murder'st troth;
Thou foul abettor! thou notorious bawd!
Thou plantest scandal and displacest laud:

---

780. **supreme fair,** the sun. 782. **misty,** so Malone; Q_{1-2}: *mustie,* retained by many editors, who justify it from contiguous phrases— *rotten damps, unwholesome breaths.* 806. **Make . . . object,** i.e., she prays that her face may never be seen. 811. **cipher,** decipher. 828. **crest-wounding,** disgraceful to the crest or cognizance. 830. **mot,** motto. 850. **toads . . . venom.** Seagar (*Shakespeare's Natural History*, pp. 306-

308) quotes from several documents attesting to the belief in the venomous quality of toads; cf. *As You Like It,* II, i, 13. 859. **barns,** stores, as in a barn. 869. **tender spring,** young shoot. 874. **Opportunity.** This account of Opportunity has details in common with Spenser's allegorical description of Occasion in *The Faerie Queene,* II, iv. 892. **smoothing,** flattering. 899. **sort,** choose. 907. **Advice . . .**

Thou ravisher, thou traitor, thou false thief,
Thy honey turns to gall, thy joy to grief!

'Thy secret pleasure turns to open shame,   890
Thy private feasting to a public fast,
Thy smoothing titles to a ragged name,
Thy sugar'd tongue to bitter wormwood taste:
Thy violent vanities can never last.
    How comes it then, vile Opportunity,
    Being so bad, such numbers seek for thee?

'When wilt thou be the humble suppliant's friend,
And bring him where his suit may be obtain'd?
When wilt thou sort an hour great strifes to end?
Or free that soul which wretchedness hath chain'd? 900
Give physic to the sick, ease to the pain'd?
    The poor, lame, blind, halt, creep, cry out for thee;
    But they ne'er meet with Opportunity.

'The patient dies while the physician sleeps;
The orphan pines while the oppressor feeds;
Justice is feasting while the widow weeps;
Advice is sporting while infection breeds:
Thou grant'st no time for charitable deeds:
    Wrath, envy, treason, rape, and murder's rages,
    Thy heinous hours wait on them as their pages.   910

'When Truth and Virtue have to do with thee,
A thousand crosses keep them from thy aid:
They buy thy help; but Sin ne'er gives a fee,
He gratis comes; and thou art well appaid
As well to hear as grant what he hath said.
    My Collatine would else have come to me
    When Tarquin did, but he was stay'd by thee.

'Guilty thou art of murder and of theft,
Guilty of perjury and subornation,
Guilty of treason, forgery, and shift,   920
Guilty of incest, that abomination;
An accessary by thine inclination
    To all sins past, and all that are to come,
    From the creation to the general doom.

'Mis-shapen Time, copesmate of ugly Night,
Swift subtle post, carrier of grisly care,
Eater of youth, false slave to false delight,
Base watch of woes, sin's pack-horse, virtue's snare;
Thou nursest all and murder'st all that are:
    O, hear me then, injurious, shifting Time!   930
    Be guilty of my death, since of my crime.

'Why hath thy servant, Opportunity,
Betray'd the hours thou gavest me to repose,
Cancell'd my fortunes, and enchained me
To endless date of never-ending woes?
Time's office is to fine the hate of foes;
    To eat up errors by opinion bred,
    Not spend the dowry of a lawful bed.

'Time's glory is to calm contending kings,
To unmask falsehood and bring truth to light,   940
To stamp the seal of time in aged things,

To wake the morn and sentinel the night,
To wrong the wronger till he render right,
    To ruinate proud buildings with thy hours,
    And smear with dust their glittering golden towers;

'To fill with worm-holes stately monuments,
To feed oblivion with decay of things,
To blot old books and alter their contents,
To pluck the quills from ancient ravens' wings,
To dry the old oak's sap and cherish springs,   950
    To spoil antiquities of hammer'd steel,
    And turn the giddy round of Fortune's wheel;

'To show the beldam daughters of her daughter,
To make the child a man, the man a child,
To slay the tiger that doth live by slaughter,
To tame the unicorn and lion wild,
To mock the subtle in themselves beguiled,
    To cheer the ploughman with increaseful crops,
    And waste huge stones with little water-drops.

'Why work'st thou mischief in thy pilgrimage,   960
Unless thou couldst return to make amends?
One poor retiring minute in an age
Would purchase thee a thousand thousand friends,
Lending him wit that to bad debtors lends:
    O, this dread night, wouldst thou one hour come
        back,
    I could prevent this storm and shun thy wrack!

'Thou ceaseless lackey to eternity,
With some mischance cross Tarquin in his flight:
Devise extremes beyond extremity,
To make him curse this cursed crimeful night: 970
Let ghastly shadows his lewd eyes affright;
    And the dire thought of his committed evil
    Shape every bush a hideous shapeless devil.

'Disturb his hours of rest with restless trances,
Afflict him in his bed with bedrid groans;
Let there bechance him pitiful mischances,
To make him moan; but pity not his moans:
Stone him with harden'd hearts, harder than stones;
    And let mild women to him lose their mildness,
    Wilder to him than tigers in their wildness.   980

'Let him have time to tear his curled hair,
Let him have time against himself to rave,
Let him have time of Time's help to despair,
Let him have time to live a loathed slave,
Let him have time a beggar's orts to crave,
    And time to see one that by alms doth live
    Disdain to him disdained scraps to give.

'Let him have time to see his friends his foes,
And merry fools to mock at him resort;
Let him have time to mark how slow time goes   990
In time of sorrow, and how swift and short
His time of folly and his time of sport;
    And ever let his unrecalling crime
    Have time to wail th' abusing of his time.

breeds. While infection is spreading, the grave rulers of the state, who ought to guard against its further progress, are careless and inattentive (Malone). Steevens thought the line alluded to the plague epidemic in London. 925. copesmate, companion. 928. watch, divided and marked only by woes (Schmidt); possibly, picket, sentinel. 936. fine, put an end to (Steevens); cf. *Troilus and Cressida*, IV, iv, 3. 950. To ... springs, to dry up the old and foster the young. 953. beldam, old woman. 958. increaseful, fruitful. 962. retiring, returning. 974. trances, visions. 981. curled hair, suggests the exquisite toilet of a prince. 985. orts, refuse, fragments. 993. unrecalling crime, crime that may not be undone.

'O Time, thou tutor both to good and bad,
Teach me to curse him that thou taught'st this ill!
At his own shadow let the thief run mad,
Himself himself seek every hour to kill!
Such wretched hands such wretched blood should
    spill;
    For who so base would such an office have   1000
    As slanderous deathsman to so base a slave?

'The baser is he, coming from a king,
To shame his hope with deeds degenerate:
The mightier man, the mightier is the thing
That makes him honour'd, or begets him hate;
For greatest scandal waits on greatest state.
    The moon being clouded presently is miss'd,
    But little stars may hide them when they list.

'The crow may bathe his coal-black wings in mire,
And unperceived fly with the filth away;   1010
But if the like the snow-white swan desire,
The stain upon his silver down will stay.
Poor grooms are sightless night, kings glorious day:
    Gnats are unnoted wheresoe'er they fly,
    But eagles gazed upon with every eye.

'Out, idle words, servants to shallow fools!
Unprofitable sounds, weak arbitrators!
Busy yourselves in skill-contending schools;
Debate where leisure serves with dull debaters;
To trembling clients be you mediators: 1020
    For me, I force not argument a straw,
    Since that my case is past the help of law.

'In vain I rail at Opportunity,
At Time, at Tarquin, and uncheerful Night;
In vain I cavil with mine infamy,
In vain I spurn at my confirm'd despite:
This helpless smoke of words doth me no right.
    The remedy indeed to do me good
    Is to let forth my foul-defiled blood.

'Poor hand, why quiver'st thou at this decree?   1030
Honour thyself to rid me of this shame;
For if I die, my honour lives in thee;
But if I live, thou livest in my defame:
Since thou couldst not defend thy loyal dame,
    And wast afeard to scratch her wicked foe,
    Kill both thyself and her for yielding so.'

This said, from her be-tumbled couch she starteth,
To find some desperate instrument of death:
But this no slaughterhouse no tool imparteth
To make more vent for passage of her breath;   1040
Which, thronging through her lips, so vanisheth
    As smoke from Ætna, that in air consumes,
    Or that which from discharged cannon fumes.

'In vain,' quoth she, 'I live, and seek in vain
Some happy mean to end a hapless life.
I fear'd by Tarquin's falchion to be slain,
Yet for the self-same purpose seek a knife:

But when I fear'd I was a loyal wife:
    So am I now: O no, that cannot be;
    Of that true type hath Tarquin rifled me.   1050

'O, that is gone for which I sought to live,
And therefore now I need not fear to die.
To clear this spot by death, at least I give
A badge of fame to slander's livery;
A dying life to living infamy:
    Poor helpless help, the treasure stol'n away,
    To burn the guiltless casket where it lay!

'Well, well, dear Collatine, thou shalt not know
The stained taste of violated troth;
I will not wrong thy true affection so,   1060
To flatter thee with an infringed oath;
This bastard graff shall never come to growth:
    He shall not boast who did thy stock pollute
    That thou art doting father of his fruit.

'Nor shall he smile at thee in secret thought,
Nor laugh with his companions at thy state;
But thou shalt know thy interest was not
    bought
Basely with gold, but stol'n from forth thy gate.
For me, I am the mistress of my fate,
    And with my trespass never will dispense,   1070
    Till life to death acquit my forced offence.

'I will not poison thee with my attaint,
Nor fold my fault in cleanly-coin'd excuses;
My sable ground of sin I will not paint,
To hide the truth of this false night's abuses:
My tongue shall utter all; mine eyes, like sluices,
    As from a mountain-spring that feeds a dale,
    Shall gush pure streams to purge my impure tale.'

By this, lamenting Philomel had ended
The well-tuned warble of her nightly sorrow,   1080
And solemn night with slow sad gait descended
To ugly hell; when, lo, the blushing morrow
Lends light to all fair eyes that light will borrow:
    But cloudy Lucrece shames herself to see,
    And therefore still in night would cloister'd be.

Revealing day through every cranny spies,
And seems to point her out where she sits weeping;
To whom she sobbing speaks: 'O eye of eyes,
Why pry'st thou through my window? leave thy
    peeping:
Mock with thy tickling beams eyes that are sleeping:
    Brand not my forehead with thy piercing light,   1091
    For day hath nought to do what 's done by night.'

Thus cavils she with every thing she sees:
True grief is fond and testy as a child,
Who wayward once, his mood with nought agrees:
Old woes, not infant sorrows, bear them mild;
Continuance tames the one; the other wild,
    Like an unpractised swimmer plunging still,
    With too much labour drowns for want of skill.

1021. **force,** attach importance to. 1054. **badge of fame,** good reputation; the metaphor is from the custom of servants wearing on their liveries badges that bore their masters' coats of arms (Malone). 1061. **flatter,** deceive. 1062. **graff,** graft, scion. 1070. **dispense** [*with*], condone by dispensation. 1071. **acquit,** atone for. 1073. **cleanly,** cleverly. 1079. **Philomel.** Cf. *Titus Andronicus*, II, iii, 43, note. 1096. **them,** themselves. **mild,** mildly, calmly. 1109. **search.** probe.

annoy, grief, injury. 1112. **sufficed,** contented. 1114. **ken,** sight; a nautical term to signify the distance that bounds the range of ordinary vision at sea. 1122. **hollow-swelling,** insincere. 1127. **dumps,** mournful melodies. 1132. **diapason,** bass notes an octave or more below the melody. 1133. **burden-wise,** in the manner of an undersong or bass. 1134. **Tereus.** Cf. *Titus Andronicus*, II, iii, 43, note. **better skill.** Malone thought the sense incomplete and suggested *with better skill;* many

So she, deep-drenched in a sea of care, 1100
Hoids disputation with each thing she views,
And to herself all sorrow doth compare;
No object but her passion's strength renews;
And as one shifts, another straight ensues:
    Sometime her grief is dumb and hath no words;
    Sometime 'tis mad and too much talk affords.

The little birds that tune their morning's joy
Make her moans mad with their sweet melody:
For mirth doth search the bottom of annoy;
Sad souls are slain in merry company; 1110
Grief best is pleased with grief's society:
    True sorrow then is feelingly sufficed
    When with like semblance it is sympathized.

'Tis double death to drown in ken of shore;
He ten times pines that pines beholding food;
To see the salve doth make the wound ache more;
Great grief grieves most at that would do it good;
Deep woes roll forward like a gentle flood,
    Who, being stopp'd, the bounding banks
        o'erflows;
    Grief dallied with nor law nor limit knows. 1120

'You mocking birds,' quoth she, 'your tunes entomb
Within your hollow-swelling feather'd breasts,
And in my hearing be you mute and dumb:
My restless discord loves no stops nor rests;
A woeful hostess brooks not merry guests:
    Relish your nimble notes to pleasing ears;
    Distress likes dumps when time is kept with tears.

'Come, Philomel, that sing'st of ravishment,
Make thy sad grove in my dishevell'd hair:
As the dank earth weeps at thy languishment, 1130
So I at each sad strain will strain a tear,
And with deep groans the diapason bear;
    For burden-wise I'll hum on Tarquin still,
    While thou on Tereus descant'st better skill.

'And whiles against a thorn thou bear'st thy part,
To keep thy sharp woes waking, wretched I,
To imitate thee well, against my heart
Will fix a sharp knife to affright mine eye;
Who, if it wink, shall thereon fall and die.
    These means, as frets upon an instrument, 1140
    Shall tune our heart-strings to true languishment.

'And for, poor bird, thou sing'st not in the day,
As shaming any eye should thee behold,
Some dark deep desert, seated from the way,
That knows not parching heat nor freezing cold,
Will we find out; and there we will unfold
    To creatures stern sad tunes, to change their
        kinds:
    Since men prove beasts, let beasts bear gentle
        minds.'

As the poor frighted deer, that stands at gaze,
Wildly determining which way to fly, 1150

Or one encompass'd with a winding maze,
That cannot tread the way out readily;
So with herself is she in mutiny,
    To live or die which of the twain were better,
    When life is shamed, and death reproach's
        debtor.

'To kill myself,' quoth she, 'alack, what were it,
But with my body my poor soul's pollution?
They that lose half with greater patience bear it
Than they whose whole is swallow'd in confusion.
That mother tries a merciless conclusion 1160
    Who, having two sweet babes, when death
        takes one,
    Will slay the other and be nurse to none.

'My body or my soul, which was the dearer,
When the one pure, the other made divine?
Whose love of either to myself was nearer,
When both were kept for heaven and Collatine?
Ay me! the bark peel'd from the lofty pine,
    His leaves will wither and his sap decay;
    So must my soul, her bark being peel'd away.

'Her house is sack'd, her quiet interrupted, 1170
Her mansion batter'd by the enemy;
Her sacred temple spotted, spoil'd, corrupted,
Grossly engirt with daring infamy:
Then let it not be call'd impiety,
    If in this blemish'd fort I make some hole
    Through which I may convey this troubled
        soul.

'Yet die I will not till my Collatine
Have heard the cause of my untimely death;
That he may vow, in that sad hour of mine,
Revenge on him that made me stop my breath. 1180
My stained blood to Tarquin I'll bequeath,
    Which by him tainted shall for him be spent,
    And as his due writ in my testament.

'My honour I'll bequeath unto the knife
That wounds my body so dishonoured.
'Tis honour to deprive dishonour'd life;
The one will live, the other being dead:
So of shame's ashes shall my fame be bred;
    For in my death I murder shameful scorn:
    My shame so dead, mine honour is new-born. 1190

'Dear lord of that dear jewel I have lost,
What legacy shall I bequeath to thee?
My resolution, love, shall be thy boast,
By whose example thou revenged mayst be.
How Tarquin must be used, read it in me:
    Myself, thy friend, will kill myself, thy foe,
    And for my sake serve thou false Tarquin so.

'This brief abridgement of my will I make:
My soul and body to the skies and ground;
My resolution, husband, do thou take; 1200
Mine honour be the knife's that makes my wound;

---

editors define it so. Wyndham takes *descant'st* as a transitive verb and *skill* as its object. Lucrece contrasts her *deep groans* uttered *burden-wise* with the *better skill* of the nightingale's treble melody. 1135. **against a thorn,** alludes to a commonplace of natural history, that the nightingale perched deliberately with a thorn against her breast to keep her awake. The wakefulness of the nightingale is a common detail of medieval romances. 1140. **frets,** bars placed on finger boards of stringed instruments to regulate the fingering. 1142. **sing'st not in the day,** one of the vulgar errors of the time; nightingales sing both by day and by night. 1144. **seated from,** situated away from. 1155. **death reproach's debtor,** elliptical: when death is the debtor of reproach. 1160. **tries . . . conclusion,** finds out if by a cruel experiment she can regain her peace of mind (Pooler). 1176. **convey,** let out.

My shame be his that did my fame confound;
  And all my fame that lives disbursed be
  To those that live, and think no shame of me.

'Thou, Collatine, shalt oversee this will;
How was I overseen that thou shalt see it!
My blood shall wash the slander of mine ill;
My life's foul deed, my life's fair end shall free it.
Faint not, faint heart, but stoutly say "So be it:"
  Yield to my hand; my hand shall conquer thee: 1210
  Thou dead, both die, and both shall victors be.'

This plot of death when sadly she had laid,
And wiped the brinish pearl from her bright eyes,
With untuned tongue she hoarsely calls her maid,
Whose swift obedience to her mistress hies;
For fleet-wing'd duty with thought's feathers flies.
  Poor Lucrece' cheeks unto her maid seem so
  As winter meads when sun doth melt their snow.

Her mistress she doth give demure good-morrow,
With soft-slow tongue, true mark of modesty, 1220
And sorts a sad look to her lady's sorrow,
For why her face wore sorrow's livery;
But durst not ask of her audaciously
  Why her two suns were cloud-eclipsed so,
  Nor why her fair cheeks over-wash'd with woe.

But as the earth doth weep, the sun being set,
Each flower moisten'd like a melting eye;
Even so the maid with swelling drops gan wet
Her circled eyne, enforced by sympathy
Of those fair suns set in her mistress' sky, 1230
  Who in a salt-waved ocean quench their light,
  Which makes the maid weep like the dewy night.

A pretty while these pretty creatures stand,
Like ivory conduits coral cisterns filling:
One justly weeps; the other takes in hand
No cause, but company, of her drops spilling:
Their gentle sex to weep are often willing;
  Grieving themselves to guess at others' smarts,
  And then they drown their eyes or break their
    hearts.

For men have marble, women waxen, minds, 1240
And therefore are they form'd as marble will;
The weak oppress'd, the impression of strange kinds
Is form'd in them by force, by fraud, or skill:
Then call them not the authors of their ill,
  No more than wax shall be accounted evil
  Wherein is stamp'd the semblance of a devil.

Their smoothness, like a goodly champaign plain,
Lays open all the little worms that creep;
In men, as in a rough-grown grove, remain
Cave-keeping evils that obscurely sleep: 1250
Through crystal walls each little mote will peep:
  Though men can cover crimes with bold stern looks,
  Poor women's faces are their own faults' books.

No man inveigh against the wither'd flower,

But chide rough winter that the flower hath kill'd:
Not that devour'd, but that which doth devour,
Is worthy blame. O, let it not be hild
Poor women's faults, that they are so fulfill'd
  With men's abuses: those proud lords, to blame,
  Make weak-made women tenants to their shame.

The precedent whereof in Lucrece view, 1261
Assail'd by night with circumstances strong
Of present death, and shame that might ensue
By that her death, to do her husband wrong:
Such danger to resistance did belong,
  That dying fear through all her body spread;
  And who cannot abuse a body dead?

By this, mild patience bid fair Lucrece speak
To the poor counterfeit of her complaining:
'My girl,' quoth she, 'on what occasion break 1270
Those tears from thee, that down thy cheeks are
    raining?
If thou dost weep for grief of my sustaining,
  Know, gentle wench, it small avails my mood:
  If tears could help, mine own would do me
    good.

'But tell me, girl, when went'—and there she stay'd
Till after a deep groan—'Tarquin from hence?'
'Madam, ere I was up,' replied the maid,
'The more to blame my sluggard negligence:
Yet with the fault I thus far can dispense;
  Myself was stirring ere the break of day, 1280
  And, ere I rose, was Tarquin gone away.

'But, lady, if your maid may be so bold,
She would request to know your heaviness.'
'O, peace!' quoth Lucrece: 'if it should be told,
The repetition cannot make it less;
For more it is than I can well express:
  And that deep torture may be call'd a hell
  When more is felt than one hath power to tell.

'Go, get me hither paper, ink, and pen:
Yet save that labour, for I have them here. 1290
What should I say? One of my husband's men
Bid thou be ready, by and by, to bear
A letter to my lord, my love, my dear:
  Bid him with speed prepare to carry it;
  The cause craves haste, and it will soon be writ.'

Her maid is gone, and she prepares to write,
First hovering o'er the paper with her quill:
Conceit and grief an eager combat fight;
What wit sets down is blotted straight with will;
This is too curious-good, this blunt and ill: 1300
  Much like a press of people at a door,
  Throng her inventions, which shall go before.

At last she thus begins: 'Thou worthy lord
Of that unworthy wife that greeteth thee,
Health to thy person! next vouchsafe t' afford—
If ever, love, thy Lucrece thou wilt see—
Some present speed to come and visit me.

1206. **overseen**, deluded, taken advantage of; quibblingly used with *oversee* (l. 1205), i.e., attend to as an executor of an estate. 1221. **sorts**, adapts, makes agree. 1234. **conduits**, alludes to the conduit spouts and fountains shaped in the form of human figures. 1257. **hild**, variant form of "held." 1261. **precedent**, proof, example. 1269. **coun-** terfeit, likeness, imitation. 1300. **curious**, fastidiously. 1309. **tedious**, painful. 1311. **uncertainly**, i.e., not in precise detail, vaguely. 1329. **Deep sounds**, depths of the sea which may be sounded. 1338. **villain**, servant. 1350. **pattern**, one who resembles dwellers in the good early times (Craig). **worn-out**, departed, i.e., golden age; cf. *As You Like*

So, I commend me from our house in grief:
My woes are tedious, though my words are brief.'

Here folds she up the tenour of her woe,   1310
Her certain sorrow writ uncertainly.
By this short schedule Collatine may know
Her grief, but not her grief's true quality:
She dares not thereof make discovery,
    Lest he should hold it her own gross abuse,
    Ere she with blood had stain'd her stain'd excuse.

Besides, the life and feeling of her passion
She hoards, to spend when he is by to hear her:
When sighs and groans and tears may grace the
    fashion
Of her disgrace, the better so to clear her   1320
From that suspicion which the world might bear her.
    To shun this blot, she would not blot the letter
    With words, till action might become them better.

To see sad sights moves more than hear them told:
For then the eye interprets to the ear
The heavy motion that it doth behold,
When every part a part of woe doth bear.
'Tis but a part of sorrow that we hear:
    Deep sounds make lesser noise than shallow fords,
    And sorrow ebbs, being blown with wind of words.

Her letter now is seal'd, and on it writ   1331
'At Ardea to my lord with more than haste.'
The post attends, and she delivers it,
Charging the sour-faced groom to hie as fast
As lagging fowls before the northern blast:
    Speed more than speed but dull and slow she deems:
    Extremity still urgeth such extremes.

The homely villain court'sies to her low;
And, blushing on her, with a steadfast eye
Receives the scroll without or yea or no,   1340
And forth with bashful innocence doth hie.
But they whose guilt within their bosoms lie
    Imagine every eye beholds their blame;
    For Lucrece thought he blush'd to see her shame:

When, silly groom! God wot, it was defect
Of spirit, life, and bold audacity.
Such harmless creatures have a true respect
To talk in deeds, while others saucily
Promise more speed, but do it leisurely:
    Even so this pattern of the worn-out age   1350
    Pawn'd honest looks, but laid no words to gage.

His kindled duty kindled her mistrust,
That two red fires in both their faces blazed;
She thought he blush'd, as knowing Tarquin's lust,
And, blushing with him, wistly on him gazed;
Her earnest eye did make him more amazed:
    The more she saw the blood his cheeks replenish,
    The more she thought he spied in her some blemish.

But long she thinks till he return again,
And yet the duteous vassal scarce is gone.   1360

The weary time she cannot entertain,
For now 'tis stale to sigh, to weep, and groan:
So woe hath wearied woe, moan tired moan,
    That she her plaints a little while doth stay,
    Pausing for means to mourn some newer way.

At last she calls to mind where hangs a piece
Of skilful painting, made for Priam's Troy;
Before the which is drawn the power of Greece,
For Helen's rape the city to destroy,
Threatening cloud-kissing Ilion with annoy;   1370
    Which the conceited painter drew so proud,
    As heaven, it seem'd, to kiss the turrets bow'd.

A thousand lamentable objects there,
In scorn of nature, art gave lifeless life:
Many a dry drop seem'd a weeping tear,
Shed for the slaughter'd husband by the wife:
The red blood reek'd, to show the painter's strife;
    And dying eyes gleam'd forth their ashy lights,
    Like dying coals burnt out in tedious nights.

There might you see the labouring pioner   1380
Begrimed with sweat, and smeared all with dust;
And from the towers of Troy there would appear
The very eyes of men through loop-holes thrust,
Gazing upon the Greeks with little lust:
    Such sweet observance in this work was had,
    That one might see those far-off eyes look sad.

In great commanders grace and majesty
You might behold, triumphing in their faces;
In youth, quick bearing and dexterity;
And here and there the painter interlaces   1390
Pale cowards, marching on with trembling paces;
    Which heartless peasants did so well resemble,
    That one would swear he saw them quake and
        tremble.

In Ajax and Ulysses, O, what art
Of physiognomy might one behold!
The face of either cipher'd either's heart;
Their face their manners most expressly told:
In Ajax' eyes blunt rage and rigour roll'd;
    But the mild glance that sly Ulysses lent
    Show'd deep regard and smiling government.   1400

There pleading might you see grave Nestor stand,
As 'twere encouraging the Greeks to fight;
Making such sober action with his hand,
That it beguiled attention, charm'd the sight:
In speech, it seem'd, his beard, all silver white,
    Wagg'd up and down, and from his lips did fly
    Thin winding breath, which purl'd up to the sky.

About him were a press of gaping faces,
Which seem'd to swallow up his sound advice;
All jointly listening, but with several graces,   1410
As if some mermaid did their ears entice,
Some high, some low, the painter was so nice;
    The scalps of many, almost hid behind,
    To jump up higher seem'd, to mock the mind.

The Rape of Lucrece

453

It, II, iii, 56. 1355. **wistly,** attentively. 1362. **stale,** wearisome repetition. 1377. **strife,** rivalry, i.e., with Nature. 1380. **pioner,** digger, miner. 1384. **lust,** pleasure, delight. 1390. **interlaces,** interweaves. 1396. **cipher'd,** showed, expressed. 1400. **deep . . . government,** profound wisdom and the complacency arising from passions

being under the command of reason (Malone). 1406. **Wagg'd,** moved. 1407. **purl'd,** flowed with a whirling motion. 1413. **scalps,** skulls, crowns of heads.

Here one man's hand lean'd on another's head,
His nose being shadow'd by his neighbour's ear;
Here one being throng'd bears back, all boll'n and
    red;
Another smother'd seems to pelt and swear;
And in their rage such signs of rage they bear,
    As, but for loss of Nestor's golden words,   1420
    It seem'd they would debate with angry swords.

For much imaginary work was there;
Conceit deceitful, so compact, so kind,
That for Achilles' image stood his spear,
Griped in an armed hand; himself, behind,
Was left unseen, save to the eye of mind:
    A hand, a foot, a face, a leg, a head,
    Stood for the whole to be imagined.

And from the walls of strong-besieged Troy
When their brave hope, bold Hector, march'd to
    field,
Stood many Trojan mothers, sharing joy   1431
To see their youthful sons bright weapons wield;
And to their hope they such odd action yield,
    That through their light joy seemed to appear,
    Like bright things stain'd, a kind of heavy fear.

And from the strand of Dardan, where they fought,
To Simois' reedy banks the red blood ran,
Whose waves to imitate the battle sought
With swelling ridges; and their ranks began
To break upon the galled shore, and than   1440
    Retire again, till, meeting greater ranks,
    They join and shoot their foam at Simois' banks.

To this well-painted piece is Lucrece come,
To find a face where all distress is stell'd.
Many she sees where cares have carved some,
But none where all distress and dolour dwell'd,
Till she despairing Hecuba beheld,
    Staring on Priam's wounds with her old eyes,
    Which bleeding under Pyrrhus' proud foot lies.

In her the painter had anatomized   1450
Time's ruin, beauty's wreck, and grim care's reign:
Her cheeks with chops and wrinkles were disguised;
Of what she was no semblance did remain:
Her blue blood changed to black in every vein,
    Wanting the spring that those shrunk pipes had fed,
    Show'd life imprison'd in a body dead.

On this sad shadow Lucrece spends her eyes,
And shapes her sorrow to the beldam's woes,
Who nothing wants to answer her but cries,
And bitter words to ban her cruel foes: 1460
The painter was no god to lend her those;
    And therefore Lucrece swears he did her wrong,
    To give her so much grief and not a tongue.

'Poor instrument,' quoth she, 'without a sound,
I'll tune thy woes with my lamenting tongue;
And drop sweet balm in Priam's painted wound,
And rail on Pyrrhus that hath done him wrong;
And with my tears quench Troy that burns so long;

And with my knife scratch out the angry eyes
Of all the Greeks that are thine enemies.   1470

'Show me the strumpet that began this stir,
That with my nails her beauty I may tear.
Thy heat of lust, fond Paris, did incur
This load of wrath that burning Troy doth bear:
Thy eye kindled the fire that burneth here;
    And here in Troy, for trespass of thine eye,
    The sire, the son, the dame, and daughter die.

'Why should the private pleasure of some one
Become the public plague of many moe?
Let sin, alone committed, light alone   1480
Upon his head that hath transgressed so;
Let guiltless souls be freed from guilty woe:
    For one's offence why should so many fall,
    To plague a private sin in general?

'Lo, here weeps Hecuba, here Priam dies,
Here manly Hector faints, here Troilus swounds,
Here friend by friend in bloody channel lies,
And friend to friend gives unadvised wounds,
And one man's lust these many lives confounds:
    Had doting Priam check'd his son's desire,   1490
    Troy had been bright with fame and not with fire.'

Here feelingly she weeps Troy's painted woes:
For sorrow, like a heavy-hanging bell,
Once set on ringing, with his own weight goes;
Then little strength rings out the doleful knell:
So Lucrece, set a-work, sad tales doth tell
    To pencill'd pensiveness and colour'd sorrow:
    She lends them words, and she their looks doth
        borrow.

She throws her eyes about the painting round,
And whom she finds forlorn she doth lament.   1500
At last she sees a wretched image bound,
That piteous looks to Phrygian shepherds lent:
His face, though full of cares, yet show'd content;
    Onward to Troy with the blunt swains he goes,
    So mild, that Patience seem'd to scorn his woes.

In him the painter labour'd with his skill
To hide deceit, and give the harmless show
An humble gait, calm looks, eyes wailing still,
A brow unbent, that seem'd to welcome woe;
Cheeks neither red nor pale, but mingled so   1510
    That blushing red no guilty instance gave,
    Nor ashy pale the fear that false hearts have.

But, like a constant and confirmed devil,
He entertain'd a show so seeming just,
And therein so ensconced his secret evil,
That jealousy itself could not mistrust
False-creeping craft and perjury should thrust
    Into so bright a day such black-faced storms,
    Or blot with hell-born sin such saint-like forms.

The well-skill'd workman this mild image drew   1520
For perjured Sinon, whose enchanting story
The credulous old Priam after slew;
Whose words like wildfire burnt the shining glory

1417. **boll'n,** swollen. 1418. **pelt,** utter angry words. 1444. **stell'd,** fixed; possibly should be read *steel'd*, i.e., engraved (Onions). 1450. **anatomized,** dissected. 1452. **chops,** chaps, cracks and lines in the skin. 1484. **in general,** publicly; i.e., to punish the general public for an individual's sin. 1488. **unadvised,** inadvertently. 1497. **pencill'd,** painted. 1502. **lent,** bestowed on. 1511. **guilty instance,** symptom of guilt (Malone). 1514. **entertain'd . . . just,** kept up an appearance of justice. 1516. **mistrust,** suspect. 1521. **enchanting.**

Of rich-built Ilion, that the skies were sorry,
  And little stars shot from their fixed places,
  When their glass fell wherein they view'd their
    faces.

This picture she advisedly perused,
And chid the painter for his wondrous skill,
Saying, some shape in Sinon's was abused;
So fair a form lodged not a mind so ill: 1530
And still on him she gazed; and gazing still,
  Such signs of truth in his plain face she spied,
  That she concludes the picture was belied.

'It cannot be,' quoth she, 'that so much guile'—
She would have said 'can lurk in such a look;'
But Tarquin's shape came in her mind the while,
And from her tongue 'can lurk' from 'cannot' took:
'It cannot be' she in that sense forsook,
  And turn'd it thus, 'It cannot be, I find,
  But such a face should bear a wicked mind: 1540

'For even as subtle Sinon here is painted,
So sober-sad, so weary, and so mild,
As if with grief or travail he had fainted,
To me came Tarquin armed; so beguiled
With outward honesty, but yet defiled
  With inward vice: as Priam him did cherish,
  So did I Tarquin; so my Troy did perish.

'Look, look, how listening Priam wets his eyes,
To see those borrow'd tears that Sinon sheds!
Priam, why art thou old and yet not wise?   1550
For every tear he falls a Trojan bleeds:
His eye drops fire, no water thence proceeds;
  Those round clear pearls of his, that move thy pity,
  Are balls of quenchless fire to burn thy city.

'Such devils steal effects from lightless hell;
For Sinon in his fire doth quake with cold,
And in that cold hot-burning fire doth dwell;
These contraries such unity do hold,
Only to flatter fools and make them bold:
  So Priam's trust false Sinon's tears doth flatter,   1560
  That he finds means to burn his Troy with water.'

Here, all enraged, such passion her assails,
That patience is quite beaten from her breast.
She tears the senseless Sinon with her nails,
Comparing him to that unhappy guest
Whose deed hath made herself herself detest:
  At last she smilingly with this gives o'er;
  'Fool, fool!' quoth she, 'his wounds will not be sore.'

Thus ebbs and flows the current of her sorrow,
And time doth weary time with her complaining.   1570
She looks for night, and then she longs for morrow,
And both she thinks too long with her remaining:
Short time seems long in sorrow's sharp sustaining:
  Though woe be heavy, yet it seldom sleeps;
  And they that watch see time how slow it creeps.

Which all this time hath overslipp'd her thought,
That she with painted images hath spent;

Being from the feeling of her own grief brought
By deep surmise of others' detriment;
Losing her woes in shows of discontent.   1580
  It easeth some, though none it ever cured,
  To think their dolour others have endured.

But now the mindful messenger, come back,
Brings home his lord and other company;
Who finds his Lucrece clad in mourning black:
And round about her tear-distained eye
Blue circles stream'd, like rainbows in the sky:
  These water-galls in her dim element
  Foretell new storms to those already spent.

Which when her sad-beholding husband saw,   1590
Amazedly in her sad face he stares:
Her eyes, though sod in tears, look'd red and raw,
Her lively colour kill'd with deadly cares.
He hath no power to ask her how she fares:
  Both stood, like old acquaintance in a trance,
  Met far from home, wondering each other's chance.

At last he takes her by the bloodless hand,
And thus begins: 'What uncouth ill event
Hath thee befall'n, that thou dost trembling stand?
Sweet love, what spite hath thy fair colour spent?   1600
Why art thou thus attired in discontent?
  Unmask, dear dear, this moody heaviness,
  And tell thy grief, that we may give redress.'

Three times with sighs she gives her sorrow fire,
Ere once she can discharge one word of woe:
At length address'd to answer his desire,
She modestly prepares to let them know
Her honour is ta'en prisoner by the foe:
  While Collatine and his consorted lords
  With sad attention long to hear her words.   1610

And now this pale swan in her watery nest
Begins the sad dirge of her certain ending;
'Few words,' quoth she, 'shall fit the trespass best,
Where no excuse can give the fault amending:
In me moe woes than words are now depending;
  And my laments would be drawn out too long,
  To tell them all with one poor tired tongue.

'Then be this all the task it hath to say:
Dear husband, in the interest of thy bed
A stranger came, and on that pillow lay   1620
Where thou wast wont to rest thy weary head;
And what wrong else may be imagined
  By foul enforcement might be done to me,
  From that, alas, thy Lucrece is not free.

'For in the dreadful dead of dark midnight,
With shining falchion in my chamber came
A creeping creature, with a flaming light,
And softly cried "Awake, thou Roman dame,
And entertain my love; else lasting shame
  On thee and thine this night I will inflict,   1630
  If thou my love's desire do contradict.

' "For some hard-favour'd groom of thine," quoth he,

*The Rape
of Lucrece*

455

bewitching. 1523. **wildfire,** gunpowder rolled up wet and set on fire.
1544. **beguiled,** disguised. 1549. **borrow'd,** counterfeited. 1584.
other company. Cf. *The Argument,* l. 18, and ll. 1731, 1734, below.
1586. **tear-distained,** tear-stained. 1588. **water-galls,** secondary rain-

bows. 1592. **sod,** scalded. 1604-1605. **Three . . . woe,** metaphor
based on the discharging of ancient firearms by means of a match
(Staunton). 1611-1612. **pale . . . ending,** alludes to the belief that
the swan sang at his death.

"Unless thou yoke thy liking to my will,
I'll murder straight, and then I'll slaughter thee
And swear I found you where you did fulfil
The loathsome act of lust, and so did kill
    The lechers in their deed: this act will be
    My fame and thy perpetual infamy."

'With this, I did begin to start and cry;
And then against my heart he sets his sword,   1640
Swearing, unless I took all patiently,
I should not live to speak another word;
So should my shame still rest upon record,
    And never be forgot in mighty Rome
    Th' adulterate death of Lucrece and her groom.

'Mine enemy was strong, my poor self weak,
And far the weaker with so strong a fear:
My bloody judge forbade my tongue to speak;
No rightful plea might plead for justice there:
His scarlet lust came evidence to swear   1650
    That my poor beauty had purloin'd his eyes;
    And when the judge is robb'd the prisoner dies.

'O, teach me how to make mine own excuse!
Or at the least this refuge let me find;
Though my gross blood be stain'd with this abuse,
Immaculate and spotless is my mind;
That was not forced; that never was inclined
    To accessary yieldings, but still pure
    Doth in her poison'd closet yet endure.'

Lo, here, the hopeless merchant of this loss,   1660
With head declined, and voice damm'd up with woe,
With sad set eyes, and wretched arms across,
From lips new-waxen pale begins to blow
The grief away that stops his answer so:
    But, wretched as he is, he strives in vain;
    What he breathes out his breath drinks up again.

As through an arch the violent roaring tide
Outruns the eye that doth behold his haste,
Yet in the eddy boundeth in his pride
Back to the strait that forced him on so fast;   1670
In rage sent out, recall'd in rage, being past:
    Even so his sighs, his sorrows, make a saw,
    To push grief on, and back the same grief draw.

Which speechless woe of his poor she attendeth,
And his untimely frenzy thus awaketh:
'Dear lord, thy sorrow to my sorrow lendeth
Another power; no flood by raining slaketh.
My woe too sensible thy passion maketh
    More feeling-painful: let it then suffice
    To drown one woe, one pair of weeping eyes.   1680

'And for my sake, when I might charm thee so
For she that was thy Lucrece, now attend me:
Be suddenly revenged on my foe,
Thine, mine, his own: suppose thou dost defend me
From what is past: the help that thou shalt lend me
    Comes all too late, yet let the traitor die;
    For sparing justice feeds iniquity.

'But ere I name him, you fair lords,' quoth she,

Speaking to those that came with Collatine,
'Shall plight your honourable faiths to me,   1690
With swift pursuit to venge this wrong of mine;
For 'tis a meritorious fair design
    To chase injustice with revengeful arms:
    Knights, by their oaths, should right poor ladies'
        harms.'

At this request, with noble disposition
Each present lord began to promise aid,
As bound in knighthood to her imposition,
Longing to hear the hateful foe bewray'd.
But she, that yet her sad task hath not said,
    The protestation stops. 'O, speak,' quoth she,   1700
    'How may this forced stain be wiped from me?

'What is the quality of mine offence,
Being constrain'd with dreadful circumstance?
May my pure mind with the foul act dispense,
My low-declined honour to advance?
May any terms acquit me from this chance?
    The poison'd fountain clears itself again;
    And why not I from this compelled stain?'

With this, they all at once began to say,
Her body's stain her mind untainted clears;   1710
While with a joyless smile she turns away
The face, that map which deep impression bears
Of hard misfortune, carved in it with tears.
    'No, no,' quoth she, 'no dame, hereafter living,
    By my excuse shall claim excuse's giving.'

Here with a sigh, as if her heart would break,
She throws forth Tarquin's name: 'He, he,' she says,
But more than 'he' her poor tongue could not speak;
Till after many accents and delays,
Untimely breathings, sick and short assays,   1720
    She utters this, 'He, he, fair lords, 'tis he,
    That guides this hand to give this wound to me.'

Even here she sheathed in her harmless breast
A harmful knife, that thence her soul unsheathed:
That blow did bail it from the deep unrest
Of that polluted prison where it breathed:
Her contrite sighs unto the clouds bequeathed
    Her winged sprite, and through her wounds doth
        fly
    Life's lasting date from cancell'd destiny.

Stone-still, astonish'd with this deadly deed,   1730
Stood Collatine and all his lordly crew;
Till Lucrece' father, that beholds her bleed,
Himself on her self-slaughter'd body threw;
And from the purple fountain Brutus drew
    The murderous knife, and, as it left the place,
    Her blood, in poor revenge, held it in chase;

And bubbling from her breast, it doth divide
In two slow rivers, that the crimson blood
Circles her body in on every side,
Who, like a late-sack'd island, vastly stood   1740
Bare and unpeopled in this fearful flood.
    Some of her blood still pure and red remain'd,
    And some look'd black, and that false Tarquin
        stain'd.

1658. accessary yieldings, i.e., as an accessory to crime. 1671. In . . .
past, alludes to the motion of the tide under old London Bridge.

1682. she, her. 1693. chase, harass, punish. 1697. imposition, injunction. 1740. vastly, far and wide. 1745. rigol, circle, ring.

About the mourning and congealed face
Of that black blood a watery rigol goes,
Which seems to weep upon the tainted place:
And ever since, as pitying Lucrece' woes,
Corrupted blood some watery token shows;
   And blood untainted still doth red abide,
   Blushing at that which is so putrified.   1750

'Daughter, dear daughter,' old Lucretius cries,
'That life was mine which thou hast here deprived.
If in the child the father's image lies,
Where shall I live now Lucrece is unlived?
Thou wast not to this end from me derived.
   If children pre-decease progenitors,
   We are their offspring, and they none of ours.

'Poor broken glass, I often did behold
In thy sweet semblance my old age new born;
But now that fair fresh mirror, dim and old,   1760
Shows me a bare-boned death by time outworn:
O, from thy cheeks my image thou hast torn,
   And shiver'd all the beauty of my glass,
   That I no more can see what once I was!

'O time, cease thou thy course and last no longer,
If they surcease to be that should survive.
Shall rotten death make conquest of the stronger
And leave the faltering feeble souls alive?
The old bees die, the young possess their hive:
   Then live, sweet Lucrece, live again and see   1770
   Thy father die, and not thy father thee!'

By this, starts Collatine as from a dream,
And bids Lucretius give his sorrow place;
And then in key-cold Lucrece' bleeding stream
He falls, and bathes the pale fear in his face,
And counterfeits to die with her a space;
   Till manly shame bids him possess his breath
   And live to be revenged on her death.

The deep vexation of his inward soul
Hath served a dumb arrest upon his tongue;   1780
Who, mad that sorrow should his use control,
Or keep him from heart-easing words so long,
Begins to talk; but through his lips do throng
   Weak words, so thick come in his poor heart's aid,
   That no man could distinguish what he said.

Yet sometime 'Tarquin' was pronounced plain,
But through his teeth, as if the name he tore.
This windy tempest, till it blow up rain,
Held back his sorrow's tide, to make it more;
At last it rains, and busy winds give o'er: 1790
   Then son and father weep with equal strife
   Who should weep most, for daughter or for wife.

The one doth call her his, the other his,
Yet neither may possess the claim they lay.
The father says 'She 's mine.' 'O, mine she is,'
Replies her husband: 'do not take away
My sorrow's interest; let no mourner say
   He weeps for her, for she was only mine,
   And only must be wail'd by Collatine.'

'O,' quoth Lucretius, 'I did give that life   1800
Which she too early and too late hath spill'd.'
'Woe, woe,' quoth Collatine, 'she was my wife,
I owed her, and 'tis mine that she hath kill'd.'
'My daughter' and 'my wife' with clamours fill'd
   The dispersed air, who, holding Lucrece' life,
   Answer'd their cries, 'my daughter' and 'my wife.'

Brutus, who pluck'd the knife from Lucrece' side,
Seeing such emulation in their woe,
Began to clothe his wit in state and pride,
Burying in Lucrece' wound his folly's show.   1810
He with the Romans was esteemed so
   As silly-jeering idiots are with kings,
   For sportive words and uttering foolish things:

But now he throws that shallow habit by,
Wherein deep policy did him disguise;
And arm'd his long-hid wits advisedly,
To check the tears in Collatinus' eyes.
'Thou wronged lord of Rome,' quoth he, 'arise:
   Let my unsounded self, supposed a fool,
   Now set thy long-experienced wit to school.   1820

'Why, Collatine, is woe the cure for woe?
Do wounds help wounds, or grief help grievous deeds?
Is it revenge to give thyself a blow
For his foul act by whom thy fair wife bleeds?
Such childish humour from weak minds proceeds:
   Thy wretched wife mistook the matter so,
   To slay herself, that should have slain her foe.

'Courageous Roman, do not steep thy heart
In such relenting dew of lamentations;
But kneel with me and help to bear thy part,   1830
To rouse our Roman gods with invocations,
That they will suffer these abominations,
   Since Rome herself in them doth stand disgraced,
   By our strong arms from forth her fair streets
      chased.

'Now, by the Capitol that we adore,
And by this chaste blood so unjustly stain'd,
By heaven's fair sun that breeds the fat earth's store,
By all our country rights in Rome maintain'd,
And by chaste Lucrece' soul that late complain'd
   Her wrongs to us, and by this bloody knife,   1840
   We will revenge the death of this true wife.'

This said, he struck his hand upon his breast,
And kiss'd the fatal knife, to end his vow;
And to his protestation urged the rest,
Who, wondering at him, did his words allow:
Then jointly to the ground their knees they bow;
   And that deep vow, which Brutus made before,
   He doth again repeat, and that they swore.

When they had sworn to this advised doom,
They did conclude to bear dead Lucrece thence;   1850
To show her bleeding body thorough Rome,
And so to publish Tarquin's foul offence:
Which being done with speedy diligence,
   The Romans plausibly did give consent
   To Tarquin's everlasting banishment.

*The Rape
of Lucrece*

457

1766. **surcease**, cease. 1774. **key-cold**, cold in death. 1776. **a space**, for a period of time. 1791. **strife**, endeavor, striving. 1819. **un**sounded, unexplored, hitherto unknown. 1845. **allow**, approve. 1854. **plausibly**, with applause.

Minor Poems

The Passionate Pilgrim

In 1599 twenty short poems were collected into a volume with the title as follows:

The Passionate Pilgrime. By William Shakespeare. At London Printed for W. Jaggard, and are to be sold by W. Leake, at the Greyhound in Paules Churchyard.[1]

A second edition seems to have perished. A third appeared in 1612, "Newly corrected and augmented." To this third edition were added "two Loue-Epistles, the first from Paris to Hellen, and Hellens answere backe againe to Paris." These additions were from Thomas Heywood's *Troia Britanica* (1609). We learn from an epistle appended to *An Apologie for Actors* (1612) that Heywood was annoyed at the theft. He says that Shakespeare was also annoyed. Shakespeare's offense may have been due to the fact that the original collection was a piracy and that it had dishonestly attributed to him the authorship of poems in which he had no share.

In point of fact, Numbers I and II are versions of sonnets cxxxviii and cxliv. Numbers III, V, and XVII are lyrics from *Love's Labour's Lost* (IV, ii, 109-122; iii, 60-73 and 101-120). Doubt has been thrown on the authenticity of all the other poems in the collection that are attributed to Shakespeare. Critics have shown a laudable desire to save various items in the collection for him, because they were thought of as worthy of his pen. Numbers VI, VII, X, XIII, XIV, and XVIII are thought of as rather too

good for anybody else in the age to have written. Longing eyes have been cast on "Crabbed Age and Youth" (No. XII) and on "When as thine eye" (No. XIX). Numbers VIII and XX are generally attributed to Richard Barnfield; XI to Bartholomew Griffin; XVIII appeared in Thomas Weelkes, *Madrigals* (1597); and XX ("Live with me, and be my love") is known to be Marlowe's, the last stanza of it being traditionally ascribed to Raleigh. Numbers XV to XX are set off by a separate title page: *Sonnets to sundry notes of Musicke.*

[1]See facsimile reproduction of *The Passionate Pilgrim* from the unique copy in the Folger Shakespeare Library with introduction by J. Q. Adams (1939).

The Phœnix and the Turtle

A poem called "The Phoenix and Turtle" is "subscribed" by William Shakespeare in a volume called *Loves Martyr: Or, Rosalins Complaint* by Robert Chester (1601). We are told on a subsidiary title page "Hereafter Follow Diuerse Poeticall Essais on the former Subiect; viz: the Turtle and Phoenix. Done by the best and chiefest of our moderne writers, with their names subscribed to their particular workes: neuer before extant."

By the phoenix is meant love and by the turtle constancy in wedded love. Chester's poem is in honor of one Sir John Salusbury of Lleweni and his wife Ursula. Shakespeare's poem, however, seems to have no bearing on the relationship between these persons and has long been an enigma to critics. Yet most of them have gladly admitted it into the Shakespeare canon. It seems to describe in striking verse and imagery a true marriage of the spirit which has been ended by death. It is a poem of shadows in spite of the apparent clarity of its expression, and has carried the minds of poetical critics into mysterious realms. The suggestion may be hazarded that *The Phoenix and the Turtle* is an example of mysticism. It has often been pointed out that the doctrine of courtly love is there, but the poem goes further than the familiar stages of platonic love, a love which rises from the sensual and the intellectual to the ideal or intuitional. *The Phoenix and the Turtle* seems to reflect a mood of spiritual unification.

A Lover's Complaint

There are only a few reasons for assigning *The Lover's Complaint* to Shakespeare. It was published in the 1609 quarto of the *Sonnets*. Perhaps Thorpe, the publisher of the *Sonnets*, meant to imply that the poem was by the same author as the *Sonnets*. *The Lover's Complaint* is written in the same meter as *Lucrece;* but it is not regarded as being truly Shakespearean in style or content. It is too labored in style and too commonplace in content to be very generally accepted as Shakespeare's. The more recent authorities have agreed that, in any case, *The Lover's Complaint* is not an early work like *Venus and Adonis* and *The Rape of Lucrece*, since its style both in vocabulary and syntax is too complicated. It may be a fragment, and it may be by another hand than Shakespeare's. It is, nevertheless, a poem of very considerable distinction and cannot be said to be unworthy of Shakespeare.

The Lover's Complaint is in the form of the traditional complaint of a maiden forsaken by her lover. Her wild, pastoral dress is described as she stands on a hill beside a river. She is joined there by a venerable and sympathetic herdsman, and for the rest of the poem she gives him a description of her false and fickle lover. The poem uses the rhetoric of the passionate pastoral. The later romances, such as Sidney's *Arcadia* and *Don Quixote*, are full of such semi-realistic pictures. This one does not arrive at any solution.

THE

Passionate Pilgrim

I.

When my love swears that she is made of truth,
I do believe her, though I know she lies,
That she might think me some untutor'd youth,
Unskilful in the world's false forgeries.
Thus vainly thinking that she thinks me young,
Although I know my years be past the best,
I smiling credit her false-speaking tongue,
Outfacing faults in love with love's ill rest.
But wherefore says my love that she is young?
And wherefore say not I that I am old?   10
O, love's best habit is a soothing tongue,
And age, in love, loves not to have years told.
    Therefore I'll lie with love, and love with me,
    Since that our faults in love thus smother'd be.

II.

Two loves I have, of comfort and despair,
That like two spirits do suggest me still;
My better angel is a man right fair,
My worser spirit a woman colour'd ill.
To win me soon to hell, my female evil
Tempteth my better angel from my side,   20
And would corrupt my saint to be a devil,
Wooing his purity with her fair pride.
And whether that my angel be turn'd fiend,
Suspect I may, yet not directly tell;
For being both to me, both to each friend,
I guess one angel in another's hell:
    The truth I shall not know, but live in doubt,
    Till my bad angel fire my good one out.

III.

Did not the heavenly rhetoric of thine eye,
'Gainst whom the world could not hold argument,   30
Persuade my heart to this false perjury?
Vows for thee broke deserve not punishment.
A woman I forswore; but I will prove,
Thou being a goddess, I forswore not thee:
My vow was earthly, thou a heavenly love;
Thy grace being gain'd cures all disgrace in me.
My vow was breath, and breath a vapour is;
Then, thou fair sun, that on this earth doth shine,
Exhale this vapour vow; in thee it is:
If broken, then it is no fault of mine.   40
    If by me broke, what fool is not so wise
    To break an oath, to win a paradise?

IV.

Sweet Cytherea, sitting by a brook
With young Adonis, lovely, fresh, and green,
Did court the lad with many a lovely look,
Such looks as none could look but beauty's queen.
She told him stories to delight his ear;
She show'd him favours to allure his eye;
To win his heart, she touch'd him here and there,—
Touches so soft still conquer chastity.   50
But whether unripe years did want conceit,
Or he refused to take her figured proffer,
The tender nibbler would not touch the bait,
But smile and jest at every gentle offer:
    Then fell she on her back, fair queen, and toward:
    He rose and ran away; ah, fool too froward!

V.

If love make me forsworn, how shall I swear to love?
O never faith could hold, if not to beauty vow'd:
Though to myself forsworn, to thee I'll constant
    prove;
Those thoughts, to me like oaks, to thee like osiers
    bow'd.   60
Study his bias leaves, and makes his book thine eyes,
Where all those pleasures live that art can
    comprehend.
If knowledge be the mark, to know thee shall suffice;
Well learned is that tongue that well can thee
    commend;
All ignorant that soul that sees thee without wonder;
Which is to me some praise, that I thy parts admire:
Thine eye Jove's lightning seems, thy voice his
    dreadful thunder,
Which, not to anger bent, is music and sweet fire.
    Celestial as thou art, O do not love that wrong,   69
    To sing heaven's praise with such an earthly tongue.

VI.

Scarce had the sun dried up the dewy morn,
And scarce the herd gone to the hedge for shade,
When Cytherea, all in love forlorn,
A longing tarriance for Adonis made
Under an osier growing by a brook,
A brook where Adon used to cool his spleen:
Hot was the day; she hotter that did look
For his approach, that often there had been.
Anon he comes, and throws his mantle by,
And stood stark naked on the brook's green brim: 80
The sun look'd on the world with glorious eye,
Yet not so wistly as this queen on him.
    He, spying her, bounced in, whereas he stood:
    'O Jove,' quoth she, 'why was not I a flood!'

VII.

Fair is my love, but not so fair as fickle;

I. A slightly varying version of Sonnet CXXXVIII. 6. **Although . . . best,** although I know she knows my years are past the best (Dowden). 8. **Outfacing,** modifies *I.* **ill rest,** inconsistency, lack of stability. 11. **habit,** demeanor, with, however, a suggestion of garb, i.e., something put on; see glossary. **soothing,** flattering.

II. A variant of Sonnet CXLIV. 15-22. **Two . . . pride,** a variation of the myth of man's good and evil angels, as presented in Marlowe's *Dr. Faustus* (Brooke). 18. **a woman colour'd ill.** This phrase is the basis of extensive conjecture as to who the "dark lady" of the Sonnets was. 25. **For . . . friend,** being both friends to me and also to each other (Feuillerat). 26. **I . . . hell,** I suspect that she (the evil angel) has him in her power. 28. **fire . . . out,** drive out fire with fire; Rollins suggests the meaning, "communicate a venereal disease."

III. From *Love's Labour's Lost,* IV, iii, 60-73. 39. **Exhale,** draw

up, as the sun draws vapor from the earth (Herford). 41. **so, so . . . as.** 42. **break,** *Love's Labour's Lost: lose.*

IV. 44. **green,** fresh, young. 45. **lovely,** amorous. 52. **take,** accept, or possibly understand (Pooler). 55. **toward,** willing. 56. **froward,** not willing to yield, perverse.

V. From *Love's Labour's Lost,* IV, ii, 109-122. 61. **Study,** the student. **bias,** particular or habitual inclination. 70. **To sing,** *Love's Labour's Lost: That sings,* which gives a clearer sense.

⊢ VI. This sonnet, following Ovid, deals with Adonis bathing in a brook; cf. *The Taming of the Shrew,* Induction, ii, 51-53. 74. **tarriance,** tarrying. 82. **wistly,** wistfully, or merely intently. 83. **whereas,** where.

VII. The theme of this poem is a faithless woman's profession of love (Dowden).

Mild as a dove, but neither true nor trusty;
Brighter than glass, and yet, as glass is, brittle;
Softer than wax, and yet, as iron, rusty:
    A lily pale, with damask dye to grace her,
    None fairer, nor none falser to deface her.   90

Her lips to mine how often hath she joined,
Between each kiss her oaths of true love swearing!
How many tales to please me hath she coined,
Dreading my love, the loss thereof still fearing!
    Yet in the midst of all her pure protestings,
    Her faith, her oaths, her tears, and all were jestings.

She burn'd with love, as straw with fire flameth;
She burn'd out love, as soon as straw outburneth;
She framed the love, and yet she foil'd the framing;
She bade love last, and yet she fell a-turning.   100
    Was this a lover, or a lecher whether?
    Bad in the best, though excellent in neither.

VIII.

If music and sweet poetry agree,
As they must needs, the sister and the brother,
Then must the love be great 'twixt thee and me,
Because thou lovest the one, and I the other.
Dowland to thee is dear, whose heavenly touch
Upon the lute doth ravish human sense;
Spenser to me, whose deep conceit is such
As, passing all conceit, needs no defence.   110
Thou lovest to hear the sweet melodious sound
That Phœbus' lute, the queen of music, makes;
And I in deep delight am chiefly drown'd
Whenas himself to singing he betakes.
    One god is god of both, as poets feign;
    One knight loves both, and both in thee remain.

IX.

Fair was the morn when the fair queen of love,
    *   *   *   *   *
Paler for sorrow than her milk-white dove,
For Adon's sake, a youngster proud and wild;   120
Her stand she takes upon a steep-up hill:
Anon Adonis comes with horn and hounds;
She, silly queen, with more than love's good will,
Forbade the boy he should not pass those grounds:
'Once,' quoth she, 'did I see a fair sweet youth
Here in these brakes deep-wounded with a boar,
Deep in the thigh, a spectacle of ruth!
See, in my thigh,' quoth she, 'here was the sore.'
    She showed hers: he saw more wounds than one,
    And blushing fled, and left her all alone.   130

X.

Sweet rose, fair flower, untimely pluck'd, soon vaded,
Pluck'd in the bud, and vaded in the spring!
Bright orient pearl, alack, too timely shaded!

Fair creature, kill'd too soon by death's sharp sting!
    Like a green plum that hangs upon a tree,
    And falls, through wind, before the fall should be.

I weep for thee, and yet no cause I have;
For why thou left'st me nothing in thy will:
And yet thou left'st me more than I did crave;
For why I craved nothing of thee still: 140
    O yes, dear friend, I pardon crave of thee,
    Thy discontent thou didst bequeath to me.

XI.

Venus, with young Adonis sitting by her
Under a myrtle shade, began to woo him:
She told the youngling how god Mars did try her,
And as he fell to her, so fell she to him.
'Even thus,' quoth she, 'the warlike god embraced
        me,'
And then she clipp'd Adonis in her arms;
'Even thus,' quoth she, 'the warlike god unlaced me,'
As if the boy should use like loving charms;   150
'Even thus,' quoth she, 'he seized on my lips,'
And with her lips on his did act the seizure:
And as she fetched breath, away he skips,
And would not take her meaning nor her pleasure.
    Ah, that I had my lady at this bay,
    To kiss and clip me till I run away!

XII.

Crabbed age and youth cannot live together:
Youth is full of pleasance, age is full of care;
Youth like summer morn, age like winter weather;
Youth like summer brave, age like winter bare.   160
Youth is full of sport, age's breath is short;
    Youth is nimble, age is lame;
Youth is hot and bold, age is weak and cold;
    Youth is wild, and age is tame.
Age, I do abhor thee; youth, I do adore thee;
    O, my love, my love is young!
Age, I do defy thee: O, sweet shepherd, hie thee,
    For methinks thou stay'st too long.

XIII.

Beauty is but a vain and doubtful good;
A shining gloss that vadeth suddenly;   170
A flower that dies when first it gins to bud;
A brittle glass that 's broken presently:
    A doubtful good, a gloss, a glass, a flower,
    Lost, vaded, broken, dead within an hour.

And as goods lost are seld or never found,
As vaded gloss no rubbing will refresh,
As flowers dead lie wither'd on the ground,
As broken glass no cement can redress,
    So beauty blemish'd once 's for ever lost,
    In spite of physic, painting, pain and cost.   180

87. **brittle.** Perhaps for the rhyme we should read *brickle*, which was a common form of "brittle" (White). 89. **damask,** pale red (Schmidt). 101. **whether,** which of the two.
    VIII. A sonnet by Barnfield. 105. **'twixt thee and me,** i.e., between Barnfield and R.L., to whom he addressed the poem. 107. **Dowland,** John Dowland (1563?-1626?), lutanist and composer. 109, 110. **conceit, conceit,** imaginative conception, play of fancy. 116. **One knight.** It has been suggested that the knight is Sir George Carey, K.G., to whom Dowland dedicated his first book of airs (Rollins).
    IX. There is apparently a line missing in this sonnet. The rhyme is with *wild* (l. 120); for the many conjectures see the Variorum. 121. **steep-up.** Cf. Sonnet VII, 5. 129. **one,** in Shakespeare's English a possible rhyme with *alone.*
    X. 131, 132. **vaded.** The forms "fade" and "vade" are distinct, not

only in spelling but in origin. The latter (from Lat. *vadere*) means "to depart, to disappear," and is therefore a stronger word than *fade*, "to lose color" (Carleton Brown).
    XI. This sonnet is believed to be the work of Bartholomew Griffin and closely resembles a sonnet (No. III) in the collection entitled *Fidessa* (1596). 153. **And,** regarded by Dyce as an error for *But*. 155. **at this bay,** in my power (Herford).
    XII. A popular song several times alluded to in the seventeenth century. 158. **pleasance,** gaiety, merriment.
    XIII. 176. **vaded.** Cf. x, 131, 132. **gloss,** variously interpreted as "polish," "faded silk," "gilding." 178. **cement,** accented on the first syllable.
    XIV. This and the following are printed as one poem in *The Passionate Pilgrim*. Malone divided them as in the text; Dowden objected

XIV.

Good night, good rest. Ah, neither be my share:
She bade good night that kept my rest away;
And daff'd me to a cabin hang'd with care,
To descant on the doubts of my decay.
   'Farewell,' quoth she, 'and come again to-morrow:'
   Fare well I could not, for I supp'd with sorrow.

Yet at my parting sweetly did she smile,
In scorn or friendship, nill I construe whether:
'T may be, she joy'd to jest at my exile,
'T may be, again to make me wander thither: 190
   'Wander,' a word for shadows like myself,
   As take the pain, but cannot pluck the pelf.

XV.

Lord, how mine eyes throw gazes to the east!
My heart doth charge the watch; the morning rise
Doth cite each moving sense from idle rest.
Not daring trust the office of mine eyes,
   While Philomela sits and sings, I sit and mark,
   And wish her lays were tuned like the lark;

For she doth welcome daylight with her ditty,
And drives away dark dismal-dreaming night: 200
The night so pack'd, I post unto my pretty;
Heart hath his hope, and eyes their wished sight;
   Sorrow changed to solace, solace mix'd with sorrow;
   For why, she sigh'd and bade me come to-morrow.

Were I with her, the night would post too soon;
But now are minutes added to the hours;
To spite me now, each minute seems a moon;
Yet not for me, shine sun to succour flowers!
   Pack night, peep day; good day, of night now
      borrow;
   Short, night, to-night, and length thyself
      to-morrow.   210

SONNETS TO SUNDRY NOTES OF MUSIC

[XVI.]

It was a lording's daughter, the fairest one of three,
That liked of her master as well as well might be,
Till looking on an Englishman, the fair'st that eye
     could see,
   Her fancy fell a-turning.
Long was the combat doubtful that love with love did
     fight,
To leave the master loveless, or kill the gallant knight:
To put in practice either, alas, it was a spite
   Unto the silly damsel!
But one must be refused; more mickle was the pain
That nothing could be used to turn them both to gain,
For of the two the trusty knight was wounded with
     disdain: 221

Alas, she could not help it!
Thus art with arms contending was victor of the day,
Which by a gift of learning did bear the maid away:
Then, lullaby, the learned man hath got the lady gay;
   For now my song is ended.

XVII.

On a day, alack the day!
Love, whose month was ever May,
Spied a blossom passing fair,
Playing in the wanton air: 230
Through the velvet leaves the wind,
All unseen, gan passage find;
That the lover, sick to death,
Wish'd himself the heaven's breath,
'Air,' quoth he, 'thy cheeks may blow;
Air, would I might triumph so!
But, alas! my hand hath sworn
Ne'er to pluck thee from thy thorn:
Vow, alack! for youth unmeet:
Youth, so apt to pluck a sweet.   240
Thou for whom Jove would swear
Juno but an Ethiope were;
And deny himself for Jove,
Turning mortal for thy love.'

[XVIII.]

My flocks feed not,
My ewes breed not,
My rams speed not,
   All is amiss:
Love's denying,
Faith's defying,   250
Heart's renying,
   Causer of this.
All my merry jigs are quite forgot,
All my lady's love is lost, God wot:
Where her faith was firmly fix'd in love,
There a nay is placed without remove.
One silly cross
Wrought all my loss;
   O frowning Fortune, cursed, fickle dame!
For now I see   260
Inconstancy
   More in women than in men remain.

In black mourn I,
All fears scorn I,
Love hath forlorn me,
   Living in thrall:
Heart is bleeding,
All help needing,
O cruel speeding,
   Fraughted with gall.   270
My shepherd's pipe can sound no deal;
My wether's bell rings doleful knell;

The Passionate Pilgrim

461

to this division. 181. **be,** is (Schmidt); are (Pooler); let neither be (Kittredge). 183. **daff'd,** put aside, turned away. **cabin,** small room, bedroom. 184. **descant,** compose variations, make musical variations (Rollins). 192. **As,** rather *who* than *which* (Kittredge).
XV. 194. **My . . . watch,** variously interpreted: my heart doth charge my eyes to watch the morning rise (Pooler); accuse the watch for marking the time so slowly (Rolfe); give notice to the watchman to proclaim the dawn (Kittredge). 205-207. **Were . . . moon.** Malone cites *Romeo and Juliet*, III, v, 44 ff.
XVI. A popular song in which a maiden hesitates in her choice between a learned man and a knight and takes the learned man. Brown connects the song with the medieval ballad theme *Disputatio inter militem et clericum.* 211. **lording's,** lord's. 212. **master,** teacher, tutor.
XVII. From *Love's Labour's Lost*, IV, iii, 101-120. 230. **wanton,**

frolicsome, sportive. 240. Brown suggests the introduction after this line of two verses from *Love's Labour's Lost* which are necessary to the sense:
    Do not call it sin in me
    That I am forsworn for thee.
XVIII. First published in a collection of madrigals by Thomas Weelkes; reprinted in *England's Helicon* (1600) as "The Unknown Shepherd's Complaint." There is an excellent contemporary manuscript of the poem, Harl. 6910, fol. 156b. 249. **Love's denying,** so Malone *et al.; The Passionate Pilgrim: Love is dying; England's Helicon: Loue is denying.* 251. **renying,** forswearing (Malone); disowning (Schmidt). 253. **jigs,** ballads and songs or dance tunes (Rollins). 270. **Fraughted,** loaded, burdened. 271. **no deal,** nothing.

My curtail dog, that wont to have play'd,
Plays not at all, but seems afraid;
My sighs so deep
Procures to weep,
    In howling wise, to see my doleful plight.
How sighs resound
Through heartless ground,
    Like a thousand vanquish'd men in bloody
        fight!   280

Clear wells spring not,
Sweet birds sing not,
Green plants bring not
    Forth their dye;
Herds stand weeping,
Flocks all sleeping,
Nymphs back peeping
    Fearfully:
All our pleasure known to us poor swains,
All our merry meetings on the plains,   290
All our evening sport from us is fled,
All our love is lost, for Love is dead.
Farewell, sweet lass,
Thy like ne'er was
    For a sweet content, the cause of all my moan:
Poor Corydon
Must live alone;
    Other help for him I see that there is none.

XIX.

When as thine eye hath chose the dame,
And stall'd the deer that thou shouldst strike,   300
Let reason rule things worthy blame,
† As well as fancy partial might:
    Take counsel of some wiser head,
    Neither too young nor yet unwed.

And when thou comest thy tale to tell,
Smooth not thy tongue with filed talk,
Lest she some subtle practice smell,—
A cripple soon can find a halt;—
    But plainly say thou lovest her well,
    And set thy person forth to sell.   310

What though her frowning brows be bent,
Her cloudy looks will calm ere night:
And then too late she will repent
That thus dissembled her delight;
    And twice desire, ere it be day,
    That which with scorn she put away.

What though she strive to try her strength,
And ban and brawl, and say thee nay,
Her feeble force will yield at length,
When craft hath taught her thus to say,   320
    'Had women been so strong as men,
    In faith, you had not had it then.'

And to her will frame all thy ways;
Spare not to spend, and chiefly there

Where thy desert may merit praise,
By ringing in thy lady's ear:
    The strongest castle, tower, and town,
    The golden bullet beats it down.

Serve always with assured trust,
And in thy suit be humble true;   330
Unless thy lady prove unjust,
Press never thou to choose anew:
    When time shall serve, be thou not slack
    To proffer, though she put thee back.

The wiles and guiles that women work,
Dissembled with an outward show,
The tricks and toys that in them lurk,
The cock that treads them shall not know.
    Have you not heard it said full oft,
    A woman's nay doth stand for nought?   340

† Think women still to strive with men,
To sin and never for to saint:
There is no heaven, by holy then,
When time with age doth them attaint.
    Were kisses all the joys in bed,
    One woman would another wed.

But, soft! enough, too much, I fear;
Lest that my mistress hear my song,
She will not stick to round me i' the ear,
To teach my tongue to be so long: 350
    Yet will she blush, here be it said,
    To hear her secrets so bewray'd.

[XX.]

Live with me, and be my love,
And we will all the pleasures prove
That hills and valleys, dales and fields,
And all the craggy mountains yields.

There will we sit upon the rocks,
And see the shepherds feed their flocks,
By shallow rivers, by whose falls
Melodious birds sing madrigals.   360

There will I make thee a bed of roses,
With a thousand fragrant posies,
A cap of flowers, and a kirtle
Embroider'd all with leaves of myrtle.

A belt of straw and ivy buds,
With coral clasps and amber studs;
And if these pleasures may thee move,
Then live with me and be my love.

LOVE'S ANSWER.

If that the world and love were young,
And truth in every shepherd's tongue,   370
These pretty pleasures might me move
To live with thee and be thy love.

---

276. **Procures,** so *The Passionate Pilgrim*; Globe *et al.*: *Procure*. The dog
procures (i.e., manages matters) so as to weep (Steevens). 279. **heartless,** possibly exhausted (Steevens).
    XIX. The text of *The Passionate Pilgrim* is poor. There exists a
much better version in a contemporary manuscript now in the Folger
Library. 300. **stall'd,** enclosed, got within range of. 302. **As . . .
might,** a difficult crux. Some editors follow Lyson's manuscript, reading
like for *might*; Furnivall suggested: *as fancy's partial might*. 306. **filed
talk,** studied or polished language (Malone). 340. **A . . . nought.**

Cf. *The Two Gentlemen of Verona*, I, ii, 55-56. 341. **Think,** expect.
342. **To . . . saint,** Folger MS.: *and not to live so like a saint*. 343. **by
holy then,** possibly, by all that's sacred (Steevens); Folger MS.: *be
holy then*. 349. **to round . . . ear,** to whisper or to tell secretly (Johnson);
some editors explain "strike me on the ear"; some follow Boswell's
conjecture: *wring mine ear*.
    XX. The first publication of Marlowe's lyric, which appeared also
in *England's Helicon* (1600), with the accompanying poem, "The
Nymph's Reply to the Shepherd," attributed to Sir Walter Raleigh;

[XXI.]

As it fell upon a day
In the merry month of May,
Sitting in a pleasant shade
Which a grove of myrtles made,
Beasts did leap, and birds did sing,
Trees did grow, and plants did spring;
Every thing did banish moan,
Save the nightingale alone: 380
She, poor bird, as all forlorn,
Lean'd her breast up-till a thorn,
And there sung the dolefull'st ditty,
That to hear it was great pity:
'Fie, fie, fie,' now would she cry;
'Tereu, tereu!' by and by;
That to hear her so complain,
Scarce I could from tears refrain;
For her griefs, so lively shown,
Made me think upon mine own.   390
Ah, thought I, thou mourn'st in vain!
None takes pity on thy pain:
Senseless trees they cannot hear thee;
Ruthless beasts they will not cheer thee:
King Pandion he is dead;
All thy friends are lapp'd in lead;
All thy fellow birds do sing,
Careless of thy sorrowing.
Even so, poor bird, like thee,
None alive will pity me.   400
Whilst as fickle Fortune smiled,
Thou and I were both beguiled.
   Every one that flatters thee
Is no friend in misery.
Words are easy, like the wind;
Faithful friends are hard to find;
Every man will be thy friend
Whilst thou hast wherewith to spend;
But if store of crowns be scant,
No man will supply thy want.   410
If that one be prodigal,
Bountiful they will him call,
And with such-like flattering,
'Pity but he were a king;'
If he be addict to vice,
Quickly him they will entice;
If to women he be bent,
They have at commandement:
But if Fortune once do frown,
Then farewell his great renown;   420
They that fawn'd on him before
Use his company no more.
He that is thy friend indeed,
He will help thee in thy need:
If thou sorrow, he will weep;
If thou wake, he cannot sleep;
Thus of every grief in heart
He with thee doth bear a part.
These are certain signs to know
Faithful friend from flattering foe.   430

THE

Phœnix and the Turtle

Let the bird of loudest lay,
On the sole Arabian tree,
Herald sad and trumpet be,
To whose sound chaste wings obey.

But thou shrieking harbinger,
Foul precurrer of the fiend,
Augur of the fever's end,
To this troop come thou not near!

From this session interdict
Every fowl of tyrant wing,   10
Save the eagle, feather'd king:
Keep the obsequy so strict.

Let the priest in surplice white,
That defunctive music can,
Be the death-divining swan,
Lest the requiem lack his right.

And thou treble-dated crow,
That thy sable gender makest
With the breath thou givest and takest,
'Mongst our mourners shalt thou go.   20

Here the anthem doth commence:
Love and constancy is dead;
Phœnix and the turtle fled
In a mutual flame from hence.

So they loved, as love in twain
Had the essence but in one;
Two distincts, division none:
Number there in love was slain.

*The Phœnix
and the Turtle*

463

many publications and manuscripts. 360. **madrigals,** pastoral songs or love songs. 360-362. Cf. *The Merry Wives of Windsor,* III, i, 17-20.
  XXI. From Richard Barnfield's *Poems in Divers Humors* (1598). 382. **up-till,** up against. 386. **Tereu.** Pooler suggests allusion to Tereus in Ovid's *Metamorphoses,* VI, 424-676. 395. **King Pandion,** the king of Athens, father of Philomela and Progne in Ovid's story. 396. **lapp'd in lead,** placed in a leaden coffin. 415. **addict,** inclined, addicted. 418. **They have.** One should understand "them," i.e., women, after *have.*

1. **the bird.** Rollins suggests the nightingale. It may be no special bird but merely the bird of loudest song. 2. **Arabian tree.** Malone cites *The Tempest,* III, iii, 22-24, and Lyly's *Euphues and his England:* "As there is but one *Phenix* in the world, so is there but one tree in Arabia where-in she buyldeth." 3. **trumpet,** trumpeter; cf. *King John,* I, i, 27-28. 4. **chaste wings,** refers not to the bird of line 1 but to the other birds summoned to the obsequies by the trumpeter bird of loudest lay (Rollins, following Fairchild). **obey,** are obedient. 5. **harbinger.** Malone defines as the "scritch-owl" and cites *A Midsummer-Night's Dream,* V, i, 383-385. 6. **precurrer,** forerunner. 14. **That . . . can,** that understands funeral music (Malone). 15. **death-divining swan,** alludes to the belief that the swan sings when it is about to die. 16. **his right,** its right (of music) (Fairchild quoted by Rollins). 17. **treble-dated crow.** The word *treble-dated* means "a comparatively large number." Pooler quotes Holland's Pliny (VII, xlviii, 180): "*Hesiodus* . . . saith forsooth, That a crow liveth 9 times as long as we; and the harts or stags 4 times as long as the crow; but the ravens thrice as long as they." 18-19. **That . . . takest.** These lines seem best explained by a quotation from *Hortus Sanitatis,* bk. iii, sec. 34, in Seager's *Natural History in Shakespeare's Time:* "They [ravens] are said to conceive and to lay eggs at the bill. The young become black on the seventh day." 27. **distincts,** separate or individual persons or things (*NED*). 28. **Number . . . slain,** refers to the mathematical dictum "one is no number." That is, by the "two" being "one" they "slay" the number (Rollins, following Adams). They are distinct and yet are made one by the power of love.

Hearts remote, yet not asunder;
Distance, and no space was seen   30
'Twixt this turtle and his queen:
But in them it were a wonder.

So between them love did shine,
That the turtle saw his right
Flaming in the phœnix' sight;
Either was the other's mine.

Property was thus appalled,
That the self was not the same;
Single nature's double name
Neither two nor one was called.   40

Reason, in itself confounded,
Saw division grow together,
To themselves yet either neither,
Simple were so well compounded,

That it cried, How true a twain
Seemeth this concordant one!
Love hath reason, reason none,
If what parts can so remain.

Whereupon it made this threne
To the phœnix and the dove,   50
Co-supremes and stars of love,
As chorus to their tragic scene.

THRENOS.

Beauty, truth, and rarity,
Grace in all simplicity,
Here enclosed in cinders lie.

Death is now the phœnix' nest;
And the turtle's loyal breast
To eternity doth rest,

Leaving no posterity:
'Twas not their infirmity,   60
It was married chastity.

Truth may seem, but cannot be:
Beauty brag, but 'tis not she;
Truth and beauty buried be.

To this urn let those repair
That are either true or fair;
For these dead birds sigh a prayer.

31. **this,** Globe: *the,* a reading due to Malone's error. 32. **But . . .
wonder,** this phenomenon, had it been seen anywhere but in them,
would have seemed wonderful. 36. **mine,** may mean "mine own"
or "rich treasure." The latter is the more probable. 37-38. **Property
. . . same.** Property is a Latinism, *proprietas,* peculiar or essential
quality; cf. *Richard II,* III, ii, 135. "Property" was appalled to find
out that personality had been destroyed, since each lover's identity was
merged into the other's and was no longer itself (Feuillerat). 41-44.
Reason . . . compounded, pure reason had seen those unlike and,
according to its insight quite incompatible, unite together. In the union
neither had an entirely separate identity, *simple,* that is, simples or
elementary elements, were so perfectly compounded or united (Fairchild, quoted by Rollins). 47-48. **Love . . . remain,** love, which
ordinarily lacks reason, is reasonable, and reason itself lacks reason if
two that are disunited nevertheless remain in union. 49. **threne,**
(and THRENOS below), lamentation, funeral song. 55. **cinders,** ashes.

From off a hill whose concave womb re-worded
A plaintful story from a sistering vale,
My spirits to attend this double voice accorded,
And down I laid to list the sad-tuned tale;
Ere long espied a fickle maid full pale,
Tearing of papers, breaking rings a-twain,
Storming her world with sorrow's wind and rain.

Upon her head a platted hive of straw,
Which fortified her visage from the sun,
Whereon the thought might think sometime it saw   10
The carcass of a beauty spent and done:
Time had not scythed all that youth begun,
Nor youth all quit; but, spite of heaven's fell rage,
Some beauty peep'd through lattice of sear'd age.

Oft did she heave her napkin to her eyne,
Which on it had conceited characters,
Laundering the silken figures in the brine
That season'd woe had pelleted in tears,
And often reading what contents it bears;
As often shrieking undistinguish'd woe,   20
In clamours of all size, both high and low.

Sometimes her levell'd eyes their carriage ride,
As they did battery to the spheres intend;
Sometime diverted their poor balls are tied
To the orbed earth; sometimes they do extend
Their view right on; anon their gazes lend
To every place at once, and, nowhere fix'd,
The mind and sight distractedly commix'd.

Her hair, nor loose nor tied in formal plat,
Proclaim'd in her a careless hand of pride;   30
For some, untuck'd, descended her sheaved hat,
Hanging her pale and pined cheek beside;
Some in her threaden fillet still did bide,
And true to bondage would not break from thence,
Though slackly braided in loose negligence.

A thousand favours from a maund she drew
Of amber, crystal, and of beaded jet,
Which one by one she in a river threw,
Upon whose weeping margent she was set;
Like usury, applying wet to wet,   40
Or monarch's hands that let not bounty fall
Where want cries some, but where excess begs all.

Of folded schedules had she many a one,

1. **re-worded,** re-echoed. 2. **sistering,** neighboring. 3. **spirits,**
pronounced as one syllable, probably "spirts." 10. **the thought,** the
mind; that which thinks. 14. **lattice,** i.e., wrinkles. 16. **conceited
characters,** fanciful or emblematic devices. 18. **pelleted,** formed into
small globules. 22. **levell'd . . . carriage,** metaphor from the aiming
and firing of a gun. 24. **diverted,** turned away. 28. **commix'd,** confused. 29. **in formal plat,** neatly braided. 30. **careless hand of pride,**
studied carelessness. 31. **sheaved hat.** Cf. l. 8, *platted hive of straw.*
33. **threaden,** made of woven threads. 36. **maund,** woven basket
with handles. 43. **schedules,** papers containing writing. 45. **posied,**
inscribed with a motto. 48. **sleided silk,** floss silk. **feat,** featly,
adroitly. **affectedly,** lovingly. 50. **fluxive,** flowing. 52. **register,**
recorder. 55. **top of,** extreme. 57. **reverend,** i.e., suggesting old

Which she perused, sigh'd, tore, and gave the flood;
Crack'd many a ring of posied gold and bone,
Bidding them find their sepulchres in mud;
Found yet moe letters sadly penn'd in blood,
With sleided silk feat and affectedly
Enswathed, and seal'd to curious secrecy.

These often bathed she in her fluxive eyes, 50
And often kiss'd, and often 'gan to tear;
Cried 'O false blood, thou register of lies,
What unapproved witness dost thou bear!
Ink would have seem'd more black and damned here!'
This said, in top of rage the lines she rents,
Big discontent so breaking their contents.

A reverend man that grazed his cattle nigh—
Sometime a blusterer, that the ruffle knew
Of court, of city, and had let go by
The swiftest hours, observed as they flew— 60
Towards this afflicted fancy fastly drew,
And, privileged by age, desires to know
In brief the grounds and motives of her woe.

So slides he down upon his grained bat,
And comely-distant sits he by her side;
When he again desires her, being sat,
Her grievance with his hearing to divide:
If that from him there may be aught applied
Which may her suffering ecstasy assuage,
'Tis promised in the charity of age. 70

'Father,' she says, 'though in me you behold
The injury of many a blasting hour,
Let it not tell your judgement I am old;
Not age, but sorrow, over me hath power:
I might as yet have been a spreading flower,
Fresh to myself, if I had self-applied
Love to myself and to no love beside.

'But, woe is me! too early I attended
A youthful suit—it was to gain my grace—
Of one by nature's outwards so commended, 80
That maidens' eyes stuck over all his face:
Love lack'd a dwelling, and made him her place;
And when in his fair parts she did abide,
She was new lodged and newly deified.

'His browny locks did hang in crooked curls;
And every light occasion of the wind
Upon his lips their silken parcels hurls.
What's sweet to do, to do will aptly find:
Each eye that saw him did enchant the mind,
For on his visage was in little drawn 90
What largeness thinks in Paradise was sawn.

'Small show of man was yet upon his chin;
His phœnix down began but to appear

Like unshorn velvet on that termless skin
Whose bare out-bragg'd the web it seem'd to wear:
Yet show'd his visage by that cost more dear;
And nice affections wavering stood in doubt
If best were as it was, or best without.

'His qualities were beauteous as his form,
For maiden-tongued he was, and thereof free; 100
Yet, if men moved him, was he such a storm
As oft 'twixt May and April is to see,
When winds breathe sweet, unruly though they be.
His rudeness so with his authorized youth
Did livery falseness in a pride of truth.

'Well could he ride, and often men would say
"That horse his mettle from his rider takes:
Proud of subjection, noble by the sway,
What rounds, what bounds, what course, what stop he
  makes!"
And controversy hence a question takes, 110
Whether the horse by him became his deed,
Or he his manage by the well-doing steed.

'But quickly on this side the verdict went:
His real habitude gave life and grace
To appertainings and to ornament,
Accomplish'd in himself, not in his case:
All aids, themselves made fairer by their place,
Came for additions; yet their purposed trim
Pieced not his grace, but were all graced by him.

'So on the tip of his subduing tongue 120
All kind of arguments and question deep,
All replication prompt, and reason strong,
For his advantage still did wake and sleep:
To make the weeper laugh, the laugher weep,
He had the dialect and different skill,
Catching all passions in his craft of will:

'That he did in the general bosom reign
Of young, of old; and sexes both enchanted,
To dwell with him in thoughts, or to remain
In personal duty, following where he haunted: 130
Consents bewitch'd, ere he desire, have granted;
And dialogued for him what he would say,
Ask'd their own wills, and made their wills obey.

'Many there were that did his picture get,
To serve their eyes, and in it put their mind;
Like fools that in th' imagination set
The goodly objects which abroad they find
Of lands and mansions, theirs in thought assign'd;
And labouring in moe pleasures to bestow them
Than the true gouty landlord which doth owe them:

'So many have, that never touch'd his hand, 141
Sweetly supposed them mistress of his heart.

age. 58. **blusterer,** boisterous fellow. **ruffle,** commotion. 61. **fancy,**
person in love. **fastly,** rapidly. 64. **grained,** pronged, forked. **bat,**
club. 69. **ecstasy,** temporary madness. 88. **to do . . . find,** i.e., will
find a doer. 89. **the mind,** i.e., of the beholder. 91. **sawn,** to be
seen; an archaism. 93. **phœnix,** suggesting his unique perfection.
94. **termless,** youthful (Pooler). 95. **bare,** bareness. 96. **cost,** perhaps
a double pun: cost, "expense" and French *coste* (*côte*), "refuse silk."
The meaning may be, his face seemed lovelier from its rich (or silken)
covering (Pooler). 102. **to see,** to be seen. 105. **livery,** dress.
pride, magnificent costume. 109. **stop,** sudden check in a horse's
"career" or trial gallop at full speed. 111-112. **Whether . . . steed,**
whether it was owing to his horsemanship that his horse acted so
becomingly or whether he seemed such a good rider because he had so

good a horse (Pooler). 114. **real,** two syllables. **habitude,** constitution, temperament. 115. **appertainings,** belongings, appurtenances.
116. **case,** the body, as enclosing the soul (Onions); conditions and
circumstances, e.g., the possession of so good a horse (Pooler). 118.
for, equivalent to "as." 119. **Pieced,** added to. 122. **replication,**
reply. 125. **dialect,** manner of expression. **different,** varied, readily
adaptable. 126. **craft of will,** skill in achieving his desires. 127.
general bosom, hearts of all. 128-130. **sexes . . . haunted,** by his
fascination he caused both men and women to think of him continually or even to live as his attendants, going where he went (Pooler).
131. **Consents,** consenting persons (Pooler); it is the subject of the
verbs *have granted* and *(have) dialogued.* 135. **in it put their mind,** let
their minds become engrossed.

My woeful self, that did in freedom stand,
And was my own fee-simple, not in part,
What with his art in youth, and youth in art,
Threw my affections in his charmed power,
Reserved the stalk and gave him all my flower.

'Yet did I not, as some my equals did,
Demand of him, nor being desired yielded;
Finding myself in honour so forbid,   150
With safest distance I mine honour shielded:
Experience for me many bulwarks builded
Of proofs new-bleeding, which remain'd the foil
Of this false jewel, and his amorous spoil.

'But, ah, who ever shunn'd by precedent
The destined ill she must herself assay?
Or forced examples, 'gainst her own content,
To put the by-past perils in her way?
Counsel may stop awhile what will not stay;
For when we rage, advice is often seen   160
By blunting us to make our wits more keen.

'Nor gives it satisfaction to our blood,
That we must curb it upon others' proof;
To be forbod the sweets that seem so good,
For fear of harms that preach in our behoof.
O appetite, from judgement stand aloof!
The one a palate hath that needs will taste,
Though Reason weep, and cry "It is thy last."

'For further I could say "This man 's untrue,"
And knew the patterns of his foul beguiling;   170
Heard where his plants in others' orchards grew,
Saw how deceits were gilded in his smiling;
Knew vows were ever brokers to defiling;
Thought characters and words merely but art,
And bastards of his foul adulterate heart.

'And long upon these terms I held my city,
Till thus he gan besiege me: "Gentle maid,
Have of my suffering youth some feeling pity,
And be not of my holy vows afraid:
That 's to ye sworn to none was ever said;   180
For feasts of love I have been call'd unto,
Till now did ne'er invite, nor never woo.

'"All my offences that abroad you see
Are errors of the blood, none of the mind;
Love made them not: with acture they may be,
Where neither party is nor true nor kind:
They sought their shame that so their shame did
        find;
And so much less of shame in me remains,
By how much of me their reproach contains.

'"Among the many that mine eyes have seen,   190
Not one whose flame my heart so much as warm'd,
Or my affection put to the smallest teen,
Or any of my leisures ever charm'd:
Harm have I done to them, but ne'er was harm'd;

Kept hearts in liveries, but mine own was free,
And reign'd, commanding in his monarchy.

'"Look here, what tributes wounded fancies sent me,
Of pallid pearls and rubies red as blood;
Figuring that they their passions likewise lent me
Of grief and blushes, aptly understood   200
In bloodless white and the encrimson'd mood;
Effects of terror and dear modesty,
Encamp'd in hearts, but fighting outwardly.

'"And, lo, behold these talents of their hair,
With twisted metal amorously impleach'd,
I have received from many a several fair,
Their kind acceptance weepingly beseech'd,
With the annexions of fair gems enrich'd,
And deep-brain'd sonnets that did amplify
Each stone's dear nature, worth, and quality.   210

'"The diamond,—why, 'twas beautiful and hard,
Whereto his invised properties did tend;
The deep-green emerald, in whose fresh regard
Weak sights their sickly radiance do amend;
The heaven-hued sapphire and the opal blend
With objects manifold: each several stone,
With wit well blazon'd, smiled or made some moan.

'"Lo, all these trophies of affections hot,
Of pensived and subdued desires the tender,
Nature hath charged me that I hoard them not,   220
But yield them up where I myself must render,
That is, to you, my origin and ender;
For these, of force, must your oblations be,
Since I their altar, you enpatron me.

'"O, then, advance of yours that phraseless hand,
Whose white weighs down the airy scale of praise;
Take all these similes to your own command,
Hallow'd with sighs that burning lungs did raise;
What me your minister, for you obeys,
Works under you; and to your audit comes   230
Their distract parcels in combined sums.

'"Lo, this device was sent me from a nun,
Or sister sanctified, of holiest note;
Which late her noble suit in court did shun,
Whose rarest havings made the blossoms dote;
For she was sought by spirits of richest coat,
But kept cold distance, and did thence remove,
To spend her living in eternal love.

'"But, O my sweet, what labour is 't to leave
The thing we have not, mastering what not strives, 240
†Playing the place which did no form receive,
Playing patient sports in unconstrained gyves?
She that her fame so to herself contrives,
The scars of battle 'scapeth by the flight,
And makes her absence valiant, not her might.

'"O, pardon me, in that my boast is true:
The accident which brought me to her eye

144. **my own fee-simple,** absolute power over myself (Malone). **in part,** a part-owner. 146. **charmed power,** i.e., he has power to charm. 155. **precedent,** advice. 156. **assay,** learn by experience (Onions). 164. **forbod,** forbidden. 174. **characters and words,** i.e., the written and spoken word. 185. **acture,** action, performance. 195. **in liveries,** i.e., the uniform of a person in service. 198. **pallid,** Globe, following Malone: *paled;* Q: *palyd.* 204. **talents,** treasures, riches. 205. **impleach'd,** intertwined. 209. **deep-brain'd,** full of profound thought

(Onions). 212. **invised,** invisible (Onions); perhaps, inspected, investigated, tried (Schmidt); possibly related to "vise." 213. **regard,** sight, view; i.e., in viewing which. 215. **blend,** usually explained as blended; perhaps "blending with" or "that blends with" in the sense of matching or resembling (Pooler). 219. **pensived,** saddened. 224. **Since . . . me,** since I am the altar, you are my patron saint. 225. **phraseless,** which there is no word to describe (Onions). 229. **What . . . obeys,** whatever obeys me, your minister, acting on your authority.

Upon the moment did her force subdue,
And now she would the caged cloister fly:
Religious love put out Religion's eye: 250
Not to be tempted, would she be immured,
And now, to tempt, all liberty procured.

'"How mighty then you are, O, hear me tell!
The broken bosoms that to me belong
Have emptied all their fountains in my well,
And mine I pour your ocean all among:
I strong o'er them, and you o'er me being strong,
Must for your victory us all congest,
As compound love to physic your cold breast.

'"My parts had power to charm a sacred nun,   260
Who, disciplined, ay, dieted in grace,
Believed her eyes when they to assail begun,
All vows and consecrations giving place:
O most potential love! vow, bond, nor space,
In thee hath neither sting, knot, nor confine,
For thou art all, and all things else are thine.

'"When thou impressest, what are precepts worth
Of stale example? When thou wilt inflame,
How coldly those impediments stand forth
Of wealth, of filial fear, law, kindred, fame!   270
†Love's arms are peace, 'gainst rule, 'gainst sense,
          'gainst shame,
And sweetens, in the suffering pangs it bears,
The aloes of all forces, shocks, and fears.

'"Now all these hearts that do on mine depend,
Feeling it break, with bleeding groans they pine;
And supplicant their sighs to you extend,
To leave the battery that you make 'gainst mine,
Lending soft audience to my sweet design,
And credent soul to that strong-bonded oath
That shall prefer and undertake my troth."   280

'This said, his watery eyes he did dismount,
Whose sights till then were levell'd on my face;
Each cheek a river running from a fount
With brinish current downward flow'd apace:
O, how the channel to the stream gave grace!
Who glazed with crystal gate the glowing roses
That flame through water which their hue encloses.

'O father, what a hell of witchcraft lies
In the small orb of one particular tear!
But with the inundation of the eyes   290
What rocky heart to water will not wear?
What breast so cold that is not warmed here?
O cleft effect! cold modesty, hot wrath,
Both fire from hence and chill extincture hath.

'For, lo, his passion, but an art of craft,
Even there resolved my reason into tears;
There my white stole of chastity I daff'd,
Shook off my sober guards and civil fears;
Appear to him, as he to me appears,

235. blossoms, the flower of the young nobility (Malone). 241. Playing, so Q; many emendations; Malone's Paling, i.e., enclosing, makes
a sort of sense. 242. unconstrained gyves, fetters imposing no restraint
(Schmidt); fetters one is not obliged to wear (Pooler). 250. Religious,
dutiful. 267. impressest, compellest. 273. aloes, bitterness. 293.
cleft, twofold. 294. extincture, extinction. 297. daff'd, doffed; i.e.,
put off.

All melting; though our drops this difference bore,   300
His poison'd me, and mine did him restore.

'In him a plenitude of subtle matter,
Applied to cautels, all strange forms receives,
Of burning blushes, or of weeping water,
Or swooning paleness; and he takes and leaves,
In either's aptness, as it best deceives,
To blush at speeches rank, to weep at woes,
Or to turn white and swoon at tragic shows:

'That not a heart which in his level came
Could 'scape the hail of his all-hurting aim,   310
Showing fair nature is both kind and tame;
And, veil'd in them, did win whom he would maim:
Against the thing he sought he would exclaim;
When he most burn'd in heart-wish'd luxury,
He preach'd pure maid, and praised cold chastity.

'Thus merely with the garment of a Grace
The naked and concealed fiend he cover'd;
That th' unexperient gave the tempter place,
Which like a cherubin above them hover'd.
Who, young and simple, would not be so lover'd?   320
Ay me! I fell; and yet do question make
What I should do again for such a sake.

'O, that infected moisture of his eye,
O, that false fire which in his cheek so glow'd,
O, that forced thunder from his heart did fly,
O, that sad breath his spongy lungs bestow'd,
O, all that borrow'd motion seeming owed,
Would yet again betray the fore-betray'd,
And new pervert a reconciled maid!'

303. cautels, crafty devices. 312. them. The antecedent is strange
forms (l. 303). 318. unexperient, unexperienced. 322. sake, inducement. 323. infected, i.e., not natural, insincere. 327. seeming owed,
seemingly owned; i.e., emotion which he seemed to have or feel.

*A courtship scene from Philip Stubbes, "Anatomy
of Abuses," 1583.*

Sonnets

In 1598 Francis Meres speaks admiringly of Shakespeare's "sugared sonnets among his private friends." The *Sonnets* were entered in the Stationers' Register by Thomas Thorpe on May 20, 1609, and published, together with *A Lover's Complaint*, by him that year. The volume has as a full page this puzzling dedication:

TO. THE. ONLIE. BEGETTER. OF. THESE. INSVING. SONNETS. MR. W. H. ALL. HAPPINESSE. AND. THAT. ETERNITIE. PROMISED. BY. OVR. EVER-LIVING. POET. WISHETH. THE. WELL-WISHING. ADVENTURER. IN. SETTING. FORTH. T. T.

"T.T." obviously stands for Thomas Thorpe. There is, so far as known, no later quarto edition; but in 1640 John Benson reissued 146 of the sonnets in a different order and with a poorer text. The text of the 1609 edition is a good one in spite of unusually numerous misprints and bad punctuation. Two of the sonnets (cxxxviii and cxliv) had been issued before in a volume printed by Jaggard in 1599, attributed to Shakespeare, and entitled *The Passionate Pilgrim*.

It has been recognized by most scholars that the volume of the *Sonnets*, as published by Thorpe, falls into two divisions: Numbers i-cxxvi seem to be addressed to a young highborn patron and friend; Numbers cxxvii-clii are addressed to, or refer to, a dark woman of beauty and malign influence. This division is in conformity to the first four lines in one of the sonnets printed by Jaggard (Number cxliv):

> Two loves I have of comfort and despair,
> Which like two spirits do suggest me still:
> The better angel is a man right fair,
> The worser spirit a woman colour'd ill.

PROBLEMS OF SHAKESPEARE'S SONNETS

No Shakespearean subject has been fraught with such perplexity as that of the *Sonnets*, and no subject has, in general, yielded less to the research and ingenuity of the scholar. One asks, in the first place, whether or not the *Sonnets* are a true cycle, or only a series of sonnet groups and individual poems; and, if it is granted that the *Sonnets* are one cycle, whether or not the arrangement in Thorpe's volume is the true one, or if a true one can be discovered. One asks, in the second place, whether or not the *Sonnets* are pure fiction, or in part fiction. Or are they wholly devoted to the expression of Shakespeare's personal reactions to situations in his own life arising from his primary affection for a man and his secondary affection for a woman? And, of course, one asks who the man and the woman were.

The *Sonnets* have the somewhat unusual characteristic of being mainly addressed to a man instead of a woman and of treating friendship instead of love as

the basal sentiment and applying to it the conventional passion of the sonnet. In spite of the difficulty, in writing sonnets, of following a thread of narrative, the same large themes recur and the groups hang together. One concludes that the *Sonnets* constitute a cycle, not, however, a completed and unified whole. One of the most convincing of modern opinions is that the *Sonnets* were written as a series of poetical epistles and gathered up, at least the first one hundred twenty-six of them, roughly in the order in which they were composed. It was for Sir Sidney Lee to call attention to the circumstance that Shakespeare's *Sonnets* partake of the nature of Renaissance sonnets in general and have a full measure of the conventionality of that conventional form. He has demonstrated this by an overpowering body of parallels. The inference from his work, one in which he did not fully share, is that Shakespeare set himself the task of composing a sonnet cycle of the ordinary mode and that that task was a literary exercise, only faintly, if at all, grounded in the circumstances of his own life. The view has found few adherents, mainly because the *Sonnets* seem too personal, too convincingly individual, to admit of a merely fictitious basis.

THE STORY OF THE SONNETS

The collection is made up of groups of sonnets, of varying length, tied together by continuity of theme but not usually joined group to group. The themes, however, frequently recur. Between these groups, and not infrequently imbedded within the groups, are some sonnets of a personal nature, whose interpretation is obscure, and others of an apparently formal or artificial character. In quality the sonnets vary greatly, from the conventional and sometimes intricately worded constructions of sonneteering commonplace to the finest and most original of all lyric verse. The collection begins with a group of twenty-six sonnets. The first seventeen are addressed (as are the first one hundred twenty-six) to a youth of nobility and beauty, who is urged to marry in order that his beauty may be perpetuated in his offspring; the next eight are on a variety of themes having to do with the poet's relation to the person addressed, and the last (Number xxvi) seems designed to accompany a gift, a "written ambassage." This sonnet serves to illustrate the poet's use of the language of love in addressing his patron, a practice seen elsewhere in Elizabethan literature. Numbers xxvii-xxxii and xlviii-lv mark periods in which the poet is absent from his friend, and lvi-lviii a period when the friend was absent from the poet. Number xxix is the sonnet beginning, "When, in disgrace with fortune and men's eyes," and Number xxx the one beginning, "When to the sessions of sweet silent thought." Numbers xxxiii-xxxv foreshadow an estrangement caused by a fault in the friend. Number xxxiii is "Full many a glorious morning have I seen." Numbers xxxviii-xlii tell specifically that the fault mentioned in Numbers xxxiii-xxxv was that the fair youth has robbed the poet of his mistress. This subject recurs at length in Numbers cxxvii-clii, the so-called Dark Lady sonnets. There is no valid reason for thinking that the reference there is not to the episode presented in xxxviii-xlii.

The sonnets from liii to lxxvii are on a variety of topics and resemble nothing so much as a series of personal letters in sonnet form. They treat the power of love and beauty, the eternizing faculty of poetry (a theme of frequent recurrence), self-love as friend's love, the evil days of the present rescued by the perfections of the friend, a vision of the poet's death (Numbers lxxi-lxxiv), the bestowal of an album. The first lines of some of the more distinguished sonnets in this division are: Number lx: "Like as the waves make towards the pebbled shore," Number lxiv: "When I have seen by Time's fell hand defaced," Number lxxiii: "That time of year thou mayst in me behold." Next comes the famous series on the "Rival Poet," Numbers lxxviii-lxxxvi. The poet reproaches his patron for the favor which has been bestowed upon some other candidate, a poet. Numbers lxxxviii-xciii continue the theme of estrangement, now a personal matter, and the loss of loving confidence rather than mere patronage. Numbers xciv-xcvi dwell obscurely on some fault committed by the friend (a subject also touched upon in Numbers lxix-lxx), and Numbers xcvii-xcix recur to the theme of absence. Numbers c-civ are a sort of apology for long silence, Number civ being a sketch of the duration of the friendship, which is seen to have been three years.

Numbers civ-cxxv are much variegated in the thoughts and emotions they express. In some cases the youth is addressed with all the lavish affection of the earlier sonnets. They celebrate his beauty and virtue and renew protests of eternal faithfulness, as if they arose from an attempt to restore a dying affection. This group of sonnets is miscellaneous in character and does not lend itself to any time scheme. Indeed, it may contain sonnets written before the main body.

Number cxxvi is not a true sonnet but a twelve-line poem in couplets, often regarded as an envoy to the series. Its connection, however, is not apparent, since it seems to repeat as an affectionate warning the frequently recurrent thought that, although the youth is still beautiful, his beauty must perish. Perhaps it foreshadows some more immediate doom.

Sonnets cxxvii-clii are mainly addressed to a woman, the Dark Lady. Perhaps they do not introduce a new element into the story, but appear in their present setting because they were so placed in the printer's manuscript. They apparently refer to the issue of love and rivalry elaborated in the first series. J. A. Fort, whose interpretation of the Sonnets is mentioned below, thinks that Numbers cxxvii, cxxviii, cxxx-cxxxii were written at a time when the mistress still favored the poet, and that Numbers cxxxv-clii represent an attempt on the poet's part to regain his mistress for himself, except, however, that Numbers cxxxviii, cxliv, and cxlvi were never intended for the mistress' eye. Numbers cliii and cliv are sonnets on Cupid, which seem superfluous, and were placed at the end no doubt by the printer's perplexity as to where they might belong.

The most recent significant study of the groupings of the Sonnets is that of Tucker Brooke.[1] He thinks that the sonnets were written in groups and sent to the friend usually on single sheets of Elizabethan paper and that later these sheets were gathered up roughly in the order of their composition and ultimately used as the basis of Thorpe's text of 1609. Brooke thought, however, that in some cases these sheets were placed in a wrong order. His attempt to replace these disarranged groups in their proper places is so reasonable and works so well in practice that we give a list of the original numbers in the order in which, according to the late Professor Brooke, they should be read: 1-35, 40-42, 36-39, 43-58, 61-65, 59-60, 66-70, 94-96, 81, 71-74, 76, 75, 77-80, 82-93, 97-108, 115-116, 113-114, 109-112, 117-128, 130-131, 150, 132, 148, 137, 139-142, 149, 143, 135-136, 145, 151, 138, 144, 133-134, 152, 147, 129, 146, 153-154.

SHAKESPEARE AND SOUTHAMPTON

It is natural that scholars in search of the fair youth of noble blood, Shakespeare's adored friend in the Sonnets, should have bethought them of Henry Wriothesley third Earl of Southampton, since the dedications of both Venus and Adonis (1593) and Lucrece (1594) furnish evidence of acquaintanceship and probably special personal relations between Shakespeare and Southampton at the very time when sonnets were being written by most English poets. Nathan Drake in Shakespeare and his Times (1817) not only suggested that Southampton was the patron and friend to whom Shakespeare addressed the Sonnets, but brought forward one of the best pieces of evidence yet discovered to prove that it was so, namely, that "the language of the Dedication to the Rape

Kingswood fo:

[1] Shakespeare's Sonnets (1936).

of Lucrece, and that part of the 26th sonnet, are almost precisely the same."

Fort has put forward in this connection the attractive idea that the first twenty-six sonnets were sent to Southampton with the copy of *Lucrece*, which was thus the "written ambassage." The Southampton theory was advocated at great length by Gerald Massey in *The Secret Drama of Shakespeare's Sonnets* (1888) and has the support of the best contemporary opinion, notably, that of the late Sir Sidney Lee.

An important recent study of the question is that of Fort,[2] who has displayed great ingenuity in fitting the various groups of the sonnets into situations in the lives of Shakespeare and Southampton during a period from the spring of the year 1593 to January or February 1601. He assumes that Southampton was the person addressed in the *Sonnets*, and sees in the Dark Lady sonnets (xxxviii-xlii, cxxvii-clii) and others, reflections of special events which indicate that the fair youth was not an imaginary person. The Rival Poet group (lxxviii-lxxxvii) indicates, he thinks, that the sonnets were addressed to a single individual; and from the parallel between the dedication of *Lucrece* and sonnet Number xxvi he concludes that there was an actual connection between Shakespeare and Southampton. From sonnet Number civ he traces the chronology of the relationship. Shakespeare shows no personal acquaintance with Southampton in the dedication to *Venus and Adonis*, and the date of its entry in the Stationers' Register (April 1593) would have been an inevitable time for such an acquaintance to have been made. Sonnet civ marks the end of the third year of their friendship. It follows then that, if Thorpe's arrangement reproduces the order in which the sonnets were written, the first one hundred four of them at least had been composed by the spring of 1596.

Fort then proceeds by the study of the absence groups and other details to distribute the various sonnets through the years 1593-1596. Sonnet cvii he dates in November 1598 on the hypothesis that it celebrates Southampton's release from prison, whither he had been consigned because of the queen's anger at his marriage with Lady Elizabeth Vernon. The year 1599, after Southampton's return from Essex' Irish expedition, occasioned a brief renewal of the intimacy between Shakespeare and his patron during which time certain of the sonnets Numbers cvii-cxxv were written. Sonnet cxxvi he regards as the conclusion of the intimacy and as a warning to Southampton against his participation in the machinations of Essex. After 1601 Southampton was a close prisoner for the rest of the queen's reign and under sentence of death for treason. In spite, however, of the considerable detail offered in support of the Southampton hypothesis, there remain serious objections to its adoption.

A confirmation of the dating of the sonnets just de-scribed is to be found in the fact that those works, plays and poems, believed to have been written during the period from 1592 to 1596, have the greatest numbers of parallels to the *Sonnets*.[3]

PEMBROKE—"MR. W. H."

The rival theory to that of Southampton is the one which makes William Herbert third Earl of Pembroke the person addressed in the *Sonnets*. He too was a brilliant youth at the court of Elizabeth in the last years of her reign. To him and his brother Philip Earl of Montgomery was dedicated the First Folio in 1623, and it is there stated that these noblemen had "prosecuted" both the plays and their author living with much favor. Thorpe's dedication of the volume of the *Sonnets* of 1609 is to "Mr. W. H.," described as "the onlie begetter of these insuing sonnets." "W. H.," it has been thought, may stand for "William Herbert," though it has also been argued that, since "W. H." may be the inverted initials of "Henry Wriothesley," they may, therefore, refer quite as well to Southampton.

Against both identifications is the objection that it would have been most unbecoming for Thorpe to have addressed either of these great noblemen in such a fashion. Many explanations of Thorpe's puzzling words have been attempted. "Onlie begetter" seems to indicate the very source of the inspiration which caused the *Sonnets* to be written. The best of these theories, itself somewhat lame, is that which identifies "Mr. W. H." with one William Hall, a person known to have supplied manuscripts to publishers. This compels us to understand the words "onlie begetter of these insuing sonnets" as meaning the sole procurer of the manuscript from which they were printed. In any case, one is inclined to believe that the manuscript came from Shakespeare or from the person to whom the sonnets were addressed. Or, perhaps, it was a transcription of a manuscript coming from one of them, since the collection as printed shows hardly a trace of formal arrangement such as might have been expected had it been intended for publication or general circulation in manuscript. Against the Pembroke theory is Pembroke's youth. He was born in 1580 and was, therefore, a mere boy during the period when the poems were being written. With him comes the identification of Mary Fitton with the Dark Lady; with Southampton comes Mrs. Davenant in that capacity. For neither identification is there so far a shred of really convincing evidence.

"THE MORTAL MOON"

A revolutionary theory about the dating of the *Sonnets*, with important discoveries about three of them, has been put forward by Leslie Hotson.[4] He points out that sonnet cvii, which contains the line,

The mortal moon hath her eclipse endur'd,

refers to the defeat of the Spanish Armada in 1588.

[2]See note 5 below.

[3]Tucker Brooke, *op. cit.*, pp. 10-17.
[4]*Shakespeare's Sonnets Dated and Other Essays* (1949), pp. 1-36.

The battle formation of the Spanish fleet was that of a crescent, a fact often mentioned at the time and for years afterwards. Secondly, he interprets sonnet cxxiii as a reference to the erection in Rome by Pope Sixtus v of four Egyptian obelisks, called in the

that the order in which Thorpe printed the sonnets is the order in which they were composed. On the other hand, Shakespeare and other poets may have been writing sonnets by 1589, and much of Shakespeare's early work may need to be moved back in date, but

From George Carleton, "A Thankfull Remembrance . . . ." 1630.

language of the day "pyramids," in the years 1586, 1587, 1588, and 1589. From the language of the sonnet, which uses such words as "newer might," "novel," and "thy registers," Hotson judges that the pope's famous architectural achievement was current news when the sonnet was written. Finally, he sees in sonnet cxxiv an allusion to the assassination of Henri III of France on August 2, 1589, and would date the sonnet in that year. There can be no reasonable doubt as to the validity of these topical allusions. That the three sonnets were written in 1589 and not a few years later, is open to question. For actual contemporaneity the second case is best. Hotson believes, moreover, that the whole cycle was complete by 1589, and this hypothesis raises serious difficulties. It seems too early for the period of sonnet writing in England, which followed the publication in 1591 of Sidney's *Astrophel and Stella* with additions from Daniel's *Delia*. That the sonnets of Shakespeare were influenced by those of Daniel as well as Sidney is pretty obvious. To have completed the main group of the *Sonnets* by 1589 would reveal a maturity in Shakespeare's style and thought far in advance, not only of *Venus and Adonis* (1593) and *The Rape of Lucrece* (1594), but of the whole group of Shakespeare's early plays. It would leave unaccounted for the striking parallels in thought and expression, cited by Brooke, between the *Sonnets* and the plays written from about 1592 to 1596. There is no assurance

that Shakespeare had completed the whole cycle by 1589 is difficult to believe. In the present state of the question it seems reasonable to think that Hotson's three sonnets and perhaps others in the group in which they occur were written before the main sequence. Until there are further discoveries one can only state this complex problem in terms of all the known factors.

With reference to the question of personal significance we may take a moderate view and believe that, although the *Sonnets* do veritably belong to the Petrarchan tradition, employ its language and its situations, and resemble the sonnets of many other poets, they are, nevertheless, sincere utterances of Shakespeare as to events in his life and embody, not only the results of his constructive imagination, but the feelings of his heart.[5]

[5]From the large body of writings about the *Sonnets* may be selected, in addition to those referred to in the notes, the following: R. M. Alden, *The Sonnets of Shakespeare*, Variorum edition (Boston, 1916); Sir Denys Bray, *The Original Order of Shakespeare's Sonnets* (1925); Edward Dowden, *Shakespeare's Sonnets* (1881); J. A. Fort, *Two Dated Sonnets of Shakespeare* (1924), "Further Notes on Shakespeare's Sonnets," *The Library*, N. S. IX, 305-325, and *A Time Scheme for Shakespeare's Sonnets* (1930); Sir Sidney Lee, *A Life of William Shakespeare* (1909), pp. 87-164, 390-461, and *Elizabethan Sonnets* (2 v. Westminster, 1904), Introduction; C. Knox Pooler, *The Sonnets* (1918), Introduction; Mrs. C. C. Stopes, *Shakespeare's Sonnets* (1904); T. G. Tucker, *The Sonnets of Shakespeare* (Cambridge, 1924), Introduction and notes. Most important of all is *A New Variorum Edition of Shakespeare: The Sonnets*, ed. Hyder E. Rollins (2 v. Philadelphia, 1944).

Sonnets

TO THE ONLIE BEGETTER OF
THESE INSUING SONNETS
MR. W. H. ALL HAPPINESSE
AND THAT ETERNITIE
PROMISED BY
OUR EVER-LIVING POET
WISHETH
THE WELL-WISHING
ADVENTURER IN
SETTING
FORTH
T. T.

I.

FROM fairest creatures we desire increase,
That thereby beauty's rose might never die,
But as the riper should by time decease,
His tender heir might bear his memory:
But thou, contracted to thine own bright eyes,
Feed'st thy light's flame with self-substantial fuel,
Making a famine where abundance lies,
Thyself thy foe, to thy sweet self too cruel.
Thou that art now the world's fresh ornament
And only herald to the gaudy spring,
Within thine own bud buriest thy content
And, tender churl, makest waste in niggarding.
  Pity the world, or else this glutton be,
  To eat the world's due, by the grave and thee.

II.

When forty winters shall besiege thy brow,
And dig deep trenches in thy beauty's field,
Thy youth's proud livery, so gazed on now,
Will be a tatter'd weed, of small worth held:
Then being ask'd where all thy beauty lies,
Where all the treasure of thy lusty days,
To say, within thine own deep-sunken eyes,
Were an all-eating shame and thriftless praise.
How much more praise deserved thy beauty's use,
If thou couldst answer 'This fair child of mine
Shall sum my count and make my old excuse,'
Proving his beauty by succession thine!
  This were to be new made when thou art old,
  And see thy blood warm when thou feel'st it cold.

III.

Look in thy glass, and tell the face thou viewest

Now is the time that face should form another;
Whose fresh repair if now thou not renewest,
Thou dost beguile the world, unbless some mother.
For where is she so fair whose unear'd womb
Disdains the tillage of thy husbandry?
Or who is he so fond will be the tomb
Of his self-love, to stop posterity?
Thou art thy mother's glass, and she in thee
Calls back the lovely April of her prime:
So thou through windows of thine age shalt see
Despite of wrinkles this thy golden time.
  But if thou live, remember'd not to be,
  Die single, and thine image dies with thee.

IV.

Unthrifty loveliness, why dost thou spend
Upon thyself thy beauty's legacy?
Nature's bequest gives nothing but doth lend,
And being frank she lends to those are free.
Then, beauteous niggard, why dost thou abuse
The bounteous largess given thee to give?
Profitless usurer, why dost thou use
So great a sum of sums, yet canst not live?
For having traffic with thyself alone,
Thou of thyself thy sweet self dost deceive.
Then how, when nature calls thee to be gone,
What acceptable audit canst thou leave?
  Thy unused beauty must be tomb'd with thee,
  Which, used, lives th' executor to be.

V.

Those hours, that with gentle work did frame
The lovely gaze where every eye doth dwell,
Will play the tyrants to the very same
And that unfair which fairly doth excel;
For never-resting time leads summer on
To hideous winter and confounds him there;
Sap check'd with frost and lusty leaves quite gone,
Beauty o'ersnow'd and bareness every where:
Then, were not summer's distillation left,
A liquid prisoner pent in walls of glass,
Beauty's effect with beauty were bereft,
Nor it nor no remembrance what it was:
  But flowers distill'd, though they with winter meet,
  Leese but their show; their substance still lives
  sweet.

VI.

Then let not winter's ragged hand deface
In thee thy summer, ere thou be distill'd:
Make sweet some vial; treasure thou some place
With beauty's treasure, ere it be self-kill'd.
That use is not forbidden usury
Which happies those that pay the willing loan;
That's for thyself to breed another thee,
Or ten times happier, be it ten for one;

Sonnets I-XVII are addressed to a young friend of the poet's. In them the young man is urged to marry so that his beauty may be perpetuated in his children.
  I. 5. **contracted,** engaged, espoused; Pooler sees a possible allusion to the fable of Narcissus; cf. *Venus and Adonis*, 161, note. 6. **self-substantial,** fuel of the substance of the flame itself (Dowden). 11. **thy content,** that which is contained in you; potential fatherhood (Pooler). 12. **makest . . . niggarding,** squander your substance by being miserly. The *Sonnets* are replete with such instances of oxymoron. 14. **by . . . thee,** by death and by your wilfully remaining childless.
  II. 4. **tatter'd weed,** worn-out garment. 8. **an all-eating . . . praise.** The phrases may be parallel: the shame of gluttony and the praise of extravagance, since you devour the world's due and are an unthrift of your beauty (Pooler). 9. **deserved,** would deserve (sub-

junctive). **use,** investment. Note with what variety this image of usury recurs in the next few sonnets (IV, 7, 13, 14; VI, 5; IX, 12), accompanied often with subtle word play.
  III. 3. **fresh repair,** healthful state. 4. **beguile,** cheat. **unbless,** withhold happiness from. 5. **unear'd,** untilled, uncultivated. 7. **will be,** i.e., that he will be (an ellipsis). 8. **self-love.** Cf. *All's Well that Ends Well*, I, i, 138-140. 9. **thy mother's glass.** Dowden takes this line (comparing XIII, 14) as an indication that the young man's father was not living—a view in which Tucker Brooke concurs. It has been urged, however, that the lines imply only that the boy resembles his mother more than his father. The same image is used in *The Rape of Lucrece*, 1758-1759 (as Malone noted) to indicate parental resemblance. 13. **remember'd not to be,** in such a way as not to be remembered. Only for the sake of being forgotten (Beeching). 14. **thine image,** any

Ten times thyself were happier than thou art,
If ten of thine ten times refigured thee:
Then what could death do, if thou shouldst depart,
Leaving thee living in posterity?
  Be not self-will'd, for thou art much too fair
  To be death's conquest and make worms thine heir.

VII.

Lo! in the orient when the gracious light
Lifts up his burning head, each under eye
Doth homage to his new-appearing sight,
Serving with looks his sacred majesty;
And having climb'd the steep-up heavenly hill,
Resembling strong youth in his middle age,
Yet mortal looks adore his beauty still,
Attending on his golden pilgrimage;
But when from highmost pitch, with weary car,
Like feeble age, he reeleth from the day,
The eyes, 'fore duteous, now converted are
From his low tract and look another way:
  So thou, thyself out-going in thy noon,
  Unlook'd on diest, unless thou get a son.

VIII.

Music to hear, why hear'st thou music sadly?
Sweets with sweets war not, joy delights in joy.
Why lovest thou that which thou receivest not gladly,
Or else receivest with pleasure thine annoy?
If the true concord of well-tuned sounds,
By unions married, do offend thine ear,
They do but sweetly chide thee, who confounds
In singleness the parts that thou shouldst bear.
Mark how one string, sweet husband to another,
Strikes each in each by mutual ordering,
Resembling sire and child and happy mother
Who all in one, one pleasing note do sing:
  Whose speechless song, being many, seeming one,
  Sings this to thee: 'thou single wilt prove none.'

IX.

Is it for fear to wet a widow's eye
That thou consumest thyself in single life?
Ah! if thou issueless shalt hap to die,
The world will wail thee, like a makeless wife;
The world will be thy widow and still weep
That thou no form of thee hast left behind,
When every private widow well may keep
By children's eyes her husband's shape in mind.
Look, what an unthrift in the world doth spend
Shifts but his place, for still the world enjoys it;
But beauty's waste hath in the world an end,
And kept unused, the user so destroys it.
  No love toward others in that bosom sits
  That on himself such murderous shame commits.

X.

For shame! deny that thou bear'st love to any,

Who for thyself art so unprovident.
Grant, if thou wilt, thou art beloved of many,
But that thou none lovest is most evident;
For thou art so possess'd with murderous hate
That 'gainst thyself thou stick'st not to conspire,
Seeking that beauteous roof to ruinate
Which to repair should be thy chief desire.
O, change thy thought, that I may change my mind!
Shall hate be fairer lodged than gentle love?
Be, as thy presence is, gracious and kind,
Or to thyself at least kind-hearted prove:
  Make thee another self, for love of me,
  That beauty still may live in thine or thee.

XI.

As fast as thou shalt wane, so fast thou growest
In one of thine, from that which thou departest;
And that fresh blood which youngly thou bestowest
Thou mayst call thine when thou from youth
      convertest.
Herein lives wisdom, beauty and increase;
Without this, folly, age and cold decay:
If all were minded so, the times should cease
And threescore year would make the world away.
Let those whom Nature hath not made for store,
Harsh, featureless and rude, barrenly perish:
Look, whom she best endow'd she gave the more;
Which bounteous gift thou shouldst in bounty
      cherish:
  She carved thee for her seal, and meant thereby
  Thou shouldst print more, not let that copy die.

XII.

When I do count the clock that tells the time,
And see the brave day sunk in hideous night;
When I behold the violet past prime,
And sable curls all silver'd o'er with white;
When lofty trees I see barren of leaves
Which erst from heat did canopy the herd,
And summer's green all girded up in sheaves
Borne on the bier with white and bristly beard,
Then of thy beauty do I question make,
That thou among the wastes of time must go,
Since sweets and beauties do themselves forsake
And die as fast as they see others grow;
  And nothing 'gainst Time's scythe can make
      defence
  Save breed, to brave him when he takes thee hence.

XIII.

O, that you were yourself! but, love, you are
No longer yours than you yourself here live:
Against this coming end you should prepare,
And your sweet semblance to some other give.
So should that beauty which you hold in lease
Find no determination; then you were

---

likeness of you.
  IV. 4. **frank,** liberal, bounteous. 8. **live,** quibble on the two
meanings, "having a livelihood" and "living in your posterity."
  V. 1-3. **Those . . . same,** an application of the Renaissance commonplace of Time as both constructive and destructive; frequent in the
Sonnets. 4. **unfair,** make unlovely; cf. *unbless,* III, 4. **fairly,** i.e., in
beauty. 9. **summer's distillation,** distilled perfume of flowers. 14.
Leese, lose.
  VI. 2. **distill'd,** i.e., dissolved in death, quibbling on the uses in
the preceding sonnet. 3. **vial,** i.e., continuing the metaphor of dis-
tilling perfume from the preceding sonnet; cf. v, 10, *walls of glass.*
treasure, enrich. 8. **ten for one,** continues the usury metaphor.
  VII. 2. **under,** earthly.
  VIII. 1. **Music to hear,** an absolute construction, a verbal noun

introducing the subject of hearing music. **sadly.** Cf. *Measure for
Measure,* IV, i, 13-15, note. 8. **In singleness,** i.e., by being unmarried.
  IX. 4. **makeless wife,** a widow.
  X. 7. **beauteous roof,** i.e., the young man's family, his house; cf.
XIII, 9. 9. **change . . . mind,** give up your aversion from marriage
that I may no longer believe that you hate mankind (Pooler). 11.
presence, appearance, bearing; a repetition of the idea in the words
fairer lodged.
  XI. 1-2. **As . . . departest.** Cf. v, 1-3. 6. **Without this,** the an-
tithesis of *Herein* (l. 5). 9. **for store,** as a source of supply (Pooler).
  XII. 6. **erst,** formerly. 11. **sweets . . . forsake,** sweetness and
beauty forsake sweet and beautiful things. 14. **Save . . . him,** except
children whose youth may set the scythe of Time at defiance.
  XIII. 6. **determination,** end.

Yourself again after yourself's decease,
When your sweet issue your sweet form should bear.
Who lets so fair a house fall to decay,
Which husbandry in honour might uphold
Against the stormy gusts of winter's day
And barren rage of death's eternal cold?
    O, none but unthrifts! Dear my love, you know
    You had a father: let your son say so.

XIV.

Not from the stars do I my judgement pluck;
And yet methinks I have astronomy,
But not to tell of good or evil luck,
Of plagues, of dearths, or seasons' quality;
Nor can I fortune to brief minutes tell,
Pointing to each his thunder, rain and wind,
Or say with princes if it shall go well,
By oft predict that I in heaven find:
But from thine eyes my knowledge I derive,
And, constant stars, in them I read such art
As truth and beauty shall together thrive,
If from thyself to store thou wouldst convert;
    Or else of thee this I prognosticate:
    Thy end is truth's and beauty's doom and date.

XV.

When I consider every thing that grows
Holds in perfection but a little moment,
That this huge stage presenteth nought but shows
Whereon the stars in secret influence comment;
When I perceive that men as plants increase,
Cheered and check'd even by the self-same sky,
Vaunt in their youthful sap, at height decrease,
And wear their brave state out of memory;
Then the conceit of this inconstant stay
Sets you most rich in youth before my sight,
Where wasteful Time debateth with Decay,
To change your day of youth to sullied night;
    And all in war with Time for love of you,
    As he takes from you, I engraft you new.

XVI.

But wherefore do not you a mightier way
Make war upon this bloody tyrant, Time?
And fortify yourself in your decay
With means more blessed than my barren rhyme?
Now stand you on the top of happy hours,
And many maiden gardens yet unset
With virtuous wish would bear your living flowers,
Much liker than your painted counterfeit:

So should the lines of life that life repair,
Which this, Time's pencil, or my pupil pen,
Neither in inward worth nor outward fair,
Can make you live yourself in eyes of men.
    To give away yourself keeps yourself still,
    And you must live, drawn by your own sweet skill.

XVII.

Who will believe my verse in time to come,
If it were fill'd with your most high deserts?
Though yet, heaven knows, it is but as a tomb
Which hides your life and shows not half your parts.
If I could write the beauty of your eyes
And in fresh numbers number all your graces,
The age to come would say 'This poet lies;
Such heavenly touches ne'er touch'd earthly faces.'
So should my papers yellow'd with their age
Be scorn'd like old men of less truth than tongue,
And your true rights be term'd a poet's rage
And stretched metre of an antique song:
    But were some child of yours alive that time,
    You should live twice; in it and in my rhyme.

XVIII.

Shall I compare thee to a summer's day?
Thou art more lovely and more temperate:
Rough winds do shake the darling buds of May,
And summer's lease hath all too short a date:
Sometime too hot the eye of heaven shines,
And often is his gold complexion dimm'd;
And every fair from fair sometime declines,
By chance or nature's changing course untrimm'd;
But thy eternal summer shall not fade
Nor lose possession of that fair thou owest;
Nor shall Death brag thou wander'st in his shade,
When in eternal lines to time thou growest:
    So long as men can breathe or eyes can see,
    So long lives this and this gives life to thee.

XIX.

Devouring Time, blunt thou the lion's paws,
And make the earth devour her own sweet brood;
Pluck the keen teeth from the fierce tiger's jaws,
And burn the long-lived phœnix in her blood;
Make glad and sorry seasons as thou fleets,
And do whate'er thou wilt, swift-footed Time,
To the wide world and all her fading sweets;
But I forbid thee one most heinous crime:
O, carve not with thy hours my love's fair brow,
Nor draw no lines there with thine antique pen;

XIV. 1. **pluck,** derive. 5. **to brief minutes,** i.e., foretell events to the precise minute. 8. **oft predict,** frequent predictions. 11-12, 14. **truth . . . convert; Thy end . . . date.** Dowden set off these examples of *such art* with quotation marks, a form which makes the structure more immediately clear.

XV. 2. **Holds in perfection,** maintains its prime. 3. **this huge stage.** Pooler notes that the metaphor of the stage and the audience is sustained through the next three lines in *comment* (l. 4) and *Cheered* and *check'd* (l. 6). 9. **inconstant stay,** constant or continual change. 11. **debateth with,** combines in battle with; *with* here implies association, not opposition, as is frequently its meaning in this idiom.

XVI. 8. **Much liker,** i.e., much more like you. 9. **lines of life,** usually explained as lineage, i.e., children. Dowden sees a play in *lines* on the meanings "lines of a picture or portrait," and "lines of verse"; living poems and pictures are children. 10. **Time's . . . pen.** Enclosed in brackets in Q; most editors read *this time's pencil,* etc. The present text construes the phrase in apposition with *this.*

XVII. 12. **stretched metre,** overstrained poetry (Dowden); poetic license (Tucker Brooke).

XVIII. This and the following sonnet develop the theme of the immortalizing power of poetry. 7. **every . . . declines.** Cf. XII, 11. 8. **untrimm'd,** stripped of ornaments. 12. **to . . . growest.** To grow to time is to be incorporated or become one with it and so to live while time lasts (Pooler).

XIX. 1. **Devouring Time.** Cf. the apostrophe to Time in *The Rape of Lucrece,* 925 ff. 5. **fleets,** fleetest. 11. **untainted,** a metaphor from tilting; a taint was a hit (Pooler).

Sonnets XX and XXI are in praise of the friend's beauty. Of XX Pooler says that it sounds as if Shakespeare had been furnished with a set of rhymes and challenged to bombast them out into a poem.

XX. 7. **hue, 'hues,'** sometimes explained as a pun on the name of William Hughes, taken by some scholars to be the W.H. of the dedication. 11. **defeated,** defrauded. 12. **to my purpose nothing,** out of line with my wishes.

XXI. Pooler thinks this sonnet belongs logically before CXXX. 1. **Muse,** poet. 4. **every fair,** every lovely thing. **rehearse,** mention. 5. **Making . . . compare,** joining in proud comparison (Dowden); uniting his *fair* to heaven by extravagant comparisons (Pooler). 8. **rondure,** sphere. 12. **gold candles,** stars. 13. **like . . . well,** like to deal in second-hand ideas (Tucker Brooke); like rumors rather than

Him in thy course untainted do allow
For beauty's pattern to succeeding men.
    Yet, do thy worst, old Time: despite thy wrong,
    My love shall in my verse ever live young.

XX.

A woman's face with Nature's own hand painted
Hast thou, the master-mistress of my passion;
A woman's gentle heart, but not acquainted
With shifting change, as is false women's fashion;
An eye more bright than theirs, less false in rolling,
Gilding the object whereupon it gazeth;
A man in hue, all 'hues' in his controlling,
Which steals men's eyes and women's souls amazeth.
And for a woman wert thou first created;
Till Nature, as she wrought thee, fell a-doting,
And by addition me of thee defeated,
By adding one thing to my purpose nothing.
    But since she prick'd thee out for women's pleasure,
    Mine be thy love and thy love's use their treasure.

XXI.

So is it not with me as with that Muse
Stirr'd by a painted beauty to his verse,
Who heaven itself for ornament doth use
And every fair with his fair doth rehearse;
Making a couplement of proud compare,
With sun and moon, with earth and sea's rich gems,
With April's first-born flowers, and all things rare
That heaven's air in this huge rondure hems.
O, let me, true in love, but truly write,
And then believe me, my love is as fair
As any mother's child, though not so bright
As those gold candles fix'd in heaven's air:
    Let them say more that like of hearsay well;
    I will not praise that purpose not to sell.

XXII.

My glass shall not persuade me I am old,
So long as youth and thou are of one date;
But when in thee time's furrows I behold,
Then look I death my days should expiate.
For all that beauty that doth cover thee
Is but the seemly raiment of my heart,
Which in thy breast doth live, as thine in me:
How can I then be elder than thou art?
O, therefore, love, be of thyself so wary
As I, not for myself, but for thee will;
Bearing thy heart, which I will keep so chary
As tender nurse her babe from faring ill.

Presume not on thy heart when mine is slain;
Thou gavest me thine, not to give back again.

XXIII.

As an unperfect actor on the stage
Who with his fear is put besides his part,
Or some fierce thing replete with too much rage,
Whose strength's abundance weakens his own heart,
So I, for fear of trust, forget to say
The perfect ceremony of love's rite,
And in mine own love's strength seem to decay,
O'ercharged with burden of mine own love's might.
O, let my books be then the eloquence
And dumb presagers of my speaking breast,
Who plead for love and look for recompense
More than that tongue that more hath more express'd.
    O, learn to read what silent love hath writ:
    To hear with eyes belongs to love's fine wit.

XXIV.

Mine eye hath play'd the painter and hath stell'd
Thy beauty's form in table of my heart;
My body is the frame wherein 'tis held,
And perspective it is best painter's art.
For through the painter must you see his skill,
To find where your true image pictured lies;
Which in my bosom's shop is hanging still,
That hath his windows glazed with thine eyes.
Now see what good turns eyes for eyes have done:
Mine eyes have drawn thy shape, and thine for me
Are windows to my breast, where-through the sun
Delights to peep, to gaze therein on thee;
    Yet eyes this cunning want to grace their art;
    They draw but what they see, know not the heart.

The Sonnets

475

XXV.

Let those who are in favour with their stars
Of public honour and proud titles boast,
Whilst I, whom fortune of such triumph bars,
Unlook'd for joy in that I honour most.
Great princes' favourites their fair leaves spread
But as the marigold at the sun's eye,
And in themselves their pride lies buried,
For at a frown they in their glory die.
The painful warrior famoused for fight,
After a thousand victories once foil'd,
Is from the book of honour razed quite,
And all the rest forgot for which he toil'd:
    Then happy I, that love and am beloved
    Where I may not remove nor be removed.

---

facts (Pooler). 14. **that ... sell.** Pooler sees this line as the converse of Proverbs 20:14: "It is naught, it is naught, saith the buyer." Malone notes parallels in *Love's Labour's Lost*, IV, iii, 240, and in *Troilus and Cressida*, IV, i, 78.

Sonnets XXII-XXV are four separate expressions of the poet's joy in his friend's love, introducing themes later elaborated (Tucker Brooke).

XXII. 4. **look I,** I foresee. **expiate,** end. 13. **Presume not on,** do not expect to receive back (Beeching).

XXIII. 5. **for fear of trust,** doubting of being trusted (Schmidt). Dowden thought the comparison was to the *unperfect actor* who dare not trust himself. He observed that in the first eight lines 5 and 6 refer to 1 and 2, 7 and 8 refer to 3 and 4. 9. **books,** the manuscript books in which he writes his *Sonnets* (Dowden); the *Sonnets* themselves (Massey); the most natural interpretation is that the poet refers to *Venus and Adonis* and *The Rape of Lucrece*, which he describes as *dumb presagers* of the love he cannot directly express, an interpretation which favors the Southampton theory (Tucker Brooke). Those who favor Sewell's emendation *looks* justify it on the ground that *books* are not *dumb presagers;* that the love which expresses itself in love poems is not silent. 10. **presagers,** those which indicate. 12. **More, more, more,** to a

greater degree; more ardors of love; more fully.

XXIV. 1. **stell'd,** fixed, installed; or possibly *steel'd,* i.e., engraved; Q: *steeld.* 4. **perspective,** optical device for producing fantastic images (Onions); a painter's highest art is to produce the illusion of distance, one thing seeming to lie behind another. You must look through the painter (my eye or myself) to see your picture, the product of his skill, which lies within him, i.e., in my heart (Dowden); the word *perspective* is used quibblingly. 7. **my bosom's shop.** The imagery is here changed; in 1-4 Shakespeare's eye is the brush, his heart the canvas, his body the frame, of his friend's picture. The second quatrain, 5-8, is connected with the first by the punning explanation of *perspective;* but by a turn of this strange kaleidoscope, the body ceases to be the frame, for part of it, viz., the bosom, has become a shop or studio in which the picture hangs. The windows of this shop are the friend's eyes looking in (Pooler). 13-14. **Yet ... heart.** Cf. *The Merchant of Venice,* III, ii, 63-69.

XXV. 4. **Unlook'd for,** neglected by the world, inconspicuous. 9. **painful,** enduring much. **fight,** Theobald's emendation of Q: *worth,* to rhyme with *quite;* he suggested as an alternative the emendation of *forth* for *quite.*

XXVI.

Lord of my love, to whom in vassalage
Thy merit hath my duty strongly knit,
To thee I send this written embassage,
To witness duty, not to show my wit:
Duty so great, which wit so poor as mine
May make seem bare, in wanting words to show it,
But that I hope some good conceit of thine
In thy soul's thought, all naked, will bestow it;
Till whatsoever star that guides my moving
Points on me graciously with fair aspect
And puts apparel on my tatter'd loving,
To show me worthy of thy sweet respect:
　　Then may I dare to boast how I do love thee;
　　Till then not show my head where thou mayst
　　　　prove me.

XXVII.

Weary with toil, I haste me to my bed,
The dear repose for limbs with travel tired;
But then begins a journey in my head,
To work my mind, when body's work's expired:
For then my thoughts, from far where I abide,
Intend a zealous pilgrimage to thee,
And keep my drooping eyelids open wide,
Looking on darkness which the blind do see:
Save that my soul's imaginary sight
Presents thy shadow to my sightless view,
Which, like a jewel hung in ghastly night,
Makes black night beauteous and her old face
　　new.
　　Lo! thus, by day my limbs, by night my mind,
　　For thee and for myself no quiet find.

XXVIII.

How can I then return in happy plight,
That am debarr'd the benefit of rest?
When day's oppression is not eased by night,
But day by night, and night by day, oppress'd?
And each, though enemies to either's reign,
Do in consent shake hands to torture me;
The one by toil, the other to complain
How far I toil, still farther off from thee.
I tell the day, to please him thou art bright
And dost him grace when clouds do blot the heaven:
So flatter I the swart-complexion'd night,
When sparkling stars twire not thou gild'st the even.

But day doth daily draw my sorrows longer
And night doth nightly make grief's strength seem
　　stronger.

XXIX.

When, in disgrace with fortune and men's eyes,
I all alone beweep my outcast state
And trouble deaf heaven with my bootless cries
And look upon myself and curse my fate,
Wishing me like to one more rich in hope,
Featured like him, like him with friends possess'd,
Desiring this man's art and that man's scope,
With what I most enjoy contented least;
Yet in these thoughts myself almost despising,
Haply I think on thee, and then my state,
Like to the lark at break of day arising
From sullen earth, sings hymns at heaven's gate;
　　For thy sweet love remember'd such wealth brings
　　That then I scorn to change my state with kings.

XXX.

When to the sessions of sweet silent thought
I summon up remembrance of things past,
I sigh the lack of many a thing I sought,
And with old woes new wail my dear time's waste:
Then can I drown an eye, unused to flow,
For precious friends hid in death's dateless night,
And weep afresh love's long since cancell'd woe,
And moan the expense of many a vanish'd sight:
Then can I grieve at grievances foregone,
And heavily from woe to woe tell o'er
The sad account of fore-bemoaned moan,
Which I new pay as if not paid before.
　　But if the while I think on thee, dear friend,
　　All losses are restored and sorrows end.

XXXI.

Thy bosom is endeared with all hearts,
Which I by lacking have supposed dead,
And there reigns love and all love's loving parts,
And all those friends which I thought buried.
How many a holy and obsequious tear
Hath dear religious love stol'n from mine eye
As interest of the dead, which now appear
But things removed that hidden in thee lie!
Thou art the grave where buried love doth live,
Hung with the trophies of my lovers gone,
Who all their parts of me to thee did give;

XXVI. This is regarded variously as an "envoy" to the twenty-five preceding sonnets and as a dedication to the next sequence (XXVI-XXXII). Its similarity in tone and phrasing to the dedication of *The Rape of Lucrece* has been frequently noted. 8. **all naked,** modifies *Duty* (l. 5). **bestow,** equip, clothe (Tyler). 9. **moving,** thought by Tyler to indicate that the poet is about to make a journey, an interpretation supported by the reference in the next sonnet to the poet's travels. The word may mean merely "living." 12. **thy,** so Malone; Q: *their,* regarded generally as a misprint; retained by some editors and explained variously as referring to (1) the stars, (2) thy soul's thought, (3) the sweet respect of the star.
　　Beginning with XXVII and continuing through the next five, the poet writes as one on a journey which takes him far from his friend. It is not unlikely that they record an actual physical separation.
　　XXVII. 6. **Intend,** direct. 11. **ghastly,** fearful. 13-14. **by day . . . find,** by day my limbs find no quiet for myself, i.e., on account of business of my own; by night my mind finds no quiet for thee, i.e., on your account, thinking of you (Dowden); this type of construction is called "chiastic," i.e., interlaced. It is not infrequent in Renaissance poetry.
　　XXVIII. 1. **plight,** state, condition. 6. **consent,** i.e., mutual agreement. 7. **to complain,** by causing me to complain. 9. **to please him.** There is some argument as to whether this phrase modifies *tell* or *bright;* the absence of any punctuation in Q leaves the line ambiguous.

12. **twire,** twinkle.
　　XXIX. 6. **Featured,** situated (Onions); more likely, formed; i.e., envying their good looks, their beauty of face. **like him, like him,** not a repetition but, as Pooler points out, "like a second man, like a third." 7. **scope,** probably implies both "range of powers" and "opportunity."
　　XXX. 1-2. **sessions . . . summon.** The metaphor is that of a court of law. Malone cites *Othello,* III, iii, 138-141. Unlike many of the sonnets this one does not sustain the figure. 4. **new wail,** lament anew. 8. **expense,** that which is spent. 9. **foregone,** past.
　　XXXI. 1. **endeared,** enhanced in value, made more precious. You have become dearer to me as representing all I have loved (Pooler). 6. **religious,** i.e., as fulfilling a duty. 7. **As interest of the dead.** The phrase carries out the idea of mourning as a duty owed to the dead. 8. **removed,** separated by time or space; i.e., absent. 12. **due of many,** i.e., the duty or obligation to many.
　　XXXII. 1. **my . . . day,** i.e., the day which will content me well. 5. **bettering of the time.** May we infer from these lines [5-6; 10] that Shakespeare had a sense of the wonderful progress of poetry in the time of Elizabeth? (Dowden). Rolfe thinks the reference is probably to the improvement to be expected in the future. 7. **Reserve,** preserve. 11. **dearer birth,** i.e., better poem, better artistic creation. 12. **To . . . equipage.** Sir Sidney Lee points out the frequency of this metaphor in Elizabethan literature. Tyler traced the line to a similar treatment of

That due of many now is thine alone:
　　Their images I loved I view in thee,
　　And thou, all they, hast all the all of me.

XXXII.

If thou survive my well-contented day,
When that churl Death my bones with dust shall cover,
And shalt by fortune once more re-survey
These poor rude lines of thy deceased lover,
Compare them with the bettering of the time,
And though they be outstripp'd by every pen,
Reserve them for my love, not for their rhyme,
Exceeded by the height of happier men.
O, then vouchsafe me but this loving thought:
'Had my friend's Muse grown with this growing age,
A dearer birth than this his love had brought,
To march in ranks of better equipage:
　　But since he died and poets better prove,
　　Theirs for their style I'll read, his for his love.'

XXXIII.

Full many a glorious morning have I seen
Flatter the mountain-tops with sovereign eye,
Kissing with golden face the meadows green,
Gilding pale streams with heavenly alchemy;
Anon permit the basest clouds to ride
With ugly rack on his celestial face,
And from the forlorn world his visage hide,
Stealing unseen to west with this disgrace:
Even so my sun one early morn did shine
With all-triumphant splendour on my brow;
But out, alack! he was but one hour mine;
The region cloud hath mask'd him from me now.
　　Yet him for this my love no whit disdaineth;
　　Suns of the world may stain when heaven's sun
　　　　staineth.

XXXIV.

Why didst thou promise such a beauteous day
And make me travel forth without my cloak,
To let base clouds o'ertake me in my way,
Hiding thy bravery in their rotten smoke?
'Tis not enough that through the cloud thou break,
To dry the rain on my storm-beaten face,
For no man well of such a salve can speak
That heals the wound and cures not the disgrace:
Nor can thy shame give physic to my grief;
Though thou repent, yet I have still the loss:

The offender's sorrow lends but weak relief
To him that bears the strong offence's cross.
　　Ah! but those tears are pearl which thy love sheds,
　　And they are rich and ransom all ill deeds.

XXXV.

No more be grieved at that which thou hast done:
Roses have thorns, and silver fountains mud;
Clouds and eclipses stain both moon and sun,
And loathsome canker lives in sweetest bud.
All men make faults, and even I in this,
Authorizing thy trespass with compare,
Myself corrupting, salving thy amiss,
Excusing thy sins more than thy sins are;
For to thy sensual fault I bring in sense—
Thy adverse party is thy advocate—
And 'gainst myself a lawful plea commence:
Such civil war is in my love and hate
　　That I an accessary needs must be
　　To that sweet thief which sourly robs from me.

XXXVI.

Let me confess that we two must be twain,
Although our undivided loves are one:
So shall those blots that do with me remain
Without thy help by me be borne alone.
In our two loves there is but one respect,
Though in our lives a separable spite,
Which though it alter not love's sole effect,
Yet doth it steal sweet hours from love's delight.
I may not evermore acknowledge thee,
Lest my bewailed guilt should do thee shame,
Nor thou with public kindness honour me,
Unless thou take that honour from thy name:
　　But do not so; I love thee in such sort
　　As, thou being mine, mine is thy good report.

XXXVII.

As a decrepit father takes delight
To see his active child do deeds of youth,
So I, made lame by fortune's dearest spite,
Take all my comfort of thy worth and truth.
For whether beauty, birth, or wealth, or wit,
Or any of these all, or all, or more,
Entitled in thy parts do crowned sit,
I make my love engrafted to this store:
So then I am not lame, poor, nor despised,
Whilst that this shadow doth such substance give

the figure in Marston's *Pygmalion* (1598); Marston was probably the borrower. **ranks . . . equipage,** thought to refer to a new school of poets—Chapman and Jonson probably.
　XXXIII. This sonnet begins a new theme. The poet has endured some indignity at the friend's hands and the friend has repented. 2. **Flatter,** explained by *sovereign;* the glance of a king is a compliment to a courtier (Pooler). The *NED* definition, "to encourage with hopeful or pleasing representations," is applicable here. 5. **permit,** to be construed as parallel with *Flatter*. 6. **rack,** mass of cloud driven before the wind in the upper air. 7. **forlorn,** accent on the first syllable. 8. **to west,** westward. 12. **region,** pertaining to the upper air. 14. **stain,** grow dim, be obscured, soiled (Pooler); cf. XXXV, 3.
　XXXIV. 4. **bravery,** finery, fine clothes. 8. **disgrace,** i.e., the scar, the disfigurement caused by his friend's harsh treatment. Pooler points out that this is the *loss* of line 10. 9. **shame,** repentance for the wrong done.
　XXXV. 3. **stain.** Cf. XXXIII, 14, note. **both moon and sun.** Fleay thought this a reference to Elizabeth (i.e., Cynthia, the moon goddess) and Southampton, with whom he assumed Shakespeare to be out of favor. 6. **Authorizing,** sanctioning, justifying. 7. **salving,** parallel in construction with *Authorizing, corrupting*, and *Excusing*. **amiss,** misdeed. 8. **Excusing . . . are,** making the excuse more than proportioned to the offense (Steevens). 9. **sensual,** pertaining to the flesh. **sense,** pertaining to the rational faculty; i.e., I reason away your offenses.

14. **sourly,** cruelly.
　XXXVI. Another series on the theme of separation begins here, interrupting the group that dwells on the wrongs suffered by the poet. Here it is the friend who has gone on a journey. 1. **twain,** parted. 3. **those blots,** several possible explanations: not moral turpitude but the professional occupation and lower social standing of the poet (Tyler); perhaps his *disgrace with fortune and men's eyes,* XXIX, whatever that may have been (Pooler); may be the darkening of soul expressed in sonnets CXLVII and CLII (Tucker Brooke). 5. **respect,** i.e., a mutual regard. 6. **separable spite,** spiteful separation (Schmidt); separating spite (Malone). The latter is warranted by Abbott's observation that adjectives in *-able* are active as well as passive.
　XXXVII. 3. **made lame.** This phrase and line 3 of LXXXIX have prompted a number of commentators to conjecture that Shakespeare was literally lame. The majority, however, agree with Dowden, who accepts the verb as figuratively used to express "a disability to join in the joyous movement of life." For other figurative occurrences of the word in Shakespeare, cf. *As You Like It*, I, iii, 6, and *Coriolanus*, IV, vii, 7. **dearest,** most bitter. 5-7. **beauty, birth,** etc. These lines are usually accepted as evidence that the *Sonnets* were addressed to a person of high rank. 7. **Entitled,** ennobled (Malone); as rightful owner by a just title (Pooler). 10. **shadow,** reflection, i.e., in the Platonic sense (Wyndham).

That I in thy abundance am sufficed
And by a part of all thy glory live.
　　Look, what is best, that best I wish in thee:
　　This wish I have; then ten times happy me!

XXXVIII.

How can my Muse want subject to invent,
While thou dost breathe, that pour'st into my verse
Thine own sweet argument, too excellent
For every vulgar paper to rehearse?
O, give thyself the thanks, if aught in me
Worthy perusal stand against thy sight;
For who 's so dumb that cannot write to thee,
When thou thyself dost give invention light?
Be thou the tenth Muse, ten times more in worth
Than those old nine which rhymers invocate;
And he that calls on thee, let him bring forth
Eternal numbers to outlive long date.
　　If my slight Muse do please these curious days,
　　The pain be mine, but thine shall be the praise.

XXXIX.

O, how thy worth with manners may I sing,
When thou art all the better part of me?
What can mine own praise to mine own self bring?
And what is 't but mine own when I praise thee?
Even for this let us divided live,
And our dear love lose name of single one,
That by this separation I may give
That due to thee which thou deservest alone.
O absence, what a torment wouldst thou prove,
Were it not thy sour leisure gave sweet leave
To entertain the time with thoughts of love,
Which time and thoughts so sweetly doth deceive,
　　And that thou teachest how to make one twain,
　　By praising him here who doth hence remain!

XL.

Take all my loves, my love, yea, take them all;
What hast thou then more than thou hadst before?
No love, my love, that thou mayst true love call;
All mine was thine before thou hadst this more.
Then if for my love thou my love receivest,
I cannot blame thee for my love thou usest;
But yet be blamed, if thou thyself deceivest
By wilful taste of what thyself refusest.
I do forgive thy robbery, gentle thief,
Although thou steal thee all my poverty;
And yet, love knows, it is a greater grief

To bear love's wrong than hate's known injury.
　　Lascivious grace, in whom all ill well shows,
　　Kill me with spites; yet we must not be foes.

XLI.

Those pretty wrongs that liberty commits,
When I am sometime absent from thy heart,
Thy beauty and thy years full well befits,
For still temptation follows where thou art.
Gentle thou art and therefore to be won,
Beauteous thou art, therefore to be assailed;
And when a woman woos, what woman's son
Will sourly leave her till she have prevailed?
Ay me! but yet thou mightst my seat forbear,
And chide thy beauty and thy straying youth,
Who lead thee in their riot even there
Where thou art forced to break a twofold truth,
　　Hers, by thy beauty tempting her to thee,
　　Thine, by thy beauty being false to me.

XLII.

That thou hast her, it is not all my grief,
And yet it may be said I loved her dearly;
That she hath thee, is of my wailing chief,
A loss in love that touches me more nearly.
Loving offenders, thus I will excuse ye:
Thou dost love her, because thou know'st I love her;
And for my sake even so doth she abuse me,
Suffering my friend for my sake to approve her.
If I lose thee, my loss is my love's gain,
And losing her, my friend hath found that loss;
Both find each other, and I lose both twain,
And both for my sake lay on me this cross:
　　But here 's the joy; my friend and I are one;
　　Sweet flattery! then she loves but me alone.

XLIII.

When most I wink, then do mine eyes best see,
For all the day they view things unrespected;
But when I sleep, in dreams they look on thee,
And darkly bright are bright in dark directed.
Then thou, whose shadow shadows doth make bright,
How would thy shadow's form form happy show
To the clear day with thy much clearer light,
When to unseeing eyes thy shade shines so!
How would, I say, mine eyes be blessed made
By looking on thee in the living day,
When in dead night thy fair imperfect shade
Through heavy sleep on sightless eyes doth stay!

XXXVIII.   Sir Sidney Lee points out the frequency in dedicatory
lines of the conceit developed in this sonnet; viz., that the patron may
claim as his own handiwork the protégé's accomplishment because he
inspires it.   1. **want . . . invent,** lack something to write about.   13.
If . . . days, possibly indicates that some means of circulation, privately,
if not by publication, was anticipated by the poet.
XXXIX.   1. **with manners,** decently, becomingly.   10. **sour,** bitter,
harsh; cf. **sourly,** XXXV, 14.
　　The three following sonnets revert to the theme of XXXIII-XXXV.
Tucker Brooke rearranges the six in a continuous series, placing
XXXVI-XXXIX after XLII. The commentators are inclined to interpret XL
(considering it with five others—XLI, XLII, CXXXIII, CXXXIV, CLXIV)
as biographically significant. Sir Sidney Lee finds here "strands of
wholly original sentiment" distinguishing these six from the rest of the
Sonnets, which for the most part are vigorous and original treatments of
stereotyped themes (see his chapter, "The Supposed Story of Intrigue
in the Sonnets," *Life,* pp. 151-160).
　　XL.   5. **my love . . . my love,** love of me . . . her whom I love
(Dowden).   7. **thyself,** so Gildon, followed by many others; Q: *this
selfe,* retained by Wyndham, who sees it as antithetical to *thyself* (l. 8);
retained also by Tucker Brooke, who explains it as "this other self of
yours."   10. **steal thee,** take for your own.   **all my property,** the poor

little that I have (Rolfe).
　　XLI.   Dowden points out that this sonnet develops the idea of line
13 of the preceding one.   2. **absent,** probably to be taken in a literal
and local as well as figurative sense (Tucker Brooke).   3. **befits.** The
subject is *wrongs* (l. 1); Abbott (333) points out the frequency in Shakespeare of the third person plural in *-s.*   5-6. **Gentle . . . assailed.**
The phrasing and the sentiment recall *1 Henry VI,* V, iii, 78-79.
12. **twofold truth,** her plighted love and your plighted friendship
(Pooler).
　　XLII.   3. **is . . . chief,** is chief cause of my lamentation.   8. **approve,**
try, test.   9. **my love's,** hers whom I love (as in LX, 5, 6).   14. **flattery,**
gratifying deception (Onions), as in *Othello,* IV, i, 133.
　　XLIII.   This picks up the theme of XXXVI-XXXIX, i.e., the friend's
absence, and continues it through XLVII.   2. **unrespected,** unnoticed.
4. **And . . . directed,** and illumined although closed are clearly directed
in the darkness (Dowden); is it possible that the phrase *darkly bright*
may mean that the eyes are bright most of all in the dark, because of
what they see in dreams? (Alden).   5. **whose . . . bright,** whose image
makes darkness bright (Pooler).   6. **thy shadow's form,** probably, the
substance of the shadow; i.e., your presence.   8. **unseeing eyes,** i.e.,
closed eyes of the dreamer.   11. **imperfect,** unsubstantial (Tyler);
perhaps indistinct as in a dream.   13. **All . . . to see,** all days are

All days are nights to see till I see thee,
And nights bright days when dreams do show thee
me.

XLIV.

If the dull substance of my flesh were thought,
Injurious distance should not stop my way;
For then despite of space I would be brought,
From limits far remote, where thou dost stay.
No matter then although my foot did stand
Upon the farthest earth removed from thee;
For nimble thought can jump both sea and land
As soon as think the place where he would be.
But, ah! thought kills me that I am not thought,
To leap large lengths of miles when thou art gone,
But that so much of earth and water wrought
I must attend time's leisure with my moan,
    Receiving nought by elements so slow
    But heavy tears, badges of either's woe.

XLV.

The other two, slight air and purging fire,
Are both with thee, wherever I abide;
The first my thought, the other my desire,
These present-absent with swift motion slide.
For when these quicker elements are gone
In tender embassy of love to thee,
My life, being made of four, with two alone
Sinks down to death, oppress'd with melancholy;
Until life's composition be recured
By those swift messengers return'd from thee,
Who even but now come back again, assured
Of thy fair health, recounting it to me:
    This told, I joy; but then no longer glad,
    I send them back again and straight grow sad.

XLVI.

Mine eye and heart are at a mortal war
How to divide the conquest of thy sight;
Mine eye my heart thy picture's sight would bar,
My heart mine eye the freedom of that right.
My heart doth plead that thou in him dost lie,—
A closet never pierced with crystal eyes—
But the defendant doth that plea deny
And says in him thy fair appearance lies.
To 'cide this title is impanneled
A quest of thoughts, all tenants to the heart,
And by their verdict is determined
The clear eye's moiety and the dear heart's part:

As thus; mine eye's due is thy outward part,
And my heart's right thy inward love of heart.

XLVII.

Betwixt mine eye and heart a league is took,
And each doth good turns now unto the other:
When that mine eye is famish'd for a look,
Or heart in love with sighs himself doth smother,
With my love's picture then my eye doth feast
And to the painted banquet bids my heart;
Another time mine eye is my heart's guest
And in his thoughts of love doth share a part:
So, either by thy picture or my love,
Thyself away art present still with me;
For thou not farther than my thoughts canst move,
And I am still with them and they with thee;
    Or, if they sleep, thy picture in my sight
    Awakes my heart to heart's and eye's delight.

XLVIII.

How careful was I, when I took my way,
Each trifle under truest bars to thrust,
That to my use it might unused stay
From hands of falsehood, in sure wards of trust!
But thou, to whom my jewels trifles are,
Most worthy comfort, now my greatest grief,
Thou, best of dearest and mine only care,
Art left the prey of every vulgar thief.
Thee have I not lock'd up in any chest,
Save where thou art not, though I feel thou art,
Within the gentle closure of my breast,
From whence at pleasure thou mayst come and
    part;
    And even thence thou wilt be stol'n, I fear,
    For truth proves thievish for a prize so dear.

XLIX.

Against that time, if ever that time come,
When I shall see thee frown on my defects,
When as thy love hath cast his utmost sum,
Call'd to that audit by advised respects;
Against that time when thou shalt strangely pass
And scarcely greet me with that sun, thine eye,
When love, converted from the thing it was,
Shall reasons find of settled gravity,—
Against that time do I ensconce me here
Within the knowledge of mine own desert,
And this my hand against myself uprear,
To guard the lawful reasons on thy part:

gloomy to behold (Steevens).
    XLIV. 4. **where,** i.e., to the place where. 6. **farthest earth removed,** that part of earth farthest removed. 11. **earth and water,** the baser elements; cf. *Antony and Cleopatra,* V, ii, 292-293; *Henry V,* III, vii, 22-23. 14. **either's.** Perhaps the salt in the tears represents the contribution of the earth; and so tears are a badge of the woe of both earth and water (Beeching).
    XLV. 4. **present-absent,** now here and immediately gone (Tucker Brooke). 8. **melancholy,** may have been pronounced *melanch'ly;* so printed by some editors. 9. **recured,** restored. 10. **those . . . thee,** suggests that the poet has just received a letter from the friend.
    The following two sonnets treat a theme that Lee points out is a favorite one with the Elizabethan sonneteers; i.e., the war between the eye and the heart. Pooler and others think it might be a continuation of XXIV, which develops the conceit of a portrait of the poet's beloved painted on his heart. Tucker Brooke finds this pair of sonnets distinguished from XXIV and from the "heart and eye" sonnets of Shakespeare's contemporaries in that they indicate "that Shakespeare has received an actual portrait of the friend and is here offering thanks for it."
    XLVI. 2. **thy sight,** the sight of you; possibly refers to the portrait. 6. **crystal,** i.e., because of their clarity. 9. **'cide,** decide; so Malone

and most editors; Q: *side* retained by some who explain "to assign to one side or another." 10. **quest,** inquest, jury.
    XLVII. 6. **painted banquet,** i.e., the picture of his beloved.
    Sonnets XLVIII-LV form another series on the poet's absence from his friend, occasioned by the poet's having gone on a second journey.
    XLVIII. 5. **to whom,** in comparison to whom. 6. **now . . . grief,** i.e., because of his absence. 12. **part,** depart.
    XLIX. 3. **cast . . . sum,** added up the sum total. A metaphor from closing accounts on a dissolution of partnership (Pooler). 4. **advised respects,** deliberate consideration of our respective circumstances (Pooler). 5. **strangely,** as a stranger. 8. **reasons . . . gravity,** find reasons for a dignified reserve (Schmidt); *settled gravity* is taken by many editors to mean "weight"; i.e., find reasons of considerable weight. 10. **desert,** absence of merit. The frequency with which this word rhymes with words like *part* indicates that that was its customary pronunciation. 11-14. **And . . . cause,** I take your part against myself by admitting that you have a legal right to disown me, since I can show no cause why you should love me (Pooler). 11. **against myself,** i.e., to take an oath, not as if with a weapon.

To leave poor me thou hast the strength of laws,
Since why to love I can allege no cause.

L.

How heavy do I journey on the way,
When what I seek, my weary travel's end,
Doth teach that ease and that repose to say
'Thus far the miles are measured from thy friend!'
The beast that bears me, tired with my woe,
Plods dully on, to bear that weight in me,
As if by some instinct the wretch did know
His rider loved not speed, being made from thee:
The bloody spur cannot provoke him on
That sometimes anger thrusts into his hide;
Which heavily he answers with a groan,
More sharp to me than spurring to his side;
    For that same groan doth put this in my mind;
    My grief lies onward and my joy behind.

LI.

Thus can my love excuse the slow offence
Of my dull bearer when from thee I speed:
From where thou art why should I haste me thence?
Till I return, of posting is no need.
O, what excuse will my poor beast then find,
When swift extremity can seem but slow?
Then should I spur, though mounted on the wind;
In winged speed no motion shall I know:
Then can no horse with my desire keep pace;
Therefore desire, of perfect'st love being made,
Shall neigh—no dull flesh—in his fiery race;
But love, for love, thus shall excuse my jade;
    Since from thee going he went wilful-slow,
    Towards thee I'll run, and give him leave to go.

LII.

So am I as the rich, whose blessed key
Can bring him to his sweet up-locked treasure,
The which he will not every hour survey,
For blunting the fine point of seldom pleasure.
Therefore are feasts so solemn and so rare,
Since, seldom coming, in the long year set,
Like stones of worth they thinly placed are,
Or captain jewels in the carcanet.
So is the time that keeps you as my chest,
Or as the wardrobe which the robe doth hide,
To make some special instant special blest,
By new unfolding his imprison'd pride.

Blessed are you, whose worthiness gives scope,
Being had, to triumph, being lack'd, to hope.

LIII.

What is your substance, whereof are you made,
That millions of strange shadows on you tend?
Since every one hath, every one, one shade,
And you, but one, can every shadow lend.
Describe Adonis, and the counterfeit
Is poorly imitated after you;
On Helen's cheek all art of beauty set,
And you in Grecian tires are painted new:
Speak of the spring and foison of the year;
The one doth shadow of your beauty show,
The other as your bounty doth appear;
And you in every blessed shape we know.
    In all external grace you have some part,
    But you like none, none you, for constant heart.

LIV.

O, how much more doth beauty beauteous seem
By that sweet ornament which truth doth give!
The rose looks fair, but fairer we it deem
For that sweet odour which doth in it live.
The canker-blooms have full as deep a dye
As the perfumed tincture of the roses,
Hang on such thorns and play as wantonly
When summer's breath their masked buds discloses:
But, for their virtue only is their show,
They live unwoo'd and unrespected fade,
Die to themselves. Sweet roses do not so;
Of their sweet deaths are sweetest odours made:
    And so of you, beauteous and lovely youth,
    When that shall fade, my verse distills your truth.

LV.

Not marble, nor the gilded monuments
Of princes, shall outlive this powerful rhyme;
But you shall shine more bright in these contents
Than unswept stone besmear'd with sluttish time.
When wasteful war shall statues overturn,
And broils root out the work of masonry,
Nor Mars his sword nor war's quick fire shall burn
The living record of your memory.
'Gainst death and all-oblivious enmity
Shall you pace forth; your praise shall still find room
Even in the eyes of all posterity
That wear this world out to the ending doom.

L. 6. **to bear,** at bearing.
LI. 1. **slow offence,** offense which consists in slowness (Beeching). 4. **posting,** hastening. 6. **swift extremity,** extreme swiftness. 10-11. **desire . . . race,** a recurrence with metaphorical application of the concept developed in XLV. 11. **dull.** Cf. *dully,* l. 6. 14. **go,** walk, as contrasted with running.
LII. This sonnet is a complement to XLVIII, where the image is that of a man locking up his treasure. 4. **For blunting,** lest it blunt. 5. **feasts,** i.e., chief festivals of the church year—e.g., Christmas, Easter, Corpus Christi, Michaelmas. 5-8. **so solemn,** etc. Malone cites *1 Henry IV,* I, ii, 229-230; and III, ii, 57-59. 8. **captain,** principal. **carcanet,** necklace of jewels. 11. **special instant,** particular moment. **special blest,** particularly blest. The image has a parallel in *1 Henry IV,* III, ii, 56-57.
LIII. 1. **substance.** Pooler finds a touch of Platonism here in the implication that the substance is divine—the idea of which the shadows are the *idola,* or representation. 2, 3, 4. **shadows, shade,** used quibblingly with the meanings "silhouette" and "picture, reflection, symbol." 2. **tend,** attend, wait upon. 5. **counterfeit,** likeness (of beauty). 8. **tires,** clothes, attire. 9. **foison,** abundance; i.e., autumn.
LIV. 2. **truth,** constancy. 8. **discloses,** causes to open. 9. **for,** because; i.e., because their appearance is their only virtue. 11. **to themselves,** i.e., without profit to others (Pooler). 14. **my,** so Malone; Q has *by,* retained by some editors. Alden thinks the Q reading may possibly be justified on the ground that "distill" is sometimes used

intransitively, meaning "trickle," "issue forth in drops."
LV. 3. **these contents,** i.e., the contents of my poems written in praise of you. 4. **unswept stone,** parallel with *contents;* i.e., *in* is to be supplied from the preceding line (Pooler). 9. **all-oblivious,** causing to be forgotten. 12. **wear . . . out,** i.e., outlast (Pooler). 13. **till . . . arise,** till the decree of the judgment day that you arise from the dead (Beeching); cf. Abbott, 284.
LVI. This, like the sonnets immediately preceding, is written in absence (Dowden). Perhaps a plea for the renewal of intimacy (Pooler). 1. **Sweet love.** The address is to the spirit of love. The friend is not directly mentioned in this sonnet (Tucker Brooke). 9. **sad interim,** i.e., the period of love's abatement or absence. 9-12. **like the ocean,** etc. The image is variously explained. Some editors see a reference to the story of Hero and Leander; others regard *the ocean* figuratively as some kind of barrier which separates lovers (even Death has been suggested); still others take *the ocean* more literally as a separating body of water—a bay or estuary which parts the shore. Alden, although he favors the last interpretation, records a suggestion of A. G. Newcomer, who thought *part* might mean "recede" or "depart from." He paraphrased as follows: Let this sad interim be only like waters that recede from their shore where, viz., by this ocean of love (dropping the image of the ocean at this point), two, *contracted new,* come daily to the banks, so that when they see the tide of love come in again, more blest may be the sight. 10. **contracted new,** Pooler, citing I, 5, explains as "lately betrothed"; Tyler regards it as indicative of the newness of

So, till the judgement that yourself arise,
You live in this, and dwell in lovers' eyes.

LVI.

Sweet love, renew thy force; be it not said
Thy edge should blunter be than appetite,
Which but to-day by feeding is allay'd,
To-morrow sharpen'd in his former might:
So, love, be thou; although to-day thou fill
Thy hungry eyes even till they wink with fullness,
To-morrow see again, and do not kill
The spirit of love with a perpetual dullness.
Let this sad interim like the ocean be
Which parts the shore, where two contracted new
Come daily to the banks, that, when they see
Return of love, more blest may be the view;
　　Else call it winter, which being full of care
　　Makes summer's welcome thrice more wish'd,
　　　　more rare.

LVII.

Being your slave, what should I do but tend
Upon the hours and times of your desire?
I have no precious time at all to spend,
Nor services to do, till you require.
Nor dare I chide the world-without-end hour
Whilst I, my sovereign, watch the clock for you,
Nor think the bitterness of absence sour
When you have bid your servant once adieu;
Nor dare I question with my jealous thought
Where you may be, or your affairs suppose,
But, like a sad slave, stay and think of nought
Save, where you are how happy you make those.
　　So true a fool is love that in your will,
　　Though you do any thing, he thinks no ill.

LVIII.

That god forbid that made me first your slave,
I should in thought control your times of pleasure,
Or at your hand the account of hours to crave,
Being your vassal, bound to stay your leisure!
O, let me suffer, being at your beck,
The imprison'd absence of your liberty;
And patience, tame to sufferance, bide each check,
Without accusing you of injury.
Be where you list, your charter is so strong
That you yourself may privilege your time
To what you will; to you it doth belong

Yourself to pardon of self-doing crime.
　　I am to wait, though waiting so be hell;
　　Not blame your pleasure, be it ill or well.

LIX.

If there be nothing new, but that which is
Hath been before, how are our brains beguiled,
Which, labouring for invention, bear amiss
The second burthen of a former child!
O, that record could with a backward look,
Even of five hundred courses of the sun,
Show me your image in some antique book,
Since mind at first in character was done!
That I might see what the old world could say
To this composed wonder of your frame;
Whether we are mended, or whether better they,
Or whether revolution be the same.
　　O, sure I am, the wits of former days
　　To subjects worse have given admiring praise.

LX.

Like as the waves make towards the pebbled shore,
So do our minutes hasten to their end;
Each changing place with that which goes before,
In sequent toil all forwards do contend.
Nativity, once in the main of light,
Crawls to maturity, wherewith being crown'd,
Crooked eclipses 'gainst his glory fight,
And Time that gave doth now his gift confound.
Time doth transfix the flourish set on youth
And delves the parallels in beauty's brow,
Feeds on the rarities of nature's truth,
And nothing stands but for his scythe to mow:
　　†And yet to times in hope my verse shall stand,
　　Praising thy worth, despite his cruel hand.

LXI.

Is it thy will thy image should keep open
My heavy eyelids to the weary night?
Dost thou desire my slumbers should be broken,
While shadows like to thee do mock my sight?
Is it thy spirit that thou send'st from thee
So far from home into my deeds to pry,
To find out shames and idle hours in me,
The scope and tenour of thy jealousy?
O, no! thy love, though much, is not so great:
It is my love that keeps mine eye awake;
Mine own true love that doth my rest defeat,

Shakespeare's friendship with W. H.
　LVII. 3. **I . . . spend.** The presumption seems to be that Shakespeare is in London and, in his friend's absence, not much employed (Tucker Brooke). 5. **world-without-end,** interminable. 10. **suppose,** make conjectures about. 13. **will.** This word, capitalized in the 1609 quarto, is regarded by some as a pun on Shakespeare's name. Dowden explains as possibly: "Love in your Will (i.e., in me) can think no ill of anything you do," and "love can discover no evil in your will." Sir Sidney Lee thinks the Elizabethan practice of capitalizing nouns too common for this instance to have any significance.
　LVIII. There is some dispute as to the probable order in which this and the preceding (LVII) should be placed. Pooler thinks LVIII should perhaps come first, the sequence of ideas being "A god made me your slave" and "being your slave, etc." Tucker Brooke regards LVIII as more likely an apology for the impatience expressed in LVII. 3. **to crave,** parallel with *control* (l. 2); *to* might be omitted or *should* (from l. 2) might be inserted instead, but the omission would create ambiguity, and the insertion would be a tedious repetition (Abbott, 416). 4. **to stay,** to await. 6. **The . . . liberty,** i.e., your absence from me, due to your independence of me, makes me as one imprisoned, dependent on (or vassal to) you. 7. **tame to,** subdued by; cf. *King Lear*, IV, vi, 225. **bide each check,** endure each rebuke. 9. **charter,** privilege or right recorded in writing. Pooler notes the loose employment of the word to denote any freedom of action. 10. **privilege,** authorize. 12. **self-doing crime,** crime committed by oneself. 14. **blame,** parallel

with *wait* (l. 13).
　LIX. Most editors discern a break in the sequence here. Tucker Brooke places this and LX after LXV, making the series LXII-LXV, LIX, LX, a series on the theme of beauty and time. 3. **labouring for invention,** striving to give birth to a new creation. 5. **record,** memory, especially memory preserved by history (Schmidt); accented on the second syllable. 8. **Since . . . done,** since thought was first expressed in writing. 10. **composed wonder,** wonderful composition (Rolfe). 11. **Whether . . . whether.** Q: *whether . . . where;* many editors write both as *whe'r;* "whether" was often monosyllabic in Elizabethan verse. 12. **revolution,** i.e., of the ages.
　LX. 4. **sequent,** one after another. 5. **main,** main body. The entrance of a child into the world at birth is an entrance into the main or ocean of light (Dowden). 6. **Crawls.** Cf. *Hamlet*, III, i, 130; the word denotes the abject condition of mankind (Tyler). 7. **Crooked,** perverse, malignant. 9. **flourish,** decoration, embellishment; the figure is possibly from penmanship, but the general meaning is, older than the scribal flourish. 10. **parallels,** wrinkles. 11. **rarities . . . truth,** rare things created by the fidelity of nature (Alden). 13. **times in hope,** times to come.
　LXI. The jealous feeling of LVII reappears (Dowden). Tucker Brooke places this sonnet after LVIII. 7. **shames and idle hours,** a hendiadys, the meaning being "to see how badly I spend my spare time" (Pooler). 8. **scope . . . jealousy,** aim and purport of your suspicion (Pooler).

To play the watchman ever for thy sake:
  For thee watch I whilst thou dost wake elsewhere,
  From me far off, with others all too near.

LXII.

Sin of self-love possesseth all mine eye
And all my soul and all my every part;
And for this sin there is no remedy,
It is so grounded inward in my heart.
Methinks no face so gracious is as mine,
No shape so true, no truth of such account;
And for myself mine own worth do define,
As I all other in all worths surmount.
But when my glass shows me myself indeed,
Beated and chopp'd with tann'd antiquity,
Mine own self-love quite contrary I read;
Self so self-loving were iniquity.
  'Tis thee, myself, that for myself I praise,
  Painting my age with beauty of thy days.

LXIII.

Against my love shall be, as I am now,
With Time's injurious hand crush'd and o'erworn;
When hours have drain'd his blood and fill'd his brow
With lines and wrinkles; when his youthful morn
Hath travell'd on to age's steepy night,
And all those beauties whereof now he 's king
Are vanishing or vanish'd out of sight,
Stealing away the treasure of his spring;
For such a time do I now fortify
Against confounding age's cruel knife,
That he shall never cut from memory
My sweet love's beauty, though my lover's life:
  His beauty shall in these black lines be seen,
  And they shall live, and he in them still green.

LXIV.

When I have seen by Time's fell hand defaced
The rich proud cost of outworn buried age;
When sometime lofty towers I see down-razed
And brass eternal slave to mortal rage;
When I have seen the hungry ocean gain
Advantage on the kingdom of the shore,
And the firm soil win of the watery main,
Increasing store with loss and loss with store;
When I have seen such interchange of state,

Or state itself confounded to decay;
Ruin hath taught me thus to ruminate,
That Time will come and take my love away.
  This thought is as a death, which cannot choose
  But weep to have that which it fears to lose.

LXV.

Since brass, nor stone, nor earth, nor boundless sea,
But sad mortality o'er-sways their power,
How with this rage shall beauty hold a plea,
Whose action is no stronger than a flower?
O, how shall summer's honey breath hold out
Against the wreckful siege of battering days,
When rocks impregnable are not so stout,
Nor gates of steel so strong, but Time decays?
O fearful meditation! where, alack,
Shall Time's best jewel from Time's chest lie hid?
Or what strong hand can hold his swift foot back?
Or who his spoil of beauty can forbid?
  O, none, unless this miracle have might,
  That in black ink my love may still shine bright.

LXVI.

Tired with all these, for restful death I cry,
As, to behold desert a beggar born,
And needy nothing trimm'd in jollity,
And purest faith unhappily forsworn,
And gilded honour shamefully misplaced,
And maiden virtue rudely strumpeted,
And right perfection wrongfully disgraced,
And strength by limping sway disabled,
And art made tongue-tied by authority,
And folly doctor-like controlling skill,
And simple truth miscall'd simplicity,
And captive good attending captain ill:
  Tired with all these, from these would I be gone,
  Save that, to die, I leave my love alone.

LXVII.

Ah! wherefore with infection should he live,
And with his presence grace impiety,
That sin by him advantage should achieve
And lace itself with his society?
Why should false painting imitate his cheek
And steal dead seeing of his living hue?
Why should poor beauty indirectly seek

12. **watchman,** one who stays awake. 13. **watch, wake.** The words were originally identical in meaning; i.e., to be awake.
LXII. 1. **Sin of self-love.** Cf. *All's Well that Ends Well*, I, i, 157. 4. **grounded . . . heart,** fixed or established inwardly. 7. **And . . . define.** Does *for myself* mean "for my own satisfaction"? (Dowden). My definition of my worth is such that, etc. (Wyndham). Several conjectures and emendations have been made to make the line construable: Delius supplied a subject (*I*) for *do;* Tucker Brooke adopts Lettsom's emendation of *so* (Elizabethan spelling *soe*) for *for* and explains "I set such a valuation on my own worth that, etc." 8. **other,** a sixteenth-century plural; see Abbott, 12. 9. **indeed,** i.e., as I actually am. 10. **Beated,** battered; Malone conjectured *Bated,* i.e., laid low. **chopp'd,** chapped, roughened. 12. **so self-loving,** i.e., to love oneself as the glass *indeed* shows him. 13. **thee, myself,** i.e., my other self.
LXIII. 1. **Against,** i.e., against the time when. 5. **steepy,** having a precipitous declivity (Schmidt); difficult to ascend (Onions); Dowden cites VII, 5, 6, and 9, 10, where the sun, likened to youth, climbs the *steep-up heavenly hill,* and like old age, *reeleth from the day.* 9. **For such a time,** etc., parallel in construction with the phrase (l. 1) *Against my love,* etc. **fortify,** raise works of defense; possibly, fortify myself, gird my strength.
LXIV. 2. **rich proud,** proud on account of its wealth. 4. **brass . . . rage.** *Mortal* may be contrasted with *eternal* in the sense of destroying as opposed to indestructible (Pooler); brass, i.e., bronze, was the enduring material for sculpture. 5-8. **When . . . store.** Lee points out the similarity of these lines to a passage in Ovid's *Metamorphoses,*

xv, 288-290. Shakespeare has used similar imagery in *The Rape of Lucrece,* 944 ff.; *1 Henry IV,* III, i, 108-111; *2 Henry IV,* III, i, 46-52. The notion is expressed also in *Timon of Athens,* the opening dialogue between Poet and Painter. 9, 10. **state, state,** condition . . . pomp or greatness (Schmidt, Beeching, Tyler); Wyndham glosses both as "condition," the first used particularly, the second in the abstract. 13. **which cannot choose,** modifies *thought.*
LXV. 1-2. **Since . . . power,** an elliptical clause: Since there is neither brass, etc., but that sad mortality o'ersways, etc. The ellipsis shows the closeness of the idea to the preceding sonnet. 4. **action,** case (for permanence); legal figure. 10. **Time's chest.** The chest of Time is the repository into which he is poetically supposed to throw those things which he designs to be forgotten (Steevens); cf. *time's wallet, Troilus and Cressida,* III, iii, 145-146, wherein he puts *alms for oblivion.* 12. **spoil,** act of spoiling; possibly, spoils, booty.
LXVI. The thoughts of death developed in the preceding series bring the poet to thoughts of his own death and his willingness to part from the world. The theme of the world's infection continues from this sonnet through LXX. 1. **all these.** The antecedent is what follows; many commentators point out the similarity to Hamlet's famous soliloquy, especially *Hamlet,* III, i, 70-75. 2. **desert,** i.e., those who have merit, as contrasted with *needy nothing* in the next line. 3. **needy nothing,** moral and mental emptiness (Tucker Brooke). **jollity,** finery. 8. **disabled,** four syllables. 10. **doctor-like,** like a learned person. 11. **simplicity,** silliness, folly.
LXVII. 1. **with infection,** i.e., the world's ills enumerated in the

Roses of shadow, since his rose is true?
Why should he live, now Nature bankrupt is,
Beggar'd of blood to blush through lively veins?
For she hath no exchequer now but his,
And, proud of many, lives upon his gains.
    O, him she stores, to show what wealth she had
    In days long since, before these last so bad.

LXVIII.

Thus is his cheek the map of days outworn,
When beauty lived and died as flowers do now,
Before these bastard signs of fair were born,
Or durst inhabit on a living brow;
Before the golden tresses of the dead,
The right of sepulchres, were shorn away,
To live a second life on second head;
Ere beauty's dead fleece made another gay:
In him those holy antique hours are seen,
Without all ornament, itself and true,
Making no summer of another's green,
Robbing no old to dress his beauty new;
    And him as for a map doth Nature store,
    To show false Art what beauty was of yore.

LXIX.

Those parts of thee that the world's eye doth view
Want nothing that the thought of hearts can mend;
All tongues, the voice of souls, give thee that due,
Uttering bare truth, even so as foes commend.
Thy outward thus with outward praise is crown'd;
But those same tongues that give thee so thine own
In other accents do this praise confound
By seeing farther than the eye hath shown.
They look into the beauty of thy mind,
And that, in guess, they measure by thy deeds;
Then, churls, their thoughts, although their eyes were
      kind,
To thy fair flower add the rank smell of weeds:
    But why thy odour matcheth not thy show,
    The soil is this, that thou dost common grow.

LXX.

That thou art blamed shall not be thy defect,
For slander's mark was ever yet the fair;
The ornament of beauty is suspect,
A crow that flies in heaven's sweetest air.

So thou be good, slander doth but approve
Thy worth the greater, being woo'd of time;
For canker vice the sweetest buds doth love,
And thou present'st a pure unstained prime.
Thou hast pass'd by the ambush of young days,
Either not assail'd or victor being charged;
Yet this thy praise cannot be so thy praise,
To tie up envy evermore enlarged:
    If some suspect of ill mask'd not thy show,
    Then thou alone kingdoms of hearts shouldst owe.

LXXI.

No longer mourn for me when I am dead
Than you shall hear the surly sullen bell
Give warning to the world that I am fled
From this vile world, with vilest worms to dwell:
Nay, if you read this line, remember not
The hand that writ it; for I love you so
That I in your sweet thoughts would be forgot
If thinking on me then should make you woe.
O, if, I say, you look upon this verse
When I perhaps compounded am with clay,
Do not so much as my poor name rehearse,
But let your love even with my life decay,
    Lest the wise world should look into your moan
    And mock you with me after I am gone.

LXXII.

O, lest the world should task you to recite
What merit lived in me, that you should love
After my death, dear love, forget me quite,
For you in me can nothing worthy prove;
Unless you would devise some virtuous lie,
To do more for me than mine own desert,
And hang more praise upon deceased I
Than niggard truth would willingly impart:
O, lest your true love may seem false in this,
That you for love speak well of me untrue,
My name be buried where my body is,
And live no more to shame nor me nor you.
    For I am shamed by that which I bring forth,
    And so should you, to love things nothing worth.

LXXIII.

That time of year thou mayst in me behold
When yellow leaves, or none, or few, do hang

---

preceding sonnet. **he,** i.e., *my love* of LXVI, 14. 4. **lace,** trim with ornament. 6. **dead seeing.** Dowden's gloss, "lifeless appearance," would better define Farmer's emendation, *dead seeming,* a reading adopted by some editors. 8. **Roses of shadow,** i.e., color of roses placed on his cheeks. 10. **Beggar'd,** modifies *Nature.* **to blush,** which blushes. 13. **stores,** keeps in store.
  LXVIII. This sonnet contrasts the real beauty of youth with artificial beauty. The subject of the sonnet is the epitome of natural beauty. 1. **map,** picture, image. 3. **bastard . . . fair,** i.e., cosmetics. 10. **itself.** Malone conjectured *himself,* thinking the antecedent to be *him* (l. 9). Pooler refers the pronoun to *holy antique hours,* singular in idea, since the phrase means "the beauty of the past"; *itself* is equivalent to "unadulterated."
  LXIX. 2. **Want . . . mend,** lack nothing which the imagination can and customarily does supply. 3. **voice of souls.** This is a Renaissance commonplace, that the tongue (power of speech) is the voice of the soul. 6. **thine own,** i.e., *that due* of line 3. 14. **soil.** Globe, following Malone, has *solve* defined as solution; Q: *solye;* the 1640 Q: *soyle;* most editors, *soil,* but explain it variously: solution (*NED*); blemish, fault (Verity, citing *Hamlet,* I, iii, 15); ground, i.e., origin, source (Tucker Brooke, who explains it as continuing the figure of the garden). **common,** stale, vulgar; Pooler quotes Case's query: "Is Shakespeare rebuking his friend for general loving, or merely . . . with gracing iniquity with his presence? Or do the slanderers stigmatize him as growing common? Probably not." Pooler cites *1 Henry IV,* III, iii, 40-41; Beeching cites *Coriolanus,* II, iii, 101.

LXX. 2. **slander's mark,** object of slander. 3. **suspect,** suspicion (as also in l. 13). 5. **So,** if only. The implied reasoning is: Slandered goodness is more than ordinarily good, for slander is evidence of beauty, and beauty of temptation (Pooler). 6. **woo'd of time,** i.e., by fashion, tempted by the world. 8. **thou . . . prime,** i.e., you have a reputation for an unspotted youth. 12. **enlarged,** at liberty. Dowden quotes a letter from J. W. Hales, who saw here a reference to Spenser's *Faerie Queene,* Bk. VI, where Calidore bound the Blatant Beast, now broken loose again and always set free; note also in Bk. II that Occasion is always being set free; so is Maleger.
  LXXI. With this sonnet the theme of death as a release from the world's ills gives place to a more contemplative mood, wherein once more the immortalizing power of poetry is the theme; not its immortalizing of the poet, but of his friend. The theme is continued through LXXIV. 14. **with me,** i.e., as they mock me.
  LXXII. 1. **task you to recite,** place upon you the task of reciting. 5. **virtuous lie,** lie about my virtue. 7. **I.** The rhyme is accountable for the pronoun. Abbott (205, 209) remarks the tendency to use *I* for *me* after the sounds *d* and *t.* 10. **untrue,** untruly.
  LXXIII. Alden calls this sonnet the finest example in the Shakespearean mode. Note the three figures of decay—autumn, sunset, and expiring fire—each occupying a quatrain; also the noble couplet of personal application.

Upon those boughs which shake against the cold,
Bare ruin'd choirs, where late the sweet birds sang.
In me thou see'st the twilight of such day
As after sunset fadeth in the west,
Which by and by black night doth take away,
Death's second self, that seals up all in rest.
In me thou see'st the glowing of such fire
That on the ashes of his youth doth lie,
As the death-bed whereon it must expire
Consumed with that which it was nourish'd by.
    This thou perceivest, which makes thy love more
       strong,
    To love that well which thou must leave ere long.

LXXIV.

But be contented: when that fell arrest
Without all bail shall carry me away,
My life hath in this line some interest,
Which for memorial still with thee shall stay.
When thou reviewest this, thou dost review
The very part was consecrate to thee:
The earth can have but earth, which is his due;
My spirit is thine, the better part of me:
So then thou hast but lost the dregs of life,
The prey of worms, my body being dead,
The coward conquest of a wretch's knife,
Too base of thee to be remembered.
    The worth of that is that which it contains,
    And that is this, and this with thee remains.

LXXV.

So are you to my thoughts as food to life,
Or as sweet-season'd showers are to the ground;
And for the peace of you I hold such strife
As 'twixt a miser and his wealth is found;
Now proud as an enjoyer and anon
Doubting the filching age will steal his treasure,
Now counting best to be with you alone,
Then better'd that the world may see my pleasure;
Sometime all full with feasting on your sight
And by and by clean starved for a look;
Possessing or pursuing no delight,
Save what is had or must from you be took.
    Thus do I pine and surfeit day by day,
    Or gluttoning on all, or all away.

LXXVI.

Why is my verse so barren of new pride,
So far from variation or quick change?
Why with the time do I not glance aside
To new-found methods and to compounds strange?

Why write I still all one, ever the same,
And deep invention in a noted weed,
That every word doth almost tell my name,
Showing their birth and where they did proceed?
O, know, sweet love, I always write of you,
And you and love are still my argument;
So all my best is dressing old words new,
Spending again what is already spent:
    For as the sun is daily new and old,
    So is my love still telling what is told.

LXXVII.

Thy glass will show thee how thy beauties wear,
Thy dial how thy precious minutes waste;
The vacant leaves thy mind's imprint will bear,
And of this book this learning mayst thou taste.
The wrinkles which thy glass will truly show
Of mouthed graves will give thee memory;
Thou by thy dial's shady stealth mayst know
Time's thievish progress to eternity.
Look, what thy memory can not contain
Commit to these waste blanks, and thou shalt find
Those children nursed, deliver'd from thy brain,
To take a new acquaintance of thy mind.
    These offices, so oft as thou wilt look,
    Shall profit thee and much enrich thy book.

LXXVIII.

So oft have I invoked thee for my Muse
And found such fair assistance in my verse
As every alien pen hath got my use
And under thee their poesy disperse.
Thine eyes that taught the dumb on high to sing
And heavy ignorance aloft to fly,
Have added feathers to the learned's wing
And given grace a double majesty.
Yet be most proud of that which I compile,
Whose influence is thine and born of thee:
In others' works thou dost but mend the style,
And arts with thy sweet graces graced be;
    But thou art all my art and dost advance
    As high as learning my rude ignorance.

LXXIX.

Whilst I alone did call upon thy aid,
My verse alone had all thy gentle grace,
But now my gracious numbers are decay'd
And my sick Muse doth give another place.
I grant, sweet love, thy lovely argument
Deserves the travail of a worthier pen,
Yet what of thee thy poet doth invent

---

4. **choirs,** that part of cathedrals where the service is said; in apposition with *boughs* (l. 3). This image was probably suggested to Shakespeare by our desolated monasteries. The resemblance between the vaulting of a Gothic aisle and an avenue of trees whose upper branches meet and form an arch overhead is too striking not to be acknowledged. When the roof of the one is shattered, and the boughs of the other leafless, the comparison becomes yet more solemn and picturesque (Steevens). 12. **that,** i.e., the ashes of what was formerly the fuel.
  LXXIV. 1. **that fell arrest,** i.e., death; Capell cites *Hamlet*, V, ii, 347-348. 3. **interest,** legal concern, right, or title. 7. **The . . . earth,** an echo, probably, of the medieval earth-upon-earth rhymes; also of the "earth to earth" phrase in the burial service of the prayer book. 11. **coward . . . knife.** Dowden cites LXIII, 10. The line also suggests some of the pictorial representations of death in the Dance of Death motifs. 12. **of thee,** by thee; modifies *remembered.* 13. **that,** the antecedent may be *line* (l. 3), which is used quibblingly, or *memorial* (l. 4).
  The three sonnets following have no apparent continuity. Tucker Brooke points out that if LXXV and LXXVI are transposed, they have some coherence; the former seems to be an expansion of the last six

lines of the latter.
  LXXV. 2. **sweet-season'd,** (of rain) soft (Onions). 3. **of you,** to be found in you (Dowden). 6. **Doubting,** suspecting, fearing. 10. **clean,** completely, absolutely. 12. **from you,** modifies both verbs, *had* and *must be took.* 14. **Or . . . or,** either . . . or. **all away,** i.e., all food being taken away.
  LXXVI. This sonnet implies on the friend's part a not unnatural restiveness at Shakespeare's plain-spokenness and abstention from the fashionable devices of eulogy (Tucker Brooke). 3. **time,** way of the world, fashion. 4. **compounds,** compound words (Onions); Lee refers the phrase to the extravagances of Shakespeare's contemporaries in inventing new words. 6. **noted weed,** dress by which it is recognizable, well-known garment. 8. **where,** from whence.
  LXXVII. Apparently these lines accompanied the gift of a book of blank pages, a memorandum book. 3. **vacant leaves,** blank pages. 4. **learning,** mental profit; what it is is explained in line 9 ff. (Tucker Brooke). 6. **mouthed,** all-devouring (Malone); gaping (Schmidt). 7. **shady stealth,** slow progress of the shadow on the dial (Onions).
  LXXVIII. With this sonnet the poet begins his complaint that his friend's patronage is being sought by other poets. The theme continues

He robs thee of and pays it thee again.
He lends thee virtue and he stole that word
From thy behaviour; beauty doth he give
And found it in thy cheek; he can afford
No praise to thee but what in thee doth live.
    Then thank him not for that which he doth say,
    Since what he owes thee thou thyself dost pay.

LXXX.

O, how I faint when I of you do write,
Knowing a better spirit doth use your name,
And in the praise thereof spends all his might,
To make me tongue-tied, speaking of your fame!
But since your worth, wide as the ocean is,
The humble as the proudest sail doth bear,
My saucy bark inferior far to his
On your broad main doth wilfully appear.
Your shallowest help will hold me up afloat,
Whilst he upon your soundless deep doth ride;
Or, being wreck'd, I am a worthless boat,
He of tall building and of goodly pride:
    Then if he thrive and I be cast away,
    The worst was this; my love was my decay.

LXXXI.

Or I shall live your epitaph to make,
Or you survive when I in earth am rotten;
From hence your memory death cannot take,
Although in me each part will be forgotten.
Your name from hence immortal life shall have,
Though I, once gone, to all the world must die:
The earth can yield me but a common grave,
When you entombed in men's eyes shall lie.
Your monument shall be my gentle verse,
Which eyes not yet created shall o'er-read,
And tongues to be your being shall rehearse
When all the breathers of this world are dead;
    You still shall live—such virtue hath my pen—
    Where breath most breathes, even in the mouths of
    men.

LXXXII.

I grant thou wert not married to my Muse
And therefore mayst without attaint o'erlook
The dedicated words which writers use
Of their fair subject, blessing every book.
Thou art as fair in knowledge as in hue,
Finding thy worth a limit past my praise,
And therefore art enforced to seek anew
Some fresher stamp of the time-bettering days.
And do so, love; yet when they have devised

What strained touches rhetoric can lend,
Thou truly fair wert truly sympathized
In true plain words by thy true-telling friend;
    And their gross painting might be better used
    Where cheeks need blood; in thee it is abused.

LXXXIII.

I never saw that you did painting need
And therefore to your fair no painting set;
I found, or thought I found, you did exceed
The barren tender of a poet's debt;
And therefore have I slept in your report,
That you yourself being extant well might show
How far a modern quill doth come too short,
Speaking of worth, what worth in you doth grow.
This silence for my sin you did impute,
Which shall be most my glory, being dumb;
For I impair not beauty being mute,
When others would give life and bring a tomb.
    There lives more life in one of your fair eyes
    Than both your poets can in praise devise.

LXXXIV.

Who is it that says most? which can say more
Than this rich praise, that you alone are you?
In whose confine immured is the store
Which should example where your equal grew.
Lean penury within that pen doth dwell
That to his subject lends not some small glory;
But he that writes of you, if he can tell
That you are you, so dignifies his story,
Let him but copy what in you is writ,
Not making worse what nature made so clear,
And such a counterpart shall fame his wit,
Making his style admired every where.
    You to your beauteous blessings add a curse,
    Being fond on praise, which makes your praises
      worse.

LXXXV.

My tongue-tied Muse in manners holds her still,
While comments of your praise, richly compiled,
Reserve their character with golden quill
And precious phrase by all the Muses filed.
I think good thoughts whilst other write good words,
And like unletter'd clerk still cry 'Amen'
To every hymn that able spirit affords
In polish'd form of well-refined pen.
Hearing you praised, I say ''Tis so, 'tis true,'
And to the most of praise add something more;
But that is in my thought, whose love to you,

to the close of LXXXVI. 3. **use,** habit; i.e., of writing in celebration of his friend. 5-6. **Thine . . . fly.** Cf. *my rude ignorance* (l. 14). 7-8. **Have . . . majesty,** a complaint of the rival poet. 9. **compile,** write, compose. 10. **influence,** inspiration; suggestion of astrological meaning. 12. **arts,** literary culture, scholarship. 13. **advance,** lift up.
    LXXIX. 5. **thy lovely argument,** the celebration of thy loveliness.
    LXXX. 2. **a better spirit,** i.e., the rival poet, whom Shakespeare admires. 4. **tongue-tied.** Hearing his friend's virtues praised has stricken the poet with awe. 10. **soundless,** unfathomable. 13. **cast away,** shipwrecked. 14. **my love . . . decay,** i.e., because it prompted me to write.
    LXXXI. After belittling his own verse, the poet here takes courage and asserts his power. 4. **in . . . part,** every quality of mine. 5. **Your . . . have.** The theme of the perpetuation of the object's name is common throughout the *Sonnets* and is found in practically all sonnet cycles. 12. **breathers,** living people; cf. *As You Like It,* III, ii, 297.
    LXXXII. 2. **attaint,** blame, discredit. 3-4. **The dedicated . . . book.** It is thought by many commentators that Shakespeare has in mind his own dedications of his poems, *Venus and Adonis* and *The Rape*

of Lucrece, to the earl of Southampton. The words, however, seem quite general. 8. **time-bettering days.** For this theme of progress in the age see XXXII, 5. 11. **truly sympathized,** faithfully described. 13. **gross painting,** extravagant compliment.
    LXXXIII. 1-2. **painting . . . painting,** a continuation of the theme of *gross painting* in the preceding sonnet. 2. **fair,** beauty. 5. **slept in your report,** made no poem about you. 14. **both your poets,** i.e., Shakespeare and the rival poet.
    LXXXIV. 3-4. **In . . . grew,** the source which should provide descendants equal to the original; possibly a continuation of the theme of I-XVII. 5-6. **Lean . . . glory,** i.e., it is a poor book that does not confer some honor on the person to whom it is dedicated. 11. **fame,** endow with fame. 14. **Being . . . worse.** The friend's doting on praise lays him open to the baser sort of panegyric.
    LXXXV. 2. **While . . . compiled,** eulogies composed in fine language. 3. **Reserve their character,** preserve their handwritings; various conjectures. 4. **filed,** polished. 11. **But that,** i.e., that which I add.

Though words come hindmost, holds his rank before.
  Then others for the breath of words respect,
  Me for my dumb thoughts, speaking in effect.

LXXXVI.

Was it the proud full sail of his great verse,
Bound for the prize of all too precious you,
That did my ripe thoughts in my brain inhearse,
Making their tomb the womb wherein they grew?
Was it his spirit, by spirits taught to write
Above a mortal pitch, that struck me dead?
No, neither he, nor his compeers by night
Giving him aid, my verse astonished.
He, nor that affable familiar ghost
Which nightly gulls him with intelligence,
As victors of my silence cannot boast;
I was not sick of any fear from thence:
  But when your countenance fill'd up his line,
  Then lack'd I matter; that enfeebled mine.

LXXXVII.

Farewell! thou art too dear for my possessing,
And like enough thou know'st thy estimate:
The charter of thy worth gives thee releasing;
My bonds in thee are all determinate.
For how do I hold thee but by thy granting?
And for that riches where is my deserving?
The cause of this fair gift in me is wanting,
And so my patent back again is swerving.
Thyself thou gavest, thy own worth then not knowing,
Or me, to whom thou gavest it, else mistaking;
So thy great gift, upon misprision growing,
Comes home again, on better judgement making.
  Thus have I had thee, as a dream doth flatter,
  In sleep a king, but waking no such matter.

LXXXVIII.

When thou shalt be disposed to set me light
And place my merit in the eye of scorn,
Upon thy side against myself I'll fight
And prove thee virtuous, though thou art forsworn.
With mine own weakness being best acquainted,
Upon thy part I can set down a story
Of faults conceal'd, wherein I am attainted,
That thou in losing me shalt win much glory:
And I by this will be a gainer too;
For bending all my loving thoughts on thee,
The injuries that to myself I do,
Doing thee vantage, double-vantage me.
  Such is my love, to thee I so belong,
  That for thy right myself will bear all wrong.

LXXXIX.

Say that thou didst forsake me for some fault,
And I will comment upon that offence;
Speak of my lameness, and I straight will halt,

Against thy reasons making no defence.
Thou canst not, love, disgrace me half so ill,
To set a form upon desired change,
As I'll myself disgrace: knowing thy will,
I will acquaintance strangle and look strange,
Be absent from thy walks, and in my tongue
Thy sweet beloved name no more shall dwell,
Lest I, too much profane, should do it wrong
And haply of our old acquaintance tell.
  For thee against myself I'll vow debate,
  For I must ne'er love him whom thou dost hate.

XC.

Then hate me when thou wilt; if ever, now;
Now, while the world is bent my deeds to cross,
Join with the spite of fortune, make me bow,
And do not drop in for an after-loss:
Ah, do not, when my heart hath 'scaped this sorrow,
Come in the rearward of a conquer'd woe;
Give not a windy night a rainy morrow,
To linger out a purposed overthrow.
If thou wilt leave me, do not leave me last,
When other petty griefs have done their spite,
But in the onset come; so shall I taste
At first the very worst of fortune's might,
  And other strains of woe, which now seem woe,
  Compared with loss of thee will not seem so.

XCI.

Some glory in their birth, some in their skill,
Some in their wealth, some in their bodies' force,
Some in their garments, though new-fangled ill,
Some in their hawks and hounds, some in their horse;
And every humour hath his adjunct pleasure,
Wherein it finds a joy above the rest:
But these particulars are not my measure;
All these I better in one general best.
Thy love is better than high birth to me,
Richer than wealth, prouder than garments' cost,
Of more delight than hawks or horses be;
And having thee, of all men's pride I boast:
  Wretched in this alone, that thou mayst take
  All this away and me most wretched make.

XCII.

But do thy worst to steal thyself away,
For term of life thou art assured mine,
And life no longer than thy love will stay,
For it depends upon that love of thine.
Then need I not to fear the worst of wrongs,
When in the least of them my life hath end.
I see a better state to me belongs
Than that which on thy humour doth depend;
Thou canst not vex me with inconstant mind,
Since that my life on thy revolt doth lie.
O, what a happy title do I find,

14. **speaking in effect,** i.e., which have the quality of speech.
  LXXXVI. This sonnet is devoted to generous praise of his rival. Some critics have seen in it an indication that Chapman was the rival poet. 1. **proud full sail.** F. J. Furnivall saw in this an allusion to Chapman's hexameters in his translation of Homer. 4. **Making . . . grew.** Cf. *Romeo and Juliet*, II, iii, 9-10. 7. **compeers by night,** spirits visiting and aiding the poet in his dreams. This has been thought to be an allusion to Chapman's *Shadow of Night* (1594), which speaks of a "heavenly familiar." 8. **astonished,** struck dumb.
  LXXXVII. 4. **determinate,** ended, expired (a legal term). 6. **riches,** wealth; a singular noun. 8. **patent,** charter granting rights of monopoly; hence, privilege. 11. **upon misprision growing,** arising out of error or mistake. 13. **as . . . flatter.** Cf. *Romeo and Juliet*, V, i, 1-5.

14. **no such matter,** nothing of the sort.
  LXXXVIII. 1. **set me light,** despise me, make light of me. 6. **Upon thy part,** in support of your opinions.
  LXXXIX. 3. **Speak of my lameness,** i.e., if you should say that I am lame; cf. xxxvii, 3, note. 6-7. **To . . . disgrace,** as to set up a pretext, which I will not acknowledge, that I should change. 8. **strangle,** put an end to. **look strange,** i.e., treat them as strangers. 9. **walks,** haunts. 13. **vow debate,** entertain hostility, quarrel.
  XC. 6. **in the rearward of,** at the end of. 13. **strains of woe,** inward feelings of woe.
  XCI. 4. **horse,** horses.
  XCII. 10. **Since . . . lie,** since if you desert me it will cost me my life.

Happy to have thy love, happy to die!
    But what 's so blessed-fair that fears no blot?
    Thou mayst be false, and yet I know it not.

XCIII.

So shall I live, supposing thou art true,
Like a deceived husband; so love's face
May still seem love to me, though alter'd new;
Thy looks with me, thy heart in other place:
For there can live no hatred in thine eye,
Therefore in that I cannot know thy change.
In many's looks the false heart's history
Is writ in moods and frowns and wrinkles strange,
But heaven in thy creation did decree
That in thy face sweet love should ever dwell;
Whate'er thy thoughts or thy heart's workings be,
Thy looks should nothing thence but sweetness tell.
    How like Eve's apple doth thy beauty grow,
    If thy sweet virtue answer not thy show!

XCIV.

They that have power to hurt and will do none,
That do not do the thing they most do show,
Who, moving others, are themselves as stone,
Unmoved, cold, and to temptation slow,
They rightly do inherit heaven's graces
And husband nature's riches from expense;
They are the lords and owners of their faces,
Others but stewards of their excellence.
The summer's flower is to the summer sweet,
Though to itself it only live and die,
But if that flower with base infection meet,
The basest weed outbraves his dignity:
    For sweetest things turn sourest by their deeds;
    Lilies that fester smell far worse than weeds.

XCV.

How sweet and lovely dost thou make the shame
Which, like a canker in the fragrant rose,
Doth spot the beauty of thy budding name!
O, in what sweets dost thou thy sins enclose!
That tongue that tells the story of thy days,
Making lascivious comments on thy sport,
Cannot dispraise but in a kind of praise;
Naming thy name blesses an ill report.
O, what a mansion have those vices got
Which for their habitation chose out thee,
Where beauty's veil doth cover every blot,
And all things turn to fair that eyes can see!
    Take heed, dear heart, of this large privilege;
    The hardest knife ill-used doth lose his edge.

XCVI.

Some say thy fault is youth, some wantonness;
Some say thy grace is youth and gentle sport;
Both grace and faults are loved of more and less;

Thou makest faults graces that to thee resort.
As on the finger of a throned queen
The basest jewel will be well esteem'd,
So are those errors that in thee are seen
To truths translated and for true things deem'd.
How many lambs might the stern wolf betray,
If like a lamb he could his looks translate!
How many gazers mightst thou lead away,
If thou wouldst use the strength of all thy state!
    But do not so; I love thee in such sort
    As, thou being mine, mine is thy good report.

XCVII.

How like a winter hath my absence been
From thee, the pleasure of the fleeting year!
What freezings have I felt, what dark days seen!
What old December's bareness every where!
And yet this time removed was summer's time,
The teeming autumn, big with rich increase,
Bearing the wanton burthen of the prime,
Like widow'd wombs after their lords' decease:
Yet this abundant issue seem'd to me
But hope of orphans and unfather'd fruit;
For summer and his pleasures wait on thee,
And, thou away, the very birds are mute;
    Or, if they sing, 'tis with so dull a cheer
    That leaves look pale, dreading the winter's near.

XCVIII.

From you have I been absent in the spring,
When proud-pied April dress'd in all his trim
Hath put a spirit of youth in every thing,
That heavy Saturn laugh'd and leap'd with him.
Yet nor the lays of birds nor the sweet smell
Of different flowers in odour and in hue
Could make me any summer's story tell,
Or from their proud lap pluck them where they grew;
Nor did I wonder at the lily's white,
Nor praise the deep vermilion in the rose;
They were but sweet, but figures of delight,
Drawn after you, you pattern of all those.
    Yet seem'd it winter still, and, you away,
    As with your shadow I with these did play:

XCIX.

The forward violet thus did I chide:
Sweet thief, whence didst thou steal thy sweet that
    smells,
If not from my love's breath? The purple pride
Which on thy soft cheek for complexion dwells
In my love's veins thou hast too grossly dyed.
The lily I condemned for thy hand,
And buds of marjoram had stol'n thy hair:
The roses fearfully on thorns did stand,
One blushing shame, another white despair;
A third, nor red nor white, had stol'n of both

XCIII. 7-8. In . . . strange. Cf. *Macbeth*, I, iv, 11-12. 14. **show**, appearance, looks.
    XCIV. 6. **expense**, waste, expenditure. 7. **They . . . faces**, they are completely masters of themselves. 14. **Lilies . . . weeds.** This line appears in the anonymous tragedy, *Edward III*, usually dated before 1595.
    XCV. 2. **canker**, worm that destroys buds and leaves. The figure is frequent in the early works of Shakespeare; cf. xxxv, 4 and lxx, 7.
    XCVI. This sonnet does not appear in *Poems*, 1640. It seems out of harmony with the poet's usually laudatory tone, but it really serves as a climax to the warnings uttered in the preceding sonnets. 3. **more and less**, great and small. 8. **translated**, transformed. 12. **the strength . . . state**, the full glory of thy strength. 13-14. **But . . . report.** Cf. xxxvi, 13-14.

XCVII. A new group of three sonnets begins here. They deal with the theme of absence. 5. **time removed**, absence. 7. **prime**, spring.
    XCVIII. 4. **That**, so that. 7. **any summer's story**, any pleasant story. 11. **but sweet . . . delight**, only sweetness, only delightful forms.
    XCIX. This sonnet has fifteen lines, the first being merely introductory. It is devoted to the figure, general among sonneteers, of the flowers stealing their beauty from the beloved. 6. **for thy hand**, i.e., because it has stolen its whiteness from thy hand. 7. **buds of marjoram.** These are dark purple red, and it may be that the reference is to color, although marjoram is noted for its sweet scent.

And to his robbery had annex'd thy breath;
But, for his theft, in pride of all his growth
A vengeful canker eat him up to death.
　　More flowers I noted, yet I none could see
　　But sweet or colour it had stol'n from thee.

C.

Where art thou, Muse, that thou forget'st so long
To speak of that which gives thee all thy might?
Spend'st thou thy fury on some worthless song,
Darkening thy power to lend base subjects light?
Return, forgetful Muse, and straight redeem
In gentle numbers time so idly spent;
Sing to the ear that doth thy lays esteem
And gives thy pen both skill and argument.
Rise, resty Muse, my love's sweet face survey,
If Time have any wrinkle graven there;
If any, be a satire to decay,
And make Time's spoils despised every where.
　　Give my love fame faster than Time wastes life;
　　So thou prevent'st his scythe and crooked knife.

CI.

O truant Muse, what shall be thy amends
For thy neglect of truth in beauty dyed?
Both truth and beauty on my love depends;
So dost thou too, and therein dignified.
Make answer, Muse: wilt thou not haply say
'Truth needs no colour, with his colour fix'd;
Beauty no pencil, beauty's truth to lay;
But best is best, if never intermix'd'?
Because he needs no praise, wilt thou be dumb?
Excuse not silence so; for 't lies in thee
To make him much outlive a gilded tomb,
And to be praised of ages yet to be.
　　Then do thy office, Muse; I teach thee how
　　To make him seem long hence as he shows now.

CII.

My love is strengthen'd, though more weak in
　　seeming;
I love not less, though less the show appear:
That love is merchandized whose rich esteeming
The owner's tongue doth publish every where.
Our love was new and then but in the spring
When I was wont to greet it with my lays,
As Philomel in summer's front doth sing
And stops her pipe in growth of riper days:
Not that the summer is less pleasant now
Than when her mournful hymns did hush the night,
But that wild music burthens every bough

And sweets grown common lose their dear delight.
　　Therefore like her I sometime hold my tongue,
　　Because I would not dull you with my song.

CIII.

Alack, what poverty my Muse brings forth,
That having such a scope to show her pride,
The argument all bare is of more worth
Than when it hath my added praise beside!
O, blame me not, if I no more can write!
Look in your glass, and there appears a face
That over-goes my blunt invention quite,
Dulling my lines and doing me disgrace.
Were it not sinful then, striving to mend,
To mar the subject that before was well?
For to no other pass my verses tend
Than of your graces and your gifts to tell;
　　And more, much more, than in my verse can sit
　　Your own glass shows you when you look in it.

CIV.

To me, fair friend, you never can be old,
For as you were when first your eye I eyed,
Such seems your beauty still. Three winters cold
Have from the forests shook three summers' pride,
Three beauteous springs to yellow autumn turn'd
In process of the seasons have I seen,
Three April perfumes in three hot Junes burn'd,
Since first I saw you fresh, which yet are green.
Ah! yet doth beauty, like a dial-hand,
Steal from his figure and no pace perceived;
So your sweet hue, which methinks still doth stand,
Hath motion and mine eye may be deceived:
　　For fear of which, hear this, thou age unbred;
　　Ere you were born was beauty's summer dead.

CV.

Let not my love be call'd idolatry,
Nor my beloved as an idol show,
Since all alike my songs and praises be
To one, of one, still such, and ever so.
Kind is my love to-day, to-morrow kind,
Still constant in a wondrous excellence;
Therefore my verse to constancy confined,
One thing expressing, leaves out difference.
'Fair, kind, and true' is all my argument,
'Fair, kind, and true' varying to other words;
And in this change is my invention spent,
Three themes in one, which wondrous scope affords.
　　'Fair, kind, and true,' have often lived alone,
　　Which three till now never kept seat in one.

---

12. **in pride . . . growth,** in his prime.
　　C.　This sonnet marks another break. The implication is that the poet has been using his pen in unworthy themes—possibly plays. 3. **fury,** poetic inspiration. 9. **resty,** inactive, inert. 11. **satire,** satirist; rebuke (Alden). 14. **prevent'st,** anticipatest, forestallest.
　　CI.　This sonnet has to do, like LXXXII-LXXXIV, with writing in praise of the friend; the main purpose is to preserve his virtues for the future. 6. **colour . . . colour,** pretense . . . hue; cf. *1 Henry VI*, II, iv, 34-36. 7. **lay,** lay in, as with a brush.
　　CII.　3. **merchandized,** degraded by being treated as "a thing of sale." 7. **Philomel,** the nightingale; regarded as feminine. 10. **mournful hymns,** reference to the tragic tale of Philomela.
　　CIII.　2. **her pride,** power of which she is proud. 3. **argument . . . bare,** subject unadorned. 7. **blunt invention,** unpolished style. 8. **Dulling,** making uninteresting. 11. **pass,** result.
　　CIV.　3. **Three winters.** J. A. Fort uses this and the following indications of the length of the friendship to date the sonnet in 1597. He supposes that Shakespeare became acquainted with Southampton in

1593, shortly before the appearance of *Venus and Adonis*. 9-10. **Ah . . . perceived,** beauty slips away like the shadow of the hand on the dial. 11. **hue,** appearance, complexion. 13. **this,** i.e., the poet's message to posterity.
　　CV.　The poet explains that he has not been guilty of idolatry, because he has celebrated in his verse the philosophic trio, the True, the Good, and the Beautiful. 4. **To . . . so.** The motto of the Wriothesley family was *Ung par tout, tout par ung*, One for all, all for one. 8. **difference.** Difference in logic divides genus from species; there has been no division in the completeness of the poet's theme. 14. **Which . . . one,** the friend alone possesses all three of the virtues.
　　CVI.　1. **wasted,** past. 2. **wights,** persons. 5. **blazon,** heraldic metaphor, meaning here "glorification." 7. **antique,** accented on the first syllable. 8. **master,** possess, control. 11. **And, for,** and because.
　　CVII.　This sonnet has been regarded as an enigma and has been thought, perhaps wrongly, to be misplaced. It seems loosely connected with the preceding sonnets. 1-2. **soul . . . world.** "Soul of the world" is a conception in the mystical philosophy of Giordano Bruno. 4. **Sup-**

CVI.

When in the chronicle of wasted time
I see descriptions of the fairest wights,
And beauty making beautiful old rhyme
In praise of ladies dead and lovely knights,
Then, in the blazon of sweet beauty's best,
Of hand, of foot, of lip, of eye, of brow,
I see their antique pen would have express'd
Even such a beauty as you master now.
So all their praises are but prophecies
Of this our time, all you prefiguring;
And, for they look'd but with divining eyes,
They had not skill enough your worth to sing:
    For we, which now behold these present days,
    Have eyes to wonder, but lack tongues to praise.

CVII.

Not mine own fears, nor the prophetic soul
Of the wide world dreaming on things to come,
Can yet the lease of my true love control,
Supposed as forfeit to a confined doom.
The mortal moon hath her eclipse endured
And the sad augurs mock their own presage;
Incertainties now crown themselves assured
And peace proclaims olives of endless age.
Now with the drops of this most balmy time
My love looks fresh, and Death to me subscribes,
Since, spite of him, I'll live in this poor rhyme,
While he insults o'er dull and speechless tribes:
    And thou in this shalt find thy monument,
    When tyrants' crests and tombs of brass are spent.

CVIII.

What's in the brain that ink may character
Which hath not figured to thee my true spirit?
What's new to speak, what new to register,
That may express my love or thy dear merit?
Nothing, sweet boy; but yet, like prayers divine,
I must each day say o'er the very same,
Counting no old thing old, thou mine, I thine,
Even as when first I hallow'd thy fair name.
So that eternal love in love's fresh case
Weighs not the dust and injury of age,
Nor gives to necessary wrinkles place,
But makes antiquity for aye his page,
    Finding the first conceit of love there bred
    Where time and outward form would show it dead.

CIX.

O, never say that I was false of heart,

Though absence seem'd my flame to qualify.
As easy might I from myself depart
As from my soul, which in thy breast doth lie:
That is my home of love: if I have ranged,
Like him that travels I return again,
Just to the time, not with the time exchanged,
So that myself bring water for my stain.
Never believe, though in my nature reign'd
All frailties that besiege all kinds of blood,
That it could so preposterously be stain'd,
To leave for nothing all thy sum of good;
    For nothing this wide universe I call,
    Save thou, my rose; in it thou art my all.

CX.

Alas, 'tis true I have gone here and there
And made myself a motley to the view,
Gored mine own thoughts, sold cheap what is most
    dear,
Made old offences of affections new;
Most true it is that I have look'd on truth
Askance and strangely: but, by all above,
These blenches gave my heart another youth,
And worse essays proved thee my best of love.
Now all is done, have what shall have no end:
Mine appetite I never more will grind
On newer proof, to try an older friend,
A god in love, to whom I am confined.
    Then give me welcome, next my heaven the best,
    Even to thy pure and most most loving breast.

CXI.

O, for my sake do you with Fortune chide,
The guilty goddess of my harmful deeds,
That did not better for my life provide
Than public means which public manners breeds.
Thence comes it that my name receives a brand,
And almost thence my nature is subdued
To what it works in, like the dyer's hand:
Pity me then and wish I were renew'd;
Whilst, like a willing patient, I will drink
Potions of eisel 'gainst my strong infection;
No bitterness that I will bitter think,
Nor double penance, to correct correction.
    Pity me then, dear friend, and I assure ye
    Even that your pity is enough to cure me.

CXII.

Your love and pity doth the impression fill
Which vulgar scandal stamp'd upon my brow;
For what care I who calls me well or ill,

---

posed . . . doom. The fears supposed his love would have an end. But it is not so (Stopes). 5. mortal moon, usually taken as a reference to Queen Elizabeth, ill or deceased. She was known as Diana, Cynthia, and other epithets of the moon goddess. Hotson explains as a reference to the Armada. See Introduction. 8. endless age, i.e., without foreseen end. 9. balmy time, spring weather. 10. subscribes, yields. 14. crests, trophies in a tomb.
    CVIII. 1. character, write. 5. sweet boy, often taken as a reference to the youthful appearance of Southampton. 7. Counting . . . thine, a summation of themes of praise—perpetuity and unity. 8. hallow'd, made sacred. Mrs. C. C. Stopes sees in the word a reminiscence of the first time Shakespeare called Southampton "Hal." 12. But . . . page, i.e., reads the same page in the book of love.
    CIX. 2. qualify, temper, moderate. 5. ranged, gone astray. 12. To . . . good, to abandon all thy virtues for a mere nothing. 14. rose, possibly the rose of the world, rosa mundi.
    CX. An interesting sonnet sometimes taken as an indictment by Shakespeare of the actor's trade. It means, however, only that he has

traveled as a player, used his private emotions as an inspiration of his art, even made new acquaintances; but has now returned to his only permanent attachment. 2. motley, parti-colored dress of the professional fool; here actor's costume. 4. Made . . . new, used his present affections to interpret old stories. 5. truth, constancy. 6. Askance, sidewise. strangely, mistrustfully. 7. blenches, swervings. 8. essays, experiments (in friendship). 10. grind, whet. 11. newer proof, further experiment. 12. god in love, i.e., his friend. 13-14. Then . . . breast. Rolfe doubts whether these lines were addressed to a man rather than to a woman.
    CXI. 1. chide, argue. 4. Than . . . breeds, a definite reference to Shakespeare's career as an actor. 5. receives a brand, is disgraced (through prejudice against his occupation). 8. renew'd, restored to what he was by nature. 10. eisel, vinegar, used as antiseptic and remedy. 12. penance, punishment. to, variant spelling of too, which gives correct reading (John S. Kenyon). Omit comma after penance.
    CXII. impression. Cf. brand, CXI, 5.

'So you o'er-green my bad, my good allow?
You are my all the world, and I must strive
To know my shames and praises from your tongue;
None else to me, nor I to none alive,
That my steel'd sense or changes right or wrong.
In so profound abysm I throw all care
Of others' voices, that my adder's sense
To critic and to flatterer stopped are.
Mark how with my neglect I do dispense:
    You are so strongly in my purpose bred
    That all the world besides methinks are dead.

CXIII.

Since I left you, mine eye is in my mind;
And that which governs me to go about
Doth part his function and is partly blind,
Seems seeing, but effectually is out;
For it no form delivers to the heart
Of bird, of flower, or shape, which it doth latch:
Of his quick objects hath the mind no part,
Nor his own vision holds what it doth catch;
For if it see the rudest or gentlest sight,
The most sweet favour or deformed'st creature,
The mountain or the sea, the day or night,
The crow or dove, it shapes them to your feature:
    Incapable of more, replete with you,
    My most true mind thus makes mine eye untrue.

CXIV.

Or whether doth my mind, being crown'd with you,
Drink up the monarch's plague, this flattery?
Or whether shall I say, mine eye saith true,
And that your love taught it this alchemy,
To make of monsters and things indigest
Such cherubins as your sweet self resemble,
Creating every bad a perfect best,
As fast as objects to his beams assemble?
O, 'tis the first; 'tis flattery in my seeing,
And my great mind most kingly drinks it up:
Mine eye well knows what with his gust is 'greeing,
And to his palate doth prepare the cup:
    If it be poison'd, 'tis the lesser sin
    That mine eye loves it and doth first begin.

CXV.

Those lines that I before have writ do lie,
Even those that said I could not love you dearer:
Yet then my judgement knew no reason why
My most full flame should afterwards burn clearer.
But reckoning time, whose million'd accidents
Creep in 'twixt vows and change decrees of kings,
Tan sacred beauty, blunt the sharp'st intents,

Divert strong minds to the course of altering things;
Alas, why, fearing of time's tyranny,
Might I not then say 'Now I love you best,'
When I was certain o'er incertainty,
Crowning the present, doubting of the rest?
    Love is a babe; then might I not say so,
    To give full growth to that which still doth grow?

CXVI.

Let me not to the marriage of true minds
Admit impediments. Love is not love
Which alters when it alteration finds,
Or bends with the remover to remove:
O, no! it is an ever-fixed mark
That looks on tempests and is never shaken;
It is the star to every wandering bark,
Whose worth 's unknown, although his height be
    taken.
Love 's not Time's fool, though rosy lips and cheeks
Within his bending sickle's compass come;
Love alters not with his brief hours and weeks,
But bears it out even to the edge of doom.
    If this be error and upon me proved,
    I never writ, nor no man ever loved.

CXVII.

Accuse me thus: that I have scanted all
Wherein I should your great deserts repay,
Forgot upon your dearest love to call,
Whereto all bonds do tie me day by day;
That I have frequent been with unknown minds
And given to time your own dear-purchased right;
That I have hoisted sail to all the winds
Which should transport me farthest from your sight.
Book both my wilfulness and errors down
And on just proof surmise accumulate;
Bring me within the level of your frown,
But shoot not at me in your waken'd hate;
    Since my appeal says I did strive to prove
    The constancy and virtue of your love.

CXVIII.

Like as, to make our appetites more keen,
With eager compounds we our palate urge,
As, to prevent our maladies unseen,
We sicken to shun sickness when we purge,
Even so, being full of your ne'er-cloying sweetness,
To bitter sauces did I frame my feeding
And, sick of welfare, found a kind of meetness
To be diseased ere that there was true needing.
Thus policy in love, to anticipate
The ills that were not, grew to faults assured

4. **o'er-green my bad,** cover my evil with green leaves; an obscure figure. 5. **all the world.** "All the world" have slandered him; his friend is not all-the-world to him. 8. **steel'd sense,** what is engraven on his sense. 10. **adder's sense.** Adders were supposed to be deaf. 12. **dispense,** excuse.
    CXIII. 2. **governs,** guides. 5. **For . . . heart,** I have no knowledge of what passes. 6. **latch,** catch or receive (the sight or sound). 12. **shapes . . . feature,** makes them resemble you.
    CXIV. 1. **crown'd with you,** i.e., elevated by reconciliation with his friend. 4. **alchemy,** science of transmuting base metals. 5. **indigest,** chaotic, formless. 6. **cherubins,** another suggestion of the youth and beauty of the friend. 10. **it,** i.e., he accepts the cup of flattery. 11. **what . . . 'greeing,** what suits the eye's taste. Steevens sees in this and the following lines an allusion to tasters for the food of kings.
    CXV. The poet evinces greater love to his friend. The former sonnets have been untruthful when they said his love had reached a maximum. Love is a babe at first but grows with time. 5. **But reckon-**

ing time, merely considering the power of Time as a destroyer. 9. **fearing of,** fearing; similar construction to *reckoning.*
    CXVI. 4. **Or . . . remove,** or inclines to inconstancy at the demand of the inconstant. 8. **Whose . . . taken.** The star has an influence over and above the determination of its altitude (for purposes of navigation). 9. **fool,** plaything. 11. **his,** i.e., Time's. 12. **But . . . doom,** endures or holds out to the very day of judgment.
    CXVII. 4. **bonds,** a pun on the legal sense of the word. 5. **unknown minds,** persons not worth knowing. 6. **And . . . right,** squandered your rights in me on temporary matters and alliances.
    CXVIII. 2. **eager,** pungent, bitter, appetizing. 3. **prevent,** anticipate. 9-12. **Thus . . . cured,** thus the attempt of love to forestall the evils of satiety had brought in sickness, when in health he had taken medicine for disease. 12. **rank of goodness,** sick with good health.
    CXIX. 1. **Siren tears,** deceitful tears of seductive women. 2. **limbecks,** vessels used in distillation. 7. **How . . . fitted,** how my eyes have popped out in convulsive fit. 10. **That . . . better.** Cf. *As You*

And brought to medicine a healthful state
Which, rank of goodness, would by ill be cured:
  But thence I learn, and find the lesson true,
  Drugs poison him that so fell sick of you.

CXIX.

What potions have I drunk of Siren tears,
Distill'd from limbecks foul as hell within,
Applying fears to hopes and hopes to fears,
Still losing when I saw myself to win!
What wretched errors hath my heart committed,
Whilst it hath thought itself so blessed never!
How have mine eyes out of their spheres been fitted
In the distraction of this madding fever!
O benefit of ill! now I find true
That better is by evil still made better;
And ruin'd love, when it is built anew,
Grows fairer than at first, more strong, far greater.
  So I return rebuked to my content
  And gain by ill thrice more than I have spent.

CXX.

That you were once unkind befriends me now,
And for that sorrow which I then did feel
Needs must I under my transgression bow,
Unless my nerves were brass or hammer'd steel.
For if you were by my unkindness shaken
As I by yours, you 've pass'd a hell of time,
And I, a tyrant, have no leisure taken
To weigh how once I suffer'd in your crime.
O, that our night of woe might have remember'd
My deepest sense, how hard true sorrow hits,
And soon to you, as you to me, then tender'd
The humble salve which wounded bosoms fits!
  But that your trespass now becomes a fee;
  Mine ransoms yours, and yours must ransom me.

CXXI.

'Tis better to be vile than vile esteem'd,
When not to be receives reproach of being,
And the just pleasure lost which is so deem'd
Not by our feeling but by others' seeing:
For why should others' false adulterate eyes
Give salutation to my sportive blood?
Or on my frailties why are frailer spies,
Which in their wills count bad what I think good?
No, I am that I am, and they that level
At my abuses reckon up their own:
I may be straight, though they themselves be bevel;
By their rank thoughts my deeds must not be shown;
  Unless this general evil they maintain,
  All men are bad, and in their badness reign.

CXXII.

Thy gift, thy tables, are within my brain
Full character'd with lasting memory,
Which shall above that idle rank remain
Beyond all date, even to eternity;
Or at the least, so long as brain and heart
Have faculty by nature to subsist;
Till each to razed oblivion yield his part
Of thee, thy record never can be miss'd.
That poor retention could not so much hold,
Nor need I tallies thy dear love to score;
Therefore to give them from me was I bold,
To trust those tables that receive thee more:
  To keep an adjunct to remember thee
  Were to import forgetfulness in me.

CXXIII.

No, Time, thou shalt not boast that I do change:
Thy pyramids built up with newer might
To me are nothing novel, nothing strange;
They are but dressings of a former sight.
Our dates are brief, and therefore we admire
What thou dost foist upon us that is old,
And rather make them born to our desire
Than think that we before have heard them told.
Thy registers and thee I both defy,
Not wondering at the present nor the past,
For thy records and what we see doth lie,
Made more or less by thy continual haste.
  This I do vow and this shall ever be;
  I will be true, despite thy scythe and thee.

CXXIV.

If my dear love were but the child of state,
It might for Fortune's bastard be unfather'd,
As subject to Time's love or to Time's hate,
Weeds among weeds, or flowers with flowers gather'd.
No, it was builded far from accident;
It suffers not in smiling pomp, nor falls
Under the blow of thralled discontent,
Whereto the inviting time our fashion calls:
It fears not policy, that heretic,
Which works on leases of short-number'd hours,
But all alone stands hugely politic,
That it nor grows with heat nor drowns with showers.
  To this I witness call the fools of time,
  Which die for goodness, who have lived for crime.

CXXV.

Were 't aught to me I bore the canopy,
With my extern the outward honouring,

Like It, II, i, 12.
  CXX. 5-6. For . . . time. The poet's greatest sorrow is character-istically that his friend has suffered. 9. our night of woe, the dark and woeful time we have endured. remember'd, reminded.
  CXXI. 2. When . . . being, when not to be vile receives the reproach of vileness. 3-4. which . . . seeing, which is measured by the opinions of others, not by my own conscience. 5-6. For . . . blood, why should others who are really wicked greet as an equal me, who am only mirthful. 8. in their wills, at their pleasure. 9. that, what. 11. bevel, out of square, crooked. 13. this general evil, this general principle of evil.
  CXXII. 2. Full . . . memory, written all over in my lasting memory. 3. above . . . rank, i.e., the rank or importance of ordinary things. 7. razed oblivion, obliterating forgetfulness. 9. retention, i.e., the book, an instrument for retaining memoranda. 10. tallies, sticks notched to serve for reckoning. 14. import, impute.
  CXXIII. 2. Thy . . . might. Taken by Hotson to refer to the erection by Pope Sixtus v of four obelisks (known as *pyramids*) in Rome in 1586 and succeeding years; see Introduction. 4. They . . . sight, they but repeat all objects in new forms; apparent assertion of the indestructibility of matter. 7-8. And . . . told, and rather hold the impression that they are our new structures than remember that we have seen them before.
  CXXIV. 1. child of state, child of rank or power; possibly circum-stance, which is always changing (Lee). 8. Whereto . . . calls. Hotson regards these lines as an allusion to the assassination of Henri III of France; see Introduction. 10. leases . . . hours, possible allusion to short-term leases granted by heretics to their friends to avoid con-fiscation of property. 11. politic, wise, prudent. 13-14. To . . . crime, I call to witness the transitory unworthy loves (sports of time; see CVI), whose death was a virtue since their life was a crime (Dowden).
  CXXV. 1. bore the canopy, i.e., honor you (or another) as those are honored over whose heads a cloth of state is carried (Pooler). 2. With . . . honouring, i.e., to honor the outward by the outward (Alden).

Or laid great bases for eternity,
Which prove more short than waste or ruining?
Have I not seen dwellers on form and favour
Lose all, and more, by paying too much rent,
For compound sweet forgoing simple savour,
Pitiful thrivers, in their gazing spent?
No, let me be obsequious in thy heart,
And take thou my oblation, poor but free,
Which is not mix'd with seconds, knows no art,
But mutual render, only me for thee.
    Hence, thou suborn'd informer! a true soul
    When most impeach'd stands least in thy
        control.

CXXVI.

O thou, my lovely boy, who in thy power
Dost hold Time's fickle glass, his sickle, hour;
Who hast by waning grown, and therein show'st
Thy lovers withering as thy sweet self grow'st;
If Nature, sovereign mistress over wrack,
As thou goest onwards, still will pluck thee back,
She keeps thee to this purpose, that her skill
May time disgrace and wretched minutes kill.
Yet fear her, O thou minion of her pleasure!
She may detain, but not still keep, her treasure:
Her audit, though delay'd, answer'd must be,
And her quietus is to render thee.

CXXVII.

492

In the old age black was not counted fair,
Or if it were, it bore not beauty's name;
But now is black beauty's successive heir,
And beauty slander'd with a bastard shame:
For since each hand hath put on nature's power,
Fairing the foul with art's false borrow'd face,
Sweet beauty hath no name, no holy bower,
But is profaned, if not lives in disgrace.
Therefore my mistress' brows are raven black,
Her eyes so suited, and they mourners seem
At such who, not born fair, no beauty lack,
Slandering creation with a false esteem:
    Yet so they mourn, becoming of their woe,
    That every tongue says beauty should look so.

CXXVIII.

How oft, when thou, my music, music play'st,
Upon that blessed wood whose motion sounds
With thy sweet fingers, when thou gently sway'st
The wiry concord that mine ear confounds,
Do I envy those jacks that nimble leap
To kiss the tender inward of thy hand,
Whilst my poor lips, which should that harvest reap,
At the wood's boldness by thee blushing stand!

To be so tickled, they would change their state
And situation with those dancing chips,
O'er whom thy fingers walk with gentle gait,
Making dead wood more blest than living lips.
    Since saucy jacks so happy are in this,
    Give them thy fingers, me thy lips to kiss.

CXXIX.

The expense of spirit in a waste of shame
Is lust in action; and till action, lust
Is perjured, murderous, bloody, full of blame,
Savage, extreme, rude, cruel, not to trust,
Enjoy'd no sooner but despised straight,
Past reason hunted, and no sooner had
Past reason hated, as a swallow'd bait
On purpose laid to make the taker mad;
Mad in pursuit and in possession so;
Had, having, and in quest to have, extreme;
A bliss in proof, and proved, a very woe;
Before, a joy proposed; behind, a dream.
    All this the world well knows; yet none knows
      well
    To shun the heaven that leads men to this hell.

CXXX.

My mistress' eyes are nothing like the sun;
Coral is far more red than her lips' red;
If snow be white, why then her breasts are dun;
If hairs be wires, black wires grow on her head.
I have seen roses damask'd, red and white,
But no such roses see I in her cheeks;
And in some perfumes is there more delight
Than in the breath that from my mistress reeks.
I love to hear her speak, yet well I know
That music hath a far more pleasing sound;
I grant I never saw a goddess go;
My mistress, when she walks, treads on the ground:
    And yet, by heaven, I think my love as rare
    As any she belied with false compare.

CXXXI.

Thou art as tyrannous, so as thou art,
As those whose beauties proudly make them
    cruel;
For well thou know'st to my dear doting heart
Thou art the fairest and most precious jewel.
Yet, in good faith, some say that thee behold
Thy face hath not the power to make love groan:
To say they err I dare not be so bold,
Although I swear it to myself alone.
And, to be sure that is not false I swear,
A thousand groans, but thinking on thy face,
One on another's neck, do witness bear
Thy black is fairest in my judgement's place.

3. Or . . . eternity, laid foundations for lasting fame. 6. by paying too much rent, by overdoing their obligations. 7. For . . . savour, foregoing actual love for the sake of obsequious flattery. 9. obsequious, devoted. 10. oblation, offering. 11. seconds, inferior parts, as of grain. 12. mutual render, fair exchange. 13. suborn'd informer, doubtful reference; possibly one of the informers mentioned in CXXI, 7, 8; possibly, false witness. 14. impeach'd, charged with treason.
CXXVI. With this sonnet (which is made up of six couplets) the first great cycle, that addressed to the friend, comes to an end. It is not in the volume of 1640. 2. fickle glass, ever-changing hourglass. Some editors retain Q reading: fickle hour. 5. wrack, ruin. Nature is mistress of decay because of her power of restoration. 10. She . . . treasure. The poet warns his friend that, although nature will keep and restore him for a time, Time will ultimately triumph over him. 11. audit, i.e., Nature's account to Time. 12. quietus, discharge, quittance.

Here begins a separate series of sonnets, apparently belonging to the same period of time as XXXIII-XLII. They are addressed to, or refer to, a dark woman who passes from loving the poet to loving the friend.
CXXVII. 1. In . . . fair. Black was traditionally associated with ugliness; cf. Love's Labour's Lost, IV, iii, 247, 261 ff. 3. successive heir, lawful successor. 9. brows. Many editors retain the Q reading eyes, i.e., eyebrows. 10. suited, clad. 12. Slandering . . . esteem, dishonoring nature by a false reputation for beauty. 13. becoming of, gracing.
CXXVIII. 5. jacks, upright pieces of wood fixed to the key-lever and fitted with a quill which plucked the strings of the virginal (Onions). 6. tender inward, delicate inside.
CXXIX. This famous sonnet, loosely connected with those that precede and follow it, deals with the ravages of lust; cf. CXLVI, note. 1. expense, expenditure, waste. 5. Enjoy'd . . . straight. Cf. The Rape of Lucrece, 211-212, 742.

In nothing art thou black save in thy deeds,
And thence this slander, as I think, proceeds.

CXXXII.

Thine eyes I love, and they, as pitying me,
Knowing thy heart torments me with disdain,
Have put on black and loving mourners be,
Looking with pretty ruth upon my pain.
And truly not the morning sun of heaven
Better becomes the grey cheeks of the east,
Nor that full star that ushers in the even
Doth half that glory to the sober west,
As those two mourning eyes become thy face:
O, let it then as well beseem thy heart
To mourn for me, since mourning doth thee grace,
And suit thy pity like in every part.
 Then will I swear beauty herself is black
 And all they foul that thy complexion lack.

CXXXIII.

Beshrew that heart that makes my heart to groan
For that deep wound it gives my friend and me!
Is 't not enough to torture me alone,
But slave to slavery my sweet'st friend must be?
Me from myself thy cruel eye hath taken,
And my next self thou harder hast engross'd:
Of him, myself, and thee, I am forsaken;
A torment thrice threefold thus to be cross'd.
Prison my heart in thy steel bosom's ward,
But then my friend's heart let my poor heart bail;
Whoe'er keeps me, let my heart be his guard;
Thou canst not then use rigour in my gaol:
 And yet thou wilt; for I, being pent in thee,
 Perforce am thine, and all that is in me.

CXXXIV.

So, now I have confess'd that he is thine,
And I myself am mortgaged to thy will,
Myself I'll forfeit, so that other mine
Thou wilt restore, to be my comfort still:
But thou wilt not, nor he will not be free,
For thou art covetous and he is kind;
He learn'd but surety-like to write for me
Under that bond that him as fast doth bind.
The statute of thy beauty thou wilt take,
Thou usurer, that put'st forth all to use,
And sue a friend came debtor for my sake;
So him I lose through my unkind abuse.
 Him have I lost; thou hast both him and me:
 He pays the whole, and yet am I not free.

CXXXV.

Whoever hath her wish, thou hast thy 'Will,'
And 'Will' to boot, and 'Will' in overplus;

More than enough am I that vex thee still,
To thy sweet will making addition thus.
Wilt thou, whose will is large and spacious,
Not once vouchsafe to hide my will in thine?
Shall will in others seem right gracious,
And in my will no fair acceptance shine?
The sea, all water, yet receives rain still
And in abundance addeth to his store;
So thou, being rich in 'Will,' add to thy 'Will'
One will of mine, to make thy large 'Will' more.
 Let no unkind, no fair beseechers kill;
 Think all but one, and me in that one 'Will.'

CXXXVI.

If thy soul check thee that I come so near,
Swear to thy blind soul that I was thy 'Will,'
And will, thy soul knows, is admitted there;
Thus far for love my love-suit, sweet, fulfil.
'Will' will fulfil the treasure of thy love,
Ay, fill it full with wills, and my will one.
In things of great receipt with ease we prove
Among a number one is reckon'd none:
Then in the number let me pass untold,
Though in thy stores' account I one must be;
For nothing hold me, so it please thee hold
That nothing me, a something sweet to thee:
 Make but my name thy love, and love that
  still,
 And then thou lovest me, for my name is 'Will.'

CXXXVII.

Thou blind fool, Love, what dost thou to mine eyes,
That they behold, and see not what they see?
They know what beauty is, see where it lies,
Yet what the best is take the worst to be.
If eyes corrupt by over-partial looks
Be anchor'd in the bay where all men ride,
Why of eyes' falsehood hast thou forged hooks,
Whereto the judgement of my heart is tied?
Why should my heart think that a several plot
Which my heart knows the wide world's common
  place?
Or mine eyes seeing this, say this is not,
To put fair truth upon so foul a face?
 In things right true my heart and eyes have err'd,
 And to this false plague are they now transferr'd.

CXXXVIII.

When my love swears that she is made of truth
I do believe her, though I know she lies,
That she might think me some untutor'd youth,
Unlearned in the world's false subtleties.
Thus vainly thinking that she thinks me young,
Although she knows my days are past the best,

CXXX. 5. **damask'd,** like a pattern in damask cloth—woven with a pattern of satin on one side. 8. **reeks,** issues as smell.

CXXXI. 1. **so as,** so. 11. **One on another's neck,** one after another. 12. **my judgement's place,** my critical opinion.

CXXXII. 4. **ruth,** pity. 12. **suit thy pity like,** clothe your pity in the same way.

CXXXIII. 6. **my next self,** my dearest friend. 8. **cross'd,** tried. 9. **steel bosom's ward,** the prison cell of thy hard heart.

CXXXIV. 3. **that other mine,** my other self. 9. **statute,** security; e.g., of a usurer. 11. **came,** i.e., who became. 12. **unkind abuse,** unnatural ill-usage.

CXXXV. This and the following sonnet ring the changes on the word *will*—desire, temper, passion, and the poet's name; possibly also the friend's name. 13. **Let . . . kill,** a puzzling line, in which *unkind* is usually taken as a noun, i.e., unkind one. Several editors favor Tyler's suggestion, "Let no unkind 'no' your beseechers kill."

CXXXVI. 5. **fulfil,** fill full. 7. **receipt,** capacity. 8. **one is reckon'd none,** variant of the common saying "one is no number." 12. **a something . . . thee.** The poet reminds his mistress that she had once held him dear. 13-14. **Make . . . Will,** love only my name (something less than loving myself), and then thou lovest me, for my name is Will, and I myself am all will, that is, all desire (Dowden). The lines may also be taken as a surrender of his mistress to his friend, also named Will.

CXXXVII. A vituperative sonnet, in which the poet blames love for blinding his eyes, so that he has chosen the worst for the best; cf. CXIII. 6. **Be . . . ride,** abuse of the mistress; cf. *common place,* l. 10. 9-10. **several . . . common,** property in private ownership and common land; cf. *Love's Labour's Lost,* II, i, 222.

CXXXVIII. This sonnet is 1 in *The Passionate Pilgrim.* 2. **believe her,** i.e., pretend to believe her.

Simply I credit her false-speaking tongue:
On both sides thus is simple truth suppress'd.
But wherefore says she not she is unjust?
And wherefore say not I that I am old?
O, love's best habit is in seeming trust,
And age in love loves not to have years told:
    Therefore I lie with her and she with me,
    And in our faults by lies we flatter'd be.

CXXXIX.

O, call not me to justify the wrong
That thy unkindness lays upon my heart;
Wound me not with thine eye but with thy tongue;
Use power with power and slay me not by art.
Tell me thou lovest elsewhere, but in my sight,
Dear heart, forbear to glance thine eye aside:
What need'st thou wound with cunning when thy
    might
Is more than my o'er-press'd defence can bide?
Let me excuse thee: ah! my love well knows
Her pretty looks have been mine enemies,
And therefore from my face she turns my foes,
That they elsewhere might dart their injuries:
    Yet do not so; but since I am near slain,
    Kill me outright with looks and rid my pain.

CXL.

Be wise as thou art cruel; do not press
My tongue-tied patience with too much disdain;
Lest sorrow lend me words and words express
The manner of my pity-wanting pain.
If I might teach thee wit, better it were,
Though not to love, yet, love, to tell me so;
As testy sick men, when their deaths be near,
No news but health from their physicians know;
For if I should despair, I should grow mad,
And in my madness might speak ill of thee:
Now this ill-wresting world is grown so bad,
Mad slanderers by mad ears believed be.
    That I may not be so, nor thou belied,
    Bear thine eyes straight, though thy proud heart go
    wide.

CXLI.

In faith, I do not love thee with mine eyes,
For they in thee a thousand errors note;
But 'tis my heart that loves what they despise,
Who in despite of view is pleased to dote;
Nor are mine ears with thy tongue's tune delighted,
Nor tender feeling, to base touches prone,
Nor taste, nor smell, desire to be invited
To any sensual feast with thee alone:
But my five wits nor my five senses can

Dissuade one foolish heart from serving thee,
Who leaves unsway'd the likeness of a man,
Thy proud heart's slave and vassal wretch to be:
    Only my plague thus far I count my gain,
    That she that makes me sin awards me pain.

CXLII.

Love is my sin and thy dear virtue hate,
Hate of my sin, grounded on sinful loving:
O, but with mine compare thou thine own state,
And thou shalt find it merits not reproving;
Or, if it do, not from those lips of thine,
That have profaned their scarlet ornaments
And seal'd false bonds of love as oft as mine,
Robb'd others' beds' revenues of their rents.
Be it lawful I love thee, as thou lovest those
Whom thine eyes woo as mine importune thee:
Root pity in thy heart, that when it grows
Thy pity may deserve to pitied be.
    If thou dost seek to have what thou dost hide,
    By self-example mayst thou be denied!

CXLIII.

Lo! as a careful housewife runs to catch
One of her feather'd creatures broke away,
Sets down her babe and makes all swift dispatch
In pursuit of the thing she would have stay,
Whilst her neglected child holds her in chase,
Cries to catch her whose busy care is bent
To follow that which flies before her face,
Not prizing her poor infant's discontent;
So runn'st thou after that which flies from thee,
Whilst I thy babe chase thee afar behind;
But if thou catch thy hope, turn back to me,
And play the mother's part, kiss me, be kind:
    So will I pray that thou mayst have thy 'Will,'
    If thou turn back, and my loud crying still.

CXLIV.

Two loves I have of comfort and despair,
Which like two spirits do suggest me still:
The better angel is a man right fair,
The worser spirit a woman colour'd ill.
To win me soon to hell, my female evil
Tempteth my better angel from my side,
And would corrupt my saint to be a devil,
Wooing his purity with her foul pride.
And whether that my angel be turn'd fiend
Suspect I may, yet not directly tell;
But being both from me, both to each friend,
I guess one angel in another's hell:
    Yet this shall I ne'er know, but live in doubt,
    Till my bad angel fire my good one out.

11. **habit,** deportment, with play on the idea of habiliment, that which is put on.
CXXXIX. 3. **Wound . . . tongue.** Cf. *Romeo and Juliet,* II, iv, 14, and *3 Henry VI,* V, vi, 26.
CXL. 4. **The . . . pain,** the nature of my pain, on which you bestow no pity. 5. **wit,** wisdom, prudence. 6. **to tell me so,** to tell me thou dost love me. 11. **ill-wresting,** misinterpreting. 13-14. **That . . . wide,** that I may not be mad and you may not be exposed, control your eyes, whatever course your heart may take.
CXLI. 6. **base touches,** sensual indulgence. 9. **five wits,** intellectual, the same in number as the five senses—the common sense, imagination, fancy, judgment, and memory. 11. **Who . . . man,** i.e., in my foolish heart, which abandons the government of my personality. 14. **pain,** punishment.
CXLII. 2. **Hate . . . loving,** implies that the mistress hates his sin only because of her own with others. 6. **profaned,** desecrated, as a temple. **scarlet ornaments,** blushes. 7. **seal'd . . . love,** i.e., with kisses; cf.

The Merchant of Venice, II, vi, 6. 8. **Robb'd . . . rents,** implication of adultery. 13-14. **If . . . denied,** if thou dost seek to have the pity thou hidst from me, thou mayst by thy own example be denied it.
CXLIII. 4. **pursuit,** accented on first syllable. 13. **will . . . Will,** pun on will, desire, and the Christian name. Whether the *Will* refers to the poet or the rival friend is a matter of doubt.
CXLIV. The second sonnet in *The Passionate Pilgrim.* It depicts the conflict in the poet's mind between his affection for his friend and his mistress. 2. **suggest,** tempt (Malone); prompt (to good or evil). 6. **Tempteth . . . side.** Cf. *Othello,* V, ii, 208. 8. **foul,** wicked. 11. **from me,** away from me. The poet suspects they are together. 14. **fire . . . out,** drive out with fire; an expression still in common use.
CXLV. A sonnet in eight-syllable meter. Critics have regarded it as out of place, or have rejected it. It has been compared to Lyly's "Cupid and my Campaspe played." 6-7. **Chiding . . . doom.** Her tongue was accustomed to dismiss her lover's guilt. 13. **'I . . . threw,** i.e., she took away the pain and danger by saying, "I do not hate you."

CXLV.

Those lips that Love's own hand did make
Breathed forth the sound that said 'I hate'
To me that languish'd for her sake;
But when she saw my woeful state,
Straight in her heart did mercy come,
Chiding that tongue that ever sweet
Was used in giving gentle doom,
And taught it thus anew to greet;
'I hate' she alter'd with an end,
That follow'd it as gentle day
Doth follow night, who like a fiend
From heaven to hell is flown away;
   'I hate' from hate away she threw,
   And saved my life, saying 'not you.'

CXLVI.

Poor soul, the centre of my sinful earth,
[Thrall to] these rebel powers that thee array,
Why dost thou pine within and suffer dearth,
Painting thy outward walls so costly gay?
Why so large cost, having so short a lease,
Dost thou upon thy fading mansion spend?
Shall worms, inheritors of this excess,
Eat up thy charge? is this thy body's end?
Then, soul, live thou upon thy servant's loss,
And let that pine to aggravate thy store;
Buy terms divine in selling hours of dross;
Within be fed, without be rich no more:
   So shalt thou feed on Death, that feeds on men,
   And Death once dead, there 's no more dying then.

CXLVII.

My love is as a fever, longing still
For that which longer nurseth the disease,
Feeding on that which doth preserve the ill,
The uncertain sickly appetite to please.
My reason, the physician to my love,
Angry that his prescriptions are not kept,
Hath left me, and I desperate now approve
Desire is death, which physic did except.
Past cure I am, now reason is past care,
And frantic-mad with evermore unrest;
My thoughts and my discourse as madmen's are,
At random from the truth vainly express'd;
   For I have sworn thee fair and thought thee bright,
   Who art as black as hell, as dark as night.

CXLVIII.

O me, what eyes hath Love put in my head,
Which have no correspondence with true sight!
Or, if they have, where is my judgement fled,
That censures falsely what they see aright?
If that be fair whereon my false eyes dote,
What means the world to say it is not so?
If it be not, then love doth well denote
Love's eye is not so true as all men's 'No.'
How can it? O, how can Love's eye be true,
That is so vex'd with watching and with tears?
No marvel then, though I mistake my view;
The sun itself sees not till heaven clears.
   O cunning Love! with tears thou keep'st me blind,
   Lest eyes well-seeing thy foul faults should find.

CXLIX.

Canst thou, O cruel! say I love thee not,
When I against myself with thee partake?
Do I not think on thee, when I forgot
Am of myself, all tyrant, for thy sake?
Who hateth thee that I do call my friend?
On whom frown'st thou that I do fawn upon?
Nay, if thou lour'st on me, do I not spend
Revenge upon myself with present moan?
What merit do I in myself respect,
That is so proud thy service to despise,
When all my best doth worship thy defect,
Commanded by the motion of thine eyes?
   But, love, hate on, for now I know thy mind;
   Those that can see thou lovest, and I am blind.

CL.

O, from what power hast thou this powerful might
With insufficiency my heart to sway?
To make me give the lie to my true sight,
And swear that brightness doth not grace the day?
Whence hast thou this becoming of things ill,
That in the very refuse of thy deeds
There is such strength and warrantise of skill
That, in my mind, thy worst all best exceeds?
Who taught thee how to make me love thee more
The more I hear and see just cause of hate?
O, though I love what others do abhor,
With others thou shouldst not abhor my state:
   If thy unworthiness raised love in me,
   More worthy I to be beloved of thee.

CLI.

Love is too young to know what conscience is;
Yet who knows not conscience is born of love?
Then, gentle cheater, urge not my amiss,
Lest guilty of my faults thy sweet self prove:
For, thou betraying me, I do betray
My nobler part to my gross body's treason;
My soul doth tell my body that he may
Triumph in love; flesh stays no farther reason;

CXLVI. A profound sonnet, not connected with the preceding, which says it is folly to adorn and feed the body instead of the mind. The body will die, but the soul will conquer death. Tucker Brooke places this sonnet and CXXIX at the end of the "Dark Lady" sequence, regarding them as moral reflections following on her dismissal. 1. **sinful earth,** the body. 2. [**Thrall to**], anonymous conjecture; Q, Globe, *et al.*, leave blank. 8. **thy charge,** that on which thou hast expended so much. 10. **aggravate,** increase. 11. **Buy terms divine,** purchase long periods of divine salvation.

CXLVII. This sonnet is associated in theme with CXLI and CXLIV— his hopeless love for an unworthy mistress. 5. **My . . . love.** Cf. *The Merry Wives of Windsor*, II, i, 5. 7-8. **I . . . except,** I, being in despair, now recognize that desire is fatal, which took exception to the teaching of physic (Stopes). 9. **cure . . . care,** an adaptation of the proverb, things past cure are past care.

CXLVIII. 4. **censures,** judges. 6. **What . . . so.** The opinion of the world refutes the warped judgment of the poet. 13. **O cunning Love,**

perhaps refers to the mistress as well as to the god of love.

CXLIX. 2. **partake,** take part (against myself). 3-4. **Do . . . sake,** it is for your sake that I neglect and tyrannize over myself. 7. **lour'st,** frown'st.

CL. Lee refers to this as a vituperative sonnet; cf. CXXXVII. The poet laments that the mistress has gained power over him, although love has made him worthy of her love. 2. **insufficiency,** lack of every virtue and charm. 5. **becoming . . . ill,** ability to render evil things attractive. 7. **warrantise of skill,** warrant or pledge of ability.

CLI. The vein of the preceding sonnet continues; cf. CXLVI. 1. **Love . . . is,** cf. CXV. 2. **Yet . . . love?** Who knows not that the power of love awakens conscience? 3. **cheater,** rogue; with possible reference to "escheater," a king's officer charged with reversions of land. 6. **My . . . treason.** She was the cause of his betraying his nobler part to the lusts of his body.

But, rising at thy name, doth point out thee
As his triumphant prize. Proud of this pride,
He is contented thy poor drudge to be,
To stand in thy affairs, fall by thy side.
　　No want of conscience hold it that I call
　　Her 'love' for whose dear love I rise and fall.

CLII.

In loving thee thou know'st I am forsworn,
But thou art twice forsworn, to me love swearing,
In act thy bed-vow broke and new faith torn
In vowing new hate after new love bearing.
But why of two oaths' breach do I accuse thee,
When I break twenty? I am perjured most;
For all my vows are oaths but to misuse thee
And all my honest faith in thee is lost,
For I have sworn deep oaths of thy deep kindness,
Oaths of thy love, thy truth, thy constancy,
And, to enlighten thee, gave eyes to blindness,
Or made them swear against the thing they see;
　　For I have sworn thee fair; more perjured I,
　　To swear against the truth so foul a lie!

———

CLIII.

Cupid laid by his brand, and fell asleep:
A maid of Dian's this advantage found,

And his love-kindling fire did quickly steep
In a cold valley-fountain of that ground;
Which borrow'd from this holy fire of Love
A dateless lively heat, still to endure,
And grew a seething bath, which yet men prove
Against strange maladies a sovereign cure.
But at my mistress' eye Love's brand new-fired,
The boy for trial needs would touch my breast;
I, sick withal, the help of bath desired,
And thither hied, a sad distemper'd guest,
　　But found no cure: the bath for my help lies
　　Where Cupid got new fire—my mistress' eyes.

CLIV.

The little Love-god lying once asleep
Laid by his side his heart-inflaming brand,
Whilst many nymphs that vow'd chaste life to keep
Came tripping by; but in her maiden hand
The fairest votary took up that fire
Which many legions of true hearts had warm'd;
And so the general of hot desire
Was sleeping by a virgin hand disarm'd.
This brand she quenched in a cool well by,
Which from Love's fire took heat perpetual,
Growing a bath and healthful remedy
For men diseased; but I, my mistress' thrall,
　　Came there for cure, and this by that I prove,
　　Love's fire heats water, water cools not love.

CLII.　9. **kindness,** affection, tenderness.　11. **to enlighten thee,**
in order to invest thee with brightness; she was a dark lady.
　　The following two sonnets have no direct connection with those
preceding. They are adaptations of epigrams in the Palatine Anthology,
Greek poems of the fifth century (translated into Latin in the sixteenth
century). The discovery was made by Hertzbert, *Shakespeare Jahrbuch,*
XIII (1878), 158-162. Malone suggested that they were early exercises

of the poet.
　　CLIII.　6. **dateless,** endless, eternal.　7. **seething bath,** spring of
hot medicinal waters.　9. **But . . . new-fired,** love has kindled his
torch at my mistress' eyes.
　　CLIV.　7. **general,** cause and commander, i.e., Cupid.　12. **thrall,**
slave, bondman.　13. **this by that,** i.e., *this* is what follows in l. 14,
by that is by my coming which failed to cure me (Pooler).

*Bombasted breeches from the time of Queen Elizabeth. A slovenly copy from the title page of
Middleton and Rowley's "Faire Quarrell," 1617.*

SHAKESPEARE'S LIFE AND WORK

The Period of Comedies
and Histories, 1595-1601

By the year 1594, Shakespeare had achieved a reputation as a poet. Possibly the greatest reputation he achieved during his lifetime was by the publication of *Venus and Adonis* and *The Rape of Lucrece*, as well as by the circulation in manuscript of the *Sonnets*. Anonymous verses prefixed to the poem *Willobie his Avisa* (1594) give us the earliest tribute to Shakespeare as a poet:

> Though *Collatine* haue deerly bought,
> To high renowne, a lasting life,
> And found, that most in vaine haue sought,
> To haue a *Faire* and *Constant* wife,
> Yet *Tarquyne* pluckt his glistering grape,
> And *Shake-speare*, paints poor *Lucrece* rape.

Some unnecessary doubt has always been attached to a more significant tribute from the hand of Edmund Spenser in *Colin Clout's Come Home Again*, written in 1594. Here Shakespeare appears as Aetion, "though last, not least," in the list of contemporary poets:

> A gentler shepheard may no where be found:
> Whose Muse, full of high thoughts inuention,
> Doth like himselfe Heroically sound.

CONTEMPORARY EVALUATION

When one considers that the writing of plays was not regarded by Shakespeare himself, or by others of his time, as literary work in a true sense, it is somewhat surprising that Shakespeare's work as a dramatist was acknowledged as generously as it was during the period from 1594 to 1601. However, in the six or seven literary allusions to Shakespeare during the period, the poems are obviously regarded as of more significance than the plays. To know the story of Shakespeare's life we should consider these references.

Of them the most important as a document, if not as a tribute, is the passage in *Palladis Tamia* (1598) by Francis Meres in which Meres declares

that the English tongue has been enriched by Sir Philip Sidney, Spenser, Daniel, Drayton, Warner, Shakespeare, Marlowe, and Chapman, even as the Greek tongue was enriched by Homer, Hesiod, and others, and the Latin tongue enriched by Virgil, Ovid, and Horace. He thinks that "the sweet witty soul of Ovid" lives in "mellifluous and honey-tongued" Shakespeare, as witnessed by his *Venus and Adonis*, his *Lucrece*, and "his sugared Sonnets among his private friends."

Meres next introduces his famous comparison of Shakespeare to the Latin tragedy writer Seneca and the Latin comedy writer Plautus. He declares that Shakespeare is as excellent among the English for both tragedy and comedy as were Seneca and Plautus, respectively, for each of the two kinds. In witness whereof he cites six comedies, all extant except one which he calls "Loves Labors Wonne," and six tragedies, or rather the two tragedies, *Titus Andronicus* and *Romeo and Juliet*, and four history plays. Elsewhere in the book Meres again mentions Shakespeare in a list of the best English writers of lyric poetry, comedy, tragedy, and love poetry.

Next to this in importance perhaps is John Weever's epigram *Ad Gulielmum Shakespeare* in *Epigrams in the Oldest Cut and the Newest Fashion*, published in 1599, but probably written before 1597:

> Honie-tong'd *Shakespeare*, when I saw thine issue,
> I swore *Apollo* got them and none other,
> Their rosie-tainted features cloth'd in tissue,
> Some heauen born goddesse said to be their mother:
> Rose-cheekt *Adonis* with his amber tresses,
> Faire fire-hot *Venus* charming him to loue her,
> Chaste *Lucretia* virgine-like her dresses,
> Prowd lust-stung *Tarquine* seeking still to proue her:
> *Romea Richard;* more, whose names I know not,
> Their sugred tongues, and power attractiue beuty
> Say they are Saints, althogh that Sts they shew not,
> For thousands vows to them subiectiue dutie:
> They burn in loue thy children. *Shakespeare* het them,
> Go, wo thy Muse more Nymphish brood beget them.

The last lines seem to indicate a desire on Weever's part that Shakespeare should write poetry rather than seek the applause of thousands by writing plays for the theater.

A somewhat similar allusion to those already given occurs in a poem called *A Remembrance of Some English Poets* in Richard Barnfield's *Poems in Divers Humors* (1598):

> And *Shakespeare* thou, whose hony-flowing Vaine,
> (Pleasing the World) thy Praises doth obtaine.
> Whose *Venus*, and whose *Lucrece* (sweete, and chaste)
> Thy Name in fames immortall Booke haue plac't.
> Liue euer you, at least in Fame liue euer:
> Well may the Bodye dye, but Fame dies neuer.

Gabriel Harvey's marginal note (see page 439) in a copy of Speght's Chaucer, made as early as 1598-1601, should also be mentioned.

THE PARNASSUS PLAYS

One of the most interesting and puzzling evidences of Shakespeare's growth in fame comes from a trilogy by Cambridge students called the Parnassus plays, usually dated in the years 1598-1602. The third of the series of three dramatic satires was the only one contemporaneously published. *The Return from Parnassus* was issued in 1606 as publicly acted by the students of St. John's College, Cambridge. The other two parts, the first of which is known as *The Pilgrimage to Parnassus*, remained in manuscript until recent times.

The Parnassus plays are made up of academic satire against the ways of the world. At one point in the second member of the trilogy (*2 Parnassus*, ed. W. D. Macray, 1886), Burbage and Kemp come in, boast of their victory over Ben Jonson, and try to recruit other poets into the service of writing plays for them. The poets are unwilling to subject their muses to the thraldom of the stage. The undergraduate authors are apparently impressed with the fame of Shakespeare. Gullio, a would-be patron of the poets, appropriates bits from Shakespeare, and Ingenioso says,

> We shall have nothing but pure Shakespeare and shreds of poetry that he hath gathered at the theatres. (ll. 1009 ff.)

And again,

> Mark, Romeo and Juliet! O monstrous theft! (l. 1015)

After Gullio has recited six lines from *Venus and Adonis* as his own, Ingenioso remarks, "Sweet Mr. Shakespeare!" (ll. 1018-1024). Later Gullio asks Ingenioso, an affected courtier, to write a poem for him:

> *Ingen.* My pen is your bounden vassal to command. But what vein would it please you to have them in?
> *Gull.* Not in a vain vein (pretty, i' faith!): make me them in two or three divers veins—in Chaucer's, Gower's, and Spenser's and Mr. Shakespeare's. Marry, I think I shall entertain those verses which run like these:
> Even as the sun with purple coloured face
> Had ta'en his last leave on the weeping morn, etc.
> O sweet Mr. Shakespeare! I'll have his picture in my study at the court. (ll. 1048 ff.)

Still later, when Ingenioso recites seven lines in imitation of *Venus and Adonis*, Gullio says,

> No more! I am one that can judge according to the proverb, "bovem ex unguibus." Ay, marry, Sir, these have some life in them! Let this duncified world esteem of Spenser and Chaucer, I'll worship sweet Mr. Shakespeare, and to honour him will lay his Venus and Adonis under my pillow, as we read of one (I do not well remember his name, but I am sure he was a king) slept with Homer under his bed's head. (ll. 1211-1227.)

Shakespeare had thus become fashionable among poetically minded young persons at the university.

SHAKESPEARE'S PRIVATE LIFE

We are also enabled to infer a good many circumstances of Shakespeare's private life from the public

A view of Poictiers. From John Speed's "Theatre of the Empire of Great Britaine," 1611. (Folger)

records which are left about him for the years 1594 to 1601. The most general of the inferences to be drawn from these records is that he was successful and prosperous. His company at the Theatre, and after 1599 at the Globe, was popular, and we may believe, in general, had the better of its rivals, the Lord Admiral's men, under Henslowe's management at the Rose. Whether Shakespeare's company is the same as the one which has been referred to as Lord Strange's

An English morris dancer.
From an ancient window in a country home
at Betley in Staffordshire. (Huntington)

company or not, they were certainly reconstituted about 1594 under the special influences of the family of Burbage. James Burbage, the father, was owner of the Theatre, Cuthbert Burbage was a manager, and Richard Burbage became the principal actor of the troupe. The Theatre operated as a sort of joint stock company of ten shares, of which the Burbages owned five and Shakespeare and four other principal actors of his company one each. Not only was Shakespeare a full sharing actor, but he was also the principal playwright of the company.

His prosperity appears in the first record of his residence in London. The tax returns, or Subsidy Rolls, of a parliamentary subsidy granted to Queen Elizabeth for the year 1596, show Shakespeare resident in the parish of St. Helen's, Bishopsgate, near the Theatre, and assessed at the respectable sum of £5. By the next year Shakespeare had evidently moved to Southwark near the Bear Garden, for the returns from Bishopsgate show his taxes delinquent. He was later located and the taxes paid.

Meantime, in August 1596, his only son Hamnet was buried at Stratford. In the Public Record Office is the summary of a deed by which Shakespeare became owner by purchase of New Place in Stratford, a house of importance and the second largest one in the town. Shakespeare's family entered the house as residents shortly after the purchase and continued there until long after Shakespeare's death. The last of his family, his granddaughter, Lady Bernard, died in 1670, and New Place was sold.

The records show that Shakespeare was also interested in the purchase of land at Shottery in 1598,

was listed among the chief holders of corn and malt in Stratford that same year, and sold a load of stone to the Stratford corporation in 1599.

More suggestive of Shakespeare's rapid rise in the world is his acquisition of the right to bear arms, or, in other words, his establishment in the rank and title of gentleman. The Herald's College in London preserves two drafts of a grant of arms to Shakespeare's father devised by one William Dethick and dated October 20, 1596. Although we may certainly believe that the application was put forward by William Shakespeare, John Shakespeare was still living, and the grant was drawn up in the father's name. The device for Shakespeare's coat-of-arms makes a somewhat easy use of the meaning of his name:

Gold on a bend sable, a spear of the first, the point steeled, proper; and for his crest or cognizance a falcon, his wings displayed, argent, standing on a wreath of his colour supporting a spear—gold—steeled as aforesaid, set upon a helmet with mantels and tassels as hath been accustomed.

According to the second document, John Shakespeare, at the height of his prosperity as a Stratford burgher, had applied twenty years before to the Herald's College for authority to bear arms. However, the family had probably not been able to meet the expense of seeing it through until William Shakespeare had made his fortune. The grant of heraldic honors to John Shakespeare was confirmed in 1599.

The Period of
Comedies and
Histories,
1595-1601

499

THE
History of the two Maids of More-clacke,

VVith the life and simple maner of IOHN
in the Hospitall.

Played by the Children of the Kings
Maiesties Reuels.

VVritten by ROBERT ARMIN, seruant to the Kings
most excellent Maiestie.

LONDON,
Printed by N.O. for *Thomas Archer,* and is to be fold at his
thop in Popes-head Pallace, 1 6 0 9,

(Huntington)

An English morris dancer.
From an ancient window in a country home
at Betley in Staffordshire. (Huntington)

Leslie Hotson has discovered in the records of the Court of the Queen's Bench, Michaelmas term 1596, a writ against William Shakespeare, Francis Langley, and others, in which one William Wayte sought "for fear of death" to have these persons bound over to keep the peace. Among earlier entries for the same term was found a similar writ sworn out by Langley against William Gardener and William Wayte. There was evidently a quarrel between two sets of persons. Langley was owner of The Swan, and he and Shakespeare were probably associated there. Gardener was a wealthy and tyrannical justice of the peace; Wayte was his stepson.

No evidence appeared as to what the quarrel was about. However, for several reasons, Hotson believes he has found in Gardener and Wayte prototypes for Justice Shallow and his Cousin Slender. Wayte was a feeble character and Gardener seems to have been a meddlesome and greedy person. Furthermore, the latter used, by right of his wife (*née* Lucy), three white luces as his coat of arms. Shakespeare, he thinks, revenged himself for persecutions at the hands of Gardener by drawing portraits of Gardener and Wayte in *2 Henry IV* and *The Merry Wives of Windsor*. The latter play must, in that case, have been written soon after the autumn of 1596. Hotson's interpretation of his discovery has been vigorously assailed.[1]

During this period Shakespeare's name appeared on the title pages of the second and third editions of *Richard II* (1598), the second edition of *Richard III* (1598), *Love's Labour's Lost* (1598), and the second edition of *Henry IV, Part One* (1599).

In 1599 William Jaggard issued a small volume containing twenty poems, five of which were certainly by Shakespeare. He attributed to Shakespeare the whole volume which bore the title, *The Passionate Pilgrim*. It contained four sonnets, two from the sonnet-cycle and two from the fourth act of *Love's*

Labour's Lost*, as well as the lyric "On a day, alack the day!" from the same play.

CONTEMPORARY DRAMA

In this particular period Shakespeare was, no doubt, in the contemporary view, the leading dramatist. The earlier group on whose work he patterned his own were either dead or silent. The great group who were to rival him and ultimately surpass him in popular favor had not yet fairly begun.

Of Jonson's earliest work little is known. A first version of *The Case is Altered* may have been written as early as 1597. For all practical purposes, however, he becomes a great new force at the end of this period with *Every Man in his Humour* in 1598 and *Every Man out of his Humour* in 1599. He began in these plays the comedy of humors or individual eccentricities, what might be called the comedy of the personal bias.

We have from George Chapman two unimportant plays of the "humors" type: *The Blind Beggar of Alexandria* in 1596 and *An Humorous Day's Mirth* in 1597. He was probably busy as a playwright during the period, but had not yet showed his characteristic vein of learning and rhetoric.

Thomas Dekker was well under way, and was writing plays for Philip Henslowe—*Old Fortunatus* and *The Shoemaker's Holiday* belong to 1599, *Patient Grissell*, to 1600. He did not have it in him to rival Shakespeare or to institute anything new, though he has his own special excellences.

Thomas Heywood, who has been called a "prose Shakespeare," was in a similar situation to that of Dekker in the service of Henslowe. Heywood's early plays are lost.

John Marston's short and rather acrid career as a dramatist was beginning. *Antonio and Mellida* belongs to 1599. His career as a satirist had begun with *The Metamorphosis of Pygmalion's Image* and *The Scourge of Villainy* in 1598.

For the rest, there were Haughton, Munday, Chettle, Daniel, Porter, and a host of persons of whom we know only the name and one or two plays. Henry Porter's *The Two Angry Women of Abingdon*, the anonymous *Edward III* and *Captain Thomas Stukeley*, and *The Merry Devil of Edmonton* (attributed to Drayton) stand out with some special significance for the study of Shakespeare. These may all be described as dramas of the Shakespearean kind. Little enough

---

[1] Leslie Hotson, *Shakespeare versus Shallow* (Boston, 1931); for comments see reviews listed in "Recent Literature of the English Renaissance," Section III, *Studies in Philology*, April Nos.

English mummers. (Huntington)

like Shakespeare in style and subjects, they are, nevertheless, more mature in sentiment and dramatic art than are the plays of Shakespeare's predecessors, and they have at their basis, like the plays of Shakespeare, a set of normal assumptions about life and about people. They are not theory ridden or strained in emotion and are neither too wild and primitive, on the one hand, nor, on the other, too much swayed by dark conceptions of the tragedy of existence or the violence of such passions as revenge and ambition. They have, in other words, in their several ways, the freedom and the wide range of the Renaissance. Dekker's plays are delightful, and even the fanciful *Old Fortunatus* has about it an atmosphere of naturalness. *Edward III* is a real history play and not one of the early chronicle plays that disguised mere story and tradition by the use of historical names and settings. *The Two Angry Women of Abingdon* is a masterpiece of realistic comedy, and even *Stukeley* is dramatically more advanced in technique than is *Tamburlaine* or *Orlando Furioso. The Merry Devil of Edmonton* has a not unworthy likeness to *The Merry Wives of Windsor* and the comic parts of the Henry IV plays, although it carries on the tradition of Greene's *Friar Bacon and Friar Bungay.*

SHAKESPEARE'S WORK

It may be worth while to call attention at this time to the great series of historical plays as possibly, from the point of view of English literature as a whole, one of Shakespeare's most important achievements. England lived for years after the defeat of the Armada in a wave of patriotic fervor, so that the people demanded, for their instruction and edification, plays on national themes. To satisfy popular taste Shakespeare supplied them, but did not do so in a mercenary or indifferent way.

The subjects were, without exception, old. Shakespeare gave them new treatment on the basis of a new and often painstaking examination of sources and on the basis of his own genius as a national poet. It will be remembered that the group of four plays beginning with *I Henry VI* and ending with *Richard III,* which comes later in historical time, was written before the group of four plays which begins with *Richard II* and ends with *Henry V.*

Another great achievement of the period is Shakespeare's mastery of comedy. With him it is not pure comedy, not a mere matter of fun or of the antics and interplay of the rogue and the fool, since there is always a serious element in the plot. Some worthy man or cause is in jeopardy. At this stage in his career, however, this element rarely threatens disaster so darkly as to color the whole play. Shakespeare's comedies are not yet tragi-comedies; still less are they problem plays. The time when he was to show doubts about the moral structure of the universe had not come. There is about the comedies of the middle period the freshness of English landscape and country and a realistic conception of the qualities of ordinary English life.

At that time no writer knew theoretically much about the depiction of character. The doctrines of this form of art did not take shape for a long time after the year 1600. But Shakespeare, if he did not know theory, was a great and natural practitioner and filled his canvas with so many varied portraits that the art of character drawing was implicit in his work. Shylock and Portia, Beatrice and Benedick, Jaques and Touchstone, Viola and Malvolio are not only great pictures in and for themselves, but great in the ways in which they stand in their groups. They fit in with their surroundings and belong with their dramatic companions. One can say that these comedies show the way in which Shakespeare looked at life.[2]

The Period of Comedies and Histories, 1595-1601

501

[2] For references on Shakespeare's Life and Work, see page 79.

COMEDIES OF THE SECOND PERIOD

THE
Merchant of Venice

A play apparently on the same subject as *The Merchant of Venice* is mentioned by Stephen Gosson in *The Schoole of Abuse*, published in 1579. Gosson is attacking stage plays, as well as poetry and music, and wishes to except two dramas from the general condemnation:

The *Iew* and *Ptoleme*, showne at the Bull, the one representing the greedinesse of worldly chusers, and bloody mindes of Usurers: The other very liuely discrybing howe seditious estates, with their owne deuises, false friendes, with their owne swoordes, and rebellious commons in their owne snares are ouerthrowne: neither with Amorous gesture wounding the eye: nor with slouenly talke hurting the eares of the chast hearers.

It is not unreasonable to conclude that the former of these plays, which concerned a Jew, bloody-minded and usurious, and had a crucial choice as a main feature of the plot, had in it not only the bond story, or the story of Shylock and Antonio, but also the casket story, or the wooing of Portia. The original source in *Il Pecorone*, to be described later, shows the ring story already a part of the bond plot. In order to complete the story, as Shakespeare tells it, it was only necessary that the elopement of Jessica should have been added in imitation of the episode of Abigail in *The Jew of Malta*, from which obviously were also taken suggestions for the character of Shylock. An allusion in Greene's *Mamillia*, about the time of the play referred to by Gosson, seems also to be to the *Jew* and may give us an earlier name for the prince of Morocco:

He which maketh choyce of bewty without vertue commits as much folly as *Critius* did, in choosing a golden boxe filled with rotten bones.

In the year 1579, Gabriel Harvey signs himself in one of his letters to Spenser as "he that is faste bownde vnto the in more obligations than any marchante in Italy to any Jew there." There is also an undated

popular ballad of *Gernutus* which tells the bond story without that of the lady or the caskets. This may well be pre-Shakespearean and may have some connection with the old play of the *Jew*.

ANTI-SEMITISM IN LONDON

There was an outbreak of prejudice against the Jews in London in 1594, in which one is tempted to see the occasion for the production of *The Merchant of Venice*.

A Portuguese Jewish physician, Dr. Roderigo Lopez, rising high in his profession, became Queen Elizabeth's physician. There was also in London one Don Antonio, a pretender to the Portuguese crown, engaged in an attempt to secure aid against Philip of Spain. The earl of Essex and the war party espoused his cause. Don Antonio had traitors among his followers who were really in the pay of King Philip. It is generally believed that they approached Dr. Lopez with the idea of bribing him to poison Don Antonio. Later, they opened negotiations with Lopez to get him to poison the queen. Lopez entertained their base proposal, saying later that he did so in order to cheat the Spanish king out of his money and leave his royal mistress untouched. In this he was probably speaking the truth. Lopez wrote to one of Philip's agents, the letter was intercepted, and Lopez was lodged in the Tower. When Lopez was tried for treason, he denied guilt, vacillated, confessed, and recanted his confession; but he was, nevertheless, sentenced to be hanged, drawn, and quartered. Queen Elizabeth, probably doubtful of his guilt, delayed the signing of his death warrant. However, anti-Semitism, easily aroused in those days, urged on the consummation of his sentence. There is a pitiful story of his attempting to address the people at his execution, of his being jeered at by the mob, and cut down alive and mutilated according to the decree.

Henslowe apparently took advantage of the popular feeling to revive *The Jew of Malta* at the Rose Theater in the summer and autumn of 1594. The earl of Essex, from whom Shakespeare seems to have drawn his political views, was Lopez' chief accuser and the friend and backer of Don Antonio. The man against whom Shylock plots is called Antonio, and we may believe that the excitement about this famous trial caused Shakespeare to write a play about a Jew. The writhings of poor Lopez may be reflected with characteristic Shakespearean sympathy in the psychology of Shylock.

THE DATE

Several considerations point, however, to a date for Shakespeare's play slightly later than the summer of the trial itself. One of these is the fact that the play is relatively mature in style, and stylistic tests would tend to place it as late as 1596. Also, a translation of Sylvain's *Orator* was published in 1596. It was a book of declamations containing among others an argument on the part of a Jew, situated as Shylock is, that he should have his pound of flesh. Shakespeare has made use of this argument; and, if he did not encounter the book until it was published in English, which seems probable, he was writing or revising the play as late as 1596. *The Merchant of Venice* is one of the six comedies cited by Meres in his *Palladis Tamia*, 1598.

PUBLICATION

The *Merchant of Venice* was entered for publication in the Stationers' Register on July 22, 1598, by James Roberts, a friend of the players, an entry probably intended to prevent piracy. It provides that the play shall not be printed without "lycence first had from the Right honorable the Lord Chamberlen." Roberts published the play in quarto form in 1600:

The most excellent Historie of the *Merchant of Venice*. VVith the extreme crueltie of *Shylocke* the Iewe towards the sayd Merchant, in cutting a iust pound of his flesh: and the obtayning of *Portia* by the choyse of three chests. *As it hath beene diuers times acted by the Lord Chamberlaine his Seruants*. Written by William Shakespeare. AT LONDON, Printed by *I. R.* for Thomas Heyes, and are to be sold in Paules Church-yard, at the signe of the Greene Dragon. 1600.

This is the first quarto, but it was long regarded as the second, because there exists another quarto edition bearing the same date. The latter is now known to have been printed, like the second quarto of *A Midsummer-Night's Dream*, by William Jaggard in 1619. The text of the First Folio seems to have been printed from the authorized playbook of Shakespeare's company, which was of course a copy of the manuscript behind the Heyes quarto of 1600.

THE SOURCES: THE BOND

There are two large component parts of the plot of *The Merchant of Venice*, and the putting of them together was a stroke of genius. As we have seen, it seems probable that this was done before Shakespeare worked on the story, although we may believe that he not only improved the juncture, but developed and interpreted the stories more fully and more dramatically than before. The first of these is the theme of the bond and the pound of flesh, an old widely distributed story resting ultimately on the provisions of Roman law which allowed creditors power over the lives and limbs of their debtors. A version is found in the thirteenth-century north English epic of *Cursor Mundi*.

A fully developed form of the bond story, with localization in Venice, is found in an Italian *novella* in a collection called *Il Pecorone* by Ser Giovanni Fiorentino. It was published in 1558, but probably written in 1378. A Venetian merchant in this story goes into debt for ten thousand ducats to a Jewish usurer on practically the same terms as those between Antonio and Shylock. His need is more real than that of Antonio. There is no effort to make the entry into the contract plausible by presenting it as a mere jest, on the ground that the merchant will be able to meet his obligation many times over before the bond falls due. Gianotto, the Bassanio of the piece, is a careless youth who wishes to proceed a third time in his attempt to win a lady of Belmonte. The lady in *Il Pecorone* is a somewhat mercenary person who has decreed that whoever enters her harbor must woo her by remaining awake throughout a night. In case of failure, the unhappy wooer must suffer his ship and all that he owns to be confiscated. She has the habit of giving her wooers a drug, so that they always go to sleep. Gianotto has failed twice, but the third time the Belmonte lady's waiting woman warns him against the drugged potion and he succeeds. In his happiness he forgets his godfather, the merchant whose life has been put in pawn for his expedition. He is awakened from his strange remissness by seeing a religious procession on St. John's day, the day on which the bond was to fall due. He departs for Venice taking with him one hundred thousand ducats, but finds the bond forfeited and the Jew inexorable. The lady too sets out from Bologna, disguised as a young lawyer. She advertises herself as a legal specialist in Venice, and, strangely enough, is selected to judge the case. There is no paving the way of probability by the invention of the learned cousin Bellario from Padua whose acumen was to thwart Shylock; this lady is clever enough to see through the matter without counsel. The Jew, disappointed of his prey, tears his bond in a rage. That finer piece of legal ingenuity by which Shakespeare's Shylock is held for having plotted against the life of a citizen, does not appear.

USURY

Not only has Shakespeare made the case rest upon Shylock's criminality, but he has contrived to give the whole trial a more general significance by depicting what were conceived to be the chief racial and religious differences between Jews and Christians. Shylock takes interest and defends the practice. His original prejudice against Antonio rests largely upon this issue, which he does not forget even while the trial is in progress. We who are used to a wide practice of interest-taking forget the legal restrictions which still in some measure hedge it about. We also forget that interest-taking is still, and was then to a greater degree, a frightful weapon in the hands of the lawless and mercenary.

Elizabethan political thinkers saw danger to the state in the taking of interest. They were glad to find it condemned in the Bible and eagerly seized upon Aristotle's description of money as barren. It was, to the men of Shakespeare's day, unnatural and sinful that money should breed money, as Antonio told Shylock. It was a contravention of the Biblical command that man should eat bread in the sweat of his brow.

The Merchant of Venice

503

The Christians of the day prided themselves on mercy as the chief article of their creed. It was often none too conspicuous in their practice, but it was, nevertheless, an ideal and a source of pride. The Jews, to whom was assigned strict adherence to law as their fundamental principle, were consequently regarded as barren of mercy. Shakespeare permeates the trial scene with this issue between justice and mercy. Shylock is given a chance to escape from his impending doom by the exercise of this exclusively Christian virtue of mercy. He refuses to exercise it, so that his blood is upon his own head. Portia grows eloquent in her plea for mercy, in words which are familiar enough. However, the student may forget the historical aspect of the subject and fail to understand the scene, because he gets no vision of the Elizabethan Christian preening himself on his superiority to the Jew.

Perhaps even the decree by which Shylock is compelled to become a Christian was popularly regarded, not as a bit of refined cruelty, but as a super act of mercy, since by that means his soul would be saved. There may have been those in the audience to whom this decree, to us a cruel and cynical piece of oppression, was looked upon in the way just described. Shakespeare was probably further along than this in his recognition of actual values, since to his characters, Gratiano and his associates, it was certainly not an act of unusual mercy, but a very good joke on Shylock.

There is nothing of the mercenary lady of Belmonte left in the charming and virtuous Portia, unless one can see it in the somewhat unsympathetic discussion of the various wooers by Portia and Nerissa, and in Portia's cavalier dismissal of Morocco and Aragon:

> A gentle riddance. Draw the curtains, go,
> Let all of his complexion choose me so,

and

> Thus hath the candle singed the moth.
> O, these deliberate fools! when they do choose,
> They have the wisdom by their wit to lose.

THE SOURCES: THE CASKETS

The story of the disposal of a lady's hand by the choice among caskets of gold, silver, and lead is also widely distributed. It appears in the Greek romance of *Barlaam and Josaphat*. Chaucer's contemporary, Gower, used it in his *Confessio Amantis*. It appears in Boccaccio's *Decameron*. In these cases it is merely a device to test wisdom.

In a story in *Gesta Romanorum* it is made a means of testing a true lover. In that version the king of Ampluy sends his daughter to marry the son of the emperor of Rome. The emperor tries out the worthiness of the lady by making her choose among three caskets: one of pure gold, studded with

gems, but containing dead men's bones—inscribed, "Whoso chooseth me shall find that he deserveth." The second is of silver, filled with earth and worms and inscribed, "Whoso chooseth me shall find that his nature desireth." The third is of lead and contains precious stones; it is inscribed, "Whoso chooseth me shall find that God has disposed to him." God directs the lady's choice, and she is received as the wife of the emperor's son. This is probably the version that came upon the stage, but Shakespeare, or the author of the old play, has given it not a religious, but a social and philosophic coloring. It is made the occasion for the exposition of the popular Renaissance theme of true love.[1]

There lies at the basis of the choice of the caskets an ancient psychology of three levels: the level of sense and appetite, the level of judgment and knowledge, and the level of understanding and will. Beasts participate with man in the exercise of the first two of these activities. The last is spiritual, so that it is only when man participates in the divine that he rises to action on that stage.

Morocco, a dark, semi-barbarous warrior, admirable in his kind, knows only enough to choose by sense and outward show. Aragon "has the wisdom by his wit to lose." He judges by the power of intellect and on the basis of knowledge. Knowing his own worth, he assumes a merit on the basis of his own clear honor. In contrast to these two, Bassanio adds humility to his choice. In the contemplation of the merit of the beloved he feels himself as nothing. The feeling of helplessness and self-sacrifice, a necessary part of all true love, makes him choose the leaden casket, whose inscription is made to read,

> Who chooseth me must give and hazard all he hath,

which "rather threateneth than doth promise aught." He discards sense and judgment and proceeds by pure understanding. This teaches him to be severed from self, passion, ingenuity, riches, and honors. He is thus one that rightly loves, having learned to choose by learning to love. There is in the very song, "Tell me where is fancy bred," a plain indication of the nature of the choice. "Fancy" meant, when applied to choosing in love, a choice by sense and appearance. Bassanio is warned against both ingenuity and sensuality. No doubt, this was to Shakespeare the principal theme of the play. Bassanio's choice comes in the middle of the third act, as if the play had been built around it.

THE STORY OF THE RINGS

As a bridge between these two stories there is a theme which unites and reinforces them both. This is the relative power and merit of love and friendship, also a frequent subject of Renaissance speculation. The bond story is made to yield a picture of the ut-

---

[1] C. R. Baskervill, "Bassanio as an Ideal Lover," *The Manly Anniversary Studies* (Chicago, 1923), pp. 90-103.

most that a man will do for his friend. Antonio offers his life as a ready and willing sacrifice.

Over against this is the picture of perfect love. To unite these two and bring them to an issue is the function of the episode of the rings. In *Il Pecorone* this was a mere addition to the bond story, but in the play it is made important. The bond story serves structurally to throw the friend into danger. The ring episode rounds out and completes the play by showing how the vows of the truest love must yield to the deep and human demands of friendship. How different is this play, as conceived by Shakespeare, from those performances in which the casket episode is slurred over and the ring episode omitted!

THE ELOPEMENT OF JESSICA

The elopement of Jessica, which is relatively less important than the themes just described, serves as a sort of plot filler, occupying gaps in the major action. It is very likely to be misconceived by readers who do not understand the background of the play. The Elizabethans did not think lightly of the stealing away of a man's daughter. Marriages were usually a matter of parental arrangement, and parental claims were fully recognized.

In this case another factor enters. Shylock the Jew is put out of the bounds of a father's rights, and it is the mystery of genius that Shakespeare should have endowed him with a father's feelings. Because he is an avaricious and malicious Jew, it is apparently thought correct enough in this play for his daughter to run away from him and to steal his gold and jewels. By becoming a Christian she saves her soul and puts herself within the pale of humanity. It is natural enough, the Elizabethans reasoned, that she should be ashamed of her father and her race. This is one of the things in the play which are shocking to modern taste, but we must blame Shakespeare and not Jessica. Her love for Lorenzo is made an ideal love, and there is not in the play, so far as one can see, the least hint of blame for her unnatural conduct. When she disappears from the window to gild herself with some more of Shylock's ducats, Gratiano is moved to exclaim in rapturous admiration, "Now, by my hood, a Gentile and no Jew." And Lorenzo takes up the theme (II, vi, 52-57):

> Beshrew me but I love her heartily;
> For she is wise, if I can judge of her,
> And fair she is, if that mine eyes be true,
> And true she is, as she hath proved herself,
> And therefore, like herself, wise, fair and true
> Shall she be placed in my constant soul.

These are not merely the rhapsodies of a lover, they are the recognized virtues of ideal Renaissance womanhood.

IS SHYLOCK INDIVIDUALIZED?

The puzzle in Shylock's relation to his daughter and in the play as a whole arises from the fact that, in spite of all this Elizabethan tradition of Shylock as a conventional villain and in spite of the recognizable anti-Semitism of the whole picture, Shakespeare has made Shylock appeal to us on the broadest possible grounds of humanity. "Hath not a Jew eyes?" he makes Shylock say (III, i, 62-68), "hath not a Jew hands, organs, dimensions, senses, affections, passions? fed with the same food, hurt with the same weapons, subject to the same diseases, healed by the same means, warmed and cooled by the same winter and summer, as a Christian is?"

Shylock appeals to us, not only as human beings, but as husbands and fathers, when he says of the ring (III, i, 126-127): "It was my turquoise; I had it of Leah when I was a bachelor: I would not have given it for a wilderness of monkeys." The audience may have laughed when Shylock said that, but to the modern reader, and possibly to Shakespeare, there is an inescapable humanizing sentiment in this recollection of Shylock's courtship. He cites the insults he has suffered, and as he leaves the stage he says (IV, i, 395-396), "I pray you, give me leave to go from hence; I am not well." It is no wonder that the play has been distorted and turned topsy-turvy by its modern interpreters.[2]

STAGE HISTORY

The stage history of *The Merchant of Venice* is important, because through it has come about a change in the conception of the play. The part of Shylock was long played as that of a pure villain rendered comic by his falling into the pit he had dug for his enemy. The actor wore a red beard like Judas and had a hooked nose.

The play was done over as *The Jew of Venice* in 1701 by George Granville, later Baron Lansdowne, to suit the taste of the Restoration. In 1741, the actor Macklin restored the Shakespearean version to the stage and laid the basis for the more humane presentation of Shylock's character. In 1814, Edmund Kean carried the sympathetic method still further. In the interpretations of Macready and Sir Henry Irving we secured the now familiar conception of Shylock as the type of a persecuted martyr and avenger.

The extent to which Shakespeare's text lends itself to this modern interpretation must be the concern of all readers of *The Merchant of Venice*. It is certain that, in order to produce the effects of the modern performance, it is necessary to cut away a great deal of Shakespeare and give a different emphasis to the play as a whole.

In the Elizabethan Stage Society's production of 1898 an attempt was made by William Poel to restore the Elizabethan conception of Shylock as a murderous villain whose defeat is, as befits a comedy, comical.

The role of Shylock offers a list of the greatest Shakespearean actors of modern times, and the role of Portia, a list of the greatest Shakespearean actresses.

[2] See H. B. Charlton, "Shakespeare's Jew," *Bulletin of the John Rylands Library*, XIX (1934), 34-38.

THE

Merchant of Venice

DRAMATIS PERSONAE

THE DUKE OF VENICE.
THE PRINCE OF MOROCCO,⎫ suitors to Portia.
THE PRINCE OF ARRAGON,⎭
ANTONIO, a merchant of Venice.
BASSANIO, his friend, suitor likewise to Portia.
SALANIO,
SALARINO,⎫ friends to Antonio and Bassanio.
GRATIANO,⎬
SALERIO,⎭
LORENZO, in love with Jessica.
SHYLOCK, a rich Jew.
TUBAL, a Jew, his friend.
LAUNCELOT GOBBO, the clown, servant to
    Shylock.
OLD GOBBO, father to Launcelot.
LEONARDO, servant to Bassanio.
BALTHASAR,⎫ servants to Portia.
STEPHANO,⎭

PORTIA, a rich heiress.
NERISSA, her waiting-maid.
JESSICA, daughter to Shylock.

Magnificoes of Venice, Officers of the Court of
    Justice, Gaoler, Servants to Portia, and other
    Attendants.

SCENE: *Partly at Venice, and partly at Belmont, the
    seat of Portia, on the Continent.*

ACT I.

SCENE I. *Venice. A street.*

Enter ANTONIO, SALARINO, *and* SALANIO.

Ant. In sooth, I know not why I am so sad:
It wearies me; you say it wearies you;
But how I caught it, found it, or came by it,
What stuff 'tis made of, whereof it is born,
I am to learn;
And such a want-wit sadness makes of me,
That I have much ado to know myself.
    Salar. Your mind is tossing on the ocean;
There, where your argosies with portly sail,
Like signiors and rich burghers on the flood,   10
Or, as it were, the pageants of the sea,
Do overpeer the petty traffickers,
That curtsy to them, do them reverence,
As they fly by them with their woven wings.
    Salan. Believe me, sir, had I such venture forth,
The better part of my affections would
Be with my hopes abroad. I should be still
Plucking the grass, to know where sits the wind,
Peering in maps for ports and piers and roads;
And every object that might make me fear   20

Misfortune to my ventures, out of doubt
Would make me sad.
    Salar.   My wind cooling my broth
Would blow me to an ague, when I thought
What harm a wind too great at sea might do.
I should not see the sandy hour-glass run,
But I should think of shallows and of flats,
And see my wealthy Andrew dock'd in sand,
Vailing her high-top lower than her ribs
To kiss her burial. Should I go to church
And see the holy edifice of stone,   30
And not bethink me straight of dangerous rocks,
Which touching but my gentle vessel's side,
Would scatter all her spices on the stream,
Enrobe the roaring waters with my silks,
And, in a word, but even now worth this,
And now worth nothing? Shall I have the thought
To think on this, and shall I lack the thought
That such a thing bechanced would make me sad?
But tell not me; I know, Antonio
Is sad to think upon his merchandise.   40
    Ant. Believe me, no: I thank my fortune for it,
My ventures are not in one bottom trusted,
Nor to one place; nor is my whole estate
Upon the fortune of this present year:
Therefore my merchandise makes me not sad.
    Salar. Why, then you are in love.
    Ant.   Fie, fie!
    Salar. Not in love neither? Then let us say you are
        sad,
Because you are not merry: and 'twere as easy
For you to laugh and leap and say you are merry,
Because you are not sad. Now, by two-headed Janus,
Nature hath framed strange fellows in her time: 51
Some that will evermore peep through their eyes
And laugh like parrots at a bag-piper,
And other of such vinegar aspect
That they'll not show their teeth in way of smile,
Though Nestor swear the jest be laughable.

Enter BASSANIO, LORENZO, *and* GRATIANO.

    Salan. Here comes Bassanio, your most noble
        kinsman,
Gratiano and Lorenzo. Fare ye well:
We leave you now with better company.
    Salar. I would have stay'd till I had made you
        merry,   60
If worthier friends had not prevented me.
    Ant. Your worth is very dear in my regard.
I take it, your own business calls on you
And you embrace the occasion to depart.
    Salar. Good morrow, my good lords.
    Bass. Good signiors both, when shall we laugh? say,
        when?
You grow exceeding strange: must it be so?
    Salar. We'll make our leisures to attend on yours.
        [*Exeunt Salarino and Salanio.*
    Lor. My Lord Bassanio, since you have found
        Antonio,

ACT I. SCENE I.   5. **am to learn,** have not learned.   9. **argosies,**
large merchant ships; word derived from Ragusa, an Italian seaport.
portly, large and full.   12. **overpeer,** tower over.   15. **venture forth,**
investment risked.   26. **flats,** sandbanks.   27. **Andrew,** name of a ship.
28. **high-top,** probably topsail.   35. **this,** probably expressed by a
gesture.   42. **bottom,** ship.   50. **two-headed Janus.** Janus, Roman god
of all beginnings, was represented by a figure with two faces, one
smiling and one sad.   54. **aspect,** look; accented on second syllable.
56. **Nestor,** a character in the *Iliad*, noted for gravity.   64. **occasion,**
opportunity.   67. **must it be so?** Must you go? or, must you show un-

We two will leave you: but at dinner-time, 70
I pray you, have in mind where we must meet.
    Bass. I will not fail you.
    Gra. You look not well, Signior Antonio;
You have too much respect upon the world:
They lose it that do buy it with much care:
Believe me, you are marvellously changed.
    Ant. I hold the world but as the world, Gratiano;
A stage where every man must play a part,
And mine a sad one.
    Gra.   Let me play the fool:
With mirth and laughter let old wrinkles come, 80
And let my liver rather heat with wine
Than my heart cool with mortifying groans.
Why should a man, whose blood is warm within,
Sit like his grandsire cut in alabaster?
Sleep when he wakes and creep into the jaundice
By being peevish? I tell thee what, Antonio—
I love thee, and it is my love that speaks—
There are a sort of men whose visages
Do cream and mantle like a standing pond,
And do a wilful stillness entertain, 90
With purpose to be dress'd in an opinion
Of wisdom, gravity, profound conceit,
As who should say 'I am Sir Oracle,
And when I ope my lips let no dog bark!'
O my Antonio, I do know of these
That therefore only are reputed wise
For saying nothing, when, I am very sure,
If they should speak, would almost damn those ears
Which, hearing them, would call their brothers fools.
I'll tell thee more of this another time: 100
But fish not, with this melancholy bait,
For this fool gudgeon, this opinion.
Come, good Lorenzo. Fare ye well awhile:
I'll end my exhortation after dinner.
    Lor. Well, we will leave you then till dinner-time:
I must be one of these same dumb wise men,
For Gratiano never lets me speak.
    Gra. Well, keep me company but two years moe,
Thou shalt not know the sound of thine own tongue.
    Ant. Farewell: I'll grow a talker for this gear. 110
    Gra. Thanks, i' faith, for silence is only
        commendable
In a neat's tongue dried and a maid not vendible.
            [*Exeunt Gratiano and Lorenzo.*
    Ant. Is that any thing now?
    Bass. Gratiano speaks an infinite deal of nothing,
more than any man in all Venice. His reasons are as
two grains of wheat hid in two bushels of chaff: you
shall seek all day ere you find them, and when you
have them, they are not worth the search.
    Ant. Well, tell me now what lady is the same
To whom you swore a secret pilgrimage, 120
That you to-day promised to tell me of?
    Bass. 'Tis not unknown to you, Antonio,
How much I have disabled mine estate,
By something showing a more swelling port
Than my faint means would grant continuance:

Nor do I now make moan to be abridged
From such a noble rate; but my chief care
Is to come fairly off from the great debts
Wherein my time something too prodigal
Hath left me gaged. To you, Antonio, 130
I owe the most, in money and in love,
And from your love I have a warranty
To unburden all my plots and purposes
How to get clear of all the debts I owe.
    Ant. I pray you, good Bassanio, let me know it;
And if it stand, as you yourself still do,
Within the eye of honour, be assured,
My purse, my person, my extremest means,
Lie all unlock'd to your occasions.
    Bass. In my school-days, when I had lost one shaft,
I shot his fellow of the self-same flight 141
The self-same way with more advised watch,
To find the other forth, and by adventuring both
I oft found both: I urge this childhood proof,
Because what follows is pure innocence.
I owe you much, and, like a wilful youth,
That which I owe is lost; but if you please
To shoot another arrow that self way
Which you did shoot the first, I do not doubt,
As I will watch the aim, or to find both 150
Or bring your latter hazard back again
And thankfully rest debtor for the first.
    Ant. You know me well, and herein spend but time
To wind about my love with circumstance;
And out of doubt you do me now more wrong
In making question of my uttermost
Than if you had made waste of all I have:
Then do but say to me what I should do
That in your knowledge may by me be done,
And I am prest unto it: therefore, speak. 160
    Bass. In Belmont is a lady richly left;
And she is fair and, fairer than that word,
Of wondrous virtues: sometimes from her eyes
I did receive fair speechless messages:
Her name is Portia, nothing undervalued
To Cato's daughter, Brutus' Portia:
Nor is the wide world ignorant of her worth,
For the four winds blow in from every coast
Renowned suitors, and her sunny locks
Hang on her temples like a golden fleece; 170
Which makes her seat of Belmont Colchos' strand,
And many Jasons come in quest of her.
O my Antonio, had I but the means
To hold a rival place with one of them,
I have a mind presages me such thrift,
That I should questionless be fortunate!
    Ant. Thou know'st that all my fortunes are at sea;
Neither have I money nor commodity
To raise a present sum: therefore go forth;
Try what my credit can in Venice do: 180
That shall be rack'd, even to the uttermost,
To furnish thee to Belmont, to fair Portia.
Go, presently inquire, and so will I,
Where money is, and I no question make

friendliness? **74. have . . . upon,** pay too much attention to. **81. heat
with wine.** Shakespeare thinks of the liver as the seat of the passions and
wine as an agency for inflaming them. **82. mortifying,** deadly. **85.
jaundice,** regarded as arising from the effects of violent passions.
89. mantle, become covered with scum. **90. wilful stillness,** obstinate
silence. **92. profound conceit,** deep thought. **99. fools.** Cf. Matthew
5:22. **102. gudgeon,** a fish used for bait. **112. neat's.** *Neat* is defined
as "cattle of the ox kind." **124. port,** style of living; see glossary.
127. rate, style of living. **130. gaged,** pledged. **143. forth,** out.
145. innocence, sometimes defined as "foolishness"; may rather mean

"ingenuousness." **153-160. You . . . speak.** This is the first indication of the friendship theme of the play. **154. wind about,** approach
circuitously. **160. prest,** ready. **161. richly left.** Bassanio's frank
avowal of his desire for Portia's fortune has caused him to be blamed as
a fortune hunter by modern critics who forget the importance of a dowry
in Renaissance consideration. **166. Brutus' Portia,** a woman famous
in ancient times for constancy and courage; she is a character in *Julius
Caesar.* **168. coast,** country. **172. Jasons.** This explains *golden fleece*
and *Colchos' strand,* above. **175. presages,** i.e., which presages; relative
pronoun omitted.

To have it of my trust or for my sake.   *[Exeunt.*

SCENE II. *Belmont. A room in* PORTIA'S *house.*

Enter PORTIA *and* NERISSA.

Por. By my troth, Nerissa, my little body is aweary of this great world.

Ner. You would be, sweet madam, if your miseries were in the same abundance as your good fortunes are: and yet, for aught I see, they are as sick that surfeit with too much as they that starve with nothing. It is no mean happiness therefore, to be seated in the mean: superfluity comes sooner by white hairs, but competency lives longer.   10

Por. Good sentences and well pronounced.

Ner. They would be better, if well followed.

Por. If to do were as easy as to know what were good to do, chapels had been churches and poor men's cottages princes' palaces. It is a good divine that follows his own instructions: I can easier teach twenty what were good to be done, than be one of the twenty to follow mine own teaching. The brain may devise laws for the blood, but a hot temper leaps o'er a cold decree: such a hare is madness the youth, to skip o'er the meshes of good counsel the cripple. But this reasoning is not in the fashion to choose me a husband. O me, the word 'choose!' I may neither choose whom I would nor refuse whom I dislike; so is the will of a living daughter curbed by the will of a dead father. Is it not hard, Nerissa, that I cannot choose one nor refuse none?   29

Ner. Your father was ever virtuous; and holy men at their death have good inspirations: therefore the lottery, that he hath devised in these three chests of gold, silver and lead, whereof who chooses his meaning chooses you, will, no doubt, never be chosen by any rightly but one who shall rightly love. But what warmth is there in your affection towards any of these princely suitors that are already come?   38

Por. I pray thee, over-name them; and as thou namest them, I will describe them; and, according to my description, level at my affection.

Ner. First, there is the Neapolitan prince.

Por. Ay, that's a colt indeed, for he doth nothing but talk of his horse; and he makes it a great appropriation to his own good parts, that he can shoe him himself. I am much afeard my lady his mother played false with a smith.   48

Ner. Then there is the County Palatine.

Por. He doth nothing but frown, as who should say 'If you will not have me, choose:' he hears merry tales and smiles not: I fear he will prove the weeping philosopher when he grows old, being so full of unmannerly sadness in his youth. I had rather be married to a death's-head with a bone in his mouth than to either of these. God defend me from these two!

Ner. How say you by the French lord, Monsieur Le Bon?   59

Por. God made him, and therefore let him pass for a man. In truth, I know it is a sin to be a mocker: but, he! why, he hath a horse better than the Neapolitan's, a better bad habit of frowning than the Count Palatine; he is every man in no man; if a throstle sing, he falls straight a capering: he will fence with his own shadow: if I should marry him, I should marry twenty husbands. If he would despise me, I would forgive him, for if he love me to madness, I shall never requite him.   70

Ner. What say you, then, to Falconbridge, the young baron of England?

Por. You know I say nothing to him, for he understands not me, nor I him: he hath neither Latin, French, nor Italian, and you will come into the court and swear that I have a poor pennyworth in the English. He is a proper man's picture, but, alas, who can converse with a dumb-show? How oddly he is suited! I think he bought his doublet in Italy, his round hose in France, his bonnet in Germany and his behaviour every where.

Ner. What think you of the Scottish lord, his neighbour?   84

Por. That he hath a neighbourly charity in him, for he borrowed a box of the ear of the Englishman and swore he would pay him again when he was able: I think the Frenchman became his surety and sealed under for another.

Ner. How like you the young German, the Duke of Saxony's nephew?   91

Por. Very vilely in the morning, when he is sober, and most vilely in the afternoon, when he is drunk: when he is best, he is a little worse than a man, and when he is worst, he is little better than a beast: an the worst fall that ever fell, I hope I shall make shift to go without him.

Ner. If he should offer to choose, and choose the right casket, you should refuse to perform your father's will, if you should refuse to accept him.   101

Por. Therefore, for fear of the worst, I pray thee, set a deep glass of rhenish wine on the contrary casket, for if the devil be within and that temptation without, I know he will choose it. I will do any thing, Nerissa, ere I'll be married to a sponge.

Ner. You need not fear, lady, the having any of these lords: they have acquainted me with their determinations; which is, indeed, to return to their home and to trouble you with no more suit, unless you may be won by some other sort than your father's imposition depending on the caskets.   115

Por. If I live to be as old as Sibylla, I will die as chaste as Diana, unless I be obtained by the manner of my father's will. I am glad this parcel of wooers are so reasonable, for there is not one among them but I dote on his very absence, and I pray God grant them a fair departure.

Ner. Do you not remember, lady, in your father's

SCENE II. 9. **comes sooner by,** brings about sooner. 11. **sentences,** maxims. 20. **blood,** thought of as a chief agent of the passions, which in turn were regarded as the enemies of reason; see glossary. 22. **meshes,** nets; allusion to hare hunting with nets. A *cripple* could not follow the hare if it skipped over the net. 23. **reasoning,** discourse, talk. 27, 28. **will, will,** volition, testament. 32. **lottery,** subject of *will,* line 35. 34. **his,** i.e., the father's. 44-48. **Ay . . . smith.** There is a rather hard tone in Portia's description of her suitors. The lady of the source was, however, much more cruel. 49. **County,** count. 51. **choose,** possibly, "do as you please." 53. **weeping philosopher,**

Heraclitus of Ephesus, who wept at everything. 65. **throstle,** thrush. 80. **suited,** dressed. **doublet,** coat. 81. **hose,** trousers. **bonnet,** hat. It was a common subject of censure in Elizabethan days that Englishmen rigged themselves out in foreign clothes. 83. **Scottish.** F has *other,* apparently substituted for *Scottish* to avoid offense to King James. 89. **became . . . another,** an allusion to the age-old alliance of the French and the Scotch against the English. The Frenchman put his seal under the Scotchman's as his surety, promising to give the Englishman another box on the ear. 96. **fall,** befall. 114. **sort,** way, manner. **imposition,** conditions imposed. 116. **Sibylla,** the Cumaean Sibyl, to time, a Venetian, a scholar and a soldier, that came hither in company of the Marquis of Montferrat?

Por. Yes, yes, it was Bassanio; as I think, he was so called.

Ner. True, madam: he, of all the men that ever my foolish eyes looked upon, was the best deserving a fair lady. 131

Por. I remember him well, and I remember him worthy of thy praise.

Enter a Serving-man.

How now! what news?

Serv. The four strangers seek for you, madam, to take their leave: and there is a forerunner come from a fifth, the Prince of Morocco, who brings word the prince his master will be here to-night. 139

Por. If I could bid the fifth welcome with so good a heart as I can bid the other four farewell, I should be glad of his approach: if he have the condition of a saint and the complexion of a devil, I had rather he should shrive me than wive me. Come, Nerissa. Sirrah, go before. Whiles we shut the gates upon one wooer, another knocks at the door. [*Exeunt.*

SCENE III. *Venice. A public place.*

Enter BASSANIO *and* SHYLOCK.

Shy. Three thousand ducats; well.

Bass. Ay, sir, for three months.

Shy. For three months; well.

Bass. For the which, as I told you, Antonio shall be bound.

Shy. Antonio shall become bound; well.

Bass. May you stead me? will you pleasure me? shall I know your answer?

Shy. Three thousand ducats for three months and Antonio bound. 10

Bass. Your answer to that.

Shy. Antonio is a good man.

Bass. Have you heard any imputation to the contrary?

Shy. Oh, no, no, no, no: my meaning in saying he is a good man is to have you understand me that he is sufficient. Yet his means are in supposition: he hath an argosy bound to Tripolis, another to the Indies; I understand, moreover, upon the Rialto, he hath a third at Mexico, a fourth for England, and other ventures he hath, squandered abroad. But ships are but boards, sailors but men: there be land-rats and water-rats, water-thieves and land-thieves, I mean pirates, and then there is the peril of waters, winds and rocks. The man is, notwithstanding, sufficient. Three thousand ducats; I think I may take his bond.

Bass. Be assured you may. 29

Shy. I will be assured I may; and, that I may be assured, I will bethink me. May I speak with Antonio?

Bass. If it please you to dine with us.

Shy. Yes, to smell pork; to eat of the habitation which your prophet the Nazarite conjured the devil into. I will buy with you, sell with you, talk with you, walk with you, and so following, but I will not eat with you, drink with you, nor pray with you. What news on the Rialto? Who is he comes here? 40

Enter ANTONIO.

Bass. This is Signior Antonio.

Shy. [*Aside*] How like a fawning publican he looks! I hate him for he is a Christian, But more for that in low simplicity He lends out money gratis and brings down The rate of usance here with us in Venice. If I can catch him once upon the hip, I will feed fat the ancient grudge I bear him. He hates our sacred nation, and he rails, Even there where merchants most do congregate, 50 On me, my bargains and my well-won thrift, Which he calls interest. Cursed be my tribe, If I forgive him!

Bass.   Shylock, do you hear?

Shy. I am debating of my present store, And, by the near guess of my memory, I cannot instantly raise up the gross Of full three thousand ducats. What of that? Tubal, a wealthy Hebrew of my tribe, Will furnish me. But soft! how many months Do you desire? [*To Ant.*] Rest you fair, good signior; 60 Your worship was the last man in our mouths.

Ant. Shylock, although I neither lend nor borrow By taking nor by giving of excess, Yet, to supply the ripe wants of my friend, I'll break a custom. Is he yet possess'd How much ye would?

Shy.   Ay, ay, three thousand ducats.

Ant. And for three months.

Shy. I had forgot; three months; you told me so. Well then, your bond; and let me see; but hear you; Methought you said you neither lend nor borrow 70 Upon advantage.

Ant.   I do never use it.

Shy. When Jacob grazed his uncle Laban's sheep— This Jacob from our holy Abram was, As his wise mother wrought in his behalf, The third possessor; ay, he was the third—

Ant. And what of him? did he take interest?

Shy. No, not take interest, not, as you would say, Directly interest: mark what Jacob did. When Laban and himself were compromised That all the eanlings which were streak'd and pied 80 Should fall as Jacob's hire, the ewes, being rank, In the end of autumn turned to the rams, And, when the work of generation was Between these woolly breeders in the act, The skilful shepherd peel'd me certain wands And, in the doing of the deed of kind, He stuck them up before the fulsome ewes,

---

whom Apollo gave as many years as there were grains in her handful of sand. 119. **parcel,** party. 141. **four.** It will be noticed that Nerissa names six suitors. Hunter suggested that four was the number of suitors in the old play which Shakespeare used as a source, and that Shakespeare himself added the Englishman and the Scotchman. 145. **shrive me,** act as my confessor.

SCENE III. 1. **ducats,** gold or silver coins of varying value. The sum asked for has been estimated by various persons from three thousand to one hundred thousand dollars. **well,** possibly interrogative. 7. **stead,** help, supply a need. 12. **good,** solvent. 19. **Rialto,** name of

the largest of the Venetian islands; here, for "exchange," "bourse." 35. **Nazarite,** Nazarene; cf. Luke 7:32, 33. 42. **publican,** Roman tax-gatherer, a term of opprobrium. 43-53. **I . . . him.** Shylock's hatred of Antonio, as it appears in this passage, is general. He does not allude so much to personal insults and injuries as to the four general grounds enumerated. 46. **usance,** usury, interest. 47. **catch . . . hip,** figure of speech from wrestling. 75. **possessor,** i.e., of God's promise. 79. **compromised,** agreed; cf. Genesis 30:35. 80. **eanlings,** young lambs or kids. **pied,** spotted. 81. **rank,** in heat; see glossary.

Who then conceiving did in eaning time
Fall parti-colour'd lambs, and those were Jacob's.
This was a way to thrive, and he was blest: 90
And thrift is blessing, if men steal it not.
    Ant. This was a venture, sir, that Jacob served for;
A thing not in his power to bring to pass,
But sway'd and fashion'd by the hand of heaven.
Was this inserted to make interest good?
Or is your gold and silver ewes and rams?
    Shy. I cannot tell; I make it breed as fast:
But note me, signior.
    Ant.   Mark you this, Bassanio,
The devil can cite Scripture for his purpose. 100
An evil soul producing holy witness
Is like a villain with a smiling cheek,
A goodly apple rotten at the heart:
O, what a goodly outside falsehood hath!
    Shy. Three thousand ducats; 'tis a good round sum.
Three months from twelve; then, let me see; the
    rate—
    Ant. Well, Shylock, shall we be beholding to you?
    Shy. Signior Antonio, many a time and oft
In the Rialto you have rated me
About my moneys and my usances:
Still have I borne it with a patient shrug, 110
For sufferance is the badge of all our tribe.
You call me misbeliever, cut-throat dog,
And spit upon my Jewish gaberdine,
And all for use of that which is mine own.
Well then, it now appears you need my help:
Go to, then; you come to me, and you say
'Shylock, we would have moneys:' you say so;
You, that did void your rheum upon my beard
And foot me as you spurn a stranger cur
Over your threshold: moneys is your suit. 120
What should I say to you? Should I not say
'Hath a dog money? is it possible
A cur can lend three thousand ducats?' Or
Shall I bend low and in a bondman's key,
With bated breath and whispering humbleness,
Say this;
'Fair sir, you spit on me on Wednesday last;
You spurn'd me such a day; another time
You call'd me dog; and for these courtesies
I'll lend you thus much moneys'? 130
    Ant. I am as like to call thee so again,
To spit on thee again, to spurn thee too.
If thou wilt lend this money, lend it not
As to thy friends; for when did friendship take
A breed for barren metal of his friend?
But lend it rather to thine enemy,
Who, if he break, thou mayst with better face
Exact the penalty.
    Shy.   Why, look you, how you storm!
I would be friends with you and have your love,
Forget the shames that you have stain'd me with, 140
Supply your present wants and take no doit
Of usance for my moneys, and you'll not hear me:
This is kind I offer.
    Bass. This were kindness.

    Shy.   This kindness will I show.
Go with me to a notary, seal me there
Your single bond; and, in a merry sport,
If you repay me not on such a day,
In such a place, such sum or sums as are
Express'd in the condition, let the forfeit
Be nominated for an equal pound 150
Of your fair flesh, to be cut off and taken
In what part of your body pleaseth me.
    Ant. Content, i' faith: I'll seal to such a bond
And say there is much kindness in the Jew.
    Bass. You shall not seal to such a bond for me:
I'll rather dwell in my necessity.
    Ant. Why, fear not, man; I will not forfeit it:
Within these two months, that's a month before
This bond expires, I do expect return
Of thrice three times the value of this bond. 160
    Shy. O father Abram, what these Christians are,
Whose own hard dealings teaches them suspect
The thoughts of others! Pray you, tell me this;
If he should break his day, what should I gain   .
By the exaction of the forfeiture?
A pound of man's flesh taken from a man
Is not so estimable, profitable neither,
As flesh of muttons, beefs, or goats. I say,
To buy his favour, I extend this friendship:
If he will take it, so; if not, adieu; 170
And, for my love, I pray you wrong me not.
    Ant. Yes, Shylock, I will seal unto this bond.
    Shy. Then meet me forthwith at the notary's;
Give him direction for this merry bond,
And I will go and purse the ducats straight,
See to my house, left in the fearful guard
Of an unthrifty knave, and presently
I will be with you.
    Ant. Hie thee, gentle Jew.   *[Exit Shylock.*
The Hebrew will turn Christian: he grows kind. 180
    Bass. I like not fair terms and a villain's mind.
    Ant. Come on: in this there can be no dismay;
My ships come home a month before the day. *[Exeunt.*

ACT II.

SCENE I. *Belmont. A room in* PORTIA'S *house.*

Flourish of cornets. Enter the PRINCE OF MOROCCO *and
his train;* PORTIA, NERISSA, *and others attending.*

    Mor. Mislike me not for my complexion,
The shadow'd livery of the burnish'd sun,
To whom I am a neighbour and near bred.
Bring me the fairest creature northward born,
Where Phœbus' fire scarce thaws the icicles,
And let us make incision for your love,
To prove whose blood is reddest, his or mine.
I tell thee, lady, this aspect of mine
Hath fear'd the valiant: by my love, I swear
The best-regarded virgins of our clime 10
Have loved it too: I would not change this hue,
Except to steal your thoughts, my gentle queen.

99-103. **The devil ... hath.** Antonio expresses the indignation which would have been most keenly felt at that time, at tampering with the Scripture. 113. **gaberdine,** cape or mantle. 135. **breed for barren metal,** an ancient argument against interest (see Introduction). F has *of* instead of *for.* 137. **Who,** from whom. **break,** fail to pay on time. 146. **single bond,** bond without other security. 153-154. **Content . . . Jew.** This ready credulity of Antonio is probably to be regarded as conventional, a thing required by the plot and not probable in daily life. Bassanio helps the stage probability by protesting. 162. **suspect,** i.e., to suspect.

ACT II. SCENE I. **7. reddest.** Red blood was regarded as a sign of courage. **14. nice direction,** dainty guidance. **17. scanted,** limited. **24. scimitar,** a sword with curved blade. **25. Sophy,** shah of Persia. **26. Solyman,** a Turkish sultan ruling 1520-1566. **32. Lichas,** a page of Hercules. **35. Alcides,** Hercules. **44. temple,** probably church, in order to take the oaths.

Por. In terms of choice I am not solely led
By nice direction of a maiden's eyes;
Besides, the lottery of my destiny
Bars me the right of voluntary choosing:
But if my father had not scanted me
And hedged me by his wit, to yield myself
His wife who wins me by that means I told you,
Yourself, renowned prince, then stood as fair   20
As any comer I have look'd on yet
For my affection.
   Mor.   Even for that I thank you:
Therefore, I pray you, lead me to the caskets
To try my fortune. By this scimitar
That slew the Sophy and a Persian prince,
That won three fields of Sultan Solyman,
I would outstare the sternest eyes that look,
Outbrave the heart most daring on the earth,
Pluck the young sucking cubs from the she-bear,
Yea, mock the lion when he roars for prey,   30
To win thee, lady. But, alas the while!
If Hercules and Lichas play at dice
Which is the better man, the greater throw
May turn by fortune from the weaker hand:
So is Alcides beaten by his page;
And so may I, blind fortune leading me,
Miss that which one unworthier may attain,
And die with grieving.
   Por.   You must take your chance,
And either not attempt to choose at all
Or swear before you choose, if you choose wrong   40
Never to speak to lady afterward
In way of marriage: therefore be advised.
   Mor. Nor will not. Come, bring me unto my
      chance.
   Por. First, forward to the temple: after dinner
Your hazard shall be made.
   Mor.   Good fortune then!
To make me blest or cursed'st among men.
                     [Cornets, and exeunt.

SCENE II. *Venice. A street.*

Enter LAUNCELOT.

   Laun. Certainly my conscience will serve me to run
from this Jew my master. The fiend is at mine elbow
and tempts me saying to me 'Gobbo, Launcelot Gobbo, good Launcelot,' or 'good Gobbo,' or 'good
Launcelot Gobbo, use your legs, take the start, run
away.' My conscience says 'No; take heed, honest
Launcelot; take heed, honest Gobbo,' or, as aforesaid,
'honest Launcelot Gobbo; do not run; scorn running
with thy heels.' Well, the most courageous fiend bids
me pack: 'Via!' says the fiend; 'away!' says the fiend;
'for the heavens, rouse up a brave mind,' says the
fiend, 'and run.' Well, my conscience, hanging about
the neck of my heart, says very wisely to me 'My
honest friend Launcelot, being an honest man's son,'
or rather an honest woman's son; for, indeed, my

father did something smack, something grow to, he
had a kind of taste; well, my conscience says 'Launcelot, budge not.' 'Budge,' says the fiend. 'Budge not,'
says my conscience. 'Conscience,' say I, 'you counsel
well;' 'Fiend,' say I, 'you counsel well:' to be ruled
by my conscience, I should stay with the Jew my
master, who, God bless the mark, is a kind of devil;
and, to run away from the Jew, I should be ruled by
the fiend, who, saving your reverence, is the devil
himself. Certainly the Jew is the very devil incarnal;
and, in my conscience, my conscience is but a kind of
hard conscience, to offer to counsel me to stay with
the Jew. The fiend gives the more friendly counsel: I
will run, fiend; my heels are at your command; I will
run.   33

Enter Old GOBBO, *with a basket.*

   Gob. Master young man, you, I pray you, which is
the way to master Jew's?
   Laun. [*Aside*] O heavens, this is my true-begotten
father! who, being more than sand-blind, high-gravel
blind, knows me not: I will try confusions with him.
   Gob. Master young gentleman, I pray you, which is
the way to master Jew's?   41
   Laun. Turn up on your right hand at the next turning, but, at the next turning of all, on your left; marry,
at the very next turning, turn of no hand, but turn
down indirectly to the Jew's house.
   Gob. By God's sonties, 'twill be a hard way to hit.
Can you tell me whether one Launcelot, that dwells
with him, dwell with him or no?   49
   Laun. Talk you of young Master Launcelot? [*Aside*]
Mark me now; now will I raise the waters. Talk you
of young Master Launcelot?
   Gob. No master, sir, but a poor man's son: his father,
though I say it, is an honest exceeding poor man and,
God be thanked, well to live.
   Laun. Well, let his father be what a' will, we talk of
young Master Launcelot.
   Gob. Your worship's friend and Launcelot, sir.
   Laun. But I pray you, ergo, old man, ergo, I beseech
you, talk you of young Master Launcelot?   60
   Gob. Of Launcelot, an 't please your mastership.
   Laun. Ergo, Master Launcelot. Talk not of Master
Launcelot, father; for the young gentleman, accord-
ing to Fates and Destinies and such odd sayings, the
Sisters Three and such branches of learning, is indeed
deceased, or, as you would say in plain terms, gone to
heaven.
   Gob. Marry, God forbid! the boy was the very staff
of my age, my very prop.   70
   Laun. Do I look like a cudgel or a hovel-post, a
staff or a prop? Do you know me, father?
   Gob. Alack the day, I know you not, young gentleman: but, I pray you, tell me, is my boy, God rest his
soul, alive or dead?
   Laun. Do you not know me, father?
   Gob. Alack, sir, I am sand-blind; I know you not.
   Laun. Nay, indeed, if you had your eyes, you might
fail of the knowing me: it is a wise father that knows

SCENE II.   3. **tempts.** The situation of the tempting fiend is a
familiar one in all medieval and Renaissance literature, perhaps commonest in morality plays.   11. **'Via!'** Italian, "begone!"   18. **something smack,** i.e., of dishonesty.   **grow to,** become an integral part of;
euphemism for "stealing."   25. **God . . . mark,** an exclamation by way
of apology for introducing something; origin of expression not understood.   37. **sand-blind,** dim-sighted.   38. **high-gravel blind,** more
than sand-blind as gravel is greater than sand.   47. **sonties,** probably a
corruption of "saints" or "sanctities."   50. **Master.** The title was
applied to gentlefolk only.   55. **well to live,** possibly Gobbo's corruption of "well-to-do."   59. **ergo,** therefore (if it means anything).   66.
Sisters Three, possibly the Muses, nine in number. Launcelot mixes
everything up; his words are a satire on pretenders to classical learning.
71. **hovel-post,** support for a hovel or open shed.

his own child. Well, old man, I will tell you news of your son: give me your blessing: truth will come to light; murder cannot be hid long; a man's son may, but at the length truth will out.

Gob. Pray you, sir, stand up: I am sure you are not Launcelot, my boy.

Laun. Pray you, let's have no more fooling about it, but give me your blessing: I am Launcelot, your boy that was, your son that is, your child that shall be. 91

Gob. I cannot think you are my son.

Laun. I know not what I shall think of that: but I am Launcelot, the Jew's man, and I am sure Margery your wife is my mother.

Gob. Her name is Margery, indeed: I'll be sworn, if thou be Launcelot, thou art mine own flesh and blood. Lord worshiped might he be! what a beard hast thou got! thou hast got more hair on thy chin than Dobbin my fill-horse has on his tail. 101

Laun. It should seem, then, that Dobbin's tail grows backward: I am sure he had more hair of his tail than I have of my face when I last saw him.

Gob. Lord, how art thou changed! How dost thou and thy master agree? I have brought him a present. How 'gree you now?

Laun. Well, well: but, for mine own part, as I have set up my rest to run away, so I will not rest till I have run some ground. My master's a very Jew: give him a present! give him a halter: I am famished in his service; you may tell every finger I have with my ribs. Father, I am glad you are come: give me your present to one Master Bassanio, who, indeed, gives rare new liveries: if I serve not him, I will run as far as God has any ground. O rare fortune! here comes the man: to him, father; for I am a Jew, if I serve the Jew any longer. 120

Enter BASSANIO, *with* LEONARDO *and other followers.*

Bass. You may do so; but let it be so hasted that supper be ready at the farthest by five of the clock. See these letters delivered; put the liveries to making, and desire Gratiano to come anon to my lodging.

[*Exit a Servant.*

Laun. To him, father.

Gob. God bless your worship!

Bass. Gramercy! wouldst thou aught with me?

Gob. Here's my son, sir, a poor boy,— 129

Laun. Not a poor boy, sir, but the rich Jew's man; that would, sir, as my father shall specify—

Gob. He hath a great infection, sir, as one would say, to serve,—

Laun. Indeed, the short and the long is, I serve the Jew, and have a desire, as my father shall specify—

Gob. His master and he, saving your worship's reverence, are scarce cater-cousins— 139

Laun. To be brief, the very truth is that the Jew, having done me wrong, doth cause me, as my father, being, I hope, an old man, shall frutify unto you—

Gob. I have here a dish of doves that I would bestow upon your worship, and my suit is—

Laun. In very brief, the suit is impertinent to myself, as your worship shall know by this honest old

man; and, though I say it, though old man, yet poor man, my father.

Bass. One speak for both. What would you? 150

Laun. Serve you, sir.

Gob. That is the very defect of the matter, sir.

Bass. I know thee well; thou hast obtain'd thy suit: Shylock thy master spoke with me this day, And hath preferr'd thee, if it be preferment To leave a rich Jew's service, to become The follower of so poor a gentleman.

Laun. The old proverb is very well parted between my master Shylock and you, sir: you have the grace of God, sir, and he hath enough. 160

Bass. Thou speak'st it well. Go, father, with thy son. Take leave of thy old master and inquire My lodging out. Give him a livery More guarded than his fellows': see it done.

Laun. Father, in. I cannot get a service, no; I have ne'er a tongue in my head. Well, if any man in Italy have a fairer table which doth offer to swear upon a book, I shall have good fortune. Go to, here's a simple line of life: here's a small trifle of wives: alas, fifteen wives is nothing! eleven widows and nine maids is a simple coming-in for one man: and then to 'scape drowning thrice, and to be in peril of my life with the edge of a feather-bed; here are simple scapes. Well, if Fortune be a woman, she's a good wench for this gear. Father, come; I'll take my leave of the Jew in the twinkling of an eye. [*Exeunt Launcelot and Old Gobbo.*

Bass. I pray thee, good Leonardo, think on this: These things being bought and orderly bestow'd, Return in haste, for I do feast to-night 180 My best-esteem'd acquaintance: hie thee, go.

Leon. My best endeavours shall be done herein.

Enter GRATIANO.

Gra. Where is your master?

Leon. Yonder, sir, he walks. [*Exit.*

Gra. Signior Bassanio!

Bass. Gratiano!

Gra. I have a suit to you.

Bass. You have obtain'd it.

Gra. You must not deny me: I must go with you to Belmont.

Bass. Why, then you must. But hear thee, Gratiano; 190 Thou art too wild, too rude and bold of voice; Parts that become thee happily enough And in such eyes as ours appear not faults; But where thou art not known, why, there they show Something too liberal. Pray thee, take pain To allay with some cold drops of modesty Thy skipping spirit, lest through thy wild behaviour I be misconstrued in the place I go to And lose my hopes.

Gra. Signior Bassanio, hear me: If I do not put on a sober habit, Talk with respect and swear but now and then, 200 Wear prayer-books in my pocket, look demurely, Nay more, while grace is saying, hood mine eyes Thus with my hat, and sigh and say 'amen,' Use all the observance of civility,

99. **beard,** Launcelot's hair. He kneels with his back to old Gobbo. 101. **fill-horse,** shaft-horse. 104. **of,** in. 110. **set . . . rest,** determined; metaphor from the card game *primero,* in which a final wager is made. 112. **very,** veritable. 128. **Gramercy,** thanks. 132. **infection,** for "affection" or "inclination." 139. **cater-cousins,** good friends; sometimes thought to have meant originally fourth cousins. 143. **frutify,**

certify. Launcelot's blunder is sometimes connected with "fructify." 146. **impertinent,** not pertaining (to). 152. **defect,** for "purport." 158. **old proverb.** The grace of God is better than riches; or the Scotch form: God's grace is gear enough. 164. **guarded,** trimmed with braided ornaments. 167. **table,** palm. 170. **trifle of wives.** "Long and deep lines from the Mount of Venus toward the line of life

Like one well studied in a sad ostent
To please his grandam, never trust me more.
   Bass. Well, we shall see your bearing.
   Gra. Nay, but I bar to-night: you shall not gauge
     me
By what we do to-night.
   Bass.   No, that were pity:
I would entreat you rather to put on   210
Your boldest suit of mirth, for we have friends
That purpose merriment. But fare you well:
I have some business.
   Gra. And I must to Lorenzo and the rest:
But we will visit you at supper-time.   [*Exeunt.*

SCENE III. *The same. A room in* SHYLOCK'S *house.*

Enter JESSICA *and* LAUNCELOT.

   Jes. I am sorry thou wilt leave my father so:
Our house is hell, and thou, a merry devil,
Didst rob it of some taste of tediousness.
But fare thee well, there is a ducat for thee:
And, Launcelot, soon at supper shalt thou see
Lorenzo, who is thy new master's guest:
Give him this letter; do it secretly;
And so farewell: I would not have my father
See me in talk with thee.   9
   Laun. Adieu! tears exhibit my tongue. Most beauti-
ful pagan, most sweet Jew! if a Christian did not play
the knave and get thee, I am much deceived. But,
adieu: these foolish drops do something drown my
manly spirit: adieu.
   Jes. Farewell, good Launcelot.   [*Exit Launcelot.*
Alack, what heinous sin is it in me
To be ashamed to be my father's child!
But though I am a daughter to his blood,
I am not to his manners. O Lorenzo,
If thou keep promise, I shall end this strife,   20
Become a Christian and thy loving wife.   [*Exit.*

SCENE IV. *The same. A street.*

Enter GRATIANO, LORENZO, SALARINO, *and* SALANIO.

   Lor. Nay, we will slink away in supper-time,
Disguise us at my lodging and return,
All in an hour.
   Gra. We have not made good preparation.
   Salar. We have not spoke us yet of torch-bearers.
   Salan. 'Tis vile, unless it may be quaintly order'd,
And better in my mind not undertook.
   Lor. 'Tis now but four o'clock: we have two hours
To furnish us.

Enter LAUNCELOT, *with a letter.*

          Friend Launcelot, what's the news?
   Laun. An it shall please you to break up this, it shall
seem to signify.   11
   Lor. I know the hand: in faith, 'tis a fair hand;

And whiter than the paper it writ on
Is the fair hand that writ.
   Gra.   Love-news, in faith.
   Laun. By your leave, sir.
   Lor. Whither goest thou?
   Laun. Marry, sir, to bid my old master the Jew to
sup to-night with my new master the Christian.
   Lor. Hold here, take this: tell gentle Jessica   20
I will not fail her; speak it privately.
Go, gentlemen,   [*Exit Launcelot.*
Will you prepare you for this masque to-night?
I am provided of a torch-bearer.
   Salar. Ay, marry, I'll be gone about it straight.
   Salan. And so will I.
   Lor.   Meet me and Gratiano
At Gratiano's lodging some hour hence.
   Salar. 'Tis good we do so.   [*Exeunt Salar. and Salan.*
   Gra. Was not that letter from fair Jessica?
   Lor. I must needs tell thee all. She hath directed   30
How I shall take her from her father's house,
What gold and jewels she is furnish'd with,
What page's suit she hath in readiness.
If e'er the Jew her father come to heaven,
It will be for his gentle daughter's sake:
And never dare misfortune cross her foot,
Unless she do it under this excuse,
That she is issue to a faithless Jew.
Come, go with me; peruse this as thou goest:
Fair Jessica shall be my torch-bearer.   [*Exeunt.* 40

SCENE V. *The same. Before* SHYLOCK'S *house.*

Enter SHYLOCK *and* LAUNCELOT.

   Shy. Well, thou shalt see, thy eyes shall be thy judge,
The difference of old Shylock and Bassanio:—
What, Jessica!—thou shalt not gormandise,
As thou hast done with me:—What, Jessica!—
And sleep and snore, and rend apparel out;—
Why, Jessica, I say!
   Laun.   Why, Jessica!
   Shy. Who bids thee call? I do not bid thee call.
   Laun. Your worship was wont to tell me that I could
do nothing without bidding.

Enter JESSICA.

   Jes. Call you? what is your will?   10
   Shy. I am bid forth to supper, Jessica:
There are my keys. But wherefore should I go?
I am not bid for love; they flatter me:
But yet I'll go in hate, to feed upon
The prodigal Christian. Jessica, my girl,
Look to my house. I am right loath to go:
There is some ill a-brewing towards my rest,
For I did dream of money-bags to-night.
   Laun. I beseech you, sir, go: my young master doth
expect your reproach.   20
   Shy. So do I his.
   Laun. And they have conspired together, I will not
say you shall see a masque; but if you do, then it was

---

signifieth so many wives."—Saunders, *Chiromancie* (Furness). 205.
sad ostent, grave appearance.
   SCENE III. 10. **exhibit,** for "restrain." 16-21. **Alack . . . wife.**
There is no evidence that Shakespeare disapproved of Jessica's frank
rejection of her father, her race, or her religion.
   SCENE IV. 5. **us,** ethical dative. 6. **'Tis vile,** it is a vulgar and

useless thing to do. **quaintly,** elegantly, tastefully. 10. **break up,**
break open.
   SCENE V. 3. **gormandise,** eat greedily. 18. **to-night,** last night.
20. **reproach,** Launcelot's blunder for "approach." Shylock takes it in
grim humor.

not for nothing that my nose fell a-bleeding on Black-Monday last at six o'clock i' the morning, falling out that year on Ash-Wednesday was four year, in the afternoon.

Shy. What, are there masques? Hear you me, Jessica:
Lock up my doors; and when you hear the drum
And the vile squealing of the wry-neck'd fife, 30
Clamber not you up to the casements then,
Nor thrust your head into the public street
To gaze on Christian fools with varnish'd faces,
But stop my house's ears, I mean my casements:
Let not the sound of shallow foppery enter
My sober house. By Jacob's staff, I swear,
I have no mind of feasting forth to-night:
But I will go. Go you before me, sirrah;
Say I will come.
Laun. I will go before, sir. Mistress, look out at window, for all this; 41
        There will come a Christian by,
        Will be worth a Jewess' eye. [*Exit.*

Shy. What says that fool of Hagar's offspring, ha?
Jes. His words were 'Farewell, mistress;' nothing else.
Shy. The patch is kind enough, but a huge feeder;
Snail-slow in profit, and he sleeps by day
More than the wild-cat: drones hive not with me;
Therefore I part with him, and part with him
To one that I would have him help to waste 50
His borrow'd purse. Well, Jessica, go in:
Perhaps I will return immediately:
Do as I bid you; shut doors after you:
Fast bind, fast find;
A proverb never stale in thrifty mind. [*Exit.*
Jes. Farewell; and if my fortune be not crost,
I have a father, you a daughter, lost. [*Exit.*

SCENE VI. *The same.*

Enter GRATIANO *and* SALARINO, *masqued.*

Gra. This is the pent-house under which Lorenzo
Desired us to make stand.
Salar.   His hour is almost past.
Gra. And it is marvel he out-dwells his hour,
For lovers ever run before the clock.
Salar. O, ten times faster Venus' pigeons fly
To seal love's bonds new-made, than they are wont
To keep obliged faith unforfeited!
Gra. That ever holds: who riseth from a feast
With that keen appetite that he sits down?
Where is the horse that doth untread again 10
His tedious measures with the unbated fire
That he did pace them first? All things that are,
Are with more spirit chased than enjoy'd.
How like a younker or a prodigal
The scarfed bark puts from her native bay,
Hugg'd and embraced by the strumpet wind!
How like the prodigal doth she return,
With over-weather'd ribs and ragged sails,
Lean, rent and beggar'd by the strumpet wind!
Salar. Here comes Lorenzo: more of this hereafter. 20

Enter LORENZO.

Lor. Sweet friends, your patience for my long abode;
Not I, but my affairs, have made you wait:
When you shall please to play the thieves for wives,
I'll watch as long for you then. Approach;
Here dwells my father Jew. Ho! who 's within?

Enter JESSICA, *above, in boy's clothes.*

Jes. Who are you? Tell me, for more certainty,
Albeit I'll swear that I do know your tongue.
Lor. Lorenzo, and thy love.
Jes. Lorenzo, certain, and my love indeed,
For who love I so much? And now who knows 30
But you, Lorenzo, whether I am yours?
Lor. Heaven and thy thoughts are witness that thou art.
Jes. Here, catch this casket; it is worth the pains.
I am glad 'tis night, you do not look on me,
For I am much ashamed of my exchange:
But love is blind and lovers cannot see
The pretty follies that themselves commit;
For if they could, Cupid himself would blush
To see me thus transformed to a boy.
Lor. Descend, for you must be my torch-bearer. 4c
Jes. What, must I hold a candle to my shames?
They in themselves, good sooth, are too too light.
Why, 'tis an office of discovery, love;
And I should be obscured.
Lor.   So are you, sweet,
Even in the lovely garnish of a boy.
But come at once;
For the close night doth play the runaway,
And we are stay'd for at Bassanio's feast.
Jes. I will make fast the doors, and gild myself
With some more ducats, and be with you straight. 50
                    [*Exit above.*
Gra. Now, by my hood, a Gentile and no Jew.
Lor. Beshrew me but I love her heartily;
For she is wise, if I can judge of her,
And fair she is, if that mine eyes be true,
And true she is, as she hath proved herself,
And therefore, like herself, wise, fair and true,
Shall she be placed in my constant soul.

Enter JESSICA, *below.*

What, art thou come? On, gentlemen; away!
Our masquing mates by this time for us stay.
          [*Exit with Jessica and Salarino.*

Enter ANTONIO.

Ant. Who 's there? 60
Gra. Signior Antonio!
Ant. Fie, fie, Gratiano! where are all the rest?
'Tis nine o'clock: our friends all stay for you.
No masque to-night: the wind is come about;
Bassanio presently will go aboard:
I have sent twenty out to seek for you.
Gra. I am glad on 't: I desire no more delight
Than to be under sail and gone to-night. [*Exeunt.*

---

25. **Black-Monday,** Easter Monday, so called, according to Stow, because of a cold and stormy Easter Monday when Edward III was besieging Paris. 29-37. **hear . . . to-night.** There is a suggestion here that Shylock distrusts Jessica. 36. **Jacob's staff.** Cf. Genesis 32:10, and Hebrews 11:21. 43. **Jewess',** so Pope; QF: *Jewes.* 44. **Hagar's offspring,** explained as "Gentile" and as "servant." 46. **patch,** fool, fellow.

SCENE VI. 1. **pent-house,** projecting roof from a house. 5. **Venus' pigeons.** Venus' chariot was drawn by doves. 14. **younker,** youth. 15. **scarfed,** decorated with flags. 43. **office of discovery,** occupation in which I shall be seen. 45. **garnish,** outfit. 53-56. **For . . . true.** The qualities given to Jessica here are those of the ideal woman; this is an indication that there is no reaction in Shakespeare's mind

SCENE VII. *Belmont. A room in* PORTIA'S *house.*

Flourish of cornets. Enter PORTIA, *with the* PRINCE OF
MOROCCO, *and their trains.*

Por. Go draw aside the curtains and discover
The several caskets to this noble prince.
Now make your choice.

Mor. The first, of gold, who this inscription bears,
'Who chooseth me shall gain what many men desire;
'The second, silver, which this promise carries,
'Who chooseth me shall get as much as he deserves;
This third, dull lead, with warning all as blunt,
'Who chooseth me must give and hazard all he hath.'
How shall I know if I do choose the right? 10

Por. The one of them contains my picture, prince:
If you choose that, then I am yours withal.

Mor. Some god direct my judgement! Let me see;
I will survey the inscriptions back again.
What says this leaden casket?
'Who chooseth me must give and hazard all he hath.'
Must give: for what? for lead? hazard for lead?
This casket threatens. Men that hazard all
Do it in hope of fair advantages:
A golden mind stoops not to shows of dross; 20
I'll then nor give nor hazard aught for lead.
What says the silver with her virgin hue?
'Who chooseth me shall get as much as he deserves.'
As much as he deserves! Pause there, Morocco,
And weigh thy value with an even hand:
If thou be'st rated by thy estimation,
Thou dost deserve enough; and yet enough
May not extend so far as to the lady:
And yet to be afeard of my deserving
Were but a weak disabling of myself. 30
As much as I deserve! Why, that's the lady;
I do in birth deserve her, and in fortunes,
In graces and in qualities of breeding;
But more than these, in love I do deserve.
What if I stray'd no further, but chose here?
Let's see once more this saying graved in gold;
'Who chooseth me shall gain what many men desire.'
Why, that's the lady; all the world desires her;
From the four corners of the earth they come,
To kiss this shrine, this mortal-breathing saint: 40
The Hyrcanian deserts and the vasty wilds
Of wide Arabia are as throughfares now
For princes to come view fair Portia:
The watery kingdom, whose ambitious head
Spits in the face of heaven, is no bar
To stop the foreign spirits, but they come,
As o'er a brook, to see fair Portia.
One of these three contains her heavenly picture.
Is 't like that lead contains her? 'Twere damnation
To think so base a thought: it were too gross 50
To rib her cerecloth in the obscure grave.
Or shall I think in silver she 's immured,
Being ten times undervalued to tried gold?
O sinful thought! Never so rich a gem
Was set in worse than gold. They have in England
A coin that bears the figure of an angel
Stamped in gold, but that's insculp'd upon;

But here an angel in a golden bed
Lies all within. Deliver me the key:
Here do I choose, and thrive I as I may! 60

Por. There, take it, prince; and if my form lie there,
Then I am yours.   [*He unlocks the golden casket.*

Mor.   O hell! what have we here?
A carrion Death, within whose empty eye
There is a written scroll! I'll read the writing.
[*Reads*] All that glisters is not gold;
    Often have you heard that told:
    Many a man his life hath sold
    But my outside to behold:
    Gilded tombs do worms infold.
    Had you been as wise as bold, 70
    Young in limbs, in judgement old,
    Your answer had not been inscroll'd:
    Fare you well; your suit is cold.

    Cold, indeed; and labour lost:
    Then, farewell, heat, and welcome, frost!
Portia, adieu. I have too grieved a heart
To take a tedious leave: thus losers part.
        [*Exit with his train. Flourish of cornets.*

Por. A gentle riddance. Draw the curtains, go.
Let all of his complexion choose me so.   [*Exeunt.*

SCENE VIII. *Venice. A street.*

Enter SALARINO *and* SALANIO.

Salar. Why, man, I saw Bassanio under sail:
With him is Gratiano gone along;
And in their ship I am sure Lorenzo is not.

Salan. The villain Jew with outcries raised the duke,
Who went with him to search Bassanio's ship.

Salar. He came too late, the ship was under sail:
But there the duke was given to understand
That in a gondola were seen together
Lorenzo and his amorous Jessica:
Besides, Antonio certified the duke 10
They were not with Bassanio in his ship.

Salan. I never heard a passion so confused,
So strange, outrageous, and so variable,
As the dog Jew did utter in the streets:
'My daughter! O my ducats! O my daughter!
Fled with a Christian! O my Christian ducats!
Justice! the law! my ducats, and my daughter!
A sealed bag, two sealed bags of ducats,
Of double ducats, stolen from me by my daughter!
And jewels, two stones, two rich and precious stones, 20
Stolen by my daughter! Justice! find the girl;
She hath the stones upon her, and the ducats.'

Salar. Why, all the boys in Venice follow him,
Crying, his stones, his daughter, and his ducats.

Salan. Let good Antonio look he keep his day,
Or he shall pay for this.

Salar.   Marry, well remember'd.
I reason'd with a Frenchman yesterday,
Who told me, in the narrow seas that part
The French and English, there miscarried

against her.
  SCENE VII. 41. **Hyrcanian.** Hyrcania was the country south of the
Caspian Sea. 49-60. **'Twere . . . may.** Morocco decides in a burst of
enthusiasm, without thought, actuated solely by the superficial view.
51. **cerecloth,** wax cloth used in embalming. 63. **carrion Death,**
death's-head. 65. **glisters,** glitters. 70. **as wise as bold.** These words

betray Morocco's error.
  SCENE VIII. 15-17. **daughter . . . ducats.** Barabas in Marlowe's
The Jew of Malta shows the same confused passion in Act I: "O girl!
O gold! O beauty! O my bliss!" 27. **reason'd,** talked with. 28.
narrow seas, probably the English Channel.

A vessel of our country richly fraught: 30
I thought upon Antonio when he told me;
And wish'd in silence that it were not his.

    Salan. You were best to tell Antonio what you hear;
Yet do not suddenly, for it may grieve him.

    Salar. A kinder gentleman treads not the earth.
I saw Bassanio and Antonio part:
Bassanio told him he would make some speed
Of his return: he answer'd, 'Do not so;
Slubber not business for my sake, Bassanio,
But stay the very riping of the time; 40
And for the Jew's bond which he hath of me,
Let it not enter in your mind of love:
Be merry, and employ your chiefest thoughts
To courtship and such fair ostents of love
As shall conveniently become you there:'
And even there, his eye being big with tears,
Turning his face, he put his hand behind him,
And with affection wondrous sensible
He wrung Bassanio's hand; and so they parted.

    Salan. I think he only loves the world for him. 50
I pray thee, let us go and find him out
And quicken his embraced heaviness
With some delight or other.

    Salar.   Do we so.   [*Exeunt.*

SCENE IX. *Belmont. A room in* PORTIA'S *house.*

Enter NERISSA *with a* Servitor.

    Ner. Quick, quick, I pray thee; draw the curtain
      straight:
The Prince of Arragon hath ta'en his oath,
And comes to his election presently.

    Flourish of cornets. Enter the PRINCE OF ARRAGON,
      PORTIA, *and their trains.*

    Por. Behold, there stand the caskets, noble prince:
If you choose that wherein I am contain'd,
Straight shall our nuptial rites be solemnized:
But if you fail, without more speech, my lord,
You must be gone from hence immediately.

    Ar. I am enjoin'd by oath to observe three things:
First, never to unfold to any one 10
Which casket 'twas I chose; next, if I fail
Of the right casket, never in my life
To woo a maid in way of marriage:
Lastly,
If I do fail in fortune of my choice,
Immediately to leave you and be gone.

    Por. To these injunctions every one doth swear
That comes to hazard for my worthless self.

    Ar. And so have I address'd me. Fortune now
To my heart's hope! Gold; silver; and base lead. 20
'Who chooseth me must give and hazard all he hath.'
You shall look fairer, ere I give or hazard.
What says the golden chest? ha! let me see:
'Who chooseth me shall gain what many men desire.'
What many men desire! that 'many' may be meant
By the fool multitude, that choose by show,

Not learning more than the fond eye doth teach;
Which pries not to the interior, but, like the martlet,
Builds in the weather on the outward wall,
Even in the force and road of casualty. 30
I will not choose what many men desire,
Because I will not jump with common spirits
And rank me with the barbarous multitudes.
Why, then to thee, thou silver treasure-house;
Tell me once more what title thou dost bear:
'Who chooseth me shall get as much as he deserves:'
And well said too; for who shall go about
To cozen fortune and be honourable
Without the stamp of merit? Let none presume
To wear an undeserved dignity. 40
O, that estates, degrees and offices
Were not derived corruptly, and that clear honour
Were purchased by the merit of the wearer!
How many then should cover that stand bare!
How many be commanded that command!
How much low peasantry would then be glean'd
From the true seed of honour! and how much honour
Pick'd from the chaff and ruin of the times
To be new-varnish'd! Well, but to my choice:
'Who chooseth me shall get as much as he deserves.' 50
I will assume desert. Give me a key for this,
And instantly unlock my fortunes here.
             [*He opens the silver casket.*

    Por. Too long a pause for that which you find there.

    Ar. What 's here? the portrait of a blinking idiot,
Presenting me a schedule! I will read it.
How much unlike art thou to Portia!
How much unlike my hopes and my deservings!
'Who chooseth me shall have as much as he deserves.'
Did I deserve no more than a fool's head?
Is that my prize? are my deserts no better? 60

    Por. To offend, and judge, are distinct offices
And of opposed natures.

    Ar.   What is here?
[*Reads*] The fire seven times tried this:
    Seven times tried that judgement is,
      That did never choose amiss.
    Some there be that shadows kiss;
    Such have but a shadow's bliss:
    There be fools alive, I wis,
    Silver'd o'er; and so was this.
    Take what wife you will to bed, 70
    I will ever be your head:
    So be gone: you are sped.

    Still more fool I shall appear
    By the time I linger here:
    With one fool's head I came to woo,
    But I go away with two.
    Sweet, adieu. I'll keep my oath,
    Patiently to bear my wroth.
           [*Exeunt Arragon and train.*

    Por. Thus hath the candle singed the moth.
O, these deliberate fools! when they do choose, 80
They have the wisdom by their wit to lose.

    Ner. The ancient saying is no heresy,
Hanging and wiving goes by destiny.

---

30. **fraught,** freighted. 39. **Slubber,** to do hastily and badly. 40. **riping of the time,** maturity.
    SCENE IX. 3. **election,** choice. 18. **hazard,** may be either a verb or a noun. 19. **address'd me,** prepared myself. 27. **Not . . . teach.** Arragon prides himself on his judgment and attempts to determine the issue on intellectual grounds. 28. **martlet,** martin. 30. **casualty,** mischance. 32. **jump,** agree; see glossary. 38. **cozen,** cheat. 41.

degrees, ranks. 44. **cover . . . bare,** i.e., put on their hats. 45. **How . . . command,** how many then should be masters that are now servants. 46. **glean'd,** culled out. 49. **new-varnish'd,** glossed over. 55. **schedule,** written paper. 61. **To . . . offices.** You have no right, having submitted your case to judgment, to object to the tribunal. 68. **I wis,** either "I know" or "certainly." It is derived from the old adverb *ywis,* often spelled as in the text. 78. **wroth,** sorrow; probably an error for

Por. Come, draw the curtain, Nerissa.

Enter a Servant.

Serv. Where is my lady?
Por. Here: what would my lord?
Serv. Madam, there is alighted at your gate
A young Venetian, one that comes before
To signify the approaching of his lord;
From whom he bringeth sensible regreets,
To wit, besides commends and courteous breath, 90
Gifts of rich value. Yet I have not seen
So likely an ambassador of love:
A day in April never came so sweet,
To show how costly summer was at hand,
As this fore-spurrer comes before his lord.
Por. No more, I pray thee: I am half afeard
Thou wilt say anon he is some kin to thee,
Thou spend'st such high-day wit in praising him.
Come, come, Nerissa; for I long to see
Quick Cupid's post that comes so mannerly. 100
Ner. Bassanio, lord Love, if thy will it be! [*Exeunt.*

ACT III.

SCENE I. *Venice. A street.*

Enter SALANIO *and* SALARINO.

Salan. Now, what news on the Rialto?
Salar. Why, yet it lives there unchecked that Antonio hath a ship of rich lading wrecked on the narrow seas; the Goodwins, I think they call the place; a very dangerous flat and fatal, where the carcases of many a tall ship lie buried, as they say, if my gossip Report be an honest woman of her word. 8
Salan. I would she were as lying a gossip in that as ever knapped ginger or made her neighbours believe she wept for the death of a third husband. But it is true, without any slips of prolixity or crossing the plain highway of talk, that the good Antonio, the honest Antonio,——O that I had a title good enough to keep his name company!—
Salar. Come, the full stop.
Salan. Ha! what sayest thou? Why, the end is, he hath lost a ship.
Salar. I would it might prove the end of his losses. 21
Salan. Let me say 'amen' betimes, lest the devil cross my prayer, for here he comes in the likeness of a Jew.

Enter SHYLOCK.

How now, Shylock! what news among the merchants?
Shy. You knew, none so well, none so well as you, of my daughter's flight.
Salar. That 's certain: I, for my part, knew the tailor that made the wings she flew withal.
Salan. And Shylock, for his own part, knew the bird was fledged; and then it is the complexion of them all to leave the dam. 33
Shy. She is damned for it.
Salar. That 's certain, if the devil may be her judge.
Shy. My own flesh and blood to rebel!

Salan. Out upon it, old carrion! rebels it at these years?
Shy. I say, my daughter is my flesh and blood. 40
Salar. There is more difference between thy flesh and hers than between jet and ivory; more between your bloods than there is between red wine and rhenish. But tell us, do you hear whether Antonio have had any loss at sea or no?
Shy. There I have another bad match: a bankrupt, a prodigal, who dare scarce show his head on the Rialto; a beggar, that was used to come so smug upon the mart; let him look to his bond: he was wont to call me usurer; let him look to his bond: he was wont to lend money for a Christian courtesy; let him look to his bond. 52
Salar. Why, I am sure, if he forfeit, thou wilt not take his flesh: what 's that good for?
Shy. To bait fish withal: if it will feed nothing else, it will feed my revenge. He hath disgraced me, and hindered me half a million; laughed at my losses, mocked at my gains, scorned my nation, thwarted my bargains, cooled my friends, heated mine enemies; and what 's his reason? I am a Jew. Hath not a Jew eyes? hath not a Jew hands, organs, dimensions, senses, affections, passions? fed with the same food, hurt with the same weapons, subject to the same diseases, healed by the same means, warmed and cooled by the same winter and summer, as a Christian is? If you prick us, do we not bleed? if you tickle us, do we not laugh? if you poison us, do we not die? and if you wrong us, shall we not revenge? If we are like you in the rest, we will resemble you in that. If a Jew wrong a Christian, what is his humility? Revenge. If a Christian wrong a Jew, what should his sufferance be by Christian example? Why, revenge. The villany you teach me, I will execute, and it shall go hard but I will better the instruction. 76

Enter a Servant.

Serv. Gentlemen, my master Antonio is at his house and desires to speak with you both.
Salar. We have been up and down to seek him.

Enter TUBAL.

Salan. Here comes another of the tribe: a third cannot be matched, unless the devil himself turn Jew.
[*Exeunt Salan., Salar., and Servant.*
Shy. How now, Tubal! what news from Genoa? hast thou found my daughter?
Tub. I often came where I did hear of her, but cannot find her. 86
Shy. Why, there, there, there, there! a diamond gone, cost me two thousand ducats in Frankfort! The curse never fell upon our nation till now; I never felt it till now: two thousand ducats in that; and other precious, precious jewels. I would my daughter were dead at my foot, and the jewels in her ear! would she were hearsed at my foot, and the ducats in her coffin! No news of them? Why, so: and I know not what 's spent in the search: why, thou loss upon loss! the thief gone with so much, and so much to find the thief; and

The Merchant of Venice
ACT III : SC I

517

"roth" (ruth). 80-81. **O . . . lose.** Portia here sums up the cause of Arragon's failure. 89. **sensible regreets,** heartfelt greeting. 90. **commends,** greetings. 92. **likely,** promising. 94. **costly,** lavish, rich. ACT III. SCENE I. 4. **Goodwins,** Goodwin Sands off the Kentish coast. 10. **knapped,** chewed. 13. **slips of,** lapses into. 23. **cross,** thwart. 32. **complexion,** natural disposition. 33. **dam,** mother bird. 46. **match,** bargain. 56-70. **He hath . . . revenge.** The appeal cannot but attract sympathy to Shylock. It is speeches like this which have brought about the modern sentimental conception of the character. 72. **humility,** humiliation he must endure. 74. **sufferance,** patience, endurance. 81. **matched,** i.e., to them. 89. **Frankfort.** There was a fair at Frankfort famous for goldsmiths' wares. 94. **hearsed,** coffined.

no satisfaction, no revenge: nor no ill luck stirring but what lights on my shoulders; no sighs but of my breathing; no tears but of my shedding. 101

Tub. Yes, other men have ill luck too: Antonio, as I heard in Genoa,—

Shy. What, what, what? ill luck, ill luck?

Tub. Hath an argosy cast away, coming from Tripolis.

Shy. I thank God, I thank God. Is 't true, is 't true?

Tub. I spoke with some of the sailors that escaped the wreck. 110

Shy. I thank thee, good Tubal: good news, good news! ha, ha! where? in Genoa?

Tub. Your daughter spent in Genoa, as I heard, in one night fourscore ducats.

Shy. Thou stickest a dagger in me: I shall never see my gold again: fourscore ducats at a sitting! fourscore ducats!

Tub. There came divers of Antonio's creditors in my company to Venice, that swear he cannot choose but break. 120

Shy. I am very glad of it: I'll plague him; I'll torture him: I am glad of it.

Tub. One of them showed me a ring that he had of your daughter for a monkey.

Shy. Out upon her! Thou torturest me, Tubal: it was my turquoise; I had it of Leah when I was a bachelor: I would not have given it for a wilderness of monkeys.

Tub. But Antonio is certainly undone. 129

Shy. Nay, that 's true, that 's very true. Go, Tubal, fee me an officer; bespeak him a fortnight before. I will have the heart of him, if he forfeit; for, were he out of Venice, I can make what merchandise I will. Go, go, Tubal, and meet me at our synagogue; go, good Tubal; at our synagogue, Tubal. [*Exeunt.*

SCENE II. *Belmont. A room in* PORTIA'S *house.*

Enter BASSANIO, PORTIA, GRATIANO, NERISSA, *and* Attendants.

Por. I pray you, tarry: pause a day or two
Before you hazard; for, in choosing wrong,
I lose your company: therefore forbear awhile.
There 's something tells me, but it is not love,
I would not lose you; and you know yourself,
Hate counsels not in such a quality.
But lest you should not understand me well,—
And yet a maiden hath no tongue but thought,—
I would detain you here some month or two
Before you venture for me. I could teach you 10
How to choose right, but I am then forsworn;
So will I never be: so may you miss me;
But if you do, you'll make me wish a sin,
That I had been forsworn. Beshrew your eyes,
They have o'erlook'd me and divided me;
One half of me is yours, the other half yours,
Mine own, I would say; but if mine, then yours,

And so all yours. O, these naughty times
Put bars between the owners and their rights!
And so, though yours, not yours. Prove it so, 20
Let fortune go to hell for it, not I.
I speak too long; but 'tis to peize the time,
To eke it and to draw it out in length,
To stay you from election.
    Bass.   Let me choose;
For as I am, I live upon the rack.
    Por. Upon the rack, Bassanio! then confess
What treason there is mingled with your love.
    Bass. None but that ugly treason of mistrust,
Which makes me fear the enjoying of my love:
There may as well be amity and life 30
'Tween snow and fire, as treason and my love.
    Por. Ay, but I fear you speak upon the rack,
Where men enforced do speak anything.
    Bass. Promise me life, and I'll confess the truth.
    Por. Well then, confess and live.
    Bass.   'Confess' and 'love'
Had been the very sum of my confession:
O happy torment, when my torturer
Doth teach me answers for deliverance!
But let me to my fortune and the caskets.
    Por. Away, then! I am lock'd in one of them: 40
If you do love me, you will find me out.
Nerissa and the rest, stand all aloof.
Let music sound while he doth make his choice;
Then, if he lose, he makes a swan-like end,
Fading in music: that the comparison
May stand more proper, my eye shall be the stream
And watery death-bed for him. He may win;
And what is music then? Then music is
Even as the flourish when true subjects bow
To a new-crowned monarch: such it is 50
As are those dulcet sounds in break of day
That creep into the dreaming bridegroom's ear
And summon him to marriage. Now he goes,
With no less presence, but with much more love,
Than young Alcides, when he did redeem
The virgin tribute paid by howling Troy
To the sea-monster: I stand for sacrifice;
The rest aloof are the Dardanian wives,
With bleared visages, come forth to view
The issue of the exploit. Go, Hercules! 60
Live thou, I live: with much much more dismay
I view the fight than thou that makest the fray.

Music, whilst BASSANIO *comments on the caskets to himself.*

SONG.
Tell me where is fancy bred,
Or in the heart or in the head?
How begot, how nourished?
    Reply, reply.
It is engender'd in the eyes,
With gazing fed; and fancy dies
In the cradle where it lies.
    Let us all ring fancy's knell: 70
    I'll begin it,—Ding, dong, bell.

126-127. **I had it . . . bachelor.** These words are given a strong coloring of sentiment and are thought to humanize Shylock because of the allusion to his wife. It must not be forgotten, however, that the turquoise was a stone of special properties, and that Shylock may have set an actual as well as a sentimental value upon it. 131. **officer,** bailiff, police sergeant. 132-134. **I will . . . will.** Shylock's desire for revenge is constantly associated with his greed of gain. SCENE II. 15. **o'erlook'd,** bewitched. 18. **naughty,** good for noth-

ing, worthless; see glossary. 22. **peize,** retard (by hanging on of weights). 44. **swan-like,** an allusion to the belief that swans sing when they come to die. 55. **Alcides.** Hercules rescued Hesione, daughter of the Trojan king, Laomedon, from a monster to which, by command of Neptune, she was about to be sacrificed. Hercules was rewarded, however, not with the lady's love, but with a famous pair of horses. 56. **howling,** lamenting. 58. **Dardanian,** Trojan. 63. **fancy,** sensuous love. The song contains a disguised warning to Bassanio not to choose by

All. Ding, dong, bell.

Bass. So may the outward shows be least themselves:
The world is still deceived with ornament.
In law, what plea so tainted and corrupt
But, being season'd with a gracious voice,
Obscures the show of evil? In religion,
What damned error, but some sober brow
Will bless it and approve it with a text,
Hiding the grossness with fair ornament? 80
There is no vice so simple but assumes
Some mark of virtue on his outward parts:
How many cowards, whose hearts are all as false
As stairs of sand, wear yet upon their chins
The beards of Hercules and frowning Mars,
Who, inward search'd, have livers white as milk;
And these assume but valour's excrement
To render them redoubted! Look on beauty,
And you shall see 'tis purchased by the weight;
Which therein works a miracle in nature, 90
Making them lightest that wear most of it:
So are those crisped snaky golden locks
Which make such wanton gambols with the wind,
Upon supposed fairness, often known
To be the dowry of a second head,
The skull that bred them in the sepulchre.
Thus ornament is but the guiled shore
To a most dangerous sea; the beauteous scarf
†Veiling an Indian beauty; in a word,
The seeming truth which cunning times put on 100
To entrap the wisest. Therefore, thou gaudy gold,
Hard food for Midas, I will none of thee;
Nor none of thee, thou pale and common drudge
'Tween man and man: but thou, thou meagre lead,
Which rather threatenest dost promise aught,
Thy paleness moves me more than eloquence;
And here choose I: joy be the consequence!

Por. [*Aside*] How all the other passions fleet to air,
As doubtful thoughts, and rash-embraced despair,
And shuddering fear, and green-eyed jealousy! 110
O love,
Be moderate; allay thy ecstasy;
In measure rein thy joy; scant this excess.
I feel too much thy blessing: make it less,
For fear I surfeit.

Bass.   What find I here?
    [*Opening the leaden casket.*
Fair Portia's counterfeit! What demi-god
Hath come so near creation? Move these eyes?
Or whether, riding on the balls of mine,
Seem they in motion? Here are sever'd lips,
Parted with sugar breath: so sweet a bar 120
Should sunder such sweet friends. Here in her hairs
The painter plays the spider and hath woven
A golden mesh to entrap the hearts of men
Faster than gnats in cobwebs: but her eyes,—
How could he see to do them? having made one,
Methinks it should have power to steal both his
And leave itself unfurnish'd. Yet look, how far
The substance of my praise doth wrong this shadow
In underprizing it, so far this shadow

Doth limp behind the substance. Here's the scroll, 130
The continent and summary of my fortune.
    [*Reads*] You that choose not by the view,
        Chance as fair and choose as true!
        Since this fortune falls to you,
        Be content and seek no new.
        If you be well pleased with this
        And hold your fortune for your bliss,
        Turn you where your lady is
        And claim her with a loving kiss.
A gentle scroll. Fair lady, by your leave; 140
I come by note, to give and to receive.
Like one of two contending in a prize,
That thinks he hath done well in people's eyes,
Hearing applause and universal shout,
Giddy in spirit, still gazing in a doubt
Whether those peals of praise be his or no;
So, thrice-fair lady, stand I, even so;
As doubtful whether what I see be true,
Until confirm'd, sign'd, ratified by you.

Por. You see me, Lord Bassanio, where I stand, 150
Such as I am: though for myself alone
I would not be ambitious in my wish,
To wish myself much better; yet, for you
I would be trebled twenty times myself;
A thousand times more fair, ten thousand times
More rich;
That only to stand high in your account,
I might in virtues, beauties, livings, friends,
Exceed account; but the full sum of me
†Is sum of something, which, to term in gross, 160
Is an unlesson'd girl, unschool'd, unpractised;
Happy in this, she is not yet so old
†But she may learn; happier than this,
She is not bred so dull but she can learn;
Happiest of all is that her gentle spirit
Commits itself to yours to be directed,
As from her lord, her governor, her king.
Myself and what is mine to you and yours
Is now converted: but now I was the lord
Of this fair mansion, master of my servants, 170
Queen o'er myself; and even now, but now,
This house, these servants and this same myself
Are yours, my lord: I give them with this ring;
Which when you part from, lose, or give away,
Let it presage the ruin of your love
And be my vantage to exclaim on you.

Bass. Madam, you have bereft me of all words,
Only my blood speaks to you in my veins;
And there is such confusion in my powers,
As, after some oration fairly spoke 180
By a beloved prince, there doth appear
Among the buzzing pleased multitude;
Where every something, being blent together,
Turns to a wild of nothing, save of joy,
Express'd and not express'd. But when this ring
Parts from this finger, then parts life from hence:
O, then be bold to say Bassanio's dead!

Ner. My lord and lady, it is now our time,
That have stood by and seen our wishes prosper,

fancy. 67. **eyes.** Love entered the heart especially through the eyes.
79. **approve,** confirm. 81. **simple,** unmixed with virtue. 84. **stairs,**
steps. 86. **livers.** The liver was thought to be the seat of courage; for it
to be deserted by the blood would be the condition of cowardice. 87.
valour's excrement, beard of a brave man. 92. **crisped,** curly. 97.
guiled, treacherous. 102. **Midas,** the Phrygian king whose touch turned
everything to gold. 104-106. **but . . . eloquence.** Bassanio rejects outward show and does not resort to reason; trusting the power of love, he

follows merely intuition. 116. **counterfeit,** portrait. 127. **unfurnish'd,**
i.e., with a companion. 141. **by note,** i.e., as directed. 142. **prize,**
contest. 157. **account,** computation. 173. **ring.** The ring, which is to
serve as a test in the love-friendship contest, is thus bestowed at the very
acme of the love plot. 176. **exclaim on,** reproach; see glossary.

To cry, good joy: good joy, my lord and lady! 190
Gra. My lord Bassanio and my gentle lady,
I wish you all the joy that you can wish;
For I am sure you can wish none from me:
And when your honours mean to solemnize
The bargain of your faith, I do beseech you,
Even at that time I may be married too.
Bass. With all my heart, so thou canst get a wife.
Gra. I thank your lordship, you have got me one.
My eyes, my lord, can look as swift as yours:
You saw the mistress, I beheld the maid; 200
You loved, I loved for intermission.
No more pertains to me, my lord, than you.
Your fortune stood upon the casket there,
And so did mine too, as the matter falls;
For wooing here until I sweat again,
And swearing till my very roof was dry
With oaths of love, at last, if promise last,
I got a promise of this fair one here
To have her love, provided that your fortune
Achieved her mistress.
Por. Is this true, Nerissa? 210
Ner. Madam, it is, so you stand pleased withal.
Bass. And do you, Gratiano, mean good faith?
Gra. Yes, faith, my lord.
Bass. Our feast shall be much honour'd in your
marriage.
Gra. We'll play with them the first boy for a thou-
sand ducats.
Ner. What, and stake down?
Gra. No; we shall ne'er win at that sport, and stake
down. 220
But who comes here? Lorenzo and his infidel?
What, and my old Venetian friend Salerio?

Enter LORENZO, JESSICA, *and* SALERIO, *a Messenger
from Venice.*

Bass. Lorenzo and Salerio, welcome hither;
If that the youth of my new interest here
Have power to bid you welcome. By your leave,
I bid my very friends and countrymen,
Sweet Portia, welcome.
Por. So do I, my lord:
They are entirely welcome.
Lor. I thank your honour. For my part, my lord,
My purpose was not to have seen you here; 230
But meeting with Salerio by the way,
He did intreat me, past all saying nay,
To come with him along.
Saler. I did, my lord;
And I have reason for it. Signor Antonio
Commends him to you. [*Gives Bassanio a letter.*
Bass. Ere I ope his letter,
I pray you, tell me how my good friend doth.
Saler. Not sick, my lord, unless it be in mind;
Nor well, unless in mind: his letter there
Will show you his estate. 239
Gra. Nerissa, cheer yon stranger; bid her welcome.
Your hand, Salerio: what's the news from Venice?
How doth that royal merchant, good Antonio?
I know he will be glad of our success;
We are the Jasons, we have won the fleece.
Saler. I would you had won the fleece that he hath
lost.

Por. There are some shrewd contents in yon same
paper,
That steals the colour from Bassanio's cheek:
Some dear friend dead; else nothing in the world
Could turn so much the constitution
Of any constant man. What, worse and worse! 250
With leave, Bassanio; I am half yourself,
And I must freely have the half of anything
That this same paper brings you.
Bass. O sweet Portia,
Here are a few of the unpleasant'st words
That ever blotted paper! Gentle lady,
When I did first impart my love to you,
I freely told you, all the wealth I had
Ran in my veins, I was a gentleman;
And then I told you true: and yet, dear lady,
Rating myself at nothing, you shall see 260
How much I was a braggart. When I told you
My state was nothing, I should then have told you
That I was worse than nothing; for, indeed,
I have engaged myself to a dear friend,
Engaged my friend to his mere enemy,
To feed my means. Here is a letter, lady;
The paper as the body of my friend,
And every word in it a gaping wound,
Issuing life-blood. But is it true, Salerio?
Have all his ventures fail'd? What, not one hit? 270
From Tripolis, from Mexico and England,
From Lisbon, Barbary and India?
And not one vessel 'scape the dreadful touch
Of merchant-marring rocks?
Saler. Not one, my lord.
Besides, it should appear, that if he had
The present money to discharge the Jew,
He would not take it. Never did I know
A creature, that did bear the shape of man,
So keen and greedy to confound a man:
He plies the duke at morning and at night, 280
And doth impeach the freedom of the state,
If they deny him justice: twenty merchants,
The duke himself, and the magnificoes
Of greatest port, have all persuaded with him;
But none can drive him from the envious plea
Of forfeiture, of justice and his bond.
Jes. When I was with him I have heard him swear
To Tubal and to Chus, his countrymen,
That he would rather have Antonio's flesh
Than twenty times the value of the sum 290
That he did owe him: and I know, my lord,
If law, authority and power deny not,
It will go hard with poor Antonio.
Por. Is it your dear friend that is thus in trouble?
Bass. The dearest friend to me, the kindest man,
The best-condition'd and unwearied spirit
In doing courtesies, and one in whom
The ancient Roman honour more appears
Than any that draws breath in Italy.
Por. What sum owes he the Jew? 300
Bass. For me three thousand ducats.
Por. What, no more?
Pay him six thousand, and deface the bond;
Double six thousand, and then treble that,
Before a friend of this description
Shall lose a hair through Bassanio's fault.

---

206. **roof,** roof of my mouth. 228. **entirely,** cordially. 235. **Com-mends him,** desires to be remembered. 239. **estate,** condition. 242. **royal merchant,** merchant prince. 249. **constitution,** state of mind or body. 250. **constant,** settled, not swayed by passion. 281. **impeach,** call in question. 283. **magnificoes,** chief men of Venice. 315. **cheer,** face. 324-325. **Notwithstanding . . . letter.** Complete self-abnegation is

First go with me to church and call me wife,
And then away to Venice to your friend;
For never shall you lie by Portia's side
With an unquiet soul. You shall have gold
To pay the petty debt twenty times over: 310
When it is paid, bring your true friend along.
My maid Nerissa and myself meantime
Will live as maids and widows. Come, away!
For you shall hence upon your wedding-day:
Bid your friends welcome, show a merry cheer:
Since you are dear bought, I will love you dear.
But let me hear the letter of your friend.   317

Bass. [*Reads*] Sweet Bassanio, my ships have all miscarried, my creditors grow cruel, my estate is very low,
my bond to the Jew is forfeit; and since in paying it,
it is impossible I should live, all debts are cleared
between you and I, if I might but see you at my death.
Notwithstanding, use your pleasure: if your love do
not persuade you to come, let not my letter.

Por. O love, dispatch all business, and be gone!

Bass. Since I have your good leave to go away,
I will make haste: but, till I come again,
No bed shall e'er be guilty of my stay,
     No rest be interposer 'twixt us twain.   [*Exeunt.* 330

SCENE III. *Venice. A street.*

Enter SHYLOCK, SALARINO, ANTONIO, *and* Gaoler.

Shy. Gaoler, look to him: tell not me of mercy;
This is the fool that lent out money gratis:
Gaoler, look to him.

Ant.   Hear me yet, good Shylock.

Shy. I'll have my bond; speak not against my bond:
I have sworn an oath that I will have my bond.
Thou call'dst me dog before thou hadst a cause;
But, since I am a dog, beware my fangs:
The duke shall grant me justice. I do wonder,
Thou naughty gaoler, that thou art so fond
To come abroad with him at his request.   10

Ant. I pray thee, hear me speak.

Shy. I'll have my bond; I will not hear thee speak:
I'll have my bond; and therefore speak no more.
I'll not be made a soft and dull-eyed fool,
To shake the head, relent, and sigh, and yield
To Christian intercessors. Follow not;
I'll have no speaking: I will have my bond.   [*Exit.*

Salar. It is the most impenetrable cur
That ever kept with men.

Ant.   Let him alone:
I'll follow him no more with bootless prayers.   20
He seeks my life; his reason well I know:
I oft deliver'd from his forfeitures
Many that have at times made moan to me;
Therefore he hates me.

Salar.   I am sure the duke
Will never grant this forfeiture to hold.

Ant. The duke cannot deny the course of law:
For the commodity that strangers have
With us in Venice, if it be denied,
Will much impeach the justice of his state;
Since that the trade and profit of the city   30
Consisteth of all nations. Therefore, go:

These griefs and losses have so bated me,
That I shall hardly spare a pound of flesh
To-morrow to my bloody creditor.
Well, gaoler, on. Pray God, Bassanio come
To see me pay his debt, and then I care not!   [*Exeunt.*

SCENE IV. *Belmont. A room in* PORTIA'S *house.*

Enter PORTIA, NERISSA, LORENZO, JESSICA, *and*
     BALTHASAR.

Lor. Madam, although I speak it in your presence,
You have a noble and a true conceit
Of god-like amity; which appears most strongly
In bearing thus the absence of your lord.
But if you knew to whom you show this honour,
How true a gentleman you send relief,
How dear a lover of my lord your husband,
I know you would be prouder of the work
Than customary bounty can enforce you.

Por. I never did repent for doing good,   10
Nor shall not now: for in companions
That do converse and waste the time together,
Whose souls do bear an equal yoke of love,
There must be needs a like proportion
Of lineaments, of manners and of spirit;
Which makes me think that this Antonio,
Being the bosom lover of my lord,
Must needs be like my lord. If it be so,
How little is the cost I have bestow'd
In purchasing the semblance of my soul   20
From out the state of hellish misery!
This comes too near the praising of myself;
Therefore no more of it: hear other things.
Lorenzo, I commit into your hands
The husbandry and manage of my house
Until my lord's return: for mine own part,
I have toward heaven breathed a secret vow
To live in prayer and contemplation,
Only attended by Nerissa here,
Until her husband and my lord's return: 30
There is a monastery two miles off;
And there will we abide. I do desire you
Not to deny this imposition;
The which my love and some necessity
Now lays upon you.

Lor.   Madam, with all my heart;
I shall obey you in all fair commands.

Por. My people do already know my mind,
And will acknowledge you and Jessica
In place of Lord Bassanio and myself.
And so farewell, till we shall meet again.   40

Lor. Fair thoughts and happy hours attend on you!

Jes. I wish your ladyship all heart's content.

Por. I thank you for your wish, and am well pleased
To wish it back on you: fare you well, Jessica.
     [*Exeunt Jessica and Lorenzo.*
Now, Balthasar,
As I have ever found thee honest-true,
So let me find thee still. Take this same letter,
And use thou all the endeavour of a man
In speed to Padua: see thou render this
Into my cousin's hand, Doctor Bellario;   50

---

here thought of as a condition of ideal friendship as well as of ideal love.
     SCENE III. 20. **bootless,** having gained nothing. 27. **commodity,**
facilities or privileges for trading.

     SCENE IV. 9. **customary bounty,** ordinary kindness. 20. **my soul,**
Bassanio. 25. **husbandry,** care of the household. **manage,** administration; see glossary. 33. **imposition,** charge imposed. 49. **render,** deliver.

And, look, what notes and garments he doth give thee,
Bring them, I pray thee, with imagined speed
Unto the tranect, to the common ferry
Which trades to Venice. Waste no time in words,
But get thee gone: I shall be there before thee.
    Balth. Madam, I go with all convenient speed. [*Exit.*
    Por. Come on, Nerissa; I have work in hand
That you yet know not of: we'll see our husbands
Before they think of us.
    Ner.   Shall they see us?
    Por. They shall, Nerissa; but in such a habit,   60
That they shall think we are accomplished
With that we lack. I'll hold thee any wager,
When we are both accoutred like young men,
I'll prove the prettier fellow of the two,
And wear my dagger with the braver grace,
And speak between the change of man and boy
With a reed voice, and turn two mincing steps
Into a manly stride, and speak of frays
Like a fine bragging youth, and tell quaint lies,
How honourable ladies sought my love,   70
Which I denying, they fell sick and died;
I could not do withal; then I'll repent,
And wish, for all that, that I had not kill'd them;
And twenty of these puny lies I'll tell,
That men shall swear I have discontinued school
Above a twelvemonth. I have within my mind
A thousand raw tricks of these bragging Jacks,
Which I will practise.
    Ner.   Why, shall we turn to men?
    Por. Fie, what a question 's that,
If thou wert near a lewd interpreter!   80
But come, I'll tell thee all my whole device
When I am in my coach, which stays for us
At the park gate; and therefore haste away,
For we must measure twenty miles to-day.   [*Exeunt.*

SCENE V. *The same. A garden.*

Enter LAUNCELOT *and* JESSICA.

    Laun. Yes, truly; for, look you, the sins of the father
are to be laid upon the children: therefore, I promise
ye, I fear you. I was always plain with you, and so
now I speak my agitation of the matter: therefore be
of good cheer, for truly I think you are damned. There
is but one hope in it that can do you any good; and
that is but a kind of bastard hope neither.
    Jes. And what hope is that, I pray thee?   10
    Laun. Marry, you may partly hope that your father
got you not, that you are not the Jew's daughter.
    Jes. That were a kind of bastard hope, indeed: so
the sins of my mother should be visited upon me.
    Laun. Truly then I fear you are damned both by
father and mother: thus when I shun Scylla, your
father, I fall into Charybdis, your mother: well, you
are gone both ways.   20
    Jes. I shall be saved by my husband; he hath made
me a Christian.
    Laun. Truly, the more to blame he: we were Chris-

tians enow before; e'en as many as could well live,
one by another. This making of Christians will raise
the price of hogs: if we grow all to be pork-eaters, we
shall not shortly have a rasher on the coals for money.

Enter LORENZO.

    Jes. I'll tell my husband, Launcelot, what you say:
here he comes.   30
    Lor. I shall grow jealous of you shortly, Launcelot,
if you thus get my wife into corners.
    Jes. Nay, you need not fear us, Lorenzo: Launcelot
and I are out. He tells me flatly, there is no mercy for
me in heaven, because I am a Jew's daughter: and he
says, you are no good member of the commonwealth,
for in converting Jews to Christians, you raise the
price of pork.   39
    Lor. I shall answer that better to the commonwealth
than you can the getting up of the negro's belly: the
Moor is with child by you, Launcelot.
    Laun. It is much that the Moor should be more than
reason: but if she be less than an honest woman, she
is indeed more than I took her for.
    Lor. How every fool can play upon the word! I
think the best grace of wit will shortly turn into
silence, and discourse grow commendable in none
only but parrots. Go in, sirrah; bid them prepare for
dinner.   52
    Laun. That is done, sir; they have all stomachs.
    Lor. Goodly Lord, what a wit-snapper are you! then
bid them prepare dinner.
    Laun. That is done too, sir; only 'cover' is the word.
    Lor. Will you cover then, sir?
    Laun. Not so, sir, neither; I know my duty.   59
    Lor. Yet more quarrelling with occasion! Wilt thou
show the whole wealth of thy wit in an instant? I pray
thee, understand a plain man in his plain meaning:
go to thy fellows; bid them cover the table, serve in
the meat, and we will come in to dinner.
    Laun. For the table, sir, it shall be served in; for the
meat, sir, it shall be covered; for your coming in to
dinner, sir, why, let it be as humours and conceits
shall govern.   [*Exit.*
    Lor. O dear discretion, how his words are suited!   70
The fool hath planted in his memory
An army of good words; and I do know
A many fools, that stand in better place,
Garnish'd like him, that for a tricksy word
Defy the matter. How cheer'st thou, Jessica?
And now, good sweet, say thy opinion,
How dost thou like the Lord Bassanio's wife?
    Jes. Past all expressing. It is very meet
The Lord Bassanio live an upright life;
For, having such a blessing in his lady,   80
He finds the joys of heaven here on earth;
†And if on earth he do not mean it, then
In reason he should never come to heaven.
Why, if two gods should play some heavenly match
And on the wager lay two earthly women,
And Portia one, there must be something else
Pawn'd with the other, for the poor rude world
Hath not her fellow.

---

52. **imagined speed,** speed of imagination, as quick as thought. 53.
tranect. Rowe conjectured *traject* (Italian *traghetto*, ferry). 61. **accomplished,** supplied. 72. **do withal,** help it. 77. **Jacks,** fellows.
    SCENE V. 3. **fear you,** i.e., for you. 5. **agitation,** for "cogitation."
19. **Scylla, Charybdis,** twin dangers of *Odyssey*, xii, 235, a rock and
a whirlpool guarding the straits between Italy and Sicily. 25. **one by**

another, together. 57. **'cover,'** two meanings: "spread the table for
the meal" and "put on your hat." 60. **quarrelling with occasion,**
answering perversely. 70. **suited,** fitted to special uses. 74. **Garnish'd,**
i.e., with words. **tricksy,** fantastic. 75. **Defy the matter,** possibly
disregard the true sense. **How cheer'st thou,** i.e., what cheer? 82.
mean it, i.e., lead an upright life.

Lor.   Even such a husband
Hast thou of me as she is for a wife.
    Jes. Nay, but ask my opinion too of that.   90
    Lor. I will anon: first, let us go to dinner.
    Jes. Nay, let me praise you while I have a stomach.
    Lor. No, pray thee, let it serve for table-talk;
Then, howsoe'er thou speak'st, 'mong other things
I shall digest it.
    Jes.   Well, I'll set you forth.   [*Exeunt.*

ACT IV.

SCENE I. *Venice. A court of justice.*

Enter the DUKE, *the* Magnificoes, ANTONIO, BASSANIO,
    GRATIANO, SALERIO, *and others.*

Duke. What, is Antonio here?
Ant. Ready, so please your grace.
Duke. I am sorry for thee: thou art come to answer
A stony adversary, an inhuman wretch
Uncapable of pity, void and empty
From any dram of mercy.
    Ant.   I have heard
Your grace hath ta'en great pains to qualify
His rigorous course; but since he stands obdurate
And that no lawful means can carry me
Out of his envy's reach, I do oppose   10
My patience to his fury, and am arm'd
To suffer, with a quietness of spirit,
The very tyranny and rage of his.
    Duke. Go one, and call the Jew into the court.
    Saler. He is ready at the door: he comes, my lord.

Enter SHYLOCK.

    Duke. Make room, and let him stand before our
        face.
Shylock, the world thinks, and I think so too,
That thou but lead'st this fashion of thy malice
To the last hour of act; and then 'tis thought
Thou 'lt show thy mercy and remorse more strange   20
Than is thy strange apparent cruelty;
And where thou now exact'st the penalty,
Which is a pound of this poor merchant's flesh,
Thou wilt not only loose the forfeiture,
But, touch'd with human gentleness and love,
Forgive a moiety of the principal;
Glancing an eye of pity on his losses,
That have of late so huddled on his back,
Enow to press a royal merchant down
And pluck commiseration of his state   30
From brassy bosoms and rough hearts of flint,
From stubborn Turks and Tartars, never train'd
To offices of tender courtesy.
We all expect a gentle answer, Jew.
    Shy. I have possess'd your grace of what I purpose;
And by our holy Sabbath have I sworn
To have the due and forfeit of my bond:
If you deny it, let the danger light
Upon your charter and your city's freedom.
You'll ask me, why I rather choose to have   40

A weight of carrion flesh than to receive
Three thousand ducats: I'll not answer that:
But, say, it is my humour: is it answer'd?
What if my house be troubled with a rat
And I be pleased to give ten thousand ducats
To have it baned? What, are you answer'd yet?
Some men there are love not a gaping pig;
Some, that are mad if they behold a cat;
And others, when the bagpipe sings i' the nose,
Cannot contain their urine: for affection,   50
Mistress of passion, sways it to the mood
Of what it likes or loathes. Now, for your answer:
As there is no firm reason to be render'd,
Why he cannot abide a gaping pig;
Why he, a harmless necessary cat;
†Why he, a woollen bag-pipe; but of force
Must yield to such inevitable shame
As to offend, himself being offended;
So can I give no reason, nor I will not,
More than a lodged hate and a certain loathing   60
I bear Antonio, that I follow thus
A losing suit against him. Are you answer'd?
    Bass. This is no answer, thou unfeeling man,
To excuse the current of thy cruelty.
    Shy. I am not bound to please thee with my answers.
    Bass. Do all men kill the things they do not love?
    Shy. Hates any man the thing he would not kill?
    Bass. Every offence is not a hate at first.
    Shy. What, wouldst thou have a serpent sting thee
        twice?
    Ant. I pray you, think you question with the Jew: 70
You may as well go stand upon the beach
And bid the main flood bate his usual height;
You may as well use question with the wolf
Why he hath made the ewe bleat for the lamb;
You may as well forbid the mountain pines
To wag their high tops and to make no noise,
When they are fretten with the gusts of heaven;
You may as well do any thing most hard,
As seek to soften that—than which what's harder?—
His Jewish heart: therefore, I do beseech you,   80
Make no more offers, use no farther means,
But with all brief and plain conveniency
Let me have judgement and the Jew his will.
    Bass. For thy three thousand ducats here is six.
    Shy. If every ducat in six thousand ducats
Were in six parts and every part a ducat,
I would not draw them; I would have my bond.
    Duke. How shalt thou hope for mercy, rendering
        none?
    Shy. What judgement shall I dread, doing no
        wrong?
You have among you many a purchased slave.   90
Which, like your asses and your dogs and mules,
You use in abject and in slavish parts,
Because you bought them: shall I say to you,
Let them be free, marry them to your heirs?
Why sweat they under burthens? let their beds
Be made as soft as yours and let their palates
Be season'd with such viands? You will answer
'The slaves are ours:' so do I answer you:

ACT IV. SCENE I. **7. qualify,** moderate. **13. tyranny,** cruelty.
18. fashion, mere form. **19. act,** action. **26. moiety,** part, portion;
see glossary. **29. Enow,** enough. **38. danger,** injury. **39. Upon . . .
freedom.** The Venetians were celebrated for their strict adherence to
law. **46. baned,** killed, especially by poison. **47. gaping pig,** explained as "pig roasted whole with its mouth open"; also as "bawling"

or "shouting," i.e., squealing. **50. affection,** mental state or inclination; see glossary. Shylock means to say that the mental state from
which passion arises may originate from mere likes and dislikes. **60.
lodged,** settled, steadfast. **certain,** definite. **77. fretten,** fretted.
87. draw, receive. **92. parts,** duties, capacities.

The pound of flesh, which I demand of him,
Is dearly bought; 'tis mine and I will have it.   100
If you deny me, fie upon your law!
There is no force in the decrees of Venice.
I stand for judgement: answer; shall I have it?
   Duke. Upon my power I may dismiss this court,
Unless Bellario, a learned doctor,
Whom I have sent for to determine this,
Come here to-day.
   Saler.   My lord, here stays without
A messenger with letters from the doctor,
New come from Padua.
   Duke. Bring us the letters; call the messenger.   110
   Bass. Good cheer, Antonio! What, man, courage
yet!
The Jew shall have my flesh, blood, bones and all,
Ere thou shalt loose for me one drop of blood.
   Ant. I am a tainted wether of the flock,
Meetest for death: the weakest kind of fruit
Drops earliest to the ground; and so let me:
You cannot better be employ'd, Bassanio,
Than to live still and write mine epitaph.

   Enter NERISSA, *dressed like a lawyer's clerk.*

   Duke. Came you from Padua, from Bellario?
   Ner. From both, my lord. Bellario greets your grace.
                                 [*Presenting a letter.*
   Bass. Why dost thou whet thy knife so earnestly?   121
   Shy. To cut the forfeiture from that bankrupt there.
   Gra. Not on thy sole, but on thy soul, harsh Jew,
Thou makest thy knife keen; but no metal can,
No, not the hangman's axe, bear half the keenness
Of thy sharp envy. Can no prayers pierce thee?
   Shy. No, none that thou hast wit enough to make.
   Gra. O, be thou damn'd, inexecrable dog!
And for thy life let justice be accused.
Thou almost makest me waver in my faith   130
To hold opinion with Pythagoras,
That souls of animals infuse themselves
Into the trunks of men: thy currish spirit
Govern'd a wolf, who, hang'd for human slaughter,
Even from the gallows did his fell soul fleet,
And, whilst thou lay'st in thy unhallow'd dam,
Infused itself in thee; for thy desires
Are wolvish, bloody, starved and ravenous.
   Shy. Till thou canst rail the seal from off my bond,
Thou but offend'st thy lungs to speak so loud: 140
Repair thy wit, good youth, or it will fall
To cureless ruin. I stand here for law.
   Duke. This letter from Bellario doth commend
A young and learned doctor to our court.
Where is he?
   Ner.   He attendeth here hard by,
To know your answer, whether you'll admit him.
   Duke. With all my heart. Some three or four of you
Go give him courteous conduct to this place.
Meantime the court shall hear Bellario's letter.   149
   Clerk. [*Reads*] Your grace shall understand that at
the receipt of your letter I am very sick: but in the in-
stant that your messenger came, in loving visitation
was with me a young doctor of Rome; his name is
Balthasar. I acquainted him with the cause in con-
troversy between the Jew and Antonio the merchant:

we turned o'er many books together: he is furnished
with my opinion; which, bettered with his own learning, the greatness whereof I cannot enough commend,
comes with him, at my importunity, to fill up your
grace's request in my stead. I beseech you, let his lack
of years be no impediment to let him lack a reverend
estimation; for I never knew so young a body with so
old a head. I leave him to your gracious acceptance,
whose trial shall better publish his commendation.
   Duke. You hear the learn'd Bellario, what he writes:
And here, I take it, is the doctor come.

   Enter PORTIA, *dressed like a doctor of laws.*

Give me your hand. Come you from old Bellario?
   Por. I did, my lord.
   Duke. You are welcome: take your place.   170
Are you acquainted with the difference
That holds this present question in the court?
   Por. I am informed throughly of the cause.
Which is the merchant here, and which the Jew?
   Duke. Antonio and old Shylock, both stand forth.
   Por. Is your name Shylock?
   Shy.   Shylock is my name.
   Por. Of a strange nature is the suit you follow;
Yet in such rule that the Venetian law
Cannot impugn you as you do proceed.
You stand within his danger, do you not?   180
   Ant. Ay, so he says.
   Por.   Do you confess the bond?
   Ant. I do.
   Por.   Then must the Jew be merciful.
   Shy. On what compulsion must I? tell me that.
   Por. The quality of mercy is not strain'd,
It droppeth as the gentle rain from heaven
Upon the place beneath: it is twice blest;
It blesseth him that gives and him that takes:
'Tis mightiest in the mightiest: it becomes
The throned monarch better than his crown;
His sceptre shows the force of temporal power,   190
The attribute to awe and majesty,
Wherein doth sit the dread and fear of kings;
But mercy is above this sceptred sway;
It is enthroned in the hearts of kings,
It is an attribute to God himself;
And earthly power doth then show likest God's
When mercy seasons justice. Therefore, Jew,
Though justice be thy plea, consider this,
That, in the course of justice, none of us
Should see salvation: we do pray for mercy;   200
And that same prayer doth teach us all to render
The deeds of mercy. I have spoke thus much
To mitigate the justice of thy plea;
Which if thou follow, this strict court of Venice
Must needs give sentence 'gainst the merchant there.
   Shy. My deeds upon my head! I crave the law,
The penalty and forfeit of my bond.
   Por. Is he not able to discharge the money?
   Bass. Yes, here I tender it for him in the court;
Yea, twice the sum: if that will not suffice,   210
I will be bound to pay it ten times o'er,
On forfeit of my hands, my head, my heart:
If this will not suffice, it must appear
That malice bears down truth. And I beseech you,

---

121. **Why . . . earnestly.** The traditional stage business at this point is
for the actor who plays the part of Shylock to be discovered whetting
his knife on the sole of his shoe.   134. **hang'd for human slaughter,** a
possible allusion to the ancient practice of trying and punishing
animals for various crimes. 135. **fleet,** flit. 140. **offend'st,** injurest.
173. **throughly,** thoroughly; see glossary. 179. **impugn,** find fault
with. 180. **danger,** power to harm; possibly a legal term. 184.
strain'd, forced, constrained; in reply to Shylock's reference to com-

Wrest once the law to your authority:
To do a great right, do a little wrong,
And curb this cruel devil of his will.

Por. It must not be; there is no power in Venice
Can alter a decree established:
'Twill be recorded for a precedent, 220
And many an error by the same example
Will rush into the state: it cannot be.

Shy. A Daniel come to judgement! yea, a Daniel!
O wise young judge, how I do honour thee!

Por. I pray you, let me look upon the bond.

Shy. Here 'tis, most reverend doctor, here it is.

Por. Shylock, there 's thrice thy money offer'd thee.

Shy. An oath, an oath, I have an oath in heaven:
Shall I lay perjury upon my soul?
No, not for Venice.

Por. Why, this bond is forfeit; 230
And lawfully by this the Jew may claim
A pound of flesh, to be by him cut off
Nearest the merchant's heart. Be merciful:
Take thrice thy money; bid me tear the bond.

Shy. When it is paid according to the tenour.
It doth appear you are a worthy judge;
You know the law, your exposition
Hath been most sound: I charge you by the law,
Whereof you are a well-deserving pillar,
Proceed to judgement: by my soul I swear 240
There is no power in the tongue of man
To alter me: I stay here on my bond.

Ant. Most heartily I do beseech the court
To give the judgement.

Por. Why then, thus it is:
You must prepare your bosom for his knife.

Shy. O noble judge! O excellent young man!

Por. For the intent and purpose of the law
Hath full relation to the penalty,
Which here appeareth due upon the bond.

Shy. 'Tis very true: O wise and upright judge! 250
How much more elder art thou than thy looks!

Por. Therefore lay bare your bosom.

Shy. Ay, his breast:
So says the bond: doth it not, noble judge?
'Nearest his heart:' those are the very words.

Por. It is so. Are there balance here to weigh
The flesh?

Shy. I have them ready.

Por. Have by some surgeon, Shylock, on your
charge,
To stop his wounds, lest he do bleed to death.

Shy. Is it so nominated in the bond?

Por. It is not so express'd: but what of that? 260
'Twere good you do so much for charity.

Shy. I cannot find it; 'tis not in the bond.

Por. You, merchant, have you any thing to say?

Ant. But little: I am arm'd and well prepared.
Give me your hand, Bassanio: fare you well!
Grieve not that I am fallen to this for you;
For herein Fortune shows herself more kind
Than is her custom: it is still her use
To let the wretched man outlive his wealth,
To view with hollow eye and wrinkled brow 270
An age of poverty; from which lingering penance
Of such misery doth she cut me off.

Commend me to your honourable wife:
Tell her the process of Antonio's end;
Say how I loved you, speak me fair in death;
And, when the tale is told, bid her be judge
Whether Bassanio had not once a love.
Repent but you that you shall lose your friend,
And he repents not that he pays your debt;
For if the Jew do cut but deep enough, 280
I'll pay it presently with all my heart.

Bass. Antonio, I am married to a wife
Which is as dear to me as life itself;
But life itself, my wife, and all the world,
Are not with me esteem'd above thy life:
I would lose all, ay, sacrifice them all
Here to this devil, to deliver you.

Por. Your wife would give you little thanks for that,
If she were by, to hear you make the offer.

Gra. I have a wife, whom, I protest, I love: 290
I would she were in heaven, so she could
Entreat some power to change this currish Jew.

Ner. 'Tis well you offer it behind her back;
The wish would make else an unquiet house.

Shy. These be the Christian husbands. I have a
daughter;
Would any of the stock of Barrabas
Had been her husband rather than a Christian! [*Aside.*
We trifle time: I pray thee, pursue sentence.

Por. A pound of that same merchant's flesh is thine:
The court awards it, and the law doth give it. 300

Shy. Most rightful judge!

Por. And you must cut this flesh from off his breast:
The law allows it, and the court awards it.

Shy. Most learned judge! A sentence! Come,
prepare!

Por. Tarry a little; there is something else.
This bond doth give thee here no jot of blood;
The words expressly are 'a pound of flesh:'
Take then thy bond, take thou thy pound of flesh;
But, in the cutting it, if thou dost shed
One drop of Christian blood, thy lands and goods 310
Are, by the laws of Venice, confiscate
Unto the state of Venice.

Gra. O upright judge! Mark, Jew: O learned judge!

Shy. Is that the law?

Por. Thyself shalt see the act:
For, as thou urgest justice, be assured
Thou shalt have justice, more than thou desirest.

Gra. O learned judge! Mark, Jew: a learned judge!

Shy. I take this offer, then; pay the bond thrice
And let the Christian go.

Bass. Here is the money.

Por. Soft! 320
The Jew shall have all justice; soft! no haste:
He shall have nothing but the penalty.

Gra. O Jew! an upright judge, a learned judge!

Por. Therefore prepare thee to cut off the flesh.
Shed thou no blood, nor cut thou less nor more
But just a pound of flesh: if thou cut'st more
Or less than a just pound, be it but so much
As makes it light or heavy in the substance,
Or the division of the twentieth part
Of one poor scruple, nay, if the scale do turn 330
But in the estimation of a hair,

---

pulsion. 214. **truth,** honesty (Johnson). 223. **Daniel.** In the Apocryphal book of *Susannah,* Daniel is the judge who rescues Susannah from her false accusers. 242. **stay . . . on,** take stand upon. 274. **process,** story; see glossary. 313. **O . . . judge.** In the modern sympathetic

presentations of the character of Shylock, it is usual to subordinate the part of Gratiano in this scene. 328. **substance,** mass or gross weight. 329-330. **division . . . scruple,** fraction of the twentieth of a scruple (20 grains apothecaries' weight).

Thou diest and all thy goods are confiscate.
Gra. A second Daniel, a Daniel, Jew!
Now, infidel, I have you on the hip.
Por. Why doth the Jew pause? take thy forfeiture.
Shy. Give me my principal, and let me go.
Bass. I have it ready for thee; here it is.
Por. He hath refused it in the open court:
He shall have merely justice and his bond.
Gra. A Daniel, still say I, a second Daniel! 340
I thank thee, Jew, for teaching me that word.
Shy. Shall I not have barely my principal?
Por. Thou shalt have nothing but the forfeiture,
To be so taken at thy peril, Jew.
Shy. Why, then the devil give him good of it!
I'll stay no longer question.
Por. Tarry, Jew:
The law hath yet another hold on you.
It is enacted in the laws of Venice,
If it be proved against an alien
That by direct or indirect attempts 350
He seek the life of any citizen,
The party 'gainst the which he doth contrive
Shall seize one half his goods; the other half
Comes to the privy coffer of the state;
And the offender's life lies in the mercy
Of the duke only, 'gainst all other voice.
In which predicament, I say, thou stand'st;
For it appears, by manifest proceeding,
That indirectly and directly too
Thou hast contrived against the very life 360
Of the defendant; and thou hast incurr'd
The danger formerly by me rehearsed.
Down therefore and beg mercy of the duke.
Gra. Beg that thou mayst have leave to hang
thyself:
And yet, thy wealth being forfeit to the state,
Thou hast not left the value of a cord;
Therefore thou must be hang'd at the state's charge.
Duke. That thou shalt see the difference of our
spirits,
I pardon thee thy life before thou ask it:
For half thy wealth, it is Antonio's; 370
The other half comes to the general state,
Which humbleness may drive unto a fine.
Por. Ay, for the state, not for Antonio.
Shy. Nay, take my life and all: pardon not that:
You take my house when you do take the prop
That doth sustain my house; you take my life
When you do take the means whereby I live.
Por. What mercy can you render him, Antonio?
Gra. A halter gratis; nothing else, for God's sake.
Ant. So please my lord the duke and all the court 380
To quit the fine for one half of his goods,
I am content; so he will let me have
The other half in use, to render it,
Upon his death, unto the gentleman
That lately stole his daughter:
Two things provided more, that, for this favour,
He presently become a Christian;
The other, that he do record a gift,
Here in the court, of all he dies possess'd,
Unto his son Lorenzo and his daughter. 390

Duke. He shall do this, or else I do recant
The pardon that I late pronounced here.
Por. Art thou contented, Jew? what dost thou say?
Shy. I am content.
Por. Clerk, draw a deed of gift.
Shy. I pray you, give me leave to go from hence;
I am not well: send the deed after me,
And I will sign it.
Duke. Get thee gone, but do it.
Gra. In christening shalt thou have two godfathers:
Had I been judge, thou shouldst have had ten more,
To bring thee to the gallows, not the font. [*Exit Shylock.*
Duke. Sir, I entreat you home with me to dinner. 401
Por. I humbly do desire your grace of pardon:
I must away this night toward Padua,
And it is meet I presently set forth.
Duke. I am sorry that your leisure serves you not.
Antonio, gratify this gentleman,
For, in my mind, you are much bound to him.
[*Exeunt Duke and his train.*
Bass. Most worthy gentleman, I and my friend
Have by your wisdom been this day acquitted
Of grievous penalties; in lieu whereof, 410
Three thousand ducats, due unto the Jew,
We freely cope your courteous pains withal.
Ant. And stand indebted, over and above,
In love and service to you evermore.
Por. He is well paid that is well satisfied;
And I, delivering you, am satisfied
And therein do account myself well paid:
My mind was never yet more mercenary.
I pray you, know me when we meet again:
I wish you well, and so I take my leave. 420
Bass. Dear sir, of force I must attempt you further:
Take some remembrance of us, as a tribute,
Not as a fee: grant me two things, I pray you,
Not to deny me, and to pardon me.
Por. You press me far, and therefore I will yield.
[*To Ant.*] Give me your gloves, I'll wear them for your
sake;
[*To Bass.*] And, for your love, I'll take this ring from
you:
Do not draw back your hand; I'll take no more;
And you in love shall not deny me this.
Bass. This ring, good sir, alas, it is a trifle! 430
I will not shame myself to give you this.
Por. I will have nothing else but only this;
And now methinks I have a mind to it.
Bass. There 's more depends on this than on the
value.
The dearest ring in Venice will I give you,
And find it out by proclamation:
Only for this, I pray you, pardon me.
Por. I see, sir, you are liberal in offers:
You taught me first to beg; and now methinks
You teach me how a beggar should be answer'd. 440
Bass. Good sir, this ring was given me by my wife;
And when she put it on, she made me vow
That I should neither sell nor give nor lose it.
Por. That 'scuse serves many men to save their gifts.
An if your wife be not a mad-woman,
And know how well I have deserved the ring,

372. **humbleness,** gentleness, tractability. 381. **quit . . . goods.** This difficult passage is variously interpreted. It seems to mean that, as the duke has seen fit to accept a fine instead of one-half of Shylock's goods, Antonio will in his turn merely take over the other half for the benefit of Lorenzo and Jessica. 387. **become a Christian.** This added penalty, frequently thought of as a piece of cynical and gratuitous cruelty, may have carried no shock to the sensibilities of the audience, who may have seen in it merely a chance for Shylock's salvation. 406. **gratify,** reward. 426. **gloves,** a customary and relatively valuable gift in Elizabethan times.

She would not hold out enemy for ever,
For giving it to me. Well, peace be with you!
                              [*Exeunt Portia and Nerissa.*
  Ant. My Lord Bassanio, let him have the ring:
Let his deservings and my love withal   450
Be valued 'gainst your wife's commandment.
  Bass. Go, Gratiano, run and overtake him;
Give him the ring, and bring him, if thou canst,
Unto Antonio's house: away! make haste.
                              [*Exit Gratiano.*
Come, you and I will thither presently;
And in the morning early will we both
Fly toward Belmont: come, Antonio.   [*Exeunt.*

SCENE II. *The same. A street.*

Enter PORTIA *and* NERISSA.

  Por. Inquire the Jew's house out, give him this deed
And let him sign it: we'll away to-night
And be a day before our husbands home:
This deed will be well welcome to Lorenzo.

Enter GRATIANO.

  Gra. Fair sir, you are well o'erta'en:
My Lord Bassanio upon more advice
Hath sent you here this ring, and doth entreat
Your company at dinner.
  Por.   That cannot be:
His ring I do accept most thankfully:
And so, I pray you, tell him: furthermore,   10
I pray you, show my youth old Shylock's house.
  Gra. That will I do.
  Ner.   Sir, I would speak with you.
[*Aside to Por.*] I'll see if I can get my husband's ring,
Which I did make him swear to keep for ever.
  Por. [*Aside to Ner.*] Thou mayst, I warrant. We shall
        have old swearing
That they did give the rings away to men;
But we'll outface them, and outswear them too.
[*Aloud*] Away! make haste: thou know'st where I will
        tarry.
  Ner. Come, good sir, will you show me to this
        house?   [*Exeunt.*

ACT V.

SCENE I. *Belmont. Avenue to* PORTIA'S *house.*

Enter LORENZO *and* JESSICA.

  Lor. The moon shines bright: in such a night as
        this,
When the sweet wind did gently kiss the trees
And they did make no noise, in such a night
Troilus methinks mounted the Troyan walls
And sigh'd his soul toward the Grecian tents,
Where Cressid lay that night.
  Jes.   In such a night
Did Thisbe fearfully o'ertrip the dew
And saw the lion's shadow ere himself

And ran dismay'd away.
  Lor.   In such a night
Stood Dido with a willow in her hand   10
Upon the wild sea banks and waft her love
To come again to Carthage.
  Jes.   In such a night
Medea gather'd the enchanted herbs
That did renew old Æson.
  Lor.   In such a night
Did Jessica steal from the wealthy Jew
And with an unthrift love did run from Venice
As far as Belmont.
  Jes.   In such a night
Did young Lorenzo swear he loved her well,
Stealing her soul with many vows of faith
And ne'er a true one.
  Lor.   In such a night   20
Did pretty Jessica, like a little shrew,
Slander her love, and he forgave it her.
  Jes. I would out-night you, did no body come;
But, hark, I hear the footing of a man.

Enter STEPHANO.

  Lor. Who comes so fast in silence of the night?
  Steph. A friend.
  Lor. A friend! what friend? your name, I pray you,
        friend?
  Steph. Stephano is my name; and I bring word
My mistress will before the break of day
Be here at Belmont: she doth stray about   30
By holy crosses, where she kneels and prays
For happy wedlock hours.
  Lor.   Who comes with her?
  Steph. None but a holy hermit and her maid.
I pray you, is my master yet return'd?
  Lor. He is not, nor we have not heard from him.
But go we in, I pray thee, Jessica,
And ceremoniously let us prepare
Some welcome for the mistress of the house.

Enter LAUNCELOT.

  Laun. Sola, sola! wo ha, ho! sola, sola!
  Lor. Who calls?   40
  Laun. Sola! did you see Master Lorenzo? Master
Lorenzo, sola, sola!
  Lor. Leave hollaing, man: here.
  Laun. Sola! where? where?
  Lor. Here.
  Laun. Tell him there's a post come from my master,
with his horn full of good news: my master will be here
ere morning.   [*Exit.*
  Lor. Sweet soul, let's in, and there expect their
        coming.
And yet no matter: why should we go in?   50
My friend Stephano, signify, I pray you,
Within the house, your mistress is at hand;
And bring your music forth into the air. [*Exit Stephano.*
How sweet the moonlight sleeps upon this bank!
Here will we sit and let the sounds of music
Creep in our ears: soft stillness and the night
Become the touches of sweet harmony.
Sit, Jessica. Look how the floor of heaven

SCENE II. 16. **old,** extraordinary.
ACT V. SCENE I. 4. **Troilus.** Cf. Chaucer, *Troilus and Criseyde*, lines
647-679. 7. **Thisbe.** The story of Pyramus and Thisbe was the subject of the play presented by Bottom and his companions in *A Midsummer-Night's Dream.* 10. **willow,** symbol of forsaken love. 11. **waft,**

beckoned. 13. **Medea,** allusion to the famous sorceress of Colchis, who
pretended to restore youth to Aeson, father of Jason, as told by Ovid.
24. **footing,** footsteps. 39. **Sola,** imitation of a postman's horn. 51.
signify, make known.

Is thick inlaid with patines of bright gold:
There's not the smallest orb which thou behold'st 60
But in his motion like an angel sings,
Still quiring to the young-eyed cherubins;
Such harmony is in immortal souls;
But whilst this muddy vesture of decay
Doth grossly close it in, we cannot hear it.

Enter Musicians.

Come, ho! and wake Diana with a hymn:
With sweetest touches pierce your mistress' ear
And draw her home with music. [*Music.*
Jes. I am never merry when I hear sweet music.
Lor. The reason is, your spirits are attentive: 70
For do but note a wild and wanton herd,
Or race of youthful and unhandled colts,
Fetching mad bounds, bellowing and neighing loud,
Which is the hot condition of their blood;
If they but hear perchance a trumpet sound,
Or any air of music touch their ears,
You shall perceive them make a mutual stand,
Their savage eyes turn'd to a modest gaze
By the sweet power of music: therefore the poet
Did feign that Orpheus drew trees, stones and floods;
Since nought so stockish, hard and full of rage, 81
But music for the time doth change his nature.
The man that hath no music in himself,
Nor is not moved with concord of sweet sounds,
Is fit for treasons, stratagems and spoils;
The motions of his spirit are dull as night
And his affections dark as Erebus:
Let no such man be trusted. Mark the music.

Enter PORTIA *and* NERISSA.

Por. That light we see is burning in my hall.
How far that little candle throws his beams! 90
So shines a good deed in a naughty world.
Ner. When the moon shone, we did not see the
 candle.
Por. So doth the greater glory dim the less:
A substitute shines brightly as a king
Until a king be by, and then his state
Empties itself, as doth an inland brook
Into the main of waters. Music! hark!
Ner. It is your music, madam, of the house.
Por. Nothing is good, I see, without respect:
Methinks it sounds much sweeter than by day. 100
Ner. Silence bestows that virtue on it, madam.
Por. The crow doth sing as sweetly as the lark
When neither is attended, and I think
The nightingale, if she should sing by day,
When every goose is cackling, would be thought
No better a musician than the wren.
How many things by season season'd are
To their right praise and true perfection!
Peace, ho! the moon sleeps with Endymion
And would not be awaked. [*Music ceases.*
Lor. That is the voice, 110
Or I am much deceived, of Portia.
Por. He knows me as the blind man knows the
 cuckoo,

By the bad voice.
Lor. Dear lady, welcome home.
Por. We have been praying for our husbands'
 healths,
Which speed, we hope, the better for our words.
Are they return'd?
Lor. Madam, they are not yet;
But there is come a messenger before,
To signify their coming.
Por. Go in, Nerissa;
Give order to my servants that they take
No note at all of our being absent hence; 120
Nor you, Lorenzo; Jessica, nor you. [*A tucket sounds.*
Lor. Your husband is at hand; I hear his trumpet:
We are no tell-tales, madam; fear you not.
Por. This night methinks is but the daylight sick;
It looks a little paler: 'tis a day,
Such as the day is when the sun is hid.

Enter BASSANIO, ANTONIO, GRATIANO, *and their*
 followers.

Bass. We should hold day with the Antipodes,
If you would walk in absence of the sun.
Por. Let me give light, but let me not be light;
For a light wife doth make a heavy husband, 130
And never be Bassanio so for me:
But God sort all! You are welcome home, my lord.
Bass. I thank you, madam. Give welcome to my
 friend.
This is the man, this is Antonio,
To whom I am so infinitely bound.
Por. You should in all sense be much bound to him,
For, as I hear, he was much bound for you.
Ant. No more than I am well acquitted of.
Por. Sir, you are very welcome to our house:
It must appear in other ways than words, 140
Therefore I scant this breathing courtesy.
Gra. [*To Ner.*] By yonder moon I swear you do me
 wrong;
In faith, I gave it to the judge's clerk:
Would he were gelt that had it, for my part,
Since you do take it, love, so much at heart.
Por. A quarrel, ho, already! what's the matter?
Gra. About a hoop of gold, a paltry ring
That she did give me, whose posy was
For all the world like cutler's poetry
Upon a knife, 'Love me, and leave me not.' 150
Ner. What talk you of the posy or the value?
You swore to me, when I did give it you,
That you would wear it till your hour of death
And that it should lie with you in your grave:
Though not for me, yet for your vehement oaths,
You should have been respective and have kept it.
Gave it a judge's clerk! no, God's my judge,
The clerk will ne'er wear hair on's face that had it.
Gra. He will, an if he live to be a man.
Ner. Ay, if a woman live to be a man. 160
Gra. Now, by this hand, I gave it to a youth,
A kind of boy, a little scrubbed boy,
No higher than thyself, the judge's clerk,
A prating boy, that begg'd it as a fee:

59. **patines,** thin, circular plates of metal. 60-65. **There's . . . hear it.** The universe was thought to be made up of revolving concentric spheres, each incorporating heavenly bodies and growing larger as the distance from the earth increased. Beyond the most distant planet was the sphere of the fixed stars, and beyond that the *primum mobile.* The spheres produced, as they moved, a harmony which the soul, itself by nature harmonious, might perceive were it not rendered dull by its covering of flesh. 62. **cherubins,** cherubim. 70. **spirits are attentive.** The spirits would be in motion within the body in merriment, whereas in sadness they would be drawn to the heart, and, as it were, busy listening. 72. **race,** herd. 77. **mutual,** common or simultaneous. 79. **poet,** possibly Ovid, with whom the story of Orpheus was a favorite

I could not for my heart deny it him.
Por. You were to blame, I must be plain with you,
To part so slightly with your wife's first gift;
A thing stuck on with oaths upon your finger
And so riveted with faith unto your flesh.
I gave my love a ring and made him swear   170
Never to part with it; and here he stands;
I dare be sworn for him he would not leave it
Nor pluck it from his finger, for the wealth
That the world masters. Now, in faith, Gratiano,
You give your wife too unkind a cause of grief:
An 'twere to me, I should be mad at it.
Bass. [*Aside*] Why, I were best to cut my left hand
    off
And swear I lost the ring defending it.
Gra. My Lord Bassanio gave his ring away
Unto the judge that begg'd it and indeed   180
Deserved it too; and then the boy, his clerk,
That took some pains in writing, he begg'd mine;
And neither man nor master would take aught
But the two rings.
Por.   What ring gave you, my lord?
Not that, I hope, which you received of me.
Bass. If I could add a lie unto a fault,
I would deny it; but you see my finger
Hath not the ring upon it; it is gone.
Por. Even so void is your false heart of truth.
By heaven, I will ne'er come in your bed   190
Until I see the ring.
Ner.   Nor I in yours
Till I again see mine.
Bass.   Sweet Portia,
If you did know to whom I gave the ring,
If you did know for whom I gave the ring
And would conceive for what I gave the ring
And how unwillingly I left the ring,
When nought would be accepted but the ring,
You would abate the strength of your displeasure.
Por. If you had known the virtue of the ring,
Or half her worthiness that gave the ring,   200
Or your own honour to contain the ring,
You would not then have parted with the ring.
What man is there so much unreasonable,
If you had pleased to have defended it
With any terms of zeal, wanted the modesty
To urge the thing held as a ceremony?
Nerissa teaches me what to believe:
I'll die for 't but some woman had the ring.
Bass. No, by my honour, madam, by my soul,
No woman had it, but a civil doctor,   210
Which did refuse three thousand ducats of me
And begg'd the ring; the which I did deny him
And suffer'd him to go displeased away;
Even he that did uphold the very life
Of my dear friend. What should I say, sweet lady?
I was enforced to send it after him;
I was beset with shame and courtesy;
My honour would not let ingratitude
So much besmear it. Pardon me, good lady;
For, by these blessed candles of the night,   220
Had you been there, I think you would have begg'd

The ring of me to give the worthy doctor.
Por. Let not that doctor e'er come near my house:
Since he hath got the jewel that I loved,
And that which you did swear to keep for me,
I will become as liberal as you;
I'll not deny him any thing I have,
No, not my body nor my husband's bed:
Know him I shall, I am well sure of it:
Lie not a night from home; watch me like Argus: 230
If you do not, if I be left alone,
Now, by mine honour, which is yet mine own,
I'll have that doctor for my bedfellow.
Ner. And I his clerk; therefore be well advised
How you do leave me to mine own protection.
Gra. Well, do you so: let not me take him, then;
For if I do, I'll mar the young clerk's pen.
Ant. I am the unhappy subject of these quarrels.
Por. Sir, grieve not you; you are welcome
    notwithstanding.
Bass. Portia, forgive me this enforced wrong;   240
And, in the hearing of these many friends,
I swear to thee, even by thine own fair eyes,
Wherein I see myself—
Por.   Mark you but that!
In both my eyes he doubly sees himself;
In each eye, one: swear by your double self,
And there 's an oath of credit.
Bass.   Nay, but hear me:
Pardon this fault, and by my soul I swear
I never more will break an oath with thee.
Ant. I once did lend my body for his wealth;
Which, but for him that had your husband's ring,   250
Had quite miscarried: I dare be bound again,
My soul upon the forfeit, that your lord
Will never more break faith advisedly.
Por. Then you shall be his surety. Give him this
And bid him keep it better than the other.
Ant. Here, Lord Bassanio; swear to keep this ring.
Bass. By heaven, it is the same I gave the doctor!
Por. I had it of him: pardon me, Bassanio;
For, by this ring, the doctor lay with me.
Ner. And pardon me, my gentle Gratiano;   260
For that same scrubbed boy, the doctor's clerk,
In lieu of this last night did lie with me.
Gra. Why, this is like the mending of highways
In summer, where the ways are fair enough:
What, are we cuckolds ere we have deserved it?
Por. Speak not so grossly. You are all amazed:
Here is a letter; read it at your leisure;
It comes from Padua, from Bellario:
There you shall find that Portia was the doctor,
Nerissa there her clerk: Lorenzo here   270
Shall witness I set forth as soon as you
And even but now return'd; I have not yet
Enter'd my house. Antonio, you are welcome;
And I have better news in store for you
Than you expect: unseal this letter soon;
There you shall find three of your argosies
Are richly come to harbour suddenly:
You shall not know by what strange accident
I chanced on this letter.

*The Merchant
of Venice*
ACT V : SC I

529

theme. 81. **stockish,** unfeeling. 87. **Erebus,** classical abode of darkness. 109. **Endymion,** shepherd of Elis who, as he slept in a cave on
Mount Latmos, was visited by Diana, the moon goddess; cf. line 66,
above. 121. *Stage Direction:* **tucket,** flourish on a trumpet. 127.
Antipodes, those who dwell on the opposite side of the globe. 132.
sort, decide. 141. **breathing courtesy,** courteous speaking. 148. **posy,**

a motto; QF: *poesie.* 156. **respective,** mindful. 162. **scrubbed,**
stunted. 164. **prating,** prattling. 176. **mad,** beside oneself with wrath.
201. **contain,** retain. 206. **ceremony,** something sacred. 210. **civil
doctor,** i.e., doctor of civil law. 230. **Argus,** i.e., with a hundred eyes.
245. **double,** deceitful. 249. **wealth,** welfare. 265. **cuckolds,** husbands
whose wives are unfaithful; see glossary.

Ant.   I am dumb.

Bass. Were you the doctor and I knew you not?   280

Gra. Were you the clerk that is to make me cuckold?

Ner. Ay, but the clerk that never means to do it,

Unless he live until he be a man.

Bass. Sweet doctor, you shall be my bedfellow:

When I am absent, then lie with my wife.

Ant. Sweet lady, you have given me life and living;

For here I read for certain that my ships

Are safely come to road.

Por.   How now, Lorenzo!

My clerk hath some good comforts too for you.

Ner. Ay, and I'll give them him without a fee.   290

There do I give to you and Jessica,

From the rich Jew, a special deed of gift,

After his death, of all he dies possess'd of.

Lor. Fair ladies, you drop manna in the way

Of starved people.

Por.   It is almost morning,

And yet I am sure you are not satisfied

Of these events at full. Let us go in;

And charge us there upon inter'gatories,

And we will answer all things faithfully.

Gra. Let it be so: the first inter'gatory   300

That my Nerissa shall be sworn on is,

Whether till the next night she had rather stay

Or go to bed now, being two hours to day:

But were the day come, I should wish it dark,

That I were couching with the doctor's clerk.

Well, while I live I'll fear no other thing

So sore as keeping safe Nerissa's ring.   [*Exeunt.*

*The Merchant
of Venice*
ACT V : SC I

530

298. **charge . . . inter'gatories,** take oath to answer all things truly, like
persons charged with contempt in the court of the Queen's Bench.

From George Carleton, "A Thankfull
Remembrance . . . . ," *1630.*

Much Ado
about Nothing

In 1600 the actors seem to have become alarmed about their stock of plays, possibly on account of the publication in garbled form of Shakespeare's *Henry V.* Several plays were entered in the Stationers' Register and ordered to be stayed, that is, not published without further authority. However, no less than four of Shakespeare's plays, all very good texts, were printed, among them *Much Ado about Nothing.* The title page of this first and only quarto edition is as follows:

Much adoe about Nothing. *As it hath been sundrie times publikely* acted by the right honourable, the Lord Chamberlaine his seruants. *Written by William Shakespeare.* LONDON. Printed by V. S. for Andrew Wise, and William Aspley. 1600.

The text of the First Folio was set up from the theatrical playbook copied from Shakespeare's revision of an earlier form of the play, which revision was used as copy for the printed quarto. The folio has the prompter's stage directions.

From the fact that Francis Meres does not mention *Much Ado* in his list in *Palladis Tamia* the play is thought to have been written after 1598, a supposition which suits the style of the play very well. However, the omission of *Much Ado about Nothing* from that list is not necessarily significant. What we know about Shakespeare's manner would lead us to think that he would be writing in just such a brilliant fashion in 1598, or in 1599 when his company was occupying the newly constructed Globe Theatre. Of the many evidences of the popularity of the play, none is better than a prefatory poem by Leonard Digges to an edition of Shakespeare's poems in 1640:

Let but *Beatrice*
And *Benedicke* be seene, loe, in a trice
The Cockpit, Galleries, Boxes, all are full.

SOURCES AND COMPOSITION

The main plot of *Much Ado about Nothing* is the story of two lovers estranged by malicious villainy. The hero is made to believe that his mistress is false to him by means of a wicked deceit, in which he thinks he sees another man entering her window. The story, which has many versions, seems to have come to Shakespeare from an Italian story of Matteo Bandello in a collection published at Lucca in 1554. Whether Shakespeare read it in the original or worked from an old play is not known. The only bit of information suggesting an old play is found in the

Revels accounts of the payment to the earl of Leicester's players in 1574 for "their matter of Panecia." Bandello's heroine is called Fenicia for Phenicia.

There is a play *Die schöne Phœnicia* (1595?) by the German dramatist Jakob Ayrer, which tells Bandello's story. It may, like so many of the German plays of the period, be based on an English original, and one concludes that this original might have served as Shakespeare's immediate source. But for lack of concrete data, the whole argument is very shadowy.

A similar plot is described in Ariosto's *Orlando Furioso*, translated into English by Harington in 1591, and is borrowed thence into Spenser's *Faerie Queene* (1590). Spenser introduces the feature of a maid dressed in her mistress' clothing, as does Shakespeare's play. Bandello's story was freely rendered into French by Belleforest in his collection known as *Histoires Tragiques* (1582).

To the already long list of sources or sources of the source—Bandello, Ariosto, Spenser, and others—there have recently been added three others: Peter Beverly's *The Historie of Ariodanto and Ieneura* (1565-1566) and George Whetstone's *The Rocke of Regard* (1576)[1]; also Della Porta's comedy, *Gli Duoi Fratelli Rivalli*[2].

There are, in point of fact, two minor plots or episodes, both apparently original with Shakespeare, which constitute the chief interest of the play—the affair of Benedick and Beatrice and the activities of Dogberry and the Watch. In Bandello there are no parts to correspond to Benedick and Beatrice, or to Dogberry. There the solution of the plot is brought about by the remorse of the villain.

EVIDENCES OF REVISION

Critics have always pointed to inconsistencies in *Much Ado about Nothing*. Claudio is too easily persuaded of Hero's guilt. His rejection of her at the altar is so cruel that he appears to be, and no doubt is, a badly plot-ridden character. That is, his actions do not conform to his character, but are forced upon him by the plot. Margaret, who is represented as being innocent of evil intention against her mistress, is not present at the wedding, where it is obvious she would have been in a position to clear up the charge against her mistress. In the quarto Innogen, the mother of Hero, appears twice in the stage directions, but plays no part in the comedy. The name is omitted in modern editions.

Recent editors of *Much Ado about Nothing*[3] have pointed out other inconsistencies in the form of the play, which seem to them to indicate that the parts of Benedick and Beatrice have been expanded in prose,

[1]C. T. Prouty, "George Whetstone, Peter Beverly, and the Sources of *Much Ado about Nothing*," *Studies in Philology*, XXXVIII (1941), 211-220.
[2]D. J. Gordon, "*Much Ado about Nothing*: A Possible Source for the Hero-Claudio Plot," *Studies in Philology*, XXXIX (1942), 279-290.
[3]Sir Arthur Quiller-Couch and John Dover Wilson, *Much Ado about Nothing*, The New Cambridge Shakespeare (1923).

and a corresponding amount cut out from the play as Shakespeare first wrote it. This play was, they think, mainly in verse and had practically the same plot. They find indications of this in various bad junctures between the old part and the new and attribute the hurried dramaturgy observable in the main plot to the abridgement it has suffered. A motive for such an alteration would, of course, be found in the popularity and interest of the Benedick-Beatrice theme. One need not suppose that Benedick and Beatrice were absent from the original play, but only that they have been made dominant in the new play. On the basis of a revision, Innogen would be explained as an omitted part. Margaret's action would be motivated pretty much as it is in Ariosto, namely, by supposing that she had let herself be flattered by her lover into donning her mistress' apparel. Perhaps even Claudio may have come out better in a more elaborate study of his remorse. Sympathy for him is diminished by the fact that the scene of his deception is known to us only by hearsay. A result, probably of revision, is that there is a greater quantity of prose in *Much Ado about Nothing* than Shakespeare had thitherto used in normal romantic comedy.

BACKGROUND

No array of words, however, can make Claudio's part, as such, plausible and palatable to a modern audience. However, it can be seen in a different and a truer way by considering the plot in the light of its times. The Italian novel dealt in sensational plots, like the rejection of an innocent maid at the altar, which suited the taste of the Renaissance. A cruelty of that kind would not be so deeply felt or seem so very unnatural if practiced on a maid unchaste or thought to be unchaste. Seeing is believing, and

Claudio thought he had seen. Shakespeare goes far toward making him attractive by showing him young, handsome, brave, a lover who falls in love at first sight, and a youth deeply smitten with contrition when he sees his mistake. But why should he offer

himself in the fifth act to be married off so casually, more or less as a matter of repayment, if he had been really so deeply grieved for the loss of Hero?

Here again, we have the opinions of the Renaissance entering the field of interpretation. We can never understand the businesslike aspect that marriage then had. There would be no particular feeling in an Elizabethan audience that Claudio should remain unmarried and forever faithful to Hero's memory. He had read his dirge and done his part and was showing a truly generous spirit in bestowing himself as a husband on, as he thought, another of Leonato's family. Then, again, what a feature is made of eavesdropping in the forced courtship of Benedick and Beatrice! Critics have actually censured Beatrice for indulging in this unladylike practice, but the manners of the times were different; eavesdropping was not regarded so seriously as it is now. In these respects and others this typical piece of Renaissance literature needs to be considered from the point of view of its own time.

SHAKESPEARE'S PART

Much Ado about Nothing gives us further insight into Shakespeare's way of depicting life, the manifestations of human character that interested or amused him, and the dramatic devices he had learned to employ with skill. His love affairs are never soft, because he was not sentimental. Also, the bright boys in his company who played women's parts could be trusted to bring out deliciously a combination of love and humor.

Benedick and Beatrice in Much Ado continue the stage situation of Biron and Rosaline in Love's Labour's Lost, though their interplay is wittier and more interesting, and there is a touch of Katharina and Petruchio in the combination. In spite of her shrewish traits, Beatrice has somehow the womanly qualities of Portia and something of the charm of Rosalind. Dogberry and his associates recall not only the constable Dull in Love's Labour's Lost but the "rude mechanicals" of A Midsummer-Night's Dream, and Dogberry's talk, with a difference, is like that of Bottom. Friar Francis, like Friar Laurence in Romeo and Juliet, supplies an element of staid and prudential wisdom. The grief for Hero recalls the grief for Juliet, while the bellicosity of Leonato and Antonio reminds us of old Capulet in his gown crying, "Give me my long sword, ho!"

COLERIDGE ON Much Ado about Nothing

These characters, situations, and devices, traditionally the stock in trade of Renaissance drama and of Shakespeare himself, are made in this play to reveal the surprises of life; as when Dogberry, contrary to all reasonable estimate of probability, is made to detect the villainy of Don John, and when Beatrice discloses in one flash her womanliness, her judgment, and her ultimate faith in Benedick in the words, "Kill Claudio."

Coleridge's paragraph,[4] describing the situation in this play, presents this feature of Shakespeare's greatness from another point of view:

The interest in the plot is always on account of the characters, not vice versa, as in almost all other writers; the plot is a mere canvas and no more. Hence arises the true justification of the same stratagem being used in regard to Benedick and Beatrice,—the vanity in each being alike. Take away from Much Ado about Nothing all that is not indispensable to the plot, either as having little to do with it, or, at best, like Dogberry and his comrades, forced into its service when any other less ingeniously absurd watchmen and night-constables would have answered the necessities of the action;— take away Benedick, Beatrice, Dogberry, and the reaction of the former on the character of Hero,—and what will remain? In other writers the main agent of the plot is always the prominent character; in Shakespeare it is so, or is not so, as the character is in itself calculated, or not calculated, to form the plot. Don John is the mainspring of the plot in this play; but he is merely shown and then withdrawn.

STAGE HISTORY

After the establishment of the two court companies at the time of the Restoration, Thomas Killigrew of the King's company and William D'Avenant (with Thomas Betterton) of the duke of York's company had divided between them the plays of the pre-Cromwellian repertory. Much Ado about Nothing and eight others of Shakespeare's plays fell to D'Avenant, who reformed them, or caused them to be reformed, according to the taste of the time. D'Avenant himself wrote The Law against Lovers (1662) making it up from Much Ado about Nothing and Measure for Measure. The former play was later unhappily combined with Molière's Princesse d'Élide by the Reverend James Miller (1737).

Rich played Shakespeare's version at Covent Garden in 1739, and Garrick, in 1748 and the years following, gained for the play a popularity it has never lost. Garrick himself was the greatest of Benedicks, and Mrs. Pritchard and Miss Pope were famous as Beatrice. The play was successful in the hands of the Kembles. Mrs. Siddons herself acted Beatrice and Mrs. Jordan was eminent in the part.

Later revivals have been no less successful. The most famous of these is that of Sir Henry Irving at the Lyceum Theater in London in 1882, on which occasion Irving played Benedick with great brilliancy. Ellen Terry gave an enchanting rendition of Beatrice, and Johnston Forbes-Robertson appeared as Claudio. There have been revivals by Beerbohm Tree, Ellen Terry, the Bensons, and many others. The play so retains its humor that it is not unusual during a performance to hear audiences laugh naturally and heartily and not because they know that it is Shakespearean comedy and supposed to be amusing.

4"Characteristics of Shakespeare's Dramas," in Lectures upon Shakespeare and other Dramatists (1884), pp. 62-63.

Much Ado about Nothing

DRAMATIS PERSONAE

DON PEDRO, prince of Arragon.
DON JOHN, his bastard brother.
CLAUDIO, a young lord of Florence.
BENEDICK, a young lord of Padua.
LEONATO, governor of Messina.
ANTONIO, his brother.
BALTHASAR, attendant on Don Pedro.
CONRADE,
BORACHIO, } followers of Don John.
FRIAR FRANCIS.
DOGBERRY, a constable.
VERGES, a headborough.
A Sexton.
A Boy.

HERO, daughter to Leonato.
BEATRICE, niece to Leonato.
MARGARET,
URSULA, } gentlewomen attending on Hero.

Messengers, Watch, Attendants, &c.

SCENE: *Messina.*

ACT I.

SCENE I. *Before* LEONATO's *house.*

Enter LEONATO, HERO, *and* BEATRICE, *with a*
Messenger.

Leon. I learn in this letter that Don Peter of Arragon comes this night to Messina.

Mess. He is very near by this: he was not three leagues off when I left him.

Leon. How many gentlemen have you lost in this action?

Mess. But few of any sort, and none of name.

Leon. A victory is twice itself when the achiever brings home full numbers. I find here that Don Peter hath bestowed much honour on a young Florentine called Claudio. 11

Mess. Much deserved on his part and equally remembered by Don Pedro: he hath borne himself beyond the promise of his age, doing, in the figure of a lamb, the feats of a lion: he hath indeed better bettered expectation than you must expect of me to tell you how.

Leon. He hath an uncle here in Messina will be very much glad of it. 19

Mess. I have already delivered him letters, and there appears much joy in him; even so much that joy could not show itself modest enough without a badge of bitterness.

Leon. Did he break out into tears?

Mess. In great measure.

Leon. A kind overflow of kindness: there are no faces truer than those that are so washed. How much better is it to weep at joy than to joy at weeping!

Beat. I pray you, is Signior Mountanto returned from the wars or no? 31

Mess. I know none of that name, lady: there was none such in the army of any sort.

Leon. What is he that you ask for, niece?

Hero. My cousin means Signior Benedick of Padua.

Mess. O, he's returned; and as pleasant as ever he was. 38

Beat. He set up his bills here in Messina and challenged Cupid at the flight; and my uncle's fool, reading the challenge, subscribed for Cupid, and challenged him at the bird-bolt. I pray you, how many hath he killed and eaten in these wars? But how many hath he killed? for indeed I promised to eat all of his killing.

Leon. Faith, niece, you tax Signior Benedick too much; but he'll be meet with you, I doubt it not.

Mess. He hath done good service, lady, in these wars. 49

Beat. You had musty victual, and he hath holp to eat it: he is a very valiant trencher-man; he hath an excellent stomach.

Mess. And a good soldier too, lady.

Beat. And a good soldier to a lady: but what is he to a lord?

Mess. A lord to a lord, a man to a man; stuffed with all honourable virtues.

Beat. It is so, indeed; he is no less than a stuffed man: but for the stuffing,—well, we are all mortal. 60

Leon. You must not, sir, mistake my niece. There is a kind of merry war betwixt Signior Benedick and her: they never meet but there's a skirmish of wit between them.

Beat. Alas! he gets nothing by that. In our last conflict four of his five wits went halting off, and now is the whole man governed with one: so that if he have wit enough to keep himself warm, let him bear it for a difference between himself and his horse; for it is all the wealth that he hath left, to be known a reasonable creature. Who is his companion now? He hath every month a new sworn brother. 73

Mess. Is't possible?

Beat. Very easily possible: he wears his faith but as the fashion of his hat; it ever changes with the next block.

Mess. I see, lady, the gentleman is not in your books.

Beat. No; an he were, I would burn my study. But, I pray you, who is his companion? Is there no young

ACT I. SCENE I. 7. **sort,** rank, or kind. **name,** reputation, or noble name. 16. **bettered,** surpassed. 23. **badge,** mark of service; here, the livery of sorrow. 30. **Mountanto.** *Montant* is an upright blow in fencing; the implication is that Benedick is a bravo. Beatrice's inquiry about him betrays a certain interest. 37. **pleasant,** jocular. 39. **bills,** placards, advertisements. 40. **challenged . . . flight,** undertook to rival Cupid as an archer. **my uncle's fool,** usually explained as a professional fool in her uncle's service; it has also been suggested that, since Beatrice herself is a jester, and *fool* is often a pet name, Beatrice is referring to herself and thus recalling an earlier flirtation with Benedick. 42. **bird-bolt,** blunt-headed arrow used for fowling. 46. **tax,** blame; see glossary. 47. **meet,** even, quits. 51. **valiant trencherman,** great eater. 59. **stuffed,** stuffed with food or anything, with play on preceding sense of "filled with." 66. **five wits,** not the five senses, but the five faculties: memory, imagination, judgment, fantasy, common wit. 70. **difference,** heraldic term, used with a play on the usual sense; see glossary. 71. **to be known,** i.e., in order that he may be known as. 73. **sworn brother,** brother in arms (*frater juratus*), an allusion to the ancient practice of swearing brotherhood. 76. **faith,** allegiance, or fidelity. 77. **block,** mold for shaping hats. 78-79. **in your books,** i.e., in favor with you, in your account books for credit.

squarer now that will make a voyage with him to the devil?

Mess. He is most in the company of the right noble Claudio.

Beat. O Lord, he will hang upon him like a disease: he is sooner caught than the pestilence, and the taker runs presently mad. God help the noble Claudio! if he have caught the Benedick, it will cost him a thousand pound ere a' be cured. 90

Mess. I will hold friends with you, lady.

Beat. Do, good friend.

Leon. You will never run mad, niece.

Beat. No, not till a hot January.

Mess. Don Pedro is approached.

Enter DON PEDRO, DON JOHN, CLAUDIO, BENEDICK, *and* BALTHASAR.

D. Pedro. Good Signior Leonato, you are come to meet your trouble: the fashion of the world is to avoid cost, and you encounter it.

Leon. Never came trouble to my house in the likeness of your grace: for trouble being gone, comfort should remain; but when you depart from me, sorrow abides and happiness takes his leave. 102

D. Pedro. You embrace your charge too willingly. I think this is your daughter.

Leon. Her mother hath many times told me so.

Bene. Were you in doubt, sir, that you asked her?

Leon. Signior Benedick, no; for then were you a child. 109

D. Pedro. You have it full, Benedick: we may guess by this what you are, being a man. Truly, the lady fathers herself. Be happy, lady; for you are like an honourable father.

Bene. If Signior Leonato be her father, she would not have his head on her shoulders for all Messina, as like him as she is.

Beat. I wonder that you will still be talking, Signior Benedick: nobody marks you.

Bene. What, my dear Lady Disdain! are you yet living? 120

Beat. Is it possible disdain should die while she hath such meet food to feed it as Signior Benedick? Courtesy itself must convert to disdain, if you come in her presence.

Bene. Then is courtesy a turncoat. But it is certain I am loved of all ladies, only you excepted: and I would I could find in my heart that I had not a hard heart; for, truly, I love none. 128

Beat. A dear happiness to women: they would else have been troubled with a pernicious suitor. I thank God and my cold blood, I am of your humour for that: I had rather hear my dog bark at a crow than a man swear he loves me.

Bene. God keep your ladyship still in that mind! so some gentleman or other shall 'scape a predestinate scratched face.

Beat. Scratching could not make it worse, an 'twere such a face as yours were.

Bene. Well, you are a rare parrot-teacher.

Beat. A bird of my tongue is better than a beast of yours. 141

Bene. I would my horse had the speed of your tongue, and so good a continuer. But keep your way, i' God's name; I have done.

Beat. You always end with a jade's trick: I know you of old.

D. Pedro. That is the sum of all, Leonato. Signior Claudio and Signior Benedick, my dear friend Leonato hath invited you all. I tell him we shall stay here at the least a month; and he heartily prays some occasion may detain us longer. I dare swear he is no hypocrite, but prays from his heart. 153

Leon. If you swear, my lord, you shall not be forsworn. [*To Don John*] Let me bid you welcome, my lord: being reconciled to the prince your brother, I owe you all duty.

D. John. I thank you: I am not of many words, but I thank you.

Leon. Please it your grace lead on? 160

D. Pedro. Your hand, Leonato; we will go together.

[*Exeunt all except Benedick and Claudio.*

Claud. Benedick, didst thou note the daughter of Signior Leonato?

Bene. I noted her not; but I looked on her.

Claud. Is she not a modest young lady?

Bene. Do you question me, as an honest man should do, for my simple true judgement; or would you have me speak after my custom, as being a professed tyrant to their sex? 170

Claud. No; I pray thee speak in sober judgement.

Bene. Why, i' faith, methinks she's too low for a high praise, too brown for a fair praise and too little for a great praise: only this commendation I can afford her, that were she other than she is, she were unhandsome; and being no other but as she is, I do not like her.

Claud. Thou thinkest I am in sport: I pray thee tell me truly how thou likest her. 180

Bene. Would you buy her, that you inquire after her?

Claud. Can the world buy such a jewel?

Bene. Yea, and a case to put it into. But speak you this with a sad brow? or do you play the flouting Jack, to tell us Cupid is a good hare-finder and Vulcan a rare carpenter? Come, in what key shall a man take you, to go in the song?

Claud. In mine eye she is the sweetest lady that ever I looked on. 190

Bene. I can see yet without spectacles and I see no such matter: there's her cousin, an she were not possessed with a fury, exceeds her as much in beauty as the first of May doth the last of December. But I hope you have no intent to turn husband, have you?

Claud. I would scarce trust myself, though I had sworn the contrary, if Hero would be my wife. 198

Bene. Is 't come to this? In faith, hath not the world one man but he will wear his cap with suspicion? Shall I never see a bachelor of threescore again? Go to, i' faith; an thou wilt needs thrust thy neck into a yoke, wear the print of it and sigh away Sundays. Look; Don Pedro is returned to seek you.

Re-enter DON PEDRO.

D. Pedro. What secret hath held you here, that you followed not to Leonato's?

Bene. I would your grace would constrain me to tell.

D. Pedro. I charge thee on thy allegiance.

Bene. You hear, Count Claudio: I can be secret as a dumb man; I would have you think so; but, on my allegiance, mark you this, on my allegiance. He is in love. With who? now that is your grace's part. Mark how short his answer is;—With Hero, Leonato's short daughter.

Claud. If this were so, so were it uttered.

Bene. Like the old tale, my lord: 'it is not so, nor 'twas not so, but, indeed, God forbid it should be so.'

Claud. If my passion change not shortly, God forbid it should be otherwise.

D. Pedro. Amen, if you love her; for the lady is very well worthy.

Claud. You speak this to fetch me in, my lord.

D. Pedro. By my troth, I speak my thought.

Claud. And, in faith, my lord, I spoke mine.

Bene. And, by my two faiths and troths, my lord, I spoke mine.

Claud. That I love her, I feel.   230

D. Pedro. That she is worthy, I know.

Bene. That I neither feel how she should be loved nor know how she should be worthy, is the opinion that fire cannot melt out of me: I will die in it at the stake.

D. Pedro. Thou wast ever an obstinate heretic in the despite of beauty.

Claud. And never could maintain his part but in the force of his will.   239

Bene. That a woman conceived me, I thank her; that she brought me up, I likewise give her most humble thanks: but that I will have a recheat winded in my forehead, or hang my bugle in an invisible baldrick, all women shall pardon me. Because I will not do them the wrong to mistrust any, I will do myself the right to trust none; and the fine is, for the which I may go the finer, I will live a bachelor.

D. Pedro. I shall see thee, ere I die, look pale with love.   250

Bene. With anger, with sickness, or with hunger, my lord, not with love: prove that ever I lose more blood with love than I will get again with drinking, pick out mine eyes with a ballad-maker's pen and hang me up at the door of a brothel-house for the sign of blind Cupid.

D. Pedro. Well, if ever thou dost fall from this faith, thou wilt prove a notable argument.

Bene. If I do, hang me in a bottle like a cat and shoot at me; and he that hits me, let him be clapped on the shoulder, and called Adam.   261

D. Pedro. Well, as time shall try: 'In time the savage bull doth bear the yoke.'

Bene. The savage bull may; but if ever the sensible Benedick bear it, pluck off the bull's horns and set them in my forehead: and let me be vilely painted, and in such great letters as they write 'Here is good horse to hire,' let them signify under my sign 'Here you may see Benedick the married man.'   270

Claud. If this should ever happen, thou wouldst be horn-mad.

D. Pedro. Nay, if Cupid have not spent all his quiver in Venice, thou wilt quake for this shortly.

Bene. I look for an earthquake too, then.

D. Pedro. Well, you will temporize with the hours. In the meantime, good Signior Benedick, repair to Leonato's: commend me to him and tell him I will not fail him at supper; for indeed he hath made great preparation.   280

Bene. I have almost matter enough in me for such an embassage; and so I commit you—

Claud. To the tuition of God: From my house, if I had it,—

D. Pedro. The sixth of July: Your loving friend, Benedick.

Bene. Nay, mock not, mock not. The body of your discourse is sometime guarded with fragments, and the guards are but slightly basted on neither: ere you flout old ends any further, examine your conscience: and so I leave you.   [*Exit.* 291

Claud. My liege, your highness now may do me good.

D. Pedro. My love is thine to teach: teach it but how, And thou shalt see how apt it is to learn Any hard lesson that may do thee good.

Claud. Hath Leonato any son, my lord?

D. Pedro. No child but Hero; she 's his only heir. Dost thou affect her, Claudio?

Claud.   O, my lord, When you went onward on this ended action, I look'd upon her with a soldier's eye,   300 That liked, but had a rougher task in hand Than to drive liking to the name of love: But now I am return'd and that war-thoughts Have left their places vacant, in their rooms Come thronging soft and delicate desires, All prompting me how fair young Hero is, Saying, I liked her ere I went to wars.

D. Pedro. Thou wilt be like a lover presently And tire the hearer with a book of words. If thou dost love fair Hero, cherish it,   310 And I will break with her and with her father And thou shalt have her. Was 't not to this end That thou began'st to twist so fine a story?

not escape from your yoke-fellow (Furness). 217. **If this . . . uttered.** If I had really confided such a secret to him, yet he would have blabbed it in this manner (Steevens). 218. **old tale,** an allusion to a children's tale in which these words occurred. 222. **otherwise,** i.e., than so. 225. **fetch me in,** take me in, cheat me. 237. **despite,** contempt. 239. **force of his will,** will, refusing to be guided by reason, which was the state of the heretic, as defined by the Schoolmen. 242-245. **but that . . . me,** women must pardon me for refusing to have my horn placed on my head (like a cuckold), where it will need no strap to sustain it. 243. **recheat,** blast blown to recall the hounds. 244. **baldrick,** strap that supports the horn. 247. **fine,** end; see glossary. 248. **go the finer,** have more to spend on fine clothes. 252. **prove that,** if you

discover. 253-254. **lose . . . drinking.** According to current theory, each sigh cost the heart a drop of blood, whereas blood was replenished by wine. 259. **bottle,** wicker basket to hold the cat used as target in shooting matches in archery. 261. **Adam,** Adam Bell, archer outlaw of the ballads. 263. **'In time . . . yoke,'** a line from Kyd's *Spanish Tragedy,* II, i, 3. 272. **horn-mad,** stark mad (from the fury of horned beasts), with allusion to cuckoldry. 274. **Venice,** noted for licentiousness. 276. **temporize . . . hours,** come to terms, or become milder, in time. 281. **matter,** wit, intelligence. 283. **tuition,** protection. 288. **guarded,** ornamented. 289. **guards,** border or trimming on a garment. 290. **old ends,** old tags, quotations. 311. **break,** open the subject. 313. **twist,** draw out the thread of.

Claud. How sweetly you do minister to love,
That know love's grief by his complexion!
But lest my liking might too sudden seem,
I would have salved it with a longer treatise.
      D. Pedro. What need the bridge much broader
            than the flood?
The fairest grant is the necessity.
Look, what will serve is fit: 'tis once, thou lovest,   320
And I will fit thee with the remedy.
I know we shall have revelling to-night:
I will assume thy part in some disguise
And tell fair Hero I am Claudio,
And in her bosom I'll unclasp my heart
And take her hearing prisoner with the force
And strong encounter of my amorous tale;
Then after to her father will I break;
And the conclusion is, she shall be thine.
In practice let us put it presently.   [*Exeunt.* 330

———————

SCENE II. *A room in* LEONATO's *house.*

Enter LEONATO *and* ANTONIO, *meeting.*

Leon. How now, brother! Where is my cousin,
your son? hath he provided this music?
      Ant. He is very busy about it. But, brother, I can
tell you strange news that you yet dreamt not of.   5
      Leon. Are they good?
      Ant. As the event stamps them: but they have a
good cover; they show well outward. The prince and
Count Claudio, walking in a thick-pleached alley in
mine orchard, were thus much overheard by a man
of mine: the prince discovered to Claudio that he
loved my niece your daughter and meant to acknowledge it this night in a dance; and if he found her
accordant, he meant to take the present time by the
top and instantly break with you of it.
      Leon. Hath the fellow any wit that told you this?
      Ant. A good sharp fellow: I will send for him; and
question him yourself.   20
      Leon. No, no; we will hold it as a dream till it
appear itself: but I will acquaint my daughter withal,
that she may be the better prepared for an answer,
if peradventure this be true. Go you and tell her of it.
[*Enter attendants.*] Cousins, you know what you have
to do. O, I cry you mercy, friend; go you with me,
and I will use your skill. Good cousin, have a care this
busy time.   [*Exeunt.*

———————

SCENE III. *The same.*

Enter DON JOHN *and* CONRADE.

Con. What the good-year, my lord! why are you
thus out of measure sad?
      D. John. There is no measure in the occasion that
breeds; therefore the sadness is without limit.

Con. You should hear reason.
      D. John. And when I have heard it, what **blessing**
brings it?
      Con. If not a present remedy, at least a patient
sufferance.   10
      D. John. I wonder that thou, being, as thou sayest
thou art, born under Saturn, goest about to apply a
moral medicine to a mortifying mischief. I cannot
hide what I am: I must be sad when I have cause
and smile at no man's jests, eat when I have stomach
and wait for no man's leisure, sleep when I am drowsy
and tend on no man's business, laugh when I am
merry and claw no man in his humour.   19
      Con. Yea, but you must not make the full show of
this till you may do it without controlment. You have
of late stood out against your brother, and he hath
ta'en you newly into his grace; where it is impossible
you should take true root but by the fair weather
that you make yourself: it is needful that you frame
the season for your own harvest.   27
      D. John. I had rather be a canker in a hedge than
a rose in his grace, and it better fits my blood to be
disdained of all than to fashion a carriage to rob love
from any: in this, though I cannot be said to be a
flattering honest man, it must not be denied but I
am a plain-dealing villain. I am trusted with a
muzzle and enfranchised with a clog; therefore I
have decreed not to sing in my cage. If I had my
mouth, I would bite; if I had my liberty, I would **do**
my liking: in the meantime let me be that I am **and**
seek not to alter me.
      Con. Can you make no use of your discontent?   40
      D. John. I make all use of it, for I use it only.
Who comes here?

Enter BORACHIO.

What news, Borachio?
      Bora. I came yonder from a great supper: the
prince your brother is royally entertained by Leonato;
and I can give you intelligence of an intended marriage.
      D. John. Will it serve for any model to build
mischief on? What is he for a fool that betroths himself to unquietness?   50
      Bora. Marry, it is your brother's right hand.
      D. John. Who? the most exquisite Claudio?
      Bora. Even he.
      D. John. A proper squire! And who and who?
which way looks he?   55
      Bora. Marry, on Hero, the daughter and heir of
Leonato.
      D. John. A very forward March-chick! How came
you to this?
      Bora. Being entertained for a perfumer, as I was
smoking a musty room, comes me the prince and
Claudio, hand in hand, in sad conference: I whipt
me behind the arras; and there heard it agreed upon
that the prince should woo Hero for himself, and

having obtained her, give her to Count Claudio.

D. John. Come, come, let us thither: this may prove food to my displeasure. That young start-up hath all the glory of my overthrow: if I can cross him any way, I bless myself every way. You are both sure, and will assist me?

Con. To the death, my lord.

D. John. Let us to the great supper: their cheer is the greater that I am subdued. Would the cook were of my mind! Shall we go prove what's to be done? 76

Bora. We'll wait upon your lordship. [*Exeunt.*

ACT II.

SCENE I. *A hall in* LEONATO's *house.*

Enter LEONATO, ANTONIO, HERO, BEATRICE, *and others.*

Leon. Was not Count John here at supper?

Ant. I saw him not.

Beat. How tartly that gentleman looks! I never can see him but I am heart-burned an hour after.

Hero. He is of a very melancholy disposition.

Beat. He were an excellent man that were made just in the midway between him and Benedick: the one is too like an image and says nothing, and the other too like my lady's eldest son, evermore tattling. 11

Leon. Then half Signior Benedick's tongue in Count John's mouth, and half Count John's melancholy in Signior Benedick's face,—

Beat. With a good leg and a good foot, uncle, and money enough in his purse, such a man would win any woman in the world, if a' could get her good-will.

Leon. By my troth, niece, thou wilt never get thee a husband, if thou be so shrewd of thy tongue. 21

Ant. In faith, she's too curst.

Beat. Too curst is more than curst: I shall lessen God's sending that way; for it is said, 'God sends a curst cow short horns;' but to a cow too curst he sends none.

Leon. So, by being too curst, God will send you no horns.

Beat. Just, if he send me no husband; for the which blessing I am at him upon my knees every morning and evening. Lord, I could not endure a husband with a beard on his face: I had rather lie in the woollen.

Leon. You may light on a husband that hath no beard.

Beat. What should I do with him? dress him in my apparel and make him my waiting-gentlewoman? He that hath a beard is more than a youth, and he that hath no beard is less than a man: and he that is more than a youth is not for me, and he that is less than a man, I am not for him: therefore I will even take sixpence in earnest of the bear-ward, and lead his apes into hell. 43

Leon. Well, then, go you into hell?

Beat. No, but to the gate; and there will the devil meet me, like an old cuckold, with horns on his head, and say 'Get you to heaven, Beatrice, get you to heaven; here's no place for you maids:' so deliver I up my apes, and away to Saint Peter for the heavens; he shows me where the bachelors sit, and there live we as merry as the day is long.

Ant. [*To Hero*] Well, niece, I trust you will be ruled by your father.

Beat. Yes, faith; it is my cousin's duty to make curtsy and say 'Father, as it please you.' But yet for all that, cousin, let him be a handsome fellow, or else make another curtsy and say 'Father, as it please me.'

Leon. Well, niece, I hope to see you one day fitted with a husband. 61

Beat. Not till God make men of some other metal than earth. Would it not grieve a woman to be over-mastered with a piece of valiant dust? to make an account of her life to a clod of wayward marl? No, uncle, I'll none: Adam's sons are my brethren; and, truly, I hold it a sin to match in my kindred.

Leon. Daughter, remember what I told you: if the prince do solicit you in that kind, you know your answer. 71

Beat. The fault will be in the music, cousin, if you be not wooed in good time: if the prince be too important, tell him there is measure in every thing and so dance out the answer. For, hear me, Hero: wooing, wedding, and repenting, is as a Scotch jig, a measure, and a cinque pace: the first suit is hot and hasty, like a Scotch jig, and full as fantastical; the wedding, mannerly-modest, as a measure, full of state and ancientry; and then comes repentance and, with his bad legs, falls into the cinque pace faster and faster, till he sink into his grave.

Leon. Cousin, you apprehend passing shrewdly.

Beat. I have a good eye, uncle; I can see a church by daylight.

Leon. The revellers are entering, brother: make good room. [*All put on their masks.*

Enter DON PEDRO, CLAUDIO, BENEDICK, BALTHASAR, DON JOHN, BORACHIO, MARGARET, URSULA, *and others, masked.*

D. Pedro. Lady, will you walk about with your friend? 90

Hero. So you walk softly and look sweetly and say nothing, I am yours for the walk; and especially when I walk away.

D. Pedro. With me in your company?

Hero. I may say so, when I please.

D. Pedro. And when please you to say so?

Hero. When I like your favour; for God defend the lute should be like the case!

D. Pedro. My visor is Philemon's roof; within the house is Jove. 100

---

start-up, upstart. 70. cross, thwart, with allusion to making the sign of the cross. 71. sure, trustworthy. 75. Would . . . mind, i.e., apparently that he might poison the food.

ACT II. SCENE I. 4. heart-burned, suffering from heartburn, affected with indigestion. 10. my . . . son, spoiled child. 22. curst, ill-tempered. 25. curst, savage, vicious. 29. Just, right, exactly so. 33. lie in the woollen, sleep between blankets. 43. bear-ward, one who keeps and exhibits a bear. Collier's emendation of QF: *Berrald.* lead . . . hell, ancient proverb: "Such as die maids do all lead apes in hell." 50. for the heavens, on my way to heaven. 51. bachelors,

unmarried persons, or possibly, unmarried women. 63. metal, substance. 66. clod . . . marl, lump of wayward earth, i.e., a man. 74. important, urgent, importunate. 78. cinque pace, lively dance, the steps of which are supposed to be based on the number five; the first five steps of the galliard (Arden ed.). 81. ancientry, old-fashioned style. 84. apprehend, understand. 90. friend, lover of both sexes. 99. visor, mask. Philemon's roof, an allusion to Ovid, *Metamorphoses,* viii. Philemon and Baucis, his wife, entertained Jupiter in their peasant cottage unawares (see *thatched,* line 102).

Hero. Why, then, your visor should be thatched.

D. Pedro. Speak low, if you speak love.

[*Drawing her aside.*

Balth. Well, I would you did like me.

Marg. So would not I, for your own sake; for I have many ill qualities.

Balth. Which is one?

Marg. I say my prayers aloud.

Balth. I love you the better: the hearers may cry, Amen. 110

Marg. God match me with a good dancer!

Balth. Amen.

Marg. And God keep him out of my sight when the dance is done! Answer, clerk.

Balth. No more words: the clerk is answered.

Urs. I know you well enough; you are Signior Antonio.

Ant. At a word, I am not.

Urs. I know you by the waggling of your head. 120

Ant. To tell you true, I counterfeit him.

Urs. You could never do him so ill-well, unless you were the very man. Here's his dry hand up and down: you are he, you are he.

Ant. At a word, I am not.

Urs. Come, come, do you think I do not know you by your excellent wit? can virtue hide itself? Go to, mum, you are he: graces will appear, and there's an end.

Beat. Will you not tell me who told you so?

Bene. No, you shall pardon me. 131

Beat. Nor will you not tell me who you are?

Bene. Not now.

Beat. That I was disdainful, and that I had my good wit out of the 'Hundred Merry Tales:'—well, this was Signior Benedick that said so.

Bene. What's he?

Beat. I am sure you know him well enough.

Bene. Not I, believe me.

Beat. Did he never make you laugh? 140

Bene. I pray you, what is he?

Beat. Why, he is the prince's jester: a very dull fool; only his gift is in devising impossible slanders: none but libertines delight in him; and the commendation is not in his wit, but in his villany; for he both pleases men and angers them, and then they laugh at him and beat him. I am sure he is in the fleet: I would he had boarded me.

Bene. When I know the gentleman, I'll tell him what you say. 151

Beat. Do, do: he'll but break a comparison or two on me; which, peradventure not marked or not laughed at, strikes him into melancholy; and then there's a partridge wing saved, for the fool will eat no supper that night. [*Music.*] We must follow the leaders.

Bene. In every good thing.

Beat. Nay, if they lead to any ill, I will leave them at the next turning. 160

[*Dance. Then exeunt all except Don John, Borachio, and Claudio.*

D. John. Sure my brother is amorous on Hero and hath withdrawn her father to break with him about it. The ladies follow her and but one visor remains.

Bora. And that is Claudio: I know him by his bearing.

D. John. Are not you Signior Benedick?

Claud. You know me well; I am he. 168

D. John. Signior, you are very near my brother in his love: he is enamoured on Hero; I pray you, dissuade him from her: she is no equal for his birth: you may do the part of an honest man in it.

Claud. How know you he loves her?

D. John. I heard him swear his affection.

Bora. So did I too; and he swore he would marry her to-night.

D. John. Come, let us to the banquet.

[*Exeunt Don John and Borachio.*

Claud. Thus answer I in name of Benedick,
But hear these ill news with the ears of Claudio. 180
'Tis certain so; the prince wooes for himself.
Friendship is constant in all other things
Save in the office and affairs of love:
Therefore all hearts in love use their own tongues;
Let every eye negotiate for itself
And trust no agent; for beauty is a witch
Against whose charms faith melteth into blood.
This is an accident of hourly proof,
Which I mistrusted not. Farewell, therefore, Hero!

Re-enter BENEDICK.

Bene. Count Claudio? 190

Claud. Yea, the same.

Bene. Come, will you go with me?

Claud. Whither?

Bene. Even to the next willow, about your own business, county. What fashion will you wear the garland of? about your neck, like an usurer's chain? or under your arm, like a lieutenant's scarf? You must wear it one way, for the prince hath got your Hero.

Claud. I wish him joy of her. 200

Bene. Why, that's spoken like an honest drovier: so they sell bullocks. But did you think the prince would have served you thus?

Claud. I pray you, leave me.

Bene. Ho! now you strike like the blind man: 'twas the boy that stole your meat, and you'll beat the post.

Claud. If it will not be, I'll leave you. [*Exit.*

Bene. Alas, poor hurt fowl! now will he creep into sedges. But that my Lady Beatrice should know me,

104, 107, 109. **Balth.,** so Theobald; QF: *Bene.* 114. **clerk,** so addressed because of Balthasar's *Amen* in preceding speeches. He is giving responses like the parish clerk. 118. **At a word,** in short. 122. **do . . . ill-well,** imitate his imperfections so perfectly. 124. **dry hand,** a sign of age. **up and down,** all over, exactly. 128. **mum,** be silent. 135. **'Hundred Merry Tales,'** a popular collection of anecdotes published by Rastell in 1526; his point is that Beatrice borrows her wit from a book of stale jests, the Joe Miller of the day. 143. **only his gift,** his only talent. **impossible,** incredible. 148. **fleet,** crowd, company. 149. **boarded,** accosted, with a play on the usual meaning. 152. **break a comparison,** make a scornful simile, innuendo. 155-157. **there's . . . night,** sarcastic thrust at Benedick, whose appetite she has before referred to. 157. **leaders,** i.e., of the dance. 169. **near,** intimate with. 178. **banquet,** course of sweetmeats following the

regular repast; dessert. 181. **certain,** certainly. 187. **faith . . . blood,** honor gives way to passion. 188. **accident,** occurrence. 194. **willow,** emblem of disappointed love. 197. **usurer's chain.** Costly chains were worn by persons of the moneyed class. 202. **drovier,** cattle dealer. 205. **like the blind man,** an allusion to the romance of Lazarillo de Tormes, in which the hero steals his master's meat and revenges himself for the beating he receives by causing the blind man to jump against a stone pillar. 210. **creep into sedges,** i.e., as wounded ducks into rushes along the river. 215. **base, though bitter.** Yale editor paraphrases: Beatrice is base, i.e., unworthy, unjust, though her words have a sting (bitterness) which base criticisms do not usually possess. Johnson emends *though* to *the.* 216. **puts . . . person,** identifies the world with herself. 217. **gives me out,** represents me. 220. **Troth,** by my faith. 221. **Lady Fame,** Dame Rumor. 222. **lodge in a warren,** and not know me! The prince's fool! Ha? It may be I go under that title because I am merry. Yea, but so I am apt to do myself wrong; I am not so reputed: it is the base, though bitter, disposition of Beatrice that puts the world into her person, and so gives me out. Well, I'll be revenged as I may.

Re-enter DON PEDRO.

D. Pedro. Now, signior, where's the count? did you see him? 219

Bene. Troth, my lord, I have played the part of Lady Fame. I found him here as melancholy as a lodge in a warren: I told him, and I think I told him true, that your grace had got the good will of this young lady; and I offered him my company to a willow-tree, either to make him a garland, as being forsaken, or to bind him up a rod, as being worthy to be whipped.

D. Pedro. To be whipped! What's his fault?

Bene. The flat transgression of a school-boy, who, being overjoyed with finding a birds' nest, shows it his companion, and he steals it. 231

D. Pedro. Wilt thou make a trust a transgression? The transgression is in the stealer.

Bene. Yet it had not been amiss the rod had been made, and the garland too; for the garland he might have worn himself, and the rod he might have bestowed on you, who, as I take it, have stolen his birds' nest.

D. Pedro. I will but teach them to sing, and restore them to the owner. 240

Bene. If their singing answer your saying, by my faith, you say honestly.

D. Pedro. The Lady Beatrice hath a quarrel to you: the gentleman that danced with her told her she is much wronged by you. 245

Bene. O, she misused me past the endurance of a block! an oak but with one green leaf on it would have answered her; my very visor began to assume life and scold with her. She told me, not thinking I had been myself, that I was the prince's jester, that I was duller than a great thaw; huddling jest upon jest with such impossible conveyance upon me that I stood like a man at a mark, with a whole army shooting at me. She speaks poniards, and every word stabs: if her breath were as terrible as her terminations, there were no living near her; she would infect to the north star. I would not marry her, though she were endowed with all that Adam had left him before he transgressed: she would have made Hercules have turned spit, yea, and have cleft his club to make the fire too. Come, talk not of her: you shall find her the infernal Ate in good apparel. I would to God some scholar would conjure her; for certainly, while she is here, a man may live as quiet in hell as in a sanc-

tuary; and people sin upon purpose, because they would go thither; so, indeed, all disquiet, horror and perturbation follows her.

D. Pedro. Look, here she comes. 270

Re-enter CLAUDIO, BEATRICE, HERO, *and* LEONATO.

Bene. Will your grace command me any service to the world's end? I will go on the slightest errand now to the Antipodes that you can devise to send me on; I will fetch you a toothpicker now from the furthest inch of Asia, bring you the length of Prester John's foot, fetch you a hair off the great Cham's beard, do you any embassage to the Pigmies, rather than hold three words' conference with this harpy. You have no employment for me? 280

D. Pedro. None, but to desire your good company.

Bene. O God, sir, here's a dish I love not: I cannot endure my Lady Tongue. [*Exit.*

D. Pedro. Come, lady, come; you have lost the heart of Signior Benedick.

Beat. Indeed, my lord, he lent it me awhile; and I gave him use for it, a double heart for his single one: marry, once before he won it of me with false dice, therefore your grace may well say I have lost it. 291

D. Pedro. You have put him down, lady, you have put him down.

Beat. So I would not he should do me, my lord, lest I should prove the mother of fools. I have brought Count Claudio, whom you sent me to seek.

D. Pedro. Why, how now, count! wherefore are you sad?

Claud. Not sad, my lord. 300

D. Pedro. How then? sick?

Claud. Neither, my lord.

Beat. The count is neither sad, nor sick, nor merry, nor well; but civil count, civil as an orange, and something of that jealous complexion.

D. Pedro. I' faith, lady, I think your blazon to be true; though, I'll be sworn, if he be so, his conceit is false. Here, Claudio, I have wooed in thy name, and fair Hero is won: I have broke with her father, and his good will obtained: name the day of marriage, and God give thee joy! 312

Leon. Count, take of me my daughter, and with her my fortunes: his grace hath made the match, and all grace say Amen to it.

Beat. Speak, count, 'tis your cue.

Claud. Silence is the perfectest herald of joy: I were but little happy, if I could say how much. Lady, as you are mine, I am yours: I give away myself for you and dote upon the exchange. 320

Beat. Speak, cousin; or, if you cannot, stop his mouth with a kiss, and let not him speak neither.

D. Pedro. In faith, lady, you have a merry heart.

Beat. Yea, my lord; I thank it, poor fool, it keeps

gamekeeper's lodge in a game preserve. **227. bind . . . rod,** tie several willow switches into a scourge. **229. flat,** absolute, downright. **241. answer. . . saying,** correspond to what you say. **244. to,** with. **246. misused,** abused. **252. huddling,** piling, heaping up. **253. impossible,** extravagant, incredible. **conveyance,** trickery. **254. man at a mark,** man who stood by the target in archery to check off the arrows. **256. terminations,** terms, expressions. **258. north star,** supposed the most remote of stars. **261. Hercules . . . spit.** Omphale put Hercules to menial tasks about the house; turning the spit was the most menial of kitchen duties. **264. Ate,** goddess of mischief or of discord. **265. scholar . . . conjure.** Scholars were supposed to have the power to control evil spirits, which had to be addressed in Latin. **275. toothpicker,** toothpick. **276. Prester John's.** Prester John was a legendary Christian king of the Far East. **277. great Cham's,** of the khan of

Tartary. **279. Pigmies,** legendary small race which beset Hercules in his sleep (*Iliad,* Bk. iii); frequently mentioned during the Renaissance. **287-291. Indeed . . . lost it.** This seems an unquestionable allusion to an earlier flirtation between Benedick and Beatrice; such an episode might have appeared in an earlier version of the play. **288, 289. double, single.** The former word seems to imply that he had her heart as well as his own, with a possible pun on the meaning of "deceitful." (It was a deceitful heart that she gave him.) The latter word seems to pun on the meanings "sincere" and "unmarried." **292. put him down,** got the better of him. **304. civil count.** Some editors place a comma between these words. **civil,** serious, grave. **civil,** pun on Seville, whence oranges came. **305. jealous complexion.** Yellow, associated with melancholy, was the accepted symbol of jealousy. **307. blazon,** description. **315. all grace,** the source of grace, God.

on the windy side of care. My cousin tells him in his ear that he is in her heart.

Claud. And so she doth, cousin. 329

Beat. Good Lord, for alliance! Thus goes every one to the world but I, and I am sunburnt; I may sit in a corner and cry heigh-ho for a husband!

D. Pedro. Lady Beatrice, I will get you one.

Beat. I would rather have one of your father's getting. Hath your grace ne'er a brother like you? Your father got excellent husbands, if a maid could come by them.

D. Pedro. Will you have me, lady? 339

Beat. No, my lord, unless I might have another for working-days: your grace is too costly to wear every day. But, I beseech your grace, pardon me: I was born to speak all mirth and no matter.

D. Pedro. Your silence most offends me, and to be merry best becomes you; for, out of question, you were born in a merry hour.

Beat. No, sure, my lord, my mother cried; but then there was a star danced, and under that was I born. Cousins, God give you joy! 350

Leon. Niece, will you look to those things I told you of?

Beat. I cry you mercy, uncle. By your grace's pardon. [*Exit.*

D. Pedro. By my troth, a pleasant-spirited lady.

Leon. There's little of the melancholy element in her, my lord: she is never sad but when she sleeps, and not ever sad then; for I have heard my daughter say, she hath often dreamed of unhappiness and waked herself with laughing. 361

D. Pedro. She cannot endure to hear tell of a husband.

Leon. O, by no means: she mocks all her wooers out of suit.

D. Pedro. She were an excellent wife for Benedick.

Leon. O Lord, my lord, if they were but a week married, they would talk themselves mad.

D. Pedro. County Claudio, when mean you to go to church? 371

Claud. To-morrow, my lord: time goes on crutches till love have all his rites.

Leon. Not till Monday, my dear son, which is hence a just seven-night; and a time too brief, too, to have all things answer my mind.

D. Pedro. Come, you shake the head at so long a breathing: but, I warrant thee, Claudio, the time shall not go dully by us. I will in the interim undertake one of Hercules' labours; which is, to bring Signior Benedick and the Lady Beatrice into a mountain of affection the one with the other. I would fain have it a match, and I doubt not but to fashion it, if you three will but minister such assistance as I shall give you direction. 386

Leon. My lord, I am for you, though it cost me ten nights' watchings.

Claud. And I, my lord.

D. Pedro. And you too, gentle Hero?

Hero. I will do any modest office, my lord, to help my cousin to a good husband. 391

D. Pedro. And Benedick is not the unhopefullest husband that I know. Thus far can I praise him; he is of a noble strain, of approved valour and confirmed honesty. I will teach you how to humour your cousin, that she shall fall in love with Benedick; and I, with your two helps, will so practise on Benedick that, in despite of his quick wit and his queasy stomach, he shall fall in love with Beatrice. If we can do this, Cupid is no longer an archer: his glory shall be ours, for we are the only love-gods. Go in with me, and I will tell you my drift. [*Exeunt.* 403

SCENE II. *The same.*

Enter DON JOHN *and* BORACHIO.

D. John. It is so; the Count Claudio shall marry the daughter of Leonato.

Bora. Yea, my lord; but I can cross it.

D. John. Any bar, any cross, any impediment will be medicinable to me: I am sick in displeasure to him, and whatsoever comes athwart his affection ranges evenly with mine. How canst thou cross this marriage?

Bora. Not honestly, my lord; but so covertly that no dishonesty shall appear in me. 10

D. John. Show me briefly how.

Bora. I think I told your lordship a year since, how much I am in the favour of Margaret, the waiting gentlewoman to Hero.

D. John. I remember.

Bora. I can, at any unseasonable instant of the night, appoint her to look out at her lady's chamber-window.

D. John. What life is in that, to be the death of this marriage? 20

Bora. The poison of that lies in you to temper. Go you to the prince your brother; spare not to tell him that he hath wronged his honour in marrying the renowned Claudio—whose estimation do you mightily hold up—to a contaminated stale, such a one as Hero.

D. John. What proof shall I make of that?

Bora. Proof enough to misuse the prince, to vex Claudio, to undo Hero and kill Leonato. Look you for any other issue? 30

D. John. Only to despite them, I will endeavour any thing.

---

327. **windy,** safe, advantageous. 331. **goes . . . world,** i.e., gets married. 332. **sunburnt,** i.e., unattractive. 333. **heigh-ho . . . husband,** title of a ballad. 344. **matter,** substance, sense. 349. **star danced,** an allusion to the belief that the sun danced at Easter. 357. **melancholy element,** i.e., earth, associated with the humor of melancholy in the old physiology; see *element* in glossary. 359. **ever.** Most editors prefer the anonymous conjecture *even.* 361. **unhappiness,** misfortune. 365. **out of suit,** out of love, with play on the legal sense of "non-suiting." 375. **a just seven-night,** exactly a week. 378. **breathing,** pause, rest. 385. **minister,** furnish, supply. 387. **am for you,** accept your proposal. 395. **approved,** tested. **honesty,** honor. 400. **queasy stomach,** squeamish taste. 403. **drift,** purpose.
SCENE II. 1. **shall,** is going to. 5. **medicinable,** medicinal. 6. **displeasure,** dislike. 7. **whatsoever . . . mine,** whatever crosses his

inclination runs parallel with mine. **ranges,** lies in the same plane; see glossary. 21. **lies in,** rests with. **temper,** mix, compound. 25. **estimation,** worth. 26. **contaminated stale,** impure harlot. 28. **misuse,** abuse; deceive. 29. **vex,** afflict. 36. **intend,** pretend. 37. **as,** i.e., saying as follows. The words between the dashes are to be understood as instructions to Don John as to what he is to say. 39. **cozened,** deceived, cheated. **semblance,** semblance only, outward appearance. 40. **that you . . . thus.** New Cambridge editor suggests that this clause be placed after *as* in line 36. 44-45. **hear . . . Claudio.** Many editors follow Theobald and read *Borachio* for *Claudio.* The present reading may be defended if one imagines that, by arrangement with Margaret, Borachio is playing the part of Claudio. D. J. Gordon points out a similar confusion in Della Porta's *Gli Duoi Fratelli Rivalli.* 50. **jealousy,** suspicion. 51. **preparation,** i.e., for the marriage. 55. **ducats,**

Bora. Go, then; find me a meet hour to draw Don Pedro and the Count Claudio alone: tell them that you know that Hero loves me; intend a kind of zeal both to the prince and Claudio, as,—in love of your brother's honour, who hath made this match, and his friend's reputation, who is thus like to be cozened with the semblance of a maid,—that you have discovered thus. They will scarcely believe this without trial: offer them instances; which shall bear no less likelihood than to see me at her chamber-window, hear me †call Margaret Hero, hear Margaret term me Claudio; and bring them to see this the very night before the intended wedding,—for in the meantime I will so fashion the matter that Hero shall be absent,—and there shall appear such seeming truth of Hero's disloyalty that jealousy shall be called assurance and all the preparation overthrown. 51

D. John. Grow this to what adverse issue it can, I will put it in practice. Be cunning in the working this, and thy fee is a thousand ducats.

Bora. Be you constant in the accusation, and my cunning shall not shame me.

D. John. I will presently go learn their day of marriage. [*Exeunt.*

SCENE III. LEONATO'S *orchard.*

Enter BENEDICK.

Bene. Boy!

Enter Boy.

Boy. Signior?

Bene. In my chamber-window lies a book: bring it hither to me in the orchard.

Boy. I am here already, sir. 5

Bene. I know that; but I would have thee hence, and here again. [*Exit Boy.*] I do much wonder that one man, seeing how much another man is a fool when he dedicates his behaviours to love, will, after he hath laughed at such shallow follies in others, become the argument of his own scorn by falling in love: and such a man is Claudio. I have known when there was no music with him but the drum and the fife; and now had he rather hear the tabor and the pipe: I have known when he would have walked ten mile a-foot to see a good armour; and now will he lie ten nights awake, carving the fashion of a new doublet. He was wont to speak plain and to the purpose, like an honest man and a soldier; and now is he turned orthography; his words are a very fantastical banquet, just so many strange dishes. May I be so converted and see with these eyes? I cannot tell; I think not: I will not be sworn but love may transform me to an oyster; but I'll take my oath on it, till

he have made an oyster of me, he shall never make me such a fool. One woman is fair, yet I am well; another is wise, yet I am well; another virtuous, yet I am well; but till all graces be in one woman, one woman shall not come in my grace. Rich she shall be, that's certain; wise, or I'll none; virtuous, or I'll never cheapen her; fair, or I'll never look on her; mild, or come not near me; noble, or not I for an angel; of good discourse, an excellent musician, and her hair shall be of what colour it please God. Ha! the prince and Monsieur Love! I will hide me in the arbour. [*Withdraws.* 38

Enter DON PEDRO, CLAUDIO, *and* LEONATO.

D. Pedro. Come, shall we hear this music?

Claud. Yea, my good lord. How still the evening is, 40 As hush'd on purpose to grace harmony!

D. Pedro. See you where Benedick hath hid himself?

Claud. O, very well, my lord: the music ended, We'll fit the kid-fox with a pennyworth.

Enter BALTHASAR *with Music.*

D. Pedro. Come, Balthasar, we'll hear that song again.

Balth. O, good my lord, tax not so bad a voice To slander music any more than once.

D. Pedro. It is the witness still of excellency To put a strange face on his own perfection. I pray thee, sing, and let me woo no more. 50

Balth. Because you talk of wooing, I will sing; Since many a wooer doth commence his suit To her he thinks not worthy, yet he wooes, Yet will he swear he loves.

D. Pedro. Now, pray thee, come; Or, if thou wilt hold longer argument, Do it in notes.

Balth. Note this before my notes; There's not a note of mine that's worth the noting.

D. Pedro. Why, these are very crotchets that he speaks; Note, notes, forsooth, and nothing. [*Air.* 59

Bene. Now, divine air! now is his soul ravished! Is it not strange that sheeps' guts should hale souls out of men's bodies? Well, a horn for my money, when all's done.

The Song.

Balth. Sigh no more, ladies, sigh no more,
  Men were deceivers ever,
  One foot in sea and one on shore,
  To one thing constant never:
  Then sigh not so, but let them go,
  And be you blithe and bonny,
  Converting all your sounds of woe 70
  Into Hey nonny, nonny.

Italian coins worth about one dollar each.
SCENE III. 5. **here already,** i.e., he will be so quick as to use no time at all. 9. **behaviours,** details of behavior. 15. **tabor . . . pipe,** symbols of peaceful merriment. 17. **armour,** suit of armor. 18. **carving,** planning. 21. **orthography,** either abstract for concrete, or, as Rowe and many editors have it, an error for "orthographer." 33. **I'll none,** I'll have none. 34. **cheapen,** ask the price of, bid for. 35, 36. **noble, angel.** Each of these words involves a pun on the meaning "a coin," a *noble* being worth 6s. 8d. and an *angel*, 10s. 37-38. **of . . . God,** i.e., of any color whatever. Some editors see an allusion to the practice of dyeing the hair. 38. **I . . . arbour.** Note the freedom with which the characters in this play indulge in eavesdropping; it was probably less objectionable as a social practice in Shakespeare's day. *Stage Direction:* F: *Enter Prince, Leonato, Claudio, and Jacke Wilson;*

Q has *Musicke* for *and Jacke Wilson.* Wilson was evidently the actor who played Balthasar. 41. **grace harmony,** do honor to music. 44. **kidfox.** Cass suggests an allusion to Spenser's *Shepheardes Calender (Eclogue* v), to the story of the kid captured by the wily fox, seeing in Benedick's situation something both of the wily fox and the innocent kid; Warburton: *hid-fox;* Onions: *cub-fox.* **pennyworth,** i.e., his money's worth. 48-49. **It . . . perfection.** It is always a proof of excellence that, in demeanor, it is unconscious, or unknowing, of its own perfection (Furness). 50. **woo,** entreat. 56. **notes,** music. 58. **crotchets,** used with play on the meanings "whim" or "fancy," and "musical notes." 59. **Note,** knows not, pretends not to know. **nothing,** with play on "noting." It has been suggested that this same pun is concealed in the title of the play, where *Nothing* would suggest "noting," or eavesdropping. 61. **sheeps' guts,** fiddle-strings.

Sing no more ditties, sing no moe,
　Of dumps so dull and heavy;
The fraud of men was ever so,
　Since summer first was leavy:
　　Then sigh not so, &c.

D. Pedro. By my troth, a good song.

Balth. And an ill singer, my lord.

D. Pedro. Ha, no, no, faith; thou singest well enough for a shift. 80

Bene. An he had been a dog that should have howled thus, they would have hanged him: and I pray God his bad voice bode no mischief. I had as lief have heard the night-raven, come what plague could have come after it.

D. Pedro. Yea, marry, dost thou hear, Balthasar? I pray thee, get us some excellent music; for to-morrow night we would have it at the Lady Hero's chamber-window.

Balth. The best I can, my lord. 90

D. Pedro. Do so: farewell. [*Exit Balthasar.*] Come hither, Leonato. What was it you told me of to-day, that your niece Beatrice was in love with Signior Benedick?

Claud. O, ay: stalk on, stalk on; the fowl sits. I did never think that lady would have loved any man.

Leon. No, nor I neither; but most wonderful that she should so dote on Signior Benedick, whom she hath in all outward behaviours seemed ever to abhor.

Bene. Is 't possible? Sits the wind in that corner?

Leon. By my troth, my lord, I cannot tell what to think of it but that she loves him with an enraged affection; it is past the infinite of thought.

D. Pedro. May be she doth but counterfeit.

Claud. Faith, like enough.

Leon. O God, counterfeit! There was never counterfeit of passion came so near the life of passion as she discovers it. 111

D. Pedro. Why, what effects of passion shows she?

Claud. Bait the hook well; this fish will bite.

Leon. What effects, my lord? She will sit you, you heard my daughter tell you how.

Claud. She did, indeed.

D. Pedro. How, how, I pray you? You amaze me: I would have thought her spirit had been invincible against all assaults of affection. 120

Leon. I would have sworn it had, my lord; especially against Benedick.

Bene. I should think this a gull, but that the white-bearded fellow speaks it: knavery cannot, sure, hide himself in such reverence.

Claud. He hath ta'en the infection: hold it up.

D. Pedro. Hath she made her affection known to Benedick?

Leon. No; and swears she never will: that 's her torment. 130

Claud. 'Tis true, indeed; so your daughter says: 'Shall I,' says she, 'that have so oft encountered him with scorn, write to him that I love him?'

Leon. This says she now when she is beginning to write to him; for she'll be up twenty times a night, and there will she sit in her smock till she have writ

a sheet of paper: my daughter tells us all. 139

Claud. Now you talk of a sheet of paper, I remember a pretty jest your daughter told us of.

Leon. O, when she had writ it and was reading it over, she found Benedick and Beatrice between the sheet?

Claud. That.

Leon. O, she tore the letter into a thousand half-pence; railed at herself, that she should be so immodest to write to one that she knew would flout her; 'I measure him,' says she, 'by my own spirit; for I should flout him, if he writ to me; yea, though I love him, I should.' 151

Claud. Then down upon her knees she falls, weeps, sobs, beats her heart, tears her hair, prays, curses; 'O sweet Benedick! God give me patience!'

Leon. She doth indeed; my daughter says so: and the ecstasy hath so much overborne her that my daughter is sometime afeard she will do a desperate outrage to herself: it is very true.

D. Pedro. It were good that Benedick knew of it by some other, if she will not discover it. 161

Claud. To what end? He would make but a sport of it and torment the poor lady worse.

D. Pedro. An he should, it were an alms to hang him. She 's an excellent sweet lady; and, out of all suspicion, she is virtuous.

Claud. And she is exceeding wise.

D. Pedro. In every thing but in loving Benedick. 169

Leon. O, my lord, wisdom and blood combatting in so tender a body, we have ten proofs to one that blood hath the victory. I am sorry for her, as I have just cause, being her uncle and her guardian.

D. Pedro. I would she had bestowed this dotage on me: I would have daffed all other respects and made her half myself. I pray you, tell Benedick of it, and hear what a' will say.

Leon. Were it good, think you? 179

Claud. Hero thinks surely she will die; for she says she will die, if he love her not, and she will die, ere she make her love known, and she will die, if he woo her, rather than she will bate one breath of her accustomed crossness. 184

D. Pedro. She doth well: if she should make tender of her love, 'tis very possible he'll scorn it; for the man, as you know all, hath a contemptible spirit.

Claud. He is a very proper man.

D. Pedro. He hath indeed a good outward happiness. 191

Claud. Before God! and, in my mind, very wise.

D. Pedro. He doth indeed show some sparks that are like wit.

Claud. And I take him to be valiant.

D. Pedro. As Hector, I assure you: and in the managing of quarrels you may say he is wise; for either he avoids them with great discretion, or undertakes them with a most Christian-like fear. 200

Leon. If he do fear God, a' must necessarily keep peace: if he break the peace, he ought to enter into a quarrel with fear and trembling.

D. Pedro. And so will he do; for the man doth fear

---

84. **night-raven,** variously identified as the owl, the night-heron, and the bittern. 86. **Yea, marry,** a continuation of Don Pedro's speech preceding Benedick's aside. 95. **stalk . . . sits,** an allusion to the practice of hunting birds by means of a stalking-horse, i.e., a horse trained to the business, or an artificial structure resembling a horse. 123. **gull,** trick, deception. 126. **hold it up,** keep up the jest. 145. **That,** that

was it. 147. **halfpence,** very tiny, silver coins. 164. **alms,** good deed. 166. **out of,** beyond. 176. **daffed,** put or thrust aside. 177. **half myself,** i.e., my wife. 188. **contemptible,** contemptuous. 190. **outward happiness,** fortunate in his good looks. 194. **wit,** sense. 206. **large,** indelicate. 210. **counsel,** consultation, deliberation. 225. **no such matter,** the reality is quite otherwise. 229. **sadly borne,** gravely

God, howsoever it seems not in him by some large jests he will make. Well, I am sorry for your niece. Shall we go seek Benedick, and tell him of her love?

Claud. Never tell him, my lord: let her wear it out with good counsel.

Leon. Nay, that's impossible: she may wear her heart out first. 210

D. Pedro. Well, we will hear further of it by your daughter: let it cool the while. I love Benedick well; and I could wish he would modestly examine himself, to see how much he is unworthy so good a lady.

Leon. My lord, will you walk? dinner is ready.

Claud. If he do not dote on her upon this, I will never trust my expectation. 220

D. Pedro. Let there be the same net spread for her; and that must your daughter and her gentlewomen carry. The sport will be, when they hold one an opinion of another's dotage, and no such matter: that's the scene that I would see, which will be merely a dumb-show. Let us send her to call him in to dinner.

[*Exeunt Don Pedro, Claudio, and Leonato.*

Bene. [*Coming forward*] This can be no trick: the conference was sadly borne. They have the truth of this from Hero. They seem to pity the lady: it seems her affections have their full bent. Love me! why, it must be requited. I hear how I am censured: they say I will bear myself proudly, if I perceive the love come from her; they say too that she will rather die than give any sign of affection. I did never think to marry: I must not seem proud: happy are they that hear their detractions and can put them to mending. They say the lady is fair; 'tis a truth, I can bear them witness; and virtuous; 'tis so, I cannot reprove it; and wise, but for loving me; by my troth, it is no addition to her wit, nor no great argument of her folly, for I will be horribly in love with her. I may chance have some odd quirks and remnants of wit broken on me, because I have railed so long against marriage: but doth not the appetite alter? a man loves the meat in his youth that he cannot endure in his age. Shall quips and sentences and these paper bullets of the brain awe a man from the career of his humour? No, the world must be peopled. When I said I would die a bachelor, I did not think I should live till I were married. Here comes Beatrice. By this day! she's a fair lady: I do spy some marks of love in her.

Enter BEATRICE.

Beat. Against my will I am sent to bid you come in to dinner.

Bene. Fair Beatrice, I thank you for your pains.

Beat. I took no more pains for those thanks than you take pains to thank me: if it had been painful, I would not have come. 261

Bene. You take pleasure then in the message?

Beat. Yea, just so much as you may take upon a knife's point and choke a daw withal. You have no stomach, signior: fare you well. [*Exit.*

Bene. Ha! 'Against my will I am sent to bid you come in to dinner;' there's a double meaning in that.

'I took no more pains for those thanks than you took pains to thank me;' that's as much as to say, Any pains that I take for you is as easy as thanks. If I do not take pity of her, I am a villain; if I do not love her, I am a Jew. I will go get her picture. [*Exit.* 273

SCENE I. LEONATO's *garden.*

Enter HERO, MARGARET, *and* URSULA.

Hero. Good Margaret, run thee to the parlour;
There shalt thou find my cousin Beatrice
Proposing with the prince and Claudio:
Whisper her ear and tell her, I and Ursula
Walk in the orchard and our whole discourse
Is all of her; say that thou overheard'st us;
And bid her steal into the pleached bower,
Where honeysuckles, ripen'd by the sun,
Forbid the sun to enter, like favourites,
Made proud by princes, that advance their pride 10
Against that power that bred it: there will she hide her,
To listen our purpose. This is thy office;
Bear thee well in it and leave us alone.

Marg. I'll make her come, I warrant you, presently.
[*Exit.*

Hero. Now, Ursula, when Beatrice doth come,
As we do trace this alley up and down,
Our talk must only be of Benedick.
When I do name him, let it be thy part
To praise him more than ever man did merit:
My talk to thee must be how Benedick 20
Is sick in love with Beatrice. Of this matter
Is little Cupid's crafty arrow made,
That only wounds by hearsay.

Enter BEATRICE, *behind.*

                      Now begin;
For look where Beatrice, like a lapwing, runs
Close by the ground, to hear our conference.

Urs. The pleasant'st angling is to see the fish
Cut with her golden oars the silver stream,
And greedily devour the treacherous bait:
So angle we for Beatrice; who even now
Is couched in the woodbine coverture. 30
Fear you not my part of the dialogue.

Hero. Then go we near her, that her ear lose nothing
Of the false sweet bait that we lay for it.
[*Approaching the bower.*
No, truly, Ursula, she is too disdainful;
I know her spirits are as coy and wild
As haggerds of the rock.

Urs.   But are you sure
That Benedick loves Beatrice so entirely?

Hero. So says the prince and my new-trothed lord.

Urs. And did they bid you tell her of it, madam?

Hero. They did entreat me to acquaint her of it; 40
But I persuaded them, if they loved Benedick,
To wish him wrestle with affection,

---

conducted. **232. bent,** degree of tension and endurance. **238. put . . . mending,** profit by them. **241. reprove,** refute. **245. quirks,** witty conceits or jokes. **249. quips,** sharp or sarcastic remarks, **sentences,** saws, maxims. **paper bullets,** i.e., taken from books. **250. career of his humour,** pursuit of his inclination. **264. choke . . . withal.** i.e., make a mouthful for a jackdaw.

ACT III. SCENE I. **3. Proposing,** conversing. **8. honeysuckles,** identified with the woodbine. **12. purpose,** discourse, conversation. **23. only . . . hearsay,** wounds by mere report. **30. woodbine coverture,** bower, or arbor, of honeysuckle. **36. haggerds,** untrained female hawks.

And never to let Beatrice know of it.
   Urs. Why did you so? Doth not the gentleman
Deserve as full as fortunate a bed
As ever Beatrice shall couch upon?
   Hero. O god of love! I know he doth deserve
As much as may be yielded to a man:
But Nature never framed a woman's heart
Of prouder stuff than that of Beatrice;   50
Disdain and scorn ride sparkling in her eyes,
Misprising what they look on, and her wit
Values itself so highly that to her
All matter else seems weak: she cannot love,
Nor take no shape nor project of affection,
She is so self-endeared.
   Urs.   Sure, I think so;
And therefore certainly it were not good
She knew his love, lest she make sport at it.
   Hero. Why, you speak truth. I never yet saw man,
How wise, how noble, young, how rarely featured,   60
But she would spell him backward: if fair-faced,
She would swear the gentleman should be her sister;
If black, why, Nature, drawing of an antique,
Made a foul blot; if tall, a lance ill-headed;
If low, an agate very vilely cut;
If speaking, why, a vane blown with all winds;
If silent, why, a block moved with none.
So turns she every man the wrong side out
And never gives to truth and virtue that
Which simpleness and merit purchaseth.   70
   Urs. Sure, sure, such carping is not commendable.
   Hero. No, not to be so odd and from all fashions
As Beatrice is, cannot be commendable:
But who dare tell her so? If I should speak,
She would mock me into air; O, she would laugh me
Out of myself, press me to death with wit.
Therefore let Benedick, like cover'd fire,
Consume away in sighs, waste inwardly:
It were a better death than die with mocks,
Which is as bad as die with tickling.   80
   Urs. Yet tell her of it: hear what she will say.
   Hero. No; rather I will go to Benedick
And counsel him to fight against his passion.
And, truly, I'll devise some honest slanders
To stain my cousin with: one doth not know
How much an ill word may empoison liking.
   Urs. O, do not do your cousin such a wrong.
She cannot be so much without true judgement—
Having so swift and excellent a wit
As she is prized to have—as to refuse   90
So rare a gentleman as Signior Benedick.
   Hero. He is the only man of Italy,
Always excepted my dear Claudio.
   Urs. I pray you, be not angry with me, madam,
Speaking my fancy: Signior Benedick,
For shape, for bearing, argument and valour,
Goes foremost in report through Italy.
   Hero. Indeed, he hath an excellent good name.
   Urs. His excellence did earn it, ere he had it.

When are you married, madam?   100
   Hero. Why, every day, to-morrow. Come, go in:
I'll show thee some attires, and have thy counsel
Which is the best to furnish me to-morrow.
   Urs. She 's limed, I warrant you: we have caught
   her, madam.
   Hero. If it proves so, then loving goes by haps:
Some Cupid kills with arrows, some with traps.
            [Exeunt Hero and Ursula.
   Beat. [*Coming forward*] What fire is in mine ears? Can
   this be true?
Stand I condemn'd for pride and scorn so much?
Contempt, farewell! and maiden pride, adieu!
No glory lives behind the back of such.   110
And, Benedick, love on; I will requite thee,
Taming my wild heart to thy loving hand:
If thou dost love, my kindness shall incite thee
To bind our loves up in a holy band;
For others say thou dost deserve, and I
Believe it better than reportingly.   *[Exit.*

SCENE II. *A room in* LEONATO's *house.*

Enter DON PEDRO, CLAUDIO, BENEDICK, *and*
   LEONATO.

   D. Pedro. I do but stay till your marriage be consummate, and then go I toward Arragon.
   Claud. I'll bring you thither, my lord, if you'll
vouchsafe me.
   D. Pedro. Nay, that would be as great a soil in the
new gloss of your marriage as to show a child his new
coat and forbid him to wear it. I will only be bold
with Benedick for his company; for, from the crown
of his head to the sole of his foot, he is all mirth: he
hath twice or thrice cut Cupid's bow-string and the
little hangman dare not shoot at him; he hath a heart
as sound as a bell and his tongue is the clapper, for
what his heart thinks his tongue speaks.   14
   Bene. Gallants, I am not as I have been.
   Leon. So say I: methinks you are sadder.
   Claud. I hope he be in love.
   D. Pedro. Hang him, truant! there 's no true drop
of blood in him, to be truly touched with love: if he
be sad, he wants money.   20
   Bene. I have the toothache.
   D. Pedro. Draw it.
   Bene. Hang it!
   Claud. You must hang it first, and draw it after-
wards.
   D. Pedro. What! sigh for the toothache?
   Leon. Where is but a humour or a worm.
   Bene. Well, every one can master a grief but he that
has it.
   Claud. Yet say I, he is in love.   30
   D. Pedro. There is no appearance of fancy in him,
unless it be a fancy that he hath to strange disguises;
as, to be a Dutchman to-day, a Frenchman to-mor-

45. **as full as,** fully as; New Cambridge (following Boas): *at full.* 52. **Misprising,** undervaluing. 55. **project,** conception, idea. 56. **self-endeared,** full of self-love. 61. **spell him backward,** say the exactly contrary thing; a possible allusion to witches' prayers, which were said backward. 63. **black,** dark. **antique** (*antic*), buffoon. 65. **agate,** diminutive person; an allusion to the small figures cut in agate for rings. 70. **simpleness,** integrity, plainness. 72. **from,** different from. 78. **Consume . . . sighs,** an allusion to the belief that each sigh costs the heart a drop of blood. 84. **some honest slanders,** slanders which do not involve her virtue. 90. **prized,** estimated. 101. **every day,**

to-morrow, every day after tomorrow. 104. **limed,** caught, as a bird in birdlime. 105. **by haps,** by chance. 107. **What . . . ears,** an allusion to the old saying that a person's ears burn when he is being discussed in his absence. 110. **No . . . such.** No good is spoken of such persons when their backs are turned. 112. **Taming . . . hand,** figure derived from the taming of the hawk by the hand of the falconer. 116. **better than reportingly,** on better evidence than mere report.
SCENE II. 3. **bring,** escort. 11. **little hangman,** playfully applied to Cupid. 27. **Where . . . worm.** Toothache was ascribed to "humors" or unhealthy secretions and to actual worms in the teeth. 36. **slops,**

row, or in the shape of two countries at once, as, a German from the waist downward, all slops, and a Spaniard from the hip upward, no doublet. Unless he have a fancy to this foolery, as it appears he hath, he is no fool for fancy, as you would have it appear he is.

Claud. If he be not in love with some woman, there is no believing old signs: a' brushes his hat o' mornings; what should that bode? 42

D. Pedro. Hath any man seen him at the barber's?

Claud. No, but the barber's man hath been seen with him, and the old ornament of his cheek hath already stuffed tennis-balls.

Leon. Indeed, he looks younger than he did, by the loss of a beard.

D. Pedro. Nay, a' rubs himself with civet: can you smell him out by that? 51

Claud. That's as much as to say, the sweet youth's in love.

D. Pedro. The greatest note of it is his melancholy.

Claud. And when was he wont to wash his face?

D. Pedro. Yea, or to paint himself? for the which, I hear what they say of him.

Claud. Nay, but his jesting spirit; which is now crept into a lute-string and now governed by stops. 62

D. Pedro. Indeed, that tells a heavy tale for him: conclude, conclude he is in love.

Claud. Nay, but I know who loves him.

D. Pedro. That would I know too: I warrant, one that knows him not.

Claud. Yes, and his ill conditions; and, in despite of all, dies for him. 69

D. Pedro. She shall be buried with her face upwards.

Bene. Yet is this no charm for the toothache. Old signior, walk aside with me: I have studied eight or nine wise words to speak to you, which these hobbyhorses must not hear. [*Exeunt Benedick and Leonato.*

D. Pedro. For my life, to break with him about Beatrice.

Claud. 'Tis even so. Hero and Margaret have by this played their parts with Beatrice; and then the two bears will not bite one another when they meet. 81

Enter DON JOHN.

D. John. My lord and brother, God save you!

D. Pedro. Good den, brother.

D. John. If your leisure served, I would speak with you.

D. Pedro. In private?

D. John. If it please you: yet Count Claudio may hear; for what I would speak of concerns him.

D. Pedro. What's the matter? 90

D. John. [*To Claudio*] Means your lordship to be married to-morrow?

D. Pedro. You know he does.

D. John. I know not that, when he knows what I know.

Claud. If there be any impediment, I pray you discover it.

D. John. You may think I love you not: let that appear hereafter, and aim better at me by that I now will manifest. For my brother, I think he holds you well, and in dearness of heart hath holp to effect your ensuing marriage;—surely suit ill spent and labour ill bestowed. 103

D. Pedro. Why, what's the matter?

D. John. I came hither to tell you; and, circumstances shortened, for she has been too long a talking of, the lady is disloyal.

Claud. Who, Hero?

D. John. Even she; Leonato's Hero, your Hero, every man's Hero. 110

Claud. Disloyal?

D. John. The word is too good to paint out her wickedness; I could say she were worse: think you of a worse title, and I will fit her to it. Wonder not till further warrant: go but with me to-night, you shall see her chamber-window entered, even the night before her wedding-day: if you love her then, tomorrow wed her; but it would better fit your honour to change your mind.

Claud. May this be so? 120

D. Pedro. I will not think it.

D. John. If you dare not trust that you see, confess not that you know: if you will follow me, I will show you enough; and when you have seen more and heard more, proceed accordingly.

Claud. If I see any thing to-night why I should not marry her to-morrow, in the congregation, where I should wed, there will I shame her.

D. Pedro. And, as I wooed for thee to obtain her, I will join with thee to disgrace her. 130

D. John. I will disparage her no farther till you are my witnesses: bear it coldly but till midnight, and let the issue show itself.

D. Pedro. O day untowardly turned!

Claud. O mischief strangely thwarting!

D. John. O plague right well prevented! so will you say when you have seen the sequel. [*Exeunt.*

SCENE III. *A street.*

Enter DOGBERRY *and* VERGES *with the* Watch.

Dog. Are you good men and true?

Verg. Yea, or else it were pity but they should suffer salvation, body and soul.

Dog. Nay, that were a punishment too good for them, if they should have any allegiance in them, being chosen for the prince's watch.

Verg. Well, give them their charge, neighbour Dogberry.

Dog. First, who think you the most desartless man to be constable? 10

First Watch. Hugh Otecake, sir, or George Seacole; for they can write and read.

Dog. Come hither, neighbour Seacole. God hath

loose breeches. **37. no doublet,** in other words, "all cloak" (Malone). **46-47. old . . . tennis-balls.** Benedick's beard has gone to stuff tennis balls. **50. civet,** perfume derived from the civet cat. **56. wash,** i.e., with cosmetics. **61. now crept.** Boas: *new crept,* followed by New Cambridge. **62. stops,** frets on the finger board. **68. ill conditions,** bad qualities. **70-71. buried . . . upwards.** Suicides were sometimes buried with their faces downwards. Beatrice will not be responsible for her own death. **75. hobby-horses,** buffoons. **78. Margaret,** mistake for *Ursula.* **83. Good den,** good evening. **90. What's the matter.** Many editors give this speech to Claudio, a highly probable

conjecture. **99. aim better at,** judge better of. **101. holds you well,** i.e., thinks well of you. **106. circumstances shortened,** without unnecessary details. **107. a talking of,** under discussion. **112. paint out,** portray in full. **115. till further warrant,** till further proof appears. **134. untowardly turned,** perversely altered.

SCENE III. **3. salvation,** blunder for "damnation." **7. charge,** instructions. **9. desartless,** for "deserving."

blessed you with a good name: to be a well-favoured man is the gift of fortune; but to write and read comes by nature. 16

Sec. Watch. Both which, master constable,—

Dog. You have: I knew it would be your answer. Well, for your favour, sir, why, give God thanks, and make no boast of it; and for your writing and reading, let that appear when there is no need of such vanity. You are thought here to be the most senseless and fit man for the constable of the watch; therefore bear you the lantern. This is your charge: you shall comprehend all vagrom men; you are to bid any man stand, in the prince's name. 27

Sec. Watch. How if a' will not stand?

Dog. Why, then, take no note of him, but let him go; and presently call the rest of the watch together and thank God you are rid of a knave.

Verg. If he will not stand when he is bidden, he is none of the prince's subjects.

Dog. True, and they are to meddle with none but the prince's subjects. You shall also make no noise in the streets; for for the watch to babble and to talk is most tolerable and not to be endured.

Watch. We will rather sleep than talk: we know what belongs to a watch. 40

Dog. Why, you speak like an ancient and most quiet watchman; for I cannot see how sleeping should offend: only, have a care that your bills be not stolen. Well, you are to call at all the ale-houses, and bid those that are drunk get them to bed.

Watch. How if they will not?

Dog. Why, then, let them alone till they are sober: if they make you not then the better answer, you may say they are not the men you took them for. 51

Watch. Well, sir.

Dog. If you meet a thief, you may suspect him, by virtue of your office, to be no true man; and, for such kind of men, the less you meddle or make with them, why, the more is for your honesty.

Watch. If we know him to be a thief, shall we not lay hands on him? 58

Dog. Truly, by your office, you may; but I think they that touch pitch will be defiled: the most peaceable way for you, if you do take a thief, is to let him show himself what he is and steal out of your company.

Verg. You have been always called a merciful man, partner.

Dog. Truly, I would not hang a dog by my will, much more a man who hath any honesty in him.

Verg. If you hear a child cry in the night, you must call to the nurse and bid her still it. 70

Watch. How if the nurse be asleep and will not hear us?

Dog. Why, then, depart in peace, and let the child wake her with crying; for the ewe that will not hear her lamb when it baes will never answer a calf when he bleats.

Verg. 'Tis very true.

Dog. This is the end of the charge:—you, constable, are to present the prince's own person: if you meet the prince in the night, you may stay him. 81

Verg. Nay, by 'r lady, that I think a' cannot.

Dog. Five shillings to one on 't, with any man that knows the statues, he may stay him: marry, not without the prince be willing; for, indeed, the watch ought to offend no man; and it is an offence to stay a man against his will.

Verg. By 'r lady, I think it be so. 89

Dog. Ha, ah, ha! Well, masters, good night: an there be any matter of weight chances, call up me: keep your fellows' counsels and your own; and good night. Come, neighbour.

Watch. Well, masters, we hear our charge: let us go sit here upon the church-bench till two, and then all to bed.

Dog. One word more, honest neighbours. I pray you, watch about Signior Leonato's door; for the wedding being there to-morrow, there is a great coil to-night. Adieu: be vigitant, I beseech you. 101

[*Exeunt Dogberry and Verges.*

Enter BORACHIO *and* CONRADE.

Bora. What, Conrade!

Watch. [*Aside*] Peace! stir not.

Bora. Conrade, I say!

Con. Here, man; I am at thy elbow.

Bora. Mass, and my elbow itched; I thought there would a scab follow.

Con. I will owe thee an answer for that: and now forward with thy tale. 109

Bora. Stand thee close, then, under this pent-house, for it drizzles rain; and I will, like a true drunkard, utter all to thee.

Watch. [*Aside*] Some treason, masters: yet stand close.

Bora. Therefore know I have earned of Don John a thousand ducats. 116

Con. Is it possible that any villany should be so dear?

Bora. Thou shouldst rather ask if it were possible any villany should be so rich; for when rich villains have need of poor ones, poor ones may make what price they will.

Con. I wonder at it.

Bora. That shows thou art unconfirmed. Thou knowest that the fashion of a doublet, or a hat, or a cloak, is nothing to a man.

Con. Yes, it is apparel.

Bora. I mean, the fashion.

Con. Yes, the fashion is the fashion. 129

Bora. Tush! I may as well say the fool's the fool. But seest thou not what a deformed thief this fashion is?

Watch. [*Aside*] I know that Deformed; a' has been a vile thief this seven year; a' goes up and down like a gentleman: I remember his name. 136

Bora. Didst thou not hear somebody?

23. **senseless,** for "sensible." 25. **comprehend,** for "apprehend." **vagrom,** vagrant. 40. **belongs to,** are the duties of. 44. **bills,** kind of pike, an ax fixed to a long pole. 54. **true,** honest. 56. **meddle or make,** have to do. **is,** it is. 101. **vigitant,** for "vigilant." 106. **Mass,** by the Mass. 107. **scab,** scurvy fellow. 111. **pent-house,** overhanging roof. 124. **unconfirmed,** inexperienced. 126. **nothing to a man,** does not make the man. 131, 133. **deformed, Deformed.** The first occurrence carries the meaning "deforming"; the second is possibly an unexplained topical allusion. 143. **Pharaoh's soldiers,** possible allusion to some picture of the Israelites passing through the Red Sea. **reechy,** dirty, filthy. 144. **god Bel's priests,** with probable allusion to the story

of Bel and the Dragon, from the Apocryphal book of *Daniel,* depicted in a stained-glass window. 145. **shaven Hercules.** There is dispute among critics as to whether the reference is to Hercules disguised as a maiden in the service of Omphale, or to some picture of a shaven Hercules which had caught Shakespeare's eye. 147. **codpiece,** article of male attire indelicately conspicuous in this tapestry. 178. **right master constable,** comic title on the pattern of "right worshipful," etc. 179. **recovered,** for "discovered." 183. **lock,** lock of hair hanging down on the left shoulder; the lovelock. 189. **let . . . to,** for "obey us and." 190. **commodity,** goods acquired. 191. **taken up,** obtained on credit. **bills,** bonds given as security, and pikes. 192. **in question,**

Con. No; 'twas the vane on the house.

Bora. Seest thou not, I say, what a deformed thief this fashion is? how giddily a' turns about all the hot bloods between fourteen and five-and-thirty? sometimes fashioning them like Pharaoh's soldiers in the reechy painting, sometime like god Bel's priests in the old church-window, sometime like the shaven Hercules in the smirched worm-eaten tapestry, where his codpiece seems as massy as his club? 147

Con. All this I see; and I see that the fashion wears out more apparel than the man. But art not thou thyself giddy with the fashion too, that thou hast shifted out of thy tale into telling me of the fashion?

Bora. Not so, neither: but know that I have to-night wooed Margaret, the Lady Hero's gentlewoman, by the name of Hero: she leans me out at her mistress' chamber-window, bids me a thousand times good night,—I tell this tale vilely:—I should first tell thee how the prince, Claudio and my master, planted and placed and possessed by my master Don John, saw afar off in the orchard this amiable encounter. 161

Con. And thought they Margaret was Hero?

Bora. Two of them did, the prince and Claudio; but the devil my master knew she was Margaret; and partly by his oaths, which first possessed them, partly by the dark night, which did deceive them, but chiefly by my villany, which did confirm any slander that Don John had made, away went Claudio enraged; swore he would meet her, as he was appointed, next morning at the temple, and there, before the whole congregation, shame her with what he saw o'er night and send her home again without a husband.

First Watch. We charge you, in the prince's name, stand!

Sec. Watch. Call up the right master constable. We have here recovered the most dangerous piece of lechery that ever was known in the commonwealth. 181

First Watch. And one Deformed is one of them: I know him; a' wears a lock.

Con. Masters, masters,—

Sec. Watch. You'll be made bring Deformed forth, I warrant you.

Con. Masters,—

First Watch. Never speak: we charge you let us obey you to go with us. 189

Bora. We are like to prove a goodly commodity, being taken up of these men's bills.

Con. A commodity in question, I warrant you. Come, we'll obey you. [*Exeunt.*

SCENE IV. HERO's *apartment.*

Enter HERO, MARGARET, *and* URSULA.

Hero. Good Ursula, wake my cousin Beatrice, and desire her to rise.

Urs. I will, lady.

Hero. And bid her come hither.

Urs. Well. [*Exit.*

Marg. Troth, I think your other rabato were better.

Hero. No, pray thee, good Meg, I'll wear this.

Marg. By my troth, 's not so good; and I warrant your cousin will say so. 10

Hero. My cousin 's a fool, and thou art another: I'll wear none but this.

Marg. I like the new tire within excellently, if the hair were a thought browner; and your gown 's a most rare fashion, i' faith. I saw the Duchess of Milan's gown that they praise so. 16

Hero. O, that exceeds, they say.

Marg. By my troth, 's but a night-gown in respect of yours: cloth o' gold, and cuts, and laced with silver, set with pearls, down sleeves, side sleeves, and skirts, round underborne with a bluish tinsel: but for a fine, quaint, graceful and excellent fashion, yours is worth ten on 't.

Hero. God give me joy to wear it! for my heart is exceeding heavy.

Marg. 'Twill be heavier soon by the weight of a man.

Hero. Fie upon thee! art not ashamed? 28

Marg. Of what, lady? of speaking honourably? Is not marriage honourable in a beggar? Is not your lord honourable without marriage? I think you would have me say, 'saving your reverence, a husband:' an bad thinking do not wrest true speaking, I'll offend nobody: is there any harm in 'the heavier for a husband'? None, I think, an it be the right husband and the right wife; otherwise 'tis light, and not heavy: ask my Lady Beatrice else; here she comes.

Enter BEATRICE.

Hero. Good morrow, coz.

Beat. Good morrow, sweet Hero. 40

Hero. Why, how now? do you speak in the sick tune?

Beat. I am out of all other tune, methinks.

Marg. Clap 's into 'Light o' love;' that goes without a burden: do you sing it, and I'll dance it.

Beat. Ye light o' love, with your heels! then, if your husband have stables enough, you'll see he shall lack no barns.

Marg. O illegitimate construction! I scorn that with my heels. 51

Beat. 'Tis almost five o'clock, cousin; 'tis time you were ready. By my troth, I am exceeding ill: heigh-ho!

Marg. For a hawk, a horse, or a husband?

Beat. For the letter that begins them all, H.

Marg. Well, an you be not turned Turk, there 's no more sailing by the star.

Beat. What means the fool, trow?

Marg. Nothing I; but God send every one their heart's desire! 61

Much Ado about Nothing
ACT III : SC IV

547

---

questionable, and about to be tried under the law.
SCENE IV. 6. **rabato,** either a ruff or collar band, or the wires which held it in place. 9. **troth, 's,** faith, it is. 13. **tire within,** headdress in the inner room, or inner trimming of hair upon the headdress. 17. **exceeds,** excels. 18. **night-gown,** dressing gown. 19. **in respect of,** compared to. **cuts,** slashes in a garment. 20. **laced,** trimmed. 20-22. **set . . . tinsel.** R. G. White explained *down sleeves* as tight-fitting sleeves to the wrist, and *side sleeves* as secondary ornamental sleeves hanging from the shoulder. Other editors, following Capell, explain that the pearls were set down the sleeves and the skirt, and were stitched on to strips of blue tinsel to set them off, *round* implying

that the pearls encircled the sleeves and skirts in a series of rings. By the other interpretation *underborne* would mean "with a lining or undergarment of tinsel." 33. **'saving . . . husband.'** Margaret pretends to beg Hero's pardon for even mentioning a husband. 34. **wrest,** misinterpret. 37. **light,** a pun on the meaning "wanton." 42. **sick tune,** tone of a sick person. 44. **'Light o' love,'** a popular song. 45. **burden,** bass accompaniment. 49. **barns,** with pun on "bairns," children. 51. **with my heels,** explained as a proverbial expression of scorn. 56. **H,** pun on "ache," pronounced "aitch." 57. **turned Turk,** proverbial for "changed completely." 58. **star,** polestar.

Hero. These gloves the count sent me; they are an excellent perfume.

Beat. I am stuffed, cousin; I cannot smell.

Marg. A maid, and stuffed! there's goodly catching of cold.

Beat. O, God help me! God help me! how long have you professed apprehension?

Marg. Ever since you left it. Doth not my wit become me rarely? 70

Beat. It is not seen enough, you should wear it in your cap. By my troth, I am sick.

Marg. Get you some of this distilled Carduus Benedictus, and lay it to your heart: it is the only thing for a qualm.

Hero. There thou prickest her with a thistle.

Beat. Benedictus! why Benedictus? you have some moral in this Benedictus. 78

Marg. Moral! no, by my troth, I have no moral meaning; I meant, plain holy-thistle. You may think perchance that I think you are in love: nay, by 'r lady, I am not such a fool to think what I list, nor I list not to think what I can, nor indeed I cannot think, if I would think my heart out of thinking, that you are in love or that you will be in love or that you can be in love. Yet Benedick was such another, and now is he become a man: he swore he would never marry, and yet now, in despite of his heart, he eats his meat without grudging: and how you may be converted I know not, but methinks you look with your eyes as other women do.

Beat. What pace is this that thy tongue keeps?

Marg. Not a false gallop. 94

Re-enter URSULA.

Urs. Madam, withdraw: the prince, the count, Signior Benedick, Don John, and all the gallants of the town, are come to fetch you to church.

Hero. Help to dress me, good coz, good Meg, good Ursula. [*Exeunt.*

SCENE V. *Another room in* LEONATO'S *house.*

Enter LEONATO, *with* DOGBERRY *and* VERGES.

Leon. What would you with me, honest neighbour?

Dog. Marry, sir, I would have some confidence with you that decerns you nearly.

Leon. Brief, I pray you; for you see it is a busy time with me.

Dog. Marry, this it is, sir.

Verg. Yes, in truth it is, sir.

Leon. What is it, my good friends? 9

Dog. Goodman Verges, sir, speaks a little off the matter: an old man, sir, and his wits are not so blunt as, God help, I would desire they were; but, in faith, honest as the skin between his brows.

Verg. Yes, I thank God I am as honest as any man living that is an old man and no honester than I.

Dog. Comparisons are odorous: palabras, neighbour Verges.

Leon. Neighbours, you are tedious. 20

Dog. It pleases your worship to say so, but we are the poor duke's officers; but truly, for mine own part, if I were as tedious as a king, I could find it in my heart to bestow it all of your worship.

Leon. All thy tediousness on me, ah?

Dog. Yea, an 'twere a thousand pound more than 'tis; for I hear as good exclamation on your worship as of any man in the city; and though I be but a poor man, I am glad to hear it. 30

Verg. And so am I.

Leon. I would fain know what you have to say.

Verg. Marry, sir, our watch to-night, excepting your worship's presence, ha' ta'en a couple of as arrant knaves as any in Messina.

Dog. A good old man, sir; he will be talking: as they say, When the age is in, the wit is out: God help us! it is a world to see. Well said, i' faith, neighbour Verges: well, God's a good man; an two men ride of a horse, one must ride behind. An honest soul, i' faith, sir; by my troth he is, as ever broke bread; but God is to be worshipped; all men are not alike; alas, good neighbour!

Leon. Indeed, neighbour, he comes too short of you.

Dog. Gifts that God gives.

Leon. I must leave you. 48

Dog. One word, sir: our watch, sir, have indeed comprehended two aspicious persons, and we would have them this morning examined before your worship.

Leon. Take their examination yourself and bring it me: I am now in great haste, as it may appear unto you.

Dog. It shall be suffigance.

Leon. Drink some wine ere you go: fare you well.

Enter a Messenger.

Mess. My lord, they stay for you to give your daughter to her husband. 60

Leon. I'll wait upon them: I am ready.

[*Exeunt Leonato and Messenger.*

Dog. Go, good partner, go, get you to Francis Seacole; bid him bring his pen and inkhorn to the gaol: we are now to examination these men.

Verg. And we must do it wisely.

Dog. We will spare for no wit, I warrant you; here's that shall drive some of them to a noncome: only get the learned writer to set down our excommunication and meet me at the gaol. [*Exeunt.*

ACT IV.

SCENE I. *A church.*

Enter DON PEDRO, DON JOHN, LEONATO, FRIAR FRANCIS, CLAUDIO, BENEDICK, HERO, BEATRICE, *and attendants.*

---

64. **stuffed,** afflicted with a cold. 68. **apprehension,** wit. 72. **wear . . . cap,** i.e., as a fool does his coxcomb. 73. **Carduus Benedictus,** the blessed thistle, noted for medicinal properties. 78. **moral,** hidden meaning. 90. **eats . . . grudging,** has a normal appetite. 94. **false gallop,** canter.
SCENE V. 3. **confidence,** possibly misused for "conference." 4. **decerns,** for "concerns." 10. **Goodman,** title of persons under the social rank of gentleman. 13-14. **honest . . . brows,** proverbial expression of

honesty, the brow being regarded as an open book. 18. **odorous,** for "odious." **palabras,** for *pocas palabras,* few words. 22. **poor duke's officers,** for "the duke's poor officers." 28. **exclamation,** possibly for "acclamation." 34. **to-night,** last night. 38. **When . . . out,** adaptation of the proverb: "When ale is in, wit is out." 39. **a world,** wonderful. 40-41. **God's . . . man,** a proverbial saying. 50. **aspicious,** for "suspicious." 56. **suffigance,** for "sufficient." 61. **wait upon,** attend. 68. **noncome,** usually taken as contraction for *non compos mentis* (not of

Leon. Come, Friar Francis, be brief; only to the plain form of marriage, and you shall recount their particular duties afterwards.

Friar. You come hither, my lord, to marry this lady.

Claud. No.

Leon. To be married to her: friar, you come to marry her.

Friar. Lady, you come hither to be married to this count. 10

Hero. I do.

Friar. If either of you know any inward impediment why you should not be conjoined, I charge you, on your souls, to utter it.

Claud. Know you any, Hero?

Hero. None, my lord.

Friar. Know you any, count?

Leon. I dare make his answer, none.

Claud. O, what men dare do! what men may do! what men daily do, not knowing what they do! 21

Bene. How now! interjections? Why, then, some be of laughing, as, ah, ha, he!

Claud. Stand thee by, friar. Father, by your leave:
Will you with free and unconstrained soul
Give me this maid, your daughter?

Leon. As freely, son, as God did give her me.

Claud. And what have I to give you back, whose worth
May counterpoise this rich and precious gift?

D. Pedro. Nothing, unless you render her again. 30

Claud. Sweet prince, you learn me noble thankfulness.
There, Leonato, take her back again:
Give not this rotten orange to your friend;
She 's but the sign and semblance of her honour.
Behold how like a maid she blushes here!
O, what authority and show of truth
Can cunning sin cover itself withal!
Comes not that blood as modest evidence
To witness simple virtue? Would you not swear,
All you that see her, that she were a maid, 40
By these exterior shows? But she is none:
She knows the heat of a luxurious bed;
Her blush is guiltiness, not modesty.

Leon. What do you mean, my lord?

Claud. Not to be married,
Not to knit my soul to an approved wanton.

Leon. Dear my lord, if you, in your own proof,
Have vanquish'd the resistance of her youth,
And made defeat of her virginity,—

Claud. I know what you would say: if I have known her,
You will say she did embrace me as a husband, 50
And so extenuate the 'forehand sin:
No, Leonato,
I never tempted her with word too large;
But, as a brother to his sister, show'd
Bashful sincerity and comely love.

Hero. And seem'd I ever otherwise to you?

Claud. Out on thee! Seeming! I will write against it:

You seem to me as Dian in her orb,
As chaste as is the bud ere it be blown;
But you are more intemperate in your blood 60
Than Venus, or those pamper'd animals
That rage in savage sensuality.

Hero. Is my lord well, that he doth speak so wide?

Leon. Sweet prince, why speak not you?

D. Pedro. What should I speak?
I stand dishonour'd, that have gone about
To link my dear friend to a common stale.

Leon. Are these things spoken, or do I but dream?

D. John. Sir, they are spoken, and these things are true.

Bene. This looks not like a nuptial.

Hero. True! O God!

Claud. Leonato, stand I here? 70
Is this the prince? is this the prince's brother?
Is this face Hero's? are our eyes our own?

Leon. All this is so: but what of this, my lord?

Claud. Let me but move one question to your daughter;
And, by that fatherly and kindly power
That you have in her, bid her answer truly.

Leon. I charge thee do so, as thou art my child.

Hero. O, God defend me! how am I beset!
What kind of catechising call you this?

Claud. To make you answer truly to your name. 80

Hero. Is it not Hero? Who can blot that name
With any just reproach?

Claud. Marry, that can Hero;
Hero itself can blot out Hero's virtue.
What man was he talk'd with you yesternight
Out at your window betwixt twelve and one?
Now, if you are a maid, answer to this.

Hero. I talk'd with no man at that hour, my lord.

D. Pedro. Why, then are you no maiden. Leonato,
I am sorry you must hear: upon mine honour,
Myself, my brother and this grieved count 90
Did see her, hear her, at that hour last night
Talk with a ruffian at her chamber-window;
Who hath indeed, most like a liberal villain,
Confess'd the vile encounters they have had
A thousand times in secret.

D. John. Fie, fie! they are not to be named, my lord,
Not to be spoke of;
There is not chastity enough in language
Without offence to utter them. Thus, pretty lady,
I am sorry for thy much misgovernment. 100

Claud. O Hero, what a Hero hadst thou been,
If half thy outward graces had been placed
About thy thoughts and counsels of thy heart!
But fare thee well, most foul, most fair! farewell,
Thou pure impiety and impious purity!
For thee I'll lock up all the gates of love,
And on my eyelids shall conjecture hang,
To turn all beauty into thoughts of harm,
And never shall it more be gracious.

Leon. Hath no man's dagger here a point for me? 110
[*Hero swoons.*

sound mind), but perhaps intended as a substitute for "nonplus." 69. **excommunication,** for "examination" or "communication."

ACT IV. SCENE I. 22. **interjections.** Benedick seems to be reminded, by Claudio's strained manner of utterance, of interjections, and proceeds to recite a tag from the current Latin grammars, *some . . . he.* 29. **counterpoise,** balance, be equivalent to. 36. **authority,** authenticity. 38. **modest evidence,** evidence of modesty. 42. **luxurious,** lascivious, lustful. 45. **approved,** convicted. 46. **in . . . proof,** in making trial

of her yourself (Wright). 51. **extenuate,** excuse, lessen. **'forehand sin,** sin of anticipating (marriage). 58. **Dian . . . orb,** Diana, goddess of chastity, enthroned in the moon. 63. **wide,** wide of the mark. 69. **True,** a reply to Don John's speech. 83. **Hero itself,** the name Hero. 100. **misgovernment,** evil conduct. 105. **pure . . . purity.** Note the oxymoron, i.e., association of words of contradictory senses. 107. **conjecture,** evil suspicion. 109. **gracious,** attractive, graceful.

Beat. Why, how now, cousin! wherefore sink you
   down?
D. John. Come, let us go. These things, come thus to
   light,
Smother her spirits up.
                  [*Exeunt Don Pedro, Don John, and Claudio.*
   Bene. How doth the lady?
   Beat.   Dead, I think. Help, uncle!
Hero! why, Hero! Uncle! Signior Benedick! Friar!
   Leon. O Fate! take not away thy heavy hand.
Death is the fairest cover for her shame
That may be wish'd for.
   Beat.   How now, cousin Hero!
   Friar. Have comfort, lady.
   Leon. Dost thou look up?   120
   Friar. Yea, wherefore should she not?
   Leon. Wherefore! Why, doth not every earthly
   thing
Cry shame upon her? Could she here deny
The story that is printed in her blood?
Do not live, Hero; do not ope thine eyes:
For, did I think thou wouldst not quickly die,
Thought I thy spirits were stronger than thy
   shames,
Myself would, on the rearward of reproaches,
Strike at thy life. Grieved I, I had but one?
Chid I for that at frugal nature's frame?   130
O, one too much by thee! Why had I one?
Why ever wast thou lovely in my eyes?
Why had I not with charitable hand
Took up a beggar's issue at my gates,
Who smirched thus and mired with infamy,
I might have said 'No part of it is mine;
This shame derives itself from unknown loins'?
But mine and mine I loved and mine I praised
And mine that I was proud on, mine so much
That I myself was to myself not mine,   140
Valuing of her,—why, she, O, she is fallen
Into a pit of ink, that the wide sea
Hath drops too few to wash her clean again
And salt too little which may season give
To her foul-tainted flesh!
   Bene.   Sir, sir, be patient.
For my part, I am so attired in wonder,
I know not what to say.
   Beat. O, on my soul, my cousin is belied!
   Bene. Lady, were you her bedfellow last night?
   Beat. No, truly not; although, until last night,   150
I have this twelvemonth been her bedfellow.
   Leon. Confirm'd, confirm'd! O, that is stronger
   made
Which was before barr'd up with ribs of iron!
Would the two princes lie, and Claudio lie,
Who loved her so, that, speaking of her foulness,
Wash'd it with tears? Hence from her! let her die.
   Friar. Hear me a little; for I have only been
Silent so long and given way unto
†This course of fortune . . .
By noting of the lady I have mark'd   160
A thousand blushing apparitions

To start into her face, a thousand innocent shames
In angel whiteness beat away those blushes;
And in her eye there hath appear'd a fire,
To burn the errors that these princes hold
Against her maiden truth. Call me a fool;
Trust not my reading nor my observations,
Which with experimental seal doth warrant
The tenour of my book; trust not my age,
My reverence, calling, nor divinity,   170
If this sweet lady lie not guiltless here
Under some biting error.
   Leon.   Friar, it cannot be.
Thou seest that all the grace that she hath left
Is that she will not add to her damnation
A sin of perjury; she not denies it:
Why seek'st thou then to cover with excuse
That which appears in proper nakedness?
   Friar. Lady, what man is he you are accused of?
   Hero. They know that do accuse me; I know none:
If I know more of any man alive   180
Than that which maiden modesty doth warrant,
Let all my sins lack mercy! O my father,
Prove you that any man with me conversed
At hours unmeet, or that I yesternight
Maintain'd the change of words with any creature,
Refuse me, hate me, torture me to death!
   Friar. There is some strange misprision in the
   princes.
   Bene. Two of them have the very bent of honour;
And if their wisdoms be misled in this,
The practice of it lives in John the bastard,   190
Whose spirits toil in frame of villanies.
   Leon. I know not. If they speak but truth of her,
These hands shall tear her; if they wrong her honour
The proudest of them shall well hear of it.
Time hath not yet so dried this blood of mine,
Nor age so eat up my invention,
Nor fortune made such havoc of my means,
Nor my bad life reft me so much of friends,
But they shall find, awaked in such a kind,
Both strength of limb and policy of mind,   200
Ability in means and choice of friends,
To quit me of them throughly.
   Friar.   Pause awhile,
And let my counsel sway you in this case.
Your daughter here the princes left for dead:
Let her awhile be secretly kept in,
And publish it that she is dead indeed;
Maintain a mourning ostentation
And on your family's old monument
Hang mournful epitaphs and do all rites
That appertain unto a burial.   210
   Leon. What shall become of this? what will this
   do?
   Friar. Marry, this well carried shall on her behalf
Change slander to remorse; that is some good:
But not for that dream I on this strange course,
But on this travail look for greater birth.
She dying, as it must be so maintain'd,
Upon the instant that she was accused,

Much Ado about Nothing
ACT IV : SC I

550

124. **blood,** blushes. 130. **frame,** established order. 140. **That . . . mine,** she was so much a part of me that by comparison I was not myself (Yale). 141. **Valuing,** when establishing the value. 144. **season,** preservative. 157-159. Text corrupt; New Cambridge omits *for . . . fortune.* 164-165. **a fire . . . burn,** an allusion to the burning of heretics. 168. **experimental seal,** stamp of experience. 169. **tenour . . . book,** what he has learned from reading. 187. **misprision,** mistake, mis-understanding. 188. **bent,** inclination of the mind. 191. **frame,** contriving. 225. **upon,** in consequence of. 227. **study of imagination,** musing, imaginative contemplation. 228. **every . . . life,** every feature of her lovely life. 231. **prospect,** range of vision. 233. **liver,** the supposed seat of the passion of love. 239. **But . . . false,** if every other aim miscarry. 242. **sort,** turn out. 245. **injuries,** insults. 247. **inwardness,** close friendship. 251. **Being that,** seeing that, since. **flow**

Shall be lamented, pitied and excused
Of every hearer: for it so falls out
That what we have we prize not to the worth 220
Whiles we enjoy it, but being lack'd and lost,
Why, then we rack the value, then we find
The virtue that possession would not show us
Whiles it was ours. So will it fare with Claudio:
When he shall hear she died upon his words,
The idea of her life shall sweetly creep
Into his study of imagination,
And every lovely organ of her life
Shall come apparell'd in more precious habit,
More moving-delicate and full of life, 230
Into the eye and prospect of his soul,
Than when she lived indeed; then shall he mourn,
If ever love had interest in his liver,
And wish he had not so accused her,
No, though he thought his accusation true.
Let this be so, and doubt not but success
Will fashion the event in better shape
Than I can lay it down in likelihood.
But if all aim but this be levell'd false,
The supposition of the lady's death 240
Will quench the wonder of her infamy:
And if it sort not well, you may conceal her,
As best befits her wounded reputation,
In some reclusive and religious life,
Out of all eyes, tongues, minds and injuries.
  Bene. Signior Leonato, let the friar advise you:
And though you know my inwardness and love
Is very much unto the prince and Claudio,
Yet, by mine honour, I will deal in this
As secretly and justly as your soul 250
Should with your body.
  Leon.   Being that I flow in grief,
The smallest twine may lead me.
  Friar. 'Tis well consented: presently away;
For to strange sores strangely they strain the cure.
Come, lady, die to live: this wedding-day
  Perhaps is but prolong'd: have patience and
    endure.   *[Exeunt all but Benedick and Beatrice.*
  Bene. Lady Beatrice, have you wept all this while?
  Beat. Yea, and I will weep a while longer.
  Bene. I will not desire that.
  Beat. You have no reason; I do it freely. 260
  Bene. Surely I do believe your fair cousin is wronged.
  Beat. Ah, how much might the man deserve of me
that would right her!
  Bene. Is there any way to show such friendship?
  Beat. A very even way, but no such friend.
  Bene. May a man do it?
  Beat. It is a man's office, but not yours.
  Bene. I do love nothing in the world so well as you:
is not that strange? 270
  Beat. As strange as the thing I know not. It were as
possible for me to say I love nothing so well as you:
but believe me not; and yet I lie not; I confess nothing,
nor I deny nothing. I am sorry for my cousin.
  Bene. By my sword, Beatrice, thou lovest me.
  Beat. Do not swear, and eat it.

  Bene. I will swear by it that you love me; and I will
make him eat it that says I love not you.
  Beat. Will you not eat your word? 280
  Bene. With no sauce that can be devised to it. I pro-
test I love thee.
  Beat. Why, then, God forgive me!
  Bene. What offence, sweet Beatrice?
  Beat. You have stayed me in a happy hour: I was
about to protest I loved you.
  Bene. And do it with all thy heart.
  Beat. I love you with so much of my heart that none
is left to protest.
  Bene. Come, bid me do any thing for thee. 290
  Beat. Kill Claudio.
  Bene. Ha! not for the wide world.
  Beat. You kill me to deny it. Farewell.
  Bene. Tarry, sweet Beatrice.
  Beat. I am gone, though I am here: there is no love
in you: nay, I pray you, let me go.
  Bene. Beatrice,—
  Beat. In faith, I will go.
  Bene. We'll be friends first.
  Beat. You dare easier be friends with me than fight
with mine enemy. 301
  Bene. Is Claudio thine enemy?
  Beat. Is he not approved in the height a villain, that
hath slandered, scorned, dishonoured my kinswoman?
O that I were a man! What, bear her in hand until
they come to take hands; and then, with public ac-
cusation, uncovered slander, unmitigated rancour,—
O God, that I were a man! I would eat his heart in
the market-place.
  Bene. Hear me, Beatrice,— 310
  Beat. Talk with a man out at a window! A proper
saying!
  Bene. Nay, but, Beatrice,—
  Beat. Sweet Hero! She is wronged, she is slandered,
she is undone.
  Bene. Beat— 316
  Beat. Princes and counties! Surely, a princely testimony, a goodly count, Count Comfect; a sweet gallant, surely! O that I were a man for his sake! or that
I had any friend would be a man for my sake! But
manhood is melted into courtesies, valour into compli-
ment, and men are only turned into tongue, and trim
ones too: he is now as valiant as Hercules that only
tells a lie and swears it. I cannot be a man with wishing, therefore I will die a woman with grieving.
  Bene. Tarry, good Beatrice. By this hand, I love thee.
  Beat. Use it for my love some other way than swearing by it. 330
  Bene. Think you in your soul the Count Claudio
hath wronged Hero?
  Beat. Yea, as sure as I have a thought or a soul.
  Bene. Enough, I am engaged; I will challenge him.
I will kiss your hand, and so I leave you. By this hand,
Claudio shall render me a dear account. As you hear
of me, so think of me. Go, comfort your cousin: I
must say she is dead: and so, farewell.   *[Exeunt.*

*Much Ado
about Nothing*
ACT IV : SC I

55I

---

in, overflow with.   254. **For . . . cure,** strange diseases require strange
and desperate cures.   256. **prolong'd,** deferred, put off.   285. **in a
happy hour,** at an appropriate moment.   291. **Kill Claudio.** This is a
famous climax in both character and plot.   295. **gone,** i.e., in spirit.
303. **in the height,** in the extreme.   306. **bear her in hand,** delude with
false hopes.   308. **uncovered,** open, unconcealed.   317. **counties,**
counts.   318. **count,** play on the title and the meaning, "declaration

of complaint in an indictment."   **Comfect,** comfit, sweetmeat.   323.
trim, nice (used ironically).   334. **Enough . . . engaged.** It is, of course,
the deeper issue over Hero's wrongs which brings Beatrice and Benedick
together and not the absurd trick that had been played on them.
336. **this hand,** i.e., Beatrice's hand.

SCENE II. *A prison.*

Enter DOGBERRY, VERGES, *and* Sexton, *in gowns; and the* Watch, *with* CONRADE *and* BORACHIO.

Dog. Is our whole dissembly appeared?

Verg. O, a stool and a cushion for the sexton.

Sex. Which be the malefactors?

Dog. Marry, that am I and my partner.

Verg. Nay, that 's certain; we have the exhibition to examine.

Sex. But which are the offenders that are to be examined? let them come before master constable.

Dog. Yea, marry, let them come before me. What is your name, friend? 11

Bora. Borachio.

Dog. Pray, write down, Borachio. Yours, sirrah?

Con. I am a gentleman, sir, and my name is Conrade.

Dog. Write down, master gentleman Conrade. Masters, do you serve God?

Con. ⎫
Bora. ⎬ Yea, sir, we hope. 19

Dog. Write down, that they hope they serve God: and write God first; for God defend but God should go before such villains! Masters, it is proved already that you are little better than false knaves; and it will go near to be thought so shortly. How answer you for yourselves?

Con. Marry, sir, we say we are none.

Dog. A marvellous witty fellow, I assure you; but I will go about with him. Come you hither, sirrah; a word in your ear: sir, I say to you, it is thought you are false knaves. 30

Bora. Sir, I say to you we are none.

Dog. Well, stand aside. 'Fore God, they are both in a tale. Have you writ down, that they are none?

Sex. Master constable, you go not the way to examine: you must call forth the watch that are their accusers.

Dog. Yea, marry, that 's the eftest way. Let the watch come forth. Masters, I charge you, in the prince's name, accuse these men. 40

First Watch. This man said, sir, that Don John, the prince's brother, was a villain.

Dog. Write down Prince John a villain. Why, this is flat perjury, to call a prince's brother villain.

Bora. Master constable,—

Dog. Pray thee, fellow, peace: I do not like thy look, I promise thee.

Sex. What heard you him say else?

Sec. Watch. Marry, that he had received a thousand ducats of Don John for accusing the Lady Hero wrongfully. 51

Dog. Flat burglary as ever was committed.

Verg. Yea, by mass, that it is.

Sex. What else, fellow?

First Watch. And that Count Claudio did mean, upon his words, to disgrace Hero before the whole assembly, and not marry her.

Dog. O villain! thou wilt be condemned into ever-lasting redemption for this.

Sex. What else? 60

Watch. This is all.

Sex. And this is more, masters, than you can deny. Prince John is this morning secretly stolen away; Hero was in this manner accused, in this very manner refused, and upon the grief of this suddenly died. Master constable, let these men be bound, and brought to Leonato's: I will go before and show him their examination. [*Exit.*

Dog. Come, let them be opinioned.

Verg. †Let them be in the hands— 70

Con. Off, coxcomb!

Dog. God 's my life, where 's the sexton? let him write down the prince's officer coxcomb. Come, bind them. Thou naughty varlet!

Con. Away! you are an ass, you are an ass.

Dog. Dost thou not suspect my place? dost thou not suspect my years? O that he were here to write me down an ass! But, masters, remember that I am an ass; though it be not written down, yet forget not that I am an ass. No, thou villain, thou art full of piety, as shall be proved upon thee by good witness. I am a wise fellow, and, which is more, an officer, and, which is more, a householder, and, which is more, as pretty a piece of flesh as any is in Messina, and one that knows the law, go to; and a rich fellow enough, go to; and a fellow that hath had losses, and one that hath two gowns and every thing hand-some about him. Bring him away. O that I had been writ down an ass! [*Exeunt.*

ACT V.

SCENE I. *Before* LEONATO'S *house.*

Enter LEONATO *and* ANTONIO.

Ant. If you go on thus, you will kill yourself;
And 'tis not wisdom thus to second grief
Against yourself.

Leon.　　　　　　　I pray thee, cease thy counsel,
Which falls into mine ears as profitless
As water in a sieve: give not me counsel;
Nor let no comforter delight mine ear
But such a one whose wrongs do suit with mine.
Bring me a father that so loved his child,
Whose joy of her is overwhelm'd like mine,
And bid him speak of patience; 10
Measure his woe the length and breadth of mine
And let it answer every strain for strain,
As thus for thus and such a grief for such,
In every lineament, branch, shape, and form:
If such a one will smile and stroke his beard,
†Bid sorrow wag, cry 'hem!' when he should
　　　groan,
Patch grief with proverbs, make misfortune drunk
With candle-wasters; bring him yet to me,

SCENE II. The stage direction here is Capell's. QF have *Enter the Constables, Borachio and the Towne clearke in gownes.* Throughout the scene in Q, Dogberry's lines are given to *Kemp* (spelled variously) except that the speech beginning in line 4 is given to *Andrew,* and the one beginning in line 69 to *Const.* Verges' speeches are headed *Cowley* or *Couley* except in line 53, where he is *Const.* Will Kemp and Richard Cowley were actors in Shakespeare's company. The appearance of the actors' names in this one scene may indicate that it is an addition to the play as originally written. 1. **dissembly,** blunder for "assembly." 5. **exhibition,** possibly for "commission" or "examination" (to exhibit). 24. **go**

near to, almost. 27. **witty,** clever, cunning. 28. **go about with,** get the better of. 33. **in a tale,** in agreement. 38. **eftest,** an unexplained blunder of Dogberry's; Theobald: *deftest;* Rowe: *easiest.* 69. **opinioned,** for "pinioned." 70-71. Text corrupt; reading due to Malone; New Cambridge: *Let them be—in the hands.* 76. **suspect,** for "respect." 81. **piety,** for "impiety." 85. **piece of flesh,** sample of humanity.

ACT V. SCENE I. 2-3. **second . . . yourself,** encourage grief which will destroy you. 12. **strain,** strong impulse of the mind. 16. **bid . . . 'hem!',** so Capell; QF: *And, sorrow, wagge, crie him;* Stevens: *And sorry wag, cry 'hem!'* 18. **candle-wasters,** those who waste candles by late

And I of him will gather patience.
But there is no such man: for, brother, men   20
Can counsel and speak comfort to that grief
Which they themselves not feel; but, tasting it,
Their counsel turns to passion, which before
Would give preceptial medicine to rage,
Fetter strong madness in a silken thread,
Charm ache with air and agony with words:
No, no; 'tis all men's office to speak patience
To those that wring under the load of sorrow,
But no man's virtue nor sufficiency
To be so moral when he shall endure   30
The like himself. Therefore give me no counsel:
My griefs cry louder than advertisement.
    Ant. Therein do men from children nothing
        differ.
    Leon. I pray thee, peace. I will be flesh and blood;
For there was never yet philosopher
That could endure the toothache patiently,
However they have writ the style of gods
And made a push at chance and sufferance.
    Ant. Yet bend not all the harm upon yourself;
Make those that do offend you suffer too.   40
    Leon. There thou speak'st reason: nay, I will do so.
My soul doth tell me Hero is belied;
And that shall Claudio know; so shall the prince
And all of them that thus dishonour her.
    Ant. Here comes the prince and Claudio hastily.

Enter DON PEDRO *and* CLAUDIO.

    D. Pedro. Good den, good den.
    Claud.   Good day to both of you.
    Leon. Hear you, my lords,—
    D. Pedro.   We have some haste, Leonato.
    Leon. Some haste, my lord! well, fare you well, my
        lord:
Are you so hasty now? well, all is one.
    D. Pedro. Nay, do not quarrel with us, good old
        man.   50
    Ant. If he could right himself with quarrelling,
Some of us would lie low.
    Claud.   Who wrongs him?
    Leon. Marry, thou dost wrong me; thou dissembler,
        thou:—
Nay, never lay thy hand upon thy sword;
I fear thee not.
    Claud.   Marry, beshrew my hand,
If it should give your age such cause of fear:
In faith, my hand meant nothing to my sword.
    Leon. Tush, tush, man; never fleer and jest at me:
I speak not like a dotard nor a fool,
As under privilege of age to brag   60
What I have done being young, or what would do
Were I not old. Know, Claudio, to thy head,
Thou hast so wrong'd mine innocent child and me
That I am forced to lay my reverence by
And, with grey hairs and bruise of many days,
Do challenge thee to trial of a man.
I say thou hast belied mine innocent child;

Thy slander hath gone through and through her
    heart,
And she lies buried with her ancestors;
O, in a tomb where never scandal slept,   70
Save this of hers, framed by thy villany!
    Claud. My villany?
    Leon.   Thine, Claudio; thine, I say.
    D. Pedro. You say not right, old man.
    Leon.   My lord, my lord,
I'll prove it on his body, if he dare,
Despite his nice fence and his active practice,
His May of youth and bloom of lustihood.
    Claud. Away! I will not have to do with you.
    Leon. Canst thou so daff me? Thou hast kill'd my
        child:
If thou kill'st me, boy, thou shalt kill a man.
    Ant. He shall kill two of us, and men indeed: 80
But that's no matter; let him kill one first;
Win me and wear me; let him answer me.
Come, follow me, boy; come, sir boy, come, follow me:
Sir boy, I'll whip you from your foining fence;
Nay, as I am a gentleman, I will.
    Leon. Brother,—
    Ant. Content yourself. God knows I loved my niece;
And she is dead, slander'd to death by villains,
That dare as well answer a man indeed
As I dare take a serpent by the tongue: 90
Boys, apes, braggarts, Jacks, milksops!
    Leon.   Brother Antony,—
    Ant. Hold you content. What, man! I know them,
        yea,
And what they weigh, even to the utmost scruple,—
Scambling, out-facing, fashion-monging boys,
That lie and cog and flout, deprave and slander,
Go anticly, show outward hideousness,
And speak off half a dozen dangerous words,
How they might hurt their enemies, if they durst;
And this is all.
    Leon. But, brother Antony,—
    Ant.   Come, 'tis no matter: 100
Do not you meddle; let me deal in this.
    D. Pedro. Gentlemen both, we will not wake your
        patience.
My heart is sorry for your daughter's death:
But, on my honour, she was charged with nothing
But what was true and very full of proof.
    Leon. My lord, my lord,—
    D. Pedro. I will not hear you.
    Leon. No? Come, brother; away! I will be heard.
    Ant. And shall, or some of us will smart for it.
            [*Exeunt Leonato and Antonio.*
    D. Pedro. See, see; here comes the man we went to
        seek.   110

Enter BENEDICK.

    Claud. Now, signior, what news?
    Bene. Good day, my lord.
    D. Pedro. Welcome, signior: you are almost come
to part almost a fray.

study; bookworms; also explained as revelers. **yet,** why then, or, yet
if you do (find such a man, bring him to me). 24. **preceptial medicine,**
medicine consisting of precepts. 26. **air,** mere breath. 28. **wring,**
writhe. 29. **sufficiency,** ability, power. 30. **moral,** prone to moralizing. 32. **advertisement,** advice, counsel. 37. **style of,** language
worthy of. 38. **push,** alternative form of "pish," expressive of indignation or contempt. **sufferance,** suffering. 49. **now,** possibly expletive,
meaning "after all that has happened," or "after my daughter is
dead." It has been thought to refer to Don Pedro's promise to stay a
month. **all is one,** it makes no difference. 53. **thou,** used contemptuously instead of the more polite "you." 57. **my hand . . . sword,** I
had no intention of using my sword. 58. **fleer,** sneer (with pretended
humility). 62. **to thy head,** to thy face. 75. **nice fence,** dexterous
swordsmanship. 76. **lustihood,** bodily vigor. 78. **daff,** put off. 82.
Win . . . me, proverbial expression. **answer me,** i.e., in a duel. 84.
foining, thrusting. 94. **Scambling,** contentious. **out-facing,** swaggering. **fashion-monging,** dandified. 95. **deprave,** detract, traduce.
96. **anticly,** fantastically. 97. **dangerous,** threatening, haughty. 102.
wake your patience, put your patience to any test.

Claud. We had like to have had our two noses snapped off with two old men without teeth.

D. Pedro. Leonato and his brother. What thinkest thou? Had we fought, I doubt we should have been too young for them.

Bene. In a false quarrel there is no true valour. I came to seek you both. 121

Claud. We have been up and down to seek thee; for we are high-proof melancholy and would fain have it beaten away. Wilt thou use thy wit?

Bene. It is in my scabbard: shall I draw it?

D. Pedro. Dost thou wear thy wit by thy side?

Claud. Never any did so, though very many have been beside their wit. I will bid thee draw, as we do the minstrels; draw, to pleasure us.

D. Pedro. As I am an honest man, he looks pale. Art thou sick, or angry? 131

Claud. What, courage, man! What though care killed a cat, thou hast mettle enough in thee to kill care.

Bene. Sir, I shall meet your wit in the career, an you charge it against me. I pray you choose another subject.

Claud. Nay, then, give him another staff: this last was broke cross.

D. Pedro. By this light, he changes more and more: I think he be angry indeed. 141

Claud. If he be, he knows how to turn his girdle.

Bene. Shall I speak a word in your ear?

Claud. God bless me from a challenge!

Bene. [*Aside to Claudio*] You are a villain; I jest not: I will make it good how you dare, with what you dare, and when you dare. Do me right, or I will protest your cowardice. You have killed a sweet lady, and her death shall fall heavy on you. Let me hear from you. 151

Claud. Well, I will meet you, so I may have good cheer.

D. Pedro. What, a feast, a feast?

Claud. I' faith, I thank him; he hath bid me to a calf's head and a capon; the which if I do not carve most curiously, say my knife's naught. Shall I not find a woodcock too?

Bene. Sir, your wit ambles well; it goes easily. 159

D. Pedro. I'll tell thee how Beatrice praised thy wit the other day. I said, thou hadst a fine wit: 'True,' said she, 'a fine little one.' 'No,' said I, 'a great wit:' 'Right,' says she, 'a great gross one.' 'Nay,' said I, 'a good wit:' 'Just,' said she, 'it hurts nobody.' 'Nay,' said I, 'the gentleman is wise:' 'Certain,' said she, 'a wise gentleman.' 'Nay,' said I, 'he hath the tongues:' 'That I believe,' said she, 'for he swore a thing to me on Monday night, which he forswore on Tuesday morning; there's a double tongue; there's two tongues.' Thus did she, an hour together, trans-shape thy particular virtues: yet at last she concluded with a sigh, thou wast the properest man in Italy. 174

Claud. For the which she wept heartily and said she cared not.

D. Pedro. Yea, that she did; but yet, for all that, an if she did not hate him deadly, she would love him dearly: the old man's daughter told us all. 180

Claud. All, all; and, moreover, God saw him when he was hid in the garden.

D. Pedro. But when shall we set the savage bull's horns on the sensible Benedick's head?

Claud. Yea, and text underneath, 'Here dwells Benedick the married man'? 186

Bene. Fare you well, boy: you know my mind. I will leave you now to your gossip-like humour: you break jests as braggarts do their blades, which, God be thanked, hurt not. My lord, for your many courtesies I thank you: I must discontinue your company: your brother the bastard is fled from Messina: you have among you killed a sweet and innocent lady. For my Lord Lackbeard there, he and I shall meet: and, till then, peace be with him. [*Exit.*

D. Pedro. He is in earnest.

Claud. In most profound earnest; and, I'll warrant you, for the love of Beatrice.

D. Pedro. And hath challenged thee. 200

Claud. Most sincerely.

D. Pedro. What a pretty thing man is when he goes in his doublet and hose and leaves off his wit!

Claud. He is then a giant to an ape; but then is an ape a doctor to such a man.

D. Pedro. But, soft you, let me be: pluck up, my heart, and be sad. Did he not say, my brother was fled? 209

Enter DOGBERRY, VERGES, *and the* Watch, *with* CONRADE *and* BORACHIO.

Dog. Come you, sir: if justice cannot tame you, she shall ne'er weigh more reasons in her balance: nay, an you be a cursing hypocrite once, you must be looked to.

D. Pedro. How now? two of my brother's men bound! Borachio one! 215

Claud. Hearken after their offence, my lord.

D. Pedro. Officers, what offence have these men done?

Dog. Marry, sir, they have committed false report; moreover, they have spoken untruth; secondarily, they are slanders; sixth and lastly, they have belied a lady; thirdly, they have verified unjust things; and, to conclude, they are lying knaves. 224

D. Pedro. First, I ask thee what they have done; thirdly, I ask thee what's their offence; sixth and lastly, why they are committed; and, to conclude, what you lay to their charge.

Claud. Rightly reasoned, and in his own division; and, by my troth, there's one meaning well suited. 231

D. Pedro. Who have you offended, masters, that you are thus bound to your answer? this learned constable is too cunning to be understood: what's your offence?

Bora. Sweet prince, let me go no farther to mine answer: do you hear me, and let this count kill me.

---

123. **high-proof,** to the highest degree. 128. **beside their wit,** out of their wits. 129. **draw,** draw as a bow across a fiddle. 136. **career,** short gallop at full speed (as in tourney). **charge,** level (as a weapon). 138. **staff,** spear shaft. 139. **broke cross,** i.e., by clumsily allowing the spear to break crosswise against his opponent's shield. 142. **turn his girdle,** explained as shifting his girdle about so that he can reach his dagger; also as a reference to wrestling, since wrestlers turned the buckles of their girdles to the back before beginning. 147-148. **Do me right,** give me satisfaction. 148. **protest,** proclaim before witnesses.

156, 158. **calf's head, capon, woodcock,** used as types of dullness. 157. **curiously,** daintily. 167. **hath the tongues,** is a linguist. 172. **trans-shape,** distort, turn the wrong side out. 189-190. **as . . . blades,** possibly, getting their blades broken without harming themselves. 202-204. **What . . . wit.** Doublet and hose formed the Elizabethan undercostume, a cloak being worn over them on formal occasions. The prince possibly means to suggest that man's wit is like a cloak which he can leave off, and go about in his natural stupidity. 205-206. **He . . . man.** He is superior to an ape in stature, but an ape is

I have deceived even your very eyes: what your wisdoms could not discover, these shallow fools have brought to light; who in the night overheard me confessing to this man how Don John your brother incensed me to slander the Lady Hero, how you were brought into the orchard and saw me court Margaret in Hero's garments, how you disgraced her, when you should marry her: my villany they have upon record; which I had rather seal with my death than repeat over to my shame. The lady is dead upon mine and my master's false accusation; and, briefly, I desire nothing but the reward of a villain. 251

D. Pedro. Runs not this speech like iron through your blood?

Claud. I have drunk poison whiles he utter'd it.

D. Pedro. But did my brother set thee on to this?

Bora. Yea, and paid me richly for the practice of it.

D. Pedro. He is composed and framed of treachery: And fled he is upon this villany.

Claud. Sweet Hero! now thy image doth appear In the rare semblance that I loved it first. 260

Dog. Come, bring away the plaintiffs: by this time our sexton hath reformed Signior Leonato of the matter: and, masters, do not forget to specify, when time and place shall serve, that I am an ass.

Verg. Here, here comes master Signior Leonato, and the sexton too.

Re-enter LEONATO *and* ANTONIO, *with the* Sexton.

Leon. Which is the villain? let me see his eyes, That, when I note another man like him, 270 I may avoid him: which of these is he?

Bora. If you would know your wronger, look on me.

Leon. Art thou the slave that with thy breath hast kill'd
Mine innocent child?

Bora. Yea, even I alone.

Leon. No, not so, villain; thou beliest thyself: Here stand a pair of honourable men; A third is fled, that had a hand in it. I thank you, princes, for my daughter's death: Record it with your high and worthy deeds: 'Twas bravely done, if you bethink you of it. 280

Claud. I know not how to pray your patience; Yet I must speak. Choose your revenge yourself; Impose me to what penance your invention Can lay upon my sin: yet sinn'd I not But in mistaking.

D. Pedro. By my soul, nor I: And yet, to satisfy this good old man, I would bend under any heavy weight That he'll enjoin me to.

Leon. I cannot bid you bid my daughter live; That were impossible: but, I pray you both, 290 Possess the people in Messina here How innocent she died; and if your love Can labour aught in sad invention, Hang her an epitaph upon her tomb

And sing it to her bones, sing it to-night: To-morrow morning come you to my house, And since you could not be my son-in-law, Be yet my nephew: my brother hath a daughter, Almost the copy of my child that 's dead, And she alone is heir to both of us: 300 Give her the right you should have given her cousin, And so dies my revenge.

Claud. O noble sir, Your over-kindness doth wring tears from me! I do embrace your offer; and dispose For henceforth of poor Claudio.

Leon. To-morrow then I will expect your coming; To-night I take my leave. This naughty man Shall face to face be brought to Margaret, Who I believe was pack'd in all this wrong, Hired to it by your brother.

Bora. No, by my soul, she was not, 310 Nor knew not what she did when she spoke to me, But always hath been just and virtuous In any thing that I do know by her.

Dog. Moreover, sir, which indeed is not under white and black, this plaintiff here, the offender, did call me ass: I beseech you, let it be remembered in his punishment. And also, the watch heard them talk of one Deformed: they say he wears a key in his ear and a lock hanging by it, and borrows money in God's name, the which he hath used so long and never paid that now men grow hard-hearted and will lend nothing for God's sake: pray you, examine him upon that point. 322

Leon. I thank thee for thy care and honest pains.

Dog. Your worship speaks like a most thankful and reverend youth; and I praise God for you.

Leon. There 's for thy pains.

Dog. God save the foundation!

Leon. Go, I discharge thee of thy prisoner, and I thank thee. 330

Dog. I leave an arrant knave with your worship; which I beseech your worship to correct yourself, for the example of others. God keep your worship! I wish your worship well; God restore you to health! I humbly give you leave to depart; and if a merry meeting may be wished, God prohibit it! Come, neighbour. [*Exeunt Dogberry and Verges.*

Leon. Until to-morrow morning, lords, farewell.

Ant. Farewell, my lords: we look for you to-morrow.

D. Pedro. We will not fail.

Claud. To-night I'll mourn with Hero.

Leon. [*To the Watch*] Bring you these fellows on. We'll talk with Margaret, 341 How her acquaintance grew with this lewd fellow.

[*Exeunt, severally.*

SCENE II. LEONATO'S *garden.*

Enter BENEDICK *and* MARGARET, *meeting.*

Bene. Pray thee, sweet Mistress Margaret, deserve

superior to him in wit. 206. **doctor,** learned man. 207. **soft you,** gently. **pluck up,** rouse thyself. 216. **Hearken after,** inquire into. 221. **landers,** for "slanderers." 223. **verified,** for "testified to." 231. **well suited,** put into many different dresses (Johnson). 233. **bound,** play on the meanings "pinioned" and "headed for a destination." **answer,** trial, account. 242. **incensed,** instigated. 249. **upon,** in consequence of. 256. **practice of it,** bringing it to pass by deceitful contrivance. 261. **plaintiffs,** for "defendants." 262. **reformed,** for "informed." 264. **specify,** for "testify" (?) 283. **me to,** on me.

300. **heir to both.** He overlooks Antonio's son mentioned in I, ii, 2. 304. **I do . . . offer.** Claudio is often censured for the readiness with which he agrees to marry another woman after his treatment of Hero, but his action can be understood if one remembers the universal custom of arranged marriages in Shakespeare's day. 313. **by,** concerning. 320. **in God's name,** a phrase of the professional beggar. 328. **God . . . foundation,** formula of those who received alms at religious houses. 342. **lewd,** wicked, worthless.

well at my hands by helping me to the speech of Beatrice.

Marg. Will you then write me a sonnet in praise of my beauty?

Bene. In so high a style, Margaret, that no man living shall come over it; for, in most comely truth, thou deservest it.

Marg. To have no man come over me! why, shall I always keep below stairs? 10

Bene. Thy wit is as quick as the greyhound's mouth; it catches.

Marg. And yours as blunt as the fencer's foils, which hit, but hurt not.

Bene. A most manly wit, Margaret; it will not hurt a woman: and so, I pray thee, call Beatrice: I give thee the bucklers.

Marg. Give us the swords; we have bucklers of our own. 19

Bene. If you use them, Margaret, you must put in the pikes with a vice; and they are dangerous weapons for maids.

Marg. Well, I will call Beatrice to you, who I think hath legs.

Bene. And therefore will come. [*Exit Margaret.*

[*Sings*]   The god of love,
           That sits above,
    And knows me, and knows me,
        How pitiful I deserve,— 29

I mean in singing; but in loving, Leander the good swimmer, Troilus the first employer of pandars, and a whole bookful of these quondam carpet-mongers, whose names yet run smoothly in the even road of a blank verse, why, they were never so truly turned over and over as my poor self in love. Marry, I cannot show it in rhyme; I have tried: I can find out no rhyme to 'lady' but 'baby,' an innocent rhyme; for 'scorn,' 'horn,' a hard rhyme; for 'school,' 'fool,' a babbling rhyme; very ominous endings: no, I was not born under a rhyming planet, nor I cannot woo in festival terms. 41

Enter BEATRICE.

Sweet Beatrice, wouldst thou come when I called thee?

Beat. Yea, signior, and depart when you bid me.

Bene. O, stay but till then!

Beat. 'Then' is spoken; fare you well now: and yet, ere I go, let me go with that I came; which is, with knowing what hath passed between you and Claudio.

Bene. Only foul words; and thereupon I will kiss thee. 51

Beat. Foul words is but foul wind, and foul wind is but foul breath, and foul breath is noisome; therefore I will depart unkissed.

Bene. Thou hast frighted the word out of his right sense, so forcible is thy wit. But I must tell thee plainly, Claudio undergoes my challenge; and either I must shortly hear from him, or I will subscribe him a coward. And, I pray thee now, tell me for which of my bad parts didst thou first fall in love with me? 61

Beat. For them all together; which maintained so

politic a state of evil that they will not admit any good part to intermingle with them. But for which of my good parts did you first suffer love for me?

Bene. Suffer love! a good epithet! I do suffer love indeed, for I love thee against my will.

Beat. In spite of your heart, I think; alas, poor heart! If you spite it for my sake, I will spite it for yours; for I will never love that which my friend hates.

Bene. Thou and I are too wise to woo peaceably.

Beat. It appears not in this confession: there's not one wise man among twenty that will praise himself. 77

Bene. An old, an old instance, Beatrice, that lived in the time of good neighbours. If a man do not erect in this age his own tomb ere he dies, he shall live no longer in monument than the bell rings and the widow weeps.

Beat. And how long is that, think you?

Bene. Question: why, an hour in clamour and a quarter in rheum: therefore is it most expedient for the wise, if Don Worm, his conscience, find no impediment to the contrary, to be the trumpet of his own virtues, as I am to myself. So much for praising myself, who, I myself will bear witness, is praiseworthy: and now tell me, how doth your cousin? 91

Beat. Very ill.

Bene. And how do you?

Beat. Very ill too.

Bene. Serve God, love me and mend. There will I leave you too, for here comes one in haste.

Enter URSULA.

Urs. Madam, you must come to your uncle. Yonder's old coil at home: it is proved my Lady Hero hath been falsely accused, the prince and Claudio mightily abused; and Don John is the author of all, who is fled and gone. Will you come presently?

Beat. Will you go hear this news, signior?

Bene. I will live in thy heart, die in thy lap and be buried in thy eyes; and moreover I will go with thee to thy uncle's. [*Exeunt.*

SCENE III. *A church.*

Enter DON PEDRO, CLAUDIO, *and three or four with tapers.*

Claud. Is this the monument of Leonato?

A Lord. It is, my lord.

Claud. [*Reading out of a scroll*]

    Done to death by slanderous tongues
        Was the Hero that here lies:
    Death, in guerdon of her wrongs,
        Gives her fame which never dies.
    So the life that died with shame
    Lives in death with glorious fame.

Hang thou there upon the tomb,
Praising her when I am dumb. 10
Now, music, sound, and sing your solemn hymn.

SCENE II. 6. **style,** play on the critical phrase for epic grandeur, "a high style," and the word "stile." 8. **comely,** good, with allusion to Margaret's beauty. 17. **I . . . bucklers.** I acknowledge myself beaten (in repartee). 21. **pikes,** spikes in the center of a shield. **vice,** screw. 26-29. **The god . . . deserve,** beginning of an old song by William Elderton (Ritson). 30. **Leander.** The tale of Hero and Leander (from the Greek of Musaeus?) had been written in part by Marlowe and completed and published by Chapman shortly before the date of this play (1598). 31. **Troilus,** hero of the tale of Troilus and Cressida. Both he and Leander are stock examples of faithful lovers. 32-33. **quondam carpet-mongers,** ancient carpet-knights. 38. **innocent,** silly. 41. **festival terms,** fanciful language (suitable for festivals). 59. **subscribe,** formally proclaim. 63. **politic,** prudently governed. 67. **epithet,** expression. 79. **time . . . neighbours,** good old times (when one's neighbors spoke well of one). 84. **Question,** that is the question. **clamour,** noise (of the bell). 85. **rheum,** tears

SONG.

Pardon, goddess of the night,
Those that slew thy virgin knight;
For the which, with songs of woe,
Round about her tomb they go.
    Midnight, assist our moan;
    Help us to sigh and groan,
      Heavily, heavily:
Graves, yawn and yield your dead,
Till death be uttered,   20
      Heavily, heavily.

Claud. Now, unto thy bones good night!
Yearly will I do this rite.
D. Pedro. Good morrow, masters; put your torches
    out:
The wolves have prey'd; and look, the gentle day,
Before the wheels of Phœbus, round about
Dapples the drowsy east with spots of grey.
Thanks to you all, and leave us: fare you well.
Claud. Good morrow, masters: each his several way.
D. Pedro. Come, let us hence, and put on other
    weeds;   30
And then to Leonato's we will go.
Claud. And Hymen now with luckier issue speed 's
Than this for whom we render'd up this woe. [*Exeunt.*

SCENE IV. *A room in* LEONATO'S *house.*

Enter LEONATO, ANTONIO, BENEDICK, BEATRICE,
  MARGARET, URSULA, FRIAR FRANCIS, *and* HERO.

Friar. Did I not tell you she was innocent?
Leon. So are the prince and Claudio, who accused
    her
Upon the error that you heard debated:
But Margaret was in some fault for this,
Although against her will, as it appears
In the true course of all the question.
Ant. Well, I am glad that all things sort so well.
Bene. And so am I, being else by faith enforced
To call young Claudio to a reckoning for it.
Leon. Well, daughter, and you gentlewomen all,   10
Withdraw into a chamber by yourselves,
And when I send for you, come hither mask'd.
                     [*Exeunt Ladies.*
The prince and Claudio promised by this hour
To visit me. You know your office, brother:
You must be father to your brother's daughter,
And give her to young Claudio.
Ant. Which I will do with confirm'd countenance.
Bene. Friar, I must entreat your pains, I think.
Friar. To do what, signior?
Bene. To bind me, or undo me; one of them.   20
Signior Leonato, truth it is, good signior,
Your niece regards me with an eye of favour.
Leon. That eye my daughter lent her: 'tis most true.
Bene. And I do with an eye of love requite her.
Leon. The sight whereof I think you had from me,
From Claudio and the prince: but what 's your will?
Bene. Your answer, sir, is enigmatical:

But, for my will, my will is your good will
May stand with ours, this day to be conjoin'd
In the state of honourable marriage: 30
In which, good friar, I shall desire your help.
Leon. My heart is with your liking.
Friar.   And my help.
Here comes the prince and Claudio.

Enter DON PEDRO *and* CLAUDIO, *and two or three
  others.*

D. Pedro. Good morrow to this fair assembly.
Leon. Good morrow, prince; good morrow, Claudio:
We here attend you. Are you yet determined
To-day to marry with my brother's daughter?
Claud. I'll hold my mind, were she an Ethiope.
Leon. Call her forth, brother; here 's the friar ready.
                      [*Exit Antonio.*
D. Pedro. Good morrow, Benedick. Why, what 's the
    matter,   40
That you have such a February face,
So full of frost, of storm and cloudiness?
Claud. I think he thinks upon the savage bull.
Tush, fear not, man; we'll tip thy horns with gold
And all Europa shall rejoice at thee,
As once Europa did at lusty Jove,
When he would play the noble beast in love.
Bene. Bull Jove, sir, had an amiable low;
And some such strange bull leap'd your father's cow,
And got a calf in that same noble feat   50
Much like to you, for you have just his bleat.
Claud. For this I owe you: here comes other
    reckonings.

Re-enter ANTONIO, *with the* Ladies *masked.*

Which is the lady I must seize upon?
Ant. This same is she, and I do give you her.
Claud. Why, then she 's mine. Sweet, let me see your
    face.
Leon. No, that you shall not, till you take her hand
Before this friar and swear to marry her.
Claud. Give me your hand: before this holy friar,
I am your husband, if you like of me.
Hero. And when I lived, I was your other wife: 60
                      [*Unmasking.*
And when you loved, you were my other husband.
Claud. Another Hero!
Hero.   Nothing certainer:
One Hero died defiled, but I do live,
And surely as I live, I am a maid.
D. Pedro. The former Hero! Hero that is dead!
Leon. She died, my lord, but whiles her slander
    lived.
Friar. All this amazement can I qualify;
When after that the holy rites are ended,
I'll tell you largely of fair Hero's death:
Meantime let wonder seem familiar,   70
And to the chapel let us presently.
Bene. Soft and fair, friar. Which is Beatrice?
Beat. [*Unmasking*] I answer to that name. What is
    your will?

(of the widow). 86-87. **Don . . . conscience.** The action of the conscience was traditionally described (in the morality plays, etc.) as the
gnawing of a worm; Mark 9:48. 100. **abused,** deceived.
    SCENE III. 5. **guerdon,** recompense. 20. **uttered,** sent abroad, put
into circulation. 25. **have prey'd,** have ceased preying. 32. **speed 's,**
favor or speed us; so Thirlby; QF: *speeds.*
    SCENE IV. 6. **question,** investigation. 7. **sort,** turn out, eventuate.
8. **by faith,** i.e., by his promise to Beatrice. 17. **confirm'd,** grave,

unmoved. 20. **undo,** ruin, with play on the meaning "untie" or
"unbind." 43. **I . . . bull,** a jocular reminiscence of the conversation
in I, i, 263 ff. (See also V, i, 83-84.) 45. **Europa,** Europe. 46.
Europa, a reference to the story of Jove's infatuation for Europa, whom
he approached in the form of a white bull and bore on his back through
the sea to the island of Crete. 52. **owe you,** i.e., an answer. 59. **like
of,** care for. 69. **largely,** at large, in full. 70. **let . . . familiar,**
restrain your wonder.

Bene. Do not you love me?

Beat. Why, no; no more than reason.

Bene. Why, then your uncle and the prince and
Claudio
Have been deceived; they swore you did.

Beat. Do not you love me?

Bene. Troth, no; no more than reason.

Beat. Why, then my cousin Margaret and Ursula
Are much deceived; for they did swear you did.

Bene. They swore that you were almost sick for me. 80

Beat. They swore that you were well-nigh dead for
me.

Bene. 'Tis no such matter. Then you do not love me?

Beat. No, truly, but in friendly recompense.

Leon. Come, cousin, I am sure you love the
gentleman.

Claud. And I'll be sworn upon 't that he loves her;
For here 's a paper written in his hand,
A halting sonnet of his own pure brain,
Fashion'd to Beatrice.

Hero. And here 's another
Writ in my cousin's hand, stolen from her pocket,
Containing her affection unto Benedick. 90

Bene. A miracle! here 's our own hands against our
hearts. Come, I will have thee; but, by this light, I
take thee for pity.

Beat. I would not deny you; but, by this good day,
I yield upon great persuasion; and partly to save your
life, for I was told you were in a consumption.

Bene. Peace! I will stop your mouth. [*Kissing her.*

D. Pedro. How dost thou, Benedick, the married
man? 100

Bene. I'll tell thee what, prince; a college of wit-
crackers cannot flout me out of my humour. Dost
thou think I care for a satire or an epigram? No: if a
man will be beaten with brains, a' shall wear nothing
handsome about him. In brief, since I do purpose to
marry, I will think nothing to any purpose that the
world can say against it; and therefore never flout at
me for what I have said against it; for man is a giddy
thing, and this is my conclusion. For thy part,
Claudio, I did think to have beaten thee; but in that
thou art like to be my kinsman, live unbruised and
love my cousin. 113

Claud. I had well hoped thou wouldst have denied
Beatrice, that I might have cudgelled thee out of thy
single life, to make thee a double-dealer; which, out
of question, thou wilt be, if my cousin do not look
exceeding narrowly to thee.

Bene. Come, come, we are friends: let 's have a
dance ere we are married, that we may lighten our
own hearts and our wives' heels.

Leon. We'll have dancing afterward. 122

Bene. First, of my word; therefore play, music.
Prince, thou art sad; get thee a wife, get thee a wife:
there is no staff more reverend than one tipped with
horn.

Enter a Messenger.

Mess. My lord, your brother John is ta'en in flight,
And brought with armed men back to Messina.

Bene. Think not on him till to-morrow: I'll devise
thee brave punishments for him. Strike up, pipers.
[*Dance. Exeunt.*

*Much Ado
about Nothing*
ACT V : SC IV

558

87. **his own pure,** purely his own.   104-105. **beaten with brains,** subjected to ridicule.   105-106. **a' shall . . . him,** i.e., so as not to attract
attention.   117. **double-dealer,** a married man and also a deceiver.

THE

Merry Wives of Windsor

The Merry Wives of Windsor is of course a comedy,
but for correct understanding it should be read in
connection with the history plays of King Henry IV.
It is inseparably linked to these by the figure of Falstaff. A tradition dating from the early years of the
eighteenth century, but universally accepted, states
that *The Merry Wives of Windsor* was written by the
special command of Queen Elizabeth. Charles Gildon in his *Remarks on the Plays of Shakespeare* (1710)
gives it in the following language:

The Fairies, in the fifth Act, make a handsome
compliment to the Queen in her Palace of Windsor,
who had obliged Shakespeare to write a Play of Sir
John Falstaff in Love, and which I am very well assured
he performed in a fortnight; a prodigious thing, when
all is so well contrived, and carried out without the least
confusion.

Literary critics have not agreed with Gildon in the
last statement. The play shows marks of haste, confusion, and unevenness.

SOURCES

The theory advanced by the most recent authorities
is that, the tradition being true, Shakespeare, possibly with the help of others, seized upon an old
comedy in the repertory of his company. Into it, with
more or less care, he thrust Sir John Falstaff and his
companions from the Henry IV plays, including Justice Shallow, who had figured popularly in *2 Henry
IV*, now provided with a Cousin Slender and an attendant Welsh Parson Evans. If this is true, the old
comedy must have dealt with bourgeois life, probably
in London, and must have had as its basis a story of a
jealous husband.

Lord Strange's men had in their repertory a
"Jealous Comedy" that has sometimes been thought
of as an original for *The Merry Wives of Windsor.* The
story of a lover detected in making love to two or
three women at the same time, as Falstaff does, occurs
in a number of Italian *novelle.* There is also to be found
the story of the deceived husband, whose wife has her
lover carried out before his eyes in a chest or a box of
feathers, as Falstaff is carried out before Ford's eyes
in the hamper of soiled linen.[1]

[1] To the six stories given by W. C. Hazlitt in *Shakespeare's Library*
(1875), Part I, Vol. III, 1–80, as resembling the plot of *The Merry
Wives of Windsor,* should be added "Of Two Brethren and their Wives"
from Barnabe Riche, *Riche his Farewell to Militarie Profession* (1581), a
tale which is in some respects the closest known analogue to *The Merry
Wives of Windsor.* See Dorothy Hart Bruce, "*The Merry Wives* and Two
Brethren," *Studies in Philology,* XXXIX, 265–278.

In any case, the basal theme of the play is Italian, and the attempts to connect it with the Henry IV plays are not altogether successful. Justice Shallow enters with a famous charge against Falstaff of having beaten his men, killed his deer, and broken open his lodge, but the charge and the Justice fade into nothing, with other odds and ends of plots. Falstaff begins like his old self, and now and then throughout shows something like the old wit. However, he who had outdone princes and chief justices, is made into a dupe by a very ordinary company of burghers. He speaks at times in so banal a way that the editors of the New Cambridge Shakespeare suggest that there may have been in his place in the old play an affected courtier, some of whose speeches have been left for poor Sir John to utter. Mistress Quickly too is quite transformed in character, though not in speech, and has apparently lost her adherence to Sir John. In fact, the play has given great dissatisfaction to the admirers of Falstaff, though it holds the stage with a deathlike grip. A well-known novelist who had seen the play at Stratford said, however, "Treated without foolish reverence in the presentation, it becomes a very good play."

TEXT AND DATE

The text has been a great puzzle. A quarto edition, printed from a stage version, played probably by a traveling company in the provinces, and sold to Thomas Creed, was published in 1602.[2] It is only about one-half as long as the text which appeared in the First Folio in 1623. The Folio text itself has undergone revision and is thought by the New Cambridge editors to have been made up for issue in the collected edition from hastily written players' parts. It may be, however, that Heminges and Condell had the Globe text recopied in a slightly different style for the use of the Folio printers. In any case, the quarto supplies some omissions in the Folio text and corrects some errors. The fact that Corporal Nym is a character in Henry V but not in the Henry IV plays, together with other considerations, has caused most critics to date the play about 1600 after the appearance of Henry V in 1599, but this is entirely too late. The Merry Wives of Windsor was performed in connection with the celebrations of the Garter Feast in the spring of 1597. This is in agreement with Leslie Hotson's interpretation of the quarrel between Shakespeare and Justice Gardener[3] and is borne out by William Bracy's discoveries in connection with the text. To place The Merry Wives of Windsor in the spring of 1597 has the effect of dating it and the Henry IV plays at an earlier

time than has been thought, and it may be that Henry V, usually regarded as fixed in the spring or summer of 1599, is earlier than we think, although that does not necessarily follow.

THE PLAY

The Merry Wives of Windsor, both in date and subject, forms a link between the history plays and the so-called "joyous comedies" of Shakespeare's second period. Yet it is impossible to fit it into the sequence of the history plays, except to say that it is later than the Henry IV plays and earlier than Henry V. The play differs radically from Much Ado about Nothing, As You Like It, and Twelfth Night. The Merry Wives of Windsor is not poetical and romantic as are these comedies, but is almost altogether in prose and is prosaic in tone. It is a comedy of social intrigue and marital jealousy written apparently for the gratification of the unsentimental tastes of courtly aristocrats who would enjoy a realistic picture of middle-class life.

The comedy is moral, and no one who understands Shakespeare's attitude toward Falstaff, particularly in 2 Henry IV, need feel that the attribution of attempted seduction and swindling is in any way a derogation of that worthy. The minor plot is ingenious, and the major and minor plots are admirably united, since the failure of mercenary aims is the theme of both of them. The neatness of Shakespeare's dramatic joinery will appear from the following summary.[4]

Shallow's cousin, Master Slender, almost the silliest character in Shakespeare, wishes to marry Mistress Anne Page. Her father wishes her to marry Slender, who is also backed by Justice Shallow and Parson Evans. "Seven hundred pounds and possibilities" is "goot gifts" says the latter. Anne's mother wishes her to marry a hot-tempered French doctor named Caius. Anne herself wishes to marry Fenton, an attractive spendthrift youth, who "has kept company with the wild prince and Poins."

Falstaff starts in to win the affections of Mrs. Ford, whose husband is very jealous, and of Mrs. Page, whose husband is not at all jealous. Falstaff writes identical love letters to each declaring that he loves her only. The women compare letters and resolve to punish him. Mrs. Ford invites him to her house.

---

[2]See William Bracy, The Merry Wives of Windsor: A Critical Study of Textual Transmission and Related Problems, University of North Carolina dissertation (1949) in process of publication by the University of Missouri Press.

[3]Leslie Hotson, Shakespeare vs. Shallow (Boston, 1931).

[4]For the many problems presented by The Merry Wives of Windsor see H. C. Hart (ed.), The Merry Wives of Windsor, Arden Shakespeare (Methuen, 1904); W. W. Greg (ed.), Shakespeare's "Merry Wives of Windsor," 1602 (Oxford, 1910); J. M. Robertson, The Problem of "The Merry Wives," Shakespeare Association (1917); A. W. Pollard and J. Dover Wilson, "The Stolne and Surreptitious Shakespearian Texts," Literary Supplement, The Times (London), Aug. 7, 1919; Sir Arthur Quiller-Couch and J. Dover Wilson (eds.), The Merry Wives of Windsor (Cambridge, 1921); T. W. Baldwin, The Organization and Personnel of the Shakespearean Company (Princeton, 1927), p. 235; J. Crofts, Shakespeare and the Post Horses (Bristol, 1937); O. J. Campbell, "The Italianate Background of The Merry Wives of Windsor," in Essays and Studies in English and Comparative Literature (Ann Arbor, 1931). See also Leslie Hotson and William Bracy as cited in preceding notes.

When he arrives, Mrs. Page rushes in to say that Mrs. Ford's irate husband is coming. They put Falstaff into a clothes basket, cover him with soiled clothes, have him carried out by their men and dumped into a ditch by the river Thames. He is even so stupid as to let her persuade him to visit her again. This time Ford comes indeed, and the women dress Falstaff up as the Witch of Brentford, against whom Ford has a violent antipathy, so that Falstaff gets soundly beaten with Ford's cudgel.

They now let Ford into the secret and both married couples arrange a third trick to play on the fat knight. With Mistress Quickly's aid he is persuaded to come as to an assignation into the forest to Herne's enchanted oak with buck's horns on his head. There children dressed as fairies dance about him, pinch him, and burn him with their torches until he confesses his folly, and what is worse, his wickedness, in words as stupid as his actions. While the fairy business is going on, Mistress Anne, who is a clever, nice girl, weds Fenton, Slender and Caius each carrying off a page dressed in girl's clothes under the impression that he is carrying off Mistress Anne as his bride. The virtue of *The Merry Wives of Windsor* is its charming treatment of ordinary life and its local color, the atmosphere of a town, and, indeed, of Windsor itself.

The *Merry Wives of Windsor* suffered relatively little at the hands of Restoration adapters. Shakespeare's play, or something like it, occupied the boards throughout the seventeenth and eighteenth centuries, though Shakespeare's actual text was probably not followed until Charles Kean's production of 1851.

In the stage history of the play we have to do with that group of actors who have had the special qualities necessary to play the part of Falstaff both in *The Merry Wives of Windsor* and the Henry IV plays. Shakespeare may have written the part for Thomas Pope, though a late tradition assigns it to John Heminges. In any case, John Lowin was famous in the part from 1603 to 1642. Betterton succeeded as Falstaff, and James Quin (1692-1766) became the most famous of all Falstaffs. John Henderson (1747-1785), George Frederick Cooke (1756-1811), Samuel Phelps, and J. H. Hackett have been successful in the part.

In recent times *The Merry Wives of Windsor* has been revived by Beerbohm Tree and Ellen Terry, the Bensons, and many others in both England and America. The play has been frequently presented by the Stratford-on-Avon Players. There is an irresistible gaiety about *The Merry Wives of Windsor* which makes it succeed on the stage where better plays fail.

THE

Merry Wives of Windsor

DRAMATIS PERSONAE

SIR JOHN FALSTAFF.
FENTON, a gentleman.
SHALLOW, a country justice.
SLENDER, cousin to Shallow.
FORD,
PAGE,} two gentlemen dwelling at Windsor.
WILLIAM PAGE, a boy, son to Page.
SIR HUGH EVANS, a Welsh parson.
DOCTOR CAIUS, a French physician.
Host of the Garter Inn.
BARDOLPH,
PISTOL,} sharpers attending on Falstaff.
NYM,
ROBIN, page to Falstaff.
SIMPLE, servant to Slender.
RUGBY, servant to Doctor Caius.

MISTRESS FORD.
MISTRESS PAGE.
ANNE PAGE, her daughter.
MISTRESS QUICKLY, servant to Doctor Caius.

Servants to Page, Ford, &c.

SCENE: *Windsor, and the neighbourhood.*

ACT I.

SCENE I. *Windsor. Before* PAGE'S *house.*

Enter JUSTICE SHALLOW, SLENDER, *and* SIR HUGH EVANS.

Shal. Sir Hugh, persuade me not; I will make a Star-chamber matter of it: if he were twenty Sir John Falstaffs, he shall not abuse Robert Shallow, esquire.

Slen. In the county of Gloucester, justice of peace and 'Coram.'

Shal. Ay, cousin Slender, and 'Custalorum.'

Slen. Ay, and 'Rato-lorum' too; and a gentleman born, master parson; who writes himself 'Armigero,' in any bill, warrant, quittance, or obligation, 'Armigero.' 11

Shal. Ay, that I do; and have done any time these three hundred years.

Slen. All his successors gone before him hath done 't; and all his ancestors that come after him may: they may give the dozen white luces in their coat.

Shal. It is an old coat.

Evans. The dozen white louses do become an old coat well; it agrees well, passant; it is a familiar beast to man, and signifies love. 21

Shal. The luce is the fresh fish; the salt fish is an old coat.

Slen. I may quarter, coz.

Shal. You may, by marrying.

Evans. It is marring indeed, if he quarter it.

Shal. Not a whit.

Evans. Yes, py'r lady: if he has a quarter of your coat, there is but three skirts for yourself, in my simple conjectures: but that is all one. If Sir John Falstaff have committed disparagements unto you, I am of the church, and will be glad to do my benevolence to make atonements and compremises between you.   33

Shal. The council shall hear it; it is a riot.

Evans. It is not meet the council hear a riot; there is no fear of Got in a riot: the council, look you, shall desire to hear the fear of Got, and not to hear a riot; take your vizaments in that.

Shal. Ha! o' my life, if I were young again, the sword should end it.   41

Evans. It is petter that friends is the sword, and end it: and there is also another device in my prain, which peradventure prings goot discretions with it: there is Anne Page, which is daughter to Master Thomas Page, which is pretty virginity.

Slen. Mistress Anne Page? She has brown hair, and speaks small like a woman.

Evans. It is that fery person for all the orld, as just as you will desire; and seven hundred pounds of moneys, and gold and silver, is her grandsire upon his death's-bed—Got deliver to a joyful resurrections!— give, when she is able to overtake seventeen years old: it were a goot motion if we leave our pribbles and prabbles, and desire a marriage between Master Abraham and Mistress Anne Page.

Slen. Did her grandsire leave her seven hundred pound?   60

Evans. Ay, and her father is make her a petter penny.

Slen. I know the young gentlewoman; she has good gifts.

Evans. Seven hundred pounds and possibilities is goot gifts.

Shal. Well, let us see honest Master Page. Is Falstaff there?

Evans. Shall I tell you a lie? I do despise a liar as I do despise one that is false, or as I despise one that is not true. The knight, Sir John, is there; and, I beseech you, be ruled by your well-willers. I will peat the door for Master Page. [*Knocks*] What, hoa! Got pless your house here!   74

Page. [*Within*] Who's there?

Enter PAGE.

Evans. Here is Got's plessing, and your friend, and Justice Shallow; and here young Master Slender, that peradventures shall tell you another tale, if matters grow to your likings.

Page. I am glad to see your worships well. I thank you for my venison, Master Shallow.   81

Shal. Master Page, I am glad to see you: much good do it your good heart! I wished your venison better; it was ill killed. How doth good Mistress Page?—and I thank you always with my heart, la! with my heart.

Page. Sir, I thank you.

Shal. Sir, I thank you; by yea and no, I do.

Page. I am glad to see you, good Master Slender.   90

Slen. How does your fallow greyhound, sir? I heard say he was outrun on Cotsall.

Page. It could not be judged, sir.

Slen. You'll not confess, you'll not confess.

Shal. That he will not. 'Tis your fault, 'tis your fault; 'tis a good dog.

Page. A cur, sir.

Shal. Sir, he's a good dog, and a fair dog: can there be more said? he is good and fair. Is Sir John Falstaff here?   100

Page. Sir, he is within; and I would I could do a good office between you.

Evans. It is spoke as a Christians ought to speak.

Shal. He hath wronged me, Master Page.

Page. Sir, he doth in some sort confess it.

Shal. If it be confessed, it is not redressed: is not that so, Master Page? He hath wronged me; indeed he hath; at a word, he hath, believe me: Robert Shallow, esquire, saith, he is wronged.   110

Page. Here comes Sir John.

Enter SIR JOHN FALSTAFF, BARDOLPH, NYM, *and* PISTOL.

Fal. Now, Master Shallow, you'll complain of me to the king?

Shal. Knight, you have beaten my men, killed my deer, and broke open my lodge.

Fal. But not kissed your keeper's daughter?

Shal. Tut, a pin! this shall be answered.

Fal. I will answer it straight; I have done all this. That is now answered.

Shal. The council shall know this.   120

Fal. 'Twere better for you if it were known in counsel: you'll be laughed at.

Evans. Pauca verba, Sir John; goot worts.

Fal. Good worts! good cabbage. Slender, I broke your head: what matter have you against me?

Slen. Marry, sir, I have matter in my head against you; and against your cony-catching rascals, Bardolph, Nym, and Pistol.

Bard. You Banbury cheese!   130

Slen. Ay, it is no matter.

Pist. How now, Mephostophilus!

Slen. Ay, it is no matter.

Nym. Slice, I say! pauca, pauca: slice! that's my humour.

Slen. Where's Simple, my man? Can you tell, cousin?

ACT I. SCENE I. 2. **a Star-chamber matter.** The court of Star Chamber, composed chiefly of the king's council, was the highest and most powerful civil court in the realm. 6. **'Coram,'** i.e., quorum, a title of certain justices whose presence was necessary to constitute a bench. 7. **'Custalorum,'** a corruption of Latin *custos rotulorum*, keeper of the rolls. 8. **'Rato-lorum,'** for *rotulorum*. 10. **'Armigero,'** esquire. 16-17. **luces in their coat.** The luce, a fresh-water fish, was displayed in the coat of arms of Sir Thomas Lucy of Charlcote, an estate near Stratford. This passage provides a basis for the deer-stalking legend considered in the biographical section of the General Introduction. Cf. Leslie Hotson, *Shakespeare Versus Shallow*, for other possible topical allusions in this passage. 19. **louses.** The pronunciations of *luce* and *louse* were sufficiently close to give the quibble point. 24. **quarter**, i.e., to arrange or display different coats of arms on one escutcheon; also, to add a coat of arms to another, or others, in this way. 33. **compremises**, a corruption of "compromises"; i.e., settlement by arbitration. 35. **The council . . . riot.** The king's council, sitting in Star Chamber, frequently concerned itself with riots. 39. **vizaments,** for "advisements," deliberations. 42. **that friends . . . sword,** i.e., that the quarrel be ended by friendly motions. 65. **possibilities,** pecuniary prospects. 72. **well-willers,** well wishers, friends. 73. **peat,** beat, knock. 84. **ill,** i.e., illegally. 92. **Cotsall,** Cotswold. 122. **in counsel,** secretly. 123. **Pauca verba,** few words. 124. **worts,** vegetables; a quibble on Sir Hugh's mispronunciation of "words." 128. **cony-catching,** cheating. 130. **Banbury cheese.** Banbury cheeses were noted for their thinness; a reference to Slender's name. 134. **Slice,** a reference to Bardolph's calling Slender a cheese.

Evans. Peace, I pray you. Now let us understand. There is three umpires in this matter, as I understand; that is, Master Page, fidelicet Master Page; and there is myself, fidelicet myself; and the three party is, lastly and finally, mine host of the Garter. 143

Page. We three, to hear it and end it between them.

Evans. Fery goot: I will make a prief of it in my note-book; and we will afterwards ork upon the cause with as great discreetly as we can.

Fal. Pistol!

Pist. He hears with ears. 150

Evans. The tevil and his tam! what phrase is this, 'He hears with ear'? why, it is affectations.

Fal. Pistol, did you pick Master Slender's purse?

Slen. Ay, by these gloves, did he, or I would I might never come in mine own great chamber again else, of seven groats in mill-sixpences, and two Edward shovel-boards, that cost me two shilling and two pence a-piece of Yead Miller, by these gloves. 161

Fal. Is this true, Pistol?

Evans. No; it is false, if it is a pick-purse.

Pist. Ha, thou mountain-foreigner! Sir John and master mine,
I combat challenge of this latten bilbo.
Word of denial in thy labras here!
Word of denial: froth and scum, thou liest!

Slen. By these gloves, then, 'twas he. 168

Nym. Be avised, sir, and pass good humours: I will say 'marry trap' with you, if you run the nuthook's humour on me; that is the very note of it.

Slen. By this hat, then, he in the red face had it; for though I cannot remember what I did when you made me drunk, yet I am not altogether an ass.

Fal. What say you, Scarlet and John?

Bard. Why, sir, for my part, I say the gentleman had drunk himself out of his five sentences. 180

Evans. It is his five senses: fie, what the ignorance is!

Bard. And being fap, sir, was, as they say, cashiered; and so conclusions passed the careires.

Slen. Ay, you spake in Latin then too; but 'tis no matter: I'll ne'er be drunk whilst I live again, but in honest, civil, godly company, for this trick: if I be drunk, I'll be drunk with those that have the fear of God, and not with drunken knaves. 190

Evans. So Got udge me, that is a virtuous mind.

Fal. You hear all these matters denied, gentlemen; you hear it.

Enter ANNE PAGE, *with wine;* MISTRESS FORD *and* MISTRESS PAGE, *following.*

Page. Nay, daughter, carry the wine in; we'll drink within. [*Exit Anne Page.*

Slen. O heaven! this is Mistress Anne Page.

Page. How now, Mistress Ford!

Fal. Mistress Ford, by my troth, you are very well met: by your leave, good mistress. [*Kisses her.*

Page. Wife, bid these gentlemen welcome. Come, we have a hot venison pasty to dinner: come, gentle-men, I hope we shall drink down all unkindness. 204

[*Exeunt all except Shal., Slen., and Evans.*

Slen. I had rather than forty shillings I had my Book of Songs and Sonnets here.

Enter SIMPLE.

How now, Simple! where have you been? I must wait on myself, must I? You have not the Book of Riddles about you, have you? 209

Sim. Book of Riddles! why, did you not lend it to Alice Shortcake upon All-hallowmas last, a fortnight afore Michaelmas?

Shal. Come, coz; come, coz; we stay for you. A word with you, coz; marry, this, coz: there is, as 'twere, a tender, a kind of tender, made afar off by Sir Hugh here. Do you understand me?

Slen. Ay, sir, you shall find me reasonable; if it be so, I shall do that that is reason.

Shal. Nay, but understand me.

Slen. So I do, sir. 220

Evans. Give ear to his motions, Master Slender: I will description the matter to you, if you be capacity of it.

Slen. Nay, I will do as my cousin Shallow says: I pray you, pardon me; he's a justice of peace in his country, simple though I stand here.

Evans. But that is not the question: the question is concerning your marriage.

Shal. Ay, there's the point, sir.

Evans. Marry, is it; the very point of it; to Mistress Anne Page. 231

Slen. Why, if it be so, I will marry her upon any reasonable demands.

Evans. But can you affection the 'oman? Let us command to know that of your mouth or of your lips; for divers philosophers hold that the lips is parcel of the mouth. Therefore, precisely, can you carry your good will to the maid?

Shal. Cousin Abraham Slender, can you love her?

Slen. I hope, sir, I will do as it shall become one that would do reason.

Evans. Nay, Got's lords and his ladies! you must speak possitable, if you can carry her your desires towards her. 245

Shal. That you must. Will you, upon good dowry, marry her?

Slen. I will do a greater thing than that, upon your request, cousin, in any reason.

Shal. Nay, conceive me, conceive me, sweet coz: what I do is to pleasure you, coz. Can you love the maid?

Slen. I will marry her, sir, at your request: but if there be no great love in the beginning, yet heaven may decrease it upon better acquaintance, when we are married and have more occasion to know one another; I hope, upon familiarity will grow more contempt: but if you say, 'Marry her,' I will marry her; that I am freely dissolved, and dissolutely. 260

140. **fidelicet,** *videlicet,* namely. 143. **Garter,** the name of an inn. 158. **groats,** coins equal to four pence; see glossary. **mill-sixpences,** coins stamped by means of the mill and press. 159. **Edward shovel-boards,** shillings coined in the reign of Edward VI, so called from their use in the gambling game of shovelboard. 160. **Yead,** dialect form of "Edward." 164. **mountain-foreigner,** Welshman. 165. **latten,** mixed metal of yellow color, resembling brass. **bilbo,** finely tempered sword of Bilbao in Spain. Pistol refers to Evans as a "brass sword." 166. **labras,** the lips; blunder for the neuter plural, *labra.* 169. **avised,** advised. **pass good humours,** do nothing ill-natured. 170. **'marry trap,'** an exclamation of insult when a man was caught in his own stratagem (Johnson). **nuthook's,** beadle's, constable's. 177. **Scarlet and John,** names of Robin Hood's companions, Will Scarlet and Little John; *Scarlet* is humorously applied to Bardolph's color. 183. **fap,** drunk. 184. **careires,** careers, short gallop at full speed; a feat in horsemanship. 191. **udge,** judge. 206. **Book of Songs and Sonnets.** This may be a reference to a manuscript book such as courtiers made, or to a volume of love poems by the earl of Surrey, Sir Thomas Wyatt, and others, published in 1557 by Tottel; it is better known to modern students as Tottel's *Miscellany.* 209. **Book of Riddles.** Such a book is mentioned as in the library of Captain Cox in *Laneham's Letter,* 1575. No copy is extant of an earlier date than 1629. 211. **All-hallowmas . . .**

Evans. It is a fery discretion answer; save the fall is in the ort 'dissolutely:' the ort is, according to our meaning, 'resolutely:' his meaning is good.

Shal. Ay, I think my cousin meant well.

Slen. Ay, or else I would I might be hanged, la!

Shal. Here comes fair Mistress Anne.

Re-enter ANNE PAGE.

Would I were young for your sake, Mistress Anne!

Anne. The dinner is on the table; my father desires your worships' company.   271

Shal. I will wait on him, fair Mistress Anne.

Evans. Od's plessed will! I will not be absence at the grace.   [*Exeunt Shallow and Evans.*

Anne. Will 't please your worship to come in, sir?

Slen. No, I thank you, forsooth, heartily; I am very well.

Anne. The dinner attends you, sir.   279

Slen. I am not a-hungry, I thank you, forsooth. Go, sirrah, for all you are my man, go wait upon my cousin Shallow. [*Exit Simple.*] A justice of peace sometime may be beholding to his friend for a man. I keep but three men and a boy yet, till my mother be dead: but what though? yet I live like a poor gentleman born.

Anne. I may not go in without your worship: they will not sit till you come.

Slen. I' faith, I'll eat nothing; I thank you as much as though I did.   291

Anne. I pray you, sir, walk in.

Slen. I had rather walk here, I thank you. I bruised my shin th' other day with playing at sword and dagger with a master of fence; three veneys for a dish of stewed prunes; and, by my troth, I cannot abide the smell of hot meat since. Why do your dogs bark so? be there bears i' the town?

Anne. I think there are, sir; I heard them talked of.

Slen. I love the sport well; but I shall as soon quarrel at it as any man in England. You are afraid, if you see the bear loose, are you not?   304

Anne. Ay, indeed, sir.

Slen. That 's meat and drink to me, now. I have seen Sackerson loose twenty times, and have taken him by the chain; but, I warrant you, the women have so cried and shrieked at it, that it passed: but women, indeed, cannot abide 'em; they are very ill-favoured rough things.

Re-enter PAGE.

Page. Come, gentle Master Slender, come; we stay for you.

Slen. I'll eat nothing, I thank you, sir.   315

Page. By cock and pie, you shall not choose, sir! come, come.

Slen. Nay, pray you, lead the way.

Page. Come on, sir.

Slen. Mistress Anne, yourself shall go first.

Anne. Not I, sir; pray you, keep on.   321

Slen. Truly, I will not go first; truly, la! I will not do you that wrong.

Anne. I pray you, sir.

Slen. I'll rather be unmannerly than troublesome. You do yourself wrong, indeed, la!   [*Exeunt.*

SCENE II. *The same.*

Enter SIR HUGH EVANS *and* SIMPLE.

Evans. Go your ways, and ask of Doctor Caius' house which is the way: and there dwells one Mistress Quickly, which is in the manner of his nurse, or his dry nurse, or his cook, or his laundry, his washer, and his wringer.

Sim. Well, sir.

Evans. Nay, it is petter yet. Give her this letter; for it is a 'oman that altogether 's acquaintance with Mistress Anne Page: and the letter is, to desire and require her to solicit your master's desires to Mistress Anne Page. I pray you, be gone: I will make an end of my dinner; there 's pippins and cheese to come.

[*Exeunt.*

SCENE III. *A room in the Garter Inn.*

Enter FALSTAFF, HOST, BARDOLPH, NYM, PISTOL, *and* ROBIN.

Fal. Mine host of the Garter!

Host. What says my bully-rook? speak scholarly and wisely.

Fal. Truly, mine host, I must turn away some of my followers.

Host. Discard, bully Hercules; cashier: let them wag; trot, trot.

Fal. I sit at ten pounds a week.   8

Host. Thou 'rt an emperor, Cæsar, Keisar, and Pheezar. I will entertain Bardolph; he shall draw, he shall tap: said I well, bully Hector?

Fal. Do so, good mine host.

Host. I have spoke; let him follow. [*To Bard.*] Let me see thee froth and lime: I am at a word; follow.
[*Exit.*

Fal. Bardolph, follow him. A tapster is a good trade: an old cloak makes a new jerkin; a withered serving-man a fresh tapster. Go; adieu.   20

Bard. It is a life that I have desired: I will thrive.

Pist. O base Hungarian wight! wilt thou the spigot wield?   [*Exit Bardolph.*

Nym. He was gotten in drink: is not the humour conceited?

Fal. I am glad I am so acquit of this tinderbox: his thefts were too open; his filching was like an unskilful singer; he kept not time.

Nym. The good humour is to steal at a minute's rest.

Pist. 'Convey,' the wise it call. 'Steal!' foh! a fico for the phrase!

Michaelmas, Simple's blunder. Michaelmas occurs in September, All-hallowmas on November 1. 244. **possitable,** the Welshman's error for "positively" (Hart). 257-258. **upon . . . contempt,** an allusion to the proverb "Familiarity breeds contempt." 279. **attends,** waits for. 296. **veneys,** thrusts in fencing. **stewed prunes,** an indelicate remark to address to a lady. Stewed prunes were associated with the "stews," or brothel houses. 307. **Sackerson,** a famous bear at the Paris Garden near the theaters on the Bankside. 316. **cock,** perversion of "God." **pie,** service book of the pre-Reformation church.

SCENE II. 1. **ask of,** inquire at. 13. **pippins and cheese.** Fruit and cheese were commonly used as desserts.

SCENE III. 2. **bully-rook,** not hyphenated in F; *bully,* gallant, fine; *rook,* a probable quibble on the meanings "the castle at chess" and "a sharper." 7. **wag,** proceed. 8. **sit at,** live on. 10. **Pheezar,** i.e., Vizier (Hart). 11. **tap,** serve as tapster. 15. **froth,** to draw liquor in such a way as to make it frothy. **lime,** adulterate wine by putting lime into it to make it sparkle. **at a word,** a man of few words (Hart). 23. **Hungarian,** a reference to discarded and cashiered soldiers from Hungary, and to the war (1593-1606) between the empire and the Turks. 31. **minute's.** Hart suggests a play on the phrase "steal a minute's rest"; Langton conjectured *minim's,* the shortest note in music; New Cambridge emends to *minim-rest.* 33. **fico,** Italian for "fig."

Fal. Well, sirs, I am almost out at heels.   34

Pist. Why, then, let kibes ensue.

Fal. There is no remedy; I must cony-catch; I must shift.

Pist. Young ravens must have food.

Fal. Which of you know Ford of this town?

Pist. I ken the wight: he is of substance good.   41

Fal. My honest lads, I will tell you what I am about.

Pist. Two yards, and more.

Fal. No quips now, Pistol! Indeed, I am in the waist two yards about; but I am now about no waste; I am about thrift. Briefly, I do mean to make love to Ford's wife: I spy entertainment in her; she discourses, she carves, she gives the leer of invitation: I can construe the action of her familiar style; and the hardest voice of her behaviour, to be Englished rightly, is, 'I am Sir John Falstaff's.'

Pist. He hath studied her will, and translated her will, out of honesty into English.

Nym. The anchor is deep: will that humour pass?

Fal. Now, the report goes she has all the rule of her husband's purse: he hath a legion of angels.   60

Pist. As many devils entertain; and 'To her, boy,' say I.

Nym. The humour rises; it is good: humour me the angels.

Fal. I have writ me here a letter to her: and here another to Page's wife, who even now gave me good eyes too, examined my parts with most judicious œillades; sometimes the beam of her view gilded my foot, sometimes my portly belly.

Pist. Then did the sun on dunghill shine.   70

Nym. I thank thee for that humour.

Fal. O, she did so course o'er my exteriors with such a greedy intention, that the appetite of her eye did seem to scorch me up like a burning-glass! Here's another letter to her: she bears the purse too; she is a region in Guiana, all gold and bounty. I will be cheater to them both, and they shall be exchequers to me; they shall be my East and West Indies, and I will trade to them both. Go bear thou this letter to Mistress Page; and thou this to Mistress Ford: we will thrive, lads, we will thrive.   82

Pist. Shall I Sir Pandarus of Troy become,
And by my side wear steel? then, Lucifer take all!

Nym. I will run no base humour: here, take the humour-letter: I will keep the haviour of reputation.

Fal. [*To Robin*] Hold, sirrah, bear you these letters tightly;
Sail like my pinnace to these golden shores.
Rogues, hence, avaunt! vanish like hailstones, go;   90
Trudge, plod away o' the hoof; seek shelter, pack!
Falstaff will learn the humour of the age,
French thrift, you rogues; myself and skirted page.
                                        [*Exeunt Falstaff and Robin.*

Pist. Let vultures gripe thy guts! for gourd and fullam holds,

And high and low beguiles the rich and poor:
Tester I'll have in pouch when thou shalt lack,
Base Phrygian Turk!

Nym. I have operations which be humours of revenge.

Pist. Wilt thou revenge?   100

Nym. By welkin and her star!

Pist. With wit or steel?

Nym. With both the humours, I:
I will discuss the humour of this love to Page.

Pist. And I to Ford shall eke unfold
        How Falstaff, varlet vile,
    His dove will prove, his gold will hold,
        And his soft couch defile.

Nym. My humour shall not cool: I will incense Page to deal with poison; I will possess him with yellowness, for the †revolt of mine is dangerous: that is my true humour.

Pist. Thou art the Mars of malecontents: I second thee; troop on.   [*Exeunt.*

SCENE IV. *A room in* DOCTOR CAIUS'S *house.*

Enter MISTRESS QUICKLY, SIMPLE, *and* RUGBY.

Quick. What, John Rugby! I pray thee, go to the casement, and see if you can see my master, Master Doctor Caius, coming. If he do, i' faith, and find any body in the house, here will be an old abusing of God's patience and the king's English.

Rug. I'll go watch.

Quick. Go; and we'll have a posset for 't soon at night, in faith, at the latter end of a sea-coal fire. [*Exit Rugby.*] An honest, willing, kind fellow, as ever servant shall come in house withal, and, I warrant you, no tell-tale nor no breed-bate: his worst fault is, that he is given to prayer; he is something peevish that way: but nobody but has his fault; but let that pass. Peter Simple, you say your name is?

Sim. Ay, for fault of a better.

Quick. And Master Slender 's your master?

Sim. Ay, forsooth.

Quick. Does he not wear a great round beard, like a glover's paring-knife?   21

Sim. No, forsooth: he hath but a little wee face, with a little yellow beard, a Cain-coloured beard.

Quick. A softly-sprighted man, is he not?

Sim. Ay, forsooth: but he is as tall a man of his hands as any is between this and his head; he hath fought with a warrener.

Quick. How say you? O, I should remember him: does he not hold up his head, as it were, and strut in his gait?   31

Sim. Yes, indeed, does he.

Quick. Well, heaven send Anne Page no worse fortune! Tell Master Parson Evans I will do what I can for your master: Anne is a good girl, and I wish—

35. **kibes,** chilblains.   40. **wight,** person.   49. **carves,** shows courtesy and affability.   52. **Englished,** expressed in English.   56. **The anchor is deep.** This phrase baffles most of the commentators. Steevens thought it might mean "his hopes are well founded"; Johnson thought *anchor* should be read *author,* taking his cue from *translated* in the preceding speech. Hart sees in the phrase Nym's acceptance of Falstaff's scheme, making the words equivalent to "the plan is fixed firmly." New Cambridge editors favor Kinnear's conjecture: *angle,* in view of *English* in the preceding speech and *angels* in the following.   60. **angels,** coins stamped with the figure of the archangel Michael.   64. **me,** the ethical dative.   68. **œillades,** amorous glances.   76. **region in Guiana.** Theobald thought this a possible compliment to Raleigh, assuming that the play

was given at court. Raleigh's *Discoverie of the Large, Rich, and Beautiful Empyre of Guiana* was published in 1596.   77. **cheater,** officer appointed to look after the king's escheats, i.e., land reverted to the crown; a quibble on the ordinary sense of "one who cheats."   83. **Sir Pandarus,** uncle of Cressida in the story of Troilus and Cressida; from his name originated the word "pander."   84. **Lucifer,** used synonymously for Satan.   86. **keep . . . reputation,** keep up good appearances.   88. **tightly,** soundly.   93. **French thrift,** alludes to the fashion of hiring French pages and of dismissing excess serving men (Hart).   94. **fullam,** a kind of false dice loaded at the corner.   96. **Tester,** sixpence.   97. **Phrygian Turk,** a term of opprobrium; cf. note to line 23 above.   98. **operations,** plans.   104. **discuss,** declare.   111. **yellowness,** jealousy.

Re-enter RUGBY.

Rug. Out, alas! here comes my master.

Quick. We shall all be shent. Run in here, good young man; go into this closet: he will not stay long. [*Shuts Simple in the closet.*] What, John Rugby! John! what, John, I say! Go, John, go inquire for my master; I doubt he be not well, that he comes not home. 43

[*Singing*] And down, down, adown-a, &c.

Enter DOCTOR CAIUS.

Caius. Vat is you sing? I do not like des toys. Pray you, go and vetch me in my closet un boitier vert, a box, a green-a box: do intend vat I speak? a green-a box.

Quick. Ay, forsooth; I'll fetch it you. [*Aside*] I am glad he went not in himself: if he had found the young man, he would have been horn-mad. 52

Caius. Fe, fe, fe, fe! ma foi, il fait fort chaud. Je m'en vais a la cour—la grande affaire.

Quick. Is it this, sir?

Caius. Oui; mette le au mon pocket: depeche, quickly. Vere is dat knave Rugby?

Quick. What, John Rugby! John!

Rug. Here, sir!

Caius. You are John Rugby, and you are Jack Rugby. Come, take-a your rapier, and come after my heel to the court. 62

Rug. 'Tis ready, sir, here in the porch.

Caius. By my trot, I tarry too long. Od's me! Qu'ai-j'oublie! dere is some simples in my closet, dat I vill not for the varld I shall leave behind.

Quick. Ay me, he'll find the young man there, and be mad!

Caius. O diable, diable! vat is in my closet? Villain! larron! [*Pulling Simple out.*] Rugby, my rapier! 72

Quick. Good master, be content.

Caius. Wherefore shall I be content-a?

Quick. The young man is an honest man.

Caius. What shall de honest man do in my closet? dere is no honest man dat shall come in my closet.

Quick. I beseech you, be not so phlegmatic. Hear the truth of it: he came of an errand to me from Parson Hugh. 81

Caius. Vell.

Sim. Ay, forsooth; to desire her to—

Quick. Peace, I pray you.

Caius. Peace-a your tongue. Speak-a your tale.

Sim. To desire this honest gentlewoman, your maid, to speak a good word to Mistress Anne Page for my master in the way of marriage.

Quick. This is all, indeed, la! but I'll ne'er put my finger in the fire, and need not. 91

Caius. Sir Hugh send-a you? Rugby, baille me some paper. Tarry you a little-a while. [*Writes.*

Quick. [*Aside to Simple*] I am glad he is so quiet: if he had been throughly moved, you should have heard him so loud and so melancholy. But notwithstanding, man, I'll do you your master what good I can: and the very yea and the no is. the French doctor, my master,—I may call him my master, look you, for I keep his house; and I wash, wring, brew, bake, scour, dress meat and drink, make the beds, and do all myself,—

Sim. [*Aside to Quickly*] 'Tis a great charge to come under one body's hand. 105

Quick. [*Aside to Simple*] Are you avised o' that? you shall find it a great charge: and to be up early and down late; but notwithstanding,—to tell you in your ear; I would have no words of it,—my master himself is in love with Mistress Anne Page: but notwithstanding that, I know Anne's mind,—that's neither here nor there.

Caius. You jack'nape, give-a this letter to Sir Hugh; by gar, it is a shallenge: I will cut his troat in de park; and I will teach a scurvy jack-a-nape priest to meddle or make. You may be gone; it is not good you tarry here. By gar, I will cut all his two stones; by gar, he shall not have a stone to throw at his dog. 119
[*Exit Simple.*

Quick. Alas, he speaks but for his friend.

Caius. It is no matter-a ver dat: do not you tell-a me dat I shall have Anne Page for myself? By gar, I vill kill de Jack priest; and I have appointed mine host of de Jarteer to measure our weapon. By gar, I will myself have Anne Page.

Quick. Sir, the maid loves you, and all shall be well. We must give folks leave to prate: what, the good-jer!

Caius. Rugby, come to the court with me. By gar, if I have not Anne Page, I shall turn your head out of my door. Follow my heels, Rugby.
[*Exeunt Caius and Rugby.*

Quick. You shall have An fool's-head of your own. No, I know Anne's mind for that: never a woman in Windsor knows more of Anne's mind than I do; nor can do more than I do with her, I thank heaven.

Fent. [*Within*] Who's within there? ho!

Quick. Who's there, I trow! Come near the house, I pray you. 141

Enter FENTON.

Fent. How now, good woman! how dost thou?

Quick. The better that it pleases your good worship to ask.

Fent. What news? how does pretty Mistress Anne?

Quick. In truth, sir, and she is pretty, and honest, and gentle; and one that is your friend, I can tell you that by the way; I praise heaven for it. 151

Fent. Shall I do any good, thinkest thou? shall I not lose my suit?

Quick. Troth, sir, all is in his hands above: but notwithstanding, Master Fenton, I'll be sworn on a book, she loves you. Have not your worship a wart above your eye?

Fent. Yes, marry, have I; what of that? 159

is dangerous. Nym means that his reaction against Falstaff for his dismissal will lead to disaster for the fat knight. 113. Mars of malecontents, i.e., a malcontent with respect to warlike matters, as contrasted with the melancholy of lovers, *et al.*

SCENE IV. 8. posset, a drink of hot milk curdled with ale or wine. 9. sea-coal, mineral coal as distinguished from charcoal. 12. breedbate, mischiefmaker. 22. wee. New Cambridge editors emend to *whey-face*, taking a cue from an error in Q_1 at line 20, *whey-colored beard.* 23. Cain-coloured, Ff: *Caine*; Q: *Kane*; most editors read *cane-coloured.* Theobald thought it referred to the pictures of Cain in old tapestries where he is given a yellow beard. 25. softly-sprighted, gentle. 26-27. as tall . . . hands. *New English Dictionary* defines *tall of one's hands* as dexterous, handy; also as stout of arms, formidable with weapons. 28. warrener, keeper of a warren, a place privileged by grant from the king for keeping certain animals. 38. shent, blamed, disgraced. 47. un boitier vert, a green box. 52. horn-mad, originally of horned beasts enraged so as to horn anyone; hence, of persons stark mad; quibblingly, mad with rage at being made a cuckold. 53-54. ma foi . . . affaire. My word, it is very hot; I am going to court—the great affair. 56. Oui . . . depeche. Yes, put it in my pocket; be quick. 61. your rapier, your master's rapier. 65. Qu'ai-j'oublie! What have I forgotten! simples, medicinal herbs. 71. larron, robber. 92. baille, give. 129. good-jer, good year; an expletive of doubtful meaning; see *NED* under "goodyear."

Quick. Well, thereby hangs a tale: good faith, it is such another Nan; but, I detest, an honest maid as ever broke bread: we had an hour's talk of that wart. I shall never laugh but in that maid's company! But indeed she is given too much to allicholy and musing: but for you—well, go to.

Fent. Well, I shall see her to-day. Hold, there's money for thee; let me have thy voice in my behalf: if thou seest her before me, commend me. 169

Quick. Will I? i' faith, that we will; and I will tell your worship more of the wart the next time we have confidence; and of other wooers.

Fent. Well, farewell; I am in great haste now.

Quick. Farewell to your worship. [*Exit Fenton.*] Truly, an honest gentleman: but Anne loves him not; for I know Anne's mind as well as another does. Out upon 't! what have I forgot? [*Exit.* 180

ACT II.

SCENE I. *Before* PAGE's *house.*

Enter MISTRESS PAGE, *with a letter.*

Mrs Page. What, have I scaped love-letters in the holiday-time of my beauty, and am I now a subject for them? Let me see. [*Reads.*

'Ask me no reason why I love you; for though Love use Reason for his precisian, he admits him not for his counsellor. You are not young, no more am I; go to then, there's sympathy: you are merry, so am I; ha, ha! then there's more sympathy: you love sack, and so do I; would you desire better sympathy? Let it suffice thee, Mistress Page,—at the least, if the love of soldier can suffice,—that I love thee. I will not say, pity me; 'tis not a soldier-like phrase: but I say, love me. By me,

Thine own true knight, 15
By day or night,
Or any kind of light,
With all his might
For thee to fight,
JOHN FALSTAFF.'

What a Herod of Jewry is this! O wicked, wicked world! One that is well-nigh worn to pieces with age to show himself a young gallant! What an unweighed behaviour hath this Flemish drunkard picked—with the devil's name!—out of my conversation, that he dares in this manner assay me? Why, he hath not been thrice in my company! What should I say to him? I was then frugal of my mirth: Heaven forgive me! Why, I'll exhibit a bill in the parliament for the putting down of men. How shall I be revenged on him? for revenged I will be, as sure as his guts are made of puddings. 32

Enter MISTRESS FORD.

Mrs Ford. Mistress Page! trust me, I was going to your house.

Mrs Page. And, trust me, I was coming to you. You look very ill.

Mrs Ford. Nay, I'll ne'er believe that; I have to show to the contrary. 38

Mrs Page. Faith, but you do, in my mind.

Mrs Ford. Well, I do then; yet I say I could show you to the contrary. O Mistress Page, give me some counsel!

Mrs Page. What's the matter, woman?

Mrs Ford. O woman, if it were not for one trifling respect, I could come to such honour!

Mrs Page. Hang the trifle, woman! take the honour. What is it? dispense with trifles; what is it?

Mrs Ford. If I would but go to hell for an eternal moment or so, I could be knighted. 50

Mrs Page. What? thou liest! Sir Alice Ford! These knights will hack; and so thou shouldst not alter the article of thy gentry.

Mrs Ford. We burn daylight: here, read, read; perceive how I might be knighted. I shall think the worse of fat men, as long as I have an eye to make difference of men's liking: and yet he would not swear; praised women's modesty; and gave such orderly and well-behaved reproof to all uncomeliness, that I would have sworn his disposition would have gone to the truth of his words; but they do no more adhere and keep place together than the Hundredth Psalm to the tune of 'Green Sleeves.' What tempest, I trow, threw this whale, with so many tuns of oil in his belly, ashore at Windsor? How shall I be revenged on him? I think the best way were to entertain him with hope, till the wicked fire of lust have melted him in his own grease. Did you ever hear the like? 70

Mrs Page. Letter for letter, but that the name of Page and Ford differs! To thy great comfort in this mystery of ill opinions, here's the twin-brother of thy letter: but let thine inherit first; for, I protest, mine never shall. I warrant he hath a thousand of these letters, writ with blank space for different names,—sure, more,—and these are of the second edition: he will print them, out of doubt; for he cares not what he puts into the press, when he would put us two. I had rather be a giantess, and lie under Mount Pelion. Well, I will find you twenty lascivious turtles ere one chaste man. 83

Mrs Ford. Why, this is the very same; the very hand, the very words. What doth he think of us?

Mrs Page. Nay, I know not: it makes me almost ready to wrangle with mine own honesty. I'll entertain myself like one that I am not acquainted withal; for, sure, unless he know some strain in me, that I know not myself, he would never have boarded me in this fury.

Mrs Ford. 'Boarding,' call you it? I'll be sure to keep him above deck. 94

Mrs Page. So will I: if he come under my hatches, I'll never to sea again. Let's be revenged on him: let's appoint him a meeting; give him a show of comfort in his suit and lead him on with a fine-baited delay, till he hath pawned his horses to mine host of the Garter.

Mrs Ford. Nay, I will consent to act any villany against him, that may not sully the chariness of our honesty. O, that my husband saw this letter! it would

---

160. **detest**, a malapropism for "protest." 164. **allicholy**, melancholy. ACT II. SCENE I. 5. **precisian**, rigid spiritual adviser; antithetical to *counselor*, i.e., worldly adviser (Hart); Globe, following Johnson: *physician.* 23. **unweighed**, inconsiderate. 26. **assay**, accost, address with proposals of love; see glossary. 29. **exhibit**, submit. 32. **puddings**, mixture of meat, herbs, etc., stuffed into intestines of animals, as sausage. 50. **moment**, period of time. 52. **hack**, of uncertain

meaning; the context suggests some indelicate reference (Onions). 53. **article of thy gentry**, character of your rank. 57. **make difference**, discriminate. **men's liking**, what men are like. 64. **'Green Sleeves,'** a popular tune to which many sets of words have been sung; cf. V, v, 22. 80. **press**, a quibble on the meanings "squeeze" and "print." 82. **lascivious turtles.** The turtle dove was proverbially chaste, i.e., faithful to its mate. 92. **boarded**, accosted, made advances to. 99. **fine-**

give eternal food to his jealousy.

Mrs Page. Why, look where he comes; and my good man too: he 's as far from jealousy as I am from giving him cause; and that I hope is an unmeasurable distance.

Mrs Ford. You are the happier woman. 110

Mrs Page. Let 's consult together against this greasy knight. Come hither. [*They retire.*

Enter FORD *with* PISTOL, *and* PAGE *with* NYM.

Ford. Well, I hope it be not so.

Pist. Hope is a curtal dog in some affairs:
Sir John affects thy wife.

Ford. Why, sir, my wife is not young.

Pist. He wooes both high and low, both rich and poor,
Both young and old, one with another, Ford;
He loves the gallimaufry: Ford, perpend.

Ford. Love my wife! 120

Pist. With liver burning hot. Prevent, or go thou,
Like Sir Actæon he, with Ringwood at thy heels:
O, odious is the name!

Ford. What name, sir?

Pist. The horn, I say. Farewell.
Take heed, have open eye, for thieves do foot by night:
Take heed, ere summer comes or cuckoo-birds do sing.
Away, Sir Corporal Nym!
Believe it, Page; he speaks sense. [*Exit.*

Ford. [*Aside*] I will be patient; I will find out this. 131

Nym. [*To Page*] And this is true; I like not the humour of lying. He hath wronged me in some humours: I should have borne the humoured letter to her; but I have a sword and it shall bite upon my necessity. He loves your wife; there 's the short and the long. My name is Corporal Nym; I speak and I avouch; 'tis true: my name is Nym and Falstaff loves your wife. Adieu. I love not the humour of bread and cheese, and there 's the humour of it. Adieu. [*Exit.*

Page. 'The humour of it,' quoth a'! here 's a fellow frights English out of his wits. 143

Ford. I will seek out Falstaff.

Page. I never heard such a drawling, affecting rogue.

Ford. If I do find it: well.

Page. I will not believe such a Cataian, though the priest o' the town commended him for a true man. 150

Ford. 'Twas a good sensible fellow: well.

Page. How now, Meg!

[*Mrs Page and Mrs Ford come forward.*

Mrs Page. Whither go you, George? Hark you.

Mrs Ford. How now, sweet Frank! why art thou melancholy?

Ford. I melancholy! I am not melancholy. Get you home, go.

Mrs Ford. Faith, thou hast some crotchets in thy head. Now, will you go, Mistress Page?

Mrs Page. Have with you. You'll come to dinner, George. [*Aside to Mrs Ford*] Look who comes yonder: she shall be our messenger to this paltry knight. 164

Mrs Ford. [*Aside to Mrs Page*] Trust me, I thought on her: she'll fit it.

Enter MISTRESS QUICKLY.

Mrs Page. You are come to see my daughter Anne?

Quick. Ay, forsooth; and, I pray, how does good Mistress Anne? 170

Mrs Page. Go in with us and see: we have an hour's talk with you.

[*Exeunt Mrs Page, Mrs Ford, and Mrs Quickly.*

Page. How now, Master Ford!

Ford. You heard what this knave told me, did you not?

Page. Yes: and you heard what the other told me?

Ford. Do you think there is truth in them?

Page. Hang 'em, slaves! I do not think the knight would offer it: but these that accuse him in his intent towards our wives are a yoke of his discarded men; very rogues, now they be out of service. 182

Ford. Were they his men?

Page. Marry, were they.

Ford. I like it never the better for that. Does he lie at the Garter?

Page. Ay, marry, does he. If he should intend this voyage towards my wife, I would turn her loose to him; and what he gets more of her than sharp words, let it lie on my head. 191

Ford. I do not misdoubt my wife; but I would be loath to turn them together. A man may be too confident: I would have nothing lie on my head: I cannot be thus satisfied.

Page. Look where my ranting host of the Garter comes: there is either liquor in his pate or money in his purse when he looks so merrily.

Enter HOST.

How now, mine host!

Host. How now, bully-rook! thou 'rt a gentleman. Cavaleiro-justice, I say! 201

Enter SHALLOW.

Shal. I follow, mine host, I follow. Good even and twenty, good Master Page! Master Page, will you go with us? we have sport in hand.

Host. Tell him, cavaleiro-justice; tell him, bully-rook.

Shal. Sir, there is a fray to be fought between Sir Hugh the Welsh priest and Caius the French doctor.

Ford. Good mine host o' the Garter, a word with you. [*Drawing him aside.*

Host. What sayest thou, my bully-rook? 213

Shal. [*To Page*] Will you go with us to behold it? My merry host hath had the measuring of their weapons; and, I think, hath appointed them contrary places; for, believe me, I hear the parson is no jester. Hark, I will tell you what our sport shall be. [*They converse apart.*

Host. Hast thou no suit against my knight, my guest-cavaleire? 221

Ford. None, I protest: but I'll give you a pottle of burnt sack to give me recourse to him and tell him my name is Brook; only for a jest.

baited, subtly alluring. 114. **curtal,** having the tail docked. 119. **gallimaufry,** promiscuous assembly. **perpend,** consider. 121. **burning hot,** an allusion to the liver as the seat of the passions. 122. **Actæon.** Cf. *Titus Andronicus,* II, iii, 63, note. **Ringwood,** one of Actæon's dogs, mentioned in Golding's translation of Ovid. 127. **cuckoo-birds,** superstitiously regarded as birds presaging ill luck in love; cf. *Love's Labour's Lost,* V, ii, 910-911. 136. **upon my necessity**

when I have need. 140. **humour . . . cheese.** Nym alludes to the scant rations he received as Falstaff's retainer. 148. **Cataian,** Cathaian, man or woman of Cathay, i.e., China; a pejorative word meaning sharper, scoundrel. 161. **Have with,** I shall go along with; see glossary. 201. **Cavaleiro,** gentleman trained in arms, a gay military man. 202-203. **Good . . . twenty,** good evening, twenty times. 221. **cavaleire,** gallant. 223. **pottle,** two-quart measure. **burnt,** heated.

Host. My hand, bully; thou shalt have egress and regress;—said I well?—and thy name shall be Brook. It is a merry knight. Will you go, †An-heires?

Shal. Have with you, mine host.

Page. I have heard the Frenchman hath good skill in his rapier. 231

Shal. Tut, sir, I could have told you more. In these times you stand on distance, your passes, stoccadoes, and I know not what: 'tis the heart, Master Page; 'tis here, 'tis here. I have seen the time, with my long sword I would have made you four tall fellows skip like rats.

Host. Here, boys, here, here! shall we wag?

Page. Have with you. I had rather hear them scold than fight. [*Exeunt Host, Shal., and Page.* 240

Ford. Though Page be a secure fool, and stands so firmly on his wife's frailty, yet I cannot put off my opinion so easily: she was in his company at Page's house; and what they made there, I know not. Well, I will look further into 't: and I have a disguise to sound Falstaff. If I find her honest, I lose not my labour; if she be otherwise, 'tis labour well bestowed. [*Exit.*

SCENE II. *A room in the Garter Inn.*

Enter FALSTAFF *and* PISTOL.

Fal. I will not lend thee a penny.

Pist. Why, then the world 's mine oyster, Which I with sword will open.

Fal. Not a penny. I have been content, sir, you should lay my countenance to pawn: I have grated upon my good friends for three reprieves for you and your coach-fellow Nym; or else you had looked through the grate, like a geminy of baboons. I am damned in hell for swearing to gentlemen my friends, you were good soldiers and tall fellows; and when Mistress Bridget lost the handle of her fan, I took 't upon mine honour thou hadst it not. 12

Pist. Didst not thou share? hadst thou not fifteen pence?

Fal. Reason, you rogue, reason: thinkest thou I'll endanger my soul gratis? At a word, hang no more about me, I am no gibbet for you. Go. A short knife and a throng! To your manor of Pickt-hatch! Go. You'll not bear a letter for me, you rogue! you stand upon your honour! Why, thou unconfinable baseness, it is as much as I can do to keep the terms of my honour precise: I, I, I myself sometimes, leaving the fear of God on the left hand and hiding mine honour in my necessity, am fain to shuffle, to hedge and to lurch; and yet you, rogue, will ensconce your rags, your cat-a-mountain looks, your red-lattice phrases, and your bold-beating oaths, under the shelter of your honour! You will not do it, you! 30

Pist. I do relent: what would thou more of man?

Enter ROBIN.

Rob. Sir, here 's a woman would speak with you.

Fal. Let her approach.

Enter MISTRESS QUICKLY.

Quick. Give your worship good morrow.

Fal. Good morrow, good wife.

Quick. Not so, an 't please your worship.

Fal. Good maid, then.

Quick. I'll be sworn, As my mother was, the first hour I was born.

Fal. I do believe the swearer. What with me? 40

Quick. Shall I vouchsafe your worship a word or two?

Fal. Two thousand, fair woman: and I'll vouchsafe thee the hearing.

Quick. There is one Mistress Ford, sir:—I pray, come a little nearer this ways:—I myself dwell with Master Doctor Caius,—

Fal. Well, on: Mistress Ford, you say,—

Quick. Your worship says very true: I pray your worship, come a little nearer this ways. 50

Fal. I warrant thee, nobody hears; mine own people, mine own people.

Quick. Are they so? God bless them and make them his servants!

Fal. Well, Mistress Ford; what of her?

Quick. Why, sir, she 's a good creature. Lord, Lord! your worship 's a wanton! Well, heaven forgive you and all of us, I pray!

Fal. Mistress Ford; come, Mistress Ford,—

Quick. Marry, this is the short and the long of it; you have brought her into such a canaries as 'tis wonderful. The best courtier of them all, when the court lay at Windsor, could never have brought her to such a canary. Yet there has been knights, and lords, and gentlemen, with their coaches, I warrant you, coach after coach, letter after letter, gift after gift; smelling so sweetly, all musk, and so rushling, I warrant you, in silk and gold; and in such alligant terms; and in such wine and sugar of the best and the fairest, that would have won any woman's heart; and, I warrant you, they could never get an eye-wink of her: I had myself twenty angels given me this morning; but I defy all angels, in any such sort, as they say, but in the way of honesty: and, I warrant you, they could never get her so much as sip on a cup with the proudest of them all: and yet there has been earls, nay, which is more, pensioners; but, I warrant you, all is one with her. 80

Fal. But what says she to me? be brief, my good she-Mercury.

Quick. Marry, she hath received your letter, for the which she thanks you a thousand times; and she gives you to notify that her husband will be absence from his house between ten and eleven.

Fal. Ten and eleven?

Quick. Ay, forsooth; and then you may come and see the picture, she says, that you wot of: Master Ford, her husband, will be from home. Alas! the sweet woman leads an ill life with him: he 's a very jealousy man: she leads a very frampold life with him, good heart. 94

---

228. **An-heires,** so F; Hart suggested *Ameers,* another oriental title, i.e., Amiras; Onions thinks it may be an error for *Mynheers,* i.e., Sirs. 233-237. **In these . . . like rats,** an allusion to the new styles in dueling; see *Shakespeare's England,* II, 392.

SCENE II. 2. **mine oyster.** To open an oyster was a metaphorical phrase for laying bare any difficult matter (Hart). 5. **countenance,** patronage. 8. **geminy,** pair. 18. **A short . . . throng,** i.e., with a

short knife one might cut purses in a crowd. 19. **Pickt-hatch,** quarter in London famous in Elizabethan times for houses of ill fame, the houses having hatches, or half doors, guarded with spikes. 21. **unconfinable,** infinite. 27. **cat-a-mountain,** leopard or panther. 28. **red-lattice phrases,** alehouse talk, from lattice painted red as the sign of an alehouse. **bold-beating,** a confusion of "bold-faced" and "browbeating." 41. **vouchsafe,** deign to grant; Quickly's error. 61.

Fal. Ten and eleven. Woman, commend me to her; I will not fail her.

Quick. Why, you say well. But I have another messenger to your worship. Mistress Page hath her hearty commendations to you too: and let me tell you in your ear, she 's as fartuous a civil modest wife, and one, I tell you, that will not miss you morning nor evening prayer, as any is in Windsor, whoe'er be the other: and she bade me tell your worship that her husband is seldom from home; but she hopes there will come a time. I never knew a woman so dote upon a man: surely I think you have charms, la; yes, in truth.

Fal. Not I, I assure thee: setting the attraction of my good parts aside I have no other charms. 111

Quick. Blessing on your heart for 't!

Fal. But, I pray thee, tell me this: has Ford's wife and Page's wife acquainted each other how they love me?

Quick. That were a jest indeed! they have not so little grace, I hope: that were a trick indeed! But Mistress Page would desire you to send her your little page, of all loves: her husband has a marvellous infection to the little page; and truly Master Page is an honest man. Never a wife in Windsor leads a better life than she does: do what she will, say what she will, take all, pay all, go to bed when she list, rise when she list, all is as she will: and truly she deserves it; for if there be a kind woman in Windsor, she is one. You must send her your page; no remedy. 127

Fal. Why, I will.

Quick. Nay, but do so, then: and, look you, he may come and go between you both; and in any case have a nay-word, that you may know one another's mind, and the boy never need to understand any thing; for 'tis not good that children should know any wickedness: old folks, you know, have discretion, as they say, and know the world.

Fal. Fare thee well: commend me to them both: there 's my purse; I am yet thy debtor. Boy, go along with this woman. [*Exeunt Mistress Quickly and Robin.*] This news distracts me! 140

Pist. This punk is one of Cupid's carriers:
Clap on more sails; pursue; up with your fights:
Give fire: she is my prize, or ocean whelm them all!
[*Exit.*

Fal. Sayest thou so, old Jack? go thy ways; I'll make more of thy old body than I have done. Will they yet look after thee? Wilt thou, after the expense of so much money, be now a gainer? Good body, I thank thee. Let them say 'tis grossly done; so it be fairly done, no matter. 150

Enter BARDOLPH.

Bard. Sir John, there 's one Master Brook below would fain speak with you, and be acquainted with you; and hath sent your worship a morning's draught of sack.

Fal. Brook is his name?

Bard. Ay, sir.

Fal. Call him in. [*Exit Bardolph.*] Such Brooks are welcome to me, that o'erflow such liquor. Ah, ha!

Mistress Ford and Mistress Page, have I encompassed you? go to; via!

Re-enter BARDOLPH, *with* FORD *disguised.*

Ford. Bless you, sir! 160

Fal. And you, sir! Would you speak with me?

Ford. I make bold to press with so little preparation upon you.

Fal. You 're welcome. What 's your will? Give us leave, drawer. [*Exit Bardolph.*

Ford. Sir, I am a gentleman that have spent much; my name is Brook.

Fal. Good Master Brook, I desire more acquaintance of you. 169

Ford. Good Sir John, I sue for yours: not to charge you; for I must let you understand I think myself in better plight for a lender than you are: the which hath something emboldened me to this unseasoned intrusion; for they say, if money go before, all ways do lie open.

Fal. Money is a good soldier, sir, and will on.

Ford. Troth, and I have a bag of money here troubles me: if you will help to bear it, Sir John, take all, or half, for easing me of the carriage.

Fal. Sir, I know not how I may deserve to be your porter. 181

Ford. I will tell you, sir, if you will give me the hearing.

Fal. Speak, good Master Brook: I shall be glad to be your servant.

Ford. Sir, I hear you are a scholar,—I will be brief with you,—and you have been a man long known to me, though I had never so good means, as desire, to make myself acquainted with you. I shall discover a thing to you, wherein I must very much lay open mine own imperfection: but, good Sir John, as you have one eye upon my follies, as you hear them unfolded, turn another into the register of your own; that I may pass with a reproof the easier, sith you yourself know how easy it is to be such an offender.

Fal. Very well, sir; proceed.

Ford. There is a gentlewoman in this town; her husband's name is Ford.

Fal. Well, sir. 200

Ford. I have long loved her, and, I protest to you, bestowed much on her; followed her with a doting observance; engrossed opportunities to meet her; fee'd every slight occasion that could but niggardly give me sight of her; not only bought many presents to give her, but have given largely to many to know what she would have given; briefly, I have pursued her as love hath pursued me; which hath been on the wing of all occasions. But whatsoever I have merited, either in my mind or in my means, meed, I am sure, I have received none; unless experience be a jewel that I have purchased at an infinite rate, and that hath taught me to say this:
'Love like a shadow flies when substance love pursues;
Pursuing that that flies, and flying what pursues.'

Fal. Have you received no promise of satisfaction at her hands?

The Merry Wives of Windsor ACT II : SC II

---

canaries, a malapropism for "quandaries" (Steevens); a quibble on "canary," suggesting that she was drunk. 68. **rushling,** i.e., rustling. 69. **alligant,** elegant. 79. **pensioners,** bodyguard to a sovereign in the royal palace. 82. **she-Mercury,** woman messenger. 94. **frampold,** disagreeable. 100. **fartuous,** mistake for "virtuous." **modest,** characterized by decency and propriety; see glossary. 102. **you,** ethical dative. 120. **infection to,** affection for. 131. **nay-word,** watchword.

140. **distracts,** perplexes, bewilders. 141. **punk,** harlot. 142. **fights,** fighting sails, i.e., screens raised during naval engagements to conceal and protect the crew. 159. **encompassed,** outwitted. **via,** go on. 203. **engrossed,** monopolized. 204. **fee'd,** employed.

Ford. Never.

Fal. Have you importuned her to such a purpose? 221

Ford. Never.

Fal. Of what quality was your love, then?

Ford. Like a fair house built on another man's ground; so that I have lost my edifice by mistaking the place where I erected it.

Fal. To what purpose have you unfolded this to me?

Ford. When I have told you that, I have told you all. Some say, that though she appear honest to me, yet in other places she enlargeth her mirth so far that there is shrewd construction made of her. Now, Sir John, here is the heart of my purpose: you are a gentleman of excellent breeding, admirable discourse, of great admittance, authentic in your place and person, generally allowed for your many war-like, court-like, and learned preparations.

Fal. O, sir! 239

Ford. Believe it, for you know it. There is money; spend it, spend it; spend more; spend all I have; only give me so much of your time in exchange of it, as to lay an amiable siege to the honesty of this Ford's wife: use your art of wooing; win her to consent to you: if any man may, you may as soon as any.

Fal. Would it apply well to the vehemency of your affection, that I should win what you would enjoy? Methinks you prescribe to yourself very preposterously. 250

Ford. O, understand my drift. She dwells so securely on the excellency of her honour, that the folly of my soul dares not present itself: she is too bright to be looked against. Now, could I come to her with any detection in my hand, my desires had instance and argument to commend themselves: I could drive her then from the ward of her purity, her reputation, her marriage-vow, and a thousand other her defences, which now are too too strongly embattled against me. What say you to 't, Sir John? 261

Fal. Master Brook, I will first make bold with your money; next, give me your hand; and last, as I am a gentleman, you shall, if you will, enjoy Ford's wife.

Ford. O good sir!

Fal. I say you shall.

Ford. Want no money, Sir John; you shall want none. 269

Fal. Want no Mistress Ford, Master Brook; you shall want none. I shall be with her, I may tell you, by her own appointment; even as you came in to me, her assistant or go-between parted from me: I say I shall be with her between ten and eleven; for at that time the jealous rascally knave her husband will be forth. Come you to me at night; you shall know how I speed.

Ford. I am blest in your acquaintance. Do you know Ford, sir? 280

Fal. Hang him, poor cuckoldly knave! I know him not: yet I wrong him to call him poor; they say the jealous wittolly knave hath masses of money; for the which his wife seems to me well-favoured. I will use her as the key of the cuckoldly rogue's coffer; and there 's my harvest-home.

Ford. I would you knew Ford, sir, that you might avoid him if you saw him. 289

Fal. Hang him, mechanical salt-butter rogue! I will stare him out of his wits; I will awe him with my cudgel: it shall hang like a meteor o'er the cuckold's horns. Master Brook, thou shalt know I will predominate over the peasant, and thou shalt lie with his wife. Come to me soon at night. Ford 's a knave, and I will aggravate his style; thou, Master Brook, shalt know him for knave and cuckold. Come to me soon at night. [*Exit.* 299

Ford. What a damned Epicurean rascal is this! My heart is ready to crack with impatience. Who says this is improvident jealousy? my wife hath sent to him; the hour is fixed; the match is made. Would any man have thought this? See the hell of having a false woman! My bed shall be abused, my coffers ransacked, my reputation gnawn at; and I shall not only receive this villanous wrong, but stand under the adoption of abominable terms, and by him that does me this wrong. Terms! names! Amaimon sounds well; Lucifer, well; Barbason, well; yet they are devils' additions, the names of fiends: but Cuckold! Wittol! —Cuckold! the devil himself hath not such a name. Page is an ass, a secure ass: he will trust his wife; he will not be jealous. I will rather trust a Fleming with my butter, Parson Hugh the Welshman with my cheese, an Irishman with my aqua-vitæ bottle, or a thief to walk my ambling gelding, than my wife with herself: then she plots, then she ruminates, then she devises; and what they think in their hearts they may effect, they will break their hearts but they will effect. God be praised for my jealousy! Eleven o'clock the hour. I will prevent this, detect my wife, be revenged on Falstaff, and laugh at Page. I will about it; better three hours too soon than a minute too late. Fie, fie, fie! cuckold! cuckold! cuckold! [*Exit.* 329

SCENE III. *A field near Windsor.*

Enter CAIUS *and* RUGBY.

Caius. Jack Rugby!

Rug. Sir?

Caius. Vat is de clock, Jack?

Rug. 'Tis past the hour, sir, that Sir Hugh promised to meet.

Caius. By gar, he has save his soul, dat he is no come; he has pray his Pible well, dat he is no come: by gar, Jack Rugby, he is dead already, if he be come.

Rug. He is wise, sir; he knew your worship would kill him, if he came. 11

Caius. By gar, de herring is no dead so as I vill kill him. Take your rapier, Jack; I vill tell you how I vill kill him.

Rug. Alas, sir, I cannot fence.

Caius. Villany, take your rapier.

Rug. Forbear; here 's company.

Enter HOST, SHALLOW, SLENDER, *and* PAGE.

Host. Bless thee, bully doctor!

---

231. **enlargeth,** gives free scope to; see glossary. 235. **admittance,** fashion, vogue. 238. **preparations,** accomplishments. 250. **preposterously,** with the natural order of things inverted. 283. **wittolly,** cuckoldly. 290. **mechanical,** engaged in manual occupation. 296. **aggravate his style,** increase or add to his title. 311. **Amaimon, Lucifer, Barbason,** names of devils; they occur in Scot's *Discoverie of Witchcraft* (1584).

SCENE III. 24. **foin,** thrust (in fencing). 25. **traverse,** march, especially backward and forward. 26. **punto,** stroke or thrust with the point of the sword. 29. **Æsculapius,** god of medicine. **Galen,** famous Greek physician. 30. **heart of elder,** opposite of "heart of oak"; the elder has no heart (Steevens). 50. **salt,** wantonness. 60. **Mounseur Mockwater.** Dr. Johnson says, "The Host means to reflect

Shal. Save you, Master Doctor Caius!

Page. Now, good master doctor! 20

Slen. Give you good morrow, sir.

Caius. Vat be all you, one, two, tree, four, come for?

Host. To see thee fight, to see thee foin, to see thee traverse; to see thee here, to see thee there; to see thee pass thy punto, thy stock, thy reverse, thy distance, thy montant. Is he dead, my Ethiopian? is he dead, my Francisco? ha, bully! What says my Æsculapius? my Galen? my heart of elder? ha! is he dead, bully stale? is he dead? 31

Caius. By gar, he is de coward Jack priest of de vorld; he is not show his face.

Host. Thou art a Castalion-King-Urinal. Hector of Greece, my boy!

Caius. I pray you, bear vitness that me have stay six or seven, two, tree hours for him, and he is no come.

Shal. He is the wiser man, master doctor: he is a curer of souls, and you a curer of bodies; if you should fight, you go against the hair of your professions. Is it not true, Master Page?

Page. Master Shallow, you have yourself been a great fighter, though now a man of peace. 44

Shal. Bodykins, Master Page, though I now be old and of the peace, if I see a sword out, my finger itches to make one. Though we are justices and doctors and churchmen, Master Page, we have some salt of our youth in us; we are the sons of women, Master Page.

Page. 'Tis true, Master Shallow.

Shal. It will be found so, Master Page. Master Doctor Caius, I am come to fetch you home. I am sworn of the peace: you have showed yourself a wise physician, and Sir Hugh hath shown himself a wise and patient churchman. You must go with me, master doctor.

Host. Pardon, guest-justice. A word, Mounseur Mockwater. 60

Caius. Mock-vater! vat is dat?

Host. Mock-water, in our English tongue, is valour, bully.

Caius. By gar, den, I have as mush mock-vater as de Englishman. Scurvy jack-dog priest! by gar, me vill cut his ears.

Host. He will clapper-claw thee tightly, bully.

Caius. Clapper-de-claw! vat is dat?

Host. That is, he will make thee amends. 70

Caius. By gar, me do look he shall clapper-de-claw me; for, by gar, me vill have it.

Host. And I will provoke him to 't, or let him wag.

Caius. Me tank you for dat.

Host. And, moreover, bully,—but first, master guest, and Master Page, and eke Cavaleiro Slender, go you through the town to Frogmore. [*Aside to them.*

Page. Sir Hugh is there, is he? 79

Host. He is there: see what humour he is in; and I will bring the doctor about by the fields. Will it do well?

Shal. We will do it.

Page, Shal., and Slen. Adieu, good master doctor.

[*Exeunt Page, Shal., and Slen.*

Caius. By gar, me vill kill de priest; for he speak for a jack-an-ape to Anne Page. 87

Host. Let him die: sheathe thy impatience, throw cold water on thy choler: go about the fields with me through Frogmore: I will bring thee where Mistress Anne Page is, at a farmhouse a-feasting; and thou shalt woo her. Cried I aim? said I well?

Caius. By gar, me dank you vor dat: by gar, I love you; and I shall procure-a you de good guest, de earl, de knight, de lords, de gentlemen, my patients.

Host. For the which I will be thy adversary toward Anne Page. Said I well?

Caius. By gar, 'tis good; vell said. 100

Host. Let us wag, then.

Caius. Come at my heels, Jack Rugby. [*Exeunt.*

ACT III.

SCENE I. *A field near Frogmore.*

Enter SIR HUGH EVANS *and* SIMPLE.

Evans. I pray you now, good Master Slender's serving-man, and friend Simple by your name, which way have you looked for Master Caius, that calls himself doctor of physic?

Sim. Marry, sir, the pittie-ward, the park-ward, every way; old Windsor way, and every way but the town way.

Evans. I most fehemently desire you you will also look that way.

Sim. I will, sir. [*Exit.* 10

Evans. 'Pless my soul, how full of chollors I am, and trempling of mind! I shall be glad if he have deceived me. How melancholies I am! I will knog his urinals about his knave's costard when I have good opportunities for the ork. 'Pless my soul! [*Sings.*

To shallow rivers, to whose falls
Melodious birds sings madrigals;
There will we make our peds of roses,
And a thousand fragrant posies. 20
To shallow—

Mercy on me! I have a great dispositions to cry.

[*Sings.*

Melodious birds sing madrigals—
When as I sat in Pabylon—
And a thousand vagram posies.
To shallow &c.

Re-enter SIMPLE.

Sim. Yonder he is coming, this way, Sir Hugh.

Evans. He 's welcome. [*Sings.*

To shallow rivers, to whose falls— 29

Heaven prosper the right! What weapons is he?

Sim. No weapons, sir. There comes my master, Master Shallow, and another gentleman, from Frogmore, over the stile, this way.

Evans. Pray you, give me my gown; or else keep it in your arms.

Enter PAGE, SHALLOW, *and* SLENDER.

---

on the inspection of urine, which made a considerable part of practical physic in that time; yet I do not see the meaning of mock-water." Farmer suggested *muck-water*, the drain of a dunghill.   92. **Cried I aim,** I applauded.

ACT III. SCENE I.   5. **pittie-ward,** evidently toward the Petty (park or other local place).   **park-ward,** toward the park, i.e., Windsor Park.   14. **knog,** knock.   **costard,** apple; humorously applied to the head.   17-20. **To shallow rivers,** etc., lines from Marlowe's *Come live with me and be my love.*   25. **vagram,** vagrant.

Shal. How now, master Parson! Good morrow, good Sir Hugh. Keep a gamester from the dice, and a good student from his book, and it is wonderful.

Slen. [*Aside*] Ah, sweet Anne Page! 40

Page. 'Save you, good Sir Hugh!

Evans. 'Pless you from his mercy sake, all of you!

Shal. What, the sword and the word! do you study them both, master parson?

Page. And youthful still! in your doublet and hose this raw rheumatic day!

Evans. There is reasons and causes for it.

Page. We are come to you to do a good office, master parson. 50

Evans. Fery well: what is it?

Page. Yonder is a most reverend gentleman, who, belike having received wrong by some person, is at most odds with his own gravity and patience that ever you saw.

Shal. I have lived fourscore years and upward; I never heard a man of his place, gravity and learning, so wide of his own respect.

Evans. What is he?

Page. I think you know him; Master Doctor Caius, the renowned French physician. 61

Evans. Got's will, and his passion of my heart! I had as lief you would tell me of a mess of porridge.

Page. Why?

Evans. He has no more knowledge in Hibocrates and Galen,—and he is a knave besides; a cowardly knave as you would desires to be acquainted withal.

Page. I warrant you, he 's the man should fight with him. 71

Slen. [*Aside*] O sweet Anne Page!

Shal. It appears so by his weapons. Keep them asunder: here comes Doctor Caius.

Enter HOST, CAIUS, *and* RUGBY.

Page. Nay, good master parson, keep in your weapon.

Shal. So do you, good master doctor.

Host. Disarm them, and let them question: let them keep their limbs whole and hack our English. 80

Caius. I pray you, let-a me speak a word with your ear. Vherefore vill you not meet-a me?

Evans. [*Aside to Caius*] Pray you, use your patience: in good time.

Caius. By gar, you are de coward, de Jack dog, John ape.

Evans. [*Aside to Caius*] Pray you, let us not be laughing-stocks to other men's humours; I desire you in friendship, and I will one way or other make you amends. [*Aloud*] I will knog your urinals about your knave's cogscomb for missing your meetings and appointments. 92

Caius. Diable! Jack Rugby,—mine host de Jarteer,—have I not stay for him to kill him? have I not, at de place I did appoint?

Evans. As I am a Christians soul now, look you, this is the place appointed: I'll be judgement by mine host of the Garter.

Host. Peace, I say, Gallia and Gaul, French and

Welsh, soul-curer and body-curer!

Caius. Ay, dat is very good; excellent.

Host. Peace, I say! hear mine host of the Garter. Am I politic? am I subtle? am I a Machiavel? Shall I lose my doctor? no; he gives me the potions and the motions. Shall I lose my parson, my priest, my Sir Hugh? no: he gives me the proverbs and the no-verbs. Give me thy hand, terrestrial; so. Give me thy hand, celestial; so. Boys of art, I have deceived you both; I have directed you to wrong places: your hearts are mighty, your skins are whole, and let burnt sack be the issue. Come, lay their swords to pawn. Follow me, lads of peace; follow, follow, follow.

Shal. Trust me, a mad host. Follow, gentlemen, follow.

Slen. [*Aside*] O sweet Anne Page!

[*Exeunt Shal., Slen., Page, and Host.*

Caius. Ha, do I perceive dat? have you make-a de sot of us, ha, ha? 119

Evans. This is well; he has made us his vlouting-stog. I desire you that we may be friends; and let us knog our prains together to be revenge on this same scall, scurvy, cogging companion, the host of the Garter.

Caius. By gar, with all my heart. He promise to bring me where is Anne Page; by gar, he deceive me too.

Evans. Well, I will smite his noddles. Pray you, follow. [*Exeunt.*

SCENE II. *A street.*

Enter MISTRESS PAGE *and* ROBIN.

Mrs Page. Nay, keep your way, little gallant; you were wont to be a follower, but now you are a leader. Whether had you rather lead mine eyes, or eye your master's heels?

Rob. I had rather, forsooth, go before you like a man than follow him like a dwarf.

Mrs Page. O, you are a flattering boy: now I see you'll be a courtier.

Enter FORD.

Ford. Well met, Mistress Page. Whither go you? 10

Mrs Page. Truly, sir, to see your wife. Is she at home?

Ford. Ay; and as idle as she may hang together, for want of company. I think, if your husbands were dead, you two would marry.

Mrs Page. Be sure of that,—two other husbands.

Ford. Where had you this pretty weathercock?

Mrs Page. I cannot tell what the dickens his name is my husband had him of. What do you call your knight's name, sirrah? 21

Rob. Sir John Falstaff.

Ford. Sir John Falstaff!

Mrs Page. He, he; I can never hit on 's name. There is such a league between my good man and he! Is your wife at home indeed?

Ford. Indeed she is.

44. **the word,** the Bible; it may possibly have an association with the phrase "the sword of the Spirit," meaning the Bible. 58. **respect,** modest deportment; see glossary. 99. **Gallia and Gaul,** Wales and France. 104. **Machiavel.** Cf. *1 Henry VI*, V, iv, 74, note. 119. **sot,** fool. 120. **vlouting-stog,** flouting-stock, i.e., laughingstock. 123. **scall,** scald, i.e., scurvy. **cogging,** cheating; see glossary. SCENE II. 13. **hang together,** i.e., as idle as she can be and still

hold together. 18. **pretty weathercock,** a reference to the page's gaudy clothes; cf. *Love's Labour's Lost*, IV, i, 97. 19. **dickens,** epithet for the devil (devilkins?). 34. **twelve score,** i.e., twelvescore paces. 35. **folly,** wantonness. **motion,** instigation. 43. **divulge,** proclaim (a person) to be. 52. **knot,** group, company. 69. **speaks holiday,** uses choice language. 70. **carry 't,** win the day; see *carry* in glossary. 73. **having,** estate; see glossary. 74. **Poins,** a character in *1* and *2*

Mrs Page. By your leave, sir: I am sick till I see her.
[*Exeunt Mrs Page and Robin.*
Ford. Has Page any brains? hath he any eyes? hath he any thinking? Sure, they sleep; he hath no use of them. Why, this boy will carry a letter twenty mile, as easy as a cannon will shoot point-blank twelve score. He pieces out his wife's inclination; he gives her folly motion and advantage: and now she's going to my wife, and Falstaff's boy with her. A man may hear this shower sing in the wind. And Falstaff's boy with her! Good plots, they are laid; and our revolted wives share damnation together. Well; I will take him, then torture my wife, pluck the borrowed veil of modesty from the so seeming Mistress Page, divulge Page himself for a secure and wilful Actæon; and to these violent proceedings all my neighbours shall cry aim. [*Clock heard.*] The clock gives me my cue, and my assurance bids me search: there I shall find Falstaff: I shall be rather praised for this than mocked; for it is as positive as the earth is firm that Falstaff is there: I will go.   50

Enter PAGE, SHALLOW, SLENDER, HOST, SIR HUGH
EVANS, CAIUS, *and* RUGBY.

Shal., Page, &c. Well met, Master Ford.
Ford. Trust me, a good knot: I have good cheer at home; and I pray you all go with me.
Shal. I must excuse myself, Master Ford.
Slen. And so must I, sir: we have appointed to dine with Mistress Anne, and I would not break with her for more money than I'll speak of.
Shal. We have lingered about a match between Anne Page and my cousin Slender, and this day we shall have our answer.   60
Slen. I hope I have your good will, father Page.
Page. You have, Master Slender; I stand wholly for you: but my wife, master doctor, is for you altogether.
Caius. Ay, be-gar; and de maid is love-a me: my nursh-a Quickly tell me so mush.
Host. What say you to young Master Fenton? he capers, he dances, he has eyes of youth, he writes verses, he speaks holiday, he smells April and May: he will carry 't, he will carry 't; 'tis in his buttons; he will carry 't.   71
Page. Not by my consent, I promise you. The gentleman is of no having: he kept company with the wild prince and Poins; he is of too high a region; he knows too much. No, he shall not knit a knot in his fortunes with the finger of my substance: if he take her, let him take her simply; the wealth I have waits on my consent, and my consent goes not that way.
Ford. I beseech you heartily, some of you go home with me to dinner: besides your cheer, you shall have sport; I will show you a monster. Master doctor, you shall go; so shall you, Master Page; and you, Sir Hugh.   83
Shal. Well, fare you well: we shall have the freer wooing at Master Page's.   [*Exeunt Shal. and Slen.*
Caius. Go home, John Rugby; I come anon.
[*Exit Rugby.*

Host. Farewell, my hearts: I will to my honest knight Falstaff, and drink canary with him.   [*Exit.*
Ford. [*Aside*] I think I shall drink in pipe-wine first with him; I'll make him dance. Will you go, gentles?
All. Have with you to see this monster.   [*Exeunt.*

SCENE III. *A room in* FORD'S *house.*

Enter MISTRESS FORD *and* MISTRESS PAGE.

Mrs Ford. What, John! What, Robert!
Mrs Page. Quickly, quickly! Is the buck-basket—
Mrs Ford. I warrant. What, Robin, I say!

Enter Servants *with a basket.*

Mrs Page. Come, come, come.
Mrs Ford. Here, set it down.
Mrs Page. Give your men the charge; we must be brief.   8
Mrs Ford. Marry, as I told you before, John and Robert, be ready here hard by in the brew-house: and when I suddenly call you, come forth, and without any pause or staggering take this basket on your shoulders: that done, trudge with it in all haste, and carry it among the whitsters in Datchet-mead, and there empty it in the muddy ditch close by the Thames side.
Mrs Page. You will do it?
Mrs Ford. I ha' told them over and over; they lack no direction. Be gone, and come when you are called.
[*Exeunt Servants.*

Mrs Page. Here comes little Robin.

Enter ROBIN.

Mrs Ford. How now, my eyas-musket! what news with you?   23
Rob. My master, Sir John, is come in at your back-door, Mistress Ford, and requests your company.
Mrs Page. You little Jack-a-Lent, have you been true to us?
Rob. Ay, I'll be sworn. My master knows not of your being here and hath threatened to put me into everlasting liberty if I tell you of it; for he swears he'll turn me away.
Mrs Page. Thou 'rt a good boy: this secrecy of thine shall be a tailor to thee and shall make thee a new doublet and hose. I'll go hide me.   36
Mrs Ford. Do so. Go tell thy master I am alone.
[*Exit Robin.*] Mistress Page, remember you your cue.
Mrs Page. I warrant thee; if I do not act it, hiss me.
[*Exit.*

Mrs Ford. Go to, then: we'll use this unwholesome humidity, this gross watery pumpion; we'll teach him to know turtles from jays.

Enter FALSTAFF.

Fal. Have I caught thee, my heavenly jewel? Why, now let me die, for I have lived long enough: this is the period of my ambition: O this blessed hour!
Mrs Ford. O sweet Sir John!   49

Fal. Mistress Ford, I cannot cog, I cannot prate, Mistress Ford. Now shall I sin in my wish: I would thy husband were dead: I'll speak it before the best lord; I would make thee my lady.

Mrs Ford. I your lady, Sir John! alas, I should be a pitiful lady!

Fal. Let the court of France show me such another. I see how thine eye would emulate the diamond: thou hast the right arched beauty of the brow that becomes the ship-tire, the tire-valiant, or any tire of Venetian admittance. 61

Mrs Ford. A plain kerchief, Sir John: my brows become nothing else; nor that well neither.

Fal. By the Lord, thou art a traitor to say so: thou wouldst make an absolute courtier; and the firm fixture of thy foot would give an excellent motion to thy gait in a semi-circled farthingale. I see what thou wert, if Fortune thy foe were not, Nature thy friend. Come, thou canst not hide it. 71

Mrs Ford. Believe me, there 's no such thing in me.

Fal. What made me love thee? let that persuade thee there 's something extraordinary in thee. Come, I cannot cog and say thou art this and that, like a many of these lisping hawthornbuds, that come like women in men's apparel, and smell like Bucklersbury in simple time; I cannot: but I love thee; none but thee; and thou deservest it. 81

Mrs Ford. Do not betray me, sir. I fear you love Mistress Page.

Fal. Thou mightst as well say I love to walk by the Counter-gate, which is as hateful to me as the reek of a lime-kiln.

Mrs Ford. Well, heaven knows how I love you; and you shall one day find it.

Fal. Keep in that mind; I'll deserve it.

Mrs Ford. Nay, I must tell you, so you do; or else I could not be in that mind. 91

Rob. [*Within*] Mistress Ford, Mistress Ford! here 's Mistress Page at the door, sweating and blowing and looking wildly, and would needs speak with you presently.

Fal. She shall not see me: I will ensconce me behind the arras.

Mrs Ford. Pray you, do so: she 's a very tattling woman. [*Falstaff hides himself.*

Re-enter MISTRESS PAGE *and* ROBIN.

What 's the matter? how now! 100

Mrs Page. O Mistress Ford, what have you done? You 're shamed, you 're overthrown, you 're undone for ever!

Mrs Ford. What 's the matter, good Mistress Page?

Mrs Page. O well-a-day, Mistress Ford! having an honest man to your husband, to give him such cause of suspicion!

Mrs Ford. What cause of suspicion?

Mrs Page. What cause of suspicion! Out upon you! how am I mistook in you! 111

Mrs Ford. Why, alas, what 's the matter?

Mrs Page. Your husband 's coming hither, woman, with all the officers in Windsor, to search for a gentleman that he says is here now in the house by your

consent, to take an ill advantage of his absence: you are undone.

Mrs Ford. 'Tis not so, I hope. 118

Mrs Page. Pray heaven it be not so, that you have such a man here! but 'tis most certain your husband 's coming, with half Windsor at his heels, to search for such a one. I come before to tell you. If you know yourself clear, why, I am glad of it; but if you have a friend here, convey, convey him out. Be not amazed; call all your senses to you; defend your reputation, or bid farewell to your good life for ever.

Mrs Ford. What shall I do? There is a gentleman my dear friend; and I fear not mine own shame so much as his peril: I had rather than a thousand pound he were out of the house. 132

Mrs Page. For shame! never stand 'you had rather' and 'you had rather:' your husband 's here at hand; bethink you of some conveyance: in the house you cannot hide him. O, how have you deceived me! Look, here is a basket: if he be of any reasonable stature, he may creep in here; and throw foul linen upon him, as if it were going to bucking: or—it is whiting-time—send him by your two men to Datchet-mead. 141

Mrs Ford. He 's too big to go in there. What shall I do?

Fal. [*Coming forward*] Let me see 't, let me see 't, O, let me see 't! I'll in, I'll in. Follow your friend's counsel. I'll in.

Mrs Page. What, Sir John Falstaff! Are these your letters, knight?

Fal. I love thee. Help me away. Let me creep in here. I'll never— 150
[*Gets into the basket; they cover him with foul linen.*

Mrs Page. Help to cover your master, boy. Call your men, Mistress Ford. You dissembling knight!

Mrs Ford. What, John! Robert! John! [*Exit Robin.*

Re-enter Servants.

Go take up these clothes here quickly. Where 's the cowl-staff? look, how you drumble! Carry them to the laundress in Datchet-mead; quickly, come.

Enter FORD, PAGE, CAIUS, *and* SIR HUGH EVANS.

Ford. Pray you, come near: if I suspect without cause, why then make sport at me; then let me be your jest; I deserve it. How now! whither bear you this? 162

Serv. To the laundress, forsooth.

Mrs Ford. Why, what have you to do whither they bear it? You were best meddle with buck-washing.

Ford. Buck! I would I could wash myself of the buck! Buck, buck, buck! Ay, buck; I warrant you, buck; and of the season too, it shall appear. [*Exeunt Servants with the basket.*] Gentlemen, I have dreamed to-night; I'll tell you my dream. Here, here, here be my keys: ascend my chambers; search, seek, find out: I'll warrant we'll unkennel the fox. Let me stop this way first. [*Locking the door.*] So, now uncape. 176

Page. Good Master Ford, be contented: you wrong yourself too much.

Ford. True, Master Page. Up, gentlemen; you shall see sport anon: follow me, gentlemen. [*Exit.*

Evans. This is fery fantastical humours and jealousies.

Caius. By gar, 'tis no the fashion of France; it is not jealous in France.

Page. Nay, follow him, gentlemen; see the issue of his search. [*Exeunt Page, Caius, and Evans.*

Mrs Page. Is there not a double excellency in this?

Mrs Ford. I know not which pleases me better, that my husband is deceived, or Sir John. 190

Mrs Page. What a taking was he in when your husband asked who was in the basket!

Mrs Ford. I am half afraid he will have need of washing; so throwing him into the water will do him a benefit.

Mrs Page. Hang him, dishonest rascal! I would all of the same strain were in the same distress.

Mrs Ford. I think my husband hath some special suspicion of Falstaff's being here; for I never saw him so gross in his jealousy till now. 201

Mrs Page. I will lay a plot to try that; and we will yet have more tricks with Falstaff: his dissolute disease will scarce obey this medicine.

Mrs Ford. Shall we send that foolish carrion, Mistress Quickly, to him, and excuse his throwing into the water; and give him another hope, to betray him to another punishment?

Mrs Page. We will do it: let him be sent for tomorrow, eight o'clock, to have amends. 210

Re-enter FORD, PAGE, CAIUS, *and* SIR HUGH EVANS.

Ford. I cannot find him: may be the knave bragged of that he could not compass.

Mrs Page. [*Aside to Mrs Ford*] Heard you that?

Mrs Ford. You use me well, Master Ford, do you?

Ford. Ay, I do so.

Mrs Ford. Heaven make you better than your thoughts!

Ford. Amen! 220

Mrs Page. You do yourself mighty wrong, Master Ford.

Ford. Ay, ay; I must bear it.

Evans. If there be any pody in the house, and in the chambers, and in the coffers, and in the presses, heaven forgive my sins at the day of judgement!

Caius. By gar, nor I too: there is no bodies.

Page. Fie, fie, Master Ford! are you not ashamed? What spirit, what devil suggests this imagination? I would not ha' your distemper in this kind for the wealth of Windsor Castle. 232

Ford. 'Tis my fault, Master Page: I suffer for it.

Evans. You suffer for a pad conscience: your wife is as honest a 'omans as I will desires among five thousand, and five hundred too.

Caius. By gar, I see 'tis an honest woman.

Ford. Well, I promised you a dinner. Come, come, walk in the Park: I pray you, pardon me; I will hereafter make known to you why I have done this. Come, wife; come, Mistress Page. I pray you, pardon me; pray heartily, pardon me. 243

Page. Let's go in, gentlemen; but, trust me, we'll mock him. I do invite you to-morrow morning to my house to breakfast: after, we'll a-birding together; I

have a fine hawk for the bush. Shall it be so?

Ford. Any thing.

Evans. If there is one, I shall make two in the company. 251

Caius. If dere be one or two, I shall make-a the turd.

Ford. Pray you, go, Master Page.

Evans. I pray you now, remembrance to-morrow on the lousy knave, mine host.

Caius. Dat is good; by gar, with all my heart!

Evans. A lousy knave, to have his gibes and his mockeries! [*Exeunt.*

SCENE IV. *A room in* PAGE'S *house.*

Enter FENTON *and* ANNE PAGE.

Fent. I see I cannot get thy father's love;
Therefore no more turn me to him, sweet Nan.

Anne. Alas, how then?

Fent.　　　　　　Why, thou must be thyself.
He doth object I am too great of birth;
And that, my state being gall'd with my expense,
I seek to heal it only by his wealth:
Besides these, other bars he lays before me,
My riots past, my wild societies;
And tells me 'tis a thing impossible
I should love thee but as a property. 10

Anne. May be he tells you true.

Fent. No, heaven so speed me in my time to come!
Albeit I will confess thy father's wealth
Was the first motive that I woo'd thee, Anne:
Yet, wooing thee, I found thee of more value
Than stamps in gold or sums in sealed bags;
And 'tis the very riches of thyself
That now I aim at.

Anne.　　　　　　Gentle Master Fenton,
Yet seek my father's love; still seek it, sir:
If opportunity and humblest suit 20
Cannot attain it, why, then,—hark you hither! [*They converse apart.*

Enter SHALLOW, SLENDER, *and* MISTRESS QUICKLY.

Shal. Break their talk, Mistress Quickly: my kinsman shall speak for himself.

Slen. I'll make a shaft or a bolt on 't: 'slid, 'tis but venturing.

Shal. Be not dismayed.

Slen. No, she shall not dismay me: I care not for that, but that I am afeard.

Quick. Hark ye; Master Slender would speak a word with you. 30

Anne. I come to him. [*Aside*] This is my father's choice.

O, what a world of vile ill-favour'd faults
Looks handsome in three hundred pounds a-year!

Quick. And how does good Master Fenton? Pray you, a word with you.

Shal. She's coming; to her, coz. O boy, thou hadst a father!

Slen. I had a father, Mistress Anne; my uncle can tell you good jests of him. Pray you, uncle, tell Mis-

---

ability. 140. **bucking,** washing. 156. **cowl-staff,** pole on which a "cowl" or basket is carried between two persons. **drumble,** be sluggish. 174. **unkennel,** reveal, unearth. 176. **uncape,** unearth (as of a fox?). 177. **be contented,** be calm; do not worry. 197. **strain,** character, kind. 255-256. **remembrance . . . host,** an allusion to

the plot carried out in IV, v.
SCENE IV. 16. **stamps in gold,** gold coins. 24. **make . . . on 't,** make a good or bad job of it; a reference to the difference in the degree of skill required for making a shaft or a bolt (Hart). **'slid,** an oath, by God's lid.

tress Anne the jest, how my father stole two geese out
of a pen, good uncle. 41

Shal. Mistress Anne, my cousin loves you.

Slen. Ay, that I do; as well as I love any woman in
Gloucestershire.

Shal. He will maintain you like a gentlewoman.

Slen. Ay, that I will, come cut and long-tail, under
the degree of a squire.

Shal. He will make you a hundred and fifty pounds
jointure. 50

Anne. Good Master Shallow, let him woo for himself.

Shal. Marry, I thank you for it; I thank you for that
good comfort. She calls you, coz: I'll leave you.

Anne. Now, Master Slender,—

Slen. Now, good Mistress Anne,—

Anne. What is your will?

Slen. My will! 'od's heartlings, that's a pretty jest
indeed! I ne'er made my will yet, I thank heaven;
I am not such a sickly creature, I give heaven praise.

Anne. I mean, Master Slender, what would you
with me?

Slen. Truly, for mine own part, I would little or
nothing with you. Your father and my uncle hath
made motions: if it be my luck, so; if not, happy man
be his dole! They can tell you how things go better
than I can: you may ask your father; here he comes.70

Enter PAGE *and* MISTRESS PAGE.

Page. Now, Master Slender: love him, daughter
Anne.
Why, how now! what does Master Fenton here?
You wrong me, sir, thus still to haunt my house:
I told you, sir, my daughter is disposed of.

Fent. Nay, Master Page, be not impatient.

Mrs Page. Good Master Fenton, come not to my
child.

Page. She is no match for you.

Fent. Sir, will you hear me?

Page. No, good Master Fenton.
Come, Master Shallow; come, son Slender, in.
Knowing my mind, you wrong me, Master Fenton. 80
[*Exeunt Page, Shal., and Slen.*

Quick. Speak to Mistress Page.

Fent. Good Mistress Page, for that I love your
daughter
In such a righteous fashion as I do,
Perforce, against all checks, rebukes and manners,
I must advance the colours of my love
And not retire: let me have your good will.

Anne. Good mother, do not marry me to yond fool.

Mrs Page. I mean it not; I seek you a better
husband.

Quick. That's my master, master doctor.

Anne. Alas, I had rather be set quick i' the earth 90
And bowl'd to death with turnips!

Mrs Page. Come, trouble not yourself. Good Master
Fenton,
I will not be your friend nor enemy:
My daughter will I question how she loves you,
And as I find her, so am I affected.
Till then farewell, sir: she must needs go in;
Her father will be angry.

Fent. Farewell, gentle mistress: farewell, Nan.
[*Exeunt Mrs Page and Anne.*

Quick. This is my doing, now: 'Nay,' said I, 'will you
cast away your child on a fool, and a physician? Look
on Master Fenton:' this is my doing. 102

Fent. I thank thee; and I pray thee, once to-night
Give my sweet Nan this ring: there's for thy pains.

Quick. Now heaven send thee good fortune! [*Exit
Fenton.*] A kind heart he hath: a woman would run
through fire and water for such a kind heart. But yet
I would my master had Mistress Anne; or I would
Master Slender had her; or, in sooth, I would Master
Fenton had her: I will do what I can for them all
three; for so I have promised, and I'll be as good as
my word; but speciously for Master Fenton. Well, I
must of another errand to Sir John Falstaff from my
two mistresses: what a beast am I to slack it! [*Exit.* 115

SCENE V. *A room in the Garter Inn.*

Enter FALSTAFF *and* BARDOLPH.

Fal. Bardolph, I say,—

Bard. Here, sir.

Fal. Go fetch me a quart of sack; put a toast in 't.
[*Exit Bard.*] Have I lived to be carried in a basket,
like a barrow of butcher's offal, and to be thrown in
the Thames? Well, if I be served such another trick,
I'll have my brains ta'en out and buttered, and give
them to a dog for a new-year's gift. The rogues
slighted me into the river with as little remorse as they
would have drowned a blind bitch's puppies, fifteen
i' the litter: and you may know by my size that I have
a kind of alacrity in sinking; if the bottom were as
deep as hell, I should down. I had been drowned, but
that the shore was shelvy and shallow,—a death that
I abhor; for the water swells a man; and what a
thing should I have been when I had been swelled!
I should have been a mountain of mummy. 18

Re-enter BARDOLPH *with sack.*

Bard. Here's Mistress Quickly, sir, to speak with
you.

Fal. Come, let me pour in some sack to the Thames
water; for my belly's as cold as if I had swallowed
snowballs for pills to cool the reins. Call her in.

Bard. Come in, woman!

Enter MISTRESS QUICKLY.

Quick. By your leave; I cry you mercy: give your
worship good morrow.

Fal. Take away these chalices. Go brew me a pottle
of sack finely. 30

Bard. With eggs, sir?

Fal. Simple of itself; I'll no pullet-sperm in my
brewage. [*Exit Bardolph.*] How now!

Quick. Marry, sir, I come to your worship from
Mistress Ford.

Fal. Mistress Ford! I have had ford enough; I was
thrown into the ford; I have my belly full of ford.

Quick. Alas the day! good heart, that was not her
fault: she does so take on with her men; they mistook
their erection. 41

---

47. **cut and long-tail,** horses or dogs with docked and long tails; i.e.,
all sorts of people. 59. **'od's,** minced form of "God's" used in oaths.
heartlings, little hearts. 68. **happy . . . dole,** may it be (his) portion
to be a happy man. 84. **checks,** reproofs; see glossary. 113. **speciously,** a malapropism for "specially."
SCENE V. 3. **toast,** piece of toast put into a drink. 9. **slighted,**

Fal. So did I mine, to build upon a foolish woman's promise.

Quick. Well, she laments, sir, for it, that it would yearn your heart to see it. Her husband goes this morning a-birding; she desires you once more to come to her between eight and nine: I must carry her word quickly: she'll make you amends, I warrant you.

Fal. Well, I will visit her: tell her so; and bid her think what a man is: let her consider his frailty, and then judge of my merit.   52

Quick. I will tell her.

Fal. Do so. Between nine and ten, sayest thou?

Quick. Eight and nine, sir.

Fal. Well, be gone: I will not miss her.

Quick. Peace be with you, sir.   [*Exit.*

Fal. I marvel I hear not of Master Brook; he sent me word to stay within: I like his money well. O, here he comes.   60

Enter FORD.

Ford. Bless you, sir!

Fal. Now, Master Brook, you come to know what hath passed between me and Ford's wife?

Ford. That, indeed, Sir John, is my business.

Fal. Master Brook, I will not lie to you: I was at her house the hour she appointed me.

Ford. And sped you, sir?

Fal. Very ill-favouredly, Master Brook.

Ford. How so, sir? Did she change her determination?   70

Fal. No, Master Brook; but the peaking Cornuto her husband, Master Brook, dwelling in a continual 'larum of jealousy, comes me in the instant of our encounter, after we had embraced, kissed, protested, and, as it were, spoke the prologue of our comedy; and at his heels a rabble of his companions, thither provoked and instigated by his distemper, and, forsooth, to search his house for his wife's love.

Ford. What, while you were there?   80

Fal. While I was there.

Ford. And did he search for you, and could not find you?

Fal. You shall hear. As good luck would have it, comes in one Mistress Page; gives intelligence of Ford's approach; and, in her invention and Ford's wife's distraction, they conveyed me into a buck-basket.

Ford. A buck-basket!   89

Fal. By the Lord, a buck-basket! rammed me in with foul shirts and smocks, socks, foul stockings, greasy napkins; that, Master Brook, there was the rankest compound of villanous smell that ever offended nostril.

Ford. And how long lay you there?   95

Fal. Nay, you shall hear, Master Brook, what I have suffered to bring this woman to evil for your good. Being thus crammed in the basket, a couple of Ford's knaves, his hinds, were called forth by their mistress to carry me in the name of foul clothes to Datchet-lane: they took me on their shoulders; met the jealous knave their master in the door, who asked them once or twice what they had in their basket: I quaked for fear, lest the lunatic knave would have searched it;

but fate, ordaining he should be a cuckold, held his hand. Well: on went he for a search, and away went I for foul clothes. But mark the sequel, Master Brook: I suffered the pangs of three several deaths; first, an intolerable fright, to be detected with a jealous rotten bell-wether; next, to be compassed, like a good bilbo, in the circumference of a peck, hilt to point, heel to head; and then, to be stopped in, like a strong distillation, with stinking clothes that fretted in their own grease: think of that,—a man of my kidney,—think of that,—that am as subject to heat as butter; a man of continual dissolution and thaw: it was a miracle to 'scape suffocation. And in the height of this bath, when I was more than half stewed in grease, like a Dutch dish, to be thrown into the Thames, and cooled, glowing hot, in that surge, like a horse-shoe; think of that,—hissing hot,—think of that, Master Brook.   124

Ford. In good sadness, sir, I am sorry that for my sake you have suffered all this. My suit then is desperate; you'll undertake her no more?

Fal. Master Brook, I will be thrown into Etna, as I have been into Thames, ere I will leave her thus. Her husband is this morning gone a-birding: I have received from her another embassy of meeting; 'twixt eight and nine is the hour, Master Brook.

Ford. 'Tis past eight already, sir.

Fal. Is it? I will then address me to my appointment. Come to me at your convenient leisure, and you shall know how I speed; and the conclusion shall be crowned with your enjoying her. Adieu. You shall have her, Master Brook; Master Brook, you shall cuckold Ford.   [*Exit.*

Ford. Hum! ha! is this a vision? is this a dream? do I sleep? Master Ford, awake! awake, Master Ford! there's a hole made in your best coat, Master Ford. This 'tis to be married! this 'tis to have linen and buck-baskets! Well, I will proclaim myself what I am: I will now take the lecher; he is at my house; he cannot 'scape me; 'tis impossible he should; he cannot creep into a halfpenny purse, nor into a pepper-box: but, lest the devil that guides him should aid him, I will search impossible places. Though what I am I cannot avoid, yet to be what I would not shall not make me tame: if I have horns to make one mad, let the proverb go with me: I'll be horn-mad.   [*Exit.*

ACT IV.

SCENE I. *A street.*

Enter MISTRESS PAGE, MISTRESS QUICKLY, *and* WILLIAM.

Mrs Page. Is he at Master Ford's already, think'st thou?

Quick. Sure he is by this, or will be presently: but, truly, he is very courageous mad about his throwing into the water. Mistress Ford desires you to come suddenly.

Mrs Page. I'll be with her by and by; I'll but bring my young man here to school. Look, where his master comes; 'tis a playing-day, I see.

---

tossed heedlessly. 10. **remorse,** pity, compassion; see glossary. 24. **reins,** loins. 29. **chalices,** wine cups. 41. **erection,** a malapropism for "direction." 71. **Cornuto,** cuckold. 112. **bilbo.** Cf. I, i, 165,

note. 116. **kidney,** temperament.
ACT IV. SCENE I. 4. **courageous,** Quickly's error for "outrageous." 9. **playing-day,** holiday.

Enter SIR HUGH EVANS.

How now, Sir Hugh! no school to-day? 10
Evans. No; Master Slender is let the boys leave to play.
Quick. Blessing of his heart!
Mrs Page. Sir Hugh, my husband says my son profits nothing in the world at his book. I pray you, ask him some questions in his accidence.
Evans. Come hither, William; hold up your head; come.
Mrs Page. Come on, sirrah; hold up your head; answer your master, be not afraid. 20
Evans. William, how many numbers is in nouns?
Will. Two.
Quick. Truly, I thought there had been one number more, because they say, ''Od's nouns.'
Evans. Peace your tattlings! What is 'fair,' William?
Will. Pulcher.
Quick. Polecats! there are fairer things than polecats, sure. 30
Evans. You are a very simplicity 'oman: I pray you, peace. What is 'lapis,' William?
Will. A stone.
Evans. And what is 'a stone,' William?
Will. A pebble.
Evans. No, it is 'lapis:' I pray you, remember in your prain.
Will. Lapis.
Evans. That is a good William. What is he, William, that does lend articles? 40
Will. Articles are borrowed of the pronoun, and be thus declined, Singulariter, nominativo, hic, hæc, hoc.
Evans. Nominativo, hig, hag, hog; pray you, mark: genitivo, hujus. Well, what is your accusative case?
Will. Accusativo, hinc.
Evans. I pray you, have your remembrance, child; accusativo, hung, hang, hog.
Quick. 'Hang-hog' is Latin for bacon, I warrant you. 51
Evans. Leave your prabbles, 'oman. What is the focative case, William?
Will. O,—vocativo, O.
Evans. Remember, William; focative is caret.
Quick. And that 's a good root.
Evans. 'Oman, forbear.
Mrs Page. Peace!
Evans. What is your genitive case plural, William? 60
Will. Genitive case!
Evans. Ay.
Will. Genitive,—horum, harum, horum.
Quick. Vengeance of Jenny's case! fie on her! never name her, child, if she be a whore.
Evans. For shame, 'oman.
Quick. You do ill to teach the child such words: he teaches him to hick and to hack, which they'll do fast enough of themselves, and to call 'horum:' fie upon you! 70
Evans. 'Oman, art thou lunatics? hast thou no understandings for thy cases and the numbers of the genders? Thou art as foolish Christian creatures as I would desires.

Mrs Page. Prithee, hold thy peace.
Evans. Show me now, William, some declensions of your pronouns.
Will. Forsooth, I have forgot.
Evans. It is qui, quæ, quod: if you forget your 'quies,' your 'quæs,' and your 'quods,' you must be preeches. Go your ways, and play; go. 81
Mrs Page. He is a better scholar than I thought he was.
Evans. He is a good sprag memory. Farewell, Mistress Page.
Mrs Page. Adieu, good Sir Hugh. [*Exit Sir Hugh*.] Get you home, boy. Come, we stay too long. [*Exeunt*.

SCENE II. *A room in* FORD's *house*.

Enter FALSTAFF *and* MISTRESS FORD.

Fal. Mistress Ford, your sorrow hath eaten up my sufferance. I see you are obsequious in your love, and I profess requital to a hair's breadth; not only, Mistress Ford, in the simple office of love, but in all the accoutrement, complement and ceremony of it. But are you sure of your husband now?
Mrs Ford. He 's a-birding, sweet Sir John.
Mrs Page. [*Within*] What, ho, gossip Ford! what, ho! 10
Mrs Ford. Step into the chamber, Sir John.
[*Exit Falstaff*.

Enter MISTRESS PAGE.

Mrs Page. How now, sweetheart! who 's at home besides yourself?
Mrs Ford. Why, none but mine own people.
Mrs Page. Indeed!
Mrs Ford. No, certainly. [*Aside to her*] Speak louder.
Mrs Page. Truly, I am so glad you have nobody here.
Mrs Ford. Why? 20
Mrs Page. Why, woman, your husband is in his old lunes again: he so takes on yonder with my husband; so rails against all married mankind; so curses all Eve's daughters, of what complexion soever; and so buffets himself on the forehead, crying, 'Peer out, peer out!' that any madness I ever yet beheld seemed but tameness, civility and patience, to this his distemper he is in now: I am glad the fat knight is not here.
Mrs Ford. Why, does he talk of him? 30
Mrs Page. Of none but him; and swears he was carried out, the last time he searched for him, in a basket; protests to my husband he is now here, and hath drawn him and the rest of their company from their sport, to make another experiment of his suspicion: but I am glad the knight is not here; now he shall see his own foolery.
Mrs Ford. How near is he, Mistress Page?
Mrs Page. Hard by; at street end; he will be here anon. 41
Mrs Ford. I am undone! The knight is here.
Mrs Page. Why then you are utterly shamed, and he 's but a dead man. What a woman are you!— Away with him, away with him! better shame than murder.

16. **accidence**, rudiments of Latin grammar. 25. **nouns**, wounds; Quickly's error. 68. **hick, hack**, Quickly's understanding of the declension of the Latin pronoun (l. 43). New Cambridge editors think this may mean "hiccup" and that Quickly may mean "get drunk"; but see II, i, 52, note. 81. **preeches**, breeched, i.e., whipped. 84. **sprag**, sprack, lively, alert. SCENE II. 2. **sufferance**, suffering, pain. 3. **obsequious**, devoted

Mrs Ford. Which way should he go? how should I bestow him? Shall I put him into the basket again?

Re-enter FALSTAFF.

Fal. No, I'll come no more i' the basket. May I not go out ere he come? 51

Mrs Page. Alas, three of Master Ford's brothers watch the door with pistols, that none shall issue out; otherwise you might slip away ere he came. But what make you here?

Fal. What shall I do? I'll creep up into the chimney.

Mrs Ford. There they always use to discharge their birding-pieces. Creep into the kiln-hole.

Fal. Where is it? 60

Mrs Ford. He will seek there, on my word. Neither press, coffer, chest, trunk, well, vault, but he hath an abstract for the remembrance of such places, and goes to them by his note: there is no hiding you in the house.

Fal. I'll go out then.

Mrs Page. If you go out in your own semblance, you die, Sir John. Unless you go out disguised— 69

Mrs Ford. How might we disguise him?

Mrs Page. Alas the day, I know not! There is no woman's gown big enough for him; otherwise he might put on a hat, a muffler and a kerchief, and so escape.

Fal. Good hearts, devise something; any extremity rather than a mischief.

Mrs Ford. My maid's aunt, the fat woman of Brentford, has a gown above.

Mrs Page. On my word, it will serve him; she 's as big as he is: and there 's her thrummed hat and her muffler too. Run up, Sir John. 81

Mrs Ford. Go, go, sweet Sir John: Mistress Page and I will look some linen for your head.

Mrs Page. Quick, quick! we'll come dress you straight: put on the gown the while. [*Exit Falstaff.*

Mrs Ford. I would my husband would meet him in this shape: he cannot abide the old woman of Brentford; he swears she 's a witch; forbade her my house and hath threatened to beat her.

Mrs Page. Heaven guide him to thy husband's cudgel, and the devil guide his cudgel afterwards! 91

Mrs Ford. But is my husband coming?

Mrs Page. Ay, in good sadness, is he; and talks of the basket too, howsoever he hath had intelligence.

Mrs Ford. We'll try that; for I'll appoint my men to carry the basket again, to meet him at the door with it, as they did last time.

Mrs Page. Nay, but he'll be here presently: let 's go dress him like the witch of Brentford.

Mrs Ford. I'll first direct my men what they shall do with the basket. Go up; I'll bring linen for him straight. [*Exit.*

Mrs Page. Hang him, dishonest varlet! we cannot misuse him enough. 105

We'll leave a proof, by that which we will do,
Wives may be merry, and yet honest too:
We do not act that often jest and laugh;
'Tis old, but true, Still swine eats all the draff. [*Exit.*

Re-enter MISTRESS FORD *with two* Servants.

Mrs Ford. Go, sirs, take the basket again on your shoulders: your master is hard at door; if he bid you set it down, obey him: quickly, dispatch. [*Exit.*

First Serv. Come, come, take it up. 113

Sec. Serv. Pray heaven it be not full of knight again.

First Serv. I hope not; I had as lief bear so much lead.

Enter FORD, PAGE, SHALLOW, CAIUS, *and* SIR HUGH EVANS.

Ford. Ay, but if it prove true, Master Page, have you any way then to unfool me again? Set down the basket, villain! Somebody call my wife. Youth in a basket! O you pandarly rascals! there 's a knot, a ging, a pack, a conspiracy against me: now shall the devil be shamed. What, wife, I say! Come, come forth! Behold what honest clothes you send forth to bleaching!

Page. Why, this passes, Master Ford; you are not to go loose any longer; you must be pinioned.

Evans. Why, this is lunatics! this is mad as a mad dog! 131

Shal. Indeed, Master Ford, this is not well, indeed.

Ford. So say I too, sir.

Re-enter MISTRESS FORD.

Come hither, Mistress Ford; Mistress Ford, the honest woman, the modest wife, the virtuous creature, that hath the jealous fool to her husband! I suspect without cause, mistress, do I?

Mrs Ford. Heaven be my witness you do, if you suspect me in any dishonesty. 140

Ford. Well said, brazen-face! hold it out. Come forth, sirrah! [*Pulling clothes out of the basket.*

Page. This passes!

Mrs Ford. Are you not ashamed? let the clothes alone.

Ford. I shall find you anon.

Evans. 'Tis unreasonable! Will you take up your wife's clothes? Come away.

Ford. Empty the basket, I say!

Mrs Ford. Why, man, why? 150

Ford. Master Page, as I am a man, there was one conveyed out of my house yesterday in this basket: why may not he be there again? In my house I am sure he is: my intelligence is true; my jealousy is reasonable. Pluck me out all the linen.

Mrs Ford. If you find a man there, he shall die a flea's death.

Page. Here 's no man.

Shal. By my fidelity, this is not well, Master Ford; this wrongs you. 161

Evans. Master Ford, you must pray, and not follow the imaginations of your own heart: this is jealousies.

Ford. Well, he 's not here I seek for.

Page. No, nor nowhere else but in your brain.

Ford. Help to search my house this one time. If I find not what I seek, show no colour for my extremity; let me for ever be your table-sport; let them say of me, 'As jealous as Ford, that searched a hollow walnut for his wife's leman.' Satisfy me once more; once more search with me.

Mrs Ford. What, ho, Mistress Page! come you and

The Merry Wives of Windsor ACT IV : SC II

579

the old woman down; my husband will come into the chamber.

Ford. Old woman! what old woman 's that?

Mrs Ford. Why, it is my maid's aunt of Brentford. 179

Ford. A witch, a quean, an old cozening quean! Have I not forbid her my house? She comes of errands, does she? We are simple men; we do not know what 's brought to pass under the profession of fortune-telling. She works by charms, by spells, by the figure, and such daubery as this is, beyond our element: we know nothing. Come down, you witch, you hag, you; come down, I say!

Mrs Ford. Nay, good, sweet husband! Good gentlemen, let him not strike the old woman. 190

Re-enter FALSTAFF *in woman's clothes, and* MISTRESS PAGE.

Mrs Page. Come, Mother Prat; come, give me your hand.

Ford. I'll prat her. [*Beating him*] Out of my door, you witch, you hag, you baggage, you polecat, you ronyon! out, out! I'll conjure you, I'll fortune-tell you. [*Exit Falstaff.*

Mrs Page. Are you not ashamed? I think you have killed the poor woman.

Mrs Ford. Nay, he will do it. 'Tis a goodly credit for you. 200

Ford. Hang her, witch!

Evans. By yea and no, I think the 'oman is a witch indeed: I like not when a 'oman has a great peard; I spy a great peard under his muffler.

Ford. Will you follow, gentlemen? I beseech you, follow; see but the issue of my jealousy: if I cry out thus upon no trail, never trust me when I open again.

Page. Let's obey his humour a little further: come, gentlemen. [*Exeunt Ford, Page, Shal., Caius, and Evans.*

Mrs Page. Trust me, he beat him most pitifully.

Mrs Ford. Nay, by the mass, that he did not; he beat him most unpitifully, methought.

Mrs Page. I'll have the cudgel hallowed and hung o'er the altar; it hath done meritorious service.

Mrs Ford. What think you? may we, with the warrant of womanhood and the witness of a good conscience, pursue him with any further revenge? 222

Mrs Page. The spirit of wantonness is, sure, scared out of him: if the devil have him not in fee-simple, with fine and recovery, he will never, I think, in the way of waste, attempt us again.

Mrs Ford. Shall we tell our husbands how we have served him? 229

Mrs Page. Yes, by all means; if it be but to scrape the figures out of your husband's brains. If they can find in their hearts the poor unvirtuous fat knight shall be any further afflicted, we two will still be the ministers.

Mrs Ford. I'll warrant they'll have him publicly shamed: and methinks there would be no period to the jest, should he not be publicly shamed.

Mrs Page. Come, to the forge with it then; shape it: I would not have things cool. [*Exeunt.*

SCENE III. *A room in the Garter Inn.*

Enter HOST *and* BARDOLPH.

Bard. Sir, the Germans desire to have three of your horses: the duke himself will be to-morrow at court, and they are going to meet him.

Host. What duke should that be comes so secretly? I hear not of him in the court. Let me speak with the gentlemen: they speak English?

Bard. Ay, sir; I'll call them to you. 9

Host. They shall have my horses; but I'll make them pay; I'll sauce them: they have had my house a week at command; I have turned away my other guests: they must come off; I'll sauce them. Come. [*Exeunt.*

SCENE IV. *A room in* FORD'S *house.*

Enter PAGE, FORD, MISTRESS PAGE, MISTRESS FORD,
    and SIR HUGH EVANS.

Evans. 'Tis one of the best discretions of a 'oman as ever I did look upon.

Page. And did he send you both these letters at an instant?

Mrs Page. Within a quarter of an hour.

Ford. Pardon me, wife. Henceforth do what thou
    wilt;
I rather will suspect the sun with cold
Than thee with wantonness: now doth thy honour
    stand,
In him that was of late an heretic,
As firm as faith.

Page.   'Tis well, 'tis well; no more: 10
Be not as extreme in submission
As in offence.
But let our plot go forward: let our wives
Yet once again, to make us public sport,
Appoint a meeting with this old fat fellow,
Where we may take him and disgrace him for it.

Ford. There is no better way than that they spoke of.

Page. How? to send him word they'll meet him in
the park at midnight? Fie, fie! he'll never come.

Evans. You say he has been thrown in the rivers and has been grievously peaten as an old 'oman: methinks there should be terrors in him that he should not come; methinks his flesh is punished, he shall have no desires.

Page. So think I too.

Mrs Ford. Devise but how you'll use him when he
    comes,
And let us two devise to bring him thither.

Mrs Page. There is an old tale goes that Herne the
    hunter,
Sometime a keeper here in Windsor forest,
Doth all the winter-time, at still midnight, 30
Walk round about an oak, with great ragg'd horns;
And there he blasts the tree and takes the cattle
And makes milch-kine yield blood and shakes a chain
In a most hideous and dreadful manner:
You have heard of such a spirit, and well you know
The superstitious idle-headed eld
Received and did deliver to our age
This tale of Herne the hunter for a truth.

Page. Why, yet there want not many that do fear
In deep of night to walk by this Herne's oak: 40
But what of this?

180. **quean,** jade, hussy. 186. **daubery,** false show. 195. **ronyon,** abusive term for a woman. 208. **upon no trail,** i.e., when there is no scent. 225. **fee-simple,** estate belonging to an owner and his heirs forever; hence, absolute possession. 226. **waste,** spoliation.

231. **figures,** fantasies, conceits.
SCENE III. 11. **sauce,** to make (a person) pay dearly. 12. **at command,** retained for their use upon their expected arrival (Hart). 13. **come off,** pay, disburse handsomely.

Mrs Ford. Marry, this is our device;
That Falstaff at that oak shall meet with us.

Page. Well, let it not be doubted but he'll come:
And in this shape when you have brought him thither,
What shall be done with him? what is your plot?

Mrs Page. That likewise have we thought upon, and
  thus:
Nan Page my daughter and my little son
And three or four more of their growth we'll dress
Like urchins, ouphes and fairies, green and white,
With rounds of waxen tapers on their heads, 50
And rattles in their hands: upon a sudden,
As Falstaff, she and I, are newly met,
Let them from forth a sawpit rush at once
With some diffused song: upon their sight,
We two in great amazedness will fly:
Then let them all encircle him about
And, fairy-like, to pinch the unclean knight,
And ask him why, that hour of fairy revel,
In their so sacred paths he dares to tread
In shape profane.

Mrs Ford. And till he tell the truth, 60
Let the supposed fairies pinch him sound
And burn him with their tapers.

Mrs Page. The truth being known,
We'll all present ourselves, dis-horn the spirit,
And mock him home to Windsor.

Ford. The children must
Be practised well to this, or they'll ne'er do 't.

Evans. I will teach the children their behaviours;
and I will be like a jack-an-apes also, to burn the
knight with my taber.

Ford. That will be excellent. I'll go buy them vizards. 70

Mrs Page. My Nan shall be the queen of all the
  fairies,
Finely attired in a robe of white.

Page. That silk will I go buy. [*Aside*] And in that
  time
Shall Master Slender steal my Nan away
And marry her at Eton. Go send to Falstaff straight.

Ford. Nay, I'll to him again in name of Brook:
He'll tell me all his purpose: sure, he'll come.

Mrs Page. Fear not you that. Go get us properties
And tricking for our fairies.

Evans. Let us about it: it is admirable pleasures and
fery honest knaveries. [*Exeunt Page, Ford, and Evans.* 81

Mrs Page. Go, Mistress Ford,
Send quickly to Sir John, to know his mind.
[*Exit Mrs Ford.*
I'll to the doctor: he hath my good will,
And none but he, to marry with Nan Page.
That Slender, though well landed, is an idiot;
And he my husband best of all affects.
The doctor is well money'd, and his friends
Potent at court: he, none but he, shall have her, 89
Though twenty thousand worthier come to crave her.
[*Exit.*

SCENE V. *A room in the Garter Inn.*

Enter HOST *and* SIMPLE.

Host. What wouldst thou have, boor? what, thick-
skin? speak, breathe, discuss; brief, short, quick, snap.

Sim. Marry, sir, I come to speak with Sir John Falstaff from Master Slender.

Host. There's his chamber, his house, his castle,
his standing-bed and truckle-bed; 'tis painted about
with the story of the Prodigal, fresh and new. Go
knock and call; he'll speak like an Anthropophaginian unto thee: knock, I say. 11

Sim. There's an old woman, a fat woman, gone up
into his chamber: I'll be so bold as stay, sir, till she
come down; I come to speak with her, indeed.

Host. Ha! a fat woman! the knight may be robbed:
I'll call. Bully knight! bully Sir John! speak from thy
lungs military: art thou there? it is thine host, thine
Ephesian, calls.

Fal. [*Above*] How now, mine host! 20

Host. Here's a Bohemian-Tartar tarries the coming down of thy fat woman. Let her descend, bully,
let her descend; my chambers are honourable: fie!
privacy? fie!

Enter FALSTAFF.

Fal. There was, mine host, an old fat woman even
now with me; but she's gone.

Sim. Pray you, sir, was't not the wise woman of
Brentford?

Fal. Ay, marry, was it, mussel-shell: what would
you with her? 30

Sim. My master, sir, Master Slender, sent to her,
seeing her go thorough the streets, to know, sir,
whether one Nym, sir, that beguiled him of a chain,
had the chain or no.

Fal. I spake with the old woman about it.

Sim. And what says she, I pray, sir?

Fal. Marry, she says that the very same man that
beguiled Master Slender of his chain cozened him
of it.

Sim. I would I could have spoken with the woman
herself; I had other things to have spoken with her
too from him. 42

Fal. What are they? let us know.

Host. Ay, come; quick.

Sim. I may not conceal them, sir.

Host. Conceal them, or thou diest.

Sim. Why, sir, they were nothing but about Mistress Anne Page; to know if it were my master's
fortune to have her or no.

Fal. 'Tis, 'tis his fortune. 50

Sim. What, sir?

Fal. To have her, or no. Go; say the woman told
me so.

Sim. May I be bold to say so, sir?

Fal. Ay, sir; like who more bold.

Sim. I thank your worship: I shall make my master
glad with these tidings. [*Exit.*

Host. Thou art clerkly, thou art clerkly, Sir John.
Was there a wise woman with thee?

Fal. Ay, that there was, mine host; one that hath
taught me more wit than ever I learned before in my
life; and I paid nothing for it neither, but was paid
for my learning. 63

Enter BARDOLPH.

SCENE IV. 1-2. **best . . . 'oman**, most discreet woman. 36. **eld**,
old age. 49. **urchins, ouphes**, terms for goblins. 54. **diffused**, confused, disorderly. 70. **vizards**, visors.
SCENE V. 8. **the Prodigal**. Cf. *2 Henry IV*, II, i, 157, where this
story is again associated with Falstaff. 10. **Anthropophaginian**, cannibal. 19. **Ephesian**, boon companion (Onions). 21. **Bohemian-
Tartar**. Cf. *Hungarian* (I, iii, 23) and *Phrygian Turk* (I, iii, 97). 29.
mussel-shell, one who gapes (Onions).

Bard. Out, alas, sir! cozenage, mere cozenage!

Host. Where be my horses? speak well of them, varletto.

Bard. Run away with the cozeners; for so soon as I came beyond Eton, they threw me off from behind one of them, in a slough of mire; and set spurs and away, like three German devils, three Doctor Faustuses. 71

Host. They are gone but to meet the duke, villain: do not say they be fled; Germans are honest men.

Enter SIR HUGH EVANS.

Evans. Where is mine host?

Host. What is the matter, sir?

Evans. Have a care of your entertainments: there is a friend of mine come to town, tells me there is three cozen-germans that has cozened all the hosts of Readins, of Maidenhead, of Colebrook, of horses and money. I tell you for good will, look you: you are wise and full of gibes and vlouting-stocks, and 'tis not convenient you should be cozened. Fare you well. 84

[*Exit.*

Enter DOCTOR CAIUS.

Caius. Vere is mine host de Jarteer?

Host. Here, master doctor, in perplexity and doubtful dilemma.

Caius. I cannot tell vat is dat: but it is tell-a me dat you make grand preparation for a duke de Jamany: by my trot, dere is no duke dat the court is know to come. I tell you for good vill: adieu. [*Exit.* 91

Host. Hue and cry, villain, go! Assist me, knight. I am undone! Fly, run, hue and cry, villain! I am undone! [*Exeunt Host and Bard.*

Fal. I would all the world might be cozened; for I have been cozened and beaten too. If it should come to the ear of the court, how I have been transformed and how my transformation hath been washed and cudgelled, they would melt me out of my fat drop by drop and liquor fishermen's boots with me: I warrant they would whip me with their fine wits till I were as crest-fallen as a dried pear. I never prospered since I forswore myself at primero. Well, if my wind were but long enough to say my prayers, I would repent.

Enter MISTRESS QUICKLY.

Now, whence come you? 106

Quick. From the two parties, forsooth.

Fal. The devil take one party and his dam the other! and so they shall be both bestowed. I have suffered more for their sakes, more than the villanous inconstancy of man's disposition is able to bear.

Quick. And have not they suffered? Yes, I warrant; speciously one of them; Mistress Ford, good heart, is beaten black and blue, that you cannot see a white spot about her. 116

Fal. What tellest thou me of black and blue? I was beaten myself into all the colours of the rainbow; and I was like to be apprehended for the witch of Brentford: but that my admirable dexterity of wit, my counterfeiting the action of an old woman, delivered me, the knave constable had set me i' the stocks, i' the common stocks, for a witch.

Quick. Sir, let me speak with you in your chamber: you shall hear how things go; and, I warrant, to your content. Here is a letter will say somewhat. Good hearts, what ado here is to bring you together! Sure, one of you does not serve heaven well, that you are so crossed. 130

Fal. Come up into my chamber. [*Exeunt.*

SCENE VI. *Another room in the Garter Inn.*

Enter FENTON *and* HOST.

Host. Master Fenton, talk not to me; my mind is heavy: I will give over all.

Fent. Yet hear me speak. Assist me in my purpose, And, as I am a gentleman, I'll give thee A hundred pound in gold more than your loss.

Host. I will hear you, Master Fenton; and I will at the least keep your counsel.

Fent. From time to time I have acquainted you With the dear love I bear to fair Anne Page; Who mutually hath answer'd my affection, 10 So far forth as herself might be her chooser, Even to my wish: I have a letter from her Of such contents as you will wonder at; The mirth whereof so larded with my matter, That neither singly can be manifested, Without the show of both; fat Falstaff Hath a great scene: the image of the jest I'll show you here at large. Hark, good mine host. To-night at Herne's oak, just 'twixt twelve and one, Must my sweet Nan present the Fairy Queen; 20 The purpose why, is here: in which disguise, While other jests are something rank on foot, Her father hath commanded her to slip Away with Slender and with him at Eton Immediately to marry: she hath consented: Now, sir, Her mother, ever strong against that match And firm for Doctor Caius, hath appointed That he shall likewise shuffle her away, While other sports are tasking of their minds, 30 And at the deanery, where a priest attends, Straight marry her: to this her mother's plot She seemingly obedient likewise hath Made promise to the doctor. Now, thus it rests: Her father means she shall be all in white, And in that habit, when Slender sees his time To take her by the hand and bid her go, She shall go with him: her mother hath intended, The better to denote her to the doctor, For they must all be mask'd and vizarded, 40 That quaint in green she shall be loose enrobed, With ribands pendent, flaring 'bout her head; And when the doctor spies his vantage ripe, To pinch her by the hand, and, on that token, The maid hath given consent to go with him.

Host. Which means she to deceive, father or mother?

Fent. Both, my good host, to go along with me: And here it rests, that you'll procure the vicar To stay for me at church 'twixt twelve and one, And, in the lawful name of marrying, 50 To give our hearts united ceremony.

Host. Well, husband your device; I'll to the vicar:
Bring you the maid, you shall not lack a priest.

Fent. So shall I evermore be bound to thee;
Besides, I'll make a present recompense.   [*Exeunt.*

ACT V.

SCENE I. *A room in the Garter Inn.*

Enter FALSTAFF *and* MISTRESS QUICKLY.

Fal. Prithee, no more prattling; go. I'll hold. This is the third time; I hope good luck lies in odd numbers. Away! go. They say there is divinity in odd numbers, either in nativity, chance, or death. Away!

Quick. I'll provide you a chain; and I'll do what I can to get you a pair of horns.

Fal. Away, I say; time wears: hold up your head, and mince.   [*Exit Mrs Quickly.*

Enter FORD.

How now, Master Brook! Master Brook, the matter will be known to-night, or never. Be you in the Park about midnight, at Herne's oak, and you shall see wonders.   13

Ford. Went you not to her yesterday, sir, as you told me you had appointed?

Fal. I went to her, Master Brook, as you see, like a poor old man: but I came from her, Master Brook, like a poor old woman. That same knave Ford, her husband, hath the finest mad devil of jealousy in him, Master Brook, that ever governed frenzy. I will tell you: he beat me grievously, in the shape of a woman; for in the shape of man, Master Brook, I fear not Goliath with a weaver's beam; because I know also life is a shuttle. I am in haste; go along with me: I'll tell you all, Master Brook. Since I plucked geese, played truant and whipped top, I knew not what 'twas to be beaten till lately. Follow me: I'll tell you strange things of this knave Ford, on whom to-night I will be revenged, and I will deliver his wife into your hand. Follow. Strange things in hand, Master Brook! Follow.   [*Exeunt.* 31

SCENE II. *Windsor Park.*

Enter PAGE, SHALLOW, *and* SLENDER.

Page. Come, come; we'll couch i' the castle-ditch till we see the light of our fairies. Remember, son Slender, my daughter.

Slen. Ay, forsooth; I have spoke with her and we have a nay-word how to know one another: I come to her in white, and cry 'mum;' she cries 'budget;' and by that we know one another.

Shal. That's good too: but what needs either your 'mum' or her 'budget?' the white will decipher her well enough. It hath struck ten o'clock.   12

Page. The night is dark; light and spirits will become it well. Heaven prosper our sport! No man means evil but the devil, and we shall know him by his horns. Let's away; follow me.   [*Exeunt.*

SCENE III. *A street leading to the Park.*

Enter MISTRESS PAGE, MISTRESS FORD, *and* DOCTOR CAIUS.

Mrs Page. Master doctor, my daughter is in green: when you see your time, take her by the hand, away with her to the deanery, and dispatch it quickly. Go before into the Park: we two must go together.

Caius. I know vat I have to do. Adieu.

Mrs Page. Fare you well, sir. [*Exit Caius.*] My husband will not rejoice so much at the abuse of Falstaff as he will chafe at the doctor's marrying my daughter: but 'tis no matter; better a little chiding than a great deal of heart-break.   11

Mrs Ford. Where is Nan now and her troop of fairies, and the Welsh devil Hugh?

Mrs Page. They are all couched in a pit hard by Herne's oak, with obscured lights; which, at the very instant of Falstaff's and our meeting, they will at once display to the night.

Mrs Ford. That cannot choose but amaze him.

Mrs Page. If he be not amazed, he will be mocked; if he be amazed, he will every way be mocked.   21

Mrs Ford. We'll betray him finely.

Mrs Page. Against such lewdsters and their lechery Those that betray them do no treachery.

Mrs Ford. The hour draws on. To the oak, to the oak!   [*Exeunt.*

SCENE IV. *Windsor Park.*

Enter SIR HUGH EVANS *disguised, with others as Fairies.*

Evans. Trib, trib, fairies; come; and remember your parts: be pold, I pray you; follow me into the pit; and when I give the watch-'ords, do as I pid you: come, come; trib, trib.   [*Exeunt.*

SCENE V. *Another part of the Park.*

Enter FALSTAFF *disguised as Herne.*

Fal. The Windsor bell hath struck twelve; the minute draws on. Now, the hot-blooded gods assist me! Remember, Jove, thou wast a bull for thy Europa; love set on thy horns. O powerful love! that, in some respects, makes a beast a man, in some other, a man a beast. You were also, Jupiter, a swan for the love of Leda. O omnipotent Love! how near the god drew to the complexion of a goose! A fault done first in the form of a beast. O Jove, a beastly fault! And then another fault in the semblance of a fowl; think on 't, Jove; a foul fault! When gods have hot backs, what shall poor men do? For me, I am here a Windsor stag; and the fattest, I think, i' the forest. Send me a cool rut-time, Jove, or who can blame me to piss my tallow? Who comes here? my doe?   17

Enter MISTRESS FORD *and* MISTRESS PAGE.

Mrs Ford. Sir John! art thou there, my deer? my male deer?

"My days are swifter than a weaver's shuttle."   26. **plucked geese** ... **whipped top**, types of boyish pranks.
SCENE II.   1. **couch**, hide.

SCENE III.   18. **amaze**, perplex.   23. **lewdsters**, lascivious persons.
SCENE V.   3, 7. **bull** ... **Europa**, **swan** ... **Leda**, references to legends of Jupiter's disguises when engaged in various amours.

Fal. My doe with the black scut! Let the sky rain potatoes; let it thunder to the tune of Green Sleeves, hail kissing-comfits and snow eringoes; let there come a tempest of provocation, I will shelter me here.   24

Mrs Ford. Mistress Page is come with me, sweetheart.

Fal. Divide me like a bribe buck, each a haunch: I will keep my sides to myself, my shoulders for the fellow of this walk, and my horns I bequeath your husbands. Am I a woodman, ha? Speak I like Herne the hunter? Why, now is Cupid a child of conscience; he makes restitution. As I am a true spirit, welcome!
                                                  [*Noise within.*

Mrs Page. Alas, what noise?
Mrs Ford. Heaven forgive our sins!
Fal. What should this be?
Mrs Ford.⎫
Mrs Page.⎭ Away, away!   [*They run off.*

Fal. I think the devil will not have me damned, lest the oil that's in me should set hell on fire; he would never else cross me thus.   40

Enter Sir Hugh Evans, *disguised as before;* Pistol, *as Hobgoblin;* Mistress Quickly, Anne Page, *and others, as Fairies, with tapers.*

Quick. Fairies, black, grey, green, and white,
You moonshine revellers, and shades of night,
You orphan heirs of fixed destiny,
Attend your office and your quality.
Crier Hobgoblin, make the fairy oyes.
Pist. Elves, list your names; silence, you airy toys.
Cricket, to Windsor chimneys shalt thou leap:
Where fires thou find'st unraked and hearths unswept,
There pinch the maids as blue as bilberry:
Our radiant queen hates sluts and sluttery.   50
Fal. They are fairies; he that speaks to them shall die:
I'll wink and couch: no man their works must eye.
                              [*Lies down upon his face.*
Evans. Where 's Bede? Go you, and where you find a maid
That, ere she sleep, has thrice her prayers said,
Raise up the organs of her fantasy;
Sleep she as sound as careless infancy:
But those as sleep and think not on their sins,
Pinch them, arms, legs, backs, shoulders, sides and shins.
Quick. About, about;
Search Windsor Castle, elves, within and out: 60
Strew good luck, ouphes, on every sacred room:
That it may stand till the perpetual doom,
In state as wholesome as in state 'tis fit,
Worthy the owner, and the owner it.
The several chairs of order look you scour
With juice of balm and every precious flower:
Each fair instalment, coat, and several crest,
With loyal blazon, evermore be blest!
And nightly, meadow-fairies, look you sing,

Like to the Garter's compass, in a ring: 70
The expressure that it bears, green let it be,
More fertile-fresh than all the field to see;
And 'Honi soit qui mal y pense' write
In emerald tufts, flowers purple, blue, and white;
Like sapphire, pearl and rich embroidery,
Buckled below fair knighthood's bending knee:
Fairies use flowers for their charactery.
Away; disperse: but till 'tis one o'clock,
Our dance of custom round about the oak
Of Herne the hunter, let us not forget.   80
Evans. Pray you, lock hand in hand; yourselves in order set;
And twenty glow-worms shall our lanterns be,
To guide our measure round about the tree.
But, stay; I smell a man of middle-earth.
Fal. Heavens defend me from that Welsh fairy, lest he transform me to a piece of cheese!
Pist. Vile worm, thou wast o'erlook'd even in thy birth.
Quick. With trial-fire touch me his finger-end:
If he be chaste, the flame will back descend
And turn him to no pain; but if he start,   90
It is the flesh of a corrupted heart.
Pist. A trial, come.
Evans.   Come, will this wood take fire?
                              [*They burn him with their tapers.*
Fal. Oh, Oh, Oh!
Quick. Corrupt, corrupt, and tainted in desire!
About him, fairies; sing a scornful rhyme;
And, as you trip, still pinch him to your time.

                              Song.
Fie on sinful fantasy!
Fie on lust and luxury!
Lust is but a bloody fire,
Kindled with unchaste desire,   100
Fed in heart, whose flames aspire
As thoughts do blow them, higher and higher.
Pinch him, fairies, mutually;
Pinch him for his villany;
Pinch him, and burn him, and turn him about,
Till candles and starlight and moonshine be out.
          [*During this song they pinch* Falstaff. Doctor
          Caius *comes one way, and steals away a boy in green;*
          Slender *another way, and takes off a boy in white;*
          and Fenton *comes, and steals away Mrs* Anne
          Page. *A noise of hunting is heard within. All the*
          Fairies run away. Falstaff *pulls off his buck's*
          head, and rises.

Enter Page, Ford, Mistress Page *and* Mistress
Ford.

Page. Nay, do not fly; I think we have watch'd you now:
Will none but Herne the hunter serve your turn?
Mrs Page. I pray you, come, hold up the jest no higher.
Now, good Sir John, how like you Windsor wives?   110

See you these, husband? do not these fair yokes
Become the forest better than the town?

Ford. Now, sir, who's a cuckold now? Master Brook,
Falstaff's a knave, a cuckoldly knave; here are his
horns, Master Brook: and, Master Brook, he hath
enjoyed nothing of Ford's but his buck-basket, his
cudgel, and twenty pounds of money, which must be
paid to Master Brook; his horses are arrested for it,
Master Brook.   119

Mrs Ford. Sir John, we have had ill luck; we could
never meet. I will never take you for my love again;
but I will always count you my deer.

Fal. I do begin to perceive that I am made an ass.

Ford. Ay, and an ox too: both the proofs are extant.

Fal. And these are not fairies? I was three or four
times in the thought they were not fairies: and yet the
guiltiness of my mind, the sudden surprise of my
powers, drove the grossness of the foppery into a received belief, in despite of the teeth of all rhyme and
reason, that they were fairies. See now how wit may
be made a Jack-a-Lent, when 'tis upon ill employment!

Evans. Sir John Falstaff, serve Got, and leave your
desires, and fairies will not pinse you.

Ford. Well said, fairy Hugh.

Evans. And leave your jealousies too, I pray you. 140

Ford. I will never mistrust my wife again, till thou
art able to woo her in good English.

Fal. Have I laid my brain in the sun and dried it,
that it wants matter to prevent so gross o'erreaching
as this? Am I ridden with a Welsh goat too? shall I
have a coxcomb of frize? 'Tis time I were choked
with a piece of toasted cheese.

Evans. Seese is not good to give putter; your belly
is all putter.   149

Fal. 'Seese' and 'putter'! have I lived to stand at the
taunt of one that makes fritters of English? This is
enough to be the decay of lust and late-walking
through the realm.   153

Mrs Page. Why, Sir John, do you think, though we
would have thrust virtue out of our hearts by the
head and shoulders and have given ourselves without
scruple to hell, that ever the devil could have made
you our delight?

Ford. What, a hodge-pudding? a bag of flax?

Mrs Page. A puffed man?   160

Page. Old, cold, withered and of intolerable entrails?

Ford. And one that is as slanderous as Satan?

Page. And as poor as Job?

Ford. And as wicked as his wife?

Evans. And given to fornications, and to taverns
and sack and wine and metheglins, and to drinkings
and swearings and starings, pribbles and prabbles? 169

Fal. Well, I am your theme: you have the start of
me; I am dejected; I am not able to answer the Welsh
flannel; ignorance itself is a plummet o'er me: use
me as you will.

Ford. Marry, sir, we'll bring you to Windsor, to one
Master Brook, that you have cozened of money, to
whom you should have been a pandar: over and
above that you have suffered, I think to repay that
money will be a biting affliction.   178

Page. Yet be cheerful, knight: thou shalt eat a
posset to-night at my house; where I will desire thee
to laugh at my wife, that now laughs at thee: tell her
Master Slender hath married her daughter.

Mrs Page. [*Aside*] Doctors doubt that: if Anne Page
be my daughter, she is, by this, Doctor Caius' wife.

Enter SLENDER.

Slen. Whoa, ho! ho, father Page!

Page. Son, how now! how now, son! have you dispatched?   189

Slen. Dispatched! I'll make the best in Gloucestershire know on 't; would I were hanged, la, else!

Page. Of what, son?

Slen. I came yonder at Eton to marry Mistress Anne
Page, and she's a great lubberly boy. If it had not
been i' the church, I would have swinged him, or he
should have swinged me. If I did not think it had
been Anne Page, would I might never stir!—and 'tis
a postmaster's boy.   199

Page. Upon my life, then, you took the wrong.

Slen. What need you tell me that? I think so, when
I took a boy for a girl. If I had been married to him,
for all he was in woman's apparel, I would not have
had him.

Page. Why, this is your own folly. Did not I tell
you how you should know my daughter by her garments?

Slen. I went to her in white, and cried 'mum,' and
she cried 'budget,' as Anne and I had appointed;
and yet it was not Anne, but a postmaster's boy.

Mrs Page. Good George, be not angry: I knew of
your purpose; turned my daughter into green; and,
indeed, she is now with the doctor at the deanery,
and there married.

Enter CAIUS.

Caius. Vere is Mistress Page? By gar, I am cozened:
I ha' married un garçon, a boy; un paysan, by gar, a
boy; it is not Anne Page: by gar, I am cozened.   220

Mrs Page. Why, did you take her in green?

Caius. Ay, by gar, and 'tis a boy: by gar, I'll raise
all Windsor.   [*Exit.*

Ford. This is strange. Who hath got the right Anne?

Page. My heart misgives me: here comes Master
Fenton.

Enter FENTON *and* ANNE PAGE.

How now, Master Fenton!

Anne. Pardon, good father! good my mother, pardon!

Page. Now, mistress, how chance you went not with
Master Slender?   231

---

of the universe, conceived of as between heaven and hell. 87. **o'er-**
look'd, bewitched, looked on with an evil eye. 103. **mutually,**
jointly, in common. 106. *Stage Direction:* **Mrs.** "Mistress" as a title of
courtesy originally referred to both married and unmarried women;
now superseded by two contracted forms, "Mrs." and "Miss," differently
pronounced. 109. **hold . . . higher,** maintain the jest no longer. 111.
these fair yokes, alluding to the horns; Hart suggests that they may
have been of oak branches, making an obvious pun. 126. **an ox.** New
Cambridge editors apply the idiom "to make an ox of someone," i.e.,
to make a fool of, with an obvious reference to the ox's horns. 132.

foppery, deceit. 145-146. **Welsh goat.** New Cambridge editors think
it alludes to Evans' costume of a satyr. Hart quotes Scot's *Discoverie of*
Witchcraft: "First as touching the divell (Bodin saith) that he dooth most
properlie and commonlie transforme himselfe into a gote." 146. **frize,**
kind of coarse woolen cloth. 153. **late-walking,** keeping late hours.
159. **hodge-pudding,** pudding made of a medley of ingredients.
167. **metheglins,** spiced drink made from wort and honey, Welsh in
origin. 173. **plummet,** a quibble on "plumbet," a woolen fabric, and
"plummet," a line for fathoming (New Cambridge). 197. **swinged,**
thrashed. 218. **garçon,** boy. 219. **paysan,** peasant.

Mrs Page. Why went you not with master doctor, maid?

Fent. You do amaze her: hear the truth of it.
You would have married her most shamefully,
Where there was no proportion held in love.
The truth is, she and I, long since contracted,
Are now so sure that nothing can dissolve us.
The offence is holy that she hath committed;
And this deceit loses the name of craft,
Of disobedience, or unduteous title, 240
Since therein she doth evitate and shun
A thousand irreligious cursed hours,
Which forced marriage would have brought upon her.

Ford. Stand not amazed; here is no remedy:
In love the heavens themselves do guide the state;
Money buys lands, and wives are sold by fate.

Fal. I am glad, though you have ta'en a special stand to strike at me, that your arrow hath glanced.

Page. Well, what remedy? Fenton, heaven give thee joy! 250
What cannot be eschew'd must be embraced.

Fal. When night-dogs run, all sorts of deer are chased.

Mrs Page. Well, I will muse no further. Master Fenton,
Heaven give you many, many merry days!
Good husband, let us every one go home,
And laugh this sport o'er by a country fire;
Sir John and all.

Ford.   Let it be so. Sir John,
To Master Brook you yet shall hold your word;
For he to-night shall lie with Mistress Ford.   [*Exeunt.*

241. **evitate,** avoid.   253. **muse,** grumble, complain.

As You Like It

A*s You Like It* was entered in the Stationers' Register, along with *Henry v*, *Every Man in His Humour*, and *Much Ado about Nothing*, as a book stayed, i.e., not printed, on August 4 of some year not given. Inasmuch as *Henry v* and *Much Ado* were published in 1600, with entries a few weeks later, there seems to be no doubt that the omitted year was 1600. *As You Like It* was possibly withheld from publication because the players were confident of being able to protect it from unauthorized publication. If so, their confidence was justified, for it was apparently not printed until the First Folio of 1623.

Attention is often called to the fact that the play is not mentioned by Meres in 1598 and that it refers in pointed terms to Marlowe's *Hero and Leander*, first published in 1598. Phebe exclaims as she beholds Rosalind disguised as Ganymede (III, v, 81-88):

Dead shepherd, now I find thy saw of might,
'Who ever loved that loved not at first sight?'

This is Shakespeare's only unquestioned allusion to a contemporary poet and may fairly be taken to indicate a tender recollection of Marlowe. Between these two dates then, 1598 and 1600, one would be disposed to place *As You Like It*. The assignment agrees well with internal evidence derived from style.

ELEMENTS OF THE STORY: *Rosalynde*

I*n As You Like It* Shakespeare followed a contemporary source, and followed it with great fidelity. Thomas Lodge (1558?-1625), poet, playwright, and novelist, wrote a long romance in order, he says in his dedication to Lord Hunsdon, to beguile the tedium of a voyage to the "Ilands of Terceras and the Canaries." He called his work "*Rosalynde: Euphues Golden Legacie.* Found after his death in his cell at Silexdra. Bequeathed to Philautus Sonnes, nursed up with their father in England." This was published in 1590 with a dedication as above and an Epistle to the Gentlemen Readers, in which Lodge remarks, "*If you like it*, so; and yet I will bee yours in duetie, if you be mine in favour," thus supplying a title for Shakespeare as well as a theme. Lodge's novel is a typical work of the English Renaissance, written in the courtly, heavily mannered style of Lyly's *Euphues*, and combining, with little thought of historical consistency, elements of the romance, the pastoral, and the native English ballad. It is also interspersed with charming lyrics.

Shakespeare discarded the euphuism, probably because it was going out of fashion by the time he wrote, but took the story over bodily, making only such modifications as he saw fit in order to change it from a novel into a play. He has compressed the action into ten days, left out an interval between the quarrel of Orlando and Oliver and the wrestling bout, caused Orlando to leave his brother's place at once, introduced the subplot before Orlando arrives in Arden, and made other similar changes. He has omitted accounts of the deathbed of Orlando's father, of a tourney which precedes the wrestling, and of various matters connected with the quarrel between the brothers. The motive of Oliver, who is called Saladyne in the story, is made, not greed to inherit Orlando's (Rosader's) lands, but jealousy of his handsome person and his popularity.

Shakespeare makes the usurping duke a brother to the banished duke, has him banish Orlando out of prejudice, and has him ultimately repent of all his wickedness. In the novel the twelve peers of France revolt against the usurper, slay him, and reseat on the throne the banished duke, or king as he is in Lodge's story.

There is also in the novel an episode of some length in which a band of robbers carry off Celia (Alinda), who is rescued by Rosader and Saladyne. Shakespeare has kept these robbers out of his peaceful woodland. Finally, Shakespeare has added all that pertains to Jaques, Touchstone, Audrey, William, Amiens, and other minor characters.

Gamelyn

Lodge himself made use of a story, not at that time printed, in a Middle English poem, *The Coke's Tale of Gamelyn*, wrongly attributed to Chaucer and found in a number of manuscripts of *The Canterbury Tales*. This is a Robin Hood story, telling of a neglected younger son who wins prizes in wrestling, quarrels with his wicked eldest brother, runs away with an old retainer, Adam Spencer, to Sherwood forest, and becomes king of the outlaws, and who, finally, has the opportunity of having his eldest brother, who was sheriff, hanged. The Robin Hood appeal of the story is still strong in the play. Shakespeare lets us feel it, not only in the songs and in the philosophy of woodland life, but also when Charles says (I, i, 120-125) of the Duke Ferdinand:

They say he is already in the forest of Arden, and a many merry men with him; and there they live like the old Robin Hood of England: they say many young gentlemen flock to him every day, and fleet the time carelessly, as they did in the golden world.

It happens that the Lord Admiral's company, the chief rivals of the Lord Chamberlain's company, had had since 1598 what must have been a very popular play, *The Downfall of Robert Earl of Huntington after called Robin Hood* by Anthony Munday, and its sequel, *The Death of Robert Earl of Huntington* by Munday and Henry Chettle. *As You Like It* was probably written in order to follow the fashion or even to serve as a counterattraction. Shakespeare probably did not know *Gamelyn*, the original Robin Hood story, but in exploiting the fashion of the forest he recurred in some matters to the older form.

PASTORALISM

Shakespeare, while toning down the element of romance and adventure, has taken full advantage of the atmosphere of the Robin Hood plays. He has also introduced another large literary component of Lodge's novel, namely, the pastoral feature. The pastoral mode had originated in the *Idylls* of Theocritus and the Sicilian Greek poets of the third century B.C., had been carried on by Virgil, and was one of the most popular kinds of ancient literature during the Renaissance. There was a great group of Italian and neo-Latin pastoral poets, some of whom were very familiar to Elizabethan Englishmen.

The best known of native pastoral works are Spenser's *Shepheardes Calender* and Sidney's *Arcadia*.

The Seven Ages of Man from Bartholomaeus Anglicus, "De Proprietatibus Rerum," 1485. See II, vii, 139 ff.

There were not only pastoral poems but pastoral romances and pastoral dramas as well. Probably the life described by Theocritus as lived by the shepherds on Mount Hybla bore some semblance to actuality. However, it had long since become purely an imaginary manner of existence and a style in literature, in which shepherds tending their clean white flocks spent their time in wandering through woods and fields, making love, and discoursing on the nature of true love, the essence of friendship, the relation of youth to age, and the vanity of dwelling in towns. To have courtiers and clowns retire to this Arcadia represented a variation, and to have Arcadia and the greenwood side by side was a complication of interests. Shakespeare has retained with reasonable effectiveness Lodge's pastoral minor plot about Corin and Silvius, Silvius and Phebe, and also Lodge's device for uniting the plots by having the proud and vain Phebe fall in love with Ganymede.

A DRAMATIZED NOVEL

The parts of Lodge's story, then, which Shakespeare has retained are somewhat descriptive and static, rather than dramatic, still having about them the quality of fiction instead of drama. The thing which he got from Lodge is a tale of true love with a charming background, rather than a sharply plotted comedy. What Shakespeare has done, besides his many minor changes, to render the story better suited to the stage, is to develop a central, crucial scene which displays the principal plot. That central incident is described in these terms by the Arden[1] editor: "Two undeclared lovers meet: the lady in disguise challenges her lover to woo her as his mistress: their courtship is thus carried on in masquerade till she is assured of his affection, when she discloses herself, and all ends happily." Shakespeare has thus given in the second scene of the third act a turning point to his comedy which, though not striking or sensational, is genuinely dramatic and delightfully comic.

SHAKESPEARE'S PART

To make a drama of this novel, Shakespeare has resorted to accessory figures. When Celia and Rosalind set out for the forest of Arden, supposed to be the forest of Ardennes in France, but really much like the forest of Arden in Warwickshire, they took with them the court fool Touchstone, one of the great original creations of Shakespeare's plays. He is a court clown and therefore in a manner a courtier; he is a city man in the presence of shepherds and rustics. "In Touchstone," says C. H. Herford, "Shakespeare for the first time utilized the professional court-fool as a medium of wit and humor."

It was probably the situation in which the clown was placed by the accident of the plot that gave Shakespeare this opportunity, and also the presence

in his company of Robert Armin, a new type of comic actor. Touchstone has in him a certain fidelity and satirical honesty which wins our sympathy. He also has more than a dash of amusing roguery, conceit, and bravado, and a vein of nonsense at once professional and spontaneous. One of the set pieces of the play is the issue, often seriously debated, between court life and sylvan or pastoral life. Touchstone, so to speak, attacks this on the flank, for he embodies certain traits of the courtier which were never meant to be brought into the debate. The one whose profession had been folly at the court becomes a philosopher in the forest.

JAQUES

Of Jaques, H. H. Furness says, "Were he really possessed of all the qualities attributed to him by his critics, we should behold a man both misanthropic and genial, sensual and refined, depraved and elevated, cynical and liberal, selfish and generous, and finally, as though to make him still more like Hamlet, we should see in him the clearly marked symptoms of incipient insanity." It is often pointed out that Jaques does nothing and is yet indispensable. He appears in the midst of a period of satire, when Jonson had set a new fashion in his Every Man in His Humour of ridiculing the foibles, eccentricities, and vices of the world.

Jonson based his work on the theory that human eccentricity is due to faulty adjustment of the four humors, or fluids, of the body, and he designated man's vagaries and peculiarities as "humors." It has been argued that Jaques is a humor character,[2] one in whom excessive melancholy is the basis of eccentricity; in fact, that he is a malcontent. When one observes what other characters think and say of Jaques, one finds a good deal to confirm this view. For example, when the First Lord tells the duke about Jaques and the deer in the first scene of the second act; when Jaques shows rudeness to Amiens in the fifth scene, and when he describes the Fool and the eminence of folly in the seventh scene of the same act. It is true that Jaques does nothing to advance the drama except to deliver his famous speech beginning "All the world's a stage" (II, vii, 139 ff.) while Orlando fetches Adam. But he is individualized and, to that degree, important.

The duke charges him (II, vii, 64-69) with having been a libertine and having plucked his melancholy as the bitter fruit of his own folly, and Jaques himself would have you believe in his dialogue with Rosalind (IV, i, 10-26) that his particular brand of melancholy is derived from a too complete knowledge of the world. His belief that there is nothing to be learned from fortunate and contented humanity, exemplified in his secession at the end to the converted duke, amounts almost to a special trait of character. Malcontent, gentle malcontent though Jaques is, he

[2]E. E. Stoll, "Hamlet, Marston and the Malcontent Type," Modern Philology, III, 281-303.

is, nevertheless, treated dramatically in this play. He is set off in contrast to the duke, to the lovers, and the Fool, and is himself delightfully parodied by the Fool and casually cast aside as a critical do-nothing by Rosalind. But he adds a sauce to the dish; for, as one might say in the words of an art critic, used about Fra Angelico's paintings, "We long for a few wolves in this impeccable sheepfold."

ROSALIND

There are no puzzles about Rosalind, it is only a question of adequate praise. "She is wit and womanliness in equal proportions," says one critic. Another calls attention to the fact that she is like Beatrice but kinder and less ironical, that she has the charm of Viola, but is more masterful, and so on. Mrs. Jameson's familiar words usually give pleasure, and they are perhaps as satisfactory as any:

Rosalind is like a compound of essences, so volatile in their nature, and so exquisitely blended, that on any attempt to analyse them, they seem to escape us. To what else shall we compare her, all-enchanting as she is?—To the silvery summer clouds, which, even while we gaze on them, shift their hues and forms, dissolving into air, and light, and rainbow showers?—To the May-morning, flush with opening blossoms and roseate dews, and 'charm of earliest birds'?—To some wild and beautiful melody, such as some shepherd boy might 'pipe to Amaryllis in the shade'?—To a mountain streamlet, now smooth as a mirror in which the skies may glass themselves, and anon leaping and sparkling in the sunshine—or rather to the very sunshine itself? for so her genial spirit touches into life and beauty whatever it shines upon!

STAGE HISTORY

The history of the play interests us because of a tradition, late but plausible, that Shakespeare acted the part of Adam in the early performances.[3] There are few traces of any interest in *As You Like It* during the seventeenth century, but the play suffered garbling at the hands of Charles Johnson in 1723, when he wrote *Love in a Forest*, a sort of amalgamation of *As You Like It, Much Ado, Twelfth Night*, and *A Midsummer-Night's Dream*. Shakespeare's play came back on the stage in 1740 with the great James Quin as Jaques and Mrs. Pritchard as Rosalind.

As You Like It is not one of Shakespeare's greatest stage plays. It is, nevertheless, charming and has always been popular. It has no really great male part, though various actors have done well as Orlando or Jaques. It does have a great woman's part, dashing, boyish, and humorous. Nearly all the greatest actresses have been successful as Rosalind: Mrs. Pritchard, Peg Woffington, Sarah Siddons, Mrs. Jordan, Laura Keene, Rose Coglan, Mary Anderson, Helen Faucit, Charlotte Cushman, Adelaide Neilson, Ada Rehan, Julia Marlowe and, more recently, Katherine Hepburn.

[3]See *Shakespeare's Life and Work, 1564-1594.*

As You Like It

DRAMATIS PERSONAE

DUKE, living in banishment.
FREDERICK, his brother, and usurper of his dominions.
AMIENS,
JAQUES, } lords attending on the banished duke.
LE BEAU, a courtier attending upon Frederick.
CHARLES, wrestler to Frederick.
OLIVER,
JAQUES, } sons of Sir Rowland de Boys.
ORLANDO,
ADAM,
DENNIS, } servants to Oliver.
TOUCHSTONE, a clown.
SIR OLIVER MARTEXT, a vicar.
CORIN,
SILVIUS, } shepherds.
WILLIAM, a country fellow, in love with Audrey.
A person representing Hymen.

ROSALIND, daughter to the banished duke.
CELIA, daughter to Frederick.
PHEBE, a shepherdess.
AUDREY, a country wench.

Lords, pages, and attendants, &c.

SCENE: *Oliver's house; Duke Frederick's court; and the Forest of Arden.*

ACT I.

SCENE I. *Orchard of* OLIVER's *house.*

Enter ORLANDO *and* ADAM.

Orl. As I remember, Adam, it was upon this fashion; bequeathed me by will but poor a thousand crowns, and, as thou sayest, charged my brother, on his blessing, to breed me well: and there begins my sadness. My brother Jaques he keeps at school, and report speaks goldenly of his profit: for my part, he keeps me rustically at home, or, to speak more properly, stays me here at home unkept; for call you that keeping for a gentleman of my birth, that differs not from the stalling of an ox? His horses are bred better; for, besides that they are fair with their feeding, they are taught their manage, and to that end riders dearly hired: but I, his brother, gain nothing under him but growth; for the which his animals on his dunghills are as much bound to him as I. Besides this nothing that he so plentifully gives me, the something that nature gave me his countenance seems to take from me: he lets me feed with his hinds, bars me the place of a brother, and, as much as in him lies, mines my gentility with my education. This is it, Adam, that grieves me; and the spirit of my father, which I think is within me, begins to mutiny against this servitude: I will no longer endure it, though yet I know no wise remedy how to avoid it.

Adam. Yonder comes my master, your brother.

Orl. Go apart, Adam, and thou shalt hear how he will shake me up. 30

Enter OLIVER.

Oli. Now, sir! what make you here?

Orl. Nothing: I am not taught to make any thing.

Oli. What mar you then, sir?

Orl. Marry, sir, I am helping you to mar that which God made, a poor unworthy brother of yours, with idleness.

Oli. Marry, sir, be better employed, and be naught awhile. 39

Orl. Shall I keep your hogs and eat husks with them? What prodigal portion have I spent, that I should come to such penury?

Oli. Know you where you are, sir?

Orl. O, sir, very well: here in your orchard.

Oli. Know you before whom, sir? 45

Orl. Ay, better than him I am before knows me. I know you are my eldest brother; and, in the gentle condition of blood, you should so know me. The courtesy of nations allows you my better, in that you are the first-born; but the same tradition takes not away my blood, were there twenty brothers betwixt us: I have as much of my father in me as you; albeit, I confess, your coming before me is nearer to his reverence.

Oli. What, boy! 55

Orl. Come, come, elder brother, you are too young in this.

Oli. Wilt thou lay hands on me, villain?

Orl. I am no villain; I am the youngest son of Sir Rowland de Boys; he was my father, and he is thrice a villain that says such a father begot villains. Wert thou not my brother, I would not take this hand from thy throat till this other had pulled out thy tongue for saying so: thou hast railed on thyself.

Adam. Sweet masters, be patient: for your father's remembrance, be at accord.

Oli. Let me go, I say. 68

Orl. I will not, till I please: you shall hear me. My father charged you in his will to give me good education: you have trained me like a peasant, obscuring and hiding from me all gentleman-like qualities. The spirit of my father grows strong in me, and I will no longer endure it: therefore allow me such exercises as may become a gentleman, or give me the poor allottery my father left me by testament; with that I will go buy my fortunes. 78

Oli. And what wilt thou do? beg, when that is spent? Well, sir, get you in: I will not long be troubled with you; you shall have some part of your will: I pray you, leave me.

Orl. I will no further offend you than becomes me for my good.

Oli. Get you with him, you old dog.

Adam. Is 'old dog' my reward? Most true, I have lost my teeth in your service. God be with my old master! he would not have spoke such a word. 89

[*Exeunt Orlando and Adam.*

Oli. Is it even so? begin you to grow upon me? I will physic your rankness, and yet give no thousand crowns neither. Holla, Dennis!

Enter DENNIS.

Den. Calls your worship?

Oli. Was not Charles, the duke's wrestler, here to speak with me?

Den. So please you, he is here at the door and importunes access to you.

Oli. Call him in. [*Exit Dennis.*] 'Twill be a good way; and to-morrow the wrestling is.

Enter CHARLES.

Cha. Good morrow to your worship. 100

Oli. Good Monsieur Charles, what's the new news at the new court?

Cha. There's no news at the court, sir, but the old news: that is, the old duke is banished by his younger brother the new duke; and three or four loving lords have put themselves into voluntary exile with him, whose lands and revenues enrich the new duke; therefore he gives them good leave to wander.

Oli. Can you tell if Rosalind, the duke's daughter, be banished with her father? 111

Cha. O, no; for the duke's daughter, her cousin, so loves her, being ever from their cradles bred together, that she would have followed her exile, or have died to stay behind her. She is at the court, and no less beloved of her uncle than his own daughter; and never two ladies loved as they do.

Oli. Where will the old duke live? 119

Cha. They say he is already in the forest of Arden, and a many merry men with him; and they there live like the old Robin Hood of England: they say many young gentlemen flock to him every day, and fleet the time carelessly, as they did in the golden world. 125

Oli. What, you wrestle to-morrow before the new duke?

Cha. Marry, do I, sir; and I came to acquaint you with a matter. I am given, sir, secretly to understand that your younger brother Orlando hath a disposition to come in disguised against me to try a fall. To-morrow, sir, I wrestle for my credit; and he that escapes me without some broken limb shall acquit him well. Your brother is but young and tender; and, for your love, I would be loath to foil him, as I must, for my own honour, if he come in: therefore, out of my love to you, I came hither to acquaint you withal, that either you might stay him from his intendment or brook such disgrace well as he shall run into, in that it is a thing of his own search and altogether against my will. 143

ACT I. SCENE I. 2. **bequeathed,** he (Orlando's father) bequeathed. 4. **on his blessing,** on pain of losing his blessing. 6. **school,** university. 7. **profit,** progress. 20. **countenance,** favor, patronage. 22. **bars me,** excludes me from. 23. **mines,** undermines. 39. **be naught awhile,** a slight malediction; possibly, efface yourself, withdraw. 41. **prodigal portion,** i.e., portion prodigally. 46. **him,** he. 48. **gentle condition of blood,** enlightened state which comes from gentle blood. 49. **courtesy of nations,** usage of civilized people. 54. **nearer to his reverence,** more worthy of the respect due him; Warburton suggested *revenue,* a reading which would account for Oliver's offense. 57. **young,** raw, inexperienced; here, indicative of Orlando's superiority at wrestling. Oliver has apparently struck him. 58. **villain,** bondman, servant. 67. **your father's remembrance,** memory of your father. 72. **obscuring and hiding,** obscuring in me, and hiding. 77. **allottery,** share, portion. 79. **thou,** used contemptuously instead of the more polite "you." 90. **grow upon,** come to take liberties with. 91. **rankness,** insolence, suggesting also the figure of *grow upon.* 115. **died to stay,** died from staying. 121. **a many,** many (as in "a dozen"); explained also as "a menie," company. 124. **fleet,** pass. 125. **golden world,** golden age, i.e., the traditional age of innocence from which man was thought to have degenerated. 134. **shall,** will inevitably. 141. **intendment,** purpose, intent. 147. **underhand means,** reasonable

Oli. Charles, I thank thee for thy love to me, which thou shalt find I will most kindly requite. I had myself notice of my brother's purpose herein and have by underhand means laboured to dissuade him from it, but he is resolute. I'll tell thee, Charles: it is the stubbornest young fellow of France, full of ambition, an envious emulator of every man's good parts, a secret and villanous contriver against me his natural brother: therefore use thy discretion; I had as lief thou didst break his neck as his finger. And thou wert best look to 't; for if thou dost him any slight disgrace or if he do not mightily grace himself on thee, he will practise against thee by poison, entrap thee by some treacherous device and never leave thee till he hath ta'en thy life by some indirect means or other; for, I assure thee, and almost with tears I speak it, there is not one so young and so villanous this day living. I speak but brotherly of him; but should I anatomize him to thee as he is, I must blush and weep and thou must look pale and wonder. 167

Cha. I am heartily glad I came hither to you. If he come to-morrow, I'll give him his payment: if ever he go alone again, I'll never wrestle for prize more: and so God keep your worship!

Oli. Farewell, good Charles. [*Exit Charles.*] Now will I stir this gamester: I hope I shall see an end of him; for my soul, yet I know not why, hates nothing more than he. Yet he 's gentle, never schooled and yet learned, full of noble device, of all sorts enchantingly beloved, and indeed so much in the heart of the world, and especially of my own people, who best know him, that I am altogether misprised: but it shall not be so long; this wrestler shall clear all: nothing remains but that I kindle the boy thither; which now I'll go about.
[*Exit.*]

SCENE II. *Lawn before the* DUKE'S *palace.*

Enter CELIA *and* ROSALIND.

Cel. I pray thee, Rosalind, sweet my coz, be merry.

Ros. Dear Celia, I show more mirth than I am mistress of; and would you yet I were merrier? Unless you could teach me to forget a banished father, you must not learn me how to remember any extraordinary pleasure.

Cel. Herein I see thou lovest me not with the full weight that I love thee. If my uncle, thy banished father, had banished thy uncle, the duke my father, so thou hadst been still with me, I could have taught my love to take thy father for mine: so wouldst thou, if the truth of thy love to me were so righteously tempered as mine is to thee. 14

Ros. Well, I will forget the condition of my estate, to rejoice in yours.

Cel. You know my father hath no child but I, nor none is like to have: and, truly, when he dies, thou shalt be his heir, for what he hath taken away from thy father perforce, I will render thee again in affection; by mine honour, I will; and when I break that oath, let me turn monster: therefore, my sweet Rose, my dear Rose, be merry. 25

Ros. From henceforth I will, coz, and devise sports. Let me see; what think you of falling in love?

Cel. Marry, I prithee, do, to make sport withal: but love no man in good earnest; nor no further in sport neither than with safety of a pure blush thou mayst in honour come off again.

Ros. What shall be our sport, then?

Cel. Let us sit and mock the good housewife Fortune from her wheel, that her gifts may henceforth be bestowed equally. 36

Ros. I would we could do so, for her benefits are mightily misplaced, and the bountiful blind woman doth most mistake in her gifts to women.

Cel. 'Tis true; for those that she makes fair she scarce makes honest, and those that she makes honest she makes very ill-favoured.

Ros. Nay, now thou goest from Fortune's office to Nature's: Fortune reigns in gifts of the world, not in the lineaments of Nature.

Enter TOUCHSTONE.

Cel. No? when Nature hath made a fair creature, may she not by Fortune fall into the fire? Though Nature hath given us wit to flout at Fortune, hath not Fortune sent in this fool to cut off the argument? 50

Ros. Indeed, there is Fortune too hard for Nature, when Fortune makes Nature's natural the cutter-off of Nature's wit.

Cel. Peradventure this is not Fortune's work neither, but Nature's; who perceiveth our natural wits too dull to reason of such goddesses and hath sent this natural for our whetstone; for always the dulness of the fool is the whetstone of the wits. How now, wit! whither wander you?

Touch. Mistress, you must come away to your father. 61

Cel. Were you made the messenger?

Touch. No, by mine honour, but I was bid to come for you.

Ros. Where learned you that oath, fool?

Touch. Of a certain knight that swore by his honour they were good pancakes and swore by his honour the mustard was naught: now I'll stand to it, the pancakes were naught and the mustard was good, and yet was not the knight forsworn. 71

Cel. How prove you that, in the great heap of your knowledge?

Ros. Ay, marry, now unmuzzle your wisdom.

Touch. Stand you both forth now: stroke your chins, and swear by your beards that I am a knave.

Cel. By our beards, if we had them, thou art. 79

Touch. By my knavery, if I had it, then I were; but if you swear by that that is not, you are not forsworn: no more was this knight, swearing by his honour, for

---

or quiet methods. 151. **emulator,** disparager. 152. **contriver,** plotter. 153. **natural brother,** brother by blood, legitimate brother. 157. **grace himself on thee,** distinguish himself at your expense. 164. **brotherly,** with a reserve proper to a brother. 165. **anatomize,** lay open in detail, analyze; F: *anathomize.* 170. **payment,** punishment. 174. **gamester,** frolicsome person. 178. **noble device,** lofty aspiration. **sorts,** classes of people. **enchantingly,** as if by the effect of enchantment. 182. **misprised,** despised. 184. **kindle,** incite (to go). **thither,** i.e., to the wrestling match.

SCENE II. 1. **sweet my coz,** my sweet cousin. 10. **so,** provided that. 12-14. **if the . . . thee,** if the composition of your love were really as

perfect as mine. 30-31. **safety . . . blush,** a degree of safety costing no more than an innocent blush. 31. **come off,** escape. 34. **housewife,** hussy; an epithet of slight contempt. 42. **ill-favouredly,** ugly, ill-favored. 49. **flout,** mock, scoff at. 53. **natural,** idiot, half-wit. 59. **whither wander you,** an allusion to the expression "wandering wits." 60. **Mistress,** not a polite title to address to a princess. 62. **messenger,** possibly, police officer. Celia says in effect, "Were you sent to arrest me?" (New Cambridge). 67. **pancakes,** fritters (which might be made of meat and so require mustard).

he never had any; or if he had, he had sworn it away before ever he saw those pancakes or that mustard.

Cel. Prithee, who is 't that thou meanest?

Touch. One that old Frederick, your father, loves.

Ros. My father's love is enough to honour him: enough! speak no more of him; you'll be whipped for taxation one of these days. 91

Touch. The more pity, that fools may not speak wisely what wise men do foolishly.

Cel. By my troth, thou sayest true; for since the little wit that fools have was silenced, the little foolery that wise men have makes a great show. Here comes Monsieur Le Beau.

Ros. With his mouth full of news.

Cel. Which he will put on us, as pigeons feed their young. 100

Ros. Then shall we be news-crammed.

Cel. All the better; we shall be the more marketable.

Enter LE BEAU.

Bon jour, Monsieur Le Beau: what 's the news?

Le Beau. Fair princess, you have lost much good sport.

Cel. Sport! of what colour?

Le Beau. What colour, madam! how shall I answer you?

Ros. As wit and fortune will. 110

Touch. Or as the Destinies decree.

Cel. Well said: that was laid on with a trowel.

Touch. Nay, if I keep not my rank,—

Ros. Thou losest thy old smell.

Le Beau. You amaze me, ladies: I would have told you of good wrestling, which you have lost the sight of.

Ros. Yet tell us the manner of the wrestling.

Le Beau. I will tell you the beginning; and, if it please your ladyships, you may see the end; for the best is yet to do; and here, where you are, they are coming to perform it.

Cel. Well, the beginning, that is dead and buried.

Le Beau. There comes an old man and his three sons,—

Cel. I could match this beginning with an old tale.

Le Beau. Three proper young men, of excellent growth and presence. 130

Ros. With bills on their necks, 'Be it known unto all men by these presents.'

Le Beau. The eldest of the three wrestled with Charles, the duke's wrestler; which Charles in a moment threw him and broke three of his ribs, that there is little hope of life in him: so he served the second, and so the third. Yonder they lie; the poor old man, their father, making such pitiful dole over them that all the beholders take his part with weeping.

Ros. Alas! 141

⌜ *Touch.* But what is the sport, monsieur, that the ladies have lost?

Le Beau. Why, this that I speak of.

Touch. Thus men may grow wiser every day: it is the first time that ever I heard breaking of ribs was sport for ladies.

Cel. Or I, I promise thee. 148

Ros. But is there any else longs to see this broken music in his sides? is there yet another dotes upon rib-breaking? Shall we see this wrestling, cousin?

Le Beau. You must, if you stay here; for here is the place appointed for the wrestling, and they are ready to perform it.

Cel. Yonder, sure, they are coming: let us now stay and see it.

Flourish. Enter DUKE FREDERICK, Lords, ORLANDO, CHARLES, *and* Attendants.

Duke F. Come on: since the youth will not be entreated, his own peril on his forwardness.

Ros. Is yonder the man? 160

Le Beau. Even he, madam.

Cel. Alas, he is too young! yet he looks successfully.

Duke F. How now, daughter and cousin! are you crept hither to see the wrestling?

Ros. Ay, my liege, so please you give us leave. 167

Duke F. You will take little delight in it, I can tell you; there is such odds in the man. In pity of the challenger's youth I would fain dissuade him, but he will not be entreated. Speak to him, ladies; see if you can move him.

Cel. Call him hither, good Monsieur Le Beau.

Duke F. Do so: I'll not be by.

Le Beau. Monsieur the challenger, the princesses call for you.

Orl. I attend them with all respect and duty.

Ros. Young man, have you challenged Charles the wrestler? 179

Orl. No, fair princess; he is the general challenger: I come but in, as others do, to try with him the strength of my youth.

Cel. Young gentleman, your spirits are too bold for your years. You have seen cruel proof of this man's strength: if you saw yourself with your eyes or knew yourself with your judgement, the fear of your adventure would counsel you to a more equal enterprise. We pray you, for your own sake, to embrace your own safety and give over this attempt. 190

Ros. Do, young sir; your reputation shall not therefore be misprised: we will make it our suit to the duke that the wrestling might not go forward.

Orl. I beseech you, punish me not with your hard thoughts; wherein I confess me much guilty, to deny so fair and excellent ladies any thing. But let your fair eyes and gentle wishes go with me to my trial: wherein if I be foiled, there is but one shamed that was never gracious; if killed, but one dead that is willing to be so: I shall do my friends no wrong, for I have none to lament me, the world no injury, for in it I have nothing; only in the world I fill up a place, which may be better supplied when I have made it empty. 206

Ros. The little strength that I have, I would it were with you.

Cel. And mine, to eke out hers.

Ros. Fare you well: pray heaven I be deceived in you! 210

89. *Ros.*, so F; Globe: *Cel.* 91. **taxation,** satire, censure; in this case directed at the reigning duke. 99. **put on,** pass off upon, communicate to. 107. **colour,** kind. 112. **laid . . . trowel,** i.e., clumsily. 131. **bills,** advertisements, proclamations. 132. **presents,** document presented, with pun on *presence.* 139. **dole,** grief, lamentation. 149. **any,** anyone. 150. **broken music,** possibly, broken musical instrument (as if the ribs were part of such an instrument). 159. **peril on,** i.e., be upon. 163. **successfully,** i.e., as if he would be successful. 169. **such odds in the**

man, such advantage on the side of the man (i.e., the wrestler, Charles, as contrasted with the youth, Orlando). 176. **princesses call,** so Theobald; F: *princess calls.* New Cambridge editors defend the F reading on the ground that Le Beau, as an adherent of the usurping duke, would recognize only one princess. 185-187. **if . . . judgement,** if you saw yourself as you really are in relation to your opponent and used your judgment. Some older editors read *our* for *your* in line 186. 192. **therefore,** on that account. **misprised,** despised. 200. **gracious,**

Cel. Your heart's desires be with you!

Cha. Come, where is this young gallant that is so desirous to lie with his mother earth?

Orl. Ready, sir; but his will hath in it a more modest working.

Duke F. You shall try but one fall.

Cha. No, I warrant your grace, you shall not entreat him to a second, that have so mightily persuaded him from a first. 219

Orl. An you mean to mock me after, you should not have mocked me before: but come your ways.

Ros. Now Hercules be thy speed, young man!

Cel. I would I were invisible, to catch the strong fellow by the leg. [*They wrestle.*

Ros. O excellent young man!

Cel. If I had a thunderbolt in mine eye, I can tell who should down. [*Shout. Charles is thrown.*

Duke F. No more, no more.

Orl. Yes, I beseech your grace: I am not yet well breathed. 230

Duke F. How dost thou, Charles?

Le Beau. He cannot speak, my lord.

Duke F. Bear him away. What is thy name, young man?

Orl. Orlando, my liege; the youngest son of Sir Rowland de Boys.

Duke F. I would thou hadst been son to some man else:
The world esteem'd thy father honourable,
But I did find him still mine enemy:
Thou shouldst have better pleased me with this deed,
Hadst thou descended from another house. 240
But fare thee well; thou art a gallant youth:
I would thou hadst told me of another father.
[*Exeunt Duke Fred., train, and Le Beau.*

Cel. Were I my father, coz, would I do this?

Orl. I am more proud to be Sir Rowland's son,
His youngest son; and would not change that calling,
To be adopted heir to Frederick.

Ros. My father loved Sir Rowland as his soul,
And all the world was of my father's mind:
Had I before known this young man his son,
I should have given him tears unto entreaties, 250
Ere he should thus have ventured.

Cel. Gentle cousin,
Let us go thank him and encourage him:
My father's rough and envious disposition
Sticks me at heart. Sir, you have well deserved:
If you do keep your promises in love
But justly, as you have exceeded all promise,
Your mistress shall be happy.

Ros. Gentleman,
[*Giving him a chain from her neck.*
Wear this for me, one out of suits with fortune,
That could give more, but that her hand lacks means.
Shall we go, coz?

Cel. Ay. Fare you well, fair gentleman.

Orl. Can I not say, I thank you? My better parts 261
Are all thrown down, and that which here stands up
Is but a quintain, a mere lifeless block.

Ros. He calls us back: my pride fell with my fortunes;
I'll ask him what he would. Did you call, sir?
Sir, you have wrestled well and overthrown
More than your enemies.

Cel. Will you go, coz?

Ros. Have with you. Fare you well.
[*Exeunt Rosalind and Celia.*

Orl. What passion hangs these weights upon my tongue?
I cannot speak to her, yet she urged conference. 270
O poor Orlando, thou art overthrown!
Or Charles or something weaker masters thee.

Re-enter LE BEAU.

Le Beau. Good sir, I do in friendship counsel you
To leave this place. Albeit you have deserved
High commendation, true applause and love,
Yet such is now the duke's condition
That he misconstrues all that you have done.
The duke is humorous: what he is indeed,
More suits you to conceive than I to speak of.

Orl. I thank you, sir: and, pray you, tell me this; 280
Which of the two was daughter of the duke
That here was at the wrestling?

Le Beau. Neither his daughter, if we judge by manners;
But yet indeed the lesser is his daughter:
The other is daughter to the banish'd duke,
And here detain'd by her usurping uncle,
To keep his daughter company; whose loves
Are dearer than the natural bond of sisters.
But I can tell you that of late this duke
Hath ta'en displeasure 'gainst his gentle niece, 290
Grounded upon no other argument
But that the people praise her for her virtues
And pity her for her good father's sake;
And, on my life, his malice 'gainst the lady
Will suddenly break forth. Sir, fare you well:
Hereafter, in a better world than this,
I shall desire more love and knowledge of you.

Orl. I rest much bounden to you: fare you well.
[*Exit Le Beau.*
Thus must I from the smoke into the smother;
From tyrant duke unto a tyrant brother: 300
But heavenly Rosalind! [*Exit.*

As You Like It
ACT I : SC III

593

SCENE III. *A room in the palace.*

Enter CELIA *and* ROSALIND.

Cel. Why, cousin! why, Rosalind! Cupid have mercy! not a word?

Ros. Not one to throw at a dog.

Cel. No, thy words are too precious to be cast away

---

looked upon with favor. 215. **working,** endeavor. 222. **come your ways,** come on. 223. **Hercules . . . speed,** may Hercules favor you. 230. **well breathed,** put into good wind. 245. **calling,** appellation, name. 249. **known,** i.e., known to be. 250. **unto,** in addition to. 254. **Sticks me at heart,** stabs me to the heart. 258. **out . . . fortune,** not wearing the livery of fortune; not in her service; or one whose suits to fortune are rejected. 263. **quintain,** wooden figure at which to tilt. 273-279. **Good . . . speak of.** Note the courtly formality of Le Beau.

276. **condition,** state of mind, disposition. 277. **misconstrues.** The F spelling *misconsters* indicates the pronunciation. 278. **humorous,** given to whims, capricious, self-willed. 284. **lesser,** so Spedding; F: *taller,* which is inconsistent with statements elsewhere (see I, iii, 117) that Rosalind is the taller of the two. In this inconsistency in the F, the New Cambridge editors find evidence of the revision of the play. 299. **smoke into the smother,** frying-pan into the fire.

upon curs; throw some of them at me; come, lame me with reasons.

Ros. Then there were two cousins laid up; when the one should be lamed with reasons and the other mad without any.

Cel. But is all this for your father? 10

Ros. No, some of it is for my child's father. O, how full of briers is this working-day world!

Cel. They are but burs, cousin, thrown upon thee in holiday foolery: if we walk not in the trodden paths, our very petticoats will catch them.

Ros. I could shake them off my coat: these burs are in my heart.

Cel. Hem them away.

Ros. I would try, if I could cry 'hem' and have him.

Cel. Come, come, wrestle with thy affections. 21

Ros. O, they take the part of a better wrestler than myself!

Cel. O, a good wish upon you! you will try in time, in despite of a fall. But, turning these jests out of service, let us talk in good earnest: is it possible, on such a sudden, you should fall into so strong a liking with old Sir Rowland's youngest son? 29

Ros. The duke my father loved his father dearly.

Cel. Doth it therefore ensue that you should love his son dearly? By this kind of chase, I should hate him, for my father hated his father dearly; yet I hate not Orlando.

Ros. No, faith, hate him not, for my sake.

Cel. Why should I not? doth he not deserve well?

Ros. Let me love him for that, and do you love him because I do. Look, here comes the duke. 41

Cel. With his eyes full of anger.

Enter DUKE FREDERICK, *with* Lords.

Duke F. Mistress, dispatch you with your safest haste
And get you from our court.

Ros.   Me, uncle?

Duke F.   You, cousin:
Within these ten days if that thou be'st found
So near our public court as twenty miles,
Thou diest for it.

Ros.   I do beseech your grace,
Let me the knowledge of my fault bear with me:
If with myself I hold intelligence
Or have acquaintance with mine own desires, 50
If that I do not dream or be not frantic,—
As I do trust I am not—then, dear uncle,
Never so much as in a thought unborn
Did I offend your highness.

Duke F.   Thus do all traitors:
If their purgation did consist in words,
They are as innocent as grace itself:
Let it suffice thee that I trust thee not.

Ros. Yet your mistrust cannot make me a traitor:
Tell me whereon the likelihood depends.

Duke F. Thou art thy father's daughter; there's enough. 60

Ros. So was I when your highness took his dukedom;

So was I when your highness banish'd him:
Treason is not inherited, my lord;
Or, if we did derive it from our friends,
What's that to me? my father was no traitor:
Then, good my liege, mistake me not so much
To think my poverty is treacherous.

Cel. Dear sovereign, hear me speak.

Duke F. Ay, Celia; we stay'd her for your sake,
Else had she with her father ranged along. 70

Cel. I did not then entreat to have her stay;
It was your pleasure and your own remorse:
I was too young that time to value her;
But now I know her: if she be a traitor,
Why so am I; we still have slept together,
Rose at an instant, learn'd, play'd, eat together,
And wheresoe'er we went, like Juno's swans,
Still we went coupled and inseparable.

Duke F. She is too subtle for thee; and her smoothness,
Her very silence and her patience 80
Speak to the people, and they pity her.
Thou art a fool: she robs thee of thy name;
And thou wilt show more bright and seem more virtuous
When she is gone. Then open not thy lips:
Firm and irrevocable is my doom
Which I have pass'd upon her; she is banish'd.

Cel. Pronounce that sentence then on me, my liege:
I cannot live out of her company.

Duke F. You are a fool. You, niece, provide yourself:
If you outstay the time, upon mine honour, 90
And in the greatness of my word, you die.

          [*Exeunt Duke Frederick and Lords.*

Cel. O my poor Rosalind, whither wilt thou go?
Wilt thou change fathers? I will give thee mine.
I charge thee, be not thou more grieved than I am.

Ros. I have more cause.

Cel.   Thou hast not, cousin;
Prithee, be cheerful: know'st thou not, the duke
Hath banish'd me, his daughter?

Ros.   That he hath not.

Cel. No, hath not? Rosalind lacks then the love
Which teacheth thee that thou and I am one:
Shall we be sunder'd? shall we part, sweet girl? 100
No: let my father seek another heir.
Therefore devise with me how we may fly,
Whither to go and what to bear with us;
And do not seek to take your change upon you,
To bear your griefs yourself and leave me out;
For, by this heaven, now at our sorrows pale,
Say what thou canst, I'll go along with thee.

Ros. Why, whither shall we go?

Cel. To seek my uncle in the forest of Arden.

Ros. Alas, what danger will it be to us, 110
Maids as we are, to travel forth so far!
Beauty provoketh thieves sooner than gold.

Cel. I'll put myself in poor and mean attire
And with a kind of umber smirch my face;
The like do you: so shall we pass along
And never stir assailants.

SCENE III. 6. **lame . . . reasons.** Rosalind has talked about throwing words at a dog and thus perhaps laming him. Celia says, "Lame me by throwing reasons at me." 12. **working-day,** trivial. 20. **cry 'hem,'** clear away with a "hem" or a cough, with a possible play on *him.* 27. **on such a sudden,** so suddenly. 37. **deserve well,** i.e., to be hated. 43. **safest haste,** speed, which is your best security. 45. **ten,** anonymous conjecture: *two.* 55. **purgation,** exculpation. 64. **friends,** relatives, kinsfolk. 70. **ranged,** roamed; see glossary. 73. **that time,** then. 77. **Juno's swans.** It has been pointed out that it was Venus and not Juno who possessed swans. 104. **change,** change of fortune. 114. **umber,** brown pigment used to disguise the face. 118. **suit,** dress. 119. **curtle-axe,** broad cutting sword. 122. **swashing,** blustering. 127. **Ganymede,** the name of Jupiter's cupbearer; used also in Lodge's *Rosalynde.* 139. **content,** contentment.

Ros.   Were it not better,
Because that I am more than common tall,
That I did suit me all points like a man?
A gallant curtle-axe upon my thigh,
A boar-spear in my hand; and—in my heart   120
Lie there what hidden woman's fear there will—
We'll have a swashing and a martial outside,
As many other mannish cowards have
That do outface it with their semblances.
    Cel. What shall I call thee when thou art a man?
    Ros. I'll have no worse a name than Jove's own
        page;
And therefore look you call me Ganymede.
But what will you be call'd?
    Cel. Something that hath a reference to my state;
No longer Celia, but Aliena.   130
    Ros. But, cousin, what if we assay'd to steal
The clownish fool out of your father's court?
Would he not be a comfort to our travel?
    Cel. He'll go along o'er the wide world with me;
Leave me alone to woo him. Let 's away,
And get our jewels and our wealth together,
Devise the fittest time and safest way
To hide us from pursuit that will be made
After my flight. Now go we in content
To liberty and not to banishment.   [*Exeunt.* 140

ACT II.

SCENE I. *The Forest of Arden.*

Enter DUKE senior, AMIENS, *and two or three* Lords,
like foresters.

    Duke S. Now, my co-mates and brothers in exile,
Hath not old custom made this life more sweet
Than that of painted pomp? Are not these woods
More free from peril than the envious court?
Here feel we but the penalty of Adam,
The seasons' difference, as the icy fang
And churlish chiding of the winter's wind,
Which, when it bites and blows upon my body,
Even till I shrink with cold, I smile and say
'This is no flattery: these are counsellors   10
That feelingly persuade me what I am.'
Sweet are the uses of adversity,
Which, like the toad, ugly and venomous,
Wears yet a precious jewel in his head;
And this our life exempt from public haunt
Finds tongues in trees, books in the running brooks,
Sermons in stones and good in every thing.
I would not change it.
    Ami.   Happy is your grace,
That can translate the stubbornness of fortune
Into so quiet and so sweet a style.   20
    Duke S. Come, shall we go and kill us venison?
And yet it irks me the poor dappled fools,
Being native burghers of this desert city,
Should in their own confines with forked heads
Have their round haunches gored.
    First Lord.   Indeed, my lord,

The melancholy Jaques grieves at that,
And, in that kind, swears you do more usurp
Than doth your brother that hath banish'd you.
To-day my Lord of Amiens and myself
Did steal behind him as he lay along   30
Under an oak whose antique root peeps out
Upon the brook that brawls along this wood:
To the which place a poor sequester'd stag,
That from the hunter's aim had ta'en a hurt,
Did come to languish, and indeed, my lord,
The wretched animal heaved forth such groans
That their discharge did stretch his leathern coat
Almost to bursting, and the big round tears
Coursed one another down his innocent nose
In piteous chase; and thus the hairy fool,   40
Much marked of the melancholy Jaques,
Stood on the extremest verge of the swift brook,
Augmenting it with tears.
    Duke S.   But what said Jaques?
Did he not moralize this spectacle?
    First Lord. O, yes, into a thousand similes.
First, for his weeping into the needless stream;
'Poor deer,' quoth he, 'thou makest a testament
As worldings do, giving thy sum of more
To that which had too much:' then, being there alone,
Left and abandon'd of his velvet friends,   50
''Tis right,' quoth he; 'thus misery doth part
The flux of company:' anon a careless herd,
Full of the pasture, jumps along by him
And never stays to greet him; 'Ay,' quoth Jaques,
'Sweep on, you fat and greasy citizens;
'Tis just the fashion: wherefore do you look
Upon that poor and broken bankrupt there?'
Thus most invectively he pierceth through
The body of the country, city, court,
Yea, and of this our life, swearing that we   60
Are mere usurpers, tyrants and what 's worse,
To fright the animals and to kill them up
In their assign'd and native dwelling-place.
    Duke S. And did you leave him in this
        contemplation?
    Sec. Lord. We did, my lord, weeping and
        commenting
Upon the sobbing deer.
    Duke S.   Show me the place:
I love to cope him in these sullen fits,
For then he 's full of matter.
    First Lord. I'll bring you to him straight.   [*Exeunt.*

SCENE II. *A room in the palace.*

Enter DUKE FREDERICK, *with* Lords.

    Duke F. Can it be possible that no man saw them?
It cannot be: some villains of my court
Are of consent and sufferance in this.
    First Lord. I cannot hear of any that did see her.
The ladies, her attendants of her chamber,
Saw her a-bed, and in the morning early
They found the bed untreasured of their mistress.

As You Like It
ACT II : SC II

595

ACT II. SCENE I. 6. **as,** such as. 13-14. **like . . . head.** The idea
that the toad was venomous comes from Pliny's *Natural History.* The
jewel referred to is the toadstone, which was thought to be in the head
of the toad. 15. **exempt,** cut off. 22. **irks,** grieves, vexes. 23.
burghers, citizens. 31. **antique,** ancient. 44. **moralize,** draw out the
hidden meaning of. 50. **velvet,** courtierlike. Velvet was the typical
dress of the courtier; a probable allusion also to the velvet of the

deer's horn. 58. **invectively,** with denunciation. 68. **matter,** sense,
substance.
SCENE II. 3. **consent and sufferance,** agreement as to course of
action and permission for events to take place without opposition;
metaphor from law.

Sec. Lord. My lord, the roynish clown, at whom so
　　oft
Your grace was wont to laugh, is also missing.
Hisperia, the princess' gentlewoman,　　　　　　　　10
Confesses that she secretly o'erheard
Your daughter and her cousin much commend
The parts and graces of the wrestler
That did but lately foil the sinewy Charles;
And she believes, wherever they are gone,
That youth is surely in their company.
　　Duke F. Send to his brother; fetch that gallant
　　hither;
If he be absent, bring his brother to me;
I'll make him find him: do this suddenly,
And let not search and inquisition quail　　　　　　20
To bring again these foolish runaways.　　　*[Exeunt.*

SCENE III. *Before* OLIVER's *house.*

Enter ORLANDO *and* ADAM, *meeting.*

Orl. Who 's there?
Adam. What, my young master? O my gentle
　　master!
O my sweet master! O you memory
Of old Sir Rowland! why, what make you here?
Why are you virtuous? why do people love you?
And wherefore are you gentle, strong and valiant?
Why would you be so fond to overcome
The bonny priser of the humorous duke?
Your praise is come too swiftly home before you.
Know you not, master, to some kind of men　　　10
Their graces serve them but as enemies?
No more do yours: your virtues, gentle master,
Are sanctified and holy traitors to you.
O, what a world is this, when what is comely
Envenoms him that bears it!
　　Orl. Why, what 's the matter?
　　Adam.　　　　　　O unhappy youth!
Come not within these doors; within this roof
The enemy of all your graces lives:
Your brother—no, no brother; yet the son—
Yet not the son, I will not call him son　　　　　　20
Of him I was about to call his father—
Hath heard your praises, and this night he means
To burn the lodging where you use to lie
And you within it: if he fail of that,
He will have other means to cut you off.
I overheard him and his practices.
This is no place; this house is but a butchery:
Abhor it, fear it, do not enter it.
　　Orl. Why, whither, Adam, wouldst thou have me
　　go?
　　Adam. No matter whither, so you come not here.　30
　　Orl. What, wouldst thou have me go and beg my
　　food?
Or with a base and boisterous sword enforce
A thievish living on the common road?
This I must do, or know not what to do:
Yet this I will not do, do how I can;

I rather will subject me to the malice
Of a diverted blood and bloody brother.
　　Adam. But do not so. I have five hundred crowns,
The thrifty hire I saved under your father,
Which I did store to be my foster-nurse　　　　　　40
When service should in my old limbs lie lame
And unregarded age in corners thrown:
Take that, and He that doth the ravens feed,
Yea, providently caters for the sparrow,
Be comfort to my age! Here is the gold;
All this I give you. Let me be your servant:
Though I look old, yet I am strong and lusty;
For in my youth I never did apply
Hot and rebellious liquors in my blood,
Nor did not with unbashful forehead woo　　　　　50
The means of weakness and debility;
Therefore my age is as a lusty winter,
Frosty, but kindly: let me go with you;
I'll do the service of a younger man
In all your business and necessities.
　　Orl. O good old man, how well in thee appears
The constant service of the antique world,
When service sweat for duty, not for meed!
Thou art not for the fashion of these times,
Where none will sweat but for promotion,　　　　　60
And having that, do choke their service up
Even with the having: it is not so with thee.
But, poor old man, thou prunest a rotten tree,
That cannot so much as a blossom yield
In lieu of all thy pains and husbandry.
But come thy ways; we'll go along together,
And ere we have thy youthful wages spent,
We'll light upon some settled low content.
　　Adam. Master, go on, and I will follow thee,
To the last gasp, with truth and loyalty.　　　　　70
From seventeen years till now almost fourscore
Here lived I, but now live here no more.
At seventeen years many their fortunes seek;
But at fourscore it is too late a week:
Yet fortune cannot recompense me better
Than to die well and not my master's debtor.　*[Exeunt.*

SCENE IV. *The Forest of Arden.*

Enter ROSALIND *for* GANYMEDE, CELIA *for* ALIENA,
　　and TOUCHSTONE.

Ros. O Jupiter, how weary are my spirits!
Touch. I care not for my spirits, if my legs were not
weary.
Ros. I could find in my heart to disgrace my man's
apparel and to cry like a woman; but I must comfort
the weaker vessel, as doublet and hose ought to show
itself courageous to petticoat: therefore courage, good
Aliena!
Cel. I pray you, bear with me; I cannot go no
further.　　　　　　　　　　　　　　　　　　　　10
Touch. For my part, I had rather bear with you
than bear you; yet I should bear no cross if I did bear
you, for I think you have no money in your purse.

---

8. **roynish**, scurvy, coarse.　17. **that gallant,** i.e., Orlando.　19. **suddenly,** speedily.　20. **inquisition,** inquiry.　**quail,** fail, slacken.　21. **again,** back.
　SCENE III.　3. **memory,** memorial, memento.　7. **to,** as to.　8. **bonny priser,** big champion or prize fighter.　14-15. **when . . . it,** i.e., as did the shirt of Nessus, or the poisoned garment sent by Medea to Creusa.　23. **use,** are wont.　27. **place,** residence, dwelling.　**butchery,**

slaughter house.　37. **diverted blood,** kinship diverted from the natural course.　39. **thrifty,** obtained by economy.　43-44. **He . . . sparrow.** See Luke 12:22-24.　57. **service,** probably, body of servants collectively.　58. **meed,** reward.　65. **lieu of,** return for.　68. **low content,** lowly contented state.　74. **too late a week,** too late by a good deal.
　SCENE IV.　1. **weary,** so Theobald; F: *merry.*　6. **weaker vessel,** woman. See I Peter 3:7.　7. **doublet and hose,** typical male attire.　13.

Ros. Well, this is the forest of Arden.

Touch. Ay, now am I in Arden; the more fool I; when I was at home, I was in a better place: but travellers must be content.

Ros. Ay, be so, good Touchstone.

Enter CORIN *and* SILVIUS.

Look you, who comes here; a young man and an old in solemn talk. 21

Cor. That is the way to make her scorn you still.

Sil. O Corin, that thou knew'st how I do love her!

Cor. I partly guess; for I have loved ere now.

Sil. No, Corin, being old, thou canst not guess,
Though in thy youth thou wast as true a lover
As ever sigh'd upon a midnight pillow:
But if thy love were ever like to mine—
As sure I think did never man love so—
How many actions most ridiculous 30
Hast thou been drawn to by thy fantasy?

Cor. Into a thousand that I have forgotten.

Sil. O, thou didst then ne'er love so heartily!
If thou remember'st not the slightest folly
That ever love did make thee run into,
Thou hast not loved:
Or if thou hast not sat as I do now,
Wearying thy hearer in thy mistress' praise,
Thou hast not loved:
Or if thou hast not broke from company 40
Abruptly, as my passion now makes me,
Thou hast not loved.
O Phebe, Phebe, Phebe! [*Exit.*

Ros. Alas, poor shepherd! searching of thy wound,
I have by hard adventure found mine own. 45

Touch. And I mine. I remember, when I was in love I broke my sword upon a stone and bid him take that for coming a-night to Jane Smile; and I remember the kissing of her batlet and the cow's dugs that her pretty chopt hands had milked; and I remember the wooing of a peascod instead of her, from whom I took two cods and, giving her them again, said with weeping tears 'Wear these for my sake.' We that are true lovers run into strange capers; but as all is mortal in nature, so is all nature in love mortal in folly.

Ros. Thou speakest wiser than thou art ware of.

Touch. Nay, I shall ne'er be ware of mine own wit till I break my shins against it. 60

Ros. Jove, Jove! this shepherd's passion
Is much upon my fashion.

Touch. And mine; but it grows something stale with me.

Cel. I pray you, one of you question yond man
If he for gold will give us any food:
I faint almost to death.

Touch. Holla, you clown!

Ros. Peace, fool: he's not thy kinsman.

Cor. Who calls?

Touch. Your betters, sir.

Cor. Else are they very wretched.

Ros. Peace, I say. Good even to you, friend.

Cor. And to you, gentle sir, and to you all. 70

Ros. I prithee, shepherd, if that love or gold

Can in this desert place buy entertainment,
Bring us where we may rest ourselves and feed:
Here's a young maid with travel much oppress'd
And faints for succour.

Cor. Fair sir, I pity her
And wish, for her sake more than for mine own,
My fortunes were more able to relieve her;
But I am shepherd to another man
And do not shear the fleeces that I graze:
My master is of churlish disposition 80
And little recks to find the way to heaven
By doing deeds of hospitality:
Besides, his cote, his flocks and bounds of feed
Are now on sale, and at our sheepcote now,
By reason of his absence, there is nothing
That you will feed on; but what is, come see,
And in my voice most welcome shall you be.

Ros. What is he that shall buy his flock and pasture?

Cor. That young swain that you saw here but
erewhile,
That little cares for buying any thing. 90

Ros. I pray thee, if it stand with honesty,
Buy thou the cottage, pasture and the flock,
And thou shalt have to pay for it of us.

Cel. And we will mend thy wages. I like this place,
And willingly could waste my time in it.

Cor. Assuredly the thing is to be sold:
Go with me: if you like upon report
The soil, the profit and this kind of life,
I will your very faithful feeder be
And buy it with your gold right suddenly. [*Exeunt.* 100

SCENE V. *The forest.*

Enter AMIENS, JAQUES, *and others.*

SONG.
Ami. Under the greenwood tree
Who loves to lie with me,
And turn his merry note
Unto the sweet bird's throat,
Come hither, come hither, come hither:
Here shall he see
No enemy
But winter and rough weather.

Jaq. More, more, I prithee, more.

Ami. It will make you melancholy, Monsieur Jaques. 11

Jaq. I thank it. More, I prithee, more. I can suck melancholy out of a song, as a weasel sucks eggs. More, I prithee, more.

Ami. My voice is ragged: I know I cannot please you.

Jaq. I do not desire you to please me; I do desire you to sing. Come, more; another stanzo: call you 'em stanzos?

Ami. What you will, Monsieur Jaques. 20

Jaq. Nay, I care not for their names; they owe me nothing. Will you sing?

cross, coin having on it a figure of a cross. 44. searching, probing. 48. a-night, by night. 50. batlet, club or bat for beating clothes in process of washing. 51. chopt, chapped. 52. peascod, pea pod; regarded as a lucky gift by rustic lovers. 56. mortal, excessive, very great. 58. ware, aware. 62. upon, after, according to. 75. for succour, for want of succor. 79. fleeces, flock. 80. churlish, niggardly, miserly. 81. recks, heeds, cares. 83. cote, shepherd's hut.

bounds of feed, limits within which he has the right of pasturage. 87. in my voice, as far as my opinion goes. 89. erewhile, a short time since. 91. stand, be consistent. 99. feeder, servant.
SCENE V. 3. turn, compose (verse, a tune). 21. names, i.e., of debts owed, signatures (to a bond).

Ami. More at your request than to please myself.

Jaq. Well then, if ever I thank any man, I'll thank you; but that they call compliment is like the encounter of two dog-apes, and when a man thanks me heartily, methinks I have given him a penny and he renders me the beggarly thanks. Come, sing; and you that will not, hold your tongues. 31

Ami. Well, I'll end the song. Sirs, cover the while; the duke will drink under this tree. He hath been all this day to look you.

Jaq. And I have been all this day to avoid him. He is too disputable for my company: I think of as many matters as he, but I give heaven thanks and make no boast of them. Come, warble, come.

SONG.

Who doth ambition shun   [*All together here.* 40
And loves to live i' the sun,
Seeking the food he eats
And pleased with what he gets,
Come hither, come hither, come hither:
    Here shall he see
      No enemy
But winter and rough weather.

Jaq. I'll give you a verse to this note that I made yesterday in despite of my invention.
Ami. And I'll sing it. 50
Jaq. Thus it goes:—

    If it do come to pass
    That any man turn ass,
    Leaving his wealth and ease,
    A stubborn will to please,
    Ducdame, ducdame, ducdame:
      Here shall he see
      Gross fools as he,
    An if he will come to me.

Ami. What's that 'ducdame'? 60
Jaq. 'Tis a Greek invocation, to call fools into a circle. I'll go sleep, if I can; if I cannot, I'll rail against all the first-born of Egypt.
Ami. And I'll go seek the duke: his banquet is prepared.   [*Exeunt severally.*

SCENE VI. *The forest.*

Enter ORLANDO *and* ADAM.

Adam. Dear master, I can go no further: O, I die for food! Here lie I down, and measure out my grave. Farewell, kind master.

Orl. Why, how now, Adam! no greater heart in thee? Live a little; comfort a little; cheer thyself a little. If this uncouth forest yield any thing savage, I will either be food for it or bring it for food to thee. Thy conceit is nearer death than thy powers. For my

sake be comfortable; hold death awhile at the arm's end: I will here be with thee presently; and if I bring thee not something to eat, I will give thee leave to die: but if thou diest before I come, thou art a mocker of my labour. Well said! thou lookest cheerly, and I'll be with thee quickly. Yet thou liest in the bleak air: come, I will bear thee to some shelter; and thou shalt not die for lack of a dinner, if there live any thing in this desert. Cheerly, good Adam!   [*Exeunt.* 20

SCENE VII. *The forest.*

A table set out. Enter DUKE senior, AMIENS, *and* Lords *like* outlaws.

Duke S. I think he be transform'd into a beast;
For I can no where find him like a man.
First Lord. My lord, he is but even now gone hence:
Here was he merry, hearing of a song.
Duke S. If he, compact of jars, grow musical,
We shall have shortly discord in the spheres.
Go, seek him: tell him I would speak with him.

Enter JAQUES.

First Lord. He saves my labour by his own approach.
Duke S. Why, how now, monsieur! what a life is this,
That your poor friends must woo your company? 10
What, you look merrily!
Jaq. A fool, a fool! I met a fool i' the forest,
A motley fool; a miserable world!
As I do live by food, I met a fool;
Who laid him down and bask'd him in the sun,
And rail'd on Lady Fortune in good terms,
In good set terms and yet a motley fool.
'Good morrow, fool,' quoth I. 'No, sir,' quoth he,
'Call me not fool till heaven hath sent me fortune:'
And then he drew a dial from his poke, 20
And, looking on it with lack-lustre eye,
Says very wisely, 'It is ten o'clock:
Thus we may see,' quoth he, 'how the world wags:
'Tis but an hour ago since it was nine,
And after one hour more 'twill be eleven;
And so, from hour to hour, we ripe and ripe,
And then, from hour to hour, we rot and rot;
And thereby hangs a tale.' When I did hear
The motley fool thus moral on the time,
My lungs began to crow like chanticleer, 30
That fools should be so deep-contemplative,
And I did laugh sans intermission
An hour by his dial. O noble fool!
A worthy fool! Motley 's the only wear.
Duke S. What fool is this?
Jaq. O worthy fool! One that hath been a courtier,
And says, if ladies be but young and fair,
They have the gift to know it: and in his brain,
Which is as dry as the remainder biscuit
After a voyage, he hath strange places cramm'd 40

With observation, the which he vents
In mangled forms. O that I were a fool!
I am ambitious for a motley coat.
   Duke S. Thou shalt have one.
   Jaq.   It is my only suit;
Provided that you weed your better judgements
Of all opinion that grows rank in them
That I am wise. I must have liberty
Withal, as large a charter as the wind,
To blow on whom I please; for so fools have;
And they that are most galled with my folly,   50
They most must laugh. And why, sir, must they so?
The 'why' is plain as way to parish church:
He that a fool doth very wisely hit
Doth very foolishly, although he smart,
Not to seem senseless of the bob: if not,
The wise man's folly is anatomized
Even by the squandering glances of the fool.
Invest me in my motley; give me leave
To speak my mind, and I will through and through
Cleanse the foul body of the infected world,   60
If they will patiently receive my medicine.
   Duke S. Fie on thee! I can tell what thou wouldst do.
   Jaq. What, for a counter, would I do but good?
   Duke S. Most mischievous foul sin, in chiding sin:
For thou thyself hast been a libertine,
As sensual as the brutish sting itself;
And all the embossed sores and headed evils,
That thou with license of free foot hast caught,
Wouldst thou disgorge into the general world.
   Jaq. Why, who cries out on pride,   70
That can therein tax any private party?
Doth it not flow as hugely as the sea,
†Till that the weary very means do ebb?
What woman in the city do I name,
When that I say the city-woman bears
The cost of princes on unworthy shoulders?
Who can come in and say that I mean her,
When such a one as she such is her neighbour?
Or what is he of basest function
That says his bravery is not on my cost,   80
Thinking that I mean him, but therein suits
His folly to the mettle of my speech?
There then; how then? what then? Let me see wherein
My tongue hath wrong'd him: if it do him right,
Then he hath wrong'd himself; if he be free,
Why then my taxing like a wild-goose flies,
Unclaim'd of any man. But who comes here?

Enter ORLANDO, *with his sword drawn.*

   Orl. Forbear, and eat no more.
   Jaq.   Why, I have eat none yet.
   Orl. Nor shalt not, till necessity be served.
   Jaq. Of what kind should this cock come of?   90
   Duke S. Art thou thus bolden'd, man, by thy
      distress,
Or else a rude despiser of good manners,
That in civility thou seem'st so empty?

   Orl. You touch'd my vein at first: the thorny point
Of bare distress hath ta'en from me the show
Of smooth civility: yet am I inland bred
And know some nurture. But forbear, I say:
He dies that touches any of this fruit
Till I and my affairs are answered.
   Jaq. An you will not be answered with reason, I
must die.   101
   Duke S. What would you have? Your gentleness
      shall force
More than your force move us to gentleness.
   Orl. I almost die for food; and let me have it.
   Duke S. Sit down and feed, and welcome to our
      table.
   Orl. Speak you so gently? Pardon me, I pray you:
I thought that all things had been savage here;
And therefore put I on the countenance
Of stern commandment. But whate'er you are
That in this desert inaccessible,   110
Under the shade of melancholy boughs,
Lose and neglect the creeping hours of time;
If ever you have look'd on better days,
If ever been where bells have knoll'd to church,
If ever sat at any good man's feast,
If ever from your eyelids wiped a tear
And know what 'tis to pity and be pitied,
Let gentleness my strong enforcement be:
In the which hope I blush, and hide my sword.
   Duke S. True is it that we have seen better days,   120
And have with holy bell been knoll'd to church
And sat at good men's feasts and wiped our eyes
Of drops that sacred pity hath engender'd:
And therefore sit you down in gentleness
And take upon command what help we have
That to your wanting may be minister'd.
   Orl. Then but forbear your food a little while,
Whiles, like a doe, I go to find my fawn
And give it food. There is an old poor man,
Who after me hath many a weary step   130
Limp'd in pure love: till he be first sufficed,
Oppress'd with two weak evils, age and hunger,
I will not touch a bit.
   Duke S.   Go find him out,
And we will nothing waste till you return.
   Orl. I thank ye; and be blest for your good
      comfort!   *[Exit.*
   Duke S. Thou seest we are not all alone unhappy:
This wide and universal theatre
Presents more woeful pageants than the scene
Wherein we play in.
   Jaq.   All the world's a stage,
And all the men and women merely players: 140
They have their exits and their entrances;
And one man in his time plays many parts,
His acts being seven ages. At first the infant,
Mewling and puking in the nurse's arms.
And then the whining school-boy, with his satchel
And shining morning face, creeping like snail

40. **places,** topics, subjects for discourse; or possibly, texts, wise bits.
48. **large . . . wind,** i.e., to blow where it listeth. 55. **Not to seem,**
so Theobald; F: *Seeme.* **bob,** jibe, taunt. 57. **squandering glances,**
random shots. 63. **counter,** type of a thing of no intrinsic value, as
a metal disk used in counting. 66. **sting,** carnal impulse. 67. **embossed,** swollen, tumid. **evils,** diseases, maladies. 71. **tax,** blame,
accuse; see glossary. 73. **weary very means,** a corrupt passage. There
are many conjectures—Singer: *wearer's very means;* Lloyd: *tributary
stream;* New Cambridge: *weary very mints,* i.e., in coining money fast
enough. 75. **city-woman,** citizen's wife. 79. **function,** office. 80.

bravery, splendor, finery. 84. **right,** justice. 93. **civility,** politeness,
code of good manners. 94. **vein,** disposition, humor. 96. **inland
bred,** i.e., civilized. 97. **nurture,** education, training. 109. **commandment,** command. 118. **my strong enforcement,** that which
strongly supports my request. 125. **upon command,** at pleasure. 132.
weak, causing weakness. 143. **At,** Capell: *As;* anonymous conjecture:
Act. 144. **Mewling,** crying feebly.

Unwillingly to school. And then the lover,
Sighing like furnace, with a woeful ballad
Made to his mistress' eyebrow. Then a soldier,
Full of strange oaths and bearded like the pard,　150
Jealous in honour, sudden and quick in quarrel,
Seeking the bubble reputation
Even in the cannon's mouth. And then the justice,
In fair round belly with good capon lined,
With eyes severe and beard of formal cut,
Full of wise saws and modern instances;
And so he plays his part. The sixth age shifts
Into the lean and slipper'd pantaloon,
With spectacles on nose and pouch on side,
His youthful hose, well saved, a world too wide　160
For his shrunk shank; and his big manly voice,
Turning again toward childish treble, pipes
And whistles in his sound. Last scene of all,
That ends this strange eventful history,
Is second childishness and mere oblivion,
Sans teeth, sans eyes, sans taste, sans every thing.

Re-enter ORLANDO, *with* ADAM.

Duke S. Welcome. Set down your venerable burden
And let him feed.
　Orl. I thank you most for him.
　　Adam.　　　So had you need:
I scarce can speak to thank you for myself.　170
　Duke S. Welcome; fall to: I will not trouble you
As yet, to question you about your fortunes.
Give us some music; and, good cousin, sing.

SONG.
　Ami. Blow, blow, thou winter wind,
　　　　Thou art not so unkind
　　　　　As man's ingratitude;
　　　　Thy tooth is not so keen,
　　　　Because thou art not seen,
　　　　　Although thy breath be rude.
Heigh-ho! sing, heigh-ho! unto the green holly:　180
Most friendship is feigning, most loving mere folly:
　　　　Then, heigh-ho, the holly!
　　　　　This life is most jolly.

　　　　Freeze, freeze, thou bitter sky,
　　　　That dost not bite so nigh
　　　　　As benefits forgot:
　　　　Though thou the waters warp,
　　　　Thy sting is not so sharp
　　　　　As friend remember'd not.
Heigh-ho! sing, &c.　190

　Duke S. If that you were the good Sir Rowland's
　　　　son,
As you have whisper'd faithfully you were,
And as mine eye doth his effigies witness
Most truly limn'd and living in your face,
Be truly welcome hither: I am the duke
That loved your father: the residue of your fortune,
Go to my cave and tell me. Good old man,
Thou art right welcome as thy master is.

Support him by the arm. Give me your hand,
And let me all your fortunes understand.　　[*Exeunt.* 200

ACT III.

SCENE I. *A room in the palace.*

Enter DUKE FREDERICK, Lords, *and* OLIVER.

　Duke F. Not see him since? Sir, sir, that cannot be:
But were I not the better part made mercy,
I should not seek an absent argument
Of my revenge, thou present. But look to it:
Find out thy brother, wheresoe'er he is;
Seek him with candle; bring him dead or living
Within this twelvemonth, or turn thou no more
To seek a living in our territory.
Thy lands and all things that thou dost call thine
Worth seizure do we seize into our hands,　10
Till thou canst quit thee by thy brother's mouth
Of what we think against thee.
　Oli. O that your highness knew my heart in this!
I never loved my brother in my life.
　Duke F. More villain thou. Well, push him out of
　　doors;
And let my officers of such a nature
Make an extent upon his house and lands:
Do this expediently and turn him going.　　[*Exeunt.*

SCENE II. *The forest.*

Enter ORLANDO, *with a paper.*

　Orl. Hang there, my verse, in witness of my love:
And thou, thrice-crowned queen of night, survey
With thy chaste eye, from thy pale sphere above,
　Thy huntress' name that my full life doth sway.
O Rosalind! these trees shall be my books
　And in their barks my thoughts I'll character;
That every eye which in this forest looks
　Shall see thy virtue witness'd every where.
Run, run, Orlando; carve on every tree
The fair, the chaste and unexpressive she.　　[*Exit.* 10

Enter CORIN *and* TOUCHSTONE.

　Cor. And how like you this shepherd's life, Master
Touchstone?
　Touch. Truly, shepherd, in respect of itself, it is a
good life; but in respect that it is a shepherd's life, it
is naught. In respect that it is solitary, I like it very
well; but in respect that it is private, it is a very vile
life. Now, in respect it is in the fields, it pleaseth me
well; but in respect it is not in the court, it is tedious.
As it is a spare life, look you, it fits my humour well;
but as there is no more plenty in it, it goes much
against my stomach. Hast any philosophy in thee,
shepherd?　23
　Cor. No more but that I know the more one sickens
the worse at ease he is; and that he that wants money,
means and content is without three good friends; that

150. **bearded . . . pard,** having bristling mustaches like the panther's
or leopard's feelers. 156. **modern,** ordinary, commonplace; see glossary. 158. **pantaloon,** ridiculous, enfeebled old man. 178. **Because
. . . seen,** i.e., because thou art an enemy that doth not brave us with
thy presence (Johnson). 180. **holly,** emblem of mirth. 187. **warp,**
apparently, freeze or ruffle (Onions). 193. **effigies,** likenesses, portraits. 194. **limn'd,** painted, portrayed.
　ACT III. SCENE I. 2. **better,** greater. 6. **Seek . . . candle.** See

Luke 15:8. 11. **quit,** acquit. **mouth,** i.e., evidence. 16. **of such a
nature,** i.e., who attend to such duties. 17. **extent,** seizure of land in
execution of a writ. 18. **expediently,** expeditiously. **turn him going,**
start him moving.
　SCENE II. 2. **thrice-crowned queen,** Diana in the three aspects of
her divinity: as Luna or Cynthia, goddess of the moon; as Diana, goddess on earth; and as Hecate or Proserpina, goddess in the lower world.
10. **unexpressive,** inexpressible. **she,** mistress, love. 31. **complain . . .**

the property of rain is to wet and fire to burn; that good pasture makes fat sheep, and that a great cause of the night is lack of the sun; that he that hath learned no wit by nature nor art may complain of good breeding or comes of a very dull kindred. 32

Touch. Such a one is a natural philosopher. Wast ever in court, shepherd?

Cor. No, truly.

Touch. Then thou art damned.

Cor. Nay, I hope.

Touch. Truly, thou art damned, like an ill-roasted egg all on one side.

Cor. For not being at court? Your reason. 40

Touch. Why, if thou never wast at court, thou never sawest good manners; if thou never sawest good manners, then thy manners must be wicked; and wickedness is sin, and sin is damnation. Thou art in a parlous state, shepherd.

Cor. Not a whit, Touchstone: those that are good manners at the court are as ridiculous in the country as the behaviour of the country is most mockable at the court. You told me you salute not at the court, but you kiss your hands: that courtesy would be uncleanly, if courtiers were shepherds. 52

Touch. Instance, briefly; come, instance.

Cor. Why, we are still handling our ewes, and their fells, you know, are greasy.

Touch. Why, do not your courtier's hands sweat? and is not the grease of a mutton as wholesome as the sweat of a man? Shallow, shallow. A better instance, I say; come.

Cor. Besides, our hands are hard. 60

Touch. Your lips will feel them the sooner. Shallow again. A more sounder instance, come.

Cor. And they are often tarred over with the surgery of our sheep; and would you have us kiss tar? The courtier's hands are perfumed with civet.

Touch. Most shallow man! thou worms-meat, in respect of a good piece of flesh indeed! Learn of the wise, and perpend: civet is of a baser birth than tar, the very uncleanly flux of a cat. Mend the instance, shepherd. 71

Cor. You have too courtly a wit for me: I'll rest.

Touch. Wilt thou rest damned? God help thee, shallow man! God make incision in thee! thou art raw.

Cor. Sir, I am a true labourer: I earn that I eat, get that I wear, owe no man hate, envy no man's happiness, glad of other men's good, content with my harm, and the greatest of my pride is to see my ewes graze and my lambs suck. 82

Touch. That is another simple sin in you, to bring the ewes and the rams together and to offer to get your living by the copulation of cattle; to be bawd to a bell-wether, and to betray a she-lamb of a twelvemonth to a crooked-pated, old, cuckoldly ram, out of all reasonable match. If thou beest not damned for this, the devil himself will have no shepherds; I cannot see else how thou shouldst 'scape. 90

Cor. Here comes young Master Ganymede, my new mistress's brother.

Enter ROSALIND, *with a paper, reading.*

Ros. From the east to western Ind,
No jewel is like Rosalind.
Her worth, being mounted on the wind,
Through all the world bears Rosalind.
All the pictures fairest lined
Are but black to Rosalind.
Let no fair be kept in mind
But the fair of Rosalind. 100

Touch. I'll rhyme you so eight years together, dinners and suppers and sleeping-hours excepted: it is the right butter-women's rank to market.

Ros. Out, fool!

Touch. For a taste:

If a hart do lack a hind,
Let him seek out Rosalind.
If the cat will after kind,
So be sure will Rosalind. 110
Winter garments must be lined,
So must slender Rosalind.
They that reap must sheaf and bind;
Then to cart with Rosalind.
Sweetest nut hath sourest rind,
Such a nut is Rosalind.
He that sweetest rose will find
Must find love's prick and Rosalind.

This is the very false gallop of verses: why do you infect yourself with them? 120

Ros. Peace, you dull fool! I found them on a tree.

Touch. Truly, the tree yields bad fruit.

Ros. I'll graff it with you, and then I shall graff it with a medlar: then it will be the earliest fruit i' the country; for you'll be rotten ere you be half ripe, and that's the right virtue of the medlar.

Touch. You have said; but whether wisely or no, let the forest judge. 130

Enter CELIA, *with a writing.*

Ros. Peace!
Here comes my sister, reading: stand aside.

Cel. [*Reads*]

Why should this a desert be?
For it is unpeopled? No;
Tongues I'll hang on every tree,
That shall civil sayings show:
Some, how brief the life of man
Runs his erring pilgrimage,
That the stretching of a span
Buckles in his sum of age; 140
Some, of violated vows
'Twixt the souls of friend and friend:
But upon the fairest boughs,
Or at every sentence end,
Will I Rosalinda write,
Teaching all that read to know

breeding, i.e., of want of good breeding. 45. **parlous,** perilous, dangerous. 49. **mockable,** deserving of ridicule. 50. **but you kiss,** without kissing. 53. **Instance,** i.e., cite an example. 55. **fells,** skin with the wool, or fleece. 69. **perpend,** reflect, consider. 75. **incision,** cutting for the purpose of letting blood. 76. **raw,** inexperienced. 77. **that,** what. 80. **harm,** ill fortune. 97. **lined,** drawn. 103. **butter-women's rank.** The rhymes, all alike, follow each other like a line of butter-women jogging along to market; conjectural for *rank:* *rack,* pace of a horse. 113. **sheaf,** make into sheaves. 119. **false gallop,** canter. 120. **infect,** pollute (either morally or physically). 125. **graff,** insert a graft. **medlar,** a fruit like a small brown-skinned apple which is eaten when decayed; a pun on "meddler." 127. **right,** true. 136. **civil sayings,** maxims of civilized life. 138. **erring,** wandering. 139. **That,** so that. 140. **Buckles,** encompasses.

The quintessence of every sprite
  Heaven would in little show.
Therefore Heaven Nature charged
  That one body should be fill'd 150
With all graces wide-enlarged:
  Nature presently distill'd
Helen's cheek, but not her heart,
  Cleopatra's majesty,
Atalanta's better part,
  Sad Lucretia's modesty.
Thus Rosalind of many parts
  By heavenly synod was devised,
Of many faces, eyes and hearts,
  To have the touches dearest prized. 160

Heaven would that she these gifts should have,
And I to live and die her slave.

Ros. O most gentle pulpiter! what tedious homily of love have you wearied your parishioners withal, and never cried 'Have patience, good people'!

Cel. How now! back, friends! Shepherd, go off a little. Go with him, sirrah.

Touch. Come, shepherd, let us make an honourable retreat; though not with bag and baggage, yet with scrip and scrippage. [*Exeunt Corin and Touchstone.* 171

Cel. Didst thou hear these verses?

Ros. O, yes, I heard them all, and more too; for some of them had in them more feet than the verses would bear.

Cel. That's no matter: the feet might bear the verses.

Ros. Ay, but the feet were lame and could not bear themselves without the verse and therefore stood lamely in the verse. 180

Cel. But didst thou hear without wondering how thy name should be hanged and carved upon these trees?

Ros. I was seven of the nine days out of the wonder before you came; for look here what I found on a palm-tree. I was never so berhymed since Pythagoras' time, that I was an Irish rat, which I can hardly remember.

Cel. Trow you who hath done this?

Ros. Is it a man?

Cel. And a chain, that you once wore, about his neck. Change you colour? 190

Ros. I prithee, who?

Cel. O Lord, Lord! it is a hard matter for friends to meet; but mountains may be removed with earthquakes and so encounter.

Ros. Nay, but who is it?

Cel. Is it possible?

Ros. Nay, I prithee now with most petitionary vehemence, tell me who it is. 200

Cel. O wonderful, wonderful, and most wonderful wonderful! and yet again wonderful, and after that, out of all hooping!

Ros. Good my complexion! dost thou think, though I am caparisoned like a man, I have a doublet and hose in my disposition? One inch of delay more is a South-sea of discovery; I prithee, tell me who is it quickly, and speak apace. I would thou couldst stammer, that thou mightst pour this concealed man out of thy mouth, as wine comes out of a narrow-mouthed bottle, either too much at once, or none at all. I prithee, take the cork out of thy mouth that I may drink thy tidings.

Cel. So you may put a man in your belly.

Ros. Is he of God's making? What manner of man? Is his head worth a hat, or his chin worth a beard?

Cel. Nay, he hath but a little beard. 219

Ros. Why, God will send more, if the man will be thankful: let me stay the growth of his beard, if thou delay me not the knowledge of his chin.

Cel. It is young Orlando, that tripped up the wrestler's heels and your heart both in an instant.

Ros. Nay, but the devil take mocking: speak, sad brow and true maid.

Cel. I' faith, coz, 'tis he.

Ros. Orlando?

Cel. Orlando. 230

Ros. Alas the day! what shall I do with my doublet and hose? What did he when thou sawest him? What said he? How looked he? Wherein went he? What makes he here? Did he ask for me? Where remains he? How parted he with thee? and when shalt thou see him again? Answer me in one word.

Cel. You must borrow me Gargantua's mouth first: 'tis a word too great for any mouth of this age's size. To say ay and no to these particulars is more than to answer in a catechism. 241

Ros. But doth he know that I am in this forest and in man's apparel? Looks he as freshly as he did the day he wrestled?

Cel. It is as easy to count atomies as to resolve the propositions of a lover; but take a taste of my finding him, and relish it with good observance. I found him under a tree, like a dropped acorn.

Ros. It may well be called Jove's tree, when it drops forth such fruit. 250

Cel. Give me audience, good madam.

Ros. Proceed.

Cel. There lay he, stretched along, like a wounded knight.

Ros. Though it be pity to see such a sight, it well becomes the ground.

Cel. Cry 'holla' to thy tongue, I prithee; it curvets unseasonably. He was furnished like a hunter. 259

Ros. O, ominous! he comes to kill my heart.

Cel. I would sing my song without a burden: thou bringest me out of tune.

Ros. Do you not know I am a woman? when I think, I must speak. Sweet, say on.

Cel. You bring me out. Soft! comes he not here?

147. **quintessence,** the fifth essence or element of the medieval alchemists, purer even than fire. 148. **in little.** In this Furness sees an allusion to the microcosm (man); the heavenly bodies would be composed of quintessence, which is here thought of as the supreme quality of a person. 151. **wide-enlarged,** spread through the world until they are concentrated in Rosalind (J. C. Smith). 155. **Atalanta's better part,** i.e., her fleetness of foot. 156. **Lucretia's.** Lucretia was the Roman lady dishonored by Tarquin, whose story Shakespeare tells in *The Rape of Lucrece.* 160. **touches,** traits. 163. **pulpiter,** so Spedding; F: *Iupiter.* 167. **back, friends.** Celia, reading, becomes aware of the others; her words are addressed to Corin and Touchstone. 170. **bag and baggage.** Note the pun on *baggage,* meaning "women." 171.

scrip and scrippage. New Cambridge editors suggest that Touchstone picks up the scrip, or writing, which Celia has been reading. 182. **should be,** was said to be. 184. **seven . . . wonder.** A wonder was said to last nine days. 187. **Pythagoras'.** Pythagoras was a Greek philosopher credited with the doctrine of the transmigration of souls. 188. **Irish rat,** reference to a current belief that Irish enchanters could rhyme rats to death. 191. **And a chain,** i.e., and with a chain. 195-196. **friends . . . encounter,** reference to the proverb, "Friends may meet, but mountains never greet." 203. **out . . . hooping,** beyond exclamations of surprise. 204. **Good my complexion,** i.e., she wishes her blushes not to betray her. 205. **caparisoned,** equipped (as of a horse). 207. **South-sea of discovery,** probable reference to the long delays of

Enter ORLANDO *and* JAQUES.

Ros. 'Tis he: slink by, and note him.

Jaq. I thank you for your company; but, good faith,
I had as lief have been myself alone.   270

Orl. And so had I; but yet, for fashion sake, I thank
you too for your society.

Jaq. God be wi' you: let 's meet as little as we can.

Orl. I do desire we may be better strangers.

Jaq. I pray you, mar no more trees with writing
love-songs in their barks.

Orl. I pray you, mar no moe of my verses with
reading them ill-favouredly.

Jaq. Rosalind is your love's name?   280

Orl. Yes, just.

Jaq. I do not like her name.

Orl. There was no thought of pleasing you when she
was christened.

Jaq. What stature is she of?

Orl. Just as high as my heart.

Jaq. You are full of pretty answers. Have you not
been acquainted with goldsmiths' wives, and conned
them out of rings?   289

Orl. Not so; but I answer you right painted cloth,
from whence you have studied your questions.

Jaq. You have a nimble wit: I think 'twas made of
Atalanta's heels. Will you sit down with me? and we
two will rail against our mistress the world and all our
misery.

Orl. I will chide no breather in the world but myself, against whom I know most faults.

Jaq. The worst fault you have is to be in love.   300

Orl. 'Tis a fault I will not change for your best
virtue. I am weary of you.

Jaq. By my troth, I was seeking for a fool when I
found you.

Orl. He is drowned in the brook: look but in, and
you shall see him.

Jaq. There I shall see mine own figure.

Orl. Which I take to be either a fool or a cipher.

Jaq. I'll tarry no longer with you: farewell, good
Signior Love.   310

Orl. I am glad of your departure: adieu, good
Monsieur Melancholy.   [*Exit Jaques.*

Ros. [*Aside to Celia*] I will speak to him like a saucy
lackey and under that habit play the knave with him.
Do you hear, forester?

Orl. Very well: what would you?

Ros. I pray you, what is 't o'clock?

Orl. You should ask me what time o' day: there 's
no clock in the forest.   319

Ros. Then there is no true lover in the forest; else
sighing every minute and groaning every hour would
detect the lazy foot of Time as well as a clock.

Orl. And why not the swift foot of Time? had not
that been as proper?

Ros. By no means, sir: Time travels in divers paces

with divers persons. I'll tell you who Time ambles
withal, who Time trots withal, who Time gallops
withal and who he stands still withal.

Orl. I prithee, who doth he trot withal?   330

Ros. Marry, he trots hard with a young maid between the contract of her marriage and the day it is
solemnized: if the interim be but a se'nnight, Time's
pace is so hard that it seems the length of seven year.

Orl. Who ambles Time withal?

Ros. With a priest that lacks Latin and a rich man
that hath not the gout, for the one sleeps easily because
he cannot study and the other lives merrily because
he feels no pain, the one lacking the burden of lean
and wasteful learning, the other knowing no burden
of heavy tedious penury; these Time ambles withal. 343

Orl. Who doth he gallop withal?

Ros. With a thief to the gallows, for though he go
as softly as foot can fall, he thinks himself too soon
there.

Orl. Who stays it still withal?

Ros. With lawyers in the vacation; for they sleep
between term and term and then they perceive not
how Time moves.   351

Orl. Where dwell you, pretty youth?

Ros. With this shepherdess, my sister; here in the
skirts of the forest, like fringe upon a petticoat.

Orl. Are you native of this place?

Ros. As the cony that you see dwell where she is
kindled.   358

Orl. Your accent is something finer than you could
purchase in so removed a dwelling.

Ros. I have been told so of many: but indeed an old
religious uncle of mine taught me to speak, who was
in his youth an inland man; one that knew courtship
too well, for there he fell in love. I have heard him
read many lectures against it, and I thank God I am
not a woman, to be touched with so many giddy
offences as he hath generally taxed their whole sex
withal.

Orl. Can you remember any of the principal evils
that he laid to the charge of women?   370

Ros. There were none principal; they were all like
one another as half-pence are, every one fault seeming monstrous till his fellow-fault came to match it.

Orl. I prithee, recount some of them.   375

Ros. No, I will not cast away my physic but on those
that are sick. There is a man haunts the forest, that
abuses our young plants with carving 'Rosalind' on
their barks; hangs odes upon hawthorns and elegies
on brambles, all, forsooth, deifying the name of Rosalind: if I could meet that fancy-monger, I would give
him some good counsel, for he seems to have the
quotidian of love upon him.   383

Orl. I am he that is so love-shaked: I pray you, tell
me your remedy.

Ros. There is none of my uncle's marks upon you:
he taught me how to know a man in love; in which

As You Like It
ACT III : SC II

603

voyages to the South Seas; many emendations; *discovery* may mean
"disclosure." 216. **of God's making,** i.e., or his tailor's. 234. **Wherein
went he,** in what clothes. 238. **Gargantua's mouth.** Gargantua is the
giant in Rabelais who swallowed five pilgrims in a salad. 241.
catechism, catechizing. 245. **atomies,** motes. 247. **relish,** taste, or
make pleasant to the palate. 248. **observance,** attention, observation.
249. **Jove's tree,** the oak. 256. **ground,** background, with play on
ordinary sense. 257. **'holla,'** stop. 258. **furnished,** equipped, dressed.
261. **burden,** undersong, bass part. 262. **bringest, puttest.** 265. **bring
me out,** put me out (of my part). 270. **myself alone,** alone, by myself.
281. **just,** just so. 289. **rings,** reference to the verses inscribed in rings,
posies. 290. **right,** true, perfect. **painted cloth,** canvas painted with

pictures (frequently scriptural) used for hangings; here, suggestive of
commonplace. 297. **breather,** living being. 331. **hard,** probably,
slow, with uneven pace. 333. **se'nnight,** week. 346. **go as softly,**
walk as slowly. 357. **cony,** rabbit. 358. **kindled,** littered, brought
forth young. 360. **removed,** remote. 362. **religious,** i.e., member of
a religious order. 364. **courtship,** play on the meaning, "knowledge
of courtly manners." 372. **half-pence.** Halfpence were almost the
only uniform coins in circulation. 382. **fancy-monger,** love-monger,
devotee of love. 383. **quotidian,** fever recurring daily (a symptom of
love); hence, *love-shaked* below.

cage of rushes I am sure you are not prisoner. 390

Orl. What were his marks?

Ros. A lean cheek, which you have not, a blue eye and sunken, which you have not, an unquestionable spirit, which you have not, a beard neglected, which you have not; but I pardon you for that, for simply your having in beard is a younger brother's revenue: then your hose should be ungartered, your bonnet unbanded, your sleeve unbuttoned, your shoe untied and every thing about you demonstrating a careless desolation; but you are no such man; you are rather point-device in your accoutrements as loving yourself than seeming the lover of any other. 403

Orl. Fair youth, I would I could make thee believe I love.

Ros. Me believe it! you may as soon make her that you love believe it; which, I warrant, she is apter to do than to confess she does: that is one of the points in the which women still give the lie to their consciences. But, in good sooth, are you he that hangs the verses on the trees, wherein Rosalind is so admired?

Orl. I swear to thee, youth, by the white hand of Rosalind, I am that he, that unfortunate he.

Ros. But are you so much in love as your rhymes speak?

Orl. Neither rhyme nor reason can express how much. 419

Ros. Love is merely a madness, and, I tell you, deserves as well a dark house and a whip as madmen do: and the reason why they are not so punished and cured is, that the lunacy is so ordinary that the whippers are in love too. Yet I profess curing it by counsel.

Orl. Did you ever cure any so? 426

Ros. Yes, one, and in this manner. He was to imagine me his love, his mistress; and I set him every day to woo me: at which time would I, being but a moonish youth, grieve, be effeminate, changeable, longing and liking, proud, fantastical, apish, shallow, inconstant, full of tears, full of smiles, for every passion something and for no passion truly any thing, as boys and women are for the most part cattle of this colour; would now like him, now loathe him; then entertain him, then forswear him; now weep for him, then spit at him; that I drave my suitor from his mad humour of love to a living humour of madness; which was, to forswear the full stream of the world and to live in a nook merely monastic. And thus I cured him; and this way will I take upon me to wash your liver as clean as a sound sheep's heart, that there shall not be one spot of love in 't.

Orl. I would not be cured, youth.

Ros. I would cure you, if you would but call me Rosalind and come every day to my cote and woo me.

Orl. Now, by the faith of my love, I will: tell me where it is. 450

Ros. Go with me to it and I'll show it you: and by the way you shall tell me where in the forest you live. Will you go?

Orl. With all my heart, good youth.

Ros. Nay, you must call me Rosalind. Come, sister, will you go? [*Exeunt.*

SCENE III. *The forest.*

Enter TOUCHSTONE *and* AUDREY; JAQUES *behind.*

Touch. Come apace, good Audrey: I will fetch up your goats, Audrey. And how, Audrey? am I the man yet? doth my simple feature content you?

Aud. Your features! Lord warrant us! what features?

Touch. I am here with thee and thy goats, as the most capricious poet, honest Ovid, was among the Goths.

Jaq. [*Aside*] O knowledge ill-inhabited, worse than Jove in a thatched house! 11

Touch. When a man's verses cannot be understood, nor a man's good wit seconded with the forward child Understanding, it strikes a man more dead than a great reckoning in a little room. Truly, I would the gods had made thee poetical.

Aud. I do not know what 'poetical' is: is it honest in deed and word? is it a true thing? 18

Touch. No, truly; for the truest poetry is the most feigning; and lovers are given to poetry, and what they swear in poetry may be said as lovers they do feign.

Aud. Do you wish then that the gods had made me poetical?

Touch. I do, truly; for thou swearest to me thou art honest: now, if thou wert a poet, I might have some hope thou didst feign.

Aud. Would you not have me honest?

Touch. No, truly, unless thou wert hard-favoured; for honesty coupled to beauty is to have honey a sauce to sugar. 31

Jaq. [*Aside*] A material fool!

Aud. Well, I am not fair; and therefore I pray the gods make me honest.

Touch. Truly, and to cast away honesty upon a foul slut were to put good meat into an unclean dish.

Aud. I am not a slut, though I thank the gods I am foul. 39

Touch. Well, praised be the gods for thy foulness! sluttishness may come hereafter. But be it as it may be, I will marry thee, and to that end I have been with Sir Oliver Martext, the vicar of the next village, who hath promised to meet me in this place of the forest and to couple us.

Jaq. [*Aside*] I would fain see this meeting.

Aud. Well, the gods give us joy! 47

Touch. Amen. A man may, if he were of a fearful heart, stagger in this attempt; for here we have no temple but the wood, no assembly but horn-beasts.

393. **blue eye,** eye having dark circles. 394. **unquestionable,** not to be questioned. 396. **having,** wealth; see glossary. 398. **bonnet,** hat. 402. **point-device,** faultless, precise. 421. **dark . . . whip,** an allusion to the common treatment of lunatics. 430. **moonish,** changeable. 439-440. **mad . . . madness,** pass from a madness of love to a real madness; Johnson read *loving* for *living* (real, not affected). 444. **liver,** seat of the emotion of love. 447-449. **I would . . . woo me.** This introduces the central comic theme in the play, which is so slight that it might not be realized. It presents a lover making love to his mistress, she being aware of the fact, he not.
SCENE III. *Stage Direction:* **Audrey,** a corruption of the name Ethelreda, whence the word "tawdry," a corruption from "St. Audrey."

5. **warrant,** assure, protect. 7, 8, 9. **goats, capricious, Goths.** Ovid (a pastoral poet; hence *goats*) was banished by Augustus to the country of the *Goths* (pun on *goats*); *capricious* is derived from Latin *capra,* she-goat. 10. **ill-inhabited,** ill-lodged. 11. **Jove in a thatched house,** an allusion to Ovid's *Metamorphoses,* viii, the story of Jupiter and Mercury lodging in the house of Baucis and Philemon. 15. **great . . . room,** great charge for lodging in a small room. Recent scholars see in this passage an allusion to the death of Marlowe, who was stabbed by Ingram Frysar at an inn at Deptford in a quarrel over a tavern reckoning, May 30, 1593. New Cambridge editors use the reference as a means of dating the original version of the play. 20. **feigning,** inventive, imaginative. 21. **may be said,** i.e., it may be said. 32. **material,** full of sense, or possibly,

But what though? Courage! As horns are odious, they are necessary. It is said, 'many a man knows no end of his goods:' right; many a man has good horns, and knows no end of them. Well, that is the dowry of his wife; 'tis none of his own getting. Horns? Even so. Poor men alone? No, no; the noblest deer hath them as huge as the rascal. Is the single man therefore blessed? No: as a walled town is more worthier than a village, so is the forehead of a married man more honourable than the bare brow of a bachelor; and by how much defence is better than no skill, by so much is a horn more precious than to want. Here comes Sir Oliver. 64

Enter SIR OLIVER MARTEXT.

Sir Oliver Martext, you are well met: will you dispatch us here under this tree, or shall we go with you to your chapel?

Sir Oli. Is there none here to give the woman?

Touch. I will not take her on gift of any man.

Sir Oli. Truly, she must be given, or the marriage is not lawful. 71

Jaq. [*Advancing*] Proceed, proceed: I'll give her.

Touch. Good even, good Master What-ye-call 't: how do you, sir? You are very well met: God 'ild you for your last company: I am very glad to see you: even a toy in hand here, sir: nay, pray be covered.

Jaq. Will you be married, motley? 79

Touch. As the ox hath his bow, sir, the horse his curb and the falcon her bells, so man hath his desires; and as pigeons bill, so wedlock would be nibbling.

Jaq. And will you, being a man of your breeding, be married under a bush like a beggar? Get you to church, and have a good priest that can tell you what marriage is: this fellow will but join you together as they join wainscot; then one of you will prove a shrunk panel and, like green timber, warp, warp. 90

Touch. [*Aside*] I am not in the mind but I were better to be married of him than of another: for he is not like to marry me well; and not being well married, it will be a good excuse for me hereafter to leave my wife.

Jaq. Go thou with me, and let me counsel thee.

Touch. Come, sweet Audrey:
We must be married, or we must live in bawdry.
Farewell, good Master Oliver: not,— 100
    O sweet Oliver,
    O brave Oliver,
    Leave me not behind thee:
but,—
        Wind away,
        Begone, I say,
    I will not to wedding with thee.
        [*Exeunt Jaques, Touchstone and Audrey.*
Sir Oli. 'Tis no matter: ne'er a fantastical knave of them all shall flout me out of my calling. [*Exit.*

SCENE IV. *The forest.*

Enter ROSALIND *and* CELIA.

Ros. Never talk to me; I will weep.

Cel. Do, I prithee; but yet have the grace to consider that tears do not become a man.

Ros. But have I not cause to weep?

Cel. As good cause as one would desire; therefore weep.

Ros. His very hair is of the dissembling colour.

Cel. Something browner than Judas's: marry, his kisses are Judas's own children. 10

Ros. I' faith, his hair is of a good colour.

Cel. An excellent colour: your chestnut was ever the only colour.

Ros. And his kissing is as full of sanctity as the touch of holy bread.

Cel. He hath bought a pair of cast lips of Diana: a nun of winter's sisterhood kisses not more religiously; the very ice of chastity is in them.

Ros. But why did he swear he would come this morning, and comes not? 21

Cel. Nay, certainly, there is no truth in him.

Ros. Do you think so?

Cel. Yes; I think he is not a pick-purse nor a horse-stealer, but for his verity in love, I do think him as concave as a covered goblet or a worm-eaten nut.

Ros. Not true in love?

Cel. Yes, when he is in; but I think he is not in. 30

Ros. You have heard him swear downright he was.

Cel. 'Was' is not 'is:' besides, the oath of a lover is no stronger than the word of a tapster; they are both the confirmer of false reckonings. He attends here in the forest on the duke your father.

Ros. I met the duke yesterday and had much question with him: he asked me of what parentage I was; I told him, of as good as he; so he laughed and let me go. But what talk we of fathers, when there is such a man as Orlando? 42

Cel. O, that 's a brave man! he writes brave verses, speaks brave words, swears brave oaths and breaks them bravely, quite traverse, athwart the heart of his lover; as a puisny tilter, that spurs his horse but on one side, breaks his staff like a noble goose: but all 's brave that youth mounts and folly guides. Who comes here?

Enter CORIN.

Cor. Mistress and master, you have oft inquired 50
After the shepherd that complain'd of love,
Who you saw sitting by me on the turf,
Praising the proud disdainful shepherdess
That was his mistress.

Cel.   Well, and what of him?

Cor. If you will see a pageant truly play'd,
Between the pale complexion of true love
And the red glow of scorn and proud disdain,
Go hence a little and I shall conduct you,

gross or carnal. 36. **foul,** ugly. 41. **foulness,** dirtiness. 43. **Sir,** usual title for a priest. 49. **stagger,** hesitate. 51. **what though?** What though it be so? 52. **necessary,** unavoidable. 58. **rascal,** deer lean and out of season. 62. **defence,** art of self-defense. 64. **than to want,** i.e., than to be without a horn. 76. **God 'ild you,** God yield you, reward you. 78. **pray be covered,** pray put on your hat. 80. **bow,** yoke. 90. **warp,** pun on the sense "go astray from the straight path" (New Cambridge). 91. **I am . . . but,** I do not know but. 108. **fantastical knave.** Capell suggests that Touchstone dances round the priest like a harlequin while he sings the ballad about Oliver.
SCENE IV. 9. **browner than Judas's,** an allusion to the traditional representation of Judas as having a red beard. 15. **holy bread,**

ordinary leavened bread which was blessed after the Eucharist and distributed to those who had not communed. 16. **cast,** cast off, discarded. 17. **Diana,** goddess of chastity. 26. **covered goblet,** i.e., a goblet having a convex top and therefore more hollow because the cover is on only when the goblet is empty. 39. **question,** conversation. 41. **what,** why. 45. **traverse,** across; with allusion to the disgrace of breaking one's lance across the body of the adversary. 46. **puisny,** petty, paltry (literally, junior). 56. **pale complexion.** Sighing was believed to draw the blood from the heart.

If you will mark it.
  Ros.   O, come, let us remove:
The sight of lovers feedeth those in love.   60
Bring us to this sight, and you shall say
I'll prove a busy actor in their play.   [*Exeunt.*

   SCENE V. *Another part of the forest.*

Enter SILVIUS *and* PHEBE.

 Sil. Sweet Phebe, do not scorn me; do not, Phebe;
Say that you love me not, but say not so
In bitterness. The common executioner,
Whose heart the accustom'd sight of death makes
  hard,
Falls not the axe upon the humbled neck
But first begs pardon: will you sterner be
†Than he that dies and lives by bloody drops?

Enter ROSALIND, CELIA, *and* CORIN, *behind.*

 Phe. I would not be thy executioner:
I fly thee, for I would not injure thee.
Thou tell'st me there is murder in mine eye: 10
'Tis pretty, sure, and very probable,
That eyes, that are the frail'st and softest things,
Who shut their coward gates on atomies,
Should be call'd tyrants, butchers, murderers!
Now I do frown on thee with all my heart;
And if mine eyes can wound, now let them kill thee:
Now counterfeit to swoon; why now fall down;
Or if thou canst not, O, for shame, for shame,
Lie not, to say mine eyes are murderers!
Now show the wound mine eye hath made in thee: 20
Scratch thee but with a pin, and there remains
Some scar of it; lean but upon a rush,
The cicatrice and capable impressure
Thy palm some moment keeps; but now mine eyes,
Which I have darted at thee, hurt thee not,
Nor, I am sure, there is no force in eyes
That can do hurt.
 Sil.   O dear Phebe,
If ever,—as that ever may be near,—
You meet in some fresh cheek the power of fancy,
Then shall you know the wounds invisible   30
That love's keen arrows make.
 Phe.   But till that time
Come not thou near me: and when that time comes,
Afflict me with thy mocks, pity me not;
As till that time I shall not pity thee.
 Ros. And why, I pray you? Who might be your
  mother,
That you insult, exult, and all at once,
Over the wretched? What though you have no
  beauty,—
As, by my faith, I see no more in you
Than without candle may go dark to bed—
Must you be therefore proud and pitiless?   40
Why, what means this? Why do you look on me?
I see no more in you than in the ordinary

Of nature's sale-work. 'Od 's my little life,
I think she means to tangle my eyes too!
No, faith, proud mistress, hope not after it:
'Tis not your inky brows, your black silk hair,
Your bugle eyeballs, nor your cheek of cream,
That can entame my spirits to your worship.
You foolish shepherd, wherefore do you follow her,
Like foggy south puffing with wind and rain? 50
You are a thousand times a properer man
Than she a woman: 'tis such fools as you
That makes the world full of ill-favour'd children:
'Tis not her glass, but you, that flatters her;
And out of you she sees herself more proper
Than any of her lineaments can show her.
But, mistress, know yourself: down on your knees,
And thank heaven, fasting, for a good man's love:
For I must tell you friendly in your ear,
Sell when you can: you are not for all markets: 60
Cry the man mercy; love him; take his offer:
Foul is most foul, being foul to be a scoffer.
So take her to thee, shepherd: fare you well.
 Phe. Sweet youth, I pray you, chide a year together:
I had rather hear you chide than this man woo.
 Ros. He 's fallen in love with your foulness and she'll
fall in love with my anger. If it be so, as fast as she
answers thee with frowning looks, I'll sauce her with
bitter words. Why look you so upon me? 70
 Phe. For no ill will I bear you.
 Ros. I pray you, do not fall in love with me,
For I am falser than vows made in wine:
Besides, I like you not. If you will know my house,
'Tis at the tuft of olives here hard by.
Will you go, sister? Shepherd, ply her hard.
Come, sister. Shepherdess, look on him better,
And be not proud: though all the world could see,
None could be so abused in sight as he.
Come, to our flock. [*Exeunt Rosalind, Celia and Corin.* 80
 Phe. Dead shepherd, now I find thy saw of might,
'Who ever loved that loved not at first sight?'
 Sil. Sweet Phebe,—
 Phe.   Ha, what say'st thou, Silvius?
 Sil. Sweet Phebe, pity me.
 Phe. Why, I am sorry for thee, gentle Silvius.
 Sil. Wherever sorrow is, relief would be:
If you do sorrow at my grief in love,
By giving love your sorrow and my grief
Were both extermined.
 Phe. Thou hast my love: is not that neighbourly? 90
 Sil. I would have you.
 Phe.   Why, that were covetousness.
Silvius, the time was that I hated thee,
And yet it is not that I bear thee love;
But since that thou canst talk of love so well,
Thy company, which erst was irksome to me,
I will endure, and I'll employ thee too:
But do not look for further recompense
Than thine own gladness that thou are employ'd.
 Sil. So holy and so perfect is my love,
And I in such a poverty of grace,   100

SCENE V. 6. **But first begs,** without first begging. 7. **Than . . .
drops,** obscure line; probable meaning: "Will you be sterner than he
(the executioner) who makes his living (lives and dies) by shedding
blood?" 11. **sure,** surely. 23. **cicatrice,** mark, impression. **impressure,** impression. 33. **mocks,** mockeries, taunts. 36. **all at once,** i.e.,
all in a breath. 39. **without candle,** i.e., your beauty is not so brilliant
that it will suffice to light you to bed. 43. **sale-work,** ready-made
work, i.e., not of the best quality. **'Od 's,** minced form of "God's,"
used in petty oaths. 47. **bugle,** tube-shaped glass bead; here, black.

48. **entame,** subdue. **to your worship,** to worship you. 50. **foggy
south.** South was the direction from which came fog and rain. 51.
properer, handsomer. 55. **out of you,** i.e., as her mirror. 62. **Foul,**
two meanings of the word played upon: Ugliness is most ugly when it is
rough and abusive. 81-82. **Dead . . . sight.** Line 82 is quoted from
Marlowe's *Hero and Leander*, Sestiad I, 176. Marlowe died on May 30,
1593; the poem was not printed until 1598. New Cambridge editors
would date the first version of the play as 1593 in part by this reference.
The publication of the poem may, of course, have occasioned the

That I shall think it a most plenteous crop
To glean the broken ears after the man
That the main harvest reaps: loose now and then
A scatter'd smile, and that I'll live upon.

Phe. Know'st thou the youth that spoke to me
  erewhile?

Sil. Not very well, but I have met him oft;
And he hath bought the cottage and the bounds
That the old carlot once was master of.

Phe. Think not I love him, though I ask for him;
'Tis but a peevish boy; yet he talks well; 110
But what care I for words? yet words do well
When he that speaks them pleases those that hear.
It is a pretty youth: not very pretty:
But, sure, he's proud, and yet his pride becomes him:
He'll make a proper man: the best thing in him
Is his complexion; and faster than his tongue
Did make offence his eye did heal it up.
He is not very tall; yet for his years he's tall:
His leg is but so so; and yet 'tis well:
There was a pretty redness in his lip, 120
A little riper and more lusty red
Than that mix'd in his cheek; 'twas just the difference
Betwixt the constant red and mingled damask.
There be some women, Silvius, had they mark'd him
In parcels as I did, would have gone near
To fall in love with him; but, for my part,
I love him not nor hate him not; and yet
I have more cause to hate him than to love him:
For what had he to do to chide at me?
He said mine eyes were black and my hair black; 130
And, now I am remember'd, scorn'd at me:
I marvel why I answer'd not again:
But that's all one; omittance is no quittance.
I'll write to him a very taunting letter,
And thou shalt bear it: wilt thou, Silvius?

Sil. Phebe, with all my heart.

Phe. I'll write it straight;
The matter's in my head and in my heart:
I will be bitter with him and passing short:
Go with me, Silvius. [*Exeunt.*

ACT IV.

SCENE I. *The forest.*

Enter ROSALIND, CELIA, *and* JAQUES.

Jaq. I prithee, pretty youth, let me be better acquainted with thee.

Ros. They say you are a melancholy fellow.

Jaq. I am so; I do love it better than laughing.

Ros. Those that are in extremity of either are abominable fellows and betray themselves to every modern censure worse than drunkards.

Jaq. Why, 'tis good to be sad and say nothing.

Ros. Why then, 'tis good to be a post. 9

Jaq. I have neither the scholar's melancholy, which is emulation, nor the musician's, which is fantastical, nor the courtier's, which is proud, nor the soldier's, which is ambitious, nor the lawyer's, which is politic, nor the lady's, which is nice, nor the lover's, which is all these: but it is a melancholy of mine own, compounded of many simples, extracted from many objects, and indeed the sundry contemplation of my travels, in which my often rumination wraps me in a most humorous sadness. 20

Ros. A traveller! By my faith, you have great reason to be sad: I fear you have sold your own lands to see other men's; then, to have seen much and to have nothing, is to have rich eyes and poor hands.

Jaq. Yes, I have gained my experience.

Ros. And your experience makes you sad: I had rather have a fool to make me merry than experience to make me sad; and to travel for it too!

Enter ORLANDO.

Orl. Good day and happiness, dear Rosalind!

Jaq. Nay, then, God be wi' you, an you talk in blank verse. [*Exit.* 32

Ros. Farewell, Monsieur Traveller: look you lisp and wear strange suits, disable all the benefits of your own country, be out of love with your nativity and almost chide God for making you that countenance you are, or I will scarce think you have swam in a gondola. Why, how now, Orlando! where have you been all this while? You a lover! An you serve me such another trick, never come in my sight more. 41

Orl. My fair Rosalind, I come within an hour of my promise.

Ros. Break an hour's promise in love! He that will divide a minute into a thousand parts and break but a part of the thousandth part of a minute in the affairs of love, it may be said of him that Cupid hath clapped him o' the shoulder, but I'll warrant him heartwhole.

Orl. Pardon me, dear Rosalind. 50

Ros. Nay, an you be so tardy, come no more in my sight: I had as lief be wooed of a snail.

Orl. Of a snail?

Ros. Ay, of a snail; for though he comes slowly, he carries his house on his head; a better jointure, I think, than you make a woman: besides, he brings his destiny with him.

Orl. What's that? 58

Ros. Why, horns, which such as you are fain to be beholding to your wives for: but he comes armed in his fortune and prevents the slander of his wife.

Orl. Virtue is no horn-maker; and my Rosalind is virtuous.

Ros. And I am your Rosalind.

Cel. It pleases him to call you so; but he hath a Rosalind of a better leer than you.

Ros. Come, woo me, woo me, for now I am in a holiday humour and like enough to consent. What would you say to me now, an I were your very very Rosalind? 71

Orl. I would kiss before I spoke.

Ros. Nay, you were better speak first, and when you

---

quotation. 89. **extermined,** exterminated. 90. **neighbourly.** This serves to take back Phebe's preceding statement, since love was divided into conjugal love and neighborly love. 100. **poverty of grace.** Love is his divinity, and love has been ungracious to him. 107. **bounds,** i.e., bounds within which he can feed stock. 108. **carlot,** peasant, countryman. 123. **constant,** uniform. **mingled damask,** striped red and white damask, i.e., the color of the damask rose (pink or rose color). 125. **In parcels,** piecemeal, in detail. 129. **what . . . do,** what business had he. 131. **am remember'd,** remember, recollect.

ACT IV. SCENE I. 14. **politic,** crafty, or insincere (out of pretended sympathy for his client). 17. **simples,** ingredients (usually herbs) of a drug. 34. **disable,** depreciate, disparage. 38. **swam in a gondola,** i.e., been in Venice. 48. **clapped . . . shoulder,** tapped on the shoulder by way of arrest. 56. **jointure,** marriage settlement. 60. **beholding,** beholden, indebted. 61. **armed . . . fortune,** i.e., with the horns of a cuckold, which it was his fate to earn. 67. **leer,** complexion, countenance.

were gravelled for lack of matter, you might take occasion to kiss. Very good orators, when they are out, they will spit; and for lovers lacking—God warn us!—matter, the cleanliest shift is to kiss.

Orl. How if the kiss be denied?

Ros. Then she puts you to entreaty, and there begins new matter. 81

Orl. Who could be out, being before his beloved mistress?

Ros. Marry, that should you, if I were your mistress, or I should think my honesty ranker than my wit.

Orl. What, of my suit?

Ros. Not out of your apparel, and yet out of your suit. Am not I your Rosalind?

Orl. I take some joy to say you are, because I would be talking of her. 91

Ros. Well, in her person I say I will not have you.

Orl. Then in mine own person I die.

Ros. No, faith, die by attorney. The poor world is almost six thousand years old, and in all this time there was not any man died in his own person, videlicet, in a love-cause. Troilus had his brains dashed out with a Grecian club; yet he did what he could to die before, and he is one of the patterns of love. Leander, he would have lived many a fair year, though Hero had turned nun, if it had not been for a hot midsummer night; for, good youth, he went but forth to wash him in the Hellespont and being taken with the cramp was drowned: and the foolish chroniclers of that age found it was 'Hero of Sestos.' But these are all lies: men have died from time to time and worms have eaten them, but not for love.

Orl. I would not have my right Rosalind of this mind, for, I protest, her frown might kill me. 110

Ros. By this hand, it will not kill a fly. But come, now I will be your Rosalind in a more coming-on disposition, and ask me what you will, I will grant it.

Orl. Then love me, Rosalind.

Ros. Yes, faith, will I, Fridays and Saturdays and all.

Orl. And wilt thou have me?

Ros. Ay, and twenty such.

Orl. What sayest thou? 120

Ros. Are you not good?

Orl. I hope so.

Ros. Why then, can one desire too much of a good thing? Come, sister, you shall be the priest and marry us. Give me your hand, Orlando. What do you say, sister?

Orl. Pray thee, marry us.

Cel. I cannot say the words.

Ros. You must begin, 'Will you, Orlando—'

Cel. Go to. Will you, Orlando, have to wife this Rosalind? 131

Orl. I will.

Ros. Ay, but when?

Orl. Why now; as fast as she can marry us.

Ros. Then you must say, 'I take thee, Rosalind, for wife.'

Orl. I take thee, Rosalind, for wife.

Ros. I might ask you for your commission; but I do take thee, Orlando, for my husband: there's a girl goes before the priest; and certainly a woman's thought runs before her actions. 141

Orl. So do all thoughts; they are winged.

Ros. Now tell me how long you would have her after you have possessed her.

Orl. For ever and a day.

Ros. Say 'a day,' without the 'ever.' No, no, Orlando; men are April when they woo, December when they wed: maids are May when they are maids, but the sky changes when they are wives. I will be more jealous of thee than a Barbary cock-pigeon over his hen, more clamorous than a parrot against rain, more new-fangled than an ape, more giddy in my desires than a monkey: I will weep for nothing, like Diana in the fountain, and I will do that when you are disposed to be merry; I will laugh like a hyen, and that when thou art inclined to sleep.

Orl. But will my Rosalind do so?

Ros. By my life, she will do as I do.

Orl. O, but she is wise. 160

Ros. Or else she could not have the wit to do this: the wiser, the waywarder: make the doors upon a woman's wit and it will out at the casement; shut that and 'twill out at the key-hole; stop that, 'twill fly with the smoke out at the chimney.

Orl. A man that had a wife with such a wit, he might say 'Wit, whither wilt?'

Ros. Nay, you might keep that check for it till you met your wife's wit going to your neighbour's bed. 171

Orl. And what wit could wit have to excuse that?

Ros. Marry, to say she came to seek you there. You shall never take her without her answer, unless you take her without her tongue. O, that woman that cannot make her fault her husband's occasion, let her never nurse her child herself, for she will breed it like a fool! 179

Orl. For these two hours, Rosalind, I will leave thee.

Ros. Alas! dear love, I cannot lack thee two hours.

Orl. I must attend the duke at dinner: by two o'clock I will be with thee again.

Ros. Ay, go your ways, go your ways; I knew what you would prove: my friends told me as much, and I thought no less: that flattering tongue of yours won me: 'tis but one cast away, and so, come, death! Two o'clock is your hour? 190

Orl. Ay, sweet Rosalind.

Ros. By my troth, and in good earnest, and so God mend me, and by all pretty oaths that are not dangerous, if you break one jot of your promise or come one minute behind your hour, I will think you the most pathetical break-promise and the most hollow lover and the most unworthy of her you call Rosalind that may be chosen out of the gross band of the unfaithful: therefore beware my censure and keep your promise.

Orl. With no less religion than if thou wert indeed my Rosalind: so adieu. 202

Ros. Well, Time is the old justice that examines all such offenders, and let Time try: adieu. [*Exit Orlando.*

Cel. You have simply misused our sex in your love-prate: we must have your doublet and hose plucked over your head, and show the world what the bird hath done to her own nest.

Ros. O coz, coz, coz, my pretty little coz, that thou didst know how many fathom deep I am in love! But it cannot be sounded: my affection hath an unknown bottom, like the bay of Portugal.

Cel. Or rather, bottomless, that as fast as you pour affection in, it runs out.   217

Ros. No, that same wicked bastard of Venus that was begot of thought, conceived of spleen and born of madness, that blind rascally boy that abuses every one's eyes because his own are out, let him be judge how deep I am in love. I'll tell thee, Aliena, I cannot be out of the sight of Orlando: I'll go find a shadow and sigh till he come.

Cel. And I'll sleep.   [*Exeunt.*

SCENE II. *The forest.*

Enter JAQUES, Lords, *and* Foresters.

Jaq. Which is he that killed the deer?

A Lord. Sir, it was I.

Jaq. Let's present him to the duke, like a Roman conqueror; and it would do well to set the deer's horns upon his head, for a branch of victory. Have you no song, forester, for this purpose?

For. Yes, sir.

Jaq. Sing it: 'tis no matter how it be in tune, so it make noise enough.   10

SONG.

For. What shall he have that kill'd the deer?
 His leather skin and horns to wear.
  Then sing him home;
    [*The rest shall bear this burden.*
 Take thou no scorn to wear the horn;
 It was a crest ere thou wast born:
  Thy father's father wore it,
  And thy father bore it:
 The horn, the horn, the lusty horn
 Is not a thing to laugh to scorn.   [*Exeunt.*

SCENE III. *The forest.*

Enter ROSALIND *and* CELIA.

Ros. How say you now? Is it not past two o'clock? and here much Orlando!

Cel. I warrant you, with pure love and troubled brain, he hath ta'en his bow and arrows and is gone forth to sleep. Look, who comes here.

Enter SILVIUS.

Sil. My errand is to you, fair youth;

My gentle Phebe bid me give you this:
I know not the contents; but, as I guess
By the stern brow and waspish action
Which she did use as she was writing of it,   10
It bears an angry tenour: pardon me;
I am but as a guiltless messenger.

Ros. Patience herself would startle at this letter
And play the swaggerer; bear this, bear all:
She says I am not fair, that I lack manners;
She calls me proud, and that she could not love me,
Were man as rare as phœnix, 'Od 's my will!
Her love is not the hare that I do hunt:
Why writes she so to me? Well, shepherd, well,
This is a letter of your own device.   20

Sil. No, I protest, I know not the contents:
Phebe did write it.

Ros.   Come, come, you are a fool
And turn'd into the extremity of love.
I saw her hand: she has a leathern hand,
A freestone-colour'd hand: I verily did think
That her old gloves were on, but 'twas her hands:
She has a huswife's hand; but that 's no matter:
I say she never did invent this letter;
This is a man's invention and his hand.

Sil. Sure, it is hers.   30

Ros. Why, 'tis a boisterous and a cruel style,
A style for challengers; why, she defies me,
Like Turk to Christian: women's gentle brain
Could not drop forth such giant-rude invention,
Such Ethiope words, blacker in their effect
Than in their countenance. Will you hear the
 letter?

Sil. So please you, for I never heard it yet;
Yet heard too much of Phebe's cruelty.

Ros. She Phebes me: mark how the tyrant writes.
           [*Reads.*
 Art thou god to shepherd turn'd,   40
 That a maiden's heart hath burn'd?
Can a woman rail thus?

Sil. Call you this railing?

Ros. [*Reads*]
 Why, thy godhead laid apart,
 Warr'st thou with a woman's heart?
Did you ever hear such railing?
 Whiles the eye of man did woo me,
 That could do no vengeance to me.
Meaning me a beast.
 If the scorn of your bright eyne   50
 Have power to raise such love in mine,
 Alack, in me what strange effect
 Would they work in mild aspect!
 Whiles you chid me, I did love;
 How then might your prayers move!
 He that brings this love to thee
 Little knows this love in me:
 And by him seal up thy mind;
 Whether that thy youth and kind
 Will the faithful offer take   60
 Of me and all that I can make;

---

miserable, or passion-moving. 201. **religion,** strict fidelity. 206. **simply misused,** absolutely slandered.
 SCENE II. The scene presents a procession of huntsmen with their kill and is full of the customs of the chase, reflecting also the heathen background of the ceremony in the decking of the chief huntsman with the hide and horns of the slain deer as a fetish. 14. **Take . . . scorn,** be not ashamed.
 SCENE III. 2. **and . . . Orlando,** ironical; Steevens: *here's much Orlando.* 5. **sleep,** unexpected turn; one would have expected her to

say "hunt." 17. **phœnix,** a fabulous bird of Arabia, the only one of its kind, which lived five hundred years and was reborn of its own ashes. 23. **turn'd,** brought. 25. **freestone-colour'd,** color of freestone, brown. 27. **huswife's hand,** i.e., hard with housework. 29. **hand,** handwriting, with play on the ordinary meaning. 35. **Ethiope,** blackamoor; here, black. 39. **Phebes,** i.e., treats cruelly. 48. **vengeance,** mischief, harm. 53. **aspect,** appearance of a planet; astrological term. 59. **youth and kind,** youthful nature.

Or else by him my love deny,
And then I'll study how to die.
Sil. Call you this chiding?
Cel. Alas, poor shepherd!
Ros. Do you pity him? no, he deserves no pity. Wilt
thou love such a woman? What, to make thee an instrument and play false strains upon thee! not to be
endured! Well, go your way to her, for I see love hath
made thee a tame snake, and say this to her: that if
she love me, I charge her to love thee; if she will not,
I will never have her unless thou entreat for her. If
you be a true lover, hence, and not a word; for here
comes more company.   [*Exit Silvius.*

Enter OLIVER.

Oli. Good morrow, fair ones: pray you, if you know,
Where in the purlieus of this forest stands
A sheep-cote fenced about with olive trees?
Cel. West of this place, down in the neighbour
  bottom:
The rank of osiers by the murmuring stream   80
Left on your right hand brings you to the place.
But at this hour the house doth keep itself;
There 's none within.
Oli. If that an eye may profit by a tongue,
Then should I know you by description;
Such garments and such years: 'The boy is fair,
Of female favour, and bestows himself
Like a ripe sister: the woman low
And browner than her brother.' Are not you
The owner of the house I did enquire for?   90
Cel. It is no boast, being ask'd, to say we are.
Oli. Orlando doth commend him to you both,
And to that youth he calls his Rosalind
He sends this bloody napkin. Are you he?
Ros. I am: what must we understand by this?
Oli. Some of my shame; if you will know of me
What man I am, and how, and why, and where
This handkercher was stain'd.
Cel.   I pray you, tell it.
Oli. When last the young Orlando parted from you
He left a promise to return again   100
Within an hour, and pacing through the forest,
Chewing the food of sweet and bitter fancy,
Lo, what befel! he threw his eye aside,
And mark what object did present itself:
Under an oak, whose boughs were moss'd with age
And high top bald with dry antiquity,
A wretched ragged man, o'ergrown with hair,
Lay sleeping on his back: about his neck
A green and gilded snake had wreathed itself,
Who with her head nimble in threats approach'd   110
The opening of his mouth; but suddenly,
Seeing Orlando, it unlink'd itself,
And with indented glides did slip away
Into a bush: under which bush's shade
A lioness, with udders all drawn dry,
Lay couching, head on ground, with catlike watch,
When that the sleeping man should stir; for 'tis
The royal disposition of that beast
To prey on nothing that doth seem as dead:

This seen, Orlando did approach the man   120
And found it was his brother, his elder brother.
Cel. O, I have heard him speak of that same
  brother;
And he did render him the most unnatural
That lived amongst men.
Oli.   And well he might so do,
For well I know he was unnatural.
Ros. But, to Orlando: did he leave him there,
Food to the suck'd and hungry lioness?
Oli. Twice did he turn his back and purposed so;
But kindness, nobler ever than revenge,
And nature, stronger than his just occasion,   130
Made him give battle to the lioness,
Who quickly fell before him: in which hurtling
From miserable slumber I awaked.
Cel. Are you his brother?
Ros.   Was 't you he rescued?
Cel. Was 't you that did so oft contrive to kill him?
Oli. 'Twas I; but 'tis not I: I do not shame
To tell you what I was, since my conversion
So sweetly tastes, being the thing I am.
Ros. But, for the bloody napkin?
Oli.   By and by.
When from the first to last betwixt us two   140
Tears our recountments had most kindly bathed,
As how I came into that desert place:—
In brief, he led me to the gentle duke,
Who gave me fresh array and entertainment,
Committing me unto my brother's love;
Who led me instantly unto his cave,
There stripp'd himself, and here upon his arm
The lioness had torn some flesh away,
Which all this while had bled; and now he fainted
And cried, in fainting, upon Rosalind.   150
Brief, I recover'd him, bound up his wound;
And, after some small space, being strong at heart,
He sent me hither, stranger as I am,
To tell this story, that you might excuse
His broken promise, and to give this napkin
Dyed in his blood unto the shepherd youth
That he in sport doth call his Rosalind.
                            [*Rosalind swoons.*
Cel. Why, how now, Ganymede! sweet Ganymede!
Oli. Many will swoon when they do look on blood.
Cel. There is more in it. Cousin Ganymede!   160
Oli. Look, he recovers.
Ros. I would I were at home.
Cel.   We'll lead you thither.
I pray you, will you take him by the arm?
Oli. Be of good cheer, youth: you a man! you lack a
man's heart.
Ros. I do so, I confess it. Ah, sirrah, a body would
think this was well counterfeited! I pray you, tell your
brother how well I counterfeited. Heigh-ho!   169
Oli. This was not counterfeit: there is too great
testimony in your complexion that it was a passion of
earnest.
Ros. Counterfeit, I assure you.
Oli. Well then, take a good heart and counterfeit to
be a man.

68. **instrument,** tool and musical instrument.   76. **fair ones,** sometimes
thought inappropriate as addressed to a boy as well as a girl, but there
is nothing against such a greeting.   77. **purlieus,** tracts of land on the
border of a forest.   79. **neighbour bottom,** neighboring dell.   80. **rank
of osiers,** row of willows.   87. **bestows,** behaves.   88. **ripe sister,**
mature or elder sister; Lettsom and New Cambridge: *forester.*   113.
indented, zigzag.   115. **udders . . . dry,** therefore fierce with hunger.

126. **to,** with regard to.   130. **just occasion,** fair chance (of revenge).
132. **hurtling,** clattering, clashing.   136. **do not shame,** am not
ashamed.   139. **for,** as regards.   141. **recountments,** relation, recital.
142. **As,** as for instance.   151. **Brief,** in brief.   **recover'd,** brought back
to consciousness or health.   166. **sirrah.** Onions suggests that this is
addressed by Rosalind to herself, since the word is frequently so used
in soliloquies.   172. **passion of earnest,** real attack.

Ros. So I do: but, i' faith, I should have been a woman by right.

Cel. Come, you look paler and paler: pray you, draw homewards. Good sir, go with us.

Oli. That will I, for I must bear answer back 180
How you excuse my brother, Rosalind.

Ros. I shall devise something: but, I pray you, commend my counterfeiting to him. Will you go? [*Exeunt.*

ACT V.

SCENE I. *The forest.*

Enter TOUCHSTONE *and* AUDREY.

Touch. We shall find a time, Audrey; patience, gentle Audrey.

Aud. Faith, the priest was good enough, for all the old gentleman's saying.

Touch. A most wicked Sir Oliver, Audrey, a most vile Martext. But, Audrey, there is a youth here in the forest lays claim to you.

Aud. Ay, I know who 'tis; he hath no interest in me in the world: here comes the man you mean. 10

Touch. It is meat and drink to me to see a clown: by my troth, we that have good wits have much to answer for; we shall be flouting; we cannot hold.

Enter WILLIAM.

Will. Good even, Audrey.

Aud. God ye good even, William.

Will. And good even to you, sir.

Touch. Good even, gentle friend. Cover thy head, cover thy head; nay, prithee, be covered. How old are you, friend? 20

Will. Five and twenty, sir.

Touch. A ripe age. Is thy name William?

Will. William, sir.

Touch. A fair name. Wast born i' the forest here?

Will. Ay, sir, I thank God.

Touch. 'Thank God;' a good answer. Art rich?

Will. Faith, sir, so so.

Touch. 'So so' is good, very good, very excellent good; and yet it is not; it is but so so. Art thou wise? 31

Will. Ay, sir, I have a pretty wit.

Touch. Why, thou sayest well. I do now remember a saying, 'The fool doth think he is wise, but the wise man knows himself to be a fool.' The heathen philosopher, when he had a desire to eat a grape, would open his lips when he put it into his mouth; meaning thereby that grapes were made to eat and lips to open. You do love this maid? 40

Will. I do, sir.

Touch. Give me your hand. Art thou learned?

Will. No, sir.

Touch. Then learn this of me: to have, is to have; for it is a figure in rhetoric that drink, being poured out of a cup into a glass, by filling the one doth empty the other; for all your writers do consent that ipse is he: now, you are not ipse, for I am he.

Will. Which he, sir? 50

Touch. He, sir, that must marry this woman. Therefore, you clown, abandon,—which is in the vulgar leave,—the society,—which in the boorish is company,—of this female,—which in the common is woman; which together is, abandon the society of this female, or, clown, thou perishest; or, to thy better understanding, diest; or, to wit, I kill thee, make thee away, translate thy life into death, thy liberty into bondage: I will deal in poison with thee, or in bastinado, or in steel; I will bandy with thee in faction; I will o'errun thee with policy; I will kill thee a hundred and fifty ways: therefore tremble, and depart.

Aud. Do, good William.

Will. God rest you merry, sir. [*Exit.* 65

Enter CORIN.

Cor. Our master and mistress seeks you; come, away, away!

Touch. Trip, Audrey! trip, Audrey! I attend, I attend. [*Exeunt.*

SCENE II. *The forest.*

Enter ORLANDO *and* OLIVER.

Orl. Is 't possible that on so little acquaintance you should like her? that but seeing you should love her? and loving woo? and, wooing, she should grant? and will you persever to enjoy her?

Oli. Neither call the giddiness of it in question, the poverty of her, the small acquaintance, my sudden wooing, nor her sudden consenting; but say with me, I love Aliena; say with her that she loves me; consent with both that we may enjoy each other: it shall be to your good; for my father's house and all the revenue that was old Sir Rowland's will I estate upon you, and here live and die a shepherd. 14

Orl. You have my consent. Let your wedding be tomorrow: thither will I invite the duke and all 's contented followers. Go you and prepare Aliena; for look you, here comes my Rosalind.

Enter ROSALIND.

Ros. God save you, brother. 20

Oli. And you, fair sister. [*Exit.*

Ros. O, my dear Orlando, how it grieves me to see thee wear thy heart in a scarf!

Orl. It is my arm.

Ros. I thought thy heart had been wounded with the claws of a lion.

Orl. Wounded it is, but with the eyes of a lady.

Ros. Did your brother tell you how I counterfeited to swoon when he showed me your handkercher? 30

Orl. Ay, and greater wonders than that.

Ros. O, I know where you are: nay, 'tis true: there was never any thing so sudden but the fight of two rams and Cæsar's thrasonical brag of 'I came, saw, and overcame:' for your brother and my sister no sooner met but they looked, no sooner looked but they loved, no sooner loved but they sighed, no sooner sighed but they asked one another the reason, no

ACT V. SCENE I. 4. **old gentleman's,** interesting comment on the age of Jaques. 12. **clown,** countryman. 13. **shall,** must. **flouting,** scoffing, expressing contempt. 16. **God ye good even,** God give you good evening. 36-40. **The heathen . . . open.** New Cambridge editors elucidate this as a way of telling William (whose mouth is probably gaping like a rustic's) that the grape (Audrey) is not for his lips. 46-47. **drink . . . other,** i.e., both Touchstone and William cannot possess

Audrey. 48. **ipse,** Latin, he himself. 60. **bastinado,** duel with cudgels. 61. **bandy,** contend. 65. **God . . . merry,** common salutation at parting.
SCENE II. 4. **persever.** Accent is on second syllable. 13. **estate,** settle as an estate, bestow. 21. **sister,** i.e., future sister-in-law. 23. **wear . . . scarf,** possible allusion to Orlando's wearing his heart on his sleeve. 32. **where you are,** what you mean. 34. **thrasonical,** boastful; from Thraso, the boaster in Terence's *Eunuchus*.

sooner knew the reason but they sought the remedy; and in these degrees have they made a pair of stairs to marriage which they will climb incontinent, or else be incontinent before marriage: they are in the very wrath of love and they will together; clubs cannot part them. 45

Orl. They shall be married to-morrow, and I will bid the duke to the nuptial. But, O, how bitter a thing it is to look into happiness through another man's eyes! By so much the more shall I to-morrow be at the height of heart-heaviness, by how much I shall think my brother happy in having what he wishes for.

Ros. Why then, to-morrow I cannot serve your turn for Rosalind?

Orl. I can live no longer by thinking. 55

Ros. I will weary you then no longer with idle talking. Know of me then, for now I speak to some purpose, that I know you are a gentleman of good conceit: I speak not this that you should bear a good opinion of my knowledge, insomuch I say I know you are; neither do I labour for a greater esteem than may in some little measure draw a belief from you, to do yourself good and not to grace me. Believe then, if you please, that I can do strange things: I have, since I was three years old, conversed with a magician, most profound in his art and yet not damnable. If you do love Rosalind so near the heart as your gesture cries it out, when your brother marries Aliena, shall you marry her: I know into what straits of fortune she is driven; and it is not impossible to me, if it appear not inconvenient to you, to set her before your eyes to-morrow human as she is and without any danger. 75

Orl. Speakest thou in sober meanings?

Ros. By my life, I do; which I tender dearly, though I say I am a magician. Therefore, put you in your best array; bid your friends; for if you will be married to-morrow, you shall, and to Rosalind, if you will. 81

Enter SILVIUS *and* PHEBE.

Look, here comes a lover of mine and a lover of hers.

Phe. Youth, you have done me much ungentleness, To show the letter that I writ to you.

Ros. I care not if I have: it is my study To seem despiteful and ungentle to you: You are there followed by a faithful shepherd; Look upon him, love him; he worships you.

Phe. Good shepherd, tell this youth what 'tis to love.

Sil. It is to be all made of sighs and tears; 90 And so am I for Phebe.

Phe. And I for Ganymede.

Orl. And I for Rosalind.

Ros. And I for no woman.

Sil. It is to be all made of faith and service; And so am I for Phebe.

Phe. And I for Ganymede.

Orl. And I for Rosalind.

Ros. And I for no woman.

Sil. It is to be all made of fantasy, 100 All made of passion and all made of wishes, All adoration, duty, and observance, All humbleness, all patience and impatience, †All purity, all trial, all observance; And so am I for Phebe.

Phe. And so am I for Ganymede.

Orl. And so am I for Rosalind.

Ros. And so am I for no woman.

Phe. If this be so, why blame you me to love you? 110

Sil. If this be so, why blame you me to love you?

Orl. If this be so, why blame you me to love you?

Ros. Who do you speak to, 'Why blame you me to love you?'

Orl. To her that is not here, nor doth not hear. 117

Ros. Pray you, no more of this; 'tis like the howling of Irish wolves against the moon. [*To Sil*.] I will help you, if I can: [*To Phe*.] I would love you, if I could. To-morrow meet me all together. [*To Phe*.] I will marry you, if ever I marry woman, and I'll be married to-morrow: [*To Orl*.] I will satisfy you, if ever I satisfied man, and you shall be married to-morrow: [*To Sil*.] I will content you, if what pleases you contents you, and you shall be married to-morrow. [*To Orl*.] As you love Rosalind, meet: [*To Sil*.] as you love Phebe, meet: and as I love no woman, I'll meet. So fare you well: I have left you commands. 131

Sil. I'll not fail, if I live.

Phe. Nor I.

Orl. Nor I. [*Exeunt*.

SCENE III. *The forest*.

Enter TOUCHSTONE *and* AUDREY.

Touch. To-morrow is the joyful day, Audrey; to-morrow will we be married.

Aud. I do desire it with all my heart; and I hope it is no dishonest desire to desire to be a woman of the world. Here come two of the banished duke's pages.

Enter two Pages.

First Page. Well met, honest gentleman.

Touch. By my troth, well met. Come, sit, sit, and a song. 9

Sec. Page. We are for you: sit i' the middle.

First Page. Shall we clap into 't roundly, without hawking or spitting or saying we are hoarse, which are the only prologues to a bad voice? 14

Sec. Page. I' faith, i' faith; and both in a tune, like two gipsies on a horse.

SONG.

It was a lover and his lass,
    With a hey, and a ho, and a hey nonino,

41. **degrees**, play on the original meaning, "steps." 42. **incontinent**, immediately. 44. **wrath**, impetuosity, ardor. 61. **insomuch**, inasmuch as. 66. **conversed**, associated. 67. **damnable**, worthy of condemnation, i.e., he was not a practicer of forbidden magic. 69. **gesture**, bearing. **cries it out**, proclaims. 74–75. **human . . . danger**, i.e., not a phantom but the real Rosalind without any of the danger generally conceived to attend the rites of incantation (Johnson). 77. **tender dearly**, value highly, a possible reference to the anti-witchcraft statutes of Elizabeth, by which witchcraft causing death was punishable by death. 102. **observance**, respect. 110. **to love**, for loving. 119. **howling . . . moon**, a probable allusion to the rebellion of the Irish rebels against Elizabeth, the Virgin Queen. 120–131. **I will . . . commands.** This

comic denouement, or unknotting of the plot complications, is unusually skillful. The audience has the flattering sense of superior understanding and at the same time has its curiosity appealed to.

SCENE III. This scene has no dramatic purpose; it serves merely as entertainment. The suggestion has been made that it is an attempt on the part of Shakespeare's theater to rival the similar attractions offered just at that time by the children at Blackfriars Theater. 4. **dishonest**, immodest. 5. **woman of the world**, married woman. 10. **sit i' the middle**, sit between us (in order to enter into the song). 11. **clap . . . roundly**, begin at once and with spirit. 13. **the only prologues**, only the prologues. 15. **both in a tune**, both in unison, or both keep in time. 20. **ring time**, time most apt for marriage. 23. **acres**, fields, or accord-

That o'er the green corn-field did pass
  In the spring time, the only pretty ring time,   20
When birds do sing, hey ding a ding, ding:
Sweet lovers love the spring.

Between the acres of the rye,
  With a hey, and a ho, and a hey nonino,
These pretty country folks would lie,
  In spring time, &c.

This carol they began that hour,
  With a hey, and a ho, and a hey nonino,
How that a life was but a flower
  In spring time, &c.   30

And therefore take the present time,
  With a hey, and a ho, and a hey nonino;
For love is crowned with the prime
  In spring time, &c.

Touch. Truly, young gentlemen, though there was
no great matter in the ditty, yet the note was very
untuneable.

First Page. You are deceived, sir: we kept time, we
lost not our time.   39

Touch. By my troth, yes; I count it but time lost to
hear such a foolish song. God be wi' you; and God
mend your voices! Come, Audrey.   [*Exeunt.*

SCENE IV. *The forest.*

Enter DUKE senior, AMIENS, JAQUES, ORLANDO,
OLIVER, *and* CELIA.

Duke S. Dost thou believe, Orlando, that the boy
Can do all this that he hath promised?

Orl. I sometimes do believe, and sometimes do not;
†As those that fear they hope, and know they fear.

Enter ROSALIND, SILVIUS, *and* PHEBE.

Ros. Patience once more, whiles our compact is
  urged:
You say, if I bring in your Rosalind,
You will bestow her on Orlando here?

Duke S. That would I, had I kingdoms to give with
  her.

Ros. And you say, you will have her, when I bring
  her?

Orl. That would I, were I of all kingdoms king.   10

Ros. You say, you'll marry me, if I be willing?

Phe. That will I, should I die the hour after.

Ros. But if you do refuse to marry me,
You'll give yourself to this most faithful shepherd?

Phe. So is the bargain.

Ros. You say, that you'll have Phebe, if she will?

Sil. Though to have her and death were both one
  thing.

Ros. I have promised to make all this matter even.
Keep you your word, O duke, to give your daughter;
You yours, Orlando, to receive his daughter: 20
Keep your word, Phebe, that you'll marry me,
Or else refusing me, to wed this shepherd:
Keep your word, Silvius, that you'll marry her,
If she refuse me: and from hence I go,
To make these doubts all even.
          [*Exeunt Rosalind and Celia.*

Duke S. I do remember in this shepherd boy
Some lively touches of my daughter's favour.

Orl. My lord, the first time that I ever saw him
Methought he was a brother to your daughter:
But, my good lord, this boy is forest-born,   30
And hath been tutor'd in the rudiments
Of many desperate studies by his uncle,
Whom he reports to be a great magician,
Obscured in the circle of this forest.

Enter TOUCHSTONE *and* AUDREY.

Jaq. There is, sure, another flood toward, and these
couples are coming to the ark. Here comes a pair of
very strange beasts, which in all tongues are called
fools.

Touch. Salutation and greeting to you all!   39

Jaq. Good my lord, bid him welcome: this is the
motley-minded gentleman that I have so often met in
the forest: he hath been a courtier, he swears.

Touch. If any man doubt that, let him put me to my
purgation. I have trod a measure; I have flattered a
lady; I have been politic with my friend, smooth with
mine enemy; I have undone three tailors; I have had
four quarrels, and like to have fought one.

Jaq. And how was that ta'en up?   50

Touch. Faith, we met, and found the quarrel was
upon the seventh cause.

Jaq. How seventh cause? Good my lord, like this
fellow.

Duke S. I like him very well.

Touch. God 'ild you, sir; I desire you of the like. I
press in here, sir, amongst the rest of the country copu-
latives, to swear and to forswear; according as marriage binds and blood breaks: a poor virgin, sir, an
ill-favoured thing, sir, but mine own; a poor humour
of mine, sir, to take that that no man else will: rich
honesty dwells like a miser, sir, in a poor house; as
your pearl in your foul oyster.   64

Duke S. By my faith, he is very swift and sententious.

Touch. According to the fool's bolt, sir, and such
dulcet diseases.

Jaq. But, for the seventh cause; how did you find
the quarrel on the seventh cause?   70

Touch. Upon a lie seven times removed:—bear
your body more seeming, Audrey:—as thus, sir. I did
dislike the cut of a certain courtier's beard: he sent me
word, if I said his beard was not cut well, he was in the
mind it was: this is called the Retort Courteous. If I

sent him word again 'it was not well cut,' he would send me word, he cut it to please himself: this is called the Quip Modest. If again 'it was not well cut,' he disabled my judgement: this is called the Reply Churlish. If again, 'it was not well cut,' he would answer, I spake not true: this is called the Reproof Valiant. If again 'it was not well cut,' he would say, I lied: this is called the Countercheck Quarrelsome: and so to the Lie Circumstantial and the Lie Direct. 86

Jaq. And how oft did you say his beard was not well cut?

Touch. I durst go no further than the Lie Circumstantial, nor he durst not give me the Lie Direct; and so we measured swords and parted. 91

Jaq. Can you nominate in order now the degrees of the lie?

Touch. O sir, we quarrel in print, by the book; as you have books for good manners: I will name you the degrees. The first, the Retort Courteous; the second, the Quip Modest; the third, the Reply Churlish; the fourth, the Reproof Valiant; the fifth, the Countercheck Quarrelsome; the sixth, the Lie with Circumstance; the seventh, the Lie Direct. All these you may avoid but the Lie Direct; and you may avoid that too, with an If. I knew when seven justices could not take up a quarrel, but when the parties were met themselves, one of them thought but of an If, as, 'If you said so, then I said so;' and they shook hands and swore brothers. Your If is the only peace-maker; much virtue in If.

Jaq. Is not this a rare fellow, my lord? he's as good at any thing and yet a fool. 110

Duke S. He uses his folly like a stalking-horse and under the presentation of that he shoots his wit.

Enter HYMEN, ROSALIND, *and* CELIA.

Still Music.

Hym. Then is there mirth in heaven,
   When earthly things made even
      Atone together.
   Good duke, receive thy daughter:
   Hymen from heaven brought her,
      Yea, brought her hither,
   That thou mightst join her hand with his   120
   Whose heart within his bosom is.

Ros. [*To Duke*] To you I give myself, for I am yours.
[*To Orl.*] To you I give myself, for I am yours.

Duke S. If there be truth in sight, you are my
   daughter.

Orl. If there be truth in sight, you are my Rosalind.

Phe. If sight and shape be true,
Why then, my love adieu!

Ros. I'll have no father, if you be not he:
I'll have no husband, if you be not he:

Nor ne'er wed woman, if you be not she.   130

Hym. Peace, ho! I bar confusion:
   'Tis I must make conclusion
      Of these most strange events:
   Here's eight that must take hands
   To join in Hymen's bands,
      If truth holds true contents.
   You and you no cross shall part:
      You and you are heart in heart:
   You to his love must accord,
      Or have a woman to your lord: 140
   You and you are sure together,
      As the winter to foul weather.
   Whiles a wedlock-hymn we sing,
   Feed yourselves with questioning;
   That reason wonder may diminish,
   How thus we met, and these things finish.

SONG.

   Wedding is great Juno's crown:
      O blessed bond of board and bed!
   'Tis Hymen peoples every town;
      High wedlock then be honoured: 150
   Honour, high honour and renown,
      To Hymen, god of every town!

Duke S. O my dear niece, welcome thou art to me!
Even daughter, welcome, in no less degree.

Phe. I will not eat my word, now thou art mine;
Thy faith my fancy to thee doth combine.

Enter JAQUES DE BOYS.

Jaq. de B. Let me have audience for a word or two:
I am the second son of old Sir Rowland,
That bring these tidings to this fair assembly.
Duke Frederick, hearing how that every day   160
Men of great worth resorted to this forest,
Address'd a mighty power; which were on foot,
In his own conduct, purposely to take
His brother here and put him to the sword:
And to the skirts of this wild wood he came;
Where meeting with an old religious man,
After some question with him, was converted
Both from his enterprise and from the world,
His crown bequeathing to his banish'd brother,
And all their lands restored to them again   170
That were with him exiled. This to be true,
I do engage my life.

Duke S.   Welcome, young man;
Thou offer'st fairly to thy brothers' wedding:
To one his lands withheld, and to the other
A land itself at large, a potent dukedom.
First, in this forest let us do those ends
That here were well begun and well begot:
And after, every of this happy number

79. **Quip,** smart jest. 80. **disabled,** disparaged. 85. **Countercheck,** rebuff; metaphor from chess. 91. **measured swords,** i.e., as preliminary to a duel. 94-95. **quarrel . . . book.** Touchstone is travestying books on the general subject of honor and arms, which dealt with occasions and circumstances of the duel. 95. **in print,** in type, and with precision (New Cambridge). **books . . . manners,** books of etiquette. 107. **swore brothers,** allusion to the practice of swearing brotherhood, becoming *fratres jurati*. 111. **stalking-horse,** a real or artificial horse under cover of which the hunter approaches his game. 112. **presentation,** semblance. 113. *Stage Direction:* **Hymen,** god of marriage. *Still Music,* soft music. 116. **Atone,** are at one. 125. **sight.** Johnson wished to read *shape* to be in accord with Phebe's *sight and shape.* 136.

If . . . contents, if truth be true. This offers a rhyme for *events* above. The quality of the verse in Hymen's song is so poor as to make many editors suspect that the lines are not Shakespeare's. 139. **accord,** agree, consent. 140. **to,** for. 141. **sure,** closely united. 147. **Juno's.** Juno was queen of gods, presiding over wedlock. 150. **High,** solemn. 154. **Even daughter,** i.e., my daughter equally with Rosalind. 156. *Stage Direction:* **Jaques de Boys,** second son of Sir Rowland de Boys (mentioned in I, i, 6); F: *Enter Second Brother;* New Cambridge editors suggest that this character had a larger part in the original form of the play. 162. **Address'd,** prepared. 163. **In . . . conduct,** under his own command. 166. **religious man,** hermit. 167. **question,** conversation. 173. **offer'st fairly,** contributest handsomely. 174. **the**

That have endured shrewd days and nights with us
Shall share the good of our returned fortune, 180
According to the measure of their states.
Meantime, forget this new-fall'n dignity
And fall into our rustic revelry.
Play, music! And you, brides and bridegrooms all,
With measure heap'd in joy, to the measures fall.
    Jaq. Sir, by your patience. If I heard you rightly,
The duke hath put on a religious life
And thrown into neglect the pompous court?
    Jaq. de B. He hath.
    Jaq. To him will I: out of these convertites 190
There is much matter to be heard and learn'd.
[*To Duke*] You to your former honour I bequeath;
Your patience and your virtue well deserves it:
[*To Orl.*] You to a love that your true faith doth
        merit:
[*To Oli.*] You to your land and love and great allies:
[*To Sil.*] You to a long and well-deserved bed:
[*To Touch.*] And you to wrangling; for thy loving
        voyage
Is but for two months victuall'd. So, to your
        pleasures:
I am for other than for dancing measures.
    Duke S. Stay, Jaques, stay. 200
    Jaq. To see no pastime I: what you would have
I'll stay to know at your abandon'd cave. [*Exit.*
    Duke S. Proceed, proceed: we will begin these rites,
As we do trust they'll end, in true delights. [*A dance.*

EPILOGUE.

Ros. It is not the fashion to see the lady the epilogue;
but it is no more unhandsome than to see the lord the
prologue. If it be true that good wine needs no bush,
'tis true that a good play needs no epilogue; yet to
good wine they do use good bushes, and good plays
prove the better by the help of good epilogues. What
a case am I in then, that am neither a good epilogue
nor cannot insinuate with you in the behalf of a good
play! I am not furnished like a beggar, therefore to
beg will not become me: my way is to conjure you;
and I'll begin with the women. I charge you, O
women, for the love you bear to men, to like as much
of this play as please you: and I charge you, O men,
for the love you bear to women—as I perceive by
your simpering, none of you hates them—that between you and the women the play may please. If I
were a woman I would kiss as many of you as had
beards that pleased me, complexions that liked me
and breaths that I defied not: and, I am sure, as
many as have good beards or good faces or sweet
breaths will, for my kind offer, when I make curtsy,
bid me farewell. [*Exeunt.* 25

Twelfth Night;

OR,

What You Will

T*welfth Night* was published first in the folio of
1623, being then licensed in the Stationers' Register
as a play not previously entered. The text is a good
one and may have been set up from the author's
manuscript. The *Diary* of John Manningham, bar-
rister of the Middle Temple, records a performance
before his society on Candlemasday, 1602:

    Feb. 2—At our feast wee had a play called 'Twelue
Night, or What you Will,' much like the Commedy of
Errores, or Menechmi in Plautus, but most like and neere
to that in Italian called *Inganni.* A good practise in it to
make the Steward beleeve his Lady widdowe was in
love with him, by counterfeyting a letter as from his
Lady in generall termes, telling him what shee liked
best in him, and prescribing his gesture in smiling, his
apparaile, &c., and then when he came to practise
making him beleeue they tooke him to be mad.

Maria's statement (III, ii, 84-86) that Malvolio
"does smile his face into more lines than is in the new
map with the augmentation of the Indies," may indicate that the play was written after the appearance in
1599 of a map by Emerie Mollineaux, to which the
description would apply. There are other indications[1] that the play appeared between 1599 and 1602,
and most critics are disposed to date it in 1600 or
1601.

Metrical and other evidence agrees with this date
very well, particularly as the play seems to show a
growth in dramatic skill. The text of the play certainly shows two strata: a poetical one presenting the
formal plot, and another, perhaps later one, largely in
prose, having to do with the deception of Malvolio
and with other special features.

NATURE OF THE COMEDY

In *Twelfth Night* Shakespeare continues the vein of
Much Ado about Nothing and *As You Like It.* He tells a
foreign love story which carries with it a good deal of
its original atmosphere. This remoteness, as of the
forest of Arden, of the setting in Illyria, mellows the
lights of his picture. In its outlines it is of the Renaissance in general, but in its details it is often purely
English. Shakespeare has thus the poetical advantages
enjoyed by the writer of romance, and at the same
time the brisk freedom of the realist in the treatment
of the ordinary course of man's experience.

[1]C. H. Coote, New Shakespeare Society *Transactions,* 1877-1879,
pp. 88-100.

It is sometimes felt that *Twelfth Night* has nothing in it so brilliant, or so moving, as have *Much Ado* and *As You Like It*. Still it has about it an evenness of tone and a perfection of detail in the depiction of ordinary life which they lack, as well as a richness of Renaissance culture not found in either of them.

COMPLEXITY OF SOURCE

Twelfth Night seems to gather materials from a dozen different related works and to combine them into one of the richest treatments of a popular theme of Renaissance literature. Morton Luce[2] enumerates a number of these works and shows reasons for believing that at least from a majority of them Shakespeare derived material.

It might be thought that Shakespeare merely followed some old play now lost and had all of this material predigested for him. However, such was not his practice, at least in the writing of history plays and probably not in the writing of other kinds of drama. Even when it is known that he was following a particular dramatic source, he also consulted the chronicles, frequently more than one of them, and, as we shall see in *King Lear*, he did not blindly follow the old play on which it is based.

There does, however, exist in *Twelfth Night* a somewhat shadowy suggestion of a dramatic source. A German comedy called *Tugend und Liebestreit*, printed in 1677, has the same major theme as *Twelfth Night*. There was also acted in Germany by English players a play on the same subject in 1608, 1626, and later dates. W. Creizenach thinks that this lost play of the English *Komödianten* was the immediate source of *Tugend und Liebestreit* and suggests that there was thus an early English comedy on the same subject as *Twelfth Night*. If such a play existed, Shakespeare may have made use of it in composing his play.[3] But on the general question Luce quotes Mark Hunter: "Gosson says in his *Plays Confuted* (1581) that comedies in Latin, French, Italian, and Spanish had been thoroughly ransacked to furnish the playhouses in London."

INDEBTEDNESS TO FOREIGN WORKS

*I*t will be noticed that Manningham shows familiarity with an Italian comedy called *Inganni*, which title might be translated "The Frauds." Hunter was led by Manningham to investigate not less than two Italian comedies called *Gl'Inganni*, one by Nicolo Secchi acted in Milan in 1547 and published at Florence in 1562, and another by Curzio Gonzaga printed in Venice in 1592. Both plays treat the story of a sister and a brother mistaken for each other, the sister being disguised as a man. In the latter of these plays the sister takes the assumed name of "Cesare," just as Viola takes the name of "Cesario."

Hunter also discovered the far more important source comedy *Gl'Ingannati*, or "The Dupes," acted in 1531 and published at Venice in 1537 in a volume entitled *Il Sacrificio, Commedia de Gl'Intronati*. The last mentioned play was long popular. It was translated into French as *Les Abusez* by Charles Estienne (Lyon, 1543), and into Latin under the name of *Lælia*,[4] for performance by students at Cambridge in 1595.

The *Gl'Inganni* plays are also probably indebted to it, as well as to at least one Spanish play. Bandello tells the story of the indistinguishable brother and sister in his *Novelle* (1554), and Belleforest after him in 1570 in *Histoires Tragiques*. Belleforest is the basis of Barnabe Riche's *Apolonius and Silla*, which has long been regarded as one of Shakespeare's principal sources; but one should not dispense with Riche's originals. Luce points out a number of striking parallels to Bandello and Belleforest and even to a prose version in Giraldi Cinthio's *Hecatommithi* (1565), from which Shakespeare was later to draw the plot of *Othello*.

In the last mentioned is introduced the feature of shipwreck as the means of the separation of brother and sister. That Barnabe Riche was actually used, either by Shakespeare or by the author of a lost play, seems confirmed by W. A. Neilson's discovery[5] that in another of Riche's stories in the same collection (*Riche, his Farwell to the Militarie Profession*, 1581), *Two Brethren and their Wives*, occurs a scene suggestive of Malvolio's imprisonment, in which a shrewish wife is cured of her humor by having it pretended that she is insane and by reciting the *Miserere* to banish the evil spirit.

The most important of any of these sources is the basal story in *Gl'Ingannati*. Fabrizio, son of a merchant, Virginio, takes his sister Lelia to Modena. Gherardo, a rich old man, wishes to marry her. She loves Flaminio, who has deserted her for Isabella, daughter of Gherardo. Lelia assumes male attire and becomes a page in the service of her fickle lover. She is employed by him to court Isabella, who falls in love with her as Olivia falls in love with Cesario. Lelia tricks her master by getting Isabella to reject him. The early attachment between Lelia and Flaminio is not retained by Shakespeare, unless one might find it in Viola's particular interest in Orsino (I, ii, 28-29). Viola's service to her master, in contrast to that of Lelia, is loyal. Fabrizio arrives in Modena, encounters Virginio and Gherardo, who have become aware of Lelia's behavior, is mistaken for Lelia, and, being thought insane because of his strange answers, is thrown into prison. The prison turns out to be Isabella's chamber, and Fabrizio and Isabella are, like Sebastian and Olivia, quickly betrothed. The solution is like that of *Twelfth Night*, Gherardo, like

[2]*Twelfth Night*, Arden Shakespeare (Methuen, 1906), Appendix I.
[3]W. Creizenach, *Schauspiele der englischen Komödianten* (1889), p. 57.

[4]G. B. Churchill and Wolfgang Keller, "Die lateinschen Universitätsdramen Englands," *Shakespeare Jahrbuch*, XXXIV, 221-325; F. S. Boas, *University Drama in the Tudor Age* (Oxford, 1914), pp. 289-297.
[5]*Atlantic Monthly*, LXXXIX, 715.

Sir Andrew Aguecheek, being the only wooer unprovided with a partner. Luce points out that in the Induction to *Il Sacrificio* is found the name *Malevolti* (evil-faced), which he thinks may have suggested the name Aguecheek; and in the same play is a character with the name *Fabio*, which may have suggested *Fabian*.

Among the minor characters in *Gl'Ingannati* are suggestions for Malvolio, Sir Toby, Feste, and Maria. In a phrase in the prologue, *La Notte di Beffania* (or Epiphany), is a suggestion for the name "Twelfth Night." We have here the household of the Lady Olivia *in posse* at least. No suggestion has been made for the source of the counterfeit letter by which Malvolio is deceived, and as a suggestion for Malvolio himself we have only the presence in the Italian play of a prig and a gull.[6] The name "Malvolio" means "evil desire, or ambition," and he is a humor character whose peculiarity, or "humor," it is to attempt to climb impertinently above his own station.

THE MATERIAL OF THE PLAY

We have in this play a study of an Elizabethan household among the nobility, servants as well as masters; its conversation, its amusements, its gossip, and its atmosphere; the hardy sea captain Antonio on the street; priests, officers, and attendants; the customs of marriage, courtship, and betrothal; drinking, jesting, and dueling. All this is English and well-nigh perfect; but there is also a large body of the material of Renaissance comedy, liable to be overlooked, which lies back of the main theme. The well-worked Italian story had been popular because it presented certain aspects of the popular theme of love. Shakespeare employed that theme and with

it we know not how much of the courtly thought about love in which it was wont to be expressed. Shakespeare, who had already written Renaissance love comedies like *The Two Gentlemen of Verona* and *The Merchant of Venice*, who was a sonneteer and a writer of amatory poetry, was entirely competent without aid of an older play to enrich the theme.

One can discover in *Twelfth Night*, as in *The Merchant of Venice*, Plato's threefold division of love, as of the senses, the intellect, and the understanding. In this case, the lowest kind of love would be exemplified in the silly and impossible courtship of Sir Andrew Aguecheek and the impertinent aspirations of Malvolio; the intellectual sort, in the sentimental self-indulgence of Orsino; and the genuine or honest love, in the self-sacrificing devotion of Viola, and to a less degree in the impulsive passions of Olivia and Sebastian. Many of the questions of love which engaged the courtly circles of Italy, France, and England[7] make their appearance in this play, forming a sort of substance for the dialogue. Especially is this true in the part of Orsino; as, for example, that music is the food of love (I, i, 1-8; II, iv, 1-14); that love is a torment to the lover (I, i, 9-23; I, iv, 26; II, iv, 15-16, etc.); that the man should be older than the woman he loves (II, iv, 29-32); that man loves more deeply than woman (II, iv, 94-106) and the reverse (II, iv, 33-36; II, iv, 119-121); that concealed love meets with no fruition (II, iv, 113-118); that scorn breeds love (III, i, 156-160); that love enters through the eye (I, v, 317); that true love is jealous (IV, iii, 27); and many others.

CHARACTERS

That *Twelfth Night* is a comedy of true love to even a greater degree than *As You Like It* no one has called in question. Critics have found in the more difficult part of Viola a sweetness entirely comparable to that of Rosalind. Usually on the stage she is made too plaintive, and it is only now and then that an actress has been able to retain the brightness, courage, and wit of the figure, which illuminate rather than conceal her wistfulness.

The singing clown Feste is also comparable to Touchstone. He is one of Shakespeare's best pictures of clownage, and the charter of freedom stated by Viola (III, i, 67-75) seems to express the conception of the possibilities of the clown's part which Shakespeare had come to hold. Feste has indeed wit "enough to play the fool." From his manipulation comes a good deal of the action of the play.

Malvolio, however, offers the most perplexing problem of interpretation to be found in the play. To see Sir Henry Irving and other tragic actors leave the stage vowing vengeance "on the whole pack

[6]Alwin Thaler has suggested (*Shakespeare Association Bulletin*, VII, 57-71) that Shakespeare may have found an original of Malvolio in one William Ffarington, steward to the earl of Derby, patron of Shakespeare's company.

[7]T. F. Crane, *Italian Social Customs of the Sixteenth Century* (New Haven, 1920), chs. XIII, VIII, XI, *et passim*; Baskervill, "Bassanio as an Ideal Lover," in *The Manly Anniversary Studies* (1923), pp. 90-103.

of you" was to have the impression of the whole comedy spoiled and to feel that a dangerous madman had been turned loose on the community. This certainly cannot have been Shakespeare's intention with reference to the part. Leonard Digges refers to Malvolio as a "cross-gartered gull," which no doubt expresses the Elizabethan conception. The fact that he is a responsible servant, well thought of by his mistress, who would not have had him miscarry for the half of her dowry and later thinks him notoriously abused, has caused him to be regarded as a meritorious man cruelly humiliated by a group of those who envied him. The virtues no doubt are there, and they are acknowledged; but actors have been disposed to forget that Malvolio aspired to his mistress' hand, which, far from being a natural and admirable ambition, was in the social thinking of the time a base fault. They also forget Olivia's own plain statement of what she thinks of his disposition (I, v, 97-104). In other words, Malvolio is to be regarded as getting pretty nearly what he deserves, especially when we are assured at the end of the play that he is to be both the plaintiff and the judge in his own cause.

STAGE HISTORY

T*welfth Night* was evidently popular in its own day if one may judge by recorded performances at court. It seems to have escaped the rehandlings of the Restoration, and, to do the critics and play adapters of that period justice, the play has fewer of the traditional Shakespearean faults, such as excessive sentiment and romance and the violation of the dramatic unities, than almost any other play in the canon.

There is no evidence of popularity, however, until its revival at Drury Lane in 1741, with Macklin as Malvolio and Mrs. Pritchard as Viola. Since that time *Twelfth Night* has appeared on the stage with a fair degree of frequency. Like *As You Like It* it is best acted when there is an actress adequate for the chief woman's part. Charles Lamb praised the "plaintive" Viola of Mrs. Jordan. Ellen Terry, Ada Rehan, Julia Marlowe, and Helen Hayes have played the part with conspicuous success. Alfred Hart suggests that the serious turn given to the part of Malvolio has been due in some measure to the fact that great tragic actors, like John Philip Kemble and Sir Henry Irving, have so often played the part.

For some reason the low comedy parts of *Twelfth Night* are almost never well done. Recent studies of the text, most recently those of J. Dover Wilson, bring out the fact that the scenes in the Lady Olivia's house and garden are full of witty allusions of all sorts. If so, they must be spoken intelligibly in order to be understood. In most performances of *Twelfth Night* these scenes are unintelligible and as grotesque as comic strips. It is said that they were not so handled in the famous production by Harley Granville-Barker at the Savoy Theater in London in 1912.

Twelfth Night;

OR,

What You Will

DRAMATIS PERSONAE

ORSINO, Duke of Illyria.
SEBASTIAN, brother to Viola.
ANTONIO, a sea captain, friend to Sebastian.
A Sea Captain, friend to Viola.
VALENTINE,
CURIO, } gentlemen attending on the Duke.
SIR TOBY BELCH, uncle to Olivia.
SIR ANDREW AGUECHEEK.
MALVOLIO, steward to Olivia.
FABIAN,
FESTE, a Clown, } servants to Olivia.

OLIVIA.
VIOLA.
MARIA, Olivia's woman.

Lords, Priests, Sailors, Officers, Musicians, and other Attendants.

SCENE: *A city in Illyria, and the sea-coast near it.*

ACT I.

SCENE I. *The* DUKE'S *palace.*

Enter DUKE, CURIO, *and other* Lords; Musicians *attending.*

Duke. If music be the food of love, play on;
Give me excess of it, that, surfeiting,
The appetite may sicken, and so die.
That strain again! it had a dying fall:
O, it came o'er my ear like the sweet sound,
That breathes upon a bank of violets,
Stealing and giving odour! Enough; no more:
'Tis not so sweet now as it was before.
O spirit of love! how quick and fresh art thou,
That, notwithstanding thy capacity   10
Receiveth as the sea, nought enters there,
Of what validity and pitch soe'er,
But falls into abatement and low price,
Even in a minute: so full of shapes is fancy
That it alone is high fantastical.
    Cur. Will you go hunt, my lord?
    Duke.   What, Curio?
    Cur. The hart.
    Duke. Why, so I do, the noblest that I have:
O, when mine eyes did see Olivia first,
Methought she purged the air of pestilence!   20
That instant was I turn'd into a hart;
And my desires, like fell and cruel hounds,
E'er since pursue me.

Enter VALENTINE.

How now! what news from her?

Val. So please my lord, I might not be admitted;
But from her handmaid do return this answer:
The element itself, till seven years' heat,
Shall not behold her face at ample view;
But, like a cloistress, she will veiled walk
And water once a day her chamber round
With eye-offending brine: all this to season   30
A brother's dead love, which she would keep fresh
And lasting in her sad remembrance.

Duke. O, she that hath a heart of that fine frame
To pay this debt of love but to a brother,
How will she love, when the rich golden shaft
Hath kill'd the flock of all affections else
That live in her; when liver, brain and heart,
These sovereign thrones, are all supplied, and fill'd
Her sweet perfections with one self king!
Away before me to sweet beds of flowers: 40
Love-thoughts lie rich when canopied with bowers.
                                        [*Exeunt.*

SCENE II. *The sea-coast.*

Enter VIOLA, *a* Captain, *and* Sailors.

Vio. What country, friends, is this?
Cap. This is Illyria, lady.
Vio. And what should I do in Illyria?
My brother he is in Elysium.
Perchance he is not drown'd: what think you,
    sailors?
Cap. It is perchance that you yourself were saved.
Vio. O my poor brother! and so perchance may he
    be.
Cap. True, madam: and, to comfort you with
    chance,
Assure yourself, after our ship did split,
When you and those poor number saved with you   10
Hung on our driving boat, I saw your brother,
Most provident in peril, bind himself,
Courage and hope both teaching him the practice,
To a strong mast that lived upon the sea;
Where, like Arion on the dolphin's back,
I saw him hold acquaintance with the waves
So long as I could see.
Vio. For saying so, there's gold:
Mine own escape unfoldeth to my hope,
Whereto thy speech serves for authority,   20
The like of him. Know'st thou this country?
Cap. Ay, madam, well; for I was bred and born
Not three hours' travel from this very place.
Vio. Who governs here?
Cap. A noble duke, in nature as in name.

Vio. What is his name?
Cap. Orsino.
Vio. Orsino! I have heard my father name him:
He was a bachelor then.
Cap. And so is now, or was so very late;   30
For but a month ago I went from hence,
And then 'twas fresh in murmur,—as, you know,
What great ones do the less will prattle of,—
That he did seek the love of fair Olivia.
Vio. What's she?
Cap. A virtuous maid, the daughter of a count
That died some twelvemonth since, then leaving her
In the protection of his son, her brother,
Who shortly also died: for whose dear love,
They say, she hath abjured the company   40
And sight of men.
Vio.   O that I served that lady
And might not be delivered to the world,
Till I had made mine own occasion mellow,
What my estate is!
Cap.   That were hard to compass;
Because she will admit no kind of suit,
No, not the duke's.
Vio. There is a fair behaviour in thee, captain;
And though that nature with a beauteous wall
Doth oft close in pollution, yet of thee
I will believe thou hast a mind that suits   50
With this thy fair and outward character.
I prithee, and I'll pay thee bounteously,
Conceal me what I am, and be my aid
For such disguise as haply shall become
The form of my intent. I'll serve this duke:
Thou shalt present me as an eunuch to him:
It may be worth thy pains; for I can sing
And speak to him in many sorts of music
That will allow me very worth his service.
What else may hap to time I will commit;   60
Only shape thou thy silence to my wit.
Cap. Be you his eunuch, and your mute I'll be:
When my tongue blabs, then let mine eyes not see.
Vio. I thank thee: lead me on.   [*Exeunt.*

SCENE III. OLIVIA'S *house.*

Enter SIR TOBY BELCH *and* MARIA.

Sir To. What a plague means my niece, to take the
death of her brother thus? I am sure care's an enemy
to life.
Mar. By my troth, Sir Toby, you must come in
earlier o' nights: your cousin, my lady, takes great
exceptions to your ill hours.
Sir To. Why, let her except, before excepted.

TITLE. **Twelfth Night,** the feast of the Epiphany, or the visit of the
Magi. It occurred on the twelfth night after Christmas. The association of this name with "What You Will" lends some plausibility to
the suggestion that the title came from the Prologue to *Gl' Ingannati*,
an Italian comedy on a similar theme, which states that the story
came from the brains of its authors "just as you draw your lots on
Twelfth Night."
ACT I. SCENE I. 1-15. **If . . . fantastical.** These opening lines reflect
Orsino's sentimentality. He is swept away by a superficial passion
which he parades but does not deeply feel. 1. **food of love.** See
Antony and Cleopatra, II, v, 1-2. 4. **fall,** cadence. 12. **validity,** value.
18. **noblest . . . have,** i.e., his noblest part, his heart. 23. **pursue me,**
reference to the story in Ovid of Actaeon, who was transformed into
a hart and killed by his own hounds. 30. **season,** keep fresh. 35.
golden shaft, i.e., of Cupid. 37. **liver, brain and heart.** In medieval
and Elizabethan psychology these organs were the seats of the passions.
39. **self,** single.

SCENE II. 2. **Illyria,** a country along the eastern shore of the
Adriatic. 4. **Elysium,** abode of the blessed dead. 8. **chance,** i.e., what
chance may bring about. 11. **driving,** drifting. 14. **lived,** kept
afloat. 15. **Arion,** a Greek poet who, when thrown into the sea by
sailors, so charmed the dolphins with his lyre that they saved him. This
was a favorite subject for pageants and paintings. 21. **like of him,** i.e.,
he, too, may be saved. 29. **bachelor.** Viola manifests a slight, possibly
feminine, interest in Orsino. 32. **murmur,** gossip. 42. **delivered,**
discovered, made known. 43. **mellow,** ready or convenient (to be made
known). 47. **behaviour.** The word means "appearance" as well as
"behavior." 51. **character,** face or features as indicating moral
qualities; see glossary. 55. **form of my intent,** nature of my purpose,
with suggestion of outward appearance in *form.* 59. **allow me,** cause
me to be acknowledged. 61. **wit,** plan, invention.
SCENE III. 7. **except, before excepted,** legal phrase, *exceptis ex-
cipiendis*, "with the exceptions before named." Sir Toby means that
enough exceptions to his behavior have already been taken.

Mar. Ay, but you must confine yourself within the modest limits of order. 9

Sir To. Confine! I'll confine myself no finer than I am: these clothes are good enough to drink in; and so be these boots too: an they be not, let them hang themselves in their own straps.

Mar. That quaffing and drinking will undo you: I heard my lady talk of it yesterday; and of a foolish knight that you brought in one night here to be her wooer.

Sir To. Who, Sir Andrew Aguecheek?

Mar. Ay, he.

Sir To. He's as tall a man as any's in Illyria.

Mar. What's that to the purpose? 21

Sir To. Why, he has three thousand ducats a year.

Mar. Ay, but he'll have but a year in all these ducats: he's a very fool and a prodigal.

Sir To. Fie, that you'll say so! he plays o' the viol-de-gamboys, and speaks three or four languages word for word without book, and hath all the good gifts of nature. 29

Mar. He hath indeed, almost natural: for besides that he's a fool, he's a great quarreller; and but that he hath the gift of a coward to allay the gust he hath in quarrelling, 'tis thought among the prudent he would quickly have the gift of a grave.

Sir To. By this hand, they are scoundrels and substractors that say so of him. Who are they?

Mar. They that add, moreover, he's drunk nightly in your company. 39

Sir To. With drinking healths to my niece: I'll drink to her as long as there is a passage in my throat and drink in Illyria: he's a coward and a coystrill that will not drink to my niece till his brains turn o' the toe like a parish-top. What, wench! Castiliano vulgo! for here comes Sir Andrew Agueface.

Enter SIR ANDREW AGUECHEEK.

Sir And. Sir Toby Belch! how now, Sir Toby Belch!

Sir To. Sweet Sir Andrew!

Sir And. Bless you, fair shrew. 50

Mar. And you too, sir.

Sir To. Accost, Sir Andrew, accost.

Sir And. What's that?

Sir To. My niece's chambermaid.

Sir And. Good Mistress Accost, I desire better acquaintance.

Mar. My name is Mary, sir.

Sir And. Good Mistress Mary Accost,—

Sir To. You mistake, knight: 'accost' is front her, board her, woo her, assail her. 60

Sir And. By my troth, I would not undertake her in this company. Is that the meaning of 'accost'?

Mar. Fare you well, gentlemen.

Sir To. An thou let part so, Sir Andrew, would thou mightst never draw sword again.

Sir And. An you part so, mistress, I would I might never draw sword again. Fair lady, do you think you have fools in hand?

Mar. Sir, I have not you by the hand. 70

Sir And. Marry, but you shall have; and here's my hand.

Mar. Now, sir, 'thought is free:' I pray you, bring your hand to the buttery-bar and let it drink.

Sir And. Wherefore, sweet-heart? what's your metaphor?

Mar. It's dry, sir.

Sir And. Why, I think so: I am not such an ass but I can keep my hand dry. But what's your jest? 80

Mar. A dry jest, sir.

Sir And. Are you full of them?

Mar. Ay, sir, I have them at my fingers' ends: marry, now I let go your hand, I am barren. [*Exit.*

Sir To. O knight, thou lackest a cup of canary: when did I see thee so put down?

Sir And. Never in your life, I think; unless you see canary put me down. Methinks sometimes I have no more wit than a Christian or an ordinary man has: but I am a great eater of beef and I believe that does harm to my wit. 91

Sir To. No question.

Sir And. An I thought that, I 'ld forswear it. I'll ride home to-morrow, Sir Toby.

Sir To. Pourquoi, my dear knight?

Sir And. What is 'pourquoi'? do or not do? I would I had bestowed that time in the tongues that I have in fencing, dancing and bear-baiting: O, had I but followed the arts!

Sir To. Then hadst thou had an excellent head of hair. 101

Sir And. Why, would that have mended my hair?

Sir To. Past question; for thou seest it will not curl by nature.

Sir And. But it becomes me well enough, does 't not?

Sir To. Excellent; it hangs like flax on a distaff; and I hope to see a housewife take thee between her legs and spin it off. 110

Sir And. Faith, I'll home to-morrow, Sir Toby: your niece will not be seen; or if she be, it's four to one she'll none of me: the count himself here hard by woos her.

Sir To. She'll none o' the count: she'll not match above her degree, neither in estate, years, nor wit; I have heard her swear 't. Tut, there's life in 't, man.

Sir And. I'll stay a month longer. I am a fellow o' the strangest mind i' the world; I delight in masques and revels sometimes altogether. 121

Sir To. Art thou good at these kickshawses, knight?

Sir And. As any man in Illyria, whatsoever he be, under the degree of my betters; and yet I will not compare with an old man.

Sir To. What is thy excellence in a galliard, knight?

---

10. **confine myself,** dress myself. 27. **viol-de-gamboys,** bass viol. 28. **without book,** by heart. Sir Andrew's complete ignorance of languages and lack of all accomplishments is one of the sources of Sir Toby's fun at his expense. 30. **natural,** with pun on the sense "born idiot." 33. **allay the gust,** moderate the pleasure. 37. **substractors,** for "detractors." 43. **coystrill,** knave, base fellow. 45. **parish-top,** a large top provided by the parish to be spun by whipping, apparently for exercise in cold weather. **Castiliano vulgo,** literally, vulgar Spaniard; possibly a slang phrase, or nonsense. 52. **Accost,** make up to. 54. **chambermaid,** lady's maid. 73. **'thought is free,'** reply to *do you think,* above. 74-75. **bring . . . drink,** said to be a proverbial phrase meaning to ask at once for a kiss and a present (Kenrick, quoted by Luce). 77. **dry,**

i.e., a sign of age and debility. 81. **dry,** dull. 83. **fingers' ends.** Sir Andrew is holding her by the hand. 86. **canary,** sack, a wine from the Canary Islands. 90. **beef,** traditional cause of dull wits. The English were frequently twitted on account of the coarseness and quantity of their food and the dullness of their wit. 95. **Pourquoi,** why. 98. **tongues,** languages and "tongs" (used for curling hair). 99. **arts.** Cf. *nature,* below. 122. **kickshawses,** corruption of the French words *quelque chose;* delicacies, fancy dishes. 126. **old man,** a puzzling reference. Furness suggests that Sir Andrew wishes to express deference to age. 128. **galliard,** lively dance in triple time. 129. **cut a caper.** Sir Andrew uses the phrase in the ordinary sense. Sir Toby makes a pun referring to *caper* sauce. 131. **back-trick,** some figure in the

Sir And. Faith, I can cut a caper.

Sir To. And I can cut the mutton to 't. 130

Sir And. And I think I have the back-trick simply as strong as any man in Illyria.

Sir To. Wherefore are these things hid? wherefore have these gifts a curtain before 'em? are they like to take dust, like Mistress Mall's picture? why dost thou not go to church in a galliard and come home in a coranto? My very walk should be a jig; I would not so much as make water but in a sink-a-pace. What dost thou mean? Is it a world to hide virtues in? I did think, by the excellent constitution of thy leg, it was formed under the star of a galliard.

Sir And. Ay, 'tis strong, and it does indifferent well in a flame-coloured stock. Shall we set about some revels?

Sir To. What shall we do else? were we not born under Taurus? 147

Sir And. Taurus! That 's sides and heart.

Sir To. No, sir; it is legs and thighs. Let me see thee caper: ha! higher: ha, ha! excellent! [*Exeunt.*

SCENE IV. *The* DUKE's *palace.*

Enter VALENTINE, *and* VIOLA *in man's attire.*

Val. If the duke continue these favours towards you, Cesario, you are like to be much advanced: he hath known you but three days, and already you are no stranger.

Vio. You either fear his humour or my negligence, that you call in question the continuance of his love: is he inconstant, sir, in his favours?

Val. No, believe me.

Vio. I thank you. Here comes the count.

Enter DUKE, CURIO, *and* Attendants.

Duke. Who saw Cesario, ho? 10

Vio. On your attendance, my lord; here.

Duke. Stand you a while aloof. Cesario,
Thou know'st no less but all; I have unclasp'd
To thee the book even of my secret soul:
Therefore, good youth, address thy gait unto her;
Be not denied access, stand at her doors,
And tell them, there thy fixed foot shall grow
Till thou have audience.

Vio.   Sure, my noble lord,
If she be so abandon'd to her sorrow
As it is spoke, she never will admit me. 20

Duke. Be clamorous and leap all civil bounds
Rather than make unprofited return.

Vio. Say I do speak with her, my lord, what then?

Duke. O, then unfold the passion of my love,
Surprise her with discourse of my dear faith:
It shall become thee well to act my woes;

She will attend it better in thy youth
Than in a nuncio's of more grave aspect.

Vio. I think not so, my lord.

Duke.   Dear lad, believe it;
For they shall yet belie thy happy years, 30
That say thou art a man: Diana's lip
Is not more smooth and rubious; thy small pipe
Is as the maiden's organ, shrill and sound,
And all is semblative a woman's part.
I know thy constellation is right apt
For this affair. Some four or five attend him;
All, if you will; for I myself am best
When least in company. Prosper well in this,
And thou shalt live as freely as thy lord,
To call his fortunes thine.

Vio.   I'll do my best 40
To woo your lady: [*Aside*] yet, a barful strife!
Whoe'er I woo, myself would be his wife.   [*Exeunt.*

SCENE V. OLIVIA's *house.*

Enter MARIA *and* CLOWN.

Mar. Nay, either tell me where thou hast been, or I will not open my lips so wide as a bristle may enter in way of thy excuse: my lady will hang thee for thy absence.

Clo. Let her hang me: he that is well hanged in this world needs to fear no colours.

Mar. Make that good.

Clo. He shall see none to fear.

Mar. A good lenten answer: I can tell thee where that saying was born, of 'I fear no colours.' 10

Clo. Where, good Mistress Mary?

Mar. In the wars; and that may you be bold to say in your foolery.

Clo. Well, God give them wisdom that have it; and those that are fools, let them use their talents.

Mar. Yet you will be hanged for being so long absent; or to be turned away, is not that as good as a hanging to you? 19

Clo. Many a good hanging prevents a bad marriage; and, for turning away, let summer bear it out.

Mar. You are resolute, then?

Clo. Not so, neither; but I am resolved on two points.

Mar. That if one break, the other will hold; or, if both break, your gaskins fall.

Clo. Apt, in good faith; very apt. Well, go thy way; if Sir Toby would leave drinking, thou wert as witty a piece of Eve's flesh as any in Illyria. 31

Mar. Peace, you rogue, no more o' that. Here comes my lady: make your excuse wisely, you were best. [*Exit.*

Clo. Wit, an 't be thy will, put me into good fooling! Those wits, that think they have thee, do very oft

---

galliard; apparently, dancing backward. 135. **Mistress Mall's picture.** It has been suggested (1) that this refers to Moll Cutpurse or some other notorious female criminal; (2) that it is Maria's picture; (3) that it is a picture of no particular person. 138. **coranto,** lively dance. 140. **sink-a-pace,** French, *cinque-pace,* a dance. 143. **under the star,** i.e., a star favorable to dancing. Men's destinies and characters were thought to be controlled by the stars. 145. **flame-coloured,** so Rowe; F: *dam'd colour'd;* Collier: *dun-coloured.* **stock,** stocking. 147, 148. **Taurus,** zodiacal sign. Sir Andrew is mistaken, since Leo governed *sides and hearts* in medical astrology.

SCENE IV. 12. **you,** addressed to the attendants. 15. **address thy gait,** go. 21. **civil bounds,** bounds of civility. 28. **nuncio's,** mes-

senger's. 30. **yet,** i.e., for a long time to come. 34. **semblative,** resembling, like. 41-42. **yet . . . wife.** Such asides as this have an important part in Shakespeare's dramatic exposition, since there are people in the audience who cannot understand by process of inference what a situation is; they need to be told. 41. **barful,** full of impediments.

SCENE V. *Stage Direction:* **Clown,** the technical word for those who played comic parts in the theater. *Fool* is more commonly used in the text to denote the jester or domestic fool. 6. **fear no colours,** fear no enemies, with pun on "colors" and "collars" (halters). 9. **lenten,** meager, scanty (like lenten fare). 27. **gaskins,** hose, breeches, held up by laces or *points;* hence Maria's quibble. 29. **Sir Toby.** The Clown hints at a match between Maria and Sir Toby.

prove fools; and I, that am sure I lack thee, may pass for a wise man: for what says Quinapalus? 'Better a witty fool than a foolish wit.' 40

Enter Lady OLIVIA *with* MALVOLIO.

God bless thee, lady!

Oli. Take the fool away.

Clo. Do you not hear, fellows? Take away the lady.

Oli. Go to, you 're a dry fool; I 'll no more of you: besides, you grow dishonest. 46

Clo. Two faults, madonna, that drink and good counsel will amend: for give the dry fool drink, then is the fool not dry: bid the dishonest man mend himself; if he mend, he is no longer dishonest; if he cannot let the botcher mend him. Any thing that 's mended is but patched: virtue that transgresses is but patched with sin; and sin that amends is but patched with virtue. If that this simple syllogism will serve, so; if it will not, what remedy? As there is no true cuckold but calamity, so beauty 's a flower. The lady bade take away the fool; therefore, I say again, take her away.

Oli. Sir, I bade them take away you. 60

Clo. Misprision in the highest degree! Lady, cucullus non facit monachum; that 's as much to say as I wear not motley in my brain. Good madonna, give me leave to prove you a fool.

Oli. Can you do it?

Clo. Dexteriously, good madonna.

Oli. Make your proof.

Clo. I must catechize you for it, madonna: good my mouse of virtue, answer me.

Oli. Well, sir, for want of other idleness, I 'll bide your proof. 71

Clo. Good madonna, why mournest thou?

Oli. Good fool, for my brother's death.

Clo. I think his soul is in hell, madonna.

Oli. I know his soul is in heaven, fool.

Clo. The more fool, madonna, to mourn for your brother's soul being in heaven. Take away the fool, gentlemen.

Oli. What think you of this fool, Malvolio? doth he not mend? 80

Mal. Yes, and shall do till the pangs of death shake him: infirmity, that decays the wise, doth ever make the better fool.

Clo. God send you, sir, a speedy infirmity, for the better increasing your folly! Sir Toby will be sworn that I am no fox; but he will not pass his word for two pence that you are no fool.

Oli. How say you to that, Malvolio? 88

Mal. I marvel your ladyship takes delight in such a barren rascal: I saw him put down the other day with an ordinary fool that has no more brain than a stone. Look you now, he 's out of his guard already; unless you laugh and minister occasion to him, he is gagged. I protest, I take these wise men, that crow so at these set kind of fools, no better than the fools' zanies. 96

Oli. O, you are sick of self-love, Malvolio, and taste with a distempered appetite. To be generous, guiltless and of free disposition, is to take those things for bird-bolts that you deem cannon-bullets: there is no slander in an allowed fool, though he do nothing but rail; nor no railing in a known discreet man, though he do nothing but reprove. 104

Clo. Now Mercury endue thee with leasing, for thou speakest well of fools!

Re-enter MARIA.

Mar. Madam, there is at the gate a young gentleman much desires to speak with you.

Oli. From the Count Orsino, is it?

Mar. I know not, madam: 'tis a fair young man, and well attended. 111

Oli. Who of my people hold him in delay?

Mar. Sir Toby, madam, your kinsman.

Oli. Fetch him off, I pray you; he speaks nothing but madman: fie on him! [*Exit Maria.*] Go you, Malvolio: if it be a suit from the count, I am sick, or not at home; what you will, to dismiss it. [*Exit Malvolio.*] Now you see, sir, how your fooling grows old, and people dislike it. 119

Clo. Thou hast spoke for us, madonna, as if thy eldest son should be a fool; whose skull Jove cram with brains! for,—here he comes,—one of thy kin has a most weak pia mater.

Enter SIR TOBY.

Oli. By mine honour, half drunk. What is he at the gate, cousin?

Sir To. A gentleman.

Oli. A gentleman! what gentleman?

Sir To. 'Tis a gentleman here—a plague o' these pickle-herring! How now, sot!

Clo. Good Sir Toby. 130

Oli. Cousin, cousin, how have you come so early by this lethargy?

Sir To. Lechery! I defy lechery. There 's one at the gate.

Oli. Ay, marry, what is he?

Sir To. Let him be the devil, an he will, I care not: give me faith, say I. Well, it 's all one. [*Exit.*

Oli. What 's a drunken man like, fool?

Clo. Like a drowned man, a fool and a mad man: one draught above heat makes him a fool; the second mads him; and a third drowns him. 141

Oli. Go thou and seek the crowner, and let him sit o' my coz; for he 's in the third degree of drink, he 's drowned: go, look after him.

Clo. He is but mad yet, madonna; and the fool shall look to the madman. [*Exit.*

Re-enter MALVOLIO.

Mal. Madam, yond young fellow swears he will speak with you. I told him you were sick; he takes on him to understand so much, and therefore comes to

39. **Quinapalus,** apparently an invented authority. 45. **dry,** dull. 46. **dishonest,** probably, ill-behaved. 52. **botcher,** mender of old clothes and shoes. 61. **Misprision,** mistake, misunderstanding, with suggestion of the legal use meaning "contempt," the arrest or imprisonment of the wrong person. 62. **cucullus . . . monachum,** the cowl does not make the monk. 63. **motley,** the many-colored garment of jesters. 69. **mouse of virtue,** term of endearment. 70. **idleness,** pastime. This and Olivia's patience at the Clown's gibe about her mourning indicate that she grows weary of her self-imposed seclusion. 91. **ordinary fool,** probably a fool from the street not regularly attached to a household.

96. **zanies,** fools' subordinates or imitators. 97. **sick of self-love.** This shows Olivia's recognition of Malvolio's self-conceit. 100. **bird-bolts,** blunt arrows for shooting small birds. 102. **allowed,** licensed. 105. **Mercury,** god of lying and thievery. **leasing,** lying. 115. **madman,** i.e., the words of madness. 123. **pia mater,** soft inner lining of the brain. 128. **here.** Sir Toby hiccoughs at this point and tries to conceal his condition. 137. **give me faith.** Sir Toby relies on faith, not works. 140. **above heat,** above the point at which the body grows warm with drinking. 142. **crowner,** coroner. 157. **sheriff's post,** post before the sheriff's door on which proclamations and notices were fixed. 165-171.

speak with you. I told him you were asleep; he seems to have a foreknowledge of that too, and therefore comes to speak with you. What is to be said to him, lady? he 's fortified against any denial.

Oli. Tell him he shall not speak with me.

Mal. Has been told so; and he says, he'll stand at your door like a sheriff's post, and be the supporter to a bench, but he'll speak with you.

Oli. What kind o' man is he?

Mal. Why, of mankind.   160

Oli. What manner of man?

Mal. Of very ill manner; he'll speak with you, will you or no.

Oli. Of what personage and years is he?

Mal. Not yet old enough for a man, nor young enough for a boy; as a squash is before 'tis a peascod, or a codling when 'tis almost an apple: 'tis with him in standing water, between boy and man. He is very well-favoured and he speaks very shrewishly; one would think his mother's milk were scarce out of him.

Oli. Let him approach: call in my gentlewoman. 173

Mal. Gentlewoman, my lady calls.   [*Exit.*

Re-enter MARIA.

Oli. Give me my veil: come, throw it o'er my face. We'll once more hear Orsino's embassy.

Enter VIOLA, *and* Attendants.

Vio. The honourable lady of the house, which is she?

Oli. Speak to me; I shall answer for her. Your will?

Vio. Most radiant, exquisite and unmatchable beauty,—I pray you, tell me if this be the lady of the house, for I never saw her: I would be loath to cast away my speech, for besides that it is excellently well penned, I have taken great pains to con it. Good beauties, let me sustain no scorn; I am very comptible, even to the least sinister usage.

Oli. Whence came you, sir?   189

Vio. I can say little more than I have studied, and that question 's out of my part. Good gentle one, give me modest assurance if you be the lady of the house, that I may proceed in my speech.

Oli. Are you a comedian?

Vio. No, my profound heart: and yet, by the very fangs of malice I swear, I am not that I play. Are you the lady of the house?

Oli. If I do not usurp myself, I am.   198

Vio. Most certain, if you are she, you do usurp yourself; for what is yours to bestow is not yours to reserve. But this is from my commission: I will on with my speech in your praise, and then show you the heart of my message.

Oli. Come to what is important in 't: I forgive you the praise.

Vio. Alas, I took great pains to study it, and 'tis poetical.   207

Oli. It is the more like to be feigned: I pray you, keep it in. I heard you were saucy at my gates, and

allowed your approach rather to wonder at you than to hear you. If you be not mad, be gone; if you have reason, be brief: 'tis not that time of moon with me to make one in so skipping a dialogue.

Mar. Will you hoist sail, sir? here lies your way.

Vio. No, good swabber; I am to hull here a little longer. Some mollification for your giant, sweet lady. Tell me your mind: I am a messenger.   220

Oli. Sure, you have some hideous matter to deliver, when the courtesy of it is so fearful. Speak your office.

Vio. It alone concerns your ear. I bring no overture of war, no taxation of homage: I hold the olive in my hand; my words are as full of peace as matter.

Oli. Yet you began rudely. What are you? what would you?   229

Vio. The rudeness that hath appeared in me have I learned from my entertainment. What I am, and what I would, are as secret as maidenhead; to your ears, divinity, to any other's, profanation.

Oli. Give us the place alone; we will hear this divinity.   [*Exeunt Maria and Attendants.*
Now, sir, what is your text?

Vio. Most sweet lady,—

Oli. A comfortable doctrine, and much may be said of it. Where lies your text?   240

Vio. In Orsino's bosom.

Oli. In his bosom! In what chapter of his bosom?

Vio. To answer by the method, in the first of his heart.

Oli. O, I have read it: it is heresy. Have you no more to say?

Vio. Good madam, let me see your face.

Oli. Have you any commission from your lord to negotiate with my face? You are now out of your text: but we will draw the curtain and show you the picture. Look you, sir, such a one I was this present: is 't not well done?   [*Unveiling.*

Vio. Excellently done, if God did all.

Oli. 'Tis in grain, sir; 'twill endure wind and weather.   256

Vio. 'Tis beauty truly blent, whose red and white Nature's own sweet and cunning hand laid on: Lady, you are the cruell'st she alive, If you will lead these graces to the grave   260 And leave the world no copy.

Oli. O, sir, I will not be so hard-hearted; I will give out divers schedules of my beauty: it shall be inventoried, and every particle and utensil labelled to my will: as, item, two lips, indifferent red; item, two grey eyes, with lids to them; item, one neck, one chin, and so forth. Were you sent hither to praise me?

Vio. I see you what you are, you are too proud; But, if you were the devil, you are fair.   270 My lord and master loves you: O, such love Could be but recompensed, though you were crown'd The nonpareil of beauty!

Oli.   How does he love me?

Vio. With adorations, fertile tears,

Not yet . . . him. Nowhere else does Malvolio speak in this vein. 166. **squash,** unripe pea pod. 167. **peascod,** pea pod. **codling,** unripe apple. 170. **shrewishly,** sharply; possibly, like a woman. 181. **Most . . . beauty.** This line is a part of Viola's prepared speech. The same style peeps out in a few places further on. 186. **con,** learn by heart. 188. **comptible,** susceptible, sensitive. 201. **from,** outside of. 213. **moon,** as affecting lunatics. 214. **skipping,** flighty, frivolous. 217. **swabber,** one who washes the decks; a nautical retort to *hoist sail* (l. 215). 218-219. **Some . . . giant,** pray pacify your giant; alluding ironically to Maria's small size. 222. **courtesy,** ceremonious introduc-

tion. 223. **office,** commission. 225. **taxation,** demand for the payment of. 239. **comfortable,** comforting. 244. **method,** i.e., your method. 253. **this present,** just now, presently. Since it was customary to hang curtains in front of pictures, Olivia in unveiling speaks as if she were displaying a picture of herself. 255. **in grain,** fast dyed. 263. **schedules,** inventories. 265. **labelled,** added as a codicil. 274. **fertile,** copious.

With groans that thunder love, with sighs of fire.

Oli. Your lord does know my mind; I cannot love
  him:
Yet I suppose him virtuous, know him noble,
Of great estate, of fresh and stainless youth;
In voices well divulged, free, learn'd and valiant;
And in dimension and the shape of nature   280
A gracious person: but yet I cannot love him;
He might have took his answer long ago.

Vio. If I did love you in my master's flame,
With such a suffering, such a deadly life,
In your denial I would find no sense;
I would not understand it.

Oli.   Why, what would you?

Vio. Make me a willow cabin at your gate,
And call upon my soul within the house;
Write loyal cantons of contemned love
And sing them loud even in the dead of night;   290
Halloo your name to the reverberate hills
And make the babbling gossip of the air
Cry out 'Olivia!' O, you should not rest
Between the elements of air and earth,
But you should pity me!

Oli.   You might do much.
What is your parentage?

Vio. Above my fortunes, yet my state is well:
I am a gentleman.

Oli.   Get you to your lord;
I cannot love him: let him send no more;
Unless, perchance, you come to me again,   300
To tell me how he takes it. Fare you well:
I thank you for your pains: spend this for me.

Vio. I am no fee'd post, lady; keep your purse:
My master, not myself, lacks recompense.
Love make his heart of flint that you shall love;
And let your fervour, like my master's, be
Placed in contempt! Farewell, fair cruelty.   [*Exit.*

Oli. 'What is your parentage?'
'Above my fortunes, yet my state is well:
I am a gentleman.' I'll be sworn thou art;   310
Thy tongue, thy face, thy limbs, actions and spirit,
Do give thee five-fold blazon: not too fast: soft, soft!
Unless the master were the man. How now!
Even so quickly may one catch the plague?
Methinks I feel this youth's perfections
With an invisible and subtle stealth
To creep in at mine eyes. Well, let it be.
What ho, Malvolio!

Re-enter MALVOLIO.

Mal.   Here, madam, at your service.

Oli. Run after that same peevish messenger,
The county's man: he left this ring behind him,   320
Would I or not: tell him I'll none of it.
Desire him not to flatter with his lord,
Nor hold him up with hopes; I am not for him:
If that the youth will come this way to-morrow,
I'll give him reasons for 't: hie thee, Malvolio.

Mal. Madam, I will.   [*Exit.*

Oli. I do I know not what, and fear to find
Mine eye too great a flatterer for my mind.
Fate, show thy force: ourselves we do not owe;
What is decreed must be, and be this so.   [*Exit.*

ACT II.

SCENE I. *The sea-coast.*

Enter ANTONIO *and* SEBASTIAN.

Ant. Will you stay no longer? nor will you not that
I go with you?

Seb. By your patience, no. My stars shine darkly
over me: the malignancy of my fate might perhaps
distemper yours; therefore I shall crave of you your
leave that I may bear my evils alone: it were a bad
recompense for your love, to lay any of them on you. 7

Ant. Let me yet know of you whither you are bound.

Seb. No, sooth, sir: my determinate voyage is mere
extravagancy. But I perceive in you so excellent a
touch of modesty, that you will not extort from me
what I am willing to keep in; therefore it charges me
in manners the rather to express myself. You must
know of me then, Antonio, my name is Sebastian,
which I called Roderigo. My father was that Sebastian of Messaline, whom I know you have heard of.
He left behind him myself and a sister, both born in
an hour: if the heavens had been pleased, would we
had so ended! but you, sir, altered that; for some hour
before you took me from the breach of the sea was my
sister drowned.   24

Ant. Alas the day!

Seb. A lady, sir, though it was said she much resembled me, was yet of many accounted beautiful:
but, though I could not with such estimable wonder
overfar believe that, yet thus far I will boldly publish
her; she bore a mind that envy could not but call fair.
She is drowned already, sir, with salt water, though I
seem to drown her remembrance again with more.   33

Ant. Pardon me, sir, your bad entertainment.

Seb. O good Antonio, forgive me your trouble.

Ant. If you will not murder me for my love, let me
be your servant.   37

Seb. If you will not undo what you have done, that
is, kill him whom you have recovered, desire it not.
Fare ye well at once: my bosom is full of kindness,
and I am yet so near the manners of my mother, that
upon the least occasion more mine eyes will tell tales
of me. I am bound to the Count Orsino's court: farewell.   [*Exit.*

Ant. The gentleness of all the gods go with thee!
I have many enemies in Orsino's court,
Else would I very shortly see thee there.
But, come what may, I do adore thee so,   48
That danger shall seem sport, and I will go.   [*Exit.*

SCENE II. *A street.*

Enter VIOLA, MALVOLIO *following.*

Mal. Were not you even now with the Countess Olivia?

Vio. Even now, sir; on a moderate pace I have since arrived but hither.

Mal. She returns this ring to you, sir: you might have saved me my pains, to have taken it away yourself. She adds, moreover, that you should put your lord into a desperate assurance she will none of him: and one thing more, that you be never so hardy to come again in his affairs, unless it be to report your lord's taking of this. Receive it so.   12

Vio. She took the ring of me: I'll none of it.

Mal. Come, sir, you peevishly threw it to her; and her will is, it should be so returned: if it be worth stooping for, there it lies in your eye; if not, be it his that finds it.   [*Exit.*

Vio. I left no ring with her: what means this lady?
Fortune forbid my outside have not charm'd her!
She made good view of me; indeed, so much,   20
That sure methought her eyes had lost her tongue,
For she did speak in starts distractedly.
She loves me, sure; the cunning of her passion
Invites me in this churlish messenger.
None of my lord's ring! why, he sent her none.
I am the man: if it be so, as 'tis,
Poor lady, she were better love a dream.
Disguise, I see, thou art a wickedness,
Wherein the pregnant enemy does much.
How easy is it for the proper-false   30
In women's waxen hearts to set their forms!
Alas, our frailty is the cause, not we!
For such as we are made of, such we be.
How will this fadge? my master loves her dearly;
And I, poor monster, fond as much on him;
And she, mistaken, seems to dote on me.
What will become of this? As I am man,
My state is desperate for my master's love;
As I am woman,—now alas the day!—
What thriftless sighs shall poor Olivia breathe!   40
O time! thou must untangle this, not I;
It is too hard a knot for me to untie!   [*Exit.*

SCENE III. OLIVIA'S *house.*

Enter SIR TOBY *and* SIR ANDREW.

Sir To. Approach, Sir Andrew: not to be abed after midnight is to be up betimes; and 'diluculo surgere,' thou know'st,—

Sir And. Nay, by my troth, I know not: but I know, to be up late is to be up late.

Sir To. A false conclusion: I hate it as an unfilled can. To be up after midnight and to go to bed then, is early: so that to go to bed after midnight is to go to

bed betimes. Does not our life consist of the four elements?   10

Sir And. Faith, so they say; but I think it rather consists of eating and drinking.

Sir To. Thou 'rt a scholar; let us therefore eat and drink. Marian, I say! a stoup of wine!

Enter CLOWN.

Sir And. Here comes the fool, i' faith.

Clo. How now, my hearts! did you never see the picture of 'we three'?

Sir To. Welcome, ass. Now let 's have a catch.   18

Sir And. By my troth, the fool has an excellent breast. I had rather than forty shillings I had such a leg, and so sweet a breath to sing, as the fool has. In sooth, thou wast in very gracious fooling last night, when thou spokest of Pigrogromitus, of the Vapians passing the equinoctial of Queubus: 'twas very good, i' faith. I sent thee sixpence for thy leman: hadst it?   26

Clo. I did impeticos thy gratillity; for Malvolio's nose is no whipstock: my lady has a white hand, and the Myrmidons are no bottle-ale houses.

Sir And. Excellent! why, this is the best fooling, when all is done. Now, a song.   31

Sir To. Come on; there is sixpence for you: let 's have a song.

Sir And. There 's a testril of me too: if one knight give a—

Clo. Would you have a love-song, or a song of good life?

Sir To. A love-song, a love-song.

Sir And. Ay, ay: I care not for good life.

Clo. [*Sings*]
  O mistress mine, where are you roaming?   40
  O, stay and hear; your true love 's coming,
    That can sing both high and low:
  Trip no further, pretty sweeting;
  Journeys end in lovers meeting,
    Every wise man's son doth know.

Sir And. Excellent good, i' faith.

Sir To. Good, good.

Clo. [*Sings*]
  What is love? 'tis not hereafter;
  Present mirth hath present laughter;
    What 's to come is still unsure: 50
  In delay there lies no plenty;
  Then come kiss me, sweet and twenty,
    Youth 's a stuff will not endure.

Sir And. A mellifluous voice, as I am true knight.

Sir To. A contagious breath.

Sir And. Very sweet and contagious, i' faith.

Sir To. To hear by the nose, it is dulcet in contagion. But shall we make the welkin dance indeed? shall we rouse the night-owl in a catch that will draw three souls out of one weaver? shall we do that?   62

Sir And. An you love me, let 's do 't: I am dog at a catch.

Clo. By 'r lady, sir, and some dogs will catch well.

the second singer takes up the first line just as the first singer is beginning the second line, and so on. 21. **leg**, probably, obeisance made by drawing back one leg and bending the other. 24-25. **Pigrogromitus . . . Queubus**, mock erudition. 26. **leman**, sweetheart. 27. **impeticos thy gratillity**, suggests "impetticoat thy gratuity." 28. **whipstock**, whip handle. It may suggest Malvolio's habit of prying into matters which he has no authority to punish. 29. **Myrmidons**, followers of Achilles; here, perhaps, taverns of high grade. **bottle-ale**, used contemptuously of taverns because they sold low-class drink. 34. **testril**, a coin worth sixpence. 37. **good life**, respectability. 40. **O mistress mine.** This song is found in several Elizabethan songbooks,

but is nevertheless thought by some authorities to be Shakespeare's. 43. **sweeting**, sweet one. 52. **sweet and twenty**, possibly meant originally "twenty times as sweet," *twenty* being used as an intensive. 59. **welkin dance**, drink till the sky seems to turn round (Johnson). 61-62. **draw . . . weaver**, usually explained as a reference to psalm-singing weavers, Protestant refugees from Belgium. There is a reference also to the Renaissance conception of the soul which was held to be threefold, the vegetal, the sensible, and the intellectual soul. 64. **dog at**, clever at.

Sir And. Most certain. Let our catch be, 'Thou knave.'

Clo. 'Hold thy peace, thou knave,' knight? I shall be constrained in 't to call thee knave, knight.　70

Sir And. 'Tis not the first time I have constrained one to call me knave. Begin, fool: it begins 'Hold thy peace.'

Clo. I shall never begin if I hold my peace.

Sir And. Good, i' faith. Come, begin.　[*Catch sung.*

Enter MARIA.

Mar. What a caterwauling do you keep here! If my lady have not called up her steward Malvolio and bid him turn you out of doors, never trust me.　79

Sir To. My lady 's a Cataian, we are politicians, Malvolio 's a Peg-a-Ramsey, and 'Three merry men be we.' Am not I consanguineous? am I not of her blood? Tillyvally. Lady! [*Sings*] 'There dwelt a man in Babylon, lady, lady!'

Clo. Beshrew me, the knight 's in admirable fooling.

Sir And. Ay, he does well enough if he be disposed, and so do I too: he does it with a better grace, but I do it more natural.　89

Sir To. [*Sings*] 'O, the twelfth day of December,'—

Mar. For the love o' God, peace!

Enter MALVOLIO.

Mal. My masters, are you mad? or what are you? Have you no wit, manners, nor honesty, but to gabble like tinkers at this time of night? Do ye make an ale-house of my lady's house, that ye squeak out your coziers' catches without any mitigation or remorse of voice? Is there no respect of place, persons, nor time in you?

Sir To. We did keep time, sir, in our catches. Sneck up!　101

Mal. Sir Toby, I must be round with you. My lady bade me tell you, that, though she harbours you as her kinsman, she 's nothing allied to your disorders. If you can separate yourself and your misdemeanours, you are welcome to the house; if not, an it would please you to take leave of her, she is very willing to bid you farewell.

Sir To. 'Farewell, dear heart, since I must needs be gone.'　110

Mar. Nay, good Sir Toby.

Clo. 'His eyes do show his days are almost done.'

Mal. Is 't even so?

Sir To. 'But I will never die.'

Clo. Sir Toby, there you lie.

Mal. This is much credit to you.

Sir To. 'Shall I bid him go?'

Clo. 'What an if you do?'

Sir To. 'Shall I bid him go, and spare not?'

Clo. 'O no, no, no, no, you dare not.'　121

Sir To. Out o' tune, sir: ye lie. Art any more than a steward? Dost thou think, because thou art virtuous, there shall be no more cakes and ale?

Clo. Yes, by Saint Anne, and ginger shall be hot i' the mouth too.

Sir To. Thou 'rt i' the right. Go, sir, rub your chain with crums. A stoup of wine, Maria!　129

Mal. Mistress Mary, if you prized my lady's favour at any thing more than contempt, you would not give means for this uncivil rule: she shall know of it, by this hand.　[*Exit.*

Mar. Go shake your ears.

Sir And. 'Twere as good a deed as to drink when a man 's a-hungry, to challenge him the field, and then to break promise with him and make a fool of him.

Sir To. Do 't, knight: I'll write thee a challenge; or I'll deliver thy indignation to him by word of mouth.

Mar. Sweet Sir Toby, be patient for to-night: since the youth of the count's was to-day with my lady, she is much out of quiet. For Monsieur Malvolio, let me alone with him: if I do not gull him into a nayword, and make him a common recreation, do not think I have wit enough to lie straight in my bed: I know I can do it.

Sir To. Possess us, possess us; tell us something of him.　150

Mar. Marry, sir, sometimes he is a kind of puritan.

Sir And. O, if I thought that, I 'ld beat him like a dog!

Sir To. What, for being a puritan? thy exquisite reason, dear knight?

Sir And. I have no exquisite reason for 't, but I have reason good enough.　158

Mar. The devil a puritan that he is, or any thing constantly, but a time-pleaser; an affected ass, that cons state without book and utters it by great swarths: the best persuaded of himself, so crammed, as he thinks, with excellencies, that it is his grounds of faith that all that look on him love him; and on that vice in him will my revenge find notable cause to work.　166

Sir To. What wilt thou do?

Mar. I will drop in his way some obscure epistles of love; wherein, by the colour of his beard, the shape of his leg, the manner of his gait, the expressure of his eye, forehead, and complexion, he shall find himself most feelingly personated. I can write very like my lady your niece: on a forgotten matter we can hardly make distinction of our hands.

Sir To. Excellent! I smell a device.

Sir And. I have 't in my nose too.

Sir To. He shall think, by the letters that thou wilt drop, that they come from my niece, and that she 's in love with him.　180

Mar. My purpose is, indeed, a horse of that colour.

Sir And. And your horse now would make him an ass.

Mar. Ass, I doubt not.

Sir And. O, 'twill be admirable!

Mar. Sport royal, I warrant you: I know my physic will work with him. I will plant you two, and

80. **Cataian,** explained as Chinese, i.e., from Cathay, suggested by *caterwauling*. **politicians,** schemers, intriguers. 81. **Peg-a-Ramsey,** common name of a tune, evidently of low character. 83. **Tillyvally,** a term of contempt, possibly from a song. 84. **'There . . . lady,'** first line of a ballad having the refrain "Lady, lady." Sir Toby's use of the word, above, suggested the song. 89. **natural,** unconsciously suggesting idiocy. 90-91. **'O . . . December.'** Kittredge suggests that this is the ballad of "Musselburgh Field" in Child's *English and Scottish Popular Ballads*, IV, 507. 101. **Sneck up!** Go hang! 109-110. **'Farewell . . . gone,'** from the ballad, "Corydon's Farewell to Phyllis." 125. **cakes and ale,** reveling (proverbial). 126. **Saint Anne,** invoked

because of her care for material welfare. 128-129. **Go . . . crums,** i.e., scour your steward's chain with crumbs; attend to your own business. 132. **give means,** i.e., by supplying drink. 133. **rule,** conduct. 146. **nayword,** byword. 147. **recreation,** laughingstock. 152. **puritan.** It was Sir Andrew's humor to hate Puritans. Shakespeare makes Maria say below that Malvolio is not a Puritan but a time-pleaser and an affected ass. It is therefore misleading to say that there is here any satire against Puritans in the figure of Malvolio. 160. **time-pleaser,** time-server, one who complies with every prevailing opinion. 161. **cons . . . book,** learns the phrases of high society by heart. 162. **best persuaded,** has the best opinion. 171. **expressure,**

let the fool make a third, where he shall find the
letter: observe his construction of it. For this night,
to bed, and dream on the event. Farewell.   [*Exit.* 192
   Sir To. Good night, Penthesilea.
   Sir And. Before me, she 's a good wench.
   Sir To. She 's a beagle, true-bred, and one that
adores me: what o' that?
   Sir And. I was adored once too.
   Sir To. Let 's to bed, knight. Thou hadst need send
for more money.
   Sir And. If I cannot recover your niece, I am a foul
way out.   201
   Sir To. Send for money, knight: if thou hast her
not i' the end, call me cut.
   Sir And. If I do not, never trust me, take it how you
will.
   Sir To. Come, come, I'll go burn some sack; 'tis too
late to go to bed now: come, knight; come, knight.
                                    [*Exeunt.*

SCENE IV. *The* Duke's *Palace.*

Enter Duke, Viola, Curio, *and others.*

   Duke. Give me some music. Now, good morrow,
     friends.
Now, good Cesario, but that piece of song,
That old and antique song we heard last night:
Methought it did relieve my passion much,
More than light airs and recollected terms
Of these most brisk and giddy-paced times:
Come, but one verse.
   Cur. He is not here, so please your lordship, that
should sing it.
   Duke. Who was it?   10
   Cur. Feste, the jester, my lord; a fool that the lady
Olivia's father took much delight in. He is about the
house.
   Duke. Seek him out, and play the tune the while.
                [*Exit Curio. Music plays.*
Come hither, boy: if ever thou shalt love,
In the sweet pangs of it remember me;
For such as I am all true lovers are,
Unstaid and skittish in all motions else,
Save in the constant image of the creature
That is beloved. How dost thou like this tune?
   Vio. It gives a very echo to the seat   21
Where Love is throned.
   Duke.   Thou dost speak masterly:
My life upon 't, young though thou art, thine eye
Hath stay'd upon some favour that it loves:
Hath it not, boy?
   Vio.   A little, by your favour.
   Duke. What kind of woman is 't?
   Vio.   Of your complexion.
   Duke. She is not worth thee, then. What years, i'
     faith?

   Vio. About your years, my lord.
   Duke. Too old, by heaven: let still the woman take
An elder than herself; so wears she to him,   31
So sways she level in her husband's heart:
For, boy, however we do praise ourselves,
Our fancies are more giddy and unfirm,
More longing, wavering, sooner lost and worn,
Than women's are.
   Vio.   I think it well, my lord.
   Duke. Then let thy love be younger than thyself,
Or thy affection cannot hold the bent;
For women are as roses, whose fair flower
Being once display'd, doth fall that very hour.   40
   Vio. And so they are: alas, that they are so;
To die, even when they to perfection grow!

       Re-enter Curio *and* Clown.

   Duke. O, fellow, come, the song we had last night.
Mark it, Cesario, it is old and plain;
The spinsters and the knitters in the sun
And the free maids that weave their thread with
     bones
Do use to chant it: it is silly sooth,
And dallies with the innocence of love,
Like the old age.
   Clo. Are you ready, sir?   50
   Duke. Ay; prithee, sing.   [*Music.*

             SONG.

   Clo. Come away, come away, death,
     And in sad cypress let me be laid;
  Fly away, fly away, breath;
     I am slain by a fair cruel maid.
  My shroud of white, stuck all with yew,
     O, prepare it!
  My part of death, no one so true
     Did share it.

  Not a flower, not a flower sweet,   60
     On my black coffin let there be strown;
  Not a friend, not a friend greet
     My poor corpse, where my bones shall be
       thrown:
  A thousand thousand sighs to save,
      Lay me, O, where
  Sad true lover never find my grave,
      To weep there!

   Duke. There 's for thy pains.
   Clo. No pains, sir; I take pleasure in singing, sir. 70
   Duke. I'll pay thy pleasure then.
   Clo. Truly, sir, and pleasure will be paid, one time
or another.
   Duke. Give me now leave to leave thee.
   Clo. Now, the melancholy god protect thee; and the
tailor make thy doublet of changeable taffeta, for thy
mind is a very opal. I would have men of such con-
stancy put to sea, that their business might be every

---

expression. 173. **personated,** described. 193. **Penthesilea,** queen of
the Amazons; another ironical allusion to Maria's stature. 195.
beagle, small hound; possibly also alluding to Maria's size. 200.
recover, win. 201. **foul way out,** explained as "out of pocket" and as
"off the track." 203. **cut,** a horse with a docked tail.
   SCENE IV. 3. **antique,** quaint. 5. **recollected terms,** artificial
expressions. 21. **seat,** i.e., the heart. 25. **stay'd . . . favour,** rested
upon some face. 30-40. **Too . . . hour.** A somewhat absurd use has
been made of this passage to prove that Shakespeare, who was younger
than his wife, is expressing a personal opinion. The idea is, of course, a
commonplace in Renaissance love literature. 31. **wears she,** adapts

herself. 32. **sways she level,** rules steadily; or possibly the figure is
drawn from scales evenly balanced. 33. **praise,** appraise. 35. **worn,**
F: *worne;* Hanmer: *won* (for *wonne*), which is probably correct. 38.
bent, degree of tension (as in archery). 46. **bones,** bobbins with which
bone-lace was made. 47. **silly sooth,** simple truth. 49. **old age,** old
times. 53. **cypress,** interpreted as meaning coffin of cypress wood, or
bier strewn with sprigs of cypress. 58-59. **My . . . it,** no one died for
love so true to love as I (Luce). 75. **melancholy god,** Saturn, if the
Clown has any god in mind. 76. **doublet,** close-fitting body garment
with or without sleeves. 77. **taffeta,** silk.

thing and their intent every where; for that's it that
always makes a good voyage of nothing. Farewell. 81
[*Exit*.

Duke. Let all the rest give place.
[*Curio and Attendants retire*.
Once more, Cesario,
Get thee to yond same sovereign cruelty:
Tell her, my love, more noble than the world,
Prizes not quantity of dirty lands;
The parts that fortune hath bestow'd upon her,
Tell her, I hold as giddily as fortune;
But 'tis that miracle and queen of gems
That nature pranks her in attracts my soul.
Vio. But if she cannot love you, sir? 90
Duke. I cannot be so answer'd.
Vio.   Sooth, but you must.
Say that some lady, as perhaps there is,
Hath for your love as great a pang of heart
As you have for Olivia: you cannot love her;
You tell her so; must she not then be answer'd?
Duke. There is no woman's sides
Can bide the beating of so strong a passion
As love doth give my heart; no woman's heart
So big, to hold so much; they lack retention.
Alas, their love may be call'd appetite, 100
No motion of the liver, but the palate,
That suffer surfeit, cloyment and revolt;
But mine is all as hungry as the sea,
And can digest as much: make no compare
Between that love a woman can bear me
And that I owe Olivia.
Vio.   Ay, but I know—
Duke. What dost thou know?
Vio. Too well what love women to men may owe:
In faith, they are as true of heart as we.
My father had a daughter loved a man, 110
As it might be, perhaps, were I a woman,
I should your lordship.
Duke.   And what's her history?
Vio. A blank, my lord. She never told her love,
But let concealment, like a worm i' the bud,
Feed on her damask cheek: she pined in thought,
And with a green and yellow melancholy
She sat like patience on a monument,
Smiling at grief. Was not this love indeed?
We men may say more, swear more: but indeed
Our shows are more than will; for still we prove 120
Much in our vows, but little in our love.
Duke. But died thy sister of her love, my boy?
Vio. I am all the daughters of my father's house,
And all the brothers too: and yet I know not.
Sir, shall I to this lady?
Duke.   Ay, that's the theme.
To her in haste; give her this jewel; say,
My love can give no place, bide no denay. [*Exeunt*.

SCENE V. OLIVIA'S *garden*.

Enter SIR TOBY, SIR ANDREW, *and* FABIAN.

Sir To. Come thy ways, Signior Fabian.
Fab. Nay, I'll come: if I lose a scruple of this sport,
let me be boiled to death with melancholy.
Sir To. Wouldst thou not be glad to have the nig-
gardly rascally sheep-biter come by some notable
shame?
Fab. I would exult, man: you know, he brought
me out o' favour with my lady about a bear-baiting
here. 10
Sir To. To anger him we'll have the bear again; and
we will fool him black and blue: shall we not, Sir
Andrew?
Sir And. An we do not, it is pity of our lives.
Sir To. Here comes the little villain.

Enter MARIA.

How now, my metal of India! 17
Mar. Get ye all three into the box-tree: Malvolio's
coming down this walk: he has been yonder i' the sun
practising behaviour to his own shadow this half
hour: observe him, for the love of mockery; for I
know this letter will make a contemplative idiot of
him. Close, in the name of jesting! Lie thou there
[*throws down a letter*]; for here comes the trout that
must be caught with tickling. [*Exit.* 26

Enter MALVOLIO.

Mal. 'Tis but fortune; all is fortune. Maria once
told me she did affect me: and I have heard herself
come thus near, that, should she fancy, it should be
one of my complexion. Besides, she uses me with a
more exalted respect than any one else that follows
her. What should I think on 't? 33
Sir To. Here's an overweening rogue!
Fab. O, peace! Contemplation makes a rare turkey-
cock of him: how he jets under his advanced plumes!
Sir And. 'Slight, I could so beat the rogue!
Sir To. Peace, I say.
Mal. To be Count Malvolio! 40
Sir To. Ah, rogue!
Sir And. Pistol him, pistol him.
Sir To. Peace, peace!
Mal. There is example for 't; the lady of the Strachy
married the yeoman of the wardrobe.
Sir And. Fie on him, Jezebel!
Fab. O, peace! now he's deeply in: look how imag-
ination blows him.
Mal. Having been three months married to her,
sitting in my state,— 50
Sir To. O, for a stone-bow, to hit him in the eye!
Mal. Calling my officers about me, in my branched
velvet gown; having come from a daybed, where I
have left Olivia sleeping,—

80-81. **for . . . nothing,** possibly ironical, meaning that such changeable
enterprise will make a good voyage come to nothing. 86. **parts,** gifts,
as wealth or rank. 87. **giddily,** carelessly, insecurely. 89. **pranks,**
adorns. 96-106. **There . . . Olivia.** The duke has just said in lines 33-36
that men are more inconstant than women. 99. **retention,** constancy,
power of retaining. 101. **liver . . . palate.** The distinction seems to be
that real love is a passion of the liver, whereas fancy (light love) is born
in the eye and nourished in the palate. 102. **That suffer,** that suffers.
That is sometimes thought to refer back to *their* (l. 100). **cloyment,**
satiety to the point of losing appetite. **revolt,** sickness, revulsion.
113. **blank,** i.e., her history is a blank. 115. **damask,** red like the
damask rose. 116. **green and yellow.** Green denoted hopefulness and
yellow jealousy; so that a green and yellow melancholy was a melan-

choly in which there was jealousy, yet hope. This accords exactly
with the state of mind of Viola (Hunter). 127. **denay,** denial.
SCENE V. 3. **boiled to death.** Melancholy being a settled passion, the
spirits descended to the intestines, carrying with them their boiling heat.
6. **sheep-biter,** sheep-killing dog. 17. **metal,** gold, probably with pun
on "mettle," spirit. 23. **contemplative,** i.e., from contemplating himself. 26. **tickling,** groping gently with the hands—a method of fishing.
28. **she,** i.e., Olivia. 30. **fancy,** fall in love. 36. **jets,** struts. 44.
lady of the Strachy, apparently a lady who had married below her
station; no satisfactory explanation. 46. **Jezebel,** a blunder of Sir
Andrew, unless, as has been suggested, we should read *her* for *him* in this
line. 48. **blows,** puffs up. 51. **stone-bow,** crossbow for shooting
stones. 54. **branched,** adorned with a figured pattern suggesting

Sir To. Fire and brimstone!

Fab. O, peace, peace!

Mal. And then to have the humour of state; and after a demure travel of regard, telling them I know my place as I would they should do theirs, to ask for my kinsman Toby,— 61

Sir To. Bolts and shackles!

Fab. O peace, peace, peace! now, now.

Mal. Seven of my people, with an obedient start, make out for him: I frown the while; and perchance wind up my watch, or play with my—some rich jewel. Toby approaches; courtesies there to me,—

Sir To. Shall this fellow live?

Fab. Though our silence be drawn from us with cars, yet peace. 71

Mal. I extend my hand to him thus, quenching my familiar smile with an austere regard of control,—

Sir To. And does not Toby take you a blow o' the lips then?

Mal. Saying, 'Cousin Toby, my fortunes having cast me on your niece give me this prerogative of speech,'—

Sir To. What, what? 80

Mal. 'You must amend your drunkenness.'

Sir To. Out, scab!

Fab. Nay, patience, or we break the sinews of our plot.

Mal. 'Besides, you waste the treasure of your time with a foolish knight,'—

Sir And. That's me, I warrant you.

Mal. 'One Sir Andrew,'—

Sir And. I knew 'twas I; for many do call me fool. 90

Mal. What employment have we here?

[Taking up the letter.

Fab. Now is the woodcock near the gin.

Sir To. O, peace! and the spirit of humours intimate reading aloud to him!

Mal. By my life, this is my lady's hand: these be her very C's, her U's and her T's; and thus makes she her great P's. It is, in contempt of question, her hand.

Sir And. Her C's, her U's and her T's: why that? 100

Mal. [*Reads*] 'To the unknown beloved, this, and my good wishes:'—her very phrases! By your leave, wax. Soft! and the impressure her Lucrece, with which she uses to seal: 'tis my lady. To whom should this be?

Fab. This wins him, liver and all.

Mal. [*Reads*]

> Jove knows I love:
> But who?
> Lips, do not move;
> No man must know. 110

'No man must know.' What follows? the numbers altered! 'No man must know:' if this should be thee, Malvolio?

Sir To. Marry, hang thee, brock!

Mal. [*Reads*]

> I may command where I adore;
> But silence, like a Lucrece knife,
> With bloodless stroke my heart doth gore:
> M, O, A, I, doth sway my life.

Fab. A fustian riddle!

Sir To. Excellent wench, say I. 120

Mal. 'M, O, A, I, doth sway my life.' Nay, but first, let me see, let me see, let me see.

Fab. What dish o' poison has she dressed him!

Sir To. And with what wing the staniel checks at it!

Mal. 'I may command where I adore.' Why, she may command me: I serve her; she is my lady. Why, this is evident to any formal capacity; there is no obstruction in this: and the end,—what should that alphabetical position portend? If I could make that resemble something in me,—Softly! M, O, A, I,—

Sir To. O, ay, make up that: he is now at a cold scent. 134

Fab. Sowter will cry upon 't for all this, though it be as rank as a fox.

Mal. M,—Malvolio; M,—why, that begins my name.

Fab. Did not I say he would work it out? the cur is excellent at faults. 140

Mal. M,—but then there is no consonancy in the sequel; that suffers under probation: A should follow, but O does.

Fab. And O shall end, I hope.

Sir To. Ay, or I'll cudgel him, and make him cry O!

Mal. And then I comes behind.

Fab. Ay, an you had any eye behind you, you might see more detraction at your heels than fortunes before you. 150

Mal. M, O, A, I; this simulation is not as the former: and yet, to crush this a little, it would bow to me, for every one of these letters are in my name. Soft! here follows prose.

[*Reads*] 'If this fall into thy hand, revolve. In my stars I am above thee; but be not afraid of greatness: some are born great, some achieve greatness and some have greatness thrust upon 'em. Thy Fates open their hands; let thy blood and spirit embrace them; and, to inure thyself to what thou art like to be, cast thy humble slough and appear fresh. Be opposite with a kinsman, surly with servants; let thy tongue tang arguments of state; put thyself into the trick of singularity: she thus advises thee that sighs for thee. Remember who commended thy yellow stockings, and wished to see thee ever cross-gartered: I say, remember. Go to, thou art made, if thou desirest to be so; if not, let me see thee a steward still, the fellow of servants, and not worthy to touch Fortune's fingers. Farewell. She that would alter services with thee, 172

THE FORTUNATE-UNHAPPY.'

branches. 55. **daybed,** sofa, couch. 58. **humour of state,** idiosyncrasies allowed to persons of rank. 59. **demure . . . regard,** grave survey of the company. 61. **Toby,** i.e., not *Sir* Toby. 66. **wind up my watch,** an impressive act in those days. 71. **cars,** used like "team of horses." 74. **regard of control,** look of authority. 82. **scab,** scurvy fellow. 92. **woodcock,** proverbial for its stupidity. **gin,** snare. 94. **intimate,** suggest. 98. **in contempt of question,** i.e., it is absurd to question it. 103. **By . . . wax,** addressed to the seal on the letter. **impressure,** impression. 104. **Lucrece,** a seal engraved with the picture of Lucrece. 114. **brock,** badger; used contemptuously. 119. **fustian,** bombastic, ridiculously pompous. 123. **dressed,** prepared for. 124. **staniel,** an inferior kind of hawk; F: *stallion,* which may be a dialectal form of the same word. 125. **checks.** A hawk "checked" when it left its

quarry and flew at a chance bird. 128. **formal capacity,** normal mind. 134. **cold scent,** cold trail. 135. **Sowter,** cobbler; probably, the name for a hound. 136. **rank as a fox,** i.e., Malvolio is so crude a hunter that he will leave the trail of a hare and follow the rank scent of a fox. 140. **faults,** breaks in the line of scent. 141. **consonancy,** consistency. 142. **probation,** when put to trial. 144. **O,** interpreted as a hempen collar (Johnson), or as a sigh (Steevens), or as an outcry of pain. 151. **simulation,** disguised meaning. 152. **crush,** force. 155. **revolve,** consider. 156. **stars,** fortunes. 159. **blood and spirit,** i.e., as the agents of passion. 161. **slough,** skin of a snake. 162. **opposite,** contradictory. 163. **tang,** sound loud with. 164. **trick of singularity,** eccentricity of manner. 167. **cross-gartered,** wearing garters above and below the knee so as to cross behind it (Onions).

Daylight and champain discovers not more: this is open. I will be proud, I will read politic authors, I will baffle Sir Toby, I will wash off gross acquaintance, I will be point-devise the very man. I do not now fool myself, to let imagination jade me; for every reason excites to this, that my lady loves me. She did commend my yellow stockings of late, she did praise my leg being cross-gartered; and in this she manifests herself to my love, and with a kind of injunction drives me to these habits of her liking. I thank my stars I am happy. I will be strange, stout, in yellow stockings, and cross-gartered, even with the swiftness of putting on. Jove and my stars be praised! Here is yet a postscript. [Reads] 'Thou canst not choose but know who I am. If thou entertainest my love, let it appear in thy smiling; thy smiles become thee well; therefore in my presence still smile, dear my sweet, I prithee.'   193

Jove, I thank thee: I will smile; I will do everything that thou wilt have me.   [Exit.

Fab. I will not give my part of this sport for a pension of thousands to be paid from the Sophy.

Sir To. I could marry this wench for this device.   200

Sir And. So could I too.

Sir To. And ask no other dowry with her but such another jest.

Sir And. Nor I neither.

Fab. Here comes my noble gull-catcher.

Re-enter MARIA.

Sir To. Wilt thou set thy foot o' my neck?

Sir And. Or o' mine either?

Sir To. Shall I play my freedom at tray-trip, and become thy bond-slave?

Sir And. I' faith, or I either?   210

Sir To. Why, thou hast put him in such a dream, that when the image of it leaves him he must run mad.

Mar. Nay, but say true; does it work upon him?

Sir To. Like aqua-vitæ with a midwife.

Mar. If you will then see the fruits of the sport, mark his first approach before my lady: he will come to her in yellow stockings, and 'tis a colour she abhors, and cross-gartered, a fashion she detests; and he will smile upon her, which will now be so unsuitable to her disposition, being addicted to a melancholy as she is, that it cannot but turn him into a notable contempt. If you will see it, follow me.   225

Sir To. To the gates of Tartar, thou most excellent devil of wit!

Sir And. I'll make one too.   [Exeunt.

ACT III.

SCENE I. OLIVIA'S *garden.*

Enter VIOLA, *and* CLOWN *with a tabor.*

Vio. Save thee, friend, and thy music: dost thou live by thy tabor?

Clo. No, sir, I live by the church.

Vio. Art thou a churchman?

Clo. No such matter, sir: I do live by the church; for I do live at my house, and my house doth stand by the church.

Vio. So thou mayst say, the king lies by a beggar, if a beggar dwell near him; or, the church stands by thy tabor, if thy tabor stand by the church.   11

Clo. You have said, sir. To see this age! A sentence is but a cheveril glove to a good wit: how quickly the wrong side may be turned outward!

Vio. Nay, that's certain; they that dally nicely with words may quickly make them wanton.

Clo. I would, therefore, my sister had had no name, sir.   20

Vio. Why, man?

Clo. Why, sir, her name's a word; and to dally with that word might make my sister wanton. But indeed words are very rascals since bonds disgraced them.

Vio. Thy reason, man?

Clo. Troth, sir, I can yield you none without words; and words are grown so false, I am loath to prove reason with them.

Vio. I warrant thou art a merry fellow and carest for nothing.   31

Clo. Not so, sir, I do care for something; but in my conscience, sir, I do not care for you: if that be to care for nothing, sir, I would it would make you invisible.

Vio. Art not thou the Lady Olivia's fool?

Clo. No, indeed, sir; the Lady Olivia has no folly: she will keep no fool, sir, till she be married; and fools are as like husbands as pilchards are to herrings; the husband's the bigger: I am indeed not her fool, but her corrupter of words.   4!

Vio. I saw thee late at the Count Orsino's.

Clo. Foolery, sir, does walk about the orb like the sun, it shines every where. I would be sorry, sir, but the fool should be as oft with your master as with my mistress: I think I saw your wisdom there.

Vio. Nay, an thou pass upon me, I'll no more with thee. Hold, there's expenses for thee.

Clo. Now Jove, in his next commodity of hair, send thee a beard!   51

Vio. By my troth, I'll tell thee, I am almost sick for one; [Aside] though I would not have it grow on my chin. Is thy lady within?

Clo. Would not a pair of these have bred, sir?

Vio. Yes, being kept together and put to use.

Clo. I would play Lord Pandarus of Phrygia, sir, to bring a Cressida to this Troilus.

Vio. I understand you, sir; 'tis well begged.   60

Clo. The matter, I hope, is not great, sir, begging but a beggar: Cressida was a beggar. My lady is within, sir. I will construe to them whence you come; who you are and what you would are out of my welkin, I might say 'element,' but the word is over-worn. [Exit.

Vio. This fellow is wise enough to play the fool;
And to do that well craves a kind of wit:
He must observe their mood on whom he jests,
The quality of persons, and the time,   70

---

174. **champain,** open country.   175. **open,** obvious.   176. **politic,** dealing with state affairs.   177. **point-devise,** extremely precise.   179. **jade,** trick.   185. **stout,** haughty.   198. **Sophy,** Shah of Persia. 208. **tray-trip,** a game with dice, success in which depended on throwing a three.   216. **aqua-vitæ,** ardent spirits.   226. **Tartar,** the infernal regions.

ACT III. SCENE I.   2. **tabor,** drum used by clowns and jesters.   13. **cheveril,** kidskin.   25. **bonds disgraced them,** i.e., were needed to make them good.   40. **pilchards,** fish resembling herring.   48. **pass upon me,**

make jokes at my expense.   50. **commodity,** supply.   55. **pair of these,** two coins like the one he had just received.   58. **Pandarus,** the go-between in the story of Troilus and Cressida; uncle to Cressida.   62. **begging . . . Cressida,** a reference to Henryson's *Testament of Cresseid* in which the heroine becomes a leper and a beggar. The Clown desires another coin to be the mate of the one he has, as Cressida, the beggar, was mate to Troilus.   65. **welkin,** sky; here used with play upon *element,* one of whose meanings was "sky."   67-75. **This . . . wit.** Note the comment on fools as a class.   71. **haggard,** untrained hawk.   75. **taint**

And, like the haggard, check at every feather
That comes before his eye. This is a practice
As full of labour as a wise man's art:
For folly that he wisely shows is fit;
But wise men, folly-fall'n, quite taint their wit.

Enter SIR TOBY *and* SIR ANDREW.

Sir To. Save you, gentleman.
Vio. And you, sir.
Sir And. Dieu vous garde, monsieur.
Vio. Et vous aussi; votre serviteur.
Sir And. I hope, sir, you are; and I am yours.   81
Sir To. Will you encounter the house? my niece is
desirous you should enter, if your trade be to her.
Vio. I am bound to your niece, sir; I mean, she is
the list of my voyage.
Sir To. Taste your legs, sir; put them to motion.
Vio. My legs do better understand me, sir, than I
understand what you mean by bidding me taste my
legs.   91
Sir To. I mean, to go, sir, to enter.
Vio. I will answer you with gait and entrance. But
we are prevented.

Enter OLIVIA *and* MARIA.

Most excellent accomplished lady, the heavens rain
odours on you!
Sir And. That youth's a rare courtier: 'Rain odours;'
well.
Vio. My matter hath no voice, lady, but to your own
most pregnant and vouchsafed ear.   100
Sir And. 'Odours,' 'pregnant' and 'vouchsafed;' I'll
get 'em all three all ready.
Oli. Let the garden door be shut, and leave me to
my hearing. [*Exeunt Sir Toby, Sir Andrew, and Maria.*]
Give me your hand, sir.
Vio. My duty, madam, and most humble service.
Oli. What is your name?
Vio. Cesario is your servant's name, fair princess.
Oli. My servant, sir! 'Twas never merry world
Since lowly feigning was call'd compliment: 110
You're servant to the Count Orsino, youth.
Vio. And he is yours, and his must needs be yours:
Your servant's servant is your servant, madam.
Oli. For him, I think not on him: for his thoughts,
Would they were blanks, rather than fill'd with me!
Vio. Madam, I come to whet your gentle thoughts
On his behalf.
Oli.   O, by your leave, I pray you,
I bade you never speak again of him:
But, would you undertake another suit,
I had rather hear you to solicit that   120
Than music from the spheres.
Vio.   Dear lady,—
Oli. Give me leave, beseech you. I did send,
After the last enchantment you did here,
A ring in chase of you: so did I abuse
Myself, my servant and, I fear me, you:
Under your hard construction must I sit,

To force that on you, in a shameful cunning,
Which you knew none of yours: what might you
        think?
Have you not set mine honour at the stake
And baited it with all the unmuzzled thoughts   130
That tyrannous heart can think? To one of your
        receiving
Enough is shown: a cypress, not a bosom,
Hideth my heart. So, let me hear you speak.
Vio. I pity you.
Oli.   That's a degree to love.
Vio. No, not a grize; for 'tis a vulgar proof,
That very oft we pity enemies.
Oli. Why, then, methinks 'tis time to smile again.
O world, how apt the poor are to be proud!
If one should be a prey, how much the better
To fall before the lion than the wolf!   [*Clock strikes.* 140
The clock upbraids me with the waste of time.
Be not afraid, good youth, I will not have you:
And yet, when wit and youth is come to harvest,
Your wife is like to reap a proper man:
There lies your way, due west.
Vio. Then westward-ho! Grace and good disposition
Attend your ladyship!
You'll nothing, madam, to my lord by me?
Oli. Stay:
I prithee, tell me what thou think'st of me.   150
Vio. That you do think you are not what you are.
Oli. If I think so, I think the same of you.
Vio. Then think you right: I am not what I am.
Oli. I would you were as I would have you be!
Vio. Would it be better, madam, than I am?
I wish it might, for now I am your fool.
Oli. O, what a deal of scorn looks beautiful
In the contempt and anger of his lip!
A murderous guilt shows not itself more soon   159
Than love that would seem hid: love's night is noon.
Cesario, by the roses of the spring,
By maidhood, honour, truth and every thing,
I love thee so, that, maugre all thy pride,
Nor wit nor reason can my passion hide.
Do not extort thy reasons from this clause,
For that I woo, thou therefore hast no cause;
But rather reason thus with reason fetter,
Love sought is good, but given unsought is better.
Vio. By innocence I swear, and by my youth,
I have one heart, one bosom and one truth,   170
And that no woman has; nor never none
Shall mistress be of it, save I alone.
And so adieu, good madam: never more
Will I my master's tears to you deplore.
Oli. Yet come again; for thou perhaps mayst move
That heart, which now abhors, to like his love. [*Exeunt.*

SCENE II. OLIVIA's *house.*

Enter SIR TOBY, SIR ANDREW, *and* FABIAN.

Sir And. No, faith, I'll not stay a jot longer.

Twelfth Night
ACT III : SC II

631

---

their wit, lose their reputation for wisdom. 78. Dieu . . . monsieur,
God keep you, sir. 79. Et . . . serviteur. And you, too; I am your
servant. 82. encounter, high-sounding word to express "enter." 87.
Taste, try. 110. lowly feigning, pretending to be of low degree.
121. music from the spheres, reference to the belief that the heavenly
bodies were fixed in hollow concentric spheres which revolved one about
the other, producing a harmony too exquisite to be heard by human
ears. 127. To force, for forcing. 129. stake. The figure of speech is
from bearbaiting. 131. receiving, capacity, intelligence. 132.

cypress, described as a thin, gauzelike material, mostly black in color.
135. grize, step corresponding to *degree* in the preceding line. 146.
westward-ho, the cry of Thames watermen to attract westward-bound
passengers. 151. That . . . are, that you think you are in love with a
man, and you are mistaken (Luce). 152. If . . . you. If I think I
lower myself, I think the same of you, i.e., that you are a nobleman in
disguise. 156. now . . . fool. You are making a fool of me, but implying, also, I am making a fool of you. 163. maugre, in spite of.

Sir To. Thy reason, dear venom, give thy reason.

Fab. You must needs yield your reason, Sir Andrew.

Sir And. Marry, I saw your niece do more favours to the count's serving-man than ever she bestowed upon me; I saw 't i' the orchard.

Sir To. Did she see thee the while, old boy? tell me that. 10

Sir And. As plain as I see you now.

Fab. This was a great argument of love in her toward you.

Sir And. 'Slight, will you make an ass o' me?

Fab. I will prove it legitimate, sir, upon the oaths of judgement and reason.

Sir To. And they have been grand-jurymen since before Noah was a sailor. 18

Fab. She did show favour to the youth in your sight only to exasperate you, to awake your dormouse valour, to put fire in your heart, and brimstone in your liver. You should then have accosted her; and with some excellent jests, fire-new from the mint, you should have banged the youth into dumbness. This was looked for at your hand, and this was balked: the double gilt of this opportunity you let time wash off, and you are now sailed into the north of my lady's opinion; where you will hang like an icicle on a Dutchman's beard, unless you do redeem it by some laudable attempt either of valour or policy. 31

Sir And. An 't be any way, it must be with valour; for policy I hate: I had as lief be a Brownist as a politician.

Sir To. Why, then, build me thy fortunes upon the basis of valour. Challenge me the count's youth to fight with him; hurt him in eleven places: my niece shall take note of it; and assure thyself, there is no love-broker in the world can more prevail in man's commendation with woman than report of valour.

Fab. There is no way but this, Sir Andrew.

Sir And. Will either of you bear me a challenge to him? 44

Sir To. Go, write it in a martial hand; be curst and brief; it is no matter how witty, so it be eloquent and full of invention: taunt him with the license of ink: if thou thou'st him some thrice, it shall not be amiss; and as many lies as will lie in thy sheet of paper, although the sheet were big enough for the bed of Ware in England, set 'em down: go, about it. Let there be gall enough in thy ink, though thou write with a goose-pen, no matter: about it. 54

Sir And. Where shall I find you?

Sir To. We'll call thee at the cubiculo: go.

[*Exit Sir Andrew.*

Fab. This is a dear manakin to you, Sir Toby.

Sir To. I have been dear to him, lad, some two thousand strong, or so.

Fab. We shall have a rare letter from him: but you'll not deliver 't? 61

Sir To. Never trust me, then; and by all means stir on the youth to an answer. I think oxen and wainropes cannot hale them together. For Andrew, if he were

opened, and you find so much blood in his liver as will clog the foot of a flea, I'll eat the rest of the anatomy.

Fab. And his opposite, the youth, bears in his visage no great presage of cruelty.

Enter MARIA.

Sir To. Look, where the youngest wren of nine comes. 71

Mar. If you desire the spleen, and will laugh yourselves into stitches, follow me. Yond gull Malvolio is turned heathen, a very renegado; for there is no Christian, that means to be saved by believing rightly, can ever believe such impossible passages of grossness. He 's in yellow stockings.

Sir To. And cross-gartered? 79

Mar. Most villanously; like a pedant that keeps a school i' the church. I have dogged him, like his murderer. He does obey every point of the letter that I dropped to betray him: he does smile his face into more lines than is in the new map with the augmentation of the Indies: you have not seen such a thing as 'tis. I can hardly forbear hurling things at him. I know my lady will strike him: if she do, he'll smile and take 't for a great favour.

Sir To. Come, bring us, bring us where he is. [*Exeunt.*

SCENE III. *A street.*

Enter SEBASTIAN *and* ANTONIO.

Seb. I would not by my will have troubled you;
But, since you make your pleasure of your pains,
I will no further chide you.

Ant. I could not stay behind you: my desire,
More sharp than filed steel, did spur me forth;
And not all love to see you, though so much
As might have drawn one to a longer voyage,
But jealousy what might befall your travel,
Being skilless in these parts; which to a stranger,
Unguided and unfriended, often prove 10
Rough and unhospitable: my willing love,
The rather by these arguments of fear,
Set forth in your pursuit.

Seb. My kind Antonio,
I can no other answer make but thanks,
†And thanks; and ever . . . . . . oft good turns
Are shuffled off with such uncurrent pay:
But, were my worth as is my conscience firm,
You should find better dealing. What 's to do?
Shall we go see the reliques of this town? 19

Ant. To-morrow, sir: best first go see your lodging.

Seb. I am not weary, and 'tis long to night:
I pray you, let us satisfy our eyes
With the memorials and the things of fame
That do renown this city.

Ant. Would you 'ld pardon me;
I do not without danger walk these streets:
Once, in a sea-fight, 'gainst the count his galleys

SCENE II. 8. **orchard**, garden. 14. **'Slight**, oath, by God's light. 21. **dormouse valour.** The dormouse was proverbially sleepy. 27. **double gilt**, twice plated; quibble on "guilt." 28. **north**, i.e., out of the warmth and sunshine of her favor. 31. **valour or policy**, frequently associated as the qualities of a nobleman; *policy* means "discretion." 34. **Brownist**, early name of the Independents, from the name of the founder, Robert Brown (1582). **politician**, intriguer. 39. **love-broker**, one who acts as an agent between lovers. 48. **thou'st**. "Thou" was used only between friends or to inferiors. 51. **bed of Ware**, a

famous bedstead capable of holding twelve persons, said to have been at the Stag Inn in Ware, Hertfordshire. 56. **cubiculo**, Italian or Latin for "lodging." 64. **wainropes**, cart ropes. 71. **nine**. Wrens have many young birds all of which are small; presumably the last hatched would be smallest. 75. **renegado**, Spanish, *renegado*, "deserter." 77. **passages of grossness**, grossly foolish tricks. 80. **pedant**, schoolmaster. 85. **new map**. This is regarded as a reference to a map published in the 1599 edition of Hakluyt's *Voyages*, which showed more of the East Indies than had ever been mapped before. The reference is used in dating the play.

I did some service; of such note indeed,
That were I ta'en here it would scarce be answer'd.
Seb. Belike you slew great number of his people.
Ant. The offence is not of such a bloody nature; 30
Albeit the quality of the time and quarrel
Might well have given us bloody argument.
It might have since been answer'd in repaying
What we took from them; which, for traffic's sake,
Most of our city did: only myself stood out;
For which, if I be lapsed in this place,
I shall pay dear.
Seb. Do not then walk too open.
Ant. It doth not fit me. Hold, sir, here's my purse.
In the south suburbs, at the Elephant,
Is best to lodge: I will bespeak our diet, 40
Whiles you beguile the time and feed your knowledge
With viewing of the town: there shall you have me.
Seb. Why I your purse?
Ant. Haply your eye shall light upon some toy
You have desire to purchase; and your store,
I think, is not for idle markets, sir.
Seb. I'll be your purse-bearer and leave you
For an hour.
Ant. To the Elephant.
Seb. I do remember. [*Exeunt.*

SCENE IV. OLIVIA's *garden.*

Enter OLIVIA *and* MARIA.

Oli. I have sent after him: he says he'll come;
How shall I feast him? what bestow of him?
For youth is bought more oft than begg'd or borrow'd.
I speak too loud.
Where is Malvolio? he is sad and civil,
And suits well for a servant with my fortunes:
Where is Malvolio?
Mar. He's coming, madam; but in very strange
manner. He is, sure, possessed, madam.
Oli. Why, what's the matter? does he rave? 10
Mar. No, madam, he does nothing but smile: your
ladyship were best to have some guard about you, if
he come; for, sure, the man is tainted in's wits.
Oli. Go call him hither. [*Exit Maria.*] I am as mad
as he,
If sad and merry madness equal be.

Re-enter MARIA, *with* MALVOLIO.

How now, Malvolio!
Mal. Sweet lady, ho, ho.
Oli. Smilest thou?
I sent for thee upon a sad occasion. 20
Mal. Sad, lady! I could be sad: this does make some
obstruction in the blood, this cross-gartering; but
what of that? if it please the eye of one, it is with me as
the very true sonnet is, 'Please one, and please all.'
Oli. Why, how dost thou, man? what is the matter
with thee?
Mal. Not black in my mind, though yellow in my
legs. It did come to his hands, and commands shall be

executed: I think we do know the sweet Roman hand.
Oli. Wilt thou go to bed, Malvolio? 32
Mal. To bed! ay, sweet-heart, and I'll come to thee.
Oli. God comfort thee! Why dost thou smile so and
kiss thy hand so oft?
Mar. How do you, Malvolio?
Mal. At your request! yes; nightingales answer
daws.
Mar. Why appear you with this ridiculous boldness
before my lady? 41
Mal. 'Be not afraid of greatness:' 'twas well writ.
Oli. What meanest thou by that, Malvolio?
Mal. 'Some are born great,'—
Oli. Ha!
Mal. 'Some achieve greatness,'—
Oli. What sayest thou?
Mal. 'And some have greatness thrust upon them.' 50
Oli. Heaven restore thee!
Mal. 'Remember who commended thy yellow
stockings,'—
Oli. Thy yellow stockings!
Mal. 'And wished to see thee cross-gartered.'
Oli. Cross-gartered!
Mal. 'Go to, thou art made, if thou desirest to be
so;'—
Oli. Am I made?
Mal. 'If not, let me see thee a servant still.' 60
Oli. Why, this is very midsummer madness.

Enter Servant.

Ser. Madam, the young gentleman of the Count
Orsino's is returned: I could hardly entreat him back:
he attends your ladyship's pleasure.
Oli. I'll come to him. [*Exit Servant.*] Good Maria, let
this fellow be looked to. Where's my cousin Toby?
Let some of my people have a special care of him: I
would not have him miscarry for the half of my
dowry. [*Exeunt Olivia and Maria.* 70
Mal. O, ho! do you come near me now? no worse
man than Sir Toby to look to me! This concurs
directly with the letter: she sends him on purpose,
that I may appear stubborn to him; for she incites me
to that in the letter. 'Cast thy humble slough,' says
she; 'be opposite with a kinsman, surly with servants;
let thy tongue tang with arguments of state; put thyself into the trick of singularity;' and consequently sets
down the manner how; as, a sad face, a reverend carriage, a slow tongue, in the habit of some sir of note,
and so forth. I have limed her; but it is Jove's doing,
and Jove make me thankful! And when she went away
now, 'Let this fellow be looked to:' fellow! not Malvolio, nor after my degree, but fellow. Why, every
thing adheres together, that no dram of a scruple, no
scruple of a scruple, no obstacle, no incredulous or
unsafe circumstance—What can be said? Nothing
that can be can come between me and the full prospect of my hopes. Well, Jove, not I, is the doer of this,
and he is to be thanked. 92

Re-enter MARIA, *with* SIR TOBY *and* FABIAN.

SCENE III. 6. **not all love,** not altogether love. 8. **jealousy,** anxiety. 9. **skilless,** ignorant, unacquainted with. 15. **And thanks,** etc. This corrupt line is usually made to read, *And thanks and ever thanks. Too oft,* etc. 17. **worth,** wealth. 19. **reliques,** antiquities. 26. **count his,** count's. 36. **lapsed,** probably, caught. 39. **Elephant,** name of an inn. 40. **diet,** dinner, food. 46. **idle markets,** unnecessary purchases.
SCENE IV. 1. **he . . . come,** i.e., suppose he says, etc. 9. **possessed,** i.e., with an evil spirit. 25. **sonnet,** song, ballad. **'Please . . . all,'** the refrain of a ballad. 28. **black . . . yellow,** possible reference to a

ballad (Collier). 33. **sweet-heart . . . thee,** possible reference to a ballad (W. J. Craig). 38. **nightingales answer daws,** i.e., I may answer you. 61. **midsummer madness,** a proverbial phrase; the midsummer moon was supposed to cause madness. 69. **miscarry,** come to harm. 71. **come near,** understand. 79. **consequently,** thereafter. 82. **limed,** caught like a bird with birdlime. 86. **fellow.** Malvolio takes the original meaning, companion; Olivia had used it in its degenerated sense. 88. **incredulous,** incredible.

Sir To. Which way is he, in the name of sanctity? If all the devils of hell be drawn in little, and Legion himself possessed him, yet I'll speak to him.

Fab. Here he is, here he is. How is 't with you, sir? how is 't with you, man?

Mal. Go off; I discard you: let me enjoy my private: go off. 100

Mar. Lo, how hollow the fiend speaks within him! did not I tell you? Sir Toby, my lady prays you to have a care of him.

Mal. Ah, ha! does she so?

Sir To. Go to, go to; peace, peace; we must deal gently with him: let me alone. How do you, Malvolio? how is 't with you? What, man! defy the devil: consider, he 's an enemy to mankind.

Mal. Do you know what you say? 110

Mar. La you, an you speak ill of the devil, how he takes it at heart! Pray God, he be not bewitched!

Fab. Carry his water to the wise woman.

Mar. Marry, and it shall be done to-morrow morning, if I live. My lady would not lose him for more than I'll say.

Mal. How now, mistress!

Mar. O Lord! 119

Sir To. Prithee, hold thy peace; this is not the way: do you not see you move him? let me alone with him.

Fab. No way but gentleness; gently, gently: the fiend is rough, and will not be roughly used.

Sir To. Why, how now, my bawcock! how dost thou, chuck?

Mal. Sir!

Sir To. Ay, Biddy, come with me. What, man! 'tis not for gravity to play at cherry-pit with Satan: hang him, foul collier! 130

Mar. Get him to say his prayers, good Sir Toby, get him to pray.

Mal. My prayers, minx!

Mar. No, I warrant you, he will not hear of godliness.

Mal. Go, hang yourselves all! you are idle shallow things: I am not of your element: you shall know more hereafter. [*Exit.*

Sir To. Is 't possible? 139

Fab. If this were played upon a stage now, I could condemn it as an improbable fiction.

Sir To. His very genius hath taken the infection of the device, man.

Mar. Nay, pursue him now, lest the device take air and taint.

Fab. Why, we shall make him mad indeed.

Mar. The house will be the quieter. 147

Sir To. Come, we'll have him in a dark room and bound. My niece is already in the belief that he 's mad: we may carry it thus, for our pleasure and his penance, till our very pastime, tired out of breath, prompt us to have mercy on him: at which time we will bring the device to the bar and crown thee for a finder of madmen. But see, but see.

Enter SIR ANDREW.

Fab. More matter for a May morning.

Sir And. Here 's the challenge, read it: I warrant there 's vinegar and pepper in 't.

Fab. Is 't so saucy? 159

Sir And. Ay, is 't, I warrant him: do but read.

Sir To. Give me. [*Reads*] 'Youth, whatsoever thou art, thou art but a scurvy fellow.'

Fab. Good, and valiant.

Sir To. [*Reads*] 'Wonder not, nor admire not in thy mind, why I do call thee so, for I will show thee no reason for 't.'

Fab. A good note; that keeps you from the blow of the law. 169

Sir To. [*Reads*] 'Thou comest to the lady Olivia, and in my sight she uses thee kindly: but thou liest in thy throat; that is not the matter I challenge thee for.'

Fab. Very brief, and to exceeding good sense—less.

Sir To. [*Reads*] 'I will waylay thee going home; where if it be thy chance to kill me,'—

Fab. Good.

Sir To. [*Reads*] 'Thou killest me like a rogue and a villain.' 180

Fab. Still you keep o' the windy side of the law: good.

Sir To. [*Reads*] 'Fare thee well; and God have mercy upon one of our souls! He may have mercy upon mine; but my hope is better, and so look to thyself. Thy friend, as thou usest him, and thy sworn enemy,
ANDREW AGUECHEEK.'
If this letter move him not, his legs cannot: I'll give 't him. 189

Mar. You may have very fit occasion for 't: he is now in some commerce with my lady, and will by and by depart.

Sir To. Go, Sir Andrew; scout me for him at the corner of the orchard like a bum-baily: so soon as ever thou seest him, draw; and, as thou drawest, swear horrible; for it comes to pass off that a terrible oath, with a swaggering accent sharply twanged off, gives manhood more approbation than ever proof itself would have earned him. Away! 200

Sir And. Nay, let me alone for swearing. [*Exit.*

Sir To. Now will not I deliver his letter: for the behaviour of the young gentleman gives him out to be of good capacity and breeding; his employment between his lord and my niece confirms no less: therefore this letter, being so excellently ignorant, will breed no terror in the youth: he will find it comes from a clodpole. But, sir, I will deliver his challenge by word of mouth; set upon Aguecheek a notable report of valour; and drive the gentleman, as I know his youth will aptly receive it, into a most hideous opinion of his rage, skill, fury and impetuosity. This will so fright them both that they will kill one another by the look, like cockatrices. 215

Re-enter OLIVIA, *with* VIOLA.

Fab. Here he comes with your niece: give them way till he take leave, and presently after him.

Sir To. I will meditate the while upon some horrid message for a challenge. 220
[*Exeunt Sir Toby, Fabian, and Maria.*

Oli. I have said too much unto a heart of stone
And laid mine honour too unchary out:
There 's something in me that reproves my fault;
But such a headstrong potent fault it is,
That it but mocks reproof.
Vio. With the same 'haviour that your passion
bears
Goes on my master's grief.
Oli. Here, wear this jewel for me, 'tis my picture;
Refuse it not; it hath no tongue to vex you;
And I beseech you come again to-morrow.   230
What shall you ask of me that I'll deny,
That honour saved may upon asking give?
Vio. Nothing but this; your true love for my master.
Oli. How with mine honour may I give him that
Which I have given to you?
Vio.   I will acquit you.
Oli. Well, come again to-morrow: fare thee well:
A fiend like thee might bear my soul to hell.   [*Exit.*

Re-enter Sir Toby *and* Fabian.

Sir To. Gentleman, God save thee.
Vio. And you, sir.   239
Sir To. That defence thou hast, betake thee to 't:
of what nature the wrongs are thou hast done him, I
know not; but thy intercepter, full of despite, bloody
as the hunter, attends thee at the orchard-end: dismount thy tuck, be yare in thy preparation, for thy
assailant is quick, skilful and deadly.
Vio. You mistake, sir; I am sure no man hath any
quarrel to me: my remembrance is very free and clear
from any image of offence done to any man.   250
Sir To. You'll find it otherwise, I assure you: therefore, if you hold your life at any price, betake you to
your guard; for your opposite hath in him what youth,
strength, skill and wrath can furnish man withal.
Vio. I pray you, sir, what is he?
Sir To. He is knight, dubbed with unhatched rapier
and on carpet consideration; but he is a devil in private brawl: souls and bodies hath he divorced three;
and his incensement at this moment is so implacable,
that satisfaction can be none but by pangs of death
and sepulchre. Hob, nob, is his word; give 't or take 't.
Vio. I will return again into the house and desire
some conduct of the lady. I am no fighter. I have
heard of some kind of men that put quarrels purposely on others, to taste their valour: belike this is a
man of that quirk.   268
Sir To. Sir, no, his indignation derives itself out of a
very competent injury: therefore, get you on and give
him his desire. Back you shall not to the house, unless
you undertake that with me which with as much
safety you might answer him: therefore, on, or strip
your sword stark naked; for meddle you must, that 's
certain, or forswear to wear iron about you.   276
Vio. This is as uncivil as strange. I beseech you, do
me this courteous office, as to know of the knight what
my offence to him is: it is something of my negligence,
nothing of my purpose.
Sir To. I will do so. Signior Fabian, stay you by this
gentleman till my return.   [*Exit.*

Vio. Pray you, sir, do you know of this matter?
Fab. I know the knight is incensed against you, even
to a mortal arbitrement; but nothing of the circumstance more.
Vio. I beseech you, what manner of man is he?   289
Fab. Nothing of that wonderful promise, to read him
by his form, as you are like to find him in the proof of
his valour. He is, indeed, sir, the most skilful, bloody
and fatal opposite that you could possibly have found
in any part of Illyria. Will you walk towards him? I
will make your peace with him if I can.
Vio. I shall be much bound to you for 't: I am one
that had rather go with sir priest than sir knight: I
care not who knows so much of my mettle. [*Exeunt.* 300

Re-enter Sir Toby, *with* Sir Andrew.

Sir To. Why, man, he 's a very devil; I have not seen
such a firago. I had a pass with him, rapier, scabbard
and all, and he gives me the stuck in with such a
mortal motion, that it is inevitable; and on the
answer, he pays you as surely as your feet hit the
ground they step on. They say he has been fencer to
the Sophy.
Sir And. Pox on 't, I'll not meddle with him.
Sir To. Ay, but he will not now be pacified: Fabian
can scarce hold him yonder.   310
Sir And. Plague on 't, an I thought he had been
valiant and so cunning in fence, I 'ld have seen him
damned ere I 'ld have challenged him. Let him let the
matter slip, and I'll give him my horse, grey Capilet.
Sir To. I'll make the motion: stand here, make a
good show on 't: this shall end without the perdition of
souls. [*Aside*] Marry, I'll ride your horse as well as I
ride you.

Re-enter Fabian *and* Viola.

[*To Fab.*] I have his horse to take up the quarrel: I
have persuaded him the youth 's a devil.   321
Fab. He is as horribly conceited of him; and pants
and looks pale, as if a bear were at his heels.
Sir To. [*To Vio.*] There 's no remedy, sir; he will
fight with you for 's oath sake: marry, he hath better
bethought him of his quarrel, and he finds that now
scarce to be worth talking of: therefore draw, for the
supportance of his vow; he protests he will not hurt
you.   330
Vio. [*Aside*] Pray God defend me! A little thing
would make me tell them how much I lack of a man.
Fab. Give ground, if you see him furious.
Sir To. Come, Sir Andrew, there 's no remedy; the
gentleman will, for his honour's sake, have one bout
with you; he cannot by the duello avoid it: but he has
promised me, as he is a gentleman and a soldier, he
will not hurt you. Come on; to 't.   340
Sir And. Pray God, he keep his oath!
Vio. I do assure you, 'tis against my will. [*They draw.*

Enter Antonio.

Ant. Put up your sword. If this young gentleman
Have done offence, I take the fault on me:

sword.   245. **yare,** ready, nimble.   257. **unhatched,** for "unhacked."
258. **carpet consideration,** i.e., he is a carpet knight, not a warrior.
263. **Hob, nob,** originally, have or have not; here, hit or miss.   265.
conduct, escort.   268. **quirk,** peculiar humor.   273. **that,** i.e., to give
satisfaction.   275. **meddle,** engage in conflict.   286. **mortal arbitrement,** trial to the death.   294. **opposite,** antagonist.   299. **sir,** commonly used as the title of priests as well as knights.   302. **firago,** thought

to be an intentional corruption of "virago."   304. **stuck in,** stoccado, a
thrust in fencing.   315. **Capilet,** evidently derived from "capel," a
nag.   320. **take up,** make up.   322. **is as horribly conceited,** has as
horrible a conception.   338. **duello,** duelling code.

If you offend him, I for him defy you.
Sir To. You, sir! why, what are you?
Ant. One, sir, that for his love dares yet do
    more   347
Than you have heard him brag to you he will.
Sir To. Nay, if you be an undertaker, I am for you.
                                      [They draw.

Enter Officers.

Fab. O good Sir Toby, hold! here come the officers.
Sir To. I'll be with you anon.
Vio. Pray, sir, put your sword up, if you please.
Sir And. Marry, will I, sir; and, for that I promised
you, I'll be as good as my word: he will bear you easily
and reins well.
First Off. This is the man; do thy office.
Sec. Off. Antonio, I arrest thee at the suit of Count
Orsino.   361
Ant. You do mistake me, sir.
First Off. No, sir, no jot; I know your favour well,
Though now you have no sea-cap on your head.
Take him away: he knows I know him well.
Ant. I must obey. [*To Vio.*] This comes with seeking
    you:
But there's no remedy; I shall answer it.
What will you do, now my necessity
Makes me to ask you for my purse? It grieves me
Much more for what I cannot do for you   370
Than what befalls myself. You stand amazed;
But be of comfort.
Sec. Off. Come, sir, away.
Ant. I must entreat of you some of that money.
Vio. What money, sir?
For the fair kindness you have show'd me here,
And, part, being prompted by your present
    trouble,
Out of my lean and low ability
I'll lend you something: my having is not much;
I'll make division of my present with you: 380
Hold, there's half my coffer.
Ant.   Will you deny me now?
Is 't possible that my deserts to you
Can lack persuasion? Do not tempt my misery,
Lest that it make me so unsound a man
As to upbraid you with those kindnesses
That I have done for you.
Vio.   I know of none;
Nor know I you by voice or any feature:
I hate ingratitude more in a man
Than lying, vainness, babbling, drunkenness,
Or any taint of vice whose strong corruption   390
Inhabits our frail blood.
Ant.   O heavens themselves!
Sec. Off. Come, sir, I pray you, go.
Ant. Let me speak a little. This youth that you see
    here
I snatch'd one half out of the jaws of death,
Relieved him with such sanctity of love,
And to his image, which methought did promise
Most venerable worth, did I devotion.

First Off. What's that to us? The time goes by:
    away!
Ant. But O how vile an idol proves this god!
Thou hast, Sebastian, done good feature shame.   400
In nature there's no blemish but the mind;
None can be call'd deform'd but the unkind:
Virtue is beauty, but the beauteous evil
Are empty trunks o'erflourish'd by the devil.
First Off. The man grows mad: away with him!
    Come, come, sir.
Ant. Lead me on.   *[Exit with Officers.*
Vio. Methinks his words do from such passion fly,
That he believes himself: so do not I.
Prove true, imagination, O, prove true,
That I, dear brother, be now ta'en for you!   410
Sir To. Come hither, knight; come hither, Fabian:
we'll whisper o'er a couplet or two of most sage saws.
Vio. He named Sebastian: I my brother know
Yet living in my glass; even such and so
In favour was my brother, and he went
Still in this fashion, colour, ornament,
For him I imitate: O, if it prove,
Tempests are kind and salt waves fresh in love.   *[Exit.*
Sir To. A very dishonest paltry boy, and more a
coward than a hare: his dishonesty appears in leaving
his friend here in necessity and denying him; and for
his cowardship, ask Fabian.
Fab. A coward, a most devout coward, religious in
it.   426
Sir And. 'Slid, I'll after him again and beat him.
Sir To. Do; cuff him soundly, but never draw thy
sword.
Sir And. An I do not,—   *[Exit.*
Fab. Come, let's see the event.   431
Sir To. I dare lay any money 'twill be nothing yet.
                                  [Exeunt.

ACT IV.

SCENE I. *Before* OLIVIA'S *house.*

Enter SEBASTIAN *and* CLOWN.

Clo. Will you make me believe that I am not sent for
you?
Seb. Go to, go to, thou art a foolish fellow:
Let me be clear of thee.
Clo. Well held out, i' faith! No, I do not know you;
nor I am not sent to you by my lady, to bid you come
speak with her; nor your name is not Master Cesario;
nor this is not my nose neither. Nothing that is so is so.
Seb. I prithee, vent thy folly somewhere else:
Thou know'st not me.   11
Clo. Vent my folly! he has heard that word of some
great man and now applies it to a fool. Vent my folly!
I am afraid this great lubber, the world, will prove a
cockney. I prithee now, ungird thy strangeness and
tell me what I shall vent to my lady: shall I vent to her
that thou art coming?
Seb. I prithee, foolish Greek, depart from me:

---

349. **undertaker,** one who takes upon himself a task or business; here,
suggests meddling. 377. **part,** partly. 379. **having,** wealth; see
glossary. 380. **present,** present store. 381. **coffer,** purse. 389. **vainness,** boastfulness. 396. **image,** what he appeared to be. 397.
venerable, worthy of honor (no reference to age). 400-404. **Thou . . .
devil.** It was a widespread belief in the Renaissance that the outward
and inward parts of man correspond in quality. 404. **o'erflourish'd,**

covered with ornamental carvings. 408. **so do not I,** may mean "I do
not believe him" or "I do not believe myself" (in the hope that has
arisen in me). 410. **That . . . you.** This is the first move in the direction
of the solution of the plot. 418. **prove,** prove true. 421. **dishonesty,**
dishonorable character. 427. **'Slid,** oath, "by God's (eye-) lid."
ACT IV. SCENE I. 15. **cockney,** effeminate or foppish fellow. 19.
Greek, jester. 24. **fourteen years' purchase,** reference to the valuation

There 's money for thee: if you tarry longer, 20
I shall give worse payment.

Clo. By my troth, thou hast an open hand. These
wise men that give fools money get themselves a good
report—after fourteen years' purchase.

Enter SIR ANDREW, SIR TOBY, *and* FABIAN.

Sir And. Now, sir, have I met you again? there 's for
you.

Seb. Why, there 's for thee, and there, and there.
Are all the people mad? 29

Sir To. Hold, sir, or I'll throw your dagger o'er the
house.

Clo. This will I tell my lady straight: I would not be
in some of your coats for two pence. [*Exit.*

Sir To. Come on, sir; hold.

Sir And. Nay, let him alone: I'll go another way to
work with him; I'll have an action of battery against
him, if there be any law in Illyria: though I struck
him first, yet it 's no matter for that.

Seb. Let go thy hand. 40

Sir To. Come, sir, I will not let you go. Come, my
young soldier, put up your iron: you are well fleshed;
come on.

Seb. I will be free from thee. What wouldst thou
now?
If thou darest tempt me further, draw thy sword.

Sir To. What, what? Nay, then I must have an
ounce or two of this malapert blood from you.

Enter OLIVIA.

Oli. Hold, Toby; on thy life I charge thee, hold!

Sir To. Madam! 50

Oli. Will it be ever thus? Ungracious wretch,
Fit for the mountains and the barbarous caves,
Where manners ne'er were preach'd! out of my sight!
Be not offended, dear Cesario.
Rudesby, be gone!
[*Exeunt Sir Toby, Sir Andrew, and Fabian.*
I prithee, gentle friend,
Let thy fair wisdom, not thy passion, sway
In this uncivil and unjust extent
Against thy peace. Go with me to my house,
And hear thou there how many fruitless pranks
This ruffian hath botch'd up, that thou thereby 60
Mayst smile at this: thou shalt not choose but go:
Do not deny. Beshrew his soul for me,
He started one poor heart of mine in thee.

Seb. What relish is in this? how runs the stream?
Or I am mad, or else this is a dream:
Let fancy still my sense in Lethe steep;
If it be thus to dream, still let me sleep!

Oli. Nay, come, I prithee; would thou 'ldst be ruled
by me!

Seb. Madam, I will.

Oli.   O, say so, and so be! [*Exeunt.*

SCENE II. OLIVIA'S *house.*

Enter MARIA *and* CLOWN.

Mar. Nay, I prithee, put on this gown and this
beard; make him believe thou art Sir Topas the
curate: do it quickly; I'll call Sir Toby the whilst. [*Exit.*

Clo. Well, I'll put it on, and I will dissemble myself
in 't; and I would I were the first that ever dissembled
in such a gown. I am not tall enough to become the
function well, nor lean enough to be thought a good
student; but to be said an honest man and a good
housekeeper goes as fairly as to say a careful man and
a great scholar. The competitors enter. 12

Enter SIR TOBY *and* MARIA.

Sir To. Jove bless thee, master Parson.

Clo. Bonos dies, Sir Toby: for, as the old hermit of
Prague, that never saw pen and ink, very wittily said
to a niece of King Gorboduc, 'That that is is;' so I,
being master Parson, am master Parson; for, what is
'that' but 'that,' and 'is' but 'is'?

Sir To. To him, Sir Topas. 20

Clo. What, ho, I say! peace in this prison!

Sir To. The knave counterfeits well; a good knave.

Mal. [*Within*] Who calls there?

Clo. Sir Topas the curate, who comes to visit Malvolio the lunatic.

Mal. Sir Topas, Sir Topas, good Sir Topas, go to my
lady.

Clo. Out, hyperbolical fiend! how vexest thou this
man! talkest thou nothing but of ladies? 30

Sir To. Well said, master Parson.

Mal. Sir Topas, never was man thus wronged: good
Sir Topas, do not think I am mad: they have laid me
here in hideous darkness.

Clo. Fie, thou dishonest Satan! I call thee by the
most modest terms; for I am one of those gentle ones
that will use the devil himself with courtesy: sayest
thou that house is dark?

Mal. As hell, Sir Topas. 39

Clo. Why, it hath bay windows transparent as
barricadoes, and the clearstores toward the south
north are as lustrous as ebony; and yet complainest
thou of obstruction?

Mal. I am not mad, Sir Topas: I say to you, this
house is dark.

Clo. Madman, thou errest: I say, there is no darkness but ignorance; in which thou art more puzzled
than the Egyptians in their fog. 48

Mal. I say, this house is as dark as ignorance,
though ignorance were as dark as hell; and I say, there
was never man thus abused. I am no more mad than
you are: make the trial of it in any constant question.

Clo. What is the opinion of Pythagoras concerning
wild fowl?

Mal. That the soul of our grandam might haply
inhabit a bird.

Clo. What thinkest thou of his opinion?

Mal. I think nobly of the soul, and no way approve
his opinion. 60

Clo. Fare thee well. Remain thou still in darkness:

---

of land at the price of twelve years' rental. The fool adds two years; see
purchase in glossary. 47. **malapert,** saucy, impudent. 55. **Rudesby,**
ruffian. 57. **extent,** attack. 60. **botch'd up,** clumsily contrived.
63. **heart,** with play on "hart." 66. **Lethe,** forgetfulness.
  SCENE II. 4. **the whilst,** in the meantime. 5. **dissemble,** disguise.
9. **said,** called. 10. **housekeeper,** good liver, hospitable person. 15.
hermit of Prague, usually thought to refer to Jerome of Prague, but

the allusion is obscure. 16. **niece of King Gorboduc.** Gorboduc was
an ancient British king; his niece is apparently an invention of the
Clown's. 29. **hyperbolical,** possibly for "diabolical." 41. **clearstores,**
upper walls of a building containing windows by which it is lighted.
48. **Egyptians . . . fog.** See Exodus 10:21, 22. 53. **constant question,**
consistent discussion. 54-55. **Pythagoras . . . wild fowl,** an opening for
the discussion of transmigration of souls, a doctrine held by Pythagoras.

thou shalt hold the opinion of Pythagoras ere I will allow of thy wits, and fear to kill a woodcock, lest thou dispossess the soul of thy grandam. Fare thee well.

Mal. Sir Topas, Sir Topas!

Sir To. My most exquisite Sir Topas!

Clo. Nay, I am for all waters.

Mar. Thou mightst have done this without thy beard and gown: he sees thee not.   70

Sir To. To him in thine own voice, and bring me word how thou findest him: I would we were well rid of this knavery. If he may be conveniently delivered, I would he were, for I am now so far in offence with my niece that I cannot pursue with any safety this sport to the upshot. Come by and by to my chamber.

[*Exeunt Sir Toby and Maria.*

Clo. [*Singing*] 'Hey, Robin, jolly Robin,
                    Tell me how thy lady does.'

Mal. Fool!   80

Clo. 'My lady is unkind, perdy.'

Mal. Fool!

Clo. 'Alas, why is she so?'

Mal. Fool, I say!

Clo. 'She loves another'—Who calls, ha?

Mal. Good fool, as ever thou wilt deserve well at my hand, help me to a candle, and pen, ink and paper: as I am a gentleman, I will live to be thankful to thee for 't.

Clo. Master Malvolio?   90

Mal. Ay, good fool.

Clo. Alas, sir, how fell you besides your five wits?

Mal. Fool, there was never man so notoriously abused: I am as well in my wits, fool, as thou art.

Clo. But as well? then you are mad indeed, if you be no better in your wits than a fool.

Mal. They have here propertied me; keep me in darkness, send ministers to me, asses, and do all they can to face me out of my wits.   101

Clo. Advise you what you say; the minister is here. Malvolio, Malvolio, thy wits the heavens restore! endeavour thyself to sleep, and leave thy vain bibble babble.

Mal. Sir Topas!

Clo. Maintain no words with him, good fellow. Who, I, sir? not I, sir. God be wi' you, good Sir Topas. Marry, amen. I will, sir, I will.

Mal. Fool, fool, fool, I say!   110

Clo. Alas, sir, be patient. What say you, sir? I am shent for speaking to you.

Mal. Good fool, help me to some light and some paper: I tell thee, I am as well in my wits as any man in Illyria.

Clo. Well-a-day that you were, sir!

Mal. By this hand, I am. Good fool, some ink, paper and light; and convey what I will set down to my lady: it shall advantage thee more than ever the bearing of letter did.   120

Clo. I will help you to 't. But tell me true, are you not mad indeed? or do you but counterfeit?

Mal. Believe me, I am not; I tell thee true.

Clo. Nay, I'll ne'er believe a madman till I see his brains. I will fetch you light and paper and ink.

Mal. Fool, I'll requite it in the highest degree: I prithee, be gone.

Clo. [*Singing*] I am gone, sir,   130
                    And anon, sir,
            I'll be with you again,
                    In a trice,
                    Like to the old Vice,
            Your need to sustain;

            Who, with dagger of lath,
            In his rage and his wrath,
                    Cries, ah, ha! to the devil:
            Like a mad lad,
            Pare thy nails, dad;   140
                    †Adieu, good man devil.   [*Exit.*

SCENE III. OLIVIA'S *garden.*

Enter SEBASTIAN.

Seb. This is the air; that is the glorious sun;
This pearl she gave me, I do feel 't and see 't;
And though 'tis wonder that enwraps me thus,
Yet 'tis not madness. Where 's Antonio, then?
I could not find him at the Elephant:
Yet there he was; and there I found this credit,
That he did range the town to seek me out.
His counsel now might do me golden service;
For though my soul disputes well with my sense,
That this may be some error, but no madness,   10
Yet doth this accident and flood of fortune
So far exceed all instance, all discourse,
That I am ready to distrust mine eyes
And wrangle with my reason that persuades me
To any other trust but that I am mad
Or else the lady 's mad; yet, if 'twere so,
She could not sway her house, command her
        followers,
Take and give back affairs and their dispatch
With such a smooth, discreet and stable bearing
As I perceive she does: there 's something in 't.   20
That is deceiveable. But here the lady comes.

Enter OLIVIA *and* Priest.

Oli. Blame not this haste of mine. If you mean well,
Now go with me and with this holy man
Into the chantry by: there, before him,
And underneath that consecrated roof,
Plight me the full assurance of your faith;
That my most jealous and too doubtful soul
May live at peace. He shall conceal it
Whiles you are willing it shall come to note,
What time we will our celebration keep   30
According to my birth. What do you say?

---

64. **woodcock.** The woodcock was a type of stupidity because it was easily caught.   68. **for all waters,** i.e., able to sail in all waters.   73. **knavery,** practical joke.   78-85. **'Hey, Robin . . . another,'** fragments of an old song.   92. **besides,** out of.   92-93. **five wits,** intellectual faculties given as common wit, imagination, fantasy, judgment, and memory.   94-95. **notoriously abused,** shamefully mistreated.   99. **propertied,** explained as "treated me as property and thrown me into the lumber-room"; may mean "have chosen to endow me with madness."   102. **Advise you,** take care. The Clown here again impersonates

Sir Topas.   112. **shent,** scolded, rebuked.   116. **Well-a-day,** alas, would that.   134. **Vice,** the buffoon of moralities and interludes; derived from *Vitia,* the minor devils or sins associated with the chief devil.   136. **dagger of lath,** symbol of the Vice, who was apparently notorious for using it for paring his nails; cf. *Henry V,* IV, iv, 75-77.
SCENE III.   15. **trust,** belief.   18. **Take and give back,** undertake and discharge.   21. **deceiveable,** deceptive.   24. **chantry,** chapel privately endowed.   27. **jealous,** anxious.   29. **Whiles,** until.   **come to note,** become known.

Seb. I'll follow this good man, and go with you;
And, having sworn truth, ever will be true.

Oli. Then lead the way, good father; and heavens
so shine,
That they may fairly note this act of mine!   [*Exeunt.*

ACT V.

SCENE I. *Before* OLIVIA'S *house.*

Enter CLOWN *and* FABIAN.

Fab. Now, as thou lovest me, let me see his letter.

Clo. Good Master Fabian, grant me another request.

Fab. Any thing.

Clo. Do not desire to see this letter.

Fab. This is, to give a dog, and in recompense desire
my dog again.

Enter DUKE, VIOLA, CURIO, *and* Lords.

Duke. Belong you to the Lady Olivia, friends?

Clo. Ay, sir; we are some of her trappings.   10

Duke. I know thee well: how dost thou, my good
fellow?

Clo. Truly, sir, the better for my foes and the worse
for my friends.

Duke. Just the contrary; the better for thy friends.

Clo. No, sir, the worse.

Duke. How can that be?   19

Clo. Marry, sir, they praise me and make an ass of
me; now my foes tell me plainly I am an ass: so that
by my foes, sir, I profit in the knowledge of myself,
and by my friends I am abused: so that, conclusions
to be as kisses, if your four negatives make your two
affirmatives, why then, the worse for my friends and
the better for my foes.

Duke. Why, this is excellent.

Clo. By my troth, sir, no; though it please you to be
one of my friends.

Duke. Thou shalt not be the worse for me: there's
gold.   31

Clo. But that it would be double-dealing, sir, I
would you could make it another.

Duke. O, you give me ill counsel.

Clo. Put your grace in your pocket, sir, for this once,
and let your flesh and blood obey it.

Duke. Well, I will be so much a sinner, to be a
double-dealer: there's another.   38

Clo. Primo, secundo, tertio, is a good play; and the
old saying is, the third pays for all: the triplex, sir, is
a good tripping measure; or the bells of Saint Bennet,
sir, may put you in mind; one, two, three.

Duke. You can fool no more money out of me at this
throw: if you will let your lady know I am here to
speak with her, and bring her along with you, it may
awake my bounty further.   47

Clo. Marry, sir, lullaby to your bounty till I come
again. I go, sir; but I would not have you to think that

my desire of having is the sin of covetousness: but, as
you say, sir, let your bounty take a nap, I will awake
it anon.   [*Exit.*

Vio. Here comes the man, sir, that did rescue me.

Enter ANTONIO *and* Officers.

Duke. That face of his I do remember well;
Yet, when I saw it last, it was besmear'd
As black as Vulcan in the smoke of war:
A bawbling vessel was he captain of,
For shallow draught and bulk unprizable;
With which such scathful grapple did he make
With the most noble bottom of our fleet,   60
That very envy and the tongue of loss
Cried fame and honour on him. What's the matter?

First Off. Orsino, this is that Antonio
That took the *Phœnix* and her fraught from Candy;
And this is he that did the *Tiger* board,
When your young nephew Titus lost his leg:
Here in the streets, desperate of shame and state,
In private brabble did we apprehend him.

Vio. He did me kindness, sir, drew on my side;
But in conclusion put strange speech upon me: 70
I know not what 'twas but distraction.

Duke. Notable pirate! thou salt-water thief!
What foolish boldness brought thee to their mercies,
Whom thou, in terms so bloody and so dear,
Hast made thine enemies?

Ant.   Orsino, noble sir,
Be pleased that I shake off these names you give me:
Antonio never yet was thief or pirate,
Though I confess, on base and ground enough,
Orsino's enemy. A witchcraft drew me hither:
That most ingrateful boy there by your side,   80
From the rude sea's enraged and foamy mouth
Did I redeem; a wreck past hope he was:
His life I gave him and did thereto add
My love, without retention or restraint,
All his in dedication; for his sake
Did I expose myself, pure for his love,
Into the danger of this adverse town;
Drew to defend him when he was beset:
Where being apprehended, his false cunning,
Not meaning to partake with me in danger,   90
Taught him to face me out of his acquaintance,
And grew a twenty years removed thing
While one would wink; denied me mine own purse,
Which I had recommended to his use
Not half an hour before.

Viol.   How can this be?

Duke. When came he to this town?

Ant. To-day, my lord; and for three months before,
No interim, not a minute's vacancy,
Both day and night did we keep company.

Enter OLIVIA *and* Attendants.

Duke. Here comes the countess: now heaven walks
on earth.   100

ACT V. SCENE I. **1. his,** i.e., Malvolio's. **23-24. conclusions . . .
kisses.** The Clown has only two negatives, which would make but one
affirmative; he needs two affirmatives and can get them if conclusions
arise like kisses, there being two pairs of lips in each kiss. **29. friends,**
probably, flatterers. The duke gives a coin to show that he is sincere.
The Clown would ask for two except for seeming to be a *double-dealer,*
i.e., insincere in his turn. **35. grace,** apparently a play on *grace* meaning "favor of God," and the title, "Your *Grace.*" **39-40. Primo,
secundo, tertio . . . all,** probably dicing terms. **41. triplex,** triple time
in music. **42. Saint Bennet,** church of St. Benedict; reference to the
sound of the church bell, which may have been embodied in a rhyme.
45. throw, i.e., of dice. **48. lullaby,** suggested by *awake,* above. **57.
bawbling,** insignificant. **58. unprizable,** of value too slight to be
estimated. **59. scathful,** destructive. **64. fraught,** cargo. **Candy,**
Candia, Crete. **67. desperate . . . state,** reckless of disgrace and position. **68. brabble,** brawl. **71. distraction,** madness. **86. pure,**
entirely. **87. Into,** unto. **adverse,** hostile. **91. face me out of,** exclude me impudently from. **94. recommended,** consigned, committed.

But for thee, fellow; fellow, thy words are madness:
Three months this youth hath tended upon me;
But more of that anon. Take him aside.
    Oli. What would my lord, but that he may not
        have,
Wherein Olivia may seem serviceable?
Cesario, you do not keep promise with me.
    Vio. Madam!
    Duke. Gracious Olivia,—
    Oli. What do you say, Cesario? Good my lord,—
    Vio. My lord would speak; my duty hushes me.   110
    Oli. If it be aught to the old tune, my lord,
It is as fat and fulsome to mine ear
As howling after music.
    Duke.   Still so cruel?
    Oli. Still so constant, lord.
    Duke. What, to perverseness? you uncivil lady,
To whose ingrate and unauspicious altars
My soul the faithfull'st offerings hath breathed out
That e'er devotion tender'd! What shall I do?
    Oli. Even what it please my lord, that shall become
        him.
    Duke. Why should I not, had I the heart to do it,   120
Like to the Egyptian thief at point of death,
Kill what I love?—a savage jealousy
That sometime savours nobly. But hear me this:
Since you to non-regardance cast my faith,
And that I partly know the instrument
That screws me from my true place in your favour,
Live you the marble-breasted tyrant still;
But this your minion, whom I know you love,
And whom, by heaven I swear, I tender dearly,
Him will I tear out of that cruel eye,   130
Where he sits crowned in his master's spite.
Come, boy, with me; my thoughts are ripe in mis-
        chief:
I'll sacrifice the lamb that I do love,
To spite a raven's heart within a dove.
    Vio. And I, most jocund, apt and willingly,
To do you rest, a thousand deaths would die.
    Oli. Where goes Cesario?
    Vio.   After him I love
More than I love these eyes, more than my life,
More, by all mores, than e'er I shall love wife.
If I do feign, you witnesses above   140
Punish my life for tainting of my love!
    Oli. Ay me, detested! how am I beguiled!
    Vio. Who does beguile you? who does do you
        wrong?
    Oli. Hast thou forgot thyself? is it so long?
Call forth the holy father.
    Duke.   Come, away!
    Oli. Whither, my lord? Cesario, husband, stay.
    Duke. Husband!
    Oli.   Ay, husband: can he that deny?
    Duke. Her husband, sirrah!
    Vio.   No, my lord, not I.
    Oli. Alas, it is the baseness of thy fear
That makes thee strangle thy propriety: 150

Fear not, Cesario; take thy fortunes up;
Be that thou know'st thou art, and then thou art
As great as that thou fear'st.

    Enter Priest.

                O, welcome, father!
Father, I charge thee, by thy reverence,
Here to unfold, though lately we intended
To keep in darkness what occasion now
Reveals before 'tis ripe, what thou dost know
Hath newly pass'd between this youth and me.
    Priest. A contract of eternal bond of love,
Confirm'd by mutual joinder of your hands,   160
Attested by the holy close of lips,
Strengthen'd by interchangement of your rings;
And all the ceremony of this compact
Seal'd in my function, by my testimony:
Since when, my watch hath told me, toward my grave
I have travell'd but two hours.
    Duke. O thou dissembling cub! what wilt thou be
When time hath sow'd a grizzle on thy case?
Or will not else thy craft so quickly grow,
That thine own trip shall be thine overthrow?   170
Farewell, and take her; but direct thy feet
Where thou and I henceforth may never meet.
    Vio. My Lord, I do protest—
    Oli.   O, do not swear!
Hold little faith, though thou hast too much fear.

    Enter SIR ANDREW.

    Sir And. For the love of God, a surgeon! Send one
presently to Sir Toby.
    Oli. What 's the matter?
    Sir And. He has broke my head across and has given
Sir Toby a bloody coxcomb too: for the love of God,
your help! I had rather than forty pound I were at
home.   181
    Oli. Who has done this, Sir Andrew?
    Sir And. The count's gentleman, one Cesario: we
took him for a coward, but he 's the very devil in-
cardinate.
    Duke. My gentleman, Cesario?
    Sir And. 'Od's lifelings, here he is! You broke my
head for nothing; and that that I did, I was set on
to do 't by Sir Toby.
    Vio. Why do you speak to me? I never hurt you: 190
You drew your sword upon me without cause;
But I bespake you fair, and hurt you not.
    Sir And. If a bloody coxcomb be a hurt, you have
hurt me: I think you set nothing by a bloody coxcomb.

    Enter SIR TOBY *and* CLOWN.

Here comes Sir Toby halting: you shall hear more:
but if he had not been in drink, he would have
tickled you othergates than he did.
    Duke. How now, gentleman! how is 't with you?   200
    Sir To. That 's all one: has hurt me, and there 's the
end on 't. Sot, didst see Dick surgeon, sot?

---

102. **Three months.** This statement is inconsistent with the hint found in
I, iv, 3; it seems reasonable, however, in this connection.   112. **fat and
fulsome,** nauseating.   121. **Egyptian thief,** allusion to the story of
Theagenes and Chariclea in the *Ethiopica,* a Greek romance by Heliodorus. The robber chief, Thyamis of Memphis, having captured
Chariclea and fallen in love with her, was attacked by a larger band of
robbers; threatened with death, he attempted to slay her first.   123.
savours nobly, is not without nobility.   136. **do you rest,** give you ease.
142. **detested,** detestable (one).   150. **strangle thy propriety,** disavow

thyself.   160. **joinder,** joining.   168. **grizzle,** gray hair.   **case,** skin, or
possibly, body as containing the soul.   170. **trip,** probably from the
trip in wrestling; here, dissembling.   174. **little,** i.e., a little.   179.
coxcomb, fool's cap with the crest of a cock; here, head.   185. **in-
cardinate,** blunder for "incarnate."   187. **'Od's lifelings,** from the
oath "By God's life."   196. **halting,** limping.   198. **othergates,** otherwise.   205. **set,** fixed, closed with drink.   206-207. **passy measures
panyn,** so F. Malone and others read *passy measures pavin,* which they
explain as connected with Italian, *passo e mezzo* (slow moving) and

Clo. O, he's drunk, Sir Toby, an hour agone; his eyes were set at eight i' the morning.

Sir To. Then he's a rogue, †and a passy measures panyn: I hate a drunken rogue.

Oli. Away with him! Who hath made this havoc with them?

Sir And. I'll help you, Sir Toby, because we'll be dressed together. 211

Sir To. Will you help? an ass-head and a coxcomb and a knave, a thin-faced knave, a gull!

Oli. Get him to bed, and let his hurt be look'd to.
    [*Exeunt Clown, Fabian, Sir Toby, and Sir Andrew.*

Enter SEBASTIAN.

Seb. I am sorry, madam, I have hurt your kinsman;
But, had it been the brother of my blood,
I must have done no less with wit and safety.
You throw a strange regard upon me, and by that
I do perceive it hath offended you: 220
Pardon me, sweet one, even for the vows
We made each other but so late ago.

Duke. One face, one voice, one habit, and two persons,
A natural perspective, that is and is not!

Seb. Antonio, O my dear Antonio!
How have the hours rack'd and tortured me,
Since I have lost thee!

Ant. Sebastian are you?

Seb.   Fear'st thou that, Antonio?

Ant. How have you made division of yourself?
An apple, cleft in two, is not more twin 230
Than these two creatures. Which is Sebastian?

Oli. Most wonderful!

Seb. Do I stand there? I never had a brother;
Nor can there be that deity in my nature,
Of here and every where. I had a sister,
Whom the blind waves and surges have devour'd.
Of charity, what kin are you to me?
What countryman? what name? what parentage?

Vio. Of Messaline: Sebastian was my father;
Such a Sebastian was my brother too, 240
So went he suited to his watery tomb:
If spirits can assume both form and suit
You come to fright us.

Seb.   A spirit I am indeed;
But am in that dimension grossly clad
Which from the womb I did participate.
Were you a woman, as the rest goes even,
I should my tears let fall upon your cheek,
And say 'Thrice-welcome, drowned Viola!'

Vio. My father had a mole upon his brow.

Seb. And so had mine. 250

Vio. And died that day when Viola from her birth
Had number'd thirteen years.

Seb. O, that record is lively in my soul!
He finished indeed his mortal act
That day that made my sister thirteen years.

Vio. If nothing lets to make us happy both
But this my masculine usurp'd attire,

Do not embrace me till each circumstance
Of place, time, fortune, do cohere and jump
That I am Viola: which to confirm, 260
I'll bring you to a captain in this town,
Where lie my maiden weeds; by whose gentle help
I was preserved to serve this noble count.
All the occurrence of my fortune since
Hath been between this lady and this lord.

Seb. [*To Olivia*] So comes it, lady, you have been mistook:
But nature to her bias drew in that.
You would have been contracted to a maid;
Nor are you therein, by my life, deceived,
You are betroth'd both to a maid and man. 270

Duke. Be not amazed; right noble is his blood.
If this be so, as yet the glass seems true,
I shall have share in this most happy wreck.
[*To Viola*] Boy, thou hast said to me a thousand times
Thou never shouldst love woman like to me.

Vio. And all those sayings will I over-swear;
And all those swearings keep as true in soul
As doth that orbed continent the fire
That severs day from night.

Duke.   Give me thy hand;
And let me see thee in thy woman's weeds. 280

Vio. The captain that did bring me first on shore
Hath my maid's garments: he upon some action
Is now in durance, at Malvolio's suit,
A gentleman, and follower of my lady's.

Oli. He shall enlarge him: fetch Malvolio hither:
And yet, alas, now I remember me,
They say, poor gentleman, he's much distract.

Re-enter CLOWN *with a letter, and* FABIAN.

A most extracting frenzy of mine own
From my remembrance clearly banish'd his.
How does he, sirrah? 290

Clo. Truly, madam, he holds Belzebub at the stave's end as well as a man in his case may do: has here writ a letter to you; I should have given 't you to-day morning, but as a madman's epistles are no gospels, so it skills not much when they are delivered.

Oli. Open 't, and read it.

Clo. Look then to be well edified when the fool delivers the madman. [*Reads*] 'By the Lord, madam,'— 300

Oli. How now! art thou mad?

Clo. No, madam, I do but read madness: an your ladyship will have it as it ought to be, you must allow Vox.

Oli. Prithee, read i' thy right wits.

Clo. So I do, madonna; but to read his right wits is to read thus: therefore perpend, my princess, and give ear.

Oli. Read it you, sirrah.   [*To Fabian.*

Fab. [*Reads*] 'By the Lord, madam, you wrong me, and the world shall know it: though you have put me into darkness and given your drunken cousin rule over me, yet have I the benefit of my senses as well as

---

pavana (a grave and stately dance). It may thus be connected with Sir Toby's impatience to have his wounds dressed. 218. **with wit and safety,** my wits looking out for my safety. 219. **strange regard,** look of estrangement. 224. **perspective,** any optical device or illusion. 235. **here and every where,** omnipresence. 241. **suited,** dressed. 244. **dimension,** body or bodily shape. **grossly clad,** i.e., in flesh. 245. **participate,** share in common with others. 246. **as . . . even,** since everything else agrees. 253. **record,** recollection. 259. **jump,** coincide, fit exactly; see glossary. 267. **nature . . . that,** nature was true

to her bent in that. 272. **glass,** i.e., the *natural perspective* of line 224. 276. **over-swear,** swear again. 278. **orbed continent,** apparently, the celestial firmament which contains, with other bodies, the sun, a fire which severs day from night. 283. **durance,** prison, captivity. 285. **enlarge,** release; see glossary. 288. **extracting,** possibly, "distracting." 295. **epistles . . . gospels,** an allusion to readings in the church service. 296. **skills,** matters. 304. **Vox.** voice; allusion unknown. 307. **perpend,** consider, attend.

your ladyship. I have your own letter that induced
me to the semblance I put on; with the which I
doubt not but to do myself much right, or you much
shame. Think of me as you please. I leave my duty a
little unthought of and speak out of my injury.
THE MADLY-USED MALVOLIO.'

Oli. Did he write this? 320
Clo. Ay, madam.
Duke. This savours not much of distraction.
Oli. See him deliver'd, Fabian; bring him hither.

[*Exit Fabian.*

My lord, so please you, these things further thought on,
To think me as well a sister as a wife,
One day shall crown the alliance on 't, so please you,
Here at my house and at my proper cost.
Duke. Madam, I am most apt to embrace your offer.
[*To Viola*] Your master quits you; and for your service
done him,
So much against the mettle of your sex, 330
So far beneath your soft and tender breeding,
And since you call'd me master for so long,
Here is my hand: you shall from this time be
Your master's mistress.
Oli. A sister! you are she.

Re-enter FABIAN, *with* MALVOLIO.

Duke. Is this the madman?
Oli. Ay, my lord, this same.
How now, Malvolio!
Mal. Madam, you have done me wrong,
Notorious wrong.
Oli. Have I, Malvolio? no.
Mal. Lady, you have. Pray you, peruse that letter.
You must not now deny it is your hand:
Write from it, if you can, in hand or phrase; 340
Or say 'tis not your seal, not your invention:
You can say none of this: well, grant it then
And tell me, in the modesty of honour,
Why you have given me such clear lights of favour,
Bade me come smiling and cross-garter'd to you,
To put on yellow stockings and to frown
Upon Sir Toby and the lighter people;
And, acting this in an obedient hope,
Why have you suffer'd me to be imprison'd,
Kept in a dark house, visited by the priest, 350
And made the most notorious geck and gull
That e'er invention play'd on? tell me why.
Oli. Alas, Malvolio, this is not my writing,
Though, I confess, much like the character:
But out of question 'tis Maria's hand.
And now I do bethink me, it was she
First told me thou wast mad; then camest in smiling,
And in such forms which here were presupposed
Upon thee in the letter. Prithee, be content:
This practice hath most shrewdly pass'd upon thee; 360
But when we know the grounds and authors of it,
Thou shalt be both the plaintiff and the judge
Of thine own cause.
Fab. Good madam, hear me speak,

And let no quarrel nor no brawl to come
Taint the condition of this present hour,
Which I have wonder'd at. In hope it shall not,
Most freely I confess, myself and Toby
Set this device against Malvolio here,
Upon some stubborn and uncourteous parts
We had conceived against him: Maria writ 370
The letter at Sir Toby's great importance;
In recompense whereof he hath married her.
How with a sportful malice it was follow'd,
May rather pluck on laughter than revenge;
If that the injuries be justly weigh'd
That have on both sides pass'd.
Oli. Alas, poor fool, how have they baffled thee!
Clo. Why, 'some are born great, some achieve
greatness, and some have greatness thrown upon
them.' I was one, sir, in this interlude; one Sir Topas,
sir; but that 's all one. 'By the Lord, fool, I am not
mad.' But do you remember? 'Madam, why laugh you
at such a barren rascal? an you smile not, he 's
gagged:' and thus the whirligig of time brings in his
revenges.
Mal. I'll be revenged on the whole pack of you. [*Exit.*
Oli. He hath been most notoriously abused.
Duke. Pursue him, and entreat him to a peace:
He hath not told us of the captain yet: 390
When that is known and golden time convents,
A solemn combination shall be made
Of our dear souls. Meantime, sweet sister,
We will not part from hence. Cesario, come;
For so you shall be, while you are a man;
But when in other habits you are seen,
Orsino's mistress and his fancy's queen.
[*Exeunt all, except Clown.*

Clo. [*Sings*]
When that I was and a little tiny boy,
With hey, ho, the wind and the rain,
A foolish thing was but a toy, 400
For the rain it raineth every day.

But when I came to man's estate,
With hey, ho, &c.
'Gainst knaves and thieves men shut their gate,
For the rain, &c.

But when I came, alas! to wive,
With hey, ho, &c.
By swaggering could I never thrive,
For the rain, &c.

But when I came unto my beds, 410
With hey, ho, &c.
With toss-pots still had drunken heads,
For the rain, &c.

A great while ago the world begun,
With hey, ho, &c.
But that 's all one, our play is done,
And we'll strive to please you every day. [*Exit.*

324. **these . . . on,** i.e., when they have been considered. 330. **mettle,**
natural disposition. 340. **from it,** differently. 343. **modesty of
honour,** sense of propriety belonging to honorable persons. 347.
lighter, less important. 351. **geck,** dupe. 358. **presupposed,** offered
beforehand for adoption. 360. **shrewdly,** cruelly. 364. **to come,** i.e.,
future brawl. 369. **Upon,** on account of. **parts,** qualities. 370.
conceived against, observed in and charged against. 371. **importance,**
importunity. 377. **baffled,** treated ignominiously. 387. **I'll . . . you.**
The reading of this line is by many modern actors so passionate and

revengeful as to spoil the effect of the comedy; this cannot have been
Shakespeare's intention. Olivia (ll. 359-363) has declared that Malvolio
shall judge his own cause; Fabian (ll. 374-376) has said that the
offense was so much on both sides that it is a matter for laughter rather
than revenge; and the duke would have them follow Malvolio to
entreat peace. Malvolio's wrongs are not, therefore, regarded as
irreparable. 391. **convents,** suits; the word elsewhere means "summons." 412. **toss-pots,** drunkards.

HISTORIES OF THE SECOND PERIOD

THE TRAGEDY OF

King Richard the Second

On August 29, 1597, Andrew Wise entered in the Stationers' Register "The Tragedye of Richard the Second," and in 1597 a quarto edition was printed for him by Valentine Simmes:

THE Tragedie of King Richard the second. *As it hath beene publikely acted by the right Honourable the Lorde Chamberlaine his Seruants.* LONDON. Printed by Valentine Simmes for Andrew Wise, and are to be sold at his shop in Paules church yard at the signe of the Angel. 1597.

The quarto text is a good one. Two more quartos appeared in 1598 with "By William Shakespeare" added to the title page. A fourth quarto, issued in 1608, adds "With new additions of the Parliament Sceane, and the deposing of King Richard, As it hath been lately acted by the Kinges Majesties seruantes, at the Globe." This quarto contained in imperfect form the famous deposition scene. However, the Folio text, set up from a playhouse manuscript, affords a better version of the deposition scene. Each quarto rests on its predecessor. As to the absence of the deposition scene from the earlier quartos, it is usually thought that it was due to the censor's taking offense at the subject. It is, however, barely possible that the deposition scene was written for the performance before the Essex outbreak and added to the fourth quarto in some irregular way.[1]

DATE

The play is mentioned by Francis Meres in 1598 as one of Shakespeare's six tragedies. The entry in the

Stationers' Register and the publication in 1597 form the latest limit for dating the play. A number of considerations point to a time late in the year 1595. Knight showed certain parallels between Shakespeare's *Richard II* and *The Civil Wars*, an epic poem written by Samuel Daniel, four books of which were published in 1595.

In the following particulars *Richard II* seems to be based on Daniel's *Civil Wars:* The queen, who was historically a child of eleven, is represented in both play and poem as a grown woman, and Daniel in his *Epistle Dedicatorie* in 1609 apologizes for taking this liberty as if he were responsible for it. Richard and Bolingbroke ride together into London instead of separately as in the chronicle. The hint which Bolingbroke gives to Pierce of Exton to kill the king is almost in Daniel's words. Daniel also puts into the king's mouth a speech suggestive of his last soliloquy in the play. Finally, in both the poem and the play Hotspur is deliberately presented as much younger than he is, in order that he may be set over against Prince Hal as a rival.

The year 1595 also agrees pretty well with stylistic evidences as to the date of *Richard II*. The play has a disproportionately large amount of rhyme for a date so late as 1595. This may possibly be accounted for on the ground that rhyme, being a conscious feature of composition, may be due to reaction or to some passing literary influence. Rhyme militates against the speech-ending test and, in some measure, against feminine endings. *Richard II* is accordingly not high in either of these respects; on the other hand, it has a full number of extra syllables in the mid-line position. There is also a good deal of the rhetorical type of blank verse, many verbal conceits, puns, and epigrams, qualities which are characteristic of Shakespeare's early work. But Shakespeare puts this kind of language mainly into the mouths of Richard and of Gaunt, as if for the purpose of marking them off from other characters. Sir E. K. Chambers has recently found a piece of evidence[2] which may confirm the date 1595, or at least show that *Richard II* was possibly a novelty in that year. In a letter dated December 9, 1595, Sir Edward Hoby invites Sir Robert Cecil to his house in Canon Row, "where, as late as shall please you, a gate for your supper shall be open, and K. Richard present himself to your view."

OTHER PLAYS ON THE SUBJECT

One has no right to say that in *Richard II* Shakespeare was not reworking an old play. If he was, however, it is certain that he proceeded as in *Richard III*, and not as in *King John*, for he resorted immediately to Holinshed, and, except for changes to agree with Daniel's *Civil Wars*, followed Holinshed with meticulous fidelity. Two minor discrepancies have, however, been thought to indicate that Shakespeare

[1]See A. W. Pollard, *A New Shakespeare Quarto: The Tragedy of Richard II . . . 1598* (1916), and on this question and on all matters of text and sources see *King Richard II*, ed. J. Dover Wilson (Cambridge, 1939), introduction, copy, and notes.

[2]*The Elizabethan Stage*, II, 194n.

had to do with an old play. In II, i, 167-168, York refers to "the prevention of poor Bolingbroke about his marriage," which is nowhere explained in the play. Again Carlisle at the end of the play is committed to the custody of the Abbot of Westminster, whereas in the Holinshed chronicle Carlisle is sent to St. Albans.

The subject was evidently familiar on the stage. There are two plays preserved which deal with the reign of Richard II, in both of which, however, there is only a superficial likeness to Shakespeare's play. *The Life and Death of Jack Straw* (1593) has to do with the peasant insurrection of 1381. *The Tragedy of Woodstock* (1591, *Shakespeare Jahrbuch*, xxxv) begins with Richard's marriage with his first queen, Anne of Bohemia, and ends with the murder of Gloucester, the point at which *Richard II* begins. On April 30, 1611, Simon Forman saw at the Globe a play, not preserved, which seems to have covered the whole period of King Richard's reign. A "booke called Perce of Extone," by Wilson, Dekker, Drayton, and Chettle, is mentioned by Henslowe in March or April 1598, when he made a part payment for the work.

POLITICAL SIGNIFICANCE

The earl of Essex, who was a friend of Shakespeare's only known patron, the earl of Southampton, made his strange uprising against Queen Elizabeth on February 7, 1601. Essex must have been a hero in Shakespeare's eyes if we may judge from his allusion to Essex's popularity and to the happy prospects of his expedition against the Irish rebels under Tyrone in the prologue to the fifth act of *Henry V*. Whatever the connection between Essex and Shakespeare may have been, Essex and Southampton spent much time seeing plays and probably exaggerated the political influence of the drama.

After Essex's disgrace and two days before that set for his rebellion, apparently as a means of stirring public sentiment, Sir Gelly Meyrick, a partisan of Essex's, arranged with Shakespeare's company for the performance of a play "of the deposing and killing of King Richard II." In the testimony of Augustine Phillips, a member of Shakespeare's company, at Essex's trial it appears that the actors considered the play "to be so old and so long out of vse that they shold have small or no Company at yt"; but in consideration of "xls more then their ordynary for yt," they played the play. Whether or not this was Shakespeare's play is a matter of doubt among critics, but most of them hold that it was.

The subject of Richard II was a sore one with the queen herself. The note of a conversation with the queen by W. Lambarde, printed by Nichols, *Progresses of Queen Elizabeth* (ed. 1788), I, A-H, page 41, says,

Her majestie fell upon the reign of King Richard II, saying, I am Richard II, know ye not that? *W. L.* Such a wicked imagination was determined and attempted by a most unkind Gent. [i.e. Essex], the most adorned creature that ever your Majestie made. *Her Majestie.* He that will forget God, will also forget his benefactors; this tragedy was played 40tie times in open streets and houses.

Since Essex did not seek the queen's death, it is argued that *Richard II* would not suit his purposes. It is to be pointed out, however, that the play does show one thing in exact line with Essex's intentions. It shows the fatal effect of ill-advisers and favorites. Essex wished to rescue the queen from her flatterers and might have indicated the necessity of so doing by depicting in the figure of her predecessor the outcome of such conduct.

RELATION TO *Edward II*

The relation of *Richard II* to Marlowe's *Edward II* is more than accidental. Marlowe had done a new and significant thing in discovering a historical character who might serve as the hero of a tragic plot and thus give the chronicle play the effect of a tragedy. Shakespeare had followed the earlier manner of Marlowe in *Richard III;* he was now to follow the later manner in *Richard II*.

The subject of Richard II is so closely parallel to that of Edward II that Shakespeare must have been put to it to avoid an uninteresting repetition. Edward II and Richard II were bad kings, both deluded by favorites, both extortioners of taxes, and both persons lacking in common judgment; both were dethroned and then murdered in prison. In connection with their downfalls there came up the question of whether or not a king might in any circumstances be dethroned, since his title came from God and his blood was doubly sacred. Marlowe presented one protagonistic figure set over against a series of secondary figures. First Gaveston is Edward's favorite; then Spencer. The part of Mortimer, who heads the rebellious nobles and wins away Edward's queen, is striking but not predominant. Mortimer is, moreover, a villain, and the issue does not fall squarely on the propriety of dethronement. Edward is misused and in some respects the victim of external circumstances.

In *Richard II* Shakespeare, either by accident or intention, introduced marked differences from Marlowe in his handling of the dethronement theme. He has in fact made dethronement the issue of the play. The judgment of critics has been warped by their habit of interpreting *Richard II* in terms of that remorse of conscience for the dethronement and murder of a king which appears in the later plays of the series, namely, in *1* and *2 Henry IV* and *Henry V;* also in the horrid significance of the event as the first cause of the civil Wars of the Roses depicted in the Henry VI plays and *Richard III*. By looking at *Richard II* within its own borders, however, one sees that in this play it is a tragedy and not a crime with which we have to do.

THE DETHRONEMENT THEME

The theme of the dethronement of kings was one in which the Renaissance took interest and found perplexity. The weight of opinion was that no degree of inefficiency or wickedness justified the rejection of God's anointed. It would be better to bear any amount of temporary oppression than to anger the Almighty by interfering with his establishment. Any recognition of the rights of the people to determine who should rule them was still to seek. Such seems to be the basis of all the plays in Shakespeare's two great series except this one, and there are some traces of it here; but, taking the play in and for itself, it must be regarded as the clearest presentation of the issue made at that time.

A manuscript play, *The Tragedy of Woodstock*, deals with the wicked self-indulgence of the king, his oppression of his people, his unworthy favorites, his own pitiful dilettantism, and his murder of his excellent and loyal uncle. It is perfectly proper to read into Shakespeare's *Richard II* the reputation of that monarch when the play was written. It was not necessary for Shakespeare to depict the evils of Richard as a ruler in order to have him condemned; he needed only to remind his audience of what they already knew. Since Shakespeare has given Richard a worthy and consistent antagonist, wronged and righteous, in Bolingbroke, the effect produced is different from that produced by Marlowe's play, and the issue of royal inviolability is more clearly raised.

RICHARD'S TRAGIC WEAKNESS

The most striking novelty in Shakespeare's tragedy is his seizing upon the weakness of King Richard's character and making it the basis of his overthrow. *Richard II* is thus in some respects the first of Shakespeare's character tragedies. We feel that Richard's tragedy is one which any man of common sense might have avoided; we do not feel that the author has depicted a fatal situation in which a hero might have been involved; there is no threat against the human state as such. All the sources suggest weakness in Richard's character, though his peculiar weakness, which is sentimentality, seems to have been Shakespeare's invention.

Shakespeare conceives of him as a sentimentalist, that is, a man whose self-consciousness takes the form of dwelling not on facts but on his conception of facts. Richard enjoys picturesque situations, reputation, and the outward shows of kingship and manliness, and neglects the essence of these qualities. He enjoys the parade and ceremony attendant upon the trial of arms at Oxford; then foolishly and inconsistently stops the duel in order to draw all eyes upon himself and his power. His sentence on Bolingbroke and Mowbray is the only means by which injustice might certainly be dealt upon both combatants. He betrays his vanity in his sensitiveness about his face and his

complexion, and his cruelty and anger when he is compelled for an instant to see himself as he is. The aged patriot Gaunt on his deathbed, after having told Richard of his faults, is thus addressed (II, i, 115-119):

> A lunatic lean-witted fool,
> Presuming on an ague's privilege,
> Darest with thy frozen admonition
> Make pale our cheek, chasing the royal blood
> With fury from his native residence.

No less to be noted are Richard's unwarranted confidence in his very name and state when he lands from Ireland, and his equally unwarranted dejection when he learns the actual situation; his base yielding to Bolingbroke when Bolingbroke had just yielded to him; his voluntary surrender of the crown for the sake of playing the dangerous role of a dethroned and deserted king; his repeated comparison of himself with the sun in heaven and with the Saviour. Shakespeare shows us that these same personal

Richard the Second

645

"The Emperor" *from Hans Holbein's* "Dance of Death," *1538. See III, ii, 155 ff.*

qualities and this same histrionic gift may be used to move the hearer, when the sentimentalist is finally stranded, when his troubles become real. In fact the most admirable thing in this poetic king is that he seems finally to discover a better nature in himself, though it manifests itself fully only in the last gallant moment of his life.

MINOR CHARACTERS

Coleridge found in the timorously loyal York an admirably drawn character. Gaunt is the champion of patriotism on the part of the subject and of righteous rule on the part of the sovereign; his great speech (II, i, 31-68) still lives in the hearts of Englishmen. Aumerle is usually condemned, for he is inconsistent, since in the first part of the play he is one of Richard's careless companions and in the latter part one of his loyal adherents, though a traitor to the established king; but one must still remember the scene of the many challenges and his "Some honest Christian trust me with a gage."

The picture of Bolingbroke with his keen, impersonal intellectuality has never had the recognition it deserves, because critics interpreting his words in the light of later plays have read guile into his actions. Richard's fall was inevitable, though Shakespeare does not exculpate Bolingbroke from treason and regicide. The point to be remembered is that, taking the play as it stands, Bolingbroke cannot be regarded as merely a usurper. It is not possible to tell clearly what Shakespeare's judgment on the dethronement issue is.

STAGE HISTORY

The statement on the title page of the fourth quarto, "As it hath been lately acted by the Kinges Majesties seruantes at the Globe," points to a revival of *Richard II* early in the reign of King James I. The issue of the later quartos (Q_5 in 1615, Q_6 in 1634) indicates for the play a certain degree of popularity in the early seventeenth century. Nahum Tate adapted it as *The Sicilian Usurper* in 1681, and a modified version by Theobald was acted in 1718 and 1738.

In more or less altered versions the play was acted repeatedly in the eighteenth and nineteenth centuries. The Shakespearean version has gradually returned to the stage. Macready, Edmund Kean, Charles Kean, Junius Brutus Booth, Edwin Booth, Beerbohm Tree, and others have played it in England and America; in Germany it has been both popular and successful.

The recent stage history of *Richard II* offers one of the great dramatic surprises of our time. In September 1937 John Gielgud, playing the part of the king, staged the play at the Queen's Theatre in London. The cast was adequate and distinguished, and London woke up to the fact that this comparatively unknown play was one of the greatest of Shakespeare's achievements. This surprising London success was paralleled and exceeded in the United States in the same year. The production in which Maurice Evans starred, ran for 171 performances in New York and the next season went on the road for a long and successful tour.

THE TRAGEDY OF

King Richard the Second

DRAMATIS PERSONAE

KING RICHARD the Second.
JOHN OF GAUNT, Duke of Lancaster,
EDMUND OF LANGLEY, Duke of York, } uncles to the King.
HENRY, surnamed BOLINGBROKE, Duke of Hereford, son to John of Gaunt; afterwards KING HENRY IV.
DUKE OF AUMERLE, son to the Duke of York.
THOMAS MOWBRAY, Duke of Norfolk.
DUKE OF SURREY.
EARL OF SALISBURY.
LORD BERKELEY.
BUSHY,
BAGOT, } servants to King Richard.
GREEN,
EARL OF NORTHUMBERLAND.
HENRY PERCY, surnamed Hotspur, his son.
LORD ROSS.
LORD WILLOUGHBY.
LORD FITZWATER.
Bishop of Carlisle.
Abbot of Westminster.
Lord Marshal.
SIR STEPHEN SCROOP.
SIR PIERCE of Exton.
Captain of a band of Welshmen.

QUEEN to King Richard.
DUCHESS OF YORK.
DUCHESS OF GLOUCESTER.
Lady attending on the Queen.

Lords, Heralds, Officers, Soldiers, two Gardeners, Keeper, Messenger, Groom, and other Attendants.

SCENE: *England and Wales.*

ACT I.

SCENE I. *London.* KING RICHARD's *palace.*

Enter KING RICHARD, JOHN OF GAUNT, *with other* Nobles *and* Attendants.

K. Rich. Old John of Gaunt, time-honour'd Lancaster,
Hast thou, according to thy oath and band,
Brought hither Henry Hereford thy bold son,
Here to make good the boisterous late appeal,
Which then our leisure would not let us hear,
Against the Duke of Norfolk, Thomas Mowbray?
Gaunt. I have, my liege.
K. Rich. Tell me, moreover, hast thou sounded him,
If he appeal the duke on ancient malice;

Or worthily, as a good subject should, 10
On some known ground of treachery in him?
Gaunt. As near as I could sift him on that argument,
On some apparent danger seen in him
Aim'd at your highness, no inveterate malice.
K. Rich. Then call them to our presence; face to
    face,
And frowning brow to brow, ourselves will hear
The accuser and the accused freely speak:
High-stomach'd are they both, and full of ire,
In rage deaf as the sea, hasty as fire.

Enter BOLINGBROKE *and* MOWBRAY.

Boling. Many years of happy days befal 20
My gracious sovereign, my most loving liege!
Mow. Each day still better other's happiness;
Until the heavens, envying earth's good hap,
Add an immortal title to your crown!
K. Rich. We thank you both: yet one but flatters us,
As well appeareth by the cause you come;
Namely, to appeal each other of high treason.
Cousin of Hereford, what dost thou object
Against the Duke of Norfolk, Thomas Mowbray?
Boling. First, heaven be the record to my speech! 30
In the devotion of a subject's love,
Tendering the precious safety of my prince,
And free from other misbegotten hate,
Come I appellant to this princely presence.
Now, Thomas Mowbray, do I turn to thee,
And mark my greeting well; for what I speak
My body shall make good upon this earth,
Or my divine soul answer it in heaven.
Thou art a traitor and a miscreant,
Too good to be so and too bad to live, 40
Since the more fair and crystal is the sky,
The uglier seem the clouds that in it fly.
Once more, the more to aggravate the note,
With a foul traitor's name stuff I thy throat;
And wish, so please my sovereign, ere I move,
What my tongue speaks my right drawn sword may
    prove.
Mow. Let not my cold words here accuse my zeal:
'Tis not the trial of a woman's war,
The bitter clamour of two eager tongues,
Can arbitrate this cause betwixt us twain; 50
The blood is hot that must be cool'd for this:
Yet can I not of such tame patience boast
As to be hush'd and nought at all to say:
First, the fair reverence of your highness curbs me
From giving reins and spurs to my free speech;
Which else would post until it had return'd
These terms of treason doubled down his throat.
Setting aside his high blood's royalty,
And let him be no kinsman to my liege,
I do defy him, and I spit at him; 60

Call him a slanderous coward and a villain:
Which to maintain I would allow him odds,
And meet him, were I tied to run afoot
Even to the frozen ridges of the Alps,
Or any other ground inhabitable,
Where ever Englishman durst set his foot.
Mean time let this defend my loyalty,
By all my hopes, most falsely doth he lie.
Boling. Pale trembling coward, there I throw my
    gage,
Disclaiming here the kindred of the king, 70
And lay aside my high blood's royalty,
Which fear, not reverence, makes thee to except.
If guilty dread have left thee so much strength
As to take up mine honour's pawn, then stoop:
By that and all the rites of knighthood else,
Will I make good against thee, arm to arm,
What I have spoke, or thou canst worse devise.
Mow. I take it up; and by that sword I swear,
Which gently laid my knighthood on my shoulder,
I'll answer thee in any fair degree, 80
Or chivalrous design of knightly trial:
And when I mount, alive may I not light,
If I be traitor or unjustly fight!
K. Rich. What doth our cousin lay to Mowbray's
    charge?
It must be great that can inherit us
So much as of a thought of ill in him.
Boling. Look, what I speak, my life shall prove it
    true;
That Mowbray hath received eight thousand nobles
In name of lendings for your highness' soldiers,
The which he hath detain'd for lewd employments, 90
Like a false traitor and injurious villain.
Besides I say and will in battle prove,
Or here or elsewhere to the furthest verge
That ever was survey'd by English eye,
That all the treasons for these eighteen years
Complotted and contrived in this land
Fetch from false Mowbray their first head and spring.
Further I say and further will maintain
Upon his bad life to make all this good,
That he did plot the Duke of Gloucester's death, 100
Suggest his soon-believing adversaries,
And consequently, like a traitor coward,
Sluiced out his innocent soul through streams of
    blood:
Which blood, like sacrificing Abel's, cries,
Even from the tongueless caverns of the earth,
To me for justice and rough chastisement;
And, by the glorious worth of my descent,
This arm shall do it, or this life be spent.
K. Rich. How high a pitch his resolution soars!
Thomas of Norfolk, what say'st thou to this? 110
Mow. O, let my sovereign turn away his face

*Richard
the Second*
ACT I : SC I

647

ACT I. SCENE I. *Stage Direction:* **London.** Holinshed places this scene at Windsor; he is followed by many editors. 1. **Old John of Gaunt,** born in 1340 at Ghent; hence the surname *Gaunt.* At this time, April 29, 1398, he was only fifty-eight, although Shakespeare represents him as being very old. 4. **appeal,** accusation, formal challenge or impeachment which the accuser was obliged to maintain in combat. 12. **sift,** discover true motives by questioning. 18. **High-stomach'd,** haughty, having an appetite for combat. 22. **other's,** the other's, of the next. 23. **hap,** fortune. 28-29. **object Against,** charge criminally against. 32. **Tendering,** holding dear. 34. **appellant,** accuser. Onions construes this as an adjective meaning "accusing or impeaching another of treason." 43. **note,** reproach. 46. **right drawn,** justly or rightly drawn. 47. **accuse my zeal,** accuse me of wanting zeal. 49. **eager,** sharp, biting. 58. **Setting . . . royalty,** disregarding Bolingbroke's royal blood. 65.

inhabitable, uninhabitable. 69. **gage,** a gauntlet as a sign of the pledge to combat. 74. **pawn,** i.e., his gage. 85. **inherit,** put in possession of. 88. **nobles,** gold coins worth twenty groats or 6s. 8d. 89. **lendings,** money advanced to soldiers when the regular pay cannot be given (Onions). 90. **lewd,** vile, base. 97. **head and spring,** synonymous words meaning "origin." 100. **Duke of Gloucester's death.** Thomas of Woodstock, duke of Gloucester, sixth (or seventh) son of Edward III and brother of John of Gaunt, was murdered at Calais in September 1397. To avenge his death is Bolingbroke's real motive. The other charges are merely trumped up, and Mowbray brushes them away in an instant (ll. 124-132); Gloucester's murder is an underlying motive throughout the earlier part of the play. 101. **Suggest,** prompt, incite; see glossary. 102. **consequently,** successively in time (not inferential). 105. **tongueless,** resonant but without articulate speech.

And bid his ears a little while be deaf,
Till I have told this slander of his blood,
How God and good men hate so foul a liar.

K. Rich. Mowbray, impartial are our eyes and ears:
Were he my brother, nay, my kingdom's heir,
As he is but my father's brother's son,
Now, by my sceptre's awe, I make a vow,
Such neighbour nearness to our sacred blood
Should nothing privilege him, nor partialize 120
The unstooping firmness of my upright soul:
He is our subject, Mowbray; so art thou:
Free speech and fearless I to thee allow.

Mow. Then, Bolingbroke, as low as to thy heart,
Through the false passage of thy throat, thou liest.
Three parts of that receipt I had for Calais
Disbursed I duly to his highness' soldiers;
The other part reserved I by consent,
For that my sovereign liege was in my debt
Upon remainder of a dear account, 130
Since last I went to France to fetch his queen:
Now swallow down that lie. For Gloucester's death,
I slew him not; but to my own disgrace
Neglected my sworn duty in that case.
For you, my noble Lord of Lancaster,
The honourable father to my foe,
Once did I lay an ambush for your life,
A trespass that doth vex my grieved soul;
But ere I last received the sacrament
I did confess it, and exactly begg'd 140
Your grace's pardon, and I hope I had it.
This is my fault: as for the rest appeal'd,
It issues from the rancour of a villain,
A recreant and most degenerate traitor:
Which in myself I boldly will defend;
And interchangeably hurl down my gage
Upon this overweening traitor's foot,
To prove myself a loyal gentleman
Even in the best blood chamber'd in his bosom.
In haste whereof, most heartily I pray 150
Your highness to assign our trial day.

K. Rich. Wrath-kindled gentlemen, be ruled by me;
Let's purge this choler without letting blood:
This we prescribe, though no physician;
Deep malice makes too deep incision;
Forget, forgive; conclude and be agreed;
Our doctors say this is no month to bleed.
Good uncle, let this end where it begun;
We'll calm the Duke of Norfolk, you your son.

Gaunt. To be a make-peace shall become my age: 160
Throw down, my son, the Duke of Norfolk's gage.

K. Rich. And, Norfolk, throw down his.

Gaunt.   When, Harry, when?
Obedience bids I should not bid again.

K. Rich. Norfolk, throw down, we bid; there is no
   boot.

Mow. Myself I throw, dread sovereign, at thy foot.
My life thou shalt command, but not my shame:
The one my duty owes; but my fair name,
Despite of death that lives upon my grave,

To dark dishonour's use thou shalt not have.
I am disgraced, impeach'd and baffled here, 170
Pierced to the soul with slander's venom'd spear,
The which no balm can cure but his heart-blood
Which breathed this poison.

K. Rich.   Rage must be withstood:
Give me his gage: lions make leopards tame.

Mow. Yea, but not change his spots: take but my
   shame,
And I resign my gage. My dear dear lord,
The purest treasure mortal times afford
Is spotless reputation: that away,
Men are but gilded loam or painted clay.
A jewel in a ten-times-barr'd-up chest 180
Is a bold spirit in a loyal breast.
Mine honour is my life; both grow in one;
Take honour from me, and my life is done:
Then, dear my liege, mine honour let me try;
In that I live and for that will I die.

K. Rich. Cousin, throw up your gage; do you begin.

Boling. O, God defend my soul from such deep sin!
Shall I seem crest-fall'n in my father's sight?
Or with pale beggar-fear impeach my height
Before this out-dared dastard? Ere my tongue 190
Shall wound my honour with such feeble wrong,
Or sound so base a parle, my teeth shall tear
The slavish motive of recanting fear,
And spit it bleeding in his high disgrace,
Where shame doth harbour, even in Mowbray's face.
                                        [Exit Gaunt.

K. Rich. We were not born to sue, but to command;
Which since we cannot do to make you friends,
Be ready, as your lives shall answer it,
At Coventry, upon Saint Lambert's day:
There shall your swords and lances arbitrate 200
The swelling difference of your settled hate:
Since we can not atone you, we shall see
Justice design the victor's chivalry.
Lord marshal, command our officers at arms
Be ready to direct these home alarms.   [Exeunt.

SCENE II. *The* DUKE OF LANCASTER'S *palace.*

Enter JOHN OF GAUNT *with the* DUCHESS OF
   GLOUCESTER.

Gaunt. Alas, the part I had in Woodstock's blood
Doth more solicit me than your exclaims,
To stir against the butchers of his life!
But since correction lieth in those hands
Which made the fault that we cannot correct,
Put we our quarrel to the will of heaven;
Who, when they see the hours ripe on earth,
Will rain hot vengeance on offenders' heads.

Duch. Finds brotherhood in thee no sharper spur?
Hath love in thy old blood no living fire? 10
Edward's seven sons, whereof thyself art one,
Were as seven vials of his sacred blood,

---

113. **slander of,** disgrace or reproach to.   126. **receipt,** thing received.
132-134. **For . . . case.** Mowbray's excuse is at the king's expense; he
vaguely hints at the king's connivance. In Holinshed Mowbray ignores
the charge.   140. **exactly,** explicitly, formally.   153. **choler,** excess of
the humor choler, anger.   **letting blood,** used with a quibble on the
sense of "mortal combat."   156. **conclude,** come to a final agreement.
157. **no month to bleed.** Spring and autumn were regarded as the
proper times to bleed patients. Ff: *time;* Q_1: *month.*   160. **make-peace,**
peacemaker.   170. **impeach'd,** called into question, discredited.

baffled, disgraced, as of a recreant knight. A part of the punishment of
coward knights was hanging by the heels, which is the original meaning
of the word.   174. **leopards.** Malone called attention to the fact,
questioned by the Clarendon Press editors, that the Norfolk crest was a
golden leopard.   189. **beggar-fear,** a beggar's fear.   **height,** high position.   190. **out-dared,** dared down, cowed.   193. **motive,** instrument.
199. **Saint Lambert's day,** September 17.   203. **design,** point out.
   SCENE II.   2. **exclaims,** exclamations.   4. **those hands,** i.e., Richard's, whom he charges with responsibility for Gloucester's death.

Or seven fair branches springing from one root:
Some of those seven are dried by nature's course,
Some of those branches by the Destinies cut;
But Thomas, my dear lord, my life, my Gloucester,
One vial full of Edward's sacred blood,
One flourishing branch of his most royal root,
Is crack'd, and all the precious liquor spilt,
Is hack'd down, and his summer leaves all faded,   20
By envy's hand and murder's bloody axe.
Ah, Gaunt, his blood was thine! that bed, that womb,
That metal, that self mould, that fashion'd thee
Made him a man; and though thou livest and
          breathest,
Yet art thou slain in him: thou dost consent
In some large measure to thy father's death,
In that thou seest thy wretched brother die,
Who was the model of thy father's life.
Call it not patience, Gaunt; it is despair:
In suffering thus thy brother to be slaughter'd,   30
Thou showest the naked pathway to thy life,
Teaching stern murder how to butcher thee:
That which in mean men we intitle patience
Is pale cold cowardice in noble breasts.
What shall I say? to safeguard thine own life,
The best way is to venge my Gloucester's death.
    Gaunt. God's is the quarrel; for God's substitute,
His deputy anointed in His sight,
Hath caused his death: the which if wrongfully,
Let heaven revenge; for I may never lift   40
An angry arm against His minister.
    Duch. Where then, alas, may I complain myself?
    Gaunt. To God, the widow's champion and defence.
    Duch. Why, then, I will. Farewell, old Gaunt.
Thou goest to Coventry, there to behold
Our cousin Hereford and fell Mowbray fight:
O, sit my husband's wrongs on Hereford's spear,
That it may enter butcher Mowbray's breast!
Or, if misfortune miss the first career,
Be Mowbray's sins so heavy in his bosom,   50
That they may break his foaming courser's back,
And throw the rider headlong in the lists,
A caitiff recreant to my cousin Hereford!
Farewell, old Gaunt: thy sometimes brother's wife
With her companion grief must end her life.
    Gaunt. Sister, farewell; I must to Coventry:
As much good stay with thee as go with me!
    Duch. Yet one word more: grief boundeth where it
          falls,
Not with the empty hollowness, but weight:
I take my leave before I have begun,   60
For sorrow ends not when it seemeth done.
Commend me to thy brother, Edmund York.
Lo, this is all:—nay, yet depart not so;
Though this be all, do not so quickly go;
I shall remember more. Bid him—ah, what?—
With all good speed at Plashy visit me.
Alack, and what shall good old York there see
But empty lodgings and unfurnish'd walls,
Unpeopled offices, untrodden stones?

And what hear there for welcome but my groans?   70
Therefore commend me; let him not come there,
To seek out sorrow that dwells every where.
Desolate, desolate, will I hence and die:
The last leave of thee takes my weeping eye.   [*Exeunt.*

SCENE III. *The lists at Coventry.*

Enter the Lord Marshal *and the* DUKE OF AUMERLE.

    Mar. My Lord Aumerle, is Harry Hereford arm'd?
    Aum. Yea, at all points; and longs to enter in.
    Mar. The Duke of Norfolk, sprightfully and bold,
Stays but the summons of the appellant's trumpet.
    Aum. Why, then, the champions are prepared, and
          stay
For nothing but his majesty's approach.

The trumpets sound, and the KING *enters with his nobles,*
GAUNT, BUSHY, BAGOT, GREEN, *and others. When
they are set, enter* MOWBRAY *in arms, defendant, with
a Herald.*

    K. Rich. Marshal, demand of yonder champion
The cause of his arrival here in arms:
Ask him his name and orderly proceed
To swear him in the justice of his cause.   10
    Mar. In God's name and the king's, say who thou
          art
And why thou comest thus knightly clad in arms,
Against what man thou comest, and what thy quarrel:
Speak truly, on thy knighthood and thy oath;
As so defend thee heaven and thy valour.
    Mow. My name is Thomas Mowbray, Duke of
          Norfolk;
Who hither come engaged by my oath—
Which God defend a knight should violate!—
Both to defend my loyalty and truth
To God, my king and my succeeding issue,   20
Against the Duke of Hereford that appeals me;
And, by the grace of God and this mine arm,
To prove him, in defending of myself,
A traitor to my God, my king, and me:
And as I truly fight, defend me heaven!

The trumpets sound. Enter BOLINGBROKE, *appellant, in
armour, with a Herald.*

    K. Rich. Marshal, ask yonder knight in arms,
Both who he is and why he cometh hither
Thus plated in habiliments of war,
And formally, according to our law,
Depose him in the justice of his cause.   30
    Mar. What is thy name? and wherefore comest thou
          hither,
Before King Richard in his royal lists?
Against whom comest thou? and what's thy quarrel?
Speak like a true knight, so defend thee heaven!
    Boling. Harry of Hereford, Lancaster and Derby
Am I; who ready here do stand in arms,
To prove, by God's grace and my body's valour,

Gaunt is more explicit in lines 37-41.   **9. Finds . . . spur.** The duchess'
argument of kinship develops into that of self-defense in lines 30 ff.
23. self mould, selfsame mold.   **28. model,** likeness; see glossary.   **36.
venge,** avenge.   **47. O . . . spear.** The duchess regards Bolingbroke as
the family champion, as he seems to have regarded himself (I, i, 104-
108).   **49. career,** the charge of the horse in the tourney or combat.
53. caitiff, cowardly.   **62. Edmund York,** Edmund of Langley, fifth son
of Edward III.   **66. Plashy,** Gloucester's seat in Essex.   **68. unfurnish'd,** bare.   **73. will I hence.** The adverb of place is used here, as
frequently in Shakespeare, without the verb of motion.
    SCENE III.   The events of this scene took place historically on Sep-
tember 16, 1398.   **3. sprightfully,** with high spirit.   **7-10. Marshal
. . . cause.** One finds here, as elsewhere in Richard's public behavior,
an illustration of what Coleridge calls his "attention to decorum and
high feeling of kingly dignity."   **28. plated,** clothed in armor.   **30.
Depose,** put under oath.

In lists, on Thomas Mowbray, Duke of Norfolk,
That he is a traitor, foul and dangerous,
To God of heaven, King Richard and to me; 40
And as I truly fight, defend me heaven!
   Mar. On pain of death, no person be so bold
Or daring-hardy as to touch the lists,
Except the marshal and such officers
Appointed to direct these fair designs.
   Boling. Lord marshal, let me kiss my sovereign's
    hand,
And bow my knee before his majesty:
For Mowbray and myself are like two men
That vow a long and weary pilgrimage;
Then let us take a ceremonious leave 50
And loving farewell of our several friends.
   Mar. The appellant in all duty greets your highness,
And craves to kiss your hand and take his leave.
   K. Rich. We will descend and fold him in our arms.
Cousin of Hereford, as thy cause is right,
So be thy fortune in this royal fight!
Farewell, my blood; which if to-day thou shed,
Lament we may, but not revenge thee dead.
   Boling. O, let no noble eye profane a tear
For me, if I be gored with Mowbray's spear: 60
As confident as is the falcon's flight
Against a bird, do I with Mowbray fight.
My loving lord, I take my leave of you;
Of you, my noble cousin, Lord Aumerle;
Not sick, although I have to do with death,
But lusty, young, and cheerly drawing breath.
Lo, as at English feasts, so I regreet
The daintiest last, to make the end most sweet:
O thou, the earthly author of my blood,
Whose youthful spirit, in me regenerate, 70
Doth with a twofold vigour lift me up
To reach at victory above my head,
Add proof unto mine armour with thy prayers;
And with thy blessings steel my lance's point,
That it may enter Mowbray's waxen coat,
And furbish new the name of John a Gaunt,
Even in the lusty haviour of his son.
   Gaunt. God in thy good cause make thee prosperous!
Be swift like lightning in the execution;
And let thy blows, doubly redoubled, 80
Fall like amazing thunder on the casque
Of thy adverse pernicious enemy:
Rouse up thy youthful blood, be valiant and live.
   Boling. Mine innocency and Saint George to thrive!
   Mow. However God or fortune cast my lot,
There lives or dies, true to King Richard's throne,
A loyal, just and upright gentleman:
Never did captive with a freer heart
Cast off his chains of bondage and embrace
His golden uncontroll'd enfranchisement, 90
More than my dancing soul doth celebrate
This feast of battle with mine adversary.
Most mighty liege, and my companion peers,
Take from my mouth the wish of happy years:

As gentle and as jocund as to jest
Go I to fight: truth hath a quiet breast.
   K. Rich. Farewell, my lord: securely I espy
Virtue with valour couched in thine eye.
Order the trial, marshal, and begin.
   Mar. Harry of Hereford, Lancaster and Derby, 100
Receive thy lance; and God defend the right!
   Boling. Strong as a tower in hope, I cry amen.
   Mar. Go bear this lance to Thomas, Duke of
    Norfolk.
   First Her. Harry of Hereford, Lancaster and Derby,
Stands here for God, his sovereign and himself,
On pain to be found false and recreant,
To prove the Duke of Norfolk, Thomas Mowbray,
A traitor to his God, his king and him;
And dares him to set forward to the fight.
   Sec. Her. Here standeth Thomas Mowbray, Duke of
    Norfolk, 110
On pain to be found false and recreant,
Both to defend himself and to approve
Henry of Hereford, Lancaster, and Derby,
To God, his sovereign and to him disloyal;
Courageously and with a free desire
Attending but the signal to begin.
   Mar. Sound, trumpets; and set forward,
    combatants.   [*A charge sounded*.
Stay, the king hath thrown his warder down.
   K. Rich. Let them lay by their helmets and their
    spears,
And both return back to their chairs again: 120
Withdraw with us: and let the trumpets sound
While we return these dukes what we decree.
                        [*A long flourish*.
Draw near,
And list what with our council we have done.
For that our kingdom's earth should not be soil'd
With that dear blood which it hath fostered;
And for our eyes do hate the dire aspect
Of civil wounds plough'd up with neighbours' sword;
And for we think the eagle-winged pride
Of sky-aspiring and ambitious thoughts, 130
With rival-hating envy, set on you
To wake our peace, which in our country's cradle
Draws the sweet infant breath of gentle sleep;
Which so roused up with boisterous untuned drums,
With harsh-resounding trumpets' dreadful bray,
And grating shock of wrathful iron arms,
Might from our quiet confines fright fair peace
And make us wade even in our kindred's blood;
Therefore, we banish you our territories:
You, cousin Hereford, upon pain of life, 140
Till twice five summers have enrich'd our fields
Shall not regreet our fair dominions,
But tread the stranger paths of banishment.
   Boling. Your will be done: this must my comfort be,
That sun that warms you here shall shine on me;
And those his golden beams to you here lent
Shall point on me and gild my banishment.

43. **daring-hardy,** daringly bold. 49. **pilgrimage.** Bolingbroke's figure carries a suggestion of future events of which he is unconscious. 59. **profane,** be profaned by. 67. **regreet,** greet, salute. 70. **regenerate,** born anew. 75. **waxen,** penetrable, soft. 77. **haviour,** behavior, deportment. 81. **amazing,** confusing, bewildering. **casque,** helmet. 95. **jest,** take part in a play or pastime. 118. **Stay . . . down.** Shakespeare fails to disclose Richard's motive here. According to Froissart, several noblemen of the king's party warned him not to let the combat proceed because the people were aroused on Bolingbroke's behalf. The victory of either knight would be perilous to the king's own safety. It is

characteristic of Richard's love of display that he should have let the ceremonies proceed to the very last possible moment. **warder,** staff or truncheon borne by the king when presiding over a trial by combat. 122. **While,** until. 125-143. **For . . . banishment.** The king's speech is confused, perhaps intentionally, perhaps because it is insincere. 134-137. **Which . . . peace.** Syntactically the antecedent of *which* is *peace*, line 132. Both the syntax and the metaphor have gone astray. Note the figurative representation of *peace*, lines 132-133. 139. **we . . . territories.** Richard shows what Gardiner calls the "unwise cunning of a madman" and takes the one course which would be sure to work injustice to both

K. Rich. Norfolk, for thee remains a heavier doom,
Which I with some unwillingness pronounce:
The sly slow hours shall not determinate   150
The dateless limit of thy dear exile;
The hopeless word of 'never to return'
Breathe I against thee, upon pain of life.

Mow. A heavy sentence, my most sovereign liege,
And all unlook'd for from your highness' mouth:
A dearer merit, not so deep a maim
As to be cast forth in the common air,
Have I deserved at your highness' hands.
The language I have learn'd these forty years,
My native English, now I must forego: 160
And now my tongue's use is to me no more
Than an unstringed viol or a harp,
Or like a cunning instrument cased up,
Or, being open, put into his hands
That knows no touch to tune the harmony:
Within my mouth you have engaol'd my tongue,
Doubly portcullis'd with my teeth and lips;
And dull unfeeling barren ignorance
Is made my gaoler to attend on me.
I am too old to fawn upon a nurse,   170
Too far in years to be a pupil now:
What is thy sentence then but speechless death,
Which robs my tongue from breathing native breath?

K. Rich. It boots thee not to be compassionate:
After our sentence plaining comes too late.

Mow. Then thus I turn me from my country's light,
To dwell in solemn shades of endless night.

K. Rich. Return again, and take an oath with thee.
Lay on our royal sword your banish'd hands;
Swear by the duty that you owe to God—   180
Our part therein we banish with yourselves—
To keep the oath that we administer:
You never shall, so help you truth and God!
Embrace each other's love in banishment;
Nor never look upon each other's face;
Nor never write, regreet, nor reconcile
This louring tempest of your home-bred hate;
Nor never by advised purpose meet
To plot, contrive, or complot any ill
'Gainst us, our state, our subjects, or our land.   190

Boling. I swear.

Mow. And I, to keep all this.

Boling. Norfolk, so far as to mine enemy:—
By this time, had the king permitted us,
One of our souls had wander'd in the air,
Banish'd this frail sepulchre of our flesh,
As now our flesh is banish'd from this land:
Confess thy treasons ere thou fly the realm;
Since thou hast far to go, bear not along
The clogging burthen of a guilty soul.   200

Mow. No, Bolingbroke: if ever I were traitor,
My name be blotted from the book of life,
And I from heaven banish'd as from hence!
But what thou art, God, thou, and I do know;
And all too soon, I fear, the king shall rue.

Farewell, my liege. Now no way can I stray;
Save back to England, all the world 's my way.   [*Exit.*

K. Rich. Uncle, even in the glasses of thine eyes
I see thy grieved heart: thy sad aspect
Hath from the number of his banish'd years   210
Pluck'd four away. [*To Boling.*] Six frozen winters
   spent,
Return with welcome home from banishment.

Boling. How long a time lies in one little word!
Four lagging winters and four wanton springs
End in a word: such is the breath of kings.

Gaunt. I thank my liege, that in regard of me
He shortens four years of my son's exile:
But little vantage shall I reap thereby;
For, ere the six years that he hath to spend
Can change their moons and bring their times about,
My oil-dried lamp and time-bewasted light   221
Shall be extinct with age and endless night;
My inch of taper will be burnt and done,
And blindfold death not let me see my son.

K. Rich. Why, uncle, thou hast many years to live.

Gaunt. But not a minute, king, that thou canst give:
Shorten my days thou canst with sullen sorrow,
And pluck nights from me, but not lend a morrow;
Thou canst help time to furrow me with age,
But stop no wrinkle in his pilgrimage;   230
Thy word is current with him for my death,
But dead, thy kingdom cannot buy my breath.

K. Rich. Thy son is banish'd upon good advice,
Whereto thy tongue a party-verdict gave:
Why at our justice seem'st thou then to lour?

Gaunt. Things sweet to taste prove in digestion sour.
You urged me as a judge; but I had rather
You would have bid me argue like a father.
O, had it been a stranger, not my child,
To smooth his fault I should have been more mild: 240
A partial slander sought I to avoid,
And in the sentence my own life destroy'd.
Alas, I look'd when some of you should say,
I was too strict to make mine own away;
But you gave leave to my unwilling tongue
Against my will to do myself this wrong.

K. Rich. Cousin, farewell; and, uncle, bid him so:
Six years we banish him, and he shall go.
          [*Flourish. Exeunt King Richard and train.*

Aum. Cousin, farewell: what presence must not
   know,
From where you do remain let paper show.   250

Mar. My lord, no leave take I; for I will ride,
As far as land will let me, by your side.

Gaunt. O, to what purpose dost thou hoard thy
   words,
That thou return'st no greeting to thy friends?

Boling. I have too few to take my leave of you,
When the tongue's office should be prodigal
To breathe the abundant dolour of the heart.

Gaunt. Thy grief is but thy absence for a time.

Boling. Joy absent, grief is present for that time.

---

men. 204-205. **But . . . rue.** The prophetic irony of this speech exposes Richard's blunder in banishing so faithful and efficient a servant. The historical Richard probably meant to recall Mowbray and make Bolingbroke's exile permanent; but such an intention is not implied in this play. 208. **glasses,** mirrors. 210. **banish'd years,** years of banishment. *Banish'd* is not a past participle, but an adjective. 211. **Pluck'd four away.** According to Holinshed the amelioration of Bolingbroke's sentence took place later, at Eltham, when the king was taking leave of Bolingbroke. Dramatically, it serves to show how Richard is imposed upon by the stronger personalities of Gaunt and Bolingbroke. 213-

215. **How . . . word.** Coleridge adds after these lines the comment, "Admirable anticipation!" 214. **wanton,** luxuriant. 230. **But . . . pilgrimage,** efface no wrinkle that comes with time. 231. **current,** i.e., as good as current coin. 234. **a party-verdict,** one person's share in a joint verdict. 241. **partial slander,** accusation of partiality. Cf. line 210. 244. **too strict to make,** i.e., in making; a gerundive use of the infinitive, common in Shakespeare. 249. **presence,** the presence chamber at court.

Gaunt. What is six winters? they are quickly gone. 260
Boling. To men in joy; but grief makes one hour ten.
Gaunt. Call it a travel that thou takest for pleasure.
Boling. My heart will sigh when I miscall it so,
Which finds it an inforced pilgrimage.
Gaunt. The sullen passage of thy weary steps
Esteem as foil wherein thou art to set
The precious jewel of thy home return.
Boling. Nay, rather, every tedious stride I make
Will but remember me what a deal of world
I wander from the jewels that I love. 270
Must I not serve a long apprenticehood
To foreign passages, and in the end,
Having my freedom, boast of nothing else
But that I was a journeyman to grief?
Gaunt. All places that the eye of heaven visits
Are to a wise man ports and happy havens.
Teach thy necessity to reason thus;
There is no virtue like necessity.
Think not the king did banish thee,
But thou the king. Woe doth the heavier sit, 280
Where it perceives it is but faintly borne.
Go, say I sent thee forth to purchase honour
And not the king exiled thee; or suppose
Devouring pestilence hangs in our air
And thou art flying to a fresher clime:
Look, what thy soul holds dear, imagine it
To lie that way thou go'st, not whence thou comest:
Suppose the singing birds musicians,
The grass whereon thou tread'st the presence strew'd,
The flowers fair ladies, and thy steps no more 290
Than a delightful measure or a dance;
For gnarling sorrow hath less power to bite
The man that mocks at it and sets it light.
Boling. O, who can hold a fire in his hand
By thinking on the frosty Caucasus?
Or cloy the hungry edge of appetite
By bare imagination of a feast?
Or wallow naked in December snow
By thinking on fantastic summer's heat?
O, no! the apprehension of the good 300
Gives but the greater feeling to the worse:
Fell sorrow's tooth doth never rankle more
Than when he bites, but lanceth not the sore.
Gaunt. Come, come, my son, I'll bring thee on thy
  way:
Had I thy youth and cause, I would not stay.
Boling. Then, England's ground, farewell; sweet
  soil, adieu;
My mother, and my nurse, that bears me yet!
Where'er I wander, boast of this I can,
Though banish'd, yet a trueborn Englishman. [*Exeunt.*

SCENE IV. *The court.*

Enter the KING, *with* BAGOT *and* GREEN *at one door;
and the* DUKE OF AUMERLE *at another.*

K. Rich. We did observe. Cousin Aumerle,
How far brought you high Hereford on his way?
Aum. I brought high Hereford, if you call him so,
But to the next highway, and there I left him.
K. Rich. And say, what store of parting tears were
  shed?
Aum. Faith, none for me; except the northeast
  wind,
Which then blew bitterly against our faces,
Awaked the sleeping rheum, and so by chance
Did grace our hollow parting with a tear.
K. Rich. What said our cousin when you parted
  with him? 10
Aum. 'Farewell:'
And, for my heart disdained that my tongue
Should so profane the word, that taught me craft
To counterfeit oppression of such grief
That words seem'd buried in my sorrow's grave.
Marry, would the word 'farewell' have lengthen'd
  hours
And added years to his short banishment,
He should have had a volume of farewells;
But since it would not, he had none of me.
K. Rich. He is our cousin, cousin; but 'tis doubt, 20
When time shall call him home from banishment,
Whether our kinsman come to see his friends.
Ourself and Bushy, Bagot here and Green
Observed his courtship to the common people;
How he did seem to dive into their hearts
With humble and familiar courtesy,
What reverence he did throw away on slaves,
Wooing poor craftsmen with the craft of smiles
And patient underbearing of his fortune,
As 'twere to banish their affects with him. 30
Off goes his bonnet to an oyster-wench;
A brace of draymen bid God speed him well
And had the tribute of his supple knee,
With 'Thanks, my countrymen, my loving friends;'
As were our England in reversion his,
And he our subjects' next degree in hope.
Green. Well, he is gone; and with him go these
  thoughts.
Now for the rebels which stand out in Ireland,
Expedient manage must be made, my liege,
Ere further leisure yield them further means 40
For their advantage and your highness' loss.
K. Rich. We will ourself in person to this war:
And, for our coffers, with too great a court
And liberal largess, are grown somewhat light,
We are inforced to farm our royal realm;
The revenue whereof shall furnish us
For our affairs in hand: if that come short,
Our substitutes at home shall have blank charters;
Whereto, when they shall know what men are rich,
They shall subscribe them for large sums of gold 50
And send them after to supply our wants;
For we will make for Ireland presently.

266. **foil,** metal surface used in setting gems to show off their luster; hence, that which sets something off to advantage. 272. **passages,** wanderings. 274. **journeyman,** laborer hired by the day; at the end of such service would come the settlement in his trade. 289. **presence strew'd,** i.e., the royal presence chamber strewn with rushes. 292. **gnarling,** snarling, growling. 299. **fantastic,** imaginary. 300. **apprehension,** idea, product of mere imagination. 302-303. **Fell . . . sore,** i.e., never poisons more than when it irritates the sore instead of lancing to cure it. 302. **rankle,** cause to fester, i.e., produce irritation by poison.
SCENE IV. 8. **rheum,** tears. 12-13. **for . . . word.** This clause is the antecedent of *that.* Aumerle says he pretended to be overcome by grief

in order to avoid saying "Farewell" to Bolingbroke. 23. **Ourself . . . Green:** so Q₅; QF: *Our selfe, and Bushy: heere. Bagot and Greene,* which may be construed by omitting punctuation except comma after *heere.* 24. **his courtship to the common people.** Compare Bolingbroke's own account, *1 Henry IV,* III, ii, 46 ff. 29. **underbearing,** bearing, enduring. 30. **affects,** affections. 35. **reversion,** right of future possession. 37. **go,** let go. 38. **rebels . . . Ireland.** Many of the colonies planted by Henry II in the "English Pale" had thrown off their allegiance and were in rebellion. 39. **Expedient manage,** expeditious management. 43. **too great a court.** Holinshed says that Richard "kept the greatest court, and mainteined the most plentifull house that euer any king in England did either before his time or since." 45. **farm,**

Enter BUSHY.

Bushy, what news?

Bushy. Old John of Gaunt is grievous sick, my lord,
Suddenly taken; and hath sent post haste
To entreat your majesty to visit him.

K. Rich. Where lies he?

Bushy. At Ely House.

K. Rich. Now put it, God, in the physician's mind
To help him to his grave immediately!　　　　　60
The lining of his coffers shall make coats
To deck our soldiers for these Irish wars.
Come, gentlemen, let's all go visit him:
Pray God we may make haste, and come too late!

All. Amen.　　　　　　　　　　　　　*[Exeunt.*

ACT II.

SCENE I. *Ely House.*

Enter JOHN OF GAUNT *sick, with the* DUKE OF YORK,
&c.

Gaunt. Will the king come, that I may breathe my
　　last
In wholesome counsel to his unstaid youth?

York. Vex not yourself, nor strive not with your
　　breath;
For all in vain comes counsel to his ear.

Gaunt. O, but they say the tongues of dying men
Enforce attention like deep harmony:
Where words are scarce, they are seldom spent in
　　vain,
For they breathe truth that breathe their words in pain.
He that no more must say is listen'd more
Than they whom youth and ease have taught to
　　glose;　　　　　　　　　　　　　　10
More are men's ends mark'd than their lives before:
　The setting sun, and music at the close,
As the last taste of sweets, is sweetest last,
Writ in remembrance more than things long past:
Though Richard my life's counsel would not hear,
My death's sad tale may yet undeaf his ear.

York. No; it is stopp'd with other flattering sounds,
As praises, of whose taste the wise are fond,
Lascivious metres, to whose venom sound
The open ear of youth doth always listen;　　　　20
Report of fashions in proud Italy,
Whose manners still our tardy apish nation
Limps after in base imitation.
Where doth the world thrust forth a vanity—
So it be new, there's no respect how vile—
That is not quickly buzz'd into his ears?
Then all too late comes counsel to be heard,
Where will doth mutiny with wit's regard.
Direct not him whose way himself will choose:

'Tis breath thou lack'st, and that breath wilt thou
　　lose.　　　　　　　　　　　　　　　30

Gaunt. Methinks I am a prophet new inspired
And thus expiring do foretell of him:
His rash fierce blaze of riot cannot last,
For violent fires soon burn out themselves;
Small showers last long, but sudden storms are short;
He tires betimes that spurs too fast betimes;
With eager feeding food doth choke the feeder:
Light vanity, insatiate cormorant,
Consuming means, soon preys upon itself.
This royal throne of kings, this scepter'd isle,　　40
This earth of majesty, this seat of Mars,
This other Eden, demi-paradise,
This fortress built by Nature for herself
Against infection and the hand of war,
This happy breed of men, this little world,
This precious stone set in the silver sea,
Which serves it in the office of a wall
Or as a moat defensive to a house,
Against the envy of less happier lands,
This blessed plot, this earth, this realm, this England,
This nurse, this teeming womb of royal kings,　　51
Fear'd by their breed and famous by their birth,
Renowned for their deeds as far from home,
For Christian service and true chivalry,
As is the sepulchre in stubborn Jewry
Of the world's ransom, blessed Mary's Son,
This land of such dear souls, this dear dear land,
Dear for her reputation through the world,
Is now leased out, I die pronouncing it,
Like to a tenement or pelting farm:　　　　　60
England, bound in with the triumphant sea,
Whose rocky shore beats back the envious siege
Of watery Neptune, is now bound in with shame,
With inky blots and rotten parchment bonds:
That England, that was wont to conquer others,
Hath made a shameful conquest of itself.
Ah, would the scandal vanish with my life,
How happy then were my ensuing death!

Enter KING RICHARD *and* QUEEN, AUMERLE, BUSHY,
　GREEN, BAGOT, ROSS, *and* WILLOUGHBY.

York. The king is come: deal mildly with his youth;
For young hot colts being †raged do rage the more.　70

Queen. How fares our noble uncle, Lancaster?

K. Rich. What comfort, man? how is't with aged
　　Gaunt?

Gaunt. O, how that name befits my composition!
Old Gaunt indeed, and gaunt in being old:
Within me grief hath kept a tedious fast;
And who abstains from meat that is not gaunt?
For sleeping England long time have I watch'd;
Watching breeds leanness, leanness is all gaunt:
The pleasure that some fathers feed upon,
Is my strict fast; I mean, my children's looks;　　80
And therein fasting, hast thou made me gaunt:

---

to let the right of collecting taxes, for a present cash payment, to the highest bidder. **48. blank charters,** ready-drawn obligations, blank spaces being left for the names of the parties and the sums they were to provide. **50. subscribe them,** make them write their names under. **58. Ely House,** palace of the bishop of Ely in Holborn.

ACT II. SCENE I. There are serious difficulties in the matter of real and dramatic time in this scene and the one which precedes it. We can suppose the lapse of only an hour or two between the scenes. In the earlier scene Bolingbroke has just departed on his exile. In II, i, 277 ff., he has been to France and is on his way back; besides, we are told (II, i, 167-168) that Richard has "prevented" him about his marriage. **2. unstaid,** thoughtless, rash. **5-16. O . . . ear.** The

rhyming measures here and elsewhere characterize Gaunt's exalted manner of speech. **9. listen'd,** listened to. **10. glose,** flatter, deceive in speech. **12. close,** harmonious chords at the end of a piece of music. **16. undeaf,** make capable of hearing. **19. venom,** pernicious, poisonous. **21. proud Italy.** Ascham, Lyly, and other sixteenth-century writers complain of the growing influence of Italian luxury. **26. buzz'd,** whispered; used contemptuously. **28. with wit's regard,** against the consideration due to reason. **38. cormorant,** glutton. **40-55. This . . . Jewry.** These lines, except line 50, were published in *England's Parnassus* (1600) and attributed to M. Dr. (Michael Drayton). **44. infection,** pollution; possibly, plague. **55. Jewry,** Judea. **60. pelting,** paltry. **70. raged,** enraged. **73. composition,** constitution.

Gaunt am I for the grave, gaunt as a grave,
Whose hollow womb inherits nought but bones.
    K. Rich. Can sick men play so nicely with their
        names?
    Gaunt. No, misery makes sport to mock itself:
Since thou dost seek to kill my name in me,
I mock my name, great king, to flatter thee.
    K. Rich. Should dying men flatter with those that
        live?
    Gaunt. No, no, men living flatter those that die.
    K. Rich. Thou, now a-dying, say'st thou flatterest
        me.   90
    Gaunt. O, no! thou diest, though I the sicker be.
    K. Rich. I am in health, I breathe, and see thee ill.
    Gaunt. Now He that made me knows I see thee ill;
Ill in myself to see, and in thee seeing ill.
Thy death-bed is no lesser than thy land
Wherein thou liest in reputation sick;
And thou, too careless patient as thou art,
Commit'st thy anointed body to the cure
Of those physicians that first wounded thee:
A thousand flatterers sit within thy crown,   100
Whose compass is no bigger than thy head;
And yet, incaged in so small a verge,
The waste is no whit lesser than thy land.
O, had thy grandsire with a prophet's eye
Seen how his son's son should destroy his sons,
From forth thy reach he would have laid thy shame,
Deposing thee before thou wert possess'd,
Which art possess'd now to depose thyself.
Why, cousin, wert thou regent of the world,
It were a shame to let this land by lease;   110
But for thy world enjoying but this land,
Is it not more than shame to shame it so?
Landlord of England art thou now, not king:
Thy state of law is bondslave to the law;
And thou—
    K. Rich.   A lunatic lean-witted fool,
Presuming on an ague's privilege,
Darest with thy frozen admonition
Make pale our cheek, chasing the royal blood
With fury from his native residence.
Now, by my seat's right royal majesty,   120
Wert thou not brother to great Edward's son,
This tongue that runs so roundly in thy head
Should run thy head from thy unreverent shoulders.
    Gaunt. O, spare me not, my brother Edward's son,
For that I was his father Edward's son;
That blood already, like the pelican,
Hast thou tapp'd out and drunkenly carous…d:
My brother Gloucester, plain well-meaning soul,
Whom fair befal in heaven 'mongst happy souls!
May be a precedent and witness good   130
That thou respect'st not spilling Edward's blood:
Join with the present sickness that I have;
And thy unkindness be like crooked age,
To crop at once a too long wither'd flower.

Live in thy shame, but die not shame with thee!
These words hereafter thy tormentors be!
Convey me to my bed, then to my grave:
Love they to live that love and honour have.
            [*Exit, borne off by his Attendants.*
    K. Rich. And let them die that age and sullens have;
For both hast thou, and both become the grave.   140
    York. I do beseech your majesty, impute his words
To wayward sickliness and age in him:
He loves you, on my life, and holds you dear
As Harry Duke of Hereford, were he here.
    K. Rich. Right, you say true: as Hereford's love, so
        his;
As theirs, so mine; and all be as it is.

Enter NORTHUMBERLAND.

    North. My liege, old Gaunt commends him to your
        majesty.
    K. Rich. What says he?
    North.   Nay, nothing; all is said:
His tongue is now a stringless instrument;
Words, life and all, old Lancaster hath spent.   150
    York. Be York the next that must be bankrupt so!
Though death be poor, it ends a mortal woe.
    K. Rich. The ripest fruit first falls, and so doth he;
His time is spent, our pilgrimage must be.
So much for that. Now for our Irish wars:
We must supplant those rough rug-headed kerns,
Which live like venom where no venom else
But only they have privilege to live.
And for these great affairs do ask some charge,
Towards our assistance we do seize to us   160
The plate, coin, revenues and moveables,
Whereof our uncle Gaunt did stand possess'd.
    York. How long shall I be patient? ah, how long
Shall tender duty make me suffer wrong?
Not Gloucester's death, nor Hereford's banishment,
Not Gaunt's rebukes, nor England's private wrongs,
Nor the prevention of poor Bolingbroke
About his marriage, nor my own disgrace,
Have ever made me sour my patient cheek,
Or bend one wrinkle on my sovereign's face.   170
I am the last of noble Edward's sons,
Of whom thy father, Prince of Wales, was first:
In war was never lion raged more fierce,
In peace was never gentle lamb more mild,
Than was that young and princely gentleman.
His face thou hast, for even so look'd he,
Accomplish'd with the number of thy hours;
But when he frown'd, it was against the French
And not against his friends; his noble hand
Did win what he did spend and spent not that   180
Which his triumphant father's hand had won;
His hands were guilty of no kindred blood,
But bloody with the enemies of his kin.
O Richard! York is too far gone with grief,
Or else he never would compare between.

83. **inherits**, possesses. 84. **Can . . . names.** Coleridge answers: "Yes! on a deathbed there is a feeling which may make all things appear but as puns and equivocations. And a passion there is that carries off its own excess by plays on words as naturally, and therefore, as appropriately to drama, as by gesticulation, looks, or tones." **nicely**, delicately, fantastically. 102. **verge**, circle, ring; technically, "the compass about the king's court which extended for twelve miles." 103. **waste**, a legal use meaning "destruction of houses, woods, lands, etc., done by a tenant to the prejudice of the heir" (Onions). 114. **state of law**, legal status as a king. 118. **Make pale our cheek.** Richard's physical sensitiveness, which caused him to turn pale readily (see III, ii, 75; III, iii, 67), is recorded by Froissart and other chroniclers. 122. **roundly**, uncere-

moniously; see glossary. 126. **pelican**, allusion to the belief that the pelican fed its young on its own blood. 139. **sullens**, moroseness, sullenness. 144. **As Harry Duke of Hereford**, i.e., as he holds Harry, etc. Richard purposely misinterprets the ambiguous speech of York. 156. **rug-headed**, rough-haired. **kerns**, Irish foot soldiers. 157. **no venom else**, allusion to the freedom of Ireland from reptiles, traditionally ascribed to St. Patrick. 163. **How . . . patient.** Although York's reproof is quite as severe as Gaunt's, it does not anger the king, since he is not planning to injure York as he is Gaunt. 166. **Gaunt's rebukes**, i.e., the rebuke given to Gaunt. 173. **raged**, may equal *enraged*, as in line 70, or we may understand a relative omitted after *lion*. 177. **Accomplish'd.** equipped. 185. **compare between**, draw com-

K. Rich. Why, uncle, what's the matter?
   York.   O my liege,
Pardon me, if you please; if not, I, pleased
Not to be pardon'd, am content withal.
Seek you to seize and gripe into your hands
The royalties and rights of banish'd Hereford?   190
Is not Gaunt dead, and doth not Hereford live?
Was not Gaunt just, and is not Harry true?
Did not the one deserve to have an heir?
Is not his heir a well-deserving son?
Take Hereford's rights away, and take from Time
His charters and his customary rights;
Let not to-morrow then ensue to-day;
Be not thyself; for how art thou a king
But by fair sequence and succession?
Now, afore God—God forbid I say true!—   200
If you do wrongfully seize Hereford's rights,
Call in the letters patents that he hath
By his attorneys-general to sue
His livery, and deny his offer'd homage,
You pluck a thousand dangers on your head,
You lose a thousand well-disposed hearts
And prick my tender patience to those thoughts
Which honour and allegiance cannot think.
   K. Rich. Think what you will, we seize into our
      hands
His plate, his goods, his money and his lands.   210
   York. I'll not be by the while: my liege, farewell:
What will ensue hereof, there's none can tell;
But by bad courses may be understood
That their events can never fall out good.   [*Exit.*
   K. Rich. Go, Bushy, to the Earl of Wiltshire straight:
Bid him repair to us to Ely House
To see this business. To-morrow next
We will for Ireland; and 'tis time, I trow:
And we create, in absence of ourself,
Our uncle York lord governor of England;   220
For he is just and always loved us well.
Come on, our queen: to-morrow must we part;
Be merry, for our time of stay is short.
   [*Flourish. Exeunt King, Queen, Aumerle, Bushy, Green,*
                           and Bagot.
   North. Well, lords, the Duke of Lancaster is dead.
   Ross. And living too; for now his son is duke.
   Willo. Barely in title, not in revenues.
   North. Richly in both, if justice had her right.
   Ross. My heart is great; but it must break with
      silence,
Ere 't be disburden'd with a liberal tongue.
   North. Nay, speak thy mind; and let him ne'er
      speak more   230
That speaks thy words again to do thee harm!
   Willo. Tends that thou wouldst speak to the Duke of
      Hereford?
If it be so, out with it boldly, man;
Quick is mine ear to hear of good towards him.
   Ross. No good at all that I can do for him;

Unless you call it good to pity him,
Bereft and gelded of his patrimony.
   North. Now, afore God, 'tis shame such wrongs are
      borne
In him, a royal prince, and many moe
Of noble blood in this declining land.   240
The king is not himself, but basely led
By flatterers; and what they will inform,
Merely in hate, 'gainst any of us all,
That will the king severely prosecute
'Gainst us, our lives, our children, and our heirs.
   Ross. The commons hath he pill'd with grievous
      taxes,
†And quite lost their hearts: the nobles hath he fined
For ancient quarrels, and quite lost their hearts.
   Willo. And daily new exactions are devised,
As blanks, benevolences, and I wot not what: 250
But what, o' God's name, doth become of this?
   North. Wars have not wasted it, for warr'd he hath not,
But basely yielded upon compromise
That which his noble ancestors achieved with blows:
More hath he spent in peace than they in wars.
   Ross. The Earl of Wiltshire hath the realm in farm.
   Willo. The king's grown bankrupt, like a broken
      man.
   North. Reproach and dissolution hangeth over him.
   Ross. He hath not money for these Irish wars,
His burthenous taxations notwithstanding,   260
But by the robbing of the banish'd duke.
   North. His noble kinsman: most degenerate king!
But, lords, we hear this fearful tempest sing,
Yet seek no shelter to avoid the storm;
We see the wind sit sore upon our sails,
And yet we strike not, but securely perish.
   Ross. We see the very wreck that we must suffer;
And unavoided is the danger now,
For suffering so the causes of our wreck.
   North. Not so; even through the hollow eyes of
      death   270
I spy life peering; but I dare not say
How near the tidings of our comfort is.
   Willo. Nay, let us share thy thoughts, as thou dost
      ours.
   Ross. Be confident to speak, Northumberland:
We three are but thyself; and, speaking so,
Thy words are but as thoughts; therefore, be bold.
   North. Then thus: I have from Port le Blanc, a bay
In Brittany, received intelligence
That Harry Duke of Hereford, Rainold Lord
      Cobham,
†.   280
That late broke from the Duke of Exeter,
His brother, Archbishop late of Canterbury,
Sir Thomas Erpingham, Sir John Ramston,
Sir John Norbery, Sir Robert Waterton and Francis
      Quoint,
All these well furnish'd by the Duke of Bretagne

---

parisons. **190. royalties,** privileges belonging to a member of the royal house. **197. ensue,** follow upon. **202. Call . . . patents.** This occurred some six weeks after Gaunt's death. **letters patents,** letters addressed by a sovereign to the patentee granting him some dignity, office, or privilege. **203. attorneys-general,** deputies, legal substitutes. **220. York lord governor.** It is the acme of Richard's tragic blindness that he should appoint to the regency a man whose loyalty was already strained to the breaking point. **227. if . . . right.** This conversation marks the beginning of the counterplot. **242. inform,** charge against (used technically); see glossary. **246. pill'd,** plundered, robbed. **247. And . . . fined.** This line is defective in meter, and is probably corrupt; Pope omitted *quite.* **250. blanks,** *cartes blanches,* referred to in

I, iv, 48. **253. basely yielded,** allusion to Richard's unpopular foreign policy of peace with France. **266. strike,** furl (of sails). **securely,** heedlessly, carelessly. **268. unavoided,** unavoidable. **280.** The break indicated here may be due to an omission of a line by the printer. Holinshed records that "the earle of Arundels sonne, named Thomas, which was kept in the duke of Exeters house, escaped out of the realme . . . and went to his vncle Thomas Arundell late archbishop of Canturburie." Malone supplying this detail from Holinshed inserts here the line, "The son of Richard Earle of Arundel." This puts the text into accord with Holinshed, since it is this Thomas and not Lord Cobham who escaped from the duke of Exeter.

With eight tall ships, three thousand men of war,
Are making hither with all due expedience
And shortly mean to touch our northern shore:
Perhaps they had ere this, but that they stay
The first departing of the king for Ireland.   290
If then we shall shake off our slavish yoke,
Imp out our drooping country's broken wing,
Redeem from broking pawn the blemish'd crown,
Wipe off the dust that hides our sceptre's gilt
And make high majesty look like itself,
Away with me in post to Ravenspurgh;
But if you faint, as fearing to do so,
Stay and be secret, and myself will go.
    Ross. To horse, to horse! urge doubts to them that
      fear.
    Willo. Hold out my horse, and I will first be there.
                                              [*Exeunt.*

SCENE II. *Windsor Castle.*

Enter QUEEN, BUSHY, *and* BAGOT.

    Bushy. Madam, your majesty is too much sad:
You promised, when you parted with the king,
To lay aside life-harming heaviness
And entertain a cheerful disposition.
    Queen. To please the king I did; to please myself
I cannot do it; yet I know no cause
Why I should welcome such a guest as grief,
Save bidding farewell to so sweet a guest
As my sweet Richard: yet again, methinks,
Some unborn sorrow, ripe in fortune's womb,   10
Is coming towards me, and my inward soul
With nothing trembles: at some thing it grieves,
More than with parting from my lord the king.
    Bushy. Each substance of a grief hath twenty
      shadows,
Which shows like grief itself, but is not so;
For sorrow's eye, glazed with blinding tears,
Divides one thing entire to many objects;
Like perspectives, which rightly gazed upon
Show nothing but confusion, eyed awry
Distinguish form: so your sweet majesty,   20
Looking awry upon your lord's departure,
Find shapes of grief, more than himself, to wail;
Which, look'd on as it is, is nought but shadows
Of what it is not. Then, thrice-gracious queen,
More than your lord's departure weep not: more 's
      not seen;
Or if it be, 'tis with false sorrow's eye,
Which for things true weeps things imaginary.
    Queen. It may be so; but yet my inward soul
Persuades me it is otherwise: howe'er it be,
I cannot but be sad; so heavy sad   30
As, though on thinking on no thought I think,
Makes me with heavy nothing faint and shrink.
    Bushy. 'Tis nothing but conceit, my gracious lady.
    Queen. 'Tis nothing less: conceit is still derived

From some forefather grief; mine is not so,
For nothing hath begot my something grief;
Or something hath the nothing that I grieve:
'Tis in reversion that I do possess;
But what it is, that is not yet known; what
I cannot name; 'tis nameless woe, I wot.   40

Enter GREEN.

    Green. God save your majesty! and well met,
      gentlemen:
I hope the king is not yet shipp'd for Ireland.
    Queen. Why hopest thou so? 'tis better hope he is;
For his designs crave haste, his haste good hope:
Then wherefore dost thou hope he is not shipp'd?
    Green. That he, our hope, might have retired his
      power,
And driven into despair an enemy's hope,
Who strongly hath set footing in this land:
The banish'd Bolingbroke repeals himself,
And with uplifted arms is safe arrived   50
At Ravenspurgh.
    Queen.   Now God in heaven forbid!
    Green. Ah, madam, 'tis too true: and that is worse,
The Lord Northumberland, his son young Henry
      Percy,
The Lords of Ross, Beaumond, and Willoughby,
With all their powerful friends, are fled to him.
    Bushy. Why have you not proclaim'd
      Northumberland
And all the rest revolted faction traitors?
    Green. We have: whereupon the Earl of Worcester
Hath broke his staff, resign'd his stewardship,
And all the household servants fled with him   60
To Bolingbroke.
    Queen. So, Green, thou art the midwife to my woe,
And Bolingbroke my sorrow's dismal heir:
Now hath my soul brought forth her prodigy,
And I, a gasping new-deliver'd mother,
Have woe to woe, sorrow to sorrow join'd.
    Bushy. Despair not, madam.
    Queen.   Who shall hinder me?
I will despair, and be at enmity
With cozening hope: he is a flatterer,
A parasite, a keeper back of death,   70
Who gently would dissolve the bands of life,
Which false hope lingers in extremity.

Enter YORK.

    Green. Here comes the Duke of York.
    Queen. With signs of war about his aged neck:
O, full of careful business are his looks!
Uncle, for God's sake, speak comfortable words.
    York. Should I do so, I should belie my thoughts:
Comfort 's in heaven; and we are on the earth,
Where nothing lives but crosses, cares and grief.
Your husband, he is gone to save far off,   80
Whilst others come to make him lose at home:
Here am I left to underprop his land,
Who, weak with age, cannot support myself:

Now comes the sick hour that his surfeit made;
Now shall he try his friends that flatter'd him.

Enter a Servant.

Serv. My lord, your son was gone before I came.
York. He was? Why, so! go all which way it will!
The nobles they are fled, the commons they are cold,
And will, I fear, revolt on Hereford's side.
Sirrah, get thee to Plashy, to my sister Gloucester; 90
Bid her send me presently a thousand pound:
Hold, take my ring.
Serv. My lord, I had forgot to tell your lordship,
To-day, as I came by, I called there;
But I shall grieve you to report the rest.
York. What is 't, knave?
Serv. An hour before I came, the duchess died.
York. God for his mercy! what a tide of woes
Comes rushing on this woeful land at once!
I know not what to do: I would to God, 100
So my untruth had not provoked him to it,
The king had cut off my head with my brother's.
What, are there no posts dispatch'd for Ireland?
How shall we do for money for these wars?
Come, sister,—cousin, I would say,—pray, pardon
  me.
Go, fellow, get thee home, provide some carts
And bring away the armour that is there. [*Exit Servant.*
Gentlemen, will you go muster men?
If I know how or which way to order these affairs
Thus thrust disorderly into my hands, 110
Never believe me. Both are my kinsmen:
The one is my sovereign, whom both my oath
And duty bids defend; the other again
Is my kinsman, whom the king hath wrong'd,
Whom conscience and my kindred bids to right.
Well, somewhat we must do. Come, cousin, I'll
Dispose of you.
Gentlemen, go, muster up your men,
And meet me presently at Berkeley.
I should to Plashy too; 120
But time will not permit: all is uneven,
And every thing is left at six and seven.
                              [*Exeunt York and Queen.*
Bushy. The wind sits fair for news to go to Ireland,
But none returns. For us to levy power
Proportionable to the enemy
Is all unpossible.
Green. Besides, our nearness to the king in love
Is near the hate of those love not the king.
Bagot. And that 's the wavering commons: for their
  love
Lies in their purses, and whoso empties them 130
By so much fills their hearts with deadly hate.
Bushy. Wherein the king stands generally
  condemn'd.
Bagot. If judgement lie in them, then so do we,
Because we ever have been near the king.
Green. Well, I will for refuge straight to Bristol
  castle:

The Earl of Wiltshire is already there.
Bushy. Thither will I with you; for little office
The hateful commons will perform for us,
Except like curs to tear us all to pieces.
Will you go along with us? 140
Bagot. No; I will to Ireland to his majesty.
Farewell: if heart's presages be not vain,
We three here part that ne'er shall meet again.
Bushy. That 's as York thrives to beat back
  Bolingbroke.
Green. Alas, poor duke! the task he undertakes
Is numbering sands and drinking oceans dry:
Where one on his side fights, thousands will fly.
Farewell at once, for once, for all, and ever.
Bushy. Well, we may meet again.
Bagot.   I fear me, never.   [*Exeunt.*

SCENE III. *Wilds in Gloucestershire.*

Enter BOLINGBROKE *and* NORTHUMBERLAND, *with
  Forces.*

Boling. How far is it, my lord, to Berkeley now?
North. Believe me, noble lord,
I am a stranger here in Gloucestershire:
These high wild hills and rough uneven ways
Draws out our miles, and makes them wearisome;
And yet your fair discourse hath been as sugar,
Making the hard way sweet and delectable.
But I bethink me what a weary way
From Ravenspurgh to Cotswold will be found
In Ross and Willoughby, wanting your company, 10
Which, I protest, hath very much beguiled
The tediousness and process of my travel:
But theirs is sweetened with the hope to have
The present benefit which I possess;
And hope to joy is little less in joy
Than hope enjoy'd: by this the weary lords
Shall make their way seem short, as mine hath done
By sight of what I have, your noble company.
Boling. Of much less value is my company
Than your good words. But who comes here? 20

Enter HENRY PERCY.

North. It is my son, young Harry Percy,
Sent from my brother Worcester, whencesoever.
Harry, how fares your uncle?
Percy. I had thought, my lord, to have learn'd his
  health of you.
North. Why, is he not with the queen?
Percy. No, my good lord; he hath forsook the court,
Broken his staff of office and dispersed
The household of the king.
North.   What was his reason?
He was not so resolved when last we spake together.
Percy. Because your lordship was proclaimed traitor.
But he, my lord, is gone to Ravenspurgh, 31
To offer service to the Duke of Hereford,
And sent me over by Berkeley, to discover

The cause of the grief can only be revealed in the future (*in reversion*).
59. **broke his staff,** i.e., in token of the resignation of his office of Lord
High Steward. Thomas Percy, earl of Worcester, brother of the earl of
Northumberland, provokes the rebellion of the Percys in *1* and *2
Henry IV.* 64. **prodigy,** monstrous birth. 69. **cozening,** cheating.
72. **lingers,** causes to linger. 74. **signs of war.** York is in armor.
76. **comfortable,** affording comfort. 86. **your son,** the duke of Aumerle,
who had accompanied Richard to Ireland. 96. **knave,** familiar
term in addressing servants (without evil significance). 97. **the duchess**

died. The death of the duchess of Gloucester is anticipated by several
months (in order to add to York's embarrassment). 122. **at six and
seven,** at sixes and sevens, in confusion. 125. **Proportionable,** pro-
portionate.
    SCENE III. 9. **Cotswold,** hilly district in Gloucestershire. 12.
tediousness and process, tedious process. 15. **joy,** enjoy. 22. **whencesoever,** from wherever.

What power the Duke of York had levied there;
Then with directions to repair to Ravenspurgh.
    North. Have you forgot the Duke of Hereford, boy?
    Percy. No, my good lord, for that is not forgot
Which ne'er I did remember: to my knowledge,
I never in my life did look on him.
    North. Then learn to know him now; this is the
        duke.   40
    Percy. My gracious lord, I tender you my service,
Such as it is, being tender, raw and young;
Which elder days shall ripen and confirm
To more approved service and desert.
    Boling. I thank thee, gentle Percy; and be sure
I count myself in nothing else so happy
As in a soul remembering my good friends;
And, as my fortune ripens with thy love,
It shall be still thy true love's recompense:
My heart this covenant makes, my hand thus seals it.
    North. How far is it to Berkeley? and what stir   51
Keeps good old York there with his men of war?
    Percy. There stands the castle, by yon tuft of trees,
Mann'd with three hundred men, as I have heard;
And in it are the Lords of York, Berkeley, and
        Seymour;
None else of name and noble estimate.

    Enter ROSS *and* WILLOUGHBY.

    North. Here come the Lords of Ross and
        Willoughby,
Bloody with spurring, fiery-red with haste.
    Boling. Welcome, my lords. I wot your love pursues
A banish'd traitor: all my treasury   60
Is yet but unfelt thanks, which more enrich'd
Shall be your love and labour's recompense.
    Ross. Your presence makes us rich, most noble lord.
    Willo. And far surmounts our labour to attain it.
    Boling. Evermore thanks, the exchequer of the poor;
Which, till my infant fortune comes to years,
Stands for my bounty. But who comes here?

    Enter BERKELEY.

    North. It is my Lord of Berkeley, as I guess.
    Berk. My Lord of Hereford, my message is to you.
    Boling. My lord, my answer is—to Lancaster;   70
And I am come to seek that name in England;
And I must find that title in your tongue,
Before I make reply to aught you say.
    Berk. Mistake me not, my lord; 'tis not my meaning
To raze one title of your honour out:
To you, my lord, I come, what lord you will,
From the most gracious regent of this land,
The Duke of York, to know what pricks you on
To take advantage of the absent time
And fright our native peace with self-born arms.   80

    Enter YORK *attended.*

    Boling. I shall not need transport my words by you;
Here comes his grace in person.

        My noble uncle!   [*Kneels.*
    York. Show me thy humble heart, and not thy knee,
Whose duty is deceivable and false.
    Boling. My gracious uncle—
    York. Tut, tut!
Grace me no grace, nor uncle me no uncle:
I am no traitor's uncle; and that word 'grace'
In an ungracious mouth is but profane.
Why have those banish'd and forbidden legs   90
Dared once to touch a dust of England's ground?
But then more 'why?' why have they dared to march
So many miles upon her peaceful bosom,
Frighting her pale-faced villages with war
And ostentation of despised arms?
Comest thou because the anointed king is hence?
Why, foolish boy, the king is left behind,
And in my loyal bosom lies his power.
Were I but now the lord of such hot youth
As when brave Gaunt, thy father, and myself   100
Rescued the Black Prince, that young Mars of men,
From forth the ranks of many thousand French,
O, then how quickly should this arm of mine,
Now prisoner to the palsy, chastise thee
And minister correction to thy fault!
    Boling. My gracious uncle, let me know my fault:
On what condition stands it and wherein?
    York. Even in condition of the worst degree,
In gross rebellion and detested treason:
Thou art a banish'd man, and here art come   110
Before the expiration of thy time,
In braving arms against thy sovereign.
    Boling. As I was banish'd, I was banish'd Hereford;
But as I come, I come for Lancaster.
And, noble uncle, I beseech your grace
Look on my wrongs with an indifferent eye:
You are my father, for methinks in you
I see old Gaunt alive; O, then, my father,
Will you permit that I shall stand condemn'd
A wandering vagabond; my rights and royalties   120
Pluck'd from my arms perforce and given away
To upstart unthrifts? Wherefore was I born?
If that my cousin king be King of England,
It must be granted I am Duke of Lancaster.
You have a son, Aumerle, my noble cousin;
Had you first died, and he been thus trod down,
He should have found his uncle Gaunt a father,
To rouse his wrongs and chase them to the bay.
I am denied to sue my livery here,
And yet my letters-patents give me leave: 130
My father's goods are all distrain'd and sold,
And these and all are all amiss employ'd.
What would you have me do? I am a subject,
And I challenge law: attorneys are denied me;
And therefore personally I lay my claim
To my inheritance of free descent.
    North. The noble duke hath been too much abused.
    Ross. It stands your grace upon to do him right.
    Willo. Base men by his endowments are made great.

---

42. **raw and young.** Henry Percy, called "Hotspur," was born in 1364; Prince Hal in 1387. Shakespeare represents them as of the same age. 45-49. **I thank . . . recompense.** Cf. *1 Henry IV*, I, iii, 251 ff., where Hotspur bitterly recalls this speech. 61. **unfelt,** impalpable, not perceived. 70. **Lancaster.** Bolingbroke will enter into no negotiations unless his proper title is given him. 79. **the absent time,** the time of absence. 80. **native,** entitled (i.e., to peace) by birth, rightful. **self-born,** indigenous, home-sprung (Clark and Wright); some editors read *self-borne,* i.e., borne for himself, not for the king. 84. **deceivable,** deceptive. 87. **Grace me no grace.** York, as he begins, intends to do

his duty by the king; later he is won over by Bolingbroke. 91. **dust, a** particle of dust. 92. **more 'why,'** more questions to ask. 114. **I come for Lancaster,** i.e., in the character of Lancaster. Compare *2 Henry IV*, IV, v, 184-186. 116. **indifferent,** impartial. 122. **unthrifts,** spendthrifts, prodigals. 128. **to the bay,** to the extremity where the hunted animal turns on its pursuers. 129. **sue my livery,** sue for legal delivery of my freehold as heir. 131. **distrain'd,** seized by legal process. 134. **challenge,** claim. 138. **stands . . . upon,** is incumbent upon. 154. **ill left,** left with inadequate means. 159. **neuter.** Neutrality on York's part is hostility to Richard; but he is practically Bolingbroke's prisoner.

York. My lords of England, let me tell you this: 140
I have had feeling of my cousin's wrongs
And labour'd all I could to do him right;
But in this kind to come, in braving arms,
Be his own carver and cut out his way,
To find out right with wrong, it may not be;
And you that do abet him in this kind
Cherish rebellion and are rebels all.
North. The noble duke hath sworn his coming is
But for his own; and for the right of that
We all have strongly sworn to give him aid; 150
And let him ne'er see joy that breaks that oath!
York. Well, well, I see the issue of these arms:
I cannot mend it, I must needs confess,
Because my power is weak and all ill left:
But if I could, by Him that gave me life,
I would attach you all and make you stoop
Unto the sovereign mercy of the king;
But since I cannot, be it known to you
I do remain as neuter. So, fare you well;
Unless you please to enter in the castle 160
And there repose you for this night.
Boling. An offer, uncle, that we will accept:
But we must win your grace to go with us
To Bristol castle, which they say is held
By Bushy, Bagot and their complices,
The caterpillars of the commonwealth,
Which I have sworn to weed and pluck away.
York. It may be I will go with you: but yet I'll
  pause;
For I am loath to break our country's laws.
Nor friends nor foes, to me welcome you are: 170
Things past redress are now with me past care. [*Exeunt.*

SCENE IV. *A camp in Wales.*

Enter SALISBURY *and a* Welsh Captain.

Cap. My Lord of Salisbury, we have stay'd ten days,
And hardly kept our countrymen together,
And yet we hear no tidings from the king;
Therefore we will disperse ourselves: farewell.
Sal. Stay yet another day, thou trusty Welshman:
The king reposeth all his confidence in thee.
Cap. 'Tis thought the king is dead; we will not stay.
The bay-trees in our country are all wither'd
And meteors fright the fixed stars of heaven;
The pale-faced moon looks bloody on the earth 10
And lean-look'd prophets whisper fearful change;
Rich men look sad and ruffians dance and leap,
The one in fear to lose what they enjoy,
The other to enjoy by rage and war:
These signs forerun the death or fall of kings.
Farewell: our countrymen are gone and fled,
As well assured Richard their king is dead. [*Exit.*
Sal. Ah, Richard, with the eyes of heavy mind
I see thy glory like a shooting star
Fall to the base earth from the firmament. 20

Thy sun sets weeping in the lowly west,
Witnessing storms to come, woe and unrest:
Thy friends are fled to wait upon thy foes,
And crossly to thy good all fortune goes. [*Exit.*

ACT III.

SCENE I. *Bristol. Before the castle.*

Enter BOLINGBROKE, YORK, NORTHUMBERLAND,
ROSS, PERCY, WILLOUGHBY, *with* BUSHY *and*
GREEN, *prisoners.*

Boling. Bring forth these men.
Bushy and Green, I will not vex your souls—
Since presently your souls must part your bodies—
With too much urging your pernicious lives,
For 'twere no charity; yet, to wash your blood
From off my hands, here in the view of men
I will unfold some causes of your deaths.
You have misled a prince, a royal king,
A happy gentleman in blood and lineaments,
By you unhappied and disfigured clean: 10
You have in manner with your sinful hours
Made a divorce betwixt his queen and him,
Broke the possession of a royal bed
And stain'd the beauty of a fair queen's cheeks
With tears drawn from her eyes by your foul wrongs.
Myself, a prince by fortune of my birth,
Near to the king in blood, and near in love
Till you did make him misinterpret me,
Have stoop'd my neck under your injuries,
And sigh'd my English breath in foreign clouds, 20
Eating the bitter bread of banishment;
Whilst you have fed upon my signories,
Dispark'd my parks and fell'd my forest woods,
From my own windows torn my household coat,
Razed out my imprese, leaving me no sign,
Save men's opinions and my living blood,
To show the world I am a gentleman.
This and much more, much more than twice all this,
Condemns you to the death. See them deliver'd over
To execution and the hand of death. 30
Bushy. More welcome is the stroke of death to me
Than Bolingbroke to England. Lords, farewell.
Green. My comfort is that heaven will take our souls
And plague injustice with the pains of hell.
Boling. My Lord Northumberland, see them
  dispatch'd.
  [*Exeunt Northumberland and others, with the prisoners.*
Uncle, you say the queen is at your house;
For God's sake, fairly let her be entreated:
Tell her I send to her my kind commends;
Take special care my greetings be deliver'd.
York. A gentleman of mine I have dispatch'd 40
With letters of your love to her at large.
Boling. Thanks, gentle uncle. Come, lords, away,
To fight with Glendower and his complices:

See line 164. 165. **Bagot.** He had gone to Ireland, not to Bristol; see
II, ii, 141. **complices,** accomplices.
  SCENE IV. 8. **bay-trees.** In this yeare . . . old baie trees withered,
and afterwards . . . grew greene againe; a strange sight, and supposed
to import some vnknowne euent (Holinshed; in second edition, 1587,
only). 11. **lean-look'd,** lean-looking. 24. **crossly,** adversely.
  ACT III. SCENE I. 4. **urging,** emphasizing as reasons (for your execu-
tions). 9. **happy,** fortunate. 10. **unhappied,** made wretched, ruined.
clean, completely. 12. **Made a divorce.** There is no basis for this
charge; but see V, i, 71 ff. It may have been suggested by the situation

in Marlowe's *Edward II.* 14. **fair queen's.** Queen Isabella, daughter
of Charles VI of France and consort of Richard II, was historically only
eleven years old at this time; see Introduction. 22. **signories,** lordships, estates. 23. **Dispark'd,** destroyed the enclosures and thrown the
parks open. 24. **my household coat,** coat of arms, frequently em-
blazoned on stained or painted windows. 25. **imprese,** device, emblematic design. 37. **entreated,** treated. 43. **Glendower.** Owen
Glendower was not at this time in arms against Bolingbroke; perhaps
Bolingbroke thinks he is the Welsh commander (see preceding scene).

Awhile to work, and after holiday.   [*Exeunt.*

SCENE II. *The coast of Wales. A castle in view.*

Drums: flourish and colours. Enter KING RICHARD, *the*
BISHOP OF CARLISLE, AUMERLE, *and Soldiers.*

K. Rich. Barkloughly castle call they this at hand?
Aum. Yea, my lord. How brooks your grace the air,
After your late tossing on the breaking seas?
K. Rich. Needs must I like it well: I weep for joy
To stand upon my kingdom once again.
Dear earth, I do salute thee with my hand,
Though rebels wound thee with their horses' hoofs:
As a long-parted mother with her child
Plays fondly with her tears and smiles in meeting,
So, weeping, smiling, greet I thee, my earth,   10
And do thee favours with my royal hands.
Feed not thy sovereign's foe, my gentle earth,
Nor with thy sweets comfort his ravenous sense;
But let thy spiders, that suck up thy venom,
And heavy-gaited toads lie in their way,
Doing annoyance to the treacherous feet
Which with usurping steps do trample thee:
Yield stinging nettles to mine enemies;
And when they from thy bosom pluck a flower,
Guard it, I pray thee, with a lurking adder   20
Whose double tongue may with a mortal touch
Throw death upon thy sovereign's enemies.
Mock not my senseless conjuration, lords:
This earth shall have a feeling and these stones
Prove armed soldiers, ere her native king
Shall falter under foul rebellion's arms.
  Car. Fear not, my lord: that Power that made you
      king
Hath power to keep you king in spite of all.
The means that heaven yields must be embraced,
And not neglected; else, if heaven would,   30
And we will not, heaven's offer we refuse,
The proffer'd means of succour and redress.
  Aum. He means, my lord, that we are too remiss;
Whilst Bolingbroke, through our security,
Grows strong and great in substance and in power.
  K. Rich. Discomfortable cousin! know'st thou not
That when the searching eye of heaven is hid,
Behind the globe, that lights the lower world,
Then thieves and robbers range abroad unseen
In murders and in outrage, boldly here;   40
But when from under this terrestrial ball
He fires the proud tops of the eastern pines
And darts his light through every guilty hole,
Then murders, treasons and detested sins,
The cloak of night being pluck'd from off their backs,
Stand bare and naked, trembling at themselves?
So when this thief, this traitor, Bolingbroke,
Who all this while hath revell'd in the night
Whilst we were wandering with the antipodes,
Shall see us rising in our throne, the east,   50
His treasons will sit blushing in his face,

Not able to endure the sight of day,
But self-affrighted tremble at his sin.
Not all the water in the rough rude sea
Can wash the balm off from an anointed king;
The breath of worldly men cannot depose
The deputy elected by the Lord:
For every man that Bolingbroke hath press'd
To lift shrewd steel against our golden crown,
God for his Richard hath in heavenly pay   60
A glorious angel: then, if angels fight,
Weak men must fall, for heaven still guards the right.

  Enter SALISBURY.

Welcome, my lord: how far off lies your power?
  Sal. Nor near nor farther off, my gracious lord,
Than this weak arm: discomfort guides my tongue
And bids me speak of nothing but despair.
One day too late, I fear me, noble lord,
Hath clouded all thy happy days on earth:
O, call back yesterday, bid time return,
And thou shalt have twelve thousand fighting men! 70
To-day, to-day, unhappy day, too late,
O'erthrows thy joys, friends, fortune and thy state:
For all the Welshmen, hearing thou wert dead,
Are gone to Bolingbroke, dispersed and fled.
  Aum. Comfort, my liege: why looks your grace so
      pale?
  K. Rich. But now the blood of twenty thousand men
Did triumph in my face, and they are fled;
And, till so much blood thither come again,
Have I not reason to look pale and dead?
All souls that will be safe fly from my side,   80
For time hath set a blot upon my pride.
  Aum. Comfort, my liege; remember who you are.
  K. Rich. I had forgot myself: am I not king?
Awake, thou coward majesty! thou sleepest.
Is not the king's name twenty thousand names?
Arm, arm, my name! a puny subject strikes
At thy great glory. Look not to the ground,
Ye favourites of a king: are we not high?
High be our thoughts: I know my uncle York
Hath power enough to serve our turn. But who comes
      here?   90

  Enter SCROOP.

  Scroop. More health and happiness betide my liege
Than can my care-tuned tongue deliver him!
  K. Rich. Mine ear is open and my heart prepared:
The worst is worldly loss thou canst unfold.
Say, is my kingdom lost? why, 'twas my care;
And what loss is it to be rid of care?
Strives Bolingbroke to be as great as we?
Greater he shall not be; if he serve God,
We'll serve Him too and be his fellow so:
Revolt our subjects? that we cannot mend;   100
They break their faith to God as well as us:
Cry woe, destruction, ruin and decay;
The worst is death, and death will have his day.
  Scroop. Glad am I that your highness is so arm'd

SCENE II. 1. **Barkloughly,** probably Harlech, a castle in Wales between Caernarvon and Aberystwyth. 4. **I weep for joy.** Shakespeare has carefully shown in him an intense love of his country, well knowing how that feeling would, in pure historic drama, redeem him in the hearts of the audience (Coleridge). 21. **double,** forked. 23. **senseless conjuration,** adjuration of senseless things. 25. **native,** entitled (to the crown) by birth, rightful. 33. **He . . . remiss.** The stern, practical bishop has attempted to bring Richard back to reality; Richard hardly understands; Aumerle interprets in this line. 34. **security,** confidence, heedlessness. 38. **that lights the lower world.**

This clause modifies *eye of heaven.* 55. **balm,** consecrated oil used in anointing a king. 58. **press'd,** impressed, forced into the ranks. 64. **near,** nearer. 65. **discomfort,** discouragement. 76. **twenty thousand men.** Holinshed puts Salisbury's force at forty thousand. 76-81. **But . . . pride.** Note that Richard's highly emotional speech is in the form of a sestet. 112. **thin,** thin-haired (Schmidt); possibly, shrunken to thinness. 114. **clap,** set briskly. **female,** weak and delicate like a woman, implying their youth. 116. **beadsmen,** almsmen whose duty it was to pray for the king. 117. **double-fatal,** doubly fatal (since the wood of the yew was used for bows and the berry as poison).

*Richard
the Second*
ACT III : SC I

66o

To bear the tidings of calamity.
Like an unseasonable stormy day,
Which makes the silver rivers drown their shores,
As if the world were all dissolved to tears,
So high above his limits swells the rage
Of Bolingbroke, covering your fearful land   110
With hard bright steel and hearts harder than steel.
White-beards have arm'd their thin and hairless
    scalps
Against thy majesty; boys, with women's voices,
Strive to speak big and clap their female joints
In stiff unwieldy arms against thy crown:
Thy very beadsmen learn to bend their bows
Of double-fatal yew against thy state;
Yea, distaff-women manage rusty bills
Against thy seat: both young and old rebel,
And all goes worse than I have power to tell.   120
    K. Rich. Too well, too well thou tell'st a tale so ill.
Where is the Earl of Wiltshire? where is Bagot?
What is become of Bushy? where is Green?
That they have let the dangerous enemy
Measure our confines with such peaceful steps?
If we prevail, their heads shall pay for it:
I warrant they have made peace with Bolingbroke.
    Scroop. Peace have they made with him indeed, my
        lord.
    K. Rich. O villains, vipers, damn'd without
        redemption!
Dogs, easily won to fawn on any man!   130
Snakes, in my heart-blood warm'd, that sting my
    heart!
Three Judases, each one thrice worse than Judas!
Would they make peace? terrible hell make war
Upon their spotted souls for this offence!
    Scroop. Sweet love, I see, changing his property,
Turns to the sourest and most deadly hate:
Again uncurse their souls; their peace is made
With heads, and not with hands: those whom you
    curse
Have felt the worst of death's destroying wound
And lie full low, graved in the hollow ground.   140
    Aum. Is Bushy, Green, and the Earl of Wiltshire
        dead?
    Scroop. Ay, all of them at Bristol lost their heads.
    Aum. Where is the duke my father with his power?
    K. Rich. No matter where; of comfort no man
        speak:
Let's talk of graves, of worms and epitaphs;
Make dust our paper and with rainy eyes
Write sorrow on the bosom of the earth,
Let's choose executors and talk of wills:
And yet not so, for what can we bequeath
Save our deposed bodies to the ground?   150
Our lands, our lives and all are Bolingbroke's,
And nothing can we call our own but death
And that small model of the barren earth
Which serves as paste and cover to our bones.
For God's sake, let us sit upon the ground
And tell sad stories of the death of kings:

How some have been deposed; some slain in war;
Some haunted by the ghosts they have deposed;
Some poison'd by their wives; some sleeping kill'd;
All murder'd: for within the hollow crown   160
That rounds the mortal temples of a king
Keeps Death his court and there the antic sits,
Scoffing his state and grinning at his pomp,
Allowing him a breath, a little scene,
To monarchize, be fear'd and kill with looks,
Infusing him with self and vain conceit,
As if this flesh which walls about our life
Were brass impregnable, and humour'd thus
Comes at the last and with a little pin
Bores through his castle wall, and farewell king!   170
Cover your heads and mock not flesh and blood
With solemn reverence: throw away respect,
Tradition, form and ceremonious duty,
For you have but mistook me all this while:
†I live with bread like you, feel want,
Taste grief, need friends: subjected thus,
How can you say to me, I am a king?
    Car. My lord, wise men ne'er sit and wail their woes,
But presently prevent the ways to wail.
To fear the foe, since fear oppresseth strength,   180
Gives in your weakness strength unto your foe,
And so your follies fight against yourself.
Fear, and be slain; no worse can come to fight:
And fight and die is death destroying death;
Where fearing dying pays death servile breath.
    Aum. My father hath a power; inquire of him,
And learn to make a body of a limb.
    K. Rich. Thou chidest me well: proud Bolingbroke,
        I come
To change blows with thee for our day of doom.
This ague fit of fear is over-blown;   190
An easy task it is to win our own.
Say, Scroop, where lies our uncle with his power?
Speak sweetly, man, although thy looks be sour.
    Scroop. Men judge by the complexion of the sky
        The state and inclination of the day:
So may you by my dull and heavy eye,
    My tongue hath but a heavier tale to say.
I play the torturer, by small and small
To lengthen out the worst that must be spoken:
Your uncle York is join'd with Bolingbroke,   200
And all your northern castles yielded up,
And all your southern gentlemen in arms
Upon his party.
    K. Rich.   Thou hast said enough.
Beshrew thee, cousin, which didst lead me forth
                                [To Aumerle,
Of that sweet way I was in to despair!
What say you now? what comfort have we now?
By heaven, I'll hate him everlastingly
That bids me be of comfort any more.
Go to Flint castle: there I'll pine away;
A king, woe's slave, shall kingly woe obey.   210
That power I have, discharge; and let them go
To ear the land that hath some hope to grow,

118. **bills,** weapons used by infantry; a *bill* was a long-handled ax with hook-shaped blade and spearhead. 122. **Bagot.** Bagot's name seems inadvertently mentioned here. The king speaks, line 132, of *three Judases;* Aumerle does not ask about Bagot in line 141. 153. **model,** may refer to Richard's own mortal body, or to the grave mound. 162. **Death.** Douce called attention to a print in the *Imagines Mortis* of a king sitting on a throne, sword in hand, surrounded by courtiers, with a grinning skeleton arising from his crown. **antic,** grotesque figure. 163. **Scoffing,** scoffing at. 164. **breath,** breathing space, moment. 166. **self and vain conceit,** selfish and vain conceit. 168. **humour'd,** having

satisfied his humor or whim (referring to Death); sometimes defined as "humored" or "indulged" (referring to the king). 176. **subjected,** made subject to grief, want, etc. 183-185. **Fear . . . breath.** To die fighting is to triumph over death; to fear death is to become its slave. 198. **by small and small,** little by little. 211. **That . . . discharge.** When Richard finds that he must fight for his kingship, he prefers to relinquish it and assume the role of the dethroned monarch; but see III, iii, 129-130. 212. **ear,** plow. **grow,** produce fruit.

For I have none: let no man speak again
To alter this, for counsel is but vain.
   Aum. My liege, one word.
   K. Rich.   He does me double wrong
That wounds me with the flatteries of his tongue.
Discharge my followers: let them hence away,
From Richard's night to Bolingbroke's fair day.
                                [*Exeunt.*

SCENE III. *Wales. Before Flint castle.*

Enter, with drum and colours, BOLINGBROKE, YORK,
  NORTHUMBERLAND, Attendants, *and forces.*

   Boling. So that by this intelligence we learn
The Welshmen are dispersed, and Salisbury
Is gone to meet the king, who lately landed
With some few private friends upon this coast.
   North. The news is very fair and good, my lord:
Richard not far from hence hath hid his head.
   York. It would beseem the Lord Northumberland
To say 'King Richard:' alack the heavy day
When such a sacred king should hide his head.
   North. Your grace mistakes; only to be brief,   10
Left I his title out.
   York.   The time hath been,
Would you have been so brief with him, he would
Have been so brief with you, to shorten you,
For taking so the head, your whole head's length.
   Boling. Mistake not, uncle, further than you should.
   York. Take not, good cousin, further than you
      should,
Lest you mistake the heavens are o'er our heads.
   Boling. I know it, uncle, and oppose not myself
Against their will. But who comes here?

   Enter PERCY.

Welcome, Harry: what, will not this castle yield?   20
   Percy. The castle royally is mann'd, my lord,
Against thy entrance.
   Boling. Royally!
Why, it contains no king?
   Percy.   Yes, my good lord,
It doth contain a king; King Richard lies
Within the limits of yon lime and stone:
And with him are the Lord Aumerle, Lord Salisbury,
Sir Stephen Scroop, besides a clergyman
Of holy reverence; who, I cannot learn.
   North. O, belike it is the Bishop of Carlisle.   30
   Boling. Noble lords,
Go to the rude ribs of that ancient castle;
Through brazen trumpet send the breath of parley
Into his ruin'd ears, and thus deliver:
Henry Bolingbroke
On both his knees doth kiss King Richard's hand
And sends allegiance and true faith of heart
To his most royal person, hither come
Even at his feet to lay my arms and power,
Provided that my banishment repeal'd   40

And lands restored again be freely granted:
If not, I'll use the advantage of my power
And lay the summer's dust with showers of blood
Rain'd from the wounds of slaughter'd Englishmen:
The which, how far off from the mind of Bolingbroke
It is, such crimson tempest should bedrench
The fresh green lap of fair King Richard's land,
My stooping duty tenderly shall show.
Go, signify as much, while here we march
Upon the grassy carpet of this plain.   50
Let's march without the noise of threatening drum,
That from this castle's tatter'd battlements
Our fair appointments may be well perused.
Methinks King Richard and myself should meet
With no less terror than the elements
Of fire and water, when their thundering shock
At meeting tears the cloudy cheeks of heaven.
Be he the fire, I'll be the yielding water:
The rage be his, whilst on the earth I rain
My waters; on the earth, and not on him.   60
March on, and mark King Richard how he looks.

   *Parle without, and answer within. Then a flourish. Enter
    on the walls,* KING RICHARD, *the* BISHOP OF
    CARLISLE, AUMERLE, SCROOP, *and* SALISBURY.

See, see, King Richard doth himself appear,
As doth the blushing discontented sun
From out the fiery portal of the east,
When he perceives the envious clouds are bent
To dim his glory and to stain the track
Of his bright passage to the occident.
   York. Yet looks he like a king: behold, his eye,
As bright as is the eagle's, lightens forth
Controlling majesty: alack, alack, for woe,   70
That any harm should stain so fair a show!
   K. Rich. We are amazed; and thus long have we
      stood
To watch the fearful bending of thy knee,   [*To North.*
Because we thought ourself thy lawful king:
And if we be, how dare thy joints forget
To pay their awful duty to our presence?
If we be not, show us the hand of God
That hath dismiss'd us from our stewardship;
For well we know, no hand of blood and bone
Can gripe the sacred handle of our sceptre,   80
Unless he do profane, steal, or usurp.
And though you think that all, as you have done,
Have torn their souls by turning them from us,
And we are barren and bereft of friends;
Yet know, my master, God omnipotent,
Is mustering in his clouds on our behalf
Armies of pestilence; and they shall strike
Your children yet unborn and unbegot,
That lift your vassal hands against my head
And threat the glory of my precious crown.   90
Tell Bolingbroke—for yond methinks he stands—
That every stride he makes upon my land
Is dangerous treason: he is come to open
The purple testament of bleeding war;

SCENE III. 6. **Richard . . . head.** The plot here diverges from
Holinshed. Richard fled to Conway Castle, where he found Salisbury.
To this place, then, Bolingbroke dispatched Northumberland, who
induced Richard to a conference, assuring him that Bolingbroke came
merely to demand his rights and advising that a parliament should be
called to restore order to the kingdom. On their riding forth from Conway, Northumberland led Richard into an ambush, by which means
Richard was taken to Flint Castle as a prisoner. Later he was taken to
Chester and to London. The divergence in plot may be accounted for by

a marginal note in Holinshed which reads: "K. Richard stealeth awaie
from his armie, and taketh the castell of Flint." 62-67. **See . . . occident,** assigned by Dyce to Percy, by Warburton and Hanmer to York;
but Bolingbroke is everywhere sensitive to Richard's personal charm.
See IV, i, 304; V, vi, 40. 81. **profane,** commit sacrilege. 83. **torn
their souls,** injured their souls by treason to the king. 93-94. **open The
purple testament,** begin to carry out a bequest of blood to England.
Blood was often said to be purple. 97. **flower of England's face,** the
blooming face of England. Cf. Daniel, *Civil Wars,* I, 118: "Th' vngodly

But ere the crown he looks for live in peace,
Ten thousand bloody crowns of mothers' sons
Shall ill become the flower of England's face,
Change the complexion of her maid-pale peace
To scarlet indignation and bedew
Her pastures' grass with faithful English blood.   100
    North. The king of heaven forbid our lord the king
Should so with civil and uncivil arms
Be rush'd upon! Thy thrice noble cousin
Harry Bolingbroke doth humbly kiss thy hand;
And by the honourable tomb he swears,
That stands upon your royal grandsire's bones,
And by the royalties of both your bloods,
Currents that spring from one most gracious head,
And by the buried hand of warlike Gaunt,
And by the worth and honour of himself,   110
Comprising all that may be sworn or said,
His coming hither hath no further scope
Than for his lineal royalties and to beg
Enfranchisement immediate on his knees:
Which on thy royal party granted once,
His glittering arms he will commend to rust,
His barbed steeds to stables, and his heart
To faithful service of your majesty.
This swears he, as he is a prince, is just;
And, as I am a gentleman, I credit him.   120
    K. Rich. Northumberland, say thus the king returns:
His noble cousin is right welcome hither;
And all the number of his fair demands
Shall be accomplish'd without contradiction:
With all the gracious utterance thou hast
Speak to his gentle hearing kind commends.
We do debase ourselves, cousin, do we not,
                              [*To Aumerle.*
To look so poorly and to speak so fair?
Shall we call back Northumberland, and send
Defiance to the traitor, and so die?   130
    Aum. No, good my lord; let's fight with gentle words
Till time lend friends and friends their helpful swords.
    K. Rich. O God, O God! that e'er this tongue of
        mine,
That laid the sentence of dread banishment
On yon proud man, should take it off again
With words of sooth! O that I were as great
As is my grief, or lesser than my name!
Or that I could forget what I have been,
Or not remember what I must be now!
Swell'st thou, proud heart? I'll give thee scope to beat,
Since foes have scope to beat both thee and me.   141
    Aum. Northumberland comes back from
        Bolingbroke.
    K. Rich. What must the king do now? must he
        submit?
The king shall do it: must he be deposed?
The king shall be contented: must he lose
The name of king? o' God's name, let it go:
I'll give my jewels for a set of beads,
My gorgeous palace for a hermitage,
My gay apparel for an almsman's gown,

My figured goblets for a dish of wood,   150
My sceptre for a palmer's walking-staff,
My subjects for a pair of carved saints
And my large kingdom for a little grave,
A little little grave, an obscure grave;
Or I'll be buried in the king's highway,
Some way of common trade, where subjects' feet
May hourly trample on their sovereign's head;
For on my heart they tread now whilst I live;
And buried once, why not upon my head?
Aumerle, thou weep'st, my tender-hearted cousin!   160
We'll make foul weather with despised tears;
Our sighs and they shall lodge the summer corn,
And make a dearth in this revolting land.
Or shall we play the wantons with our woes,
And make some pretty match with shedding tears?
As thus, to drop them still upon one place,
Till they have fretted us a pair of graves
Within the earth; and, therein laid,—there lies
Two kinsmen digg'd their graves with weeping eyes.
Would not this ill do well? Well, well, I see   170
I talk but idly, and you laugh at me.
Most mighty prince, my Lord Northumberland,
What says King Bolingbroke? will his majesty
Give Richard leave to live till Richard die?
You make a leg, and Bolingbroke says ay.
    North. My lord, in the base court he doth attend
To speak with you; may it please you to come down.
    K. Rich. Down, down I come; like glistering
        Phaethon,
Wanting the manage of unruly jades.
In the base court? Base court, where kings grow base,
To come at traitors' calls and do them grace.   181
In the base court? Come down? Down, court! down,
        king!
For night-owls shriek where mounting larks should
        sing.   [*Exeunt from above.*
    Boling. What says his majesty?
    North.   Sorrow and grief of heart
Makes him speak fondly, like a frantic man:
Yet he is come.

Enter KING RICHARD *and his attendants below.*

    Boling. Stand all apart,
And show fair duty to his majesty.   [*He kneels down.*
My gracious lord,—
    K. Rich. Fair cousin, you debase your princely
        knee   190
To make the base earth proud with kissing it:
Me rather had my heart might feel your love
Than my unpleased eye see your courtesy.
Up, cousin, up; your heart is up, I know,
Thus high at least, although your knee be low.
    Boling. My gracious lord, I come but for mine own.
    K. Rich. Your own is yours, and I am yours, and all.
    Boling. So far be mine, my most redoubted lord,
As my true service shall deserve your love.
    K. Rich. Well you deserve: they well deserve to
        have,   200

bloodshed that . . . did marre the flowre of thy chiefe pride . . ." The
abundance of Richard's metaphors is startling. Blood, which disfigures
war and also the heads of ten thousand Englishmen, stains purple the
will or testament, makes the face of England scarlet with indignation,
and bedews the grass of the pastures. 102. **civil,** used in civil strife.
uncivil, barbarous, violent. 114. **Enfranchisement,** restoration to the
rights of a freeman. 116. **commend,** give over. 117. **barbed,** armed.
136. **sooth,** cajolery, flattery. 143. **What must the king,** etc. The king
characteristically throws away his advantage; Bolingbroke would have

had to put his forces at the king's command or incur the responsibility
of seizing him. 162. **lodge,** beat down. 167. **fretted,** eaten away,
worn. 175. **make a leg,** assent by making an obeisance or curtsy.
176. **base court,** outer or lower court of a castle. 178. **glistering,**
glistening. **Phaethon,** son of Apollo, who, unable to control the
horses of the sun, was hurled from the chariot by Jupiter. 179. **jades,**
worthless horses. 192. **Me rather had,** a construction resulting from
a combination of "me were liefer" and "I had rather."

That know the strong'st and surest way to get.
Uncle, give me your hands: nay, dry your eyes;
Tears show their love, but want their remedies.
Cousin, I am too young to be your father,
Though you are old enough to be my heir.
What you will have, I'll give, and willing too;
For do we must what force will have us do.
Set on towards London, cousin, is it so?
    Boling. Yea, my good lord.
    K. Rich.   Then I must not say no.
                                     [Flourish. Exeunt.

SCENE IV. *Langley. The* DUKE OF YORK's *garden.*

Enter the QUEEN *and two* Ladies.

    Queen. What sport shall we devise here in this
        garden,
To drive away the heavy thought of care?
    Lady. Madam, we'll play at bowls.
    Queen. 'Twill make me think the world is full of rubs,
And that my fortune runs against the bias.
    Lady. Madam, we'll dance.
    Queen. My legs can keep no measure in delight,
When my poor heart no measure keeps in grief:
Therefore, no dancing, girl; some other sport.
    Lady. Madam, we'll tell tales.   10
    Queen. Of sorrow or of joy?
    Lady.   Of either, madam.
    Queen. Of neither, girl:
For if of joy, being altogether wanting,
It doth remember me the more of sorrow;
Or if of grief, being altogether had,
It adds more sorrow to my want of joy:
For what I have I need not to repeat;
And what I want it boots not to complain.
    Lady. Madam, I'll sing.
    Queen.   'Tis well that thou hast cause;
But thou shouldst please me better, wouldst thou
    weep.   20
    Lady. I could weep, madam, would it do you good.
    Queen. And I could sing, would weeping do me
    good,
And never borrow any tear of thee.

Enter a Gardener, *and two* Servants.

But stay, here come the gardeners:
Let's step into the shadow of these trees.
My wretchedness unto a row of pins,
They'll talk of state; for every one doth so
Against a change; woe is forerun with woe.
                      [Queen and Ladies retire.
    Gard. Go, bind thou up yon dangling apricocks,
Which, like unruly children, make their sire   30
Stoop with oppression of their prodigal weight:
Give some supportance to the bending twigs.
Go thou, and like an executioner,
Cut off the heads of too fast growing sprays
That look too lofty in our commonwealth:
All must be even in our government.
You thus employ'd, I will go root away

The noisome weeds, which without profit suck
The soil's fertility from wholesome flowers.
    Serv. Why should we in the compass of a pale   40
Keep law and form and due proportion,
Showing, as in a model, our firm estate,
When our sea-walled garden, the whole land,
Is full of weeds, her fairest flowers choked up,
Her fruit-trees all unpruned, her hedges ruin'd,
Her knots disorder'd and her wholesome herbs
Swarming with caterpillars?
    Gard.   Hold thy peace:
He that hath suffer'd this disorder'd spring
Hath now himself met with the fall of leaf:
The weeds which his broad-spreading leaves did
    shelter,   50
That seem'd in eating him to hold him up,
Are pluck'd up root and all by Bolingbroke,
I mean the Earl of Wiltshire, Bushy, Green.
    Serv. What, are they dead?
    Gard.   They are; and Bolingbroke
Hath seized the wasteful king. O, what pity is it
That he had not so trimm'd and dress'd his land
As we this garden! We at time of year
Do wound the bark, the skin of our fruit-trees,
Lest, being over-proud in sap and blood,
With too much riches it confound itself: 60
Had he done so to great and growing men,
They might have lived to bear and he to taste
Their fruits of duty: superfluous branches
We lop away, that bearing boughs may live:
Had he done so, himself had borne the crown,
Which waste of idle hours hath quite thrown down.
    Serv. What, think you then the king shall be
    deposed?
    Gard. Depress'd he is already, and deposed
'Tis doubt he will be: letters came last night
To a dear friend of the good Duke of York's,   70
That tell black tidings.
    Queen. O, I am press'd to death through want of
    speaking!   *[Coming forward.*
Thou, old Adam's likeness, set to dress this garden,
How dares thy harsh rude tongue sound this
    unpleasing news?
What Eve, what serpent, hath suggested thee
To make a second fall of cursed man?
Why dost thou say King Richard is deposed?
Darest thou, thou little better thing than earth,
Divine his downfall? Say, where, when, and how,
Camest thou by this ill tidings? speak, thou wretch. 80
    Gard. Pardon me, madam: little joy have I
To breathe this news; yet what I say is true.
King Richard, he is in the mighty hold
Of Bolingbroke: their fortunes both are weigh'd:
In your lord's scale is nothing but himself,
And some few vanities that make him light;
But in the balance of great Bolingbroke,
Besides himself, are all the English peers,
And with that odds he weighs King Richard down.
Post you to London, and you will find it so;   90
I speak no more than every one doth know.
    Queen. Nimble mischance, that art so light of foot,

203. **Tears . . . remedies,** tears show love, but offer no remedies. 204.
too . . . father. Bolingbroke was born in 1367, and Richard a few
months later in 1368.
    SCENE IV. 14. **remember,** remind. 28. **Against,** just before. 29.
apricocks, apricots. 40. **pale,** enclosure. 46. **knots,** laid-out garden
plots. 69. **doubt,** doubtful. 72. **press'd to death,** allusion to the
peine forte et dure, inflicted by pressure of heavy weights upon the chests

of indicted persons who refused to plead. 79. **Divine,** foretell prophetically. 93. **embassage,** message. 105. **rue,** "herb of grace," a
plant symbolical of repentance, ruth, or sorrow for another's misery.
    ACT IV. SCENE I. *Stage Direction: Westminster Hall.* It had just
been rebuilt by King Richard's orders. 1. **Call forth Bagot.** Bolingbroke lends dignity to his usurpation by thus bringing forward at
once the issue which drove him to revolt. 5. **timeless,** untimely. 10.

Doth not thy embassage belong to me,
And am I last that knows it? O, thou think'st
To serve me last, that I may longest keep
Thy sorrow in my breast. Come, ladies, go,
To meet at London London's king in woe.
What, was I born to this, that my sad look
Should grace the triumph of great Bolingbroke?
Gardener, for telling me these news of woe,   100
Pray God the plants thou graft'st may never grow.
                            [Exeunt Queen and Ladies.
   Gard. Poor queen! so that thy state might be no
       worse,
I would my skill were subject to thy curse.
Here did she fall a tear; here in this place
I'll set a bank of rue, sour herb of grace:
Rue, even for ruth, here shortly shall be seen,
In the remembrance of a weeping queen.   *[Exeunt.*

ACT IV.

SCENE I. *Westminster Hall.*

Enter, as to the Parliament, BOLINGBROKE, AUMERLE,
NORTHUMBERLAND, PERCY, FITZWATER, SURREY,
the BISHOP OF CARLISLE, *the* ABBOT OF WESTMIN-
STER, *and another* Lord, Herald, Officers,
and BAGOT.

Boling. Call forth Bagot.
Now, Bagot, freely speak thy mind;
What thou dost know of noble Gloucester's death,
Who wrought it with the king, and who perform'd
The bloody office of his timeless end.
   Bagot. Then set before my face the Lord Aumerle.
   Boling. Cousin, stand forth, and look upon that man.
   Bagot. My Lord Aumerle, I know your daring
       tongue
Scorns to unsay what once it hath deliver'd.
In that dead time when Gloucester's death was
       plotted,   10
I heard you say, 'Is not my arm of length,
That reacheth from the restful English court
As far as Calais, to mine uncle's head?'
Amongst much other talk, that very time,
I heard you say that you had rather refuse
The offer of an hundred thousand crowns
Than Bolingbroke's return to England;
Adding withal, how blest this land would be
In this your cousin's death.
   Aum.   Princes and noble lords,
What answer shall I make to this base man?   20
Shall I so much dishonour my fair stars,
On equal terms to give him chastisement?
Either I must, or have mine honour soil'd
With the attainder of his slanderous lips.
There is my gage, the manual seal of death,
That marks thee out for hell: I say, thou liest,
And will maintain what thou hast said is false
In thy heart-blood, though being all too base
To stain the temper of my knightly sword.
   Boling. Bagot, forbear; thou shalt not take it up.   30

   Aum. Excepting one, I would he were the best
In all this presence that hath moved me so.
   Fitz. If that thy valour stand on sympathy,
There is my gage, Aumerle, in gage to thine:
By that fair sun which shows me where thou stand'st,
I heard thee say, and vauntingly thou spakest it,
That thou wert cause of noble Gloucester's death.
If thou deny'st it twenty times, thou liest;
And I will turn thy falsehood to thy heart,
Where it was forged, with my rapier's point.   40
   Aum. Thou darest not, coward, live to see that day.
   Fitz. Now, by my soul, I would it were this hour.
   Aum. Fitzwater, thou art damn'd to hell for this.
   Percy. Aumerle, thou liest; his honour is as true
In this appeal as thou art all unjust;
And that thou art so, there I throw my gage,
To prove it on thee to the extremest point
Of mortal breathing: seize it, if thou darest.
   Aum. An if I do not, may my hands rot off
And never brandish more revengeful steel   50
Over the glittering helmet of my foe!
   Another Lord. I task the earth to the like, forsworn
       Aumerle;
And spur thee on with full as many lies
As may be holloa'd in thy treacherous ear
From sun to sun: there is my honour's pawn;
Engage it to the trial, if thou darest.
   Aum. Who sets me else? by heaven, I'll throw at all:
I have a thousand spirits in one breast,
To answer twenty thousand such as you.
   Surrey. My Lord Fitzwater, I do remember well   60
The very time Aumerle and you did talk.
   Fitz. 'Tis very true: you were in presence then;
And you can witness with me this is true.
   Surrey. As false, by heaven, as heaven itself is true.
   Fitz. Surrey, thou liest.
   Surrey.   Dishonourable boy!
That lie shall lie so heavy on my sword,
That it shall render vengeance and revenge
Till thou the lie-giver and that lie do lie
In earth as quiet as thy father's skull:
In proof whereof, there is my honour's pawn;   70
Engage it to the trial, if thou darest.
   Fitz. How fondly dost thou spur a forward horse!
If I dare eat, or drink, or breathe, or live,
I dare meet Surrey in a wilderness,
And spit upon him, whilst I say he lies,
And lies, and lies: there is my bond of faith,
To tie thee to my strong correction.
As I intend to thrive in this new world,
Aumerle is guilty of my true appeal:
Besides, I heard the banish'd Norfolk say   80
That thou, Aumerle, didst send two of thy men
To execute the noble duke at Calais.
   Aum. Some honest Christian trust me with a gage,
That Norfolk lies: here do I throw down this,
If he may be repeal'd, to try his honour.
   Boling. These differences shall all rest under gage
Till Norfolk be repeal'd: repeal'd he shall be,
And, though mine enemy, restored again
To all his lands and signories: when he 's return'd,

dead, deathlike. 14. **that very time.** This seems to be a mistake;
Gloucester's death occurred before Bolingbroke left England. 21.
stars, i.e., his sphere or fortune. 24. **attainder,** dishonoring accusation.
25. **manual seal of death,** death warrant. 33. **sympathy,** correspondence, or equality, of blood or rank. 52. **task the earth,** charge the
earth with the task of bearing my gage. 53. **full as many lies,** giving
the lie as many times. 56. **Engage,** take up (a pledge). 57. **sets,**

challenges to a game (properly, by laying down stakes). 60. **Surrey,**
Richard's nephew, who with Aumerle represents the Yorkist faction.
67. **vengeance and revenge,** possibly tautological, meaning "furious
revenge." 80. **Besides, I heard,** etc. John Hall, a groom of Mowbray's
at Calais, confessed on October 18, 1399, that he and two servants
murdered Gloucester. They were sent, Mowbray told him, by Aumerle.
85. **repeal'd,** recalled from exile.

Against Aumerle we will enforce his trial. 90
   Car. That honourable day shall ne'er be seen.
Many a time hath banish'd Norfolk fought
For Jesu Christ in glorious Christian field,
Streaming the ensign of the Christian cross
Against black pagans, Turks, and Saracens;
And toil'd with works of war, retired himself
To Italy; and there at Venice gave
His body to that pleasant country's earth,
And his pure soul unto his captain Christ,
Under whose colours he had fought so long. 100
   Boling. Why, bishop, is Norfolk dead?
   Car. As surely as I live, my lord.
   Boling. Sweet peace conduct his sweet soul to the
      bosom
Of good old Abraham! Lords appellants,
Your differences shall all rest under gage
Till we assign you to your days of trial.

Enter YORK, *attended.*

   York. Great Duke of Lancaster, I come to thee
From plume-pluck'd Richard; who with willing soul
Adopts thee heir, and his high sceptre yields
To the possession of thy royal hand: 110
Ascend his throne, descending now from him;
And long live Henry, fourth of that name!
   Boling. In God's name, I'll ascend the regal throne.
   Car. Marry, God forbid!
Worst in this royal presence may I speak,
Yet best beseeming me to speak the truth.
Would God that any in this noble presence
Were enough noble to be upright judge
Of noble Richard! then true noblesse would
Learn him forbearance from so foul a wrong. 120
What subject can give sentence on his king?
And who sits here that is not Richard's subject?
Thieves are not judged but they are by to hear,
Although apparent guilt be seen in them;
And shall the figure of God's majesty,
His captain, steward, deputy-elect,
Anointed, crowned, planted many years,
Be judged by subject and inferior breath,
And he himself not present? O, forfend it, God,
That in a Christian climate souls refined 130
Should show so heinous, black, obscene a deed!
I speak to subjects, and a subject speaks,
Stirr'd up by God, thus boldly for his king.
My Lord of Hereford here, whom you call king,
Is a foul traitor to proud Hereford's king:
And if you crown him, let me prophesy:
The blood of English shall manure the ground,
And future ages groan for this foul act;
Peace shall go sleep with Turks and infidels,
And in this seat of peace tumultuous wars 140
Shall kin with kin and kind with kind confound;
Disorder, horror, fear and mutiny

Shall here inhabit, and this land be call'd
The field of Golgotha and dead men's skulls.
O, if you raise this house against this house,
It will the woefullest division prove
That ever fell upon this cursed earth.
Prevent it, resist it, let it not be so,
Lest child, child's children, cry against you 'woe!'
   North. Well have you argued, sir; and, for your pains,
Of capital treason we arrest you here. 151
My Lord of Westminster, be it your charge
To keep him safely till his day of trial.
May it please you, lords, to grant the commons' suit.
   Boling. Fetch hither Richard, that in common view
He may surrender; so we shall proceed
Without suspicion.
   York.   I will be his conduct.   [*Exit.*
   Boling. Lords, you that here are under our arrest,
Procure your sureties for your days of answer.
Little are we beholding to your love, 160
And little look'd for at your helping hands.

Re-enter YORK, *with* RICHARD, *and* Officers *bearing
the regalia.*

   K. Rich. Alack, why am I sent for to a king,
Before I have shook off the regal thoughts
Wherewith I reign'd? I hardly yet have learn'd
To insinuate, flatter, bow, and bend my limbs:
Give sorrow leave awhile to tutor me
To this submission. Yet I well remember
The favours of these men: were they not mine?
Did they not sometime cry, 'all hail!' to me?
So Judas did to Christ: but he, in twelve, 170
Found truth in all but one; I, in twelve thousand,
     none.
God save the king! Will no man say amen?
Am I both priest and clerk? well then, amen.
God save the king! although I be not he;
And yet, amen, if heaven do think him me.
To do what service am I sent for hither?
   York. To do that office of thine own good will
Which tired majesty did make thee offer,
The resignation of thy state and crown
To Henry Bolingbroke. 180
   K. Rich. Give me the crown. Here, cousin, seize the
     crown;
Here, cousin;
On this side my hand, and on that side yours.
Now is this golden crown like a deep well
That owes two buckets, filling one another,
The emptier ever dancing in the air,
The other down, unseen and full of water:
That bucket down and full of tears am I,
Drinking my griefs, whilst you mount up on high.
   Boling. I thought you had been willing to resign. 190
   K. Rich. My crown I am; but still my griefs
     are mine:

91-100. That . . . long. This year (1399) Thomas Mowbraie, Duke of Norffolke, died in exile at Venice (Holinshed). Norffolk . . . died at Venice in his return from Jerusalem (Stow, *Annals*). 94. **streaming,** causing to stream. 96. **toil'd,** wearied. 104. **good old Abraham.** See Luke 16:22. Note Bolingbroke's exultation in dismissing the subject of the murder of Gloucester; it has served his purpose. Aumerle is left with the suspicion of guilt upon him, but he is not brought to trial. **Lords appellants,** lords who appear as formal accusers. 108. **plume-pluck'd,** humbled. 113. **In . . . throne.** Shakespeare gives no ground for Henry's claim; in Holinshed he claims the throne as descended from Henry III according to a false tradition that his ancestor, Edward Crouchback, was older than his brother Edward I, but was set aside on account of physical deformity. 114. **Marry, God forbid,** etc. Carlisle's

speech, according to Holinshed, from whom it is largely taken, was made on October 22, three weeks before the deposition. 119. **noblesse,** noble birth, nobleness. 131. **obscene,** odious, repulsive. 141. **kin,** relationship (of family). **kind,** relationship (of race and nation). 152. **My . . . charge.** Carlisle was committed to the Abbey of St. Albans and some months later transferred to the Abbey of Westminster. 154-318. Omitted from Q_{1-3}. That they belonged originally to the play is clear from line 321. 154. **commons' suit.** Probable reference to a demand that Bolingbroke ascend the throne. No such suit is known, though Holinshed says that the commons favored him. 156-157. **we . . . suspicion.** The deposition scene is without historical basis. Richard signed, perhaps under compulsion, an act of abdication, but before witnesses in the Tower. Daniel (*Civil Wars*) gives an elaborate description

You may my glories and my state depose,
But not my griefs; still am I king of those.
  Boling. Part of your cares you give me with your
    crown.
  K. Rich. Your cares set up do not pluck my cares
    down.
My care is loss of care, by old care done;
Your care is gain of care, by new care won:
The cares I give I have, though given away;
They tend the crown, yet still with me they stay.
  Boling. Are you contented to resign the crown?   200
  K. Rich. Ay, no; no, ay; for I must nothing be;
Therefore no no, for I resign to thee.
Now mark me, how I will undo myself:
I give this heavy weight from off my head
And this unwieldy sceptre from my hand,
The pride of kingly sway from out my heart;
With mine own tears I wash away my balm,
With mine own hands I give away my crown,
With mine own tongue deny my sacred state,
With mine own breath release all duteous oaths: 210
All pomp and majesty I do forswear;
My manors, rents, revenues I forego;
My acts, decrees, and statutes I deny:
God pardon all oaths that are broke to me!
God keep all vows unbroke are made to thee!
Make me, that nothing have, with nothing grieved,
And thou with all pleased, that hast all achieved!
Long mayst thou live in Richard's seat to sit,
And soon lie Richard in an earthy pit!
God save King Henry, unking'd Richard says,   220
And send him many years of sunshine days!
What more remains?
  North.   No more, but that you read
These accusations and these grievous crimes
Committed by your person and your followers
Against the state and profit of this land;
That, by confessing them, the souls of men
May deem that you are worthily deposed.
  K. Rich. Must I do so? and must I ravel out
My weaved-up folly? Gentle Northumberland,
If thy offences were upon record,   230
Would it not shame thee in so fair a troop
To read a lecture of them? If thou wouldst,
There shouldst thou find one heinous article,
Containing the deposing of a king
And cracking the strong warrant of an oath,
Mark'd with a blot, damn'd in the book of heaven:
Nay, all of you that stand and look upon,
Whilst that my wretchedness doth bait myself,
Though some of you with Pilate wash your hands
Showing an outward pity; yet you Pilates   240
Have here deliver'd me to my sour cross,
And water cannot wash away your sin.
  North. My lord, dispatch; read o'er these articles.
  K. Rich. Mine eyes are full of tears, I cannot see:

And yet salt water blinds them not so much
But they can see a sort of traitors here.
Nay, if I turn mine eyes upon myself,
I find myself a traitor with the rest;
For I have given here my soul's consent
To undeck the pompous body of a king;   250
Made glory base and sovereignty a slave,
Proud majesty a subject, state a peasant.
  North. My lord,—
  K. Rich. No lord of thine, thou haught insulting
    man,
Nor no man's lord; I have no name, no title,
No, not that name was given me at the font,
But 'tis usurp'd: alack the heavy day,
That I have worn so many winters out,
And know not now what name to call myself!
O that I were a mockery king of snow,   260
Standing before the sun of Bolingbroke,
To melt myself away in water-drops!
Good king, great king, and yet not greatly good,
An if my word be sterling yet in England,
Let it command a mirror hither straight,
That it may show me what a face I have,
Since it is bankrupt of his majesty.
  Boling. Go some of you and fetch a looking-glass.
              [*Exit an attendant.*
  North. Read o'er this paper while the glass doth
    come.
  K. Rich. Fiend, thou torment'st me ere I come to
    hell!   270
  Boling. Urge it no more, my Lord Northumberland.
  North. The commons will not then be satisfied.
  K. Rich. They shall be satisfied: I'll read enough,
When I do see the very book indeed
Where all my sins are writ, and that's myself.

Re-enter Attendant, *with a glass.*

Give me the glass, and therein will I read.
No deeper wrinkles yet? hath sorrow struck
So many blows upon this face of mine,
And made no deeper wounds? O flattering glass,
Like to my followers in prosperity,   280
Thou dost beguile me! Was this face the face
That every day under his household roof
Did keep ten thousand men? was this the face
That, like the sun, did make beholders wink?
Was this the face that faced so many follies,
And was at last out-faced by Bolingbroke?
A brittle glory shineth in this face:
As brittle as the glory is the face;
              [*Dashes the glass against the ground.*
For there it is, crack'd in a hundred shivers.
Mark, silent king, the moral of this sport,   290
How soon my sorrow hath destroy'd my face.
  Boling. The shadow of your sorrow hath destroy'd
The shadow of your face.

of the scene.   160-161. **Little . . . hands.** These lines seem to be an
aside.   160. **beholding,** obliged, indebted.   165. **insinuate,** wheedle,
ingratiate oneself.   176. **To . . . hither.** Observe the two levels of
Richard's speech; when he is not under stress of emotion, has no part to
play, he speaks with unusual flatness. See lines 181, 203, 222; and V, v,
5.   195. **cares.** Three meanings of "care" are involved in the word play
which follows: "care" in the sense of responsibility; in the sense of duty
or task; in the sense of grief.   201-202. **Ay,** i.e., I. But *I* = nothing; therefore *Ay* = I = no.   204-221. **I give. . .days.** The speech follows with some
faithfulness the formula of abdication, as recorded in the Rolls of Parliament.   210. **duteous oaths;** so F; Q_{3-4} and Globe: *duty's rites.*   215.
are made; so F; Q_{3-4} and Globe: *that swear.*   220. **Henry,** so F; Q_{3-4}
and Globe: *Harry.*   232-233. **wouldst . . . shouldst.** In modern usage

these words would be reversed.   239. **wash your hands.** See Matthew
27:24. Richard persistently compares himself with Christ; see also
III, ii, 24, 61; IV, i, 170.   254. **haught,** haughty, proud.   255. **I have
no name,** an allusion to a story, circulated by the Lancastrian party,
that Richard was not the son of the Black Prince, but of a canon of
Bordeaux.   260. **mockery,** counterfeit.   271. **Urge it no more.**
Herford points this out as "another touch which brings out Bolingbroke's absence of personal rancor toward Richard. He aims at power
and is stern or clement as policy, not passion, determines."   292-293.
The . . . face. Your sentimental show of sorrow has destroyed your
image in the glass. Note in the lines following, first, Richard's generous
appreciation of a fine phrase, and, second, the readiness with which he
turns aside its practical application to himself.

K. Rich. Say that again.
The shadow of my sorrow! ha! let's see:
'Tis very true, my grief lies all within;
And these external manners of laments
Are merely shadows to the unseen grief
That swells with silence in the tortured soul;
There lies the substance: and I thank thee, king,
For thy great bounty, that not only givest   300
Me cause to wail but teachest me the way
How to lament the cause. I'll beg one boon,
And then be gone and trouble you no more.
Shall I obtain it?
  Boling.   Name it, fair cousin.
  K. Rich. 'Fair cousin'? I am greater than a king:
For when I was a king, my flatterers
Were then but subjects; being now a subject,
I have a king here to my flatterer.
Being so great, I have no need to beg.
  Boling. Yet ask.   310
  K. Rich. And shall I have?
  Boling. You shall.
  K. Rich. Then give me leave to go.
  Boling. Whither?
  K. Rich. Whither you will, so I were from your
    sights.
  Boling. Go, some of you convey him to the Tower.
  K. Rich. O, good! convey? conveyers are you all,
That rise thus nimbly by a true king's fall.
    [*Exeunt King Richard, some Lords, and a Guard.*
  Boling. On Wednesday next we solemnly set down
Our coronation: lords, prepare yourselves.   320
    [*Exeunt all except the Bishop of Carlisle, the Abbot of
                 Westminster, and Aumerle.*
  Abbot. A woeful pageant have we here beheld.
  Car. The woe's to come; the children yet unborn
Shall feel this day as sharp to them as thorn.
  Aum. You holy clergymen, is there no plot
To rid the realm of this pernicious blot?
  Abbot. My lord,
Before I freely speak my mind herein,
You shall not only take the sacrament
To bury mine intents, but also to effect
Whatever I shall happen to devise.   330
I see your brows are full of discontent,
Your hearts of sorrow and your eyes of tears:
Come home with me to supper; and I'll lay
A plot shall show us all a merry day.   [*Exeunt.*

ACT V.

SCENE I. *London. A street leading to the Tower.*

Enter QUEEN *and* Ladies.

  Queen. This way the king will come; this is the way
To Julius Cæsar's ill-erected tower,
To whose flint bosom my condemned lord
Is doom'd a prisoner by proud Bolingbroke:

Here let us rest, if this rebellious earth
Have any resting for her true king's queen.

  Enter RICHARD *and* Guard.

But soft, but see, or rather do not see,
My fair rose wither: yet look up, behold,
That you in pity may dissolve to dew,
And wash him fresh again with true-love tears.   10
Ah, thou, the model where old Troy did stand,
Thou map of honour, thou King Richard's tomb,
And not King Richard; thou most beauteous inn,
Why should hard-favour'd grief be lodged in thee,
When triumph is become an alehouse guest?
  K. Rich. Join not with grief, fair woman, do not so,
To make my end too sudden: learn, good soul,
To think our former state a happy dream;
From which awaked, the truth of what we are
Shows us but this: I am sworn brother, sweet,   20
To grim Necessity, and he and I
Will keep a league till death. Hie thee to France
And cloister thee in some religious house:
Our holy lives must win a new world's crown,
Which our profane hours here have stricken down.
  Queen. What, is my Richard both in shape and
    mind
Transform'd and weaken'd? hath Bolingbroke
    deposed
Thine intellect? hath he been in thy heart?
The lion dying thrusteth forth his paw,
And wounds the earth, if nothing else, with rage   30
To be o'erpower'd; and wilt thou, pupil-like,
Take thy correction mildly, kiss the rod,
And fawn on rage with base humility,
Which art a lion and a king of beasts?
  K. Rich. A king of beasts, indeed; if aught but beasts,
I had been still a happy king of men.
Good sometime queen, prepare thee hence for France:
Think I am dead and that even here thou takest,
As from my death-bed, thy last living leave.
In winter's tedious nights sit by the fire   40
With good old folks and let them tell thee tales
Of woeful ages long ago betid;
And ere thou bid good night, to quit their griefs,
Tell thou the lamentable tale of me
And send the hearers weeping to their beds:
For why, the senseless brands will sympathize
The heavy accent of thy moving tongue
And in compassion weep the fire out;
And some will mourn in ashes, some coal-black,
For the deposing of a rightful king.   50

  Enter NORTHUMBERLAND *and* others.

  North. My lord, the mind of Bolingbroke is changed;
You must to Pomfret, not unto the Tower.
And, madam, there is order ta'en for you;
With all swift speed you must away to France.
  K. Rich. Northumberland, thou ladder wherewithal
The mounting Bolingbroke ascends my throne,
The time shall not be many hours of age

---

308. **to my flatterer,** as, or in the capacity of, my flatterer. 313.
Then . . . go. Richard throws away his last small chance to make terms
for himself. 316. **convey,** escort. 317. **convey,** steal, with a play
upon the normal sense of the word.
  ACT V. SCENE I. 1. **This . . . come.** There is no historical authority
for this interview between Richard and the queen; they did not meet
again after Richard left for Ireland. In Daniel, *Civil Wars*, II, 89-94,
the queen visits him in prison, and there is a striking parallel to Daniel
in the passage (II, 66 ff.) where she watches the king ride into the city.

2. **Julius Cæsar's.** The Tower, ascribed by tradition to Julius Caesar,
was built by William the Conqueror to hold the city in subordination.
ill-erected, erected for evil ends, or under evil auspices. 8. **My fair
rose.** Hotspur calls Richard *that sweet lovely rose, 1 Henry IV*, I, iii, 175.
11. **thou . . . stand,** thou ruined majesty that resemblest the desolate
waste where Troy once stood (Malone). 12. **map of honour,** i.e.,
the mere outline. 13. **inn,** mansion, abode (with some sense, however,
of its more common meaning). 20. **sworn brother,** allusion to the
fratres jurati of chivalry. 24. **new world's,** heaven's. 42. **betid,** past.

More than it is ere foul sin gathering head
Shall break into corruption: thou shalt think,
Though he divide the realm and give thee half, 60
It is too little, helping him to all;
And he shall think that thou, which know'st the way
To plant unrightful kings, wilt know again,
Being ne'er so little urged, another way
To pluck him headlong from the usurped throne.
The love of wicked men converts to fear;
That fear to hate, and hate turns one or both
To worthy danger and deserved death.
    North. My guilt be on my head, and there an end.
Take leave and part; for you must part forthwith. 70
    K. Rich. Doubly divorced! Bad men, you violate
A twofold marriage, 'twixt my crown and me,
And then betwixt me and my married wife.
Let me unkiss the oath 'twixt thee and me;
And yet not so, for with a kiss 'twas made.
Part us, Northumberland; I towards the north,
Where shivering cold and sickness pines the clime;
My wife to France: from whence, set forth in pomp,
She came adorned hither like sweet May,
Sent back like Hallowmas or short'st of day. 80
    Queen. And must we be divided? must we part?
    K. Rich. Ay, hand from hand, my love, and heart
        from heart.
    Queen. Banish us both and send the king with me.
    North. That were some love but little policy.
    Queen. Then whither he goes, thither let me go.
    K. Rich. So two, together weeping, make one woe.
Weep thou for me in France, I for thee here;
Better far off than near, be ne'er the near.
Go, count thy way with sighs; I mine with groans.
    Queen. So longest way shall have the longest moans.
    K. Rich. Twice for one step I'll groan, the way
        being short, 91
And piece the way out with a heavy heart.
Come, come, in wooing sorrow let's be brief,
Since, wedding it, there is such length in grief:
One kiss shall stop our mouths, and dumbly part;
Thus give I mine, and thus take I thy heart.
    Queen. Give me mine own again; 'twere no good
        part
To take on me to keep and kill thy heart.
So, now I have mine own again, be gone,
That I may strive to kill it with a groan. 100
    K. Rich. We make woe wanton with this fond delay:
Once more, adieu; the rest let sorrow say. [*Exeunt.*

SCENE II. *The* DUKE OF YORK'S *palace.*

Enter YORK *and his* DUCHESS.

    Duch. My lord, you told me you would tell the rest,
When weeping made you break the story off,
Of our two cousins coming into London.
    York. Where did I leave?
    Duch.   At that sad stop, my lord,

Where rude misgovern'd hands from windows' tops
Threw dust and rubbish on King Richard's head.
    York. Then, as I said, the duke, great Bolingbroke,
Mounted upon a hot and fiery steed
Which his aspiring rider seem'd to know,
With slow but stately pace kept on his course, 10
Whilst all tongues cried 'God save thee, Bolingbroke!'
You would have thought the very windows spake,
So many greedy looks of young and old
Through casements darted their desiring eyes
Upon his visage, and that all the walls
With painted imagery had said at once
'Jesu preserve thee! welcome, Bolingbroke!'
Whilst he, from the one side to the other turning,
Bareheaded, lower than his proud steed's neck,
Bespake them thus: 'I thank you, countrymen:' 20
And thus still doing, thus he pass'd along.
    Duch. Alack, poor Richard! where rode he the
        whilst?
    York. As in a theatre, the eyes of men,
After a well-graced actor leaves the stage,
Are idly bent on him that enters next,
Thinking his prattle to be tedious;
Even so, or with much more contempt, men's eyes
Did scowl on gentle Richard; no man cried 'God
        save him!'
No joyful tongue gave him his welcome home:
But dust was thrown upon his sacred head; 30
Which with such gentle sorrow he shook off,
His face still combating with tears and smiles,
The badges of his grief and patience,
That had not God, for some strong purpose, steel'd
The hearts of men, they must perforce have melted
And barbarism itself have pitied him.
But heaven hath a hand in these events,
To whose high will we bound our calm contents.
To Bolingbroke are we sworn subjects now,
Whose state and honour I for aye allow. 40
    Duch. Here comes my son Aumerle.
    York.   Aumerle that was;
But that is lost for being Richard's friend,
And, madam, you must call him Rutland now:
I am in parliament pledge for his truth
And lasting fealty to the new made king.

Enter AUMERLE.

    Duch. Welcome, my son: who are the violets now
That strew the green lap of the new come spring?
    Aum. Madam, I know not, nor I greatly care not:
God knows I had as lief be none as one.
    York. Well, bear you well in this new spring of time,
Lest you be cropp'd before you come to prime. 51
What news from Oxford? hold those justs and
        triumphs?
    Aum. For aught I know, my lord, they do.
    York. You will be there, I know.
    Aum. If God prevent not, I purpose so.
    York. What seal is that, that hangs without thy
        bosom?

43. **quit their griefs,** make return for their tragic tales. 52. **Pomfret,** Pontefract in Yorkshire, twenty-two miles from York. 53. **order ta'en,** arrangements made. 55. **Northumberland, thou ladder,** etc. Henry recalls this speech, quoting lines 55 and 56 in altered form, in *2 Henry IV*, III, i, 70. 59. **corruption,** putrid matter, pus. 66. **converts,** changes to, turns to. 74. **unkiss,** annul with a kiss (regarded as the seal of a ceremonial bond). 77. **pines,** afflicts, distresses. 80. **Hallowmas,** All Saints' Day (November 1); regarded as the beginning of winter; ten days later in the old calendar than

it is now. 88. **Better . . . near,** better be far off than near and yet be unable to meet. The second *near* is the old short comparative form for "nearer."
    SCENE II. 4. **leave,** leave off. 20. **Bespake,** spoke to. 25. **idly,** indifferently. 40. **allow,** acknowledge. 41. **Aumerle that was.** Aumerle, with others of Richard's party, lost all titles and honors conferred upon him by King Richard. 46-47. **who are . . . spring?** Who are the favorites of the new king?

Yea, look'st thou pale? let me see the writing.
   Aum. My lord, 'tis nothing.
   York.   No matter, then, who see it:
I will be satisfied; let me see the writing.
   Aum. I do beseech your grace to pardon me: 60
It is a matter of small consequence,
Which for some reasons I would not have seen.
   York. Which for some reasons, sir, I mean to see.
I fear, I fear,—
   Duch.   What should you fear?
'Tis nothing but some bond, that he is enter'd into
For gay apparel 'gainst the triumph day.
   York. Bound to himself! what doth he with a bond
That he is bound to? Wife, thou art a fool.
Boy, let me see the writing.
   Aum. I do beseech you, pardon me; I may not
      show it.   70
   York. I will be satisfied; let me see it, I say.
                 [*He plucks it out of his bosom and reads it.*
Treason! foul treason! Villain! traitor! slave!
   Duch. What is the matter, my lord?
   York. Ho! who is within there?

Enter a Servant.

                Saddle my horse.
God for his mercy, what treachery is here!
   Duch. Why, what is it, my lord?
   York. Give me my boots, I say; saddle my horse.
                       [*Exit Servant.*
Now, by mine honour, by my life, by my troth,
I will appeach the villain.
   Duch.   What is the matter?
   York. Peace, foolish woman.   80
   Duch. I will not peace. What is the matter, Aumerle?
   Aum. Good mother, be content; it is no more
Than my poor life must answer.
   Duch.   Thy life answer!
   York. Bring me my boots: I will unto the king.

Re-enter Servant *with boots.*

   Duch. Strike him, Aumerle. Poor boy, thou art
      amazed.
Hence, villain! never more come in my sight.
   York. Give me my boots, I say.
   Duch. Why, York, what wilt thou do?
Wilt thou not hide the trespass of thine own?
Have we more sons? or are we like to have?   90
Is not my teeming date drunk up with time?
And wilt thou pluck my fair son from mine age,
And rob me of a happy mother's name?
Is he not like thee? is he not thine own?
   York. Thou fond mad woman,
Wilt thou conceal this dark conspiracy?
A dozen of them here have ta'en the sacrament,
And interchangeably set down their hands,
To kill the king at Oxford.
   Duch.   He shall be none;
We'll keep him here: then what is that to him?   100

   York. Away, fond woman! were he twenty times my
      son,
I would appeach him.
   Duch.   Hadst thou groan'd for him
As I have done, thou wouldst be more pitiful.
But now I know thy mind; thou dost suspect
That I have been disloyal to thy bed,
And that he is a bastard, not thy son:
Sweet York, sweet husband, be not of that mind:
He is as like thee as a man may be,
Not like to me, or any of my kin,
And yet I love him.
   York.   Make way, unruly woman! [*Exit.*
   Duch. After, Aumerle! mount thee upon his horse;111
Spur post, and get before him to the king,
And beg thy pardon ere he do accuse thee.
I'll not be long behind; though I be old,
I doubt not but to ride as fast as York:
And never will I rise up from the ground
Till Bolingbroke have pardon'd thee. Away, be gone!
                         [*Exeunt.*

SCENE III. *A royal palace.*

Enter BOLINGBROKE, PERCY, *and other* Lords.

   Boling. Can no man tell me of my unthrifty son?
'Tis full three months since I did see him last:
If any plague hang over us, 'tis he.
I would to God, my lords, he might be found:
Inquire at London, 'mongst the taverns there,
For there, they say, he daily doth frequent,
With unrestrained loose companions,
Even such, they say, as stand in narrow lanes,
And beat our watch, and rob our passengers;
Which he, young wanton and effeminate boy,   10
Takes on the point of honour to support
So dissolute a crew.
   Percy. My lord, some two days since I saw the prince,
And told him of those triumphs held at Oxford.
   Boling. And what said the gallant?
   Percy. His answer was, he would unto the stews,
And from the common'st creature pluck a glove,
And wear it as a favour; and with that
He would unhorse the lustiest challenger.
   Boling. As dissolute as desperate; yet through both 20
I see some sparks of better hope, which elder years
May happily bring forth. But who comes here?

Enter AUMERLE.

   Aum. Where is the king?
   Boling. What means our cousin, that he stares and
      looks
So wildly?
   Aum. God save your grace! I do beseech your
      majesty,
To have some conference with your grace alone.

Boling. Withdraw yourselves, and leave us here
    alone.   *[Exeunt Percy and Lords.*
What is the matter with our cousin now?
    Aum. For ever may my knees grow to the earth,   30
My tongue cleave to my roof within my mouth,
Unless a pardon ere I rise or speak.
    Boling. Intended or committed was this fault?
If on the first, how heinous e'er it be,
To win thy after-love I pardon thee.
    Aum. Then give me leave that I may turn the key,
That no man enter till my tale be done.
    Boling. Have thy desire.
    York. [*Within*] My liege, beware; look to thyself;
Thou hast a traitor in thy presence there.   40
    Boling. Villain, I'll make thee safe.   [*Drawing.*
    Aum. Stay thy revengeful hand; thou hast no cause
    to fear.
    York. [*Within*] Open the door, secure, foolhardy
    king:
Shall I for love speak treason to thy face?
Open the door, or I will break it open.

Enter YORK.

    Boling. What is the matter, uncle? speak;
Recover breath; tell us how near is danger,
That we may arm us to encounter it.
    York. Peruse this writing here, and thou shalt know
The treason that my haste forbids me show.   50
    Aum. Remember, as thou read'st, thy promise
    pass'd:
I do repent me; read not my name there;
My heart is not confederate with my hand.
    York. It was, villain, ere thy hand did set it down.
I tore it from the traitor's bosom, king;
Fear, and not love, begets his penitence:
Forget to pity him, lest thy pity prove
A serpent that will sting thee to the heart.
    Boling. O heinous, strong and bold conspiracy!
O loyal father of a treacherous son!   60
Thou sheer, immaculate and silver fountain,
From whence this stream through muddy passages
Hath held his current and defiled himself!
Thy overflow of good converts to bad,
And thy abundant goodness shall excuse
This deadly blot in thy digressing son.
    York. So shall my virtue be his vice's bawd;
And he shall spend mine honour with his shame,
As thriftless sons their scraping fathers' gold.
Mine honour lives when his dishonour dies,   70
Or my shamed life in his dishonour lies:
Thou kill'st me in his life; giving him breath,
The traitor lives, the true man 's put to death.
    Duch. [*Within*] What ho, my liege! for God's sake,
    let me in.
    Boling. What shrill-voiced suppliant makes this
    eager cry?
    Duch. A woman, and thy aunt, great king; 'tis I.
Speak with me, pity me, open the door:

A beggar begs that never begg'd before.
    Boling. Our scene is alter'd from a serious thing,
And now changed to 'The Beggar and the King.'   80
My dangerous cousin, let your mother in:
I know she is come to pray for your foul sin.
    York. If thou do pardon, whosoever pray,
More sins for this forgiveness prosper may.
This fester'd joint cut off, the rest rest sound;
This let alone will all the rest confound.

Enter DUCHESS.

    Duch. O king, believe not this hard-hearted man!
Love loving not itself none other can.
    York. Thou frantic woman, what dost thou make
    here?
Shall thy old dugs once more a traitor rear?   90
    Duch. Sweet York, be patient. Hear me, gentle liege.
                                    [*Kneels.*
    Boling. Rise up, good aunt.
    Duch.   Not yet, I thee beseech:
For ever will I walk upon my knees,
And never see day that the happy sees,
Till thou give joy; until thou bid me joy,
By pardoning Rutland, my transgressing boy.
    Aum. Unto my mother's prayers I bend my knee.
    York. Against them both my true joints bended be.
Ill mayst thou thrive, if thou grant any grace!
    Duch. Pleads he in earnest? look upon his face;   100
His eyes do drop no tears, his prayers are in jest;
His words come from his mouth, ours from our breast:
He prays but faintly and would be denied;
We pray with heart and soul and all beside:
His weary joints would gladly rise, I know;
Our knees shall kneel till to the ground they grow:
His prayers are full of false hypocrisy;
Ours of true zeal and deep integrity.
Our prayers do out-pray his; then let them have
That mercy which true prayer ought to have.   110
    Boling. Good aunt, stand up.
    Duch.   Nay, do not say, 'stand up;'
Say 'pardon' first, and afterwards 'stand up.'
An if I were thy nurse, thy tongue to teach,
'Pardon' should be the first word of thy speech.
I never long'd to hear a word till now;
Say 'pardon,' king; let pity teach thee how:
The word is short, but not so short as sweet;
No word like 'pardon' for kings' mouths so meet.
    York. Speak it in French, king; say 'pardonne moi.'
    Duch. Dost thou teach pardon pardon to destroy? 120
Ah, my sour husband, my hard-hearted lord,
That set'st the word itself against the word!
Speak 'pardon' as 'tis current in our land;
The chopping French we do not understand.
Thine eye begins to speak; set thy tongue there;
Or in thy piteous heart plant thou thine ear;
That hearing how our plaints and prayers do pierce,
Pity may move thee 'pardon' to rehearse.
    Boling. Good aunt, stand up.

broke's feelings may be further understood from *1 Henry IV*, I, i, 78-90;
and the tavern view of the matter from the same play, II, iv, 114-121.
16. **stews,** houses of ill fame.   22. **happily,** haply; possibly, combining
also the modern sense of the word.   43. **secure,** unsuspecting, heedless.
44. **speak . . . face,** i.e., by calling him *secure* and *foolhardy*.   58. **serpent,**
allusion to the fable of the *Countryman and the Viper*. See also III, ii, 131.
61-66. **Thou . . . son.** Chambers quotes a parallel passage from Lyly's
Euphues (Arbor ed., page 191): "As the water that springeth from the
fountain's head," etc.   61. **sheer,** clear, pure.   66. **digressing,** transgressing.   80. **'The Beggar and the King,'** one of the many allusions in
Shakespeare to the ballad of *King Cophetua and the Beggar Maid*; see
Love's Labour's Lost, I, ii, 114 ff.; *Romeo and Juliet*, II, i, 14; *2 Henry IV*,
V, iii, 106.   81. **My dangerous cousin,** another example of Bolingbroke's sarcastic humor used so freely above in his interviews with
Richard.   88. **Love . . . can.** He who does not love his own kin can
love no one else, not even the king.   119. **'pardonne moi,'** excuse me
(affectedly polite refusal).   124. **chopping,** jerky, shifting suddenly;
possibly, changing (the sense of words).

Duch.   I do not sue to stand;
Pardon is all the suit I have in hand.   130
    Boling. I pardon him, as God shall pardon me.
    Duch. O happy vantage of a kneeling knee!
Yet am I sick for fear: speak it again;
Twice saying 'pardon' doth not pardon twain,
But makes one pardon strong.
    Boling.   With all my heart
I pardon him.
    Duch.   A god on earth thou art.
    Boling. But for our trusty brother-in-law and the
        abbot,
With all the rest of that consorted crew,
Destruction straight shall dog them at the heels.
Good uncle, help to order several powers   140
To Oxford, or where'er these traitors are:
They shall not live within this world, I swear,
But I will have them, if I once know where.
Uncle, farewell: and, cousin too, adieu:
Your mother well hath pray'd, and prove you true.
    Duch. Come, my old son: I pray God make thee
        new.   [*Exeunt.*

SCENE IV. *The same.*

Enter EXTON *and* Servant.

    Exton. Didst thou not mark the king, what words he
        spake,
'Have I no friend will rid me of this living fear?'
Was it not so?
    Ser.   These were his very words.
    Exton. 'Have I no friend?' quoth he: he spake it
        twice,
And urged it twice together, did he not?
    Serv. He did.
    Exton. And speaking it, he wistly look'd on me;
As who should say, 'I would thou wert the man
That would divorce this terror from my heart;'
Meaning the king at Pomfret. Come, let's go: 10
I am the king's friend, and will rid his foe.   [*Exeunt.*

SCENE V. *Pomfret castle.*

Enter KING RICHARD.

    K. Rich. I have been studying how I may compare
This prison where I live unto the world:
And for because the world is populous
And here is not a creature but myself,
I cannot do it; yet I'll hammer it out.
My brain I'll prove the female to my soul,
My soul the father; and these two beget
A generation of still-breeding thoughts,
And these same thoughts people this little world,
In humours like the people of this world,   10
For no thought is contented. The better sort,
As thoughts of things divine, are intermix'd
With scruples and do set the word itself
Against the word:
As thus, 'Come, little ones,' and then again,
'It is as hard to come as for a camel
To thread the postern of a small needle's eye.'
Thoughts tending to ambition, they do plot
Unlikely wonders; how these vain weak nails
May tear a passage through the flinty ribs   20
Of this hard world, my ragged prison walls,
And, for they cannot, die in their own pride.
Thoughts tending to content flatter themselves
That they are not the first of fortune's slaves,
Nor shall not be the last; like silly beggars
Who sitting in the stocks refuge their shame,
That many have and others must sit there;
And in this thought they find a kind of ease,
Bearing their own misfortunes on the back
Of such as have before endured the like.   30
Thus play I in one person many people,
And none contented: sometimes am I king;
Then treasons make me wish myself a beggar,
And so I am: then crushing penury
Persuades me I was better when a king;
Then am I king'd again: and by and by
Think that I am unking'd by Bolingbroke,
And straight am nothing: but whate'er I be,
Nor I nor any man that but man is
With nothing shall be pleased, till he be eased   40
With being nothing. Music do I hear?   [*Music.*
Ha, ha! keep time: how sour sweet music is,
When time is broke and no proportion kept!
So is it in the music of men's lives.
And here have I the daintiness of ear
To check time broke in a disorder'd string;
But for the concord of my state and time
Had not an ear to hear my true time broke.
I wasted time, and now doth time waste me;
For now hath time made me his numbering clock: 50
My thoughts are minutes; and with sighs they jar
Their watches on unto mine eyes, the outward watch,
Whereto my finger, like a dial's point,
Is pointing still, in cleansing them from tears.
Now sir, the sound that tells what hour it is
Are clamorous groans, which strike upon my heart,
Which is the bell: so sighs and tears and groans
Show minutes, times, and hours: but my time
Runs posting on in Bolingbroke's proud joy,
While I stand fooling here, his Jack o' the clock.   60
This music mads me; let it sound no more;
For though it have holp madmen to their wits,
In me it seems it will make wise men mad.
Yet blessing on his heart that gives it me!
For 'tis a sign of love; and love to Richard
Is a strange brooch in this all-hating world.

---

130. **suit,** petition (with play upon the term as used at cards). 137. **our trusty brother-in-law,** i.e., John, earl of Huntingdon, who had married Bolingbroke's sister Elizabeth. 138. **consorted,** confederate. 145. **prove you true.** Aumerle, as duke of York, died leading the van at Agincourt.
    SCENE IV. 7. **And speaking it,** etc. Cf. Daniel's *Civil Wars,* II, 57:

      "And wisht that some would so his life esteeme,
      As *ridde* him of these feares wherein he stood:
      And there-with eyes a knight, that then was by,
      Who soone could learne his lesson by his eye."

    SCENE V. 1. **I have been studying,** etc. Daniel (III, 64-69) presents Richard soliloquizing, "Conferring captiue-Crownes with freedome poore," somewhat in the spirit of this passage. 5. **I'll hammer it out.** Richard has an artist's determination to express his idea. 21. **ragged,** rugged. 26. **refuge,** comfort. 50. **numbering clock.** Henley explains thus: " . . . his sighs correspond to the jarring of the pendulum, which, at the same time that it watches or numbers the seconds, marks also their progress in minutes on the dial or outward watch, to which the king compares his eyes; and their want of figures is supplied by a succession of tears, or, to use the expression of Milton, minute-drops; his finger, by as regularly wiping these tears

Enter a Groom of the Stable.

Groom. Hail, royal prince!
K. Rich.   Thanks, noble peer;
The cheapest of us is ten groats too dear.
What art thou? and how comest thou hither,
Where no man never comes but that sad dog   70
That brings me food to make misfortune live?
Groom. I was a poor groom of thy stable, king,
When thou wert king; who, travelling towards York,
With much ado at length have gotten leave
To look upon my sometimes royal master's face.
O, how it yearn'd my heart when I beheld
In London streets, that coronation-day,
When Bolingbroke rode on roan Barbary,
That horse that thou so often hast bestrid,
That horse that I so carefully have dress'd!   80
K. Rich. Rode he on Barbary? Tell me, gentle friend,
How went he under him?
Groom. So proudly as if he disdain'd the ground.
K. Rich. So proud that Bolingbroke was on his back!
That jade hath eat bread from my royal hand;
This hand hath made him proud with clapping him.
Would he not stumble? would he not fall down,
Since pride must have a fall, and break the neck
Of that proud man that did usurp his back?
Forgiveness, horse! why do I rail on thee,   90
Since thou, created to be awed by man,
Wast born to bear? I was not made a horse;
And yet I bear a burthen like an ass,
Spur-gall'd and tired by jauncing Bolingbroke.

Enter Keeper, *with a dish.*

Keep. Fellow, give place; here is no longer stay.
K. Rich. If thou love me, 'tis time thou wert away.
Groom. What my tongue dares not, that my heart
     shall say.   [*Exit.*
Keep. My lord, will 't please you to fall to?
K. Rich. Taste of it first, as thou art wont to do.   99
Keep. My lord, I dare not: Sir Pierce of Exton, who
lately came from the king, commands the contrary.
K. Rich. The devil take Henry of Lancaster and
     thee!
Patience is stale, and I am weary of it. [*Beats the keeper.*
Keep. Help, help, help!

Enter EXTON *and* Servants, *armed.*

K. Rich. How now! what means death in this rude
     assault?
Villain, thy own hand yields thy death's instrument.
     [*Snatching an axe from a Servant and killing him.*
Go thou, and fill another room in hell.
     [*He kills another. Then Exton strikes him down.*
That hand shall burn in never-quenching fire
That staggers thus my person. Exton, thy fierce hand
Hath with the king's blood stain'd the king's own land.
Mount, mount, my soul! thy seat is up on high;   112

Whilst my gross flesh sinks downward, here to die.
                                            [*Dies.*

Exton. As full of valour as of royal blood:
Both have I spill'd; O would the deed were good!
For now the devil, that told me I did well,
Says that this deed is chronicled in hell.
This dead king to the living king I'll bear:
Take hence the rest, and give them burial here.
                                         [*Exeunt.*

SCENE VI. *Windsor castle.*

Flourish. Enter BOLINGBROKE, YORK, *with other* Lords,
     and Attendants.

Boling. Kind uncle York, the latest news we hear
Is that the rebels have consumed with fire
Our town of Cicester in Gloucestershire;
But whether they be ta'en or slain we hear not.

Enter NORTHUMBERLAND.

Welcome, my lord: what is the news?
North. First, to thy sacred state wish I all happiness.
The next news is, I have to London sent
The heads of Oxford, Salisbury, Blunt, and Kent:
The manner of their taking may appear
At large discoursed in this paper here.   10
Boling. We thank thee, gentle Percy, for thy pains;
And to thy worth will add right worthy gains.

Enter FITZWATER.

Fitz. My lord, I have from Oxford sent to London
The heads of Brocas and Sir Bennet Seely,
Two of the dangerous consorted traitors
That sought at Oxford thy dire overthrow.
Boling. Thy pains, Fitzwater, shall not be forgot;
Right noble is thy merit, well I wot.

Enter PERCY, *and the* BISHOP OF CARLISLE.

Percy. The grand conspirator, Abbot of Westminster,
With clog of conscience and sour melancholy   20
Hath yielded up his body to the grave;
But here is Carlisle living, to abide
Thy kingly doom and sentence of his pride.
Boling. Carlisle, this is your doom:
Choose out some secret place, some reverend room,
More than thou hast, and with it joy thy life;
So as thou livest in peace, die free from strife:
For though mine enemy thou hast ever been,
High sparks of honour in thee have I seen.

Enter EXTON, *with persons bearing a coffin.*

Exton. Great king, within this coffin I present   30
Thy buried fear: herein all breathless lies
The mightiest of thy greatest enemies,
Richard of Bordeaux, by me hither brought.

*Richard
the Second*

ACT V : SC VI

673

---

away performs the office of the dial point; his clamorous groans are
the sounds that tell the hour." 51. **jar,** tick. 60. **Jack o' the clock,**
a figure which struck the bell on a clock. 62. **holp madmen to their
wits,** probable allusion to the story of the cure of Saul by David. 66.
brooch, ornament (worn in a man's hat). 68. **ten groats too dear.**
There is a pun on *royal* and *noble* in the preceding lines. Though a royal
(10s.) is worth 10 groats (ten times 4d.) more than a noble (6s. 8d.) is,
a noble itself is 10 groats too high a price for either Richard or the
Groom. 76. **yearn'd,** vexed, grieved. 78. **roan Barbary.** Boswell-
Stone suggests that the story of "roan Barbary" may come from an
account repeated in Froissart of a greyhound, Mathe, which forsook

his old master, Richard, and followed Bolingbroke. 94. **Spur-gall'd
and tired.** Q: *Spurr'd, gall'd, and tired.* **gall'd,** annoyed; literally, made
sore by rubbing. **jauncing,** making prance up and down (of a horse);
here, hard-riding. 108. **room,** a particular place assigned to a person.
115. **O . . . good!** It is said, that sir Piers of Exton, after he had thus
slaine him, wept right bitterlie, as one stricken with the pricke of
a giltie conscience, for murthering him, whome he had so long time
obeied as king (Holinshed).
SCENE VI. 8. **Oxford.** No such name occurs in Holinshed; F reads
Spencer. Shakespeare antedates the death of Richard, since the conspiracy was put down before his death. 15. **consorted,** confederate.

Boling. Exton, I thank thee not; for thou hast
    wrought
A deed of slander with thy fatal hand
Upon my head and all this famous land.
    Exton. From your own mouth, my lord, did I this
    deed.
    Boling. They love not poison that do poison need,
Nor do I thee: though I did wish him dead,
I hate the murderer, love him murdered.   40
The guilt of conscience take thou for thy labour,
But neither my good word nor princely favour:
With Cain go wander thorough shades of night,
And never show thy head by day nor light.
Lords, I protest, my soul is full of woe,
That blood should sprinkle me to make me grow:
Come, mourn with me for that I do lament,
And put on sullen black incontinent:
I'll make a voyage to the Holy Land,
To wash this blood off from my guilty hand: 50
March sadly after; grace my mournings here;
In weeping after this untimely bier.   [*Exeunt.*

34. **Exton, I thank thee not.** There is no mention of Henry's repudia-
tion of Exton in any of the *Chronicles*. Daniel, *Civil Wars*, III, 79, has
a vague parallel. 48. **incontinent,** immediately. 49-50. **I'll . . .
hand.** Henry never fulfilled his vow, though he had it always in mind;
see *1 Henry IV*, I, i, 19 ff.; *2 Henry IV*, III, i, 108; IV, iv, 3; v, 210 ff.
and 233 ff. 52. **In . . . bier.** Richard probably died in January 1400;
he was buried at Pomfret. His body was then carried to London,
displayed in Cheapside and St. Paul's on March 12, 1400, and buried
in an obscure grave at Langley. Through the piety of Henry v, his
body was placed in the tomb in Westminster Abbey that Richard
himself had built for his first queen, Anne of Bohemia.

*Richard
the Second*
ACT V : SC VI

674

THE

Henry the Fourth Plays

An edition of *1 Henry IV* was published in quarto
by P. S. for Andrew Wise in 1598 with the following
title:

THE HISTORY OF HENRIE THE FOVRTH;
With the battell at Shrewsburie, *betweene the King and Lord*
Henry Percy, surnamed Henrie Hotspur of the North.
With the humorous conceits of Sir Iohn Falstalffe. AT
LONDON, Printed by *P. S.* for *Andrew Wise,* dwelling
in Paules Churchyard, at the signe of the Angell. 1598.

It had been entered in the Stationers' Register on
February 25th of that year.

In 1600 there came out, also in quarto:

THE Second part of Henrie the fourth, continuing
to his death, *and coronation of Henrie* the fift. With the
humours of sir Iohn Fal*staffe, and swaggering* Pistoll. *As
it hath been sundrie times publikely* acted by the right honourable, the Lord Chamberlaine his seruants. *Written
by William Shakespeare.* LONDON. Printed by V. S. for
Andrew Wise, and William Aspley. 1600.

This had been entered in the Stationers' Register
on August 23, 1600. There are two issues of the

second part under this date and title, the first of which
omits the first scene of the third act.

No less than eight quarto editions of *1 Henry IV*
appeared. The Folio text was set from the playhouse
manuscript, not from a quarto. There was only
one quarto publication of *2 Henry IV*, and a distinct
text from that of the quarto is used for the Folio.
The quarto texts of both parts of the play are good,
and the publishers were respectable. The texts they
used probably came from the playhouse.

FALSTAFF AND OLDCASTLE

How the plays came to be printed is a matter of
interesting speculation. It was possibly from a desire
to protect the plays from piracy, but also it may have
been in order to advertise a correction. There is
evidence of a serious offense against Lord Cobham
because in the first versions of these plays the famous
fat knight was called Sir John Oldcastle and not Sir
John Falstaff. Lord Cobham was a descendant of
Sir John Oldcastle, an honorable nobleman and a
Wycliffe martyr, whom the religious prejudices of
the intervening time had made into a hypocrite,
a wine-bibber, and a misleader of the young prince
who subsequently became King Henry v.

The tradition had been embodied in the source of
these plays, one of the oldest of chronicle plays, preserved in a degenerate version known as *The Famous
Victories of Henry V* (1598). The depiction had probably given no offense, or remained unnoticed, in the
old play. However, when Shakespeare's play sprang
into popularity, Lord Cobham's resentment was
natural. Shakespeare therefore revised his play and
changed the name of his comic hero to Sir John
Falstaff, perhaps a modification of the name Sir
John Fastolfe, a character who is made to play a
coward's part in *1 Henry VI*. Scholars after Shakespeare's death called attention to the fact that he
had also done historical injustice to Sir John Fastolfe,
but the name was at least less offensive than that of
Sir John Oldcastle.

The Lord Admiral's men, the rival company to
the players at the Globe, put on the stage a chronicle
play in two parts intended to mete out full justice to
the Lollard martyr, *The History of the Life of Sir John
Oldcastle, Lord Cobham, with his Martyrdom.* The important playwrights Munday, Wilson, Drayton, and
Hathway were the authors, and the first part of it
was published in 1600. The year seems significant,
for Shakespeare not only revised his plays but made
public denial of the identification of Falstaff and
Oldcastle in the epilogue to *2 Henry IV*, sent to the
printers that year. "For Oldcastle died a martyr,
and this is not the man," he says.

The revision was not so careful that traces of the
old name may not be found, not only in *1* and *2
Henry IV*, but more doubtfully also in *The Merry
Wives of Windsor*, which in that case must have been
written before the early part of the year 1598. In
1 Henry IV (I, ii, 47-48) the prince addresses Falstaff

as "my old lad of the castle," and in *2 Henry IV* (I, ii, 137) the catch-name *Old.* has been left standing before one of Falstaff's speeches in the quarto edition. Various cases have also been pointed out in which the name Oldcastle completes a line of verse which has been left one syllable short by the substitution of Falstaff for Oldcastle.

The Famous Victories AND THE "OLDCASTLE" PLAYS

There was, at least as early as 1588, a play acted by the queen's men on the life of King Henry V.[1] It covered the same ground historically as is covered by *1* and *2 Henry IV* and *Henry V*. In the year of theatrical readjustments, 1594, the queen's company, according to Henslowe, "broke & went into the contrey to play" and are never heard of in London again. Nearly all of their repertory of plays seems to have been disposed of to the printers. However, part of it fell into the hands of the Lord Admiral's company, including no doubt a copy of the old Henry V play, for Henslowe records a new play (or revision) called "harey the V" acted at the Rose on November 28, 1595, and subsequently thirteen times between that date and July 15, 1596.

On May 14, 1594, a printer of no standing called Thomas Creed entered in the Stationers' Register *The Famous victories of HENRYE the FFYFTH containinge the honorable battell of Agincourt.* If he published the play at once, no copy has survived. He issued without further entry *The Famous Victories of Henry V* in 1598. This is not the old Henry V play, but is a corrupt and badly degenerated version of it. In other words, it is not the immediate source from which Shakespeare worked, but is derived from that source. Indeed, there is very little of Oldcastle besides his name in the badly abridged *The Famous Victories.*

A copy of the old Henry V play must have come into the hands of Shakespeare or his company. Working on this, he wrote first a play on Henry IV in two parts. The plays were largely in verse and in them Falstaff was known as Oldcastle. These "Oldcastle" plays were probably written in the blank verse style somewhat in the manner of *King John* and *Richard II*. The prose in these plays was no doubt of the common clownage type which still appears in *1 Henry IV*, II, i. The popularity of the Oldcastle parts caused Shakespeare to expand them and enrich them in the free prose style of the Falstaff scenes. His first version was, however, probably a one-part play which he later expanded into two parts.

Morgan finds unmistakable evidence of this curtailment and abundant signs of the rehandling in prose of comic scenes which were formerly in verse. Imbedded in the prose of the comic scenes of *1 Henry IV* he finds some two hundred lines of verse. The verse remnants are mainly found in those passages which we know from *The Famous Victories* go back to

the original Henry V play. They are fewest in the freest and most typical passages of Falstaffian humor. There are few evidences of original verse in the Shallow-Silence parts of *2 Henry IV*. Those parts would, therefore, belong mainly to the latest revision.

THE HISTORICAL PLOT

The originals of *1* and *2 Henry IV*, as Shakespeare first wrote them, would not have been inconsiderable plays, for they probably contained the historical plots as they now stand. These plots have merely lost a certain amount of material by excision. Sir John Oldcastle in verse would have been a poor substitute for Falstaff in prose as we have him; but the serious plots have no doubt lost something of their original fullness. Hotspur probably did not appear in the old Henry V play, so that Shakespeare has built a new heroic drama connected with Hotspur around the career of the young prince.

To do this he went to the second edition of Holinshed's *Chronicles of England, Scotland, and Ireland* (1587), and to Daniel's *Civil Wars*, and, although he has followed his sources with faithfulness as to fact, he has illuminated them in marvelous fashion. From Holinshed comes the main historical business of both parts: the insurrection of Harry Percy, the rebellion of York, Bardolph, Hastings, and Mowbray, the dishonest defeat of the rebels at Gaultree, and the troubles and sorrows of Henry IV. Probably from Daniel he has taken the conception of Hotspur as a youth of Prince Hal's age, the rescue of the king by the prince during the battle of Shrewsbury, the absence of the Welsh from that conflict, and the idea that Henry IV suffered a nemesis in his conscience for his usurpation of the throne.

Much of the serious plot comes also from the old Henry V play; for example, the king's trouble about his wayward son, the incident of Hal's removal of the crown and the reconciliation which follows, and finally the rejection of his wild companions after his coronation. In some cases the same theme appears in more than one source, and Shakespeare before writing seems characteristically to have gone over the whole field of his material.

FALSTAFF

Falstaff has been regarded as a character of puzzling complexity. To what extent the twice-depicted Oldcastle, who lies back of him, may be shining inconsistently through his fat bulk nobody can tell. In any case, his earlier forms will keep us from the fallacy of thinking of him either as an actual character such as occurs in history, or as struck out at one forging from a clear-cut and definite pattern in Shakespeare's brain.

Falstaff is, from the point of view of literary history, an accident, a very happy accident, which will not bear the analysis of the critics. We cannot, in the light of his origin, expect meticulous consistency, or even believe that Shakespeare, by original concep-

---

[1]See A. E. Morgan, *Some Problems of Shakespeare's "Henry the Fourth"* (The Shakespeare Association, 1924), which is followed in this section.

tion, made him inconsistent. Falstaff is inconsistent but has the inconsistency of life itself. He is in point of fact the first great synthetic character in modern drama.

Falstaff happened into the drama from a greatly varied body of antecedent circumstances. He is not accounted for, as one body of critics would have us believe, by considering him as a traditional stage rogue and jester, although he plays every trick known to that species; nor is he accounted for as a combination of traditional rogue and gull. He is still less, however, to be accounted for by those other critics who persist in thinking of him as a man as real as Sir Walter Raleigh and a character whose every word, act, experience, and thought arise by his creator's deliberate design.[2]

STAGE HISTORY

The Henry IV plays must both have been popular during the lifetime of their author and probably until the closing of the theaters in 1642. Although there are few known references to actual performances, *1 Henry IV* went through eight quarto editions, and no plays are more frequently alluded to than the Henry IV plays.[3]

After the Restoration *1 Henry IV* was soon revived, Pepys having seen the play with varying approval no less than five times. The Restoration and the eighteenth century were the Falstaff era.

Betterton played Hotspur until 1700 and then won a great reputation as an actor of Falstaff, playing the part in *1* and *2 Henry IV* and *The Merry Wives of Windsor*, as did James Quin, who has come down in stage history as one of the greatest actors in that part. Garrick played Hotspur none too successfully and later succeeded better as the king in *2 Henry IV*. John Henderson was so great a Falstaff that it was thought that he rivaled Quin. John Philip Kemble played Hotspur successfully in 1802, and in 1804 he and his brother Charles played the parts of the king and the prince in the second part. George Bartley (1782?-1858) was probably the most famous of the Falstaffs of the nineteenth century. In 1896 and 1914 Tree, although not well suited to the part, played the Falstaff of *1 Henry IV* with success, and in 1939 Maurice Evans played the part in a brilliant revival in New York.

The first part was played now and then in the nineteenth century in England and America, but the second part almost never. Both parts were played by Phelps at Sadler's Wells about the middle of the nineteenth century and by the Benson company at the Stratford Memorial Theater in 1906.

[2]The student should read for varying points of view on Falstaff: Schücking, Stoll (*Modern Philology*, XII, 197-240), Bradley ("The Rejection of Falstaff," in *Oxford Lectures*), Brandes, Dowden, and other critics. See also John James Elson, "The Non-Shakespearean *Richard II* and Shakespeare's *Henry IV, Part I*," *Studies in Philology*, XXXII (1935), 177-188. See especially the inclusive work, *The Fortunes of Falstaff* by J. Dover Wilson (Cambridge, 1943).
[3]R. P. Cowl, *Some Echoes in Elizabethan Drama of Shakespeare's "King Henry the Fourth"* (1926).

THE FIRST PART OF
King Henry the Fourth

DRAMATIS PERSONAE

KING HENRY the Fourth.
HENRY, Prince of Wales, } sons to the King.
JOHN of Lancaster,
EARL OF WESTMORELAND.
SIR WALTER BLUNT.
THOMAS PERCY, Earl of Worcester.
HENRY PERCY, Earl of Northumberland.
HENRY PERCY, surnamed HOTSPUR, his son.
EDMUND MORTIMER, Earl of March.
RICHARD SCROOP, Archbishop of York.
ARCHIBALD, Earl of DOUGLAS.
OWEN GLENDOWER.
SIR RICHARD VERNON.
SIR JOHN FALSTAFF.
SIR MICHAEL, a friend to the Archbishop of York.
POINS.
GADSHILL.
PETO.
BARDOLPH.

LADY PERCY, wife to Hotspur, and sister to Mortimer.
LADY MORTIMER, daughter to Glendower, and wife to Mortimer.
MISTRESS QUICKLY, hostess of a tavern in Eastcheap.

Lords, Officers, Sheriff, Vintner, Chamberlain, Drawers, two Carriers, Travellers, and Attendants.

SCENE: *England.*

ACT I.

SCENE I. *London. The palace.*

Enter KING HENRY, LORD JOHN OF LANCASTER, *the* EARL OF WESTMORELAND, SIR WALTER BLUNT, *and others.*

King. So shaken as we are, so wan with care,
Find we a time for frighted peace to pant,
And breathe short-winded accents of new broils
To be commenced in strands afar remote.
†No more the thirsty entrance of this soil
Shall daub her lips with her own children's blood;
No more shall trenching war channel her fields,
Nor bruise her flowerets with the armed hoofs
Of hostile paces: those opposed eyes,
Which, like the meteors of a troubled heaven,   10
All of one nature, of one substance bred,
Did lately meet in the intestine shock

And furious close of civil butchery
Shall now, in mutual well-beseeming ranks,
March all one way and be no more opposed
Against acquaintance, kindred and allies:
The edge of war, like an ill-sheathed knife,
No more shall cut his master. Therefore, friends,
As far as to the sepulchre of Christ,
Whose soldier now, under whose blessed cross   20
We are impressed and engaged to fight,
Forthwith a power of English shall we levy;
Whose arms were moulded in their mothers' womb
To chase these pagans in those holy fields
Over whose acres walk'd those blessed feet
Which fourteen hundred years ago were nail'd
For our advantage on the bitter cross.
But this our purpose now is twelve month old,
And bootless 'tis to tell you we will go:
Therefore we meet not now. Then let me hear   30
Of you, my gentle cousin Westmoreland,
What yesternight our council did decree
In forwarding this dear expedience.
    West. My liege, this haste was hot in question,
And many limits of the charge set down
But yesternight: when all athwart there came
A post from Wales loaden with heavy news;
Whose worst was, that the noble Mortimer,
Leading the men of Herefordshire to fight
Against the irregular and wild Glendower,   40
Was by the rude hands of that Welshman taken,
A thousand of his people butchered;
Upon whose dead corpse there was such misuse,
Such beastly shameless transformation,
By those Welshwomen done as may not be
Without much shame retold or spoken of.
    King. It seems then that the tidings of this broil
Brake off our business for the Holy Land.
    West. This match'd with other did, my gracious
        lord;
For more uneven and unwelcome news   50
Came from the north and thus it did import:
On Holy-rood day, the gallant Hotspur there,
Young Harry Percy and brave Archibald,
That ever-valiant and approved Scot,
At Holmedon met,
Where they did spend a sad and bloody hour;
As by discharge of their artillery,
And shape of likelihood, the news was told;
For he that brought them, in the very heat
And pride of their contention did take horse,   60
Uncertain of the issue any way.
    King. Here is a dear, a true industrious friend,
Sir Walter Blunt, new lighted from his horse,
Stain'd with the variation of each soil
Betwixt that Holmedon and this seat of ours;
And he hath brought us smooth and welcome news.
The Earl of Douglas is discomfited:
Ten thousand bold Scots, two and twenty knights,
Balk'd in their own blood did Sir Walter see

On Holmedon's plains. Of prisoners, Hotspur took   70
Mordake the Earl of Fife, and eldest son
To beaten Douglas; and the Earl of Athol,
Of Murray, Angus, and Menteith:
And is not this an honourable spoil?
A gallant prize? ha, cousin, is it not?
    West. In faith,
It is a conquest for a prince to boast of.
    King. Yea, there thou makest me sad and makest
        me sin
In envy that my Lord Northumberland
Should be the father to so blest a son,   80
A son who is the theme of honour's tongue;
Amongst a grove, the very straightest plant;
Who is sweet Fortune's minion and her pride:
Whilst I, by looking on the praise of him,
See riot and dishonour stain the brow
Of my young Harry. O that it could be proved
That some night-tripping fairy had exchanged
In cradle-clothes our children where they lay,
And call'd mine Percy, his Plantagenet!
Then would I have his Harry, and he mine.   90
But let him from my thoughts. What think you, coz,
Of this young Percy's pride? the prisoners,
Which he in this adventure hath surprised,
To his own use he keeps; and sends me word,
I shall have none but Mordake Earl of Fife.
    West. This is his uncle's teaching: this is Worcester,
Malevolent to you in all aspects;
Which makes him prune himself, and bristle up
The crest of youth against your dignity.
    King. But I have sent for him to answer this;   100
And for this cause awhile we must neglect
Our holy purpose to Jerusalem.
Cousin, on Wednesday next our council we
Will hold at Windsor; so inform the lords:
But come yourself with speed to us again;
For more is to be said and to be done
Than out of anger can be uttered.
    West. I will, my liege.   [*Exeunt.*

1 Henry IV
ACT I : SC II

677

SCENE II. *London. An apartment of the Prince's.*

Enter the PRINCE OF WALES *and* FALSTAFF.

    Fal. Now, Hal, what time of day is it, lad?
    Prince. Thou art so fat-witted, with drinking of old
sack and unbuttoning thee after supper and sleeping
upon benches after noon, that thou hast forgotten to
demand that truly which thou wouldst truly know.
What a devil hast thou to do with the time of the day?
Unless hours were cups of sack and minutes capons
and clocks the tongues of bawds and dials the signs of
leaping-houses and the blessed sun himself a fair hot
wench in flame-coloured taffeta, I see no reason why
thou shouldst be so superfluous to demand the time
of the day.   13

ACT I. SCENE I. 5. **entrance**, i.e., mouth. 9. **opposed**, hostile (of enemies). 13. **close**, encounter. 19. **As far as to.** There is an idea of motion in the word *levy*, line 22. 28. **twelve month**, a year; used collectively. 33. **dear expedience**, urgent expedition. 34. **hot in question**, being hotly debated. 35. **limits of the charge**, military arrangements; possibly, estimates of expense. 36. **athwart**, frustrating, interrupting. 38. **worst**, i.e., worst news. 40. **irregular**, lawless. 43-46. **Upon . . . spoken of.** Holinshed also says that the outrages are unmentionable. 49. **This . . . other**, this piece of news matched with another. 50. **uneven**, embarrassing. 55. **Holmedon**, Humbleton, a

town in Northumberland. 57. **by**, i.e., judging from. 64. **the variation of each**, every kind of. 66. **smooth**, flattering, pleasant. 69. **Balk'd**, heaped up in balks or ridges. 71. **Mordake.** This Murdoch, earl of Fife, was the son of the regent of Scotland. Shakespeare follows the text of Holinshed in which a comma was omitted after the word *governour*: "Mordacke earl of Fife, son to the governour Archembald earl Dowglas." 95. **none but Mordake.** Since the prisoner in question was of royal blood, being grandson to Robert II, Hotspur could not claim him as his prisoner. 97. **Malevolent, aspects**, astrological terms. 98. **prune**, preen (as a bird its feathers).

Fal. Indeed, you come near me now, Hal; for we that take purses go by the moon and the seven stars, and not by Phœbus, he, 'that wandering knight so fair.' And, I prithee, sweet wag, when thou art king, as, God save thy grace,—majesty I should say, for grace thou wilt have none,— 20

Prince. What, none?

Fal. No, by my troth, not so much as will serve to be prologue to an egg and butter.

Prince. Well, how then? come, roundly, roundly.

Fal. Marry, then, sweet wag, when thou art king, let not us that are squires of the night's body be called thieves of the day's beauty: let us be Diana's foresters, gentlemen of the shade, minions of the moon; and let men say we be men of good government, being governed, as the sea is, by our noble and chaste mistress the moon, under whose countenance we steal. 33

Prince. Thou sayest well, and it holds well too; for the fortune of us that are the moon's men doth ebb and flow like the sea, being governed, as the sea is, by the moon. As, for proof, now: a purse of gold most resolutely snatched on Monday night and most dissolutely spent on Tuesday morning; got with swearing 'Lay by' and spent with crying 'Bring in;' now in as low an ebb as the foot of the ladder and by and by in as high a flow as the ridge of the gallows. 43

Fal. By the Lord, thou sayest true, lad. And is not my hostess of the tavern a most sweet wench?

Prince. As the honey of Hybla, my old lad of the castle. And is not a buff jerkin a most sweet robe of durance? 49

Fal. How now, how now, mad wag! what, in thy quips and thy quiddities? what a plague have I to do with a buff jerkin?

Prince. Why, what a pox have I to do with my hostess of the tavern?

Fal. Well, thou hast called her to a reckoning many a time and oft.

Prince. Did I ever call for thee to pay thy part?

Fal. No; I'll give thee thy due, thou hast paid all there. 60

Prince. Yea, and elsewhere, so far as my coin would stretch; and where it would not, I have used my credit.

Fal. Yea, and so used it that, were it not here apparent that thou art heir apparent—But, I prithee, sweet wag, shall there be gallows standing in England when thou art king? and resolution thus fobbed as it is with the rusty curb of old father antic the law? Do not thou, when thou art king, hang a thief. 70

Prince. No; thou shalt.

Fal. Shall I? O rare! By the Lord, I'll be a brave judge.

Prince. Thou judgest false already: I mean, thou shalt have the hanging of the thieves and so become a rare hangman.

Fal. Well, Hal, well; and in some sort it jumps

with my humour as well as waiting in the court, I can tell you.

Prince. For obtaining of suits? 80

Fal. Yea, for obtaining of suits, whereof the hangman hath no lean wardrobe. 'Sblood, I am as melancholy as a gib cat or a lugged bear.

Prince. Or an old lion, or a lover's lute.

Fal. Yea, or the drone of a Lincolnshire bagpipe.

Prince. What sayest thou to a hare, or the melancholy of Moor-ditch? 88

Fal. Thou hast the most unsavoury similes and art indeed the most comparative, rascalliest, sweet young prince. But, Hal, I prithee, trouble me no more with vanity. I would to God thou and I knew where a commodity of good names were to be bought. An old lord of the council rated me the other day in the street about you, sir, but I marked him not; and yet he talked very wisely, but I regarded him not; and yet he talked wisely, and in the street too.

Prince. Thou didst well; for wisdom cries out in the streets, and no man regards it. 100

Fal. O, thou hast damnable iteration and art indeed able to corrupt a saint. Thou hast done much harm upon me, Hal; God forgive thee for it! Before I knew thee, Hal, I knew nothing; and now am I, if a man should speak truly, little better than one of the wicked. I must give over this life, and I will give it over: by the Lord, an I do not, I am a villain: I'll be damned for never a king's son in Christendom.

Prince. Where shall we take a purse to-morrow, Jack? 111

Fal. 'Zounds, where thou wilt, lad; I'll make one; an I do not, call me villain and baffle me.

Prince. I see a good amendment of life in thee; from praying to purse-taking.

Fal. Why, Hal, 'tis my vocation, Hal; 'tis no sin for a man to labour in his vocation. 117

Enter POINS.

Poins! Now shall we know if Gadshill have set a match. O, if men were to be saved by merit, what hole in hell were hot enough for him? This is the most omnipotent villain that ever cried 'Stand' to a true man.

Prince. Good morrow, Ned.

Poins. Good morrow, sweet Hal. What says Monsieur Remorse? what says Sir John Sack and Sugar? Jack! how agrees the devil and thee about thy soul, that thou soldest him on Good-Friday last for a cup of Madeira and a cold capon's leg? 129

Prince. Sir John stands to his word, the devil shall have his bargain; for he was never yet a breaker of proverbs: he will give the devil his due.

Poins. Then art thou damned for keeping thy word with the devil.

Prince. Else he had been damned for cozening the devil. 137

SCENE II. **14. come near me now.** Prince Hal's speech has been full of extravagant abuse; Falstaff parries by taking it in a sense of his own. **16. the seven stars,** the Pleiades. **17-18. 'that . . . fair,'** a line from some ballad. **23. prologue,** punning allusion to grace before meat. **24. roundly,** out with it. It is a wit combat. **27-29. squires . . . beauty.** Note the euphuistic balance. Falstaff talks in the style of a courtier. **40. 'Lay by,'** a cry of highwaymen, like "Hands up!" **41. 'Bring in,'** i.e., the orders in the tavern. **47. Hybla,** a mountain region in Sicily near Syracuse, famed for honey. **48. old lad of the castle,** a pun on the name, Sir John Oldcastle, borne by Falstaff in the earlier versions of the Henry IV plays. **buff jerkin,** a leather jacket worn by officers of the law; a *robe of durance* in two senses, since *durance* means "imprison-

ment" and "durability." **51. quips,** jests. **quiddities,** subtleties of speech. **68. fobbed,** cheated. **69. antic,** the buffoon of the old plays. **78. waiting in the court,** in a double sense, as a courtier and a judge. **80. suits,** suits at court and suits of clothes. **82. 'Sblood,** an oath. **83. gib cat,** tomcat. **lugged bear,** bear dragged by a rope. **88. Moor-ditch,** a foul ditch draining Moorfields. **99. wisdom cries out,** etc., an allusion to Proverbs 1:20-24. **103. much harm upon me.** Oldcastle was traditionally a religious hypocrite and a Lollard, or follower of John Wycliffe; Falstaff retains his faculty for insincere repentance. **112. 'Zounds,** an oath, "God's wounds." **113. baffle,** hang up by the heels as a recreant knight. **116. vocation,** a cant term for religious conversion. **118. Gadshill,** an old name appearing

Poins. But, my lads, my lads, to-morrow morning, by four o'clock, early at Gadshill! there are pilgrims going to Canterbury with rich offerings, and traders riding to London with fat purses: I have vizards for you all; you have horses for yourselves: Gadshill lies to-night in Rochester: I have bespoke supper to-morrow night in Eastcheap: we may do it as secure as sleep. If you will go, I will stuff your purses full of crowns; if you will not, tarry at home and be hanged.

Fal. Hear ye, Yedward; if I tarry at home and go not, I'll hang you for going. 150

Poins. You will, chops?

Fal. Hal, wilt thou make one?

Prince. Who, I rob? I a thief? not I, by my faith.

Fal. There 's neither honesty, manhood, nor good fellowship in thee, nor thou camest not of the blood royal, if thou darest not stand for ten shillings. 158

Prince. Well then, once in my days I'll be a madcap.

Fal. Why, that 's well said.

Prince. Well, come what will, I'll tarry at home.

Fal. By the Lord, I'll be a traitor then, when thou art king.

Prince. I care not.

Poins. Sir John, I prithee, leave the prince and me alone: I will lay him down such reasons for this adventure that he shall go. 169

Fal. Well, God give thee the spirit of persuasion and him the ears of profiting, that what thou speakest may move and what he hears may be believed, that the true prince may, for recreation sake, prove a false thief; for the poor abuses of the time want countenance. Farewell: you shall find me in Eastcheap.

Prince. Farewell, thou latter spring! farewell, All-hallown summer! [*Exit Falstaff.* 178

Poins. Now, my good sweet honey lord, ride with us to-morrow: I have a jest to execute that I cannot manage alone. Falstaff, Bardolph, Peto and Gadshill shall rob those men that we have already waylaid; yourself and I will not be there; and when they have the booty, if you and I do not rob them, cut this head off from my shoulders.

Prince. How shall we part with them in setting forth? 188

Poins. Why, we will set forth before or after them, and appoint them a place of meeting, wherein it is at our pleasure to fail, and then will they adventure upon the exploit themselves; which they shall have no sooner achieved, but we'll set upon them.

Prince. Yea, but 'tis like that they will know us by our horses, by our habits and by every other appointment, to be ourselves. 198

Poins. Tut! our horses they shall not see; I'll tie them in the wood; our vizards we will change after we leave them: and, sirrah, I have cases of buckram for the nonce, to immask our noted outward garments.

Prince. Yea, but I doubt they will be too hard for us.

Poins. Well, for two of them, I know them to be as

true-bred cowards as ever turned back; and for the third, if he fight longer than he sees reason, I'll forswear arms. The virtue of this jest will be, the incomprehensible lies that this same fat rogue will tell us when we meet at supper: how thirty, at least, he fought with; what wards, what blows, what extremities he endured; and in the reproof of this lies the jest. 213

Prince. Well, I'll go with thee: provide us all things necessary and meet me to-morrow night in Eastcheap; there I'll sup. Farewell.

Poins. Farewell, my lord. [*Exit.*

Prince. I know you all, and will awhile uphold
The unyoked humour of your idleness:
Yet herein will I imitate the sun, 220
Who doth permit the base contagious clouds
To smother up his beauty from the world,
That, when he please again to be himself,
Being wanted, he may be more wonder'd at,
By breaking through the foul and ugly mists
Of vapours that did seem to strangle him.
If all the year were playing holidays,
To sport would be as tedious as to work;
But when they seldom come, they wish'd for come,
And nothing pleaseth but rare accidents. 230
So, when this loose behaviour I throw off
And pay the debt I never promised,
By how much better than my word I am,
By so much shall I falsify men's hopes;
And like bright metal on a sullen ground,
My reformation, glittering o'er my fault,
Shall show more goodly and attract more eyes
Than that which hath no foil to set it off.
I'll so offend, to make offence a skill;
Redeeming time when men think least I will. [*Exit.* 240

SCENE III. *London. The palace.*

Enter the KING, NORTHUMBERLAND, WORCESTER, HOTSPUR, SIR WALTER BLUNT, *with others.*

King. My blood hath been too cold and temperate,
Unapt to stir at these indignities,
And you have found me; for accordingly
You tread upon my patience: but be sure
I will from henceforth rather be myself,
Mighty and to be fear'd, than my condition;
Which hath been smooth as oil, soft as young down,
And therefore lost that title of respect
Which the proud soul ne'er pays but to the proud.

Wor. Our house, my sovereign liege, little deserves
The scourge of greatness to be used on it; 11
And that same greatness too which our own hands
Have holp to make so portly.

North. My lord,—

King. Worcester, get thee gone; for I do see

1 Henry IV
ACT I : SC III

679

in *The Famous Victories*, apparently from a hill southeast of London, notorious for highway robberies. 119. **set a match,** arranged a robbery. In the old play Gadshill is called a "setter." 142. **vizards,** masks. 149. **Yedward,** Edward; a colloquialism. 151. **chops,** apparently alluding to Falstaff's fat jaws. 170, 171. **spirit of persuasion, ears of profiting,** cant phrases of religious connotation. 178. **All-hallow summer.** Falstaff's summer (his youth) has lasted to All Saints' Day, November 1st. 182. **Bardolph, Peto,** so Theobald; QF: *Harvey, Rossill,* probably names of actors. 201. **cases,** suits. 202. **noted,** known. 208. **incomprehensible lies.** This passage serves dramatically as a preparation for the great fourth scene of the second act. 218-240. **I know . . . will.** This soliloquy is often misinterpreted. Some consider

Prince Hal a prig; others say that he, like his father, is a schemer, or that he makes a lame attempt to convince himself that he is justifiable. In point of fact, the author is merely talking to his audience and telling them his plans for his hero. Here, as is often the case in soliloquies, the speaker's character should not be judged by inferences from what he says; only the face value of the dramatist's words should be accepted.
SCENE III. 3. **found me,** i.e., found me so. 13. **portly,** prosperous, with a suggestion of overprosperity. 14. **My lord.** Northumberland is apparently about to protest against Worcester's impertinence; he is Worcester's brother and the head of the house of Percy, but he would not remind the king so obviously that they have seated him on his throne.

Danger and disobedience in thine eye:
O, sir, your presence is too bold and peremptory,
And majesty might never yet endure
The moody frontier of a servant brow.
You have good leave to leave us: when we need   20
Your use and counsel, we shall send for you.[*Exit Wor.*
You were about to speak.   [*To North.*
    North.   Yea, my good lord.
Those prisoners in your highness' name demanded,
Which Harry Percy here at Holmedon took,
Were, as he says, not with such strength denied
As is deliver'd to your majesty:
Either envy, therefore, or misprision
Is guilty of this fault and not my son.
    Hot. My liege, I did deny no prisoners.
But I remember, when the fight was done,   30
When I was dry with rage and extreme toil,
Breathless and faint, leaning upon my sword,
Came there a certain lord, neat, and trimly dress'd,
Fresh as a bridegroom; and his chin new reap'd
Show'd like a stubble-land at harvest-home;
He was perfumed like a milliner;
And 'twixt his finger and his thumb he held
A pouncet-box, which ever and anon
He gave his nose and took 't away again;
Who therewith angry, when it next came there,   40
Took it in snuff; and still he smiled and talk'd,
And as the soldiers bore dead bodies by,
He call'd them untaught knaves, unmannerly,
To bring a slovenly unhandsome corse
Betwixt the wind and his nobility.
With many holiday and lady terms
He question'd me; amongst the rest, demanded
My prisoners in your majesty's behalf.
I then, all smarting with my wounds being cold,
To be so pester'd with a popinjay,   50
Out of my grief and my impatience,
Answer'd neglectingly I know not what,
He should, or he should not; for he made me mad
To see him shine so brisk and smell so sweet
And talk so like a waiting-gentlewoman
Of guns and drums and wounds,—God save the
    mark!—
And telling me the sovereign'st thing on earth
Was parmaceti for an inward bruise;
And that it was great pity, so it was,
This villanous salt-petre should be digg'd   60
Out of the bowels of the harmless earth,
Which many a good tall fellow had destroy'd
So cowardly; and but for these vile guns,
He would himself have been a soldier.
This bald unjointed chat of his, my lord,
I answer'd indirectly, as I said;
And I beseech you, let not his report
Come current for an accusation
Betwixt my love and your high majesty.
    Blunt. The circumstance consider'd, good my lord,
Whate'er Lord Harry Percy then had said   71
To such a person and in such a place,

At such a time, with all the rest retold,
May reasonably die and never rise
To do him wrong or any way impeach
What then he said, so he unsay it now.
    King. Why, yet he doth deny his prisoners,
But with proviso and exception,
That we at our own charge shall ransom straight
His brother-in-law, the foolish Mortimer;   80
Who, on my soul, hath wilfully betray'd
The lives of those that he did lead to fight
Against that great magician, damn'd Glendower,
Whose daughter, as we hear, the Earl of March
Hath lately married. Shall our coffers, then,
Be emptied to redeem a traitor home?
Shall we buy treason? and indent with fears,
When they have lost and forfeited themselves?
No, on the barren mountains let him starve;
For I shall never hold that man my friend   90
Whose tongue shall ask me for one penny cost
To ransom home revolted Mortimer.
    Hot. Revolted Mortimer!
He never did fall off, my sovereign liege,
But by the chance of war: to prove that true
Needs no more but one tongue for all those wounds,
Those mouthed wounds, which valiantly he took,
When on the gentle Severn's sedgy bank,
In single opposition, hand to hand,
He did confound the best part of an hour   100
In changing hardiment with great Glendower:
Three times they breathed and three times did they
    drink,
Upon agreement, of swift Severn's flood;
Who then, affrighted with their bloody looks,
Ran fearfully among the trembling reeds,
And hid his crisp head in the hollow bank
Bloodstained with these valiant combatants.
Never did base and rotten policy
Colour her working with such deadly wounds;
Nor never could the noble Mortimer   110
Receive so many, and all willingly:
Then let not him be slander'd with revolt.
    King. Thou dost belie him, Percy, thou dost belie
    him;
He never did encounter with Glendower:
I tell thee,
He durst as well have met the devil alone
As Owen Glendower for an enemy.
Art thou not ashamed? But, sirrah, henceforth
Let me not hear you speak of Mortimer:
Send me your prisoners with the speediest means   120
Or you shall hear in such a kind from me
As will displease you. My Lord Northumberland,
We license your departure with your son.
Send us your prisoners, or you will hear of it.
    [*Exeunt King Henry, Blunt, and train.*
    Hot. An if the devil come and roar for them,
I will not send them: I will after straight
And tell him so; for I will ease my heart,
Albeit I make a hazard of my head.

19. **moody**, passionate, angry. **frontier**, outwork or fortification; here with play on the word *front* or *brow.* 27. **misprision**, misunderstanding. 29-69. **My . . . majesty.** Hotspur's speech, containing the famous description of the fop, is humorous, appealing, and not unfriendly. One must always feel that the stubborn directness of King Henry, reminiscent of the same quality in the Bolingbroke of *Richard II*, is most unfortunate. 35. **harvest-home**, end of harvest, fields being neat and bare. 36. **milliner**, man dealing in fancy articles. 38. **pouncet-box**, perfume box with perforated lid. 46. **lady**, ladylike. 50. **popinjay**, parrot. 56. **God save the mark.** Probably originally a formula to avert evil

omen; here, an expression of impatience. 58. **parmaceti**, spermaceti, sperm from the whale. 80, 84. **Mortimer, Earl of March.** There were two Edmund Mortimers, Shakespeare confuses them and combines their stories. It was the uncle (1378-1409?) who was captured by Glendower and married Glendower's daughter; it was the nephew (1391-1425), fourth earl of March, who had been proclaimed heir to King Richard II. 101. **hardiment**, bravery, daring. 118. **Art . . . sirrah.** It is the king's turn to wax insulting. Not only does he reject Hotspur's noble defense of his brother-in-law, Mortimer, but he reflects on Hotspur's sincerity and addresses him as "sirrah." The effect of this is to enrage Hotspur.

North. What, drunk with choler? stay and pause
    awhile:
Here comes your uncle.

          Re-enter WORCESTER.

Hot.   Speak of Mortimer!   130
'Zounds, I will speak of him; and let my soul
Want mercy, if I do not join with him:
Yea, on his part I'll empty all these veins,
And shed my dear blood drop by drop in the dust,
But I will lift the down-trod Mortimer
As high in the air as this unthankful king,
As this ingrate and canker'd Bolingbroke.
  North. Brother, the king hath made your nephew
    mad.
  Wor. Who struck this heat up after I was gone?
  Hot. He will, forsooth, have all my prisoners;   140
And when I urged the ransom once again
Of my wife's brother, then his cheek look'd pale,
And on my face he turn'd an eye of death,
Trembling even at the name of Mortimer.
  Wor. I cannot blame him: was not he proclaim'd
By Richard that dead is the next of blood?
  North. He was; I heard the proclamation:
And then it was when the unhappy king,—
Whose wrongs in us God pardon!—did set forth
Upon his Irish expedition;   150
From whence he intercepted did return
To be deposed and shortly murdered.
  Wor. And for whose death we in the world's wide
    mouth
Live scandalized and foully spoken of.
  Hot. But, soft, I pray you; did King Richard then
Proclaim my brother Edmund Mortimer
Heir to the crown?
  North.   He did; myself did hear it.
  Hot. Nay, then I cannot blame his cousin king,
That wish'd him on the barren mountains starve.
But shall it be, that you, that set the crown   160
Upon the head of this forgetful man
And for his sake wear the detested blot
Of murderous subornation, shall it be,
That you a world of curses undergo,
Being the agents, or base second means,
The cords, the ladder, or the hangman rather?
O, pardon me that I descend so low,
To show the line and the predicament
Wherein you range under this subtle king;
Shall it for shame be spoken in these days,   170
Or fill up chronicles in time to come,
That men of your nobility and power
Did gage them both in an unjust behalf,
As both of you—God pardon it!—have done,
To put down Richard, that sweet lovely rose,
And plant this thorn, this canker, Bolingbroke?
And shall it in more shame be further spoken,
That you are fool'd, discarded and shook off
By him for whom these shames ye underwent?
No; yet time serves wherein you may redeem   180

Your banish'd honours and restore yourselves
Into the good thoughts of the world again,
Revenge the jeering and disdain'd contempt
Of this proud king, who studies day and night
To answer all the debt he owes to you
Even with the bloody payment of your deaths:
Therefore, I say,—
  Wor.   Peace, cousin, say no more:
And now I will unclasp a secret book,
And to your quick-conceiving discontents
I'll read you matter deep and dangerous,   190
As full of peril and adventurous spirit
As to o'er-walk a current roaring loud
On the unsteadfast footing of a spear.
  Hot. If he fall in, good night! or sink or swim:
Send danger from the east unto the west,
So honour cross it from the north to south,
And let them grapple: O, the blood more stirs
To rouse a lion than to start a hare!
  North. Imagination of some great exploit
Drives him beyond the bounds of patience.   200
  Hot. By heaven, methinks it were an easy leap,
To pluck bright honour from the pale-faced moon,
Or dive into the bottom of the deep,
Where fathom-line could never touch the ground,
And pluck up drowned honour by the locks;
So he that doth redeem her thence might wear
Without corrival all her dignities:
But out upon this half-faced fellowship!
  Wor. He apprehends a world of figures here,
But not the form of what he should attend.   210
Good cousin, give me audience for a while.
  Hot. I cry you mercy.
  Wor.   Those same noble Scots
That are your prisoners,—
  Hot.   I'll keep them all;
By God, he shall not have a Scot of them;
No, if a Scot would save his soul, he shall not:
I'll keep them, by this hand.
  Wor.   You start away
And lend no ear unto my purposes.
Those prisoners you shall keep.
  Hot.   Nay, I will; that's flat:
He said he would not ransom Mortimer;
Forbad my tongue to speak of Mortimer;   220
But I will find him when he lies asleep,
And in his ear I'll holla 'Mortimer!'
Nay,
I'll have a starling shall be taught to speak
Nothing but 'Mortimer,' and give it him,
To keep his anger still in motion.
  Wor. Hear you, cousin; a word.
  Hot. All studies here I solemnly defy,
Save how to gall and pinch this Bolingbroke:
And that same sword-and-buckler Prince of Wales, 230
But that I think his father loves him not
And would be glad he met with some mischance,
I would have him poison'd with a pot of ale.
  Wor. Farewell, kinsman: I'll talk to you

and in the dialogue which follows we see him caught in the madness of
the passion of anger. 137. **canker'd,** spoiled, malignant. 145-152.
I . . . murdered. These lines and the dialogue as a whole serve to
connect this play with *Richard II* and to make clear the political situation back of the revolt. .163. **subornation,** oath-breaking, treason.
164. **a world of curses.** Treason against the king was treason against
God. 168. **predicament,** category. 176. **canker,** canker rose, dog rose.
183. **disdain'd,** disdainful. 199. **Imagination . . . exploit.** It will be
noticed that Northumberland thinks of Hotspur as beside himself,
insane; and so, according to the theory of passions which prevailed

at the time, he was. This line gives the theory of the effect of a
fixed idea, which lies back of the madness of Lear and Othello. 207.
corrival, rival, competitor. 208. **half-faced,** half-hearted. Shakespeare
represents Hotspur as actuated by chivalry exaggerated to the point
of madness. 226. **in motion,** i.e., he will not allow the spirits of anger
to settle or be diverted. 230. **sword-and-buckler,** arms improper for a
prince, who should carry rapier and dagger. 233. **poison'd.** This has
been called malicious; it is only part of Hotspur's madness.

When you are better temper'd to attend.

 North. Why, what a wasp-stung and impatient fool
Art thou to break into this woman's mood,
Tying thine ear to no tongue but thine own!

 Hot. Why, look you, I am whipp'd and scourged
  with rods,
Nettled and stung with pismires, when I hear 240
Of this vile politician, Bolingbroke.
In Richard's time,—what do you call the place?—
A plague upon it, it is in Gloucestershire;
'Twas where the madcap duke his uncle kept,
His uncle York; where I first bow'd my knee
Unto this king of smiles, this Bolingbroke,—
'Sblood!—
When you and he came back from Ravenspurgh.

 North. At Berkley castle.

 Hot. You say true: 250
Why, what a candy deal of courtesy
This fawning greyhound then did proffer me!
Look, 'when his infant fortune came to age,'
And 'gentle Harry Percy,' and 'kind cousin;'
O, the devil take such cozeners! God forgive me!
Good uncle, tell your tale; I have done.

 Wor. Nay, if you have not, to it again;
We will stay your leisure.

 Hot.   I have done, i' faith.

 Wor. Then once more to your Scottish prisoners.
Deliver them up without their ransom straight, 260
And make the Douglas' son your only mean
For powers in Scotland; which, for divers reasons
Which I shall send you written, be assured,
Will easily be granted. You, my lord,

          [*To Northumberland.*

Your son in Scotland being thus employ'd,
Shall secretly into the bosom creep
Of that same noble prelate, well beloved,
The archbishop.

 Hot. Of York, is it not?

 Wor. True; who bears hard 270
His brother's death at Bristol, the Lord Scroop.
I speak not this in estimation,
As what I think might be, but what I know
Is ruminated, plotted and set down,
And only stays but to behold the face
Of that occasion that shall bring it on.

 Hot. I smell it: upon my life, it will do well.

 North. Before the game is afoot, thou still let'st slip.

 Hot. Why, it cannot choose but be a noble plot:
And then the power of Scotland and of York, 280
To join with Mortimer, ha?

 Wor.   And so they shall.

 Hot. In faith, it is exceedingly well aim'd.

 Wor. And 'tis no little reason bids us speed,
To save our heads by raising of a head;
For, bear ourselves as even as we can,
The king will always think him in our debt,
And think we think ourselves unsatisfied,
Till he hath found a time to pay us home:

And see already how he doth begin
To make us strangers to his looks of love. 290

 Hot. He does, he does: we'll be revenged on him.

 Wor. Cousin, farewell: no further go in this
Than I by letters shall direct your course.
When time is ripe, which will be suddenly,
I'll steal to Glendower and Lord Mortimer;
Where you and Douglas and our powers at once,
As I will fashion it, shall happily meet,
To bear our fortunes in our own strong arms,
Which now we hold at much uncertainty.

 North. Farewell, good brother: we shall thrive, I
  trust. 300

 Hot. Uncle, adieu: O, let the hours be short
Till fields and blows and groans applaud our sport!

             [*Exeunt.*

ACT II.

SCENE I. *Rochester. An inn yard.*

Enter a Carrier *with a lantern in his hand.*

 First Car. Heigh-ho! an it be not four by the day,
I'll be hanged: Charles' wain is over the new chimney,
and yet our horse not packed. What, ostler!

 Ost. [*Within*] Anon, anon.

 First Car. I prithee, Tom, beat Cut's saddle, put a
few flocks in the point; poor jade, is wrung in the
withers out of all cess.

Enter another Carrier.

 Sec. Car. Peas and beans are as dank here as a dog,
and that is the next way to give poor jades the bots:
this house is turned upside down since Robin Ostler
died. 12

 First Car. Poor fellow, never joyed since the price
of oats rose; it was the death of him.

 Sec. Car. I think this be the most villanous house in
all London road for fleas: I am stung like a tench.

 First Car. Like a tench! by the mass, there is ne'er
a king christen could be better bit than I have been
since the first cock. 20

 Sec. Car. Why, they will allow us ne'er a jordan, and
then we leak in your chimney; and your chamber-lie
breeds fleas like a loach.

 First Car. What, ostler! come away and be hanged!
come away.

 Sec. Car. I have a gammon of bacon and two razes of
ginger, to be delivered as far as Charing-cross. 28

 First Car. God's body! the turkeys in my pannier
are quite starved. What, ostler! A plague on thee!
hast thou never an eye in thy head? canst not hear?
An 'twere not as good deed as drink, to break the
pate on thee, I am a very villain. Come, and be
hanged! hast no faith in thee?

Enter GADSHILL.

Gads. Good morrow, carriers. What 's o'clock?

First Car. I think it be two o'clock.

Gads. I prithee, lend me thy lantern, to see my gelding in the stable.

First Car. Nay, by God, soft; I know a trick worth two of that, i' faith. 41

Gads. I pray thee, lend me thine.

Sec. Car. Ay, when? canst tell? Lend me thy lantern, quoth he? marry, I'll see thee hanged first.

Gads. Sirrah carrier, what time do you mean to come to London?

Sec. Car. Time enough to go to bed with a candle, I warrant thee. Come, neighbour Mugs, we'll call up the gentlemen: they will along with company, for they have great charge. [*Exeunt Carriers.*

Gads. What, ho! chamberlain! 52

Cham. [*Within*] At hand, quoth pick-purse.

Gads. That 's even as fair as—at hand, quoth the chamberlain; for thou variest no more from picking of purses than giving direction doth from labouring; thou layest the plot how.

Enter Chamberlain.

Cham. Good morrow, Master Gadshill. It holds current that I told you yesternight: there 's a franklin in the wild of Kent hath brought three hundred marks with him in gold: I heard him tell it to one of his company last night at supper; a kind of auditor; one that hath abundance of charge too, God knows what. They are up already, and call for eggs and butter: they will away presently.

Gads. Sirrah, if they meet not with Saint Nicholas' clerks, I'll give thee this neck. 69

Cham. No, I'll none of it: I pray thee, keep that for the hangman; for I know thou worshippest Saint Nicholas as truly as a man of falsehood may.

Gads. What talkest thou to me of the hangman? if I hang, I'll make a fat pair of gallows; for if I hang, old Sir John hangs with me, and thou knowest he is no starveling. Tut! there are other Trojans that thou dreamest not of, the which for sport sake are content to do the profession some grace; that would, if matters should be looked into, for their own credit sake, make all whole. I am joined with no foot land-rakers, no long-staff sixpenny strikers, none of these mad mustachio purple-hued malt-worms; but with nobility and tranquillity, burgomasters and great oneyers, such as can hold in, such as will strike sooner than speak, and speak sooner than drink, and drink sooner than pray: and yet, 'zounds, I lie; for they pray continually to their saint, the commonwealth; or rather, not pray to her, but prey on her, for they ride up and down on her and make her their boots. 91

Cham. What, the commonwealth their boots? will she hold out water in foul way?

Gads. She will, she will; justice hath liquored her. We steal as in a castle, cocksure; we have the receipt of fern-seed, we walk invisible.

Cham. Nay, by my faith, I think you are more beholding to the night than to fern-seed for your walking invisible.

Gads. Give me thy hand: thou shalt have a share in our purchase, as I am a true man. 101

Cham. Nay, rather let me have it, as you are a false thief.

Gads. Go to; 'homo' is a common name to all men. Bid the ostler bring my gelding out of the stable. Farewell, you muddy knave. [*Exeunt.*

SCENE II. *The highway, near Gadshill.*

Enter PRINCE HENRY *and* POINS.

Poins. Come, shelter, shelter: I have removed Falstaff's horse, and he frets like a gummed velvet.

Prince. Stand close.

Enter FALSTAFF.

Fal. Poins! Poins, and be hanged! Poins!

Prince. Peace, ye fat-kidneyed rascal! what a brawling dost thou keep!

Fal. Where 's Poins, Hal?

Prince. He is walked up to the top of the hill: I'll go seek him. 9

Fal. I am accursed to rob in that thief's company: the rascal hath removed my horse, and tied him I know not where. If I travel but four foot by the squier further afoot, I shall break my wind. Well, I doubt not but to die a fair death for all this, if I 'scape hanging for killing that rogue. I have forsworn his company hourly any time this two and twenty years, and yet I am bewitched with the rogue's company. If the rascal have not given me medicines to make me love him, I'll be hanged; it could not be else; I have drunk medicines. Poins! Hal! a plague upon you both! Bardolph! Peto! I'll starve ere I'll rob a foot further. An 'twere not as good a deed as drink, to turn true man and to leave these rogues, I am the veriest varlet that ever chewed with a tooth. Eight yards of uneven ground is threescore and ten miles afoot with me; and the stony-hearted villains know it well enough: a plague upon it when thieves cannot be true one to another! [*They whistle.*] Whew! A plague upon you all! Give me my horse, you rogues; give me my horse, and be hanged!

Prince. Peace, ye fat-guts! lie down; lay thine ear close to the ground and list if thou canst hear the tread of travellers.

Fal. Have you any levers to lift me up again, being down? 'Sblood, I'll not bear mine own flesh so far afoot again for all the coin in thy father's exchequer. What a plague mean ye to colt me thus? 40

Prince. Thou liest; thou art not colted, thou art uncolted.

Fal. I prithee, good Prince Hal, help me to my horse, good king's son.

1 Henry IV
ACT II : SC II

683

---

weald (wooded region) of Kent. 62. **marks,** coins of the value in that day of 13s. 6d. 65. **charge,** tavern bill. 68. **Saint Nicholas' clerks,** highwaymen. St. Nicholas was vulgarly supposed the patron of thieves. 77. **Trojans,** slang for "thieves." 81. **foot land-rakers,** footpads. 82. **long-staff sixpenny strikers,** robbers with long staves who would knock down their victims for sixpence. 83. **mustachio purple-hued malt-worms,** common drunkards with mustaches stained with drink. 85. **oneyers,** many conjectures; possibly, a coinage from *ones* with pun on *owner* (White). 91. **boots,** booty, with pun on "boots." 95. **liquored,** made waterproof by oiling, and made drunk. 96. **of fern-seed,** i.e.,

of becoming invisible, since fern seed was popularly supposed to render its possessor invisible. 104. **'homo,'** apparently a definition from the Latin grammar, meaning here, "Don't call names." The scene would suggest to sober-minded people the danger of a situation in which robbery would have royal patronage.

SCENE II. 2. **frets,** chafes, with pun on another meaning of the word applying to velvet with the nap awry. 13. **squier,** square, measure. 20. **medicines,** ridiculous allusion to love potions. 25. **turn true man,** turn honest man; possibly, turn informer. 40. **colt,** cheat.

Prince. Out, ye rogue! shall I be your ostler?

Fal. Go hang thyself in thine own heir-apparent garters! If I be ta'en, I'll peach for this. An I have not ballads made on you all and sung to filthy tunes, let a cup of sack be my poison: when a jest is so forward, and afoot too! I hate it.

Enter GADSHILL, BARDOLPH *and* PETO *with him.*

Gads. Stand.

Fal. So I do, against my will. 52

Poins. O, 'tis our setter: I know his voice. Bardolph, what news?

Bard. Case ye, case ye; on with your vizards: there's money of the king's coming down the hill; 'tis going to the king's exchequer.

Fal. You lie, ye rogue; 'tis going to the king's tavern.

Gads. There's enough to make us all. 60

Fal. To be hanged.

Prince. Sirs, you four shall front them in the narrow lane; Ned Poins and I will walk lower: if they 'scape from your encounter, then they light on us.

Peto. How many be there of them?

Gads. Some eight or ten.

Fal. 'Zounds, will they not rob us?

Prince. What, a coward, Sir John Paunch?

Fal. Indeed, I am not John of Gaunt, your grandfather; but yet no coward, Hal. 71

Prince. Well, we leave that to the proof.

Poins. Sirrah Jack, thy horse stands behind the hedge: when thou needest him, there thou shalt find him. Farewell, and stand fast.

Fal. Now cannot I strike him, if I should be hanged.

Prince. Ned, where are our disguises?

Poins. Here, hard by: stand close.

[*Exeunt Prince and Poins.*

Fal. Now, my masters, happy man be his dole, say I: every man to his business. 81

Enter the Travellers.

First Trav. Come, neighbour: the boy shall lead our horses down the hill; we'll walk afoot awhile, and ease our legs.

Thieves. Stand!

Travellers. Jesus bless us!

Fal. Strike; down with them; cut the villains' throats: ah! whoreson caterpillars! bacon-fed knaves! they hate us youth: down with them; fleece them. 90

Travellers. O, we are undone, both we and ours for ever!

Fal. Hang ye, gorbellied knaves, are ye undone? No, ye fat chuffs; I would your store were here! On, bacons, on! What, ye knaves! young men must live. You are grandjurors, are ye? we'll jure ye, 'faith.

[*Here they rob them and bind them. Exeunt.*

Re-enter PRINCE HENRY *and* POINS.

Prince. The thieves have bound the true men. Now could thou and I rob the thieves and go merrily to London, it would be argument for a week, laughter for a month and a good jest for ever.

Poins. Stand close; I hear them coming.

Enter the Thieves again.

Fal. Come, my masters, let us share, and then to horse before day. An the Prince and Poins be not two arrant cowards, there's no equity stirring: there's no more valour in that Poins than in a wild-duck.

Prince. Your money!

Poins. Villains! 110

[*As they are sharing, the Prince and Poins set upon them; they all run away; and Falstaff, after a blow or two, runs away too, leaving the booty behind them.*

Prince. Got with much ease. Now merrily to horse:
The thieves are all scatter'd and possess'd with fear
So strongly that they dare not meet each other;
Each takes his fellow for an officer.
Away, good Ned. Falstaff sweats to death,
And lards the lean earth as he walks along:
Were 't not for laughing, I should pity him.

Poins. How the fat rogue roar'd! [*Exeunt.*

SCENE III. *Warkworth castle.*

Enter HOTSPUR, *solus, reading a letter.*

Hot. 'But, for mine own part, my lord, I could be well contented to be there, in respect of the love I bear your house.' He could be contented: why is he not, then? In respect of the love he bears our house: he shows in this, he loves his own barn better than he loves our house. Let me see some more. 'The purpose you undertake is dangerous;'—why, that's certain: 'tis dangerous to take a cold, to sleep, to drink; but I tell you, my lord fool, out of this nettle, danger, we pluck this flower, safety. 'The purpose you undertake is dangerous; the friends you have named uncertain; the time itself unsorted; and your whole plot too light for the counterpoise of so great an opposition.' Say you so, say you so? I say unto you again, you are a shallow cowardly hind, and you lie. What a lackbrain is this! By the Lord, our plot is a good plot as ever was laid; our friends true and constant: a good plot, good friends, and full of expectation; an excellent plot, very good friends. What a frosty-spirited rogue is this! Why, my lord of York commends the plot and the general course of the action. 'Zounds, an I were now by this rascal, I could brain him with his lady's fan. Is there not my father, my uncle and myself? lord Edmund Mortimer, my lord of York and Owen Glendower? is there not besides the Douglas? have I not all their letters to meet me in arms by the ninth of the next month? and are they not some of them set forward already? What a pagan rascal is this! an infidel! Ha! you shall see now in very sincerity of fear and cold heart, will he to the king and lay open all our proceedings. O, I could divide myself and go to buffets, for moving such a dish of skim milk with so honourable an action! Hang him! let him tell the king: we are prepared. I will set forward to-night.

---

47. **garters,** an allusion to a proverbial expression about hanging oneself in one's garters, with a pun on the Order of the Garter. 53. **setter,** arranger of the robbery. 55. **Case ye,** put on your disguises. 80. **happy man be his dole,** may happiness be his portion. 88. **caterpillars,** those who thrive off the commonwealth. 93. **gorbellied,** big-bellied. 94. **chuffs,** churls, rich but miserly. 95. **bacons,** swine. 107. **equity,** justice; variously interpreted. 116. **lards the lean earth,** an allusion to the practice on the part of butchers of inserting fat into lean meat. "Sweat" was not distinguished from fat. 118. **fat,** introduced by Neilson from a fragmentary Q$_1$; not in Globe.

SCENE III. 56. **basilisks,** large cannon. **culverin,** long cannon. 58. **currents,** occurrences. 61-67. **beads . . . not.** The physiological aspects of violent passion recorded here are in line with the psychology of the time. 74. **esperance,** hope; the motto of the Percy family. 88.

Enter LADY PERCY.

How now, Kate! I must leave you within these two
    hours.
   Lady. O, my good lord, why are you thus alone?   40
For what offence have I this fortnight been
A banish'd woman from my Harry's bed?
Tell me, sweet lord, what is 't that takes from thee
Thy stomach, pleasure and thy golden sleep?
Why dost thou bend thine eyes upon the earth,
And start so often when thou sit'st alone?
Why hast thou lost the fresh blood in thy cheeks;
And given my treasures and my rights of thee
To thick-eyed musing and cursed melancholy?
In thy faint slumbers I by thee have watch'd,   50
And heard thee murmur tales of iron wars;
Speak terms of manage to thy bounding steed;
Cry 'Courage! to the field!' And thou hast talk'd
Of sallies and retires, of trenches, tents,
Of palisadoes, frontiers, parapets,
Of basilisks, of cannon, culverin,
Of prisoners' ransom and of soldiers slain,
And all the currents of a heady fight.
Thy spirit within thee hath been so at war
And thus hath so bestirr'd thee in thy sleep,   60
That beads of sweat have stood upon thy brow,
Like bubbles in a late-disturbed stream;
And in thy face strange motions have appear'd,
Such as we see when men restrain their breath
On some great sudden hest. O, what portents are
    these?
Some heavy business hath my lord in hand,
And I must know it, else he loves me not.
   Hot. What, ho!

Enter Servant.
            Is Gilliams with the packet gone?
   Serv. He is, my lord, an hour ago.
   Hot. Hath Butler brought those horses from the
    sheriff?   70
   Serv. One horse, my lord, he brought even now.
   Hot. What horse? a roan, a crop-ear, is it not?
   Serv. It is, my lord.
   Hot.   That roan shall be my throne.
Well, I will back him straight: O esperance!
Bid Butler lead him forth into the park.   [*Exit Servant.*
   Lady. But hear you, my lord.
   Hot. What say'st thou, my lady?
   Lady. What is it carries you away?
   Hot. Why, my horse, my love, my horse.
   Lady. Out, you mad-headed ape!   80
A weasel hath not such a deal of spleen
As you are toss'd with. In faith,
I'll know your business, Harry, that I will.
I fear my brother Mortimer doth stir
About his title, and hath sent for you
To line his enterprize: but if you go,—
   Hot. So far afoot, I shall be weary, love.
   Lady. Come, come, you paraquito, answer me
Directly unto this question that I ask:
In faith, I'll break thy little finger, Harry,   90
An if thou wilt not tell me all things true.

   Hot. Away,
Away, you trifler! Love! I love thee not,
I care not for thee, Kate: this is no world
To play with mammets and to tilt with lips:
We must have bloody noses and crack'd crowns,
And pass them current too. God 's me, my horse!
What say'st thou, Kate? what would'st thou have
    with me?
   Lady. Do you not love me? do you not, indeed?
Well, do not then; for since you love me not,   100
I will not love myself. Do you not love me?
Nay, tell me if you speak in jest or no.
   Hot. Come, wilt thou see me ride?
And when I am o' horseback, I will swear
I love thee infinitely. But hark you, Kate:
I must not have you henceforth question me
Whither I go, nor reason whereabout:
Whither I must, I must; and, to conclude,
This evening must I leave you, gentle Kate.
I know you wise, but yet no farther wise   110
Than Harry Percy's wife: constant you are,
But yet a woman: and for secrecy,
No lady closer; for I well believe
Thou wilt not utter what thou dost not know;
And so far will I trust thee, gentle Kate.
   Lady. How! so far?
   Hot. Not an inch further. But hark you, Kate:
Whither I go, thither shall you go too;
To-day will I set forth, to-morrow you.
Will this content you, Kate?
   Lady.   It must of force. [*Exeunt.* 120

1 Henry IV
ACT II : SC IV

685

SCENE IV. *The Boar's-Head Tavern, Eastcheap.*

Enter the PRINCE, *and* POINS.

   Prince. Ned, prithee, come out of that fat room, and
lend me thy hand to laugh a little.
   Poins. Where hast been, Hal?
   Prince. With three or four loggerheads amongst
three or four score hogsheads. I have sounded the
very base-string of humility. Sirrah, I am sworn
brother to a leash of drawers; and can call them all
by their christen names, as Tom, Dick, and Francis.
They take it already upon their salvation, that though
I be but Prince of Wales, yet I am the king of courtesy;
and tell me flatly I am no proud Jack, like Falstaff,
but a Corinthian, a lad of mettle, a good boy, by the
Lord, so they call me, and when I am king of England, I shall command all the good lads in Eastcheap.
They call drinking deep, dyeing scarlet; and when
you breathe in your watering, they cry 'hem!' and
bid you play it off. To conclude, I am so good a
proficient in one quarter of an hour, that I can
drink with any tinker in his own language during my
life. I tell thee, Ned, thou hast lost much honour,
that thou wert not with me in this action. But, sweet
Ned,—to sweeten which name of Ned, I give thee
this pennyworth of sugar, clapped even now into

---

paraquito, little parrot; term of endearment. 90. **break thy little
finger.** She probably squeezes his folded little finger. 95. **mammets,**
dolls; or else breasts. 96. **crowns,** obvious pun on the coin called a
"crown." 120. **It must of force.** Some critics have unnecessarily seen
in this interview evidence of cruelty on Hotspur's part and lack of
marital confidence.
   SCENE IV. 1. **fat,** vat. 4. **loggerheads,** blockheads. 7. **sworn**

brother, allusion to the practice of becoming *fratres jurati.* **leash of
drawers,** i.e., three waiters (like three greyhounds). 13. **Corinthian,**
gay fellow, with suggestion of profligacy. 18. **watering,** drinking.
20-21. **tinker . . . language.** Tinkers' language was cant or jargon, and
tinkers were proverbial drinkers.

my hand by an under-skinker, one that never spake other English in his life than 'Eight shillings and sixpence,' and 'You are welcome,' with this shrill addition, 'Anon, anon, sir! Score a pint of bastard in the Half-moon,' or so. But, Ned, to drive away the time till Falstaff come, I prithee, do thou stand in some by-room, while I question my puny drawer to what end he gave me the sugar; and do thou never leave calling 'Francis,' that his tale to me may be nothing but 'Anon.' Step aside, and I'll show thee a precedent.

Poins. Francis!
Prince. Thou art perfect.   39
Poins. Francis!   [*Exit Poins.*

Enter FRANCIS.

Fran. Anon, anon, sir. Look down into the Pomgarnet, Ralph.
Prince. Come hither, Francis.
Fran. My lord?
Prince. How long hast thou to serve, Francis?
Fran. Forsooth, five years, and as much as to—
Poins. [*Within*] Francis!
Fran. Anon, anon, sir.   49
Prince. Five year! by'r lady, a long lease for the clinking of pewter. But, Francis, darest thou be so valiant as to play the coward with thy indenture and show it a fair pair of heels and run from it?
Fran. O Lord, sir, I'll be sworn upon all the books in England, I could find in my heart.
Poins. [*Within*] Francis!
Fran. Anon, sir.
Prince. How old art thou, Francis?
Fran. Let me see—about Michaelmas next I shall be—   61
Poins. [*Within*] Francis!
Fran. Anon, sir. Pray stay a little, my lord.
Prince. Nay, but hark you, Francis: for the sugar thou gavest me, 'twas a pennyworth, was't not?
Fran. O Lord, I would it had been two!
Prince. I will give thee for it a thousand pound: ask me when thou wilt, and thou shalt have it.   70
Poins. [*Within*] Francis!
Fran. Anon, anon.
Prince. Anon, Francis? No, Francis; but to-morrow, Francis; or Francis, o' Thursday; or indeed, Francis, when thou wilt. But, Francis!
Fran. My lord?
Prince. Wilt thou rob this leathern jerkin, crystal-button, not-pated, agate-ring, puke-stocking, caddis-garter, smooth-tongue, Spanish-pouch,—   80
Fran. O Lord, sir, who do you mean?
Prince. Why, then, your brown bastard is your only drink; for look you, Francis, your white canvas doublet will sully: in Barbary, sir, it cannot come to so much.
Fran. What, sir?
Poins. [*Within*] Francis!

Prince. Away, you rogue! dost thou not hear them call?   89
[*Here they both call him; the drawer stands amazed, not knowing which way to go.*

Enter Vintner.

Vint. What, standest thou still, and hearest such a calling? Look to the guests within. [*Exit Francis.*] My lord, old Sir John, with half-a-dozen more, are at the door: shall I let them in?
Prince. Let them alone awhile, and then open the door. [*Exit Vintner.*] Poins!

Re-enter POINS.

Poins. Anon, anon, sir.
Prince. Sirrah, Falstaff and the rest of the thieves are at the door: shall we be merry?   99
Poins. As merry as crickets, my lad. But hark ye; what cunning match have you made with this jest of the drawer? come, what's the issue?
Prince. I am now of all humours that have showed themselves humours since the old days of goodman Adam to the pupil age of this present twelve o'clock at midnight.

Re-enter FRANCIS.

What's o'clock, Francis?
Fran. Anon, anon, sir.   [*Exit.* 109
Prince. That ever this fellow should have fewer words than a parrot, and yet the son of a woman! His industry is up-stairs and down-stairs; his eloquence the parcel of a reckoning. I am not yet of Percy's mind, the Hotspur of the north; he that kills me some six or seven dozen of Scots at a breakfast, washes his hands, and says to his wife 'Fie upon this quiet life! I want work.' 'O my sweet Harry,' says she, 'how many hast thou killed to-day?' 'Give my roan horse a drench,' says he; and answers 'Some fourteen,' an hour after; 'a trifle, a trifle.' I prithee, call in Falstaff: I'll play Percy, and that damned brawn shall play Dame Mortimer his wife. 'Rivo!' says the drunkard. Call in ribs, call in tallow.   125

Enter FALSTAFF, GADSHILL, BARDOLPH, *and* PETO; FRANCIS *following with wine.*

Poins. Welcome, Jack: where hast thou been?
Fal. A plague of all cowards, I say, and a vengeance too! marry, and amen! Give me a cup of sack, boy. Ere I lead this life long, I'll sew nether stocks and mend them and foot them too. A plague of all cowards! Give me a cup of sack, rogue. Is there no virtue extant?   [*He drinks.*
Prince. Didst thou never see Titan kiss a dish of butter? pitiful-hearted Titan, that melted at the sweet tale of the sun's! if thou didst, then behold that compound.   136
Fal. You rogue, here's lime in this sack too: there is nothing but roguery to be found in villanous man: yet a coward is worse than a cup of sack with lime in

26. **under-skinker,** under-tapster. 31. **bastard,** sweet Spanish wine. **Half-moon,** name of a room in the inn. 35. **puny,** in the ordinary sense with a pun on the original *puisné,* younger son, applied to the second drawer. 37. **precedent,** example. The spectacle of the young prince disporting himself among drawers may have been delightful to the popular mind, but the scene has lost much of its humor. 78. **not-pated,** crop-haired. **puke-stocking,** dark-colored stocking. 79. **caddis-garter,** worsted garter. Since garters were worn in sight, they needed to be of better stuff than common worsted. The prince's epithets

seem to apply to the vintner, the boy's master. 82-85. **Why . . . much.** The prince talks complete nonsense in order to bewilder Francis. 106. **goodman,** a sort of familiar title. **pupil age,** i.e., the day is young. 113. **parcel,** item. 124. **'Rivo!'** An interjection of doubtful meaning; certainly bacchanalian. 130. **nether stocks,** stockings. 134. **pitiful-hearted Titan.** Theobald suggested *butter* for *Titan,* which still seems the best way to explain this apparently contradictory passage. 137. **lime in this sack,** i.e., used as a preservative. 143. **shotten herring,** a herring that has cast its roe and is thin. 147. **weaver,** allusion to psalm-it. A villanous coward! Go thy ways, old Jack; die when thou wilt, if manhood, good manhood, be not forgot upon the face of the earth, then am I a shotten herring. There live not three good men unhanged in England; and one of them is fat and grows old: God help the while! a bad world, I say. I would I were a weaver; I could sing psalms or any thing. A plague of all cowards, I say still.

Prince. How now, wool-sack! what mutter you? 149

Fal. A king's son! If I do not beat thee out of thy kingdom with a dagger of lath, and drive all thy subjects afore thee like a flock of wild-geese, I'll never wear hair on my face more. You Prince of Wales!

Prince. Why, you whoreson round man, what's the matter?

Fal. Are not you a coward? answer me to that: and Poins there?

Poins. 'Zounds, ye fat paunch, and ye call me coward, by the Lord, I'll stab thee. 160

Fal. I call thee coward! I'll see thee damned ere I call thee coward: but I would give a thousand pound I could run as fast as thou canst. You are straight enough in the shoulders, you care not who sees your back: call you that backing of your friends? A plague upon such backing! give me them that will face me. Give me a cup of sack: I am a rogue, if I drunk to-day.

Prince. O villain! thy lips are scarce wiped since thou drunkest last. 171

Fal. All's one for that. [*He drinks.*] A plague of all cowards, still say I.

Prince. What's the matter?

Fal. What's the matter! there be four of us here have ta'en a thousand pound this day morning.

Prince. Where is it, Jack? where is it?

Fal. Where is it! taken from us it is: a hundred upon poor four of us. 180

Prince. What, a hundred, man?

Fal. I am a rogue, if I were not at half-sword with a dozen of them two hours together. I have 'scaped by miracle. I am eight times thrust through the doublet, four through the hose; my buckler cut through and through; my sword hacked like a hand-saw—ecce signum! I never dealt better since I was a man: all would not do. A plague of all cowards! Let them speak: if they speak more or less than truth, they are villains and the sons of darkness. 191

Prince. Speak, sirs; how was it?

Gads. We four set upon some dozen—

Fal. Sixteen at least, my lord.

Gads. And bound them.

Peto. No, no, they were not bound.

Fal. You rogue, they were bound, every man of them; or I am a Jew else, an Ebrew Jew.

Gads. As we were sharing, some six or seven fresh men set upon us— 200

Fal. And unbound the rest, and then come in the other.

Prince. What, fought you with them all?

Fal. All! I know not what you call all; but if I fought not with fifty of them, I am a bunch of radish: if there were not two or three and fifty upon poor old Jack, then am I no two-legged creature.

Prince. Pray God you have not murdered some of them. 210

Fal. Nay, that's past praying for: I have peppered two of them; two I am sure I have paid, two rogues in buckram suits. I tell thee what, Hal, if I tell thee a lie, spit in my face, call me horse. Thou knowest my old ward; here I lay, and thus I bore my point. Four rogues in buckram let drive at me—

Prince. What, four? thou saidst but two even now.

Fal. Four, Hal; I told thee four. 220

Poins. Ay, ay, he said four.

Fal. These four came all a-front, and mainly thrust at me. I made me no more ado but took all their seven points in my target, thus.

Prince. Seven? why, there were but four even now.

Fal. In buckram?

Poins. Ay, four, in buckram suits.

Fal. Seven, by these hilts, or I am a villain else. 230

Prince. Prithee, let him alone; we shall have more anon.

Fal. Dost thou hear me, Hal?

Prince. Ay, and mark thee too, Jack.

Fal. Do so, for it is worth the listening to. These nine in buckram that I told thee of—

Prince. So, two more already.

Fal. Their points being broken,—

Poins. Down fell their hose. 239

Fal. Began to give me ground: but I followed me close, came in foot and hand; and with a thought seven of the eleven I paid.

Prince. O monstrous! eleven buckram men grown out of two!

Fal. But, as the devil would have it, three misbegotten knaves in Kendal green came at my back and let drive at me; for it was so dark, Hal, that thou couldst not see thy hand.

Prince. These lies are like their father that begets them; gross as a mountain, open, palpable. Why, thou clay-brained guts, thou knotty-pated fool, thou whoreson, obscene, greasy tallow-catch,— 253

Fal. What, art thou mad? art thou mad? is not the truth the truth?

Prince. Why, how couldst thou know these men in Kendal green, when it was so dark thou couldst not see thy hand? come, tell us your reason: what sayest thou to this?

Poins. Come, your reason, Jack, your reason. 260

Fal. What, upon compulsion? 'Zounds, an I were at the strappado, or all the racks in the world, I would not tell you on compulsion. Give you a reason on compulsion! if reasons were as plentiful as blackberries, I would give no man a reason upon compulsion, I. 266

Prince. I'll be no longer guilty of this sin; this san-

1 Henry IV
ACT II : SC IV

687

---

singing Protestants from Flanders, mainly weavers. 151. **dagger of lath.** The Vice in the interludes was so armed, as no doubt other clowns were. 161-163. **I call . . . canst.** This is a typical example of Falstaff's method of turning aside an issue and at the same time maintaining his point. 182. **half-sword,** fighting at close quarters. 187. **ecce signum,** behold the proof; familiar words from the Mass. 213. **buckram,** coarse linen cloth stiffened. 215. **ward,** guard in fencing. 223. **mainly,** powerfully. 224. **target,** shield; see glossary. 238. **points.** Falstaff uses *points* to mean "swords"; Poins' reply introduces a pun on the same

word meaning the "laces" by which the hose were attached to the doublet and so supported. 240. **followed me,** a sort of reflexive or middle voice. 246. **Kendal green,** green cloth worn by foresters. 253. **tallow-catch,** explained as "tallow-tub," and as "tallow-keech," a roll of fat delivered by the butcher to the tallow chandler. It has been pointed out that such breathless strings of epithets of abuse are characteristic of Latin comedy. 264. **reason . . . blackberries.** Falstaff not only avoids the issue, but also turns it into a jest by punning on the word "raisins," which was pronounced nearly like *reasons.*

guine coward, this bed-presser, this horseback-breaker, this huge hill of flesh,—

Fal. 'Sblood, you starveling, you elf-skin, you dried neat's tongue, you bull's pizzle, you stock-fish! O for breath to utter what is like thee! you tailor's-yard, you sheath, you bow-case, you vile standing-tuck,—

Prince. Well, breathe awhile, and then to it again: and when thou hast tired thyself in base comparisons, hear me speak but this. 277

Poins. Mark, Jack.

Prince. We two saw you four set on four and bound them, and were masters of their wealth. Mark now, how a plain tale shall put you down. Then did we two set on you four; and, with a word, out-faced you from your prize, and have it; yea, and can show it you here in the house: and, Falstaff, you carried your guts away as nimbly, with as quick dexterity, and roared for mercy and still run and roared, as ever I heard bull-calf. What a slave art thou, to hack thy sword as thou hast done, and then say it was in fight! What trick, what device, what starting-hole, canst thou now find out to hide thee from this open and apparent shame? 293

Poins. Come, let's hear, Jack; what trick hast thou now?

Fal. By the Lord, I knew ye as well as he that made ye. Why, hear you, my masters: was it for me to kill the heir-apparent? should I turn upon the true prince? why, thou knowest I am as valiant as Hercules: but beware instinct; the lion will not touch the true prince. Instinct is a great matter; I was now a coward on instinct. I shall think the better of myself and thee during my life; I for a valiant lion, and thou for a true prince. But, by the Lord, lads, I am glad you have the money. Hostess, clap to the doors: watch to-night, pray to-morrow. Gallants, lads, boys, hearts of gold, all the titles of good fellowship come to you! What, shall we be merry? shall we have a play extempore?

Prince. Content; and the argument shall be thy running away. 311

Fal. Ah, no more of that, Hal, an thou lovest me!

Enter Hostess.

Host. O Jesu, my lord the prince!

Prince. How now, my lady the hostess! what sayest thou to me?

Host. Marry, my lord, there is a nobleman of the court at door would speak with you: he says he comes from your father. 319

Prince. Give him as much as will make him a royal man, and send him back again to my mother.

Fal. What manner of man is he?

Host. An old man.

Fal. What doth gravity out of his bed at midnight? Shall I give him his answer?

Prince. Prithee, do, Jack.

Fal. 'Faith, and I'll send him packing. [*Exit.*

Prince. Now, sirs: by 'r lady, you fought fair; so did you, Peto; so did you, Bardolph: you are lions too,

you ran away upon instinct, you will not touch the true prince; no, fie! 332

Bard. 'Faith, I ran when I saw others run.

Prince. 'Faith, tell me now in earnest, how came Falstaff's sword so hacked?

Peto. Why, he hacked it with his dagger, and said he would swear truth out of England but he would make you believe it was done in fight, and persuaded us to do the like. 339

Bard. Yea, and to tickle our noses with spear-grass to make them bleed, and then to beslubber our garments with it and swear it was the blood of true men. I did that I did not this seven year before, I blushed to hear his monstrous devices.

Prince. O villain, thou stolest a cup of sack eighteen years ago, and wert taken with the manner, and ever since thou hast blushed extempore. Thou hadst fire and sword on thy side, and yet thou rannest away: what instinct hadst thou for it? 350

Bard. My lord, do you see these meteors? do you behold these exhalations?

Prince. I do.

Bard. What think you they portend?

Prince. Hot livers and cold purses.

Bard. Choler, my lord, if rightly taken.

Prince. No, if rightly taken, halter.

Re-enter FALSTAFF.

Here comes lean Jack, here comes bare-bone. How now, my sweet creature of bombast! How long is 't ago, Jack, since thou sawest thine own knee? 361

Fal. My own knee! when I was about thy years, Hal, I was not an eagle's talon in the waist; I could have crept into any alderman's thumb-ring: a plague of sighing and grief! it blows a man up like a bladder. There's villanous news abroad: here was Sir John Bracy from your father; you must to the court in the morning. That same mad fellow of the north, Percy, and he of Wales, that gave Amamon the bastinado and made Lucifer cuckold and swore the devil his true liegeman upon the cross of a Welsh hook—what a plague call you him? 373

Poins. O, Glendower.

Fal. Owen, Owen, the same; and his son-in-law Mortimer, and old Northumberland, and that sprightly Scot of Scots, Douglas, that runs o' horse-back up a hill perpendicular,—

Prince. He that rides at high speed and with his pistol kills a sparrow flying. 380

Fal. You have hit it.

Prince. So did he never the sparrow.

Fal. Well, that rascal hath good mettle in him; he will not run.

Prince. Why, what a rascal art thou then, to praise him so for running!

Fal. O' horseback, ye cuckoo; but afoot he will not budge a foot.

Prince. Yes, Jack, upon instinct. 389

Fal. I grant ye, upon instinct. Well, he is there too, and one Mordake, and a thousand blue-caps more:

272. **stock-fish**, dried cod. 274. **standing-tuck**, rapier standing on end. 283. **out-faced**, frightened. 290. **starting-hole**, point of shelter (like a rabbit's hole). The most famous of all Falstaff's evasions follows. 321. **royal**. The man is a noble (6s. 8d.); give him 3s. 4d. and he will be a *royal* (10s.) *man*. 348. **fire . . . side**. Bardolph is a drunkard, and his flaming face is continually harped upon. 355. **Hot . . . purses**, livers made hot by drink, and purses made empty by spending. 357. **halter**. The pun is on "collar" pronounced like *choler*. 359.

bombast, cotton padding. 370. **Amamon**, name of a demon. **bastinado**, cudgel, or a beating with a cudgel. 372. **cross of a Welsh hook**, cross formed by the axhead and the shaft in the Welsh halberd. 374. **O**, possibly an abbreviation of *Owen*. 380. **pistol**. There were, of course, no pistols in the time of King Henry's reign. 392. **blue-caps**, Scottish soldiers. 414. **particulars**, details of a private nature; see glossary. 418. **joined-stool**, a stool made by a joiner, hence, of rough workmanship. 426. **King Cambyses' vein**, allusion to Thomas

Worcester is stolen away to-night; thy father's beard is turned white with the news: you may buy land now as cheap as stinking mackerel.

Prince. Why, then, it is like, if there come a hot June and this civil buffeting hold, we shall buy maidenheads as they buy hob-nails, by the hundreds.

Fal. By the mass, lad, thou sayest true; it is like we shall have good trading that way. But tell me, Hal, art not thou horrible afeard? thou being heir-apparent, could the world pick thee out three such enemies again as that fiend Douglas, that spirit Percy, and that devil Glendower? Art thou not horribly afraid? doth not thy blood thrill at it?

Prince. Not a whit, i' faith; I lack some of thy instinct. 409

Fal. Well, thou wilt be horribly chid to-morrow when thou comest to thy father: if thou love me, practise an answer.

Prince. Do thou stand for my father, and examine me upon the particulars of my life.

Fal. Shall I? content: this chair shall be my state, this dagger my sceptre, and this cushion my crown. 417

Prince. Thy state is taken for a joined-stool, thy golden sceptre for a leaden dagger, and thy precious rich crown for a pitiful bald crown!

Fal. Well, an the fire of grace be not quite out of thee, now shalt thou be moved. Give me a cup of sack to make my eyes look red, that it may be thought I have wept; for I must speak in passion, and I will do it in King Cambyses' vein. 426

Prince. Well, here is my leg.

Fal. And here is my speech. Stand aside, nobility.

Host. O Jesu, this is excellent sport, i' faith!

Fal. Weep not, sweet queen; for trickling tears are vain.

Host. O, the father, how he holds his countenance!

Fal. For God's sake, lords, convey my tristful queen; For tears do stop the flood-gates of her eyes.

Host. O Jesu, he doth it as like one of these harlotry players as ever I see! 437

Fal. Peace, good pint-pot; peace, good tickle-brain. Harry, I do not only marvel where thou spendest thy time, but also how thou art accompanied: for though the camomile, the more it is trodden on the faster it grows, yet youth, the more it is wasted the sooner it wears. That thou art my son, I have partly thy mother's word, partly my own opinion, but chiefly a villanous trick of thine eye and a foolish hanging of thy nether lip, that doth warrant me. If then thou be son to me, here lies the point; why, being son to me, art thou so pointed at? Shall the blessed sun of heaven prove a micher and eat blackberries? a question not to be asked. Shall the son of England prove a thief and take purses? a question to be asked. There is a thing, Harry, which thou hast often heard of and it is known to many in our land by the name of pitch: this pitch, as ancient writers do report, doth defile; so doth the company thou keepest: for, Harry, now I do not speak to thee in drink but in tears, not in pleasure but in passion, not

in words only, but in woes also: and yet there is a virtuous man whom I have often noted in thy company, but I know not his name. 461

Prince. What manner of man, an it like your majesty?

Fal. A goodly portly man, i' faith, and a corpulent; of a cheerful look, a pleasing eye and a most noble carriage; and, as I think, his age some fifty, or, by 'r lady, inclining to three score; and now I remember me, his name is Falstaff: if that man should be lewdly given, he deceiveth me; for, Harry, I see virtue in his looks. If then the tree may be known by the fruit, as the fruit by the tree, then, peremptorily I speak it, there is virtue in that Falstaff: him keep with, the rest banish. And tell me now, thou naughty varlet, tell me, where hast thou been this month?

Prince. Dost thou speak like a king? Do thou stand for me, and I'll play my father. 478

Fal. Depose me? if thou dost it half so gravely, so majestically, both in word and matter, hang me up by the heels for a rabbit-sucker or a poulter's hare.

Prince. Well, here I am set.

Fal. And here I stand: judge, my masters.

Prince. Now, Harry, whence come you?

Fal. My noble lord, from Eastcheap.

Prince. The complaints I hear of thee are grievous.

Fal. 'Sblood, my lord, they are false: nay, I'll tickle ye for a young prince, i' faith. 489

Prince. Swearest thou, ungracious boy? henceforth ne'er look on me. Thou art violently carried away from grace: there is a devil haunts thee in the likeness of an old fat man; a tun of man is thy companion. Why dost thou converse with that trunk of humours, that bolting-hutch of beastliness, that swollen parcel of dropsies, that huge bombard of sack, that stuffed cloak-bag of guts, that roasted Manningtree ox with the pudding in his belly, that reverend vice, that grey iniquity, that father ruffian, that vanity in years? Wherein is he good, but to taste sack and drink it? wherein neat and cleanly, but to carve a capon and eat it? wherein cunning, but in craft? wherein crafty, but in villany? wherein villanous, but in all things? wherein worthy, but in nothing?

Fal. I would your grace would take me with you: whom means your grace?

Prince. That villanous abominable misleader of youth, Falstaff, that old white-bearded Satan.

Fal. My lord, the man I know. 510

Prince. I know thou dost.

Fal. But to say I know more harm in him than in myself, were to say more than I know. That he is old, the more the pity, his white hairs do witness it; but that he is, saving your reverence, a whoremaster, that I utterly deny. If sack and sugar be a fault, God help the wicked! if to be old and merry be a sin, then many an old host that I know is damned: if to be fat be to be hated, then Pharaoh's lean kine are to be loved. No, my good lord; banish Peto, banish Bardolph, banish Poins: but for sweet Jack Falstaff, kind Jack Falstaff, true Jack Falstaff, valiant Jack Falstaff,

1 Henry IV
ACT II : SC IV

689

Preston's bombastic tragedy *Cambises*, still preserved. 427. **leg,** bow. 434. **tristful,** sorrowing. 437. **harlotry,** vagabond. 439. **tickle-brain,** strong drink. 441. **camomile.** This parodies an actual passage in Lyly's *Euphues* and exaggerates the balance and alliteration of the style. 450. **micher,** truant. 456-457. **pitch . . . defile,** an allusion to the familiar proverb from Ecclesiasticus 13:1, about the defilement of touching pitch. This proverb appears also in Lyly's *Euphues.* 480. **rabbit-sucker,** sucking rabbit. 481. **poulter's,** poulterer's. 495. **bolting-**

hutch, bin for bolted meal. 497. **bombard,** leathern drinking vessel. 498. **Manningtree ox.** Manningtree, a town in Essex, had noted fairs where, no doubt, oxen were roasted whole. 499-500. **vice . . . iniquity.** These terms suggest another feature of Manningtree, which was the acting of morality plays; the word *vanity* also suggests a character in such plays. 521. **Pharaoh's lean kine.** See Genesis 41:3-4.

and therefore more valiant, being, as he is, old Jack
Falstaff, banish not him thy Harry's company,
banish not him thy Harry's company: banish plump
Jack, and banish all the world. 527

Prince. I do, I will. [*A knocking heard.*
[*Exeunt Hostess, Francis, and Bardolph.*

Re-enter BARDOLPH, *running.*

Bard. O, my lord, my lord! the sheriff with a most
monstrous watch is at the door.

Fal. Out, ye rogue! Play out the play: I have much
to say in the behalf of that Falstaff.

Re-enter the Hostess.

Host. O Jesu, my lord, my lord!

Prince. Heigh, heigh! the devil rides upon a fiddlestick: what 's the matter?

Host. The sheriff and all the watch are at the door:
they are come to search the house. Shall I let them in?

Fal. Dost thou hear, Hal? never call a true piece of
gold a counterfeit: thou art essentially mad, without
seeming so. 541

Prince. And thou a natural coward, without instinct.

Fal. I deny your major: if you will deny the sheriff,
so; if not, let him enter: if I become not a cart as well
as another man, a plague on my bringing up! I hope
I shall as soon be strangled with a halter as another.

Prince. Go, hide thee behind the arras: the rest walk
up above. Now, my masters, for a true face and good
conscience. 551

Fal. Both which I have had: but their date is out,
and therefore I'll hide me.

Prince. Call in the sheriff.

[*Exeunt all except the Prince and Peto.*

Enter Sheriff *and the* Carrier.

Now, master sheriff, what is your will with me?

Sher. First, pardon me, my lord. A hue and cry
Hath follow'd certain men unto this house.

Prince. What men?

Sher. One of them is well known, my gracious lord,
A gross fat man.

Car. As fat as butter. 560

Prince. The man, I do assure you, is not here;
For I myself at this time have employ'd him.
And, sheriff, I will engage my word to thee
That I will, by to-morrow dinner-time,
Send him to answer thee, or any man,
For any thing he shall be charged withal:
And so let me entreat you leave the house.

Sher. I will, my lord. There are two gentlemen
Have in this robbery lost three hundred marks.

Prince. It may be so: if he have robb'd these men, 570
He shall be answerable; and so farewell.

Sher. Good night, my noble lord.

Prince. I think it is good morrow, is it not?

Sher. Indeed, my lord, I think it be two o'clock.

[*Exeunt Sheriff and Carrier.*

Prince. This oily rascal is known as well as Paul's.
Go, call him forth.

Peto. Falstaff!—Fast asleep behind the arras, and
snorting like a horse. 578

Prince. Hark, how hard he fetches breath. Search
his pockets. [*He searcheth his pockets, and findeth certain
papers.*] What hast thou found?

Peto. Nothing but papers, my lord.

Prince. Let 's see what they be: read them.

Peto. [*Reads*]

Item, A capon, ... 2s. 2d.
Item, Sauce, ... 4d.
Item, Sack, two gallons, . . 5s. 8d.
Item, Anchovies and sack after
supper, ... 2s. 6d.
Item, Bread, ... ob. 590

Prince. O monstrous! but one half-pennyworth of
bread to this intolerable deal of sack! What there is
else, keep close; we'll read it at more advantage:
there let him sleep till day. I'll to the court in the
morning. We must all to the wars, and thy place
shall be honourable. I'll procure this fat rogue a
charge of foot; and I know his death will be a march
of twelve-score. The money shall be paid back again
with advantage. Be with me betimes in the morning;
and so, good morrow, Peto. 601

Peto. Good morrow, good my lord. [*Exeunt.*

ACT III.

SCENE I. *Bangor. The Archdeacon's house.*

Enter HOTSPUR, WORCESTER, MORTIMER, *and*
GLENDOWER.

Mort. These promises are fair, the parties sure,
And our induction full of prosperous hope.

Hot. Lord Mortimer, and cousin Glendower,
Will you sit down?
And uncle Worcester: a plague upon it!
I have forgot the map.

Glend. No, here it is.
Sit, cousin Percy; sit, good cousin Hotspur,
For by that name as oft as Lancaster
Doth speak of you, his cheek looks pale and with
A rising sigh he wisheth you in heaven. 10

Hot. And you in hell, as oft as he hears Owen
Glendower spoke of.

Glend. I cannot blame him: at my nativity
The front of heaven was full of fiery shapes,
Of burning cressets; and at my birth
The frame and huge foundation of the earth
Shaked like a coward.

Hot. Why, so it would have done at the same season,
if your mother's cat had but kittened, though yourself
had never been born. 20

Glend. I say the earth did shake when I was born.

Hot. And I say the earth was not of my mind,
If you suppose as fearing you it shook.

Glend. The heavens were all on fire, the earth did
tremble.

Hot. O, then the earth shook to see the heavens on
fire,

And not in fear of your nativity.
Diseased nature oftentimes breaks forth
In strange eruptions; oft the teeming earth
Is with a kind of colic pinch'd and vex'd
By the imprisoning of unruly wind   30
Within her womb; which, for enlargement striving,
Shakes the old beldam earth and topples down
Steeples and moss-grown towers. At your birth
Our grandam earth, having this distemperature,
In passion shook.
    Glend.   Cousin, of many men
I do not bear these crossings. Give me leave
To tell you once again that at my birth
The front of heaven was full of fiery shapes,
The goats ran from the mountains, and the herds
Were strangely clamorous to the frighted fields.   40
These signs have mark'd me extraordinary;
And all the courses of my life do show
I am not in the roll of common men.
Where is he living, clipp'd in with the sea
That chides the banks of England, Scotland, Wales,
Which calls me pupil, or hath read to me?
And bring him out that is but woman's son
Can trace me in the tedious ways of art
And hold me pace in deep experiments.
    Hot. I think there's no man speaks better Welsh.
I'll to dinner.   51
    Mort. Peace, cousin Percy; you will make him mad.
    Glend. I can call spirits from the vasty deep.
    Hot. Why, so can I, or so can any man;
But will they come when you do call for them?
    Glend. Why, I can teach you, cousin, to command
The devil.
    Hot. And I can teach thee, coz, to shame the devil
By telling truth: tell truth and shame the devil.
If thou have power to raise him, bring him hither,   60
And I'll be sworn I have power to shame him hence.
O, while you live, tell truth and shame the devil!
    Mort. Come, come, no more of this unprofitable
    chat.
    Glend. Three times hath Henry Bolingbroke made
    head
Against my power; thrice from the banks of Wye
And sandy-bottom'd Severn have I sent him
Bootless home and weather-beaten back.
    Hot. Home without boots, and in foul weather too!
How 'scapes he agues, in the devil's name?
    Glend. Come, here's the map: shall we divide our
    right   70
According to our threefold order ta'en?
    Mort. The archdeacon hath divided it
Into three limits very equally:
England, from Trent and Severn hitherto,
By south and east is to my part assign'd:
All westward, Wales beyond the Severn shore,
And all the fertile land within that bound,
To Owen Glendower: and, dear coz, to you
The remnant northward, lying off from Trent.
And our indentures tripartite are drawn;   80
Which being sealed interchangeably,

A business that this night may execute,
To-morrow, cousin Percy, you and I
And my good Lord of Worcester will set forth
To meet your father and the Scottish power,
As is appointed us, at Shrewsbury.
My father Glendower is not ready yet,
Nor shall we need his help these fourteen days.
Within that space you may have drawn together
Your tenants, friends and neighbouring gentlemen.   90
    Glend. A shorter time shall send me to you, lords:
And in my conduct shall your ladies come;
From whom you now must steal and take no leave,
For there will be a world of water shed
Upon the parting of your wives and you.
    Hot. Methinks my moiety, north from Burton here,
In quantity equals not one of yours:
See how this river comes me cranking in,
And cuts me from the best of all my land
A huge half-moon, a monstrous cantle out.   100
I'll have the current in this place damm'd up;
And here the smug and silver Trent shall run
In a new channel, fair and evenly;
It shall not wind with such a deep indent,
To rob me of so rich a bottom here.
    Glend. Not wind? it shall, it must; you see it doth.
    Mort. Yea, but
Mark how he bears his course, and runs me up
With like advantage on the other side;
Gelding the opposed continent as much   110
As on the other side it takes from you.
    Wor. Yea, but a little charge will trench him here
And on this north side win this cape of land;
And then he runs straight and even.
    Hot. I'll have it so: a little charge will do it.
    Glend. I'll not have it alter'd.
    Hot.   Will not you?
    Glend. No, nor you shall not.
    Hot.   Who shall say me nay?
    Glend. Why, that will I.
    Hot. Let me not understand you, then; speak it in
Welsh.   120
    Glend. I can speak English, lord, as well as you;
For I was train'd up in the English court;
Where, being but young, I framed to the harp
Many an English ditty lovely well
And gave the tongue a helpful ornament,
A virtue that was never seen in you.
    Hot. Marry,
And I am glad of it with all my heart:
I had rather be a kitten and cry mew
Than one of these same metre ballad-mongers;   130
I had rather hear a brazen canstick turn'd,
Or a dry wheel grate on the axle-tree;
And that would set my teeth nothing on edge,
Nothing so much as mincing poetry:
'Tis like the forced gait of a shuffling nag.
    Glend. Come, you shall have Trent turn'd.
    Hot. I do not care: I'll give thrice so much land
To any well-deserving friend;
But in the way of bargain, mark ye me,

believed in Glendower's powers in spite of making him ridiculous. 14.
front, face; see glossary. 22-23. **And . . . shook.** Hotspur ridicules
Glendower and does not hesitate to affront him, although Glendower is
his ally. 27-35. **Diseased . . . shook.** These lines give the currently
accepted scientific explanation of earthquakes. 48. **trace,** follow,
keep pace. 72. **archdeacon,** an official of an Episcopal diocese. The
divisions of the Kingdom are really very ancient; they appear in
Geoffrey of Monmouth's *Chronicle*, and are those into which King Lear
divided his kingdom. 87. **father,** father-in-law. 98. **comes me
cranking in,** comes bending in on my share; *me* is an ethical dative.
100. **cantle,** piece. 122-126. **For . . . you.** Glendower had indeed been
bred in the English court; he shows a characteristic Welsh pride in
being a poet, and Hotspur an equally characteristic scorn of the fine
arts. 131. **canstick,** candlestick. 139-140. **But . . . hair.** Hotspur here
describes his splenetic humor. He was generous, but his generosity
could never be the result of justice or reason.

I'll cavil on the ninth part of a hair. 140
Are the indentures drawn? shall we be gone?
　Glend. The moon shines fair; you may away by
　　night:
I'll haste the writer and withal
Break with your wives of your departure hence:
I'am afraid my daughter will run mad,
So much she doteth on her Mortimer.　　[*Exit.*
　Mort. Fie, cousin Percy! how you cross my father!
　Hot. I cannot choose: sometime he angers me
With telling me of the moldwarp and the ant,
Of the dreamer Merlin and his prophecies, 150
And of a dragon and a finless fish,
A clip-wing'd griffin and a moulten raven,
A couching lion and a ramping cat,
And such a deal of skimble-skamble stuff
As puts me from my faith. I tell you what;
He held me last night at least nine hours
In reckoning up the several devils' names
That were his lackeys: I cried 'hum,' and 'well, go to,'
But mark'd him not a word. O, he is as tedious
As a tired horse, a railing wife; 160
Worse than a smoky house: I had rather live
With cheese and garlic in a windmill, far,
Than feed on cates and have him talk to me
In any summer-house in Christendom.
　Mort. In faith, he is a worthy gentleman,
Exceedingly well read, and profited
In strange concealments, valiant as a lion
And wondrous affable and as bountiful
As mines of India. Shall I tell you, cousin?
He holds your temper in a high respect 170
And curbs himself even of his natural scope
When you come 'cross his humour; faith, he does:
I warrant you, that man is not alive
Might so have tempted him as you have done,
Without the taste of danger and reproof:
But do not use it oft, let me entreat you.
　Wor. In faith, my lord, you are too wilful-blame;
And since your coming hither have done enough
To put him quite beside his patience.
You must needs learn, lord, to amend this fault: 180
Though sometimes it show greatness, courage,
　　blood,—
And that 's the dearest grace it renders you,—
Yet oftentimes it doth present harsh rage,
Defect of manners, want of government,
Pride, haughtiness, opinion and disdain:
The least of which haunting a nobleman
Loseth men's hearts and leaves behind a stain
Upon the beauty of all parts besides,
Beguiling them of commendation.
　Hot. Well, I am school'd: good manners be your
　　speed! 190
Here come our wives, and let us take our leave.

　　Re-enter GLENDOWER *with the ladies.*

　Mort. This is the deadly spite that angers me;
My wife can speak no English, I no Welsh.

　Glend. My daughter weeps: she will not part
　　with you;
She'll be a soldier too, she'll to the wars.
　Mort. Good father, tell her that she and my aunt
　　Percy
Shall follow in your conduct speedily.
　[*Glendower speaks to her in Welsh, and she answers him*
　　　　　　　　　　　　　　　　　　　in the same.
　Glend. She is desperate here; a peevish self-will'd
harlotry, one that no persuasion can do good upon.
　　　　　　　　　　　　[*The lady speaks in Welsh.*
　Mort. I understand thy looks: that pretty Welsh 201
Which thou pour'st down from these swelling heavens
I am too perfect in; and, but for shame,
In such a parley should I answer thee.
　　　　　　　　[*The lady speaks again in Welsh.*
I understand thy kisses and thou mine,
And that 's a feeling disputation:
But I will never be a truant, love,
Till I have learn'd thy language; for thy tongue
Makes Welsh as sweet as ditties highly penn'd,
Sung by a fair queen in a summer's bower, 210
With ravishing division, to her lute.
　Glend. Nay, if you melt, then will she run mad.
　　　　　　　　[*The lady speaks again in Welsh.*
　Mort. O, I am ignorance itself in this!
　Glend. She bids you on the wanton rushes lay you
　　down
And rest your gentle head upon her lap,
And she will sing the song that pleaseth you
And on your eyelids crown the god of sleep,
Charming your blood with pleasing heaviness,
Making such difference 'twixt wake and sleep
As is the difference betwixt day and night 220
The hour before the heavenly-harness'd team
Begins his golden progress in the east.
　Mort. With all my heart I'll sit and hear her sing:
By that time will our book, I think, be drawn.
　Glend. Do so;
And those musicians that shall play to you
Hang in the air a thousand leagues from hence,
And straight they shall be here: sit, and attend.
　Hot. Come, Kate, thou art perfect in lying down:
come, quick, quick, that I may lay my head in thy lap.
　Lady P. Go, ye giddy goose.　　　[*Music plays.* 232
　Hot. Now I perceive the devil understands Welsh;
And 'tis no marvel he is so humorous.
By 'r lady, he is a good musician.
　Lady P. Then should you be nothing but musical,
for you are altogether governed by humours. Lie still,
ye thief, and hear the lady sing in Welsh.
　Hot. I had rather hear Lady, my brach, howl in
Irish. 241
　Lady P. Wouldst thou have thy head broken?
　Hot. No.
　Lady P. Then be still.
　Hot. Neither; 'tis a woman's fault.
　Lady P. Now God help thee!
　Hot. To the Welsh lady's bed.
　Lady P. What 's that?

1 Henry IV
ACT III : SC I

692

143. writer, the scrivener who would be drawing the indentures.　**144.**
Break with, communicate with.　**149. moldwarp,** mole. Holinshed
tells us that the division was arranged because of a prophecy which
represented King Henry as the mole and the others as the dragon, the
lion, and the wolf, who should divide the land among them.　**150.**
Merlin, the traditional bard and prophet of the Welsh.　**152. griffin,**
a fabulous beast.　**153. ramping,** rampant, advancing on its hind legs.
154. skimble-skamble, confused and foolish.　**177-189. In . . . com-**

mendation. Worcester's reproof expresses an ideal of noble courtesy
and is important in the understanding of the situation.　**177. wilful-**
blame, willfully guilty.　**199. harlotry,** silly wench.　**206. disputation,**
conversation.　**211. division,** variation (in music).　**214. wanton,**
soft, luxurious.　**224. book,** document, indentures.　**234. humorous,**
capricious.　**240. brach,** bitch hound.　**252-253. you swear . . . wife.**
Hotspur prefers more violent oaths in accordance with the fashion
of the time, when even the queen herself swore vigorously.　253.

Hot. Peace! she sings. [*Here the lady sings a Welsh song.*

Hot. Come, Kate, I'll have your song too.

Lady P. Not mine, in good sooth. 251

Hot. Not yours, in good sooth! Heart! you swear
like a comfit-maker's wife. 'Not you, in good sooth,'
and 'as true as I live,' and 'as God shall mend me,'
and 'as sure as day,'
And givest such sarcenet surety for thy oaths,
As if thou never walk'st further than Finsbury.
Swear me, Kate, like a lady as thou art,
A good mouth-filling oath, and leave 'in sooth,'
And such protest of pepper-gingerbread, 260
To velvet-guards and Sunday-citizens.
Come, sing.

Lady P. I will not sing.

Hot. 'Tis the next way to turn tailor, or be redbreast teacher. An the indentures be drawn, I'll away
within these two hours; and so, come in when ye
will. [*Exit.*

Glend. Come, come, Lord Mortimer; you are as
 slow
As hot Lord Percy is on fire to go.
By this our book is drawn; we'll but seal, 270
And then to horse immediately.

Mort. With all my heart. [*Exeunt.*

SCENE II. *London. The palace.*

Enter the KING, PRINCE OF WALES, *and others.*

King. Lords, give us leave; the Prince of Wales
 and I
Must have some private conference: but be near at
 hand,
For we shall presently have need of you. [*Exeunt Lords.*
I know not whether God will have it so,
For some displeasing service I have done,
That, in his secret doom, out of my blood
He'll breed revengement and a scourge for me;
But thou dost in thy passages of life
Make me believe that thou art only mark'd
For the hot vengeance and the rod of heaven 10
To punish my mistreadings. Tell me else,
Could such inordinate and low desires,
Such poor, such bare, such lewd, such mean attempts,
Such barren pleasures, rude society,
As thou art match'd withal and grafted to,
Accompany the greatness of thy blood
And hold their level with thy princely heart?

Prince. So please your majesty, I would I could
Quit all offences with as clear excuse
As well as I am doubtless I can purge 20
Myself of many I am charged withal:
Yet such extenuation let me beg,
As, in reproof of many tales devised,
Which oft the ear of greatness needs must hear,
By smiling pick-thanks and base newsmongers,
I may, for some things true, wherein my youth
Hath faulty wander'd and irregular,
Find pardon on my true submission.

King. God pardon thee! yet let me wonder, Harry,
At thy affections, which do hold a wing 30
Quite from the flight of all thy ancestors.
Thy place in council thou hast rudely lost,
Which by thy younger brother is supplied,
And art almost an alien to the hearts
Of all the court and princes of my blood:
The hope and expectation of thy time
Is ruin'd, and the soul of every man
Prophetically doth forethink thy fall.
Had I so lavish of my presence been,
So common-hackney'd in the eyes of men, 40
So stale and cheap to vulgar company,
Opinion, that did help me to the crown,
Had still kept loyal to possession
And left me in reputeless banishment,
A fellow of no mark nor likelihood.
By being seldom seen, I could not stir
But like a comet I was wonder'd at;
That men would tell their children 'This is he;'
Others would say 'Where, which is Bolingbroke?'
And then I stole all courtesy from heaven, 50
And dress'd myself in such humility
That I did pluck allegiance from men's hearts,
Loud shouts and salutations from their mouths,
Even in the presence of the crowned king.
Thus did I keep my person fresh and new;
My presence, like a robe pontifical,
Ne'er seen but wonder'd at: and so my state,
Seldom but sumptuous, showed like a feast
And won by rareness such solemnity.
The skipping king, he ambled up and down 60
With shallow jesters and rash bavin wits,
Soon kindled and soon burnt; carded his state,
Mingled his royalty with capering fools,
Had his great name profaned with their scorns
And gave his countenance, against his name,
To laugh at gibing boys and stand the push
Of every beardless vain comparative,
Grew a companion to the common streets,
Enfeoff'd himself to popularity;
That, being daily swallow'd by men's eyes, 70
They surfeited with honey and began
To loathe the taste of sweetness, whereof a little
More than a little is by much too much.
So when he had occasion to be seen,
He was but as the cuckoo is in June,
Heard, not regarded; seen, but with such eyes
As, sick and blunted with community,
Afford no extraordinary gaze,
Such as is bent on sun-like majesty
When it shines seldom in admiring eyes; 80
But rather drowsed and hung their eyelids down,
Slept in his face and render'd such aspect
As cloudy men use to their adversaries,
Being with his presence glutted, gorged and full.
And in that very line, Harry, standest thou;
For thou hast lost thy princely privilege
With vile participation: not an eye
But is a-weary of thy common sight,

---

comfit-maker's, confectioner's. 256. **sarcenet,** soft, from the silken
material known as "sarcenet." 257. **Finsbury,** an archery ground outside Moorgate, resorted to by citizens. 261. **velvet-guards,** wearers of
velvet trimmings. 264. **turn tailor.** Tailors were noted for singing.
 SCENE II. 1. **give us leave,** leave us. 25. **pick-thanks,** flatterers.
43. **to possession,** i.e., to Richard II's sovereignty. 50. **stole . . .
heaven.** He assumed a bearing of the utmost graciousness. 60.
skipping, flighty. 61. **bavin,** brushwood, soon burnt out. 62. **carded,**

debased; a term applied to the adulteration of wool. 65. **name,** i.e.,
dignity. 66. **stand the push,** undergo the attack. 67. **comparative,**
rival (in wit). 69. **Enfeoff'd,** gave himself up to. The king is expressing
the current view of royal dignity and policy with reference to the
populace. 77. **community,** commonness. 87. **vile participation,**
base association or companionship.

Save mine, which hath desired to see thee more;
Which now doth that I would not have it do, 90
Make blind itself with foolish tenderness.
    Prince. I shall hereafter, my thrice gracious lord,
Be more myself.
    King.   For all the world
As thou art to this hour was Richard then
When I from France set foot at Ravenspurgh,
And even as I was then is Percy now.
Now, by my sceptre and my soul to boot,
He hath more worthy interest to the state
Than thou the shadow of succession;
For of no right, nor colour like to right, 100
He doth fill fields with harness in the realm,
Turns head against the lion's armed jaws,
And, being no more in debt to years than thou,
Leads ancient lords and reverend bishops on
To bloody battles and to bruising arms.
What never-dying honour hath he got
Against renowned Douglas! whose high deeds,
Whose hot incursions and great name in arms
Holds from all soldiers chief majority
And military title capital 110
Through all the kingdoms that acknowledge Christ:
Thrice hath this Hotspur, Mars in swathling clothes,
This infant warrior, in his enterprizes
Discomfited great Douglas, ta'en him once,
Enlarged him and made a friend of him,
To fill the mouth of deep defiance up
And shake the peace and safety of our throne.
And what say you to this? Percy, Northumberland,
The Archbishop's grace of York, Douglas, Mortimer,
Capitulate against us and are up. 120
But wherefore do I tell these news to thee?
Why, Harry, do I tell thee of my foes,
Which art my near'st and dearest enemy?
Thou that art like enough, through vassal fear,
Base inclination and the start of spleen,
To fight against me under Percy's pay,
To dog his heels and curtsy at his frowns,
To show how much thou art degenerate.
    Prince. Do not think so; you shall not find it so:
And God forgive them that so much have sway'd 130
Your majesty's good thoughts away from me!
I will redeem all this on Percy's head
And in the closing of some glorious day
Be bold to tell you that I am your son;
When I will wear a garment all of blood
And stain my favours in a bloody mask,
Which, wash'd away, shall scour my shame with it:
And that shall be the day, whene'er it lights,
That this same child of honour and renown,
This gallant Hotspur, this all-praised knight, 140
And your unthought-of Harry chance to meet.
For every honour sitting on his helm,
Would they were multitudes, and on my head
My shames redoubled! for the time will come,
That I shall make this northern youth exchange
His glorious deeds for my indignities.
Percy is but my factor, good my lord,
To engross up glorious deeds on my behalf;

And I will call him to so strict account,
That he shall render every glory up, 150
Yea, even the slightest worship of his time,
Or I will tear the reckoning from his heart.
This, in the name of God, I promise here:
The which if He be pleased I shall perform,
I do beseech your majesty may salve
The long-grown wounds of my intemperance:
If not, the end of life cancels all bands;
And I will die a hundred thousand deaths
Ere break the smallest parcel of this vow.
    King. A hundred thousand rebels die in this: 160
Thou shalt have charge and sovereign trust herein.

Enter BLUNT.

How now, good Blunt? thy looks are full of speed.
    Blunt. So hath the business that I come to speak of.
Lord Mortimer of Scotland hath sent word
That Douglas and the English rebels met
The eleventh of this month at Shrewsbury:
A mighty and a fearful head they are,
If promises be kept on every hand,
As ever offer'd foul play in a state.
    King. The Earl of Westmoreland set forth to-day; 170
With him my son, Lord John of Lancaster;
For this advertisement is five days old:
On Wednesday next, Harry, you shall set forward;
On Thursday we ourselves will march: our meeting
Is Bridgenorth: and, Harry, you shall march
Through Gloucestershire; by which account,
Our business valued, some twelve days hence
Our general forces at Bridgenorth shall meet.
Our hands are full of business: let 's away;
Advantage feeds him fat, while men delay. [*Exeunt.* 180

_____

SCENE III. *Eastcheap. The Boar's-Head Tavern.*

Enter FALSTAFF *and* BARDOLPH.

    Fal. Bardolph, am I not fallen away vilely since
this last action? do I not bate? do I not dwindle?
Why, my skin hangs about me like an old lady's loose
gown; I am withered like an old apple-john. Well,
I'll repent, and that suddenly, while I am in some
liking; I shall be out of heart shortly, and then I shall
have no strength to repent. An I have not forgotten
what the inside of a church is made of, I am a pepper-
corn, a brewer's horse: the inside of a church! Company, villanous company, hath been the spoil of me. 12
    Bard. Sir John, you are so fretful, you cannot live
long.
    Fal. Why, there is it: come sing me a bawdy song;
make me merry. I was as virtuously given as a
gentleman need to be; virtuous enough; swore little;
diced not above seven times a week; went to a
bawdy-house not above once in a quarter—of an
hour; paid money that I borrowed, three or four
times; lived well and in good compass: and now I
live out of all order, out of all compass. 23
    Bard. Why, you are so fat, Sir John, that you
must needs be out of all compass, out of all reasonable
compass, Sir John.

Fal. Do thou amend thy face, and I'll amend my life: thou art our admiral, thou bearest the lantern in the poop, but 'tis in the nose of thee; thou art the Knight of the Burning Lamp. 30

Bard. Why, Sir John, my face does you no harm.

Fal. No, I'll be sworn; I make as good use of it as many a man doth of a Death's-head or a memento mori: I never see thy face but I think upon hell-fire and Dives that lived in purple; for there he is in his robes, burning, burning. If thou wert any way given to virtue, I would swear by thy face; my oath should be 'By this fire, that's God's angel:' but thou art altogether given over; and wert indeed, but for the light in thy face, the son of utter darkness. When thou rannest up Gadshill in the night to catch my horse, if I did not think thou hadst been an ignis fatuus or a ball of wildfire, there's no purchase in money. O, thou art a perpetual triumph, an ever-lasting bonfire-light! Thou hast saved me a thousand marks in links and torches, walking with thee in the night betwixt tavern and tavern: but the sack that thou hast drunk me would have bought me lights as good cheap at the dearest chandler's in Europe. I have maintained that salamander of yours with fire any time this two and thirty years; God reward me for it! 56

Bard. 'Sblood, I would my face were in your belly!

Fal. God-a-mercy! so should I be sure to be heart-burned.

Enter HOSTESS.

How now, Dame Partlet the hen! have you inquired yet who picked my pocket? 61

Host. Why, Sir John, what do you think, Sir John? do you think I keep thieves in my house? I have searched, I have inquired, so has my husband, man by man, boy by boy, servant by servant: the tithe of a hair was never lost in my house before.

Fal. Ye lie, hostess: Bardolph was shaved and lost many a hair; and I'll be sworn my pocket was picked. Go to, you are a woman, go.

Host. Who, I? no; I defy thee: God's light, I was never called so in mine own house before.

Fal. Go to, I know you well enough.

Host. No, Sir John; you do not know me, Sir John. I know you, Sir John: you owe me money, Sir John; and now you pick a quarrel to beguile me of it: I bought you a dozen of shirts to your back. 78

Fal. Dowlas, filthy dowlas: I have given them away to bakers' wives, and they have made bolters of them.

Host. Now, as I am a true woman, holland of eight shillings an ell. You owe money here besides, Sir John, for your diet and by-drinkings, and money lent you, four and twenty pound.

Fal. He had his part of it; let him pay.

Host. He? alas, he is poor; he hath nothing. 88

Fal. How! poor? look upon his face; what call you rich? let them coin his nose, let them coin his cheeks: I'll not pay a denier. What, will you make a younker of me? shall I not take mine ease in mine inn but I shall have my pocket picked? I have lost a seal-ring of my grandfather's worth forty mark.

Host. O Jesu, I have heard the prince tell him, I know not how oft, that that ring was copper!

Fal. How! the prince is a Jack, a sneak-cup: 'sblood, an he were here, I would cudgel him like a dog, if he would say so. 101

Enter the PRINCE *and* PETO, *marching, and* FALSTAFF *meets them playing on his truncheon like a fife.*

How now, lad! is the wind in that door, i' faith? must we all march?

Bard. Yea, two and two, Newgate fashion.

Host. My lord, I pray you, hear me.

Prince. What sayest thou, Mistress Quickly? How doth thy husband? I love him well; he is an honest man.

Host. Good my lord, hear me.

Fal. Prithee, let her alone, and list to me.

Prince. What sayest thou, Jack? 111

Fal. The other night I fell asleep here behind the arras and had my pocket picked: this house is turned bawdy-house; they pick pockets.

Prince. What didst thou lose, Jack?

Fal. Wilt thou believe me, Hal? three or four bonds of forty pound a-piece, and a seal-ring of my grand-father's.

Prince. A trifle, some eight-penny matter. 119

Host. So I told him, my lord; and I said I heard your grace say so: and, my lord, he speaks most vilely of you, like a foul-mouthed man as he is; and said he would cudgel you.

Prince. What! he did not?

Host. There's neither faith, truth, nor womanhood in me else.

Fal. There's no more faith in thee than in a stewed prune; nor no more truth in thee than in a drawn fox; and for womanhood, Maid Marian may be the deputy's wife of the ward to thee. Go, you thing, go. 131

Host. Say, what thing! what thing?

Fal. What thing? why, a thing to thank God on.

Host. I am no thing to thank God on, I would thou shouldst know it; I am an honest man's wife: and, setting thy knighthood aside, thou art a knave to call me so.

Fal. Setting thy womanhood aside, thou art a beast to say otherwise. 140

Host. Say, what beast, thou knave, thou?

Fal. What beast! why, an otter.

Prince. An otter, Sir John! why an otter?

Fal. Why, she's neither fish nor flesh; a man knows not where to have her.

Host. Thou art an unjust man in saying so: thou or any man knows where to have me, thou knave, thou!

Prince. Thou sayest true, hostess; and he slanders thee most grossly. 150

Host. So he doth you, my lord; and said this other day you ought him a thousand pound.

Prince. Sirrah, do I owe you a thousand pound?

Fal. A thousand pound, Hal! a million: thy love is worth a million: thou owest me thy love.

to in Luke 16:19-31. 39. **'By . . . angel,'** allusion to Psalms 104:4 and Hebrews 1:7. 44-45. **ignis fatuus,** will-o'-the-wisp. 48. **links,** torches. 51. **good cheap,** cheap. 53. **salamander,** a fabled monster able to live in fire. 60. **Partlet,** traditional name of a hen. 79. **Dowlas,** a coarse kind of linen. 81. **bolters,** cloths for sifting meal. 82. **holland,** fine linen. 83. **ell,** a measure of a yard and a quarter. 91. **denier,** one twelfth of a sou; type of very small coin. 92. **younker,** youth,

greenhorn. 99. **sneak-cup.** Nares defines this as "one who shirks his liquor"; Johnson modifies to *sneak-up,* meaning "a sneak." 104. **Newgate,** famous city prison in London. 129. **drawn fox,** fox driven from cover and wily in getting back. 152. **ought,** owed.

Host. Nay, my lord, he called you Jack, and said he would cudgel you.

Fal. Did I, Bardolph? 160

Bard. Indeed, Sir John, you said so.

Fal. Yea, if he said my ring was copper.

Prince. I say 'tis copper: darest thou be as good as thy word now?

Fal. Why, Hal, thou knowest, as thou art but man, I dare: but as thou art prince, I fear thee as I fear the roaring of the lion's whelp.

Prince. And why not as the lion?

Fal. The king himself is to be feared as the lion: dost thou think I'll fear thee as I fear thy father? nay, an I do, I pray God my girdle break. 171

Prince. O, if it should, how would thy guts fall about thy knees! But, sirrah, there's no room for faith, truth, nor honesty in this bosom of thine; it is all filled up with guts and midriff. Charge an honest woman with picking thy pocket! why, thou whoreson, impudent, embossed rascal, if there were anything in thy pocket but tavern-reckonings, memorandums of bawdy-houses, and one poor penny-worth of sugar-candy to make thee long-winded, if thy pocket were enriched with any other injuries but these, I am a villain: and yet you will stand to it; you will not pocket up wrong: art thou not ashamed? 184

Fal. Dost thou hear, Hal? thou knowest in the state of innocency Adam fell; and what should poor Jack Falstaff do in the days of villany? Thou seest I have more flesh than another man, and therefore more frailty. You confess then, you picked my pocket? 190

Prince. It appears so by the story.

Fal. Hostess, I forgive thee: go, make ready break-fast; love thy husband, look to thy servants, cherish thy guests: thou shalt find me tractable to any honest reason: thou seest I am pacified still. Nay, prithee, be gone. [*Exit Hostess.*] Now, Hal, to the news at court: for the robbery, lad, how is that answered?

Prince. O, my sweet beef, I must still be good angel to thee: the money is paid back again. 200

Fal. O, I do not like that paying back; 'tis a double labour.

Prince. I am good friends with my father and may do any thing.

Fal. Rob me the exchequer the first thing thou doest, and do it with unwashed hands too.

Bard. Do, my lord.

Prince. I have procured thee, Jack, a charge of foot.

Fal. I would it had been of horse. Where shall I find one that can steal well? O for a fine thief, of the age of two and twenty or thereabouts! I am heinously unprovided. Well, God be thanked for these rebels, they offend none but the virtuous: I laud them, I praise them.

Prince. Bardolph!

Bard. My lord? 217

Prince. Go bear this letter to Lord John of Lancaster, to my brother John; this to my Lord of Westmore-land. [*Exit Bardolph.*] Go, Peto, to horse, to horse; for

thou and I have thirty miles to ride yet ere dinner time. [*Exit Peto.*] Jack, meet me to-morrow in the Temple hall at two o'clock in the afternoon. There shalt thou know thy charge; and there receive Money and order for their furniture. The land is burning; Percy stands on high; And either we or they must lower lie. [*Exit.*

Fal. Rare words! brave world! Hostess, my breakfast, come! O, I could wish this tavern were my drum! [*Exit.* 230

ACT IV.

SCENE I. *The rebel camp near Shrewsbury.*

Enter HOTSPUR, WORCESTER, *and* DOUGLAS.

Hot. Well said, my noble Scot: if speaking truth
In this fine age were not thought flattery,
Such attribution should the Douglas have,
As not a soldier of this season's stamp
Should go so general current through the world.
By God, I cannot flatter; I do defy
The tongues of soothers; but a braver place
In my heart's love hath no man than yourself:
Nay, task me to my word; approve me, lord.

Doug. Thou art the king of honour: 10
No man so potent breathes upon the ground
But I will beard him.

Hot. Do so, and 'tis well.

Enter a Messenger *with letters.*

What letters hast thou there?—I can but thank you.

Mess. These letters come from your father.

Hot. Letters from him! why comes he not himself?

Mess. He cannot come, my lord; he is grievous sick.

Hot. 'Zounds! how has he the leisure to be sick
In such a justling time? Who leads his power?
Under whose government come they along?

Mess. His letters bear his mind, not I, my lord. 20

Wor. I prithee, tell me, doth he keep his bed?

Mess. He did, my lord, four days ere I set forth;
And at the time of my departure thence
He was much fear'd by his physicians.

Wor. I would the state of time had first been whole
Ere he by sickness had been visited:
His health was never better worth than now.

Hot. Sick now! droop now! this sickness doth infect
The very life-blood of our enterprise;
'Tis catching hither, even to our camp. 30
†He writes me here, that inward sickness—
And that his friends by deputation could not
So soon be drawn, nor did he think it meet
To lay so dangerous and dear a trust
On any soul removed but on his own.
Yet doth he give us bold advertisement,
That with our small conjunction we should on,
To see how fortune is disposed to us;
For, as he writes, there is no quailing now,
Because the king is certainly possess'd 40

177. **embossed,** swollen (with fat). 182. **injuries,** used by the prince in allusion to the pocketing of injuries, i.e., failing to resent them. 192. **Hostess, I forgive thee.** This most comic line is an indication of Falstaff's mastery. 206. **with unwashed hands,** at once. 226. **furniture,** equipment, provision. 230. **drum.** Possibly Falstaff means to say that he could wish that he might recruit his soldiers by means of this tavern.

ACT IV. SCENE I. 3. **attribution,** praise. 4-5. **stamp . . . current,**

a figure of speech derived from coining. 7. **soothers,** flatterers. 9. **task . . . word,** challenge me to make good my word. **approve,** test. 18. **justling,** jostling, busy. 36. **advertisement,** counsel, advice. 37. **conjunction,** joint force, with allusion to the conjunction of planets. 44. **want,** i.e., the lack of him. 47. **cast,** throw of the dice. **main,** number called by the caster before the dice are thrown. 51. **list,** limit; see glossary. 53. **reversion,** part of an estate yet to be inherited; hope of future profit. 61. **hair,** kind, nature. 69. **offering side,** side

I Henry IV
ACT III : SC III

696

Of all our purposes. What say you to it?
  Wor. Your father's sickness is a maim to us.
  Hot. A perilous gash, a very limb lopp'd off:
And yet, in faith, it is not; his present want
Seems more than we shall find it: were it good
To set the exact wealth of all our states
All at one cast? to set so rich a main
On the nice hazard of one doubtful hour?
It were not good; †for therein should we read
The very bottom and the soul of hope, 50
The very list, the very utmost bound
Of all our fortunes.
  Doug.   'Faith, and so we should;
Where now remains a sweet reversion:
†We may boldly spend upon the hope of what
Is to come in:
A comfort of retirement lives in this.
  Hot. A rendezvous, a home to fly unto,
If that the devil and mischance look big
Upon the maidenhead of our affairs.
  Wor. But yet I would your father had been here. 60
The quality and hair of our attempt
Brooks no division: it will be thought
By some, that know not why he is away,
That wisdom, loyalty and mere dislike
Of our proceedings kept the earl from hence:
And think how such an apprehension
May turn the tide of fearful faction
And breed a kind of question in our cause;
For well you know we of the offering side
Must keep aloof from strict arbitrement, 70
And stop all sight-holes, every loop from whence
The eye of reason may pry in upon us:
This absence of your father's draws a curtain,
That shows the ignorant a kind of fear
Before not dreamt of.
  Hot.   You strain too far.
I rather of his absence make this use:
It lends a lustre and more great opinion,
A larger dare to our great enterprise,
Than if the earl were here; for men must think,
If we without his help can make a head 80
To push against a kingdom, with his help
We shall o'erturn it topsy-turvy down.
Yet all goes well, yet all our joints are whole.
  Doug. As heart can think: there is not such a word
Spoke of in Scotland as this term of fear.

Enter Sir Richard Vernon.

  Hot. My cousin Vernon! welcome, by my soul.
  Ver. Pray God my news be worth a welcome, lord.
The Earl of Westmoreland, seven thousand strong,
Is marching hitherwards; with him Prince John.
  Hot. No harm: what more?
  Ver.   And further, I have learn'd, 90
The king himself in person is set forth,
Or hitherwards intended speedily,
With strong and mighty preparation.
  Hot. He shall be welcome too. Where is his son,
The nimble-footed madcap Prince of Wales,

And his comrades, that daff'd the world aside,
And bid it pass?
  Ver.   All furnish'd, all in arms;
†All plumed like estridges that with the wind
Baited like eagles having lately bathed;
Glittering in golden coats, like images; 100
As full of spirit as the month of May,
And gorgeous as the sun at midsummer;
Wanton as youthful goats, wild as young bulls.
I saw young Harry, with his beaver on,
His cuisses on his thighs, gallantly arm'd,
Rise from the ground like feather'd Mercury,
And vaulted with such ease into his seat,
As if an angel dropp'd down from the clouds,
To turn and wind a fiery Pegasus
And witch the world with noble horsemanship. 110
  Hot. No more, no more: worse than the sun in
      March,
This praise doth nourish agues. Let them come;
They come like sacrifices in their trim,
And to the fire-eyed maid of smoky war
All hot and bleeding will we offer them:
The mailed Mars shall on his altar sit
Up to the ears in blood. I am on fire
To hear this rich reprisal is so nigh
And yet not ours. Come, let me taste my horse,
Who is to bear me like a thunderbolt 120
Against the bosom of the Prince of Wales:
Harry to Harry shall, hot horse to horse,
Meet and ne'er part till one drop down a corse.
O that Glendower were come!
  Ver.   There is more news:
I learn'd in Worcester, as I rode along,
He cannot draw his power this fourteen days.
  Doug. That's the worst tidings that I hear of yet.
  Wor. Ay, by my faith, that bears a frosty sound.
  Hot. What may the king's whole battle reach unto?
  Ver. To thirty thousand.
  Hot.   Forty let it be: 130
My father and Glendower being both away,
The powers of us may serve so great a day.
Come, let us take a muster speedily:
Doomsday is near; die all, die merrily.
  Doug. Talk not of dying: I am out of fear
Of death or death's hand for this one-half year.
                                    [*Exeunt.*

1 Henry IV
ACT IV : SC II

697

SCENE II. *A public road near Coventry.*

Enter Falstaff *and* Bardolph.

  Fal. Bardolph, get thee before to Coventry; fill me
a bottle of sack: our soldiers shall march through;
we'll to Sutton Co'fil' to-night.
  Bard. Will you give me money, captain?
  Fal. Lay out, lay out.
  Bard. This bottle makes an angel.
  Fal. An if it do, take it for thy labour; and if it
make twenty, take them all; I'll answer the coinage.
Bid my lieutenant Peto meet me at town's end. 10

which attacks. 70. **arbitrement,** just inquiry or investigation. 96. **daff'd,** put aside with a gesture. 97. **furnish'd,** equipped. 98. **like estridges,** a reference to ostrich plumes on crests. 99. **Baited.** Most editors prefer *bated,* meaning "beating the wings impatiently." 100. **images.** Images (of saints, etc.) were dressed in splendid robes for holidays. 104. **beaver,** visor (of helmet). 105. **cuisses,** armor for the thighs. 109. **wind a fiery Pegasus,** turn or wheel like the winged horse of Greek mythology. 110. **witch,** bewitch. 111-112. **worse . . . agues.**

Your praise causes me worse pain than the agues of March. 113. **trim,** fine apparel, trappings. 118. **reprisal,** prize.
SCENE II. 3. **Sutton Co'fil',** Sutton Coldfield in Warwickshire near Coventry. 6. **makes an angel,** i.e., that I have spent. **angel,** coin worth ten shillings.

Bard. I will, captain: farewell. [*Exit.*

Fal. If I be not ashamed of my soldiers, I am a soused gurnet. I have misused the king's press damnably. I have got, in exchange of a hundred and fifty soldiers, three hundred and odd pounds. I press me none but good householders, yeomen's sons; inquire me out contracted bachelors, such as had been asked twice on the banns; such a commodity of warm slaves, as had as lieve hear the devil as a drum; such as fear the report of a caliver worse than a struck fowl or a hurt wild-duck. I pressed me none but such toasts-and-butter, with hearts in their bellies no bigger than pins' heads, and they have bought out their services; and now my whole charge consists of ancients, corporals, lieutenants, gentlemen of companies, slaves as ragged as Lazarus in the painted cloth, where the glutton's dogs licked his sores; and such as indeed were never soldiers, but discarded unjust serving-men, younger sons to younger brothers, revolted tapsters and ostlers trade-fallen, the cankers of a calm world and a long peace, ten times more dishonourable ragged than an old faced ancient: and such have I, to fill up the rooms of them that have bought out their services, that you would think that I had a hundred and fifty tattered prodigals lately come from swine-keeping, from eating draff and husks. A mad fellow met me on the way and told me I had unloaded all the gibbets and pressed the dead bodies. No eye hath seen such scarecrows. I'll not march through Coventry with them, that's flat: nay, and the villains march wide betwixt the legs, as if they had gyves on; for indeed I had the most of them out of prison. There's but a shirt and a half in all my company; and the half shirt is two napkins tacked together and thrown over the shoulders like a herald's coat without sleeves; and the shirt, to say the truth, stolen from my host at Saint Alban's, or the red-nose innkeeper of Daventry. But that's all one; they'll find linen enough on every hedge. 52

Enter the PRINCE *and* WESTMORELAND.

Prince. How now, blown Jack! how now, quilt!

Fal. What, Hal! how now, mad wag! what a devil dost thou in Warwickshire? My good Lord of Westmoreland, I cry you mercy: I thought your honour had already been at Shrewsbury. 59

West. Faith, Sir John, 'tis more than time that I were there, and you too; but my powers are there already. The king, I can tell you, looks for us all: we must away all night.

Fal. Tut, never fear me: I am as vigilant as a cat to steal cream.

Prince. I think, to steal cream indeed, for thy theft hath already made thee butter. But tell me, Jack, whose fellows are these that come after?

Fal. Mine, Hal, mine. 69

Prince. I did never see such pitiful rascals.

Fal. Tut, tut; good enough to toss; food for powder, food for powder; they'll fill a pit as well as better: tush, man, mortal men, mortal men.

West. Ay, but, Sir John, methinks they are exceeding poor and bare, too beggarly.

Fal. 'Faith, for their poverty, I know not where they had that; and for their bareness, I am sure they never learned that of me.

Prince. No, I'll be sworn; unless you call three fingers on the ribs bare. But, sirrah, make haste: Percy is already in the field. 81

Fal. What, is the king encamped?

West. He is, Sir John: I fear we shall stay too long.

Fal. Well,
To the latter end of a fray and the beginning of a
    feast
Fits a dull fighter and a keen guest. [*Exeunt.*

SCENE III. *The rebel camp near Shrewsbury.*

Enter HOTSPUR, WORCESTER, DOUGLAS, *and* VERNON.

Hot. We'll fight with him to-night.

Wor.   It may not be.

Doug. You give him then advantage.

Ver.   Not a whit.

Hot. Why say you so? looks he not for supply?

Ver. So do we.

Hot.   His is certain, ours is doubtful.

Wor. Good cousin, be advised; stir not to-night.

Ver. Do not, my lord.

Doug.   You do not counsel well:
You speak it out of fear and cold heart.

Ver. Do me no slander, Douglas: by my life,
And I dare well maintain it with my life,
If well-respected honour bid me on, 10
I hold as little counsel with weak fear
As you, my lord, or any Scot that this day lives:
Let it be seen to-morrow in the battle
Which of us fears.

Doug.   Yea, or to-night.

Ver.   Content.

Hot. To-night, say I.

Ver. Come, come, it may not be. I wonder much,
Being men of such great leading as you are,
That you foresee not what impediments
Drag back our expedition: certain horse
Of my cousin Vernon's are not yet come up: 20
Your uncle Worcester's horse came but to-day;
And now their pride and mettle is asleep,
Their courage with hard labour tame and dull,
That not a horse is half the half of himself.

Hot. So are the horses of the enemy
In general, journey-bated and brought low:
The better part of ours are full of rest.

Wor. The number of the king exceedeth ours:
For God's sake, cousin, stay till all come in.
        [*The trumpet sounds a parley.*

Enter SIR WALTER BLUNT.

Blunt. I come with gracious offers from the king, 30
If you vouchsafe me hearing and respect.

Hot. Welcome, Sir Walter Blunt; and would to God
You were of our determination!
Some of us love you well; and even those some

1 Henry IV
ACT IV : SC II

698

---

13. **soused gurnet,** a kind of fish pickled; opprobrious. 14. **king's press,** royal warrant for the impressment of troops. 16. **yeomen's,** small freeholders'. 17. **contracted,** engaged to be married. 21. **caliver,** musket or harquebus. **struck,** wounded. 26. **ancients,** standardbearers. 28. **painted cloth,** hangings for a room; in this case painted with the story of Lazarus, Luke 16:20. 32. **cankers,** worms which destroy leaves and buds; used figuratively. 34. **old faced ancient,** defined as an old standard mended with new cloth, or as a standard presenting an old aspect. Cambridge reads *old feaz'd,* meaning "frayed." 37. **prodigals.** See Luke 15:15-16. 39. **draff,** hogwash. 44. **gyves,** fetters. 50,51. **Saint Alban's, Daventry,** towns on the road from London to Coventry. 53. **blown,** swollen, inflated. 71. **toss,** i.e., on a pike.

Envy your great deservings and good name,
Because you are not of our quality,
But stand against us like an enemy.
    Blunt. And God defend but still I should stand so,
So long as out of limit and true rule
You stand against anointed majesty. 40
But to my charge. The king hath sent to know
The nature of your griefs, and whereupon
You conjure from the breast of civil peace
Such bold hostility, teaching his duteous land
Audacious cruelty. If that the king
Have any way your good deserts forgot,
Which he confesseth to be manifold,
He bids you name your griefs; and with all speed
You shall have your desires with interest
And pardon absolute for yourself and these 50
Herein misled by your suggestion.
    Hot. The king is kind; and well we know the king
Knows at what time to promise, when to pay.
My father and my uncle and myself
Did give him that same royalty he wears;
And when he was not six and twenty strong,
Sick in the world's regard, wretched and low,
A poor unminded outlaw sneaking home,
My father gave him welcome to the shore;
And when he heard him swear and vow to God 60
He came but to be Duke of Lancaster,
To sue his livery and beg his peace,
With tears of innocency and terms of zeal,
My father, in kind heart and pity moved,
Swore him assistance and perform'd it too.
Now when the lords and barons of the realm
Perceived Northumberland did lean to him,
The more and less came in with cap and knee;
Met him in boroughs, cities, villages,
Attended him on bridges, stood in lanes, 70
Laid gifts before him, proffer'd him their oaths,
Gave him their heirs, as pages follow'd him
Even at the heels in golden multitudes.
He presently, as greatness knows itself,
Steps me a little higher than his vow
Made to my father, while his blood was poor,
Upon the naked shore at Ravenspurgh;
And now, forsooth, takes on him to reform
Some certain edicts and some strait decrees
That lie too heavy on the commonwealth, 80
Cries out upon abuses, seems to weep
Over his country's wrongs; and by this face,
This seeming brow of justice, did he win
The hearts of all that he did angle for;
Proceeded further; cut me off the heads
Of all the favourites that the absent king
In deputation left behind him here,
When he was personal in the Irish war.
    Blunt. Tut, I came not to hear this.
    Hot.   Then to the point.
In short time after, he deposed the king; 90
Soon after that, deprived him of his life;
And in the neck of that, task'd the whole state;
To make that worse, suffer'd his kinsman March,
Who is, if every owner were well placed,

Indeed his king, to be engaged in Wales,
There without ransom to lie forfeited;
Disgraced me in my happy victories,
Sought to entrap me by intelligence;
Rated mine uncle from the council-board;
In rage dismiss'd my father from the court; 100
Broke oath on oath, committed wrong on wrong,
And in conclusion drove us to seek out
This head of safety; and withal to pry
Into his title, the which we find
Too indirect for long continuance.
    Blunt. Shall I return this answer to the king?
    Hot. Not so, Sir Walter: we'll withdraw awhile.
Go to the king; and let there be impawn'd
Some surety for a safe return again,
And in the morning early shall my uncle 110
Bring him our purposes: and so farewell.
    Blunt. I would you would accept of grace and love.
    Hot. And may be so we shall.
    Blunt.   Pray God you do.   [*Exeunt.*

SCENE IV. *York. The* ARCHBISHOP'S *palace.*

Enter the ARCHBISHOP OF YORK *and* SIR MICHAEL.

    Arch. Hie, good Sir Michael; bear this sealed brief
With winged haste to the lord marshal;
This to my cousin Scroop, and all the rest
To whom they are directed. If you knew
How much they do import, you would make haste.
    Sir M. My good lord,
I guess their tenour.
    Arch.   Like enough you do.
To-morrow, good Sir Michael, is a day
Wherein the fortune of ten thousand men
Must bide the touch; for, sir, at Shrewsbury, 10
As I am truly given to understand,
The king with mighty and quick-raised power
Meets with Lord Harry: and, I fear, Sir Michael,
What with the sickness of Northumberland,
Whose power was in the first proportion,
And what with Owen Glendower's absence thence,
Who with them was a rated sinew too
And comes not in, o'er-ruled by prophecies,
I fear the power of Percy is too weak
To wage an instant trial with the king. 20
    Sir M. Why, my good lord, you need not fear;
There is Douglas and Lord Mortimer.
    Arch. No, Mortimer is not there.
    Sir M. But there is Mordake, Vernon, Lord Harry
    Percy,
And there is my Lord of Worcester and a head
Of gallant warriors, noble gentlemen.
    Arch. And so there is: but yet the king hath drawn
The special head of all the land together:
The Prince of Wales, Lord John of Lancaster,
The noble Westmoreland and warlike Blunt; 30
And many moe corrivals and dear men
Of estimation and command in arms.
    Sir M. Doubt not, my lord, they shall be well
    opposed.

SCENE III. 10. **well-respected,** well weighed or considered. 26. **journey-bated,** tired from the journey. 51. **suggestion,** prompting to evil. 62. **sue his livery,** sue as an heir come of age for the delivery of his lands held by the crown. 68. **more and less,** persons of all ranks. 88. **personal,** in person. 92. **task'd,** laid taxes upon. 98. **intelligence,** secret information, i.e., from spies. 103. **head of safety,** armed force

for their protection.
    SCENE IV. 1. **brief,** letter, dispatch. 10. **bide the touch,** put to the test (like gold). 17. **rated sinew,** main strength or support reckoned upon. 31. **moe corrivals,** more partners in the enterprise. 32. **estimation,** reputation, importance.

Arch. I hope no less, yet needful 'tis to fear;
And, to prevent the worst, Sir Michael, speed:
For if Lord Percy thrive not, ere the king
Dismiss his power, he means to visit us,
For he hath heard of our confederacy,
And 'tis but wisdom to make strong against him:
Therefore make haste. I must go write again 40
To other friends; and so farewell, Sir Michael. [*Exeunt.*

ACT V.

SCENE I. *The* KING'S *camp near Shrewsbury.*

Enter the KING, PRINCE OF WALES, LORD JOHN OF
LANCASTER, EARL OF WESTMORELAND, SIR
WALTER BLUNT, *and* FALSTAFF.

King. How bloodily the sun begins to peer
Above yon busky hill! the day looks pale
At his distemperature.
Prince.   The southern wind
Doth play the trumpet to his purposes,
And by his hollow whistling in the leaves
Foretells a tempest and a blustering day.
King. Then with the losers let it sympathise,
For nothing can seem foul to those that win.
[*The trumpet sounds.*

Enter WORCESTER *and* VERNON.

How now, my Lord of Worcester! 'tis not well
That you and I should meet upon such terms 10
As now we meet. You have deceived our trust,
And made us doff our easy robes of peace,
To crush our old limbs in ungentle steel:
This is not well, my lord, this is not well.
What say you to it? will you again unknit
This churlish knot of all-abhorred war?
And move in that obedient orb again
Where you did give a fair and natural light,
And be no more an exhaled meteor,
A prodigy of fear and a portent 20
Of broached mischief to the unborn times?
Wor. Hear me, my liege:
For mine own part, I could be well content
To entertain the lag-end of my life
With quiet hours; for I do protest,
I have not sought the day of this dislike.
King. You have not sought it! how comes it, then?
Fal. Rebellion lay in his way, and he found it.
Prince. Peace, chewet, peace!
Wor. It pleased your majesty to turn your looks 30
Of favour from myself and all our house;
And yet I must remember you, my lord,
We were the first and dearest of your friends.
For you my staff of office did I break
In Richard's time; and posted day and night
To meet you on the way, and kiss your hand,
When yet you were in place and in account
Nothing so strong and fortunate as I.
It was myself, my brother and his son,
That brought you home and boldly did outdare 40

The dangers of the time. You swore to us,
And you did swear that oath at Doncaster,
That you did nothing purpose 'gainst the state;
Nor claim no further than your new-fall'n right,
The seat of Gaunt, dukedom of Lancaster:
To this we swore our aid. But in short space
It rain'd down fortune showering on your head;
And such a flood of greatness fell on you,
What with our help, what with the absent king,
What with the injuries of a wanton time, 50
The seeming sufferances that you had borne,
And the contrarious winds that held the king
So long in his unlucky Irish wars
That all in England did repute him dead:
And from this swarm of fair advantages
You took occasion to be quickly woo'd
To gripe the general sway into your hand;
Forgot your oath to us at Doncaster;
And being fed by us you used us so
As that ungentle gull, the cuckoo's bird, 60
Useth the sparrow; did oppress our nest;
Grew by our feeding to so great a bulk
That even our love durst not come near your sight
For fear of swallowing; but with nimble wing
We were enforced, for safety sake, to fly
Out of your sight and raise this present head;
Whereby we stand opposed by such means
As you yourself have forged against yourself
By unkind usage, dangerous countenance,
And violation of all faith and troth 70
Sworn to us in your younger enterprise.
King. These things indeed you have articulate,
Proclaim'd at market-crosses, read in churches,
To face the garment of rebellion
With some fine colour that may please the eye
Of fickle changelings and poor discontents,
Which gape and rub the elbow at the news
Of hurlyburly innovation:
And never yet did insurrection want
Such water-colours to impaint his cause; 80
Nor moody beggars, starving for a time
Of pellmell havoc and confusion.
Prince. In both your armies there is many a soul
Shall pay full dearly for this encounter,
If once they join in trial. Tell your nephew,
The Prince of Wales doth join with all the world
In praise of Henry Percy: by my hopes,
This present enterprise set off his head,
I do not think a braver gentleman,
More active-valiant or more valiant-young, 90
More daring or more bold, is now alive
To grace this latter age with noble deeds.
For my part, I may speak it to my shame,
I have a truant been to chivalry;
And so I hear he doth account me too;
Yet this before my father's majesty—
I am content that he shall take the odds
Of his great name and estimation,
And will, to save the blood on either side,
Try fortune with him in a single fight. 100
King. And, Prince of Wales, so dare we venture thee,

ACT V. SCENE I. 2. **busky,** bosky, bushy. 3. **distemperature,** ill-humor, or possibly, inclemency. 17. **orb,** orbit, sphere of action. 19. **exhaled,** drawn forth or engendered by the sun. 21. **broached,** already begun. 29. **chewet,** chough, jackdaw; piece of fried pie. 51. **sufferances,** suffering, distress. 60. **gull,** unfledged nestling. **cuckoo's bird,** allusion to the cuckoo's habit of laying its

eggs in the sparrow's nest. 72. **articulate,** set forth, specified. 74. **face,** trim, adorn. 78. **innovation,** disturbance, commotion. 88. **set off his head,** taken from his account. 111. **wait on us,** are in attendance upon us. 126. **thou . . . death,** proverbial, with a pun on "debt." 130-144. **Yea, but . . . catechism.** Falstaff's famous soliloquy on honor, though characteristic of him, is to be regarded, in some measure, as a

Albeit considerations infinite
Do make against it. No, good Worcester, no,
We love our people well; even those we love
That are misled upon your cousin's part;
And, will they take the offer of our grace,
Both he and they and you, yea, every man
Shall be my friend again and I'll be his:
So tell your cousin, and bring me word
What he will do: but if he will not yield, 110
Rebuke and dread correction wait on us
And they shall do their office. So, be gone;
We will not now be troubled with reply:
We offer fair; take it advisedly.
                    [*Exeunt Worcester and Vernon.*
    Prince. It will not be accepted, on my life:
The Douglas and the Hotspur both together
Are confident against the world in arms.
    King. Hence, therefore, every leader to his charge;
For, on their answer, will we set on them:
And God befriend us, as our cause is just! 120
        [*Exeunt all but the Prince of Wales and Falstaff.*
    Fal. Hal, if thou see me down in the battle and
bestride me, so; 'tis a point of friendship.
    Prince. Nothing but a colossus can do thee that
friendship. Say thy prayers, and farewell.
    Fal. I would 'twere bed-time, Hal, and all well.
    Prince. Why, thou owest God a death. [*Exit.*
    Fal. 'Tis not due yet; I would be loath to pay him
before his day. What need I be so forward with him
that calls not on me? Well, 'tis no matter; honour
pricks me on. Yea, but how if honour prick me off
when I come on? how then? Can honour set to a leg?
no: or an arm? no: or take away the grief of a wound?
no. Honour hath no skill in surgery, then? no. What is
honour? a word. What is in that word honour? what is
that honour? air. A trim reckoning! Who hath it? he
that died o' Wednesday. Doth he feel it? no. Doth he
hear it? no. 'Tis insensible, then? Yea, to the dead. But
will it not live with the living? no. Why? detraction
will not suffer it. Therefore I'll none of it. Honour is a
mere scutcheon: and so ends my catechism. [*Exit.* 144

SCENE II. *The rebel camp.*

Enter WORCESTER *and* VERNON.

    Wor. O, no, my nephew must not know, Sir
        Richard,
The liberal and kind offer of the king.
    Ver. 'Twere best he did.
    Wor.   Then are we all undone.
It is not possible, it cannot be,
The king should keep his word in loving us;
He will suspect us still and find a time
To punish this offence in other faults:
Suspicion all our lives shall be stuck full of eyes;
For treason is but trusted like the fox,
Who, ne'er so tame, so cherish'd and lock'd up, 10
Will have a wild trick of his ancestors.
Look how we can, or sad or merrily,
Interpretation will misquote our looks,

And we shall feed like oxen at a stall,
The better cherish'd, still the nearer death.
My nephew's trespass may be well forgot;
It hath the excuse of youth and heat of blood,
And an adopted name of privilege,
A hare-brain'd Hotspur, govern'd by a spleen:
All his offences live upon my head 20
And on his father's; we did train him on,
And, his corruption being ta'en from us,
We, as the spring of all, shall pay for all.
Therefore, good cousin, let not Harry know,
In any case, the offer of the king.
    Ver. Deliver what you will; I'll say 'tis so.
Here comes your cousin.

Enter HOTSPUR *and* DOUGLAS.

    Hot. My uncle is return'd:
Deliver up my Lord of Westmoreland.
Uncle, what news? 30
    Wor. The king will bid you battle presently.
    Doug. Defy him by the Lord of Westmoreland.
    Hot. Lord Douglas, go you and tell him so.
    Doug. Marry, and shall, and very willingly. [*Exit.*
    Wor. There is no seeming mercy in the king.
    Hot. Did you beg any? God forbid!
    Wor. I told him gently of our grievances,
Of his oath-breaking; which he mended thus,
By now forswearing that he is forsworn:
He calls us rebels, traitors; and will scourge 40
With haughty arms this hateful name in us.

Re-enter DOUGLAS.

    Doug. Arm, gentlemen; to arms! for I have thrown
A brave defiance in King Henry's teeth,
And Westmoreland, that was engaged, did bear it;
Which cannot choose but bring him quickly on.
    Wor. The Prince of Wales stepp'd forth before the
        king,
And, nephew, challenged you to single fight.
    Hot. O, would the quarrel lay upon our heads,
And that no man might draw short breath to-day
But I and Harry Monmouth! Tell me, tell me, 50
How show'd his tasking? seem'd it in contempt?
    Ver. No, by my soul; I never in my life
Did hear a challenge urged more modestly,
Unless a brother should a brother dare
To gentle exercise and proof of arms.
He gave you all the duties of a man;
Trimm'd up your praises with a princely tongue,
Spoke your deservings like a chronicle,
Making you ever better than his praise
By still dispraising praise valued with you; 60
And, which became him like a prince indeed,
He made a blushing cital of himself;
And chid his truant youth with such a grace
As if he master'd there a double spirit
Of teaching and of learning instantly.
There did he pause: but let me tell the world,
If he outlive the envy of this day,
England did never owe so sweet a hope,
So much misconstrued in his wantonness.

1 Henry IV
ACT V : SC II

701

---

speech inserted to amuse the audience.   131. **prick me off,** probably,
mark me off as one dead.   143. **scutcheon,** emblem or hatchment
carried in funerals. It was the lowest form of symbol, having no pennon
or other insignia.
    SCENE II.   18. **adopted name of privilege.** The meaning is that
Hotspur has taken a nickname, "hotspur," to justify his rashness.   51.

tasking, challenge.   52-69. **I . . . wantonness.** This praise in the mouth
of Hal's enemies is hardly in character, but is conventionally introduced
to inform the audience.   62. **cital,** impeachment.

Hot. Cousin, I think thou art enamoured 70
On his follies: never did I hear
Of any prince so wild a libertine.
But be he as he will, yet once ere night
I will embrace him with a soldier's arm,
That he shall shrink under my courtesy.
Arm, arm with speed: and, fellows, soldiers, friends,
Better consider what you have to do
Than I, that have not well the gift of tongue,
Can lift your blood up with persuasion.

Enter a Messenger.

Mess. My lord, here are letters for you. 80
Hot. I cannot read them now.
O gentlemen, the time of life is short!
To spend that shortness basely were too long,
If life did ride upon a dial's point,
Still ending at the arrival of an hour.
An if we live, we live to tread on kings;
If die, brave death, when princes die with us!
Now, for our consciences, the arms are fair,
When the intent of bearing them is just.

Enter another Messenger.

Mess. My lord, prepare; the king comes on apace. 90
Hot. I thank him, that he cuts me from my tale,
For I profess not talking; only this—
Let each man do his best: and here draw I
A sword, whose temper I intend to stain
With the best blood that I can meet withal
In the adventure of this perilous day.
Now, Esperance! Percy! and set on.
Sound all the lofty instruments of war,
And by that music let us all embrace;
For, heaven to earth, some of us never shall 100
A second time do such a courtesy.
[The trumpets sound. They embrace, and exeunt.

SCENE III. *Plain between the camps.*

The KING *enters with his power. Alarum to the battle.
Then enter* DOUGLAS *and* SIR WALTER BLUNT.

Blunt. What is thy name, that in the battle thus
Thou crossest me? what honour dost thou seek
Upon my head?
Doug. Know then, my name is
Douglas;
And I do haunt thee in the battle thus
Because some tell me that thou art a king.
Blunt. They tell thee true.
Doug. The Lord of Stafford dear to-day hath bought
Thy likeness, for instead of thee, King Harry,
This sword hath ended him: so shall it thee,
Unless thou yield thee as my prisoner. 10
Blunt. I was not born a yielder, thou proud Scot;
And thou shalt find a king that will revenge
Lord Stafford's death. *[They fight. Douglas kills Blunt.*

Enter HOTSPUR.

Hot. O Douglas, hadst thou fought at Holmedon
thus,
I never had triumph'd upon a Scot.

Doug. All 's done, all 's won; here breathless lies the
king.
Hot. Where?
Doug. Here.
Hot. This, Douglas? no: I know this face full well:
A gallant knight he was, his name was Blunt; 20
Semblably furnish'd like the king himself.
Doug. A fool go with thy soul, whither it goes!
A borrow'd title hast thou bought too dear:
Why didst thou tell me that thou wert a king?
Hot. The king hath many marching in his coats.
Doug. Now, by my sword, I will kill all his coats;
I'll murder all his wardrobe, piece by piece,
Until I meet the king.
Hot. Up, and away!
Our soldiers stand full fairly for the day. *[Exeunt. 29*

Alarum. Enter FALSTAFF, *solus.*

Fal. Though I could 'scape shot-free at London, I
fear the shot here; here 's no scoring but upon the
pate. Soft! who are you? Sir Walter Blunt: there 's
honour for you! here 's no vanity! I am as hot as
molten lead, and as heavy too: God keep lead out of
me! I need no more weight than mine own bowels. I
have led my ragamuffins where they are peppered:
there 's not three of my hundred and fifty left alive;
and they are for the town's end, to beg during life.
But who comes here? 40

Enter the PRINCE.

Prince. What, stand'st thou idle here? lend me thy
sword:
Many a nobleman lies stark and stiff
Under the hoofs of vaunting enemies,
Whose deaths are yet unrevenged: I prithee, lend me
thy sword.
Fal. O Hal, I prithee, give me leave to breathe
awhile. Turk Gregory never did such deeds in arms
as I have done this day. I have paid Percy, I have
made him sure.
Prince. He is, indeed; and living to kill thee. I
prithee, lend me thy sword. 50
Fal. Nay, before God, Hal, if Percy be alive, thou
get'st not my sword; but take my pistol, if thou wilt.
Prince. Give it me: what, is it in the case?
Fal. Ay, Hal; 'tis hot, 'tis hot; there 's that will sack
a city.
[The Prince draws it out, and finds it to be a bottle of sack.
Prince. What, is it a time to jest and dally now? 58
[He throws the bottle at him. Exit.
Fal. Well, if Percy be alive, I'll pierce him. If he
do come in my way, so: if he do not, if I come in his
willingly, let him make a carbonado of me. I like not
such grinning honour as Sir Walter hath: give me life:
which if I can save, so; if not, honour comes unlooked
for, and there 's an end. *[Exit.*

SCENE IV. *Another part of the field.*

Alarum. Excursions. Enter the KING, *the* PRINCE, LORD
JOHN OF LANCASTER, *and* EARL OF WEST-
MORELAND.

King. I prithee,

---

84. **dial's point,** hand of watch or clock.
SCENE III. 21. **Semblably furnish'd,** similarly accoutered. 30. **shot-
free,** scot-free, without paying. 31. **scoring,** marking up of charges
(often on the inn door). 46. **Turk Gregory,** a sort of combined allusion

to the famous pope Gregory the Great, and to the Grand Turk. 59.
Percy...pierce. Current pronunciation probably rendered the pun more
obvious than it is now. 62. **carbonado,** meat scored across for broiling.
SCENE IV. 5. **make up,** go forward. 6. **amaze,** alarm. 22. **mainte-**

Harry, withdraw thyself; thou bleed'st too much.
Lord John of Lancaster, go you with him.
   Lan. Not I, my lord, unless I did bleed too.
   Prince. I beseech your majesty, make up,
Lest your retirement do amaze your friends.
   King. I will do so.
My Lord of Westmoreland, lead him to his tent.
   West. Come, my lord, I'll lead you to your tent.
   Prince. Lead me, my lord? I do not need your help:
And God forbid a shallow scratch should drive   11
The Prince of Wales from such a field as this,
Where stain'd nobility lies trodden on,
And rebels' arms triumph in massacres!
   Lan. We breathe too long: come, cousin
     Westmoreland,
Our duty this way lies; for God's sake, come.
          [Exeunt Prince John and Westmoreland.
   Prince. By God, thou hast deceived me, Lancaster;
I did not think thee lord of such a spirit:
Before, I loved thee as a brother, John;
But now, I do respect thee as my soul.   20
   King. I saw him hold Lord Percy at the point
With lustier maintenance than I did look for
Of such an ungrown warrior.
   Prince.   O, this boy
Lends mettle to us all!   *[Exit.*

Enter DOUGLAS.

   Doug. Another king! they grow like Hydra's heads:
I am the Douglas, fatal to all those
That wear those colours on them: what art thou,
That counterfeit'st the person of a king?
   King. The king himself; who, Douglas, grieves at
     heart
So many of his shadows thou hast met   30
And not the very king. I have two boys
Seek Percy and thyself about the field:
But, seeing thou fall'st on me so luckily,
I will assay thee: so, defend thyself.
   Doug. I fear thou art another counterfeit;
And yet, in faith, thou bear'st thee like a king:
But mine I am sure thou art, whoe'er thou be,
And thus I win thee.
    [They fight; the King being in danger, re-enter Prince
                      of Wales.
   Prince. Hold up thy head, vile Scot, or thou art like
Never to hold it up again! the spirits   40
Of valiant Shirley, Stafford, Blunt, are in my arms:
It is the Prince of Wales that threatens thee;
Who never promiseth but he means to pay.
                [They fight: Douglas flies.
Cheerly, my lord: how fares your grace?
Sir Nicholas Gawsey hath for succour sent,
And so hath Clifton: I'll to Clifton straight.
   King. Stay, and breathe awhile:
Thou hast redeem'd thy lost opinion,
And show'd thou makest some tender of my life,
In this fair rescue thou hast brought to me.   50
   Prince. O God! they did me too much injury
That ever said I hearken'd for your death.
If it were so, I might have let alone
The insulting hand of Douglas over you,
Which would have been as speedy in your end

As all the poisonous potions in the world
And saved the treacherous labour of your son.
   King. Make up to Clifton: I'll to Sir Nicholas
     Gawsey.   *[Exit.*

Enter HOTSPUR.

   Hot. If I mistake not, thou art Harry Monmouth.
   Prince. Thou speak'st as if I would deny my name. 60
   Hot. My name is Harry Percy.
   Prince.   Why, then I see
A very valiant rebel of the name.
I am the Prince of Wales; and think not, Percy,
To share with me in glory any more:
Two stars keep not their motion in one sphere;
Nor can one England brook a double reign,
Of Harry Percy and the Prince of Wales.
   Hot. Nor shall it, Harry; for the hour is come
To end the one of us; and would to God
Thy name in arms were now as great as mine!   70
   Prince. I'll make it greater ere I part from thee;
And all the budding honours on thy crest
I'll crop, to make a garland for my head.
   Hot. I can no longer brook thy vanities. *[They fight.*

Enter FALSTAFF.

   Fal. Well said, Hal! to it, Hal! Nay, you shall find
no boy's play here, I can tell you.

Re-enter DOUGLAS; *he fights with* FALSTAFF, *who falls down*
   as if he were dead, and exit DOUGLAS. HOTSPUR
        is wounded, and falls.

   Hot. O, Harry, thou hast robb'd me of my youth!
I better brook the loss of brittle life
Than those proud titles thou hast won of me;
They wound my thoughts worse than thy sword my
     flesh: 80
But thought's the slave of life, and life time's fool;
And time, that takes survey of all the world,
Must have a stop. O, I could prophesy,
But that the earthy and cold hand of death
Lies on my tongue: no, Percy, thou art dust,
And food for—   *[Dies.*
   Prince. For worms, brave Percy: fare thee well, great
     heart!
Ill-weaved ambition, how much art thou shrunk!
When that this body did contain a spirit,
A kingdom for it was too small a bound;   90
But now two paces of the vilest earth
Is room enough: this earth that bears thee dead
Bears not alive so stout a gentleman.
If thou wert sensible of courtesy,
I should not make so dear a show of zeal:
But let my favours hide thy mangled face;
And, even in thy behalf, I'll thank myself
For doing these fair rites of tenderness.
Adieu, and take thy praise with thee to heaven!
Thy ignominy sleep with thee in the grave,   100
But not remember'd in thy epitaph!
         [He spieth Falstaff on the ground.
What, old acquaintance! could not all this flesh
Keep in a little life? Poor Jack, farewell!
I could have better spared a better man:
O, I should have a heavy miss of thee,
If I were much in love with vanity!

---

nance, bearing, demeanor.   **25. Hydra's heads,** allusion to the Lernean
Hydra, whose heads grew again as fast as they were cut off.   **49. makest
some tender,** hast some care for.   **52. hearken'd,** listened (as for welcome intelligence).   **65. Two . . . sphere,** proverbial allusion to the

fact that each planet has its own orbit.   **81-83. But . . . stop.** Thought
ends with life, and life is ended by time; and time, though it serve
as the measure for the world, must itself come to an end.   **96. favours,**
knots of ribbon.

Death hath not struck so fat a deer to-day,
Though many dearer, in this bloody fray.
Embowell'd will I see thee by and by:
Till then in blood by noble Percy lie.   [*Exit.* 110
  Fal. [*Rising up*] Embowelled! if thou embowel me
to-day, I'll give you leave to powder me and eat me
too to-morrow. 'Sblood, 'twas time to counterfeit,
or that hot termagant Scot had paid me scot and lot
too. Counterfeit? I lie, I am no counterfeit: to die, is
to be a counterfeit; for he is but the counterfeit of a
man who hath not the life of a man: but to counterfeit
dying, when a man thereby liveth, is to be no counterfeit, but the true and perfect image of life indeed.
The better part of valour is discretion; in the which
better part I have saved my life. 'Zounds, I am afraid
of this gunpowder Percy, though he be dead: how,
if he should counterfeit too and rise? by my faith, I
am afraid he would prove the better counterfeit.
Therefore I'll make him sure; yea, and I'll swear I
killed him. Why may not he rise as well as I? Nothing
confutes me but eyes, and nobody sees me. Therefore,
sirrah [*stabbing him*], with a new wound in your
thigh, come you along with me.   132
                  [*Takes up Hotspur on his back.*

Re-enter the PRINCE OF WALES *and* LORD JOHN OF
LANCASTER.

  Prince. Come, brother John; full bravely hast thou
    flesh'd
Thy maiden sword.
  Lan.   But, soft! whom have we here?
Did you not tell me this fat man was dead?
  Prince. I did; I saw him dead,
Breathless and bleeding on the ground. Art thou alive?
Or is it fantasy that plays upon our eyesight?
I prithee, speak; we will not trust our eyes
Without our ears: thou art not what thou seem'st. 140
  Fal. No, that's certain; I am not a double man: but
if I be not Jack Falstaff, then am I a Jack. There is
Percy [*throwing the body down*]: if your father will do
me any honour, so; if not, let him kill the next Percy
himself. I look to be either earl or duke, I can assure
you.
  Prince. Why, Percy I killed myself and saw thee
    dead.
  Fal. Didst thou? Lord, Lord, how this world is
given to lying! I grant you I was down and out of
breath; and so was he: but we rose both at an instant
and fought a long hour by Shrewsbury clock. If I
may be believed, so; if not, let them that should
reward valour bear the sin upon their own heads.
I'll take it upon my death, I gave him this wound in
the thigh: if the man were alive and would deny it,
'zounds, I would make him eat a piece of my sword.
  Lan. This is the strangest tale that ever I heard.
  Prince. This is the strangest fellow, brother John.
Come, bring your luggage nobly on your back: 160
For my part, if a lie may do thee grace,
I'll gild it with the happiest terms I have.
                        [*A retreat is sounded.*
The trumpet sounds retreat; the day is ours.

Come, brother, let us to the highest of the field,
To see what friends are living, who are dead.
          [*Exeunt Prince of Wales and Lancaster.*
  Fal. I'll follow, as they say, for reward. He that
rewards me, God reward him! If I do grow great,
I'll grow less; for I'll purge, and leave sack, and live
cleanly as a nobleman should do.   [*Exit.*

SCENE V. *Another part of the field.*

The trumpets sound. Enter the KING, PRINCE OF WALES,
LORD JOHN OF LANCASTER, EARL OF WEST-
MORELAND, *with* WORCESTER *and* VERNON
prisoners.

  King. Thus ever did rebellion find rebuke.
Ill-spirited Worcester! did not we send grace,
Pardon and terms of love to all of you?
And wouldst thou turn our offers contrary?
Misuse the tenour of thy kinsman's trust?
Three knights upon our party slain to-day,
A noble earl and many a creature else
Had been alive this hour,
If like a Christian thou hadst truly borne
Betwixt our armies true intelligence.   10
  Wor. What I have done my safety urged me to;
And I embrace this fortune patiently,
Since not to be avoided it falls on me.
  King. Bear Worcester to the death and Vernon too:
Other offenders we will pause upon.
          [*Exeunt Worcester and Vernon, guarded.*
How goes the field?
  Prince. The noble Scot, Lord Douglas, when he saw
The fortune of the day quite turn'd from him,
The noble Percy slain, and all his men
Upon the foot of fear, fled with the rest;   20
And falling from a hill, he was so bruised
That the pursuers took him. At my tent
The Douglas is; and I beseech your grace
I may dispose of him.
  King.   With all my heart.
  Prince. Then, brother John of Lancaster, to you
This honourable bounty shall belong:
Go to the Douglas, and deliver him
Up to his pleasure, ransomless and free:
His valour shown upon our crests to-day
Hath taught us how to cherish such high deeds   30
Even in the bosom of our adversaries.
  Lan. I thank your grace for this high courtesy,
Which I shall give away immediately.
  King. Then this remains, that we divide our power.
You, son John, and my cousin Westmoreland
Towards York shall bend you with your dearest speed,
To meet Northumberland and the prelate Scroop,
Who, as we hear, are busily in arms:
Myself and you, son Harry, will towards Wales,
To fight with Glendower and the Earl of March.   40
Rebellion in this land shall lose his sway,
Meeting the check of such another day:
And since this business so fair is done,
Let us not leave till all our own be won.   [*Exeunt.*

THE SECOND PART OF
King Henry the Fourth

DRAMATIS PERSONAE

RUMOUR, the Presenter.
KING HENRY the Fourth.
HENRY, PRINCE OF WALES,
    afterwards King Henry V.,
THOMAS, DUKE OF CLARENCE, } his sons.
PRINCE JOHN OF LANCASTER,
PRINCE HUMPHREY OF GLOUCESTER,
EARL OF WARWICK.
EARL OF WESTMORELAND.
EARL OF SURREY.
GOWER.
HARCOURT.
BLUNT.
Lord Chief-Justice of the King's Bench.
A Servant of the Chief-Justice.
EARL OF NORTHUMBERLAND.
SCROOP, Archbishop of York.
LORD MOWBRAY.
LORD HASTINGS.
LORD BARDOLPH.
SIR JOHN COLEVILE.
TRAVERS and MORTON, retainers of
    Northumberland.
SIR JOHN FALSTAFF.
His Page.
BARDOLPH.
PISTOL.
POINS.
PETO.
SHALLOW, } country justices.
SILENCE,
DAVY, Servant to Shallow.
MOULDY, SHADOW, WART, FEEBLE, and
    BULLCALF, recruits.
FANG and SNARE, sheriff's officers.

LADY NORTHUMBERLAND.
LADY PERCY.
MISTRESS QUICKLY, hostess of a tavern in
    Eastcheap.
DOLL TEARSHEET.

Lords and Attendants; Porter, Drawers,
    Beadles, Grooms, &c.
A Dancer, speaker of the epilogue.

SCENE: *England.*

INDUCTION.

Warkworth. Before the castle.

Enter Rumour, *painted full of tongues.*

Rum. Open your ears; for which of you will stop
The vent of hearing when loud Rumour speaks?

I, from the orient to the drooping west,
Making the wind my post-horse, still unfold
The acts commenced on this ball of earth:
Upon my tongues continual slanders ride,
The which in every language I pronounce,
Stuffing the ears of men with false reports.
I speak of peace, while covert enmity
Under the smile of safety wounds the world: 10
And who but Rumour, who but only I,
Make fearful musters and prepared defence,
Whiles the big year, swoln with some other grief,
Is thought with child by the stern tyrant war,
And no such matter? Rumour is a pipe
Blown by surmises, jealousies, conjectures,
And of so easy and so plain a stop
That the blunt monster with uncounted heads,
The still-discordant wavering multitude,
Can play upon it. But what need I thus   20
My well-known body to anatomize
Among my household? Why is Rumour here?
I run before King Harry's victory;
Who in a bloody field by Shrewsbury
Hath beaten down young Hotspur and his troops,
Quenching the flame of bold rebellion
Even with the rebels' blood. But what mean I
To speak so true at first? my office is
To noise abroad that Harry Monmouth fell
Under the wrath of noble Hotspur's sword,   30
And that the king before the Douglas' rage
Stoop'd his anointed head as low as death.
This have I rumour'd through the peasant towns
Between that royal field of Shrewsbury
And this worm-eaten hold of ragged stone,
Where Hotspur's father, old Northumberland,
Lies crafty-sick: the posts come tiring on,
And not a man of them brings other news
Than they have learn'd of me: from Rumour's
    tongues
They bring smooth comforts false, worse than true
    wrongs.   [*Exit.* 40

ACT I.

SCENE I. *The same.*

Enter LORD BARDOLPH.

L. Bard. Who keeps the gate here, ho?

The Porter *opens the gate.*
           Where is the earl?
Port. What shall I say you are?
L. Bard.   Tell thou the earl
That the Lord Bardolph doth attend him here.
    Port. His lordship is walk'd forth into the orchard:
Please it your honour, knock but at the gate,
And he himself will answer.

The Second Part of King Henry the Fourth. The play is supposed to open
immediately after the Battle of Shrewsbury, in which Henry Percy, or
Hotspur, and the Scottish earl of Douglas have been overthrown. We
are concerned first of all with the news of the battle.
    INDUCTION. *Stage Direction:* **Rumour . . . tongues.** Rumor wears a
symbolic costume. Virgil describes her as full of eyes, ears, and tongues
(*Aeneid,* iv, 174). 17. **stop,** hole in wind instruments. 18. **blunt,**
stupid, dull-witted. 21. **anatomize,** lay open minutely, explain. 33.
peasant, rural, or provincial. 35. **hold,** stronghold. 37. **crafty-sick,**
feigning sickness.
    ACT I. SCENE I. 2. **What,** etc., of what name and station.

Enter NORTHUMBERLAND.

L. Bard. Here comes the earl.
                                 [*Exit Porter.*
   North. What news, Lord Bardolph? every minute
      now
Should be the father of some stratagem:
The times are wild; contention, like a horse
Full of high feeding, madly hath broke loose   10
And bears down all before him.
   L. Bard. Noble earl,
I bring you certain news from Shrewsbury.
   North. Good, an God will!
   L. Bard. As good as heart can wish:]
The king is almost wounded to the death;
And, in the fortune of my lord your son,
Prince Harry slain outright; and both the Blunts
Kill'd by the hand of Douglas; young Prince John
And Westmoreland and Stafford fled the field;
And Harry Monmouth's brawn, the hulk Sir John,
Is prisoner to your son: O, such a day,   20
So fought, so follow'd and so fairly won,
Came not till now to dignify the times,
Since Cæsar's fortunes!
   North. How is this derived?
Saw you the field? came you from Shrewsbury?
   L. Bard. I spake with one, my lord, that came from
      thence,
A gentleman well bred and of good name,
That freely render'd me these news for true.
   North. Here comes my servant Travers, whom I sent
On Tuesday last to listen after news.

Enter TRAVERS.

   L. Bard. My lord, I over-rode him on the way;   30
And he is furnish'd with no certainties
More than he haply may retail from me.
   North. Now, Travers, what good tidings comes with
      you?
   Tra. My lord, Sir John Umfrevile turn'd me back
With joyful tidings; and, being better horsed,
Out-rode me. After him came spurring hard
A gentleman, almost forspent with speed,
That stopp'd by me to breathe his bloodied horse.
He ask'd the way to Chester; and of him
I did demand what news from Shrewsbury: 40
He told me that rebellion had bad luck
And that young Harry Percy's spur was cold.
With that, he gave his able horse the head,
And bending forward struck his armed heels
Against the panting sides of his poor jade
Up to the rowel-head, and starting so
He seem'd in running to devour the way,
Staying no longer question.
   North. Ha! Again:
Said he young Harry Percy's spur was cold?
Of Hotspur Coldspur? that rebellion   50
Had met ill luck?
   L. Bard. My lord, I'll tell you what;
If my young lord your son have not the day,
Upon mine honour, for a silken point
I'll give my barony: never talk of it.

   North. Why should that gentleman that rode by
      Travers
Give then such instances of loss?
   L. Bard. Who, he?
He was some hilding fellow that had stolen
The horse he rode on, and, upon my life,
Spoke at a venture. Look, here comes more news.

Enter MORTON.

   North. Yea, this man's brow, like to a title-leaf,   60
Foretells the nature of a tragic volume:
So looks the strand whereon the imperious flood
Hath left a witness'd usurpation.
Say, Morton, didst thou come from Shrewsbury?
   Mor. I ran from Shrewsbury, my noble lord;
Where hateful death put on his ugliest mask
To fright our party.
   North. How doth my son and brother?
Thou tremblest; and the whiteness in thy cheek
Is apter than thy tongue to tell thy errand.
Even such a man, so faint, so spiritless,   70
So dull, so dead in look, so woe-begone,
Drew Priam's curtain in the dead of night,
And would have told him half his Troy was burnt;
But Priam found the fire ere he his tongue,
And I my Percy's death ere thou report'st it.
This thou wouldst say, 'Your son did thus and thus;
Your brother thus: so fought the noble Douglas:'
Stopping my greedy ear with their bold deeds:
But in the end, to stop my ear indeed,
Thou hast a sigh to blow away this praise,   80
Ending with 'Brother, son, and all are dead.'
   Mor. Douglas is living, and your brother, yet;
But, for my lord your son,—
   North. Why, he is dead.
See what a ready tongue suspicion hath!
He that but fears the thing he would not know
Hath by instinct knowledge from others' eyes
That what he fear'd is chanced. Yet speak, Morton;
Tell thou an earl his divination lies,
And I will take it as a sweet disgrace
And make thee rich for doing me such wrong.   90
   Mor. You are too great to be by me gainsaid:
Your spirit is too true, your fears too certain.
   North. Yet, for all this, say not that Percy 's dead.
I see a strange confession in thine eye:
Thou shakest thy head and hold'st it fear or sin
To speak a truth. If he be slain, say so;
The tongue offends not that reports his death:
And he doth sin that doth belie the dead,
Not he which says the dead is not alive.
Yet the first bringer of unwelcome news   100
Hath but a losing office, and his tongue
Sounds ever after as a sullen bell,
Remember'd tolling a departing friend.
   L. Bard. I cannot think, my lord, your son is dead.
   Mor. I am sorry I should force you to believe
That which I would to God I had not seen;
But these mine eyes saw him in bloody state,
Rendering faint quittance, wearied and outbreathed,
To Harry Monmouth; whose swift wrath beat down

8. **stratagem**, deed of violence. 15. **in the fortune of,** by the good fortune of. 19. **brawn,** fleshy part of the body; an allusion to Falstaff's fatness. 21. **follow'd,** carried through. 37. **forspent,** exhausted. 38. **bloodied,** i.e., with spurring. 45. **jade,** tired horse. 46. **rowel-head,** the end of the spur, in which the barbed wheel turns. 53. **point,** lace for fastening hose to doublet. 57. **hilding,** good-for-nothing. 63. **witness'd usurpation.** evidence of its ravages. 72. **Priam's.** Priam was

the king of Troy. 91. **gainsaid,** contradicted. 103. **tolling,** ringing the passing bell for. 108. **quittance,** requital, i.e., resistance. 112. **In few,** in few words. 114. **bruited,** noised abroad, reported. 116. **metal,** courage, temperament. 120. **enforcement,** compulsion. 128. **appearance,** i.e., warriors dressed like the king. 129. **'Gan vail,** began to abate or lower (his courage). 141. **buckle,** bend (under stress). 144. **grief . . . grief,** hardship . . . sorrow. 147. **quoif,** close-

The never-daunted Percy to the earth,   110
From whence with life he never more sprung up.
In few, his death, whose spirit lent a fire
Even to the dullest peasant in his camp,
Being bruited once, took fire and heat away
From the best-temper'd courage in his troops;
For from his metal was his party steel'd;
Which once in him abated, all the rest
Turn'd on themselves, like dull and heavy lead:
And as the thing that's heavy in itself,
Upon enforcement flies with greatest speed,   120
So did our men, heavy in Hotspur's loss,
Lend to this weight such lightness with their fear
That arrows fled not swifter toward their aim
Than did our soldiers, aiming at their safety,
Fly from the field. Then was that noble Worcester
Too soon ta'en prisoner; and that furious Scot,
The bloody Douglas, whose well-labouring sword
Had three times slain the appearance of the king,
'Gan vail his stomach and did grace the shame
Of those that turn'd their backs, and in his flight,   130
Stumbling in fear, was took. The sum of all
Is that the king hath won, and hath sent out
A speedy power to encounter you, my lord,
Under the conduct of young Lancaster
And Westmoreland. This is the news at full.
    North. For this I shall have time enough to mourn.
In poison there is physic; and these news,
Having been well, that would have made me sick,
Being sick, have in some measure made me well:
And as the wretch, whose fever-weaken'd joints,   140
Like strengthless hinges, buckle under life,
Impatient of his fit, breaks like a fire
Out of his keeper's arms, even so my limbs,
Weaken'd with grief, being now enraged with grief,
Are thrice themselves. Hence, therefore, thou nice
        crutch!
A scaly gauntlet now with joints of steel
Must glove this hand: and hence, thou sickly quoif!
Thou art a guard too wanton for the head
Which princes, flesh'd with conquest, aim to hit.
Now bind my brows with iron; and approach   150
The ragged'st hour that time and spite dare bring
To frown upon the enraged Northumberland!
Let heaven kiss earth! now let not Nature's hand
Keep the wild flood confined! let order die!
And let this world no longer be a stage
To feed contention in a lingering act;
But let one spirit of the first-born Cain
Reign in all bosoms, that, each heart being set
On bloody courses, the rude scene may end,
And darkness be the burier of the dead!   160
    Tra. This strained passion doth you wrong, my lord.
    L. Bard. Sweet earl, divorce not wisdom from your
        honour.
    Mor. The lives of all your loving complices
Lean on your health; the which, if you give o'er
To stormy passion, must perforce decay.
You cast the event of war, my noble lord,
And summ'd the account of chance, before you said
'Let us make head.' It was your presurmise,

That, in the dole of blows, your son might drop:
You knew he walk'd o'er perils, on an edge,   170
More likely to fall in than to get o'er;
You were advised his flesh was capable
Of wounds and scars and that his forward spirit
Would lift him where most trade of danger ranged:
Yet did you say 'Go forth;' and none of this,
Though strongly apprehended, could restrain
The stiff-borne action: what hath then befallen,
Or what hath this bold enterprise brought forth,
More than that being which was like to be?
    L. Bard. We all that are engaged to this loss   180
Knew that we ventured on such dangerous seas
That if we wrought out life 'twas ten to one;
And yet we ventured, for the gain proposed
Choked the respect of likely peril fear'd;
And since we are o'erset, venture again.
Come, we will all put forth, body and goods.
    Mor. 'Tis more than time: and, my most noble lord,
I hear for certain, and do speak the truth,
The gentle Archbishop of York is up
With well-appointed powers: he is a man   190
Who with a double surety binds his followers.
My lord your son had only but the corpse,
But shadows and the shows of men, to fight;
For that same word, rebellion, did divide
The action of their bodies from their souls;
And they did fight with queasiness, constrain'd,
As men drink potions, that their weapons only
Seem'd on our side; but, for their spirits and souls,
This word, rebellion, it had froze them up,
As fish are in a pond. But now the bishop   200
Turns insurrection to religion:
Supposed sincere and holy in his thoughts,
He 's followed both with body and with mind;
And doth enlarge his rising with the blood
Of fair King Richard, scraped from Pomfret stones;
Derives from heaven his quarrel and his cause;
Tells them he doth bestride a bleeding land,
Gasping for life under great Bolingbroke;
And more and less do flock to follow him.
    North. I knew of this before; but, to speak truth,   210
This present grief had wiped it from my mind.
Go in with me; and counsel every man
The aptest way for safety and revenge:
Get posts and letters, and make friends with speed:
Never so few, and never yet more need.   [*Exeunt.*

SCENE II. *London. A street.*

Enter FALSTAFF, *with his* Page *bearing his sword and
    buckler.*

Fal. Sirrah, you giant, what says the doctor to my
water?
    Page. He said, sir, the water itself was a good
healthy water; but, for the party that owed it, he
might have more diseases than he knew for.   6
    Fal. Men of all sorts take a pride to gird at me: the
brain of this foolish-compounded clay, man, is not

able to invent any thing that tends to laughter, more than I invent or is invented on me: I am not only witty in myself, but the cause that wit is in other men. I do here walk before thee like a sow that hath overwhelmed all her litter but one. If the prince put thee into my service for any other reason than to set me off, why then I have no judgement. Thou whoreson mandrake, thou art fitter to be worn in my cap than to wait at my heels. I was never manned with an agate till now: but I will inset you neither in gold nor silver, but in vile apparel, and send you back again to your master, for a jewel,—the juvenal, the prince your master, whose chin is not yet fledged. I will sooner have a beard grow in the palm of my hand than he shall get one on his cheek; and yet he will not stick to say his face is a face-royal: God may finish it when he will, 'tis not a hair amiss yet: he may keep it still at a face-royal, for a barber shall never earn sixpence out of it; and yet he'll be crowing as if he had writ man ever since his father was a bachelor. He may keep his own grace, but he's almost out of mine, I can assure him. What said Master Dombledon about the satin for my short cloak and my slops? 34

Page. He said, sir, you should procure him better assurance than Bardolph: he would not take his band and yours; he liked not the security.

Fal. Let him be damned, like the glutton! pray God his tongue be hotter! A whoreson Achitophel! a rascally yea-forsooth knave! to bear a gentleman in hand, and then stand upon security! The whoreson smooth-pates do now wear nothing but high shoes, and bunches of keys at their girdles; and if a man is through with them in honest taking up, then they must stand upon security. I had as lief they would put ratsbane in my mouth as offer to stop it with security. I looked a' should have sent me two and twenty yards of satin, as I am a true knight, and he sends me security. Well, he may sleep in security; for he hath the horn of abundance, and the lightness of his wife shines through it: and yet cannot he see, though he have his own lanthorn to light him. Where's Bardolph? 55

Page. He's gone into Smithfield to buy your worship a horse.

Fal. I bought him in Paul's, and he'll buy me a horse in Smithfield: an I could get me but a wife in the stews, I were manned, horsed, and wived. 61

Enter the Lord Chief-Justice *and* Servant.

Page. Sir, here comes the nobleman that committed the prince for striking him about Bardolph.

Fal. Wait close; I will not see him.

Ch. Just. What's he that goes there?

Serv. Falstaff, an't please your lordship.

Ch. Just. He that was in question for the robbery? 69

Serv. He, my lord: but he hath since done good service at Shrewsbury; and, as I hear, is now going

with some charge to the Lord John of Lancaster.

Ch. Just. What, to York? Call him back again.

Serv. Sir John Falstaff!

Fal. Boy, tell him I am deaf.

Page. You must speak louder; my master is deaf. 79

Ch. Just. I am sure he is, to the hearing of any thing good. Go, pluck him by the elbow; I must speak with him.

Serv. Sir John!

Fal. What! a young knave, and begging! Is there not wars? is there not employment? doth not the king lack subjects? do not the rebels need soldiers? Though it be a shame to be on any side but one, it is worse shame to beg than to be on the worst side, were it worse than the name of rebellion can tell how to make it. 90

Serv. You mistake me, sir.

Fal. Why, sir, did I say you were an honest man? setting my knighthood and my soldiership aside, I had lied in my throat, if I had said so.

Serv. I pray you, sir, then set your knighthood and your soldiership aside; and give me leave to tell you, you lie in your throat, if you say I am any other than an honest man.

Fal. I give thee leave to tell me so! I lay aside that which grows to me! If thou gettest any leave of me, hang me; if thou takest leave, thou wert better be hanged. You hunt counter: hence! avaunt! 103

Serv. Sir, my lord would speak with you.

Ch. Just. Sir John Falstaff, a word with you.

Fal. My good lord! God give your lordship good time of day. I am glad to see your lordship abroad: I heard say your lordship was sick: I hope your lordship goes abroad by advice. Your lordship, though not clean past your youth, hath yet some smack of age in you, some relish of the saltness of time; and I most humbly beseech your lordship to have a reverent care of your health.

Ch. Just. Sir John, I sent for you before your expedition to Shrewsbury. 116

Fal. An't please your lordship, I hear his majesty is returned with some discomfort from Wales.

Ch. Just. I talk not of his majesty: you would not come when I sent for you. 121

Fal. And I hear, moreover, his highness is fallen into this same whoreson apoplexy.

Ch. Just. Well, God mend him! I pray you, let me speak with you.

Fal. This apoplexy is, as I take it, a kind of lethargy, an't please your lordship; a kind of sleeping in the blood, a whoreson tingling.

Ch. Just. What tell you me of it? be it as it is. 130

Fal. It hath it original from much grief, from study and perturbation of the brain: I have read the cause of his effects in Galen: it is a kind of deafness.

Ch. Just. I think you are fallen into the disease; for you hear not what I say to you.

Fal. Very well, my lord, very well: rather, an't

11-13. **I am . . . men,** a masterly comment on Falstaff. 18. **mandrake,** a poisonous plant whose root was supposed to resemble the human figure. 20. **agate,** small figure cut in agate for jewelry. 21. **inset,** set. 23. **juvenal,** youth. 28. **face-royal,** face of the king on the *royal,* a coin, with pun (l. 30) on *royal face.* 34. **slops,** loose breeches. 39. **glutton,** a reference to the parable of Dives (Luke 16:19-31). 41. **Achitophel,** counselor of Absalom (II Samuel, Chap. 15-17). **yea-forsooth,** contemptuous allusion to polite oaths. 42. **bear . . . in hand,** delude with false hopes. 43. **smooth-pates,** allusion to the short hair of tradesmen. 46. **taking up,** obtaining on credit. 52. **horn,** an allusion to the cuckold's horn, as also in *lanthorn* below. 56. **Smithfield,** famous then

as now as a livestock market. 58. **Paul's,** St. Paul's Cathedral, resort of serving-men seeking employment. 60. **stews,** houses of ill fame. 68. **in question,** under judicial examination. 70. **done good service.** This passage is cited by those who insist that Falstaff was a man of courage. 100. **grows to,** is an integral part of. 103. **hunt counter,** a hunting term meaning "run backward on the trail." 111. **smack of age,** the savor of age. 118. **discomfort,** grief of mind. 123. **apoplexy,** paralysis. 131. **it original,** its origin. 133. **Galen,** the famous Greek authority on medicine. 141. **punish . . . heels,** punish in the stocks. 148-149. **dram of a scruple,** small portion of doubt, with puns on *dram* and *scruple* as weights. 154-156. **As I . . . come.** Falstaff means to say please you, it is the disease of not listening, the malady of not marking, that I am troubled withal. 140

Ch. Just. To punish you by the heels would amend the attention of your ears; and I care not if I do become your physician.

Fal. I am as poor as Job, my lord, but not so patient: your lordship may minister the potion of imprisonment to me in respect of poverty; but how should I be your patient to follow your prescriptions, the wise may make some dram of a scruple, or indeed a scruple itself.

Ch. Just. I sent for you, when there were matters against you for your life, to come speak with me. 153

Fal. As I was then advised by my learned counsel in the laws of this land-service, I did not come.

Ch. Just. Well, the truth is, Sir John, you live in great infamy.

Fal. He that buckles him in my belt cannot live in less.

Ch. Just. Your means are very slender, and your waste is great. 160

Fal. I would it were otherwise; I would my means were greater, and my waist slenderer.

Ch. Just. You have misled the youthful prince.

Fal. The young prince hath misled me: I am the fellow with the great belly, and he my dog.

Ch. Just. Well, I am loath to gall a new-healed wound: your day's service at Shrewsbury hath a little gilded over your night's exploit on Gad's-hill: you may thank the unquiet time for your quiet o'er-posting that action. 171

Fal. My lord?

Ch. Just. But since all is well, keep it so: wake not a sleeping wolf.

Fal. To wake a wolf is as bad as to smell a fox.

Ch. Just. What! you are as a candle, the better part burnt out.

Fal. A wassail candle, my lord, all tallow: if I did say of wax, my growth would approve the truth. 181

Ch. Just. There is not a white hair on your face but should have his effect of gravity.

Fal. His effect of gravy, gravy, gravy.

Ch. Just. You follow the young prince up and down, like his ill angel. 186

Fal. Not so, my lord; your ill angel is light; but I hope he that looks upon me will take me without weighing: and yet, in some respects, I grant, I cannot go: I cannot tell. Virtue is of so little regard in these costermonger times that true valour is turned bear-herd: pregnancy is made a tapster, and hath his quick wit wasted in giving reckonings: all the other gifts appertinent to man, as the malice of this age shapes them, are not worth a gooseberry. You that are old consider not the capacities of us that are young; you do measure the heat of our livers with the bitterness of your galls: and we that are in the vaward of our youth, I must confess, are wags too. 200

Ch. Just. Do you set down your name in the scroll

of youth, that are written down old with all the characters of age? Have you not a moist eye? a dry hand? a yellow cheek? a white beard? a decreasing leg? an increasing belly? is not your voice broken? your wind short? your chin double? your wit single? and every part about you blasted with antiquity? and will you yet call yourself young? Fie, fie, fie, Sir John! 209

Fal. My lord, I was born about three of the clock in the afternoon, with a white head and something a round belly. For my voice, I have lost it with halloing and singing of anthems. To approve my youth further, I will not: the truth is, I am only old in judgement and understanding; and he that will caper with me for a thousand marks, let him lend me the money, and have at him! For the box of the ear that the prince gave you, he gave it like a rude prince, and you took it like a sensible lord. I have checked him for it, and the young lion repents; marry, not in ashes and sackcloth, but in new silk and old sack. 223

Ch. Just. Well, God send the prince a better companion!

Fal. God send the companion a better prince! I cannot rid my hands of him.

Ch. Just. Well, the king hath severed you and Prince Harry: I hear you are going with Lord John of Lancaster against the Archbishop and the Earl of Northumberland. 230

Fal. Yea; I thank your pretty sweet wit for it. But look you pray, all you that kiss my lady Peace at home, that our armies join not in a hot day; for, by the Lord, I take but two shirts out with me, and I mean not to sweat extraordinarily: if it be a hot day, and I brandish any thing but a bottle, I would I might never spit white again. There is not a danger-ous action can peep out his head but I am thrust upon it: well, I cannot last ever: but it was alway yet the trick of our English nation, if they have a good thing, to make it too common. If ye will needs say I am an old man, you should give me rest. I would to God my name were not so terrible to the enemy as it is: I were better to be eaten to death with a rust than to be scoured to nothing with per-petual motion. 246

Ch. Just. Well, be honest, be honest; and God bless your expedition!

Fal. Will your lordship lend me a thousand pound to furnish me forth?

Ch. Just. Not a penny, not a penny; you are too impatient to bear crosses. Fare you well: commend me to my cousin Westmoreland.

[*Exeunt Chief-Justice and Servant.*

Fal. If I do, fillip me with a three-man beetle. A man can no more separate age and covetousness than a' can part young limbs and lechery: but the gout galls the one, and the pox pinches the other; and so both the degrees prevent my curses. Boy! 260

that his counsel, learned in the laws of military service, has advised him that while he was so engaged he was not liable to arrest. 170. **o'er-posting**, escaping the consequences of. 175. **smell a fox**, suspect something, smell a mouse. 179. **wassail candle**, candle lighted up at a feast. 183. **his effect**, i.e., its effect as the outward sign of gravity. Falstaff pretends to hear the word as *gravy*, the pronunciation of which would be much closer to *gravity* than now. 186. **ill angel**, an evil attendant spirit. Falstaff quibbles on the other sense of the word meaning "a clipped angel," a coin worth 6s. 8d., current at 10s. 190. **cannot go**, i.e., walk, with pun on the meaning "pass current." 191. **costermonger**, commercial; used contemptuously. 192. **pregnancy**,

quickness (of wit). 194. **appertinent**, belonging to, becoming to. 198-199. **heat . . . galls.** The liver was the source of vegetative spirits and active in youth; the gall was the seat of melancholy and prevalent in age. 200. **vaward**, vanguard, early part. 206. **single**, weak, with play on *double*, strong. 214. **approve**, prove. 217. **marks**, coins worth 13s. 4d. 219. **box of the ear.** This event of the striking of the Chief-Justice by the young prince is important in *The Famous Victories;* Shakespeare does not depict the scene. 238. **spit white.** Spitting white is a sign of thirst. 253. **crosses**, quibble on bearing affliction and receiving money; money was often marked with a figure of the cross. 255. **fillip . . . beetle**, tap me with a mallet wielded by three men.

Page. Sir?

Fal. What money is in my purse?

Page. Seven groats and two pence.

Fal. I can get no remedy against this consumption of the purse: borrowing only lingers and lingers it out, but the disease is incurable. Go bear this letter to my Lord of Lancaster; this to the prince; this to the Earl of Westmoreland; and this to old Mistress Ursula, whom I have weekly sworn to marry since I perceived the first white hair on my chin. About it: you know where to find me. [*Exit Page.*] A pox of this gout! or, a gout of this pox! for the one or the other plays the rogue with my great toe. 'Tis no matter if I do halt; I have the wars for my colour, and my pension shall seem the more reasonable. A good wit will make use of any thing: I will turn diseases to commodity. [*Exit.*

SCENE III. *York. The* ARCHBISHOP'S *palace*.

Enter the ARCHBISHOP, *the* LORDS HASTINGS, MOWBRAY, *and* BARDOLPH.

Arch. Thus have you heard our cause and know
　　our means;
And, my most noble friends, I pray you all,
Speak plainly your opinions of our hopes:
And first, lord marshal, what say you to it?

Mowb. I well allow the occasion of our arms;
But gladly would be better satisfied
How in our means we should advance ourselves
To look with forehead bold and big enough
Upon the power and puissance of the king.

Hast. Our present musters grow upon the file 10
To five and twenty thousand men of choice;
And our supplies live largely in the hope
Of great Northumberland, whose bosom burns
With an incensed fire of injuries.

L. Bard. The question then, Lord Hastings,
　　standeth thus;
Whether our present five and twenty thousand
May hold up head without Northumberland?

Hast. With him, we may.

L. Bard. 　　　　　　Yea, marry, there's the point:
But if without him we be thought too feeble,
My judgement is, we should not step too far 20
Till we had his assistance by the hand;
For in a theme so bloody-faced as this
Conjecture, expectation, and surmise
Of aids incertain should not be admitted.

Arch. 'Tis very true, Lord Bardolph; for indeed
It was young Hotspur's case at Shrewsbury.

L. Bard. It was, my lord; who lined himself with
　　hope,
Eating the air on promise of supply,
Flattering himself in project of a power
Much smaller than the smallest of his thoughts: 30
And so, with great imagination

Proper to madmen, led his powers to death
And winking leap'd into destruction.

Hast. But, by your leave, it never yet did hurt
To lay down likelihoods and forms of hope.

L. Bard. †Yes, if this present quality of war,
Indeed the instant action: a cause on foot
Lives so in hope as in an early spring
We see the appearing buds; which to prove fruit,
Hope gives not so much warrant as despair 40
That frosts will bite them. When we mean to build,
We first survey the plot, then draw the model;
And when we see the figure of the house,
Then must we rate the cost of the erection;
Which if we find outweighs ability,
What do we then but draw anew the model
In fewer offices, or at last desist
To build at all? Much more, in this great work,
Which is almost to pluck a kingdom down
And set another up, should we survey 50
The plot of situation and the model,
Consent upon a sure foundation,
Question surveyors, know our own estate,
How able such a work to undergo,
To weigh against his opposite; or else
We fortify in paper and in figures,
Using the names of men instead of men:
Like one that draws the model of a house
Beyond his power to build it; who, half through,
Gives o'er and leaves his part-created cost 60
A naked subject to the weeping clouds
And waste for churlish winter's tyranny.

Hast. Grant that our hopes, yet likely of fair birth,
Should be still-born, and that we now possess'd
The utmost man of expectation,
I think we are a body strong enough,
Even as we are, to equal with the king.

L. Bard. What, is the king but five and twenty
　　thousand?

Hast. To us no more; nay, not so much, Lord
　　Bardolph.
For his divisions, as the times do brawl, 70
Are in three heads: one power against the French,
And one against Glendower; perforce a third
Must take up us: so is the unfirm king
In three divided; and his coffers sound
With hollow poverty and emptiness.

Arch. That he should draw his several strengths
　　together
And come against us in full puissance,
Need not be dreaded.

Hast. 　　　　　　If he should do so,
He leaves his back unarm'd, the French and Welsh
Baying him at the heels: never fear that. 80

L. Bard. Who is it like should lead his forces hither?

Hast. The Duke of Lancaster and Westmoreland;
Against the Welsh, himself and Harry Monmouth:
But who is substituted 'gainst the French,
I have no certain notice.

---

279. **commodity,** profit.

SCENE III. 7. **in,** with. 22. **theme,** business. 27. **lined,** strengthened. 29. **project . . . power,** anticipation of an armed force. 35. **forms of hope,** shapes that hope assumes. 36-41. **Yes . . . them.** These lines have been variously interpreted. The following interpretation is from the Yale Shakespeare: Lord Hastings has just been remonstrating with Lord Bardolph for his pessimism, saying that hope never injured any cause. Lord Bardolph replies: "Yes, it does—if, for example, this present business of war (indeed this very action now contemplated, this cause that is now on foot), lives merely on such desperate hopes as buds

which appear too early in the spring; for hope gives less warrant that these buds will become fruit than despair gives that the frosts will destroy them." If we read *Yes, if,* in line 36 as *Yet is,* and understand *which* as the subject of *Lives,* in line 38, we obtain a fair sense. 47. **offices,** apartments devoted to household business. 54. **undergo,** undertake; see glossary. 55. **opposite,** opponent. 60. **part-created cost,** partly finished splendor. 67. **equal with,** cope on equal terms with. 73. **take up,** encounter, oppose. 76. **several strengths,** various armies. 80. **Baying him,** driving him to bay. 91. **fond many,** foolish multitude. 94. **trimm'd in,** furnished with. 109. **draw,** assemble,

Arch.   Let us on,
And publish the occasion of our arms.
The commonwealth is sick of their own choice;
Their over-greedy love hath surfeited:
An habitation giddy and unsure
Hath he that buildeth on the vulgar heart.   90
O thou fond many, with what loud applause
Didst thou beat heaven with blessing Bolingbroke,
Before he was what thou wouldst have him be!
And being now trimm'd in thine own desires,
Thou, beastly feeder, art so full of him,
That thou provokest thyself to cast him up.
So, so, thou common dog, didst thou disgorge
Thy glutton bosom of the royal Richard;
And now thou wouldst eat thy dead vomit up,
And howl'st to find it. What trust is in these times? 100
They that, when Richard lived, would have him die,
Are now become enamour'd on his grave:
Thou, that threw'st dust upon his goodly head
When through proud London he came sighing on
After the admired heels of Bolingbroke,
Criest now 'O earth, yield us that king again,
And take thou this!' O thoughts of men accursed!
Past and to come seems best; things present worst.

    Mowb. Shall we go draw our numbers and set on? 109
    Hast. We are time's subjects, and time bids be gone.
                                     [*Exeunt.*

ACT II.

SCENE I. *London. A street.*

Enter Hostess, FANG *and his* Boy *with her, and* SNARE
    following.

    Host. Master Fang, have you entered the action?
    Fang. It is entered.
    Host. Where 's your yeoman? Is 't a lusty yeoman?
will a' stand to 't?
    Fang. Sirrah, where 's Snare?
    Host. O Lord, ay! good Master Snare.
    Snare. Here, here.
    Fang. Snare, we must arrest Sir John Falstaff.
    Host. Yea, good Master Snare; I have entered him
and all.   11
    Snare. It may chance cost some of us our lives, for
he will stab.
    Host. Alas the day! take heed of him; he stabbed
me in mine own house, and that most beastly: in good
faith, he cares not what mischief he does, if his
weapon be out: he will foin like any devil; he will
spare neither man, woman, nor child.
    Fang. If I can close with him, I care not for his
thrust.   21
    Host. No, nor I neither: I'll be at your elbow.
    Fang. An I but fist him once; and a' come but
within my vice,—
    Host. I am undone by his going; I warrant you,

he 's an infinitive thing upon my score. Good Master
Fang, hold him sure: good Master Snare, let him
not 'scape. A' comes continuantly to Pie-corner—
saving your manhoods—to buy a saddle; and he is
indited to dinner to the Lubber's-head in Lumbert
street, to Master Smooth's the silkman: I pray ye,
since my exion is entered and my case so openly
known to the world, let him be brought in to his
answer. A hundred mark is a long one for a poor lone
woman to bear: and I have borne, and borne, and
borne, and have been fubbed off, and fubbed off, and
fubbed off, from this day to that day, that it is a
shame to be thought on. There is no honesty in such
dealing; unless a woman should be made an ass and
a beast, to bear every knave's wrong. Yonder he
comes; and that arrant malmsey-nose knave, Bardolph, with him. Do your offices, do your offices:
Master Fang and Master Snare, do me, do me, do
me your offices.   45

    Enter FALSTAFF, Page, *and* BARDOLPH.

    Fal. How now! whose mare 's dead? what 's the
matter?
    Fang. Sir John, I arrest you at the suit of Mistress
Quickly.   49
    Fal. Away, varlets! Draw, Bardolph: cut me off the
villain's head: throw the quean in the channel.
    Host. Throw me in the channel! I'll throw thee in
the channel. Wilt thou? wilt thou? thou bastardly
rogue! Murder, murder! Ah, thou honey-suckle
villain! wilt thou kill God's officers and the king's?
Ah, thou honey-seed rogue! thou art a honey-seed, a
man-queller, and a woman-queller.
    Fal. Keep them off, Bardolph.   60
    Fang. A rescue! a rescue!
    Host. Good people, bring a rescue or two. Thou
wo 't, wo 't thou? thou wo 't, wo 't ta? do, do, thou
rogue! do, thou hemp-seed!
    Fal. Away, you scullion! you rampallian! you
fustilarian! I'll tickle your catastrophe.

    Enter the LORD CHIEF-JUSTICE, *and his men.*

    Ch. Just. What is the matter? keep the peace here,
ho!
    Host. Good my lord, be good to me. I beseech you,
stand to me.   70
    Ch. Just. How now, Sir John! what are you brawling
here?
Doth this become your place, your time and business?
You should have been well on your way to York.
Stand from him, fellow: wherefore hang'st upon him?
    Host. O my most worshipful lord, an 't please your
grace, I am a poor widow of Eastcheap, and he is
arrested at my suit.
    Ch. Just. For what sum?   78
    Host. It is more than for some, my lord; it is for all,
all I have. He hath eaten me out of house and home;
he hath put all my substance into that fat belly of his:

---

muster. **set on,** march.

ACT II. SCENE I. 4. **yeoman,** sheriff's officer. 11. **entered,** brought
action against in court. 18. **foin,** thrust in fencing. 23. **fist,** i.e.,
seize. 24. **vice,** grip. 25. **going,** i.e., without paying. 26. **infinitive,**
for "infinite," endless. 29. **continuantly,** for "incontinently," immediately. 31. **indited,** for "invited." **Lubber's-head,** blunder for
"Libbard's-head" (Leopard's-head Inn). 32. **Lumbert,** for "Lombard." 33. **exion,** action, lawsuit. 35. **A hundred . . . one.** The mark
was 13s. 4d; possible puns on the *hundred mark* as a distance, and on *one*
and "ow'n" (owing). 37. **fubbed off,** for "fobbed off," i.e., put off

with excuses. 42. **malmsey-nose,** red-nosed. 51. **quean,** jade, hussy.
52. **channel,** street gutter. 56. **honey-suckle,** for "homicidal." 58.
honey-seed, for "homicide." 59. **man-queller,** murderer. 63. **wo 't
thou?** Wilt thou? 64. **hemp-seed,** a possible allusion to the hangman's
rope; "hempseed" was commonly associated with invisibility. 65.
scullion, a term of abuse. **rampallian,** ruffian; usually applied to men.
66. **fustilarian,** a comic formation on the word "fustilugs," a fat,
frowsy woman (Onions).

but I will have some of it out again, or I will ride thee o' nights like the mare.

Fal. I think I am as like to ride the mare, if I have any vantage of ground to get up.

Ch. Just. How comes this, Sir John? Fie! what man of good temper would endure this tempest of exclamation? Are you not ashamed to enforce a poor widow to so rough a course to come by her own? 90

Fal. What is the gross sum that I owe thee?

Host. Marry, if thou wert an honest man, thyself and the money too. Thou didst swear to me upon a parcel-gilt goblet, sitting in my Dolphin-chamber, at the round table, by a sea-coal fire, upon Wednesday in Wheeson week, when the prince broke thy head for liking his father to a singing-man of Windsor, thou didst swear to me then, as I was washing thy wound, to marry me and make me my lady thy wife. Canst thou deny it? Did not goodwife Keech, the butcher's wife, come in then and call me gossip Quickly? coming in to borrow a mess of vinegar; telling us she had a good dish of prawns; whereby thou didst desire to eat some; whereby I told thee they were ill for a green wound? And didst thou not, when she was gone down stairs, desire me to be no more so familiarity with such poor people; saying that ere long they should call me madam? And didst thou not kiss me and bid me fetch thee thirty shillings? I put thee now to thy book-oath: deny it, if thou canst. 112

Fal. My lord, this is a poor mad soul; and she says up and down the town that her eldest son is like you: she hath been in good case, and the truth is, poverty hath distracted her. But for these foolish officers, I beseech you I may have redress against her.

Ch. Just. Sir John, Sir John, I am well acquainted with your manner of wrenching the true cause the false way. It is not a confident brow, nor the throng of words that come with such more than impudent sauciness from you, can thrust me from a level consideration: you have, as it appears to me, practised upon the easy-yielding spirit of this woman, and made her serve your uses both in purse and in person.

Host. Yea, in truth, my lord. 128

Ch. Just. Pray thee, peace. Pay her the debt you owe her, and unpay the villany you have done her: the one you may do with sterling money, and the other with current repentance.

Fal. My lord, I will not undergo this sneap without reply. You call honourable boldness impudent sauciness: if a man will make courtesy and say nothing, he is virtuous: no, my lord, my humble duty remembered, I will not be your suitor. I say to you, I do desire deliverance from these officers, being upon hasty employment in the king's affairs. 140

Ch. Just. You speak as having power to do wrong: but answer in the effect of your reputation, and satisfy the poor woman.

Fal. Come hither, hostess.

Enter GOWER.

Ch. Just. Now, Master Gower, what news?

Gow. The king, my lord, and Harry Prince of Wales Are near at hand: the rest the paper tells.

Fal. As I am a gentleman.

Host. Faith, you said so before.

Fal. As I am a gentleman. Come, no more words of it. 151

Host. By this heavenly ground I tread on, I must be fain to pawn both my plate and the tapestry of my dining-chambers.

Fal. Glasses, glasses, is the only drinking: and for thy walls, a pretty slight drollery, or the story of the Prodigal, or the German hunting in water-work, is worth a thousand of these bed-hangings and these fly-bitten tapestries. Let it be ten pound, if thou canst. Come, and 'twere not for thy humours, there's not a better wench in England. Go, wash thy face, and draw the action. Come, thou must not be in this humour with me; dost not know me? come, come, I know thou wast set on to this. 165

Host. Pray thee, Sir John, let it be but twenty nobles: i' faith, I am loath to pawn my plate, so God save me, la!

Fal. Let it alone; I'll make other shift: you'll be a fool still. 170

Host. Well, you shall have it, though I pawn my gown. I hope you'll come to supper. You'll pay me all together?

Fal. Will I live? [*To Bardolph*] Go, with her, with her; hook on, hook on.

Host. Will you have Doll Tearsheet meet you at supper?

Fal. No more words; let's have her.

[*Exeunt Hostess, Bardolph, Officers, and Boy.*

Ch. Just. I have heard better news.

Fal. What's the news, my lord? 180

Ch. Just. Where lay the king last night?

Gow. At Basingstoke, my lord.

Fal. I hope, my lord, all's well: what is the news, my lord?

Ch. Just. Come all his forces back?

Gow. No; fifteen hundred foot, five hundred horse, Are march'd up to my lord of Lancaster, Against Northumberland and the Archbishop.

Fal. Comes the king back from Wales, my noble lord?

Ch. Just. You shall have letters of me presently: 190 Come, go along with me, good Master Gower.

Fal. My lord!

Ch. Just. What's the matter?

Fal. Master Gower, shall I entreat you with me to dinner?

Gow. I must wait upon my good lord here; I thank you, good Sir John.

Ch. Just. Sir John, you loiter here too long, being you are to take soldiers up in counties as you go. 200

Fal. Will you sup with me, Master Gower?

Ch. Just. What foolish master taught you these manners, Sir John?

Fal. Master Gower, if they become me not, he was

<hr>

84. **mare,** nightmare. 94. **parcel-gilt,** partly gilt. 95. **Dolphin-chamber,** one of the fanciful names for chambers in inns. 96. **sea-coal,** bituminous coal, brought in by sea. **Wheeson,** Whitsun. 97. **liking,** likening. 101. **goodwife,** title of married women; *Keech* means "a lump of tallow." 102. **gossip,** familiar term applied to a female friend. 104. **mess of vinegar,** enough vinegar for one meal. 105. **prawns,** crustaceans like large shrimp. 115. **in good case,** well-to-do. 132. **current repentance,** genuine repentance; allusion to current coin.

134. **sneap,** reproof, snub. 142. **effect of,** manner becoming. 155. **Glasses . . . drinking.** It is a question of selling her cups of silver and pewter and using glasses for serving drinks. 156. **drollery,** comic picture. 158. **water-work,** water color, i.e., a picture of a German hunting scene. 162. **draw,** withdraw. 167. **nobles,** coins current at 6s. 8d. 175. **hook on,** follow her. 182. **Basingstoke,** a town in Hampshire fifty miles from London. 199. **being . . . up,** seeing that you are to levy soldiers. 207. **tap for tap,** tit for tat. 208. **lighten,** enlighten;

a fool that taught them me. This is the right fencing grace, my lord; tap for tap, and so part fair.

Ch. Just. Now the Lord lighten thee! thou art a great fool. [*Exeunt.*

SCENE II. *London. Another street.*

Enter PRINCE HENRY *and* POINS.

Prince. Before God, I am exceeding weary.

Poins. Is 't come to that? I had thought weariness durst not have attached one of so high blood.

Prince. Faith, it does me; though it discolours the complexion of my greatness to acknowledge it. Doth it not show vilely in me to desire small beer?

Poins. Why, a prince should not be so loosely studied as to remember so weak a composition. 9

Prince. Belike then my appetite was not princely got; for, by my troth, I do now remember the poor creature, small beer. But, indeed, these humble considerations make me out of love with my greatness. What a disgrace is it to me to remember thy name! or to know thy face to-morrow! or to take note how many pair of silk stockings thou hast, viz. these, and those that were thy peach-coloured ones! or to bear the inventory of thy shirts, as, one for superfluity, and another for use! But that the tennis-court-keeper knows better than I; for it is a low ebb of linen with thee when thou keepest not racket there; as thou hast not done a great while, because the rest of thy low countries have made a shift to eat up thy holland: and God knows, whether those that bawl out the ruins of thy linen shall inherit his kingdom: but the midwives say the children are not in the fault; whereupon the world increases, and kindreds are mightily strengthened. 30

Poins. How ill it follows, after you have laboured so hard, you should talk so idly! Tell me, how many good young princes would do so, their fathers being so sick as yours at this time is?

Prince. Shall I tell thee one thing, Poins?

Poins. Yes, faith; and let it be an excellent good thing.

Prince. It shall serve among wits of no higher breeding than thine.

Poins. Go to; I stand the push of your one thing that you will tell. 41

Prince. Marry, I tell thee, it is not meet that I should be sad, now my father is sick: albeit I could tell to thee, as to one it pleases me, for fault of a better, to call my friend, I could be sad, and sad indeed too.

Poins. Very hardly upon such a subject.

Prince. By this hand, thou thinkest me as far in the devil's book as thou and Falstaff for obduracy and persistency: let the end try the man. But I tell thee, my heart bleeds inwardly that my father is so sick: and keeping such vile company as thou art hath in reason taken from me all ostentation of sorrow. 54

Poins. The reason?

Prince. What wouldst thou think of me, if I should weep?

Poins. I would think thee a most princely hypocrite.

Prince. It would be every man's thought; and thou art a blessed fellow to think as every man thinks: never a man's thought in the world keeps the roadway better than thine: every man would think me an hypocrite indeed. And what accites your most worshipful thought to think so?

Poins. Why, because you have been so lewd and so much engraffed to Falstaff. 67

Prince. And to thee.

Poins. By this light, I am well spoke on; I can hear it with mine own ears: the worst that they can say of me is that I am a second brother and that I am a proper fellow of my hands; and those two things, I confess, I cannot help. By the mass, here comes Bardolph.

Enter BARDOLPH *and* Page.

Prince. And the boy that I gave Falstaff: a' had him from me Christian; and look, if the fat villain have not transformed him ape. 77

Bard. God save your grace!

Prince. And yours, most noble Bardolph!

Bard. Come, you virtuous ass, you bashful fool, must you be blushing? wherefore blush you now? What a maidenly man-at-arms are you become! Is 't such a matter to get a pottle-pot's maidenhead? 83

Page. A' calls me e'en now, my lord, through a red lattice, and I could discern no part of his face from the window: at last I spied his eyes, and methought he had made two holes in the ale-wife's new petticoat and so peeped through.

Prince. Has not the boy profited? 90

Bard. Away, you whoreson upright rabbit, away!

Page. Away, you rascally Althæa's dream, away!

Prince. Instruct us, boy; what dream, boy?

Page. Marry, my lord, Althæa dreamed she was delivered of a fire-brand; and therefore I call him her dream.

Prince. A crown's worth of good interpretation: there 'tis, boy. 100

Poins. O, that this good blossom could be kept from cankers! Well, there is sixpence to preserve thee.

Bard. An you do not make him hanged among you, the gallows shall have wrong.

Prince. And how doth thy master, Bardolph?

Bard. Well, my lord. He heard of your grace's coming to town: there 's a letter for you.

Poins. Delivered with good respect. And how doth the martlemas, your master? 110

Bard. In bodily health, sir.

Poins. Marry, the immortal part needs a physician; but that moves not him: though that be sick, it dies not.

Prince. I do allow this wen to be as familiar with me as my dog; and he holds his place; for look you how he writes. 117

---

with side reference to Falstaff's weight.
    SCENE II. 7. **small beer,** weak kind of beer. 9. **studied,** versed, inclined. 10. **Belike,** I suppose. 25. **holland,** a kind of linen; pun on "Holland" as a low country. 26. **bawl out,** bawl in swaddling clothes made out of Poins' old shirts (Herford). 40. **push,** attack, onset. 49. **devil's book,** devil's favor, or devil's debt. 65. **accites,** excites. 67. **engraffed,** closely attached to. 71. **a second brother,** as a second brother he would have no inheritance. 72-73. **proper . . . hands,**

capital fellow in using my hands (for stealing?). 83. **pottle-pot's,** two-quart tankard's. 93. **Althæa's dream.** Althaea dreamed that her newborn son would live only so long as a brand on the fire lasted. The Page mistakenly relates Hecuba's dream. 99. **crown's worth,** five shillings. 102. **cankers,** worms which destroy buds and leaves. 103. **to preserve thee,** allusion to the cross on the sixpence. 110. **martlemas,** Martinmas (November 11); probably short for "Martinmas beef." Beeves were regularly slaughtered and salted at that season.

Poins. [*Reads*] 'John Falstaff, knight,'— every man must know that, as oft as he has occasion to name himself: even like those that are kin to the king; for they never prick their finger but they say, 'There's some of the king's blood spilt.' 'How comes that?' says he, that takes upon him not to conceive. The answer is as ready as a borrower's cap, 'I am the king's poor cousin, sir.' 126

Prince. Nay, they will be kin to us, or they will fetch it from Japhet. But to the letter:

Poins. [*Reads*] 'Sir John Falstaff, knight, to the son of the king, nearest his father, Harry Prince of Wales, greeting.' Why, this is a certificate.

Prince. Peace! 133

Poins. [*Reads*] 'I will imitate the honourable Romans in brevity:' he sure means brevity in breath, short-winded. 'I commend me to thee, I commend thee, and I leave thee. Be not too familiar with Poins; for he misuses thy favours so much, that he swears thou art to marry his sister Nell. Repent at idle times as thou mayest; and so, farewell. 141

'Thine, by yea and no, which is as much as to say, as thou usest him, JACK FALSTAFF with my familiars, JOHN with my brothers and sisters, and SIR JOHN with all Europe.'

My lord, I'll steep this letter in sack and make him eat it.

Prince. That's to make him eat twenty of his words. But do you use me thus, Ned? must I marry your sister? 151

Poins. God send the wench no worse fortune! But I never said so.

Prince. Well, thus we play the fools with the time, and the spirits of the wise sit in the clouds and mock us. Is your master here in London?

Bard. Yea, my lord.

Prince. Where sups he? doth the old boar feed in the old frank? 160

Bard. At the old place, my lord, in Eastcheap.

Prince. What company?

Page. Ephesians, my lord, of the old church.

Prince. Sup any women with him?

Page. None, my lord, but old Mistress Quickly and Mistress Doll Tearsheet.

Prince. What pagan may that be?

Page. A proper gentlewoman, sir, and a kinswoman of my master's. 170

Prince. Even such kin as the parish heifers are to the town bull. Shall we steal upon them, Ned, at supper?

Poins. I am your shadow, my lord; I'll follow you.

Prince. Sirrah, you boy, and Bardolph, no word to your master that I am yet come to town: there's for your silence.

Bard. I have no tongue, sir. 179

Page. And for mine, sir, I will govern it.

Prince. Fare you well; go. [*Exeunt Bardolph and Page.*] This Doll Tearsheet should be some road.

Poins. I warrant you, as common as the way between Saint Alban's and London.

Prince. How might we see Falstaff bestow himself

to-night in his true colours, and not ourselves be seen?

Poins. Put on two leathern jerkins and aprons, and wait upon him at his table as drawers. 191

Prince. From a God to a bull? a heavy descension! it was Jove's case. From a prince to a prentice? a low transformation! that shall be mine; for in every thing the purpose must weigh with the folly. Follow me, Ned. [*Exeunt.*

SCENE III. *Warkworth. Before the castle.*

Enter NORTHUMBERLAND, LADY NORTHUMBERLAND, *and* LADY PERCY.

North. I pray thee, loving wife, and gentle daughter,
Give even way unto my rough affairs:
Put not you on the visage of the times
And be like them to Percy troublesome.

Lady N. I have given over, I will speak no more:
Do what you will; your wisdom be your guide.

North. Alas, sweet wife, my honour is at pawn;
And, but my going, nothing can redeem it.

Lady P. O yet, for God's sake, go not to these wars!
The time was, father, that you broke your word, 10
When you were more endear'd to it than now;
When your own Percy, when my heart's dear Harry,
Threw many a northward look to see his father
Bring up his powers; but he did long in vain.
Who then persuaded you to stay at home?
There were two honours lost, yours and your son's.
For yours, the God of heaven brighten it!
For his, it stuck upon him as the sun
In the grey vault of heaven, and by his light
Did all the chivalry of England move 20
To do brave acts: he was indeed the glass
Wherein the noble youth did dress themselves:
He had no legs that practised not his gait;
And speaking thick, which nature made his blemish,
Became the accents of the valiant;
For those that could speak low and tardily
Would turn their own perfection to abuse,
To seem like him: so that in speech, in gait,
In diet, in affections of delight,
In military rules, humours of blood, 30
He was the mark and glass, copy and book,
That fashion'd others. And him, O wondrous him!
O miracle of men! him did you leave,
Second to none, unseconded by you,
To look upon the hideous god of war
In disadvantage; to abide a field
Where nothing but the sound of Hotspur's name
Did seem defensible: so you left him.
Never, O never, do his ghost the wrong
To hold your honour more precise and nice 40
With others than with him! let them alone:
The marshal and the archbishop are strong:
Had my sweet Harry had but half their numbers,
To-day might I, hanging on Hotspur's neck,
Have talk'd of Monmouth's grave.

---

118. **Poins.** [*Reads*]. From this point Q and F assign the reading of the letter to the prince, which is probably correct; the change to Poins is due to Hanmer. 128. **Japhet,** one of the sons of Noah (Genesis 10:2-5). 135. **Romans.** Warburton suggested *Roman* as an allusion to Caesar's "I came, I saw, I conquered." 160. **frank,** sty, pen. 164. **Ephesians,** cant term for good fellows. **old church,** allusion to the ancient and authoritative church at Ephesus. 168. **pagan,** courtesan; a cant name. 186. **bestow,** behave. 192. **heavy descension,** grievous descent.

193. **Jove's case,** an allusion to Jupiter, who for love of Europa transformed himself into a bull. 196. **weigh with,** counterbalance.
SCENE III. 11. **endear'd,** pledged. 19. **grey,** used to describe the dull or cold light of a cloudy day. 20. **chivalry,** men-at-arms. 24. **thick.** Most authorities define as "quickly" or "fast"; it probably refers to stammering. 38. **defensible,** able to make defense. 57. **came,** became. 61. **recordation,** remembrance. 64. **still-stand,** standstill.
SCENE IV. 2. **apple-johns,** a kind of apple said to keep two years

North.   Beshrew your heart,
Fair daughter, you do draw my spirits from me
With new lamenting ancient oversights.
But I must go and meet with danger there,
Or it will seek me in another place
And find me worse provided.
    Lady N.   O, fly to Scotland,   50
Till that the nobles and the armed commons
Have of their puissance made a little taste.
    Lady P. If they get ground and vantage of the king,
Then join you with them, like a rib of steel,
To make strength stronger; but, for all our loves,
First let them try themselves. So did your son;
He was so suffer'd: so came I a widow;
And never shall have length of life enough
To rain upon remembrance with mine eyes,
That it may grow and sprout as high as heaven,   60
For recordation to my noble husband.
    North. Come, come, go in with me. 'Tis with my
        mind
As with the tide swell'd up unto his height,
That makes a still-stand, running neither way:
Fain would I go to meet the archbishop,
But many thousand reasons hold me back.
I will resolve for Scotland: there am I,
Till time and vantage crave my company.   [*Exeunt.*

SCENE IV. *London. The Boar's-head Tavern in Eastcheap.*

    Enter two Drawers.

    First Draw. What the devil hast thou brought
there? apple-johns? thou knowest Sir John cannot
endure an apple-john.
    Sec. Draw. Mass, thou sayest true. The prince once
set a dish of apple-johns before him, and told him
there were five more Sir Johns, and, putting off his
hat, said 'I will now take my leave of these six dry,
round, old, withered knights.' It angered him to the
heart: but he hath forgot that.   10
    First Draw. Why, then, cover, and set them down:
and see if thou canst find out Sneak's noise; Mistress
Tearsheet would fain hear some music. Dispatch:
the room where they supped is too hot; they'll come
in straight.
    Sec. Draw. Sirrah, here will be the prince and
Master Poins anon; and they will put on two of our
jerkins and aprons; and Sir John must not know of it:
Bardolph hath brought word.   20
    First Draw. By the mass, here will be old Utis:
it will be an excellent stratagem.
    Sec. Draw. I'll see if I can find out Sneak.   [*Exit.*

    Enter Hostess *and* DOLL TEARSHEET.

    Host. I' faith, sweetheart, methinks now you are in
an excellent good temperality: your pulsidge beats
as extraordinarily as heart would desire; and your
color, I warrant you, is as red as any rose, in good
truth, la! But, i' faith, you have drunk too much

canaries; and that's a marvelous searching wine, and
it perfumes the blood ere one can say 'What's this?'
How do you now?   32
    Dol. Better than I was: hem!
    Host. Why, that's well said; a good heart's worth
gold. Lo, here comes Sir John.

    Enter FALSTAFF.

    Fal. [*Singing*] 'When Arthur first in court'—Empty
the jordan. [*Exit First Drawer.*]—[*Singing*] 'And was
a worthy king.' How now, Mistress Doll!
    Host. Sick of a calm; yea, good faith.   40
    Fal. So is all her sect; an they be once in a calm,
they are sick.
    Dol. You muddy rascal, is that all the comfort you
give me?
    Fal. You make fat rascals, Mistress Doll.
    Dol. I make them! gluttony and diseases make
them; I make them not.
    Fal. If the cook help to make the gluttony, you
help to make the diseases, Doll: we catch of you, Doll,
we catch of you; grant that, my poor virtue, grant
that.   51
    Dol. Yea, joy, our chains and our jewels.
    Fal. 'Your brooches, pearls, and ouches:' for to
serve bravely is to come halting off, you know: to
come off the breach with his pike bent bravely,
and to surgery bravely; to venture upon the charged
chambers bravely,—
    Dol. Hang yourself, you muddy conger, hang
yourself!   59
    Host. By my troth, this is the old fashion; you two
never meet but you fall to some discord: you are
both, i' good truth, as rheumatic as two dry toasts:
you cannot one bear with another's confirmities.
What the good-year! one must bear, and that must
be you: you are the weaker vessel, as they say, the
emptier vessel.   66
    Dol. Can a weak empty vessel bear such a huge
full hogshead? there's a whole merchant's venture
of Bourdeaux stuff in him; you have not seen a hulk
better stuffed in the hold. Come, I'll be friends with
thee, Jack: thou art going to the wars; and whether
I shall ever see thee again or no, there is nobody cares.

    Re-enter First Drawer.

    First Draw. Sir, Ancient Pistol's below, and would
speak with you.
    Dol. Hang him, swaggering rascal! let him not
come hither: it is the foul-mouthed'st rogue in
England.   78
    Host. If he swagger, let him not come here: no, by
my faith; I must live among my neighbours; I'll no
swaggerers: I am in good name and fame with the
very best: shut the door; there comes no swaggerers
here: I have not lived all this while, to have swaggering now: shut the door, I pray you.
    Fal. Dost thou hear, hostess?
    Host. Pray ye, pacify yourself, Sir John: there
comes no swaggerers here.

and to be in perfect condition when shriveled and withered. 13.
Sneak's noise, band of musicians. 21. **old Utis,** rare fun. *Utas* was the
term of eight days or the eighth day after a feast; hence, a period of
merrymaking. 25. **temperality,** for "temper," or "temperature." 26.
pulsidge, for "pulse." **extraordinarily,** for "ordinarily." 30. **canaries,**
light, sweet wine from the Canary Islands. 40. **calm,** probably pun on
"qualm." 45. **fat rascals.** A *rascal* was a lean deer; used here with pun
on "rascal" meaning "good-for-nothing." 53. **ouches,** gems, or jewels.

The line is from a ballad. 58. **conger,** conger eel; applied abusively.
62. **rheumatic.** This is a misused term; she probably meant to say
"choleric." 64. **confirmities,** for "infirmities." **What . . . year,** expletive; no special meaning. 69. **Bourdeaux stuff,** wine. 74. **Ancient,**
ensign, standard-bearer; a common military title. 79. **swagger,** bluster.

Fal. Dost thou hear? it is mine ancient.   89

Host. Tilly-fally, Sir John, ne'er tell me: your ancient swaggerer comes not in my doors. I was before Master Tisick, the debuty, t' other day; and, as he said to me, 'twas no longer ago than Wednesday last, 'I' good faith, neighbour Quickly,' says he; Master Dumbe, our minister was by then; 'neighbour Quickly,' says he, 'receive those that are civil; for,' said he, 'you are in an ill name:' now a' said so, I can tell whereupon; 'for,' says he, 'you are an honest woman, and well thought on; therefore take heed what guests you receive: receive,' says he, 'no swaggering companions.' There comes none here: you would bless you to hear what he said: no, I'll no swaggerers.   104

Fal. He's no swaggerer, hostess; a tame cheater, i' faith; you may stroke him as gently as a puppy greyhound: he'll not swagger with a Barbary hen, if her feathers turn back in any show of resistance. Call him up, drawer.   [*Exit First Drawer.* 109

Host. Cheater, call you him? I will bar no honest man my house, nor no cheater: but I do not love swaggering, by my troth; I am the worse, when one says swagger: feel, masters, how I shake; look you, I warrant you.

Dol. So you do, hostess.

Host. Do I? yea, in very truth, do I, an 'twere an aspen leaf: I cannot abide swaggerers.

Enter PISTOL, BARDOLPH, *and* Page.

Pist. God save you, Sir John!   119

Fal. Welcome, Ancient Pistol. Here, Pistol, I charge you with a cup of sack: do you discharge upon mine hostess.

Pist. I will discharge upon her, Sir John, with two bullets.

Fal. She is pistol-proof, sir; you shall hardly offend her.

Host. Come, I'll drink no proofs nor no bullets: I'll drink no more than will do me good, for no man's pleasure, I.

Pist. Then to you, Mistress Dorothy; I will charge you.   131

Dol. Charge me! I scorn you, scurvy companion. What! you poor, base, rascally, cheating, lack-linen mate! Away, you mouldy rogue, away! I am meat for your master.

Pist. I know you, Mistress Dorothy.   136

Dol. Away, you cut-purse rascal! you filthy bung, away! by this wine, I'll thrust my knife in your mouldy chaps, an you play the saucy cuttle with me. Away, you bottle-ale rascal! you basket-hilt stale juggler, you! Since when, I pray you, sir? God's light, with two points on your shoulder? much!   143

Pist. God let me not live, but I will murder your ruff for this.

Fal. No more, Pistol; I would not have you go off here: discharge yourself of our company, Pistol.

Host. No, good Captain Pistol; not here, sweet captain.   150

Dol. Captain! thou abominable damned cheater, art thou not ashamed to be called captain? An captains were of my mind, they would truncheon you out, for taking their names upon you before you have earned them. You a captain! you slave, for what? for tearing a poor whore's ruff in a bawdy-house? He a captain! hang him, rogue! he lives upon mouldy stewed prunes and dried cakes. A captain! God's light, these villains will make the word as odious as the word 'occupy;' which was an excellent good word before it was ill sorted: therefore captains had need look to 't.   162

Bard. Pray thee, go down, good ancient.

Fal. Hark thee hither, Mistress Doll.

Pist. Not I: I tell thee what, Corporal Bardolph, I could tear her: I'll be revenged of her.

Page. Pray thee, go down.

Pist. I'll see her damned first; to Pluto's damned lake, by this hand, to the infernal deep, with Erebus and tortures vile also. Hold hook and line, say I. Down, down, dogs! down, faitors! Have we not Hiren here?   173

Host. Good Captain Peesel, be quiet; 'tis very late, i' faith: I beseek you now, aggravate your choler.

Pist. These be good humours, indeed! Shall
    pack-horses
And hollow pamper'd jades of Asia,
Which cannot go but thirty mile a-day,
Compare with Cæsars, and with Cannibals,   180
And Trojan Greeks? nay, rather damn them with
King Cerberus; and let the welkin roar.
Shall we fall foul for toys?

Host. By my troth, captain, these are very bitter words.

Bard. Be gone, good ancient: this will grow to a brawl anon.

Pist. Die men like dogs! give crowns like pins! Have we not Hiren here?   189

Host. O' my word, captain, there 's none such here. What the good-year! do you think I would deny her? For God's sake, be quiet.

Pist. Then feed, and be fat, my fair Calipolis. Come, give 's some sack.
'Si fortune me tormente, sperato me contento.'
Fear we broadsides? no, let the fiend give fire:
Give me some sack: and, sweetheart, lie thou there.
    [*Laying down his sword.*
Come we to full points here; and are etceteras
    nothing?

Fal. Pistol, I would be quiet.   199

Pist. Sweet knight, I kiss thy neif: what! we have seen the seven stars.

---

90. **Tilly-fally,** expression of contempt. 92. **Tisick,** suggests an elderly citizen with a cough. 93. **debuty,** deputy of the ward; a grave citizen charged with the good conduct of his ward. 96. **Master Dumbe.** Ministers who were not permitted to preach were said to be dumb. 105. **tame cheater,** one who won at gaming by cheating; probably acted also as decoy. The Cambridge editors suggest *cheetah,* the hunting leopard. 108. **Barbary hen,** guinea hen. 110. **Cheater,** rogue, as above; Mistress Quickly understands the word as *escheator,* an officer of the king's exchequer. 131. **charge,** pledge, drink to. 138. **bung,** pickpocket. 140. **cuttle,** cutthroat or cutpurse. 141. **basket-hilt,** sword hilt with protector for the hand; evidently a term of contempt, possibly suggesting a sword trickster or a braggart swordsman. 142. **God's light,** by God's light. 143. **points,** tags for securing armor. **much,** ironical for "not much," or "no." 145. **ruff,** large frilled collar. 154. **truncheon,** staff

carried by captains. 169-173. **I'll see . . . here.** This is the first of the characteristic ranting speeches of this famous character. His allusions are to old plays in the heroic drama; it is his "humor" to allude to them. 173. **faitors,** impostors, cheats; doubtful meaning here. **Hiren,** an allusion to a lost play by Peele, *Turkish Mahomet and the Fair Greek. Hiren* is Irene. 175. **beseek,** beseech. **aggravate,** blunder for "moderate." 177. **humours,** freaks of conduct; current slang. 177-179. **Shall . . . a-day,** misquotation from Marlowe's *Second Part of Tamburlaine,* IV, iv, 1-2. 193. **Then . . . Calipolis,** burlesque of a line in Peele's *Battle of Alcazar.* 195. **'Si . . . contento,'** if fortune torments me, hope contents me. It is not clear what language Pistol is speaking, Italian or Spanish. The Cambridge editors think he is reading the motto on his sword. Such a saying was widely current. 198. **full points,** full stop. 200. **neif,** fist. 201. **seven stars,** Pleiades. 203.

Dol. For God's sake, thrust him down stairs: I cannot endure such a fustian rascal.

Pist. Thrust him down stairs! know we not Galloway nags?

Fal. Quoit him down, Bardolph, like a shove-groat shilling: nay, an a' do nothing but speak nothing, a' shall be nothing here.

Bard. Come, get you down stairs. 209

Pist. What! shall we have incision? shall we imbrue?
[*Snatching up his sword.*
Then death rock me asleep, abridge my doleful days!
Why, then, let grievous, ghastly, gaping wounds
Untwine the Sisters Three! Come, Atropos, I say!

Host. Here 's goodly stuff toward!

Fal. Give me my rapier, boy.

Dol. I pray thee, Jack, I pray thee, do not draw.

Fal. Get you down stairs.
[*Drawing, and driving Pistol out.*
Host. Here 's a goodly tumult! I'll forswear keeping house, afore I'll be in these tirrits and frights. So; murder, I warrant now. Alas, alas! put up your naked weapons, put up your naked weapons. 223
[*Exeunt Pistol and Bardolph.*
Dol. I pray thee, Jack, be quiet; the rascal 's gone. Ah, you whoreson little valiant villain, you!

Host. Are you not hurt i' the groin? methought a' made a shrewd thrust at your belly.

Re-enter BARDOLPH.

Fal. Have you turned him out o' doors?

Bard. Yea, sir. The rascal 's drunk: you have hurt him, sir, i' the shoulder. 231

Fal. A rascal! to brave me!

Dol. Ah, you sweet little rogue, you! Alas, poor ape, how thou sweatest! come, let me wipe thy face; come on, you whoreson chops: ah, rogue! i' faith, I love thee: thou art as valorous as Hector of Troy, worth five of Agamemnon, and ten times better than the Nine Worthies: ah, villain!

Fal. A rascally slave! I will toss the rogue in a blanket. 241

Dol. Do, an thou darest for thy heart: an thou dost, I'll canvass thee between a pair of sheets.

Enter Music.

Page. The music is come, sir.

Fal. Let them play. Play, sirs. Sit on my knee, Doll. A rascal bragging slave! the rogue fled from me like quicksilver. 248

Dol. I' faith, and thou followedst him like a church. Thou whoreson little tidy Bartholomew boar-pig, when wilt thou leave fighting o' days and foining o' nights, and begin to patch up thine old body for heaven?

Enter, behind, PRINCE HENRY *and* POINS, *disguised.*

Fal. Peace, good Doll! do not speak like a death's-head; do not bid me remember mine end.

Dol. Sirrah, what humour 's the prince of?

Fal. A good shallow young fellow: a' would have made a good pantler, a' would ha' chipped bread well.

Dol. They say Poins has a good wit. 260

Fal. He a good wit? hang him, baboon! his wit 's as thick as Tewksbury mustard; there 's no more conceit in him than is in a mallet.

Dol. Why does the prince love him so, then?

Fal. Because their legs are both of a bigness, and a' plays at quoits well, and eats conger and fennel, and drinks off candles' ends for flap-dragons, and rides the wild-mare with the boys, and jumps upon joined-stools, and swears with a good grace, and wears his boots very smooth, like unto the sign of the leg, and breeds no bate with telling of discreet stories; and such other gambol faculties a' has, that show a weak mind and an able body, for the which the prince admits him: for the prince himself is such another; the weight of a hair will turn the scales between their avoirdupois. 277

Prince. Would not this nave of a wheel have his ears cut off?

Poins. Let 's beat him before his whore.

Prince. Look, whether the withered elder hath not his poll clawed like a parrot.

Poins. Is it not strange that desire should so many years outlive performance?

Fal. Kiss me, Doll.

Prince. Saturn and Venus this year in conjunction! what says the almanac to that?

Poins. And, look, whether the fiery Trigon, his man, be not lisping to his master's old tables, his note-book, his counsel-keeper. 290

Fal. Thou dost give me flattering busses.

Dol. By my troth, I kiss thee with a most constant heart.

Fal. I am old, I am old.

Dol. I love thee better than I love e'er a scurvy young boy of them all.

Fal. What stuff wilt have a kirtle of? I shall receive money o' Thursday: shalt have a cap to-morrow. A merry song, come: it grows late; we'll to bed. Thou 'lt forget me when I am gone. 300

Dol. By my troth, thou 'lt set me a-weeping, and thou sayest so: prove that ever I dress myself handsome till thy return: well, hearken at the end.

Fal. Some sack, Francis.

Prince. }
Poins. } Anon, anon, sir.   [*Coming forward.*

Fal. Ha! a bastard son of the king's? And art not thou Poins his brother?

Prince. Why, thou globe of sinful continents, what a life dost thou lead! 310

---

fustian, nonsensical. 205. **Galloway nags,** an inferior breed of horses. 206. **Quoit,** throw. 207. **shove-groat shilling,** an Edward VI shilling used in shove-groat, a game in which the coins were shoved toward a mark. 208. **speak nothing,** talk nonsense. **be nothing here,** be gone from here. 210. **incision,** bloodshed. **imbrue,** shed blood. 211. **death . . . asleep,** quotation from a current poem about Anne Boleyn. 213. **Sisters Three,** allusion to the three Fates, Clotho, Lachesis, and Atropos. Atropos severed the thread of life. 221. **tirrits,** possibly "terrors." 236. **chops,** fat jaws. 237. **Hector of Troy,** leader of the Trojans; the type of valor. 238. **Agamemnon,** leader of the Greeks at Troy. 239. **Nine Worthies,** traditional group of the nine greatest men; usually three Christians, three pagans, and three Jews: e.g., Arthur, Charlemagne, Godfrey of Boulogne; Hector, Alexander, Julius Caesar; Joshua, David, Judas Maccabaeus. 250. **Bartholomew boar-pig,**

allusion to roast pig at Bartholomew fair. 258. **pantler,** servant in charge of a pantry. 262. **Tewksbury mustard.** Tewkesbury was famous for mustard. 267. **fennel,** yellow-flowered herb used in pickles and sauces. 268. **flap-dragons,** raisins snatched out of burning spirits and swallowed in the game of snapdragon. **wild-mare,** seesaw. 269. **joined-stools,** stools made by joiners. 271. **breeds no bate,** causes no strife. 272. **gambol,** sportive. 278. **nave,** hub; reference to Falstaff's rotundity. 286. **conjunction,** two planets in the same direction as viewed from the earth. 288. **fiery Trigon,** a division of the zodiac consisting of Aries, Leo, and Sagittarius. Poins alludes to Bardolph's complexion. Bardolph is apparently kissing Dame Quickly. 291. **busses,** kisses. 297. **kirtle,** gown or petticoat. 304. **hearken at,** wait for.

Fal. A better than thou: I am a gentleman; thou art a drawer.

Prince. Very true, sir; and I come to draw you out by the ears.

Host. O, the Lord preserve thy good grace! by my troth, welcome to London. Now, the Lord bless that sweet face of thine! O Jesu, are you come from Wales?

Fal. Thou whoreson mad compound of majesty, by this light flesh and corrupt blood, thou art welcome. 321

Dol. How, you fat fool! I scorn you.

Poins. My lord, he will drive you out of your revenge and turn all to a merriment, if you take not the heat.

Prince. You whoreson candle-mine, you, how vilely did you speak of me even now before this honest, virtuous, civil gentlewoman!

Host. God's blessing of your good heart! and so she is, by my troth. 330

Fal. Didst thou hear me?

Prince. Yea, and you knew me, as you did when you ran away by Gad's-hill: you knew I was at your back, and spoke it on purpose to try my patience.

Fal. No, no, no; not so; I did not think thou wast within hearing.

Prince. I shall drive you then to confess the wilful abuse; and then I know how to handle you.

Fal. No abuse, Hal, o' mine honour; no abuse. 340

Prince. Not to dispraise me, and call me pantler and bread-chipper and I know not what?

Fal. No abuse, Hal.

Poins. No abuse?

Fal. No abuse, Ned, i' the world; honest Ned, none. I dispraised him before the wicked, that the wicked might not fall in love with him; in which doing, I have done the part of a careful friend and a true subject, and thy father is to give me thanks for it. No abuse, Hal: none, Ned, none: no, faith, boys, none. 351

Prince. See now, whether pure fear and entire cowardice doth not make thee wrong this virtuous gentlewoman to close with us. Is she of the wicked? is thine hostess here of the wicked? or is thy boy of the wicked? or honest Bardolph, whose zeal burns in his nose, of the wicked? 358

Poins. Answer, thou dead elm, answer.

Fal. The fiend hath pricked down Bardolph irrecoverable; and his face is Lucifer's privy-kitchen, where he doth nothing but roast malt-worms. For the boy, there is a good angel about him; but the devil outbids him too.

Prince. For the women?

Fal. For one of them, she is in hell already, and burns poor souls. For the other, I owe her money; and whether she be damned for that, I know not.

Host. No, I warrant you. 369

Fal. No, I think thou art not; I think thou art quit for that. Marry, there is another indictment upon thee, for suffering flesh to be eaten in thy house, contrary to the law; for the which I think thou wilt howl.

Host. All victuallers do so: what's a joint of mutton or two in a whole Lent?

Prince. You, gentlewoman,—

Dol. What says your grace?

Fal. His grace says that which his flesh rebels against. [*Knocking within.* 380

Host. Who knocks so loud at door? Look to the door there, Francis.

Enter PETO.

Prince. Peto, how now! what news?

Peto. The king your father is at Westminster;
And there are twenty weak and wearied posts
Come from the north: and, as I came along,
I met and overtook a dozen captains,
Bare-headed, sweating, knocking at the taverns,
And asking every one for Sir John Falstaff. 389

Prince. By heaven, Poins, I feel me much to blame,
So idly to profane the precious time,
When tempest of commotion, like the south
Borne with black vapour, doth begin to melt
And drop upon our bare unarmed heads.
Give me my sword and cloak. Falstaff, good night.
[*Exeunt Prince Henry, Poins, Peto, and Bardolph.*

Fal. Now comes in the sweetest morsel of the night, and we must hence and leave it unpicked. [*Knocking within.*] More knocking at the door!

Re-enter BARDOLPH.

How now! what's the matter? 400

Bard. You must away to court, sir, presently;
A dozen captains stay at door for you.

Fal. [*To the Page*] Pay the musicians, sirrah. Farewell, hostess; farewell, Doll. You see, my good wenches, how men of merit are sought after: the undeserver may sleep, when the man of action is called on. Farewell, good wenches: if I be not sent away post, I will see you again ere I go.

Dol. I cannot speak; if my heart be not ready to burst,—well, sweet Jack, have a care of thyself.

Fal. Farewell, farewell. [*Exeunt Falstaff and Bardolph.*

Host. Well, fare thee well: I have known thee twenty nine years, come peascod-time; but an honester and truer-hearted man,—well, fare thee well.

Bard. [*Within*] Mistress Tearsheet!

Host. What's the matter?

Bard. [*Within*] Bid Mistress Tearsheet come to my master. 419

Host. O, run, Doll, run; run, good Doll: come. [*She comes blubbered.*] Yea, will you come, Doll? [*Exeunt.*

ACT III.

SCENE I. *Westminster. The palace.*

Enter the KING *in his nightgown, with a* Page.

King. Go call the Earls of Surrey and of Warwick;
But, ere they come, bid them o'er-read these letters,
And well consider of them: make good speed.
[*Exit Page.*

---

325. **heat,** start. 326. **candle-mine,** magazine of tallow. 346-348. **I dispraised . . . him.** This is a bit of the cant of puritanism which Falstaff uses as a mock excuse. 354. **close,** come to terms, agree. 360. **pricked down,** marked, or designated. 363. **malt-worms,** topers. 364. **good angel,** an allusion to the belief in spirits of good and evil which accompanied man. 372. **flesh to be eaten,** allusion to enactments to prevent the sale of meat in Lent. 379. **grace,** used quibblingly on the meanings "royal grace" and "heavenly grace." 392. **south,** south wind, regarded as a breeder of tempests. 393. **Borne with,** laden with. 421. *Stage Direction:* **blubbered,** disfigured with weeping.

ACT III. SCENE I. *Stage Direction:* **nightgown,** dressing gown. 5-31. **O sleep . . . crown.** This is one of the better known passages of the

How many thousand of my poorest subjects
Are at this hour asleep! O sleep, O gentle sleep,
Nature's soft nurse, how have I frighted thee,
That thou no more wilt weigh my eyelids down
And steep my senses in forgetfulness?
Why rather, sleep, liest thou in smoky cribs,
Upon uneasy pallets stretching thee   10
And hush'd with buzzing night-flies to thy slumber,
Than in the perfumed chambers of the great,
Under the canopies of costly state,
And lull'd with sound of sweetest melody?
O thou dull god, why liest thou with the vile
In loathsome beds, and leavest the kingly couch
A watch-case or a common 'larum-bell?
Wilt thou upon the high and giddy mast
Seal up the ship-boy's eyes, and rock his brains
In cradle of the rude imperious surge   20
And in the visitation of the winds,
Who take the ruffian billows by the top,
Curling their monstrous heads and hanging them
With deafening clamour in the slippery clouds,
That, with the hurly, death itself awakes?
Canst thou, O partial sleep, give thy repose
To the wet sea-boy in an hour so rude,
And in the calmest and most stillest night,
With all appliances and means to boot,
Deny it to a king? Then happy low, lie down!   30
Uneasy lies the head that wears a crown.

Enter WARWICK *and* SURREY.

War. Many good morrows to your majesty!
King. Is it good morrow, lords?
War. 'Tis one o'clock, and past.
King. Why, then, good morrow to you all, my lords.
Have you read o'er the letters that I sent you?
War. We have, my liege.
King. Then you perceive the body of our kingdom
How foul it is; what rank diseases grow,
And with what danger, near the heart of it.   40
War. It is but as a body yet distemper'd;
Which to his former strength may be restored
With good advice and little medicine:
My Lord Northumberland will soon be cool'd.
King. O God! that one might read the book of fate,
And see the revolution of the times
Make mountains level, and the continent,
Weary of solid firmness, melt itself
Into the sea! and, other times, to see
The beachy girdle of the ocean   50
Too wide for Neptune's hips; how chances mock,
And changes fill the cup of alteration
With divers liquors! O, if this were seen,
The happiest youth, viewing his progress through,
What perils past, what crosses to ensue,
Would shut the book, and sit him down and die.
'Tis not ten years gone
Since Richard and Northumberland, great friends,
Did feast together, and in two years after
Were they at wars: it is but eight years since   60
This Percy was the man nearest my soul,
Who like a brother toil'd in my affairs

And laid his love and life under my foot,
Yea, for my sake, even to the eyes of Richard
Gave him defiance. But which of you was by—
You, cousin Nevil, as I may remember—[*To Warwick.*
When Richard, with his eye brimful of tears,
Then check'd and rated by Northumberland,
Did speak these words, now proved a prophecy?
'Northumberland, thou ladder by the which   70
My cousin Bolingbroke ascends my throne;'
Though then, God knows, I had no such intent,
But that necessity so bow'd the state
That I and greatness were compell'd to kiss:
'The time shall come,' thus did he follow it,
'The time will come, that foul sin, gathering head,
Shall break into corruption:' so went on,
Foretelling this same time's condition
And the division of our amity.
War. There is a history in all men's lives,   80
Figuring the nature of the times deceased;
The which observed, a man may prophesy,
With a near aim, of the main chance of things
As yet not come to life, which in their seeds
And weak beginnings lie intreasured.
Such things become the hatch and brood of time;
And by the necessary form of this
King Richard might create a perfect guess
That great Northumberland, then false to him,
Would of that seed grow to a greater falseness;   90
Which should not find a ground to root upon,
Unless on you.
King.   Are these things then necessities?
Then let us meet them like necessities:
And that same word even now cries out on us:
They say the bishop and Northumberland
Are fifty thousand strong.
War.   It cannot be, my lord;
Rumour doth double, like the voice and echo,
The numbers of the fear'd. Please it your grace
To go to bed. Upon my soul, my lord,
The powers that you already have sent forth   100
Shall bring this prize in very easily.
To comfort you the more, I have received
A certain instance that Glendower is dead.
Your majesty hath been this fortnight ill,
And these unseason'd hours perforce must add
Unto your sickness.
King.   I will take your counsel:
And were these inward wars out of hand,
We would, dear lords, unto the Holy Land.   [*Exeunt.*

SCENE II. *Gloucestershire. Before* JUSTICE SHALLOW's *house.*

Enter SHALLOW *and* SILENCE, *meeting;* MOULDY,
  SHADOW, WART, FEEBLE, BULLCALF, *a Servant or*
  two with them.

Shal. Come on, come on, come on, sir; give me
your hand, sir, give me your hand, sir: an early
stirrer, by the rood! And how doth my good cousin
Silence?

play, having a beauty independent of its appropriateness in the mouth
of the weary king. 9. **cribs,** hovels. 15. **dull,** drowsy. **vile,** i.e.,
in rank. 17. **watch-case,** sentry box. 24. **slippery,** i.e., giving the
waves nothing to hold by. 25. **hurly,** tumult. 28. **most stillest,** double
superlative, as often in Shakespeare. 30. **low,** humble. 39. **foul,**
infected. 47. **continent,** dry land. 56. **shut the book,** expression of

despair. He would shut the book of his future. 64. **to the eyes,** to the
face. 67. **Richard.** See *Richard II,* V, i, 55 ff. 81. **Figuring,** sym-
bolizing. 85. **intreasured,** in store. 87. **necessary form,** logical
necessity. 105. **unseason'd,** unseasonable.
  SCENE II. 1. **Come on.** In Shallow's repetitions there is a suggestion
of fussiness and possibly old age. 3. **rood,** cross.

Sil. Good morrow, good cousin Shallow.

Shal. And how doth my cousin, your bedfellow? and your fairest daughter and mine, my god-daughter Ellen?

Sil. Alas, a black ousel, cousin Shallow! 9

Shal. By yea and nay, sir, I dare say my cousin William is become a good scholar: he is at Oxford still, is he not?

Sil. Indeed, sir, to my cost.

Shal. A' must, then, to the inns o' court shortly. I was once of Clement's Inn, where I think they will talk of mad Shallow yet.

Sil. You were called 'lusty Shallow' then, cousin. 18

Shal. By the mass, I was called any thing; and I would have done any thing indeed too, and roundly too. There was I, and Little John Doit of Stafford-shire, and black George Barnes, and Francis Pick-bone, and Will Squele, a Cotswold man; you had not four such swinge-bucklers in all the inns o' court again: and I may say to you, we knew where the bona-robas were and had the best of them all at commandment. Then was Jack Falstaff, now Sir John, a boy, and page to Thomas Mowbray, Duke of Norfolk.

Sil. This Sir John, cousin, that comes hither anon about soldiers? 31

Shal. The same Sir John, the very same. I see him break Skogan's head at the court-gate, when a' was a crack not thus high: and the very same day did I fight with one Sampson Stockfish, a fruiterer, behind Gray's Inn. Jesu, Jesu, the mad days that I have spent! and to see how many of my old acquaintance are dead!

Sil. We shall all follow, cousin. 39

Shal. Certain, 'tis certain; very sure, very sure: death, as the Psalmist saith, is certain to all; all shall die. How a good yoke of bullocks at Stamford fair?

Sil. By my troth, I was not there.

Shal. Death is certain. Is old Double of your town living yet?

Sil. Dead, sir. 47

Shal. Jesu, Jesu, dead! a' drew a good bow; and dead! a' shot a fine shoot: John a Gaunt loved him well, and betted much money on his head. Dead! a' would have clapped i' the clout at twelve score; and carried you a forehand shaft a fourteen and fourteen and a half, that it would have done a man's heart good to see. How a score of ewes now?

Sil. Thereafter as they be: a score of good ewes may be worth ten pounds.

Shal. And is old Double dead?

Sil. Here come two of Sir John Falstaff's men, as I think. 60

Enter BARDOLPH *and one with him.*

Bard. Good morrow, honest gentlemen: I beseech you, which is Justice Shallow?

Shal. I am Robert Shallow, sir; a poor esquire of this county, and one of the king's justices of the peace: what is your good pleasure with me?

Bard. My captain, sir, commends him to you; my

captain, Sir John Falstaff, a tall gentleman, by heaven, and a most gallant leader. 68

Shal. He greets me well, sir. I knew him a good backsword man. How doth the good knight? may I ask how my lady his wife doth?

Bard. Sir, pardon; a soldier is better accommodated than with a wife.

Shal. It is well said, in faith, sir; and it is well said indeed too. Better accommodated! it is good; yea, indeed, is it: good phrases are surely, and ever were, very commendable. Accommodated! it comes of 'accommodo:' very good; a good phrase. 79

Bard. Pardon me, sir; I have heard the word. Phrase call you it? by this good day, I know not the phrase; but I will maintain the word with my sword to be a soldier-like word, and a word of exceeding good command, by heaven. Accommodated; that is, when a man is, as they say, accommodated; or when a man is, being, whereby a' may be thought to be accommodated; which is an excellent thing.

Shal. It is very just. 89

Enter FALSTAFF.

Look, here comes good Sir John. Give me your good hand, give me your worship's good hand: by my troth, you like well and bear your years very well: welcome, good Sir John.

Fal. I am glad to see you well, good Master Robert Shallow: Master Surecard, as I think?

Shal. No, Sir John; it is my cousin Silence, in commission with me.

Fal. Good Master Silence, it well befits you should be of the peace.

Sil. Your good worship is welcome. 100

Fal. Fie! this is hot weather, gentlemen. Have you provided me here half a dozen sufficient men?

Shal. Marry, have we, sir. Will you sit?

Fal. Let me see them, I beseech you.

Shal. Where 's the roll? where 's the roll? where 's the roll? Let me see, let me see, let me see. So, so, so, so, so, so, so: yea, marry, sir: Ralph Mouldy! Let them appear as I call; let them do so, let them do so. Let me see; where is Mouldy? 111

Moul. Here, an 't please you.

Shal. What think you, Sir John? a good-limbed fellow; young, strong, and of good friends.

Fal. Is thy name Mouldy?

Moul. Yea, an 't please you.

Fal. 'Tis the more time thou wert used.

Shal. Ha, ha, ha! most excellent, i' faith! things that are mouldy lack use: very singular good! in faith, well said, Sir John, very well said. 120

Fal. Prick him.

Moul. I was pricked well enough before, an you could have let me alone: my old dame will be undone now for one to do her husbandry and her drudgery: you need not to have pricked me; there are other men fitter to go out than I.

Fal. Go to: peace, Mouldy; you shall go. Mouldy, it is time you were spent.

Moul. Spent! 129

9. **ousel,** blackbird. 15. **Clement's Inn,** one of the inns of court, or colleges of law. 17. **lusty,** merry. 24. **Cotswold,** Cotswold Hills; a region famous for athletic sports. 25. **swinge-bucklers,** roisterers, swashbucklers. 27. **bona-robas,** showily dressed wantons. 29. **page to Thomas Mowbray.** Both Sir John Oldcastle (Falstaff's original) and Sir John Fastolfe (for whom Falstaff was renamed) were pages to the

duke of Norfolk, who figures in the play *Richard II.* 33. **Skogan.** There was a court jester to Edward IV whose name was John Skogan, and a jestbook known as "Skogan's Jests." 34. **crack,** pert little boy. 42. **How,** how much. 52. **clapped i' the clout,** hit the bull's-eye. **twelve score,** i.e., yards. 53. **forehand shaft,** arrow used for shooting straight before one. 70. **backsword man,** singlestick fencer. 72. **accom-**

Shal. Peace, fellow, peace; stand aside: know you where you are? For the other, Sir John: let me see: Simon Shadow!

Fal. Yea, marry, let me have him to sit under: he 's like to be a cold soldier.

Shal. Where 's Shadow?

Shad. Here, sir.

Fal. Shadow, whose son art thou?

Shad. My mother's son, sir.

Fal. Thy mother's son! like enough, and thy father's shadow: so the son of the female is the shadow of the male: it is often so, indeed; but much of the father's substance!

Shal. Do you like him, Sir John? 143

Fal. Shadow will serve for summer; prick him, for we have a number of shadows to fill up the muster-book.

Shal. Thomas Wart!

Fal. Where 's he?

Wart. Here, sir.

Fal. Is thy name Wart? 150

Wart. Yea, sir.

Fal. Thou art a very ragged wart.

Shal. Shall I prick him down, Sir John?

Fal. It were superfluous; for his apparel is built upon his back and the whole frame stands upon pins: prick him no more.

Shal. Ha, ha, ha! you can do it, sir; you can do it: I commend you well. Francis Feeble!

Fee. Here, sir.

Fal. What trade art thou, Feeble? 160

Fee. A woman's tailor, sir.

Shal. Shall I prick him, sir?

Fal. You may: but if he had been a man's tailor, he 'ld ha' pricked you. Wilt thou make as many holes in an enemy's battle as thou hast done in a woman's petticoat? 166

Fee. I will do my good will, sir: you can have no more.

Fal. Well said, good woman's tailor! well said, courageous Feeble! thou wilt be as valiant as the wrathful dove or most magnanimous mouse. Prick the woman's tailor: well, Master Shallow; deep, Master Shallow.

Fee. I would Wart might have gone, sir.

Fal. I would thou wert a man's tailor, that thou mightst mend him and make him fit to go. I cannot put him to a private soldier that is the leader of so many thousands: let that suffice, most forcible Feeble.

Fee. It shall suffice, sir. 180

Fal. I am bound to thee, reverend Feeble. Who is next?

Shal. Peter Bullcalf o' the green!

Fal. Yea, marry, let 's see Bullcalf.

Bull. Here, sir.

Fal. 'Fore God, a likely fellow! Come, prick me Bullcalf till he roar again.

Bull. O Lord! good my lord captain,—

Fal. What, dost thou roar before thou art pricked? 190

Bull. O Lord, sir! I am a diseased man.

Fal. What disease hast thou?

Bull. A whoreson cold, sir, a cough, sir, which I caught with ringing in the king's affairs upon his coronation-day, sir.

Fal. Come, thou shalt go to the wars in a gown; we will have away thy cold; and I will take such order that thy friends shall ring for thee. Is here all? 199

Shal. Here is two more called than your number; you must have but four here, sir: and so, I pray you, go in with me to dinner.

Fal. Come, I will go drink with you, but I cannot tarry dinner. I am glad to see you, by my troth, Master Shallow.

Shal. O, Sir John, do you remember since we lay all night in the windmill in Saint George's field?

Fal. No more of that, good Master Shallow, no more of that.

Shal. Ha! 'twas a merry night. And is Jane Night-work alive? 211

Fal. She lives, Master Shallow.

Shal. She never could away with me.

Fal. Never, never; she would always say she could not abide Master Shallow.

Shal. By the mass, I could anger her to the heart. She was then a bona-roba. Doth she hold her own well?

Fal. Old, old, Master Shallow. 219

Shal. Nay, she must be old; she cannot choose but be old; certain she 's old; and had Robin Nightwork by old Nightwork before I came to Clement's Inn.

Sil. That 's fifty five years ago.

Shal. Ha, cousin Silence, that thou hadst seen that that this knight and I have seen! Ha, Sir John, said I well?

Fal. We have heard the chimes at midnight, Master Shallow. 229

Shal. That we have, that we have, that we have; in faith, Sir John, we have: our watchword was 'Hem boys!' Come, let 's to dinner; come, let 's to dinner: Jesus, the days that we have seen! Come, come. [*Exeunt Falstaff and the Justices.*

Bull. Good Master Corporate Bardolph, stand my friend; and here 's four Harry ten shillings in French crowns for you. In very truth, sir, I had as lief be hanged, sir, as go: and yet, for mine own part, sir, I do not care; but rather, because I am unwilling, and, for mine own part, have a desire to stay with my friends; else, sir, I did not care, for mine own part, so much. 242

Bard. Go to; stand aside.

Moul. And, good master corporal captain, for my old dame's sake, stand my friend: she has nobody to do any thing about her when I am gone; and she is old, and cannot help herself: you shall have forty, sir.

Bard. Go to; stand aside. 249

Fee. By my troth, I care not; a man can die but once: we owe God a death: I'll ne'er bear a base mind: an 't be my destiny, so; an 't be not, so: no man is too good to serve 's prince; and let it go which way it will, he that dies this year is quit for the next.

Bard. Well said; thou 'rt a good fellow.

Fee. Faith, I'll bear no base mind.

modated, furnished, equipped; a bit of fine language on Bardolph's part. 92. **like well**, are in good condition. 95. **Surecard**, boon companion. 99. **of the peace**, i.e., a magistrate; reference to the name *Silence*. 103. **sufficient**, fit for service. 122. **pricked**, dressed; with quibble on the meaning, "marked, or designated, for service." 144-146. **Shadow . . . muster-book**, an allusion to the practice of employing false muster lists and drawing pay for imaginary soldiers. 177. **to, in** the character of. 178. **thousands**, i.e., of vermin. 207. **Saint George's field**, open space between Lambeth and Southwark; a muster ground. 213. **away with**, get on with. 235. **Corporate**, for "corporal." 236. **Harry ten shillings**, i.e., coined in the reign of Henry VII; current at half the face value. The reference is anachronistic. 248. **forty**, i.e., shillings.

Re-enter FALSTAFF *and the* Justices.

Fal. Come, sir, which men shall I have?

Shal. Four of which you please.

Bard. Sir, a word with you: I have three pound to free Mouldy and Bullcalf. 261

Fal. Go to; well.

Shal. Come, Sir John, which four will you have?

Fal. Do you choose for me.

Shal. Marry, then, Mouldy, Bullcalf, Feeble and Shadow.

Fal. Mouldy and Bullcalf: for you, Mouldy, stay at home till you are past service: and for your part, Bullcalf, grow till you come unto it: I will none of you.

Shal. Sir John, Sir John, do not yourself wrong: they are your likeliest men, and I would have you served with the best. 274

Fal. Will you tell me, Master Shallow, how to choose a man? Care I for the limb, the thewes, the stature, bulk, and big assemblance of a man! Give me the spirit, Master Shallow. Here 's Wart; you see what a ragged appearance it is: a' shall charge you and discharge you with the motion of a pewterer's hammer, come off and on swifter than he that gibbets on the brewer's bucket. And this same half-faced fellow, Shadow; give me this man: he presents no mark to the enemy; the foeman may with as great aim level at the edge of a penknife. And for a retreat; how swiftly will this Feeble the woman's tailor run off! O, give me the spare men, and spare me the great ones. Put me a caliver into Wart's hand, Bardolph. 290

Bard. Hold, Wart, traverse; thus, thus, thus.

Fal. Come, manage me your caliver. So; very well: go to: very good, exceeding good. O, give me always a little, lean, old, chapt, bald shot. Well said, i' faith, Wart; thou 'rt a good scab: hold, there 's a tester for thee.

Shal. He is not his craft's master; he doth not do it right. I remember at Mile-end Green, when I lay at Clement's Inn,—I was then Sir Dagonet in Arthur's show,—there was a little quiver fellow, and a' would manage you his piece thus; and a' would about and about, and come you in and come you in: 'rah, tah, tah,' would a' say; 'bounce' would a' say; and away again would a' go, and again would a' come: I shall ne'er see such a fellow. 306

Fal. These fellows will do well, Master Shallow. God keep you, Master Silence: I will not use many words with you. Fare you well, gentlemen both: I thank you: I must a dozen mile to-night. Bardolph, give the soldiers coats.

Shal. Sir John, the Lord bless you! God prosper your affairs! God send us peace! At your return visit our house; let our old acquaintance be renewed: peradventure I will with ye to the court. 316

Fal. 'Fore God, I would you would, Master Shallow.

Shal. Go to; I have spoke at a word. God keep you.

Fal. Fare you well, gentle gentlemen. [*Exeunt Justices.*] On, Bardolph; lead the men away. [*Exeunt Bardolph, Recruits, &c.*] As I return, I will fetch off these justices: I do see the bottom of Justice Shallow. Lord, Lord, how subject we old men are to this vice of lying! This same starved justice hath done nothing but prate to me of the wildness of his youth, and the feats he hath done about Turnbull Street; and every third word a lie, duer paid to the hearer than the Turk's tribute. I do remember him at Clement's Inn like a man made after supper of a cheese-paring: when a' was naked, he was, for all the world, like a forked radish, with a head fantastically carved upon it with a knife: a' was so forlorn, that his dimensions to any thick sight were invincible: a' was the very genius of famine; yet lecherous as a monkey, and the whores called him mandrake: a' came ever in the rearward of the fashion, and sung those tunes to the overscutched huswives that he heard the carmen whistle, and sware they were his fancies or his good-nights. And now is this Vice's dagger become a squire, and talks as familiarly of John a Gaunt as if he had been sworn brother to him; and I'll be sworn a' ne'er saw him but once in the Tilt-yard; and then he burst his head for crowding among the marshal's men. I saw it, and told John a Gaunt he beat his own name; for you might have thrust him and all his apparel into an eel-skin; the case of a treble hautboy was a mansion for him, a court: and now has he land and beefs. Well, I'll be acquainted with him, if I return; and it shall go hard but I will make him a philosopher's two stones to me: if the young dace be a bait for the old pike, I see no reason in the law of nature but I may snap at him. Let time shape, and there an end. [*Exit.* 358

ACT IV.

SCENE I. *Yorkshire. Gaultree Forest.*

Enter the ARCHBISHOP OF YORK, MOWBRAY, HASTINGS, *and others.*

Arch. What is this forest call'd?

Hast. 'Tis Gaultree Forest, an 't shall please your grace.

Arch. Here stand, my lords; and send discoverers forth

To know the numbers of our enemies.

Hast. We have sent forth already.

Arch.   'Tis well done.

My friends and brethren in these great affairs,

I must acquaint you that I have received

New-dated letters from Northumberland;

Their cold intent, tenour and substance, thus:

Here doth he wish his person, with such powers 10

As might hold sortance with his quality,

2 Henry IV
ACT III : SC II

722

---

277. **assemblance,** appearance. 280, 281. **charge, discharge, come off and on,** terms in the drilling of troops. 282. **gibbets on,** hangs as on a gibbet; a reference to the skill of brewer's men in swinging buckets upon the gibbet or yoke which they wore on their shoulders. 290. **caliver,** light musket or harquebus. 291. **traverse,** march. 295. **shot,** marksman. 296. **scab,** scurvy fellow. **tester,** sixpence. 298-300. **I remember . . . show.** There was an exhibition of archery held annually at Mile-end Green called "Arthur's show"; in this show Shallow played the part of Sir Dagonet, King Arthur's fool. 301. **quiver,** nimble. 304. **'bounce,'** bang. 319. **at a word,** briefly and sincerely. 324. **fetch**

off, get the better of. 325. **see . . . Shallow.** The character of Shallow, which became immediately popular on the London stage, afforded the opportunity not only of laughing at a stupid and pompous country justice, but of presenting the ancient spectacle of the fool being fleeced by the rogue. 329. **Turnbull Street,** a street in Clerkenwell, ill-reputed. 330. **Turk's tribute.** Much of Christendom was paying tribute to the sultan of Turkey. 336. **forlorn,** meager, thin. 339. **mandrake,** root of a plant, the white mandrake, said to resemble the body of a man; said also to be an emblem of incontinence. 340. **overscutched huswives,** outworn prostitutes. 342. **fancies . . . good-nights,**

The which he could not levy; whereupon
He is retired, to ripe his growing fortunes,
To Scotland: and concludes in hearty prayers
That your attempts may overlive the hazard
And fearful meeting of their opposite.
   Mowb. Thus do the hopes we have in him touch
     ground
And dash themselves to pieces.

Enter a Messenger.

   Hast.   Now, what news?
   Mess. West of this forest, scarcely off a mile,
In goodly form comes on the enemy;   20
And, by the ground they hide, I judge their number
Upon or near the rate of thirty thousand.
   Mowb. The just proportion that we gave them out.
Let us sway on and face them in the field.
   Arch. What well-appointed leader fronts us here?

Enter WESTMORELAND.

   Mowb. I think it is my Lord of Westmoreland.
   West. Health and fair greeting from our general,
The prince, Lord John and Duke of Lancaster.
   Arch. Say on, my Lord of Westmoreland, in peace:
What doth concern your coming?
   West.   Then, my lord,   30
Unto your grace do I in chief address
The substance of my speech. If that rebellion
Came like itself, in base and abject routs,
Led on by bloody youth, guarded with rags,
And countenanced by boys and beggary,
I say, if damn'd commotion so appear'd,
In his true, native and most proper shape,
You, reverend father, and these noble lords
Had not been here, to dress the ugly form
Of base and bloody insurrection   40
With your fair honours. You, lord archbishop,
Whose see is by a civil peace maintain'd,
Whose beard the silver hand of peace hath touch'd,
Whose learning and good letters peace hath tutor'd,
Whose white investments figure innocence,
The dove and very blessed spirit of peace,
Wherefore do you so ill translate yourself
Out of the speech of peace that bears such grace,
Into the harsh and boisterous tongue of war;
Turning your books to †graves, your ink to blood,   50
Your pens to lances and your tongue divine
To a loud trumpet and a point of war?
   Arch. Wherefore do I this? so the question stands.
Briefly to this end: we are all diseased,
And with our surfeiting and wanton hours
Have brought ourselves into a burning fever,
And we must bleed for it; of which disease
Our late king, Richard, being infected, died.
But, my most noble Lord of Westmoreland,
I take not on me here as a physician,   60
Nor do I as an enemy to peace
Troop in the throngs of military men;

But rather show awhile like fearful war,
To diet rank minds sick of happiness
And purge the obstructions which begin to stop
Our very veins of life. Hear me more plainly.
I have in equal balance justly weigh'd
What wrongs our arms may do, what wrongs we
     suffer,
And find our griefs heavier than our offences.
We see which way the stream of time doth run,   70
And are enforced from our most quiet there
By the rough torrent of occasion;
And have the summary of all our griefs,
When time shall serve, to show in articles;
Which long ere this we offer'd to the king,
And might by no suit gain our audience:
When we are wrong'd and would unfold our griefs,
We are denied access unto his person
Even by those men that most have done us wrong.
The dangers of the days but newly gone,   80
Whose memory is written on the earth
With yet appearing blood, and the examples
Of every minute's instance, present now,
Hath put us in these ill-beseeming arms,
Not to break peace or any branch of it,
But to establish here a peace indeed,
Concurring both in name and quality.
   West. When ever yet was your appeal denied?
Wherein have you been galled by the king?
What peer hath been suborn'd to grate on you,   90
That you should seal this lawless bloody book
Of forged rebellion with a seal divine
And consecrate commotion's bitter edge?
   Arch. †My brother general, the commonwealth,
To brother born an household cruelty,
I make my quarrel in particular.
   West. There is no need of any such redress;
Or if there were, it not belongs to you.
   Mowb. Why not to him in part, and to us all
That feel the bruises of the days before,   100
And suffer the condition of these times
To lay a heavy and unequal hand
Upon our honours?
   West.   O, my good Lord Mowbray,
Construe the times to their necessities,
And you shall say indeed, it is the time,
And not the king, that doth you injuries.
Yet for your part, it not appears to me
Either from the king or in the present time
That you should have an inch of any ground
To build a grief on: were you not restored   110
To all the Duke of Norfolk's signories,
Your noble and right well remember'd father's?
   Mowb. What thing, in honour, had my father lost,
That need to be revived and breathed in me?
The king that loved him, as the state stood then,
Was force perforce compell'd to banish him:
And then that Henry Bolingbroke and he,
Being mounted and both roused in their seats,

2 Henry IV
ACT IV : SC I

723

love songs, of which he claims authorship. 343. **Vice's dagger.** The Vice, or comic character of the morality plays, was armed with a wooden dagger. 351. **hautboy,** oboe. 355. **philosopher's two stones,** i.e., yield twice as much as the philosopher's stone, which would produce boundless wealth. 356. **young dace . . . old pike.** The fish dace, or luce, was the pike's food; this passage has been thought to allude to Shakespeare's animosity for Sir Thomas Lucy of Charlecote. See Shakespeare's Life and Work 1564-1594.
   ACT IV. SCENE I. 2. **Gaultree Forest,** ancient forest of Galtres north of York. 11. **hold sortance,** accord. 15. **overlive,** outlive. 24. **sway on,** move on. 34. **bloody,** passionate. **guarded,** adorned,

trimmed. 36. **commotion,** tumult, sedition. 42. **civil,** orderly, law-abiding. 45. **investments,** clothes, vestments. 50. **graves,** Hanmer: *glaives;* Steevens: *greaves;* Vaughan: *gloves.* 52. **point of war,** trumpet, signal of war. 69. **griefs,** grievances. 89. **galled,** injured, made sore with chafing. 90. **suborn'd . . . on,** induced by secret plot to annoy. 94-96. **My . . . particular.** This is a corrupt text of which the sense seems to be: I make this my quarrel on both public and private grounds, that is, because of the sufferings of the commonwealth and of my own family at the hands of the king (Yale); see *particular* in glossary. 117ff. These lines give the subject of the play *Richard II.*

Their neighing coursers daring of the spur,
Their armed staves in charge, their beavers down, 120
Their eyes of fire sparkling through sights of steel
And the loud trumpet blowing them together,
Then, then, when there was nothing could have
    stay'd
My father from the breast of Bolingbroke,
O, when the king did throw his warder down,
His own life hung upon the staff he threw;
Then threw he down himself and all their lives
That by indictment and by dint of sword
Have since miscarried under Bolingbroke.
    West. You speak, Lord Mowbray, now you know
        not what. 130
The Earl of Hereford was reputed then
In England the most valiant gentleman:
Who knows on whom fortune would then have
    smiled?
But if your father had been victor there,
He ne'er had borne it out of Coventry:
For all the country in a general voice
Cried hate upon him; and all their prayers and love
Were set on Hereford, whom they doted on
And bless'd and graced indeed, more than the king.
But this is mere digression from my purpose. 140
Here come I from our princely general
To know your griefs; to tell you from his grace
That he will give you audience; and wherein
It shall appear that your demands are just,
You shall enjoy them, every thing set off
That might so much as think you enemies.
    Mowb. But he hath forced us to compel this offer;
And it proceeds from policy, not love.
    West. Mowbray, you overween to take it so;
This offer comes from mercy, not from fear: 150
For, lo! within a ken our army lies,
Upon mine honour, all too confident
To give admittance to a thought of fear.
Our battle is more full of names than yours,
Our men more perfect in the use of arms,
Our armour all as strong, our cause the best;
Then reason will our hearts should be as good:
Say you not then our offer is compell'd.
    Mowb. Well, by my will we shall admit no parley.
    West. That argues but the shame of your offence: 160
A rotten case abides no handling.
    Hast. Hath the Prince John a full commission,
In very ample virtue of his father,
To hear and absolutely to determine
Of what conditions we shall stand upon?
    West. That is intended in the general's name:
I muse you make so slight a question.
    Arch. Then take, my Lord of Westmoreland, this
        schedule,
For this contains our general grievances:
Each several article herein redress'd, 170
All members of our cause, both here and hence,
That are insinew'd to this action,
Acquitted by a true substantial form

And present execution of our wills
To us and to our purposes confined,
We come within our awful banks again
And knit our powers to the arm of peace.
    West. This will I show the general. Please you, lords,
In sight of both our battles we may meet;
And either end in peace, which God so frame! 180
Or to the place of difference call the swords
Which must decide it.
    Arch.   My lord, we will do so.
                            [*Exit West.*
    Mowb. There is a thing within my bosom tells me
That no conditions of our peace can stand.
    Hast. Fear you not that: if we can make our peace
Upon such large terms and so absolute
As our conditions shall consist upon,
Our peace shall stand as firm as rocky mountains.
    Mowb. Yea, but our valuation shall be such
That every slight and false-derived cause, 190
Yea, every idle, nice and wanton reason
Shall to the king taste of this action;
That, were our royal faiths martyrs in love,
We shall be winnow'd with so rough a wind
That even our corn shall seem as light as chaff
And good from bad find no partition.
    Arch. No, no, my lord. Note this; the king is weary
Of dainty and such picking grievances:
For he hath found to end one doubt by death
Revives two greater in the heirs of life, 200
And therefore will he wipe his tables clean
And keep no tell-tale to his memory
That may repeat and history his loss
To new remembrance; for full well he knows
He cannot so precisely weed this land
As his misdoubts present occasion:
His foes are so enrooted with his friends
That, plucking to unfix an enemy,
He doth unfasten so and shake a friend:
So that this land, like an offensive wife 210
That hath enraged him on to offer strokes,
As he is striking, holds his infant up
And hangs resolved correction in the arm
That was uprear'd to execution.
    Hast. Besides, the king hath wasted all his rods
On late offenders, that he now doth lack
The very instruments of chastisement:
So that his power, like to a fangless lion,
May offer, but not hold.
    Arch.   'Tis very true;
And therefore be assured, my good lord marshal, 220
If we do now make our atonement well,
Our peace will, like a broken limb united,
Grow stronger for the breaking.
    Mowb.   Be it so.
Here is return'd my Lord of Westmoreland.

                Re-enter WESTMORELAND.

    West. The prince is here at hand: pleaseth your
        lordship

To meet his grace just distance 'tween our armies.
Mowb. Your grace of York, in God's name, then,
    set forward.
Arch. Before, and greet his grace: my lord, we come.
                              [Exeunt.

SCENE II. *Another part of the forest.*

Enter, from one side, MOWBRAY, *attended; afterwards
the* ARCHBISHOP, HASTINGS, *and others: from the
other side,* PRINCE JOHN OF LANCASTER, *and*
WESTMORELAND; *Officers, and others with them.*

Lan. You are well encounter'd here, my cousin
    Mowbray:
Good day to you, gentle lord archbishop;
And so to you, Lord Hastings, and to all.
My Lord of York, it better show'd with you
When that your flock, assembled by the bell,
Encircled you to hear with reverence
Your exposition on the holy text
Than now to see you here an iron man,
Cheering a rout of rebels with your drum,
Turning the word to sword and life to death.   10
That man that sits within a monarch's heart,
And ripens in the sunshine of his favour,
Would he abuse the countenance of the king,
Alack, what mischiefs might he set abroach
In shadow of such greatness! With you, lord bishop,
It is even so. Who hath not heard it spoken
How deep you were within the books of God?
To us the speaker in his parliament;
To us the imagined voice of God himself;
The very opener and intelligencer   20
Between the grace, the sanctities of heaven
And our dull workings. O, who shall believe
But you misuse the reverence of your place,
Employ the countenance and grace of heaven,
As a false favourite doth his prince's name,
In deeds dishonourable? You have ta'en up,
Under the counterfeited zeal of God,
The subjects of his substitute, my father,
And both against the peace of heaven and him
Have here up-swarm'd them.
Arch.   Good my Lord of Lancaster, 30
I am not here against your father's peace;
But, as I told my Lord of Westmoreland,
The time misorder'd doth, in common sense,
Crowd us and crush us to this monstrous form,
To hold our safety up. I sent your grace
The parcels and particulars of our grief,
The which hath been with scorn shoved from the
    court,
Whereon this Hydra son of war is born;
Whose dangerous eyes may well be charm'd asleep
With grant of our most just and right desires,   40
And true obedience, of this madness cured,
Stoop tamely to the foot of majesty.
Mowb. If not, we ready are to try our fortunes

To the last man.
Hast.   And though we here fall down,
We have supplies to second our attempt:
If they miscarry, theirs shall second them;
And so success of mischief shall be born
And heir from heir shall hold this quarrel up
Whiles England shall have generation.
Lan. You are too shallow, Hastings, much too
    shallow,   50
To sound the bottom of the after-times.
West. Pleaseth your grace to answer them directly
How far forth you do like their articles.
Lan. I like them all, and do allow them well,
And swear here, by the honour of my blood,
My father's purposes have been mistook,
And some about him have too lavishly
Wrested his meaning and authority.
My lord, these griefs shall be with speed redress'd;
Upon my soul, they shall. If this may please you,   60
Discharge your powers unto their several counties,
As we will ours: and here between the armies
Let's drink together friendly and embrace,
That all their eyes may bear those tokens home
Of our restored love and amity.
Arch. I take your princely word for these redresses.
Lan. I give it you, and will maintain my word:
And thereupon I drink unto your grace.
Hast. Go, captain, and deliver to the army
This news of peace: let them have pay, and part: 70
I know it will well please them. Hie thee, captain.
                            [Exit Officer.
Arch. To you, my noble Lord of Westmoreland.
West. I pledge your grace; and, if you knew what
    pains
I have bestow'd to breed this present peace,
You would drink freely: but my love to ye
Shall show itself more openly hereafter.
Arch. I do not doubt you.
West.   I am glad of it.
Health to my lord and gentle cousin, Mowbray.
Mowb. You wish me health in very happy season;
For I am, on the sudden, something ill.   80
Arch. Against ill chances men are ever merry;
But heaviness foreruns the good event.
West. Therefore be merry, coz; since sudden sorrow
Serves to say thus, 'some good thing comes
    to-morrow.'
Arch. Believe me, I am passing light in spirit.
Mowb. So much the worse, if your own rule be true.
                          [Shouts within.
Lan. The word of peace is render'd: hark, how they
    shout!
Mowb. This had been cheerful after victory.
Arch. A peace is of the nature of a conquest;
For then both parties nobly are subdued,   90
And neither party loser.
Lan.   Go, my lord,
And let our army be discharged too.
                     [Exit Westmoreland.

please. 226. **just,** exact. 228. **Before,** i.e., go before.
   SCENE II. 8. **iron man,** warrior clad in armor. 14. **set abroach,** set
on foot, begin. 17. **within the books,** in the good graces. 18. **speaker,**
allusion to the speaker of Parliament, who acted as the voice or
interpreter of the house. 20. **opener,** revealer. **intelligencer,** interpreter, secret agent. 22. **dull workings,** stupid endeavors. 27. **zeal.**
Herford suggests a play on "seal." 28. **substitute,** deputy. Note the
current theory of the position and function of the king. In this speech
the prince gives a preliminary justification of the breach of faith with

the rebels, whom he regarded as outside the pale of rectitude. 33.
time misorder'd, disorders of the time. 36. **parcels,** items, parts.
38. **Hydra.** The Lernaean Hydra was a fabulous monster with several
heads; when one was cut off, others grew in its place. 42. **Stoop tamely,**
yield, submit; a metaphor from falconry. 45. **supplies,** forces in
reserve. 49. **generation,** issue, offspring. 54. **allow,** approve, sanction.
81. **Against,** when about to face.

And, good my lord, so please you, let our trains
March by us, that we may peruse the men
We should have coped withal.
　　Arch. 　　　　　　Go, good Lord Hastings,
And, ere they be dismiss'd, let them march by.
　　　　　　　　　　　　　　　　[*Exit Hastings.*
　　Lan. I trust, lords, we shall lie to-night together.

Re-enter WESTMORELAND.

Now cousin, wherefore stands our army still?
　　West. The leaders, having charge from you to stand,
Will not go off until they hear you speak. 　　　100
　　Lan. They know their duties.

Re-enter HASTINGS.

　　Hast. My lord, our army is dispersed already:
Like youthful steers unyoked, they take their courses
East, west, north, south; or, like a school broke up,
Each hurries toward his home and sporting-place.
　　West. Good tidings, my Lord Hastings; for the
　　　　which
I do arrest thee, traitor, of high treason:
And you, lord archbishop, and you, lord Mowbray,
Of capital treason I attach you both.
　　Mowb. Is this proceeding just and honourable? 　110
　　West. Is your assembly so?
　　Arch. Will you thus break your faith?
　　Lan. 　　　　　I pawn'd thee none:
I promised you redress of these same grievances
Whereof you did complain; which, by mine honour,
I will perform with a most Christian care.
But for you, rebels, look to taste the due
Meet for rebellion and such acts as yours.
Most shallowly did you these arms commence,
Fondly brought here and foolishly sent hence.
Strike up our drums, pursue the scatter'd stray: 　120
God, and not we, hath safely fought to-day.
Some guard these traitors to the block of death,
Treason's true bed and yielder up of breath. 　[*Exeunt.*

<hr>

SCENE III. *Another part of the forest.*

Alarum. Excursions. Enter FALSTAFF *and* COLEVILE,
　meeting.

　　Fal. What's your name, sir? of what condition are
you, and of what place, I pray?
　　Cole. I am a knight, sir; and my name is Colevile of
the dale.
　　Fal. Well, then, Colevile is your name, a knight is
your degree, and your place the dale: Colevile shall
be still your name, a traitor your degree, and the
dungeon your place, a place deep enough; so shall
you be still Colevile of the dale. 　　　　　　　10
　　Cole. Are not you Sir John Falstaff?
　　Fal. As good a man as he, sir, whoe'er I am. Do ye
yield, sir? or shall I sweat for you? If I do sweat, they
are the drops of thy lovers, and they weep for thy

death: therefore rouse up fear and trembling, and do
observance to my mercy.
　　Cole. I think you are Sir John Falstaff, and in that
thought yield me. 　　　　　　　　　　　　　　19
　　Fal. I have a whole school of tongues in this belly
of mine, and not a tongue of them all speaks any other
word but my name. An I had but a belly of any
indifferency, I were simply the most active fellow in
Europe: my womb, my womb, my womb, undoes
me. Here comes our general.

Enter PRINCE JOHN OF LANCASTER, WESTMORELAND,
　BLUNT, *and others.*

　　Lan. The heat is past; follow no further now:
Call in the powers, good cousin Westmoreland.
　　　　　　　　　　　　[*Exit Westmoreland.*
Now, Falstaff, where have you been all this while?
When every thing is ended, then you come: 　　30
These tardy tricks of yours will, on my life,
One time or other break some gallows' back.
　　Fal. I would be sorry, my lord, but it should be
thus: I never knew yet but rebuke and check was the
reward of valour. Do you think me a swallow, an
arrow, or a bullet? have I, in my poor and old motion,
the expedition of thought? I have speeded hither
with the very extremest inch of possibility; I have
foundered nine score and odd posts: and here,
travel-tainted as I am, have, in my pure and immaculate valour, taken Sir John Colevile of the dale,
a most furious knight and valorous enemy. But what
of that? he saw me, and yielded; that I may justly
say, with the hook-nosed fellow of Rome, 'I came,
saw, and overcame.' 　　　　　　　　　　　　47
　　Lan. It was more of his courtesy than your deserving.
　　Fal. I know not: here is he, and here I yield him:
and I beseech your grace, let it be booked with the
rest of this day's deeds; or, by the Lord, I will have
it in a particular ballad else, with mine own picture
on the top on 't, Colevile kissing my foot: to the
which course if I be enforced, if you do not all show
like gilt two-pences to me, and I in the clear sky of
fame o'ershine you as much as the full moon doth
the cinders of the element, which show like pins'
heads to her, believe not the word of the noble:
therefore let me have right, and let desert mount. 　61
　　Lan. Thine's too heavy to mount.
　　Fal. Let it shine, then.
　　Lan. Thine's too thick to shine.
　　Fal. Let it do something, my good lord, that may
do me good, and call it what you will.
　　Lan. Is thy name Colevile?
　　Cole. It is, my lord.
　　Lan. A famous rebel art thou, Colevile.
　　Fal. And a famous true subject took him. 　　70
　　Cole. I am, my lord, but as my betters are
That led me hither: had they been ruled by me,
You should have won them dearer than you have.
　　Fal. I know how they sold themselves: but thou,

<hr>

94. **peruse,** survey. 95. **coped withal,** encountered, fought with. 109. **capital,** punishable by death. 112-123. **I . . . breath.** Prince John's perfidy seems nowhere to be censured by Shakespeare; this possibly finds its explanation in the theory of the time with regard to rebels. To modern ears the prince's words seem false indeed. 112. **pawn'd,** pledged. 118. **shallowly,** without adequate cause. 120. **stray,** stragglers.
　　SCENE III. 2. **condition,** rank. 14. **drops,** tears. 17. **observance,** reverence, homage. 23. **indifferency,** moderate size. 25. **womb,** belly.

27. **heat,** pursuit, race. 38. **expedition,** speed. 41. **posts,** post horses. 46. **hook-nosed fellow of Rome,** Julius Caesar. 53. **particular ballad,** allusion to the practice of having broadside ballads written and published. 58. **cinders of the element,** defined as "stars," more probably the moon's surface when lighted by earthshine only. 64. **thick,** dim. 82. **dispatch we,** let us hasten. 92-135. **I would . . . to sack.** This famous speech on the virtue of sack will be found to embody the current physiological conception of the action and virtue of wine in the human system. There is back of it, however, the idea that Falstaff is too

like a kind fellow, gavest thyself away gratis; and I thank thee for thee.

Re-enter WESTMORELAND.

Lan. Now, have you left pursuit?

West. Retreat is made and execution stay'd.

Lan. Send Colevile with his confederates
To York, to present execution: 80
Blunt, lead him hence; and see you guard him sure.
    [*Exeunt Blunt and others with Colevile.*
And now dispatch we toward the court, my lords:
I hear the king my father is sore sick:
Our news shall go before us to his majesty,
Which, cousin, you shall bear to comfort him,
And we with sober speed will follow you.

Fal. My lord, I beseech you, give me leave to go
Through Gloucestershire: and, when you come to
   court,
Stand my good lord, pray, in your good report.

Lan. Fare you well, Falstaff: I, in my condition,   90
Shall better speak of you than you deserve.
    [*Exeunt all but Falstaff.*

Fal. I would you had but the wit: 'twere better than your dukedom. Good faith, this same young sober-blooded boy doth not love me; nor a man cannot make him laugh; but that's no marvel, he drinks no wine. There's never none of these demure boys come to any proof; for thin drink doth so over-cool their blood, and making many fish-meals, that they fall into a kind of male green-sickness; and then when they marry, they get wenches: they are gener-ally fools and cowards; which some of us should be too, but for inflammation. A good sherris-sack hath a two-fold operation in it. It ascends me into the brain; dries me there all the foolish and dull and crudy vapours which environ it; makes it apprehensive, quick, forgetive, full of nimble fiery and delectable shapes; which, delivered o'er to the voice, the tongue, which is the birth, becomes excellent wit. The second property of your excellent sherris is, the warming of the blood; which, before cold and settled, left the liver white and pale, which is the badge of pusillani-mity and cowardice; but the sherris warms it and makes it course from the inwards to the parts extreme: it illumineth the face, which as a beacon gives warn-ing to all the rest of this little kingdom, man, to arm; and then the vital commoners and inland petty spirits muster me all to their captain, the heart, who, great and puffed up with this retinue, doth any deed of courage; and this valour comes of sherris. So that skill in the weapon is nothing without sack, for that sets it a-work; and learning a mere hoard of gold kept by a devil, till sack commences it and sets it in act and use. Hereof comes it that Prince Harry is valiant; for the cold blood he did naturally inherit of his father, he hath, like lean, sterile and bare land, manured, husbanded and tilled with excellent en-deavour of drinking good and good store of fertile sherris, that he is become very hot and valiant. If I

had a thousand sons, the first humane principle I would teach them should be, to forswear thin pota-tions and to addict themselves to sack.   135

Enter BARDOLPH.

How now, Bardolph?

Bard. The army is discharged all and gone.

Fal. Let them go. I'll through Gloucestershire; and there will I visit Master Robert Shallow, esquire: I have him already tempering between my finger and my thumb, and shortly will I seal with him. Come away.   [*Exeunt.*

SCENE IV. *Westminster. The Jerusalem Chamber.*

Enter the KING, *the* PRINCES THOMAS OF CLARENCE *and* HUMPHREY OF GLOUCESTER, WARWICK, *and others.*

King. Now, lords, if God doth give successful end
To this debate that bleedeth at our doors,
We will our youth lead on to higher fields
And draw no swords but what are sanctified.
Our navy is address'd, our power collected,
Our substitutes in absence well invested,
And every thing lies level to our wish:
Only, we want a little personal strength;
And pause us, till these rebels, now afoot,
Come underneath the yoke of government.   10

War. Both which we doubt not but your majesty
'hall soon enjoy.

King.   Humphrey, my son of Gloucester,
here is the prince your brother?

Glou. I think he's gone to hunt, my lord, at Windsor.

King. And how accompanied?

Glou.   I do not know, my lord.

King. Is not his brother, Thomas of Clarence, with
him?

Glou. No, my good lord; he is in presence here.

Clar. What would my lord and father?

King. Nothing but well to thee, Thomas of Clarence.
How chance thou art not with the prince thy brother?
He loves thee, and thou dost neglect him, Thomas;   21
Thou hast a better place in his affection
Than all thy brothers: cherish it, my boy,
And noble offices thou mayst effect
Of mediation, after I am dead,
Between his greatness and thy other brethren:
Therefore omit him not; blunt not his love,
Nor lose the good advantage of his grace
By seeming cold or careless of his will;
For he is gracious, if he be observed: 30
He hath a tear for pity and a hand
Open as day for melting charity:
Yet notwithstanding, being incensed, he's flint,
As humorous as winter and as sudden
As flaws congealed in the spring of day.
His temper, therefore, must be well observed:
Chide him for faults, and do it reverently,
When you perceive his blood inclined to mirth;

---

excessive in his own practice to be a proper proponent of the cause. 97. **come to any proof,** turn out well. 100. **green-sickness,** kind of anemia affecting young women. 103. **inflammation,** excitement with liquor. 106. **crudy,** defined as "thick"; wet and cold vapors were conducive to dullness. 107. **apprehensive,** quick to perceive. **for-getive,** seems to mean "inventive"; it has been connected with "forge." 118. **little kingdom,** microcosm. Man was thought of as a microcosm corresponding in parts and qualities to the universe, or macrocosm. 140. **tempering,** softening (like a piece of wax).

SCENE IV. 3. **higher fields.** He will lead them on a crusade. 5. **address'd,** ready, prepared. 6. **substitutes,** deputies. **invested,** i.e., with power. 7. **level,** conformable. 30. **observed,** paid proper respect. 32. **melting,** tearful. 33. **flint,** i.e., in emitting fire. 34. **humorous,** unpredictable in action. 35. **flaws,** defined as "snow" (Onions), or as blades of ice seen at the edge of water on winter mornings (Yale); see glossary. **spring of day,** early morning. 36. **temper,** disposition, mood.

But, being moody, give him line and scope,
Till that his passions, like a whale on ground, 40
Confound themselves with working. Learn this,
   Thomas,
And thou shalt prove a shelter to thy friends,
A hoop of gold to bind thy brothers in,
That the united vessel of their blood,
Mingled with venom of suggestion—
As, force perforce, the age will pour it in—
Shall never leak, though it do work as strong
As aconitum or rash gunpowder.
   Clar. I shall observe him with all care and love.
   King. Why art thou not at Windsor with him,
     Thomas? 50
   Clar. He is not there to-day; he dines in London.
   King. And how accompanied? canst thou tell that?
   Clar. With Poins, and other his continual followers.
   King. Most subject is the fattest soil to weeds;
And he, the noble image of my youth,
Is overspread with them: therefore my grief
Stretches itself beyond the hour of death:
The blood weeps from my heart when I do shape
In forms imaginary the unguided days
And rotten times that you shall look upon 60
When I am sleeping with my ancestors.
For when his headstrong riot hath no curb,
When rage and hot blood are his counsellors,
When means and lavish manners meet together,
O, with what wings shall his affections fly
Towards fronting peril and opposed decay!
   War. My gracious lord, you look beyond him quite:
The prince but studies his companions
Like a strange tongue, wherein, to gain the language,
'Tis needful that the most immodest word 70
Be look'd upon and learn'd; which once attain'd,
Your highness knows, comes to no further use
But to be known and hated. So, like gross terms,
The prince will in the perfectness of time
Cast off his followers; and their memory
Shall as a pattern or a measure live,
By which his grace must mete the lives of others,
Turning past evils to advantages.
   King. 'Tis seldom when the bee doth leave her
     comb
In the dead carrion.

Enter WESTMORELAND.

          Who's here? Westmoreland? 80
   West. Health to my sovereign, and new happiness
Added to that that I am to deliver!
Prince John your son doth kiss your grace's hand:
Mowbray, the Bishop Scroop, Hastings and all
Are brought to the correction of your law;
There is not now a rebel's sword unsheathed,
But Peace puts forth her olive every where.
The manner how this action hath been borne
Here at more leisure may your highness read,
With every course in his particular. 90
   King. O Westmoreland, thou art a summer bird,
Which ever in the haunch of winter sings

The lifting up of day.

Enter HARCOURT.

          Look, here's more news.
   Har. From enemies heaven keep your majesty;
And, when they stand against you, may they fall
As those that I am come to tell you of!
The Earl Northumberland and the Lord Bardolph,
With a great power of English and of Scots,
Are by the sheriff of Yorkshire overthrown:
The manner and true order of the fight 100
This packet, please it you, contains at large.
   King. And wherefore should these good news make
     me sick?
Will Fortune never come with both hands full,
But write her fair words still in foulest letters?
She either gives a stomach and no food;
Such are the poor, in health; or else a feast
And takes away the stomach; such are the rich,
That have abundance and enjoy it not.
I should rejoice now at this happy news;
And now my sight fails, and my brain is giddy: 110
O me! come near me; now I am much ill.
   Glou. Comfort, your majesty!
   Clar.   O my royal father!
   West. My sovereign lord, cheer up yourself, look up.
   War. Be patient, princes; you do know, these fits
Are with his highness very ordinary.
Stand from him, give him air; he'll straight be well.
   Clar. No, no, he cannot long hold out these pangs:
The incessant care and labour of his mind
Hath wrought the mure that should confine it in
So thin that life looks through and will break out. 120
   Glou. The people fear me; for they do observe
Unfather'd heirs and loathly births of nature:
The seasons change their manners, as the year
Had found some months asleep and leap'd them over.
   Clar. The river hath thrice flow'd, no ebb between;
And the old folk, time's doting chronicles,
Say it did so a little time before
That our great-grandsire, Edward, sick'd and died.
   War. Speak lower, princes, for the king recovers.
   Glou. This apoplexy will certain be his end. 130
   King. I pray you, take me up, and bear me hence
Into some other chamber: softly, pray.   [*Exeunt.*

SCENE V. *Another chamber.*

The KING *lying on a bed:* CLARENCE, GLOUCESTER,
WARWICK, *and others in attendance.*

   King. Let there be no noise made, my gentle friends;
Unless some dull and favourable hand
Will whisper music to my weary spirit.
   War. Call for the music in the other room.
   King. Set me the crown upon my pillow here.
   Clar. His eye is hollow, and he changes much.
   War. Less noise, less noise!

Enter PRINCE HENRY.

Prince. Who saw the Duke of Clarence?
Clar. I am here, brother, full of heaviness.
Prince. How now! rain within doors, and none
    abroad!
How doth the king? 10
Glou. Exceeding ill.
Prince. Heard he the good news yet!
Tell it him.
    Glou. He alter'd much upon the hearing it.
    Prince. If he be sick with joy, he'll recover without
physic.
    War. Not so much noise, my lords: sweet prince,
    speak low;
The king your father is disposed to sleep.
    Clar. Let us withdraw into the other room.
    War. Will 't please your grace to go along with us?
    Prince. No; I will sit and watch here by the king. 20
                [*Exeunt all but the Prince.*
Why doth the crown lie there upon his pillow,
Being so troublesome a bedfellow?
O polish'd perturbation! golden care!
That keep'st the ports of slumber open wide
To many a watchful night! sleep with it now!
Yet not so sound and half so deeply sweet
As he whose brow with homely biggen bound
Snores out the watch of night. O majesty!
When thou dost pinch thy bearer, thou dost sit
Like a rich armour worn in heat of day, 30
That scalds with safety. By his gates of breath
There lies a downy feather which stirs not:
Did he suspire, that light and weightless down
Perforce must move. My gracious lord! my father!
This sleep is sound indeed; this is a sleep
That from this golden rigol hath divorced
So many English kings. Thy due from me
Is tears and heavy sorrows of the blood,
Which nature, love, and filial tenderness,
Shall, O dear father, pay thee plenteously: 40
My due from thee is this imperial crown,
Which, as immediate from thy place and blood,
Derives itself to me. Lo, here it sits,
Which God shall guard: and put the world's whole
    strength
Into one giant arm, it shall not force
This lineal honour from me: this from thee
Will I to mine leave, as 'tis left to me.   [*Exit.*
    King. Warwick! Gloucester! Clarence!

Re-enter WARWICK, GLOUCESTER, CLARENCE,
and the rest.

    Clar. Doth the king call?
    War. What would your majesty? How fares your
    grace? 50
    King. Why did you leave me here alone, my lords?
    Clar. We left the prince my brother here, my liege,
Who undertook to sit and watch by you.
    King. The Prince of Wales! Where is he? let me see
    him:
He is not here.
    War. This door is open; he is gone this way.

Glou. He came not through the chamber where we
    stay'd.
    King. Where is the crown? who took it from my
    pillow?
    War. When we withdrew, my liege, we left it here.
    King. The prince hath ta'en it hence: go, seek him
    out. 60
Is he so hasty that he doth suppose
My sleep my death?
Find him, my Lord of Warwick; chide him hither.
                [*Exit Warwick.*
This part of his conjoins with my disease,
And helps to end me. See, sons, what things you are!
How quickly nature falls into revolt
When gold becomes her object!
For this the foolish over-careful fathers
Have broke their sleep with thoughts, their brains
    with care,
Their bones with industry; 70
For this they have engross'd and piled up
The canker'd heaps of strange-achieved gold;
For this they have been thoughtful to invest
Their sons with arts and martial exercises:
When, like the bee, tolling from every flower
The virtuous sweets,
Our thighs pack'd with wax, our mouths with honey,
We bring it to the hive, and, like the bees,
Are murdered for our pains. This bitter taste
Yield his engrossments to the ending father. 80

Re-enter WARWICK.

Now, where is he that will not stay so long
Till his friend sickness hath determined me?
    War. My lord, I found the prince in the next room,
Washing with kindly tears his gentle cheeks,
With such a deep demeanour in great sorrow
That tyranny, which never quaff'd but blood,
Would, by beholding him, have wash'd his knife
With gentle eye-drops. He is coming hither.
    King. But wherefore did he take away the crown?

Re-enter PRINCE HENRY.

Lo, where he comes. Come hither to me, Harry. 90
Depart the chamber, leave us here alone.
          [*Exeunt Warwick and the rest.*
    Prince. I never thought to hear you speak again.
    King. Thy wish was father, Harry, to that thought:
I stay too long by thee, I weary thee.
Dost thou so hunger for mine empty chair
That thou wilt needs invest thee with my honours
Before thy hour be ripe? O foolish youth!
Thou seek'st the greatness that will overwhelm thee.
Stay but a little; for my cloud of dignity
Is held from falling with so weak a wind 100
That it will quickly drop: my day is dim.
Thou hast stolen that which after some few hours
Were thine without offence; and at my death
Thou hast seal'd up my expectation:
Thy life did manifest thou lovedst me not,
And thou wilt have me die assured of it.

which Shakespeare follows Holinshed in recording portents in nature.
  SCENE V. 2. **dull,** soft, soothing. 3. **music.** The medical practice
of the time attributed healing power to music. 6. **changes,** changes
color, turns pale. 23. **perturbation,** agitation by the passions; here
used to mean the cause of agitation. 25. **watchful,** wakeful. **sleep
with it,** i.e., if you can. 27. **biggen,** nightcap. 28. **watch of night,**
period of night. 31. **scalds,** burns (while providing safety). 33. **suspire,** breathe. 36. **rigol,** circle, crown. 38. **blood,** usually taken as
  meaning the source of tears and sorrows; probably, parenthood, blood-
kinship. 42. **immediate,** passing in direct succession. 64. **part,** act,
action; or role (?). **conjoins,** unites, joins. 69. **thoughts,** cares. 71.
engross'd, amassed. 72. **canker'd,** corroded, tarnished. **strange-
achieved,** gained in strange ways. 75. **tolling,** taking as toll; so Q;
F and Globe: *culling.* 79. **Are . . . pains.** It is the drones, not the
worker bees, that are murdered. 80. **engrossments,** stored-up treasures.
82. **determined,** ended, put an end to.

Thou hidest a thousand daggers in thy thoughts,
Which thou hast whetted on thy stony heart,
To stab at half an hour of my life.
What! canst thou not forbear me half an hour? 110
Then get thee gone and dig my grave thyself,
And bid the merry bells ring to thine ear
That thou art crowned, not that I am dead.
Let all the tears that should bedew my hearse
Be drops of balm to sanctify thy head:
Only compound me with forgotten dust;
Give that which gave thee life unto the worms.
Pluck down my officers, break my decrees;
For now a time is come to mock at form:
Harry the Fifth is crown'd: up, vanity! 120
Down, royal state! all you sage counsellors, hence!
And to the English court assemble now,
From every region, apes of idleness!
Now, neighbour confines, purge you of your scum:
Have you a ruffian that will swear, drink, dance,
Revel the night, rob, murder, and commit
The oldest sins the newest kind of ways?
Be happy, he will trouble you no more;
England shall double gild his treble guilt,
England shall give him office, honour, might; 130
For the fifth Harry from curb'd license plucks
The muzzle of restraint, and the wild dog
Shall flesh his tooth on every innocent.
O my poor kingdom, sick with civil blows!
When that my care could not withhold thy riots,
What wilt thou do when riot is thy care?
O, thou wilt be a wilderness again,
Peopled with wolves, thy old inhabitants!
    Prince. O, pardon me, my liege! but for my tears,
The moist impediments unto my speech, 140
I had forestall'd this dear and deep rebuke
Ere you with grief had spoke and I had heard
The course of it so far. There is your crown;
And He that wears the crown immortally
Long guard it yours! If I affect it more
Than as your honour and as your renown,
Let me no more from this obedience rise,
Which my most inward true and duteous spirit
Teacheth, this prostrate and exterior bending.
God witness with me, when I here came in, 150
And found no course of breath within your majesty,
How cold it struck my heart! If I do feign,
O, let me in my present wildness die
And never live to show the incredulous world
The noble change that I have purposed!
Coming to look on you, thinking you dead,
And dead almost, my liege, to think you were,
I spake unto this crown as having sense,
And thus upbraided it: 'The care on thee depending
Hath fed upon the body of my father; 160
Therefore, thou best of gold art worst of gold:
Other, less fine in carat, is more precious,
Preserving life in medicine potable;
But thou, most fine, most honour'd, most renown'd,

Hath eat thy bearer up.' Thus, my most royal liege,
Accusing it, I put it on my head,
To try with it, as with an enemy
That had before my face murder'd my father,
The quarrel of a true inheritor.
But if it did infect my blood with joy, 170
Or swell my thoughts to any strain of pride;
If any rebel or vain spirit of mine
Did with the least affection of a welcome
Give entertainment to the might of it,
Let God for ever keep it from my head
And make me as the poorest vassal is
That doth with awe and terror kneel to it!
    King. O my son,
God put it in thy mind to take it hence,
That thou mightst win the more thy father's love, 180
Pleading so wisely in excuse of it!
Come hither, Harry, sit thou by my bed;
And hear, I think, the very latest counsel
That ever I shall breathe. God knows, my son,
By what by-paths and indirect crook'd ways
I met this crown; and I myself know well
How troublesome it sat upon my head.
To thee it shall descend with better quiet,
Better opinion, better confirmation;
For all the soil of the achievement goes 190
With me into the earth. It seem'd in me
But as an honour snatch'd with boisterous hand,
And I had many living to upbraid
My gain of it by their assistances;
Which daily grew to quarrel and to bloodshed,
Wounding supposed peace: all these bold fears
Thou see'st with peril I have answered;
For all my reign hath been but as a scene
Acting that argument: and now my death
Changes the mode; for what in me was purchased, 200
Falls upon thee in a more fairer sort;
So thou the garland wear'st successively.
Yet, though thou stand'st more sure than I could do,
Thou art not firm enough, since griefs are green;
And all my friends, which thou must make thy friends,
Have but their stings and teeth newly ta'en out;
By whose fell working I was first advanced
And by whose power I well might lodge a fear
To be again displaced: which to avoid,
I cut them off; and had a purpose now, 210
To lead out many to the Holy Land,
Lest rest and lying still might make them look
Too near unto my state. Therefore, my Harry,
Be it thy course to busy giddy minds
With foreign quarrels; that action, hence borne out,
May waste the memory of the former days.
More would I, but my lungs are wasted so
That strength of speech is utterly denied me.
How I came by the crown, O God forgive;
And grant it may with thee in true peace live! 220
    Prince. My gracious liege,
You won it, wore it, kept it, gave it me;

2 Henry IV
ACT IV : SC V

730

110. **forbear,** spare. 115. **balm,** consecrated oil used in anointing the king at his coronation. 119. **form,** laws, orderly usages. 120. **vanity,** folly. 124. **neighbour confines,** territories of neighboring countries. 136. **care,** special study. 141. **dear and deep,** heartfelt and severe. 144. **immortally,** eternally. 147. **obedience,** obeisance. 148. **inward,** sincere. 162. **carat,** standard of fineness in gold. **precious,** double meaning suggesting, besides the usual sense, the idea of curing. 163. **medicine potable,** potable gold, an elixir, thought from Galen's time to possess magical power to cure. 169. **inheritor,** owner. 171. **strain,** height of emotion. 172. **vain,** vainglorious.

188. **quiet,** by some defined as "conscience"; more probably, peace and acquiescence. 200. **mode,** key in which music is written; here suggestive of "mood," state of mind. 201. **sort,** manner, way. 202. **successively,** by right of succession. 204. **green,** fresh. 207. **fell working,** evil effort. 214-216. **Be . . . days.** The idea expressed in these lines was a commonly held political doctrine of the time. 215. **hence,** in other lands. 216. **waste,** efface, obliterate. 231. **makes a period,** comes to an end, rounds out a whole (as a sentence ends). 234. **lodging,** apartment. 235. **Jerusalem,** a chamber adjoining the south-west tower of Westminster Abbey, so called perhaps from tapestries

Then plain and right must my possession be:
Which I with more than with a common pain
'Gainst all the world will rightfully maintain.

Enter LORD JOHN OF LANCASTER.

King. Look, look, here comes my John of Lancaster.
Lan. Health, peace, and happiness to my royal
father!
King. Thou bring'st me happiness and peace, son
John;
But health, alack, with youthful wings is flown
From this bare wither'd trunk: upon thy sight   230
My worldly business makes a period.
Where is my Lord of Warwick?
Prince.   My Lord of Warwick!

Re-enter WARWICK, *and others.*

King. Doth any name particular belong
Unto the lodging where I first did swoon?
War. 'Tis call'd Jerusalem, my noble lord.
King. Laud be to God! even there my life must end.
It hath been prophesied to me many years,
I should not die but in Jerusalem;
Which vainly I supposed the Holy Land:
But bear me to that chamber; there I'll lie;   240
In that Jerusalem shall Harry die.   [*Exeunt.*

ACT V.

SCENE I. *Gloucestershire.* SHALLOW's *house.*

Enter SHALLOW, FALSTAFF, BARDOLPH, *and* Page.

Shal. By cock and pie, sir, you shall not away to-
night. What, Davy, I say!
Fal. You must excuse me, Master Robert Shallow.
Shal. I will not excuse you; you shall not be excused;
excuses shall not be admitted; there is no excuse shall
serve; you shall not be excused. Why, Davy!

Enter DAVY.

Davy. Here, sir.   9
Shal. Davy, Davy, Davy, Davy, let me see, Davy;
let me see, Davy; let me see: yea, marry, William
cook, bid him come hither. Sir John, you shall not be
excused.
Davy. Marry, sir, thus; those precepts cannot be
served: and, again, sir, shall we sow the headland
with wheat?
Shal. With red wheat, Davy. But for William cook:
are there no young pigeons?
Davy. Yes, sir. Here is now the smith's note for
shoeing and plough-irons.   20
Shal. Let it be cast and paid. Sir John, you shall not
be excused.
Davy. Now, sir, a new link to the bucket must needs
be had: and, sir, do you mean to stop any of William's

wages, about the sack he lost the other day at Hinckley fair?
Shal. A' shall answer it. Some pigeons, Davy, a
couple of short-legged hens, a joint of mutton, and
any pretty little tiny kickshaws, tell William cook.   30
Davy. Doth the man of war stay all night, sir?
Shal. Yea, Davy. I will use him well: a friend i' the
court is better than a penny in purse. Use his men
well, Davy; for they are arrant knaves, and will back-
bite.
Davy. No worse than they are backbitten, sir; for
they have marvellous foul linen.
Shal. Well conceited, Davy: about thy business,
Davy.   40
Davy. I beseech you, sir, to countenance William
Visor of Woncot against Clement Perkes of the hill.
Shal. There is many complaints, Davy, against that
Visor: that Visor is an arrant knave, on my knowledge.
Davy. I grant your worship that he is a knave, sir;
but yet, God forbid, sir, but a knave should have
some countenance at his friend's request. An honest
man, sir, is able to speak for himself, when a knave is
not. I have served your worship truly, sir, this eight
years; and if I cannot once or twice in a quarter
bear out a knave against an honest man, I have but
a very little credit with your worship. The knave
is mine honest friend, sir; therefore, I beseech your
worship, let him be countenanced.   57
Shal. Go to; I say he shall have no wrong. Look
about, Davy. [*Exit Davy.*] Where are you, Sir John?
Come, come, come, off with your boots. Give me
your hand, Master Bardolph.
Bard. I am glad to see your worship.
Shal. I thank thee with all my heart, kind Master
Bardolph: and welcome, my tall fellow [*to the Page*].
Come, Sir John.   66
Fal. I'll follow you, good Master Robert Shallow.
[*Exit Shallow.*] Bardolph, look to our horses. [*Exeunt
Bardolph and Page.*] If I were sawed into quantities, I
should make four dozen of such bearded hermits'
staves as Master Shallow. It is a wonderful thing to
see the semblable coherence of his men's spirits and
his: they, by observing of him, do bear themselves
like foolish justices; he, by conversing with them, is
turned into a justice-like serving-man: their spirits
are so married in conjunction with the participation
of society that they flock together in consent, like so
many wild-geese. If I had a suit to Master Shallow, I
would humour his men with the imputation of being
near their master: if to his men, I would curry with
Master Shallow that no man could better command
his servants. It is certain that either wise bearing or
ignorant carriage is caught, as men take diseases,
one of another: therefore let men take heed of their
company. I will devise matter enough out of this
Shallow to keep Prince Harry in continual laughter
the wearing out of six fashions, which is four terms,

---

hung there which depicted matters connected with Jerusalem. This
chamber was the traditional place of the king's death, and its occurrence
there was regarded as the fulfillment of the prophecy referred to.
ACT V. SCENE I.   1. **cock and pie,** a trivial oath.   2. **What,** an exclamation of impatience.   14. **precepts,** writs requiring something to
be done.   16. **headland,** strip of plowed land at the end of furrows;
Q: *hade land,* which might mean "high land."   26. **Hinckley,** market
town in Leicestershire.   29. **kickshaws,** fancy dishes; from French
quelque chose.   39. **Well conceited,** ingeniously punned.   41. **countenance,** favor.   42, 43. **Visor, Perkes.** Madden identified these names

in Gloucestershire records. It is therefore thought that Shakespeare
must have had intimate knowledge of Gloucestershire.   53. **bear out,**
testify in favor of.   59. **Look about,** look sharp, be on the alert.   65.
tall fellow, brave man; applied jocularly to the diminutive page.   70.
quantities, fragments.   73. **semblable coherence,** similar or complete
agreement.   75. **conversing,** associating.   79. **consent,** agreement.
82. **curry with,** employ flattery with.   85. **carriage,** demeanor,
behavior.   90. **terms,** i.e., of court.

or two actions, and a' shall laugh without inter-
vallums. O, it is much that a lie with a slight oath
and a jest with a sad brow will do with a fellow that
never had the ache in his shoulders! O, you shall see
him laugh till his face be like a wet cloak ill laid up! 95
Shal. [*Within*] Sir John!
Fal. I come, Master Shallow; I come, Master
Shallow. [*Exit.*

SCENE II. *Westminster. The palace.*

Enter WARWICK *and the* LORD CHIEF-JUSTICE, *meeting.*

War. How now, my lord chief-justice! whither
away?
Ch. Just. How doth the king?
War. Exceeding well; his cares are now all ended.
Ch. Just. I hope, not dead.
War. He 's walk'd the way of nature;
And to our purposes he lives no more.
Ch. Just. I would his majesty had call'd me with
him:
The service that I truly did his life
Hath left me open to all injuries.
War. Indeed I think the young king loves you not.
Ch. Just. I know he doth not, and do arm myself 10
To welcome the condition of the time,
Which cannot look more hideously upon me
Than I have drawn it in my fantasy.

Enter LANCASTER, CLARENCE, GLOUCESTER,
WESTMORELAND, *and others.*

War. Here come the heavy issue of dead Harry:
O that the living Harry had the temper
Of him, the worst of these three gentlemen!
How many nobles then should hold their places,
That must strike sail to spirits of vile sort!
Ch. Just. O God, I fear all will be overturn'd! 19
Lan. Good morrow, cousin Warwick, good morrow.
Glou.
Clar. } Good morrow, cousin.
Lan. We meet like men that had forgot to speak.
War. We do remember; but our argument
Is all too heavy to admit much talk.
Lan. Well, peace be with him that hath made us
heavy!
Ch. Just. Peace be with us, lest we be heavier!
Glou. O, good my lord, you have lost a friend
indeed;
And I dare swear you borrow not that face
Of seeming sorrow, it is sure your own.
Lan. Though no man be assured what grace to find,
You stand in coldest expectation: 31
I am the sorrier; would 'twere otherwise.
Clar. Well, you must now speak Sir John Falstaff
fair;
Which swims against your stream of quality.
Ch. Just. Sweet princes, what I did, I did in honour,

Led by the impartial conduct of my soul;
And never shall you see that I will beg
A ragged and forestall'd remission.
If truth and upright innocency fail me,
I'll to the king my master that is dead, 40
And tell him who hath sent me after him.
War. Here comes the prince.

Enter KING HENRY *the Fifth, attended.*

Ch. Just. Good morrow; and God save your
majesty!
King. This new and gorgeous garment, majesty,
Sits not so easy on me as you think.
Brothers, you mix your sadness with some fear:
This is the English, not the Turkish court;
Not Amurath an Amurath succeeds,
But Harry Harry. Yet be sad, good brothers,
For, by my faith, it very well becomes you: 50
Sorrow so royally in you appears
That I will deeply put the fashion on
And wear it in my heart: why then, be sad;
But entertain no more of it, good brothers,
Than a joint burden laid upon us all.
For me, by heaven, I bid you be assured,
I'll be your father and your brother too;
Let me but bear your love, I'll bear your cares:
Yet weep that Harry 's dead; and so will I;
But Harry lives, that shall convert those tears 60
By number into hours of happiness.
Princes. We hope no other from your majesty.
King. You all look strangely on me: and you most;
You are, I think, assured I love you not.
Ch. Just. I am assured, if I be measured rightly,
Your majesty hath no just cause to hate me.
King. No!
How might a prince of my great hopes forget
So great indignities you laid upon me?
What! rate, rebuke, and roughly send to prison 70
The immediate heir of Englend! Was this easy?
May this be wash'd in Lethe, and forgotten?
Ch. Just. I then did use the person of your father;
The image of his power lay then in me:
And, in the administration of his law,
Whiles I was busy for the commonwealth,
Your highness pleased to forget my place,
The majesty and power of law and justice,
The image of the king whom I presented,
And struck me in my very seat of judgement; 80
Whereon, as an offender to your father,
I gave bold way to my authority
And did commit you. If the deed were ill,
Be you contented, wearing now the garland,
To have a son set your decrees at nought,
To pluck down justice from your awful bench,
To trip the course of law and blunt the sword
That guards the peace and safety of your person;
Nay, more, to spurn at your most royal image
And mock your workings in a second body. 90

Question your royal thoughts, make the case yours;
Be now the father and propose a son,
Hear your own dignity so much profaned,
See your most dreadful laws so loosely slighted,
Behold yourself so by a son disdain'd;
And then imagine me taking your part
And in your power soft silencing your son:
After this cold considerance, sentence me;
And, as you are a king, speak in your state
What I have done that misbecame my place, 100
My person, or my liege's sovereignty.
 King. You are right, justice, and you weigh this well;
Therefore still bear the balance and the sword:
And I do wish your honours may increase,
Till you do live to see a son of mine
Offend you and obey you, as I did.
So shall I live to speak my father's words:
'Happy am I, that have a man so bold,
That dares do justice on my proper son;
And not less happy, having such a son, 110
That would deliver up his greatness so
Into the hands of justice.' You did commit me:
For which, I do commit into your hand
The unstained sword that you have used to bear;
With this remembrance, that you use the same
With the like bold, just and impartial spirit
As you have done 'gainst me. There is my hand.
You shall be as a father to my youth:
My voice shall sound as you do prompt mine ear,
And I will stoop and humble my intents 120
To your well-practised wise directions.
And, princes all, believe me, I beseech you;
My father is gone wild into his grave,
For in his tomb lie my affections;
And with his spirit sadly I survive,
To mock the expectation of the world,
To frustrate prophecies and to raze out
Rotten opinion, who hath writ me down
After my seeming. The tide of blood in me
Hath proudly flow'd in vanity till now: 130
Now doth it turn and ebb back to the sea,
Where it shall mingle with the state of floods
And flow henceforth in formal majesty.
Now call we our high court of parliament:
And let us choose such limbs of noble counsel,
That the great body of our state may go
In equal rank with the best govern'd nation;
That war, or peace, or both at once, may be
As things acquainted and familiar to us;
In which you, father, shall have foremost hand. 140
Our coronation done, we will accite,
As I before remember'd, all our state:
And, God consigning to my good intents,
No prince nor peer shall have just cause to say,
God shorten Harry's happy life one day! [*Exeunt.*

SCENE III. *Gloucestershire.* SHALLOW's *orchard.*

Enter FALSTAFF, SHALLOW, SILENCE, DAVY,
 BARDOLPH, *and the* Page.

Shal. Nay, you shall see my orchard, where, in an arbour, we will eat a last year's pippin of my own graffing, with a dish of caraways, and so forth: come, cousin Silence: and then to bed.

Fal. 'Fore God, you have here a goodly dwelling and a rich.

Shal. Barren, barren, barren; beggars all, beggars all, Sir John: marry, good air. Spread, Davy; spread, Davy: well said, Davy. 10

Fal. This Davy serves you for good uses; he is your serving-man and your husband.

Shal. A good varlet, a good varlet, a very good varlet, Sir John: by the mass, I have drunk too much sack at supper: a good varlet. Now sit down, now sit down: come, cousin.

Sil. Ah, sirrah! quoth-a, we shall
Do nothing but eat, and make good cheer, [*Singing.*
And praise God for the merry year;
When flesh is cheap and females dear, 20
And lusty lads roam here and there
   So merrily,
And ever among so merrily.

Fal. There's a merry heart! Good Master Silence, I'll give you a health for that anon.

Shal. Give Master Bardolph some wine, Davy. 27

Davy. Sweet sir, sit; I'll be with you anon; most sweet sir, sit. Master page, good master page, sit. Proface! What you want in meat, we'll have in drink: but you must bear; the heart's all.   [*Exit.*

Shal. Be merry, Master Bardolph; and, my little soldier there, be merry.

Sil. Be merry, be merry, my wife has all; [*Singing.*
For women are shrews, both short and tall:
'Tis merry in hall when beards wag all,
  And welcome merry Shrove-tide.
Be merry, be merry.

Fal. I did not think Master Silence had been a man of this mettle. 41

Sil. Who, I? I have been merry twice and once ere now.

Re-enter DAVY.

Davy. There's a dish of leather-coats for you.
     [*To Bardolph.*

Shal. Davy!

Davy. Your worship! I'll be with you straight [*to Bardolph*]. A cup of wine, sir?

Sil. A cup of wine that's brisk and fine, [*Singing.*
And drink unto the leman mine;
  And a merry heart lives long-a. 50

Fal. Well said, Master Silence.

Sil. An we shall be merry, now comes in the sweet o' the night.

Fal. Health and long life to you, Master Silence.

Sil. Fill the cup, and let it come; [*Singing.*
 I'll pledge you a mile to the bottom.

---

has disappeared with his father's death, that wildness is buried along with his father. **127. raze out**, erase. **129. After my seeming**, according to what I seemed. **132. state of floods**, majesty of ocean. **135. limbs**, members. **137. equal rank**, step by step. **141. accite**, summon. **142. remember'd**, mentioned. **143. consigning to**, sanctioning.
 SCENE III. **3. graffing**, grafting. **4. caraways**, sweetmeats containing caraway seeds. **9. Spread**, spread the cloth. **said**, done. **12. husband**, manager of the household. **13. varlet**, servant; normally used in a bad sense, but here affectionately. **17. quoth-a**, said he (the singer). **23. ever among**, all the while. **30. Proface**, formula

of welcome to a meal, meaning "May it do you good." **30-31. What . . . drink**, a proverbial saying. **31. bear**, be forbearing, excuse the deficiencies of the entertainment. **37. 'Tis . . . all**, an old English proverb. **38. Shrove-tide**, the day before Ash Wednesday; a season of merrymaking. **42. twice and once**, adverbial expression denoting something like "now and again." **44. leather-coats**, russet apples. **48. brisk**, agreeably sharp to the taste. **49. leman**, sweetheart. **57. mile**, i.e., if it were a mile.

Shal. Honest Bardolph, welcome: if thou wantest any thing, and wilt not call, beshrew thy heart. Welcome, my little tiny thief [*to the Page*], and welcome indeed too. I'll drink to Master Bardolph, and to all the cavaleros about London.   63

Davy. I hope to see London once ere I die.

Bard. An I might see you there, Davy,—

Shal. By the mass, you'll crack a quart together, ha! will you not, Master Bardolph?

Bard. Yea, sir, in a pottle-pot.

Shal. By God's liggens, I thank thee: the knave will stick by thee, I can assure thee that. A' will not out; he is true bred.   71

Bard. And I'll stick by him, sir.

Shal. Why, there spoke a king. Lack nothing: be merry. [*Knocking within.*] Look who's at door there, ho! who knocks?   [*Exit Davy.*

Fal. Why, now you have done me right.
                    [*To Silence, seeing him take off a bumper.*

Sil.   Do me right,   [*Singing.*
          And dub me knight:
               Samingo.

Is't not so?   80

Fal. 'Tis so.

Sil. Is't so? Why then, say an old man can do somewhat.

Re-enter DAVY.

Davy. An't please your worship, there's one Pistol come from the court with news.

Fal. From the court! let him come in.

Enter PISTOL.

How now, Pistol!

Pist. Sir John, God save you!   88

Fal. What wind blew you hither, Pistol?

Pist. Not the ill wind which blows no man to good. Sweet knight, thou art now one of the greatest men in this realm.

Sil. By'r lady, I think a' be, but goodman Puff of Barson.

Pist. Puff!

Puff in thy teeth, most recreant coward base!
Sir John, I am thy Pistol and thy friend,
And helter-skelter have I rode to thee,
And tidings do I bring and lucky joys
And golden times and happy news of price.   100

Fal. I pray thee now, deliver them like a man of this world.

Pist. A foutre for the world and worldlings base! I speak of Africa and golden joys.

Fal. O base Assyrian knight, what is thy news? Let King Cophetua know the truth thereof.

Sil. And Robin Hood, Scarlet, and John. [*Singing.*

Pist. Shall dunghill curs confront the Helicons? And shall good news be baffled? Then, Pistol, lay thy head in Furies' lap.   110

Shal. Honest gentleman, I know not your breeding.

Pist. Why then, lament therefore.

Shal. Give me pardon, sir: if, sir, you come with news from the court, I take it there's but two ways, either to utter them, or to conceal them. I am, sir, under the king, in some authority.

Pist. Under which king, Besonian? speak, or die.

Shal. Under King Harry.

Pist.   Harry the Fourth? or Fifth?   120

Shal. Harry the Fourth.

Pist.   A foutre for thine office!
Sir John, thy tender lambkin now is king;
Harry the Fifth's the man. I speak the truth:
When Pistol lies, do this; and fig me, like
The bragging Spaniard.

Fal. What, is the old king dead?

Pist. As nail in door: the things I speak are just.

Fal. Away, Bardolph! saddle my horse. Master Robert Shallow, choose what office thou wilt in the land, 'tis thine. Pistol, I will double-charge thee with dignities.   131

Bard. O joyful day!
I would not take a knighthood for my fortune.

Pist. What! I do bring good news.

Fal. Carry Master Silence to bed. Master Shallow, my Lord Shallow,—be what thou wilt; I am fortune's steward—get on thy boots: we'll ride all night. O sweet Pistol! Away, Bardolph! [*Exit Bard.*] Come, Pistol, utter more to me; and withal devise something to do thyself good. Boot, boot, Master Shallow: I know the young king is sick for me. Let us take any man's horses; the laws of England are at my commandment. Blessed are they that have been my friends; and woe to my lord chief-justice!   145

Pist. Let vultures vile seize on his lungs also!
'Where is the life that late I led?' say they:
Why, here it is; welcome these pleasant days! [*Exeunt.*

SCENE IV. *London. A street.*

Enter Beadles, *dragging in* HOSTESS QUICKLY *and* DOLL TEARSHEET.

Host. No, thou arrant knave; I would to God that I might die, that I might have thee hanged: thou hast drawn my shoulder out of joint.

First Bead. The constables have delivered her over to me; and she shall have whipping-cheer enough, I warrant her: there hath been a man or two lately killed about her.   7

Dol. Nut-hook, nut-hook, you lie. Come on; I'll tell thee what, thou damned tripe-visaged rascal, an the child I now go with do miscarry, thou wert better thou hadst struck thy mother, thou paper-faced villain.

Host. O the Lord, that Sir John were come! he would make this a bloody day to somebody. But I pray God the fruit of her womb miscarry!

First Bead. If it do, you shall have a dozen of

---

63. **cavaleros,** cavaliers. 69. **liggens,** an original oath of Shallow's. 71. **will not out,** will not fail you. 77. **Do me right,** pledge me. 78-79. **dub . . . Samingo,** fragment of a drinking song, with an allusion to the selection of one to be dubbed knight in the drinking bout; *Samingo* is a refrain; it appears also as "San Domingo." 83. **somewhat,** something. 93. **but,** except. **goodman Puff of Barson,** an allusion to some fat man not known. 102. **man of this world,** ordinary man. 103. **foutre,** a contemptuous expression. 104. **Africa,** fabled for wealth. 106. **Cophetua.** King Cophetua married a beggar maid according to the popular ballad, *King Cophetua and the Beggar-Maid.* 107. **And . . . John,** a scrap from the ballad, *Robin Hood and the Pinner*

of Wakefield. 108. **Helicons.** Helicon was the abode of the Muses; Pistol resents the intrusion of Robin Hood. 109. **baffled,** treated with contumely. 112. **breeding,** parentage, rank. 119. **Besonian,** beggar; probably a low, beggarly soldier. Shallow is thus designated because of his assertion of authority. 124. **do this.** Pistol makes a vulgar gesture, said to consist in thrusting the thumb between the first and middle finger; in any case, to make such gesture was called *to fig.* 142-145. **Let us . . . chief-justice.** Those who take seriously the danger to the realm from Falstaff before his rejection stress this passage. 147. **'Where . . . led,'** fragment of a ballad.
SCENE IV. 3. **shoulder out of joint,** a reference to the rough methods

cushions again; you have but eleven now. Come, I charge you both go with me; for the man is dead that you and Pistol beat amongst you.   19

Dol. I'll tell you what, you thin man in a censer, I will have you as soundly swinged for this,—you blue-bottle rogue, you filthy famished correctioner, if you be not swinged, I'll forswear half-kirtles.

First Bead. Come, come, you she knight-errant, come.

Host. O God, that right should thus overcome might! Well, of sufferance comes ease.

Dol. Come, you rogue, come; bring me to a justice.   30

Host. Ay, come, you starved blood-hound.

Dol. Goodman death, goodman bones!

Host. Thou atomy, thou!

Dol. Come, you thin thing; come, you rascal.

First Bead. Very well.   [*Exeunt.*

———————————

SCENE V. *A public place near Westminster Abbey.*

Enter two GROOMS, *strewing rushes.*

First Groom. More rushes, more rushes.

Sec. Groom. The trumpets have sounded twice.

First Groom. 'Twill be two o'clock ere they come from the coronation: dispatch, dispatch.   [*Exeunt.*

Enter FALSTAFF, SHALLOW, PISTOL, BARDOLPH, *and* Page.

Fal. Stand here by me, Master Robert Shallow; I will make the king do you grace: I will leer upon him as a' comes by; and do but mark the countenance that he will give me.

Pist. God bless thy lungs, good knight.   9

Fal. Come here, Pistol; stand behind me. O, if I had had time to have made new liveries, I would have bestowed the thousand pound I borrowed of you. But 'tis no matter; this poor show doth better: this doth infer the zeal I had to see him.

Shal. It doth so.

Fal. It shows my earnestness of affection,—

Shal. It doth so.

Fal. My devotion,—

Shal. It doth, it doth, it doth.   20

Fal. As it were, to ride day and night; and not to deliberate, not to remember, not to have patience to shift me,—

Shal. It is best, certain.

Fal. But to stand stained with travel, and sweating with desire to see him; thinking of nothing else, putting all affairs else in oblivion, as if there were nothing else to be done but to see him.   29

Pist. 'Tis 'semper idem,' for 'obsque hoc nihil est:' 'tis all in every part.

Shal. 'Tis so, indeed.

Pist. My knight, I will inflame thy noble liver, And make thee rage.

Thy Doll, and Helen of thy noble thoughts, Is in base durance and contagious prison; Haled thither By most mechanical and dirty hand: Rouse up revenge from ebon den with fell Alecto's snake, For Doll is in. Pistol speaks nought but truth.   40

Fal. I will deliver her.
          [*Shouts within, and the trumpets sound.*

Pist. There roar'd the sea, and trumpet-clangor sounds.

Enter the KING *and his train, the* LORD CHIEF-JUSTICE *among them.*

Fal. God save thy grace, King Hal! my royal Hal!

Pist. The heavens thee guard and keep, most royal imp of fame!

Fal. God save thee, my sweet boy!

King. My lord chief-justice, speak to that vain man.

Ch. Just. Have you your wits? know you what 'tis you speak?

Fal. My king! my Jove! I speak to thee, my heart!   50

King. I know thee not, old man: fall to thy prayers; How ill white hairs become a fool and jester! I have long dream'd of such a kind of man, So surfeit-swell'd, so old and so profane; But, being awaked, I do despise my dream. Make less thy body hence, and more thy grace; Leave gormandizing; know the grave doth gape For thee thrice wider than for other men. Reply not to me with a fool-born jest: Presume not that I am the thing I was;   60 For God doth know, so shall the world perceive, That I have turn'd away my former self; So will I those that kept me company. When thou dost hear I am as I have been, Approach me, and thou shalt be as thou wast, The tutor and the feeder of my riots; Till then, I banish thee, on pain of death, As I have done the rest of my misleaders, Not to come near our person by ten mile. For competence of life I will allow you,   70 That lack of means enforce you not to evil: And, as we hear you do reform yourselves, We will, according to your strengths and qualities, Give you advancement. Be it your charge, my lord, To see perform'd the tenour of our word. Set on.   [*Exeunt King, &c.*

Fal. Master Shallow, I owe you a thousand pound.

Shal. Yea, marry, Sir John; which I beseech you to let me have home with me.   80

Fal. That can hardly be, Master Shallow. Do not you grieve at this; I shall be sent for in private to him: look you, he must seem thus to the world: fear not your advancements; I will be the man yet that shall make you great.

Shal. I cannot well perceive how, unless you should give me your doublet and stuff me out with straw. I beseech you, good Sir John, let me have five hundred of my thousand.

Fal. Sir, I will be as good as my word: this that you heard was but a colour. 91

Shal. A colour that I fear you will die in, Sir John.

Fal. Fear no colours: go with me to dinner: come, Lieutenant Pistol; come, Bardolph: I shall be sent for soon at night.

 Re-enter PRINCE JOHN, *the* LORD CHIEF-JUSTICE;
   Officers *with them.*

Ch. Just. Go, carry Sir John Falstaff to the Fleet: Take all his company along with him.

Fal. My lord, my lord,—

Ch. Just. I cannot now speak: I will hear you soon. Take them away. 101

Pist. Si fortuna me tormenta, spero contenta.
  [Exeunt all but Prince John and the Chief-Justice.

Lan. I like this fair proceeding of the king's: He hath intent his wonted followers Shall all be very well provided for; But all are banish'd till their conversations Appear more wise and modest to the world.

Ch. Just. And so they are.

Lan. The king hath call'd his parliament, my lord.

Ch. Just. He hath. 110

Lan. I will lay odds that, ere this year expire, We bear our civil swords and native fire As far as France: I heard a bird so sing, Whose music, to my thinking, pleased the king. Come, will you hence?   *[Exeunt.*

EPILOGUE.

Spoken by a Dancer.

First my fear; then my courtesy; last my speech. My fear is, your displeasure; my courtesy, my duty; and my speech, to beg your pardons. If you look for a good speech now, you undo me: for what I have to say is of mine own making; and what indeed I should say will, I doubt, prove mine own marring. But to the purpose, and so to the venture. Be it known to you, as it is very well, I was lately here in the end of a displeasing play, to pray your patience for it and to promise you a better. I meant indeed to pay you with this; which, if like an ill venture it come unluckily home, I break, and you, my gentle creditors, lose. Here I promised you I would be and here I commit my body to your mercies: bate me some and I will pay you some and, as most debtors do, promise you infinitely. 18

If my tongue cannot entreat you to acquit me, will you command me to use my legs? and yet that were but light payment, to dance out of your debt. But a good conscience will make any possible satisfaction, and so would I. All the gentlewomen here

have forgiven me: if the gentlemen will not, then the gentlemen do not agree with the gentlewomen, which was never seen before in such an assembly. 27

One word more, I beseech you. If you be not too much cloyed with fat meat, our humble author will continue the story, with Sir John in it, and make you merry with fair Katharine of France: where, for any thing I know, Falstaff shall die of a sweat, unless already a' be killed with your hard opinions; for Oldcastle died a martyr, and this is not the man. My tongue is weary; when my legs are too, I will bid you good night: and so kneel down before you; but, indeed, to pray for the queen. 38

28. **One word more.** If, as seems probable, there was an epilogue written to be spoken by a dancer in the play in its first Shakespearean form (where Falstaff was called Oldcastle), this last paragraph was added at the time of revision. 31. **Sir John in it.** Shakespeare evidently intended to introduce Falstaff into a play on Henry v and, subsequent to the writing of this Epilogue, gave up the intention. Coleridge suggested that Falstaff had no place in the new world of glorious enthusiasm and patriotic fervor which opened with the coronation of King Henry v. In any case, this promise in the Epilogue is very hard to reconcile with a theory of the very early composition of *Henry V*. It is not ordinarily thought that the revision from Oldcastle to Falstaff was made very long before the publication of the Q of *1 Henry IV* (1598), and yet a quarto version of *Henry V*, printed in 1600, depicts the death of Falstaff before the opening of the French campaign. 34. **Oldcastle died a martyr.** It is supposed with good reason, since there was an extensive controversy, that the Lord Cobham of the day resented the caricature of his ancestor, Sir John Oldcastle, Lollard martyr under Henry v (1417), and that this Epilogue, together with the change of the name to *Falstaff*, was intended to placate him. 38. **pray for the queen,** a customary way to end plays.

THE LIFE OF

King Henry the Fifth

The only reliable text of *Henry v* is that of the First Folio of 1623. On August 4, 1600, the play was entered in the Stationers' Register with *As You Like It* and *Much Ado about Nothing* to be "staied." If this was intended to prevent piracy it did not, in the case of *Henry v*, succeed, for a corrupt version was issued that year by Thomas Millington and John Busby without stationers' license. This quarto is a wretched thing without the choruses and without many important passages including three scenes (I, i; III, i; IV, ii). It bears no evidence of having been printed from a prompt copy. It was republished in 1602 and again by Jaggard in 1619 with the fictitious date of 1608, when he was projecting a collection of Shakespeare's plays. No corrected and augmented copy of the play seems to have been issued in quarto form. It has been suggested, without great probability, that an actor who played the part of the governor of Harfleur made up the version for the printers, since in the midst of the disorder of other roles his part is relatively correct. However this may be, it seems quite

94. **colours,** pretenses, with quibble on the meaning "standard" or "enemy." 96. **soon at night,** toward evening. 97. **Fleet,** Fleet Prison on what is now Farrington Street. 102. **Si . . . contenta.** See note on II, iv, 195, above.
 EPILOGUE. 1. **courtesy,** curtsy. 10. **displeasing play.** No satisfactory explanation has ever been offered. W. J. Lawrence suggested Ben Jonson's *Every Man out of His Humour.* 13. **venture,** probable allusion to the ventures of merchant vessels. Any voyage might prove a losing venture. **break,** become bankrupt. 16. **bate me some,** let me off from some portion of the debt.

certain that the quarto is not based on the Folio version as we have it.[1]

DATE

It is usually thought that *Henry V* was written between April 15 and September 28, 1599, because of an allusion in the chorus of the fifth act (ll. 29-34) to an expedition to Ireland led by the earl of Essex.

The campaign resulted in disaster, a fact which was evidently unknown when the lines were written. The play is not included in Meres' list in 1598, although *Henry IV* appears there. The promise of the epilogue to *2 Henry IV* that "our humble author will continue the story, with Sir John in it, and make you merry with fair Katharine of France," not realized as regards Sir John, is a part of the Oldcastle apology and points as we have seen to 1598, indicating that *Henry V* had not yet been written. There is also the allusion in the chorus of the first act (ll. 12-14) to "this wooden O" which seems to be the Globe Theatre, thought to have been ready for occupancy in the season of 1599.[2] The choruses may, of course, be later than the rest of the play; it is possible, therefore, that they are part of a revision of the play by Shakespeare in 1599.

SOURCES

The serious events of the story come from Holinshed's *Chronicles* (1587), which Shakespeare followed

with some license, but faithfully upon the whole. Holinshed recounts the more glorious features of the conquest of France. Henry advances an outrageous, but undoubtedly sincere, claim to the crown of France and a better one to certain provinces of that kingdom anciently belonging to his family. Fearful of waging an unjust war, he consults the leading churchmen of his land, who reassure him. It is shrewdly pointed out by the ecclesiastics that by supporting the king in his foreign war they may prevent the execution of a bill in parliament for confiscating their lands. Henry quells a treason in the form of a plot against his life by three of his favorite courtiers. He invades France and captures Harfleur; advances with a small and ill-provided army toward Calais and is forced by his misfortunes to reap the harvest of glory at Agincourt; so much in regular order from Holinshed.

Shakespeare then omits Henry's far more important second campaign, three years in length, and all intervening events. He closes his play with the Treaty of Troyes and Henry's betrothal to the Princess Katharine. Suggestions for the episode of the tennis balls, Pistol's capture of the French soldier, and Henry's wooing of Katharine come from the old Henry V play.[3]

The connections with the Henry IV plays are closely made. In the first scene of the first act the churchmen talk over with approval Henry's reformation. In the third scene of the second act the Hostess gives her memorable account of the death of Falstaff. Pistol, Bardolph, the Hostess, and the Boy are brought over from *2 Henry IV*. To them is added Nym, so "humorous" a character that he seems intended to ridicule the vogue of humor characters. To the comic side Shakespeare also adds four soldiers, typical of the four British races, Fluellen, Macmorris, Captain Jamy, and Williams. In a famous comic scene he assigns to the Welshman Fluellen the dramatic function of exposing the braggart soldier Pistol.

THE THEME

Henry V is essentially epic in theme. Business of council and state, war, peace negotiations, and a courtship, all occupying the hero's mind during a single scene, are narrative rather than dramatic. *Henry V* is, nevertheless, remarkable as a chronicle play in that it remains a block of history, a series of disconnected scenes, and is at the same time a unit. The unity is achieved in some measure by centering the interest upon Henry himself, particularly as a figure at the Battle of Agincourt, but also by various other devices. The choruses bridge over the intervals between the main events of the play, each selected event standing out as a piece of splendid pageantry.

The play, by its appeal to the imagination, fulfills

---

[1]Pollard, *Folios and Quartos*, p. 81, and *Shakespeare's Fight with the Pirates* (Cambridge, 1920); H. T. Price, *The Text of Henry V* (Newcastle-under-Lyme, 1920); Adams, *A Life of William Shakespeare*, pp. 518-519, 525-532; Hardin Craig, "The Relation of the First Quarto Version to the First Folio Version of Shakespeare's *Henry V*," *Philological Quarterly*, VI (1927), 225-234; Evelyn M. Albright, "The Folio Version of *Henry V*," *PMLA*, XLIII (1928), 722-756; Chambers, *William Shakespeare*, I, 388-396.
[2]Chambers, *The Elizabethan Stage*, II, 414-434.

[3]See Introduction to *1* and *2 Henry IV*.

an artistic law of the chronicle play. Shakespeare realized his artistic difficulties in the shaping of his materials for the theater, and the choruses are full of apology.

Piece out our imperfections with your thoughts,

he says; and again:

And so our scene must to the battle fly;
Where—O for pity!—we shall much disgrace
With four or five most vile and ragged foils,
Right ill-disposed in brawl ridiculous,
The name of Agincourt.

And yet in no history play is the difficulty of presenting a wide range of historical events so well overcome. This is in part achieved by a feature of the play appropriate to its spectacular quality, namely, its oratory. *Henry v* has not the poetical oratory of *Richard II*, nor the popular oratory of *Julius Caesar*, but a clear and practical eloquence of its own (I, ii, 259-310; III, i, 1-34; III, vi, 148-175; IV, iii, 18-67, 90-125). Passages of pure and beautiful poetry add to the effect (II, ii, 126-144; IV, vi, 7-32), which is in no small measure due to the exalted declamatory tone of the choruses.

HENRY V

It is the figure of Henry v, however, on which most pains have been lavished. To know the king in *Henry v* one must also know Prince Hal and his career as Shakespeare conceived it in *1* and *2 Henry IV*. One should also know Bolingbroke from those plays and from *Richard II*, and the politics of all the plays. Henry has learned much from his past, so that he appears in *Henry v* with certain established traits and qualities, no doubt conceived of as due to his life experience. He is prudent and conscientious (I, ii; IV, i). The duties of kingship and not its frivolities and amenities are shown in him. He is just and unflinching in the enforcement of law and discipline (II, ii; III, iii; III, vi, 113-120). He is a man of most pronounced devotion to great objects outside of himself, modest, humble, honest, religious, sympathetic with all classes of men, with a man-to-man way of regarding his fellows which was, and is, one of the noblest traits of his race.

So naturally are these traits made to grow up in the prince and king, so well are they accounted for in the course of events, that one forgets that there lies back of them the most important theme in the social and political thinking of the Renaissance, namely, the ideal prince. One thinks at once of the three great classics of the Renaissance that are still best known to the modern world: Castiglione's *Il Cortegiano* (1528), translated into English by Hoby as *The Courtier* (1561), Elyot's *The Governour* (1531), and Machiavelli's *The Prince* (1516). No subject interested the Renaissance so much as the training and character of statesmen.

In the Tudor time it was thought most necessary, most essential, to have educated rulers and thus to uphold the standard of righteousness in public men and affairs. The ethics of the time was largely a public ethics, so that the best men of the age were saturated in the literature of the courtier, the governor, and the prince. The most weighty of ancient classics often contributed to this interest. Plato's *Republic* and Aristotle's *Politics* are concerned with the education of the philosopher prince, as are Xenophon's *Cyropaedia* and Quintilian's *Institutes;* Castiglione had based his work in some measure on Cicero's *De Oratore*.

Henry's princely virtues, as enumerated and depicted in *Henry v*, are the recognizable and customary group. One cannot but believe that he was deliberately conceived of as the embodiment of these ideals. "Never was such a sudden scholar made. Hear him but reason on divinity, debate of commonwealth affairs, discourse of war, or any cause of policy, the Gordian knot of it he will unloose, familiar as his garter. The prince obscured his contemplation under the veil of wildness; but, no doubt, it grew like the summer grass."

STAGE HISTORY

Henry v must certainly have been popular in its own day, if for no other reason than because it impresses us as the finest expression of Elizabethan patriotism. A funeral elegy written in honor of the contemporary actor, Richard Burbage, connects him with the part of Henry. There is no other known contemporary allusion.

The play was apparently neglected until well into the eighteenth century, at least two adaptations having proved short-lived. Garrick presented Shakespeare's play at Drury Lane in 1747 and surprised the world by leaving the part of the heroic king to Barry while he himself recited the part of the Chorus. In 1761 came a characteristic revival of *Henry v* by John Rich (1682?-1761), pantomimist and theatrical manager, at Covent Garden. The play was there treated as a spectacle, which fashion has been followed. In Charles Kean's presentation at the Princess' Theatre in 1850 the siege of Harfleur was staged with the utmost attention to historical accuracy, Henry's return to London was presented, not in the words of the Chorus, but as an actual royal entry, and Mrs. Kean recited the part of the Chorus costumed as Clio, the Muse of History. Similar features likewise appeared in Richard Mansfield's famous American production in 1900. John Philip Kemble, Edmund Kean, Charles Kean, William Macready, Samuel Phelps, and Lewis Waller have acted the part of King Henry, usually with some show of elaboration and ornament. The widely popular and much admired film version of *Henry v*, produced and directed by Sir Laurence Olivier, in which he also played the title role, was perhaps the greatest success ever achieved in the presentation of a Shakespearean play in moving pictures.

THE LIFE OF
King Henry the Fifth

DRAMATIS PERSONAE

KING HENRY the Fifth.
DUKE OF GLOUCESTER, } brothers to the King.
DUKE OF BEDFORD,
DUKE OF EXETER, uncle to the King.
DUKE OF YORK, cousin to the King.
EARLS OF SALISBURY, WESTMORELAND, and
  WARWICK.
ARCHBISHOP OF CANTERBURY.
BISHOP OF ELY.
EARL OF CAMBRIDGE.
LORD SCROOP.
SIR THOMAS GREY.
SIR THOMAS ERPINGHAM, GOWER, FLUELLEN,
  MACMORRIS, JAMY, officers in King Henry's
  army.
BATES, COURT, WILLIAMS, soldiers in the same.
PISTOL, NYM, BARDOLPH.
Boy.
A Herald.

CHARLES the Sixth, King of France.
LEWIS, the Dauphin.
DUKES OF BURGUNDY, ORLEANS, and BOURBON.
The Constable of France.
RAMBURES and GRANDPRÉ, French Lords.
Governor of Harfleur.
MONTJOY, a French Herald.
Ambassadors to the King of England.

ISABEL, Queen of France.
KATHARINE, daughter to Charles and Isabel.
ALICE, a lady attending on her.
Hostess of a tavern in Eastcheap, formerly
  Mistress Quickly, and now married to Pistol.

Lords, Ladies, Officers, Soldiers, Citizens,
  Messengers, and Attendants.

Chorus.

SCENE: *England; afterwards France.*

PROLOGUE.

Enter Chorus.

Chor. O for a Muse of fire, that would ascend
The brightest heaven of invention,
A kingdom for a stage, princes to act
And monarchs to behold the swelling scene!
Then should the warlike Harry, like himself,
Assume the port of Mars; and at his heels,
Leash'd in like hounds, should famine, sword and
  fire
Crouch for employment. But pardon, gentles all,

The flat unraised spirits that have dared
On this unworthy scaffold to bring forth   10
So great an object: can this cockpit hold
The vasty fields of France? or may we cram
Within this wooden O the very casques
That did affright the air at Agincourt?
O, pardon! since a crooked figure may
Attest in little place a million;
And let us, ciphers to this great accompt,
On your imaginary forces work.
Suppose within the girdle of these walls
Are now confined two mighty monarchies,   20
Whose high upreared and abutting fronts
The perilous narrow ocean parts asunder:
Piece out our imperfections with your thoughts;
Into a thousand parts divide one man,
And make imaginary puissance;
Think, when we talk of horses, that you see them
Printing their proud hoofs i' the receiving earth;
For 'tis your thoughts that now must deck our kings,
Carry them here and there; jumping o'er times,
Turning the accomplishment of many years   30
Into an hour-glass: for the which supply,
Admit me Chorus to this history;
Who prologue-like your humble patience pray,
Gently to hear, kindly to judge, our play.   [*Exit.*

ACT I.

SCENE I. *London. An ante-chamber*
in the KING'S *palace.*

Enter the ARCHBISHOP OF CANTERBURY, *and the*
  BISHOP OF ELY.

Cant. My lord, I'll tell you; that self bill is urged,
Which in the eleventh year of the last king's reign
Was like, and had indeed against us pass'd,
But that the scambling and unquiet time
Did push it out of farther question.
  Ely. But how, my lord, shall we resist it now?
  Cant. It must be thought on. If it pass against us,
We lose the better half of our possession:
For all the temporal lands which men devout
By testament have given to the church   10
Would they strip from us; being valued thus:
As much as would maintain, to the king's honour,
Full fifteen earls and fifteen hundred knights,
Six thousand and two hundred good esquires;
And, to relief of lazars and weak age,
Of indigent faint souls past corporal toil,
A hundred almshouses right well supplied;
And to the coffers of the king beside,
A thousand pounds by the year: thus runs the bill.
  Ely. This would drink deep.
  Cant.   'Twould drink the cup and all. 20

PROLOGUE. **Chorus.** It will be noticed that the Chorus carries part
of the action in *Henry V* and that Shakespeare uses it to win the sympathy of the audience for his theatrical limitations.   7. **famine, sword**
and fire. According to Holinshed, Henry told the people of Rouen that
Bellona, the goddess of battle, had three handmaidens attendant upon
her called "blood, fire, and famine."   10. **scaffold,** stage.   11. **cockpit.**
Elizabethan theaters were used for cockfighting. One of them was
called the Cockpit.   13. **O,** refers to a round theater such as the Globe.
casques, helmets.   16. **Attest,** stand for.   17. **accompt,** account.   18.
imaginary forces, forces of imagination. Shakespeare recognizes here
the part the audience must have in the play.   22. **narrow ocean,** the
English Channel.   31. **supply,** service.
ACT I. SCENE I.   1. **self,** same.   4. **scambling,** unsettled.   15. **lazars,**
lepers.

Ely. But what prevention?
Cant. The king is full of grace and fair regard.
Ely. And a true lover of the holy church.
Cant. The courses of his youth promised it not.
The breath no sooner left his father's body,
But that his wildness, mortified in him,
Seem'd to die too; yea, at that very moment
Consideration, like an angel, came
And whipp'd the offending Adam out of him,
Leaving his body as a paradise, 30
To envelope and contain celestial spirits.
Never was such a sudden scholar made;
Never came reformation in a flood,
With such a heady currance, scouring faults;
Nor never Hydra-headed wilfulness
So soon did lose his seat and all at once
As in this king.
    Ely.   We are blessed in the change.
    Cant. Hear him but reason in divinity,
And all-admiring with an inward wish
You would desire the king were made a prelate: 40
Hear him debate of commonwealth affairs,
You would say it hath been all in all his study:
List his discourse of war, and you shall hear
A fearful battle render'd you in music:
Turn him to any cause of policy,
The Gordian knot of it he will unloose,
Familiar as his garter: that, when he speaks,
The air, a charter'd libertine, is still,
And the mute wonder lurketh in men's ears,
To steal his sweet and honey'd sentences; 50
So that the art and practic part of life
Must be the mistress to this theoric:
Which is a wonder how his grace should glean it,
Since his addiction was to courses vain,
His companies unletter'd, rude and shallow,
His hours fill'd up with riots, banquets, sports,
And never noted in him any study,
Any retirement, any sequestration
From open haunts and popularity.
    Ely. The strawberry grows underneath the nettle 60
And wholesome berries thrive and ripen best
Neighbour'd by fruit of baser quality:
And so the prince obscured his contemplation
Under the veil of wildness; which, no doubt,
Grew like the summer grass, fastest by night,
Unseen, yet crescive in his faculty.
    Cant. It must be so; for miracles are ceased;
And therefore we must needs admit the means
How things are perfected.
    Ely.   But, my good lord,
How now for mitigation of this bill 70
Urged by the commons? Doth his majesty
Incline to it, or no?
    Cant.   He seems indifferent,
Or rather swaying more upon our part
Than cherishing the exhibiters against us;
For I have made an offer to his majesty,
Upon our spiritual convocation

And in regard of causes now in hand,
Which I have open'd to his grace at large,
As touching France, to give a greater sum
Than ever at one time the clergy yet 80
Did to his predecessors part withal.
    Ely. How did this offer seem received, my lord?
    Cant. With good acceptance of his majesty;
Save that there was not time enough to hear,
As I perceived his grace would fain have done,
The severals and unhidden passages
Of his true titles to some certain dukedoms
And generally to the crown and seat of France
Derived from Edward, his great-grandfather.
    Ely. What was the impediment that broke this off? 90
    Cant. The French ambassador upon that instant
Craved audience; and the hour, I think, is come
To give him hearing: is it four o'clock?
    Ely. It is.
    Cant. Then go we in, to know his embassy;
Which I could with a ready guess declare,
Before the Frenchman speak a word of it.
    Ely. I'll wait upon you, and I long to hear it.[*Exeunt.*

SCENE II. *The same. The Presence chamber.*

Enter KING HENRY, GLOUCESTER, BEDFORD,
    EXETER, WARWICK, WESTMORELAND, *and*
    Attendants.

    K. Hen. Where is my gracious Lord of Canterbury?
    Exe. Not here in presence.
    K. Hen.   Send for him, good uncle.
    West. Shall we call in the ambassador, my liege?
    K. Hen. Not yet, my cousin: we would be resolved,
Before we hear him, of some things of weight
That task our thoughts, concerning us and France.

Enter the ARCHBISHOP OF CANTERBURY, *and the*
    BISHOP OF ELY.

    Cant. God and his angels guard your sacred throne
And make you long become it!
    K. Hen.   Sure, we thank you.
My learned lord, we pray you to proceed
And justly and religiously unfold 10
Why the law Salique that they have in France
Or should, or should not, bar us in our claim:
And God forbid, my dear and faithful lord,
That you should fashion, wrest, or bow your reading,
Or nicely charge your understanding soul
With opening titles miscreate, whose right
Suits not in native colours with the truth;
For God doth know how many now in health
Shall drop their blood in approbation
Of what your reverence shall incite us to. 20
Therefore take heed how you impawn our person,
How you awake our sleeping sword of war:
We charge you, in the name of God, take heed;
For never two such kingdoms did contend
Without much fall of blood; whose guiltless drops

---

29. **offending Adam,** original sin. Henry's offenses have been driven out of him as Adam was driven out of Paradise. 34. **heady currance,** headlong current. 35. **Hydra-headed,** an allusion to the Lernaean Hydra overcome by Hercules. 38-47. **Hear . . . garter.** These lines enumerate the principal subjects of princely education. Note that policy (statecraft) as well as war held a recognized place. 46. **Gordian knot,** an allusion to the knot of Gordius, of which it was foretold that whoever should untie it would rule Asia. Alexander solved the problem by

cutting the knot. 47. **Familiar,** familiarly. **that,** so that. 48. **charter'd libertine,** one privileged to lead a dissolute life. 51. **practic,** practical. 52. **theoric,** theory. 55. **companies,** companions. 57. **noted,** denoted. 59. **popularity,** intercourse with low society. 63. **obscured,** concealed. 66. **crescive,** tending to grow. 74. **exhibiters,** those who introduce bills in Parliament. 79. **to give a greater sum.** An underlying motive of the churchmen in urging on the French war is here disclosed. 86. **unhidden passages,** plain facts.

Are every one a woe, a sore complaint
'Gainst him whose wrongs give edge unto the swords
That make such waste in brief mortality.
Under this conjuration speak, my lord;
For we will hear, note and believe in heart   30
That what you speak is in your conscience wash'd
As pure as sin with baptism.
    Cant. Then hear me, gracious sovereign, and you
        peers,
That owe yourselves, your lives and services
To this imperial throne. There is no bar
To make against your highness' claim to France
But this, which they produce from Pharamond,
'In terram Salicam mulieres ne succedant:'
'No woman shall succeed in Salique land:'
Which Salique land the French unjustly glose   40
To be the realm of France, and Pharamond
The founder of this law and female bar.
Yet their own authors faithfully affirm
That the land Salique is in Germany,
Between the floods of Sala and of Elbe;
Where Charles the Great, having subdued the Saxons,
There left behind and settled certain French;
Who, holding in disdain the German women
For some dishonest manners of their life,
Establish'd this law; to wit, no female   50
Should be inheritrix in Salique land:
Which Salique, as I said, 'twixt Elbe and Sala,
Is at this day in Germany call'd Meisen.
Then doth it well appear the Salique law
Was not devised for the realm of France;
Nor did the French possess the Salique land
Until four hundred one and twenty years
After defunction of King Pharamond,
Idly supposed the founder of this law;
Who died within the year of our redemption   60
Four hundred twenty-six; and Charles the Great
Subdued the Saxons, and did seat the French
Beyond the river Sala, in the year
Eight hundred five. Besides, their writers say,
King Pepin, which deposed Childeric,
Did, as heir general, being descended
Of Blithild, which was daughter to King Clothair,
Make claim and title to the crown of France.
Hugh Capet also, who usurp'd the crown
Of Charles the duke of Lorraine, sole heir male   70
Of the true line and stock of Charles the Great,
To find his title with some shows of truth,
Though, in pure truth, it was corrupt and naught,
Convey'd himself as heir to the Lady Lingare,
Daughter to Charlemain, who was the son
To Lewis the emperor, and Lewis the son
Of Charles the Great. Also King Lewis the Tenth,
Who was sole heir to the usurper Capet,
Could not keep quiet in his conscience,
Wearing the crown of France, till satisfied   80
That fair Queen Isabel, his grandmother,
Was lineal of the Lady Ermengare,
Daughter to Charles the foresaid duke of Lorraine:

By the which marriage the line of Charles the Great
Was re-united to the crown of France.
So that, as clear as is the summer's sun,
King Pepin's title and Hugh Capet's claim,
King Lewis his satisfaction, all appear
To hold in right and title of the female:
So do the kings of France unto this day;   90
Howbeit they would hold up this Salique law
To bar your highness claiming from the female,
And rather choose to hide them in a net
Than amply to imbar their crooked titles
Usurp'd from you and your progenitors.
    K. Hen. May I with right and conscience make this
        claim?
    Cant. The sin upon my head, dread sovereign!
For in the book of Numbers is it writ,
When the man dies, let the inheritance
Descend unto the daughter. Gracious lord,   100
Stand for your own; unwind your bloody flag;
Look back into your mighty ancestors:
Go, my dread lord, to your great-grandsire's tomb,
From whom you claim; invoke his warlike spirit,
And your great-uncle's, Edward the Black Prince,
Who on the French ground play'd a tragedy,
Making defeat on the full power of France,
Whiles his most mighty father on a hill
Stood smiling to behold his lion's whelp
Forage in blood of French nobility.   110
O noble English, that could entertain
With half their forces the full pride of France
And let another half stand laughing by,
All out of work and cold for action!
    Ely. Awake remembrance of these valiant dead
And with your puissant arm renew their feats:
You are their heir; you sit upon their throne;
The blood and courage that renowned them
Runs in your veins; and my thrice-puissant liege
Is in the very May-morn of his youth,   120
Ripe for exploits and mighty enterprises.
    Exe. Your brother kings and monarchs of the earth
Do all expect that you should rouse yourself,
As did the former lions of your blood.
    West. They know your grace hath cause and means
        and might;
So hath your highness; never king of England
Had nobles richer and more loyal subjects,
Whose hearts have left their bodies here in England
And lie pavilion'd in the fields of France.
    Cant. O, let their bodies follow, my dear liege,   130
With blood and sword and fire to win your right;
In aid whereof we of the spiritualty
Will raise your highness such a mighty sum
As never did the clergy at one time
Bring in to any of your ancestors.
    K. Hen. We must not only arm to invade the
        French,
But lay down our proportions to defend
Against the Scot, who will make road upon us
With all advantages.

SCENE II. 8-32. **Sure . . . baptism.** Shakespeare wishes to indicate in this scene the extreme uprightness of his hero. 11. **law Salique.** Shakespeare brings in what Neilson calls "a show of expert advice," in order that Henry may go to the war with a clear conscience. 15. **nicely,** strictly. 16. **opening,** examining. **miscreate,** improperly framed. 21. **impawn,** pledge. 40. **glose,** explain. 58. **defunction,** death. 61. **Charles the Great,** Charlemagne. 66. **heir general,** heir to the whole kingdom. 72. **find,** to provide or trace out. 75. **Charle-**

main, Charles the Bald. 82. **lineal of,** descended from. 88. **Lewis his,** Lewis'. 93. **net,** possibly expressive of something easily seen through; also explained as "a tangle of contradictions." 94. **imbar,** secure; sometimes defined as "exclude." 98. **Numbers.** See Numbers 27:8. 107. **defeat,** ruin; see glossary. 108. **his most mighty father.** Holinshed gives the story of Edward III's watching the Battle of Crécy (1346) as recounted in the text. 114. **cold for action,** cold for want of action. 137. **lay down our proportions,** set down the proper numbers.

Cant. They of those marches, gracious sovereign, 140
Shall be a wall sufficient to defend
Our inland from the pilfering borderers.
  K. Hen. We do not mean the coursing snatchers
      only,
But fear the main intendment of the Scot,
Who hath been still a giddy neighbour to us;
For you shall read that my great-grandfather
Never went with his forces into France
But that the Scot on his unfurnish'd kingdom
Came pouring, like the tide into a breach,
With ample and brim fulness of his force, 150
Galling the gleaned land with hot assays,
Girding with grievous siege castles and towns;
That England, being empty of defence,
Hath shook and trembled at the ill neighbourhood.
  Cant. She hath been then more fear'd than harm'd,
      my liege;
For hear her but exampled by herself:
When all her chivalry hath been in France
And she a mourning widow of her nobles,
She hath herself not only well defended
But taken and impounded as a stray 160
The King of Scots; whom she did send to France,
To fill King Edward's fame with prisoner kings
And make her chronicle as rich with praise
As is the ooze and bottom of the sea
With sunken wreck and sumless treasuries.
  West. But there 's a saying very old and true,
      'If that you will France win,
          Then with Scotland first begin:'
For once the eagle England being in prey,
To her unguarded nest the weasel Scot 170
Comes sneaking and so sucks her princely eggs,
Playing the mouse in absence of the cat,
To tear and havoc more than she can eat.
  Exe. It follows then the cat must stay at home:
Yet that is but a crush'd necessity,
Since we have locks to safeguard necessaries,
And pretty traps to catch the petty thieves.
While that the armed hand doth fight abroad,
The advised head defends itself at home;
For government, though high and low and lower, 180
Put into parts, doth keep in one consent,
Congreeing in a full and natural close,
Like music.
  Cant.   Therefore doth heaven divide
The state of man in divers functions,
Setting endeavour in continual motion;
To which is fixed, as an aim or butt,
Obedience: for so work the honey-bees,
Creatures that by a rule in nature teach
The act of order to a peopled kingdom.
They have a king and officers of sorts; 190
Where some, like magistrates, correct at home,
Others, like merchants, venture trade abroad,
Others, like soldiers, armed in their stings,
Make boot upon the summer's velvet buds,
Which pillage they with merry march bring home
To the tent-royal of their emperor;

Who, busied in his majesty, surveys
The singing masons building roofs of gold,
The civil citizens kneading up the honey,
The poor mechanic porters crowding in 200
Their heavy burdens at his narrow gate,
The sad-eyed justice, with his surly hum,
Delivering o'er to executors pale
The lazy yawning drone. I this infer,
That many things, having full reference
To one consent, may work contrariously:
As many arrows, loosed several ways,
Come to one mark; as many ways meet in one town;
As many fresh streams meet in one salt sea;
As many lines close in the dial's centre; 210
So may a thousand actions, once afoot,
End in one purpose, and be all well borne
Without defeat. Therefore to France, my liege.
Divide your happy England into four;
Whereof take you one quarter into France,
And you withal shall make all Gallia shake.
If we, with thrice such powers left at home,
Cannot defend our own doors from the dog,
Let us be worried and our nation lose
The name of hardiness and policy. 220
  K. Hen. Call in the messengers sent from the
      Dauphin.   [*Exeunt some Attendants.*
Now are we well resolved; and, by God's help,
And yours, the noble sinews of our power,
France being ours, we'll bend it to our awe,
Or break it all to pieces: or there we'll sit,
Ruling in large and ample empery
O'er France and all her almost kingly dukedoms,
Or lay these bones in an unworthy urn,
Tombless, with no remembrance over them:
Either our history shall with full mouth 230
Speak freely of our acts, or else our grave,
Like Turkish mute, shall have a tongueless mouth,
Not worshipp'd with a waxen epitaph.

  Enter Ambassadors *of France.*

Now are we well prepared to know the pleasure
Of our fair cousin Dauphin; for we hear
Your greeting is from him, not from the king.
  First Amb. May 't please your majesty to give us
      leave
Freely to render what we have in charge;
Or shall we sparingly show you far off
The Dauphin's meaning and our embassy? 240
  K. Hen. We are no tyrant, but a Christian king;
Unto whose grace our passion is as subject
As are our wretches fetter'd in our prisons:
Therefore with frank and with uncurbed plainness
Tell us the Dauphin's mind.
  First Amb.   Thus, then, in few.
Your highness, lately sending into France,
Did claim some certain dukedoms, in the right
Of your great predecessor, King Edward the Third.
In answer of which claim, the prince our master
Says that you savour too much of your youth, 250
And bids you be advised there 's nought in France

---

140. **marches,** borders. 143. **coursing snatchers,** mounted raiders.
144. **intendment,** plan. 151. **gleaned,** stripped (of defenders). **assays,**
assaults. 160. **impounded as a stray.** David Bruce was captured and
imprisoned in 1346 while Edward III was in France. 173. **havoc,**
the signal for slaughter; here, destroy. 175. **crush'd,** forced. 182.
Congreeing, agreeing together. **close,** cadence. 184-204. **The state
. . . drone.** This elaborate comparison of human society to a hive of
bees is a familiar Renaissance theme. It expresses the current political

theory of the naturalness of rank and class and the necessity of order.
202. **sad-eyed,** grave-eyed. 203. **executors,** executioners. 216.
Gallia, Latin name for France. 220. **hardiness and policy,** bravery
and statesmanship, the two highest virtues of a king. 221. **Dauphin,**
heir apparent to the French throne. 226. **empery,** dominion. 233.
waxen epitaph, allusion to the custom of affixing epitaphs to tombs.
It is explained that the epitaph was stuck on with wax. 252. **galliard,**
a lively dance. 255. **tun,** a cask. Holinshed speaks of "a barrel of

That can be with a nimble galliard won;
You cannot revel into dukedoms there.
He therefore sends you, meeter for your spirit,
This tun of treasure; and, in lieu of this,
Desires you let the dukedoms that you claim
Hear no more of you. This the Dauphin speaks.

   K. Hen. What treasure, uncle?
   Exe.   Tennis-balls, my liege.
   K. Hen. We are glad the Dauphin is so pleasant with
      us;

His present and your pains we thank you for: 260
When we have match'd our rackets to these balls,
We will, in France, by God's grace, play a set
Shall strike his father's crown into the hazard.
Tell him he hath made a match with such a wrangler
That all the courts of France will be disturb'd
With chaces. And we understand him well,
How he comes o'er us with our wilder days,
Not measuring what use we made of them.
We never valued this poor seat of England;
And therefore, living hence, did give ourself   270
To barbarous license; as 'tis ever common
That men are merriest when they are from home.
But tell the Dauphin I will keep my state,
Be like a king and show my sail of greatness
When I do rouse me in my throne of France:
For that I have laid by my majesty
And plodded like a man for working-days,
But I will rise there with so full a glory
That I will dazzle all the eyes of France,
Yea, strike the Dauphin blind to look on us.   280
And tell the pleasant prince this mock of his
Hath turn'd his balls to gun-stones; and his soul
Shall stand sore charged for the wasteful vengeance
That shall fly with them: for many a thousand widows
Shall this his mock mock out of their dear husbands;
Mock mothers from their sons, mock castles down;
And some are yet ungotten and unborn
That shall have cause to curse the Dauphin's scorn.
But this lies all within the will of God,
To whom I do appeal; and in whose name   290
Tell you the Dauphin I am coming on,
To venge me as I may and to put forth
My rightful hand in a well-hallow'd cause.
So get you hence in peace; and tell the Dauphin
His jest will savour but of shallow wit,
When thousands weep more than did laugh at it.
Convey them with safe conduct. Fare you well.
                          [Exeunt Ambassadors.

   Exe. This was a merry message.
   K. Hen. We hope to make the sender blush at it.
Therefore, my lords, omit no happy hour   300
That may give furtherance to our expedition;
For we have now no thought in us but France,
Save those to God, that run before our business.
Therefore let our proportions for these wars
Be soon collected and all things thought upon
That may with reasonable swiftness add
More feathers to our wings; for, God before,
We'll chide this Dauphin at his father's door.

Therefore let every man now task his thought,
That this fair action may on foot be brought.   310
                          [Exeunt. Flourish.

ACT II.

PROLOGUE.

Flourish. Enter Chorus.

   Chor. Now all the youth of England are on fire,
And silken dalliance in the wardrobe lies:
Now thrive the armourers, and honour's thought
Reigns solely in the breast of every man:
They sell the pasture now to buy the horse,
Following the mirror of all Christian kings,
With winged heels, as English Mercuries.
For now sits Expectation in the air,
And hides a sword from hilts unto the point
With crowns imperial, crowns and coronets,   10
Promised to Harry and his followers.
The French, advised by good intelligence
Of this most dreadful preparation,
Shake in their fear and with pale policy
Seek to divert the English purposes.
O England! model to thy inward greatness,
Like little body with a mighty heart,
What mightst thou do, that honour would thee do,
Were all thy children kind and natural!
But see thy fault! France hath in thee found out   20
A nest of hollow bosoms, which he fills
With treacherous crowns; and three corrupted men,
One, Richard Earl of Cambridge, and the second,
Henry Lord Scroop of Masham, and the third,
Sir Thomas Grey, knight, of Northumberland,
Have, for the gilt of France,—O guilt indeed!—
Confirm'd conspiracy with fearful France;
And by their hands this grace of kings must die,
If hell and treason hold their promises,
Ere he take ship for France, and in Southampton.   30
Linger your patience on; †and we'll digest
The abuse of distance; force a play:
The sum is paid; the traitors are agreed;
The king is set from London; and the scene
Is now transported, gentles, to Southampton;
There is the playhouse now, there must you sit:
And thence to France shall we convey you safe,
And bring you back, charming the narrow seas
To give you gentle pass; for, if we may,
We'll not offend one stomach with our play.   40
But, till the king come forth, and not till then,
Unto Southampton do we shift our scene.   *[Exit.*

SCENE I. *London. A street.*

Enter Corporal NYM *and* Lieutenant BARDOLPH.

   Bard. Well met, Corporal Nym.
   Nym. Good morrow, Lieutenant Bardolph.
   Bard. What, are Ancient Pistol and you friends yet?

Paris balls." 263. **hazard,** in tennis, the side of the court into which
the ball is served. 264. **wrangler,** stubborn adversary. 266. **chaces.**
A *chace* is the second bound of a ball which the opponent fails to return;
obvious pun on "chase." 267. **comes o'er,** taunts. 269-280. **We
. . . us.** The king speaks ironically to the disadvantage of England,
suggesting that his mind is fixed on France. 269. **seat,** throne. 270.
living hence, not frequenting the royal court. 282. **gun-stones,** cannon
balls.

ACT II. PROLOGUE. 18. **would,** would have. 22. **crowns,** crown
pieces. 26. **gilt,** gold. 31-32. **digest The abuse of distance,** overcome
the difficulties of representing distance. 32. **force a play,** make a play
in spite of difficulties. 41-42. **But . . . scene.** The meaning is that
the scene will be shifted to Southampton, but not until the king comes
forth.
SCENE I. 3. **Ancient,** ensign.

Nym. For my part, I care not: I say little; but when time shall serve, there shall be smiles; but that shall be as it may. I dare not fight; but I will wink and hold out mine iron: it is a simple one; but what though? it will toast cheese, and it will endure cold as another man's sword will: and there's an end. 11

Bard. I will bestow a breakfast to make you friends; and we'll be all three sworn brothers to France: let it be so, good Corporal Nym.

Nym. Faith, I will live so long as I may, that's the certain of it; and when I cannot live any longer, I will do as I may: that is my rest, that is the rendezvous of it.

Bard. It is certain, corporal, that he is married to Nell Quickly: and certainly she did you wrong; for you were troth-plight to her. 21

Nym. I cannot tell: things must be as they may: men may sleep, and they may have their throats about them at that time; and some say knives have edges. It must be as it may: though patience be a tired mare, yet she will plod. There must be conclusions. Well, I cannot tell. 27

Enter PISTOL *and* Hostess.

Bard. Here comes Ancient Pistol and his wife: good corporal, be patient here. How now, mine host Pistol!

Pist. Base tike, call'st thou me host?
Now, by this hand, I swear, I scorn the term;
Nor shall my Nell keep lodgers.

Host. No, by my troth, not long; for we cannot lodge and board a dozen or fourteen gentlewomen that live honestly by the prick of their needles, but it will be thought we keep a bawdy house straight. [*Nym and Pistol draw.*] O well a day, Lady, if he be not drawn now! we shall see wilful adultery and murder committed. 40

Bard. Good lieutenant! good corporal! offer nothing here.

Nym. Pish!

Pist. Pish for thee, Iceland dog! thou prick-ear'd cur of Iceland!

Host. Good Corporal Nym, show thy valour, and put up your sword.

Nym. Will you shog off? I would have you solus.

Pist. 'Solus,' egregious dog? O viper vile!
The 'solus' in thy most mervailous face; 50
The 'solus' in thy teeth, and in thy throat,
And in thy hateful lungs, yea, in thy maw, perdy,
And, which is worse, within thy nasty mouth!
I do retort the 'solus' in thy bowels;
For I can take, and Pistol's cock is up,
And flashing fire will follow. 56

Nym. I am not Barbason; you cannot conjure me. I have an humour to knock you indifferently well. If you grow foul with me, Pistol, I will scour you with my rapier, as I may, in fair terms: if you would walk off, I would prick your guts a little, in good terms, as I may: and that's the humour of it.

Pist. O braggart vile and damned furious wight!

The grave doth gape, and doting death is near;
Therefore exhale.

Bard. Hear me, hear me what I say: he that strikes the first stroke, I'll run him up to the hilts, as I am a soldier. [*Draws.*

Pist. An oath of mickle might; and fury shall abate.
Give me thy fist, thy fore-foot to me give: 71
Thy spirits are most tall.

Nym. I will cut thy throat, one time or other, in fair terms: that is the humour of it.

Pist. 'Couple a gorge!'
That is the word. I thee defy again.
O hound of Crete, think'st thou my spouse to get?
No; to the spital go,
And from the powdering-tub of infamy
Fetch forth the lazar kite of Cressid's kind, 80
Doll Tearsheet she by name, and her espouse:
I have, and I will hold, the quondam Quickly
For the only she; and—pauca, there's enough.
Go to.

Enter the Boy.

Boy. Mine host Pistol, you must come to my master, and you, hostess: he is very sick, and would to bed. Good Bardolph, put thy face between his sheets, and do the office of a warming-pan. Faith, he's very ill.

Bard. Away, you rogue! 90

Host. By my troth, he'll yield the crow a pudding one of these days. The king has killed his heart. Good husband, come home presently.

[*Exeunt Hostess and Boy.*

Bard. Come, shall I make you two friends? We must to France together: why the devil should we keep knives to cut one another's throats?

Pist. Let floods o'erswell, and fiends for food howl on!

Nym. You'll pay me the eight shillings I won of you at betting?

Pist. Base is the slave that pays. 100

Nym. That now I will have: that's the humour of it.

Pist. As manhood shall compound: push home.

[*They draw.*

Bard. By this sword, he that makes the first thrust, I'll kill him; by this sword, I will.

Pist. Sword is an oath, and oaths must have their course.

Bard. Corporal Nym, an thou wilt be friends, be friends: an thou wilt not, why, then, be enemies with me too. Prithee, put up.

Nym. I shall have my eight shillings I won of you at betting? 111

Pist. A noble shalt thou have, and present pay;
And liquor likewise will I give to thee,
And friendship shall combine, and brotherhood:
I'll live by Nym, and Nym shall live by me;
Is not this just? for I shall sutler be
Unto the camp, and profits will accrue.
Give me thy hand.

Nym. I shall have my noble?

Pist. In cash most justly paid. 120
Nym. Well, then, that 's the humour of 't.

Re-enter Hostess.

Host. As ever you came of women, come in quickly to Sir John. Ah, poor heart! he is so shaked of a burning quotidian tertian, that it is most lamentable to behold. Sweet men, come to him.

Nym. The king hath run bad humours on the knight; that 's the even of it.

Pist. Nym, thou hast spoke the right; His heart is fracted and corroborate. 130

Nym. The king is a good king: but it must be as it may; he passes some humours and careers.

Pist. Let us condole the knight; for, lambkins, we will live.

SCENE II. *Southampton. A council-chamber.*

Enter EXETER, BEDFORD, *and* WESTMORELAND.

Bed. 'Fore God, his grace is bold, to trust these traitors.

Exe. They shall be apprehended by and by.

West. How smooth and even they do bear themselves!
As if allegiance in their bosoms sat,
Crowned with faith and constant loyalty.

Bed. The king hath note of all that they intend,
By interception which they dream not of.

Exe. Nay, but the man that was his bedfellow,
Whom he hath dull'd and cloy'd with gracious favours,
That he should, for a foreign purse, so sell 10
His sovereign's life to death and treachery.

Trumpets sound. Enter KING HENRY, SCROOP, CAMBRIDGE, GREY, *and* Attendants.

K. Hen. Now sits the wind fair, and we will aboard.
My Lord of Cambridge, and my kind Lord of Masham,
And you, my gentle knight, give me your thoughts:
Think you not that the powers we bear with us
Will cut their passage through the force of France,
Doing the execution and the act
For which we have in head assembled them?

Scroop. No doubt, my liege, if each man do his best.

K. Hen. I doubt not that; since we are well persuaded 20
We carry not a heart with us from hence
That grows not in a fair consent with ours,
Nor leave not one behind that doth not wish
Success and conquest to attend on us.

Cam. Never was monarch better fear'd and loved
Than is your majesty: there 's not, I think, a subject
That sits in heart-grief and uneasiness
Under the sweet shade of your government.

Grey. True: those that were your father's enemies
Have steep'd their galls in honey and do serve you 30

With hearts create of duty and of zeal.

K. Hen. We therefore have great cause of thankfulness;
And shall forget the office of our hand,
Sooner than quittance of desert and merit
According to the weight and worthiness.

Scroop. So service shall with steeled sinews toil,
And labour shall refresh itself with hope,
To do your grace incessant services.

K. Hen. We judge no less. Uncle of Exeter,
Enlarge the man committed yesterday, 40
That rail'd against our person: we consider
It was excess of wine that set him on;
And on his more advice we pardon him.

Scroop. That 's mercy, but too much security:
Let him be punish'd, sovereign, lest example
Breed, by his sufferance, more of such a kind.

K. Hen. O, let us yet be merciful.

Cam. So may your highness, and yet punish too.

Grey. Sir,
You show great mercy, if you give him life, 50
After the taste of much correction.

K. Hen. Alas, your too much love and care of me
Are heavy orisons 'gainst this poor wretch!
If little faults, proceeding on distemper,
Shall not be wink'd at, how shall we stretch our eye
When capital crimes, chew'd, swallow'd and digested,
Appear before us? We'll yet enlarge that man,
Though Cambridge, Scroop and Grey, in their dear care
And tender preservation of our person,
Would have him punish'd. And now to our French causes: 60
Who are the late commissioners?

Cam. I one, my lord:
Your highness bade me ask for it to-day.

Scroop. So did you me, my liege.

Grey. And I, my royal sovereign.

K. Hen. Then, Richard Earl of Cambridge, there is yours;
There yours, Lord Scroop of Masham; and, sir knight,
Grey of Northumberland, this same is yours:
Read them; and know, I know your worthiness.
My Lord of Westmoreland, and uncle Exeter, 70
We will aboard to night. Why, how now, gentlemen!
What see you in those papers that you lose
So much complexion? Look ye, how they change!
Their cheeks are paper. Why, what read you there,
That hath so cowarded and chased your blood
Out of appearance?

Cam. I do confess my fault;
And do submit me to your highness' mercy.

Grey.
Scroop. } To which we all appeal.

K. Hen. The mercy that was quick in us but late,
By your own counsel is suppress'd and kill'd: 80
You must not dare, for shame, to talk of mercy;
For your own reasons turn into your bosoms,

Henry
the Fifth
ACT II : SC II

745

As dogs upon their masters, worrying you.
See you, my princes and my noble peers,
These English monsters! My Lord of Cambridge here,
You know how apt our love was to accord
To furnish him with all appertinents
Belonging to his honour; and this man
Hath, for a few light crowns, lightly conspired,
And sworn unto the practices of France,   90
To kill us here in Hampton: to the which
This knight, no less for bounty bound to us
Than Cambridge is, hath likewise sworn. But, O,
What shall I say to thee, Lord Scroop? thou cruel,
Ingrateful, savage and inhuman creature!
Thou that didst bear the key of all my counsels,
That knew'st the very bottom of my soul,
That almost mightst have coin'd me into gold,
Wouldst thou have practised on me for thy use!
May it be possible, that foreign hire   100
Could out of thee extract one spark of evil
That might annoy my finger? 'tis so strange,
That, though the truth of it stands off as gross
As black and white, my eye will scarcely see it.
Treason and murder ever kept together,
As two yoke-devils sworn to either's purpose,
Working so grossly in a natural cause,
That admiration did not hoop at them:
But thou, 'gainst all proportion, didst bring in
Wonder to wait on treason and on murder: 110
And whatsoever cunning fiend it was
That wrought upon thee so preposterously
Hath got the voice in hell for excellence:
All other devils that suggest by treasons
Do botch and bungle up damnation
With patches, colours, and with forms being fetch'd
From glistering semblances of piety;
But he that temper'd thee bade thee stand up,
Gave thee no instance why thou shouldst do treason,
Unless to dub thee with the name of traitor.   120
If that same demon that hath gull'd thee thus
Should with his lion gait walk the whole world,
He might return to vasty Tartar back,
And tell the legions 'I can never win
A soul so easy as that Englishman's.'
O, how hast thou with jealousy infected
The sweetness of affiance! Show men dutiful?
Why, so didst thou: seem they grave and learned?
Why, so didst thou: come they of noble family?
Why, so didst thou: seem they religious?   130
Why, so didst thou: or are they spare in diet,
Free from gross passion or of mirth or anger,
Constant in spirit, not swerving with the blood,
Garnish'd and deck'd in modest complement,
Not working with the eye without the ear,
And but in purged judgement trusting neither?
Such and so finely bolted didst thou seem:
And thus thy fall hath left a kind of blot,
To mark the full-fraught man and best indued
With some suspicion. I will weep for thee;   140
For this revolt of thine, methinks, is like
Another fall of man. Their faults are open:

Arrest them to the answer of the law;
And God acquit them of their practices!

Exe. I arrest thee of high treason, by the name of
Richard Earl of Cambridge.
I arrest thee of high treason, by the name of Henry
Lord Scroop of Masham.
I arrest thee of high treason, by the name of Thomas
Grey, knight, of Northumberland.   150
Scroop. Our purposes God justly hath discover'd;
And I repent my fault more than my death;
Which I beseech your highness to forgive,
Although my body pay the price of it.
Cam. For me, the gold of France did not seduce;
Although I did admit it as a motive
The sooner to effect what I intended:
But God be thanked for prevention;
Which I in sufferance heartily will rejoice,
Beseeching God and you to pardon me.   160
Grey. Never did faithful subject more rejoice
At the discovery of most dangerous treason
Than I do at this hour joy o'er myself,
Prevented from a damned enterprise:
My fault, but not my body, pardon, sovereign.
K. Hen. God quit you in his mercy! Hear your
    sentence.
You have conspired against our royal person,
Join'd with an enemy proclaim'd and from his coffers
Received the golden earnest of our death;
Wherein you would have sold your king to slaughter,
His princes and his peers to servitude,   171
His subjects to oppression and contempt
And his whole kingdom into desolation.
Touching our person seek we no revenge;
But we our kingdom's safety must so tender,
Whose ruin you have sought, that to her laws
We do deliver you. Get you therefore hence,
Poor miserable wretches, to your death:
The taste whereof, God of his mercy give
You patience to endure, and true repentance   180
Of all your dear offences! Bear them hence.
            [*Exeunt Cambridge, Scroop and Grey, guarded.*
Now, lords, for France; the enterprise whereof
Shall be to you, as us, like glorious.
We doubt not of a fair and lucky war,
Since God so graciously hath brought to light
This dangerous treason lurking in our way
To hinder our beginnings. We doubt not now
But every rub is smoothed on our way.
Then forth, dear countrymen: let us deliver
Our puissance into the hand of God,   190
Putting it straight in expedition.
Cheerly to sea; the signs of war advance:
No king of England, if not king of France.   [*Exeunt.*

SCENE III. *London. Before a tavern.*

Enter PISTOL, Hostess, NYM, BARDOLPH, *and* BOY.

Host. Prithee, honey-sweet husband, let me bring
thee to Staines.

Pist. No; for my manly heart doth yearn.
Bardolph, be blithe: Nym, rouse thy vaunting veins:
Boy, bristle thy courage up; for Falstaff he is dead,
And we must yearn therefore.

Bard. Would I were with him, wheresome'er he is,
either in heaven or in hell! 8

Host. Nay, sure, he's not in hell: he's in Arthur's
bosom, if ever man went to Arthur's bosom. A' made
a finer end and went away an it had been any christom
child; a' parted even just between twelve and one,
even at the turning o' the tide: for after I saw him
fumble with the sheets and play with flowers and
smile upon his fingers' ends, I knew there was but one
way; for his nose was as sharp as a pen, and a' babbled
of green fields. 'How now, Sir John!' quoth I: 'what,
man! be o' good cheer.' So a' cried out, 'God, God,
God!' three or four times. Now I, to comfort him, bid
him a' should not think of God; I hoped there was no
need to trouble himself with any such thoughts yet.
So a' bade me lay more clothes on his feet: I put my
hand into the bed and felt them, and they were as
cold as any stone; then I felt to his knees, and they
were as cold as any stone, and so upward and upward, and all was as cold as any stone.

Nym. They say he cried out of sack.

Host. Ay, that a' did. 30

Bard. And of women.

Host. Nay, that a' did not.

Boy. Yes, that a' did; and said they were devils
incarnate.

Host. A' could never abide carnation; 'twas a
colour he never liked.

Boy. A' said once, the devil would have him about
women.

Host. A' did in some sort, indeed, handle women;
but then he was rheumatic, and talked of the whore of
Babylon. 41

Boy. Do you not remember, a' saw a flea stick upon
Bardolph's nose, and a' said it was a black soul burning in hell-fire?

Bard. Well, the fuel is gone that maintained that
fire: that's all the riches I got in his service.

Nym. Shall we shog? the king will be gone from
Southampton.

Pist. Come, let's away. My love, give me thy lips.
Look to my chattels and my movables: 50
Let senses rule; the word is 'Pitch and Pay:'
Trust none;
For oaths are straws, men's faiths are wafer-cakes,
And hold-fast is the only dog, my duck:
Therefore, Caveto be thy counsellor.
Go, clear thy crystals. Yoke-fellows in arms,
Let us to France; like horse-leeches, my boys,
To suck, to suck, the very blood to suck!

Boy. And that's but unwholesome food, they
    say. 60

Pist. Touch her soft mouth, and march.

Bard. Farewell, hostess. [*Kissing her.*

Nym. I cannot kiss, that is the humour of it; but,
adieu.

Pist. Let housewifery appear: keep close, I thee
    command.

Host. Farewell; adieu. [*Exeunt.*

SCENE IV. *France. The* KING's *palace.*

Flourish. Enter the FRENCH KING, *the* DAUPHIN, *the*
DUKES OF BERRI *and* BRETAGNE, *the* CONSTABLE,
and others.

Fr. King. Thus comes the English with full power
    upon us;
And more than carefully it us concerns
To answer royally in our defences.
Therefore the Dukes of Berri and of Bretagne,
Of Brabant and of Orleans, shall make forth,
And you, Prince Dauphin, with all swift dispatch,
To line and new repair our towns of war
With men of courage and with means defendant;
For England his approaches makes as fierce
As waters to the sucking of a gulf. 10
It fits us then to be as provident
As fear may teach us out of late examples
Left by the fatal and neglected English
Upon our fields.

Dau.   My most redoubted father,
It is most meet we arm us 'gainst the foe;
For peace itself should not so dull a kingdom,
Though war nor no known quarrel were in question,
But that defences, musters, preparations,
Should be maintain'd, assembled and collected,
As were a war in expectation. 20
Therefore, I say 'tis meet we all go forth
To view the sick and feeble parts of France:
And let us do it with no show of fear;
No, with no more than if we heard that England
Were busied with a Whitsun morris-dance:
For, my good liege, she is so idly king'd,
Her sceptre so fantastically borne
By a vain, giddy, shallow, humorous youth,
That fear attends her not.

Con.   O peace, Prince Dauphin!
You are too much mistaken in this king: 30
Question your grace the late ambassadors,
With what great state he heard their embassy,
How well supplied with noble counsellors,
How modest in exception, and withal
How terrible in constant resolution,
And you shall find his vanities forespent
Were but the outside of the Roman Brutus,
Covering discretion with a coat of folly;
As gardeners do with ordure hide those roots
That shall first spring and be most delicate. 40

Dau. Well, 'tis not so, my lord high constable;
But though we think it so, it is no matter:
In cases of defence 'tis best to weigh
The enemy more mighty than he seems:
So the proportions of defence are fill'd;
Which of a weak and niggardly projection

---

probably the latter, since, if the child died, the chrisom was used as a
shroud. 18. **a' babbled of green fields.** This line contains Theobald's
famous emendation. F has *and a Table of greene fields.* Falstaff would seem
to have been reciting the Twenty-third Psalm. 44. **black soul burning
in hell-fire,** a reminiscence of the play of Doomsday in the mystery
plays. 51. **senses,** possibly, common sense. 'Pitch and Pay,' proverbial for "cash payment"; supposed to be derived from a rule at Cloth-
Hall in London that, when a bale of cloth was deposited (*pitched*), a

penny must be paid. 54. **hold-fast.** Cf. the proverb, "Brag is a good
dog, but hold-fast is a better." 55. **Caveto,** be cautious; Latin imperative of *caveo.* 56. **clear thy crystals,** wipe thine eyes.
SCENE IV. 25. **Whitsun morris-dance,** dance performed on various
holidays by persons in fancy costumes. 28. **humorous,** capricious. 34.
exception, making objections. 37. **Brutus.** The elder Brutus pretended
insanity in order to overthrow the Tarquins. 46. **Which . . . projection,** i.e., defense is futile if calculated on a niggardly scale.

Doth, like a miser, spoil his coat with scanting
A little cloth.
Fr. King.   Think we King Harry
    strong;
And, princes, look you strongly arm to meet him.
The kindred of him hath been flesh'd upon us;   50
And he is bred out of that bloody strain
That haunted us in our familiar paths:
Witness our too much memorable shame
When Cressy battle fatally was struck,
And all our princes captived by the hand
Of that black name, Edward, Black Prince of Wales;
Whiles that his mountain sire, on mountain standing,
Up in the air, crown'd with the golden sun,
Saw his heroical seed, and smiled to see him,
Mangle the work of nature and deface   60
The patterns that by God and by French fathers
Had twenty years been made. This is a stem
Of that victorious stock; and let us fear
The native mightiness and fate of him.

Enter a Messenger.

Mess. Ambassadors from Harry King of England
Do crave admittance to your majesty.
    Fr. King. We'll give them present audience. Go, and
      bring them.   [*Exeunt Messenger and certain Lords.*
You see this chase is hotly follow'd, friends.
    Dau. Turn head, and stop pursuit; for coward
      dogs
Most spend their mouths when what they seem to
    threaten   70
Runs far before them. Good my sovereign,
Take up the English short, and let them know
Of what a monarchy you are the head:
Self-love, my liege, is not so vile a sin
As self-neglecting.

    Re-enter Lords, *with* EXETER *and train.*

    Fr. King.   From our brother England?
    Exe. From him; and thus he greets your majesty.
He wills you, in the name of God Almighty,
That you divest yourself, and lay apart
The borrow'd glories that by gift of heaven,
By law of nature and of nations, 'long   80
To him and to his heirs; namely, the crown
And all wide-stretched honours that pertain
By custom and the ordinance of times
Unto the crown of France. That you may know
'Tis no sinister nor no awkward claim,
Pick'd from the worm-holes of long-vanish'd days,
Nor from the dust of old oblivion raked,
He sends you this most memorable line,
In every branch truly demonstrative;
Willing you overlook this pedigree: 90
And when you find him evenly derived
From his most famed of famous ancestors,
Edward the Third, he bids you then resign
Your crown and kingdom, indirectly held
From him the native and true challenger.
    Fr. King. Or else what follows?
    Exe. Bloody constraint; for if you hide the crown

Even in your hearts, there will he rake for it:
Therefore in fierce tempest is he coming,
In thunder and in earthquake, like a Jove,   100
That, if requiring fail, he will compel;
And bids you, in the bowels of the Lord,
Deliver up the crown, and to take mercy
On the poor souls for whom this hungry war
Opens his vasty jaws; and on your head
Turning the widows' tears, the orphans' cries,
The dead men's blood, the pining maidens' groans,
For husbands, fathers and betrothed lovers,
That shall be swallow'd in this controversy.
This is his claim, his threatening, and my message;   110
Unless the Dauphin be in presence here,
To whom expressly I bring greeting too.
    Fr. King. For us, we will consider of this further:
To-morrow shall you bear our full intent
Back to our brother England.
    Dau.   For the Dauphin,
I stand here for him: what to him from England?
    Exe. Scorn and defiance; slight regard, contempt,
And any thing that may not misbecome
The mighty sender, doth he prize you at.
Thus says my king; an if your father's highness   120
Do not, in grant of all demands at large,
Sweeten the bitter mock you sent his majesty,
He'll call you to so hot an answer of it,
That caves and womby vaultages of France
Shall chide your trespass and return your mock
In second accent of his ordnance.
    Dau. Say, if my father render fair return,
It is against my will; for I desire
Nothing but odds with England: to that end,
As matching to his youth and vanity,   130
I did present him with the Paris balls.
    Exe. He'll make your Paris Louvre shake for it,
Were it the mistress-court of mighty Europe:
And, be assured, you'll find a difference,
As we his subjects have in wonder found,
Between the promise of his greener days
And these he masters now: now he weighs time
Even to the utmost grain: that you shall read
In your own losses, if he stay in France.
    Fr. King. To-morrow shall you know our mind at
      full.   140
    Exe. Dispatch us with all speed, lest that our king
Come here himself to question our delay;
For he is footed in this land already.
    Fr. King. You shall be soon dispatch'd with fair
      conditions:
A night is but small breath and little pause
To answer matters of this consequence.
                        [*Flourish. Exeunt.*

ACT III.

PROLOGUE.

Enter Chorus.

Chor. Thus with imagined wing our swift scene flies

48-64. **Think . . . him.** This is a passage of exaggerated patriotism on
Shakespeare's part, the tendency of which is to belittle the enemy. It is
inconceivable that the French should talk so. There is much of this
chauvinism in *Henry V.*   64. **fate,** what he is destined to do.   70. **spend
their mouths,** bay.   80. **law of nature and of nations.** This seems to be a
reference to the current theory that international law is derived from
the law of nature. **'long,** belong.   88. **line,** pedigree.   91. **evenly,**

directly.   102. **bowels,** mercy. Cf. Philippians 1:8.   124. **womby
vaultages,** deep caverns.   131. **Paris balls,** tennis balls.   132. **Louvre,**
the French royal palace.   136. **greener,** younger, cruder.
    ACT III. PROLOGUE.   1. **imagined wing,** wings of imagination.   14.
rivage, banks.   18. **to sternage,** astern.   33. **linstock,** staff holding a
gunner's match. *Stage Direction: chambers,* small cannon.
    SCENE I.   6-17. **Then . . . height.** This passage indicates Shake-

In motion of no less celerity
Than that of thought. Suppose that you have seen
The well-appointed king at Hampton pier
Embark his royalty; and his brave fleet
With silken streamers the young Phœbus fanning:
Play with your fancies, and in them behold
Upon the hempen tackle ship-boys climbing;
Hear the shrill whistle which doth order give
To sounds confused; behold the threaden sails,   10
Borne with the invisible and creeping wind,
Draw the huge bottoms through the furrow'd sea,
Breasting the lofty surge: O, do but think
You stand upon the rivage and behold
A city on the inconstant billows dancing;
For so appears this fleet majestical,
Holding due course to Harfleur. Follow, follow:
Grapple your minds to sternage of this navy,
And leave your England, as dead midnight still,
Guarded with grandsires, babies and old women,   20
Either past or not arrived to pith and puissance;
For who is he, whose chin is but enrich'd
With one appearing hair, that will not follow
These cull'd and choice-drawn cavaliers to France?
Work, work your thoughts, and therein see a siege;
Behold the ordnance on their carriages,
With fatal mouths gaping on girded Harfleur.
Suppose the ambassador from the French comes back;
Tells Harry that the king doth offer him
Katharine his daughter, and with her, to dowry,   30
Some petty and unprofitable dukedoms.
The offer likes not: and the nimble gunner
With linstock now the devilish cannon touches,
        [Alarum, and chambers go off.
And down goes all before them. Still be kind,
And eke out our performance with your mind.   [Exit.

SCENE I. *France. Before Harfleur.*

Alarum. Enter KING HENRY, EXETER, BEDFORD,
GLOUCESTER, *and* Soldiers, *with scaling-ladders.*

K. Hen. Once more unto the breach, dear friends,
        once more;
Or close the wall up with our English dead.
In peace there's nothing so becomes a man
As modest stillness and humility:
But when the blast of war blows in our ears,
Then imitate the action of the tiger;
Stiffen the sinews, summon up the blood,
Disguise fair nature with hard-favour'd rage;
Then lend the eye a terrible aspect;
Let it pry through the portage of the head   10
Like the brass cannon; let the brow o'erwhelm it
As fearfully as doth a galled rock
O'erhang and jutty his confounded base,
Swill'd with the wild and wasteful ocean.
Now set the teeth and stretch the nostril wide,
Hold hard the breath and bend up every spirit
To his full height. On, on, you noblest English,
Whose blood is fet from fathers of war-proof!

Fathers that, like so many Alexanders,
Have in these parts from morn till even fought   20
And sheathed their swords for lack of argument:
Dishonour not your mothers; now attest
That those whom you call'd fathers did beget you.
Be copy now to men of grosser blood,
And teach them how to war. And you, good yeomen,
Whose limbs were made in England, show us here
The mettle of your pasture; let us swear
That you are worth your breeding; which I doubt
        not;
For there is none of you so mean and base,
That hath not noble lustre in your eyes.   30
I see you stand like greyhounds in the slips,
Straining upon the start. The game's afoot:
Follow your spirit, and upon this charge
Cry 'God for Harry, England, and Saint George!'
        [Exeunt. Alarum, and chambers go off.

SCENE II. *The same.*

Enter NYM, BARDOLPH, PISTOL, *and* BOY.

Bard. On, on, on, on, on! to the breach, to the
breach!
Nym. Pray thee, corporal, stay: the knocks are too
hot; and, for mine own part, I have not a case of lives:
the humour of it is too hot, that is the very plain-song
of it.
Pist. The plain-song is most just; for humours do
        abound:
Knocks go and come; God's vassals drop and die;
        And sword and shield,
        In bloody field,   10
        Doth win immortal fame.
Boy. Would I were in an alehouse in London! I
would give all my fame for a pot of ale and safety.
Pist. And I:
        If wishes would prevail with me,
        My purpose should not fail with me,
        But thither would I hie.
Boy. As duly, but not as truly,
        As bird doth sing on bough.   20

Enter FLUELLEN.

Flu. Up to the breach, you dogs! avaunt, you
cullions!   [*Driving them forward.*
Pist. Be merciful, great duke, to men of mould.
Abate thy rage, abate thy manly rage,
Abate thy rage, great duke!
Good bawcock, bate thy rage; use lenity, sweet
        chuck!
Nym. These be good humours! your honour wins
bad humours.   [*Exeunt all but Boy.* 28
Boy. As young as I am, I have observed these three
swashers. I am boy to them all three: but all they
three, though they would serve me, could not be man
to me; for indeed three such antics do not amount to a
man. For Bardolph, he is white-livered and red-faced;
by the means whereof a' faces it out, but fights not.
For Pistol, he hath a killing tongue and a quiet sword;

---

speare's theory of the operations of the passions. Everywhere he entertains the idea that the spiritual depends upon the physical state. 10.
portage, porthole. 11. **o'erwhelm,** project over. 12. **galled,** washed
away, undermined. 13. **jutty,** overhang. 14. **Swill'd,** washed. 18.
fet, fetched. **war-proof,** proved in war. 27. **mettle of your pasture,**
quality of your breeding (literally, "feeding"). 31. **slips,** leashes.
    SCENE II. 5. **case,** set. 6. **plain-song,** air without any variations.

Nym probably means "that is the truth of the matter." 22. **cullions,**
rascals. 23. **men of mould,** mere mortals. 26. **bawcock,** French, *beau
coq,* fine fellow. **chuck,** a term of endearment. 30. **swashers,** swashbucklers. 33. **antics,** grotesque figures. 34. **white-livered,** cowardly.
In extreme fear the blood was thought to sink below the liver, leaving
it bloodless.

by the means whereof a' breaks words, and keeps whole weapons. For Nym, he hath heard that men of few words are the best men; and therefore he scorns to say his prayers, lest a' should be thought a coward: but his few bad words are matched with as few good deeds; for a' never broke any man's head but his own, and that was against a post when he was drunk. They will steal any thing, and call it purchase. Bardolph stole a lute-case, bore it twelve leagues, and sold it for three half-pence. Nym and Bardolph are sworn brothers in filching, and in Calais they stole a fire-shovel: I knew by that piece of service the men would carry coals. They would have me as familiar with men's pockets as their gloves or their handkerchers: which makes much against my manhood, if I should take from another's pocket to put into mine; for it is plain pocketing up of wrongs. I must leave them, and seek some better service: their villany goes against my weak stomach, and therefore I must cast it up. [*Exit.* 57

Re-enter FLUELLEN, GOWER *following.*

Gow. Captain Fluellen, you must come presently to the mines; the Duke of Gloucester would speak with you. 60

Flu. To the mines! tell you the duke, it is not so good to come to the mines; for, look you, the mines is not according to the disciplines of the war: the concavities of it is not sufficient; for, look you, th' athversary, you may discuss unto the duke, look you, is digt himself four yard under the countermines: by Cheshu, I think a' will plow up all, if there is not better directions. 68

Gow. The Duke of Gloucester, to whom the order of the siege is given, is altogether directed by an Irishman, a very valiant gentleman, i' faith.

Flu. It is Captain Macmorris, is it not?

Gow. I think it be. 73

Flu. By Cheshu, he is an ass, as in the world: I will verify as much in his beard: he has no more directions in the true disciplines of the wars, look you, of the Roman disciplines, than is a puppy-dog.

Enter MACMORRIS *and* Captain JAMY.

Gow. Here a' comes; and the Scots captain, Captain Jamy, with him. 80

Flu. Captain Jamy is a marvellous falorous gentleman, that is certain; and of great expedition and knowledge in th' aunchient wars, upon my particular knowledge of his directions: by Cheshu, he will maintain his argument as well as any military man in the world, in the disciplines of the pristine wars of the Romans.

Jamy. I say gud-day, Captain Fluellen.

Flu. God-den to your worship, good Captain James. 90

Gow. How now, Captain Macmorris! have you

quit the mines? have the pioners given o'er?

Mac. By Chrish, la! tish ill done: the work ish give over, the trompet sound the retreat. By my hand, I swear, and my father's soul, the work ish ill done; it ish give over: I would have blowed up the town, so Chrish save me, la! in an hour: O, tish ill done, tish ill done; by my hand, tish ill done! 99

Flu. Captain Macmorris, I beseech you now, will you voutsafe me, look you, a few disputations with you, as partly touching or concerning the disciplines of the war, the Roman wars, in the way of argument, look you, and friendly communication; partly to satisfy my opinion, and partly for the satisfaction, look you, of my mind, as touching the direction of the military discipline; that is the point.

Jamy. It sall be vary gud, gud feith, gud captains bath: and I sall quit you with gud leve, as I may pick occasion; that sall I, marry. 111

Mac. It is no time to discourse, so Chrish save me: the day is hot, and the weather, and the wars, and the king, and the dukes: it is no time to discourse. The town is beseeched, and the trumpet call us to the breach; and we talk, and, be Chrish, do nothing: 'tis shame for us all: so God sa' me, 'tis shame to stand still; it is shame, by my hand: and there is throats to be cut, and works to be done; and there ish nothing done, so Chrish sa' me, la! 121

Jamy. By the mess, ere theise eyes of mine take themselves to slomber, ay'll de gud service, or ay'll lig i' the grund for it; ay, or go to death; and ay'll pay 't as valorously as I may, that sall I suerly do, that is the breff and the long. Marry, I wad full fain hear some question 'tween you tway.

Flu. Captain Macmorris, I think, look you, under your correction, there is not many of your nation— 131

Mac. Of my nation! What ish my nation? Ish a villain, and a bastard, and a knave, and a rascal— What ish my nation? Who talks of my nation?

Flu. Look you, if you take the matter otherwise than is meant, Captain Macmorris, peradventure I shall think you do not use me with that affability as in discretion you ought to use me, look you; being as good a man as yourself, both in the disciplines of war, and in the derivation of my birth, and in other particularities. 142

Mac. I do not know you so good a man as myself: so Chrish save me, I will cut off your head.

Gow. Gentlemen both, you will mistake each other.

Jamy. A! that 's a foul fault. [*A parley sounded.*

Gow. The town sounds a parley. 149

Flu. Captain Macmorris, when there is more better opportunity to be required, look you, I will be so bold as to tell you I know the disciplines of war; and there is an end. [*Exeunt.*

SCENE III. *The same. Before the gates.*

The Governor *and some* Citizens *on the walls; the*
English forces below. Enter KING HENRY *and his*
train.

K. Hen. How yet resolves the governor of the town?
This is the latest parle we will admit:
Therefore to our best mercy give yourselves;
Or like to men proud of destruction
Defy us to our worst: for, as I am a soldier,
A name that in my thoughts becomes me best,
If I begin the battery once again,
I will not leave the half-achieved Harfleur
Till in her ashes she lie buried.
The gates of mercy shall be all shut up,   10
And the flesh'd soldier, rough and hard of heart,
In liberty of bloody hand shall range
With conscience wide as hell, mowing like grass
Your fresh-fair virgins and your flowering infants.
What is it then to me, if impious war,
Array'd in flames like to the prince of fiends,
Do, with his smirch'd complexion, all fell feats
Enlink'd to waste and desolation?
What is 't to me, when you yourselves are cause,
If your pure maidens fall into the hand   20
Of hot and forcing violation?
What rein can hold licentious wickedness
When down the hill he holds his fierce career?
We may as bootless spend our vain command
Upon the enraged soldiers in their spoil
As send precepts to the leviathan
To come ashore. Therefore, you men of Harfleur,
Take pity of your town and of your people,
Whiles yet my soldiers are in my command;
Whiles yet the cool and temperate wind of grace   30
O'erblows the filthy and contagious clouds
Of heady murder, spoil and villany.
If not, why, in a moment look to see
The blind and bloody soldier with foul hand
Defile the locks of your shrill-shrieking daughters;
Your fathers taken by the silver beards,
And their most reverend heads dash'd to the walls,
Your naked infants spitted upon pikes,
Whiles the mad mothers with their howls confused
Do break the clouds, as did the wives of Jewry   40
At Herod's bloody-hunting slaughtermen.
What say you? will you yield, and this avoid,
Or, guilty in defence, be thus destroy'd?

Gov. Our expectation hath this day an end:
The Dauphin, whom of succours we entreated,
Returns us that his powers are yet not ready
To raise so great a siege. Therefore, great king,
We yield our town and lives to thy soft mercy.
Enter our gates; dispose of us and ours;
For we no longer are defensible.   50

K. Hen. Open your gates. Come, uncle Exeter,
Go you and enter Harfleur; there remain,
And fortify it strongly 'gainst the French:
Use mercy to them all. For us, dear uncle,
The winter coming on and sickness growing
Upon our soldiers, we will retire to Calais.
To-night in Harfleur will we be your guest;
To-morrow for the march are we addrest.
       [*Flourish. The king and his train enter the town.*

SCENE IV. *The* FRENCH KING'S *palace.*

Enter KATHARINE *and* ALICE.

Kath. Alice, tu as été en Angleterre, et tu parles bien
le langage.

Alice. Un peu, madame.

Kath. Je te prie, m'enseignez; il faut que j'apprenne
à parler. Comment appelez-vous la main en Anglois?

Alice. La main? elle est appelée de hand.

Kath. De hand. Et les doigts?

Alice. Les doigts? ma foi, j'oublie les doigts; mais je
me souviendrai. Les doigts? je pense qu'ils sont ap-
pelés de fingres; oui, de fingres.   11

Kath. La main, de hand; les doigts, de fingres. Je
pense que je suis le bon écolier; j'ai gagné deux mots
d'Anglois vîtement. Comment appelez-vous les ongles?

Alice. Les ongles? nous les appelons de nails.

Kath. De nails. Écoutez; dites-moi, si je parle bien:
de hand, de fingres, et de nails.

Alice. C'est bien dit, madame; il est fort bon
Anglois.   20

Kath. Dites-moi l'Anglois pour le bras.

Alice. De arm, madame.

Kath. Et le coude?

Alice. De elbow.

Kath. De elbow. Je m'en fais la répétition de tous les
mots que vous m'avez appris dès à présent.

Alice. Il est trop difficile, madame, comme je pense.

Kath. Excusez-moi, Alice; écoutez: de hand, de
fingres, de nails, de arma, de bilbow.

Alice. De elbow, madame.   32

Kath. O Seigneur Dieu, je m'en oublie! de elbow.
Comment appelez-vous le col?

Alice. De neck, madame.

Kath. De nick. Et le menton?

Alice. De chin.

Kath. De sin. Le col, de nick; le menton, de sin.   39

Alice. Oui. Sauf votre honneur, en vérite, vous
prononcez les mots aussi droit que les natifs d'Angleterre.

Kath. Je ne doute point d'apprendre, par la grace de
Dieu, et en peu de temps.

Alice. N'avez vous pas déjà oublié ce que je vous ai
enseigné?

Henry
the Fifth
ACT III : SC IV

75I

---

clever scholar; I have learned two English words in no time. What do
you call *les ongles?*
    Alice. Les ongles? We call them de nails.
    Kath. De nails. Listen; tell me whether or not I speak correctly:
de hand, de fingres, and de nails.
    Alice. That is correct, my lady; it is very good English.
    Kath. Tell me the English for *le bras.*
    Alice. De arm, my lady.
    Kath. And *le coude?*
    Alice. De elbow.
    Kath. De elbow. I am going to repeat all the words you have taught
me so far.
    Alice. It is too hard, my lady, I fear.
    Kath. Pardon me, Alice; listen: de hand, de fingres, de nails, de

arma, de bilbow.
    Alice. De elbow, my lady.
    Kath. O Lord, I can't remember! de elbow. What do you call *le col?*
    Alice. De neck, my lady.
    Kath. De nick. And *le menton?*
    Alice. De chin.
    Kath. De sin. *Le col,* de nick; *le menton,* de sin.
    Alice. Yes. On my word, really you pronounce the words just as
English people themselves do.
    Kath. I have no doubt that I shall learn, with God's help, in a very
short time.
    Alice. Have you not already forgotten what I have taught you?

Kath. Non, je reciterai à vous promptement: de hand, de fingres, de mails,—

Alice. De nails, madame.

Kath. De nails, de arm, de ilbow.

Alice. Sauf votre honneur, de elbow.   50

Kath. Ainsi dis-je; de elbow, de nick, et de sin. Comment appelez-vous le pied et la robe?

Alice. De foot, madame; et de coun.

Kath. De foot et de coun! O Seigneur Dieu! ce sont mots de son mauvais, corruptible, gros, et impudique, et non pour les dames d'honneur d'user: je ne voudrais prononcer ces mots devant les seigneurs de France pour tout le monde. Foh! le foot et le coun! Néanmoins, je réciterai une autre fois ma leçon ensemble: de hand, de fingres, de nails, de arm, de elbow, de nick, de sin, de foot, de coun.

Alice. Excellent, madame!

Kath. C'est assez pour une fois: allons-nous à dîner.

[*Exeunt.*

SCENE V. *The same.*

Enter the KING OF FRANCE, *the* DAUPHIN, *the* DUKE OF BOURBON, *the* CONSTABLE OF FRANCE, *and others.*

Fr. King. 'Tis certain he hath pass'd the river
       Somme.

Con. And if he be not fought withal, my lord,
Let us not live in France; let us quit all
And give our vineyards to a barbarous people.

Dau. O Dieu vivant! shall a few sprays of us,
The emptying of our fathers' luxury,
Our scions, put in wild and savage stock,
Spirt up so suddenly into the clouds,
And overlook their grafters?

Bour. Normans, but bastard Normans, Norman
       bastards!   10
Mort de ma vie! if they march along
Unfought withal, but I will sell my dukedom,
To buy a slobbery and a dirty farm
In that nook-shotten isle of Albion.

Con. Dieu de batailles! where have they this mettle?
Is not their climate foggy, raw and dull,
On whom, as in despite, the sun looks pale,
Killing their fruit with frowns? Can sodden water,
A drench for sur-rein'd jades, their barley-broth,
Decoct their cold blood to such valiant heat?   20
And shall our quick blood, spirited with wine,
Seem frosty? O, for honour of our land,
Let us not hang like roping icicles
Upon our houses' thatch, whiles a more frosty people
Sweat drops of gallant youth in our rich fields!
Poor we may call them in their native lords.

Dau. By faith and honour,
Our madams mock at us, and plainly say
Our mettle is bred out and they will give
Their bodies to the lust of English youth   30
To new-store France with bastard warriors.

Bour. They bid us to the English dancing-schools,
And teach lavoltas high and swift corantos;
Saying our grace is only in our heels,
And that we are most lofty runaways.

Fr. King. Where is Montjoy the herald? speed him
       hence:
Let him greet England with our sharp defiance.
Up, princes! and, with spirit of honour edged
More sharper than your swords, hie to the field:
Charles Delabreth, high constable of France;   40
You Dukes of Orleans, Bourbon, and of Berri,
Alençon, Brabant, Bar, and Burgundy;
Jaques Chatillon, Rambures, Vaudemont,
Beaumont, Grandpré, Roussi, and Fauconberg,
Foix, Lestrale, Bouciqualt, and Charolois;
High dukes, great princes, barons, lords and knights,
For your great seats now quit you of great shames.
Bar Harry England, that sweeps through our land
With pennons painted in the blood of Harfleur:
Rush on his host, as doth the melted snow   50
Upon the valleys, whose low vassal seat
The Alps doth spit and void his rheum upon:
Go down upon him, you have power enough,
And in a captive chariot into Rouen
Bring him our prisoner.

Con.   This becomes the great.
Sorry am I his numbers are so few,
His soldiers sick and famish'd in their march,
For I am sure, when he shall see our army,
He'll drop his heart into the sink of fear
And for achievement offer us his ransom.   60

Fr. King. Therefore, lord constable, haste on
       Montjoy,
And let him say to England that we send
To know what willing ransom he will give.
Prince Dauphin, you shall stay with us in Rouen.

Dau. Not so, I do beseech your majesty.

Fr. King. Be patient, for you shall remain with us.
Now forth, lord constable and princes all,
And quickly bring us word of England's fall.   [*Exeunt.*

SCENE VI. *The English camp in Picardy.*

Enter GOWER *and* FLUELLEN, *meeting.*

Gow. How now, Captain Fluellen! come you from the bridge?

Flu. I assure you, there is very excellent services committed at the bridge.

Gow. Is the Duke of Exeter safe?

Flu. The Duke of Exeter is as magnanimous as Agamemnon; and a man that I love and honour with my soul, and my heart, and my duty, and my life, and my living, and my uttermost power: he is not—God be praised and blessed!—any hurt in the world; but keeps the bridge most valiantly, with excellent discipline. There is an aunchient lieutenant there at the pridge, I think in my very conscience he is as valiant

Kath. No, I shall recite to you at once: de hand, de fingres, de mails—
Alice. De nails, my lady.
Kath. De nails, de arm, de ilbow.
Alice. By your leave, de elbow.
Kath. That's what I said; de elbow, de nick, and de sin. What do you call *le pied* and *la robe*?
Alice. De foot, my lady; and de coun.
Kath. De foot and de coun! O Lord! those are naughty words, wicked, coarse, and immodest, and are not fit to be used by nice ladies; I wouldn't say those words before French gentlemen for the whole world. Bah! le foot and le coun! Nevertheless, I shall recite my whole lesson once more: de hand, de fingres, de nails, de arm, de elbow, de nick, de sin, de foot, de coun.
Alice. Excellent, my lady.
Kath. That's enough for one time; let's go to dinner.
SCENE V. 5. **sprays,** branches. 6. **luxury,** lust. 9. **overlook,** rise above. **grafters,** trees from which scions are taken. 14. **nook-shotten,**

a man as Mark Antony; and he is a man of no estimation in the world; but I did see him do as gallant
service.

Gow. What do you call him?

Flu. He is called Aunchient Pistol.

Gow. I know him not.   20

Enter PISTOL.

Flu. Here is the man.

Pist. Captain, I thee beseech to do me favours:
The Duke of Exeter doth love thee well.

Flu. Ay, I praise God; and I have merited some
love at his hands.

Pist. Bardolph, a soldier, firm and sound of heart,
And of buxom valour, hath, by cruel fate,
And giddy Fortune's furious fickle wheel,
That goddess blind,
That stands upon the rolling restless stone—   30

Flu. By your patience, Aunchient Pistol. Fortune is
painted blind, with a muffler afore her eyes, to signify
to you that Fortune is blind; and she is painted also
with a wheel, to signify to you, which is the moral of it,
that she is turning, and inconstant, and mutability,
and variation: and her foot, look you, is fixed upon a
spherical stone, which rolls, and rolls, and rolls: in
good truth, the poet makes a most excellent description of it: Fortune is an excellent moral.   40

Pist. Fortune is Bardolph's foe, and frowns on him;
For he hath stolen a pax, and hanged must a' be:
A damned death!
Let gallows gape for dog; let man go free
And let not hemp his wind-pipe suffocate:
But Exeter hath given the doom of death
For pax of little price.
Therefore, go speak; the duke will hear thy voice;
And let not Bardolph's vital thread be cut
With edge of penny cord and vile reproach: 50
Speak, captain, for his life, and I will thee requite.

Flu. Aunchient Pistol, I do partly understand your
meaning.

Pist. Why then, rejoice therefore.

Flu. Certainly, aunchient, it is not a thing to rejoice
at: for if, look you, he were my brother, I would desire
the duke to use his good pleasure, and put him to
execution; for discipline ought to be used.

Pist. Die and be damn'd! and figo for thy
    friendship!   60

Flu. It is well.

Pist. The fig of Spain!   [*Exit.*

Flu. Very good.

Gow. Why, this is an arrant counterfeit rascal; I
remember him now; a bawd, a cutpurse.

Flu. I'll assure you, a' uttered as prave words at the
pridge as you shall see in a summer's day. But it is
very well; what he has spoke to me, that is well, I
warrant you, when time is serve.   69

Gow. Why, 'tis a gull, a fool, a rogue, that now and
then goes to the wars, to grace himself at his return
into London under the form of a soldier. And such

fellows are perfect in the great commanders' names:
and they will learn you by rote where services were
done; at such and such a sconce, at such a breach, at
such a convoy; who came off bravely, who was shot,
who disgraced, what terms the enemy stood on; and
this they con perfectly in the phrase of war, which they
trick up with new-tuned oaths: and what a beard of
the general's cut and a horrid suit of the camp will do
among foaming bottles and ale-washed wits, is wonderful to be thought on. But you must learn to know
such slanders of the age, or else you may be marvellously mistook.   85

Flu. I tell you what, Captain Gower; I do perceive
he is not the man that he would gladly make show to
the world he is: if I find a hole in his coat, I will tell
him my mind. [*Drum heard.*] Hark you, the king is
coming, and I must speak with him from the pridge. 91

Drum and colours. Enter KING HENRY, GLOUCESTER,
    and Soldiers.

God pless your majesty!

K. Hen. How now, Fluellen! camest thou from the
    bridge?

Flu. Ay, so please your majesty. The Duke of
Exeter has very gallantly maintained the pridge: the
French is gone off, look you; and there is gallant and
most prave passages; marry, th' athversary was have
possession of the pridge; but he is enforced to retire,
and the Duke of Exeter is master of the pridge: I can
tell your majesty, the duke is a prave man.   101

K. Hen. What men have you lost, Fluellen?

Flu. The perdition of th' athversary hath been very
great, reasonable great: marry, for my part, I think
the duke hath lost never a man, but one that is like to
be executed for robbing a church, one Bardolph, if
your majesty know the man: his face is all bubukles,
and whelks, and knobs, and flames o' fire: and his lips
blows at his nose, and it is like a coal of fire, sometimes
plue and sometimes red; but his nose is executed, and
his fire 's out.   111

K. Hen. We would have all such offenders so cut off:
and we give express charge, that in our marches
through the country, there be nothing compelled
from the villages, nothing taken but paid for, none of
the French upbraided or abused in disdainful language; for when lenity and cruelty play for a kingdom, the gentler gamester is the soonest winner.   120

Tucket. Enter MONTJOY.

Mont. You know me by my habit.

K. Hen. Well then I know thee: what shall I know
    of thee?

Mont. My master's mind.

K. Hen. Unfold it.

Mont. Thus says my king: Say thou to Harry of
England: Though we seemed dead, we did but sleep:
advantage is a better soldier than rashness. Tell him
we could have rebuked him at Harfleur, but that we
thought not good to bruise an injury till it were full

full of nooks and angles. **18. sodden,** boiled. **19. sur-rein'd jades,**
overridden horses. **barley-broth,** beer. **20. Decoct,** warm up. **23.
roping,** hanging down like a rope. **33. lavoltas, corantos,** fashionable
dances. **36. Montjoy,** title of the chief herald of France. Shakespeare
apparently took it for a name. **52. void his rheum,** spit.
SCENE VI. **2. bridge.** According to Holinshed, the French were
beaten in their attempt to break down the bridge over the Ternois. **13.
aunchient lieutenant.** Fluellen, who is at this time impressed with Pistol,
gives him two titles. **27. buxom,** lively. **42. pax.** Holinshed describes

the object stolen as a *pyx*, the vessel containing the consecrated host.
Shakespeare may have changed this into *pax*, a plate stamped with a
picture of Christ, since the offense would be less shocking. **60. figo,**
fig. **70. gull,** dupe. **76. sconce,** a fort. **103. perdition,** losses.
108. bubukles. Fluellen confuses "bubo" and "carbuncle." **109.
whelks,** boils. **110-111. and his lips . . . fire.** This is the last of the
many jokes about Bardolph's fiery face. **120.** *Stage Direction:* **Tucket,**
trumpet signal. **121. habit,** tabard, herald's coat.

ripe: now we speak upon our cue, and our voice is imperial: England shall repent his folly, see his weakness, and admire our sufferance. Bid him therefore consider of his ransom; which must proportion the losses we have borne, the subjects we have lost, the disgrace we have digested; which in weight to reanswer, his pettiness would bow under. For our losses, his exchequer is too poor; for the effusion of our blood, the muster of his kingdom too faint a number; and for our disgrace, his own person, kneeling at our feet, but a weak and worthless satisfaction. To this add defiance: and tell him, for conclusion, he hath betrayed his followers, whose condemnation is pronounced. So far my king and master; so much my office. 145

K. Hen. What is thy name? I know thy quality.

Mont. Montjoy.

K. Hen. Thou dost thy office fairly. Turn thee back,
And tell thy king I do not seek him now;
But could be willing to march on to Calais 150
Without impeachment: for, to say the sooth,
Though 'tis no wisdom to confess so much
Unto an enemy of craft and vantage,
My people are with sickness much enfeebled,
My numbers lessen'd, and those few I have
Almost no better than so many French;
Who when they were in health, I tell thee, herald,
I thought upon one pair of English legs
Did march three Frenchmen. Yet, forgive me, God,
That I do brag thus! This your air of France 160
Hath blown that vice in me; I must repent.
Go therefore, tell thy master here I am;
My ransom is this frail and worthless trunk,
My army but a weak and sickly guard;
Yet, God before, tell him we will come on,
Though France himself and such another neighbour
Stand in our way. There 's for thy labour, Montjoy.
Go, bid thy master well advise himself:
If we may pass, we will; if we be hinder'd,
We shall your tawny ground with your red blood 170
Discolour: and so, Montjoy, fare you well.
The sum of all our answer is but this:
We would not seek a battle, as we are;
Nor, as we are, we say we will not shun it:
So tell your master.

Mont. I shall deliver so. Thanks to your highness.
[*Exit.*

Glou. I hope they will not come upon us now.

K. Hen. We are in God's hand, brother, not in theirs.
March to the bridge; it now draws toward night:
Beyond the river we'll encamp ourselves, 180
And on to-morrow bid them march away. [*Exeunt.*

SCENE VII. *The French camp, near Agincourt.*

Enter the CONSTABLE OF FRANCE, *the* LORD
RAMBURES, ORLEANS, DAUPHIN, *with others.*

Con. Tut! I have the best armour of the world. Would it were day!

Orl. You have an excellent armour; but let my horse have his due.

Con. It is the best horse of Europe.

Orl. Will it never be morning?

Dau. My Lord of Orleans, and my lord high constable, you talk of horse and armour?

Orl. You are as well provided of both as any prince in the world. 10

Dau. What a long night is this! I will not change my horse with any that treads but on four pasterns. Ça, ha! he bounds from the earth, as if his entrails were hairs; le cheval volant, the Pegasus, chez les narines de feu! When I bestride him, I soar, I am a hawk: he trots the air; the earth sings when he touches it; the basest horn of his hoof is more musical than the pipe of Hermes.

Orl. He 's of the colour of the nutmeg. 20

Dau. And of the heat of the ginger. It is a beast for Perseus: he is pure air and fire; and the dull elements of earth and water never appear in him, but only in patient stillness while his rider mounts him: he is indeed a horse; and all other jades you may call beasts.

Con. Indeed, my lord, it is a most absolute and excellent horse.

Dau. It is the prince of palfreys; his neigh is like the bidding of a monarch and his countenance enforces homage. 31

Orl. No more, cousin.

Dau. Nay, the man hath no wit that cannot, from the rising of the lark to the lodging of the lamb, vary deserved praise on my palfrey: it is a theme as fluent as the sea: turn the sands into eloquent tongues, and my horse is argument for them all: 'tis a subject for a sovereign to reason on, and for a sovereign's sovereign to ride on; and for the world, familiar to us and unknown, to lay apart their particular functions and wonder at him. I once writ a sonnet in his praise and began thus: 'Wonder of nature,'— 43

Orl. I have heard a sonnet begin so to one's mistress.

Dau. Then did they imitate that which I composed to my courser, for my horse is my mistress.

Orl. Your mistress bears well.

Dau. Me well; which is the prescript praise and perfection of a good and particular mistress.

Con. Nay, for methought yesterday your mistress shrewdly shook your back. 52

Dau. So perhaps did yours.

Con. Mine was not bridled.

Dau. O then belike she was old and gentle; and you rode, like a kern of Ireland, your French hose off, and in your strait strossers. 57

Con. You have good judgement in horsemanship.

Dau. Be warned by me, then: they that ride so and ride not warily, fall into foul bogs. I had rather have my horse to my mistress.

Con. I had as lief have my mistress a jade.

Dau. I tell thee, constable, my mistress wears his own hair.

Con. I could make as true a boast as that, if I had a sow to my mistress.

---

136. **re-answer,** be an equivalent for. 151. **impeachment,** hindrance. SCENE VII. 14. **hairs,** used as stuffing for tennis balls. 15-16. **le cheval . . . feu,** the flying horse, Pegasus, with nostrils breathing fire. 19. **pipe of Hermes.** Hermes charmed Argus to sleep with playing on his pipe. 34. **lodging,** lying down. 49. **prescript,** regular. 52.

shrewdly, viciously. 56. **kern,** foot soldier. 57. **strossers,** trousers. French hose were wide. 68-69. '**Le chien . . . bourbier.**' Cf. II Peter 2:22. 90. **faced . . . way,** put to shame. 93. **go to hazard,** bet. 121. **hooded valour.** The hawk was kept hooded to prevent it from beating its wings (baiting); here the implication is that the prince will prepare

Dau. 'Le chien est retourné à son propre vomisse-
ment, et la truie lavée au bourbier:' thou makest use
of any thing.   70

Con. Yet do I not use my horse for my mistress, or
any such proverb so little kin to the purpose.

Ram. My lord constable, the armour that I saw in
your tent to-night, are those stars or suns upon it?

Con. Stars, my lord.

Dau. Some of them will fall to-morrow, I hope.

Con. And yet my sky shall not want.

Dau. That may be, for you bear a many super-
fluously, and 'twere more honour some were away.   81

Con. Even as your horse bears your praises; who
would trot as well, were some of your brags dismounted.

Dau. Would I were able to load him with his
desert! Will it never be day? I will trot to-morrow a
mile, and my way shall be paved with English faces. 88

Con. I will not say so, for fear I should be faced out
of my way: but I would it were morning; for I would
fain be about the ears of the English.

Ram. Who will go to hazard with me for twenty
prisoners?

Con. You must first go yourself to hazard, ere you
have them.

Dau. 'Tis midnight; I'll go arm myself.   [*Exit.*

Orl. The Dauphin longs for morning.

Ram. He longs to eat the English.

Con. I think he will eat all he kills.   100

Orl. By the white hand of my lady, he 's a gallant
prince.

Con. Swear by her foot, that she may tread out the
oath.

Orl. He is simply the most active gentleman of
France.

Con. Doing is activity; and he will still be doing.

Orl. He never did harm, that I heard of.

Con. Nor will he do none to-morrow: he will keep that
good name still.   111

Orl. I know him to be valiant.

Con. I was told that by one that knows him better
than you.

Orl. What 's he?

Con. Marry, he told me so himself; and he said he
cared not who knew it.

Orl. He needs not; it is no hidden virtue in him.   119

Con. By my faith, sir, but it is; never any body saw
it but his lackey: 'tis a hooded valour; and when it
appears, it will bate.

Orl. Ill will never said well.

Con. I will cap that proverb with 'There is flattery
in friendship.'

Orl. And I will take up that with 'Give the devil his
due.'

Con. Well placed: there stands your friend for the
devil: have at the very eye of that proverb with 'A
pox of the devil.'   130

Orl. You are the better at proverbs, by how much
'A fool's bolt is soon shot.'

Con. You have shot over.

Orl. 'Tis not the first time you were overshot.

Enter a Messenger.

Mess. My lord high constable, the English lie within
fifteen hundred paces of your tents.

Con. Who hath measured the ground?

Mess. The Lord Grandpré.

Con. A valiant and most expert gentleman. Would
it were day! Alas, poor Harry of England! he longs not
for the dawning as we do.   141

Orl. What a wretched and peevish fellow is this
king of England, to mope with his fat-brained followers so far out of his knowledge!

Con. If the English had any apprehension, they
would run away.

Orl. That they lack; for if their heads had any
intellectual armour, they could never wear such
heavy head-pieces.   149

Ram. That island of England breeds very valiant
creatures; their mastiffs are of unmatchable courage.

Orl. Foolish curs, that run winking into the mouth
of a Russian bear and have their heads crushed like
rotten apples! You may as well say, that 's a valiant
flea that dare eat his breakfast on the lip of a lion.

Con. Just, just; and the men do sympathize with the
mastiffs in robustious and rough coming on, leaving
their wits with their wives: and then give them great
meals of beef and iron and steel, they will eat like
wolves and fight like devils.   163

Orl. Ay, but these English are shrewdly out of beef.

Con. Then shall we find to-morrow they have only
stomachs to eat and none to fight. Now is it time to
arm: come, shall we about it?

Orl. It is now two o'clock: but, let me see, by ten
We shall have each a hundred Englishmen.   [*Exeunt.*

ACT IV.

PROLOGUE.

Enter Chorus.

Chor. Now entertain conjecture of a time
When creeping murmur and the poring dark
Fills the wide vessel of the universe.
From camp to camp through the foul womb of night
The hum of either army stilly sounds,
That the fix'd sentinels almost receive
The secret whispers of each other's watch:
Fire answers fire, and through their paly flames
Each battle sees the other's umber'd face;
Steed threatens steed, in high and boastful neighs   10
Piercing the night's dull ear; and from the tents
The armourers, accomplishing the knights,
With busy hammers closing rivets up,
Give dreadful note of preparation:
The country cocks do crow, the clocks do toll,
And the third hour of drowsy morning name.
Proud of their numbers and secure in soul,
The confident and over-lusty French
Do the low-rated English play at dice;
And chide the cripple tardy-gaited night   20

---

for flight. 123-132. **Ill will . . . shot,** an example of the game of
proverb capping. 145. **apprehension,** as used by the constable it means
"sense" and "sense of danger." Orleans takes it to mean "sense" or
"perception" only. 153-155. **Foolish curs . . . apples,** a picturesque
reference to the courage of the dogs in the cruel sport of bearbaiting.

ACT IV. PROLOGUE. 2. **poring,** straining the eyes to see. 9. **umber'd,**
shadowed, possibly by firelight. 12. **accomplishing,** equipping. 13.
rivets. Parts of the armor might be riveted together even after it had
been donned. 18. **over-lusty,** merry.

Who, like a foul and ugly witch, doth limp
So tediously away. The poor condemned English,
Like sacrifices, by their watchful fires
Sit patiently and inly ruminate
The morning's danger, and their gesture sad
Investing lank-lean cheeks and war-worn coats
Presenteth them unto the gazing moon
So many horrid ghosts. O now, who will behold
The royal captain of this ruin'd band
Walking from watch to watch, from tent to tent,　　30
Let him cry 'Praise and glory on his head!'
For forth he goes and visits all his host,
Bids them good morrow with a modest smile
And calls them brothers, friends and countrymen.
Upon his royal face there is no note
How dread an army hath enrounded him;
Nor doth he dedicate one jot of colour
Unto the weary and all-watched night,
But freshly looks and over-bears attaint
With cheerful semblance and sweet majesty;　　40
That every wretch, pining and pale before,
Beholding him, plucks comfort from his looks:
A largess universal like the sun
His liberal eye doth give to every one,
Thawing cold fear, that mean and gentle all
Behold, as may unworthiness define,
A little touch of Harry in the night.
And so our scene must to the battle fly;
Where—O for pity!—we shall much disgrace
With four or five most vile and ragged foils,　　50
Right ill-disposed in brawl ridiculous,
The name of Agincourt. Yet sit and see,
Minding true things by what their mockeries be. [*Exit.*

SCENE I. *The English camp at Agincourt.*

Enter KING HENRY, BEDFORD, *and* GLOUCESTER.

K. Hen. Gloucester, 'tis true that we are in great
　　danger;
The greater therefore should our courage be.
Good morrow, brother Bedford. God Almighty!
There is some soul of goodness in things evil,
Would men observingly distil it out.
For our bad neighbour makes us early stirrers,
Which is both healthful and good husbandry:
Besides, they are our outward consciences,
And preachers to us all, admonishing
That we should dress us fairly for our end.　　10
Thus may we gather honey from the weed,
And make a moral of the devil himself.

Enter ERPINGHAM.

Good morrow, old Sir Thomas Erpingham:
A good soft pillow for that good white head
Were better than a churlish turf of France.
Erp. Not so, my liege: this lodging likes me better,
Since I may say 'Now lie I like a king.'
K. Hen. 'Tis good for men to love their present
　　pains
Upon example; so the spirit is eased:

And when the mind is quicken'd, out of doubt,　　20
The organs, though defunct and dead before,
Break up their drowsy grave and newly move,
With casted slough and fresh legerity.
Lend me thy cloak, Sir Thomas. Brothers both,
Commend me to the princes in our camp;
Do my good morrow to them, and anon
Desire them all to my pavilion.
Glou. We shall, my liege.
Erp. Shall I attend your grace?
K. Hen.　　　　　No, my good knight,
Go with my brothers to my lords of England:　　30
I and my bosom must debate a while,
And then I would no other company.
Erp. The Lord in heaven bless thee, noble Harry!
　　　　　　　　　　[*Exeunt all but King.*
K. Hen. God-a-mercy, old heart! thou speak'st
　　cheerfully.

Enter PISTOL.

Pist. Qui va là?
K. Hen. A friend.
Pist. Discuss unto me; art thou officer?
Or art thou base, common and popular?
K. Hen. I am a gentleman of a company.
Pist. Trail'st thou the puissant pike?　　40
K. Hen. Even so. What are you?
Pist. As good a gentleman as the emperor.
K. Hen. Then you are a better than the king.
Pist. The king 's a bawcock, and a heart of gold,
A lad of life, an imp of fame;
Of parents good, of fist most valiant:
I kiss his dirty shoe, and from heart-string
I love the lovely bully. What is thy name?
K. Hen. Harry le Roy.
Pist. Le Roy! a Cornish name: art thou of Cornish
　　crew?　　50
K. Hen. No, I am a Welshman.
Pist. Know'st thou Fluellen?
K. Hen. Yes.
Pist. Tell him, I'll knock his leek about his pate
Upon Saint Davy's day.
K. Hen. Do not you wear your dagger in your cap
that day, lest he knock that about yours.
Pist. Art thou his friend?
K. Hen. And his kinsman too.
Pist. The figo for thee, then!　　60
K. Hen. I thank you: God be with you!
Pist. My name is Pistol call'd.　　[*Exit.*
K. Hen. It sorts well with your fierceness.

Enter FLUELLEN *and* GOWER.

Gow. Captain Fluellen!
Flu. So! in the name of Jesu Christ, speak lower. It
is the greatest admiration in the universal world,
when the true and aunchient prerogatifes and laws of
the wars is not kept: if you would take the pains but
to examine the wars of Pompey the Great, you shall
find, I warrant you, that there is no tiddle taddle nor
pibble pabble in Pompey's camp; I warrant you, you
shall find the ceremonies of the wars, and the cares of

it, and the forms of it, and the sobriety of it, and the modesty of it, to be otherwise. 75

Gow. Why, the enemy is loud; you hear him all night.

Flu. If the enemy is an ass and a fool and a prating coxcomb, is it meet, think you, that we should also, look you, be an ass and a fool and a prating coxcomb? in your own conscience, now? 81

Gow. I will speak lower.

Flu. I pray you and beseech you that you will.
[*Exeunt Gower and Fluellen.*

K. Hen. Though it appear a little out of fashion,
There is much care and valour in this Welshman.

Enter three soldiers, JOHN BATES, ALEXANDER COURT, *and* MICHAEL WILLIAMS.

Court. Brother John Bates, is not that the morning which breaks yonder?

Bates. I think it be: but we have no great cause to desire the approach of day. 90

Will. We see yonder the beginning of the day, but I think we shall never see the end of it. Who goes there?

K. Hen. A friend.

Will. Under what captain serve you?

K. Hen. Under Sir Thomas Erpingham.

Will. A good old commander and a most kind gentleman: I pray you, what thinks he of our estate?

K. Hen. Even as men wrecked upon a sand, that look to be washed off the next tide. 101

Bates. He hath not told his thought to the king?

K. Hen. No; nor is it not meet he should. For, though I speak to you, I think the king is but a man, as I am: the violet smells to him as it doth to me; the element shows to him as it doth to me; all his senses have but human conditions: his ceremonies laid by, in his nakedness he appears but a man; and though his affections are higher mounted than ours, yet, when they stoop, they stoop with the like wing. Therefore when he sees reason of fears, as we do, his fears, out of doubt, be of the same relish as ours are: yet, in reason, no man should possess him with any appearance of fear, lest he, by showing it, should dishearten his army. 117

Bates. He may show what outward courage he will; but I believe, as cold a night as 'tis, he could wish himself in Thames up to the neck; and so I would he were, and I by him, at all adventures, so we were quit here.

K. Hen. By my troth, I will speak my conscience of the king: I think he would not wish himself any where but where he is.

Bates. Then I would he were here alone; so should he be sure to be ransomed, and a many poor men's lives saved. 128

K. Hen. I dare say you love him not so ill, to wish him here alone, howsoever you speak this to feel other men's minds: methinks I could not die any where so contented as in the king's company; his cause being just and his quarrel honourable.

Will. That 's more than we know.

Bates. Ay, or more than we should seek after; for we

know enough, if we know we are the king's subjects: if his cause be wrong, our obedience to the king wipes the crime of it out of us. 139

Will. But if the cause be not good, the king himself hath a heavy reckoning to make, when all those legs and arms and heads, chopped off in a battle, shall join together at the latter day and cry all 'We died at such a place;' some swearing, some crying for a surgeon, some upon their wives left poor behind them, some upon the debts they owe, some upon their children rawly left. I am afeard there are few die well that die in a battle; for how can they charitably dispose of any thing, when blood is their argument? Now, if these men do not die well, it will be a black matter for the king that led them to it; whom to disobey were against all proportion of subjection. 153

K. Hen. So, if a son that is by his father sent about merchandise do sinfully miscarry upon the sea, the imputation of his wickedness, by your rule, should be imposed upon his father that sent him: or if a servant, under his master's command transporting a sum of money, be assailed by robbers and die in many irreconciled iniquities, you may call the business of the master the author of the servant's damnation: but this is not so: the king is not bound to answer the particular endings of his soldiers, the father of his son, nor the master of his servant; for they purpose not their death, when they purpose their services. Besides, there is no king, be his cause never so spotless, if it come to the arbitrement of swords, can try it out with all unspotted soldiers: some peradventure have on them the guilt of premeditated and contrived murder; some, of beguiling virgins with the broken seals of perjury; some, making the wars their bulwark, that have before gored the gentle bosom of peace with pillage and robbery. Now, if these men have defeated the law and outrun native punishment, though they can outstrip men, they have no wings to fly from God: war is his beadle, war is his vengeance; so that here men are punished for before-breach of the king's laws in now the king's quarrel: where they feared the death, they have borne life away; and where they would be safe, they perish: then if they die unprovided, no more is the king guilty of their damnation than he was before guilty of those impieties for the which they are now visited. Every subject's duty is the king's; but every subject's soul is his own. Therefore should every soldier in the wars do as every sick man in his bed, wash every mote out of his conscience: and dying so, death is to him advantage; or not dying, the time was blessedly lost wherein such preparation was gained: and in him that escapes, it were not sin to think that, making God so free an offer, He let him outlive that day to see His greatness and to teach others how they should prepare. 196

Will. 'Tis certain, every man that dies ill, the ill upon his own head, the king is not to answer it.

Bates. I do not desire he should answer for me; and yet I determine to fight lustily for him.

K. Hen. I myself heard the king say he would not be ransomed.

border of Wales; it seems to have been thought of as a Welsh city. 54-55. **leek . . . day.** On St. David's Day, March 1, the leek was worn in memory of a Welsh victory over the Saxons, since St. David, the Welsh leader, had commanded his followers to wear leeks in their caps on that occasion. The leek is therefore a patriotic emblem. 81. **conscience,** inmost thought. 107. **shows,** looks. 112. **stoop,** swoop down. 147. **rawly,** without provision. 153. **proportion of subjection,** proper duty

of a subject. 154-196. **So, if . . . prepare.** The king's speech presents the customary case made out for those responsible for war. Battle becomes God's instrument for punishing the guilty. Such speculations are not infrequent in the literature of the time. Henry continues his discourse on the responsibilities and cares of kingship in lines 247-301. 155. **sinfully miscarry,** die in their sins. 173. **bulwark,** refuge. 176. **native,** at home. 183. **unprovided,** unprepared.

Will. Ay, he said so, to make us fight cheerfully: but when our throats are cut, he may be ransomed, and we ne'er the wiser.

K. Hen. If I live to see it, I will never trust his word after. 208

Will. You pay him then. That's a perilous shot out of an elder-gun, that a poor and a private displeasure can do against a monarch! you may as well go about to turn the sun to ice with fanning in his face with a peacock's feather. You'll never trust his word after! come, 'tis a foolish saying.

K. Hen. Your reproof is something too round: I should be angry with you, if the time were convenient.

Will. Let it be a quarrel between us, if you live. 220

K. Hen. I embrace it.

Will. How shall I know thee again?

K. Hen. Give me any gage of thine, and I will wear it in my bonnet: then, if ever thou darest acknowledge it, I will make it my quarrel.

Will. Here's my glove: give me another of thine.

K. Hen. There. 228

Will. This will I also wear in my cap: if ever thou come to me and say, after to-morrow, 'This is my glove,' by this hand, I will take thee a box on the ear.

K. Hen. If ever I live to see it, I will challenge it.

Will. Thou darest as well be hanged.

K. Hen. Well, I will do it, though I take thee in the king's company.

Will. Keep thy word: fare thee well.

Bates. Be friends, you English fools, be friends: we have French quarrels enow, if you could tell how to reckon. 241

K. Hen. Indeed, the French may lay twenty French crowns to one, they will beat us; for they bear them on their shoulders: but it is no English treason to cut French crowns, and to-morrow the king himself will be a clipper. [*Exeunt Soldiers.*

Upon the king! let us our lives, our souls,
Our debts, our careful wives,
Our children and our sins lay on the king!
We must bear all. O hard condition, 250
Twin-born with greatness, subject to the breath
Of every fool, whose sense no more can feel
But his own wringing! What infinite heart's-ease
Must kings neglect, that private men enjoy!
And what have kings, that privates have not too,
Save ceremony, save general ceremony?
And what art thou, thou idol ceremony?
What kind of god art thou, that suffer'st more
Of mortal griefs than do thy worshippers?
What are thy rents? what are thy comings in? 260
O ceremony, show me but thy worth!
What is thy soul of adoration?
Art thou aught else but place, degree and form,
Creating awe and fear in other men?
Wherein thou art less happy being fear'd
Than they in fearing.
What drink'st thou oft, instead of homage sweet,
But poison'd flattery? O, be sick, great greatness,
And bid thy ceremony give thee cure!

Think'st thou the fiery fever will go out 270
With titles blown from adulation?
Will it give place to flexure and low bending?
Canst thou, when thou command'st the beggar's knee,
Command the health of it? No, thou proud dream,
That play'st so subtly with a king's repose;
I am a king that find thee, and I know
'Tis not the balm, the sceptre and the ball,
The sword, the mace, the crown imperial,
The intertissued robe of gold and pearl,
The farced title running 'fore the king, 280
The throne he sits on, nor the tide of pomp
That beats upon the high shore of this world,
No, not all these, thrice-gorgeous ceremony,
Not all these, laid in bed majestical,
Can sleep so soundly as the wretched slave,
Who with a body fill'd and vacant mind
Gets him to rest, cramm'd with distressful bread;
Never sees horrid night, the child of hell,
But, like a lackey, from the rise to set
Sweats in the eye of Phœbus and all night 290
Sleeps in Elysium; next day after dawn,
Doth rise and help Hyperion to his horse,
And follows so the ever-running year,
With profitable labour, to his grave:
And, but for ceremony, such a wretch,
Winding up days with toil and nights with sleep,
Had the fore-hand and vantage of a king.
The slave, a member of the country's peace,
Enjoys it; but in gross brain little wots
What watch the king keeps to maintain the peace, 300
Whose hours the peasant best advantages.

Re-enter ERPINGHAM.

Erp. My lord, your nobles, jealous of your absence,
Seek through your camp to find you.

K. Hen.   Good old knight,
Collect them all together at my tent:
I'll be before thee.

Erp.   I shall do 't, my lord. [*Exit.*

K. Hen. O God of battles! steel my soldiers' hearts;
Possess them not with fear; take from them now
The sense of reckoning, if the opposed numbers
Pluck their hearts from them. Not to-day, O Lord,
O, not to-day, think not upon the fault 310
My father made in compassing the crown!
I Richard's body have interred new;
And on it have bestow'd more contrite tears
Than from it issued forced drops of blood:
Five hundred poor I have in yearly pay,
Who twice a-day their wither'd hands hold up
Toward heaven, to pardon blood; and I have built
Two chantries, where the sad and solemn priests
Sing still for Richard's soul. More will I do;
Though all that I can do is nothing worth, 320
Since that my penitence comes after all,
Imploring pardon.

Re-enter GLOUCESTER.

210. **elder-gun,** popgun made from a hollowed branch of elder. 217. **round,** direct, brusque; see glossary. 245. **crowns,** double pun on *crown* meaning "coin" and *crown* meaning "head." 246. **clipper,** one who mutilates coins by clipping the edges. 253. **wringing,** suffering. 262. **soul of adoration,** essence of the adoration (paid thee). 271. **blown,** breathed. 276. **find,** find out. 280. **farced,** stuffed with pompous phrases. 287. **distressful,** earned by hard work. 291. **Elysium,** the abode of the blessed. 292. **Hyperion,** the sun god. The

peasant is up before the sun. 298. **member,** sharer. 302. **jealous of,** apprehensive because of. 306-322. **O . . . pardon.** This passage contains the principal evidence of Shakespeare's presentation of his hero as a religious man. The fault the king refers to is the deposition and murder of Richard II, a theme which runs through all the plays of this series.
SCENE II. 2. **Montez à cheval!** To horse! 4-6. **Via . . . Orleans.** The dauphin, admiring his horse, says, "Begone, water and earth." He apparently thinks of his horse as being made only of the elements of

Glou. My liege!
K. Hen. My brother Gloucester's voice? Ay;
I know thy errand, I will go with thee:
The day, my friends and all things stay for me.[*Exeunt.*

SCENE II. *The French camp.*

Enter the DAUPHIN, ORLEANS, RAMBURES, *and others.*

Orl. The sun doth gild our armour; up, my lords!
Dau. Montez à cheval! My horse! varlet! laquais!
ha!
Orl. O brave spirit!
Dau. Via! les eaux et la terre.
Orl. Rien puis? l'air et le feu.
Dau. Ciel, cousin Orleans.

Enter CONSTABLE.

Now, my lord constable!
Con. Hark, how our steeds for present service neigh!
Dau. Mount them, and make incision in their hides,
That their hot blood may spin in English eyes,   10
And dout them with superfluous courage, ha!
Ram. What, will you have them weep our horses'
blood?
How shall we, then, behold their natural tears?

Enter Messenger.

Mess. The English are embattled, you French peers.
Con. To horse, you gallant princes! straight to
horse!
Do but behold yon poor and starved band,
And your fair show shall suck away their souls,
Leaving them but the shales and husks of men.
There is not work enough for all our hands;
Scarce blood enough in all their sickly veins   20
To give each naked curtle-axe a stain,
That our French gallants shall to-day draw out,
And sheathe for lack of sport: let us but blow on them,
The vapour of our valour will o'erturn them.
'Tis positive 'gainst all exceptions, lords,
That our superfluous lackeys and our peasants,
Who in unnecessary action swarm
About our squares of battle, were enow
To purge this field of such a hilding foe,
Though we upon this mountain's basis by   30
Took stand for idle speculation:
But that our honours must not. What 's to say?
A very little little let us do,
And all is done. Then let the trumpets sound
The tucket sonance and the note to mount;
For our approach shall so much dare the field
That England shall couch down in fear and yield.

Enter GRANDPRÉ.

Grand. Why do you stay so long, my lords of France?
Yon island carrions, desperate of their bones,
Ill-favouredly become the morning field: 40
Their ragged curtains poorly are let loose,
And our air shakes them passing scornfully:

Big Mars seems bankrupt in their beggar'd host
And faintly through a rusty beaver peeps:
The horsemen sit like fixed candlesticks,
With torch-staves in their hand; and their poor jades
Lob down their heads, dropping the hides and hips,
The gum down-roping from their pale-dead eyes,
And in their pale dull mouths the gimmal bit
Lies foul with chew'd grass, still and motionless;   50
And their executors, the knavish crows,
Fly o'er them, all impatient for their hour.
Description cannot suit itself in words
To demonstrate the life of such a battle
In life so lifeless as it shows itself.
Con. They have said their prayers, and they stay for
death.
Dau. Shall we go send them dinners and fresh suits
And give their fasting horses provender,
And after fight with them?
Con. I stay but for my guidon: to the field!   60
I will the banner from a trumpet take,
And use it for my haste. Come, come, away!
The sun is high, and we outwear the day.   [*Exeunt.*

SCENE III. *The English camp.*

Enter GLOUCESTER, BEDFORD, EXETER, ERPINGHAM,
with all his host: SALISBURY *and* WESTMORELAND.

Glou. Where is the king?
Bed. The king himself is rode to view their battle.
West. Of fighting men they have full three score
thousand.
Exe. There 's five to one; besides, they all are fresh.
Sal. God's arm strike with us! 'tis a fearful odds.
God be wi' you, princes all; I'll to my charge:
If we no more meet till we meet in heaven,
Then, joyfully, my noble Lord of Bedford,
My dear Lord Gloucester, and my good Lord Exeter,
And my kind kinsman, warriors all, adieu!   10
Bed. Farewell, good Salisbury; and good luck go
with thee!
Exe. Farewell, kind lord; fight valiantly to-day:
And yet I do thee wrong to mind thee of it,
For thou art framed of the firm truth of valour.
                           [*Exit Salisbury.*
Bed. He is as full of valour as of kindness;
Princely in both.

Enter the KING.

West.   O that we now had here
But one ten thousand of those men in England
That do no work to-day!
K. Hen.   What 's he that wishes so?
My cousin Westmoreland? No, my fair cousin:
If we are mark'd to die, we are enow   20
To do our country loss; and if to live,
The fewer men, the greater share of honour.
God's will! I pray thee, wish not one man more.
By Jove, I am not covetous for gold,
Nor care I who doth feed upon my cost;

---

fire and air. Orleans, with the same thought in mind, says in effect, "There is nothing [in him] then but air and fire." The dauphin replies, "There is also heaven." 9. **incision,** i.e., with spurs. 11. **dout,** put out. 18. **shales,** shells. 21. **curtle-axe,** cutlass, short sword. 29. **hilding,** worthless, base. 35. **tucket sonance,** trumpet call. 36. **dare,** cause to stare, to be stupefied. 41. **curtains,** colors, banners. 44. **beaver,** visor. 46. **torch-staves,** staves to fix candles on. 47. **Lob,** hang down. 49. **gimmal,** double or made of double rings; so Johnson;

F: *Iymold;* Arden editor reads *gimmal'd,* meaning "made of links." 61. **trumpet,** trumpeter; the action is sometimes explained as taking a banderole, or little fringed flag, from a trumpet.
  SCENE III. 18-67. **What's . . . day.** Henry's famous speech contrasts strongly in its dignity and manliness with the boastful frivolity of the French.

It yearns me not if men my garments wear;
Such outward things dwell not in my desires:
But if it be a sin to covet honour,
I am the most offending soul alive.
No, faith, my coz, wish not a man from England: 30
God's peace! I would not lose so great an honour
As one man more, methinks, would share from me
For the best hope I have. O, do not wish one more!
Rather proclaim it, Westmoreland, through my host,
That he which hath no stomach to this fight,
Let him depart; his passport shall be made
And crowns for convoy put into his purse:
We would not die in that man's company
That fears his fellowship to die with us.
This day is call'd the feast of Crispian: 40
He that outlives this day, and comes safe home,
Will stand a tip-toe when this day is named,
And rouse him at the name of Crispian.
He that shall live this day, and see old age,
Will yearly on the vigil feast his neighbours,
And say 'To-morrow is Saint Crispian:'
Then will he strip his sleeve and show his scars,
And say 'These wounds I had on Crispin's day.'
Old men forget; yet all shall be forgot,
But he'll remember with advantages 50
What feats he did that day: then shall our names,
Familiar in his mouth as household words,
Harry the king, Bedford and Exeter,
Warwick and Talbot, Salisbury and Gloucester,
Be in their flowing cups freshly remember'd.
This story shall the good man teach his son;
And Crispin Crispian shall ne'er go by,
From this day to the ending of the world,
But we in it shall be remembered;
We few, we happy few, we band of brothers; 60
For he to-day that sheds his blood with me
Shall be my brother; be he ne'er so vile,
This day shall gentle his condition:
And gentlemen in England now a-bed
Shall think themselves accursed they were not here,
And hold their manhoods cheap whiles any speaks
That fought with us upon Saint Crispin's day.

Re-enter SALISBURY.

Sal. My sovereign lord, bestow yourself with speed:
The French are bravely in their battles set,
And will with all expedience charge on us. 70
K. Hen. All things are ready, if our minds be so.
West. Perish the man whose mind is backward now!
K. Hen. Thou dost not wish more help from
   England, coz?
West. God's will! my liege, would you and I alone,
Without more help, could fight this royal battle!
K. Hen. Why, now thou hast unwish'd five
   thousand men;
Which likes me better than to wish us one.
You know your places: God be with you all!

Tucket. Enter MONTJOY.

Mont. Once more I come to know of thee, King
   Harry,
If for thy ransom thou wilt now compound, 80
Before thy most assured overthrow:
For certainly thou art so near the gulf,
Thou needs must be englutted. Besides, in mercy,
The constable desires thee thou wilt mind
Thy followers of repentance; that their souls
May make a peaceful and a sweet retire
From off these fields, where, wretches, their poor
   bodies
Must lie and fester.
K. Hen.   Who hath sent thee now?
Mont. The Constable of France.
K. Hen. I pray thee, bear my former answer back: 90
Bid them achieve me and then sell my bones.
Good God! why should they mock poor fellows thus?
The man that once did sell the lion's skin
While the beast lived, was killed with hunting him.
A many of our bodies shall no doubt
Find native graves; upon the which, I trust,
Shall witness live in brass of this day's work:
And those that leave their valiant bones in France,
Dying like men, though buried in your dunghills,
They shall be famed; for there the sun shall greet
   them, 100
And draw their honours reeking up to heaven;
Leaving their earthly parts to choke your clime,
The smell whereof shall breed a plague in France.
Mark then abounding valour in our English,
That being dead, like to the bullet's grazing,
Break out into a second course of mischief,
Killing in relapse of mortality.
Let me speak proudly: tell the constable
We are but warriors for the working-day;
Our gayness and our gilt are all besmirch'd 110
With rainy marching in the painful field;
There 's not a piece of feather in our host—
Good argument, I hope, we will not fly—
And time hath worn us into slovenry:
But, by the mass, our hearts are in the trim;
And my poor soldiers tell me, yet ere night
They'll be in fresher robes, or they will pluck
The gay new coats o'er the French soldiers' heads
And turn them out of service. If they do this,—
As, if God please, they shall,—my ransom then 120
Will soon be levied. Herald, save thou thy labour;
Come thou no more for ransom, gentle herald:
They shall have none, I swear, but these my joints;
Which if they have as I will leave 'em them,
Shall yield them little, tell the constable.
Mont. I shall, King Harry. And so fare thee well:
Thou never shalt hear herald any more.   [*Exit.*
K. Hen. I fear thou 'lt once more come again for
   ransom.

Enter YORK.

York. My lord, most humbly on my knee I beg

26. **yearns,** grieves. 37. **crowns for convoy,** travel pay. 39. **That
. . . us,** that is afraid to risk his life in our company. 40. **Crispian.**
Crispinus and Crispianus were martyrs in France in the fourth century;
they were shoemakers by trade and became the patron saints of that
craft. 45. **vigil,** evening before a feast day. 50. **advantages,** additions
of his own. 63. **gentle,** raise to the rank of gentleman. 70. **expedience,**
speed. 83. **englutted,** swallowed up. 96. **native,** in their own
land. 105. **grazing,** glancing off. 107. **Killing . . . mortality,** killing
(their foes) as they fall back (decompose) into their elements. 130.
vaward, vanguard.

SCENE IV. The battle has, so to speak, been fought in anticipation.

This is the only bit of actual conflict. If it has any dramatic value, it
may suggest the greatness of a victory in which the cowardly Pistol
might make so easy a capture. 2-3. **Je . . . qualité.** I think that you
are a gentleman of high rank. Most of Pistol's replies are nonsense.
4. **calmie custure me.** These words are perhaps derived from the refrain
of a popular song, supposed to be Irish, "Calen o custure me" (Young
maiden, my treasure). 8. **Perpend,** attend to, consider. 9. **fox,**
sword. 12-13. **O . . . moi!** Oh, have mercy! pity on me! 14.
Moy. Pistol, not understanding the French, imagines that a coin is
referred to. 15. **rim,** midriff, diaphragm. 17-18. **Est-il . . . bras?** Is
there no way to escape the strength of your arm? 26. **Écoutez . . .**

The leading of the vaward. 130
   K. Hen. Take it, brave York. Now, soldiers, march
     away:
And how thou pleasest, God, dispose the day! [*Exeunt.*

SCENE IV. *The field of battle.*

Alarum. Excursions. Enter PISTOL, French Soldier, *and*
   Boy.

   Pist. Yield, cur!
   Fr. Sol. Je pense que vous êtes gentilhomme de
bonne qualité.
   Pist. Qualtitie calmie custure me! Art thou a
gentleman? what is thy name? discuss.
   Fr. Sol. O Seigneur Dieu!
   Pist. O, Signieur Dew should be a gentleman:
Perpend my words, O Signieur Dew, and mark;
O Signieur Dew, thou diest on point of fox,
Except, O signieur, thou do give to me 10
Egregious ransom.
   Fr. Sol. O, prenez miséricorde! ayez pitié de moi!
   Pist. Moy shall not serve; I will have forty moys;
Or I will fetch thy rim out at thy throat
In drops of crimson blood.
   Fr. Sol. Est-il impossible d'échapper la force de ton
bras?
   Pist. Brass, cur!
Thou damned and luxurious mountain goat, 20
Offer'st me brass?
   Fr. Sol. O pardonnez moi!
   Pist. Say'st thou me so? is that a ton of moys?
Come hither, boy: ask me this slave in French
What is his name.
   Boy. Écoutez: comment êtes-vous appelé?
   Fr. Sol. Monsieur le Fer.
   Boy. He says his name is Master Fer.
   Pist. Master Fer! I'll fer him, and firk him, and
ferret him: discuss the same in French unto him. 31
   Boy. I do not know the French for fer, and ferret,
and firk.
   Pist. Bid him prepare; for I will cut his throat.
   Fr. Sol. Que dit-il, monsieur?
   Boy. Il me commande de vous dire que vous faites
vous prêt; car ce soldat ici est disposé tout à cette
heure de couper votre gorge.
   Pist. Owy, cuppele gorge, permafoy.
Peasant, unless thou give me crowns, brave crowns; 40
Or mangled shalt thou be by this my sword.
   Fr. Sol. O, je vous supplie, pour l'amour de Dieu,
me pardonner! Je suis gentilhomme de bonne maison:
gardez ma vie, et je vous donnerai deux cents écus.
   Pist. What are his words?
   Boy. He prays you to save his life: he is a gentleman
of a good house; and for his ransom he will give you
two hundred crowns.
   Pist. Tell him my fury shall abate, and I 50

The crowns will take.
   Fr. Sol. Petit monsieur, que dit-il?
   Boy. Encore qu'il est contre son jurement de pardonner aucun prisonnier, néanmoins, pour les écus
que vous l'avez promis, il est content de vous donner
la liberté, le franchisement.
   Fr. Sol. Sur mes genoux je vous donne mille re-
mercîmens; et je m'estime heureux que je suis tombé
entre les mains d'un chevalier, je pense, le plus brave,
vaillant, et très distingué seigneur d'Angleterre. 61
   Pist. Expound unto me, boy.
   Boy. He gives you, upon his knees, a thousand
thanks; and he esteems himself happy that he hath
fallen into the hands of one, as he thinks, the most
brave, valorous, and thrice-worthy signieur of England.
   Pist. As I suck blood, I will some mercy show.
Follow me! 69
   Boy. Suivez-vous le grand capitaine. [*Exeunt Pistol,
and French Soldier.*] I did never know so full a voice
issue from so empty a heart: but the saying is true,
'The empty vessel makes the greatest sound.' Bardolph and Nym had ten times more valour than this
roaring devil i' the old play, that every one may pare
his nails with a wooden dagger; and they are both
hanged; and so would this be, if he durst steal any
thing adventurously. I must stay with the lackeys,
with the luggage of our camp: the French might have
a good prey of us, if he knew of it; for there is none to
guard it but boys. [*Exit.*

SCENE V. *Another part of the field.*

Enter CONSTABLE, ORLEANS, BOURBON, DAUPHIN,
   and RAMBURES.

   Con. O diable!
   Orl. O seigneur! le jour est perdu, tout est perdu!
   Dau. Mort de ma vie! all is confounded, all!
Reproach and everlasting shame
Sits mocking in our plumes. O méchante fortune!
Do not run away. [*A short alarum.*
   Con.   Why, all our ranks are broke.
   Dau. O perdurable shame! let's stab ourselves.
Be these the wretches that we play'd at dice for?
   Orl. Is this the king we sent to for his ransom?
   Bour. Shame and eternal shame, nothing but shame!
Let us die in honour: once more back again; 11
And he that will not follow Bourbon now,
Let him go hence, and with his cap in hand,
Like a base pandar, hold the chamber-door
Whilst by a slave, no gentler than my dog,
His fairest daughter is contaminated.
   Con. Disorder, that hath spoil'd us, friend us now!
Let us on heaps go offer up our lives.
   Orl. We are enow yet living in the field
To smother up the English in our throngs, 20

---

appelé? Listen: what is your name? 29. **firk,** trounce. 30. **ferret,**
probably, worry like a ferret. 35-38. **Que . . . gorge.** What does he
say, sir? *Boy:* He bids me tell you that you must prepare yourself,
because this soldier intends to cut your throat immediately. 42-45.
O . . . écus. Oh, I pray you, for the love of God, to pardon me. I am a
gentleman of a good house; preserve my life, and I shall give you two
hundred crowns. 52-56. **Petit . . . franchisement.** What does he say,
little sir? *Boy:* I tell you again that it is against his oath to pardon any
prisoner; nevertheless for the sake of the crowns you have promised, he
is willing to give you your liberty, your freedom. 57-61. **Sur . . .
d'Angleterre.** On my knees I give you a thousand thanks; and I

consider myself happy that I have fallen into the hands of a knight, as
I think, the bravest, most valiant and distinguished gentleman in
England. 70. **Suivez-vous . . . capitaine.** Follow the great captain.
76. **old play,** an allusion probably to moralities or interludes rather than
the mystery plays. The Vice is traditionally associated with the wooden
dagger; this passage would indicate that he had long nails.
SCENE V. 2. **O . . . perdu!** O sir, the day is lost, all is lost! 7.
perdurable, everlasting.

If any order might be thought upon.

Bour. The devil take order now! I'll to the throng:
Let life be short; else shame will be too long. [*Exeunt.*

SCENE VI. *Another part of the field.*

Alarums. Enter KING HENRY *and forces,* EXETER, *and others.*

K. Hen. Well have we done, thrice valiant
    countrymen,
But all 's not done; yet keep the French the field.

Exe. The Duke of York commends him to your
    majesty.

K. Hen. Lives he, good uncle? thrice within this
    hour
I saw him down; thrice up again, and fighting;
From helmet to the spur all blood he was.

Exe. In which array, brave soldier, doth he lie,
Larding the plain; and by his bloody side,
Yoke-fellow to his honour-owing wounds,
The noble Earl of Suffolk also lies.   10
Suffolk first died: and York, all haggled over,
Comes to him, where in gore he lay insteep'd,
And takes him by the beard; kisses the gashes
That bloodily did yawn upon his face;
And cries aloud 'Tarry, dear cousin Suffolk!
My soul shall thine keep company to heaven;
Tarry, sweet soul, for mine, then fly abreast,
As in this glorious and well-foughten field
We kept together in our chivalry!'
Upon these words I came and cheer'd him up: 20
He smiled me in the face, raught me his hand,
And, with a feeble gripe, says 'Dear my lord,
Commend my service to my sovereign.'
So did he turn and over Suffolk's neck
He threw his wounded arm and kiss'd his lips;
And so espoused to death, with blood he seal'd
A testament of noble-ending love.
The pretty and sweet manner of it forced
Those waters from me which I would have stopp'd;
But I had not so much of man in me,   30
And all my mother came into mine eyes
And gave me up to tears.

K. Hen.   I blame you not;
For, hearing this, I must perforce compound
With mistful eyes, or they will issue too.   [*Alarum.*
But, hark! what new alarum is this same?
The French have reinforced their scatter'd men:
Then every soldier kill his prisoners:
Give the word through.   [*Exeunt.*

SCENE VII. *Another part of the field.*

Enter FLUELLEN *and* GOWER.

Flu. Kill the poys and the luggage! 'tis expressly
against the law of arms: 'tis as arrant a piece of
knavery, mark you now, as can be offer 't; in your
conscience, now, is it not?

Gow. 'Tis certain there 's not a boy left alive; and the

cowardly rascals that ran from the battle ha' done
this slaughter: besides, they have burned and carried
away all that was in the king's tent; wherefore the
king, most worthily, hath caused every soldier to cut
his prisoner's throat. O, 'tis a gallant king!   11

Flu. Ay, he was porn at Monmouth, Captain
Gower. What call you the town's name where Alexander the Pig was born?

Gow. Alexander the Great.

Flu. Why, I pray you, is not pig great? the pig, or
the great, or the mighty, or the huge, or the magnanimous, are all one reckonings, save the phrase is a little
variations.

Gow. I think Alexander the Great was born in
Macedon: his father was called Philip of Macedon, as
I take it.   22

Flu. I think it is in Macedon where Alexander is
porn. I tell you, captain, if you look in the maps of the
'orld, I warrant you sall find, in the comparisons between Macedon and Monmouth, that the situations,
look you, is both alike. There is a river in Macedon;
and there is also moreover a river at Monmouth: it is
called Wye at Monmouth; but it is out of my prains
what is the name of the other river; but 'tis all one,
'tis alike as my fingers is to my fingers, and there is
salmons in both. If you mark Alexander's life well,
Harry of Monmouth's life is come after it indifferent
well; for there is figures in all things. Alexander, God
knows, and you know, in his rages, and his furies, and
his wraths, and his cholers, and his moods, and his
displeasures, and his indignations, and also being a
little intoxicates in his prains, did, in his ales and his
angers, look you, kill his best friend, Cleitus.   41

Gow. Our king is not like him in that: he never
killed any of his friends.

Flu. It is not well done, mark you now, to take the
tales out of my mouth, ere it is made and finished. I
speak but in the figures and comparisons of it: as
Alexander killed his friend Cleitus, being in his ales
and his cups; so also Harry Monmouth, being in his
right wits and his good judgements, turned away the
fat knight with the great-belly doublet: he was full of
jests, and gipes, and knaveries, and mocks; I have
forgot his name.   53

Gow. Sir John Falstaff.

Flu. That is he: I'll tell you there is good men porn
at Monmouth.

Gow. Here comes his majesty.

Alarum. Enter KING HENRY, *and forces;* WARWICK,
    GLOUCESTER, EXETER, *and others.*

K. Hen. I was not angry since I came to France
Until this instant. Take a trumpet, herald;
Ride thou unto the horsemen on yon hill: 60
If they will fight with us, bid them come down,
Or void the field; they do offend our sight:
If they'll do neither, we will come to them,
And make them skirr away, as swift as stones
Enforced from the old Assyrian slings:
Besides, we'll cut the throats of those we have,
And not a man of them that we shall take
Shall taste our mercy. Go and tell them so.

SCENE VI.   9. **honour-owing,** honor-owing, honorable.   21. **raught,**
past tense of *reach.*   31. **mother,** the tenderer part of me.   37. **kill his
prisoners.** This follows Holinshed, who says that Henry, alarmed by
the outcry of the lackeys and boys of the camp, feared a new attack and
ordered the prisoners killed as a means of precaution. Gower, Scene

VII, 9-10, attributes the king's action to revenge.
  SCENE VII.   35. **figures,** probably, analogies, points of comparison.
41. **Cleitus,** one of the generals of Alexander the Great.   51. **great-
belly doublet,** a long waistcoat then in style.   54. **Sir John Falstaff,**
the last allusion to the fat knight. One cannot escape the impression

Enter MONTJOY.

Exe. Here comes the herald of the French, my liege.
Glo. His eyes are humbler than they used to be. 70
K. Hen. How now! what means this, herald? know'st
    thou not
That I have fined these bones of mine for ransom?
Comest thou again for ransom?
Mont.   No, great king:
I come to thee for charitable license,
That we may wander o'er this bloody field
To book our dead, and then to bury them;
To sort our nobles from our common men.
For many of our princes—woe the while!—
Lie drown'd and soak'd in mercenary blood;
So do our vulgar drench their peasant limbs 80
In blood of princes; and their wounded steeds
Fret fetlock deep in gore and with wild rage
Yerk out their armed heels at their dead masters,
Killing them twice. O, give us leave, great king,
To view the field in safety and dispose
Of their dead bodies!
K. Hen.   I tell thee truly, herald,
I know not if the day be ours or no;
For yet a many of your horsemen peer
And gallop o'er the field.
Mont.   The day is yours. 89
K. Hen. Praised be God, and not our strength, for it!
What is this castle call'd that stands hard by?
Mont. They call it Agincourt.
K. Hen. Then call we this the field of Agincourt,
Fought on the day of Crispin Crispianus.
Flu. Your grandfather of famous memory, an't
please your majesty, and your great-uncle Edward
the Plack Prince of Wales, as I have read in the
chronicles, fought a most prave pattle here in France.
K. Hen. They did, Fluellen. 100
Flu. Your majesty says very true: if your majesties
is remembered of it, the Welshmen did good service
in a garden where leeks did grow, wearing leeks in
their Monmouth caps; which, your majesty know,
to this hour is an honourable badge of the service; and
I do believe your majesty takes no scorn to wear
the leek upon Saint Tavy's day.
K. Hen. I wear it for a memorable honour;
For I am Welsh, you know, good countryman. 110
Flu. All the water in Wye cannot wash your
majesty's Welsh plood out of your pody, I can tell
you that: God pless it and preserve it, as long as it
pleases his grace, and his majesty too!
K. Hen. Thanks, good my countryman.
Flu. By Jeshu, I am your majesty's countryman, I
care not who know it; I will confess it to all the 'orld:
I need not to be ashamed of your majesty, praised be
God, so long as your majesty is an honest man. 120
K. Hen. God keep me so! Our heralds go with him:
Bring me just notice of the numbers dead
On both our parts. Call yonder fellow hither.
     [*Points to Williams. Exeunt Heralds with Montjoy.*
Exe. Soldier, you must come to the king.
K. Hen. Soldier, why wearest thou that glove in thy
cap?

Will. An 't please your majesty, 'tis the gage of one
that I should fight withal, if he be alive.
K. Hen. An Englishman? 129
Will. An 't please your majesty, a rascal that
swaggered with me last night; who, if alive and ever
dare to challenge this glove, I have sworn to take him
a box o' th' ear: or if I can see my glove in his cap,
which he swore, as he was a soldier, he would wear if
alive, I will strike it out soundly.
K. Hen. What think you, Captain Fluellen? is it fit
this soldier keep his oath?
Flu. He is a craven and a villain else, an 't please
your majesty, in my conscience. 140
K. Hen. It may be his enemy is a gentleman of great
sort, quite from the answer of his degree.
Flu. Though he be as good a gentleman as the
devil is, as Lucifer and Belzebub himself, it is necessary, look your grace, that he keep his vow and his
oath: if he be perjured, see you now, his reputation is
as arrant a villain and a Jacksauce, as ever his black
shoe trod upon God's ground and his earth, in my
conscience, la! 150
K. Hen. Then keep thy vow, sirrah, when thou
meetest the fellow.
Will. So I will, my liege, as I live.
K. Hen. Who servest thou under?
Will. Under Captain Gower, my liege.
Flu. Gower is a good captain, and is good knowledge and literatured in the wars.
K. Hen. Call him hither to me, soldier.
Will. I will, my liege.   [*Exit.* 159
K. Hen. Here, Fluellen, wear thou this favour for me
and stick it in thy cap: when Alençon and myself were
down together, I plucked this glove from his helm: if
any man challenge this, he is a friend to Alençon, and
an enemy to our person; if thou encounter any such,
apprehend him, an thou dost me love.
Flu. Your grace doo's me as great honours as can
be desired in the hearts of his subjects: I would fain
see the man, that has but two legs, that shall find himself aggriefed at this glove; that is all; but I would
fain see it once, an please God of his grace that I
might see. 171
K. Hen. Knowest thou Gower?
Flu. He is my dear friend, an please you.
K. Hen. Pray thee, go seek him, and bring him to
my tent.
Flu. I will fetch him.   [*Exit.*
K. Hen. My Lord of Warwick, and my brother
    Gloucester,
Follow Fluellen closely at the heels:
The glove which I have given him for a favour 180
May haply purchase him a box o' th' ear;
It is the soldier's; I by bargain should
Wear it myself. Follow, good cousin Warwick:
If that the soldier strike him, as I judge
By his blunt bearing he will keep his word,
Some sudden mischief may arise of it;
For I do know Fluellen valiant
And, touch'd with choler, hot as gunpowder,
And quickly will return an injury:
Follow, and see there be no harm between them. 190

that in Shakespeare's thought the rejection of Falstaff was a matter of
some importance. 62. **void,** leave. 64. **skirr,** scurry. 65. **Enforced,**
discharged. 72. **fined,** agreed to pay as a fine or ransom. 76. **book,**
Globe (following Collier): *look.* 79. **mercenary,** of mercenary soldiers.
83. **Yerk,** kick. 88. **peer,** appear. 148. **Jacksauce,** saucy knave. 161-

166. **when Alençon . . . love.** This rather crude jest of the king's,
contrived at such a solemn moment, is an example of Shakespeare's
mixture of the serious and the comic, the ground of much adverse
criticism by continental writers. 188. **choler,** anger.

Go you with me, uncle of Exeter.   [*Exeunt.*

SCENE VIII. *Before* KING HENRY'S *pavilion*.

Enter GOWER *and* WILLIAMS.

Will. I warrant it is to knight you, captain.

Enter FLUELLEN.

Flu. God's will and his pleasure, captain, I beseech
you now, come apace to the king: there is more good
toward you peradventure than is in your knowledge
to dream of.

Will. Sir, know you this glove?

Flu. Know the glove! I know the glove is a glove.

Will. I know this; and thus I challenge it.
     [*Strikes him.*

Flu. 'Sblood! an arrant traitor as any is in the
universal world, or in France, or in England!   11

Gow. How now, sir! you villain!

Will. Do you think I'll be forsworn?

Flu. Stand away, Captain Gower; I will give
treason his payment into plows, I warrant you.

Will. I am no traitor.

Flu. That's a lie in thy throat. I charge you in his
majesty's name, apprehend him: he's a friend of the
Duke Alençon's.   19

Enter WARWICK *and* GLOUCESTER.

War. How now, how now! what's the matter?

Flu. My Lord of Warwick, here is—praised be God
for it!—a most contagious treason come to light, look
you, as you shall desire in a summer's day. Here is his
majesty.

Enter KING HENRY *and* EXETER.

K. Hen. How now! what's the matter?

Flu. My liege, here is a villain and a traitor, that,
look your grace, has struck the glove which your
majesty is take out of the helmet of Alençon.   28

Will. My liege, this was my glove; here is the fellow
of it; and he that I gave it to in change promised to
wear it in his cap: I promised to strike him, if he did:
I met this man with my glove in his cap, and I have
been as good as my word.

Flu. Your majesty hear now, saving your majesty's
manhood, what an arrant, rascally, beggarly, lousy
knave it is: I hope your majesty is pear me testimony
and witness, and will avouchment, that this is the
glove of Alençon, that your majesty is give me; in
your conscience, now.   40

K. Hen. Give me thy glove, soldier: look, here is the
fellow of it.
'Twas I, indeed, thou promised'st to strike;
And thou hast given me most bitter terms.

Flu. And please your majesty, let his neck answer
for it, if there is any martial law in the world.

K. Hen. How canst thou make me satisfaction?

Will. All offences, my lord, come from the heart:
never came any from mine that might offend your
majesty.   51

K. Hen. It was ourself thou didst abuse.

Will. Your majesty came not like yourself: you
appeared to me but as a common man; witness the
night, your garments, your lowliness; and what your
highness suffered under that shape, I beseech you take
it for your own fault and not mine: for had you been
as I took you for, I made no offence; therefore, I beseech your highness, pardon me.   60

K. Hen. Here, uncle Exeter, fill this glove with
    crowns,
And give it to this fellow. Keep it, fellow;
And wear it for an honour in thy cap
Till I do challenge it. Give him the crowns:
And, captain, you must needs be friends with him.

Flu. By this day and this light, the fellow has mettle
enough in his belly. Hold, there is twelve pence for
you; and I pray you to serve God, and keep you out
of prawls, and prabbles, and quarrels, and dissensions,
and, I warrant you, it is the better for you.   71

Will. I will none of your money.

Flu. It is with a good will; I can tell you, it will serve
you to mend your shoes: come, wherefore should you
be so pashful? your shoes is not so good: 'tis a good
silling, I warrant you, or I will change it.

Enter an English Herald.

K. Hen. Now, herald, are the dead number'd?

Her. Here is the number of the slaughter'd French.

K. Hen. What prisoners of good sort are taken,
    uncle?   80

Exe. Charles Duke of Orleans, nephew to the king;
John Duke of Bourbon, and Lord Bouciqualt:
Of other lords and barons, knights and squires,
Full fifteen hundred, besides common men.

K. Hen. This note doth tell me of ten thousand
    French
That in the field lie slain: of princes, in this number,
And nobles bearing banners, there lie dead
One hundred twenty-six: added to these,
Of knights, esquires, and gallant gentlemen,
Eight thousand and four hundred; of the which,   90
Five hundred were but yesterday dubb'd knights:
So that, in these ten thousand they have lost,
There are but sixteen hundred mercenaries;
The rest are princes, barons, lords, knights, squires,
And gentlemen of blood and quality.
The names of those their nobles that lie dead:
Charles Delabreth, high constable of France;
Jacques of Chatillon, admiral of France;
The master of the cross-bows, Lord Rambures;
Great Master of France, the brave Sir Guichard
    Dolphin,   100
John Duke of Alençon, Anthony Duke of Brabant,
The brother to the Duke of Burgundy,
And Edward Duke of Bar: of lusty earls,
Grandpré and Roussi, Fauconberg and Foix,
Beaumont and Marle, Vaudemont and Lestrale.
Here was a royal fellowship of death!
Where is the number of our English dead?
    [*Herald shews him another paper.*
Edward the Duke of York, the Earl of Suffolk,

SCENE VIII. 53-60. **Your . . . me.** The situation is saved by these
manly words of the common soldier. 85-117. **This . . . thine.** The
catalog of the slain is straight from Holinshed. Neilson calls attention
to the return of the act to the high level of the king's piety. 110. **name,**
rank, importance.

ACT V. Between Acts IV and V there is historically an interval of

about five years during which Henry made a second campaign in
France and brought the French to terms in the Treaty of Troyes.
  PROLOGUE. *Stage Direction*: **Chorus.** In modern presentations of the
play, notably in that of Mansfield, the return to London described in
this prologue is made the basis for great spectacular display. 10.
Pales, impales, surrounds. 12. **whiffler,** an usher heading the proces-

Sir Richard Ketly, Davy Gam, esquire:
None else of name; and of all other men   110
But five and twenty. O God, thy arm was here;
And not to us, but to thy arm alone,
Ascribe we all! When, without stratagem,
But in plain shock and even play of battle,
Was ever known so great and little loss
On one part and on the other? Take it, God,
For it is none but thine!
    Exe.   'Tis wonderful!
    K. Hen. Come, go we in procession to the village:
And be it death proclaimed through our host
To boast of this or take that praise from God   120
Which is his only.
    Flu. Is it not lawful, an please your majesty, to tell
how many is killed?
    K. Hen. Yes, captain; but with this acknowl-
        edgement,
That God fought for us.
    Flu. Yes, my conscience, he did us great good.
    K. Hen. Do we all holy rites;
Let there be sung 'Non nobis' and 'Te Deum;'
The dead with charity enclosed in clay:
And then to Calais; and to England then;   130
Where ne'er from France arrived more happy men.
                                      [*Exeunt.*

ACT V.

PROLOGUE.

Enter Chorus.

    Chor. Vouchsafe to those that have not read the
        story,
That I may prompt them: and of such as have,
I humbly pray them to admit the excuse
Of time, of numbers and due course of things,
Which cannot in their huge and proper life
Be here presented. Now we bear the king
Toward Calais: grant him there; there seen,
Heave him away upon your winged thoughts
Athwart the sea. Behold, the English beach
Pales in the flood with men, with wives and boys, 10
Whose shouts and claps out-voice the deep-mouth'd
    sea,
Which like a mighty whiffler 'fore the king
Seems to prepare his way: so let him land,
And solemnly see him set on to London.
So swift a pace hath thought that even now
You may imagine him upon Blackheath;
Where that his lords desire him to have borne
His bruised helmet and his bended sword
Before him through the city: he forbids it,
Being free from vainness and self-glorious pride; 20
Giving full trophy, signal and ostent
Quite from himself to God. But now behold,
In the quick forge and working-house of thought,
How London doth pour out her citizens!
The mayor and all his brethren in best sort,
Like to the senators of the antique Rome,

With the plebeians swarming at their heels,
Go forth and fetch their conquering Cæsar in:
As by a lower but loving likelihood,
Were now the general of our gracious empress,   30
As in good time he may, from Ireland coming,
Bringing rebellion broached on his sword,
How many would the peaceful city quit,
To welcome him! much more, and much more cause,
Did they this Harry. Now in London place him;
As yet the lamentation of the French
Invites the King of England's stay at home;
The emperor 's coming in behalf of France,
To order peace between them; and omit
All the occurrences, whatever chanced,   40
Till Harry 's back-return again to France:
There must we bring him; and myself have play'd
The interim, by remembering you 'tis past.
Then brook abridgement, and your eyes advance,
After your thoughts, straight back again to France.
                                  [*Exit.*

    SCENE I. *France. The English camp.*

Enter FLUELLEN *and* GOWER.

    Gow. Nay, that 's right; but why wear you your
leek to-day? Saint Davy's day is past.
    Flu. There is occasions and causes why and where-
fore in all things: I will tell you, asse my friend,
Captain Gower: the rascally, scauld, beggarly, lousy,
pragging knave, Pistol, which you and yourself and
all the world know to be no petter than a fellow, look
you now, of no merits, he is come to me and prings me
pread and salt yesterday, look you, and bid me eat my
leek: it was in a place where I could not breed no
contention with him; but I will be so bold as to wear
it in my cap till I see him once again, and then I will
tell him a little piece of my desires.   14

Enter PISTOL.

    Gow. Why, here he comes, swelling like a turkey-
cock.
    Flu. 'Tis no matter for his swellings nor his turkey-
cocks. God pless you, Aunchient Pistol! you scurvy,
lousy knave, God pless you!
    Pist. Ha! art thou bedlam? dost thou thirst, base
      Trojan,   20
To have me fold up Parca's fatal web?
Hence! I am qualmish at the smell of leek.
    Flu. I peseech you heartily, scurvy, lousy knave, at
my desires, and my requests, and my petitions, to eat,
look you, this leek: because, look you, you do not love
it, nor your affections and your appetites and your
disgestions doo's not agree with it, I would desire you
to eat it.
    Pist. Not for Cadwallader and all his goats.
    Flu. There is one goat for you. [*Strikes him.*] Will
you be so good, scauld knave, as eat it?   31
    Pist. Base Trojan, thou shalt die.
    Flu. You say very true, scauld knave, when God's
will is: I will desire you to live in the mean time, and

---

sion to clear the way. 21. **signal,** token (of victory). **ostent,** external
show. 29–35. **As . . . him,** one of the few unquestionable allusions by
Shakespeare to contemporary events. The earl of Essex had left London
on his Irish expedition on March 27, 1599; he returned unsuccessful
and under a cloud on September 28 of the same year. These lines,
therefore, must have been written between the dates mentioned. 32,

broached, transfixed, spitted. 38. **emperor 's.** The Holy Roman Emperor, Sigismund, came to England on behalf of France in May 1416.
SCENE I. 6. **scauld,** scurvy. 20. **bedlam,** crazy. **Trojan,** dissolute
fellow; a current term of contempt. 21. **Parca's.** The fates, or Parcae,
spun the web of life. 29. **Cadwallader,** last king of the Welsh. Pistol
makes the customary taunt that the Welsh were goatherds.

eat your victuals: come, there is sauce for it. [*Strikes him.*] You called me yesterday mountain-squire; but I will make you to-day a squire of low degree. I pray you, fall to: if you can mock a leek, you can eat a leek.

Gow. Enough, captain: you have astonished him. 41

Flu. I say, I will make him eat some part of my leek, or I will peat his pate four days. Bite, I pray you; it is good for your green wound and your ploody coxcomb.

Pist. Must I bite?

Flu. Yes, certainly, and out of doubt and out of question too, and ambiguities.

Pist. By this leek, I will most horribly revenge: I eat and eat, I swear— 50

Flu. Eat, I pray you: will you have some more sauce to your leek? there is not enough leek to swear by.

Pist. Quiet thy cudgel; thou dost see I eat.

Flu. Much good do you, scauld knave, heartily. Nay, pray you, throw none away; the skin is good for your broken coxcomb. When you take occasions to see leeks hereafter, I pray you, mock at 'em; that is all.

Pist. Good. 60

Flu. Ay, leeks is good: hold you, there is a groat to heal your pate.

Pist. Me a groat!

Flu. Yes, verily and in truth, you shall take it; or I have another leek in my pocket, which you shall eat.

Pist. I take thy groat in earnest of revenge.

Flu. If I owe you any thing, I will pay you in cudgels: you shall be a woodmonger, and buy nothing of me but cudgels. God b' wi' you, and keep you, and heal your pate. [*Exit.*

Pist. All hell shall stir for this. 71

Gow. Go, go; you are a counterfeit cowardly knave. Will you mock at an ancient tradition, begun upon an honourable respect, and worn as a memorable trophy of predeceased valour and dare not avouch in your deeds any of your words? I have seen you gleeking and galling at this gentleman twice or thrice. You thought, because he could not speak English in the native garb, he could not therefore handle an English cudgel: you find it otherwise; and henceforth let a Welsh correction teach you a good English condition. Fare ye well. [*Exit.*

Pist. Doth Fortune play the huswife with me now? News have I, that my Nell is dead i' the spital Of malady of France; And there my rendezvous is quite cut off. Old I do wax; and from my weary limbs Honour is cudgelled. Well, bawd I'll turn, 90 And something lean to cutpurse of quick hand. To England will I steal, and there I'll steal: And patches will I get unto these cudgell'd scars, And swear I got them in the Gallia wars. [*Exit.*

SCENE II. *France. A royal palace.*

Enter, at one door, KING HENRY, EXETER, BEDFORD, GLOUCESTER, WARWICK, WESTMORELAND, *and*

other Lords; *at another, the* FRENCH KING, QUEEN ISABEL, *the* PRINCESS KATHARINE, ALICE *and other* Ladies; *the* DUKE OF BURGUNDY, *and his train.*

K. Hen. Peace to this meeting, wherefore we are met!
Unto our brother France, and to our sister,
Health and fair time of day; joy and good wishes
To our most fair and princely cousin Katharine;
And, as a branch and member of this royalty,
By whom this great assembly is contrived,
We do salute you, Duke of Burgundy;
And, princes French, and peers, health to you all!

Fr. King. Right joyous are we to behold your face,
Most worthy brother England; fairly met: 10
So are you, princes English, every one.

Q. Isa. So happy be the issue, brother England,
Of this good day and of this gracious meeting,
As we are now glad to behold your eyes;
Your eyes, which hitherto have borne in them
Against the French, that met them in their bent,
The fatal balls of murdering basilisks:
The venom of such looks, we fairly hope,
Have lost their quality, and that this day
Shall change all griefs and quarrels into love. 20

K. Hen. To cry amen to that, thus we appear.

Q. Isa. You English princes all, I do salute you.

Bur. My duty to you both, on equal love,
Great Kings of France and England! That I have labour'd,
With all my wits, my pains and strong endeavours,
To bring your most imperial majesties
Unto this bar and royal interview,
Your mightiness on both parts best can witness.
Since then my office hath so far prevail'd
That, face to face and royal eye to eye, 30
You have congreeted, let it not disgrace me,
If I demand, before this royal view,
What rub or what impediment there is,
Why that the naked, poor and mangled Peace,
Dear nurse of arts, plenties and joyful births,
Should not in this best garden of the world,
Our fertile France, put up her lovely visage?
Alas, she hath from France too long been chased,
And all her husbandry doth lie on heaps,
Corrupting in it own fertility. 40
Her vine, the merry cheerer of the heart,
Unpruned dies; her hedges even-pleach'd,
Like prisoners wildly over-grown with hair,
Put forth disorder'd twigs; her fallow leas
The darnel, hemlock and rank fumitory
Doth root upon, while that the coulter rusts
That should deracinate such savagery;
The even mead, that erst brought sweetly forth
The freckled cowslip, burnet and green clover,
Wanting the scythe, all uncorrected, rank, 50
Conceives by idleness and nothing teems
But hateful docks, rough thistles, kecksies, burs,
Losing both beauty and utility.
And as our vineyards, fallows, meads and hedges,

---

37. **mountain-squire,** an allusion to the mountainous surface of Wales. 38. **squire of low degree,** allusion to a medieval romance, *The Squire of Low Degree.* 40. **astonished,** terrified. 78. **gleeking and galling,** gibing and scoffing. 85. **huswife,** hussy. 86. **Nell,** F: *Doll;* text follows Capell on the ground that Mistress Quickly's name was Nell. **spital,** hospital. 94. **And . . . wars.** Here one places Johnson's famous note: "The comic scenes of The History of Henry the Fourth and Fifth are now at an end, and all the comic personages are now dismissed.

Falstaff and Mrs. Quickly are dead; Nym and Bardolph are hanged; Gadshill was lost immediately after the robbery; Poins and Peto have vanished since, one knows not how; and Pistol is now beaten into obscurity. I believe every reader regrets their departure."

SCENE II. 1. **wherefore,** an account of which (the peace). 16. **bent,** gaze. 17. **basilisks,** a large cannon. Note that *balls* is probably a pun on "eyeballs." 27. **bar,** court. 31. **congreeted,** greeted each other. 40. **it,** its. 42. **even-pleach'd,** smoothly intertwined. 44. **fallow,** un-

Defective in their natures, grow to wildness,
Even so our houses and ourselves and children
Have lost, or do not learn for want of time,
The sciences that should become our country;
But grow like savages,—as soldiers will
That nothing do but meditate on blood,—   60
To swearing and stern looks, defused attire
And every thing that seems unnatural.
Which to reduce into our former favour
You are assembled: and my speech entreats
That I may know the let, why gentle Peace
Should not expel these inconveniences
And bless us with her former qualities.

K. Hen. If, Duke of Burgundy, you would the peace,
Whose want gives growth to the imperfections
Which you have cited, you must buy that peace   70
With full accord to all our just demands;
Whose tenours and particular effects
You have enscheduled briefly in your hands.

Bur. The king hath heard them; to the which as yet
There is no answer made.

K. Hen.   Well then the peace,
Which you before so urged, lies in his answer.

Fr. King. I have but with a cursory eye
O'erglanced the articles: pleaseth your grace
To appoint some of your council presently
To sit with us once more, with better heed   80
To re-survey them, we will suddenly
Pass our accept and peremptory answer.

K. Hen. Brother, we shall. Go, uncle Exeter,
And brother Clarence, and you, brother Gloucester,
Warwick and Huntingdon, go with the king;
And take with you free power to ratify,
Augment, or alter, as your wisdoms best
Shall see advantageable for our dignity,
Any thing in or out of our demands,
And we'll consign thereto. Will you, fair sister,   90
Go with the princes, or stay here with us?

Q. Isa. Our gracious brother, I will go with them:
Haply a woman's voice may do some good,
When articles too nicely urged be stood on.

K. Hen. Yet leave our cousin Katharine here with
        us:
She is our capital demand, comprised
Within the fore-rank of our articles.

Q. Isa. She hath good leave.

     [*Exeunt all except Henry, Katharine, and Alice.*
K. Hen.   Fair Katharine, and most fair,
Will you vouchsafe to teach a soldier terms
Such as will enter at a lady's ear   100
And plead his love-suit to her gentle heart?

Kath. Your majesty shall mock at me; I cannot
speak your England.

K. Hen. O fair Katharine, if you will love me
soundly with your French heart, I will be glad to
hear you confess it brokenly with your English
tongue. Do you like me, Kate?

Kath. Pardonnez-moi, I cannot tell vat is 'like me.'

K. Hen. An angel is like you, Kate, and you are like
an angel.   111

Kath. Que dit-il? que je suis semblable à les anges?

Alice. Oui, vraiment, sauf votre grace, ainsi dit-il.

K. Hen. I said so, dear Katharine; and I must not
blush to affirm it.

Kath. O bon Dieu! les langues des hommes sont
pleines de tromperies.

K. Hen. What says she, fair one? that the tongues of
men are full of deceits?   121

Alice. Oui, dat de tongues of de mans is be full of
deceits: dat is de princess.

K. Hen. The princess is the better Englishwoman. I'
faith, Kate, my wooing is fit for thy understanding: I
am glad thou canst speak no better English; for, if
thou couldst, thou wouldst find me such a plain king
that thou wouldst think I had sold my farm to buy my
crown. I know no ways to mince it in love, but directly to say 'I love you:' then if you urge me farther
than to say 'do you in faith?' I wear out my suit. Give
me your answer; i' faith, do: and so clap hands and a
bargain: how say you, lady?   134

Kath. Sauf votre honneur, me understand vell.

K. Hen. Marry, if you would put me to verses or to
dance for your sake, Kate, why you undid me: for
the one, I have neither words nor measure, and for
the other, I have no strength in measure, yet a
reasonable measure in strength. If I could win a lady
at leap-frog, or by vaulting into my saddle with my
armour on my back, under the correction of bragging
be it spoken, I should quickly leap into a wife. Or if I
might buffet for my love, or bound my horse for her
favours, I could lay on like a butcher and sit like a
jack-an-apes, never off. But, before God, Kate, I cannot look greenly nor gasp out my eloquence, nor I
have no cunning in protestation; only downright
oaths, which I never use till urged, nor never break for
urging. If thou canst love a fellow of this temper, Kate,
whose face is not worth sunburning, that never looks
in his glass for love of any thing he sees there, let thine
eye be thy cook. I speak to thee plain soldier: if thou
canst love me for this, take me; if not, to say to thee
that I shall die, is true; but for thy love, by the Lord,
no; yet I love thee too. And while thou livest, dear
Kate, take a fellow of plain and uncoined constancy;
for he perforce must do thee right, because he hath
not the gift to woo in other places: for these fellows
of infinite tongue, that can rhyme themselves into
ladies' favours, they do always reason themselves out
again. What! a speaker is but a prater; a rhyme is but
a ballad. A good leg will fall; a straight back will
stoop; a black beard will turn white; a curled pate
will grow bald; a fair face will wither; a full eye will
wax hollow: but a good heart, Kate, is the sun and the
moon; or rather the sun and not the moon; for it
shines bright and never changes, but keeps his course
truly. If thou would have such a one, take me; and
take me, take a soldier; take a soldier, take a king.
And what sayest thou then to my love? speak, my fair,
and fairly, I pray thee.

Kath. Is it possible dat I sould love de enemy of
France?   179

---

cultivated. **leas,** meadows. 45. **darnel,** a weed. **fumitory,** a weed
with a bitter taste. 47. **deracinate,** root out. 48. **erst,** formerly. 49.
burnet, an herb. 51. **teems,** grows. 52. **kecksies,** dry-stemmed plants,
possibly dried hemlock stalks. 54. **fallows,** land plowed and left lying.
61. **defused,** disordered. 72. **Whose . . . effects,** whose general purport
and specific details. 73. **enscheduled,** drawn up in writing. 77.
cursorary, cursory, hasty. 81. **suddenly,** speedily. 90. **consign,** agree,
subscribe. 94. **nicely,** with insistence on detail. **stood on,** insisted

on. 112-115. **Que . . . dit-il.** What does he say? That I am like the
angels? *Alice:* Yes truly, save your grace, he says so. 133. **clap,** clasp.
145. **buffet,** box. 146. **bound,** make prance. 148. **jack-an-apes,**
monkey. 156. **cook.** Probably the meaning is that she must dress him
with fine qualities as a cook dresses meat. 161. **uncoined,** not coined
for circulation; therefore, fixed, steady. 167. **fall,** shrink.

K. Hen. No; it is not possible you should love the enemy of France, Kate: but, in loving me, you should love the friend of France; for I love France so well that I will not part with a village of it; I will have it all mine; and, Kate, when France is mine and I am yours, then yours is France and you are mine.

Kath. I cannot tell vat is dat.

K. Hen. No, Kate? I will tell thee in French; which I am sure will hang upon my tongue like a new-married wife about her husband's neck, hardly to be shook off. Je quand sur le possession de France, et quand vous avez le possession de moi,—let me see, what then? Saint Denis be my speed!—donc votre est France et vous êtes mienne. It is as easy for me, Kate, to conquer the kingdom as to speak so much more French: I shall never move thee in French, unless it be to laugh at me. 198

Kath. Sauf votre honneur, le François que vous parlez, il est meilleur que l' Anglois lequel je parle.

K. Hen. No, faith, is 't not, Kate: but thy speaking of my tongue, and I thine, most truly-falsely, must needs be granted to be much at one. But, Kate, dost thou understand thus much English, canst thou love me?

Kath. I cannot tell. 207

K. Hen. Can any of your neighbours tell, Kate? I'll ask them. Come, I know thou lovest me: and at night, when you come into your closet, you'll question this gentlewoman about me; and I know, Kate, you will to her dispraise those parts in me that you love with your heart: but, good Kate, mock me mercifully; the rather, gentle princess, because I love thee cruelly. If ever thou beest mine, Kate, as I have a saving faith within me tells me thou shalt, I get thee with scambling, and thou must therefore needs prove a good soldier-breeder: shall not thou and I, between Saint Denis and Saint George, compound a boy, half French, half English, that shall go to Constantinople and take the Turk by the beard? shall we not? what sayest thou, my fair flower-de-luce? 224

Kath. I do not know dat.

K. Hen. No; 'tis hereafter to know, but now to promise: do but now promise, Kate, you will endeavour for your French part of such a boy; and for my English moiety take the word of a king and a bachelor. How answer you, la plus belle Katharine du monde, mon très cher et devin déesse?

Kath. Your majestee ave fausse French enough to deceive de most sage demoiselle dat is en France. 235

K. Hen. Now, fie upon my false French! By mine honour, in true English, I love thee, Kate: by which honour I dare not swear thou lovest me; yet my blood begins to flatter me that thou dost, notwithstanding the poor and untempering effect of my visage. Now, beshrew my father's ambition! he was thinking of civil wars when he got me: therefore was I created with a stubborn outside, with an aspect of iron, that, when I come to woo ladies, I fright them. But, in faith, Kate, the elder I wax, the better I shall appear: my comfort is, that old age, that ill layer up of beauty, can do no more spoil upon my face: thou hast me, if thou hast me, at the worst; and thou shalt wear me, if thou

wear me, better and better: and therefore tell me, most fair Katharine, will you have me? Put off your maiden blushes; avouch the thoughts of your heart with the looks of an empress; take me by the hand, and say 'Harry of England, I am thine:' which word thou shalt no sooner bless mine ear withal, but I will tell thee aloud 'England is thine, Ireland is thine, France is thine, and Henry Plantagenet is thine;' who, though I speak it before his face, if he be not fellow with the best king, thou shalt find the best king of good fellows. Come, your answer in broken music; for thy voice is music and thy English broken; therefore, queen of all, Katharine, break thy mind to me in broken English; wilt thou have me?

Kath. Dat is as it sall please de roi mon père.

K. Hen. Nay, it will please him well, Kate; it shall please him, Kate.

Kath. Den it sall also content me. 270

K. Hen. Upon that I kiss your hand, and I call you my queen.

Kath. Laissez, mon seigneur, laissez, laissez: ma foi, je ne veux point que vous abaissiez votre grandeur en baisant la main d'une de votre seigneurie indigne serviteur; excusez-moi, je vous supplie, mon très-puissant seigneur.

K. Hen. Then I will kiss your lips, Kate. 278

Kath. Les dames et demoiselles pour être baisées devant leur noces, il n'est pas la coutume de France.

K. Hen. Madam my interpreter, what says she?

Alice. Dat it is not be de fashion pour les ladies of France,—I cannot tell vat is baiser en Anglish.

K. Hen. To kiss.

Alice. Your majesty entendre bettre que moi.

K. Hen. It is not the fashion for the maids in France to kiss before they are married, would she say?

Alice. Oui, vraiment. 292

K. Hen. O Kate, nice customs curtsy to great kings. Dear Kate, you and I cannot be confined within the weak list of a country's fashion: we are the makers of manners, Kate; and the liberty that follows our places stops the mouth of all find-faults; as I will do yours, for upholding the nice fashion of your country in denying me a kiss: therefore, patiently and yielding. [*Kissing her.*] You have witchcraft in your lips, Kate: there is more eloquence in a sugar touch of them than in the tongues of the French council; and they should sooner persuade Harry of England than a general petition of monarchs. Here comes your father. 306

Re-enter the FRENCH KING *and his* QUEEN, BURGUNDY, *and other* Lords.

Bur. God save your majesty! my royal cousin, teach you our princess English?

K. Hen. I would have her learn, my fair cousin, how perfectly I love her; and that is good English.

Bur. Is she not apt?

K. Hen. Our tongue is rough, coz, and my condition is not smooth; so that, having neither the voice nor the heart of flattery about me, I cannot so conjure up the spirit of love in her, that he will appear in his true likeness. 317

192-195. **Je quand . . . mienne.** When I have possession of France, and you have possession of me . . . then France is yours and you are mine. 194. **Saint Denis,** patron saint of France. 199-201. **Sauf . . . parle.** Save your honor, the French that you speak is better than the English that I speak. 218. **scambling,** scrambling, struggling. 224. **flower-de-luce,** fleur-de-lis, the emblem of France. 231-232. **la plus . . . déesse,** the most beautiful Katharine in the world, my very dear and divine

goddess. 241. **untempering,** unwinsome. 262. **broken music,** music in parts for different instruments. 273-277. **Laissez . . . seigneur.** Don't, my lord, don't, don't; by my faith, I do not wish you to lower your greatness by kissing the hand of your unworthy servant; excuse me, I beg you, my most powerful lord. 279-281. **Les dames . . . France.** It is not customary in France for ladies and young girls to be kissed before their marriage. 288. **Your . . . moi.** Your majesty

Bur. Pardon the frankness of my mirth, if I answer you for that. If you would conjure in her, you must make a circle; if conjure up love in her in his true likeness, he must appear naked and blind. Can you blame her then, being a maid yet rosed over with the virgin crimson of modesty, if she deny the appearance of a naked blind boy in her naked seeing self? It were, my lord, a hard condition for a maid to consign to.

K. Hen. Yet they do wink and yield, as love is blind and enforces.

Bur. They are then excused, my lord, when they see not what they do. 330

K. Hen. Then, good my lord, teach your cousin to consent winking.

Bur. I will wink on her to consent, my lord, if you will teach her to know my meaning: for maids, well summered and warm kept, are like flies at Bartholomew-tide, blind, though they have their eyes; and then they will endure handling, which before would not abide looking on. 338

K. Hen. This moral ties me over to time and a hot summer; and so I shall catch the fly, your cousin, in the latter end and she must be blind too.

Bur. As love is, my lord, before it loves.

K. Hen. It is so: and you may, some of you, thank love for my blindness, who cannot see many a fair French city for one fair French maid that stands in my way.

Fr. King. Yes, my lord, you see them perspectively, the cities turned into a maid; for they are all girdled with maiden walls that war hath never entered. 350

K. Hen. Shall Kate be my wife?

Fr. King. So please you.

K. Hen. I am content; so the maiden cities you talk of may wait on her: so the maid that stood in the way for my wish shall show me the way to my will.

Fr. King. We have consented to all terms of reason.

K. Hen. Is 't so, my lords of England?

West. The king hath granted every article: 360
His daughter first, and then in sequel all,
According to their firm proposed natures.

Exe. Only he hath not yet subscribed this: Where your majesty demands, that the King of France, having any occasion to write for matter of grant, shall name your highness in this form and with this addition, in French, Notre très-cher fils Henri, Roi d'Angleterre, Héritier de France; and thus in Latin, Præclarissimus filius noster Henricus, Rex Angliæ, et Hæres Franciæ. 370

Fr. King. Nor this I have not, brother, so denied,
But your request shall make me let it pass.

K. Hen. I pray you then, in love and dear alliance,
Let that one article rank with the rest;
And thereupon give me your daughter.

Fr. King. Take her, fair son, and from her blood
    raise up
Issue to me; that the contending kingdoms
Of France and England, whose very shores look pale
With envy of each other's happiness,
May cease their hatred, and this dear conjunction 380
Plant neighbourhood and Christian-like accord

In their sweet bosoms, that never war advance
His bleeding sword 'twixt England and fair France.

All. Amen!

K. Hen. Now, welcome, Kate: and bear me witness
    all,
That here I kiss her as my sovereign queen. [*Flourish.*

Q. Isa. God, the best maker of all marriages,
Combine your hearts in one, your realms in one!
As man and wife, being two, are one in love,
So be there 'twixt your kingdoms such a spousal, 390
That never may ill office, or fell jealousy,
Which troubles oft the bed of blessed marriage,
Thrust in between the paction of these kingdoms,
To make divorce of their incorporate league;
That English may as French, French Englishmen,
Receive each other. God speak this Amen!

All. Amen!

K. Hen. Prepare we for our marriage: on which day,
My Lord of Burgundy, we'll take your oath,
And all the peers', for surety of our leagues. 400
Then shall I swear to Kate, and you to me;
And may our oaths well kept and prosperous be!
[*Sennet. Exeunt.*

EPILOGUE.

Enter Chorus.

Chor. Thus far, with rough and all-unable pen,
    Our bending author hath pursued the story,
In little room confining mighty men,
    Mangling by starts the full course of their glory.
Small time, but in that small most greatly lived
    This star of England: Fortune made his sword;
By which the world's best garden he achieved,
    And of it left his son imperial lord.
Henry the Sixth, in infant bands crown'd King
    Of France and England, did this king succeed; 10
Whose state so many had the managing,
    That they lost France and made his England bleed:
Which oft our stage hath shown; and, for their sake,
In your fair minds let this acceptance take. [*Exit.*

393. **paction,** alliance, compact.
EPILOGUE. 2. **bending,** i.e., under the weight of his task. 13. **Which . . . shown,** a reference to the three parts of *King Henry VI,* which were written probably about 1591-1592 and may have been revived about the time that *Henry V* was on the stage. The older plays show some evidence of late revision.

understands better than I. 292. **Oui, vraiment.** Yes, truly. 326. **consign,** agree. 336. **Bartholomew-tide,** St. Bartholomew's Day, August 24. 347. **perspectively,** distorted by a perspective glass. 368. **fils,** son. 369. **Héritier,** heir. **Præclarissimus,** most renowned. Shakespeare repeats an error in Holinshed for *praecarissimus,* i.e., most dear.

A TRAGEDY OF THE

SECOND PERIOD

Julius Cæsar

The only early publication of *Julius Caesar* is that of the First Folio, where it is placed among the tragedies and called *The Tragedie of Julius Caesar.* In the table of contents it appears as *The Life and Death of Julius Caesar*, as if it were there thought of as a history play, which in some respects it is. The text of the Folio is good. John Weever's *Mirror of Martyrs*, written as a defense of Sir John Oldcastle, probably in 1599, alludes to the play in these lines:

> The many-headed multitude were drawn
> By Brutus' speech that Cæsar was ambitious;
> When eloquent Mark Anthony had shown
> His virtues, who but Brutus then was vicious?
> Man's memory with new forgets the old;
> One tale is good until another's told.

Thomas Platter, a physician visiting London from Basel, crossed the river and saw about two o'clock in the afternoon in a "thatch-roofed building the tragedy of the first emperor Julius Caesar" on September 21, 1599. This would point to the Globe Theatre and to *Julius Caesar* as a new play.[1] Ben Jonson's *Everyman in his Humour*, also acted in 1599, quotes *Et tu Brute!* somewhat derisively, and remarks that "reason long since is fled to animals," which seems to allude to Antony's

> O judgement! thou art fled to brutish beasts,
> And men have lost their reason. (III, ii, 109-110.)

These references indicate that the play belongs to the year 1599, or slightly earlier.

SOURCE

The men of the Renaissance were greatly interested in the figures of Roman history. Caesar particularly caught their attention and appealed to their imaginations. They endorsed the idea of empire, and, although they probably understood and to some degree appreciated the idea of republicanism, it seemed to them an impossible dream.

Probably Caesar, Cicero, Antony, Cleopatra, Augustus, and the whole story of the breakdown of the Roman republic and the establishment of the glorious Roman empire, were as familiar to an Elizabethan audience as they are to us, and were relatively much more important. The Elizabethan world, which as yet had not seen Cromwell and Washington, looked to antiquity for stories of political significance, events which had ideas back of them.

The chief means of rendering familiar the stories of the great men of Greece and Rome was Plutarch's *Lives of the Noble Grecians and Romans*. Plutarch was a clever Greek, who lived from about 46 A.D. to 120 A.D., lectured on philosophy in Rome, and wrote forty-six parallel lives of Grecians and Romans arranged in twos for comparison, Cicero being paired with Demosthenes, Theseus with Romulus, Caesar with Alexander, and so forth. Plutarch's purpose was not primarily historical, but moral and fictional.

His book had a good deal of the engrossing interest of fiction and far more authority, for Plutarch was a moralist and a great observer of life. His theory of biography was that a man's character is often more

Julius Caesar

clearly revealed in his idle moments, his petty tastes, and offhand conversation than in his battles and public actions and utterances.

Plutarch, who was a literary artist of great skill, found in Jacques Amyot, who translated the *Lives* into French in 1559, a person able to render him appreciatively; in turn, in Sir Thomas North another equally good translator who, though he did not go to Plutarch's Greek, was able to put Amyot's French into racy and effective English. North's translation was issued in 1579 and must have been well known to Shakespeare, particularly since an edition was issued in 1595 from the press of his fellow townsman, Richard Field.

Shakespeare, who had already used Plutarch in the composition of *A Midsummer-Night's Dream*, was always willing to let well enough alone. He therefore made use of Plutarch's gold without trying to gild it. He respected Holinshed's chronicles insofar, we may believe, as he respected the general truth of history as he understood it, but Holinshed was only an annalist of poor enough tradition and little art. Plutarch, on the other hand, gave Shakespeare scene by scene the very texture of what he was to say. Plutarch is the main reason for the carefully detailed portraits of the persons in the play of *Julius Caesar*, and it may be that from Plutarch Shakespeare learned much of the art of dramatic portraiture and the complexity of human motive.

JULIUS CAESAR AND PLUTARCH

At any rate, it is easy to point out as we go through the play how Shakespeare has repeated event after

[1]G. Binz, "Londoner Theater und Schauspiele im Jahre 1599," *Anglia*, XXII, 456; Chambers, *The Elizabethan Stage*, II, 364-366; *Thomas Platters des Jüngeren Englandfahrt im Jahre 1599*, edited by Hans Hecht (Halle, 1929); English translation (1937).

event from Plutarch's lives of Caesar, Brutus, and Antony. For example, the behavior and fate of the tribunes Flavius and Marullus; the offering of the crown to Caesar and the reception by the mob of his refusal of it; the formation of the conspiracy with the inclusion of Ligarius and the exclusion of Cicero; Brutus' whole course of conduct with his gradual yielding to persuasion and his refusal to bind the conspirators with oaths; all the circumstances of Caesar's debate with himself, his wife, and with Decius Brutus as to whether or not he should go to the senate house on the fatal Ides of March; and so on throughout the play.

It must not be thought that Shakespeare does not improve on Plutarch, for Shakespeare makes the story more vividly dramatic. Consider how much more frightful the supernatural portents which precede the death of Caesar are rendered by having the hardy Casca with his drawn sword in his hand tremble and start as he recounts them. Then again, the greatest scene in the play, that in which Antony over the body of Caesar incites the mob to vengeance, seems to be Shakespeare's own. One of the most interesting things in Shakespeare's version is the way in which he has caught Plutarch's delineation of Brutus and Cassius in terms of the philosophies which they held and has made these philosophies illuminate their parts as characters in the play.

Stoicism is quite the most respectable of the ancient creeds and Brutus is a Stoic who believes in right for right's sake. We say he is an idealist. He steels himself against the strokes of fate and carries the medicine for his own wounds. He follows his ideals to the end, though he wrecks the conspiracy and ultimately takes his own life, for he finds ruin at last too great for Stoicism.

Cassius, on the other hand, is an Epicurean, not the vulgar pleasure lover whom moderns have made typical of the sect, but an Epicurean as anciently conceived, a practical man, one who faces facts and tests all things, even the ambition of Caesar, in terms of their effects on him himself. His strength is less than that of Brutus, because his philosophy is a philosophy of pliability. Brutus is "yoke-fellow to a lamb."

JULIUS CAESAR

Singularly enough the one respect in which Shakespeare seems to differ most from Plutarch is in the conception of Julius Caesar himself. Shakespeare's Caesar is arrogant—said to be—and boastful, inconsistent and petulant, vain and deaf, superstitious and self-deluding. In Plutarch he is a far nobler and more impressive character. Here then is something which obviously requires explanation.

We are asked by the ordinary critics to believe that Shakespeare has given us in the portrait of Caesar a picture of decaying power. However, the matter goes deeper than this, even if we believe that

Shakespeare ever worked in a way which would have caused him to invent a thing for which there was no warrant in fact.

Julius Caesar was a popular theme on the stage of the sixteenth century in Holland, Italy, France, and England. He had acquired a perfectly well-known stage character not unlike that in Shakespeare. Caesar had been made the hero of various Senecan tragedies, traceable from the Latin *Julius Caesar* of Muret and its French adaptation *César* by Jacques Grévin to Sir William Alexander's *Julius Caesar* and the anonymous *Caesar and Pompey, or the Tragedy of Caesar's Revenge* (1592-1596).[2] Caesar's pride and blindness, even his superstition, were in these plays the tragic weaknesses over which brooded the vengeance of the gods.

It is easy to see why the play is called "Julius Caesar." Not only was the fall of Julius Caesar the most important event of the ancient world, but the play in its first major movement is actually his tragedy. His glorious successes belong to an earlier phase of the story.

The theme of Julius Caesar was usually a tragedy in two parts, the first part dealing with the overthrow of Pompey and the death of Caesar and the second part with Caesar's revenge. In the latter, Caesar's spirit returns to demand vengeance and is not laid to rest until his enemies are destroyed. It may be that *Julius Caesar* is in some measure a combination of these two themes, but mainly a play of Caesar's revenge. In other words, it has a Senecan background which still makes itself felt. In the light of this it will be seen that Caesar alive is a condensed and hasty picture of a smitten tragic hero, but that the importance of Caesar dead is fully recognized.

The play is named for Caesar dead, who dying becomes the most potent character in the play. The editor of the Tudor edition quotes from North's translation of a *Comparison of Alexander and Caesar*: "He lived in the person of his successor, Augustus, who . . . established a monarchy the which . . . hath continued many hundreds of years," a statement which seems to express Shakespeare's conception of Caesar's primacy.

These ideas appear as a formative pattern in a whole series of Plutarchan subjects. The Greek idea of nemesis afforded a conception of human life that gave to generations of thinkers a general notion about the careers of great men. Their lives were seen to present a rhythm like that of nature—origin, maturity, and decay; flood tide and ebb tide; youth, manhood, and old age, and so on. A hero climbed to power and paused on the summit. Then the gods, grown jealous, struck him down. For example, if one imagines that Caius Marius, who had overthrown the enemies of the Gracchi, found his fate in Sulla, then

²Harry Morgan Ayres, "Shakespeare's *Julius Cæsar* in the Light of Some Other Versions," *PMLA*, XXV, 183-227; "Caesar's Revenge," *ibid.*, XXX, 771-787.

a play of Marius and Sulla would show Sulla crescent and Marius cadent. A play of Sulla and Pompey would show Pompey rising and Sulla falling. In a play of Caesar and Pompey, Pompey would be cadent as Caesar rose, and again Caesar would fall as Brutus rose, Brutus would fall as Antony rose. It will thus be seen that *Julius Caesar* embodies two of these actions, both affecting Brutus. Caesar appears only as a declining hero and Antony only as a rising hero. *Julius Caesar* is thus a complete play of Brutus, who in his rise to power brings in a declining Caesar and a rising Antony. We shall see this Antony cadent in the play of *Antony and Cleopatra*, in which Octavius is crescent.

STAGE HISTORY

Julius Caesar, perhaps because of its stately classical qualities, escaped mutilation by the Restoration adapters and revisers of Shakespeare,[3] though John Sheffield, first duke of Buckingham and Normandy (1648-1721), rewrote according to the current ideas of dramatic propriety *Julius Caesar* as two plays, *Julius Caesar* and *Marcus Brutus*.

The play as Shakespeare wrote it, dealing in moral and philosophic fashion with ideas of governing, appeals to men of affairs and statesmen. It is a play for the grave and thoughtful, and its gravity and judicial tone, its political speculation, its clearness and purity (what was called its classical quality), caused it to become a favorite with the playgoers of the Restoration and the eighteenth century. Its vigorous declamatory passages also had an appeal.

Betterton created the role of Brutus, and the greatest actors since his time have played one or other of the five first-rate parts. Of Betterton's acting of Brutus, Colley Cibber says, "When the Betterton-Brutus was provoked in his dispute with Cassius, his spirit flew only to his eye; his steady look alone supplied that terror which he disdained an intemperance in his voice should rise to." Barton Booth, James Quin, John Philip Kemble, Junius Brutus Booth, Charles Kean, and Beerbohm Tree have been distinguished as Brutus.

Because of the number of important parts *Julius Caesar* has been a great play for combinations of great actors, all-star casts. In the performance at Covent Garden in 1838 Macready acted Brutus; Phelps, Cassius; and Vandenhoff and Elton, Antony. On the American stage Edwin Booth and Lawrence Barrett were magnificent as Brutus and Cassius.

In more recent times the Brutus of Richard Mansfield, the Antony of Beerbohm Tree, of Henry Ainley, and of William Faversham have met with great success. A performance directed by Orson Welles in 1937 attracted much attention. It was in modern dress and had anti-fascist bearings. A company directed by Margaret Webster was on the boards in 1949-1950.

---
[3]F. W. Kilbourne, *Alterations and Adaptations of Shakespeare* (Boston, 1906); Hazelton Spencer, *Shakespeare Improved* (Cambridge, 1928).

Julius Cæsar

DRAMATIS PERSONÆ

JULIUS CÆSAR.
OCTAVIUS CÆSAR,
MARCUS ANTONIUS, } triumvirs after the death of Julius Cæsar.
M. ÆMILIUS LEPIDUS,
CICERO,
PUBLIUS, } senators.
POPILIUS LENA,
MARCUS BRUTUS,
CASSIUS,
CASCA,
TREBONIUS, } conspirators against Julius Cæsar.
LIGARIUS,
DECIUS BRUTUS,
METELLUS CIMBER,
CINNA,
FLAVIUS and MARULLUS, tribunes.
ARTEMIDORUS of Cnidos, a teacher of Rhetoric.
A Soothsayer.
CINNA, a poet. Another Poet.
LUCILIUS,
TITINIUS,
MESSALA, } friends to Brutus and Cassius.
Young CATO,
VOLUMNIUS,
VARRO,
CLITUS,
CLAUDIUS, } servants to Brutus.
STRATO,
LUCIUS,
DARDANIUS,
PINDARUS, servant to Cassius.

CALPURNIA, wife to Cæsar.
PORTIA, wife to Brutus.

Senators, Citizens, Guards, Attendants, &c.

SCENE: *Rome: the neighbourhood of Sardis: the neighbourhood of Philippi.*

ACT I.

SCENE I. *Rome. A street.*

Enter FLAVIUS, MARULLUS, *and certain* Commoners.

Flav. Hence! home, you idle creatures, get you
    home:
Is this a holiday? what! know you not,
Being mechanical, you ought not walk
Upon a labouring day without the sign
Of your profession? Speak, what trade art thou?
    First Com. Why, sir, a carpenter.
    Mar. Where is thy leather apron and thy rule?
What dost thou with thy best apparel on?
You, sir, what trade are you?
    Sec. Com. Truly, sir, in respect of a fine workman,
I am but, as you would say, a cobbler.

9

Mar. But what trade art thou? answer me directly.

Sec. Com. A trade, sir, that, I hope, I may use with a safe conscience; which is, indeed, sir, a mender of bad soles.

Mar. What trade, thou knave? thou naughty knave, what trade?

Sec. Com. Nay, I beseech you, sir, be not out with me: yet, if you be out, sir, I can mend you.

Mar. What meanest thou by that? mend me, thou saucy fellow!   21

Sec. Com. Why, sir, cobble you.

Flav. Thou art a cobbler, art thou?

Sec. Com. Truly, sir, all that I live by is with the awl: I meddle with no tradesman's matters, nor women's matters, but with awl. I am, indeed, sir, a surgeon to old shoes; when they are in great danger, I recover them. As proper men as ever trod upon neat's leather have gone upon my handiwork.   30

Flav. But wherefore art not in thy shop to-day?
Why dost thou lead these men about the streets?

Sec. Com. Truly, sir, to wear out their shoes, to get myself into more work. But, indeed, sir, we make holiday, to see Cæsar and to rejoice in his triumph.

Mar. Wherefore rejoice? What conquest brings he home?
What tributaries follow him to Rome,
To grace in captive bonds his chariot-wheels?
You blocks, you stones, you worse than senseless
    things!   40
O you hard hearts, you cruel men of Rome,
Knew you not Pompey? Many a time and oft
Have you climb'd up to walls and battlements,
To towers and windows, yea, to chimney-tops,
Your infants in your arms, and there have sat
The live-long day, with patient expectation,
To see great Pompey pass the streets of Rome:
And when you saw his chariot but appear,
Have you not made an universal shout,
That Tiber trembled underneath her banks,   50
To hear the replication of your sounds
Made in her concave shores?
And do you now put on your best attire?
And do you now cull out a holiday?
And do you now strew flowers in his way
That comes in triumph over Pompey's blood?
Be gone!
Run to your houses, fall upon your knees,
Pray to the gods to intermit the plague
That needs must light on this ingratitude.   60

Flav. Go, go, good countrymen, and, for this fault,
Assemble all the poor men of your sort;
Draw them to Tiber banks, and weep your tears
Into the channel, till the lowest stream
Do kiss the most exalted shores of all.
                                   [*Exeunt all the Commoners.*

See, whether their basest metal be not moved;
They vanish tongue-tied in their guiltiness.
Go you down that way towards the Capitol;
This way will I: disrobe the images,
If you do find them deck'd with ceremonies.   70
    Mar. May we do so?
You know it is the feast of Lupercal.
    Flav. It is no matter; let no images
Be hung with Cæsar's trophies. I'll about,
And drive away the vulgar from the streets:
So do you too, where you perceive them thick.
These growing feathers pluck'd from Cæsar's wing
Will make him fly an ordinary pitch,
Who else would soar above the view of men
And keep us all in servile fearfulness.   [*Exeunt.* 80

SCENE II. *A public place.*

Flourish. Enter CÆSAR; ANTONY, *for the course;*
    CALPURNIA, PORTIA, DECIUS, CICERO, BRUTUS,
    CASSIUS, *and* CASCA; *a great crowd following, among*
    them a Soothsayer.

Cæs. Calpurnia!
Casca.   Peace, ho! Cæsar speaks.
Cæs.   Calpurnia!
Cal. Here, my lord.
Cæs. Stand you directly in Antonius' way,
When he doth run his course. Antonius!
    Ant. Cæsar, my lord?
    Cæs. Forget not, in your speed, Antonius,
To touch Calpurnia; for our elders say,
The barren, touched in this holy chase,
Shake off their sterile curse.
    Ant.   I shall remember:
When Cæsar says 'do this,' it is perform'd.   10
    Cæs. Set on; and leave no ceremony out. [*Flourish.*
Sooth. Cæsar!
    Cæs. Ha! who calls?
    Casca. Bid every noise be still: peace yet again!
    Cæs. Who is it in the press that calls on me?
I hear a tongue, shriller than all the music,
Cry 'Cæsar!' Speak; Cæsar is turn'd to hear.
    Sooth. Beware the ides of March.
    Cæs.   What man is that?
    Bru. A soothsayer bids you beware the ides of
    March.
    Cæs. Set him before me; let me see his face.   20
    Cas. Fellow, come from the throng; look upon
    Cæsar.
    Cæs. What say'st thou to me now? speak once again.
    Sooth. Beware the ides of March.
    Cæs. He is a dreamer; let us leave him: pass.
        [*Sennet. Exeunt all except Brutus and Cassius.*
    Cas. Will you go see the order of the course?

ACT I. SCENE I.   3. **mechanical,** of the class of mechanics or artisans. 4. **sign,** garb and implements. 18. **out,** i.e., of temper. 26. **with awl,** F: *withal,* without punctuation after the word; many editors: *with all.* There is thus a pun on the word *withal* meaning "nevertheless." 29. **neat's.** *Neat* means "cattle of the ox kind." 36. **triumph.** Caesar had just overthrown the sons of Pompey in Spain at the Battle of Munda (March 17, 45 B.C.). He is celebrating his triumph, which is resented because it is over Romans and not foreign enemies (cf. l. 56, below). The triumph is disguised by the celebration of the feast of the Lupercalia. 42. **Pompey.** Caesar had overthrown the great soldier, Pompey, at the Battle of Pharsalia in 48 B.C., and Pompey had been murdered in Egypt. This story was itself the subject of various tragedies. In the dramatic treatment of the whole theme the tragedy of Pompey had been a first part, and the tragedy of Caesar a second part. In this lies

the reason for the name of this play. 50. **her.** The Roman custom was to speak of Father Tiber, but the English feeling for rivers as feminine here prevails. 51. **replication,** echo. 70. **ceremonies,** ceremonial trappings. 72. **Lupercal,** a feast of purification in honor of Pan celebrated from ancient times in Rome on February 15 of each year. The celebrants, called *Luperci,* raced around the Palatine Hill and the Circus carrying thongs of goatskin called *februa* (whence *February*). With the thongs they struck those who came in their way. Women so lashed were cured of barrenness; hence Caesar's wish that Antony would strike Calpurnia (I, ii, 6-8).
SCENE II.   9. **sterile curse,** curse of sterility. 17. **Cæsar.** Caesar's referring to himself in the third person suggests a royal habit. It was, however, his custom in his *Commentaries.* 18. **ides of March,** March 15. 25. **order of the course,** performance of the race.

Bru. Not I.

Cas. I pray you, do.

Bru. I am not gamesome: I do lack some part
Of that quick spirit that is in Antony.
Let me not hinder, Cassius, your desires; 30
I'll leave you.

Cas. Brutus, I do observe you now of late:
I have not from your eyes that gentleness
And show of love as I was wont to have:
You bear too stubborn and too strange a hand
Over your friend that loves you.

Bru. Cassius,
Be not deceived: if I have veil'd my look,
I turn the trouble of my countenance
Merely upon myself. Vexed I am
Of late with passions of some difference, 40
Conceptions only proper to myself,
Which give some soil perhaps to my behaviours;
But let not therefore my good friends be grieved—
Among which number, Cassius, be you one—
Nor construe any further my neglect,
Than that poor Brutus, with himself at war,
Forgets the shows of love to other men.

Cas. Then, Brutus, I have much mistook your
passion;
By means whereof this breast of mine hath buried
Thoughts of great value, worthy cogitations. 50
Tell me, good Brutus, can you see your face?

Bru. No, Cassius; for the eye sees not itself,
But by reflection, by some other things.

Cas. 'Tis just:
And it is very much lamented, Brutus,
That you have no such mirrors as will turn
Your hidden worthiness into your eye,
That you might see your shadow. I have heard,
Where many of the best respect in Rome,
Except immortal Cæsar, speaking of Brutus 60
And groaning underneath this age's yoke,
Have wish'd that noble Brutus had his eyes.

Bru. Into what dangers would you lead me, Cassius,
That you would have me seek into myself
For that which is not in me?

Cas. Therefore, good Brutus, be prepared to hear:
And since you know you cannot see yourself
So well as by reflection, I, your glass,
Will modestly discover to yourself
That of yourself which you yet know not of. 70
And be not jealous on me, gentle Brutus;
Were I a common laugher, or did use
To stale with ordinary oaths my love
To every new protester; if you know
That I do fawn on men and hug them hard
And after scandal them, or if you know
That I profess myself in banqueting
To all the rout, then hold me dangerous.

[*Flourish, and shout.*

Bru. What means this shouting? I do fear, the
people
Choose Cæsar for their king.

Cas. Ay, do you fear it? 80
Then must I think you would not have it so.

Bru. I would not, Cassius; yet I love him well.
But wherefore do you hold me here so long?
What is it that you would impart to me?
If it be aught toward the general good,
Set honour in one eye and death i' the other,
And I will look on both indifferently:
For let the gods so speed me as I love
The name of honour more than I fear death.

Cas. I know that virtue to be in you, Brutus, 90
As well as I do know your outward favour.
Well, honour is the subject of my story.
I cannot tell what you and other men
Think of this life; but, for my single self,
I had as lief not be as live to be
In awe of such a thing as I myself.
I was born free as Cæsar; so were you:
We both have fed as well, and we can both
Endure the winter's cold as well as he:
For once, upon a raw and gusty day, 100
The troubled Tiber chafing with her shores,
Cæsar said to me 'Darest thou, Cassius, now
Leap in with me into this angry flood,
And swim to yonder point?' Upon the word,
Accoutred as I was, I plunged in
And bade him follow; so indeed he did.
The torrent roar'd, and we did buffet it
With lusty sinews, throwing it aside
And stemming it with hearts of controversy;
But ere we could arrive the point proposed, 110
Cæsar cried 'Help me, Cassius, or I sink!'
I, as Æneas, our great ancestor,
Did from the flames of Troy upon his shoulder
The old Anchises bear, so from the waves of Tiber
Did I the tired Cæsar. And this man
Is now become a god, and Cassius is
A wretched creature and must bend his body,
If Cæsar carelessly but nod on him.
He had a fever when he was in Spain,
And when the fit was on him, I did mark 120
How he did shake: 'tis true, this god did shake:
His coward lips did from their colour fly,
And that same eye whose bend doth awe the world
Did lose his lustre: I did hear him groan:
Ay, and that tongue of his that bade the Romans
Mark him and write his speeches in their books,
Alas, it cried 'Give me some drink, Titinius,'
As a sick girl. Ye gods, it doth amaze me
A man of such a feeble temper should
So get the start of the majestic world 130
And bear the palm alone. [*Shout. Flourish.*

Bru. Another general shout!
I do believe that these applauses are
For some new honours that are heap'd on Cæsar.

Cas. Why, man, he doth bestride the narrow world
Like a Colossus, and we petty men
Walk under his huge legs and peep about
To find ourselves dishonourable graves.
Men at some time are masters of their fates:
The fault, dear Brutus, is not in our stars, 140
But in ourselves, that we are underlings.
Brutus and Cæsar: what should be in that 'Cæsar'?

28. **gamesome,** fond of sports. 35. **stubborn,** rough. 40. **of some difference,** conflicting. 41. **only proper,** peculiar, relating merely. 42. **give . . . to,** sully. 49. **By means whereof,** i.e., by which mistake. 71. **jealous on,** suspicious of. 73. **stale,** render stale. 74. **protester,** i.e., one who protests friendship. 76. **scandal,** slander. 77. **profess myself,** make declarations of friendship. 82. **I love him well.** It is necessary to

remember this idea, placed so early and so emphatically, in order to understand Shakespeare's conception of the deed that Brutus was to do. Friendship ranked high in Elizabethan thought. 87. **indifferently,** impartially. 109. **hearts of controversy,** competing courage. 123. **bend,** glance. 136. **Colossus,** the gigantic statue which stood astride the entrance to the harbor of Rhodes. 155. **walls,** so Rowe. Many

Why should that name be sounded more than yours?
Write them together, yours is as fair a name;
Sound them, it doth become the mouth as well;
Weigh them, it is as heavy; conjure with 'em,
Brutus will start a spirit as soon as Cæsar.
Now, in the names of all the gods at once,
Upon what meat doth this our Cæsar feed,
That he is grown so great? Age, thou art shamed! 150
Rome, thou hast lost the breed of noble bloods!
When went there by an age, since the great flood,
But it was famed with more than with one man?
When could they say till now, that talk'd of Rome,
That her wide walls encompass'd but one man?
Now is it Rome indeed and room enough,
When there is in it but one only man.
O, you and I have heard our fathers say,
There was a Brutus once that would have brook'd
The eternal devil to keep his state in Rome 160
As easily as a king.
    Bru. That you do love me, I am nothing jealous;
What you would work me to, I have some aim:
How I have thought of this and of these times,
I shall recount hereafter; for this present,
I would not, so with love I might entreat you,
Be any further moved. What you have said
I will consider; what you have to say
I will with patience hear, and find a time
Both meet to hear and answer such high things. 170
Till then, my noble friend, chew upon this:
Brutus had rather be a villager
Than to repute himself a son of Rome
Under these hard conditions as this time
Is like to lay upon us.
    Cas. I am glad that my weak words
Have struck but thus much show of fire from Brutus.
    Bru. The games are done and Cæsar is returning.
    Cas. As they pass by, pluck Casca by the sleeve;
And he will, after his sour fashion, tell you 180
What hath proceeded worthy note to-day.

Re-enter CÆSAR *and his Train.*

    Bru. I will do so. But, look you, Cassius,
The angry spot doth glow on Cæsar's brow,
And all the rest look like a chidden train:
Calpurnia's cheek is pale; and Cicero
Looks with such ferret and such fiery eyes
As we have seen him in the Capitol,
Being cross'd in conference by some senators.
    Cas. Casca will tell us what the matter is.
    Cæs. Antonius! 190
    Ant. Cæsar?
    Cæs. Let me have men about me that are fat;
Sleek-headed men and such as sleep o' nights;
Yond Cassius has a lean and hungry look;
He thinks too much: such men are dangerous.
    Ant. Fear him not, Cæsar; he 's not dangerous;
He is a noble Roman and well given.
    Cæs. Would he were fatter! But I fear him not:
Yet if my name were liable to fear,
I do not know the man I should avoid 200
So soon as that spare Cassius. He reads much;

He is a great observer and he looks
Quite through the deeds of men; he loves no plays,
As thou dost, Antony; he hears no music;
Seldom he smiles, and smiles in such a sort
As if he mock'd himself and scorn'd his spirit
That could be moved to smile at any thing.
Such men as he be never at heart's ease
Whiles they behold a greater than themselves,
And therefore are they very dangerous. 210
I rather tell thee what is to be fear'd
Than what I fear; for always I am Cæsar.
Come on my right hand, for this ear is deaf,
And tell me truly what thou think'st of him.
    [*Sennet. Exeunt Cæsar and all his Train, but Casca.*
    Casca. You pull'd me by the cloak; would you speak
        with me?
    Bru. Ay, Casca; tell us what hath chanced to-day,
That Cæsar looks so sad.
    Casca. Why, you were with him, were you not?
    Bru. I should not then ask Casca what had chanced.
    Casca. Why, there was a crown offered him: and
being offered him, he put it by with the back of his
hand, thus; and then the people fell a-shouting.
    Bru. What was the second noise for?
    Casca. Why, for that too.
    Cas. They shouted thrice: what was the last cry
        for?
    Casca. Why, for that too.
    Bru. Was the crown offered him thrice?
    Casca. Ay, marry, was 't, and he put it by thrice,
every time gentler than other, and at every putting-by
mine honest neighbours shouted. 231
    Cas. Who offered him the crown?
    Casca. Why, Antony.
    Bru. Tell us the manner of it, gentle Casca.
    Casca. I can as well be hanged as tell the manner
of it: it was mere foolery; I did not mark it. I saw
Mark Antony offer him a crown;—yet 'twas not a
crown neither, 'twas one of these coronets;—and, as
I told you, he put it by once: but, for all that, to my
thinking, he would fain have had it. Then he offered
it to him again; then he put it by again: but, to my
thinking, he was very loath to lay his fingers off it.
And then he offered it the third time; he put it the
third time by: and still as he refused it, the rabblement hooted and clapped their chopped hands and
threw up their sweaty night-caps and uttered such a
deal of stinking breath because Cæsar refused the
crown that it had almost choked Cæsar; for he
swounded and fell down at it: and for mine own part,
I durst not laugh, for fear of opening my lips and
receiving the bad air. 252
    Cas. But, soft, I pray you: what, did Cæsar swound?
    Casca. He fell down in the market-place, and foamed
at mouth, and was speechless.
    Bru. 'Tis very like: he hath the falling sickness.
    Cas. No, Cæsar hath it not; but you and I
And honest Casca, we have the falling sickness. 258
    Casca. I know not what you mean by that; but, I
am sure, Cæsar fell down. If the tag-rag people did
not clap him and hiss him, according as he pleased

editions follow F and read *walks*, explained as a reference to the famous
paved ways of the Romans. The Arden editor offers an explanation of
walks as tracts of garden, park, or forest, adding that ancient Rome was
almost entirely surrounded by a "green girdle of gardens and pleasure
grounds." 159. **Brutus,** Lucius Junius Brutus, who expelled the Tarquins and founded the Roman Republic (509 B.C.). 163. **aim,** inkling.

186. **ferret,** ferretlike, i.e., small and red. 197. **given,** disposed. 204.
hears no music, regarded as a sign of a morose and treacherous character.
238. **coronets,** chaplets, garlands. 246. **chopped,** chapped. 247. **night-
caps,** scornful allusion to the *pileus,* a cap worn by the populace. Patricians
went bareheaded. 249. **swounded,** fainted. 258. **falling sickness,**
epilepsy. 261. **tag-rag,** literally rag; customarily applied to the rabble.

and displeased them, as they use to do the players in the theatre, I am no true man.

Bru. What said he when he came unto himself? 264

Casca. Marry, before he fell down, when he perceived the common herd was glad he refused the crown, he plucked me ope his doublet and offered them his throat to cut. An I had been a man of any occupation, if I would not have taken him at a word, I would I might go to hell among the rogues. And so he fell. When he came to himself again, he said, If he had done or said any thing amiss, he desired their worships to think it was his infirmity. Three or four wenches, where I stood, cried 'Alas, good soul!' and forgave him with all their hearts: but there's no heed to be taken of them; if Cæsar had stabbed their mothers, they would have done no less.

Bru. And after that, he came, thus sad, away?

Casca. Ay. 280

Cas. Did Cicero say any thing?

Casca. Ay, he spoke Greek.

Cas. To what effect?

Casca. Nay, an I tell you that, I'll ne'er look you i' the face again: but those that understood him smiled at one another and shook their heads; but, for mine own part, it was Greek to me. I could tell you more news too: Marullus and Flavius, for pulling scarfs off Cæsar's images, are put to silence. Fare you well. There was more foolery yet, if I could remember it. 291

Cas. Will you sup with me to-night, Casca?

Casca. No, I am promised forth.

Cas. Will you dine with me to-morrow?

Casca. Ay, if I be alive and your mind hold and your dinner worth the eating.

Cas. Good: I will expect you.

Casca. Do so. Farewell, both.   [*Exit.*

Bru. What a blunt fellow is this grown to be! He was quick mettle when he went to school. 300

Cas. So is he now in execution Of any bold or noble enterprise, However he puts on this tardy form. This rudeness is a sauce to his good wit, Which gives men stomach to digest his words With better appetite.

Bru. And so it is. For this time I will leave you: To-morrow, if you please to speak with me, I will come home to you; or, if you will, Come home to me, and I will wait for you. 310

Cas. I will do so: till then, think of the world.
                              [*Exit Brutus.*

Well, Brutus, thou art noble; yet, I see, Thy honourable metal may be wrought From that it is disposed: therefore it is meet That noble minds keep ever with their likes; For who so firm that cannot be seduced? Cæsar doth bear me hard; but he loves Brutus: If I were Brutus now and he were Cassius, He should not humour me. I will this night, In several hands, in at his windows throw, 320 As if they came from several citizens, Writings all tending to the great opinion

That Rome holds of his name; wherein obscurely Cæsar's ambition shall be glanced at: And after this let Cæsar seat him sure; For we will shake him, or worse days endure.   [*Exit.*

SCENE III. *The same. A street.*

Thunder and lightning. Enter, from opposite sides,
CASCA, *with his sword drawn, and* CICERO.

Cic. Good even, Casca: brought you Cæsar home? Why are you breathless? and why stare you so?

Casca. Are not you moved, when all the sway of earth Shakes like a thing unfirm? O Cicero, I have seen tempests, when the scolding winds Have rived the knotty oaks, and I have seen The ambitious ocean swell and rage and foam, To be exalted with the threatening clouds: But never till to-night, never till now, Did I go through a tempest dropping fire. 10 Either there is a civil strife in heaven, Or else the world, too saucy with the gods, Incenses them to send destruction.

Cic. Why, saw you any thing more wonderful?

Casca. A common slave—you know him well by sight— Held up his left hand, which did flame and burn Like twenty torches join'd, and yet his hand, Not sensible of fire, remain'd unscorch'd. Besides—I ha' not since put up my sword— Against the Capitol I met a lion, 20 Who glared upon me, and went surly by, Without annoying me: and there were drawn Upon a heap a hundred ghastly women, Transformed with their fear; who swore they saw Men all in fire walk up and down the streets. And yesterday the bird of night did sit Even at noon-day upon the market-place, Hooting and shrieking. When these prodigies Do so conjointly meet, let not men say 'These are their reasons; they are natural;' 30 For, I believe, they are portentous things Unto the climate that they point upon.

Cic. Indeed, it is a strange-disposed time: But men may construe things after their fashion, Clean from the purpose of the things themselves. Comes Cæsar to the Capitol to-morrow?

Casca. He doth; for he did bid Antonius Send word to you he would be there to-morrow.

Cic. Good night then, Casca: this disturbed sky Is not to walk in.

Casca.   Farewell, Cicero. [*Exit Cicero.* 40

Enter CASSIUS.

Cas. Who's there?

Casca.   A Roman.

Cas.   Casca, by your voice.

Casca. Your ear is good. Cassius, what night is this!

Cas. A very pleasing night to honest men.

Casca. Who ever knew the heavens menace so?

267. **ope,** open. 268. **doublet,** Elizabethan jacket. 269. **occupation,** handicraft. 287. **Greek to me.** This famous phrase arose from Casca's old Roman dislike for foreign culture. 288. **scarfs,** fillets. 290. **put to silence,** probably, dismissed from office and banished. 293. **promised forth,** engaged to dine out. 303. **However,** however much. **tardy form,** sluggishness. 312-326. **Well . . . endure.** It cannot be that Shakespeare thought of Cassius as a base man, yet the role he plays here is the villain's role in many plays. There may be an underlying accept-

ance of the world-wide belief that the assassination of Caesar was one of the calamities of history, and the agent of such a catastrophe might well be thought a villain. 317. **bear me hard,** dislike me.
SCENE III. 1. **brought,** escorted. 3. **sway,** probably, weight. 18. **Not sensible of fire,** i.e., not feeling it. 22-23. **drawn Upon a heap,** huddled together. **ghastly,** pallid. 26. **bird of night,** owl, a bird of evil omen. 28. **prodigies,** portents. 32. **climate,** region. 35. **Clean . . . purpose,** contrary to the import or meaning. 42. **what night,** what

Cas. Those that have known the earth so full of
    faults.
For my part, I have walk'd about the streets,
Submitting me unto the perilous night,
And, thus unbraced, Casca, as you see,
Have bared my bosom to the thunder-stone;
And when the cross blue lightning seem'd to open   50
The breast of heaven, I did present myself
Even in the aim and very flash of it.
    Casca. But wherefore did you so much tempt the
    heavens?
It is the part of men to fear and tremble,
When the most mighty gods by tokens send
Such dreadful heralds to astonish us.
    Cas. You are dull, Casca, and those sparks of life
That should be in a Roman you do want,
Or else you use not. You look pale and gaze
And put on fear and cast yourself in wonder,   60
To see the strange impatience of the heavens:
But if you would consider the true cause
Why all these fires, why all these gliding ghosts,
Why birds and beasts from quality and kind,
Why old men fool and children calculate,
Why all these things change from their ordinance
Their natures and preformed faculties
To monstrous quality,—why, you shall find
That heaven hath infused them with these spirits,
To make them instruments of fear and warning   70
Unto some monstrous state.
Now could I, Casca, name to thee a man
Most like this dreadful night,
That thunders, lightens, opens graves, and roars
As doth the lion in the Capitol,
A man no mightier than thyself or me
In personal action, yet prodigious grown
And fearful, as these strange eruptions are.
    Casca. 'Tis Cæsar that you mean; is it not, Cassius?
    Cas. Let it be who it is: for Romans now   80
Have thews and limbs like to their ancestors;
But, woe the while! our fathers' minds are dead,
And we are govern'd with our mothers' spirits;
Our yoke and sufferance show us womanish.
    Casca. Indeed, they say the senators to-morrow
Mean to establish Cæsar as a king;
And he shall wear his crown by sea and land,
In every place, save here in Italy.
    Cas. I know where I will wear this dagger then;
Cassius from bondage will deliver Cassius: 90
Therein, ye gods, you make the weak most strong;
Therein, ye gods, you tyrants do defeat:
Nor stony tower, nor walls of beaten brass,
Nor airless dungeon, nor strong links of iron,
Can be retentive to the strength of spirit;
But life, being weary of these worldly bars,
Never lacks power to dismiss itself.
If I know this, know all the world besides,
That part of tyranny that I do bear
I can shake off at pleasure.   [*Thunder still*.
    Casca.   So can I: 100
So every bondman in his own hand bears

The power to cancel his captivity.
    Cas. And why should Cæsar be a tyrant then?
Poor man! I know he would not be a wolf,
But that he sees the Romans are but sheep:
He were no lion, were not Romans hinds.
Those that with haste will make a mighty fire
Begin it with weak straws: what trash is Rome,
What rubbish and what offal, when it serves
For the base matter to illuminate   110
So vile a thing as Cæsar! But, O grief,
Where hast thou led me? I perhaps speak this
Before a willing bondman; then I know
My answer must be made. But I am arm'd,
And dangers are to me indifferent.
    Casca. You speak to Casca, and to such a man
That is no fleering tell-tale. Hold, my hand:
Be factious for redress of all these griefs,
And I will set this foot of mine as far
As who goes farthest.
    Cas.   There 's a bargain made.   120
Now know you, Casca, I have moved already
Some certain of the noblest-minded Romans
To undergo with me an enterprise
Of honourable-dangerous consequence;
And I do know, by this, they stay for me
In Pompey's porch: for now, this fearful night,
There is no stir or walking in the streets;
And the complexion of the element
In favour's like the work we have in hand,
Most bloody, fiery, and most terrible.   130
    Casca. Stand close awhile, for here comes one in
    haste.
    Cas. 'Tis Cinna; I do know him by his gait;
He is a friend.

Enter CINNA.

                Cinna, where haste you so?
    Cin. To find out you. Who 's that? Metellus Cimber?
    Cas. No, it is Casca; one incorporate
To our attempts. Am I not stay'd for, Cinna?
    Cin. I am glad on 't. What a fearful night is this!
There 's two or three of us have seen strange sights.
    Cas. Am I not stay'd for? tell me.
    Cin.   Yes, you are.
O Cassius, if you could   140
But win the noble Brutus to our party—
    Cas. Be you content: good Cinna, take this paper,
And look you lay it in the prætor's chair,
Where Brutus may but find it; and throw this
In at his window; set this up with wax
Upon old Brutus' statue: all this done,
Repair to Pompey's porch, where you shall find us.
Is Decius Brutus and Trebonius there?
    Cin. All but Metellus Cimber; and he 's gone
To seek you at your house. Well, I will hie,   150
And so bestow these papers as you bade me.
    Cas. That done, repair to Pompey's theatre.
                         [*Exit Cinna*.
Come, Casca, you and I will yet ere day
See Brutus at his house: three parts of him

a night. 48. **unbraced,** with doublet unfastened. 49. **thunder-stone.**
Thunderbolts were supposed to be composed of solid bodies. 60. **put
on,** show signs of. 65. **fool,** so Grant White; F: *Fooles,* retained by
many editors, the line being punctuated with commas after *men* and *fools.*
In that case we should understand *old men* as meaning "dotards." **calculate,** prophesy. 66. **ordinance,** ordinary character and nature. 81.
thews, sinews, muscles. 84. **yoke and sufferance,** patience under the
yoke. 106. **hinds,** females of the red deer; also, servants, rustics. 117.

fleering, mocking, sneering. 118. **factious,** active as a partisan. 126.
Pompey's porch, a magnificent colonnade built by Pompey in 55 B.C.,
and attached to his great open theater. The recesses along the sides were
convenient for such meetings. 135. **incorporate,** admitted as a member.
143. **prætor's chair,** official seat of the praetor, a Roman magistrate
ranking next below the consul. Brutus was praetor. 146. **old Brutus'.**
Brutus was reputed to be a descendant of Lucius Junius Brutus.

Is ours already, and the man entire
Upon the next encounter yields him ours.
    Casca. O, he sits high in all the people's hearts:
And that which would appear offence in us,
His countenance. like richest alchemy,
Will change to virtue and to worthiness.   160
    Cas. Him and his worth and our great need of him
You have right well conceited. Let us go,
For it is after midnight; and ere day
We will awake him and be sure of him.   *[Exeunt.*

ACT II.

SCENE I. *Rome. Brutus's orchard.*

Enter BRUTUS.

    Bru. What, Lucius, ho!
I cannot, by the progress of the stars,
Give guess how near to day. Lucius, I say!
I would it were my fault to sleep so soundly.
When, Lucius, when? awake, I say! what, Lucius!

Enter LUCIUS.

    Luc. Call'd you, my lord?
    Bru. Give me a taper in my study, Lucius:
When it is lighted, come and call me here.
    Luc. I will, my lord.   *[Exit.*
    Bru. It must be by his death: and for my part,   10
I know no personal cause to spurn at him,
But for the general. He would be crown'd:
How that might change his nature, there's the
    question.
It is the bright day that brings forth the adder;
And that craves wary walking. Crown him?—that;—
And then, I grant, we put a sting in him,
That at his will he may do danger with.
The abuse of greatness is, when it disjoins
Remorse from power: and, to speak truth of Cæsar,
I have not known when his affections sway'd   20
More than his reason. But 'tis a common proof,
That lowliness is young ambition's ladder,
Whereto the climber-upward turns his face;
But when he once attains the upmost round,
He then unto the ladder turns his back,
Looks in the clouds, scorning the base degrees
By which he did ascend. So Cæsar may.
Then, lest he may, prevent. And, since the quarrel
Will bear no colour for the thing he is,
Fashion it thus; that what he is, augmented,   30
Would run to these and these extremities:
And therefore think him as a serpent's egg
Which, hatch'd, would, as his kind, grow mischievous,
And kill him in the shell.

Re-enter LUCIUS.

    Luc. The taper burneth in your closet, sir.
Searching the window for a flint, I found
This paper, thus seal'd up; and, I am sure,

It did not lie there when I went to bed.
        [Gives him the letter.
    Bru. Get you to bed again; it is not day.
Is not to-morrow, boy, the ides of March?   40
    Luc. I know not, sir.
    Bru. Look in the calendar, and bring me word.
    Luc. I will, sir.   *[Exit.*
    Bru. The exhalations whizzing in the air
Give so much light that I may read by them.
        [Opens the letter and reads.
'Brutus, thou sleep'st: awake, and see thyself.
Shall Rome, &c. Speak, strike, redress!
Brutus, thou sleep'st: awake!'
Such instigations have been often dropp'd
Where I have took them up.   50
'Shall Rome, &c.' Thus must I piece it out:
Shall Rome stand under one man's awe? What,
    Rome?
My ancestors did from the streets of Rome
The Tarquin drive, when he was call'd a king.
'Speak, strike, redress!' Am I entreated
To speak and strike? O Rome, I make thee promise;
If the redress will follow, thou receivest
Thy full petition at the hand of Brutus!

Re-enter LUCIUS.

    Luc. Sir, March is wasted fourteen days.
        [Knocking within.
    Bru. 'Tis good. Go to the gate; somebody knocks.   60
        [Exit Lucius.
Since Cassius first did whet me against Cæsar,
I have not slept.
Between the acting of a dreadful thing
And the first motion, all the interim is
Like a phantasma, or a hideous dream:
The Genius and the mortal instruments
Are then in council; and the state of man,
Like to a little kingdom, suffers then
The nature of an insurrection.

Re-enter LUCIUS.

    Luc. Sir, 'tis your brother Cassius at the door,   70
Who doth desire to see you.
    Bru.   Is he alone?
    Luc. No, sir, there are moe with him.
    Bru.   Do you know them?
    Luc. No, sir; their hats are pluck'd about their ears,
And half their faces buried in their cloaks,
That by no means I may discover them
By any mark of favour.
    Bru.   Let 'em enter.   *[Exit Lucius.*
They are the faction. O conspiracy,
Shamest thou to show thy dangerous brow by night,
When evils are most free? O, then by day
Where wilt thou find a cavern dark enough   80
To mask thy monstrous visage? Seek none, conspiracy;
Hide it in smiles and affability:
For if thou path, thy native semblance on,
Not Erebus itself were dim enough
To hide thee from prevention.

159. **alchemy,** chemistry, the chief object of which was the transmutation of metals. 162. **conceited,** conceived, grasped.
    ACT II. SCENE I. 12. **general,** i.e., for the sake of the general welfare.
15-27. **Crown . . . ascend.** This is a condensed statement of Brutus'
motive. By *affections* (l. 20) he means "passions," but it need not be
understood that he means to compliment Caesar; rather, he means to
say that Caesar has those cold-blooded qualities which will make him

disregard pity (*Remorse*, l. 19) when he is in power. 36. **flint,** i.e., with
which to strike a light. 44. **exhalations,** meteors. 63-69. **Between . . .**
insurrection. This is one of the most perfect expressions in Shakespeare
of the psychology of warring emotions, hesitation, and inward conflict.
The *Genius* is used to signify the soul; the *mortal instruments* are the
spirits, which are the agents of reason and the will. 67. **state of man,**
familiar designation of man as a microcosm. 70. **brother.** Cassius had

Enter the conspirators, CASSIUS, CASCA, DECIUS, CINNA, METELLUS CIMBER, *and* TREBONIUS.

Cas. I think we are too bold upon your rest:
Good morrow, Brutus; do we trouble you?
Bru. I have been up this hour, awake all night.
Know I these men that come along with you?
Cas. Yes, every man of them, and no man here 90
But honours you; and every one doth wish
You had but that opinion of yourself
Which every noble Roman bears of you.
This is Trebonius.
Bru.   He is welcome hither.
Cas. This, Decius Brutus.
Bru.   He is welcome too.
Cas. This, Casca; this, Cinna; and this, Metellus
    Cimber.
Bru. They are all welcome.
What watchful cares do interpose themselves
Betwixt your eyes and night?
Cas. Shall I entreat a word? 100
                  [*Brutus and Cassius whisper.*
Dec. Here lies the east: doth not the day break here?
Casca. No.
Cin. O, pardon, sir, it doth; and yon gray lines
That fret the clouds are messengers of day.
Casca. You shall confess that you are both deceived.
Here, as I point my sword, the sun arises,
Which is a great way growing on the south,
Weighing the youthful season of the year.
Some two months hence up higher toward the north
He first presents his fire; and the high east 110
Stands, as the Capitol, directly here.
Bru. Give me your hands all over, one by one.
Cas. And let us swear our resolution.
Bru. No, not an oath: if not the face of men,
The sufferance of our souls, the time's abuse,—
If these be motives weak, break off betimes,
And every man hence to his idle bed;
So let high-sighted tyranny range on,
Till every man drop by lottery. But if these,
As I am sure they do, bear fire enough 120
To kindle cowards and to steel with valour
The melting spirits of women, then, countrymen,
What need we any spur but our own cause,
To prick us to redress? what other bond
Than secret Romans, that have spoke the word,
And will not palter? and what other oath
Than honesty to honesty engaged,
That this shall be, or we will fall for it?
Swear priests and cowards and men cautelous,
Old feeble carrions and such suffering souls 130
That welcome wrongs; unto bad causes swear
Such creatures as men doubt; but do not stain
The even virtue of our enterprise,
Nor the insuppressive mettle of our spirits,
To think that or our cause or our performance
Did need an oath; when every drop of blood
That every Roman bears, and nobly bears,
Is guilty of a several bastardy,

If he do break the smallest particle
Of any promise that hath pass'd from him. 140
Cas. But what of Cicero? shall we sound him?
I think he will stand very strong with us.
Casca. Let us not leave him out.
Cin.   No, by no means.
Met. O, let us have him, for his silver hairs
Will purchase us a good opinion
And buy men's voices to commend our deeds:
It shall be said, his judgement ruled our hands;
Our youths and wildness shall no whit appear,
But all be buried in his gravity.
Bru. O, name him not: let us not break with him; 150
For he will never follow any thing
That other men begin.
Cas.   Then leave him out.
Casca. Indeed he is not fit.
Dec. Shall no man else be touch'd but only Cæsar?
Cas. Decius, well urged: I think it is not meet,
Mark Antony, so well beloved of Cæsar,
Should outlive Cæsar: we shall find of him
A shrewd contriver; and, you know, his means,
If he improve them, may well stretch so far
As to annoy us all: which to prevent, 160
Let Antony and Cæsar fall together.
Bru. Our course will seem too bloody, Caius Cassius,
To cut the head off and then hack the limbs,
Like wrath in death and envy afterwards;
For Antony is but a limb of Cæsar:
Let us be sacrificers, but not butchers, Caius.
We all stand up against the spirit of Cæsar;
And in the spirit of men there is no blood:
O, that we then could come by Cæsar's spirit,
And not dismember Cæsar! But, alas, 170
Cæsar must bleed for it! And, gentle friends,
Let 's kill him boldly, but not wrathfully;
Let 's carve him as a dish fit for the gods,
Not hew him as a carcass fit for hounds:
And let our hearts, as subtle masters do,
Stir up their servants to an act of rage,
And after seem to chide 'em. This shall make
Our purpose necessary and not envious:
Which so appearing to the common eyes,
We shall be call'd purgers, not murderers. 180
And for Mark Antony, think not of him;
For he can do no more than Cæsar's arm
When Cæsar's head is off.
Cas.   Yet I fear him;
For in the ingrafted love he bears to Cæsar—
Bru. Alas, good Cassius, do not think of him:
If he love Cæsar, all that he can do
Is to himself, take thought and die for Cæsar:
And that were much he should; for he is given
To sports, to wildness and much company.
Treb. There is no fear in him; let him not die; 190
For he will live, and laugh at this hereafter.
                     [*Clock strikes.*
Bru. Peace! count the clock.
Cas.   The clock hath stricken three.
Treb. 'Tis time to part.

---

married the sister of Brutus. 83. **path,** proceed. 84. **Erebus,** the region of darkness between earth and Hades. 104. **fret,** mark with interlacing lines. 107. **growing on,** toward. 114. **not an oath.** Brutus is thus refusing a genuine means of security in view of the importance of oaths to conspirators and the penalties which befell those who broke them. 115. **sufferance,** state of suffering. 118. **high-sighted,** haughty. 125. **secret,** conspiring. 126. **palter,** use trickery.

129. **cautelous,** deceitful. 130. **suffering,** long-suffering. 134. **insuppressive,** not to be suppressed. 138. **several bastardy,** individual act dishonoring its origin. 150. **break with,** tell to, confide in. 153. **fit.** Plutarch tells us that they feared Cicero lacked courage and that they thought him too old; he was sixty-three. 160. **annoy,** injure. 187. **take thought,** despond. 188. **much he should,** a good deal for him to do. 192. **clock.** Striking clocks were not invented until the Middle Ages.

Cas.   But it is doubtful yet,
Whether Cæsar will come forth to-day, or no;
For he is superstitious grown of late,
Quite from the main opinion he held once
Of fantasy, of dreams and ceremonies:
It may be, these apparent prodigies,
The unaccustom'd terror of this night,
And the persuasion of his augurers,   200
May hold him from the Capitol to-day.
   Dec. Never fear that: if he be so resolved,
I can o'ersway him; for he loves to hear
That unicorns may be betray'd with trees,
And bears with glasses, elephants with holes,
Lions with toils and men with flatterers;
But when I tell him he hates flatterers,
He says he does, being then most flattered.
Let me work;
For I can give his humour the true bent,   210
And I will bring him to the Capitol.
   Cas. Nay, we will all of us be there to fetch him.
   Bru. By the eighth hour: is that the uttermost?
   Cin. Be that the uttermost, and fail not then.
   Met. Caius Ligarius doth bear Cæsar hard,
Who rated him for speaking well of Pompey:
I wonder none of you have thought of him.
   Bru. Now, good Metellus, go along by him:
He loves me well, and I have given him reasons;
Send him but hither, and I'll fashion him.   220
   Cas. The morning comes upon 's: we'll leave you,
    Brutus.
And, friends, disperse yourselves; but all remember
What you have said, and show yourselves true
    Romans.
   Bru. Good gentlemen, look fresh and merrily;
Let not our looks put on our purposes,
But bear it as our Roman actors do,
With untired spirits and formal constancy:
And so good morrow to you every one.
                  [*Exeunt all but Brutus.*
Boy! Lucius! Fast asleep? It is no matter!
Enjoy the honey-heavy dew of slumber: 230
Thou hast no figures nor no fantasies,
Which busy care draws in the brains of men;
Therefore thou sleep'st so sound.

   Enter PORTIA.

   Por.   Brutus, my lord!
   Bru. Portia, what mean you? wherefore rise you
    now?
It is not for your health thus to commit
Your weak condition to the raw cold morning.
   Por. Nor for yours neither. You 've ungently, Brutus,
Stole from my bed: and yesternight, at supper,
You suddenly arose, and walk'd about,
Musing and sighing, with your arms across,   240
And when I ask'd you what the matter was,
You stared upon me with ungentle looks;
I urged you further; then you scratch'd your head,
And too impatiently stamp'd with your foot;
Yet I insisted, yet you answer'd not,
But, with an angry wafture of your hand,

Gave sign for me to leave you: so I did;
Fearing to strengthen that impatience
Which seem'd too much enkindled, and withal
Hoping it was but an effect of humour,   250
Which sometime hath his hour with every man.
It will not let you eat, nor talk, nor sleep,
And could it work so much upon your shape
As it hath much prevail'd on your condition,
I should not know you, Brutus. Dear my lord,
Make me acquainted with your cause of grief.
   Bru. I am not well in health, and that is all.
   Por. Brutus is wise, and, were he not in health,
He would embrace the means to come by it.
   Bru. Why, so I do. Good Portia, go to bed.   260
   Por. Is Brutus sick? and is it physical
To walk unbraced and suck up the humours
Of the dank morning? What, is Brutus sick,
And will he steal out of his wholesome bed,
To dare the vile contagion of the night
And tempt the rheumy and unpurged air
To add unto his sickness? No, my Brutus;
You have some sick offence within your mind,
Which, by the right and virtue of my place,
I ought to know of: and, upon my knees,   270
I charm you, by my once-commended beauty,
By all your vows of love and that great vow
Which did incorporate and make us one,
That you unfold to me, yourself, your half,
Why you are heavy, and what men to-night
Have had resort to you: for here have been
Some six or seven, who did hide their faces
Even from darkness.
   Bru.   Kneel not, gentle Portia.
   Por. I should not need, if you were gentle Brutus.
Within the bond of marriage, tell me, Brutus,   280
Is it excepted I should know no secrets
That appertain to you? Am I yourself
But, as it were, in sort or limitation,
To keep with you at meals, comfort your bed,
And talk to you sometimes? Dwell I but in the suburbs
Of your good pleasure? If it be no more,
Portia is Brutus' harlot, not his wife.
   Bru. You are my true and honourable wife,
As dear to me as are the ruddy drops
That visit my sad heart.   290
   Por. If this were true, then should I know this secret.
I grant I am a woman; but withal
A woman that Lord Brutus took to wife:
I grant I am a woman; but withal
A woman well-reputed, Cato's daughter.
Think you I am no stronger than my sex,
Being so father'd and so husbanded?
Tell me your counsels, I will not disclose 'em:
I have made strong proof of my constancy,
Giving myself a voluntary wound   300
Here, in the thigh: can I bear that with patience,
And not my husband's secrets?
   Bru.   O ye gods,
Render me worthy of this noble wife! [*Knocking within.*
Hark, hark! one knocks: Portia, go in awhile;
And by and by thy bosom shall partake

---

196. **main,** probably, prevailing or general rather than strong. 204.
unicorns . . . betray'd, i.e., by having the unicorn imprison himself by
driving his horn into a tree as he charged at the hunter. 205. **glasses,**
mirrors. There was a myth to the effect that bears could be dazzled and
tamed by means of mirrors. **holes,** pitfalls. 206. **toils,** nets, snares.
210. **bent,** inclination of the mind. 218. **by him,** by way of his house.

227. **formal constancy,** steadfast manner. 246. **wafture,** act of waving.
253-254. **shape . . . condition,** i.e., outward appearance . . . inner state
of mind. 266. **rheumy,** i.e., causing colds, or possibly, rheumatism.
unpurged, not purified (by the sun). 271. **charm,** entreat. 295.
Cato's daughter. Portia was the daughter of Cato the Younger. 300.
voluntary wound. Plutarch recounts of Portia that in order to give

The secrets of my heart.
All my engagements I will construe to thee,
All the charactery of my sad brows:
Leave me with haste. [*Exit Portia.*] Lucius, who's that
    knocks?

        Re-enter LUCIUS *with* LIGARIUS.

Luc. Here is a sick man that would speak with you.
Bru. Caius Ligarius, that Metellus spake of.   311
Boy, stand aside. Caius Ligarius! how?
Lig. Vouchsafe good morrow from a feeble tongue.
Bru. O, what a time have you chose out, brave
    Caius,
To wear a kerchief! Would you were not sick!
Lig. I am not sick, if Brutus have in hand
Any exploit worthy the name of honour.
Bru. Such an exploit have I in hand, Ligarius,
Had you a healthful ear to hear of it.
Lig. By all the gods that Romans bow before,   320
I here discard my sickness! Soul of Rome!
Brave son, derived from honourable loins!
Thou, like an exorcist, hast conjured up
My mortified spirit. Now bid me run,
And I will strive with things impossible;
Yea, get the better of them. What's to do?
Bru. A piece of work that will make sick men whole.
Lig. But are not some whole that we must make
    sick?
Bru. That must we also. What it is, my Caius,
I shall unfold to thee, as we are going   330
To whom it must be done.
Lig.   Set on your foot,
And with a heart new-fired I follow you,
To do I know not what: but it sufficeth
That Brutus leads me on.
Bru.   Follow me, then.   [*Exeunt.*

         SCENE II. *Cæsar's house.*

Thunder and lightning. Enter CÆSAR, *in his night-gown.*

Cæs. Nor heaven nor earth have been at peace
    to-night:
Thrice hath Calpurnia in her sleep cried out,
'Help, ho! they murder Cæsar!' Who's within?

    Enter a Servant.

Serv. My lord?
Cæs. Go bid the priests do present sacrifice
And bring me their opinions of success.
Serv. I will, my lord.   [*Exit.*

    Enter CALPURNIA.

Cal. What mean you, Cæsar? think you to walk
    forth?
You shall not stir out of your house to-day.
Cæs. Cæsar shall forth: the things that threaten'd
    me   10
Ne'er look'd but on my back; when they shall see
The face of Cæsar, they are vanished.
Cal. Cæsar, I never stood on ceremonies,

Yet now they fright me. There is one within,
Besides the things that we have heard and seen,
Recounts most horrid sights seen by the watch.
A lioness hath whelped in the streets;
And graves have yawn'd, and yielded up their dead;
Fierce fiery warriors fought upon the clouds,
In ranks and squadrons and right form of war,   20
Which drizzled blood upon the Capitol;
The noise of battle hurtled in the air,
Horses did neigh, and dying men did groan,
And ghosts did shriek and squeal about the streets.
O Cæsar! these things are beyond all use,
And I do fear them.
Cæs.   What can be avoided
Whose end is purposed by the mighty gods?
Yet Cæsar shall go forth; for these predictions
Are to the world in general as to Cæsar.
Cal. When beggars die, there are no comets seen;   30
The heavens themselves blaze forth the death of
    princes.
Cæs. Cowards die many times before their deaths;
The valiant never taste of death but once.
Of all the wonders that I yet have heard,
It seems to me most strange that men should fear;
Seeing that death, a necessary end,
Will come when it will come.

    Re-enter Servant.

         What say the augurers?
Serv. They would not have you to stir forth to-day.
Plucking the entrails of an offering forth,
They could not find a heart within the beast.   40
Cæs. The gods do this in shame of cowardice:
Cæsar should be a beast without a heart,
If he should stay at home to-day for fear.
No, Cæsar shall not: danger knows full well
That Cæsar is more dangerous than he:
We are two lions litter'd in one day,
And I the elder and more terrible:
And Cæsar shall go forth.
Cal.   Alas, my lord,
Your wisdom is consumed in confidence.
Do not go forth to-day: call it my fear   50
That keeps you in the house, and not your own.
We'll send Mark Antony to the senate-house;
And he shall say you are not well to-day:
Let me, upon my knee, prevail in this.
Cæs. Mark Antony shall say I am not well;
And, for thy humour, I will stay at home.

    Enter DECIUS.

Here's Decius Brutus, he shall tell them so.
Dec. Cæsar, all hail! good morrow, worthy Cæsar:
I come to fetch you to the senate-house.
Cæs. And you are come in very happy time,   60
To bear my greeting to the senators
And tell them that I will not come to-day:
Cannot, is false, and that I dare not, falser:
I will not come to-day: tell them so, Decius.
Cal. Say he is sick.
Cæs.   Shall Cæsar send a lie?

-----

proof of her sincerity she gave herself a great gash in the thigh with a
little razor. **309. who's,** who is it. **313. Vouchsafe,** deign to accept.
315. kerchief, headdress; *to wear a kerchief* meant "to be ill." **323.
exorcist,** conjurer. **324. mortified,** deadened.
    SCENE II. *Stage Direction:* **night-gown,** dressing gown. **13. stood on
ceremonies,** attached importance to omens. **17-24. A lioness . . .**

streets. Similar enumerations of portents are made in I, iii, in *Hamlet*,
I, i, and elsewhere in Shakespeare. These portents are very ancient
and seem to be connected with the Fifteen Signs of Judgment appearing frequently in medieval literature. Most of the omens here mentioned
are from Plutarch. **22. hurtled,** clashed (of weapons).

Have I in conquest stretch'd mine arm so far,
To be afeard to tell graybeards the truth?
Decius, go tell them Cæsar will not come.
    Dec. Most mighty Cæsar, let me know some cause,
Lest I be laugh'd at when I tell them so.   70
    Cæs. The cause is in my will: I will not come;
That is enough to satisfy the senate.
But for your private satisfaction,
Because I love you, I will let you know:
Calpurnia here, my wife, stays me at home:
She dreamt to-night she saw my statua,
Which, like a fountain with an hundred spouts,
Did run pure blood; and many lusty Romans
Came smiling, and did bathe their hands in it:
And these does she apply for warnings, and portents,
And evils imminent; and on her knee   81
Hath begg'd that I will stay at home to-day.
    Dec. This dream is all amiss interpreted;
It was a vision fair and fortunate:
Your statue spouting blood in many pipes,
In which so many smiling Romans bathed,
Signifies that from you great Rome shall suck
Reviving blood, and that great men shall press
For tinctures, stains, relics and cognizance.
This by Calpurnia's dream is signified.   90
    Cæs. And this way have you well expounded it.
    Dec. I have, when you have heard what I can say:
And know it now: the senate have concluded
To give this day a crown to mighty Cæsar.
If you shall send them word you will not come,
Their minds may change. Besides, it were a mock
Apt to be render'd, for some one to say
'Break up the senate till another time,
When Cæsar's wife shall meet with better dreams.'
If Cæsar hide himself, shall they not whisper   100
'Lo, Cæsar is afraid'?
Pardon me, Cæsar; for my dear dear love
To your proceeding bids me tell you this;
And reason to my love is liable.
    Cæs. How foolish do your fears seem now,
        Calpurnia!
I am ashamed I did yield to them.
Give me my robe, for I will go.

Enter PUBLIUS, BRUTUS, LIGARIUS, METELLUS, CASCA,
    TREBONIUS, *and* CINNA.

And look where Publius is come to fetch me.
    Pub. Good morrow, Cæsar.
    Cæs.   Welcome, Publius.
What, Brutus, are you stirr'd so early too?   110
Good morrow, Casca. Caius Ligarius,
Cæsar was ne'er so much your enemy
As that same ague which has made you lean.
What is 't o'clock?
    Bru.   Cæsar, 'tis strucken eight.
    Cæs. I thank you for your pains and courtesy.

Enter ANTONY.

See! Antony, that revels long o' nights,
Is notwithstanding up. Good morrow, Antony.
    Ant. So to most noble Cæsar.

    Cæs.   Bid them prepare within:
I am to blame to be thus waited for.
Now, Cinna: now, Metellus: what, Trebonius!   120
I have an hour's talk in store for you;
Remember that you call on me to-day:
Be near me, that I may remember you.
    Treb. Cæsar, I will: [*Aside*] and so near will I be,
That your best friends shall wish I had been further.
    Cæs. Good friends, go in, and taste some wine with
        me;
And we, like friends, will straightway go together.
    Bru. [*Aside*] That every like is not the same, O
        Cæsar,
The heart of Brutus yearns to think upon!   [*Exeunt.*

SCENE III. *A street near the Capitol.*

Enter ARTEMIDORUS, *reading a paper.*

    Art. 'Cæsar, beware of Brutus; take heed of Cassius;
come not near Casca; have an eye to Cinna; trust not
Trebonius; mark well Metellus Cimber: Decius
Brutus loves thee not: thou hast wronged Caius
Ligarius. There is but one mind in all these men, and
it is bent against Cæsar. If thou beest not immortal,
look about you: security gives way to conspiracy
The mighty gods defend thee! Thy lover,

                        'ARTEMIDORUS.'

Here will I stand till Cæsar pass along,   11
And as a suitor will I give him this.
My heart laments that virtue cannot live
Out of the teeth of emulation.
If thou read this, O Cæsar, thou mayst live;
If not, the Fates with traitors do contrive.   [*Exit.*

SCENE IV. *Another part of the same street, before
the house of Brutus.*

Enter PORTIA *and* LUCIUS.

    Por. I prithee, boy, run to the senate-house;
Stay not to answer me, but get thee gone:
Why dost thou stay?
    Luc.   To know my errand, madam.
    Por. I would have had thee there, and here again,
Ere I can tell thee what thou shouldst do there.
O constancy, be strong upon my side,
Set a huge mountain 'tween my heart and tongue!
I have a man's mind, but a woman's might.
How hard it is for women to keep counsel!
Art thou here yet?
    Luc.   Madam, what should I do?   10
Run to the Capitol, and nothing else?
And so return to you, and nothing else?
    Por. Yes, bring me word, boy, if thy lord look well,
For he went sickly forth: and take good note
What Cæsar doth, what suitors press to him.
Hark, boy! what noise is that?
    Luc. I hear none, madam.
    Por.   Prithee, listen well;

---

76. **to-night,** last night. **statua,** statue. 89. **tinctures,** explained as
alluding to the practice of dipping handkerchiefs in the blood of
martyrs, or as healing medicines. **stains,** patches of color or "assimi-
lable traces (tinges) of Cæsar's qualities" (Mason). **relics,** remembrances, sacred mementos. **cognizance,** heraldic emblems. 96. **mock,**
jibe. 103. **proceeding,** career. 104. **liable,** under the sway of.

SCENE III. 8. **security,** want of caution. 10. **lover,** friend. 14.
emulation, grudge against the superiority of others.
SCENE IV. 37. **void,** empty.
ACT III. SCENE I. *Stage Direction:* **Capitol.** The scene is not located
in F, but is indicated by the text. Shakespeare implies (l. 12) that
Cæsar was assassinated in the Capitol, but it is clear from Plutarch

I heard a bustling rumour, like a fray,
And the wind brings it from the Capitol.
   Luc. Sooth, madam, I hear nothing.   20

   Enter the Soothsayer.

   Por. Come hither, fellow: which way hast thou
     been?
   Sooth. At mine own house, good lady.
   Por. What is 't o'clock?
   Sooth.   About the ninth hour, lady.
   Por. Is Cæsar yet gone to the Capitol?
   Sooth. Madam, not yet: I go to take my stand,
To see him pass on to the Capitol.
   Por. Thou hast some suit to Cæsar, hast thou not?
   Sooth. That I have, lady: if it will please Cæsar
To be so good to Cæsar as to hear me,
I shall beseech him to befriend himself.   30
   Por. Why, know'st thou any harm 's intended
     towards him?
   Sooth. None that I know will be, much that I fear
     may chance.
Good morrow to you. Here the street is narrow:
The throng that follows Cæsar at the heels,
Of senators, of prætors, common suitors,
Will crowd a feeble man almost to death:
I'll get me to a place more void, and there
Speak to great Cæsar as he comes along.   [*Exit.*
   Por. I must go in. Ay me, how weak a thing
The heart of woman is! O Brutus,   40
The heavens speed thee in thine enterprise!
Sure, the boy heard me: Brutus hath a suit
That Cæsar will not grant. O, I grow faint.
Run, Lucius, and commend me to my lord;
Say I am merry: come to me again,
And bring me word what he doth say to thee.
                   [*Exeunt severally.*

ACT III.

SCENE I. *Rome. Before the Capitol; the Senate sitting
above.*

A crowd of people; among them ARTEMIDORUS *and the*
Soothsayer. *Flourish. Enter* CÆSAR, BRUTUS,
CASSIUS, CASCA, DECIUS, METELLUS, TREBONIUS,
CINNA, ANTONY, LEPIDUS, POPILIUS, PUBLIUS,
and others.

   Cæs. [*To the Soothsayer*] The ides of March are come.
   Sooth. Ay, Cæsar; but not gone.
   Art. Hail, Cæsar! read this schedule.
   Dec. Trebonius doth desire you to o'er-read,
At your best leisure, this his humble suit.
   Art. O Cæsar, read mine first; for mine 's a suit
That touches Cæsar nearer: read it, great Cæsar.
   Cæs. What touches us ourself shall be last served.
   Art. Delay not, Cæsar; read it instantly.
   Cæs. What, is the fellow mad?
   Pub.   Sirrah, give place.   10
   Cas. What, urge you your petitions in the street?
Come to the Capitol.

CÆSAR goes up to the Senate-House, the rest following.

   Pop. I wish your enterprise to-day may thrive.
   Cas. What enterprise, Popilius?
   Pop.   Fare you well. [*Advances to Cæsar.*
   Bru. What said Popilius Lena?
   Cas. He wish'd to-day our enterprise might thrive.
I fear our purpose is discovered.
   Bru. Look, how he makes to Cæsar: mark him.
   Cas. Casca, be sudden, for we fear prevention.
Brutus, what shall be done? If this be known,   20
Cassius or Cæsar never shall turn back,
For I will slay myself.
   Bru.   Cassius, be constant:
Popilius Lena speaks not of our purposes;
For, look, he smiles, and Cæsar doth not change.
   Cas. Trebonius knows his time; for, look you,
     Brutus,
He draws Mark Antony out of the way.
         [*Exeunt Antony and Trebonius.*
   Dec. Where is Metellus Cimber? Let him go,
And presently prefer his suit to Cæsar.
   Bru. He is address'd: press near and second him.
   Cin. Casca, you are the first that rears your hand.   30
   Cæs. Are we all ready? What is now amiss
That Cæsar and his senate must redress?
   Met. Most high, most mighty, and most puissant
     Cæsar,
Metellus Cimber throws before thy seat
An humble heart,—   [*Kneeling.*
   Cæs.   I must prevent thee, Cimber.
These couchings and these lowly courtesies
Might fire the blood of ordinary men,
And turn pre-ordinance and first decree
Into the law of children. Be not fond,
To think that Cæsar bears such rebel blood   40
That will be thaw'd from the true quality
With that which melteth fools; I mean, sweet words,
Low-crooked court'sies and base spaniel-fawning.
Thy brother by decree is banished:
If thou dost bend and pray and fawn for him,
I spurn thee like a cur out of my way.
Know, Cæsar doth not wrong, nor without cause
Will he be satisfied.
   Met. Is there no voice more worthy than my own,
To sound more sweetly in great Cæsar's ear   50
For the repealing of my banish'd brother?
   Bru. I kiss thy hand, but not in flattery, Cæsar;
Desiring thee that Publius Cimber may
Have an immediate freedom of repeal.
   Cæs. What, Brutus!
   Cas.   Pardon, Cæsar; Cæsar, pardon:
As low as to thy foot doth Cassius fall,
To beg enfranchisement for Publius Cimber.
   Cæs. I could be well moved, if I were as you;
If I could pray to move, prayers would move me:
But I am constant as the northern star,   60
Of whose true-fix'd and resting quality
There is no fellow in the firmament.
The skies are painted with unnumber'd sparks,
They are all fire and every one doth shine,

---

that it was in the portico of Pompey's theater, where the Senate was
sitting. 3. **schedule,** written scroll. 8. **What . . . served.** Caesar's
pride is admirable but is made the source of his downfall. That he
does not read the paper is usually regarded as an element of fate in
the tragedy, but the idea just expressed is more truly Shakespearean.
29. **address'd,** ready. 41. **thaw'd from the true quality.** The idea is

that the cool brain governed by reason might be visited by various
intruding spirits (carrying with them heat) and so thawed. 47-48.
Know . . . satisfied. Ben Jonson ridicules these lines in his *Discoveries,*
where he says, "Caesar did never wrong but with just cause." Such
may have been the original text or its reading on the stage, but the F
reading is intelligible.

But there 's but one in all doth hold his place:
So in the world; 'tis furnish'd well with men,
And men are flesh and blood, and apprehensive;
Yet in the number I do know but one
That unassailable holds on his rank,
Unshaked of motion: and that I am he,   70
Let me a little show it, even in this;
That I was constant Cimber should be banish'd,
And constant do remain to keep him so.
    Cin. O Cæsar,—
    Cæs.   Hence! wilt thou lift up Olympus?
    Dec. Great Cæsar,—
    Cæs.   Doth not Brutus bootless kneel?
    Casca. Speak, hands, for me!
           [*Casca first, then the other Conspirators and Marcus*
                      Brutus stab Cæsar.
    Cæs. Et tu, Brute! Then fall, Cæsar!   [*Dies.*
    Cin. Liberty! Freedom! Tyranny is dead!
Run hence, proclaim, cry it about the streets.
    Cas. Some to the common pulpits, and cry out   80
'Liberty, freedom, and enfranchisement!'
    Bru. People and senators, be not affrighted;
Fly not; stand still: ambition's debt is paid.
    Casca. Go to the pulpit, Brutus.
    Dec.   And Cassius too.
    Bru. Where 's Publius?
    Cin. Here, quite confounded with this mutiny.
    Met. Stand fast together, lest some friend of Cæsar's
Should chance—
    Bru. Talk not of standing. Publius, good cheer;
There is no harm intended to your person,   90
Nor to no Roman else: so tell them, Publius.
    Cas. And leave us, Publius; lest that the people,
Rushing on us, should do your age some mischief.
    Bru. Do so: and let no man abide this deed,
But we the doers.

    Re-enter TREBONIUS.

    Cas.   Where is Antony?
    Tre. Fled to his house amazed:
Men, wives and children stare, cry out and run
As it were doomsday.
    Bru.   Fates, we will know your pleasures:
That we shall die, we know; 'tis but the time
And drawing days out, that men stand upon.   100
    Cas. Why, he that cuts off twenty years of life
Cuts off so many years of fearing death.
    Bru. Grant that, and then is death a benefit:
So are we Cæsar's friends, that have abridged
His time of fearing death. Stoop, Romans, stoop,
And let us bathe our hands in Cæsar's blood
Up to the elbows, and besmear our swords:
Then walk we forth, even to the market-place,
And, waving our red weapons o'er our heads,
Let 's all cry, 'Peace, freedom and liberty!'   110
    Cas. Stoop, then, and wash. How many ages hence
Shall this our lofty scene be acted over
In states unborn and accents yet unknown!
    Bru. How many times shall Cæsar bleed in sport,
That now on Pompey's basis lies along
No worthier than the dust!

    Cas.   So oft as that shall be,
So often shall the knot of us be call'd
The men that gave their country liberty.
    Dec. What, shall we forth?
    Cas.   Ay, every man away:
Brutus shall lead; and we will grace his heels   120
With the most boldest and best hearts of Rome.

    Enter a Servant.

    Bru. Soft! who comes here? A friend of Antony's.
    Serv. Thus, Brutus, did my master bid me kneel;
Thus did Mark Antony bid me fall down;
And, being prostrate, thus he bade me say:
Brutus is noble, wise, valiant, and honest;
Cæsar was mighty, bold, royal, and loving:
Say I love Brutus, and I honour him;
Say I fear'd Cæsar, honour'd him and loved him.
If Brutus will vouchsafe that Antony   130
May safely come to him, and be resolved
How Cæsar hath deserved to lie in death,
Mark Antony shall not love Cæsar dead
So well as Brutus living; but will follow
The fortunes and affairs of noble Brutus
Thorough the hazards of this untrod state
With all true faith. So says my master Antony.
    Bru. Thy master is a wise and valiant Roman;
I never thought him worse.
Tell him, so please him come unto this place,   140
He shall be satisfied; and, by my honour,
Depart untouch'd.
    Serv.   I'll fetch him presently.   [*Exit.*
    Bru. I know that we shall have him well to friend.
    Cas. I wish we may: but yet have I a mind
That fears him much; and my misgiving still
Falls shrewdly to the purpose.
    Bru. But here comes Antony.

    Re-enter ANTONY.

           Welcome, Mark Antony.
    Ant. O mighty Cæsar! dost thou lie so low?
Are all thy conquests, glories, triumphs, spoils,
Shrunk to this little measure? Fare thee well.   150
I know not, gentlemen, what you intend,
Who else must be let blood, who else is rank:
If I myself, there is no hour so fit
As Cæsar's death's hour, nor no instrument
Of half that worth as those your swords, made rich
With the most noble blood of all this world.
I do beseech ye, if you bear me hard,
Now, whilst your purpled hands do reek and smoke,
Fulfil your pleasure. Live a thousand years,
I shall not find myself so apt to die: 160
No place will please me so, no mean of death,
As here by Cæsar, and by you cut off,
The choice and master spirits of this age.
    Bru. O Antony, beg not your death of us.
Though now we must appear bloody and cruel,
As, by our hands and this our present act,
You see we do, yet see you but our hands
And this the bleeding business they have done:
Our hearts you see not; they are pitiful;

67. **apprehensive,** sensitive, i.e., quick to perceive or learn. 69. **rank,** place, in line or file, position. 77. **Et tu, Brute.** These words, the exact origin of which is not known, are so striking in their condensed significance that they have maintained their Latin form unchanged. 80. **common pulpits,** public rostra. 97. **wives,** women. 100. **drawing days out,** prolonging their lives. **stand upon,** lay emphasis upon.

115. **Pompey's basis,** pedestal of Pompey's statue. 118. **liberty.** Shakespeare here exploits the glory of tyrannicide, so much so that the play in its political aspect may be said to turn on that issue. 143. **to friend,** for a friend. 146. **Falls . . . purpose,** hits the mark precisely. 152. **let blood,** bled. **rank,** plethoric or full-blooded. 157. **bear . . . hard,** bear ill-will to. 160. **apt,** ready, prepared. 177·178.

And pity to the general wrong of Rome— 170
As fire drives out fire, so pity pity—
Hath done this deed on Cæsar. For your part,
To you our swords have leaden points, Mark Antony:
†Our arms, in strength of malice, and our hearts
Of brothers' temper, do receive you in
With all kind love, good thoughts, and reverence.
 Cas. Your voice shall be as strong as any man's
In the disposing of new dignities.
 Bru. Only be patient till we have appeased
The multitude, beside themselves with fear, 180
And then we will deliver you the cause,
Why I, that did love Cæsar when I struck him,
Have thus proceeded.
 Ant.   I doubt not of your wisdom.
Let each man render me his bloody hand:
First, Marcus Brutus, will I shake with you;
Next, Caius Cassius, do I take your hand;
Now, Decius Brutus, yours; now yours, Metellus;
Yours, Cinna; and, my valiant Casca, yours;
Though last, not least in love, yours, good Trebonius.
Gentlemen all,—alas, what shall I say? 190
My credit now stands on such slippery ground,
That one of two bad ways you must conceit me,
Either a coward or a flatterer.
That I did love thee, Cæsar, O, 'tis true:
If then thy spirit look upon us now,
Shall it not grieve thee dearer than thy death,
To see thy Antony making his peace,
Shaking the bloody fingers of thy foes,
Most noble! in the presence of thy corse?
Had I as many eyes as thou hast wounds, 200
Weeping as fast as they stream forth thy blood,
It would become me better than to close
In terms of friendship with thine enemies.
Pardon me, Julius! Here wast thou bay'd, brave hart;
Here didst thou fall; and here thy hunters stand,
Sign'd in thy spoil, and crimson'd in thy lethe.
O world, thou wast the forest to this hart;
And this, indeed, O world, the heart of thee.
How like a deer, strucken by many princes,
Dost thou here lie! 210
 Cas. Mark Antony,—
 Ant.   Pardon me, Caius Cassius:
The enemies of Cæsar shall say this;
Then, in a friend, it is cold modesty.
 Cas. I blame you not for praising Cæsar so;
But what compact mean you to have with us?
Will you be prick'd in number of our friends;
Or shall we on, and not depend on you?
 Ant. Therefore I took your hands, but was, indeed,
Sway'd from the point, by looking down on Cæsar.
Friends am I with you all and love you all, 220
Upon this hope, that you shall give me reasons
Why and wherein Cæsar was dangerous.
 Bru. Or else were this a savage spectacle:
Our reasons are so full of good regard
That were you, Antony, the son of Cæsar,
You should be satisfied.
 Ant.   That's all I seek:
And am moreover suitor that I may

Produce his body to the market-place;
And in the pulpit, as becomes a friend,
Speak in the order of his funeral. 230
 Bru. You shall, Mark Antony.
 Cas.   Brutus, a word with you.
[*Aside to Bru.*] You know not what you do: do not consent
That Antony speak in his funeral:
Know you how much the people may be moved
By that which he will utter?
 Bru.   By your pardon;
I will myself into the pulpit first,
And show the reason of our Cæsar's death:
What Antony shall speak, I will protest
He speaks by leave and by permission,
And that we are contented Cæsar shall 240
Have all true rites and lawful ceremonies.
It shall advantage more than do us wrong.
 Cas. I know not what may fall; I like it not.
 Bru. Mark Antony, here, take you Cæsar's body.
You shall not in your funeral speech blame us,
But speak all good you can devise of Cæsar,
And say you do 't by our permission;
Else shall you not have any hand at all
About his funeral: and you shall speak
In the same pulpit whereto I am going, 250
After my speech is ended.
 Ant.   Be it so;
I do desire no more.
 Bru. Prepare the body then, and follow us.
       [*Exeunt all but Antony.*
 Ant. O, pardon me, thou bleeding piece of earth,
That I am meek and gentle with these butchers!
Thou art the ruins of the noblest man
That ever lived in the tide of times.
Woe to the hand that shed this costly blood!
Over thy wounds now do I prophesy,—
Which, like dumb mouths, do ope their ruby lips, 260
To beg the voice and utterance of my tongue—
A curse shall light upon the †limbs of men;
Domestic fury and fierce civil strife
Shall cumber all the parts of Italy;
Blood and destruction shall be so in use
And dreadful objects so familiar
That mothers shall but smile when they behold
Their infants quarter'd with the hands of war;
All pity choked with custom of fell deeds:
And Cæsar's spirit, ranging for revenge, 270
With Ate by his side come hot from hell,
Shall in these confines with a monarch's voice
Cry 'Havoc,' and let slip the dogs of war;
That this foul deed shall smell above the earth
With carrion men, groaning for burial.

 Enter a Servant.

You serve Octavius Cæsar, do you not?
 Serv. I do, Mark Antony.
 Ant. Cæsar did write for him to come to Rome.
 Serv. He did receive his letters, and is coming;
And bid me say to you by word of mouth— 280
O Cæsar!—   [*Seeing the body.*

Your . . . dignities. Cassius better understands Antony's motives when he offers him a voice in distributing the offices. **204. bay'd,** brought to bay. **hart,** stag, with pun on *heart.* **206. Sign'd in,** marked with the signs of. **lethe,** death. **207-210. O world . . . lie.** Shakespeare seems to have meant to depict real grief and indignation in Antony. **216. prick'd in,** set down, marked off on a list. **224.**

regard, possibly, design, intention. **230. order,** course. **232. You know not what you do.** Plutarch calls attention to this as the second error which Brutus committed; the first was that he failed to have Antony killed as well as Cæsar. **238. protest,** announce. **268. quarter'd,** slaughtered. **271. Ate,** goddess of revenge. **273. 'Havoc,'** the signal for sack, pillage, and slaughter. **274. That,** so that.

Ant. Thy heart is big, get thee apart and weep.
Passion, I see, is catching; for mine eyes,
Seeing those beads of sorrow stand in thine,
Began to water. Is thy master coming?
 Serv. He lies to-night within seven leagues of Rome.
 Ant. Post back with speed, and tell him what hath
  chanced:
Here is a mourning Rome, a dangerous Rome,
No Rome of safety for Octavius yet;
Hie hence, and tell him so. Yet, stay awhile;   290
Thou shalt not back till I have borne this corse
Into the market-place: there shall I try,
In my oration, how the people take
The cruel issue of these bloody men;
According to the which, thou shalt discourse
To young Octavius of the state of things.
Lend me your hand.   [*Exeunt with Cæsar's body.*

SCENE II. *The Forum.*

Enter BRUTUS *and* CASSIUS, *and a throng of* Citizens.

Citizens. We will be satisfied; let us be satisfied.
 Bru. Then follow me, and give me audience, friends.
Cassius, go you into the other street,
And part the numbers.
Those that will hear me speak, let 'em stay here;
Those that will follow Cassius, go with him;
And public reasons shall be rendered
Of Cæsar's death.
 First Cit.   I will hear Brutus speak.
 Sec. Cit. I will hear Cassius; and compare their
  reasons,
When severally we hear them rendered.   10
  [*Exit Cassius, with some of the Citizens. Brutus goes*
        into the pulpit.
 Third. Cit. The noble Brutus is ascended: silence!
 Bru. Be patient till the last.
Romans, countrymen, and lovers! hear me for my
cause, and be silent, that you may hear: believe me
for mine honour, and have respect to mine honour,
that you may believe: censure me in your wisdom,
and awake your senses, that you may the better judge.
If there be any in this assembly, any dear friend of
Cæsar's, to him I say, that Brutus' love to Cæsar was
no less than his. If then that friend demand why
Brutus rose against Cæsar, this is my answer:—Not
that I loved Cæsar less, but that I loved Rome more.
Had you rather Cæsar were living and die all slaves,
than that Cæsar were dead, to live all free men? As
Cæsar loved me, I weep for him; as he was fortunate,
I rejoice at it; as he was valiant, I honour him: but, as
he was ambitious, I slew him. There is tears for his
love; joy for his fortune; honour for his valour; and
death for his ambition. Who is here so base that
would be a bondman? If any, speak; for him have I
offended. Who is here so rude that would not be a
Roman? If any, speak; for him have I offended.
Who is here so vile that will not love his country?
If any, speak; for him have I offended. I pause for a
reply.   37

All. None, Brutus, none.
 Bru. Then none have I offended. I have done no
more to Cæsar than you shall do to Brutus. The
question of his death is enrolled in the Capitol; his
glory not extenuated, wherein he was worthy, nor
his offences enforced, for which he suffered death. 44

Enter ANTONY *and others, with* CÆSAR's *body.*

Here comes his body, mourned by Mark Antony:
who, though he had no hand in his death, shall
receive the benefit of his dying, a place in the com-
monwealth; as which of you shall not? With this I
depart,—that, as I slew my best lover for the good of
Rome, I have the same dagger for myself, when it
shall please my country to need my death.
 All. Live, Brutus! live, live!   53
 First Cit. Bring him with triumph home unto his
  house.
 Sec. Cit. Give him a statue with his ancestors.
 Third Cit. Let him be Cæsar.
 Fourth Cit.   Cæsar's better parts
Shall be crown'd in Brutus.
 First Cit.   We'll bring him to his house
With shouts and clamours.
 Bru.   My countrymen,—
 Sec. Cit. Peace, silence! Brutus speaks.
 First Cit.   Peace, ho!
 Bru. Good countrymen, let me depart alone, 60
And, for my sake, stay here with Antony:
Do grace to Cæsar's corpse, and grace his speech
Tending to Cæsar's glories; which Mark Antony,
By our permission, is allow'd to make.
I do entreat you, not a man depart,
Save I alone, till Antony have spoke.   [*Exit.*
 First Cit. Stay, ho! and let us hear Mark Antony.
 Third Cit. Let him go up into the public chair;
We'll hear him. Noble Antony, go up.
 Ant. For Brutus' sake, I am beholding to you. 70
       [*Goes into the pulpit.*
 Fourth Cit. What does he say of Brutus?
 Third Cit.   He says, for Brutus' sake,
He finds himself beholding to us all.
 Fourth Cit. 'Twere best he speak no harm of Brutus
  here.
 First Cit. This Cæsar was a tyrant.
 Third Cit.   Nay, that's certain:
We are blest that Rome is rid of him.
 Sec. Cit. Peace! let us hear what Antony can say.
 Ant. You gentle Romans,—
 Citizens.   Peace, ho! let us hear him.
 Ant. Friends, Romans, countrymen, lend me your
  ears;
I come to bury Cæsar, not to praise him.
The evil that men do lives after them;   80
The good is oft interred with their bones;
So let it be with Cæsar. The noble Brutus
Hath told you Cæsar was ambitious:
If it were so, it was a grievous fault,
And grievously hath Cæsar answer'd it.
Here, under leave of Brutus and the rest—
For Brutus is an honourable man;

---

294. **issue**, deed.
 SCENE II. 4. **part**, divide; see glossary. 10. **severally**, individually.
12-37. **Be . . . reply.** The speech of Brutus is in careful sententious
prose. It is Shakespeare's attempt to reproduce in style what Plutarch
means when he says, "He counterfeited that brief compendious manner
of speech of the Lacedaemonians." In content the speech is original

with Shakespeare. 33. **rude**, barbarous. 41. **question of**, judicial
inquiry into. 42. **extenuated**, minimized. 43. **enforced**, enlarged
upon. 78-257. **Friends . . . such another.** Plutarch gives a brief
description of Antony's oration and its effect, telling how Antony moved
the audience and displayed to them Cæsar's bloody garments. Appian
tells of an image of Caesar in wax with three and twenty wounds; and

So are they all, all honourable men—
Come I to speak in Cæsar's funeral.
He was my friend, faithful and just to me: 90
But Brutus says he was ambitious;
And Brutus is an honourable man.
He hath brought many captives home to Rome,
Whose ransoms did the general coffers fill:
Did this in Cæsar seem ambitious?
When that the poor have cried, Cæsar hath wept:
Ambition should be made of sterner stuff:
Yet Brutus says he was ambitious;
And Brutus is an honourable man.
You all did see that on the Lupercal   100
I thrice presented him a kingly crown,
Which he did thrice refuse: was this ambition?
Yet Brutus says he was ambitious;
And, sure, he is an honourable man.
I speak not to disprove what Brutus spoke,
But here I am to speak what I do know.
You all did love him once, not without cause:
What cause withholds you then, to mourn for him?
O judgement! thou art fled to brutish beasts,
And men have lost their reason. Bear with me;   110
My heart is in the coffin there with Cæsar,
And I must pause till it come back to me.
    First Cit. Methinks there is much reason in his
    sayings.
    Sec. Cit. If thou consider rightly of the matter,
Cæsar has had great wrong.
    Third Cit.   Has he, masters?
I fear there will a worse come in his place.
    Fourth Cit. Mark'd ye his words? He would not take
    the crown;
Therefore 'tis certain he was not ambitious.
    First Cit. If it be found so, some will dear abide it.
    Sec. Cit. Poor soul! his eyes are red as fire with
    weeping.   120
    Third Cit. There 's not a nobler man in Rome than
    Antony.
    Fourth Cit. Now mark him, he begins again to speak.
    Ant. But yesterday the word of Cæsar might
Have stood against the world; now lies he there,
And none so poor to do him reverence.
O masters, if I were disposed to stir
Your hearts and minds to mutiny and rage,
I should do Brutus wrong, and Cassius wrong,
Who, you all know, are honourable men:
I will not do them wrong; I rather choose   130
To wrong the dead, to wrong myself and you,
Than I will wrong such honourable men.
But here 's a parchment with the seal of Cæsar;
I found it in his closet, 'tis his will:
Let but the commons hear this testament—
Which, pardon me, I do not mean to read—
And they would go and kiss dead Cæsar's wounds
And dip their napkins in his sacred blood,
Yea, beg a hair of him for memory,
And, dying, mention it within their wills,   140
Bequeathing it as a rich legacy
Unto their issue.
    Fourth Cit. We'll hear the will: read it, Mark Antony.

    All. The will, the will! we will hear Cæsar's will.
    Ant. Have patience, gentle friends, I must not
    read it;
It is not meet you know how Cæsar loved you.
You are not wood, you are not stones, but men;
And, being men, hearing the will of Cæsar,
It will inflame you, it will make you mad:
'Tis good you know not that you are his heirs;   150
For, if you should, O, what would come of it!
    Fourth Cit. Read the will; we'll hear it, Antony;
You shall read us the will, Cæsar's will.
    Ant. Will you be patient? will you stay awhile?
I have o'ershot myself to tell you of it:
I fear I wrong the honourable men
Whose daggers have stabb'd Cæsar; I do fear it.
    Fourth Cit. They were traitors: honourable men!
    All. The will! the testament!
    Sec. Cit. They were villains, murderers: the will!
    read the will.   160
    Ant. You will compel me, then, to read the will?
Then make a ring about the corpse of Cæsar,
And let me show you him that made the will.
Shall I descend? and will you give me leave?
    Several Cit. Come down.
    Sec. Cit. Descend.
    Third Cit. You shall have leave.   [*Antony comes down.*
    Fourth Cit. A ring; stand round.
    First Cit. Stand from the hearse, stand from the
    body.
    Sec. Cit. Room for Antony, most noble Antony.   170
    Ant. Nay, press not so upon me; stand far off.
    Several Cit. Stand back; room; bear back.
    Ant. If you have tears, prepare to shed them now.
You all do know this mantle: I remember
The first time ever Cæsar put it on;
'Twas on a summer's evening, in his tent,
That day he overcame the Nervii:
Look, in this place ran Cassius' dagger through:
See what a rent the envious Casca made:
Through this the well-beloved Brutus stabb'd;   180
And as he pluck'd his cursed steel away,
Mark how the blood of Cæsar follow'd it,
As rushing out of doors, to be resolved
If Brutus so unkindly knock'd, or no;
For Brutus, as you know, was Cæsar's angel:
Judge, O you gods, how dearly Cæsar loved him!
This was the most unkindest cut of all;
For when the noble Cæsar saw him stab,
Ingratitude, more strong than traitors' arms,
Quite vanquish'd him: then burst his mighty heart; 190
And, in his mantle muffling up his face,
Even at the base of Pompey's statua,
Which all the while ran blood, great Cæsar fell.
O, what a fall was there, my countrymen!
Then I, and you, and all of us fell down,
Whilst bloody treason flourish'd over us.
O, now you weep; and, I perceive, you feel
The dint of pity: these are gracious drops.
Kind souls, what, weep you when you but behold
Our Cæsar's vesture wounded? Look you here,   200
Here is himself, marr'd, as you see, with traitors.

Julius Cæsar
ACT III : SC II

Dion furnishes hints for Antony's praise of Caesar's liberality and Caesar's
betrayal by his friends. The oration is sometimes thought to illustrate the
"Asiatic" or florid style as opposed to the "Greek" or classical style
used by Brutus. 93. **captives.** It has been estimated that Caesar and
Pompey sold a million captives into slavery. 169. **hearse,** bier. 177.
Nervii, the Belgian tribe whose defeat is described in Caesar's *Gallic*

War, II, xv-xxvii. 185. **angel,** guardian spirit. 187. **most unkindest,**
the most familiar of Shakespeare's double superlatives. 191. **muffling
up.** This detail showing the dignity of Caesar's death appears in almost
every version of the story from ancient times on.

First Cit. O piteous spectacle!
Sec. Cit. O noble Cæsar!
Third Cit. O woful day!
Fourth Cit. O traitors, villains!
First Cit. O most bloody sight!
Sec. Cit. We will be revenged.
All. Revenge! About! Seek! Burn! Fire! Kill! Slay!
Let not a traitor live!
   Ant. Stay, countrymen.   210
   First Cit. Peace there! hear the noble Antony.
   Sec. Cit. We'll hear him, we'll follow him, we'll die
with him.
   Ant. Good friends, sweet friends, let me not stir
      you up
To such a sudden flood of mutiny.
They that have done this deed are honourable:
What private griefs they have, alas, I know not,
That made them do it: they are wise and honourable,
And will, no doubt, with reasons answer you.
I come not, friends, to steal away your hearts: 220
I am no orator, as Brutus is;
But, as you know me all, a plain blunt man,
That love my friend; and that they know full well
That gave me public leave to speak of him:
For I have neither wit, nor words, nor worth,
Action, nor utterance, nor the power of speech,
To stir men's blood: I only speak right on;
I tell you that which you yourselves do know;
Show you sweet Cæsar's wounds, poor poor dumb
      mouths,
And bid them speak for me: but were I Brutus,   230
And Brutus Antony, there were an Antony
Would ruffle up your spirits and put a tongue
In every wound of Cæsar that should move
The stones of Rome to rise and mutiny.
   All. We'll mutiny.
   First Cit. We'll burn the house of Brutus.
   Third Cit. Away, then! come, seek the conspirators.
   Ant. Yet hear me, countrymen; yet hear me speak.
   All. Peace, ho! Hear Antony. Most noble Antony!
   Ant. Why, friends, you go to do you know not what:
Wherein hath Cæsar thus deserved your loves?   241
Alas, you know not: I must tell you, then:
You have forgot the will I told you of.
   All. Most true. The will! Let's stay and hear the
      will.
   Ant. Here is the will, and under Cæsar's seal.
To every Roman citizen he gives,
To every several man, seventy five drachmas.
   Sec. Cit. Most noble Cæsar! We'll revenge his death.
   Third Cit. O royal Cæsar!
   Ant. Hear me with patience.   250
   All. Peace, ho!
   Ant. Moreover, he hath left you all his walks,
His private arbours and new-planted orchards,
On this side Tiber; he hath left them you,
And to your heirs for ever, common pleasures,
To walk abroad, and recreate yourselves.
Here was a Cæsar! when comes such another?
   First Cit. Never, never. Come, away, away!
We'll burn his body in the holy place,

And with the brands fire the traitors' houses.   260
Take up the body.
   Sec. Cit. Go fetch fire.
   Third Cit. Pluck down benches.
   Fourth Cit. Pluck down forms, windows, any thing.
          [*Exeunt Citizens with the body.*
   Ant. Now let it work. Mischief, thou art afoot,
Take thou what course thou wilt!

Enter a Servant.

      How now, fellow!
   Serv. Sir, Octavius is already come to Rome.
   Ant. Where is he?
   Serv. He and Lepidus are at Cæsar's house.
   Ant. And thither will I straight to visit him: 270
He comes upon a wish. Fortune is merry,
And in this mood will give us any thing.
   Serv. I heard him say, Brutus and Cassius
Are rid like madmen through the gates of Rome.
   Ant. Belike they had some notice of the people,
How I had moved them. Bring me to Octavius.
          [*Exeunt.*

SCENE III. *A street.*

Enter CINNA *the poet.*

   Cin. I dreamt to-night that I did feast with Cæsar,
And things unluckily charge my fantasy:
I have no will to wander forth of doors,
Yet something leads me forth.

Enter Citizens.

   First Cit. What is your name?
   Sec. Cit. Whither are you going?
   Third Cit. Where do you dwell?
   Fourth Cit. Are you a married man or a bachelor?
   Sec. Cit. Answer every man directly.   10
   First Cit. Ay, and briefly.
   Fourth Cit. Ay, and wisely.
   Third Cit. Ay, and truly, you were best.
   Cin. What is my name? Whither am I going?
Where do I dwell? Am I a married man or a bachelor?
Then, to answer every man directly and briefly,
wisely and truly: wisely I say, I am a bachelor.
   Sec. Cit. That's as much as to say, they are fools
that marry: you'll bear me a bang for that, I fear.
Proceed; directly.   21
   Cin. Directly, I am going to Cæsar's funeral.
   First Cit. As a friend or an enemy?
   Cin. As a friend.
   Sec. Cit. That matter is answered directly.
   Fourth Cit. For your dwelling—briefly.
   Cin. Briefly, I dwell by the Capitol.
   Third Cit. Your name, sir, truly.
   Cin. Truly, my name is Cinna.
   First Cit. Tear him to pieces; he's a conspirator.   31
   Cin. I am Cinna the poet, I am Cinna the poet.
   Fourth Cit. Tear him for his bad verses, tear him
for his bad verses.
   Cin. I am not Cinna the conspirator.

---

225. **wit,** understanding, intelligence. 226. **Action,** gesture. 243. **will.** Antony's holding back the mob serves to increase their impatience. His action might be compared to the bending and careful aiming of a great bow. 247. **drachmas,** Greek coins of small denomination probably equivalent to the Roman denarius (a silver coin worth about twenty cents). It is variously estimated that Caesar's gift would amount to from ten to one hundred dollars for each citizen. 255. **pleasures,** pleasure gardens (in which). 264. **forms,** benches. 275. **Belike,** likely enough.

ACT IV. SCENE I. 1. **prick'd,** indicated by a mark; appropriate to the use of the stylus on waxen tablets. 6. **spot,** puncture with a stylus. 8-9. **Fetch . . . legacies,** i.e., by killing off some of the legatees. 14.

Fourth Cit. It is no matter, his name 's Cinna; pluck but his name out of his heart, and turn him going.   39

Third Cit. Tear him, tear him! Come, brands, ho! fire-brands: to Brutus', to Cassius'; burn all: some to Decius' house, and some to Casca's; some to Ligarius': away, go!   [*Exeunt.*

ACT IV.

SCENE I. *A house in Rome.*

ANTONY, OCTAVIUS, *and* LEPIDUS, *seated at a table.*

Ant. These many, then, shall die; their names are
   prick'd.
Oct. Your brother too must die; consent you,
   Lepidus?
Lep. I do consent,—
Oct.   Prick him down, Antony.
Lep. Upon condition Publius shall not live,
Who is your sister's son, Mark Antony.
Ant. He shall not live; look, with a spot I damn him.
But, Lepidus, go you to Cæsar's house;
Fetch the will hither, and we shall determine
How to cut off some charge in legacies.
   Lep. What, shall I find you here?   10
   Oct. Or here, or at the Capitol.   [*Exit Lepidus.*
   Ant. This is a slight unmeritable man,
Meet to be sent on errands: is it fit,
The three-fold world divided, he should stand
One of the three to share it?
   Oct.   So you thought him;
And took his voice who should be prick'd to die,
In our black sentence and proscription.
   Ant. Octavius, I have seen more days than you:
And though we lay these honours on this man,
To ease ourselves of divers slanderous loads,   20
He shall but bear them as the ass bears gold,
To groan and sweat under the business,
Either led or driven, as we point the way;
And having brought our treasure where we will,
Then take we down his load, and turn him off,
Like to the empty ass, to shake his ears,
And graze in commons.
   Oct.   You may do your will;
But he 's a tried and valiant soldier.
   Ant. So is my horse, Octavius; and for that
I do appoint him store of provender: 30
It is a creature that I teach to fight,
To wind, to stop, to run directly on,
His corporal motion govern'd by my spirit.
And, in some taste, is Lepidus but so;
He must be taught and train'd and bid go forth;
A barren-spirited fellow; one that feeds
On abjects, orts and imitations,
Which, out of use and staled by other men,
Begin his fashion: do not talk of him,
But as a property. And now, Octavius,   40
Listen great things:—Brutus and Cassius
Are levying powers: we must straight make head:
Therefore let our alliance be combined,

†Our best friends made, our means stretch'd;
And let us presently go sit in council,
How covert matters may be best disclosed,
And open perils surest answered.
   Oct. Let us do so: for we are at the stake,
And bay'd about with many enemies;
And some that smile have in their hearts, I fear,   50
Millions of mischiefs.   [*Exeunt.*

SCENE II. *Camp near Sardis. Before Brutus's tent.*

Drum. Enter BRUTUS, LUCILIUS, LUCIUS, *and* Soldiers;
   TITINIUS *and* PINDARUS *meeting them.*

Bru. Stand, ho!
Lucil. Give the word, ho! and stand.
Bru. What now, Lucilius! is Cassius near?
Lucil. He is at hand; and Pindarus is come
To do you salutation from his master.
   Bru. He greets me well. Your master, Pindarus,
In his own change, or by ill officers,
Hath given me some worthy cause to wish
Things done, undone: but, if he be at hand,
I shall be satisfied.
   Pin.   I do not doubt   10
But that my noble master will appear
Such as he is, full of regard and honour.
   Bru. He is not doubted. A word, Lucilius;
How he received you, let me be resolved.
   Lucil. With courtesy and with respect enough;
But not with such familiar instances,
Nor with such free and friendly conference,
As he hath used of old.
   Bru.   Thou hast described
A hot friend cooling: ever note, Lucilius,
When love begins to sicken and decay,   20
It useth an enforced ceremony.
There are no tricks in plain and simple faith;
But hollow men, like horses hot at hand,
Make gallant show and promise of their mettle;
But when they should endure the bloody spur,
They fall their crests, and, like deceitful jades,
Sink in the trial. Comes his army on?
   Lucil. They mean this night in Sardis to be
      quarter'd;
The greater part, the horse in general,
Are come with Cassius.
   Bru.   Hark! he is arrived.   30
                              [*Low march within.*
March gently on to meet him.

Enter CASSIUS *and his powers.*

Cas. Stand, ho!
Bru. Stand, ho! Speak the word along.
First Sol. Stand!
Sec. Sol. Stand!
Third Sol. Stand!
Cas. Most noble brother, you have done me wrong.
Bru. Judge me, you gods! wrong I mine enemies?
And, if not so, how should I wrong a brother?
Cas. Brutus, this sober form of yours hides wrongs;

---

three-fold, signifying either division into three parts or as made up of Europe, Asia, and Africa. 27. **commons,** common land. 32. **wind,** turn (horse trainer's term). 37. **On . . . imitations,** so Staunton; F: *On Objects, Arts, and Imitations.* In this reading *objects* would be explained as "objects of interest," *arts* as "works of art." In the text: *abjects,* things to be cast away; *orts,* fragments, refuse bits. 38.

staled, made common or cheap. 39. **fashion,** newest fashion. 48. **at the stake,** a figure from bearbaiting.
   SCENE II. 7. **change,** i.e., in his feelings. 12. **regard and honour,** honorable regard. 23. **hollow,** insincere. **hot at hand,** restless when held in. 26. **jades,** worthless horses.

And when you do them—
    Bru.   Cassius, be content;   41
Speak your griefs softly: I do know you well.
Before the eyes of both our armies here,
Which should perceive nothing but love from us,
Let us not wrangle: bid them move away;
Then in my tent, Cassius, enlarge your griefs,
And I will give you audience.
    Cas.   Pindarus,
Bid our commanders lead their charges off
A little from this ground.
    Bru. Lucilius, do you the like; and let no man   50
Come to our tent till we have done our conference.
Let Lucius and Titinius guard our door.   *[Exeunt.*

SCENE III. *Brutus's tent.*

Enter BRUTUS *and* CASSIUS.

    Cas. That you have wrong'd me doth appear in this:
You have condemn'd and noted Lucius Pella
For taking bribes here of the Sardians;
Wherein my letters, praying on his side,
Because I knew the man, were slighted off.
    Bru. You wrong'd yourself to write in such a case.
    Cas. In such a time as this it is not meet
That every nice offence should bear his comment.
    Bru. Let me tell you, Cassius, you yourself
Are much condemn'd to have an itching palm;   10
To sell and mart your offices for gold
To undeservers.
    Cas.   I an itching palm!
You know that you are Brutus that speak this,
Or, by the gods, this speech were else your last.
    Bru. The name of Cassius honours this corruption,
And chastisement doth therefore hide his head.
    Cas. Chastisement!
    Bru. Remember March, the ides of March
      remember:
Did not great Julius bleed for justice' sake?
What villain touch'd his body, that did stab,   20
And not for justice? What, shall one of us,
That struck the foremost man of all this world
But for supporting robbers, shall we now
Contaminate our fingers with base bribes,
And sell the mighty space of our large honours
For so much trash as may be grasped thus?
I had rather be a dog, and bay the moon,
Than such a Roman.
    Cas.   Brutus, bait not me;
I'll not endure it: you forget yourself,
To hedge me in; I am a soldier, I,   30
Older in practice, abler than yourself
To make conditions.
    Bru.   Go to; you are not, Cassius.
    Cas. I am.
    Bru. I say you are not.
    Cas. Urge me no more, I shall forget myself;
Have mind upon your health, tempt me no farther.
    Bru. Away, slight man!

    Cas. Is 't possible?
    Bru.   Hear me, for I will speak.
Must I give way and room to your rash choler?
Shall I be frighted when a madman stares?   40
    Cas. O ye gods, ye gods! must I endure all this?
    Bru. All this! ay, more: fret till your proud heart
      break;
Go show your slaves how choleric you are,
And make your bondmen tremble. Must I budge?
Must I observe you? must I stand and crouch
Under your testy humour? By the gods,
You shall digest the venom of your spleen,
Though it do split you; for, from this day forth,
I'll use you for my mirth, yea, for my laughter,
When you are waspish.
    Cas.   Is it come to this?   50
    Bru. You say you are a better soldier:
Let it appear so; make your vaunting true,
And it shall please me well: for mine own part,
I shall be glad to learn of noble men.
    Cas. You wrong me every way; you wrong me,
      Brutus;
I said, an elder soldier, not a better:
Did I say 'better'?
    Bru.   If you did, I care not.
    Cas. When Cæsar lived, he durst not thus have
      moved me.
    Bru. Peace, peace! you durst not so have tempted
      him.
    Cas. I durst not!   60
    Bru. No.
    Cas. What, durst not tempt him!
    Bru.   For your life you durst not.
    Cas. Do not presume too much upon my love;
I may do that I shall be sorry for.
    Bru. You have done that you should be sorry for.
There is no terror, Cassius, in your threats,
For I am arm'd so strong in honesty
That they pass by me as the idle wind,
Which I respect not. I did send to you
For certain sums of gold, which you denied me: 70
For I can raise no money by vile means:
By heaven, I had rather coin my heart,
And drop my blood for drachmas, than to wring
From the hard hands of peasants their vile trash
By any indirection: I did send
To you for gold to pay my legions,
Which you denied me: was that done like Cassius?
Should I have answer'd Caius Cassius so?
When Marcus Brutus grows so covetous,
To lock such rascal counters from his friends,   80
Be ready, gods, with all your thunderbolts;
Dash him to pieces!
    Cas.   I denied you not.
    Bru. You did.
    Cas. I did not: he was but a fool that brought
My answer back. Brutus hath rived my heart:
A friend should bear his friend's infirmities,
But Brutus makes mine greater than they are.
    Bru. I do not, till you practise them on me.
    Cas. You love me not.

SCENE III. 2. **noted**, marked for disgrace. **Lucius Pella**, a Roman
praetor in Sardis; detail from Plutarch. 4. **on his side**, in his behalf.
5. **slighted off**, put slightingly aside. 8. **bear his comment**, be made
the object of scrutiny. 10. **to have**, for having. **itching**, covetous.
11. **mart**, market. 15. **corruption**, dishonesty in public office. 26.
trash. It is a part of Brutus' stoic philosophy to despise money. 27.

bay, bark at. 28. **bait**, F: *baite;* Theobald: *bay*, followed by Globe,
with the meaning "bring me not to bay." 32. **make condition**, i.e.,
deal with his subordinates. 45. **observe**, pay reverence to. 71. **vile
means**, may allude to Cassius' extortions of money from the Rhodians;
mentioned by Plutarch. 75. **indirection**, irregular or unjust means.
80. **rascal counters**, worthless pelf. 85. **rived**, cleft. 102. **Plutus'**.

Bru.   I do not like your faults.
Cas. A friendly eye could never see such faults.   90
Bru. A flatterer's would not, though they do appear
As huge as high Olympus.
Cas. Come, Antony, and young Octavius, come,
Revenge yourselves alone on Cassius,
For Cassius is aweary of the world;
Hated by one he loves; braved by his brother;
Check'd like a bondman; all his faults observed,
Set in a note-book, learn'd, and conn'd by rote,
To cast into my teeth. O, I could weep
My spirit from mine eyes! There is my dagger,   100
And here my naked breast; within, a heart
Dearer than Plutus' mine, richer than gold:
If that thou be'st a Roman, take it forth;
I, that denied thee gold, will give my heart:
Strike, as thou didst at Cæsar; for, I know,
When thou didst hate him worst, thou lovedst him
  better
Than ever thou lovedst Cassius.
Bru.   Sheathe your dagger:
Be angry when you will, it shall have scope;
Do what you will, dishonour shall be humour.
O Cassius, you are yoked with a lamb   110
That carries anger as the flint bears fire;
Who, much enforced, shows a hasty spark,
And straight is cold again.
Cas.   Hath Cassius lived
To be but mirth and laughter to his Brutus,
When grief, and blood ill-temper'd, vexeth him?
Bru. When I spoke that, I was ill-temper'd too.
Cas. Do you confess so much? Give me your hand.
Bru. And my heart too.
Cas.   O Brutus!
Bru.   What's the matter?
Cas. Have not you love enough to bear with me,
When that rash humour which my mother gave me   120
Makes me forgetful?
Bru.   Yes, Cassius; and, from hence-
  forth,
When you are over-earnest with your Brutus,
He'll think your mother chides, and leave you so.
Poet. [*Within*] Let me go in to see the generals;
There is some grudge between 'em, 'tis not meet
They be alone.
Lucil. [*Within*] You shall not come to them.
Poet. [*Within*] Nothing but death shall stay me.

Enter Poet, *followed by* LUCILIUS, TITINIUS, *and* LUCIUS.

Cas. How now! what's the matter?
Poet. For shame, you generals! what do you mean?
Love, and be friends, as two such men should be;   131
For I have seen more years, I'm sure, than ye.
Cas. Ha, ha! how vilely doth this cynic rhyme!
Bru. Get you hence, sirrah; saucy fellow, hence!
Cas. Bear with him, Brutus; 'tis his fashion.
Bru. I'll know his humour, when he knows his time:
What should the wars do with these jigging fools?
Companion, hence!
Cas.   Away, away, be gone! [*Exit Poet.*
Bru. Lucilius and Titinius, bid the commanders

Prepare to lodge their companies to-night.   140
Cas. And come yourselves, and bring Messala with
  you
Immediately to us.   [*Exeunt Lucilius and Titinius.*
Bru.   Lucius, a bowl of wine!
                                            [*Exit Lucius.*
Cas. I did not think you could have been so angry.
Bru. O Cassius, I am sick of many griefs.
Cas. Of your philosophy you make no use,
If you give place to accidental evils.
Bru. No man bears sorrow better. Portia is dead.
Cas. Ha! Portia!
Bru. She is dead.
Cas. How 'scaped I killing when I cross'd you so? 150
O insupportable and touching loss!
Upon what sickness?
Bru.   Impatient of my absence,
And grief that young Octavius with Mark Antony
Have made themselves so strong:—for with her death
That tidings came;—with this she fell distract,
And, her attendants absent, swallow'd fire.
Cas. And died so?
Bru.   Even so.
Cas.   O ye immortal gods!

Re-enter LUCIUS, *with wine and taper.*

Bru. Speak no more of her. Give me a bowl of wine.
In this I bury all unkindness, Cassius.
Cas. My heart is thirsty for that noble pledge.   160
Fill, Lucius, till the wine o'erswell the cup;
I cannot drink too much of Brutus' love.
Bru. Come in, Titinius!   [*Exit Lucius.*

Re-enter TITINIUS, *with* MESSALA.

                          Welcome, good Messala.
Now sit we close about this taper here,
And call in question our necessities.
Cas. Portia, art thou gone?
Bru.   No more, I pray you.
Messala, I have here received letters,
That young Octavius and Mark Antony
Come down upon us with a mighty power,
Bending their expedition toward Philippi.   170
Mes. Myself have letters of the selfsame tenour.
Bru. With what addition?
Mes. That by proscription and bills of outlawry,
Octavius, Antony, and Lepidus,
Have put to death an hundred senators.
Bru. Therein our letters do not well agree;
Mine speak of seventy senators that died
By their proscriptions, Cicero being one.
Cas. Cicero one!
Mes.   Cicero is dead,
And by that order of proscription.   180
Had you your letters from your wife, my lord?
Bru. No, Messala.
Mes. Nor nothing in your letters writ of her?
Bru. Nothing, Messala.
Mes.   That, methinks, is strange.
Bru. Why ask you? hear you aught of her in yours?
Mes. No, my lord.

Plutus was the god of riches.   115. **ill-temper'd,** i.e., with humors.
133. **cynic,** rude fellow.   136. **time,** proper time.   146. **accidental,**
incidental.   156. **swallow'd fire.** Plutarch: "Portia . . . took hot
burning coals and cast them in her mouth, and kept her mouth so close
that she choked herself."   165. **call in question,** examine into.   184.
Nothing, Messala. It is not clear why Brutus withholds his knowledge
of Portia's death. It may be a detail indicative of his stoical habit of
suppressing grief. It can hardly be that he is hoping to have the report
contradicted.

Bru. Now, as you are a Roman, tell me true.

Mes. Then like a Roman bear the truth I tell:
For certain she is dead, and by strange manner.

Bru. Why, farewell, Portia. We must die, Messala:
With meditating that she must die once,   191
I have the patience to endure it now.

Mes. Even so great men great losses should endure.

Cas. I have as much of this in art as you,
But yet my nature could not bear it so.

Bru. Well, to our work alive. What do you think
Of marching to Philippi presently?

Cas. I do not think it good.

Bru.   Your reason?

Cas.   This it is:
'Tis better that the enemy seek us:
So shall he waste his means, weary his soldiers,   200
Doing himself offence; whilst we, lying still,
Are full of rest, defence, and nimbleness.

Bru. Good reasons must, of force, give place to
    better.
The people 'twixt Philippi and this ground
Do stand but in a forced affection;
For they have grudged us contribution:
The enemy, marching along by them,
By them shall make a fuller number up,
Come on refresh'd, new-added, and encouraged;
From which advantage shall we cut him off,   210
If at Philippi we do face him there,
These people at our back.

Cas.   Hear me, good brother.

Bru. Under your pardon. You must note beside,
That we have tried the utmost of our friends,
Our legions are brim-full, our cause is ripe:
The enemy increaseth every day;
We, at the height, are ready to decline.
There is a tide in the affairs of men,
Which, taken at the flood, leads on to fortune;
Omitted, all the voyage of their life   220
Is bound in shallows and in miseries.
On such a full sea are we now afloat;
And we must take the current when it serves,
Or lose our ventures.

Cas.   Then, with your will, go on;
We'll along ourselves, and meet them at Philippi.

Bru. The deep of night is crept upon our talk,
And nature must obey necessity;
Which we will niggard with a little rest.
There is no more to say?

Cas.   No more. Good night:
Early to-morrow will we rise, and hence.   230

Bru. Lucius! [*Enter Lucius.*] My gown. [*Exit Lucius.*]
    Farewell, good Messala:
Good night, Titinius. Noble, noble Cassius,
Good night, and good repose.

Cas.   O my dear brother!
This was an ill beginning of the night:
Never come such division 'tween our souls!
Let it not, Brutus.

Bru.   Every thing is well.

Cas. Good night, my lord.

Bru.   Good night, good brother.

Tit. Mes. Good night, Lord Brutus.

Bru.   Farewell, every one.
              [*Exeunt all but Brutus.*

Re-enter Lucius, *with the gown.*

Give me the gown. Where is thy instrument?

Luc. Here in the tent.

Bru.   What, thou speak'st drowsily?   240
Poor knave, I blame thee not; thou art o'er-watch'd.
Call Claudius and some other of my men;
I'll have them sleep on cushions in my tent.

Luc. Varro and Claudius!

Enter Varro *and* Claudius.

Var. Calls my lord?

Bru. I pray you, sirs, lie in my tent and sleep;
It may be I shall raise you by and by
On business to my brother Cassius.

Var. So please you, we will stand and watch your
    pleasure.

Bru. I will not have it so: lie down, good sirs;   250
It may be I shall otherwise bethink me.
Look, Lucius, here's the book I sought for so;
I put it in the pocket of my gown.
            [*Var. and Clau. lie down.*

Luc. I was sure your lordship did not give it me.

Bru. Bear with me, good boy, I am much forgetful.
Canst thou hold up thy heavy eyes awhile,
And touch thy instrument a strain or two?

Luc. Ay, my lord, an 't please you.

Bru.   It does, my boy:
I trouble thee too much, but thou art willing.

Luc. It is my duty, sir.   260

Bru. I should not urge thy duty past thy might;
I know young bloods look for a time of rest.

Luc. I have slept, my lord, already.

Bru. It was well done; and thou shalt sleep again;
I will not hold thee long: if I do live,
I will be good to thee.   [*Music, and a song.*
This is a sleepy tune. O murderous slumber,
Lay'st thou thy leaden mace upon my boy,
That plays thee music? Gentle knave, good night;
I will not do thee so much wrong to wake thee: 270
If thou dost nod, thou break'st thy instrument;
I'll take it from thee; and, good boy, good night.
Let me see, let me see; is not the leaf turn'd down
Where I left reading? Here it is, I think.

Enter the Ghost of Cæsar.

How ill this taper burns! Ha! who comes here?
I think it is the weakness of mine eyes
That shapes this monstrous apparition.
It comes upon me. Art thou any thing?
Art thou some god, some angel, or some devil,
That makest my blood cold and my hair to stare?   280
Speak to me what thou art.

Ghost. Thy evil spirit, Brutus.

Bru. Why comest thou?

Ghost. To tell thee thou shalt see me at Philippi.

Bru. Well; then I shall see thee again?

Ghost. Ay, at Philippi.

191. **once,** at some time. 194. **art,** acquired faculty. 196. **alive,** concerning us as living. 209. **new-added,** newly increased. 224. **ventures,** investments (of enterprises at sea). 228. **niggard,** treat in a niggardly fashion. 231. **gown,** dressing gown. 239. **instrument,** lute. 241. **knave,** boy. 267. **murderous,** producing the likeness of death. 268. **mace,** staff, club. 275. **How . . . burns.** It is a part of the machinery of apparitions that lights burn low and blue. 280. **stare,** stand on end. 287. **Why . . . then.** In view of superstitious terror, greater in Shakespeare's day than ours, this line presents an example of marvelous courage.

Bru. Why, I will see thee at Philippi, then.
                                                  [*Exit Ghost.*
Now I have taken heart thou vanishest:
Ill spirit, I would hold more talk with thee.
Boy, Lucius! Varro! Claudius! Sirs, awake!   290
Claudius!
    Luc. The strings, my lord, are false.
    Bru. He thinks he still is at his instrument.
Lucius, awake!
    Luc. My lord?
    Bru. Didst thou dream, Lucius, that thou so criedst
        out?
    Luc. My lord, I do not know that I did cry.
    Bru. Yes, that thou didst: didst thou see any thing?
    Luc. Nothing, my lord.
    Bru. Sleep again, Lucius. Sirrah Claudius!   300
[*To Var.*] Fellow thou, awake!
    Var. My lord?
    Clau. My lord?
    Bru. Why did you so cry out, sirs, in your sleep?
    Var. Clau. Did we, my lord?
    Bru.   Ay: saw you any thing?
    Var. No, my lord, I saw nothing.
    Clau.   Nor I, my lord.
    Bru. Go and commend me to my brother Cassius;
Bid him set on his powers betimes before,
And we will follow.
    Var. Clau.   It shall be done, my lord.
                                                  [*Exeunt.*

ACT V.

SCENE I. *The plains of Philippi.*

Enter OCTAVIUS, ANTONY, *and their* army.

    Oct. Now, Antony, our hopes are answered:
You said the enemy would not come down,
But keep the hills and upper regions;
It proves not so: their battles are at hand;
They mean to warn us at Philippi here,
Answering before we do demand of them.
    Ant. Tut, I am in their bosoms, and I know
Wherefore they do it: they could be content
To visit other places; and come down
With fearful bravery, thinking by this face   10
To fasten in our thoughts that they have courage;
But 'tis not so.

Enter a Messenger.

    Mess.   Prepare you, generals:
The enemy comes on in gallant show;
Their bloody sign of battle is hung out,
And something to be done immediately.
    Ant. Octavius, lead your battle softly on,
Upon the left hand of the even field.
    Oct. Upon the right hand I; keep thou the left.
    Ant. Why do you cross me in this exigent?
    Oct. I do not cross you; but I will do so.   [*March.* 20

Drum. Enter BRUTUS, CASSIUS, *and their* Army;
    LUCILIUS, TITINIUS, MESSALA, *and others.*

    Bru. They stand, and would have parley.
    Cas. Stand fast, Titinius: we must out and talk.
    Oct. Mark Antony, shall we give sign of battle?
    Ant. No, Cæsar, we will answer on their charge.
Make forth; the generals would have some words.
    Oct. Stir not until the signal.
    Bru. Words before blows: is it so, countrymen?
    Oct. Not that we love words better, as you do.
    Bru. Good words are better than bad strokes,
        Octavius.
    Ant. In your bad strokes, Brutus, you give good
        words: 30
Witness the hole you made in Cæsar's heart,
Crying 'Long live! hail, Cæsar!'
    Cas.   Antony,
The posture of your blows are yet unknown;
But for your words, they rob the Hybla bees,
And leave them honeyless.
    Ant.   Not stingless too.
    Bru. O, yes, and soundless too;
For you have stol'n their buzzing, Antony,
And very wisely threat before you sting.
    Ant. Villains, you did not so, when your vile daggers
Hack'd one another in the sides of Cæsar: 40
You show'd your teeth like apes, and fawn'd like
        hounds,
And bow'd like bondmen, kissing Cæsar's feet;
Whilst damned Casca, like a cur, behind
Struck Cæsar on the neck. O you flatterers!
    Cas. Flatterers! Now, Brutus, thank yourself:
This tongue had not offended so to-day,
If Cassius might have ruled.
    Oct. Come, come, the cause: if arguing make us
        sweat,
The proof of it will turn to redder drops.
Look;   50
I draw a sword against conspirators;
When think you that the sword goes up again?
Never, till Cæsar's three and thirty wounds
Be well avenged; or till another Cæsar
Have added slaughter to the sword of traitors.
    Bru. Cæsar, thou canst not die by traitors' hands,
Unless thou bring'st them with thee.
    Oct.   So I hope;
I was not born to die on Brutus' sword.
    Bru. O, if thou wert the noblest of thy strain,
Young man, thou couldst not die more honourable.   60
    Cas. A peevish schoolboy, worthless of such honour,
Join'd with a masker and a reveller!
    Ant. Old Cassius still!
    Oct.   Come, Antony, away!
Defiance, traitors, hurl we in your teeth:
If you dare fight to-day, come to the field;
If not, when you have stomachs.
            [*Exeunt Octavius, Antony, and their army.*
    Cas. Why, now, blow wind, swell billow and swim
        bark!
The storm is up, and all is on the hazard.
    Bru. Ho, Lucilius! hark, a word with you.
    Lucil.   [*Standing forth*] My lord?
            [*Brutus and Lucilius converse apart.*

ACT V. SCENE I.   5. **warn,** summon.   7. **bosoms,** secret councils.   10.
fearful bravery, cowardly bravado.   **face,** pretense.   14. **bloody sign
of battle.** Plutarch describes this as an "arming scarlet coat."   17.
even, probably, evenly divided rather than level.   19. **exigent,**
emergency.   20. **I will do so,** i.e., as I said.   21. **parley,** conference.

Dramatists have to fight many of their battles in words. This battle
takes the form of a peculiarly unbecoming verbal row.   24. **answer on
their charge,** attack when they attack.   34. **Hybla,** a mountain near
Syracuse, famous in pastoral poetry.   41. **show'd your teeth,** i.e., in
smiles.   48. **cause,** issue at stake.

Cas. Messala!

Mes.   [*Standing forth*] What says my
   general?   70

Cas. Messala,
This is my birth-day; as this very day
Was Cassius born. Give me thy hand, Messala:
Be thou my witness that against my will,
As Pompey was, am I compell'd to set
Upon one battle all our liberties.
You know that I held Epicurus strong
And his opinion: now I change my mind,
And partly credit things that do presage.
Coming from Sardis, on our former ensign   80
Two mighty eagles fell, and there they perch'd,
Gorging and feeding from our soldiers' hands;
Who to Philippi here consorted us:
This morning are they fled away and gone;
And in their steads do ravens, crows and kites,
Fly o'er our heads and downward look on us,
As we were sickly prey: their shadows seem
A canopy most fatal, under which
Our army lies, ready to give up the ghost.

Mes. Believe not so.

Cas.   I but believe it partly;   90
For I am fresh of spirit and resolved
To meet all perils very constantly.

Bru. Even so, Lucilius.

Cas.   Now, most noble Brutus,
The gods to-day stand friendly, that we may,
Lovers in peace, lead on our days to age!
But since the affairs of men rest still incertain,
Let's reason with the worst that may befall.
If we do lose this battle, then is this
The very last time we shall speak together:
What are you then determined to do?   100

Bru. Even by the rule of that philosophy
By which I did blame Cato for the death
Which he did give himself, I know not how,
But I do find it cowardly and vile,
For fear of what might fall, so to prevent
The time of life: arming myself with patience
To stay the providence of some high powers
That govern us below.

Cas.   Then, if we lose this battle,
You are contented to be led in triumph
Thorough the streets of Rome?   110

Bru. No, Cassius, no: think not, thou noble Roman,
That ever Brutus will go bound to Rome;
He bears too great a mind. But this same day
Must end that work the ides of March begun;
And whether we shall meet again I know not.
Therefore our everlasting farewell take:
For ever, and for ever, farewell, Cassius!
If we do meet again, why, we shall smile;
If not, why then, this parting was well made.

Cas. For ever, and for ever, farewell, Brutus!   120
If we do meet again, we'll smile indeed;
If not, 'tis true this parting was well made.

Bru. Why, then, lead on. O, that a man might
   know

The end of this day's business ere it come!
But it sufficeth that the day will end,
And then the end is known. Come, ho! away! [*Exeunt.*

SCENE II. *The same. The field of battle.*

Alarum. Enter BRUTUS *and* MESSALA.

Bru. Ride, ride, Messala, ride, and give these bills
Unto the legions on the other side.   [*Loud alarum.*
Let them set on at once; for I perceive
But cold demeanour in Octavius' wing,
And sudden push gives them the overthrow.
Ride, ride, Messala: let them all come down. [*Exeunt.*

SCENE III. *Another part of the field.*

Alarums. Enter CASSIUS *and* TITINIUS.

Cas. O, look, Titinius, look, the villains fly!
Myself have to mine own turn'd enemy:
This ensign here of mine was turning back;
I slew the coward, and did take it from him.

Tit. O Cassius, Brutus gave the word too early;
Who, having some advantage on Octavius,
Took it too eagerly: his soldiers fell to spoil,
Whilst we by Antony are all enclosed.

Enter PINDARUS.

Pin. Fly further off, my lord, fly further off;
Mark Antony is in your tents, my lord: 10
Fly, therefore, noble Cassius, fly far off.

Cas. This hill is far enough. Look, look, Titinius;
Are those my tents where I perceive the fire?

Tit. They are, my lord.

Cas.   Titinius, if thou lovest me,
Mount thou my horse, and hide thy spurs in him,
Till he have brought thee up to yonder troops,
And here again; that I may rest assured
Whether yon troops are friend or enemy.

Tit. I will be here again, even with a thought. [*Exit.*

Cas. Go, Pindarus, get higher on that hill;   20
My sight was ever thick; regard Titinius,
And tell me what thou notest about the field.
             [*Pindarus ascends the hill.*
This day I breathed first: time is come round,
And where I did begin, there shall I end;
My life is run his compass. Sirrah, what news?

Pin. [*Above*] O my lord!

Cas. What news?

Pin. [*Above*] Titinius is enclosed round about
With horsemen, that make to him on the spur;
Yet he spurs on. Now they are almost on him. 30
Now, Titinius! Now some light. O, he lights too.
He's ta'en. [*Shout.*] And, hark! they shout for joy.

Cas. Come down, behold no more.
O, coward that I am, to live so long,
To see my best friend ta'en before my face!

PINDARUS *descends.*

Come hither, sirrah:
In Parthia did I take thee prisoner;
And then I swore thee, saving of thy life,
That whatsoever I did bid thee do,
Thou shouldst attempt it. Come now, keep thine
    oath;   40
Now be a freeman: and with this good sword,
That ran through Cæsar's bowels, search this bosom.
Stand not to answer: here, take thou the hilts;
And, when my face is cover'd, as 'tis now,
Guide thou the sword. [*Pindarus stabs him.*] Cæsar,
    thou art revenged,
Even with the sword that kill'd thee.   [*Dies.*
    Pin. So, I am free; yet would not so have been,
Durst I have done my will. O Cassius,
Far from this country Pindarus shall run,
Where never Roman shall take note of him.   [*Exit.* 50

    Re-enter TITINIUS *with* MESSALA.

    Mes. It is but change, Titinius; for Octavius
Is overthrown by noble Brutus' power,
As Cassius' legions are by Antony.
    Tit. These tidings will well comfort Cassius.
    Mes. Where did you leave him?
    Tit.   All disconsolate,
With Pindarus his bondman, on this hill.
    Mes. Is not that he that lies upon the ground?
    Tit. He lies not like the living. O my heart!
    Mes. Is not that he?
    Tit.   No, this was he, Messala,
But Cassius is no more. O setting sun,   60
As in thy red rays thou dost sink to night,
So in his red blood Cassius' day is set;
The sun of Rome is set! Our day is gone;
Clouds, dews, and dangers come; our deeds are done!
Mistrust of my success hath done this deed.
    Mes. Mistrust of good success hath done this deed.
O hateful error, melancholy's child,
Why dost thou show to the apt thoughts of men
The things that are not? O error, soon conceived,
Thou never comest unto a happy birth,   70
But kill'st the mother that engender'd thee!
    Tit. What, Pindarus! where art thou, Pindarus?
    Mes. Seek him, Titinius, whilst I go to meet
The noble Brutus, thrusting this report
Into his ears; I may say, thrusting it;
For piercing steel and darts envenomed
Shall be as welcome to the ears of Brutus
As tidings of this sight.
    Tit.   Hie you, Messala,
And I will seek for Pindarus the while.   [*Exit Messala.*
Why didst thou send me forth, brave Cassius?   80
Did I not meet thy friends? and did not they
Put on my brows this wreath of victory,
And bid me give it thee? Didst thou not hear their
    shouts?
Alas, thou hast misconstrued every thing!
But, hold thee, take this garland on thy brow;
Thy Brutus bid me give it thee, and I
Will do his bidding. Brutus, come apace,

And see how I regarded Caius Cassius.
By your leave, gods:—this is a Roman's part:
Come, Cassius' sword, and find Titinius' heart.   90
        [*Kills himself.*

    Alarum. Re-enter MESSALA, *with* BRUTUS, *young* CATO,
    STRATO, VOLUMNIUS, *and* LUCILIUS.

    Bru. Where, where, Messala, doth his body lie?
    Mes. Lo, yonder, and Titinius mourning it.
    Bru. Titinius' face is upward.
    Cato.   He is slain.
    Bru. O Julius Cæsar, thou art mighty yet!
Thy spirit walks abroad, and turns our swords
In our own proper entrails.   [*Low alarums.*
    Cato.   Brave Titinius!
Look, whether he have not crown'd dead Cassius!
    Bru. Are yet two Romans living such as these?
The last of all the Romans, fare thee well!
It is impossible that ever Rome   100
Should breed thy fellow. Friends, I owe more tears
To this dead man than you shall see me pay.
I shall find time, Cassius, I shall find time.
Come, therefore, and to Thasos send his body:
His funerals shall not be in our camp,
Lest it discomfort us. Lucilius, come;
And come, young Cato; let us to the field.
Labeo and Flavius, set our battles on:
'Tis three o'clock; and, Romans, yet ere night
We shall try fortune in a second fight.   [*Exeunt.* 110

    SCENE IV. *Another part of the field.*

    Alarum. Enter fighting, Soldiers *of both armies; then*
    BRUTUS, *young* CATO, LUCILIUS, *and others.*

    Bru. Yet, countrymen, O, yet hold up your heads!
    Cato. What bastard doth not? Who will go with me?
I will proclaim my name about the field:
I am the son of Marcus Cato, ho!
A foe to tyrants, and my country's friend;
I am the son of Marcus Cato, ho!
    Bru. And I am Brutus, Marcus Brutus, I;
Brutus, my country's friend; know me for Brutus!
        [*Exit.*
    Lucil. O young and noble Cato, art thou down?
Why, now thou diest as bravely as Titinius;   10
And mayst be honour'd, being Cato's son.
    First Sold. Yield, or thou diest.
    Lucil.   Only I yield to die:
There is so much that thou wilt kill me straight;
    [*Offering money.*
Kill Brutus, and be honour'd in his death.
    First Sold. We must not. A noble prisoner!
    Sec. Sold. Room, ho! Tell Antony, Brutus is ta'en.
    First Sold. I'll tell the news. Here comes the general.

    Enter ANTONY.

Brutus is ta'en, Brutus is ta'en, my lord.
    Ant. Where is he?

---

dim. 31. **lights**, alights. 37. **Parthia**, allusion to the campaign of
Crassus in Parthia, 53 B.C., in which Plutarch states that Cassius had
captured Pindarus. 38. **swore thee**, made thee swear. 49. **Pindarus
shall run.** Plutarch states that Pindarus was never seen again. 51.
change, exchange. 65. **Mistrust**, i.e., on Cassius' part. 68. **apt**,
liable to be impressed. 104. **Thasos**, an island off the coast of Thrace.

106. **discomfort**, discourage. 110. **second fight.** The second battle
was, in point of fact, twenty days later.
SCENE IV. 7-8. **And I . . . Brutus.** This speech is unassigned in F.
It is sometimes assigned to Lucilius, who, in lines 12-14 below, pretends
to be Brutus as an act of devotion to his master. 9. **Cato**, a son of
Marcus Cato, whose death is recounted by Plutarch.

Lucil. Safe, Antony; Brutus is safe enough: 20
I dare assure thee that no enemy
Shall ever take alive the noble Brutus:
The gods defend him from so great a shame!
When you do find him, or alive or dead,
He will be found like Brutus, like himself.
 Ant. This is not Brutus, friend; but, I assure
  you,
A prize no less in worth: keep this man safe;
Give him all kindness: I had rather have
Such men my friends than enemies. Go on,
And see whether Brutus be alive or dead; 30
And bring us word unto Octavius' tent
How every thing is chanced. [*Exeunt.*

SCENE V. *Another part of the field.*

Enter BRUTUS, DARDANIUS, CLITUS, STRATO, *and*
 VOLUMNIUS.

 Bru. Come, poor remains of friends, rest on this
  rock.
 Cli. Statilius show'd the torch-light, but, my lord,
He came not back: he is or ta'en or slain.
 Bru. Sit thee down, Clitus: slaying is the word;
It is a deed in fashion. Hark thee, Clitus. [*Whispers.*
 Cli. What, I, my lord? No, not for all the world.
 Bru. Peace then! no words.
 Cli. I'll rather kill myself.
 Bru. Hark thee, Dardanius. [*Whispers.*
 Dar. Shall I do such a deed?
 Cli. O Dardanius!
 Dar. O Clitus! 10
 Cli. What ill request did Brutus make to thee?
 Dar. To kill him, Clitus. Look, he meditates.
 Cli. Now is that noble vessel full of grief,
That it runs over even at his eyes.
 Bru. Come hither, good Volumnius; list a word.
 Vol. What says my lord?
 Bru. Why, this, Volumnius:
The ghost of Cæsar hath appear'd to me
Two several times by night; at Sardis once,
And, this last night, here in Philippi fields:
I know my hour is come.
 Vol. Not so, my lord. 20
 Bru. Nay, I am sure it is, Volumnius.
Thou seest the world, Volumnius, how it goes;
Our enemies have beat us to the pit: [*Low alarums.*
It is more worthy to leap in ourselves,
Than tarry till they push us. Good Volumnius,
Thou know'st that we two went to school together:
Even for that our love of old, I prithee,
Hold thou my sword-hilts, whilst I run on it.
 Vol. That 's not an office for a friend, my lord.
 [*Alarum still.*
 Cli. Fly, fly, my lord; there is no tarrying here. 30
 Bru. Farewell to you; and you; and you, Volumnius.
Strato, thou hast been all this while asleep;

Farewell to thee too, Strato. Countrymen,
My heart doth joy that yet in all my life
I found no man but he was true to me.
I shall have glory by this losing day
More than Octavius and Mark Antony
By this vile conquest shall attain unto.
So fare you well at once; for Brutus' tongue
Hath almost ended his life's history: 40
Night hangs upon mine eyes; my bones would rest,
That have but labour'd to attain this hour.
 [*Alarum. Cry within,* 'Fly, fly, fly!'
 Cli. Fly, my lord, fly.
 Bru. Hence! I will follow.
 [*Exeunt Clitus, Dardanius, and Volumnius.*
I prithee, Strato, stay thou by thy lord:
Thou art a fellow of a good respect;
Thy life hath had some smatch of honour in it:
Hold then my sword, and turn away thy face,
While I do run upon it. Wilt thou, Strato?
 Stra. Give me your hand first. Fare you well, my
  lord.
 Bru. Farewell, good Strato. [*Runs on his sword.*]
 Cæsar, now be still: 50
I kill'd not thee with half so good a will. [*Dies.*

Alarum. Retreat. Enter OCTAVIUS, ANTONY, MESSALA,
 LUCILIUS, *and the army.*

 Oct. What man is that?
 Mes. My master's man. Strato, where is thy
  master?
 Stra. Free from the bondage you are in, Messala:
The conquerors can but make a fire of him;
For Brutus only overcame himself,
And no man else hath honour by his death.
 Lucil. So Brutus should be found. I thank thee,
  Brutus,
That thou hast proved Lucilius' saying true.
 Oct. All that served Brutus, I will entertain them. 60
Fellow, wilt thou bestow thy time with me?
 Stra. Ay, if Messala will prefer me to you.
 Oct. Do so, good Messala.
 Mes. How died my master, Strato?
 Stra. I held the sword, and he did run on it.
 Mes. Octavius, then take him to follow thee,
That did the latest service to my master.
 Ant. This was the noblest Roman of them all:
All the conspirators save only he
Did that they did in envy of great Cæsar; 70
He only, in a general honest thought
And common good to all, made one of them.
His life was gentle, and the elements
So mix'd in him that Nature might stand up
And say to all the world 'This was a man!'
 Oct. According to his virtue let us use him,
With all respect and rites of burial.
Within my tent his bones to-night shall lie,
Most like a soldier, order'd honourably.
So call the field to rest; and let 's away, 80
To part the glories of this happy day. [*Exeunt.*

SCENE V. 23. **pit,** the last ditch (proverbial). 33-35. **Countrymen
. . . me.** These almost mystical words of Brutus, partly explained in
the lines which follow as referring to his fame, have a much wider and
deeper import. It is the case of a great leader, defeated, overthrown,
and rejected, and yet forever triumphant in the ideals he has held. 46.
smatch, smack, flavor. 68-75. **This . . . man.** This famous eulogy is
based upon a statement by Plutarch that Antony cast his embroidered
cloak over Brutus' body and paid the cost of Brutus' burial, and upon

Plutarch's statement in his summary of the character of Brutus that
even Brutus' enemies confessed that he had had no other intent but to
restore the ancient institutions of Rome. 73. **gentle,** a favorite word
with Shakespeare meaning "true," "cultured," "affable"; it was often
applied to Shakespeare himself by his contemporaries. **elements.**
Man as a microcosm was made up of earth, air, fire, and water, whose
qualities were mingled in Brutus in due proportions. 80. **field,** army
in the field. 81. **part,** share.

SHAKESPEARE'S LIFE AND WORK

The Period of the Tragedies, 1602-1608

When the Globe, the most famous of the London public playhouses, was built in 1599, one-half interest in the property was assigned to the brothers Cuthbert and Richard Burbage; the other half to five actors, Shakespeare, Kemp, Pope, Phillips, and Heminges. Kemp had left the company by 1600 and in 1602 was with the earl of Worcester's men. His place as leading comic actor was taken by Robert Armin, a man of some culture and the author of a book on comedy. With this change there was also a change in the nature of the comic parts introduced into Shakespeare's plays. The parts of Dogberry, Launcelot Gobbo, and Bottom had been written to suit Kemp's talent for old-fashioned clownage. For Armin, Shakespeare invented such refinements in the art as are represented by Touchstone, Feste, Lavache in *All's Well that Ends Well*, and the Fool in *King Lear*.

There were other changes in the composition of the company, which are reflected in Shakespeare's adaptation of his parts to the histrionic talent at his disposal. Changes occurred also in the ownership of the shares, so that the value of Shakespeare's proportional share of the Globe varied from time to time.

From the year 1599 to 1602 there occurred the War of the Theaters, a theatrical struggle begun by Ben Jonson and carried on by means of satirical dramas. In *Everyman out of his Humour* (1599) Jonson ridiculed Marston, Daniel, and others, who, he says in the *Conversations with Drummond*, had for three years "provoked him with their petulant styles on every stage." More immediately he had taken offense at *The Scourge of Villainy* (1598), a verse satire in which Marston directly satirized Jonson under the name of Torquatus.

The Children of the Chapel Royal, who occupied the theater which Burbage had built in Blackfriars, and the Children of Paul's, who probably acted in their own singing school in St. Paul's churchyard, assumed extraordinary importance. They had at their command the pen of Jonson himself, as well as of Chapman and others who catered to the current popular taste for social satire.

On the other side was Marston, and apparently Shakespeare, although it is impossible to determine exactly what part Shakespeare took in the affair. If he wrote anything directly applicable, it has been lost or destroyed. The tone of the famous passage in *Hamlet* (II, ii, 328-379) is kindly and remonstrant rather than otherwise. Apparently he does not think it well that professionals should be driven off the London stage and compelled to take the road because of the quarrels among playwrights and actors and the sudden infatuation on the part of the public for the boy actors.

A passage in the second part of *The Return from Parnassus* (December 1601?) seems to indicate that Shakespeare had worsted Jonson in satirical encounter.[1] In one scene (IV, v) Kemp and Burbage are represented as coming to Cambridge to recruit actors from among the students:

Kempe. Few of the university men pen plays well. They smell too much of that writer, Ovid, and that writer, Metamorphosis, and talk much of Proserpina and Jupiter. Why, here's our fellow Shakespeare puts them all down; ay, and Ben Jonson too. O that Ben Jonson is a pestilent fellow: he brought up Horace giving the poets a pill, but our fellow Shakespeare hath given him a purge that made him bewray his credit.
Burbage. It is a shrewd fellow indeed. . . .

Whatever may have been the outcome of the War of the Theaters, and it is not likely to have been important, the Lord Chamberlain's company maintained its lead in the dramatic profession, throughout the later years of Queen Elizabeth's reign, and in 1603 became the King's Servants. Some of the greatest dramatists of the age, including Ben Jonson, wrote for this company, and Jonson and Shakespeare were intimate friends.

[1]See Chambers, *William Shakespeare*, I, 71-72, for further references.

NOMEN HERBAF MANDRAGORA

A mandrake, as pictured in a book of herbs, 1484. (Huntington)

That Shakespeare and his colleagues were adopted as the King's Servants within ten days after King James' arrival in London is witnessed by a document of instructions, preserved at the Public Record Office, from the king to his Keeper of the Privy Seal. It is dated May 17, 1603, and endorsed "The Players' Privilege." Shakespeare, Burbage, Phillips, Heminges, Condell, Sly, Armin, and Cowley are mentioned by name; and with them Lawrence Fletcher, an actor who had played before the king and the Scottish court in 1599 and 1601. They are given the usual privileges of exercising their art anywhere within the kingdom and are henceforth to be known as the King's Company. As the King's Servants, the principal members of the troupe were also appointed to the honorary rank of Grooms of the Royal Chamber. We therefore find them duly recorded in the Accounts of the Master of the Wardrobe on March 15, 1604, as recipients of the customary grants of red cloth, so that they, dressed in the royal livery, might take part in the approaching coronation procession of King James. The same men are mentioned in these grants as in the Players' Privilege. Shakespeare's name stands second in the former document and first in the latter. In a somewhat similar manner the king's players, as Grooms of the Royal Chamber, were called in attendance on the Spanish ambassador at Somerset House in August 1604.

For the end of that year and the beginning of the next the Revels Accounts have an unusually ample entry of plays performed at Whitehall. In the entry Shakespeare's plays predominate. They include *Othello*, *The Merry Wives of Windsor*, *Measure for Measure*, the "Play of Errors," *Love's Labour's Lost*, *Henry V*, and *The Merchant of Venice*. Three of these are marked in a column headed "The poets which made the plays" with the name *Shaxberd*. Final *e* in the Elizabethan handwriting is easily mistaken for final *d*, so that the entry as given is either a misreading of the present entry or a miswriting of some earlier notes in which the word had been written "Shaxbere" or "Shaxpere." The authenticity of this entry is often called in question, since some scholars regard it as a forgery. However, the grounds for regarding it as a forgery are hardly adequate, and its general appropriateness and consistency make it entirely worthy of credence.

In the will of Shakespeare's fellow actor and member of the king's company, Augustine Phillips, probated May 4, 1605, there is a bequest of "a thirty shillings piece of gold" to "my fellow, William Shakespeare," with similar bequests to Condell, Beeston, Fletcher, and other members of the troupe.

BIOGRAPHICAL

Meantime during the period there are a number of records concerned with Shakespeare as a man of property. On May 1, 1602, John and William Combe conveyed to Shakespeare one hundred seven acres of land in the parish of Old Stratford. It is notable that the deed was delivered to Shakespeare's brother Gilbert and not to the poet, who was probably at that time occupied in London. On September 28th of the same year Shakespeare acquired title in copyhold (a form of tenure limited by the superior claims of a lord of the manor) of a cottage and land opposite New Place in Stratford, "one cottage and one garden by estimation a quarter of an acre."

There are also records of a somewhat complicated speculation into which Shakespeare entered in 1605. He purchased an interest in the tithes of Stratford and adjacent villages from one Ralph Huband for the considerable sum of four hundred and twenty pounds. This is an instance of the strange fiduciary customs of Shakespeare's times. The collection of money originally levied for the support of the church under a tithe law had become a private and negotiable right belonging to certain persons who had contracted for such taxes by the payment of a fixed sum, and who reimbursed themselves and derived a profit by the collection of as much as they could of the total amount due under the law. Huband seems to have owned one-half interest in certain kinds of tithes in certain villages, which half, or "moiety," Shakespeare bought. Probably between January and March 1609, there was issued, as appears from the Stratford Corporation Records, a complaint by Shakespeare and others to the Lord Chancellor of England reciting the full history of the leasing of the Stratford tithes and praying that certain other titheholders be required to come into the High Court of Chancery and make answer to the complaints alleged, namely, that they have not paid their proportional part of an annual rental of £27 13s. 4d. on the whole property in the tithes to one Henry Barker. Barker thus had the right to recover possession from the three dozen and more other titheholders. In bringing this suit Shakespeare acted the part of a public-spirited citizen and brought a much muddled business association into a state of order.[2]

The Stratford Burial Register shows the death of Shakespeare's father in 1601, of his brother Edmund in 1607, and of his mother in 1608. The Stratford Marriage Register and the Stratford Baptismal Register contribute respectively records of the marriage of Shakespeare's daughter Susanna to Dr. John Hall and the baptism in Trinity Church of Elizabeth, daughter to John Hall, and Shakespeare's first grandchild.

LITERARY ALLUSIONS

Literary allusions to Shakespeare had by this time become fairly frequent. For example, Anthony Scoloker in the epistle prefatory to *Diaphantus, or the Passions of Love* (1604) says,

It should be like the never-too-well-read Arcadia . . . or to come home to the vulgar's element like Friendly Shakespeare's tragedies, where the comedian rides when the tragedian stands on tip-toe: 'faith it should please all, like Prince Hamlet.

The great antiquarian William Camden includes Shakespeare's name among important modern poets in his casual list in *Remains* (1605):

These may suffice for some poetical descriptions of our ancient poets; if I would come to our time, what a world could I present to you out of Sir Philip Sidney, Ed. Spenser, Samuel Daniel, Hugh Holland, Ben: Jonson, Th. Campion, Mich. Drayton, George Chapman, John Marston, William Shakespeare, and other most pregnant wits of these our times, whom succeeding ages may justly admire.

The plays also come in for a share of allusions, the greatest stir being created by the Henry IV plays. Falstaff and Justice Shallow had established their popularity. The Prologue to *Sir John Oldcastle* (1599) exclaimed indignantly:

It is no pamper'd glutton we present,
Nor aged counselor to youthful sin,
But one whose virtue shone above the rest,
A valiant martyr and a virtuous peer.

A letter (1600) from Sir Charles Percy, detained in the country, to a friend in London says, "If I stay here long in this fashion, at my return I think you will find me so dull that I shall be taken for Justice Silence or Justice Shallow. . . . [The news you send me] though perhaps they will not exempt me from the

opinion of a Justice Shallow in London, yet, I assure you, they will make me pass for a very sufficient gentleman in Gloucestershire." Again the postscript to a letter from the countess of Southampton to her husband, dated the 8th of July, possibly 1599, shows a quaint reflection of the popularity of *2 Henry IV*:

All the news I can send you that I think will make you merry is that I read in a letter from London that Sir John Falstaff is by his mistress, Dame Pintpot, made father of a goodly miller's thumb, a boy that's all head and very little body; but this is a secret.

Also from the second part of *The Return from Parnassus*, in which the actor Burbage is represented as trying out for the stage a student called Philomusus, comes the following bit of dialogue:

Burbage. I like your face and the proportion of your body for Richard the Third. I pray you, Mr. Philomusus, let me see you act a little of it.
Philomosus. "Now is the winter of our discontent
Made glorious summer by the sun of York."
Burbage. Very well, I assure you!

A striking event in the history of Shakespeare's plays during this period was a performance of *Richard II* two days before the abortive rebellion of the earl of

Frontispiece from "The Arte of Archerie," 1634. (Huntington)

[2]Tucker Brooke, "Shakespeare's Moiety of the Stratford Tithes," *MLN*, XL, 462-469.

Essex on February 7, 1601. The performance was arranged for with Shakespeare's company by Sir Gelly Meyrick, a partisan of Essex, with the idea that, by presenting on the stage the story of a ruler who had been ruined by unworthy favorites, public sympathy would be aroused for Essex, whose object was to remove his political enemies from the favor of the queen.

One of the really curious references is found in the notes of a certain Captain Keeling, commander of the East India Company's ship *Dragon*, off Sierra Leone, in the years 1607 and 1608:

September 5. I sent the interpreter, according to his desire, aboard the *Hector*, where he broke fast and after came aboard me, where we gave the tragedy of *Hamlet*.

September 30. Captain Hawkins dined with me, where my companions acted *King Richard the Second*.

March 31. I invited Captain Hawkins to a fish dinner, and had *Hamlet* acted aboard me; which I permit to keep my people from idleness and unlawful games or sleep.

OTHER DRAMA OF THE PERIOD

A second great outburst of dramatic activity occurred after 1600. Shakespeare bridges a gap between Marlowe and Jonson and himself participates in the new movement. Indeed, the first decade of the seventeenth century in England is a period conspicuous in the world's literature for what was accomplished in the drama. There have been preserved from that time perhaps fifty plays which have some claim to be considered interesting or important. A new set of dramatists, most of whom had already learned the art of playwriting, were at work, animated by

From the title page of Heywood's "Philocothonista," 1635. (Folger)

a new spirit and encouraged as never before by noble and royal favor. There were relatively few new subjects, but there was an extraordinary intensification in the treatment of old themes. The English drama, coming at the end of the period of the European Renaissance, had taken over a group of subjects, a set of literary themes, and a psychology and ethics, personal and social, which it continued to exploit.

The whole period covered was not a long one. We have many single dramatists who worked almost all the way through the Elizabethan and Jacobean drama, in close connection with one another and with the same public before them. What the drama of Kyd, Marlowe, and Greene was at the beginning, such the drama in some sense remained until the end, with, of course, changes in emphasis, further discoveries of dramatic ideas, and a constant development in power.

In the earliest period we saw the adoption by Shakespeare in *A Comedy of Errors* of the clear lines of structure in both plot and character of Italianate Latin comedy. This continues in the second period in Shakespeare's *Twelfth Night*, and in the third period, in Jonson's *Volpone* and *The Alchemist*, and Chapman's *All Fools*.

There is likewise a renewed interest in the theme of revenge, begun by Thomas Kyd in *The Spanish Tragedy* and no doubt always in use by dramatists after that. It becomes the tragedy of blood and intrigue, as exemplified in Marston's *Antonio's Revenge* (1599), Shakespeare's *Hamlet*, Chettle's *Hoffman, or The Revenge of a Father* (1602?), *The Revenger's Tragedy* (1606-1607?), attributed to Cyril Tourneur, Webster's *The White Devil* (possibly before 1610), and others.

Death was the only known ending for a tragedy, and we have it, gruesome and inevitable, not only in the tragedy of intrigue but especially exploited in murder plays. *Arden of Feversham* is reflected in *A Yorkshire Tragedy*, sometimes attributed to Shakespeare, and in *Macbeth* itself.

Domestic drama, finding its roots in such plays as *Wily Beguiled* (1596?), *The Two Angry Women of Abingdon* (before 1598) by Henry Porter, and *The Merry Devil of Edmonton* (1603?), takes on great vitality in Thomas Heywood's *A Woman Killed with Kindness* (1603), Thomas Dekker's *The Honest Whore* (1604), Shakespeare's *Othello* and *King Lear*, and is a feature of many of the tragedies of blood and intrigue. *Othello* and *King Lear* are, of course, courtly and deal with persons of high standing in the ancient tradition of tragedy, which is not at all like the tragedies of contemporary crime and humble life, such as *The Yorkshire Tragedy* and *A Woman Killed with Kindness;* but *Othello* and *King Lear*, along with their greater issues, introduce family relations and in this respect resemble what are called domestic tragedies.

The dramatists saw potentialities for disaster in the maladjustment of the social relationships of the sexes, in conjugal unfaithfulness, marital jealousy, avarice as a motive in marriage, the profligacy of men, and the unchastity of women. Woman begins to come into the center of dramatic interest, where she remained in the decade following 1610. She begins to be regarded in the ways characteristic of a disillusioned and degenerate society; that is, as the unfortunate victim of man's lust and greed, as a martyr in the cause of hapless love, or as the embodiment of unchastity.

The older romance goes on as pastoralism, or as adventure, which latter we see in Heywood's *Fortune by Land and Sea* (1603?), a sort of chronicle play, and his *Fair Maid of the West* (1603?). It is against these, and, we may believe, many far worse plays, that Beaumont directs his satire in *The Knight of the Burning Pestle* (1607). To this romantic impulse belongs *Pericles* (1607-1608), a play to whose influence much importance must be attached.

The ransacking of classical literature continued with unabated zeal, not only for satiric method and the reinforcement of opinion, but for subjects, as for example, in Heywood's *The Rape of Lucrece* (1608), Webster's *Appius and Virginia* (1608?), Jonson's *Sejanus* (1603), and Shakespeare's *Coriolanus* and *Antony and Cleopatra*. But no classification based on subject matter or theme really classifies, for every possible combination seems to occur; so we must turn again to a consideration of individual dramatists.

INDIVIDUAL DRAMATISTS

Of newer developments after 1600 there seem to be two of greatest importance. One is the adoption of a realistic, often satiric, point of view. Dekker, Heywood, Jonson, Rowley, and Middleton are the realists of the period. They fall into two definite groups. Jonson became the exponent of satire and criticism. He not only learned the method and practiced it with the utmost skill, but he taught others to practice it. He achieves in his comedies from *Everyman in his Humour* (1598) to *Bartholomew Fair* (1614) a genuine greatness in pure comedy, cool, objective, Aristophanic, and executed with the maturity of touch that characterizes the great veterans of literature like John Dryden. There is no form of writing which Jonson cannot do well, lyric, tragic, comic, or expository.

The realism of Dekker is very different. He came to his knowledge of the world by a hard road. So obscure, so disorganized, so wretched was his life that we know neither the date of his birth nor of his death. We know only that his life was largely wasted. Lamb's words, "He had poetry enough for anything," are trite, but almost universally admitted to be true. We catch a glimpse of him as Henslowe's hack in 1598, but that very year the curious Meres mentions him as eminent for tragedy. Always in debt and often in prison, he acquired a wide knowledge of the seamy side of life and a vast pity for it, an appreciation of the sweetness, even the dignity, of simple and lowly life, and a talent for exquisite simple expression in

prose, rhyme, and blank verse. *The Shoemaker's Holiday* (1599), *The Honest Whore*, particularly the second part (1605?), *Westward Ho* (1604) and *Northward Ho* (1605) (in both of which he collaborated with Webster), and other plays express his qualities.

Middleton combines something of the objectivity of Jonson with the intimacy of Dekker in such plays as *Michaelmas Term*, *A Trick to Catch the Old One*, and *A Mad World, my Masters*, all of which were probably written between 1604 and 1606.

Illustration for a book of medicine, 1588.
From Clowes' "Proved Practices for All Young Chirurgians." (Folger)

The other new feature of the period is a growing use of psychology. As stated earlier in the introduction to this volume, the dramatists and other writers of the end of the sixteenth and the beginning of the seventeenth centuries became suddenly, almost morbidly, aware of the implications of ancient psychology with reference to man's earthly life. They saw him in an unstable position not from fate or external force only, but from his liability to be overcome by the passions of his own soul. Reason and the passions were at war, and for the passions to dominate might mean madness, ecstasy, tragic error, and disaster; or folly, eccentricity, and incongruous maladjustment. The mixture within the man of the four humors—blood, phlegm, choler, and bile—determined temperament. An overabundance of one humor made the individual too sanguine, too

A vagabond minstrel in stocks.
From one of the "Roxburghe Ballads."

phlegmatic, too choleric, or too melancholy. He thus became the creature of a ruling passion. The segregation of these qualities in their combinations and their varied effects gave Jonson and his followers the basis for the portrayal of types and the occasion for satire.

In tragedy the psychological factor was not a matter of temperament but of the indulgence of a passion such as anger, revenge, jealousy, ambition, avarice, or lust. *Coriolanus* is a study of pride, *Hamlet* (in part at least) of melancholy, *Macbeth* of ambition, *Othello* of jealousy, and so on. The psychological interest that appears in Shakespeare during this his greatest period appears also in his contemporaries. It is, nevertheless, a mistake to believe that Shakespeare was ever mechanical in his treatment of character and that he was ever so dominated by the stoical psychology of the passions that he ceased to center his interest on human beings as such. Elizabethan psychology was always for Shakespeare mainly a medium of communication and a way of talking about human nature.

SHAKESPEARE'S WORK

What circumstances may there have been in Shakespeare's private life or in the complexion of his thought that might have caused him to turn his great powers during the years from 1603 to 1607 to the production of tragedy? So far as we can see he was extremely prosperous and successful. His bereavements were natural and inevitable, and the worst one, the death of his only son, was some years behind him. It is certain that he read Montaigne's *Essays*, published in the translation of John Florio in 1603.[3] They deepened his thinking, no doubt, but they did not necessarily give to his thought a despairing cast. Essex, who may have been his political leader, had met his death in 1602. Southampton, who was certainly at an earlier time his friend and

patron, had been released from prison and was enjoying the favor of the new king. All that can be said is that Shakespeare came, in the course of his life's experience, to a deeper, more comprehensive, and ultimately less secure view of man's destiny, and chose to devote his talent to the displaying of this philosophy in tragedies on the stage. It does not sufficiently account for Shakespeare's work to say that tragedy became the fashion of the London stage. Such a thing may have started him in the vein, no doubt it did. However, his depiction of man in relation to the tragic possibilities of existence is too momentous to be regarded merely as a fashion of the stage. In the eye of Shakespearean tragedy man is unstable, unassured, and unassurable.

If it were only a question of the tragedies, one might say that Shakespeare deliberately turned his artist's mind toward the terrible, and was himself relatively unaffected; but we have also to do with three rather mirthless dramas which Dowden described as serious, dark, and ironical. In *All's Well that Ends Well* he revamped, with no great care, enthusiasm, or consistency, an old Renaissance comedy, of somewhat the same nature as *The Two Gentlemen of Verona*. *All's Well that Ends Well* was possibly originally called *Love's Labour's Won*, the play mentioned by Meres, which Shakespeare probably had written in the early nineties. *Measure for Measure* he wrote about 1604 on the basis of *Promos and Cassandra*, a drama by George Whetstone, and an Italian tale by Giraldi Cinthio. *Troilus and Cressida* comes somewhere between 1599 and 1609.

The three plays present a world in which sex relations are awry. No one of them is without disillusion, dark irony, and wistful melancholy. Illicit love sets the action going or twists it from its natural course. In *All's Well that Ends Well* and in *Measure for Measure*, virtue wins a decided victory. In *Troilus and Cressida* it suffers defeat. Because of the nature of these plays and their appearance in the period of profound tragedies, Dowden described Shakespeare's work from 1600 to 1607 as written *de profundis* or "out of the depths." *Troilus and Cressida* and *Measure for Measure* are suggestive of the pessimism of *Hamlet*, *Macbeth*, and *King Lear*. To this period, rather than to that of *Macbeth* and *Antony and Cleopatra*, *Timon of Athens* seems in temper and style to belong.

As we sketch the comedies it will be seen that, to some extent at least, *All's Well that Ends Well* and *Measure for Measure* have in them a faith in womanly purity equal to that which appears in *Othello* and *King Lear*. What makes them seem out of harmony is the fact that, with situations which call for tragedy as loudly as anything in the tragedies mentioned, we are nevertheless provided with happy endings. Of *Troilus and Cressida* one can only say that, in so far as it is a love story, it is more bitter in its conception of womanly faithlessness than is any tragedy.[4]

[3]G. C. Taylor, *Shakespeare's Debt to Montaigne* (Cambridge, 1925); J. M. Robertson, *Montaigne and Shakespeare* (1897).

[4]For references on Shakespeare's life and work see page 79.

COMEDIES OF THE THIRD PERIOD

All's Well that Ends Well

All's Well that Ends Well was published first in the folio edition of 1623. We are reasonably certain that there had been no earlier edition of the play, because it is one of those mentioned in the Stationers' Register on November 8, 1623, as not previously entered for publication. There is no certain external evidence about the play until this entry.

From the fact that Love's Labour's Won is listed by Francis Meres in Palladis Tamia in 1598 as one of Shakespeare's comedies there has, however, arisen a fascinating problem in connection with All's Well that Ends Well. It would appear from Meres' list that there existed in 1598 a Shakespearean comedy now lost. Its title suggests that it may have been a companion piece to Love's Labour's Lost and for that reason probably an early comedy. The play, however, may have been preserved, but under a different name. Attempts have, accordingly, been made to prove that All's Well that Ends Well is Love's Labour's Won revised and renamed. In favor of this is the fact that the old name would suit the theme of All's Well that Ends Well and its source, which is one of the stories in Boccaccio's Decameron. The story belongs to the third day in that work, on which were told tales of lovers who had, in order to gain their ends, overcome apparently insuperable obstacles. Such obstacles were overcome by Helena in the plot of All's Well that Ends Well. There is also a passage in the play which seems to allude to the earlier title. Helena says to Bertram (V, iii, 314-315):

> This is done:
> Will you be mine, now you are doubly won?

Internal evidence, moreover, gives overwhelming proof that All's Well that Ends Well was written at two different times. A large part of the principal story appears in rhymed couplets. There are letters in sonnet form, lyrical dialogue, puns and conceits. All of these things are regarded as characteristic of Shakespeare's early style. Interspersed with these rhetorical parts are passages of blank verse closely compacted in thought and free with reference to the limits of the line. This is Shakespeare's later style.

Because of the unmistakable presence of these two styles most critics have assigned the original composition to about 1590-1592 and the revision to about 1602-1603. Resemblances in spirit and tone as well as in sentiment and style to Hamlet and Measure for Measure have caused the selection of the latter date.

It is, however, only fair to say that important scholars have insisted that Love's Labour's Won is to be identified with Much Ado about Nothing, or with The Taming of the Shrew, and that the two styles of All's Well should both be dated much later. This theory dates the original composition about 1598-1600 and the revision about 1607. The most recent conjecture is that of Leslie Hotson, who thinks that the lost play, Love's Labour's Won, was Troilus and Cressida.[1]

HELENA AND BERTRAM

There has been great difference of opinion among critics as regards the character of Helena. Coleridge spoke of her as Shakespeare's "loveliest creation." Others have considered her actions in the play as despicable, since she is forced by the plot of the original story to thrust herself on an unwilling bridegroom and later to resort to what, from the modern point of view, is rather base intrigue in order to compel her husband to accept her as his wife. Shaw regards her as a quite modern case of woman as wooer and pursuer. Nothing can be done to prevent the anachronistic reflections of readers and critics. It can be shown, however, that to Shakespeare and his contemporaries Helena was justifiable; indeed, that she was clever and admirable in what she did to win a husband and that she displayed virtue and constancy in meeting the hard terms laid upon her by Bertram. Helena was, in Elizabethan eyes, a good woman. From this point of view the matter becomes fairly simple.

There were two episodes in the tale as told by Boccaccio, both derived from medieval folk story.[2] The first of these has to do with the theme of healing the king of France of his obstinate fistula. There are other stories of such healings. Boccaccio makes it the means by which Helena, a lowborn maiden, acquires for herself a husband of superior rank, a spectacle always dear to the popular heart. It is notable that in Boccaccio's tale Beltramo, the Bertram of the piece, objects to marrying Giletta (Helena) merely on the ground that he does not wish to ally himself with a wife of inferior social position. By Shakespeare's time more liberal ideas of what constituted true nobility were abroad. Therefore, the French king argues with Bertram (II, iii, 124-151) that

[1]See *Shakespeare's Sonnets Dated and Other Essays* (1949), pp. 37-56.
[2]See the excellent analysis of this question by W. W. Lawrence, *Shakespeare's Problem Comedies* (1931), pp. 32-77.

Helena has raised herself to a level of high nobility by what she has done, since "Good alone is good without a name."

The second episode is that of the fulfillment of the tasks. Here too there is a large body of parallel folk stories. These tasks are selected, after the medieval

All's Well that Ends Well

804

fashion, as well-nigh impossible of accomplishment. They thus offer a challenge to the exercise of the qualities which constituted Virtue. Helena, like other heroines so situated, meets the challenge. To do so was to demonstrate that she was a woman of noble spirit. The trick by which she entered her husband's bed, not an admirable action from the modern point of view, would have caused no feeling of impropriety in a sixteenth-century audience. It would have seemed entirely proper since Bertram was Helena's lawfully wedded husband.

The changes in social point of view which had taken place between Boccaccio's time and Shakespeare's bore heavily on Bertram. It was understandable that Beltramo should have objected to marrying beneath his station. The king had a perfect right to dispose of his hand without persuasion or argument. Beltramo's violation of his marriage vows was to some extent sanctioned by the customs of courtly society. On these bases he might accept Giletta in joyous admiration after she had fulfilled his hard requirements, and he does so.

But with Bertram the issues are different. Social classes were no longer so rigidly demarcated. There was a greater right of free choice in matrimony, and adultery was less readily condoned. The result of these changes is the blackening of Bertram's

character. His actions are no longer readily defensible, and Shakespeare does not try to defend him. Shakespeare does, however, resort to certain devices which, from a human point of view, serve to lighten his guilt. In the end of the play Shakespeare provides for genuine repentance. In a highly complicated denouement, original with Shakespeare, Bertram lies, evades, and puts himself in seeming hazard until he finally comes to some realization of the nature of his conduct and looks upon Helena as a deliverer. Despite all of their romanticism the Elizabethan audiences were, in purely human relations, more realistic than we are. They would, therefore, have been more ready than our age to forgive Bertram for his trespasses.

Shakespeare, also, has apparently wished us to conceive of Bertram as very young and misled by the sinister rascal Parolles. The relation between Bertram and Parolles brings into operation an important line of Renaissance thought. It was customary to denounce, as a social danger, the corruption of princes and noblemen by flatterers and men of base nature. This situation arises in the case of Falstaff and Prince Hal and elsewhere.[3]

THE PLAY

The actual telling of the story will make the situations of the principal characters more obvious. The scene of *All's Well that Ends Well*, like its source in Boccaccio, is laid in France and in Tuscany. The heroine is Helena, orphan daughter of a distinguished physician, Gerard of Narbonne. After her father's death Helena has been taken into the household of the countess of Rousillon, a wise and charming old woman. The countess is Shakespeare's creation, she has no parallel in Boccaccio's story. Helena has fallen in love with the handsome Bertram, son to the countess. Her love is, of course, hopeless because of differences in birth and fortune between them. She loves a "bright particular star" and "hopes to wed it." It is her doctrine, however, that:

> Our remedies oft in ourselves do lie,
> Which we ascribe to heaven.

Her opportunity comes in the illness of the king of France. His incurable "fistula" has baffled all physicians. Helena with a recipe of her father's sets out for the French court, whither Bertram has already gone. She hopes to heal the king and thus elevate herself to a station sufficiently noble for her to wed Bertram. She is aided in her enterprise with the advice and sympathy of the countess and of Lafeu, a frank and kindly old nobleman, who is a friend of the countess. Lafeu is another Shakespearean addition.

With Bertram is Parolles, a boaster and a coward, whom in the revision of the play Shakespeare has

[3]C. R. Baskervill, "The Quarrel between Benedick and Beatrice," *A Memorial Volume to Shakespeare and Harvey.* University of Texas Publications No. 1701 (Austin, 1917), pp. 89-96.

made somewhat responsible for Bertram's misdeeds. Shakespeare perhaps felt that if Bertram is to hold any part of our sympathies, some excuse for his action must be provided.

Helena succeeds in healing the French king. As a reward she is ennobled and given the privilege of choosing a husband from among the lords in attendance at the king's court. She promptly chooses Bertram. Bertram has been anxious to get away from home into the great world. Helena is revolting to him as part of the life of which he has grown tired. At first he refuses to marry her, but for fear of the king's displeasure finally accepts her as his wife. He behaves very badly in the matter, concealing from her the blow which he intends to strike. Under the influence of Parolles he runs away to the Italian wars, leaving for Helena a letter in which he declares that he will not live with her as a husband until she can obtain a certain ring from his finger and prove that she is with child by him—which will never be.

The second act shows plain evidences of the two different styles. When the scenes are devoted to the original story of Helena's healing the king and winning a husband, couplets seem to carry the burden; whereas interruptions and additions appear in mature blank verse or in prose. Note, for example, the sudden change to rhyme at line 133 of the first scene of the second act and at line 79 of the third scene of the same act and, in the lines which follow, the interspersal of speeches by Lafeu in prose, as if they were additions.

During his soldiering in Italy the cowardice of Parolles is exposed, so that even Bertram must recognize it. Helena appears in Italy and by means of the clever intrigue of the source in Boccaccio succeeds in carrying out the hard and humiliating terms of Bertram's letter. All the parties return again to Rousillon, the plot is revealed, Bertram is convinced (put in jeopardy of his life, indeed, for his falsity), and accepts Helena, saying to the king:

> If she, my liege, can make me know this clearly,
> I'll love her dearly, ever, ever dearly.

HISTORY OF THE PLAY

All's Well that Ends Well has never been popular on the stage and obviously could not be. It has been revived rarely except on those occasions when, for the sake of paying homage to the master dramatist, all of the plays in the canon have been put on the stage.

Its literary life, however, is not inconsiderable. Helena is universally admired. The domestic atmosphere of the household of the countess of Rousillon, the countess herself, the kindly, cynical old Lafeu, the grateful king, the vulgar, bitter Fool, even the braggart Parolles, all serve to keep alive a badly mixed up and patched up play. This is not to say, however, that various revivals of All's Well that Ends Well have not been greatly enjoyed by discriminating persons.

All's Well that Ends Well

DRAMATIS PERSONAE

KING OF FRANCE.
DUKE OF FLORENCE.
BERTRAM, Count of Rousillon.
LAFEU, an old lord.
PAROLLES, a follower of Bertram.
Steward, } servants to the Countess of Rousillon.
Clown, }
A Page.

COUNTESS OF ROUSILLON, mother to Bertram.
HELENA, a gentlewoman protected by the Countess.
An old Widow of Florence.
DIANA, daughter to the Widow.
VIOLENTA, } neighbours and friends to the
MARIANA, } Widow.

Lords, Officers, Soldiers, &c., French and Florentine.

SCENE: *Rousillon; Paris; Florence; Marseilles.*

ACT I.

SCENE I. *Rousillon. The* COUNT'S *palace.*

Enter BERTRAM, *the* COUNTESS OF ROUSILLON, HELENA, *and* LAFEU, *all in black.*

Count. In delivering my son from me, I bury a second husband.

Ber. And I in going, madam, weep o'er my father's death anew: but I must attend his majesty's command, to whom I am now in ward, evermore in subjection.

Laf. You shall find of the king a husband, madam; you, sir, a father: he that so generally is at all times good must of necessity hold his virtue to you; whose worthiness would stir it up where it wanted rather than lack it where there is such abundance. 12

Count. What hope is there of his majesty's amendment?

Laf. He hath abandoned his physicians, madam; under whose practices he hath persecuted time with hope, and finds no other advantage in the process but only the losing of hope by time.

Count. This young gentlewoman had a father,—O, that 'had'! how sad a passage 'tis!—whose skill was almost as great as his honesty; had it stretched so far, would have made nature immortal, and death should have play for lack of work. Would, for the king's sake, he were living! I think it would be the death of the king's disease.

Laf. How called you the man you speak of, madam?

Count. He was famous, sir, in his profession, and it was his great right to be so: Gerard de Narbon. 31

Laf. He was excellent indeed, madam: the king very lately spoke of him admiringly and mourningly:

he was skilful enough to have lived still, if knowledge could be set up against mortality.

Ber. What is it, my good lord, the king languishes of?

Laf. A fistula, my lord.

Ber. I heard not of it before. 40

Laf. I would it were not notorious. Was this gentlewoman the daughter of Gerard de Narbon?

Count. His sole child, my lord, and bequeathed to my overlooking. I have those hopes of her good that her education promises; her dispositions she inherits, which makes fair gifts fairer; for where an unclean mind carries virtuous qualities, there commendations go with pity; they are virtues and traitors too: in her they are the better for their simpleness; she derives her honesty and achieves her goodness. 52

Laf. Your commendations, madam, get from her tears.

Count. 'Tis the best brine a maiden can season her praise in. The remembrance of her father never approaches her heart but the tyranny of her sorrows takes all livelihood from her cheek. No more of this, Helena; go to, no more; lest it be rather thought you affect a sorrow than have it. 61

Hel. I do affect a sorrow indeed, but I have it too.

Laf. Moderate lamentation is the right of the dead, excessive grief the enemy to the living.

Count. If the living be enemy to the grief, the excess makes it soon mortal.

Ber. Madam, I desire your holy wishes.

Laf. How understand we that?

Count. Be thou blest, Bertram, and succeed thy father 70
In manners, as in shape! thy blood and virtue
Contend for empire in thee, and thy goodness
Share with thy birthright! Love all, trust a few,
Do wrong to none: be able for thine enemy
Rather in power than use, and keep thy friend
Under thy own life's key: be check'd for silence,
But never tax'd for speech. What heaven more will,
That thee may furnish and my prayers pluck down,
Fall on thy head! Farewell, my lord;
'Tis an unseason'd courtier; good my lord, 80
Advise him.

Laf. He cannot want the best
That shall attend his love.

Count. Heaven bless him! Farewell, Bertram. [*Exit.*

Ber. [*To Helena*] The best wishes that can be forged in your thoughts be servants to you! Be comfortable to my mother, your mistress, and make much of her.

Laf. Farewell, pretty lady: you must hold the credit of your father. [*Exeunt Bertram and Lafeu.*

Hel. O, were that all! I think not on my father; 90
And these great tears grace his remembrance more

Than those I shed for him. What was he like?
I have forgot him: my imagination
Carries no favour in 't but Bertram's.
I am undone: there is no living, none,
If Bertram be away. 'Twere all one
That I should love a bright particular star
And think to wed it, he is so above me:
In his bright radiance and collateral light
Must I be comforted, not in his sphere. 100
The ambition in my love thus plagues itself:
The hind that would be mated by the lion
Must die for love. 'Twas pretty, though a plague,
To see him every hour; to sit and draw
His arched brows, his hawking eye, his curls,
In our heart's table; heart too capable
Of every line and trick of his sweet favour:
But now he 's gone, and my idolatrous fancy
Must sanctify his reliques. Who comes here?

Enter PAROLLES.

[*Aside*] One that goes with him: I love him for his
sake; 110
And yet I know him a notorious liar,
Think him a great way fool, solely a coward;
Yet these fix'd evils sit so fit in him,
That they take place, when virtue's steely bones
†Look bleak i' the cold wind: withal, full oft we see
Cold wisdom waiting on superfluous folly.

Par. Save you, fair queen!

Hel. And you, monarch!

Par. No.

Hel. And no. 120

Par. Are you meditating on virginity?

Hel. Ay. You have some stain of soldier in you: let me ask you a question. Man is enemy to virginity; how may we barricado it against him?

Par. Keep him out.

Hel. But he assails; and our virginity, though valiant, in the defence yet is weak: unfold to us some warlike resistance.

Par. There is none: man, sitting down before you, will undermine you and blow you up.

Hel. Bless our poor virginity from underminers and blowers up! Is there no military policy, how virgins might blow up men? 133

Par. Virginity being blown down, man will quicklier be blown up: marry, in blowing him down again, with the breach yourselves made, you lose your city. It is not politic in the commonwealth of nature to preserve virginity. Loss of virginity is rational increase and there was never virgin got till virginity was first lost. That you were made of is metal to make virgins. Virginity by being once lost

---

may be ten times found; by being ever kept, it is ever lost: 'tis too cold a companion; away with 't! 144

Hel. I will stand for 't a little, though therefore I die a virgin.

Par. There 's little can be said in 't; 'tis against the rule of nature. To speak on the part of virginity, is to accuse your mothers; which is most infallible disobedience. He that hangs himself is a virgin: virginity murders itself; and should be buried in highways out of all sanctified limit, as a desperate offendress against nature. Virginity breeds mites, much like a cheese; consumes itself to the very paring, and so dies with feeding his own stomach. Besides, virginity is peevish, proud, idle, made of self-love, which is the most inhibited sin in the canon. Keep it not; you cannot choose but lose by 't: out with 't! within ten year it will make itself ten, which is a goodly increase; and the principal itself not much the worse: away with 't! 161

Hel. How might one do, sir, to lose it to her own liking?

Par. Let me see: marry, ill, to like him that ne'er it likes. 'Tis a commodity will lose the gloss with lying; the longer kept, the less worth: off with 't while 'tis vendible; answer the time of request. Virginity, like an old courtier, wears her cap out of fashion: richly suited, but unsuitable: just like the brooch and the tooth-pick, which wear not now. Your date is better in your pie and your porridge than in your cheek: and your virginity, your old virginity, is like one of our French withered pears, it looks ill, it eats drily; marry, 'tis a withered pear; it was formerly better; marry, yet 'tis a withered pear: will you any thing with it?

Hel. †Not my virginity yet . . . . .
There shall your master have a thousand loves, 180
A mother and a mistress and a friend,
A phœnix, captain and an enemy,
A guide, a goddess, and a sovereign,
A counsellor, a traitress, and a dear;
His humble ambition, proud humility,
His jarring concord, and his discord dulcet,
His faith, his sweet disaster; with a world
Of pretty, fond, adoptious christendoms,
That blinking Cupid gossips. Now shall he—
I know not what he shall. God send him well! 190
The court 's a learning place, and he is one—

Par. What one, i' faith?

Hel. That I wish well. 'Tis pity—

Par. What 's pity?

Hel. That wishing well had not a body in 't,
Which might be felt; that we, the poorer born,
Whose baser stars do shut us up in wishes,

Might with effects of them follow our friends,
And show what we alone must think, which never
Returns us thanks. 200

Enter Page.

Page. Monsieur Parolles, my lord calls for you. [*Exit.*

Par. Little Helen, farewell: if I can remember thee, I will think of thee at court.

Hel. Monsieur Parolles, you were born under a charitable star.

Par. Under Mars, I.

Hel. I especially think, under Mars.

Par. Why under Mars?

Hel. The wars have so kept you under that you must needs be born under Mars. 210

Par. When he was predominant.

Hel. When he was retrograde, I think, rather.

Par. Why think you so?

Hel. You go so much backward when you fight.

Par. That 's for advantage.

Hel. So is running away, when fear proposes the safety: but the composition that your valour and fear makes in you is a virtue of a good wing, and I like the wear well. 219

Par. I am so full of businesses, I cannot answer thee acutely. I will return perfect courtier; in the which, my instruction shall serve to naturalize thee, so thou wilt be capable of a courtier's counsel and understand what advice shall thrust upon thee; else thou diest in thine unthankfulness, and thine ignorance makes thee away: farewell. When thou hast leisure, say thy prayers; when thou hast none, remember thy friends: get thee a good husband, and use him as he uses thee: so, farewell. [*Exit.* 230

Hel. Our remedies oft in ourselves do lie,
Which we ascribe to heaven: the fated sky
Gives us free scope, only doth backward pull
Our slow designs when we ourselves are dull.
What power is it which mounts my love so high,
That makes me see, and cannot feed mine eye?
The mightiest space in fortune nature brings
To join like likes and kiss like native things.
Impossible be strange attempts to those
That weigh their pains in sense and do suppose 240
What hath been cannot be: who ever strove
To show her merit, that did miss her love?
The king's disease—my project may deceive me,
But my intents are fix'd and will not leave me. [*Exit.*

SCENE II. *Paris. The* KING'S *palace.*

Flourish of cornets. Enter the KING OF FRANCE, *with letters, and divers Attendants.*

probably a reference to the "first and great commandment" as read in the liturgy after the decalogue—i.e., that you love your neighbor as yourself. Charron characterizes self-love as "the plague of mankinde, the capitall enemie of wisdome, the true gangreene and corruption of the soul." (*Of Wisdom*, Bk. II, Ch. i.) 167. **with lying,** i.e., unused, possibly with quibble. 168-169. **the time of request,** when there is demand. 170. **suited,** trimmed. 171. **brooch,** jeweled ornament. **tooth-pick,** usually associated with foppish manners; cf. *King John*, I, i, 190. 172. **date,** pun on the fruit and the meaning "time of life." 179. **Not . . . yet.** This is Helena's answer to Parolles' question. It is sometimes thought that the prose dialogue is an interpolation and that the splicing of the text has resulted here in the loss of several lines following this one. 181-184. **A mother . . . a dear,** terms of endearment with which Helena imagines Bertram will address his thousand loves. 181. **mother,** identified by Herford with "mauther," a provincial word for a maid. 188. **adoptious christendoms,** pet names. 189. **gossips,** is godfather to. 198. **them,** i.e., wishes. 211. **predominant,**

in the ascendant, ruling; i.e., in that sign of the zodiac which is just rising above the horizon. 212. **retrograde,** moving apparently in a direction contrary to the order of the signs of the zodiac, or from east to west (Onions); cf. *1 Henry VI*, I, ii, 1-2, note. 218. **of a good wing,** strong in flight; said of a falcon or of an arrow. 223. **naturalize,** familiarize. 226-227. **makes . . . away,** destroys, puts an end to. 232. **fated,** invested with the power of destiny. 237-238. **The mightiest . . . things.** Helena's resolve is apparent in the change in metaphor: whereas above (ll. 96-100) she thinks of their relative positions in terms of the natural phenomenon of the celestial spheres, the space between which nothing can bridge, now she thinks of herself and Bertram as so similar in affections that they naturally will be drawn together. 239. **Impossible,** inconceivable. 240. **That weigh . . . sense,** i.e., that consider their efforts rationally, not imaginatively.

King. The Florentines and Senoys are by the ears;
Have fought with equal fortune and continue
A braving war.
　First Lord. So 'tis reported, sir.
　King. Nay, 'tis most credible; we here receive it
A certainty, vouch'd from our cousin Austria,
With caution that the Florentine will move us
For speedy aid; wherein our dearest friend
Prejudicates the business and would seem
To have us make denial.
　First Lord.　　　　　　His love and wisdom,
Approved so to your majesty, may plead　　　　　　10
For amplest credence.
　King.　　　　　　He hath arm'd our answer,
And Florence is denied before he comes:
Yet, for our gentlemen that mean to see
The Tuscan service, freely have they leave
To stand on either part.
　Sec. Lord.　　　　　　It well may serve
A nursery to our gentry, who are sick
For breathing and exploit.
　King.　　　　　　What's he comes here?

Enter BERTRAM, LAFEU, *and* PAROLLES.

　First Lord. It is the Count Rousillon, my good lord,
Young Bertram.
　King. Youth, thou bear'st thy father's face;
Frank nature, rather curious than in haste,　　　　20
Hath well composed thee. Thy father's moral parts
Mayst thou inherit too! Welcome to Paris.
　Ber. My thanks and duty are your majesty's.
　King. I would I had that corporal soundness now,
As when thy father and myself in friendship
First tried our soldiership! He did look far
Into the service of the time and was
Disci=pled of the bravest: he lasted long;
But on us both did haggish age steal on
And wore us out of act. It much repairs me　　　30
To talk of your good father. In his youth
He had the wit which I can well observe
To-day in our young lords; but they may jest
Till their own scorn return to them unnoted
Ere they can hide their levity in honour:
†So like a courtier, contempt nor bitterness
Were in his pride or sharpness; if they were,
His equal had awaked them, and his honour,
Clock to itself, knew the true minute when
Exception bid him speak, and at this time　　　40
His tongue obey'd his hand: who were below him
He used as creatures of another place
And bow'd his eminent top to their low ranks,
Making them proud of his humility,
†In their poor praise he humbled. Such a man
Might be a copy to these younger times;
Which, follow'd well, would demonstrate them now
But goers backward.
　Ber.　　　　　　His good remembrance, sir,
Lies richer in your thoughts than on his tomb;

So in approof lives not his epitaph　　　　　　50
As in your royal speech.
　King. Would I were with him! He would always
　　say—
Methinks I hear him now; his plausive words
He scatter'd not in ears, but grafted them,
To grow there and to bear,—'Let me not live,'—
This his good melancholy oft began,
On the catastrophe and heel of pastime,
When it was out,—'Let me not live,' quoth he,
'After my flame lacks oil, to be the snuff
Of younger spirits, whose apprehensive senses　　60
All but new things disdain; whose judgements are
Mere fathers of their garments; whose constancies
Expire before their fashions.' This he wish'd:
I after him do after him wish too,
Since I nor wax nor honey can bring home,
I quickly were dissolved from my hive,
To give some labourers room.
　Sec. Lord.　　　　　　You are loved, sir;
They that least lend it you shall lack you first.
　King. I fill a place, I know 't. How long is 't, count,
Since the physician at your father's died?　　　70
He was much famed.
　Ber.　　　　　　Some six months since, my lord.
　King. If he were living, I would try him yet.
Lend me an arm; the rest have worn me out
With several applications: nature and sickness
Debate it at their leisure. Welcome, count;
My son's no dearer.
　Ber.　　　　　　Thank your majesty.
　　　　　　　　　　　　　　[Exeunt. Flourish.

───────────────────

SCENE III. *Rousillon. The* COUNT's *palace.*

Enter COUNTESS, Steward, *and* Clown.

　Count. I will now hear; what say you of this gentlewoman?
　Stew. Madam, the care I have had to even your
content, I wish might be found in the calendar of
my past endeavours; for then we wound our modesty
and make foul the clearness of our deservings, when
of ourselves we publish them.　　　　　　7
　Count. What does this knave here? Get you gone,
sirrah: the complaints I have heard of you I do not all
believe: 'tis my slowness that I do not; for I know
you lack not folly to commit them, and have ability
enough to make such knaveries yours.
　Clo. 'Tis not unknown to you, madam, I am a
poor fellow.
　Count. Well, sir.
　Clo. No, madam, 'tis not so well that I am poor,
though many of the rich are damned: but, if I may
have your ladyship's good will to go to the world,
Isbel the woman and I will do as we may.　　　21
　Count. Wilt thou needs be a beggar?
　Clo. I do beg your good will in this case.

SCENE II. 1. **Senoys,** natives of Siena. **by the ears,** at variance,
quarreling. 3. **braving war,** war of taunts and challenges. 8. **Prejudicates,** passes judgment beforehand. 10. **Approved,** demonstrated
by proofs. 16. **nursery,** training school. 16-17. **sick For,** i.e., for want
of. 17. **breathing,** vigorous exercise. 27. **service,** military affairs.
30. **repairs,** refreshes. 33-35. **but they . . . honour.** Your father
(says the king) had the same airy flights of satirical wit with the young
lords of the present time, but they do not what he did, hide their
unnoted (i.e., disregarded) levity in honor, cover petty faults with
great merit (Johnson). 36. **courtier,** perfect gentleman. 41. **his,** i.e.,
the clock's. 42. **creatures . . . place,** people of a different (i.e., more

elevated) station; cf. *Hamlet,* II, ii, 556-558. 45. **humbled,** i.e.,
humbled himself. 50. **approof,** approbation. 53. **plausive,** pleasing
(Brigstocke, citing *Hamlet,* I, iv, 30). 57. **catastrophe . . . pastime,**
i.e., pastime drawing to a close. 58. **it,** i.e., pastime. 59. **snuff,**
candle end. 60. **apprehensive,** quick to perceive. 61-62. **whose
judgements . . . garments,** i.e., they employ their judgments in de-
signing fashionable clothes. 64. **I after . . . wish too,** I, surviving him,
wish as he did. 66. **were dissolved,** optative subjunctive; see Abbott,
301. 68. **lend it.** The antecedent is *love,* implied in the verb, line 67
(New Cambridge).
　SCENE III. 3. **to even your content,** make my endeavors balance with

Count. In what case?

Clo. In Isbel's case and mine own. Service is no heritage: and I think I shall never have the blessing of God till I have issue o' my body; for they say barnes are blessings.

Count. Tell me thy reason why thou wilt marry. 29

Clo. My poor body, madam, requires it: I am driven on by the flesh; and he must needs go that the devil drives.

Count. Is this all your worship's reason?

Clo. Faith, madam, I have other holy reasons, such as they are.

Count. May the world know them?

Clo. I have been, madam, a wicked creature, as you and all flesh and blood are; and, indeed, I do marry that I may repent.

Count. Thy marriage, sooner than thy wickedness. 41

Clo. I am out o' friends, madam; and I hope to have friends for my wife's sake.

Count. Such friends are thine enemies, knave.

Clo. You 're shallow, madam, in great friends; for the knaves come to do that for me which I am aweary of. He that ears my land spares my team and gives me leave to in the crop; if I be his cuckold, he 's my drudge: he that comforts my wife is the cherisher of my flesh and blood; he that cherishes my flesh and blood loves my flesh and blood; he that loves my flesh and blood is my friend: ergo, he that kisses my wife is my friend. If men could be contented to be what they are, there were no fear in marriage; for young Charbon the puritan and old Poysam the papist, howsome'er their hearts are severed in religion, their heads are both one; they may joul horns together, like any deer i' the herd. 59

Count. Wilt thou ever be a foul-mouthed and calumnious knave?

Clo. A prophet I, madam; and I speak the truth the next way:

    For I the ballad will repeat,
      Which men full true shall find;
    Your marriage comes by destiny,
      Your cuckoo sings by kind.

Count. Get you gone, sir; I'll talk with you more anon.

Stew. May it please you, madam, that he bid Helen come to you: of her I am to speak. 71

Count. Sirrah, tell my gentlewoman I would speak with her; Helen, I mean.

Clo. Was this fair face the cause, quoth she,
    Why the Grecians sacked Troy?
    Fond done, done fond,
      Was this King Priam's joy?
    With that she sighed as she stood,
    With that she sighed as she stood,
      And gave this sentence then; 80
    Among nine bad if one be good,
    Among nine bad if one be good,
      There 's yet one good in ten.

Count. What, one good in ten? you corrupt the song, sirrah.

Clo. One good woman in ten, madam; which is a purifying o' the song: would God would serve the world so all the year! we 'ld find no fault with the tithe-woman, if I were the parson. One in ten, quoth a'! An we might have a good woman born but one every blazing star, or at an earthquake, 'twould mend the lottery well: a man may draw his heart out, ere a' pluck one. 93

Count. You'll be gone, sir knave, and do as I command you.

Clo. That man should be at woman's command, and yet no hurt done! Though honesty be no puritan, yet it will do no hurt; it will wear the surplice of humility over the black gown of a big heart. I am going, forsooth: the business is for Helen to come hither. [*Exit.*

Count. Well, now.

Stew. I know, madam, you love your gentlewoman entirely.

Count. Faith, I do: her father bequeathed her to me; and she herself, without other advantage, may lawfully make title to as much love as she finds: there is more owing her than is paid; and more shall be paid her than she 'll demand. 109

Stew. Madam, I was very late more near her than I think she wished me: alone she was, and did communicate to herself her own words to her own ears; she thought, I dare vow for her, they touched not any stranger sense. Her matter was, she loved your son: Fortune, she said, was no goddess, that had put such difference betwixt their two estates; Love no god, that would not extend his might, only where qualities were level; Dian no queen of virgins, that would suffer her poor knight surprised, without rescue in the first assault or ransom afterward. This she delivered in the most bitter touch of sorrow that e'er I heard virgin exclaim in: which I held my duty speedily to acquaint you withal; sithence, in the loss that may happen, it concerns you something to know it. 125

Count. You have discharged this honestly; keep it to yourself: many likelihoods informed me of this before, which hung so tottering in the balance that I could neither believe nor misdoubt. Pray you, leave me: stall this in your bosom; and I thank you for your honest care: I will speak with you further anon.
[*Exit Steward.*

Enter HELENA.

Even so it was with me when I was young:
    If ever we are nature's, these are ours; this thorn
Doth to our rose of youth rightly belong;
    Our blood to us, this to our blood is born;
It is the show and seal of nature's truth,
Where love's strong passion is impress'd in youth:
By our remembrances of days foregone, 140

your wishes (Brigstocke). 4. **calendar,** record. 7. **we publish,** a hint to the countess to dismiss the clown. 19-20. **go to the world,** give up the life of a celibate. 28. **barnes,** children. 34. **holy reasons,** in antithesis to both the *world,* the *flesh,* and the *devil* (ll. 20, 31, 32). 45. **shallow . . . in,** a superficial judge of. 48. **in,** a verb, to get in; i.e., harvest the crop. 55, 56. **Charbon, Poysam,** corruptions of *Chairbonne,* good meat, and *Poisson,* fish, the fast-day diets of Puritans and Catholics respectively. 58. **joul,** dash, knock. 63. **next,** nearest; i.e., speak the truth most directly. 89. **tithe-woman,** an allusion to the practice **of paying** tithes "in kind," not in money; cf. *Romeo and Juliet,* I, iv, 79. 97-100. **Though honesty . . . big heart,** a variant on the conventional slur at the Puritans who demurred at obedience to some of the rubrics and canons pertaining to public worship; some of them, to *do no hurt,* conformed in some respects such as wearing the surplice; nevertheless they wore it over the black Genevan gown customarily worn by Calvinistic Protestants on the Continent. 100. **big heart,** proud spirit. 120. **surprised,** to be surprised. 124. **sithence,** since. 135. **these,** i.e., the pangs of love, signs of which the countess sees manifested in Helena.

†Such were our faults, or then we thought them none.
Her eye is sick on 't: I observe her now.
    Hel. What is your pleasure, madam?
    Count.   You know, Helen,
I am a mother to you.
    Hel. Mine honourable mistress.
    Count.   Nay, a mother:
Why not a mother? When I said 'a mother,'
Methought you saw a serpent: what 's in 'mother,'
That you start at it? I say, I am your mother;
And put you in the catalogue of those
That were enwombed mine: 'tis often seen   150
Adoption strives with nature and choice breeds
A native slip to us from foreign seeds:
You ne'er oppress'd me with a mother's groan,
Yet I express to you a mother's care:
God's mercy, maiden! does it curd thy blood
To say I am thy mother? What 's the matter,
That this distemper'd messenger of wet,
The many-colour'd Iris, rounds thine eye?
Why? that you are my daughter?
    Hel.   That I am not.
    Count. I say, I am your mother.
    Hel.   Pardon, madam;   160
The Count Rousillon cannot be my brother:
I am from humble, he from honour'd name;
No note upon my parents, his all noble:
My master, my dear lord he is; and I
His servant live, and will his vassal die:
He must not be my brother.
    Count.   Nor I your mother?
    Hel. You are my mother, madam; would you
        were,—
So that my lord your son were not my brother,—
Indeed my mother! or were you both our mothers,
I care no more for than I do for heaven,   170
So I were not his sister. Can 't no other,
But, I your daughter, he must be my brother?
    Count. Yes, Helen, you might be my daughter-in-
    law:
God shield you mean it not! daughter and mother
So strive upon your pulse. What, pale again?
My fear hath catch'd your fondness: now I see
The mystery of your loneliness, and find
Your salt tears' head: now to all sense 'tis gross
You love my son; invention is ashamed,
Against the proclamation of thy passion,   180
To say thou dost not: therefore tell me true;
But tell me then, 'tis so; for, look, thy cheeks
Confess it, th' one to th' other; and thine eyes
See it so grossly shown in thy behaviours
That in their kind they speak it: only sin
And hellish obstinacy tie thy tongue,
That truth should be suspected. Speak, is 't so?
If it be so, you have wound a goodly clew;
If it be not, forswear 't: howe'er, I charge thee,

As heaven shall work in me for thine avail,   190
To tell me truly.
    Hel.   Good madam, pardon me!
    Count. Do you love my son?
    Hel.   Your pardon, noble mistress!
    Count. Love you my son?
    Hel.   Do not you love him, madam?
    Count. Go not about; my love hath in 't a bond,
Whereof the world takes note: come, come, disclose
The state of your affection; for your passions
Have to the full appeach'd.
    Hel.   Then, I confess,
Here on my knee, before high heaven and you,
That before you, and next unto high heaven,
I love your son.   200
My friends were poor, but honest; so 's my love:
Be not offended; for it hurts not him
That he is loved of me: I follow him not
By any token of presumptuous suit;
Nor would I have him till I do deserve him;
Yet never know how that desert should be.
I know I love in vain, strive against hope;
Yet in this captious and intenible sieve
I still pour in the waters of my love
And lack not to lose still: thus, Indian-like,   210
Religious in mine error, I adore
The sun, that looks upon his worshipper,
But knows of him no more. My dearest madam,
Let not your hate encounter with my love
For loving where you do: but if yourself,
Whose aged honour cites a virtuous youth,
Did ever in so true a flame of liking
Wish chastely and love dearly, that your Dian
Was both herself and love; O, then, give pity
To her, whose state is such that cannot choose   220
But lend and give where she is sure to lose;
That seeks not to find that her search implies,
But riddle-like lives sweetly where she dies!
    Count. Had you not lately an intent,—speak truly,—
To go to Paris?
    Hel.   Madam, I had.
    Count.   Wherefore? tell true.
    Hel. I will tell truth; by grace itself I swear.
You know my father left me some prescriptions
Of rare and proved effects, such as his reading
And manifest experience had collected
For general sovereignty; and that he will'd me   230
In heedfull'st reservation to bestow them,
As notes whose faculties inclusive were
More than they were in note: amongst the rest
There is a remedy, approved, set down,
To cure the desperate languishings whereof
The king is render'd lost.
    Count.   This was your motive
For Paris, was it? speak.
    Hel. My lord your son made me to think of this;

152. **slip**, grafting. 158. **Iris**, Juno's messenger; also the rainbow.
163. **note**, distinction. 178. **gross**, palpable, apparent. 188. **clew**,
ball of thread (used figuratively). 197. **appeach'd**, informed against.
201. **friends**, kinfolk. 208. **captious**, deceptive. **intenible**, incapable
of holding. 210. **lack not**, do not cease (Brigstocke). 216. **cites**,
bespeaks, gives evidence of. 222. **implies**, involves. 229. **manifest
experience**, i.e., the practice, in antithesis to the theory (reading).
230. **general sovereignty**, general efficacy and use. 232. **notes**,
prescriptions. 233. **note**, writing. 247. **Embowell'd**, emptied.
    ACT II. SCENE I. 6. **After . . . soldiers**, usually explained as "after
having become seasoned soldiers"; the New Cambridge editors punctuate: *After, well-entered soldiers*, taking *After* with *return*. 12-14. **let**

higher . . . monarchy. *Higher Italy* has been taken to mean (1) the
knightly class in antithesis to *worthy Frenchmen;* (2) Tuscany, of which
Florence and Siena are cities. *The last monarchy* has been explained as
the Roman monarchy; the New Cambridge editors think it refers to
the decline of the house of the Medici after the death of Cosimo in
1574, citing the social demoralization of Florence. They paraphrase:
"except those Tuscans (*those bated*) who adhere to the decadent fortunes
and vices of the Medicis." 16. **questant**, seeker. 17. **cry you loud**,
proclaim you loudly. 23. **Come . . . me.** Some stage business accompanies this speech for which F gives no guidance. Most editors follow
either Pope, who has the king leave the stage, or Capell, who has him
retire to a couch. The words may be addressed to Bertram (Pope) or to

Else Paris and the medicine and the king
Had from the conversation of my thoughts   240
Haply been absent then.
   Count.   But think you, Helen,
If you should tender your supposed aid,
He would receive it? he and his physicians
Are of a mind; he, that they cannot help him,
They, that they cannot help: how shall they credit
A poor unlearned virgin, when the schools,
Embowell'd of their doctrine, have left off
The danger to itself?
   Hel.   There's something in 't,
More than my father's skill, which was the greatest
Of his profession, that his good receipt   250
Shall for my legacy be sanctified
By the luckiest stars in heaven: and, would your
     honour
But give me leave to try success, I 'ld venture
The well-lost life of mine on his grace's cure
By such a day and hour.
   Count.   Dost thou believe 't?
   Hel. Ay, madam, knowingly.
   Count. Why, Helen, thou shalt have my leave and
     love,
Means and attendants and my loving greetings
To those of mine in court: I'll stay at home
And pray God's blessing into thy attempt: 260
Be gone to-morrow; and be sure of this,
What I can help thee to thou shalt not miss.   [*Exeunt.*

ACT II.

SCENE I. *Paris. The* KING's *Palace.*

Flourish of cornets. Enter the KING, *attended with divers
   young* Lords *taking leave for the Florentine war;*
   BERTRAM, *and* PAROLLES.

   King. Farewell, young lords; these warlike
     principles
Do not throw from you: and you, my lords, farewell:
Share the advice betwixt you; if both gain, all
The gift doth stretch itself as 'tis received,
And is enough for both.
   First Lord.   'Tis our hope, sir,
After well enter'd soldiers, to return
And find your grace in health.
   King. No, no, it cannot be; and yet my heart
Will not confess he owes the malady
That doth my life besiege. Farewell, young lords;   10
Whether I live or die, be you the sons
Of worthy Frenchmen: let higher Italy,—
†Those bated that inherit but the fall
Of the last monarchy,—see that you come
Not to woo honour, but to wed it; when

The bravest questant shrinks, find what you seek,
That fame may cry you loud: I say, farewell.
   Sec. Lord. Health, at your bidding, serve your
     majesty!
   King. Those girls of Italy, take heed of them:
They say, our French lack language to deny,   20
If they demand: beware of being captives,
Before you serve.
   Both.   Our hearts receive your warnings.
   King. Farewell. Come hither to me.   [*Exit, attended.*
   First Lord. O my sweet lord, that you will stay
     behind us!
   Par. 'Tis not his fault, the spark.
   Sec. Lord.   O, 'tis brave wars!
   Par. Most admirable: I have seen those wars.
   Ber. I am commanded here, and kept a coil with
'Too young' and 'the next year' and ''tis too early.'
   Par. An thy mind stand to 't boy, steal away
     bravely.
   Ber. I shall stay here the forehorse to a smock,   30
Creaking my shoes on the plain masonry,
Till honour be bought up and no sword worn
But one to dance with! By heaven, I'll steal away.
   First Lord. There's honour in the theft.
   Par.   Commit it, count.
   Sec. Lord. I am your accessary; and so, farewell.
   Ber. I grow to you, and our parting is a tortured
body.
   First Lord. Farewell, captain.
   Sec. Lord. Sweet Monsieur Parolles!   39
   Par. Noble heroes, my sword and yours are kin.
Good sparks and lustrous, a word, good metals: you
shall find in the regiment of the Spinii one Captain
Spurio, with his cicatrice, an emblem of war, here
on his sinister cheek; it was this very sword en-
trenched it: say to him, I live; and observe his
reports for me.
   First Lord. We shall, noble captain.   [*Exeunt Lords.*
   Par. Mars dote on you for his novices! what will
ye do?
   Ber. Stay: the king.   50

   Re-enter KING. BERTRAM *and* PAROLLES *retire.*

   Par. [*To Ber.*] Use a more spacious ceremony to the
noble lords; you have restrained yourself within the
list of too cold an adieu: be more expressive to them:
for they wear themselves in the cap of the time, there
do muster true gait, eat, speak, and move under the
influence of the most received star; and though the
devil lead the measure, such are to be followed: after
them, and take a more dilated farewell.
   Ber. And I will do so.   60
   Par. Worthy fellows; and like to prove most
sinewy sword-men.   [*Exeunt Bertram and Parolles.*

   Enter LAFEU.

attendants (Theobald). The New Cambridge editors follow Theobald and add the stage direction, "he swoons and is carried to the couch, before which curtains are drawn." Cf. l. 50 below, note. 25. **spark,** foppish or elegant young man, a beau. 27. **kept a coil,** pestered. 30. **forehorse . . . smock,** i.e., ushering in and squiring ladies (Schmidt); the leader in a team of horses driven by a woman (New Cambridge); a *forehorse* is the lead horse of a team. 32. **Till . . . up,** till opportunity for winning honor in the wars is past. 33. **one to dance with,** light ornamental weapon. 43. **Spinii,** casual reference. **cicatrice,** scar. 50. **Stay: the king.** F, without stage direction, reads: *Stay the King.* So punctuated it would mean "support or wait on the king"; Brigstocke so explains it. Pope, followed by others, punctuated: *Stay; the king,* ex-

plaining as "I shall stay; the king wills it." The Cambridge editors, taking *Stay* as a word of caution, punctuate as here and explain, "The ushers in attendance throw open the folding doors at the back of the stage, Bertram and Parolles retire close to one of the side doors, and while they are speaking together the king is borne in upon his couch to the front of the stage." 55. **muster true gait,** set an example of proper conduct. 56. **influence,** supposed flowing from the stars of an ethereal fluid acting upon the characters and destinies of men; see glossary. 57. **received,** fashionable. 59. **dilated,** expressed at length.

Laf. [*Kneeling*] Pardon, my lord, for me and for my
   tidings.
King. I'll fee thee to stand up.
Laf. Then here 's a man stands, that has brought his
   pardon.
I would you had kneel'd, my lord, to ask me mercy,
And that at my bidding you could so stand up.
   King. I would I had; so I had broke thy pate,
And ask'd thee mercy for 't.
   Laf. Good faith, across: but, my good lord, 'tis
   thus;   70
Will you be cured of your infirmity?
   King. No.
   Laf. O, will you eat no grapes, my royal fox?
Yes, but you will my noble grapes, an if
My royal fox could reach them: I have seen a
   medicine
That 's able to breathe life into a stone,
Quicken a rock, and make you dance canary
With spritely fire and motion; whose simple touch
Is powerful to araise King Pepin, nay,
To give great Charlemain a pen in 's hand   80
And write to her a love-line.
   King.   What 'her' is this?
   Laf. Why, Doctor She: my lord, there 's one
   arrived,
If you will see her: now, by my faith and honour,
If seriously I may convey my thoughts
In this my light deliverance, I have spoke
With one that, in her sex, her years, profession,
Wisdom and constancy, hath amazed me more
Than I dare blame my weakness: will you see her,
For that is her demand, and know her business?
That done, laugh well at me.
   King.   Now, good Lafeu,   90
Bring in the admiration; that we with thee
May spend our wonder too, or take off thine
By wondering how thou took'st it.
   Laf.   Nay, I'll fit you,
And not be all day neither.   [*Exit.*
   King. Thus he his special nothing ever prologues.

    Re-enter LAFEU, *with* HELENA.

   Laf. Nay, come your ways.
   King.   This haste hath wings indeed.
   Laf. Nay, come your ways;
This is his majesty; say your mind to him:
A traitor you do look like; but such traitors
His majesty seldom fears: I am Cressid's uncle, 100
That dare leave two together; fare you well.   [*Exit.*
   King. Now, fair one, does your business follow us?
   Hel. Ay, my good lord.
Gerard de Narbon was my father;
In what he did profess, well found.
   King.   I knew him.
   Hel. The rather will I spare my praises towards
   him;
Knowing him is enough. On 's bed of death
Many receipts he gave me; chiefly one,

Which, as the dearest issue of his practice,
And of his old experience the only darling,   110
He bade me store up, as a triple eye,
Safer than mine own two, more dear; I have so;
And, hearing your high majesty is touch'd
With that malignant cause wherein the honour
Of my dear father's gift stands chief in power,
I come to tender it and my appliance
With all bound humbleness.
   King.   We thank you, maiden;
But may not be so credulous of cure,
When our most learned doctors leave us and
The congregated college have concluded   120
That labouring art can never ransom nature
From her inaidible estate; I say we must not
So stain our judgement, or corrupt our hope,
To prostitute our past-cure malady
To empirics, or to dissever so
Our great self and our credit, to esteem
A senseless help when help past sense we deem.
   Hel. My duty then shall pay me for my pains:
I will no more enforce mine office on you;
Humbly entreating from your royal thoughts   130
A modest one, to bear me back again.
   King. I cannot give thee less, to be call'd
   grateful:
Thou thought'st to help me; and such thanks I
   give
As one near death to those that wish him live:
But what at full I know, thou know'st no part,
I knowing all my peril, thou no art.
   Hel. What I can do can do no hurt to try,
Since you set up your rest 'gainst remedy.
He that of greatest works is finisher
Oft does them by the weakest minister: 140
So holy writ in babes hath judgement shown,
When judges have been babes; great floods have
   flown
From simple sources, and great seas have dried
When miracles have by the greatest been denied.
Oft expectation fails and most oft there
Where most it promises, and oft it hits
Where hope is coldest and despair most fits.
   King. I must not hear thee; fare thee well, kind
   maid;
Thy pains not used must by thyself be paid:
Proffers not took reap thanks for their reward. 150
   Hel. Inspired merit so by breath is barr'd:
It is not so with Him that all things knows
As 'tis with us that square our guess by shows;
But most it is presumption in us when
The help of heaven we count the act of men.
Dear sir, to my endeavours give consent;
Of heaven, not me, make an experiment.
I am not an impostor that proclaim
Myself against the level of mine aim;
But know I think and think I know most sure 160
My art is not past power nor you past cure.
   King. Art thou so confident? within what space

64. **I'll fee . . . up.** Those who retain this reading explain it in one of two ways: (1) the king, referring to his inability to rise, says to Lafeu, "I'll fee thee to help me to stand"; (2) referring to Lafeu's having knelt, he bids him rise. Lafeu's speech indicates that the latter is the more likely. Some editors accept Theobald's emendation: *I see thee . . . .* 70. **Good faith, across,** a metaphor from tilting; to break a lance *across* one's opponent is the act of an unskillful tilter. 75. **medicine,** physician. 77. **canary,** lively Spanish dance. 79. **araise,** raise from the dead. 85. **deliverance,** utterance, delivery. 86. **profession,** what she professes to be. 93. **fit,** satisfy. 96. **come your**

ways, come along. 100. **Cressid's uncle,** Pandarus, in the story of Troilus and Cressida, who acted as a go-between for the lovers. 105. **well found,** well skilled. 120. **congregated college,** college of physicians, who kept quacks from practice. 125. **empirics,** quack doctors. 127. **past sense,** past realization or perception. 138. **set . . . rest,** stake your all; a figure from gambling. 151. **by breath,** i.e., by spoken words. 153. **square . . . shows,** make decisions on the basis of appearances; in antithesis to the king's words, line 127. 158-159. **proclaim . . . aim,** claim more than I can accomplish. 163. **great'st grace,** divine grace. 168. **pilot's glass,** sandglass measuring half an hour;

Hopest thou my cure?
Hel.   The great'st grace lending grace,
Ere twice the horses of the sun shall bring
Their fiery torcher his diurnal ring,
Ere twice in murk and occidental damp
Moist Hesperus hath quench'd his sleepy lamp,
Or four and twenty times the pilot's glass
Hath told the thievish minutes how they pass,
What is infirm from your sound parts shall fly,   170
Health shall live free and sickness freely die.
King. Upon thy certainty and confidence
What darest thou venture?
Hel.   Tax of impudence,
A strumpet's boldness, a divulged shame
Traduced by odious ballads: my maiden's name
Sear'd otherwise; nay, worse—if worse—extended
With vilest torture let my life be ended.
King. Methinks in thee some blessed spirit doth
     speak
His powerful sound within an organ weak:
And what impossibility would slay   180
In common sense, sense saves another way.
Thy life is dear; for all that life can rate
Worth name of life in thee hath estimate,
Youth, beauty, wisdom, courage, all
That happiness and prime can happy call:
Thou this to hazard needs must intimate
Skill infinite or monstrous desperate.
Sweet practiser, thy physic I will try,
That ministers thine own death if I die.
Hel. If I break time, or flinch in property   190
Of what I spoke, unpitied let me die,
And well deserved: not helping, death 's my fee;
But, if I help, what do you promise me?
King. Make thy demand.
Hel.   But will you make it even?
King. Ay, by my sceptre and my hopes of heaven.
Hel. Then shalt thou give me with thy kingly
     hand
What husband in thy power I will command:
Exempted be from me the arrogance
To choose from forth the royal blood of France,
My low and humble name to propagate   200
With any branch or image of thy state;
But such a one, thy vassal, whom I know
Is free for me to ask, thee to bestow.
King. Here is my hand; the premises observed,
Thy will by my performance shall be served:
So make the choice of thy own time, for I,
Thy resolved patient, on thee still rely.
More should I question thee, and more I must,
Though more to know could not be more to trust,
From whence thou camest, how tended on: but rest   210
Unquestion'd welcome and undoubted blest.
Give me some help here, ho! If thou proceed
As high as word, my deed shall match thy meed.
                      [*Flourish. Exeunt.*

---

hourglasses may have been used by seamen at this early date (*Shakespeare's England*, I, 164.) 173. **Tax,** accusation. 181. **common sense,** ututored perception. **sense,** the rational faculty. 190. **break,** infringe, fail to keep. **flinch,** yield (my purpose) or turn aside from (my promises). **in property,** in any particular.

     SCENE II. 1-2. **put you . . . breeding,** test your good manners. 3. **lowly taught,** taught to keep my place. 5-6. **make you special,** do you indicate specially. 6. **put off,** set aside. 9. **put it off,** carry it off. 23. **French crown,** probably used quibblingly: a coin and the *corona veneris,* a scab on the head, symptomatic of the "French disease," as

SCENE II. *Rousillon. The* COUNT'S *palace.*

Enter COUNTESS *and* CLOWN.

Count. Come on, sir; I shall now put you to the height of your breeding.
Clo. I will show myself highly fed and lowly taught: I know my business is but to the court.
Count. To the court! why, what place make you special, when you put off that with such contempt? But to the court!   7
Clo. Truly, madam, if God have lent a man any manners, he may easily put it off at court: he that cannot make a leg, put off 's cap, kiss his hand and say nothing, has neither leg, hands, lip, nor cap; and indeed such a fellow, to say precisely, were not for the court; but for me, I have an answer will serve all men.
Count. Marry, that 's a bountiful answer that fits all questions.
Clo. It is like a barber's chair that fits all buttocks, the pin-buttock, the quatch-buttock, the brawn buttock, or any buttock.
Count. Will your answer serve fit to all questions?   21
Clo. As fit as ten groats is for the hand of an attorney, as your French crown for your taffeta punk, as Tib's rush for Tom's forefinger, as a pancake for Shrove Tuesday, a morris for May-day, as the nail to his hole, the cuckold to his horn, as a scolding quean to a wrangling knave, as the nun's lip to the friar's mouth, nay, as the pudding to his skin.
Count. Have you, I say, an answer of such fitness for all questions?   31
Clo. From below your duke to beneath your constable, it will fit any question.
Count. It must be an answer of most monstrous size that must fit all demands.
Clo. But a trifle neither, in good faith, if the learned should speak truth of it: here it is, and all that belongs to 't. Ask me if I am a courtier: it shall do you no harm to learn.   39
Count. To be young again, if we could: I will be a fool in question, hoping to be the wiser by your answer. I pray you, sir, are you a courtier?
Clo. O Lord, sir! There 's a simple putting off. More, more, a hundred of them.
Count. Sir, I am a poor friend of yours, that loves you.
Clo. O Lord, sir! Thick, thick, spare not me.
Count. I think, sir, you can eat none of this homely meat.   49
Clo. O Lord, sir! Nay, put me to 't, I warrant you.
Count. You were lately whipped, sir, as I think.
Clo. O Lord, sir! spare not me.
Count. Do you cry, 'O Lord, sir!' at your whipping, and 'spare not me'? Indeed your 'O Lord, sir!' is very sequent to your whipping: you would answer very well to a whipping, if you were but bound to 't.
Clo. I ne'er had worse luck in my life in my 'O Lord, sir!' I see things may serve long, but not serve ever.   61

syphilis was sometimes called. (*Shakespeare's England*, I, 438.) 23-24. **taffeta punk,** prostitute finely dressed. 24. **Tib's rush,** a possible reference to a folk custom of placing a ring made of rush on the woman's finger in a marriage without benefit of clergy. 25. **morris,** morris dance. 27. **quean,** jade. 43. **O Lord, sir,** a foppish phrase in vogue at King James' court. Farmer finds it ridiculed in other contemporary passages. 47. **Thick,** quickly.

Count. I play the noble housewife with the time,
To entertain 't so merrily with a fool.
   Clo. O Lord, sir! why, there 't serves well again.
   Count. An end, sir; to your business. Give Helen
this,
And urge her to a present answer back:
Commend me to my kinsmen and my son:
This is not much.
   Clo. Not much commendation to them.   70
   Count. Not much employment for you: you under-
stand me?
   Clo. Most fruitfully: I am there before my legs.
   Count. Haste you again.   [*Exeunt severally.*

SCENE III. *Paris. The* KING'S *palace.*

Enter BERTRAM, LAFEU, *and* PAROLLES.

   Laf. They say miracles are past; and we have our
philosophical persons, to make modern and familiar,
things supernatural and causeless. Hence is it that
we make trifles of terrors, ensconcing ourselves into
seeming knowledge, when we should submit our-
selves to an unknown fear.
   Par. Why, 'tis the rarest argument of wonder that
hath shot out in our latter times.
   Ber. And so 'tis.
   Laf. To be relinquished of the artists,—   10
   Par. So I say.
   Laf. Both of Galen and Paracelsus.
   Par. So I say.
   Laf. Of all the learned and authentic fellows,—
   Par. Right; so I say.
   Laf. That gave him out incurable,—
   Par. Why, there 'tis; so say I too.
   Laf. Not to be helped,—
   Par. Right: as 'twere, a man assured of a—
   Laf. Uncertain life, and sure death.   20
   Par. Just, you say well; so would I have said.
   Laf. I may truly say, it is a novelty to the world.
   Par. It is, indeed: if you will have it in showing,
you shall read it in—what do ye call there?
   Laf. A showing of a heavenly effect in an earthly
actor.
   Par. That 's it; I would have said the very same .   30
   Laf. Why, your dolphin is not lustier: 'fore me, I
speak in respect—
   Par. Nay, 'tis strange, 'tis very strange, that is the
brief and the tedious of it; and he 's of a most facinerious spirit that will not acknowledge it to be the—
   Laf. Very hand of heaven.
   Par. Ay, so I say.
   Laf. In a most weak—[*pausing*] and debile minister, great power, great transcendence: which
should, indeed, give us a further use to be made than
alone the recovery of the king, as to be—[*pausing*]
generally thankful.   44
   Par. I would have said it; you say well. Here comes
the king.

Enter KING, HELENA, *and* Attendants. LAFEU *and*
   PAROLLES *retire.*

   Laf. Lustig, as the Dutchman says: I 'll like a maid
the better, whilst I have a tooth in my head: why,
he 's able to lead her a coranto.
   Par. Mort du vinaigre! is not this Helen?   50
   Laf. 'Fore God, I think so.
   King. Go, call before me all the lords in court.
Sit, my preserver, by thy patient's side;
And with this healthful hand, whose banish'd sense
Thou hast repeal'd, a second time receive
The confirmation of my promised gift,
Which but attends thy naming.

Enter three or four Lords.

Fair maid, send forth thine eye: this youthful parcel
Of noble bachelors stand at my bestowing,
O'er whom both sovereign power and father's voice   60
I have to use: thy frank election make;
Thou hast power to choose, and they none to forsake.
   Hel. To each of you one fair and virtuous mistress
Fall, when Love please! marry, to each, but one!
   Laf. I 'ld give bay Curtal and his furniture,
My mouth no more were broken than these boys',
And writ as little beard.
   King.   Peruse them well:
Not one of those but had a noble father.
   Hel. Gentlemen,   69
Heaven hath through me restored the king to health.
   All. We understand it, and thank heaven for you.
   Hel. I am a simple maid, and therein wealthiest,
That I protest I simply am a maid.
Please it your majesty, I have done already:
The blushes in my cheeks thus whisper me,
'We blush that thou shouldst choose; but, be refused,
Let the white death sit on thy cheek for ever;
We 'll ne'er come there again.'
   King.   Make choice; and, see,
Who shuns thy love shuns all his love in me.
   Hel. Now, Dian, from thy altar do I fly,   80
And to imperial Love, that god most high,
Do my sighs stream. Sir, will you hear my suit?
   First Lord. And grant it.
   Hel.   Thanks, sir; all the rest is mute.
   Laf. I had rather be in this choice than throw
ames-ace for my life.
   Hel. The honour, sir, that flames in your fair eyes,
Before I speak, too threateningly replies:
Love make your fortunes twenty times above
Her that so wishes and her humble love!
   Sec. Lord. No better, if you please.
   Hel.   My wish receive,   90
Which great Love grant! and so, I take my leave.
   Laf. Do all they deny her? An they were sons of
mine, I 'd have them whipped; or I would send them
to the Turk, to make eunuchs of.
   Hel. Be not afraid that I your hand should take;
I 'll never do you wrong for your own sake:
Blessing upon your vows! and in your bed

SCENE III.   4. **ensconcing**, taking refuge, fortifying.   10. **artists, i.e.**,
the physicians.   12. **Galen**, Greek physician of the second century.
Paracelsus, Swiss physician of the sixteenth century.   14. **authentic
fellows**, those properly licensed to practice.   25. **showing,** writing.
31. **dolphin**, the fish; supposed by some to mean the dauphin of France.
34. **the brief . . . it.** Cf. the modern phrase "the short and the long of
it."   35. **facinerious**, infamous.   39. **debile**, weak.   47. **Lustig,**
German word for "merry."   49. **coranto**, lively dance.   50. **Mort du**

vinaigre, possibly an oath by the vinegar in Christ's wounds; literally,
death of the vinegar.   61. **frank election,** uninhibited choice.   65.
bay . . . furniture, my horse and his trappings.   66. **My mouth . . .
broken,** i.e., if I had all my teeth.   67. **writ,** laid claim to.   83. **all
. . . mute,** I have nothing more to say to you.   85. **ames-ace,** two aces;
the lowest possible throw in dice—i.e., barely escape death (New
Cambridge).   92. **Do all . . . her.** None of them have denied her, or
deny her afterwards, but Bertram. The scene must be so regulated that

Find fairer fortune, if you ever wed!

Laf. These boys are boys of ice, they'll none have her: sure, they are bastards to the English; the French ne'er got 'em. 101

Hel. You are too young, too happy, and too good, To make yourself a son out of my blood.

Fourth Lord. Fair one, I think not so.

Laf. There 's one grape yet; I am sure thy father drunk wine: but if thou be'st not an ass, I am a youth of fourteen; I have known thee already.

Hel. [*To Bertram*] I dare not say I take you; but I give
Me and my service, ever whilst I live, 110
Into your guiding power. This is the man.

King. Why, then, young Bertram, take her; she 's thy wife.

Ber. My wife, my liege! I shall beseech your highness, In such a business give me leave to use
The help of mine own eyes.

King.   Know'st thou not, Bertram,
What she has done for me?

Ber.   Yes, my good lord;
But never hope to know why I should marry her.

King. Thou know'st she has raised me from my sickly bed.

Ber. But follows it, my lord, to bring me down
Must answer for your raising? I know her well: 120
She had her breeding at my father's charge.
A poor physician's daughter my wife! Disdain
Rather corrupt me ever!

King. 'Tis only title thou disdain'st in her, the which
I can build up. Strange is it that our bloods,
Of colour, weight, and heat, pour'd all together,
Would quite confound distinction, yet stand off
In differences so mighty. If she be
All that is virtuous, save what thou dislikest,
A poor physician's daughter, thou dislikest 130
Of virtue for the name: but do not so:
From lowest place when virtuous things proceed,
The place is dignified by the doer's deed:
Where great additions swell 's, and virtue none,
It is a dropsied honour. Good alone
Is good without a name. Vileness is so:
The property by what it is should go,
Not by the title. She is young, wise, fair;
In these to nature she 's immediate heir,
And these breed honour: that is honour's scorn, 140
Which challenges itself as honour's born
And is not like the sire: honours thrive,
When rather from our acts we them derive
Than our foregoers: the mere word 's a slave
Debosh'd on every tomb, on every grave
A lying trophy, and as oft is dumb
Where dust and damn'd oblivion is the tomb
Of honour'd bones indeed. What should be said?
If thou canst like this creature as a maid,
I can create the rest: virtue and she 150
Is her own dower; honour and wealth from me.

Ber. I cannot love her, nor will strive to do 't.

King. Thou wrong'st thyself, if thou shouldst strive to choose.

Hel. That you are well restored, my lord, I'm glad: Let the rest go.

King. My honour 's at the stake; which to defeat, I must produce my power. Here, take her hand,
Proud scornful boy, unworthy this good gift;
That dost in vile misprision shackle up
My love and her desert; that canst not dream, 160
We, poising us in her defective scale,
Shall weigh thee to the beam; that wilt not know,
It is in us to plant thine honour where
We please to have it grow. Check thy contempt:
Obey our will, which travails in thy good:
Believe not thy disdain, but presently
Do thine own fortunes that obedient right
Which both thy duty owes and our power claims;
Or I will throw thee from my care for ever
Into the staggers and the careless lapse 170
Of youth and ignorance; both my revenge and hate
Loosing upon thee, in the name of justice,
Without all terms of pity. Speak; thine answer.

Ber. Pardon, my gracious lord; for I submit
My fancy to your eyes: when I consider
What great creation and what dole of honour
Flies where you bid it, I find that she, which late
Was in my nobler thoughts most base, is now
The praised of the king; who, so ennobled,
Is as 'twere born so.

King.   Take her by the hand, 180
And tell her she is thine: to whom I promise
A counterpoise, if not to thy estate
A balance more replete.

Ber.   I take her hand.

King. Good fortune and the favour of the king
Smile upon this contract; whose ceremony
Shall seem expedient on the now-born brief,
And be perform'd to-night: the solemn feast
Shall more attend upon the coming space,
Expecting absent friends. As thou lovest her,
Thy love 's to me religious; else, does err. 190
[*Exeunt all but Lafeu and Parolles.*

Laf. [*Advancing*] Do you hear, monsieur? a word with you.

Par. Your pleasure, sir?

Laf. Your lord and master did well to make his recantation.

Par. Recantation! My lord! my master!

Laf. Ay; is it not a language I speak?

Par. A most harsh one, and not to be understood without bloody succeeding. My master!

Laf. Are you companion to the Count Rousillon? 201

Par. To any count, to all counts, to what is man.

Laf. To what is count's man: count's master is of another style.

Par. You are too old, sir; let it satisfy you, you are too old.

Laf. I must tell thee, sirrah, I write man; to which title age cannot bring thee. 209

Par. What I dare too well do, I dare not do.

Lafeu and Parolles talk at a distance, where they may see what passes between Helena and the lords, but not hear it, so that they know not by whom the refusal is made (Johnson). 106. **drunk wine,** i.e., was red-blooded. 122-123. **Disdain . . . me,** i.e., people's disdain for me. 134. **swell 's,** swell us. 141. **challenges itself,** claims itself to be. 145. **Debosh'd,** debauched. 159. **misprision,** contempt. 170. **staggers,** giddy or wild conduct. 186. **now-born brief,** contract just arranged. 196. **Recantation.** Parolles, as Bertram's man, takes umbrage at Lafeu's

slur against his master's honor. 199. **succeeding,** consequences; i.e., a duel. 202. **count, counts.** Parolles reminds Lafeu of his inferior rank. 203, 204. **man, count's man.** Parolles means (l. 202) to imply that Lafeu is no man; Lafeu turns the slur against Parolles, using *man* to signify servant, referring to the latter's relation to Bertram.

Laf. I did think thee, for two ordinaries, to be a pretty wise fellow; thou didst make tolerable vent of thy travel; it might pass: yet the scarfs and the bannerets about thee did manifoldly dissuade me from believing thee a vessel of too great a burthen. I have now found thee; when I lose thee again, I care not: yet art thou good for nothing but taking up; and that thou 'rt scarce worth.

Par. Hadst thou not the privilege of antiquity upon thee,—   221

Laf. Do not plunge thyself too far in anger, lest thou hasten thy trial; which if—Lord have mercy on thee for a hen! So, my good window of lattice, fare thee well: thy casement I need not open, for I look through thee. Give me thy hand.

Par. My lord, you give me most egregious indignity.

Laf. Ay, with all my heart; and thou art worthy of it.   231

Par. I have not, my lord, deserved it.

Laf. Yes, good faith, every dram of it; and I will not bate thee a scruple.

Par. Well, I shall be wiser.

Laf. Even as soon as thou canst, for thou hast to pull at a smack o' the contrary. If ever thou be'st bound in thy scarf and beaten, thou shalt find what it is to be proud of thy bondage. I have a desire to hold my acquaintance with thee, or rather my knowledge, that I may say in the default, he is a man I know.   242

Par. My lord, you do me most insupportable vexation.

Laf. I would it were hell-pains for thy sake, and my poor doing eternal: for doing I am past; as I will by thee, in what motion age will give me leave.   [*Exit.*

Par. Well, thou hast a son shall take this disgrace off me; scurvy, old, filthy, scurvy lord! Well, I must be patient; there is no fettering of authority. I'll beat him, by my life, if I can meet him with any convenience, an he were double and double a lord. I'll have no more pity of his age than I would have of—I'll beat him, an if I could but meet him again.   256

Re-enter LAFEU.

Laf. Sirrah, your lord and master 's married; there 's news for you: you have a new mistress.

Par. I most unfeignedly beseech your lordship to make some reservation of your wrongs: he is my good lord: whom I serve above is my master.   261

Laf. Who? God?

Par. Ay, sir.

Laf. The devil it is that 's thy master. Why dost thou garter up thy arms o' this fashion? dost make hose of thy sleeves? do other servants so? Thou wert best set thy lower part where thy nose stands. By mine honour, if I were but two hours younger, I 'ld beat thee: methinks, thou art a general offence, and every man should beat thee: I think thou wast created for men to breathe themselves upon thee.

Par. This is hard and undeserved measure, my lord.   271

Laf. Go to, sir; you were beaten in Italy for picking a kernel out of a pomegranate; you are a vagabond and no true traveller: you are more saucy with lords and honourable personages than the commission of your birth and virtue gives you heraldry. You are not worth another word, else I 'ld call you knave. I leave you.   [*Exit.* 281

Par. Good, very good; it is so then: good, very good; let it be concealed awhile.

Re-enter BERTRAM.

Ber. Undone, and forfeited to cares for ever!

Par. What 's the matter, sweet-heart?

Ber. Although before the solemn priest I have
      sworn,
I will not bed her.

Par. What, what, sweet-heart?

Ber. O my Parolles, they have married me! I'll to
the Tuscan wars, and never bed her.   290

Par. France is a dog-hole, and it no more merits
The tread of a man's foot: to the wars!

Ber. There 's letters from my mother: what the
import is, I know not yet.

Par. Ay, that would be known. To the wars, my
      boy, to the wars!
He wears his honour in a box unseen,
That hugs his kicky-wicky here at home,
Spending his manly marrow in her arms,
Which should sustain the bound and high curvet
Of Mars's fiery steed. To other regions   300
France is a stable; we that dwell in 't jades;
Therefore, to the war!

Ber. It shall be so: I'll send her to my house,
Acquaint my mother with my hate to her,
And wherefore I am fled; write to the king
That which I durst not speak: his present gift
Shall furnish me to those Italian fields,
Where noble fellows strike: war is no strife
To the dark house and the detested wife.

Par. Will this capriccio hold in thee? art sure?   310

Ber. Go with me to my chamber, and advise me.
I'll send her straight away: to-morrow
I'll to the wars, she to her single sorrow.

Par. Why, these balls bound; there 's noise in it.
  'Tis hard:
A young man married is a man that 's marr'd:
Therefore away, and leave her bravely; go:
The king has done you wrong: but, hush, 'tis so.
                                                              [*Exeunt.*

SCENE IV. *Paris. The* KING's *palace.*

Enter HELENA *and* CLOWN.

Hel. My mother greets me kindly: is she well?

Clo. She is not well; but yet she has her health: she 's very merry; but yet she is not well: but thanks be given, she 's very well and wants nothing i' the world; but yet she is not well.

Hel. If she be very well, what does she ail, that she 's not very well?

211. **ordinaries**, meals. 220. **privilege of antiquity**, referring to his advanced age. 237. **smack**, a taste, a draught. **the contrary**, i.e., of wisdom (l. 235)—folly. 241. **in the default**, at need. 246. **my poor doing**, referring to Parolles' *you do me*, etc. (l. 243). 253. **convenience**, advantage. 293. **letters**, i.e., a letter. 307. **furnish me**. Knights customarily provided themselves with trappings and armed retainers when enlisting in warlike enterprises. 310. **capriccio**, caprice. 314.

these balls bound. Parolles compares Bertram's words to good tennis balls, which rebound with a noise.
SCENE IV. 2. **not well**, an adaptation of the Elizabethan euphemism by which the dead were spoken of as "well"; cf. *2 Henry IV*, V, ii, 3; *Antony and Cleopatra*, II, v, 31-33. 24. **shakes out**, referring to his loose, wagging tongue. 32. **found thee**, found you out. 34. **in yourself**, by yourself. 45. **Whose want**, the lack of which; the antecedent of

Clo. Truly, she's very well indeed, but for two things.

Hel. What two things? 10

Clo. One, that she's not in heaven, whither God send her quickly! the other, that she's in earth, from whence God send her quickly!

Enter PAROLLES.

Par. Bless you, my fortunate lady!

Hel. I hope, sir, I have your good will to have mine own good fortunes.

Par. You had my prayers to lead them on; and to keep them on, have them still. O, my knave, how does my old lady?

Clo. So that you had her wrinkles and I her money, I would she did as you say. 21

Par. Why, I say nothing.

Clo. Marry, you are the wiser man; for many a man's tongue shakes out his master's undoing: to say nothing, to do nothing, to know nothing, and to have nothing, is to be a great part of your title; which is within a very little of nothing.

Par. Away! thou'rt a knave.

Clo. You should have said, sir, before a knave thou'rt a knave; that's, before me thou'rt a knave: this had been truth, sir. 31

Par. Go to, thou art a witty fool; I have found thee.

Clo. Did you find me in yourself, sir? or were you taught to find me? The search, sir, was profitable; and much fool may you find in you, even to the world's pleasure and the increase of laughter.

Par. A good knave, i' faith, and well fed.

Madam, my lord will go away to-night; 40
A very serious business calls on him.
The great prerogative and rite of love,
Which, as your due, time claims, he does
    acknowledge;
But puts it off to a compell'd restraint;
Whose want, and whose delay, is strew'd with sweets,
Which they distil now in the curbed time,
To make the coming hour o'erflow with joy
And pleasure drown the brim.

Hel.   What's his will else?

Par. That you will take your instant leave o' the
    king,
And make this haste as your own good proceeding, 50
Strengthen'd with what apology you think
May make it probable need.

Hel.   What more commands he?

Par. That, having this obtain'd, you presently
Attend his further pleasure.

Hel. In every thing I wait upon his will.

Par. I shall report it so.

Hel.   I pray you. [*Exit Parolles.*] Come,
    sirrah.   [*Exeunt.*

SCENE V. *Paris. The* KING's *palace.*

Enter LAFEU *and* BERTRAM.

Laf. But I hope your lordship thinks not him a soldier.

Ber. Yes, my lord, and of very valiant approof.

Laf. You have it from his own deliverance.

Ber. And by other warranted testimony.

Laf. Then my dial goes not true: I took this lark for a bunting.

Ber. I do assure you, my lord, he is very great in knowledge and accordingly valiant. 9

Laf. I have then sinned against his experience and transgressed against his valour; and my state that way is dangerous, since I cannot yet find in my heart to repent. Here he comes: I pray you, make us friends; I will pursue the amity.

Enter PAROLLES.

Par. [*To Bertram*] These things shall be done, sir.

Laf. Pray you, sir, who's his tailor?

Par. Sir?

Laf. O, I know him well, I, sir; he, sir,'s a good workman, a very good tailor. 21

Ber. [*Aside to Par.*] Is she gone to the king?

Par. She is.

Ber. Will she away to-night?

Par. As you'll have her.

Ber. I have writ my letters, casketed my treasure,
Given order for our horses; and to-night,
When I should take possession of the bride,
End ere I do begin. 29

Laf. A good traveller is something at the latter end of a dinner; but one that lies three thirds and uses a known truth to pass a thousand nothings with, should be once heard and thrice beaten. God save you, captain.

Ber. Is there any unkindness between my lord and you, monsieur?

Par. I know not how I have deserved to run into my lord's displeasure. 38

Laf. You have made shift to run into 't, boots and spurs and all, like him that leaped into the custard; and out of it you'll run again, rather than suffer question for your residence.

Ber. It may be you have mistaken him, my lord.

Laf. And shall do so ever, though I took him at 's prayers. Fare you well, my lord; and believe this of me, there can be no kernel in this light nut; the soul of this man is his clothes. Trust him not in matter of heavy consequence; I have kept of them tame, and know their natures. Farewell, monsieur: I have spoken better of you †than you have or will to deserve at my hand; but we must do good against evil. [*Exit.* 53

Par. An idle lord, I swear.

Ber. I think so.

Par. Why, do you not know him?

Ber. Yes, I do know him well, and common speech
Gives him a worthy pass. Here comes my clog.

Enter HELENA.

Hel. I have, sir, as I was commanded from you,
Spoke with the king and have procured his leave 60
For present parting; only he desires

All's Well
that Ends Well
ACT II : SC V

817

---

whose is the idea of line 42. 46. curbed time, usually explained as restraints of time. The New Cambridge editors explain the metaphor to be drawn from the process of distillation, the curbed time being conceived as the confined vessel or still in which the process is carried on. 52. probable need, a specious appearance of necessity (Johnson).
SCENE V. 7. lark, bunting, birds so nearly alike as to be confused by the casual observer. 30. good traveller, referring to their previous quarrel (II, iii, 212-213). 39-42. You have . . . residence. Lafeu taunts Parolles with his braggartlike conduct at their previous meeting. 40. leaped . . . custard. Theobald points out the "foolery practised at city entertainments" of having a clown jump into a large, deep custard. 49-50. I have . . . tame, I have kept tame animals of this kind (New Cambridge).

Some private speech with you.
  Ber.   I shall obey his will.
You must not marvel, Helen, at my course,
Which holds not colour with the time, nor does
The ministration and required office
On my particular. Prepared I was not
For such a business; therefore am I found
So much unsettled: this drives me to entreat you
That presently you take your way for home;
And rather muse than ask why I entreat you,   70
For my respects are better than they seem
And my appointments have in them a need
Greater than shows itself at the first view
To you that know them not. This to my mother:
                        [*Giving a letter.*
'Twill be two days ere I shall see you, so
I leave you to your wisdom.
  Hel.   Sir, I can nothing say,
But that I am your most obedient servant.
  Ber. Come, come, no more of that.
  Hel.   And ever shall
With true observance seek to eke out that
Wherein toward me my homely stars have fail'd   80
To equal my great fortune.
  Ber.   Let that go:
My haste is very great: farewell; hie home.
  Hel. Pray, sir, your pardon.
  Ber.   Well, what would you say?
  Hel. I am not worthy of the wealth I owe,
Nor dare I say 'tis mine, and yet it is;
But, like a timorous thief, most fain would steal
What law does vouch mine own.
  Ber.   What would you have?
  Hel. Something; and scarce so much: nothing,
     indeed.
I would not tell you what I would, my lord:
Faith, yes;   90
Strangers and foes do sunder, and not kiss.
  Ber. I pray you, stay not, but in haste to horse.
  Hel. I shall not break your bidding, good my lord.
  Ber. Where are my other men, monsieur? Farewell.
                        [*Exit Helena.*
Go thou toward home; where I will never come
Whilst I can shake my sword or hear the drum.
Away, and for our flight.
  Par.   Bravely, coragio!   [*Exeunt.*

ACT III.

SCENE I. *Florence. The* DUKE'S *palace.*

Flourish. Enter the DUKE *of Florence, attended; the
     two Frenchmen, with a troop of soldiers.*

  Duke. So that from point to point now have you
     heard
The fundamental reasons of this war,
Whose great decision hath much blood let forth
And more thirsts after.
  First Lord.   Holy seems the quarrel
Upon your grace's part; black and fearful
On the opposer.

  Duke. Therefore we marvel much our cousin
     France
Would in so just a business shut his bosom
Against our borrowing prayers.
  Sec. Lord.   Good my lord,
The reasons of our state I cannot yield,   10
But like a common and an outward man,
That the great figure of a council frames
By self-unable motion: therefore dare not
Say what I think of it, since I have found
Myself in my incertain grounds to fail
As often as I guess'd.
  Duke.   Be it his pleasure.
  First Lord. But I am sure the younger of our nature,
That surfeit on their ease, will day by day
Come here for physic.
  Duke.   Welcome shall they be;
And all the honours that can fly from us   20
Shall on them settle. You know your places well;
When better fall, for your avails they fell:
To-morrow to the field.   [*Flourish. Exeunt.*

SCENE II. *Rousillon. The* COUNT'S *palace.*

Enter COUNTESS *and* CLOWN.

  Count. It hath happened all as I would have had it,
save that he comes not along with her.
  Clo. By my troth, I take my young lord to be a
very melancholy man.
  Count. By what observance, I pray you?
  Clo. Why, he will look upon his boot and sing;
mend the ruff and sing; ask questions and sing; pick
his teeth and sing. I know a man that had this trick
of melancholy sold a goodly manor for a song.   10
  Count. Let me see what he writes, and when he
means to come.   [*Opening a letter.*
  Clo. I have no mind to Isbel since I was at court:
our old ling and our Isbels o' the country are nothing
like your old ling and your Isbels o' the court: the
brains of my Cupid's knocked out, and I begin to
love, as an old man loves money, with no stomach.
  Count. What have we here?
  Clo. E'en that you have there.   [*Exit.* 20
  Count. [*Reads*] I have sent you a daughter-in-law:
she hath recovered the king, and undone me. I have
wedded her, not bedded her; and sworn to make the
'not' eternal. You shall hear I am run away: know it
before the report come. If there be breadth enough in
the world, I will hold a long distance. My duty to you.
                    Your unfortunate son,
                              BERTRAM.
This is not well, rash and unbridled boy,   30
To fly the favours of so good a king;
To pluck his indignation on thy head
By the misprising of a maid too virtuous
For the contempt of empire.

Re-enter CLOWN.

  Clo. O madam, yonder is heavy news within between two soldiers and my young lady!
  Count. What is the matter?

71. **respects,** motives. 72. **appointments,** purposes. 97. **coragio,**
courage.
ACT III. SCENE I. 3. **decision,** combat to decide an issue. 10.
yield, communicate, produce. 11. **outward,** not having intimate
knowledge of things. 12. **the great . . . council.** The New Cambridge

editors explain this as an astrological metaphor, defining *figure* as a
scheme or table showing the disposition of the heavens at a given time.
13. **self-unable,** impotent. 17. **nature,** kind—by birth and position;
i.e., young lords. 22. **When better fall,** i.e., better places fall vacant
(Brigstocke).

*All's Well
that Ends Well*
ACT II : SC V

818

Clo. Nay, there is some comfort in the news, some comfort; your son will not be killed so soon as I thought he would.   40

Count. Why should he be killed?

Clo. So say I, madam, if he run away, as I hear he does: the danger is in standing to 't; that 's the loss of men, though it be the getting of children. Here they come will tell you more: for my part, I only hear your son was run away.   [*Exit.*

Enter HELENA *and two* Gentlemen.

First Gent. Save you, good madam.

Hel. Madam, my lord is gone, for ever gone.

Sec. Gent. Do not say so.

Count. Think upon patience. Pray you, gentlemen, 50
I have felt so many quirks of joy and grief,
That the first face of neither, on the start,
Can woman me unto 't: where is my son, I pray you?

Sec. Gent. Madam, he 's gone to serve the duke of
   Florence:
We met him thitherward; for thence we came,
And, after some dispatch in hand at court,
Thither we bend again.   57

Hel. Look on his letter, madam; here 's my passport.
[*Reads*] When thou canst get the ring upon my finger which never shall come off, and show me a child begotten of thy body that I am father to, then call me husband: but in such a 'then' I write a 'never.'
This is a dreadful sentence.

Count. Brought you this letter, gentlemen?

First Gent.   Ay, madam;
And for the contents' sake are sorry for our pains.

Count. I prithee, lady, have a better cheer;
If thou engrossest all the griefs are thine,
Thou robb'st me of a moiety: he was my son;
But I do wash his name out of my blood,   70
And thou art all my child. Towards Florence is he?

Sec. Gent. Ay, madam.

Count.   And to be a soldier?

Sec. Gent. Such is his noble purpose; and, believe 't,
The duke will lay upon him all the honour
That good convenience claims.

Count.   Return you thither?

First Gent. Ay, madam, with the swiftest wing of
   speed.

Hel. [*Reads*] Till I have no wife, I have nothing in
   France.
'Tis bitter.

Count. Find you that there?

Hel.   Ay, madam.

First Gent. 'Tis but the boldness of his hand, haply,
which his heart was not consenting to.   80

Count. Nothing in France, until he have no wife!
There 's nothing here that is too good for him
But only she; and she deserves a lord
That twenty such rude boys might tend upon
And call her hourly mistress. Who was with him?

First Gent. A servant only, and a gentleman
Which I have sometime known.

Count.   Parolles, was it not?

First Gent. Ay, my good lady, he.

Count. A very tainted fellow, and full of wickedness.

My son corrupts a well-derived nature   90
With his inducement.

First Gent.   Indeed, good lady,
The fellow has a deal of that too much,
Which holds him much to have.

Count. You 're welcome, gentlemen.
I will entreat you, when you see my son,
To tell him that his sword can never win
The honour that he loses: more I 'll entreat you
Written to bear along.

Sec. Gent.   We serve you, madam,
In that and all your worthiest affairs.

Count. Not so, but as we change our courtesies. 100
Will you draw near?   [*Exeunt Countess and Gentlemen.*

Hel. 'Till I have no wife, I have nothing in France.'
Nothing in France, until he has no wife!
Thou shalt have none, Rousillon, none in France;
Then hast thou all again. Poor lord! is 't I
That chase thee from thy country and expose
Those tender limbs of thine to the event
Of the none-sparing war? and is it I
That drive thee from the sportive court, where thou
Wast shot at with fair eyes, to be the mark   110
Of smoky muskets? O you leaden messengers,
That ride upon the violent speed of fire,
†Fly with false aim; move the still-peering air,
That sings with piercing; do not touch my lord.
Whoever shoots at him, I set him there;
Whoever charges on his forward breast,
I am the caitiff that do hold him to 't;
And, though I kill him not, I am the cause
His death was so effected: better 'twere
I met the ravin lion when he roar'd   120
With sharp constraint of hunger; better 'twere
That all the miseries which nature owes
Were mine at once. No, come thou home, Rousillon,
Whence honour but of danger wins a scar,
As oft it loses all: I will be gone;
My being here it is that holds thee hence:
Shall I stay here to do 't? no, no, although
The air of paradise did fan the house
And angels officed all: I will be gone,
That pitiful rumour may report my flight,   130
To consolate thine ear. Come, night; end, day!
For with the dark, poor thief, I 'll steal away. [*Exit.*

SCENE III. *Florence. Before the* DUKE's *palace.*

Flourish. Enter the DUKE *of Florence,* BERTRAM,
PAROLLES, *Soldiers, Drum, and* Trumpets.

Duke. The general of our horse thou art; and we,
Great in our hope, lay our best love and credence
Upon thy promising fortune.

Ber.   Sir, it is
A charge too heavy for my strength, but yet
We 'll strive to bear it for your worthy sake
To the extreme edge of hazard.

Duke.   Then go thou forth;
And fortune play upon thy prosperous helm,
As thy auspicious mistress!

Ber.   This very day,

SCENE II. 14. **ling,** salted codfish. 33. **misprising,** despising. 53. **woman me,** bend or subdue me like a woman. 68. **griefs are,** griefs that are; common elliptical usage. 75. **convenience,** propriety. 91. **inducement,** influence (Brigstocke). 93. **holds him,** is of use or advantage to him. 100. **Not so . . . courtesies,** i.e., only as we serve each

other—I by giving you entertainment. 113. **still-peering,** so F; F₂₋₄: *still piecing;* Steevens' emendation *still-piecing,* the most favored, is adopted by the New Cambridge editors, who define it "ever repairing or joining up again." 121. **constraint,** compulsion.
SCENE III. 6. **hazard,** peril.

Great Mars, I put myself into thy file:
Make me but like my thoughts, and I shall prove   10
A lover of thy drum, hater of love.   [*Exeunt.*

SCENE IV. *Rousillon. The* COUNT's *palace.*

Enter COUNTESS *and* Steward.

Count. Alas! and would you take the letter of her?
Might you not know she would do as she has done,
By sending me a letter? Read it again.
Stew. [*Reads*]
I am Saint Jaques' pilgrim, thither gone:
    Ambitious love hath so in me offended,
That barefoot plod I the cold ground upon,
    With sainted vow my faults to have amended.
Write, write, that from the bloody course of war
    My dearest master, your dear son, may hie:
Bless him at home in peace, whilst I from far   10
    His name with zealous fervour sanctify:
His taken labours bid him me forgive;
    I, his despiteful Juno, sent him forth
From courtly friends, with camping foes to live,
    Where death and danger dogs the heels of worth:
He is too good and fair for death and me;
    Whom I myself embrace, to set him free.
Count. Ah, what sharp stings are in her mildest
    words!
Rinaldo, you did never lack advice so much,
As letting her pass so: had I spoke with her,   20
I could have well diverted her intents,
Which thus she hath prevented.
Stew.   Pardon me, madam:
If I had given you this at over-night,
She might have been o'erta'en; and yet she writes,
Pursuit would be but vain.
Count.   What angel shall
Bless this unworthy husband? he cannot thrive,
Unless her prayers, whom heaven delights to hear
And loves to grant, reprieve him from the wrath
Of greatest justice. Write, write, Rinaldo,
To this unworthy husband of his wife;   30
Let every word weigh heavy of her worth
That he does weigh too light: my greatest grief,
Though little he do feel it, set down sharply.
Dispatch the most convenient messenger:
When haply he shall hear that she is gone,
He will return; and hope I may that she,
Hearing so much, will speed her foot again,
Led hither by pure love: which of them both
Is dearest to me, I have no skill in sense
To make distinction: provide this messenger: 40
My heart is heavy and mine age is weak;
Grief would have tears, and sorrow bids me speak.
                                [*Exeunt.*

SCENE V. *Florence. Without the walls. A tucket afar off.*

Enter an old Widow *of Florence,* DIANA, VIOLENTA,
    and MARIANA, *with other* Citizens.

Wid. Nay, come; for if they do approach the city,
we shall lose all the sight.
Dia. They say the French count has done most
honourable service.
Wid. It is reported that he has taken their greatest
commander; and that with his own hand he slew the
duke's brother. [*Tucket.*] We have lost our labour;
they are gone a contrary way: hark! you may know
by their trumpets.   9
Mar. Come, let 's return again, and suffice ourselves
with the report of it. Well, Diana, take heed of this
French earl: the honour of a maid is her name; and
no legacy is so rich as honesty.
Wid. I have told my neighbour how you have been
solicited by a gentleman his companion.
Mar. I know that knave; hang him! one Parolles: a
filthy officer he is in those suggestions for the young
earl. Beware of them, Diana; their promises, entice-
ments, oaths, tokens, and all these engines of lust, are
not the things they go under: many a maid hath been
seduced by them; and the misery is, example, that so
terrible shows in the wreck of maidenhood, cannot
for all that dissuade succession, but that they are
limed with the twigs that threaten them. I hope I
need not to advise you further; but I hope your own
grace will keep you where you are, though there were
no further danger known but the modesty which is
so lost.   30
Dia. You shall not need to fear me.
Wid. I hope so.

Enter HELENA, *disguised like a Pilgrim.*

Look, here comes a pilgrim: I know she will lie at
my house; thither they send one another: I'll question
her. God save you, pilgrim! whither are you bound?
Hel. To Saint Jaques le Grand.
Where do the palmers lodge, I do beseech you?
Wid. At the Saint Francis here beside the port.
Hel. Is this the way?   40
Wid. Ay, marry, is 't. [*A march afar.*] Hark you!
    they come this way.
If you will tarry, holy pilgrim,
But till the troops come by,
I will conduct you where you shall be lodged;
The rather, for I think I know your hostess
As ample as myself.
Hel.   Is it yourself?
Wid. If you shall please so, pilgrim.
Hel. I thank you, and will stay upon your leisure.
Wid. You came, I think, from France?
Hel.   I did so.
Wid. Here you shall see a countryman of yours   50
That has done worthy service.
Hel.   His name, I pray you.
Dia. The Count Rousillon: know you such a one?
Hel. But by the ear, that hears most nobly of him:
His face I know not.
Dia.   Whatsome'er he is,
He 's bravely taken here. He stole from France,
As 'tis reported, for the king had married him
Against his liking: think you it is so?
Hel. Ay, surely, mere the truth: I know his lady.

*All's Well
that Ends Well*
ACT III : SC III

820

9. **file,** army.
    SCENE IV. 4. **Saint Jaques' pilgrim.** The pilgrim's costume was a
favorite disguise for lovers; cf. *Romeo and Juliet,* I, v, 99; *Hamlet,* IV,
v, 23-26. Some commentators have sought to identify the shrine
toward which Helena is bent with that of St. James of Compostella in

Spain. 11. **sanctify,** honor as holy. 13. **despiteful Juno,** an allusion
to Juno's pursuit of Hercules. 17. **Whom,** i.e., *death.* 40. **provide,**
equip.
    SCENE V. *Stage Direction:* **tucket,** preliminary signal given on a
trumpet. 22. **go under,** pretend to be. 23-25. **example . . . succes-**

Dia. There is a gentleman that serves the count
Reports but coarsely of her.
 Hel.   What 's his name?   60
 Dia. Monsieur Parolles.
 Hel.   O, I believe with him,
In argument of praise, or to the worth
Of the great count himself, she is too mean
To have her name repeated: all her deserving
Is a reserved honesty, and that
I have not heard examined.
 Dia.   Alas, poor lady!
'Tis a hard bondage to become the wife
Of a detesting lord.
 Wid. I warrant, good creature, wheresoe'er she is,
Her heart weighs sadly: this young maid might do her
A shrewd turn, if she pleased.
 Hel.   How do you mean?   71
May be the amorous count solicits her
In the unlawful purpose.
 Wid.   He does indeed;
And brokes with all that can in such a suit
Corrupt the tender honour of a maid:
But she is arm'd for him and keeps her guard
In honestest defence.
 Mar.   The gods forbid else!
 Wid. So, now they come: \

Drum and Colours. Enter BERTRAM, PAROLLES, *and the
 whole army.*

That is Antonio, the duke's eldest son;
That, Escalus.
 Hel.   Which is the Frenchman?
 Dia.   He;   80
That with the plume: 'tis a most gallant fellow.
I would he loved his wife: if he were honester
He were much goodlier: is 't not a handsome
  gentleman?
 Hel. I like him well.
 Dia. 'Tis pity he is not honest: yond 's that same
  knave
That leads him to these places: were I his lady,
I would poison that vile rascal.
 Hel.   Which is he?
 Dia. That jack-an-apes with scarfs: why is he
melancholy?
 Hel. Perchance he 's hurt i' the battle.   90
 Par. Lose our drum! well.
 Mar. He 's shrewdly vexed at something: look, he
has spied us.
 Wid. Marry, hang you!
 Mar. And your courtesy, for a ring-carrier!
      [*Exeunt Bertram, Parolles, and army.*
 Wid. The troop is past. Come, pilgrim, I will bring
  you
Where you shall host: of enjoin'd penitents
There 's four or five, to great Saint Jaques bound,
Already at my house.
 Hel.   I humbly thank you:
Please it this matron and this gentle maid   100
To eat with us to-night, the charge and thanking
Shall be for me; and, to requite you further,
I will bestow some precepts of this virgin

Worthy the note.
 Both.   We'll take your offer kindly.
              [*Exeunt.*

SCENE VI. *Camp before Florence.*

Enter BERTRAM *and the two French* Lords.

 Sec. Lord. Nay, good my lord, put him to 't; let him
have his way.
 First Lord. If your lordship find him not a hilding,
hold me no more in your respect.
 Sec. Lord. On my life, my lord, a bubble.
 Ber. Do you think I am so far deceived in him?
 Sec. Lord. Believe it, my lord, in mine own direct
knowledge, without any malice, but to speak of him
as my kinsman, he 's a most notable coward, an
infinite and endless liar, an hourly promise-breaker,
the owner of no one good quality worthy your lordship's entertainment.   13
 First Lord. It were fit you knew him; lest, reposing
too far in his virtue, which he hath not, he might at
some great and trusty business in a main danger fail
you.
 Ber. I would I knew in what particular action to
try him.   19
 First Lord. None better than to let him fetch off his
drum, which you hear him so confidently undertake
to do.
 Sec. Lord. I, with a troop of Florentines, will suddenly surprise him; such I will have, whom I am sure
he knows not from the enemy: we will bind and hoodwink him so, that he shall suppose no other but that
he is carried into the leaguer of the adversaries, when
we bring him to our own tents. Be but your lordship
present at his examination: if he do not, for the promise of his life and in the highest compulsion of base
fear, offer to betray you and deliver all the intelligence
in his power against you, and that with the divine
forfeit of his soul upon oath, never trust my judgement in any thing.   34
 First Lord. O, for the love of laughter, let him fetch
his drum; he says he has a stratagem for 't: when your
lordship sees the bottom of his success in 't, and to
what metal this counterfeit lump of ore will be melted,
if you give him not John Drum's entertainment, your
inclining cannot be removed. Here he comes.

Enter PAROLLES.

 Sec. Lord. [*Aside to Ber.*] O, for the love of laughter,
hinder not the honour of his design: let him fetch off
his drum in any hand.
 Ber. How now, monsieur! this drum sticks sorely in
your disposition.
 First Lord. A pox on 't, let it go; 'tis but a drum.   49
 Par. 'But a drum'! is 't 'but a drum'? A drum so
lost! There was excellent command,—to charge in
with our horse upon our own wings, and to rend our
own soldiers!
 First Lord. That was not to be blamed in the command of the service: it was a disaster of war that

---

sion, cannot dissuade another from a similar course. **46. ample,** fully,
completely. **65. reserved,** well guarded. **95. ring-carrier,** go-
between. **97. host,** lodge. **enjoin'd,** obligated by oath.
 SCENE VI. **4. hilding,** good-for-nothing. **20. fetch off,** recapture.
26. hoodwink, blindfold. **27. leaguer,** camp. **41. John Drum's**

entertainment, a probable allusion to the satirical comedy *Jack Drum's
Entertainment*, reputedly by Marston, produced in 1600 in connection
with War of the Theaters. *Drum's entertainment* (cf. *Tom Drum*, V, iii,
322 below) is a phrase frequent in Elizabethan writings to indicate
hard physical abuse.

Cæsar himself could not have prevented, if he had been there to command.

Ber. Well, we cannot greatly condemn our success: some dishonour we had in the loss of that drum; but it is not to be recovered. 60

Par. It might have been recovered.

Ber. It might; but it is not now.

Par. It is to be recovered: but that the merit of service is seldom attributed to the true and exact performer, I would have that drum or another, or 'hic jacet.'

Ber. Why, if you have a stomach, to 't, monsieur: if you think your mystery in stratagem can bring this instrument of honour again into his native quarter, be magnanimous in the enterprise and go on; I will grace the attempt for a worthy exploit: if you speed well in it, the duke shall both speak of it, and extend to you what further becomes his greatness, even to the utmost syllable of your worthiness. 75

Par. By the hand of a soldier, I will undertake it.

Ber. But you must not now slumber in it.

Par. I'll about it this evening: and I will presently pen down my dilemmas, encourage myself in my certainty, put myself into my mortal preparation; and by midnight look to hear further from me.

Ber. May I be bold to acquaint his grace you are gone about it?

Par. I know not what the success will be, my lord; but the attempt I vow.

Ber. I know thou 'rt valiant; and, to the possibility of thy soldiership, will subscribe for thee. Farewell. 90

Par. I love not many words. [*Exit.*

Sec. Lord. No more than a fish loves water. Is not this a strange fellow, my lord, that so confidently seems to undertake this business, which he knows is not to be done; damns himself to do and dares better be damned than to do 't?

First Lord. You do not know him, my lord, as we do: certain it is, that he will steal himself into a man's favour and for a week escape a great deal of discoveries; but when you find him out, you have him ever after. 101

Ber. Why, do you think he will make no deed at all of this that so seriously he does address himself unto?

Sec. Lord. None in the world; but return with an invention and clap upon you two or three probable lies: but we have almost embossed him; you shall see his fall to-night; for indeed he is not for your lordship's respect. 109

First Lord. We'll make you some sport with the fox ere we case him. He was first smoked by the old lord Lafeu: when his disguise and he is parted, tell me what a sprat you shall find him; which you shall see this very night.

Sec. Lord. I must go look my twigs: he shall be caught.

Ber. Your brother he shall go along with me.

Sec. Lord. As 't please your lordship; I'll leave you. [*Exit.*

Ber. Now will I lead you to the house, and show you 118
The lass I spoke of.

First Lord. But you say she 's honest.

Ber. That 's all the fault: I spoke with her but once
And found her wondrous cold; but I sent to her,
By this same coxcomb that we have i' the wind,
Tokens and letters which she did re-send;
And this is all I have done. She 's a fair creature:
Will you go see her?

First Lord. With all my heart, my lord.
[*Exeunt.*

SCENE VII. *Florence. The* Widow's *house.*

Enter HELENA *and* Widow.

Hel. If you misdoubt me that I am not she,
I know not how I shall assure you further,
But I shall lose the grounds I work upon.

Wid. Though my estate be fallen, I was well born,
Nothing acquainted with these businesses;
And would not put my reputation now
In any staining act.

Hel. Nor would I wish you.
First, give me trust, the count he is my husband,
And what to your sworn counsel I have spoken
Is so from word to word; and then you cannot, 10
By the good aid that I of you shall borrow,
Err in bestowing it.

Wid. I should believe you;
For you have show'd me that which well approves
You 're great in fortune.

Hel. Take this purse of gold,
And let me buy your friendly help thus far,
Which I will over-pay and pay again
When I have found it. The count he wooes your daughter,
Lays down his wanton siege before her beauty,
Resolved to carry her: let her in fine consent,
As we'll direct her how 'tis best to bear it. 20
Now his important blood will nought deny
That she'll demand: a ring the county wears,
That downward hath succeeded in his house
From son to son, some four or five descents
Since the first father wore it: this ring he holds
In most rich choice; yet in his idle fire,
To buy his will, it would not seem too dear,
Howe'er repented after.

Wid. Now I see
The bottom of your purpose.

Hel. You see it lawful, then: it is no more, 30
But that your daughter, ere she seems as won,
Desires this ring; appoints him an encounter;
In fine, delivers me to fill the time,
Herself most chastely absent: after this,
To marry her, I'll add three thousand crowns
To what is past already.

Wid. I have yielded:
Instruct my daughter how she shall persever,
That time and place with this deceit so lawful
May prove coherent. Every night he comes
With musics of all sorts and songs composed 40
To her unworthiness: it nothing steads us
To chide him from our eaves; for he persists

---

66. **'hic jacet,'** here lies; the beginning phrase of tomb inscriptions. 68. **mystery,** skill. 80. **pen . . . dilemmas,** encourage myself in my certainty, i.e., by writing down all the contrary arguments in order to argue them out in my own favor (Brigstocke). 81-82. **mortal preparation,** extreme unction. 88. **possibility,** capacity. 107. **embossed,**

foaming at the mouth from exhaustion; figure from the chase. 111. **case,** surround. **smoked,** found out. 115. **look my twigs,** a figure from catching birds by liming the twigs.
SCENE VII. 17. **it,** i.e., fortune. 21. **important,** importunate. 26. **most rich choice,** highest estimation.

As if his life lay on 't.
Hel.   Why then to-night
Let us assay our plot; which, if it speed,
Is wicked meaning in a lawful deed
And lawful meaning in a lawful act,
Where both not sin, and yet a sinful fact:
But let 's about it.   [*Exeunt.*

ACT IV.

SCENE I. *Without the Florentine camp.*

Enter Second French Lord, *with five or six other*
    Soldiers *in ambush.*

Sec. Lord. He can come no other way but by this
hedge-corner. When you sally upon him, speak what
terrible language you will: though you understand it
not yourselves, no matter; for we must not seem to
understand him, unless some one among us whom
we must produce for an interpreter.

First Sold. Good captain, let me be the interpreter.

Sec. Lord. Art not acquainted with him? knows he
not thy voice?   11

First Sold. No, sir, I warrant you.

Sec. Lord. But what linsey-woolsey hast thou to
speak to us again?

First Sold. E'en such as you speak to me.

Sec. Lord. He must think us some band of strangers
i' the adversary's entertainment. Now he hath a
smack of all neighbouring languages; therefore we
must every one be a man of his own fancy, not to
know what we speak one to another; so we seem to
know, is to know straight our purpose: choughs'
language, gabble enough, and good enough. As for
you, interpreter, you must seem very politic. But
couch, ho! here he comes, to beguile two hours in a
sleep, and then to return and swear the lies he forges. 26

Enter PAROLLES.

Par. Ten o'clock: within these three hours 'twill be
time enough to go home. What shall I say I have
done? It must be a very plausive invention that
carries it: they begin to smoke me; and disgraces
have of late knocked too often at my door. I find my
tongue is too foolhardy; but my heart hath the fear
of Mars before it and of his creatures, not daring the
reports of my tongue.

Sec. Lord. This is the first truth that e'er thine own
tongue was guilty of.   36

Par. What the devil should move me to undertake
the recovery of this drum, being not ignorant of the
impossibility, and knowing I had no such purpose?
I must give myself some hurts, and say I got them in
exploit: yet slight ones will not carry it; they will
say, 'Came you off with so little?' and great ones I
dare not give. Wherefore, what 's the instance?
Tongue, I must put you into a butter-woman's
mouth and buy myself another of Bajazet's mule, if
you prattle me into these perils.   47

Sec. Lord. Is it possible he should know what he is,
and be that he is?

Par. I would the cutting of my garments would
serve the turn, or the breaking of my Spanish sword.

Sec. Lord. We cannot afford you so.

Par. Or the baring of my beard; and to say it was
in stratagem.

Sec. Lord. 'Twould not do.

Par. Or to drown my clothes, and say I was stripped.

Sec. Lord. Hardly serve.

Par. Though I swore I leaped from the window of
the citadel—   61

Sec. Lord. How deep?

Par. Thirty fathom.

Sec. Lord. Three great oaths would scarce make that
be believed.

Par. I would I had any drum of the enemy's: I
would swear I recovered it.

Sec. Lord. You shall hear one anon.

Par. A drum now of the enemy's,—   [*Alarum within.*

Sec. Lord. Throca movousus, cargo, cargo, cargo. 71

All. Cargo, cargo, cargo, villianda par corbo, cargo.

Par. O, ransom, ransom! do not hide mine eyes.
             [*They seize and blindfold him.*

First Sold. Boskos thromuldo boskos.

Par. I know you are the Muskos' regiment:
And I shall lose my life for want of language:
If there be here German, or Dane, low Dutch,
Italian, or French, let him speak to me; I'll
Discover that which shall undo the Florentine.   80

First Sold. Boskos vauvado: I understand thee, and
can speak thy tongue. Kerelybonto, sir, betake thee
to thy faith, for seventeen poniards are at thy bosom.

Par. O!

First Sold. O, pray, pray, pray! Manka revania
dulche.

Sec. Lord. Oscorbidulchos volivorco.

First Sold. The general is content to spare thee yet;
And, hoodwink'd as thou art, will lead thee on   90
To gather from thee: haply thou mayst inform
Something to save thy life.

Par.   O, let me live!
And all the secrets of our camp I'll show,
Their force, their purposes; nay, I'll speak that
Which you will wonder at.

First Sold.   But wilt thou faithfully?

Par. If I do not, damn me.

First Sold. Acordo linta.
Come on; thou art granted space.
      [*Exit, with Parolles guarded. A short alarum within.*

Sec. Lord. Go, tell the Count Rousillon, and my
    brother,
We have caught the woodcock, and will keep him
    muffled   100
Till we do hear from them.

Sec. Sold.   Captain, I will.

Sec. Lord. A' will betray us all unto ourselves:
Inform on that.

Sec. Sold. So I will, sir.

Sec. Lord. Till then I'll keep him dark and safely
    lock'd.   [*Exeunt.*

SCENE II. *Florence. The* Widow's *house.*

ACT IV. SCENE I.   13. **linsey-woolsey,** a fabric woven from wool and
flax; figuratively, nonsense.   22. **choughs',** small, chattering species
of the crow family, the jackdaw.   46. **Bajazet's mule,** generally
regarded as corrupt. *Balaam's mule, Bajazeth's mute* have been conjectured. The New Cambridge editors emend to *Bajazet's mate,* i.e.,
Bajazet's wife Zabina in Marlowe's *Tamburlaine,* a termagant, whose
tongue will outdo the butter woman's.   54. **baring,** shaving.   55. **in
stratagem,** in executing the stratagem.   76. **Muskos',** Muscovites.
91. **gather,** get information.   **inform,** give form to; see glossary.

Enter BERTRAM *and* DIANA.

Ber. They told me that your name was Fontibell.
Dia. No, my good lord, Diana.
Ber.   Titled goddess;
And worth it, with addition! But, fair soul,
In your fine frame hath love no quality?
If the quick fire of youth light not your mind,
You are no maiden, but a monument:
When you are dead, you should be such a one
As you are now, for you are cold and stern;
And now you should be as your mother was
When your sweet self was got.   10
Dia. She then was honest.
Ber.   So should you be.
Dia.   No:
My mother did but duty; such, my lord,
As you owe to your wife.
Ber.   No more o' that;
I prithee, do not strive against my vows:
I was compell'd to her; but I love thee
By love's own sweet constraint, and will for ever
Do thee all rights of service.
Dia.   Ay, so you serve us
Till we serve you; but when you have our roses,
You barely leave our thorns to prick ourselves
And mock us with our bareness.
Ber.   How have I sworn!   20
Dia. 'Tis not the many oaths that makes the truth,
But the plain single vow that is vow'd true.
What is not holy, that we swear not by,
But take the High'st to witness: then, pray you,
           tell me,
If I should swear by God's great attributes,
I loved you dearly, would you believe my oaths,
When I did love you ill? This has no holding,
To swear by him whom I protest to love,
That I will work against him: therefore your oaths
Are words and poor conditions, but unseal'd,   30
At least in my opinion.
Ber.   Change it, change it;
Be not so holy-cruel: love is holy;
And my integrity ne'er knew the crafts
That you do charge men with. Stand no more off,
But give thyself unto my sick desires,
Who then recover: say thou art mine, and ever
My love as it begins shall so persever.
Dia. †I see that men make ropes in such a scarre
That we'll forsake ourselves. Give me that ring.
Ber. I'll lend it thee, my dear; but have no power   40
To give it from me.
Dia.   Will you not, my lord?
Ber. It is an honour 'longing to our house,
Bequeathed down from many ancestors;
Which were the greatest obloquy i' the world
In me to lose.
Dia.   Mine honour 's such a ring:
My chastity 's the jewel of our house,
Bequeathed down from many ancestors;
Which were the greatest obloquy i' the world
In me to lose: thus your own proper wisdom
Brings in the champion Honour on my part,   50
Against your vain assault.

Ber.   Here, take my ring:
My house, mine honour, yea, my life, be thine,
And I'll be bid by thee.
Dia. When midnight comes, knock at my
           chamber-window:
I'll order take my mother shall not hear.
Now will I charge you in the band of truth,
When you have conquer'd my yet maiden bed,
Remain there but an hour, nor speak to me:
My reasons are most strong; and you shall know
           them
When back again this ring shall be deliver'd: 60
And on your finger in the night I'll put
Another ring, that what in time proceeds
May token to the future our past deeds.
Adieu, till then; then, fail not. You have won
A wife of me, though there my hope be done.
Ber. A heaven on earth I have won by wooing thee.
                                        [*Exit.*

Dia. For which live long to thank both heaven and
           me!
You may so in the end.
My mother told me just how he would woo,
As if she sat in 's heart; she says all men   70
Have the like oaths: he had sworn to marry me
When his wife 's dead; therefore I'll lie with him
When I am buried. Since Frenchmen are so braid,
Marry that will, I live and die a maid:
Only in this disguise I think 't no sin
To cozen him that would unjustly win.   [*Exit.*

SCENE III. *The Florentine camp.*

Enter the two French Lords *and some two or three*
           Soldiers.

First Lord. You have not given him his mother's
letter?
Sec. Lord. I have delivered it an hour since: there is
something in 't that stings his nature; for on the
reading it he changed almost into another man.
First Lord. He has much worthy blame laid upon
him for shaking off so good a wife and so sweet a lady.
Sec. Lord. Especially he hath incurred the everlasting displeasure of the king, who had even tuned
his bounty to sing happiness to him. I will tell you a
thing, but you shall let it dwell darkly with you.   13
First Lord. When you have spoken it, 'tis dead, and
I am the grave of it.
Sec. Lord. He hath perverted a young gentlewoman
here in Florence, of a most chaste renown; and this
night he fleshes his will in the spoil of her honour: he
hath given her his monumental ring, and thinks
himself made in the unchaste composition.   22
First Lord. Now, God delay our rebellion! as we are
ourselves, what things are we!
Sec. Lord. Merely our own traitors. And as in the
common course of all treasons, we still see them
reveal themselves, till they attain to their abhorred
ends, so he that in this action contrives against his
own nobility, in his proper stream o'erflows himself.   30
First Lord. Is it not meant damnable in us, to be

SCENE II. **27. holding,** consistency. **36. Who.** The antecedent is
desires. **38. ropes . . . scarre,** so Ff. *hopes . . . affairs* (Rowe); *hopes
. . . scene* (Malone); *rapes . . . scour* (New Cambridge), *scour* meaning

"a sudden onset." **73. braid,** Scotch form of *broad,* i.e., loose (New
Cambridge).
SCENE III. **24. are ourselves,** unaided by God (Brigstocke). 37.

trumpeters of our unlawful intents? We shall not then have his company to-night?

Sec. Lord. Not till after midnight; for he is dieted to his hour.

First Lord. That approaches apace; I would gladly have him see his company anatomized, that he might take a measure of his own judgements, wherein so curiously he had set this counterfeit. 40

Sec. Lord. We will not meddle with him till he come; for his presence must be the whip of the other.

First Lord. In the mean time, what hear you of these wars?

Sec. Lord. I hear there is an overture of peace.

First Lord. Nay, I assure you, a peace concluded.

Sec. Lord. What will Count Rousillon do then? will he travel higher, or return again into France? 51

First Lord. I perceive, by this demand, you are not altogether of his council.

Sec. Lord. Let it be forbid, sir; so should I be a great deal of his act.

First Lord. Sir, his wife some two months since fled from his house: her pretence is a pilgrimage to Saint Jaques le Grand; which holy undertaking with most austere sanctimony she accomplished; and, there residing, the tenderness of her nature became as a prey to her grief; in fine, made a groan of her last breath, and now she sings in heaven. 63

Sec. Lord. How is this justified?

First Lord. The stronger part of it by her own letters, which makes her story true, even to the point of her death: her death itself, which could not be her office to say is come, was faithfully confirmed by the rector of the place.

Sec. Lord. Hath the count all this intelligence? 70

First Lord. Ay, and the particular confirmations, point from point, to the full arming of the verity.

Sec. Lord. I am heartily sorry that he'll be glad of this.

First Lord. How mightily sometimes we make us comforts of our losses!

Sec. Lord. And how mightily some other times we drown our gain in tears! The great dignity that his valour hath here acquired for him shall at home be encountered with a shame as ample. 82

First Lord. The web of our life is of a mingled yarn, good and ill together: our virtues would be proud, if our faults whipped them not; and our crimes would despair, if they were not cherished by our virtues.

Enter a Messenger.

How now! where 's your master?

Serv. He met the duke in the street, sir, of whom he hath taken a solemn leave: his lordship will next morning for France. The duke hath offered him letters of commendations to the king. 92

Sec. Lord. They shall be no more than needful there, if they were more than they can commend.

First Lord. They cannot be too sweet for the king's tartness. Here 's his lordship now.

Enter BERTRAM.

How now, my lord! is 't not after midnight?

Ber. I have to-night dispatched sixteen businesses,

a month's length a-piece, by an abstract of success: I have congied with the duke, done my adieu with his nearest; buried a wife, mourned for her; writ to my lady mother I am returning; entertained my convoy; and between these main parcels of dispatch effected many nicer needs: the last was the greatest, but that I have not ended yet.

Sec. Lord. If the business be of any difficulty, and this morning your departure hence, it requires haste of your lordship. 109

Ber. I mean, the business is not ended, as fearing to hear of it hereafter. But shall we have this dialogue between the fool and the soldier? Come, bring forth this counterfeit module, has deceived me, like a double-meaning prophesier.

Sec. Lord. Bring him forth: has sat i' the stocks all night, poor gallant knave. 117

Ber. No matter; his heels have deserved it, in usurping his spurs so long. How does he carry himself?

Sec. Lord. I have told your lordship already, the stocks carry him. But to answer you as you would be understood; he weeps like a wench that had shed her milk: he hath confessed himself to Morgan, whom he supposes to be a friar, from the time of his remembrance to this very instant disaster of his setting i' the stocks: and what think you he hath confessed?

Ber. Nothing of me, has a'? 129

Sec. Lord. His confession is taken, and it shall be read to his face: if your lordship be in 't, as I believe you are, you must have the patience to hear it.

Enter PAROLLES *guarded, and* First Soldier.

Ber. A plague upon him! muffled! he can say nothing of me: hush, hush!

First Lord. Hoodman comes! Portotartarosa.

First Sold. He calls for the tortures: what will you say without 'em?

Par. I will confess what I know without constraint: if ye pinch me like a pasty, I can say no more. 141

First Sold. Bosko chimurcho.

First Lord. Boblibindo chicurmurco.

First Sold. You are a merciful general. Our general bids you answer to what I shall ask you out of a note.

Par. And truly, as I hope to live.

First Sold. [*Reads*] 'First demand of him how many horse the duke is strong.' What say you to that? 150

Par. Five or six thousand; but very weak and unserviceable: the troops are all scattered, and the commanders very poor rogues, upon my reputation and credit and as I hope to live.

First Sold. Shall I set down your answer so?

Par. Do: I'll take the sacrament on 't, how and which way you will.

Ber. All 's one to him. What a past-saving slave is this! 159

First Lord. You 're deceived, my lord: this is Monsieur Parolles, the gallant militarist,—that was his own phrase,—that had the whole theoric of war in the knot of his scarf, and the practice in the chape of his dagger.

Sec. Lord. I will never trust a man again for keeping his sword clean, nor believe he can have every thing in him by wearing his apparel neatly.

---

company, companion. anatomized, dissected, analyzed. 40. this counterfeit, refers to Parolles; cf. l. 113. 50. travel higher, i.e., go to the mountainous districts of Italy—Tuscany; cf. II, i, 12. 59.

sanctimony, holiness. 64. justified, made certain. 69. rector, governor. 114. module, mere image. 136. Hoodman comes, customary call in the game of blindman's buff when the blindfold man enters the ring.

First Sold. Well, that 's set down. 169

Par. Five or six thousand horse, I said,—I will say true,—or thereabouts, set down, for I'll speak truth.

First Lord. He 's very near the truth in this.

Ber. But I con him no thanks for 't, in the nature he delivers it.

Par. Poor rogues, I pray you, say.

First Sold. Well, that 's set down.

Par. I humbly thank you, sir: a truth 's a truth, the rogues are marvellous poor. 179

First Sold. [*Reads*] 'Demand of him, of what strength they are a-foot.' What say you to that?

Par. By my troth, sir, if I were to live this present hour, I will tell true. Let me see: Spurio, a hundred and fifty; Sebastian, so many; Corambus, so many; Jaques, so many; Guiltian, Cosmo, Lodowick, and Gratii, two hundred and fifty each; mine own company, Chitopher, Vaumond, Bentii, two hundred and fifty each: so that the muster-file, rotten and sound, upon my life, amounts not to fifteen thousand poll; half of the which dare not shake the snow from off their cassocks, lest they shake themselves to pieces.

Ber. What shall be done to him? 194

First Lord. Nothing, but let him have thanks. Demand of him my condition, and what credit I have with the duke.

First Sold. Well, that 's set down. [*Reads*] 'You shall demand of him, whether one Captain Dumain be i' the camp, a Frenchman; what his reputation is with the duke; what his valour, honesty, and expertness in wars; or whether he thinks it were not possible, with well-weighing sums of gold, to corrupt him to a revolt.' What say you to this? what do you know of it?

Par. I beseech you, let me answer to the particular of the inter'gatories: demand them singly.

First Sold. Do you know this Captain Dumain? 210

Par. I know him: a' was a botcher's 'prentice in Paris, from whence he was whipped for getting the shrieve's fool with child,—a dumb innocent, that could not say him nay.

Ber. Nay, by your leave, hold your hands; though I know his brains are forfeit to the next tile that falls.

First Sold. Well, is this captain in the duke of Florence's camp?

Par. Upon my knowledge, he is, and lousy. 220

First Lord. Nay, look not so upon me; we shall hear of your lordship anon.

First Sold. What is his reputation with the duke?

Par. The duke knows him for no other but a poor officer of mine; and writ to me this other day to turn him out o' the band: I think I have his letter in my pocket.

First Sold. Marry, we'll search. 229

Par. In good sadness, I do not know; either it is there, or it is upon a file with the duke's other letters in my tent.

First Sold. Here 'tis; here 's a paper: shall I read it to you?

Par. I do not know if it be it or no.

Ber. Our interpreter does it well.

First Lord. Excellently.

First Sold. [*Reads*] 'Dian, the count 's a fool, and full of gold,'— 238

Par. That is not the duke's letter, sir; that is an advertisement to a proper maid in Florence, one Diana, to take heed of the allurement of one Count Rousillon, a foolish idle boy, but for all that very ruttish: I pray you, sir, put it up again.

First Sold. Nay, I'll read it first, by your favour.

Par. My meaning in 't, I protest, was very honest in the behalf of the maid; for I knew the young count to be a dangerous and lascivious boy, who is a whale to virginity and devours up all the fry it finds. 250

Ber. Damnable both-sides rogue!

First Sold. [*Reads*] 'When he swears oaths, bid him drop gold, and take it;
After he scores, he never pays the score:
Half won is match well made; match, and well make it;
He ne'er pays after-debts, take it before;
And say a soldier, Dian, told thee this,
Men are to mell with, boys are not to kiss:
For count of this, the count 's a fool, I know it,
Who pays before, but not when he does owe it.
    Thine, as he vowed to thee in thine ear,
                                    PAROLLES.'

Ber. He shall be whipped through the army with this rhyme in 's forehead.

Sec. Lord. This is your devoted friend, sir, the manifold linguist and the armipotent soldier.

Ber. I could endure any thing before but a cat, and now he 's a cat to me.

First Sold. I perceive, sir, by the general's looks, we shall be fain to hang you. 269

Par. My life, sir, in any case: not that I am afraid to die; but that, my offences being many, I would repent out the remainder of nature: let me live, sir, in a dungeon, i' the stocks, or any where, so I may live.

First Sold. We'll see what may be done, so you confess freely; therefore, once more to this Captain Dumain: you have answered to his reputation with the duke and to his valour: what is his honesty? 279

Par. He will steal, sir, an egg out of a cloister: for rapes and ravishments he parallels Nessus: he professes not keeping of oaths; in breaking 'em he is stronger than Hercules: he will lie, sir, with such volubility, that you would think truth were a fool: drunkenness is his best virtue, for he will be swine-drunk; and in his sleep he does little harm, save to his bed-clothes about him; but they know his conditions and lay him in straw. I have but little more to say, sir, of his honesty: he has every thing that an honest man should not have; what an honest man should have, he has nothing. 292

First Lord. I begin to love him for this.

Ber. For this description of thine honesty? A pox upon him for me, he 's more and more a cat.

First Sold. What say you to his expertness in war?

Par. Faith, sir, has led the drum before the English tragedians; to belie him, I will not, and more of his soldiership I know not; except, in that country he had the honour to be the officer at a place there called Mile-end, to instruct for the doubling of files: I would do the man what honour I can, but of this I am not certain. 304

211. **botcher's**, mender's, especially a tailor who makes repairs. 213. **shrieve's**, sheriff's. 240. **advertisement**, advice, counsel. 257. **mell**, meddle. 265. **armipotent**, powerful in arms. 272. **remainder of nature**, i.e., what is left of my life. 281. **Nessus**, a centaur who offered

violence to the wife of Hercules. 298-299. **led . . . tragedians.** It was a custom of actors to parade the street before the performance of a play. 302. **Mile-end**, place near London where the trainbands were regularly exercised. 311. **quart d'écu**, eight pence. 333. **supposition,**

First Lord. He hath out-villained villany so far, that the rarity redeems him.

Ber. A pox on him, he 's a cat still.

First Sold. His qualities being at this poor price, I need not to ask you if gold will corrupt him to revolt.

Par. Sir, for a quart d'écu he will sell the fee-simple of his salvation, the inheritance of it; and cut the entail from all remainders, and a perpetual succession for it perpetually.

First Sold. What 's his brother, the other Captain Dumain?

Sec. Lord. Why does he ask him of me?

First Sold. What 's he? 318

Par. E'en a crow o' the same nest; not altogether so great as the first in goodness, but greater a great deal in evil: he excels his brother for a coward, yet his brother is reputed one of the best that is: in a retreat he outruns any lackey; marry, in coming on he has the cramp.

First Sold. If your life be saved, will you undertake to betray the Florentine?

Par. Ay, and the captain of his horse, Count Rousillon.

First Sold. I'll whisper with the general, and know his pleasure. 330

Par. [*Aside*] I'll no more drumming; a plague of all drums! Only to seem to deserve well, and to beguile the supposition of that lascivious young boy the count, have I run into this danger. Yet who would have suspected an ambush where I was taken?

First Sold. There is no remedy, sir, but you must die: the general says, you that have so traitorously discovered the secrets of your army and made such pestiferous reports of men very nobly held, can serve the world for no honest use; therefore you must die. Come, headsman, off with his head.

Par. O Lord, sir, let me live, or let me see my death!

First Sold. That shall you, and take your leave of all your friends. [*Unblinding him.*] So, look about you: know you any here?

Ber. Good morrow, noble captain.

Sec. Lord. God bless you, Captain Parolles. 350

First Lord. God save you, noble captain.

Sec. Lord. Captain, what greeting will you to my Lord Lafeu? I am for France.

First Lord. Good captain, will you give me a copy of the sonnet you writ to Diana in behalf of the Count Rousillon? an I were not a very coward, I 'ld compel it of you: but fare you well.

[*Exeunt Bertram and Lords.*

First Sold. You are undone, captain, all but your scarf; that has a knot on 't yet. 359

Par. Who cannot be crushed with a plot?

First Sold. If you could find out a country where but women were that had received so much shame, you might begin an impudent nation. Fare ye well, sir; I am for France too: we shall speak of you there.

[*Exit, with Soldiers.*

Par. Yet am I thankful: if my heart were great,
'Twould burst at this. Captain I'll be no more;
But I will eat and drink, and sleep as soft
As captain shall: simply the thing I am
Shall make me live. Who knows himself a braggart, 370

Let him fear this, for it will come to pass
That every braggart shall be found an ass.
Rust, sword! cool, blushes! and, Parolles, live
Safest in shame! being fool'd, by foolery thrive!
There 's place and means for every man alive.
I'll after them. [*Exit.*

SCENE IV. *Florence. The* Widow's *house.*

Enter HELENA, Widow, *and* DIANA.

Hel. That you may well perceive I have not
   wrong'd you,
One of the greatest in the Christian world
Shall be my surety; 'fore whose throne 'tis needful,
Ere I can perfect mine intents, to kneel:
Time was, I did him a desired office,
Dear almost as his life; which gratitude
Through flinty Tartar's bosom would peep forth,
And answer, thanks: I duly am inform'd
His grace is at Marseilles; to which place
We have convenient convoy. You must know, 10
I am supposed dead: the army breaking,
My husband hies him home; where, heaven aiding,
And by the leave of my good lord the king,
We'll be before our welcome.

Wid.   Gentle madam,
You never had a servant to whose trust
Your business was more welcome.

Hel.   Nor you, mistress,
Ever a friend whose thoughts more truly labour
To recompense your love: doubt not but heaven
Hath brought me up to be your daughter's dower,
As it hath fated her to be my motive 20
And helper to a husband. But, O strange men!
That can such sweet use make of what they hate,
When saucy trusting of the cozen'd thoughts
Defiles the pitchy night: so lust doth play
With what it loathes for that which is away.
But more of this hereafter. You, Diana,
Under my poor instructions yet must suffer
Something in my behalf.

Dia.   Let death and honesty
Go with your impositions, I am yours
Upon your will to suffer.

Hel.   Yet, I pray you: 30
But with the word the time will bring on summer,
When briers shall have leaves as well as thorns,
And be as sweet as sharp. We must away;
Our waggon is prepared, and time revives us:
ALL'S WELL THAT ENDS WELL: still the fine 's the
   crown;
Whate'er the course, the end is the renown. [*Exeunt.*

SCENE V. *Rousillon. The* COUNT's *palace.*

Enter COUNTESS, LAFEU, *and* CLOWN.

Laf. No, no, no, your son was misled with a snipt-taffeta fellow there, whose villanous saffron would have made all the unbaked and doughy youth of a

suspicion. 366. **great,** full or "big" with emotion or pride.
  SCENE IV. 11. **breaking,** demobilizing. 20. **motive,** promoter, instigator.
  SCENE V. 2. **snipt-taffeta,** wearing notched or serrated garments of

taffeta. **saffron,** vegetable coloring used in making pastry; applied here to the fashionable wearing of yellow.

nation in his colour: your daughter-in-law had been alive at this hour, and your son here at home, more advanced by the king than by that red-tailed humble-bee I speak of. 7

Count. I would I had not known him; it was the death of the most virtuous gentlewoman that ever nature had praise for creating. If she had partaken of my flesh, and cost me the dearest groans of a mother, I could not have owed her a more rooted love.

Laf. 'Twas a good lady, 'twas a good lady: we may pick a thousand salads ere we light on such another herb.

Clo. Indeed, sir, she was the sweet-marjoram of the salad, or rather, the herb of grace.

Laf. They are not herbs, you knave; they are nose-herbs. 20

Clo. I am no great Nebuchadnezzar, sir; I have not much skill in grass.

Laf. Whether dost thou profess thyself, a knave or a fool?

Clo. A fool, sir, at a woman's service, and a knave at a man's.

Laf. Your distinction?

Clo. I would cozen the man of his wife and do his service. 30

Laf. So you were a knave at his service, indeed.

Clo. And I would give his wife my bauble, sir, to do her service.

Laf. I will subscribe for thee, thou art both knave and fool.

Clo. At your service.

Laf. No, no, no.

Clo. Why, sir, if I cannot serve you, I can serve as great a prince as you are.

Laf. Who 's that? a Frenchman? 40

Clo. Faith, sir, a' has an English name; but his fisnomy is more hotter in France than there.

Laf. What prince is that?

Clo. The black prince, sir; alias, the prince of darkness; alias, the devil.

Laf. Hold thee, there 's my purse: I give thee not this to suggest thee from thy master thou talkest of; serve him still. 48

Clo. I am a woodland fellow, sir, that always loved a great fire; and the master I speak of ever keeps a good fire. But, sure, he is the prince of the world; let his nobility remain in 's court. I am for the house with the narrow gate, which I take to be too little for pomp to enter: some that humble themselves may; but the many will be too chill and tender, and they'll be for the flowery way that leads to the broad gate and the great fire. 57

Laf. Go thy ways, I begin to be aweary of thee; and I tell thee so before, because I would not fall out with thee. Go thy ways: let my horses be well looked to, without any tricks.

Clo. If I put any tricks upon 'em, sir, they shall be jades' tricks; which are their own right by the law of nature. [*Exit*.

Laf. A shrewd knave and an unhappy.

Count. So he is. My lord that 's gone made himself

much sport out of him: by his authority he remains here, which he thinks is a patent for his sauciness; and, indeed, he has no pace, but runs where he will. 71

Laf. I like him well; 'tis not amiss. And I was about to tell you, since I heard of the good lady's death and that my lord your son was upon his return home, I moved the king my master to speak in the behalf of my daughter; which, in the minority of them both, his majesty, out of a self-gracious remembrance, did first propose: his highness hath promised me to do it: and, to stop up the displeasure he hath conceived against your son, there is no fitter matter. How does your ladyship like it? 82

Count. With very much content, my lord; and I wish it happily effected.

Laf. His highness comes post from Marseilles, of as able body as when he numbered thirty: he will be here to-morrow, or I am deceived by him that in such intelligence hath seldom failed.

Count. It rejoices me, that I hope I shall see him ere I die. I have letters that my son will be here to-night: I shall beseech your lordship to remain with me till they meet together. 91

Laf. Madam, I was thinking with what manners I might safely be admitted.

Count. You need but plead your honourable privilege.

Laf. Lady, of that I have made a bold charter; but I thank my God it holds yet.

Re-enter CLOWN.

Clo. O madam, yonder 's my lord your son with a patch of velvet on 's face: whether there be a scar under 't or no, the velvet knows; but 'tis a goodly patch of velvet: his left cheek is a cheek of two pile and a half, but his right cheek is worn bare.

Laf. A scar nobly got, or a noble scar, is a good livery of honour; so belike is that.

Clo. But it is your carbonadoed face.

Laf. Let us go see your son, I pray you: I long to talk with the young noble soldier. 109

Clo. Faith, there 's a dozen of 'em, with delicate fine hats and most courteous feathers, which bow the head and nod at every man. [*Exeunt*.

ACT V.

SCENE I. *Marseilles. A street.*

Enter HELENA, Widow, *and* DIANA, *with two* Attendants.

Hel. But this exceeding posting day and night
Must wear your spirits low; we cannot help it:
But since you have made the days and nights as one
To wear your gentle limbs in my affairs,
Be bold you do so grow in my requital
As nothing can unroot you. In happy time;

Enter a Gentleman.

This man may help me to his majesty's ear,
If he would spend his power. God save you, sir.

19. **not herbs.** The New Cambridge editors emend to *knot-herbs*, i.e., garden flowers used in knot gardens—ingeniously designed flower beds (cf. *curious-knotted garden, Love's Labour's Lost*, I, i, 249); Rowe and others emended to *not salad herbs*. 20. **nose-herbs,** fragrant herbs used for bouquets, not salads. 21-22. **Nebuchadnezzar . . . grass.** Cf. Daniel

4:5, the account of Nebuchadnezzar's dream and its fulfillment—that his heart became like the beasts', his dwelling with the wild asses, and his food grass. 32. **bauble,** stick carried by a court fool. 41. **English name,** i.e., the Black Prince. 42. **fisnomy,** physiognomy. 107. **carbonadoed,** scored across with gashes (as meat for broiling).

Gent. And you.

Hel. Sir, I have seen you in the court of France. 10

Gent. I have been sometimes there.

Hel. I do presume, sir, that you are not fallen
From the report that goes upon your goodness;
And therefore, goaded with most sharp occasions,
Which lay nice manners by, I put you to
The use of your own virtues, for the which
I shall continue thankful.

Gent. What 's your will?

Hel. That it will please you
To give this poor petition to the king,
And aid me with that store of power you have 20
To come into his presence.

Gent. The king 's not here.

Hel. Not here, sir!

Gent. Not, indeed:
He hence removed last night and with more haste
Than is his use.

Wid. Lord, how we lose our pains!

Hel. ALL'S WELL THAT ENDS WELL yet,
Though time seem so adverse and means unfit.
I do beseech you, whither is he gone?

Gent. Marry, as I take it, to Rousillon;
Whither I am going.

Hel. I do beseech you, sir,
Since you are like to see the king before me, 30
Commend the paper to his gracious hand,
Which I presume shall render you no blame
But rather make you thank your pains for it.
I will come after you with what good speed
Our means will make us means.

Gent. This I'll do for you.

Hel. And you shall find yourself to be well thank'd,
Whate'er falls more. We must to horse again.
Go, go, provide. [*Exeunt.*

SCENE II. *Rousillon. Before the* COUNT's *palace.*

Enter CLOWN, *and* PAROLLES, *following.*

Par. Good Monsieur Lavache, give my Lord Lafeu
this letter: I have ere now, sir, been better known to
you, when I have held familiarity with fresher
clothes; but I am now, sir, muddied in fortune's
mood, and smell somewhat strong of her strong displeasure.

Clo. Truly, fortune's displeasure is but sluttish, if
it smell so strongly as thou speakest of: I will henceforth eat no fish of fortune's buttering. Prithee, allow
the wind. 10

Par. Nay, you need not to stop your nose, sir; I
spake but by a metaphor.

Clo. Indeed, sir, if your metaphor stink, I will stop
my nose; or against any man's metaphor. Prithee,
get thee further.

Par. Pray you, sir, deliver me this paper.

Clo. Foh! prithee, stand away: a paper from fortune's close-stool to give to a nobleman! Look, here
he comes himself. 19

Enter LAFEU.

Here is a purr of fortune's, sir, or of fortune's cat,—
but not a musk-cat,—that has fallen into the unclean
fishpond of her displeasure, and, as he says, is
muddied withal: pray you, sir, use the carp as you
may; for he looks like a poor, decayed, ingenious,
foolish, rascally knave. I do pity his distress in my
similes of comfort and leave him to your lordship. [*Exit.*

Par. My lord, I am a man whom fortune hath
cruelly scratched. 29

Laf. And what would you have me to do? 'Tis too
late to pare her nails now. Wherein have you played
the knave with fortune, that she should scratch you,
who of herself is a good lady and would not have
knaves thrive long under her? There 's a quart d'écu
for you: let the justices make you and fortune friends:
I am for other business.

Par. I beseech your honour to hear me one single
word.

Laf. You beg a single penny more: come, you shall
ha 't; save your word. 40

Par. My name, my good lord, is Parolles.

Laf. You beg more than 'word,' then. Cox my
passion! give me your hand. How does your drum?

Par. O my good lord, you were the first that found
me!

Laf. Was I, in sooth? and I was the first that lost
thee.

Par. It lies in you, my lord, to bring me in some
grace, for you did bring me out. 50

Laf. Out upon thee, knave! dost thou put upon me
at once both the office of God and the devil? One
brings thee in grace and the other brings thee out.
[*Trumpets sound.*] The king 's coming; I know by his
trumpets. Sirrah, inquire further after me; I had
talk of you last night: though you are a fool and a
knave, you shall eat; go to, follow.

Par. I praise God for you. [*Exeunt.* 59

SCENE III. *Rousillon. The* COUNT's *palace.*

Flourish. Enter KING, COUNTESS, LAFEU, *the two*
French Lords, *with* Attendants.

King. We lost a jewel of her; and our esteem
Was made much poorer by it: but your son,
As mad in folly, lack'd the sense to know
Her estimation home.

Count. 'Tis past, my liege;
And I beseech your majesty to make it
Natural rebellion, done i' the blaze of youth;
When oil and fire, too strong for reason's force,
O'erbears it and burns on.

King. My honour'd lady,
I have forgiven and forgotten all;
Though my revenges were high bent upon him, 10
And watch'd the time to shoot.

Laf. This I must say,
But first I beg my pardon, the young lord
Did to his majesty, his mother and his lady
Offence of mighty note; but to himself
The greatest wrong of all. He lost a wife
Whose beauty did astonish the survey

All's Well
that Ends Well
ACT V : SC III

829

ACT V. SCENE I. 5. **bold,** sure.
SCENE II. 10. **allow the wind,** let me have the windward side of you.
25. **ingenious,** tricky. 35. **for you.** Here the New Cambridge editors
insert the stage direction "he gives him a coin"; after *save your word*
(l. 40) they insert "he gives him another coin." 41-42. **Parolles . . .**

'**word,**' a pun on Parolles' name, which suggests the French *parole,* meaning "word." 42. **Cox,** a perversion of *God's,* sometimes spelled *Cock's.*
SCENE III. 1. **esteem,** estimated value. 6-8. **Natural . . . O'er-**
bears it. Cf. the countess' characterization of Bertram, I, i, 71-72.

Of richest eyes, whose words all ears took captive,
Whose dear perfection hearts that scorn'd to serve
Humbly call'd mistress.
    King.   Praising what is lost
Makes the remembrance dear. Well, call him hither;
We are reconciled, and the first view shall kill   21
All repetition: let him not ask our pardon;
The nature of his great offence is dead,
And deeper than oblivion we do bury
The incensing relics of it: let him approach,
A stranger, no offender; and inform him
So 'tis our will he should.
    Gent.   I shall, my liege.   [*Exit.*
    King. What says he to your daughter? have you
      spoke?
    Laf. All that he is hath reference to your highness.
    King. Then shall we have a match. I have letters
      sent me   30
That set him high in fame.

Enter BERTRAM.

    Laf.   He looks well on 't.
    King. I am not a day of season,
For thou mayst see a sunshine and a hail
In me at once: but to the brightest beams
Distracted clouds give way; so stand thou forth;
The time is fair again.
    Ber.   My high-repented blames,
Dear sovereign, pardon to me.
    King.   All is whole;
Not one word more of the consumed time.
Let 's take the instant by the forward top;
For we are old, and on our quick'st decrees   40
The inaudible and noiseless foot of Time
Steals ere we can effect them. You remember
The daughter of this lord?
    Ber. Admiringly, my liege, at first
I stuck my choice upon her, ere my heart
Durst make too bold a herald of my tongue:
Where the impression of mine eye infixing,
Contempt his scornful perspective did lend me,
Which warp'd the line of every other favour;
Scorn'd a fair colour, or express'd it stolen;   50
Extended or contracted all proportions
To a most hideous object: thence it came
That she whom all men praised and whom myself,
Since I have lost, have loved, was in mine eye
The dust that did offend it.
    King.   Well excused:
That thou didst love her, strikes some scores away
From the great compt: but love that comes too late,
Like a remorseful pardon slowly carried,
To the great sender turns a sour offence,
Crying, 'That 's good that 's gone.' Our rash faults   60
Make trivial price of serious things we have,
Not knowing them until we know their grave:
Oft our displeasures, to ourselves unjust,
Destroy our friends and after weep their dust:
†Our own love waking cries to see what 's done,
While shameful hate sleeps out the afternoon.
Be this sweet Helen's knell, and now forget her.
Send forth your amorous token for fair Maudlin:

The main consents are had; and here we'll stay
To see our widower's second marriage-day.   70
    Count. Which better than the first, O dear heaven,
      bless!
Or, ere they meet, in me, O nature, cesse!
    Laf. Come on, my son, in whom my house's name
Must be digested, give a favour from you
To sparkle in the spirits of my daughter,
That she may quickly come. [*Bertram gives a ring.*] By
      my old beard,
And every hair that 's on 't, Helen, that 's dead,
Was a sweet creature: such a ring as this,
The last that e'er I took her leave at court,
I saw upon her finger.
    Ber.   Hers it was not.   80
    King. Now, pray you, let me see it; for mine eye,
While I was speaking, oft was fasten'd to 't.
This ring was mine; and, when I gave it Helen,
I bade her, if her fortunes ever stood
Necessitied to help, that by this token
I would relieve her. Had you that craft, to reave her
Of what should stead her most?
    Ber.   My gracious sovereign,
Howe'er it pleases you to take it so,
The ring was never hers.
    Count.   Son, on my life,
I have seen her wear it; and she reckon'd it   90
At her life's rate.
    Laf.   I am sure I saw her wear it.
    Ber. You are deceived, my lord; she never saw it:
In Florence was it from a casement thrown me,
Wrapp'd in a paper, which contain'd the name
Of her that threw it: noble she was, and thought
I stood ingag'd: but when I had subscribed
To mine own fortune and inform'd her fully
I could not answer in that course of honour
As she had made the overture, she ceased
In heavy satisfaction and would never   100
Receive the ring again.
    King.   Plutus himself,
That knows the tinct and multiplying medicine,
Hath not in nature's mystery more science
Than I have in this ring: 'twas mine, 'twas Helen's,
Whoever gave it you. Then, if you know
That you are well acquainted with yourself,
Confess 'twas hers, and by what rough enforcement
You got it from her; she call'd the saints to surety
That she would never put it from her finger,
Unless she gave it to yourself in bed,   110
Where you have never come, or sent it us
Upon her great disaster.
    Ber.   She never saw it.
    King. Thou speak'st it falsely, as I love mine honour;
And makest conjectural fears to come into me,
Which I would fain shut out. If it should prove
That thou art so inhuman,—'twill not prove so;—
And yet I know not: thou didst hate her deadly,
And she is dead; which nothing, but to close
Her eyes myself, could win me to believe,
More than to see this ring. Take him away.   120
                    [*Guards seize Bertram.*
My fore-past proofs, howe'er the matter fall,

---

22. **repetition,** mention of what is past. 32. **day of season,** seasonable day. 36. **blames,** i.e., faults for which I am to blame. 48. **perspective,** a metaphor from the optical glass for producing distorted images. 57. **compt,** reckoning. 66. **shameful hate,** so F; Globe: *shame full late;* Brigstocke's paraphrase: Hate has done its best and now sleeps at

ease. 72. **cesse,** cease. 74. **digested,** amalgamated. 85. **Necessitied to,** in need of. 96. **ingag'd,** not pledged; the prefix has negative force; so F; Globe: *engaged.* 100. **heavy satisfaction,** doleful resignation. 101. **Plutus,** the god of wealth. 102. **tinct . . . medicine,** the alchemical process of transmuting base metals into gold. 103. **science,** knowledge.

Shall tax my fears of little vanity,
Having vainly fear'd too little. Away with him!
We'll sift this matter further.
 Ber.   If you shall prove
This ring was ever hers, you shall as easy
Prove that I husbanded her bed in Florence,
Where yet she never was.   [*Exit, guarded*.
 King. I am wrapp'd in dismal thinkings.

 Enter a Gentleman.

 Gent.   Gracious sovereign,
Whether I have been to blame or no, I know not:
Here 's a petition from a Florentine,   130
Who hath for four or five removes come short
To tender it herself. I undertook it,
Vanquish'd thereto by the fair grace and speech
Of the poor suppliant, who by this I know
Is here attending: her business looks in her
With an importing visage; and she told me,
In a sweet verbal brief, it did concern
Your highness with herself.   138
 King. [*Reads*] Upon his many protestations to
marry me when his wife was dead, I blush to say it,
he won me. Now is the Count Rousillon a widower:
his vows are forfeited to me, and my honour 's paid
to him. He stole from Florence, taking no leave, and I
follow him to his country for justice: grant it me, O
king! in you it best lies; otherwise a seducer flourishes,
and a poor maid is undone.   DIANA CAPILET.
 Laf. I will buy me a son-in-law in a fair, and toll for
this: I'll none of him.
 King. The heavens have thought well on thee,
  Lafeu,   150
To bring forth this discovery. Seek these suitors:
Go speedily and bring again the count.
I am afeard the life of Helen, lady,
Was foully snatch'd.
 Count.   Now, justice on the doers!

 Re-enter BERTRAM, *guarded*.

 King. I wonder, sir, sith wives are monsters to you,
And that you fly them as you swear them lordship,
Yet you desire to marry.

 Enter Widow *and* DIANA.

       What woman 's that?
 Dia. I am, my lord, a wretched Florentine,
Derived from the ancient Capilet:
My suit, as I do understand, you know,   160
And therefore know how far I may be pitied.
 Wid. I am her mother, sir, whose age and honour
Both suffer under this complaint we bring,
And both shall cease, without your remedy.
 King. Come hither, count; do you know these
  women?
 Ber. My lord, I neither can nor will deny
But that I know them: do they charge me further?
 Dia. Why do you look so strange upon your wife?
 Ber. She 's none of mine, my lord.
 Dia.   If you shall marry,
You give away this hand, and that is mine; 170
You give away heaven's vows, and those are mine;
You give away myself, which is known mine;

For I by vow am so embodied yours,
That she which marries you must marry me,
Either both or none.
 Laf. Your reputation comes too short for my
daughter; you are no husband for her.
 Ber. My lord, this is a fond and desperate creature,
Whom sometime I have laugh'd with: let your
  highness
Lay a more noble thought upon mine honour 180
Than for to think that I would sink it here.
 King. Sir, for my thoughts, you have them ill to
  friend
Till your deeds gain them: fairer prove your honour
Than in my thought it lies.
 Dia.   Good my lord,
Ask him upon his oath, if he does think
He had not my virginity.
 King. What say'st thou to her?
 Ber.   She 's impudent, my lord,
And was a common gamester to the camp.
 Dia. He does me wrong, my lord; if I were so,
He might have bought me at a common price: 190
Do not believe him. O, behold this ring,
Whose high respect and rich validity
Did lack a parallel; yet for all that
He gave it to a commoner o' the camp,
If I be one.
 Count.   He blushes, and 'tis it:
Of six preceding ancestors, that gem,
Conferr'd by testament to the sequent issue,
Hath it been owed and worn. This is his wife;
That ring 's a thousand proofs.
 King.   Methought you said
You saw one here in court could witness it. 200
 Dia. I did, my lord, but loath am to produce
So bad an instrument: his name 's Parolles.
 Laf. I saw the man to-day, if man he be.
 King. Find him, and bring him hither.
            [*Exit an Attendant*.
 Ber.   What of him?
He 's quoted for a most perfidious slave,
With all the spots o' the world tax'd and debosh'd;
Whose nature sickens but to speak a truth.
Am I or that or this for what he'll utter,
That will speak any thing?
 King.   She hath that ring of yours.
 Ber. I think she has: certain it is I liked her, 210
And boarded her i' the wanton way of youth:
She knew her distance and did angle for me,
Madding my eagerness with her restraint,
As all impediments in fancy's course
Are motives of more fancy; and, in fine,
Her infinite cunning, with her modern grace,
Subdued me to her rate: she got the ring;
And I had that which any inferior might
At market-price have bought.
 Dia.   I must be patient:
You, that have turn'd off a first so noble wife, 220
May justly diet me. I pray you yet;
Since you lack virtue, I will lose a husband;
Send for your ring, I will return it home,
And give me mine again.

---

114. **conjectural,** suspicious. 121. **fore-past,** previous. 122. **of little
vanity,** of not much substance. 149. **toll for,** take out a license for
selling. 182. **to friend,** as a friend. 188. **gamester,** prostitute. 197.
sequent issue, the next heir. 211. **boarded,** accosted. 221. **diet,**
restrict, cause to conform (Onions); be loath or weary of (Malone);

deprive, i.e., of the rites of love (Collins); the New Cambridge editors
derive it from *dieta* (medieval Latin), a day's work and wage, and
explain: send me packing after a day's work.

Ber. I have it not.

King. What ring was yours, I pray you?

Dia. Sir, much like
The same upon your finger.

King. Know you this ring? this ring was his of late.

Dia. And this was it I gave him, being abed.

King. The story then goes false, you threw it him
Out of a casement.

Dia. I have spoke the truth. 230

Enter PAROLLES.

Ber. My lord, I do confess the ring was hers.

King. You boggle shrewdly, every feather starts you.
Is this the man you speak of?

Dia. Ay, my lord.

King. Tell me, sirrah, but tell me true, I charge you,
Not fearing the displeasure of your master,
Which on your just proceeding I'll keep off,
By him and by this woman here what know you?

Par. So please your majesty, my master hath been
an honourable gentleman: tricks he hath had in him,
which gentlemen have. 240

King. Come, come, to the purpose: did he love this
woman?

Par. Faith, sir, he did love her; but how?

King. How, I pray you?

Par. He did love her, sir, as a gentleman loves a
woman.

King. How is that?

Par. He loved her, sir, and loved her not.

King. As thou art a knave, and no knave.
What an equivocal companion is this! 250

Par. I am a poor man, and at your majesty's command.

Laf. He's a good drum, my lord, but a naughty
orator.

Dia. Do you know he promised me marriage?

Par. Faith, I know more than I'll speak.

King. But wilt thou not speak all thou knowest?

Par. Yes, so please your majesty. I did go between
them, as I said; but more than that, he loved her: for
indeed he was mad for her, and talked of Satan and
of Limbo and of Furies and I know not what: yet
I was in that credit with them at that time that I
knew of their going to bed, and of other motions, as
promising her marriage, and things which would
derive me ill will to speak of; therefore I will not
speak what I know. 267

King. Thou hast spoken all already, unless thou
canst say they are married: but thou art too fine in
thy evidence; therefore stand aside. This ring, you
say, was yours?

Dia. Ay, my good lord.

King. Where did you buy it? or who gave it you?

Dia. It was not given me, nor I did not buy it.

King. Who lent it you?

Dia. It was not lent me neither.

King. Where did you find it, then?

Dia. I found it not.

King. If it were yours by none of all these ways,
How could you give it him?

Dia. I never gave it him.

Laf. This woman's an easy glove, my lord; she
goes off and on at pleasure.

King. This ring was mine; I gave it his first wife. 280

Dia. It might be yours or hers, for aught I know.

King. Take her away; I do not like her now;
To prison with her: and away with him.
Unless thou tell'st me where thou hadst this ring,
Thou diest within this hour.

Dia. I'll never tell you.

King. Take her away.

Dia. I'll put in bail, my liege.

King. I think thee now some common customer.

Dia. By Jove, if ever I knew man, 'twas you.

King. Wherefore hast thou accused him all this
while.

Dia. Because he's guilty, and he is not guilty: 290
He knows I am no maid, and he'll swear to't;
I'll swear I am a maid, and he knows not.
Great king, I am no strumpet, by my life;
I am either maid, or else this old man's wife.

King. She does abuse our ears: to prison with her.

Dia. Good mother, fetch my bail. Stay, royal sir:
  [*Exit Widow.*
The jeweller that owes the ring is sent for,
And he shall surety me. But for this lord,
Who hath abused me, as he knows himself,
Though yet he never harm'd me, here I quit him: 300
He knows himself my bed he hath defiled;
And at that time he got his wife with child:
Dead though she be, she feels her young one kick:
So there's my riddle: one that's dead is quick:
And now behold the meaning.

Re-enter Widow, *with* HELENA.

King. Is there no exorcist
Beguiles the truer office of mine eyes?
Is't real that I see?

Hel. No, my good lord;
'Tis but the shadow of a wife you see,
The name and not the thing.

Ber. Both, both. O, pardon!

Hel. O my good lord, when I was like this maid, 310
I found you wondrous kind. There is your ring;
And, look you, here's your letter; this it says:
'When from my finger you can get this ring
And are by me with child,' &c. This is done:
Will you be mine, now you are doubly won?

Ber. If she, my liege, can make me know this
  clearly,
I'll love her dearly, ever, ever dearly.

Hel. If it appear not plain and prove untrue,
Deadly divorce step between me and you!
O my dear mother, do I see you living? 320

Laf. Mine eyes smell onions; I shall weep anon:
[*To Parolles*] Good Tom Drum, lend me a
  handkercher: so,
I thank thee: wait on me home, I'll make sport
  with thee:
Let thy courtesies alone, they are scurvy ones.

King. Let us from point to point this story know,
To make the even truth in pleasure flow.
[*To Diana*] If thou be'st yet a fresh uncropped flower,
Choose thou thy husband, and I'll pay thy dower;
For I can guess that by thy honest aid
Thou kept'st a wife herself, thyself a maid. 330
Of that and all the progress, more and less,
Resolvedly more leisure shall express:
All yet seems well; and if it end so meet,

232. **boggle,** waver. 270. **fine,** subtle. 332. **Resolvedly,** so that all
doubts are removed.

The bitter past, more welcome is the sweet. [*Flourish.*

EPILOGUE.

King. The king 's a beggar, now the play is done:
All is well ended, if this suit be won,
That you express content; which we will pay,
With strife to please you, day exceeding day:
Ours be your patience then, and yours our parts;
Your gentle hands lend us, and take our hearts.   340
[*Exeunt.*

Measure for Measure

King James VI of Scotland arrived in London on May 7, 1603, to succeed Queen Elizabeth on the throne of England. Plays had been prohibited at the queen's death on March 24, but were allowed again on May 9. On May 19 the Lord Chamberlain's Company was licensed as the King's Company and placed under royal patronage. About this time the plague began raging in the city, and on May 26 the theaters were closed. Shakespeare's company then traveled in the country.

Also because of the plague, King James remained absent from the city, staying first at Wilton and then at Hampton Court, thus delaying his royal entry into London until March 15, 1604. On that occasion the leading members of the King's Company, as Grooms of the Royal Chamber, received liveries and took part in the ceremony.

When the theaters opened on April 9, 1604, Shakespeare's company had probably its first great opportunity to win the new king's favor. A Revels Office account, the authenticity of which has long been debated but is now usually admitted, has been preserved which gives a list of plays presented before and after Christmas of that year. "John Heminges one of his Majesties players" was paid for plays performed by the King's Company. They included "Mesure for Mesur by Shaxberd."

DATE

If *Measure for Measure* was not written for this occasion, it must at least have been very extensively revised. In I, i, 67-72, is a possible allusion to King James' well-advertised modesty, for the duke remarks that though he loves the people, he does not "like to stage me to their eyes." Malone saw in the use of the word "sweat" (I, ii, 84) an allusion to the recent plague. And Pompey's speech at the beginning of IV, iii, seems to refer to the recently proclaimed "statute of stabbing." Parts of the play at least and its general temper and style associate it with *Othello.* Everything seems to point to 1604 as the date of composition. *Measure for Measure* appeared in print for the first time in the Folio of 1623, and like *All's*

Well that Ends Well was one of the plays entered in the Stationers' Register on November 8, 1623, as never having been printed or licensed.

SOURCE

As to sources Shakespeare seems to have taken his characteristic pains. It used to be said that *Measure for Measure* rests solely on a play called *Promos and Cassandra* by George Whetstone (1578). However, more recent and more careful studies seem to indicate that Shakespeare in writing *Measure for Measure* consulted not only Whetstone's play but Whetstone's translation in prose of the same narrative from Giraldi Cinthio's *Hecatommithi,* the story in the *Hecatommithi* itself, and even *Epitia,* an Italian play by Giraldi.

THE PLAY

Measure for Measure has a realistic plot which probably originated in occurrences in actual life. This gives to the play a superior degree of natural passion. The scene is laid in Vienna and is so marked in the Folio. That city is suffering greatly from lawlessness, particularly sexual vice. The duke who is the governor of the city seems to despair of enforcing the laws himself. He, therefore, turns over the government of the city to a deputy, Angelo, a severe moralist with a great reputation for uprightness, but with at least one breach of promise in his past. It is sometimes thought, on inadequate grounds, that the duke gave up his government in order to expose the professional reformer and to indicate that reforming a city by the exaction of penalties is not proper. The duke goes away on a pretended journey and presently returns disguised as a friar to correct the injuries done by his pious substitute.

Neither the duke's motive nor the natural character of Angelo can be told with certainty. Until his conversion at the end of the play, it seems best to regard Angelo as a man essentially cruel, insincere, and selfish. The duke should be looked upon as one of the first of Shakespeare's self-possessed and dominant men whose wisdom embraces all aspects of the general and particular issues of the action.

The story of the play, widely known over Europe for at least two centuries, arises out of Angelo's rigid enforcement of a law which makes it a capital offense to beget an illegitimate child. Claudio has offended with Juliet, to whom he was betrothed. His chaste and beautiful sister Isabella goes to Angelo to plead for her brother's life. Angelo, who prides himself on being above all temptation, makes to Isabella the base proposal that he will spare Claudio's life if she will yield to his lust. She scorns him, then visits her brother in prison feeling sure that Claudio will die rather than see her sacrifice her honor. This gives occasion for one of Shakespeare's famous scenes, albeit a somewhat pessimistic one. At first Claudio declares he will "encounter darkness as a bride" and hug it in his arms; but later he sees it differently and makes his cringing, eloquent speech:

> Ay, but to die, and go we know not where;
> To lie in cold obstruction and to rot.

He desires Isabella to yield, but she bids him perish in his ignominy.

At this point the duke, who knows what has happened, begins to operate the machine, and the course of the original plot changes. The duke's participation in the earlier part of the action is Shakespeare's addition to the story. It has been suggested by W. W. Lawrence[1] that in his new role in the romantic plot the duke discharges the function of the State as represented in dukes and kings and that of the Church as exemplified by Friar Laurence in *Romeo and Juliet* and Friar Francis in *Much Ado about Nothing*.

The duke arranges to have Isabella pretend to consent to Angelo's proposal. However, the duke substitutes for her Mariana, a former betrothed of Angelo, whom he had rejected because she had lost her fortune. Angelo thus consummates his marriage with Mariana. It helps this bad plot to remember that a betrothal had the validity of a marriage, but nothing can save the plot from its ingrained unpleasantness. Angelo decrees, in spite of his apparent victory, that Claudio shall die. But before the execution can be achieved, the duke reveals himself, resumes his authority, and proceeds to set everything to rights. Claudio is forgiven and marries Juliet. Angelo formally weds Mariana. Isabella and the duke are betrothed. The immoral but lifelike people in the underplot, whom Claudio's imprisonment has brought into the story, are also all forgiven.

It may be questioned, and often has been, whether the ends of justice are satisfied in the forgiveness and rehabilitation of Angelo, as also whether marriage to him is, after all, a remedy for the troubles of Mariana. The best answer seems to be that of Lawrence, who says, "The same marvelous processes which lead to the forgiveness of erring male characters, and their conversion to the paths of rectitude, also automatically make them perfect husbands."

As Shakespeare first wrote the play he seems to have followed the story as told by Whetstone in *Promos and Cassandra* with greater fidelity than appears in the present version. Those parts of the plot which differ most from Whetstone bear the marks of being additions and changes. According to Whetstone, Cassandra (Isabella) yields to the evil proposal of Promos (Angelo), who even then condemns her brother to death. The brother escapes from prison through the mercy of his jailer, the king (duke) returns, exposes Promos, condemns him to marry the wronged Cassandra and to suffer death. Cassandra then pleads for his life and he is spared.

What apparently happened is this: When Shakespeare, with his constant faith in the chastity of noble women, considered Whetstone's story of Cassandra, he decided that she would never have yielded up her honor. He then proceeded with the story of his Isabella's integrity and its immediate

consequences. Up to that point (III, i) he wrote his drama brilliantly, but then cast about for means of making a comedy out of this threatening plot. He had to end the play with one or more happy marriages, a device which was his customary resort in comedy, and in producing the desired result he introduced a number of inconsistencies.

There is nothing in Whetstone's play which corresponds to Mariana and her relation to Angelo. This is the very part which appears on textual grounds to have been introduced into the play after it was first written. Moreover, it is perfectly plain that in the use of the device of the unrecognized wife Shakespeare was borrowing from his own play of *All's Well that Ends Well*, where a similar ruse is resorted to in Helena's behalf. There are verbal parallels between *Measure for Measure* and *All's Well* that confirm this. The effect of the introduction of the Mariana episode is to ameliorate the plot; for bad as the story is in *Measure for Measure*, it is worse in *Promos and Cassandra*.[2]

Measure for Measure is a poor play from the points of view of structure, subject matter, dramatic consistency, and the characterization of minor figures. One would not say that the minor characters are badly done, but they are a rather unpleasant lot and most of them seem imitative of earlier creations. Lucio, a sort of variant of Parolles, is the best. On the other hand, it contains some of Shakespeare's finest dramatic poetry. Isabella is one of Shakespeare's greatest women. Angelo too is extremely well done. The duke, although often misunderstood because of an anachronistic interpretation, becomes, if seen with the eyes of Shakespeare's age, a character of poise and wisdom.[3]

STAGE HISTORY

Measure for Measure in spite of its touches of beauty remains one of Shakespeare's worst plays. Its badness, however, has not prevented it from having great popularity on the stage. It was acted, often in modified form, in the late seventeenth century, and was extremely popular with the great Shakespearean actors of the eighteenth and early nineteenth centuries. Colley Cibber, Garrick, Mrs. Siddons, Miss O'Neill, John Philip Kemble, and Macready, all appeared in it. Miss Neilson revived it in London and New York in 1876 and 1880 respectively, and there are those still living who have seen one or more of Madame Modjeska's revivals.

Tyrone Guthrie has produced the play twice at the Old Vic" in London, in 1933 and 1937, with great success. In 1933 Charles Laughton played Angelo, and Flora Robson, Isabella. The performance of the Stratford Players, seen in this country, was excellent; but the drama is always played in the dark and is gloomy and unpropitious.

---

[1]*Shakespeare's Problem Comedies*, pp. 78-121.

[2]See R. H. Wilson, "The Mariana Plot of *Measure for Measure*," *Philological Quarterly*, IX, 341-350.
[3]On the whole subject of the interpretation of *Measure for Measure* the student should see R. W. Chambers, *The Jacobean Shakespeare and Measure for Measure* (1938).

Measure for Measure

DRAMATIS PERSONAE

VINCENTIO, the Duke.
ANGELO, Deputy.
ESCALUS, an ancient Lord.
CLAUDIO, a young gentleman.
LUCIO, a fantastic.
Two other gentlemen.
PROVOST.
THOMAS,
PETER, } two friars.
A Justice.
VARRIUS.
ELBOW, a simple constable.
FROTH, a foolish gentleman.
POMPEY, servant to Mistress Overdone.
ABHORSON, an executioner.
BARNARDINE, a dissolute prisoner.

ISABELLA, sister to Claudio.
MARIANA, betrothed to Angelo.
JULIET, beloved of Claudio.
FRANCISCA, a nun.
MISTRESS OVERDONE, a bawd.

Lords, Officers, Citizens, Boy, and
    Attendants.

SCENE: *Vienna.*

ACT I.

SCENE I. *An apartment in the* DUKE'S *palace.*

Enter DUKE, ESCALUS, Lords *and* Attendants.

Duke. Escalus.
Escal. My lord.
Duke. Of government the properties to unfold,
Would seem in me to affect speech and discourse;
Since I am put to know that your own science
Exceeds, in that, the lists of all advice
My strength can give you: then no more remains,
†But that to your sufficiency
. . . . as your worth is able,
And let them work. The nature of our people,   10
Our city's institutions, and the terms
For common justice, you 're as pregnant in
As art and practice hath enriched any
That we remember. There is our commission,
From which we would not have you warp. Call hither,
I say, bid come before us Angelo.   [*Exit an Attendant.*
What figure of us think you he will bear?
For you must know, we have with special soul
Elected him our absence to supply,
Lent him our terror, dress'd him with our love,   20
And given his deputation all the organs
Of our own power: what think you of it?
Escal. If any in Vienna be of worth

To undergo such ample grace and honour,
It is Lord Angelo.
Duke.   Look where he comes.

Enter ANGELO.

Ang. Always obedient to your grace's will,
I come to know your pleasure.
Duke.   Angelo,
There is a kind of character in thy life,
That to the observer doth thy history
Fully unfold. Thyself and thy belongings   30
Are not thine own so proper as to waste
Thyself upon thy virtues, they on thee.
Heaven doth with us as we with torches do,
Not light them for themselves; for if our virtues
Did not go forth of us, 'twere all alike
As if we had them not. Spirits are not finely touch'd
But to fine issues, nor Nature never lends
The smallest scruple of her excellence
But, like a thrifty goddess, she determines
Herself the glory of a creditor,   40
Both thanks and use. But I do bend my speech
To one that can my part in him advertise;
Hold therefore, Angelo:—
In our remove be thou at full ourself;
Mortality and mercy in Vienna
Live in thy tongue and heart: old Escalus,
Though first in question, is thy secondary.
Take thy commission.
Ang.   Now, good my lord,
Let there be some more test made of my mettle,
Before so noble and so great a figure   50
Be stamp'd upon it.
Duke.   No more evasion:
We have with a leaven'd and prepared choice
Proceeded to you; therefore take your honours.
Our haste from hence is of so quick condition
That it prefers itself and leaves unquestion'd
Matters of needful value. We shall write to you,
As time and our concernings shall importune,
How it goes with us, and do look to know
What doth befall you here. So, fare you well:
To the hopeful execution do I leave you   60
Of your commissions.
Ang.   Yet give leave, my lord,
That we may bring you something on the way.
Duke. My haste may not admit it;

DRAMATIS PERSONAE. 5. **a fantastic,** one who has fanciful ideas
or indulges in wild notions.
ACT I. SCENE I.   4. **to affect . . . discourse,** to be in love with my
own voice. 5. **put to know,** forced to admit. **science,** knowledge.
6. **that,** i.e., *properties of government* (l. 3). 8-9. **But . . . able.** The
passage appears in F as a single line. Several unsuccessful attempts
at emendation have been made; Theobald inserted after *sufficiency*
the phrase *you add due diligency.* The most plausible explanation is
that something has been deleted or has been inadvertently omitted by
the printer. 8. **sufficiency,** fitness for office. 11-12. **terms . . .
justice,** the terms of court. 17. **figure,** representation. 18. **with
special soul,** with sincerest intentions or sentiments. 20. **Lent . . .
terror,** commissioned him with authority to administer punishments.
21. **his deputation,** him as deputy. 24. **undergo,** bear the weight of.
36. **touch'd,** endowed. 37. **issues,** purposes. 39. **determines,** requests.
40. **Herself,** for herself. 42. **advertise,** inform. 44. **at full,** in every
respect. 45-46. **Mortality . . . heart,** your word is the only law
respecting sentence of life and death. 49. **mettle,** so F; Globe: *metal.*
52. **leaven'd,** fermented; i.e., well-considered. 54-55. **Our . . . itself,**
the cause for my hasty departure is so urgent (*quick*) that it takes
precedence over all other matters. 55. **unquestion'd,** not yet considered. 57. **importune,** make urgent. 60. **hopeful execution,** transferred modifier; i.e., I hopefully leave you. 62. **bring you something,**
accompany you a short distance.

Nor need you, on mine honour, have to do
With any scruple; your scope is as mine own,
So to enforce or qualify the laws
As to your soul seems good. Give me your hand:
I'll privily away. I love the people,
But do not like to stage me to their eyes:
Though it do well, I do not relish well   70
Their loud applause and Aves vehement;
Nor do I think the man of safe discretion
That does affect it. Once more, fare you well.

    Ang. The heavens give safety to your purposes!
    Escal. Lead forth and bring you back in happiness!
    Duke. I thank you. Fare you well.   [*Exit.*
    Escal. I shall desire you, sir, to give me leave
To have free speech with you; and it concerns me
To look into the bottom of my place:
A power I have, but of what strength and nature   80
I am not yet instructed.
    Ang. 'Tis so with me. Let us withdraw together,
And we may soon our satisfaction have
Touching that point.
    Escal. I'll wait upon your honour.   [*Exeunt.*

SCENE II. *A street.*

Enter LUCIO *and two* Gentlemen.

    Lucio. If the duke with the other dukes come not to
composition with the King of Hungary, why then all
the dukes fall upon the king.
    First Gent. Heaven grant us its peace, but not the
King of Hungary's!
    Sec. Gent. Amen.
    Lucio. Thou concludest like the sanctimonious pi-
rate, that went to sea with the Ten Commandments, but scraped one out of the table.
    Sec. Gent. 'Thou shalt not steal'?   10
    Lucio. Ay, that he razed.
    First Gent. Why, 'twas a commandment to com-
mand the captain and all the rest from their functions:
they put forth to steal. There's not a soldier of us all,
that, in the thanksgiving before meat, do relish the
petition well that prays for peace.
    Sec. Gent. I never heard any soldier dislike it.
    Lucio. I believe thee; for I think thou never wast
where grace was said.   20
    Sec. Gent. No? a dozen times at least.
    First Gent. What, in metre?
    Lucio. In any proportion or in any language.
    First Gent. I think, or in any religion.
    Lucio. Ay, why not? Grace is grace, despite of all
controversy: as, for example, thou thyself art a
wicked villain, despite of all grace.
    First Gent. Well, there went but a pair of shears
between us.

    Lucio. I grant; as there may between the lists and
the velvet. Thou art the list.   31
    First Gent. And thou the velvet: thou art good
velvet; thou 'rt a three-piled piece, I warrant thee:
I had as lief be a list of an English kersey as be piled,
as thou art piled, for a French velvet. Do I speak
feelingly now?
    Lucio. I think thou dost; and, indeed, with most
painful feeling of thy speech: I will, out of thine own
confession, learn to begin thy health; but, whilst I
live, forget to drink after thee.   40
    First Gent. I think I have done myself wrong, have I
not?
    Sec. Gent. Yes, that thou hast, whether thou art
tainted or free.
    Lucio. Behold, behold, where Madam Mitigation
comes! I have purchased as many diseases under her
roof as come to—
    Sec. Gent. To what, I pray?
    Lucio. Judge.
    Sec. Gent. To three thousand dolours a year.   50
    First Gent. Ay, and more.
    Lucio. A French crown more.
    First Gent. Thou art always figuring diseases in me;
but thou art full of error; I am sound.
    Lucio. Nay, not as one would say, healthy; but so
sound as things that are hollow: thy bones are hollow;
impiety has made a feast of thee.

Enter MISTRESS OVERDONE.

    First Gent. How now! which of your hips has the
most profound sciatica?   59
    Mrs Ov. Well, well; there's one yonder arrested
and carried to prison was worth five thousand of
you all.
    Sec. Gent. Who's that, I pray thee?
    Mrs Ov. Marry, sir, that's Claudio, Signior Claudio.
    First Gent. Claudio to prison? 'tis not so.
    Mrs Ov. Nay, but I know 'tis so: I saw him arrested,
saw him carried away; and, which is more, within
these three days his head to be chopped off.   70
    Lucio. But, after all this fooling, I would not have it
so. Art thou sure of this?
    Mrs Ov. I am too sure of it: and it is for getting
Madam Julietta with child.
    Lucio. Believe me, this may be: he promised to meet
me two hours since, and he was ever precise in
promise-keeping.
    Sec. Gent. Besides, you know, it draws something
near to the speech we had to such a purpose.
    First Gent. But, most of all, agreeing with the proc-
lamation.   81
    Lucio. Away! let's go learn the truth of it.
            [*Exeunt Lucio and Gentlemen.*
    Mrs Ov. Thus, what with the war, what with the

64-65. **Nor . . . scruple,** you need have no misgivings. 68-69. **I'll
privily away,** etc. This passage is usually explained as a complimentary
reference to King James' dislike for crowds. The compliment is repeated
in I, iii, 8-10, and in II, iv, 24-30. The fact that James issued an
edict against his subjects' crowding to wish him well on his entrance
to London in 1603 and the further fact that this play was presented
before the king (1604) give credence to this explanation. 72. **safe,**
sound, sane. 79. **the bottom . . . place,** the extent of my commission
and authority.
    SCENE II. 4. **its,** one of the few instances in Shakespeare of this
form of the possessive; cf. *his* in glossary. 22. **in metre,** i.e., a grace
in verse; probably suggested by the rhythm of the Second Gentleman's reply. 28-29. **there . . . between us,** we're of the same stuff.

31. **lists,** selvages. 33. **three-piled.** The New Cambridge editors
suggest that the Gentleman quibbles in *piled* on the meaning "the
downy nap [on velvet]" and the word *piled-pilled* or *peeled,* i.e., hairless,
bald, with reference to the French disease; cf. *All's Well that Ends Well,*
II, ii, 23, note. 35. **kersey,** a coarse, cheap fabric. 36. **feelingly,**
to the purpose. 37-40. **I think . . . thee.** Lucio's reply is a quibble
on *feelingly;* i.e., the Gentleman speaks with most painful feeling
because his mouth is affected by the French disease; hence Lucio will
not drink from the same cup after him. 50. **dolours,** quibble on
"dollars." 84. **the sweat,** sweating sickness; a form of the plague. 85.
custom-shrunk, having fewer customers. 91. **peculiar,** privately
owned. 98. **houses,** brothels. 118. **Provost,** officer charged with
apprehension, custody, and punishment of offenders. 126. **words of**

sweat, what with the gallows and what with poverty,
I am custom-shrunk.

Enter POMPEY.

How now! what 's the news with you?

Pom. Yonder man is carried to prison.

Mrs Ov. Well; what has he done?

Pom. A woman.

Mrs Ov. But what 's his offence? 90

Pom. Groping for trouts in a peculiar river.

Mrs Ov. What, is there a maid with child by him?

Pom. No, but there 's a woman with maid by him.
You have not heard of the proclamation, have you?

Mrs Ov. What proclamation, man?

Pom. All houses in the suburbs of Vienna must be
plucked down.

Mrs Ov. And what shall become of those in the
city? 101

Pom. They shall stand for seed: they had gone
down too, but that a wise burgher put in for them.

Mrs Ov. But shall all our houses of resort in the
suburbs be pulled down?

Pom. To the ground, mistress.

Mrs Ov. Why, here 's a change indeed in the commonwealth! What shall become of me?

Pom. Come; fear not you: good counsellors lack no
clients: though you change your place, you need not
change your trade; I'll be your tapster still. Courage!
there will be pity taken on you: you that have worn
your eyes almost out in the service, you will be considered.

Mrs Ov. What 's to do here, Thomas tapster? let 's
withdraw.

Pom. Here comes Signior Claudio, led by the provost to prison; and there 's Madam Juliet. [*Exeunt.*

Enter PROVOST, CLAUDIO, JULIET, *and* Officers.

Claud. Fellow, why dost thou show me thus to the
world? 120
Bear me to prison, where I am committed.

Prov. I do it not in evil disposition,
But from Lord Angelo by special charge.

Claud. Thus can the demigod Authority
Make us pay down for our offence by weight
The words of heaven; on whom it will, it will;
On whom it will not, so; yet still 'tis just.

Re-enter LUCIO *and two* Gentlemen.

Lucio. Why, how now, Claudio! whence comes this
restraint?

Claud. From too much liberty, my Lucio, liberty:
As surfeit is the father of much fast, 130
So every scope by the immoderate use
Turns to restraint. Our natures do pursue,
Like rats that ravin down their proper bane,
A thirsty evil; and when we drink we die.

Lucio. If I could speak so wisely under an arrest, I

would send for certain of my creditors: and yet, to
say the truth, I had as lief have the foppery of freedom
as the morality of imprisonment. What 's thy offence,
Claudio?

Claud. What but to speak of would offend again. 140

Lucio. What, is 't murder?

Claud. No.

Lucio. Lechery?

Claud. Call it so.

Prov. Away, sir! you must go.

Claud. One word, good friend. Lucio, a word with
you.

Lucio. A hundred, if they'll do you any good.
Is lechery so look'd after?

Claud. Thus stands it with me: upon a true contract
I got possession of Julietta's bed: 150
You know the lady; she is fast my wife,
Save that we do the denunciation lack
Of outward order: this we came not to,
Only for propagation of a dower
Remaining in the coffer of her friends,
From whom we thought it meet to hide our love
Till time had made them for us. But it chances
The stealth of our most mutual entertainment
With character too gross is writ on Juliet.

Lucio. With child, perhaps?

Claud.   Unhappily, even so. 160
And the new deputy now for the duke—
Whether it be the fault and glimpse of newness,
Or whether that the body public be
A horse whereon the governor doth ride,
Who, newly in the seat, that it may know
He can command, lets it straight feel the spur;
Whether the tyranny be in his place,
Or in his eminence that fills it up,
I stagger in:—but this new governor
Awakes me all the enrolled penalties 170
Which have, like unscour'd armour, hung by the wall
So long that nineteen zodiacs have gone round
And none of them been worn; and, for a name,
Now puts the drowsy and neglected act
Freshly on me: 'tis surely for a name.

Lucio. I warrant it is: and thy head stands so tickle
on thy shoulders that a milkmaid, if she be in love,
may sigh it off. Send after the duke and appeal to him.

Claud. I have done so, but he 's not to be found. 180
I prithee, Lucio, do me this kind service:
This day my sister should the cloister enter
And there receive her approbation:
Acquaint her with the danger of my state;
Implore her, in my voice, that she make friends
To the strict deputy; bid herself assay him:
I have great hope in that; for in her youth
There is a prone and speechless dialect,
Such as move men; beside, she hath prosperous art
When she will play with reason and discourse, 190

heaven. Hart quotes Henley's observation: "To this uncontrollable
power (*Authority*) the poet applies a passage from St. Paul to the Romans
9:15-18, '. . . I will have mercy on whom I will have mercy . . . and
whom he will he hardeneth.' These are the words of heaven." 128.
whence . . . restraint. The New Cambridge editors call attention to the
fact that Lucio has already been acquainted with Claudio's offense
(ll. 73-74). They find the sudden changes from prose to verse in the
scene, combined with this discrepancy, to be indicative of revision.
133. their proper, belonging exclusively to them. 151. fast my wife,
i.e., by precontract. Formal betrothal was legally regarded as making a
valid marriage. Cf. IV, i, 71-75, where the duke urges Mariana to
comply in the plot to save Claudio on the grounds of her precontract
with Angelo. 152. denunciation, formal declaration. 154. propa-

gation, increase. 157. made them for us, disposed them (*friends*) in
our favor. 159. character too gross, letters too large. 162. the fault
. . . newness, imperfection awaiting upon the sudden and unaccustomed
brightness or flash of novelty (Hart). The New Cambridge editors note
E. Maunde Thompson's suggestion (made privately) that *fault* may be
a printer's misreading of *foill*, i.e., a mirror, which gives us "a picture of
Angelo looking at himself in the glass in his new Deputy-costume."
172. nineteen zodiacs, nineteen years. 177. tickle, uncertain. 188.
prone, eager. The phrase is taken commonly as a hendiadys—speech-
lessly prone, i.e., speaking eagerly without words (Onions). 189.
prosperous art, skill or ability to gain favorable results.

And well she can persuade.

Lucio. I pray she may; as well for the encouragement of the like, which else would stand under grievous imposition, as for the enjoying of thy life, who I would be sorry should be thus foolishly lost at a game of tick-tack. I'll to her.

Claud. I thank you, good friend Lucio.

Lucio. Within two hours.

Claud. Come, officer, away! [*Exeunt.*

SCENE III. *A monastery.*

Enter DUKE *and* FRIAR THOMAS.

Duke. No, holy father; throw away that thought;
Believe not that the dribbling dart of love
Can pierce a complete bosom. Why I desire thee
To give me secret harbour, hath a purpose
More grave and wrinkled than the aims and ends
Of burning youth.

Fri. T. May your grace speak of it?

Duke. My holy sir, none better knows than you
How I have ever loved the life removed
And held in idle price to haunt assemblies
Where youth, and cost, and witless bravery keeps. 10
I have deliver'd to Lord Angelo,
A man of stricture and firm abstinence,
My absolute power and place here in Vienna,
And he supposes me travell'd to Poland;
For so I have strew'd it in the common ear,
And so it is received. Now, pious sir,
You will demand of me why I do this?

Fri. T. Gladly, my lord.

Duke. We have strict statutes and most biting laws,
The needful bits and curbs to headstrong weeds, 20
Which for this nineteen years we have let slip;
Even like an o'ergrown lion in a cave,
That goes not out to prey. Now, as fond fathers,
Having bound up the threatening twigs of birch,
Only to stick it in their children's sight
For terror, not to use, in time the rod
Becomes more mock'd than fear'd; so our decrees,
Dead to infliction, to themselves are dead;
And liberty plucks justice by the nose;
The baby beats the nurse, and quite athwart 30
Goes all decorum.

Fri. T. It rested in your grace
To unloose this tied-up justice when you pleased:
And it in you more dreadful would have seem'd
Than in Lord Angelo.

Duke. I do fear, too dreadful:
Sith 'twas my fault to give the people scope,
'Twould be my tyranny to strike and gall them
For what I bid them do: for we bid this be done,
When evil deeds have their permissive pass
And not the punishment. Therefore indeed, my
father,
I have on Angelo imposed the office; 40
Who may, in the ambush of my name, strike home,
†And yet my nature never in the fight
To do it slander. And to behold his sway,

I will, as 'twere a brother of your order,
Visit both prince and people: therefore, I prithee,
Supply me with the habit and instruct me
How I may formally in person bear me
Like a true friar. Moe reasons for this action
At our more leisure shall I render you;
Only, this one: Lord Angelo is precise; 50
Stands at a guard with envy; scarce confesses
That his blood flows, or that his appetite
Is more to bread than stone: hence shall we see,
If power change purpose, what our seemers be. [*Exeunt.*

SCENE IV. *A nunnery.*

Enter ISABELLA *and* FRANCISCA.

Isab. And have you nuns no farther privileges?

Fran. Are not these large enough?

Isab. Yes, truly: I speak not as desiring more;
But rather wishing a more strict restraint
Upon the sisterhood, the votarists of Saint Clare.

Lucio. [*Within*] Ho! Peace be in this place!

Isab. Who 's that which calls?

Fran. It is a man's voice. Gentle Isabella,
Turn you the key, and know his business of him;
You may, I may not; you are yet unsworn.
When you have vow'd, you must not speak with men
But in the presence of the prioress: 11
Then, if you speak, you must not show your face,
Or, if you show your face, you must not speak.
He calls again; I pray you, answer him. [*Exit.*

Isab. Peace and prosperity! Who is 't that calls?

Enter LUCIO.

Lucio. Hail, virgin, if you be, as those cheek-roses
Proclaim you are no less! Can you so stead me
As bring me to the sight of Isabella,
A novice of this place and the fair sister
To her unhappy brother Claudio? 20

Isab. Why 'her unhappy brother'? let me ask,
The rather for I now must make you know
I am that Isabella and his sister.

Lucio. Gentle and fair, your brother kindly greets
you:
Not to be weary with you, he 's in prison.

Isab. Woe me! for what?

Lucio. For that which, if myself might be his judge,
He should receive his punishment in thanks:
He hath got his friend with child.

Isab. Sir, make me not your story.

Lucio. It is true. 30
I would not—though 'tis my familiar sin
With maids to seem the lapwing and to jest,
Tongue far from heart—play with all virgins so:
I hold you as a thing ensky'd and sainted,
By your renouncement an immortal spirit,
And to be talk'd with in sincerity,
As with a saint.

Isab. You do blaspheme the good in mocking me.

Lucio. Do not believe it. Fewness and truth, 'tis
thus:

---

196. **tick-tack,** a form of backgammon in which pegs were driven into holes.
    SCENE III. 2. **dribbling,** falling short or wide of the mark. 9. **idle,** unprofitable. 10. **cost,** costly things. 12. **stricture,** strictness. 21. **nineteen,** F: *foureteene.* 28. **Dead to infliction,** dead in that they are not executed. 43. **it,** i.e., nature; so Hanmer; Globe, following F: *in.* 50. **precise,** puritanical. 51. **Stands at a guard,** acts cautiously.

SCENE IV. 30. **make . . . story,** don't spin tales to me (Hart); don't make me a dupe (New Cambridge editors, who see a quibble on *story* in Lucio's retort). 32. **lapwing,** peewit or plover, with reference to its habit of running away from its nest in order to draw away enemies. 39. **Fewness and truth,** in few words and truly. 43. **foison,** plentiful harvest. 51-52. **Bore . . . action,** kept us in expectation of some action.

Your brother and his lover have embraced: 40
As those that feed grow full, as blossoming time
That from the seedness the bare fallow brings
To teeming foison, even so her plenteous womb
Expresseth his full tilth and husbandry.
    Isab. Some one with child by him? My cousin
    Juliet?
    Lucio. Is she your cousin?
    Isab. Adoptedly; as school-maids change their
    names
By vain though apt affection.
    Lucio.   She it is.
    Isab. O, let him marry her.
    Lucio.   This is the point.
The duke is very strangely gone from hence; 50
Bore many gentlemen, myself being one,
In hand and hope of action: but we do learn
By those that know the very nerves of state,
His givings-out were of an infinite distance
From his true-meant design. Upon his place,
And with full line of his authority,
Governs Lord Angelo; a man whose blood
Is very snow-broth; one who never feels
The wanton stings and motions of the sense,
But doth rebate and blunt his natural edge 60
With profits of the mind, study and fast.
He—to give fear to use and liberty,
Which have for long run by the hideous law,
As mice by lions—hath pick'd out an act,
Under whose heavy sense your brother's life
Falls into forfeit: he arrests him on it;
And follows close the rigour of the statute,
To make him an example. All hope is gone,
Unless you have the grace by your fair prayer
To soften Angelo: and that's my pith of business 70
'Twixt you and your poor brother.
    Isab. Doth he so seek his life?
    Lucio.   Has censured him
Already; and, as I hear, the provost hath
A warrant for his execution.
    Isab. Alas! what poor ability's in me
To do him good?
    Lucio.   Assay the power you have.
    Isab. My power? Alas, I doubt—
    Lucio.   Our doubts are traitors
And make us lose the good we oft might win
By fearing to attempt. Go to Lord Angelo,
And let him learn to know, when maidens sue, 80
Men give like gods; but when they weep and kneel,
All their petitions are as freely theirs
As they themselves would owe them.
    Isab. I'll see what I can do.
    Lucio.   But speedily.
    Isab. I will about it straight;
No longer staying but to give the mother
Notice of my affair. I humbly thank you:
Commend me to my brother: soon at night
I'll send him certain word of my success.
    Lucio. I take my leave of you.
    Isab.   Good sir, adieu.   [*Exeunt.* 90

---

60. **rebate,** abate.
    ACT II. SCENE I. 6. **fall,** fell; i.e., cause to fall. 22. **what knows,**
so F; Globe, following Rowe: *what know;* New Cambridge: *who knows.*
There is no need to emend either the pronoun or the verb. Third person
present plurals in *s* and *es* are common in Shakespeare; cf. Abbott,
333. Moreover, the cold impersonality of Angelo's speech is charac-

ACT II.

SCENE I. *A hall in* ANGELO'S *house.*

Enter ANGELO, ESCALUS, *and a* Justice, Provost,
    Officers, *and other* Attendants, *behind.*

    Ang. We must not make a scarecrow of the
    law,
Setting it up to fear the birds of prey,
And let it keep one shape, till custom make it
Their perch and not their terror.
    Escal.   Ay, but yet
Let us be keen, and rather cut a little,
Than fall, and bruise to death. Alas, this gentleman,
Whom I would save, had a most noble father!
Let but your honour know,
Whom I believe to be most strait in virtue,
That, in the working of your own affections, 10
Had time cohered with place or place with wishing,
Or that the resolute acting of your blood
Could have attain'd the effect of your own purpose,
Whether you had not sometime in your life
Err'd in this point which now you censure him,
And pull'd the law upon you.
    Ang. 'Tis one thing to be tempted, Escalus,
Another thing to fall. I not deny,
The jury, passing on the prisoner's life,
May in the sworn twelve have a thief or two 20
Guiltier than him they try. What's open made to
    justice,
That justice seizes: what knows the laws
That thieves do pass on thieves? 'Tis very pregnant,
The jewel that we find, we stoop and take't
Because we see it; but what we do not see
We tread upon, and never think of it.
You may not so extenuate his offence
For I have had such faults; but rather tell me,
When I, that censure him, do so offend,
Let mine own judgement pattern out my death, 30
And nothing come in partial. Sir, he must die.
    Escal. Be it as your wisdom will.
    Ang.   Where is the provost?
    Prov. Here, if it like your honour.
    Ang.   See that Claudio
Be executed by nine to-morrow morning:
Bring him his confessor, let him be prepared;
For that's the utmost of his pilgrimage.   [*Exit Provost.*
    Escal. [*Aside*] Well, heaven forgive him! and forgive
    us all!
Some rise by sin, and some by virtue fall:
†Some run from brakes of vice, and answer none:
And some condemned for a fault alone. 40

    Enter ELBOW, *and* Officers *with* FROTH *and* POMPEY.

    Elb. Come, bring them away: if these be good
people in a commonweal that do nothing but use
their abuses in common houses, I know no law: bring
them away.
    Ang. How now, sir! What's your name? and what's
the matter?
    Elb. If it please your honour, I am the poor duke's

---

teristic of his tyranny. He is emphasizing the importance of the law as
an absolute thing, and he asks here, "What does the law know of those
who enforce it?" The law, he urges, is not to be identified and confused
with its enforcers. 28. **For,** because. 31. **And . . . partial,** let there
be no partiality. 36. **utmost,** furthest point. 39. **vice,** so Rowe;
Globe, following F: *ice.*

constable, and my name is Elbow: I do lean upon justice, sir, and do bring in here before your good honour two notorious benefactors. 50

Ang. Benefactors? Well; what benefactors are they? are they not malefactors?

Elb. If it please your honour, I know not well what they are: but precise villains they are, that I am sure of; and void of all profanation in the world that good Christians ought to have.

Escal. This comes off well; here's a wise officer.

Ang. Go to: what quality are they of? Elbow is your name? why dost thou not speak, Elbow? 60

Pom. He cannot, sir; he's out at elbow.

Ang. What are you, sir?

Elb. He, sir! a tapster, sir; parcel-bawd; one that serves a bad woman; whose house, sir, was, as they say, plucked down in the suburbs; and now she professes a hot-house, which, I think, is a very ill house too.

Escal. How know you that?

Elb. My wife, sir, whom I detest before heaven and your honour,— 70

Escal. How? thy wife?

Elb. Ay, sir; whom, I thank heaven, is an honest woman,—

Escal. Dost thou detest her therefore?

Elb. I say, sir, I will detest myself also, as well as she, that this house, if it be not a bawd's house, it is pity of her life, for it is a naughty house.

Escal. How dost thou know that, constable? 79

Elb. Marry, sir, by my wife; who, if she had been a woman cardinally given, might have been accused in fornication, adultery, and all uncleanliness there.

Escal. By the woman's means?

Elb. Ay, sir, by Mistress Overdone's means: but as she spit in his face, so she defied him.

Pom. Sir, if it please your honour, this is not so.

Elb. Prove it before these varlets here, thou honourable man; prove it.

Escal. Do you hear how he misplaces? 90

Pom. Sir, she came in great with child; and longing, saving your honour's reverence, for stewed prunes; sir, we had but two in the house, which at that very distant time stood, as it were, in a fruit-dish, a dish of some three-pence; your honours have seen such dishes; they are not China dishes, but very good dishes,—

Escal. Go to, go to: no matter for the dish, sir.

Pom. No, indeed, sir, not of a pin; you are therein in the right: but to the point. As I say, this Mistress Elbow, being, as I say, with child, and being great-bellied, and longing, as I said, for prunes; and having but two in the dish, as I said, Master Froth here, this very man, having eaten the rest, as I said, and, as I say, paying for them very honestly; for, as you know, Master Froth, I could not give you three-pence again.

Froth. No, indeed.

Pom. Very well; you being then, if you be remembered, cracking the stones of the foresaid prunes,— 111

Froth. Ay, so I did indeed.

Pom. Why, very well; I telling you then, if you be remembered, that such a one and such a one were

past cure of the thing you wot of, unless they kept very good diet, as I told you,—

Froth. All this is true.

Pom. Why, very well, then,—

Escal. Come, you are a tedious fool: to the purpose. What was done to Elbow's wife, that he hath cause to complain of? Come me to what was done to her. 121

Pom. Sir, your honour cannot come to that yet.

Escal. No, sir, nor I mean it not.

Pom. Sir, but you shall come to it, by your honour's leave. And, I beseech you, look into Master Froth here, sir; a man of fourscore pound a year; whose father died at Hallowmas: was't not at Hallowmas, Master Froth?

Froth. All-hallond eve. 130

Pom. Why, very well; I hope here be truths. He, sir, sitting, as I say, in a lower chair, sir; 'twas in the Bunch of Grapes, where indeed you have a delight to sit, have you not?

Froth. I have so; because it is an open room and good for winter.

Pom. Why, very well, then; I hope here be truths.

Ang. This will last out a night in Russia,
When nights are longest there: I'll take my leave, 140
And leave you to the hearing of the cause;
Hoping you'll find good cause to whip them all.

Escal. I think no less. Good morrow to your
    lordship.   [*Exit Angelo.*
Now, sir, come on: what was done to Elbow's wife, once more?

Pom. Once, sir? there was nothing done to her once.

Elb. I beseech you, sir, ask him what this man did to my wife.

Pom. I beseech your honour, ask me. 150

Escal. Well, sir; what did this gentleman to her?

Pom. I beseech you, sir, look in this gentleman's face. Good Master Froth, look upon his honour; 'tis for a good purpose. Doth your honour mark his face?

Escal. Ay, sir, very well.

Pom. Nay, I beseech you, mark it well.

Escal. Well, I do so.

Pom. Doth your honour see any harm in his face? 161

Escal. Why, no.

Pom. I'll be supposed upon a book, his face is the worst thing about him. Good, then; if his face be the worst thing about him, how could Master Froth do the constable's wife any harm? I would know that of your honour.

Escal. He's in the right. Constable, what say you to it?

Elb. First, an it like you, the house is a respected house; next, this is a respected fellow; and his mistress is a respected woman. 169

Pom. By this hand, sir, his wife is a more respected person than any of us all.

Elb. Varlet, thou liest; thou liest, wicked varlet! the time is yet to come that she was ever respected with man, woman, or child.

Pom. Sir, she was respected with him before he married with her.

Escal. Which is the wiser here? Justice or Iniquity? Is this true? 181

---

54. **precise,** puritanical; possibly one of Elbow's malapropisms. 55. **profanation,** malapropism for "profession." 57. **comes off well,** turns out well (Onions); is well told (Durham, following Johnson). 63. **parcel-bawd,** partly, i.e., he follows two trades—tapster and bawd. 69. **detest,** possibly for "protest." 81. **cardinally,** malapropism for "carnally." 90. **misplaces,** uses words in the wrong place. 92-93. **stewed prunes,** associated with prostitutes; cf. *stews,* meaning "houses of prostitution." 99. **pin,** used to denote an insignificant trifle. 120. **done.** Cf. the use of this word at I, ii, 88; Pompey so understands it here. 121. **me,** the ethical dative. 130. **All-hallond eve,** Halloween. 132.

Elb. O thou caitiff! O thou varlet! O thou wicked Hannibal! I respected with her before I was married to her! If ever I was respected with her, or she with me, let not your worship think me the poor duke's officer. Prove this, thou wicked Hannibal, or I'll have mine action of battery on thee.

Escal. If he took you a box o' the ear, you might have your action of slander too. 190

Elb. Marry, I thank your good worship for it. What is 't your worship's pleasure I shall do with this wicked caitiff?

Escal. Truly, officer, because he hath some offences in him that thou wouldst discover if thou couldst, let him continue in his courses till thou knowest what they are.

Elb. Marry, I thank your worship for it. Thou seest, thou wicked varlet, now, what 's come upon thee: thou art to continue now, thou varlet; thou art to continue. 201

Escal. Where were you born, friend?

Froth. Here in Vienna, sir.

Escal. Are you of fourscore pounds a year?

Froth. Yes, an 't please you, sir.

Escal. So. What trade are you of, sir?

Pom. A tapster; a poor widow's tapster.

Escal. Your mistress' name?

Pom. Mistress Overdone.

Escal. Hath she had any more than one husband? 211

Pom. Nine, sir; Overdone by the last.

Escal. Nine! Come hither to me, Master Froth. Master Froth, I would not have you acquainted with tapsters: they will draw you, Master Froth, and you will hang them. Get you gone, and let me hear no more of you.

Froth. I thank your worship. For mine own part, I never come into any room in a taphouse, but I am drawn in. 220

Escal. Well, no more of it, Master Froth: farewell. [*Exit Froth.*] Come you hither to me, Master tapster. What 's your name, Master tapster?

Pom. Pompey.

Escal. What else?

Pom. Bum, sir.

Escal. Troth, and your bum is the greatest thing about you; so that in the beastliest sense you are Pompey the Great. Pompey, you are partly a bawd, Pompey, howsoever you colour it in being a tapster, are you not? come, tell me true: it shall be the better for you. 233

Pom. Truly, sir, I am a poor fellow that would live.

Escal. How would you live, Pompey? by being a bawd? What do you think of the trade, Pompey? is it a lawful trade?

Pom. If the law would allow it, sir.

Escal. But the law will not allow it, Pompey; nor it shall not be allowed in Vienna. 241

Pom. Does your worship mean to geld and splay all the youth of the city?

Escal. No, Pompey.

Pom. Truly, sir, in my poor opinion, they will to 't then. If your worship will take order for the drabs and the knaves, you need not to fear the bawds.

Escal. There are pretty orders beginning, I can tell you: it is but heading and hanging.

Pom. If you head and hang all that offend that way but for ten year together, you'll be glad to give out a commission for more heads: if this law hold in Vienna ten year, I'll rent the fairest house in it after three-pence a bay: if you live to see this come to pass, say Pompey told you so. 256

Escal. Thank you, good Pompey; and, in requital of your prophecy, hark you, I advise you, let me not find you before me again upon any complaint whatsoever; no, not for dwelling where you do: if I do, Pompey, I shall beat you to your tent, and prove a shrewd Cæsar to you; in plain dealing, Pompey, I shall have you whipt: so, for this time, Pompey, fare you well.

Pom. I thank your worship for your good counsel: [*Aside*] but I shall follow it as the flesh and fortune shall better determine. 268

Whip me? No, no; let carman whip his jade:

The valiant heart 's not whipt out of his trade. [*Exit.*

Escal. Come hither to me, Master Elbow; come hither, Master constable. How long have you been in this place of constable?

Elb. Seven year and a half, sir.

Escal. I thought, by your readiness in the office, you had continued in it some time. You say, seven years together?

Elb. And a half, sir. 274

Escal. Alas, it hath been great pains to you. They do you wrong to put you so oft upon 't: are there not men in your ward sufficient to serve it?

Elb. Faith, sir, few of any wit in such matters: as they are chosen, they are glad to choose me for them; I do it for some piece of money, and go through with all.

Escal. Look you bring me in the names of some six or seven, the most sufficient of your parish.

Elb. To your worship's house, sir?

Escal. To my house. Fare you well. [*Exit Elbow.*
What 's o'clock, think you? 290

Just. Eleven, sir.

Escal. I pray you home to dinner with me.

Just. I humbly thank you.

Escal. It grieves me for the death of Claudio;
But there 's no remedy.

Just. Lord Angelo is severe.

Escal. It is but needful:
Mercy is not itself, that oft looks so;
Pardon is still the nurse of second woe:
But yet,—poor Claudio! There is no remedy.
Come, sir. [*Exeunt.* 300

SCENE II. *Another room in the same.*

Enter PROVOST *and a* Servant.

Serv. He 's hearing of a cause; he will come straight:
I'll tell him of you.

Prov. Pray you, do. [*Exit Servant.*] I'll
know
His pleasure; may be he will relent. Alas,
He hath but as offended in a dream!

lower chair, possibly easy chair (Steevens). 133. the Bunch of Grapes, the name of a room. It was not uncommon to designate particular rooms in inns by such names. 135. open, public. 163. supposed, malapropism for "deposed," i.e., sworn. 180. Justice or Iniquity, the officer or the prisoner. 183. Hannibal, for "cannibal." 215. draw, used with multiple quibble in the senses of "disembowel," "empty"—i.e., of his belongings, and (l. 220) "cheat"—i.e., take in. 250. heading, beheading. 255. bay, division of a house included under one gable. 263. Cæsar. Escalus refers to Caesar's defeat of Pompey at Pharsalus. SCENE II. 4. He, i.e., Claudio.

All sects, all ages smack of this vice; and he
To die for 't!

Enter ANGELO.

Ang. Now, what 's the matter, provost?
Prov. Is it your will Claudio shall die to-morrow?
Ang. Did not I tell thee yea? hadst thou not order?
Why dost thou ask again?
Prov. Lest I might be too rash:
Under your good correction, I have seen, 10
When, after execution, judgement hath
Repented o'er his doom.
Ang. Go to; let that be mine:
Do you your office, or give up your place,
And you shall well be spared.
Prov. I crave your honour's pardon.
What shall be done, sir, with the groaning Juliet?
She 's very near her hour.
Ang. Dispose of her
To some more fitter place, and that with speed.

Re-enter Servant.

Serv. Here is the sister of the man condemn'd
Desires access to you.
Ang. Hath he a sister?
Prov. Ay, my good lord; a very virtuous maid, 20
And to be shortly of a sisterhood,
If not already.
Ang. Well, let her be admitted.
[*Exit Servant.*
See you the fornicatress be removed:
Let her have needful, but not lavish, means;
There shall be order for 't.

Enter ISABELLA *and* LUCIO.

Prov. God save your honour!
Ang. Stay a little while. [*To Isab.*] You 're welcome:
what 's your will?
Isab. I am a woeful suitor to your honour,
Please but your honour hear me.
Ang. Well; what 's your suit?
Isab. There is a vice that most I do abhor,
And most desire should meet the blow of justice; 30
For which I would not plead, but that I must;
For which I must not plead, but that I am
At war 'twixt will and will not.
Ang. Well; the matter?
Isab. I have a brother is condemn'd to die:
I do beseech you, let it be his fault,
And not my brother.
Prov. [*Aside*] Heaven give thee moving
graces!
Ang. Condemn the fault, and not the actor of it?
Why, every fault 's condemn'd ere it be done:
Mine were the very cipher of a function,
To fine the faults whose fine stands in record, 40
And let go by the actor.
Isab. O just but severe law!
I had a brother, then. Heaven keep your honour!
Lucio. [*Aside to Isab.*] Give 't not o'er so: to him
again, entreat him;
Kneel down before him, hang upon his gown:
You are too cold; if you should need a pin,

You could not with more tame a tongue desire it:
To him, I say!
Isab. Must he needs die?
Ang. Maiden, no remedy.
Isab. Yes; I do think that you might pardon him,
And neither heaven nor man grieve at the mercy. 50
Ang. I will not do 't.
Isab. But can you, if you would?
Ang. Look, what I will not, that I cannot do.
Isab. But might you do 't, and do the world no
wrong,
If so your heart were touch'd with that remorse
As mine is to him?
Ang. He 's sentenced; 'tis too late.
Lucio. [*Aside to Isab.*] You are too cold.
Isab. Too late? why, no; I, that do speak a word,
May call it back again. Well, believe this,
No ceremony that to great ones 'longs,
Not the king's crown, nor the deputed sword, 60
The marshal's truncheon, nor the judge's robe,
Become them with one half so good a grace
As mercy does.
If he had been as you and you as he,
You would have slipt like him; but he, like you,
Would not have been so stern.
Ang. Pray you, be gone.
Isab. I would to heaven I had your potency,
And you were Isabel! should it then be thus?
No; I would tell what 'twere to be a judge,
And what a prisoner.
Lucio. [*Aside to Isab.*] Ay, touch him;
there 's the vein. 70
Ang. Your brother is a forfeit of the law,
And you but waste your words.
Isab. Alas, alas!
Why, all the souls that were forfeit once;
And He that might the vantage best have took
Found out the remedy. How would you be,
If He, which is the top of judgement, should
But judge you as you are? O, think on that;
And mercy then will breathe within your lips,
Like man new made.
Ang. Be you content, fair maid;
It is the law, not I condemn your brother: 80
Were he my kinsman, brother, or my son,
It should be thus with him: he must die to-morrow.
Isab. To-morrow! O, that 's sudden! Spare him,
spare him!
He 's not prepared for death. Even for our kitchens
We kill the fowl of season: shall we serve heaven
With less respect than we do minister
To our gross selves? Good, good my lord, bethink you;
Who is it that hath died for this offence?
There 's many have committed it.
Lucio. [*Aside to Isab.*] Ay, well said.
Ang. The law hath not been dead, though it hath
slept: 90
Those many had not dared to do that evil,
If the first that did the edict infringe
Had answer'd for his deed: now 'tis awake,
Takes note of what is done; and, like a prophet,
Looks in a glass, that shows what future evils,
Either new, or by remissness new-conceived,

---

5. **sects,** classes of people, ranks. 10. **Under . . . correction,** i.e., allow
me to say. 23. **fornicatress,** i.e., Juliet. 35. **let . . . fault,** i.e., let the
fault die. 39. **cipher,** nonentity, a mere nothing. 40. **fine, fine,**

punish, punishment. 43. **Give 't . . . so,** don't give up so soon. 61.
truncheon, staff borne by military officers. 71. **forfeit,** person handed
over to the law or to death. 75-77. **How would . . . you are.** Cf. *Hamlet*

And so in progress to be hatch'd and born,
Are now to have no successive degrees,
But, ere they live, to end.
   Isab.   Yet show some pity.
   Ang. I show it most of all when I show justice;   100
For then I pity those I do not know,
Which a dismiss'd offence would after gall;
And do him right that, answering one foul wrong,
Lives not to act another. Be satisfied;
Your brother dies to-morrow; be content.
   Isab. So you must be the first that gives this sentence,
And he, that suffers. O, it is excellent
To have a giant's strength; but it is tyrannous
To use it like a giant.
   Lucio.   [*Aside to Isab.*] That 's well said.
   Isab. Could great men thunder   110
As Jove himself does, Jove would ne'er be quiet,
For every pelting, petty officer
Would use his heaven for thunder;
Nothing but thunder! Merciful Heaven,
Thou rather with thy sharp and sulphurous bolt
Split'st the unwedgeable and gnarled oak
Than the soft myrtle: but man, proud man,
Drest in a little brief authority,
Most ignorant of what he 's most assured,
His glassy essence, like an angry ape,   120
Plays such fantastic tricks before high heaven
As make the angels weep; who, with our spleens,
Would all themselves laugh mortal.
   Lucio. [*Aside to Isab.*] O, to him, to him, wench! he
    will relent;
He 's coming; I perceive 't.
   Prov.   [*Aside*] Pray heaven she win him!
   Isab. We cannot weigh our brother with ourself:
Great men may jest with saints; 'tis wit in them,
But in the less foul profanation.
   Lucio. Thou 'rt i' the right, girl; more o' that.
   Isab. That in the captain 's but a choleric word,   130
Which in the soldier is flat blasphemy.
   Lucio. [*Aside to Isab.*] Art avised o' that? more on 't.
   Ang. Why do you put these sayings upon me?
   Isab. Because authority, though it err like others,
Hath yet a kind of medicine in itself,
That skins the vice o' the top. Go to your bosom;
Knock there, and ask your heart what it doth know
That 's like my brother's fault: if it confess
A natural guiltiness such as is his,
Let it not sound a thought upon your tongue   140
Against my brother's life.
   Ang.   [*Aside*] She speaks, and 'tis
Such sense, that my sense breeds with it. Fare you
    well.
   Isab. Gentle my lord, turn back.
   Ang. I will bethink me: come again to-morrow.
   Isab. Hark how I'll bribe you: good my lord, turn
    back.
   Ang. How! bribe me?
   Isab. Ay, with such gifts that heaven shall share
    with you.
   Lucio. [*Aside to Isab.*] You had marr'd all else.
   Isab. Not with fond shekels of the tested gold,
Or stones whose rates are either rich or poor   150
As fancy values them; but with true prayers

That shall be up at heaven and enter there
Ere sun-rise, prayers from preserved souls,
From fasting maids whose minds are dedicate
To nothing temporal.
   Ang.   Well; come to me to-morrow.
   Lucio. [*Aside to Isab.*] Go to; 'tis well; away!
   Isab. Heaven keep your honour safe!
   Ang.   [*Aside*] Amen:
For I am that way going to temptation,
Where prayers cross.
   Isab.   At what hour to-morrow
Shall I attend your lordship?
   Ang.   At any time 'fore noon.   160
   Isab. 'Save your honour!
           [*Exeunt Isabella, Lucio, and Provost.*
   Ang.   From thee, even from thy virtue!
What 's this, what 's this? Is this her fault or mine?
The tempter or the tempted, who sins most?
Ha!
Not she; nor doth she tempt: but it is I
That, lying by the violet in the sun,
Do as the carrion does, not as the flower,
Corrupt with virtuous season. Can it be
That modesty may more betray our sense
Than woman's lightness? Having waste ground
    enough,   170
Shall we desire to raze the sanctuary
And pitch our evils there? O, fie, fie, fie!
What dost thou, or what art thou, Angelo?
Dost thou desire her foully for those things
That make her good? O, let her brother live:
Thieves for their robbery have authority
When judges steal themselves. What, do I love her,
That I desire to hear her speak again,
And feast upon her eyes? What is 't I dream on?
O cunning enemy, that, to catch a saint,   180
With saints dost bait thy hook! Most dangerous
Is that temptation that doth goad us on
To sin in loving virtue: never could the strumpet,
With all her double vigour, art and nature,
Once stir my temper; but this virtuous maid
Subdues me quite. Ever till now,
When men were fond, I smiled and wonder'd how.
                      [*Exit.*

<hr>

SCENE III. *A room in a prison.*

Enter, severally, DUKE *disguised as a friar, and* PROVOST.

   Duke. Hail to you, provost! so I think you are.
   Prov. I am the provost. What 's your will, good friar?
   Duke. Bound by my charity and my blest order,
I come to visit the afflicted spirits
Here in the prison. Do me the common right
To let me see them and to make me know
The nature of their crimes, that I may minister
To them accordingly.
   Prov. I would do more than that, if more were
    needful.

Enter JULIET.

Look, here comes one: a gentlewoman of mine,   10
Who, falling in the flaws of her own youth,

II, ii, 554-556. **76. top of judgement,** supreme judge. **79. Like man new made,** i.e., new created by salvation, born again. **95. glass,** crystal ball into which one gazes to learn the future. **98. successive degrees,** successors. **112. pelting,** paltry. **120. glassy essence,** fragile nature. **123. laugh mortal,** i.e., excessively. **132. avised,** informed. **136. skins . . . top,** covers over with skin. **168. virtuous,** beneficial.

Hath blister'd her report: she is with child;
And he that got it, sentenced; a young man
More fit to do another such offence
Than die for this.
    Duke. When must he die?
    Prov.   As I do think, to-morrow.
I have provided for you: stay awhile,   [*To Juliet.*
And you shall be conducted.
    Duke. Repent you, fair one, of the sin you carry?
    Jul. I do; and bear the shame most patiently.   20
    Duke. I'll teach you how you shall arraign your
    conscience,
And try your penitence, if it be sound,
Or hollowly put on.
    Jul.   I'll gladly learn.
    Duke. Love you the man that wrong'd you?
    Jul. Yes, as I love the woman that wrong'd him.
    Duke. So then it seems your most offenceful act
Was mutually committed?
    Jul.   Mutually.
    Duke. Then was your sin of heavier kind than his.
    Jul. I do confess it, and repent it, father.   29
    Duke. 'Tis so, daughter: but lest you do repent,
As that the sin hath brought you to this shame,
Which sorrow is always toward ourselves, not heaven,
Showing we would not spare heaven as we love it,
But as we stand in fear,—
    Jul. I do repent me, as it is an evil,
And take the shame with joy.
    Duke.   There rest.
Your partner, as I hear, must die to-morrow,
And I am going with instruction to him.
Grace go with you, Benedicite!   [*Exit.*
    Jul. Must die to-morrow! O injurious love,   40
That respites me a life, whose very comfort
Is still a dying horror!
    Prov.   'Tis pity of him.   [*Exeunt.*

SCENE IV. *A room in* ANGELO'S *house.*

Enter ANGELO.

    Ang. When I would pray and think, I think and
    pray
To several subjects. Heaven hath my empty words;
Whilst my invention, hearing not my tongue,
Anchors on Isabel: Heaven in my mouth,
As if I did but only chew his name;
And in my heart the strong and swelling evil
Of my conception. The state, whereon I studied,
Is like a good thing, being often read,
Grown fear'd and tedious; yea, my gravity,
Wherein—let no man hear me—I take pride,   10
Could I with boot change for an idle plume,
Which the air beats for vain. O place, O form,
How often dost thou with thy case, thy habit,

Wrench awe from fools and tie the wiser souls
To thy false seeming! Blood, thou art blood:
Let's write good angel on the devil's horn;
'Tis not the devil's crest.

Enter a Servant.

         How now! who's there?
    Serv. One Isabel, a sister, desires access to you.
    Ang. Teach her the way. [*Exit Serv.*] O heavens!
Why does my blood thus muster to my heart,   20
Making both it unable for itself,
And dispossessing all my other parts
Of necessary fitness?
So play the foolish throngs with one that swoons;
Come all to help him, and so stop the air
By which he should revive: and even so
The general, subject to a well-wish'd king,
Quit their own part, and in obsequious fondness
Crowd to his presence, where their untaught love
Must needs appear offence.

Enter ISABELLA.

         How now, fair maid?   30
    Isab. I am come to know your pleasure.
    Ang. That you might know it, would much better
    please me
Than to demand what 'tis. Your brother cannot live.
    Isab. Even so. Heaven keep your honour!
    Ang. Yet may he live awhile; and, it may be,
As long as you or I: yet he must die.
    Isab. Under your sentence?
    Ang. Yea.
    Isab. When, I beseech you? that in his reprieve,
Longer or shorter, he may be so fitted   40
That his soul sicken not.
    Ang. Ha! fie, these filthy vices! It were as good
To pardon him that hath from nature stolen
A man already made, as to remit
Their saucy sweetness that do coin heaven's image
In stamps that are forbid: 'tis all as easy
Falsely to take away a life true made
As to put metal in restrained means
To make a false one.
    Isab. 'Tis set down so in heaven, but not in earth.   50
    Ang. Say you so? then I shall pose you quickly.
Which had you rather, that the most just law
Now took your brother's life; or, to redeem him,
Give up your body to such sweet uncleanness
As she that he hath stain'd?
    Isab.   Sir, believe this,
I had rather give my body than my soul.
    Ang. I talk not of your soul: our compell'd sins
Stand more for number than for accompt.
    Isab.   How say you?
    Ang. Nay, I'll not warrant that; for I can speak
Against the thing I say. Answer to this: 60

SCENE III.   12. **report,** reputation.   31, 33, 34. **As that, as,** because. 41. **respites,** i.e., prolongs, does not forfeit. The law imposed the death penalty on the offending man but not on the woman.
    SCENE IV.   9. **fear'd,** so F, a reading hard to construe; Hanmer: *sear'd;* New Cambridge, following Hudson: *sere* (spelled *Seare,* mistaken for *fear'd*).   15. **Blood, thou art blood.** Angelo may refer to his fleshly nature or to his passions. To Shakespeare's audience the word probably connoted both ideas; see *blood* in glossary.   16. **angel.** Angelo is punning on his own name.   20-23. **Why . . . fitness.** According to Elizabethan psychology and physiology, this is what happens to a victim of passion. Normally the blood passes from the veins into the heart where from it "spirit" is engendered which is conveyed by the arteries to the other parts and becomes "the instrument of the soul, to

perform all his actions." Under the sway of passion, however, the blood rushes (*musters*) to the heart, and the parts of the soul, having "more motion and heat than is needful for them, change and become hurtful." (Burton, *Anatomy of Melancholy,* I, 1, ii, 2; Charron, *Of Wisdom,* Bk. I, Ch. xviii.)   27. **general,** public, multitude.   43-44. **To . . . made,** to pardon a murderer.   45. **saucy,** wanton.   48. **metal.** Cf. I, i, 49. **restrained,** prohibited, illicit. **means,** F: *meanes;* Malone: *moulds;* Steevens: *mints,* adopted by the New Cambridge editors, who point out that it is paleographically possible, since a sixteenth-century spelling was *ments,* which could be mistaken for *menes. Mints,* furthermore, makes the metaphor consistent; cf. *As You Like It,* II, vii, 73, note. 57-58. **compell'd . . . accompt.** Sins committed under compulsion are not held against us so much as those we do freely; hence their number

I, now the voice of the recorded law,
Pronounce a sentence on your brother's life:
Might there not be a charity in sin
To save this brother's life?
   Isab.   Please you to do 't,
I'll take it as a peril to my soul,
It is no sin at all, but charity.
   Ang. Pleased you to do 't at peril of your soul,
Were equal poise of sin and charity.
   Isab. That I do beg his life, if it be sin,
Heaven let me bear it! you granting of my suit,   70
If that be sin, I'll make it my morn prayer
To have it added to the faults of mine,
And nothing of your answer.
   Ang.   Nay, but hear me.
Your sense pursues not mine: either you are ignorant,
Or seem so craftily; and that 's not good.
   Isab. Let me be ignorant, and in nothing good,
But graciously to know I am no better.
   Ang. Thus wisdom wishes to appear most bright
When it doth tax itself; as these black masks
Proclaim an enshield beauty ten times louder   80
Than beauty could, display'd. But mark me;
To be received plain, I'll speak more gross:
Your brother is to die.
   Isab. So.
   Ang. And his offence is so, as it appears,
Accountant to the law upon that pain.
   Isab. True.
   Ang. Admit no other way to save his life,—
As I subscribe not that, nor any other,
But in the loss of question,—that you, his sister,   90
Finding yourself desired of such a person,
Whose credit with the judge, or own great place,
Could fetch your brother from the manacles
Of the all-building law; and that there were
No earthly mean to save him, but that either
You must lay down the treasures of your body
To this supposed, or else to let him suffer;
What would you do?
   Isab. As much for my poor brother as myself:
That is, were I under the terms of death,   100
The impression of keen whips I 'ld wear as rubies,
And strip myself to death, as to a bed
That longing have been sick for, ere I 'ld yield
My body up to shame.
   Ang.   Then must your brother die.
   Isab. And 'twere the cheaper way:
Better it were a brother died at once,
Than that a sister, by redeeming him,
Should die for ever.
   Ang. Were not you then as cruel as the sentence
That you have slander'd so?   110
   Isab. Ignomy in ransom and free pardon
Are of two houses: lawful mercy
Is nothing kin to foul redemption.

   Ang. You seem'd of late to make the law a tyrant;
And rather proved the sliding of your brother
A merriment than a vice.
   Isab. O, pardon me, my lord; it oft falls out,
To have what we would have, we speak not what we
    mean:
I something do excuse the thing I hate,
For his advantage that I dearly love.   120
   Ang. We are all frail.
   Isab.   Else let my brother die,
If not a feodary, but only he
Owe and succeed thy weakness.
   Ang. Nay, women are frail too.
   Isab. Ay, as the glasses where they view themselves;
Which are as easy broke as they make forms.
Women! Help Heaven! men their creation mar
In profiting by them. Nay, call us ten times frail;
For we are soft as our complexions are,
And credulous to false prints.
   Ang.   I think it well;   130
And from this testimony of your own sex,—
Since I suppose we are made to be no stronger
Than faults may shake our frames,—let me be bold;
I do arrest your words. Be that you are,
That is, a woman; if you be more, you 're none;
If you be one, as you are well express'd
By all external warrants, show it now,
By putting on the destined livery.
   Isab. I have no tongue but one: gentle my lord,
Let me entreat you speak the former language.   140
   Ang. Plainly conceive, I love you.
   Isab. My brother did love Juliet,
And you tell me that he shall die for it.
   Ang. He shall not, Isabel, if you give me love.
   Isab. I know your virtue hath a license in 't,
Which seems a little fouler than it is,
To pluck on others.
   Ang.   Believe me, on mine honour,
My words express my purpose.
   Isab. Ha! little honour to be much believed,
And most pernicious purpose! Seeming, seeming!   150
I will proclaim thee, Angelo; look for 't:
Sign me a present pardon for my brother,
Or with an outstretch'd throat I'll tell the world
    aloud
What man thou art.
   Ang.   Who will believe thee, Isabel?
My unsoil'd name, the austereness of my life,
My vouch against you, and my place i' the state,
Will so your accusation overweigh,
That you shall stifle in your own report
And smell of calumny. I have begun,
And now I give my sensual race the rein: 160
Fit thy consent to my sharp appetite;
Lay by all nicety and prolixious blushes,
That banish what they sue for; redeem thy brother

is more significant than their seriousness. 59. **that**, i.e., the idea expressed in lines 57-58. 77. **graciously**, through divine grace. 79. **these black masks**, a metaphor to signify pretense of ignorance or modesty; *these* is probably generic, although it has been taken to have particular reference to (1) the masks worn by ladies in the audience; (2) the black costume worn by Isabella; and (3) Jonson's *Masque of Blackness*, which the New Cambridge editors think likely, finding evidence here for their theory of revision. 80. **enshield**, enshielded, protected, i.e., behind the *black masks*. 82. **received plain**, plainly understood. **gross**, plainly. 86. **Accountant**, accountable. 89. **subscribe**, admit, acknowledge. 90. **in . . . question**, in idle conversation (Malone). Singer conjectured *loose* for *loss*, which is explainable as "freedom." The New Cambridge editors think this reading quite

probable and see in it a play on the use of *loose* as an archery term for the discharge of an arrow. 106. **died at once**, i.e., physical death as contrasted to the death of the soul through sin. 111. **Ignomy**, ignominy. 122-123. **If . . . weakness**, if he, not as a sharer of the weakness of all men, but unique in this respect, is the only man to possess this inclination to sin. 122. **feodary**, associate, i.e., one of the whole group of mankind. 123. **thy**, spoken to Angelo not as an individual but as of the class; this is plain from Angelo's response (l. 124). 127. **men . . . mar**, men debase their nature. 130. **credulous . . . prints**, susceptible to false impressions. 134. **arrest**, take as security. 145-147. **your virtue . . . others**, you, although virtuous, are pretending foul purposes in order to mislead (*pluck on*) me. 156. **vouch**, testimony. 160. **race**, natural or inherited disposition. 162. **prolixious**, tedious.

By yielding up thy body to my will;
Or else he must not only die the death,
But thy unkindness shall his death draw out
To lingering sufferance. Answer me to-morrow,
Or, by the affection that now guides me most,
I'll prove a tyrant to him. As for you,
Say what you can, my false o'erweighs your true. [*Exit.*
  Isab. To whom should I complain? Did I tell this, 171
Who would believe me? O perilous mouths,
That bear in them one and the self-same tongue,
Either of condemnation or approof;
Bidding the law make court'sy to their will;
Hooking both right and wrong to the appetite,
To follow as it draws! I'll to my brother:
Though he hath fall'n by prompture of the blood,
Yet hath he in him such a mind of honour,
That, had he twenty heads to tender down   180
On twenty bloody blocks, he 'ld yield them up,
Before his sister should her body stoop
To such abhorr'd pollution.
Then, Isabel, live chaste, and, brother, die:
More than our brother is our chastity.
I'll tell him yet of Angelo's request,
And fit his mind to death, for his soul's rest.   [*Exit.*

ACT III.

SCENE I. *A room in the prison.*

Enter DUKE *disguised as before,* CLAUDIO, *and* PROVOST.

Duke. So then you hope of pardon from Lord
   Angelo?
  Claud. The miserable have no other medicine
But only hope:
I 've hope to live, and am prepared to die.
  Duke. Be absolute for death; either death or life
Shall thereby be the sweeter. Reason thus with life:
If I do lose thee, I do lose a thing
That none but fools would keep: a breath thou art,
Servile to all the skyey influences,
That dost this habitation, where thou keep'st,   10
Hourly afflict: merely, thou art death's fool;
For him thou labour'st by thy flight to shun
And yet runn'st toward him still. Thou art not noble;
For all the accommodations that thou bear'st
Are nursed by baseness. Thou 'rt by no means valiant;
For thou dost fear the soft and tender fork
Of a poor worm. Thy best of rest is sleep,
And that thou oft provokest; yet grossly fear'st
Thy death, which is no more. Thou art not thyself;
For thou exist'st on many a thousand grains   20
That issue out of dust. Happy thou art not;
For what thou hast not, still thou strivest to get,
And what thou hast, forget'st. Thou art not certain;
For thy complexion shifts to strange effects,
After the moon. If thou art rich, thou 'rt poor;
For, like an ass whose back with ingots bows,
Thou bear'st thy heavy riches but a journey,

And death unloads thee. Friend hast thou none;
For thine own bowels, which do call thee sire,
The mere effusion of thy proper loins,   30
Do curse the gout, serpigo, and the rheum,
For ending thee no sooner. Thou hast nor youth nor
   age,
But, as it were, an after-dinner's sleep,
Dreaming on both; for all thy blessed youth
Becomes as aged, and doth beg the alms
Of palsied eld; and when thou art old and rich,
Thou hast neither heat, affection, limb, nor beauty,
To make thy riches pleasant. What 's yet in this
That bears the name of life? Yet in this life
Lie hid moe thousand deaths: yet death we fear,   40
That makes these odds all even.
  Claud.   I humbly thank you.
To sue to live, I find I seek to die;
And, seeking death, find life: let it come on.
  Isab. [*Within*] What, ho! Peace here; grace and
   good company!
  Prov. Who 's there? come in: the wish deserves a
   welcome.
  Duke. Dear sir, ere long I'll visit you again.
  Claud. Most holy sir, I thank you.

Enter ISABELLA.

  Isab. My business is a word or two with Claudio.
  Prov. And very welcome. Look, signior, here 's your
   sister.
  Duke. Provost, a word with you.   50
  Prov. As many as you please.
  Duke. Bring me to hear them speak, where I may
be concealed.   [*Exeunt Duke and Provost.*
  Claud. Now, sister, what 's the comfort?
  Isab.   Why,
As all comforts are; most good, most good indeed.
Lord Angelo, having affairs to heaven,
Intends you for his swift ambassador,
Where you shall be an everlasting leiger:
Therefore your best appointment make with speed;   60
To-morrow you set on.
  Claud.   Is there no remedy?
  Isab. None, but such remedy as, to save a head,
To cleave a heart in twain.
  Claud.   But is there any?
  Isab. Yes, brother, you may live:
There is a devilish mercy in the judge,
If you'll implore it, that will free your life,
But fetter you till death.
  Claud.   Perpetual durance?
  Isab. Ay, just; perpetual durance, a restraint,
Though all the world's vastidity you had,
To a determined scope.
  Claud.   But in what nature?   70
  Isab. In such a one as, you consenting to 't,
Would bark your honour from that trunk you bear,
And leave you naked.
  Claud.   Let me know the point.
  Isab. O, I do fear thee, Claudio; and I quake,

ACT III. SCENE I.   5. **absolute,** free from imperfection.   7-41. **If I do lose,** etc. The duke's indirect apostrophe to Life becomes merged, as the speech proceeds, with his direct instructions to Claudio. It is not easy to keep clear the distinction between the abstraction apostrophized and the young man who is the embodiment of that abstraction.   14. **accommodations,** conveniences.   23-25. **Thou . . . moon,** Life (personified) is of a temperament as variable as the constantly changing moon.   23. **certain,** steadfast.   24. **effects,** appearances, manifestations.   26. **ingots,** metal cast into molds.   31. **serpigo,** skin eruption.

rheum, morbid defluxion of humors; also catarrh.   59. **leiger,** ambassador.   60. **appointment,** preparation.   67. **durance,** imprisonment.   68-70. **restraint . . . scope,** confinement to fixed limit or bounds.   69. **vastidity,** immensity.   72. **bark,** strip.   75. **feverous life.** Cf. the modern phrase "a hectic life."   **entertain,** maintain, keep up (Onions); endure (Hart); possibly, desire.   82. **fetch,** derive.   91. **emmew,** drive a fowl into the water; misprint for *enew* (so printed by some editors).   93. **cast,** vomited.   94, 97. **prenzie,** so F; the word is unknown elsewhere. *Princely, priestly, primsie* are suggested conjectures. Hart connects

Lest thou a feverous life shouldst entertain,
And six or seven winters more respect
Than a perpetual honour. Darest thou die?
The sense of death is most in apprehension;
And the poor beetle, that we tread upon,
In corporal sufferance finds a pang as great   80
As when a giant dies.
   Claud.   Why give you me this shame?
Think you I can a resolution fetch
From flowery tenderness? If I must die,
I will encounter darkness as a bride,
And hug it in mine arms.
   Isab. There spake my brother; there my father's
     grave
Did utter forth a voice. Yes, thou must die:
Thou art too noble to conserve a life
In base appliances. This outward-sainted deputy,
Whose settled visage and deliberate word   90
Nips youth i' the head and follies doth emmew
As falcon doth the fowl, is yet a devil;
His filth within being cast, he would appear
A pond as deep as hell.
   Claud.   The prenzie Angelo!
   Isab. O, 'tis the cunning livery of hell,
The damned'st body to invest and cover
In prenzie guards! Dost thou think, Claudio?
If I would yield him my virginity,
Thou mightst be freed.
   Claud.   O heavens! it cannot be.
   Isab. Yes, he would give 't thee, from this rank
     offence,   100
So to offend him still. This night 's the time
That I should do what I abhor to name,
Or else thou diest to-morrow.
   Claud.   Thou shalt not do 't.
   Isab. O, were it but my life,
I 'ld throw it down for your deliverance
As frankly as a pin.
   Claud.   Thanks, dear Isabel.
   Isab. Be ready, Claudio, for your death to-morrow.
   Claud. Yes. Has he affections in him,
That thus can make him bite the law by the nose,
When he would force it? Sure, it is no sin;   110
Or of the deadly seven it is the least.
   Isab. Which is the least?
   Claud. If it were damnable, he being so wise,
Why would he for the momentary trick
Be perdurably fined? O Isabel!
   Isab. What says my brother?
   Claud.   Death is a fearful thing.
   Isab. And shamed life a hateful.
   Claud. Ay, but to die, and go we know not where;
To lie in cold obstruction and to rot;
This sensible warm motion to become   120
A kneaded clod; and the delighted spirit
To bathe in fiery floods, or to reside
In thrilling region of thick-ribbed ice;
To be imprison'd in the viewless winds,
And blown with restless violence round about

The pendent world; or to be worse than worst
Of those that lawless and incertain thought
Imagine howling: 'tis too horrible!
The weariest and most loathed worldly life
That age, ache, penury and imprisonment   130
Can lay on nature is a paradise
To what we fear of death.
   Isab. Alas, alas!
   Claud.   Sweet sister, let me live:
What sin you do to save a brother's life,
Nature dispenses with the deed so far
That it becomes a virtue.
   Isab.   O you beast!
O faithless coward! O dishonest wretch!
Wilt thou be made a man out of my vice?
Is 't not a kind of incest, to take life   139
From thine own sister's shame? What should I think?
Heaven shield my mother play'd my father fair!
For such a warped slip of wilderness
Ne'er issued from his blood. Take my defiance!
Die, perish! Might but my bending down
Reprieve thee from thy fate, it should proceed:
I'll pray a thousand prayers for thy death,
No word to save thee.
   Claud. Nay, hear me, Isabel.
   Isab.   O, fie, fie, fie!
Thy sin 's not accidental, but a trade.
Mercy to thee would prove itself a bawd: 150
'Tis best that thou diest quickly.
   Claud.   O hear me, Isabella!

           Re-enter DUKE.

   Duke. Vouchsafe a word, young sister, but one
     word.
   Isab. What is your will?
   Duke. Might you dispense with your leisure, I would
by and by have some speech with you: the satisfaction I would require is likewise your own benefit.   157
   Isab. I have no superfluous leisure; my stay must be
stolen out of other affairs; but I will attend you awhile.
                                   [Walks apart.
   Duke. Son, I have overheard what hath passed between you and your sister. Angelo had never the purpose to corrupt her; only he hath made an assay of
her virtue to practise his judgement with the disposition of natures: she, having the truth of honour
in her, hath made him that gracious denial which he
is most glad to receive. I am confessor to Angelo, and
I know this to be true; therefore prepare yourself to
death: do not satisfy your resolution with hopes that
are fallible: to-morrow you must die; go to your
knees and make ready.   172
   Claud. Let me ask my sister pardon. I am so out of
love with life that I will sue to be rid of it.
   Duke. Hold you there: farewell. [*Exit Claudio.*] Provost, a word with you!

           Re-enter PROVOST.

   Prov. What 's your will, father?

---

it with "prim," i.e., overnice; the New Cambridge editors favor *proxy* (Bulloch's conjecture) for line 94 and some word corresponding with "priestly" for line 97; they offer *prosne* or *prozne* (i.e., homily). 115. **perdurably,** lastingly. 119. **obstruction,** cessation of the vital functions. 121. **delighted spirit,** spirit once or now capable of delight. 122-128. **fiery . . . howling.** Keightly in his comment on *Paradise Lost,* II, 587-595, observes the currency in the Middle Ages of the idea of hell as consisting in alternations between the extremes of cold and heat; he finds it to come from the Jewish commentators. It is found in Dante's

Inferno and in the description of hell in the *Faust-Book* (1587). 123. **thrilling,** causing one to shiver. 142. **warped,** perverse. **slip,** scion. **wilderness,** worthlessness. 154. **Might you,** etc. Up to this point the verse scene is marked by broken lines and textual difficulties which indicate cuts and revisions. The sudden change to prose at this point suggests that the remainder of the scene has been rewritten. The New Cambridge editors call attention to verse fossils; e.g., lines 215, 233, 234, and the last speech of the scene. 164-165. **to practise . . . natures,** to test his ability to judge people's characters.

Duke. That now you are come, you will be gone. Leave me awhile with the maid: my mind promises with my habit no loss shall touch her by my company.

Prov. In good time.   183

[*Exit Provost. Isabella comes forward.*

Duke. The hand that hath made you fair hath made you good: the goodness that is cheap in beauty makes beauty brief in goodness; but grace, being the soul of your complexion, shall keep the body of it ever fair. The assault that Angelo hath made to you, fortune hath conveyed to my understanding; and, but that frailty hath examples for his falling, I should wonder at Angelo. How will you do to content this substitute, and to save your brother?   193

Isab. I am now going to resolve him: I had rather my brother die by the law than my son should be unlawfully born. But, O, how much is the good duke deceived in Angelo! If ever he return and I can speak to him, I will open my lips in vain, or discover his government.

Duke. That shall not be much amiss: yet, as the matter now stands, he will avoid your accusation; he made trial of you only. Therefore fasten your ear on my advisings: to the love I have in doing good a remedy presents itself. I do make myself believe that you may most uprighteously do a poor wronged lady a merited benefit; redeem your brother from the angry law; do no stain to your own gracious person; and much please the absent duke, if peradventure he shall ever return to have hearing of this business.   211

Isab. Let me hear you speak farther. I have spirit to do any thing that appears not foul in the truth of my spirit.

Duke. Virtue is bold, and goodness never fearful. Have you not heard speak of Mariana, the sister of Frederick the great soldier who miscarried at sea?

Isab. I have heard of the lady, and good words went with her name.   220

Duke. She should this Angelo have married; was affianced to her by oath, and the nuptial appointed: between which time of the contract and limit of the solemnity, her brother Frederick was wrecked at sea, having in that perished vessel the dowry of his sister. But mark how heavily this befell to the poor gentlewoman: there she lost a noble and renowned brother, in his love toward her ever most kind and natural; with him, the portion and sinew of her fortune, her marriage-dowry; with both, her combinate husband, this well-seeming Angelo.   232

Isab. Can this be so? did Angelo so leave her?

Duke. Left her in her tears, and dried not one of them with his comfort; swallowed his vows whole, pretending in her discoveries of dishonour: in few, bestowed her on her own lamentation, which she yet wears for his sake; and he, a marble to her tears, is washed with them, but relents not.

Isab. What a merit were it in death to take this poor maid from the world! What corruption in this life, that it will let this man live! But how out of this can she avail?   243

Duke. It is a rupture that you may easily heal: and the cure of it not only saves your brother, but keeps you from dishonour in doing it.

Isab. Show me how, good father.

Duke. This forenamed maid hath yet in her the continuance of her first affection: his unjust unkindness, that in all reason should have quenched her love, hath, like an impediment in the current, made it more violent and unruly. Go you to Angelo; answer his requiring with a plausible obedience; agree with his demands to the point; only refer yourself to this advantage, first, that your stay with him may not be long; that the time may have all shadow and silence in it; and the place answer to convenience. This being granted in course,—and now follows all,—we shall advise this wronged maid to stead up your appointment, go in your place; if the encounter acknowledge itself hereafter, it may compel him to her recompense: and here, by this, is your brother saved, your honour untainted, the poor Mariana advantaged, and the corrupt deputy scaled. The maid will I frame and make fit for his attempt. If you think well to carry this as you may, the doubleness of the benefit defends the deceit from reproof. What think you of it?   272

Isab. The image of it gives me content already; and I trust it will grow to a most prosperous perfection.

Duke. It lies much in your holding up. Haste you speedily to Angelo: if for this night he entreat you to his bed, give him promise of satisfaction. I will presently to Saint Luke's: there, at the moated grange, resides this dejected Mariana. At that place call upon me; and dispatch with Angelo, that it may be quickly.   279

Isab. I thank you for this comfort. Fare you well, good father.   [*Exeunt severally.*

SCENE II. *The street before the prison.*

Enter, on one side, DUKE *disguised as before; on the other,* ELBOW, *and* Officers *with* POMPEY.

Elb. Nay, if there be no remedy for it, but that you will needs buy and sell men and women like beasts, we shall have all the world drink brown and white bastard.

Duke. O heavens! what stuff is here?

Pom. 'Twas never merry world since, of two usuries, the merriest was put down, and the worser allowed by order of law a furred gown to keep him warm; and furred with fox and lamb-skins too, to signify, that craft, being richer than innocency, stands for the facing.   11

Elb. Come your way, sir. 'Bless you, good father friar.

---

192. **this substitute,** i.e., the deputy, Angelo. 231. **combinate husband,** i.e., betrothed; cf. I, ii, 151, note. 237. **bestowed . . . lamentation,** left to her grief, with quibble on *bestowed* meaning "gave in marriage." 253. **plausible,** acceptable. 261-262. **if the . . . hereafter,** i.e., if she should become pregnant. 276. **Saint Luke's,** a casual place reference. 278. **dispatch,** settle, conclude (business).

SCENE II. F has no scene division here. It was first introduced by Capell. This scene is characterized, like the last, by changes from verse to prose, the latter frequently containing what the New Cambridge editors describe as "verse fossils," particularly in the Escalus episode

(ll. 201-274). The absence of any trace of these verse fossils in the Lucio episode (ll. 45-195) suggests that it was a complete recasting. 4. **bastard,** sweet Spanish wine (used quibblingly). 6-7. **two usuries,** i.e., moneylending (*the worser*) and procuring (*the merriest*). 9. **furred . . . lamb-skins,** characteristic trimmings of usurers' gowns. 14. **brother father,** the duke's retort to Elbow's *father friar* (i.e., father brother). 41. **From our . . . free,** so F; there are no satisfactory conjectures. Some editors adopt F2: *Free from our,* etc. 42. **His . . . cord.** Elbow hints at Pompey's liability to hang, at the same time referring to the cord about the duke's waist—in his habit of friar. 47.

Duke. And you, good brother father. What offence hath this man made you, sir?

Elb. Marry, sir, he hath offended the law: and, sir, we take him to be a thief too, sir; for we have found upon him, sir, a strange picklock, which we have sent to the deputy.

Duke. Fie, sirrah! a bawd, a wicked bawd! 20
The evil that thou causest to be done,
That is thy means to live. Do thou but think
What 'tis to cram a maw or clothe a back
From such a filthy vice: say to thyself,
From their abominable and beastly touches
I drink, I eat, array myself, and live.
Canst thou believe thy living is a life,
So stinkingly depending? Go mend, go mend.

Pom. Indeed, it does stink in some sort, sir; but yet, sir, I would prove— 30

Duke. Nay, if the devil have given thee proofs for sin, Thou wilt prove his. Take him to prison, officer:
Correction and instruction must both work
Ere this rude beast will profit.

Elb. He must before the deputy, sir; he has given him warning: the deputy cannot abide a whoremaster: if he be a whoremonger, and comes before him, he were as good go a mile on his errand.

Duke. That we were all, as some would seem to be, †From our faults, as faults from seeming, free! 41

Elb. His neck will come to your waist,—a cord, sir.

Pom. I spy comfort; I cry bail. Here's a gentleman and a friend of mine.

Enter LUCIO.

Lucio. How now, noble Pompey! What, at the wheels of Cæsar? art thou led in triumph? What, is there none of Pygmalion's images, newly made woman, to be had now, for putting the hand in the pocket and extracting it clutched? What reply, ha? What sayest thou to this tune, matter and method? Is 't not drowned i' the last rain, ha? What sayest thou, Trot? Is the world as it was, man? Which is the way? Is it sad, and few words? or how? The trick of it?

Duke. Still thus, and thus; still worse! 55

Lucio. How doth my dear morsel, thy mistress? Procures she still, ha?

Pom. Troth, sir, she hath eaten up all her beef, and she is herself in the tub.

Lucio. Why, 'tis good; it is the right of it; it must be so: ever your fresh whore and your powdered bawd: an unshunned consequence; it must be so. Art going to prison, Pompey?

Pom. Yes, faith, sir.

Lucio. Why, 'tis not amiss, Pompey. Farewell: go say I sent thee thither. For debt, Pompey? or how?

Elb. For being a bawd, for being a bawd. 68

Lucio. Well, then, imprison him: if imprisonment be the due of a bawd, why, 'tis his right: bawd is he doubtless, and of antiquity too; bawd-born. Farewell, good Pompey. Commend me to the prison, Pompey:

you will turn good husband now, Pompey; you will keep the house.

Pom. I hope, sir, your good worship will be my bail.

Lucio. No, indeed, will I not, Pompey; it is not the wear. I will pray, Pompey, to increase your bondage: if you take it not patiently, why, your mettle is the more. Adieu, trusty Pompey. 'Bless you, friar. 81

Duke. And you.

Lucio. Does Bridget paint still, Pompey, ha?

Elb. Come your ways, sir; come.

Pom. You will not bail me, then, sir?

Lucio. Then, Pompey, nor now. What news abroad, friar? what news?

Elb. Come your ways, sir; come.

Lucio. Go to kennel, Pompey; go. [*Exeunt Elbow, Pompey and Officers.*] What news, friar, of the duke? 91

Duke. I know none. Can you tell me of any?

Lucio. Some say he is with the Emperor of Russia; other some, he is in Rome: but where is he, think you?

Duke. I know not where; but wheresoever, I wish him well.

Lucio. It was a mad fantastical trick of him to steal from the state, and usurp the beggary he was never born to. Lord Angelo dukes it well in his absence; he puts transgression to 't. 101

Duke. He does well in 't.

Lucio. A little more lenity to lechery would do no harm in him: something too crabbed that way, friar.

Duke. It is too general a vice, and severity must cure it.

Lucio. Yes, in good sooth, the vice is of a great kindred; it is well allied: but it is impossible to extirp it quite, friar, till eating and drinking be put down. They say this Angelo was not made by man and woman after this downright way of creation: is it true, think you? 113

Duke. How should he be made, then?

Lucio. Some report a sea-maid spawned him; some, that he was begot between two stock-fishes. But it is certain that when he makes water his urine is congealed ice; that I know to be true: †and he is a motion generative; that's infallible.

Duke. You are pleasant, sir, and speak apace. 120

Lucio. Why, what a ruthless thing is this in him, for the rebellion of a codpiece to take away the life of a man! Would the duke that is absent have done this? Ere he would have hanged a man for the getting a hundred bastards, he would have paid for the nursing a thousand: he had some feeling of the sport; he knew the service, and that instructed him to mercy.

Duke. I never heard the absent duke much detected for women; he was not inclined that way. 130

Lucio. O, sir, you are deceived.

Duke. 'Tis not possible.

Lucio. Who, not the duke? yes, your beggar of fifty; and his use was to put a ducat in her clack-dish: the duke had crotchets in him. He would be drunk too; that let me inform you.

Pygmalion's images, possibly a glance at Marston's *Metamorphosis of Pygmalion's Image* (1598), a poem ordered to be burned on account of its indecency. 52. **Trot,** contemptuous term for an old woman; cf. *The Taming of the Shrew,* I, ii, 80. 59. **in the tub,** i.e., a victim of venereal disease, so designated from the sweating-tub treatment to which victims were subjected. 62. **powdered,** salted; salt was put into the baths (cf. preceding note); hence arise the puns on *salt* meaning "wanton, lecherous." 73. **good husband,** thrifty manager. 80. **mettle,** spirit, with quibble on "metal," i.e., the irons with which he will be shackled. 108-109. **is . . . kindred,** belongs to a numerous race. 110. **extirp,**

eradicate. 115. **sea-maid,** mermaid. 116. **stock-fishes,** dried codfish. 119. **motion generative,** a puppet appearing to be generative or possessed of generative powers. 122. **codpiece,** an appendage to the front of close-fitting hose or breeches worn by men in the sixteenth century, often ornamented and indelicately conspicuous. 135. **clack-dish,** wooden dish with a lid, carried by beggars and "clacked" to attract attention. **crotchets,** whims, fancies.

Duke. You do him wrong, surely.

Lucio. Sir, I was an inward of his. A shy fellow was the duke: and I believe I know the cause of his withdrawing. 140

Duke. What, I prithee, might be the cause?

Lucio. No, pardon; 'tis a secret must be locked within the teeth and the lips: but this I can let you understand, the greater file of the subject held the duke to be wise.

Duke. Wise! why, no question but he was.

Lucio. A very superficial, ignorant, unweighing fellow. 147

Duke. Either this is envy in you, folly, or mistaking: the very stream of his life and the business he hath helmed must upon a warranted need give him a better proclamation. Let him be but testimonied in his own bringings-forth, and he shall appear to the envious a scholar, a statesman and a soldier. Therefore you speak unskilfully; or if your knowledge be more it is much darkened in your malice.

Lucio. Sir, I know him, and I love him.

Duke. Love talks with better knowledge, and knowledge with dearer love. 160

Lucio. Come, sir, I know what I know.

Duke. I can hardly believe that, since you know not what you speak. But, if ever the duke return, as our prayers are he may, let me desire you to make your answer before him. If it be honest you have spoke, you have courage to maintain it: I am bound to call upon you; and, I pray you, your name?

Lucio. Sir, my name is Lucio; well known to the duke. 170

Duke. He shall know you better, sir, if I may live to report you.

Lucio. I fear you not.

Duke. O, you hope the duke will return no more; or you imagine me too unhurtful an opposite. But indeed I can do you little harm; you'll forswear this again.

Lucio. I'll be hanged first: thou art deceived in me, friar. But no more of this. Canst thou tell if Claudio die to-morrow or no? 180

Duke. Why should he die, sir?

Lucio. Why? For filling a bottle with a tun-dish. I would the duke we talk of were returned again: this ungenitured agent will unpeople the province with continency; sparrows must not build in his houseeaves, because they are lecherous. The duke yet would have dark deeds darkly answered; he would never bring them to light: would he were returned! Marry, this Claudio is condemned for untrussing. Farewell, good friar: I prithee, pray for me. The duke, I say to thee again, would eat mutton on Fridays. He 's not past it yet, and I say to thee, he would mouth with a beggar, though she smelt brown bread and garlic: say that I said so. Farewell. [*Exit.*

Duke. No might nor greatness in mortality

Can censure 'scape; back-wounding calumny
The whitest virtue strikes. What king so strong
Can tie the gall up in the slanderous tongue?
But who comes here? 200

Enter Escalus, Provost, *and* Officers *with* Mistress Overdone.

Escal. Go; away with her to prison!

Mrs Ov. Good my lord, be good to me; your honour is accounted a merciful man; good my lord.

Escal. Double and treble admonition, and still forfeit in the same kind! This would make mercy swear and play the tyrant.

Prov. A bawd of eleven years' continuance, may it please your honour. 209

Mrs Ov. My lord, this is one Lucio's information against me. Mistress Kate Keepdown was with child by him in the duke's time; he promised her marriage: his child is a year and a quarter old, come Philip and Jacob: I have kept it myself; and see how he goes about to abuse me!

Escal. That fellow is a fellow of much license: let him be called before us. Away with her to prison! Go to; no more words. [*Exeunt Officers with Mistress Ov.*] Provost, my brother Angelo will not be altered: Claudio must die to-morrow: let him be furnished with divines, and have all charitable preparation. If my brother wrought by my pity, it should not be so with him. 222

Prov. So please you, this friar hath been with him, and advised him for the entertainment of death.

Escal. Good even, good father.

Duke. Bliss and goodness on you!

Escal. Of whence are you?

Duke. Not of this country, though my chance is now
To use it for my time: I am a brother
Of gracious order, late come from the See
In special business from his holiness.

Escal. What news abroad i' the world? 234

Duke. None, but that there is so great a fever on goodness, that the dissolution of it must cure it: novelty is only in request; and it is as dangerous to be aged in any kind of course, as it is virtuous to be constant in any undertaking. There is scarce truth enough alive to make societies secure; but security enough to make fellowships accurst: much upon this riddle runs the wisdom of the world. This news is old enough, yet it is every day's news. I pray you, sir, of what disposition was the duke? 244

Escal. One that, above all other strifes, contended especially to know himself.

Duke. What pleasure was he given to?

Escal. Rather rejoicing to see another merry, than merry at any thing which professed to make him rejoice: a gentleman of all temperance. But leave we him to his events, with a prayer they may prove prosperous; and let me desire to know how you find

138. **inward,** intimate acquaintance. 144. **file,** number. 147. **unweighing,** thoughtless. 151. **upon . . . need,** if a warrant is needed. 175. **too . . . opposite,** too harmless an adversary. 182. **tun-dish,** funnel. 184. **ungenitured,** impotent. 188. **darkly answered,** not made public. 192. **mutton,** quibble on the meaning "prostitute." 214. **Philip and Jacob,** feast of St. Philip and St. Jacob, May 1. 232. **the See,** Rome. 256. **sinister,** unfair, unjust. 269. **straitness,** strictness. 277-278. **Pattern . . . virtue go,** so F; Johnson rewrote: *Patterning Himself . . . In grace to stand, in virtue go.* Hart emended *and to an* (i.e., *if*), which gives the sense, "if virtue fail elsewhere." 287-290. **How . . . things.** Of the many conjectures none is convincing. Hart's note suggests a solution: "In these two short lines (287-288) of eleven words,

three begin with 'ma.' Perhaps only two should so begin, and the other should be 'my' not 'may'. The compositor's eye may have become confused. The duke is condemning Angelo with the utmost severity. He is the more indignant that his likeness (representative), compacted in sin, is practising on these wicked opportunities to work out important matters of life and death by such vain and guileful methods. Cobweb was constantly used at this time of craft and deceit."

ACT IV. SCENE I. 4. **mislead,** i.e., mislead one to expect the morning. 8-9. **whose . . . discontent.** Mariana is implying a length of association impossible with the time scheme as it now stands. This fact and other difficulties in the treatment of the Mariana plot indicate that it was of later composition than the main lines of the play. Cf. Introduction.

Claudio prepared. I am made to understand that
you have lent him visitation.   255
    Duke. He professes to have received no sinister
measure from his judge, but most willingly humbles
himself to the determination of justice: yet had he
framed to himself, by the instruction of his frailty,
many deceiving promises of life; which I by my good
leisure have discredited to him, and now is he resolved to die.
    Escal. You have paid the heavens your function,
and the prisoner the very debt of your calling. I have
laboured for the poor gentleman to the extremest
shore of my modesty: but my brother justice have I
found so severe, that he hath forced me to tell him he
is indeed Justice.   267
    Duke. If his own life answer the straitness of his
proceeding, it shall become him well; wherein if he
chance to fail, he hath sentenced himself.
    Escal. I am going to visit the prisoner. Fare you
well.
    Duke. Peace be with you! [*Exeunt Escalus and Provost.*
He who the sword of heaven will bear
Should be as holy as severe;
Pattern in himself to know,
†Grace to stand, and virtue go;
More nor less to others paying
Than by self-offences weighing.   280
Shame to him whose cruel striking
Kills for faults of his own liking!
Twice treble shame on Angelo,
To weed my vice and let his grow!
O, what may man within him hide,
Though angel on the outward side!
†How may likeness made in crimes,
Making practice on the times,
To draw with idle spiders' strings
Most ponderous and substantial things!   290
Craft against vice I must apply:
With Angelo to-night shall lie
His old betrothed but despised;
†So disguise shall, by the disguised,
Pay with falsehood false exacting,
And perform an old contracting.   [*Exit.*

ACT IV.

SCENE I. *The moated grange at* ST LUKE'S.

Enter MARIANA *and a* BOY.

BOY *sings.*

Take, O, take those lips away,
    That so sweetly were forsworn;
And those eyes, the break of day,
    Lights that do mislead the morn:
But my kisses bring again, bring again;
Seals of love, but seal'd in vain, seal'd in vain.

Mari. Break off thy song, and haste thee quick
    away:
Here comes a man of comfort, whose advice
Hath often still'd my brawling discontent.   [*Exit Boy.*

    Enter DUKE *disguised as before.*

I cry you mercy, sir; and well could wish   10
You had not found me here so musical:
Let me excuse me, and believe me so,
My mirth it much displeased, but pleased my woe.
    Duke. 'Tis good; though music oft hath such a
    charm
To make bad good, and good provoke to harm.
I pray you, tell me, hath any body inquired for me
here to-day? much upon this time have I promised
here to meet.
    Mari. You have not been inquired after: I have sat
here all day.   20

    Enter ISABELLA.

    Duke. I do constantly believe you. The time is come
even now. I shall crave your forbearance a little:
may be I will call upon you anon, for some advantage
to yourself.
    Mari. I am always bound to you.   [*Exit.*
    Duke. Very well met, and well come.
What is the news from this good deputy?
    Isab. He hath a garden circummured with brick,
Whose western side is with a vineyard back'd;
And to that vineyard is a planched gate,   30
That makes his opening with this bigger key:
This other doth command a little door
Which from the vineyard to the garden leads;
There have I made my promise
Upon the heavy middle of the night
To call upon him.
    Duke. But shall you on your knowledge find this
    way?
    Isab. I have ta'en a due and wary note upon 't:
With whispering and most guilty diligence,
In action all of precept, he did show me   40
The way twice o'er.
    Duke.   Are there no other tokens
Between you 'greed concerning her observance?
    Isab. No, none, but only a repair i' the dark;
And that I have possess'd him my most stay
Can be but brief; for I have made him know
I have a servant comes with me along,
That stays upon me, whose persuasion is
I come about my brother.
    Duke.   'Tis well borne up.
I have not yet made known to Mariana
A word of this. What, ho! within! come forth!   50

    Re-enter MARIANA.

I pray you, be acquainted with this maid;
She comes to do you good.

13-15. **My . . . harm.** These lines reflect the Renaissance conception
of the psychological effects of music; cf. Burton's description: "As
[music] is acceptable and conducing to most, so especially to a melancholy man; provided always, his disease proceed not originally from it,
that he be not some light *Inamorato*, some idle phantastick, who capers
in conceit all the day long, and thinks of nothing else but how to
make Jigs, Sonnets, Madrigals, in commendation of his Mistress.
In such cases Musick is most pernicious, as a spur to a free horse
will make him run himself blind, or break his wind . . . for Musick
enchants, it will make such melancholy persons mad, and the sound
of those Jigs and Horn-pipes will not be removed out of the ears a
week after. *Plato* for this reason forbids Musick and wine to all young
men, because they are most part amorous, lest one fire increase another.
Many men are melancholy by hearing Musick, but it is a pleasing
melancholy that it causeth; and therefore to such as are discontent,
in woe, fear, sorrow, or dejected, it is a most present remedy; it expels
cares, alters their grieved minds, and easeth in an instant." (*Anatomy
of Melancholy*, II, 2, vi, 3.) 21. **constantly,** confidently. 28. **circum-
mured,** walled about. 30. **planched,** made of boards. 40. **In . . .
precept,** i.e., Angelo accompanied his actions with much argument.
43. **repair,** act of going or coming to a place. 44. **my most stay,** my
stay at most.

Isab.　　　　　　　I do desire the like.

Duke. Do you persuade yourself that I respect you?

Mari. Good friar, I know you do, and have found it.

Duke. Take, then, this your companion by the hand,
Who hath a story ready for your ear.
I shall attend your leisure: but make haste;
The vaporous night approaches.

Mari. Will 't please you walk aside?
　　　　　　　　[*Exeunt Mariana and Isabella.*

Duke. O place and greatness! millions of false eyes　60
Are stuck upon thee: volumes of report
Run with these false and most contrarious quests
Upon thy doings: thousand escapes of wit
Make thee the father of their idle dreams
And rack thee in their fancies.

Re-enter MARIANA *and* ISABELLA.

　　　　　　　Welcome, how agreed?

Isab. She'll take the enterprise upon her, father,
If you advise it.

Duke. 　　　　　　　It is not my consent,
But my entreaty too.

Isab. 　　　　　　　Little have you to say
When you depart from him, but, soft and low,
'Remember now my brother.'

Mari. 　　　　　　Fear me not.　　　　　　70

Duke. Nor, gentle daughter, fear you not at all.
He is your husband on a pre-contract:
To bring you thus together, 'tis no sin,
Sith that the justice of your title to him
Doth flourish the deceit. Come, let us go.
Our corn 's to reap, for yet our tithe 's to sow. [*Exeunt.*

SCENE II. *A room in the prison.*

Enter PROVOST *and* POMPEY.

Prov. Come hither, sirrah. Can you cut off a man's
head?

Pom. If the man be a bachelor, sir, I can; but if he
be a married man, he 's his wife's head, and I can
never cut off a woman's head.

Prov. Come, sir, leave me your snatches, and yield
me a direct answer. To-morrow morning are to die
Claudio and Barnardine. Here is in our prison a
common executioner, who in his office lacks a helper:
if you will take it on you to assist him, it shall redeem
you from your gyves; if not, you shall have your full
time of imprisonment and your deliverance with an
unpitied whipping, for you have been a notorious
bawd.　　　　　　14

Pom. Sir, I have been an unlawful bawd time out of
mind; but yet I will be content to be a lawful hangman. I would be glad to receive some instruction
from my fellow partner.

Prov. What, ho! Abhorson! Where 's Abhorson,
there?　　　　　　21

Enter ABHORSON.

Abhor. Do you call, sir?

Prov. Sirrah, here 's a fellow will help you to-morrow
in your execution. If you think it meet, compound
with him by the year, and let him abide here with
you; if not, use him for the present and dismiss him.
He cannot plead his estimation with you; he hath
been a bawd.

Abhor. A bawd, sir? fie upon him! he will discredit
our mystery.　　　　　　30

Prov. Go to, sir; you weigh equally; a feather will
turn the scale.　　　　　　[*Exit.*

Pom. Pray, sir, by your good favour,—for surely,
sir, a good favour you have, but that you have a
hanging look,—do you call, sir, your occupation a
mystery?

Abhor. Ay, sir; a mystery.　　　　　　37

Pom. Painting, sir, I have heard say, is a mystery;
and your whores, sir, being members of my occupation, using painting, do prove my occupation a
mystery: but what mystery there should be in hanging, if I should be hanged, I cannot imagine.

Abhor. Sir, it is a mystery.

Pom. Proof?

Abhor. Every true man's apparel fits your thief:
if it be too little for your thief, your true man thinks
it big enough; if it be too big for your thief, your
thief thinks it little enough: so every true man's
apparel fits your thief.　　　　　　50

Re-enter PROVOST.

Prov. Are you agreed?

Pom. Sir, I will serve him; for I do find your hangman is a more penitent trade than your bawd; he
doth oftener ask forgiveness.

Prov. You, sirrah, provide your block and your
axe to-morrow four o'clock.

Abhor. Come on, bawd; I will instruct thee in my
trade; follow.

Pom. I do desire to learn, sir: and I hope, if you
have occasion to use me for your own turn, you shall
find me yare; for truly, sir, for your kindness I owe
you a good turn.　　　　　　62

Prov. Call hither Barnardine and Claudio:
　　　　　[*Exeunt Pompey and Abhorson.*
The one has my pity; not a jot the other,
Being a murderer, though he were my brother.

Enter CLAUDIO.

Look, here 's the warrant, Claudio, for thy death:
'Tis now dead midnight, and by eight to-morrow
Thou must be made immortal. Where 's Barnardine?

Claud. As fast lock'd up in sleep as guiltless labour
When it lies starkly in the traveller's bones:　　70
He will not wake.

Prov. 　　　　　　Who can do good on him?
Well, go, prepare yourself. [*Knocking within.*] But, hark,
　　what noise?

60-61. **millions . . . thee,** an allusion to the eyelike markings of the
peacock's plumage, a bird significant of pride and display. Warburton
noted that this passage (ll. 60-65) can follow consecutively III, ii, 196-
200. The reference to *false and most contrarious quests* (l. 62) has point
in III, ii, where it refers to the false reports of Lucio. The insertion
of a portion of the speech here is taken by some editors as indicative
of revision, something being needed here for filler while Isabella
and Mariana converse offstage. 62. **quests,** inquiries. 63. **escapes,**
sallies (of wit). 65. **rack,** distort. 72. **pre-contract.** Cf. I, ii, 151,
note. 75. **flourish,** embellish. 76. **tithe 's,** i.e., our tenth, our

profit.
SCENE II. 6. **snatches,** smart repartee. 12. **gyves,** fetters, shackles.
27-28. **plead his estimation,** claim any respect on account of his reputation. 30. **mystery,** craft, occupation. 38-50. **Painting, sir . . . your
thief.** Pompey's argument is: Painting is a craft, whores use painting,
therefore their trade is a craft or respectable mystery. And since he
belongs to a kindred occupation, both Pompey's and Overdone's
occupations rank as mysteries. Abhorson replies, similarly I can show
that thieves' and hangmen's trades belong to the dignity of a mystery.
A fitter of apparel's occupation is a mystery (a tailor's craft); a thief

Heaven give your spirits comfort! [*Exit Claudio.*] By
    and by.
I hope it is some pardon or reprieve
For the most gentle Claudio.

Enter DUKE *disguised as before.*

                Welcome, father.
Duke. The best and wholesomest spirits of the night
Envelope you, good Provost! Who call'd here of late?
Prov. None, since the curfew rung.
Duke. Not Isabel?
Prov.   No.
Duke.   They will, then, ere 't be long.
Prov. What comfort is for Claudio?   80
Duke. There 's some in hope.
Prov.   It is a bitter deputy.
Duke. Not so, not so; his life is parallel'd
Even with the stroke and line of his great justice:
He doth with holy abstinence subdue
That in himself which he spurs on his power
To qualify in others: were he meal'd with that
Which he corrects, then were he tyrannous;
But this being so, he 's just.   [*Knocking within.*
            Now are they come.   [*Exit Provost.*
This is a gentle provost: seldom when   89
The steeled gaoler is the friend of men.[*Knocking within.*
How now! what noise? That spirit 's possess'd with
    haste
That wounds the unsisting postern with these strokes.

Re-enter PROVOST.

Prov. There he must stay until the officer
Arise to let him in: he is call'd up.
Duke. Have you no countermand for Claudio yet,
But he must die to-morrow?
Prov.   None, sir, none.
Duke. As near the dawning, provost, as it is,
You shall hear more ere morning.
Prov.   Happily
You something know; yet I believe there comes
No countermand; no such example have we: 100
Besides, upon the very siege of justice
Lord Angelo hath to the public ear
Profess'd the contrary.

Enter a MESSENGER.

                This is his lordship's man.
Duke. And here comes Claudio's pardon.
Mes. [*Giving a paper.*] My lord hath sent you this
note; and by me this further charge, that you swerve
not from the smallest article of it, neither in time,
matter, or other circumstance. Good morrow; for, as
I take it, it is almost day.
Prov. I shall obey him.   [*Exit Messenger.*
Duke. [*Aside*] This is his pardon, purchased by such
    sin   111
For which the pardoner himself is in.
Hence hath offence his quick celerity,

When it is borne in high authority:
When vice makes mercy, mercy 's so extended,
That for the fault's love is the offender friended.
Now, sir, what news?
Prov. I told you. Lord Angelo, belike thinking me
remiss in mine office, awakens me with this unwonted
putting-on; methinks strangely, for he hath not used
it before.   121
Duke. Pray you, let 's hear.
Prov. [*Reads*]
'Whatsoever you may hear to the contrary, let
Claudio be executed by four of the clock; and in the
afternoon Barnardine: for my better satisfaction, let
me have Claudio's head sent me by five. Let this be
duly performed; with a thought that more depends
on it than we must yet deliver. Thus fail not to do
your office, as you will answer it at your peril.'   130
What say you to this, sir?
Duke. What is that Barnardine who is to be exe-
cuted in the afternoon?
Prov. A Bohemian born, but here nursed up and
bred; one that is a prisoner nine years old.
Duke. How came it that the absent duke had not
either delivered him to his liberty or executed him?
I have heard it was ever his manner to do so.   139
Prov. His friends still wrought reprieves for him:
and, indeed, his fact, till now in the government of
Lord Angelo, came not to an undoubtful proof.
Duke. It is now apparent?
Prov. Most manifest, and not denied by himself.
Duke. Hath he borne himself penitently in prison?
how seems he to be touched?
Prov. A man that apprehends death no more dreadfully but as a drunken sleep; careless, reckless, and
fearless of what 's past, present, or to come; insensible
of mortality, and desperately mortal.   152
Duke. He wants advice.
Prov. He will hear none: he hath evermore had the
liberty of the prison; give him leave to escape hence,
he would not: drunk many times a day, if not many
days entirely drunk. We have very oft awaked him,
as if to carry him to execution, and showed him a
seeming warrant for it: it hath not moved him at all.
Duke. More of him anon. There is written in your
brow, provost, honesty and constancy: if I read it not
truly, my ancient skill beguiles me; but, in the boldness of my cunning, I will lay my self in hazard.
Claudio, whom here you have warrant to execute, is
no greater forfeit to the law than Angelo who hath
sentenced him. To make you understand this in a
manifested effect, I crave but four days' respite; for
the which you are to do me both a present and a
dangerous courtesy.   172
Prov. Pray, sir, in what?
Duke. In the delaying death.
Prov. Alack, how may I do it, having the hour
limited, and an express command, under penalty, to
deliver his head in the view of Angelo? I may make

---

fits himself from every true man, therefore his business is a mystery.
And I, the hangman, find the thief's apparel big enough for my use,
who am a true man, so that I am also a member of the thief's occupation or mystery (Hart). Abhorson (ll. 46-50) refers to the custom
of the executioner's taking the garments of those executed. 54. **he
doth . . . forgiveness.** The executioner perfunctorily asked forgiveness
of those whose lives he was about to take. 56. **to-morrow four o'clock.**
Cf. *by eight to-morrow* (l. 67); the contradiction is accompanied by
the fact that the first reference is in a prose passage, the second in
a verse passage. 60. **use me . . . turn,** i.e., cut off your head. 61.

yare, ready. 70. **starkly,** stiffly. 86. **qualify,** modify. **meal'd,**
spotted, stained. 92. **unsisting,** unassisting (Hart). **postern,** back
door. 101. **siege,** seat. 125. **better satisfaction,** greater assurance.
135. **a prisoner . . . old,** nine years a prisoner. 152-153. **insensible
. . . mortal,** indifferent to death and without hope of immortality.
167. **forfeit to the law.** Cf. II, ii, 71, note. 169. **in a . . . effect,** by
means of concrete proof.

my case as Claudio's, to cross this in the smallest. 179

Duke. By the vow of mine order I warrant you, if my instructions may be your guide. Let this Barnardine be this morning executed, and his head borne to Angelo.

Prov. Angelo hath seen them both, and will discover the favour.

Duke. O, death 's a great disguiser; and you may add to it. Shave the head, and tie the beard; and say it was the desire of the penitent to be so bared before his death: you know the course is common. If any thing fall to you upon this, more than thanks and good fortune, by the saint whom I profess, I will plead against it with my life.

Prov. Pardon me, good father; it is against my oath.

Duke. Were you sworn to the duke, or to the deputy?

Prov. To him, and to his substitutes.

Duke. You will think you have made no offence, if the duke avouch the justice of your dealing? 201

Prov. But what likelihood is in that?

Duke. Not a resemblance, but a certainty. Yet since I see you fearful, that neither my coat, integrity, nor persuasion can with ease attempt you, I will go further than I meant, to pluck all fears out of you. Look you, sir, here is the hand and seal of the duke: you know the character, I doubt not; and the signet is not strange to you.

Prov. I know them both. 210

Duke. The contents of this is the return of the duke: you shall anon over-read it at your pleasure; where you shall find, within these two days he will be here. This is a thing that Angelo knows not; for he this very day receives letters of strange tenour; perchance of the duke's death; perchance entering into some monastery; but, by chance, nothing of what is writ. Look, the unfolding star calls up the shepherd. Put not yourself into amazement how these things should be: all difficulties are but easy when they are known. Call your executioner, and off with Barnardine's head: I will give him a present shrift and advise him for a better place. Yet you are amazed; but this shall absolutely resolve you. Come away; it is almost clear dawn. [*Exeunt.* 226

SCENE III. *Another room in the same.*

Enter POMPEY.

Pom. I am as well acquainted here as I was in our house of profession: one would think it were Mistress Overdone's own house, for here be many of her old customers. First, here 's young Master Rash; he 's in for a commodity of brown paper and old ginger, nine-score and seventeen pounds; of which he made five marks, ready money: marry, then ginger was not much in request, for the old women were all dead. Then is there here one Master Caper, at the

suit of Master Three-pile the mercer, for some four suits of peach-coloured satin, which now peaches him a beggar. Then have we here young Dizy, and young Master Deep-vow, and Master Copper-spur, and Master Starve-lackey the rapier and dagger man, and young Drop-heir that killed lusty Pudding, and Master Forthlight the tilter, and brave Master Shooty the great traveller, and wild Half-can that stabbed Pots, and, I think, forty more; all great doers in our trade, and are now 'for the Lord's sake.' 21

Enter ABHORSON.

Abhor. Sirrah, bring Barnardine hither.

Pom. Master Barnardine! you must rise and be hanged, Master Barnardine!

Abhor. What, ho, Barnardine!

Bar. [*Within*] A pox o' your throats! Who makes that noise there? What are you?

Pom. Your friends, sir; the hangman. You must be so good, sir, to rise and be put to death.

Bar. [*Within*] Away, you rogue, away! I am sleepy. 31

Abhor. Tell him he must awake, and that quickly too.

Pom. Pray, Master Barnardine, awake till you are executed, and sleep afterwards.

Abhor. Go in to him, and fetch him out.

Pom. He is coming, sir, he is coming; I hear his straw rustle.

Abhor. Is the axe upon the block, sirrah?

Pom. Very ready, sir. 40

Enter BARNARDINE.

Bar. How now, Abhorson? what 's the news with you?

Abhor. Truly, sir, I would desire you to clap into your prayers; for, look you, the warrant 's come.

Bar. You rogue, I have been drinking all night; I am not fitted for 't.

Pom. O, the better, sir; for he that drinks all night, and is hanged betimes in the morning, may sleep the sounder all the next day. 50

Abhor. Look you, sir; here comes your ghostly father: do we jest now, think you?

Enter DUKE *disguised as before.*

Duke. Sir, induced by my charity, and hearing how hastily you are to depart, I am come to advise you, comfort you and pray with you.

Bar. Friar, not I: I have been drinking hard all night, and I will have more time to prepare me, or they shall beat out my brains with billets: I will not consent to die this day, that 's certain.

Duke. O, sir, you must: and therefore I beseech you Look forward on the journey you shall go. 61

Bar. I swear I will not die to-day for any man's persuasion.

Duke. But hear you.

Bar. Not a word: if you have any thing to say to

me, come to my ward; for thence will not I to-day.
[Exit.
Duke. Unfit to live or die: O gravel heart!
After him, fellows; bring him to the block.
[Exeunt Abhorson and Pompey.

Enter PROVOST.

Prov. Now, sir, how do you find the prisoner?   70
Duke. A creature unprepared, unmeet for death;
And to transport him in the mind he is
Were damnable.
Prov.   Here in the prison, father,
There died this morning of a cruel fever
One Ragozine, a most notorious pirate,
A man of Claudio's years; his beard and head
Just of his colour. What if we do omit
This reprobate till he were well inclined;
And satisfy the deputy with the visage
Of Ragozine, more like to Claudio?   80
Duke. O, 'tis an accident that heaven provides!
Dispatch it presently; the hour draws on
Prefix'd by Angelo: see this be done,
And sent according to command; whiles I
Persuade this rude wretch willingly to die.
Prov. This shall be done, good father, presently.
But Barnardine must die this afternoon:
And how shall we continue Claudio,
To save me from the danger that might come
If he were known alive?
Duke.   Let this be done.   90
Put them in secret holds, both Barnardine and
    Claudio:
Ere twice the sun hath made his journal greeting
To the under generation, you shall find
Your safety manifested.
Prov. I am your free dependant.
Duke. Quick, dispatch, and send the head to
    Angelo.   [Exit Provost.
Now will I write letters to Angelo,—
The provost, he shall bear them,—whose contents
Shall witness to him I am near at home,
And that, by great injunctions, I am bound   100
To enter publicly: him I'll desire
To meet me at the consecrated fount
A league below the city; and from thence,
By cold gradation and well-balanced form,
We shall proceed with Angelo.

Re-enter PROVOST.

Prov. Here is the head; I'll carry it myself.
Duke. Convenient is it. Make a swift return;
For I would commune with you of such things
That want no ear but yours.
Prov.   I'll make all speed.   [Exit.
Isab. [Within] Peace, ho, be here!   110
Duke. The tongue of Isabel. She 's come to know
If yet her brother's pardon be come hither:
But I will keep her ignorant of her good,

To make her heavenly comforts of despair,
When it is least expected.

Enter ISABELLA.

Isab.   Ho, by your leave!
Duke. Good morning to you, fair and gracious
    daughter.
Isab. The better, given me by so holy a man.
Hath yet the deputy sent my brother's pardon?
Duke. He hath released him, Isabel, from the world:
His head is off and sent to Angelo.   120
Isab. Nay, but it is not so.
Duke. It is no other: show your wisdom, daughter,
In your close patience.
Isab. O, I will to him and pluck out his eyes!
Duke. You shall not be admitted to his sight.
Isab. Unhappy Claudio! wretched Isabel!
Injurious world! most damned Angelo!
Duke. This nor hurts him nor profits you a jot;
Forbear it therefore; give your cause to heaven.
Mark what I say, which you shall find   130
By every syllable a faithful verity:
The duke comes home to-morrow; nay, dry your eyes;
One of our convent, and his confessor,
Gives me this instance: already he hath carried
Notice to Escalus and Angelo,
Who do prepare to meet him at the gates,
There to give up their power. If you can, pace your
    wisdom
In that good path that I would wish it go,
And you shall have your bosom on this wretch,
Grace of the duke, revenges to your heart,   140
And general honour.
Isab.   I am directed by you.
Duke. This letter, then, to Friar Peter give;
'Tis that he sent me of the duke's return:
Say, by this token, I desire his company
At Mariana's house to-night. Her cause and yours
I'll perfect him withal, and he shall bring you
Before the duke, and to the head of Angelo
Accuse him home and home. For my poor self,
I am combined by a sacred vow
And shall be absent. Wend you with this letter: 150
Command these fretting waters from your eyes
With a light heart; trust not my holy order,
If I pervert your course. Who 's here?

Enter LUCIO.

Lucio. Good even. Friar, where 's the provost?
Duke. Not within, sir.
Lucio. O pretty Isabella, I am pale at mine heart to
see thine eyes so red: thou must be patient. I am fain
to dine and sup with water and bran; I dare not for
my head fill my belly; one fruitful meal would set
me to 't. But they say the duke will be here to-morrow.
By my troth, Isabel, I loved thy brother: if the old
fantastical duke of dark corners had been at home, he
had lived.   [Exit Isabella. 165

live. 92. **journal,** daily. 93. **the under,** so Hanmer; F: *yond;* Pope:
yonder; New Cambridge: *th'under,* from W. W. Greg's suggestion
(privately made) that Shakespeare wrote *ye onder. Under* may mean the
antipodes, or merely the human race—the generation under heaven.
Hart keeps *yond,* defining as "those beyond the prison walls." 97. **to
Angelo.** The New Cambridge editors think this a mistake, since Angelo
was not to meet the duke *at the consecrated fount a league below the city,*
but at the city gates (cf. ll. 135-137 below). The compositor's eye
probably caught the phrase *to Angelo* from the end of the preceding
line. 100. **great injunctions,** powerful precedent. 104. **By cold**

gradation, not eagerly and passionately, as my feelings would prompt
me (Schmidt). **well-balanced form.** Some editors retain F: *weal(e)
balanced,* which Schmidt defines as "kept in a just proportion by reasons
of state." 107. **Convenient,** timely. 117. **better,** i.e., comparative of
Good in the preceding line. 123. **In your close patience,** by enduring
your grief secretly. 139. **bosom,** desire. 146. **perfect,** acquaint
completely. 157-158. **I am . . . heart,** i.e., from sighing, since sighs
cost the heart loss of blood. 159. **fain,** compelled.

Duke. Sir, the duke is marvellous little beholding to your reports; but the best is, he lives not in them.

Lucio. Friar, thou knowest not the duke so well as I do: he 's a better woodman than thou takest him for.

Duke. Well, you'll answer this one day. Fare ye well.

Lucio. Nay, tarry; I'll go along with thee: I can tell thee pretty tales of the duke.

Duke. You have told me too many of him already, sir, if they be true; if not true, none were enough.

Lucio. I was once before him for getting a wench with child. 180

Duke. Did you such a thing?

Lucio. Yes, marry, did I: but I was fain to forswear it; they would else have married me to the rotten medlar.

Duke. Sir, your company is fairer than honest. Rest you well.

Lucio. By my troth, I'll go with thee to the lane's end: if bawdy talk offend you, we'll have very little of it. Nay, friar, I am a kind of burr; I shall stick.

[*Exeunt.*

SCENE IV. *A room in* ANGELO'S *house.*

Enter ANGELO *and* ESCALUS.

Escal. Every letter he hath writ hath disvouched other.

Ang. In most uneven and distracted manner. His actions show much like to madness: pray heaven his wisdom be not tainted! And why meet him at the gates, and redeliver our authorities there?

Escal. I guess not.

Ang. And why should we proclaim it in an hour before his entering, that if any crave redress of injustice, they should exhibit their petitions in the street? 12

Escal. He shows his reason for that: to have a dispatch of complaints, and to deliver us from devices hereafter, which shall then have no power to stand against us.

Ang. Well, I beseech you, let it be proclaimed betimes i' the morn; I'll call you at your house: give notice to such men of sort and suit as are to meet him.

Escal. I shall, sir. Fare you well. 21

Ang. Good night. [*Exit Escalus.*

This deed unshapes me quite, makes me unpregnant
And dull to all proceedings. A deflower'd maid!
And by an eminent body that enforced
The law against it! But that her tender shame
Will not proclaim against her maiden loss,
How might she tongue me! Yet reason dares her no;
For my authority bears of a credent bulk,
That no particular scandal once can touch 30
But it confounds the breather. He should have lived,
Save that his riotous youth, with dangerous sense,
Might in the times to come have ta'en revenge,
By so receiving a dishonour'd life
With ransom of such shame. Would yet he had lived!
Alack, when once our grace we have forgot,

Nothing goes right: we would, and we would not.

[*Exit.*

SCENE V. *Fields without the town.*

Enter DUKE *in his own habit, and* FRIAR PETER.

Duke. These letters at fit time deliver me:

[*Giving letters.*

The provost knows our purpose and our plot.
The matter being afoot, keep your instruction,
And hold you ever to our special drift;
Though sometimes you do blench from this to that,
As cause doth minister. Go call at Flavius' house,
And tell him where I stay: give the like notice
To Valentinus, Rowland, and to Crassus,
And bid them bring the trumpets to the gate;
But send me Flavius first.

Fri. P.   It shall be speeded well. [*Exit.* 10

Enter VARRIUS.

Duke. I thank thee, Varrius; thou hast made good haste:
Come, we will walk. There 's other of our friends
Will greet us here anon, my gentle Varrius.   [*Exeunt.*

SCENE VI. *Street near the city gate.*

Enter ISABELLA *and* MARIANA.

Isab. To speak so indirectly I am loath:
I would say the truth; but to accuse him so,
That is your part: yet I am advised to do it;
He says, to veil full purpose.

Mari.   Be ruled by him.

Isab. Besides, he tells me that, if peradventure
He speak against me on the adverse side,
I should not think it strange; for 'tis a physic
That 's bitter to sweet end.

Mari. I would Friar Peter—

Isab.   O, peace! the friar is come.   9

Enter FRIAR PETER.

Fri. P. Come, I have found you out a stand most fit,
Where you may have such vantage on the duke,
He shall not pass you. Twice have the trumpets sounded;
The generous and gravest citizens
Have hent the gates, and very near upon
The duke is entering: therefore, hence, away! [*Exeunt.*

ACT V.

SCENE I. *The city gate.*

MARIANA *veiled,* ISABELLA, *and* FRIAR PETER, *at their stand. Enter* DUKE, VARRIUS, LORDS, ANGELO, ESCALUS, LUCIO, PROVOST, *Officers, and* Citizens, *at several doors.*

Duke. My very worthy cousin, fairly met!
Our old and faithful friend, we are glad to see you.

Ang. } Happy return be to your royal grace!
Escal.
Duke. Many and hearty thankings to you both.
We have made inquiry of you; and we hear
Such goodness of your justice, that our soul
Cannot but yield you forth to public thanks,
Forerunning more requital.
 Ang.   You make my bonds still greater.
 Duke. O, your desert speaks loud; and I should
  wrong it,
To lock it in the wards of covert bosom,   10
When it deserves, with characters of brass,
A forted residence 'gainst the tooth of time
And razure of oblivion. Give me your hand,
And let the subject see, to make them know
That outward courtesies would fain proclaim
Favours that keep within. Come, Escalus,
You must walk by us on our other hand;
And good supporters are you.

 FRIAR PETER *and* ISABELLA *come forward.*

 Fri. P. Now is your time: speak loud and kneel be-
  fore him.
 Isab. Justice, O royal duke! Vail your regard   20
Upon a wrong'd, I would fain have said, a maid!
O worthy prince, dishonour not your eye
By throwing it on any other object
Till you have heard me in my true complaint
And given me justice, justice, justice, justice!
 Duke. Relate your wrongs; in what? by whom? be
  brief.
Here is Lord Angelo shall give you justice:
Reveal yourself to him.
 Isab.   O worthy duke,
You bid me seek redemption of the devil:
Hear me yourself; for that which I must speak   30
Must either punish me, not being believed,
Or wring redress from you. Hear me, O hear me, here!
 Ang. My lord, her wits, I fear me, are not firm:
She hath been a suitor to me for her brother
Cut off by course of justice,—
 Isab.   By course of justice!
 Ang. And she will speak most bitterly and strange.
 Isab. Most strange, but yet most truly, will I speak:
That Angelo 's forsworn; is it not strange?
That Angelo 's a murderer; is 't not strange?
That Angelo is an adulterous thief,   40
An hypocrite, a virgin-violator;
Is it not strange and strange?
 Duke.   Nay, it is ten times strange.
 Isab. It is not truer he is Angelo
Than this is all as true as it is strange:
Nay, it is ten times true; for truth is truth
To the end of reckoning.
 Duke.   Away with her! Poor soul,
She speaks this in the infirmity of sense.
 Isab. O prince, I conjure thee, as thou believest
There is another comfort than this world,
That thou neglect me not, with that opinion   50
That I am touch'd with madness! Make not
  impossible
That which but seems unlike: 'tis not impossible

But one, the wicked'st caitiff on the ground,
May seem as shy, as grave, as just, as absolute
As Angelo; even so may Angelo,
In all his dressings, characts, titles, forms,
Be an arch-villain; believe it, royal prince:
If he be less, he 's nothing; but he 's more,
Had I more name for badness.
 Duke.   By mine honesty,
If she be mad,—as I believe no other,—   60
Her madness hath the oddest frame of sense,
Such a dependency of thing on thing,
As e'er I heard in madness.
 Isab.   O gracious duke,
Harp not on that, nor do not banish reason
For inequality; but let your reason serve
To make the truth appear where it seems hid,
And hide the false seems true.
 Duke.   Many that are not mad
Have, sure, more lack of reason. What would you say?
 Isab. I am the sister of one Claudio,
Condemn'd upon the act of fornication   70
To lose his head; condemn'd by Angelo:
I, in probation of a sisterhood,
Was sent to by my brother; one Lucio
As then the messenger,—
 Lucio.   That 's I, an 't like your grace:
I came to her from Claudio, and desired her
To try her gracious fortune with Lord Angelo
For her poor brother's pardon.
 Isab.   That 's he indeed.
 Duke. You were not bid to speak.
 Lucio.   No, my good lord;
Nor wish'd to hold my peace.
 Duke.   I wish you now, then;
Pray you, take note of it: and when you have   80
A business for yourself, pray heaven you then
Be perfect.
 Lucio.   I warrant your honour.
 Duke. The warrant 's for yourself; take heed to 't.
 Isab. This gentleman told somewhat of my tale,—
 Lucio. Right.
 Duke. It may be right; but you are i' the wrong
To speak before your time. Proceed.
 Isab.   I went
To this pernicious caitiff deputy,—
 Duke. That 's somewhat madly spoken.
 Isab.   Pardon it;
The phrase is to the matter.   90
 Duke. Mended again. The matter; proceed.
 Isab. In brief, to set the needless process by,
How I persuaded, how I pray'd, and kneel'd,
How he refell'd me, and how I replied,—
For this was of much length,—the vile conclusion
I now begin with grief and shame to utter:
He would not, but by gift of my chaste body
To his concupiscible intemperate lust,
Release my brother; and, after much debatement,
My sisterly remorse confutes mine honour,   100
And I did yield to him: but the next morn betimes,
His purpose surfeiting, he sends a warrant
For my poor brother's head.
 Duke.   This is most likely!

*Measure
for Measure*
ACT V : SC I

857

SCENE VI. 13. **generous,** highborn. 14. **hent,** reached, occupied.
ACT V. SCENE I. 12. **forted,** fortified. 13. **razure,** effacement.
47. **in . . . sense,** out of a sick mind. 56. **characts,** distinctive marks.
62. **a dependency of thing on thing,** coherence. 65. **inequality,**
injustice. 92. **to . . . by,** not to dwell on the story; see *process* in glossary.

94. **refell'd,** repelled. 98. **concupiscible,** lustful. 103. **This . . .
likely.** The duke feigns contempt for Isabella's story in order to fortify
Angelo's confidence in denying Isabella.

Isab. O, that it were as like as it is true!

Duke. By heaven, fond wretch, thou know'st not
    what thou speak'st,
Or else thou art suborn'd against his honour
In hateful practice. First, his integrity
Stands without blemish. Next, it imports no reason
That with such vehemency he should pursue
Faults proper to himself: if he had so offended,   110
He would have weigh'd thy brother by himself
And not have cut him off. Some one hath set you on:
Confess the truth, and say by whose advice
Thou camest here to complain.

Isab.   And is this all?
Then, O you blessed ministers above,
Keep me in patience, and with ripen'd time
Unfold the evil which is here wrapt up
In countenance! Heaven shield your grace from woe,
As I, thus wrong'd, hence unbelieved go!

Duke. I know you 'ld fain be gone. An officer!   120
To prison with her! Shall we thus permit
A blasting and a scandalous breath to fall
On him so near us? This needs must be a practice.
Who knew of your intent and coming hither?

Isab. One that I would were here, Friar Lodowick.

Duke. A ghostly father, belike. Who knows that
    Lodowick?

Lucio. My lord, I know him; 'tis a meddling friar;
I do not like the man: had he been lay, my lord,
For certain words he spake against your grace
In your retirement, I had swinged him soundly.   130

Duke. Words against me! this is a good friar,
    belike!
And to set on this wretched woman here
Against our substitute! Let this friar be found.

Lucio. But yesternight, my lord, she and that friar,
I saw them at the prison: a saucy friar,
A very scurvy fellow.

Fri. P. Blessed be your royal grace!
I have stood by, my lord, and I have heard
Your royal ear abused. First, hath this woman
Most wrongfully accused your substitute,   140
Who is as free from touch or soil with her
As she from one ungot.

Duke.   We did believe no less.
Know you that Friar Lodowick that she speaks of?

Fri. P. I know him for a man divine and holy;
Not scurvy, nor a temporary meddler,
As he 's reported by this gentleman;
And, on my trust, a man that never yet
Did, as he vouches, misreport your grace.

Lucio. My lord, most villanously; believe it.   149

Fri. P. Well, he in time may come to clear himself;
But at this instant he is sick, my lord,
Of a strange fever. Upon his mere request,
Being come to knowledge that there was complaint
Intended 'gainst Lord Angelo, came I hither,
To speak, as from his mouth, what he doth know
Is true and false; and what he with his oath
And all probation will make up full clear,
Whensoever he 's convented. First, for this woman,
To justify this worthy nobleman,
So vulgarly and personally accused,   160

Her shall you hear disproved to her eyes,
Till she herself confess it.

Duke.   Good friar, let 's hear it.
    [Isabella is carried off guarded; and Mariana comes
                              forward.
Do you not smile at this, Lord Angelo?
O heaven, the vanity of wretched fools!
Give us some seats. Come, cousin Angelo;
In this I'll be impartial; be you judge
Of your own cause. Is this the witness, friar?
First, let her show her face, and after speak.

Mari. Pardon, my lord; I will not show my face
Until my husband bid me.   170

Duke. What, are you married?

Mari. No, my lord.

Duke. Are you a maid?

Mari. No, my lord.

Duke. A widow, then?

Mari. Neither, my lord.

Duke. Why, you are nothing then: neither maid,
widow, nor wife?

Lucio. My lord, she may be a punk; for many of
them are neither maid, widow, nor wife.   180

Duke. Silence that fellow: I would he had some
    cause
To prattle for himself.

Lucio. Well, my lord.

Mari. My lord, I do confess I ne'er was married;
And I confess besides I am no maid:
I have known my husband; yet my husband
Knows not that ever he knew me.

Lucio. He was drunk then, my lord: it can be no
better.

Duke. For the benefit of silence, would thou wert
so too!   191

Lucio. Well, my lord.

Duke. This is no witness for Lord Angelo.

Mari. Now I come to 't, my lord:
She that accuses him of fornication,
In self-same manner doth accuse my husband,
And charges him, my lord, with such a time
When I'll depose I had him in mine arms
With all the effect of love.

Ang. Charges she more than me?

Mari.   Not that I know.   200

Duke. No? you say your husband.

Mari. Why, just, my lord, and that is Angelo,
Who thinks he knows that he ne'er knew my body,
But knows he thinks that he knows Isabel's.

Ang. This is a strange abuse. Let 's see thy face.

Mari. My husband bids me; now I will unmask.
                            [Unveiling.
This is that face, thou cruel Angelo,
Which once thou sworest was worth the looking on;
This is the hand which, with a vow'd contract,
Was fast belock'd in thine; this is the body   210
That took away the match from Isabel,
And did supply thee at thy garden-house
In her imagined person.

Duke.   Know you this woman?

Lucio. Carnally, she says.

Duke.   Sirrah, no more!

118. **countenance**, pretense. 142. **ungot**, unborn. 158. **convented**,
summoned. 162. **Till . . . hear it.** This line anticipates action (or a
speech) which does not subsequently occur. The New Cambridge
editors think the text has been tampered with here and corroborate
their guess with the observation that there is no exit for Isabella at

this point in F, although she is referred to as *gone* (l. 242) and re-enters
at line 281. 172. **No, my lord.** The New Cambridge editors call
attention to the drop to prose here, anticipating Lucio's prose speech
embedded in this verse portion of the scene. In their headnote to the
scene they remark that Lucio's use at times of verse indicates that he

Lucio. Enough, my lord.

Ang. My lord, I must confess I know this woman:
And five years since there was some speech of
    marriage
Betwixt myself and her; which was broke off,
Partly for that her promised proportions
Came short of composition, but in chief   220
For that her reputation was disvalued
In levity: since which time of five years
I never spake with her, saw her, nor heard from her,
Upon my faith and honour.

Mari.   Noble prince,
As there comes light from heaven and words from
    breath,
As there is sense in truth and truth in virtue,
I am affianced this man's wife as strongly
As words could make up vows: and, my good lord,
But Tuesday night last gone in 's garden-house
He knew me as a wife. As this is true,   230
Let me in safety raise me from my knees;
Or else for ever be confixed here,
A marble monument!

Ang.   I did but smile till now:
Now, good my lord, give me the scope of justice;
My patience here is touch'd. I do perceive
These poor informal women are no more
But instruments of some more mightier member
That sets them on: let me have way, my lord,
To find this practice out.

Duke.   Ay, with my heart;
And punish them to your height of pleasure.   240
Thou foolish friar, and thou pernicious woman,
Compact with her that 's gone, think'st thou thy oaths,
Though they would swear down each particular saint,
Were testimonies against his worth and credit
That 's seal'd in approbation? You, Lord Escalus,
Sit with my cousin; lend him your kind pains
To find out this abuse, whence 'tis derived.
There is another friar that set them on;
Let him be sent for.   249

Fri. P. Would he were here, my lord! for he indeed
Hath set the women on to this complaint:
Your provost knows the place where he abides
And he may fetch him.

Duke.   Go do it instantly. [*Exit Provost.*
And you, my noble and well-warranted cousin,
Whom it concerns to hear this matter forth,
Do with your injuries as seems you best,
In any chastisement: I for a while will leave you;
But stir not you till you have well determined
Upon these slanderers.

Escal. My lord, we'll do it throughly. [*Exit Duke.* 260
Signior Lucio, did not you say you knew that Friar
Lodowick to be a dishonest person?

Lucio. 'Cucullus non facit monachum:' honest in
nothing but in his clothes; and one that hath spoke
most villanous speeches of the duke.

Escal. We shall entreat you to abide here till he
come and enforce them against him: we shall find
this friar a notable fellow.

Lucio. As any in Vienna, on my word.   269

Escal. Call that same Isabel here once again: I

would speak with her. [*Exit an Attendant.*] Pray you,
my lord, give me leave to question; you shall see how
I'll handle her.

Lucio. Not better than he, by her own report.

Escal. Say you?

Lucio. Marry, sir, I think, if you handled her
privately, she would sooner confess: perchance,
publicly, she'll be ashamed.

Escal. I will go darkly to work with her.

Lucio. That 's the way; for women are light at
midnight.   281

Re-enter OFFICERS *with* ISABELLA*; and* PROVOST *with the*
DUKE *in his friar's habit.*

Escal. Come on, mistress: here 's a gentlewoman
denies all that you have said.

Lucio. My lord, here comes the rascal I spoke of;
here with the provost.

Escal. In very good time: speak not you to him till
we call upon you.

Lucio. Mum.

Escal. Come, sir: did you set these women on to
slander Lord Angelo? they have confessed you did. 291

Duke. 'Tis false.

Escal. How! know you where you are?

Duke. Respect to your great place! and let the devil
Be sometime honour'd for his burning throne!
Where is the duke? 'tis he should hear me speak.

Escal. The duke 's in us; and we will hear you
    speak:
Look you speak justly.

Duke. Boldly, at least. But, O, poor souls,
Come you to seek the lamb here of the fox?   300
Good night to your redress! Is the duke gone?
Then is your cause gone too. The duke 's unjust,
Thus to retort your manifest appeal,
And put your trial in the villain's mouth
Which here you come to accuse.

Lucio. This is the rascal; this is he I spoke of.

Escal. Why, thou unreverend and unhallow'd friar,
Is 't not enough thou hast suborn'd these women
To accuse this worthy man, but, in foul mouth
And in the witness of his proper ear,   310
To call him villain? and then to glance from him
To the duke himself, to tax him with injustice?
Take him hence; to the rack with him! We'll touse
    you
Joint by joint, but we will know his purpose.
What, 'unjust'!

Duke.   Be not so hot; the duke
Dare no more stretch this finger of mine than he
Dare rack his own: his subject am I not,
Nor here provincial. My business in this state
Made me a looker on here in Vienna,
Where I have seen corruption boil and bubble   320
Till it o'er-run the stew; laws for all faults,
But faults so countenanced, that the strong statutes
Stand like the forfeits in a barber's shop,
As much in mock as mark.

Escal. Slander to the state! Away with him to
    prison!

Ang. What can you vouch against him, Signior Lucio?

was an original character (i.e., before revision took place) in the scene
and that his prose speeches are usually attended by prose speeches of
other characters. 219. **proportions**, dowry. 236. **informal**, without
form or composure. 243. **swear down**, i.e., call down to witness.
263. **'Cucullus . . . monachum,'** a cowl doesn't make a monk; a nice

bit of dramatic irony. 279. **darkly**, in private. 280. **light**, wanton,
unchaste. 313. **touse**, tear. 323. **forfeits**, i.e., the extracted teeth of
patients (barbers also were tooth-drawers) strung and hung on the
walls (Hart, who notes *most biting laws*, I, iii, 19).

Is this the man that you did tell us of?

Lucio. 'Tis he, my lord. Come hither, goodman baldpate: do you know me? 329

Duke. I remember you, sir, by the sound of your voice: I met you at the prison, in the absence of the duke.

Lucio. O, did you so? And do you remember what you said of the duke?

Duke. Most notedly, sir.

Lucio. Do you so, sir? And was the duke a flesh-monger, a fool, and a coward, as you then reported him to be?

Duke. You must, sir, change persons with me, ere you make that my report: you, indeed, spoke so of him; and much more, much worse. 341

Lucio. O thou damnable fellow! Did not I pluck thee by the nose for thy speeches?

Duke. I protest I love the duke as I love myself.

Ang. Hark, how the villain would close now, after his treasonable abuses!

Escal. Such a fellow is not to be talked withal. Away with him to prison! Where is the provost? Away with him to prison! lay bolts enough upon him: let him speak no more. Away with those giglots too, and with the other confederate companion! 352

Duke. [*To Provost*] Stay, sir; stay awhile.

Ang. What, resists he? Help him, Lucio.

Lucio. Come, sir; come, sir; come, sir; foh, sir! Why, you bald-pated, lying rascal, you must be hooded, must you? Show your knave's visage, with a pox to you! show your sheep-biting face, and be hanged an hour! Will 't not off? 360

[*Pulls off the friar's hood, and discovers the Duke.*

Duke. Thou art the first knave that e'er madest a duke.

First, provost, let me bail these gentle three. [*To Lucio*] Sneak not away, sir; for the friar and you Must have a word anon. Lay hold on him.

Lucio. This may prove worse than hanging.

Duke. [*To Escalus*] What you have spoke I pardon: sit you down: We'll borrow place of him. [*To Angelo*] Sir, by your leave. Hast thou or word, or wit, or impudence, That yet can do thee office? If thou hast, Rely upon it till my tale be heard, 370 And hold no longer out.

Ang. O my dread lord, I should be guiltier than my guiltiness, To think I can be undiscernible, When I perceive your grace, like power divine, Hath look'd upon my passes. Then, good prince, No longer session hold upon my shame, But let my trial be mine own confession: Immediate sentence then and sequent death Is all the grace I beg.

Duke. Come hither, Mariana. Say, wast thou e'er contracted to this woman? 380

Ang. I was, my lord.

Duke. Go take her hence, and marry her instantly. Do you the office, friar; which consummate, Return him here again. Go with him, provost.

[*Exeunt Angelo, Mariana, Friar Peter and Provost.*

Escal. My lord, I am more amazed at his dishonour

Than at the strangeness of it.

Duke. Come hither, Isabel. Your friar is now your prince: as I was then Advertising and holy to your business, Not changing heart with habit, I am still Attorney'd at your service.

Isab. O, give me pardon, 390 That I, your vassal, have employ'd and pain'd Your unknown sovereignty!

Duke. You are pardon'd, Isabel: And now, dear maid, be you as free to us. Your brother's death, I know, sits at your heart; And you may marvel why I obscured myself, Labouring to save his life, and would not rather Make rash remonstrance of my hidden power Than let him so be lost. O most kind maid, It was the swift celerity of his death, Which I did think with slower foot came on, 400 That brain'd my purpose. But, peace be with him! That life is better life, past fearing death, Than that which lives to fear: make it your comfort, So happy is your brother.

Isab. I do, my lord.

Re-enter ANGELO, MARIANA, FRIAR PETER, *and* PROVOST.

Duke. For this new-married man approaching here, Whose salt imagination yet hath wrong'd Your well defended honour, you must pardon For Mariana's sake: but as he adjudged your brother,— Being criminal, in double violation Of sacred chastity and of promise-breach 410 Thereon dependent, for your brother's life,— The very mercy of the law cries out Most audible, even from his proper tongue, 'An Angelo for Claudio, death for death!' Haste still pays haste, and leisure answers leisure; Like doth quit like, and MEASURE still FOR MEASURE. Then, Angelo, thy fault 's thus manifested; Which, though thou wouldst deny, denies thee vantage. We do condemn thee to the very block Where Claudio stoop'd to death, and with like haste. 420 Away with him!

Mari. O my most gracious lord, I hope you will not mock me with a husband.

Duke. It is your husband mock'd you with a husband. Consenting to the safeguard of your honour, I thought your marriage fit; else imputation, For that he knew you, might reproach your life And choke your good to come: for his possessions, Although by confiscation they are ours, We do instate and widow you withal, To buy you a better husband.

Mari. O my dear lord, 430 I crave no other, nor no better man.

Duke. Never crave him; we are definitive.

Mari. Gentle my liege,— [*Kneeling.*

Duke. You do but lose your labour. Away with him to death! [*To Lucio*] Now, sir, to you.

---

346. **close,** come to terms. 352. **giglots,** wanton women. 373. **un-discernible,** not to be seen through (Schmidt). 375. **passes,** demeanor,

conduct. 397. **remonstrance,** manifestation. 401. **brain'd,** defeated. 406. **salt,** lecherous. 425. **imputation,** reputation. 429. **widow,** settle

Mari. O my good lord! Sweet Isabel, take my
  part;
Lend me your knees, and all my life to come
I'll lend you all my life to do you service.
  Duke. Against all sense you do importune her:
Should she kneel down in mercy of this fact,
Her brother's ghost his paved bed would break, 440
And take her hence in horror.
  Mari.   Isabel,
Sweet Isabel, do yet but kneel by me;
Hold up your hands, say nothing; I'll speak all.
They say, best men are moulded out of faults;
And, for the most, become much more the better
For being a little bad: so may my husband.
O Isabel, will you not lend a knee?
  Duke. He dies for Claudio's death.
  Isab.   Most bounteous sir, [*Kneeling.*
Look, if it please you, on this man condemn'd,
As if my brother lived: I partly think 450
A due sincerity govern'd his deeds,
Till he did look on me: since it is so,
Let him not die. My brother had but justice,
In that he did the thing for which he died:
For Angelo,
His act did not o'ertake his bad intent,
And must be buried but as an intent
That perish'd by the way: thoughts are no subjects;
Intents but merely thoughts.
  Mari.   Merely, my lord.
  Duke. Your suit 's unprofitable; stand up, I say. 460
I have bethought me of another fault.
Provost, how came it Claudio was beheaded
At an unusual hour?
  Prov.   It was commanded so.
  Duke. Had you a special warrant for the deed?
  Prov. No, my good lord; it was by private message.
  Duke. For which I do discharge you of your office:
Give up your keys.
  Prov.   Pardon me, noble lord:
I thought it was a fault, but knew it not;
Yet did repent me, after more advice:
For testimony whereof, one in the prison, 470
That should by private order else have died,
I have reserved alive.
  Duke.   What 's he?
  Prov.   His name is Barnardine.
  Duke. I would thou hadst done so by Claudio.
Go fetch him hither; let me look upon him.
                              [*Exit Provost.*
  Escal. I am sorry, one so learned and so wise
As you, Lord Angelo, have still appear'd,
Should slip so grossly, both in the heat of blood,
And lack of temper'd judgement afterward.
  Ang. I am sorry that such sorrow I procure:
And so deep sticks it in my penitent heart 480
That I crave death more willingly than mercy;
'Tis my deserving, and I do entreat it.

  Re-enter PROVOST, *with* BARNARDINE, CLAUDIO *muffled,*
            and JULIET.

  Duke. Which is that Barnardine?
  Prov.   This, my lord.
  Duke. There was a friar told me of this man.
Sirrah, thou art said to have a stubborn soul,

That apprehends no further than this world,
And squarest thy life according. Thou 'rt condemn'd:
But, for those earthly faults, I quit them all;
And pray thee take this mercy to provide
For better times to come. Friar, advise him; 490
I leave him to your hand. What muffled fellow 's
  that?
  Prov. This is another prisoner that I saved,
Who should have died when Claudio lost his head;
As like almost to Claudio as himself. [*Unmuffles Claudio.*
  Duke. [*To Isabella*] If he be like your brother, for
  his sake
Is he pardon'd; and, for your lovely sake,
Give me your hand and say you will be mine,
He is my brother too: but fitter time for that.
By this Lord Angelo perceives he 's safe;
Methinks I see a quickening in his eye. 500
Well, Angelo, your evil quits you well:
Look that you love your wife; her worth worth yours.
I find an apt remission in myself;
And yet here 's one in place I cannot pardon.
[*To Lucio*] You, sirrah, that knew me for a fool, a
  coward,
One all of luxury, an ass, a madman;
Wherein have I so deserved of you,
That you extol me thus? 508
  Lucio. 'Faith, my lord, I spoke it but according to
the trick. If you will hang me for it, you may; but I
had rather it would please you I might be whipt.
  Duke. Whipt first, sir, and hanged after.
Proclaim it, provost, round about the city,
Is any woman wrong'd by this lewd fellow,
As I have heard him swear himself there 's one
Whom he begot with child, let her appear,
And he shall marry her: the nuptial finish'd,
Let him be whipt and hang'd. 519
  Lucio. I beseech your highness, do not marry me to
a whore. Your highness said even now, I made you a
duke: good my lord, do not recompense me in making
me a cuckold.
  Duke. Upon mine honour, thou shalt marry her.
Thy slanders I forgive; and therewithal
Remit thy other forfeits. Take him to prison;
And see our pleasure herein executed.
  Lucio. Marrying a punk, my lord, is pressing to
death, whipping, and hanging.
  Duke. Slandering a prince deserves it. 530
                    [*Exeunt Officers with Lucio.*
She, Claudio, that you wrong'd, look you restore.
Joy to you, Mariana! Love her, Angelo:
I have confess'd her and I know her virtue.
Thanks, good friend Escalus, for thy much goodness:
There 's more behind that is more gratulate.
Thanks, provost, for thy care and secrecy:
We shall employ thee in a worthier place.
Forgive him, Angelo, that brought you home
The head of Ragozine for Claudio's:
The offence pardons itself. Dear Isabel, 540
I have a motion much imports your good;
Whereto if you'll a willing ear incline,
What 's mine is yours and what is yours is mine.
So, bring us to our palace; where we'll show
What 's yet behind, that 's meet you all should know.
                              [*Exeunt.*

a jointure upon. 487. **squarest**, regulatest. 501. **quits**, rewards,
requites. 508. **extol**, proclaim. 509-510. **according to the trick**, as a
joke. 528-529. **pressing to death**, i.e., by having heavy weights
placed on the chest. 535. **gratulate**, gratifying.

TRAGEDIES OF THE
THIRD PERIOD

Troilus and Cressida

An entry in the Stationers' Register for February 7, 1603, gives an approximate date for *Troilus and Cressida*. A publisher named James Roberts entered his copy to print, "when he hath got sufficient authority for it, the book of Troilus and Cressida as it is acted by Lord Chamberlain's men." It is not known why he lacked authority. Perhaps he was acting in behalf of the players and attempting to prevent the piracy of the play.

It was reëntered to R. Bonian and H. Walley on January 28, 1609, and printed that year. It seems almost certain that the printing was unauthorized, for the title page appears in two somewhat inconsistent forms. The texts are in all particulars exactly the same, but what appears to be the earlier has this title:

THE Historie of Troylus *and* Cresseida. *As it was acted by the Kings Maiesties* seruants at the Globe. *Written by* William Shakespeare. LONDON. Imprinted by *G. Eld* for *R. Bonian* and *H. Walley*, and are to be sold at the spred Eagle in Paules Church-yeard, ouer against the great North doore. 1609.

The second issue substitutes for the first part of the title the following:

The Famous Historie of Troylus *and* Cresseid. *Excellently expressing the beginning* of their loues, with the conceited wooing of *Pandarus* Prince of *Licia*.

This second issue has a thing unique among Shakespearean quartos, namely, a preface or epistle to the reader beginning, "A Neuer writer, to a neuer reader. Newes." It declares that the play is "neuer stal'd with the Stage, neuer clapper-clawd with the palmes of the vulgar." It also declares that the play is published against "the grand possessors wills." The new title page and the epistle seem to be designed to evade the consequences of publishing a play to which the publishers had no proper title.

Troilus and Cressida stands in the First Folio between the "Histories" and the "Tragedies" and is not listed in the table of contents, possibly because the editors were having difficulty in securing the right to print it. *Troilus and Cressida* has been generally associated by students of Shakespeare with *All's Well that Ends Well* and *Measure for Measure* and treated as a "bitter" comedy. This offers the only excuse for placing the play with comedies. It can be said that *Troilus and Cressida* was regarded as a tragedy by the editors of the First Folio and that the story, embracing the death of Hector and the downfall of Troy, was regarded as tragic.

DATE

The subject was an extremely familiar one in sixteenth-century drama and literature. A comedy called *Troilus and Pandarus* was performed at court in 1515, and there are records of other plays on the subject. Henslowe's *Diary* for 1599 shows that Dekker and Chettle were preparing for Henslowe a play to be called *Troylles and Cresseda* (Henslowe's spelling), though when it was finished it was called *Agamemnon*. This can hardly have been the play referred to in *Histriomastix* (a play written by Marston in 1599 apparently on the basis of a still older play), for this reference seems to connect Shakespeare with the subject of Troilus and Cressida before the end of the century:

> *Troy.*—Come, Cressida, my cresset light,
> Thy face doth shine both day and night,
> Behold, behold thy garter blue
> Thy knight his valiant elbow wears,
> That when he *shakes* his furious *speare*,
> The foe, in shivering fearful sort,
> May lay him down in death to snort.

Our present version of the play may not be Shakespeare's first version but a rewriting to remove from it the traces of the controversy connected with the War of the Theaters.

The prologue to the play, as given in the folio version, alludes unmistakably to Jonson's *Poetaster*, which appeared in the summer of 1601. In the light of this and of the first entry in the Stationers' Register, one concludes the play in its final form was probably written about 1601-1602.

The play comes from the period of the end of the war between the regular companies and the children's companies but is not a part of that controversy, though possibly an earlier version, referred to in *Histriomastix*, was. Fleay's attempt to connect it with that quarrel by identifying Jonson with Ajax and Marston with Thersites is not regarded by Shakespeare scholars as successful, but has points in its favor.

The folio text of 1623 seems to have been printed from a copy of the 1609 quarto which had been used as a prompt book in the theater, supplied with stage directions, and subjected to revisions and emendations. It was not, however, printed without frequent reference to a playhouse manuscript, older and of greater authority.

No play in Shakespeare has perhaps been more misunderstood than has *Troilus and Cressida*. Critics have been perplexed by it, and it has had no stage career. Dowden was so uncertain as to the significance of *Troilus and Cressida* that he declined to discuss it in the first edition of *Shakespeare, his Mind and Art*. Later, in the preface to the third edition, he wrote, "I now believe this strange and difficult play was a last attempt to continue comedy, made when Shakespeare had ceased to be able to smile genially and when he must be either ironical or taking a deep, passionate, and tragical view of life." "It is," he says, "the comedy of disillusion." From a point of view which insists on interpreting Shakespeare's plays as reflections of his private life and of his attitude toward the world, this theory is no doubt inescapable. In other words, if one must believe that when Shakespeare wrote tragedy he felt tragically about the world as it affected him and his fellow human beings, then *Troilus and Cressida* could have arisen only from an embittered mind.[1]

SOURCES

The tale of Troilus and his love Cressida is the proverbial case of the fickle woman who deserts a faithful lover. It came originally as an offshoot of the tale of Troy,[2] not as told by Homer in the *Iliad*, but as invented by Benoit de Ste.-Maure in *Le Roman de Troie* in the twelfth century and amplified into a long poem *Il Filostrato* by Boccaccio before the middle of the fourteenth century, and by Chaucer in *Troilus and Creseyde* later in the same century. Chaucer told the story sympathetically; his Criseyde is something more than a faithless woman. But Chaucer's treatment is only one of many and by no means the most influential of the group. Cressida underwent great degeneration between Chaucer and Shakespeare and became the type of the woman false in love, a tradition of which Shakespeare reveals a consciousness. The reference to Cressida's leprosy is no doubt due to Henryson's *Testament of Cresseid*, a Scottish sequel to Chaucer, which presents a pitiful picture of Cresseid as a beggar and a diseased and abandoned prostitute.

Shakespeare seems to have done in the case of

Troilus and Cressida what he also did in the characterization of Julius Caesar and of Cleopatra. He interpreted his character according to the current tradition and not according to his source. He probably took his material in part from *Troilus and Creseyde*, but he followed Chaucer in substance, not at all in spirit. This medieval love story he retold with a frankness and cynicism no greater than the events justify and no more realistically than it had been told before. He placed it against a background of the siege of Troy, and here again he is baffling and unsatisfactory to modern taste.

We draw our conceptions of the Trojan War from Homer. Shakespeare probably knew some part of Chapman's translation of the *Iliad*[3] and made some use of it, particularly in the characterization of Thersites; but what he really followed in both event and sympathy was the medieval romance of Troy. He followed Raoul le Fevre's *Receuil des Histoires de Troye*, as translated and published by Caxton, and probably also Lydgate's *Troy Book*, translated from Guido delle Colonne's *Historia Trojana*. The medieval origin of *Troilus and Cressida* has imparted to it more of the atmosphere of chivalry than is to be felt in any other Shakespearean play. The negotiations, set speeches, challenges, fights, boastings, love-loyalties, and protestations of honorable sentiment must have made the play and the subject agreeable to the Renaissance, which was always unwilling to admit the decay of chivalry. To look at *Troilus and Cressida* as a rich, varied, and interesting, indeed, heroic and sensational spectacle is perhaps better than to involve ourselves too deeply in questions of moral significance in the interpretation of the play.

These romances do not present the fall of Troy as merely the result of a war of antiquity. They render it personal and immediate. They sympathize with the Trojans. The English, the Italians, the French, and even the Scandinavians—all imitating the Romans—regarded the Trojans as their ancestors and conceived of the Greeks as crafty, cowardly, and brutal enemies. Hence, it is easy to see that Shakespeare and his audience sided with the Trojans.

Shakespeare serves the Greeks much better than the tradition warranted. Thersites is a "deformed and scurrilous Greek," Ajax a stupid bully, Achilles a selfish coward, and Menelaus a somewhat ignoble figure. But, on the other hand, Agamemnon is a sagacious and dignified commander of troops, Nestor a sage, and Ulysses one of Shakespeare's real triumphs in the creation of manly character. Ulysses is so statesmanlike, so shrewd, so wise, and withal so kindly that he suggests one of the statesmen for whom Elizabeth's reign was celebrated. Among the Trojans, who are as a whole much more admirable than the Greeks, Hector is a truly noble figure, offsetting Ulysses on the Greek side; and Troilus, a model of

---

[1]See W. W. Lawrence, *Shakespeare's Problem Comedies* (1931). See also H. B. Charlton, "The Dark Comedies," *Bulletin of the John Rylands Library*, XXI (1937), 78-128.

[2]See J. S. P. Tatlock, *PMLA*, XXX, 672-670; W. W. Lawrence, *Shakespearean Studies*, Columbia University (1916), pp. 187-211; H. E. Rollins, *PMLA*, XXXII, 383-429; P. Alexander, 4 *Library*, IX, 267-286; see also O. J. Campbell, *Shakespeare's Satire* (1943), pp. 98-120, where *Troilus and Cressida* is treated as a "comicall satyre."

[3]Chapman published an installment of seven books of his translation of Homer's *Iliad* in 1598.

love and courage, suggests Romeo. The play presents a wealth of Renaissance learning.

THE PLAY

Shakespeare has devoted thought to the political and social aspects of the war between the Greeks and the Trojans and has made the most of the wisdom of Ulysses and the nobility of Hector. Without the conventions and ideals of courtly love, such as permeate Chaucer's *Troilus and Creseyde*, Shakespeare, in spite of his chivalric atmosphere, could do little with the tale itself, which when transferred into the midst of the moral standards of his time, is merely disappointing. The situation within the play will be made clear by the following summary.

Troilus loves Cressida with a deep and unselfish love. He wins her through the despicable services of her uncle Pandarus, not, however, until she has displayed the arts of the coquette in order to inflame his love. This tale of illicit love is set over against the love of Paris for Helen, the stolen wife of the Greek Menelaus.

As the play opens the Greeks are torn by dissension, so that they cannot succeed in capturing Troy. Achilles is enraged at Agamemnon, the Greek general, and is sulking in his tent in company with his beloved Patroclus, as in the *Iliad*. Ulysses tries with all his wisdom and eloquence to make peace between them and heal the breach. The issue of the play arises when Hector, the principal warrior among the Trojans, challenges some Grecian to single combat. The Greeks select Ajax as their representative in the hope of arousing Achilles to action by appealing to his jealousy of Ajax; it is in vain.

The Trojan leaders debate on the propriety of returning Helen to her former husband and thus ending the war. Hector wishes to do this, but Troilus stands out against it; so that in spite of the warnings of their sister Cassandra, a prophetess whose fate it is to have her prophecies disregarded, Hector gives in to Troilus and Paris and the war goes on.

Calchas, the father of Cressida, a Trojan renegade to the Greeks, who has left his daughter behind him in Troy, provides for an exchange of prisoners, so that he may regain his daughter Cressida by exchanging her for the Trojan Antenor. Diomedes has charge of the exchange. Cressida parts from Troilus with renewed oaths of everlasting love, in which she seems to be sincere, and accompanies Diomedes. When she arrives in the Greek camp, she kisses the Greeks all round, disgusting Ulysses, who sees her for what she is. Diomedes, breaking through the thin veneer of her coquetry, takes Cressida for his mistress. Then occur feastings between Greeks and Trojans in the Greek camp. Ulysses accompanies Troilus to Calchas' tent, where Troilus overhears Cressida's carryings on with Diomedes. Troilus returns to Troy disillusioned and bitter.

On the next morning Hector slays Patroclus, who was wearing the armor of Achilles. At this Achilles

goes to battle. He does not, however, meet Hector in fair fight, but surrounds him with the Myrmidons and murders him; then he ties his body to the tail of his horse and drags it about the walls of Troy.

Achilles binding the wounds of his friend Patroklos, from a Greek vase painting.

The play ends with a curse delivered by Troilus against Pandarus, the go-between. Troilus goes forth to die in battle.

On the basis of this sorry tale critics have been led to believe that Shakespeare was satirizing the heroes of antiquity, pricked on thereto by his jealousy of Chapman the translator of Homer; but the idea is absurd. Shakespeare has merely put on the stage the medieval Troy story, and has elevated rather than debased the tale in so doing.

STAGE HISTORY

Dryden rewrote Shakespeare's *Troilus and Cressida* in 1679 under the title *Troilus and Cressida; or, Truth Found too Late*. He took great pains to adapt the play to the refined tastes of his age. Dryden was an excellent workman and, although one resents his tampering with the work of his betters, his version is not without merit. In it Cressida is true to Troilus, encourages Diomedes only in order to assist her father to escape from the Greek camp, and, when reproached by Troilus for infidelity, slays herself. *Troilus and Cressida* has almost no further stage history. However, if one may judge from the revival by the Cambridge Dramatic Society in 1922, and the performance at the Shakespeare Memorial Theatre in 1948, *Troilus and Cressida* has unexploited possibilities as a stage play.

Troilus and Cressida

DRAMATIS PERSONAE

PRIAM, king of Troy.
HECTOR,
TROILUS,
PARIS, } his sons.
DEIPHOBUS,
HELENUS,
MARGARELON, a bastard son of Priam.
ÆNEAS,
ANTENOR, } Trojan commanders.
CALCHAS, a Trojan priest, taking part with the Greeks.
PANDARUS, uncle to Cressida.
AGAMEMNON, the Grecian general.
MENELAUS, his brother.
ACHILLES,
AJAX,
ULYSSES,
NESTOR, } Grecian princes.
DIOMEDES,
PATROCLUS,
THERSITES, a deformed and scurrilous Grecian.
ALEXANDER, servant to Cressida.
Servant to Troilus.
Servant to Paris.
Servant to Diomedes.

HELEN, wife to Menelaus.
ANDROMACHE, wife to Hector.
CASSANDRA, daughter to Priam, a prophetess.
CRESSIDA, daughter to Calchas.

Trojan and Greek Soldiers, and Attendants.

SCENE: *Troy, and the Grecian camp before it.*

PROLOGUE.

IN Troy, there lies the scene. From isles of Greece
The princes orgulous, their high blood chafed,
Have to the port of Athens sent their ships,
Fraught with the ministers and instruments
Of cruel war: sixty and nine, that wore
Their crownets regal, from the Athenian bay
Put forth toward Phrygia; and their vow is made
To ransack Troy, within whose strong immures
The ravish'd Helen, Menelaus' queen,
With wanton Paris sleeps; and that 's the quarrel.   10
To Tenedos they come;
And the deep-drawing barks do there disgorge
Their warlike fraughtage: now on Dardan plains
The fresh and yet unbruised Greeks do pitch
Their brave pavilions: Priam's six-gated city,
Dardan, and Tymbria, Helias, Chetas, Troien,
And Antenorides, with massy staples
And corresponsive and fulfilling bolts,
Sperr up the sons of Troy.

Now expectation, tickling skittish spirits,   20
On one and other side, Trojan and Greek,
Sets all on hazard: and hither am I come
A prologue arm'd, but not in confidence
Of author's pen or actor's voice, but suited
In like conditions as our argument,
To tell you, fair beholders, that our play
Leaps o'er the vaunt and firstlings of those broils,
Beginning in the middle, starting thence away
To what may be digested in a play.
Like or find fault; do as your pleasures are: 30
Now good or bad, 'tis but the chance of war.

ACT I.

SCENE I. *Troy. Before Priam's palace.*

Enter TROILUS *armed, and* PANDARUS.

Tro. Call here my varlet; I'll unarm again:
Why should I war without the walls of Troy,
That find such cruel battle here within?
Each Trojan that is master of his heart,
Let him to field; Troilus, alas! hath none.
 Pan. Will this gear ne'er be mended?
 Tro. The Greeks are strong and skilful to their
    strength,
Fierce to their skill and to their fierceness valiant;
But I am weaker than a woman's tear,
Tamer than sleep, fonder than ignorance,   10
Less valiant than the virgin in the night
And skilless as unpractised infancy.
 Pan. Well, I have told you enough of this: for my part, I'll not meddle nor make no further. He that will have a cake out of the wheat must needs tarry the grinding.
 Tro. Have I not tarried?
 Pan. Ay, the grinding; but you must tarry the bolting.
 Tro. Have I not tarried?
 Pan. Ay, the bolting, but you must tarry the leavening.   20
 Tro. Still have I tarried.
 Pan. Ay, to the leavening; but here 's yet in the word 'hereafter' the kneading, the making of the cake, the heating of the oven and the baking; nay, you must stay the cooling too, or you may chance to burn your lips.

PROLOGUE. 2. **orgulous**, proud. 4. **ministers**, agents. 6. **crownets**, coronets, i.e., garlands, chaplets; here probably the equivalent of "crown." 7. **Phrygia**, district in Asia Minor, identified by the Roman poets—hence in Renaissance poetry—with Troy. 8. **immures**, walls. 11. **Tenedos**, small island in the Aegean Sea off the coast of Asia Minor. 13. **fraughtage**, cargo. **Dardan**, Trojan, from Dardanus—son of Zeus and Electra, daughter of Atlas—according to legend, the ancestor of the Trojan race. 18. **corresponsive**, answering. 19. **Sperr**, close. 23-25. **A prologue . . . argument.** I am armed not as a belligerent actor or author, but as representing the warlike theme of the play. 27. **vaunt**, van, beginning. **firstlings**, first-fruits.
ACT I. SCENE I. 1. **varlet**, gentleman's son in the service of a knight or a prince; probably free from any connotation of contempt. 5. **none**, i.e., heart. 7-8. **The Greeks . . . valiant.** These lines illustrate the mature Shakespeare's peculiar compactness of style. The series of ideas here is like a series of involutes in their intricacy and closeness of expression and idea. When the lines are footnoted by equating *to* with "in addition to," assuming that the reader will make the substitution, they are reduced to their mere literal significance, as if the involutes had been pulled out into a straight but limp and uninteresting line. The idea is not an unusual or complex one, but its expression is compact and interesting. As one of Troilus' first utterances, it helps to make us aware of his personality and of his overwrought emotional state. 7. **to**, in addition to, but see Abbott (187), who explains "in proportion to." 16. **tarry**, wait for.

Tro. Patience herself, what goddess e'er she be,
Doth lesser blench at sufferance than I do.
At Priam's royal table do I sit;
And when fair Cressid comes into my thoughts,— 30
So, traitor! 'When she comes!' When is she thence?

Pan. Well, she looked yesternight fairer than ever I
saw her look, or any woman else.

Tro. I was about to tell thee:—when my heart,
As wedged with a sigh, would rive in twain,
Lest Hector or my father should perceive me,
I have, as when the sun doth light a storm,
Buried this sigh in wrinkle of a smile:
But sorrow, that is couch'd in seeming gladness,
Is like that mirth fate turns to sudden sadness. 40

Pan. An her hair were not somewhat darker than
Helen's—well, go to—there were no more comparison
between the women: but, for my part, she is my
kinswoman; I would not, as they term it, praise her:
but I would somebody had heard her talk yesterday,
as I did. I will not dispraise your sister Cassandra's
wit, but—

Tro. O Pandarus! I tell thee, Pandarus,—
When I do tell thee, there my hopes lie drown'd,
Reply not in how many fathoms deep 50
They lie indrench'd. I tell thee I am mad
In Cressid's love: thou answer'st 'she is fair;'
Pour'st in the open ulcer of my heart
Her eyes, her hair, her cheek, her gait, her voice,
Handlest in thy discourse; O, that her hand,
In whose comparison all whites are ink,
Writing their own reproach, to whose soft seizure
The cygnet's down is harsh and spirit of sense
Hard as the palm of ploughman: this thou tell'st me,
As true thou tell'st me, when I say I love her; 60
But, saying thus, instead of oil and balm,
Thou lay'st in every gash that love hath given me
The knife that made it.

Pan. I speak no more than truth.

Tro. Thou dost not speak so much.

Pan. Faith, I'll not meddle in 't. Let her be as she is:
if she be fair, 'tis the better for her; an she be not, she
has the mends in her own hands.

Tro. Good Pandarus, how now, Pandarus!

Pan. I have had my labour for my travail; ill-
thought on of her and ill-thought on of you; gone
between and between, but small thanks for my labour.

Tro. What, art thou angry, Pandarus? what, with
me?

Pan. Because she 's kin to me, therefore she 's not
so fair as Helen: an she were not kin to me, she would
be as fair on Friday as Helen is on Sunday. But what
care I? I care not an she were a black-a-moor; 'tis all
one to me. 80

Tro. Say I she is not fair?

Pan. I do not care whether you do or no. She 's a
fool to stay behind her father; let her to the Greeks;
and so I'll tell her the next time I see her: for my
part, I'll meddle nor make no more i' the matter.

Tro. Pandarus,—
Pan. Not I.
Tro. Sweet Pandarus,—
Pan. Pray you, speak no more to me: I will leave
all as I found it, and there an end. 91
[*Exit Pandarus. An alarum.*
Tro. Peace, you ungracious clamours! peace, rude
sounds!
Fools on both sides! Helen must needs be fair,
When with your blood you daily paint her thus.
I cannot fight upon this argument;
It is too starved a subject for my sword.
But Pandarus,—O gods, how do you plague me!
I cannot come to Cressid but by Pandar;
And he 's as tetchy to be woo'd to woo,
As she is stubborn-chaste against all suit. 100
Tell me, Apollo, for thy Daphne's love,
What Cressid is, what Pandar, and what we?
Her bed is India; there she lies, a pearl:
Between our Ilium and where she resides,
Let it be call'd the wild and wandering flood,
Ourself the merchant, and this sailing Pandar
Our doubtful hope, our convoy and our bark.

Alarum. Enter ÆNEAS.

Æne. How now, Prince Troilus! wherefore not
afield?
Tro. Because not there: this woman's answer sorts,
For womanish it is to be from thence. 110
What news, Æneas, from the field to-day?
Æne. That Paris is returned home and hurt.
Tro. By whom, Æneas?
Æne.   Troilus, by Menelaus.
Tro. Let Paris bleed: 'tis but a scar to scorn;
Paris is gored with Menelaus' horn.   [*Alarum.*
Æne. Hark, what good sport is out of town to-day!
Tro. Better at home, if 'would I might' were 'may.'
But to the sport abroad: are you bound thither?
Æne. In all swift haste.
Tro.   Come, go we then together.
[*Exeunt.*

SCENE II. *The same. A street.*

Enter CRESSIDA *and* ALEXANDER.

Cres. Who were those went by?
Alex.   Queen Hecuba and Helen.
Cres. And whither go they?
Alex.   Up to the eastern tower,
Whose height commands as subject all the vale,
To see the battle. Hector, whose patience
Is, as a virtue fix'd, to-day was moved:
He chid Andromache and struck his armorer,
And, like as there were husbandry in war,
Before the sun rose he was harness'd light,
And to the field goes he; where every flower

27-28. **Patience . . . I do.** I have a greater capacity for suffering than
patience herself. 28. **blench,** shy from. 35. **as wedged,** as if entered
by a wedge; cf. I, iii, 316. 41-63. **An her hair,** etc. This humorously
incongruous alternation between the lovelorn blank verse of Troilus
and the tantalizing prose of Pandarus has the tone of "debunking"
the passion of love. The tone is continued in Pandarus' following
dialogue with Cressida. 47. **Cassandra's wit,** refers to Cassandra's
gift of prophecy, bestowed on her by Apollo out of his love for her.
Because she slighted his love, he added to the gift the condition that
her prophecies would never be believed. 51. **indrench'd,** immersed.
55. **discourse.** Globe has comma; Q has colon. 57. **seizure,** clasp; i.e.,

hand clasp. 58. **spirit of sense,** most exquisite power of sensibility
(Johnson); sense or sensibility itself (Schmidt). 68. **mends,** remedy;
Johnson thought the line referred to cosmetics; Steevens paraphrased,
"She may make the best of it." 83. **her father.** Cressida's father,
Calchas, was a Trojan priest who, advised by the oracle of Apollo
that Troy would fall, fled to the Greeks. 95. **upon this argument,**
for this cause, i.e., Paris' cause, with quibbling allusion, probably,
to the phrase "to fight on an empty stomach." 99. **tetchy,** fretful,
peevish. 101. **Apollo,** i.e., in his role of god of music and poetry.
Mention of his love for Daphne is appropriate here because she successfully eluded him. 109. **sorts,** is appropriate. 112-113. **Paris . . -**

Did, as a prophet, weep what it foresaw 10
In Hector's wrath.

Cres. What was his cause of anger?

Alex. The noise goes, this: there is among the
Greeks
A lord of Trojan blood, nephew to Hector;
They call him Ajax.

Cres. Good; and what of him?

Alex. They say he is a very man per se,
And stands alone.

Cres. So do all men, unless they are drunk, sick, or
have no legs. 18

Alex. This man, lady, hath robbed many beasts of
their particular additions; he is as valiant as the lion,
churlish as the bear, slow as the elephant: a man into
whom nature hath so crowded humours that his
valour is crushed into folly, his folly sauced with discretion: there is no man hath a virtue that he hath
not a glimpse of, nor any man an attaint but he
carries some stain of it: he is melancholy without
cause, and merry against the hair: he hath the joints
of every thing, but every thing so out of joint that he
is a gouty Briareus, many hands and no use, or purblind Argus, all eyes and no sight. 31

Cres. But how should this man, that makes me
smile, make Hector angry?

Alex. They say he yesterday coped Hector in the
battle and struck him down, the disdain and shame
whereof hath ever since kept Hector fasting and
waking.

Cres. Who comes here?

Alex. Madam, your uncle Pandarus.

Enter PANDARUS.

Cres. Hector 's a gallant man. 40

Alex. As may be in the world, lady.

Pan. What 's that? what 's that?

Cres. Good morrow, uncle Pandarus.

Pan. Good morrow, cousin Cressid: what do you
talk of? Good morrow, Alexander. How do you,
cousin? When were you at Ilium?

Cres. This morning, uncle.

Pan. What were you talking of when I came? Was
Hector armed and gone ere ye came to Ilium? Helen
was not up, was she? 50

Cres. Hector was gone, but Helen was not up.

Pan. E'en so: Hector was stirring early.

Cres. That were we talking of, and of his anger.

Pan. Was he angry?

Cres. So he says here.

Pan. True, he was so: I know the cause too: he'll
lay about him to-day, I can tell them that: and
there 's Troilus will not come far behind him; let
them take heed of Troilus, I can tell them that too. 61

Cres. What, is he angry too?

Pan. Who, Troilus? Troilus is the better man of the
two.

Cres. O Jupiter! there 's no comparison.

Pan. What, not between Troilus and Hector?
Do you know a man if you see him?

Cres. Ay, if I ever saw him before and knew him.

Pan. Well, I say Troilus is Troilus. 70

Cres. Then you say as I say; for, I am sure, he is not
Hector.

Pan. No, nor Hector is not Troilus in some degrees.

Cres. 'Tis just to each of them; he is himself.

Pan. Himself! Alas, poor Troilus! I would he were.

Cres. So he is.

Pan. Condition, I had gone barefoot to India. 80

Cres. He is not Hector.

Pan. Himself! no, he 's not himself: would a' were
himself! Well, the gods are above; time must friend
or end: well, Troilus, well: I would my heart were
in her body. No, Hector is not a better man than
Troilus.

Cres. Excuse me.

Pan. He is elder.

Cres. Pardon me, pardon me. 89

Pan. Th' other 's not come to 't; you shall tell me
another tale, when th' other 's come to 't. Hector
shall not have his wit this year.

Cres. He shall not need it, if he have his own.

Pan. Nor his qualities.

Cres. No matter.

Pan. Nor his beauty.

Cres. 'Twould not become him; his own 's better.

Pan. You have no judgement, niece: Helen herself
swore th' other day, that Troilus, for a brown favour
—for so 'tis, I must confess,—not brown neither,—

Cres. No, but brown.

Pan. 'Faith, to say truth, brown and not brown.

Cres. To say the truth, true and not true.

Pan. She praised his complexion above Paris.

Cres. Why, Paris hath colour enough.

Pan. So he has. 109

Cres. Then Troilus should have too much: if she
praised him above, his complexion is higher than his;
he having colour enough, and the other higher, is too
flaming a praise for a good complexion. I had as lief
Helen's golden tongue had commended Troilus for a
copper nose.

Pan. I swear to you, I think Helen loves him better
than Paris.

Cres. Then she 's a merry Greek indeed. 118

Pan. Nay, I am sure she does. She came to him th'
other day into the compassed window,—and, you
know, he has not past three or four hairs on his chin,—

Cres. Indeed, a tapster's arithmetic may soon bring
his particulars therein to a total.

Pan. Why, he is very young: and yet will he, within
three pound, lift as much as his brother Hector.

Cres. Is he so young a man and so old a lifter? 129

Pan. But to prove to you that Helen loves him: she
came and puts me her white hand to his cloven chin—

Cres. Juno have mercy! how came it cloven?

Pan. Why, you know, 'tis dimpled: I think his

Menelaus, alludes to the duel (related in *Iliad,* III) between Paris and
Menelaus, stopped by Venus' interference. 114. **a scar to scorn.**
The phrase plays on the two ideas, a wound not sufficiently serious to
be regarded, and a scar in return for Paris' scorn for Menelaus. 116.
out of town, outside the walls.

SCENE II. 5. **Is . . . fix'd,** is of the nature of a fixed, unshakable
virtue (Deighton); the pointing follows F; Globe: *Is, as a virtue, fix'd.*
7. **husbandry,** i.e., as if the principles of husbandry applied to war.
8. **light,** i.e., in light armor. 15. **per se,** i.e., unique. 26. **attaint,**
the opposite of virtue (l. 25); any defect of character. 28. **against
the hair,** contrary to natural tendency. 30. **Briareus,** Greek mytho-

logical monster with fifty heads and one hundred hands. 31. **Argus,**
a monster with one hundred eyes. 46. **Ilium,** the palace. 58. **lay
about him,** fight vigorously. 73. **in some,** by several. 80. **I had gone,**
contrary to fact subjunctive; i.e., he is himself if I have gone, etc.
115. **copper,** red. 118. **Greek,** grig, i.e., a cunning person, a sharper.
120. **compassed,** curved. 123. **tapster's,** proverbially a poor reckoner;
cf. *Love's Labour's Lost,* I, ii, 43. 129. **lifter,** quibble on the meaning
"thief."

smiling becomes him better than any man in all Phrygia.

Cres. O, he smiles valiantly.

Pan. Does he not?

Cres. O yes, an 'twere a cloud in autumn.

Pan. Why, go to, then: but to prove to you that Helen loves Troilus,— 141

Cres. Troilus will stand to the proof, if you'll prove it so.

Pan. Troilus! why, he esteems her no more than I esteem an addle egg.

Cres. If you love an addle egg as well as you love an idle head, you would eat chickens i' the shell.

Pan. I cannot choose but laugh, to think how she tickled his chin: indeed, she has a marvellous white hand, I must needs confess,— 151

Cres. Without the rack.

Pan. And she takes upon her to spy a white hair on his chin.

Cres. Alas, poor chin! many a wart is richer.

Pan. But there was such laughing! Queen Hecuba laughed that her eyes ran o'er.

Cres. With mill-stones.

Pan. And Cassandra laughed.

Cres. But there was more temperate fire under the pot of her eyes: did her eyes run o'er too? 161

Pan. And Hector laughed.

Cres. At what was all this laughing?

Pan. Marry, at the white hair that Helen spied on Troilus' chin.

Cres. An 't had been a green hair, I should have laughed too.

Pan. They laughed not so much at the hair as at his pretty answer.

Cres. What was his answer? 170

Pan. Quoth she, 'Here 's but two and fifty hairs on your chin, and one of them is white.'

Cres. This is her question.

Pan. That 's true; make no question of that. 'Two and fifty hairs,' quoth he, 'and one white: that white hair is my father, and all the rest are his sons.' 'Jupiter!' quoth she, 'which of these hairs is Paris my husband?' 'The forked one,' quoth he, 'pluck 't out, and give it him.' But there was such laughing! and Helen so blushed, and Paris so chafed, and all the rest so laughed, that it passed. 181

Cres. So let it now; for it has been a great while going by.

Pan. Well, cousin, I told you a thing yesterday; think on 't.

Cres. So I do.

Pan. I'll be sworn 'tis true; he will weep you, an 'twere a man born in April.

Cres. And I'll spring up in his tears, an 'twere a nettle against May.— [*A retreat sounded.* 191

Pan. Hark! they are coming from the field: shall we stand up here, and see them as they pass toward Ilium? good niece, do, sweet niece Cressida.

Cres. At your pleasure.

Pan. Here, here, here 's an excellent place; here

we may see most bravely: I'll tell you them all by their names as they pass by; but mark Troilus above the rest. 200

Cres. Speak not so loud.

Æneas *passes.*

Pan. That 's Æneas: is not that a brave man? he 's one of the flowers of Troy, I can tell you: but mark Troilus; you shall see anon.

Antenor *passes.*

Cres. Who 's that?

Pan. That 's Antenor: he has a shrewd wit, I can tell you; and he 's a man good enough: he 's one o' the soundest judgements in Troy, whosoever, and a proper man of person. When comes Troilus? I'll show you Troilus anon: if he see me, you shall see him nod at me. 211

Cres. Will he give you the nod?

Pan. You shall see.

Cres. If he do, the rich shall have more.

Hector *passes.*

Pan. That 's Hector, that, that, look you, that; there 's a fellow! Go thy way, Hector! There 's a brave man, niece. O brave Hector! Look how he looks! there 's a countenance! is 't not a brave man?

Cres. O, a brave man! 220

Pan. Is a' not? it does a man's heart good. Look you what hacks are on his helmet! look you yonder, do you see? look you there: there 's no jesting; there 's laying on, take 't off who will, as they say: there be hacks!

Cres. Be those with swords?

Pan. Swords! any thing, he cares not; an the devil come to him, it 's all one; by God's lid, it does one's heart good. Yonder comes Paris, yonder comes Paris.

Paris *passes.*

Look ye yonder, niece; is 't not a gallant man too, is 't not? Why, this is brave now. Who said he came hurt home to-day? he 's not hurt: why, this will do Helen's heart good now, ha! Would I could see Troilus now! You shall see Troilus anon.

Helenus *passes.*

Cres. Who 's that?

Pan. That 's Helenus. I marvel where Troilus is. That 's Helenus. I think he went not forth to-day. That 's Helenus. 240

Cres. Can Helenus fight, uncle?

Pan. Helenus? no. Yes, he'll fight indifferent well. I marvel where Troilus is. Hark! do you not hear the people cry 'Troilus'? Helenus is a priest.

Cres. What sneaking fellow comes yonder?

Troilus *passes.*

Pan. Where? yonder? that 's Deiphobus. 'Tis Troilus! there 's a man, niece! Hem! Brave Troilus! the prince of chivalry!

142. **stand . . . proof,** i.e., will not shrink from the test. 175. **Two and fifty.** Priam had fifty sons. Theobald emended to *one and fifty.* Some commentators assume that the bastard Margarelon is to be included among the sons of Priam. 178. **forked,** i.e., he has cuckold's horns. 189. **an 'twere,** as if he were. 191. **against,** in expectation of. 212. **give . . . nod,** a term in the game of cards called noddy, a word which also signifies "a fool." Cressida means to call Pandarus a noddy, and says he shall by more nods be made more significantly a fool

(Singer). 214. **the rich . . . more,** i.e., it will not make you rich (Schmidt). 224. **laying on,** evidence of blows exchanged. 228. **by God's lid,** an oath by God's eyelid. 283. **ward, lie,** technical terms in fencing. 312. **wooing,** i.e., being wooed. 314. **That she,** that woman. 319. **Achievement . . . beseech,** i.e., to achieve (to win a woman) is to command her; unwon, she must be besought.

Scene iii. The scene has an epic tone; this is due to the long fig-urative speeches, which give it the ceremoniousness of an epic counsel.

Cres. Peace, for shame, peace! 250

Pan. Mark him; note him. O brave Troilus! Look well upon him, niece: look you how his sword is bloodied, and his helm more hacked than Hector's, and how he looks, and how he goes! O admirable youth! he ne'er saw three and twenty. Go thy way, Troilus, go thy way! Had I a sister were a grace, or a daughter a goddess, he should take his choice. O admirable man! Paris? Paris is dirt to him; and, I warrant, Helen, to change, would give an eye to boot.

Cres. Here come more. 261

Forces pass.

Pan. Asses, fools, dolts! chaff and bran, chaff and bran! porridge after meat! I could live and die i' the eyes of Troilus. Ne'er look, ne'er look; the eagles are gone: crows and daws, crows and daws! I had rather be such a man as Troilus than Agamemnon and all Greece.

Cres. There is among the Greeks Achilles, a better man than Troilus.

Pan. Achilles! a drayman, a porter, a very camel. 271

Cres. Well, well.

Pan. 'Well, well!' Why, have you any discretion? have you any eyes? do you know what a man is? Is not birth, beauty, good shape, discourse, manhood, learning, gentleness, virtue, youth, liberality, and such like, the spice and salt that season a man?

Cres. Ay, a minced man: and then to be baked with no date in the pie, for then the man's date 's out. 281

Pan. You are such a woman! one knows not at what ward you lie.

Cres. Upon my back, to defend my belly; upon my wit, to defend my wiles; upon my secrecy, to defend mine honesty; my mask, to defend my beauty; and you, to defend all these: and at all these wards I lie, at a thousand watches.

Pan. Say one of your watches. 290

Cres. Nay, I'll watch you for that; and that 's one of the chiefest of them too: if I cannot ward what I would not have hit, I can watch you for telling how I took the blow; unless it swell past hiding, and then it 's past watching.

Pan. You are such another!

Enter TROILUS'S *Boy.*

Boy. Sir, my lord would instantly speak with you.

Pan. Where?

Boy. At your own house; there he unarms him. 301

Pan. Good boy, tell him I come. [*Exit Boy.*
I doubt he be hurt. Fare ye well, good niece.

Cres. Adieu, uncle.

Pan. I'll be with you, niece, by and by.

Cres. To bring, uncle?

Pan. Ay, a token from Troilus.

Cres. By the same token, you are a bawd.
[*Exit Pandarus.*
Words, vows, gifts, tears, and love's full sacrifice,
He offers in another's enterprise:
But more in Troilus thousand fold I see 310

Than in the glass of Pandar's praise may be;
Yet hold I off. Women are angels, wooing:
Things won are done; joy's soul lies in the doing.
That she beloved knows nought that knows not this:
Men prize the thing ungain'd more than it is:
That she was never yet that ever knew
Love got so sweet as when desire did sue.
Therefore this maxim out of love I teach:
Achievement is command; ungain'd, beseech: 319
Then though my heart's content firm love doth bear,
Nothing of that shall from mine eyes appear. [*Exeunt.*

SCENE III. *The Grecian camp. Before Agamemnon's tent.*

Sennet. Enter AGAMEMNON, NESTOR, ULYSSES,
MENELAUS, *and others.*

Agam. Princes,
What grief hath set the jaundice on your cheeks?
The ample proposition that hope makes
In all designs begun on earth below
Fails in the promised largeness: checks and disasters
Grow in the veins of actions highest rear'd,
As knots, by the conflux of meeting sap,
Infect the sound pine and divert his grain
Tortive and errant from his course of growth.
Nor, princes, is it matter new to us 10
That we come short of our suppose so far
That after seven years' siege yet Troy walls stand;
Sith every action that hath gone before,
Whereof we have record, trial did draw
Bias and thwart, not answering the aim,
And that unbodied figure of the thought
That gave 't surmised shape. Why then, you princes,
Do you with cheeks abash'd behold our works,
And call them shames? which are indeed nought else
But the protractive trials of great Jove 20
To find persistive constancy in men:
The fineness of which metal is not found
In fortune's love; for then the bold and coward,
The wise and fool, the artist and unread,
The hard and soft, seem all affined and kin:
But, in the wind and tempest of her frown,
Distinction, with a broad and powerful fan,
Puffing at all, winnows the light away;
And what hath mass or matter, by itself
Lies rich in virtue and unmingled. 30
Nest. With due observance of thy godlike seat,
Great Agamemnon, Nestor shall apply
Thy latest words. In the reproof of chance
Lies the true proof of men: the sea being smooth,
How many shallow bauble boats dare sail
Upon her patient breast, making their way
With those of nobler bulk!
But let the ruffian Boreas once enrage
The gentle Thetis, and anon behold 39
The strong-ribb'd bark through liquid mountains cut,
Bounding between the two moist elements,

---

3. **proposition,** offer (Onions); promise held out (Deighton). 5-6. **checks . . . rear'd,** reflects the ancient idea that calamity always attends greatness. 9. **Tortive,** distorted. **errant,** wandering. 11. **suppose,** expectation. 13-17. **Sith . . . shape.** Delius noted that *trial* is the subject, *action* the object. Paradise paraphrases: Since trial has drawn awry and crosswise every previous action of which we have record, so that it has not corresponded to the aim of its originator nor to the impalpable shape which it assumed in thought. 14. **record,** accent on second syllable. 24. **artist,** scholar. 25. **affined,** related. 26. **her.** The antecedent is *fortune's* (l. 23). 30. **unmingled,** unalloyed. 31. **godlike,** because Agamemnon is king. 35. **bauble,** toy. 38. **Boreas,** the north wind. 39. **Thetis,** a sea deity, mother of Achilles. 41. **moist elements,** air and water.

Like Perseus' horse: where 's then the saucy boat
Whose weak untimber'd sides but even now
Co-rivall'd greatness? Either to harbour fled,
Or made a toast for Neptune. Even so
Doth valour's show and valour's worth divide
In storms of fortune; for in her ray and brightness
The herd hath more annoyance by the breese
Than by the tiger; but when the splitting wind
Makes flexible the knees of knotted oaks, 50
And flies fled under shade, why, then the thing of
    courage
As roused with rage with rage doth sympathize,
And with an accent tuned in selfsame key
Retorts to chiding fortune.
    Ulyss.   Agamemnon,
Thou great commander, nerve and bone of Greece,
Heart of our numbers, soul and only spirit,
In whom the tempers and the minds of all
Should be shut up, hear what Ulysses speaks.
Besides the applause and approbation
The which, [*To Agamemnon*] most mighty for thy
    place and sway, 60
[*To Nestor*] And thou most reverend for thy
    stretch'd-out life
I give to both your speeches, which were such
As Agamemnon and the hand of Greece
Should hold up high in brass, and such again
As venerable Nestor, hatch'd in silver,
Should with a bond of air, strong as the axle-tree
On which heaven rides, knit all the Greekish ears
To his experienced tongue, yet let it please both,
Thou great, and wise, to hear Ulysses speak.
    Agam. Speak, Prince of Ithaca; and be 't of less
    expect 70
That matter needless, of importless burden,
Divide thy lips, than we are confident,
When rank Thersites opes his mastic jaws,
We shall hear music, wit and oracle.
    Ulyss. Troy, yet upon his basis, had been down,
And the great Hector's sword had lack'd a master,
But for these instances.
The specialty of rule hath been neglected:
And, look, how many Grecian tents do stand
Hollow upon this plain, so many hollow factions. 80
When that the general is not like the hive
To whom the foragers shall all repair,
What honey is expected? Degree being vizarded,
The unworthiest shows as fairly in the mask.
The heavens themselves, the planets and this centre
Observe degree, priority and place,
Insisture, course, proportion, season, form,

Office and custom, in all line of order;
And therefore is the glorious planet Sol
In noble eminence enthroned and sphered 90
Amidst the other; whose medicinable eye
Corrects the ill aspects of planets evil,
And posts, like the commandment of a king,
Sans check to good and bad: but when the planets
In evil mixture to disorder wander,
What plagues and what portents! what mutiny!
What raging of the sea! shaking of earth!
Commotion in the winds! frights, changes, horrors,
Divert and crack, rend and deracinate
The unity and married calm of states 100
Quite from their fixure! O, when degree is shaked,
Which is the ladder to all high designs,
The enterprise is sick! How could communities,
Degrees in schools and brotherhoods in cities,
Peaceful commerce from dividable shores,
The primogenitive and due of birth,
Prerogative of age, crowns, sceptres, laurels,
But by degree, stand in authentic place?
Take but degree away, untune that string,
And, hark, what discord follows! each thing meets 110
In mere oppugnancy: the bounded waters
Should lift their bosoms higher than the shores
And make a sop of all this solid globe:
Strength should be lord of imbecility,
And the rude son should strike his father dead:
Force should be right; or rather, right and wrong,
Between whose endless jar justice resides,
Should lose their names, and so should justice too.
Then every thing includes itself in power,
Power into will, will into appetite; 120
And appetite, an universal wolf,
So doubly seconded with will and power,
Must make perforce an universal prey,
And last eat up himself. Great Agamemnon,
This chaos, when degree is suffocate,
Follows the choking.
And this neglection of degree it is
That by a pace goes backward, with a purpose
It hath to climb. The general 's disdain'd
By him one step below, he by the next, 130
That next by him beneath; so every step,
Exampled by the first pace that is sick
Of his superior, grows to an envious fever
Of pale and bloodless emulation:
And 'tis this fever that keeps Troy on foot,
Not her own sinews. To end a tale of length,
Troy in our weakness stands, not in her strength.
    Nest. Most wisely hath Ulysses here discover'd

42. **Perseus' horse,** Pegasus, a winged horse which sprang from the blood of Medusa when Perseus cut off her head. The horse was given to Bellerophon by the gods. It is associated, however, with Perseus, probably because Ovid relates that the latter hero was mounted on Pegasus when he rescued Andromeda from the sea monster. **saucy,** presumptuous, rashly venturing. 45. **toast,** rich morsel to be swallowed (Schmidt). 48. **breese,** gadfly. 51. **fled,** are fled. **thing of courage,** any courageous thing. 64. **brass,** frequently used as a type of durability. 65. **hatch'd,** thinly streaked, referring to Nestor's gray hair. 66. **bond of air,** his breath—words. 70-74. **be 't . . . oracle,** i.e., we should expect unimportant matter from you just as we should expect music, wit, and oracle from Thersites. 70. **expect,** expectation. 73. **mastic,** gum, resin exuding from bark, used medicinally, sometimes for filling teeth. Onions explains as a possible misprint for *mastice,* dialect form of "mastiff," or possibly the equivalent to "massive"; Grant White suggested that it may be an adjective formed from "mastix," a scourge. 78. **specialty of rule,** particular rights of supreme authority (Johnson). 80. **Hollow,** empty, groundless, unnecessary. 83. **Degree,** here the equivalent of authority. Below (l. 86) the word has a more

cosmological import, where it reflects the Renaissance belief (inherited from Plato) that the world achieved its stability by means of the gradation of all created things. The social and political implication of this conception is that human beings are born to a designated station or degree to which they must adhere with mutual respect and the responsibilities of which they must accept if society and government are to remain stable. Renaissance writers were fond of pointing out analogies between the civil organization and any natural or cosmological manifestations of some kind of order or degree. This passage (ll. 85-134) is not only Shakespeare's fullest and most eloquent statement of this concept, but also one of the most distinguished in all Renaissance literature. 85. **this centre,** the earth. 87. **Insisture,** steady continuance in their path. 91. **medicinable,** healing. 92. **aspects,** relative positions of the heavenly bodies as they appear to an observer on the earth's surface at a given time, and the influence attributed thereto. 95. **mixture,** conjunction. 99. **deracinate,** uproot. 101. **fixure,** stability. 102. **ladder . . . designs,** means by which all lofty purposes are realized. 105. **dividable,** separated. 113. **sop,** pulp. 114. **imbecility,** weakness. 116-117. **right . . . resides,** refers to the

The fever whereof all our power is sick.

Agam. The nature of the sickness found, Ulysses, 140
What is the remedy?

Ulyss. The great Achilles, whom opinion crowns
The sinew and the forehand of our host,
Having his ear full of his airy fame,
Grows dainty of his worth and in his tent
Lies mocking our designs: with him Patroclus
Upon a lazy bed the livelong day
Breaks scurril jests,
And with ridiculous and awkward action,
Which, slanderer, he imitation calls, 150
He pageants us. Sometime, great Agamemnon,
Thy topless deputation he puts on,
And, like a strutting player, whose conceit
Lies in his hamstring, and doth think it rich
To hear the wooden dialogue and sound
'Twixt his stretch'd footing and the scaffoldage,—
Such to-be-pitied and o'er-wrested seeming
He acts thy greatness in: and when he speaks,
'Tis like a chime a-mending; with terms unsquared,
Which, from the tongue of roaring Typhon dropp'd,
Would seem hyperboles. At this fusty stuff 161
The large Achilles, on his press'd bed lolling,
From his deep chest laughs out a loud applause;
Cries 'Excellent! 'tis Agamemnon just.
Now play me Nestor; hem, and stroke thy beard,
As he being drest to some oration.'
That's done, as near as the extremest ends
Of parallels, as like as Vulcan and his wife:
Yet god Achilles still cries 'Excellent!
'Tis Nestor right. Now play him me, Patroclus, 170
Arming to answer in a night alarm.'
And then, forsooth, the faint defects of age
Must be the scene of mirth; to cough and spit,
And, with a palsy-fumbling on his gorget,
Shake in and out the rivet: and at this sport
Sir Valour dies; cries 'O, enough, Patroclus;
Or give me ribs of steel! I shall split all
In pleasure of my spleen.' And in this fashion,
All our abilities, gifts, natures, shapes,
Severals and generals of grace exact, 180
Achievements, plots, orders, preventions,
Excitements to the field, or speech for truce,
Success or loss, what is or is not, serves
As stuff for these two to make paradoxes.

Nest. And in the imitation of these twain—
Who, as Ulysses says, opinion crowns
With an imperial voice—many are infect.
Ajax is grown self-will'd, and bears his head
In such a rein, in full as proud a place

As broad Achilles; keeps his tent like him; 190
Makes factious feasts; rails on our state of war,
Bold as an oracle, and sets Thersites,
A slave whose gall coins slanders like a mint,
To match us in comparisons with dirt,
To weaken and discredit our exposure,
How rank soever rounded in with danger.

Ulyss. They tax our policy, and call it cowardice,
Count wisdom as no member of the war,
Forestall prescience and esteem no act
But that of hand: the still and mental parts, 200
That do contrive how many hands shall strike,
When fitness calls them on, and know by measure
Of their observant toil the enemies' weight,—
Why, this hath not a finger's dignity:
They call this bed-work, mappery, closet-war;
So that the ram that batters down the wall,
For the great swing and rudeness of his poise,
They place before his hand that made the engine,
Or those that with the fineness of their souls
By reason guide his execution. 210

Nest. Let this be granted, and Achilles' horse
Makes many Thetis' sons. [*A tucket.*

Agam. What trumpet? look, Menelaus.

Men. From Troy.

Enter ÆNEAS.

Agam. What would you 'fore our tent?

Æne. Is this great Agamemnon's tent, I pray you?

Agam. Even this.

Æne. May one, that is a herald and a prince,
Do a fair message to his kingly ears?

Agam. With surety stronger than Achilles' arm 220
'Fore all the Greekish heads, which with one voice
Call Agamemnon head and general.

Æne. Fair leave and large security. How may
A stranger to those most imperial looks
Know them from eyes of other mortals?

Agam. How!

Æne. Ay;
I ask, that I might waken reverence,
And bid the cheek be ready with a blush
Modest as morning when she coldly eyes
The youthful Phœbus: 230
Which is that god in office, guiding men?
Which is the high and mighty Agamemnon?

Agam. This Trojan scorns us; or the men of Troy
Are ceremonious courtiers.

Æne. Courtiers as free, as debonair, unarm'd,
As bending angels; that's their fame in peace:
But when they would seem soldiers, they have galls,

desirability of adhering to the golden mean. 119-124. **Then . . .
himself.** This metaphor is the converse of the figure of the microcosm,
or man as a little world. Here the faculties and passsions of the soul
are imputed to the universe and misgovernment in states is explained
in physiological terms. 119. **includes,** resolves itself in the end into
(Deighton); encloses within limits (*NED,* citing this passage). 132.
sick, envious. 143. **forehand,** upper hand or advantage. 144. **airy,**
unsubstantial. 145. **dainty of,** i.e., he overestimates his own worth.
148. **scurril,** indecent. 151. **pageants,** dramatizes, mimics. 152.
topless deputation, supreme power deputed to thee (Rolfe); dignity as
Jove's substitute (Schmidt). 153-154. **like . . . hamstring,** i.e., his
ability as an actor is not in his faculties but in his legs; implies, perhaps,
an artificial strut. 156. **'Twixt . . . scaffoldage,** between the floor and
roof of the stage; i.e., he is impressed by the echo of his own voice.
159. **a-mending.** He who has been in the tower of a church while the
chimes were repairing, will never wish a second time to be present at
so dissonantly noisy an operation (Steevens). **terms,** notes. **unsquared,** unadapted to their subject as stones are unfitted to the purposes of architecture while they are yet unsquared (Steevens). 160.

Typhon, Greek mythological monster with a hundred heads which
breathed fire. He made war against the gods and was destroyed by one
of Zeus' thunderbolts. 161. **fusty,** pertaining to fustian, i.e., bombastic
language. 168. **Vulcan . . . wife,** the ugliest god, and Venus, the most
beautiful goddess. 174. **gorget,** piece of armor for the throat. 176.
Sir Valour, contemptuously refers to Achilles' reputation. 180.
Severals . . . exact, well-ordered gifts, individual and general (Delius).
183. **what is or is not,** i.e., all our positive qualities and all our defects
of character or conduct. 184. **paradoxes,** absurdities (Deighton).
186-187. **opinion . . . voice,** i.e., they virtually rule the Greek forces
because of the high regard in which they are held. 195. **our exposure,**
the danger to which we are exposed. 197. **tax,** blame, censure; see
glossary. 199. **Forestall,** condemn beforehand (Paradise). **prescience,** foresight; or perhaps measures taken as a result of foresight.
202. **fitness,** readiness. 203. **their.** The antecedent is *mental parts*
(l. 200). 209. **fineness . . . souls,** the idea is the opposite to mere
physical action; perhaps brain-work. 212. **many Thetis' sons,** i.e.,
many Achilleses. *Stage Direction:* **tucket,** signal given on a trumpet.
235. **debonair,** gentle, meek. 237. **galls,** spirit to resent injury.

Good arms, strong joints, true swords; and, Jove's
  accord,
Nothing so full of heart. But peace, Æneas,
Peace, Trojan; lay thy finger on thy lips!   240
The worthiness of praise distains his worth,
If that the praised himself bring the praise forth:
But what the repining enemy commends,
That breath fame blows; that praise, sole pure,
  transcends.
  Agam. Sir, you of Troy, call you yourself Æneas?
  Æne. Ay, Greek, that is my name.
  Agam. What 's your affair, I pray you?
  Æne. Sir, pardon; 'tis for Agamemnon's ears.
  Agam. He hears nought privately that comes from
  Troy.
  Æne. Nor I from Troy come not to whisper him: 250
I bring a trumpet to awake his ear,
To set his sense on the attentive bent,
And then to speak.
  Agam.   Speak frankly as the wind;
It is not Agamemnon's sleeping hour:
That thou shalt know, Trojan, he is awake,
He tells thee so himself.
  Æne.   Trumpet, blow loud,
Send thy brass voice through all these lazy tents;
And every Greek of mettle, let him know,
What Troy means fairly shall be spoke aloud.

                           [*Trumpet sounds.*

We have, great Agamemnon, here in Troy   260
A prince call'd Hector,—Priam is his father,—
Who in this dull and long-continued truce
Is rusty grown: he bade me take a trumpet,
And to this purpose speak. Kings, princes, lords!
If there be one among the fair'st of Greece
That holds his honour higher than his ease,
That seeks his praise more than he fears his peril,
That knows his valour, and knows not his fear,
That loves his mistress more than in confession,
With truant vows to her own lips he loves,   270
And dare avow her beauty and her worth
In other arms than hers,—to him this challenge.
Hector, in view of Trojans and of Greeks,
Shall make it good, or do his best to do it,
He hath a lady, wiser, fairer, truer,
Than ever Greek did compass in his arms,
And will to-morrow with his trumpet call
Midway between your tents and walls of Troy,
To rouse a Grecian that is true in love:
If any come, Hector shall honour him;   280
If none, he'll say in Troy when he retires,
The Grecian dames are sunburnt and not worth
The splinter of a lance. Even so much.
  Agam. This shall be told our lovers, Lord Æneas;
If none of them have soul in such a kind,
We left them all at home: but we are soldiers;
And may that soldier a mere recreant prove,
That means not, hath not, or is not in love!
If then one is, or hath, or means to be,
That one meets Hector; if none else, I am he.   290
  Nest. Tell him of Nestor, one that was a man

When Hector's grandsire suck'd: he is old now;
But if there be not in our Grecian host
One noble man that hath one spark of fire,
To answer for his love, tell him from me
I'll hide my silver beard in a gold beaver
And in my vantbrace put this wither'd brawn,
And meeting him will tell him that my lady
Was fairer than his grandam and as chaste
As may be in the world: his youth in flood,   300
I'll prove this truth with my three drops of blood.
  Æne. Now heavens forbid such scarcity of youth!
  Ulyss. Amen.
  Agam. Fair Lord Æneas, let me touch your hand;
To our pavilion shall I lead you, sir.
Achilles shall have word of this intent;
So shall each lord of Greece, from tent to tent:
Yourself shall feast with us before you go
And find the welcome of a noble foe.
                  [*Exeunt all but Ulysses and Nestor.*
  Ulyss. Nestor!   310
  Nest. What says Ulysses?
  Ulyss. I have a young conception in my brain;
Be you my time to bring it to some shape.
  Nest. What is 't?
  Ulyss. This 'tis:
Blunt wedges rive hard knots: the seeded pride
That hath to this maturity blown up
In rank Achilles must or now be cropp'd,
Or, shedding, breed a nursery of like evil,
To overbulk us all.
  Nest.   Well, and how?   320
  Ulyss. This challenge that the gallant Hector sends,
However it is spread in general name,
Relates in purpose only to Achilles.
  Nest. The purpose is perspicuous even as substance,
Whose grossness little characters sum up:
And, in the publication, make no strain,
But that Achilles, were his brain as barren
As banks of Libya,—though, Apollo knows,
'Tis dry enough,—will, with great speed of judgement,
Ay, with celerity, find Hector's purpose   330
Pointing on him.
  Ulyss. And wake him to the answer, think you?
  Nest. Yes, 'tis most meet: whom may you else
  oppose,
That can from Hector bring his honour off,
If not Achilles? Though 't be a sportful combat,
Yet in the trial much opinion dwells;
For here the Trojans taste our dear'st repute
With their finest palate: and trust to me, Ulysses,
Our imputation shall be oddly poised
In this wild action; for the success,   340
Although particular, shall give a scantling
Of good or bad unto the general;
And in such indexes, although small pricks
To their subsequent volumes, there is seen
The baby figure of the giant mass
Of things to come at large. It is supposed
He that meets Hector issues from our choice;
And choice, being mutual act of all our souls,

Makes merit her election, and doth boil,
As 'twere from forth us all, a man distill'd 350
Out of our virtues; who miscarrying,
What heart receives from hence the conquering part,
To steel a strong opinion to themselves?
Which entertain'd, limbs are his instruments,
In no less working than are swords and bows
Directive by the limbs.
    Ulyss. Give pardon to my speech:
Therefore 'tis meet Achilles meet not Hector.
Let us, like merchants, show our foulest wares,
And think, perchance, they'll sell; if not, 360
The lustre of the better yet to show,
Shall show the better. Do not consent
That ever Hector and Achilles meet;
For both our honour and our shame in this
Are dogg'd with two strange followers.
    Nest. I see them not with my old eyes: what are
        they?
    Ulyss. What glory our Achilles shares from Hector,
Were he not proud, we all should share with him:
But he already is too insolent;
And we were better parch in Afric sun 370
Than in the pride and salt scorn of his eyes,
Should he 'scape Hector fair: if he were foil'd,
Why then, we did our main opinion crush
In taint of our best man. No, make a lottery;
And, by device, let blockish Ajax draw
The sort to fight with Hector: among ourselves
Give him allowance for the better man;
For that will physic the great Myrmidon
Who broils in loud applause, and make him fall
His crest that prouder than blue Iris bends. 380
If the dull brainless Ajax come safe off,
We'll dress him up in voices: if he fail,
Yet go we under our opinion still
That we have better men. But, hit or miss,
Our project's life this shape of sense assumes:
Ajax employ'd plucks down Achilles' plumes.
    Nest. Ulysses,
Now I begin to relish thy advice;
And I will give a taste of it forthwith
To Agamemnon: go we to him straight. 390
Two curs shall tame each other: pride alone
Must tarre the mastiffs on, as 'twere their bone.
                        [Exeunt.

ACT II.

SCENE I. *A part of the Grecian camp.*

Enter AJAX *and* THERSITES.

    Ajax. Thersites!
    Ther. Agamemnon, how if he had boils? full, all
over, generally?
    Ajax. Thersites!
    Ther. And those boils did run? say so: did not the
general run then? were not that a botchy core?
    Ajax. Dog!

    Ther. Then would come some matter from him; I
see none now. 10
    Ajax. Thou bitch-wolf's son, canst thou not hear?
[*Beating him*] Feel, then.
    Ther. The plague of Greece upon thee, thou mon-
grel beef-witted lord!
    Ajax. Speak then, thou vinewedst leaven, speak:
I will beat thee into handsomeness.
    Ther. I shall sooner rail thee into wit and holiness:
but, I think, thy horse will sooner con an oration than
thou learn a prayer without book. Thou canst strike,
canst thou? a red murrain o' thy jade's tricks! 21
    Ajax. Toadstool, learn me the proclamation.
    Ther. Dost thou think I have no sense, thou strikest
me thus?
    Ajax. The proclamation!
    Ther. Thou art proclaimed a fool, I think.
    Ajax. Do not, porpentine, do not: my fingers itch.
    Ther. I would thou didst itch from head to foot and
I had the scratching of thee; I would make thee the
loathsomest scab in Greece. When thou art forth in
the incursions, thou strikest as slow as another.
    Ajax. I say, the proclamation!
    Ther. Thou grumblest and railest every hour on
Achilles, and thou art as full of envy at his greatness
as Cerberus is at Proserpina's beauty, ay, that thou
barkest at him.
    Ajax. Mistress Thersites!
    Ther. Thou shouldst strike him. 40
    Ajax. Cobloaf!
    Ther. He would pun thee into shivers with his fist,
as a sailor breaks a biscuit.
    Ajax. [*Beating him*] You whoreson cur!
    Ther. Do, do.
    Ajax. Thou stool for a witch!
    Ther. Ay, do, do; thou sodden-witted lord! thou
hast no more brain than I have in mine elbows; an
assinego may tutor thee: thou scurvy-valiant ass!
thou art here but to thrash Trojans; and thou art
bought and sold among those of any wit, like a
barbarian slave. If thou use to beat me, I will begin
at thy heel, and tell what thou art by inches, thou
thing of no bowels, thou!
    Ajax. You dog!
    Ther. You scurvy lord!
    Ajax. [*Beating him*] You cur!
    Ther. Mars his idiot! do, rudeness; do, camel;
do, do. 59

Enter ACHILLES *and* PATROCLUS.

    Achil. Why, how now, Ajax! wherefore do you thus?
How now, Thersites! what's the matter, man?
    Ther. You see him there, do you?
    Achil. Ay; what's the matter?
    Ther. Nay, look upon him.
    Achil. So I do: what's the matter?
    Ther. Nay, but regard him well.
    Achil. 'Well!' why, I do so.
    Ther. But yet you look not well upon him; for,
whosoever you take him to be, he is Ajax. 70

---

376. **sort,** lot. 378. **the great Myrmidon,** i.e., Achilles, so called here
because accompanied by a band of Myrmidon warriors—a tribe living
in Thessaly. 379. **broils in,** is excited by. 392. **tarre,** provoke, incite.
ACT II. SCENE I. 6. **botchy core,** central hard mass of a boil or
tumor. 9. **matter,** sense, with quibble. 14. **mongrel.** His mother was
a Trojan; cf. II, ii, 77, note. 15. **vinewedst,** most moldy. 22. **learn
me,** find out for me. 27. **porpentine,** porcupine. 32. **forth in the
incursions,** abroad engaging in battle. 37. **Cerberus,** three-headed

dog which guarded the entrance to Hades. **Proserpina,** queen of
Hades. 41. **Cobloaf,** small round loaf; a bun. 42. **pun,** pound. 46.
stool for a witch, an abusive term of uncertain significance; Grey
thought it might refer to some of the apparatus for torturing witches,
such as the ducking stool. 49. **assinego,** little ass. 54. **of no bowels,**
merciless. 58. **Mars his,** Mars'.

Achil. I know that, fool.

Ther. Ay, but that fool knows not himself.

Ajax. Therefore I beat thee.

Ther. Lo, lo, lo, lo, what modicums of wit he utters! his evasions have ears thus long. I have bobbed his brain more than he has beat my bones: I will buy nine sparrows for a penny, and his pia mater is not worth the ninth part of a sparrow. This lord, Achilles, Ajax, who wears his wit in his belly and his guts in his head, I'll tell you what I say of him.   81

Achil. What?

Ther. I say, this Ajax—   *[Ajax offers to beat him.*

Achil. Nay, good Ajax.

Ther. Has not so much wit—

Achil. Nay, I must hold you.

Ther. As will stop the eye of Helen's needle, for whom he comes to fight.

Achil. Peace, fool!   89

Ther. I would have peace and quietness, but the fool will not: he there: that he: look you there.

Ajax. O thou damned cur! I shall—

Achil. Will you set your wit to a fool's?

Ther. No, I warrant you; for a fool's will shame it.

Patr. Good words, Thersites.

Achil. What 's the quarrel?

Ajax. I bade the vile owl go learn me the tenour of the proclamation, and he rails upon me.   100

Ther. I serve thee not.

Ajax. Well, go to, go to.

Ther. I serve here voluntary.

Achil. Your last service was sufferance, 'twas not voluntary: no man is beaten voluntary: Ajax was here the voluntary, and you as under an impress.

Ther. E'en so; a great deal of your wit, too, lies in your sinews, or else there be liars. Hector shall have a great catch, if he knock out either of your brains: a' were as good crack a fusty nut with no kernel.   112

Achil. What, with me too, Thersites?

Ther. There 's Ulysses and old Nestor, whose wit was mouldy ere your grandsires had nails on their toes, yoke you like draught-oxen and make you plough up the wars.

Achil. What, what?

Ther. Yes, good sooth: to, Achilles! to, Ajax! to!   120

Ajax. I shall cut out your tongue.

Ther. 'Tis no matter; I shall speak as much as thou afterwards.

Patr. No more words, Thersites; peace!

Ther. I will hold my peace when Achilles' brach bids me, shall I?

Achil. There 's for you, Patroclus.

Ther. I will see you hanged, like clotpoles, ere I come any more to your tents: I will keep where there is wit stirring and leave the faction of fools.   *[Exit.* 130

Patr. A good riddance.

Achil. Marry, this, sir, is proclaim'd through all our host:

That Hector, by the fifth hour of the sun,

Will with a trumpet 'twixt our tents and Troy

To-morrow morning call some knight to arms

That hath a stomach: and such a one that dare

Maintain—I know not what: 'tis trash. Farewell.

Ajax. Farewell. Who shall answer him?

Achil. I know not: 'tis put to lottery; otherwise   140

He knew his man.

Ajax. O, meaning you. I will go learn more of it.

                                        [Exeunt.

SCENE II. *Troy. A room in Priam's palace.*

Enter PRIAM, HECTOR, TROILUS, PARIS, *and* HELENUS.

Pri. After so many hours, lives, speeches spent,

Thus once again says Nestor from the Greeks:

'Deliver Helen, and all damage else—

As honour, loss of time, travail, expense,

Wounds, friends, and what else dear that is consumed

In hot digestion of this cormorant war—

Shall be struck off.' Hector, what say you to 't?

Hect. Though no man lesser fears the Greeks than I

As far as toucheth my particular,

Yet, dread Priam,   10

There is no lady of more softer bowels,

More spongy to suck in the sense of fear,

More ready to cry out 'Who knows what follows?'

Than Hector is: the wound of peace is surety,

Surety secure; but modest doubt is call'd

The beacon of the wise, the tent that searches

To the bottom of the worst. Let Helen go:

Since the first sword was drawn about this question,

Every tithe soul, 'mongst many thousand dismes,

Hath been as dear as Helen; I mean, of ours: 20

If we have lost so many tenths of ours,

To guard a thing not ours nor worth to us,

Had it our name, the value of one ten,

What merit 's in that reason which denies

The yielding of her up?

Tro.   Fie, fie, my brother!

Weigh you the worth and honour of a king

So great as our dread father in a scale

Of common ounces? will you with counters sum

The past proportion of his infinite?

And buckle in a waist most fathomless   30

With spans and inches so diminutive

As fears and reasons? fie, for godly shame!

Hel. No marvel, though you bite so sharp at reasons,

You are so empty of them. Should not our father

Bear the great sway of his affairs with reasons,

Because your speech hath none that tells him so?

Tro. You are for dreams and slumbers, brother
priest;

You fur your gloves with reason. Here are your
reasons:

You know an enemy intends you harm;

You know a sword employ'd is perilous,   40

And reason flies the object of all harm:

Who marvels then, when Helenus beholds

A Grecian and his sword, if he do set

---

75. **have ears thus long,** are those of an ass.   77. **pia mater,** used loosely for "brain."   94. **set your wit to,** match wits with.   111. **fusty,** moldy.   126. **brach,** bitch hound.   128. **clotpoles,** blockheads.   134. **fifth hour,** eleven o'clock.   141. **knew,** subjunctive, would know.   SCENE II.   6. **cormorant,** gluttonous.   11. **bowels,** considered as the seat of tenderness and pity.   14. **the wound . . . surety,** i.e., a sense of security is dangerous to peace.   16. **tent,** probe.   19. **Every tithe soul,** every soul exacted by the war as a tithe.   **dismes,** tenths (of men sacrificed).   23. **our name,** i.e., the name of Trojan, which Helen has

not.   28. **counters,** pieces of coin-shaped metal used in calculation.   29. **past . . . infinite,** his infinitude past all comparison.   37-50. **You . . . deject.** This tirade shows Troilus to be a person in whom the passion of love has brought about a rejection of reason; he deliberately follows the rule of impulse.   38. **You . . . reason,** a hyperbolical way of saying, you demand reason—or rely on reason—for everything.   45. **chidden Mercury.** Mercury as Jove's errand boy was subject to his chiding.   46. **disorb'd,** removed from its sphere.   58-60. **the will . . . merit,** the will which attributes qualities to what it loves is foolish

The very wings of reason to his heels
And fly like chidden Mercury from Jove,
Or like a star disorb'd? Nay, if we talk of reason,
Let 's shut our gates and sleep: manhood and honour
Should have hare-hearts, would they but fat their
    thoughts
With this cramm'd reason: reason and respect
Make livers pale and lustihood deject. 50
  Hect. Brother, she is not worth what she doth cost
The holding.
  Tro.   What is aught, but as 'tis valued?
  Hect. But value dwells not in particular will;
It holds his estimate and dignity
As well wherein 'tis precious of itself
As in the prizer: 'tis mad idolatry
To make the service greater than the god;
And the will dotes that is attributive
To what infectiously itself affects,
Without some image of the affected merit. 60
  Tro. I take to-day a wife, and my election
Is led on in the conduct of my will;
My will enkindled by mine eyes and ears,
Two traded pilots 'twixt the dangerous shores
Of will and judgement: how may I avoid,
Although my will distaste what it elected,
The wife I chose? there can be no evasion
To blench from this and to stand firm by honour:
We turn not back the silks upon the merchant, 69
When we have soil'd them, nor the remainder viands
We do not throw in unrespective sieve,
Because we now are full. It was thought meet
Paris should do some vengeance on the Greeks:
Your breath of full consent bellied his sails;
The seas and winds, old wranglers, took a truce
And did him service: he touch'd the ports desired,
And for an old aunt whom the Greeks held captive,
He brought a Grecian queen, whose youth and
    freshness
Wrinkles Apollo's, and makes stale the morning.
Why keep we her? the Grecians keep our aunt: 80
Is she worth keeping? why, she is a pearl,
Whose price hath launch'd above a thousand ships,
And turn'd crown'd kings to merchants,
If you'll avouch 'twas wisdom Paris went—
As you must needs, for you all cried 'Go, go,'—
If you'll confess he brought home noble prize—
As you must needs, for you all clapp'd your hands,
And cried 'Inestimable!'— why do you now
The issue of your proper wisdoms rate,
And do a deed that fortune never did, 90
Beggar the estimation which you prized
Richer than sea and land? O, theft most base,
That we have stol'n what we do fear to keep!
But, thieves, unworthy of a thing so stol'n,
That in their country did them that disgrace,
We fear to warrant in our native place!
  Cas. [*Within*] Cry, Trojans, cry!
  Pri.   What noise? what shriek is this?
  Tro. 'Tis our mad sister, I do know her voice.

  Cas. [*Within*] Cry, Trojans!
  Hect. It is Cassandra.   100

  Enter CASSANDRA, *raving.*

  Cas. Cry, Trojans, cry! lend me ten thousand eyes,
And I will fill them with prophetic tears.
  Hect. Peace, sister, peace!
  Cas. Virgins and boys, mid-age and wrinkled eld,
Soft infancy, that nothing canst but cry,
Add to my clamours! let us pay betimes
A moiety of that mass of moan to come.
Cry, Trojans, cry! practise your eyes with tears!
Troy must not be, nor goodly Ilion stand;
Our firebrand brother, Paris, burns us all.   110
Cry, Trojans, cry! a Helen and a woe:
Cry, cry! Troy burns, or else let Helen go.   [*Exit.*
  Hect. Now, youthful Troilus, do not these high
    strains
Of divination in our sister work
Some touches of remorse? or is your blood
So madly hot that no discourse of reason,
Nor fear of bad success in a bad cause,
Can qualify the same?
  Tro.   Why, brother Hector,
We may not think the justness of each act
Such and no other than event doth form it,   120
Nor once deject the courage of our minds,
Because Cassandra 's mad: her brain-sick raptures
Cannot distaste the goodness of a quarrel
Which hath our several honours all engaged
To make it gracious. For my private part,
I am no more touch'd than all Priam's sons:
And Jove forbid there should be done amongst us
Such things as might offend the weakest spleen
To fight for and maintain!
  Par. Else might the world convince of levity   130
As well my undertakings as your counsels:
But I attest the gods, your full consent
Gave wings to my propension and cut off
All fears attending on so dire a project.
For what, alas, can these my single arms?
What propugnation is in one man's valour,
To stand the push and enmity of those
This quarrel would excite? Yet, I protest,
Were I alone to pass the difficulties
And had as ample power as I have will,   140
Paris should ne'er retract what he hath done,
Nor faint in the pursuit.
  Pri.   Paris, you speak
Like one besotted on your sweet delights:
You have the honey still, but these the gall;
So to be valiant is no praise at all.
  Par. Sir, I propose not merely to myself
The pleasures such a beauty brings with it;
But I would have the soil of her fair rape
Wiped off, in honourable keeping her.
What treason were it to the ransack'd queen,
Disgrace to your great worths and shame to me,   150
Now to deliver her possession up

unless there is present some evidence (*image*) of the merit or qualities
attributed. 61. **I take to-day a wife,** etc. Troilus, in stating Paris' case,
is also stating his own credo about love. 64. **traded,** practiced, skillful
in their trade. 71. **unrespective sieve,** i.e., one that cares not what
is thrown into it. 77. **an old aunt,** Hesione, Priam's sister, rescued
from the wrath of Poseidon by Hercules and bestowed by him on the
Greek, Telamon, father of Ajax. 79. **Wrinkles Apollo's,** makes
Apollo look old and ugly by comparison. 82. **Whose . . . ships,**
echoes the famous line from Marlowe's *Faustus:* "Was this the face that

launched a thousand ships?" 83. **turn'd . . . merchants,** made kings
like merchants seeking a rare pearl. 91. **Beggar,** make valueless. 105.
nothing canst, can do nothing. 108. **practise . . . tears,** learn to weep
(Schmidt). 123. **distaste,** render distasteful. 125. **gracious,** righteous,
pious, holy. 128-129. **offend . . . fight,** offend to the extent of making
(someone) fight. 133. **propension,** propensity. 136. **propugnation,**
defense. 139. **pass,** experience, undergo. 141. **retract,** disavow.
148. **rape,** abduction. 150. **ransack'd,** carried off.

On terms of base compulsion! Can it be
That so degenerate a strain as this
Should once set footing in your generous bosoms?
There 's not the meanest spirit on our party
Without a heart to dare or sword to draw
When Helen is defended, nor none so noble
Whose life were ill bestow'd or death unfamed
Where Helen is the subject; then, I say,   160
Well may we fight for her whom, we know well,
The world's large spaces cannot parallel.
   Hect. Paris and Troilus, you have both said well,
And on the cause and question now in hand
Have glozed, but superficially; not much
Unlike young men, whom Aristotle thought
Unfit to hear moral philosophy:
The reasons you allege do more conduce
To the hot passion of distemper'd blood
Than to make up a free determination   170
'Twixt right and wrong, for pleasure and revenge
Have ears more deaf than adders to the voice
Of any true decision. Nature craves
All dues be render'd to their owners: now,
What nearer debt in all humanity
Than wife is to the husband? If this law
Of nature be corrupted through affection,
And that great minds, of partial indulgence
To their benumbed wills, resist the same,
There is a law in each well-order'd nation   180
To curb those raging appetites that are
Most disobedient and refractory.
If Helen then be wife to Sparta's king,
As it is known she is, these moral laws
Of nature and of nations speak aloud
To have her back return'd: thus to persist
In doing wrong extenuates not wrong,
But makes it much more heavy. Hector's opinion
Is this in way of truth; yet ne'ertheless,
My spritely brethren, I propend to you   190
In resolution to keep Helen still,
For 'tis a cause that hath no mean dependance
Upon our joint and several dignities.
   Tro. Why, there you touch'd the life of our design:
Were it not glory that we more affected
Than the performance of our heaving spleens,
I would not wish a drop of Trojan blood
Spent more in her defence. But, worthy Hector,
She is a theme of honour and renown,
A spur to valiant and magnanimous deeds,   200
Whose present courage may beat down our foes,
And fame in time to come canonize us;
For, I presume, brave Hector would not lose
So rich advantage of a promised glory
As smiles upon the forehead of this action
For the wide world's revenue.
   Hect.   I am yours,
You valiant offspring of great Priamus.
I have a roisting challenge sent amongst

The dull and factious nobles of the Greeks
Will strike amazement to their drowsy spirits: 210
I was advertised their great general slept,
Whilst emulation in the army crept:
This, I presume, will wake him.   [*Exeunt.*

SCENE III. *The Grecian camp. Before Achilles' tent.*

Enter THERSITES, *solus.*

   Ther. How now, Thersites! what, lost in the labyrinth of thy fury! Shall the elephant Ajax carry it
thus? he beats me, and I rail at him: O, worthy
satisfaction! would it were otherwise; that I could
beat him, whilst he railed at me. 'Sfoot, I'll learn to
conjure and raise devils, but I'll see some issue of
my spiteful execrations. Then there 's Achilles, a rare
enginer! If Troy be not taken till these two undermine it, the walls will stand till they fall of themselves.
O thou great thunder-darter of Olympus, forget that
thou art Jove, the king of gods, and, Mercury, lose all
the serpentine craft of thy caduceus, if ye take not
that little little less than little wit from them that
they have! which short-armed ignorance itself knows
is so abundant scarce, it will not in circumvention
deliver a fly from a spider, without drawing their
massy irons and cutting the web. After this, the
vengeance on the whole camp! or rather, the bone-
ache! for that, methinks, is the curse dependant on
those that war for a placket. I have said my prayers
and devil Envy say Amen. What ho! my Lord
Achilles!   23

Enter PATROCLUS.

   Patr. Who 's there? Thersites! Good Thersites,
come in and rail.
   Ther. If I could have remembered a gilt counterfeit, thou wouldst not have slipped out of my contemplation: but it is no matter; thyself upon thyself!
The common curse of mankind, folly and ignorance, be thine in great revenue! heaven bless
thee from a tutor, and discipline come not near
thee! Let thy blood be thy direction till thy death!
then if she that lays thee out says thou art a fair corse,
I'll be sworn and sworn upon 't she never shrouded
any but lazars. Amen. Where 's Achilles?
   Patr. What, art thou devout? wast thou in prayer?
   Ther. Ay: the heavens hear me!   40

Enter ACHILLES.

   Achil. Who 's there?
   Patr. Thersites, my lord.
   Achil. Where, where? Art thou come? why, my
cheese, my digestion, why hast thou not served thyself
in to my table so many meals? Come, what 's Agamemnon?

---

165. **glozed,** commented on. 167. **moral philosophy.** Aristotle says this of political philosophy in the *Nichomachean Ethics.* Shakespeare's line is paralleled by a sentence in Bacon's *Advancement of Learning,* Book II: "Is not the opinion of Aristotle worthy to be regarded wherein he saith that young men are not fit auditors of moral philosophy?" This similarity of apparent error is advanced in support of the Baconian theory of authorship. Sir Sidney Lee (*Life of Shakespeare,* App. II) points out that both Bacon and Shakespeare relied, in all probability, on a summary paraphrase of Aristotle's *Ethics,* translated from Italian and published in 1547, in which *political* as referring to civil society is made the equivalent of *moral* as understood in the Renaissance period. 172. **adders.** Cf. *2 Henry VI,* III, ii, 76, note. 178-179. **great . . . wills,**

great minds indulgent (through partiality) to their wills benumbed (i.e., rendered impotent) by affection. 178. **of,** out of. 190. **spritely,** full of spirit. **propend,** incline. 199. **a theme of honour.** Troilus' statement is an appeal to honor, which is not controlled by prudence. 202. **canonize,** enroll among famous persons. 206. **revenue,** accent on second syllable. 208. **roisting,** blustering, bullying. 211. **their great general,** Achilles. 212. **emulation,** ambitious or jealous rivalry.
   SCENE III. 4. **worthy satisfaction,** adequate revenge (used contemptuously). 6. **'Sfoot,** an oath by God's foot. 8. **enginer,** crafty deviser of military schemes (used contemptuously). 13-14. **the serpentine . . . caduceus,** alludes to Mercury's wand, having two serpents twined round it; also to the wisdom of serpents. 18. **massy irons,**

Ther. Thy commander, Achilles. Then tell me, Patroclus, what's Achilles?

Patr. Thy lord, Thersites: then tell me, I pray thee, what's thyself? 50

Ther. Thy knower, Patroclus: then tell me, Patroclus, what art thou?

Patr. Thou mayst tell that knowest.

Achil. O, tell, tell.

Ther. I'll decline the whole question. Agamemnon commands Achilles; Achilles is my lord; I am Patroclus' knower, and Patroclus is a fool.

Patr. You rascal!

Ther. Peace, fool! I have not done. 60

Achil. He is a privileged man. Proceed, Thersites.

Ther. Agamemnon is a fool; Achilles is a fool; Thersites is a fool, and, as aforesaid, Patroclus is a fool.

Achil. Derive this; come.

Ther. Agamemnon is a fool to offer to command Achilles; Achilles is a fool to be commanded of Agamemnon; Thersites is a fool to serve such a fool, and Patroclus is a fool positive. 70

Patr. Why am I a fool?

Ther. Make that demand of the prover. It suffices me thou art. Look you, who comes here?

Achil. Patroclus, I'll speak with nobody. Come in with me, Thersites. [*Exit.*

Ther. Here is such patchery, such juggling and such knavery! all the argument is a cuckold and a whore; a good quarrel to draw emulous factions and bleed to death upon. Now, the dry serpigo on the subject! and war and lechery confound all! [*Exit.* 81

Enter AGAMEMNON, ULYSSES, NESTOR, DIOMEDES, *and* AJAX.

Agam. Where is Achilles?

Patr. Within his tent; but ill disposed, my lord.

Agam. Let it be known to him that we are here.
He shent our messengers; and we lay by
Our appertainments, visiting of him:
Let him be told so; lest perchance he think
We dare not move the question of our place,
Or know not what we are.

Patr.   I shall say so to him. [*Exit.* 90

Ulyss. We saw him at the opening of his tent:
He is not sick.

Ajax. Yes, lion-sick, sick of proud heart: you may call it melancholy, if you will favour the man; but, by my head, 'tis pride: but why, why? let him show us the cause. A word, my lord. [*Takes Agamemnon aside.*

Nest. What moves Ajax thus to bay at him?

Ulyss. Achilles hath inveigled his fool from him. 100

Nest. Who, Thersites?

Ulyss. He.

Nest. Then will Ajax lack matter, if he have lost his argument.

Ulyss. No, you see, he is his argument that has his argument, Achilles.

Nest. All the better; their fraction is more our wish than their faction: but it was a strong composure a fool could disunite.

Ulyss. The amity that wisdom knits not, folly may easily untie. Here comes Patroclus.

Re-enter PATROCLUS.

Nest. No Achilles with him.

Ulyss. The elephant hath joints, but none for courtesy: his legs are legs for necessity, not for flexure.

Patr. Achilles bids me say, he is much sorry,
If any thing more than your sport and pleasure
Did move your greatness and this noble state
To call upon him; he hopes it is no other
But for your health and your digestion sake, 120
An after-dinner's breath.

Agam.   Hear you, Patroclus:
We are too well acquainted with these answers:
But his evasion, wing'd thus swift with scorn,
Cannot outfly our apprehensions.
Much attribute he hath, and much the reason
Why we ascribe it to him; yet all his virtues,
Not virtuously on his own part beheld,
Do in our eyes begin to lose their gloss,
Yea, like fair fruit in an unwholesome dish,
Are like to rot untasted. Go and tell him, 130
We come to speak with him; and you shall not sin,
If you do say we think him over-proud
And under-honest, in self-assumption greater
Than in the note of judgement; and worthier than
      himself
Here tend the savage strangeness he puts on,
Disguise the holy strength of their command,
And underwrite in an observing kind
His humorous predominance; yea, watch
His pettish lunes, his ebbs, his flows, as if
The passage and whole carriage of this action 140
Rode on his tide. Go tell him this, and add,
That if he overhold his price so much,
We'll none of him; but let him, like an engine
Not portable, lie under this report:
'Bring action hither, this cannot go to war:
A stirring dwarf we do allowance give
Before a sleeping giant.' Tell him so.

Patr. I shall; and bring his answer presently. [*Exit.*

Agam. In second voice we'll not be satisfied;
We come to speak with him. Ulysses, enter you. 150
      [*Exit Ulysses.*

Ajax. What is he more than another?

Agam. No more than what he thinks he is.

Ajax. Is he so much? Do you not think he thinks himself a better man than I am?

Agam. No question.

Ajax. Will you subscribe his thought, and say he is?

Agam. No, noble Ajax; you are as strong, as valiant, as wise, no less noble, much more gentle, and altogether more tractable. 160

Troilus and Cressida
ACT II : SC III

877

swords, in contrast to cobwebs. 20. **bone-ache,** another name for venereal disease. 22. **placket,** used to signify a woman. 28. **slipped,** quibble on "slip," counterfeit coin. 32. **bless thee from,** bless by protecting thee from. 36. **lazars,** lepers, from the biblical leper, Lazarus. 44. **cheese,** supposed, proverbially, to aid digestion. 55. **decline,** go through in order from beginning to end, as when inflecting a noun. 61. **privileged man.** Fools were privileged to speak without restraint. 66. **Derive,** give the origin of; the grammatical metaphor is continued here and also in line 70. 70. **positive,** i.e., absolute. 77. **patchery,** knavery. 78. **all the argument,** issue of the war. 79. **emulous,** envious. 81 **serpigo,** skin eruption. 86. **shent,** rebuked; literally, injured. 87. **appertainments,** rights, prerogatives. 93.

lion-sick, sick with pride. 107. **fraction,** discord. **faction,** union. 109. **composure,** union (contemptuously). 113. **elephant hath joints.** A vulgar error mentioned often in the sixteenth century regarding natural history was to the effect that elephants had no joints. 118. **this noble state,** i.e., the distinguished men accompanying Agamemnon. 124. **apprehensions,** understanding. 125. **attribute,** credit, reputation. 134. **Than . . . judgement,** than true judges know him to be (Schmidt); than in the distinctive mark of judgment (Deighton). 137. **underwrite,** submit to (as observers). 138. **humorous predominance,** whim caused by unbalanced humors. 139. **lunes,** lunacies, freaks.

Ajax. Why should a man be proud? How doth pride grow? I know not what pride is.

Agam. Your mind is the clearer, Ajax, and your virtues the fairer. He that is proud eats up himself: pride is his own glass, his own trumpet, his own chronicle; and whatever praises itself but in the deed, devours the deed in the praise.

Ajax. I do hate a proud man, as I hate the engendering of toads. 170

Nest. Yet he loves himself: is 't not strange? [*Aside.*

Re-enter ULYSSES.

Ulyss. Achilles will not to the field to-morrow.

Agam. What 's his excuse?

Ulyss. He doth rely on none,
But carries on the stream of his dispose
Without observance or respect of any,
In will peculiar and in self-admission.

Agam. Why will he not upon our fair request
Untent his person and share the air with us?

Ulyss. Things small as nothing, for request's sake only,
He makes important: possess'd he is with greatness, 180
And speaks not to himself but with a pride
That quarrels at self-breath: imagined worth
Holds in his blood such swoln and hot discourse
That 'twixt his mental and his active parts
Kingdom'd Achilles in commotion rages
And batters down himself: what should I say?
He is so plaguy proud that the death-tokens of it
Cry 'No recovery.'

Agam. Let Ajax go to him.
Dear lord, go you and greet him in his tent:
'Tis said he holds you well, and will be led 190
At your request a little from himself.

Ulyss. O Agamemnon, let it not be so!
We'll consecrate the steps that Ajax makes
When they go from Achilles: shall the proud lord
That bastes his arrogance with his own seam
And never suffers matter of the world
Enter his thoughts, save such as do revolve
And ruminate himself, shall he be worshipp'd
Of that we hold an idol more than he?
No, this thrice worthy and right valiant lord 200
Must not so stale his palm, nobly acquired;
Nor, by my will, assubjugate his merit,
As amply titled as Achilles is,
By going to Achilles:
That were to enlard his fat already pride
And add more coals to Cancer when he burns
With entertaining great Hyperion.
This lord go to him! Jupiter forbid,
And say in thunder 'Achilles go to him.'

Nest. [*Aside to Dio.*] O, this is well; he rubs the vein of him. 210

Dio. [*Aside to Nest.*] And how his silence drinks up this applause!

Ajax. If I go to him, with my armed fist
I'll pash him o'er the face.

Agam. O, no, you shall not go.

Ajax. An a' be proud with me, I'll pheeze his pride.
Let me go to him.

Ulyss. Not for the worth that hangs upon our quarrel.

Ajax. A paltry, insolent fellow!

Nest. How he describes himself!

Ajax. Can he not be sociable? 220

Ulyss. The raven chides blackness.

Ajax. I'll let his humours blood.

Agam. He will be the physician that should be the patient.

Ajax. An all men were o' my mind,—

Ulyss. Wit would be out of fashion.

Ajax. A' should not bear it so, a' should eat swords first: shall pride carry it?

Nest. An 'twould, you 'ld carry half.

Ulyss. A' would have ten shares. 230

Ajax. I will knead him; I'll make him supple.

Nest. He 's not yet through warm: force him with praises: pour in, pour in; his ambition is dry.

Ulyss. [*To Agam.*] My lord, you feed too much on this dislike.

Nest. Our noble general, do not do so.

Dio. You must prepare to fight without Achilles.

Ulyss. Why, 'tis this naming of him does him harm.
Here is a man—but 'tis before his face; 240
I will be silent.

Nest. Wherefore should you so?
He is not emulous, as Achilles is.

Ulyss. Know the whole world, he is as valiant.

Ajax. A whoreson dog, that shall palter thus with us!
Would he were a Trojan!

Nest. What a vice were it in Ajax now,—

Ulyss. If he were proud,—

Dio. Or covetous of praise,—

Ulyss. Ay, or surly borne,—

Dio. Or strange, or self-affected! 250

Ulyss. Thank the heavens, lord, thou art of sweet composure;
Praise him that got thee, she that gave thee suck:
Famed be thy tutor, and thy parts of nature
Thrice famed, beyond all erudition:
But he that disciplined thy arms to fight,
Let Mars divide eternity in twain,
And give him half: and, for thy vigour,
Bull-bearing Milo his addition yield
To sinewy Ajax. I will not praise thy wisdom,
Which, like a bourn, a pale, a shore, confines 260
Thy spacious and dilated parts: here 's Nestor;
Instructed by the antiquary times,
He must, he is, he cannot but be wise:
But pardon, father Nestor, were your days
As green as Ajax' and your brain so temper'd,
You should not have the eminence of him,
But be as Ajax.

Ajax. Shall I call you father?

Nest. Ay, my good son.

Dio. Be ruled by him, Lord Ajax.

Ulyss. There is no tarrying here; the hart Achilles
Keeps thicket. Please it our great general 270

---

176. **will peculiar,** i.e., his own independent will. **self-admission,** self-approbation. 184. **mental . . . parts,** his mind and body. 187. **it.** The antecedent is "pride," implied in the phrase *plaguy proud.* 195. **bastes,** moistens (as roasting meat with melted fat). **seam,** fat, grease. 201. **stale . . . acquired,** sully his nobly won honor. 202. **assubjugate,** reduce to subjection. 206-207. **add . . . Hyperion.** Cancer is the sign of the zodiac into which the sun enters at midsummer. The lines mean "add a fire to the heat of midsummer." 207. **Hyperion,**

the sun god. 210. **vein,** humor, disposition. 213. **pash,** smash. 215. **pheeze,** drive or frighten away. 222. **let . . . blood,** bleed him (as a physician) to cure his excessive humors. 232. **through,** thoroughly. 253. **parts of nature,** natural gifts; i.e., are far more famous than any acquired abilities. 258. **Milo,** celebrated athlete of phenomenal strength. 273. **main,** full force.

ACT III. SCENE I. 11. **know . . . better,** i.e., know it to be improved. 15. **in . . . grace,** i.e., in the way of salvation because he desires to be

To call together all his state of war;
Fresh kings are come to Troy: to-morrow
We must with all our main of power stand fast:
And here 's a lord,—come knights from east to west,
And cull their flower, Ajax shall cope the best.
    Agam. Go we to council. Let Achilles sleep:
Light boats sail swift, though greater hulks draw
    deep.   [*Exeunt.*

ACT III.

SCENE I. *Troy. Priam's palace.*

Enter a Servant *and* PANDARUS.

Pan. Friend, you! pray you, a word: do not you
follow the young Lord Paris?

Serv. Ay, sir, when he goes before me.

Pan. You depend upon him, I mean?

Serv. Sir, I do depend upon the lord.

Pan. You depend upon a noble gentleman; I must
needs praise him.

Serv. The lord be praised!

Pan. You know me, do you not?

Serv. Faith, sir, superficially.   10

Pan. Friend, know me better; I am the Lord
Pandarus.

Serv. I hope I shall know your honour better.

Pan. I do desire it.

Serv. You are in the state of grace.

Pan. Grace! not so, friend; honour and lordship are
my titles. [*Music within.*] What music is this?

Serv. I do but partly know, sir: it is music in parts.   20

Pan. Know you the musicians?

Serv. Wholly, sir.

Pan. Who play they to?

Serv. To the hearers, sir.

Pan. At whose pleasure, friend?

Serv. At mine, sir, and theirs that love music.

Pan. Command, I mean, friend.

Serv. Who shall I command, sir?

Pan. Friend, we understand not one another: I am
too courtly and thou art too cunning. At whose
request do these men play?   31

Serv. That 's to 't indeed, sir: marry, sir, at the
request of Paris my lord, who 's there in person;
with him, the mortal Venus, the heart-blood of
beauty, love's invisible soul,—

Pan. Who, my cousin Cressida?

Serv. No, sir, Helen: could you not find out that
by her attributes?

Pan. It should seem, fellow, that thou hast not
seen the Lady Cressida. I come to speak with Paris
from the Prince Troilus: I will make a complimental
assault upon him, for my business seethes.   43

Serv. Sodden business! there 's a stewed phrase
indeed!

Enter PARIS *and* HELEN, *attended.*

Pan. Fair be to you, my lord, and to all this fair

company! fair desires, in all fair measure, fairly guide
them! especially to you, fair queen! fair thoughts be
your fair pillow!

Helen. Dear lord, you are full of fair words.

Pan. You speak your fair pleasure, sweet queen.
Fair prince, here is good broken music.

Par. You have broke it, cousin: and, by my life,
you shall make it whole again; you shall piece it
out with a piece of your performance. Nell, he is full
of harmony.   56

Pan. Truly, lady, no.

Helen. O, sir,—

Pan. Rude, in sooth; in good sooth, very rude.

Par. Well said, my lord! well, you say so in fits.

Pan. I have business to my lord, dear queen. My
lord, will you vouchsafe me a word?

Helen. Nay, this shall not hedge us out: we'll hear
you sing, certainly.

Pan. Well, sweet queen, you are pleasant with me.
But, marry, thus, my lord: my dear lord and most
esteemed friend, your brother Troilus,—   70

Helen. My Lord Pandarus; honey-sweet lord,—

Pan. Go to, sweet queen, go to:—commends himself
most affectionately to you,—

Helen. You shall not bob us out of our melody: if
you do, our melancholy upon your head!

Pan. Sweet queen, sweet queen! that 's a sweet
queen, i' faith.

Helen. And to make a sweet lady sad is a sour
offence.   80

Pan. Nay, that shall not serve your turn; that shall
it not, in truth, la. Nay, I care not for such words;
no, no. And, my lord, he desires you, that if the king
call for him at supper, you will make his excuse.

Helen. My Lord Pandarus,—

Pan. What says my sweet queen, my very very
sweet queen?

Par. What exploit 's in hand? where sups he to-
night?   90

Helen. Nay, but, my lord,—

Pan. What says my sweet queen? My cousin will
fall out with you. You must not know where he sups.

Par. I'll lay my life, with my disposer Cressida.

Pan. No, no, no such matter; you are wide: come,
your disposer is sick.

Par. Well, I'll make excuse.   99

Pan. Ay, good my lord. Why should you say Cressida? no, your poor disposer 's sick.

Par. I spy.

Pan. You spy! what do you spy? Come, give me an
instrument. Now, sweet queen.

Helen. Why, this is kindly done.

Pan. My niece is horribly in love with a thing you
have, sweet queen.

Helen. She shall have it, my lord, if it be not my
lord Paris.

Pan. He! no, she'll none of him; they two are
twain.   111

Helen. Falling in, after falling out, may make them
three.

---

better. Pandarus answers to the idea of grace as a courtly title applicable to a duke. 35. **love's invisible soul,** the very essence or spirit
of love, personified in Helen. 42. **complimental,** courteous. 44.
stewed, quibbling reference to stews, brothels. 52. **broken music,**
music arranged for parts, with quibble. 59. **Rude,** discordant.
Pandarus deprecates his musical talents. 62. **in fits,** perhaps a quibble
on *fit* as "division of a song." 75. **bob,** cheat. 92-94. **My cousin
. . . sups.** QF assign the last sentence of this speech to Helen. Hanmer
assigned it to Pandarus. Deighton questions the relevance of the words
My cousin will fall out with you to this context. He thinks they have
greater appropriateness at line 111 after *twain,* where they give point
to Helen's *Falling in, after falling out,* etc. 95. **disposer,** she who disposes
or inclines me to mirth (Dyce). 111. **twain,** parted, i.e., not in accord.

Pan. Come, come, I'll hear no more of this; I'll sing you a song now.

Helen. Ay, ay, prithee now. By my troth, sweet lord, thou hast a fine forehead.

Pan. Ay, you may, you may.

Helen. Let thy song be love: this love will undo us all. O Cupid, Cupid, Cupid! 120

Pan. Love! ay, that it shall, i' faith.

Par. Ay, good now, love, love, nothing but love.

Pan. In good troth, it begins so. [*Sings.*

Love, love, nothing but love, still more!
For, O, love's bow
Shoots buck and doe:
The shaft confounds,
Not that it wounds,
But tickles still the sore. 130
These lovers cry Oh! oh! they die!
Yet that which seems the wound to kill,
Doth turn oh! oh! to ha! ha! he!
So dying love lives still:
Oh! oh! a while, but ha! ha! ha!
Oh! oh! groans out for ha! ha! ha!
Heigh-ho!

Helen. In love, i' faith, to the very tip of the nose. 139

Par. He eats nothing but doves, love, and that breeds hot blood, and hot blood begets hot thoughts, and hot thoughts beget hot deeds, and hot deeds is love.

Pan. Is this the generation of love? hot blood, hot thoughts, and hot deeds? Why, they are vipers: is love a generation of vipers? Sweet lord, who 's a-field to-day?

Par. Hector, Deiphobus, Helenus, Antenor, and all the gallantry of Troy: I would fain have armed to-day, but my Nell would not have it so. How chance my brother Troilus went not? 151

Helen. He hangs the lip at something: you know all, Lord Pandarus.

Pan. Not I, honey-sweet queen. I long to hear how they sped to-day. You 'll remember your brother's excuse?

Par. To a hair.

Pan. Farewell, sweet queen.

Helen. Commend me to your niece.

Pan. I will, sweet queen. [*Exit.* 160
[*A retreat sounded.*

Par. They 're come from field: let us to Priam's hall,
To greet the warriors. Sweet Helen, I must woo you
To help unarm our Hector: his stubborn buckles,
With these your white enchanting fingers touch'd,
Shall more obey than to the edge of steel
Or force of Greekish sinews; you shall do more
Than all the island kings,—disarm great Hector.

Helen. 'Twill make us proud to be his servant, Paris;
Yea, what he shall receive of us in duty
Gives us more palm in beauty than we have, 170
Yea, overshines ourself.

Par. Sweet, above thought I love thee. [*Exeunt.*

SCENE II. *The same. Pandarus' orchard.*

Enter PANDARUS *and* TROILUS' Boy, *meeting.*

Pan. How now! where 's thy master? at my cousin Cressida's?

Boy. No, sir; he stays for you to conduct him thither.

Pan. O, here he comes.

Enter TROILUS.

How now, how now!

Tro. Sirrah, walk off. [*Exit Boy.*

Pan. Have you seen my cousin?

Tro. No, Pandarus: I stalk about her door,
Like a strange soul upon the Stygian banks 10
Staying for waftage. O, be thou my Charon,
And give me swift transportance to those fields
Where I may wallow in the lily-beds
Proposed for the deserver! O gentle Pandarus,
From Cupid's shoulder pluck his painted wings,
And fly with me to Cressid!

Pan. Walk here i' the orchard, I'll bring her straight. [*Exit.*

Tro. I am giddy; expectation whirls me round.
The imaginary relish is so sweet 20
That it enchants my sense: what will it be,
When that the watery palate tastes indeed
Love's thrice repured nectar? death, I fear me,
Swooning destruction, or some joy too fine,
Too subtle-potent, tuned too sharp in sweetness,
For the capacity of my ruder powers:
I fear it much; and I do fear besides,
That I shall lose distinction in my joys;
As doth a battle, when they charge on heaps
The enemy flying. 30

Re-enter PANDARUS.

Pan. She 's making her ready, she'll come straight: you must be witty now. She does so blush, and fetches her wind so short, as if she were frayed with a sprite: I'll fetch her. It is the prettiest villain: she fetches her breath as short as a new-ta'en sparrow. [*Exit.*

Tro. Even such a passion doth embrace my bosom:
My heart beats thicker than a feverous pulse;
And all my powers do their bestowing lose,
Like vassalage at unawares encountering 40
The eye of majesty.

Re-enter PANDARUS *with* CRESSIDA.

Pan. Come, come, what need you blush? shame 's a baby. Here she is now: swear the oaths now to her that you have sworn to me. What, are you gone again? you must be watched ere you be made tame, must you? Come your ways, come your ways; an you draw backward, we'll put you i' the fills. Why do you not speak to her? Come, draw this curtain, and let 's see your picture. Alas the day, how loath you are to offend daylight! an 'twere dark, you' ld close sooner. So, so; rub on, and kiss the mistress. How now! a kiss in fee-farm! build there, carpenter; the air is sweet. Nay, you shall fight your hearts out ere I part you. The falcon as the tercel, for all the ducks i' the river: go to, go to. 56

Tro. You have bereft me of all words, lady.

---

140. **doves.** Burton names the flesh of doves as one of the causes of melancholy. 167. **island kings,** kings of Grecian islands. 170. **more palm,** i.e., more honor.

SCENE II. 10-11. **a strange . . . Charon,** refers to the Greek mythological conception of the fate of departed souls who had to wait on the banks of the Styx or the Acheron until the boatman Charon ferried them across to the infernal regions. 14. **Proposed,** promised. 28.

lose . . . joys, be unable to distinguish one delight from another. 32. **witty,** smart, knowing. 34. **frayed,** frightened. **sprite,** ghost. 38. **thicker,** faster. 39. **bestowing,** self-control. 48. **fills,** shafts of a cart. 49-50. **Come, draw . . . picture,** remove your veil and let us see your face. 52. **kiss the mistress,** touch the central target; term from bowls; *mistress* is analogous to "master," short for "master bowl," a small bowl placed as a mark for players to aim at. 53. **fee-farm,** grant of

Pan. Words pay no debts, give her deeds: but she'll bereave you o' the deeds too, if she call your activity in question. What, billing again? Here 's 'In witness whereof the parties interchangeably'—Come in, come in: I'll go get a fire. [*Exit.*

Cres. Will you walk in, my lord?

Tro. O Cressida, how often have I wished me thus!

Cres. Wished, my lord! The gods grant,—O my lord!

Tro. What should they grant? what makes this pretty abruption? What too curious dreg espies my sweet lady in the fountain of our love? 71

Cres. More dregs than water, if my fears have eyes.

Tro. Fears make devils of cherubins; they never see truly.

Cres. Blind fear, that seeing reason leads, finds safer footing than blind reason stumbling without fear: to fear the worst oft cures the worse.

Tro. O, let my lady apprehend no fear: in all Cupid's pageant there is presented no monster. 81

Cres. Nor nothing monstrous neither?

Tro. Nothing, but our undertakings; when we vow to weep seas, live in fire, eat rocks, tame tigers; thinking it harder for our mistress to devise imposition enough than for us to undergo any difficulty imposed. This is the monstruosity in love, lady, that the will is infinite and the execution confined, that the desire is boundless and the act a slave to limit. 90

Cres. They say all lovers swear more performance than they are able and yet reserve an ability that they never perform, vowing more than the perfection of ten and discharging less than the tenth part of one. They have the voice of lions and the act of hares, are they not monsters?

Tro. Are there such? such are not we: praise us as we are tasted, allow us as we prove; our head shall go bare till merit crown it: no perfection in reversion shall have a praise in present: we will not name desert before his birth, and, being born, his addition shall be humble. Few words to fair faith: Troilus shall be such to Cressid as what envy can say worst shall be a mock for his truth, and what truth can speak truest not truer than Troilus. 106

Cres. Will you walk in, my lord?

Re-enter PANDARUS.

Pan. What, blushing still? have you not done talking yet?

Cres. Well, uncle, what folly I commit, I dedicate to you. 111

Pan. I thank you for that: if my lord get a boy of you, you'll give him me. Be true to my lord: if he flinch, chide me for it.

Tro. You know now your hostages; your uncle's word and my firm faith.

Pan. Nay, I'll give my word for her too: our kindred, though they be long ere they are wooed, they are constant being won: they are burs, I can tell you; they'll stick where they are thrown. 120

Cres. Boldness comes to me now, and brings me heart.

Prince Troilus, I have loved you night and day
For many weary months.

Tro. Why was my Cressid then so hard to win?

Cres. Hard to seem won: but I was won, my lord,
With the first glance that ever—pardon me—
If I confess much, you will play the tyrant.
I love you now; but not, till now, so much
But I might master it: in faith, I lie;
My thoughts were like unbridled children, grown 130
Too headstrong for their mother. See, we fools!
Why have I blabb'd? who shall be true to us,
When we are so unsecret to ourselves?
But, though I loved you well, I woo'd you not:
And yet, good faith, I wish'd myself a man,
Or that we women had men's privilege
Of speaking first. Sweet, bid me hold my tongue,
For in this rapture I shall surely speak
The thing I shall repent. See, see, your silence,
Cunning in dumbness, from my weakness draws 140
My very soul of counsel! stop my mouth.

Tro. And shall, albeit sweet music issues thence.

Pan. Pretty, i' faith.

Cres. My lord, I do beseech you, pardon me;
'Twas not my purpose, thus to beg a kiss:
I am ashamed. O heavens! what have I done?
For this time will I take my leave, my lord.

Tro. Your leave, sweet Cressid!

Pan. Leave! an you take leave till to-morrow morning,— 150

Cres. Pray you, content you.

Tro. What offends you, lady?

Cres. Sir, mine own company.

Tro. You cannot shun Yourself.

Cres. Let me go and try:
I have a kind of self resides with you;
But an unkind self, that itself will leave,
To be another's fool. I would be gone:
Where is my wit? I know not what I speak.

Tro. Well know they what they speak that speak so wisely.

Cres. Perchance, my lord, I show more craft than love; 160
And fell so roundly to a large confession,
To angle for your thoughts: but you are wise,
Or else you love not, for to be wise and love
Exceeds man's might; that dwells with gods above.

Tro. O that I thought it could be in a woman—
As, if it can, I will presume in you—
To feed for aye her lamp and flames of love;
To keep her constancy in plight and youth,
Outliving beauty's outward, with a mind
That doth renew swifter than blood decays! 170
Or that persuasion could but thus convince me,
That my integrity and truth to you
Might be affronted with the match and weight
Of such a winnow'd purity in love;
How were I then uplifted! but, alas!
I am as true as truth's simplicity
And simpler than the infancy of truth.

Cres. In that I'll war with you.

lands in fee, that is, forever; i.e., a kiss of endless duration. 55-56. **The falcon . . . tercel,** the female hawk against the male, as in a wager; i.e., Cressida is a match for Troilus. 80-81. **no fear . . . no monster,** may refer to figures in masques or similar entertainments. 83-87. **when we vow,** etc. Malone saw in these monstrous vows an allusion to the extravagant boasts of Orlando Furioso, hero of Ariosto's romance. 98. **tasted,** tried, proved. **allow,** acknowledge. 99-100. **no . . .**

reversion, no promise of perfection to come. 104-105. **what envy . . . his truth,** the worst envy can do is to mock Troilus' loyalty. 106. **than,** Globe, by error: *that.* 141. **counsel,** my inmost thoughts. 157. **fool,** dupe; possibly with a quibble on "fool" used as a term of endearment. 168. **To . . . youth,** to keep her pledged constancy fresh. 170. **blood decays,** passions wane. 173. **affronted,** confronted.

Tro.   O virtuous fight,
When right with right wars who shall be most right!
True swains in love shall in the world to come   180
Approve their truths by Troilus: when their rhymes,
Full of protest, of oath and big compare,
Want similes, truth tired with iteration,
As true as steel, as plantage to the moon,
As sun to day, as turtle to her mate,
As iron to adamant, as earth to the centre,
Yet, after all comparisons of truth,
As truth's authentic author to be cited,
'As true as Troilus' shall crown up the verse,
And sanctify the numbers.
    Cres.   Prophet may you be!   190
If I be false, or swerve a hair from truth,
When time is old and hath forgot itself,
When waterdrops have worn the stones of Troy,
And blind oblivion swallow'd cities up,
And mighty states characterless are grated
To dusty nothing, yet let memory,
From false to false, among false maids in love,
Upbraid my falsehood! when they 've said 'as false
As air, as water, wind, or sandy earth,
As fox to lamb, as wolf to heifer's calf,   200
Pard to the hind, or stepdame to her son,'
'Yea,' let them say, to stick the heart of falsehood,
'As false as Cressid.'
    Pan. Go to, a bargain made: seal it, seal it; I'll be
the witness. Here I hold your hand, here my cousin's.
If ever you prove false one to another, since I have
taken such pains to bring you together, let all pitiful
goers-between be called to the world's end after my
name; call them all Pandars; let all constant men be
Troiluses, all false women Cressids, and all brokers-
between Pandars! say, amen.   211
    Tro. Amen.
    Cres. Amen.
    Pan. Amen. Whereupon I will show you a chamber
with a bed; which bed, because it shall not speak of
your pretty encounters, press it to death: away!
And Cupid grant all tongue-tied maidens here
Bed, chamber, Pandar to provide this gear!   [*Exeunt.*

SCENE III. *The Grecian camp. Before Achilles' tent.*

Enter AGAMEMNON, ULYSSES, DIOMEDES, NESTOR,
    AJAX, MENELAUS, *and* CALCHAS.

    Cal. Now, princes, for the service I have done you,
The advantage of the time prompts me aloud
To call for recompense. Appear it to your mind
†That, through the sight I bear in things to come,
I have abandon'd Troy, left my possession,
Incurr'd a traitor's name; exposed myself,
From certain and possess'd conveniences,
To doubtful fortunes; sequestering from me all
That time, acquaintance, custom and condition

Made tame and most familiar to my nature,   10
And here, to do you service, am become
As new into the world, strange, unacquainted:
I do beseech you, as in way of taste,
To give me now a little benefit,
Out of those many register'd in promise,
Which, you say, live to come in my behalf.
    Agam. What wouldst thou of us, Trojan? make
        demand.
    Cal. You have a Trojan prisoner, call'd Antenor,
Yesterday took: Troy holds him very dear.
Oft have you—often have you thanks therefore—   20
Desired my Cressid in right great exchange,
Whom Troy hath still denied: but this Antenor,
I know, is such a wrest in their affairs
That their negotiations all must slack,
Wanting his manage; and they will almost
Give us a prince of blood, a son of Priam,
In change of him: let him be sent, great princes,
And he shall buy my daughter; and her presence
Shall quite strike off all service I have done,
In most accepted pain.
    Agam.   Let Diomedes bear him,   30
And bring us Cressid hither: Calchas shall have
What he requests of us. Good Diomed,
Furnish you fairly for this interchange:
Withal bring word if Hector will to-morrow
Be answer'd in his challenge: Ajax is ready.
    Dio. This shall I undertake; and 'tis a burden
Which I am proud to bear.

                    [*Exeunt Diomedes and Calchas.*

Enter ACHILLES *and* PATROCLUS, *before their tent.*

    Ulyss. Achilles stands i' the entrance of his tent:
Please it our general to pass strangely by him,
As if he were forgot; and, princes all,   40
Lay negligent and loose regard upon him:
I will come last. 'Tis like he'll question me
Why such unplausive eyes are bent on him:
If so, I have derision medicinable,
To use between your strangeness and his pride,
Which his own will shall have desire to drink:
It may do good: pride hath no other glass
To show itself but pride, for supple knees
Feed arrogance and are the proud man's fees.
    Agam. We'll execute your purpose, and put on   50
A form of strangeness as we pass along:
So do each lord, and either greet him not,
Or else disdainfully, which shall shake him more
Than if not look'd on. I will lead the way.
    Achil. What, comes the general to speak with me?
You know my mind, I 'll fight no more 'gainst Troy.
    Agam. What says Achilles? would he aught with us?
    Nest. Would you, my lord, aught with the general?
    Achil. No.
    Nest. Nothing, my lord.   60
    Agam. The better.   [*Exeunt Agamemnon and Nestor.*

182. **protest,** protestation. **big compare,** extravagant comparisons.
184. **plantage . . . moon,** vegetation waxing in growth with the moon.
186. **as earth . . . centre,** perhaps, as faithfully as earth remains in the
center; sometimes taken to hint at the Copernican hypothesis. 195.
characterless are grated, i.e., all record of their greatness obliterated.
197. **From . . . love,** from one false one to another false one among
maids in love who are false (Deighton).
    SCENE III. 2-3. **aloud To call,** to give vocal utterance. 4. **in
things to come,** so F_4; QF_{1-3}: *in things to love;* Tannenbaum (*Shakespeare
Association Bulletin,* VII, 76-77) justifies the F_4 text here on paleo-
graphical grounds: "From other errors in the Shakspere canon we
know that his Roman *c* (a letter which many Elizabethans preferred to

the secretary *c*) was sometimes mistaken for an *l;* also, that Shakspere's
m, n, and *v* (*u*) were often indistinguishable." 8. **sequestering,** separating, removing. 10. **Made . . . nature,** accustomed my nature to.
16. **live to come,** i.e., are actually forthcoming. 21. **right great
exchange,** i.e., exchange for distinguished captives. 23. **wrest,** tuning
key. 30. **In most accepted pain,** in pains (troubles, hardships) which
I have accepted most willingly. 33. **Furnish you fairly,** provide
yourself well. 39. **strangely,** i.e., as one who pretends to be a stranger.
43. **unplausive,** disapproving. 44. **derision,** pretended seriousness
(Deighton). 48. **To show itself,** in which to see its image. 48-49. **for
supple . . . fees,** arrogance feeds on obsequious bending of knees, and
such knee-bending is the fee exacted by pride. 84. **slippery,** inconstant.

Achil. Good day, good day.

Men. How do you? how do you? [*Exit.*

Achil. What, does the cuckold scorn me?

Ajax. How now, Patroclus!

Achil. Good morrow, Ajax.

Ajax. Ha?

Achil. Good morrow.

Ajax. Ay, and good next day too. [*Exit.*

Achil. What mean these fellows? Know they not
 Achilles? 70

Patr. They pass by strangely: they were used to
 bend,
To send their smiles before them to Achilles;
To come as humbly as they used to creep
To holy altars.

Achil.   What, am I poor of late?
'Tis certain, greatness, once fall'n out with fortune,
Must fall out with men too: what the declined is
He shall as soon read in the eyes of others
As feel in his own fall; for men, like butterflies,
Show not their mealy wings but to the summer,
And not a man, for being simply man, 80
Hath any honour, but honour for those honours
That are without him, as place, riches, favour,
Prizes of accident as oft as merit:
Which when they fall, as being slippery standers,
The love that lean'd on them as slippery too,
Do one pluck down another and together
Die in the fall. But 'tis not so with me:
Fortune and I are friends: I do enjoy
At ample point all that I did possess,
Save these men's looks; who do, methinks, find out 90
Something not worth in me such rich beholding
As they have often given. Here is Ulysses:
I'll interrupt his reading.
How now, Ulysses!

Ulyss.   Now, great Thetis' son!

Achil. What are you reading?

Ulyss.   A strange fellow here
Writes me: 'That man, how dearly ever parted,
How much in having, or without or in,
Cannot make boast to have that which he hath,
Nor feels not what he owes, but by reflection;
As when his virtues shining upon others 100
Heat them and they retort that heat again
To the first giver.'

Achil.   This is not strange, Ulysses.
The beauty that is borne here in the face
The bearer knows not, but commends itself
To others' eyes; nor doth the eye itself,
That most pure spirit of sense, behold itself,
Not going from itself; but eye to eye opposed
Salutes each other with each other's form;
For speculation turns not to itself,
Till it hath travell'd and is mirror'd there 110
Where it may see itself. This is not strange at all.

Ulyss. I do not strain at the position,—

It is familiar,—but at the author's drift;
Who, in his circumstance, expressly proves
That no man is the lord of any thing,
Though in and of him there be much consisting,
Till he communicate his parts to others;
Nor doth he of himself know them for aught
Till he behold them form'd in the applause
Where they 're extended; who, like an arch,
 reverberates 120
The voice again, or, like a gate of steel
Fronting the sun, receives and renders back
His figure and his heat. I was much wrapt in this;
And apprehended here immediately
The unknown Ajax.
Heavens, what a man is there! a very horse,
That has he knows not what. Nature, what things
 there are
Most abject in regard and dear in use!
What things again most dear in the esteem
And poor in worth! Now shall we see to-morrow— 130
An act that very chance doth throw upon him—
Ajax renown'd. O heavens, what some men do,
While some men leave to do!
How some men creep in skittish fortune's hall,
Whiles others play the idiots in her eyes!
How one man eats into another's pride,
While pride is fasting in his wantonness!
To see these Grecian lords!—why, even already
They clap the lubber Ajax on the shoulder,
As if his foot were on brave Hector's breast 140
And great Troy shrieking.

Achil. I do believe it; for they pass'd by me
As misers do by beggars, neither gave to me
Good word nor look: what, are my deeds forgot?

Ulyss. Time hath, my lord, a wallet at his back,
Wherein he puts alms for oblivion,
A great-sized monster of ingratitudes:
Those scraps are good deeds past; which are devour'd
As fast as they are made, forgot as soon
As done: perseverance, dear my lord, 150
Keeps honour bright: to have done is to hang
Quite out of fashion, like a rusty mail
In monumental mockery. Take the instant way;
For honour travels in a strait so narrow,
Where one but goes abreast: keep then the path;
For emulation hath a thousand sons
That one by one pursue: if you give way,
Or hedge aside from the direct forthright,
Like to an enter'd tide, they all rush by
And leave you hindmost; 160
Or, like a gallant horse fall'n in first rank,
Lie there for pavement to the abject rear,
O'er-run and trampled on: then what they do in
 present,
Though less than yours in past, must o'ertop yours;
For time is like a fashionable host
That slightly shakes his parting guest by the hand,

89. **At ample point,** to the full.　91. **Something . . . beholding,** something in me not worthy of such high respect.　95. **strange fellow.** Churton Collins noted that Plato is the strange fellow. The sentiments to which Ulysses gives utterance are from the *Dialogues.* 101. **retort,** reflect.　106. **most . . . sense,** the most exquisite sense; cf. I, i, 58. 109. **speculation,** power of sight.　112. **strain at,** find difficulty in. 112, 113. **position, drift,** the generalization and the application of it. 116. **Though . . . consisting,** although in him there are qualities from which much may be expected.　120. **extended,** magnified.　**who.** The antecedent is *applause.*　125. **unknown Ajax,** Ajax, wanting in true self-knowledge (Clarke); Deighton compares line 127, *That has he knows not what.* 128. **abject in regard,** of low esteem.　**dear in use,** of

practical value. 132, 133. **do,** implies activity; i.e., some men are energetic, some are inactivity itself.　134. **creep,** keep out of sight (Johnson).　136-137. **How . . . wantonness.** Achilles is he who fasts; who capriciously [in his wantonness] abstains from those active exertions which would furnish new food for his pride (Malone).　153. **instant way,** the way which lies immediately before you now.　154. **strait,** narrow pass.　157. **one by one pursue,** follow one another in single file.　158. **forthright,** straight path.　162. **abject rear,** those who follow abjectly in the rear.　166. **slightly,** carelessly.

And with his arms outstretch'd, as he would fly,
Grasps in the comer: welcome ever smiles,
And farewell goes out sighing. O, let not virtue seek
Remuneration for the thing it was; 170
For beauty, wit,
High birth, vigour of bone, desert in service,
Love, friendship, charity, are subjects all
To envious and calumniating time.
One touch of nature makes the whole world kin,
That all with one consent praise new-born gawds,
Though they are made and moulded of things past,
And give to dust that is a little gilt
More laud than gilt o'er-dusted.
The present eye praises the present object: 180
Then marvel not, thou great and complete man,
That all the Greeks begin to worship Ajax;
Since things in motion sooner catch the eye
Than what not stirs. The cry went once on thee,
And still it might, and yet it may again,
If thou wouldst not entomb thyself alive
And case thy reputation in thy tent;
Whose glorious deeds, but in these fields of late,
Made emulous missions 'mongst the gods themselves
And drave great Mars to faction.
    Achil.   Of this my privacy 190
I have strong reasons.
    Ulyss.   But 'gainst your privacy
The reasons are more potent and heroical:
'Tis known, Achilles, that you are in love
With one of Priam's daughters.
    Achil.   Ha! known!
    Ulyss. Is that a wonder?
The providence that 's in a watchful state
Knows almost every grain of Plutus' gold,
Finds bottom in the uncomprehensive deeps,
Keeps place with thought and almost, like the gods,
Does thoughts unveil in their dumb cradles. 200
There is a mystery—with whom relation
Durst never meddle—in the soul of state;
Which hath an operation more divine
Than breath or pen can give expressure to:
All the commerce that you have had with Troy
As perfectly is ours as yours, my lord;
And better would it fit Achilles much
To throw down Hector than Polyxena:
But it must grieve young Pyrrhus now at home,
When fame shall in our islands sound her trump, 210
And all the Greekish girls shall tripping sing,
'Great Hector's sister did Achilles win,
But our great Ajax bravely beat down him.'
Farewell, my lord: I as your lover speak;
The fool slides o'er the ice that you should break. [*Exit.*
    Patr. To this effect, Achilles, have I moved you:
A woman impudent and mannish grown
Is not more loathed than an effeminate man
In time of action. I stand condemn'd for this;
They think my little stomach to the war 220
And your great love to me restrains you thus:

Sweet, rouse yourself; and the weak wanton Cupid
Shall from your neck unloose his amorous fold,
And, like a dew-drop from the lion's mane,
Be shook to air.
    Achil.   Shall Ajax fight with Hector?
    Patr. Ay, and perhaps receive much honour by him.
    Achil. I see my reputation is at stake;
My fame is shrewdly gored.
    Patr.   O, then, beware;
Those wounds heal ill that men do give themselves:
Omission to do what is necessary 230
Seals a commission to a blank of danger;
And danger, like an ague, subtly taints
Even then when we sit idly in the sun.
    Achil. Go call Thersites hither, sweet Patroclus:
I'll send the fool to Ajax and desire him
To invite the Trojan lords after the combat
To see us here unarm'd: I have a woman's longing,
An appetite that I am sick withal,
To see great Hector in his weeds of peace,
To talk with him and to behold his visage, 240
Even to my full of view.

Enter THERSITES.

              A labour saved!
    Ther. A wonder!
    Achil. What?
    Ther. Ajax goes up and down the field, asking for
himself.
    Achil. How so?
    Ther. He must fight singly to-morrow with Hector,
and is so prophetically proud of an heroical cudgelling
that he raves in saying nothing.
    Achil. How can that be? 250
    Ther. Why, he stalks up and down like a peacock,—
a stride and a stand: ruminates like an hostess that
hath no arithmetic but her brain to set down her
reckoning: bites his lip with a politic regard, as who
should say 'There were wit in this head, an 'twould
out;' and so there is, but it lies as coldly in him as fire
in a flint, which will not show without knocking.
The man 's undone for ever; for if Hector break not
his neck i' the combat, he'll break 't himself in vain-
glory. He knows not me: I said 'Good morrow, Ajax;'
and he replies 'Thanks, Agamemnon.' What think
you of this man that takes me for the general? He 's
grown a very land-fish, languageless, a monster.
A plague of opinion! a man may wear it on both
sides, like a leather jerkin. 266
    Achil. Thou must be my ambassador to him,
Thersites.
    Ther. Who, I? why, he'll answer nobody; he pro-
fesses not answering: speaking is for beggars; he
wears his tongue in 's arms. I will put on his presence:
let Patroclus make demands to me, you shall see the
pageant of Ajax.
    Achil. To him, Patroclus: tell him I humbly desire
the valiant Ajax to invite the most valorous Hector to

come unarmed to my tent, and to procure safe-conduct for his person of the magnanimous and most illustrious six-or-seven-times-honoured captain-general of the Grecian army, Agamemnon, et cetera. Do this. 280

Patr. Jove bless great Ajax!

Ther. Hum!

Patr. I come from the worthy Achilles,—

Ther. Ha!

Patr. Who most humbly desires you to invite Hector to his tent,—

Ther. Hum!

Patr. And to procure safe-conduct from Agamemnon.

Ther. Agamemnon! 290

Patr. Ay, my lord.

Ther. Ha!

Patr. What say you to 't?

Ther. God b' wi' you, with all my heart.

Patr. Your answer, sir.

Ther. If to-morrow be a fair day, by eleven o'clock it will go one way or other: howsoever, he shall pay for me ere he has me.

Patr. Your answer, sir.

Ther. Fare you well, with all my heart. 300

Achil. Why, but he is not in this tune, is he?

Ther. No, but he 's out o' tune thus. What music will be in him when Hector has knocked out his brains, I know not; but, I am sure, none, unless the fiddler Apollo get his sinews to make catlings on.

Achil. Come, thou shalt bear a letter to him straight.

Ther. Let me bear another to his horse; for that 's the more capable creature. 310

Achil. My mind is troubled, like a fountain stirr'd; And I myself see not the bottom of it.

[*Exeunt Achilles and Patroclus.*

Ther. Would the fountain of your mind were clear again, that I might water an ass at it! I had rather be a tick in a sheep than such a valiant ignorance. [*Exit.*

ACT IV.

SCENE I. *Troy. A street.*

Enter, from one side, ÆNEAS, *and* Servant *with a torch; from the other,* PARIS, DEIPHOBUS, ANTENOR, DIOMEDES, *and others, with torches.*

Par. See, ho! who is that there?

Dei. It is the Lord Æneas.

Æne. Is the prince there in person? Had I so good occasion to lie long As you, Prince Paris, nothing but heavenly business Should rob my bed-mate of my company.

Dio. That 's my mind too. Good morrow, Lord Æneas.

Par. A valiant Greek, Æneas,—take his hand,— Witness the process of your speech, wherein

You told how Diomed, a whole week by days, Did haunt you in the field.

Æne. Health to you, valiant sir, 10 During all question of the gentle truce; But when I meet you arm'd, as black defiance As heart can think or courage execute.

Dio. The one and other Diomed embraces. Our bloods are now in calm; and, so long, health! But when contention and occasion meet, By Jove, I'll play the hunter for thy life With all my force, pursuit and policy.

Æne. And thou shalt hunt a lion, that will fly With his face backward. In humane gentleness, 20 Welcome to Troy! now, by Anchises' life, Welcome, indeed! By Venus' hand I swear, No man alive can love in such a sort The thing he means to kill more excellently.

Dio. We sympathise: Jove, let Æneas live, If to my sword his fate be not the glory, A thousand complete courses of the sun! But, in mine emulous honour, let him die, With every joint a wound, and that to-morrow!

Æne. We know each other well. 30

Dio. We do; and long to know each other worse.

Par. This is the most despiteful gentle greeting, The noblest hateful love, that e'er I heard of. What business, lord, so early?

Æne. I was sent for to the king; but why, I know not.

Par. His purpose meets you: 'twas to bring this Greek To Calchas' house, and there to render him, For the enfreed Antenor, the fair Cressid: Let 's have your company, or, if you please, Haste there before us: I constantly do think— 40 Or rather, call my thought a certain knowledge— My brother Troilus lodges there to-night: Rouse him and give him note of our approach, With the whole quality wherefore: I fear We shall be much unwelcome.

Æne. That I assure you: Troilus had rather Troy were borne to Greece Than Cressid borne from Troy.

Par. There is no help; The bitter disposition of the time Will have it so. On, lord; we'll follow you.

Æne. Good morrow, all. [*Exit with Servant.* 50

Par. And tell me, noble Diomed, faith, tell me true, Even in the soul of sound good-fellowship, Who, in your thoughts, merits fair Helen best, Myself or Menelaus?

Dio. Both alike: He merits well to have her, that doth seek her, Not making any scruple of her soilure, With such a hell of pain and world of charge, And you as well to keep her, that defend her, Not palating the taste of her dishonour, With such a costly loss of wealth and friends: 60

---

him. 305. **the fiddler Apollo,** i.e., as god of music. 306. **catlings,** catgut, of which strings for instruments were made.

ACT IV. SCENE I. 8. **Witness...speech,** let the burden of your speech bear witness (Paradise). 9. **a whole week by days,** every day for a week. 11. **question,** discussion, parley (allowed by the truce). 12. **black defiance,** parallel in structure with *Health* (l. 10). 16. **when ...meet,** when the battle gives us opportunity. 21, 22. **Anchises' life, Venus' hand.** Diomedes, with the aid of Minerva, had wounded Venus in the hand. Warburton thought that this oath was used to insinuate Aeneas' resentment. Anchises and Venus were his parents.

23. **in such a sort,** to such a degree. 24. **excellently,** modifies *kill.* 28. **emulous,** ambitious; a transferred epithet. Diomedes is ambitious for such an honor. 31. **worse,** perhaps, in worse condition, wounded, or dead, or deprived of honor; may be simply oxymoron. 40. **constantly do think,** am confirmed in the thought. 44. **the...wherefore,** with all the reasons and circumstances. 57. **With ... charge,** modifies *seek* (l. 55); refers to the hardships of the war.

He, like a puling cuckold, would drink up
The lees and dregs of a flat tamed piece;
You, like a lecher, out of whorish loins
Are pleased to breed out your inheritors:
Both merits poised, each weighs nor less nor more;
But he as he, the heavier for a whore.
 Par. You are too bitter to your country-woman.
 Dio. She 's bitter to her country: hear me, Paris:
For every false drop in her bawdy veins
A Grecian's life hath sunk; for every scruple 70
Of her contaminated carrion weight,
A Trojan hath been slain: since she could speak,
She hath not given so many good words breath
As for her Greeks and Trojans suffer'd death.
 Par. Fair Diomed, you do as chapmen do,
Dispraise the thing that you desire to buy:
But we in silence hold this virtue well,
We'll but commend what we intend to sell.
Here lies our way.   [*Exeunt.*

  SCENE II. *The same. Court of Pandarus' house.*

Enter TROILUS *and* CRESSIDA.

 Tro. Dear, trouble not yourself: the morn is cold.
 Cres. Then, sweet my lord, I'll call mine uncle
  down;
He shall unbolt the gates.
 Tro.   Trouble him not;
To bed, to bed: sleep kill those pretty eyes,
And give as soft attachment to thy senses
As infants' empty of all thought!
 Cres.   Good morrow, then.
 Tro. I prithee now, to bed.
 Cres.   Are you a-weary of me?
 Tro. O Cressida! but that the busy day,
Waked by the lark, hath roused the ribald crows,
And dreaming night will hide our joys no longer, 10
I would not from thee.
 Cres.   Night hath been too brief.
 Tro. Beshrew the witch! with venomous wights she
  stays
As tediously as hell, but flies the grasps of love
With wings more momentary-swift than thought.
You will catch cold, and curse me.
 Cres.   Prithee, tarry:
You men will never tarry.
O foolish Cressid! I might have still held off,
And then you would have tarried. Hark! there 's one
  up.
 Pan. [*Within*] What, 's all the doors open here?
 Tro. It is your uncle.   20
 Cres. A pestilence on him! now will he be mocking:
I shall have such a life!

Enter PANDARUS.

 Pan. How now, how now! how go maidenheads?
Here, you maid! where 's my cousin Cressid?
 Cres. Go hang yourself, you naughty mocking
  uncle!
You bring me to do, and then you flout me too.

 Pan. To do what? to do what? let her say what:
what have I brought you to do?
 Cres. Come, come, beshrew your heart! you'll ne'er
  be good,   30
Nor suffer others.
 Pan. Ha, ha! Alas, poor wretch! ah, poor capocchia!
hast not slept to-night? would he not, a naughty man,
let it sleep? a bugbear take him!
 Cres. Did not I tell you? Would he were knock'd i'
  the head!   [*Knocking within.*
Who 's that at door? good uncle, go and see.
My lord, come you again into my chamber:
You smile and mock me, as if I meant naughtily.
 Tro. Ha, ha!   39
 Cres. Come, you are deceived, I think of no such
  thing.   [*Knocking within.*
How earnestly they knock! Pray you, come in:
I would not for half Troy have you seen here.
    [*Exeunt Troilus and Cressida.*
 Pan. Who 's there? what 's the matter? will you
beat down the door? How now! what 's the matter?

Enter ÆNEAS.

 Æne. Good morrow, lord, good morrow.
 Pan. Who 's there? my Lord Æneas! By my troth,
I knew you not: what news with you so early?
 Æne. Is not Prince Troilus here?
 Pan. Here! what should he do here? 50
 Æne. Come, he is here, my lord; do not deny him:
It doth import him much to speak with me.
 Pan. Is he here, say you? 'tis more than I know,
I'll be sworn: for my own part, I came in late. What
should he do here?
 Æne. Who!—nay, then: come, come, you'll do
him wrong ere you 're ware: you'll be so true to him,
to be false to him: do not you know of him, but yet
go fetch him hither; go.

Re-enter TROILUS.

 Tro. How now! what 's the matter? 60
 Æne. My lord, I scarce have leisure to salute you,
My matter is so rash: there is at hand
Paris your brother, and Deiphobus,
The Grecian Diomed, and our Antenor
Deliver'd to us; and for him forthwith,
Ere the first sacrifice, within this hour,
We must give up to Diomedes' hand
The Lady Cressida.
 Tro.   Is it so concluded?
 Æne. By Priam and the general state of Troy:
They are at hand and ready to effect it. 70
 Tro. How my achievements mock me!
I will go meet them: and, my Lord Æneas,
We met by chance; you did not find me here.
 Æne. Good, good, my lord; the secrets of nature
Have not more gift in taciturnity.
    [*Exeunt Troilus and Æneas.*
 Pan. Is 't possible? no sooner got but lost? The devil
take Antenor! the young prince will go mad: a
plague upon Antenor! I would they had broke 's
neck!

Re-enter CRESSIDA.

Cres. How now! what's the matter? who was here? 81
Pan. Ah, ah!
Cres. Why sigh you so profoundly? where 's my
lord? gone! Tell me, sweet uncle, what 's the matter?
Pan. Would I were as deep under the earth as I am
above!
Cres. O the gods! what 's the matter?
Pan. Prithee, get thee in: would thou hadst ne'er
been born! I knew thou wouldst be his death. O,
poor gentleman! A plague upon Antenor!
Cres. Good uncle, I beseech you, on my knees I
beseech you, what 's the matter?
Pan. Thou must be gone, wench, thou must be
gone; thou art changed for Antenor: thou must to
thy father, and be gone from Troilus: 'twill be his
death; 'twill be his bane; he cannot bear it.
Cres. O you immortal gods! I will not go. 100
Pan. Thou must.
Cres. I will not, uncle: I have forgot my father;
I know no touch of consanguinity;
No kin, no love, no blood, no soul so near me
As the sweet Troilus. O you gods divine!
Make Cressid's name the very crown of falsehood,
If ever she leave Troilus! Time, force, and death,
Do to this body what extremes you can;
But the strong base and building of my love
Is as the very centre of the earth, 110
Drawing all things to it. I'll go in and weep,—
Pan. Do, do.
Cres. Tear my bright hair and scratch my praised
    cheeks,
Crack my clear voice with sobs and break my heart
With sounding Troilus. I will not go from Troy.
                                                    [*Exeunt.*

SCENE III. *The same. Street before Pandarus' house.*

Enter PARIS, TROILUS, ÆNEAS, DEIPHOBUS, ANTENOR,
    and DIOMEDES.

Par. It is great morning, and the hour prefix'd
Of her delivery to this valiant Greek
Comes fast upon. Good my brother Troilus,
Tell you the lady what she is to do,
And haste her to the purpose.
Tro.   Walk into her house;
I'll bring her to the Grecian presently:
And to his hand when I deliver her,
Think it an altar, and thy brother Troilus
A priest there offering to it his own heart. [*Exit.*
Par. I know what 'tis to love; 10
And would, as I shall pity, I could help!
Please you walk in, my lords.
                                                    [*Exeunt.*

SCENE IV. *The same. Pandarus' house.*

Enter PANDARUS *and* CRESSIDA.

Pan. Be moderate, be moderate.
Cres. Why tell you me of moderation?
The grief is fine, full, perfect, that I taste,
And violenteth in a sense as strong
As that which causeth it: how can I moderate it?
If I could temporise with my affection,
Or brew it to a weak and colder palate,
The like allayment could I give my grief:
My love admits no qualifying dross;
No more my grief, in such a precious loss. 10
Pan. Here, here, here he comes.

Enter TROILUS.

Ah, sweet ducks!
Cres. O Troilus! Troilus!   [*Embracing him.*
Pan. What a pair of spectacles is here! Let me em-
brace too. 'O heart,' as the goodly saying is,
    '——O heart, heavy heart,
        Why sigh'st thou without breaking?'
where he answers again,
        'Because thou canst not ease thy smart 20
        By friendship nor by speaking.'
There was never a truer rhyme. Let us cast away
nothing, for we may live to have need of such a verse:
we see it, we see it. How now, lambs?
Tro. Cressid, I love thee in so strain'd a purity,
That the bless'd gods, as angry with my fancy,
More bright in zeal than the devotion which
Cold lips blow to their deities, take thee from me.
Cres. Have the gods envy? 30
Pan. Ay, ay, ay, ay; 'tis too plain a case.
Cres. And is it true that I must go from Troy?
Tro. A hateful truth.
Cres.   What, and from Troilus too?
Tro. From Troy and Troilus.
Cres.   Is it possible?
Tro. And suddenly; where injury of chance
Puts back leave-taking, justles roughly by
All time of pause, rudely beguiles our lips
Of all rejoindure, forcibly prevents
Our lock'd embrasures, strangles our dear vows
Even in the birth of our own labouring breath: 40
We two, that with so many thousand sighs
Did buy each other, must poorly sell ourselves
With the rude brevity and discharge of one.
Injurious time now with a robber's haste
Crams his rich thievery up, he knows not how:
As many farewells as be stars in heaven,
With distinct breath and consign'd kisses to them,
He fumbles up into a loose adieu,
And scants us with a single famish'd kiss,
Distasted with the salt of broken tears. 50
Æne. [*Within*] My lord, is the lady ready?
Tro. Hark! you are call'd: some say the Genius so
Cries 'come' to him that instantly must die.
Bid them have patience; she shall come anon.
Pan. Where are my tears? rain, to lay this wind, or
my heart will be blown up by the root. [*Exit.*
Cres. I must then to the Grecians?
Tro.   No remedy.
Cres. A woful Cressid 'mongst the merry Greeks!
When shall we see again? 59
Tro. Hear me, my love: be thou but true of heart,—
Cres. I true! how now! what wicked deem is this?
Tro. Nay, we must use expostulation kindly,

answer to Pandarus' exhortation to be moderate. **4. violenteth**, is
violent. **26. strain'd**, purified as by filtering. **35. injury of chance**,
injurious Fortune. **38. rejoindure**, reunion. **47. consign'd**, added by
way of ratification (Onions). **49. scants us**, puts us off with. **50.
Distasted**, rendered distasteful. **52. Genius**, attendant spirit supposed
to be allotted to a person at birth. **55-56. rain . . . wind.** Cf. *Macbeth*,
I, vii, 25; *Lucrece*, 1788. **58. merry Greeks.** Cf. I, ii, 118. **61. deem**,
thought. **62. expostulation**, opportunity for discourse.

For it is parting from us:
I speak not 'be thou true,' as fearing thee,
For I will throw my glove to Death himself,
That there's no maculation in thy heart:
But 'be thou true,' say I, to fashion in
My sequent protestation; be thou true,
And I will see thee.
    Cres. O, you shall be exposed, my lord, to dangers 70
As infinite as imminent! but I'll be true.
    Tro. And I'll grow friend with danger. Wear this
      sleeve.
    Cres. And you this glove. When shall I see you?
    Tro. I will corrupt the Grecian sentinels,
To give thee nightly visitation.
But yet be true.
    Cres.   O heavens! 'be true' again!
    Tro. Hear why I speak it, love:
The Grecian youths are full of quality;
They're loving, well composed with gifts of nature,
Flowing and swelling o'er with arts and exercise: 80
How novelty may move, and parts with person,
Alas, a kind of godly jealousy—
Which, I beseech you, call a virtuous sin—
Makes me afeard.
    Cres.   O heavens! you love me not.
    Tro. Die I a villain, then!
In this I do not call your faith in question
So mainly as my merit: I cannot sing,
Nor heel the high lavolt, nor sweeten talk,
Nor play at subtle games; fair virtues all, 89
To which the Grecians are most prompt and pregnant:
But I can tell that in each grace of these
There lurks a still and dumb-discoursive devil
That tempts most cunningly: but be not tempted.
    Cres. Do you think I will?
    Tro. No.
But something may be done that we will not:
And sometimes we are devils to ourselves,
When we will tempt the frailty of our powers,
Presuming on their changeful potency.
    Æne. [*Within*] Nay, good my lord,—
    Tro.   Come, kiss; and let us part. 100
    Par. [*Within*] Brother Troilus!
    Tro.   Good brother, come you hither;
And bring Æneas and the Grecian with you.
    Cres. My lord, will you be true?
    Tro. Who, I? alas, it is my vice, my fault:
Whiles others fish with craft for great opinion,
I with great truth catch mere simplicity;
Whilst some with cunning gild their copper crowns,
With truth and plainness I do wear mine bare.
Fear not my truth: the moral of my wit
Is 'plain and true;' there's all the reach of it. 110

    Enter ÆNEAS, PARIS, ANTENOR, DEIPHOBUS, *and*
      DIOMEDES.

Welcome, Sir Diomed! here is the lady
Which for Antenor we deliver you:
At the port, lord, I'll give her to thy hand;
And by the way possess thee what she is.

Entreat her fair; and, by my soul, fair Greek,
If e'er thou stand at mercy of my sword,
Name Cressid, and thy life shall be as safe
As Priam is in Ilion.
    Dio.   Fair Lady Cressid,
So please you, save the thanks this prince expects:
The lustre in your eye, heaven in your cheek, 120
Pleads your fair usage; and to Diomed
You shall be mistress, and command him wholly.
    Tro. Grecian, thou dost not use me courteously,
To shame the zeal of my petition to thee
In praising her: I tell thee, lord of Greece,
She is as far high-soaring o'er thy praises
As thou unworthy to be call'd her servant.
I charge thee use her well, even for my charge;
For, by the dreadful Pluto, if thou dost not,
Though the great bulk Achilles be thy guard, 130
I'll cut thy throat.
    Dio.   O, be not moved, Prince Troilus:
Let me be privileged by my place and message,
To be a speaker free; when I am hence,
I'll answer to my lust: and know you, lord,
I'll nothing do on charge: to her own worth
She shall be prized; but that you say 'be 't so,'
I'll speak it in my spirit and honour, 'no.'
    Tro. Come, to the port. I'll tell thee, Diomed,
This brave shall oft make thee to hide thy head.
Lady, give me your hand, and, as we walk, 140
To our own selves bend we our needful talk.
        [*Exeunt Troilus, Cressida, and Diomedes.*
                    [*Trumpet within.*
    Par. Hark! Hector's trumpet.
    Æne.   How have we spent this morning!
The prince must think me tardy and remiss,
That swore to ride before him to the field.
    Par. 'Tis Troilus' fault: come, come, to field with
      him.
    Dei. Let us make ready straight.
    Æne. Yea, with a bridegroom's fresh alacrity,
Let us address to tend on Hector's heels:
The glory of our Troy doth this day lie
On his fair worth and single chivalry.   [*Exeunt.* 150

SCENE V. *The Grecian camp. Lists set out.*

Enter AJAX, *armed;* AGAMEMNON, ACHILLES,
    PATROCLUS, MENELAUS, ULYSSES, NESTOR, *and*
    others.

    Agam. Here art thou in appointment fresh and fair,
Anticipating time. With starting courage,
Give with thy trumpet a loud note to Troy,
Thou dreadful Ajax; that the appalled air
May pierce the head of the great combatant
And hale him hither.
    Ajax.   Thou, trumpet, there's my purse.
Now crack thy lungs, and split thy brazen pipe:
Blow, villain, till thy sphered bias cheek
Outswell the colic of puff'd Aquilon: 9

---

66. **maculation,** stain of impurity. 67. **to fashion in,** to contrive to
put in or insert. 81. **parts,** mental attributes. **persons,** personal
appearance. 82, 83. **godly jealousy, virtuous sin,** instances of
oxymoron. 88. **lavolt,** lively dance for two. 90. **prompt,** inclined.
92. **dumb-discoursive,** eloquently silent. 96. **will not,** do not desire.
98. **tempt,** test, try. 99. **Presuming . . . potency,** not counting on their
instability. 105. **others fish with craft,** probably a veiled allusion to
Ulysses. 109. **moral,** maxim. 110. **reach,** sphere to which an agency

or power is limited. 134. **I'll answer . . . lust,** I'll follow my own
desires. 142. **spent,** consumed by using. 148. **address,** get ready.
    SCENE V. 1. **appointment,** equipment, accouterment. 2. **time.
With.** The punctuation is that of QF; Globe, following Theobald:
time with. **starting courage,** bold defiance (Deighton). 6. **trumpet,**
trumpeter. 9. **Aquilon,** the north wind. 20-21. **particular . . .
general,** i.e., private, in his own person, not as the general of the army,
with quibble on *general.* 24. **that winter,** alludes to Nestor's old age.

Come, stretch thy chest, and let thy eyes spout blood;
Thou blow'st for Hector.   [*Trumpet sounds.*
  Ulyss. No trumpet answers.
  Achil.   'Tis but early days.
  Agam. Is not yond Diomed, with Calchas' daughter?
  Ulyss. 'Tis he, I ken the manner of his gait;
He rises on the toe: that spirit of his
In aspiration lifts him from the earth.

Enter DIOMEDES, *with* CRESSIDA.

  Agam. Is this the Lady Cressid?
  Dio.   Even she.
  Agam. Most dearly welcome to the Greeks, sweet
    lady.
  Nest. Our general doth salute you with a kiss.
  Ulyss. Yet is the kindness but particular;   20
'Twere better she were kiss'd in general.
  Nest. And very courtly counsel: I'll begin.
So much for Nestor.
  Achil. I'll take that winter from your lips, fair lady:
Achilles bids you welcome.
  Men. I had good argument for kissing once.
  Patr. But that's no argument for kissing now;
For thus popp'd Paris in his hardiment,
And parted thus you and your argument.
  Ulyss. O deadly gall, and theme of all our scorns!   30
For which we lose our heads to gild his horns.
  Patr. The first was Menelaus' kiss; this, mine:
Patroclus kisses you.
  Men.   O, this is trim!
  Patr. Paris and I kiss evermore for him.
  Men. I'll have my kiss, sir. Lady, by your leave.
  Cres. In kissing, do you render or receive?
  Patr. Both take and give.
  Cres.   I'll make my match to live,
The kiss you take is better than you give;
Therefore no kiss.   39
  Men. I'll give you boot, I'll give you three for one.
  Cres. You 're an odd man; give even, or give none.
  Men. An odd man, lady! every man is odd.
  Cres. No, Paris is not; for you know 'tis true,
That you are odd, and he is even with you.
  Men. You fillip me o' the head.
  Cres.   No, I'll be sworn.
  Ulyss. It were no match, your nail against his horn.
May I, sweet lady, beg a kiss of you?
  Cres. You may.
  Ulyss.   I do desire it.
  Cres.   Why, beg, then.
  Ulyss. Why then for Venus' sake, give me a kiss,
When Helen is a maid again, and his.   50
  Cres. I am your debtor, claim it when 'tis due.
  Ulyss. Never 's my day, and then a kiss of you.
  Dio. Lady, a word: I'll bring you to your father.
                    [*Exit with Cressida.*
  Nest. A woman of quick sense.
  Ulyss.   Fie, fie upon her!
There 's language in her eye, her cheek, her lip,
Nay, her foot speaks; her wanton spirits look out
At every joint and motive of her body.

O, these encounterers, so glib of tongue,
That give accosting welcome ere it comes,
And wide unclasp the tables of their thoughts   60
To every ticklish reader! set them down
For sluttish spoils of opportunity
And daughters of the game.   [*Trumpet within.*
  All. The Trojans' trumpet.
  Agam.   Yonder comes the troop.

Enter HECTOR, *armed;* ÆNEAS, TROILUS, *and other*
    Trojans, *with* Attendants.

  Æne. Hail, all you state of Greece! what shall be
    done
To him that victory commands? or do you purpose
A victor shall be known? will you the knights
Shall to the edge of all extremity
Pursue each other, or shall be divided
By any voice or order of the field?   70
Hector bade ask.
  Agam.   Which way would Hector have
    it?
  Æne. He cares not; he'll obey conditions.
  Achil. 'Tis done like Hector; but securely done,
A little proudly, and great deal misprizing
The knight opposed.
  Æne.   If not Achilles, sir,
What is your name?
  Achil.   If not Achilles, nothing.
  Æne. Therefore Achilles: but, whate'er, know this:
In the extremity of great and little,
Valour and pride excel themselves in Hector;
The one almost as infinite as all,   80
The other blank as nothing. Weigh him well,
And that which looks like pride is courtesy.
This Ajax is half made of Hector's blood:
In love whereof, half Hector stays at home;
Half heart, half hand, half Hector comes to seek
This blended knight, half Trojan and half Greek.
  Achil. A maiden battle, then? O, I perceive you.

Re-enter DIOMEDES.

  Agam. Here is Sir Diomed. Go, gentle knight,
Stand by our Ajax: as you and Lord Æneas
Consent upon the order of their fight,   90
So be it; either to the uttermost,
Or else a breath: the combatants being kin
Half stints their strife before their strokes begin.
                    [*Ajax and Hector enter the lists.*
  Ulyss. They are opposed already.
  Agam. What Trojan is that same that looks so
    heavy?
  Ulyss. The youngest son of Priam, a true knight,
Not yet mature, yet matchless, firm of word,
Speaking in deeds and deedless in his tongue;
Not soon provoked nor being provoked soon calm'd;
His heart and hand both open and both free;   100
For what he has he gives, what thinks he shows;
Yet gives he not till judgement guide his bounty,
Nor dignifies an impair thought with breath;
Manly as Hector, but more dangerous;

---

28. **hardiment,** bold exploits, boldness. 37. **I'll . . . to live,** I'll wager
my life. 41. **odd.** Deighton sees a play here on the meaning "single,"
i.e., no longer having a wife. 57. **motive,** moving limb or organ. 58.
encounterers, forward persons. 59. **accosting,** so Theobald; FQ: *a
coasting,* i.e., assailing, attacking (*NED*). 61. **ticklish,** wanton. 62.
sluttish . . . opportunity, corrupt wenches, of whose chastity every
opportunity may make a prey (Johnson). 63. **daughters of the game,**
i.e., prostitutes. 73. **securely,** confidently. 74. **misprizing,** despising.

78-79. **In . . . Hector,** Hector's valor excels in the extreme of greatness, his pride in the extreme of littleness. 83. **Ajax . . . blood.**
Cf. II, ii, 77, note. 87. **maiden battle,** one without bloodshed. 94.
opposed, facing each other ready for the contest. 103. **impair,** unsuitable.

For Hector in his blaze of wrath subscribes
To tender objects, but he in heat of action
Is more vindicative than jealous love:
They call him Troilus, and on him erect
A second hope, as fairly built as Hector.
Thus says Æneas; one that knows the youth   110
Even to his inches, and with private soul
Did in great Ilion thus translate him to me.
                [*Alarum. Hector and Ajax fight.*
  Agam. They are in action.
  Nest. Now, Ajax, hold thine own!
  Tro.   Hector, thou sleep'st;
Awake thee!
  Agam. His blows are well disposed: there, Ajax!
  Dio. You must no more.   [*Trumpets cease.*
  Æne.   Princes, enough, so please you.
  Ajax. I am not warm yet; let us fight again.
  Dio. As Hector pleases.
  Hect.   Why, then will I no more:
Thou art, great lord, my father's sister's son,   120
A cousin-german to great Priam's seed;
The obligation of our blood forbids
A gory emulation 'twixt us twain:
Were thy commixtion Greek and Trojan so
That thou couldst say 'This hand is Grecian all,
And this is Trojan; the sinews of this leg
All Greek, and this all Troy; my mother's blood
Runs on the dexter cheek, and this sinister
Bounds in my father's;' by Jove multipotent,   129
Thou shouldst not bear from me a Greekish member
Wherein my sword had not impressure made
Of our rank feud: but the just gods gainsay
That any drop thou borrow'dst from thy mother,
My sacred aunt, should by my mortal sword
Be drain'd! Let me embrace thee, Ajax:
By him that thunders, thou hast lusty arms;
Hector would have them fall upon him thus:
Cousin, all honour to thee!
  Ajax.   I thank thee, Hector:
Thou art too gentle and too free a man:
I came to kill thee, cousin, and bear hence   140
A great addition earned in thy death.
  Hect. Not Neoptolemus so mirable,
On whose bright crest Fame with her loud'st Oyes
Cries 'This is he,' could promise to himself
A thought of added honour torn from Hector.
  Æne. There is expectance here from both the sides,
What further you will do.
  Hect.   We'll answer it;
The issue is embracement: Ajax, farewell.
  Ajax. If I might in entreaties find success—
As seld I have the chance—I would desire   150
My famous cousin to our Grecian tents.
  Dio. 'Tis Agamemnon's wish, and great Achilles
Doth long to see unarm'd the valiant Hector.
  Hect. Æneas, call my brother Troilus to me,
And signify this loving interview
To the expecters of our Trojan part;
Desire them home. Give me thy hand, my cousin;
I will go eat with thee and see your knights.
  Ajax. Great Agamemnon comes to meet us here.

 Hect. The worthiest of them tell me name by name;
But for Achilles, mine own searching eyes   161
Shall find him by his large and portly size.
  Agam. Worthy of arms! as welcome as to one
That would be rid of such an enemy;
But that's no welcome: understand more clear.
What's past and what's to come is strew'd with
    husks
And formless ruin of oblivion;
But in this extant moment, faith and troth,
Strain'd purely from all hollow bias-drawing,
Bids thee, with most divine integrity,   170
From heart of very heart, great Hector, welcome.
  Hect. I thank thee, most imperious Agamemnon.
  Agam. [*To Troilus*] My well-famed lord of Troy, no
    less to you.
  Men. Let me confirm my princely brother's
    greeting:
You brace of warlike brothers, welcome hither.
  Hect. Who must we answer?
  Æne.   The noble Menelaus.
  Hect. O, you, my lord? by Mars his gauntlet, thanks!
Mock not, that I affect the untraded oath;
Your quondam wife swears still by Venus' glove:
She's well, but bade me not commend her to you.   180
  Men. Name her not now, sir; she's a deadly theme.
  Hect. O, pardon; I offend.
  Nest. I have, thou gallant Trojan, seen thee oft
Labouring for destiny make cruel way
Through ranks of Greekish youth, and I have seen
    thee,
As hot as Perseus, spur thy Phrygian steed,
Despising many forfeits and subduements,
When thou hast hung thy advanced sword i' the air,
Not letting it decline on the declined,
That I have said to some my standers by   190
'Lo, Jupiter is yonder, dealing life!'
And I have seen thee pause and take thy breath,
When that a ring of Greeks have hemm'd thee in,
Like an Olympian wrestling: this have I seen;
But this thy countenance, still lock'd in steel,
I never saw till now. I knew thy grandsire,
And once fought with him: he was a soldier good;
But, by great Mars, the captain of us all,
Never like thee. Let an old man embrace thee;
And, worthy warrior, welcome to our tents.   200
  Æne. 'Tis the old Nestor.
  Hect. Let me embrace thee, good old chronicle,
That hast so long walk'd hand in hand with time:
Most reverend Nestor, I am glad to clasp thee.
  Nest. I would my arms could match thee in
    contention,
As they contend with thee in courtesy.
  Hect. I would they could.
  Nest. Ha!
By this white beard, I'ld fight with thee to-morrow.
Well, welcome, welcome!—I have seen the time.   210
  Ulyss. I wonder now how yonder city stands
When we have here her base and pillar by us.
  Hect. I know your favour, Lord Ulysses, well.
Ah, sir, there's many a Greek and Trojan dead,

107. **vindicative,** vindictive. 111. **Even . . . inches,** every inch of
him. 128. **sinister,** a reference to the bar sinister. 142. **Neoptolemus,**
evidently intended for Achilles; this is the name of Achilles' son.
mirable, marvelous. 143. **Oyes,** hear; call of the public crier. 150.
seld, seldom. 156. **expecters . . . part,** Trojans awaiting the outcome.
162. **portly,** stately, dignified. 163. **as to one,** as is possible to one.

169. **Strain'd,** refined, purged. **hollow bias-drawing,** insincerities,
obliquities, such as the bias gives the bowl. 178. **untraded,** unhack-
neyed; i.e., that his use of a new, eccentric oath is an affectation. 184.
Labouring for destiny, employed in the service of fate, putting people
to death. 187. **Despising . . . subduements,** scorning to slay those
who had already surrendered or were unable to resist. 202. **chronicle.**

Since first I saw yourself and Diomed
In Ilion, on your Greekish embassy.

Ulyss. Sir, I foretold you then what would ensue:
My prophecy is but half his journey yet;
For yonder walls, that pertly front your town,   219
Yond towers, whose wanton tops do buss the clouds,
Must kiss their own feet.

Hect.   I must not believe you:
There they stand yet, and modestly I think,
The fall of every Phrygian stone will cost
A drop of Grecian blood: the end crowns all,
And that old common arbitrator, Time,
Will one day end it.

Ulyss.   So to him we leave it.
Most gentle and most valiant Hector, welcome:
After the general, I beseech you next
To feast with me and see me at my tent.

Achil. I shall forestall thee, Lord Ulysses, thou!   230
Now, Hector, I have fed mine eyes on thee;
I have with exact view perused thee, Hector,
And quoted joint by joint.

Hect.   Is this Achilles?

Achil. I am Achilles.

Hect. Stand fair, I pray thee: let me look on thee.

Achil. Behold thy fill.

Hect.   Nay, I have done already.

Achil. Thou art too brief: I will the second time,
As I would buy thee, view thee limb by limb.

Hect. O, like a book of sport thou 'lt read me o'er;
But there 's more in me than thou understand'st.   240
Why dost thou so oppress me with thine eye?

Achil. Tell me, you heavens, in which part of his
        body
Shall I destroy him? whether there, or there, or there?
That I may give the local wound a name
And make distinct the very breach whereout
Hector's great spirit flew: answer me, heavens!

Hect. It would discredit the blest gods, proud man,
To answer such a question: stand again:
Think'st thou to catch my life so pleasantly
As to prenominate in nice conjecture   250
Where thou wilt hit me dead?

Achil.   I tell thee, yea.

Hect. Wert thou an oracle to tell me so,
I 'ld not believe thee. Henceforth guard thee well;
For I'll not kill thee there, nor there, nor there;
But, by the forge that stithied Mars his helm,
I'll kill thee every where, yea, o'er and o'er.
You wisest Grecians, pardon me this brag;
His insolence draws folly from my lips;
But I'll endeavour deeds to match these words,
Or may I never—

Ajax.   Do not chafe thee, cousin: 260
And you, Achilles, let these threats alone,
Till accident or purpose bring you to 't:
You may have every day enough of Hector,
If you have stomach; the general state, I fear,
Can scarce entreat you to be odd with him.

Hect. I pray you, let us see you in the field:
We have had pelting wars, since you refused
The Grecians' cause.

Achil.   Dost thou entreat me, Hector?
To-morrow do I meet thee, fell as death;
To-night all friends.

Hect.   Thy hand upon that match.   270

Agam. First, all you peers of Greece, go to my tent;
There in the full convive we: afterwards,
As Hector's leisure and your bounties shall
Concur together, severally entreat him.
Beat loud the tabourines, let the trumpets blow,
That this great soldier may his welcome know.
              [*Exeunt all except Troilus and Ulysses.*

Tro. My Lord Ulysses, tell me, I beseech you,
In what place of the field doth Calchas keep?

Ulyss. At Menelaus' tent, most princely Troilus:
There Diomed doth feast with him to-night;   280
Who neither looks upon the heaven nor earth,
But gives all gaze and bent of amorous view
On the fair Cressid.

Tro. Shall I, sweet lord, be bound to you so much,
After we part from Agamemnon's tent,
To bring me thither?

Ulyss.   You shall command me, sir.
As gentle tell me, of what honour was
This Cressida in Troy? Had she no lover there
That wails her absence?

Tro. O, sir, to such as boasting show their scars   290
A mock is due. Will you walk on, my lord?
She was beloved, she loved; she is, and doth:
But still sweet love is food for fortune's tooth. [*Exeunt.*

ACT V.

SCENE I. *The Grecian camp. Before Achilles' tent.*

Enter ACHILLES *and* PATROCLUS.

Achil. I'll heat his blood with Greekish wine
        to-night,
Which with my scimitar I'll cool to-morrow.
Patroclus, let us feast him to the height.

Patr. Here comes Thersites.

Enter THERSITES.

Achil.   How now, thou core of envy!
Thou crusty batch of nature, what 's the news?

Ther. Why, thou picture of what thou seemest, and
idol of idiot-worshippers, here 's a letter for thee.

Achil. From whence, fragment?

Ther. Why, thou full dish of fool, from Troy.   10

Patr. Who keeps the tent now?

Ther. The surgeon's box, or the patient's wound.

Patr. Well said, adversity! and what need these
tricks?

Ther. Prithee, be silent, boy; I profit not by thy
talk: thou art thought to be Achilles' male varlet.

Patr. Male varlet, you rogue! what 's that?

Ther. Why, his masculine whore. Now, the rotten
diseases of the south, the guts-griping, ruptures,
catarrhs, loads o' gravel i' the back, lethargies, cold
palsies, raw eyes, dirt-rotten livers, wheezing lungs,
bladders full of imposthume, sciaticas, limekilns i' the

As an old man he is the repository of the events of the past. 219.
front, i.e., that are the front of. 239. **book of sport**, possibly a jest
book, or any book of light entertainment. 255. **stithied**, forged. 265.
be odd, be at odds. 267. **pelting**, paltry. 272. **convive**, feast together.
274. **entreat**, entertain.
ACT V. SCENE I. 5. **crusty . . . nature**, i.e., as a batch of crusty

bread. 12. **surgeon's box.** Thersites puns on *tent* (l. 11), i.e., a roll
of lint for cleansing a wound. 24. **imposthume**, abscess. 25. **limekilns**, burning sensations.

palm, incurable bone-ache, and the rivelled fee-simple
of the tetter, take and take again such preposterous
discoveries!

Patr. Why, thou damnable box of envy, thou,
what meanest thou to curse thus?   30

Ther. Do I curse thee?

Patr. Why, no, you ruinous butt, you whoreson
indistinguishable cur, no.

Ther. No! why art thou then exasperate, thou idle
immaterial skein of sleave-silk, thou green sarcenet
flap for a sore eye, thou tassel of a prodigal's purse,
thou? Ah, how the poor world is pestered with such
waterflies, diminutives of nature!

Patr. Out, gall!   40

Ther. Finch-egg!

Achil. My sweet Patroclus, I am thwarted quite
From my great purpose in to-morrow's battle.
Here is a letter from Queen Hecuba,
A token from her daughter, my fair love,
Both taxing me and gaging me to keep
An oath that I have sworn. I will not break it:
Fall Greeks; fail fame; honour or go or stay;
My major vow lies here, this I'll obey.
Come, come, Thersites, help to trim my tent: 50
This night in banqueting must all be spent.
Away, Patroclus!   [*Exeunt Achilles and Patroclus.*

Ther. With too much blood and too little brain,
these two may run mad; but, if with too much brain
and too little blood they do, I'll be a curer of madmen. Here 's Agamemnon, an honest fellow enough,
and one that loves quails; but he has not so much
brain as ear-wax: and the goodly transformation of
Jupiter there, his brother, the bull,—the primitive
statue, and oblique memorial of cuckolds; a thrifty
shoeing-horn in a chain, hanging at his brother's leg,
—to what form but that he is, should wit larded with
malice and malice forced with wit turn him to? To
an ass, were nothing; he is both ass and ox: to an ox,
were nothing; he is both ox and ass. To be a dog,
a mule, a cat, a fitchew, a toad, a lizard, an owl, a
puttock, or a herring without a roe, I would not care;
but to be Menelaus! I would conspire against destiny.
Ask me not what I would be, if I were not Thersites;
for I care not to be the louse of a lazar, so I were not
Menelaus. Hoy-day! spirits and fires!   73

Enter HECTOR, TROILUS, AJAX, AGAMEMNON,
    ULYSSES, NESTOR, MENELAUS, *and* DIOMEDES,
    with lights.

Agam. We go wrong, we go wrong.

Ajax.   No, yonder 'tis;
There, where we see the lights.

Hect.   I trouble you.

Ajax. No, not a whit.

Ulyss.   Here comes himself to guide you.

Re-enter ACHILLES.

Achil. Welcome, brave Hector; welcome, princes
all.

Agam. So now, fair Prince of Troy, I bid good night.
Ajax commands the guard to tend on you.   79

Hect. Thanks and good night to the Greeks' general.

Men. Good night, my lord.

Hect.   Good night, sweet Lord
    Menelaus.

Ther. Sweet draught: 'sweet' quoth 'a! sweet sink,
sweet sewer.

Achil. Good night and welcome, both at once, to
    those
That go or tarry.

Agam. Good night. [*Exeunt Agamemnon and Menelaus.*

Achil. Old Nestor tarries; and you too, Diomed,
Keep Hector company an hour or two.

Dio. I cannot, lord; I have important business,
The tide whereof is now. Good night, great Hector.   90

Hect. Give me your hand.

Ulyss. [*Aside to Troilus*] Follow his torch; he goes to
    Calchas' tent:
I'll keep you company.

Tro.   Sweet sir, you honour me.

Hect. And so, good night.
        [*Exit Diomedes; Ulysses and Troilus following.*

Achil.   Come, come, enter my tent.
        [*Exeunt Achilles, Hector, Ajax, and Nestor.*

Ther. That same Diomed 's a false-hearted rogue,
a most unjust knave; I will no more trust him when he
leers than I will a serpent when he hisses: he will
spend his mouth, and promise, like Brabbler the
hound; but when he performs, astronomers foretell
it; it is prodigious, there will come some change; the
sun borrows of the moon, when Diomed keeps his
word. I will rather leave to see Hector, than not to
dog him: they say he keeps a Trojan drab, and uses
the traitor Calchas' tent: I'll after. Nothing but
lechery! all incontinent varlets!   [*Exit.* 106

SCENE II. *The same. Before Calchas' tent.*

Enter DIOMEDES.

Dio. What, are you up here, ho? speak.

Cal. [*Within*] Who calls?

Dio. Diomed. Calchas, I think. Where 's your
    daughter?

Cal. [*Within*] She comes to you.

Enter TROILUS *and* ULYSSES, *at a distance; after them,*
    THERSITES.

Ulyss. Stand where the torch may not discover us.

Enter CRESSIDA.

Tro. Cressid comes forth to him.

Dio.   How now, my charge!

Cres. Now, my sweet guardian! Hark, a word with
    you.   [*Whispers.*

Tro. Yea, so familiar!

Ulyss. She will sing any man at first sight.

Ther. And any man may sing her, if he can take
her cliff; she 's noted.   11

Dio. Will you remember?

Cres. Remember! yes.

Dio. Nay, but do, then;
And let your mind be coupled with your words.

*Troilus
and Cressida*
ACT V : SC I

892

26. **rivelled**, wrinkled. **fee-simple**, absolute possession, i.e., incurable
disease. 27. **tetter**, skin disease. 35. **sleave-silk**, floss-silk. 36.
sarcenet, fine, soft silk. 57. **quails**, cant term for prostitutes. 59-
60. **transformation . . . bull**, alludes to the myth of Jupiter's rape of
Europa, whom he encountered in a meadow after changing himself

into a bull. Thersites has in mind the bull's horns; cf. V, vii, 10, 12.
60. **oblique memorial**, indirect reminder. 61. **shoeing-horn**, shoe-
horn; emblem of a subservient fool. 67. **fitchew**, polecat. 68.
puttock, bird of prey of the kite kind. **herring . . . roe.** Cf. *Romeo and
Juliet*, II, iv, 39. 71. **care not to be**, would as soon be. 98. **spend**

Tro. What should she remember?

Ulyss. List.

Cres. Sweet honey Greek, tempt me no more to folly.

Ther. Roguery!

Dio. Nay, then,— 20

Cres. I'll tell you what,—

Dio. Foh, foh! come, tell a pin: you are forsworn.

Cres. In faith, I cannot: what would you have me do?

Ther. A juggling trick,—to be secretly open.

Dio. What did you swear you would bestow on me?

Cres. I prithee, do not hold me to mine oath;
Bid me do any thing but that, sweet Greek.

Dio. Good night.

Tro. Hold, patience!

Ulyss. How now, Trojan! 30

Cres. Diomed,—

Dio. No, no, good night: I'll be your fool no more.

Tro. Thy better must.

Cres. Hark, one word in your ear.

Tro. O plague and madness!

Ulyss. You are moved, prince; let us depart, I pray you,
Lest your displeasure should enlarge itself
To wrathful terms: this place is dangerous;
The time right deadly; I beseech you, go.

Tro. Behold, I pray you!

Ulyss. Nay, good my lord, go off: 40
You flow to great distraction; come, my lord.

Tro. I pray thee, stay.

Ulyss. You have not patience; come.

Tro. I pray you, stay; by hell and all hell's torments,
I will not speak a word!

Dio. And so, good night.

Cres. Nay, but you part in anger.

Tro. Doth that grieve thee?
O wither'd truth!

Ulyss. Why, how now, lord!

Tro. By Jove,
I will be patient.

Cres. Guardian!—why, Greek!

Dio. Foh, foh! adieu; you palter.

Cres. In faith, I do not: come hither once again.

Ulyss. You shake, my lord, at something: will you go? 50
You will break out.

Tro. She strokes his cheek!

Ulyss. Come, come.

Tro. Nay, stay; by Jove, I will not speak a word:
There is between my will and all offences
A guard of patience: stay a little while.

Ther. How the devil Luxury, with his fat rump and
potato-finger, tickles these together! Fry, lechery, fry!

Dio. But will you, then?

Cres. In faith, I will, la; never trust me else.

Dio. Give me some token for the surety of it. 60

Cres. I'll fetch you one. [*Exit.*

Ulyss. You have sworn patience.

Tro. Fear me not, sweet lord;
I will not be myself, nor have cognition
Of what I feel: I am all patience.

Re-enter CRESSIDA.

Ther. Now the pledge; now, now, now!

Cres. Here, Diomed, keep this sleeve.

Tro. O beauty! where is thy faith?

Ulyss. My lord,—

Tro. I will be patient; outwardly I will.

Cres. You look upon that sleeve; behold it well.
He loved me—O false wench!—Give 't me again. 70

Dio. Whose was 't?

Cres. It is no matter, now I have 't again.
I will not meet with you to-morrow night:
I prithee, Diomed, visit me no more.

Ther. Now she sharpens: well said, whetstone!

Dio. I shall have it.

Cres. What, this?

Dio. Ay, that.

Cres. O, all you gods! O pretty, pretty pledge!
Thy master now lies thinking in his bed
Of thee and me, and sighs, and takes my glove,
And gives memorial dainty kisses to it, 80
As I kiss thee. Nay, do not snatch it from me;
He that takes that doth take my heart withal.

Dio. I had your heart before, this follows it.

Tro. I did swear patience.

Cres. You shall not have it, Diomed; faith, you shall not;
I'll give you something else.

Dio. I will have this: whose was it?

Cres. It is no matter.

Dio. Come, tell me whose it was.

Cres. 'Twas one's that loved me better than you will.
But, now you have it, take it.

Dio. Whose was it? 90

Cres. By all Diana's waiting-women yond,
And by herself, I will not tell you whose.

Dio. To-morrow will I wear it on my helm,
And grieve his spirit that dares not challenge it.

Tro. Wert thou the devil, and worest it on thy horn,
It should be challenged.

Cres. Well, well, 'tis done, 'tis past: and yet it is not;
I will not keep my word.

Dio. Why, then, farewell;
Thou never shalt mock Diomed again.

Cres. You shall not go: one cannot speak a word, 100
But it straight starts you.

Dio. I do not like this fooling.

Ther. Nor I, by Pluto: but that that likes not you
pleases me best.

Dio. What, shall I come? the hour?

Cres. Ay, come:—O Jove!—do come:—I shall be plagued.

Dio. Farewell till then.

Cres. Good night: I prithee, come.
[*Exit Diomedes.*
Troilus, farewell! one eye yet looks on thee;
But with my heart the other eye doth see.
Ah, poor our sex! this fault in us I find,
The error of our eye directs our mind: 110
What error leads must err; O, then conclude
Minds sway'd by eyes are full of turpitude. [*Exit.*

Ther. A proof of strength she could not publish more,

---

his mouth, bay without scenting the game. 103. **leave to see,** cease gazing on. **him,** i.e., Diomedes.

SCENE II. 9. **sing ... at first sight,** i.e., without previous practice or acquaintance. 11. **cliff,** clef, key. **noted,** set to music, with quibble on the meaning "stigmatized," i.e., in bad repute. 41. **flow,** rise and overflow. 48. **palter,** use trickery. 56. **potato-finger.** Potatoes were accounted stimulants to lechery; cf. *The Merry Wives of Windsor,* V, v, 21. 91. **Diana's.** Ironically, Cressida swears by the goddess of chastity.

Unless she said 'My mind is now turn'd whore.'
   Ulyss. All 's done, my lord.
   Tro.   It is.
   Ulyss.   Why stay we, then?
   Tro. To make a recordation to my soul
Of every syllable that here was spoke.
But if I tell how these two did co-act,
Shall I not lie in publishing a truth?
Sith yet there is a credence in my heart,   120
An esperance so obstinately strong,
That doth invert the attest of eyes and ears,
As if those organs had deceptious functions,
Created only to calumniate.
Was Cressid here?
   Ulyss.   I cannot conjure, Trojan.
   Tro. She was not, sure.
   Ulyss.   Most sure she was.
   Tro. Why, my negation hath no taste of madness.
   Ulyss. Nor mine, my lord: Cressid was here but
    now.
   Tro. Let it not be believed for womanhood!
Think, we had mothers; do not give advantage 130
To stubborn critics, apt, without a theme,
For depravation, to square the general sex
By Cressid's rule: rather think this not Cressid.
   Ulyss. What hath she done, prince, that can soil our
    mothers?
   Tro. Nothing at all, unless that this were she.
   Ther. Will he swagger himself out on 's own eyes?
   Tro. This she? no, this is Diomed's Cressida:
If beauty have a soul, this is not she;
If souls guide vows, if vows be sanctimonies,
If sanctimony be the gods' delight,   140
If there be rule in unity itself,
This is not she. O madness of discourse,
That cause sets up with and against itself!
Bi-fold authority! where reason can revolt
Without perdition, and loss assume all reason
Without revolt: this is, and is not, Cressid.
Within my soul there doth conduce a fight
Of this strange nature that a thing inseparate
Divides more wider than the sky and earth,
And yet the spacious breadth of this division 150
Admits no orifex for a point as subtle
As Ariachne's broken woof to enter.
Instance, O instance! strong as Pluto's gates;
Cressid is mine, tied with the bonds of heaven:
Instance, O instance! strong as heaven itself;
The bonds of heaven are slipp'd, dissolved, and
    loosed;
And with another knot, five-finger-tied,
The fractions of her faith, orts of her love,
The fragments, scraps, the bits and greasy relics
Of her o'er-eaten faith, are bound to Diomed. 160
   Ulyss. May worthy Troilus be half attach'd
With that which here his passion doth express?
   Tro. Ay, Greek; and that shall be divulged well
In characters as red as Mars his heart
Inflamed with Venus: never did young man fancy
With so eternal and so fix'd a soul.

Hark, Greek: as much as I do Cressid love,
So much by weight hate I her Diomed:
That sleeve is mine that he'll bear on his helm;
Were it a casque composed by Vulcan's skill, 170
My sword should bite it: not the dreadful spout
Which shipmen do the hurricano call,
Constringed in mass by the almighty sun,
Shall dizzy with more clamour Neptune's ear
In his descent than shall my prompted sword
Falling on Diomed.
   Ther. He'll tickle it for his concupy.
   Tro. O Cressid! O false Cressid! false, false, false!
Let all untruths stand by thy stained name,
And they'll seem glorious.
   Ulyss.   O, contain yourself; 180
Your passion draws ears hither.

Enter ÆNEAS.

   Æne. I have been seeking you this hour, my lord:
Hector, by this, is arming him in Troy;
Ajax, your guard, stays to conduct you home.
   Tro. Have with you, prince. My courteous lord,
    adieu.
Farewell, revolted fair! and, Diomed,
Stand fast, and wear a castle on thy head!
   Ulyss. I'll bring you to the gates.
   Tro. Accept distracted thanks.
            [Exeunt Troilus, Æneas, and Ulysses.
   Ther. Would I could meet that rogue Diomed! I
would croak like a raven; I would bode, I would
bode. Patroclus will give me any thing for the in-
telligence of this whore: the parrot will not do more
for an almond than he for a commodious drab.
Lechery, lechery; still, wars and lechery; nothing else
holds fashion: a burning devil take them!   *[Exit.*

SCENE III. *Troy. Before Priam's palace.*

Enter HECTOR and ANDROMACHE.

   And. When was my lord so much ungently
    temper'd,
To stop his ears against admonishment?
Unarm, unarm, and do not fight to-day.
   Hect. You train me to offend you; get you in:
By all the everlasting gods, I'll go!
   And. My dreams will, sure, prove ominous to the
    day.
   Hect. No more, I say.

Enter CASSANDRA.

   Cas.   Where is my brother Hector?
   And. Here, sister; arm'd, and bloody in intent.
Consort with me in loud and dear petition,
Pursue we him on knees; for I have dream'd   10
Of bloody turbulence, and this whole night
Hath nothing been but shapes and forms of slaughter.
   Cas. O, 'tis true.
   Hect.   Ho! bid my trumpet sound.

121. **esperance,** hope. 132-133. **square . . . rule,** make Cressida the
standard by which all womankind is measured. 136. **swagger.** Thersites regards Troilus' passionate self-deception as swaggering. **on,** of.
139. **sanctimonies,** sacred things. 147. **conduce,** take place. 151. **orifex,** orifice. 152. **Ariachne's broken woof,** spider's web. Some have
thought that Shakespeare had here confused Arachne with Ariadne (we
need the four syllables for the meter), whose clew may have been in his mind;
cf. *The Two Gentlemen of Verona,* IV, iv, 172, note. 157. **five-finger-tied,**

a knot tied by giving her hand to Diomedes (Johnson). 158. **orts,** refuse, fragments. 161-162. **be half attach'd With,** have half the feeling
of. 170. **casque,** headpiece, helmet. 173. **Constringed,** compressed.
177. **concupy,** lust. 187. **castle,** fortress. 192. **bode,** warn, prognosticate.
    SCENE III. 21. **would give,** want to give. 26. **keeps the weather of,**
keeps to the windward side of. 27. **the dear man,** earnest, sincere person; so Q; Globe, following Pope: *the brave man.* 34. **brushes,** hostile
encounters. 37. **vice of mercy,** an instance of oxymoron. 38. **better**

Cas. No notes of sally, for the heavens, sweet
   brother.
Hect. Be gone, I say: the gods have heard me swear.
Cas. The gods are deaf to hot and peevish vows:
They are polluted offerings, more abhorr'd
Than spotted livers in the sacrifice.
And. O, be persuaded! do not count it holy
To hurt by being just: it is as lawful,   20
For we would give much, to use violent thefts,
And rob in the behalf of charity.
Cas. It is the purpose that makes strong the vow;
But vows to every purpose must not hold:
Unarm, sweet Hector.
Hect.   Hold you still, I say;
Mine honour keeps the weather of my fate:
Life every man holds dear; but the dear man
Holds honour far more precious-dear than life.

Enter TROILUS.

How now, young man! mean'st thou to fight
   to-day?
And. Cassandra, call my father to persuade.   30
                   [*Exit Cassandra.*
Hect. No, faith, young Troilus; doff thy harness,
   youth;
I am to-day i' the vein of chivalry:
Let grow thy sinews till their knots be strong,
And tempt not yet the brushes of the war.
Unarm thee, go, and doubt thou not, brave boy,
I'll stand to-day for thee and me and Troy.
Tro. Brother, you have a vice of mercy in you,
Which better fits a lion than a man.
Hect. What vice is that, good Troilus? chide me for
   it.
Tro. When many times the captive Grecian falls,   40
Even in the fan and wind of your fair sword,
You bid them rise, and live.
Hect. O, 'tis fair play.
Tro.   Fool's play, by heaven, Hector.
Hect. How now! how now!
Tro.   For the love of all the gods,
Let 's leave the hermit pity with our mothers,
And when we have our armours buckled on,
The venom'd vengeance ride upon our swords,
Spur them to ruthful work, rein them from ruth.
Hect. Fie, savage, fie!
Tro.   Hector, then 'tis wars.
Hect. Troilus, I would not have you fight to-day.   50
Tro. Who should withhold me?
Not fate, obedience, nor the hand of Mars
Beckoning with fiery truncheon my retire;
Not Priamus and Hecuba on knees,
Their eyes o'ergalled with recourse of tears;
Nor you, my brother, with your true sword drawn,
Opposed to hinder me, should stop my way,
But by my ruin.

Re-enter CASSANDRA, *with* PRIAM.

Cas. Lay hold upon him, Priam, hold him fast:
He is thy crutch; now if thou lose thy stay,   60

Thou on him leaning, and all Troy on thee,
Fall all together.
Pri.   Come, Hector, come, go back:
Thy wife hath dream'd; thy mother hath had visions;
Cassandra doth foresee; and I myself
Am like a prophet suddenly enrapt
To tell thee that this day is ominous:
Therefore, come back.
Hect.   Æneas is a-field;
And I do stand engaged to many Greeks,
Even in the faith of valour, to appear
This morning to them.
Pri.   Ay, but thou shalt not go.   70
Hect. I must not break my faith.
You know me dutiful; therefore, dear sir,
Let me not shame respect; but give me leave
To take that course by your consent and voice,
Which you do here forbid me, royal Priam.
Cas. O Priam, yield not to him!
And.   Do not, dear father.
Hect. Andromache, I am offended with you:
Upon the love you bear me, get you in.
                 [*Exit Andromache.*
Tro. This foolish, dreaming, superstitious girl
Makes all these bodements.
Cas.   O, farewell, dear Hector!   80
Look, how thou diest! look, how thy eye turns pale!
Look, how thy wounds do bleed at many vents!
Hark, how Troy roars! how Hecuba cries out!
How poor Andromache shrills her dolours forth!
Behold, distraction, frenzy and amazement,
Like witless antics, one another meet,
And all cry, Hector! Hector 's dead! O Hector!
Tro. Away! away!
Cas. Farewell: yet, soft! Hector, I take my leave:
Thou dost thyself and all our Troy deceive.   [*Exit.* 90
Hect. You are amazed, my liege, at her exclaim:
Go in and cheer the town: we'll forth and fight,
Do deeds worth praise and tell you them at night.
Pri. Farewell: the gods with safety stand about
   thee!   [*Exeunt severally Priam and Hector. Alarums.*
Tro. They are at it, hark! Proud Diomed, believe,
I come to lose my arm, or win my sleeve.

Enter PANDARUS.

Pan. Do you hear, my lord? do you hear?
Tro. What now?
Pan. Here 's a letter come from yond poor girl.
Tro. Let me read.   100
Pan. A whoreson tisick, a whoreson rascally tisick
so troubles me, and the foolish fortune of this girl;
and what one thing, what another, that I shall leave
you one o' these days: and I have a rheum in mine
eyes too, and such an ache in my bones that, unless a
man were cursed, I cannot tell what to think on 't.
What says she there?
Tro. Words, words, mere words, no matter from the
   heart;
The effect doth operate another way. [*Tearing the letter.*
Go, wind, to wind, there turn and change together. 110

My love with words and errors still she feeds;
But edifies another with her deeds.   [*Exeunt severally.*

SCENE IV. *Plains between Troy and the Grecian camp.*

Alarums: excursions. Enter THERSITES.

Ther. Now they are clapper-clawing one another;
I'll go look on. That dissembling abominable varlet,
Diomed, has got that same scurvy doting foolish
young knave's sleeve of Troy there in his helm: I
would fain see them meet; that that same young
Trojan ass, that loves the whore there, might send
that Greekish whoremasterly villain, with the sleeve,
back to the dissembling luxurious drab, of a sleeveless
errand. O' the t'other side, the policy of those crafty
swearing rascals, that stale old mouse-eaten dry
cheese, Nestor, and that same dog-fox, Ulysses, is not
proved worth a blackberry: they set me up, in policy,
that mongrel cur, Ajax, against that dog of as bad a
kind, Achilles: and now is the cur Ajax prouder than
the cur Achilles, and will not arm to-day; whereupon
the Grecians begin to proclaim barbarism, and policy
grows into an ill opinion. Soft! here comes sleeve, and
t'other.

Enter DIOMEDES, TROILUS *following.*

Tro. Fly not; for shouldst thou take the river Styx, 20
I would swim after.
Dio.   Thou dost miscall retire:
I do not fly, but advantageous care
Withdrew me from the odds of multitude:
Have at thee!
    Ther. Hold thy whore, Grecian!—now for thy
whore, Trojan!—now the sleeve, now the sleeve!
            [*Exeunt Troilus and Diomedes, fighting.*

Enter HECTOR.

Hect. What art thou, Greek? art thou for Hector's
    match?
Art thou of blood and honour?
    Ther. No, no, I am a rascal; a scurvy railing knave;
a very filthy rogue.   31
    Hect. I do believe thee: live.   [*Exit.*
    Ther. God-a-mercy, that thou wilt believe me; but
a plague break thy neck for frighting me! What's
become of the wenching rogues? I think they have
swallowed one another: I would laugh at that
miracle: yet, in a sort, lechery eats itself. I'll seek
them.   [*Exit.*

SCENE V. *Another part of the plains.*

Enter DIOMEDES *and a* Servant.

Dio. Go, go, my servant, take thou Troilus' horse;
Present the fair steed to my lady Cressid:
Fellow, commend my service to her beauty;
Tell her I have chastised the amorous Trojan,
And am her knight by proof.
    Serv.   I go, my lord.   [*Exit.*

Enter AGAMEMNON.

Agam. Renew, renew! The fierce Polydamas
Hath beat down Menon: bastard Margarelon
Hath Doreus prisoner,
And stands colossus-wise, waving his beam,
Upon the pashed corses of the kings   10
Epistrophus and Cedius: Polyxenes is slain,
Amphimachus and Thoas deadly hurt,
Patroclus ta'en or slain, and Palamedes
Sore hurt and bruised: the dreadful Sagittary
Appals our numbers: haste we, Diomed,
To reinforcement, or we perish all.

Enter NESTOR.

Nest. Go, bear Patroclus' body to Achilles;
And bid the snail-paced Ajax arm for shame.
There is a thousand Hectors in the field:
Now here he fights on Galathe his horse,   20
And there lacks work; anon he's there afoot,
And there they fly or die, like scaled sculls
Before the belching whale; then is he yonder,
And there the strawy Greeks, ripe for his edge,
Fall down before him, like the mower's swath:
Here, there, and every where, he leaves and takes,
Dexterity so obeying appetite
That what he will he does, and does so much
That proof is call'd impossibility.   29

Enter ULYSSES.

Ulyss. O, courage, courage, princes! great Achilles
Is arming, weeping, cursing, vowing vengeance:
Patroclus' wounds have roused his drowsy blood,
Together with his mangled Myrmidons,
That noseless, handless, hack'd and chipp'd, come to
    him,
Crying on Hector. Ajax hath lost a friend
And foams at mouth, and he is arm'd and at it,
Roaring for Troilus, who hath done to-day
Mad and fantastic execution,
Engaging and redeeming of himself
With such a careless force and forceless care   40
As if that luck, in very spite of cunning,
Bade him win all.

Enter AJAX.

Ajax. Troilus! thou coward Troilus!   [*Exit.*
Dio.   Ay, there, there.
Nest. So, so, we draw together.

Enter ACHILLES.

Achil.   Where is this Hector?
Come, come, thou boy-queller, show thy face;
Know what it is to meet Achilles angry:
Hector! where's Hector? I will none but Hector.
                                            [*Exeunt.*

SCENE VI. *Another part of the plains.*

Enter AJAX.

Ajax. Troilus, thou coward Troilus, show thy head!

Enter DIOMEDES.

SCENE IV. 1. **clapper-clawing,** mauling, thrashing; cf. the use of
this term in the Preface to the second issue of Q (see Introduction).
9. **sleeveless,** futile. 18. **proclaim barbarism,** set up the authority of
ignorance, to declare that they will be governed by policy no longer
(Johnson). 21. **miscall retire,** call my retirement by a wrong name.
23. **odds of multitude,** i.e., the odds of fighting among too many are

against a successful hand-to-hand combat. 28. **for Hector's match,**
ready for a match with Hector.
    SCENE V. 9. **colossus-wise,** i.e., like the statue of Apollo at Rhodes,
which, according to an unfounded tradition, was said to have its feet
placed on two moles which formed the harbor entrance so that ships
passed between its legs. It was demolished by an earthquake in the

Dio. Troilus, I say! where 's Troilus?
Ajax.   What wouldst thou?
Dio. I would correct him.
Ajax. Were I the general, thou shouldst have my
    office
Ere that correction. Troilus, I say! what, Troilus!

Enter TROILUS.

Tro. O traitor Diomed! turn thy false face, thou
    traitor,
And pay thy life thou owest me for my horse!
Dio. Ha, art thou there?
Ajax. I'll fight with him alone: stand, Diomed.
Dio. He is my prize; I will not look upon.   10
Tro. Come, both you cogging Greeks; have at you
    both!   [*Exeunt, fighting.*

Enter HECTOR.

Hect. Yea, Troilus? O, well fought, my youngest
    brother!

Enter ACHILLES.

Achil. Now do I see thee, ha! have at thee, Hector!
Hect. Pause, if thou wilt.
Achil. I do disdain thy courtesy, proud Trojan:
Be happy that my arms are out of use:
My rest and negligence befriends thee now,
But thou anon shalt hear of me again;
Till when, go seek thy fortune.   [*Exit.*
Hect.   Fare thee well:
I would have been much more a fresher man,   20
Had I expected thee. How now, my brother!

Re-enter TROILUS.

Tro. Ajax hath ta'en Æneas: shall it be?
No, by the flame of yonder glorious heaven,
He shall not carry him: I'll be ta'en too,
Or bring him off: fate, hear me what I say!
I reck not though I end my life to-day.   [*Exit.*

Enter one in sumptuous armour.

Hect. Stand, stand, thou Greek; thou art a goodly
    mark:
No? wilt thou not? I like thy armour well;
I'll frush it and unlock the rivets all,
But I'll be master of it: wilt thou not, beast, abide?   30
Why, then fly on, I'll hunt thee for thy hide.   [*Exeunt.*

SCENE VII. *Another part of the plains.*

Enter ACHILLES, *with* Myrmidons.

Achil. Come here about me, you my Myrmidons;
Mark what I say. Attend me where I wheel:
Strike not a stroke, but keep yourselves in breath:
And when I have the bloody Hector found,
Empale him with your weapons round about;
In fellest manner execute your aims.
Follow me, sirs, and my proceedings eye:
It is decreed Hector the great must die.   [*Exeunt.*

Enter MENELAUS *and* PARIS, *fighting: then* THERSITES.

Ther. The cuckold and the cuckold-maker are at it.
Now, bull! now, dog! 'Loo, Paris, 'loo! now my
double-henned sparrow! 'loo, Paris, 'loo! The bull has
the game: ware horns, ho! [*Exeunt Paris and Menelaus.*

Enter MARGARELON.

Mar. Turn, slave, and fight.
Ther. What art thou?
Mar. A bastard son of Priam's.   15
Ther. I am a bastard too; I love bastards: I am a
bastard begot, bastard instructed, bastard in mind,
bastard in valour, in every thing illegitimate. One
bear will not bite another, and wherefore should one
bastard? Take heed, the quarrel 's most ominous to
us: if the son of a whore fight for a whore, he tempts
judgement: farewell, bastard.   [*Exit.*
Mar. The devil take thee, coward!   [*Exit.*

SCENE VIII. *Another part of the plains.*

Enter HECTOR.

Hect. Most putrefied core, so fair without,
Thy goodly armour thus hath cost thy life.
Now is my day's work done; I'll take good breath:
Rest, sword; thou hast thy fill of blood and death.
    [*Puts off his helmet and hangs his shield behind him.*

Enter ACHILLES *and* Myrmidons.

Achil. Look, Hector, how the sun begins to set;
How ugly night comes breathing at his heels:
Even with the vail and darking of the sun,
To close the day up, Hector's life is done.
Hect. I am unarm'd; forego this vantage, Greek.
Achil. Strike, fellows, strike; this is the man I seek.   10
    [*Hector falls.*
So, Ilion, fall thou next! now, Troy, sink down!
Here lies thy heart, thy sinews, and thy bone.
On, Myrmidons, and cry you all amain,
'Achilles hath the mighty Hector slain.'
    [*A retreat sounded.*
Hark! a retire upon our Grecian part.
Myr. The Trojan trumpets sound the like, my lord.
Achil. The dragon wing of night o'erspreads the
    earth,
And, stickler-like, the armies separates.
My half-supp'd sword, that frankly would have fed,
Pleased with this dainty bait, thus goes to bed.   20
    [*Sheathes his sword.*
Come, tie his body to my horse's tail;
Along the field I will the Trojan trail.   [*Exeunt.*

SCENE IX. *Another part of the plains.*

Enter AGAMEMNON, AJAX, MENELAUS, NESTOR,
DIOMEDES, *and others, marching. Shouts within.*

Agam. Hark! hark! what shout is that?
Nest. Peace, drums!
[*Within*] Achilles! Achilles! Hector 's slain! Achilles!
Dio. The bruit is, Hector 's slain, and by Achilles.

third century B.C. **beam,** sword. 14. **Sagittary,** literally, the archer;
a centaur, i.e., a monster half man, half horse, who according to
medieval legends fought in the Trojan War against the Greeks. 22.
sculls, schools (of fish). 40. **forceless care,** easy dexterity (Deighton).
45. **boy-queller,** boy killer; i.e., he has slain Patroclus.
    SCENE VI. 29. **frush,** bruise.

SCENE VII. 10. **'Loo,** cry to incite dogs to the chase. 11. **double-
henned sparrow,** alludes to Helen's belonging to two men; she "doubles"
as wife to both.
    SCENE VIII. 18. **stickler-like,** like an umpire.

Ajax. If it be so, yet bragless let it be;
Great Hector was a man as good as he.
  Agam. March patiently along: let one be sent
To pray Achilles see us at our tent.
If in his death the gods have us befriended,
Great Troy is ours, and our sharp wars are ended. 10
                    [*Exeunt, marching.*

SCENE X. *Another part of the plains.*

Enter ÆNEAS *and* Trojans.

  Æne. Stand, ho! yet are we masters of the field:
Never go home; here starve we out the night.

Enter TROILUS.

  Tro. Hector is slain.
  All.   Hector! the gods forbid!
  Tro. He 's dead; and at the murderer's horse's tail,
In beastly sort, dragg'd through the shameful field.
Frown on, you heavens, effect your rage with speed!
Sit, gods, upon your thrones, and smile at Troy!
I say, at once let your brief plagues be mercy,
And linger not our sure destructions on!
  Æne. My lord, you do discomfort all the host. 10
  Tro. You understand me not that tell me so:
I do not speak of flight, of fear, of death,
But dare all imminence that gods and men
Address their dangers in. Hector is gone:
Who shall tell Priam so, or Hecuba?
Let him that will a screech-owl aye be call'd,
Go in to Troy, and say there, Hector 's dead:
There is a word will Priam turn to stone;
Make wells and Niobes of the maids and wives,
Cold statues of the youth, and, in a word, 20
Scare Troy out of itself. But, march away:
Hector is dead; there is no more to say.
Stay yet. You vile abominable tents,
Thus proudly pight upon our Phrygian plains,
Let Titan rise as early as he dare.
I'll through and through you! and, thou great-sized
    coward,
No space of earth shall sunder our two hates:
I'll haunt thee like a wicked conscience still,
That mouldeth goblins swift as frenzy's thoughts.
Strike a free march to Troy! with comfort go: 30
Hope of revenge shall hide our inward woe.
            [*Exeunt Æneas and Trojans.*

As TROILUS *is going out, enter, from the other side,*
    PANDARUS.

  Pan. But hear you, hear you!
  Tro. Hence, broker-lackey! ignomy and shame
Pursue thy life, and live aye with thy name!   [*Exit.*
  Pan. A goodly medicine for my aching bones! O
world! world! world! thus is the poor agent despised!
O traitors and bawds, how earnestly are you set
a-work, and how ill requited! why should our en-

SCENE IX. 5. **bragless,** without gloating.
SCENE X. 13. **imminence,** impending evil. 16. **screech-owl,** traditional prognosticator of death. 19. **Niobes.** Niobe boasted that her
six sons and six daughters made her superior to Latona, mother of
Apollo and Diana, for which she was punished by seeing them put to
death by the arrows of these two deities. While weeping she was changed
into a stone, but her tears continued to flow from the rock. 24. **pight,**
pitched. 28. **conscience,** almost synonymous with imagination; it
carries the double suggestion that the sense of guilt makes the imagination conjure up goblins. 34. **live . . . name.** Cf. III, ii, 208-210.

---

deavour be so loved and the performance so loathed?
what verse for it? what instance for it? Let me see: 41

  Full merrily the humble-bee doth sing,
  Till he hath lost his honey and his sting;
  And being once subdued in armed tail,
  Sweet honey and sweet notes together fail.

Good traders in the flesh, set this in your painted
cloths.

  As many as be here of pandar's hall,
  Your eyes, half out, weep out at Pandar's fall;
  Or if you cannot weep, yet give some groans, 50
  Though not for me, yet for your aching bones.
  Brethren and sisters of the hold-door trade,
  Some two months hence my will shall here be made:
  It should be now, but that my fear is this,
  Some galled goose of Winchester would hiss:
  Till then I'll sweat and seek about for eases,
  And at that time bequeathe you my diseases.   [*Exit.*

46. **your painted cloths,** hangings worked or painted with designs.
52. **hold-door trade,** prostitution. 55. **galled . . . Winchester,** one
having a venereal disease; so called because the brothels of Southwark
were under the jurisdiction of the bishop of Winchester.

Hamlet, Prince of Denmark

The first edition of *Hamlet,* a quarto, has the following title page:

THE Tragicall Historie of HAMLET *Prince of Denmarke.* By William Shake-speare. As it hath beene diuerse
times acted by his Highnesse seruants in the Cittie of
London: as also in the two Vniuersities of Cambridge
and Oxford, and elsewhere. At London printed for
N. L. and Iohn Trundell. 1603.

The second quarto has this title page:

THE Tragicall Historie of HAMLET, *Prince of Denmarke.* By William Shakespeare. Newly imprinted and
enlarged to almost as much againe as it was, according
to the true and perfect Coppie. AT LONDON, Printed
by I. R. for N. L. and are to be sold at his shoppe vnder
Saint Dunstons Church in Fleet-street. 1604.

"N. L." is Nicholas Ling and "I. R." is James
Roberts. On July 26, 1602, Roberts had entered in
the Stationers' Register "A Booke called the Revenge
of Hamlett Prince of Denmarke as yt was latelie
Acted by the Lord Chamberlayne his servantes."
Roberts' name is not mentioned on the title page of
the first quarto, and the book, which seems to have
been Ling's property, was assigned from his estate in

1607 to John Smethwick. Either Ling forestalled Roberts in the issue of the first quarto and they subsequently made terms with each other in the issue of the second, Ling as printer and Roberts as publisher, or they were partners in both enterprises. Roberts had a good position in the trade and was to all appearances a friend of the players, since he enjoyed the privilege of printing the players' bills. He did not, however, print Q_1. Less is known about Ling, whose record is not good. Q_1 has all the marks of being "stolne and surreptitious," but Q_1 is merely a version of Shakespeare's first *Hamlet* degenerated by actors on the provincial stage, and Q_2 is a revision of that original in better form.

There was never a second issue of Q_1. Additional copies of Q_2 were issued with a change of date to 1605. John Smethwick printed a third edition (Q_4) in 1611, and later an undated quarto series of no less than four others was issued before the end of the seventeenth century.

The Folio prints what is regarded as a distinct text from the quartos. Though it resembles the second quarto, it is evidently a playhouse copy possibly abridged for acting. At any rate, it contains eighty-five lines not in Q_2 and omits 218 lines which are in Q_2.

VERSIONS

Before considering the question of date it is necessary to consider the nature of Q_1. The earliest known copy of it was discovered by Sir Henry Bunbury in 1823. It was first regarded as an imperfect reproduction of an earlier version of the text as we have it in Q_2 and the First Folio. Later, following Collier in 1843, it came to be regarded as a badly botched version of the true text taken down in the theater by a shorthand writer and made ready for the press by that person or by an indifferent poet employed to revise it. This is still the view of notable scholars.[1]

Of recent years, however, the first view has been more and more positively stated and argued for.[2] J. M. Robertson believed that certain passages in Q_1 are actually borrowed from an old play of Hamlet by Thomas Kyd. Dover Wilson, anticipated in part by Henry David Gray, has put forward the hypothesis that Shakespeare made a revision of Kyd's play in

1591-1592, with a brief transcript for the road in 1593. He has also offered the suggestion, now widely accepted, that in the piracy of Q_1 we have to do not with a stenographer-pirate, but with an actor-pirate, some dishonest member of Shakespeare's company who had been earlier the purveyor to the printer of other bad quartos.

Wilson thinks he has discovered traces of the pirate in the fact that the roles which he played are used as the starting point for the reconstruction of the play, his parts being more correctly given and the scenes in which he appeared being best remembered. According to this theory, the pirate played in succession the parts of Marcellus, Voltimand, a Player, second Gravedigger, Churlish Priest, and English Ambassador.

F. G. Hubbard and E. E. Stoll give reasons to show that Shakespeare wrote the tragedy twice and that Q_1 is, therefore, a corruption of his first draft. G. I. Duthie[3] believes that all of the parts of Q_1 not corresponding to Q_2 have been made up by actors. These reasons are independent of the theory of how Q_1 came into existence. Q_1 is a stage version and shows the marks of the prompter's hand. It may be that it was made up by oral cooperation among the actors, and the better memory of certain actors may account for the superiority of the text of certain roles to others.

Hubbard investigated the readings of the text of Q_1 in their relation to the readings of other quartos and the folios and showed the independence and authenticity of that version. Stoll finds positive evidence of a plot revision of the original of Q_1 in the direction of compactness and increase of dramatic interest; in the shifting of the "Get thee to a nunnery" scene, together with the "To be or not to be" soliloquy which precedes it (III, i, 56-196), from the second act to the third; in the absence from Q_1 of Hamlet's soliloquy (IV, iv, 32-66), "How all occasions do inform against me," and of the passage (III, iv, 202-210) about "hoisting the enginer with his own petar"; in the changes in the interview with his mother by which she is less involved in Hamlet's plot for revenge; and in other matters.

DATE

Hamlet is not mentioned by Meres in 1598. Since it was always a famous play, it probably would have been mentioned if Shakespeare had written his version by that time. In both quartos the play contains an allusion to the child actors and the War of the Theaters (II, ii, 340-379). This allusion could not have been made before 1598 when the Children of the Chapel Royal began to act at Blackfriars and probably points to 1599-1601, when they had become serious rivals of the adult companies and forced these companies to leave London for the provinces.

[1]W. Creizenach, "Hamletfragen," *Shakespeare Jahrbuch*, XLII, 76-85; B. A. P. Van Dam, *The Text of Shakespeare's "Hamlet"* (1924).

[2]Adams, *Life of William Shakespeare*, pp. 520-521; F. S. Boas, *The Works of Thomas Kyd* (1901), Introduction; F. G. Hubbard, *The First Quarto Edition of Shakespeare's "Hamlet"* (Madison, 1920), and "The Readings of the First Quarto of *Hamlet*," *PMLA*, XXXVIII, 792-822; Pollard, *Shakespeare's Fight with the Pirates* (Cambridge, 1920); J. M. Robertson, *The Problem of "Hamlet"* (1919); E. E. Stoll, *Hamlet: An Historical and Comparative Study* (Minneapolis, 1919); J. D. Wilson, "The Copy for *Hamlet*, 1603," and "The *Hamlet* Transcript, 1593," *The Library*, July and October, 1918; H. D. Gray, "The First Quarto of *Hamlet*," *Modern Language Review*, X, 171-180, "Thomas Kyd and the First Quarto of *Hamlet*," *PMLA*, XLII, 721-735, and "Reconstruction of a Lost Play," *Philological Quarterly*, VII, 254-274. See *The Tragedy of Hamlet*. A critical edition of the Second Quarto, 1604, by Thomas Marc Parrott and Hardin Craig (Princeton, 1938); edition of *Hamlet* by J. D. Wilson (1936); Paul S. Conklin, *A History of Hamlet Criticism* (1947).

[3]*The "Bad" Quarto of Hamlet* (Cambridge, 1941), *passim*.

There is a reference to *Hamlet* in Harvey's *Marginalia* which was made possibly between 1598 and 1601[4]; and we have the entry of the play in the Stationers' Register in 1602. The original of Q_1 may, therefore, date from 1598-1601, Q_2 from 1603-1604, unless, of course, Q_1 is to be regarded merely as a pirated version of Q_2.

It is also important to note that there was a revival of the "tragedy of blood" during these years. Henslowe's company revived *The Spanish Tragedy* in 1597. In 1601 and 1602 Henslowe paid Ben Jonson for "adicyons" to that play. Marston wrote revenge plays for the Children of Paul's, Chettle and others for Henslowe's company, and it is natural enough to suppose that Shakespeare may have been called upon to recast the famous old revenge play of Hamlet for his company.

THE OLD *Hamlet*

There are unmistakable traces of an early revenge play called *Hamlet*. It is alluded to by Thomas Nashe in his *Epistle to the Gentlemen Students of Both Universities*, prefixed to Greene's *Menaphon* (1589). It was acted at Newington Butts on June 9, 1594, while the Lord Admiral's and the Lord Chamberlain's companies were acting there under Henslowe's management. In Thomas Lodge's pamphlet *Wits miserie, and the Worlds madnesse, discovering the Devils incarnate of this Age* (1596), one of his evil spirits, "Hate-Virtue, a foul lubber," "looks as pale as the visard of the Ghost, which cried so miserably at the theator, *Hamlet reuenge*." "My name's Hamlet reuenge," exclaims a character in Dekker's *Satiromastix* (1602), as if the phrase was a sort of catch word.

The passage in Nashe's *Epistle* has been made to yield a suggestion as to the authorship of the old play. Nashe, like Greene in *A Groatsworth of Wit*, is criticizing the actors and certain dramatists who write for them:

. . . I'le turne backe to my first text of Studies of delight, and talke a little in friendship with a few of our triuiall translators. It is a common practise now a dayes amongst a sort of shifting companions, that runne through euery Art and thriue by none, to leaue the trade of *Nouerint*, whereto they were borne, and busie themselues with the endeuours of Art, that could scarcely Latinize their neck verse if they should haue neede; yet English *Seneca* read by Candlelight yeelds many good sentences, as *Blood is a begger*, and so forth; and if you intreate him faire in a frostie morning, hee will affoord you whole Hamlets, I should say handfuls of Tragicall speeches. But O griefe! *Tempus edax rerum*, whats that will last alwayes? The Sea exhaled by droppes will in continuance bee drie, and *Seneca*, let blood line by line and page by page, at length must needes die to our Stage; which makes his famished followers to imitate the Kidde in *Æsop*, who, enamoured with the Foxes newfangles,

forsooke all hopes of life to leape into a newe occupation; and these men, renouncing all possibilities of credite or estimation, to intermeddle with Italian Translations . . .

Many of the allusions in this peculiar passage have never been explained. However, it does point to a play of *Hamlet* in the Senecan style, done by a person who was born to the trade of noverint, or scrivener,

who occupied himself in translations, was evidently not a university man, but ground out his work like a hack writer by candlelight. Thomas Kyd fulfills these conditions. He was the most Senecan of Elizabethan dramatists; he translated at least two works from the French; his father was a scrivener; and his name seems to be glanced at in the allusion to the "Kidde in Æsop." Moreover, his only absolutely authentic original play, *The Spanish Tragedy*, bears in its theme and its devices the very closest resemblance to *Hamlet*. Malone denied the authorship of the old *Hamlet* to Shakespeare, and Fleay attributed the play to Kyd. Since that time many critics have written on the question, and Fleay's attribution, particularly in the light of this obscure passage, is pretty generally accepted.[5]

Fratricide Punished

Among the many English plays which entered Germany in the period from 1590 to 1600 is one called *Hamlet*. It was acted at Dresden by a company of English actors under John Green in 1626. What seems to be a late modernized version of it (1710) is preserved under the name *Der bestrafte Brudermord (Fratricide Punished)*. It tells the Hamlet story pretty much as we know it, but with certain characteristics which connect it with the pre-Shakespearean period, such as an explanatory prologue, spoken by Alecto, in the manner of Seneca and of Kyd in *The Spanish Tragedy*. The character Polonius is called Corambis in Q_1, and in *Fratricide Punished* the court chamberlain is called Corambus. So far as the story can be made

[4]See Leo Kirschbaum, "The Date of Shakespeare's *Hamlet*," *Studies in Philology*, XXXIV (1937), 168-175.

[5]Fleay, *Biographical Chronicle of the English Drama*, s. v. Kyd, ii, 26; G. Sarrazin, *Thomas Kyd und Sein Kreis* (Berlin, 1892); Boas, *Works of Thomas Kyd*; Robertson, *The Problem of "Hamlet"*; Chambers, *The Elizabethan Stage*, III, 397, IV, 234. But see McKerrow, *The Works of Thomas Nashe* (1904-1910), III, 311, IV, 444, and Chambers, *William Shakespeare*, I, 422-423.

out in its degenerated form, it is closer to the first quarto than to the second and is all the way through more primitive in its appeal than either. We know from other sources that the old play had in it a ghost demanding revenge, a scene on a "frostie morning" like that on the battlements of Elsinore, and that it was Senecan. In the German play, as also probably in the old *Hamlet*, there are the secret murder and adultery revealed to the son by the return of the wronged man's ghost; the feigned madness, treated comically; delay and self-reproach; attempts by the court chamberlain, the lady with eavesdroppers, and the hero's mother to discover the cause of Hamlet's madness; the play-within-the-play; the sparing of the king while at prayer in order to slay his soul as well as his body; the unintentional killing of the court chamberlain; the voyage to England; Ophelia's madness; the fencing bout with poisoned foils and the poisoned drink; and the final combination of vengeance and death in the last scene.

SAXO AND BELLEFOREST

There was a Hamlet-saga alluded to in Scandinavian literature at least as early as the tenth century. Indeed, there is a great body of critical writing devoted to Hamlet as the story appeared long before the sixteenth century.[6]

Saxo Grammaticus wrote between 1180 and 1208 his *Historia Danica*. In this, like Geoffrey of Monmouth in England, he gathered up legends and traditions and made them into a connected history. In his third and fourth books he gives us the history of Amlethus, or Hamlet. Horwendil, the father of Hamlet, is murdered by his brother Fengon, who marries Horwendil's wife Gerutha. Hamlet pretends to be foolish in order to secure revenge, but his folly is the mask of an almost superhuman cunning. A woman is put in his way in order that he may betray his true state of mind through love of her, but he is too shrewd to give himself away. He has an interview with his mother, also planned to make him betray himself, and during the interview kills an eavesdropper who is covered with a quilt. Fengon sends Hamlet to England bearing a letter to the English king by the terms of which Hamlet is to be put to death. He has with him two companions. He alters the letter, inserting their names, and they suffer death in his stead. He returns to Denmark, sets fire to the hall, slays his uncle and all his courtiers, makes a speech to the people, and ascends the throne. The story has a long sequel, which does not appear in the play. Hamlet returns to England, marries two differ-

ent wives, and by the second of them is betrayed to death. There is no Laertes, no Fortinbras, no duel, no ghost, no play-within-a-play. Thomas Kyd could have invented these things, for they were all well within the range of his technique. Hamlet is a heroic figure in Saxo, who saw in him a marvelous combination of wit and bravery.

Saxo's story was freely translated into French by Belleforest and included in his *Histoires Tragiques* (1570), a book which Shakespeare must have known. A translation of Belleforest's story was issued in 1608 by Thomas Pavier with the title *The Hystorie of Hamblet*, but that publication draws certain details from the play and seems rather to have been occasioned by its popularity than to have been its source.

DIFFICULTIES OF THE STORY

We have seen that the old play had a reputation for noise and fury and that the story was crude and savage. Of it Shakespeare has made the subtlest and most refined of all his works. The bloodshed is still there. Fortinbras exclaims about the slaughter at the end,

> Such a sight as this
> Becomes the field, but here shows much amiss.

Hamlet's deeds are full of the old ferocity, although there is always a slight shock connected with having it pointed out. He treats Ophelia as if she were the decoy for an ambush of murderous villains, although to us she is palpably innocent. He refrains from killing the king at his prayers, because he is not content with killing his body, but wishes that:

> his soul may be as damn'd and black
> As hell, whereto it goes.

He stabs Polonius with the frank but rather cruel explanation,

> Thou wretched, rash, intruding fool, farewell!
> I took thee for thy better.

He sends Rosencrantz and Guildenstern to their death in England with no compunction; and he shows a lion's courage in the last act in carrying through his revenge and as he dies, in wresting the cup from the hand of Horatio:

> Give me the cup; let go; by heaven, I'll have 't.

But how different is the total impression made by this character and this play from that of the source! This difference of impression constitutes the problem of *Hamlet* criticism. It was characteristic of Shakespeare that, when he wrote a revenge play, he should write it in an original way; for, although he followed the fashion of his time, he did not follow it in the way of common men.

---

[6]Gollancz, *The Sources of "Hamlet"* (1926); Josef Schick, *Corpus Hamleticum* (Berlin, 1912, 1934); Kemp Malone, *The Literary History of "Hamlet"* (Heidelberg, 1923); Oliver Elton, "On Saxo's Hamlet," Appendix to *The First Nine Books of the Danish History of Saxo Grammaticus* (1894).

There were difficulties in the story when he undertook it, which the refinements he wrought in it rather increased than lessened. To have had the king surrounded by an armed guard, so that access to his person was impossible without finesse, would have made Hamlet's pretense of insanity plausible. It was so in Saxo and Belleforest, and we may believe also in some measure in Kyd, since guards are mentioned in *Fratricide Punished*, but apparently it did not suit Shakespeare to write a tragedy in which the tragic obstacles were physical. Thus Hamlet's delay is unmotivated, since when the ghost appears and its mandate is accepted, there is no obstacle to serve as an excuse for delay except only that Hamlet shall become convinced of his mandate for revenge. The great chain of being would place upon him, as God's vicegerent, the duty of vengeance—the punishment of the murderer and the dethronement of the usurper. This would constitute his responsibility. The fact that Hamlet's is a righteous vengeance is often forgotten; as also is true with reference to revenge tragedy in general. Revenge might be a sacred duty, indeed it was usually so, in part at least; or it might be a sinful indulgence. When Hamlet has become convinced of his duty by means of the play within the play, he himself is subject to attack, and his opportunity for an easy vengeance is lost.

ROMANTIC INTERPRETATION

No critic seems to have noticed that there was anything wrong with Hamlet's will, his power to act, until the period of the Romantic movement. Then, by reconceiving the situation and by making the most of his self-reproaches, the critics gave us a new Hamlet. On this assumption critics have written eloquently and enriched the world with new thoughts on the nature of voluntary action. They have found motives for Hamlet's inaction and for his actions which Shakespeare never dreamed of, made of Hamlet a type of whole races, and have found a Hamlet in every human soul.

There is no objection to this if one knows what one is doing; but no one can surpass the original consistency of Shakespeare's Danish prince. Despite this, there are great modern names on the side of romantic interpretation. Goethe found the play representative of "the effects of a great action laid upon a soul unfit for the performance of it—an oak tree planted in a costly jar." Coleridge saw in Hamlet "an overbalance in the contemplative faculty, one who vacillates from sensibility, and procrastinates from thought, and loses the power of action in the energy of resolve."

Some critics now offer more objective criticisms. In general, however, the world has taken Hamlet to its heart and made of him its representative both in vacillation and in ultimate nobility. Nor would one say that they are wrong; but it is they and

not Shakespeare who have conceived the tale in this romantic way.

HAMLET'S PROBLEM

No theoretical solution of Hamlet's mystery so far proposed is entirely satisfactory. We may perhaps get closer to the truth by asking why *Hamlet* has such an irresistible general appeal. Hamlet cannot be explained away, and the reason seems to be that he is perhaps the most representative character in all dramatic literature. One might well ask whether critics have not overstressed the individual psychology of Hamlet and given to his self-reproaches too intimate and personal a bearing.

Hamlet's situation as a grief-stricken hero caught in the toils of innumerable difficulties and dangers is typical. Cardan and other moralists of the Renaissance say that all men are in like case with Hamlet and that the remedy lies in the curing of the mind so that it will rise above the trials of life. They reproach man for allowing himself to become "lapsed in time and passion" so that he habitually lets go "the important acting of a dread command," and suffers his mind to become tainted with worldly considerations and cowardice. These are Hamlet's reproaches against himself and are to be interpreted as exemplifying the common fate of all men. Hamlet is not weak as an individual; he is merely the representative of weak humanity. He rebukes himself, not for his own faults, but for those of all mankind. Men look at Hamlet and see a picture of themselves, for deep in the heart of man is a consciousness of the frailty of the clay of which he is made.

The significance of Hamlet's struggle is thus profound. Its background is human calamity, which Hamlet conquers by overcoming his human cowardice and his human fears. He reaches a point where he is able to defy the augury of death and see that "readiness is all." To appreciate the truth of the picture one must ask, even in this age, who are the absolutely brave? Who are those that can call themselves completely happy and completely strong? The idea that Hamlet was struggling through great adversity to attain fortitude puts his famous praise of Horatio (III, ii, 59-79) in exactly the right perspective. Hamlet meant, not to confess his own proper weakness when he so delineated Horatio, but to express the ideal of his own character and the goal of his own striving.[7]

STAGE HISTORY

The anonymous *A Funeral Elegy on the Death of the famous Actor, Richard Burbage* connects him with the parts of Hamlet, Othello, and King Lear. This is

[7]See the editor's "Hamlet's Book," *Huntington Library Bulletin*, No. 6 (November 1934), 17-37; also John E. Hankins, *The Character of Hamlet and Other Essays*, University of North Carolina Press, 1941.

borne out by other traditions, and there is no doubt that Burbage was the first great Hamlet. Nicholas Rowe, Shakespeare's first editor, states (1709) that "the top of his [Shakespeare's] performance was the Ghost in his own *Hamlet*."

After the Restoration *Hamlet* fell into excellent hands. Thomas Betterton appeared in the play in D'Avenant's (the duke of York's) company at the new theater in Lincoln's Inn Fields on August 24, 1661, and thenceforward for many years helped, by his greatness as an actor, to secure the vogue of *Hamlet* through the succeeding centuries and to save the play from mutilation. "I never," says Colley Cibber, "heard a line in tragedy come from Betterton, wherein my judgment, my ear, and my imagination were not fully satisfied." It is said that Betterton was instructed in playing the part of Hamlet by D'Avenant, who remembered the playing of Joseph Taylor, an actor in Shakespeare's company before the closing of the theaters in 1642. There is thus a continuity in theatrical tradition in the acting of *Hamlet*.

David Garrick was famous as Hamlet, though his version was rather badly garbled in the fifth act. Readers of *Tom Jones* will remember the visit of Jones and Partridge to the playhouse (Bk. XVI, ch. v) and Partridge's contempt for the naturalness of Garrick: "I am sure, if I had seen a ghost, I should have looked in the very same manner and done just as he did." John Philip Kemble continued the Garrick tradition into the nineteenth century, when there occurred a famous rivalry between him and his younger contemporary Edmund Kean. Kemble acted the part with evenness of tone and dignity of bearing and Kean anticipated the passionate eccentricity with which we are familiar on the modern stage. Macready and Phelps, both well known in the part of Hamlet, continued the older tradition, whereas Booth and Irving followed the methods of Kean. Forbes-Robertson's playing of *Hamlet* was a combination of the two styles. It had beauty and dignity and, at the same time, naturalness and wit. Kean, Irving (with Ellen Terry as Ophelia), and Forbes-Robertson all made tours to America, and the great American Hamlet, Edwin Booth, played successfully in Europe.

After about 1900 E. H. Sothern (later with Julia Marlowe as Ophelia) played *Hamlet* frequently in America, as did Robert Mantell.

The playing of *Hamlet* with the actors wearing modern clothes was an interesting novelty of the season 1925-1926 in London and New York, there being almost general testimony to the effect that the play lost little or none of its charm when so presented.

In the most recent years John Gielgud and Maurice Evans have both won distinction in the character of Hamlet. The latter played in an uncut version.

Hamlet stays on the stage. It is possibly, in its own appeal, the greatest of stage plays, and to act the part of Hamlet successfully has been, and is, the goal of tragic actors.

Hamlet, Prince of Denmark

DRAMATIS PERSONAE

CLAUDIUS, king of Denmark.
HAMLET, son to the late, and nephew to the present king.
POLONIUS, lord chamberlain.
HORATIO, friend to Hamlet.
LAERTES, son to Polonius.
VOLTIMAND,
CORNELIUS,
ROSENCRANTZ, } courtiers.
GUILDENSTERN,
OSRIC,
A Gentleman,
A Priest.
MARCELLUS, } officers.
BERNARDO,
FRANCISCO, a soldier.
REYNALDO, servant to Polonius.
Players.
Two Clowns, grave-diggers.
FORTINBRAS, prince of Norway.
A Captain.
English Ambassadors.

GERTRUDE, queen of Denmark, and mother to Hamlet.
OPHELIA, daughter to Polonius.

Lords, Ladies, Officers, Soldiers, Sailors, Messengers, and other Attendants.
Ghost of Hamlet's Father.

SCENE: *Denmark.*

Hamlet
ACT I : SC 1

903

ACT I.

SCENE I. *Elsinore. A platform before the castle.*

FRANCISCO *at his post. Enter to him* BERNARDO.

Ber. Who's there?
Fran. Nay, answer me: stand, and unfold yourself.
Ber. Long live the king!
Fran. Bernardo?
Ber. He.
Fran. You come most carefully upon your hour.
Ber. 'Tis now struck twelve; get thee to bed, Francisco.
Fran. For this relief much thanks: 'tis bitter cold, And I am sick at heart.
Ber. Have you had quiet guard?
Fran.   Not a mouse stirring.   10
Ber. Well, good night.
If you do meet Horatio and Marcellus,
The rivals of my watch, bid them make haste.
Fran. I think I hear them. Stand, ho! Who's there?

Enter HORATIO *and* MARCELLUS.

Hor. Friends to this ground.

Mar. And liegemen to the Dane.
Fran. Give you good night.
Mar. O, farewell, honest soldier:
Who hath relieved you?
Fran. Bernardo has my place.
Give you good night. [*Exit.*
Mar. Holla! Bernardo!
Ber. Say,
What, is Horatio there?
Hor. A piece of him. 19
Ber. Welcome, Horatio: welcome, good Marcellus.
Mar. What, has this thing appear'd again to-night?
Ber. I have seen nothing.
Mar. Horatio says 'tis but our fantasy,
And will not let belief take hold of him
Touching this dreaded sight, twice seen of us:
Therefore I have entreated him along
With us to watch the minutes of this night;
That if again this apparition come,
He may approve our eyes and speak to it.
Hor. Tush, tush, 'twill not appear.
Ber. Sit down awhile; 30
And let us once again assail your ears,
That are so fortified against our story
What we have two nights seen.
Hor. Well, sit we down,
And let us hear Bernardo speak of this.
Ber. Last night of all,
When yond same star that 's westward from the pole
Had made his course to illume that part of heaven
Where now it burns, Marcellus and myself,
The bell then beating one,—

Enter Ghost.

Mar. Peace, break thee off; look, where it comes
again! 40
Ber. In the same figure, like the king that 's dead.
Mar. Thou art a scholar; speak to it, Horatio.
Ber. Looks it not like the king? mark it, Horatio.
Hor. Most like: it harrows me with fear and wonder.
Ber. It would be spoke to.
Mar. Question it, Horatio.
Hor. What art thou that usurp'st this time of night,
Together with that fair and warlike form
In which the majesty of buried Denmark
Did sometimes march? by heaven I charge thee,
speak!
Mar. It is offended.
Ber. See, it stalks away! 50
Hor. Stay! speak, speak! I charge thee, speak!
[*Exit Ghost.*
Mar. 'Tis gone, and will not answer.
Ber. How now, Horatio! you tremble and look pale:
Is not this something more than fantasy?
What think you on 't?
Hor. Before my God, I might not this believe

Without the sensible and true avouch
Of mine own eyes.
Mar. Is it not like the king?
Hor. As thou art to thyself:
Such was the very armour he had on 60
When he the ambitious Norway combated;
So frown'd he once, when, in an angry parle,
He smote the sledded Polacks on the ice.
'Tis strange.
Mar. Thus twice before, and jump at this dead
hour,
With martial stalk hath he gone by our watch.
Hor. In what particular thought to work I know not;
But in the gross and scope of my opinion,
This bodes some strange eruption to our state.
Mar. Good now, sit down, and tell me, he that
knows, 70
Why this same strict and most observant watch
So nightly toils the subject of the land,
And why such daily cast of brazen cannon,
And foreign mart for implements of war;
Why such impress of shipwrights, whose sore task
Does not divide the Sunday from the week;
What might be toward, that this sweaty haste
Doth make the night joint-labourer with the day:
Who is 't that can inform me?
Hor. That can I;
At least, the whisper goes so. Our last king, 80
Whose image even but now appear'd to us,
Was, as you know, by Fortinbras of Norway,
Thereto prick'd on by a most emulate pride,
Dared to the combat; in which our valiant Hamlet—
For so this side of our known world esteem'd him—
Did slay this Fortinbras; who, by a seal'd compact,
Well ratified by law and heraldry,
Did forfeit, with his life, all those his lands
Which he stood seized of, to the conqueror:
Against the which, a moiety competent 90
Was gaged by our king; which had return'd
To the inheritance of Fortinbras,
Had he been vanquisher; as, by the same covenant,
And carriage of the article design'd,
His fell to Hamlet. Now, sir, young Fortinbras,
Of unimproved mettle hot and full,
Hath in the skirts of Norway here and there
Shark'd up a list of lawless resolutes,
For food and diet, to some enterprise
That hath a stomach in 't; which is no other— 100
As it doth well appear unto our state—
But to recover of us, by strong hand
And terms compulsatory, those foresaid lands
So by his father lost: and this, I take it,
Is the main motive of our preparations,
The source of this our watch and the chief head
Of this post-haste and romage in the land.
Ber. I think it be no other but e'en so:

ACT I. SCENE I. *Stage Direction:* **platform,** a level space on the battlements of the royal castle at Elsinore, a Danish seaport; now Helsingör. 2. **me.** This is emphatic, since Francisco is the sentry. 3. **Long live the king,** evidently the password, though Horatio and Marcellus use a different one in line 15. 16. **Give you,** God give you. 19. **piece of him,** a casual answer implying flippancy. 29. **approve,** corroborate, justify. 36. **yond same star,** probably part of the constellation of the Great Bear, since this was used to tell time by. 42. **scholar.** Exorcisms were performed in Latin, which Horatio an educated man would be able to speak. 44. **harrows,** lacerates the feelings. 45. **It . . . to.** A ghost could not speak until spoken to. **Question,** speak to. 63. **smote,** defeated. **sledded Polacks,** Polanders using sledges. The earl of Rochester (1761) explained *sleaded* (Q₁F) or

sledded (Q₂) as "loaded with lead" and *pollax* (Q₁,₂F) as "pole-ax," the idea being that the elder Hamlet dashed his pole-ax against the ice while engaged in a parley; this is upheld by Schmidt and others. 68. **gross and scope,** general drift. 70. **Good now,** an expression denoting entreaty or expostulation. 72. **toils,** causes or makes to toil. **subject,** people, subjects. 73. **cast,** casting, founding. 74. **mart,** buying and selling, traffic. 75. **impress,** impressment. 83. **prick'd on,** incited. **emulate,** ambitious. 87. **law and heraldry,** civil law and also the courts of chivalry. 89. **seized,** possessed. 90. **moiety competent,** adequate or sufficient portion. 93. **covenant.** The Q₂ reading, *comart,* has been interpreted by some editors as meaning "joint bargain." 94. **carriage,** import, bearing. 96. **unimproved,** not turned to account. **hot and full,** full of fight. 98. **Shark'd up,** got together in haphazard fashion.

Well may it sort that this portentous figure
Comes armed through our watch; so like the king 110
That was and is the question of these wars.
    Hor. A mote it is to trouble the mind's eye.
In the most high and palmy state of Rome,
A little ere the mightiest Julius fell,
The graves stood tenantless and the sheeted dead
Did squeak and gibber in the Roman streets:
†As stars with trains of fire and dews of blood,
Disasters in the sun; and the moist star
Upon whose influence Neptune's empire stands
Was sick almost to doomsday with eclipse: 120
And even the like precurse of fear'd events,
As harbingers preceding still the fates
And prologue to the omen coming on,
Have heaven and earth together demonstrated
Unto our climatures and countrymen.—
But soft, behold! lo, where it comes again!

            Re-enter Ghost.

I'll cross it, though it blast me. Stay, illusion!
If thou hast any sound, or use of voice,
Speak to me:
If there be any good thing to be done, 130
That may to thee do ease and grace to me,
Speak to me: *[Cock crows.*
If thou art privy to thy country's fate,
Which, happily, foreknowing may avoid,
O, speak!
Or if thou hast uphoarded in thy life
Extorted treasure in the womb of earth,
For which, they say, you spirits oft walk in death,
Speak of it: stay, and speak! Stop it, Marcellus.
    Mar. Shall I strike at it with my partisan? 140
    Hor. Do, if it will not stand.
    Ber.   'Tis here!
    Hor.   'Tis here!
    Mar. 'Tis gone!   *[Exit Ghost.*
We do it wrong, being so majestical,
To offer it the show of violence;
For it is, as the air, invulnerable,
And our vain blows malicious mockery.
    Ber. It was about to speak, when the cock crew.
    Hor. And then it started like a guilty thing
Upon a fearful summons. I have heard,
The cock, that is the trumpet to the morn, 150
Doth with his lofty and shrill-sounding throat
Awake the god of day; and, at his warning,
Whether in sea or fire, in earth or air,
The extravagant and erring spirit hies
To his confine: and of the truth herein
This present object made probation.
    Mar. It faded on the crowing of the cock.
Some say that ever 'gainst that season comes
Wherein our Saviour's birth is celebrated,
The bird of dawning singeth all night long: 160

And then, they say, no spirit dare stir abroad;
The nights are wholesome; then no planets strike,
No fairy takes, nor witch hath power to charm,
So hallow'd and so gracious is the time.
    Hor. So have I heard and do in part believe it.
But, look, the morn, in russet mantle clad,
Walks o'er the dew of yon high eastward hill:
Break we our watch up; and by my advice,
Let us impart what we have seen to-night
Unto young Hamlet; for, upon my life, 170
This spirit, dumb to us, will speak to him.
Do you consent we shall acquaint him with it,
As needful in our loves, fitting our duty?
    Mar. Let's do 't, I pray; and I this morning know
Where we shall find him most conveniently.   *[Exeunt.*

        SCENE II. *A room of state in the castle.*

Enter the KING, QUEEN, HAMLET, POLONIUS,
   LAERTES, VOLTIMAND, CORNELIUS, Lords, *and*
   Attendants.

    King. Though yet of Hamlet our dear brother's
        death
The memory be green, and that it us befitted
To bear our hearts in grief and our whole kingdom
To be contracted in one brow of woe,
Yet so far hath discretion fought with nature
That we with wisest sorrow think on him,
Together with remembrance of ourselves.
Therefore our sometime sister, now our queen,
The imperial jointress to this warlike state,
Have we, as 'twere with a defeated joy,— 10
With an auspicious and a dropping eye,
With mirth in funeral and with dirge in marriage,
In equal scale weighing delight and dole,—
Taken to wife: nor have we herein barr'd
Your better wisdoms, which have freely gone
With this affair along. For all, our thanks.
Now follows, that you know, young Fortinbras,
Holding a weak supposal of our worth,
Or thinking by our late dear brother's death
Our state to be disjoint and out of frame, 20
Colleagued with the dream of his advantage,
He hath not fail'd to pester us with message,
Importing the surrender of those lands
Lost by his father, with all bonds of law,
To our most valiant brother. So much for him.
Now for ourself and for this time of meeting:
Thus much the business is: we have here writ
To Norway, uncle of young Fortinbras,—
Who, impotent and bed-rid, scarcely hears
Of this his nephew's purpose,—to suppress 30
His further gait herein; in that the levies,
The lists and full proportions, are all made

---

resolutes, desperadoes.   99. **food and diet,** no pay but their keep.   107.
romage, bustle, commotion.   113. **palmy state,** triumphant sovereignty.
117. **As . . . blood.** This abrupt transition suggests that matter is
possibly omitted between lines 116 and 117.   **stars . . . fire,** i.e., comets.
118. **Disasters,** unfavorable aspects.   **moist star,** the moon, governing
tides.   119. **Neptune's empire,** the sea.   120. **sick . . . doomsday.**
See Matthew 24:20; Revelation 6:12.   121. **precurse,** heralding.
fear'd, Collier: *feard;* Q_2: *feare;* Globe: *fierce,* after Q_4: *fearce.*   127.
cross, meet, face; thus bringing down the evil influence on the person
who crosses it.   133-139. **If . . . it.** Horatio recites the traditional
reasons why ghosts might walk.   140. **partisan,** long-handled spear
with a blade having lateral projections.   147. **cock crew.** According
to traditional ghost lore, spirits returned to their confines at cockcrow

154. **extravagant and erring,** wandering. Both words mean the same
thing.   155. **confine,** place of confinement.   156. **probation,** proof,
trial.   162. **planets strike.** It was thought that planets were malignant
and might strike travelers by night.   164. **gracious,** full of goodness.
    SCENE II. *Stage Direction:* **Polonius:** Q_2 *counsaile: as Polonius,* which
may be for *counsailor Polonius.* Chambers suggests a printer's endeavor
to make sense of *Corambis* (name of Polonius in Q_1), left in the manuscript along with the new name.   9. **jointress,** dowager, widow who
holds an estate settled on her to be enjoyed after her husband's death.
17. **that,** that which.   18. **weak supposal,** low estimate.   20. **disjoint,**
distracted, out of joint.   **frame,** order.   21. **Colleagued,** added to.
dream . . . advantage, visionary hope of success.   23. **Importing,**
purporting, pertaining to.   31. **gait,** proceeding.

Out of his subject: and we here dispatch
You, good Cornelius, and you, Voltimand,
For bearers of this greeting to old Norway;
Giving to you no further personal power
To business with the king, more than the scope
Of these delated articles allow.
Farewell, and let your haste commend your duty.

Cor.
Vol. } In that and all things will we show our duty. 40

King. We doubt it nothing: heartily farewell.
                    [*Exeunt Voltimand and Cornelius.*
And now, Laertes, what's the news with you?
You told us of some suit; what is 't, Laertes?
You cannot speak of reason to the Dane,
And lose your voice: what wouldst thou beg, Laertes,
That shall not be my offer, not thy asking?
The head is not more native to the heart,
The hand more instrumental to the mouth,
Than is the throne of Denmark to thy father.
What wouldst thou have, Laertes?

Laer.   My dread lord, 50
Your leave and favour to return to France;
From whence though willingly I came to Denmark,
To show my duty in your coronation,
Yet now, I must confess, that duty done,
My thoughts and wishes bend again toward France
And bow them to your gracious leave and pardon.

King. Have you your father's leave? What says
    Polonius?

Pol. He hath, my lord, wrung from me my slow
    leave
By laboursome petition, and at last
Upon his will I seal'd my hard consent: 60
I do beseech you, give him leave to go.

King. Take thy fair hour, Laertes; time be thine,
And thy best graces spend it at thy will!
But now, my cousin Hamlet, and my son,—

Ham. [*Aside*] A little more than kin, and less than
    kind.

King. How is it that the clouds still hang on you?

Ham. Not so, my lord; I am too much i' the sun.

Queen. Good Hamlet, cast thy nighted colour off,
And let thine eye look like a friend on Denmark.
Do not for ever with thy vailed lids 70
Seek for thy noble father in the dust:
Thou know'st 'tis common; all that lives must die,
Passing through nature to eternity.

Ham. Ay, madam, it is common.

Queen.   If it be,
Why seems it so particular with thee?

Ham. Seems, madam! nay, it is; I know not 'seems.'
'Tis not alone my inky cloak, good mother,
Nor customary suits of solemn black,
Nor windy suspiration of forced breath,
No, nor the fruitful river in the eye, 80
Nor the dejected 'haviour of the visage,
Together with all forms, moods, shapes of grief,
That can denote me truly: these indeed seem,

For they are actions that a man might play:
But I have that within which passeth show;
These but the trappings and the suits of woe.

King. 'Tis sweet and commendable in your nature,
    Hamlet,
To give these mourning duties to your father:
But, you must know, your father lost a father;
That father lost, lost his, and the survivor bound 90
In filial obligation for some term
To do obsequious sorrow: but to persever
In obstinate condolement is a course
Of impious stubbornness; 'tis unmanly grief;
It shows a will most incorrect to heaven,
A heart unfortified, a mind impatient,
An understanding simple and unschool'd:
For what we know must be and is as common
As any the most vulgar thing to sense,
Why should we in our peevish opposition 100
Take it to heart? Fie! 'tis a fault to heaven,
A fault against the dead, a fault to nature,
To reason most absurd; whose common theme
Is death of fathers, and who still hath cried,
From the first corse till he that died to-day,
'This must be so.' We pray you, throw to earth
This unprevailing woe, and think of us
As of a father: for let the world take note,
You are the most immediate to our throne;
And with no less nobility of love 110
Than that which dearest father bears his son,
Do I impart toward you. For your intent
In going back to school in Wittenberg,
It is most retrograde to our desire:
And we beseech you, bend you to remain
Here, in the cheer and comfort of our eye,
Our chiefest courtier, cousin, and our son.

Queen. Let not thy mother lose her prayers, Hamlet:
I pray thee, stay with us; go not to Wittenberg.

Ham. I shall in all my best obey you, madam. 120

King. Why, 'tis a loving and a fair reply:
Be as ourself in Denmark. Madam, come;
This gentle and unforced accord of Hamlet
Sits smiling to my heart: in grace whereof,
No jocund health that Denmark drinks to-day,
But the great cannon to the clouds shall tell,
And the king's rouse the heaven shall bruit again,
Re-speaking earthly thunder. Come away.
                    [*Exeunt all but Hamlet.*

Ham. O, that this too too sullied flesh would melt,
Thaw and resolve itself into a dew! 130
Or that the Everlasting had not fix'd
His canon 'gainst self-slaughter! O God! God!
How weary, stale, flat and unprofitable,
Seem to me all the uses of this world!
Fie on 't! ah fie! 'tis an unweeded garden,
That grows to seed; things rank and gross in nature
Possess it merely. That it should come to this!
But two months dead: nay, not so much, not two:
So excellent a king; that was, to this,

33. **subject,** subjects (collectively). 38. **delated,** expressly stated. 44.
the Dane, Danish king. 45. **lose your voice,** speak in vain. 47.
native, closely connected, related. 48. **instrumental,** serviceable.
56. **leave and pardon,** permission to depart. 62. **Take . . . hour,** enjoy
the privileges of youth. 65. **A little . . . kind,** my relation to you has
become more than kinship warrants; it has also become unnatural.
67. **I am . . . sun.** The senses seem to be: I am too much out of doors,
I am too much in the sun of your grace (ironical), I am too much of a
son to you. Johnson suggested an allusion to the proverb, "Out of
heaven's blessing into the warm sun," i.e., Hamlet is out of house and

home in being deprived of the kingship. 74. **Ay . . . common,** it is
common, but it hurts nevertheless; possibly a reference to the commonplace quality of the queen's remark. 78. **customary suits,** suits
prescribed by custom for mourning. 79. **windy suspiration,** heavy
sighing. **forced breath,** i.e., by the distress of the heart. 92. **obsequious,** dutiful. 93. **condolement,** sorrowing. 95. **incorrect,** untrained, uncorrected. 99. **vulgar thing,** common experience. 107.
unprevailing, unavailing. 109. **most immediate,** next in succession.
110. **nobility,** high degree. 112. **impart.** The object is apparently *love*
(l. 110). 113. **Wittenberg,** famous German university founded in 1502.

Hyperion to a satyr; so loving to my mother 140
That he might not beteem the winds of heaven
Visit her face too roughly. Heaven and earth!
Must I remember? why, she would hang on him,
As if increase of appetite had grown
By what it fed on: and yet, within a month—
Let me not think on 't—Frailty, thy name is woman!—
A little month, or ere those shoes were old
With which she follow'd my poor father's body,
Like Niobe, all tears:—why she, even she—
O God! a beast, that wants discourse of reason, 150
Would have mourn'd longer—married with my uncle,
My father's brother, but no more like my father
Than I to Hercules: within a month:
Ere yet the salt of most unrighteous tears
Had left the flushing in her galled eyes,
She married. O, most wicked speed, to post
With such dexterity to incestuous sheets!
It is not nor it cannot come to good:
But break, my heart; for I must hold my tongue.

Enter HORATIO, MARCELLUS, *and* BERNARDO.

Hor. Hail to your lordship!
Ham.   I am glad to see you well: 160
Horatio,—or I do forget myself.
   Hor. The same, my lord, and your poor servant
      ever.
Ham. Sir, my good friend; I'll change that name
      with you:
And what make you from Wittenberg, Horatio?
Marcellus?
   Mar. My good lord—
   Ham. I am very glad to see you. Good even, sir.
But what, in faith, make you from Wittenberg?
   Hor. A truant disposition, good my lord.
   Ham. I would not hear your enemy say so, 170
Nor shall you do mine ear that violence,
To make it truster of your own report
Against yourself: I know you are no truant.
But what is your affair in Elsinore?
We'll teach you to drink deep ere you depart.
   Hor. My lord, I came to see your father's funeral.
   Ham. I pray thee, do not mock me, fellow-student;
I think it was to see my mother's wedding.
   Hor. Indeed, my lord, it follow'd hard upon.
   Ham. Thrift, thrift, Horatio! the funeral baked
      meats 180
Did coldly furnish forth the marriage tables.
Would I had met my dearest foe in heaven
Or ever I had seen that day, Horatio!
My father!—methinks I see my father.
   Hor. Where, my lord?
   Ham.   In my mind's eye, Horatio.
   Hor. I saw him once; he was a goodly king.
   Ham. He was a man, take him for all in all,
I shall not look upon his like again.
   Hor. My lord, I think I saw him yesternight.
   Ham. Saw? who? 190

   Hor. My lord, the king your father.
   Ham.   The king my father!
   Hor. Season your admiration for a while
With an attent ear, till I may deliver,
Upon the witness of these gentlemen,
This marvel to you.
   Ham.   For God's love, let me hear.
   Hor. Two nights together had these gentlemen,
Marcellus and Bernardo, on their watch,
In the dead vast and middle of the night,
Been thus encounter'd. A figure like your father,
Armed at point exactly, cap-a-pe, 200
Appears before them, and with solemn march
Goes slow and stately by them: thrice he walk'd
By their oppress'd and fear-surprised eyes,
Within his truncheon's length; whilst they, distill'd
Almost to jelly with the act of fear,
Stand dumb and speak not to him. This to me
In dreadful secrecy impart they did;
And I with them the third night kept the watch:
Where, as they had deliver'd, both in time,
Form of the thing, each word made true and good, 210
The apparition comes: I knew your father;
These hands are not more like.
   Ham.   But where was this?
   Mar. My lord, upon the platform where we
      watch'd.
   Ham. Did you not speak to it?
   Hor.   My lord, I did;
But answer made it none: yet once methought
It lifted up it head and did address
Itself to motion, like as it would speak;
But even then the morning cock crew loud,
And at the sound it shrunk in haste away,
And vanish'd from our sight.
   Ham.   'Tis very strange. 220
   Hor. As I do live, my honour'd lord, 'tis true;
And we did think it writ down in our duty
To let you know of it.
   Ham. Indeed, indeed, sirs, but this troubles me.
Hold you the watch to-night?
   Mar. ⎫
   Ber. ⎭   We do, my lord.
   Ham. Arm'd, say you?
   Mar. ⎫
   Ber. ⎭   Arm'd, my lord.
   Ham. From top to toe?
   Mar. ⎫
   Ber. ⎭   My lord, from head to foot.
   Ham. Then saw you not his face?
   Hor. O, yes, my lord; he wore his beaver up. 230
   Ham. What, look'd he frowningly?
   Hor. A countenance more in sorrow than in anger.
   Ham. Pale or red?
   Hor. Nay, very pale.
   Ham.   And fix'd his eyes upon you?
   Hor. Most constantly.
   Ham.   I would I had been there.

114. **retrograde,** contrary. 115. **bend you,** incline yourself; imperative.
127. **rouse,** draft of liquor. **heaven,** so Q_2; F and Globe: *heavens.*
bruit again, echo. 129. **sullied,** so Furness and Cambridge; Qq:
sallied; F and Globe: *solid.* 137. **merely,** completely, entirely. 140.
Hyperion, god of the sun in the older regime of ancient gods; here,
probably Apollo. 141. **beteem,** allow. 149. **Niobe,** Tantalus'
daughter, who boasted that she had more sons and daughters than Leto;
for this Apollo and Artemis slew her children. She was turned into
stone by Zeus on Mount Sipylus. 150. **discourse of reason,** process or
faculty of reason. 157. **dexterity,** facility. 163. **I'll . . . you,** I'll be
your servant, you shall be my friend (Johnson); also explained as "I'll
exchange the name of friend with you." 179. **hard,** close. 180. **baked
meats,** meat pies. 182. **dearest,** direst. The adjective *dear* in Shakespeare has two different origins: O. E. *dēore,* "beloved," and O. E.
dēor, "fierce." *Dearest* is the superlative of the second. 192. **Season
your admiration,** restrain your astonishment. 200. **cap-a-pe,** from
head to foot. 203. **oppress'd,** distressed. 204. **truncheon,** officer's
staff. **distill'd,** softened, weakened. 205. **act,** action. 216. **it,** its.
222. **writ down.** Q_1 has *right done,* regarded as an evidence of stenographic reporting. 230. **beaver,** visor on the helmet.

Hor. It would have much amazed you.

Ham. Very like, very like. Stay'd it long?

Hor. While one with moderate haste might tell a
hundred.

Mar.
Ber. } Longer, longer.

Hor. Not when I saw 't.

Ham. His beard was grizzled,—no? 240

Hor. It was, as I have seen it in his life,
A sable silver'd.

Ham. I will watch to-night;
Perchance 'twill walk again.

Hor. I warrant it will.

Ham. If it assume my noble father's person,
I'll speak to it, though hell itself should gape
And bid me hold my peace. I pray you all,
If you have hitherto conceal'd this sight,
Let it be tenable in your silence still;
And whatsoever else shall hap to-night,
Give it an understanding, but no tongue: 250
I will requite your loves. So, fare you well:
Upon the platform, 'twixt eleven and twelve,
I'll visit you.

All. Our duty to your honour.

Ham. Your loves, as mine to you: farewell.

[*Exeunt all but Hamlet.*

My father's spirit in arms! all is not well;
I doubt some foul play: would the night were come!
Till then sit still, my soul: foul deeds will rise,
Though all the earth o'erwhelm them, to men's eyes.

[*Exit.*

SCENE III. *A room in Polonius' house.*

Enter LAERTES *and* OPHELIA.

Laer. My necessaries are embark'd: farewell:
And, sister, as the winds give benefit
And convoy is assistant, do not sleep,
But let me hear from you.

Oph. Do you doubt that?

Laer. For Hamlet and the trifling of his favour,
Hold it a fashion and a toy in blood,
A violet in the youth of primy nature,
Forward, not permanent, sweet, not lasting,
The perfume and suppliance of a minute;
No more.

Oph. No more but so?

Laer. Think it no more: 10
For nature, crescent, does not grow alone
In thews and bulk, but, as this temple waxes,
The inward service of the mind and soul
Grows wide withal. Perhaps he loves you now,
And now no soil nor cautel doth besmirch
The virtue of his will: but you must fear,
His greatness weigh'd, his will is not his own;

For he himself is subject to his birth:
He may not, as unvalued persons do,
Carve for himself; for on his choice depends 20
The sanity and health of this whole state;
And therefore must his choice be circumscribed
Unto the voice and yielding of that body
Whereof he is the head. Then if he says he loves you,
It fits your wisdom so far to believe it
As he in his particular act and place
May give his saying deed; which is no further
Than the main voice of Denmark goes withal.
Then weigh what loss your honour may sustain,
If with too credent ear you list his songs, 30
Or lose your heart, or your chaste treasure open
To his unmaster'd importunity.
Fear it, Ophelia, fear it, my dear sister,
And keep you in the rear of your affection,
Out of the shot and danger of desire.
The chariest maid is prodigal enough,
If she unmask her beauty to the moon:
Virtue itself 'scapes not calumnious strokes:
The canker galls the infants of the spring,
Too oft before their buttons be disclosed, 40
And in the morn and liquid dew of youth
Contagious blastments are most imminent.
Be wary then; best safety lies in fear:
Youth to itself rebels, though none else near.

Oph. I shall the effect of this good lesson keep,
As watchman to my heart. But, good my brother,
Do not, as some ungracious pastors do,
Show me the steep and thorny way to heaven;
Whiles, like a puff'd and reckless libertine,
Himself the primrose path of dalliance treads, 50
And recks not his own rede.

Laer. O, fear me not.
I stay too long: but here my father comes.

Enter POLONIUS.

A double blessing is a double grace;
Occasion smiles upon a second leave.

Pol. Yet here, Laertes! aboard, aboard, for shame!
The wind sits in the shoulder of your sail,
And you are stay'd for. There; my blessing with thee!
And these few precepts in thy memory
Look thou character. Give thy thoughts no tongue,
Nor any unproportion'd thought his act. 60
Be thou familiar, but by no means vulgar.
Those friends thou hast, and their adoption tried,
Grapple them to thy soul with hoops of steel;
But do not dull thy palm with entertainment
Of each new-hatch'd, unfledged comrade. Beware
Of entrance to a quarrel, but being in,
Bear 't that the opposed may beware of thee.
Give every man thy ear, but few thy voice;
Take each man's censure, but reserve thy judgement.
Costly thy habit as thy purse can buy, 70

242. **sable,** black color.
SCENE III. 3. **convoy is assistant,** means of conveyance are at hand.
6. **fashion,** custom, prevailing usage. **toy in blood,** passing amorous
fancy. 7. **primy,** in its prime. 8. **Forward,** precocious. 9. **suppliance of a minute,** diversion to fill up a minute. 10. **so.** Q₂F place a
period after this word. The punctuation concerns the extent to which
Ophelia is obedient to Laertes' suggestion. 11. **crescent,** growing,
waxing. 12. **thews,** bodily strength. **temple,** body. 15. **soil,** blemish.
cautel, crafty device. 16. **virtue . . . will,** good intentions. 21.
sanity, so Theobald; Q₂: *safty;* F: *sanctity;* Globe: *safety.* 23. **voice
and yielding,** support, approval. 27. **deed,** effect. 32. **unmaster'd,**
unrestrained. 36. **chariest,** most scrupulously modest. 39. **The
canker . . . spring,** the cankerworm destroys the young plants of spring.
40. **buttons,** buds. **disclosed,** opened. 41. **liquid dew,** i.e., time when

dew is fresh. 42. **blastments,** blights. 47. **ungracious,** graceless. 49.
puff'd, bloated. 51. **recks,** heeds. **rede,** counsel. 53. **double,** i.e.,
Laertes has already bade his father good-by. 54. **Occasion,** opportunity. 58. **precepts.** Many parallels have been found to the series of
maxims which follows, one of the closest being that in Lyly's *Euphues.*
59. **Look,** so Q₂; Globe, following F: *See.* 60. **unproportion'd,** inordinate. 61. **vulgar,** common. 64. **dull thy palm,** make thyself less
sensitive to true hospitality. 65. **unfledged,** immature. 71. **express'd
in fancy,** fantastical in design. 74. **Are . . . that.** Onions defines *chief* as
"in chief," "mainly," "principally." Rowe and Delius omit *of* and place
a comma after *generous.* Collier changes *chief* to *choice. Chief* is usually
taken as a substantive meaning "head," "eminence." 77. **husbandry,**
thrift. 81. **season,** mature. 94. **put on,** impressed on. 99, 103.
tenders, offers. 102. **Unsifted,** untried. 106. **tenders,** promises to

But not express'd in fancy; rich, not gaudy;
For the apparel oft proclaims the man,
And they in France of the best rank and station
†Are of a most select and generous chief in that.
Neither a borrower nor a lender be;
For loan oft loses both itself and friend,
And borrowing dulls the edge of husbandry.
This above all: to thine own self be true,
And it must follow, as the night the day,
Thou canst not then be false to any man.   80
Farewell: my blessing season this in thee!
   Laer. Most humbly do I take my leave, my lord.
   Pol. The time invites you; go; your servants tend.
   Laer. Farewell, Ophelia; and remember well
What I have said to you.
   Oph.   'Tis in my memory lock'd,
And you yourself shall keep the key of it.
   Laer. Farewell.   [*Exit.*
   Pol. What is 't, Ophelia, he hath said to you?
   Oph. So please you, something touching the Lord
   Hamlet.
   Pol. Marry, well bethought: 90
'Tis told me, he hath very oft of late
Given private time to you; and you yourself
Have of your audience been most free and bounteous:
If it be so, as so 't is put on me,
And that in way of caution, I must tell you,
You do not understand yourself so clearly
As it behoves my daughter and your honour.
What is between you? give me up the truth.
   Oph. He hath, my lord, of late made many tenders
Of his affection to me.   100
   Pol. Affection! pooh! you speak like a green girl,
Unsifted in such perilous circumstance.
Do you believe his tenders, as you call them?
   Oph. I do not know, my lord, what I should think.
   Pol. Marry, I'll teach you: think yourself a baby;
That you have ta'en these tenders for true pay,
Which are not sterling. Tender yourself more dearly;
Or—not to crack the wind of the poor phrase,
Running it thus—you'll tender me a fool.
   Oph. My lord, he hath importuned me with love   110
In honourable fashion.
   Pol. Ay, fashion you may call it; go to, go to.
   Oph. And hath given countenance to his speech, my
   lord,
With almost all the holy vows of heaven.
   Pol. Ay, springes to catch woodcocks. I do know,
When the blood burns, how prodigal the soul
Lends the tongue vows: these blazes, daughter,
Giving more light than heat, extinct in both,
Even in their promise, as it is a-making,
You must not take for fire. From this time   120
Be somewhat scanter of your maiden presence;
Set your entreatments at a higher rate
Than a command to parley. For Lord Hamlet,

Believe so much in him, that he is young,
And with a larger tether may he walk
Than may be given you: in few, Ophelia,
Do not believe his vows; for they are brokers,
Not of that dye which their investments show,
But mere implorators of unholy suits,
Breathing like sanctified and pious bawds,   130
The better to beguile. This is for all:
I would not, in plain terms, from this time forth,
Have you so slander any moment leisure,
As to give words or talk with the Lord Hamlet.
Look to 't, I charge you: come your ways.
   Oph. I shall obey, my lord.   [*Exeunt.*

SCENE IV. *The platform.*

Enter HAMLET, HORATIO, *and* MARCELLUS.

   Ham. The air bites shrewdly; it is very cold.
   Hor. It is a nipping and an eager air.
   Ham. What hour now?
   Hor.   I think it lacks of twelve.
   Mar. No, it is struck.
   Hor. Indeed? I heard it not: then it draws near the
   season
Wherein the spirit held his wont to walk.
      [*A flourish of trumpets, and ordnance shot off, within.*
What does this mean, my lord?
   Ham. The king doth wake to-night and takes his
   rouse,
Keeps wassail, and the swaggering up-spring reels;
And, as he drains his draughts of Rhenish down,   10
The kettle-drum and trumpet thus bray out
The triumph of his pledge.
   Hor.   Is it a custom?
   Ham. Ay, marry, is 't:
But to my mind, though I am native here
And to the manner born, it is a custom
More honour'd in the breach than the observance.
This heavy-headed revel east and west
Makes us traduced and tax'd of other nations:
They clepe us drunkards, and with swinish phrase
Soil our addition; and indeed it takes   20
From our achievements, though perform'd at height,
The pith and marrow of our attribute.
So, oft it chances in particular men,
That for some vicious mole of nature in them,
As, in their birth—wherein they are not guilty,
Since nature cannot choose his origin—
By the o'ergrowth of some complexion,
Oft breaking down the pales and forts of reason,
Or by some habit that too much o'er-leavens
The form of plausive manners, that these men,   30
Carrying, I say, the stamp of one defect,
Being nature's livery, or fortune's star,—
Their virtues else—be they as pure as grace,

As infinite as man may undergo—
Shall in the general censure take corruption
From that particular fault: the dram of †eale
Doth all the noble substance †of a doubt
To his own scandal.
    Hor.   Look, my lord, it comes!

    Enter Ghost.

    Ham. Angels and ministers of grace defend us!
Be thou a spirit of health or goblin damn'd,   40
Bring with thee airs from heaven or blasts from hell,
Be thy intents wicked or charitable,
Thou comest in such a questionable shape
That I will speak to thee: I'll call thee Hamlet,
King, father, royal Dane: O, answer me!
Let me not burst in ignorance; but tell
Why thy canonized bones, hearsed in death,
Have burst their cerements; why the sepulchre,
Wherein we saw thee quietly interr'd,
Hath oped his ponderous and marble jaws,   50
To cast thee up again. What may this mean,
That thou, dead corse, again in complete steel
Revisit'st thus the glimpses of the moon,
Making night hideous; and we fools of nature
So horridly to shake our disposition
With thoughts beyond the reaches of our souls?
Say, why is this? wherefore? what should we do?
                    [Ghost beckons Hamlet.
    Hor. It beckons you to go away with it,
As if it some impartment did desire
To you alone.
    Mar.   Look, with what courteous
      action   60
It waves you to a more removed ground:
But do not go with it.
    Hor.   No, by no means.
    Ham. It will not speak; then I will follow it.
    Hor. Do not, my lord.
    Ham.   Why, what should be the fear?
I do not set my life at a pin's fee;
And for my soul, what can it do to that,
Being a thing immortal as itself?
It waves me forth again: I'll follow it.
    Hor. What if it tempt you toward the flood, my
      lord,
Or to the dreadful summit of the cliff   70
That beetles o'er his base into the sea,
And there assume some other horrible form,
Which might deprive your sovereignty of reason
And draw you into madness? think of it:
The very place puts toys of desperation,
Without more motive, into every brain
That looks so many fathoms to the sea
And hears it roar beneath.
    Ham.   It waves me still.
Go on; I'll follow thee.

Mar. You shall not go, my lord.
Ham.   Hold off your hands.   80
Hor. Be ruled; you shall not go.
Ham.   My fate cries out,
And makes each petty artery in this body
As hardy as the Nemean lion's nerve.
Still am I call'd. Unhand me, gentlemen.
By heaven, I'll make a ghost of him that lets me!
I say, away! Go on; I'll follow thee.
                [Exeunt Ghost and Hamlet.
    Hor. He waxes desperate with imagination.
    Mar. Let 's follow; 'tis not fit thus to obey him.
    Hor. Have after. To what issue will this come?
    Mar. Something is rotten in the state of Denmark. 90
    Hor. Heaven will direct it.
    Mar.   Nay, let 's follow him.   *[Exeunt.*

SCENE V. *Another part of the platform.*

Enter GHOST *and* HAMLET.

Ham. Whither wilt thou lead me? speak; I'll go no
    further.
Ghost. Mark me.
Ham.   I will.
Ghost.   My hour is almost come,
When I to sulphurous and tormenting flames
Must render up myself.
    Ham.   Alas, poor ghost!
    Ghost. Pity me not, but lend thy serious hearing
To what I shall unfold.
    Ham.   Speak; I am bound to hear.
    Ghost. So art thou to revenge, when thou shalt hear.
    Ham. What?
    Ghost. I am thy father's spirit,
Doom'd for a certain term to walk the night,   10
And for the day confined to fast in fires,
Till the foul crimes done in my days of nature
Are burnt and purged away. But that I am forbid
To tell the secrets of my prison-house,
I could a tale unfold whose lightest word
Would harrow up thy soul, freeze thy young blood,
Make thy two eyes, like stars, start from their spheres,
Thy knotted and combined locks to part
And each particular hair to stand an end,
Like quills upon the fretful porpentine: 20
But this eternal blazon must not be
To ears of flesh and blood. List, list, O, list!
If thou didst ever thy dear father love—
    Ham. O God!
    Ghost. Revenge his foul and most unnatural murder.
    Ham. Murder!
    Ghost. Murder most foul, as in the best it is;
But this most foul, strange and unnatural.
    Ham. Haste me to know 't, that I, with wings as
    swift

36-38. **the dram . . . scandal,** a famous crux; *dram of eale* has had various interpretations, the preferred one being probably, "a dram of evil." The following emendations of *of a doubt* have been offered: (1) *oft adoubt* or *adout* (often erase or "do out"), (2) *antidote* (counteract). Dowden suggests that *scandal* may be a verb to be read with *Doth,* giving the general interpretation, "Out of a mere doubt or suspicion the dram of evil degrades in reputation all the noble substance to its own [substance]." 39. **ministers of grace,** messengers of God. 43. **questionable,** inviting question or conversation. 47. **canonized,** buried according to the canons of the church. **hearsed,** coffined. 48. **cerements,** grave-clothes. 49. **interr'd,** so Qq; F: *enurn'd;* Globe: *inurn'd.* 53. **glimpses of the moon,** the earth by night. 54. **fools of nature,** persons limited in intelligence by nature. 59. **impartment,**

communication. 61. **removed,** remote. 71. **beetles o'er,** overhangs threateningly. 73. **deprive . . . reason,** take away the sovereignty of your reason. It was thought that evil spirits would sometimes assume the form of departed spirits in order to work madness in a human creature. 75. **toys of desperation,** freakish notions of suicide. 83. **Nemean lion's.** The Nemean lion was one of the monsters slain by Hercules. **nerve,** sinew, tendon. The point is that the arteries which were carrying the spirits out into the body were functioning and were as stiff and hard as the sinews of the lion. 89. **issue,** outcome. 91. **it,** i.e., the outcome. SCENE v. 1. **Whither,** Q_2: *Whether;* F and Globe: *Where.* 11. **fast,** probably, do without food. It has been sometimes taken in the sense of doing general penance. 17. **spheres,** orbits. 18. **knotted,** perhaps, intricately arranged (Onions). **combined,** tied, bound. 20. **fretful,**

As meditation or the thoughts of love,   30
May sweep to my revenge.
     Ghost.   I find thee apt;
And duller shouldst thou be than the fat weed
That roots itself in ease on Lethe wharf,
Wouldst thou not stir in this. Now, Hamlet, hear:
'Tis given out that, sleeping in my orchard,
A serpent stung me; so the whole ear of Denmark
Is by a forged process of my death
Rankly abused: but know, thou noble youth,
The serpent that did sting thy father's life
Now wears his crown.
     Ham.   O my prophetic soul!   40
My uncle!
     Ghost. Ay, that incestuous, that adulterate beast,
With witchcraft of his wit, with traitorous gifts,—
O wicked wit and gifts, that have the power
So to seduce!—won to his shameful lust
The will of my most seeming-virtuous queen:
O Hamlet, what a falling-off was there!
From me, whose love was of that dignity
That it went hand in hand even with the vow
I made to her in marriage, and to decline   50
Upon a wretch whose natural gifts were poor
To those of mine!
But virtue, as it never will be moved,
Though lewdness court it in a shape of heaven,
So lust, though to a radiant angel link'd,
Will sate itself in a celestial bed,
And prey on garbage.
But, soft! methinks I scent the morning air;
Brief let me be. Sleeping within my orchard,
My custom always of the afternoon,   60
Upon my secure hour thy uncle stole,
With juice of cursed hebenon in a vial,
And in the porches of my ears did pour
The leperous distilment; whose effect
Holds such an enmity with blood of man
That swift as quicksilver it courses through
The natural gates and alleys of the body,
And with a sudden vigour it doth posset
And curd, like eager droppings into milk,
The thin and wholesome blood: so did it mine;   70
And a most instant tetter bark'd about,
Most lazar-like, with vile and loathsome crust,
All my smooth body.
Thus was I, sleeping, by a brother's hand
Of life, of crown, of queen, at once dispatch'd:
Cut off even in the blossoms of my sin,
Unhousel'd, disappointed, unaneled,
No reckoning made, but sent to my account
With all my imperfections on my head:
O, horrible! O, horrible! most horrible!   80
If thou hast nature in thee, bear it not;
Let not the royal bed of Denmark be
A couch for luxury and damned incest.

But, howsoever thou pursuest this act,
Taint not thy mind, nor let thy soul contrive
Against thy mother aught: leave her to heaven
And to those thorns that in her bosom lodge,
To prick and sting her. Fare thee well at once!
The glow-worm shows the matin to be near,
And 'gins to pale his uneffectual fire: 90
Adieu, adieu! Hamlet, remember me.   [*Exit.*
     Ham. O all you host of heaven! O earth! what else?
And shall I couple hell? O, fie! Hold, hold, my heart;
And you, my sinews, grow not instant old,
But bear me stiffly up. Remember thee!
Ay, thou poor ghost, while memory holds a seat
In this distracted globe. Remember thee!
Yea, from the table of my memory
I'll wipe away all trivial fond records,
All saws of books, all forms, all pressures past,   100
That youth and observation copied there;
And thy commandment all alone shall live
Within the book and volume of my brain,
Unmix'd with baser matter: yes, by heaven!
O most pernicious woman!
O villain, villain, smiling, damned villain!
My tables,—meet it is I set it down,
That one may smile, and smile, and be a villain;
At least I'm sure it may be so in Denmark: [*Writing.*
So, uncle, there you are. Now to my word;   110
It is 'Adieu, adieu! remember me.'
I have sworn 't.
     Mar.⎫
     Hor.⎭ [*Within*] My lord, my lord,—
     Mar.   [*Within*] Lord Hamlet,—
     Hor.   [*Within*] Heaven secure him!
     Ham. So be it!
     Hor. [*Within*] Hillo, ho, ho, my lord!
     Ham. Hillo, ho, ho, boy! come, bird, come.

Enter HORATIO *and* MARCELLUS.

     Mar. How is 't, my noble lord?
     Hor.   What news, my lord?
     Ham. O, wonderful!
     Hor.   Good my lord, tell it.
     Ham. No; you'll reveal it.
     Hor. Not I, my lord, by heaven.
     Mar.   Nor I, my lord.   120
     Ham. How say you, then; would heart of man once
          think it?
But you'll be secret?
     Hor. ⎫
     Mar. ⎭   Ay, by heaven, my lord.
     Ham. There's ne'er a villain dwelling in all
          Denmark
But he's an arrant knave.
     Hor. There needs no ghost, my lord, come from the
          grave
To tell us this.

so Q_1F; Q_2: *fearefull,* which is defensible. **porpentine,** porcupine.
21. **eternal blazon,** promulgation or proclamation of eternity, revelation of the hereafter. 25. **unnatural,** i.e., pertaining to fratricide.
32. **fat weed.** Many suggestions have been offered as to the particular
plant intended, including asphodel; probably, a general figure for
plants growing along rotting wharves and piles. 33. **Lethe wharf,** bank
of the river of forgetfulness in Hades. 42. **adulterate,** adulterous.
61. **secure,** confident, unsuspicious. 62. **hebenon,** generally supposed
to mean henbane. Elze conjectured *hemlock;* Nicholson, *ebenus,* meaning
"yew." 64. **leperous,** causing leprosy. 68. **posset,** coagulate, curdle.
69. **eager,** sour, acid. 72. **lazar-like,** leperlike. 75. **dispatch'd,**
suddenly bereft. 77. **Unhousel'd,** without having received the sacrament. **disappointed,** unready, without equipment for the last journey.

unaneled, without having received extreme unction. 80. **O . . .
horrible.** Many editors give this line to Hamlet; Garrick and Sir Henry
Irving spoke it in that part. 83. **luxury,** lechery. 85. **Taint . . .
mind,** probably, deprave not thy character, do nothing except in the
pursuit of a natural revenge. 89. **matin,** morning. 90. **uneffectual
fire,** cold light. 93. **couple,** add. 97. **distracted globe,** confused
head. 100. **pressures,** impressions stamped. 107. **tables,** probably a
small portable writing-tablet carried at the belt. 110. **word,** watchword. 115. **Hillo, ho, ho,** a falconer's call to a hawk in air. 124.
arrant, thoroughgoing.

Ham. Why, right; you are i' the right;
And so, without more circumstance at all,
I hold it fit that we shake hands and part:
You, as your business and desire shall point you;
For every man has business and desire, 130
Such as it is; and for mine own poor part,
Look you, I'll go pray.
    Hor. These are but wild and whirling words, my
      lord.
    Ham. I'm sorry they offend you, heartily;
Yes, 'faith, heartily.
    Hor.   There's no offence, my lord.
    Ham. Yes, by Saint Patrick, but there is, Horatio,
And much offence too. Touching this vision here,
It is an honest ghost, that let me tell you:
For your desire to know what is between us,
O'ermaster 't as you may. And now, good friends, 140
As you are friends, scholars and soldiers,
Give me one poor request.
    Hor. What is 't, my lord? we will.
    Ham. Never make known what you have seen
      to-night.
    Hor. }
    Mar. } My lord, we will not.
    Ham.   Nay, but swear 't.
    Hor.   In faith,
My lord, not I.
    Mar.   Nor I, my lord, in faith.
    Ham. Upon my sword.
    Mar.   We have sworn, my lord, already.
    Ham. Indeed, upon my sword, indeed.
    Ghost. [*Beneath*] Swear.
    Ham. Ah, ha, boy! say'st thou so? art thou there,
      truepenny? 150
Come on—you hear this fellow in the cellarage—
Consent to swear.
    Hor.   Propose the oath, my lord.
    Ham. Never to speak of this that you have seen,
Swear by my sword.
    Ghost. [*Beneath*] Swear.
    Ham. Hic et ubique? then we'll shift our ground.
Come hither, gentlemen,
And lay your hands again upon my sword:
Swear by my sword,
Never to speak of this that you have heard. 160
    Ghost. [*Beneath*] Swear by his sword.
    Ham. Well said, old mole! canst work i' the earth so
    fast?
A worthy pioner! Once more remove, good friends.
    Hor. O day and night, but this is wondrous strange!
    Ham. And therefore as a stranger give it welcome.
There are more things in heaven and earth, Horatio,
Than are dreamt of in your philosophy.
But come;
Here, as before, never, so help you mercy,
How strange or odd soe'er I bear myself, 170
As I perchance hereafter shall think meet

To put an antic disposition on,
That you, at such times seeing me, never shall,
With arms encumber'd thus, or this head-shake,
Or by pronouncing of some doubtful phrase,
As 'Well, well, we know,' or 'We could, an if we
    would,'
Or 'If we list to speak,' or 'There be, an if they might,'
Or such ambiguous giving out, to note
That you know aught of me: this not to do,
So grace and mercy at your most need help you, 180
Swear.
    Ghost. [*Beneath*] Swear.
    Ham. Rest, rest, perturbed spirit! [*They swear*]. So,
    gentlemen,
With all my love I do commend me to you:
And what so poor a man as Hamlet is
May do, to express his love and friending to you,
God willing, shall not lack. Let us go in together;
And still your fingers on your lips, I pray.
The time is out of joint: O cursed spite,
That ever I was born to set it right! 190
Nay, come, let's go together.   [*Exeunt.*

ACT II.

SCENE I. *A room in Polonius' house.*

Enter POLONIUS *and* REYNALDO.

Pol. Give him this money and these notes, Reynaldo.
Rey. I will, my lord.
Pol. You shall do marvellous wisely, good Reynaldo,
Before you visit him, to make inquire
Of his behaviour.
    Rey.   My lord, I did intend it.
    Pol. Marry, well said; very well said. Look you, sir,
Inquire me first what Danskers are in Paris;
And how, and who, what means, and where they
    keep,
What company, at what expense; and finding
By this encompassment and drift of question 10
That they do know my son, come you more nearer
Than your particular demands will touch it:
Take you, as 'twere, some distant knowledge of him;
As thus, 'I know his father and his friends,
And in part him:' do you mark this, Reynaldo?
    Rey. Ay, very well, my lord.
    Pol. 'And in part him; but' you may say 'not well:
But, if 't be he I mean, he's very wild;
Addicted so and so:' and there put on him
What forgeries you please; marry, none so rank 20
As may dishonour him; take heed of that;
But, sir, such wanton, wild and usual slips
As are companions noted and most known
To youth and liberty.
    Rey.   As gaming, my lord.

Pol. Ay, or drinking, fencing, swearing, quarrelling,
Drabbing: you may go so far.
    Rey. My lord, that would dishonour him.
    Pol. 'Faith, no; as you may season it in the charge.
You must not put another scandal on him,
That he is open to incontinency;   30
That 's not my meaning: but breathe his faults so
    quaintly
That they may seem the taints of liberty,
The flash and outbreak of a fiery mind,
A savageness in unreclaimed blood,
Of general assault.
    Rey.   But, my good lord,—
    Pol. Wherefore should you do this?
    Rey.   Ay, my lord,
I would know that.
    Pol.   Marry, sir, here 's my drift;
And, I believe, it is a fetch of wit:
You laying these slight sullies on my son,
As 'twere a thing a little soil'd i' the working,   40
Mark you,
Your party in converse, him you would sound,
Having ever seen in the prenominate crimes
The youth you breathe of guilty, be assured
He closes with you in this consequence;
'Good sir,' or so, or 'friend,' or 'gentleman,'
According to the phrase or the addition
Of man and country.
    Rey.   Very good, my lord.
    Pol. And then, sir, does he this—he does—what
was I about to say? By the mass, I was about to say
something: where did I leave?   51
    Rey. At 'closes in the consequence,' at 'friend or so,'
and 'gentleman.'
    Pol. At 'closes in the consequence,' ay, marry;
He closes thus: 'I know the gentleman;
I saw him yesterday, or t' other day,
Or then, or then; with such, or such; and, as you say,
There was a' gaming; there o'ertook in 's rouse;
There falling out at tennis:' or perchance,
'I saw him enter such a house of sale,'   60
Videlicet, a brothel, or so forth.
See you now;
Your bait of falsehood takes this carp of truth:
And thus do we of wisdom and of reach,
With windlasses and with assays of bias,
By indirections find directions out:
So by my former lecture and advice,
Shall you my son. You have me, have you not?
    Rey. My lord, I have.
    Pol.   God be wi' you; fare you well.
    Rey. Good my lord!   70
    Pol. Observe his inclination in yourself.
    Rey. I shall, my lord.
    Pol. And let him ply his music.
    Rey.   Well, my lord.
    Pol. Farewell!   [*Exit Reynaldo.*

Enter OPHELIA.

            How now, Ophelia! what 's the matter?
    Oph. O, my lord, my lord, I have been so affrighted!
    Pol. With what, i' the name of God?
    Oph. My lord, as I was sewing in my closet,
Lord Hamlet, with his doublet all unbraced;
No hat upon his head; his stockings foul'd,
Ungarter'd, and down-gyved to his ancle;   80
Pale as his shirt; his knees knocking each other;
And with a look so piteous in purport
As if he had been loosed out of hell
To speak of horrors,—he comes before me.
    Pol. Mad for thy love?
    Oph.   My lord, I do not know;
But truly, I do fear it.
    Pol.   What said he?
    Oph. He took me by the wrist and held me hard;
Then goes he to the length of all his arm;
And, with his other hand thus o'er his brow,
He falls to such perusal of my face   90
As he would draw it. Long stay'd he so;
At last, a little shaking of mine arm
And thrice his head thus waving up and down,
He raised a sigh so piteous and profound
As it did seem to shatter all his bulk
And end his being: that done, he lets me go:
And, with his head over his shoulder turn'd,
He seem'd to find his way without his eyes;
For out o' doors he went without their helps,
And, to the last, bended their light on me.   100
    Pol. Come, go with me: I will go seek the king.
This is the very ecstasy of love,
Whose violent property fordoes itself
And leads the will to desperate undertakings
As oft as any passion under heaven
That does afflict our natures. I am sorry.
What, have you given him any hard words of late?
    Oph. No, my good lord, but, as you did command,
I did repel his letters and denied
His access to me.
    Pol.   That hath made him mad. 110
I am sorry that with better heed and judgement
I had not quoted him: I fear'd he did but trifle,
And meant to wreck thee; but, beshrew my jealousy!
By heaven, it is as proper to our age
To cast beyond ourselves in our opinions
As it is common for the younger sort
To lack discretion. Come, go we to the king:
This must be known; which, being kept close, might
    move
More grief to hide than hate to utter love.   [*Exeunt.*

SCENE II. *A room in the castle.*

Enter KING, QUEEN, ROSENCRANTZ, GUILDENSTERN,
    and Attendants.

---

all untrained youth. 38. **fetch of wit,** clever trick. The F reading, *fetch of warrant,* would mean "a warranted device." 43. **ever,** at any time. **prenominate,** before-mentioned. 45. **closes . . . consequence,** agrees with you in this conclusion. 49-51. **And then . . . leave.** Malone's arrangement of Q₂F as prose is probably correct, since Polonius is represented as letting his mind wander in confusion. 58. **o'ertook in 's rouse,** overcome by drink. 61. **Videlicet,** namely. 64. **reach,** capacity, ability. 65. **windlasses,** i.e., circuitous paths. **assays of bias,** attempts that resemble the course of the bowl, which, being weighted on one side, has a curving motion. 66. **indirections,** devious courses. **directions,** straight courses, i.e., the truth. 67. **lecture,** admonition. 71. **Observe . . . yourself,** in your own person, not by spies (Johnson),

or conform your own conduct to his inclination (Clarendon Press); or test him by studying yourself. 73. **ply his music,** probably to be taken literally. 77. **closet,** private chamber. 78. **doublet,** close-fitting coat. **unbraced,** unfastened. 80. **down-gyved,** fallen to the ankles (like gyves or fetters). 95. **bulk,** body. 103. **property,** nature. **fordoes,** destroys. 113. **beshrew my jealousy,** curse my suspicion. 115. **cast beyond,** overshoot, miscalculate. 118-119. **might . . . love,** i.e., I might cause more grief to others by hiding the knowledge of Hamlet's love to Ophelia than hatred to me and mine by telling of it. 119. After this line Q₂ has *Come.*

King. Welcome, dear Rosencrantz and
    Guildenstern!
Moreover that we much did long to see you,
The need we have to use you did provoke
Our hasty sending. Something have you heard
Of Hamlet's transformation; so call it,
Sith nor the exterior nor the inward man
Resembles that it was. What it should be,
More than his father's death, that thus hath put him
So much from the understanding of himself,
I cannot dream of: I entreat you both,   10
That, being of so young days brought up with him,
And sith so neighbour'd to his youth and haviour,
That you vouchsafe your rest here in our court
Some little time: so by your companies
To draw him on to pleasures, and to gather,
So much as from occasion you may glean,
Whether aught, to us unknown, afflicts him thus,
That, open'd, lies within our remedy.
    Queen. Good gentlemen, he hath much talk'd of
    you;
And sure I am two men there are not living   20
To whom he more adheres. If it will please you
To show us so much gentry and good will
As to expend your time with us awhile,
For the supply and profit of our hope,
Your visitation shall receive such thanks
As fits a king's remembrance.
    Ros.   Both your majesties
Might, by the sovereign power you have of us,
Put your dread pleasures more into command
Than to entreaty.
    Guil.   But we both obey,
And here give up ourselves, in the full bent   30
To lay our service freely at your feet,
To be commanded.
    King. Thanks, Rosencrantz and gentle Guildenstern.
    Queen. Thanks, Guildenstern and gentle
    Rosencrantz:
And I beseech you instantly to visit
My too much changed son. Go, some of you,
And bring these gentlemen where Hamlet is.
    Guil. Heavens make our presence and our practices
Pleasant and helpful to him!
    Queen.   Ay, amen!
    [*Exeunt Rosencrantz, Guildenstern, and some Attendants.*

Enter POLONIUS.

    Pol. The ambassadors from Norway, my good lord,
Are joyfully return'd.   41
    King. Thou still hast been the father of good news.
    Pol. Have I, my lord? I assure my good liege,
I hold my duty, as I hold my soul,
Both to my God and to my gracious king:
And I do think, or else this brain of mine
Hunts not the trail of policy so sure
As it hath used to do, that I have found
The very cause of Hamlet's lunacy.
    King. O, speak of that; that do I long to hear.   50

    Pol. Give first admittance to the ambassadors;
My news shall be the fruit to that great feast.
    King. Thyself do grace to them, and bring them in.
        [*Exit Polonius.*
He tells me, my dear Gertrude, he hath found
The head and source of all your son's distemper.
    Queen. I doubt it is no other but the main;
His father's death, and our o'erhasty marriage.
    King. Well, we shall sift him.

Re-enter POLONIUS, *with* VOLTIMAND *and* CORNELIUS.

    Welcome, my good friends!
Say, Voltimand, what from our brother Norway?
    Volt. Most fair return of greetings and desires.   60
Upon our first, he sent out to suppress
His nephew's levies; which to him appear'd
To be a preparation 'gainst the Polack;
But, better look'd into, he truly found
It was against your highness: whereat grieved,
That so his sickness, age and impotence
Was falsely borne in hand, sends out arrests
On Fortinbras; which he, in brief, obeys;
Receives rebuke from Norway, and in fine
Makes vow before his uncle never more   70
To give the assay of arms against your majesty.
Whereon old Norway, overcome with joy,
Gives him three score thousand crowns in annual fee,
And his commission to employ those soldiers,
So levied as before, against the Polack:
With an entreaty, herein further shown,[*Giving a paper.*
That it might please you to give quiet pass
Through your dominions for this enterprise,
On such regards of safety and allowance
As therein are set down.
    King.   It likes us well;   80
And at our more consider'd time we'll read,
Answer, and think upon this business.
Meantime we thank you for your well-took labour:
Go to your rest; at night we'll feast together:
Most welcome home!   [*Exeunt Voltimand and Cornelius.*
    Pol.   This business is well ended.
My liege, and madam, to expostulate
What majesty should be, what duty is,
Why day is day, night night, and time is time,
Were nothing but to waste night, day and time.
Therefore, since brevity is the soul of wit,   90
And tediousness the limbs and outward flourishes,
I will be brief: your noble son is mad:
Mad call I it; for, to define true madness,
What is 't but to be nothing else but mad?
But let that go.
    Queen.   More matter, with less art.
    Pol. Madam, I swear I use no art at all.
That he is mad, 'tis true: 'tis true 'tis pity;
And pity 'tis 'tis true: a foolish figure;
But farewell it, for I will use no art.
Mad let us grant him, then: and now remains   100
That we find out the cause of this effect,
Or rather say, the cause of this defect,

SCENE II. 11. **of . . . days,** from such early youth. 13. **vouchsafe your rest,** please to stay. 22. **gentry,** courtesy. 24. **supply and profit,** aid and successful outcome. 30. **in . . . bent,** to the utmost degree of our mental capacity. 56. **main,** chief point, principal concern. 67. **borne in hand,** deluded. 71. **assay,** assault, trial (of arms). 73. **three score,** so Q₂; Globe, following F: *three.* 79. **safety and allowance,** pledges of safety to the country and terms of permission for the troops to pass. 81. **consider'd,** suitable for deliberation. 90. **wit,** sound sense or judgment. 91. **flourishes,** ostentatious embellishments. 98. **figure,** figure of speech. 105. **Perpend,** consider. 120. **ill . . . numbers,** unskilled at writing verses. 121. **reckon,** number metrically, scan (Yale). 124. **machine,** bodily frame. 126. **more above,** moreover. 127. **fell out,** occurred. **means,** opportunities (of access). 136. **play'd . . . table-book,** i.e., remained shut up, concealed his information. 137. **given . . . winking,** given my heart a signal to keep silent. 140. **bespeak,** address. 141. **out . . . star,** above thee in position. 146. **repelled,** so Q₂; F and Globe: *repulsed.* 148. **watch,** state of sleeplessness. 149. **lightness,** light-headedness. **declension,**

For this effect defective comes by cause:
Thus it remains, and the remainder thus.
Perpend.
I have a daughter—have while she is mine—
Who, in her duty and obedience, mark,
Hath given me this: now gather, and surmise. [*Reads.*
'To the celestial and my soul's idol, the most beauti-
fied Ophelia,'— 110
That's an ill phrase, a vile phrase; 'beautified' is a vile
phrase: but you shall hear. Thus: [*Reads.*
'In her excellent white bosom, these, &c.'
   Queen. Came this from Hamlet to her?
   Pol. Good madam, stay awhile; I will be faithful.
                                      [*Reads.*

    'Doubt thou the stars are fire;
      Doubt that the sun doth move;
      Doubt truth to be a liar;
      But never doubt I love. 119

    'O dear Ophelia, I am ill at these numbers; I
have not art to reckon my groans: but that I love thee
best, O most best, believe it. Adieu.
    'Thine evermore, most dear lady, whilst this
                   machine is to him, HAMLET.'
This, in obedience, hath my daughter shown me,
And more above, hath his solicitings,
As they fell out by time, by means and place,
All given to mine ear.
   King.   But how hath she
Received his love?
   Pol.   What do you think of me?
   King. As of a man faithful and honourable. 130
   Pol. I would fain prove so. But what might you
think,
When I had seen this hot love on the wing—
As I perceived it, I must tell you that,
Before my daughter told me—what might you,
Or my dear majesty your queen here, think,
If I had play'd the desk or table-book,
Or given my heart a winking, mute and dumb,
Or look'd upon this love with idle sight;
What might you think? No, I went round to work,
And my young mistress thus I did bespeak: 140
'Lord Hamlet is a prince, out of thy star;
This must not be:' and then I prescripts gave her,
That she should lock herself from his resort,
Admit no messengers, receive no tokens.
Which done, she took the fruits of my advice;
And he, repelled—a short tale to make—
Fell into a sadness, then into a fast,
Thence to a watch, thence into a weakness,
Thence to a lightness, and, by this declension,
Into the madness wherein now he raves, 150
And all we mourn for.
   King.   Do you think 'tis this?
   Queen. It may be, very like.
   Pol. Hath there been such a time—I'd fain know
that—
That I have positively said ''Tis so,'
When it proved otherwise?

   King.   Not that I know.
   Pol. [*Pointing to his head and shoulder*] Take this from
this, if this be otherwise:
If circumstances lead me, I will find
Where truth is hid, though it were hid indeed
Within the centre.
   King.   How may we try it further?
   Pol. You know, sometimes he walks four hours
together 160
Here in the lobby.
   Queen.   So he does indeed.
   Pol. At such a time I'll loose my daughter to him:
Be you and I behind an arras then;
Mark the encounter: if he love her not
And be not from his reason fall'n thereon,
Let me be no assistant for a state,
But keep a farm and carters.
   King.   We will try it.
   Queen. But, look, where sadly the poor wretch
comes reading.
   Pol. Away, I do beseech you, both away:
I'll board him presently.
            [*Exeunt King, Queen, and Attendants.*

   Enter HAMLET, *reading.*
                O, give me leave: 170
How does my good Lord Hamlet?
   Ham. Well, God-a-mercy.
   Pol. Do you know me, my lord?
   Ham. Excellent well; you are a fishmonger.
   Pol. Not I, my lord.
   Ham. Then I would you were so honest a man.
   Pol. Honest, my lord!
   Ham. Ay, sir; to be honest, as this world goes, is to
be one man picked out of ten thousand.
   Pol. That's very true, my lord. 180
   Ham. For if the sun breed maggots in a dead dog,
being a god kissing carrion,—Have you a daughter?
   Pol. I have, my lord.
   Ham. Let her not walk i' the sun: conception is a
blessing: but not as your daughter may conceive.
Friend, look to 't.
   Pol. [*Aside*] How say you by that? Still harping on
my daughter: yet he knew me not at first; he said I
was a fishmonger: he is far gone: and truly in my
youth I suffered much extremity for love; very near
this. I'll speak to him again. What do you read, my
lord?
   Ham. Words, words, words.
   Pol. What is the matter, my lord? 195
   Ham. Between who?
   Pol. I mean, the matter that you read, my lord.
   Ham. Slanders, sir: for the satirical rogue says here
that old men have grey beards, that their faces are
wrinkled, their eyes purging thick amber and plum-
tree gum and that they have a plentiful lack of wit,
together with most weak hams: all which, sir, though
I most powerfully and potently believe, yet I hold it
not honesty to have it thus set down, for yourself, sir,

decline, deterioration. 152. **like,** so Q₂; Globe, following F: *likely.*
159. **centre,** middle point of the earth. 163. **arras,** hanging, tapestry.
164. **encounter,** style or manner of address, behavior. 170. **board,**
accost. 174. **fishmonger,** an opprobrious expression possibly meaning
"bawd," "procurer." 182. **god kissing carrion,** the sun god shining on
a dead body. The Q₂F reading, *good kissing carrion,* some editors explain
as "carrion fit for kissing by the sun." Hamlet is supposed to be reading
the matter from the book he is carrying. 185. **i' the sun,** in the sunshine of princely favors (Chambers). **conception,** quibble on "under-

standing" and "pregnancy." 188. **by,** concerning. 191. **far gone,**
Globe, following F, repeats *far gone.* 195. **matter,** substance. 196.
Between who. Hamlet deliberately takes *matter* as meaning "basis of
dispute"; modern usage demands *whom* instead of *who.* 198. **satirical
rogue.** Warburton saw an allusion to the tenth satire of Juvenal. In
point of fact there were dozens of books in circulation in Shakespeare's
time which contained such descriptions of old age, but we need not
assume that Shakespeare supposed Hamlet to be carrying any particular
book. 200. **purging,** discharging. 205. **honesty,** decency.

should be old as I am, if like a crab you could go backward.

Pol. [*Aside*] Though this be madness, yet there is method in 't. Will you walk out of the air, my lord?

Ham. Into my grave. 210

Pol. Indeed, that is out o' the air. [*Aside*] How pregnant sometimes his replies are! a happiness that often madness hits on, which reason and sanity could not so prosperously be delivered of. I will leave him, and suddenly contrive the means of meeting between him and my daughter.—My honourable lord, I will most humbly take my leave of you.

Ham. You cannot, sir, take from me any thing that I will more willingly part withal: except my life, except my life, except my life. 221

Pol. Fare you well, my lord.

Ham. These tedious old fools!

Enter ROSENCRANTZ *and* GUILDENSTERN.

Pol. You go to seek the Lord Hamlet; there he is.

Ros. [*To Polonius*] God save you, sir! ⌈*Exit Polonius.*

Guil. My honoured lord!

Ros. My most dear lord!

Ham. My excellent good friends! How dost thou, Guildenstern? Ah, Rosencrantz! Good lads, how do ye both? 230

Ros. As the indifferent children of the earth.

Guil. Happy, in that we are not over-happy; On fortune's cap we are not the very button.

Ham. Nor the soles of her shoe?

Ros. Neither, my lord.

Ham. Then you live about her waist, or in the middle of her favours?

Guil. 'Faith, her privates we.

Ham. In the secret parts of fortune? O, most true; she is a strumpet. What 's the news? 240

Ros. None, my lord, but that the world 's grown honest.

Ham. Then is doomsday near: but your news is not true. Let me question more in particular: what have you, my good friends, deserved at the hands of fortune, that she sends you to prison hither?

Guil. Prison, my lord!

Ham. Denmark 's a prison.

Ros. Then is the world one. 250

Ham. A goodly one; in which there are many confines, wards and dungeons, Denmark being one o' the worst.

Ros. We think not so, my lord.

Ham. Why, then, 'tis none to you; for there is nothing either good or bad, but thinking makes it so: to me it is a prison.

Ros. Why then, your ambition makes it one; 'tis too narrow for your mind. 259

Ham. O God, I could be bounded in a nutshell and count myself a king of infinite space, were it not that I have bad dreams.

Guil. Which dreams indeed are ambition, for the very substance of the ambitious is merely the shadow of a dream.

Ham. A dream itself is but a shadow.

Ros. Truly, and I hold ambition of so airy and light a quality that it is but a shadow's shadow. 268

Ham. Then are our beggars bodies, and our monarchs and outstretched heroes the beggars' shadows. Shall we to the court? for, by my fay, I cannot reason.

Ros. ⎱ We'll wait upon you.
Guil. ⎰

Ham. No such matter: I will not sort you with the rest of my servants, for, to speak to you like an honest man, I am most dreadfully attended. But, in the beaten way of friendship, what make you at Elsinore?

Ros. To visit you, my lord; no other occasion. 279

Ham. Beggar that I am, I am even poor in thanks; but I thank you: and sure, dear friends, my thanks are too dear a halfpenny. Were you not sent for? Is it your own inclining? Is it a free visitation? Come, deal justly with me: come, come; nay, speak.

Guil. What should we say, my lord?

Ham. Why, any thing, but to the purpose. You were sent for; and there is a kind of confession in your looks which your modesties have not craft enough to colour: I know the good king and queen have sent for you. 291

Ros. To what end, my lord?

Ham. That you must teach me. But let me conjure you, by the rights of our fellowship, by the consonancy of our youth, by the obligation of our ever-preserved love, and by what more dear a better proposer could charge you withal, be even and direct with me, whether you were sent for, or no?

Ros. [*Aside to Guil.*] What say you? 300

Ham. [*Aside*] Nay, then, I have an eye of you.—If you love me, hold not off.

Guil. My lord, we were sent for.

Ham. I will tell you why; so shall my anticipation prevent your discovery, and your secrecy to the king and queen moult no feather. I have of late—but wherefore I know not—lost all my mirth, forgone all custom of exercises; and indeed it goes so heavily with my disposition that this goodly frame, the earth, seems to me a sterile promontory, this most excellent canopy, the air, look you, this brave o'erhanging firmament, this majestical roof fretted with golden fire, why, it appears no other thing to me than a foul and pestilent congregation of vapours. What a piece of work is a man! how noble in reason! how infinite in faculty! in form and moving how express and ad-

213. **happiness,** felicity of expression. 214. **prosperously,** successfully. 231. **indifferent,** ordinary. 252. **confines,** places of confinement. 264. **very . . . ambitious,** that seemingly most substantial thing which the ambitious pursue (Hudson). 272. **fay,** faith. **reason,** argue. 273. **wait upon,** accompany. 274. **sort,** class. 276. **dreadfully attended,** poorly provided with servants. 277. **in the . . . friendship,** as a matter of course among friends. 282. **a,** i.e., at a. 294. **conjure,** adjure, entreat. 295. **consonancy of our youth,** the fact that we are of the same age. 297. **better proposer,** one more skillful in finding proposals. 305. **prevent your discovery,** forestall your disclosure. 313. **fretted,** adorned. 317. **faculty,** capacity. 318. **express,** well-framed (?) exact (?) 319. **apprehension,** understanding. 321. **quintessence,** the fifth essence of ancient philosophy, supposed to be the substance of the heavenly bodies and to be latent in all things. 329. **lenten,** meager. 330. **coted,** overtook and passed beyond. 334. **foil and target,** sword and shield; see *target* in glossary. 336. **humorous man,** actor who

takes the part of the humor characters. 338. **tickle o' the sere,** easy on the trigger. 338-340. **the lady . . . for 't,** the lady (fond of talking) shall have opportunity to talk, blank verse or no blank verse. 344. **residence,** remaining in one place. 346. **inhibition,** formal prohibition (from acting plays in the city or, possibly, at court). 347. **innovation.** The allusion is either to the introduction into plays of satire on persons or to the introduction of the Children of the Revels into Blackfriars Theatre (January 1603). The actors have been forced to take to the road by two things—some "inhibition" and the rivalry of the children. 352-379. **How . . . load too.** The passage (omitted from Qq) is the famous one dealing with the War of the Theaters (1599-1602), namely, the rivalry between the children's companies and the adult actors. 354. **aery,** nest. 355. **eyases,** young hawks. 355-356. **cry . . . question,** speak in a high key dominating conversation (Clarendon Press); clamor forth the height of controversy (Dowden); probably "excel" (cf. l. 459); perhaps intended to decry leaders of the dramatic mirable! in action how like an angel! in apprehension how like a god! the beauty of the world! the paragon of animals! And yet, to me, what is this quintessence of dust? man delights not me: no, nor woman neither, though by your smiling you seem to say so.   323

Ros. My lord, there was no such stuff in my thoughts.

Ham. Why did you laugh then, when I said 'man delights not me'?

Ros. To think, my lord, if you delight not in man, what lenten entertainment the players shall receive from you: we coted them on the way; and hither are they coming, to offer you service.   331

Ham. He that plays the king shall be welcome; his majesty shall have tribute of me; the adventurous knight shall use his foil and target; the lover shall not sigh gratis; the humorous man shall end his part in peace; the clown shall make those laugh whose lungs are tickle o' the sere; and the lady shall say her mind freely, or the blank verse shall halt for 't. What players are they?   340

Ros. Even those you were wont to take delight in, the tragedians of the city.

Ham. How chances it they travel? their residence, both in reputation and profit, was better both ways.

Ros. I think their inhibition comes by the means of the late innovation.

Ham. Do they hold the same estimation they did when I was in the city? are they so followed?   350

Ros. No, indeed, are they not.

Ham. How comes it? do they grow rusty?

Ros. Nay, their endeavour keeps in the wonted pace: but there is, sir, an aery of children, little eyases, that cry out on the top of question, and are most tyrannically clapped for 't: these are now the fashion, and so berattle the common stages—so they call them—that many wearing rapiers are afraid of goose-quills and dare scarce come thither.   360

Ham. What, are they children? who maintains 'em? how are they escoted? Will they pursue the quality no longer than they can sing? will they not say afterwards, if they should grow themselves to common players—as it is most like, if their means are no better —their writers do them wrong, to make them exclaim against their own succession?   368

Ros. 'Faith, there has been much to do on both sides; and the nation holds it no sin to tarre them to controversy: there was, for a while, no money bid for argument, unless the poet and the player went to cuffs in the question.

Ham. Is 't possible?

Guil. O, there has been much throwing about of brains.

Ham. Do the boys carry it away?

Ros. Ay, that they do, my lord; Hercules and his load too.   379

Ham. It is not very strange; for mine uncle is king of Denmark, and those that would make mows at him while my father lived, give twenty, forty, fifty, an hundred ducats a-piece for his picture in little. 'Sblood, there is something in this more than natural, if philosophy could find it out.   385

[*Flourish of trumpets within.*

Guil. There are the players.

Ham. Gentlemen, you are welcome to Elsinore. Your hands, come then: the appurtenance of welcome is fashion and ceremony: let me comply with you in this garb, lest my extent to the players, which, I tell you, must show fairly outward, should more appear like entertainment than yours. You are welcome: but my uncle-father and aunt-mother are deceived.   394

Guil. In what, my dear lord?

Ham. I am but mad north-north-west: when the wind is southerly I know a hawk from a handsaw.

Re-enter POLONIUS.

Pol. Well be with you, gentlemen!

Ham. Hark you, Guildenstern; and you too: at each ear a hearer: that great baby you see there is not yet out of his swaddling-clouts.   401

Ros. Happily he 's second time come to them; for they say an old man is twice a child.

Ham. I will prophesy he comes to tell me of the players; mark it. You say right, sir: o' Monday morning; 'twas so indeed.

Pol. My lord, I have news to tell you.

Ham. My lord, I have news to tell you. When Roscius was an actor in Rome,—   410

Pol. The actors are come hither, my lord.

Ham. Buz, buz!

Pol. Upon mine honour,—

Ham. Then came each actor on his ass,—

Pol. The best actors in the world, either for tragedy, comedy, history, pastoral, pastoral-comical, historical-pastoral, tragical-historical, tragical-comical-historical-pastoral, scene individable, or poem unlimited: Seneca cannot be too heavy, nor Plautus too light. For the law of writ and the liberty, these are the only men.   421

Ham. O Jephthah, judge of Israel, what a treasure hadst thou!

Pol. What a treasure had he, my lord?

Ham. Why,

'One fair daughter, and no more,
The which he loved passing well.'

Pol. [*Aside*] Still on my daughter.

Ham. Am I not i' the right, old Jephthah?

profession. 356. **tyrannically,** outrageously. 358. **berattle,** fill with din. **common stages,** public theaters. 359. **many wearing rapiers,** many men of fashion, who were afraid to patronize the common players for fear of being satirized by the poets who wrote for the children. 360. **goose-quills,** i.e., satire. 362. **escoted,** maintained. 363-364. **no longer . . . sing,** i.e., until their voices change. 365. **common,** regular. 368. **succession,** future careers. 370. **tarre,** set on (as dogs). 372. **argument,** probably, plot for a play. 373. **went to cuffs,** came to blows. **question,** controversy. 377. **carry it away,** win the day. 378-379. **Hercules . . . load,** regarded as an allusion to the sign of the Globe Theatre, which was Hercules bearing the world on his shoulder. 382. **ducats,** gold coins worth 9s. 4d. 383. **in little,** in miniature. 390. **comply,** observe the formalities of courtesy. **garb,** manner. 391. **extent,** showing of kindness. 396. **I am . . . north-north-west,** I am only partly mad, i.e., in only one point of the compass. 397. **handsaw.** Hanmer's proposed reading *hernshaw* would mean "heron"; *hand-*

saw may be an early corruption of *hernshaw*. Another view regards *hawk* as the variant of *hack,* a tool of the pickax type, and *handsaw* as a saw operated by hand. 401. **swaddling-clouts,** cloths in which to wrap a newborn baby. 407. **o' Monday morning,** said to mislead Polonius. 410. **Roscius,** a famous Roman actor. 412. **Buz, buz,** according to Blackstone, an interjection used at Oxford to denote stale news. 414. **Then . . . ass,** probably a quotation, not identified. 418. **scene individable,** a play observing the unity of place. **poem unlimited,** a play disregarding the unities of time and place. 419. **Seneca,** writer of Latin tragedies, model of early Elizabethan writers of tragedy. **Plautus,** writer of Latin comedy. 420. **law . . . liberty,** obligation to be faithful to the text of written plays and freedom to improvise (Hudson); pieces written according to rules and without rules, i.e., "classical" and "romantic" dramas (Chambers). 422. **Jephthah . . . Israel.** A popular ballad of *Jephthah's Daughter* has been preserved in several forms.

Pol. If you call me Jephthah, my lord, I have a
daughter that I love passing well. 431
Ham. Nay, that follows not.
Pol. What follows, then, my lord?
Ham. Why,
    'As by lot, God wot,'
and then, you know,
    'It came to pass, as most like it was,'—
the first row of the pious chanson will show you more;
for look, where my abridgement comes. 439

Enter four or five Players.

You are welcome, masters; welcome, all. I am glad
to see thee well. Welcome, good friends. O, my old
friend! thy face is valanced since I saw thee last:
comest thou to beard me in Denmark? What, my
young lady and mistress! By 'r lady, your ladyship
is nearer to heaven than when I saw you last, by the
altitude of a chopine. Pray God, your voice, like a
piece of uncurrent gold, be not cracked within the
ring. Masters, you are all welcome. We'll e'en to 't
like French falconers, fly at any thing we see: we'll
have a speech straight: come, give us a taste of your
quality; come, a passionate speech. 452
First Play. What speech, my lord?
Ham. I heard thee speak me a speech once, but it
was never acted; or, if it was, not above once; for the
play, I remember, pleased not the million; 'twas
caviare to the general: but it was—as I received it,
and others, whose judgements in such matters cried
in the top of mine—an excellent play, well digested
in the scenes, set down with as much modesty as
cunning. I remember, one said there were no sallets
in the lines to make the matter savoury, nor no matter
in the phrase that might indict the author of affectation; but called it an honest method, as wholesome as
sweet, and by very much more handsome than fine.
One speech in it I chiefly loved: 'twas Æneas' tale to
Dido; and thereabout of it especially, where he speaks
of Priam's slaughter: if it live in your memory, begin
at this line: let me see, let me see— 471
    'The rugged Pyrrhus, like the Hyrcanian beast,'—
it is not so:—it begins with Pyrrhus:—
    'The rugged Pyrrhus, he whose sable arms,
Black as his purpose, did the night resemble
When he lay couched in the ominous horse,
Hath now this dread and black complexion
    smear'd
With heraldry more dismal; head to foot
Now is he total gules; horridly trick'd
With blood of fathers, mothers, daughters, sons, 480
Baked and impasted with the parching streets,
That lend a tyrannous and damned light
To their lord's murder: roasted in wrath and fire,
And thus o'er-sized with coagulate gore,
With eyes like carbuncles, the hellish Pyrrhus

Old grandsire Priam seeks.'
So, proceed you.
Pol. 'Fore God, my lord, well spoken, with good
accent and good discretion.
First Play.   'Anon he finds him 490
Striking too short at Greeks; his antique sword,
Rebellious to his arm, lies where it falls,
Repugnant to command: unequal match'd,
Pyrrhus at Priam drives; in rage strikes wide;
But with the whiff and wind of his fell sword
The unnerved father falls. Then senseless Ilium,
Seeming to feel this blow, with flaming top
Stoops to his base, and with a hideous crash
Takes prisoner Pyrrhus' ear: for, lo! his sword,
Which was declining on the milky head 500
Of reverend Priam, seem'd i' the air to stick:
So, as a painted tyrant, Pyrrhus stood,
And like a neutral to his will and matter,
Did nothing.
But, as we often see, against some storm,
A silence in the heavens, the rack stand still,
The bold winds speechless and the orb below
As hush as death, anon the dreadful thunder
Doth rend the region, so, after Pyrrhus' pause,
Aroused vengeance sets him new a-work; 510
And never did the Cyclops' hammers fall
On Mars's armour forged for proof eterne
With less remorse than Pyrrhus' bleeding sword
Now falls on Priam.
Out, out, thou strumpet, Fortune! All you gods,
In general synod, take away her power;
Break all the spokes and fellies from her wheel,
And bowl the round nave down the hill of heaven,
As low as to the fiends!'
Pol. This is too long. 520
Ham. It shall be to the barber's, with your beard.
Prithee, say on: he 's for a jig or a tale of bawdry, or
he sleeps: say on: come to Hecuba.
First Play. 'But who, O, who had seen the mobled
queen—'
Ham. 'The mobled queen?'
Pol. That 's good; 'mobled queen' is good.
First Play. 'Run barefoot up and down, threatening
    the flames
With bisson rheum; a clout upon that head
Where late the diadem stood, and for a robe, 530
About her lank and all o'er-teemed loins,
A blanket, in the alarm of fear caught up;
Who this had seen, with tongue in venom steep'd,
'Gainst Fortune's state would treason have
    pronounced;
But if the gods themselves did see her then
When she saw Pyrrhus make malicious sport
In mincing with his sword her husband's limbs,
The instant burst of clamour that she made,
Unless things mortal move them not at all,

---

437. **like,** probable. 438. **row,** possibly, stanza. **pious chanson,**
scriptural ballad. 439. **abridgement comes,** opportunity comes for
cutting short the conversation. 442. **valanced,** fringed (with a beard).
447. **chopine,** kind of shoe raised by the thickness of the heel; worn in
Italy, particularly at Venice. 448. **uncurrent,** not passable as lawful
coinage. 449. **cracked within the ring.** In the center of coins were
rings enclosing the sovereign's head; if the coin was cracked within this
ring, it was unfit for currency. 457. **caviare to the general,** not relished
by the multitude (like caviare). 459. **cried in the top of,** spoke with
greater authority than. 461. **cunning,** skill. 462. **sallets,** salads; here,
spicy improprieties. 464. **indict,** convict. 466-467. **as wholesome
. . . fine.** Its beauty was not that of elaborate ornament, but that of
order and proportion (Chambers). 468. **Æneas' tale to Dido.** The lines

recited by the player are imitated from Marlowe and Nashe's *Dido
Queen of Carthage* (II, i, 214 ff.). They are written in such a way that the
conventionality of the play within a play is raised above that of ordinary
drama. 472. **Pyrrhus,** a Greek hero in the Trojan War. **Hyrcanian
beast,** the tiger; see Virgil, *Aeneid,* IV, 266. 476. **ominous horse,**
Trojan horse. 479. **gules,** red; a heraldic term. **trick'd,** spotted,
smeared. 481. **impasted,** made into a paste. 484. **o'er-sized,** covered
as with size or glue. 493. **Repugnant,** offering resistance. 496. **Then
senseless Ilium,** insensible Troy. 502. **painted tyrant,** tyrant in a
picture. 503. **matter,** task. 505. **against,** before. 506. **rack,** mass of
clouds. 509. **region,** sky. 512. **proof eterne,** eternal resistance to
assault. 516. **synod,** assembly. 517. **fellies,** pieces of wood forming
the rim of a wheel. 518. **nave,** hub. 522. **jig,** comic performance

Would have made milch the burning eyes
    of heaven,   540
And passion in the gods.'
Pol. Look, whether he has not turned his colour
and has tears in 's eyes. Pray you, no more.

Ham. 'Tis well; I'll have thee speak out the rest
soon. Good my lord, will you see the players well
bestowed? Do you hear, let them be well used; for
they are the abstract and brief chronicles of the time:
after your death you were better have a bad epitaph
than their ill report while you live.   551

Pol. My lord, I will use them according to their
desert.

Ham. God's bodykins, man, much better: use
every man after his desert, and who should 'scape
whipping? Use them after your own honour and
dignity: the less they deserve, the more merit is in
your bounty. Take them in.

Pol. Come, sirs.   559

Ham. Follow him, friends: we'll hear a play to-
morrow. [*Exit Polonius with all the Players but the First.*]
Dost thou hear me, old friend; can you play the
Murder of Gonzago?

First Play. Ay, my lord.

Ham. We'll ha 't to-morrow night. You could, for
a need, study a speech of some dozen or sixteen lines,
which I would set down and insert in 't, could you not?

First Play. Ay, my lord.   569

Ham. Very well. Follow that lord; and look you
mock him not. [*Exit First Player.*] My good friends,
I'll leave you till night: you are welcome to Elsinore.

Ros. Good my lord!

Ham. Ay, so, God be wi' ye; [*Exeunt Rosencrantz and
    Guildenstern.*] Now I am alone.

O, what a rogue and peasant slave am I!
Is it not monstrous that this player here,
But in a fiction, in a dream of passion,
Could force his soul so to his own conceit
That from her working all his visage wann'd,   580
Tears in his eyes, distraction in 's aspect,
A broken voice, and his whole function suiting
With forms to his conceit? and all for nothing!
For Hecuba!
What 's Hecuba to him, or he to Hecuba,
That he should weep for her? What would he do,
Had he the motive and the cue for passion
That I have? He would drown the stage with tears
And cleave the general ear with horrid speech,
Make mad the guilty and appal the free,   590
Confound the ignorant, and amaze indeed
The very faculties of eyes and ears.
Yet I,
A dull and muddy-mettled rascal, peak,
Like John-a-dreams, unpregnant of my cause,
And can say nothing; no, not for a king,
Upon whose property and most dear life

A damn'd defeat was made. Am I a coward?
Who calls me villain? breaks my pate across?
Plucks off my beard, and blows it in my face?   600
Tweaks me by the nose? gives me the lie i' the throat,
As deep as to the lungs? who does me this?
Ha!
'Swounds, I should take it: for it cannot be
But I am pigeon-liver'd and lack gall
To make oppression bitter, or ere this
I should have fatted all the region kites
With this slave's offal: bloody, bawdy villain!
Remorseless, treacherous, lecherous, kindless villain!
O, vengeance!   610
Why, what an ass am I! This is most brave,
That I, the son of a dear father murder'd,
Prompted to my revenge by heaven and hell,
Must, like a whore, unpack my heart with words,
And fall a-cursing, like a very drab,
A scullion!
Fie upon 't! foh! About, my brain! I have heard
That guilty creatures sitting at a play
Have by the very cunning of the scene
Been struck so to the soul that presently   620
They have proclaim'd their malefactions;
For murder, though it have no tongue, will speak
With most miraculous organ. I'll have these players
Play something like the murder of my father
Before mine uncle: I'll observe his looks;
I'll tent him to the quick: if he but blench,
I know my course. The spirit that I have seen
May be the devil: and the devil hath power
To assume a pleasing shape; yea, and perhaps
Out of my weakness and my melancholy,   630
As he is very potent with such spirits,
Abuses me to damn me: I'll have grounds
More relative than this: the play 's the thing
Wherein I'll catch the conscience of the king.   [*Exit.*

ACT III.

SCENE I. *A room in the castle.*

Enter KING, QUEEN, POLONIUS, OPHELIA,
    ROSENCRANTZ, *and* GUILDENSTERN.

King. And can you, by no drift of conference,
Get from him why he puts on this confusion,
Grating so harshly all his days of quiet
With turbulent and dangerous lunacy?

Ros. He does confess he feels himself distracted;
But from what cause he will by no means speak.

Guil. Nor do we find him forward to be sounded,
But, with a crafty madness, keeps aloof,
When we would bring him on to some confession
Of his true state.

Queen.   Did he receive you well?   10

Ros. Most like a gentleman.

given at the end or in an interval of a play. 523. **bawdry,** indecency.
Hecuba, wife of Priam, king of Troy. 525. **mobled,** muffled. 529.
bisson rheum, blinding tears. **clout,** piece of cloth. 531. **o'er-
teemed,** worn out with bearing children. 534. **pronounced,** proclaimed. 540. **milch,** moist with tears. 542. **turned,** changed. 548.
abstract, summary account. 554. **bodykins,** diminutive form of the
oath, "by God's body." 567. **dozen or sixteen lines.** Critics have
amused themselves by trying to locate Hamlet's lines. Lucianus' speech,
III, ii, 266, ff., is the best guess. 576. **peasant,** base. 580. **wann'd,**
grew pale. 582-583. **his whole . . . conceit,** his whole being responded
with forms to suit his thought. 594. **muddy-mettled,** dull-spirited.
peak, mope, pine. 595. **John-a-dreams,** an expression occurring elsewhere in Elizabethan literature to indicate a dreamer. **unpregnant of,**

not quickened by. 597. **property,** proprietorship (of crown and life).
605. **pigeon-liver'd.** The pigeon was supposed to secrete no gall; if
Hamlet, so he says, had had gall, he would have felt the bitterness of
oppression, and avenged it. 607. **region kites,** kites of the air. 609.
kindless, unnatural. 615. **drab,** prostitute. 616. **scullion,** kitchen
servant; Q_2: *stallyon*, which is defensible; see *NED* under *stallion* 3.
617. **About,** about it, or turn thou right about. 626. **tent,** probe.
blench, quail, flinch. 628. **May be the devil.** Hamlet's suspicion is
properly grounded in the belief of the time. 631. **spirits,** humors. 633.
relative, closely related, definite. **this,** i.e., the ghost's story.

ACT III. SCENE I. 1. **drift of conference,** device of conversation; so
Q_2; Globe, following F: *circumstance.* 7. **forward,** willing.

Guil. But with much forcing of his disposition.

Ros. Niggard of question; but, of our demands,
Most free in his reply.

Queen. Did you assay him
To any pastime?

Ros. Madam, it so fell out, that certain players
We o'er-raught on the way: of these we told him;
And there did seem in him a kind of joy
To hear of it: they are about the court,
And, as I think, they have already order   20
This night to play before him.

Pol. 'Tis most true:
And he beseech'd me to entreat your majesties
To hear and see the matter.

King. With all my heart; and it doth much content me
To hear him so inclined.
Good gentlemen, give him a further edge,
And drive his purpose on to these delights.

Ros. We shall, my lord.
                    [*Exeunt Rosencrantz and Guildenstern.*

King. Sweet Gertrude, leave us too;
For we have closely sent for Hamlet hither,
That he, as 'twere by accident, may here   30
Affront Ophelia:
Her father and myself, lawful espials,
Will so bestow ourselves that, seeing, unseen,
We may of their encounter frankly judge,
And gather by him, as he is behaved,
If 't be the affliction of his love or no
That thus he suffers for.

Queen. I shall obey you.
And for your part, Ophelia, I do wish
That your good beauties be the happy cause
Of Hamlet's wildness: so shall I hope your virtues   40
Will bring him to his wonted way again,
To both your honours.

Oph. Madam, I wish it may. [*Exit Queen.*

Pol. Ophelia, walk you here. Gracious, so please you,
We will bestow ourselves. [*To Ophelia*] Read on this book;
That show of such an exercise may colour
Your loneliness. We are oft to blame in this,—
'Tis too much proved—that with devotion's visage
And pious action we do sugar o'er
The devil himself.

King. [*Aside*] O, 'tis too true!
How smart a lash that speech doth give my conscience!   50
The harlot's cheek, beautied with plastering art,
Is not more ugly to the thing that helps it
Than is my deed to my most painted word:
O heavy burthen!

Pol. I hear him coming: let 's withdraw, my lord.
                    [*Exeunt King and Polonius.*

Enter HAMLET.

Ham. To be, or not to be: that is the question:
Whether 'tis nobler in the mind to suffer
The slings and arrows of outrageous fortune,
Or to take arms against a sea of troubles,
And by opposing end them? To die: to sleep;   60
No more; and by a sleep to say we end
The heart-ache and the thousand natural shocks
That flesh is heir to, 'tis a consummation
Devoutly to be wish'd. To die, to sleep;
To sleep: perchance to dream: ay, there 's the rub;
For in that sleep of death what dreams may come
When we have shuffled off this mortal coil,
Must give us pause: there 's the respect
That makes calamity of so long life;
For who would bear the whips and scorns of time,   70
The oppressor's wrong, the proud man's contumely,
The pangs of despised love, the law's delay,
The insolence of office and the spurns
That patient merit of the unworthy takes,
When he himself might his quietus make
With a bare bodkin? who would fardels bear,
To grunt and sweat under a weary life,
But that the dread of something after death,
The undiscover'd country from whose bourn
No traveller returns, puzzles the will   80
And makes us rather bear those ills we have
Than fly to others that we know not of?
Thus conscience does make cowards of us all;
And thus the native hue of resolution
Is sicklied o'er with the pale cast of thought,
And enterprises of great pitch and moment
With this regard their currents turn awry,
And lose the name of action.—Soft you now!
The fair Ophelia! Nymph, in thy orisons
Be all my sins remember'd.

Oph. Good my lord,   90
How does your honour for this many a day?

Ham. I humbly thank you; well, well, well.

Oph. My lord, I have remembrances of yours,
That I have longed long to re-deliver;
I pray you, now receive them.

Ham. No, not I;
I never gave you aught.

Oph. My honour'd lord, you know right well you did;
And, with them, words of so sweet breath composed
As made the things more rich: their perfume lost,
Take these again; for to the noble mind   100
Rich gifts wax poor when givers prove unkind.
There, my lord.

Ham. Ha, ha! are you honest?

Oph. My lord?

Ham. Are you fair?

Oph. What means your lordship?

12. **forcing of his disposition,** i.e., against his will. 13. **Niggard of question,** sparing of conversation. 17. **o'er-raught,** overtook. 26. **edge,** incitement. 28. **too,** so F; Q_2: *two*. 29. **closely,** secretly. 31. **Affront,** confront. 32. **lawful espials,** legitimate spies. 40. **wildness,** madness. 43. **Gracious,** your grace (addressed to the king). 45. **exercise,** act of devotion. 52. **to,** compared to. **thing,** i.e., the cosmetic. 54. **O heavy burthen.** The king's sudden repentance serves to convince the audience of his guilt. It is to be noted also that the current theory of psychology provided for sudden changes such as this by the ready movement of spirits to the heart. 59. **sea.** The mixed metaphor of this speech has often been commented on; Theobald's emendation *siege* has sometimes been spoken on the stage. 67. **shuffled,** sloughed, cast. **coil,** usually means "turmoil"; here, possibly "body" (conceived of as wound about the soul like rope); *clay, soil, veil,* have been suggested

as emendations. 69. **of . . . life,** so long lived. 70. **time,** the world. 72. **despised,** rejected. 73. **office,** office-holders. **spurns,** insults. 75. **quietus,** acquittance; here, death. 76. **bare bodkin,** mere dagger; *bare* is sometimes understood as "unsheathed." **fardels,** burdens. 79. **bourn,** boundary. 83. **conscience,** probably, inhibition by the faculty of reason restraining the will from doing wrong. 84. **native hue,** natural color; metaphor derived from the color of the face. 85. **sicklied o'er,** given a sickly tinge. **cast,** shade of color. 86. **moment,** importance. 87. **regard,** respect, consideration. **currents,** courses. 89. **orisons,** prayers. 103-108. **are you . . . beauty.** *Honest* meaning "truthful" (l. 103) and "chaste" (l. 107), and *fair* meaning "just, honorable" (l. 105) and "beautiful" (l. 107) are not mere quibbles; the speech has the irony of a *double entendre.* 108. **your honesty,** your chastity. **discourse to,** familiar intercourse with. 110. **commerce,**

Ham. That if you be honest and fair, your honesty should admit no discourse to your beauty.

Oph. Could beauty, my lord, have better commerce than with honesty? 110

Ham. Ay, truly; for the power of beauty will sooner transform honesty from what it is to a bawd than the force of honesty can translate beauty into his likeness: this was sometime a paradox, but now the time gives it proof. I did love you once.

Oph. Indeed, my lord, you made me believe so.

Ham. You should not have believed me; for virtue cannot so inoculate our old stock but we shall relish of it: I loved you not. 120

Oph. I was the more deceived.

Ham. Get thee to a nunnery: why wouldst thou be a breeder of sinners? I am myself indifferent honest; but yet I could accuse me of such things that it were better my mother had not borne me: I am very proud, revengeful, ambitious, with more offences at my beck than I have thoughts to put them in, imagination to give them shape, or time to act them in. What should such fellows as I do crawling between earth and heaven? We are arrant knaves, all; believe none of us. Go thy ways to a nunnery. Where 's your father? 133

Oph. At home, my lord.

Ham. Let the doors be shut upon him, that he may play the fool no where but in 's own house. Farewell.

Oph. O, help him, you sweet heavens!

Ham. If thou dost marry, I'll give thee this plague for thy dowry: be thou as chaste as ice, as pure as snow, thou shalt not escape calumny. Get thee to a nunnery, go: farewell. Or, if thou wilt needs marry, marry a fool; for wise men know well enough what monsters you make of them. To a nunnery, go, and quickly too. Farewell. 146

Oph. O heavenly powers, restore him!

Ham. I have heard of your paintings too, well enough; God has given you one face, and you make yourselves another: you jig, you amble, and you lisp, and nick-name God's creatures, and make your wantonness your ignorance. Go to, I'll no more on 't; it hath made me mad. I say, we will have no more marriages: those that are married already, all but one, shall live; the rest shall keep as they are. To a nunnery, go. [*Exit.*

Oph. O, what a noble mind is here o'er-thrown!
The courtier's, soldier's, scholar's, eye, tongue, sword;
The expectancy and rose of the fair state, 160
The glass of fashion and the mould of form,
The observed of all observers, quite, quite down!
And I, of ladies most deject and wretched,
That suck'd the honey of his music vows,
Now see that noble and most sovereign reason,
Like sweet bells jangled, out of tune and harsh;
That unmatch'd form and feature of blown youth
Blasted with ecstasy: O, woe is me,

To have seen what I have seen, see what I see!

Re-enter KING *and* POLONIUS.

King. Love! his affections do not that way tend; 170
Nor what he spake, though it lack'd form a little,
Was not like madness. There 's something in his soul,
O'er which his melancholy sits on brood;
And I do doubt the hatch and the disclose
Will be some danger: which for to prevent,
I have in quick determination
Thus set it down: he shall with speed to England,
For the demand of our neglected tribute:
Haply the seas and countries different
With variable objects shall expel 180
This something-settled matter in his heart,
Whereon his brains still beating puts him thus
From fashion of himself. What think you on 't?

Pol. It shall do well: but yet do I believe
The origin and commencement of his grief
Sprung from neglected love. How now, Ophelia!
You need not tell us what Lord Hamlet said;
We heard it all. My lord, do as you please;
But, if you hold it fit, after the play
Let his queen mother all alone entreat him 190
To show his grief: let her be round with him;
And I'll be placed, so please you, in the ear
Of all their conference. If she find him not,
To England send him, or confine him where
Your wisdom best shall think.

King. It shall be so:
Madness in great ones must not unwatch'd go. [*Exeunt.*

SCENE II. *A hall in the castle.*

Enter HAMLET *and* Players.

Ham. Speak the speech, I pray you, as I pronounced it to you, trippingly on the tongue: but if you mouth it, as many of your players do, I had as lief the town-crier spoke my lines. Nor do not saw the air too much with your hand, thus, but use all gently; for in the very torrent, tempest, and, as I may say, the whirlwind of your passion, you must acquire and beget a temperance that may give it smoothness. O, it offends me to the soul to hear a robustious periwig-pated fellow tear a passion to tatters, to very rags, to split the ears of the groundlings, who for the most part are capable of nothing but inexplicable dumb-shows and noise: I would have such a fellow whipped for o'er-doing Termagant; it out-herods Herod: pray you, avoid it.

First Play. I warrant your honour. 17

Ham. Be not too tame neither, but let your own discretion be your tutor: suit the action to the word, the word to the action; with this special observance, that you o'er-step not the modesty of nature: for any thing so overdone is from the purpose of playing, whose end, both at the first and now, was and is, to hold, as 't were, the mirror up to nature; to show virtue her own feature, scorn her own image, and the very age and body of the time his form and pressure. Now this overdone, or come tardy off, though it make the unskilful laugh, cannot but make the judicious grieve; the censure of the which one must in your allowance o'erweigh a whole theatre of others. O, there be players that I have seen play, and heard others praise, and that highly, not to speak it profanely, that, neither having the accent of Christians nor the gait of Christian, pagan, nor man, have so strutted and bellowed that I have thought some of nature's journeymen had made men and not made them well, they imitated humanity so abominably.   40

First Play. I hope we have reformed that indifferently with us, sir.

Ham. O, reform it altogether. And let those that play your clowns speak no more than is set down for them; for there be of them that will themselves laugh, to set on some quantity of barren spectators to laugh too; though, in the mean time, some necessary question of the play be then to be considered: that 's villanous, and shows a most pitiful ambition in the fool that uses it. Go, make you ready.   [*Exeunt Players.*

Enter POLONIUS, ROSENCRANTZ, *and* GUILDENSTERN.

How now, my lord! will the king hear this piece of work?

Pol. And the queen too, and that presently.

Ham. Bid the players make haste.   [*Exit Polonius.* Will you two help to hasten them?

Ros. } We will, my lord.
Guil. }

[*Exeunt Rosencrantz and Guildenstern.*

Ham. What ho! Horatio!

Enter HORATIO.

Hor. Here, sweet lord, at your service.

Ham. Horatio, thou art e'en as just a man
As e'er my conversation coped withal.   60

Hor. O, my dear lord,—

Ham.   Nay, do not think I flatter;
For what advancement may I hope from thee
That no revenue hast but thy good spirits,
To feed and clothe thee? Why should the poor be
    flatter'd?
No, let the candied tongue lick absurd pomp,
And crook the pregnant hinges of the knee
Where thrift may follow fawning. Dost thou hear?
Since my dear soul was mistress of her choice
And could of men distinguish her election,
S' hath seal'd thee for herself; for thou hast been   70
As one, in suffering all, that suffers nothing,
A man that fortune's buffets and rewards
Hast ta'en with equal thanks: and blest are those

Whose blood and judgement are so well commeddled,
That they are not a pipe for fortune's finger
To sound what stop she please. Give me that man
That is not passion's slave, and I will wear him
In my heart's core, ay, in my heart of heart,
As I do thee.—Something too much of this.—
There is a play to-night before the king;   80
One scene of it comes near the circumstance
Which I have told thee of my father's death:
I prithee, when thou seest that act afoot,
Even with the very comment of thy soul
Observe mine uncle: if his occulted guilt
Do not itself unkennel in one speech,
It is a damned ghost that we have seen,
And my imaginations are as foul
As Vulcan's stithy. Give him heedful note;
For I mine eyes will rivet to his face,   90
And after we will both our judgements join
In censure of his seeming.

Hor.   Well, my lord:
If he steal aught the whilst this play is playing,
And 'scape detecting, I will pay the theft.

Ham. They are coming to the play; I must be idle:
Get you a place.

Danish march. A flourish. Enter KING, QUEEN,
    POLONIUS, OPHELIA, ROSENCRANTZ,
    GUILDENSTERN, *and others*.

King. How fares our cousin Hamlet?

Ham. Excellent, i' faith; of the chameleon's dish: I eat the air, promise-crammed: you cannot feed capons so.   100

King. I have nothing with this answer, Hamlet; these words are not mine.

Ham. No, nor mine now. [*To Polonius*] My lord, you played once i' the university, you say?

Pol. That did I, my lord; and was accounted a good actor.

Ham. What did you enact?

Pol. I did enact Julius Cæsar: I was killed i' the Capitol; Brutus killed me.

Ham. It was a brute part of him to kill so capital a calf there. Be the players ready?   111

Ros. Ay, my lord; they stay upon your patience.

Queen. Come hither, my dear Hamlet, sit by me.

Ham. No, good mother, here 's metal more attractive.

Pol. [*To the King*] O, ho! do you mark that?

Ham. Lady, shall I lie in your lap?

[*Lying down at Ophelia's feet.*

Oph. No, my lord.   120

Ham. I mean, my head upon your lap?

Oph. Ay, my lord.

Ham. Do you think I meant country matters?

Oph. I think nothing, my lord.

Ham. That 's a fair thought to lie between maids' legs.

Oph. What is, my lord?

26. **very age,** actual generation. 27. **pressure,** stamp, impressed character. 28. **come tardy off,** inadequately done. 31. **which one,** one of whom. 38. **journeymen,** laborers not yet masters in their trade. 40. **abominably.** Q₂F: *abhominably,* a word thought to be derived from *ab homine,* a circumstance which brings out better the contrast with *humanity.* 41. **indifferently,** fairly, tolerably. 43. **clowns.** The parts spoken by clowns were often not written down at all, and their jests were no doubt interruptions in serious plays. Writing definite parts for them (and making them stick to their parts) was apparently progressive during Shakespeare's career.

44. **of,** i.e., some among them. 46. **barren,** i.e., of wit. 59. **just,** honest, honorable. 63. **revenue,** accent on second syllable. 67. **thrift,** profit. 69-70. Text follows Q₂; Globe, following F, places comma after *distinguish* and reads *Hath.* 74. **commeddled,** so Q₂; Globe, following F: *commingled.* 76. **stop,** hole in a wind instrument for controlling the sound. 84. **very . . . soul,** inward and sagacious criticism (Dowden). 85. **occulted,** hidden. 87. **damned,** in league with Satan. 89. **stithy,** smithy, place of *stiths* (anvils). 92. **censure . . . seeming,** judgment of his appearance or behavior. 95. **idle,** crazy, or not attending to any-

Ham. Nothing.

Oph. You are merry, my lord.

Ham. Who, I? 130

Oph. Ay, my lord.

Ham. O God, your only jig-maker. What should a man do but be merry? for, look you, how cheerfully my mother looks, and my father died within these two hours.

Oph. Nay, 'tis twice two months, my lord. 136

Ham. So long? Nay then, let the devil wear black, for I'll have a suit of sables. O heavens! die two months ago, and not forgotten yet? Then there 's hope a great man's memory may outlive his life half a year: but, by 'r lady, he must build churches, then; or else shall he suffer not thinking on, with the hobby-horse, whose epitaph is 'For, O, for, O, the hobby-horse is forgot.' 145

Hautboys play. The dumb-show enters.

Enter a King *and a* Queen *very lovingly; the* Queen *embracing him, and he her. She kneels, and makes show of protestation unto him. He takes her up, and declines his head upon her neck: lays him down upon a bank of flowers: she, seeing him asleep, leaves him. Anon comes in a fellow, takes off his crown, kisses it, and pours poison in the* King's *ears, and exit. The* Queen *returns; finds the* King *dead, and makes passionate action. The* Poisoner, *with some two or three* Mutes, *comes in again, seeming to lament with her. The dead body is carried away. The* Poisoner *wooes the* Queen *with gifts: she seems loath and unwilling awhile, but in the end accepts his love.* [*Exeunt.*

Oph. What means this, my lord?

Ham. Marry, this is miching mallecho; it means mischief.

Oph. Belike this show imports the argument of the play. 150

Enter Prologue.

Ham. We shall know by this fellow: the players cannot keep counsel; they'll tell all.

Oph. Will he tell us what this show meant?

Ham. Ay, or any show that you'll show him: be not you ashamed to show, he'll not shame to tell you what it means.

Oph. You are naught, you are naught: I'll mark the play.

Pro. For us, and for our tragedy,
　　Here stooping to your clemency, 160
　　We beg your hearing patiently. [*Exit.*

Ham. Is this a prologue, or the posy of a ring?

Oph. 'Tis brief, my lord.

Ham. As woman's love.

Enter two Players, King *and* Queen.

P. King. Full thirty times hath Phœbus' cart gone
　　round
Neptune's salt wash and Tellus' orbed ground,

And thirty dozen moons with borrow'd sheen
About the world have times twelve thirties been,
Since love our hearts and Hymen did our hands
Unite commutual in most sacred bands. 170

P. Queen. So many journeys may the sun and moon
Make us again count o'er ere love be done!
But, woe is me, you are so sick of late,
So far from cheer and from your former state,
That I distrust you. Yet, though I distrust,
Discomfort you, my lord, it nothing must:
For women's fear and love holds quantity;
In neither aught, or in extremity.
Now, what my love is, proof hath made you know;
And as my love is sized, my fear is so: 180
Where love is great, the littlest doubts are fear;
Where little fears grow great, great love grows there.

P. King. 'Faith, I must leave thee, love, and shortly
　　too;
My operant powers their functions leave to do:
And thou shalt live in this fair world behind,
Honour'd, beloved; and haply one as kind
For husband shalt thou—

P. Queen. 　　　　　O, confound the rest!
Such love must needs be treason in my breast:
In second husband let me be accurst!
None wed the second but who kill'd the first. 190

Ham. [*Aside*] Wormwood, wormwood.

P. Queen. The instances that second marriage move
Are base respects of thrift, but none of love:
A second time I kill my husband dead,
When second husband kisses me in bed.

P. King. I do believe you think what now you speak;
But what we do determine oft we break.
Purpose is but the slave to memory,
Of violent birth, but poor validity:
Which now, like fruit unripe, sticks on the tree; 200
But fall, unshaken, when they mellow be.
Most necessary 'tis that we forget
To pay ourselves what to ourselves is debt:
What to ourselves in passion we propose,
The passion ending, doth the purpose lose.
The violence of either grief or joy
Their own enactures with themselves destroy:
Where joy most revels, grief doth most lament;
Grief joys, joy grieves, on slender accident.
This world is not for aye, nor 'tis not strange 210
That even our loves should with our fortunes change;
For 'tis a question left us yet to prove,
Whether love lead fortune, or else fortune love.
The great man down, you mark his favourite flies;
The poor advanced makes friends of enemies.
And hitherto doth love on fortune tend;
For who not needs shall never lack a friend,
And who in want a hollow friend doth try,
Directly seasons him his enemy.
But, orderly to end where I begun, 220
Our wills and fates do so contrary run
That our devices still are overthrown;

thing serious. 98. **chameleon's dish.** Chameleons were supposed to feed on air. 101. **have . . . with,** make nothing of. 102. **are not mine,** mean nothing to me. 132. **your only,** only your. **jig-maker,** composer of jigs (song and dance). 138. **suit of sables,** garments trimmed with the fur of the sable, with a quibble on *sable* meaning "black." 143. **suffer . . . on,** undergo oblivion. 144-145. **'For . . . forgot,'** verse of a song occurring also in *Love's Labour's Lost,* III, i, 30. The hobbyhorse was a character in the Morris Dance. 145. *Stage Direction:* **Hautboys,** wooden double-reed instruments of high pitch. 147. **miching mallecho,**

sneaking mischief, so Malone; Q2: *munching Mallico;* F: *miching Malicho.* 160. **stooping,** bowing. 162. **posy,** motto. 166. **salt wash,** the sea. **Tellus'.** Tellus was a goddess personifying the earth (*orbed ground*). 167. **borrow'd,** i.e., reflected. 169. **Hymen,** god of matrimony. 170. **commutual,** intensely mutual. 175. **distrust,** am anxious about. 176. After this line Q2 has *For women feare too much, euen as they love.* 177. **holds quantity,** keeps proportion between. 184. **operant,** active. **leave,** cease. 207. **enactures,** fulfillments. 210. **aye,** ever. 218. **who,** whoever. 219. **seasons,** matures, ripens.

Our thoughts are ours, their ends none of our own:
So think thou wilt no second husband wed;
But die thy thoughts when thy first lord is dead.
P. Queen. Nor earth to me give food, nor heaven
    light!
Sport and repose lock from me day and night!
To desperation turn my trust and hope!
An anchor's cheer in prison be my scope!
Each opposite that blanks the face of joy   230
Meet what I would have well and it destroy!
Both here and hence pursue me lasting strife,
If, once a widow, ever I be wife!
Ham. If she should break it now!
P. King. 'Tis deeply sworn. Sweet, leave me here
    awhile;
My spirits grow dull, and fain I would beguile
The tedious day with sleep.   [*Sleeps.*
P. Queen.   Sleep rock thy brain!
And never come mischance between us twain! [*Exit.*
Ham. Madam, how like you this play?
Queen. The lady doth protest too much, methinks.240
Ham. O, but she'll keep her word.
King. Have you heard the argument? Is there no
offence in 't?
Ham. No, no, they do but jest, poison in jest; no of-
fence i' the world.
King. What do you call the play?
Ham. The Mouse-trap. Marry, how? Tropically.
This play is the image of a murder done in Vienna:
Gonzago is the duke's name; his wife, Baptista: you
shall see anon; 't is a knavish piece of work: but what
o' that? your majesty and we that have free souls, it
touches us not: let the galled jade wince, our withers
are unwrung.   253

Enter LUCIANUS.

This is one Lucianus, nephew to the king.
Oph. You are as good as a chorus, my lord.
Ham. I could interpret between you and your love,
if I could see the puppets dallying.
Oph. You are keen, my lord, you are keen.
Ham. It would cost you a groaning to take off my
edge.   260
Oph. Still better, and worse.
Ham. So you must take your husbands. Begin,
murderer; pox, leave thy damnable faces, and begin.
Come: 'the croaking raven doth bellow for revenge.'
Luc. Thoughts black, hands apt, drugs fit, and time
    agreeing;
Confederate season, else no creature seeing;
Thou mixture rank, of midnight weeds collected,
With Hecate's ban thrice blasted, thrice infected,
Thy natural magic and dire property,   270
On wholesome life usurp immediately.
          [*Pours the poison into the sleeper's ears.*
Ham. He poisons him i' the garden for 's estate. His

name 's Gonzago: the story is extant, and writ in
choice Italian: you shall see anon how the murderer
gets the love of Gonzago's wife.
Oph. The king rises.
Ham. What, frighted with false fire!
Queen. How fares my lord?
Pol. Give o'er the play.
King. Give me some light: away!   280
All. Lights, lights, lights!
          [*Exeunt all but Hamlet and Horatio.*
Ham. Why, let the stricken deer go weep,
          The hart ungalled play;
          For some must watch, while some must sleep:
          So runs the world away.
Would not this, sir, and a forest of feathers—if the
rest of my fortunes turn Turk with me—with two
Provincial roses on my razed shoes, get me a fellow-
ship in a cry of players, sir?
Hor. Half a share.   290
Ham. A whole one, I.
          For thou dost know, O Damon dear,
              This realm dismantled was
          Of Jove himself; and now reigns here
              A very, very—pajock.
Hor. You might have rhymed.
Ham. O good Horatio, I'll take the ghost's word for
a thousand pound. Didst perceive?
Hor. Very well, my lord.
Ham. Upon the talk of the poisoning?   300
Hor. I did very well note him.
Ham. Ah, ha! Come, some music! come, the
recorders!
          For if the king like not the comedy,
              Why then, belike, he likes it not, perdy.
Come, some music!

Re-enter ROSENCRANTZ *and* GUILDENSTERN.

Guil. Good my lord, vouchsafe me a word with you.
Ham. Sir, a whole history.
Guil. The king, sir,—   310
Ham. Ay, sir, what of him?
Guil. Is in his retirement marvellous distempered.
Ham. With drink, sir?
Guil. No, my lord, rather with choler.
Ham. Your wisdom should show itself more richer
to signify this to his doctor; for, for me to put him to
his purgation would perhaps plunge him into far
more choler.   319
Guil. Good my lord, put your discourse into some
frame and start not so wildly from my affair.
Ham. I am tame, sir: pronounce.
Guil. The queen, your mother, in most great afflic-
tion of spirit, hath sent me to you.
Ham. You are welcome.   325
Guil. Nay, good my lord, this courtesy is not of the
right breed. If it shall please you to make me a whole-

223. **ends**, results. 229. **An anchor's**, an anchorite's. **cheer**, fare;
sometimes printed as *chair*. 230. **opposite**, adversary. **blanks**, causes
to *blanch* or grow pale. 248. **Tropically**, figuratively. The Q_1 reading,
trapically, suggests a pun on *trap* in *Mouse-trap* (l. 247). 249. **Gonzago**.
In 1538 Luigi Gonzago murdered the duke of Urbano by pouring
poisoned lotion in his ears. 253. **galled jade**, horse whose hide is
rubbed by saddle or harness. **withers**, the part between the horse's
shoulder blades. **unwrung**, not wrung or twisted. 255. **chorus**. In
many Elizabethan plays the action was explained by an actor known as
the "chorus"; at a puppet show the actor who explained the action was
known as an "interpreter," as indicated by the lines following. 261.
Still . . . worse, more keen, less decorous (Caldecott). 263. **pox**, an
imprecation. 264-265. **'the croaking . . . revenge,'** possibly reminiscent of the *True Tragedie of Richard the Third:* "The screeking raven sits

croaking for revenge. Whole herds of beasts come bellowing for revenge."
267. **Confederate**, conspiring (to assist the murderer). 269. **Hecate**,
the goddess of witchcraft. **ban**, curse. 277. **false fire**, fireworks, or a
blank discharge. 282-285. **Why . . . away**, probably from an old
ballad, with allusion to the popular belief that a wounded deer retires
to weep and die. Cf. *As You Like It*, II, i, 66. 286. **this**, i.e., the play.
feathers, allusion to the plumes which Elizabethan actors were fond of
wearing. 287. **turn Turk with**, go back on. 288. **two Provincial
roses**, rosettes of ribbon like the roses of Provins near Paris, or else the
roses of Provence. **razed**, cut, slashed (by way of ornament). 289.
fellowship . . . players, partnership in a theatrical company. **cry**,
pack (as of hounds). 290. **Half a share**, allusion to the custom in
dramatic companies of dividing the ownership into a number of shares
among the householders. 292-295. **For . . . very**, probably from an old

some answer, I will do your mother's commandment: if not, your pardon and my return shall be the end of my business.

Ham. Sir, I cannot. 331

Guil. What, my lord?

Ham. Make you a wholesome answer; my wit's diseased: but, sir, such answer as I can make, you shall command; or, rather, as you say, my mother: therefore no more, but to the matter: my mother, you say,—

Ros. Then thus she says; your behaviour hath struck her into amazement and admiration. 339

Ham. O wonderful son, that can so astonish a mother! But is there no sequel at the heels of this mother's admiration? Impart.

Ros. She desires to speak with you in her closet, ere you go to bed.

Ham. We shall obey, were she ten times our mother. Have you any further trade with us?

Ros. My lord, you once did love me.

Ham. So I do still, by these pickers and stealers. 349

Ros. Good my lord, what is your cause of distemper? you do, surely, bar the door upon your own liberty, if you deny your griefs to your friend.

Ham. Sir, I lack advancement.

Ros. How can that be, when you have the voice of the king himself for your succession in Denmark?

Ham. Ay, sir, but 'While the grass grows,'—the proverb is something musty. 359

Re-enter Players *with recorders.*

O, the recorders! let me see one. To withdraw with you:—why do you go about to recover the wind of me, as if you would drive me into a toil?

Guil. O, my lord, if my duty be too bold, my love is too unmannerly.

Ham. I do not well understand that. Will you play upon this pipe?

Guil. My lord, I cannot.

Ham. I pray you.

Guil. Believe me, I cannot.

Ham. I do beseech you. 370

Guil. I know no touch of it, my lord.

Ham. 'Tis as easy as lying: govern these ventages with your fingers and thumb, give it breath with your mouth, and it will discourse most eloquent music. Look you, these are the stops.

Guil. But these cannot I command to any utterance of harmony; I have not the skill. 378

Ham. Why, look you now, how unworthy a thing you make of me! You would play upon me; you would seem to know my stops; you would pluck out the heart of my mystery; you would sound me from my lowest note to the top of my compass: and there is much music, excellent voice, in this little organ; yet cannot you make it speak. 'Sblood, do you think I am

easier to be played on than a pipe? Call me what instrument you will, though you can fret me, yet you cannot play upon me.

Enter POLONIUS.

God bless you, sir! 390

Pol. My lord, the queen would speak with you, and presently.

Ham. Do you see yonder cloud that 's almost in shape of a camel?

Pol. By the mass, and 'tis like a camel, indeed.

Ham. Methinks it is like a weasel.

Pol. It is backed like a weasel.

Ham. Or like a whale?

Pol. Very like a whale. 399

Ham. Then I will come to my mother by and by. They fool me to the top of my bent. I will come by and by.

Pol. I will say so.

Ham. By and by is easily said. [*Exit Polonius.* Leave me, friends. [*Exeunt all but Hamlet.*

'Tis now the very witching time of night,
When churchyards yawn and hell itself breathes out
Contagion to this world: now could I drink hot blood,
And do such bitter business as the day
Would quake to look on. Soft! now to my mother. 410
O heart, lose not thy nature; let not ever
The soul of Nero enter this firm bosom:
Let me be cruel, not unnatural:
I will speak daggers to her, but use none;
My tongue and soul in this be hypocrites;
How in my words soever she be shent,
To give them seals never, my soul, consent! [*Exit.*

SCENE III. *A room in the castle.*

Enter KING, ROSENCRANTZ, *and* GUILDENSTERN.

King. I like him not, nor stands it safe with us
To let his madness range. Therefore prepare you;
I your commission will forthwith dispatch,
And he to England shall along with you:
The terms of our estate may not endure
Hazard so near us as doth hourly grow
Out of his lunacies.

Guil.   We will ourselves provide:
Most holy and religious fear it is
To keep those many many bodies safe
That live and feed upon your majesty. 10

Ros. The single and peculiar life is bound,
With all the strength and armour of the mind,
To keep itself from noyance; but much more
That spirit upon whose weal depend and rest
The lives of many. The cease of majesty
Dies not alone; but, like a gulf, doth draw
What 's near it with it: it is a massy wheel,

ballad having to do with Damon and Pythias. 293. **dismantled,** stripped, divested. 295. **pajock,** peacock (a bird with a bad reputation). Skeat suggested that the word was *patchock,* diminutive of *patch,* clown. 303. **recorders,** wind instruments of the flute kind. 305. **perdy,** corruption of *par dieu.* 315. **choler,** bilious disorder, with quibble on the sense "anger." 321. **frame,** order. 328. **wholesome,** sensible. 337. **matter,** matter in hand. 349. **pickers and stealers,** hands, so called from the catechism, "to keep my hands from picking and stealing." 356. **voice,** support. 358. **'While . . . grows.'** The rest of the proverb is "the silly horse starves." Hamlet may be destroyed while he is waiting for the succession to the kingdom (Malone). 360. **withdraw,** speak in private. 361. **recover the wind,** get to the windward side. 362. **toil,** snare. 363-364. **if . . . unmannerly,** if I am using an unmannerly boldness, it is my love which occasions it. 373. **ventages,** stops of the

recorders. 384. **compass,** range of voice. 385. **organ,** musical instrument, i.e., the pipe. 388. **fret,** quibble on meaning "irritate" and the piece of wood, gut, or metal which regulates the fingering. 401. **top of my bent,** limit of endurance, i.e., extent to which a bow may be bent. 402. **by and by,** immediately. 406. **witching time,** i.e., time when spells are cast. 412. **Nero,** murderer of his mother, Agrippina. 416. **shent,** rebuked. 417. **give them seals,** confirm with deeds.

SCENE III. 3. **dispatch,** prepare. 5. **terms,** condition, circumstances. **estate,** state. 7. **lunacies,** so F; Q₂: *browes;* Parrott and Craig: *braves.* 11. **single and peculiar,** individual and private. 13. **noyance,** harm. 16. **gulf,** whirlpool.

Fix'd on the summit of the highest mount,
To whose huge spokes ten thousand lesser things
Are mortised and adjoin'd; which, when it falls, 20
Each small annexment, petty consequence,
Attends the boisterous ruin. Never alone
Did the king sigh, but with a general groan.

King. Arm you, I pray you, to this speedy voyage;
For we will fetters put about this fear,
Which now goes too free-footed.

Ros. }
Guil. }   We will haste us.

[*Exeunt Rosencrantz and Guildenstern.*

Enter POLONIUS.

Pol. My lord, he's going to his mother's closet:
Behind the arras I'll convey myself,
To hear the process; I'll warrant she'll tax him
    home:
And, as you said, and wisely was it said, 30
'Tis meet that some more audience than a mother,
Since nature makes them partial, should o'erhear
The speech, of vantage. Fare you well, my liege:
I'll call upon you ere you go to bed,
And tell you what I know.

King.   Thanks, dear my lord.

[*Exit Polonius.*

O, my offence is rank, it smells to heaven;
It hath the primal eldest curse upon 't,
A brother's murder. Pray can I not,
Though inclination be as sharp as will:
My stronger guilt defeats my strong intent; 40
And, like a man to double business bound,
I stand in pause where I shall first begin,
And both neglect. What if this cursed hand
Were thicker than itself with brother's blood,
Is there not rain enough in the sweet heavens
To wash it white as snow? Whereto serves mercy
But to confront the visage of offence?
And what's in prayer but this two-fold force,
To be forestalled ere we come to fall,
Or pardon'd being down? Then I'll look up; 50
My fault is past. But, O, what form of prayer
Can serve my turn? 'Forgive me my foul murder'?
That cannot be: since I am still possess'd
Of those effects for which I did the murder,
My crown, mine own ambition and my queen.
May one be pardon'd and retain the offence?
In the corrupted currents of this world
Offence's gilded hand may shove by justice,
And oft 'tis seen the wicked prize itself
Buys out the law: but 'tis not so above; 60
There is no shuffling, there the action lies
In his true nature; and we ourselves compell'd,
Even to the teeth and forehead of our faults,
To give in evidence. What then? what rests?
Try what repentance can: what can it not?

Yet what can it when one can not repent?
O wretched state! O bosom black as death!
O limed soul, that, struggling to be free,
Art more engaged! Help, angels! Make assay!
Bow, stubborn knees; and, heart with strings of steel,
Be soft as sinews of the new-born babe! 71
All may be well.   [*Retires and kneels.*

Enter HAMLET.

Ham. Now might I do it pat, now he is praying;
And now I'll do 't. And so he goes to heaven;
And so am I revenged. That would be scann'd:
A villain kills my father; and for that,
I, his sole son, do this same villain send
To heaven.
O, this is hire and salary, not revenge.
He took my father grossly, full of bread; 80
With all his crimes broad blown, as flush as May;
And how his audit stands who knows save heaven?
But in our circumstance and course of thought,
'Tis heavy with him: and am I then revenged,
To take him in the purging of his soul,
When he is fit and season'd for his passage?
No!
Up, sword; and know thou a more horrid hent:
When he is drunk asleep, or in his rage,
Or in the incestuous pleasure of his bed; 90
At gaming, swearing, or about some act
That has no relish of salvation in 't;
Then trip him, that his heels may kick at heaven,
And that his soul may be as damn'd and black
As hell, whereto it goes. My mother stays:
This physic but prolongs thy sickly days. [*Exit.*

King. [*Rising*] My words fly up, my thoughts
    remain below:
Words without thoughts never to heaven go. [*Exit.*

SCENE IV. *The Queen's closet.*

Enter QUEEN *and* POLONIUS.

Pol. He will come straight. Look you lay home to
    him:
Tell him his pranks have been too broad to bear with,
And that your grace hath screen'd and stood between
Much heat and him. I'll sconce me even here.
Pray you, be round with him.

Ham. [*Within*] Mother, mother, mother!

Queen.   I'll warrant you,
Fear me not: withdraw, I hear him coming.

[*Polonius hides behind the arras.*

Enter HAMLET.

Ham. Now, mother, what's the matter?
Queen. Hamlet, thou hast thy father much offended.
Ham. Mother, you have my father much offended. 10

24. **Arm,** prepare. 25. **about,** so Q₂; Globe, following F: *upon*. 28. **arras,** screen of tapestry placed around the walls of household apartments. **convey,** implication of secrecy; *convey* was often used to mean "steal." 29. **tax him home,** reprove him severely. 39. **sharp as will,** i.e., his desire is as strong as his determination. 47. **confront,** oppose directly. 49. **forestalled,** prevented. 55. **ambition,** i.e., realization of ambition. 56. **offence,** benefit accruing from offense. 57. **currents,** courses. 58. **gilded hand,** hand offering gold as a bribe. 59. **wicked prize,** prize won by wickedness. 61. **shuffling,** escape by trickery. **lies,** is sustainable. 63. **teeth and forehead,** very face. 64. **rests,** remains. 68. **limed,** caught as with birdlime. 69. **assay,** trial. 73-95. **Now might . . . goes.** This may be described as the crucial passage in the interpretation of Hamlet's character. One school of critics, following Coleridge, has held that Hamlet fails to kill the king

because of weakness of will; this group regards what he says as merely so many excuses for not doing his duty. A more recent and undoubtedly a sounder group take Hamlet's reasons literally, saying that, like other heroes of revenge tragedies, he wishes to make his vengeance equivalent and complete. 75. **would be scann'd,** needs to be looked into. 79. **hire and salary,** so F; Q₂: *base and silly,* which can be defended; Wilson: *bait and salary.* 80. **full of bread,** allusion to Ezekiel 16:49. 81. **broad blown,** in full bloom. **flush,** lusty. 83. **in . . . course,** as we see it in our mortal situation. 86. **fit . . . passage,** i.e., reconciled to heaven by forgiveness of his sins. 88. **hent,** seizing; or, more probably, occasion of seizure. 89. **drunk asleep,** in a drunken sleep. 91. **At . . . swearing,** so F; Q₂: *At game, a swearing,* which makes sense if read *a-swearing.* 96. **physic,** purging (by prayer).

SCENE IV. 2. **broad,** unrestrained. 4. **Much heat,** i.e., the king's

Queen. Come, come, you answer with an idle tongue.
Ham. Go, go, you question with a wicked tongue.
Queen. Why, how now , Hamlet!
Ham.   What 's the matter now?
Queen. Have you forgot me?
Ham.   No, by the rood, not so:
You are the queen, your husband's brother's wife;
And—would it were not so!—you are my mother.
    Queen. Nay, then, I'll set those to you that can
        speak.
    Ham. Come, come, and sit you down; you shall not
        budge;
You go not till I set you up a glass
Where you may see the inmost part of you.   20
    Queen. What wilt thou do? thou wilt not murder
        me?
Help, help, ho!
    Pol. [*Behind*] What, ho! help, help, help!
    Ham. [*Drawing*] How now! a rat? Dead, for a ducat,
        dead!   [*Makes a pass through the arras.*
    Pol. [*Behind*] O, I am slain!   [*Falls and dies.*
    Queen. O me, what hast thou done?
    Ham.   Nay, I know not:
Is it the king?
    Queen. O, what a rash and bloody deed is this!
    Ham. A bloody deed! almost as bad, good mother,
As kill a king, and marry with his brother.
    Queen. As kill a king!
    Ham.   Ay, lady, 'twas my word.   30
                [*Lifts up the arras and discovers Polonius.*
Thou wretched, rash, intruding fool, farewell!
I took thee for thy better: take thy fortune;
Thou find'st to be too busy is some danger.
Leave wringing of your hands: peace! sit you down,
And let me wring your heart; for so I shall,
If it be made of penetrable stuff,
If damned custom have not brass'd it so
That it be proof and bulwark against sense.
    Queen. What have I done, that thou darest wag thy
        tongue
In noise so rude against me?
    Ham.   Such an act   40
That blurs the grace and blush of modesty,
Calls virtue hypocrite, takes off the rose
From the fair forehead of an innocent love
And sets a blister there, makes marriage-vows
As false as dicers' oaths: O, such a deed
As from the body of contraction plucks
The very soul, and sweet religion makes
A rhapsody of words: heaven's face doth glow;
Yea, this solidity and compound mass,
With heated visage, as against the doom,   50
Is thought-sick at the act.
    Queen.   Ay me, what act,
That roars so loud, and thunders in the index?
    Ham. Look here, upon this picture, and on this.

The counterfeit presentment of two brothers.
See, what a grace was seated on this brow;
Hyperion's curls; the front of Jove himself;
An eye like Mars, to threaten and command;
A station like the herald Mercury
New-lighted on a heaven-kissing hill;
A combination and a form indeed,   60
Where every god did seem to set his seal,
To give the world assurance of a man:
This was your husband. Look you now, what follows:
Here is your husband; like a mildew'd ear,
Blasting his wholesome brother. Have you eyes?
Could you on this fair mountain leave to feed,
And batten on this moor? Ha! have you eyes?
You cannot call it love; for at your age
The hey-day in the blood is tame, it 's humble,   69
And waits upon the judgement: and what judgement
Would step from this to this? Sense, sure, you have,
Else could you not have motion; but sure, that sense
Is apoplex'd; for madness would not err,
Nor sense to ecstasy was ne'er so thrall'd
But it reserved some quantity of choice,
To serve in such a difference. What devil was 't
That thus hath cozen'd you at hoodman-blind?
Eyes without feeling, feeling without sight,
Ears without hands or eyes, smelling sans all,
Or but a sickly part of one true sense   80
Could not so mope.
O shame! where is thy blush? Rebellious hell,
If thou canst mutine in a matron's bones,
To flaming youth let virtue be as wax,
And melt in her own fire: proclaim no shame
When the compulsive ardour gives the charge,
Since frost itself as actively doth burn
And reason pandars will.
    Queen.   O Hamlet, speak no more:
Thou turn'st mine eyes into my very soul;
And there I see such black and grained spots   90
As will not leave their tinct.
    Ham.   Nay, but to live
In the rank sweat of an enseamed bed,
Stew'd in corruption, honeying and making love
Over the nasty sty,—
    Queen.   O, speak to me no more;
These words, like daggers, enter in mine ears;
No more, sweet Hamlet!
    Ham.   A murderer and a villain;
A slave that is not twentieth part the tithe
Of your precedent lord; a vice of kings;
A cutpurse of the empire and the rule,
That from a shelf the precious diadem stole,   100
And put it in his pocket!
    Queen.   No more!
    Ham. A king of shreds and patches,—

Enter GHOST.

anger. **sconce,** hide. 9-10. **thy father, my father,** i.e., Claudius, the elder Hamlet. 14. **rood,** cross. 26. **Is it the king.** The fact that Hamlet thinks he is stabbing the king is an indication that he does not lack will to carry out his revenge. 37. **brass'd,** brazened, hardened. 44. **sets a blister,** brands as a harlot. 46. **contraction,** betrothal. 48. **rhapsody,** string. 49. **this . . . mass,** the earth itself. 50. **heated,** so Q_2; Globe, following F: *tristful.* **doom,** Last Judgment. 51. **thought-sick,** sick with anxiety. 52. **index,** prelude or preface. 54. **counterfeit presentment,** portrayed representation; on the stage the portraits are sometimes presented as miniatures, sometimes as pictures on the wall. 56. **Hyperion,** the sun god. 58. **station,** manner of standing. 62. **assurance,** pledge, guarantee. 64. **mildew'd ear.** See Genesis 41:5-7. 67. **batten,** grow fat. **moor,** barren upland. 69. **hey-day,** state of excitement. 71-72. **Sense . . . motion.** Sense and

motion are functions of the middle or sensible soul, the possession of sense being the basis of motion. 73. **apoplex'd,** paralyzed. Mental derangement was thus of three sorts: apoplexy, ecstasy, and diabolic possession. 74. **thrall'd,** enslaved. 75. **quantity of choice,** fragment of the power to choose. 77. **cozen'd,** tricked, cheated. **hoodman-blind,** blindman's buff. 81. **mope,** be in a depressed, spiritless state, act aimlessly. 83. **mutine,** mutiny, rebel. 86. **charge,** order, command. 88. **reason pandars will.** The normal and proper situation was one in which reason guided the will in the direction of good; here, reason is perverted and leads in the direction of evil. 90. **grained,** dyed in grain. 92. **enseamed,** loaded with grease, greased. 98. **precedent lord,** i.e., the elder Hamlet. **vice of kings,** buffoon of kings; a reference to the Vice, or clown, of the morality plays and interludes. 102. **shreds and patches,** i.e., motley, the traditional costume of the Vice.

Save me, and hover o'er me with your wings,
You heavenly guards! What would your gracious
    figure?
    Queen. Alas, he 's mad!
    Ham. Do you not come your tardy son to chide,
That, lapsed in time and passion, lets go by
The important acting of your dread command?
O, say!
    Ghost. Do not forget: this visitation   110
Is but to whet thy almost blunted purpose.
But, look, amazement on thy mother sits:
O, step between her and her fighting soul:
Conceit in weakest bodies strongest works:
Speak to her, Hamlet.
    Ham.   How is it with you, lady?
    Queen. Alas, how is 't with you,
That you do bend your eye on vacancy
And with the incorporal air do hold discourse?
Forth at your eyes your spirits wildly peep;
And, as the sleeping soldiers in the alarm,   120
Your bedded hair, like life in excrements,
Start up, and stand an end. O gentle son,
Upon the heat and flame of thy distemper
Sprinkle cool patience. Whereon do you look?
    Ham. On him, on him! Look you, how pale he
    glares!
His form and cause conjoin'd, preaching to stones,
Would make them capable. Do not look upon me;
Lest with this piteous action you convert
My stern effects: then what I have to do
Will want true colour; tears perchance for blood.   130
    Queen. To whom do you speak this?
    Ham.   Do you see nothing there?
    Queen. Nothing at all; yet all that is I see.
    Ham. Nor did you nothing hear?
    Queen.   No, nothing but ourselves.
    Ham. Why, look you there! look, how it steals away!
My father, in his habit as he lived!
Look, where he goes, even now, out at the portal!
                    [*Exit Ghost.*
    Queen. This is the very coinage of your brain:
This bodiless creation ecstasy
Is very cunning in.
    Ham.   Ecstasy!
My pulse, as yours, doth temperately keep time,   140
And makes as healthful music: it is not madness
That I have utter'd: bring me to the test,
And I the matter will re-word, which madness
Would gambol from. Mother, for love of grace,
Lay not that flattering unction to your soul,
That not your trespass, but my madness speaks:
It will but skin and film the ulcerous place,
Whiles rank corruption, mining all within,
Infects unseen. Confess yourself to heaven;
Repent what 's past; avoid what is to come;   150
And do not spread the compost on the weeds,

To make them ranker. Forgive me this my virtue;
For in the fatness of these pursy times
Virtue itself of vice must pardon beg,
Yea, curb and woo for leave to do him good.
    Queen. O Hamlet, thou hast cleft my heart in twain.
    Ham. O, throw away the worser part of it,
And live the purer with the other half.
Good night: but go not to mine uncle's bed;
Assume a virtue, if you have it not.   160
That monster, custom, who all sense doth eat,
Of habits devil, is angel yet in this,
That to the use of actions fair and good
He likewise gives a frock or livery,
That aptly is put on. Refrain to-night,
And that shall lend a kind of easiness
To the next abstinence: the next more easy;
For use almost can change the stamp of nature,
†And either . . . the devil, or throw him out
With wondrous potency. Once more, good night: 170
And when you are desirous to be bless'd,
I'll blessing beg of you. For this same lord,
                [*Pointing to Polonius.*
I do repent: but heaven hath pleased it so,
To punish me with this and this with me,
That I must be their scourge and minister.
I will bestow him, and will answer well
The death I gave him. So, again, good night.
I must be cruel, only to be kind:
Thus bad begins and worse remains behind.
One word more, good lady.
    Queen.   What shall I do?   180
    Ham. Not this, by no means, that I bid you do:
Let the bloat king tempt you again to bed;
Pinch wanton on your cheek; call you his mouse;
And let him, for a pair of reechy kisses,
Or paddling in your neck with his damn'd fingers,
Make you to ravel all this matter out,
That I essentially am not in madness,
But mad in craft. 'Twere good you let him know;
For who, that 's but a queen, fair, sober, wise,
Would from a paddock, from a bat, a gib,   190
Such dear concernings hide? who would do so?
No, in despite of sense and secrecy,
Unpeg the basket on the house's top,
Let the birds fly, and, like the famous ape,
To try conclusions, in the basket creep,
And break your own neck down.
    Queen. Be thou assured, if words be made of breath,
And breath of life, I have no life to breathe
What thou hast said to me.
    Ham. I must to England; you know that?
    Queen.   Alack,   200
I had forgot: 'tis so concluded on.
    Ham. There 's letters seal'd: and my two
    schoolfellows,
Whom I will trust as I will adders fang'd,

107. **lapsed . . . passion,** having suffered time to slip and passion to cool (Johnson); also explained as "engrossed in casual events and lapsed into mere fruitless passion, so that he no longer entertains a rational purpose." 108. **important,** urgent. 112. **amazement,** frenzy, distraction. 118. **incorporal,** immaterial. 121. **bedded,** laid in smooth layers. **excrements.** The hair was considered an excrement or voided part of the body. 122. **an,** on. 126. **conjoin'd,** united. 128-129. **convert . . . effects,** divert me from my stern duty. For *effects* Singer conjectures *affects* (affections of the mind). 130. **want true colour,** lack good reason so that (with a play on the normal sense of *colour*) I shall shed tears instead of blood. 143. **re-word,** repeat in words. 144. **gambol,** skip away. 145. **unction,** ointment used medicinally or as a rite; suggestion that forgiveness for sin may not be so

easily achieved. 148. **mining,** working under the surface. 150. **what is to come,** i.e., the sins of the future. 151. **compost,** manure. 152. **this my virtue,** this virtue of mine, i.e., in reproving you. 153. **fatness,** grossness. **pursy,** short-winded, corpulent. 155. **curb,** bow, bend the knee. 169. Defective line usually emended by inserting *master* after *either*, following Q4 and early editors. 171. **be bless'd,** become blessed, i.e., repentant. 182. **bloat,** bloated. 184. **reechy,** dirty, filthy. 187. **essentially,** in my essential nature. 190. **paddock,** toad. **gib,** tomcat. 191. **dear concernings,** important affairs. 194. **the famous ape.** A letter from Sir John Suckling seems to supply other details of the story, otherwise not identified: "It is the story of the jackanapes and the partridges; thou starest after a beauty till it be lost to thee, then let'st out another, and starest after that till it is gone

They bear the mandate; they must sweep my way,
And marshal me to knavery. Let it work;
For 'tis the sport to have the enginer
Hoist with his own petar: and 't shall go hard
But I will delve one yard below their mines,
And blow them at the moon: O, 'tis most sweet,
When in one line two crafts directly meet.   210
This man shall set me packing:
I'll lug the guts into the neighbour room.
Mother, good night. Indeed this counsellor
Is now most still, most secret and most grave,
Who was in life a foolish prating knave.
Come, sir, to draw toward an end with you.
Good night, mother.
   [Exeunt severally; Hamlet dragging in Polonius.

ACT IV.

 Scene I. *A room in the castle.*

Enter King, Queen, Rosencrantz, *and*
 Guildenstern.

King. There's matter in these sighs, these profound
  heaves:
You must translate: 'tis fit we understand them.
Where is your son?
 Queen. Bestow this place on us a little while.
    [Exeunt Rosencrantz and Guildenstern.
Ah, mine own lord, what have I seen to-night!
 King. What, Gertrude? How does Hamlet?
 Queen. Mad as the sea and wind, when both contend
Which is the mightier: in his lawless fit,
Behind the arras hearing something stir,
Whips out his rapier, cries, 'A rat, a rat!'   10
And, in this brainish apprehension, kills
The unseen good old man.
 King.   O heavy deed!
It had been so with us, had we been there:
His liberty is full of threats to all;
To you yourself, to us, to every one.
Alas, how shall this bloody deed be answer'd?
It will be laid to us, whose providence
Should have kept short, restrain'd and out of haunt,
This mad young man: but so much was our love,
We would not understand what was most fit;   20
But, like the owner of a foul disease,
To keep it from divulging, let it feed
Even on the pith of life. Where is he gone?
 Queen. To draw apart the body he hath kill'd:
O'er whom his very madness, like some ore
Among a mineral of metals base,
Shows itself pure; he weeps for what is done.
 King. O Gertrude, come away!
The sun no sooner shall the mountains touch,
But we will ship him hence: and this vile deed   30

We must, with all our majesty and skill,
Both countenance and excuse. Ho, Guildenstern!

 Re-enter Rosencrantz *and* Guildenstern.

Friends both, go join you with some further aid:
Hamlet in madness hath Polonius slain,
And from his mother's closet hath he dragg'd him:
Go seek him out; speak fair, and bring the body
Into the chapel. I pray you, haste in this.
    [Exeunt Rosencrantz and Guildenstern.
Come, Gertrude, we'll call up our wisest friends;
And let them know, both what we mean to do,
†And what 's untimely done   40
Whose whisper o'er the world's diameter,
As level as the cannon to his blank,
Transports his poison'd shot, may miss our name,
And hit the woundless air. O, come away!
My soul is full of discord and dismay.   *[Exeunt.*

 Scene II. *Another room in the castle.*

Enter Hamlet.

Ham. Safely stowed.
 Ros.⎫
 Guil.⎬ *[Within]* Hamlet! Lord Hamlet!
Ham. But soft, what noise? who calls on Hamlet?
O, here they come.

 Enter Rosencrantz *and* Guildenstern.

 Ros. What have you done, my lord, with the dead
  body?
 Ham. Compounded it with dust, whereto 'tis kin.
 Ros. Tell us where 'tis, that we may take it thence
And bear it to the chapel.
 Ham. Do not believe it.
 Ros. Believe what?   10
 Ham. That I can keep your counsel and not mine
own. Besides, to be demanded of a sponge! what
replication should be made by the son of a king?
 Ros. Take you me for a sponge, my lord?
 Ham. Ay, sir, that soaks up the king's countenance,
his rewards, his authorities. But such officers do the
king best service in the end: he keeps them, like an
ape an apple, in the corner of his jaw; first mouthed,
to be last swallowed: when he needs what you have
gleaned, it is but squeezing you, and, sponge, you
shall be dry again.   23
 Ros. I understand you not, my lord.
 Ham. I am glad of it: a knavish speech sleeps in a
foolish ear.
 Ros. My lord, you must tell us where the body is,
and go with us to the king.
 Ham. The body is with the king, but the king is not
with the body. The king is a thing—   30
 Guil. A thing, my lord!

---

too." 195. **conclusions,** experiments. 204. **sweep my way,** clear my
path. 206. **enginer,** constructor of military works, or possibly,
artilleryman. 207. **Hoist,** blown up. **petar,** defined as a small
engine of war used to blow in a door or make a breach, and as a case
filled with explosive materials. 210. **two crafts,** two acts of guile,
with quibble on the sense of "two ships." 211. **set me packing,** set me
to making schemes, and set me to lugging (him), and, possibly, send
me off in a hurry. 216. **draw,** come, with quibble on literal sense.
 Act IV. Scene I. 11. **brainish,** headstrong, passionate. **apprehension,** conception, imagination. 17. **providence,** foresight. 18. **short,**
i.e., on a short tether. **out of haunt,** secluded. 22. **divulging,** becoming evident. 26. **mineral,** mine. 40. Defective line; Capell and
others: *so, haply, slander;* Theobald and others: *for, haply, slander;*

other conjectures. 41. **diameter,** extent from side to side. 42. **level,**
straight. **blank,** white spot in the center of a target. 44. **woundless,**
invulnerable.
 Scene II. 11. **keep your counsel.** Hamlet is aware of their treachery
but says nothing about it. 13. **replication,** reply. 17. **authorities,**
authoritative backing. 19. **like . . . apple,** so Farmer; F: *like an
ape* (Globe); Q₂: *like an apple.* 29-30. **The body . . . body.** There are
many interpretations; possibly, "The body lies in death with the
king, my father; but my father walks disembodied" (Dowden); or
"Claudius has the bodily possession of kingship, but kingliness, or
justice of inheritance, is not with him." Yale editor explains, "The
King is still alive (i.e., with *his* body), but he is not with the dead body
(i.e., Polonius)."

Ham. Of nothing: bring me to him. Hide fox, and all after.   [*Exeunt.*

SCENE III. *Another room in the castle.*

Enter KING, *attended.*

King. I have sent to seek him, and to find the body.
How dangerous is it that this man goes loose!
Yet must not we put the strong law on him:
He's loved of the distracted multitude,
Who like not in their judgement, but their eyes;
And where 'tis so, the offender's scourge is weigh'd,
But never the offence. To bear all smooth and even,
This sudden sending him away must seem
Deliberate pause: diseases desperate grown
By desperate appliance are relieved,   10
Or not at all.

Enter ROSENCRANTZ.

                    How now! what hath befall'n?
Ros. Where the dead body is bestow'd, my lord,
We cannot get from him.
King.   But where is he?
Ros. Without, my lord; guarded, to know your
    pleasure.
King. Bring him before us.
Ros. Ho, Guildenstern! bring in my lord.

Enter HAMLET *and* GUILDENSTERN.

King. Now, Hamlet, where's Polonius?
Ham. At supper.
King. At supper! where?   19
Ham. Not where he eats, but where he is eaten: a certain convocation of politic worms are e'en at him. Your worm is your only emperor for diet: we fat all creatures else to fat us, and we fat ourselves for maggots: your fat king and your lean beggar is but variable service, two dishes, but to one table: that's the end.
King. Alas, alas!
Ham. A man may fish with the worm that hath eat of a king, and eat of the fish that hath fed of that worm.   30
King. What dost thou mean by this?
Ham. Nothing but to show you how a king may go a progress through the guts of a beggar.
King. Where is Polonius?
Ham. In heaven; send thither to see: if your messenger find him not there, seek him i' the other place yourself. But indeed, if you find him not within this month, you shall nose him as you go up the stairs into the lobby.
King. Go seek him there.   [*To some Attendants.* 40
Ham. He will stay till you come.   [*Exeunt Attendants.*
King. Hamlet, this deed, for thine especial safety,—
Which we do tender, as we dearly grieve
For that which thou hast done,—must send thee hence

With fiery quickness: therefore prepare thyself;
The bark is ready, and the wind at help,
The associates tend, and everything is bent
For England.
Ham.   For England!
King.   Ay, Hamlet.
Ham.   Good.
King. So is it, if thou knew'st our purposes.
Ham. I see a cherub that sees them. But, come; for England! Farewell, dear mother.
King. Thy loving father, Hamlet.   52
Ham. My mother: father and mother is man and wife; man and wife is one flesh; and so, my mother. Come, for England!   [*Exit.*
King. Follow him at foot; tempt him with speed
    aboard;
Delay it not; I'll have him hence to-night:
Away! for every thing is seal'd and done
That else leans on the affair: pray you, make haste.
                    [*Exeunt Rosencrantz and Guildenstern.*
And, England, if my love thou hold'st at aught—   60
As my great power thereof may give thee sense,
Since yet thy cicatrice looks raw and red
After the Danish sword, and thy free awe
Pays homage to us— thou mayst not coldly set
Our sovereign process; which imports at full,
By letters congruing to that effect,
The present death of Hamlet. Do it, England;
For like the hectic in my blood he rages,
And thou must cure me: till I know 'tis done,
Howe'er my haps, my joys were ne'er begun.   [*Exit.* 70

SCENE IV. *A plain in Denmark.*

Enter FORTINBRAS, *a* Captain, *and* Soldiers, *marching.*

For. Go, captain, from me greet the Danish king;
Tell him that, by his license, Fortinbras
Craves the conveyance of a promised march
Over his kingdom. You know the rendezvous.
If that his majesty would aught with us,
We shall express our duty in his eye;
And let him know so.
Cap.   I will do 't, my lord.
For. Go softly on.   [*Exeunt Fortinbras and Soldiers.*

Enter HAMLET, ROSENCRANTZ, GUILDENSTERN, *and others.*

Ham. Good sir, whose powers are these?
Cap. They are of Norway, sir.   10
Ham. How purposed, sir, I pray you?
Cap. Against some part of Poland.
Ham. Who commands them, sir?
Cap. The nephew to old Norway, Fortinbras.
Ham. Goes it against the main of Poland, sir,
Or for some frontier?
Cap. Truly to speak, and with no addition,
We go to gain a little patch of ground

32-33. **Hide . . . after,** an old signal cry in the game of hide-and-seek.
SCENE III. 4. **distracted,** i.e., without power of forming logical judgments. 6. **scourge,** punishment. **weigh'd,** taken into consideration. 9. **Deliberate pause,** considered action. 21. **convocation . . . worms,** allusion to the Diet of Worms (1521). **politic,** crafty. 25. **variable service,** a variety of dishes. 33. **progress,** royal journey of state. 43. **tender,** regard, hold dear. 50 **cherub.** Cherubim are angels of knowledge (Dowden). 56. **at foot,** close behind, at heel. 63. **free awe,** awe still felt, but no longer enforced by arms. 68. **hectic,** fever. 70. **haps,** fortunes.

SCENE IV. 2. **license,** leave. 3. **conveyance,** escort, convoy. 6. **in his eye,** in his presence. 8. **softly,** slowly. 15. **main,** country itself. 20. **farm it,** take a lease of it. 22. **fee,** fee simple. 26. **debate . . . straw,** settle this trifling matter. 27. **imposthume,** purulent abscess or swelling. 32. **occasions,** incidents, events. **inform against,** generally defined as "show," "betray" (i.e., his tardiness); more probably *inform* means "take shape," as in *Macbeth,* II, i, 48. 34. **market of his time,** the best use he makes of his time, or, that for which he sells his time (Johnson). 39. **fust,** grow moldy. 58. **Excitements of,** incentives to. 61. **trick,** toy, trifle. 62. **plot,** i.e., of ground.

That hath in it no profit but the name.
To pay five ducats, five, I would not farm it;   20
Nor will it yield to Norway or the Pole
A ranker rate, should it be sold in fee.
    Ham. Why, then the Polack never will defend it.
    Cap. Yes, it is already garrison'd.
    Ham. Two thousand souls and twenty thousand
        ducats
Will not debate the question of this straw:
This is the imposthume of much wealth and peace,
That inward breaks, and shows no cause without
Why the man dies. I humbly thank you, sir.
    Cap. God be wi' you, sir.   [*Exit.*
    Ros.   Will 't please you go, my lord?   30
    Ham. I'll be with you straight. Go a little before.
                            [*Exeunt all except Hamlet.*
How all occasions do inform against me,
And spur my dull revenge! What is a man,
If his chief good and market of his time
Be but to sleep and feed? a beast, no more.
Sure, he that made us with such large discourse,
Looking before and after, gave us not
That capability and god-like reason
To fust in us unused. Now, whether it be
Bestial oblivion, or some craven scruple   40
Of thinking too precisely on the event,
A thought which, quarter'd, hath but one part
        wisdom
And ever three parts coward, I do not know
Why yet I live to say 'This thing 's to do;'
Sith I have cause and will and strength and means
To do 't. Examples gross as earth exhort me:
Witness this army of such mass and charge
Led by a delicate and tender prince,
Whose spirit with divine ambition puff'd
Makes mouths at the invisible event,   50
Exposing what is mortal and unsure
To all that fortune, death and danger dare,
Even for an egg-shell. Rightly to be great
Is not to stir without great argument,
But greatly to find quarrel in a straw
When honour 's at the stake. How stand I then,
That have a father kill'd, a mother stain'd,
Excitements of my reason and my blood,
And let all sleep? while, to my shame, I see
The imminent death of twenty thousand men,   60
That, for a fantasy and trick of fame,
Go to their graves like beds, fight for a plot
Whereon the numbers cannot try the cause,
Which is not tomb enough and continent
To hide the slain? O, from this time forth,
My thoughts be bloody, or be nothing worth!   [*Exit.*

SCENE V. *Elsinore. A room in the castle.*

Enter QUEEN, HORATIO, *and a* Gentleman.

Queen. I will not speak with her.

Gent. She is importunate, indeed distract:
Her mood will needs be pitied.
    Queen.   What would she have?
    Gent. She speaks much of her father; says she hears
There 's tricks i' the world; and hems, and beats her
        heart;
Spurns enviously at straws; speaks things in doubt,
That carry but half sense: her speech is nothing,
Yet the unshaped use of it doth move
The hearers to collection; they yawn at it,
And botch the words up fit to their own thoughts;   10
Which, as her winks, and nods, and gestures yield
        them,
Indeed would make one think there might be thought,
Though nothing sure, yet much unhappily.
    Hor. 'Twere good she were spoken with: for she
        may strew
Dangerous conjectures in ill-breeding minds.
    Queen. Let her come in.   [*Exit Horatio.*
To my sick soul, as sin's true nature is,
Each toy seems prologue to some great amiss:
So full of artless jealousy is guilt,
It spills itself in fearing to be spilt.   20

    Re-enter HORATIO, *with* OPHELIA.

    Oph. Where is the beauteous majesty of Denmark?
    Queen. How now, Ophelia!
    Oph. [*Sings*] How should I your true love know
                From another one?
            By his cockle hat and staff,
                And his sandal shoon.
    Queen. Alas, sweet lady, what imports this song?
    Oph. Say you? nay, pray you, mark.
    [*Sings*]   He is dead and gone, lady,
                He is dead and gone;   30
                At his head a grass-green turf,
                At his heels a stone.
    Queen. Nay, but, Ophelia,—
    Oph. Pray you, mark
    [*Sings*] White his shroud as the mountain snow,—

    Enter KING.

    Queen. Alas, look here, my lord.
    Oph. [*Sings*] Larded all with flowers;
            Which bewept to the grave did not go
                With true-love showers.
    King. How do you, pretty lady?   40
    Oph. Well, God 'ild you! They say the owl was a
baker's daughter. Lord, we know what we are, but
know not what we may be. God be at your table!
    King. Conceit upon her father.
    Oph. Pray you, let 's have no words of this; but
when they ask you what it means, say you this:
    [*Sings*] To-morrow is Saint Valentine's day,
            All in the morning betime,
            And I a maid at your window,   50
                To be your Valentine.
            Then up he rose, and donn'd his clothes,

SCENE V. 5. **tricks,** deceptions. **heart,** i.e., breast. 6. **Spurns
. . . straws,** kicks spitefully at small objects in her path. 8. **unshaped,**
unformed, artless. 9. **collection,** inference. **yawn,** wonder; so Q2;
Globe, following F: *aim.* 10. **botch,** patch. 11. **yield,** deliver,
bring forth (her words). 13. **much unhappily,** expressive of much
unhappiness. 15. **ill-breeding minds,** minds bent on mischief. 18.
great amiss, calamity, disaster. 19-20. **So . . . spilt,** guilt is so full
of suspicion that it unskillfully betrays itself in fearing to be betrayed
(Onions). 25. **cockle hat,** hat with cockleshell stuck in it as a sign
that the wearer had been a pilgrim to the shrine of St. James of

Compostella. The pilgrim's garb was a conventional disguise for lovers.
26. **shoon,** shoes. 37. **Larded . . . flowers,** so Q2; Globe, following
F: *Larded with sweet flowers.* **Larded,** decorated. 38. **not,** so Q2F;
Globe, following Pope, omits. 41. **God 'ild,** God yield or reward.
42. **owl,** reference to a monkish legend that a baker's daughter was
turned into an owl for refusing bread to the Saviour; quoted by Douce.
51. **Valentine.** This song alludes to the belief that the first girl seen
by a man on the morning of this day was his valentine or truelove
(Halliwell).

And dupp'd the chamber-door;
Let in the maid, that out a maid
Never departed more.
King. Pretty Ophelia!
Oph. Indeed, la, without an oath, I'll make an end
on 't:
[*Sings*] By Gis and by Saint Charity,
Alack, and fie for shame! 60
Young men will do 't, if they come to 't;
By cock, they are to blame.
Quoth she, before you tumbled me,
You promised me to wed.
So would I ha' done, by yonder sun,
An thou hadst not come to my bed.
King. How long hath she been thus?
Oph. I hope all will be well. We must be patient:
but I cannot choose but weep, to think they should
lay him i' the cold ground. My brother shall know of
it: and so I thank you for your good counsel. Come,
my coach! Good night, ladies; good night, sweet
ladies; good night, good night. [*Exit.* 74
King. Follow her close; give her good watch, I pray
you. [*Exit Horatio.*
O, this is the poison of deep grief; it springs
All from her father's death. O Gertrude, Gertrude,
When sorrows come, they come not single spies,
But in battalions. First, her father slain:
Next, your son gone; and he most violent author 80
Of his own just remove: the people muddied,
Thick and unwholesome in their thoughts and
whispers,
For good Polonius' death; and we have done but
greenly,
In hugger-mugger to inter him: poor Ophelia
Divided from herself and her fair judgement,
Without the which we are pictures, or mere beasts:
Last, and as much containing as all these,
Her brother is in secret come from France;
Feeds on his wonder, keeps himself in clouds,
And wants not buzzers to infect his ear 90
With pestilent speeches of his father's death;
Wherein necessity, of matter beggar'd,
Will nothing stick our person to arraign
In ear and ear. O my dear Gertrude, this,
Like to a murdering-piece, in many places
Gives me superfluous death. [*A noise within.*
Queen. Alack, what noise is this?
King. Where are my Switzers? Let them guard the
door.

Enter another Gentleman.

What is the matter?
Gent. Save yourself, my lord:
The ocean, overpeering of his list,
Eats not the flats with more impetuous haste 100
Than young Laertes, in a riotous head,
O'erbears your officers. The rabble call him lord;
And, as the world were now but to begin,
Antiquity forgot, custom not known,

The ratifiers and props of every word,
They cry 'Choose we: Laertes shall be king:'
Caps, hands, and tongues, applaud it to the clouds:
'Laertes shall be king, Laertes king!'
Queen. How cheerfully on the false trail they cry!
O, this is counter, you false Danish dogs! 110
King. The doors are broke. [*Noise within.*

Enter LAERTES, *armed;* Danes *following.*

Laer. Where is this king? Sirs, stand you all without.
Danes. No, let 's come in.
Laer. I pray you, give me leave.
Danes. We will, we will. [*They retire without the door.*
Laer. I thank you: keep the door. O thou vile king,
Give me my father!
Queen. Calmly, good Laertes.
Laer. That drop of blood that 's calm proclaims me
bastard,
Cries cuckold to my father, brands the harlot
Even here, between the chaste unsmirched brow
Of my true mother.
King. What is the cause, Laertes, 120
That thy rebellion looks so giant-like?
Let him go, Gertrude; do not fear our person:
There 's such divinity doth hedge a king,
That treason can but peep to what it would,
Acts little of his will. Tell me, Laertes,
Why thou art thus incensed. Let him go, Gertrude.
Speak, man.
Laer. Where is my father?
King. Dead.
Queen. But not by him.
King. Let him demand his fill.
Laer. How came he dead? I'll not be juggled with:
To hell, allegiance! vows, to the blackest devil! 131
Conscience and grace, to the profoundest pit!
I dare damnation. To this point I stand,
That both the worlds I give to negligence,
Let come what comes; only I'll be revenged
Most throughly for my father.
King. Who shall stay you?
Laer. My will, not all the world:
And for my means, I'll husband them so well,
They shall go far with little.
King. Good Laertes,
If you desire to know the certainty 140
Of your dear father's death, is 't writ in your revenge,
That, swoopstake, you will draw both friend and foe,
Winner and loser?
Laer. None but his enemies.
King. Will you know them then?
Laer. To his good friends thus wide I'll ope my
arms;
And like the kind life-rendering pelican,
Repast them with my blood.
King. Why, now you speak
Like a good child and a true gentleman.
That I am guiltless of your father's death,
And am most sensibly in grief for it, 150

53. **dupp'd**, opened. 59. **Gis**, Jesus. 62. **cock**, perversion of "God"
in oaths. 83. **greenly**, foolishly. 84. **hugger-mugger**, secret haste.
89. **in clouds**, invisible. 90. **buzzers**, gossipers. 93. **nothing stick**,
not hesitate. 94. **In ear and ear**, in everybody's ears. 95. **murdering-
piece**, small cannon or mortar; suggestion of numerous missiles fired.
97. **Switzers**, Swiss guards, mercenaries. 99. **overpeering**, overflowing. 105. **word**, probably, title or custom; *ward, weal,* and *work*
have been suggested as emendations. 110. **counter**, a hunting term
meaning to follow the trail in a direction opposite to that which the

game has taken. 124. **peep**, look. **would**, wishes to do. 134. **give
to negligence.** He despises both the here and the hereafter. 137. **My
will.** He will not be stopped except by his own will. 142. **swoopstake**,
literally, drawing the whole stake at once, i.e., indiscriminately. 146.
pelican, reference to the belief that the pelican feeds its young with its
own blood. 147. **Repast**, feed. 151. **'pear**, so Q₂; Globe, following F:
pierce. 154. **heat**, probably the heat generated by the passion of grief.
172. **wheel**, spinning wheel as accompaniment to the song (Onions);
refrain (Steevens). **false steward.** The story is unknown. 175. **rosemary,**

It shall as level to your judgement 'pear
As day does to your eye.
 Danes.   [*Within*] Let her come in.
 Laer. How now! what noise is that?

     Re-enter OPHELIA.

O heat, dry up my brains! tears seven times salt,
Burn out the sense and virtue of mine eye!
By heaven, thy madness shall be paid with weight,
Till our scale turn the beam. O rose of May!
Dear maid, kind sister, sweet Ophelia!
O heavens! is 't possible, a young maid's wits
Should be as mortal as an old man's life? 160
Nature is fine in love, and where 'tis fine,
It sends some precious instance of itself
After the thing it loves.
 Oph. [*Sings*]
  They bore him barefaced on the bier;
  Hey non nonny, nonny, hey nonny;
  And in his grave rain'd many a tear:—
Fare you well, my dove!
 Laer. Hadst thou thy wits, and didst persuade
  revenge,
It could not move thus.
 Oph. [*Sings*] You must sing a-down a-down, 170
  An you call him a-down-a.
O, how the wheel becomes it! It is the false steward,
that stole his master's daughter.
 Laer. This nothing 's more than matter.
 Oph. There 's rosemary, that 's for remembrance;
pray, love, remember: and there is pansies, that 's for
thoughts.
 Laer. A document in madness, thoughts and re-
membrance fitted. 179
 Oph. There 's fennel for you, and columbines:
there 's rue for you; and here 's some for me: we may
call it herb of grace o' Sundays: O, you must wear
your rue with a difference. There 's a daisy: I
would give you some violets, but they withered all
when my father died: they say he made a good
end,—
 [*Sings*] For bonny sweet Robin is all my joy.
 Laer. Thought and affliction, passion, hell itself,
She turns to favour and to prettiness.
 Oph. [*Sings*] And will he not come again? 190
  And will he not come again?
  No, no, he is dead:
  Go to thy death-bed:
  He never will come again.

  His beard was as white as snow,
  All flaxen was his poll:
  He is gone, he is gone,
  And we cast away moan:
  God ha' mercy on his soul!
And of all Christian souls, I pray God. God be wi' ye.
         [*Exit.*
 Laer. Do you see this, O God? 201
 King. Laertes, I must commune with your grief,

Or you deny me right. Go but apart,
Make choice of whom your wisest friends you will,
And they shall hear and judge 'twixt you and me:
If by direct or by collateral hand
They find us touch'd, we will our kingdom give,
Our crown, our life, and all that we call ours,
To you in satisfaction; but if not,
Be you content to lend your patience to us, 210
And we shall jointly labour with your soul
To give it due content.
 Laer.   Let this be so;
His means of death, his obscure funeral—
No trophy, sword, nor hatchment o'er his bones,
No noble rite nor formal ostentation—
Cry to be heard, as 'twere from heaven to earth,
That I must call 't in question.
 King.   So you shall;
And where the offence is let the great axe fall.
I pray you, go with me.   [*Exeunt.*

SCENE VI. *Another room in the castle.*

Enter HORATIO *and a* Servant.

 Hor. What are they that would speak with me?
 Serv. Sailors, sir: they say they have letters for you.
 Hor. Let them come in. [*Exit Servant.*
I do not know from what part of the world
I should be greeted, if not from lord Hamlet.

    Enter Sailors.

 First Sail. God bless you, sir.
 Hor. Let him bless thee too.
 First Sail. He shall, sir, an 't please him. There 's a
letter for you, sir; it comes from the ambassador that
was bound for England; if your name be Horatio, as
I am let to know it is. 11
 Hor. [*Reads*] 'Horatio, when thou shalt have overlooked this, give these fellows some means to the king:
they have letters for him. Ere we were two days old at
sea, a pirate of very warlike appointment gave us
chase. Finding ourselves too slow of sail, we put on a
compelled valour, and in the grapple I boarded them:
on the instant they got clear of our ship; so I alone
became their prisoner. They have dealt with me like
thieves of mercy: but they knew what they did; I am
to do a good turn for them. Let the king have the
letters I have sent; and repair thou to me with as
much speed as thou wouldst fly death. I have words
to speak in thine ear will make thee dumb; yet are
they much too light for the bore of the matter. These
good fellows will bring thee where I am. Rosencrantz
and Guildenstern hold their course for England: of
them I have much to tell thee. Farewell. 30
   'He that thou knowest thine, HAMLET.'
Come, I will make you way for these your letters;
And do 't the speedier, that you may direct me
To him from whom you brought them. [*Exeunt.*

---

used as a symbol of remembrance both at weddings and at funerals.
177. **pansies,** emblems of love and courtship. Cf. French *pensées.* 178.
document, piece of instruction or lesson. 180. **fennel,** emblem of
flattery. **columbines,** emblem of unchastity (?) or ingratitude (?)
181. **rue,** emblem of repentance. It was usually mingled with holy
water and then known as *herb of grace.* F and Globe: *herb-grace.* Ophelia
is probably playing on the two meanings of *rue,* "repentant" and "even
for ruth (pity)"; the former signification is for the queen, the latter for
herself. 184. **daisy,** emblem of dissembling, faithlessness. **violets,**

emblems of faithfulness. 187. **For . . . joy,** probably a line from a Robin
Hood ballad. 188. **Thought,** melancholy thought. 190. **And . . .
again.** This song appeared in the songbooks as "The Merry Milkmaids'
Dumps." 196. **poll,** head. 198. **cast away,** shipwrecked. 203. **right,**
my rights. 206. **collateral,** indirect. 207. **touch'd,** implicated. 214.
hatchment, tablet displaying the armorial bearings of a deceased person.
 SCENE VI. 14. **means,** means of access. 21. **thieves of mercy,**
merciful thieves. 27. **bore,** caliber, importance.

SCENE VII. *Another room in the castle.*

Enter KING *and* LAERTES.

King. Now must your conscience my acquittance
    seal,
And you must put me in your heart for friend,
Sith you have heard, and with a knowing ear,
That he which hath your noble father slain
Pursued my life.
    Laer.   It well appears: but tell me
Why you proceeded not against these feats,
So criminal and so capital in nature,
As by your safety, wisdom, all things else,
You mainly were stirr'd up.
    King.   O, for two special reasons;
Which may to you, perhaps, seem much unsinew'd, 10
But yet to me they are strong. The queen his mother
Lives almost by his looks; and for myself—
My virtue or my plague, be it either which—
She 's so conjunctive to my life and soul,
That, as the star moves not but in his sphere,
I could not but by her. The other motive,
Why to a public count I might not go,
Is the great love the general gender bear him;
Who, dipping all his faults in their affection,
Would, like the spring that turneth wood to stone, 20
Convert his gyves to graces; so that my arrows,
Too slightly timber'd for so loud a wind,
Would have reverted to my bow again,
And not where I had aim'd them.
    Laer. And so have I a noble father lost;
A sister driven into desperate terms,
Whose worth, if praises may go back again,
Stood challenger on mount of all the age
For her perfections: but my revenge will come.
    King. Break not your sleeps for that: you must not
    think   30
That we are made of stuff so flat and dull
That we can let our beard be shook with danger
And think it pastime. You shortly shall hear more:
I loved your father, and we love ourself;
And that, I hope, will teach you to imagine—

Enter a Messenger.

How now! what news?
    Mess.   Letters, my lord, from Hamlet:
This to your majesty; this to the queen.
    King. From Hamlet! who brought them?
    Mess. Sailors, my lord, they say; I saw them not:
They were given me by Claudio; he received them 40
Of him that brought them.
    King.   Laertes, you shall hear them.
Leave us.   *[Exit Messenger.*
[*Reads*] 'High and mighty, You shall know I am set
naked on your kingdom. To-morrow shall I beg leave

to see your kingly eyes: when I shall, first asking your
pardon thereunto, recount the occasion of my sudden
and more strange return.   'HAMLET.'
What should this mean? Are all the rest come back? 50
Or is it some abuse, and no such thing?
    Laer. Know you the hand?
    King.   'Tis Hamlet's character. 'Naked!'
And in a postscript here, he says 'alone.'
Can you advise me?
    Laer. I 'm lost in it, my lord. But let him come;
It warms the very sickness in my heart,
That I shall live and tell him to his teeth,
'Thus didst thou.'
    King.   If it be so, Laertes—
As how should it be so? how otherwise?—
Will you be ruled by me?
    Laer.   Ay, my lord;   60
So you will not o'errule me to a peace.
    King. To thine own peace. If he be now return'd,
As checking at his voyage, and that he means
No more to undertake it, I will work him
To an exploit, now ripe in my device,
Under the which he shall not choose but fall:
And for his death no wind of blame shall breathe,
But even his mother shall uncharge the practice
And call it accident.
    Laer.   My lord, I will be ruled;
The rather, if you could devise it so   70
That I might be the organ.
    King.   It falls right.
You have been talk'd of since your travel much,
And that in Hamlet's hearing, for a quality
Wherein, they say, you shine: your sum of parts
Did not together pluck such envy from him
As did that one, and that, in my regard,
Of the unworthiest siege.
    Laer.   What part is that, my lord?
    King. A very riband in the cap of youth,
Yet needful too; for youth no less becomes
The light and careless livery that it wears   80
Than settled age his sables and his weeds,
Importing health and graveness. Two months since,
Here was a gentleman of Normandy:—
I 've seen myself, and served against, the French,
And they can well on horseback: but this gallant
Had witchcraft in 't; he grew unto his seat;
And to such wondrous doing brought his horse,
As had he been incorpsed and demi-natured
With the brave beast: so far he topp'd my thought,
That I, in forgery of shapes and tricks,   90
Come short of what he did.
    Laer.   A Norman was 't?
    King. A Norman.
    Laer. Upon my life, Lamond.
    King.   The very same.

SCENE VII. 1. **conscience,** knowledge that this is true. 7. **criminal,**
so Q2; Globe, following F: *crimeful.* **capital,** punishable by death. 9.
mainly, greatly. 10. **unsinew'd,** weak. 14. **conjunctive,** comformable
(the next line suggesting planetary conjunction). 15. **sphere,** the
hollow sphere in which, according to Ptolemaic astronomy, the planets
were supposed to move. 17. **count,** account, reckoning. 18. **general
gender,** common people. 20. **spring,** i.e., one heavily charged with
lime. 21. **gyves,** fetters; here, faults, or possibly, punishments inflicted
(on him). 22. **slightly timber'd,** light. **loud,** strong. For *loud a
wind* Jennens would retain the Q2 reading *loved Arm'd,* explaining, "one
so loved and armed with the affections of the people"; for *so loud a wind*
Elze suggests *solid arms* to agree with his reading *grieves* (for *gyves*) in
line 21. 26. **terms,** state, condition. 27. **go back,** i.e., to Ophelia's
former virtues. 28. **on mount,** set up on high (Onions), mounted
(on horseback). **of all the age,** qualifies *challenger* and not *mount.*

37. **to the queen.** One hears no more of the letter to the queen. 40.
Claudio. This character does not appear in the play. 44. **naked,**
unprovided (with retinue). 59. **As . . . otherwise?** How can this
(Hamlet's return) be true? (yet) how otherwise than true (since we
have the evidence of his letter)? Some editors read *How should it not be
so,* etc., making the words refer to Laertes' desire to meet with Hamlet.
63. **checking at,** used in falconry of a hawk's leaving the quarry to fly
at a chance bird. 68. **uncharge the practice,** not object to the stratagem. 71. **organ,** agent, instrument. 77. **siege,** rank. 81. **sables,**
rich garments. 85. **can well,** are skilled. 88. **incorpsed and demi-
natured,** of one body and nearly of one nature (like the centaur). 89.
topp'd, surpassed. 90. **forgery,** invention. 93. **Lamond.** This refers
possibly to Pietro Monte, instructor to Louis XII's master of the horse
(Hudson). 96. **confession,** report. 98. **art and exercise,** skillful
exercise. **defence,** science of defense in sword practice. 101. **scrimers,**

Laer. I know him well: he is the brooch indeed
And gem of all the nation.
King. He made confession of you,
And gave you such a masterly report
For art and exercise in your defence
And for your rapier most especial,
That he cried out, 'twould be a sight indeed, 100
If one could match you: the scrimers of their nation,
He swore, had neither motion, guard, nor eye,
If you opposed them. Sir, this report of his
Did Hamlet so envenom with his envy
That he could nothing do but wish and beg
Your sudden coming o'er, to play with him.
Now, out of this,—
Laer. What out of this, my lord?
King. Laertes, was your father dear to you?
Or are you like the painting of a sorrow,
A face without a heart?
Laer. Why ask you this? 110
King. Not that I think you did not love your father;
But that I know love is begun by time;
And that I see, in passages of proof,
Time qualifies the spark and fire of it.
There lives within the very flame of love
A kind of wick or snuff that will abate it;
And nothing is at a like goodness still;
For goodness, growing to a plurisy,
Dies in his own too much: that we would do,
We should do when we would; for this 'would'
  changes 120
And hath abatements and delays as many
As there are tongues, are hands, are accidents;
And then this 'should' is like a spendthrift sigh,
That hurts by easing. But, to the quick o' the ulcer:—
Hamlet comes back: what would you undertake,
To show yourself your father's son in deed
More than in words?
Laer. To cut his throat i' the church.
King. No place, indeed, should murder sanctuarize;
Revenge should have no bounds. But, good Laertes,
Will you do this, keep close within your chamber. 130
Hamlet return'd shall know you are come home:
We'll put on those shall praise your excellence
And set a double varnish on the fame
The Frenchman gave you, bring you in fine together
And wager on your heads: he, being remiss,
Most generous and free from all contriving,
Will not peruse the foils; so that, with ease,
Or with a little shuffling, you may choose
A sword unbated, and in a pass of practice
Requite him for your father.
Laer. I will do 't: 140
And, for that purpose, I'll anoint my sword.
I bought an unction of a mountebank,
So mortal that, but dip a knife in it,

Where it draws blood no cataplasm so rare,
Collected from all simples that have virtue
Under the moon, can save the thing from death
That is but scratched withal: I'll touch my point
With this contagion, that, if I gall him slightly,
It may be death.
King. Let 's further think of this;
Weigh what convenience both of time and means 150
May fit us to our shape: if this should fail,
And that our drift look through our bad performance,
'Twere better not assay'd: therefore this project
Should have a back or second, that might hold,
If this should blast in proof. Soft! let me see:
We'll make a solemn wager on your cunnings:
I ha 't:
When in your motion you are hot and dry—
As make your bouts more violent to that end—
And that he calls for drink, I'll have prepared him 160
A chalice for the nonce, whereon but sipping,
If he by chance escape your venom'd stuck,
Our purpose may hold there.

Enter QUEEN.

  How now, sweet queen!
Queen. One woe doth tread upon another's heel,
So fast they follow: your sister 's drown'd, Laertes.
Laer. Drown'd! O, where?
Queen. There is a willow grows aslant a brook,
That shows his hoar leaves in the glassy stream;
There with fantastic garlands did she make
Of crow-flowers, nettles, daisies, and long purples 170
That liberal shepherds give a grosser name,
But our cold maids do dead men's fingers call them:
There, on the pendent boughs her coronet weeds
Clambering to hang, an envious sliver broke;
When down her weedy trophies and herself
Fell in the weeping brook. Her clothes spread wide;
And, mermaid-like, awhile they bore her up:
Which time she chanted snatches of old tunes;
As one incapable of her own distress,
Or like a creature native and indued 180
Unto that element: but long it could not be
Till that her garments, heavy with their drink,
Pull'd the poor wretch from her melodious lay
To muddy death.
Laer. Alas then, she is drown'd?
Queen. Drown'd, drown'd.
Laer. Too much of water hast thou, poor Ophelia,
And therefore I forbid my tears: but yet
It is our trick; nature her custom holds,
Let shame say what it will: when these are gone,
The woman will be out. Adieu, my lord: 190
I have a speech of fire, that fain would blaze,
But that this folly douts it. [*Exit.*
King. Let 's follow, Gertrude:

fencers. 106. **play,** fence. 113. **passages of proof,** proved instances.
118. **plurisy,** excess, plethora. 119. **in his own too much,** of its own
excess. 121. **abatements,** diminutions. 122. **accidents,** occurrences,
incidents. 123. **spendthrift,** an allusion to the belief that each sigh
cost the heart a drop of blood. 124. **quick o' the ulcer,** heart of the
difficulty. 128. **sanctuarize,** protect from punishment; allusion to the
right of sanctuary with which certain religious places were invested.
139. **unbated,** not blunted, having no button. **pass of practice,** treacherous thrust. 142. **mountebank,** quack doctor. 144. **cataplasm,**
plaster or poultice. 145. **simples,** herbs. 146. **Under the moon,** i.e.,
when collected by moonlight to add to their medicinal value. 148.
gall, graze, wound. 151. **shape,** part we propose to act. 152. **drift
. . . performance,** intention be disclosed by our bungling. 155. **blast
in proof,** burst in the test (like a cannon). 156. **cunnings,** skills. The
F reading, *commings,* is explained by Caldecott and Knight as "bouts at

fence." 161. **chalice,** cup. 162. **stuck,** thrust (from *stoccado*). 167.
willow, for its significance of forsaken love. **aslant a,** so F; Q₂:
ascaunt (variant of "askance") *the.* 168. **hoar,** white (i.e., on the
underside). 169. **make,** so Q₂; Globe, following F, *come.* 170. **crow-
flowers,** buttercups. **long purples,** early purple orchis. 171. **liberal,**
probably, free-spoken. 173. **coronet,** made into a chaplet. 174.
sliver, branch. 175. **weedy,** i.e., of plants. 178. **tunes,** so Q₁F; Q₂:
laudes. 179. **incapable,** lacking capacity to apprehend. 180. **indued,**
endowed with qualities fitting her for living in water. 186-187. **Too
. . . tears,** an illustration of the fact that puns were not inappropriate
under any circumstance in Shakespeare's time. 188. **trick,** way. 189-
190. **when . . . out,** when my tears are all shed, the woman in me will
be satisfied. 192. **douts,** does out, extinguishes.

How much I had to do to calm his rage!
Now fear I this will give it start again;
Therefore let 's follow. [Exeunt.

ACT V.

SCENE I. A churchyard.

Enter two Clowns, with spades, &c.

First Clo. Is she to be buried in Christian burial that wilfully seeks her own salvation?

Sec. Clo. I tell thee she is; and therefore make her grave straight: the crowner hath sat on her, and finds it Christian burial.

First Clo. How can that be, unless she drowned herself in her own defence?

Sec. Clo. Why, 'tis found so. 8

First Clo. It must be 'se offendendo;' it cannot be else. For here lies the point: if I drown myself wittingly, it argues an act: and an act hath three branches; it is, to act, to do, and to perform: argal, she drowned herself wittingly. 14

Sec. Clo. Nay, but hear you, goodman delver,—

First Clo. Give me leave. Here lies the water; good: here stands the man; good: if the man go to this water, and drown himself, it is, will he, nill he, he goes,—mark you that; but if the water come to him and drown him, he drowns not himself: argal, he that is not guilty of his own death shortens not his own life.

Sec. Clo. But is this law? 23

First Clo. Ay, marry, is 't; crowner's quest law.

Sec. Clo. Will you ha' the truth on 't? If this had not been a gentlewoman, she should have been buried out o' Christian burial.

First Clo. Why, there thou say'st: and the more pity that great folk should have countenance in this world to drown or hang themselves, more than their even Christian. Come, my spade. There is no ancient gentlemen but gardeners, ditchers, and grave-makers: they hold up Adam's profession.

Sec. Clo. Was he a gentleman?

First Clo. A' was the first that ever bore arms.

Sec. Clo. Why, he had none. 39

First Clo. What, art a heathen? How dost thou understand the Scripture? The Scripture says 'Adam digged:' could he dig without arms? I'll put another question to thee: if thou answerest me not to the purpose, confess thyself—

Sec. Clo. Go to.

First Clo. What is he that builds stronger than either the mason, the shipwright, or the carpenter?

Sec. Clo. The gallows-maker; for that frame outlives a thousand tenants. 50

First Clo. I like thy wit well, in good faith: the gallows does well; but how does it well? it does well

to those that do ill: now thou dost ill to say the gallows is built stronger than the church: argal, the gallows may do well to thee. To 't again, come.

Sec. Clo. 'Who builds stronger than a mason, a shipwright, or a carpenter?'

First Clo. Ay, tell me that, and unyoke.

Sec. Clo. Marry, now I can tell. 60

First Clo. To 't.

Sec. Clo. Mass, I cannot tell.

Enter HAMLET and HORATIO, at a distance.

First Clo. Cudgel thy brains no more about it, for your dull ass will not mend his pace with beating; and, when you are asked this question next, say 'a grave-maker:' the houses that he makes last till doomsday. Go, get thee in, and fetch me a stoup of liquor. [Exit Sec. Clown.
[He digs, and sings.

In youth, when I did love, did love,
    Methought it was very sweet, 70
To contract, O, the time, for, ah, my behove,
    O, methought, there was nothing meet.

Ham. Has this fellow no feeling of his business, that he sings at grave-making?

Hor. Custom hath made it in him a property of easiness.

Ham. 'Tis e'en so: the hand of little employment hath the daintier sense.

First Clo. [Sings]
    But age, with his stealing steps,
        Hath claw'd me in his clutch, 80
    And hath shipped me into the land,
        As if I had never been such. [Throws up a skull.

Ham. That skull had a tongue in it, and could sing once: how the knave jowls it to the ground, as if it were Cain's jaw-bone, that did the first murder! It might be the pate of a politician, which this ass now o'er-reaches; one that would circumvent God, might it not?

Hor. It might, my lord. 89

Ham. Or of a courtier; which could say 'Good morrow, sweet lord! How dost thou, good lord?' This might be my lord such-a-one, that praised my lord such-a-one's horse, when he meant to beg it; might it not?

Hor. Ay, my lord.

Ham. Why, e'en so: and now my Lady Worm's; chapless, and knocked about the mazzard with a sexton's spade: here 's fine revolution, an we had the trick to see 't. Did these bones cost no more the breeding, but to play at loggats with 'em? mine ache to think on 't. 101

First Clo. [Sings]
    A pick-axe, and a spade, a spade,
        For and a shrouding sheet:
    O, a pit of clay for to be made
        For such a guest is meet. [Throws up another skull.

Hamlet
ACT IV : SC VII

936

ACT V. SCENE I. *Stage Direction:* **Clowns.** The word *clown* was used to denote peasants as well as humorous characters; here applied to the rustic type of clown. 4. **straight,** straightway, immediately; Johnson interprets "from east to west in a direct line, parallel with the church." **crowner,** coroner. 9. **'se offendendo,'** for *se defendendo,* term used in verdicts of justifiable homicide. 11. **wittingly,** intentionally. 12. **three branches,** parody of legal phraseology. 13. **argal,** corruption of *ergo,* therefore. 15. **delver,** digger. 24. **quest,** inquest. 29. **there thou say'st,** that's right. 31. **countenance,** privilege. 32. **even,** fellow. 35. **hold up,** maintain, continue. 44. **confess thyself,** "and be hanged" completes the proverb. 45. **Go to,** perhaps, "begin," or some other form of concession. 59. **unyoke,** after this great effort

you may unharness the team of your wits (Dowden). 62. **Mass,** by the Mass. 68. **in, and,** so Q_2; F: *to Yaughan,* probably a London tavern keeper. **stoup,** two-quart measure. 69. **In . . . love.** This and the two following stanzas, with nonsensical variations, are from a poem attributed to Lord Vaux and printed in *Tottel's Miscellany* (1557). The *O* and *ah* are possibly grunts of the digger or (Clarendon Press) represent drawling notes. 71. **behove,** benefit. 76. **property of easiness,** a peculiarity that now is easy. 81. **into,** so Q_2; Globe, following F: *intil.* 84. **jowls,** dashes. 85. **Cain's jaw-bone,** allusion to the old tradition that Cain slew Abel with the jawbone of an ass. 87. **politician,** schemer, plotter. **o'er-reaches,** quibble on the literal sense and the sense "circumvent"; the F reading, *o'er Offices,* Onions

Ham. There 's another: why may not that be the skull of a lawyer? Where be his quiddities now, his quillets, his cases, his tenures, and his tricks? why does he suffer this rude knave now to knock him about the sconce with a dirty shovel, and will not tell him of his action of battery? Hum! This fellow might be in 's time a great buyer of land, with his statutes, his recognizances, his fines, his double vouchers, his recoveries: is this the fine of his fines, and the recovery of his recoveries, to have his fine pate full of fine dirt? will his vouchers vouch him no more of his purchases, and double ones too, than the length and breadth of a pair of indentures? The very conveyances of his lands will hardly lie in this box; and must the inheritor himself have no more, ha?　121

Hor. Not a jot more, my lord.

Ham. Is not parchment made of sheep-skins?

Hor. Ay, my lord, and of calf-skins too.

Ham. They are sheep and calves which seek out assurance in that. I will speak to this fellow. Whose grave 's this, sirrah?

First Clo. Mine, sir.

[*Sings*] O, a pit of clay for to be made
　　　　　　For such a guest is meet.　130

Ham. I think it be thine, indeed; for thou liest in 't.

First Clo. You lie out on 't, sir, and therefore it is not yours: for my part, I do not lie in 't, and yet it is mine.

Ham. Thou dost lie in 't, to be in 't and say it is thine: 'tis for the dead, not for the quick; therefore thou liest.

First Clo. 'Tis a quick lie, sir; 'twill away again, from me to you.　140

Ham. What man dost thou dig it for?

First Clo. For no man, sir.

Ham. What woman, then?

First Clo. For none, neither.

Ham. Who is to be buried in 't?

First Clo. One that was a woman, sir; but, rest her soul, she 's dead.　147

Ham. How absolute the knave is! we must speak by the card, or equivocation will undo us. By the Lord, Horatio, these three years I have taken note of it; the age is grown so picked that the toe of the peasant comes so near the heel of the courtier, he galls his kibe. How long hast thou been a grave-maker?

First Clo. Of all the days i' the year, I came to 't that day that our last king Hamlet overcame Fortinbras.　157

Ham. How long is that since?

First Clo. Cannot you tell that? every fool can tell that: it was the very day that young Hamlet was born; he that is mad, and sent into England.

Ham. Ay, marry, why was he sent into England?

First Clo. Why, because he was mad: he shall recover his wits there; or, if he do not, it 's no great matter there.

Ham. Why?

First Clo. 'Twill not be seen in him there; there the men are as mad as he.　170

Ham. How came he mad?

First Clo. Very strangely, they say.

Ham. How strangely?

First Clo. Faith, e'en with losing his wits.

Ham. Upon what ground?

First Clo. Why, here in Denmark: I have been sexton here, man and boy, thirty years.

Ham. How long will a man lie i' the earth ere he rot?

First Clo. I' faith, if he be not rotten before he die— as we have many pocky corses now-a-days, that will scarce hold the laying in—he will last you some eight year or nine year: a tanner will last you nine year.　184

Ham. Why he more than another?

First Clo. Why, sir, his hide is so tanned with his trade, that he will keep out water a great while; and your water is a sore decayer of your whoreson dead body. Here 's a skull now hath lain you i' th' earth three and twenty years.　191

Ham. Whose was it?

First Clo. A whoreson mad fellow's it was: whose do you think it was?

Ham. Nay, I know not.

First Clo. A pestilence on him for a mad rogue! a' poured a flagon of Rhenish on my head once. This same skull, sir, was Yorick's skull, the king's jester.

Ham. This?　200

First Clo. E'en that.

Ham. Let me see. [*Takes the skull.*] Alas, poor Yorick! I knew him, Horatio: a fellow of infinite jest, of most excellent fancy: he hath borne me on his back a thousand times; and now, how abhorred in my imagination it is! my gorge rises at it. Here hung those lips that I have kissed I know not how oft. Where be your gibes now? your gambols? your songs? your flashes of merriment, that were wont to set the table on a roar? Not one now, to mock your own grinning? quite chap-fallen? Now get you to my lady's chamber, and tell her, let her paint an inch thick, to this favour she must come; make her laugh at that. Prithee, Horatio, tell me one thing.

Hor. What 's that, my lord?

Ham. Dost thou think Alexander looked o' this fashion i' the earth?

Hor. E'en so.　220

Ham. And smelt so? pah!　　　　[*Puts down the skull.*

Hor. E'en so, my lord.

Ham. To what base uses we may return, Horatio! Why may not imagination trace the noble dust of Alexander, till he find it stopping a bung-hole?

Hor. 'Twere to consider too curiously, to consider so.

Ham. No, faith, not a jot; but to follow him thither with modesty enough, and likelihood to lead it: as thus: Alexander died, Alexander was buried, Alex-

ander returneth into dust; the dust is earth; of earth
we make loam; and why of that loam, whereto he
was converted, might they not stop a beer-barrel?
　　Imperious Cæsar, dead and turn'd to clay,
　　Might stop a hole to keep the wind away:
　　O, that that earth, which kept the world in awe,
　　Should patch a wall to expel the winter's flaw!
But soft! but soft! aside: here comes the king, 　　240

　　　Enter Priests, *&c. in procession; the Corpse of* OPHELIA,
　　　LAERTES *and* Mourners, *following;* KING, QUEEN,
　　　their trains, &c.

The queen, the courtiers: who is this they follow?
And with such maimed rites? This doth betoken
The corse they follow did with desperate hand
Fordo it own life: 'twas of some estate.
Couch we awhile, and mark.　　*[Retiring with Horatio.*
　　Laer. What ceremony else?
　　Ham.　　　　　　That is Laertes,
A very noble youth: mark.
　　Laer. What ceremony else?
　　First Priest. Her obsequies have been as far enlarged
As we have warranty: her death was doubtful;　　250
And, but that great command o'ersways the order,
She should in ground unsanctified have lodged
Till the last trumpet; for charitable prayers,
Shards, flints and pebbles should be thrown on her:
Yet here she is allow'd her virgin crants,
Her maiden strewments and the bringing home
Of bell and burial.
　　Laer. Must there no more be done?
　　First Priest.　　　　No more be done:
We should profane the service of the dead
To sing a requiem and such rest to her　　260
As to peace-parted souls.
　　Laer.　　　　Lay her i' the earth:
And from her fair and unpolluted flesh
May violets spring! I tell thee, churlish priest,
A ministering angel shall my sister be,
When thou liest howling.
　　Ham.　　　　What, the fair Ophelia!
　　Queen. Sweets to the sweet: farewell!
　　　　　　　　　　　[Scattering flowers.
I hoped thou shouldst have been my Hamlet's wife;
I thought thy bride-bed to have deck'd, sweet maid,
And not have strew'd thy grave.
　　Laer.　　　　O, treble woe
Fall ten times treble on that cursed head,　　270
Whose wicked deed thy most ingenious sense
Deprived thee of! Hold off the earth awhile,
Till I have caught her once more in mine arms:
　　　　　　　　　　[Leaps into the grave.
Now pile your dust upon the quick and dead,
Till of this flat a mountain you have made,
To o'ertop old Pelion, or the skyish head
Of blue Olympus.

　　Ham.　　　　*[Advancing]* What is he whose
　　　grief
Bears such an emphasis? whose phrase of sorrow
Conjures the wandering stars, and makes them stand
Like wonder-wounded hearers? This is I,　　280
Hamlet the Dane.　　　　*[Leaps into the grave.*
　　Laer.　　　　The devil take thy soul!
　　　　　　　　　　[Grappling with him.
　　Ham. Thou pray'st not well.
I prithee, take thy fingers from my throat;
For, though I am not splenitive and rash,
Yet have I in me something dangerous,
Which let thy wiseness fear: hold off thy hand.
　　King. Pluck them asunder.
　　Queen.　　　　Hamlet, Hamlet!
　　All. Gentlemen,—
　　Hor.　　　　Good my lord, be quiet.
　　　*[The Attendants part them, and they come out
　　　　　　　　　　　of the grave.*
　　Ham. Why, I will fight with him upon this theme
Until my eyelids will no longer wag.　　290
　　Queen. O my son, what theme?
　　Ham. I loved Ophelia: forty thousand brothers
Could not, with all their quantity of love,
Make up my sum. What wilt thou do for her?
　　King. O, he is mad, Laertes.
　　Queen. For love of God, forbear him.
　　Ham. 'Swounds, show me what thou 'lt do:
Woo 't weep? woo 't fight? woo 't fast? woo 't tear
　　thyself?
Woo 't drink up eisel? eat a crocodile?
I'll do 't. Dost thou come here to whine?　　300
To outface me with leaping in her grave?
Be buried quick with her, and so will I:
And, if thou prate of mountains, let them throw
Millions of acres on us, till our ground,
Singeing his pate against the burning zone,
Make Ossa like a wart! Nay, an thou 'lt mouth,
I'll rant as well as thou.
　　Queen.　　　　This is mere madness:
And thus awhile the fit will work on him;
Anon, as patient as the female dove,
When that her golden couplets are disclosed,　　310
His silence will sit drooping.
　　Ham.　　　　Hear you, sir;
What is the reason that you use me thus?
I loved you ever: but it is no matter;
Let Hercules himself do what he may,
The cat will mew and dog will have his day.　　*[Exit.*
　　King. I pray you, good Horatio, wait upon him.
　　　　　　　　　　　[Exit Horatio.
[To Laertes] Strengthen your patience in our last
　　night's speech;
We'll put the matter to the present push.
Good Gertrude, set some watch over your son.
This grave shall have a living monument:　　320

An hour of quiet shortly shall we see;
Till then, in patience our proceeding be.   [*Exeunt.*

SCENE II. *A hall in the castle.*

Enter HAMLET *and* HORATIO.

Ham. So much for this, sir: now shall you see the
    other;
You do remember all the circumstance?
  Hor. Remember it, my lord!
  Ham. Sir, in my heart there was a kind of fighting,
That would not let me sleep: methought I lay
Worse than the mutines in the bilboes. Rashly,
And praised be rashness for it, let us know,
Our indiscretion sometimes serves us well,
When our deep plots do pall: and that should teach us
There 's a divinity that shapes our ends,   10
Rough-hew them how we will,—
  Hor.   That is most certain.
  Ham. Up from my cabin,
My sea-gown scarf'd about me, in the dark
Groped I to find out them; had my desire,
Finger'd their packet, and in fine withdrew
To mine own room again; making so bold,
My fears forgetting manners, to unseal
Their grand commission; where I found, Horatio,—
O royal knavery!—an exact command,
Larded with many several sorts of reasons   20
Importing Denmark's health and England's too,
With, ho! such bugs and goblins in my life,
That, on the supervise, no leisure bated,
No, not to stay the grinding of the axe,
My head should be struck off.
  Hor.   Is 't possible?
  Ham. Here 's the commission: read it at more
    leisure.
But wilt thou hear me how I did proceed?
  Hor. I beseech you.
  Ham. Being thus be-netted round with villanies,—
Ere I could make a prologue to my brains,   30
They had begun the play—I sat me down,
Devised a new commission, wrote it fair:
I once did hold it, as our statists do,
A baseness to write fair and labour'd much
How to forget that learning, but, sir, now
It did me yeoman's service: wilt thou know
The effect of what I wrote?
  Hor.   Ay, good my lord.
  Ham. An earnest conjuration from the king,
As England was his faithful tributary,
As love between them like the palm might flourish,   40
As peace should still her wheaten garland wear
And stand a comma 'tween their amities,
And many such-like 'As'es of great charge,

That, on the view and knowing of these contents,
Without debatement further, more or less,
He should the bearers put to sudden death,
Not shriving-time allow'd.
  Hor.   How was this seal'd?
  Ham. Why, even in that was heaven ordinant.
I had my father's signet in my purse,
Which was the model of that Danish seal;   50
Folded the writ up in form of the other,
Subscribed it, gave 't the impression, placed it safely,
The changeling never known. Now, the next day
Was our sea-fight; and what to this was sequent
Thou know'st already.
  Hor. So Guildenstern and Rosencrantz go to 't.
  Ham. Why, man, they did make love to this
    employment;
They are not near my conscience; their defeat
Does by their own insinuation grow:
'Tis dangerous when the baser nature comes   60
Between the pass and fell incensed points
Of mighty opposites.
  Hor.   Why, what a king is this!
  Ham. Does it not, thinks 't thee, stand me now
    upon—
He that hath kill'd my king and whored my mother,
Popp'd in between the election and my hopes,
Thrown out his angle for my proper life,
And with such cozenage—is 't not perfect conscience,
To quit him with this arm? and is 't not to be damn'd,
To let this canker of our nature come
In further evil?   70
  Hor. It must be shortly known to him from England
What is the issue of the business there.
  Ham. It will be short: the interim is mine;
And a man's life 's no more than to say 'One.'
But I am very sorry, good Horatio,
That to Laertes I forgot myself;
For, by the image of my cause, I see
The portraiture of his: I'll court his favours:
But, sure, the bravery of his grief did put me
Into a towering passion.
  Hor.   Peace! who comes here?   80

Enter OSRIC.

  Osr. Your lordship is right welcome back to Denmark.
  Ham. I humbly thank you, sir. Dost know this
water-fly?
  Hor. No, my good lord.
  Ham. Thy state is the more gracious; for 'tis a vice
to know him. He hath much land, and fertile: let a
beast be lord of beasts, and his crib shall stand at the
king's mess: 'tis a chough; but, as I say, spacious in
the possession of dirt.   90
  Osr. Sweet lord, if your lordship were at leisure, I
should impart a thing to you from his majesty.

---

coarse, high-collered, and short-sleeved gowne, reaching down to the
mid-leg, and used most by seamen and saylors" (Cotgrave, quoted by
Singer). 15. **Finger'd,** pilfered, filched. 20. **Larded,** interspersed.
22. **such . . . life,** such imaginary dangers if I were allowed to live, or
such exaggeration of the actual facts of life. **bugs,** bugbears. 23.
supervise, perusal. **leisure bated,** delay allowed. 30-31. **prologue
. . . play,** i.e., before I could begin to think, my mind had made its
decision. 33. **statists,** statesmen. 34. **fair,** in a clear hand. 36.
yeoman's, i.e., faithful. 41. **wheaten garland,** symbol of peace. 42.
comma, smallest break or separation (Gollancz). Here *amity* begins and
amity ends the period, and *peace* stands between like a dependent clause
(Dowden). 43. **'As'es,** probably the "whereases" of a formal document, with play on the word *ass*. **charge,** import, and burden. 47.

shriving-time, time for absolution. 48. **ordinant,** directing. 54.
sequent, subsequent. 59. **insinuation,** interference. 61. **pass,** thrust.
fell incensed, fiercely angered. 63. **stand,** become incumbent. 65.
election. The Danish throne was filled by election. 66. **angle,** fish-
hook. 67. **cozenage,** trickery. 69. **canker,** ulcer, or possibly the worm
which destroys buds and leaves. 79. **bravery,** bravado. 84. **water-
fly,** vain or busily idle person. 88. **lord of beasts.** Cf. Genesis 1:26, 28.
89. **his crib . . . mess,** he shall eat at the king's table, i.e., be one of the
group of persons (usually four) constituting a *mess* at a banquet.
90. **chough,** probably, chattering jackdaw; also explained as *chuff,*
provincial boor or churl.

Ham. I will receive it, sir, with all diligence of spirit. Put your bonnet to his right use; 'tis for the head.

Osr. I thank your lordship, it is very hot.

Ham. No, believe me, 'tis very cold; the wind is northerly. 99

Osr. It is indifferent cold, my lord, indeed.

Ham. But yet methinks it is very sultry and hot for my complexion.

Osr. Exceedingly, my lord; it is very sultry,—as 'twere,—I cannot tell how. But, my lord, his majesty bade me signify to you that he has laid a great wager on your head: sir, this is the matter,—

Ham. I beseech you, remember— 108

[*Hamlet moves him to put on his hat.*

Osr. Nay, good my lord; for mine ease, in good faith. Sir, here is newly come to court Laertes; believe me, an absolute gentleman, full of most excellent differences, of very soft society and great showing: indeed, to speak feelingly of him, he is the card or calendar of gentry, for you shall find in him the continent of what part a gentleman would see. 116

Ham. Sir, his definement suffers no perdition in you; though, I know, to divide him inventorially would dizzy the arithmetic of memory, †and yet but yaw neither, in respect of his quick sail. But, in the verity of extolment, I take him to be a soul of great article; and his infusion of such dearth and rareness, as, to make true diction of him, his semblable is his mirror; and who else would trace him, his umbrage, nothing more. 126

Osr. Your lordship speaks most infallibly of him.

Ham. The concernancy, sir? why do we wrap the gentleman in our more rawer breath?

Osr. Sir? 130

Hor. Is 't not possible to understand in another tongue? You will do 't, sir, really.

Ham. What imports the nomination of this gentleman?

Osr. Of Laertes?

Hor. His purse is empty already; all 's golden words are spent.

Ham. Of him, sir.

Osr. I know you are not ignorant— 139

Ham. I would you did, sir; yet, in faith, if you did, it would not much approve me. Well, sir?

Osr. You are not ignorant of what excellence Laertes is—

Ham. I dare not confess that, lest I should compare with him in excellence; but, to know a man well, were to know himself.

Osr. I mean, sir, for his weapon; but in the imputation laid on him by them, in his meed he 's unfellowed.

Ham. What 's his weapon?

Osr. Rapier and dagger.

Ham. That 's two of his weapons: but, well.

Osr. The king, sir, hath wagered with him six

Barbary horses: against the which he has imponed, as I take it, six French rapiers and poniards, with their assigns, as girdle, hangers, and so: three of the carriages, in faith, are very dear to fancy, very responsive to the hilts, most delicate carriages, and of very liberal conceit. 160

Ham. What call you the carriages?

Hor. I knew you must be edified by the margent ere you had done.

Osr. The carriages, sir, are the hangers.

Ham. The phrase would be more german to the matter, if we could carry cannon by our sides: I would it might be hangers till then. But, on: six Barbary horses against six French swords, their assigns, and three liberal-conceited carriages; that 's the French bet against the Danish. Why is this 'imponed,' as you call it? 171

Osr. The king, sir, hath laid, that in a dozen passes between yourself and him, he shall not exceed you three hits: he hath laid on twelve for nine; and it would come to immediate trial, if your lordship would vouchsafe the answer.

Ham. How if I answer 'no'?

Osr. I mean, my lord, the opposition of your person in trial. 179

Ham. Sir, I will walk here in the hall: if it please his majesty, 't is the breathing time of day with me; let the foils be brought, the gentleman willing, and the king hold his purpose, I will win for him an I can; if not, I will gain nothing but my shame and the odd hits. 185

Osr. Shall I re-deliver you e'en so?

Ham. To this effect, sir; after what flourish your nature will.

Osr. I commend my duty to your lordship.

Ham. Yours, yours. [*Exit Osric.*] He does well to commend it himself; there are no tongues else for 's turn.

Hor. This lapwing runs away with the shell on his head. 194

Ham. He did comply with his dug, before he sucked it. Thus has he—and many more of the same breed that I know the drossy age dotes on—only got the tune of the time and out of an habit of encounter; a kind of yesty collection, which carries them through and through the most †fann'd and winnowed opinions; and do but blow them to their trial, the bubbles are out. 202

Enter a Lord.

Lord. My lord, his majesty commended him to you by young Osric, who brings back to him, that you attend him in the hall: he sends to know if your pleasure hold to play with Laertes, or that you will take longer time.

Ham. I am constant to my purposes; they follow

the king's pleasure: if his fitness speaks, mine is ready;
now or whensoever, provided I be so able as now.   211
Lord. The king and queen and all are coming down.
Ham. In happy time.
Lord. The queen desires you to use some gentle
entertainment to Laertes before you fall to play.
Ham. She well instructs me.   [*Exit Lord.*
Hor. You will lose this wager, my lord.   219
Ham. I do not think so; since he went into France,
I have been in continual practice; I shall win at the
odds. But thou wouldst not think how ill all 's here
about my heart: but it is no matter.
Hor. Nay, good my lord,—
Ham. It is but foolery; but it is such a kind of gain-
giving, as would perhaps trouble a woman.
Hor. If your mind dislike any thing, obey it: I will
forestal their repair hither, and say you are not fit.   229
Ham. Not a whit, we defy augury: there 's a special
providence in the fall of a sparrow. If it be now, 'tis
not to come; if it be not to come, it will be now; if it
be not now, yet it will come: the readiness is all: since
no man has aught of what he leaves, what is 't to
leave betimes? Let be.   235

Enter KING, QUEEN, LAERTES, *Lords,* OSRIC, *and*
Attendants *with foils, &c.*

King. Come, Hamlet, come, and take this hand
from me. [*The King puts Laertes' hand into Hamlet's.*
Ham. Give me your pardon, sir: I 've done you
wrong;
But pardon 't, as you are a gentleman.
This presence knows,
And you must needs have heard, how I am punish'd
With sore distraction. What I have done,   241
That might your nature, honour and exception
Roughly awake, I here proclaim was madness.
Was 't Hamlet wrong'd Laertes? Never Hamlet:
If Hamlet from himself be ta'en away,
And when he 's not himself does wrong Laertes,
Then Hamlet does it not, Hamlet denies it.
Who does it, then? His madness: if 't be so,
Hamlet is of the faction that is wrong'd;
His madness is poor Hamlet's enemy.   250
Sir, in this audience,
Let my disclaiming from a purposed evil
Free me so far in your most generous thoughts,
That I have shot mine arrow o'er the house,
And hurt my brother.
Laer.   I am satisfied in nature,
Whose motive, in this case, should stir me most
To my revenge: but in my terms of honour
I stand aloof; and will no reconcilement,
Till by some elder masters, of known honour,
I have a voice and precedent of peace,   260
To keep my name ungored. But till that time,
I do receive your offer'd love like love,

And will not wrong it.
Ham.   I embrace it freely;
And will this brother's wager frankly play.
Give us the foils. Come on.
Laer.   Come, one for me.
Ham. I'll be your foil, Laertes: in mine ignorance
Your skill shall, like a star i' the darkest night,
Stick fiery off indeed.
Laer.   You mock me, sir.
Ham. No, by this hand.
King. Give them the foils, young Osric. Cousin
Hamlet,   270
You know the wager?
Ham.   Very well, my lord;
Your grace hath laid the odds o' the weaker side.
King. I do not fear it; I have seen you both:
But since he is better'd, we have therefore odds.
Laer. This is too heavy, let me see another.
Ham. This likes me well. These foils have all a
length?   [*They prepare to play.*
Osr. Ay, my good lord.
King. Set me the stoups of wine upon that table.
If Hamlet give the first or second hit,
Or quit in answer of the third exchange,   280
Let all the battlements their ordnance fire;
The king shall drink to Hamlet's better breath;
And in the cup an union shall he throw,
Richer than that which four successive kings
In Denmark's crown have worn. Give me the cups;
And let the kettle to the trumpet speak,
The trumpet to the cannoneer without,
The cannons to the heavens, the heavens to earth,
'Now the king drinks to Hamlet.' Come, begin:
And you, the judges, bear a wary eye.   290
Ham. Come on, sir.
Laer.   Come, my lord.   [*They play.*
Ham.   One.
Laer.   No.
Ham.   Judgement.
Osr. A hit, a very palpable hit.
Laer.   Well; again.
King. Stay; give me drink. Hamlet, this pearl is
thine;
Here 's to thy health.
      [*Trumpets sound, and cannon shot off within.*
        Give him the cup.
Ham. I'll play this bout first; set it by awhile.
Come. [*They play.*] Another hit; what say you?
Laer. A touch, a touch, I do confess 't.
King. Our son shall win.
Queen.   He 's fat, and scant of breath.
Here, Hamlet, take my napkin, rub thy brows:
The queen carouses to thy fortune, Hamlet.   300
Ham. Good madam!
King.   Gertrude, do not drink.
Queen. I will, my lord; I pray you, pardon me.

---

exercise period.   193. **lapwing,** peewit; note its wiliness in drawing a
visitor away from its nest and its supposed habit of running about when
newly hatched with its head in the shell; Ruth Cline suggests allusion
to Osric's hat.   195. **did comply with his dug,** paid compliments to his
mother's breast.   197. **drossy,** frivolous.   198. **tune,** temper, mood.
199. **out of an,** so Q_2; F (Globe): *outward.* **habit of encounter,**
demeanor of social intercourse.   **yesty,** frothy.   201. **fann'd and
winnowed,** Q_2: *prophane and trennowed*; F: *fond and winnowed* (trivial and
sensible; so Globe, following W. J. Craig); text follows Warburton.
202. **blow . . . out,** i.e., put them to the test, and their ignorance is
exposed.   214. **In happy time,** a phrase of courtesy.   222. **at the odds,**
with the balance of advantage in my favor.   226. **gain-giving,** misgiving.   233-235. Text follows Caldecott.   239. **presence,** royal

assembly.   242. **exception,** disapproval.   255. **brother.** With reference
to the F reading, *mother,* Dowden calls attention to Gertrude's request
to *use some gentle entertainment* to Laertes.   **nature,** i.e., he is personally
satisfied, but his honor must be satisfied by the rules of the code of honor.
260. **voice,** authoritative pronouncement.   266. **foil,** quibble on the
two senses, "background which sets something off," and "blunted rapier
for fencing."   268. **Stick fiery off,** stand out brilliantly.   283. **union,**
pearl.   286. **kettle,** kettledrum.   293. **pearl,** i.e., the poison.   297.
confess 't, Q_2: *confest;* F (Globe): *confess.*   298. **fat.** There is a tradition
that *fat* describes Richard Burbage, the original Hamlet, known to have
been corpulent. Many editors define it as "soft, out of training." It has
been recently suggested that *fat* means "sweaty." Emendations *faint*
and *hot* have been proposed.   300. **carouses,** drinks a toast.

King. [*Aside*] It is the poison'd cup: it is too late.
Ham. I dare not drink yet, madam; by and by.
Queen. Come, let me wipe thy face.
Laer. My lord, I'll hit him now.
King.   I do not think 't.
Laer. [*Aside*] And yet 'tis almost 'gainst my
  conscience.
Ham. Come, for the third, Laertes: you but dally;
I pray you, pass with your best violence;
I am afeard you make a wanton of me.   310
  Laer. Say you so? come on.   [*They play.*
  Osr. Nothing, neither way.
  Laer. Have at you now!
    [*Laertes wounds Hamlet; then, in scuffling, they change
                    rapiers, and Hamlet wounds Laertes.*
King.   Part them; they are incensed.
Ham. Nay, come, again.   [*The Queen falls.*
Osr.   Look to the queen there, ho!
Hor. They bleed on both sides. How is it, my lord?
Osr. How is 't, Laertes?
Laer. Why, as a woodcock to mine own springe,
  Osric;
I am justly kill'd with mine own treachery.
  Ham. How does the queen?
King.   She swounds to see them bleed.
Queen. No, no, the drink, the drink,—O my dear
  Hamlet,—   320
The drink, the drink! I am poison'd.   [*Dies.*
  Ham. O villany! Ho! let the door be lock'd:
Treachery! Seek it out.
  Laer. It is here, Hamlet: Hamlet, thou art slain;
No medicine in the world can do thee good;
In thee there is not half an hour of life;
The treacherous instrument is in thy hand,
Unbated and envenom'd: the foul practice
Hath turn'd itself on me; lo, here I lie,
Never to rise again: thy mother's poison'd: 330
I can no more: the king, the king's to blame.
  Ham. The point envenom'd too!
Then, venom, to thy work.   [*Stabs the King.*
  All. Treason! treason!
King. O, yet defend me, friends; I am but hurt.
Ham. Here, thou incestuous, murderous, damned
  Dane,
Drink off this potion. Is thy union here?
Follow my mother.   [*King dies.*
  Laer.   He is justly served;
It is a poison temper'd by himself.
Exchange forgiveness with me, noble Hamlet: 340
Mine and my father's death come not upon thee,
Nor thine on me!   [*Dies.*
  Ham. Heaven make thee free of it! I follow thee.
I am dead, Horatio. Wretched queen, adieu!
You that look pale and tremble at this chance,
That are but mutes or audience to this act,
Had I but time—as this fell sergeant, death,
Is strict in his arrest—O, I could tell you—
But let it be. Horatio, I am dead;

Thou livest; report me and my cause aright   350
To the unsatisfied.
  Hor.   Never believe it:
I am more an antique Roman than a Dane:
Here 's yet some liquor left.
  Ham.   As thou 'rt a man,
Give me the cup: let go; by heaven, I'll have 't.
O God! Horatio, what a wounded name,
Things standing thus unknown, shall live behind me!
If thou didst ever hold me in thy heart,
Absent thee from felicity awhile,
And in this harsh world draw thy breath in pain,
To tell my story.   [*March afar off, and shot within.*
            What warlike noise is this?   360
  Osr. Young Fortinbras, with conquest come from
  Poland,
To the ambassadors of England gives
This warlike volley.
  Ham.   O, I die, Horatio;
The potent poison quite o'er-crows my spirit:
I cannot live to hear the news from England;
But I do prophesy the election lights
On Fortinbras: he has my dying voice;
So tell him, with the occurrents, more and less,
Which have solicited. The rest is silence.   [*Dies.*
  Hor. Now cracks a noble heart. Good night, sweet
  prince;   370
And flights of angels sing thee to thy rest!
Why does the drum come hither?   [*March within.*

Enter FORTINBRAS, *the* English Ambassadors, *and
  others.*

  Fort. Where is this sight?
Hor.   What is it ye would see?
If aught of woe or wonder, cease your search.
  Fort. This quarry cries on havoc. O proud death,
What feast is toward in thine eternal cell,
That thou so many princes at a shot
So bloodily hast struck?
  First Amb.   The sight is dismal;
And our affairs from England come too late:
The ears are senseless that should give us hearing,   380
To tell him his commandment is fulfill'd,
That Rosencrantz and Guildenstern are dead:
Where should we have our thanks?
  Hor.   Not from his mouth,
Had it the ability of life to thank you:
He never gave commandment for their death.
But since, so jump upon this bloody question,
You from the Polack wars, and you from England,
Are here arrived, give order that these bodies
High on a stage be placed to the view;
And let me speak to the yet unknowing world   390
How these things came about: so shall you hear
Of carnal, bloody, and unnatural acts,
Of accidental judgements, casual slaughters,
Of deaths put on by cunning and forced cause,
And, in this upshot, purposes mistook

310. **wanton,** spoiled child. 313. *Stage Direction:* **in scuffling, they change rapiers.** Occurs in F and indicates that at the Globe Theatre the exchange was played as a chance occurrence and was not, as Friesen suggests, a part of the regular tactics of fence. Actors have adopted various methods of exchanging rapiers. Sir Johnston Forbes-Robertson's way was very convincing. He got scratched, grew suspicious, disarmed Laertes, and forced the exchange. 314. **ho.** Supposed by Staunton to be a signal to stop the combat. 317. **woodcock,** as type of stupidity or as decoy. **springe,** trap, snare. 319. **swounds,** swoons. 328. **Unbated,** not blunted with a button. 339. **temper'd,** mixed. 346. **mutes,** per-

formers in a play who speak no words. 347. **sergeant,** sheriff's officer. Chambers takes the word to mean the officer who enforces a judgment of a tribunal or the commands of a person in authority. 352. **Roman.** It was the Roman custom to follow masters in death (Yale). 355. **God,** so Q_2; F (Globe): *good.* 364. **o'er-crows,** triumphs over. 368. **occurrents,** events, incidents. 369. **solicited,** moved, urged. 375. **quarry,** heap of dead. **cries on havoc,** calls for merciless slaughter. 376. **eternal,** used to express extreme abhorrence. 383. **his mouth,** i.e., the king's. 386. **question,** dispute. 389. **stage,** platform. 392-396. **Of carnal . . . heads.** The words bear detailed reference to the tragic issues of the play.

Fall'n on the inventors' heads: all this can I
Truly deliver.
    Fort.   Let us haste to hear it,
And call the noblest to the audience.
For me, with sorrow I embrace my fortune:
I have some rights of memory in this kingdom,   400
Which now to claim my vantage doth invite me.
    Hor. Of that I shall have also cause to speak,
And from his mouth whose voice will draw on more:
But let this same be presently perform'd,
Even while men's minds are wild; lest more
        mischance,
On plots and errors, happen.
    Fort.   Let four captains
Bear Hamlet, like a soldier, to the stage;
For he was likely, had he been put on,
To have proved most royal: and, for his passage,
The soldiers' music and the rites of war   410
Speak loudly for him.
Take up the bodies: such a sight as this
Becomes the field, but here shows much amiss.
Go, bid the soldiers shoot.
        [*A dead march. Exeunt, bearing off the dead bodies;*
            after which a peal of ordnance is shot off.

400. **of memory,** traditional, remembered.   403. **draw on more,** lead
more to speak.   406. **On,** on account of, or possibly, on top of, in
addition to.   409. **royal,** so Q_2; F (Globe): *royally.* **passage,** death.
413. **field,** i.e., of battle.

Othello,
the Moor of Venice

A quarto edition of *Othello* came out in 1622, the
year before the issue of the play among "the Tragedies" in the First Folio. It bore the following title
page:

THE Tragœdy of Othello, The Moore of Venice.
As it hath beene diuerse times acted at the Globe, *and at the*
Black Friers, *by his Maiesties Seruants. Written by* VVilliam
Shakespeare. *LONDON,* Printed by *N. O.* for *Thomas
Walkley,* and are to be sold at his shop, at the Eagle and
Child, in Brittans Bursse. 1622.

Walkley, who had entered the play in the Stationers'
Register on October 6, 1621, supplies a short preface,
"The Stationer to the Reader," which contains
nothing of interest except that "the Authors name is
sufficient to vent his worke."

The First Folio and the quarto present the same
version of the play of *Othello* with no more differences
than can be accounted for by copying and printing
and by cuts for dramatic purposes in the quarto,
which was printed from a prompt copy. The quarto
has been cut for acting, not heavily but in a typical
way, by the omission of long speeches and parts of

long speeches of small dramatic value. The quarto is
about 190 lines shorter than the folio, if the computation is made on actual discourse and not on printed
lines. The two texts may rest on a common original,
or the quarto may have been printed from Shakespeare's manuscript, the peculiarities of which, in a few
instances, the quarto seems to reproduce. Why two
copies, both apparently theatrical copies, should have
been prepared is not clear. The manuscript behind
the quarto, which because of its retention of oaths
banned by the *Act of Abuses* (1606) is judged to be the
older, may have been lost or misplaced for a time. A
second quarto (1630) was printed from the first and
a third (1655) from the second.

DATE

O*thello* is dated, with a good deal of unanimity, in
the year 1604. Malone stated that it was acted that
year. He had evidently seen an entry in the account
books of the Revels Office, printed later by Peter
Cunningham (1842) but subsequently long regarded
as a forgery, since the leaf containing the entry had
been torn out of its proper place. It was left for
Ernest Law, who subjected the entry to careful tests
and to the opinions of handwriting experts, to prove
it genuine and to clear the name of the unfortunate
Cunningham from the charge of forgery.[1]

The entry in question is a curious one, showing
payments to the King's Majesty's players on Hallow-
mas Day (November 1), 1604, for "a play in the
Banketinge house att Whitehall called The Moore of
Venis." On the Sunday following, *The Merry Wives of
Windsor* was presented; on St. Stephen's Day, *Measure
for Measure*; on Innocent's night, "The plaie of
Errors," the last two mentioned being attributed to
"Shaxberd."

General considerations of style and technique
would lead one to think that *Othello* must have been a
new play at that time. The first quarto seems to
reflect the early stage of the play in its retention in the
text of oaths which, in accordance with the statute of
1606 against the use of the name of God profanely in
plays, have been carefully expunged from the folio
text. Almost no other considerations affecting the
question of date have ever been urged.

SOURCE

O*thello* is one of the very few plays of Shakespeare
for which no dramatic source is known or suspected.
He seems to have worked directly from a novel in a
popular collection of Giraldi Cinthio's *Hecatommithi*
(1565).[2] No translation of this story is known to have

[1]*Some Supposed Shakespeare Forgeries* (1911); *More about Shakespeare
Forgeries* (1913). But see S. A. Tannenbaum, *Shakespeare Forgeries in the
Revels Accounts* (1928).
[2]For other suggestions as to sources see A. H. Krappe, "The Source
of *Othello,* Act III, sc. ii, ll. 157-161," *Modern Language Review,* XIII,
44-45, and Lillian Winstanley, "*Othello*" as the Tragedy of Italy (1924).

been made into English, so that Shakespeare must have worked from the Italian, or from the French translation of 1584.

If in *Julius Caesar* and elsewhere Shakespeare showed a disposition to be faithful to good sources, here at least he shows an equal disposition to change bad ones. Such a transmutation of base metal into gold as he effects in Giraldi's tale is hardly to be found in the study of literary history.

In Giraldi's version we find in the service of Venice a warlike Moor who has married, in spite of the opposition of her relatives, a lovely Venetian lady named Disdemona. She had fallen in love with him not from erring fancy but for his noble qualities. They lived together in Venice happily until the Moor was sent to military command at Cyprus. Disdemona insisted on accompanying him. With him he took also his ensign, an intriguing scoundrel, very handsome, a boaster, and a coward. The ensign fell in love with Disdemona, who rejected his advances because of her love for her husband.

The ensign's love was turned to hatred so that he formed a plot to ruin her by accusing her of infidelity to her husband. A captain in Othello's command was the object of the ensign's malignity. This captain soon afterwards struck and wounded a sentry and was discharged from his command. Disdemona interceded for him, a fact that gave the ensign a chance to further his plot. He aroused the Moor to jealous fury by having him see, but not overhear, a conversation with the captain, which the Moor wrongly supposed was about the captain's relations with Disdemona. The ensign finally confirmed the Moor's suspicions by showing in the possession of a lady connected with the captain a handkerchief of special beauty that the ensign had caused to be stolen from Disdemona and had left on the captain's bed. The instrument for this theft was the ensign's own child, and almost the most striking scene in the tale is the picture of the ensign carrying his child to Disdemona and, while she caresses the child, stealing the handkerchief.

At the Moor's request the ensign promised to kill the captain, wounded him, and then joined the Moor in Disdemona's chamber, where they beat her to death "with a stocking filled with sand." The Moor diverted suspicion from himself by pulling down the ceiling of the room and giving it out that the lady had been killed by a falling beam. He was, however, so filled with remorse that he turned on the ensign, degraded him, and drove him out of his service. The ensign revealed the crime to the captain, who made it known to the Venetian senate. The Moor was arrested, tortured, tried, and banished, and later was slain by Disdemona's relatives. Later also, and for another cause, the ensign was put to the torture and died from the effects. No names are used in the story except that of Disdemona.

Giraldi's story is thought to be connected with a certain Venetian nobleman, Christopher Moro,

commandant in Cyprus, who returned to Venice in 1508 after having lost his wife. The tale was at any rate regarded as practically contemporary, and the play retains from its source a realistic manner and atmosphere not elsewhere found in Shakespeare's tragedies. T. M. Parrott makes the interesting suggestion that Othello reflects the vogue of the domestic tragedy, pointing out that Heywood's *A Woman Killed with Kindness* belongs to the year 1603.[3]

As Shakespeare first wrote *Othello* he apparently followed Giraldi's story in providing Cassio (Giraldi's Captain) with both a wife and a mistress. Later he decided on what are sufficiently obvious grounds to dispense with the wife as unnecessary or in the way and proceeded to obliterate the part. Some of it he gave to Bianca, but not every trace of the first version is removed from the play; as, for example, Iago's otherwise inexplicable verse about Cassio (I, i, 21):

> A fellow almost damn'd in a fair wife

and Bianca's words, possibly originally written for Cassio's wife (V, i, 122-123):

> I am no strumpet; but of life as honest
> As you that thus abuse me.

The first quarto shows bibliographical evidences of this revision in interruption of meter and in mislining of verse.

THE PLOT

The plot of *Othello* is thus an intrigue of a conventional character; that is, it depends for its acceptance by the audience on the granting of belief by them that such a thing might occur. E. E. Stoll has argued that the issue in *Othello* rests on the convention of "the calumniator believed."[4] He has contended strongly against the widely current views of those who would find in Othello, when he falls a victim to Iago's treachery, a rational psychology in the modern sense, whether this is done by supposing that in spite of Othello's statement that he was "not easily jealous," he had a predisposition to jealousy, or that he was blinded by passion; or indeed that Othello was intended to be so stupid as to be taken in by Iago, if we are to suppose him to be at the same time a wise statesman, an experienced soldier, and a master among men.

Shakespeare obviously presents the figure of a noble, simple, sensible, efficient man suddenly assailed and overthrown by the base passion of jealousy. He depicts, as almost nowhere else in literature, the power and pathos of such a figure. He asks his audience to believe, moreover, as in all conscience it must be believed of such a man, that

---

[3]T. M. Parrott, Introduction to *Othello* in the Tudor Shakespeare.
[4]E. E. Stoll, *Othello: an Historical and Comparative Study* (Minneapolis, 1915).

he was not prone to jealousy. Against Othello he pits a character especially conceived to win our artistic belief that he might delude Othello even in such matters as the treason of his wife and his best friend. Of course, an Othello in real life would be, by his very character and experience, particularly likely to have been loyal and just to his wife and his best friend, to have come to an understanding with his precious wife and heard her story if any such suspicion arose, and since he was a man of arms, to have had it out with Cassio sword to sword. The fact remains, however, that Othello, though not easily jealous or at all likely to be made jealous by the means employed, is furiously jealous.

Iago is represented as a man of perfect reputation; not even his own wife knows his concealed diabolical nature. The whole play rings with the words, "honest Iago." If we go to life, instead of remaining within the ample and sufficient confines of art, we have to think it unlikely, to say the least, that such a man could have such a reputation, that he could so easily take in his dupe Roderigo, much less his shrewd wife Emilia, or his manly and experienced commander.

Desdemona and Cassio remain silent under the exigencies of the plot when it would have been altogether more natural for them to speak. Emilia, although she knows her husband has the handkerchief, fails to say anything about it even when she sees that its loss is occasioning trouble to her beloved mistress.

These are defects in the story, if you will, but they are not necessarily defects in the play; they are the hard terms of the bond. It may certainly be said that, partly because of the close limits of his task, as well as by the nature of his rather sordid story of domestic intrigue, Shakespeare has gone further here in refined dramatic skill, in poetry of inexhaustible truth and beauty, and in the expression of the depths of human passion, than perhaps in any other play. In the very nature of tragedy one finds another reason for exculpating Othello from the charge of unnatural stupidity or from the exigencies of mere literary convention. It is an ancient law of both tragedy and epic that nothing may debase the hero below the level of human sympathy and respect. The ultimate blame must not rest on the hero. It may rest on error or fate or, as in the case of Othello, on the machinations of a villain.

WORKMANSHIP

On the stage Shakespeare's play asks no favors of anybody. *Othello* is very true to the psychology of the passions as Shakespeare knew it. Shakespeare was not a psychologist, but it reinforces his plausibility to observe that in his conception the passions were savage instincts in every human soul, and no character was proof against them. He knew that men of tragic possibilities are prone to passion. These perturbations were a chief source of danger, for they might seize upon a man and shove reason from its seat. We must realize too that, according to the theory of the time, passions in the heart might change with the suddenness of the emptying and filling of a cup, so that no man was safe from jealousy or other evil passion. When the irascible passions get control, excess, fury, and madness result. Iago, after his words about "trifles light as air," even gives away his psychological method when he says (III, iii, 325-329):

> The Moor already changes with my poison:
> Dangerous conceits are, in their natures, poisons,
> Which at the first are scarce found to distaste,
> But with a little act upon the blood,
> Burn like the mines of sulphur.

These "dangerous conceits," images of Desdemona's wickedness and Othello's disgrace, are the means by which Iago keeps Othello's emotions all agog, and prevents the better, reasonable nature of the Moor from reassuming its control. By these means Othello's conduct and situation are made plausible, so that the great first conception of Othello remains throughout, however much it may be shaken. It appears in his grief: "O, Iago, the pity of it, Iago!" And again in his moving reminiscences (III, iii, 348-354):

> Farewell the tranquil mind! farewell content!
> Farewell the plumed troop, and the big wars,
> That make ambition virtue! O, farewell!
> Farewell the neighing steed, and the shrill trump,
> The spirit-stirring drum, the ear-piercing fife,
> The royal banner, and all quality,
> Pride, pomp and circumstance of glorious war!

It asserts itself again gloriously at the end of the play in the hero's full awareness of the nature of his deed and in his death. His soldiership goes with him, even in his fury, in the form of a blunt and immediate habit of acting on his resolution. In fact Shakespeare never forgets the fundamental conception of his character.

IAGO

On Iago, the instrument of Othello's ruin, Shakespeare has lavished a wealth of dramatic skill. Iago's subtlety and cleverness are such as to lead many critics to think that Othello's actions are completely accounted for by the supreme diabolism of his adversary. That this is sufficient for the stage no one who has seen a great Iago can ever seriously call in question; as for example, "the plausible cunning and indescribable malignity of Edwin Booth" in the character of Iago. To what extent Shakespeare regarded Iago as a demon in human form, having no motive and needing none, since he had chosen evil as his good, has long been in debate.

The Renaissance could conceive, better than we, of complete human depravity. It thought of historical

Othello

945

characters, like Richard III and Cesare Borgia, as all bad. This doctrine was derived wrongly from Machiavelli's *Prince*. Machiavelli himself became the symbol of such human diabolism.[5] Iago has the outlook and the main traits of the Machiavel, though certainly he is more individualized than Richard III and than Edmund in *King Lear*.

Nevertheless, Iago has personal motives which he expresses more than once, and it is doubtful if their force has been realized since Coleridge's phrase about "the motive hunting of a motiveless malignity" became current. Iago is a soldier of the mercenary type familiar to the Renaissance. He has learned his soldiership in the field and has all of the hatred of the theoretical soldier that those so trained often acquire. He has also the professional soldier's belief in the ultimate justice of promotion by seniority, "old gradation," as he calls it. He has worked hard, or at least has kept his service record unspotted, in order that he may achieve promotion, and it has been denied him on what to him are contemptible and infuriating terms. He has even tried the use of influence to secure advancement (I, i, 8-17):

> Three great ones of the city,
> In personal suit to make me his lieutenant,
> Off-capp'd to him: and, by the faith of man,
> I know my price, I am worth no worse a place:
> But he, as loving his own pride and purposes,
> Evades them, with a bombast circumstance
> Horribly stuff'd with epithets of war;
> And, in conclusion,
> Nonsuits my mediators; for, 'Certes,' says he,
> 'I have already chose my officer.'

Iago shows all the way through complete presence of mind and self-control, as if he had been conceived of as having undergone the most rigorous military discipline.

These traits fit in with his opportunism, his pride of intellect, and his skill; he does not plan far ahead, but lives, soldier-like, from task to task and from day to day. As for the rumors of evil relations between Othello and Emilia, which he himself does not believe and yet determines to avenge, his words seem to imply that "mere suspicion in that kind," since it touches a man's reputation abroad, must be treated as if it were the truth. Iago is a man very tender of his reputation. Parrott thus states this view:

This motive has a twofold aspect: on the one hand his dominating sense of superiority to his fellows, on the other his craving to demonstrate this superiority by making them his puppets. Regarded in this light, Iago's motives appear perfectly adequate to account for his inception of the plot. Wounded pride and lust of power are not commonly regarded as weak impulses to action. It must be remembered, moreover, that Iago enters upon this intrigue without realizing its full and fatal consequences. There is not a hint that he originally contemplated the double murder of Cassio and Desde-

mona. Apparently all that he anticipated was such action on the part of Othello as should secure his own immediate ends. . . . Too much has been written on the superhuman intellect of Iago. It is plain, I think, to any one who regards the play as a whole, that Iago, with all his gifts, was a limited and unimaginative intelligence. As a soldier he must have been a brilliant tactician, but a wretched strategist.[6]

STAGE HISTORY

Few Shakespearean plays have more brilliant stage histories than *Othello*. The effectiveness of the style of the tragedy, its almost unique reliance on the art of the actor, and the fact that it has two great parts set over against each other as protagonist and antagonist are the elements of its greatness as a stage play.

Othello was Burbage's part, and he was succeeded in the role in Shakespeare's company by Field. Joseph Taylor played Iago. There are an unusual number of performances of *Othello* recorded in the years preceding the closing of the theaters in 1642, and the play was one of the first revived after the Restoration.

Pepys, the diarist, saw it with Burt in the title role at the Cockpit on October 11, 1660. Malone states that Desdemona was the first of Shakespeare's female parts to be played by a woman. Betterton was splendid as Othello, and, singularly enough, James Quin, the famous Falstaff, was popular in the part. Garrick was relatively unsuccessful as Othello, and one thinks that he should have essayed the role of Iago instead.

In 1785 Mrs. Siddons played Desdemona to her brother John Philip Kemble's Othello at Drury Lane Theater in London.

Edmund Kean was apparently transcendent as Othello, and his praises ring through all the criticism of the time. Two occasions in his acting of the part may be worth mentioning. When he visited America in 1826 he played Othello opposite the Iago of the brilliant young actor Edwin Forrest, later himself famous as Othello. Three weeks before Kean's death he broke down in mortal illness on the stage while playing Othello with his son Charles Kean as Iago.

Several great occasions in the playing of *Othello* are connected with the career of Edwin Booth, who played both Othello and Iago supremely well and was able to alternate the two parts. In 1881 Booth and Irving, with Ellen Terry as Desdemona, played an engagement at the Lyceum Theater in London and frequently exchanged the two principal parts. In 1886 Booth played Iago at the Academy of Music in New York to the Othello of the illustrious Italian actor Salvini. Tree, Forbes-Robertson, and William Faversham have revived *Othello* during the present century and the acting of the part of Othello by Paul Robeson has met with much praise.

[5]E. S. Meyer, *Machiavelli and the Elizabethan Drama* (Weimar, 1897).

[6]*Op. cit.*, pp. xviii-xix.

Othello,
the Moor of Venice

DRAMATIS PERSONAE

DUKE OF VENICE.
BRABANTIO, a senator.
Other Senators.
GRATIANO, brother to Brabantio.
LODOVICO, kinsman to Brabantio.
OTHELLO, a noble Moor in the service of the
  Venetian state.
CASSIO, his lieutenant.
IAGO, his ancient.
RODERIGO, a Venetian gentleman.
MONTANO, Othello's predecessor in the
  government of Cyprus.
Clown, servant to Othello.

DESDEMONA, daughter to Brabantio and wife to
  Othello.
EMILIA, wife to Iago.
BIANCA, mistress to Cassio.

Sailor, Messenger, Herald, Officers,
  Gentlemen, Musicians, and Attendants.

SCENE: *Venice: a Sea-port in Cyprus.*

ACT I.

SCENE I. *Venice. A street.*

Enter RODERIGO *and* IAGO.

Rod. Tush! never tell me; I take it much unkindly
That thou, Iago, who hast had my purse
As if the strings were thine, shouldst know of this.
Iago. 'Sblood, but you will not hear me:
If ever I did dream of such a matter,
Abhor me.
   Rod. Thou told'st me thou didst hold him in thy
     hate.
   Iago. Despise me, if I do not. Three great ones of the
     city,
In personal suit to make me his lieutenant,
Off-capp'd to him: and, by the faith of man,   10
I know my price, I am worth no worse a place:
But he, as loving his own pride and purposes,
Evades them, with a bombast circumstance
Horribly stuff'd with epithets of war;
And, in conclusion,
Nonsuits my mediators; for, 'Certes,' says he,
'I have already chose my officer.'
And what was he?
Forsooth, a great arithmetician,
One Michael Cassio, a Florentine,   20
†A fellow almost damn'd in a fair wife;
That never set a squadron in the field,
Nor the division of a battle knows
More than a spinster; unless the bookish theoric,

Wherein the toged consuls can propose
As masterly as he: mere prattle, without practice,
Is all his soldiership. But he, sir, had the election:
And I, of whom his eyes had seen the proof
At Rhodes, at Cyprus and on other grounds
Christian and heathen, must be be-lee'd and calm'd 30
By debitor and creditor: this counter-caster,
He, in good time, must his lieutenant be,
And I—God bless the mark!—his Moorship's ancient.
   Rod. By heaven, I rather would have been his
     hangman.
   Iago. Why, there's no remedy; 'tis the curse of
     service,
Preferment goes by letter and affection,
And not by old gradation, where each second
Stood heir to the first. Now, sir, be judge yourself,
Whether I in any just term am affined
To love the Moor.
   Rod.   I would not follow him then.   40
   Iago. O, sir, content you;
I follow him to serve my turn upon him:
We cannot all be masters, nor all masters
Cannot be truly follow'd. You shall mark
Many a duteous and knee-crooking knave,
That, doting on his own obsequious bondage,
Wears out his time, much like his master's ass,
For nought but provender, and when he's old,
     cashier'd:
Whip me such honest knaves. Others there are
Who, trimm'd in forms and visages of duty,   50
Keep yet their hearts attending on themselves,
And, throwing but shows of service on their lords,
Do well thrive by them and when they have lined
     their coats
Do themselves homage: these fellows have some soul;
And such a one do I profess myself. For, sir,
It is as sure as you are Roderigo,
Were I the Moor, I would not be Iago:
In following him, I follow but myself;
Heaven is my judge, not I for love and duty,
But seeming so, for my peculiar end: 60
For when my outward action doth demonstrate
The native act and figure of my heart
In compliment extern, 'tis not long after
But I will wear my heart upon my sleeve
For daws to peck at: I am not what I am.
   Rod. What a full fortune does the thick-lips owe,
If he can carry 't thus!
   Iago.   Call up her father,
Rouse him: make after him, poison his delight,
Proclaim him in the streets; incense her kinsmen,

ACT I. SCENE I.   4. **'Sblood,** an oath, "by God's blood." 8. **great ones of the city.** Iago means to indicate his importance in the community; this is suggested also by his use of the word *worth* in line 11. 19. **arithmetician,** a man whose military knowledge was merely theoretical, based on books of tactics. 20. **Florentine,** i.e., a commercial person. Florence was celebrated for business. 21. **A . . . wife.** Cassio has no wife; *wife* is sometimes taken to mean "woman." Possibly in Shakespeare's first version of the play Cassio had a wife as he did in the source. 23. **division,** disposition of a battle line. 24. **theoric,** theory. 25. **toged,** wearing the toga. **propose,** discuss. 29. **Rhodes, Cyprus,** islands in the Mediterranean south of Asia Minor, long subject to contention between the Venetians and the Turks. 31. **counter-caster,** a sort of bookkeeper; contemptuous term. 32. **in good time,** forsooth. 33. **God bless the mark,** anciently, a pious interjection to avert evil omens. **ancient,** standardbearer, ensign. 37. **old gradation,** seniority. Iago here expresses a characteristic prejudice of professional soldiers. 39. **affined,** bound. 41-55. **O, sir . . . myself.** These lines are an expression of Iago's ethics. 57. **Were . . . Iago.** Were I in the position of the Moor, I should not feel as Iago feels. 63. **compliment extern,** outward civility. 66. **thick-lips,** probably African.

And, though he in a fertile climate dwell, 70
Plague him with flies: though that his joy be joy,
Yet throw such changes of vexation on 't,
As it may lose some colour.
    Rod. Here is her father's house; I'll call aloud.
    Iago. Do, with like timorous accent and dire yell
As when, by night and negligence, the fire
Is spied in populous cities.
    Rod. What, ho, Brabantio! Signior Brabantio, ho!
    Iago. Awake! what, ho, Brabantio! thieves! thieves!
    thieves!
Look to your house, your daughter and your bags! 80
Thieves! thieves!

BRABANTIO *appears above, at a window.*

    Bra. What is the reason of this terrible summons?
What is the matter there?
    Rod. Signior, is all your family within?
    Iago. Are your doors lock'd?
    Bra.   Why, wherefore ask you this?
    Iago. 'Zounds, sir, you 're robb'd; for shame, put on
    your gown;
Your heart is burst, you have lost half your soul;
Even now, now, very now, an old black ram
Is tupping your white ewe. Arise, arise;
Awake the snorting citizens with the bell, 90
Or else the devil will make a grandsire of you:
Arise, I say.
    Bra.   What, have you lost your wits?
    Rod. Most reverend signior, do you know my voice?
    Bra. Not I: what are you?
    Rod. My name is Roderigo.
    Bra.   The worser welcome:
I have charged thee not to haunt about my doors:
In honest plainness thou hast heard me say
My daughter is not for thee; and now, in madness,
Being full of supper and distempering draughts,
Upon malicious bravery, dost thou come 100
To start my quiet.
    Rod. Sir, sir, sir,—
    Bra.   But thou must needs be sure
My spirit and my place have in them power
To make this bitter to thee.
    Rod.   Patience, good sir.
    Bra. What tell'st thou me of robbing? this is Venice;
My house is not a grange.
    Rod.   Most grave Brabantio,
In simple and pure soul I come to you.
    Iago. 'Zounds, sir, you are one of those that will
not serve God, if the devil bid you. Because we come
to do you service and you think we are ruffians, you'll
have your daughter covered with a Barbary horse;
you'll have your nephews neigh to you; you'll have
coursers for cousins and gennets for germans. 114
    Bra. What profane wretch art thou?
    Iago. I am one, sir, that comes to tell you your
daughter and the Moor are now making the beast
with two backs.
    Bra. Thou art a villain.
    Iago.   You are—a senator.
    Bra. This thou shalt answer; I know thee, Roderigo.

    Rod. Sir, I will answer any thing. But, I beseech
    you, 121
If 't be your pleasure and most wise consent,
As partly I find it is, that your fair daughter,
At this odd-even and dull watch o' the night,
Transported, with no worse nor better guard
But with a knave of common hire, a gondolier,
To the gross clasps of a lascivious Moor,—
If this be known to you and your allowance,
We then have done you bold and saucy wrongs;
But if you know not this, my manners tell me 130
We have your wrong rebuke. Do not believe
That, from the sense of all civility,
I thus would play and trifle with your reverence:
Your daughter, if you have not given her leave,
I say again, hath made a gross revolt;
Tying her duty, beauty, wit and fortunes
In an extravagant and wheeling stranger
Of here and every where. Straight satisfy yourself:
If she be in her chamber or your house,
Let loose on me the justice of the state 140
For thus deluding you.
    Bra.   Strike on the tinder, ho!
Give me a taper! call up all my people!
This accident is not unlike my dream:
Belief of it oppresses me already.
Light, I say! light!   [*Exit above.*
    Iago.   Farewell; for I must leave you:
It seems not meet, nor wholesome to my place,
To be produced—as, if I stay, I shall—
Against the Moor: for, I do know, the state,
However this may gall him with some check,
Cannot with safety cast him, for he 's embark'd 150
With such loud reason to the Cyprus wars,
Which even now stand in act, that, for their souls,
Another of his fathom they have none,
To lead their business: in which regard,
Though I do hate him as I do hell-pains,
Yet, for necessity of present life,
I must show out a flag and sign of love,
Which is indeed but sign. That you shall surely find
    him,
Lead to the Sagittary the raised search;
And there will I be with him. So, farewell.   [*Exit.* 160

Enter, below, BRABANTIO, *and* Servants *with torches.*

    Bra. It is too true an evil: gone she is;
And what 's to come of my despised time
Is nought but bitterness. Now, Roderigo,
Where didst thou see her? O unhappy girl!
With the Moor, say'st thou? Who would be a father!
How didst thou know 'twas she? O, she deceives me
Past thought! What said she to you? Get more tapers:
Raise all my kindred. Are they married, think you?
    Rod. Truly, I think they are.
    Bra. O heaven! How got she out? O treason of the
    blood! 170
Fathers, from hence trust not your daughters' minds
By what you see them act. Is there not charms
By which the property of youth and maidhood
May be abused? Have you not read, Roderigo,

---

75. **timorous,** used ironically. 90. **snorting,** snoring. 100. **bravery,**
defiance, bravado. 101. **start,** startle. 106. **grange,** farmhouse.
112. **nephews,** grandsons. 113. **gennets,** small Spanish horses. 114.
germans, near relatives. 124. **odd-even,** about midnight. 128.
allowance, permission. 132. **from,** contrary to. 137. **extravagant,**
wandering. **wheeling,** wandering, vagabond. 141. **tinder,** charred
linen kept in a metal box, and ignited by a spark from flint and steel.

143. **accident,** occurrence, event. 150. **cast,** dismiss. 159. **Sagittary,**
probably an inn. 172. **Is,** are. 173. **property,** special quality. 176.
you, Roderigo. 183. **officers of night,** police.
    SCENE II. 5. **yerk'd,** stabbed. 12. **magnifico,** Venetian grandee.
13. **effect,** influence. **potential,** powerful. 14. **double,** forcible, or
twice as forcible. 18. **signiory,** governing body of Venice. 22. **siege,**
rank. **demerits,** deserts. 23. **unbonneted,** on equal terms. 31. **My**

Of some such thing?
  Rod.   Yes, sir, I have indeed.
  Bra. Call up my brother. O, would you had had
     her!
Some one way, some another. Do you know
Where we may apprehend her and the Moor?
  Rod. I think I can discover him, if you please
To get good guard and go along with me.   180
  Bra. Pray you, lead on. At every house I'll call;
I may command at most. Get weapons, ho!
And raise some special officers of night.
On, good Roderigo: I'll deserve your pains. [*Exeunt.*

SCENE II. *Another street.*

Enter OTHELLO, IAGO, *and* Attendants *with torches.*

  Iago. Though in the trade of war I have slain men,
Yet do I hold it very stuff o' the conscience
To do no contrived murder: I lack iniquity
Sometimes to do me service: nine or ten times
I had thought to have yerk'd him here under the ribs.
  Oth. 'Tis better as it is.
  Iago.   Nay, but he prated,
And spoke such scurvy and provoking terms
Against your honour
That, with the little godliness I have,
I did full hard forbear him. But, I pray you, sir,   10
Are you fast married? Be assured of this,
That the magnifico is much beloved,
And hath in his effect a voice potential
As double as the duke's: he will divorce you;
Or put upon you what restraint and grievance
The law, with all his might to enforce it on,
Will give him cable.
  Oth.   Let him do his spite;
My services which I have done the signiory
Shall out-tongue his complaints. 'Tis yet to know,—
Which, when I know that boasting is an honour,   20
I shall promulgate—I fetch my life and being
From men of royal siege, and my demerits
May speak unbonneted to as proud a fortune
As this that I have reach'd: for know, Iago,
But that I love the gentle Desdemona,
I would not my unhoused free condition
Put into circumscription and confine
For the sea's worth. But, look! what lights come yond?
  Iago. Those are the raised father and his friends:
You were best go in.
  Oth.   Not I; I must be found: 30
My parts, my title and my perfect soul
Shall manifest me rightly. Is it they?
  Iago. By Janus, I think no.

Enter CASSIO, *and certain* Officers *with torches.*

  Oth. The servants of the duke, and my lieutenant.
The goodness of the night upon you, friends!
What is the news?
  Cas.   The duke does greet you, general,
And he requires your haste-post-haste appearance,
Even on the instant.

  Oth.   What is the matter, think you?
  Cas. Something from Cyprus, as I may divine:
It is a business of some heat: the galleys   40
Have sent a dozen sequent messengers
This very night at one another's heels,
And many of the consuls, raised and met,
Are at the duke's already: you have been hotly call'd
   for;
When, being not at your lodging to be found,
The senate hath sent about three several quests
To search you out.
  Oth.   'Tis well I am found by you.
I will but spend a word here in the house,
And go with you.   [*Exit.*
  Cas.   Ancient, what makes he here?
  Iago. 'Faith, he to-night hath boarded a land
   carack: 50
If it prove lawful prize, he 's made for ever.
  Cas. I do not understand.
  Iago.   He 's married.
  Cas.   To who?

Re-enter OTHELLO.

  Iago. Marry, to—Come, captain, will you go?
  Oth.   Have with you.
  Cas. Here comes another troop to seek for you.
  Iago. It is Brabantio. General, be advised;
He comes to bad intent.

Enter BRABANTIO, RODERIGO, *and* Officers *with
torches and weapons.*

  Oth.   Holla! stand there!
  Rod. Signior, it is the Moor.
  Bra.   Down with him, thief!
     [*They draw on both sides.*
  Iago. You, Roderigo! come, sir, I am for you.
  Oth. Keep up your bright swords, for the dew will
   rust them.
Good signior, you shall more command with years   60
Than with your weapons.
  Bra. O thou foul thief, where hast thou stow'd my
   daughter?
Damn'd as thou art, thou hast enchanted her;
For I'll refer me to all things of sense,
If she in chains of magic were not bound,
Whether a maid so tender, fair and happy,
So opposite to marriage that she shunn'd
The wealthy curled darlings of our nation,
Would ever have, to incur a general mock,
Run from her guardage to the sooty bosom   70
Of such a thing as thou, to fear, not to delight.
Judge me the world, if 'tis not gross in sense
That thou hast practised on her with foul charms,
Abused her delicate youth with drugs or minerals
That weaken motion: I'll have 't disputed on;
'Tis probable and palpable to thinking.
I therefore apprehend and do attach thee
For an abuser of the world, a practiser
Of arts inhibited and out of warrant.
Lay hold upon him: if he do resist,   80
Subdue him at his peril.

. . . **soul,** my merits, my reputation, and my unblemished honor.   41.
sequent, successive.   43. **consuls,** senators.   50. **carack,** large merchant
ship.   59. **Keep . . . them.** In most stage versions of *Othello* the hero
enters for the first time at this point; it is a brilliant stage entrance.   70.
guardage, guardianship.   72. **gross in sense,** easily discernible in
apprehension or perception.   74. **minerals,** medicine, poison.   75.
weaken motion, lessen the power of movement; since inward promptings

of all sorts were dependent on sense. Brabantio therefore thinks that
Desdemona's unnatural conduct is due to drugs.   **disputed on,** argued
in court by professional counsel.   78. **abuser of the world,** corrupter
of society.   79. **inhibited,** prohibited.

Oth.   Hold your hands,
Both you of my inclining, and the rest:
Were it my cue to fight, I should have known it
Without a prompter. Where will you that I go
To answer this your charge?
    Bra.   To prison, till fit time
Of law and course of direct session
Call thee to answer.
    Oth.   What if I do obey?
How may the duke be therewith satisfied,
Whose messengers are here about my side,
Upon some present business of the state   90
To bring me to him?
    First Off.   'Tis true, most worthy signior;
The duke 's in council, and your noble self,
I am sure, is sent for.
    Bra.   How! the duke in council!
In this time of the night! Bring him away:
Mine 's not an idle cause: the duke himself,
Or any of my brothers of the state,
Cannot but feel this wrong as 'twere their own;
For if such actions may have passage free,
Bond-slaves and pagans shall our statesmen be.
                                [Exeunt.

SCENE III. *A council-chamber.*

The DUKE *and* Senators *sitting at a table;* Officers
    attending.

Duke. There is no composition in these news
That gives them credit.
    First Sen.   Indeed, they are
    disproportion'd;
My letters say a hundred and seven galleys.
    Duke. And mine, a hundred and forty.
    Sec. Sen.   And mine, two hundred:
But though they jump not on a just account,—
As in these cases, where the aim reports,
'Tis oft with difference—yet do they all confirm
A Turkish fleet, and bearing up to Cyprus.
    Duke. Nay, it is possible enough to judgement:
I do not so secure me in the error,   10
But the main article I do approve
In fearful sense.
    Sailor.   *[Within]* What, ho! what, ho!
    what, ho!
    First Off. A messenger from the galleys.

Enter a Sailor.

    Duke.   Now, what 's the business?
    Sail. The Turkish preparation makes for Rhodes;
So was I bid report here to the state
By Signior Angelo.
    Duke. How say you by this change?
    First Sen.   This cannot be,
By no assay of reason: 'tis a pageant,
To keep us in false gaze. When we consider
The importancy of Cyprus to the Turk,   20
And let ourselves again but understand,
That as it more concerns the Turk than Rhodes,

So may he with more facile question bear it,
For that it stands not in such warlike brace,
But altogether lacks the abilities
That Rhodes is dress'd in: if we make thought of this,
We must not think the Turk is so unskilful
To leave that latest which concerns him first,
Neglecting an attempt of ease and gain,
To wake and wage a danger profitless.   30
    Duke. Nay, in all confidence, he 's not for Rhodes.
    First Off. Here is more news.

Enter a Messenger.

    Mess. The Ottomites, reverend and gracious,
Steering with due course towards the isle of Rhodes,
Have there injointed them with an after fleet.
    First Sen. Ay, so I thought. How many, as you guess?
    Mess. Of thirty sail: and now they do re-stem
Their backward course, bearing with frank
    appearance
Their purposes toward Cyprus. Signior Montano,
Your trusty and most valiant servitor,   40
With his free duty recommends you thus,
And prays you to believe him.
    Duke. 'Tis certain, then, for Cyprus.
Marcus Luccicos, is not he in town?
    First Sen. He 's now in Florence.
    Duke. Write from us to him; post-post-haste
    dispatch.
    First Sen. Here comes Brabantio and the valiant
    Moor.

Enter BRABANTIO, OTHELLO, IAGO, RODERIGO, *and*
    Officers.

    Duke. Valiant Othello, we must straight employ you
Against the general enemy Ottoman.
[To Brabantio] I did not see you; welcome, gentle
    signior;   50
We lack'd your counsel and your help to-night.
    Bra. So did I yours. Good your grace, pardon me;
Neither my place nor aught I heard of business
Hath raised me from my bed, nor doth the general
    care
Take hold on me, for my particular grief
Is of so flood-gate and o'erbearing nature
That it engluts and swallows other sorrows
And it is still itself.
    Duke.   Why, what 's the matter?
    Bra. My daughter! O, my daughter!
    Duke and Sen.   Dead?
    Bra.   Ay, to me;
She is abused, stol'n from me, and corrupted   60
By spells and medicines bought of mountebanks;
For nature so preposterously to err,
Being not deficient, blind, or lame of sense,
Sans witchcraft could not.
    Duke. Whoe'er he be that in this foul proceeding
Hath thus beguiled your daughter of herself
And you of her, the bloody book of law
You shall yourself read in the bitter letter
After your own sense, yea, though our proper son
Stood in your action.

---

82. **inclining,** following, party.   86. **course of direct session,** regular
legal proceedings.   99. **Bond-slaves and pagans,** contemptuous references to Othello's past history.
    SCENE III.   2. **disproportion'd,** inconsistent.   6. **aim,** conjecture.
10. **secure me,** feel myself secure.   11. **main article,** i.e., that the
Turkish fleet is threatening.   18. **assay,** test.   23. **more facile question,**

greater facility of effort.   24. **brace,** state of defense.   37. **re-stem,**
steer again.   57. **engluts,** engulfs.   70. **Stood . . . action,** was under
your accusation.   83. **pith,** strength, vigor.   89. **patience,** sufferance,
permission.   95-96. **motion . . . herself,** inward impulses blushed
at themselves.   103. **vouch,** assert.   111-112. **Did . . . affections.**
The possibility of such enchantment is accepted by the court; it would

Bra. Humbly I thank your grace.   70
Here is the man, this Moor, whom now, it seems,
Your special mandate for the state-affairs
Hath hither brought.
     Duke and Sen. We are very sorry for 't.
     Duke. [*To Othello*] What, in your own part, can you
          say to this?
     Bra. Nothing, but this is so.
     Oth. Most potent, grave, and reverend signiors,
My very noble and approved good masters,
That I have ta'en away this old man's daughter,
It is most true; true, I have married her:
The very head and front of my offending   80
Hath this extent, no more. Rude am I in my speech,
And little bless'd with the soft phrase of peace;
For since these arms of mine had seven years' pith,
Till now some nine moons wasted, they have used
Their dearest action in the tented field,
And little of this great world can I speak,
More than pertains to feats of broil and battle,
And therefore little shall I grace my cause
In speaking for myself. Yet, by your gracious patience,
I will a round unvarnish'd tale deliver   90
Of my whole course of love; what drugs, what
          charms,
What conjuration and what mighty magic,
For such proceeding I am charged withal,
I won his daughter.
     Bra.   A maiden never bold;
Of spirit so still and quiet, that her motion
Blush'd at herself; and she, in spite of nature,
Of years, of country, credit, every thing,
To fall in love with what she fear'd to look on!
It is a judgement maim'd and most imperfect
That will confess perfection so could err   100
Against all rules of nature, and must be driven
To find out practices of cunning hell,
Why this should be. I therefore vouch again
That with some mixtures powerful o'er the blood,
Or with some dram conjured to this effect,
He wrought upon her.
     Duke.   To vouch this, is no proof,
Without more wider and more overt test
Than these thin habits and poor likelihoods
Of modern seeming do prefer against him.
     First Sen. But, Othello, speak: 110
Did you by indirect and forced courses
Subdue and poison this young maid's affections?
Or came it by request and such fair question
As soul to soul affordeth?
     Oth.   I do beseech you,
Send for the lady to the Sagittary,
And let her speak of me before her father:
If you do find me foul in her report,
The trust, the office I do hold of you,
Not only take away, but let your sentence
Even fall upon my life.
     Duke.   Fetch Desdemona hither.   120
     Oth. Ancient, conduct them; you best know the
          place.   [*Exeunt Iago and Attendants.*
And, till she come, as truly as to heaven

I do confess the vices of my blood,
So justly to your grave ears I'll present
How I did thrive in this fair lady's love,
And she in mine.
     Duke. Say it, Othello.
     Oth. Her father loved me; oft invited me;
Still question'd me the story of my life,
From year to year, the battles, sieges, fortunes,   130
That I have pass'd.
I ran it through, even from my boyish days,
To the very moment that he bade me tell it;
Wherein I spake of most disastrous chances,
Of moving accidents by flood and field,
Of hair-breadth scapes i' the imminent deadly breach,
Of being taken by the insolent foe
And sold to slavery, of my redemption thence
And portance in my travels' history:
Wherein of antres vast and deserts idle,   140
Rough quarries, rocks and hills whose heads touch
          heaven,
It was my hint to speak,—such was the process;
And of the Cannibals that each other eat,
The Anthropophagi and men whose heads
Do grow beneath their shoulders. This to hear
Would Desdemona seriously incline:
But still the house-affairs would draw her thence:
Which ever as she could with haste dispatch,
She 'ld come again, and with a greedy ear
Devour up my discourse: which I observing,   150
Took once a pliant hour, and found good means
To draw from her a prayer of earnest heart
That I would all my pilgrimage dilate,
Whereof by parcels she had something heard,
But not intentively: I did consent,
And often did beguile her of her tears,
When I did speak of some distressful stroke
That my youth suffer'd. My story being done,
She gave me for my pains a world of sighs:
She swore, in faith, 'twas strange, 'twas passing
          strange,   160
'Twas pitiful, 'twas wondrous pitiful:
She wish'd she had not heard it, yet she wish'd
That heaven had made her such a man: she thank'd
          me,
And bade me, if I had a friend that loved her,
I should but teach him how to tell my story,
And that would woo her. Upon this hint I spake:
She loved me for the dangers I had pass'd,
And I loved her that she did pity them.
This only is the witchcraft I have used:
Here comes the lady; let her witness it.   170

     Enter DESDEMONA, IAGO, *and* Attendants.

     Duke. I think this tale would win my daughter too.
Good Brabantio,
Take up this mangled matter at the best:
Men do their broken weapons rather use
Than their bare hands.
     Bra.   I pray you, hear her speak:
If she confess that she was half the wooer,
Destruction on my head, if my bad blame

---

be as readily accepted by an Elizabethan audience. The English Parliament of the year 1604 denounced by law the employment of magic to secure love.   136. **imminent,** i.e., impending parts when a gap has been made in a fortification.   139. **portance,** conduct.   140. **antres,** caverns.   **idle,** barren, unprofitable.   142. **hint,** occasion.   143. **eat,** ate.   144. **Anthropophagi,** man-eaters, a term from Pliny's *Natural*

History.   144-145. **whose . . . shoulders.** Tales of tribes of headless men appear in Pliny and in the voyages of travelers, such as Raleigh's *Discovery of Guiana.*   153. **dilate,** relate in detail.   155. **intentively,** attentively.   163. **her,** i.e., for her.

Light on the man! Come hither, gentle mistress:
Do you perceive in all this noble company
Where most you owe obedience?
    Des.   My noble father,   180
I do perceive here a divided duty:
To you I am bound for life and education;
My life and education both do learn me
How to respect you; you are the lord of duty;
I am hitherto your daughter: but here 's my husband,
And so much duty as my mother show'd
To you, preferring you before her father,
So much I challenge that I may profess
Due to the Moor my lord.
    Bra.   God be wi' you! I have done.
Please it your grace, on to the state-affairs: 190
I had rather to adopt a child than get it.
Come hither, Moor:
I here do give thee that with all my heart
Which, but thou hast already, with all my heart
I would keep from thee. For your sake, jewel,
I am glad at soul I have no other child;
For thy escape would teach me tyranny,
To hang clogs on them. I have done, my lord.
    Duke. Let me speak like yourself, and lay a sentence,
Which, as a grise or step, may help these lovers   200
Into your favour.
When remedies are past, the griefs are ended
By seeing the worst, which late on hopes depended.
To mourn a mischief that is past and gone
Is the next way to draw new mischief on.
What cannot be preserved when fortune takes,
Patience her injury a mockery makes.
The robb'd that smiles steals something from the
    thief;
He robs himself that spends a bootless grief.
    Bra. So let the Turk of Cyprus us beguile;   210
We lose it not, so long as we can smile.
He bears the sentence well that nothing bears
But the free comfort which from thence he hears,
But he bears both the sentence and the sorrow
That, to pay grief, must of poor patience borrow.
These sentences, to sugar, or to gall,
Being strong on both sides, are equivocal:
But words are words; I never yet did hear   218
That the bruised heart was pierced through the ear.
I humbly beseech you, proceed to the affairs of state.
    Duke. The Turk with a most mighty preparation
makes for Cyprus. Othello, the fortitude of the place
is best known to you; and though we have there a
substitute of most allowed sufficiency, yet opinion, a
sovereign mistress of effects, throws a more safer voice
on you: you must therefore be content to slubber the
gloss of your new fortunes with this more stubborn
and boisterous expedition.
    Oth. The tyrant custom, most grave senators,   230
Hath made the flinty and steel couch of war
My thrice-driven bed of down: I do agnize

A natural and prompt alacrity
I find in hardness, and do undertake
These present wars against the Ottomites.
Most humbly therefore bending to your state,
I crave fit disposition for my wife,
Due reference of place and exhibition,
With such accommodation and besort
As levels with her breeding.
    Duke.   If you please,   240
Be 't at her father's.
    Bra.   I'll not have it so.
    Oth. Nor I.
    Des.   Nor I; I would not there reside,
To put my father in impatient thoughts
By being in his eye. Most gracious duke,
To my unfolding lend your prosperous ear;
And let me find a charter in your voice,
To assist my simpleness.
    Duke. What would you, Desdemona?
    Des. That I did love the Moor to live with him,
My downright violence and storm of fortunes   250
May trumpet to the world: my heart 's subdued
Even to the very quality of my lord:
I saw Othello's visage in his mind,
And to his honours and his valiant parts
Did I my soul and fortunes consecrate.
So that, dear lords, if I be left behind,
A moth of peace, and he go to the war,
The rites for which I love him are bereft me,
And I a heavy interim shall support
By his dear absence. Let me go with him.   260
    Oth. Let her have your voices.
Vouch with me, heaven, I therefore beg it not,
To please the palate of my appetite,
Nor to comply with heat—the young affects
In me defunct—and proper satisfaction,
But to be free and bounteous to her mind:
And heaven defend your good souls, that you think
I will your serious and great business scant
For she is with me: no, when light-wing'd toys
Of feather'd Cupid seel with wanton dullness   270
My speculative and officed instruments,
That my disports corrupt and taint my business,
Let housewives make a skillet of my helm,
And all indign and base adversities
Make head against my estimation!
    Duke. Be it as you shall privately determine,
Either for her stay or going: the affair cries haste,
And speed must answer it.
    First Sen. You must away to-night.
    Oth.   With all my heart.   279
    Duke. At nine i' the morning here we'll meet again.
Othello, leave some officer behind,
And he shall our commission bring to you;
With such things else of quality and respect
As doth import you.
    Oth.   So please your grace, my ancient;

---

181. **divided duty.** Desdemona recognizes that she still owes a duty to
her father even after marriage. 190. **on to,** i.e., proceed with. 195. **For
your sake,** on your account. 199. **like yourself,** i.e., in a like strain of
resignation. 200. **grise,** step. 202-220. **When . . . state.** The sententious matter in this passage is cast into rhyme, as not infrequently in
Shakespeare. 205. **next,** nearest. 213. **comfort,** i.e., the consolation
that it may be borne with patience. 223. **fortitude,** strength. 225.
allowed, acknowledged. 228. **slubber,** soil, sully. 232. **thrice-driven,**
thrice sifted. **agnize,** confess. 234. **hardness,** hardship. 238. **exhibition,** allowance. 239. **besort,** suitable company. 245. **prosperous,**
propitious. 246. **charter,** privilege. 247. **simpleness,** simplicity. 258.

rites. Some editors read *rights.* 264. **affects,** inclinations, desires. 270.
seel, in falconry, to make blind by sewing up the eyes of the hawk in
training. 271. **speculative,** having ability to see. **officed,** official,
active; Q: *active.* 272. **That,** so that. **disports,** pastime. **taint,** impair.
273. **skillet,** defined as "a small kettle"; usually means "a frying pan
of the older style." 274. **indign,** unworthy, shameful. 275. **estimation,** reputation. 284. **import,** concern. 290. **delighted,** delightful.
293-294. **Look to her, Moor,** etc., a tragic premonition delivered
casually. 295. **Honest Iago,** an evidence of Iago's carefully built
reputation. 306. **incontinently,** immediately. 313. **four times seven.**
Clarke expresses surprise that Iago should be so young and so versed

A man he is of honesty and trust:
To his conveyance I assign my wife,
With what else needful your good grace shall think
To be sent after me.
        Duke.   Let it be so.
Good night to every one. [*To Brab.*] And, noble
        signior,
If virtue no delighted beauty lack,   290
Your son-in-law is far more fair than black.
        First Sen. Adieu, brave Moor; use Desdemona well.
        Bra. Look to her, Moor, if thou hast eyes to see:
She has deceived her father, and may thee.
                [*Exeunt Duke, Senators, Officers, &c.*
        Oth. My life upon her faith! Honest Iago,
My Desdemona must I leave to thee:
I prithee, let thy wife attend on her;
And bring them after in the best advantage.
Come, Desdemona; I have but an hour
Of love, of worldly matters and direction,   300
To spend with thee: we must obey the time.
                [*Exeunt Othello and Desdemona.*
        Rod. Iago,—
        Iago. What say'st thou, noble heart?
        Rod. What will I do, thinkest thou?
        Iago. Why, go to bed, and sleep.
        Rod. I will incontinently drown myself.
        Iago. If thou dost, I shall never love thee after.
Why, thou silly gentleman!
        Rod. It is silliness to live when to live is torment;
and then have we a prescription to die when death is
our physician.   311
        Iago. O villanous! I have looked upon the world for
four times seven years; and since I could distinguish
betwixt a benefit and an injury, I never found man
that knew how to love himself. Ere I would say, I
would drown myself for the love of a guinea-hen,
I would change my humanity with a baboon.
        Rod. What should I do? I confess it is my shame to
be so fond; but it is not in my virtue to amend it.   321
        Iago. Virtue! a fig! 'tis in ourselves that we are thus or
thus. Our bodies are our gardens, to the which our
wills are gardeners; so that if we will plant nettles, or
sow lettuce, set hyssop and weed up thyme, supply it
with one gender of herbs, or distract it with many,
either to have it sterile with idleness, or manured
with industry, why, the power and corrigible authority of this lies in our wills. If the balance of our
lives had not one scale of reason to poise another of
sensuality, the blood and baseness of our natures
would conduct us to most preposterous conclusions:
but we have reason to cool our raging motions, our
carnal stings, our unbitted lusts, whereof I take this
that you call love to be a sect or scion.   337
        Rod. It cannot be.
        Iago. It is merely a lust of the blood and a permis-
sion of the will. Come, be a man. Drown thyself!
drown cats and blind puppies. I have professed me

thy friend and I confess me knit to thy deserving with
cables of perdurable toughness; I could never better
stead thee than now. Put money in thy purse; follow
thou the wars; defeat thy favour with an usurped
beard; I say, put money in thy purse. It cannot be
that Desdemona should long continue her love to
the Moor,—put money in thy purse,—nor he his to
her: it was a violent commencement, and thou shalt
see an answerable sequestration:—put but money in
thy purse. These Moors are changeable in their wills:
—fill thy purse with money:—the food that to him
now is as luscious as locusts, shall be to him shortly as
bitter as coloquintida. She must change for youth:
when she is sated with his body, she will find the
error of her choice: she must have change, she must:
therefore put money in thy purse. If thou wilt needs
damn thyself, do it a more delicate way than drowning. Make all the money thou canst: if sanctimony
and a frail vow betwixt an erring barbarian and a
super-subtle Venetian be not too hard for my wits
and all the tribe of hell, thou shalt enjoy her; therefore make money. A pox of drowning thyself! it is
clean out of the way: seek thou rather to be hanged
in compassing thy joy than to be drowned and go
without her.
        Rod. Wilt thou be fast to my hopes, if I depend on
the issue?   370
        Iago. Thou art sure of me:—go, make money:—I
have told thee often, and I re-tell thee again and
again, I hate the Moor: my cause is hearted; thine
hath no less reason. Let us be conjunctive in our
revenge against him; if thou canst cuckold him, thou
dost thyself a pleasure, me a sport. There are many
events in the womb of time which will be delivered.
Traverse! go, provide thy money. We will have more
of this to-morrow. Adieu.   380
        Rod. Where shall we meet i' the morning?
        Iago. At my lodging.
        Rod. I'll be with thee betimes.
        Iago. Go to; farewell. Do you hear, Roderigo?
        Rod. What say you?
        Iago. No more of drowning, do you hear?
        Rod. I am changed: I'll go sell all my land.   [*Exit.*
        Iago. Thus do I ever make my fool my purse;
For I mine own gain'd knowledge should profane,   390
If I would time expend with such a snipe,
But for my sport and profit. I hate the Moor;
And it is thought abroad, that 'twixt my sheets
He has done my office: I know not if 't be true;
But I, for mere suspicion in that kind,
Will do as if for surety. He holds me well;
The better shall my purpose work on him.
Cassio 's a proper man: let me see now:
To get his place and to plume up my will
In double knavery—How, how?—Let 's see:—   400
After some time, to abuse Othello's ear
That he is too familiar with his wife.

---

in worldly ways. Twenty-eight was, however, a maturer age in
Shakespeare's time.   **322. Virtue! a fig.** This passage states the ethics,
the infidelity, of selfishness.   **325. hyssop,** an herb of the mint family.
327. gender, kind.   **328. idleness,** want of cultivation.   **334-335.
reason . . . motions.** Iago understands the warfare between reason and
sensuality, but his ethics are totally inverted; reason works in him not
good, as it should according to natural law, but evil, which he has
chosen for his good.   **337. sect,** cutting.   **344. perdurable,** very
durable.   **346. defeat thy favour,** disguise thy face.   **351. answerable
sequestration,** a separation corresponding.   **354. locusts,** of doubtful
meaning; defined as fruit of the carob tree (Matthew 3:4), as honey-

suckle, and as lollipops or sugar-sticks.   **355. coloquintida** colocynth,
or bitter apple.   **362. erring,** wandering, vagabond.   **374. hearted,**
fixed in the heart.   **375. conjunctive,** united.   **379. Traverse,** go
(military term).   **391. snipe,** gull, fool.   **392-410. I hate . . . light.**
This is the passage about which Coleridge used his famous phrase, "the
motive-hunting of a motiveless malignity." It is to be doubted, however,
if Shakespeare thought of Iago's villainy as completely gratuitous. He
here recites two motives of supreme potency with Iago: his professional
displacement, and the fact that he has been made the subject of scandal
because of Othello; reputation was to him of supreme importance.
399. plume up, glorify.   **402. he,** i.e., Cassio.

He hath a person and a smooth dispose
To be suspected, framed to make women false.
The Moor is of a free and open nature,
That thinks men honest that but seem to be so,
And will as tenderly be led by the nose
As asses are.
I have 't. It is engender'd. Hell and night   409
Must bring this monstrous birth to the world's light.
                                        [*Exit.*

ACT II.

SCENE I. *A Sea-port in Cyprus. An open place near the quay.*

Enter MONTANO *and two* Gentlemen.

Mon. What from the cape can you discern at sea?
First Gent. Nothing at all: it is a high-wrought flood;
I cannot, 'twixt the heaven and the main,
Descry a sail.
Mon. Methinks the wind hath spoke aloud at land;
A fuller blast ne'er shook our battlements:
If it hath ruffian'd so upon the sea,
What ribs of oak, when mountains melt on them,
Can hold the mortise? What shall we hear of this?
Sec. Gent. A segregation of the Turkish fleet: 10
For do but stand upon the foaming shore,
The chidden billow seems to pelt the clouds;
The wind-shaked surge, with high and monstrous
        mane,
Seems to cast water on the burning bear,
And quench the guards of the ever-fixed pole:
I never did like molestation view
On the enchafed flood.
Mon.   If that the Turkish fleet
Be not enshelter'd and embay'd, they are drown'd;
It is impossible they bear it out.

Enter a third Gentleman.

Third Gent. News, lads! our wars are done.   20
The desperate tempest hath so bang'd the Turks,
That their designment halts: a noble ship of Venice
Hath seen a grievous wreck and sufferance
On most part of their fleet.
Mon. How! is this true?
Third Gent.   The ship is here put in,
A Veronesa; Michael Cassio,
Lieutenant to the warlike Moor Othello,
Is come on shore: the Moor himself at sea,
And is in full commission here for Cyprus.
Mon. I am glad on 't; 'tis a worthy governor.   30
Third Gent. But this same Cassio, though he speak of
        comfort
Touching the Turkish loss, yet he looks sadly,
And prays the Moor be safe; for they were parted
With foul and violent tempest.
Mon.   Pray heavens he be;
For I have served him, and the man commands
Like a full soldier. Let 's to the seaside, ho!
As well to see the vessel that 's come in
As to throw out our eyes for brave Othello,
Even till we make the main and the aerial blue

An indistinct regard.
Third Gent.   Come, let 's do so;   40
For every minute is expectancy
Of more arrivance.

Enter CASSIO.

Cas. Thanks, you the valiant of this warlike isle,
That so approve the Moor! O, let the heavens
Give him defence against the elements,
For I have lost him on a dangerous sea.
Mon. Is he well shipp'd?
Cas. His bark is stoutly timber'd, and his pilot
Of very expert and approved allowance;
Therefore my hopes, not surfeited to death,   50
Stand in bold cure. [*A cry within* 'A sail, a sail, a sail!'

Enter a fourth Gentleman.

Cas. What noise?
Fourth Gent. The town is empty; on the brow o' the
        sea
Stand ranks of people, and they cry 'A sail!'
Cas. My hopes do shape him for the governor.
                                        [*Guns heard.*
Sec. Gent. They do discharge their shot of courtesy:
Our friends at least.
Cas.   I pray you, sir, go forth,
And give us truth who 'tis that is arrived.
Sec. Gent. I shall.   [*Exit.*
Mon. But, good lieutenant, is your general wived?   60
Cas. Most fortunately: he hath achieved a maid
That paragons description and wild fame;
One that excels the quirks of blazoning pens,
And in the essential vesture of creation
Does tire the ingener.

Re-enter second Gentleman.

              How now! who has put in?
Sec. Gent. 'Tis one Iago, ancient to the general.
Cas. Has had most favourable and happy speed:
Tempests themselves, high seas and howling winds,
The gutter'd rocks and congregated sands,—
Traitors ensteep'd to clog the guiltless keel,—   70
As having sense of beauty, do omit
Their mortal natures, letting go safely by
The divine Desdemona.
Mon.   What is she?
Cas. She that I spake of, our great captain's captain,
Left in the conduct of the bold Iago,
Whose footing here anticipates our thoughts
A se'nnight's speed. Great Jove, Othello guard,
And swell his sail with thine own powerful breath,
That he may bless this bay with his tall ship,
Make love's quick pants in Desdemona's arms,   80
Give renew'd fire to our extinct spirits,
And bring all Cyprus comfort!

Enter DESDEMONA, EMILIA, IAGO, RODERIGO, *and*
        Attendants.

              O, behold,
The riches of the ship is come on shore!
Ye men of Cyprus, let her have your knees.

---

403. **dispose,** external manner. 405-408. **The Moor . . . are.** This tribute to Othello, and other such speeches, must be regarded as a dramatic convention intended to give information to the audience. No villain would talk this way in real life. 409. **Hell and night.** Note Iago's allegiance to the devil.

ACT II. SCENE I. 7. **ruffian'd,** raged. 9. **mortise,** the socket hollowed out in fitting timbers. 10. **segregation,** dispersion. 14. **bear,** a

constellation. 15. **quench the guards,** overwhelm the guards of the pole, i.e., the constellation of Boötes. 17. **enchafed,** angry. 22. **designment,** enterprise. 23. **sufferance,** disaster. 36. **full,** perfect. 39-40. **make . . . regard,** cause the blue of the sea and the air to grow indistinct in our view. 42. **arrivance,** arrival. 49. **allowance,** reputation. 62. **paragons,** surpasses. 63. **quirks,** witty conceits. **blazoning,** setting forth honorably in words. 64. **vesture of creation,** the real

Hail to thee, lady! and the grace of heaven,
Before, behind thee and on every hand,
Enwheel thee round!

Des. I thank you, valiant Cassio.
What tidings can you tell me of my lord?

Cas. He is not yet arrived: nor know I aught
But that he 's well and will be shortly here.   90

Des. O, but I fear—How lost you company?

Cas. The great contention of the sea and skies
Parted our fellowship—But, hark! a sail.

                [*Within* 'A sail, a sail!' *Guns heard.*

Sec. Gent. They give their greeting to the citadel:
This likewise is a friend.

Cas. See for the news. [*Exit Gentleman.*
Good ancient, you are welcome. [*To Emilia*] Welcome, mistress:
Let it not gall your patience, good Iago,
That I extend my manners; 'tis my breeding   99
That gives me this bold show of courtesy. [*Kissing her.*

Iago. Sir, would she give you so much of her lips
As of her tongue she oft bestows on me,
You 'ld have enough.

Des. Alas, she has no speech.

Iago. In faith, too much;
I find it still, when I have list to sleep:
Marry, before your ladyship, I grant,
She puts her tongue a little in her heart,
And chides with thinking.

Emil. You have little cause to say so.

Iago. Come on, come on; you are pictures out of
    doors,   110
Bells in your parlours, wild-cats in your kitchens,
Saints in your injuries, devils being offended,
Players in your housewifery, and housewives in your
    beds.

Des. O, fie upon thee, slanderer!

Iago. Nay, it is true, or else I am a Turk:
You rise to play and go to bed to work.

Emil. You shall not write my praise.

Iago. No, let me not.

Des. What wouldst thou write of me, if thou
    shouldst praise me?

Iago. O gentle lady, do not put me to 't;
For I am nothing, if not critical.   120

Des. Come on, assay. There 's one gone to the
    harbour?

Iago. Ay, madam.

Des. I am not merry; but I do beguile
The thing I am, by seeming otherwise.
Come, how wouldst thou praise me?

Iago. I am about it; but indeed my invention
Comes from my pate as birdlime does from frize;
It plucks out brains and all: but my Muse labours,
And thus she is deliver'd.
If she be fair and wise, fairness and wit,   130
The one 's for use, the other useth it.

Des. Well praised! How if she be black and witty?

Iago. If she be black, and thereto have a wit,
She'll find a white that shall her blackness fit.

Des. Worse and worse.

Emil. How if fair and foolish?

Iago. She never yet was foolish that was fair;
For even her folly help'd her to an heir.

Des. These are old fond paradoxes to make fools
laugh i' the alehouse. What miserable praise hast thou
for her that 's foul and foolish?   141

Iago. There 's none so foul and foolish thereunto,
But does foul pranks which fair and wise ones do.

Des. O heavy ignorance! thou praisest the worst
best. But what praise couldst thou bestow on a deserving woman indeed, one that, in the authority of
her merit, did justly put on the vouch of very malice
itself?

Iago. She that was ever fair and never proud,
Had tongue at will and yet was never loud,   150
Never lack'd gold and yet went never gay,
Fled from her wish and yet said 'Now I may,'
She that being anger'd, her revenge being nigh,
Bade her wrong stay and her displeasure fly,
She that in wisdom never was so frail
To change the cod's head for the salmon's tail,
She that could think and ne'er disclose her mind,
See suitors following and not look behind,
She was a wight, if ever such wight were,—

Des. To do what?   160

Iago. To suckle fools and chronicle small beer.

Des. O most lame and impotent conclusion! Do
not learn of him, Emilia, though he be thy husband.
How say you, Cassio? is he not a most profane and
liberal counsellor?

Cas. He speaks home, madam: you may relish
him more in the soldier than in the scholar.

Iago. [*Aside*] He takes her by the palm: ay, well
said, whisper: with as little a web as this will I ensnare as great a fly as Cassio. Ay, smile upon her, do;
I will gyve thee in thine own courtship. You say true;
'tis so, indeed: if such tricks as these strip you out
of your lieutenantry, it had been better you had not
kissed your three fingers so oft, which now again you
are most apt to play the sir in. Very good; well
kissed! an excellent courtesy! 'tis so, indeed. Yet again
your fingers to your lips? would they were clysterpipes for your sake! [*Trumpet within.*] The Moor! I
know his trumpet.   180

Cas. 'Tis truly so.

Des. Let 's meet him and receive him.

Cas. Lo, where he comes!

Enter OTHELLO *and* Attendants.

Oth. O my fair warrior!

Des. My dear Othello!

Oth. It gives me wonder great as my content
To see you here before me. O my soul's joy!
If after every tempest come such calms,
May the winds blow till they have waken'd death!
And let the labouring bark climb hills of seas
Olympus-high and duck again as low   190
As hell 's from heaven! If it were now to die,
'Twere now to be most happy; for, I fear,
My soul hath her content so absolute
That not another comfort like to this
Succeeds in unknown fate.

Othello
ACT II : SC J

955

qualities with which creation has invested her (Johnson). 65. **ingener,**
inventor. 69. **gutter'd,** jagged, trenched. 70. **ensteep'd,** lying under
water. 77. **se'nnight's,** week's. 113. **housewives,** huzzies. 120.
critical, censorious. 127. **birdlime,** sticky substance smeared on twigs
to catch small birds. **frize,** coarse woolen cloth. 130-161. **If she
. . . beer.** This is an illustration of the familiar game of wit-combat
as practiced in Shakespeare's time. 134. **white,** a fair person, with
word-play on "wight." 148. **put on the vouch,** challenge the testimony. 156. **To change . . . tail,** to exchange a delicacy for mere
refuse. 161. **chronicle small beer,** keep petty household accounts.
166. **speaks home,** i.e., without reserve. 171. **gyve,** fetter, shackle.
172. **courtship,** courtesy. 175. **kissed your three fingers.** He kisses his
own hand as a token of reverence. 176. **the sir,** i.e., the fine gentleman. 179. **clyster-pipes,** tubes used for injections.

Des. The heavens forbid
But that our loves and comforts should increase,
Even as our days do grow!
Oth. Amen to that, sweet powers!
I cannot speak enough of this content;
It stops me here; it is too much of joy: 199
And this, and this, the greatest discords be [*Kissing her.*
That e'er our hearts shall make!
Iago. [*Aside*] O, you are well tuned
now!
But I'll set down the pegs that make this music,
As honest as I am.
Oth. Come, let us to the castle.
News, friends; our wars are done, the Turks are
drown'd.
How does my old acquaintance of this isle?
Honey, you shall be well desired in Cyprus;
I have found great love amongst them. O my sweet,
I prattle out of fashion, and I dote
In mine own comforts. I prithee, good Iago,
Go to the bay and disembark my coffers: 210
Bring thou the master to the citadel;
He is a good one, and his worthiness
Does challenge much respect. Come, Desdemona,
Once more, well met at Cyprus.
[*Exeunt Othello, Desdemona, and Attendants.*
Iago. Do thou meet me presently at the harbour.
Come hither. If thou be'st valiant,—as, they say, base
men being in love have then a nobility in their
natures more than is native to them,—list me. The
lieutenant tonight watches on the court of guard:—
first, I must tell thee this—Desdemona is directly in
love with him. 221
Rod. With him! why, 'tis not possible.
Iago. Lay thy finger thus, and let thy soul be instructed. Mark me with what violence she first loved
the Moor, but for bragging and telling her fantastical
lies: and will she love him still for prating? let not thy
discreet heart think it. Her eye must be fed; and what
delight shall she have to look on the devil? When the
blood is made dull with the act of sport, there should
be, again to inflame it and to give satiety a fresh
appetite, loveliness in favour, sympathy in years,
manners and beauties; all which the Moor is defective
in: now, for want of these required conveniences, her
delicate tenderness will find itself abused, begin to
heave the gorge, disrelish and abhor the Moor; very
nature will instruct her in it and compel her to some
second choice. Now, sir, this granted,—as it is a most
pregnant and unforced position—who stands so
eminent in the degree of this fortune as Cassio does? a
knave very voluble; no further conscionable than in
putting on the mere form of civil and humane seeming, for the better compassing of his salt and most
hidden loose affection? why, none; why, none: a
slipper and subtle knave, a finder of occasions, that
has an eye can stamp and counterfeit advantages,
though true advantage never present itself; a devilish
knave. Besides, the knave is handsome, young, and
hath all those requisites in him that folly and green
minds look after: a pestilent complete knave; and the
woman hath found him already. 253

Rod. I cannot believe that in her; she 's full of most
blessed condition.
Iago. Blessed fig's-end! the wine she drinks is made
of grapes: if she had been blessed, she would never
have loved the Moor. Blessed pudding! Didst thou
not see her paddle with the palm of his hand? didst
not mark that?
Rod. Yes, that I did; but that was but courtesy. 262
Iago. Lechery, by this hand; an index and obscure
prologue to the history of lust and foul thoughts.
They met so near with their lips that their breaths
embraced together. Villanous thoughts, Roderigo!
when these mutualities so marshal the way, hard at
hand comes the master and main exercise, the incorporate conclusion, Pish! But, sir, be you ruled by
me: I have brought you from Venice. Watch you
to-night; for the command, I'll lay 't upon you.
Cassio knows you not. I'll not be far from you: do
you find some occasion to anger Cassio, either by
speaking too loud, or tainting his discipline; or from
what other course you please, which the time shall
more favourably minister. 277
Rod. Well.
Iago. Sir, he is rash and very sudden in choler, and
haply may strike at you: provoke him, that he may;
for even out of that will I cause these of Cyprus to
mutiny; whose qualification shall come into no true
taste again but by the displanting of Cassio. So shall
you have a shorter journey to your desires by the
means I shall then have to prefer them; and the
impediment most profitably removed, without the
which there were no expectation of our prosperity.
Rod. I will do this, if I can bring it to any oppor-
tunity. 290
Iago. I warrant thee. Meet me by and by at the
citadel: I must fetch his necessaries ashore. Farewell.
Rod. Adieu. [*Exit.*
Iago. That Cassio loves her, I do well believe it;
That she loves him, 'tis apt and of great credit:
The Moor, howbeit that I endure him not,
Is of a constant, loving, noble nature,
And I dare think he'll prove to Desdemona
A most dear husband. Now, I do love her too; 300
Not out of absolute lust, though peradventure
I stand accountant for as great a sin,
But partly led to diet my revenge,
For that I do suspect the lusty Moor
Hath leap'd into my seat; the thought whereof
Doth, like a poisonous mineral, gnaw my inwards;
And nothing can or shall content my soul
Till I am even'd with him, wife for wife,
Or failing so, yet that I put the Moor
At least into a jealousy so strong 310
That judgement cannot cure. Which thing to do,
If this poor trash of Venice, whom I trash
For his quick hunting, stand the putting on,
I'll have our Michael Cassio on the hip,
Abuse him to the Moor in the rank garb—
For I fear Cassio with my night-cap too—
Make the Moor thank me, love me and reward me,
For making him egregiously an ass
And practising upon his peace and quiet

202. **set down the pegs**, lower the pitch of the strings, i.e., disturb
the harmony. 219. **court of guard**, guardhouse. 242. **conscionable**,
conscientious. 244. **salt**, licentious. 246. **slipper**, slippery. 275.
tainting, disparaging. 283. **qualification**, condition. 291. **by and by**,
immediately. 296. **apt**, natural. **credit**, credibility. 312. **trash**,

worthless thing. **trash**, hold in check. This use of the word is as a
hunting term. 313. **putting on**, incitement to quarrel. 314. **on the
hip**, at an advantage (wrestling term).
SCENE II. 10. **offices**, rooms where food and drink were kept.
SCENE III. 2. **stop**, restraint. 14. **cast**, dismissed. 30. **stoup**,

Even to madness. 'Tis here, but yet confused: 320
Knavery's plain face is never seen till used.   [*Exit.*

SCENE II. *A street.*

Enter a Herald *with a proclamation;* People *following.*

Her. It is Othello's pleasure, our noble and valiant
general, that, upon certain tidings now arrived,
importing the mere perdition of the Turkish fleet,
every man put himself into triumph; some to dance,
some to make bonfires, each man to what sport and
revels his addiction leads him: for, besides these
beneficial news, it is the celebration of his nuptial.
So much was his pleasure should be proclaimed. All
offices are open, and there is full liberty of feasting
from this present hour of five till the bell have told
eleven. Heaven bless the isle of Cyprus and our noble
general Othello!   [*Exeunt.*

SCENE III. *A hall in the castle.*

Enter OTHELLO, DESDEMONA, CASSIO, *and*
Attendants.

Oth. Good Michael, look you to the guard to-night:
Let's teach ourselves that honourable stop,
Not to outsport discretion.
Cas. Iago hath direction what to do;
But, notwithstanding, with my personal eye
Will I look to 't.
Oth.   Iago is most honest.
Michael, good night: to-morrow with your earliest
Let me have speech with you. [*To Desdemona*] Come,
    my dear love,
The purchase made, the fruits are to ensue;
That profit 's yet to come 'tween me and you.   10
Good night. [*Exeunt Othello, Desdemona, and Attendants.*

Enter IAGO.

Cas. Welcome, Iago; we must to the watch.
Iago. Not this hour, lieutenant; 'tis not yet ten
o' the clock. Our general cast us thus early for the
love of his Desdemona; who let us not therefore
blame: he hath not yet made wanton the night with
her; and she is sport for Jove.
Cas. She 's a most exquisite lady.
Iago. And, I'll warrant her, full of game.
Cas. Indeed, she 's a most fresh and delicate creature.   21
Iago. What an eye she has! methinks it sounds a
parley of provocation.
Cas. An inviting eye; and yet methinks right
modest.
Iago. And when she speaks, is it not an alarum to
love?
Cas. She is indeed perfection.
Iago. Well, happiness to their sheets! Come,
lieutenant, I have a stoup of wine; and here without
are a brace of Cyprus gallants that would fain have a
measure to the health of black Othello.

Cas. Not to-night, good Iago: I have very poor and
unhappy brains for drinking: I could well wish
courtesy would invent some other custom of entertainment.
Iago. O, they are our friends; but one cup: I'll
drink for you.   39
Cas. I have drunk but one cup to-night, and that
was craftily qualified too, and, behold, what inno-
vation it makes here: I am unfortunate in the
infirmity, and dare not task my weakness with any
more.
Iago. What, man! 'tis a night of revels: the gallants
desire it.
Cas. Where are they?
Iago. Here at the door; I pray you, call them in.
Cas. I'll do 't; but it dislikes me.   [*Exit.*
Iago. If I can fasten but one cup upon him,   50
With that which he hath drunk to-night already,
He'll be as full of quarrel and offence
As my young mistress' dog. Now, my sick fool
    Roderigo,
Whom love hath turn'd almost the wrong side
    out,
To Desdemona hath to-night caroused
Potations pottle-deep; and he 's to watch:
Three lads of Cyprus, noble swelling spirits,
That hold their honours in a wary distance,
The very elements of this warlike isle,
Have I to-night fluster'd with flowing cups,   60
And they watch too. Now, 'mongst this flock of
    drunkards,
Am I to put our Cassio in some action
That may offend the isle.—But here they come:
If consequence do but approve my dream,
My boat sails freely, both with wind and stream.

Re-enter CASSIO; *with him* MONTANO *and* Gentlemen;
    Servants following with wine.

Cas. 'Fore God, they have given me a rouse already.
Mon. Good faith, a little one; not past a pint, as I
am a soldier.
Iago. Some wine, ho!   70
[*Sings*] And let me the canakin clink, clink;
        And let me the canakin clink:
            A soldier 's a man;
            A life 's but a span;
        Why, then, let a soldier drink.
Some wine, boys!
Cas. 'Fore God, an excellent song.
Iago. I learned it in England, where, indeed, they
are most potent in potting: your Dane, your German,
and your swag-bellied Hollander—Drink, ho!—are
nothing to your English.   81
Cas. Is your Englishman so expert in his drinking?
Iago. Why, he drinks you, with facility, your Dane
dead drunk; he sweats not to overthrow your Almain;
he gives your Hollander a vomit, ere the next pottle
can be filled.
Cas. To the health of our general!
Mon. I am for it, lieutenant; and I'll do you justice.
Iago. O sweet England!   91
    King Stephen was a worthy peer,

Othello
ACT II : SC III

957

---

measure of liquor, two quarts. **35-37. I could . . . entertainment.**
This sentence expresses the current opinion that it was polite and proper
to drink socially. **41. craftily qualified,** slyly diluted, i.e., by Cassio
himself. **42. innovation,** disturbance. **56. pottle-deep,** to the bottom
of the tankard. **58. hold . . . distance,** i.e., are extremely sensitive

of their honor. **61. watch,** are members of the guard. **64. approve,**
confirm. **67. rouse,** full draft of liquor. **71. canakin,** small drinking
vessel. **86. Almain,** German. **89-90. I'll . . . justice,** i.e., drink as
much as you. **92-99. King . . . thee,** a version of a popular ballad,
found also in the *Percy Folio.*

His breeches cost him but a crown;
He held them sixpence all too dear,
    With that he call'd the tailor lown.

He was a wight of high renown,
    And thou art but of low degree:
'Tis pride that pulls the country down;
    Then take thine auld cloak about thee.
Some wine, ho!   100
    Cas. Why, this is a more exquisite song than the other.
    Iago. Will you hear 't again?
    Cas. No; for I hold him to be unworthy of his place that does those things. Well, God's above all; and there be souls must be saved, and there be souls must not be saved.
    Iago. It's true, good lieutenant.
    Cas. For mine own part,—no offence to the general, nor any man of quality,—I hope to be saved.   111
    Iago. And so do I too, lieutenant.
    Cas. Ay, but, by your leave, not before me; the lieutenant is to be saved before the ancient. Let's have no more of this; let's to our affairs.—Forgive us our sins!—Gentlemen, let's look to our business. Do not think, gentlemen, I am drunk: this is my ancient; this is my right hand, and this is my left: I am not drunk now; I can stand well enough, and speak well enough.   120
    All. Excellent well.
    Cas. Why, very well then; you must not think then that I am drunk.   [*Exit.*
    Mon. To the platform, masters; come, let's set the watch.
    Iago. You see this fellow that is gone before;
He is a soldier fit to stand by Cæsar
And give direction: and do but see his vice;
'Tis to his virtue a just equinox,
The one as long as the other: 'tis pity of him.   130
I fear the trust Othello puts him in,
On some odd time of his infirmity,
Will shake this island.
    Mon.   But is he often thus?
    Iago. 'Tis evermore the prologue to his sleep:
He'll watch the horologe a double set,
If drink rock not his cradle.
    Mon.   It were well
The general were put in mind of it.
Perhaps he sees it not; or his good nature
Prizes the virtue that appears in Cassio,
And looks not on his evils: is not this true?   140

Enter RODERIGO.

    Iago. [*Aside to him*] How now, Roderigo!
I pray you, after the lieutenant; go.   [*Exit Roderigo.*
    Mon. And 'tis great pity that the noble Moor
Should hazard such a place as his own second
With one of an ingraft infirmity:
It were an honest action to say
So to the Moor.
    Iago.   Not I, for this fair island:
I do love Cassio well; and would do much
To cure him of this evil—But, hark! what noise?
                          [*Cry within:* 'Help! help!'

Re-enter CASSIO, *driving in* RODERIGO.

    Cas. You rogue! you rascal!
    Mon.   What's the matter, lieutenant?
    Cas. A knave teach me my duty!   151
I'll beat the knave into a twiggen bottle.
    Rod. Beat me!
    Cas.   Dost thou prate, rogue? [*Striking Roderigo.*
    Mon.   Nay, good lieutenant;
                                      [*Staying him.*
I pray you, sir, hold your hand.
    Cas.   Let me go, sir,
Or I'll knock you o'er the mazzard.
    Mon.   Come, come, you're drunk.
    Cas. Drunk!   [*They fight.*
    Iago. [*Aside to Roderigo*] Away, I say; go out, and cry
    a mutiny.   [*Exit Roderigo.*
Nay, good lieutenant,—alas, gentlemen;—
Help, ho!—Lieutenant,—sir,—Montano,—sir;—
Help, masters!—Here's a goodly watch indeed!   160
                                      [*Bell rings.*
Who's that which rings the bell?—Diablo, ho!
The town will rise: God's will, lieutenant, hold!
You will be shamed for ever.

Re-enter OTHELLO *and* Attendants.

    Oth.   What is the matter here?
    Mon. 'Zounds, I bleed still; I am hurt to the death.
                                      [*Faints.*
    Oth. Hold, for your lives!
    Iago. Hold, ho! Lieutenant,—sir,—Montano,—
    gentlemen,—
Have you forgot all sense of place and duty?
Hold! the general speaks to you; hold, hold, for
    shame!
    Oth. Why, how now, ho! from whence ariseth this?
Are we turn'd Turks, and to ourselves do that   170
Which heaven hath forbid the Ottomites?
For Christian shame, put by this barbarous brawl:
He that stirs next to carve for his own rage
Holds his soul light; he dies upon his motion.
Silence that dreadful bell: it frights the isle
From her propriety. What is the matter, masters?
Honest Iago, that look'st dead with grieving,
Speak, who began this? on thy love, I charge thee.
    Iago. I do not know: friends all but now, even now,
In quarter, and in terms like bride and groom   180
Devesting them for bed; and then, but now—
As if some planet had unwitted men—
Swords out, and tilting one at other's breast,
In opposition bloody. I cannot speak
Any beginning to this peevish odds;
And would in action glorious I had lost
Those legs that brought me to a part of it!
    Oth. How comes it, Michael, you are thus forgot?
    Cas. I pray you, pardon me; I cannot speak.
    Oth. Worthy Montano, you were wont be civil;   190
The gravity and stillness of your youth
The world hath noted, and your name is great
In mouths of wisest censure: what's the matter,
That you unlace your reputation thus
And spend your rich opinion for the name
Of a night-brawler? give me answer to it.
    Mon. Worthy Othello, I am hurt to danger:

95. **lown**, lout, loon. 129. **equinox**, equal length of days and nights; used figuratively to mean "counterpart." 135. **horologe**, clock. **double set**, twice around. 145. **ingraft**, ingrafted, inveterate. 152. **twiggen**, covered with woven twigs. 155. **mazzard**, head. 161. **Diablo**, the

Devil; a scrap of Spanish. 170. **turn'd Turks**, changed completely for the worse; proverbial. 173. **carve for**, indulge. 176. **propriety**, proper state or condition. 180. **In quarter**, on terms. 194. **unlace**, degrade. 205-207. **My blood . . . way.** This is the first indication of Othello's

Your officer, Iago, can inform you,—
While I spare speech, which something now offends
   me,—
Of all that I do know: nor know I aught   200
By me that 's said or done amiss this night;
Unless self-charity be sometimes a vice,
And to defend ourselves it be a sin
When violence assails us.
    Oth.   Now, by heaven,
My blood begins my safer guides to rule;
And passion, having my best judgement collied,
Assays to lead the way: if I once stir,
Or do but lift this arm, the best of you
Shall sink in my rebuke. Give me to know
How this foul rout began, who set it on;   210
And he that is approved in this offence,
Though he had twinn'd with me, both at a birth,
Shall lose me. What! in a town of war,
Yet wild, the people's hearts brimful of fear,
To manage private and domestic quarrel,
In night, and on the court and guard of safety!
'Tis monstrous. Iago, who began 't?
    Mon. If partially affined, or leagued in office,
Thou dost deliver more or less than truth,
Thou art no soldier.
    Iago.   Touch me not so near: 220
I had rather have this tongue cut from my mouth
Than it should do offence to Michael Cassio;
Yet, I persuade myself, to speak the truth
Shall nothing wrong him. Thus it is, general.
Montano and myself being in speech,
There comes a fellow crying out for help;
And Cassio following him with determined sword,
To execute upon him. Sir, this gentleman
Steps in to Cassio, and entreats his pause:
Myself the crying fellow did pursue,   230
Lest by his clamour—as it so fell out—
The town might fall in fright: he, swift of foot,
Outran my purpose; and I return'd the rather
For that I heard the clink and fall of swords,
And Cassio high in oath; which till to-night
I ne'er might say before. When I came back—
For this was brief—I found them close together,
At blow and thrust; even as again they were
When you yourself did part them.
More of this matter cannot I report: 240
But men are men; the best sometimes forget:
Though Cassio did some little wrong to him,
As men in rage strike those that wish them best,
Yet surely Cassio, I believe, received
From him that fled some strange indignity,
Which patience could not pass.
    Oth.   I know, Iago,
Thy honesty and love doth mince this matter,
Making it light to Cassio. Cassio, I love thee;
But never more be officer of mine.

    Re-enter DESDEMONA, *attended.*

Look, if my gentle love be not raised up!   250
I'll make thee an example.
    Des.   What 's the matter?
    Oth. All 's well now, sweeting; come away to bed.
Sir, for your hurts, myself will be your surgeon:

Lead him off.   [*To Montano, who is led off.*
Iago, look with care about the town,
And silence those whom this vile brawl distracted.
Come, Desdemona: 'tis the soldiers' life
To have their balmy slumbers waked with strife.
            [*Exeunt all but Iago and Cassio.*
    Iago. What, are you hurt, lieutenant?
    Cas. Ay, past all surgery.   260
    Iago. Marry, heaven forbid!
    Cas. Reputation, reputation, reputation! O, I have
lost my reputation! I have lost the immortal part of
myself, and what remains is bestial. My reputation,
Iago, my reputation!
    Iago. As I am an honest man, I thought you had
received some bodily wound; there is more sense in
that than in reputation. Reputation is an idle and
most false imposition; oft got without merit, and lost
without deserving: you have lost no reputation at all,
unless you repute yourself such a loser. What, man!
there are ways to recover the general again: you are
but now cast in his mood, a punishment more in
policy than in malice; even so as one would beat his
offenceless dog to affright an imperious lion: sue to
him again, and he 's yours.   277
    Cas. I will rather sue to be despised than to deceive
so good a commander with so slight, so drunken, and
so indiscreet an officer. Drunk? and speak parrot?
and squabble? swagger? swear? and discourse fustian
with one's own shadow? O thou invisible spirit of
wine, if thou hast no name to be known by, let us
call thee devil!
    Iago. What was he that you followed with your
sword? What had he done to you?
    Cas. I know not.
    Iago. Is 't possible?   288
    Cas. I remember a mass of things, but nothing
distinctly; a quarrel, but nothing wherefore. O God,
that men should put an enemy in their mouths to steal
away their brains! that we should, with joy, pleasance,
revel and applause, transform ourselves into beasts!
    Iago. Why, but you are now well enough: how
came you thus recovered?
    Cas. It hath pleased the devil drunkenness to give
place to the devil wrath: one unperfectness shows me
another, to make me frankly despise myself.   300
    Iago. Come, you are too severe a moraler: as the
time, the place, and the condition of this country
stands, I could heartily wish this had not befallen;
but, since it is as it is, mend it for your own good.
    Cas. I will ask him for my place again; he shall tell
me I am a drunkard! Had I as many mouths as
Hydra, such an answer would stop them all. To be
now a sensible man, by and by a fool, and presently a
beast! O strange! Every inordinate cup is unblessed
and the ingredient is a devil.   312
    Iago. Come, come, good wine is a good familiar
creature, if it be well used: exclaim no more against it.
And, good lieutenant, I think you think I love you.
    Cas. I have well approved it, sir. I drunk!   317
    Iago. You or any man living may be drunk at a
time, man. I'll tell you what you shall do. Our
general's wife is now the general: I may say so in this
respect, for that he hath devoted and given up himself

psychology; he is a man whose judgment may be overthrown by his
passion. 206. **collied,** darkened. 211. **approved in,** found guilty of.
216. **court and guard,** spot and guarding place, i.e., the main guardhouse.
218. **affined,** bound by a tie. 228. **execute,** give effect to (his anger).

281. **speak parrot,** talk nonsense; *discourse fustian,* below, has the same
meaning. 299. **unperfectness,** imperfection. 308. **Hydra,** the Lernaean Hydra, a monster with many heads, slain by Hercules as the second
of his twelve labors. 311. **unblessed,** accursed. 317. **approved,** proved.

to the contemplation, mark, and denotement of her
parts and graces: confess yourself freely to her; importune her help to put you in your place again: she
is of so free, so kind, so apt, so blessed a disposition,
she holds it a vice in her goodness not to do more than
she is requested: this broken joint between you and
her husband entreat her to splinter; and, my fortunes
against any lay worth naming, this crack of your
love shall grow stronger than it was before.   331

 Cas. You advise me well.

 Iago. I protest, in the sincerity of love and honest
kindness.

 Cas. I think it freely; and betimes in the morning I
will beseech the virtuous Desdemona to undertake for
me: I am desperate of my fortunes if they check me
here.

 Iago. You are in the right. Good night, lieutenant;
I must to the watch.   340

 Cas. Good night, honest Iago.   [*Exit.*

 Iago. And what 's he then that says I play the
  villain?
When this advice is free I give and honest,
Probal to thinking and indeed the course
To win the Moor again? For 'tis most easy
The inclining Desdemona to subdue
In any honest suit: she 's framed as fruitful
As the free elements. And then for her
To win the Moor—were 't to renounce his baptism,
All seals and symbols of redeemed sin,   350
His soul is so enfetter'd to her love,
That she may make, unmake, do what she list,
Even as her appetite shall play the god
With his weak function. How am I then a villain
To counsel Cassio to this parallel course,
Directly to his good? Divinity of hell!
When devils will the blackest sins put on,
They do suggest at first with heavenly shows,
As I do now: for whiles this honest fool
Plies Desdemona to repair his fortunes   360
And she for him pleads strongly to the Moor,
I'll pour this pestilence into his ear,
That she repeals him for her body's lust;
And by how much she strives to do him good,
She shall undo her credit with the Moor.
So will I turn her virtue into pitch,
And out of her own goodness make the net
That shall enmesh them all.

Re-enter Roderigo.

   How now, Roderigo!   368

 Rod. I do follow here in the chase, not like a hound
that hunts, but one that fills up the cry. My money is
almost spent; I have been to-night exceedingly well
cudgelled; and I think the issue will be, I shall have so
much experience for my pains, and so, with no money
at all and a little more wit, return again to Venice.

 Iago. How poor are they that have not patience!
What wound did ever heal but by degrees?
Thou know'st we work by wit, and not by witchcraft;
And wit depends on dilatory time.
Does 't not go well? Cassio hath beaten thee,   380
And thou, by that small hurt, hast cashier'd Cassio:

Though other things grow fair against the sun,
Yet fruits that blossom first will first be ripe:
Content thyself awhile. By the mass, 'tis morning;
Pleasure and action make the hours seem short.
Retire thee; go where thou art billeted:
Away, I say; thou shalt know more hereafter:
Nay, get thee gone. [*Exit Roderigo.*] Two things are to
  be done:
My wife must move for Cassio to her mistress;
I'll set her on;   390
Myself the while to draw the Moor apart,
And bring him jump when he may Cassio find
Soliciting his wife: ay, that 's the way:
Dull not device by coldness and delay.   [*Exit.*

ACT III.

SCENE I. *Before the castle.*

Enter Cassio *and some* Musicians.

 Cas. Masters, play here; I will content your pains;
Something that 's brief; and bid 'Good morrow,
  general.'   [*Music.*

Enter Clown.

 Clo. Why, masters, have your instruments been in
Naples, that they speak i' the nose thus?

 First Mus. How, sir, how!

 Clo. Are these, I pray you, wind-instruments?

 First Mus. Ay, marry, are they, sir.

 Clo. O, thereby hangs a tail.

 First Mus. Whereby hangs a tale, sir?   9

 Clo. Marry, sir, by many a wind-instrument that I
know. But, masters, here 's money for you: and the
general so likes your music, that he desires you, for
love's sake, to make no more noise with it.

 First Mus. Well, sir, we will not.

 Clo. If you have any music that may not be heard,
to 't again: but, as they say, to hear music the general
does not greatly care.

 First Mus. We have none such, sir.

 Clo. Then put up your pipes in your bag, for I'll
away: go; vanish into air; away! [*Exeunt Musicians.* 21

 Cas. Dost thou hear, my honest friend?

 Clo. No, I hear not your honest friend; I hear you.

 Cas. Prithee, keep up thy quillets. There 's a poor
piece of gold for thee: if the gentlewoman that
attends the general's wife be stirring, tell her there 's
one Cassio entreats her a little favour of speech: wilt
thou do this?

 Clo. She is stirring, sir: if she will stir hither, I shall
seem to notify unto her.   31

 Cas. Do, good my friend.   [*Exit Clown.*

Enter Iago.

   In happy time, Iago.

 Iago. You have not been a-bed, then?

 Cas. Why, no; the day had broke
Before we parted. I have made bold, Iago,
To send in to your wife: my suit to her
Is, that she will to virtuous Desdemona

---

323. **denotement,** observation; QF: *devotement,* which is possibly
correct. 329. **splinter,** bind with splints. 330. **lay,** stake, wager.
344. **Probal,** probable. 346. **inclining,** favorably disposed. 355.
parallel, probably, corresponding to his best interest. 356. **Divinity
of hell.** This is another significant alignment of Iago with the powers

of evil. 363. **repeals him,** i.e., attempts to get him restored. 371.
cry, pack. 381. **cashier'd,** dismissed from service.
 ACT III. SCENE I. 1. **content,** reward. 4. **speak i' the nose,** i.e., like
Neapolitans, who spoke a nasal dialect. 31. **seem to,** a current colloquialism having no particular meaning. 43. **Florentine,** i.e., even a

Procure me some access.
Iago. I'll send her to you presently;
And I'll devise a mean to draw the Moor
Out of the way, that your converse and business   40
May be more free.
Cas. I humbly thank you for 't. [*Exit Iago.*] I never
    knew
A Florentine more kind and honest.

Enter EMILIA.

Emil. Good morrow, good lieutenant: I am sorry
For your displeasure; but all will sure be well.
The general and his wife are talking of it;
And she speaks for you stoutly: the Moor replies,
That he you hurt is of great fame in Cyprus
And great affinity and that in wholesome wisdom
He might not but refuse you, but he protests he loves
    you   50
And needs no other suitor but his likings
To take the safest occasion by the front
To bring you in again.
Cas. Yet, I beseech you,
If you think fit, or that it may be done,
Give me advantage of some brief discourse
With Desdemona alone.
Emil. Pray you, come in:
I will bestow you where you shall have time
To speak your bosom freely.
Cas. I am much bound to you.   [*Exeunt.*

SCENE II. *A room in the castle.*

Enter OTHELLO, IAGO, *and* Gentlemen.

Oth. These letters give, Iago, to the pilot;
And by him do my duties to the senate:
That done, I will be walking on the works;
Repair there to me.
Iago. Well, my good lord, I'll do 't.
Oth. This fortification, gentlemen, shall we see 't?
Gent. We'll wait upon your lordship.   [*Exeunt.*

SCENE III. *The garden of the castle.*

Enter DESDEMONA, CASSIO, *and* EMILIA.

Des. Be thou assured, good Cassio, I will do
All my abilities in thy behalf.
Emil. Good madam, do: I warrant it grieves my
    husband,
As if the case were his.
Des. O, that 's an honest fellow. Do not doubt,
    Cassio,
But I will have my lord and you again
As friendly as you were.
Cas. Bounteous madam,
Whatever shall become of Michael Cassio,
He 's never any thing but your true servant.
Des. I know 't; I thank you. You do love my lord: 10
You have known him long; and be you well assured
He shall in strangeness stand no further off

Than in a politic distance.
Cas. Ay, but, lady,
That policy may either last so long,
Or feed upon such nice and waterish diet,
Or breed itself so out of circumstance,
That, I being absent and my place supplied,
My general will forget my love and service.
Des. Do not doubt that; before Emilia here
I give thee warrant of thy place: assure thee,   20
If I do vow a friendship, I'll perform it
To the last article: my lord shall never rest;
I'll watch him tame and talk him out of patience;
His bed shall seem a school, his board a shrift;
I'll intermingle every thing he does
With Cassio's suit: therefore be merry, Cassio;
For thy solicitor shall rather die
Than give thy cause away.
Emil. Madam, here comes my lord.
Cas. Madam, I'll take my leave.   30
Des. Why, stay, and hear me speak.
Cas. Madam, not now: I am very ill at ease,
Unfit for mine own purposes.
Des. Well, do your discretion.   [*Exit Cassio.*

Enter OTHELLO *and* IAGO.

Iago. Ha! I like not that.
Oth. What dost thou say?
Iago. Nothing, my lord: or if—I know not what.
Oth. Was not that Cassio parted from my wife?
Iago. Cassio, my lord! No, sure, I cannot think it,
That he would steal away so guilty-like,
Seeing you coming.
Oth. I do believe 'twas he.   40
Des. How now, my lord!
I have been talking with a suitor here,
A man that languishes in your displeasure.
Oth. Who is 't you mean?
Des. Why, your lieutenant, Cassio. Good my lord,
If I have any grace or power to move you,
His present reconciliation take;
For if he be not one that truly loves you,
That errs in ignorance and not in cunning,
I have no judgement in an honest face: 50
I prithee, call him back.
Oth. Went he hence now?
Des. Ay, sooth; so humbled
That he hath left part of his grief with me,
To suffer with him. Good love, call him back.
Oth. Not now, sweet Desdemona; some other time.
Des. But shall 't be shortly?
Oth. The sooner, sweet, for you.
Des. Shall 't be to-night at supper?
Oth. No, not to-night.
Des. To-morrow dinner, then?
Oth. I shall not dine at home;
I meet the captains at the citadel.
Des. Why, then, to-morrow night; or Tuesday
    morn;   60
On Tuesday noon, or night; on Wednesday morn:
I prithee, name the time, but let it not
Exceed three days: in faith, he 's penitent;
And yet his trespass, in our common reason—

Othello

ACT III : SC III

961

Florentine; Iago was a Venetian, Cassio a Florentine. 49. **affinity,**
kindred, family connection. 52. **by the front,** i.e., by the forelock.
    SCENE II. 3. **works,** earthworks, fortifications.
    SCENE III. 12. **strangeness,** distant behavior. 16. **breed . . . cir-
cumstance,** increase itself so on account of accidents. 23. **watch him**

tame, tame him by keeping him from sleeping (a term from falconry).
24. **shrift,** confession. 28. **away,** up. 35. **I . . . that.** Iago, as an
opportunist, seizes every advantageous detail. 64. **common reason,**
everyday judgments.

Save that, they say, the wars must make examples
Out of their best—is not almost a fault
To incur a private check. When shall he come?
Tell me, Othello: I wonder in my soul,
What you would ask me, that I should deny,
Or stand so mammering on. What! Michael Cassio, 70
That came a-wooing with you, and so many a time,
When I have spoke of you dispraisingly,
Hath ta'en your part; to have so much to do
To bring him in! Trust me, I could do much,—
  Oth. Prithee, no more: let him come when he will;
I will deny thee nothing.
  Des.   Why, this is not a boon;
'Tis as I should entreat you wear your gloves,
Or feed on nourishing dishes, or keep you warm,
Or sue to you to do a peculiar profit
To your own person: nay, when I have a suit   80
Wherein I mean to touch your love indeed,
It shall be full of poise and difficult weight
And fearful to be granted.
  Oth.   I will deny thee nothing:
Whereon, I do beseech thee, grant me this,
To leave me but a little to myself.
  Des. Shall I deny you? no: farewell, my lord.
  Oth. Farewell, my Desdemona: I'll come to thee
    straight.
  Des. Emilia, come. Be as your fancies teach you;
Whate'er you be, I am obedient.
                    [*Exeunt Desdemona and Emilia.*
  Oth. Excellent wretch! Perdition catch my soul,   90
But I do love thee! and when I love thee not,
Chaos is come again.
  Iago. My noble lord,—
  Oth.   What dost thou say, Iago?
  Iago. Did Michael Cassio, when you woo'd my lady,
Know of your love?
  Oth. He did, from first to last: why dost thou ask?
  Iago. But for a satisfaction of my thought;
No further harm.
  Oth.   Why of thy thought, Iago?
  Iago. I did not think he had been acquainted with
    her.
  Oth. O, yes; and went between us very oft.   100
  Iago. Indeed!
  Oth. Indeed! ay, indeed: discern'st thou aught in
    that?
Is he not honest?
  Iago.   Honest, my lord!
  Oth.   Honest! ay, honest.
  Iago. My lord, for aught I know.
  Oth. What dost thou think?
  Iago.   Think, my lord!
  Oth.   Think, my lord!
By heaven, he echoes me,
As if there were some monster in his thought
Too hideous to be shown. Thou dost mean something:
I heard thee say even now, thou likedst not that,
When Cassio left my wife: what didst not like?   110
And when I told thee he was of my counsel
In my whole course of wooing, thou criedst 'Indeed!'
And didst contract and purse thy brow together,

As if thou then hadst shut up in thy brain
Some horrible conceit: if thou dost love me,
Show me thy thought.
  Iago. My lord, you know I love you.
  Oth.   I think thou dost;
And, for I know thou 'rt full of love and honesty,
And weigh'st thy words before thou givest them
    breath,
Therefore these stops of thine fright me the more: 120
For such things in a false disloyal knave
Are tricks of custom, but in a man that 's just
They are close delations, working from the heart
That passion cannot rule.
  Iago.   For Michael Cassio,
I dare be sworn I think that he is honest.
  Oth. I think so too.
  Iago.   Men should be what they seem;
Or those that be not, would they might seem none!
  Oth. Certain, men should be what they seem.
  Iago. Why, then, I think Cassio 's an honest man.
  Oth. Nay, yet there 's more in this: 130
I prithee, speak to me as to thy thinkings,
As thou dost ruminate, and give thy worst of thoughts
The worst of words.
  Iago.   Good my lord, pardon me:
Though I am bound to every act of duty,
I am not bound to that all slaves are free to.
Utter my thoughts? Why, say they are vile and false;
As where 's that palace whereinto foul things
Sometimes intrude not? who has a breast so pure,
But some uncleanly apprehensions
Keep leets and law-days and in session sit   140
With meditations lawful?
  Oth. Thou dost conspire against thy friend, Iago,
If thou but think'st him wrong'd and makest his ear
A stranger to thy thoughts.
  Iago.   I do beseech you—
Though I perchance am vicious in my guess,
As, I confess, it is my nature's plague
To spy into abuses, and oft my jealousy
Shapes faults that are not—that your wisdom yet,
From one that so imperfectly conceits,
Would take no notice, nor build yourself a trouble   150
Out of his scattering and unsure observance.
It were not for your quiet nor your good,
Nor for my manhood, honesty, or wisdom,
To let you know my thoughts.
  Oth.   What dost thou mean?
  Iago. Good name in man and woman, dear my
    lord,
Is the immediate jewel of their souls:
Who steals my purse steals trash; 'tis something,
    nothing;
'Twas mine, 'tis his, and has been slave to thousands;
But he that filches from me my good name
Robs me of that which not enriches him   160
And makes me poor indeed.
  Oth. By heaven, I'll know thy thoughts.
  Iago. You cannot, if my heart were in your hand;
Nor shall not, whilst 'tis in my custody.
  Oth. Ha!

---

70. **mammering on,** wavering; originally, *stammering.* 82. **poise,** weight, heaviness. 90. **wretch,** term of affectionate endearment with a connotation of pity. 123. **close delations,** secret or involuntary accusations; Q: *denotements,* which is close to the sense. 140. **Keep leets,** hold courts. **law-days,** court-days. 145. **vicious,** wrong. 147.

jealousy, suspicion of evil. 149. **conceits,** judges. 173. **fineless,** boundless. 182. **exsufflicate and blown,** unsubstantial and inflated. 198. **secure,** free from uneasiness. 200. **self-bounty,** inherent or natural goodness. 201. **our country disposition.** Iago speaks insidiously as an experienced Venetian. 209. **seeming,** false appearance.

Iago.   O. beware, my lord, of jealousy;
It is the green-eyed monster which doth mock
The meat it feeds on: that cuckold lives in bliss
Who, certain of his fate, loves not his wronger;
But, O, what damned minutes tells he o'er
Who dotes, yet doubts, suspects, yet strongly loves! 170
     Oth. O misery!
     Iago. Poor and content is rich and rich enough,
But riches fineless is as poor as winter
To him that ever fears he shall be poor.
Good heaven, the souls of all my tribe defend
From jealousy!
     Oth.   Why, why is this?
Think'st thou I 'ld make a life of jealousy,
To follow still the changes of the moon
With fresh suspicions? No; to be once in doubt
Is once to be resolved: exchange me for a goat,   180
When I shall turn the business of my soul
To such exsufflicate and blown surmises,
Matching thy inference. 'Tis not to make me jealous
To say my wife is fair, feeds well, loves company,
Is free of speech, sings, plays and dances well;
Where virtue is, these are more virtuous:
Nor from mine own weak merits will I draw
The smallest fear or doubt of her revolt;
For she had eyes, and chose me. No, Iago;
I'll see before I doubt; when I doubt, prove;   190
And on the proof, there is no more but this,—
Away at once with love or jealousy!
     Iago. I am glad of it; for now I shall have reason
To show the love and duty that I bear you
With franker spirit: therefore, as I am bound,
Receive it from me. I speak not yet of proof.
Look to your wife; observe her well with Cassio;
Wear your eye thus, not jealous nor secure:
I would not have your free and noble nature,
Out of self-bounty, be abused; look to 't: 200
I know our country disposition well;
In Venice they do let heaven see the pranks
They dare not show their husbands; their best
     conscience
Is not to leave 't undone, but keep 't unknown.
     Oth. Dost thou say so?
     Iago. She did deceive her father, marrying you;
And when she seem'd to shake and fear your looks,
She loved them most.
     Oth.   And so she did.
     Iago.   Why, go to then;
She that, so young, could give out such a seeming,
To seel her father's eyes up close as oak—   210
He thought 'twas witchcraft—but I am much to
     blame;
I humbly do beseech you of your pardon
For too much loving you.
     Oth.   I am bound to thee for ever.
     Iago. I see this hath a little dash'd your spirits.
     Oth. Not a jot, not a jot.
     Iago.   I' faith, I fear it has.
I hope you will consider what is spoke
Comes from my love. But I do see you 're moved:
I am to pray you not to strain my speech

To grosser issues nor to larger reach
Than to suspicion.   220
     Oth. I will not.
     Iago.   Should you do so, my lord,
My speech should fall into such vile success
As my thoughts aim not at. Cassio 's my worthy
     friend—
My lord, I see you 're moved.
     Oth.   No, not much moved:
I do not think but Desdemona 's honest.
     Iago. Long live she so! and long live you to think so!
     Oth. And yet, how nature erring from itself,—
     Iago. Ay, there 's the point: as—to be bold with
          you—
Not to affect many proposed matches
Of her own clime, complexion, and degree,   230
Whereto we see in all things nature tends—
Foh! one may smell in such a will most rank,
Foul disproportion, thoughts unnatural.
But pardon me; I do not in position
Distinctly speak of her; though I may fear
Her will, recoiling to her better judgement,
May fall to match you with her country forms
And happily repent.
     Oth.   Farewell, farewell:
If more thou dost perceive, let me know more;
Set on thy wife to observe: leave me, Iago.   240
     Iago. [*Going*] My lord, I take my leave.
     Oth. Why did I marry? This honest creature
          doubtless
Sees and knows more, much more, than he unfolds.
     Iago. [*Returning*] My Lord, I would I might entreat
          your honour
To scan this thing no further; leave it to time:
Though it be fit that Cassio have his place,
For, sure, he fills it up with great ability,
Yet, if you please to hold him off awhile,
You shall by that perceive him and his means:
Note, if your lady strain his entertainment   250
With any strong or vehement importunity;
Much will be seen in that. In the mean time,
Let me be thought too busy in my fears—
As worthy cause I have to fear I am—
And hold her free, I do beseech your honour.
     Oth. Fear not my government.
     Iago. I once more take my leave.   [*Exit.*
     Oth. This fellow 's of exceeding honesty,
And knows all qualities, with a learned spirit,
Of human dealings. If I do prove her haggard,   260
Though that her jesses were my dear heartstrings,
I 'ld whistle her off and let her down the wind,
To prey at fortune. Haply, for I am black
And have not those soft parts of conversation
That chamberers have, or for I am declined
Into the vale of years,—yet that 's not much—
She 's gone. I am abused; and my relief
Must be to loathe her. O curse of marriage,
That we can call these delicate creatures ours,
And not their appetites! I had rather be a toad,   270
And live upon the vapour of a dungeon,
Than keep a corner in the thing I love

210. **seel,** blind (a term from falconry). 232. **will,** sensuality. 233.
disproportion, abnormality. 234. **position,** formal assertion. 236.
recoiling to, falling back upon, or recoiling against. 237. **fall to,**
apply (herself) to. **country forms,** probably, after the manner of her
country. 238. **repent,** i.e., of her marriage. 250. **strain his enter-**
tainment, urge his reinstatement. 255. **hold her free,** regard her as
innocent. 256. **government,** self-control. 260. **haggard,** wild, intractable; a haggard was a wild female hawk caught when in her adult
plumage. 261. **jesses,** straps fastened around the legs of a trained
hawk. 263. **at fortune,** at random. 265. **chamberers,** gallants.

For others' uses. Yet, 'tis the plague of great ones;
Prerogatived are they less than the base;
'Tis destiny unshunnable, like death:
Even then this forked plague is fated to us
When we do quicken. Desdemona comes:

Re-enter DESDEMONA *and* EMILIA.

If she be false, O, then heaven mocks itself!
I'll not believe 't.
  Des.   How now, my dear Othello!
Your dinner, and the generous islanders   280
By you invited, do attend your presence.
  Oth. I am to blame.
  Des.   Why do you speak so faintly?
Are you not well?
  Oth. I have a pain upon my forehead here.
  Des. 'Faith, that 's with watching; 'twill away
    again:
Let me but bind it hard, within this hour
It will be well.
  Oth.   Your napkin is too little:
    [*He puts the handkerchief from him; and it drops.*
Let it alone. Come, I'll go in with you.
  Des. I am very sorry that you are not well.
    [*Exeunt Othello and Desdemona.*
  Emil. I am glad I have found this napkin: 290
This was her first remembrance from the Moor:
My wayward husband hath a hundred times
Woo'd me to steal it; but she so loves the token,
For he conjured her she should ever keep it,
That she reserves it evermore about her
To kiss and talk to. I'll have the work ta'en out,
And give 't Iago: what he will do with it
Heaven knows, not I;
I nothing but to please his fantasy.

Re-enter Iago.

  Iago. How now! what do you here alone? 300
  Emil. Do not you chide; I have a thing for you.
  Iago. A thing for me? it is a common thing—
  Emil. Ha!
  Iago. To have a foolish wife.
  Emil. O, is that all? What will you give me now
For that same handkerchief?
  Iago.   What handkerchief?
  Emil. What handkerchief!
Why, that the Moor first gave to Desdemona;
That which so often you did bid me steal.
  Iago. Hast stol'n it from her? 310
  Emil. No, 'faith; she let it drop by negligence,
And, to the advantage, I, being here, took 't up.
Look, here it is.
  Iago.   A good wench; give it me.
  Emil. What will you do with 't, that you have been
    so earnest
To have me filch it?
  Iago.   [*Snatching it*] Why, what 's that
    to you?
  Emil. If it be not for some purpose of import,
Give 't me again: poor lady, she'll run mad
When she shall lack it.
  Iago. Be not acknown on 't; I have use for it.

Go, leave me.   [*Exit Emilia.* 320
I will in Cassio's lodging lose this napkin,
And let him find it. Trifles light as air
Are to the jealous confirmations strong
As proofs of holy writ: this may do something.
The Moor already changes with my poison:
Dangerous conceits are, in their natures, poisons,
Which at the first are scarce found to distaste,
But with a little act upon the blood,
Burn like the mines of sulphur. I did say so:
Look, where he comes!

Re-enter OTHELLO.

    Not poppy, nor mandragora, 330
Nor all the drowsy syrups of the world,
Shall ever medicine thee to that sweet sleep
Which thou owedst yesterday.
  Oth.   Ha! ha! false to me?
  Iago. Why, how now, general! no more of that.
  Oth. Avaunt! be gone! thou hast set me on the rack:
I swear 'tis better to be much abused
Than but to know 't a little.
  Iago.   How now, my lord!
  Oth. What sense had I of her stol'n hours of lust?
I saw 't not, thought it not, it harm'd not me:
I slept the next night well, was free and merry; 340
I found not Cassio's kisses on her lips:
He that is robb'd, not wanting what is stol'n,
Let him not know 't, and he 's not robb'd at all.
  Iago. I am sorry to hear this.
  Oth. I had been happy, if the general camp,
Pioners and all, had tasted her sweet body,
So I had nothing known. O, now, for ever
Farewell the tranquil mind! farewell content!
Farewell the plumed troop, and the big wars,
That make ambition virtue! O, farewell! 350
Farewell the neighing steed, and the shrill trump,
The spirit-stirring drum, the ear-piercing fife,
The royal banner, and all quality,
Pride, pomp and circumstance of glorious war!
And, O you mortal engines, whose rude throats
The immortal Jove's dread clamours counterfeit,
Farewell! Othello's occupation 's gone!
  Iago. Is 't possible, my lord?
  Oth. Villain, be sure thou prove my love a whore,
Be sure of it; give me the ocular proof; 360
Or, by the worth of man's eternal soul,
Thou hadst been better have been born a dog
Than answer my waked wrath!
  Iago.   Is 't come to this?
  Oth. Make me to see 't; or, at the least, so prove it,
That the probation bear no hinge nor loop
To hang a doubt on; or woe upon thy life!
  Iago. My noble lord,—
  Oth. If thou dost slander her and torture me,
Never pray more; abandon all remorse;
On horror's head horrors accumulate; 370
Do deeds to make heaven weep, all earth amazed;
For nothing canst thou to damnation add
Greater than that.
  Iago.   O grace! O heaven forgive me!
Are you a man? have you a soul or sense?

Othello
ACT III : SC III

964

---

274. **Prerogatived,** privileged. 276. **forked,** an allusion to the horns
of the cuckold. 277. **quicken,** receive life. 280. **generous,** noble.
293. **to steal it.** Pilfering was so customary in Shakespeare's time
that Queen Elizabeth's suite would despoil the noblemen who entertained her on her progresses. 296. **work ta'en out,** design copied.

319. **Be . . . on 't,** do not confess knowledge of it. 328. **act,** action,
working. 346. **Pioners,** sappers, a low grade of soldiers. 354. **circumstance,** attendant fact; here, formal display; see glossary. 355. **mortal
engines** i.e., cannon. 370. **horrors,** object of *accumulate.* 404. **salt,**
wanton, sensual. 406. **imputation,** i.e., opinion founded on strong

God be wi' you; take mine office. O wretched fool,
That livest to make thine honesty a vice!
O monstrous world! Take note, take note, O world,
To be direct and honest is not safe.
I thank you for this profit; and from hence
I'll love no friend, sith love breeds such offence.   380
    Oth. Nay, stay: thou shouldst be honest.
    Iago. I should be wise, for honesty 's a fool
And loses that it works for.
    Oth.   By the world,
I think my wife be honest and think she is not;
I think that thou art just and think thou art not.
I'll have some proof. Her name, that was as fresh
As Dian's visage, is now begrimed and black
As mine own face. If there be cords, or knives,
Poison, or fire, or suffocating streams,
I'll not endure it. Would I were satisfied!   390
    Iago. I see, sir, you are eaten up with passion:
I do repent me that I put it to you.
You would be satisfied?
    Oth.   Would! nay, I will.
    Iago. And may: but, how? how satisfied, my lord?
Would you, the supervisor, grossly gape on—
Behold her topp'd?
    Oth.   Death and damnation! O!
    Iago. It were a tedious difficulty, I think,
To bring them to that prospect: damn them then,
If ever mortal eyes do see them bolster
More than their own! What then? how then?   400
What shall I say? Where 's satisfaction?
It is impossible you should see this,
Were they as prime as goats, as hot as monkeys,
As salt as wolves in pride, and fools as gross
As ignorance made drunk. But yet, I say,
If imputation and strong circumstances,
Which lead directly to the door of truth,
Will give you satisfaction, you may have 't.
    Oth. Give me a living reason she 's disloyal.
    Iago. I do not like the office: 410
But, sith I am enter'd in this cause so far,
Prick'd to 't by foolish honesty and love,
I will go on. I lay with Cassio lately;
And, being troubled with a raging tooth,
I could not sleep.
There are a kind of men so loose of soul,
That in their sleeps will mutter their affairs:
One of this kind is Cassio:
In sleep I heard him say 'Sweet Desdemona,
Let us be wary, let us hide our loves;'   420
And then, sir, would he gripe and wring my hand,
Cry 'O sweet creature!' and then kiss me hard,
As if he pluck'd up kisses by the roots
That grew upon my lips: then laid his leg
Over my thigh, and sigh'd, and kiss'd; and then
Cried 'Cursed fate that gave thee to the Moor!'
    Oth. O monstrous! monstrous!
    Iago.   Nay, this was but his dream.
    Oth. But this denoted a foregone conclusion:
'Tis a shrewd doubt, though it be but a dream.
    Iago. And this may help to thicken other proofs   430
That do demonstrate thinly.
    Oth.   I'll tear her all to pieces.

    Iago. Nay, but be wise: yet we see nothing done;
She may be honest yet. Tell me but this,
Have you not sometimes seen a handkerchief
Spotted with strawberries in your wife's hand?
    Oth. I gave her such a one; 'twas my first gift.
    Iago. I know not that: but such a handkerchief—
I am sure it was your wife's—did I to-day
See Cassio wipe his beard with.
    Oth.   If it be that,—
    Iago. If it be that, or any that was hers,   440
It speaks against her with the other proofs.
    Oth. O, that the slave had forty thousand lives!
One is too poor, too weak for my revenge.
Now do I see 'tis true. Look here, Iago;
All my fond love thus do I blow to heaven.
'Tis gone.
Arise, black vengeance, from thy hollow cell!
Yield up, O love, thy crown and hearted throne
To tyrannous hate! Swell, bosom, with thy fraught,
For 'tis of aspics' tongues!
    Iago.   Yet be content.   450
    Oth. O, blood, blood, blood!
    Iago. Patience, I say; your mind perhaps may
        change.
    Oth. Never, Iago. Like to the Pontic sea,
Whose icy current and compulsive course
Ne'er feels retiring ebb, but keeps due on
To the Propontic and the Hellespont,
Even so my bloody thoughts, with violent pace,
Shall ne'er look back, ne'er ebb to humble love,
Till that a capable and wide revenge
Swallow them up. Now, by yond marble heaven,   460
[*Kneels*] In the due reverence of a sacred vow
I here engage my words.
    Iago.   Do not rise yet.
[*Kneels*] Witness, you ever-burning lights above,
You elements that clip us round about,
Witness that here Iago doth give up
The execution of his wit, hands, heart,
To wrong'd Othello's service! Let him command,
And to obey shall be in me remorse,
What bloody business ever.   [*They rise.*
    Oth.   I greet thy love,
Not with vain thanks, but with acceptance bounteous,
And will upon the instant put thee to 't: 471
Within these three days let me hear thee say
That Cassio 's not alive.
    Iago. My friend is dead; 'tis done at your request:
But let her live.
    Oth. Damn her, lewd minx! O, damn her!
Come, go with me apart; I will withdraw,
To furnish me with some swift means of death
For the fair devil. Now art thou my lieutenant.
    Iago. I am your own for ever.   [*Exeunt.* 480

SCENE IV. *Before the castle.*

Enter DESDEMONA, EMILIA, *and* Clown.

    Des. Do you know, sirrah, where Lieutenant Cassio
lies?
    Clo. I dare not say he lies any where.

---

circumstantial evidence (Schmidt).   428. **foregone conclusion,** previous
trial or experience (not used in our sense).   448. **hearted,** fixed in the
heart.   449. **fraught,** freight, burden.   450. **aspics',** venomous serpents'.   453-456. **Pontic . . . Propontic . . . Hellespont.** Steevens
refers to Holland's *Pliny,* bk. II, ch. 97 (1601): "And the sea Pontus

euermore floweth and runneth out into Propontic, but the sea neuer
retireth backe againe within Pontus [the Black Sea]."   460. **marble,**
i.e., gleaming like marble.   466. **execution,** exercise.   468. **remorse,**
pity for Othello's wrongs.

Des. Why, man?

Clo. He 's a soldier, and for one to say a soldier lies, is stabbing.

Des. Go to: where lodges he?

Clo. To tell you where he lodges, is to tell you where I lie.

Des. Can any thing be made of this? 10

Clo. I know not where he lodges, and for me to devise a lodging and say he lies here or he lies there, were to lie in mine own throat.

Des. Can you inquire him out, and be edified by report?

Clo. I will catechize the world for him; that is, make questions, and by them answer.

Des. Seek him, bid him come hither: tell him I have moved my lord on his behalf, and hope all will be well. 20

Clo. To do this is within the compass of man's wit; and therefore I will attempt the doing it. [*Exit.*

Des. Where should I lose that handkerchief, Emilia?

Emil. I know not, madam.

Des. Believe me, I had rather have lost my purse
Full of crusadoes: and, but my noble Moor
Is true of mind and made of no such baseness
As jealous creatures are, it were enough
To put him to ill thinking.

Emil. Is he not jealous?

Des. Who, he? I think the sun where he was born 30
Drew all such humours from him.

Emil. Look, where he comes.

Des. I will not leave him now till Cassio
Be call'd to him.

Enter OTHELLO.

How is 't with you, my lord?

Oth. Well, my good lady. [*Aside*] O, hardness to
    dissemble!—
How do you, Desdemona?

Des. Well, my good lord.

Oth. Give me your hand: this hand is moist, my
    lady.

Des. It yet hath felt no age nor known no sorrow.

Oth. This argues fruitfulness and liberal heart:
Hot, hot, and moist: this hand of yours requires
A sequester from liberty, fasting and prayer, 40
Much castigation, exercise devout;
For here 's a young and sweating devil here,
That commonly rebels. 'Tis a good hand,
A frank one.

Des. You may, indeed, say so;
For 'twas that hand that gave away my heart.

Oth. A liberal hand: the hearts of old gave hands;
But our new heraldry is hands, not hearts.

Des. I cannot speak of this. Come now, your
    promise.

Oth. What promise, chuck? 49

Des. I have sent to bid Cassio come speak with you.

Oth. I have a salt and sorry rheum offends me;
Lend me thy handkerchief.

Des. Here, my lord.

Oth. That which I gave you.

Des. I have it not about me.

Oth. Not?

Des. No, indeed, my lord.

Oth. That is a fault.
That handkerchief
Did an Egyptian to my mother give;
She was a charmer, and could almost read
The thoughts of people: she told her, while she kept it,
'Twould make her amiable and subdue my father
Entirely to her love, but if she lost it 60
Or made a gift of it, my father's eye
Should hold her loathed and his spirits should hunt
After new fancies: she, dying, gave it me;
And bid me, when my fate would have me wive,
To give it her. I did so: and take heed on 't;
Make it a darling like your precious eye;
To lose 't or give 't away were such perdition
As nothing else could match.

Des. Is 't possible?

Oth. 'Tis true: there 's magic in the web of it:
A sibyl, that had number'd in the world 70
The sun to course two hundred compasses,
In her prophetic fury sew'd the work;
The worms were hallow'd that did breed the silk;
And it was dyed in mummy which the skilful
Conserved of maidens' hearts.

Des. Indeed! is 't true?

Oth. Most veritable; therefore look to 't well.

Des. Then would to God that I had never seen 't!

Oth. Ha! wherefore?

Des. Why do you speak so startingly and rash?

Oth. Is 't lost? is 't gone? speak, is it out o' the way? 80

Des. Heaven bless us!

Oth. Say you?

Des. It is not lost; but what an if it were?

Oth. How!

Des. I say, it is not lost.

Oth. Fetch 't, let me see 't.

Des. Why, so I can, sir, but I will not now.
This is a trick to put me from my suit:
Pray you, let Cassio be received again.

Oth. Fetch me the handkerchief: my mind misgives.

Des. Come, come; 90
You'll never meet a more sufficient man.

Oth. The handkerchief!

Des. I pray, talk me of Cassio.

Oth. The handkerchief!

Des. A man that all his time
Hath founded his good fortunes on your love,
Shared dangers with you,—

Oth. The handkerchief!

Des. In sooth, you are to blame.

Oth. Away! [*Exit.*

Emil. Is not this man jealous?

Des. I ne'er saw this before. 100
Sure, there 's some wonder in this handkerchief:
I am most unhappy in the loss of it.

Emil. 'Tis not a year or two shows us a man:
They are all but stomachs, and we all but food;
They eat us hungerly, and when they are full,

SCENE IV. 26. **crusadoes,** Portuguese gold coins. 40. **sequester,** separation, sequestration. 47. **new . . . hearts.** This is thought by Warburton and some later critics to allude to the creation of a new order of baronets by King James I in 1611, the arms for which were a hand gules on a field argent. More probably, however, it is a current expression referring to marriages in which there is a joining of hands without the giving of hearts. 51. **sorry rheum,** painful tears. 56. **Egyptian,** gypsy. 70-71. **had number'd . . . compasses.** "We say, I counted the clock to strike four; so she numbered the sun to course, to run two hundred compasses, two hundred annual circuits" (Johnson).

They belch us. Look you, Cassio and my husband!

Enter CASSIO *and* IAGO.

Iago. There is no other way; 'tis she must do 't:
And, lo, the happiness! go, and importune her.
 Des. How now, good Cassio! what 's the news with
  you?
 Cas. Madam, my former suit: I do beseech you 110
That by your virtuous means I may again
Exist, and be a member of his love
Whom I with all the office of my heart
Entirely honour: I would not be delay'd.
If my offence be of such mortal kind
That nor my service past, nor present sorrows,
Nor purposed merit in futurity,
Can ransom me into his love again,
But to know so must be my benefit;
So shall I clothe me in a forced content, 120
And shut myself up in some other course,
To fortune's alms.
 Des.   Alas, thrice-gentle Cassio!
My advocation is not now in tune;
My lord is not my lord; nor should I know him,
Were he in favour as in humour alter'd.
So help me every spirit sanctified,
As I have spoken for you all my best
And stood within the blank of his displeasure
For my free speech! you must awhile be patient:
What I can do I will; and more I will 130
Than for myself I dare: let that suffice you.
 Iago. Is my lord angry?
 Emil.   He went hence but now,
And certainly in strange unquietness.
 Iago. Can he be angry? I have seen the cannon,
When it hath blown his ranks into the air,
And, like the devil, from his very arm
Puff'd his own brother:—and can he be angry?
Something of moment then: I will go meet him:
There 's matter in 't indeed, if he be angry.
 Des. I prithee, do so.   [*Exit Iago.*
    Something, sure, of state, 140
Either from Venice, or some unhatch'd practice
Made demonstrable here in Cyprus to him,
Hath puddled his clear spirit; and in such cases
Men's natures wrangle with inferior things,
Though great ones are their object. 'Tis even so;
For let our finger ache, and it indues
Our other healthful members even to that sense
Of pain: nay, we must think men are not gods,
Nor of them look for such observances
As fit the bridal. Beshrew me much, Emilia, 150
I was, unhandsome warrior as I am,
Arraigning his unkindness with my soul;
But now I find I had suborn'd the witness,
And he 's indicted falsely.
 Emil. Pray heaven it be state-matters, as you think,
And no conception nor no jealous toy
Concerning you.
 Des. Alas the day! I never gave him cause.
 Emil. But jealous souls will not be answer'd so;
They are not ever jealous for the cause, 160

But jealous for they are jealous: 'tis a monster
Begot upon itself, born on itself.
 Des. Heaven keep that monster from Othello's
  mind!
 Emil. Lady, amen.
 Des. I will go seek him. Cassio, walk here about:
If I do find him fit, I'll move your suit
And seek to effect it to my uttermost.
 Cas. I humbly thank your ladyship.
    [*Exeunt Desdemona and Emilia.*

Enter BIANCA.

 Bian. Save you, friend Cassio!
 Cas.   What make you from home?
How is it with you, my most fair Bianca? 170
I' faith, sweet love, I was coming to your house.
 Bian. And I was going to your lodging, Cassio.
What, keep a week away? seven days and nights?
Eight score eight hours? and lovers' absent hours,
More tedious than the dial eight score times?
O weary reckoning!
 Cas.   Pardon me, Bianca:
I have this while with leaden thoughts been press'd;
But I shall, in a more continuate time,
Strike off this score of absence. Sweet Bianca,
   [*Giving her Desdemona's handkerchief.*
Take me this work out.
 Bian.   O Cassio, whence came this? 180
This is some token from a newer friend:
To the felt absence now I feel a cause:
Is 't come to this? Well, well.
 Cas.   Go to, woman!
Throw your vile guesses in the devil's teeth,
From whence you have them. You are jealous now
That this is from some mistress, some remembrance:
No, in good troth, Bianca.
 Bian.   Why, whose is it?
 Cas. I know not, sweet: I found it in my chamber.
I like the work well: ere it be demanded—
As like enough it will—I 'ld have it copied: 190
Take it, and do 't; and leave me for this time.
 Bian. Leave you! wherefore?
 Cas. I do attend here on the general;
And think it no addition, nor my wish,
To have him see me woman'd.
 Bian.   Why, I pray you?
 Cas. Not that I love you not.
 Bian.   But that you do not love me.
I pray you, bring me on the way a little,
And say if I shall see you soon at night.
 Cas. 'Tis but a little way that I can bring you;
For I attend here: but I'll see you soon. 200
 Bian. 'Tis very good; I must be circumstanced.
    [*Exeunt.*

ACT IV.

SCENE I. *Cyprus. Before the castle.*

Enter OTHELLO *and* IAGO.

---

74. **mummy,** medicinal or magical preparation from the flesh of mummified bodies. 75. **Conserved of,** preserved out of. 119. **to know . . . benefit,** to know that my case is hopeless will end my vain endeavor. 123. **advocation,** advocacy. 128. **blank,** white spot in the center of a target; here, range. 143. **puddled,** sullied the purity of.

146. **indues,** brings to the same condition. 151. **unhandsome,** unfair. 156. **conception,** mere fancy. 178. **continuate,** uninterrupted. Q: *conuenient.* 180. **Take . . . out,** i.e., copy this embroidery for me. 201. **circumstanced,** governed by circumstances.

Iago. Will you think so?
Oth.   Think so, Iago!
Iago.   What,
To kiss in private?
Oth.   An unauthorized kiss.
Iago. Or to be naked with her friend in bed
An hour or more, not meaning any harm?
Oth. Naked in bed, Iago, and not mean harm!
It is hypocrisy against the devil:
They that mean virtuously, and yet do so,
The devil their virtue tempts, and they tempt heaven.
Iago. So they do nothing, 'tis a venial slip:
But if I give my wife a handkerchief,—   10
Oth. What then?
Iago. Why, then, 'tis hers, my lord; and, being hers,
She may, I think, bestow 't on any man.
Oth. She is protectress of her honour too:
May she give that?
Iago. Her honour is an essence that 's not seen;
They have it very oft that have it not:
But, for the handkerchief,—
Oth. By heaven, I would most gladly have forgot it.
Thou said'st—O, it comes o'er my memory,   20
As doth the raven o'er the infected house,
Boding to all—he had my handkerchief.
Iago. Ay, what of that?
Oth.   That 's not so good now.
Iago.   What,
If I had said I had seen him do you wrong?
Or heard him say,—as knaves be such abroad,
Who having, by their own importunate suit,
Or voluntary dotage of some mistress,
Convinced or supplied them, cannot choose
But they must blab—
Oth.   Hath he said any thing?
Iago. He hath, my lord; but be you well assured,   30
No more than he'll unswear.
Oth.   What hath he said?
Iago. 'Faith, that he did—I know not what he did.
Oth. What? what?
Iago. Lie—
Oth.   With her?
Iago.   With her, on her; what you
          will.
Oth. Lie with her! lie on her! We say lie on her,
when they belie her. Lie with her! that 's fulsome.—
Handkerchief—confessions—handkerchief!—To con-
fess, and be hanged for his labour;—first, to be
hanged, and then to confess.—I tremble at it. Nature
would not invest herself in such shadowing passion
without some instruction. It is not words that shake
me thus. Pish! Noses, ears, and lips.—Is 't possible?—
Confess—handkerchief!—O devil!   [*Falls in a trance.*
Iago. Work on,
My medicine, work! Thus credulous fools are caught;
And many worthy and chaste dames even thus,
All guiltless, meet reproach. What, ho! my lord!
My lord, I say! Othello!

Enter CASSIO.

How now, Cassio!

Cas. What 's the matter?   50
Iago. My lord is fall'n into an epilepsy:
This is his second fit; he had one yesterday.
Cas. Rub him about the temples.
Iago.   No, forbear;
The lethargy must have his quiet course:
If not, he foams at mouth and by and by
Breaks out to savage madness. Look, he stirs:
Do you withdraw yourself a little while,
He will recover straight: when he is gone,
I would on great occasion speak with you. [*Exit Cassio.*
How is it, general? have you not hurt your head?   60
Oth. Dost thou mock me?
Iago.   I mock you! no, by heaven.
Would you would bear your fortune like a man!
Oth. A horned man 's a monster and a beast.
Iago. There 's many a beast then in a populous city,
And many a civil monster.
Oth. Did he confess it?
Iago.   Good sir, be a man;
Think every bearded fellow that 's but yoked
May draw with you: there 's millions now alive
That nightly lie in those unproper beds
Which they dare swear peculiar: your case is better.   70
O, 'tis the spite of hell, the fiend's arch-mock,
To lip a wanton in a secure couch,
And to suppose her chaste! No, let me know;
And knowing what I am, I know what she shall be.
Oth. O, thou art wise; 'tis certain.
Iago.   Stand you awhile apart;
Confine yourself but in a patient list.
Whilst you were here o'erwhelmed with your grief—
A passion most unsuiting such a man—
Cassio came hither: I shifted him away,
And laid good 'scuse upon your ecstasy,   80
Bade him anon return and here speak with me;
The which he promised. Do but encave yourself,
And mark the fleers, the gibes, and notable scorns,
That dwell in every region of his face;
For I will make him tell the tale anew,
Where, how, how oft, how long ago, and when
He hath, and is again to cope your wife:
I say, but mark his gesture. Marry, patience;
Or I shall say you are all in all in spleen,
And nothing of a man.
Oth.   Dost thou hear, Iago?   90
I will be found most cunning in my patience;
But—dost thou hear?—most bloody.
Iago.   That 's not amiss;
But yet keep time in all. Will you withdraw?
          [*Othello retires.*
Now will I question Cassio of Bianca,
A housewife that by selling her desires
Buys herself bread and clothes: it is a creature
That dotes on Cassio; as 'tis the strumpet's plague
To beguile many and be beguiled by one:
He, when he hears of her, cannot refrain
From the excess of laughter. Here he comes: 100

Re-enter CASSIO.

As he shall smile, Othello shall go mad;

ACT IV. SCENE I.   1. **Will you think so.** It will be noticed that Iago
has made enormous progress in his attack on the peace of mind of
Othello in the interval between acts; Othello has become utterly
credulous.   21. **raven . . . house,** allusion to the belief that the raven
hovered over a house of sickness or infection.   28. **Convinced or
supplied,** i.e., mistresses gained by importunity and those who doted

voluntarily.   40-42. **Nature . . . instruction,** i.e., my jealousy cannot
be merely the result of natural imagination, but must have some foundation in fact.   54. **lethargy,** unconscious condition.   65. **civil,** i.e., in
civilized society.   69. **unproper,** not belonging exclusively to an
individual. The meaning "improper" is post-Shakespearean.   70.
peculiar, private, one's own.   76. **patient list,** within the bounds of

And his unbookish jealousy must construe
Poor Cassio's smiles, gestures and light behaviour,
Quite in the wrong. How do you now, lieutenant?

Cas. The worser that you give me the addition
Whose want even kills me.

Iago. Ply Desdemona well, and you are sure on 't.
[*Speaking lower*] Now, if this suit lay in Bianca's power,
How quickly should you speed!

Cas.   Alas, poor caitiff!

Oth. Look, how he laughs already!   110

Iago. I never knew woman love man so.

Cas. Alas, poor rogue! I think, i' faith, she loves me.

Oth. Now he denies it faintly, and laughs it out.

Iago. Do you hear, Cassio?

Oth.   Now he importunes him
To tell it o'er : go to; well said, well said.

Iago. She gives it out that you shall marry her :
Do you intend it?

Cas. Ha, ha, ha!   120

Oth. Do you triumph, Roman? do you triumph?

Cas. I marry her! what? a customer! Prithee, bear
some charity to my wit; do not think it so unwholesome. Ha, ha, ha!

Oth. So, so, so, so : they laugh that win.

Iago. 'Faith, the cry goes that you shall marry her.

Cas. Prithee, say true.

Iago. I am a very villain else.

Oth. Have you scored me? Well.   130

Cas. This is the monkey's own giving out : she is
persuaded I will marry her, out of her own love and
flattery, not out of my promise.

Oth. Iago beckons me; now he begins the story.

Cas. She was here even now; she haunts me in
every place. I was the other day talking on the sea-
bank with certain Venetians; and thither comes the
bauble, and, by this hand, she falls me thus about my
neck—   140

Oth. Crying, 'O dear Cassio!' as it were : his gesture
imports it.

Cas. So hangs, and lolls, and weeps upon me; so
hales, and pulls me : ha, ha, ha!

Oth. Now he tells how she plucked him to my
chamber. O, I see that nose of yours, but not that dog
I shall throw it to.

Cas. Well, I must leave her company.

Iago. Before me! look, where she comes.

Cas. 'Tis such another fitchew! marry, a perfumed
one.   151

Enter BIANCA.

What do you mean by this haunting of me?

Bian. Let the devil and his dam haunt you! What
did you mean by that same handkerchief you gave me
even now? I was a fine fool to take it. I must take out
the work?—A likely piece of work, that you should
find it in your chamber, and not know who left it
there! This is some minx's token, and I must take out
the work? There; give it your hobby-horse : wheresoever you had it, I'll take out no work on 't.   161

Cas. How now, my sweet Bianca! how now! how
now!

Oth. By heaven, that should be my handkerchief!

Bian. An you'll come to supper to-night, you may;
an you will not, come when you are next prepared for.
    [*Exit.*

Iago. After her, after her.

Cas. 'Faith, I must; she'll rail in the street else.   171

Iago. Will you sup there?

Cas. 'Faith, I intend so.

Iago. Well, I may chance to see you; for I would
very fain speak with you.

Cas. Prithee, come; will you?

Iago. Go to; say no more.   [*Exit Cassio.*

Oth. [*Advancing*] How shall I murder him, Iago?

Iago. Did you perceive how he laughed at his vice?

Oth. O Iago!   182

Iago. And did you see the handkerchief?

Oth. Was that mine?

Iago. Yours, by this hand : and to see how he prizes
the foolish woman your wife! she gave it him, and he
hath given it his whore.

Oth. I would have him nine years a-killing. A fine
woman! a fair woman! a sweet woman!

Iago. Nay, you must forget that.   190

Oth. Ay, let her rot, and perish, and be damned
to-night; for she shall not live : no, my heart is turned
to stone; I strike it, and it hurts my hand. O, the
world hath not a sweeter creature : she might lie by
an emperor's side and command him tasks.

Iago. Nay, that 's not your way.

Oth. Hang her! I do but say what she is : so delicate
with her needle : an admirable musician : O! she will
sing the savageness out of a bear : of so high and
plenteous wit and invention :—   201

Iago. She 's the worse for all this.

Oth. O, a thousand thousand times : and then, of so
gentle a condition!

Iago. Ay, too gentle.

Oth. Nay, that 's certain : but yet the pity of it,
Iago! O Iago, the pity of it, Iago!

Iago. If you are so fond over her iniquity, give her
patent to offend; for, if it touch not you, it comes near
nobody.   210

Oth. I will chop her into messes : cuckold me!

Iago. O, 'tis foul in her.

Oth. With mine officer!

Iago. That 's fouler.

Oth. Get me some poison, Iago; this night : I'll not
expostulate with her, lest her body and beauty unprovide my mind again : this night, Iago.   219

Iago. Do it not with poison, strangle her in her bed,
even the bed she hath contaminated.

Oth. Good, good : the justice of it pleases : very good.

Iago. And for Cassio, let me be his undertaker : you
shall hear more by midnight.

Oth. Excellent good. [*A trumpet within.*] What
    trumpet is that same?

Iago. Something from Venice, sure. 'Tis Lodovico
Come from the duke : and, see, your wife is with him.

Enter LODOVICO, DESDEMONA, *and* Attendants.

Lod. Save you, worthy general!

patience; see glossary. 82. **encave,** conceal. 83. **fleers,** sneers. 93.
keep time, use judgment and order. Iago here seems to betray a little
uneasiness with reference to the forces he has awakened. 102. **unbookish,** ignorant. 121. **Roman.** The epithet arises from the association of the Romans with the idea of triumph. 122. **customer,** prostitute. 130, **scored me,** made up my reckoning, or branded me. 139.

bauble, foolish person, trifler. 149. **Before me!** On my soul! 150.
fitchew, polecat (as a lustful animal?). 160. **hobby-horse,** lover.
197. **your way,** i.e., the way you should think of her. 209. **patent,**
license. 211. **messes,** dishes of food. 218. **unprovide,** weaken, unfit.
224. **let . . . undertaker,** i.e., let me settle with him.

Oth.   With all my heart, sir.

Lod. The duke and senators of Venice greet you.   230
                         [*Gives him a letter.*

Oth. I kiss the instrument of their pleasures.
                 [*Opens the letter, and reads.*

Des. And what's the news, good cousin Lodovico?

Iago. I am very glad to see you, signior;
Welcome to Cyprus.

Lod. I thank you. How does Lieutenant Cassio?

Iago. Lives, sir.

Des. Cousin, there's fall'n between him and my
      lord
An unkind breach: but you shall make all well.

Oth. Are you sure of that?

Des. My lord?

Oth. [*Reads*] 'This fail you not to do, as you will—'

Lod. He did not call; he's busy in the paper.   241
Is there division 'twixt my lord and Cassio?

Des. A most unhappy one: I would do much
To atone them, for the love I bear to Cassio.

Oth. Fire and brimstone!

Des.   My lord?

Oth.   Are you wise?

Des. What, is he angry?

Lod.   May be the letter moved him;
For, as I think, they do command him home,
Deputing Cassio in his government.

Des. Trust me, I am glad on 't.

Oth.   Indeed!

Des.   My lord?

Oth. I am glad to see you mad.

Des.   Why, sweet Othello,—   250

Oth. [*Striking her*] Devil!

Des. I have not deserved this.

Lod. My lord, this would not be believed in Venice,
Though I should swear I saw 't: 'tis very much:
Make her amends; she weeps.

Oth.   O devil, devil!
If that the earth could teem with woman's tears,
Each drop she falls would prove a crocodile.
Out of my sight!

Des.   I will not stay to offend you. [*Going.*

Lod. Truly, an obedient lady:
I do beseech your lordship, call her back.   260

Oth. Mistress!

Des.   My lord?

Oth.   What would you with her, sir?

Lod. Who, I, my lord?

Oth. Ay; you did wish that I would make her turn:
Sir, she can turn, and turn, and yet go on,
And turn again; and she can weep, sir, weep;
And she's obedient, as you say, obedient,
Very obedient. Proceed you in your tears.
Concerning this, sir,—O well-painted passion!—
I am commanded home. Get you away;
I'll send for you anon. Sir, I obey the mandate,   270
And will return to Venice. Hence, avaunt!
                     [*Exit Desdemona.*
Cassio shall have my place. And, sir, to-night,
I do entreat that we may sup together:
You are welcome, sir, to Cyprus.—Goats and
      monkeys!   [*Exit.*

Lod. Is this the noble Moor whom our full senate
Call all in all sufficient? Is this the nature
Whom passion could not shake? whose solid virtue
The shot of accident, nor dart of chance,
Could neither graze nor pierce?

Iago.   He is much changed.

Lod. Are his wits safe? is he not light of brain?   280

Iago. He's that he is: I may not breathe my censure
What he might be: if what he might he is not,
I would to heaven he were!

Lod.   What, strike his wife!

Iago. 'Faith, that was not so well; yet would I knew
That stroke would prove the worst!

Lod.   Is it his use?
Or did the letters work upon his blood,
And new-create this fault?

Iago.   Alas, alas!
It is not honesty in me to speak
What I have seen and known. You shall observe him,
And his own courses will denote him so   290
That I may save my speech: do but go after,
And mark how he continues.

Lod. I am sorry that I am deceived in him.   [*Exeunt.*

SCENE II. *A room in the castle.*

Enter OTHELLO *and* EMILIA.

Oth. You have seen nothing then?

Emil. Nor ever heard, nor ever did suspect.

Oth. Yes, you have seen Cassio and she together.

Emil. But then I saw no harm, and then I heard
Each syllable that breath made up between them.

Oth. What, did they never whisper?

Emil.   Never, my lord.

Oth. Nor send you out o' the way?

Emil. Never.

Oth. To fetch her fan, her gloves, her mask, nor
      nothing?

Emil. Never, my lord.   10

Oth. That's strange.

Emil. I durst, my lord, to wager she is honest,
Lay down my soul at stake: if you think other,
Remove your thought; it doth abuse your bosom.
If any wretch have put this in your head,
Let heaven requite it with the serpent's curse!
For, if she be not honest, chaste, and true,
There's no man happy; the purest of their wives
Is foul as slander.

Oth.   Bid her come hither: go.
                     [*Exit Emilia.*
She says enough; yet she's a simple bawd   20
That cannot say as much. This is a subtle whore,
A closet lock and key of villanous secrets:
And yet she'll kneel and pray; I have seen her do 't.

Enter DESDEMONA *with* EMILIA.

Des. My lord, what is your will?

Oth.   Pray, chuck, come hither.

Des. What is your pleasure?

Oth.   Let me see your eyes;
Look in my face.

---

248. **government**, office.   257. **prove a crocodile**, i.e., by weeping crocodile tears; it was believed the crocodile shed tears over the body of the man he was eating.   268. **well-painted passion**, well-simulated emotion.   286. The purpose of Othello's recall is not clear.   SCENE II.   16. **serpent's curse.** Cf. Genesis 3:14.   22. **closet lock**

and key, complete storeroom.   27. **function**, profession.   30. **mystery**, trade, occupation.   41. **O . . . away.** Othello's rejection of testimony in the form of the assurance he would most like to receive is often regarded as an example of the dramatic convention of the "calumniator believed."   48. **they**, heavenly powers.   54-55. **A . . . at.** Othello

Des. What horrible fancy 's this?
Oth. [*To Emilia*] Some of your function, mistress;
Leave procreants alone and shut the door;
Cough, or cry 'hem', if any body come:
Your mystery, your mystery: nay, dispatch. 30
[*Exit Emilia.*
Des. Upon my knees, what doth your speech
import?
I understand a fury in your words,
But not the words.
Oth. Why, what art thou?
Des. Your wife, my lord; your true
And loyal wife.
Oth. Come, swear it, damn thyself;
Lest, being like one of heaven, the devils themselves
Should fear to seize thee: therefore be double damn'd:
Swear thou art honest.
Des. Heaven doth truly know it.
Oth. Heaven truly knows that thou art false as hell.
Des. To whom, my lord? with whom? how am I
false? 40
Oth. O Desdemona! away! away! away!
Des. Alas the heavy day! Why do you weep?
Am I the motive of these tears, my lord?
If haply you my father do suspect
An instrument of this your calling back,
Lay not your blame on me: if you have lost him,
Why, I have lost him too.
Oth. Had it pleased heaven
To try me with affliction; had they rain'd
All kinds of sores and shames on my bare head,
Steep'd me in poverty to the very lips, 50
Given to captivity me and my utmost hopes,
I should have found in some place of my soul
A drop of patience: but, alas, to make me
A fixed figure for the time of scorn
To point his slow unmoving finger at!
Yet could I bear that too; well, very well:
But there, where I have garner'd up my heart,
Where either I must live, or bear no life;
The fountain from the which my current runs,
Or else dries up; to be discarded thence! 60
Or keep it as a cistern for foul toads
To knot and gender in! Turn thy complexion there,
Patience, thou young and rose-lipp'd cherubin,—
Ay, there, look grim as hell!
Des. I hope my noble lord esteems me honest.
Oth. O, ay; as summer flies are in the shambles,
That quicken even with blowing. O thou weed,
Who art so lovely fair and smell'st so sweet
That the sense aches at thee, would thou hadst ne'er
been born!
Des. Alas, what ignorant sin have I committed? 70
Oth. Was this fair paper, this most goodly book,
Made to write 'whore' upon? What committed!
Committed! O thou public commoner!
I should make very forges of my cheeks,
That would to cinders burn up modesty,
Did I but speak thy deeds. What committed!
Heaven stops the nose at it and the moon winks,
The bawdy wind that kisses all it meets
Is hush'd within the hollow mine of earth,

And will not hear it. What committed! 80
Impudent strumpet!
Des. By heaven, you do me wrong.
Oth. Are not you a strumpet?
Des. No, as I am a Christian:
If to preserve this vessel for my lord
From any other foul unlawful touch
Be not to be a strumpet, I am none.
Oth. What, not a whore?
Des. No, as I shall be saved.
Oth. Is 't possible?
Des. O, heaven forgive us!
Oth. I cry you mercy, then:
I took you for that cunning whore of Venice
That married with Othello. [*Raising his voice*] You,
mistress, 90
That have the office opposite to Saint Peter,
And keep the gate of hell!

Re-enter EMILIA.

You, you, ay, you!
We have done our course; there 's money for your
pains:
I pray you, turn the key and keep our counsel. [*Exit.*
Emil. Alas, what does this gentleman conceive?
How do you, madam? how do you, my good lady?
Des. 'Faith, half asleep.
Emil. Good madam, what 's the matter with my
lord?
Des. With who?
Emil. Why, with my lord, madam. 100
Des. Who is thy lord?
Emil. He that is yours, sweet lady.
Des. I have none: do not talk to me, Emilia;
I cannot weep; nor answer have I none,
But what should go by water. Prithee, tonight
Lay on my bed my wedding sheets: remember;
And call thy husband hither.
Emil. Here 's a change indeed! [*Exit.*
Des. 'Tis meet I should be used so, very meet.
How have I been behaved, that he might stick
The small'st opinion on my least misuse?

Re-enter EMILIA *with* IAGO.

Iago. What is your pleasure, madam? How is 't with
you? 110
Des. I cannot tell. Those that do teach young babes
Do it with gentle means and easy tasks:
He might have chid me so; for, in good faith,
I am a child to chiding.
Iago. What 's the matter, lady?
Emil. Alas, Iago, my lord hath so bewhored her,
Thrown such despite and heavy terms upon her,
As true hearts cannot bear.
Des. Am I that name, Iago?
Iago. What name, fair lady?
Des. Such as she says my lord did say I was.
Emil. He call'd her whore: a beggar in his drink 120
Could not have laid such terms upon his callet.
Iago. Why did he so?
Des. I do not know; I am sure I am none such.
Iago. Do not weep, do not weep. Alas the day!

possibly thinks of himself as a man set in a pillory at whom the scornful world points in mockery. There seems to be a comparison with the sundial, whose gnomon, or indicator, becomes the finger of scornful time. For *unmoving* some editors adopt the F reading, *and moving.* 62. **gender,** engender. **Turn thy complexion,** grow pale. At such an object do thou, patience, thyself change color; at this do thou, even thou, rosy cherub as thou art, look grim as hell (Johnson). 73. **commoner,** prostitute. 83. **vessel,** body; I Thessalonians 4:4. 104. **go by water,** be expressed by tears. 109. **misuse,** evil conduct. 116. **despite,** contempt, scorn. 119. **says.** F: *said.* 121. **callet,** lewd woman.

Emil. Hath she forsook so many noble matches,
Her father and her country and her friends,
To be call'd whore? would it not make one weep?
    Des. It is my wretched fortune.
    Iago.   Beshrew him for 't!
How comes this trick upon him?
    Des.   Nay, heaven doth know.
    Emil. I will be hang'd, if some eternal villain,   130
Some busy and insinuating rogue,
Some cogging, cozening slave, to get some office,
Have not devised this slander; I'll be hang'd else.
    Iago. Fie, there is no such man; it is impossible.
    Des. If any such there be, heaven pardon him!
    Emil. A halter pardon him! and hell gnaw his
        bones!
Why should he call her whore? who keeps her
        company?
What place? what time? what form? what likelihood?
The Moor 's abused by some most villanous knave,
Some base notorious knave, some scurvy fellow.   140
O heaven, that such companions thou 'ldst unfold,
And put in every honest hand a whip
To lash the rascals naked through the world
Even from the east to the west!
    Iago.   Speak within door.
    Emil. O, fie upon them! Some such squire he was
That turn'd your wit the seamy side without,
And made you to suspect me with the Moor.
    Iago. You are a fool; go to.
    Des.   O good Iago,
What shall I do to win my lord again?
Good friend, go to him; for, by this light of heaven, 150
I know not how I lost him. Here I kneel:
If e'er my will did trespass 'gainst his love,
Either in discourse of thought or actual deed,
Or that mine eyes, mine ears, or any sense,
Delighted them in any other form;
Or that I do not yet, and ever did,
And ever will—though he do shake me off
To beggarly divorcement—love him dearly,
Comfort forswear me! Unkindness may do much;
And his unkindness may defeat my life,   160
But never taint my love. I cannot say 'whore:'
It doth abhor me now I speak the word;
To do the act that might the addition earn
Not the world's mass of vanity could make me.
    Iago. I pray you, be content; 'tis but his humour:
The business of the state does him offence,
And he does chide with you.
    Des. If 'twere no other,—
    Iago.   'Tis but so, I warrant.
                        [Trumpets within.
Hark, how these instruments summon to supper!
The messengers of Venice stay the meat;   170
Go in, and weep not; all things shall be well.
                [Exeunt Desdemona and Emilia.

Enter RODERIGO.

How now, Roderigo!
    Rod. I do not find that thou dealest justly with me.
    Iago. What in the contrary?   175
    Rod. Every day thou daffest me with some device,

Iago; and rather, as it seems to me now, keepest from
me all conveniency than suppliest me with the least
advantage of hope. I will indeed no longer endure it,
nor am I yet persuaded to put up in peace what
already I have foolishly suffered.
    Iago. Will you hear me, Roderigo?
    Rod. 'Faith, I have heard too much, for your words
and performances are no kin together.
    Iago. You charge me most unjustly.   186
    Rod. With nought but truth. I have wasted myself
out of my means. The jewels you have had from me
to deliver to Desdemona would half have corrupted a
votarist: you have told me she hath received them
and returned me expectations and comforts of sudden
respect and acquaintance, but I find none.
    Iago. Well; go to; very well.
    Rod. Very well! go to! I cannot go to, man; nor 'tis
not very well: nay, I think it is scurvy, and begin to
find myself fopped in it.
    Iago. Very well.
    Rod. I tell you 'tis not very well. I will make myself
known to Desdemona: if she will return me my jewels,
I will give over my suit and repent my unlawful
solicitation; if not, assure yourself I will seek satisfaction of you.
    Iago. You have said now.   204
    Rod. Ay, and said nothing but what I protest
intendment of doing.
    Iago. Why, now I see there 's mettle in thee, and
even from this instant do build on thee a better
opinion than ever before. Give me thy hand, Roderigo: thou hast taken against me a most just exception;
but yet, I protest, I have dealt most directly in thy
affair.
    Rod. It hath not appeared.   213
    Iago. I grant indeed it hath not appeared, and your
suspicion is not without wit and judgement. But,
Roderigo, if thou hast that in thee indeed, which I
have greater reason to believe now than ever, I mean
purpose, courage and valour, this night show it: if
thou the next night following enjoy not Desdemona,
take me from this world with treachery and devise
engines for my life.
    Rod. Well, what is it? is it within reason and com-
pass?
    Iago. Sir, there is especial commission come from
Venice to depute Cassio in Othello's place.
    Rod. Is that true? why, then Othello and Desde-
mona return again to Venice.   228
    Iago. O, no; he goes into Mauritania and takes
away with him the fair Desdemona, unless his
abode be lingered here by some accident: wherein
none can be so determinate as the removing of Cassio.
    Rod. How do you mean, removing of him?
    Iago. Why, by making him uncapable of Othello's
place; knocking out his brains.
    Rod. And that you would have me to do?   237
    Iago. Ay, if you dare do yourself a profit and a right.
He sups to-night with a harlotry, and thither will I
go to him: he knows not yet of his honourable fortune.
If you will watch his going thence, which I will
fashion to fall out between twelve and one, you may

---

132. **cogging,** cheating with loaded dice. 144. **Speak . . . door,** i.e., not
so loud; Q: *dores.* 170. **stay the meat,** are waiting for supper. 176.
daffest me, puttest me off with an excuse. 178. **conveniency,** advantage, opportunity. 181. **put up,** submit to. 197. **fopped,** fooled, duped.
204. **You . . . now,** well said, quite right (Schmidt). 206. **intendment,**
purpose, intention. 221. **engines,** defined as "instruments of torture,"
and as "devices of plots" (against my life). 229. **Mauritania,** Roman
name of northwest Africa, supposed land of the Moors. 232. **determinate,** decisive. 239. **harlotry,** courtesan. 249. **high supper-time,**
defined as "high time for supper"; *high* probably means "quite."

take him at your pleasure: I will be near to second your attempt, and he shall fall between us. Come, stand not amazed at it, but go along with me; I will show you such a necessity in his death that you shall think yourself bound to put it on him. It is now high supper-time, and the night grows to waste: about it. 250

Rod. I will hear further reason for this.

Iago. And you shall be satisfied.   [*Exeunt.*

SCENE III. *Another room in the castle.*

Enter OTHELLO, LODOVICO, DESDEMONA, EMILIA, *and* Attendants.

Lod. I do beseech you, sir, trouble yourself no further.

Oth. O, pardon me; 'twill do me good to walk.

Lod. Madam, good night; I humbly thank your ladyship.

Des. Your honour is most welcome.

Oth.   Will you walk, sir?

O,—Desdemona,—

Des. My lord?

Oth. Get you to bed on the instant; I will be re-turned forthwith: dismiss your attendant there: look it be done.

Des. I will, my lord.   10

[*Exeunt Othello, Lodovico, and Attendants.*

Emil. How goes it now? he looks gentler than he did.

Des. He says he will return incontinent:
He hath commanded me to go to bed,
And bade me to dismiss you.

Emil.   Dismiss me!

Des. It was his bidding; therefore, good Emilia,
Give me my nightly wearing, and adieu:
We must not now displease him.

Emil. I would you had never seen him!   18

Des. So would not I: my love doth so approve him,
That even his stubbornness, his checks, his frowns,—
Prithee, unpin me,—have grace and favour in them.

Emil. I have laid those sheets you bade me on the bed.

Des. All 's one. Good faith, how foolish are our minds!
If I do die before thee, prithee, shroud me
In one of those same sheets.

Emil.   Come, come, you talk.

Des. My mother had a maid call'd Barbara:
She was in love, and he she loved proved mad
And did forsake her: she had a song of 'willow;'
An old thing 'twas, but it express'd her fortune,
And she died singing it: that song to-night   30
Will not go from my mind; I have much to do,
But to go hang my head all at one side,
And sing it like poor Barbara. Prithee, dispatch.

Emil. Shall I go fetch your night-gown?

Des.   No, unpin me here.
This Lodovico is a proper man.

Emil. A very handsome man.

Des. He speaks well.

Emil. I know a lady in Venice would have walked barefoot to Palestine for a touch of his nether lip.   40

Des. [*Singing*] The poor soul sat sighing by a sycamore tree,
Sing all a green willow;
Her hand on her bosom, her head on her knee,
Sing willow, willow, willow:
The fresh streams ran by her, and murmur'd her moans;
Sing willow, willow, willow;
Her salt tears fell from her, and soften'd the stones;—
Lay by these:—
[*Singing*] Sing willow, willow, willow;
Prithee, hie thee; he'll come anon:—   50
[*Singing*] Sing all a green willow must be my garland.
Let nobody blame him; his scorn I approve,—
Nay, that 's not next.—Hark! who is 't that knocks?

Emil. It 's the wind.

Des. [*Singing*] I call'd my love false love; but what said he then?
Sing willow, willow, willow:
If I court moe women, you'll couch with moe men.—
So, get thee gone; good night. Mine eyes do itch;
Doth that bode weeping?

Emil.   'Tis neither here nor there.

Des. I have heard it said so. O, these men, these men!   60
Dost thou in conscience think,—tell me, Emilia,—
That there be women do abuse their husbands
In such gross kind?

Emil.   There be some such, no question.

Des. Wouldst thou do such a deed for all the world?

Emil. Why, would not you?

Des.   No, by this heavenly light!

Emil. Nor I neither by this heavenly light; I might do 't as well i' the dark.

Des. Wouldst thou do such a deed for all the world?

Emil. The world 's a huge thing: it is a great price
For a small vice.

Des. In troth, I think thou wouldst not.   70

Emil. In troth, I think I should; and undo 't when I had done. Marry, I would not do such a thing for a joint-ring, nor for measures of lawn, nor for gowns, petticoats, nor caps, nor any petty exhibition; but, for the whole world,—why, who would not make her husband a cuckold to make him a monarch? I should venture purgatory for 't.

Des. Beshrew me, if I would do such a wrong
For the whole world.   79

Emil. Why, the wrong is but a wrong i' the world; and having the world for your labour, 'tis a wrong in your own world, and you might quickly make it right.

Des. I do not think there is any such woman.

Emil. Yes, a dozen; and as many to the vantage as would store the world they played for.
But I do think it is their husbands' faults
If wives do fall: say that they slack their duties,
And pour our treasures into foreign laps,
Or else break out in peevish jealousies,   90
Throwing restraint upon us; or say they strike us,
Or scant our former having in despite;

SCENE III. 12. **incontinent,** immediately. 20. **stubbornness,** roughness, harshness. 32. **But to,** not to. 34. **night-gown,** dressing-gown. 41-57. **The poor soul,** etc. Desdemona's song is a popular ballad apparently well known in Shakespeare's time. In the versions preserved the forsaken lover is a man. Shakespeare has changed it to apply to Desdemona, and has made it personal by introducing the pathetic little sketch of Barbara, her mother's maid. 73. **joint-ring,** a ring made in separable halves as a lover's token. 75. **exhibition,** gift, present. 85-86. **to the vantage,** in addition, to boot. 92. **despite,** spite.

Why, we have galls, and though we have some grace,
Yet have we some revenge. Let husbands know
Their wives have sense like them: they see and smell
And have their palates both for sweet and sour,
As husbands have. What is it that they do
When they change us for others? Is it sport?
I think it is: and doth affection breed it?
I think it doth: is 't frailty that thus errs? 100
It is so too: and have not we affections,
Desires for sport, and frailty, as men have?
Then let them use us well: else let them know,
The ills we do, their ills instruct us so.
   Des. Good night, good night: heaven me such uses
     send,
Not to pick bad from bad, but by bad mend!   [*Exeunt*.

ACT V.

SCENE I. *Cyprus. A street*.

Enter IAGO *and* RODERIGO.

Iago. Here, stand behind this bulk; straight will he
   come:
Wear thy good rapier bare, and put it home:
Quick, quick; fear nothing; I'll be at thy elbow:
It makes us, or it mars us; think on that,
And fix most firm thy resolution.
   Rod. Be near at hand; I may miscarry in 't.
   Iago. Here, at thy hand: be bold, and take thy
   stand.   [*Retires*.
   Rod. I have no great devotion to the deed;
And yet he hath given me satisfying reasons:
'Tis but a man gone. Forth, my sword: he dies.   10
   Iago. I have rubb'd this young quat almost to the
   sense,
And he grows angry. Now, whether he kill Cassio,
Or Cassio him, or each do kill the other,
Every way makes my gain: live Roderigo,
He calls me to a restitution large
Of gold and jewels that I bobb'd from him,
As gifts to Desdemona;
It must not be: if Cassio do remain,
He hath a daily beauty in his life
That makes me ugly; and, besides, the Moor   20
May unfold me to him; there stand I in much peril:
No, he must die. But so: I hear him coming.

Enter CASSIO.

   Rod. I know his gait, 'tis he.—Villain, thou diest!
               [*Makes a pass at Cassio*.
   Cas. That thrust had been mine enemy indeed,
But that my coat is better than thou know'st:
I will make proof of thine. [*Draws, and wounds Roderigo*.
   Rod.   O, I am slain!
   [*Iago from behind wounds Cassio in the leg, and exit*.
   Cas. I am maim'd for ever. Help, ho! murder!
   murder!   [*Falls*.

Enter OTHELLO.

   Oth. The voice of Cassio: Iago keeps his word.
   Rod. O, villain that I am!

   Oth.   It is even so.
   Cas. O, help, ho! light! a surgeon!   30
   Oth. 'Tis he:—O brave Iago, honest and just,
That hast such noble sense of thy friend's wrong!
Thou teachest me. Minion, your dear lies dead,
And your unblest fate hies: strumpet, I come.
Forth of my heart those charms, thine eyes, are
   blotted:
Thy bed, lust-stain'd, shall with lust's blood be
   spotted.   [*Exit*.

Enter LODOVICO *and* GRATIANO.

   Cas. What, ho! no watch? no passage? murder!
   murder!
   Gra. 'Tis some mischance; the cry is very direful.
   Cas. O, help!
   Lod. Hark!   40
   Rod. O wretched villain!
   Lod. Two or three groan: it is a heavy night:
These may be counterfeits: let 's think 't unsafe
To come in to the cry without more help.
   Rod. Nobody come? then shall I bleed to death.
   Lod. Hark!

Re-enter IAGO, *with a light*.

   Gra. Here 's one comes in his shirt, with light and
   weapons.
   Iago. Who 's there? whose noise is this that cries on
   murder?
   Lod. We do not know.
   Iago.   Did not you hear a cry?
   Cas. Here, here! for heaven's sake, help me!
   Iago.   What 's the matter?   50
   Gra. This is Othello's ancient, as I take it.
   Lod. The same indeed; a very valiant fellow.
   Iago. What are you here that cry so grievously?
   Cas. Iago? O, I am spoil'd, undone by villains!
Give me some help.
   Iago. O me, lieutenant! what villains have done
   this?
   Cas. I think that one of them is hereabout,
And cannot make away.
   Iago.   O treacherous villains!
What are you there? come in, and give some help.
           [*To Lodovico and Gratiano*.
   Rod. O, help me here!   60
   Cas. That 's one of them.
   Iago.   O murderous slave! O villain!
             [*Stabs Roderigo*.
   Rod. O damn'd Iago! O inhuman dog!
   Iago. Kill men i' the dark!—Where be these
   bloody thieves?—
How silent is this town!—Ho! murder! murder!—
What may you be? are you of good or evil?
   Lod. As you shall prove us, praise us.
   Iago. Signior Lodovico?
   Lod. He, sir.
   Iago. I cry you mercy. Here 's Cassio hurt by
   villains.
   Gra. Cassio!   70
   Iago. How is 't, brother!
   Cas. My leg is cut in two.

93. **galls,** are capable of resenting injury and insult. **grace,** i.e., to forgive.
  ACT V. SCENE I. 1. **bulk,** framework projecting from the front of a shop. 11. **quat,** pimple, pustule; used contemptuously. **to the sense,** to the quick. 16. **bobb'd,** filched cunningly. 25. **coat,** coat of mail.

37. **passage,** people passing. 42. **heavy,** thick, cloudy. 48. **cries on,** cries out. 65. **What,** who. 82. **chair,** sedan chair. 85. **trash,** worthless thing, i.e., Bianca. 106. **gastness,** terror, ghastliness. 129. **fordoes,** undoes, ruins. Iago's uneasiness is again apparent in this scene.

Iago. Marry, heaven forbid!
Light, gentlemen: I'll bind it with my shirt.

Enter BIANCA.

Bian. What is the matter, ho? who is 't that cried?
Iago. Who is 't that cried?
Bian. O my dear Cassio! my sweet Cassio!
O Cassio, Cassio, Cassio!
Iago. O notable strumpet! Cassio, may you suspect
Who they should be that have thus mangled you?
Cas. No.   80
Gra. I am sorry to find you thus: I have been to
seek you.
Iago. Lend me a garter. So. O, for a chair,
To bear him easily hence!
Bian. Alas, he faints! O Cassio, Cassio, Cassio!
Iago. Gentlemen all, I do suspect this trash
To be a party in this injury.
Patience awhile, good Cassio. Come, come;
Lend me a light. Know we this face or no?
Alas, my friend and my dear countryman
Roderigo! no:—yes, sure:—O heaven! Roderigo.   90
Gra. What, of Venice?
Iago. Even he, sir: did you know him?
Gra.   Know him! ay.
Iago. Signior Gratiano? I cry you gentle pardon;
These bloody accidents must excuse my manners,
That so neglected you.
Gra.   I am glad to see you.
Iago. How do you, Cassio? O, a chair, a chair!
Gra. Roderigo!
Iago. He, he, 'tis he. [*A chair brought in.*] O, that's
well said; the chair.
Some good man bear him carefully from hence;
I'll fetch the general's surgeon. [*To Bianca*] For you,
mistress,   100
Save you your labour. He that lies slain here, Cassio,
Was my dear friend: what malice was between you?
Cas. None in the world; nor do I know the man.
Iago. [*To Bian.*] What, look you pale? O, bear him
out o' the air.   [*Cassio and Roderigo are borne off.*
Stay you, good gentlemen. Look you pale, mistress?
Do you perceive the gastness of her eye?
Nay, if you stare, we shall hear more anon.
Behold her well; I pray you, look upon her:
Do you see, gentlemen? nay, guiltiness will speak,
Though tongues were out of use.   110

Enter EMILIA.

Emil. 'Las, what's the matter? what's the matter,
husband?
Iago. Cassio hath here been set on in the dark
By Roderigo and fellows that are scaped:
He's almost slain, and Roderigo dead.
Emil. Alas, good gentleman! alas, good Cassio!
Iago. This is the fruit of whoring. Prithee, Emilia,
Go know of Cassio where he supp'd to-night.
[*To Bianca*] What, do you shake at that?
Bian. He supp'd at my house; but I therefore shake
not.
Iago. O, did he so? I charge you, go with me.   120
Emil. Fie, fie upon thee, strumpet!

Bian. I am no strumpet; but of life as honest
As you that thus abuse me.
Emil.   As I! foh! fie upon thee!
Iago. Kind gentlemen, let's go see poor Cassio
dress'd.
Come, mistress, you must tell 's another tale.
Emilia, run you to the citadel,
And tell my lord and lady what hath happ'd.
Will you go on? I pray. [*Aside*] This is the night
That either makes me or fordoes me quite.   [*Exeunt.*

SCENE II. *A bedchamber in the castle:* DESDEMONA *in bed
asleep; a light burning.*

Enter OTHELLO.

Oth. It is the cause, it is the cause, my soul,—
Let me not name it to you, you chaste stars!—
It is the cause. Yet I'll not shed her blood;
Nor scar that whiter skin of hers than snow,
And smooth as monumental alabaster.
Yet she must die, else she'll betray more men.
Put out the light, and then put out the light:
If I quench thee, thou flaming minister,
I can again thy former light restore,
Should I repent me: but once put out thy light,   10
Thou cunning'st pattern of excelling nature,
I know not where is that Promethean heat
That can thy light relume. When I have pluck'd the
rose,
I cannot give it vital growth again,
It must needs wither: I'll smell it on the tree.
                                                             [*Kissing her.*
Ah, balmy breath, that dost almost persuade
Justice to break her sword! One more, one more.
Be thus when thou art dead, and I will kill thee,
And love thee after. One more, and this the last:
So sweet was ne'er so fatal. I must weep,   20
But they are cruel tears: this sorrow's heavenly;
It strikes where it doth love. She wakes.
Des. Who's there? Othello?
Oth.   Ay, Desdemona.
Des. Will you come to bed, my lord?
Oth. Have you pray'd to-night, Desdemona?
Des.   Ay, my lord.
Oth. If you bethink yourself of any crime
Unreconciled as yet to heaven and grace,
Solicit for it straight.
Des. Alas, my lord, what do you mean by that?
Oth. Well, do it, and be brief; I will walk by: 30
I would not kill thy unprepared spirit;
No; heaven forfend! I would not kill thy soul.
Des. Talk you of killing?
Oth.   Ay, I do.
Des.   Then heaven
Have mercy on me!
Oth.   Amen, with all my heart!
Des. If you say so, I hope you will not kill me.
Oth. Hum!
Des. And yet I fear you; for you are fatal then
When your eyes roll so: why I should fear I know not,
Since guiltiness I know not; but yet I feel I fear.

SCENE II. 1. **It is the cause.** If Othello's words are taken quite
generally to mean that he defends his act on the grounds of pure
justice, one must suppose a shift in the sense after the first line, for
it in line 2 seems to refer to Desdemona's supposed unchastity. The
passage has caused much perplexity. 12. **Promethean heat,** divine
fire; allusion to the theft of fire from heaven by Prometheus. 13.
relume, rekindle. 21. **this . . . heavenly,** this tenderness, with which
I lament the punishment which justice compels me to inflict, is a holy
passion (Johnson).

Oth. Think on thy sins.

Des.   They are loves I bear to you.   40

Oth. Ay, and for that thou diest.

Des. That death 's unnatural that kills for loving.
Alas, why gnaw you so your nether lip?
Some bloody passion shakes your very frame:
These are portents; but yet I hope, I hope,
They do not point on me.

Oth.   Peace, and be still!

Des. I will so. What 's the matter?

Oth. That handkerchief which I so loved and gave
thee
Thou gavest to Cassio.

Des.   No, by my life and soul!
Send for the man, and ask him.

Oth.   Sweet soul, take heed,   50
Take heed of perjury; thou art on thy deathbed.

Des. Ay, but not yet to die.

Oth.   Yes, presently:
Therefore confess thee freely of thy sin;
For to deny each article with oath
Cannot remove nor choke the strong conception
That I do groan withal. Thou art to die.

Des. Then Lord have mercy on me!

Oth.   I say, amen.

Des. And have you mercy too! I never did
Offend you in my life; never loved Cassio
But with such general warranty of heaven   60
As I might love; I never gave him token.

Oth. By heaven, I saw my handkerchief in 's hand.
O perjured woman! thou dost stone my heart,
And makest me call what I intend to do
A murder, which I thought a sacrifice:
I saw the handkerchief.

Des.   He found it then;
I never gave it him: send for him hither;
Let him confess a truth.

Oth.   He hath confess'd.

Des. What, my lord?

Oth. That he hath used thee.

Des.   How? unlawfully?

Oth.   Ay.   70

Des. He will not say so.

Oth.   No, his mouth is stopp'd;
Honest Iago hath ta'en order for 't.

Des. O! my fear interprets: what, is he dead?

Oth. Had all his hairs been lives, my great revenge
Had stomach for them all.

Des. Alas! he is betray'd and I undone.

Oth. Out, strumpet! weep'st thou for him to my
face?

Des. O, banish me, my lord, but kill me not!

Oth. Down, strumpet!

Des. Kill me to-morrow: let me live to-night!   80

Oth. Nay, if you strive,—

Des. But half an hour!

Oth.   Being done, there is no pause.

Des. But while I say one prayer!

Oth.   It is too late.   [*He stifles her.*

Emil. [*Within*] My lord, my lord! what, ho! my
lord, my lord!

Oth. What noise is this? Not dead? not yet quite
dead?
I that am cruel am yet merciful;
I would not have thee linger in thy pain:
So, so.

Emil. [*Within*] What, ho! my lord, my lord!

Oth.   Who 's there?

Emil. [*Within*] O, good my lord, I would speak a
word with you!   90

Oth. Yes: 'tis Emilia. By and by. She 's dead.
'Tis like she comes to speak of Cassio's death.—
The noise was here. Ha! no more moving?
Still as the grave. Shall she come in? were 't good?—
I think she stirs again:—no. What 's best to do?
If she come in, she'll sure speak to my wife:
My wife! my wife! what wife? I have no wife.
O, insupportable! O heavy hour!
Methinks it should be now a huge eclipse
Of sun and moon, and that the affrighted globe   100
Should yawn at alteration.

Emil.   [*Within*] I do beseech you
That I may speak with you, O, good my lord!

Oth. I had forgot thee: O, come in, Emilia:
Soft; by and by. Let me the curtains draw.
Where art thou?   [*Unlocks the door.*

Enter EMILIA.

                    What 's the matter with thee now?

Emil. O, my good lord, yonder 's foul murders
done!

Oth. What, now?

Emil. But now, my lord.

Oth. It is the very error of the moon;
She comes more nearer earth than she was wont,   110
And makes men mad.

Emil. Cassio, my lord, hath kill'd a young Venetian
Call'd Roderigo.

Oth.   Roderigo kill'd!
And Cassio kill'd!

Emil.   No, Cassio is not kill'd.

Oth. Not Cassio kill'd! then murder 's out of tune,
And sweet revenge grows harsh.

Des. O, falsely, falsely murder'd!

Emil.   Alas, what cry is that?

Oth. That! what?

Emil. Out, and alas! that was my lady's voice.
Help! help, ho! help! O lady, speak again!   120
Sweet Desdemona! O sweet mistress, speak!

Des. A guiltless death I die.

Emil. O, who hath done this deed?

Des. Nobody; I myself. Farewell:
Commend me to my kind lord: O, farewell!   [*Dies.*

Oth. Why, how should she be murder'd?

Emil.   Alas, who knows?

Oth. You heard her say herself, it was not I.

Emil. She said so: I must needs report the truth.

Oth. She 's, like a liar, gone to burning hell:
'Twas I that kill'd her.

Emil.   O, the more angel she,   130
And you the blacker devil!

Oth. She turn'd to folly, and she was a whore.

---

55. **conception,** plan, intention. 63. **stone,** turn to stone, harden; Othello means that he will be tempted to kill her in sheer anger because of her perjury. 72. **ta'en order,** taken measures. 82. **Being . . . pause,** i.e., when the execution of the deed has once begun, there is no stopping. 88. **So, so.** The stage tradition, dating apparently from the time of Garrick, is for Othello to stab Desdemona. There is,

however, no necessity for assuming such an action, and it is more likely that he renews his attempt to smother her (Parrott). 101. **yawn,** gape in amazement, i.e., there would be an earthquake, since according to Pliny, earthquakes often happen during eclipses. **at alteration,** at the change. 109. **error,** aberration, irregularity. 132. **folly,** unchastity. 145. **chrysolite,** the golden stone; a name given to various

Emil. Thou dost belie her, and thou art a devil.

Oth. She was false as water.

Emil.   Thou art rash as fire, to say
That she was false: O, she was heavenly true!

Oth. Cassio did top her; ask thy husband else.
O, I were damn'd beneath all depth in hell,
But that I did proceed upon just grounds
To this extremity. Thy husband knew it all.

Emil. My husband!   140

Oth. Thy husband.

Emil. That she was false to wedlock?

Oth. Ay, with Cassio. Nay, had she been true,
If heaven would make me such another world
Of one entire and perfect chrysolite,
I 'ld not have sold her for it.

Emil. My husband!

Oth.   Ay, 'twas he that told me first:
An honest man he is, and hates the slime
That sticks on filthy deeds.

Emil.   My husband!

Oth. What needs this iteration, woman? I say thy
   husband.   150

Emil. O mistress, villany hath made mocks with
   love!
My husband say that she was false!

Oth.   He, woman;
I say thy husband: dost understand the word?
My friend, thy husband, honest, honest Iago.

Emil. If he say so, may his pernicious soul
Rot half a grain a day! he lies to the heart:
She was too fond of her most filthy bargain.

Oth. Ha!

Emil. Do thy worst:
This deed of thine is no more worthy heaven   160
Than thou wast worthy her.

Oth.   Peace, you were best.

Emil. Thou hast not half that power to do me harm
As I have to be hurt. O gull! O dolt!
As ignorant as dirt! thou hast done a deed—
I care not for thy sword; I'll make thee known,
Though I lost twenty lives.—Help! help, ho! help!
The Moor hath kill'd my mistress! Murder! murder!

Enter MONTANO, GRATIANO, IAGO, *and others.*

Mon. What is the matter? How now, general!

Emil. O, are you come, Iago? you have done well,
That men must lay their murders on your neck.   170

Gra. What is the matter?

Emil. Disprove this villain, if thou be'st a man:
He says thou told'st him that his wife was false:
I know thou didst not, thou 'rt not such a villain:
Speak, for my heart is full.

Iago. I told him what I thought, and told no more
Than what he found himself was apt and true.

Emil. But did you ever tell him she was false?

Iago. I did.

Emil. You told a lie; an odious, damned lie;   180
Upon my soul, a lie, a wicked lie.
She false with Cassio!—did you say with Cassio?

Iago. With Cassio, mistress. Go to, charm your
   tongue.

Emil. I will not charm my tongue; I am bound to
   speak:
My mistress here lies murder'd in her bed,—

All. O heavens forfend!

Emil. And your reports have set the murder on.

Oth. Nay, stare not, masters: it is true, indeed.

Gra. 'Tis a strange truth.

Mon. O monstrous act!

Emil.   Villany, villany, villany!   190
I think upon 't, I think: I smell 't: O villany!—
I thought so then:—I'll kill myself for grief:—
O villany, villany!

Iago. What, are you mad? I charge you, get you
   home.

Emil. Good gentlemen, let me have leave to speak:
'Tis proper I obey him, but not now.
Perchance, Iago, I will ne'er go home.

Oth. O! O! O!   [*He falls on the bed.*

Emil.   Nay, lay thee down and roar;
For thou hast kill'd the sweetest innocent
That e'er did lift up eye.

Oth.   [*Rising*] O, she was foul!   200
I scarce did know you, uncle: there lies your niece,
Whose breath, indeed, these hands have newly
   stopp'd:
I know this act shows horrible and grim.

Gra. Poor Desdemona! I am glad thy father 's dead:
Thy match was mortal to him, and pure grief
Shore his old thread in twain: did he live now,
This sight would make him do a desperate turn,
Yea, curse his better angel from his side,
And fall to reprobation.

Oth. 'Tis pitiful; but yet Iago knows   210
That she with Cassio hath the act of shame
A thousand times committed; Cassio confess'd it:
And she did gratify his amorous works
With that recognizance and pledge of love
Which I first gave her; I saw it in his hand:
It was a handkerchief, an antique token
My father gave my mother.

Emil. O heaven! O heavenly powers!

Iago. Come, hold your peace.

Emil.   'Twill out, 'twill out: I peace!
No, I will speak as liberal as the north: 220
Let heaven and men and devils, let them all,
All, all, cry shame against me, yet I'll speak.

Iago. Be wise, and get you home.

Emil.   I will not. [*Iago offers to stab Emilia.*

Gra.   Fie!
Your sword upon a woman?

Emil. O thou dull Moor! that handkerchief thou
   speak'st of
I found by fortune and did give my husband;
For often, with a solemn earnestness,
More than indeed belong'd to such a trifle,
He begg'd of me to steal it.

Iago.   Villanous whore!

Emil. She give it Cassio! no, alas! I found it,   230
And I did give 't my husband.

Iago.   Filth, thou liest!

Emil. By heaven, I do not, I do not, gentlemen.

---

precious stones of green color. 150. **iteration,** so Q; F: *iterance,* which
is possibly to be preferred. 151. **made mocks with,** derided, made sport
of. 163. **to be hurt,** i.e., to endure hurting. 177. **apt,** natural, likely.
183. **charm,** keep silent. 192. **then,** i.e., at some earlier time, probably
IV, ii, 130-144, when she suspected the machinations of *some eternal
villain:* she did not, however, suspect Iago until this moment. 206.

Shore, cut. 209. **reprobation,** damnation, rejection by God; so Q;
F: *reprobance,* possibly to be preferred. 214. **recognizance,** token.
217. **My . . . mother.** This statement is hardly consistent with that in
III, iv, 56. 220. **liberal as the north,** freely as the north wind. 226.
fortune, chance.

O murderous coxcomb! what should such a fool
Do with so good a woman?
 Oth.   Are there no stones in heaven
But what serve for the thunder?—Precious villain!
 [He runs at Iago: Iago, from behind, stabs Emilia, and exit.
 Gra. The woman falls; sure, he hath kill'd his wife.
 Emil. Ay, ay: O, lay me by my mistress' side.
 Gra. He's gone, but his wife's kill'd.
 Mon. 'Tis a notorious villain. Take you this weapon,
Which I have here recover'd from the Moor: 240
Come, guard the door without; let him not pass,
But kill him rather. I'll after that same villain,
For 'tis a damned slave. *[Exeunt Montano and Gratiano.*
 Oth.   I am not valiant neither,
But every puny whipster gets my sword:
But why should honour outlive honesty?
Let it go all.
 Emil. What did thy song bode, lady?
Hark, canst thou hear me? I will play the swan,
And die in music. *[Singing]* Willow, willow, willow.—
Moor, she was chaste; she loved thee, cruel Moor;
So come my soul to bliss, as I speak true;   250
So speaking as I think, I die, I die.   *[Dies.*
 Oth. I have another weapon in this chamber;
It is a sword of Spain, the ice-brook's temper:—
O, here it is. Uncle, I must come forth.
 Gra. *[Within]* If thou attempt it, it will cost thee
 dear:
Thou hast no weapon, and perforce must suffer.
 Oth. Look in upon me then and speak with me,
Or, naked as I am, I will assault thee.

Re-enter GRATIANO.

 Gra. What is the matter?
 Oth.   Behold, I have a weapon;
A better never did itself sustain   260
Upon a soldier's thigh: I have seen the day,
That, with this little arm and this good sword,
I have made my way through more impediments
Than twenty times your stop: but, O vain boast!
Who can control his fate? 'tis not so now.
Be not afraid, though you do see me weapon'd;
Here is my journey's end, here is my butt,
And very sea-mark of my utmost sail.
Do you go back dismay'd? 'tis a lost fear;
Man but a rush against Othello's breast,   270
And he retires. Where should Othello go?
Now, how dost thou look now? O ill-starr'd wench!
Pale as thy smock! when we shall meet at compt,
This look of thine will hurl my soul from heaven,
And fiends will snatch at it. Cold, cold, my girl!
Even like thy chastity. O cursed slave!
Whip me, ye devils,
From the possession of this heavenly sight!
Blow me about in winds! roast me in sulphur!
Wash me in steep-down gulfs of liquid fire!   280
O Desdemona! Desdemona! dead!
Oh! Oh! Oh!

 Enter LODOVICO, MONTANO, CASSIO *carried in a chair,*
 and Officers *with* IAGO, *prisoner.*

 Lod. Where is this rash and most unfortunate man?
 Oth. That's he that was Othello: here I am.
 Lod. Where is that viper? bring the villain forth.
 Oth. I look down towards his feet; but that's a
 fable.
If that thou be'st a devil, I cannot kill thee.
              [Wounds Iago.
 Lod. Wrench his sword from him.
 Iago.   I bleed, sir; but not kill'd.
 Oth. I am not sorry neither: I'ld have thee live;
For, in my sense, 'tis happiness to die.   290
 Lod. O thou Othello, that wert once so good,
Fall'n in the practice of a damned slave,
What shall be said to thee?
 Oth.   Why, any thing:
An honourable murderer, if you will;
For nought I did in hate, but all in honour.
 Lod. This wretch hath part confess'd his villany:
Did you and he consent in Cassio's death?
 Oth. Ay.
 Cas. Dear general, I never gave you cause.
 Oth. I do believe it, and I ask you pardon.   300
Will you, I pray, demand that demi-devil
Why he hath thus ensnared my soul and body?
 Iago. Demand me nothing: what you know, you
 know:
From this time forth I never will speak word.
 Lod. What, not to pray?
 Gra.   Torments will ope your lips.
 Oth. Well, thou dost best.
 Lod. Sir, you shall understand what hath befall'n,
Which, as I think, you know not. Here is a letter
Found in the pocket of the slain Roderigo;
And here another: the one of them imports   310
The death of Cassio to be undertook
By Roderigo.
 Oth. O villain!
 Cas.   Most heathenish and most gross!
 Lod. Now here's another discontented paper,
Found in his pocket too; and this, it seems,
Roderigo meant to have sent this damned villain;
But that belike Iago in the interim
Came in and satisfied him.
 Oth.   O the pernicious caitiff!
How came you, Cassio, by that handkerchief
That was my wife's?
 Cas.   I found it in my chamber: 320
And he himself confess'd but even now
That there he dropp'd it for a special purpose
Which wrought to his desire.
 Oth.   O fool! fool! fool!
 Cas. There is besides in Roderigo's letter,
How he upbraids Iago, that he made him
Brave me upon the watch; whereon it came
That I was cast: and even but now he spake,
After long seeming dead, Iago hurt him,
Iago set him on.
 Lod. You must forsake this room, and go with us: 330
Your power and your command is taken off,
And Cassio rules in Cyprus. For this slave,

233. **coxcomb,** fool; addressed to Othello. 234. **stones in heaven,** thunderbolts. It was supposed that real stones fell with the thunder and caused the damage. 244. **whipster,** contemptible fellow. 245. **honour outlive honesty.** Othello realizes that he has done a shameful deed; he asks why his reputation for valor should endure. 253. **ice-brook's temper,** usually defined as "tempered in ice-cold water." F has *Ice brookes,* Q: *Isebrookes;* Onions notes that *Isebrooke* is the Elizabethan form for *Innsbruck,* once noted for fine steel. 258. **naked,** unarmed.

264. **your stop,** what you can stop. 267. **butt,** mark for archery, goal, limit. 268. **sea-mark,** beacon. 270. **Man,** provide, as in manning a gun. 273. **compt,** account, judgment day. 286. **towards his feet,** i.e., to see if they were cloven like a devil's. 304. **From . . . word.** Iago has all the way through the self-command of a soldier; his refusal to speak is characteristic. 314. **discontented,** expressing dissatisfaction. 318. **caitiff,** wretch. 331. **taken off,** taken away.

If there be any cunning cruelty
That can torment him much and hold him long,
It shall be his. You shall close prisoner rest,
Till that the nature of your fault be known
To the Venetian state. Come, bring him away.
   Oth. Soft you; a word or two before you go.
I have done the state some service, and they know 't.
No more of that. I pray you, in your letters,   340
When you shall these unlucky deeds relate,
Speak of me as I am; nothing extenuate,
Nor set down aught in malice: then must you speak
Of one that loved not wisely but too well;
Of one not easily jealous, but being wrought,
Perplex'd in the extreme; of one whose hand,
Like the base Indian, threw a pearl away
Richer than all his tribe; of one whose subdued eyes,
Albeit unused to the melting mood,
Drop tears as fast as the Arabian trees   350
Their medicinal gum. Set you down this;
And say besides, that in Aleppo once,
Where a malignant and a turban'd Turk
Beat a Venetian and traduced the state,
I took by the throat the circumcised dog,
And smote him, thus.   [*Stabs himself.*
   Lod. O bloody period!
   Gra.   All that 's spoke is marr'd.
   Oth. I kiss'd thee ere I kill'd thee: no way but this;
Killing myself, to die upon a kiss.   359
               [*Falls on the bed, and dies.*
   Cas. This did I fear, but thought he had no weapon;
For he was great of heart.
   Lod.   [*To Iago*] O Spartan dog,
More fell than anguish, hunger, or the sea!
Look on the tragic loading of this bed;
This is thy work: the object poisons sight;
Let it be hid. Gratiano, keep the house,
And seize upon the fortunes of the Moor,
For they succeed on you. To you, lord governor,
Remains the censure of this hellish villain;
The time, the place, the torture: O, enforce it!
Myself will straight aboard; and to the state   370
This heavy act with heavy heart relate.   [*Exeunt.*

342. **extenuate,** diminish, depreciate; the idea is contrasted with the thought of *malice* in the following line. 346. **Perplex'd,** confounded, distracted. 347. **Indian,** so Q and F_{2-3-4}; F_1: *Iudean,* which has been defended by some editors as an allusion to Herod, who slew Miriamne in a fit of jealousy, or as an allusion to Judas Iscariot, the betrayer of Christ. Coleridge thought that Othello compares himself to a rude Indian—American savage. If *Indian* is correct, there may be back of the reading some story that we do not know. 350-351. **tears . . . gum.** Back of the comparison of tears to Arabian gums lies Pliny's description of the aromatic wealth of Arabia. 351. **medicinal,** so Q; F: *medicinable,* which is possibly original. 352. **Aleppo,** a Turkish city where the Venetians had special trading privileges. It is stated that it was immediate death for a Christian to strike a Turk in Aleppo; Othello risked his life for the honor of Venice. 357. **period,** termination, conclusion. 361. **Spartan dog.** Spartan dogs were noted for their savagery.

King Lear

O n November 26, 1607, there was properly entered in the Stationers' Register by Nathaniel Butter and John Busby *A Booke called Master William Shakespeare his historye of Kinge Lear, as yt was played before the Kinges maiestie at Whitehall vppon Sainct Ste-* *phens night at Christmas Last, by his maieties servantes playinge vsually at the Globe on the Banksyde*. The next year Q_1 was issued, with the title page:

M. William Shak-speare: *HIS* True Chronicle Historie of the life and death of King LEAR and his three Daughters. *With the vnfortunate life of* Edgar, *sonne* and heire to the Earle of Gloster, and his sullen and assumed humor of TOM of Bedlam: *As it was played before the Kings Maiestie at Whitehall vpon S. Stephans night in Christmas Hollidayes.* By his Maiesties Seruants playing vsually at the Gloabe on the Bancke-side. *LONDON,* Printed for *Nathaniel Butter,* and are to be sold at his shop in *Pauls* Church-yard at the signe of the Pide Bull neere St. *Austins* Gate. 1608.

How Butter and Busby, who were not very reputable printers, were able to make this apparently authorized issue is not clear. They seem to have printed from a copy which was particularly illegible. Some of the sheets were corrected after others had been printed off, so that it follows that in different copies of the same edition there are both corrected and uncorrected sheets.[1]

Pollard thought that the text of the play in the First Folio was set up from a copy of this quarto with, however, the correction from a manuscript of certain sheets which were present in the playhouse quarto in the uncorrected form.[2] It is certain, however, that the Folio editors made use throughout of an independent manuscript text in their possession, since their text omits about three hundred lines contained in the quarto and adds over a hundred not found in the quarto, and since their text shows constant verbal variation from the quarto text and many changes clearly designed for stage presentation. Because of significant common errors in the two texts, W. W. Greg thinks that the copy for the Folio was a quarto corrected to conform to the stage manuscript.[3] As to the nature of the copy from which the quarto was set, there is a widely current opinion to the effect that Q_1 is to be regarded as a "bad" quarto derived from the good text represented by the Folio version by some process of oral transmission, possibly stenography. These theories are unnecessary, since it is perfectly clear that the quarto text is, in spite of its corruptions, too good, too near what Shakespeare wrote, to be classified as a "bad" quarto.

The correct explanation of the relation of the quarto and the Folio versions is probably this: Shakespeare's manuscript, having been revised by him and thereby rendered somewhat illegible, was copied. The revised manuscript got into the hands of the printers and was issued as the quarto. The clean

[1]See W. W. Greg, "The Date of *King Lear* and Shakespeare's Use of Earlier Versions of the Story," *The Library,* XX (1940), 377-400; *The Variants in the First Quarto of "King Lear"* (Oxford, 1940).
[2]*Folios and Quartos,* p. 53.
[3]See W. W. Greg, "The Function of Bibliography in Literary Criticism Illustrated in a Study of the Text of *King Lear," Neophilologus,* XVIII (1933), 241-262; *The Editorial Problem in Shakespeare* (Oxford, 1942), pp. 88-101.

copy stayed in the playhouse, underwent further alteration, and became ultimately the text of the play in the Folio.[4] There exists another quarto also dated 1608, but really printed in 1619 by Jaggard

An Abraham Man or Tom o' Bedlam.

and Pavier when they were intending to issue a collection of Shakespeare's plays. For some reason, not fully known, they gave this and the quartos of several other plays their original dates of publication.

DATE

The entry quoted from the Stationers' Register shows that *King Lear* was written before December 26, St. Stephen's Day, 1606. Shakespeare drew the names of Edgar's fiends and other slight matters from Harsnet's *Declaration of Popish Impostures*. This book was published in 1603, hence, *King Lear* could not have been written before that date.

One other circumstance may fix the date still more closely by giving an indication of the time when the tragedy began to make a stir as a popular play. An anonymous play, *The True Chronicle History of King Leir, and his three daughters, Gonorill, Ragan, and Cordella*, was fished up, entered in the Stationers' Register, and published in 1605. It had already been entered in the Stationers' Register in 1594, but apparently not published. The entry of 1605 (May 8) speaks of the book as "the Tragecall historie of king Leir, etc." The play is not a tragedy and the way it is described, as well as the fact of its publication, may very well be due to the reputation of Shakespeare's play. The year

1605 is thus indicated as the year when Shakespeare's play was staged. *King Lear* is in Shakespeare's late, highly condensed style, so that internal evidence would also place it in the very middle of his tragical period.

SOURCES

For his sources Shakespeare went not only to *King Leir*, based on Holinshed, but to Holinshed himself, to *The Mirror for Magistrates*, to the *Faerie Queene*, and possibly to Warner's *Albion's England*. The plot of Gloucester and his sons, which stands as a parallel to the Lear story, he found in Sidney's *Arcadia*. The basis of the main story is a folk tale about a love test set by a father for his three daughters, the youngest of whom replies too frankly to suit the jealous father. She is disinherited, but finally turns out to be the only daughter whose filial piety was sincere. Geoffrey of Monmouth had placed this story in *Historia Regum Britanniae*, written about 1135; it had become, in poems and chronicles, a regular part of the history of England. Wilfred Perrett thinks that Shakespeare consulted Geoffrey himself; but when the full list of sources including Geoffrey is considered, one has little enough of *King Lear* as we know it.[5]

The *Arcadia* is, however, a rich and varied work, which served as an important source of ideas as well as events. The story of King Lear did not originally have a tragic ending, since by the intervention of the French king, Lear was restored to his throne and reigned until his death. Cordelia's end, according to the chronicle, was tragic. Her misfortune, however, did not come until after the death of Lear when she was dethroned and murdered by her wicked nephews. In the original story Lear does not give his whole kingdom away, but retains part of it. He is not so much overthrown by his daughters as by his sons-in-law, who rebel against him to get his kingdom. He goes to France for aid and gets it.

The True Chronicle History of King Leir is a rather bright and cheerful play. It furnished events for Shakespeare's *King Lear*, but it did not furnish tone, atmosphere, the deeper significances of the play, and the tragic concept. These came from the story of the "Paphlagonian unkinde King, and his kinde sonne" as narrated in the tenth chapter of the second book of Sidney's *Arcadia*. The story of the Paphlagonian king is tragic, that of the old King Leir is not. The concept or pattern of Sidney's story is the tragic consequences of filial ingratitude. That concept is taken over from *Arcadia* and applied to the Lear story. The genesis of the tragedy of *King Lear* is to be found in the story of the blind king of Paphlagonia; that is, the tragic possibilities of filial ingratitude came from the reading of *Arcadia*, not from familiarity with the old *King Leir*. Sidney provides active cruelty,

[4]Madeleine Doran, *The Text of King Lear* (Stanford University Press, 1931); J. Q. Adams, "The Quarto of *King Lear* and Shorthand," *Modern Philology*, XXXI (1933), 135-163; Madeleine Doran, "The Quarto of *King Lear* and Bright's Shorthand," *Modern Philology*, XXXIII (1935), 139-157; W. W. Greg, as cited in footnotes 1 and 3.

[5]Wilfred Perrett, *The Story of King Lear* (Berlin, 1904); Madeleine Doran, "Elements in the Composition of *King Lear*," *Studies in Philology*, XXX (1933), 34-58; See W. W. Greg, "The Date of *King Lear* and Shakespeare's Use of Earlier Versions of the Story," *The Library*, XX (1940), 377-400.

filial ingratitude in dreadful form, base deceit, and dark intrigue. He furnishes the themes of hunted fugitives, exposure to storm, a cave of refuge (which may be the hovel), blindness, danger, destitution, and, more than all, the deepest possible reflection on tragic folly and the worthlessness of miserable life. Finally, in Sidney, the prototype of Gloucester dies.

Perhaps the greatest contribution of *Arcadia* to *King Lear* is the element of sinful and dangerous intrigue. From the fifteenth chapter of the second book of *Arcadia*, which treats of the story of Plangus, come by plain suggestion the machinations by means of which Edmund undermines and uproots Edgar.[6] By means similar to those used by Edmund against Edgar the corrupt stepmother achieves the downfall and banishment of Plangus. From that story also comes the suggestion for the disagreeably appropriate liaison between Edmund and the wicked daughters of King Lear.

It was a stroke of genius that made Shakespeare combine two stories so different in their tone and yet so closely parallel in their course as that of the old King Leir and the blind king of Paphlagonia. He knit these stories together with a naturalness which will always be amazing, but his general task may be described as that of permeating the Lear story with the tragic quality and temper of the Gloucester story. The tragedy as tragedy is to be found in the tale from *Arcadia*. Shakespeare retains from the old play the sweetness of Cordelia and the faithfulness of Kent (Perillus). The stoutness in the character of the aged Lear is yet to be accounted for, since the Leir of the old play is merely pathetic. Few parts of *King Lear*, or of any of Shakespeare's plays, seem to have been invented outright. There is the figure of the Fool, a traditional part written no doubt for Robert Armin, the trial by combat, no very difficult thing to invent, and the change from British defeat to British victory. When, however, it is said that this change from defeat to victory is an indication of Shakespeare's own patriotic feeling, one has a right to demur. Shakespeare apparently needed to make this change in order to entangle Lear and Cordelia in the mesh of his tragedy. In other words, the British victory serves Shakespeare as a device for the carrying out of his tragic purpose. This is not, however, intended to minimize the structural magnificence of *King Lear* or the greatness of its characterization, but merely to describe the way in which Shakespeare seems to have worked. The idea of plot invention was still undeveloped, and, in any case, the greatest geniuses seem to exemplify Poe's dictum: "To originate is carefully, patiently, and understandingly to combine."

POLITICAL BACKGROUNDS

Critics have found in Shakespeare's changes and additions justification and enrichment of the theme.

However, to accept the masterpiece in this way is not the full story, and it detracts nothing from Shakespeare's art to discover whence his thoughts, feelings, and moral judgments may in some measure have come.

Lilian Winstanley published a series of studies in which she attempted to show that *Hamlet, Macbeth,* and *King Lear* reflect immediately the matters of most absorbing political interest to Englishmen in the early years of the reign of James I.[7] Without accepting her entire list of multifarious parallels between the three tragedies and state papers, Huguenot memoirs, accounts of the Gunpowder Plot, and histories, memorials, and letters of Mary Queen of Scots, with accounts of current French politics and the massacre of St. Bartholomew, or without accepting her general conclusion that Shakespeare meant his tragedies as vast allegories of political import, one may nevertheless admit that she has opened up a background of plot, intrigue, fear, murder, and violence which undoubtedly did occupy the minds of the men of that time, and that this background is one which Shakespeare in his great tragedies reflected. She thinks that Lear was meant to typify both Darnley, the father of James I, and Coligny, the victim of Catharine de' Medici; that the daughters represent Queen Mary; that Oswald is Rizzio, and that Edmund stands for Bothwell. These parallels in violence, if not in event, give us an insight into royal intrigue and crime, into the state of a kingdom such as that of Scotland or France at such a period, and, particularly, into the world-scheme according to which Shakespeare and the men of his time saw order grow out of, or lapse back into, chaos. Back of *King Lear* lies also the question of political power with its lures and its dangers that appears in *Gorboduc* and the plays of Marlowe, Chapman, and Jonson.

ETHICAL INTERPRETATION

Nature in Renaissance thinking is power, growth, generation. Left alone, it is chaos; combed, subdued, and directed by man's law and God's law, it is civilization and order. A crime against nature is the most heinous of all crimes. Consider the following statement of the doctrine in Wilson's *Arte of Rhetorique* a passage derived from Cicero, and its applicability to *King Lear:*[8]

. . . the wisdome of Princes, and the feare of Gods threate, which was vttered by his worde, forced men by a lawe, both to allowe things confirmed by nature, and to beare with old custome, or els they should not onely

---

[6]See D. M. McKeithan, "*King Lear* and Sidney's *Arcadia*," *Studies in English*, No. 14 (1934) (Austin, Texas), pp. 45-49.

[7]Lilian Winstanley, *Hamlet and the Scottish Succession* (Cambridge, 1921); *Macbeth, King Lear, and Contemporary History* (Cambridge, 1922). See also various writings on the political use of the stage: Richard Simpson, New Shakespeare Society 1874, pp. 371 ff., pp. 396 ff.; T. S. Graves, *Modern Philology*, IX, 545 ff.; XIV, 525 ff.; *Anglia*, XXXVIII, 137 ff.; R. W. Bond, edition of Lyly's works; Feuillerat, *John Lyly* (1910); Edith Rickert, *Modern Philology*, XXI, 53-87, 133-154.

[8]*Wilson's Arte of Rhetorique*, edited by G. H. Mair (Oxford, 1909), p. 32.

suffer in body temporall punishment, but also lose their soules for euer. Nature is a right that phantasie hath not framed, but God hath graffed and giuen man power thereunto, whereof these are deriued:

> Religion, and acknowledging of God.
> Naturall loue to our children, and other.
> Thankfulnesse to all men.
> Stoutnesse, both to withstand and reuenge.
> Reuerence to the superior.
> Assured and constant trueth in things.

When Lear gives over the sovereignty of his kingdom to the wicked, chaos comes again. The voice of the Fool, no less than the practical voice of the wise Kent, rings out through the earlier part of the play to make this situation clear. Point by point the play presents, to the accompaniment of wars and the rebellion of subjects, evidences of the violation of natural fundamentals: the sympathetic agony of nature, portents, extremes in violence, beggary, and insanity. The cruelty and tyranny of Regan and Goneril and the wickedness of Edmund violate "the naturall loue to our children, and other." Edmund, himself under "the plague of custom" because of his illegitimacy, declares that nature (that is, chaotic nature) is his goddess: "Now, gods, stand up for bastards!" (I, ii, 1-22).

The royal state of the king, the embodiment of authority and honor, is lost, and the loyal service of Kent is rejected in favor of the base flattery of Oswald (II, ii); thus is the "reuerence to the superior" put to naught. As to thankfulness to all men, Lear has "given all," and ingratitude, the "marble-hearted fiend," has established itself in the family and the kingdom. Kent and Cordelia, who stand for "assured and constant trueth in things," are banished and disgraced. Even "stoutnesse, both to withstand and reuenge," is not forgotten in the conduct of Edgar and the kingliness of Lear (II, iv, 275-281).

> You see me here, you gods, a poor old man,
> As full of grief as age; wretched in both!
> If it be you that stir these daughters' hearts
> Against their father, fool me not so much
> To bear it tamely; touch me with noble anger,
> And let not women's weapons, water-drops,
> Stain my man's cheeks!

Finally, "religion, and acknowledging of God" are not forgotten in the moral system of this play. Lear is a pagan, close to nature, so that the stars and the gods are never off his lips. The faith of the good men of the play is a religious faith, though pagan, like that of Albany when he hears of the death of Cornwall (IV, ii, 78-81):

> This shows you are above,
> You justicers, that these our nether crimes
> So speedily can venge!

Edmund, on the other hand, scorning the heavenly influence of the stars, is obviously an infidel (I, ii, 128-145).

King Lear, then, pictures, in the tragedy of a king, who is also kingship, and of a father, who is also fatherhood, the return to chaos in a kingdom and a royal family, the ruin of the centers and, therefore, of the whole body politic. This is the ultimate idea of evil in the philosophy of the Renaissance.

STAGE HISTORY

K*ing Lear*, possibly the greatest of Shakespeare's tragedies, has not been completely fortunate in its stage history. It is supposed that the part of Lear was written for Richard Burbage. There are few, if any, traces of performance before the closing of the theaters in 1642. However, the play must have been well known, for it was quickly revived after the Restoration, Betterton probably playing in Shakespeare's version.

This was, however, completely superseded by Nahum Tate's adaptation (1681), which held the stage until 1838, when Macready restored the original. Tate resorted to a no longer appropriate happy ending to the play, about which Charles Lamb made his famous remark:

A happy ending!—as if the martyrdom that Lear has gone through, the flaying of his feelings alive, did not make a fair dismissal from the stage of life the only decorous thing for him.

Garrick restored part of Shakespeare's text in the place of Tate's lines, and Kean restored Shakespeare's tragic ending; but Betterton, Garrick, Spranger Barry, Kemble, and Kean himself retained either all or part of Tate's alterations.

Tate gave the tragedy a happy ending with the idea that the stage should show truth and virtue always triumphant. He banished the Fool as too indecorous for tragedy and constructed a love plot between Edgar and Cordelia resulting in their betrothal. Lear was restored to all of his kingdom except Albany's share.

When one thinks of the play in this form one wonders at the triumphs of the great tragic actors. Betterton and Garrick were famous in the part of Lear. When Kean was praised for his brilliancy in *Othello*, he said, "The London audience have no notion of what I can do until they see me over the dead body of Cordelia." Kean, it will be remembered, restored the tragic ending.

There were also some great Lears in the nineteenth century, Samuel Phelps, John McCullough, Edwin Forrest, Edwin Booth, and Sir Henry Irving (1892). In more recent times it has rarely been possible to see the play except in the excellent work of Robert Mantell. Quite recently Sir Laurence Olivier played Lear at the London Old Vic and in 1950 John Gielgud played the part at the Shakespeare Memorial Theatre at Stratford. There have been other performances, for the play seems to have grown popular. Louis Calhern played Lear in New York in the 1951 season.

King Lear

DRAMATIS PERSONAE

LEAR, king of Britain.
KING OF FRANCE.
DUKE OF BURGUNDY.
DUKE OF CORNWALL.
DUKE OF ALBANY.
EARL OF KENT.
EARL OF GLOUCESTER.
EDGAR, son to Gloucester.
EDMUND, bastard son to Gloucester.
CURAN, a courtier.
Old Man, tenant to Gloucester.
Doctor.
Fool.
OSWALD, steward to Goneril.
A Captain employed by Edmund.
Gentleman attendant on Cordelia.
A Herald.
Servants to Cornwall.

GONERIL,
REGAN,   } daughters to Lear.
CORDELIA,

Knights of Lear's train, Captains,
    Messengers, Soldiers, and Attendants.

SCENE: *Britain.*

ACT I.

SCENE I. *King Lear's palace.*

Enter KENT, GLOUCESTER, *and* EDMUND.

Kent. I thought the king had more affected the
Duke of Albany than Cornwall.

Glou. It did always seem so to us: but now, in the
division of the kingdom, it appears not which of the
dukes he values most; for equalities are so weighed,
that curiosity in neither can make choice of either's
moiety.

Kent. Is not this your son, my lord?

Glou. His breeding, sir, hath been at my charge:
I have so often blushed to acknowledge him, that now
I am brazed to it.   11

Kent. I cannot conceive you.

Glou. Sir, this young fellow's mother could: whereupon she grew round-wombed, and had, indeed, sir,
a son for her cradle ere she had a husband for her
bed. Do you smell a fault?

Kent. I cannot wish the fault undone, the issue of it
being so proper.   18

Glou. But I have, sir, a son by order of law, some
year elder than this, who yet is no dearer in my
account: though this knave came something saucily
into the world before he was sent for, yet was his
mother fair; there was good sport at his making, and

the whoreson must be acknowledged. Do you know
this noble gentleman, Edmund?

Edm. No, my lord.

Glou. My lord of Kent: remember him hereafter as
my honourable friend.

Edm. My services to your lordship.

Kent. I must love you, and sue to know you better. 31

Edm. Sir, I shall study deserving.

Glou. He hath been out nine years, and away he
shall again. The king is coming.

Sennet. Enter KING LEAR, CORNWALL, ALBANY,
    GONERIL, REGAN, CORDELIA, *and* Attendants.

Lear. Attend the lords of France and Burgundy,
    Gloucester.

Glou. I shall, my liege. [*Exeunt Gloucester and Edmund.*

Lear. Meantime we shall express our darker purpose.
Give me the map there. Know that we have divided
In three our kingdom: and 'tis our fast intent
To shake all cares and business from our age;   40
Conferring them on younger strengths, while we
Unburthen'd crawl toward death. Our son of
    Cornwall,
And you, our no less loving son of Albany,
We have this hour a constant will to publish
Our daughters' several dowers, that future strife
May be prevented now. The princes, France and
    Burgundy,
Great rivals in our youngest daughter's love,
Long in our court have made their amorous sojourn,
And here are to be answer'd. Tell me, my
    daughters,—
Since now we will divest us, both of rule,   50
Interest of territory, cares of state,—
Which of you shall we say doth love us most?
That we our largest bounty may extend
Where nature doth with merit challenge. Goneril,
Our eldest-born, speak first.

Gon. Sir, I love you more than words can wield the
    matter;
Dearer than eye-sight, space, and liberty;
Beyond what can be valued, rich or rare;
No less than life, with grace, health, beauty, honour;
As much as child e'er loved, or father found;   60
A love that makes breath poor, and speech unable;
Beyond all manner of so much I love you.

Cor. [*Aside*] What shall Cordelia do? Love, and be
    silent.

Lear. Of all these bounds, even from this line to this,
With shadowy forests and with champains rich'd,
With plenteous rivers and wide-skirted meads,
We make thee lady: to thine and Albany's issue
Be this perpetual. What says our second daughter,
Our dearest Regan, wife to Cornwall? Speak.

Reg. Sir, I am made   70
Of the self-same metal that my sister is,
And prize me at her worth. In my true heart
I find she names my very deed of love;
Only she comes too short: that I profess
Myself an enemy to all other joys,

ACT I. SCENE I. 5. **equalities,** equivalences (in the lands assigned).
6. **curiosity,** nicety, close scrutiny. 11. **brazed,** hardened. 39.
fast intent, firm intention. 44. **constant,** fixed. 54. **Where . . .
challenge,** where both natural affection and merit claim it as due. 56.
wield the matter, avail in expressing. 64. **bounds.** The division of
Lear's kingdom seems to be a traditional one; it appears also in *1 Henry
IV,* III, i, 70 ff. 65. **shadowy,** shady. **champains,** plains. 73. **deed
of love,** love in very deed. 74. **that,** in that.

Which the most precious square of sense possesses;
And find I am alone felicitate
In your dear highness' love.
    Cor.   [*Aside*] Then poor Cordelia!
And yet not so; since, I am sure, my love 's
More richer than my tongue.   80
    Lear. To thee and thine hereditary ever
Remain this ample third of our fair kingdom;
No less in space, validity, and pleasure,
Than that conferr'd on Goneril. Now, our joy,
Although the last, not least; to whose young love
The vines of France and milk of Burgundy
Strive to be interess'd; what can you say to draw
A third more opulent than your sisters? Speak.
    Cor. Nothing, my lord.
    Lear. Nothing!   90
    Cor. Nothing.
    Lear. Nothing will come of nothing: speak again.
    Cor. Unhappy that I am, I cannot heave
My heart into my mouth: I love your majesty
According to my bond; nor more nor less.
    Lear. How, how, Cordelia! mend your speech a
      little,
Lest it may mar your fortunes.
    Cor.   Good my lord,
You have begot me, bred me, loved me: I
Return those duties back as are right fit,
Obey you, love you, and most honour you.   100
Why have my sisters husbands, if they say
They love you all? Haply, when I shall wed,
That lord whose hand must take my plight shall carry
Half my love with him, half my care and duty:
Sure, I shall never marry like my sisters,
To love my father all.
    Lear. But goes thy heart with this?
    Cor.   Ay, good my lord.
    Lear. So young, and so untender?
    Cor. So young, my lord, and true.
    Lear. Let it be so; thy truth, then, be thy dower. 110
For, by the sacred radiance of the sun,
The mysteries of Hecate, and the night;
By all the operation of the orbs
From whom we do exist, and cease to be;
Here I disclaim all my paternal care,
Propinquity and property of blood,
And as a stranger to my heart and me
Hold thee, from this, for ever. The barbarous
    Scythian,
Or he that makes his generation messes
To gorge his appetite, shall to my bosom   120
Be as well neighbour'd, pitied, and relieved,
As thou my sometime daughter.
    Kent.   Good my liege,—
    Lear. Peace, Kent!
Come not between the dragon and his wrath.
I loved her most, and thought to set my rest
On her kind nursery. Hence, and avoid my sight!
So be my grave my peace, as here I give
Her father's heart from her! Call France; who stirs?
Call Burgundy. Cornwall and Albany,

With my two daughters' dowers digest this third: 130
Let pride, which she calls plainness, marry her.
I do invest you jointly with my power,
Pre-eminence, and all the large effects
That troop with majesty. Ourself, by monthly course,
With reservation of an hundred knights,
By you to be sustain'd, shall our abode
Make with you by due turns. Only we still retain
The name, and all the additions to a king;
The sway, revenue, execution of the rest,
Beloved sons, be yours: which to confirm,   140
This coronet part betwixt you.   [*Giving the crown.*
    Kent.   Royal Lear,
Whom I have ever honour'd as my king,
Loved as my father, as my master follow'd,
As my great patron thought on in my prayers,—
    Lear. The bow is bent and drawn, make from the
      shaft.
    Kent. Let it fall rather, though the fork invade
The region of my heart: be Kent unmannerly,
When Lear is mad. What wilt thou do, old man?
Think'st thou that duty shall have dread to speak,
When power to flattery bows? To plainness honour 's
      bound,   150
When majesty stoops to folly. Reverse thy doom;
And, in thy best consideration, check
This hideous rashness: answer my life my judgement,
Thy youngest daughter does not love thee least;
Nor are those empty-hearted whose low sound
Reverbs no hollowness.
    Lear.   Kent, on thy life, no more.
    Kent. My life I never held but as a pawn
To wage against thy enemies; nor fear to lose it,
Thy safety being the motive.
    Lear.   Out of my sight!
    Kent. See better, Lear; and let me still remain   160
The true blank of thine eye.
    Lear. Now, by Apollo,—
    Kent.   Now, by Apollo, king,
Thou swear'st thy gods in vain.
    Lear.   O, vassal! miscreant!
                  [*Laying his hand on his sword.*
    Alb. ⎱
    Corn.⎰ Dear sir, forbear.
    Kent. Do;
Kill thy physician, and the fee bestow
Upon thy foul disease. Revoke thy doom;
Or, whilst I can vent clamour from my throat,
I'll tell thee thou dost evil.
    Lear.   Hear me, recreant!
On thine allegiance, hear me!   170
Since thou hast sought to make us break our vow,
Which we durst never yet, and with strain'd pride
To come between our sentence and our power,
Which nor our nature nor our place can bear,
Our potency made good, take thy reward.
Five days we do allot thee, for provision
To shield thee from diseases of the world;
And on the sixth to turn thy hated back
Upon our kingdom: if, on the tenth day following,

Thy banish'd trunk be found in our dominions,   180
The moment is thy death. Away! by Jupiter,
This shall not be revoked.
   Kent. Fare thee well, king: sith thus thou wilt
       appear,
Freedom lives hence, and banishment is here.
[*To Cordelia*] The gods to their dear shelter take thee,
       maid,
That justly think'st, and hast most rightly said!
[*To Regan and Goneril*] And your large speeches may
       your deeds approve,
That good effects may spring from words of love.
Thus Kent, O princes, bids you all adieu;
He'll shape his old course in a country new.   [*Exit.* 190

       Flourish. Re-enter GLOUCESTER, *with*
       FRANCE, BURGUNDY, *and* Attendants.

   Glou. Here 's France and Burgundy, my noble lord.
   Lear. My lord of Burgundy,
We first address towards you, who with this king
Hath rivall'd for our daughter: what, in the least,
Will you require in present dower with her,
Or cease your quest of love?
   Bur.   Most royal majesty,
I crave no more than what your highness offer'd,
Nor will you tender less.
   Lear.   Right noble Burgundy,
When she was dear to us, we did hold her so;
But now her price is fall'n. Sir, there she stands: 200
If aught within that little seeming substance,
Or all of it, with our displeasure pieced,
And nothing more, may fitly like your grace,
She 's there, and she is yours.
   Bur.   I know no answer.
   Lear. Will you, with those infirmities she owes,
Unfriended, new-adopted to our hate,
Dower'd with our curse, and stranger'd with our oath,
Take her, or leave her?
   Bur.   Pardon me, royal sir;
Election makes not up on such conditions.
   Lear. Then leave her, sir; for, by the power that
       made me,   210
I tell you all her wealth. [*To France*] For you, great
       king,
I would not from your love make such a stray,
To match you where I hate; therefore beseech you
To avert your liking a more worthier way
Than on a wretch whom nature is ashamed
Almost to acknowledge hers.
   France.   This is most strange,
That she, that even but now was your best object,
The argument of your praise, balm of your age,
Most best, most dearest, should in this trice of time
Commit a thing so monstrous, to dismantle   220
So many folds of favour. Sure, her offence
Must be of such unnatural degree,
That monsters it, or your fore-vouch'd affection
Fall'n into taint: which to believe of her,
Must be a faith that reason without miracle
Could never plant in me.

   Cor.   I yet beseech your majesty,—
If for I want that glib and oily art,
To speak and purpose not; since what I well intend,
I'll do 't before I speak,—that you make known
It is no vicious blot, murder, or foulness,   230
No unchaste action, or dishonour'd step,
That hath deprived me of your grace and favour;
But even for want of that for which I am richer,
A still-soliciting eye, and such a tongue
As I am glad I have not, though not to have it
Hath lost me in your liking.
   Lear.   Better thou
Hadst not been born than not to have pleased me
       better.
   France. Is it but this,—a tardiness in nature
Which often leaves the history unspoke
That it intends to do? My lord of Burgundy,   240
What say you to the lady? Love 's not love
When it is mingled with regards that stand
Aloof from the entire point. Will you have her?
She is herself a dowry.
   Bur.   Royal Lear,
Give but that portion which yourself proposed,
And here I take Cordelia by the hand,
Duchess of Burgundy.
   Lear. Nothing: I have sworn; I am firm.
   Bur. I am sorry, then, you have so lost a father
That you must lose a husband.
   Cor.   Peace be with Burgundy!   250
Since that respects of fortune are his love,
I shall not be his wife.
   France. Fairest Cordelia, that art most rich, being
       poor;
Most choice, forsaken; and most loved, despised!
Thee and thy virtues here I seize upon:
Be it lawful I take up what 's cast away.
Gods, gods! 'tis strange that from their cold'st neglect
My love should kindle to inflamed respect.
Thy dowerless daughter, king, thrown to my chance,
Is queen of us, of ours, and our fair France: 260
Not all the dukes of waterish Burgundy
Can buy this unprized precious maid of me.
Bid them farewell, Cordelia, though unkind:
Thou losest here, a better where to find.
   Lear. Thou hast her, France: let her be thine; for we
Have no such daughter, nor shall ever see
That face of hers again. Therefore be gone
Without our grace, our love, our benison.
Come, noble Burgundy.
       [*Flourish. Exeunt all but France, Goneril, Regan,
                                              and Cordelia.*
   France. Bid farewell to your sisters.   270
   Cor. The jewels of our father, with wash'd eyes
Cordelia leaves you: I know you what you are;
And like a sister am most loath to call
Your faults as they are named. Use well our father:
To your professed bosoms I commit him:
But yet, alas, stood I within his grace,
I would prefer him to a better place.
So, farewell to you both.

---

162. **by Apollo.** The play of *King Lear* is rather carefully pagan in all
of its externals.   172. **strain'd,** excessive.   175. **Our potency made
good,** our authority being maintained.   177. **diseases,** troubles, dis-
comforts.   193. **address,** address ourself.   201. **seeming,** probably,
specious, insincere; taken also with *little* to mean "seemingly small."
202. **pieced,** added.   207. **stranger'd,** estranged.   209. **Election . . .
up,** choice comes to no decision.   212. **make such a stray,** stray so far.
223. **monsters,** makes monstrous.   **fore-vouch'd,** hitherto affirmed.

224. **taint,** decay.   234. **still-soliciting,** ever-begging.   242. **regards,**
considerations.   261. **waterish,** well-watered (with rivers); used contemptuously, water being the symbol of fickleness.   262. **unprized,**
not appreciated, or priceless.   264. **here . . . where,** used as nouns.
275. **professed,** i.e., full of professions (avowals).

Reg. Prescribe not us our duties.

Gon.   Let your study
Be to content your lord, who hath received you   280
At fortune's alms. You have obedience scanted,
And well are worth the want that you have wanted.

Cor. Time shall unfold what plaited cunning hides:
Who cover faults, at last shame them derides.
Well may you prosper!

France.   Come, my fair Cordelia.
                    [*Exeunt France and Cordelia.*

Gon. Sister, it is not a little I have to say of what
most nearly appertains to us both. I think our father
will hence to-night.

Reg. That's most certain, and with you; next
month with us.   290

Gon. You see how full of changes his age is; the observation we have made of it hath not been little: he
always loved our sister most; and with what poor
judgement he hath now cast her off appears too
grossly.

Reg. 'Tis the infirmity of his age: yet he hath ever
but slenderly known himself.   297

Gon. The best and soundest of his time hath been
but rash; then must we look to receive from his age,
not alone the imperfections of long-engraffed condition, but therewithal the unruly waywardness that
infirm and choleric years bring with them.

Reg. Such unconstant starts are we like to have
from him as this of Kent's banishment.

Gon. There is further compliment of leave-taking
between France and him. Pray you, let's hit together: if our father carry authority with such dispositions as he bears, this last surrender of his will but
offend us.   310

Reg. We shall further think on't.

Gon. We must do something, and i' the heat. [*Exeunt.*

SCENE II. *The Earl of Gloucester's castle.*

Enter EDMUND, *with a letter.*

Edm. Thou, nature, art my goddess; to thy law
My services are bound. Wherefore should I
Stand in the plague of custom, and permit
The curiosity of nations to deprive me,
For that I am some twelve or fourteen moonshines
Lag of a brother? Why bastard? wherefore base?
When my dimensions are as well compact,
My mind as generous, and my shape as true,
As honest madam's issue? Why brand they us
With base? with baseness? bastardy? base, base?   10
Who, in the lusty stealth of nature, take
More composition and fierce quality
Than doth, within a dull, stale, tired bed,
Go to the creating a whole tribe of fops,
Got 'tween asleep and wake? Well, then,
Legitimate Edgar, I must have your land:

Our father's love is to the bastard Edmund
As to the legitimate: fine word,—legitimate!
Well, my legitimate, if this letter speed,
And my invention thrive, Edmund the base   20
Shall top the legitimate. I grow; I prosper:
Now, gods, stand up for bastards!

Enter GLOUCESTER.

Glou. Kent banish'd thus! and France in choler
     parted!
And the king gone to-night! subscribed his power!
Confined to exhibition! All this done
Upon the gad! Edmund, how now! what news?

Edm. So please your lordship, none.
                    [*Putting up the letter.*

Glou. Why so earnestly seek you to put up that
     letter?

Edm. I know no news, my lord.

Glou. What paper were you reading?   30

Edm. Nothing, my lord.

Glou. No? What needed, then, that terrible dispatch of it into your pocket? the quality of nothing
hath not such need to hide itself. Let's see: come, if it
be nothing, I shall not need spectacles.

Edm. I beseech you, sir, pardon me: it is a letter
from my brother, that I have not all o'er-read; and
for so much as I have perused, I find it not fit for
your o'er-looking.   40

Glou. Give me the letter, sir.

Edm. I shall offend, either to detain or give it. The
contents, as in part I understand them, are to blame.

Glou. Let's see, let's see.

Edm. I hope, for my brother's justification, he
wrote this but as an essay or taste of my virtue.

Glou. [*Reads*] 'This policy and reverence of age
makes the world bitter to the best of our times; keeps
our fortunes from us till our oldness cannot relish
them. I begin to find an idle and fond bondage in the
oppression of aged tyranny; who sways, not as it hath
power, but as it is suffered. Come to me, that of this
I may speak more. If our father would sleep till I
waked him, you should enjoy half his revenue for
ever, and live the beloved of your brother,
                                        EDGAR.'
Hum—conspiracy!—'Sleep till I waked him,—you
should enjoy half his revenue,'—My son Edgar! Had
he a hand to write this? a heart and brain to breed it
in?—When came this to you? who brought it?   62

Edm. It was not brought me, my lord; there's the
cunning of it; I found it thrown in at the casement of
my closet.

Glou. You know the character to be your brother's?

Edm. If the matter were good, my lord, I durst
swear it were his; but, in respect of that, I would fain
think it were not.   70

Glou. It is his.

Edm. It is his hand, my lord; but I hope his heart is
not in the contents.

King Lear
ACT I : SC I

986

---

281. **At,** i.e., priced at. 282. **well . . . wanted,** well deserve the lack
of affection which you yourself have shown; *want* may, however, refer
to her dowry. 283. **plaited,** folded, insincere. 295. **grossly,** obviously.
298. **time,** lifetime. 301. **long-engraffed condition,** long-implanted
habit. Goneril's case against Lear, which seems in this explanatory
scene to be Shakespeare's, is (1) that "he hath ever but slenderly
known himself" (self-knowledge was a Renaissance ideal), (2) that he
has the infirmity of old age, and (3) that he is habituated to self-
indulgence. 308. **hit,** agree. 310. **offend,** harm, injure. 312. **i' the
heat,** i.e., while the iron is hot.

SCENE II.   1. **nature,** natural force; also, course of life undisciplined
by culture.   3. **plague,** vexatious injustice. Warburton suggested
plage meaning "place," "boundary."   4. **curiosity,** nicety, fastidious-
ness.   5. **moonshines,** months.   6. **Lag of,** later than.   7. **dimensions,**
bodily parts or proportions.   **compact,** knit together.   24. **subscribed,**
surrendered.   25. **exhibition,** allowance.   26. **Upon the gad,** suddenly,
as if pricked by a gad.   32. **terrible,** terrified.   47. **essay,** assay, trial.
48. **policy and reverence of,** i.e., policy of reverencing; hendiadys, a
construction common in *King Lear.*   65. **closet,** private room.   77.
declining, becoming feeble.   82. **detested,** detestable.   89. **where,**

Glou. Hath he never heretofore sounded you in this business?

Edm. Never, my lord: but I have heard him oft maintain it to be fit, that, sons at perfect age, and fathers declining, the father should be as ward to the son, and the son manage his revenue.   79

Glou. O villain, villain! His very opinion in the letter! Abhorred villain! Unnatural, detested, brutish villain! worse than brutish! Go, sirrah, seek him; I'll apprehend him: abominable villain! Where is he?

Edm. I do not well know, my lord. If it shall please you to suspend your indignation against my brother till you can derive from him better testimony of his intent, you shall run a certain course; where, if you violently proceed against him, mistaking his purpose, it would make a great gap in your own honour, and shake in pieces the heart of his obedience. I dare pawn down my life for him, that he hath wrote this to feel my affection to your honour, and to no further pretence of danger.   95

Glou. Think you so?

Edm. If your honour judge it meet, I will place you where you shall hear us confer of this, and by an auricular assurance have your satisfaction; and that without any further delay than this very evening.   101

Glou. He cannot be such a monster—

Edm. Nor is not, sure.

Glou. To his father, that so tenderly and entirely loves him. Heaven and earth! Edmund, seek him out; wind me into him, I pray you: frame the business after your own wisdom. I would unstate myself, to be in a due resolution.

Edm. I will seek him, sir, presently; convey the business as I shall find means, and acquaint you withal.   111

Glou. These late eclipses in the sun and moon portend no good to us: though the wisdom of nature can reason it thus and thus, yet nature finds itself scourged by the sequent effects: love cools, friendship falls off, brothers divide: in cities, mutinies; in countries, discord; in palaces, treason; and the bond cracked 'twixt son and father. This villain of mine comes under the prediction; there's son against father: the king falls from bias of nature; there's father against child. We have seen the best of our time: machinations, hollowness, treachery, and all ruinous disorders, follow us disquietly to our graves. Find out this villain, Edmund; it shall lose thee nothing; do it carefully. And the noble and true-hearted Kent banished! his offence, honesty! 'Tis strange.   [*Exit.* 127

Edm. This is the excellent foppery of the world, that, when we are sick in fortune,—often the surfeit of our own behaviour,—we make guilty of our disasters the sun, the moon, and the stars: as if we were villains by necessity; fools by heavenly compulsion; knaves, thieves, and treachers, by spherical predominance; drunkards, liars, and adulterers, by an enforced obedience of planetary influence; and all that we are evil in, by a divine thrusting on: an admirable evasion of whoremaster man, to lay his goatish disposition to the charge of a star! My father compounded with my mother under the dragon's tail; and my nativity was under Ursa major; so that it follows, I am rough and lecherous. Tut, I should have been that I am, had the maidenliest star in the firmament twinkled on my bastardizing. Edgar—

Enter EDGAR.

and pat he comes like the catastrophe of the old comedy: my cue is villanous melancholy, with a sigh like Tom o' Bedlam. O, these eclipses do portend these divisions! fa, sol, la, mi.

Edg. How now, brother Edmund! what serious contemplation are you in?   151

Edm. I am thinking, brother, of a prediction I read this other day, what should follow these eclipses.

Edg. Do you busy yourself about that?

Edm. I promise you, the effects he writes of succeed unhappily; as of unnaturalness between the child and the parent; death, dearth, dissolutions of ancient amities; divisions in state, menaces and maledictions against king and nobles; needless diffidences, banishment of friends, dissipation of cohorts, nuptial breaches, and I know not what.   163

Edg. How long have you been a sectary astronomical?

Edm. Come, come; when saw you my father last?

Edg. Why, the night gone by.

Edm. Spake you with him?

Edg. Ay, two hours together.   170

Edm. Parted you in good terms? Found you no displeasure in him by word or countenance?

Edg. None at all.

Edm. Bethink yourself wherein you may have offended him: and at my entreaty forbear his presence till some little time hath qualified the heat of his displeasure; which at this instant so rageth in him, that with the mischief of your person it would scarcely allay.

Edg. Some villain hath done me wrong.   180

Edm. That's my fear. I pray you, have a continent forbearance till the speed of his rage goes slower; and, as I say, retire with me to my lodging, from whence I will fitly bring you to hear my lord speak: pray ye, go; there's my key: if you do stir abroad, go armed.

Edg. Armed, brother!

Edm. Brother, I advise you to the best; go armed: I am no honest man if there be any good meaning towards you: I have told you what I have seen and heard; but faintly, nothing like the image and horror of it: pray you, away.

Edg. Shall I hear from you anon?

Edm. I do serve you in this business.   [*Exit Edgar.*
A credulous father! and a brother noble,
Whose nature is so far from doing harms,

whereas. 95. **pretence,** intention, purpose. 106. **wind me into him,** insinuate yourself into his confidence; *me* is an ethical dative. 108. **unstate myself,** give up my position and dignity. **due resolution,** actual certainty. 109. **convey,** manage with secrecy. 112-127. **These . . . strange.** The fact that there were eclipses of the sun and moon in the autumn of 1605 has been regarded as an indication of the date of the play; also the references to discord, mutinies, and treason have been thought to refer to the Gunpowder Plot (Nov. 5, 1605). 114. **wisdom of nature,** natural science. 115. **sequent,** consequent, following. 128. **foppery,** foolishness. 131. **disasters,** unfavorable aspects.

134. **treachers,** traitors. **spherical predominance,** ascendancy of planets. Edmund's denial of planetary influence must be set down as a sort of religious infidelity. 148. **Tom o' Bedlam.** See II, iii, 14, note below. 157. **succeed,** come to pass. 161. **diffidences,** distrust of others. 162. **dissipation of cohorts,** breaking up of military organizations; probably corrupt; *disputation* or *dissension of consorts* has been suggested. 164. **sectary astronomical,** student of astrology. 178. **mischief of,** harm to. 179. **allay,** be allayed. 182. **continent,** restraining.

That he suspects none; on whose foolish honesty
My practices ride easy! I see the business.
Let me, if not by birth, have lands by wit:
All with me 's meet that I can fashion fit.   [*Exit.* 200

SCENE III. *The Duke of Albany's palace.*

Enter GONERIL, *and* OSWALD, *her steward.*

Gon. Did my father strike my gentleman for chiding
of his fool?
Osw. Yes, madam.
Gon. By day and night he wrongs me; every hour
He flashes into one gross crime or other,
That sets us all at odds: I'll not endure it:
His knights grow riotous, and himself upbraids us
On every trifle. When he returns from hunting,
I will not speak with him; say I am sick:
If you come slack of former services,
You shall do well; the fault of it I'll answer.   10
Osw. He 's coming, madam; I hear him.
                                        [*Horns within.*
Gon. Put on what weary negligence you please,
You and your fellows; I 'ld have it come to question:
If he dislike it, let him to our sister,
Whose mind and mine, I know, in that are one,
Not to be over-ruled. Idle old man,
That still would manage those authorities
That he hath given away! Now, by my life,
Old fools are babes again; and must be used
With checks as flatteries,—when they are seen
    abused.   20
Remember what I tell you.
Osw.   Well, madam.
Gon. And let his knights have colder looks among
    you;
What grows of it, no matter; advise your fellows so:
I would breed from hence occasions, and I shall
That I may speak: I'll write straight to my sister,
To hold my very course. Prepare for dinner. [*Exeunt.*

SCENE IV. *A hall in the same.*

Enter KENT, *disguised.*

Kent. If but as well I other accents borrow,
That can my speech defuse, my good intent
May carry through itself to that full issue
For which I razed my likeness. Now, banish'd Kent,
If thou canst serve where thou dost stand condemn'd,
So may it come, thy master, whom thou lovest,
Shall find thee full of labours.

Horns within. Enter LEAR, Knights, *and* Attendants.

Lear. Let me not stay a jot for dinner; go get it
ready. [*Exit an Attendant.*] How now! what art thou? 10
Kent. A man, sir.
Lear. What dost thou profess? what wouldst thou
with us?

Kent. I do profess to be no less than I seem; to serve
him truly that will put me in trust; to love him that is
honest; to converse with him that is wise, and says
little; to fear judgement; to fight when I cannot
choose; and to eat no fish.
Lear. What art thou?
Kent. A very honest-hearted fellow, and as poor as
the king.   21
Lear. If thou be as poor for a subject as he is for a
king, thou art poor enough. What wouldst thou?
Kent. Service.
Lear. Who wouldst thou serve?
Kent. You.
Lear. Dost thou know me, fellow?
Kent. No, sir; but you have that in your counte-
nance which I would fain call master.   30
Lear. What 's that?
Kent. Authority.
Lear. What services canst thou do?
Kent. I can keep honest counsel, ride, run, mar a
curious tale in telling it, and deliver a plain message
bluntly: that which ordinary men are fit for, I am
qualified in; and the best of me is diligence.
Lear. How old art thou?   39
Kent. Not so young, sir, to love a woman for singing,
nor so old to dote on her for any thing: I have years
on my back forty eight.
Lear. Follow me; thou shalt serve me: if I like thee
no worse after dinner, I will not part from thee yet.
Dinner, ho, dinner! Where 's my knave? my fool? Go
you, and call my fool hither.   [*Exit an Attendant.*

Enter OSWALD.

You, you, sirrah, where 's my daughter?
Osw. So please you,—   [*Exit.*
Lear. What says the fellow there? Call the clotpoll
back. [*Exit a Knight.*] Where 's my fool, ho? I think
the world 's asleep.   52

Re-enter Knight.

How now! where 's that mongrel?
Knight. He says, my lord, your daughter is not well.
Lear. Why came not the slave back to me when I
called him?
Knight. Sir, he answered me in the roundest manner, he would not.
Lear. He would not!   60
Knight. My lord, I know not what the matter is;
but, to my judgement, your highness is not entertained with that ceremonious affection as you were
wont; there 's a great abatement of kindness appears
as well in the general dependants as in the duke himself also and your daughter.
Lear. Ha! sayest thou so?
Knight. I beseech you, pardon me, my lord, if I be
mistaken; for my duty cannot be silent when I think
your highness wronged.   71
Lear. Thou but rememberest me of mine own conception: I have perceived a most faint neglect of late;
which I have rather blamed as mine own jealous

SCENE III. 16. **Idle,** foolish, silly. 20. **With . . . abused.** The line,
probably corrupt, yields a sort of meaning if one understands *as* to
mean "as well as," *they* to refer to *Old fools,* and *abused* to mean "deceived" or "misguided." 24. **breed from hence occasions.** One sees in
Goneril greater initiative than in Regan.
SCENE IV. 2. **defuse,** confuse; hence, disguise. 4. **razed,** erased.
12. **What . . . profess?** What is thy profession? 18. **eat no fish.**
Warburton's explanation is usually followed: Roman Catholics, who

observed the custom of eating fish on Fridays, were thought of as
enemies of the government. 51. **clotpoll,** blockhead. 72. **rememberest,** remindest. 74. **faint,** slight, or indifferent, half-hearted. 75.
jealous curiosity, overscrupulous regard for his own dignity. 76.
pretence, intention, purpose. 92. **bandy,** strike a ball to and fro, as in
tennis; here figurative, give and take. 95. **football player.** Football
was a rough, dangerous, public sport without organization or officials,
and under statutory ban; it was played in the streets by the worst

curiosity than as a very pretence and purpose of unkindness: I will look further into 't. But where 's my fool? I have not seen him this two days.

Knight. Since my young lady 's going into France, sir, the fool hath much pined away.

Lear. No more of that; I have noted it well. Go you, and tell my daughter I would speak with her. [*Exit an Attendant.*] Go you, call hither my fool. 80

[*Exit an Attendant.*

Re-enter OSWALD.

O, you sir, you, come you hither, sir: who am I, sir?

Osw. My lady's father.

Lear. 'My lady's father'! my lord's knave: you whoreson dog! you slave! you cur!

Osw. I am none of these, my lord; I beseech your pardon. 91

Lear. Do you bandy looks with me, you rascal?

[*Striking him.*

Osw. I'll not be struck, my lord.

Kent. Nor tripped neither, you base foot-ball player.

[*Tripping up his heels.*

Lear. I thank thee, fellow; thou servest me, and I'll love thee.

Kent. Come, sir, arise, away! I'll teach you differences: away, away! If you will measure your lubber's length again, tarry: but away! go to; have you wisdom? so. [*Pushes Oswald out.* 102

Lear. Now, my friendly knave, I thank thee: there 's earnest of thy service. [*Giving Kent money.*

Enter Fool.

Fool. Let me hire him too: here 's my coxcomb.

[*Offering Kent his cap.*

Lear. How now, my pretty knave! how dost thou?

Fool. Sirrah, you were best take my coxcomb.

Kent. Why, fool? 110

Fool. Why, for taking one's part that 's out of favour: nay, an thou canst not smile as the wind sits, thou 'lt catch cold shortly: there, take my coxcomb: why, this fellow has banished two on 's daughters, and did the third a blessing against his will; if thou follow him, thou must needs wear my coxcomb. How now, nuncle! Would I had two coxcombs and two daughters!

Lear. Why, my boy? 119

Fool. If I gave them all my living, I 'ld keep my coxcombs myself. There 's mine; beg another of thy daughters.

Lear. Take heed, sirrah; the whip.

Fool. Truth 's a dog must to kennel; he must be whipped out, when Lady the brach may stand by the fire and stink.

Lear. A pestilent gall to me!

Fool. Sirrah, I'll teach thee a speech.

Lear. Do.

Fool. Mark it, nuncle: 130

   Have more than thou showest,
   Speak less than thou knowest,
   Lend less than thou owest,

   Ride more than thou goest,
   Learn more than thou trowest,
   Set less than thou throwest;
   Leave thy drink and thy whore,
   And keep in-a-door,
   And thou shalt have more
   Than two tens to a score. 140

Kent. This is nothing, fool.

Fool. Then 'tis like the breath of an unfee'd lawyer; you gave me nothing for 't. Can you make no use of nothing, nuncle?

Lear. Why, no, boy; nothing can be made out of nothing.

Fool. [*To Kent*] Prithee, tell him, so much the rent of his land comes to: he will not believe a fool.

Lear. A bitter fool! 150

Fool. Dost thou know the difference, my boy, between a bitter fool and a sweet fool?

Lear. No, lad; teach me.

Fool. That lord that counsell'd thee
   To give away thy land,
   Come place him here by me,
   Do thou for him stand:
   The sweet and bitter fool
   Will presently appear;
   The one in motley here, 160
   The other found out there.

Lear. Dost thou call me fool, boy?

Fool. All thy other titles thou hast given away; that thou wast born with.

Kent. This is not altogether fool, my lord.

Fool. No, faith, lords and great men will not let me; if I had a monopoly out, they would have part on 't: and ladies too, they will not let me have all fool to myself; they'll be snatching. Give me an egg, nuncle, and I'll give thee two crowns. 171

Lear. What two crowns shall they be?

Fool. Why, after I have cut the egg i' the middle, and eat up the meat, the two crowns of the egg. When thou clovest thy crown i' the middle, and gavest away both parts, thou borest thy ass on thy back o'er the dirt: thou hadst little wit in thy bald crown, when thou gavest thy golden one away. If I speak like myself in this, let him be whipped that first finds it so. 180

[*Singing*] Fools had ne'er less wit in a year;
   For wise men are grown foppish,
   They know not how their wits to wear,
   Their manners are so apish.

Lear. When were you wont to be so full of songs, sirrah?

Fool. I have used it, nuncle, ever since thou madest thy daughters thy mother: for when thou gavest them the rod, and put'st down thine own breeches, 190

[*Singing*] Then they for sudden joy did weep,
   And I for sorrow sung,
   That such a king should play bo-peep,
   And go the fools among.

Prithee, nuncle, keep a schoolmaster that can teach thy fool to lie: I would fain learn to lie.

element of the population. 105. **coxcomb,** fool's cap. 117. **nuncle,** contraction of "mine uncle," customary address of the licensed fool to his superior. 120. **living,** property. 125. **brach,** a female hound. 131. **showest,** seemest to have. 134. **goest,** i.e., on foot. 136. **Set . . . throwest,** stake less at dice than you have a chance to throw, i.e., don't bet all you can. 138. **in-a-door,** at home. 154. **That lord.** A lord, Skalliger, in the old play of *King Leir* is apparently referred to; no such advice is given Lear in this play. 160. **motley,** the particolored dress

of the fool. 167. **monopoly.** This allusion would be well understood, since the granting of monopolies by King James was a current abuse. **out,** taken out, granted. 182. **foppish,** foolish. 191-194. **Then . . . among.** These lines, and probably others below, are no doubt taken from old songs.

Lear. An you lie, sirrah, we'll have you whipped. 198

Fool. I marvel what kin thou and thy daughters are: they'll have me whipped for speaking true, thou 'lt have me whipped for lying; and sometimes I am whipped for holding my peace. I had rather be any kind o' thing than a fool: and yet I would not be thee, nuncle; thou hast pared thy wit o' both sides, and left nothing i' the middle: here comes one o' the parings.

Enter GONERIL.

Lear. How now, daughter! what makes that frontlet on? Methinks you are too much of late i' the frown. 209

Fool. Thou wast a pretty fellow when thou hadst no need to care for her frowning; now thou art an O without a figure: I am better than thou art now; I am a fool, thou art nothing. [*To Gon.*] Yes, forsooth, I will hold my tongue; so your face bids me, though you say nothing. Mum, mum,

　　He that keeps nor crust nor crum,
　　Weary of all, shall want some.

[*Pointing to Lear*] That 's a shealed peascod.

Gon. Not only, sir, this your all-licensed fool, 220
But other of your insolent retinue
Do hourly carp and quarrel; breaking forth
In rank and not-to-be-endured riots. Sir,
I had thought, by making this well known unto you,
To have found a safe redress; but now grow fearful,
By what yourself too late have spoke and done,
That you protect this course, and put it on
By your allowance; which if you should, the fault
Would not 'scape censure, nor the redresses sleep,
Which, in the tender of a wholesome weal, 230
Might in their working do you that offence,
Which else were shame, that then necessity
Will call discreet proceeding.

Fool. For, you know, nuncle,

　　The hedge-sparrow fed the cuckoo so long,
　　That it had it head bit off by it young.

So, out went the candle, and we were left darkling.

Lear. Are you our daughter?

Gon. Come, sir,
I would you would make use of that good wisdom, 240
Whereof I know you are fraught; and put away
These dispositions, that of late transform you
From what you rightly are.

Fool. May not an ass know when the cart draws the horse? Whoop, Jug! I love thee.

Lear. Doth any here know me? This is not Lear:
Doth Lear walk thus? speak thus? Where are his eyes?
Either his notion weakens, his discernings
Are lethargied—Ha! waking? 'tis not so.
Who is it that can tell me who I am? 250

Fool. Lear's shadow.

Lear. I would learn that; for, by the marks of sovereignty, knowledge, and reason, I should be false persuaded I had daughters.

Fool. Which they will make an obedient father.

Lear. Your name, fair gentlewoman?

Gon. This admiration, sir, is much o' the savour

Of other your new pranks. I do beseech you
To understand my purposes aright: 260
As you are old and reverend, you should be wise.
Here do you keep a hundred knights and squires;
Men so disorder'd, so debosh'd and bold,
That this our court, infected with their manners,
Shows like a riotous inn: epicurism and lust
Make it more like a tavern or a brothel
Than a graced palace. The shame itself doth speak
For instant remedy: be then desired
By her, that else will take the thing she begs,
A little to disquantity your train; 270
And the remainder, that shall still depend,
To be such men as may besort your age,
And know themselves and you.

Lear.　　　　　　　Darkness and devils!
Saddle my horses; call my train together.
Degenerate bastard! I'll not trouble thee:
Yet have I left a daughter.

Gon. You strike my people; and your disorder'd rabble
Make servants of their betters.

Enter ALBANY.

Lear. Woe, that too late repents,—[*To Alb.*] O, sir, are you come?
Is it your will? Speak, sir. Prepare my horses. 280
Ingratitude, thou marble-hearted fiend,
More hideous when thou show'st thee in a child
Than the sea-monster!

Alb.　　　　　　Pray, sir, be patient.

Lear. [*To Gon.*] Detested kite! thou liest:
My train are men of choice and rarest parts,
That all particulars of duty know,
And in the most exact regard support
The worships of their name. O most small fault,
How ugly didst thou in Cordelia show!
That, like an engine, wrench'd my frame of nature 290
From the fix'd place; drew from my heart all love,
And added to the gall. O Lear, Lear, Lear!
Beat at this gate, that let thy folly in, [*Striking his head.*
And thy dear judgement out! Go, go, my people.

Alb. My lord, I am guiltless, as I am ignorant
Of what hath moved you.

Lear.　　　　　　It may be so, my lord.
Hear, nature, hear; dear goddess, hear!
Suspend thy purpose, if thou didst intend
To make this creature fruitful!
Into her womb convey sterility! 300
Dry up in her the organs of increase;
And from her derogate body never spring
A babe to honour her! If she must teem,
Create her child of spleen; that it may live,
And be a thwart disnatured torment to her!
Let it stamp wrinkles in her brow of youth;
With cadent tears fret channels in her cheeks;
Turn all her mother's pains and benefits
To laughter and contempt; that she may feel
How sharper than a serpent's tooth it is 310

208. **frontlet,** a band worn on the forehead; forehead; here, frowning visage. 212. **O without a figure,** cipher of no value unless joined to a figure. 219. **shealed peascod,** shelled pea pod. 221. **other,** others. 227. **put it on,** encourage it. 228. **allowance,** approval. 229. **nor the redresses sleep,** punishment for the riotous conduct of Lear's attendants will be inflicted. 230. **tender . . . weal,** preservation of the peace of the state. 232-233. **necessity . . . proceeding,** i.e., everyone will justify her because of the necessity of the action. 236. **it.** The second and third *its* are possessives. 237. **darkling,** in the dark. 241. **fraught,**

filled. 245. **Whoop, Jug! I love thee,** regarded as a quotation from an old song; used by the Fool to cover up his impertinence. *Jug,* probably, Joan. 248. **notion,** intellectual power. 255. **Which,** whom. 263. **debosh'd,** debauched. 265. **epicurism,** luxury. 267. **graced,** honorable. 270. **disquantity,** diminish. 271. **depend,** be dependents. 272. **besort,** befit. 283. **sea-monster,** possible allusion to the hippopotamus, reputed in Egyptian mythology to be a monster of ingratitude; the whale has also been suggested. W. J. Craig suggests that no particular monster is meant, but that the allusion is to the monsters of classical

To have a thankless child! Away, away!   [*Exit.*
  Alb. Now, gods that we adore, whereof comes this?
  Gon. Never afflict yourself to know the cause;
But let his disposition have that scope
That dotage gives it.

Re-enter LEAR.

  Lear. What, fifty of my followers at a clap!
Within a fortnight!
  Alb.   What's the matter, sir?
  Lear. I'll tell thee: [*To Gon.*] Life and death! I am
    ashamed
That thou hast power to shake my manhood thus;
That these hot tears, which break from me perforce,
Should make thee worth them. Blasts and fogs upon
    thee!   321
The untented woundings of a father's curse
Pierce every sense about thee! Old fond eyes,
Beweep this cause again, I'll pluck ye out,
And cast you, with the waters that you lose,
To temper clay. Yea, is it come to this?
Let it be so: yet have I left a daughter,
Who, I am sure, is kind and comfortable:
When she shall hear this of thee, with her nails
She'll flay thy wolvish visage. Thou shalt find   330
That I'll resume the shape which thou dost think
I have cast off for ever: thou shalt, I warrant thee.
    [*Exeunt Lear, Kent, and Attendants.*
  Gon. Do you mark that, my lord?
  Alb. I cannot be so partial, Goneril,
To the great love I bear you,—
  Gon. Pray you, content. What, Oswald, ho!
[*To the Fool*] You, sir, more knave than fool, after your
    master.
  Fool. Nuncle Lear, nuncle Lear, tarry and take the
fool with thee.
      A fox, when one has caught her,   340
      And such a daughter,
      Should sure to the slaughter,
      If my cap would buy a halter:
      So the fool follows after.   [*Exit.*
  Gon. This man hath had good counsel:—a hundred
    knights!
'Tis politic and safe to let him keep
At point a hundred knights: yes, that, on every dream,
Each buzz, each fancy, each complaint, dislike,
He may enguard his dotage with their powers,
And hold our lives in mercy. Oswald, I say!   350
  Alb. Well, you may fear too far.
  Gon.   Safer than trust too far:
Let me still take away the harms I fear,
Not fear still to be taken: I know his heart.
What he hath utter'd I have writ my sister:
If she sustain him and his hundred knights,
When I have show'd the unfitness,—

Re-enter OSWALD.

      How now, Oswald!
What, have you writ that letter to my sister?

  Osw. Yes, madam.
  Gon. Take you some company, and away to horse:
Inform her full of my particular fear;   360
And thereto add such reasons of your own
As may compact it more. Get you gone;
And hasten your return. [*Exit Oswald.*] No, no, my
    lord,
This milky gentleness and course of yours
Though I condemn not, yet, under pardon,
You are much more attask'd for want of wisdom
Than praised for harmful mildness.
  Alb. How far your eyes may pierce I cannot tell:
Striving to better, oft we mar what's well.
  Gon. Nay, then—   370
  Alb. Well, well; the event.   [*Exeunt.*

————————

SCENE V. *Court before the same.*

Enter LEAR, KENT, *and* Fool.

  Lear. Go you before to Gloucester with these letters.
Acquaint my daughter no further with any thing you
know than comes from her demand out of the letter.
If your diligence be not speedy, I shall be there afore
you.
  Kent. I will not sleep, my lord, till I have delivered
your letter.   [*Exit.*
  Fool. If a man's brains were in 's heels, were 't not
in danger of kibes?
  Lear. Ay, boy.   10
  Fool. Then, I prithee, be merry; thy wit shall ne'er
go slip-shod.
  Lear. Ha, ha, ha!
  Fool. Shalt see thy other daughter will use thee
kindly; for though she's as like this as a crab's like
an apple, yet I can tell what I can tell.
  Lear. Why, what canst thou tell, my boy?
  Fool. She will taste as like this as a crab does to a
crab. Thou canst tell why one's nose stands i' the
middle on 's face?   20
  Lear. No.
  Fool. Why, to keep one's eyes of either side 's nose;
that what a man cannot smell out, he may spy into.
  Lear. I did her wrong—
  Fool. Canst tell how an oyster makes his shell?
  Lear. No.
  Fool. Nor I neither; but I can tell why a snail has a
house.   30
  Lear. Why?
  Fool. Why, to put his head in; not to give it away to
his daughters, and leave his horns without a case.
  Lear. I will forget my nature. So kind a father! Be
my horses ready?
  Fool. Thy asses are gone about 'em. The reason why
the seven stars are no more than seven is a pretty
reason.
  Lear. Because they are not eight?   40
  Fool. Yes, indeed: thou wouldst make a good fool.

---

mythology. **287. in . . . regard,** with extreme care. **288. worships,**
honors. **290. engine,** possibly machines for razing houses. **297. nature
. . . goddess.** This is the first of Lear's terrible curses. **302. derogate,**
debased. **305. thwart,** contrary. **disnatured,** without natural affection. **307. cadent,** falling. **322. untented,** not cleansed with lint, and
therefore liable to fester. **328. comfortable,** willing to comfort. **347.
At point,** under arms. **348. buzz,** idle rumor. **349. enguard,** surround
with a guard. **353. taken,** overtaken (by the *harms*). **362. compact,**
confirm. **364. This . . . yours,** the cowardly weakness of your course.

366. attask'd, taken to task, blamed. **371. the event,** time will show.
  SCENE V. **9. kibes,** chilblains, or ulcerated sores on the heels. **12.
slip-shod,** in slippers. There are no brains, thinks the Fool, in Lear's
heels when they are on their way to visit Regan. **15. kindly,** double
sense: according to filial nature and according to her own nature. **16.
a crab's . . . apple,** seems proverbial for "a crab-apple's an apple."
25. her. Lear again thinks of Cordelia. **38. seven stars,** the Pleiades.

Lear. To take 't again perforce! Monster ingratitude!

Fool. If thou wert my fool, nuncle, I 'ld have thee beaten for being old before thy time.

Lear. How 's that?

Fool. Thou shouldst not have been old till thou hadst been wise.

Lear. O, let me not be mad, not mad, sweet heaven! Keep me in temper: I would not be mad! 51

Enter Gentleman.

How now! are the horses ready?

Gent. Ready, my lord.

Lear. Come, boy.

Fool. She that 's a maid now, and laughs at my departure,
Shall not be a maid long, unless things be cut shorter.
[*Exeunt.*

ACT II.

SCENE I. *The Earl of Gloucester's castle.*

Enter EDMUND, *and* CURAN *meets him.*

Edm. Save thee, Curan.

Cur. And you, sir. I have been with your father, and given him notice that the Duke of Cornwall and Regan his duchess will be here with him this night.

Edm. How comes that?

Cur. Nay, I know not. You have heard of the news abroad; I mean the whispered ones, for they are yet but ear-bussing arguments?

Edm. Not I: pray you, what are they? 10

Cur. Have you heard of no likely wars toward, 'twixt the Dukes of Cornwall and Albany?

Edm. Not a word.

Cur. You may do, then, in time. Fare you well, sir.
[*Exit.*

Edm. The duke be here to-night? The better! best!
This weaves itself perforce into my business.
My father hath set guard to take my brother;
And I have one thing, of a queasy question,
Which I must act: briefness and fortune, work! 20
Brother, a word; descend: brother, I say!

Enter EDGAR.

My father watches: O sir, fly this place;
Intelligence is given where you are hid;
You have now the good advantage of the night:
Have you not spoken 'gainst the Duke of Cornwall?
He 's coming hither; now, i' the night, i' the haste,
And Regan with him: have you nothing said
Upon his party 'gainst the Duke of Albany?
Advise yourself.

Edg.   I am sure on 't, not a word.

Edm. I hear my father coming: pardon me; 30

In cunning I must draw my sword upon you:
Draw; seem to defend yourself; now quit you well.
Yield: come before my father. Light, ho, here!
Fly, brother. Torches, torches! So, farewell.
[*Exit Edgar.*
Some blood drawn on me would beget opinion
[*Wounds his arm.*
Of my more fierce endeavour: I have seen drunkards
Do more than this in sport. Father, father!
Stop, stop! No help?

Enter GLOUCESTER, *and* Servants *with torches.*

Glou. Now, Edmund, where 's the villain? 39

Edm. Here stood he in the dark, his sharp sword out,
Mumbling of wicked charms, conjuring the moon
To stand auspicious mistress,—

Glou.   But where is he?

Edm. Look, sir, I bleed.

Glou.   Where is the villain, Edmund?

Edm. Fled this way, sir. When by no means he could—

Glou. Pursue him, ho! Go after. [*Exeunt some Servants.*] By no means what?

Edm. Persuade me to the murder of your lordship;
But that I told him, the revenging gods
'Gainst parricides did all their thunders bend;
Spoke, with how manifold and strong a bond
The child was bound to the father; sir, in fine, 50
Seeing how loathly opposite I stood
To his unnatural purpose, in fell motion,
With his prepared sword, he charges home
My unprovided body, lanced mine arm:
But when he saw my best alarum'd spirits,
Bold in the quarrel's right, roused to the encounter,
Or whether gasted by the noise I made,
Full suddenly he fled.

Glou.   Let him fly far:
Not in this land shall he remain uncaught;
And found—dispatch. The noble duke my master, 60
My worthy arch and patron, comes to-night:
By his authority I will proclaim it,
That he which finds him shall deserve our thanks,
Bringing the murderous caitiff to the stake;
He that conceals him, death.

Edm. When I dissuaded him from his intent,
And found him pight to do it, with curst speech
I threaten'd to discover him: he replied,
'Thou unpossessing bastard! dost thou think,
If I would stand against thee, could the reposure 70
Of any trust, virtue, or worth in thee
Make thy words faith'd? No: what I should deny,—
As this I would; ay, though thou didst produce
My very character,—I 'ld turn it all
To thy suggestion, plot, and damned practice:
And thou must make a dullard of the world,
If they not thought the profits of my death
Were very pregnant and potential spurs

---

50. **let . . . mad.** Lear thus marks his first symptom of coming madness. It will be noted that he thinks of madness as the loss of the even balance of spirits, i.e., temper, and as the forgetting of his nature.
ACT II. SCENE I. 1. **Save thee,** i.e., God save thee. 8. **ear-bussing,** so Q₁; Globe, following F: *ear-kissing*; lightly whispered. 19. **queasy question,** hazardous, or ticklish, nature. 20. **briefness,** promptitude. 28. **Upon his party,** possibly, on his (i.e., Cornwall's) side. This would be confusing; Edmund is credited with making it so in order to frighten Edgar. It may mean, "Have you said nothing about the party Cornwall is forming against Albany?" 29. **Advise yourself,** probably, recollect. 31. **cunning,** pretense. 35. **beget,** create (for me). 51. **loathly**

opposite, loathingly opposed. 52. **fell motion,** deadly thrust. 54. **lanced,** wounded. 55. **best alarum'd,** thoroughly aroused to action as by a trumpet. 57. **gasted,** frightened. 60. **dispatch,** I will dispatch him. 61. **arch,** chief. 64. **caitiff,** so Q₁; Globe, following F: *coward.* **stake,** an allusion to tying prisoners to a stake, or a figure from bear-baiting. 67. **pight,** determined. 69. **unpossessing,** unable to inherit, beggarly. 70. **I would,** I should. **could the reposure,** so Q₁; Globe, following F: *would the reposal.* 72. **faith'd,** believed. 76. **make . . . world,** think the world an idiot. 77. **If . . . thought,** if they had not thought. 79. **Strong and fasten'd,** obdurate and confirmed. 99. **consort,** set, company. 101. **put . . . on,** incited him to. 102. **waste**

To make thee seek it.'

Glou.   Strong and fasten'd villain!
Would he deny his letter? I never got him.   80
                [*Tucket within.*
Hark, the duke's trumpets! I know not why he comes.
All ports I'll bar; the villain shall not 'scape;
The duke must grant me that: besides, his picture
I will send far and near, that all the kingdom
May have due note of him; and of my land,
Loyal and natural boy, I'll work the means
To make thee capable.

Enter CORNWALL, REGAN, *and* Attendants.

Corn. How now, my noble friend! since I came
    hither,
Which I can call but now, I have heard strange news.

Reg. If it be true, all vengeance comes too short   90
Which can pursue the offender. How dost, my lord?

Glou. O, madam, my old heart is crack'd, is crack'd!

Reg. What, did my father's godson seek your life?
He whom my father named? your Edgar?

Glou. O, lady, lady, shame would have it hid!

Reg. Was he not companion with the riotous knights
That tend upon my father?

Glou. I know not, madam: 'tis too bad, too bad.

Edm. Yes, madam, he was of that consort.

Reg. No marvel, then, though he were ill affected :100
'Tis they have put him on the old man's death,
To have the waste and spoil of his revenues.
I have this present evening from my sister
Been well inform'd of them; and with such cautions,
That if they come to sojourn at my house,
I'll not be there.

Corn.   Nor I, assure thee, Regan.
Edmund, I hear that you have shown your father
A child-like office.

Edm.   'Twas my duty, sir.

Glou. He did bewray his practice; and received
This hurt you see, striving to apprehend him.   110

Corn. Is he pursued?

Glou.   Ay, my good lord.

Corn. If he be taken, he shall never more
Be fear'd of doing harm: make your own purpose,
How in my strength you please. For you, Edmund,
Whose virtue and obedience doth this instant
So much commend itself, you shall be ours:
Natures of such deep trust we shall much need;
You we first seize on.

Edm.   I shall serve you, sir,
Truly, however else.

Glou.   For him I thank your grace.

Corn. You know not why we came to visit you,—   120

Reg. Thus out of season, threading dark-eyed night:
Occasions, noble Gloucester, of some poise,
Wherein we must have use of your advice:
Our father he hath writ, so hath our sister,
Of differences, which I least thought it fit

To answer from our home; the several messengers
From hence attend dispatch. Our good old friend,
Lay comforts to your bosom; and bestow
Your needful counsel to our business,
Which craves the instant use.

Glou.   I serve you, madam: 130
Your graces are right welcome.   [*Exeunt.*

SCENE II. *Before Gloucester's castle.*

Enter KENT *and* OSWALD, *severally.*

Osw. Good dawning to thee, friend: art of this
house?

Kent. Ay.

Osw. Where may we set our horses?

Kent. I' the mire.

Osw. Prithee, if thou lovest me, tell me.

Kent. I love thee not.

Osw. Why, then, I care not for thee.

Kent. If I had thee in Lipsbury pinfold, I would
make thee care for me.   10

Osw. Why dost thou use me thus? I know thee not.

Kent. Fellow, I know thee.

Osw. What dost thou know me for?

Kent. A knave; a rascal; an eater of broken meats;
a base, proud, shallow, beggarly, three-suited,
hundred-pound, filthy, worsted-stocking knave; a
lily-livered, action-taking knave, a whoreson, glass-
gazing, superserviceable, finical rogue; one-trunk-inheriting slave; one that wouldst be a bawd, in way of
good service, and art nothing but the composition of
a knave, beggar, coward, pandar, and the son and
heir of a mongrel bitch: one whom I will beat into
clamorous whining, if thou deniest the least syllable of
thy addition.

Osw. Why, what a monstrous fellow art thou, thus
to rail on one that is neither known of thee nor
knows thee!   29

Kent. What a brazen-faced varlet art thou, to deny
thou knowest me! Is it two days ago since I tripped
up thy heels, and beat thee before the king? Draw,
you rogue: for, though it be night, yet the moon
shines; I'll make a sop o' the moonshine of you: draw,
you whoreson cullionly barber-monger, draw.
               [*Drawing his sword.*

Osw. Away! I have nothing to do with thee.   37

Kent. Draw, you rascal: you come with letters
against the king; and take vanity the puppet's part
against the royalty of her father: draw, you rogue, or
I'll so carbonado your shanks: draw, you rascal;
come your ways.

Osw. Help, ho! murder! help!

Kent. Strike, you slave; stand, rogue, stand; you
neat slave, strike.   [*Beating him.*

Osw. Help, ho! murder! murder!   46

King Lear
ACT II : SC II

993

---

and spoil, so Q₁; Globe, following F: *expense and waste.* **109. bewray,**
disclose. **114. in my strength,** by my power and authority. **For,** as
for. **121. threading,** passing through (as thread through the eye of a
needle). **122. poise,** weight, importance. **125. which,** the letter.
127. attend dispatch, wait to be dispatched.
   SCENE II. **9. Lipsbury pinfold.** This phrase is unexplained. *Pinfold*
means "pound for stray animals." Critics have tried to see in it an
allusion to the prize ring; Nares supposes the allusion may be to the
teeth within the pinfold of the lips. **17. three-suited,** probable allusion
to three suits a year allowed to servants. **hundred-pound,** possible
allusion to the minimum property qualification for the status of gentleman; sometimes seen as a reference to James 1's wholesale creation of
knights. **worsted-stocking,** too poor and menial to wear silk stockings.
18. action-taking, settling quarrels by resort to law instead of arms,
cowardly. **19. glass-gazing,** fond of looking in the mirror. **superserviceable,** officious. **20. finical,** excessively particular, probably,
in dress. **one-trunk-inheriting,** possessing effects sufficient for one
trunk only. **35. sop o' the moonshine,** supposed punning allusion
to a dish called "eggs in moonshine." **36. cullionly barber-monger,**
base frequenter of barber shops, fop. **39-40. vanity the puppet's
part.** Vanity was a character in the morality plays. **41. carbonado,**
cut you crosswise like meat for broiling. **45. neat,** foppish.

Enter EDMUND, *with his rapier drawn*, CORNWALL,
  REGAN, GLOUCESTER, *and* Servants.

Edm. How now! What's the matter?

Kent. With you, goodman boy, an you please:
come, I'll flesh ye: come on, young master.

Glou. Weapons! arms! What's the matter here? 51

Corn. Keep peace, upon your lives;
He dies that strikes again. What is the matter?

Reg. The messengers from our sister and the king.

Corn. What is your difference? speak.

Osw. I am scarce in breath, my lord.

Kent. No marvel, you have so bestirred your valour.
You cowardly rascal, nature disclaims in thee: a
tailor made thee. 60

Corn. Thou art a strange fellow: a tailor make a
man?

Kent. Ay, a tailor, sir: a stone-cutter or a painter
could not have made him so ill, though he had been
but two hours at the trade.

Corn. Speak yet, how grew your quarrel?

Osw. This ancient ruffian, sir, whose life I have
spared at suit of his gray beard,— 68

Kent. Thou whoreson zed! thou unnecessary letter!
My lord, if you will give me leave, I will tread this
unbolted villain into mortar, and daub the walls of a
jakes with him. Spare my gray beard, you wagtail?

Corn. Peace, sirrah!
You beastly knave, know you no reverence?

Kent. Yes, sir; but anger hath a privilege.

Corn. Why art thou angry?

Kent. That such a slave as this should wear a sword,
Who wears no honesty. Such smiling rogues as these,
Like rats, oft bite the holy cords a-twain 80
Which are too intrinse t' unloose; smooth every
          passion
That in the natures of their lords rebel;
Bring oil to fire, snow to their colder moods;
Renege, affirm, and turn their halcyon beaks
With every gale and vary of their masters,
Knowing nought, like dogs, but following.
A plague upon your epileptic visage!
Smile you my speeches, as I were a fool?
Goose, if I had you upon Sarum plain,
I 'ld drive ye cackling home to Camelot. 90

Corn. What, art thou mad, old fellow?

Glou. How fell you out? say that.

Kent. No contraries hold more antipathy
Than I and such a knave.

Corn. Why dost thou call him knave? What's his
          offence?

Kent. His countenance likes me not.

Corn. No more, perchance, does mine, nor his, nor
          hers.

Kent. Sir, 'tis my occupation to be plain:
I have seen better faces in my time
Than stands on any shoulder that I see 100

Before me at this instant.

Corn.   This is some fellow,
Who, having been praised for bluntness, doth affect
A saucy roughness, and constrains the garb
Quite from his nature: he cannot flatter, he,
An honest mind and plain, he must speak truth!
An they will take it, so; if not, he 's plain.
These kind of knaves I know, which in this plainness
Harbour more craft and more corrupter ends
Than twenty silly ducking observants
That stretch their duties nicely. 110

Kent. Sir, in good sooth, in sincere verity,
Under the allowance of your great aspect,
Whose influence, like the wreath of radiant fire
On flickering Phœbus' front,—

Corn.   What mean'st by this?

Kent. To go out of my dialect, which you discom-
mend so much. I know, sir, I am no flatterer: he that
beguiled you in a plain accent was a plain knave;
which for my part I will not be; though I should win
your displeasure to entreat me to 't. 120

Corn. What was the offence you gave him?

Osw. I never gave him any:
It pleased the king his master very late
To strike at me, upon his misconstruction;
When he, conjunct, and flattering his displeasure,
Tripp'd me behind; being down, insulted, rail'd,
And put upon him such a deal of man,
That worthied him, got praises of the king
For him attempting who was self-subdued;
And, in the fleshment of this dread exploit, 130
Drew on me here again.

Kent.   None of these rogues and
          cowards
But Ajax is their fool.

Corn.   Fetch forth the stocks!
You stubborn ancient knave, you reverend braggart,
We'll teach you—

Kent.   Sir, I am too old to learn:
Call not your stocks for me: I serve the king;
On whose employment I was sent to you:
You shall do small respect, show too bold malice
Against the grace and person of my master,
Stocking his messenger.

Corn. Fetch forth the stocks! As I have life and
          honour, 140
There shall he sit till noon.

Reg. Till noon! till night, my lord; and all night too.

Kent. Why, madam, if I were your father's dog,
You should not use me so.

Reg.   Sir, being his knave, I will.

Corn. This is a fellow of the self-same colour
Our sister speaks of. Come, bring away the stocks!
                              [*Stocks brought out.*

Glou. Let me beseech your grace not to do so:
His fault is much, and the good king his master
Will check him for 't: your purposed low correction

47. **matter.** Kent takes the secondary meaning, "cause for quarrel."
48. **goodman boy,** contemptuously. 60. **disclaims in,** disowns. 69.
zed, the letter Z, a Greek character; in the spelling of English words,
known but unnecessary, and often not included in dictionaries.
71. **unbolted,** unsifted; hence, coarse. 73. **wagtail,** name of a
bird; epithet to denote pertness. 75. **beastly,** in literal sense, beastlike.
80. **holy cords,** natural bonds of affection. 81. **intrinse,** defined as
"entangled" and as "very tightly drawn." **smooth,** flatter, humor. 84.
Renege, deny. **halcyon beaks.** The halcyon or kingfisher, if hung up,
would turn his beak against the wind. 85. **vary,** variation. 87.
epileptic, indication of Oswald's visage, pale with fright and distorted
with a grin. 89-90. **Sarum . . . Camelot.** The allusion is to Sarum

plain, the Salisbury plain (where large flocks of geese were bred), and
to Camelot, the seat of King Arthur and his Round Table, said to have
been at Cadbury and at Winchester. 100. **shoulder,** the part of the
back between the shoulders (W. J. Craig). 101. **some,** a (sort of).
103-104. **constrains . . . nature,** assumes by an effort a bearing or
manner of speech which is wholly unnatural 109. **ducking observants,**
bowing, obsequious courtiers. 110. **nicely,** punctiliously. 111. **Sir, in
good sooth,** etc., Kent assumes the speech of courtly decorum. 124.
misconstruction, misunderstanding (me). 125. **conjunct,** joined,
united with him. 127. **put . . . man,** acted like such a hero. 128.
worthied, won reputation. 129. **attempting,** assailing. 130. **fleshment,** excitement resulting from a first success. 132. **Ajax is their fool,**

Is such as basest and contemned'st wretches 150
For pilferings and most common trespasses
Are punish'd with: the king must take it ill,
That he 's so slightly valued in his messenger,
Should have him thus restrain'd.
    Corn.   I'll answer that.
    Reg. My sister may receive it much more worse,
To have her gentleman abused, assaulted,
For following her affairs. Put in his legs.
                    [*Kent is put in the stocks.*
Come, my good lord, away.
                    [*Exeunt all but Gloucester and Kent.*
    Glou. I am sorry for thee, friend; 'tis the duke's
    pleasure,
Whose disposition, all the world well knows, 160
Will not be rubb'd nor stopp'd: I'll entreat for thee.
    Kent. Pray, do not, sir: I have watched and travell'd
    hard;
Some time I shall sleep out, the rest I'll whistle.
A good man's fortune may grow out at heels:
Give you good morrow!
    Glou. The duke 's to blame in this; 'twill be ill
    taken.   [*Exit.*
    Kent. Good king, that must approve the common
    saw,
Thou out of heaven's benediction comest
To the warm sun!
Approach, thou beacon to this under globe, 170
That by thy comfortable beams I may
Peruse this letter! Nothing almost sees miracles
But misery: I know 'tis from Cordelia,
Who hath most fortunately been inform'd
Of my obscured course; and shall find time
†From this enormous state, seeking to give
Losses their remedies. All weary and o'er-watch'd,
Take vantage, heavy eyes, not to behold
This shameful lodging.
Fortune, good night: smile once more; turn thy
    wheel!   [*Sleeps.* 180

SCENE III. *A wood.*

Enter EDGAR.

    Edg. I heard myself proclaim'd;
And by the happy hollow of a tree
Escaped the hunt. No port is free; no place,
That guard, and most unusual vigilance,
Does not attend my taking. Whiles I may 'scape,
I will preserve myself: and am bethought
To take the basest and most poorest shape
That ever penury, in contempt of man,
Brought near to beast: my face I'll grime with filth;
Blanket my loins; elf all my hair in knots; 10
And with presented nakedness out-face
The winds and persecutions of the sky.
The country gives me proof and precedent

Of Bedlam beggars, who, with roaring voices,
Strike in their numb'd and mortified bare arms
Pins, wooden pricks, nails, sprigs of rosemary;
And with this horrible object, from low farms,
Poor pelting villages, sheep-cotes, and mills,
Sometime with lunatic bans, sometime with prayers,
Enforce their charity. Poor Turlygod! poor Tom! 20
That 's something yet: Edgar I nothing am.   [*Exit.*

SCENE IV. *Before Gloucester's castle. Kent in the stocks.*

Enter LEAR, Fool, *and* Gentleman.

    Lear. 'Tis strange that they should so depart from
    home,
And not send back my messenger.
    Gent.   As I learn'd,
The night before there was no purpose in them
Of this remove.
    Kent.   Hail to thee, noble master!
    Lear. Ha!
Makest thou this shame thy pastime?
    Kent.   No, my lord.
    Fool. Ha, ha! he wears cruel garters. Horses are tied
by the heads, dogs and bears by the neck, monkeys
by the loins, and men by the legs: when a man 's
over-lusty at legs, then he wears wooden nether-
stocks.   11
    Lear. What 's he that hath so much thy place
    mistook
To set thee here?
    Kent.   It is both he and she;
Your son and daughter.
    Lear. No.
    Kent. Yes.
    Lear. No, I say.
    Kent. I say, yea.
    Lear. No, no, they would not.
    Kent. Yes, they have.   20
    Lear. By Jupiter, I swear, no.
    Kent. By Juno, I swear, ay.
    Lear.   They durst not do 't;
They could not, would not do 't; 'tis worse than
    murder,
To do upon respect such violent outrage:
Resolve me, with all modest haste, which way
Thou mightst deserve, or they impose, this usage,
Coming from us.
    Kent.   My lord, when at their home
I did commend your highness' letters to them,
Ere I was risen from the place that show'd
My duty kneeling, came there a reeking post, 30
Stew'd in his haste, half breathless, panting forth
From Goneril his mistress salutations;
Deliver'd letters, spite of intermission,
Which presently they read: on whose contents,
They summon'd up their meiny, straight took horse;

Ajax, traditional braggart, is outdone by them in boasting. **138. grace . . . master,** who as a messenger Kent represented. 161. **rubb'd,** hindered, obstructed; term from bowls. 163. **sleep out,** sleep through. 165. **Give you,** i.e., God give you. 167. **approve,** prove true. **saw,** proverb: "To run out of God's blessing into the warm sun," meaning "to go from better to worse." 171. **comfortable,** useful. 175-177. **and . . . remedies,** an obscure passage. Daniel's conjecture of *she'll* for *shall* makes a sort of sense. 177. **o'er-watch'd,** exhausted with watching.
    SCENE III. 3. **port,** means of exit. 5. **attend,** watch, wait for. 6. **am bethought,** it has occurred to me. 10. **elf,** tangle into elf-locks. 14. **Bedlam beggars,** called also "Tom o' Bedlams" and "Abraham men"; they were lunatic patients of Bethlehem Hospital turned out to

beg for their bread. Dekker in the *Bellman of London,* 1608, gives a description of their characteristics which closely parallels the one in the text. 15. **mortified,** numbed, insensible. 16. **wooden pricks,** skewers. 17. **object,** appearance. **low,** lowly. 18. **pelting,** paltry, petty. 19. **bans,** curses. 20. **Turlygod,** meaning unknown; Warburton proposed *Turlipin,* the name of an order of mad beggars in France. 21. **nothing,** probably, not at all, in no respect.
    SCENE IV. 4. **remove,** change of residence (of royalty). 7. **cruel.** Q: *crewell,* a double meaning: (1) "unkind," (2) "crewel," a thin yarn of which garters were made. 11. **nether-stocks,** stockings. 24. **upon respect,** deliberately. 28. **commend,** deliver, commit. 33. **spite of intermission,** in spite of interrupting me. 35. **meiny,** household.

Commanded me to follow, and attend
The leisure of their answer; gave me cold looks:
And meeting here the other messenger,
Whose welcome, I perceived, had poison'd mine,—
Being the very fellow that of late   40
Display'd so saucily against your highness,—
Having more man than wit about me, drew:
He raised the house with loud and coward cries.
Your son and daughter found this trespass worth
The shame which here it suffers.

Fool. Winter 's not gone yet, if the wild-geese fly
that way.

   Fathers that wear rags
    Do make their children blind;
   But fathers that bear bags   50
    Shall see their children kind.
   Fortune, that arrant whore,
   Ne'er turns the key to the poor.

But, for all this, thou shalt have as many dolours for
thy daughters as thou canst tell in a year.

Lear. O, how this mother swells up toward my
 heart!
Hysterica passio, down, thou climbing sorrow,
Thy element 's below! Where is this daughter?

Kent. With the earl, sir, here within.

Lear.   Follow me not;
Stay here.   [*Exit.* 60

Gent. Made you no more offence but what you speak
of?

Kent. None.
How chance the king comes with so small a train?

Fool. An thou hadst been set i' the stocks for that
question, thou hadst well deserved it.

Kent. Why, fool?

Fool. We'll set thee to school to an ant, to teach
thee there 's no labouring i' the winter. All that follow
their noses are led by their eyes but blind men; and
there 's not a nose among twenty but can smell him
that 's stinking. Let go thy hold when a great wheel
runs down a hill, lest it break thy neck with following
it; but the great one that goes up the hill, let him
draw thee after. When a wise man gives thee better
counsel, give me mine again: I would have none but
knaves follow it, since a fool gives it.

   That sir which serves and seeks for gain,
    And follows but for form,   80
   Will pack when it begins to rain,
    And leave thee in the storm.
   But I will tarry; the fool will stay,
    And let the wise man fly:
   The knave turns fool that runs away;
    The fool no knave, perdy.

Kent. Where learned you this, fool?

Fool. Not i' the stocks, fool.

   Re-enter LEAR, *with* GLOUCESTER.

Lear. Deny to speak with me? They are sick? they
 are weary?
They have travell'd all the night? Mere fetches;   90

The images of revolt and flying off.
Fetch me a better answer.

Glou.   My dear lord,
You know the fiery quality of the duke;
How unremoveable and fix'd he is
In his own course.

Lear. Vengeance! plague! death! confusion!
Fiery? what quality? Why, Gloucester, Gloucester,
I 'ld speak with the Duke of Cornwall and his wife.

Glou. Well, my good lord, I have inform'd them so.

Lear. Inform'd them! Dost thou understand me,
 man?   100

Glou. Ay, my good lord.

Lear. The king would speak with Cornwall; the
 dear father
Would with his daughter speak, commands her
 service:
Are they inform'd of this? My breath and blood!
Fiery? the fiery duke? Tell the hot duke that—
No, but not yet: may be he is not well:
Infirmity doth still neglect all office
Whereto our health is bound; we are not ourselves
When nature, being oppress'd, commands the mind
To suffer with the body: I'll forbear;   110
And am fall'n out with my more headier will,
To take the indisposed and sickly fit
For the sound man. Death on my state! wherefore
       [*Looking on Kent.*
Should he sit here? This act persuades me
That this remotion of the duke and her
Is practice only. Give me my servant forth.
Go tell the duke and 's wife I 'ld speak with them,
Now, presently: bid them come forth and hear me,
Or at their chamber-door I'll beat the drum
Till it cry sleep to death.   120

Glou. I would have all well betwixt you. [*Exit.*

Lear. O me, my heart, my rising heart! but, down!

Fool. Cry to it, nuncle, as the cockney did to the
eels when she put 'em i' the paste alive; she knapped
'em o' the coxcombs with a stick, and cried 'Down,
wantons, down!' 'Twas her brother that, in pure
kindness to his horse, buttered his hay.

 Enter CORNWALL, REGAN, GLOUCESTER, *and*
  Servants.

Lear. Good morrow to you both.

Corn.   Hail to your grace!
      [*Kent is set at liberty.*

Reg. I am glad to see your highness.   130

Lear. Regan, I think you are; I know what reason
I have to think so: if thou shouldst not be glad,
I would divorce me from thy mother's tomb,
Sepulchring an adultress. [*To Kent*] O, are you free?
Some other time for that. Beloved Regan,
Thy sister 's naught: O Regan, she hath tied
Sharp-tooth'd unkindness, like a vulture, here:
      [*Points to his heart.*
I can scarce speak to thee; thou 'lt not believe
With how depraved a quality—O Regan!

Reg. I pray you, sir, take patience: I have hope   140

---

41. **Display'd,** behaved ostentatiously. 42. **drew,** i.e., my sword. 55. **dolours,** griefs, with pun on "dollars." 56, 57. **mother, Hysterica passio,** a disease, apparently called by both these names, accompanied by a sense of strangulation. Lear mistakes the epigastric discomfort of extreme grief for the disease. 64. **chance,** chances it. 79. **sir,** great person. 81. **pack,** take himself off. 90. **fetches,** pretexts, dodges. 91. **flying off,** desertion. 111-112. **am . . . take,** am wrong because of my more impetuous will in taking. 115. **remotion,** removal. 120. **cry**

sleep to death, i.e., put an end to sleep. 123. **cockney,** a word of disputed origin and meaning. It is said to have meant a pampered, affected woman, a spoiled child, a milksop; the passage here suggests the meaning "cook." 125. **knapped 'em.** Q: *rapt um;* Steevens preferred the Q reading because *knap* means properly "to break asunder." **coxcombs,** heads. 140-142. **I have . . . duty.** The passage does not construe literally; the sense is plain. 150. **confine,** assigned boundary. 151. **discretion,** discreet person. 155. **how . . . house,** how this would be

You less know how to value her desert
Than she to scant her duty.
   Lear.   Say, how is that?
   Reg. I cannot think my sister in the least
Would fail her obligation: if, sir, perchance
She have restrain'd the riots of your followers,
'Tis on such ground, and to such wholesome end,
As clears her from all blame.
   Lear. My curses on her!
   Reg.   O, sir, you are old;
Nature in you stands on the very verge
Of her confine: you should be ruled and led   150
By some discretion, that discerns your state
Better than you yourself. Therefore, I pray you,
That to our sister you do make return;
Say you have wrong'd her, sir.
   Lear.   Ask her forgiveness?
Do you but mark how this becomes the house:
'Dear daughter, I confess that I am old;   [*Kneeling.*
Age is unnecessary: on my knees I beg
That you'll vouchsafe me raiment, bed, and food.'
   Reg. Good sir, no more; these are unsightly tricks:
Return you to my sister.
   Lear.   [*Rising*] Never, Regan: 160
She hath abated me of half my train;
Look'd black upon me; struck me with her tongue,
Most serpent-like, upon the very heart:
All the stored vengeances of heaven fall
On her ingrateful top! Strike her young bones,
You taking airs, with lameness!
   Corn.   Fie, sir, fie!
   Lear. You nimble lightnings, dart your blinding
   flames
Into her scornful eyes! Infect her beauty,
You fen-suck'd fogs, drawn by the powerful sun,
To fall and blast her pride!   170
   Reg. O the blest gods! so will you wish on me,
When the rash mood is on.
   Lear. No, Regan, thou shalt never have my curse:
Thy tender-hefted nature shall not give
Thee o'er to harshness: her eyes are fierce; but thine
Do comfort and not burn. 'Tis not in thee
To grudge my pleasures, to cut off my train,
To bandy hasty words, to scant my sizes,
And in conclusion to oppose the bolt
Against my coming in: thou better know'st   180
The offices of nature, bond of childhood,
Effects of courtesy, dues of gratitude;
Thy half o' the kingdom hast thou not forgot,
Wherein I thee endow'd.
   Reg.   Good sir, to the purpose.
   Lear. Who put my man i' the stocks?   [*Tucket within.*
   Corn.   What trumpet 's that?
   Reg. I know 't, my sister's: this approves her letter,
That she would soon be here.

Enter OSWALD.

            Is your lady come?
   Lear. This is a slave, whose easy-borrow'd pride
Dwells in the fickle grace of her he follows.

Out, varlet, from my sight!
   Corn.   What means your grace?   190
   Lear. Who stock'd my servant? Regan, I have good
   hope
Thou didst not know on 't. Who comes here? O
   heavens,

Enter GONERIL.

If you do love old men, if your sweet sway
Allow obedience, if yourselves are old,
Make it your cause; send down, and take my part!
[*To Gon.*] Art not ashamed to look upon this beard?
O Regan, wilt thou take her by the hand?
   Gon. Why not by the hand, sir? How have I
   offended?
All 's not offence that indiscretion finds
And dotage terms so.
   Lear.   O sides, you are too tough;   200
Will you yet hold? How came my man i' the stocks?
   Corn. I set him there, sir: but his own disorders
Deserved much less advancement.
   Lear.   You! did you?
   Reg. I pray you, father, being weak, seem so.
If, till the expiration of your month,
You will return and sojourn with my sister,
Dismissing half your train, come then to me:
I am now from home, and out of that provision
Which shall be needful for your entertainment.
   Lear. Return to her, and fifty men dismiss'd?   210
No, rather I abjure all roofs, and choose
To wage against the enmity o' the air;
To be a comrade with the wolf and owl,—
Necessity's sharp pinch! Return with her?
Why, the hot-blooded France, that dowerless took
Our youngest born, I could as well be brought
To knee his throne, and, squire-like, pension beg
To keep base life afoot. Return with her?
Persuade me rather to be slave and sumpter
To this detested groom.   [*Pointing at Oswald.*
   Gon.   At your choice, sir.   220
   Lear. I prithee, daughter, do not make me mad:
I will not trouble thee, my child; farewell:
We'll no more meet, no more see one another:
But yet thou art my flesh, my blood, my daughter;
Or rather a disease that 's in my flesh,
Which I must needs call mine: thou art a boil,
A plague-sore, an embossed carbuncle,
In my corrupted blood. But I'll not chide thee;
Let shame come when it will, I do not call it:
I do not bid the thunder-bearer shoot,   230
Nor tell tales of thee to high-judging Jove:
Mend when thou canst; be better at thy leisure:
I can be patient; I can stay with Regan,
I and my hundred knights.
   Reg.   Not altogether so:
I look'd not for you yet, nor am provided
For your fit welcome. Give ear, sir, to my sister;
For those that mingle reason with your passion
Must be content to think you old, and so—
But she knows what she does.

---

suitable to our position. 165. **ingrateful top,** ungrateful head. **young
bones,** i.e., unborn child. 169. **fen-suck'd.** It was supposed that the
sun sucked up poisons from fens or marshes. 174. **tender-hefted,** set in
a tender, delicate frame (Wright); gentle. 178. **sizes,** allowances.
180-183. **thou . . . forgot.** Note that Lear enumerates what are ethically
the pillars of society. 186. **approves,** confirms. 188. **easy-borrow'd,**
put on without justification; hyphen comes from Theobald; perhaps
easy has an independent meaning, "cool," "impudent." 191. **stock'd,**
put into the stocks. 195. **Make . . . cause,** make my cause yours. 200.
sides . . . tough. This is not figurative but indicates belief in an actual
swelling of the heart so that it might break through the sides. 212.
wage, wage war. 215. **hot-blooded,** passionate, angry. In I, ii, 23,
France is said to have "in choler parted," his blood heated by passion.
217. **knee,** fall on my knees before. 219. **sumpter,** pack horse; hence,
drudge. 227. **embossed,** swollen, tumid. 230. **thunder-bearer,** Jupiter.

Lear.　　　　　Is this well spoken?

Reg. I dare avouch it, sir: what, fifty followers?　240
Is it not well? What should you need of more?
Yea, or so many, sith that both charge and danger
Speak 'gainst so great a number? How, in one house,
Should many people, under two commands,
Hold amity? 'Tis hard; almost impossible.

Gon. Why might not you, my lord, receive
　attendance
From those that she calls servants or from mine?

Reg. Why not, my lord? If then they chanced to
　slack you,
We could control them. If you will come to me,—
For now I spy a danger,—I entreat you　250
To bring but five and twenty: to no more
Will I give place or notice.

Lear. I gave you all—

Reg.　　　　　And in good time you gave it.

Lear. Made you my guardians, my depositaries;
But kept a reservation to be follow'd
With such a number. What, must I come to you
With five and twenty, Regan? said you so?

Reg. And speak 't again, my lord; no more with me.

Lear. Those wicked creatures yet do look
　well-favour'd,
When others are more wicked; not being the worst　260
Stands in some rank of praise. [*To Gon.*] I'll go with
　thee:
Thy fifty yet doth double five-and-twenty,
And thou art twice her love.

Gon.　　　　　Hear me, my lord:
What need you five and twenty, ten, or five,
To follow in a house where twice so many
Have a command to tend you?

Reg.　　　　　What need one?

Lear. O, reason not the need: our basest beggars
Are in the poorest thing superfluous:
Allow not nature more than nature needs,
Man's life 's as cheap as beast's: thou art a lady;　270
If only to go warm were gorgeous,
Why, nature needs not what thou gorgeous wear'st,
Which scarcely keeps thee warm. But, for true need,—
You heavens, give me that patience, patience I need!
You see me here, you gods, a poor old man,
As full of grief as age; wretched in both!
If it be you that stir these daughters' hearts
Against their father, fool me not so much
To bear it tamely; touch me with noble anger,
And let not women's weapons, water-drops,　280
Stain my man's cheeks! No, you unnatural hags,
I will have such revenges on you both,
That all the world shall—I will do such things,—
What they are, yet I know not; but they shall be
The terrors of the earth. You think I'll weep;
No, I'll not weep:
I have full cause of weeping; but this heart
Shall break into a hundred thousand flaws,

Or ere I'll weep. O fool, I shall go mad!
　　[*Exeunt Lear, Gloucester, Kent, and Fool. Storm
　　　　　　　　　　　　　　and tempest.*

Corn. Let us withdraw; 'twill be a storm.　290

Reg. This house is little: the old man and his people
Cannot be well bestow'd.

Gon. 'Tis his own blame; hath put himself from rest,
And must needs taste his folly.

Reg. For his particular, I'll receive him gladly,
But not one follower.

Gon.　　　　　So am I purposed.
Where is my lord of Gloucester?

Corn. Follow'd the old man forth: he is return'd.

　　　　Re-enter GLOUCESTER.

Glou. The king is in high rage.

Corn.　　　　　Whither is he going?

Glou. He calls to horse; but will I know not whither.

Corn. 'Tis best to give him way; he leads himself.　301

Gon. My lord, entreat him by no means to stay.

Glou. Alack, the night comes on, and the bleak
　winds
Do sorely ruffle; for many miles about
There 's scarce a bush.

Reg.　　　　　O, sir, to wilful men,
The injuries that they themselves procure
Must be their schoolmasters. Shut up your doors:
He is attended with a desperate train;
And what they may incense him to, being apt
To have his ear abused, wisdom bids fear.　310

Corn. Shut up your doors, my lord; 'tis a wild night:
My Regan counsels well: come out o' the storm.
　　　　　　　　　　　　　　[*Exeunt.*

　　　　　　　　　　ACT III.

　　　　　SCENE I. *A heath.*

Storm still. Enter KENT *and a* Gentleman, *meeting.*

Kent. Who 's there, besides foul weather?

Gent. One minded like the weather, most unquietly.

Kent. I know you. Where 's the king?

Gent. Contending with the fretful element;
Bids the wind blow the earth into the sea,
Or swell the curled waters 'bove the main,
That things might change or cease; tears his white
　hair,
Which the impetuous blasts, with eyeless rage,
Catch in their fury, and make nothing of;
Strives in his little world of man to out-scorn　10
The to-and-fro-conflicting wind and rain.
This night, wherein the cub-drawn bear would couch,
The lion and the belly-pinched wolf
Keep their fur dry, unbonneted he runs,
And bids what will take all.

Kent.　　　　　But who is with him?

---

240. **avouch,** acknowledge.　245. **Hold amity,** maintain friendship.
248. **slack,** be careless in their attendance on.　252. **notice,** countenance.
254. **my guardians.** Lear understands his contract to be that the
daughters were guardians, or stewardesses, of his realm under him.
259-260. **Those . . . wicked.** Bad as Goneril is, there is a more exquisite
quality of cruelty in Regan.　266. **tend,** wait on.　**What need one.**
Lear's answer (ll. 267 ff.) is in some respects an expression of the underlying theme of the story: Why *reason,* i.e., discuss, the *need,* since it is not
a question of need? It is a spiritual, not a temporal, matter which is
involved.　274. **patience.** Patience seems to have been a term for the
counterbalance which reason might set up against the passions.　279.
noble anger. One cannot understand either the character of Lear or the

significance of his story without a sound conception of righteous
indignation as a noble virtue; with it is connected the ethical propriety
of revenge.　285. **terrors of the earth.** Note the artistic effect of vague
suggestion at this moment of extreme tension.　292. **bestow'd,** lodged.
293. **blame,** fault.　295. **For his particular,** as for him individually.
304. **ruffle,** bluster.　308. **desperate train,** body of desperate followers.
309. **incense him to,** incite him to undertake.
ACT III. SCENE I.　6. **main,** mainland.　10. **little world of man,** the
microcosm; allusion to the theory that man is an epitome of the macrocosm, or universe, and moves in accordance with its laws and influences.　12. **cub-drawn,** famished, with udders sucked dry.　**couch,** lie
close.　18. **upon . . . note,** on the strength of what I know.　19. **Com-**

Gent. None but the fool; who labours to out-jest
His heart-struck injuries.
   Kent.   Sir, I do know you;
And dare, upon the warrant of my note,
Commend a dear thing to you. There is division,
Although as yet the face of it be cover'd   20
With mutual cunning, 'twixt Albany and Cornwall;
Who have—as who have not, that their great stars
Throned and set high?—servants, who seem no less,
Which are to France the spies and speculations
Intelligent of our state; what hath been seen,
Either in snuffs and packings of the dukes,
Or the hard rein which both of them have borne
Against the old kind king; or something deeper,
Whereof perchance these are but furnishings;
But, true it is, from France there comes a power   30
Into this scatter'd kingdom; who already,
Wise in our negligence, have secret feet
In some of our best ports, and are at point
To show their open banner. Now to you:
If on my credit you dare build so far
To make your speed to Dover, you shall find
Some that will thank you, making just report
Of how unnatural and bemadding sorrow
The king hath cause to plain.
I am a gentleman of blood and breeding;   40
And, from some knowledge and assurance, offer
This office to you.
   Gent. I will talk further with you.
   Kent.   No, do not.
For confirmation that I am much more
Than my out-wall, open this purse, and take
What it contains. If you shall see Cordelia,—
As fear not but you shall,—show her this ring;
And she will tell you who your fellow is
That yet you do not know. Fie on this storm!
I will go seek the king.   50
   Gent. Give me your hand: have you no more to say?
   Kent. Few words, but, to effect, more than all yet;
That, when we have found the king,—in which your
     pain
That way, I'll this,—he that first lights on him
Holla the other.   *[Exeunt severally.*

SCENE II. *Another part of the heath. Storm still.*

Enter LEAR *and* Fool.

   Lear. Blow, winds, and crack your cheeks! rage!
     blow!
You cataracts and hurricanoes, spout
Till you have drench'd our steeples, drown'd the
     cocks!
You sulphurous and thought-executing fires,
Vaunt-couriers to oak-cleaving thunderbolts,
Singe my white head! And thou, all-shaking thunder,
Smite flat the thick rotundity o' the world!

Crack nature's moulds, all germens spill at once,
That make ingrateful man!   9
   Fool. O nuncle, court holy-water in a dry house is
better than this rain-water out o' door. Good nuncle,
in, and ask thy daughters' blessing: here 's a night
pities neither wise man nor fool.
   Lear. Rumble thy bellyful! Spit, fire! spout, rain!
Nor rain, wind, thunder, fire, are my daughters:
I tax not you, you elements, with unkindness;
I never gave you kingdom, call'd you children,
You owe me no subscription: then let fall
Your horrible pleasure; here I stand, your slave,
A poor, infirm, weak, and despised old man: 20
But yet I call you servile ministers,
That have with two pernicious daughters join'd
Your high engender'd battles 'gainst a head
So old and white as this. O! O! 'tis foul!
   Fool. He that has a house to put 's head in has a
good head-piece.
          The cod-piece that will house
            Before the head has any,
          The head and he shall louse;
            So beggars marry many.   30
          The man that makes his toe
            What he his heart should make
          Shall of a corn cry woe,
            And turn his sleep to wake.
For there was never yet fair woman but she made
mouths in a glass.
   Lear. No, I will be the pattern of all patience;
I will say nothing.

Enter KENT.

   Kent. Who 's there?
   Fool. Marry, here 's grace and a cod-piece; that 's a
wise man and a fool.   41
   Kent. Alas, sir, are you here? things that love night
Love not such nights as these; the wrathful skies
Gallow the very wanderers of the dark,
And make them keep their caves: since I was man,
Such sheets of fire, such bursts of horrid thunder,
Such groans of roaring wind and rain, I never
Remember to have heard: man's nature cannot carry
The affliction nor the fear.
   Lear.   Let the great gods,
That keep this dreadful pother o'er our heads,   50
Find out their enemies now. Tremble, thou wretch,
That hast within thee undivulged crimes,
Unwhipp'd of justice: hide thee, thou bloody hand;
Thou perjured, and thou simular man of virtue
That art incestuous: caitiff, to pieces shake,
That under covert and convenient seeming
Hast practised on man's life: close pent-up guilts,
Rive your concealing continents, and cry
These dreadful summoners grace. I am a man
More sinn'd against than sinning.
   Kent.   Alack, bare-headed!   60

mend, entrust. 24. **speculations,** scouts, spies. Johnson conjectured
speculators. 26. **snuffs,** quarrels. 29. **furnishings,** outward shows. 31.
scatter'd, divided. 33. **at point,** ready. 38. **bemadding,** distracting.
39. **plain,** complain of. 45. **out-wall,** exterior. 52. **to effect,** to the
purpose. 53-54. **your pain That way,** laborious quest (take you)
that way.
   SCENE II. 2. **hurricanoes,** waterspouts. 3. **cocks,** weathercocks. 4.
thought-executing, probably, acting with the quickness of thought.
5. **Vaunt-couriers,** forerunners. 8. **germens,** germs, seeds. **spill,**
destroy. 10. **court holy-water,** flattery. 18. **subscription,** allegiance.
23. **high engender'd battles,** battalions levied in the heavens. 27-34.
The cod-piece . . . wake. A man who prefers a mean member in place of

a vital one shall suffer enduring pain where others would suffer merely a
twinge. Lear had preferred Regan and Goneril to Cordelia (Furness).
40. **cod-piece,** the front part of the close-fitting hose worn by men; here
applied by the Fool to himself. 44. **Gallow,** frighten, terrify. 49. **Let
the great gods,** etc. An expression of Lear's faith in the power of the
gods, or, as we should say, God; it is the symbol of the retention of his
sanity. When he loses his reason he loses also his faith in divinity. 50.
pother, turmoil. 54. **simular man,** pretender. 56. **seeming,** hypocrisy. 58-59. **cry . . . grace,** pray for mercy at the hands of the officers
of divine justice. A *summoner* was the police officer of an ecclesiastical
court. 60. **More sinn'd against than sinning.** This famous phrase
is a perfect indication that Lear is still sane.

Gracious my lord, hard by here is a hovel;
Some friendship will it lend you 'gainst the tempest:
Repose you there; while I to this hard house—
More harder than the stones whereof 'tis raised;
Which even but now, demanding after you,
Denied me to come in—return, and force
Their scanted courtesy.
    Lear.   My wits begin to turn.
Come on, my boy: how dost, my boy? art cold?
I am cold myself. Where is this straw, my fellow?
The art of our necessities is strange,   70
That can make vile things precious. Come, your
    hovel.
Poor fool and knave, I have one part in my heart
That 's sorry yet for thee.
    Fool. [*Singing*] He that has and a little tiny wit,—
        With hey, ho, the wind and the rain,—
        Must make content with his fortunes fit,
        For the rain it raineth every day.
    Lear. True, my good boy. Come, bring us to this
    hovel.   [*Exeunt Lear and Kent.*
    Fool. This is a brave night to cool a courtezan.
I'll speak a prophecy ere I go: 80
    When priests are more in word than matter;
    When brewers mar their malt with water;
    When nobles are their tailors' tutors;
    No heretics burn'd, but wenches' suitors;
    When every case in law is right;
    No squire in debt, nor no poor knight;
    When slanders do not live in tongues;
    Nor cutpurses come not to throngs;
    When usurers tell their gold i' the field;
    And bawds and whores do churches build;   90
    Then shall the realm of Albion
    Come to great confusion:
    Then comes the time, who lives to see 't,
    That going shall be used with feet.
This prophecy Merlin shall make; for I live before his
    time.   [*Exit.*

SCENE III. *Gloucester's castle.*

Enter GLOUCESTER *and* EDMUND.

    Glou. Alack, alack, Edmund, I like not this un-
natural dealing. When I desired their leave that I
might pity him, they took from me the use of mine
own house; charged me, on pain of their perpetual
displeasure, neither to speak of him, entreat for him,
nor any way sustain him.
    Edm. Most savage and unnatural!   7
    Glou. Go to; say you nothing. There 's a division
betwixt the dukes; and a worse matter than that: I
have received a letter this night; 'tis dangerous to be
spoken; I have locked the letter in my closet: these
injuries the king now bears will be revenged home;
there 's part of a power already footed: we must in-

cline to the king. I will seek him, and privily relieve
him: go you and maintain talk with the duke, that my
charity be not of him perceived: if he ask for me, I am
ill, and gone to bed. Though I die for it, as no less is
threatened me, the king my old master must be relieved. There is some strange thing toward, Edmund;
pray you, be careful.   [*Exit.* 21
    Edm. This courtesy, forbid thee, shall the duke
Instantly know; and of that letter too:
This seems a fair deserving, and must draw me
That which my father loses; no less than all:
The younger rises when the old doth fall.   [*Exit.*

SCENE IV. *The heath. Before a hovel.*

Enter LEAR, KENT, *and* Fool.

    Kent. Here is the place, my lord; good my lord,
    enter:
The tyranny of the open night 's too rough
For nature to endure.   [*Storm still.*
    Lear.   Let me alone.
    Kent. Good my lord, enter here.
    Lear.   Wilt break my heart?
    Kent. I had rather break mine own. Good my lord,
    enter.
    Lear. Thou think'st 'tis much that this contentious
    storm
Invades us to the skin: so 'tis to thee;
But where the greater malady is fix'd,
The lesser is scarce felt. Thou 'ldst shun a bear;
But if thy flight lay toward the raging sea,   10
Thou 'ldst meet the bear i' the mouth. When the
    mind 's free,
The body 's delicate: the tempest in my mind
Doth from my senses take all feeling else
Save what beats there. Filial ingratitude!
Is it not as this mouth should tear this hand
For lifting food to 't? But I will punish home:
No, I will weep no more. In such a night
To shut me out! Pour on; I will endure.
In such a night as this! O Regan, Goneril!
Your old kind father, whose frank heart gave all,— 20
O, that way madness lies; let me shun that;
No more of that.
    Kent.   Good my lord, enter here.
    Lear. Prithee, go in thyself; seek thine own ease:
This tempest will not give me leave to ponder
On things would hurt me more. But I'll go in.
[*To the Fool*] In, boy; go first. You houseless
    poverty,—
Nay, get thee in. I'll pray, and then I'll sleep.
          [*Fool goes in.*
Poor naked wretches, wheresoe'er you are,
That bide the pelting of this pitiless storm,
How shall your houseless heads and unfed sides,   30
Your loop'd and window'd raggedness, defend you

---

63. **hard,** cruel. 65. **Which,** i.e., the owners of the house. **demanding,** I inquiring. 67. **My wits begin to turn,** a premonition followed by an expression of more than Lear's normal sanity, since it is his first reflection of sympathy for others. 80-95. **I'll . . . time.** Omitted in Q and usually regarded as an interpolation in the text of F. Merlin was a magician of King Arthur's court; a prophecy of Merlin, somewhat like these lines, is found in Holinshed and other places.

    SCENE III. 14. **footed,** landed. 22. **courtesy, forbid thee,** i.e., this kindness to Lear you were forbidden to show. 24. **fair deserving,** meritorious action.

    SCENE IV. 8. **greater malady.** There was a familiar belief that one passion might drive out or allay another. 28-36. **Poor naked wretches,**

etc. Lear's error has been a violation of that law of nature which is called justice. His sufferings have brought him round to a complete recognition and expression of general distributive justice. This quality, we may suppose, was in his nature, but his obstinacy and self-conceit had stifled it. 29. **bide,** endure. 31. **loop'd and window'd,** full of openings like windows and loopholes. 35. **superflux,** superfluity, a word suggestive of the ethics of ownership in society. 49-50. **Hast . . . this.** Lear can interpret only in terms of his own great sorrow; the passage illustrates obsession and is still sound psychologically, or psychiatrically. 59. **five wits,** the five mental faculties: common wit, imagination, fantasy, judgment, memory. 61. **star-blasting,** blighting by influence of the stars. 69. **pendulous,** suspended. 77.

From seasons such as these? O, I have ta'en
Too little care of this! Take physic, pomp;
Expose thyself to feel what wretches feel,
That thou mayst shake the superflux to them,
And show the heavens more just.

Edg. [*Within*] Fathom and half, fathom and half!
Poor Tom! [*The Fool runs out from the hovel.*

Fool. Come not in here, nuncle, here 's a spirit.
Help me, help me! 40

Kent. Give me thy hand. Who 's there?

Fool. A spirit, a spirit: he says his name 's poor Tom.

Kent. What art thou that dost grumble there i' the
straw? Come forth.

Enter EDGAR *disguised as a madman.*

Edg. Away! the foul fiend follows me!
Through the sharp hawthorn blows the cold wind.
Hum! go to thy cold bed, and warm thee.

Lear. Hast thou given all to thy two daughters?
And art thou come to this? 50

Edg. Who gives any thing to poor Tom? whom the
foul fiend hath led through fire and through flame,
through ford and whirlpool, o'er bog and quagmire;
that hath laid knives under his pillow, and halters in
his pew; set ratsbane by his porridge; made him
proud of heart, to ride on a bay trotting-horse over
four-inched bridges, to course his own shadow for a
traitor. Bless thy five wits! Tom 's a-cold,—O, do de,
do de, do de. Bless thee from whirlwinds, star-blasting,
and taking! Do poor Tom some charity, whom the
foul fiend vexes: there could I have him now,—and
there,—and there again, and there. [*Storm still.*

Lear. What, have his daughters brought him to this
pass? 65
Couldst thou save nothing? Didst thou give them all?

Fool. Nay, he reserved a blanket, else we had been
all shamed.

Lear. Now, all the plagues that in the pendulous air
Hang fated o'er men's faults light on thy daughters! 70

Kent. He hath no daughters, sir.

Lear. Death, traitor! nothing could have subdued
nature
To such a lowness but his unkind daughters.
Is it the fashion, that discarded fathers
Should have thus little mercy on their flesh?
Judicious punishment! 'twas this flesh begot
Those pelican daughters.

Edg. Pillicock sat on Pillicock-hill:
Halloo, halloo, loo, loo!

Fool. This cold night will turn us all to fools and
madmen. 81

Edg. Take heed o' the foul fiend: obey thy parents;
keep thy word justly; swear not; commit not with
man's sworn spouse; set not thy sweet heart on proud
array. Tom 's a-cold.

Lear. What hast thou been? 86

Edg. A serving-man, proud in heart and mind; that

curled my hair; wore gloves in my cap; served the lust
of my mistress' heart, and did the act of darkness with
her; swore as many oaths as I spake words, and broke
them in the sweet face of heaven: one that slept in the
contriving of lust, and waked to do it: wine loved I
deeply, dice dearly; and in woman out-paramoured
the Turk: false of heart, light of ear, bloody of hand;
hog in sloth, fox in stealth, wolf in greediness, dog in
madness, lion in prey. Let not the creaking of shoes
nor the rustling of silks betray thy poor heart to
woman: keep thy foot out of brothels, thy hand out of
plackets, thy pen from lenders' books, and defy the
foul fiend. 101
Still through the hawthorn blows the cold wind:
Says suum, mun, ha, no, nonny.
Dolphin my boy, my boy, sessa! let him trot by.
[*Storm still.*

Lear. Why, thou wert better in thy grave than to
answer with thy uncovered body this extremity of the
skies. Is man no more than this? Consider him well.
Thou owest the worm no silk, the beast no hide, the
sheep no wool, the cat no perfume. Ha! here 's three
on 's are sophisticated! Thou art the thing itself:
unaccommodated man is no more but such a poor,
bare, forked animal as thou art. Off, off, you lendings!
come, unbutton here. [*Tearing off his clothes.*

Fool. Prithee, nuncle, be contented; 'tis a naughty
night to swim in. Now a little fire in a wild field were
like an old lecher's heart; a small spark, all the rest
on 's body cold. Look, here comes a walking fire. 119

Enter GLOUCESTER, *with a torch.*

Edg. This is the foul fiend Flibbertigibbet: he begins at curfew, and walks till the first cock; he gives
the web and the pin, squints the eye, and makes the
hare-lip; mildews the white wheat, and hurts the
poor creature of earth.
S. Withold footed thrice the old;
He met the night-mare, and her nine-fold;
    Bid her alight,
    And her troth plight,
And, aroint thee, witch, aroint thee!

Kent. How fares your grace? 130

Lear. What 's he?

Kent. Who 's there? What is 't you seek?

Glou. What are you there? Your names?

Edg. Poor Tom; that eats the swimming frog, the
toad, the tadpole, the wall-newt and the water; that
in the fury of his heart, when the foul fiend rages, eats
cow-dung for sallets; swallows the old rat and the
ditch-dog; drinks the green mantle of the standing
pool; who is whipped from tithing to tithing, and
stock-punished, and imprisoned; who hath had three
suits to his back, six shirts to his body, horse to ride,
and weapon to wear; 143
But mice and rats, and such small deer,
Have been Tom's food for seven long year.

---

pelican, greedy; a reference to the belief that young pelicans fed on
the flesh of their mother's breasts. 78. **Pillicock,** from an old rhyme
(suggested by *pillicock*). *Pillicock* seems to have been used to mean
"darling." 88. **gloves,** as his mistress' favors. 95. **light of ear,**
foolishly credulous (Schmidt), frivolous (Onions). 103-104. **suum . . .
sessa,** imitative of the wind. 104. **Dolphin my boy,** a slang phrase, or
bit of song. 110. **cat,** civet cat. 111. **sophisticated,** clad in the
trappings of civilized life; Schmidt defines as "adulterated." 112.
unaccommodated man, man unprovided with clothes and necessaries,
also man without social modification. 114. **Off, off, you lendings.** It
may be said that Lear plunges logically into insanity. This is the climax
of his story. He is convinced that chaos is come again, that it is not God's

world; reason is dethroned and faith abandoned. 120. **Flibbertigibbet,**
a fiend whose name Shakespeare borrowed from Harsnet's *Declaration*
(1603). 122. **web and the pin,** cataract of the eye. **squints,** makes to
squint. 124. **white wheat,** approaching ripeness. 125. **S. Withold,**
understood as a corruption of St. Vitalis, who is said to have been
invoked against nightmare. **footed thrice the old,** thrice traversed the
wold (tract of hilly upland). 126. **nine-fold,** nine familiars; suggestive
also certainly of nine foals. 129. **aroint thee,** begone. 135. **wall-newt,**
lizard. 136. **water,** i.e., water newt. 137. **sallets,** salads. 140.
tithing to tithing, i.e., from one ward or parish to another. **stock-
punished,** punished by being put into the stocks. 144. **deer,** probably,
animals generally.

Beware my follower. Peace, Smulkin; peace, thou
fiend!

Glou. What, hath your grace no better company?

Edg. The prince of darkness is a gentleman:
Modo he's call'd, and Mahu.

Glou. Our flesh and blood is grown so vile, my lord,
That it doth hate what gets it. 151

Edg. Poor Tom's a-cold.

Glou. Go in with me: my duty cannot suffer
To obey in all your daughters' hard commands:
Though their injunction be to bar my doors,
And let this tyrannous night take hold upon you,
Yet have I ventured to come seek you out,
And bring you where both fire and food is ready.

Lear. First let me talk with this philosopher.
What is the cause of thunder? 160

Kent. Good my lord, take his offer; go into the
house.

Lear. I'll talk a word with this same learned
Theban.
What is your study?

Edg. How to prevent the fiend, and to kill vermin.

Lear. Let me ask you one word in private.

Kent. Importune him once more to go, my lord;
His wits begin to unsettle.

Glou.   Canst thou blame him? [*Storm still.*
His daughters seek his death; ah, that good Kent!
He said it would be thus, poor banish'd man! 169
Thou say'st the king grows mad; I'll tell thee, friend,
I am almost mad myself: I had a son,
Now outlaw'd from my blood; he sought my life,
But lately, very late: I loved him, friend:
No father his son dearer: truth to tell thee,
The grief hath crazed my wits. What a night's this!
I do beseech your grace,—

Lear.   O, cry you mercy, sir.
Noble philosopher, your company.

Edg. Tom's a-cold.

Glou. In, fellow, there, into the hovel: keep thee
warm.

Lear. Come, let's in all.

Kent.   This way, my lord.

Lear.   With him; 180
I will keep still with my philosopher.

Kent. Good my lord, soothe him; let him take the
fellow.

Glou. Take him you on.

Kent. Sirrah, come on; go along with us.

Lear. Come, good Athenian.

Glou. No words, no words: hush.

Edg. Child Rowland to the dark tower came,
His word was still,—Fie, foh, and fum,
I smell the blood of a British man. [*Exeunt.*

SCENE V. *Gloucester's castle.*

Enter CORNWALL *and* EDMUND.

Corn. I will have my revenge ere I depart his house.

Edm. How, my lord, I may be censured, that nature
thus gives way to loyalty, something fears me to think
of.

Corn. I now perceive, it was not altogether your
brother's evil disposition made him seek his death;
but a provoking merit, set a-work by a reproveable
badness in himself. 9

Edm. How malicious is my fortune, that I must repent to be just! This is the letter he spoke of, which
approves him an intelligent party to the advantages of
France. O heavens! that this treason were not, or not
I the detector!

Corn. Go with me to the duchess.

Edm. If the matter of this paper be certain, you
have mighty business in hand.

Corn. True or false, it hath made thee earl of
Gloucester. Seek out where thy father is, that he may
be ready for our apprehension. 20

Edm. [*Aside*] If I find him comforting the king, it
will stuff his suspicion more fully.—I will persevere in
my course of loyalty, though the conflict be sore between that and my blood.

Corn. I will lay trust upon thee; and thou shalt find
a dearer father in my love. [*Exeunt.*

SCENE VI. *A chamber in a farmhouse adjoining the castle.*

Enter GLOUCESTER, LEAR, KENT, Fool, *and* EDGAR.

Glou. Here is better than the open air; take it
thankfully. I will piece out the comfort with what
addition I can: I will not be long from you.

Kent. All the power of his wits have given way to his
impatience: the gods reward your kindness! 6
[*Exit Gloucester.*

Edg. Fraterretto calls me; and tells me Nero is an
angler in the lake of darkness. Pray, innocent, and
beware the foul fiend.

Fool. Prithee, nuncle, tell me whether a madman
be a gentleman or a yeoman? 11

Lear. A king, a king!

Fool. No, he's a yeoman that has a gentleman to
his son; for he's a mad yeoman that sees his son a
gentleman before him.

Lear. To have a thousand with red burning spits
Come hissing in upon 'em,—

Edg. The foul fiend bites my back.

Fool. He's mad that trusts in the tameness of a
wolf, a horse's health, a boy's love, or a whore's oath. 21

Lear. It shall be done; I will arraign them straight.
[*To Edgar*] Come, sit thou here, most learned justicer;
[*To the Fool*] Thou, sapient sir, sit here. Now, you she
foxes!

Edg. Look, where he stands and glares!
Wantest thou eyes at trial, madam?
Come o'er the bourn, Bessy, to me,—

---

146. **Smulkin,** another name occurring in Harsnet. 149. **Modo,
Mahu,** two superior fiends in Harsnet. 162. **learned Theban,** possibly
a current phrase to indicate a philosopher. 182. **soothe,** humor,
indulge. 187. **Child Rowland,** etc., fragments of the ballad *Child
Rowland and Burd Ellen.* The theme of Browning's *Childe Roland to the
Dark Tower Came* is derived from these lines.
SCENE V. 8. **provoking merit,** etc., i.e., a forward-looking merit
(in Edgar) incited by the badness of Gloucester. 12. **approves him,**
proves him to be. **intelligent,** aware (in the legal sense).
SCENE VI. 7. **Fraterretto,** another of the fiends from Harsnet. 8.
Nero is an angler, pointed out as an allusion to Rabelais, ii, 30, where

Nero is described as a fiddler and Trajan as an angler. 9. **innocent,**
simpleton, fool. 15. **gentleman before him.** It has been often pointed
out that this passage has a strange applicability to Shakespeare himself, since he had seen to it that his father, John Shakespeare, was
granted arms by the College of Heralds in 1599. 23. **justicer,** judge.
26. **Wantest . . . trial,** meaning doubtful. Possibly Edgar alludes to
the staring fiend. 27. **Come . . . me,** first line of a ballad by William
Birche (1558). 32. **Hopdance,** a fiend. 33. **white herring,** fresh
herring or pickled herring; at any rate, not a red herring. **Croak,**
make a rumbling sound in the stomach to denote hunger. 37. **evidence,**
witnesses. 39. **yoke-fellow,** partner. 40. **Bench,** sit on the judgment

Fool. Her boat hath a leak,
    And she must not speak
    Why she dares not come over to thee.   30
  Edg. The foul fiend haunts poor Tom in the voice
of a nightingale. Hopdance cries in Tom's belly for
two white herring. Croak not, black angel; I have no
food for thee.
  Kent. How do you, sir? Stand you not so amazed:
Will you lie down and rest upon the cushions?
  Lear. I'll see their trial first. Bring in the evidence.
[*To Edgar*] Thou robed man of justice, take thy place;
[*To the Fool*] And thou, his yoke-fellow of equity,
Bench by his side: [*To Kent*] you are o' the
    commission,   40
Sit you too.
  Edg. Let us deal justly.
    Sleepest or wakest thou, jolly shepherd?
      Thy sheep be in the corn;
    And for one blast of thy minikin mouth,
      Thy sheep shall take no harm.
Pur! the cat is gray.
  Lear. Arraign her first; 'tis Goneril. I here take my
oath before this honourable assembly, she kicked the
poor king her father.   50
  Fool. Come hither, mistress. Is your name Goneril?
  Lear. She cannot deny it.
  Fool. Cry you mercy, I took you for a joint-stool.
  Lear. And here 's another, whose warp'd looks
    proclaim
What store her heart is made on. Stop her there!
Arms, arms, sword, fire! Corruption in the place!
False justicer, why hast thou let her 'scape?
  Edg. Bless thy five wits!   60
  Kent. O pity! Sir, where is the patience now,
That you so oft have boasted to retain?
  Edg. [*Aside*] My tears begin to take his part so
    much,
They'll mar my counterfeiting.
  Lear. The little dogs and all,
Tray, Blanch, and Sweet-heart, see, they bark at me.
  Edg. Tom will throw his head at them.
Avaunt, you curs!
    Be thy mouth or black or white,
    Tooth that poisons if it bite;   70
    Mastiff, greyhound, mongrel grim,
    Hound or spaniel, brach or lym,
    Or bobtail tike or trundle-tail,
    Tom will make them weep and wail:
    For, with throwing thus my head,
    Dogs leap the hatch, and all are fled.
Do de, de, de. Sessa! Come, march to wakes and fairs
and market-towns. Poor Tom, thy horn is dry.   79
  Lear. Then let them anatomize Regan; see what
breeds about her heart. Is there any cause in nature
that makes these hard hearts? [*To Edgar*] You, sir, I
entertain for one of my hundred; only I do not like
the fashion of your garments: you will say they are
Persian attire; but let them be changed.

  Kent. Now, good my lord, lie here and rest awhile.
  Lear. Make no noise, make no noise; draw the cur-
tains: so, so, so. We'll go to supper i' the morning.
So, so, so.   91
  Fool. And I'll go to bed at noon.

              Re-enter GLOUCESTER.

  Glou. Come hither, friend: where is the king my
    master?
  Kent. Here, sir; but trouble him not, his wits are
    gone.
  Glou. Good friend, I prithee, take him in thy arms;
I have o'erheard a plot of death upon him:
There is a litter ready; lay him in 't,
And drive towards Dover, friend, where thou shalt
    meet
Both welcome and protection. Take up thy master:
If thou shouldst dally half an hour, his life,   100
With thine, and all that offer to defend him,
Stand in assured loss: take up, take up;
And follow me, that will to some provision
Give thee quick conduct.
  Kent.   Oppressed nature sleeps:
This rest might yet have balm'd thy broken sinews,
Which, if convenience will not allow,
Stand in hard cure. [*To the Fool*] Come, help to bear
    thy master;
Thou must not stay behind.
  Glou.   Come, come, away.
                     [*Exeunt all but Edgar.*
  Edg. When we our betters see bearing our woes,
We scarcely think our miseries our foes.   110
Who alone suffers suffers most i' the mind,
Leaving free things and happy shows behind:
But then the mind much sufferance doth o'erskip,
When grief hath mates, and bearing fellowship.
How light and portable my pain seems now,
When that which makes me bend makes the king
    bow,
He childed as I father'd! Tom, away!
Mark the high noises; and thyself bewray,
When false opinion, whose wrong thought defiles thee,
In thy just proof, repeals and reconciles thee.   120
What will hap more to-night, safe 'scape the king!
Lurk, lurk.   [*Exit.*

        SCENE VII. *Gloucester's castle.*

  Enter CORNWALL, REGAN, GONERIL, EDMUND, *and*
    Servants.

  Corn. Post speedily to my lord your husband; show
him this letter: the army of France is landed. Seek out
the villain Gloucester.   [*Exeunt some of the Servants.*
  Reg. Hang him instantly.
  Gon. Pluck out his eyes.
  Corn. Leave him to my displeasure. Edmund, keep
you our sister company: the revenges we are bound to

---

seat. **o' the commission,** a justice of peace. 45. **minikin,** pretty,
dainty. 47. **Pur.** Perhaps for the sound of a cat, or the name of a
demon, or both. There is a fiend in Harsnet named Purre. 55. **joint-
stool,** chair made by a joiner, possibly ornamented. The expression has
a proverbial meaning not understood on which the Fool is punning in
his reference to the stool Lear has placed before them to represent
Goneril. 57. **store,** probably, material; Theobald conjectured *stone*.
63. **Edg. [*Aside*].** Edgar's counterfeiting has been so perfect that this
is needed to remind the audience that it is counterfeit. 72. **lym,**
lymmer, a species of bloodhound which runs by scent. 73. **tike,** small
dog, cur. **trundle-tail,** curly tail. 76. **hatch,** lower half of a divided

door. 86. **Persian attire,** rich, gorgeous attire (ironical). 96. **upon,**
against. 102. **Stand in assured loss,** will assuredly be lost. 105.
balm'd, cured, healed. 109-122. **When . . . lurk.** These lines do not
appear in F. Their genuineness is sometimes questioned, but such
general comment for the enlightenment of the audience is not unusual.
113. **sufferance,** suffering. 114. **bearing,** tribulation. 115. **portable,**
endurable. 117. **He . . . father'd,** he has found the same cruelty in
his children which I found in my father. 118. **bewray,** betray, reveal.
120. **repeals,** recalls, restores. 121. **What . . . king!** Whatever else
happens, may the king escape!

take upon your traitorous father are not fit for your beholding. Advise the duke, where you are going, to a most festinate preparation: we are bound to the like. Our posts shall be swift and intelligent betwixt us. Farewell, dear sister: farewell, my lord of Gloucester.

Enter OSWALD.

How now! where 's the king? 14
   Osw. My lord of Gloucester hath convey'd him hence:
Some five or six and thirty of his knights,
Hot questrists after him, met him at gate;
Who, with some other of the lords dependants,
Are gone with him towards Dover; where they boast
To have well-armed friends.
   Corn.   Get horses for your mistress. 20
   Gon. Farewell, sweet lord, and sister.
   Corn. Edmund, farewell.
               [Exeunt Goneril, Edmund, and Oswald.
        Go seek the traitor Gloucester,
Pinion him like a thief, bring him before us.
                  [Exeunt other Servants.
Though well we may not pass upon his life
Without the form of justice, yet our power
Shall do a courtesy to our wrath, which men
May blame, but not control. Who 's there? the traitor?

Enter GLOUCESTER, *brought in by two or three.*

   Reg. Ingrateful fox! 'tis he.
   Corn. Bind fast his corky arms.
   Glou. What mean your graces? Good my friends, consider 30
You are my guests: do me no foul play, friends.
   Corn. Bind him, I say.   *[Servants bind him.*
   Reg.   Hard, hard. O filthy traitor!
   Glou. Unmerciful lady as you are, I 'm none.
   Corn. To this chair bind him. Villain, thou shalt find—   *[Regan plucks his beard.*
   Glou. By the kind gods, 'tis most ignobly done
To pluck me by the beard.
   Reg. So white, and such a traitor!
   Glou.   Naughty lady,
These hairs, which thou dost ravish from my chin,
Will quicken, and accuse thee: I am your host:
With robbers' hands my hospitable favours 40
You should not ruffle thus. What will you do?
   Corn. Come, sir, what letters had you late from France?
   Reg. Be simple answerer, for we know the truth.
   Corn. And what confederacy have you with the traitors
Late footed in the kingdom?
   Reg. To whose hands have you sent the lunatic king?
Speak.
   Glou.   I have a letter guessingly set down,
Which came from one that 's of a neutral heart,

And not from one opposed.
   Corn.   Cunning.
   Reg.   And false.
   Corn. Where hast thou sent the king? 50
   Glou. To Dover.
   Reg. Wherefore to Dover? Wast thou not charged at peril—
   Corn. Wherefore to Dover? Let him first answer that.
   Glou. I am tied to the stake, and I must stand the course.
   Reg. Wherefore to Dover, sir?
   Glou. Because I would not see thy cruel nails
Pluck out his poor old eyes; nor thy fierce sister
In his anointed flesh stick boarish fangs.
The sea, with such a storm as his bare head
In hell-black night endured, would have buoy'd up, 60
And quench'd the stelled fires:
Yet, poor old heart, he holp the heavens to rain.
If wolves had at thy gate howl'd that stern time,
Thou shouldst have said 'Good porter, turn the key,'
All cruels else subscribed: but I shall see
The winged vengeance overtake such children.
   Corn. See 't shalt thou never. Fellows, hold the chair.
Upon these eyes of thine I 'll set my foot.
   Glou. He that will think to live till he be old,
Give me some help! O cruel! O you gods! 70
   Reg. One side will mock another; the other too.
   Corn. If you see vengeance,—
   First Serv.   Hold your hand, my lord:
I have served you ever since I was a child;
But better service have I never done you
Than now to bid you hold.
   Reg.   How now, you dog!
   First Serv. If you did wear a beard upon your chin,
I 'd shake it on this quarrel. What do you mean?
   Corn. My villain!   *[They draw and fight.*
   First Serv. Nay, then, come on, and take the chance of anger.
   Reg. Give me thy sword. A peasant stand up thus! 80
          [Takes a sword, and runs at him behind.
   First Serv. O, I am slain! My lord, you have one eye left
To see some mischief on him. O!   *[Dies.*
   Corn. Lest it see more, prevent it. Out, vile jelly!
Where is thy lustre now?
   Glou. All dark and comfortless. Where 's my son Edmund?
Edmund, enkindle all the sparks of nature,
To quit this horrid act.
   Reg.   Out, treacherous villain!
Thou call'st on him that hates thee: it was he
That made the overture of thy treasons to us;
Who is too good to pity thee. 90
   Glou. O my follies! then Edgar was abused.
Kind gods, forgive me that, and prosper him!
   Reg. Go thrust him out at gates, and let him smell
His way to Dover. [*Exit one with Gloucester.*] How is 't, my lord? how look you?

SCENE VII. 9-10. **Advise . . . to,** i.e., advise him to make. 10. **festinate,** hasty. 11. **bound,** ready. 12. **intelligent,** serviceable in bearing intelligence. 13. **my . . . Gloucester,** i.e., Edmund. In line 15 the reference is to Gloucester himself. 17. **questrists,** searchers. 24. **pass upon,** pass sentence upon. 29. **corky,** withered with age. 39. **quicken,** come to life. 40. **hospitable favours.** Gloucester appeals to the sacredness of hospitality; the meaning is "the features of me, your host." 43. **simple answerer,** straightforward answerer. F has *simple*

answer'd, i.e., straightforward in your answers. 54. **tied to the stake,** like a bear to be baited with dogs. 60. **buoy'd,** lifted itself. 61. **stelled,** fixed; sometimes defined as "starry." 63. **stern,** so F; Q: *heard that dearn.* Many editors follow Capell, *howl'd that dearn,* in which *dearn* means "dire," "dreary." 65. **All . . . subscribed,** all their usual cruelties condoned or forgiven; so Q; F: *subscribe,* which may mean: all other cruel creatures show forgiveness except you. 66. **winged vengeance.** Note Gloucester's faith in the rectitude of the gods;

Corn. I have received a hurt: follow me, lady.
Turn out that eyeless villain; throw this slave
Upon the dunghill. Regan, I bleed apace:
Untimely comes this hurt: give me your arm.
                              [*Exit Cornwall, led by Regan.*
Sec. Serv. I'll never care what wickedness I do,
If this man come to good.
Third Serv.   If she live long,   100
And in the end meet the old course of death,
Women will all turn monsters.
Sec. Serv. Let 's follow the old earl, and get the
              Bedlam
To lead him where he would: his roguish madness
Allows itself to any thing.
Third Serv. Go thou: I'll fetch some flax and whites
              of eggs
To apply to his bleeding face. Now, heaven help him!
                              [*Exeunt severally.*

ACT IV.

SCENE I. *The heath.*

Enter EDGAR.

Edg. Yet better thus, and known to be contemn'd,
Than still contemn'd and flatter'd. To be worst,
The lowest and most dejected thing of fortune,
Stands still in esperance, lives not in fear:
The lamentable change is from the best;
The worst returns to laughter. Welcome, then,
Thou unsubstantial air that I embrace!
The wretch that thou hast blown unto the worst
Owes nothing to thy blasts. But who comes here?

Enter GLOUCESTER, *led by an* Old Man.

My father, poorly led? World, world, O world!   10
But that thy strange mutations make us hate thee,
Life would not yield to age.
Old Man. O, my good lord, I have been your
tenant, and your father's tenant, these fourscore years.
Glou. Away, get thee away; good friend, be gone:
Thy comforts can do me no good at all;
Thee they may hurt.
Old Man. Alack, sir, you cannot see your way.
Glou. I have no way, and therefore want no eyes;   20
I stumbled when I saw: full oft 'tis seen,
Our means secure us, and our mere defects
Prove our commodities. O dear son Edgar,
The food of thy abused father's wrath!
Might I but live to see thee in my touch,
I 'ld say I had eyes again!
Old Man.   How now! Who 's there?
Edg. [*Aside*] O gods! Who is 't can say 'I am at the
              worst'?
I am worse than e'er I was.
Old Man.   'Tis poor mad Tom.
Edg. [*Aside*] And worse I may be yet: the worst is
              not
So long as we can say 'This is the worst.'   30

Old Man. Fellow, where goest?
Glou.   Is it a beggar-man?
Old Man. Madman and beggar too.
Glou. He has some reason, else he could not beg.
I' the last night's storm I such a fellow saw;
Which made me think a man a worm: my son
Came then into my mind; and yet my mind
Was then scarce friends with him: I have heard more
              since.
As flies to wanton boys, are we to the gods,
They kill us for their sport.
Edg.   [*Aside*] How should this be?
Bad is the trade that must play fool to sorrow,   40
Angering itself and others.—Bless thee, master!
Glou. Is that the naked fellow?
Old Man.   Ay, my lord.
Glou. Then, prithee, get thee gone: if, for my sake,
Thou wilt o'ertake us, hence a mile or twain,
I' the way toward Dover, do it for ancient love;
And bring some covering for this naked soul,
Who I'll entreat to lead me.
Old Man.   Alack, sir, he is mad.
Glou. 'Tis the times' plague, when madmen lead the
              blind.
Do as I bid thee, or rather do thy pleasure;
Above the rest, be gone.   50
Old Man. I'll bring him the best 'parel that I have,
Come on 't what will.   [*Exit.*
Glou. Sirrah, naked fellow,—
Edg. Poor Tom 's a-cold. [*Aside*] I cannot daub it
              further.
Glou. Come hither, fellow.
Edg. [*Aside*] And yet I must.—Bless thy sweet eyes,
              they bleed.   56
Glou. Know'st thou the way to Dover?
Edg. Both stile and gate, horse-way and foot-path.
Poor Tom hath been scared out of his good wits:
bless thee, good man's son, from the foul fiend! five
fiends have been in poor Tom at once; of lust, as
Obidicut; Hobbididance, prince of dumbness;
Mahu, of stealing; Modo, of murder; Flibbertigibbet,
of mopping and mowing, who since possesses cham-
bermaids and waiting-women. So, bless thee, master!
Glou. Here, take this purse, thou whom the heavens'
              plagues
Have humbled to all strokes: that I am wretched
Makes thee the happier: heavens, deal so still!
Let the superfluous and lust-dieted man,   70
That slaves your ordinance, that will not see
Because he doth not feel, feel your power quickly;
So distribution should undo excess,
And each man have enough. Dost thou know Dover?
Edg. Ay, master.
Glou. There is a cliff, whose high and bending head
Looks fearfully in the confined deep:
Bring me but to the very brim of it,
And I'll repair the misery thou dost bear
With something rich about me: from that place   80
I shall no leading need.
Edg.   Give me thy arm:

note also that in this speech he twice suggests ironically his own fate.
78. **villain,** servant, bondman. 89. **overture,** disclosure. 98. **Untimely,** inopportunely. 101. **old,** customary, natural. 103. **Bedlam,**
Bedlamite, lunatic.
  ACT IV. SCENE I. 3. **dejected . . . of,** debased or humbled by. 4.
esperance, hope. 11. **mutations,** changes, variations. 22. **Our means
secure us,** our resources make us overconfident. 23. **commodities,**
benefits. 38-39. **As . . . sport.** This is a clear statement of Gloucester's

loss of faith, which he signalizes (l. 76) by forming a plan to commit
suicide. 51. **'parel,** apparel. 54. **daub it further,** keep up the disguise. 62-64. **Obidicut . . . Flibbertigibbet,** fiends borrowed, as
before, from Harsnet. 65. **mopping and mowing,** making grimaces
and mouths. 70. **superfluous,** having a superfluity. **lust-dieted,**
probably, feeding luxuriously. 71. **slaves your ordinance,** i.e., makes
the laws of heaven his slaves. 73. **distribution,** the principle of distributive justice in ethics.

Poor Tom shall lead thee. [*Exeunt.*

SCENE II. *Before the Duke of Albany's palace.*

Enter GONERIL *and* EDMUND.

Gon. Welcome, my lord: I marvel our mild husband
Not met us on the way.

Enter OSWALD.

               Now, where 's your master?
Osw. Madam, within; but never man so changed.
I told him of the army that was landed;
He smiled at it: I told him you were coming;
His answer was 'The worse:' of Gloucester's treachery,
And of the loyal service of his son,
When I inform'd him, then he call'd me sot,
And told me I had turn'd the wrong side out:
What most he should dislike seems pleasant to him; 10
What like, offensive.
    Gon.   [*To Edm.*] Then shall you go no
    further.
It is the cowish terror of his spirit,
That dares not undertake: he'll not feel wrongs
Which tie him to an answer. Our wishes on the way
May prove effects. Back, Edmund, to my brother;
Hasten his musters and conduct his powers:
I must change arms at home, and give the distaff
Into my husband's hands. This trusty servant
Shall pass between us: ere long you are like to hear,
If you dare venture in your own behalf, 20
A mistress's command. Wear this; spare speech;
                    [*Giving a favour.*
Decline your head: this kiss, if it durst speak,
Would stretch thy spirits up into the air:
Conceive, and fare thee well.
    Edm. Yours in the ranks of death.
    Gon.   My most dear Gloucester!
                    [*Exit Edmund.*
O, the difference of man and man!
To thee a woman's services are due:
My fool usurps my body.
    Osw.   Madam, here comes my lord. [*Exit.*

Enter ALBANY.

    Gon. I have been worth the whistle.
    Alb.   O Goneril!
You are not worth the dust which the rude wind 30
Blows in your face. I fear your disposition:
That nature, which contemns it origin,
Cannot be border'd certain in itself;
She that herself will sliver and disbranch
From her material sap, perforce must wither
And come to deadly use.
    Gon. No more; the text is foolish.
    Alb. Wisdom and goodness to the vile seem vile:
Filths savour but themselves. What have you done?
Tigers, not daughters, what have you perform'd? 40

A father, and a gracious aged man,
Whose reverence even the head-lugg'd bear would
    lick,
Most barbarous, most degenerate! have you madded.
Could my good brother suffer you to do it?
A man, a prince, by him so benefited!
If that the heavens do not their visible spirits
Send quickly down to tame these vile offences,
It will come,
Humanity must perforce prey on itself,
Like monsters of the deep.
    Gon.   Milk-liver'd man! 50
That bear'st a cheek for blows, a head for wrongs:
Who hast not in thy brows an eye discerning
Thine honour from thy suffering; that not know'st
Fools do those villains pity who are punish'd
Ere they have done their mischief. Where 's thy drum?
France spreads his banners in our noiseless land,
With plumed helm thy state begins to threat;
Whiles thou, a moral fool, sit'st still, and criest
'Alack, why does he so?'
    Alb.   See thyself, devil!
Proper deformity seems not in the fiend 60
So horrid as in woman.
    Gon.   O vain fool!
    Alb. Thou changed and self-cover'd thing, for
    shame,
Be-monster not thy feature. Were 't my fitness
To let these hands obey my blood,
They are apt enough to dislocate and tear
Thy flesh and bones: howe'er thou art a fiend,
A woman's shape doth shield thee.
    Gon. Marry, your manhood now—

Enter a Messenger.

    Alb. What news?
    Mess. O, my good lord, the Duke of Cornwall 's
    dead; 70
Slain by his servant, going to put out
The other eye of Gloucester.
    Alb.   Gloucester's eyes!
    Mess. A servant that he bred, thrill'd with remorse,
Opposed against the act, bending his sword
To his great master; who, thereat enraged,
Flew on him, and amongst them fell'd him dead;
But not without that harmful stroke, which since
Hath pluck'd him after.
    Alb.   This shows you are above,
You justicers, that these our nether crimes
So speedily can venge! But, O poor Gloucester! 80
Lost he his other eye?
    Mess.   Both, both, my lord.
This letter, madam, craves a speedy answer;
'Tis from your sister.
    Gon. [*Aside*] One way I like this well;
But being widow, and my Gloucester with her,
May all the building in my fancy pluck
Upon my hateful life: another way,

SCENE II. 1. **mild,** used ironically. 8. **sot,** fool. 9. **turn'd the
wrong side out,** put a wrong interpretation on the matter. 12. **cowish,**
cowardly. 13-14. **he'll . . . answer,** i.e., in his cowardice he will
ignore injuries he ought to resent. 14. **Our . . . way,** my wishes
expressed to you on the way. 15. **prove effects,** come to pass. 17.
arms, distaff, i.e., she must turn warrior and give into Albany's hands
the *arms,* or insignia, of housewifery. 24. **Conceive,** understand, take
my meaning. 28. **My . . . body,** so F; Q₁ (uncorr. copies): *my foote
. . . body;* Q₁ (corr. copies): *A toole . . . bed;* Q₂: *my foote . . . head.* 29.
whistle. She alludes to the proverb: "It is a poor dog that is not

worth the whistling." 32. **it,** its. 33. **border'd,** kept within bounds.
34. **sliver,** tear off. 35. **material sap,** nourishing substance. 39.
savour but, care only for. 42. **head-lugg'd,** dragged by the head and
infuriated. 43. **madded,** driven mad. 47. **offences,** offenders. 50.
Milk-liver'd, cowardly. 56. **noiseless,** peaceful, having none of the
bustle of war. 58. **moral,** moralizing. 60. **Proper,** i.e., the deformity
appropriate to the fiend. 62. **self-cover'd,** having the true self concealed. 63. **Be-monster . . . feature,** do not, being fiend, take on the
outward form of woman. **my fitness,** suitable for me. 66. **howe'er,**
although. 68. **now.** Some copies of Q have *mew,* as an exclamation of

The news is not so tart.—I'll read, and answer. [*Exit.*
  Alb. Where was his son when they did take his eyes?
  Mess. Come with my lady hither.
  Alb.   He is not here.   90
  Mess. No, my good lord; I met him back again.
  Alb. Knows he the wickedness?
  Mess. Ay, my good lord; 'twas he inform'd against
    him;
And quit the house on purpose, that their punishment
Might have the freer course.
  Alb.   Gloucester, I live
To thank thee for the love thou show'dst the king,
And to revenge thine eyes. Come hither, friend:
Tell me what more thou know'st.   [*Exeunt.*

SCENE III. *The French camp near Dover.*

Enter KENT *and a* Gentleman.

  Kent. Why the King of France is so suddenly gone
back know you the reason?
  Gent. Something he left imperfect in the state, which
since his coming forth is thought of; which imports to
the kingdom so much fear and danger, that his per-
sonal return was most required and necessary.
  Kent. Who hath he left behind him general?
  Gent. The Marshal of France, Monsieur La Far.   10
  Kent. Did your letters pierce the queen to any
demonstration of grief?
  Gent. Ay, sir; she took them, read them in my
    presence;
And now and then an ample tear trill'd down
Her delicate cheek: it seem'd she was a queen
Over her passion; who, most rebel-like,
Sought to be king o'er her.
  Kent.   O, then it moved her.
  Gent. Not to a rage: patience and sorrow strove
Who should express her goodliest. You have seen
Sunshine and rain at once: her smiles and tears   20
†Were like a better way: those happy smilets,
That play'd on her ripe lip, seem'd not to know
What guests were in her eyes; which parted thence,
As pearls from diamonds dropp'd. In brief,
Sorrow would be a rarity most beloved,
If all could so become it.
  Kent.   Made she no verbal question?
  Gent. 'Faith, once or twice she heaved the name of
    'father'
Pantingly forth, as if it press'd her heart;
Cried 'Sisters! sisters! Shame of ladies! sisters!
Kent! father! sisters! What, i' the storm? i' the night?30
Let pity not be believed!' There she shook
The holy water from her heavenly eyes,
And clamour moisten'd: then away she started
To deal with grief alone.
  Kent.   It is the stars,
The stars above us, govern our conditions;
Else one self mate and mate could not beget

Such different issues. You spoke not with her since?
  Gent. No.
  Kent. Was this before the king return'd?
  Gent.   No, since.
  Kent. Well, sir, the poor distressed Lear 's i' the
    town;   40
Who sometime, in his better tune, remembers
What we are come about, and by no means
Will yield to see his daughter.
  Gent.   Why, good sir?
  Kent. A sovereign shame so elbows him: his own
    unkindness,
That stripp'd her from his benediction, turn'd her
To foreign casualties, gave her dear rights
To his dog-hearted daughters, these things sting
His mind so venomously, that burning shame
Detains him from Cordelia.
  Gent.   Alack, poor gentleman!
  Kent. Of Albany's and Cornwall's powers you heard
    not?   50
  Gent. 'Tis so, they are afoot.
  Kent. Well, sir, I'll bring you to our master Lear,
And leave you to attend him: some dear cause
Will in concealment wrap me up awhile;
When I am known aright, you shall not grieve
Lending me this acquaintance. I pray you, go
Along with me.   [*Exeunt.*

SCENE IV. *The same. A tent.*

Enter, with drum and colours, CORDELIA, Doctor, *and*
  Soldiers.

  Cor. Alack, 'tis he: why, he was met even now
As mad as the vex'd sea; singing aloud;
Crown'd with rank fumiter and furrow-weeds,
With bur-docks, hemlock, nettles, cuckoo-flowers,
Darnel, and all the idle weeds that grow
In our sustaining corn. A century send forth;
Search every acre in the high-grown field,
And bring him to our eye. [*Exit an Officer.*] What can
    man's wisdom
In the restoring his bereaved sense?
He that helps him take all my outward worth.   10
  Doct. There is means, madam:
Our foster-nurse of nature is repose,
The which he lacks; that to provoke in him,
Are many simples operative, whose power
Will close the eye of anguish.
  Cor.   All blest secrets,
All you unpublish'd virtues of the earth,
Spring with my tears! be aidant and remediate
In the good man's distress! Seek, seek for him;
Lest his ungovern'd rage dissolve the life
That wants the means to lead it.

Enter a Messenger.

  Mess.   News, madam;   20

---

disgust. 73. **remorse,** pity. 74-75. **bending . . . To,** directing his
sword against. 78-79. **This . . . justicers,** premonition of ultimate
justice. 88. **tart,** painful, grievous. 91. **back,** going back.
  SCENE III. 5. **imports,** portends. 14. **trill'd,** trickled. 21. **like
a better way,** possibly, better than this. **smilets,** smiles. 22. **ripe,**
probably, red (W. J. Craig). 27. **heaved,** breathed out. 34. **It is the
stars.** One of the many expressions in the play of the inscrutability
of Providence. 36. **and mate,** Q: *and make,* which would mean "marital
partner." 41. **better tune,** saner moments. 44. **elbows,** thrusts away,
or possibly, stands at his elbow. 45. **turn'd,** expelled.

SCENE IV. 3. **fumiter,** the weed "earth-smoke." **furrow-weeds,**
weeds growing in the furrows of plowed land. 4. **bur-docks.** Q: *hor-
docks.* Some editors follow Collier: *hoar-docks,* i.e., white-leaved. **cuckoo-
flowers,** possibly, cowslips. 5. **Darnel,** a weed of the grass kind. The
plants mentioned in this passage are probably selected because of their
bitter and poisonous quality. 6. **sustaining,** giving sustenance.
century, usually interpreted as a troop of 100 men, as in the Roman
army; also taken to mean "sentry" or "scout." 8. **wisdom,** science.
9. **bereaved,** snatched away. 14. **simples,** medicinal plants. **operative,** effective. 17. **aidant and remediate,** helpful and remedial.

The British powers are marching hitherward.
   Cor. 'Tis known before; our preparation stands
In expectation of them. O dear father,
It is thy business that I go about;
Therefore great France
My mourning and important tears hath pitied.
No blown ambition doth our arms incite,
But love, dear love, and our aged father's right:
Soon may I hear and see him!   [*Exeunt.*

SCENE V. *Gloucester's castle.*

Enter REGAN *and* OSWALD.

   Reg. But are my brother's powers set forth?
   Osw.   Ay, madam.
   Reg. Himself in person there?
   Osw.   Madam, with much ado:
Your sister is the better soldier.
   Reg. Lord Edmund spake not with your lord at
      home?
   Osw. No, madam.
   Reg. What might import my sister's letter to him?
   Osw. I know not, lady.
   Reg. 'Faith, he is posted hence on serious matter.
It was great ignorance, Gloucester's eyes being out,
To let him live: where he arrives he moves   10
All hearts against us: Edmund, I think, is gone,
In pity of his misery, to dispatch
His nighted life; moreover, to descry
The strength o' the enemy.
   Osw. I must needs after him, madam, with my
      letter.
   Reg. Our troops set forth to-morrow: stay with us;
The ways are dangerous.
   Osw.   I may not, madam:
My lady charged my duty in this business.
   Reg. Why should she write to Edmund? Might not
      you
Transport her purposes by word? Belike,   20
Something—I know not what: I'll love thee much,
Let me unseal the letter.
   Osw.   Madam, I had rather—
   Reg. I know your lady does not love her husband;
I am sure of that: and at her late being here
She gave strange œillades and most speaking looks
To noble Edmund. I know you are of her bosom.
   Osw. I, madam?
   Reg. I speak in understanding; you are, I know 't:
Therefore I do advise you, take this note:
My lord is dead; Edmund and I have talk'd;   30
And more convenient is he for my hand
Than for your lady's: you may gather more.
If you do find him, pray you, give him this;
And when your mistress hears thus much from you,
I pray, desire her call her wisdom to her.
So, fare you well.
If you do chance to hear of that blind traitor,

King Lear
<small>ACT IV : SC IV</small>

1008

Preferment falls on him that cuts him off.
   Osw. Would I could meet him, madam! I should
      show
What party I do follow.
   Reg.   Fare thee well.   [*Exeunt.* 40

SCENE VI. *Fields near Dover.*

Enter GLOUCESTER, *and* EDGAR *dressed like a peasant.*

   Glou. When shall we come to the top of that same
      hill?
   Edg. You do climb up it now: look, how we labour.
   Glou. Methinks the ground is even.
   Edg.   Horrible steep.
Hark, do you hear the sea?
   Glou.   No, truly.
   Edg. Why, then, your other senses grow imperfect
By your eyes' anguish.
   Glou.   So may it be, indeed:
Methinks thy voice is alter'd; and thou speak'st
In better phrase and matter than thou didst.
   Edg. You 're much deceived: in nothing am I
      changed   9
But in my garments.
   Glou.   Methinks you 're better spoken.
   Edg. Come on, sir; here 's the place: stand still.
      How fearful
And dizzy 'tis, to cast one's eyes so low!
The crows and choughs that wing the midway air
Show scarce so gross as beetles: half way down
Hangs one that gathers samphire, dreadful trade!
Methinks he seems no bigger than his head:
The fishermen, that walk upon the beach,
Appear like mice; and yond tall anchoring bark,
Diminish'd to her cock; her cock, a buoy
Almost too small for sight: the murmuring surge,   20
That on the unnumber'd idle pebbles chafes,
Cannot be heard so high. I'll look no more;
Lest my brain turn, and the deficient sight
Topple down headlong.
   Glou.   Set me where you stand.
   Edg. Give me your hand: you are now within a foot
Of the extreme verge: for all beneath the moon
Would I not leap upright.
   Glou.   Let go my hand.
Here, friend, 's another purse; in it a jewel
Well worth a poor man's taking: fairies and gods
Prosper it with thee! Go thou farther off;   30
Bid me farewell, and let me hear thee going.
   Edg. Now fare you well, good sir.
   Glou.   With all my heart.
   Edg. Why I do trifle thus with his despair
Is done to cure it.
   Glou.   [*Kneeling*] O you mighty gods!
This world I do renounce, and, in your sights,
Shake patiently my great affliction off:
If I could bear it longer, and not fall

---

26. **important,** importunate. 27. **blown,** puffed up with pride.
  SCENE V. 6. **import,** to bear as its purport, to express (Onions).
11-14. **Edmund . . . enemy.** Note the irony which reveals Edmund's
real reason as it states his pretended one. 20. **word,** word of mouth.
Belike, it may be. 25. **œillades,** amorous glances. 26. **of her bosom,**
in her confidence. 29. **take this note,** take note of this. 30. **have
talk'd,** are affianced to one another (W. J. Craig).
  SCENE VI. 11-24. **here 's . . . headlong.** This famous passage might
almost be taken to symbolize the want of scenery on Shakespeare's own
stage; his atmosphere had to be in large measure the creation of his
poetry. 13. **choughs,** jackdaws. 15. **samphire,** an herb called sea-

fennel and the herb of St. Pierre, used for pickles. 19. **cock,** cock-boat.
21. **unnumber'd,** innumerable. 33-80. **Why . . . thoughts.** This
passage has important moral and theological import. Its plain teaching
is against suicide; in that, as in other matters, the play is Christian
in spite of its pagan setting; see lines 75-77. 38. **opposeless,** irresistible. 39. **snuff,** useless residue; the metaphor is taken from the
smoking wick of a candle. 47. **pass,** die. 53. **at each,** end to end.
57. **bourn,** limit, boundary. 58. **a-height,** on high. **shrill-gorged,**
shrill-throated. 71. **whelk'd,** explained as "twisted"; also as "swollen,
as with whelks or knobs." **enridged,** furrowed. 73. **clearest,** most
righteous. 74. **men's impossibilities,** things impossible to men.

To quarrel with your great opposeless wills,
My snuff and loathed part of nature should
Burn itself out. If Edgar live, O, bless him!   40
Now, fellow, fare thee well.   [*He falls forward.*
    Edg.   Gone, sir: farewell.
And yet I know not how conceit may rob
The treasury of life, when life itself
Yields to the theft: had he been where he thought,
By this, had thought been past. Alive or dead?
Ho, you sir! friend! Hear you, sir! speak!
Thus might he pass indeed: yet he revives.
What are you, sir?
    Glou.   Away, and let me die.
    Edg. Hadst thou been aught but gossamer, feathers,
          air,
So many fathom down precipitating,   50
Thou 'dst shiver'd like an egg: but thou dost breathe;
Hast heavy substance; bleed'st not; speak'st; art
          sound.
Ten masts at each make not the altitude
Which thou hast perpendicularly fell:
Thy life 's a miracle. Speak yet again.
    Glou. But have I fall'n, or no?
    Edg. From the dread summit of this chalky bourn.
Look up a-height; the shrill-gorged lark so far
Cannot be seen or heard: do but look up.
    Glou. Alack, I have no eyes.   60
Is wretchedness deprived that benefit,
To end itself by death? 'Twas yet some comfort,
When misery could beguile the tyrant's rage,
And frustrate his proud will.
    Edg.   Give me your arm:
Up: so. How is 't? Feel you your legs? You stand.
    Glou. Too well, too well.
    Edg.   This is above all strangeness.
Upon the crown o' the cliff, what thing was that
Which parted from you?
    Glou.   A poor unfortunate beggar.
    Edg. As I stood here below, methought his eyes
Were two full moons; he had a thousand noses,   70
Horns whelk'd and waved like the enridged sea:
It was some fiend; therefore, thou happy father,
Think that the clearest gods, who make them honours
Of men's impossibilities, have preserved thee.
    Glou. I do remember now: henceforth I'll bear
Affliction till it do cry out itself
'Enough, enough,' and die. That thing you speak of,
I took it for a man; often 'twould say
'The fiend, the fiend:' he led me to that place.
    Edg. Bear free and patient thoughts. But who comes
          here?   80

Enter LEAR, *fantastically dressed with wild flowers.*

The safer sense will ne'er accommodate
His master thus.
    Lear. No, they cannot touch me for coining;
I am the king himself.
    Edg. O thou side-piercing sight!   85

    Lear. Nature 's above art in that respect. There 's
your press-money. That fellow handles his bow like a
crow-keeper: draw me a clothier's yard. Look, look, a
mouse! Peace, peace; this piece of toasted cheese will
do 't. There 's my gauntlet; I'll prove it on a giant.
Bring up the brown bills. O, well flown, bird! i' the
clout, i' the clout: hewgh! Give the word.
    Edg. Sweet marjoram.
    Lear. Pass.
    Glou. I know that voice.   96
    Lear. Ha! Goneril, with a white beard! They
flattered me like a dog; and told me I had white hairs
in my beard ere the black ones were there. To say
'ay' and 'no' to every thing that I said!—'Ay' and
'no' too was no good divinity. When the rain came to
wet me once, and the wind to make me chatter; when
the thunder would not peace at my bidding; there I
found 'em, there I smelt 'em out. Go to, they are not
men o' their words: they told me I was every thing;
'tis a lie, I am not ague-proof.   107
    Glou. The trick of that voice I do well remember:
Is 't not the king?
    Lear.   Ay, every inch a king:
When I do stare, see how the subject quakes.   110
I pardon that man's life. What was thy cause?
Adultery?
Thou shalt not die: die for adultery! No:
The wren goes to 't, and the small gilded fly
Does lecher in my sight.
Let copulation thrive; for Gloucester's bastard son
Was kinder to his father than my daughters
Got 'tween the lawful sheets.
To 't, luxury, pell-mell! for I lack soldiers.
Behold yond simpering dame,   120
Whose face between her forks presages snow;
That minces virtue, and does shake the head
To hear of pleasure's name;
The fitchew, nor the soiled horse, goes to 't
With a more riotous appetite.
Down from the waist they are Centaurs,
Though women all above:
But to the girdle do the gods inherit,
Beneath is all the fiends';
There 's hell, there 's darkness, there 's the sulphurous
          pit,   130
Burning, scalding, stench, consumption; fie, fie, fie!
pah, pah! Give me an ounce of civet, good apothe-
cary, to sweeten my imagination: there 's money for
thee.
    Glou. O, let me kiss that hand!
    Lear. Let me wipe it first; it smells of mortality.
    Glou. O ruin'd piece of nature! This great world
Shall so wear out to nought. Dost thou know me?
    Lear. I remember thine eyes well enough. Dost
thou squiny at me? No, do thy worst, blind Cupid;
I'll not love. Read thou this challenge; mark but the
penning of it.   142
    Glou. Were all the letters suns, I could not see one.

(marginal note, right column)

King Lear
ACT IV : SC VI

1009

80. **free**, probably, free from fear. 81. **safer**, saner. **accommodate**,
furnish, equip. 83. **touch**, arrest, prosecute. 87. **press-money**,
bonus given soldiers when they were pressed into service. 88. **crow-
keeper**, scarecrow; or possibly, crow-frightener. 89. **clothier's yard**,
arrow the length of a cloth yard. 92. **brown bills**, soldiers carrying
pikes, or the pikes themselves. **well flown, bird**. Lear may think he
is hawking, or he may be speaking of the flight of an arrow. 93.
clout, target. **word**, password. 98-107. **They flattered . . . ague-
proof**. This strangely sane passage echoes one of the themes of the play,
namely, the wickedness of flattery. 104. **peace**, hold its peace. 108.
trick, peculiar characteristic. 109. **Ay, every inch a king**. Gloucester's

words bring Lear back to the recollection of his kingly state, and he
begins to speak in blank verse, irregular to correspond to his wandering
sanity. The whole passage is full of the deepest social pessimism.
It is the reflection in Lear's crazed mind of the chaos, domestic and
political, wrought in the state by wickedness in high places. 119.
luxury, lust. 124. **fitchew**, polecat. **soiled horse**, horse turned out
to grass. 126. **Centaurs**, fabulous monsters, half man, half horse.
128. **But**, only. **inherit**, possess. 137. **piece**, masterpiece. 140.
squiny, squint, look askance.

Edg. I would not take this from report; it is,
And my heart breaks at it.
Lear. Read.
Glou. What, with the case of eyes? 147
Lear. O, ho, are you there with me? No eyes in your head, nor no money in your purse? Your eyes are in a heavy case, your purse in a light: yet you see how this world goes.
Glou. I see it feelingly. 152
Lear. What, art mad? A man may see how this world goes with no eyes. Look with thine ears: see how yond justice rails upon yond simple thief. Hark, in thine ear: change places; and, handy-dandy, which is the justice, which is the thief? Thou hast seen a farmer's dog bark at a beggar?
Glou. Ay, sir. 160
Lear. And the creature run from the cur? There thou mightst behold the great image of authority: a dog's obeyed in office.
Thou rascal beadle, hold thy bloody hand!
Why dost thou lash that whore? Strip thine own back;
Thou hotly lust'st to use her in that kind
For which thou whipp'st her. The usurer hangs the
    cozener.
Through tatter'd clothes small vices do appear;
Robes and furr'd gowns hide all. Plate sin with gold,
And the strong lance of justice hurtless breaks; 170
Arm it in rags, a pigmy's straw does pierce it.
None does offend, none, I say, none; I'll able 'em:
Take that of me, my friend, who have the power
To seal the accuser's lips. Get thee glass eyes;
And, like a scurvy politician, seem
To see the things thou dost not. Now, now, now, now:
Pull off my boots: harder, harder: so.
Edg. O, matter and impertinency mix'd!
Reason in madness!
Lear. If thou wilt weep my fortunes, take my eyes. 180
I know thee well enough; thy name is Gloucester:
Thou must be patient; we came crying hither:
Thou know'st, the first time that we smell the air,
We wawl and cry. I will preach to thee: mark.
Glou. Alack, alack the day!
Lear. When we are born, we cry that we are come
To this great stage of fools: this' a good block;
It were a delicate stratagem, to shoe
A troop of horse with felt: I'll put 't in proof;
And when I have stol'n upon these sons-in-law, 190
Then, kill, kill, kill, kill, kill, kill!

Enter a Gentleman, *with* Attendants.

Gent. O, here he is: lay hand upon him. Sir,
Your most dear daughter—
Lear. No rescue? What, a prisoner? I am even
The natural fool of fortune. Use me well;
You shall have ransom. Let me have surgeons;
I am cut to the brains.
Gent.   You shall have any thing.
Lear. No seconds? all myself?
Why, this would make a man a man of salt,
To use his eyes for garden water-pots, 200

Ay, and laying autumn's dust.
Gent.   Good sir,—
Lear. I will die bravely, like a bridegroom. What!
I will be jovial: come, come; I am a king,
My masters, know you that.
Gent. You are a royal one, and we obey you.
Lear. Then there's life in 't. Nay, if you get it, you shall get it with running. Sa, sa, sa, sa.
    [*Exit running; Attendants follow.*
Gent. A sight most pitiful in the meanest wretch,
Past speaking of in a king! Thou hast one daughter,
Who redeems nature from the general curse 210
Which twain have brought her to.
Edg. Hail, gentle sir.
Gent.   Sir, speed you: what's your
    will?
Edg. Do you hear aught, sir, of a battle toward?
Gent. Most sure and vulgar: every one hears that,
Which can distinguish sound.
Edg.   But, by your favour,
How near 's the other army?
Gent. Near and on speedy foot; the main descry
Stands on the hourly thought.
Edg.   I thank you, sir: that's all.
Gent. Though that the queen on special cause is
    here,
Her army is moved on.
Edg.   I thank you, sir.   [*Exit Gent.* 220
Glou. You ever-gentle gods, take my breath from
    me;
Let not my worser spirit tempt me again
To die before you please!
Edg.   Well pray you, father.
Glou. Now, good sir, what are you?
Edg. A most poor man, made tame to fortune's
    blows;
Who, by the art of known and feeling sorrows,
Am pregnant to good pity. Give me your hand,
I'll lead you to some biding.
Glou.   Hearty thanks:
The bounty and the benison of heaven
To boot, and boot!

Enter OSWALD.

Osw.   A proclaim'd prize! Most
    happy! 230
That eyeless head of thine was first framed flesh
To raise my fortunes. Thou old unhappy traitor,
Briefly thyself remember: the sword is out
That must destroy thee.
Glou.   Now let thy friendly hand
Put strength enough to 't.   [*Edgar interposes.*
Osw.   Wherefore, bold peasant,
Darest thou support a publish'd traitor? Hence;
Lest that the infection of his fortune take
Like hold on thee. Let go his arm.
Edg. Chill not let go, zir, without vurther 'casion. 240
Osw. Let go, slave, or thou diest!
Edg. Good gentleman, go your gait, and let poor volk pass. An chud ha' bin zwaggered out of my life,

147. **case,** mere sockets. 148. **are . . . me?** Is that what you refer to? 157. **handy-dandy,** take your choice of hands, as in a well-known child's game. 161-171. **And the . . . pierce it.** Into these ravings should be read the conception of a state resting upon authority solely, and this state fallen into ruin because the holders of this divinely constituted authority are themselves corrupt. 167. **cozener,** cheater. 172. **able,** give warrant to. 175. **politician,** trickster. 187. **this',** this is. **block,** probably, hat, from the form on which it was molded.

199. **man of salt,** of salt tears. 212. **speed you,** God speed you. 214. **vulgar,** in everyone's mouth, generally known. 215. **Which,** who. 217-218. **the main . . . thought,** the full view of the main body is expected every hour. 226. **feeling,** heartfelt, deep. 228. **biding,** abiding place. 230. **To boot, and boot,** i.e., in addition (to my thanks), I wish you the bounty of heaven. 233. **thyself remember,** confess thy sins. 239. **Chill,** I will. Edgar adopts a dialect, apparently of the south country. 242. **go your gait,** go your own way. 243. **An chud,**

'twould not ha' bin zo long as 'tis by a vortnight. Nay, come not near th' old man; keep out, che vor ye, or ise try whether your costard or my ballow be the harder: chill be plain with you.

Osw. Out, dunghill!

Edg. Chill pick your teeth, zir: come; no matter vor your foins.   [*They fight, and Edgar knocks him down.* 251

Osw. Slave, thou hast slain me: villain, take my
  purse:
If ever thou wilt thrive, bury my body;
And give the letters which thou find'st about me
To Edmund earl of Gloucester; seek him out
Upon the British party: O, untimely death!   [*Dies.*

Edg. I know thee well: a serviceable villain;
As duteous to the vices of thy mistress
As badness would desire.

Glou.   What, is he dead?

Edg. Sit you down, father; rest you.   260
Let 's see these pockets: the letters that he speaks of
May be my friends. He 's dead; I am only sorry
He had no other death's-man. Let us see:
Leave, gentle wax; and, manners, blame us not:
To know our enemies' minds, we 'ld rip their hearts;
Their papers, is more lawful.   266

[*Reads*] 'Let our reciprocal vows be remembered.
You have many opportunities to cut him off: if your
will want not, time and place will be fruitfully
offered. There is nothing done, if he return the conqueror: then am I the prisoner, and his bed my gaol;
from the loathed warmth whereof deliver me, and
supply the place for your labour.

  'Your—wife, so I would say—
    'Affectionate servant,   'GONERIL.'
O undistinguish'd space of woman's will!
A plot upon her virtuous husband's life;
And the exchange my brother! Here, in the sands,   280
Thee I'll rake up, the post unsanctified
Of murderous lechers: and in the mature time
With this ungracious paper strike the sight
Of the death-practised duke: for him 'tis well
That of thy death and business I can tell.

Glou. The king is mad: how stiff is my vile sense,
That I stand up, and have ingenious feeling
Of my huge sorrows! Better I were distract:
So should my thoughts be sever'd from my griefs,
And woes by wrong imaginations lose   290
The knowledge of themselves.

Edg.   Give me your hand:
                    [*Drum afar off.*
Far off, methinks, I hear the beaten drum:
Come, father, I'll bestow you with a friend.   [*Exeunt.*

SCENE VII. *A tent in the French camp.* LEAR *on a bed asleep, soft music playing;* Gentleman, *and others attending.*

Enter CORDELIA, KENT, *and* Doctor.

Cor. O thou good Kent, how shall I live and work,
To match thy goodness? My life will be too short,
And every measure fail me.

Kent. To be acknowledged, madam, is o'er-paid.
All my reports go with the modest truth;
Nor more nor clipp'd, but so.

Cor.   Be better suited:
These weeds are memories of those worser hours:
I prithee, put them off.

Kent.   Pardon me, dear madam;
Yet to be known shortens my made intent:
My boon I make it, that you know me not   10
Till time and I think meet.

Cor. Then be 't so, my good lord. [*To the Doctor*] How
  does the king?

Doct. Madam, sleeps still.

Cor. O you kind gods,
Cure this great breach in his abused nature!
The untuned and jarring senses, O, wind up
Of this child-changed father!

Doct.   So please your majesty
That we may wake the king: he hath slept long.

Cor. Be govern'd by your knowledge, and proceed
I' the sway of your own will. Is he array'd?   20

Gent. Ay, madam; in the heaviness of his sleep
We put fresh garments on him.

Doct. Be by, good madam, when we do awake him;
I doubt not of his temperance.

Cor.   Very well.

Doct. Please you, draw near. Louder the music
  there!

Cor. O my dear father! Restoration hang
Thy medicine on my lips; and let this kiss
Repair those violent harms that my two sisters
Have in thy reverence made!

Kent.   Kind and dear princess!

Cor. Had you not been their father, these white
  flakes   30
Had challenged pity of them. Was this a face
To be opposed against the warring winds?
To stand against the deep dread-bolted thunder?
In the most terrible and nimble stroke
Of quick, cross lightning? to watch—poor perdu!—
With this thin helm? Mine enemy's dog,
Though he had bit me, should have stood that night
Against my fire; and wast thou fain, poor father,
To hovel thee with swine, and rogues forlorn,
In short and musty straw? Alack, alack!   40
'Tis wonder that thy life and wits at once
Had not concluded all. He wakes; speak to him.

Doct. Madam, do you; 'tis fittest.

Cor. How does my royal lord? How fares your
  majesty?

Lear. You do me wrong to take me out o' the grave:
Thou art a soul in bliss; but I am bound
Upon a wheel of fire, that mine own tears
Do scald like molten lead.

Cor.   Sir, do you know me?

Lear. You are a spirit, I know: when did you die?

Cor. Still, still, far wide!   50

Doct. He 's scarce awake: let him alone awhile.

Lear. Where have I been? Where am I? Fair
  daylight?

---

if I could. 246. **che vor ye,** I warn you. 247. **ise,** I shall. **costard,** an apple, slang for "head." **ballow,** cudgel. 249. **dunghill,** person of the lowest extraction. 251. **foins,** thrusts in fencing. 263. **death's-man,** executioner. 264. **Leave,** by your leave. 270. **fruitfully,** amply, fully. 276. **servant,** lover. 278. **undistinguish'd . . . will,** incalculable range of woman's appetite. 281. **rake up,** cover up. 283. **ungracious,** wicked. 284. **death-practised,** whose death is plotted. 287. **ingenious,** conscious. 288. **distract,** distracted, crazy.

SCENE VII. 6. **clipp'd,** curtailed. **suited,** dressed. 7. **memories,** remembrances. 9. **made intent,** carefully thought-out purpose. 17. **child-changed,** changed (in mind) by children's cruelty. 24. **temperance,** sanity. 33. **dread-bolted,** furnished with the dreadful thunderstone. 35. **perdu,** soldier placed in a position of peculiar danger. 42. **concluded all,** come to an end all together.

I am mightily abused. I should e'en die with pity,
To see another thus. I know not what to say.
I will not swear these are my hands: let's see;
I feel this pin prick. Would I were assured
Of my condition!
 Cor.   O, look upon me, sir,
And hold your hands in benediction o'er me:
No, sir, you must not kneel.
 Lear.   Pray, do not mock me:
I am a very foolish fond old man,   60
Fourscore and upward, not an hour more nor less;
And, to deal plainly,
I fear I am not in my perfect mind.
Methinks I should know you, and know this man;
Yet I am doubtful: for I am mainly ignorant
What place this is; and all the skill I have
Remembers not these garments; nor I know not
Where I did lodge last night. Do not laugh at me;
For, as I am a man, I think this lady
To be my child Cordelia.
 Cor.   And so I am, I am.   70
 Lear. Be your tears wet? yes, 'faith. I pray, weep not:
If you have poison for me, I will drink it.
I know you do not love me; for your sisters
Have, as I do remember, done me wrong:
You have some cause, they have not.
 Cor.   No cause, no cause.
 Lear. Am I in France?
 Kent.   In your own kingdom, sir.
 Lear. Do not abuse me.
 Doct. Be comforted, good madam: the great rage,
You see, is kill'd in him: and yet it is danger
To make him even o'er the time he has lost. 80
Desire him to go in; trouble him no more
Till further settling.
 Cor. Will 't please your highness walk?
 Lear.   You must bear with me:
Pray you now, forget and forgive: I am old and
  foolish.   *[Exeunt all but Kent and Gentleman.*
 Gent. Holds it true, sir, that the Duke of Cornwall
was so slain?
 Kent. Most certain, sir.
 Gent. Who is conductor of his people?
 Kent. As 'tis said, the bastard son of Gloucester. 90
 Gent. They say Edgar, his banished son, is with the
Earl of Kent in Germany.
 Kent. Report is changeable. 'Tis time to look about;
the powers of the kingdom approach apace.
 Gent. The arbitrement is like to be bloody. Fare you
well, sir.   *[Exit.*
 Kent. My point and period will be throughly
  wrought, .
Or well or ill, as this day's battle 's fought. *[Exit.* 99

ACT V.

SCENE I. *The British camp, near Dover.*

Enter, with drum and colours, EDMUND, REGAN,
 Gentlemen, *and* Soldiers.

Eam. Know of the duke if his last purpose hold,
Or whether since he is advised by aught
To change the course: he 's full of alteration
And self-reproving: bring his constant pleasure.
      [To a Gentleman, who goes out.
 Reg. Our sister's man is certainly miscarried.
 Edm. 'Tis to be doubted, madam.
 Reg.   Now, sweet lord,
You know the goodness I intend upon you:
Tell me—but truly—but then speak the truth,
Do you not love my sister?
 Edm.   In honour'd love.
 Reg. But have you never found my brother's way 10
To the forfended place?
 Edm.   That thought abuses you.
 Reg. I am doubtful that you have been conjunct
And bosom'd with her, as far as we call hers.
 Edm. No, by mine honour, madam.
 Reg. I never shall endure her: dear my lord,
Be not familiar with her.
 Edm.   Fear me not:
She and the duke her husband!

Enter, with drum and colours, ALBANY, GONERIL, *and*
 Soldiers.

 Gon. [*Aside*] I had rather lose the battle than that
  sister
Should loosen him and me.
 Alb. Our very loving sister, well be-met. 20
Sir, this I hear; the king is come to his daughter,
With others whom the rigour of our state
Forced to cry out. Where I could not be honest,
I never yet was valiant: for this business,
It toucheth us, as France invades our land,
Not bolds the king, with others, whom, I fear,
Most just and heavy causes make oppose.
 Edm. Sir, you speak nobly.
 Reg.   Why is this reason'd?
 Gon. Combine together 'gainst the enemy;
For these domestic and particular broils 30
Are not the question here.
 Alb.   Let 's then determine
With the ancient of war on our proceedings.
 Edm. I shall attend you presently at your tent.
 Reg. Sister, you'll go with us?
 Gon. No.
 Reg. 'Tis most convenient; pray you, go with us.
 Gon. [*Aside*] O, ho, I know the riddle.—I will go.

As they are going out, enter EDGAR *disguised.*

 Edg. If e'er your grace had speech with man so
  poor,
Hear me one word.
 Alb.   I'll overtake you. Speak.
     [Exeunt all but Albany and Edgar.
 Edg. Before you fight the battle, ope this letter. 40
If you have victory, let the trumpet sound
For him that brought it: wretched though I seem,
I can produce a champion that will prove
What is avouched there. If you miscarry,

King Lear
ACT IV : SC VII

1012

---

65. **mainly,** perfectly. 73-75. **I know . . . not.** This pathetic passage is not merely the strugglings of Lear's mind back to recognition; it is also a momentary restoration of the bargain-and-sale ethics which characterized the partition of his kingdom. 80. **even o'er,** give an account of, go over in his mind. 82. **settling,** composing of his mind. 95. **arbitrement,** decision by arms. 98. **period,** end aimed at.
 ACT V. SCENE I. 4. **constant pleasure,** settled decision. 5. **miscarried,** lost, perished. 9. **honour'd,** honorable. 11. **forfended,**

forbidden. 12. **conjunct,** joined. 13. **bosom'd with her,** in her confidence; suggesting also her embraces. 26. **Not . . . others,** not because France encourages the king and others. 27. **heavy causes,** weighty reasons. **make oppose,** compel to fight (against us). 32. **ancient of war,** veteran soldiers. 36. **convenient,** proper, befitting. 44. **avouched,** formally asserted. **miscarry,** perish, come to destruction. 50. **o'erlook,** peruse. 53. **discovery,** reconnoitering. 54. **greet the time,** face the situation. 56. **jealous,** suspicious. 61. **carry out my**

Your business of the world hath so an end,
And machination ceases. Fortune love you!
    Alb. Stay till I have read the letter.
    Edg.   I was forbid it.
When time shall serve, let but the herald cry,
And I'll appear again.
    Alb. Why, fare thee well: I will o'erlook thy paper. 50
                               [Exit Edgar.

          Re-enter EDMUND.

    Edm. The enemy 's in view; draw up your powers.
Here is the guess of their true strength and forces
By diligent discovery; but your haste
Is now urged on you.
    Alb.   We will greet the time.   *[Exit.*
    Edm. To both these sisters have I sworn my love;
Each jealous of the other, as the stung
Are of the adder. Which of them shall I take?
Both? one? or neither? Neither can be enjoy'd,
If both remain alive: to take the widow
Exasperates, makes mad her sister Goneril;   60
And hardly shall I carry out my side,
Her husband being alive. Now then we'll use
His countenance for the battle; which being done,
Let her who would be rid of him devise
His speedy taking off. As for the mercy
Which he intends to Lear and to Cordelia,
The battle done, and they within our power,
Shall never see his pardon; for my state
Stands on me to defend, not to debate.   *[Exit.* 69

    SCENE II. *A field between the two camps.*

Alarum within. Enter, with drum and colours, LEAR,
CORDELIA, *and* Soldiers, *over the stage; and exeunt.*

Enter EDGAR *and* GLOUCESTER.

    Edg. Here, father, take the shadow of this tree
For your good host; pray that the right may thrive:
If ever I return to you again,
I'll bring you comfort.
    Glou.   Grace go with you, sir!
                               [Exit Edgar.

Alarum and retreat within. Re-enter EDGAR.

    Edg. Away, old man; give me thy hand; away!
King Lear hath lost, he and his daughter ta'en:
Give me thy hand; come on.
    Glou. No farther, sir; a man may rot even here.
    Edg. What, in ill thoughts again? Men must endure
Their going hence, even as their coming hither: 10
Ripeness is all: come on.
    Glou.   And that 's true too.   *[Exeunt.*

    SCENE III. *The British camp near Dover.*

Enter, in conquest, with drum and colours, EDMUND;
    LEAR *and* CORDELIA, *prisoners;* Captain, Soldiers,
    &c.

    Edm. Some officers take them away: good guard,
Until their greater pleasures first be known
That are to censure them.
    Cor.   We are not the first
Who, with best meaning, have incurr'd the worst.
For thee, oppressed king, am I cast down;
Myself could else out-frown false fortune's frown.
Shall we not see these daughters and these sisters?
    Lear. No, no, no, no! Come, let 's away to prison:
We two alone will sing like birds i' the cage:
When thou dost ask me blessing, I'll kneel down,   10
And ask of thee forgiveness: so we'll live,
And pray, and sing, and tell old tales, and laugh
At gilded butterflies, and hear poor rogues
Talk of court news; and we'll talk with them too,
Who loses and who wins; who 's in, who 's out;
And take upon 's the mystery of things,
As if we were God's spies: and we'll wear out,
In a wall'd prison, packs and sects of great ones,
That ebb and flow by the moon.
    Edm.   Take them away.
    Lear. Upon such sacrifices, my Cordelia,   20
The gods themselves throw incense. Have I caught
    thee?
He that parts us shall bring a brand from heaven,
And fire us hence like foxes. Wipe thine eyes;
The good-years shall devour them, flesh and fell,
Ere they shall make us weep: we'll see 'em starve first.
Come.   *[Exeunt Lear and Cordelia, guarded.*
    Edm. Come hither, captain; hark.
Take thou this note [*giving a paper*]; go follow them to
    prison:
One step I have advanced thee; if thou dost
As this instructs thee, thou dost make thy way
To noble fortunes: know thou this, that men   30
Are as the time is: to be tender-minded
Does not become a sword: thy great employment
Will not bear question; either say thou 'lt do 't,
Or thrive by other means.
    Capt.   I'll do 't, my lord.
    Edm. About it; and write happy when thou hast
    done.
Mark, I say, instantly; and carry it so
As I have set it down.
    Capt. I cannot draw a cart, nor eat dried oats;
If it be man's work, I'll do it.   *[Exit.*

Flourish. Enter ALBANY, GONERIL, REGAN, *another*
    Captain, *and* Soldiers.

    Alb. Sir, you have shown to-day your valiant strain,
And fortune led you well: you have the captives   41
That were the opposites of this day's strife:
We do require them of you, so to use them
As we shall find their merits and our safety
May equally determine.
    Edm.   Sir, I thought it fit
To send the old and miserable king
To some retention and appointed guard;
Whose age has charms in it, whose title more,
To pluck the common bosom on his side,

---

side, win my game; possibly a figure from cards. 68-69. **my state . . .
debate,** my position depends upon maintenance by force, not on debate.
   SCENE II. 9-11. **Men . . . all,** a stern utterance of the doctrine of
fortitude, repeatedly applied to poor Gloucester. It must be said,
however, that fortitude is the crowning quality of Edgar's character.
11. **Ripeness,** readiness.
   SCENE III. 13. **gilded butterflies,** courtiers. 17. **wear out,** forget,
efface from memory. 18. **sects,** parties. 23. **fire . . . foxes,** i.e., as

foxes are driven out of their holes by fire and smoke; reminiscent of
Samson's stratagem, Judges 15:4. 24. **good-years,** apparently a
general word for evil; thought sometimes to be the name of a disease.
Compare, however, the story of Pharaoh's dream, Genesis 41. **flesh
and fell,** flesh and skin. 33. **bear question,** be argued about. 35.
write happy, call yourself happy. 47. **retention,** custody. 49. **common
bosom,** the affection of the mob.

And turn our impress'd lances in our eyes 50
Which do command them. With him I sent the
    queen;
My reason all the same; and they are ready
To-morrow, or at further space, to appear
Where you shall hold your session. At this time
We sweat and bleed: the friend hath lost his friend;
And the best quarrels, in the heat, are cursed
By those that feel their sharpness:
The question of Cordelia and her father
Requires a fitter place.
    Alb.   Sir, by your patience,
I hold you but a subject of this war, 60
Not as a brother.
    Reg.   That's as we list to grace him.
Methinks our pleasure might have been demanded,
Ere you had spoke so far. He led our powers;
Bore the commission of my place and person;
The which immediacy may well stand up,
And call itself your brother.
    Gon.   Not so hot:
In his own grace he doth exalt himself,
More than in your addition.
    Reg.   In my rights,
By me invested, he compeers the best. 69
    Gon. That were the most, if he should husband you.
    Reg. Jesters do oft prove prophets.
    Gon.   Holla, holla!
That eye that told you so look'd but a-squint.
    Reg. Lady, I am not well; else I should answer
From a full-flowing stomach. General,
Take thou my soldiers, prisoners, patrimony;
Dispose of them, of me; the walls are thine:
Witness the world, that I create thee here
My lord and master.
    Gon.   Mean you to enjoy him?
    Alb. The let-alone lies not in your good will.
    Edm. Nor in thine, lord.
    Alb.   Half-blooded fellow, yes. 80
    Reg. [*To Edmund*] Let the drum strike, and prove
    my title thine.
    Alb. Stay yet; hear reason. Edmund, I arrest thee
On capital treason; and, in thine attaint,
This gilded serpent [*pointing to Gon.*]. For your claim,
    fair sister,
I bar it in the interest of my wife;
'Tis she is sub-contracted to this lord,
And I, her husband, contradict your bans.
If you will marry, make your loves to me,
My lady is bespoke.
    Gon.   An interlude!
    Alb. Thou art arm'd, Gloucester: let the trumpet
    sound: 90
If none appear to prove upon thy head
Thy heinous, manifest, and many treasons,
There is my pledge [*throwing down a glove*]; I'll prove
    it on thy heart,
Ere I taste bread, thou art in nothing less
Than I have here proclaim'd thee.
    Reg.   Sick, O, sick!
    Gon. [*Aside*] If not, I'll ne'er trust medicine.

    Edm. There's my exchange [*throwing down a glove*]:
    what in the world he is
That names me traitor, villain-like he lies:
Call by thy trumpet: he that dares approach,
On him, on you, who not? I will maintain 100
My truth and honour firmly.
    Alb. A herald, ho!
    Edm.   A herald, ho, a herald!
    Alb. Trust to thy single virtue; for thy soldiers,
All levied in my name, have in my name
Took their discharge.
    Reg.   My sickness grows upon me.
    Alb. She is not well; convey her to my tent.
                    [*Exit Regan, led.*

Enter a Herald.

Come hither, herald,—Let the trumpet sound,—
And read out this. 108
    Capt. Sound, trumpet!   [*A trumpet sounds.*
    Her. [*Reads*] 'If any man of quality or degree within
the lists of the army will maintain upon Edmund,
supposed Earl of Gloucester, that he is a manifold
traitor, let him appear by the third sound of the
trumpet: he is bold in his defence.'
    Edm. Sound!   [*First trumpet.*
    Her. Again!   [*Second trumpet.*
    Her. Again!   [*Third trumpet.*
                [*Trumpet answers within.*

Enter EDGAR, *at the third sound, armed, with a trumpet*
    before him.

    Alb. Ask him his purposes, why he appears
Upon this call o' the trumpet.
    Her.   What are you?
Your name, your quality? and why you answer 120
This present summons?
    Edg.   Know, my name is lost;
By treason's tooth bare-gnawn and canker-bit:
Yet am I noble as the adversary
I come to cope.
    Alb.   Which is that adversary?
    Edg. What's he that speaks for Edmund Earl of
    Gloucester?
    Edm. Himself: what say'st thou to him?
    Edg.   Draw thy sword,
That, if my speech offend a noble heart,
Thy arm may do thee justice: here is mine.
Behold, it is the privilege of mine honours,
My oath, and my profession: I protest, 130
Maugre thy strength, youth, place, and eminence,
Despite thy victor sword and fire-new fortune,
Thy valour and thy heart, thou art a traitor;
False to thy gods, thy brother, and thy father;
Conspirant 'gainst this high-illustrious prince;
And, from the extremest upward of thy head
To the descent and dust below thy foot,
A most toad-spotted traitor. Say thou 'No,'
This sword, this arm, and my best spirits, are bent
To prove upon thy heart, whereto I speak, 140
Thou liest.
    Edm.   In wisdom I should ask thy name;

---

50. **impress'd lances,** weapons of troops impressed into service. 58.
question, cause. 64. **commission,** warrant as representative. 65. **immediacy,** next in authority, or nearness of his being my agent. 69.
compeers, is equal with. 72. **That ... a-squint,** reference to a proverb:
Love being jealous makes a good eye look asquint. 74. **full-flowing**

stomach, full tide of angry rejoinder. 76. **the walls are thine,** probably
a phrase signifying complete surrender; many conjectures. 80. **Half-
blooded,** partly of mean blood. 83. **attaint,** impeachment. 89. **interlude,** play, i.e., you are melodramatic. 105. **Took,** taken, received.
107. **trumpet,** trumpeter. 112. **supposed,** pretended. 119. **What,**

But, since thy outside looks so fair and warlike,
And that thy tongue some say of breeding breathes,
What safe and nicely I might well delay
By rule of knighthood, I disdain and spurn:
Back do I toss these treasons to thy head;
With the hell-hated lie o'erwhelm thy heart;
Which, for they yet glance by and scarcely bruise,
This sword of mine shall give them instant way,
Where they shall rest for ever. Trumpets, speak!   150
     [Alarums. They fight. Edmund falls.
 Alb. Save him, save him!
 Gon.   This is practice, Gloucester:
By the law of arms thou wast not bound to answer
An unknown opposite; thou art not vanquish'd,
But cozen'd and beguiled.
 Alb.   Shut your mouth, dame,
Or with this paper shall I stop it. Hold, sir;
Thou worse than any name, read thine own evil:
No tearing, lady; I perceive you know it.
     [Gives the letter to Edmund.
 Gon. Say, if I do, the laws are mine, not thine:
Who can arraign me for 't?
 Alb.   Most monstrous! oh!
Know'st thou this paper?
 Gon.   Ask me not what I know. [Exit. 160
 Alb. Go after her: she 's desperate; govern her.
 Edm. What you have charged me with, that have I
  done;
And more, much more; the time will bring it out:
'Tis past, and so am I. But what art thou
That hast this fortune on me? If thou 'rt noble,
I do forgive thee.
 Edg.   Let 's exchange charity.
I am no less in blood than thou art, Edmund;
If more, the more thou hast wrong'd me.
My name is Edgar, and thy father's son.
The gods are just, and of our pleasant vices   170
Make instruments to plague us:
The dark and vicious place where thee he got
Cost him his eyes.
 Edm.   Thou hast spoken right, 'tis true;
The wheel is come full circle; I am here.
 Alb. Methought thy very gait did prophesy
A royal nobleness: I must embrace thee:
Let sorrow split my heart, if ever I
Did hate thee or thy father!
 Edg.   Worthy prince, I know 't.
 Alb. Where have you hid yourself?
How have you known the miseries of your father?   180
 Edg. By nursing them, my lord. List a brief tale;
And when 'tis told, O, that my heart would burst!
The bloody proclamation to escape,
That follow'd me so near,—O, our lives' sweetness!
That we the pain of death would hourly die
Rather than die at once!—taught me to shift
Into a madman's rags; to assume a semblance
That very dogs disdain'd: and in this habit
Met I my father with his bleeding rings,
Their precious stones new lost; became his guide,   190
Led him, begg'd for him, saved him from despair;
Never,—O fault!—reveal'd myself unto him,

Until some half-hour past, when I was arm'd:
Not sure, though hoping, of this good success,
I ask'd his blessing, and from first to last
Told him my pilgrimage: but his flaw'd heart,
Alack, too weak the conflict to support!
'Twixt two extremes of passion, joy and grief,
Burst smilingly.
 Edm.   This speech of yours hath moved
 me,
And shall perchance do good: but speak you on;   200
You look as you had something more to say.
 Alb. If there be more, more woeful, hold it in;
For I am almost ready to dissolve,
Hearing of this.
 Edg.   This would have seem'd a period
To such as love not sorrow; but another,
To amplify too much, would make much more,
And top extremity.
Whilst I was big in clamour came there in a man,
Who, having seen me in my worst estate,
Shunn'd my abhorr'd society; but then, finding   210
Who 'twas that so endured, with his strong arms
He fasten'd on my neck, and bellow'd out
As he 'ld burst heaven; threw him on my father;
Told the most piteous tale of Lear and him
That ever ear received: which in recounting
His grief grew puissant, and the strings of life
Began to crack: twice then the trumpets sounded,
And there I left him tranced.
 Alb.   But who was this?
 Edg. Kent, sir, the banish'd Kent; who in disguise
Follow'd his enemy king, and did him service   220
Improper for a slave.

 Enter a Gentleman, with a bloody knife.

 Gent. Help, help, O, help!
 Edg.   What kind of help?
 Alb.   Speak, man.
 Edg. What means that bloody knife?
 Gent.   'Tis hot, it smokes;
It came even from the heart of—O, she 's dead!
 Alb. Who dead? speak, man.
 Gent. Your lady, sir, your lady: and her sister
By her is poisoned; she hath confess'd it.
 Edm. I was contracted to them both: all three
Now marry in an instant.
 Edg.   Here comes Kent.
 Alb. Produce their bodies, be they alive or dead: 230
This judgement of the heavens, that makes us tremble,
Touches us not with pity.   [Exit Gentleman.

 Enter KENT.

      O, is this he?
The time will not allow the compliment
Which very manners urges.
 Kent.   I am come
To bid my king and master aye good night:
Is he not here?
 Alb.   Great thing of us forgot!
Speak, Edmund, where 's the king? and where 's
 Cordelia?

---

who. 122. **canker-bit**, withered, i.e., bitten by the caterpillar. 131.
Maugre, in spite of. 132. **fire-new**, freshly gained. 136. **upward**, top.
138. **toad-spotted**, venomous, or having spots of infamy. 141. **wisdom**,
prudence; i.e., Edmund might have demanded that his adversary be his
equal in rank. 143. **say**, flavor, indication; possibly for "assay," proof.

146. **head**, i.e., to thy teeth. 147. **hell-hated**, hated as hell is hated.
161. **govern**, restrain. 165. **fortune**, victory, success. 174. **wheel**,
wheel of fortune. 189. **rings**, sockets. 192. **fault**, mistake. 196.
flaw'd, cracked, damaged by a flaw. 218. **tranced**, entranced, senseless.
236. **forgot**, forgotten. There is an improbability in this forgetfulness.

See'st thou this object, Kent?
>[*The bodies of Goneril and Regan are brought in.*
Kent. Alack, why thus?
Edm. Yet Edmund was beloved:
The one the other poison'd for my sake, 240
And after slew herself.
Alb. Even so. Cover their faces.
Edm. I pant for life: some good I mean to do,
Despite of mine own nature. Quickly send,
Be brief in it, to the castle; for my writ
Is on the life of Lear and on Cordelia:
Nay, send in time.
Alb. Run, run, O, run!
Edg. To who, my lord? Who hath the office? send
Thy token of reprieve.
Edm. Well thought on: take my sword, 250
Give it the captain.
Alb. Haste thee, for thy life.
>[*Exit Edgar.*
Edm. He hath commission from thy wife and me
To hang Cordelia in the prison, and
To lay the blame upon her own despair,
That she fordid herself.
Alb. The gods defend her! Bear him hence awhile.
>[*Edmund is borne off.*

Re-enter LEAR, *with* CORDELIA *dead in his arms;* EDGAR,
Captain, *and others following.*

Lear. Howl, howl, howl, howl! O, you are men of
stones:
Had I your tongues and eyes, I 'ld use them so
That heaven's vault should crack. She 's gone for
ever!
I know when one is dead, and when one lives; 260
She 's dead as earth. Lend me a looking-glass;
If that her breath will mist or stain the stone,
Why, then she lives.
Kent. Is this the promised end?
Edg. Or image of that horror?
Alb. Fall, and cease!
Lear. This feather stirs; she lives! if it be so,
It is a chance which does redeem all sorrows
That ever I have felt.
Kent. [*Kneeling*] O my good master!
Lear. Prithee, away.
Edg. 'Tis noble Kent, your friend.
Lear. A plague upon you, murderers, traitors all!
I might have saved her; now she 's gone for ever! 270
Cordelia, Cordelia! stay a little. Ha!
What is 't thou say'st? Her voice was ever soft,
Gentle, and low, an excellent thing in woman.
I kill'd the slave that was a-hanging thee.
Capt. 'Tis true, my lords, he did.
Lear. Did I not, fellow?
I have seen the day, with my good biting falchion
I would have made them skip: I am old now,
And these same crosses spoil me. Who are you?
Mine eyes are not o' the best: I'll tell you straight.
Kent. If fortune brag of two she loved and hated, 280
One of them we behold.

Lear. This is a dull sight. Are you not Kent?
Kent. The same,
Your servant Kent. Where is your servant Caius?
Lear. He 's a good fellow, I can tell you that;
He'll strike, and quickly too: he 's dead and rotten.
Kent. No, my good lord; I am the very man,—
Lear. I'll see that straight.
Kent. That, from your first of difference and decay,
Have follow'd your sad steps.
Lear. You are welcome hither.
Kent. Nor no man else: all 's cheerless, dark, and
deadly. 290
Your eldest daughters have fordone themselves,
And desperately are dead.
Lear. Ay, so I think.
Alb. He knows not what he says: and vain it is
That we present us to him.
Edg. Very bootless.

Enter a Captain.

Capt. Edmund is dead, my lord.
Alb. That 's but a trifle here.
You lords and noble friends, know our intent.
What comfort to this great decay may come
Shall be applied: for us, we will resign,
During the life of this old majesty,
To him our absolute power: [*To Edgar and Kent*] you,
to your rights; 300
With boot, and such addition as your honours
Have more than merited. All friends shall taste
The wages of their virtue, and all foes
The cup of their deservings. O, see, see!
Lear. And my poor fool is hang'd! No, no, no life!
Why should a dog, a horse, a rat, have life,
And thou no breath at all? Thou 'lt come no more,
Never, never, never, never, never!
Pray you, undo this button: thank you, sir.
Do you see this? Look on her, look, her lips, 310
Look there, look there! [*Dies.*
Edg. He faints! My lord, my lord!
Kent. Break, heart; I prithee, break!
Edg. Look up, my lord.
Kent. Vex not his ghost: O, let him pass! he hates
him much
That would upon the rack of this tough world
Stretch him out longer.
Edg. He is gone, indeed.
Kent. The wonder is, he hath endured so long:
He but usurp'd his life.
Alb. Bear them from hence. Our present business
Is general woe. [*To Kent and Edgar*] Friends of my
soul, you twain
Rule in this realm, and the gored state sustain. 320
Kent. I have a journey, sir, shortly to go;
My master calls me, I must not say no.
Alb. The weight of this sad time we must obey;
Speak what we feel, not what we ought to say.
The oldest hath borne most: we that are young
Shall never see so much, nor live so long.
>[*Exeunt, with a dead march.*

King Lear
ACT V : SC III

1016

243-244. **some good . . . nature.** It is made clear to us in the first act that Edmund, born outside the pale of social organization, is adverse and hostile to the laws of gods and men; he repents and is therefore not an inhuman monster; note the implication of line 239. 255. **forbid,** destroyed. 262. **mist,** becloud. **stone,** crystal (of which the mirror is made). 263. **end,** Last Judgment. 264. **Fall, and cease.** Possibly, let the heavens fall and all things cease. 276. **falchion,** sword; properly, a sword curved at the point with the edge on the convex side. 288.

first of difference, beginning of your change of fortune for the worst. 292. **desperately,** in despair. 305. **my poor fool,** i.e., Cordelia. It has sometimes been wrongly thought that this refers to the Fool, but *fool*, as here used, is a term of endearment. 313-315. **he hates . . . longer.** These words of Kent's seem a complete rejoinder to those amiable critics of the eighteenth century who took delight in Tate's version, in which Cordelia was permitted to come back to life, and Lear was restored to his throne.

Timon of Athens

A play belonging to this period, most obscure in its history, is *Timon of Athens*. It has been assumed for nearly a century that in this play we have a work for which Shakespeare is only partly responsible. However, critics have not been able to agree as to whether Shakespeare revised the incomplete work of another man, or whether another man revised the incomplete work of Shakespeare.

The most plausible hypothesis of multiple authorship is that of T. M. Parrott,[1] who sees in it a play begun by Shakespeare, completed after his death by the poet-dramatist Chapman, and then cut down and prepared for the stage by some actor-dramatist, possibly Field. It is hard to see in the play either the style of Chapman, which is well known, or that of Field. The irregular and inharmonious parts are too bad to be regarded as the work of competent revisers. *Timon of Athens* seems rather to remain an unfinished piece, and it is not difficult to believe that it is all the work of Shakespeare. Some parts are carefully finished; other parts are first drafts roughly sketched in and never worked over into final form. Note, for example, the carefully wrought portraits of the Poet and the Painter in the first scene of the play as contrasted with the rough and hasty presentation of the same characters in the first scene of the fifth act.

SOURCE

Shakespeare found the story in Plutarch's *Life of Antony*. He may also have amplified it by reference to the dialogue, *Timon the Misanthrope*, by the Greek satirist, Lucian, since a number of passages recall Lucian's words. There is also an old play on Timon which he may have known.

Timon of Athens, in spite of its fragmentary and imperfect form, shows that it is conceived of in the Shakespearean way. It again presents the contrast between the man of action and the man of inaction; as in Bolingbroke and Richard II, or Fortinbras and Hamlet. Timon refuses to act and the conduct of Alcibiades suggests that of Coriolanus. Indeed, *Timon of Athens* has much in common with *Coriolanus* and *Antony and Cleopatra*, plays which are more convinced in their pessimism about human nature than those earlier in the same period. They depict the rulers of the earth as putting appetite before duty, the populace as a mere rabble, the world of courts and business as given over to dishonesty and selfishness, and men of sense and virtue, like Enobarbus and Menenius

Agrippa, as speaking only to deaf ears. In *Timon of Athens*, as in these Plutarchan plays, passion and reason are still at war—passion now grown old, violent, and sordid, and reason become selfish and cold-blooded.

STRUCTURE AND CHARACTERIZATION

Structurally *Timon of Athens* has a feature of excellence sometimes overlooked. It presents three types of misanthropy, or rather, three ways of reacting to the baseness of one's fellow men. Apemantus is a professional misanthrope. He refuses to admit the possibility of human virtue. He is fixed in his attitude, expects nothing, and enjoys his unhappiness. Timon becomes a misanthrope for specific reasons and on the basis of experience. Pessimism is a discovery that he makes, and he sinks into it as into a bog. He is an idealist whose faith is broken. Alcibiades also suffers wrong, but he believes at least in himself and sets about the rectification of his wrongs. This last-mentioned part is not well developed in the play, but it offers at many points an illuminating contrast to that of Timon. It is to be regretted that we know so little of Alcibiades, who, inferior to Timon, has a strength of common men that Timon lacks.

In spite of these structural features which indicate the presence of Shakespeare's hand, *Timon of Athens* is dramatically not an effective play. The very fact that the characters are so clearly typed is in part responsible for this ineffectiveness. Apemantus is the cynic, Alcibiades the unreflective doer of deeds. The Poet, the Painter, and others in the early scenes are typical patron seekers. There are thieves, prostitutes, flattering courtiers, and parasites—all professionals. Timon himself, though intended to represent the unbiased individual, stands too much alone; he is so presented as to suggest a typical human reaction to man's ingratitude. This characterization by types might have been rendered dramatically effective by individualized and humanized plot situations. But Timon's tragedy is not involved in any domestic relationships as is Othello's or King Lear's; there is here no emotional conflict as in *Romeo and Juliet*, no dilemma as in *Hamlet*, no moral struggle as in *Macbeth*, no passion for an ideal as in *Julius Caesar*.

All of the great tragedies of Shakespeare have issues which arise out of the heart. Timon, however, never has to choose between his affections and his duty. He has no loyalties which are put under strain; he has no binding human ties whatever—no parents, no children, no social connections. In the early part of the play he represents the extreme of generosity, which is prodigality. His folly is somewhat like that of Lear. The shock of disillusionment, however, brings different effects. This is because in Lear's case the causes as well as the effects are modified by the human relationships involved. Timon's conduct is made the logical consequence of his unwisdom.

[1] *The Problem of "Timon of Athens,"* The Shakespeare Association, 1923. For a differing view see Una Ellis-Fermor, "*Timon of Athens:* an Unfinished Play," *Review of English Studies*, XVIII (1942), 270-283; on the whole question see Chambers, *William Shakespeare*, I, 480-484.

Finding no salvation in any kind of mean, he moves to another and a worse extreme, so that in the end he stands there not as a great tragic spectacle inspiring an audience with feelings of pity and terror, but as a symbol of a kind of ethical perversion.

After the first three acts the hero becomes inactive, a mere sufferer, and the minor plot does not, as in *King Lear*, come to the rescue of the major plot. The puzzling fifth scene of the third act seems to be part of an unrecorded minor plot which somehow found fulfillment in the design of the last scene of the fourth act, where Timon finds the gold and confronts in turn Alcibiades, Apemantus, and Flavius, the faithful steward.

THE THEME AND ITS SIGNIFICANCE

As a result of these features—the typed characters and the dehumanized plot—*Timon of Athens* is distinguished by its predominantly didactic tone. This tone is set in the first scene by the Poet, who in recounting the contents of his poem foretells Timon's downfall. Timon's deterioration of character is marked by his perverse restatement of a number of accepted ethical doctrines of the Renaissance, reinterpreted in terms of the villainy of human nature. The concept of social gradation, described by Ulysses in *Troilus and Cressida* as the "ladder to all high design," becomes in Timon's ethics a ladder where "every grise of fortune is smooth'd [*i.e.*, flattered] by that below"; and the universe, instead of exemplifying for him the principle of gratitude, shows him that in nature "each thing's a thief." Thus his misanthropy expresses itself in cosmic terms. As the

A pedlar from a ballad in the Pepysian Collection.

Senators say of him at his withdrawal from the scene, "his discontents are unremovably coupled to nature." Timon acts according to his conviction that "there's nothing level in our cursed natures but direct villany." Consequently, he is more civil to wrongdoers and wreakers of vengeance than to decent people and those who are "respectable" like the Poet and the Painter. He gives gold to those who come frankly asking for it—thieves and prostitutes; but to those who come flattering him, hoping to be rewarded, he gives only abuse. Indeed, by the time the Senators approach, humbly and honestly wishing to make amends, he is so warped in his mind that he sees no difference between their motives and those of the flatterers.

Timon's disillusionment, therefore, and his subsequent conduct become the theme of the play. However, unmodified as it is by any human involvements, it is dramatically unconvincing. It may be that during the early years of the seventeenth century (1601-1606) Shakespeare was preoccupied, if not actually obsessed, with the theme of disillusionment. This note is present, certainly, in *Troilus and Cressida*, *Measure for Measure*, *Hamlet*, and *King Lear*. Perhaps he felt after writing *King Lear* that the issue was cosmic, that it went beyond the bounds of human intercourse; perhaps *Timon of Athens* is an attempt at a play which develops a theory. If so, Shakespeare found that such a theme, to be dramatically effective, must treat the interrelationships of men and, divorced from these, has no dramatic meaning. For these reasons he may have lost interest in the play and have left it in its present uneven and incomplete form.

It is not possible to date *Timon of Athens* with any certainty. Because the style of the parts always attributed to Shakespeare is not in his latest manner and because it continues and exaggerates the pessimism of *King Lear*, it has been placed in this edition next after that play. There is only one very poor original text of *Timon of Athens*, that of the First Folio of 1623.

STAGE HISTORY

The stage history of *Timon of Athens* is almost a blank. There is no evidence that the play was acted before it was printed. It has been played only rarely since, and, so far as can be ascertained, always in a modified version. The play had some attention during the seventeenth and eighteenth centuries in Thomas Shadwell's adaptation (1678). It was acted at Drury Lane Theater in 1816 in what may have been an abridged form of the original. Phelps played *Timon of Athens* with Shakespeare's text in 1851; Benson revived it at Stratford in 1892; it was played at the "Old Vic" in London in 1922. A more recent important production was at the Westminster Theater in 1935, with Ernest Milton playing the part of Timon. The performance by the players of the Birmingham Repertory Theatre in 1947 had the merit of establishing sympathy for Timon in the first act as a man of generous, hospitable, and humane nature, so that one could see embodied in him a favorite Renaissance ideal.

Timon of Athens

DRAMATIS PERSONAE

TIMON, of Athens.
LUCIUS,
LUCULLUS, } flattering lords.
SEMPRONIUS,
VENTIDIUS, one of Timon's false friends.
ALCIBIADES, an Athenian captain.
APEMANTUS, a churlish philosopher.
FLAVIUS, steward to Timon.
Poet, Painter, Jeweller, and Merchant.
An old Athenian.
FLAMINIUS,
LUCILIUS, } servants to Timon.
SERVILIUS,
CAPHIS,
PHILOTUS,
TITUS, } servants to Timon's
LUCIUS, } creditors.
HORTENSIUS,
And others,
A Page. A Fool. Three Strangers.

PHRYNIA, } mistresses to Alcibiades.
TIMANDRA,

Cupid and Amazons in the mask.

Other Lords, Senators, Officers, Soldiers,
Banditti, and Attendants.

SCENE: *Athens, and the neighbouring woods.*

ACT I.

SCENE I. *Athens. A hall in Timon's house.*

Enter Poet, Painter, Jeweller, Merchant, *and others,
at several doors.*

Poet. Good day, sir.
Pain.   I am glad you 're well.
Poet. I have not seen you long: how goes the world?
Pain. It wears, sir, as it grows.
Poet.   Ay, that 's well known:
But what particular rarity? what strange,
Which manifold record not matches? See,
Magic of bounty! all these spirits thy power
Hath conjured to attend. I know the merchant.
Pain. I know them both; th' other 's a jeweller.
Mer. O, 'tis a worthy lord.
Jew.   Nay, that 's most fix'd.
Mer. A most incomparable man, breathed, as it
were,   10
To an untirable and continuate goodness:
He passes.
Jew.   I have a jewel here—
Mer. O, pray, let 's see 't: for the Lord Timon, sir?
Jew. If he will touch the estimate: but, for that—

Poet. [*Reciting to himself*] 'When we for recompense
     have praised the vile,
It stains the glory in that happy verse
Which aptly sings the good.'
Mer.   'Tis a good form.
                     [*Looking at the jewel.*
Jew. And rich: here is a water, look ye.
Pain. You are rapt, sir, in some work, some
     dedication
To the great lord.
Poet.   A thing slipp'd idly from me.   20
Our poesy is as a gum, which oozes
From whence 'tis nourish'd: the fire i' the flint
Shows not till it be struck; our gentle flame
Provokes itself and like the current flies
Each bound it chafes. What have you there?
Pain. A picture, sir. When comes your book forth?
Poet. Upon the heels of my presentment, sir.
Let 's see your piece.
Pain.   'Tis a good piece.
Poet. So 'tis: this comes off well and excellent.
Pain. Indifferent.
Poet.   Admirable: how this grace   30
Speaks his own standing! what a mental power
This eye shoots forth! how big imagination
Moves in this lip! to the dumbness of the gesture
One might interpret.
Pain. It is a pretty mocking of the life.
Here is a touch; is 't good?
Poet.   I will say of it,
It tutors nature: artificial strife
Lives in these touches, livelier than life.

Enter certain Senators, *and pass over.*

Pain. How this lord is follow'd!
Poet. The senators of Athens: happy man!   40
Pain. Look, more!
Poet. You see this confluence, this great flood of
     visitors.
I have, in this rough work, shaped out a man,
Whom this beneath world doth embrace and hug
With amplest entertainment: my free drift
Halts not particularly, but moves itself
In a wide sea of wax: no levell'd malice

ACT I. SCENE I.   2. **long,** for a long time.   3. **wears . . . grows,** the Renaissance commonplace of the constant movement of nature between destruction and repair; cf. *Sonnet* lxiv, 8.   4. **what strange,** what rarity. 5. **Which . . . matches,** which is not matched in any of the manifold written records.   6. **Magic of bounty,** an apostrophe to the abstract concept or personification of bounty, not identified precisely in the poet's mind with Timon himself; rather, Timon and his bounty are distinct in the minds of the sycophantic followers, since it is his generosity, not his personality, that attracts them. The concept of magic may be used deliberately to suggest the ephemeral aspect of Timon's affluence as well as of his popularity; his followers are like conjured spirits, now here, now vanished. The notion of magic as an evil thing contrasts with those firmly established ethical concepts against which Timon revolts after his disillusionment; cf. Introduction.   10. **breathed,** inured by exercise.   14. **estimate,** i.e., the valuation, fixed price. 18. **water,** luster of a diamond.   24. **Provokes itself,** i.e., is self-generating.   27. **Upon . . . presentment,** as soon as I have presented it; alludes to the custom of poets to present their books to wealthy patrons in return for which they were often rewarded with gifts of money.   29. **comes off,** turns out.   30. **Indifferent,** moderate, fair. 30-31. **how . . . standing,** how the graceful attitude of this figure proclaims that it stands firm on its own centre, or gives evidence in favor of its own fixture. *Grace* is introduced as bearing witness to propriety (Steevens).   32. **Imagination,** the painter's creative power. 33-34. **to . . . interpret,** i.e., the very gestures depicted are eloquent. 45. **drift,** design.   46. **Halts not particularly,** doesn't concern itself with any one individually.   47. **sea of wax.** Some editors think this alludes to writing on a wax tablet with a stylus; others, that *wax* signifies growth, i.e., a waxing sea; Deighton conjectured *waste* (sp. *wast*).

Infects one comma in the course I hold;
But flies an eagle flight, bold and forth on,
Leaving no tract behind. 50
  Pain. How shall I understand you?
  Poet.   I will unbolt to you.
You see how all conditions, how all minds,
As well of glib and slippery creatures as
Of grave and austere quality, tender down
Their services to Lord Timon: his large fortune
Upon his good and gracious nature hanging
Subdues and properties to his love and tendance
All sorts of hearts; yea, from the glass-faced flatterer
To Apemantus, that few things loves better
Than to abhor himself: even he drops down 60
The knee before him and returns in peace
Most rich in Timon's nod.
  Pain.   I saw them speak together.
  Poet. Sir, I have upon a high and pleasant hill
Feign'd Fortune to be throned: the base o' the mount
Is rank'd with all deserts, all kind of natures,
That labour on the bosom of this sphere
To propagate their states: amongst them all,
Whose eyes are on this sovereign lady fix'd,
One do I personate of Lord Timon's frame,
Whom Fortune with her ivory hand wafts to her; 70
Whose present grace to present slaves and servants
Translates his rivals.
  Pain.   'Tis conceived to scope.
This throne, this Fortune, and this hill, methinks,
With one man beckon'd from the rest below,
Bowing his head against the steepy mount
To climb his happiness, would be well express'd
In our condition.
  Poet.   Nay, sir, but hear me on.
All those which were his fellows but of late,
Some better than his value, on the moment
Follow his strides, his lobbies fill with tendance, 80
Rain sacrificial whisperings in his ear,
Make sacred even his stirrup, and through him
Drink the free air.
  Pain.   Ay, marry, what of these?
  Poet. When Fortune in her shift and change of
  mood
Spurns down her late beloved, all his dependants
Which labour'd after him to the mountain's top
Even on their knees and hands, let him slip down,
Not one accompanying his declining foot.
  Pain. 'Tis common:
A thousand moral paintings I can show 90
That shall demonstrate these quick blows of Fortune's
More pregnantly than words. Yet you do well
To show Lord Timon that mean eyes have seen
The foot above the head.

 Trumpets sound. Enter LORD TIMON, *addressing himself*
 courteously to every suitor; a Messenger *from*
 VENTIDIUS *talking with him;* LUCILIUS *and other*
 servants following.

  Tim.   Imprison'd is he, say you?
  Mess. Ay, my good lord: five talents is his debt,
His means most short, his creditors most strait:

Your honourable letter he desires
To those have shut him up; which failing,
Periods his comfort.
  Tim.   Noble Ventidius! Well;
I am not of that feather to shake off 100
My friend when he must need me. I do know him
A gentleman that well deserves a help:
Which he shall have: I'll pay the debt, and free him.
  Mess. Your lordship ever binds him.
  Tim. Commend me to him: I will send his ransom;
And being enfranchised, bid him come to me.
'Tis not enough to help the feeble up,
But to support him after. Fare you well.
  Mess. All happiness to your honour!   [*Exit.*

 Enter an old Athenian.

  Old Ath. Lord Timon, hear me speak.
  Tim.   Freely, good father. 110
  Old Ath. Thou hast a servant named Lucilius.
  Tim. I have so: what of him?
  Old Ath. Most noble Timon, call the man before
  thee.
  Tim. Attends he here, or no? Lucilius!
  Luc. Here, at your lordship's service.
  Old Ath. This fellow here, Lord Timon, this thy
  creature,
By night frequents my house. I am a man
That from my first have been inclined to thrift;
And my estate deserves an heir more raised
Than one which holds a trencher.
  Tim.   Well; what further? 120
  Old Ath. One only daughter have I, no kin else,
On whom I may confer what I have got:
The maid is fair, o' the youngest for a bride,
And I have bred her at my dearest cost
In qualities of the best. This man of thine
Attempts her love: I prithee, noble lord,
Join with me to forbid him her resort;
Myself have spoke in vain.
  Tim.   The man is honest.
  Old Ath. Therefore he will be, Timon: 130
His honesty rewards him in itself;
It must not bear my daughter.
  Tim.   Does she love him?
  Old Ath. She is young and apt:
Our own precedent passions do instruct us
What levity 's in youth.
  Tim.   [*To Lucilius*] Love you the
  maid?
  Luc. Ay, my good lord, and she accepts of it.
  Old Ath. If in her marriage my consent be missing,
I call the gods to witness, I will choose
Mine heir from forth the beggars of the world,
And dispossess her all.
  Tim.   How shall she be endow'd,
If she be mated with an equal husband? 140
  Old Ath. Three talents on the present; in future, all.
  Tim. This gentleman of mine hath served me long:
To build his fortune I will strain a little,
For 'tis a bond in men. Give him thy daughter:
What you bestow, in him I'll counterpoise,

---

48. **comma,** a term of rhetoric meaning a short member of a sentence.
51. **unbolt,** disclose. 57. **properties,** appropriates. 58. **glass-faced
flatterer,** one that shows in his look, as by reflection, the looks of his
patron (Johnson). 65. **rank'd,** filled with ranks of. **deserts,** degrees
of merit. 67. **propagate,** enlarge. 69. **frame,** appearance. 71-72.
Whose . . . rivals, i.e., whose gracious presence transforms his rivals
immediately into slaves and servants. 72. **to scope,** to the purpose.

76-77. **would . . . condition,** would find a striking parallel in our
state (Schmidt). 79. **better than his value,** his superiors. 90. **moral
paintings,** allegorical depictions. 93. **mean eyes,** man of low degree.
94. **foot above the head,** highest and lowest changing places. 95.
talents, probably Attic talents of silver, units of money worth perhaps
$1000. 96. **strait,** severe, exacting. 98. **which failing,** the lack of
which. 99. **Periods,** puts an end to. 126. **Attempts,** tries to win.

And make him weigh with her.
   Old Ath.   Most noble lord,
Pawn me to this your honour, she is his.
   Tim. My hand to thee; mine honour on my
      promise.
   Luc. Humbly I thank your lordship: never may
That state or fortune fall into my keeping,   150
Which is not owed to you!
             [*Exeunt Lucilius and Old Athenian.*
   Poet. Vouchsafe my labour, and long live your
      lordship!
   Tim. I thank you; you shall hear from me anon:
Go not away. What have you there, my friend?
   Pain. A piece of painting, which I do beseech
Your lordship to accept.
   Tim.   Painting is welcome.
The painting is almost the natural man;
For since dishonour traffics with man's nature,
He is but outside: these pencill'd figures are
Even such as they give out. I like your work;   160
And you shall find I like it: wait attendance
Till you hear further from me.
   Pain.   The gods preserve ye!
   Tim. Well fare you, gentleman: give me your hand;
We must needs dine together. Sir, your jewel
Hath suffer'd under praise.
   Jew.   What, my lord! dispraise?
   Tim. A mere satiety of commendations.
If I should pay you for 't as 'tis extoll'd,
It would unclew me quite.
   Jew.   My lord, 'tis rated
As those which sell would give: but you well know,
Things of like value differing in the owners   170
Are prized by their masters: believe 't, dear lord,
You mend the jewel by the wearing it.
   Tim. Well mock'd.
   Mer. No, my good lord; he speaks the common
      tongue,
Which all men speak with him.
   Tim. Look, who comes here: will you be chid?

Enter APEMANTUS.

   Jew. We'll bear, with your lordship.
   Mer.   He'll spare none.
   Tim. Good morrow to thee, gentle Apemantus!
   Apem. Till I be gentle, stay thou for thy good
      morrow;   179
When thou art Timon's dog, and these knaves honest.
   Tim. Why dost thou call them knaves? thou know'st
      them not.
   Apem. Are they not Athenians?
   Tim. Yes.
   Apem. Then I repent not.
   Jew. You know me, Apemantus?
   Apem. Thou know'st I do: I call'd thee by thy name.
   Tim. Thou art proud, Apemantus.
   Apem. Of nothing so much as that I am not like
Timon.   190
   Tim. Whither art going?
   Apem. To knock out an honest Athenian's brains.
   Tim. That 's a deed thou 'lt die for.

   Apem. Right, if doing nothing be death by the law.
   Tim. How likest thou this picture, Apemantus?
   Apem. The best, for the innocence.
   Tim. Wrought he not well that painted it?   200
   Apem. He wrought better that made the painter;
and yet he 's but a filthy piece of work.
   Pain. You 're a dog.
   Apem. Thy mother 's of my generation: what 's she,
if I be a dog?
   Tim. Wilt dine with me, Apemantus?
   Apem. No; I eat not lords.
   Tim. An thou shouldst, thou 'ldst anger ladies.
   Apem. O, they eat lords; so they come by great
bellies.   210
   Tim. That 's a lascivious apprehension.
   Apem. So thou apprehendest it: take it for thy
labour.
   Tim. How dost thou like this jewel, Apemantus?
   Apem. Not so well as plain-dealing, which will not
cost a man a doit.
   Tim. What dost thou think 'tis worth?
   Apem. Not worth my thinking. How now, poet!   220
   Poet. How now, philosopher!
   Apem. Thou liest.
   Poet. Art not one?
   Apem. Yes.
   Poet. Then I lie not.
   Apem. Art not a poet?
   Poet. Yes.
   Apem. Then thou liest: look in thy last work, where
thou hast feigned him a worthy fellow.
   Poet. That 's not feigned; he is so.   230
   Apem. Yes, he is worthy of thee, and to pay thee for
thy labour: he that loves to be flattered is worthy o'
the flatterer. Heavens, that I were a lord!
   Tim. What wouldst do then, Apemantus?
   Apem. E'en as Apemantus does now; hate a lord
with my heart.
   Tim. What, thyself?
   Apem. Ay.
   Tim. Wherefore?   240
   Apem. †That I had no angry wit to be a lord. Art
not thou a merchant?
   Mer. Ay, Apemantus.
   Apem. Traffic confound thee, if the gods will not!
   Mer. If traffic do it, the gods do it.
   Apem. Traffic 's thy god; and thy god confound
thee!

Trumpet sounds. Enter a Messenger.

   Tim. What trumpet 's that?
   Mess. 'Tis Alcibiades, and some twenty horse,   250
All of companionship.
   Tim. Pray, entertain them; give them guide to us.
              [*Exeunt some Attendants.*
You must needs dine with me: go not you hence
Till I have thank'd you: when dinner 's done,
Show me this piece. I am joyful of your sights.

Enter ALCIBIADES, *with the rest.*

Most welcome, sir!

---

132. **apt,** easily taught. 140. **If . . . husband,** if her husband's fortune
equal her dowry. 150. **That,** i.e., any. 157-160. **The painting . . .
out.** This remark is to be held in mind in connection with Timon's
disillusionment (IV, iii) about man's pretense to virtue and the *direct
villany* of the thief and the prostitute. 164-165. **your . . . praise.**
Timon means that excess of praise—*satiety of commendations*—has made
its sale less easy. 168. **unclew,** unwind, i.e., ruin. 169. **As . . . give,**

at a price which merchants would pay, i.e., at cost. 171. **by their
masters,** i.e., as their masters are respected; the gem will increase in
value because Timon will wear it. 199. **innocence,** i.e., Apemantus
would say, "at least it is innocuous." 204. **generation,** species.
241. **That . . . lord,** i.e., he would lack angry wit sufficient to condemn
the status of being a lord. 244. **Traffic,** business. 251. **All of companionship,** all belonging to the same party.

Apem.   So, so, there!
Aches contract and starve your supple joints!
That there should be small love 'mongst these sweet
      knaves,
And all this courtesy! The strain of man 's bred out
Into baboon and monkey.   260
    Alcib. Sir, you have saved my longing, and I feed
Most hungerly on your sight.
    Tim.   Right welcome, sir!
Ere we depart, we'll share a bounteous time
In different pleasures. Pray you, let us in.
                    [*Exeunt all except Apemantus.*

    Enter two Lords.
    First Lord. What time o' day is 't, Apemantus?
    Apem. Time to be honest.
    First Lord. That time serves still.
    Apem. The most accursed thou, that still omitt'st it.
    Sec. Lord. Thou art going to Lord Timon's feast? 270
    Apem. Ay, to see meat fill knaves and wine heat
      fools.
    Sec. Lord. Fare thee well, fare thee well.
    Apem. Thou art a fool to bid me farewell twice.
    Sec. Lord. Why, Apemantus?
    Apem. Shouldst have kept one to thyself, for I mean
to give thee none.
    First Lord. Hang thyself!
    Apem. No, I will do nothing at thy bidding: make
thy requests to thy friend.
    Sec. Lord. Away, unpeaceable dog, or I'll spurn
thee hence!   281
    Apem. I will fly, like a dog, the heels o' the ass. [*Exit.*
    First Lord. He 's opposite to humanity. Come, shall
      we in,
And taste Lord Timon's bounty? he outgoes
The very heart of kindness.
    Sec. Lord. He pours it out; Plutus, the god of gold,
Is but his steward: no meed, but he repays
Sevenfold above itself; no gift to him,
But breeds the giver a return exceeding   290
All use of quittance.
    First Lord.   The noblest mind he carries
That ever govern'd man.
    Sec. Lord. Long may he live in fortunes! Shall we in?
    First Lord. I'll keep you company.   [*Exeunt.*

    SCENE II. *A banqueting-room in Timon's house.*

    Hautboys playing loud music. A great banquet served in;
    FLAVIUS *and others attending; then enter* LORD
    TIMON, ALCIBIADES, Lords, Senators, *and*
    VENTIDIUS. *Then comes, dropping after all,*
    APEMANTUS, *discontentedly, like himself.*

    Ven. Most honour'd Timon,
It hath pleased the gods to remember my father's age,
And call him to long peace.
He is gone happy, and has left me rich:

Then, as in grateful virtue I am bound
To your free heart, I do return those talents,
Doubled with thanks and service, from whose help
I derived liberty.
    Tim.   O, by no means,
Honest Ventidius; you mistake my love:
I gave it freely ever; and there 's none   10
Can truly say he gives, if he receives:
If our betters play at that game, we must not dare
To imitate them; faults that are rich are fair.
    Ven. A noble spirit!
    Tim.   Nay, my lords,
        [*They all stand ceremoniously looking on Timon.*
Ceremony was but devised at first
To set a gloss on faint deeds, hollow welcomes,
Recanting goodness, sorry ere 'tis shown;
But where there is true friendship, there needs none.
Pray, sit; more welcome are ye to my fortunes
Than my fortunes to me.   [*They sit.* 20
    First Lord. My lord, we always have confess'd it.
    Apem. Ho, ho, confess'd it! hang'd it, have you not?
    Tim. O, Apemantus, you are welcome.
    Apem.   No;
You shall not make me welcome:
I come to have thee thrust me out of doors.
    Tim. Fie, thou 'rt a churl; ye 've got a humour there
Does not become a man; 'tis much to blame.
They say, my lords, 'ira furor brevis est;' but yond
man is ever angry. Go, let him have a table by himself,
for he does neither affect company, nor is he fit for 't,
indeed.   31
    Apem. Let me stay at thine apperil, Timon: I come
to observe; I give thee warning on 't.
    Tim. I take no heed of thee; thou 'rt an Athenian,
therefore welcome: I myself would have no power;
prithee, let my meat make thee silent.
    Apem. I scorn thy meat; 'twould choke me, for I
should ne'er flatter thee. O you gods, what a number
of men eat Timon, and he sees 'em not! It grieves me
to see so many dip their meat in one man's blood;
and all the madness is, he cheers them up too.   43
I wonder men dare trust themselves with men:
Methinks they should invite them without knives;
Good for their meat, and safer for their lives.
There 's much example for 't; the fellow that sits next
him now, parts bread with him, pledges the breath of
him in a divided draught, is the readiest man to kill
him: 't has been proved. If I were a huge man, I
should fear to drink at meals;   51
Lest they should spy my windpipe's dangerous notes:
Great men should drink with harness on their throats.
    Tim. My lord, in heart; and let the health go
      round.
    Sec. Lord. Let it flow this way, my good lord.
    Apem. Flow this way! A brave fellow! he keeps his
tides well. Those healths will make thee and thy state
look ill, Timon. Here 's that which is too weak to be a
sinner, honest water, which ne'er left man i' the mire:

This and my food are equals; there 's no odds: 61
Feasts are too proud to give thanks to the gods.

Apemantus' grace.

Immortal gods, I crave no pelf;
I pray for no man but myself:
Grant I may never prove so fond,
To trust man on his oath or bond;
Or a harlot, for her weeping;
Or a dog, that seems a-sleeping;
Or a keeper with my freedom;
Or my friends, if I should need 'em. 70
Amen. So fall to 't:
Rich men sin, and I eat root. [*Eats and drinks.*
Much good †dich thy good heart, Apemantus!

Tim. Captain Alcibiades, your heart 's in the field now.

Alcib. My heart is ever at your service, my lord.

Tim. You had rather be at a breakfast of enemies than a dinner of friends. 79

Alcib. So they were bleeding-new, my lord, there 's no meat like 'em: I could wish my best friend at such a feast.

Apem. Would all those flatterers were thine enemies then, that then thou mightst kill 'em and bid me to 'em!

First Lord. Might we but have that happiness, my lord, that you would once use our hearts, whereby we might express some part of our zeals, we should think ourselves for ever perfect. 90

Tim. O, no doubt, my good friends, but the gods themselves have provided that I shall have much help from you: how had you been my friends else? why have you that charitable title from thousands, did not you chiefly belong to my heart? I have told more of you to myself than you can with modesty speak in your own behalf; and thus far I confirm you. O you gods, think I, what need we have any friends, if we should ne'er have need of 'em? they were the most needless creatures living, should we ne'er have use for 'em, and would most resemble sweet instruments hung up in cases that keep their sounds to themselves. Why, I have often wished myself poorer, that I might come nearer to you. We are born to do benefits: and what better or properer can we call our own than the riches of our friends? O, what a precious comfort 'tis, to have so many, like brothers, commanding one another's fortunes! O joy, e'en made away ere 't can be born! Mine eyes cannot hold out water, methinks: to forget their faults, I drink to you. 112

Apem. Thou weepest to make them drink, Timon.

Sec. Lord. Joy had the like conception in our eyes
And at that instant like a babe sprung up.

Apem. Ho, ho! I laugh to think that babe a bastard.

Third Lord. I promise you, my lord, you moved me much.

Apem. Much! [*Tucket, within.*

Tim. What means that trump? 120

Enter a Servant.

How now?

Serv. Please you, my lord, there are certain ladies most desirous of admittance.

Tim. Ladies! what are their wills?

Serv. There comes with them a forerunner, my lord, which bears that office, to signify their pleasures.

Tim. I pray, let them be admitted.

Enter CUPID.

Cup. Hail to thee, worthy Timon, and to all
That of his bounties taste! The five best senses
Acknowledge thee their patron; and come freely 130
To gratulate thy plenteous bosom: th' ear,
Taste, touch and smell, pleased from thy table rise;
They only now come but to feast thine eyes.

Tim. They 're welcome all; let 'em have kind
admittance:
Music, make their welcome! [*Exit Cupid.*

First Lord. You see, my lord, how ample you 're
beloved.

Music. Re-enter CUPID, *with a mask of* Ladies *as Amazons, with lutes in their hands, dancing and playing.*

Apem. Hoy-day, what a sweep of vanity comes this
way!
They dance! they are mad women.
Like madness is the glory of this life,
As this pomp shows to a little oil and root. 140
We make ourselves fools, to disport ourselves;
And spend our flatteries, to drink those men
Upon whose age we void it up again,
With poisonous spite and envy.
Who lives that 's not depraved or depraves?
Who dies, that bears not one spurn to their graves
Of their friends' gift?
I should fear those that dance before me now
Would one day stamp upon me: 't has been done;
Men shut their doors against a setting sun. 150

The Lords *rise from table, with much adoring of* TIMON; *and to show their loves, each singles out an* Amazon, *and all dance, men with women, a lofty strain or two to the hautboys, and cease.*

Tim. You have done our pleasures much grace, fair
ladies,
Set a fair fashion on our entertainment,
Which was not half so beautiful and kind;
You have added worth unto 't and lustre,
And entertain'd me with mine own device;
I am to thank you for 't.

First Lady. My lord, you take us even at the best.

Apem. 'Faith, for the worst is filthy; and would not
hold taking, I doubt me.

Tim. Ladies, there is an idle banquet attends you: 160
Please you to dispose yourselves.

All Ladies. Most thankfully, my lord.
[*Exeunt Cupid and Ladies.*

my tears. 126. **pleasures,** wishes. 137. **sweep of vanity,** troop of vain creatures. 138. **they are mad women.** Steevens quotes Stubbes' *Anatomy of Abuses:* "*Dauncers* thought to be *mad men*," and again: "And as in all feasts and pastimes dauncing is the last, so it is the extream of all other vice." 139-140. **Like madness . . . root.** The word *like* in this place does not express *resemblance,* but *equality.* Apemantus does not mean to say that the glory of this life was like madness, but it was *just as much madness* in the eye of reason, as the pomp appeared to be when compared to the frugal repast of a philosopher (M. Mason). 142-144. **And . . . envy,** and lavish our flatteries in order to swallow down those upon whom, when old, we cast up our surfeit in the shape of poisonous spite and envy (Deighton). 145. **depraved,** vilified, slandered. 147. **gift,** giving. 150. **Men . . . sun.** Cf. North's Plutarch (*Life of Pompey*), where is related Pompey's retort to Sulla's threat of resistance: Pompey "told him frankly again how men did honour the rising, not the setting of the sun." 153. **kind,** favorable (Onions); suitable (Deighton). 155. **with mine own device.** The mask appears to have been designed by Timon to surprise his guests (Johnson). 160. **idle,** trifling, slight.

Tim. Flavius.
Flav. My lord?
Tim. The little casket bring me hither.
Flav. Yes, my lord. More jewels yet! [*Aside.*
There is no crossing him in 's humour;
Else I should tell him well, i' faith, I should,
When all 's spent, he 'ld be cross'd then, an he could.
'Tis pity bounty had not eyes behind,
That man might ne'er be wretched for his mind. [*Exit.*
First Lord. Where be our men? 171
Serv. Here, my lord, in readiness.
Sec. Lord. Our horses!

Re-enter FLAVIUS, *with the casket.*

Tim. O my friends,
I have one word to say to you: look you, my good
lord,
I must entreat you, honour me so much
As to advance this jewel; accept it and wear it,
Kind my lord.
First Lord. I am so far already in your gifts,—
All. So are we all.

Enter a Servant.

Serv. My lord, there are certain nobles of the
senate 180
Newly alighted, and come to visit you.
Tim. They are fairly welcome.
Flav. I beseech your honour,
Vouchsafe me a word; it does concern you near.
Tim. Near! why then, another time I'll hear thee:
I prithee, let 's be provided to show them
entertainment.
Flav. [*Aside*] I scarce know how.

Enter a second Servant.

Sec. Serv. May it please your honour, Lord Lucius,
Out of his free love, hath presented to you
Four milk-white horses, trapp'd in silver.
Tim. I shall accept them fairly; let the presents 190
Be worthily entertain'd.

Enter a third Servant.

How now! what news?
Third Serv. Please you, my lord, that honourable
gentleman, Lord Lucullus, entreats your company
to-morrow to hunt with him, and has sent your
honour two brace of greyhounds.
Tim. I'll hunt with him; and let them be received,
Not without fair reward.
Flav. [*Aside*] What will this come to?
He commands us to provide, and give great gifts,
And all out of an empty coffer:
Nor will he know his purse, or yield me this, 200
To show him what a beggar his heart is,
Being of no power to make his wishes good:
His promises fly so beyond his state
That what he speaks is all in debt; he owes
For every word: he is so kind that he now
Pays interest for 't; his land 's put to their books.

Well, would I were gently put out of office
Before I were forced out!
Happier is he that has no friend to feed
Than such that do e'en enemies exceed. 210
I bleed inwardly for my lord. [*Exit.*
Tim. You do yourselves
Much wrong, you bate too much of your own merits:
Here, my lord, a trifle of our love.
Sec. Lord. With more than common thanks I will
receive it.
Third Lord. O, he 's the very soul of bounty!
Tim. And now I remember, my lord, you gave
Good words the other day of a bay courser
I rode on: it is yours, because you liked it.
Sec. Lord. O, I beseech you, pardon me, my lord,
in that.
Tim. You may take my word, my lord; I know, no
man 220
Can justly praise but what he does affect:
I weigh my friend's affection with mine own;
I'll tell you true. I'll call to you.
All Lords. O, none so welcome.
Tim. I take all and your several visitations
So kind to heart, 'tis not enough to give;
Methinks, I could deal kingdoms to my friends,
And ne'er be weary. Alcibiades,
Thou art a soldier, therefore seldom rich;
It comes in charity to thee: for all thy living
Is 'mongst the dead, and all the lands thou hast 230
Lie in a pitch'd field.
Alcib. Ay, defiled land, my lord.
First Lord. We are so virtuously bound—
Tim. And so
Am I to you.
Sec. Lord. So infinitely endear'd—
Tim. All to you. Lights, more lights!
First Lord. The best of happiness,
Honour and fortunes, keep with you, Lord Timon!
Tim. Ready for his friends.
[*Exeunt all but Apemantus and Timon.*
Apem. What a coil 's here!
Serving of becks and jutting-out of bums!
I doubt whether their legs be worth the sums 238
That are given for 'em. Friendship 's full of dregs:
Methinks, false hearts should never have sound legs.
Thus honest fools lay out their wealth on court'sies.
Tim. Now, Apemantus, if thou wert not sullen,
I would be good to thee.
Apem. No, I'll nothing: for if I should be bribed
too, there would be none left to rail upon thee, and
then thou wouldst sin the faster. Thou givest so long,
Timon, I fear me thou wilt give away thyself in paper
shortly: what need these feasts, pomps and vain-
glories? 249
Tim. Nay, an you begin to rail on society once, I
am sworn not to give regard to you. Farewell; and
come with better music. [*Exit.*
Apem. So:
Thou wilt not hear me now; thou shalt not then:
I'll lock thy heaven from thee.

---

167. **tell him well,** use plain language; so F; Globe, following Rowe: *tell him—well.* Editors adopting Rowe's punctuation think such direct language indecorous for a servant; but see the steward's speeches at II, ii, 8, *I must be round with him,* and II, ii, 142-147, *At many . . . I . . . pray'd you,* etc. 168. **cross'd,** quibbling on the meanings "thwarted" and "provided with coins having on them the representation of a cross." 170. **for his mind,** on account of his intentions. 176. **advance,** make more worthy; i.e., by possessing it; cf. I, i, 170-172. 200. **yield**

me this, grant me opportunity. 202. **Being,** modifies *heart.* 212. **bate too much of,** belittle too much. 223. **call to,** call on (Malone); appeal to (Delius). 231. **defiled land,** quibble on "pitch'd field." 237. **becks,** nods, bows. 238. **their legs,** curtsies. 248. **paper,** bonds, promises to pay.

ACT II. SCENE I. 10. **No porter.** Johnson thought a line was lost here "in which the behaviour of a surly porter was described." As Farmer pointed out, sternness was characteristic of a porter; Mason

O, that men's ears should be
To counsel deaf, but not to flattery!   [*Exit.*

ACT II.

SCENE I. *A Senator's house.*

Enter Senator, *with papers in his hand.*

Sen. And late, five thousand: to Varro and to
   Isidore
He owes nine thousand; besides my former sum,
Which makes it five and twenty. Still in motion
Of raging waste? It cannot hold; it will not.
If I want gold, steal but a beggar's dog,
And give it Timon, why, the dog coins gold.
If I would sell my horse, and buy twenty more
Better than he, why, give my horse to Timon,
Ask nothing, give it him, it foals me, straight,
And able horses. No porter at his gate,   10
But rather one that smiles and still invites
All that pass by. It cannot hold; no reason
Can sound his state in safety. Caphis, ho!
Caphis, I say!

Enter CAPHIS.

Caph.   Here, sir; what is your pleasure?
Sen. Get on your cloak, and haste you to Lord
   Timon;
Importune him for my moneys; be not ceased
With slight denial, nor then silenced when—
'Commend me to your master'—and the cap
Plays in the right hand, thus: but tell him,
My uses cry to me, I must serve my turn   20
Out of mine own; his days and times are past
And my reliances on his fracted dates
Have smit my credit: I love and honour him,
But must not break my back to heal his finger;
Immediate are my needs, and my relief
Must not be toss'd and turn'd to me in words,
But find supply immediate. Get you gone:
Put on a most importunate aspect,
A visage of demand; for, I do fear,
When every feather sticks in his own wing,   30
Lord Timon will be left a naked gull,
Which flashes now a phœnix. Get you gone.
Caph. I go, sir.
Sen. 'I go, sir!'—Take the bonds along with you,
And have the dates in compt.
Caph.   I will, sir.
Sen.   Go.   [*Exeunt.*

SCENE II. *The same. A hall in Timon's house.*

Enter FLAVIUS, *with many bills in his hand.*

Flav. No care, no stop! so senseless of expense,
That he will neither know how to maintain it,
Nor cease his flow of riot: takes no account
How things go from him, nor resumes no care

Of what is to continue: never mind
Was to be so unwise, to be so kind.
What shall be done? he will not hear, till feel:
I must be round with him, now he comes from
   hunting.
Fie, fie, fie, fie!

Enter CAPHIS, *and the* Servants *of* ISIDORE *and* VARRO.

Caph.   Good even, Varro: what,
You come for money?
Var. Serv.   Is 't not your business too? 10
Caph. It is: and yours too, Isidore?
Isid. Serv.   It is so.
Caph. Would we were all discharged!
Var. Serv.   I fear it.
Caph. Here comes the lord.

Enter TIMON, ALCIBIADES, *and* Lords, *&c.*

Tim. So soon as dinner 's done, we'll forth again,
My Alcibiades. With me? what is your will?
Caph. My lord, here is a note of certain dues.
Tim. Dues! Whence are you?
Caph.   Of Athens here, my lord.
Tim. Go to my steward.
Caph. Please it your lordship, he hath put me off
To the succession of new days this month: 20
My master is awaked by great occasion
To call upon his own, and humbly prays you
That with your other noble parts you'll suit
In giving him his right.
Tim.   Mine honest friend,
I prithee, but repair to me next morning.
Caph. Nay, good my lord,—
Tim.   Contain thyself, good friend.
Var. Serv. One Varro's servant, my good lord,—
Isid. Serv.   From Isidore;
He humbly prays your speedy payment.
Caph. If you did know, my lord, my master's
   wants—
Var. Serv. 'Twas due on forfeiture, my lord, six
   weeks   30
And past.
Isid. Serv. Your steward puts me off, my lord;
And I am sent expressly to your lordship.
Tim. Give me breath.
I do beseech you, good my lords, keep on;
I'll wait upon you instantly.
                    [*Exeunt Alcibiades and Lords.*
                    [*To Flav.*] Come hither: pray you,
How goes the world, that I am thus encounter'd
With clamorous demands of date-broke bonds,
And the detention of long-since-due debts,
Against my honour?
Flav.   Please you, gentlemen,   40
The time is unagreeable to this business:
Your importunacy cease till after dinner,
That I may make his lordship understand
Wherefore you are not paid.
Tim. Do so, my friends. See them well entertain'd.
                    [*Exit.*

added, further, that *one* does not refer to *porter* but means "a person."
13. **sound,** so F; i.e., by sounding find it to be safe; Globe, following
Johnson: *found.* 16. **be not ceased,** do not allow yourself to be
silenced. 20. **uses,** needs. 22. **fracted,** broken; i.e., failure to meet
payments on notes due; cf. II, ii, 38, *date-broke bonds.* 27. **immediate,**
immediately. 30. **When . . . wing,** when everything is in the hands
of its rightful possessor. 31. **gull,** quibble on the meanings "unfledged bird" and "dupe." 35. **in compt,** in reckoning; Theobald's

addition to text.
   SCENE II. 2. **know how,** set his mind to knowing how. 6. **Was . . .
kind,** to be so unwise in order to be so kind. 12. **discharged,** paid.
fear it, am apprehensive about our being paid. 20. **this month,** for a
month; i.e., he has put me off from one day to another all month.
23. **with . . . parts,** in conformity to your otherwise noble nature.

Flav. Pray, draw near. [*Exit.*

Enter APEMANTUS *and* Fool.

Caph. Stay, stay, here comes the fool with Apemantus: let 's ha' some sport with 'em.

Var. Serv. Hang him, he'll abuse us.

Isid. Serv. A plague upon him, dog! 50

Var. Serv. How dost, fool?

Apem. Dost dialogue with thy shadow?

Var. Serv. I speak not to thee.

Apem. No, 'tis to thyself. [*To the Fool*] Come away.

Isid. Serv. There 's the fool hangs on your back already.

Apem. No, thou stand'st single, thou 'rt not on him yet.

Caph. Where 's the fool now? 59

Apem. He last asked the question. Poor rogues, and usurers' men! bawds between gold and want!

All Serv. What are we, Apemantus?

Apem. Asses.

All Serv. Why?

Apem. That you ask me what you are, and do not know yourselves. Speak to 'em, fool.

Fool. How do you, gentlemen?

All Serv. Gramercies, good fool: how does your mistress? 70

Fool. She 's e'en setting on water to scald such chickens as you are. Would we could see you at Corinth!

Apem. Good! gramercy.

Enter Page.

Fool. Look you, here comes my mistress' page.

Page. [*To the Fool*] Why, how now, captain! what do you in this wise company? How dost thou, Apemantus?

Apem. Would I had a rod in my mouth, that I might answer thee profitably. 80

Page. Prithee, Apemantus, read me the superscription of these letters: I know not which is which.

Apem. Canst not read?

Page. No.

Apem. There will little learning die then, that day thou art hanged. This is to Lord Timon; this to Alcibiades. Go; thou wast born a bastard, and thou 't die a bawd. 89

Page. Thou wast whelped a dog, and thou shalt famish a dog's death. Answer not: I am gone. [*Exit.*

Apem. E'en so thou outrunnest grace. Fool, I will go with you to Lord Timon's.

Fool. Will you leave me there?

Apem. If Timon stay at home. You three serve three usurers?

All Serv. Ay; would they served us!

Apem. So would I,—as good a trick as ever hangman served thief. 100

Fool. Are you three usurers' men?

All Serv. Ay, fool.

Fool. I think no usurer but has a fool to his servant: my mistress is one, and I am her fool. When men come to borrow of your masters, they approach sadly,

and go away merry; but they enter my mistress' house merrily, and go away sadly: the reason of this?

Var. Serv. I could render one. 109

Apem. Do it then, that we may account thee a whoremaster and a knave; which notwithstanding, thou shalt be no less esteemed.

Var. Serv. What is a whoremaster, fool?

Fool. A fool in good clothes, and something like thee. 'Tis a spirit: sometime 't appears like a lord; sometime like a lawyer; sometime like a philosopher, with two stones moe than 's artificial one: he is very often like a knight; and, generally, in all shapes that man goes up and down in from fourscore to thirteen, this spirit walks in. 121

Var. Serv. Thou art not altogether a fool.

Fool. Nor thou altogether a wise man: as much foolery as I have, so much wit thou lackest.

Apem. That answer might have become Apemantus.

All Serv. Aside, aside; here comes Lord Timon.

Re-enter TIMON *and* FLAVIUS.

Apem. Come with me, fool, come.

Fool. I do not always follow lover, elder brother and woman; sometime the philosopher. 131
[*Exeunt Apemantus and Fool.*

Flav. Pray you, walk near: I'll speak with you anon. [*Exeunt Servants.*

Tim. You make me marvel: wherefore ere this time
Had you not fully laid my state before me,
That I might so have rated my expense,
As I had leave of means?

Flav.   You would not hear me,
At many leisures I proposed.

Tim.   Go to:
Perchance some single vantages you took,
When my indisposition put you back;
And that unaptness made your minister, 140
Thus to excuse yourself.

Flav.   O my good lord,
At many times I brought in my accounts,
Laid them before you; you would throw them off,
And say, you found them in mine honesty.
When, for some trifling present, you have bid me
Return so much, I have shook my head and wept;
Yea, 'gainst the authority of manners, pray'd you
To hold your hand more close: I did endure
Not seldom, nor no slight checks, when I have
Prompted you in the ebb of your estate 150
And your great flow of debts. My loved lord,
†Though you hear now, too late—yet now 's a time—
The greatest of your having lacks a half
To pay your present debts.

Tim.   Let all my land be sold.

Flav. 'Tis all engaged, some forfeited and gone;
And what remains will hardly stop the mouth
Of present dues: the future comes apace:
What shall defend the interim? and at length
How goes our reckoning?

Tim. To Lacedæmon did my land extend. 160

Flav. O my good lord, the world is but a word:

Were it all yours to give it in a breath,
How quickly were it gone!
  Tim.   You tell me true.
  Flav. If you suspect my husbandry or falsehood,
Call me before the exactest auditors
And set me on the proof. So the gods bless me,
When all our offices have been oppress'd
With riotous feeders, when our vaults have wept
With drunken spilth of wine, when every room
Hath blazed with lights and bray'd with minstrelsy, 170
I have retired me to a wasteful cock,
And set mine eyes at flow.
  Tim.   Prithee, no more.
  Flav. Heavens, have I said, the bounty of this lord!
How many prodigal bits have slaves and peasants
This night englutted! Who is not Timon's?
What heart, head, sword, force, means, but is Lord
    Timon's?
Great Timon, noble, worthy, royal Timon!
Ah, when the means are gone that buy this praise,
The breath is gone whereof this praise is made:
Feast-won, fast-lost; one cloud of winter showers,   180
These flies are couch'd.
  Tim.   Come, sermon me no further:
No villanous bounty yet hath pass'd my heart;
Unwisely, not ignobly, have I given.
Why dost thou weep? Canst thou the conscience lack,
To think I shall lack friends? Secure thy heart;
If I would broach the vessels of my love,
And try the argument of hearts by borrowing,
Men and men's fortunes could I frankly use
As I can bid thee speak.
  Flav.   Assurance bless your thoughts!
  Tim. And, in some sort, these wants of mine are
    crown'd,   190
That I account them blessings; for by these
Shall I try friends: you shall perceive how you
Mistake my fortunes; I am wealthy in my friends.
Within there! Flaminius! Servilius!

Enter FLAMINIUS, SERVILIUS, *and other* Servants.

  Servants. My lord? my lord?
  Tim. I will dispatch you severally; you to Lord
Lucius; to Lord Lucullus you: I hunted with his
honour to-day: you, to Sempronius: commend me to
their loves, and, I am proud, say, that my occasions
have found time to use 'em toward a supply of money:
let the request be fifty talents.   202
  Flam. As you have said, my lord.
  Flav. [*Aside*] Lord Lucius and Lucullus? hum!
  Tim. Go you, sir, to the senators—
Of whom, even to the state's best health, I have
Deserved this hearing—bid 'em send o' the instant
A thousand talents to me.
  Flav.   I have been bold—
For that I knew it the most general way—
To them to use your signet and your name;   210
But they do shake their heads, and I am here
No richer in return.
  Tim.   Is 't true? can 't be?

Flav. They answer, in a joint and corporate voice,
That now they are at fall, want treasure, cannot
Do what they would; are sorry—you are
    honourable,—
But yet they could have wish'd—they know not—
Something hath been amiss—a noble nature
May catch a wrench—would all were well—'tis
    pity;—
And so, intending other serious matters,
After distasteful looks and these hard fractions,   220
With certain half-caps and cold-moving nods
They froze me into silence.
  Tim.   You gods, reward them!
Prithee, man, look cheerly. These old fellows
Have their ingratitude in them hereditary:
Their blood is caked, 'tis cold, it seldom flows;
'Tis lack of kindly warmth they are not kind;
And nature, as it grows again toward earth,
Is fashion'd for the journey, dull and heavy.
[*To a Serv.*] Go to Ventidius. [*To Flav.*] Prithee, be
    not sad,
Thou art true and honest; ingeniously I speak,   230
No blame belongs to thee. [*To Ser.*] Ventidius lately
Buried his father; by whose death he 's stepp'd
Into a great estate: when he was poor,
Imprison'd and in scarcity of friends,
I clear'd him with five talents: greet him from me;
Bid him suppose some good necessity
Touches his friend, which craves to be remember'd
With those five talents [*Exit Ser.*]. [*To Flav.*] That
    had, give 't these fellows
To whom 'tis instant due. Ne'er speak, or think,
That Timon's fortunes 'mong his friends can sink.   240
  Flav. I would I could not think it: that thought is
    bounty's foe;
Being free itself, it thinks all others so.   [*Exeunt.*

ACT III.

SCENE I. *A room in Lucullus' house.*

FLAMINIUS *waiting. Enter a* Servant *to him.*

  Serv. I have told my lord of you; he is coming down
to you.
  Flam. I thank you, sir.

Enter LUCULLUS.

  Serv. Here 's my lord.
  Lucul. [*Aside*] One of Lord Timon's men? a gift, I
warrant. Why, this hits right; I dreamt of a silver
basin and ewer to-night. Flaminius, honest Flaminius;
you are very respectively welcome, sir. Fill me some
wine. [*Exit Servant.*] And how does that honourable,
complete, free-hearted gentleman of Athens, thy very
bountiful good lord and master?   11
  Flam. His health is well, sir.
  Lucul. I am right glad that his health is well, sir:
and what hast thou there under thy cloak, pretty
Flaminius?

---

cock, faucet. 175-177. **Who is not Timon's,** etc. Flavius is scornfully
recalling the empty pledges of loyalty that he has overheard during
these extravagant feasts. 181. **couch'd,** lying concealed. 191. **That,**
so that. 196. **severally,** on different errands. 206. **state's best
health,** i.e., for my services in behalf of the state's welfare; cf. IV, iii,
93-95, where Alcibiades refers to Timon's sword and fortune offered
in the defense of Athens. 210. **To . . . name,** i.e., Timon's friends
have drawn on his fortune to pay their debts. 213. **joint . . . voice,**

in unanimous agreement. 220. **fractions,** broken sentences. 230.
ingeniously, frankly. 238. **That had,** when you have that. 241. **that
thought,** i.e., the thought that his fortunes cannot sink when he has
friends to sustain them.

ACT III, SCENE I. 7. **respectively,** with due respect.

Flam. 'Faith, nothing but an empty box, sir; which, in my lord's behalf, I come to entreat your honour to supply; who, having great and instant occasion to use fifty talents, hath sent to your lordship to furnish him, nothing doubting your present assistance therein. 21

Lucul. La, la, la la! 'nothing doubting,' says he? Alas, good lord! a noble gentleman 'tis, if he would not keep so good a house. Many a time and often I ha' dined with him, and told him on 't, and come again to supper to him, of purpose to have him spend less, and yet he would embrace no counsel, take no warning by my coming. Every man has his fault, and honesty is his: I ha' told him on 't, but I could ne'er get him from 't. 31

Re-enter Servant, *with wine.*

Serv. Please your lordship, here is the wine.

Lucul. Flaminius, I have noted thee always wise. Here 's to thee.

Flam. Your lordship speaks your pleasure.

Lucul. I have observed thee always for a towardly prompt spirit—give thee thy due—and one that knows what belongs to reason; and canst use the time well, if the time use thee well: good parts in thee. [*To Serv.*] Get you gone, sirrah [*Exit Serv.*]. Draw nearer, honest Flaminius. Thy lord 's a bountiful gentleman: but thou art wise; and thou knowest well enough, although thou comest to me, that this is no time to lend money, especially upon bare friendship, without security. Here 's three solidares for thee: good boy, wink at me, and say thou sawest me not. Fare thee well.

Flam. Is 't possible the world should so much differ, And we alive that lived? Fly, damned baseness, 50 To him that worships thee! [*Throwing the money back.*

Lucul. Ha! now I see thou art a fool, and fit for thy master. [*Exit.*

Flam. May these add to the number that may scald thee!
Let molten coin be thy damnation,
Thou disease of a friend, and not himself!
Has friendship such a faint and milky heart,
It turns in less than two nights? O you gods,
I feel my master's passion! this slave,
Unto his honour, has my lord's meat in him: 60
Why should it thrive and turn to nutriment,
When he is turn'd to poison?
O, may diseases only work upon 't!
And, when he 's sick to death, let not that part of nature
Which my lord paid for, be of any power
To expel sickness, but prolong his hour! [*Exit.*

SCENE II. *A public place.*

Enter LUCIUS, *with three* Strangers.

Luc. Who, the Lord Timon? he is my very good friend, and an honourable gentleman.

First Stran. We know him for no less, though we are but strangers to him. But I can tell you one thing, my lord, and which I hear from common rumours: now Lord Timon's happy hours are done and past, and his estate shrinks from him.

Luc. Fie, no, do not believe it; he cannot want for money. 10

Sec. Stran. But believe you this, my lord, that, not long ago, one of his men was with the Lord Lucullus to borrow so many talents, nay, urged extremely for 't and showed what necessity belonged to 't, and yet was denied.

Luc. How!

Sec. Stran. I tell you, denied, my lord.

Luc. What a strange case was that! now, before the gods, I am ashamed on 't. Denied that honourable man! there was very little honour showed in 't. For my own part, I must needs confess, I have received some small kindnesses from him, as money, plate, jewels and such-like trifles, nothing comparing to his; yet, had he mistook him and sent to me, I should ne'er have denied his occasion so many talents. 26

Enter SERVILIUS.

Ser. See, by good hap, yonder 's my lord; I have sweat to see his honour. My honoured lord,—
[*To Lucius.*

Luc. Servilius! you are kindly met, sir. Fare thee well: commend me to thy honourable virtuous lord, my very exquisite friend.

Ser. May it please your honour, my lord hath sent—

Luc. Ha! what has he sent? I am so much endeared to that lord; he 's ever sending: how shall I thank him, thinkest thou? And what has he sent now?

Ser. Has only sent his present occasion now, my lord; requesting your lordship to supply his instant use with so many talents. 41

Luc. I know his lordship is but merry with me; †He cannot want fifty five hundred talents.

Ser. But in the mean time he wants less, my lord. If his occasion were not virtuous, I should not urge it half so faithfully.

Luc. Dost thou speak seriously, Servilius?

Ser. Upon my soul, 'tis true, sir.

Luc. What a wicked beast was I to disfurnish myself against such a good time, when I might ha' shown myself honourable! how unluckily it happened, that I should purchase the day before for a little part, and undo a great deal of honour! Servilius, now, before the gods, I am not able to do,—the more beast, I say: —I was sending to use Lord Timon myself, these gentlemen can witness; but I would not, for the wealth of Athens, I had done 't now. Commend me bountifully to his good lordship; and I hope his honour will conceive the fairest of me, because I have no power to be kind: and tell him this from me, I

24. **keep . . . house**, be so lavish in his housekeeping. 26-27. **of purpose . . . him,** purposely to urge him. 29. **honesty,** liberality. 35. **Your lordship . . . pleasure,** a complimentary reply: it pleases your lordship to say so. 37. **towardly prompt,** quick to meet another's thoughts (Deighton). 46. **solidares,** small coins. 54-55. **May . . . damnation.** Stories appear to be common of avaricious men punished with tortures by means of molten metal. Steevens cites three: Mithridates' treatment of M. Aquilius; Lazarus' description in the *Kalender of Shepherdes* (see Oskar Sommer's reprint of the Paris edition, 1503, e₄, verso) of covetous men in hell being thrown into kettles of boiling lead and oil; and a black-letter ballad entitled *The Dead Man's Song.* Mason cites the

story of Crassus and the Parthians, who are said to have poured molten gold down his throat. 58. **turns,** sours, with quibble on the idea of "turn" as in turncoat. 59. **feel . . . passion,** feel the anger which my master is going to feel.
SCENE II. 25. **mistook,** misdoubted. 28. **I have sweat,** i.e., I have been hurrying. 36. **endeared,** bound by obligation. 43. **He cannot . . . talents,** a hyperbolical expression: he must be worth 5500 talents, i.e., he has at least that much, defining *want* as "lack." 45. **were not virtuous,** were due to a fault instead of a virtue, i.e., generosity. 52-53. **purchase . . . part,** several attempts at emendation: Theobald read *dirt* for *part,* Johnson, *park;* Jackson transposes the *and* following

count it one of my greatest afflictions, say, that I
cannot pleasure such an honourable gentleman. Good
Servilius, will you befriend me so far, as to use mine
own words to him? 65

Ser. Yes, sir, I shall.

Luc. I'll look you out a good turn, Servilius.
                                    [*Exit Servilius.*

True, as you said, Timon is shrunk indeed;
And he that 's once denied will hardly speed.   [*Exit.*

   First Stran. Do you observe this, Hostilius?
   Sec. Stran.   Ay, too well. 70
   First Stran. Why, this is the world's soul; and just of
      the same piece
Is every flatterer's spirit. Who can call him
His friend that dips in the same dish? for, in
My knowing, Timon has been this lord's father,
And kept his credit with his purse,
Supported his estate; nay, Timon's money
Has paid his men their wages: he ne'er drinks,
But Timon's silver treads upon his lip;
And yet—O, see the monstrousness of man
When he looks out in an ungrateful shape!— 80
He does deny him, in respect of his,
What charitable men afford to beggars.

   Third Stran. Religion groans at it.
   First Stran.   For mine own part,
I never tasted Timon in my life,
Nor came any of his bounties over me,
To mark me for his friend; yet, I protest,
For his right noble mind, illustrious virtue
And honourable carriage,
Had his necessity made use of me,
I would have put my wealth into donation, 90
And the best half should have return'd to him,
So much I love his heart: but, I perceive,
Men must learn now with pity to dispense;
For policy sits above conscience.   [*Exeunt.*

SCENE III. *A room in Sempronius' house.*

Enter SEMPRONIUS, *and a* Servant *of* TIMON'S.

Sem. Must he needs trouble me in 't,—hum!
   —'bove all others?
He might have tried Lord Lucius or Lucullus;
And now Ventidius is wealthy too,
Whom he redeem'd from prison: all these
Owe their estates unto him.
   Serv.   My lord,
They have all been touch'd and found base metal, for
They have all denied him.
   Sem.   How! have they denied him?
Has Ventidius and Lucullus denied him?
And does he send to me? Three? hum!
It shows but little love or judgement in him: 10
Must I be his last refuge? His friends, like physicians,
†Thrive, give him over: must I take the cure upon
   me?

Has much disgraced me in 't; I 'm angry at him,
That might have known my place: I see no sense for 't,
But his occasions might have woo'd me first;
For, in my conscience, I was the first man
That e'er received gift from him:
And does he think so backwardly of me now,
That I'll requite it last? No:
So it may prove an argument of laughter 20
To the rest, and 'mongst lords I be thought a fool.
I 'ld rather than the worth of thrice the sum,
Had sent to me first, but for my mind's sake;
I'd such a courage to do him good. But now return,
And with their faint reply this answer join;
Who bates mine honour shall not know my coin. [*Exit.*

   Serv. Excellent! Your lordship 's a goodly villain.
The devil knew not what he did when he made man
politic; he crossed himself by 't: and I cannot think
but, in the end, the villanies of man will set him clear.
How fairly this lord strives to appear foul! takes
virtuous copies to be wicked, like those that under hot
ardent zeal would set whole realms on fire:
Of such a nature is his politic love.
This was my lord's best hope; now all are fled,
Save only the gods: now his friends are dead,
Doors, that were ne'er acquainted with their wards
Many a bounteous year, must be employ'd
Now to guard sure their master. 40
And this is all a liberal course allows;
Who cannot keep his wealth must keep his house. [*Exit.*

SCENE IV. *The same. A hall in Timon's house.*

Enter two Servants *of* VARRO, *and the* Servant *of*
   LUCIUS, *meeting* TITUS, HORTENSIUS, *and other*
   Servants *of* TIMON'S *creditors, waiting his coming out.*

First Var. Serv. Well met; good morrow, Titus and
   Hortensius.
Tit. The like to you, kind Varro.
Hor.   Lucius!
What, do we meet together?
Luc. Serv.   Ay, and I think
One business does command us all; for mine
Is money.
Tit. So is theirs and ours.

Enter PHILOTUS.

Luc. Serv.   And Sir Philotus too!
Phi. Good day at once.
Luc. Serv.   Welcome, good brother.
What do you think the hour?
Phi.   Labouring for nine.
Luc. Serv. So much?
Phi.   Is not my lord seen yet?
Luc. Serv.   Not yet.
Phi. I wonder on 't; he was wont to shine at seven. 10
Luc. Serv. Ay, but the days are wax'd shorter with
   him:

*Timon
of Athens*
ACT III : SC IV

1029

---

this phrase to read *and for a little part;* Onions (citing *NED*) defines
purchase as "exert oneself," which removes all difficulties. 63. **pleasure,**
gratify. 71. **soul,** real essence, vital principle. 81-82. **He . . . beggars.**
Considering his possessions, he (Lucius) denies Timon the mere pittance
that a charitable man would give a beggar. 90. **put . . . donation,**
made my wealth accessible for distribution, as converting non-negoti-
able goods into negotiable.
   SCENE III. 6. **touch'd,** metaphor derived from testing metals with a
touchstone to see if they are gold. 12. **Thrive, give,** many emendations: Pope: *Three give;* Theobald: *Thriv'd, give;* Hanmer: *Tried give;*
Johnson: *Thrice give;* Mitford: *Have given;* Deighton explains the

difficulty as an ellipsis: physicians (who) thrive, give. 23. **Had,** i.e.,
he had. **my mind's sake,** for the sake of my own satisfaction. 24.
courage, desire, inclination. 26. **Who bates,** whoever abates. 29.
crossed. Johnson saw a play on the meanings "exempted from evil"
(i.e., by signing of the cross) and "out of debt" (crossed himself off the
books). 31. **fairly,** completely, plausibly; probably a quibble on these
two meanings plus the antithesis to *foul.* 32. **copies,** patterns, examples.
38. **wards,** bolts; i.e., were never locked. 42. **keep his house,** stay
indoors; with quibble.
   SCENE IV. 10. **to shine at seven.** This metaphor of the sun, continued
in the next speech, ironically echoes Timon's figure earlier (I, ii, 150).

You must consider that a prodigal course
Is like the sun's; but not, like his, recoverable.
I fear 'tis deepest winter in Lord Timon's purse;
That is, one may reach deep enough, and yet
Find little.
    Phi.   I am of your fear for that.
    Tit. I'll show you how to observe a strange event.
Your lord sends now for money.
    Hor.   Most true, he does.
    Tit. And he wears jewels now of Timon's gift,
For which I wait for money.   20
    Hor. It is against my heart.
    Luc. Serv.   Mark, how strange it shows,
Timon in this should pay more than he owes:
And e'en as if your lord should wear rich jewels,
And send for money for 'em.
    Hor. I 'm weary of this charge, the gods can witness:
I know my lord hath spent of Timon's wealth,
And now ingratitude makes it worse than stealth.
    First Var. Serv. Yes, mine 's three thousand crowns:
      what 's yours?
    Luc. Serv. Five thousand mine.
    First Var. Serv. 'Tis much deep: and it should seem
      by the sum,   30
Your master's confidence was above mine;
Else, surely, his had equall'd.

    Enter FLAMINIUS.

    Tit. One of Lord Timon's men.
    Luc. Serv. Flaminius! Sir, a word: pray, is my lord
ready to come forth?
    Flam. No, indeed, he is not.
    Tit. We attend his lordship; pray, signify so much.
    Flam. I need not tell him that; he knows you are too
diligent.   [*Exit.* 40

    Enter FLAVIUS *in a cloak, muffled.*

    Luc. Serv. Ha! is not that his steward muffled so?
He goes away in a cloud: call him, call him.
    Tit. Do you hear, sir?
    Sec. Var. Serv. By your leave, sir,—
    Flav. What do ye ask of me, my friend?
    Tit. We wait for certain money here, sir.
    Flav.   Ay,
If money were as certain as your waiting,
'Twere sure enough.
Why then preferr'd you not your sums and bills,
When your false masters eat of my lord's meat?   50
Then they could smile and fawn upon his debts
And take down the interest into their gluttonous
    maws.
You do yourselves but wrong to stir me up;
Let me pass quietly:
Believe 't, my lord and I have made an end;
I have no more to reckon, he to spend.
    Luc. Serv. Ay, but this answer will not serve.
    Flav. If 'twill not serve, 'tis not so base as you;
For you serve knaves.   [*Exit.*
    First Var. Serv. How! what does his cashiered wor-
ship mutter?   61
    Sec. Var. Serv. No matter what; he 's poor, and
that 's revenge enough. Who can speak broader than

he that has no house to put his head in? such may rail
against great buildings.

    Enter SERVILIUS.

    Tit. O, here 's Servilius; now we shall know some
answer.
    Ser. If I might beseech you, gentlemen, to repair
some other hour, I should derive much from 't; for,
take 't of my soul, my lord leans wondrously to discontent: his comfortable temper has forsook him; he 's
much out of health, and keeps his chamber.   73
    Luc. Serv. Many do keep their chambers are not sick:
And, if it be so far beyond his health,
Methinks he should the sooner pay his debts,
And make a clear way to the gods.
    Ser.   Good gods!
    Tit. We cannot take this for answer, sir.
    Flam. [*Within*] Servilius, help! My lord! my lord!

    Enter TIMON, *in a rage;* FLAMINIUS *following.*

    Tim. What, are my doors opposed against my
      passage?   80
Have I been ever free, and must my house
Be my retentive enemy, my gaol?
The place which I have feasted, does it now,
Like all mankind, show me an iron heart?
    Luc. Serv. Put in now, Titus.
    Tit. My lord, here is my bill.
    Luc. Serv. Here 's mine.
    Hor. And mine, my lord.
    Both Var. Serv. And ours, my lord.
    Phi. All our bills.   90
    Tim. Knock me down with 'em: cleave me to the
      girdle.
    Luc. Serv. Alas, my lord,—
    Tim. Cut my heart in sums.
    Tit. Mine, fifty talents.
    Tim. Tell out my blood.
    Luc. Serv. Five thousand crowns, my lord.
    Tim. Five thousand drops pays that. What yours?—
      and yours?
    First Var. Serv. My lord,—
    Sec. Var. Serv. My lord,—   99
    Tim. Tear me, take me, and the gods fall upon you!
                         [*Exit.*
    Hor. 'Faith, I perceive our masters may throw their
caps at their money: these debts may well be called
desperate ones, for a madman owes 'em.   [*Exeunt.*

    Re-enter TIMON *and* FLAVIUS.

    Tim. They have e'en put my breath from me, the
      slaves.
Creditors? devils!
    Flav. My dear lord,—
    Tim. What if it should be so?
    Flav. My lord,—
    Tim. I'll have it so. My steward!
    Flav. Here, my lord.   110
    Tim. So fitly? Go, bid all my friends again,
Lucius, Lucullus, and Sempronius:
All, sirrah, all:
I'll once more feast the rascals.

---

21. **against my heart,** contrary to my feelings.   27. **stealth,** theft.   42. **in a cloud,** quibble on the meanings "muffled" and "in a surly humor."   64. **broader,** quibble on "more freely" and "more in the open."   69. **repair,** return.   71. **comfortable,** cheerful.   77. **make . . . gods,** i.e., pay all his debts before he dies.   83. **place . . . feasted,** Timon's mis-

anthropy extends to the personification of his own house, where he has been so lavish.   91. **Knock, cleave.** Timon plays on *bills* as weapons.   SCENE V.   5. **compassion to the senate,** i.e., may the senate have compassion.   12. **stepp'd into the law,** incurred the penalties of the law.   14. **setting . . . aside,** not considering his ill-fated action.   17. **buys out,**

Flav.   O my lord,
You only speak from your distracted soul;
There is not so much left, to furnish out
A moderate table.
    Tim.   Be 't not in thy care; go,
I charge thee, invite them all: let in the tide
Of knaves once more; my cook and I'll provide.
                                  [Exeunt.

SCENE V. *The same. The senate-house.*

The Senate sitting.

First Sen. My lord, you have my voice to it; the
    fault 's
Bloody; 'tis necessary he should die:
Nothing emboldens sin so much as mercy.
    Sec. Sen. Most true; the law shall bruise him.

Enter ALCIBIADES, *with* Attendants.

    Alcib. Honour, health, and compassion to the
    senate!
    First Sen. Now, captain?
    Alcib. I am an humble suitor to your virtues;
For pity is the virtue of the law,
And none but tyrants use it cruelly.
It pleases time and fortune to lie heavy   10
Upon a friend of mine, who, in hot blood,
Hath stepp'd into the law, which is past depth
To those that, without heed, do plunge into 't.
He is a man, setting his fate aside,
Of comely virtues:
Nor did he soil the fact with cowardice—
An honour in him which buys out his fault—
But with a noble fury and fair spirit,
Seeing his reputation touch'd to death,
He did oppose his foe: 20
And with such sober and unnoted passion
He did behave his anger, ere 'twas spent,
As if he had but proved an argument.
    First Sen. You undergo too strict a paradox,
Striving to make an ugly deed look fair:
Your words have took such pains as if they labour'd
To bring manslaughter into form and set quarrelling
Upon the head of valour; which indeed
Is valour misbegot and came into the world
When sects and factions were newly born: 30
He 's truly valiant that can wisely suffer
The worst that man can breathe, and make his
        wrongs
His outsides, to wear them like his raiment, carelessly,
And ne'er prefer his injuries to his heart,
To bring it into danger.
If wrongs be evils and enforce us kill,
What folly 'tis to hazard life for ill!
    Alcib. My lord,—
    First Sen.   You cannot make gross sins
    look clear:
To revenge is no valour, but to bear.
    Alcib. My lords, then, under favour, pardon me,   40
If I speak like a captain.
Why do fond men expose themselves to battle,

And not endure all threats? sleep upon 't,
And let the foes quietly cut their throats,
Without repugnancy? If there be
Such valour in the bearing, what make we
Abroad? why then, women are more valiant
That stay at home, if bearing carry it,
And the ass more captain than the lion, the felon
Loaden with irons wiser than the judge,   50
If wisdom be in suffering. O my lords,
As you are great, be pitifully good:
Who cannot condemn rashness in cold blood?
To kill, I grant, is sin's extremest gust;
But, in defence, by mercy, 'tis most just.
To be in anger is impiety;
But who is man that is not angry?
Weigh but the crime with this.
    Sec. Sen. You breathe in vain.
    Alcib.   In vain! his service done
At Lacedæmon and Byzantium   60
Were a sufficient briber for his life.
    First Sen. What 's that?
    Alcib. I say, my lords, he has done fair service,
And slain in fight many of your enemies:
How full of valour did he bear himself
In the last conflict, and made plenteous wounds!
    Sec. Sen. He has made too much plenty with 'em;
He 's a sworn rioter: he has a sin that often
Drowns him, and takes his valour prisoner:
If there were no foes, that were enough   70
To overcome him: in that beastly fury
He has been known to commit outrages,
And cherish factions: 'tis inferr'd to us,
His days are foul and his drink dangerous.
    First Sen. He dies.
    Alcib.   Hard fate! he might have died
    in war.
My lords, if not for any parts in him—
Though his right arm might purchase his own time
And be in debt to none—yet, more to move you,
Take my deserts to his, and join 'em both:
And, for I know your reverend ages love   80
Security, I'll pawn my victories, all
My honours to you, upon his good returns.
If by this crime he owes the law his life,
Why, let the war receive 't in valiant gore;
For law is strict, and war is nothing more.
    First Sen. We are for law: he dies; urge it no more,
On height of our displeasure: friend or brother,
He forfeits his own blood that spills another.
    Alcib. Must it be so? it must not be. My lords,
I do beseech you, know me.   90
    Sec. Sen. How!
    Alcib. Call me to your remembrances.
    Third Sen.   What!
    Alcib. I cannot think but your age has forgot me;
It could not else be, I should prove so base,
To sue, and be denied such common grace:
My wounds ache at you.
    First Sen.   Do you dare our anger?
'Tis in few words, but spacious in effect;
We banish thee for ever.
    Alcib.   Banish me!

Timon
of Athens
ACT III : SC V

1031

---

redeems. 22. **behave,** control. 24. **undergo,** take upon yourself to
demonstrate. 27. **bring . . . form,** make murder appear orderly, or
according to form. 34. **prefer,** advance; metaphor from the practice
of recommending someone for honor or advancement. 45. **repugnancy,** resistance. 54. **sin's extremest gust,** the relish of extremest sin;

Malone defined *gust* as outburst. 55. **by mercy,** by a merciful interpretation of law (Malone). 61. **briber,** pleader. 77. **Though . . .
time,** his ability in war should purchase his freedom, i.e., let him die
a natural death. 97. **spacious in effect,** of great import, with quibble
on the limitless world to which Alcibiades is banished.

Banish your dotage; banish usury,
That makes the senate ugly.   100
    First Sen. If, after two days' shine, Athens contain
        thee,
Attend our weightier judgement. And, not to swell
    our spirit,
He shall be executed presently.   [*Exeunt Senators.*
    Alcib. Now the gods keep you old enough; that you
        may live
Only in bone, that none may look on you!
I 'm worse than mad: I have kept back their foes,
While they have told their money and let out
Their coin upon large interest, I myself
Rich only in large hurts. All those for this?
Is this the balsam that the usuring senate   110
Pours into captains' wounds? Banishment!
It comes not ill; I hate not to be banish'd;
It is a cause worthy my spleen and fury,
That I may strike at Athens. I'll cheer up
My discontented troops, and lay for hearts.
'Tis honour with most lands to be at odds;
Soldiers should brook as little wrongs as gods.   [*Exit.*

SCENE VI. *The same. A banqueting-room in Timon's house.*

Music. Tables set out: Servants *attending. Enter divers*
    Lords, Senators *and others, at several doors.*

First Lord. The good time of day to you, sir.
    Sec. Lord. I also wish it to you. I think this honour-
able lord did but try us this other day.
    First Lord. Upon that were my thoughts tiring,
when we encountered: I hope it is not so low with
him as he made it seem in the trial of his several
friends.
    Sec. Lord. It should not be, by the persuasion of his
new feasting.   9
    First Lord. I should think so: he hath sent me an
earnest inviting, which many my near occasions did
urge me to put off; but he hath conjured me beyond
them, and I must needs appear.
    Sec. Lord. In like manner was I in debt to my im-
portunate business, but he would not hear my excuse.
I am sorry, when he sent to borrow of me, that my
provision was out.
    First Lord. I am sick of that grief too, as I under-
stand how all things go.   20
    Sec. Lord. Every man here 's so. What would he
have borrowed of you?
    First Lord. A thousand pieces.
    Sec. Lord. A thousand pieces!
    First Lord. What of you?
    Sec. Lord. He sent to me, sir,—Here he comes.

Enter TIMON *and* Attendants.

    Tim. With all my heart, gentlemen both; and how
fare you?
    First Lord. Ever at the best, hearing well of your
lordship.   30

    Sec. Lord. The swallow follows not summer more
willing than we your lordship.
    Tim. [*Aside*] Nor more willingly leaves winter; such
summer-birds are men. Gentlemen, our dinner will
not recompense this long stay: feast your ears with
the music awhile, if they will fare so harshly o' the
trumpet's sound; we shall to 't presently.
    First Lord. I hope it remains not unkindly with your
lordship that I returned you an empty messenger.   41
    Tim. O, sir, let it not trouble you.
    Sec. Lord. My noble lord,—
    Tim. Ah, my good friend, what cheer?
    Sec. Lord. My most honourable lord, I am e'en sick
of shame, that, when your lordship this other day sent
to me, I was so unfortunate a beggar.
    Tim. Think not on 't, sir.
    Sec. Lord. If you had sent but two hours before,—   51
    Tim. Let it not cumber your better remembrance.
[*The banquet brought in.*] Come, bring in all together.
    Sec. Lord. All covered dishes!
    First Lord. Royal cheer, I warrant you.
    Third Lord. Doubt not that, if money and the season
can yield it.
    First Lord. How do you? What 's the news?
    Third Lord. Alcibiades is banished: hear you of it? 61
    First and Sec. Lord. Alcibiades banished!
    Third Lord. 'Tis so, be sure of it.
    First Lord. How! how!
    Sec. Lord. I pray you, upon what?
    Tim. My worthy friends, will you draw near?
    Third Lord. I'll tell you more anon. Here 's a noble
feast toward.
    Sec. Lord. This is the old man still.
    Third Lord. Will 't hold? will 't hold?   70
    Sec. Lord. It does: but time will—and so—
    Third Lord. I do conceive.
    Tim. Each man to his stool, with that spur as he
would to the lip of his mistress: your diet shall be in
all places alike. Make not a city feast of it, to let the
meat cool ere we can agree upon the first place: sit,
sit. The gods require our thanks.   77

    You great benefactors, sprinkle our society with
thankfulness. For your own gifts, make yourselves
praised: but reserve still to give, lest your deities be
despised. Lend to each man enough, that one need
not lend to another; for, were your godheads to
borrow of men, men would forsake the gods. Make
the meat be beloved more than the man that gives it.
Let no assembly of twenty be without a score of
villains: if there sit twelve women at the table, let a
dozen of them be—as they are. †The rest of your fees,
O gods—the senators of Athens, together with the
common lag of people—what is amiss in them, you
gods, make suitable for destruction. For these my
present friends, as they are to me nothing, so in
nothing bless them, and to nothing are they welcome.

Uncover, dogs, and lap.   95
    [*The dishes are uncovered and seen to be full of warm water.*

---

105. **Only in bone,** i.e., mere skeletons. 115. **lay for hearts,** endeavor
to win their affection. 116. **at odds,** at variance, in disagreement.
    SCENE VI. 5. **tiring,** preying upon, i.e., busily engaged. 8-9. **by
the . . . feasting,** i.e., as his new feasting persuades me to believe.
11-12. **near occasions,** urgent necessities or business. 38. **to 't,** i.e., to
the dinner. 47-48. **so unfortunate a beggar,** so unfortunate as to be
out of ready resources. 69. **This . . . still,** this is the same (generous)
Timon. 75. **city feast,** formal occasion. 77. **first place,** place of
honor. 89. **fees,** i.e., as for the rest of your gifts or benefactions.

90. **lag,** followers. 91-92. **what . . . destruction,** what doesn't at
present deserve destroying, make suitable for destruction. Timon
suggests by implication that only the wrong is right; right is amiss and
must be corrected and brought into line with all other evil so that it may
fulfill its destiny, which is destruction. 101. **you with flatteries,** so F;
Globe, following Warburton and Hanmer: *with your flatteries.* **flatteries,**
i.e., the unworthy or undeserved fruits of Timon's bounty. 107. **Cap
and knee slaves,** men obsequious with their caps and curtsies. **minute-
jacks,** fickle persons, jacks (i.e., mannikins which strike a bell on the

*Timon
of Athens*
ACT III : SC V

1032

Some speak. What does his lordship mean?
Some other. I know not.
  Tim. May you a better feast never behold,
You knot of mouth-friends! smoke and luke-warm
            water
Is your perfection. This is Timon's last; 100
Who, stuck and spangled you with flatteries,
Washes it off, and sprinkles in your faces
Your reeking villany.   [*Throwing the water in their faces.*
          Live loathed and long,
Most smiling, smooth, detested parasites,
Courteous destroyers, affable wolves, meek bears,
You fools of fortune, trencher-friends, time's flies,
Cap and knee slaves, vapours, and minute-jacks!
Of man and beast the infinite malady
Crust you quite o'er! What, dost thou go?
Soft! take thy physic first—thou too—and thou;— 110
Stay, I will lend thee money, borrow none.
      [*Throws the dishes at them, and drives them out.*
What, all in motion? Henceforth be no feast,
Whereat a villain 's not a welcome guest.
Burn, house! sink, Athens! henceforth hated be
Of Timon, man, and all humanity!   [*Exit.*

          Re-enter the Lords, Senators, *&c.*

  First Lord. How now, my lords!
  Sec. Lord. Know you the quality of Lord Timon's
fury?
  Third Lord. Push! did you see my cap?
  Fourth Lord. I have lost my gown. 120
  First Lord. He 's but a mad lord, and nought but
humour sways him. He gave me a jewel th' other day,
and now he has beat it out of my hat: did you see my
jewel?
  Third Lord. Did you see my cap?
  Sec. Lord. Here 'tis.
  Fourth Lord. Here lies my gown.
  First Lord. Let 's make no stay.
  Sec. Lord. Lord Timon 's mad.
  Third Lord.   I feel 't upon my bones.
  Fourth Lord. One day he gives us diamonds, next
    day stones.   [*Exeunt.*

ACT IV.

SCENE I. *Without the walls of Athens.*

Enter TIMON.

  Tim. Let me look back upon thee. O thou wall,
That girdlest in those wolves, dive in the earth,
And fence not Athens! Matrons, turn incontinent!
Obedience fail in children! slaves and fools,
Pluck the grave wrinkled senate from the bench,
And minister in their steads! to general filths
Convert o' the instant, green virginity,
Do 't in your parents' eyes! bankrupts, hold fast;
Rather than render back, out with your knives,
And cut your trusters' throats! bound servants, steal! 10

Large-handed robbers your grave masters are,
And pill by law. Maid, to thy master's bed;
Thy mistress is o' the brothel! Son of sixteen,
Pluck the lined crutch from thy old limping sire,
With it beat out his brains! Piety, and fear,
Religion to the gods, peace, justice, truth,
Domestic awe, night-rest, and neighbourhood,
Instruction, manners, mysteries, and trades,
Degrees, observances, customs, and laws,
Decline to your confounding contraries, 20
And let confusion live! Plagues, incident to men,
Your potent and infectious fevers heap
On Athens, ripe for stroke! Thou cold sciatica,
Cripple our senators, that their limbs may halt
As lamely as their manners! Lust and liberty
Creep in the minds and marrows of our youth,
That 'gainst the stream of virtue they may strive,
And drown themselves in riot! Itches, blains,
Sow all the Athenian bosoms; and their crop
Be general leprosy! Breath infect breath, 30
That their society, as their friendship, may
Be merely poison! Nothing I'll bear from thee,
But nakedness, thou detestable town!
Take thou that too, with multiplying bans!
Timon will to the woods; where he shall find
The unkindest beast more kinder than mankind.
The gods confound—hear me, you good gods all—
The Athenians both within and out that wall!
And grant, as Timon grows, his hate may grow
To the whole race of mankind, high and low! 40
Amen.   [*Exit.*

Timon
of Athens
ACT IV : SC II

1033

SCENE II. *Athens. A room in Timon's house.*

Enter FLAVIUS, *with two or three* Servants.

  First Serv. Hear you, master steward, where 's our
    master?
Are we undone? cast off? nothing remaining?
  Flav. Alack, my fellows, what should I say to you?
Let me be recorded by the righteous gods,
I am as poor as you.
  First Serv.   Such a house broke!
So noble a master fall'n! All gone! and not
One friend to take his fortune by the arm,
And go along with him!
  Sec. Serv.   As we do turn our backs
From our companion thrown into his grave,
So his familiars to his buried fortunes 10
Slink all away, leave their false vows with him,
Like empty purses pick'd; and his poor self,
A dedicated beggar to the air,
With his disease of all-shunn'd poverty,
Walks, like contempt, alone. More of our fellows.

Enter other Servants.

  Flav. All broken implements of a ruin'd house.
  Third Serv. Yet do our hearts wear Timon's livery;
That see I by our faces; we are fellows still,

---

outside of a clock) which vary with every minute. 108. **the infinite
malady,** every loathsome disease, infinite as the number is (Deighton).
115. Most editions including Globe leave this line without punctuation; F has comma after *man.* 119. **Push,** pshaw.
    ACT IV. SCENE I. 3. **fence,** quibble on the meanings "enclose" and
"defend." 6. **general filths,** common prostitutes. 12. **pill,** pillage.
14. **lined,** stuffed, padded. 15-21. **Piety . . . live,** another of Timon's
statements contrary to the accepted ethics of the age; such contraries
come more and more to be the burden of his misanthropic reflection.

17. **Domestic awe,** respect for the head of a household. **neighbourhood,** neighborliness. 20. **Decline,** i.e., may all these virtues give
way to their opposites. 25. **liberty,** licentiousness. 32. **merely,** i.e.,
unadulterated, nothing but.
    SCENE II. 10. **his familiars . . . fortunes,** those familiar with him
when he was fortunate. 13. **dedicated . . . air,** a beggar dedicated to
homelessness.

Serving alike in sorrow: leak'd is our bark,
And we, poor mates, stand on the dying deck, 20
Hearing the surges threat: we must all part
Into this sea of air.
    Flav.   Good fellows all,
The latest of my wealth I'll share amongst you.
Wherever we shall meet, for Timon's sake,
Let 's yet be fellows; let 's shake our heads, and say,
As 'twere a knell unto our master's fortunes,
'We have seen better days.' Let each take some;
Nay, put out all your hands. Not one word more:
Thus part we rich in sorrow, parting poor.
              [*Servants embrace, and part several ways.*
O, the fierce wretchedness that glory brings us! 30
Who would not wish to be from wealth exempt,
Since riches point to misery and contempt?
Who would be so mock'd with glory? or to live
But in a dream of friendship?
To have his pomp and all what state compounds
But only painted, like his varnish'd friends?
Poor honest lord, brought low by his own heart,
Undone by goodness! Strange, unusual blood,
When man's worst sin is, he does too much good!
Who, then, dares to be half so kind again? 40
For bounty, that makes gods, does still mar men.
My dearest lord, bless'd, to be most accursed,
Rich, only to be wretched, thy great fortunes
Are made thy chief afflictions. Alas, kind lord!
He 's flung in rage from this ingrateful seat
Of monstrous friends, nor has he with him to
Supply his life, or that which can command it.
I'll follow and inquire him out:
I'll ever serve his mind with my best will;
Whilst I have gold, I'll be his steward still.   [*Exit.* 50

———————

SCENE III. *Woods and cave, near the sea-shore.*

Enter TIMON, *from the cave.*

    Tim. O blessed breeding sun, draw from the earth
Rotten humidity; below thy sister's orb
Infect the air! Twinn'd brothers of one womb,
Whose procreation, residence, and birth,
Scarce is dividant, touch them with several fortunes;
The greater scorns the lesser: not nature,
To whom all sores lay siege, can bear great fortune,
But by contempt of nature.
Raise me this beggar, and deny 't that lord;
The senator shall bear contempt hereditary, 10
The beggar native honour.
It is the pasture lards the rother's sides,
The want that makes him lean. Who dares, who dares,
In purity of manhood stand upright,
And say 'This man 's a flatterer'? if one be,
So are they all; for every grise of fortune
Is smooth'd by that below: the learned pate

Ducks to the golden fool: all 's obliquy;
There 's nothing level in our cursed natures,
But direct villany. Therefore, be abhorr'd 20
All feasts, societies, and throngs of men!
His semblable, yea, himself, Timon disdains:
Destruction fang mankind! Earth, yield me roots!
                       [*Digging.*
Who seeks for better of thee, sauce his palate
With thy most operant poison! What is here?
Gold? yellow, glittering, precious gold? No, gods,
I am no idle votarist: roots, you clear heavens!
Thus much of this will make black white, foul fair,
Wrong right, base noble, old young, coward valiant.
Ha, you gods! why this? what this, you gods? Why,
    this 30
Will lug your priests and servants from your sides,
Pluck stout men's pillows from below their heads:
This yellow slave
Will knit and break religions, bless the accursed,
Make the hoar leprosy adored, place thieves
And give them title, knee and approbation
With senators on the bench: this is it
That makes the wappen'd widow wed again;
She, whom the spital-house and ulcerous sores
Would cast the gorge at, this embalms and spices 40
To the April day again. Come, damned earth,
Thou common whore of mankind, that put'st odds
Among the rout of nations, I will make thee
Do thy right nature. [*March afar off.*] Ha! a drum?
    Thou 'rt quick,
But yet I'll bury thee: thou 'lt go, strong thief,
When gouty keepers of thee cannot stand.
Nay, stay thou out for earnest.   [*Keeping some gold.*

Enter ALCIBIADES, *with drum and fife, in warlike manner;*
    PHRYNIA *and* TIMANDRA.

    Alcib. What art thou there? speak.
    Tim. A beast, as thou art. The canker gnaw thy
    heart,
For showing me again the eyes of man! 50
    Alcib. What is thy name? Is man so hateful to thee,
That art thyself a man?
    Tim. I am Misanthropos, and hate mankind.
For thy part, I do wish thou wert a dog,
That I might love thee something.
    Alcib.   I know thee well;
But in thy fortunes am unlearn'd and strange.
    Tim. I know thee too; and more than that I know
    thee,
I not desire to know. Follow thy drum;
With man's blood paint the ground, gules, gules:
Religious canons, civil laws are cruel; 60
Then what should war be? This fell whore of thine
Hath in her more destruction than thy sword,
For all her cherubin look.
    Phr.   Thy lips rot off!

33. **or to live,** i.e., or who would live. 35. **all . . . compounds,** that which constitutes dignity. 46-47. **nor . . . life,** he has nothing to maintain himself. 49. **serve his mind,** execute his wishes.

    SCENE III. 2. **Rotten humidity,** damp causing rot (Rolfe). **thy sister's,** i.e., the moon. Apollo, god of the sun, was twin brother to Diana, goddess of the moon. 5. **dividant,** separate. **touch,** test. 6, 8. **nature,** quibble on the meanings "human nature" and "beings of like nature" (Deighton, who thinks Timon conceives of great fortune as a sore). 10. **bear contempt hereditary,** endure contempt as something inherited, i.e., proper to their position. 12. **rother's,** ox's. 16. **grise,** step. 17. **smooth'd,** flattered. 18. **all's obliquy,** i.e., deviating from the right; so F; Globe, following Pope: *all is oblique.* The image in this passage cumulates by the logic of suggestion. Timon thinks first of the conduct of an individual toward his superior, then of another:

he sees them as forming a series which becomes "the ladder to all high design" set askew, and he sums up the image in the phrase, *all's obliquy.* 19. **level,** direct; the contrary to *obliquy.* 22. **His semblable,** his own kind. 23. **fang,** seize. 25. **operant,** active, potent. 27. **no idle votarist,** no trifler in my vows. 32. **Pluck . . . heads,** i.e., men who have strength yet remaining to struggle with their distemper. This alludes to an old custom of drawing away the pillow from under the heads of men in their last agonies to make their departure easier (Warburton). 35. **place thieves,** give thievery a recognized status. 38. **wappen'd,** worn out; possible misprint for *wapper'd,* fatigued. 40-41. **embalms . . . again,** restores to the freshness of an April day. 42-43. **Thou . . . nations,** i.e., gold stirs up strife among nations and makes them behave like individuals that make up the rabble. 44. **thy right nature,** i.e., the *right nature* of the *common whore of mankind;* Timon

Tim. I will not kiss thee; then the rot returns
To thine own lips again.
   Alcib. How came the noble Timon to this change?
   Tim. As the moon does, by wanting light to give:
But then renew I could not, like the moon;
There were no suns to borrow of.
   Alcib.   Noble Timon,
What friendship may I do thee?
   Tim.   None, but to   70
Maintain my opinion.
   Alcib.   What is it, Timon?
   Tim. Promise me friendship, but perform none: if
thou wilt not promise, the gods plague thee, for thou
art a man! if thou dost perform, confound thee, for
thou art a man!
   Alcib. I have heard in some sort of thy miseries.
   Tim. Thou saw'st them, when I had prosperity.
   Alcib. I see them now; then was a blessed time.
   Tim. As thine is now, held with a brace of harlots.
   Timan. Is this the Athenian minion, whom the
     world   80
Voiced so regardfully?
   Tim.   Art thou Timandra?
   Timan. Yes.
   Tim. Be a whore still: they love thee not that use
     thee;
Give them diseases, leaving with thee their lust.
Make use of thy salt hours: season the slaves
For tubs and baths; bring down rose-cheeked youth
To the tub-fast and the diet.
   Timan.   Hang thee, monster!
   Alcib. Pardon him, sweet Timandra; for his wits
Are drown'd and lost in his calamities.
I have but little gold of late, brave Timon,   90
The want whereof doth daily make revolt
In my penurious band: I have heard, and grieved,
How cursed Athens, mindless of thy worth,
Forgetting thy great deeds, when neighbour states,
But for thy sword and fortune, trod upon them,—
   Tim. I prithee, beat thy drum, and get thee gone.
   Alcib. I am thy friend, and pity thee, dear Timon.
   Tim. How dost thou pity him whom thou dost
     trouble?
I had rather be alone.
   Alcib.   Why, fare thee well.
Here is some gold for thee.
   Tim.   Keep it, I cannot eat it.   100
   Alcib. When I have laid proud Athens on a heap,—
   Tim. Warr'st thou 'gainst Athens?
   Alcib.   Ay, Timon, and have cause.
   Tim. The gods confound them all in thy conquest;
And thee after, when thou hast conquer'd!
   Alcib. Why me, Timon?
   Tim.   That, by killing of villains,
Thou wast born to conquer my country.
Put up thy gold: go on,—here 's gold,—go on;

Be as a planetary plague, when Jove
Will o'er some high-viced city hang his poison
In the sick air: let not thy sword skip one: 110
Pity not honour'd age for his white beard;
He is an usurer: strike me the counterfeit matron;
It is her habit only that is honest,
Herself 's a bawd: let not the virgin's cheek
Make soft thy trenchant sword; for those milk-paps,
That through the window-bars bore at men's eyes,
Are not within the leaf of pity writ,
But set them down horrible traitors: spare not the
     babe,
Whose dimpled smiles from fools exhaust their mercy;
Think it a bastard, whom the oracle   120
Hath doubtfully pronounced thy throat shall cut,
And mince it sans remorse: swear against objects;
Put armour on thine ears and on thine eyes;
Whose proof, nor yells of mothers, maids, nor babes,
Nor sight of priests in holy vestments bleeding,
Shall pierce a jot. There 's gold to pay thy soldiers:
Make large confusion; and, thy fury spent,
Confounded be thyself! Speak not, be gone.
   Alcib. Hast thou gold yet? I'll take the gold thou
     givest me,
Not all thy counsel.   130
   Tim. Dost thou, or dost thou not, heaven's curse
     upon thee!
   Phr. and Timan. Give us some gold, good Timon:
     hast thou more?
   Tim. Enough to make a whore forswear her trade,
And to make whores, a bawd. Hold up, you sluts,
Your aprons mountant: you are not oathable,—
Although, I know, you'll swear, terribly swear
Into strong shudders and to heavenly agues
The immortal gods that hear you,—spare your oaths,
I'll trust to your conditions: be whores still;
And he whose pious breath seeks to convert you,   140
Be strong in whore, allure him, burn him up;
Let your close fire predominate his smoke,
And be no turncoats: yet may your pains, six months,
Be quite contrary: and thatch your poor thin roofs
With burthens of the dead;—some that were hang'd,
No matter:—wear them, betray with them: whore
     still;
Paint till a horse may mire upon your face:
A pox of wrinkles!
   Phr. and Timan. Well, more gold: what then?
Believe 't, that we'll do any thing for gold.   150
   Tim. Consumptions sow
In hollow bones of man; strike their sharp shins,
And mar men's spurring. Crack the lawyer's voice,
That he may never more false title plead,
Nor sound his quillets shrilly: hoar the flamen,
That scolds against the quality of flesh,
And not believes himself: down with the nose,
Down with it flat; take the bridge quite away

is anticipating the use he put the gold to later in the scene (Deighton).
53. **Misanthropos,** hater of mankind. 59. **gules,** heraldic name for
"red." 76. **in some sort,** i.e., I have heard something. 81. **regardfully,** respectfully. 85. **salt,** lecherous. 86. **tubs and baths,** allusion
to the treatments for venereal diseases, as is also *tub-fast* (l. 87). 93.
mindless, careless, unmindful. 108. **planetary plague,** allusion to
the superstitious belief in the malignant influence of planets. 109.
high-viced, extremely vicious. 116. **window-bars,** i.e., laced bodices.
119. **exhaust,** draw forth. 122. **mince,** slash, cut in small pieces;
not uncommonly applied to murdering persons (*NED*). **swear
against objects,** take an oath against yielding to concrete appeals to
the senses; i.e., steel yourself against pity. 133-134. **Enough . . .
bawd,** enough to make a whore leave whoring and a bawd leave making
whores (Johnson). 135. **mountant,** rising; a heraldic term. **oathable,**

to be believed on your oath (Deighton). 142. **close,** possible quibble
on the meanings "secret," i.e., concealed disease, and "concentrated."
143-144. **yet . . . contrary,** various explanations: six months in houses
of correction (Steevens); six months recuperating from the ravaging
effects of your profession (Warburton); Deighton conjectures the reading *paint-sized mouths*; the sense of the whole passage may be construed
as, "Cheer up! in six months you will have achieved murder." 148.
A pox of wrinkles, don't worry about the wrinkles; i.e., because the
paint will cover them. 151-152. **Consumptions . . . bones,** i.e., the
bones will be made hollow by the disease of pox. 155. **hoar,** make
rotten. **flamen,** priest. 156. **scolds . . . flesh,** alludes to the custom of
priests examining the flesh of sacrificial victims for omens.

Of him that, his particular to foresee,
Smells from the general weal: make curl'd-pate
    ruffians bald; 160
And let the unscarr'd braggarts of the war
Derive some pain from you: plague all;
That your activity may defeat and quell
The source of all erection. There's more gold:
Do you damn others, and let this damn you,
And ditches grave you all!
    Phr. and Timan. More counsel with more money,
      bounteous Timon.
    Tim. More whore, more mischief first; I have given
      you earnest.
    Alcib. Strike up the drum towards Athens! Farewell,
      Timon:
If I thrive well, I'll visit thee again. 170
    Tim. If I hope well, I'll never see thee more.
    Alcib. I never did thee harm.
    Tim. Yes, thou spokest well of me.
    Alcib.   Call'st thou that harm?
    Tim. Men daily find it. Get thee away, and take
Thy beagles with thee.
    Alcib.   We but offend him. Strike!
    [*Drum beats. Exeunt Alcibiades, Phrynia, and*
                         Timandra.
    Tim. That nature, being sick of man's unkindness,
Should yet be hungry! Common mother, thou,
                              [*Digging.*
Whose womb unmeasurable, and infinite breast,
Teems, and feeds all; whose self-same mettle,
Whereof thy proud child, arrogant man, is puff'd, 180
Engenders the black toad and adder blue,
The gilded newt and eyeless venom'd worm,
With all the abhorred births below crisp heaven
Whereon Hyperion's quickening fire doth shine;
Yield him, who all thy human sons doth hate,
From forth thy plenteous bosom, one poor root!
Ensear thy fertile and conceptious womb,
Let it no more bring out ingrateful man!
Go great with tigers, dragons, wolves, and bears;
Teem with new monsters, whom thy upward face 190
Hath to the marbled mansion all above
Never presented!—O, a root,—dear thanks!—
Dry up thy marrows, vines, and plough-torn leas;
Whereof ingrateful man, with liquorish draughts
And morsels unctuous, greases his pure mind,
That from it all consideration slips!

Enter APEMANTUS.

More man? plague, plague!
    Apem. I was directed hither: men report
Thou dost affect my manners, and dost use them. 199
    Tim. 'Tis, then, because thou dost not keep a dog,
Whom I would imitate: consumption catch thee!
    Apem. This is in thee a nature but infected;
A poor unmanly melancholy sprung
From change of fortune. Why this spade? this place?
This slave-like habit? and these looks of care?
Thy flatterers yet wear silk, drink wine, lie soft;
Hug their diseased perfumes, and have forgot

That ever Timon was. Shame not these woods,
By putting on the cunning of a carper.
Be thou a flatterer now, and seek to thrive 210
By that which has undone thee: hinge thy knee,
And let his very breath, whom thou 'lt observe,
Blow off thy cap; praise his most vicious strain,
And call it excellent: thou wast told thus;
Thou gavest thine ears like tapsters that bid welcome
To knaves and all approachers: 'tis most just
That thou turn rascal; hadst thou wealth again,
Rascals should have 't. Do not assume my likeness.
    Tim. Were I like thee, I 'ld throw away myself.
    Apem. Thou hast cast away thyself, being like
      thyself; 220
A madman so long, now a fool. What, think'st
That the bleak air, thy boisterous chamberlain,
Will put thy shirt on warm? will these moss'd trees,
That have outlived the eagle, page thy heels,
And skip where thou point'st out? will the cold
    brook,
Candied with ice, caudle thy morning taste,
To cure thy o'er-night's surfeit? Call the creatures
Whose naked natures live in all the spite
Of wreakful heaven, whose bare unhoused trunks,
To the conflicting elements exposed, 230
Answer mere nature; bid them flatter thee;
O, thou shalt find—
    Tim.   A fool of thee: depart.
    Apem. I love thee better now than e'er I did.
    Tim. I hate thee worse.
    Apem.   Why?
    Tim.   Thou flatter'st misery.
    Apem. I flatter not; but say thou art a caitiff.
    Tim. Why dost thou seek me out?
    Apem.   To vex thee.
    Tim. Always a villain's office or a fool's.
Dost please thyself in 't?
    Apem.   Ay.
    Tim.   What! a knave too?
    Apem. If thou didst put this sour-cold habit on
To castigate thy pride, 'twere well: but thou 240
Dost it enforcedly; thou 'ldst courtier be again,
Wert thou not beggar. Willing misery
Outlives incertain pomp, is crown'd before:
The one is filling still, never complete;
The other, at high wish: best state, contentless,
Hath a distracted and most wretched being,
Worse than the worst, content.
Thou shouldst desire to die, being miserable.
    Tim. Not by his breath that is more miserable.
Thou art a slave, whom Fortune's tender arm 250
With favour never clasp'd; but bred a dog.
Hadst thou, like us from our first swath, proceeded
The sweet degrees that this brief world affords
To such as may the passive drugs of it
Freely command, thou wouldst have plunged thyself
In general riot; melted down thy youth
In different beds of lust; and never learn'd
The icy precepts of respect, but follow'd
The sugar'd game before thee. But myself,

159. **his particular to foresee,** in order to look out for his own interests. 160. **Smells from,** metaphor from hounds following the scent of game; *to smell from* is to leave or lose the scent. 174. **find it,** i.e., find it harmful to be well spoken of. 175. **beagles,** i.e., beagle hounds, fawning followers—the prostitutes. 182. **newt,** a small salamander. **eyeless venom'd worm,** the blindworm; cf. *Macbeth*, IV, i, 16; *A Midsummer-Night's Dream*, II, ii, 11. 184. **Hyperion's,** i.e., the sun's. 187. **Ensear,** dry up. 196. **consideration,** regard for others, or for other things than sensual

pleasures (Deighton); possibly, reflection, rationality; cf. *Henry V*, I, i, 28. 202. **but infected,** i.e., he isn't to the manner born; his pessimism is induced by misery; it is not philosophical, hence it is insincere. 207. **diseased perfumes,** diseased perfumed mistresses (Malone). 209. **By . . . carper.** Apemantus objects not to Timon's philosophy but to his behavior. 221-223. **think'st . . . warm,** alludes to the practice of having a servant warm one's garment by the fire. 226. **caudle,** provide with a caudle, i.e., a hot spiced drink. 228. **in,** exposed

Who had the world as my confectionary,   260
The mouths, the tongues, the eyes and hearts of men
At duty, more than I could frame employment,
That numberless upon me stuck as leaves
Do on the oak, have with one winter's brush
Fell from their boughs and left me open, bare
For every storm that blows: I, to bear this,
That never knew but better, is some burden:
Thy nature did commence in sufferance, time
Hath made thee hard in 't. Why shouldst thou hate
     men?
They never flatter'd thee: what hast thou given?   270
If thou wilt curse, thy father, that poor rag,
Must be thy subject, who in spite put stuff
To some she beggar and compounded thee
Poor rogue hereditary. Hence, be gone!
If thou hadst not been born the worst of men,
Thou hadst been a knave and flatterer.
     Apem.   Art thou proud yet?
     Tim. Ay, that I am not thee.
     Apem.   I, that I was
No prodigal.
     Tim.   I, that I am one now:
Were all the wealth I have shut up in thee,
I 'ld give thee leave to hang it. Get thee gone.   280
That the whole life of Athens were in this!
Thus would I eat it.   [*Eating a root.*
     Apem.   Here; I will mend thy feast.
                              [*Offering him a root.*
     Tim. First mend my company, take away thyself.
     Apem. So I shall mend mine own, by the lack of
     thine.
     Tim. 'Tis not well mended so, it is but botch'd;
If not, I would it were.
     Apem. What wouldst thou have to Athens?
     Tim. Thee thither in a whirlwind. If thou wilt,
Tell them there I have gold; look, so I have.
     Apem. Here is no use for gold.
     Tim.   The best and truest;   290
For here it sleeps, and does no hired harm.
     Apem. Where liest o' nights, Timon?
     Tim.   Under that 's above me.
Where feed'st thou o' days, Apemantus?
     Apem. Where my stomach finds meat; or, rather,
where I eat it.
     Tim. Would poison were obedient and knew my
mind!
     Apem. Where wouldst thou send it?
     Tim. To sauce thy dishes.   299
     Apem. The middle of humanity thou never knewest,
but the extremity of both ends: when thou wast in
thy gilt and thy perfume, they mocked thee for too
much curiosity; in thy rags thou knowest none, but
art despised for the contrary. There 's a medlar for
thee, eat it.
     Tim. On what I hate I feed not.
     Apem. Dost hate a medlar?
     Tim. Ay, though it look like thee.
     Apem. An thou hadst hated meddlers sooner, thou
shouldst have loved thyself better now. What man

didst thou ever know unthrift that was beloved after
his means?   312
     Tim. Who, without those means thou talkest of,
didst thou ever know beloved?
     Apem. Myself.
     Tim. I understand thee; thou hadst some means to
keep a dog.
     Apem. What things in the world canst thou nearest
compare to thy flatterers?   319
     Tim. Women nearest; but men, men are the things
themselves. What wouldst thou do with the world,
Apemantus, if it lay in thy power?
     Apem. Give it the beasts, to be rid of the men.
     Tim. Wouldst thou have thyself fall in the con-
fusion of men, and remain a beast with the beasts?   326
     Apem. Ay, Timon.
     Tim. A beastly ambition, which the gods grant thee
t' attain to! If thou wert the lion, the fox would
beguile thee: if thou wert the lamb, the fox would eat
thee: if thou wert the fox, the lion would suspect thee,
when peradventure thou wert accused by the ass: if
thou wert the ass, thy dulness would torment thee,
and still thou livedst but as a breakfast to the wolf: if
thou wert the wolf, thy greediness would afflict thee,
and oft thou shouldst hazard thy life for thy dinner:
wert thou the unicorn, pride and wrath would confound thee and make thine own self the conquest of
thy fury: wert thou a bear, thou wouldst be killed by
the horse: wert thou a horse, thou wouldst be seized
by the leopard: wert thou a leopard, thou wert
german to the lion and the spots of thy kindred were
jurors on thy life: all thy safety were remotion and
thy defence absence. What beast couldst thou be, that
were not subject to a beast? and what a beast art thou
already, that seest not thy loss in transformation!   349
     Apem. If thou couldst please me with speaking to
me, thou mightst have hit upon it here: the commonwealth of Athens is become a forest of beasts.
     Tim. How has the ass broke the wall, that thou art
out of the city?
     Apem. Yonder comes a poet and a painter: the
plague of company light upon thee! I will fear to
catch it and give way: when I know not what else
to do, I'll see thee again.   359
     Tim. When there is nothing living but thee, thou
shalt be welcome. I had rather be a beggar's dog than
Apemantus.
     Apem. Thou art the cap of all the fools alive.
     Tim. Would thou wert clean enough to spit upon!
     Apem. A plague on thee! thou art too bad to curse.
     Tim. All villains that do stand by thee are pure.
     Apem. There is no leprosy but what thou speak'st.
     Tim. If I name thee.
I'll beat thee, but I should infect my hands.
     Apem. I would my tongue could rot them off!   370
     Tim. Away, thou issue of a mangy dog!
Choler does kill me that thou art alive;
I swound to see thee.
     Apem.   Would thou wouldst burst!
     Tim.   Away,

Timon
of Athens
ACT IV : SC III

1037

Thou tedious rogue! I am sorry I shall lose
A stone by thee.   [*Throws a stone at him.*
   Apem.   Beast!
   Tim.   Slave!
   Apem.   Toad!
   Tim.   Rogue, rogue, rogue!
I am sick of this false world, and will love nought
But even the mere necessities upon 't.
Then, Timon, presently prepare thy grave;
Lie where the light foam of the sea may beat
Thy grave-stone daily: make thine epitaph,   380
That death in me at others' lives may laugh.
[*To the gold*] O thou sweet king-killer, and dear
    divorce
'Twixt natural son and sire! thou bright defiler
Of Hymen's purest bed! thou valiant Mars!
Thou ever young, fresh, loved and delicate wooer,
Whose blush doth thaw the consecrated snow
That lies on Dian's lap! thou visible god,
That solder'st close impossibilities,
And makest them kiss! that speak'st with every
    tongue,
To every purpose! O thou touch of hearts!   390
Think, thy slave man rebels, and by thy virtue
Set them into confounding odds, that beasts
May have the world in empire!
   Apem.   Would 'twere so!
But not till I am dead. I'll say thou 'st gold:
Thou wilt be throng'd to shortly.
   Tim.   Throng'd to!
   Apem.   Ay.
   Tim. Thy back, I prithee.
   Apem.   Live, and love thy misery.   396
   Tim. Long live so, and so die. [*Exit Apemantus.*] I
    am quit.
Moe things like men! Eat, Timon, and abhor them.

Enter Banditti.

   First Ban. Where should he have this gold? It is
some poor fragment, some slender ort of his remain-
der: the mere want of gold, and the falling-from of his
friends, drove him into this melancholy.
   Sec. Ban. It is noised he hath a mass of treasure.
   Third Ban. Let us make the assay upon him: if he
care not for 't, he will supply us easily; if he covet-
ously reserve it, how shall 's get it?
   Sec. Ban. True; for he bears it not about him, 'tis
hid.
   First Ban. Is not this he?   410
   Banditti. Where?
   Sec. Ban. 'Tis his description.
   Third Ban. He; I know him.
   Banditti. Save thee, Timon.
   Tim. Now, thieves?
   Banditti. Soldiers, not thieves.
   Tim. Both too; and women's sons.
   Banditti. We are not thieves, but men that much do
want.
   Tim. Your greatest want is, you want much of
meat.   419

Why should you want? Behold, the earth hath roots;
Within this mile break forth a hundred springs;
The oaks bear mast, the briers scarlet hips;
The bounteous housewife, nature, on each bush
Lays her full mess before you. Want! why want?
   First Ban. We cannot live on grass, on berries,
    water,
As beasts and birds and fishes.
   Tim. Nor on the beasts themselves, the birds, and
    fishes;
You must eat men. Yet thanks I must you con
That you are thieves profess'd, that you work not
In holier shapes: for there is boundless theft   430
In limited professions. Rascal thieves,
Here 's gold. Go, suck the subtle blood o' the grape,
Till the high fever seethe your blood to froth,
And so 'scape hanging: trust not the physician;
His antidotes are poison, and he slays
Moe than you rob: take wealth and lives together;
Do villany, do, since you protest to do 't,
Like workmen. I'll example you with thievery:
The sun 's a thief, and with his great attraction
Robs the vast sea: the moon 's an arrant thief,   440
And her pale fire she snatches from the sun:
The sea 's a thief, whose liquid surge resolves
The moon into salt tears: the earth 's a thief,
That feeds and breeds by a composture stolen
From general excrement: each thing 's a thief:
The laws, your curb and whip, in their rough power
Have uncheck'd theft. Love not yourselves: away,
Rob one another. There 's more gold. Cut throats:
All that you meet are thieves: to Athens go,
Break open shops; nothing can you steal,   450
But thieves do lose it: steal no less for this
I give you; and gold confound you howsoe'er!
Amen.
   Third Ban. Has almost charmed me from my pro-
fession, by persuading me to it.
   First Ban. 'Tis in the malice of mankind that he
thus advises us; not to have us thrive in our mystery.
   Sec. Ban. I'll believe him as an enemy, and give
over my trade.   460
   First Ban. Let us first see peace in Athens: there is
no time so miserable but a man may be true.
                              [*Exeunt Banditti.*

Enter FLAVIUS.

   Flav. O you gods!
Is yond despised and ruinous man my lord?
Full of decay and failing? O monument
And wonder of good deeds evilly bestow'd!
What an alteration of honour
Has desperate want made!
What viler thing upon the earth than friends   470
Who can bring noblest minds to basest ends!
How rarely does it meet with this time's guise,
When man was wish'd to love his enemies!
Grant I may ever love, and rather woo
Those that would mischief me than those that do!
Has caught me in his eye: I will present

My honest grief unto him; and, as my lord,
Still serve him with my life. My dearest master!
   Tim. Away! what art thou?
   Flav.   Have you forgot me, sir?
   Tim. Why dost ask that? I have forgot all men;   480
Then, if thou grant'st thou 'rt a man, I have forgot
    thee.
   Flav. An honest poor servant of yours.
   Tim. Then I know thee not:
I never had honest man about me, I; all
I kept were knaves, to serve in meat to villains.
   Flav. The gods are witness,
Ne'er did poor steward wear a truer grief
For his undone lord than mine eyes for you.
   Tim. What, dost thou weep? Come nearer. Then I
    love thee,
Because thou art a woman, and disclaim'st   490
Flinty mankind; whose eyes do never give
But thorough lust and laughter. Pity 's sleeping:
Strange times, that weep with laughing, not with
    weeping!
   Flav. I beg of you to know me, good my lord,
To accept my grief and whilst this poor wealth lasts
To entertain me as your steward still.
   Tim. Had I a steward
So true, so just, and now so comfortable?
It almost turns my dangerous nature mild.
Let me behold thy face. Surely, this man   500
Was born of woman.
Forgive my general and exceptless rashness,
You perpetual-sober gods! I do proclaim
One honest man—mistake me not—but one;
No more, I pray,—and he 's a steward.
How fain would I have hated all mankind!
And thou redeem'st thyself: but all, save thee,
I fell with curses.
Methinks thou art more honest now than wise;
For, by oppressing and betraying me,   510
Thou mightst have sooner got another service:
For many so arrive at second masters,
Upon their first lord's neck. But tell me true—
For I must ever doubt, though ne'er so sure—
Is not thy kindness subtle, covetous,
If not a usuring kindness, and, as rich men deal gifts,
Expecting in return twenty for one?
   Flav. No, my most worthy master; in whose breast
Doubt and suspect, alas, are placed too late:
You should have fear'd false times when you did feast:
Suspect still comes where an estate is least.   521
That which I show, heaven knows, is merely love,
Duty and zeal to your unmatched mind,
Care of your food and living; and, believe it,
My most honour'd lord,
For any benefit that points to me,
Either in hope or present, I 'ld exchange
For this one wish, that you had power and wealth
To requite me, by making rich yourself.
   Tim. Look thee, 'tis so! Thou singly honest man,   530
Here, take: the gods out of my misery
Have sent thee treasure. Go, live rich and happy;

But thus condition'd: thou shalt build from men;
Hate all, curse all, show charity to none,
But let the famish'd flesh slide from the bone,
Ere thou relieve the beggar; give to dogs
What thou deny'st to men; let prisons swallow 'em,
Debts wither 'em to nothing; be men like blasted
    woods,
And may diseases lick up their false bloods!
And so farewell and thrive.
   Flav.   O, let me stay,   540
And comfort you, my master.
   Tim.   If thou hatest curses,
Stay not; fly, whilst thou art blest and free:
Ne'er see thou man, and let me ne'er see thee.
          [Exit Flavius. Timon retires to his cave.

ACT V.

SCENE I. *The woods. Before Timon's cave.*

Enter Poet *and* Painter; TIMON *watching them from
his cave.*

   Pain. As I took note of the place, it cannot be far
where he abides.
   Poet. What 's to be thought of him? does the
rumour hold for true, that he 's so full of gold?
   Pain. Certain: Alcibiades reports it; Phrynia and
Timandra had gold of him: he likewise enriched poor
straggling soldiers with great quantity: 'tis said he
gave unto his steward a mighty sum.
   Poet. Then this breaking of his has been but a try
for his friends.   11
   Pain. Nothing else: you shall see him a palm in
Athens again, and flourish with the highest. Therefore
'tis not amiss we tender our loves to him, in this supposed distress of his: it will show honestly in us; and is
very likely to load our purposes with what they
travail for, if it be a just and true report that goes of
his having.
   Poet. What have you now to present unto him?
   Pain. Nothing at this time but my visitation: only I
will promise him an excellent piece.   21
   Poet. I must serve him so too, tell him of an intent
that 's coming toward him.
   Pain. Good as the best. Promising is the very air o'
the time: it opens the eyes of expectation: performance is ever the duller for his act; and, but in the
plainer and simpler kind of people, the deed of saying
is quite out of use. To promise is most courtly and
fashionable: performance is a kind of will or testament which argues a great sickness in his judgement
that makes it.   *[Timon comes from his cave, behind.*
   Tim. [*Aside*] Excellent workman! thou canst not
paint a man so bad as is thyself.   33
   Poet. I am thinking what I shall say I have provided for him: it must be a personating of himself; a
satire against the softness of prosperity, with a discovery of the infinite flatteries that follow youth and
opulency.

Tim. [*Aside*] Must thou needs stand for a villain in thine own work? wilt thou whip thine own faults in other men? Do so, I have gold for thee.

Poet. Nay, let 's seek him:
Then do we sin against our own estate,
When we may profit meet, and come too late.

Pain. True;
When the day serves, before black-corner'd night,
Find what thou want'st by free and offer'd light. Come.

Tim. [*Aside*] I'll meet you at the turn. What a god 's
gold, 50
That he is worshipp'd in a baser temple
Than where swine feed!
'Tis thou that rigg'st the bark and plough'st the foam,
Settlest admired reverence in a slave:
To thee be worship! and thy saints for aye
Be crown'd with plagues that thee alone obey!
Fit I meet them. [*Coming forward.*

Poet. Hail, worthy Timon!

Pain. Our late noble master!

Tim. Have I once lived to see two honest men?

Poet. Sir, 60
Having often of your open bounty tasted,
Hearing you were retired, your friends fall'n off,
Whose thankless natures—O abhorred spirits!—
Not all the whips of heaven are large enough:
What! to you,
Whose star-like nobleness gave life and influence
To their whole being! I am rapt and cannot cover
The monstrous bulk of this ingratitude
With any size of words.

Tim. Let it go naked, men may see 't the better: 70
You that are honest, by being what you are,
Make them best seen and known.

Pain. He and myself
Have travail'd in the great shower of your gifts,
And sweetly felt it.

Tim. Ay, you are honest men.

Pain. We are hither come to offer you our service.

Tim. Most honest men! Why, how shall I requite
you?
Can you eat roots, and drink cold water? no.

Both. What we can do, we'll do, to do you service.

Tim. Ye 're honest men: ye 've heard that I have
gold;
I am sure you have: speak truth; ye 're honest men. 80

Pain. So it is said, my noble lord; but therefore
Came not my friend nor I.

Tim. Good honest men! Thou draw'st a counterfeit
Best in all Athens: thou 'rt, indeed, the best;
Thou counterfeit'st most lively.

Pain. So, so, my lord.

Tim. E'en so, sir, as I say. And, for thy fiction,
Why, thy verse swells with stuff so fine and smooth
That thou art even natural in thine art.
But, for all this, my honest-natured friends,
I must needs say you have a little fault: 90
Marry, 'tis not monstrous in you, neither wish I
You take much pains to mend.

Both. Beseech your honour

To make it known to us.

Tim. You'll take it ill.

Both. Most thankfully, my lord.

Tim. Will you, indeed?

Both. Doubt it not, worthy lord.

Tim. There 's never a one of you but trusts a knave,
That mightily deceives you.

Both. Do we, my lord?

Tim. Ay, and you hear him cog, see him dissemble,
Know his gross patchery, love him, feed him,
Keep in your bosom: yet remain assured 100
That he 's a made-up villain.

Pain. I know none such, my lord.

Poet. Nor I.

Tim. Look you, I love you well; I'll give you gold,
Rid me these villains from your companies:
Hang them or stab them, drown them in a draught,
Confound them by some course, and come to me,
I'll give you gold enough.

Both. Name them, my lord, let 's know them.

Tim. You that way and you this, but two in
company;
Each man apart, all single and alone, 110
Yet an arch-villain keeps him company.
If where thou art two villains shall not be,
Come not near him. If thou wouldst not reside
But where one villain is, then him abandon.
Hence, pack! there 's gold; you came for gold, ye
slaves:
[*To Painter*] You have work'd for me; there 's
payment for you: hence!
[*To Poet*] You are an alchemist; make gold of that.
Out, rascal dogs!
[*Beats them out, and then retires to his cave.*

Enter FLAVIUS *and two* Senators.

Flav. It is in vain that you would speak with Timon;
For he is set so only to himself 120
That nothing but himself which looks like man
Is friendly with him.

First Sen. Bring us to his cave:
It is our part and promise to the Athenians
To speak with Timon.

Sec. Sen. At all times alike
Men are not still the same: 'twas time and griefs
That framed him thus: time, with his fairer hand,
Offering the fortunes of his former days,
The former man may make him. Bring us to him,
And chance it as it may.

Flav. Here is his cave.
Peace and content be here! Lord Timon! Timon! 130
Look out, and speak to friends: the Athenians,
By two of their most reverend senate, greet thee:
Speak to them, noble Timon.

TIMON *comes from his cave.*

Tim. Thou sun, that comfort'st, burn! Speak, and
be hang'd:
For each true word, a blister! and each false
Be as a cauterizing to the root o' the tongue,
Consuming it with speaking!

47. **black-corner'd night,** night which darkens corners; i.e., makes it hard to find things. 51. **temple,** the human body. 54. **admired . . . slave,** reverence in an admiring slave. 66. **star-like . . . influence,** an astrological metaphor: whose nobility of character was of such power as to influence men's destinies. 67. **rapt,** literally, caught, possessed; equivalent to the loose use today of "overwhelmed." 83. **counterfeit,**

picture, likeness, with quibble in line 85. 88. **natural,** i.e., true to your own nature, which is deceitful. 99. **patchery,** knavery. 105. **draught,** cesspool, sink. 115-117. **there 's . . . that.** Timon gives not gold but abuse to the least sincere of his visitors. He refers here to the beating he is giving them. 118. *Stage Direction: Enter . . . Senators.* This episode shows Timon so much warped in his understanding that

First Sen. Worthy Timon,—
Tim. Of none but such as you, and you of Timon.
First Sen. The senators of Athens greet thee, Timon.
Tim. I thank them; and would send them back the
plague, 140
Could I but catch it for them.
First Sen. O, forget
What we are sorry for ourselves in thee.
The senators with one consent of love
Entreat thee back to Athens; who have thought
On special dignities, which vacant lie
For thy best use and wearing.
Sec. Sen. They confess
Toward thee forgetfulness too general, gross:
Which now the public body, which doth seldom
Play the recanter, feeling in itself
A lack of Timon's aid, hath sense withal 150
Of it own fail, restraining aid to Timon;
And send forth us, to make their sorrow'd render,
Together with a recompense more fruitful
Than their offence can weigh down by the dram;
Ay, even such heaps and sums of love and wealth
As shall to thee blot out what wrongs were theirs
And write in thee the figures of their love,
Ever to read them thine.
Tim. You witch me in it;
Surprise me to the very brink of tears:
Lend me a fool's heart and a woman's eyes, 160
And I'll beweep these comforts, worthy senators.
First Sen. Therefore, so please thee to return with us
And of our Athens, thine and ours, to take
The captainship, thou shalt be met with thanks,
Allow'd with absolute power and thy good name
Live with authority: so soon we shall drive back
Of Alcibiades the approaches wild,
Who, like a boar too savage, doth root up
His country's peace.
Sec. Sen. And shakes his threatening
sword
Against the walls of Athens.
First Sen. Therefore, Timon,— 170
Tim. Well, sir, I will; therefore, I will, sir; thus:
If Alcibiades kill my countrymen,
Let Alcibiades know this of Timon,
That Timon cares not. But if he sack fair Athens,
And take our goodly aged men by the beards,
Giving our holy virgins to the stain
Of contumelious, beastly, mad-brain'd war,
Then let him know, and tell him Timon speaks it,
In pity of our aged and our youth,
I cannot choose but tell him, that I care not, 180
And let him take 't at worst; for their knives care not,
While you have throats to answer: for myself,
There's not a whittle in the unruly camp
But I do prize it at my love before
The reverend'st throat in Athens. So I leave you
To the protection of the prosperous gods,
As thieves to keepers.
Flav. Stay not, all's in vain.
Tim. Why, I was writing of my epitaph;
It will be seen to-morrow: my long sickness

Of health and living now begins to mend, 190
And nothing brings me all things. Go, live still;
Be Alcibiades your plague, you his,
And last so long enough!
First Sen. We speak in vain.
Tim. But yet I love my country, and am not
One that rejoices in the common wreck,
As common bruit doth put it.
First Sen. That's well spoke.
Tim. Commend me to my loving countrymen,—
First Sen. These words become your lips as they pass
thorough them.
Sec. Sen. And enter in our ears like great triumphers
In their applauding gates.
Tim. Commend me to them, 200
And tell them that, to ease them of their griefs,
Their fears of hostile strokes, their aches, losses,
Their pangs of love, with other incident throes
That nature's fragile vessel doth sustain
In life's uncertain voyage, I will some kindness do
them:
I'll teach them to prevent wild Alcibiades' wrath.
First Sen. I like this well; he will return again.
Tim. I have a tree, which grows here in my close,
That mine own use invites me to cut down,
And shortly must I fell it: tell my friends, 210
Tell Athens, in the sequence of degree
From high to low throughout, that whoso please
To stop affliction, let him take his haste,
Come hither, ere my tree hath felt the axe,
And hang himself. I pray you, do my greeting.
Flav. Trouble him no further; thus you still shall
find him.
Tim. Come not to me again: but say to Athens,
Timon hath made his everlasting mansion
Upon the beached verge of the salt flood;
Who once a day with his embossed froth 220
The turbulent surge shall cover: thither come,
And let my grave-stone be your oracle.
Lips, let sour words go by and language end:
What is amiss plague and infection mend!
Graves only be men's works and death their gain!
Sun, hide thy beams! Timon hath done his reign.
[*Retires to his cave.*
First Sen. His discontents are unremoveably
Coupled to nature.
Sec. Sen. Our hope in him is dead: let us return,
And strain what other means is left unto us 230
In our dear peril.
First Sen. It requires swift foot. [*Exeunt.*

SCENE II. *Before the walls of Athens.*

Enter two Senators *and a* Messenger.

First Sen. Thou hast painfully discover'd: are his
files
As full as thy report?
Mess. I have spoke the least:
Besides, his expedition promises
Present approach.

Sec. Sen. We stand much hazard, if they bring not
    Timon.
Mess. I met a courier, one mine ancient friend;
Whom, though in general part we were opposed,
†Yet our old love made a particular force,
And made us speak like friends: this man was riding
From Alcibiades to Timon's cave,   10
With letters of entreaty, which imported
His fellowship i' the cause against your city,
In part for his sake moved.
    First Sen.   Here come our brothers.

    Enter the Senators *from* TIMON.

    Third Sen. No talk of Timon, nothing of him expect.
The enemies' drum is heard, and fearful scouring
Doth choke the air with dust: in, and prepare:
Ours is the fall, I fear; our foes the snare.   [*Exeunt.*

SCENE III. *The woods. Timon's cave, and a rude tomb seen.*

    Enter a Soldier, *seeking* TIMON.

    Sold. By all description this should be the place.
Who's here? speak, ho! No answer! What is this?
Timon is dead, who hath outstretch'd his span:
Some beast rear'd this; there does not live a man.
Dead, sure; and this his grave. What's on this tomb
I cannot read; the character I'll take with wax:
Our captain hath in every figure skill,
An aged interpreter, though young in days:
Before proud Athens he's set down by this,
Whose fall the mark of his ambition is.   [*Exit.* 10

SCENE IV. *Before the walls of Athens.*

    Trumpets sound. Enter ALCIBIADES *with his powers.*

    Alcib. Sound to this coward and lascivious town
Our terrible approach.   [*A parley sounded.*

    Enter Senators *on the walls.*

Till now you have gone on and fill'd the time
With all licentious measure, making your wills
The scope of justice; till now myself and such
As slept within the shadow of your power
Have wander'd with our traversed arms and breathed
Our sufferance vainly: now the time is flush,
When crouching marrow in the bearer strong
Cries of itself 'No more:' now breathless wrong   10
Shall sit and pant in your great chairs of ease,
And pursy insolence shall break his wind
With fear and horrid flight.
    First Sen.   Noble and young,
When thy first griefs were but a mere conceit,
Ere thou hadst power or we had cause of fear,
We sent to thee, to give thy rages balm,
To wipe out our ingratitude with loves

Above their quantity.
    Sec. Sen.   So did we woo
Transformed Timon to our city's love
By humble message and by promised means: 20
We were not all unkind, nor all deserve
The common stroke of war.
    First Sen.   These walls of ours
Were not erected by their hands from whom
You have received your griefs; nor are they such
That these great towers, trophies and schools should
    fall
For private faults in them.
    Sec. Sen.   Nor are they living
Who were the motives that you first went out;
Shame that they wanted cunning, in excess
Hath broke their hearts. March, noble lord,
Into our city with thy banners spread: 30
By decimation, and a tithed death—
If thy revenges hunger for that food
Which nature loathes—take thou the destined tenth,
And by the hazard of the spotted die
Let die the spotted.
    First Sen.   All have not offended;
For those that were, it is not square to take
On those that are, revenges: crimes, like lands,
Are not inherited. Then, dear countryman,
Bring in thy ranks, but leave without thy rage:
Spare thy Athenian cradle and those kin   40
Which in the bluster of thy wrath must fall
With those that have offended: like a shepherd,
Approach the fold and cull the infected forth,
But kill not all together.
    Sec. Sen.   What thou wilt,
Thou rather shalt enforce it with thy smile
Than hew to 't with thy sword.
    First Sen.   Set but thy foot
Against our rampired gates, and they shall ope;
So thou wilt send thy gentle heart before,
To say thou 'lt enter friendly.
    Sec. Sen.   Throw thy glove,
Or any token of thine honour else,   50
That thou wilt use the wars as thy redress
And not as our confusion, all thy powers
Shall make their harbour in our town, till we
Have seal'd thy full desire.
    Alcib.   Then there's my glove;
Descend, and open your uncharged ports:
Those enemies of Timon's and mine own
Whom you yourselves shall set out for reproof
Fall and no more: and, to atone your fears
With my more noble meaning, not a man
Shall pass his quarter, or offend the stream   60
Of regular justice in your city's bounds,
But shall be render'd to your public laws
At heaviest answer.
    Both.   'Tis most nobly spoken.
    Alcib. Descend, and keep your words.
       [*The Senators descend, and open the gates.*

Enter Soldier.

Sold. My noble general, Timon is dead;
Entomb'd upon the very hem o' the sea;
And on his grave-stone this insculpture, which
With wax I brought away, whose soft impression
Interprets for my poor ignorance.
   Alcib. [*Reads the epitaph*] 'Here lies a wretched corse,
    of wretched soul bereft: 70
Seek not my name: a plague consume you wicked
    caitiffs left!
Here lie I, Timon; who, alive, all living men did hate:
Pass by and curse thy fill, but pass and stay not here
    thy gait.'
These well express in thee thy latter spirits:
Though thou abhorr'dst in us our human griefs,
Scorn'dst our brain's flow and those our droplets
    which
From niggard nature fall, yet rich conceit
Taught thee to make vast Neptune weep for aye
On thy low grave, on faults forgiven. Dead
Is noble Timon: of whose memory   80
Hereafter more. Bring me into your city,
And I will use the olive with my sword,
Make war breed peace, make peace stint war,
    make each
Prescribe to other as each other's leech.
Let our drums strike.   [*Exeunt.*

76. **brain's flow,** tears.

Macbeth

Macbeth is one of the greatest of Shakespeare's
plays, and, at the same time, a play for which we
have one of the worst texts. Its first printing in the
folio of 1623 offers a text which is thought to have
been cut down for stage presentation and contaminated with the work of another man. Doubts have
been expressed as to the authenticity of various
passages. These doubts have reduced themselves to
certainty in the case of the scene containing the long
speech of Hecate and the song (III, v), a similar
later speech and song (IV, i, 39-43), and the speech
of the first witch in the same scene (125-132). These
lines are different in style and not in harmony with
Shakespeare's conception of the witches as it appears
elsewhere in the play. They closely resemble the
style of certain passages of Thomas Middleton's *The
Witch*, dating probably after 1613. Moreover, the
two songs, "Come away, come away" and "Black
spirits, and white," are found in Middleton's play.
The Restoration adaptation of *Macbeth*, probably by
Sir William D'Avenant, gives the songs in full as in
The Witch.

It is generally believed that Middleton, who was
younger than Shakespeare and also wrote for the
King's Company, was engaged on the occasion of

some revival of *Macbeth* to adapt the play to a somewhat different form of dramatic entertainment, one
in which there would be songs and dances by witches.
Possibly to make room for ballet features, the precious
dramatic craftsmanship of Shakespeare was cut
away. Therefore, certain passages of the text are
hopelessly corrupt and obscure, certain matters of the
plot are inconsistent, and the story of Macbeth's
reign is told more barely and scantily than one would
believe possible in the author who had just written
King Lear.[1]

DATE

Dr. Simon Forman, a quack and astrologer, had the
interesting habit of visiting the theater and noting
down the plots of plays which he saw "for common
Pollicie"; that is, for what he might learn from them.
He saw *Macbeth* on the second of April 1610, at the
Globe, and gives a rather full but not very accurate
summary of the plot.[2] This cannot, however, have
been the first performance. *The Puritan, or The Widow
of Watling Street*, published in 1607, contains a line
suggestive of Banquo's ghost: "Instead of a jester
we'll have a ghost in a white sheet sit at the upper
end of the table." This play for several reasons
is thought to belong to the year 1606.

Macbeth is filled to overflowing with matters which
would be agreeable to King James. Oldys, the
antiquary, records a tradition that the king wrote
Shakespeare a letter that possibly commanded him
to write this play, since it develops the king's royal
descent from Fleance the son of Banquo, and thus
from all the line of British kings back to Brute. The
play also stresses the king's divine right as indicated
by his possession of the royal touch to cure the king's
evil, a power reasserted by James in 1605 (IV, iii,
140-159).

James had been proclaimed "King of Great
Britain, France, and Ireland," on October 24, 1604,
and was for the next few years anxious to carry out
the complete union of England and Scotland as Great
Britain; hence the "twofold balls and treble sceptres"
of the show of kings (IV, i, 112-121). The Porter's
"farmer, that hanged himself on the expectation of
plenty" (II, iii, 5), has been thought to reflect the not
unusual agricultural situation of the season of 1606,
when, though crops were good, prices were low; and
his other allusion to the "equivocator, that could
swear in both scales against either scale," has been
taken pretty generally as referring to the trial of
Garnet in March 1606, for complicity in the Gunpowder Plot, which had been discovered in November
1605.

---

[1]But see Alwin Thaler, "The 'Lost Scenes' of *Macbeth*," *PMLA*, XL
(1934), 835-847.
  [2]The authenticity of Forman's diary has been called in question; see
The Tragedy of Macbeth, edited by J. Q. Adams (Boston, 1931), pp. 293-
298; S. A. Tannenbaum, *Shakespearian Scraps and other Elizabethan Fragments* (1933), pp. 1-35; for refutation see J. Dover Wilson, "Authenticity
of Simon Forman's *Booke of Plaies*," *Review of English Studies*, XXIII
(1947), 193-197.

A peculiar bit of evidence is that of an entertainment presented before the king during a progress to Oxford on August 27, 1605. At the gates of St. John's

Macbeth being crowned. From Holinshed's Chronicles.

College three youths, representing nymphs or sybils, or, as we should say from the play, witches, prophesied the reign of Banquo's descendants and delivered orations in Latin and English. The king, as descendant of Banquo, may have been so well pleased with this testimonial to the acceptance of him as the extender of the Arthurian empire to the entire island of Britain in accordance with supernatural prophecy, that he may have desired to see the subject treated more at large.

Sir E. K. Chambers suggests that *Macbeth* was produced on the occasion of the visit of the king of Denmark to England in July 1606.[3]

SOURCE

There can be no doubt that the subject of the triumph of Banquo's offspring was recognized as one of the greatest interest to the king and to those Englishmen who were loyal to the Scottish succession, as most Englishmen were. Especially in *Macbeth* there was foreshadowed the triumph of Protestantism and insular independence, since the play carried as a story the theme of the escape and survival of the royal seed when it was beset by murder, usurpation, and tyranny.

For the material of this story Shakespeare went to Holinshed's *Chronicles;* in the first instance to the account of the reigns of Duncan and Macbeth, in the second, to the chronicle of King Duff. From the former comes the story of Macbeth's rise and fall and most matter pertaining to Banquo and Macduff. From the latter he borrowed the story of how Donwald, a man whom King Duff never suspected, murdered King Duff in the castle of Forres. Having, with the aid of his wife, drugged the two chamberlains who lay

with the king, Donwald, although he greatly abhorred the deed and did it only at the instigation of his wife, induced four of his servants to cut the king's throat. When morning came, he slew the chamberlains and cleared himself of the crime by his power and authority, though not without being suspected by certain noblemen because of his overdiligence. There were great portents in the kingdom that year both of sun and moon; certain horses in Lothian ate their own flesh; and a "sparhauke" was strangled by an owl.

Thirdly, from the chronicle of King Kenneth, who had murdered Malcolm Duff, is drawn the idea of a voice, which Kenneth heard as he lay in his bed at night, warning him of the sure detection of his crime, so that he was filled with dread and passed the night without any sleep.

Finally, from the chronicle of King Edward the Confessor comes the account of how that saintly monarch cured the king's evil by his touch, and the story of Siward's invasion of Scotland in which he overthrew Macbeth. The chronicle of King Macbeth contains within it the story of Macduff. In the beginning of the chronicle of Robert II there is even a suggestion for the show of eight Stuart kings (IV, i, 110 ff.).

These Scottish chronicles were for Shakespeare a brilliant and spirited source, far better than the chronicles of English kings that he had used earlier in his career. Holinshed's compilation had drawn on the Latin of Hector Boece (1527), and to him probably is to be attributed the vividness of the narratives. Boece had drawn from Fordun, a historian of the fourteenth century.

SHAKESPEARE'S ADDITIONS

It will be observed that Shakespeare treats the chronicles with great freedom, combining as he does the reigns of two different kings. Besides this great transposition, his most important changes are the increase in importance of the part played by Lady Macbeth, the development, even beyond the superstitious chroniclers, of the supernatural element, and the addition of particular detail.

Lillian Winstanley argues, from an elaborate series of parallel passages from contemporary documents, that the play was particularly designed to please King James not only in the matter of its emphasis upon his descent from the prophetically established royal line, evident in the vision of kings and in the power of touch for the king's evil, but also in the matter of the inheritance by King James of the united crowns of England and Scotland.[4]

THE WITCHES

Belief in witchcraft was widespread and general in the sixteenth century. King James himself was a firm

[3]Edition of *Macbeth*, Arden Shakespeare (Heath); *William Shakespeare*, I, 471-476. See also for contemporary allusions Arthur N. Stunz, "The Date of *Macbeth*," *ELH*, IX (1942), 95-105.

[4]*Macbeth, King Lear and Contemporary History* (Cambridge, 1922), pp. 37-115.

believer in witchcraft and was an authority on the subject to the extent that when Reginald Scot wrote *The Discovery of Witchcraft* (1584) against the belief in witches, King James considered Scot's opinions "damnable," and wrote his *Demonologie* (1597) to confute them. It is also said that he ordered all copies of Scot's book to be burned. Scot gives a good deal of detail about sorcery, and it is usually thought that Shakespeare drew on his book for the witchlore in *Macbeth*. Shakespeare knew Harsnet's *Declaration of Egregious Popish Impostures* (1603), as is shown by *King Lear*.

It has long been thought with very good reason that some of the witchlore in *Macbeth* comes from accounts of various Scottish witch trials published about 1590. Scotch witches had the power of prophecy through their master spirits and were guilty of the practices described in *Macbeth*. They raised storms, beset vessels at sea, danced ceremonial dances in threes, made witch-broth quite like that in *Macbeth*, and, particularly, sailed the sea in sieves. They were serious and dangerous creatures, and often deluded the unsuspecting by telling them partial truths. The "weird sisters," although they are made up externally like the witches of vulgar superstition, are thought of by Holinshed as "goddesses of destiny, . . . nymphs, or feiries," who had the knowledge of prophecy. In Shakespeare they are, however, of the evil one, and not impartial like fates or norns. It is still a question to what extent Shakespeare meant that the free will of Macbeth was interfered with by "supernatural soliciting."

Holinshed's chronicle of King Macbeth has incorporated two very ancient pieces of folklore, namely, the story of the moving forest and the one of the man not born of woman. Shakespeare's use of them is exactly the same as that of Holinshed, for we are told there that Macbeth "by this prophecie put all fear out of his heart."

THE GREATNESS OF *Macbeth*

Macbeth is the play, more perhaps than any other, in which Shakespeare has been thought to challenge comparison with Aeschylus. His plot is bare, free from disturbing episodes, and perfectly unified from a dramatic standpoint, having also what Sir E. K. Chambers calls "unity of the philosophic idea." The two great personages are both cast in noble mold, both consistently conceived of and perfectly adjusted the one to the other.

Macbeth is man yielding to temptation and plunging deeper and deeper into sin. Lady Macbeth is woman in the nature of her ambitions (as far as one can see, largely for her husband and for social position), in her sense of the importance of tangible things and of bearing and deportment, and in her methods with her husband. Both are in a large way typical. Perhaps Macbeth, as conceived of by Elizabethan audiences, would be more immediately con-

demned as a villain than he is by us. Ambition to them was fundamentally a sin, and the idea of surrendering one's soul to the devil was more immediately horrible. The persons of a king and of a guest had about them an especial sanctity, and Macbeth murders his king who is also his guest. Well may he speak of:

> mine eternal jewel
> Given to the common enemy of man. . . .

When Macbeth expresses the wish that:

> this blow
> Might be the be-all and the end-all here,
> But here, upon this bank and shoal of time,
> We 'ld jump the life to come,

he seems to place every reliance upon the earthly life and to sacrifice every manly ideal and every hope of heaven to a wicked ambition; but, in so doing, he does not rid himself of the fear of human justice. The element of earthly fear in his composition is large. He seems rather to be preyed upon throughout by dread of punishment, by horrible dreams, startings, and agonies, than moved by any spiritualized remorse or repentance. *Macbeth* thus becomes a drama of fear, horror, and the most perturbing passions.

Elizabethan psychology understood that these perturbations must be controlled if there were to be efficient and successful actions. Lady Macbeth is better able to dominate her feelings, so that her breakdown comes only when the load has grown too heavy for her body and her will to bear. The passions were localized in Elizabethan psychology, as indeed their manifestations are, in the members of the body—in hair, hands, limbs—so that one recalls the modern theory of the emotions as arising from physical states when one hears Lady Macbeth's fiery admonitions to her husband; she fully understands that emotional control depends on bodily quiescence (III, iv, 63-67):

> O, these flaws and starts,
> Impostors to true fear, would well become
> A woman's story at a winter's fire,
> Authorized by her grandam. Shame itself!
> Why do you make such faces?

STAGE HISTORY

Macbeth, as we have seen, had suffered some corruption before its publication in the First Folio of 1623, a corruption which introduced into it an element of light opera—songs and a ballet of witches. What had begun thus early was carried yet further after the Restoration. D'Avenant wrote more songs for *Macbeth* and modified much of its condensed and weighty English into something commonplace and flat. Betterton appeared in D'Avenant's version at the theater in Lincoln's Inn Fields, where Pepys saw the play three times and commended it ominously for "variety." In 1672 Matthew Locke (1630?-1677) composed witch music for D'Avenant's version.

Garrick gave himself great credit for restoring Shakespeare's play to the stage, but in point of fact he did not completely restore it. He retained the witch songs and by writing a dying speech for Macbeth kept himself on the stage until the end. He was, however, famous as Macbeth, and one hears that in the dagger scene he was especially impressive and that in the murder scene his face "grew whiter and whiter." Mrs. Pritchard was his Lady Macbeth.

Macklin is remembered for having costumed himself and his fellows in Highland garb instead of the military uniforms with tie-wigs that were customary at the time.

The Kembles achieved great success in *Macbeth*. John Philip Kemble was Macbeth; Charles Kemble, Macduff; and their sister, Mrs. Siddons, Lady Macbeth. Kemble had no actor enter as the ghost of Banquo in the banquet scene, but made of it a ghost of the mind of Macbeth; in this he was followed by Macready, Booth, and Irving.

Lady Macbeth was the most famous part of the most famous of Shakespearean actresses, Mrs. Siddons. Reynolds painted her as "The Tragic Muse," and Galt speaks of the "low deep accent of apprehension, or of conscious conspiracy which she sustained throughout [the part of Lady Macbeth], especially as it influenced the utterance of her Medean invocation to the:

> spirits
> That tend on mortal thought,

and still more in the subsequent scene, where she chastises with her valour the hesitation of Macbeth."

Edmund Kean dispensed with the clap-trap of the witches and followed Shakespeare's conception of them as spirits of malign power and dignity. Macbeth was Macready's greatest role, and he was possibly the greatest of Macbeths. He was supported by Helen Faucit in the character of Lady Macbeth. Samuel Phelps restored (1847) Shakespeare's text. Irving played *Macbeth* first in 1875, and in 1896 in partnership with Ellen Terry brought the play to America. He conceived of Macbeth as a remorseless villain, a conception which gave room for Miss Terry's sympathetic interpretation of Lady Macbeth.

Revivals of the play have been frequent in later years. Those of Beerbohm Tree, Mrs. Patrick Campbell, Violet Vanbrugh, Charlotte Cushman, Madame Modjeska, and Sothern and Marlowe have been noteworthy. *Macbeth* has been popular on the German stage and even on those of France and Italy. *Macbeth* has been played a number of time in recent years. John Gielgud has appeared in the title role, and Godfrey Tearle's playing of the part at the Shakespeare Memorial Theatre at Stratford in the season of 1949 was noteworthy for the way he humanized Macbeth and made of him, as indeed he was, a good man gone wrong. A distinguished performance of *Macbeth* was that of Maurice Evans and Judith Anderson in New York in 1941-1942.

Macbeth

DRAMATIS PERSONAE

DUNCAN, king of Scotland.
MALCOLM, } his sons.
DONALBAIN, }
MACBETH, } generals of the king's army.
BANQUO, }
MACDUFF, }
LENNOX, }
ROSS, }
MENTEITH, } noblemen of Scotland.
ANGUS, }
CAITHNESS, }
FLEANCE, son to Banquo.
SIWARD, Earl of Northumberland, general of the English forces.
Young SIWARD, his son.
SEYTON, an officer attending on Macbeth.
Boy, son to Macduff.
An English Doctor.
A Scotch Doctor.
A Soldier.
A Porter.
An Old Man.

LADY MACBETH.
LADY MACDUFF.
Gentlewoman attending on Lady Macbeth.

HECATE.
Three Witches.
Apparitions.

Lords, Gentlemen, Officers, Soldiers, Murderers, Attendants, and Messengers.

SCENE: *Scotland: England.*

ACT I.

SCENE I. *A desert place.*

Thunder and lightning. Enter three Witches.

First Witch. When shall we three meet again
In thunder, lightning, or in rain?
Sec. Witch. When the hurlyburly 's done,
When the battle 's lost and won.
Third Witch. That will be ere the set of sun.
First Witch. Where the place?
Sec. Witch.   Upon the heath.
Third Witch. There to meet with Macbeth.
First Witch. I come, Graymalkin!
Sec. Witch. Paddock calls.
Third Witch. Anon.
All. Fair is foul, and foul is fair:
Hover through the fog and filthy air.   [*Exeunt.*

10

SCENE II. *A camp near Forres.*

Alarum within. Enter DUNCAN, MALCOLM, DONALBAIN,
LENNOX, *with* Attendants, *meeting a bleeding*
Sergeant.

Dun. What bloody man is that? He can report,
As seemeth by his plight, of the revolt
The newest state.
Mal. This is the sergeant
Who like a good and hardy soldier fought
'Gainst my captivity. Hail, brave friend!
Say to the king the knowledge of the broil
As thou didst leave it.
Ser. Doubtful it stood;
As two spent swimmers, that do cling together
And choke their art. The merciless Macdonwald—
Worthy to be a rebel, for to that   10
The multiplying villanies of nature
Do swarm upon him—from the western isles
Of kerns and gallowglasses is supplied;
And fortune, on his damned quarrel smiling,
Show'd like a rebel's whore: but all 's too weak:
For brave Macbeth—well he deserves that name—
Disdaining fortune, with his brandish'd steel,
Which smoked with bloody execution,
Like valour's minion carved out his passage
Till he faced the slave;   20
†Which ne'er shook hands, nor bade farewell to him,
Till he unseam'd him from the nave to the chaps,
And fix'd his head upon our battlements.
Dun. O valiant cousin! worthy gentleman!
Ser. As whence the sun 'gins his reflection
Shipwrecking storms and direful thunders break,
So from that spring whence comfort seem'd to come
Discomfort swells. Mark, king of Scotland, mark:
No sooner justice had with valour arm'd
Compell'd these skipping kerns to trust their heels,   30
But the Norweyan lord surveying vantage,
With furbish'd arms and new supplies of men
Began a fresh assault.
Dun. Dismay'd not this
Our captains, Macbeth and Banquo?
Ser. Yes;
As sparrows eagles, or the hare the lion.
If I say sooth, I must report they were
As cannons overcharged with double cracks, so they
Doubly redoubled strokes upon the foe:
Except they meant to bathe in reeking wounds,
Or memorize another Golgotha,   40
I cannot tell.
But I am faint, my gashes cry for help.
Dun. So well thy words become thee as thy wounds;

They smack of honour both. Go get him surgeons.
        [*Exit Sergeant, attended.*
Who comes here?

Enter Ross.
Mal. The worthy thane of Ross.
Len. What a haste looks through his eyes! So should
    he look
That seems to speak things strange.
Ross. God save the king!
Dun. Whence camest thou, worthy thane?
Ross. From Fife, great king;
Where the Norweyan banners flout the sky
And fan our people cold. Norway himself,   50
With terrible numbers,
Assisted by that most disloyal traitor
The thane of Cawdor, began a dismal conflict;
Till that Bellona's bridegroom, lapp'd in proof,
Confronted him with self-comparisons,
Point against point rebellious, arm 'gainst arm,
Curbing his lavish spirit: and, to conclude,
The victory fell on us.
Dun. Great happiness!
Ross. That now
Sweno, the Norways' king, craves composition;
Nor would we deign him burial of his men   60
Till he disbursed at Saint Colme's inch
Ten thousand dollars to our general use.
Dun. No more that thane of Cawdor shall deceive
Our bosom interest: go pronounce his present death,
And with his former title greet Macbeth.
Ross. I'll see it done.
Dun. What he hath lost noble Macbeth hath won.
        [*Exeunt.*

Macbeth
ACT I : SC III

1047

SCENE III. *A heath near Forres.*

Thunder. Enter the three Witches.

First Witch. Where hast thou been, sister?
Sec. Witch. Killing swine.
Third Witch. Sister, where thou?
First Witch. A sailor's wife had chestnuts in her lap,
And munch'd, and munch'd, and munch'd:— 'Give
    me,' quoth I:
'Aroint thee, witch!' the rump-fed ronyon cries.
Her husband 's to Aleppo gone, master o' the Tiger:
But in a sieve I'll thither sail,
And, like a rat without a tail,
I'll do, I'll do, and I'll do.   10
Sec. Witch. I'll give thee a wind.
First Witch. Thou 'rt kind.

Third Witch. And I another.
First Witch. I myself have all the other,
And the very ports they blow,
All the quarters that they know
I' the shipman's card.
I will drain him dry as hay:
Sleep shall neither night nor day
Hang upon his pent-house lid;   20
He shall live a man forbid:
Weary se'nnights nine times nine
Shall he dwindle, peak and pine:
Though his bark cannot be lost,
Yet it shall be tempest-tost.
Look what I have.
    Sec. Witch. Show me, show me.
    First Witch. Here I have a pilot's thumb,
Wreck'd as homeward he did come.   [*Drum within.*
    Third Witch. A drum, a drum!   30
Macbeth doth come.
    All. The weird sisters, hand in hand,
Posters of the sea and land,
Thus do go about, about:
Thrice to thine and thrice to mine
And thrice again, to make up nine.
Peace! the charm 's wound up.

Enter MACBETH *and* BANQUO.

    Macb. So foul and fair a day I have not seen.
    Ban. How far is 't call'd to Forres? What are these
So wither'd and so wild in their attire,   40
That look not like the inhabitants o' the earth,
And yet are on 't? Live you? or are you aught
That man may question? You seem to understand me,
By each at once her choppy finger laying
Upon her skinny lips: you should be women,
And yet your beards forbid me to interpret
That you are so.
    Macb.   Speak, if you can: what are
you?
    First Witch. All hail, Macbeth! hail to thee, thane of
Glamis!
    Sec. Witch. All hail, Macbeth! hail to thee, thane of
Cawdor!
    Third Witch. All hail, Macbeth, that shalt be king
hereafter!   50
    Ban. Good sir, why do you start; and seem to fear
Things that do sound so fair? I' the name of truth,
Are ye fantastical, or that indeed
Which outwardly ye show? My noble partner
You greet with present grace and great prediction
Of noble having and of royal hope,
That he seems rapt withal: to me you speak not.
If you can look into the seeds of time,
And say which grain will grow and which will not,
Speak then to me, who neither beg nor fear   60
Your favours nor your hate.
    First Witch. Hail!
    Sec. Witch. Hail!

Third Witch. Hail!
First Witch. Lesser than Macbeth, and greater.
Sec. Witch. Not so happy, yet much happier.
Third Witch. Thou shalt get kings, though thou be
none:
So all hail, Macbeth and Banquo!
    First Witch. Banquo and Macbeth, all hail!
    Macb. Stay, you imperfect speakers, tell me more: 70
By Sinel's death I know I am thane of Glamis;
But how of Cawdor? the thane of Cawdor lives,
A prosperous gentleman; and to be king
Stands not within the prospect of belief,
No more than to be Cawdor. Say from whence
You owe this strange intelligence? or why
Upon this blasted heath you stop our way
With such prophetic greeting? Speak, I charge you.
                                        [*Witches vanish.*
    Ban. The earth hath bubbles, as the water has,
And these are of them. Whither are they vanish'd?   80
    Macb. Into the air; and what seem'd corporal
melted
As breath into the wind. Would they had stay'd!
    Ban. Were such things here as we do speak about?
Or have we eaten on the insane root
That takes the reason prisoner?
    Macb. Your children shall be kings.
    Ban.   You shall be king.
    Macb. And thane of Cawdor too: went it not so?
    Ban. To the selfsame tune and words. Who 's here?

Enter ROSS *and* ANGUS.

    Ross. The king hath happily received, Macbeth,
The news of thy success; and when he reads   90
Thy personal venture in the rebels' fight,
His wonders and his praises do contend
Which should be thine or his: silenced with that,
In viewing o'er the rest o' the selfsame day,
He finds thee in the stout Norweyan ranks,
Nothing afeard of what thyself didst make,
Strange images of death. As thick as hail
Came post with post; and every one did bear
Thy praises in his kingdom's great defence,
And pour'd them down before him.
    Ang.   We are sent   100
To give thee from our royal master thanks;
Only to herald thee into his sight,
Not pay thee.
    Ross. And, for an earnest of a greater honour,
He bade me, from him, call thee thane of Cawdor:
In which addition, hail, most worthy thane!
For it is thine.
    Ban.   What, can the devil speak true?
    Macb. The thane of Cawdor lives: why do you
dress me
In borrow'd robes?
    Ang.   Who was the thane lives yet;
But under heavy judgement bears that life   110
Which he deserves to lose. Whether he was combined

15. **blow,** blow upon. 17. **shipman's card,** compass card, or a chart.
20. **pent-house lid,** eyelid. 21. **forbid,** accursed. 22. **se'nnights,**
weeks. 32. **weird,** connected with fate. 33. **Posters of,** travelers
over. 53. **fantastical,** creatures of fantasy or imagination. 54. **show,**
appear. 71. **Sinel's.** Sinel was Macbeth's father. **Glamis,** now a
village near Perth; pronounced by the Scotch as a monosyllable
rhyming with "alms." 72. **the . . . lives.** This is the first of the strange
inconsistencies between the second scene and the third. Macbeth
cannot have been ignorant of the events in which he himself took part.
This is explained as forgetfulness on Shakespeare's part, and also,

more probably, as due to the play's having been tampered with by
another hand. This scene is organic and in good verse; the second scene
is confused, but it is hard to believe that there is none of the work of
Shakespeare in it. 81. **corporal,** bodily. 84. **insane root,** root causing
insanity. The root of hemlock may be referred to since the eating of it
was supposed to cause men to see visions. 96. **Nothing afeard,** not
at all afraid. 108-129. **The . . . gentlemen.** Ross has informed Duncan
(I, ii, 48-62) of Cawdor's overthrow, and Macbeth had defeated him;
yet both here seem ignorant of the event. 112. **line,** strengthen. 126.
deepest consequence, matters of the greatest importance. 129. **im-**

With those of Norway, or did line the rebel
With hidden help and vantage, or that with both
He labour'd in his country's wreck, I know not;
But treasons capital, confess'd and proved,
Have overthrown him.
   Macb. [*Aside*] Glamis, and thane of Cawdor!
The greatest is behind. [*To Ross and Angus*] Thanks for
   your pains.
[*To Ban.*] Do you not hope your children shall be
   kings,
When those that gave the thane of Cawdor to me
Promised no less to them?
   Ban.   That trusted home   120
Might yet enkindle you unto the crown,
Besides the thane of Cawdor. But 'tis strange:
And oftentimes, to win us to our harm,
The instruments of darkness tell us truths,
Win us with honest trifles, to betray 's
In deepest consequence.
Cousins, a word, I pray you.
   Macb.   [*Aside*] Two truths are told,
As happy prologues to the swelling act
Of the imperial theme.—I thank you, gentlemen.
[*Aside*] This supernatural soliciting   130
Cannot be ill, cannot be good: if ill,
Why hath it given me earnest of success,
Commencing in a truth? I am thane of Cawdor:
If good, why do I yield to that suggestion
Whose horrid image doth unfix my hair
And make my seated heart knock at my ribs,
Against the use of nature? Present fears
Are less than horrible imaginings:
My thought, whose murder yet is but fantastical,
Shakes so my single state of man that function   140
Is smother'd in surmise, and nothing is
But what is not.
   Ban.   Look, how our partner 's rapt.
   Macb. [*Aside*] If chance will have me king, why,
   chance may crown me,
Without my stir.
   Ban.   New honours come upon him,
Like our strange garments, cleave not to their
   mould
But with the aid of use.
   Macb.   [*Aside*] Come what come may,
Time and the hour runs through the roughest day.
   Ban. Worthy Macbeth, we stay upon your leisure.
   Macb. Give me your favour: my dull brain was
   wrought
With things forgotten. Kind gentlemen, your pains 150
Are register'd where every day I turn
The leaf to read them. Let us toward the king.
Think upon what hath chanced, and, at more time,
The interim having weigh'd it, let us speak
Our free hearts each to other.
   Ban.   Very gladly.
   Macb. Till then, enough. Come, friends.   [*Exeunt.*

SCENE IV. *Forres. The palace.*

Flourish. Enter DUNCAN, MALCOLM, DONALBAIN,
   LENNOX, *and* Attendants.

   Dun. Is execution done on Cawdor? Are not
Those in commission yet return'd?
   Mal.   My liege,
They are not yet come back. But I have spoke
With one that saw him die: who did report
That very frankly he confess'd his treasons,
Implor'd your highness' pardon and set forth
A deep repentance: nothing in his life
Became him like the leaving it; he died
As one that had been studied in his death
To throw away the dearest thing he owed,   10
As 'twere a careless trifle.
   Dun.   There 's no art
To find the mind's construction in the face:
He was a gentleman on whom I built
An absolute trust.

   Enter MACBETH, BANQUO, ROSS, *and* ANGUS.
              O worthiest cousin!
The sin of my ingratitude even now
Was heavy on me: thou art so far before
That swiftest wing of recompense is slow
To overtake thee. Would thou hadst less deserved,
That the proportion both of thanks and payment
Might have been mine! only I have left to say,   20
More is thy due than more than all can pay.
   Macb. The service and the loyalty I owe,
In doing it, pays itself. Your highness' part
Is to receive our duties; and our duties
Are to your throne and state children and servants,
Which do but what they should, by doing every thing
Safe toward your love and honour.
   Dun.   Welcome hither:
I have begun to plant thee, and will labour
To make thee full of growing. Noble Banquo,
That hast no less deserved, nor must be known   30
No less to have done so, let me infold thee
And hold thee to my heart.
   Ban.   There if I grow,
The harvest is your own.
   Dun.   My plenteous joys,
Wanton in fulness, seek to hide themselves
In drops of sorrow. Sons, kinsmen, thanes,
And you whose places are the nearest, know
We will establish our estate upon
Our eldest, Malcolm, whom we name hereafter
The Prince of Cumberland; which honour must
Not unaccompanied invest him only,   40
But signs of nobleness, like stars, shall shine
On all deservers. From hence to Inverness,
And bind us further to you.
   Macb. The rest is labour, which is not used for you:
I'll be myself the harbinger and make joyful
The hearing of my wife with your approach;

perial theme, theme of empire. 130. supernatural soliciting, temptation by supernatural beings. 134. suggestion. Macbeth is imaginative,
and, therefore, ambitious; it is on the imaginative side of his nature
that he is assailed. 135. unfix my hair, make it stand on end. 140.
single state of man, whole being; an obvious allusion to the doctrine
of the microcosm, according to which the being of man is a counterpart
of the macrocosm, or universe. 140-142. function . . . not, power of
action is lost in speculation and only unreal imaginings have (for me)
any reality. 144. stir, bestirring (myself). come, i.e., which have
come. 153. at more time, at a time of greater leisure. 155. Our free

hearts, our hearts freely.
   SCENE IV. 2. commission, those having warrant to see to the execution of Cawdor. 11. careless, uncared for. 22-27. The . . . honour.
One need not consider this speech devoid of sincerity. Macbeth has
indeed plotted to murder the king, but has resolved to leave the issue
to chance; his words have a loyal sound. 27. Safe toward, securely
directed toward. 37. establish our estate, fix the succession of our
state. 42. Inverness, the seat of Macbeth's castle. 45. harbinger,
forerunner, messenger.

So humbly take my leave.
    Dun.   My worthy Cawdor!
    Macb. [*Aside*] The Prince of Cumberland! that is a
    step
On which I must fall down, or else o'erleap,
For in my way it lies. Stars, hide your fires;   50
Let not light see my black and deep desires:
The eye wink at the hand; yet let that be,
Which the eye fears, when it is done, to see.   [*Exit.*
    Dun. True, worthy Banquo; he is full so valiant,
And in his commendations I am fed;
It is a banquet to me. Let 's after him,
Whose care is gone before to bid us welcome:
It is a peerless kinsman.   [*Flourish. Exeunt.*

SCENE V. *Inverness. Macbeth's castle.*

Enter LADY MACBETH, *reading a letter.*

    Lady M. 'They met me in the day of success; and I
have learned by the perfectest report, they have more
in them than mortal knowledge. When I burned in
desire to question them further, they made themselves
air, into which they vanished. Whiles I stood rapt in
wonder of it, came missives from the king, who all-
hailed me "Thane of Cawdor;" by which title, before,
these weird sisters saluted me, and referred me to the
coming on of time, with "Hail, king that shalt be!"
This have I thought good to deliver thee, my dearest
partner of greatness, that thou mightst not lose the
dues of rejoicing, by being ignorant of what greatness
is promised thee. Lay it to thy heart, and farewell.'
Glamis thou art, and Cawdor; and shalt be
What thou art promised: yet do I fear thy nature;
It is too full o' the milk of human kindness
To catch the nearest way: thou wouldst be great;
Art not without ambition, but without   20
The illness should attend it: what thou wouldst
    highly,
That wouldst thou holily; wouldst not play false,
And yet wouldst wrongly win: thou 'ldst have, great
    Glamis,
That which cries 'Thus thou must do, if thou have it;
And that which rather thou dost fear to do
Than wishest should be undone.' Hie thee hither,
That I may pour my spirits in thine ear;
And chastise with the valour of my tongue
All that impedes thee from the golden round,
Which fate and metaphysical aid doth seem   30
To have thee crown'd withal.

Enter a Messenger.

             What is your tidings?
    Mess. The king comes here to-night.
    Lady M.   Thou 'rt mad to say it:
Is not thy master with him? who, were 't so,
Would have inform'd for preparation.

    Mess. So please you, it is true: our thane is coming:
One of my fellows had the speed of him,
Who, almost dead for breath, had scarcely more
Than would make up his message.
    Lady M.   Give him tending;
He brings great news.   [*Exit Messenger.*
         The raven himself is hoarse
That croaks the fatal entrance of Duncan   40
Under my battlements. Come, you spirits
That tend on mortal thoughts, unsex me here,
And fill me from the crown to the toe top-full
Of direst cruelty! make thick my blood;
Stop up the access and passage to remorse,
That no compunctious visitings of nature
Shake my fell purpose, nor keep peace between
The effect and it! Come to my woman's breasts,
And take my milk for gall, you murdering ministers,
Wherever in your sightless substances   50
You wait on nature's mischief! Come, thick night,
And pall thee in the dunnest smoke of hell,
That my keen knife see not the wound it makes,
Nor heaven peep through the blanket of the dark,
To cry 'Hold, hold!'

Enter MACBETH.

         Great Glamis! worthy Cawdor!
Greater than both, by the all-hail hereafter!
Thy letters have transported me beyond
This ignorant present, and I feel now
The future in the instant.
    Macb.   My dearest love,
Duncan comes here to-night.
    Lady M.   And when goes hence?   60
    Macb. To-morrow, as he purposes.
    Lady M.   O, never
Shall sun that morrow see!
Your face, my thane, is as a book where men
May read strange matters. To beguile the time,
Look like the time; bear welcome in your eye,
Your hand, your tongue: look like the innocent
    flower,
But be the serpent under 't. He that 's coming
Must be provided for: and you shall put
This night's great business into my dispatch;
Which shall to all our nights and days to come   70
Give solely sovereign sway and masterdom.
    Macb. We will speak further.
    Lady M.   Only look up clear;
To alter favour ever is to fear:
Leave all the rest to me.   [*Exeunt.*

SCENE VI. *Before Macbeth's castle.*

Hautboys and torches. Enter DUNCAN, MALCOLM,
    DONALBAIN, BANQUO, LENNOX, MACDUFF, ROSS,
    ANGUS, *and* Attendants.

50. **in my way it lies.** Prince of Cumberland was the title of the heir
apparent to Duncan's throne. The monarchy was not hereditary, and
Macbeth had a right to believe that he himself might be chosen as
Duncan's successor; he here states the issue as to whether or not he will
interfere with the course of circumstance. 52. **eye wink at the hand.**
Fairchild discovers in this an allusion to an emblem in Alciatus which
pictures an eye set in a hand to symbolize attention to one's deeds.
   SCENE V. 7. **missives,** messengers. 18. **milk of human kindness,**
gentleness of human nature. Macbeth is Duncan's *peerless kinsman* (I, iv,
58), and this is another testimony to the uprightness of his character
when the play begins. 21. **illness,** evil. 24-26. **That . . . undone.** Many
editors end the quotation after *it*, which refers to the crown. A meaning
for the passage can be had by understanding *that which* in line 25 as
meaning "that's what." 29. **golden round,** the crown. 30. **meta-**

physical, supernatural. 36. **had the speed of,** outstripped. 42. **tend
. . . thoughts,** are the instruments of deadly or murderous thoughts.
The spirits conveying various passions were the tools of thought.
44-45. **make . . . remorse.** By making the blood thick it would be less
able to flow out in generous passions and thus awaken remorse or pity.
46. **compunctious . . . nature,** natural feelings of pity and conscience.
49. **murdering ministers,** evil angels. 50. **sightless,** invisible. 52.
pall, envelope. **dunnest,** darkest. 72. **clear,** serenely. 73. **To . . .
fear,** to change the aspect of one's face is always to feel fear.
   SCENE VI. 3. **gentle senses,** a case of transferred epithet. It is the
air which seems gentle to the senses. 6. **jutty,** projection of wall
or building. 7. **coign of vantage,** convenient corner, i.e., for nesting.
10. **delicate,** delicious. 11. **follows,** attends. **sometime,** sometimes.
13. **God 'ild us,** God reward us, i.e., thank us. Duncan means that,

Dun. This castle hath a pleasant seat; the air
Nimbly and sweetly recommends itself
Unto our gentle senses.
Ban.   This guest of summer,
The temple-haunting martlet, does approve,
By his loved mansionry, that the heaven's breath
Smells wooingly here: no jutty, frieze,
Buttress, nor coign of vantage, but this bird
Hath made his pendent bed and procreant cradle:
Where they most breed and haunt, I have observed,
The air is delicate.

Enter LADY MACBETH.

Dun.   See, see, our honour'd hostess! 10
The love that follows us sometime is our trouble,
Which still we thank as love. Herein I teach you
How you shall bid God 'ild us for your pains,
And thank us for your trouble.
Lady M.   All our service
In every point twice done and then done double
Were poor and single business to contend
Against those honours deep and broad wherewith
Your majesty loads our house: for those of old,
And the late dignities heap'd up to them,
We rest your hermits.
Dun.   Where 's the thane of Cawdor? 20
We coursed him at the heels, and had a purpose
To be his purveyor: but he rides well;
And his great love, sharp as his spur, hath holp him
To his home before us. Fair and noble hostess,
We are your guest to-night.
Lady M.   Your servants ever
Have theirs, themselves and what is theirs, in compt,
To make their audit at your highness' pleasure,
Still to return your own.
Dun.   Give me your hand;
Conduct me to mine host: we love him highly,
And shall continue our graces towards him.   30
By your leave, hostess.   [*Exeunt.*

SCENE VII. *Macbeth's castle.*

Hautboys and torches. Enter a Sewer, *and divers*
Servants *with dishes and service, and pass over the*
stage. Then enter MACBETH.

Macb. If it were done when 'tis done, then 'twere
    well
It were done quickly: if the assassination
Could trammel up the consequence, and catch
With his surcease success; that but this blow
Might be the be-all and the end-all here,
But here, upon this bank and shoal of time,
We 'ld jump the life to come. But in these cases
We still have judgement here; that we but teach
Bloody instructions, which, being taught, return

To plague the inventor: this even-handed justice   10
Commends the ingredients of our poison'd chalice
To our own lips. He 's here in double trust;
First, as I am his kinsman and his subject,
Strong both against the deed; then, as his host,
Who should against his murderer shut the door,
Not bear the knife myself. Besides, this Duncan
Hath borne his faculties so meek, hath been
So clear in his great office, that his virtues
Will plead like angels, trumpet-tongued, against
The deep damnation of his taking-off;   20
And pity, like a naked new-born babe,
Striding the blast, or heaven's cherubim, horsed
Upon the sightless couriers of the air,
Shall blow the horrid deed in every eye,
That tears shall drown the wind. I have no spur
To prick the sides of my intent, but only
Vaulting ambition, which o'erleaps itself
And falls on the other.

Enter LADY MACBETH.

                         How now! what news?
Lady M. He has almost supp'd: why have you left
    the chamber?
Macb. Hath he ask'd for me?
Lady M.   Know you not he has?   30
Macb. We will proceed no further in this business:
He hath honour'd me of late; and I have bought
Golden opinions from all sorts of people,
Which would be worn now in their newest gloss,
Not cast aside so soon.
Lady M.   Was the hope drunk
Wherein you dress'd yourself? hath it slept since?
And wakes it now, to look so green and pale
At what it did so freely? From this time
Such I account thy love. Art thou afeard
To be the same in thine own act and valour   40
As thou art in desire? Wouldst thou have that
Which thou esteem'st the ornament of life,
And live a coward in thine own esteem,
Letting 'I dare not' wait upon 'I would,'
Like the poor cat i' the adage?
Macb.   Prithee, peace:
I dare do all that may become a man;
Who dares do more is none.
Lady M.   What beast was 't, then,
That made you break this enterprise to me?
When you durst do it, then you were a man;
And, to be more than what you were, you would   50
Be so much more the man. Nor time nor place
Did then adhere, and yet you would make both:
They have made themselves, and that their fitness
    now
Does unmake you. I have given suck, and know
How tender 'tis to love the babe that milks me:
I would, while it was smiling in my face,

---

since he is there because he loves them, they should thank him even for the trouble he causes them. **16. single,** small, inconsiderable. **16-17. contend Against,** vie with. **20. rest,** remain. **hermits,** i.e., those who will pray for you like hermits or beadsmen. **22. purveyor,** an officer sent ahead of the king to provide for his entertainment; here, forerunner. **26. in compt,** under obligation (to serve the king).

SCENE VII. *Stage Direction:* **Hautboys,** wooden double-reed musical instruments. **Sewer,** chief servant who directed the placing of dishes on the table, or the servant who acted as taster and guard against poison. **3. trammel up,** entangle in a net, prevent. **4. surcease,** cessation. **6. shoal,** so Theobald; F: *schoole,* which may be construed with *bank* (meaning bench) and with lines 8-10. **17. faculties,** prerogatives. **20. taking-off,** murder. Macbeth is perfectly conscious of the

nature of his sin. **28. other,** i.e., the other side of my intent. **45. adage,** "The cate would eate fyshe, and would not wet her feete" (Heywood). **47-51. beast . . . man,** if you are a man, it must have been a beast that prompted you to *break* (disclose) this enterprise to me; if it is unmanly to do the deed, it was unmanly to suggest it. Note that it was Macbeth who had suggested the murder. A well-known teacher of Shakespeare identifies Lady Macbeth's method as the universal feminine method of persuading men: (1) You do not love me (l. 39). (2) You are afraid (ll. 39-45). (3) If I were a man, I would do it (ll. 56-58). Surely one must also add: (4) You said you would do it (ll. 58-59). **52. adhere,** agree, suit.

Have pluck'd my nipple from his boneless gums,
And dash'd the brains out, had I so sworn as you
Have done to this.
  Macb.   If we should fail?
  Lady M.   We fail!
But screw your courage to the sticking-place,   60
And we'll not fail. When Duncan is asleep—
Whereto the rather shall his day's hard journey
Soundly invite him—his two chamberlains
Will I with wine and wassail so convince
That memory, the warder of the brain,
Shall be a fume, and the receipt of reason
A limbeck only: when in swinish sleep
Their drenched natures lie as in a death,
What cannot you and I perform upon
The unguarded Duncan? what not put upon   70
His spongy officers, who shall bear the guilt
Of our great quell?
  Macb.   Bring forth men-children only;
For thy undaunted mettle should compose
Nothing but males. Will it not be received,
When we have mark'd with blood those sleepy two
Of his own chamber and used their very daggers,
That they have done 't?
  Lady M.   Who dares receive it other,
As we shall make our griefs and clamour roar
Upon his death?
  Macb.   I am settled, and bend up
Each corporal agent to this terrible feat.   80
Away, and mock the time with fairest show:
False face must hide what the false heart doth know.
                                    [*Exeunt.*

ACT II.

SCENE I. *Court of Macbeth's castle.*

Enter BANQUO, *and* FLEANCE *bearing a torch before him.*

  Ban. How goes the night, boy?
  Fle. The moon is down; I have not heard the clock.
  Ban. And she goes down at twelve.
  Fle.   I take 't, 'tis later, sir.
  Ban. Hold, take my sword. There 's husbandry in
      heaven;
Their candles are all out. Take thee that too.
A heavy summons lies like lead upon me,
And yet I would not sleep: merciful powers,
Restrain in me the cursed thoughts that nature
Gives way to in repose!

Enter MACBETH, *and a* Servant *with a torch.*
            Give me my sword.
Who 's there?   10
  Macb. A friend.
  Ban. What, sir, not yet at rest? The king 's a-bed:
He hath been in unusual pleasure, and

Sent forth great largess to your offices.
This diamond he greets your wife withal,
By the name of most kind hostess; and shut up
In measureless content.
  Macb.   Being unprepared,
Our will became the servant to defect;
Which else should free have wrought.
  Ban.   All 's well.
I dreamt last night of the three weird sisters: 20
To you they have show'd some truth.
  Macb.   I think not of them:
Yet, when we can entreat an hour to serve,
We would spend it in some words upon that business,
If you would grant the time.
  Ban.   At your kind'st leisure.
  Macb. If you shall cleave to my consent, when 'tis,
It shall make honour for you.
  Ban.   So I lose none
In seeking to augment it, but still keep
My bosom franchised and allegiance clear,
I shall be counsell'd.
  Macb.   Good repose the while!
  Ban. Thanks, sir: the like to you!   30
                        [*Exeunt Banquo and Fleance.*
  Macb. Go bid thy mistress, when my drink is ready,
She strike upon the bell. Get thee to bed. [*Exit Servant.*
Is this a dagger which I see before me,
The handle toward my hand? Come, let me clutch
      thee.
I have thee not, and yet I see thee still.
Art thou not, fatal vision, sensible
To feeling as to sight? or art thou but
A dagger of the mind, a false creation,
Proceeding from the heat-oppressed brain?
I see thee yet, in form as palpable   40
As this which now I draw.
Thou marshall'st me the way that I was going;
And such an instrument I was to use.
Mine eyes are made the fools o' the other senses,
Or else worth all the rest; I see thee still,
And on thy blade and dudgeon gouts of blood,
Which was not so before. There 's no such thing:
It is the bloody business which informs
Thus to mine eyes. Now o'er the one half-world
Nature seems dead, and wicked dreams abuse   50
The curtain'd sleep; witchcraft celebrates
Pale Hecate's offerings, and wither'd murder,
Alarum'd by his sentinel, the wolf,
Whose howl 's his watch, thus with his stealthy
      pace,
With Tarquin's ravishing strides, towards his design
Moves like a ghost. Thou sure and firm-set earth,
Hear not my steps, which way they walk, for fear
Thy very stones prate of my whereabout,
And take the present horror from the time,
Which now suits with it. Whiles I threat, he lives: 60
Words to the heat of deeds too cold breath gives.
                                    [*A bell rings.*

60. **sticking-place,** probably a metaphor from the tightening of the strings of a musical instrument. 64. **wassail,** carousal, drink. **convince,** overpower. 65-67. **warder . . . only.** The brain was divided into three ventricles, imagination in front, memory at the back, and between them the seat of reason. The fumes of wine would deaden memory and judgment. 67. **limbeck,** alembic, still. 70. **put upon,** attribute to. 71. **spongy,** drunken. 72. **quell,** murder. 74. **received,** as truth. 77. **other,** otherwise. 79. **settled,** determined. 79-80. **bend . . . feat.** The language all the way through the passage about the deed is not primarily figurative, but drawn from current psychology. A stiffly

maintained head of passion is necessary for action. *To alter favour ever is to fear* (I, v, 73); hence, the bodily agents must be immovable, the blood thick, and the passage to remorse closed.
  ACT II. SCENE I. 4. **husbandry,** economy. 14. **offices,** servants' quarters. Some editors read *officers.* 25. **If . . . 'tis.** If you give me your support when the fulfillment occurs. 28. **franchised,** free (from guilt). **clear,** unstained. 46. **dudgeon,** hilt of a dagger. **gouts,** drops. 52. **Hecate's.** Hecate was the goddess of witchcraft.
  SCENE II. 1. **bold.** Lady Macbeth has deliberately taken wine to bolster up her courage; this is denied by some critics. 5. **grooms,**

I go, and it is done; the bell invites me.
Hear it not, Duncan; for it is a knell
That summons thee to heaven or to hell.   [*Exit.*

SCENE II. *The same.*

Enter LADY MACBETH.

Lady M. That which hath made them drunk hath
    made me bold;
What hath quench'd them hath given me fire. Hark!
    Peace!
It was the owl that shriek'd, the fatal bellman,
Which gives the stern'st good-night. He is about it:
The doors are open; and the surfeited grooms
Do mock their charge with snores: I have drugg'd
    their possets,
That death and nature do contend about them,
Whether they live or die.
    Macb. [*Within*] Who's there? what, ho!
    Lady M. Alack, I am afraid they have awaked,   10
And 'tis not done. The attempt and not the deed
Confounds us. Hark! I laid their daggers ready;
He could not miss 'em. Had he not resembled
My father as he slept, I had done 't.

Enter MACBETH.

          My husband!
Macb. I have done the deed. Didst thou not hear a
    noise?
    Lady M. I heard the owl scream and the crickets
    cry.
Did not you speak?
    Macb.   When?
    Lady M.   Now.
    Macb.   As I descended?
    Lady M. Ay.
    Macb. Hark!
Who lies i' the second chamber?
    Lady M.   Donalbain.   20
    Macb. This is a sorry sight.   [*Looking on his hands.*
    Lady M. A foolish thought, to say a sorry sight.
    Macb. There's one did laugh in's sleep, and one
    cried 'Murder!'
That they did wake each other: I stood and heard
    them:
But they did say their prayers, and address'd them
Again to sleep.
    Lady M. There are two lodged together.
    Macb. One cried 'God bless us!' and 'Amen' the
    other;
As they had seen me with these hangman's hands.
Listening their fear, I could not say 'Amen,'
When they did say 'God bless us!'
    Lady M.   Consider it not so deeply.   30
    Macb. But wherefore could not I pronounce
    'Amen'?
I had most need of blessing, and 'Amen'

Stuck in my throat.
    Lady M.   These deeds must not be
    thought
After these ways; so, it will make us mad.
    Macb. Methought I heard a voice cry 'Sleep no
    more!
Macbeth does murder sleep,' the innocent sleep,
Sleep that knits up the ravell'd sleave of care,
The death of each day's life, sore labour's bath,
Balm of hurt minds, great nature's second course,
Chief nourisher in life's feast,—
    Lady M.   What do you mean?   40
    Macb. Still it cried 'Sleep no more!' to all the house:
'Glamis hath murder'd sleep, and therefore Cawdor
Shall sleep no more; Macbeth shall sleep no more.'
    Lady M. Who was it that thus cried? Why, worthy
    thane,
You do unbend your noble strength, to think
So brainsickly of things. Go get some water,
And wash this filthy witness from your hand.
Why did you bring these daggers from the place?
They must lie there: go carry them; and smear
The sleepy grooms with blood.
    Macb.   I'll go no more: 50
I am afraid to think what I have done;
Look on 't again I dare not.
    Lady M.   Infirm of purpose!
Give me the daggers: the sleeping and the dead
Are but as pictures: 'tis the eye of childhood
That fears a painted devil. If he do bleed,
I'll gild the faces of the grooms withal;
For it must seem their guilt.   [*Exit. Knocking within.*
    Macb.   Whence is that knocking?
How is 't with me, when every noise appals me?
What hands are here? ha! they pluck out mine eyes.
Will all great Neptune's ocean wash this blood   60
Clean from my hand? No, this my hand will rather
The multitudinous seas incarnadine,
Making the green one red.

Re-enter LADY MACBETH.

    Lady M. My hands are of your colour; but I shame
To wear a heart so white. [*Knocking within.*] I hear a
    knocking
At the south entry: retire we to our chamber:
A little water clears us of this deed:
How easy is it, then! Your constancy
Hath left you unattended. [*Knocking within.*] Hark!
    more knocking.
Get on your nightgown, lest occasion call us,   70
And show us to be watchers. Be not lost
So poorly in your thoughts.
    Macb. To know my deed, 'twere best not know
    myself.   [*Knocking within.*
Wake Duncan with thy knocking! I would thou
    couldst!   [*Exeunt.*

---

servants. 6. **possets,** hot milk poured on ale or wine and spiced, a bedtime drink common at the time. 13-14. **Had . . . done 't.** This, one of the few personal touches in the part of Lady Macbeth, prepares us for the terrible effect her crime was yet to have upon her. 21. **sorry,** wretched. 25. **address'd them,** settled themselves. 26. **two,** possibly, Malcolm and Donalbain thus half-awakened by their father's murder. 29. **Listening,** listening to. 34. **it will make us mad.** This idea of the effect of obsession on sanity is firmly fixed in Shakespeare's psychology. 37. **ravell'd sleave,** tangled unwrought silk. 39. **second course.** Ordinary feasts had two courses; only the more elaborate ones had

three; hence, the second course was the *chief nourisher* and the conclusion of the feast. 46. **brainsickly,** insanely, madly. 56-57. **gild . . . guilt.** The pun would be more obvious to Shakespeare's audience than to us, for gold was ordinarily thought of as red. 62. **incarnadine,** make red. 63. **one red,** one all-pervading red. F has *Making the Greene one, Red,* which some editors have followed. 64. **shame,** am ashamed. 68-69. **Your . . . unattended,** your firmness has deserted you. 70. **nightgown,** dressing gown. 72. **poorly,** dejectedly. 73. **To . . . deed.** It were better to be lost in my thoughts than to have consciousness of my deed.

SCENE III. *The same.*

Knocking within. Enter a Porter.

Porter. Here 's a knocking indeed! If a man were porter of hell-gate, he should have old turning the key. [*Knocking within.*] Knock, knock, knock! Who 's there, i' the name of Beelzebub? Here 's a farmer, that hanged himself on the expectation of plenty: come in time; have napkins enow about you; here you'll sweat for 't. [*Knocking within.*] Knock, knock! Who 's there, in the other devil's name? Faith, here 's an equivocator, that could swear in both the scales against either scale; who committed treason enough for God's sake, yet could not equivocate to heaven: O, come in, equivocator. [*Knocking within.*] Knock, knock, knock! Who 's there? Faith, here 's an English tailor come hither, for stealing out of a French hose: come in, tailor; here you may roast your goose. [*Knocking within.*] Knock, knock; never at quiet! What are you? But this place is too cold for hell. I'll devil-porter it no further: I had thought to have let in some of all professions that go the primrose way to the everlasting bonfire. [*Knocking within.*] Anon, anon! I pray you, remember the porter.

[*Opens the gate.*]

Enter MACDUFF *and* LENNOX.

Macd. Was it so late, friend, ere you went to bed, That you do lie so late?

Port. 'Faith, sir, we were carousing till the second cock: and drink, sir, is a great provoker of three things.

Macd. What three things does drink especially provoke? 30

Port. Marry, sir, nose-painting, sleep, and urine. Lechery, sir, it provokes, and unprovokes; it provokes the desire, but it takes away the performance: therefore, much drink may be said to be an equivocator with lechery: it makes him, and it mars him; it sets him on, and it takes him off; it persuades him, and disheartens him; makes him stand to, and not stand to; in conclusion, equivocates him in a sleep, and, giving him the lie, leaves him. 40

Macd. I believe drink gave thee the lie last night.

Port. That it did, sir, i' the very throat on me: but I requited him for his lie; and, I think, being too strong for him, though he took up my legs sometime, yet I made a shift to cast him.

Macd. Is thy master stirring?

Enter MACBETH.

Our knocking has awaked him; here he comes.

Len. Good morrow, noble sir.
Macb.   Good morrow, both.
Macd. Is the king stirring, worthy thane?
Macb.   Not yet. 50
Macd. He did command me to call timely on him: I have almost slipp'd the hour.

Macb.   I'll bring you to him.
Macd. I know this is a joyful trouble to you; But yet 'tis one.
Macb. The labour we delight in physics pain. This is the door.
Macd.   I'll make so bold to call, For 'tis my limited service.   [*Exit.*
Len. Goes the king hence to-day?
Macb.   He does: he did appoint so.
Len. The night has been unruly: where we lay, Our chimneys were blown down; and, as they say, 60 Lamentings heard i' the air; strange screams of death, And prophesying with accents terrible Of dire combustion and confused events New hatch'd to the woeful time: the obscure bird Clamour'd the livelong night: some say, the earth Was feverous and did shake.
Macb.   'Twas a rough night.
Len. My young remembrance cannot parallel A fellow to it.

Re-enter MACDUFF.

Macd. O horror, horror, horror! Tongue nor heart Cannot conceive nor name thee!
Macb.⎫
Len. ⎬   What 's the matter? 70
Macd. Confusion now hath made his masterpiece! Most sacrilegious murder hath broke ope The Lord's anointed temple, and stole thence The life o' the building!
Macb.   What is 't you say? the life?
Len. Mean you his majesty?
Macd. Approach the chamber, and destroy your sight With a new Gorgon: do not bid me speak; See, and then speak yourselves.

[*Exeunt Macbeth and Lennox.*]

      Awake, awake!
Ring the alarum-bell. Murder and treason!
Banquo and Donalbain! Malcolm! awake! 80
Shake off this downy sleep, death's counterfeit,
And look on death itself! up, up, and see
The great doom's image! Malcolm! Banquo!
As from your graves rise up, and walk like sprites,
To countenance this horror! Ring the bell. [*Bell rings.*

Enter LADY MACBETH.

Lady M. What 's the business, That such a hideous trumpet calls to parley The sleepers of the house? speak, speak!
Macd.   O gentle lady, 'Tis not for you to hear what I can speak: The repetition, in a woman's ear, 90 Would murder as it fell.

Enter BANQUO.

      O Banquo, Banquo, Our royal master's murder'd!
Lady M.   Woe, alas!

SCENE III. 2. **porter of hell-gate.** The game the porter plays with himself is based on the mystery play, *Harrowing of Hell*, in which Christ knocks at the gate of Hell, supplied, we may believe, with a humorous porter. 3. **old,** colloquial use, as in "a high old time." 5-6. **Here 's a farmer . . . plenty.** This is thought to allude to the conditions of the year 1606 when there were abundant harvests and low prices. 7. **come in time,** you have come in good time. 10. **equivocator.** This is regarded as an allusion to the trial of the Jesuit Henry Garnet for treason in the spring of 1606, and to the doctrine of equivocation said to have been presented in his defense; according to this doctrine a lie was not a lie if the utterer had in his mind a different meaning in which the utterance was true. 17. **French hose,** very narrow breeches and therefore hard for the tailor to steal cloth from when he made them. 18. **goose,** tailor's smoothing iron. 27. **cock,** cockcrow. 51. **timely,** betimes, early. 52. **slipp'd,** let slip. 55. **physics,** cures. 57. **limited,** appointed. 64. **obscure bird,** owl, the bird of darkness. 71. **Confusion,** destruction. 73. **The Lord's anointed temple,** allusion to the king as God's anointed representative. 77. **Gorgon,** allusion to the monsters of Greek mythology whose look turned the beholders to stone. 85. **countenance,** be in keeping with. 98. **mortality,** mortal life.

What, in our house?
  Ban.   Too cruel any where.
Dear Duff, I prithee, contradict thyself,
And say it is not so.

  Re-enter MACBETH *and* LENNOX, *with* ROSS.

  Macb. Had I but died an hour before this chance,
I had lived a blessed time; for, from this instant,
There 's nothing serious in mortality:
All is but toys: renown and grace is dead;
The wine of life is drawn, and the mere lees   100
Is left this vault to brag of.

  Enter MALCOLM *and* DONALBAIN.

  Don. What is amiss?
  Macb.   You are, and do not know 't:
The spring, the head, the fountain of your blood
Is stopp'd; the very source of it is stopp'd.
  Macd. Your royal father 's murdered.
  Mal.   O, by whom?
  Len. Those of his chamber, as it seem'd, had done 't:
Their hands and faces were all badged with blood;
So were their daggers, which unwiped we found
Upon their pillows:
They stared, and were distracted; no man's life   110
Was to be trusted with them.
  Macb. O, yet I do repent me of my fury,
That I did kill them.
  Macd.   Wherefore did you so?
  Macb. Who can be wise, amazed, temperate and
    furious,
Loyal and neutral, in a moment? No man:
The expedition of my violent love
Outrun the pauser, reason. Here lay Duncan,
His silver skin laced with his golden blood;
And his gash'd stabs look'd like a breach in nature
For ruin's wasteful entrance: there, the murderers, 120
Steep'd in the colours of their trade, their daggers
Unmannerly breech'd with gore: who could refrain,
That had a heart to love, and in that heart
Courage to make 's love known?
  Lady M.   Help me hence, ho!
  Macd. Look to the lady.
  Mal.   [*Aside to Don.*] Why do we hold
    our tongues,
That most may claim this argument for ours?
  Don. [*Aside to Mal.*] What should be spoken here,
    where our fate,
Hid in an auger-hole, may rush, and seize us?
Let 's away;
Our tears are not yet brew'd.
  Mal.   [*Aside to Don.*] Nor our strong
    sorrow   130
Upon the foot of motion.
  Ban.   Look to the lady:
                [Lady Macbeth is carried out.
And when we have our naked frailties hid,
That suffer in exposure, let us meet,

And question this most bloody piece of work,
To know it further. Fears and scruples shake us:
In the great hand of God I stand; and thence
Against the undivulged pretence I fight
Of treasonous malice.
  Macd.   And so do I.
  All.   So all.
  Macb. Let 's briefly put on manly readiness,
And meet i' the hall together.
  All.   Well contented.   140
                [Exeunt all but Malcolm and Donalbain.
  Mal. What will you do? Let 's not consort with
    them:
To show an unfelt sorrow is an office
Which the false man does easy. I'll to England.
  Don. To Ireland, I; our separated fortune
Shall keep us both the safer: where we are,
There 's daggers in men's smiles: the near in blood,
The nearer bloody.
  Mal.   This murderous shaft that 's
    shot
Hath not yet lighted, and our safest way
Is to avoid the aim. Therefore, to horse;
And let us not be dainty of leave-taking,   150
But shift away: there 's warrant in that theft
Which steals itself, when there 's no mercy left. [*Exeunt.*

  SCENE IV. *Outside Macbeth's castle.*

  Enter ROSS *and an old Man.*

  Old M. Threescore and ten I can remember well:
Within the volume of which time I have seen
Hours dreadful and things strange; but this sore night
Hath trifled former knowings.
  Ross.   Ah, good father,
Thou seest, the heavens, as troubled with man's act,
Threaten his bloody stage: by the clock, 'tis day,
And yet dark night strangles the travelling lamp:
Is 't night's predominance, or the day's shame,
That darkness does the face of earth entomb,
When living light should kiss it?
  Old M.   'Tis unnatural,   10
Even like the deed that 's done. On Tuesday last,
A falcon, towering in her pride of place,
Was by a mousing owl hawk'd at and kill'd.
  Ross. And Duncan's horses—a thing most strange
    and certain—
Beauteous and swift, the minions of their race,
Turn'd wild in nature, broke their stalls, flung out,
Contending 'gainst obedience, as they would make
War with mankind.
  Old M.   'Tis said they eat each other.
  Ross. They did so, to the amazement of mine eyes
That look'd upon 't. Here comes the good Macduff.   20

  Enter MACDUFF.

How goes the world, sir, now?

---

107. **badged,** marked as with a badge or emblem. 116. **expedition,**
haste. 122. **breech'd,** covered to the hilts with gore (as with breeches).
124. **Help me hence, ho!** This timely fainting of Lady Macbeth is
usually taken as pretense in order to make a diversion in behalf of her
husband, but it need not be so understood. 128. **in an auger-hole,** in
some obscure place. 136-138. **and thence . . . malice.** With God's help
I will fight against the as-yet-unknown purpose which prompted this
treason. If Banquo here suspects Macbeth, nothing comes of it, for
when we next see him he is a loyal servant to the new king. 139.
manly readiness, men's clothing, or armor. 143. **easy,** easily. 146.

near, nearer, i.e., the nearer in relationship the greater the danger
of being murdered. 148. **lighted,** descended.
  SCENE IV. 4. **trifled . . . knowings,** made trivial all former knowledge.
8. **predominance,** ascendancy, superior influence (of a heavenly body).
12. **towering,** soaring (term in falconry). **place,** pitch, highest point in
the falcon's flight. 14. **horses,** pronounced as one syllable, indicating
the old form of the plural then in common use.

Macd.   Why, see you not?
Ross. Is 't known who did this more than bloody
    deed?
Macd. Those that Macbeth hath slain.
Ross.   Alas, the day!
What good could they pretend?
Macd.   They were suborn'd:
Malcolm and Donalbain, the king's two sons,
Are stol'n away and fled; which puts upon them
Suspicion of the deed.
Ross.   'Gainst nature still!
Thriftless ambition, that wilt ravin up
Thine own life's means! Then 'tis most like
The sovereignty will fall upon Macbeth.   30
Macd. He is already named, and gone to Scone
To be invested.
Ross.   Where is Duncan's body?
Macd. Carried to Colmekill,
The sacred storehouse of his predecessors,
And guardian of their bones.
Ross.   Will you to Scone?
Macd. No, cousin, I'll to Fife.
Ross.   Well, I will thither.
Macd. Well, may you see things well done there:
    adieu!
Lest our old robes sit easier than our new!
Ross. Farewell, father.
Old M. God's benison go with you; and with those
That would make good of bad, and friends of foes!   41
                                        [*Exeunt.*

ACT III.

SCENE I. *Forres. The palace.*

Enter BANQUO.

Ban. Thou hast it now: king, Cawdor, Glamis, all,
As the weird women promised, and, I fear,
Thou play'dst most foully for 't: yet it was said
It should not stand in thy posterity,
But that myself should be the root and father
Of many kings. If there come truth from them—
As upon thee, Macbeth, their speeches shine—
Why, by the verities on thee made good,
May they not be my oracles as well,
And set me up in hope? But hush! no more.   10

Sennet sounded. Enter MACBETH, *as king,* LADY
    MACBETH, *as queen,* LENNOX, ROSS, Lords, Ladies,
    and Attendants.

Macb. Here 's our chief guest.
Lady M.   If he had been forgotten,
It had been as a gap in our great feast,
And all-thing unbecoming.
Macb. To-night we hold a solemn supper, sir,
And I'll request your presence.
Ban.   Let your highness

Command upon me; to the which my duties
Are with a most indissoluble tie
For ever knit.
Macb. Ride you this afternoon?
Ban. Ay, my good lord.   20
Macb. We should have else desired your good
    advice,
Which still hath been both grave and prosperous,
In this day's council; but we'll take to-morrow.
Is 't far you ride?
Ban. As far, my lord, as will fill up the time
'Twixt this and supper: go not my horse the better,
I must become a borrower of the night
For a dark hour or twain.
Macb.   Fail not our feast.
Ban. My lord, I will not.
Macb. We hear, our bloody cousins are bestow'd   30
In England and in Ireland, not confessing
Their cruel parricide, filling their hearers
With strange invention: but of that to-morrow,
When therewithal we shall have cause of state
Craving us jointly. Hie you to horse: adieu,
Till you return at night. Goes Fleance with you?
Ban. Ay, my good lord: our time does call upon 's.
Macb. I wish your horses swift and sure of foot;
And so I do commend you to their backs.
Farewell.   [*Exit Banquo.* 40
Let every man be master of his time
Till seven at night: to make society
The sweeter welcome, we will keep ourself
Till supper-time alone: while then, God be with you!
                    [*Exeunt all but Macbeth, and an attendant.*
Sirrah, a word with you: attend those men
Our pleasure?
Atten. They are, my lord, without the palace gate.
Macb. Bring them before us.   [*Exit Attendant.*
                    To be thus is nothing;
But to be safely thus.—Our fears in Banquo
Stick deep; and in his royalty of nature   50
Reigns that which would be fear'd: 'tis much he
    dares;
And, to that dauntless temper of his mind,
He hath a wisdom that doth guide his valour
To act in safety. There is none but he
Whose being I do fear: and, under him,
My Genius is rebuked; as, it is said,
Mark Antony's was by Cæsar. He chid the sisters
When first they put the name of king upon me,
And bade them speak to him: then prophet-like
They hail'd him father to a line of kings: 60
Upon my head they placed a fruitless crown,
And put a barren sceptre in my gripe,
Thence to be wrench'd with an unlineal hand,
No son of mine succeeding. If 't be so,
For Banquo's issue have I filed my mind;
For them the gracious Duncan have I murder'd;
Put rancours in the vessel of my peace
Only for them; and mine eternal jewel

---

24. **pretend,** intend, design.   **suborn'd,** procured to do an evil action.
28. **ravin up,** devour ravenously.   31. **Scone,** ancient royal city of
Scotland near Perth. The stone of Scone, on which Jacob rested his
head at Bethel, was carried to England by Edward I. It has ever since
formed a part of the coronation chair of English kings in Westminster
Abbey.   33. **Colmekill,** Icolmkill, i.e., Cell of St. Columba, the barren
islet of Iona in the Western Islands, a sacred spot where the kings were
buried; here called a *storehouse.*   40. **benison,** blessing.
    ACT III. SCENE I.   7. **shine,** are brilliantly manifest.   13. **all-thing,**
in every way.   14. **solemn,** ceremonious.   30. **bestow'd,** lodged.   34.

cause **of state,** questions of state.   44. **while,** till.   48-49. **To ... thus.**
This is explained in several ways, of which the following is perhaps
correct: "To be thus (i.e., on the throne) is nothing unless we are
safely on the throne."   52-54. **to that ... safety.** Macbeth here attributes to Banquo the perfect virtue of courage.   56. **My Genius.**
This passage is a borrowing from Plutarch's *Life of Antony;* Antony's
good angel was abashed before that of Octavius. Cf. *Antony and Cleopatra,*
II, iii.   62. **gripe,** grasp.   65. **filed,** defiled.   68-69. **mine ... man.**
Macbeth had understood his bargain when he professed a willingness to
jump the life to come (I, vii, 7); he here acknowledges it.   71. **list,** lists, place

Given to the common enemy of man,
To make them kings, the seed of Banquo kings! 70
Rather than so, come fate into the list,
And champion me to the utterance! Who 's there?

Re-enter Attendant, *with two* Murderers.

Now go to the door, and stay there till we call.
[*Exit Attendant.*
Was it not yesterday we spoke together?
  First Mur. It was, so please your highness.
  Macb.   Well then, now
Have you consider'd of my speeches? Know
That it was he in the times past which held you
So under fortune, which you thought had been
Our innocent self: this I made good to you
In our last conference, pass'd in probation with you, 80
How you were borne in hand, how cross'd, the
    instruments,
Who wrought with them, and all things else that
    might
To half a soul and to a notion crazed
Say 'Thus did Banquo.'
  First Mur.   You made it known to us.
  Macb. I did so, and went further, which is now
Our point of second meeting. Do you find
Your patience so predominant in your nature
That you can let this go? Are you so gospell'd
To pray for this good man and for his issue,
Whose heavy hand hath bow'd you to the grave 90
And beggar'd yours for ever?
  First Mur.   We are men, my liege.
  Macb. Ay, in the catalogue ye go for men;
As hounds and greyhounds, mongrels, spaniels, curs,
Shoughs, water-rugs and demi-wolves are clept
All by the name of dogs: the valued file
Distinguishes the swift, the slow, the subtle,
The housekeeper, the hunter, every one
According to the gift which bounteous nature
Hath in him closed, whereby he does receive
Particular addition, from the bill 100
That writes them all alike: and so of men.
Now, if you have a station in the file,
Not i' the worst rank of manhood, say 't;
And I will put that business in your bosoms,
Whose execution takes your enemy off,
Grapples you to the heart and love of us,
Who wear our health but sickly in his life,
Which in his death were perfect.
  Sec. Mur.   I am one, my liege,
Whom the vile blows and buffets of the world
Have so incensed that I am reckless what 110
I do to spite the world.
  First Mur.   And I another
So weary with disasters, tugg'd with fortune,
That I would set my life on any chance,
To mend it, or be rid on 't.
  Macb.   Both of you
Know Banquo was your enemy.

  Both Mur.   True, my lord.
  Macb. So is he mine; and in such bloody distance,
That every minute of his being thrusts
Against my near'st of life: and though I could
With barefaced power sweep him from my sight
And bid my will avouch it, yet I must not, 120
For certain friends that are both his and mine,
Whose loves I may not drop, but wail his fall
Who I myself struck down; and thence it is,
That I to your assistance do make love,
Masking the business from the common eye
For sundry weighty reasons.
  Sec. Mur.   We shall, my lord,
Perform what you command us.
  First Mur.   Though our lives—
  Macb. Your spirits shine through you. Within this
    hour at most
I will advise you where to plant yourselves;
Acquaint you with the perfect spy o' the time, 130
The moment on 't; for 't must be done to-night,
And something from the palace; always thought
That I require a clearness: and with him—
To leave no rubs nor botches in the work—
Fleance his son, that keeps him company,
Whose absence is no less material to me
Than is his father's, must embrace the fate
Of that dark hour. Resolve yourselves apart:
I'll come to you anon.
  Both Mur.   We are resolved, my lord.
  Macb. I'll call upon you straight: abide within. 140
                   [*Exeunt Murderers.*
It is concluded. Banquo, thy soul's flight,
If it find heaven, must find it out to-night.   [*Exit.*

SCENE II. *The palace.*

Enter LADY MACBETH *and a* Servant.

  Lady M. Is Banquo gone from court?
  Serv. Ay, madam, but returns again to-night.
  Lady M. Say to the king, I would attend his leisure
For a few words.
  Serv.   Madam, I will.   [*Exit.*
  Lady M.   Nought 's had, all 's
    spent,
Where our desire is got without content:
'Tis safer to be that which we destroy
Than by destruction dwell in doubtful joy.

Enter MACBETH.

How now, my lord! why do you keep alone,
Of sorriest fancies your companions making, 9
Using those thoughts which should indeed have died
With them they think on? Things without all remedy
Should be without regard: what 's done is done.
  Macb. We have scotch'd the snake, not kill'd it:
She'll close and be herself, whilst our poor malice
Remains in danger of her former tooth.

of combat. **72. champion me,** fight with me in single combat. **to the utterance,** to the last extremity; French *à l'outrance.* **80. probation,** proof, i.e., in detail. **81. borne in hand,** deceived (by false promises). **83. notion,** mind. **88. gospell'd,** imbued with the gospel spirit. **94. Shoughs,** a kind of shaggy dog, called also *shocks.* **water-rugs,** rough water dogs (?) **demi-wolves,** apparently a crossbreed with the wolf. **clept,** called. **95. valued file,** list classified according to value. **97. housekeeper,** watchdog. **100. Particular . . . bill,** particular qualification apart from the catalog. **112. tugg'd with,** pulled about by (as in wrestling). It is plain that these are not professional murderers, but

desperate men. **116. distance,** hostility. **118. near'st of life,** most vital interests. **120. avouch,** warrant, i.e., destroy him as an act of royal will. **128. Your . . . you,** i.e., the spirits of hatred and revenge rise into their faces. **130. perfect spy o' the time,** knowledge or espial of the exact time; many conjectures. **132. thought,** being borne in mind. **133. clearness,** freedom from suspicion.
    SCENE II. **13. scotch'd,** cut, gashed, so Theobald; F: *scotch'd,* which had perhaps the same meaning (Neilson).

But let the frame of things disjoint, both the worlds
    suffer,
Ere we will eat our meal in fear and sleep
In the affliction of these terrible dreams
That shake us nightly: better be with the dead,
Whom we, to gain our peace, have sent to peace,   20
Than on the torture of the mind to lie
In restless ecstasy. Duncan is in his grave;
After life's fitful fever he sleeps well;
Treason has done his worst: nor steel, nor poison,
Malice domestic, foreign levy, nothing,
Can touch him further.
    Lady M.   Come on;
Gentle my lord, sleek o'er your rugged looks;
Be bright and jovial among your guests to-night.
    Macb. So shall I, love; and so, I pray, be you:
Let your remembrance apply to Banquo;   30
Present him eminence, both with eye and tongue:
†Unsafe the while, that we
Must lave our honours in these flattering streams,
And make our faces vizards to our hearts,
Disguising what they are.
    Lady M.   You must leave this.
    Macb. O, full of scorpions is my mind, dear wife!
Thou know'st that Banquo, and his Fleance, lives.
    Lady M. But in them nature's copy 's not eterne.
    Macb. There 's comfort yet; they are assailable;
Then be thou jocund: ere the bat hath flown   40
His cloister'd flight, ere to black Hecate's summons
The shard-borne beetle with his drowsy hums
Hath rung night's yawning peal, there shall be done
A deed of dreadful note.
    Lady M.   What 's to be done?
    Macb. Be innocent of the knowledge, dearest chuck,
Till thou applaud the deed. Come, seeling night,
Scarf up the tender eye of pitiful day;
And with thy bloody and invisible hand
Cancel and tear to pieces that great bond
Which keeps me pale! Light thickens; and the crow   50
Makes wing to the rooky wood:
Good things of day begin to droop and drowse;
Whiles night's black agents to their preys do rouse.
Thou marvell'st at my words: but hold thee still:
Things bad begun make strong themselves by ill.
So, prithee, go with me.   [*Exeunt.*

SCENE III. *A park near the palace.*

Enter three Murderers.

First Mur. But who did bid thee join with us?
Third Mur.   Macbeth.
Sec. Mur. He needs not our mistrust, since he
    delivers
Our offices and what we have to do
To the direction just.
    First Mur.   Then stand with us.

The west yet glimmers with some streaks of day.
Now spurs the lated traveller apace
To gain the timely inn; and near approaches
The subject of our watch.
    Third Mur.   Hark! I hear horses.
    Ban. [*Within*] Give us a light there, ho!
    Sec. Mur.   Then 'tis he: the rest
That are within the note of expectation   10
Already are i' the court.
    First Mur.   His horses go about.
    Third Mur. Almost a mile: but he does usually,
So all men do, from hence to the palace gate
Make it their walk.
    Sec. Mur.   A light, a light!

Enter BANQUO, *and* FLEANCE *with a torch.*
    Third Mur.   'Tis he.
    First Mur. Stand to 't.
    Ban. It will be rain to-night.
    First Mur.   Let it come down.
                    [*They set upon Banquo.*
    Ban. O, treachery! Fly, good Fleance, fly, fly, fly!
Thou mayst revenge. O slave!   [*Dies. Fleance escapes.*
    Third Mur. Who did strike out the light?
    First Mur.   Was 't not the way?
    Third Mur. There 's but one down; the son is fled.
    Sec. Mur.   We have lost   20
Best half of our affair.
    First Mur. Well, let 's away, and say how much is
    done.   [*Exeunt.*

SCENE IV. *The same. Hall in the palace.*

A banquet prepared. Enter MACBETH, LADY MACBETH,
ROSS, LENNOX, Lords, *and* Attendants.

    Macb. You know your own degrees; sit down: at
    first
And last the hearty welcome.
    Lords.   Thanks to your majesty.
    Macb. Ourself will mingle with society,
And play the humble host.
Our hostess keeps her state, but in best time
We will require her welcome.
    Lady M. Pronounce it for me, sir, to all our friends;
For my heart speaks they are welcome.

First Murderer *appears at the door.*
    Macb. See, they encounter thee with their hearts'
    thanks.
Both sides are even: here I'll sit i' the midst: 10
Be large in mirth; anon we'll drink a measure
The table round. [*Approaching the door.*] There 's blood
    upon thy face.
    Mur. 'Tis Banquo's then.
    Macb. 'Tis better thee without than he within.
Is he dispatch'd?
    Mur. My lord, his throat is cut; that I did for him.

16. **frame of things,** universe. **both the worlds suffer,** heaven and earth perish. 27. **sleek o'er,** smooth. 31. **Present him eminence,** distinguish him with favor. Macbeth has apparently not confided his plot to his wife, yet it is hard to see why he gives her these directions. 32-33. **Unsafe . . . streams,** we are unsafe so long as we have to keep our dignities unsullied by means of flattery. The text is probably corrupt. 34. **vizards,** masks. 38. **nature's copy,** lease of life (i.e., by copyhold); possibly, man. **eterne,** perpetual. 42. **shard-borne,** borne on shards, or horny wing cases. 43. **yawning,** drowsy. 44. **note,** significance. 45. **chuck,** term of endearment. 46. **seeling,** eye-closing. Night is pictured here as a falconer sewing up the eyes of day lest it should struggle

against the deed that is to be done (Parrott). 47. **Scarf-up,** blindfold. 49. **bond,** Banquo's lease of life. 51. **rooky,** full of rooks.
    SCENE III. 2-3. **He . . . offices,** we need not mistrust him, since he reports upon our business. 4. **To,** according to. **just,** exactly. That is, they know he comes from Macbeth; it has been thought by certain ingenious critics that the Third Murderer is Macbeth. 6. **lated,** belated. 10. **note of expectation,** list of those expected.
    SCENE IV. 1. **degrees,** ranks. 1-2. **at first And last,** from the beginning to the end (of the feast). 6. **require,** request. 14. **'Tis better . . . within.** It is better for it to be on the outside of thee than on the inside of him; sometimes explained as "better that his blood shou'.

Macb. Thou art the best o' the cut-throats: yet he 's good
That did the like for Fleance: if thou didst it,
Thou art the nonpareil.
Mur. Most royal sir,
Fleance is 'scaped. 20
Macb. Then comes my fit again: I had else been perfect,
Whole as the marble, founded as the rock,
As broad and general as the casing air:
But now I am cabin'd, cribb'd, confined, bound in
To saucy doubts and fears. But Banquo 's safe?
Mur. Ay, my good lord: safe in a ditch he bides,
With twenty trenched gashes on his head;
The least a death to nature.
Macb. Thanks for that.
There the grown serpent lies; the worm that 's fled
Hath nature that in time will venom breed, 30
No teeth for the present. Get thee gone: to-morrow
We'll hear, ourselves, again. [*Exit Murderer.*
Lady M. My royal lord,
You do not give the cheer: the feast is sold
That is not often vouch'd, while 'tis a-making,
'Tis given with welcome: to feed were best at home;
From thence the sauce to meat is ceremony;
Meeting were bare without it.
Macb. Sweet remembrancer!
Now, good digestion wait on appetite,
And health on both!
Len. May 't please your highness sit.
[*The Ghost of Banquo enters, and sits in Macbeth's place.*

Macb. Here had we now our country's honour roof'd, 40
Were the graced person of our Banquo present;
Who may I rather challenge for unkindness
Than pity for mischance!
Ross. His absence, sir,
Lays blame upon his promise. Please 't your highness
To grace us with your royal company.
Macb. The table 's full.
Len. Here is a place reserved, sir.
Macb. Where?
Len. Here, my good lord. What is 't that moves your highness?
Macb. Which of you have done this?
Lords. What, my good lord?
Macb. Thou canst not say I did it: never shake 50
Thy gory locks at me.
Ross. Gentlemen rise; his highness is not well.
Lady M. Sit, worthy friends: my lord is often thus,
And hath been from his youth: pray you, keep seat;
The fit is momentary; upon a thought
He will again be well: if much you note him,
You shall offend him and extend his passion:
Feed, and regard him not. Are you a man?
Macb. Ay, and a bold one, that dare look on that
Which might appal the devil.

Lady M. O proper stuff! 60
This is the very painting of your fear:
This is the air-drawn dagger which, you said,
Led you to Duncan. O, these flaws and starts,
Impostors to true fear, would well become
A woman's story at a winter's fire,
Authorized by her grandam. Shame itself!
Why do you make such faces? When all 's done,
You look but on a stool.
Macb. Prithee, see there! behold! look! lo! how say you?
Why, what care I? If thou canst nod, speak too. 70
If charnel-houses and our graves must send
Those that we bury back, our monuments
Shall be the maws of kites. [*Ghost vanishes.*
Lady M. What, quite unmann'd in folly?
Macb. If I stand here, I saw him.
Lady M. Fie, for shame!
Macb. Blood hath been shed ere now, i' the olden time,
Ere humane statute purged the gentle weal;
Ay, and since too, murders have been perform'd
Too terrible for the ear: the time has been,
That, when the brains were out, the man would die,
And there an end; but now they rise again, 80
With twenty mortal murders on their crowns,
And push us from our stools: this is more strange
Than such a murder is.
Lady M. My worthy lord,
Your noble friends do lack you.
Macb. I do forget.
Do not muse at me, my most worthy friends;
I have a strange infirmity, which is nothing
To those that know me. Come, love and health to all;
Then I'll sit down. Give me some wine; fill full.
I drink to the general joy o' the whole table,
And to our dear friend Banquo, whom we miss; 90
Would he were here! to all, and him, we thirst,
And all to all.
Lords. Our duties, and the pledge.

Re-enter Ghost.

Macb. Avaunt! and quit my sight! let the earth hide thee!
Thy bones are marrowless, thy blood is cold;
Thou hast no speculation in those eyes
Which thou dost glare with!
Lady M. Think of this, good peers,
But as a thing of custom: 'tis no other;
Only it spoils the pleasure of the time.
Macb. What man dare, I dare:
Approach thou like the rugged Russian bear, 100
The arm'd rhinoceros, or the Hyrcan tiger;
Take any shape but that, and my firm nerves
Shall never tremble: or be alive again,
And dare me to the desert with thy sword;
†If trembling I inhabit then, protest me

be on thy face than he in this room." 20. **Fleance is 'scaped.** If *Macbeth* is regarded as a tragedy of fate, this must be taken as marking its turning point. 23. **casing,** enveloping. 24-25. **bound in To,** confined along with. 25. **saucy,** sharp (Koppel); impudent (Schmidt). 26. **bides,** lies. 29. **worm,** small serpent. 32. **hear, ourselves,** talk it over. 34. **vouch'd,** assurance given that it is not sold like a meal at an inn. 40. **roof'd,** under one roof. 41. **graced,** gracious. 42. **Who may I,** whom I hope I may. 55. **upon a thought,** in a moment. 57. **extend,** prolong. 60. **O proper stuff!** O veritable nonsense! 64. **to,** compared with. 73. **maws,** stomachs. If the body were devoured by kites, the ghost could not rise. 76. **humane.** This spelling carried

both meanings: "appertaining to mankind" and "befitting man." **purged . . . weal,** cleansed the commonwealth of violence and made it gentle. 81. **mortal murders,** deadly wounds. 84. **lack,** miss. 91. **thirst,** desire to drink. 92. **all to all,** all good wishes to all. 93. **Avaunt!** Note the recoil to the courage of desperation, which Macbeth was to show again in the last moment of his life. 95. **speculation,** light of living intellect; also defined as "power of sight." 100-101. **bear . . . tiger.** Bears of Russia and tigers of Hyrcania were types of ferocity. 101. **arm'd,** sheathed in armor. 105. **If . . . then,** if then I tremble (i.e., put on trembling as a garment). Some editors prefer the reading due to Pope and Steevens: *If trembling I inhibit thee.*

The baby of a girl. Hence, horrible shadow!
Unreal mockery, hence! [*Ghost vanishes.*
                    Why, so: being gone,
I am a man again. Pray you, sit still.
  Lady M. You have displaced the mirth, broke the
      good meeting,
With most admired disorder.
  Macb.   Can such things be,   110
And overcome us like a summer's cloud,
Without our special wonder? You make me strange
Even to the disposition that I owe,
When now I think you can behold such sights,
And keep the natural ruby of your cheeks,
When mine is blanch'd with fear.
  Ross.   What sights, my lord?
  Lady M. I pray you, speak not; he grows worse and
      worse;
Question enrages him. At once, good night:
Stand not upon the order of your going,
But go at once.
  Len.   Good night; and better health   120
Attend his majesty!
  Lady M.   A kind good night to all!
        [*Exeunt all but Macbeth and Lady M.*
  Macb. It will have blood; they say, blood will have
      blood:
Stones have been known to move and trees to speak;
Augurs and understood relations have
By magot-pies and choughs and rooks brought forth
The secret'st man of blood. What is the night?
  Lady M. Almost at odds with morning, which is
      which.
  Macb. How say'st thou, that Macduff denies his
      person
At our great bidding?
  Lady M.   Did you send to him, sir?
  Macb. I hear it by the way; but I will send: 130
There 's not a one of them but in his house
I keep a servant fee'd. I will to-morrow,
And betimes I will, to the weird sisters:
More shall they speak; for now I am bent to know,
By the worst means, the worst. For mine own good,
All causes shall give way: I am in blood
Stepp'd in so far that, should I wade no more,
Returning were as tedious as go o'er:
Strange things I have in head, that will to hand;
Which must be acted ere they may be scann'd.   140
  Lady M. You lack the season of all natures, sleep.
  Macb. Come, we'll to sleep. My strange and
      self-abuse
Is the initiate fear that wants hard use:
We are yet but young in deed.   [*Exeunt.*

─────────

SCENE V. A Heath.

Thunder. Enter the three Witches, *meeting* HECATE.

  First Witch. Why, how now, Hecate! you look
      angerly.

Macbeth
ACT III : SC IV

1060

  Hec. Have I not reason, beldams as you are,
Saucy and overbold? How did you dare
To trade and traffic with Macbeth
In riddles and affairs of death;
And I, the mistress of your charms,
The close contriver of all harms,
Was never call'd to bear my part,
Or show the glory of our art?
And, which is worse, all you have done   10
Hath been but for a wayward son,
Spiteful and wrathful, who, as others do,
Loves for his own ends, not for you.
But make amends now: get you gone,
And at the pit of Acheron
Meet me i' the morning: thither he
Will come to know his destiny:
Your vessels and your spells provide,
Your charms and every thing beside.
I am for the air; this night I'll spend   20
Unto a dismal and a fatal end:
Great business must be wrought ere noon:
Upon the corner of the moon
There hangs a vaporous drop profound;
I'll catch it ere it come to ground:
And that distill'd by magic sleights
Shall raise such artificial sprites
As by the strength of their illusion
Shall draw him on to his confusion:
He shall spurn fate, scorn death, and bear   30
His hopes 'bove wisdom, grace and fear:
And you all know, security
Is mortals' chiefest enemy.
    [*Music and a song within:* 'Come away, come
                    away,' &c.
Hark! I am call'd; my little spirit, see,
Sits in a foggy cloud, and stays for me.   [*Exit.*
  First Witch. Come, let 's make haste; she'll soon be
      back again.   [*Exeunt.*

─────────

SCENE VI. Forres. The palace.

Enter LENNOX *and another* Lord.

  Len. My former speeches have but hit your
      thoughts,
Which can interpret further: only, I say,
Things have been strangely borne. The gracious
      Duncan
Was pitied of Macbeth: marry, he was dead:
And the right-valiant Banquo walk'd too late;
Whom, you may say, if 't please you, Fleance kill'd,
For Fleance fled: men must not walk too late.
Who cannot want the thought how monstrous
It was for Malcolm and for Donalbain
To kill their gracious father? damned fact!   10
How it did grieve Macbeth! did he not straight
In pious rage the two delinquents tear,
That were the slaves of drink and thralls of sleep?

<hr>

106. **baby of a girl,** (puny) infant of an immature mother; some editors
prefer "*girl's doll.*" 109. **displaced,** banished. 119. **Stand . . . order,**
do not wait for the ceremonies. 123. **Stones,** thought to be an allusion
to rocking-stones or great stones so balanced on their foundations that
they can be rocked with little effort. 124. **Augurs,** probably, auguries.
understood relations, secret mystical connections. 125. **magot-pies,**
magpies. 141. **season,** seasoning, relish. 142. **self-abuse,** self-delu-
sion. 143. **initiate,** of the beginner. **use,** experience. Macbeth will
accustom himself to crime and thus grow indifferent and bold. His

new theory is already signalized by his trembling defiance of Banquo's
ghost, his independence of Lady Macbeth, and his half-formed plot
against Macduff.

  SCENE V. Practically all critics agree that this scene is not by
Shakespeare. 15. **Acheron,** a river of hell. 24. **profound,** ready to
drop (?) of deep significance (?) 27. **artificial,** produced by magical
arts. 32. **security,** confidence, overconfidence.

  SCENE VI. 8. **want the thought,** help thinking. 13. **thralls,** slaves.
21. **from,** on account of. **broad,** open, plain. 22. **tyrant's,** usurper's.

Was not that nobly done? Ay, and wisely too;
For 'twould have anger'd any heart alive
To hear the men deny 't. So that, I say,
He has borne all things well: and I do think
That had he Duncan's sons under his key—
As, an 't please heaven, he shall not—they should find
What 'twere to kill a father; so should Fleance. 20
But, peace! for from broad words and 'cause he fail'd
His presence at the tyrant's feast, I hear
Macduff lives in disgrace: sir, can you tell
Where he bestows himself?
   Lord.   The son of Duncan,
From whom this tyrant holds the due of birth,
Lives in the English court, and is received
Of the most pious Edward with such grace
That the malevolence of fortune nothing
Takes from his high respect: thither Macduff
Is gone to pray the holy king, upon his aid 30
To wake Northumberland and warlike Siward:
That, by the help of these—with Him above
To ratify the work—we may again
Give to our tables meat, sleep to our nights,
Free from our feasts and banquets bloody knives,
Do faithful homage and receive free honours:
All which we pine for now: and this report
Hath so exasperate the king that he
Prepares for some attempt of war.
   Len.   Sent he to Macduff?
   Lord. He did: and with an absolute 'Sir, not I,' 40
The cloudy messenger turns me his back,
And hums, as who should say 'You'll rue the time
That clogs me with this answer.'
   Len.   And that well might
Advise him to a caution, to hold what distance
His wisdom can provide. Some holy angel
Fly to the court of England and unfold
His message ere he come, that a swift blessing
May soon return to this our suffering country
Under a hand accursed!
   Lord.   I'll send my prayers with him.
                                      [*Exeunt.*

ACT IV.

SCENE I. *A cavern. In the middle, a boiling cauldron.*

Thunder. Enter the three Witches.

First Witch. Thrice the brinded cat hath mew'd.
Sec. Witch. Thrice and once the hedge-pig whined.
Third Witch. Harpier cries 'Tis time, 'tis time.
First Witch. Round about the cauldron go;
In the poison'd entrails throw.
†Toad, that under cold stone
Days and nights has thirty one
Swelter'd venom sleeping got,
Boil thou first i' the charmed pot.
   All. Double, double toil and trouble; 10

Fire burn, and cauldron bubble.
   Sec. Witch. Fillet of a fenny snake,
In the cauldron boil and bake;
Eye of newt and toe of frog,
Wool of bat and tongue of dog,
Adder's fork and blind-worm's sting,
Lizard's leg and howlet's wing,
For a charm of powerful trouble,
Like a hell-broth boil and bubble.
   All. Double, double toil and trouble; 20
Fire burn and cauldron bubble.
   Third Witch. Scale of dragon, tooth of wolf,
Witches' mummy, maw and gulf
Of the ravin'd salt-sea shark,
Root of hemlock digg'd i' the dark,
Liver of blaspheming Jew,
Gall of goat, and slips of yew
Sliver'd in the moon's eclipse,
Nose of Turk and Tartar's lips,
Finger of birth-strangled babe 30
Ditch-deliver'd by a drab,
Make the gruel thick and slab:
Add thereto a tiger's chaudron,
For the ingredients of our cauldron.
   All. Double, double toil and trouble;
Fire burn and cauldron bubble.
   Sec. Witch. Cool it with a baboon's blood,
Then the charm is firm and good.

Enter HECATE *to the other three Witches.*

   Hec. O, well done! I commend your pains;
And every one shall share i' the gains: 40
And now about the cauldron sing,
Like elves and fairies in a ring,
Enchanting all that you put in.
             [*Music and a song:* 'Black spirits,' &c.
                         [*Hecate retires.*
   Sec. Witch. By the pricking of my thumbs,
Something wicked this way comes.
             Open, locks,
             Whoever knocks!

Enter MACBETH.

   Macb. How now, you secret, black, and midnight hags!
What is 't you do?
   All.   A deed without a name.
   Macb. I conjure you, by that which you profess, 50
Howe'er you come to know it, answer me:
Though you untie the winds and let them fight
Against the churches; though the yesty waves
Confound and swallow navigation up;
Though bladed corn be lodged and trees blown down;
Though castles topple on their warders' heads;
Though palaces and pyramids do slope
Their heads to their foundations; though the treasure
Of nature's germens tumble all together,
Even till destruction sicken; answer me 60
To what I ask you.

27. **Edward,** Edward the Confessor. 30. **upon his aid,** in aid of Malcolm. 35. **Free . . . feasts,** free our feasts from. 36. **free,** freely bestowed, or the honors pertaining to freemen. 40. **absolute,** curt, peremptory. 41. **cloudy,** sullen. 48-49. **suffering country Under,** country suffering under.

ACT IV. SCENE I. 1. **brinded,** marked with streaks (as by fire), brindled. 2. **hedge-pig,** hedgehog. 3. **Harpier,** form doubtful, probably intended for "harpy." 6. **cold,** two syllables. 8. **venom.** The toad was commonly thought to be venomous. 16. **fork,** forked

tongue. **blind-worm,** a harmless kind of snake also called slowworm. 17. **howlet's,** owl's. 23. **gulf,** gullet. 24. **ravin'd,** ravenous. 28. **Sliver'd,** broken off (as a branch). 32. **slab,** viscous, thick. 33. **chaudron,** entrails. 39-43. **O . . . in.** These lines are universally regarded as non-Shakespearean. 53. **yesty,** foamy. 55. **bladed,** in the blade, still green. **corn,** general name for wheat and other grains. **lodged,** thrown down, laid. 59. **nature's germens,** seeds or elements, from which nature operates. 60. **sicken,** be surfeited.

First Witch.　　　　　Speak.
Sec. Witch.　　　　　　Demand.
Third Witch.　　　　　　　　We'll answer.
First Witch. Say, if thou 'dst rather hear it from our
　mouths,
Or from our masters?
Macb.　　　　　Call 'em; let me see 'em.
First Witch. Pour in sow's blood, that hath eaten
Her nine farrow; grease that 's sweaten
From the murderer's gibbet throw
Into the flame.
All.　　　　　Come, high or low;
Thyself and office deftly show!

Thunder. First Apparition : *an armed Head.*

Macb. Tell me, thou unknown power,—
First Witch.　　　　He knows thy thought:
Hear his speech, but say thou nought.　　　　70
First App. Macbeth! Macbeth! Macbeth! beware
　Macduff;
Beware the thane of Fife. Dismiss me. Enough.
　　　　　　　　　　　　　　　　[*Descends.*
Macb. Whate'er thou art, for thy good caution,
　thanks;
Thou hast harp'd my fear aright: but one word
　more,—
First Witch. He will not be commanded: here 's
　another,
More potent than the first.

Thunder. Second Apparition : *a bloody Child.*

Sec. App. Macbeth! Macbeth! Macbeth!
Macb. Had I three ears, I 'ld hear thee.
Sec. App. Be bloody, bold, and resolute; laugh to
　scorn
The power of man, for none of woman born　　80
Shall harm Macbeth.　　　　　　[*Descends.*
Macb. Then live, Macduff: what need I fear of thee?
But yet I'll make assurance double sure,
And take a bond of fate: thou shalt not live;
That I may tell pale-hearted fear it lies,
And sleep in spite of thunder.

Thunder. Third Apparition : *a Child crowned, with a
　tree in his hand.*

　　　　　What is this
That rises like the issue of a king,
And wears upon his baby-brow the round
And top of sovereignty?
All.　　　　　Listen, but speak not to 't.　89
Third App. Be lion-mettled, proud; and take no care
Who chafes, who frets, or where conspirers are :
Macbeth shall never vanquish'd be until
Great Birnam wood to high Dunsinane hill
Shall come against him.　　　　　[*Descends.*
Macb.　　　　That will never be :
Who can impress the forest, bid the tree
Unfix his earth-bound root? Sweet bodements! good!

Rebellion's head, rise never till the wood
Of Birnam rise, and our high-placed Macbeth
Shall live the lease of nature, pay his breath
To time and mortal custom. Yet my heart　　100
Throbs to know one thing: tell me, if your art
Can tell so much: shall Banquo's issue ever
Reign in this kingdom?
All.　　　　　Seek to know no more.
Macb. I will be satisfied: deny me this,
And an eternal curse fall on you! Let me know.
Why sinks that cauldron? and what noise is this?
　　　　　　　　　　　　　　　　[*Hautboys.*

First Witch. Show!
Sec. Witch. Show!
Third Witch. Show!
All. Show his eyes, and grieve his heart;　　110
Come like shadows, so depart!

A show of Eight Kings, *the last with a glass in his hand;
　Banquo's Ghost following.*

Macb. Thou art too like the spirit of Banquo: down!
Thy crown does sear mine eye-balls. And thy hair,
Thou other gold-bound brow, is like the first.
A third is like the former. Filthy hags!
Why do you show me this? A fourth! Start, eyes!
What, will the line stretch out to the crack of doom?
Another yet! A seventh! I'll see no more:
And yet the eighth appears, who bears a glass
Which shows me many more; and some I see　　120
That two-fold balls and treble sceptres carry:
Horrible sight! Now, I see, 'tis true;
For the blood-bolter'd Banquo smiles upon me,
And points at them for his. [*Apparitions vanish.*] What,
　is this so?
First Witch. Ay, sir, all this is so: but why
Stands Macbeth thus amazedly?
Come, sisters, cheer we up his sprites,
And show the best of our delights:
I'll charm the air to give a sound,
While you perform your antic round;　　130
That this great king may kindly say,
Our duties did his welcome pay.
　　　　[*Music. The Witches dance, and then vanish, with
　　　　　　　　　　　　　　　　　Hecate.*

Macb. Where are they? Gone? Let this pernicious
　hour
Stand aye accursed in the calendar!
Come in, without there!

Enter LENNOX.

Len.　　　　　What 's your grace's will?
Macb. Saw you the weird sisters?
Len.　　　　　No, my lord.
Macb. Came they not by you?
Len.　　　　　No, indeed, my lord.
Macb. Infected be the air whereon they ride;
And damn'd all those that trust them! I did hear
The galloping of horse: who was 't came by?　　140

65. **nine farrow,** litter of nine. 68. *Stage Direction:* **armed Head.** This symbolizes the head of Macbeth cut off by Macduff and presented by him to Malcolm. 74. **harp'd,** hit, touched. 76. *Stage Direction:* **bloody Child.** This symbolizes Macduff (see V, viii, 15-16). 83. **double,** doubly. 86. *Stage Direction:* **Child . . . hand.** This third apparition symbolizes Malcolm, the royal child. 88-89. **round . . . sovereignty,** seems to allude to the shape of a crown as made up of a lower round and a top part, and also to the rounding out and culmination in sovereignty. 93. **Birnam, Dunsinane.** Birnam is a hill near Dunkeld, twelve miles from Dunsinane, which is seven miles from

Perth. 95. **impress,** like soldiers. 96. **bodements,** prophecies. 99. **lease of nature,** natural period. 106. **noise,** music. 112. **Thou . . . Banquo.** This would be the first in the succession of Scottish kings down to James I, therefore Fleance, whose coronation was the thing most dreaded by Macbeth. 117. **crack of doom,** possibly, thunder announcing Doomsday. 121. **two-fold balls,** a probable reference to the double coronation of James at Scone and Westminster, as king of England and Scotland. **treble sceptres,** almost certainly refers to James' assumed title of King of Great Britain, France, and Ireland. 123. **blood-bolter'd,** having his hair matted with blood. 125-135. **Ay**

Len. 'Tis two or three, my lord, that bring you
  word
Macduff is fled to England.
  Macb.   Fled to England!
  Len. Ay, my good lord.
  Macb. Time, thou anticipatest my dread exploits:
The flighty purpose never is o'ertook
Unless the deed go with it: from this moment
The very firstlings of my heart shall be
The firstlings of my hand. And even now,
To crown my thoughts with acts, be it thought and
  done:
The castle of Macduff I will surprise;   150
Seize upon Fife; give to the edge o' the sword
His wife, his babes, and all unfortunate souls
That trace him in his line. No boasting like a fool:
This deed I'll do before this purpose cool.
But no more sights!—Where are these gentlemen?
Come, bring me where they are.   [*Exeunt.*

SCENE II. *Fife. Macduff's castle.*

Enter LADY MACDUFF, *her* Son, *and* Ross.

  L. Macd. What had he done, to make him fly the
  land?
  Ross. You must have patience, madam.
  L. Macd.   He had none:
His flight was madness: when our actions do not,
Our fears do make us traitors.
  Ross.   You know not
Whether it was his wisdom or his fear.
  L. Macd. Wisdom! to leave his wife, to leave his
  babes,
His mansion and his titles in a place
From whence himself does fly? He loves us not;
He wants the natural touch: for the poor wren,
The most diminutive of birds, will fight,   10
Her young ones in her nest, against the owl.
All is the fear and nothing is the love;
As little is the wisdom, where the flight
So runs against all reason.
  Ross.   My dearest coz,
I pray you, school yourself: but for your husband,
He is noble, wise, judicious, and best knows
The fits o' the season. I dare not speak much further;
But cruel are the times, when we are traitors
And do not know ourselves, when we hold rumour
From what we fear, yet know not what we fear,   20
But float upon a wild and violent sea
Each way and move. I take my leave of you:
Shall not be long but I'll be here again:
Things at the worst will cease, or else climb upward
To what they were before. My pretty cousin,
Blessing upon you!
  L. Macd. Father'd he is, and yet he's fatherless.
  Ross. I am so much a fool, should I stay longer,

It would be my disgrace and your discomfort:
I take my leave at once.   [*Exit.*
  L. Macd.   Sirrah, your father's dead:
And what will you do now? How will you live?   31
  Son. As birds do, mother.
  L. Macd.   What, with worms and flies?
  Son. With what I get, I mean; and so do they.
  L. Macd. Poor bird! thou 'ldst never fear the net
  nor lime,
The pitfall nor the gin.
  Son. Why should I, mother? Poor birds they are not
  set for.
My father is not dead, for all your saying.
  L. Macd. Yes, he is dead: how wilt thou do for a
  father?
  Son. Nay, how will you do for a husband?   39
  L. Macd. Why, I can buy me twenty at any market.
  Son. Then you'll buy 'em to sell again.
  L. Macd. Thou speak'st with all thy wit; and yet, i'
  faith,
With wit enough for thee.
  Son. Was my father a traitor, mother?
  L. Macd. Ay, that he was.
  Son. What is a traitor?
  L. Macd. Why, one that swears and lies.
  Son. And be all traitors that do so?
  L. Macd. Every one that does so is a traitor, and
must be hanged.   50
  Son. And must they all be hanged that swear and
lie?
  L. Macd. Every one.
  Son. Who must hang them?
  L. Macd. Why, the honest men.
  Son. Then the liars and swearers are fools, for there
are liars and swearers enow to beat the honest men
and hang up them.
  L. Macd. Now, God help thee, poor monkey! But
how wilt thou do for a father?   60
  Son. If he were dead, you 'ld weep for him: if you
would not, it were a good sign that I should quickly
have a new father.
  L. Macd. Poor prattler, how thou talk'st!

Enter a Messenger.

  Mess. Bless you, fair dame! I am not to you known,
Though in your state of honour I am perfect.
I doubt some danger does approach you nearly:
If you will take a homely man's advice,
Be not found here; hence, with your little ones.
To fright you thus, methinks, I am too savage;   70
To do worse to you were fell cruelty,
Which is too nigh your person. Heaven preserve you!
I dare abide no longer.   [*Exit.*
  L. Macd.   Whither should I fly?
I have done no harm. But I remember now
I am in this earthly world; where to do harm
Is often laudable, to do good sometime
Accounted dangerous folly: why then, alas,

... **there.** These lines are also held to be spurious. 130. **antic round,**
grotesque dance in a circle. 145. **flighty,** fleeting. 153. **trace,** follow.
  SCENE II. 2. **He had none.** Patience was the virtue by which the
faculties were controlled; hence, *His flight was madness* (l. 3). 7. **titles,**
possessions. 9. **touch,** affection, feeling. 17. **fits o' the season,** violent
disorders of the time. 19. **know ourselves,** know ourselves (or possibly,
each other) to be traitors. Owing to Macbeth's system of espionage
even good men have grown suspicious of each other. **hold,** accept,
believe. 22. **Each . . . move,** many emendations; Theobald: *Each
way and wave;* Capell: *And move each way;* Cambridge eds.: *Each way*

and none. 23. **Shall,** it shall. 34. **lime,** birdlime. 35. **gin,** snare.
36. **they,** the snares. 47. **swears and lies,** swears allegiance and breaks
his oath. 61-63. **If he . . . father.** This is an example of Shakespeare's
treatment of children. The child has a precocity appropriate only to
grown people, and yet his ideas are offered in a childish way. There
was no knowledge of the psychology of childhood in Shakespeare's
day. 66. **in . . . honour,** with your honorable rank. **perfect,** perfectly acquainted.

Do I put up that womanly defence,
To say I have done no harm?

Enter Murderers.

           What are these faces?
First Mur. Where is your husband?   80
L. Macd. I hope, in no place so unsanctified
Where such as thou mayst find him.
First Mur.   He 's a traitor.
Son. Thou liest, thou shag-hair'd villain!
First Mur.   What, you egg!
                           [*Stabbing him*.

Young fry of treachery!
Son.   He has kill'd me, mother:
Run away, I pray you!   [*Dies*.
        [*Exit Lady Macduff, crying* 'Murder!' *Exeunt*
                Murderers, following her.

SCENE III. *England. Before the King's palace*.

Enter MALCOLM *and* MACDUFF.

Mal. Let us seek out some desolate shade, and there
Weep our sad bosoms empty.
    Macd.   Let us rather
Hold fast the mortal sword, and like good men
Bestride our down-fall'n birthdom: each new morn
New widows howl, new orphans cry, new sorrows
Strike heaven on the face, that it resounds
As if it felt with Scotland and yell'd out
Like syllable of dolour.
    Mal.   What I believe I'll wail,
What know believe, and what I can redress,
As I shall find the time to friend, I will.   10
What you have spoke, it may be so perchance.
This tyrant, whose sole name blisters our tongues,
Was once thought honest: you have loved him well;
He hath not touch'd you yet. I am young; but
    something
You may deserve of him through me, and wisdom
To offer up a weak poor innocent lamb
To appease an angry god.
    Macd. I am not treacherous.
    Mal.   But Macbeth is.
A good and virtuous nature may recoil   19
In an imperial charge. But I shall crave your pardon;
That which you are my thoughts cannot transpose:
Angels are bright still, though the brightest fell:
Though all things foul would wear the brows of
    grace,
Yet grace must still look so.
    Macd.   I have lost my hopes.
    Mal. Perchance even there where I did find my
    doubts.
Why in that rawness left you wife and child,
Those precious motives, those strong knots of love,
Without leave-taking? I pray you,
Let not my jealousies be your dishonours,
But mine own safeties. You may be rightly just,   30

Whatever I shall think.
    Macd.   Bleed, bleed, poor country!
Great tyranny! lay thou thy basis sure,
For goodness dare not check thee: wear thou thy
    wrongs;
The title is affeer'd! Fare thee well, lord:
I would not be the villain that thou think'st
For the whole space that 's in the tyrant's grasp,
And the rich East to boot.
    Mal.   Be not offended:
I speak not as in absolute fear of you.
I think our country sinks beneath the yoke;
It weeps, it bleeds; and each new day a gash   40
Is added to her wounds: I think withal
There would be hands uplifted in my right;
And here from gracious England have I offer
Of goodly thousands: but, for all this,
When I shall tread upon the tyrant's head,
Or wear it on my sword, yet my poor country
Shall have more vices than it had before,
More suffer and more sundry ways than ever,
By him that shall succeed.
    Macd.   What should he be?
    Mal. It is myself I mean: in whom I know   50
All the particulars of vice so grafted
That, when they shall be open'd, black Macbeth
Will seem as pure as snow, and the poor state
Esteem him as a lamb, being compared
With my confineless harms.
    Macd.   Not in the legions
Of horrid hell can come a devil more damn'd
In evils to top Macbeth.
    Mal.   I grant him bloody,
Luxurious, avaricious, false, deceitful,
Sudden, malicious, smacking of every sin
That has a name: but there 's no bottom, none,   60
In my voluptuousness: your wives, your daughters,
Your matrons and your maids, could not fill up
The cistern of my lust, and my desire
All continent impediments would o'erbear
That did oppose my will: better Macbeth
Than such an one to reign.
    Macd.   Boundless intemperance
In nature is a tyranny; it hath been
The untimely emptying of the happy throne
And fall of many kings. But fear not yet
To take upon you what is yours: you may   70
Convey your pleasures in a spacious plenty,
And yet seem cold, the time you may so hoodwink.
We have willing dames enough; there cannot be
That vulture in you, to devour so many
As will to greatness dedicate themselves,
Finding it so inclined.
    Mal.   With this there grows
In my most ill-composed affection such
A stanchless avarice that, were I king,
I should cut off the nobles for their lands,
Desire his jewels and this other's house: 80
And my more-having would be as a sauce
To make me hunger more; that I should forge

83. **egg,** used contemptuously of the young. 84. **fry,** swarm of young fishes; contemptuously used.
    SCENE III. 2. **Weep . . . empty.** Up to line 117 Malcolm suspects Macduff of being an emissary of Macbeth sent thither to ensnare him; he is testing out Macduff. 4. **Bestride,** stand over in defense. **birthdom,** fatherland. 10. **to friend,** for my friend. 12. **sole,** mere. 19. **recoil,** fall away, degenerate. 20. **imperial charge,** royal command. 24. **so,** like grace. 26. **rawness,** haste, unpreparedness. 34. **affeer'd,**

confirmed, certified. 43. **England,** king of England. 48. **sundry,** various. 49. **What,** who. 52. **open'd,** unfolded (like buds). 55. **my confineless harms,** the boundless injuries I shall inflict. 58. **Luxurious,** lustful. 59. **Sudden,** violent, passionate. 64. **continent,** restraining. 67. **tyranny,** usurpation. 69. **yet,** nevertheless. 71. **Convey,** manage with secrecy. 72. **the time . . . hoodwink,** you may so deceive the age. 77. **ill-composed affection,** evil disposition. 78. **stanchless,** insatiable. 86. **summer-seeming,** passing away with youth, transitory. 88.

Quarreïs unjust against the good and loyal,
Destroying them for wealth.
    Macd.   This avarice
Sticks deeper, grows with more pernicious root
Than summer-seeming lust, and it hath been
The sword of our slain kings: yet do not fear;
Scotland hath foisons to fill up your will,
Of your mere own: all these are portable,
With other graces weigh'd.   90
    Mal. But I have none: the king-becoming graces,
As justice, verity, temperance, stableness,
Bounty, perseverance, mercy, lowliness,
Devotion, patience, courage, fortitude,
I have no relish of them, but abound
In the division of each several crime,
Acting it many ways. Nay, had I power, I should
Pour the sweet milk of concord into hell,
Uproar the universal peace, confound
All unity on earth.
    Macd.   O Scotland, Scotland!   100
    Mal. If such a one be fit to govern, speak:
I am as I have spoken.
    Macd.   Fit to govern!
No, not to live. O nation miserable,
With an untitled tyrant bloody-scepter'd,
When shalt thou see thy wholesome days again,
Since that the truest issue of thy throne
By his own interdiction stands accursed,
And does blaspheme his breed? Thy royal father
Was a most sainted king: the queen that bore thee,
Oftener upon her knees than on her feet,   110
Died every day she lived. Fare thee well!
These evils thou repeat'st upon thyself
Have banish'd me from Scotland. O my breast,
Thy hope ends here!
    Mal.   Macduff, this noble passion,
Child of integrity, hath from my soul
Wiped the black scruples, reconciled my thoughts
To thy good truth and honour. Devilish Macbeth
By many of these trains hath sought to win me
Into his power, and modest wisdom plucks me
From over-credulous haste: but God above   120
Deal between thee and me! for even now
I put myself to thy direction, and
Unspeak mine own detraction, here abjure
The taints and blames I laid upon myself,
For strangers to my nature. I am yet
Unknown to woman, never was forsworn,
Scarcely have coveted what was mine own,
At no time broke my faith, would not betray
The devil to his fellow, and delight
No less in truth than life: my first false speaking   130
Was this upon myself: what I am truly,
Is thine and my poor country's to command:
Whither indeed, before thy here-approach,
Old Siward, with ten thousand warlike men,
Already at a point, was setting forth.
Now we'll together; and the chance of goodness
Be like our warranted quarrel! Why are you silent?
    Macd. Such welcome and unwelcome things at once

'Tis hard to reconcile.

Enter a Doctor.

    Mal. Well; more anon.—Comes the king forth, I
    pray you?   140
    Doct. Ay, sir; there are a crew of wretched souls
That stay his cure: their malady convinces
The great assay of art; but at his touch—
Such sanctity hath heaven given his hand—
They presently amend.
    Mal.   I thank you, doctor. [*Exit Doctor.*
    Macd. What 's the disease he means?
    Mal.   'Tis call'd the evil:
A most miraculous work in this good king;
Which often, since my here-remain in England,
I have seen him do. How he solicits heaven,
Himself best knows: but strangely-visited people,   150
All swoln and ulcerous, pitiful to the eye,
The mere despair of surgery, he cures,
Hanging a golden stamp about their necks,
Put on with holy prayers: and 'tis spoken,
To the succeeding royalty he leaves
The healing benediction. With this strange virtue,
He hath a heavenly gift of prophecy,
And sundry blessings hang about his throne,
That speak him full of grace.

Enter ROSS.

    Macd.   See, who comes here?
    Mal. My countryman; but yet I know him not.   160
    Macd. My ever-gentle cousin, welcome hither.
    Mal. I know him now. Good God, betimes
    remove
The means that makes us strangers!
    Ross.   Sir, amen.
    Macd. Stands Scotland where it did?
    Ross.   Alas, poor country!
Almost afraid to know itself. It cannot
Be call'd our mother, but our grave; where nothing,
But who knows nothing, is once seen to smile;
Where sighs and groans and shrieks that rend the air
Are made, not mark'd; where violent sorrow seems
A modern ecstasy: the dead man's knell   170
Is there scarce ask'd for who; and good men's lives
Expire before the flowers in their caps,
Dying or ere they sicken.
    Macd.   O, relation
Too nice, and yet too true!
    Mal.   What 's the newest grief?
    Ross. That of an hour's age doth hiss the speaker:
Each minute teems a new one.
    Macd.   How does my wife?
    Ross. Why, well.
    Macd.   And all my children?
    Ross.   Well too.
    Macd. The tyrant has not batter'd at their peace?
    Ross. No; they were well at peace when I did leave
    'em.   179
    Macd. Be not a niggard of your speech: how goes 't?
    Ross. When I came hither to transport the tidings,

foisons, resources. 89. **your mere own,** what is absolutely your own.
portable, bearable. 90. **With,** against. 91. **king-becoming graces.**
The list which follows is a typical enumeration of the princely virtues
of the Renaissance. 95. **relish of,** flavor or trace of. 104. **untitled,**
lacking rightful title. 107. **interdiction,** authoritative exclusion.
108. **blaspheme,** slander, defame. 111. **Died . . . lived,** lived a life
of daily mortification (Delius). 118. **trains,** plots, artifices. 126.
forsworn, perjured. 135. **at a point,** ready, prepared. 136. **chance of**

goodness, chance of success. 141. **crew,** company. 142. **convinces,**
conquers. 143. **assay of art,** efforts of medical skill. 146. **evil,** disease,
i.e., scrofula. The passage is an obvious compliment to James I, who
claimed the miraculous power of the royal touch. 150. **strangely-
visited,** afflicted by strange diseases. 153. **stamp,** coin (hung around
the necks of the persons touched). 166. **nothing,** nobody. 167. **once,**
ever. 170. **modern ecstasy,** commonplace excitement. 175. **hiss,** cause
to be hissed. 176. **teems,** teems with. 177. **children,** three syllables.

Which I have heavily borne, there ran a rumour
Of many worthy fellows that were out;
Which was to my belief witness'd the rather,
For that I saw the tyrant's power a-foot:
Now is the time of help; your eye in Scotland
Would create soldiers, make our women fight,
To doff their dire distresses.
    Mal.   Be 't their comfort
We are coming thither: gracious England hath
Lent us good Siward and ten thousand men;   190
An older and a better soldier none
That Christendom gives out.
    Ross.   Would I could answer
This comfort with the like! But I have words
That would be howl'd out in the desert air,
Where hearing should not latch them.
    Macd.   What concern they?
The general cause? or is it a fee-grief
Due to some single breast?
    Ross.   No mind that 's honest
But in it shares some woe; though the main part
Pertains to you alone.
    Macd.   If it be mine,
Keep it not from me, quickly let me have it.   200
    Ross. Let not your ears despise my tongue for ever,
Which shall possess them with the heaviest sound
That ever yet they heard.
    Macd.   Hum! I guess at it.
    Ross. Your castle is surprised; your wife and babes
Savagely slaughter'd: to relate the manner,
Were, on the quarry of these murder'd deer,
To add the death of you.
    Mal.   Merciful heaven!
What, man! ne'er pull your hat upon your brows;
Give sorrow words: the grief that does not speak
Whispers the o'er-fraught heart and bids it break.   210
    Macd. My children too?
    Ross.   Wife, children, servants, all
That could be found.
    Macd.   And I must be from thence!
My wife kill'd too?
    Ross.   I have said.
    Mal.   Be comforted:
Let 's make us medicines of our great revenge,
To cure this deadly grief.
    Macd. He has no children. All my pretty ones?
Did you say all? O hell-kite! All?
What, all my pretty chickens and their dam
At one fell swoop?
    Mal. Dispute it like a man.
    Macd.   I shall do so;   220
But I must also feel it as a man:
I cannot but remember such things were,
That were most precious to me. Did heaven look on,
And would not take their part? Sinful Macduff,
They were all struck for thee! naught that I am,
Not for their own demerits, but for mine,
Fell slaughter on their souls. Heaven rest them now!
    Mal. Be this the whetstone of your sword: let grief

Convert to anger; blunt not the heart, enrage it.
    Macd. O, I could play the woman with mine eyes 230
And braggart with my tongue! But, gentle heavens,
Cut short all intermission; front to front
Bring thou this fiend of Scotland and myself;
Within my sword's length set him; if he 'scape,
Heaven forgive him too!
    Mal.   This tune goes manly.
Come, go we to the king; our power is ready;
Our lack is nothing but our leave: Macbeth
Is ripe for shaking, and the powers above
Put on their instruments. Receive what cheer you
    may:
The night is long that never finds the day.   [*Exeunt.* 240

ACT V.

SCENE I. *Dunsinane. Ante-room in the castle.*

Enter a Doctor of Physic *and a* Waiting-
    Gentlewoman.

Doct. I have two nights watched with you, but can
perceive no truth in your report. When was it she
last walked?

Gent. Since his majesty went into the field, I have
seen her rise from her bed, throw her nightgown upon
her, unlock her closet, take forth paper, fold it, write
upon 't, read it, afterwards seal it, and again return
to bed; yet all this while in a most fast sleep.   9

Doct. A great perturbation in nature, to receive at
once the benefit of sleep, and do the effects of watching! In this slumbery agitation, besides her walking
and other actual performances, what, at any time,
have you heard her say?

Gent. That, sir, which I will not report after her.

Doct. You may to me: and 'tis most meet you
should.

Gent. Neither to you nor any one, having no witness
to confirm my speech.   21

Enter LADY MACBETH, *with a taper.*

Lo you, here she comes! This is her very guise; and,
upon my life, fast asleep. Observe her; stand close.

Doct. How came she by that light?

Gent. Why, it stood by her: she has light by her
continually; 'tis her command.

Doct. You see, her eyes are open.

Gent. Ay, but their sense is shut.

Doct. What is it she does now? Look, how she rubs
her hands.   31

Gent. It is an accustomed action with her, to seem
thus washing her hands: I have known her continue
in this a quarter of an hour.

Lady M. Yet here 's a spot.

Doct. Hark! she speaks: I will set down what comes
from her, to satisfy my remembrance the more
strongly.   38

Lady M. Out, damned spot! out, I say!—One: two:

---

why, then 'tis time to do 't.—Hell is murky!—Fie, my
lord, fie! a soldier, and afeard? What need we fear
who knows it, when none can call our power to
account?—Yet who would have thought the old man
to have had so much blood in him.

Doct. Do you mark that?

Lady M. The thane of Fife had a wife: where is she
now?—What, will these hands ne'er be clean?—No
more o' that, my lord, no more o' that: you mar all
with this starting. 50

Doct. Go to, go to; you have known what you
should not.

Gent. She has spoke what she should not, I am sure
of that: heaven knows what she has known.

Lady M. Here 's the smell of the blood still: all the
perfumes of Arabia will not sweeten this little hand.
Oh, oh, oh!

Doct. What a sigh is there! The heart is sorely
charged. 60

Gent. I would not have such a heart in my bosom for
the dignity of the whole body.

Doct. Well, well, well,—

Gent. Pray God it be, sir.

Doct. This disease is beyond my practice: yet I
have known those which have walked in their sleep
who have died holily in their beds.

Lady M. Wash your hands, put on your nightgown;
look not so pale.—I tell you yet again, Banquo 's
buried; he cannot come out on 's grave. 71

Doct. Even so?

Lady M. To bed, to bed! there 's knocking at the
gate: come, come, come, come, give me your hand.
What 's done cannot be undone.—To bed, to bed,
to bed! [*Exit.*

Doct. Will she go now to bed?

Gent. Directly.

Doct. Foul whisperings are abroad: unnatural deeds
Do breed unnatural troubles: infected minds 80
To their deaf pillows will discharge their secrets:
More needs she the divine than the physician.
God, God forgive us all! Look after her;
Remove from her the means of all annoyance,
And still keep eyes upon her. So, good night:
My mind she has mated, and amazed my sight.
I think, but dare not speak.

Gent. Good night, good doctor. [*Exeunt.*

SCENE II. *The country near Dunsinane.*

Drum and colours. Enter MENTEITH, CAITHNESS,
ANGUS, LENNOX, *and* Soldiers.

Ment. The English power is near, led on by
   Malcolm,
His uncle Siward and the good Macduff:
Revenges burn in them; for their dear causes
Would to the bleeding and the grim alarm
Excite the mortified man.

Ang. Near Birnam wood
Shall we well meet them; that way are they coming.

Caith. Who knows if Donalbain be with his
   brother?

Len. For certain, sir, he is not: I have a file
Of all the gentry: there is Siward's son,
And many unrough youths that even now 10
Protest their first of manhood.

Ment. What does the tyrant?

Caith. Great Dunsinane he strongly fortifies:
Some say he 's mad; others that lesser hate him
Do call it valiant fury: but, for certain,
He cannot buckle his distemper'd cause
Within the belt of rule.

Ang. Now does he feel
His secret murders sticking on his hands;
Now minutely revolts upbraid his faith-breach;
Those he commands move only in command,
Nothing in love: now does he feel his title 20
Hang loose about him, like a giant's robe
Upon a dwarfish thief.

Ment. Who then shall blame
His pester'd senses to recoil and start,
When all that is within him does condemn
Itself for being there?

Caith. Well, march we on,
To give obedience where 'tis truly owed:
Meet we the medicine of the sickly weal,
And with him pour we in our country's purge
Each drop of us.

Len. Or so much as it needs,
To dew the sovereign flower and drown the weeds. 30
Make we our march towards Birnam. [*Exeunt, marching.*

SCENE III. *Dunsinane. A room in the castle.*

Enter MACBETH, Doctor, *and* Attendants.

Macb. Bring me no more reports; let them fly all:
Till Birnam wood remove to Dunsinane,
I cannot taint with fear. What 's the boy Malcolm?
Was he not born of woman? The spirits that know
All mortal consequences have pronounced me thus:
'Fear not, Macbeth; no man that 's born of woman
Shall e'er have power upon thee.' Then fly, false
   thanes,
And mingle with the English epicures:
The mind I sway by and the heart I bear
Shall never sag with doubt nor shake with fear. 10

Enter a Servant.

The devil damn thee black, thou cream-faced loon!
Where got'st thou that goose look?

Serv. There is ten thousand—

Macb. Geese, villain?

Serv. Soldiers, sir.

Macb. Go, prick thy face, and over-red thy fear,
Thou lily-liver'd boy. What soldiers, patch?
Death of thy soul! those linen cheeks of thine

---

60. **sorely charged,** heavily burdened with passions. 71. **on 's,** of his.
84. **annoyance,** i.e., harming herself. 86. **mated,** bewildered, stupefied.
   SCENE II. 4. **alarm,** call to battle. 5. **mortified,** paralyzed. . 8. **file,**
list, roster. 10. **unrough,** beardless. 11. **Protest,** assert publicly. 18.
minutely, happening every minute. 23. **pester'd,** troubled, embarrassed. **recoil,** fall away, degenerate. 27. **medicine,** i.e., Malcolm.
30. **dew,** bedew.
   SCENE III. 1. **them,** the thanes. 3. **taint,** become inbued with (an
undesirable quality). 5. **mortal consequences,** what befalls man.

Cuningham prefers either *consequents* or (following Singer) *consequence*,
both of which are metrically better than the text. 8. **epicures,** luxury-
loving persons. Holinshed refers to the introduction of luxurious habits
of living by the English into Scotland. 9. **sway by,** am directed or
swayed by. 11. **loon,** stupid fellow. 14. **over-red,** redden over. The
servant's blood has all retired into his lower abdomen on account of
his fear, so that he is very pale and there is no blood in his liver, where
his courage should have resided—hence, *lily-liver'd* (l. 15). 15. **patch,**
domestic fool; here used contemptuously.

Are counsellors to fear. What soldiers, whey-face?
Serv. The English force, so please you.
Macb. Take thy face hence. [*Exit Servant.*
　　　　　Seyton!—I am sick at heart,
When I behold—Seyton, I say!—This push　　　20
Will cheer me ever, or disseat me now.
I have lived long enough: my way of life
Is fall'n into the sear, the yellow leaf;
And that which should accompany old age,
As honour, love, obedience, troops of friends,
I must not look to have; but, in their stead,
Curses, not loud but deep, mouth-honour, breath,
Which the poor heart would fain deny, and dare not.
Seyton!

Enter SEYTON.

Sey. What is your gracious pleasure?
Macb. 　　　　　What news more?　　　30
Sey. All is confirm'd, my lord, which was reported.
Macb. I'll fight till from my bones my flesh be
　　hack'd.
Give me my armour.
Sey. 　　　　　'Tis not needed yet.
Macb. I'll put it on.
Send out moe horses; skirr the country round;
Hang those that talk of fear. Give me mine armour.
How does your patient, doctor?
Doct. 　　　　　Not so sick, my lord,
As she is troubled with thick-coming fancies,
That keep her from her rest.
Macb. 　　　　　Cure her of that.
Canst thou not minister to a mind diseased,　　40
Pluck from the memory a rooted sorrow,
Raze out the written troubles of the brain
And with some sweet oblivious antidote
Cleanse the stuff'd bosom of that perilous stuff
Which weighs upon the heart?
Doct. 　　　　　Therein the patient
Must minister to himself.
Macb. Throw physic to the dogs; I'll none of it.
Come, put mine armour on; give me my staff.
Seyton, send out. Doctor, the thanes fly from me.
Come, sir, dispatch. If thou couldst, doctor, cast　　50
The water of my land, find her disease,
And purge it to a sound and pristine health,
I would applaud thee to the very echo,
That should applaud again.—Pull 't off, I say.—
What rhubarb, senna, or what purgative drug,
Would scour these English hence? Hear'st thou of
　　them?
Doct. Ay, my good lord; your royal preparation
Makes us hear something.
Macb. 　　　　　Bring it after me.
I will not be afraid of death and bane,
Till Birnam forest come to Dunsinane.　　60
Doct. [*Aside*] Were I from Dunsinane away and
　　clear,
Profit again should hardly draw me here. [*Exeunt.*

SCENE IV. *Country near Birnam wood.*

Drum and colours. Enter MALCOLM, *old* SIWARD *and his*
　Son, MACDUFF, MENTEITH, CAITHNESS, ANGUS,
　LENNOX, ROSS, *and* Soldiers, *marching.*

Mal. Cousins, I hope the days are near at hand
That chambers will be safe.
Ment. 　　　　　We doubt it nothing.
Siw. What wood is this before us?
Ment. 　　　　　The wood of Birnam.
Mal. Let every soldier hew him down a bough
And bear 't before him: thereby shall we shadow
The numbers of our host and make discovery
Err in report of us.
Soldiers. 　　　　　It shall be done.
Siw. We learn no other but the confident tyrant
Keeps still in Dunsinane, and will endure
Our setting down before 't.
Mal. 　　　　　'Tis his main hope:　　10
For where there is advantage to be given,
Both more and less have given him the revolt,
And none serve with him but constrained things
Whose hearts are absent too.
Macd. 　　　　　Let our just censures
Attend the true event, and put we on
Industrious soldiership.
Siw. 　　　　　The time approaches
That will with due decision make us know
What we shall say we have and what we owe.
Thoughts speculative their unsure hopes relate,
But certain issue strokes must arbitrate:　　20
Towards which advance the war. [*Exeunt, marching.*

SCENE V. *Dunsinane. Within the castle.*

Enter MACBETH, SEYTON, *and* Soldiers, *with drum and*
　colours.

Macb. Hang out our banners on the outward walls:
The cry is still 'They come:' our castle's strength
Will laugh a siege to scorn: here let them lie
Till famine and the ague eat them up:
Were they not forced with those that should be ours,
We might have met them dareful, beard to beard,
And beat them backward home. [*A cry of women within.*
　　　　　What is that noise?
Sey. It is the cry of women, my good lord. [*Exit.*
Macb. I have almost forgot the taste of fears:
The time has been, my senses would have cool'd　　10
To hear a night-shriek; and my fell of hair
Would at a dismal treatise rouse and stir
As life were in 't: I have supp'd full with horrors;
Direness, familiar to my slaughterous thoughts,
Cannot once start me.

Re-enter SEYTON.
　　　Wherefore was that cry?

Sey. The queen, my lord, is dead.

Macb. She should have died hereafter;
There would have been a time for such a word.
To-morrow, and to-morrow, and to-morrow,
Creeps in this petty pace from day to day   20
To the last syllable of recorded time,
And all our yesterdays have lighted fools
The way to dusty death. Out, out, brief candle!
Life's but a walking shadow, a poor player
That struts and frets his hour upon the stage
And then is heard no more: it is a tale
Told by an idiot, full of sound and fury,
Signifying nothing.

Enter a Messenger.

Thou comest to use thy tongue; thy story quickly.

Mess. Gracious my lord,   30
I should report that which I say I saw,
But know not how to do it.

Macb.   Well, say, sir.

Mess. As I did stand my watch upon the hill,
I look'd toward Birnam, and anon, methought,
The wood began to move.

Macb.   Liar and slave!

Mess. Let me endure your wrath, if 't be not so:
Within this three mile may you see it coming;
I say, a moving grove.

Macb.   If thou speak'st false,
Upon the next tree shalt thou hang alive,
Till famine cling thee: if thy speech be sooth,   40
I care not if thou dost for me as much.
I pull in resolution, and begin
To doubt the equivocation of the fiend
That lies like truth: 'Fear not, till Birnam wood
Do come to Dunsinane:' and now a wood
Comes toward Dunsinane. Arm, arm, and out!
If this which he avouches does appear,
There is nor flying hence nor tarrying here.
I 'gin to be aweary of the sun,
And wish the estate o' the world were now undone.   50
Ring the alarum-bell! Blow, wind! come, wrack!
At least we'll die with harness on our back.   [*Exeunt*.

SCENE VI. *Dunsinane. Before the castle.*

Drum and colours. Enter MALCOLM, *old* SIWARD,
MACDUFF, *and their* Army, *with boughs*.

Mal. Now near enough: your leavy screens throw
          down,
And show like those you are. You, worthy uncle,
Shall, with my cousin, your right-noble son,
Lead our first battle: worthy Macduff and we
Shall take upon 's what else remains to do,
According to our order.

Siw.   Fare you well.
Do we but find the tyrant's power to-night,
Let us be beaten, if we cannot fight.

Macd. Make all our trumpets speak; give them all
          breath,
Those clamorous harbingers of blood and death.   10
          [*Exeunt*.

SCENE VII. *Another part of the field.*

Alarums. Enter MACBETH.

Macb. They have tied me to a stake; I cannot fly,
But, bear-like, I must fight the course. What 's he
That was not born of woman? Such a one
Am I to fear, or none.

Enter young SIWARD.

Yo. Siw. What is thy name?

Macb.   Thou 'lt be afraid to hear it.

Yo. Siw. No; though thou call'st thyself a hotter
          name
Than any is in hell.

Macb.   My name 's Macbeth.

Yo. Siw. The devil himself could not pronounce a
          title
More hateful to mine ear.

Macb.   No, nor more fearful.

Yo. Siw. Thou liest, abhorred tyrant; with my
          sword   10
I'll prove the lie thou speak'st.
          [*They fight and young Siward is slain.*

Macb.   Thou wast born of woman.
But swords I smile at, weapons laugh to scorn,
Brandish'd by man that 's of a woman born.   [*Exit*.

Alarums. Enter MACDUFF.

Macd. That way the noise is. Tyrant, show thy face!
If thou be'st slain and with no stroke of mine,
My wife and children's ghosts will haunt me still.
I cannot strike at wretched kerns, whose arms
Are hired to bear their staves: either thou, Macbeth,
Or else my sword with an unbatter'd edge
I sheathe again undeeded. There thou shouldst be;   20
By this great clatter, one of greatest note
Seems bruited. Let me find him, fortune!
And more I beg not.   [*Exit. Alarums*.

Enter MALCOLM *and old* SIWARD.

Siw. This way, my lord; the castle 's gently
          render'd:
The tyrant's people on both sides do fight;
The noble thanes do bravely in the war;
The day almost itself professes yours,
And little is to do.

Mal.   We have met with foes
That strike beside us.

Siw.   Enter, sir, the castle.
          [*Exeunt. Alarums*.

SCENE VIII. *Another part of the field.*

Enter MACBETH.

Macb. Why should I play the Roman fool, and die

On mine own sword? whiles I see lives, the gashes
Do better upon them.

Enter MACDUFF.

Macd.   Turn, hell-hound, turn!
Macb. Of all men else I have avoided thee:
But get thee back; my soul is too much charged
With blood of thine already.
Macd.   I have no words:
My voice is in my sword: thou bloodier villain
Than terms can give thee out!   [*They fight.*
Macb.   Thou losest labour:
As easy mayst thou the intrenchant air
With thy keen sword impress as make me bleed: 10
Let fall thy blade on vulnerable crests;
I bear a charmed life, which must not yield
To one of woman born.
Macd.   Despair thy charm;
And let the angel whom thou still hast served
Tell thee, Macduff was from his mother's womb
Untimely ripp'd.
Macb. Accursed be that tongue that tells me so,
For it hath cow'd my better part of man!
And be these juggling fiends no more believed,
That palter with us in a double sense;   20
That keep the word of promise to our ear,
And break it to our hope. I'll not fight with thee.
Macd. Then yield thee, coward,
And live to be the show and gaze o' the time:
We'll have thee, as our rarer monsters are,
Painted upon a pole, and underwrit,
'Here may you see the tyrant.'
Macb.   I will not yield,
To kiss the ground before young Malcolm's feet,
And to be baited with the rabble's curse.
Though Birnam wood be come to Dunsinane,   30
And thou opposed, being of no woman born,
Yet I will try the last. Before my body
I throw my warlike shield. Lay on, Macduff,
And damn'd be him that first cries 'Hold, enough!'
                    [*Exeunt, fighting. Alarums.*

Retreat. Flourish. Enter, with drum and colours,
     MALCOLM, *old* SIWARD, ROSS, *the other* Thanes,
     and Soldiers.

Mal. I would the friends we miss were safe arrived.
Siw. Some must go off: and yet, by these I see,
So great a day as this is cheaply bought.
Mal. Macduff is missing, and your noble son.
Ross. Your son, my lord, has paid a soldier's debt:
He only lived but till he was a man;   40
The which no sooner had his prowess confirm'd
In the unshrinking station where he fought,
But like a man he died.
Siw.   Then he is dead?
Ross. Ay, and brought off the field: your cause of
     sorrow

Must not be measured by his worth, for then
It hath no end.
Siw.   Had he his hurts before?
Ross. Ay, on the front.
Siw.   Why then, God's soldier be he!
Had I as many sons as I have hairs,
I would not wish them to a fairer death:
And so, his knell is knoll'd.
Mal.   He 's worth more sorrow,   50
And that I'll spend for him.
Siw.   He 's worth no more:
They say he parted well, and paid his score:
And so, God be with him! Here comes newer comfort.

Re-enter MACDUFF, *with* MACBETH's *head.*

Macd. Hail, king! for so thou art: behold, where
     stands
The usurper's cursed head: the time is free:
I see thee compass'd with thy kingdom's pearl,
That speak my salutation in their minds;
Whose voices I desire aloud with mine:
Hail, King of Scotland!
All.   Hail, King of Scotland! [*Flourish.*
Mal. We shall not spend a large expense of time   60
Before we reckon with your several loves,
And make us even with you. My thanes and kinsmen,
Henceforth be earls, the first that ever Scotland
In such an honour named. What 's more to do,
Which would be planted newly with the time,
As calling home our exiled friends abroad
That fled the snares of watchful tyranny;
Producing forth the cruel ministers
Of this dead butcher and his fiend-like queen,
Who, as 'tis thought, by self and violent hands   70
Took off her life; this, and what needful else
That calls upon us, by the grace of Grace,
We will perform in measure, time and place:
So, thanks to all at once and to each one,
Whom we invite to see us crown'd at Scone.
                    [*Flourish. Exeunt.*

56. **thy kingdom's pearl,** the flower of thy kingdom.   63. **Henceforth be earls,** a detail from Holinshed. *Earl* was an English title.   70. **self and violent,** her own violent.

9. **intrenchant,** invulnerable, indivisible.   14. **angel,** evil angel, Macbeth's genius.   18. **cow'd . . . man,** subdued my soul, or spirit, or mind. Macbeth's invulnerability was, in some measure, his belief in his invulnerability.   20. **palter . . . sense,** equivocate with us.   26. **Painted upon a pole,** i.e., painted on a board suspended on a pole.   30-34. **Though . . . enough.** Macbeth's recoil to courage would be explained in the psychology of the time as the setting up in him of a new impulse of passion. His repugnance to submission drives out his craven fear.   34. *Stage Direction: Exeunt, fighting.* F has *Enter fighting and Macbeth slain,* which is inconsistent with the stage direction after line 53. It may, however, indicate that at some early performances Macbeth was slain on the stage.   42. **unshrinking station,** post from which he did not shrink.

The three witches, as pictured in Holinshed's "Chronicles."

Antony and Cleopatra

There is a difference of opinion as to whether *Antony and Cleopatra* belongs to 1606 or 1607, but there is practically no doubt that it belongs to one or the other year. It represents, along with *Coriolanus*, a return to Plutarch for source material, and is usually considered earlier than that play. It was entered in the Register of the Stationers' Company along with *Pericles* on May 20, 1608, by Edward Blount. No issue of the texts followed these entries, which were possibly intended to forestall illegal publication. If so, the entry was not successful in the case of *Pericles*, since that play came out in quarto form with a different publisher in 1609. *Antony and Cleopatra* did not appear in print until the publication of the First Folio in 1623, when it was relicensed as if it had never been entered before.

The best piece of evidence for 1606 or 1607 comes from its relation to Samuel Daniel's tragedy *Cleopatra*. This was first published in 1594 and is a drama on the classical model. It is made up largely of soliloquy and of long speeches and is moralistic and reflective in tone. It tells the story of Cleopatra after the death of Antony, and Shakespeare seems to have known the play. On the other hand, Daniel seems to have remodeled his play under the influence of Shakespeare's *Antony and Cleopatra*, publishing it as "newly altered" in 1607. In the new version he uses dialogue more freely than in the old and makes a greater use than he had before of some of the characters who appear in Shakespeare's play. There are even a few rather striking parallels to *Antony and Cleopatra* in the verse of the new play.[1]

Also Barnabe Barnes' *The Divils Charter*, acted early in 1607, contains what seems to be a parody of the death scene of Cleopatra where she applies the asp to her breast. *Macbeth*, on which Shakespeare was at work at about the same time, shows some familiarity (III, i, 54-57) with the life of Antony in Plutarch.

SOURCES

Shakespeare must have known Daniel's *Cleopatra* and the countess of Pembroke's *Antonius, a Tragedie*, which had been Daniel's model for his first version. Perhaps Shakespeare knew other plays now lost, for the subject was well known on the stage. The countess of Pembroke's play is a translation of Robert Garnier's *Marc Antoine*. Étienne Jodelle had written *Cléopâtre Captive* in the middle of the sixteenth century. Other French, English, and German plays on Cleopatra are also known.

Back of the Renaissance there lies a large body of Cleopatra literature, for Antony and Cleopatra had taken their place among the world's famous lovers. This is important to remember in considering Shakespeare's use of Plutarch. Although he went to the life of Antony in Plutarch's *Lives of the Noble Grecians and Romans*, and followed it very closely as regards the Cleopatra of the final act, he did not get from it his initial conception of this character.

CLEOPATRA

In Plutarch Antony is blamed for falling victim to infatuation and throwing away the world for love of Cleopatra. Plutarch is mainly interested in the downfall of the great Roman and its significance in politics, history, and morals. He dwells on the magnificence of Cleopatra, tells about her gifts of gold and silver, the sumptuousness of her household, the splendor of her feasts, how eight wild boars were roasted whole in the kitchen of Antony, and so on. Cleopatra is beautiful, flattering, charming; but she is also great. She ruled a kingdom unaided; she was cultured; she knew many languages; and, characteristically, Plutarch tells a good deal about her humor and describes the sports and amusements of Antony and Cleopatra in Alexandria.

Now, when we come to Shakespeare we find him with a different conception. To him the Cleopatra of the first three acts is fickle, vain, mercenary, unscrupulous, and the living embodiment of sensuality. This is easily illustrated from the second, third, and fifth scenes of the first act, and all through, at least as far as the thirteenth scene of the third act. But when we pass that point we have to do with a different person. She seems suddenly to possess womanly fidelity, is steadfast and resolute, and, being left to occupy the stage alone in the last act, advances to a heroic death.

L. L. Schücking[2] has argued that Shakespeare has not been consistent in the portraiture of the character, for he started out with one conception and ended with another, knowing, no doubt, that on the stage the inconsistency would not be apparent. Schücking insists that, if Shakespeare had thought of the character of the first three acts as the same as that of the last two, some evidence of that better nature would have been revealed earlier. It is impossible, he thinks, that any woman of the nature of the first Cleopatra could have manifested the qualities of the later one.

There is this to be said in favor of his contention. Shakespeare had to tell a complicated double story, and the play is perhaps not worked down to the fine point of connection that marks *Macbeth* and *Coriolanus*. But that is as far as one can go, for Shakespeare never worked with greater artistry, and the play has every

Antony and Cleopatra

1071

---

[1] R. H. Case, *The Tragedy of Antony and Cleopatra*, Arden Shakespeare (Methuen), Introduction.

[2] *Character Problems in Shakespeare's Plays* (1922), pp. 119 ff.

sign of life. To be sure, after the middle of the play, Shakespeare more or less puts Plutarch on the stage. There is a multitude of short scenes which reproduce the source almost literally, so that the play seems comparatively confused in its dramaturgy. This multiplicity of scenes, however, would be not only allowable, but effective on the Elizabethan stage with its freely changing scenes. It is often spoken of as a chronicle play in form and is said to lack, except in its great figures, the quality of tragedy.

Shakespeare had two conflicting ideas to present, the one derived from the popular conception of Cleopatra as the mistress of sensual love and the other the Plutarchan story of the woman who loved Antony so well that she followed him to the shades of death. It may be that in the earlier part of the play, which is dramatically so much more carefully done, he was following the first of these ideas, and that in the later part he was plunging hurriedly through the second. The question to be decided is whether Shakespeare gives us anything to show that he meant Cleopatra to be so profoundly moved by the misfortunes of Antony that her nature was changed. There is in the source no clear provision of such a conversion, and it is very unlike Shakespeare to leave such a matter obscure.

There is, however, a clear and powerful marking of the moment of the change. It is the scene of Antony's rage when he thinks wrongly that Cleopatra has withdrawn her fleet from the battle and has caused his defeat. She feels the scourge of his tongue when he says (III, xiii, 116-122),

> I found you as a morsel cold upon
> Dead Cæsar's trencher; nay, you were a fragment
> Of Cneius Pompey's; besides what hotter hours,
> Unregister'd in vulgar fame, you have
> Luxuriously pick'd out: for, I am sure,
> Though you can guess what temperance should be,
> You know not what it is.

Under his reproaches she is perfectly meek. "O, is't come to this?" "I must stay his time." "Not know me yet?" These are her replies, and from that moment she has her new nobility. Many critics find in her holding back part of her treasure, in her blandishments of Octavius, and in her false message to Antony that she was dead, a basis for the belief that she was

Asps. From Gesner's "Historia Animalium," 1603.

still the old Cleopatra, anxious at any cost to save her life, even willing to secure another lover in the crafty Octavius; but to construe it so is to read things into the text that are not there. Plutarch makes it perfectly clear that Cleopatra had resolved to die: "Cleopatra finely deceiveth Octavius Cæsar, as though she desired to live." In the tenets of Elizabethan psychology, and perhaps in life itself, there is no difficulty in conceiving of the possibility of such a sudden change.

ANTONY

Antony is superbly and consistently presented, and here Plutarch and his values are Shakespeare's guide. The play is Antony's to the end of the fourth act. Antony is a great soldier and a man of vast ability, but his greatness suffers eclipse before our eyes when he lets his passion betray his reason. His decisions are unwise, and he has Enobarbus and others to tell him so; but he persists in the error of his ways. He is guided by Cleopatra in matters where absolute primacy should be his. As he rallies from his self-occasioned defeats, his old greatness comes momentarily out like great flashes of lightning. We have Enobarbus, who interprets and sets off Antony, to tell us how little they signify. Antony has said (III, xiii, 191-194):

> Come on, my queen;
> There's sap in 't yet. The next time I do fight,
> I'll make death love me; for I will contend
> Even with his pestilent scythe.

Enobarbus observes (ll. 195-201):

> Now he'll outstare the lightning. To be furious,
> Is to be frighted out of fear; and in that mood
> The dove will peck the estridge; and I see still,
> A diminution in our captain's brain
> Restores his heart: when valour preys on reason,
> It eats the sword it fights with. I will seek
> Some way to leave him.

A WORK OF GENIUS

Antony and Cleopatra is a work of the most magnificent poetry—boldness in the use of words, startling imagery, imagination penetrating into the recesses of the human soul, unequaled variety of emotions, and a texture so rich that the play is like a gorgeous tapestry. It reminded Dowden of "a room splendid with the colors of Titian and Paul Veronese."

The minor characters, quite apart from the two great figures, are vivid enough to give distinction to any drama. There is the cool, clear-headed, determined politician Octavius, who seems to have no personal feeling except for his sister. There is Octavia herself, something of a pawn in the game of state, but a good woman and much of a lady. There are Lepidus, who has had greatness thrust upon him; Sextus Pompeius, an almost great son of a great father, with his clever henchman Menas; Scarus among Antony's followers, who in his few words reveals immortal courage.

But the greatest of all the minor characters is Enobarbus, whose career as given in the play is a genuine tragedy. He is Shakespeare's mouthpiece, a common man who knows the truth and has the courage to speak it. Even the puppets of Cleopatra's household are vividly realized, perfectly human—Mardian, the eunuch; Seleucus, the treacherous steward; Charmian, a mere figurine, but faithful unto death. Even the Clown who brings the "odd worm" in which there is "no goodness," is instinct with life.

STAGE HISTORY

Antony and Cleopatra has not been frequently played on the stage or, as a whole, successfully. Dryden's *All for Love, or the World Lost* (1678) differs from other Restoration treatments of Shakespeare. It is not so much an adaptation of *Antony and Cleopatra* as an independent dramatization of the same subject on Dryden's lines. He took great pains with it and was proud of the result. He wrote in blank verse, observed the unities of time, place, and action with some fidelity, and achieved a far superior unity, if unity be considered narrowly. However, on the other hand, what he gained in the narrow field he lost in the broad one. *Antony and Cleopatra* is a drama of a world empire, with Antony bestriding it like a colossus, and all its variation reflected in the "infinite variety" of Cleopatra. In Dryden's version Antony chiefly suffers, becoming a "bankrupt of honor and fortune." Clownage, thought to be too strong an element in Enobarbus, is banished with him. Cleopatra is tamed.

This version, which is, in spite of what has been said, a truly noble work, superseded *Antony and Cleopatra* on the stage for many years. Garrick tried unsuccessfully to revive Shakespeare's version in 1758. Macready likewise failed in 1833. The performance of Samuel Phelps in 1849 was the first modern success in the performance of Shakespeare's play. He played Antony to crowded houses throughout the season. Isabella Dallas Glyn (1823-1889), a tragic actress of stately bearing and excellent elocution, was his Cleopatra; she again appeared in this part at Drury Lane Theatre in 1873.

Since the middle of the nineteenth century there have been all told perhaps a dozen revivals of *Antony and Cleopatra* in England and America. The most successful was that of Beerbohm Tree (1906-1907) at His Majesty's Theatre in London, on which occasion Tree played Antony, Constance Collier, Cleopatra, and Basil Gill, Octavius. Other notable performances are those of Kyrle Bellew and Mrs. Potter in New York in 1889, Charles Coghlan and Mrs. Langtry in London in 1890, and Sothern and Marlowe in 1910. *Antony and Cleopatra* was well acted at the "Old Vic" in London in the season of 1933-1934, and in New York in 1947 with great public approval by Godfrey Tearle and Katharine Cornell. There have been other recent performances.

Antony and Cleopatra

DRAMATIS PERSONAE

MARK ANTONY,
OCTAVIUS CÆSAR, } triumvirs.
M. ÆMILIUS LEPIDUS,
SEXTUS POMPEIUS.
DOMITIUS ENOBARBUS,
VENTIDIUS,
EROS,
SCARUS, } friends to Antony.
DERCETAS,
DEMETRIUS,
PHILO,

MECÆNAS,
AGRIPPA,
DOLABELLA,
PROCULEIUS, } friends to Cæsar.
THYREUS,
GALLUS,

MENAS,
MENECRATES, } friends to Pompey.
VARRIUS,
TAURUS, lieutenant-general to Cæsar.
CANIDIUS, lieutenant-general to Antony.
SILIUS, an officer in Ventidius's army.
EUPHRONIUS, an ambassador from Antony to Cæsar.
ALEXAS,
MARDIAN, a Eunuch, } attendants on Cleopatra.
SELEUCUS,
DIOMEDES,
A Soothsayer.
A Clown.

CLEOPATRA, queen of Egypt.
OCTAVIA, sister to Cæsar and wife to Antony.
CHARMIAN, } attendants on Cleopatra.
IRAS,

Officers, Soldiers, Messengers, and other Attendants.

SCENE: *In several parts of the Roman empire.*

ACT I.

SCENE I. *Alexandria. A room in Cleopatra's palace.*

Enter DEMETRIUS *and* PHILO.

Phi. Nay, but this dotage of our general's
O'erflows the measure: those his goodly eyes,
That o'er the files and musters of the war
Have glow'd like plated Mars, now bend, now turn,
The office and devotion of their view
Upon a tawny front: his captain's heart,
Which in the scuffles of great fights hath burst
The buckles on his breast, reneges all temper,

And is become the bellows and the fan
To cool a gipsy's lust.

Flourish. Enter ANTONY, CLEOPATRA, *her Ladies, the
Train, with Eunuchs fanning her.*

Look, where they come: 10
Take but good note, and you shall see in him
The triple pillar of the world transform'd
Into a strumpet's fool: behold and see.
    Cleo. If it be love indeed, tell me how much.
    Ant. There's beggary in the love that can be
reckon'd.
    Cleo. I'll set a bourn how far to be beloved.
    Ant. Then must thou needs find out new heaven,
new earth.

Enter an Attendant.

    Att. News, my good lord, from Rome.
    Ant.   Grates me: the sum.
    Cleo. Nay, hear them, Antony:
Fulvia perchance is angry; or, who knows 20
If the scarce-bearded Cæsar have not sent
His powerful mandate to you, 'Do this, or this;
Take in that kingdom, and enfranchise that;
Perform 't, or else we damn thee.'
    Ant.   How, my love!
    Cleo. Perchance! nay, and most like:
You must not stay here longer, your dismission
Is come from Cæsar; therefore hear it, Antony.
Where's Fulvia's process? Cæsar's I would say? both?
Call in the messengers. As I am Egypt's queen,
Thou blushest, Antony; and that blood of thine 30
Is Cæsar's homager: else so thy cheek pays shame
When shrill-tongued Fulvia scolds. The messengers!
    Ant. Let Rome in Tiber melt, and the wide arch
Of the ranged empire fall! Here is my space.
Kingdoms are clay: our dungy earth alike
Feeds beast as man: the nobleness of life
Is to do thus; when such a mutual pair   [*Embracing.*
And such a twain can do 't, in which I bind,
On pain of punishment, the world to weet
We stand up peerless.
    Cleo.   Excellent falsehood! 40
Why did he marry Fulvia, and not love her?
I'll seem the fool I am not; Antony
Will be himself.
    Ant.   But stirr'd by Cleopatra.
Now, for the love of Love and her soft hours,
Let's not confound the time with conference harsh:
There's not a minute of our lives should stretch
Without some pleasure now. What sport to-night?
    Cleo. Hear the ambassadors.
    Ant.   Fie, wrangling queen!
Whom every thing becomes, to chide, to laugh,
To weep; whose every passion fully strives 50
To make itself, in thee, fair and admired!
No messenger, but thine; and all alone
To-night we'll wander through the streets and note
The qualities of people. Come, my queen;

Last night you did desire it: speak not to us.
                    [*Exeunt Ant. and Cleo. with their train.*
    Dem. Is Cæsar with Antonius prized so slight?
    Phi. Sir, sometimes, when he is not Antony,
He comes too short of that great property
Which still should go with Antony.
    Dem.   I am full sorry
That he approves the common liar, who 60
Thus speaks of him at Rome: but I will hope
Of better deeds to-morrow. Rest you happy!   [*Exeunt.*

SCENE II. *The same. Another room.*

Enter CHARMIAN, IRAS, ALEXAS, *and a* Soothsayer.

    Char. Lord Alexas, sweet Alexas, most any thing
Alexas, almost most absolute Alexas, where's the
soothsayer that you praised so to the queen? O, that I
knew this husband, which, you say, must charge his
horns with garlands!
    Alex. Soothsayer!
    Sooth. Your will?
    Char. Is this the man? Is 't you, sir, that know
things?
    Sooth. In nature's infinite book of secrecy
A little I can read.
    Alex.   Show him your hand. 10

Enter ENOBARBUS.

    Eno. Bring in the banquet quickly; wine enough
Cleopatra's health to drink.
    Char. Good sir, give me good fortune.
    Sooth. I make not, but foresee.
    Char. Pray, then, foresee me one.
    Sooth. You shall be yet far fairer than you are.
    Char. He means in flesh.
    Iras. No, you shall paint when you are old.
    Char. Wrinkles forbid!
    Alex. Vex not his prescience; be attentive. 20
    Char. Hush!
    Sooth. You shall be more beloving than beloved.
    Char. I had rather heat my liver with drinking.
    Alex. Nay, hear him.
    Char. Good now, some excellent fortune! Let me be
married to three kings in a forenoon, and widow them
all: let me have a child at fifty, to whom Herod of
Jewry may do homage: find me to marry me with
Octavius Cæsar, and companion me with my mistress.
    Sooth. You shall outlive the lady whom you serve.
    Char. O excellent! I love long life better than figs.
    Sooth. You have seen and proved a fairer former
fortune
Than that which is to approach.
    Char. Then belike my children shall have no names:
prithee, how many boys and wenches must I have?
    Sooth. If every of your wishes had a womb,
And fertile every wish, a million.
    Char. Out, fool! I forgive thee for a witch. 40
    Alex. You think none but your sheets are privy to
your wishes.

ACT I. SCENE I. 4. **plated**, clothed in armor. 5. **office**, service.
6. **tawny**, yellowish brown. 8. **reneges**, renounces. **temper**, self-
restraint. 10. **gipsy's**, suggests that Cleopatra was an Egyptian, and
also used as an opprobrious epithet. 12. **triple**, third; allusion to the
Triumvirate composed of Antony, Lepidus, and Octavius Caesar. 16.
bourn, boundary. 18. **Grates me**, it vexes me. **the sum**, i.e., be brief.
20. **Fulvia**, Antony's wife, of whom Cleopatra is jealous. 23. **Take in**,
conquer. **enfranchise**, set free. 26. **dismission**, dismissal. 31. **homager**, vassal. 34. **ranged**, ordered, or possibly, extended. 37. **mutual**,

exchanging equal love. 39. **weet**, wit, know. 43. **stirr'd**, moved,
excited. The meaning depends somewhat on lines 40-42, which Johnson
thought were spoken as an aside. 60. **approves**, corroborates.
    SCENE II. 11. **banquet**, dessert. 23. **with drinking**, with wine rather
than love. 28. **Herod of Jewry**, the pattern of a blustering tyrant, so
presented in the mystery plays. She would like such a son. 29. **find me**,
by examining my hand. 32. **better than figs**, probably a proverbial
expression, although no citations are forthcoming. Malone saw in this
an allusion to the asp in the basket of figs in Act V. Many commenta-

Char. Nay, come, tell Iras hers.

Alex. We'll know all our fortunes.

Eno. Mine, and most of our fortunes, to-night, shall be—drunk to bed.

Iras. There's a palm presages chastity, if nothing else.

Char. E'en as the o'erflowing Nilus presageth famine.

Iras. Go, you wild bedfellow, you cannot soothsay.

Char. Nay, if an oily palm be not a fruitful prognostication, I cannot scratch mine ear. Prithee, tell her but a worky-day fortune.

Sooth. Your fortunes are alike.

Iras. But how, but how? give me particulars.

Sooth. I have said.

Iras. Am I not an inch of fortune better than she? 60

Char. Well, if you were but an inch of fortune better than I, where would you choose it?

Iras. Not in my husband's nose.

Char. Our worser thoughts heavens mend! Alexas,— come, his fortune, his fortune! O, let him marry a woman that cannot go, sweet Isis, I beseech thee! and let her die too, and give him a worse! and let worse follow worse, till the worst of all follow him laughing to his grave, fifty-fold a cuckold! Good Isis, hear me this prayer, though thou deny me a matter of more weight; good Isis, I beseech thee! 70

Iras. Amen. Dear goddess, hear that prayer of the people! for, as it is a heart-breaking to see a handsome man loose-wived, so it is a deadly sorrow to behold a foul knave uncuckolded: therefore, dear Isis, keep decorum, and fortune him accordingly!

Char. Amen. 79

Alex. Lo, now, if it lay in their hands to make me a cuckold, they would make themselves whores, but they'ld do't!

Eno. Hush! here comes Antony.

Char. Not he; the queen.

Enter CLEOPATRA.

Cleo. Saw you my lord?

Eno. No, lady.

Cleo. Was he not here?

Char. No, madam.

Cleo. He was disposed to mirth; but on the sudden
A Roman thought hath struck him. Enobarbus!

Eno. Madam?

Cleo. Seek him, and bring him hither. Where's Alexas?

Alex. Here, at your service. My lord approaches. 90

Cleo. We will not look upon him: go with us. [*Exeunt.*

Enter ANTONY *with a* Messenger *and* Attendants.

Mess. Fulvia thy wife first came into the field.

Ant. Against my brother Lucius?

Mess. Ay:
But soon that war had end, and the time's state
Made friends of them, jointing their force 'gainst
    Cæsar;

Whose better issue in the war, from Italy,
Upon the first encounter, drave them.

Ant. Well, what worst?

Mess. The nature of bad news infects the teller.

Ant. When it concerns the fool or coward. On: 100
Things that are past are done with me. 'Tis thus;
Who tells me true, though in his tale lie death,
I hear him as he flatter'd.

Mess. Labienus—
This is stiff news—hath, with his Parthian force,
Extended Asia from Euphrates;
His conquering banner shook from Syria
To Lydia and to Ionia;
Whilst—

Ant. Antony, thou wouldst say,—

Mess. O, my lord!

Ant. Speak to me home, mince not the general tongue:
Name Cleopatra as she is call'd in Rome; 110
Rail thou in Fulvia's phrase; and taunt my faults
With such full license as both truth and malice
Have power to utter. O, then we bring forth weeds,
When our quick minds lie still; and our ills told us
Is as our earing. Fare thee well awhile.

Mess. At your noble pleasure. [*Exit.*

Ant. From Sicyon, ho, the news! Speak there!

First Att. The man from Sicyon,—is there such an one?

Sec. Att. He stays upon your will.

Ant. Let him appear.
These strong Egyptian fetters I must break, 120
Or lose myself in dotage.

Enter another Messenger.
    What are you?

Sec. Mess. Fulvia thy wife is dead.

Ant. Where died she?

Sec. Mess. In Sicyon:
Her length of sickness, with what else more serious
Importeth thee to know, this bears. [*Gives a letter.*

Ant. Forbear me. [*Exit Sec. Messenger.*
There's a great spirit gone! Thus did I desire it:
What our contempt doth often hurl from us,
We wish it ours again; the present pleasure,
By revolution lowering, does become
The opposite of itself: she's good, being gone; 130
The hand could pluck her back that shoved her on.
I must from this enchanting queen break off:
Ten thousand harms, more than the ills I know,
My idleness doth hatch. How now! Enobarbus!

Re-enter ENOBARBUS.

Eno. What's your pleasure, sir?

Ant. I must with haste from hence.

Eno. Why, then, we kill all our women: we see how mortal an unkindness is to them; if they suffer our departure, death's the word.

Ant. I must be gone. 140

Eno. Under a compelling occasion, let women die:

tors interpret the soothsayer's words in terms of the outcome of the play. 38. **every of,** every one of. 40. **I forgive . . . witch,** probably I forgive thee because thou art a wizard; possibly, I have no opinion of your powers as a soothsayer. 53. **oily palm,** sweaty or moist palm; indication of a wanton disposition. 55. **worky-day,** ordinary. 67. **Isis,** Egyptian goddess of earth and fertility. 87. **Roman thought.** Schmidt explains as "a thought of Rome"; possibly to be explained as "a thought of duty and virtue." 96. **jointing,** uniting. 103. **Labienus,** emissary of Brutus and Cassius to Orodes, king of Parthia; after Philippi

he became the commander of the Parthian forces. 105. **Extended,** seized upon; legal phrase. **Euphrates,** accented on first syllable. 109. **general tongue,** common report. 111. **Fulvia's phrase.** Plutarch says she was of a "peevish, crooked, and troublesome nature." 114-115. **our ills . . . earing,** telling us our faults improves us as plowing improves land run to weeds. 117. **Sicyon,** ancient city of Greece. 125. **Forbear me,** leave me. 129. **By revolution lowering,** growing worse by the revolution of time. 131. **could,** would be willing to.

it were pity to cast them away for nothing; though, between them and a great cause, they should be esteemed nothing. Cleopatra, catching but the least noise of this, dies instantly; I have seen her die twenty times upon far poorer moment: I do think there is mettle in death, which commits some loving act upon her, she hath such a celerity in dying.

Ant. She is cunning past man's thought. 150

Eno. Alack, sir, no; her passions are made of nothing but the finest part of pure love: we cannot call her winds and waters sighs and tears; they are greater storms and tempests than almanacs can report: this cannot be cunning in her; if it be, she makes a shower of rain as well as Jove.

Ant. Would I had never seen her! 158

Eno. O, sir, you had then left unseen a wonderful piece of work; which not to have been blest withal would have discredited your travel.

Ant. Fulvia is dead.

Eno. Sir?

Ant. Fulvia is dead.

Eno. Fulvia!

Ant. Dead. 166

Eno. Why, sir, give the gods a thankful sacrifice. When it pleaseth their deities to take the wife of a man from him, it shows to man the tailors of the earth; comforting therein, that when old robes are worn out, there are members to make new. If there were no more women but Fulvia, then had you indeed a cut, and the case to be lamented: this grief is crowned with consolation; your old smock brings forth a new petticoat: and indeed the tears live in an onion that should water this sorrow. 177

Ant. The business she hath broached in the state Cannot endure my absence.

Eno. And the business you have broached here cannot be without you; especially that of Cleopatra's, which wholly depends on your abode. 182

Ant. No more light answers. Let our officers Have notice what we purpose. I shall break The cause of our expedience to the queen, And get her leave to part. For not alone The death of Fulvia, with more urgent touches, Do strongly speak to us; but the letters too Of many our contriving friends in Rome Petition us at home: Sextus Pompeius 190 Hath given the dare to Cæsar, and commands The empire of the sea: our slippery people, Whose love is never link'd to the deserver Till his deserts are past, begin to throw Pompey the Great and all his dignities Upon his son; who, high in name and power, Higher than both in blood and life, stands up For the main soldier: whose quality, going on, The sides o' the world may danger: much is breeding, Which, like the courser's hair, hath yet but life, 200 And not a serpent's poison. Say, our pleasure, To such whose place is under us, requires

Our quick remove from hence.

Eno. I shall do 't. [*Exeunt.*

SCENE III. *The same. Another room.*

Enter CLEOPATRA, CHARMIAN, IRAS, *and* ALEXAS.

Cleo. Where is he?

Char. I did not see him since.

Cleo. See where he is, who 's with him, what he does:
I did not send you: if you find him sad,
Say I am dancing; if in mirth, report
That I am sudden sick: quick, and return. [*Exit Alexas.*

Char. Madam, methinks, if you did love him dearly,
You do not hold the method to enforce
The like from him.

Cleo. What should I do, I do not?

Char. In each thing give him way, cross him in nothing.

Cleo. Thou teachest like a fool; the way to lose him.

Char. Tempt him not so too far; I wish, forbear: 11
In time we hate that which we often fear.
But here comes Antony.

Enter ANTONY.

Cleo. I am sick and sullen.

Ant. I am sorry to give breathing to my purpose,—

Cleo. Help me away, dear Charmian; I shall fall:
It cannot be thus long, the sides of nature
Will not sustain it.

Ant. Now, my dearest queen,—

Cleo. Pray you, stand farther from me.

Ant. What 's the matter?

Cleo. I know, by that same eye, there 's some good news.
What says the married woman? You may go: 20
Would she had never given you leave to come!
Let her not say 'tis I that keep you here:
I have no power upon you; hers you are.

Ant. The gods best know,—

Cleo. O, never was there queen
So mightily betray'd! yet at the first
I saw the treasons planted.

Ant. Cleopatra,—

Cleo. Why should I think you can be mine and true,
Though you in swearing shake the throned gods,
Who have been false to Fulvia? Riotous madness,
To be entangled with those mouth-made vows, 30
Which break themselves in swearing!

Ant. Most sweet queen,—

Cleo. Nay, pray you, seek no colour for your going,
But bid farewell, and go: when you sued staying,
Then was the time for words: no going then;
Eternity was in our lips and eyes,
Bliss in our brows' bent; none our parts so poor,
But was a race of heaven: they are so still,
Or thou, the greatest soldier of the world,

146. **upon . . . moment,** for less important reasons. 150. **cunning,** clever in dissembling. 169-172. **it shows . . . new.** Many explanations of this obscure passage; Johnson's is as good as any: "It shows man the tailors of the earth comforting him in this . . . that the deities have made other women to take her place." *Members* may, however, mean "persons." 182. **abode,** staying. 185. **expedience,** expedition, or haste. 187. **urgent touches,** pressing feelings or motives. 189. **Of . . . friends,** many friends working in our interest. 190. **Petition us at home,** i.e., to come home. **Sextus Pompeius,** son of Pompey the Great and now leader of the party opposed to Caesar. 194-196. **throw . . . Upon,**

bestow . . . upon. 197. **blood and life,** mettle and vitality. 198. **main,** principal. 199. **sides,** frame. **danger,** endanger. 200. **like . . . hair,** allusion to the popular belief that a horsehair put into water will turn to a snake.

SCENE III. 8. **like,** same. 10. Collier, followed by many editors, punctuates this line with commas after *teachest* and *fool.* 14. **breathing,** utterance. 16. **sides of nature,** i.e., her body cannot contain her swelling heart, and she will die. Enobarbus has already borne testimony to her use of this device. 20. **married woman,** i.e., Fulvia. 26. **planted,** probably in the gardener's sense. 37. **race of heaven,** of

Art turn'd the greatest liar.

Ant.   How now, lady!

Cleo. I would I had thy inches; thou shouldst know
There were a heart in Egypt.

Ant.   Hear me, queen: 41
The strong necessity of time commands
Our services awhile; but my full heart
Remains in use with you. Our Italy
Shines o'er with civil swords: Sextus Pompeius
Makes his approaches to the port of Rome:
Equality of two domestic powers
Breed scrupulous faction: the hated, grown to
   strength,
Are newly grown to love: the condemn'd Pompey,
Rich in his father's honour, creeps apace 50
Into the hearts of such as have not thrived
Upon the present state, whose numbers threaten;
And quietness, grown sick of rest, would purge
By any desperate change: my more particular,
And that which most with you should safe my going,
Is Fulvia's death.

Cleo. Though age from folly could not give me
   freedom,
It does from childishness: can Fulvia die?

Ant. She 's dead, my queen:
Look here, and at thy sovereign leisure read 60
The garboils she awaked; at the last, best:
See when and where she died.

Cleo.   O most false love!
Where be the sacred vials thou shouldst fill
With sorrowful water? Now I see, I see,
In Fulvia's death, how mine received shall be.

Ant. Quarrel no more, but be prepared to know
The purposes I bear; which are, or cease,
As you shall give the advice. By the fire
That quickens Nilus' slime, I go from hence
Thy soldier, servant; making peace or war 70
As thou affect'st.

Cleo.   Cut my lace, Charmian, come;
But let it be: I am quickly ill, and well,
So Antony loves.

Ant.   My precious queen, forbear;
And give true evidence to his love, which stands
An honourable trial.

Cleo.   So Fulvia told me.
I prithee, turn aside and weep for her;
Then bid adieu to me, and say the tears
Belong to Egypt: good now, play one scene
Of excellent dissembling; and let it look
Like perfect honour.

Ant.   You'll heat my blood: no more. 80

Cleo. You can do better yet; but this is meetly.

Ant. Now, by my sword,—

Cleo.   And target. Still he mends;
But this is not the best. Look, prithee, Charmian,
How this Herculean Roman does become
The carriage of his chafe.

Ant. I'll leave you, lady.

Cleo.   Courteous lord, one word.
Sir, you and I must part, but that 's not it:
Sir, you and I have loved, but there 's not it;
That you know well: something it is I would,—
O, my oblivion is a very Antony, 90
And I am all forgotten.

Ant.   But that your royalty
Holds idleness your subject, I should take you
For idleness itself.

Cleo.   'Tis sweating labour
To bear such idleness so near the heart
As Cleopatra this. But, sir, forgive me;
Since my becomings kill me, when they do not
Eye well to you: your honour calls you hence;
Therefore be deaf to my unpitied folly,
And all the gods go with you! upon your sword
Sit laurel victory! and smooth success 100
Be strew'd before your feet!

Ant.   Let us go. Come;
Our separation so abides, and flies,
That thou, residing here, go'st yet with me,
And I, hence fleeting, here remain with thee.
Away!   [*Exeunt.*

SCENE IV. *Rome. Cæsar's house.*

Enter OCTAVIUS CÆSAR, *reading a letter,* LEPIDUS,
   and their Train.

Cæs. You may see, Lepidus, and henceforth
   know,
It is not Cæsar's natural vice to hate
Our great competitor: from Alexandria
This is the news: he fishes, drinks, and wastes
The lamps of night in revel; is not more manlike
Than Cleopatra; nor the queen of Ptolemy
More womanly than he; hardly gave audience, or
Vouchsafed to think he had partners: you shall find
   there
A man who is the abstract of all faults
That all men follow.

Lep.   I must not think there are 10
Evils enow to darken all his goodness:
His faults in him seem as the spots of heaven,
More fiery by night's blackness; hereditary,
Rather than purchased; what he cannot change,
Than what he chooses.

Cæs. You are too indulgent. Let us grant, it is not
Amiss to tumble on the bed of Ptolemy;
To give a kingdom for a mirth; to sit
And keep the turn of tippling with a slave;
To reel the streets at noon, and stand the buffet 20
With knaves that smell of sweat: say this becomes
   him,—
As his composure must be rare indeed
Whom these things cannot blemish,—yet must
   Antony
No way excuse his soils, when we do bear

---

heavenly origin; defined also as "smack or flavor of heaven." **44. in
use,** i.e., in usufruct, for use. **48. scrupulous,** cautious, or carping.
53. purge, be restored to activity (as by medicinal purgation). **55. safe,**
make safe. **61. garboils,** disturbances, commotions. **63. sacred vials,**
alluding to the supposed custom of the Romans of putting bottles filled
with tears in the tombs of the departed. **71. lace,** cord fastening up
the bodice. **73. So,** if only. **74. evidence,** testimony, i.e., by her
behavior. **78. Egypt,** the queen of Egypt. **81. meetly,** fairly good.
84. Herculean. Antony claimed descent from Anton, son of Hercules.
84-85. does . . . chafe, lends grace to his angry deportment. **90-91. my**

. . . **forgotten,** my forgetful memory is like Antony, and, like him,
has forgotten my power over it. **91-92. your . . . subject,** if you did
not consciously employ trifling (banter) to serve your royal purposes.
97. Eye, appear to the eye.
    SCENE IV. **3. competitor,** associate. **6. Ptolemy,** allusion to Cleo-
patra's brother, to whom she had been married according to Egyptian
custom. She was supposed to have poisoned him. **9. abstract,** epitome.
20. reel, stagger along. **22. composure,** composition, temperament.
24. soils, blemishes.

So great weight in his lightness. If he fill'd
His vacancy with his voluptuousness,
Full surfeits, and the dryness of his bones,
Call on him for 't: but to confound such time,
That drums him from his sport, and speaks as loud
As his own state and ours,—'tis to be chid 30
As we rate boys, who, being mature in knowledge,
Pawn their experience to their present pleasure,
And so rebel to judgement.

Enter a Messenger.

Lep.   Here 's more news.
Mess. Thy biddings have been done; and every
    hour,
Most noble Cæsar, shalt thou have report
How 'tis abroad. Pompey is strong at sea;
And it appears he is beloved of those
That only have fear'd Cæsar: to the ports
The discontents repair, and men's reports
Give him much wrong'd.
Cæs.   I should have known no less. 40
It hath been taught us from the primal state,
That he which is was wish'd until he were;
And the ebb'd man, ne'er loved till ne'er worth love,
Comes dear'd by being lack'd. This common body,
Like to a vagabond flag upon the stream,
Goes to and back, lackeying the varying tide,
To rot itself with motion.
Mess.   Cæsar, I bring thee word,
Menecrates and Menas, famous pirates,
Make the sea serve them, which they ear and wound
With keels of every kind: many hot inroads 50
They make in Italy; the borders maritime
Lack blood to think on 't, and flush youth revolt:
No vessel can peep forth, but 'tis as soon
Taken as seen; for Pompey's name strikes more
Than could his war resisted.
Cæs.   Antony,
Leave thy lascivious wassails. When thou once
Wast beaten from Modena, where thou slew'st
Hirtius and Pansa, consuls, at thy heel
Did famine follow; whom thou fought'st against,
Though daintily brought up, with patience more 60
Than savages could suffer: thou didst drink
The stale of horses, and the gilded puddle
Which beasts would cough at: thy palate then did
    deign
The roughest berry on the rudest hedge;
Yea, like the stag, when snow the pasture sheets,
The barks of trees thou browsed'st; on the Alps
It is reported thou didst eat strange flesh,
Which some did die to look on: and all this—
It wounds thine honour that I speak it now—
Was borne so like a soldier, that thy cheek 70
So much as lank'd not.
Lep.   'Tis pity of him.
Cæs. Let his shames quickly
Drive him to Rome: 'tis time we twain
Did show ourselves i' the field; and to that end
Assemble we immediate council: Pompey

Thrives in our idleness.
Lep.   To-morrow, Cæsar,
I shall be furnish'd to inform you rightly
Both what by sea and land I can be able
To front this present time.
Cæs.   Till which encounter,
It is my business too. Farewell.   80
Lep. Farewell, my lord: what you shall know
    meantime
Of stirs abroad, I shall beseech you, sir,
To let me be partaker.
Cæs.   Doubt not, sir;
I knew it for my bond.   [*Exeunt.*

SCENE V. *Alexandria. Cleopatra's palace.*

Enter CLEOPATRA, CHARMIAN, IRAS, *and* MARDIAN.

Cleo. Charmian!
Char. Madam?
Cleo. Ha, ha!
Give me to drink mandragora.
Char.   Why, madam?
Cleo. That I might sleep out this great gap of time
My Antony is away.
Char.   You think of him too much.
Cleo. O, 'tis treason!
Char.   Madam, I trust, not so.
Cleo. Thou, eunuch Mardian!
Mar.   What 's your highness' pleasure?
Cleo. Not now to hear thee sing; I take no pleasure
In aught an eunuch has: 'tis well for thee, 10
That, being unseminar'd, thy freer thoughts
May not fly forth of Egypt. Hast thou affections?
Mar. Yes, gracious madam.
Cleo. Indeed!
Mar. Not in deed, madam; for I can do nothing
But what indeed is honest to be done:
Yet have I fierce affections, and think
What Venus did with Mars.
Cleo.   O Charmian,
Where think'st thou he is now? Stands he, or sits he?
Or does he walk? or is he on his horse? 20
O happy horse, to bear the weight of Antony!
Do bravely, horse! for wot'st thou whom thou movest?
The demi-Atlas of this earth, the arm
And burgonet of men. He 's speaking now,
Or murmuring 'Where 's my serpent of old Nile?'
For so he calls me: now I feed myself
With most delicious poison. Think on me,
That am with Phœbus' amorous pinches black,
And wrinkled deep in time? Broad-fronted Cæsar,
When thou wast here above the ground, I was 30
A morsel for a monarch: and great Pompey
Would stand and make his eyes grow in my brow;
There would he anchor his aspect and die
With looking on his life.

Enter ALEXAS.

Alex.   Sovereign of Egypt, hail!

25. **lightness,** levity, with play on literal meaning. 25-28. **If . . . for 't,**
if he filled his idle hours with voluptuousness, gluttony, and the ruin
of his health, let him pay for it. 40. **Give him,** represent him as. 42.
That . . . were, that the man in power was desired until he obtained
it. 43. **ebb'd,** decayed in fortune. 44. **Comes dear'd,** becomes
endeared. 45. **flag,** iris. 46. **lackeying,** following like a lackey.
49. **ear,** plow. 52. **Lack blood,** turn pale. **flush,** lusty. 54. **strikes,**
destroys. 56. **wassails,** carousals. 56-71. **When . . . not,** a passage
closely following Plutarch and serving to improve our opinion of
Antony by displaying his romantic virtues. 62. **gilded,** covered with
red or yellow slime. 71. **lank'd,** became thin. 84. **bond,** bounden duty.
SCENE V. 4. **mandragora,** juice of the mandrake (a narcotic). 11.
unseminar'd, deprived of virility. 23. **demi-Atlas.** She disregards
Lepidus as a triumvir. 24. **burgonet,** light casque or steel cap.
29. **Cæsar,** Julius Caesar. 33. **aspect,** look, glance. 36. **medicine,**
drug, elixir; possibly, physician. 37. **tinct,** color. 48. **arm-gaunt.**

Cleo. How much unlike art thou Mark Antony!
Yet, coming from him, that great medicine hath
With his tinct gilded thee.
How goes it with my brave Mark Antony?
   Alex. Last thing he did, dear queen,
He kiss'd,—the last of many doubled kisses,—   40
This orient pearl. His speech sticks in my heart.
   Cleo. Mine ear must pluck it thence.
   Alex.   'Good friend,' quoth he,
'Say, the firm Roman to great Egypt sends
This treasure of an oyster; at whose foot,
To mend the petty present, I will piece
Her opulent throne with kingdoms; all the east,
Say thou, shall call her mistress.' So he nodded,
†And soberly did mount an arm-gaunt steed,
Who neigh'd so high, that what I would have spoke
Was beastly dumb'd by him.
   Cleo.   What, was he sad or merry?   50
   Alex. Like to the time o' the year between the
      extremes
Of hot and cold, he was nor sad nor merry.
   Cleo. O well-divided disposition! Note him,
Note him, good Charmian, 'tis the man; but note
      him:
He was not sad, for he would shine on those
That make their looks by his; he was not merry,
Which seem'd to tell them his remembrance lay
In Egypt with his joy; but between both:
O heavenly mingle! Be'st thou sad or merry,
The violence of either thee becomes,   60
So does it no man else. Met'st thou my posts?
   Alex. Ay, madam, twenty several messengers:
Why do you send so thick?
   Cleo.   Who's born that day
When I forget to send to Antony,
Shall die a beggar. Ink and paper, Charmian.
Welcome, my good Alexas. Did I, Charmian,
Ever love Cæsar so?
   Char.   O that brave Cæsar!
   Cleo. Be choked with such another emphasis!
Say, the brave Antony.
   Char.   The valiant Cæsar!
   Cleo. By Isis, I will give thee bloody teeth,   70
If thou with Cæsar paragon again
My man of men.
   Char.   By your most gracious pardon,
I sing but after you.
   Cleo.   My salad days,
When I was green in judgement: cold in blood,
To say as I said then! But, come, away;
Get me ink and paper!
He shall have every day a several greeting,
Or I'll unpeople Egypt.   [*Exeunt.*

ACT II.

SCENE I. *Messina. Pompey's house.*

Enter POMPEY, MENECRATES, *and* MENAS, *in warlike*
manner.

Pom. If the great gods be just, they shall assist
The deeds of justest men.
   Mene.   Know, worthy Pompey,
That what they do delay, they not deny.
   Pom. Whiles we are suitors to their throne, decays
The thing we sue for.
   Mene.   We, ignorant of ourselves,
Beg often our own harms, which the wise powers
Deny us for our good; so find we profit
By losing of our prayers.
   Pom.   I shall do well:
The people love me, and the sea is mine;
My powers are crescent, and my auguring hope   10
Says it will come to the full. Mark Antony
In Egypt sits at dinner, and will make
No wars without doors: Cæsar gets money where
He loses hearts: Lepidus flatters both,
Of both is flatter'd; but he neither loves,
Nor either cares for him.
   Men.   Cæsar and Lepidus
Are in the field: a mighty strength they carry.
   Pom. Where have you this? 'tis false.
   Men.   From Silvius, sir.
   Pom. He dreams: I know they are in Rome
      together,
Looking for Antony. But all the charms of love,   20
Salt Cleopatra, soften thy waned lip!
Let witchcraft join with beauty, lust with both!
Tie up the libertine in a field of feasts,
Keep his brain fuming; Epicurean cooks
Sharpen with cloyless sauce his appetite;
That sleep and feeding may prorogue his honour
Even till a Lethe'd dulness!

Enter VARRIUS.

        How now, Varrius!
   Var. This is most certain that I shall deliver:
Mark Antony is every hour in Rome
Expected: since he went from Egypt 'tis   30
A space for further travel.
   Pom.   I could have given less matter
A better ear. Menas, I did not think
This amorous surfeiter would donn'd his helm
For such a petty war: his soldiership
Is twice the other twain: but let us rear
The higher our opinion, that our stirring
Can from the lap of Egypt's widow pluck
The ne'er-lust-wearied Antony.
   Men.   I cannot hope
Cæsar and Antony shall well greet together:
His wife that's dead did trespasses to Cæsar;   40
His brother warr'd upon him; although, I think,
Not moved by Antony.
   Pom.   I know not, Menas,
How lesser enmities may give way to greater.
Were't not that we stand up against them all,
'Twere pregnant they should square between
      themselves;
For they have entertained cause enough
To draw their swords: but how the fear of us

gaunt from bearing arms in warlike service, or with gaunt limbs;
many emendations. 50. **dumb'd**, silenced. 71. **paragon**, compare on
equal terms. 73-75. **My salad . . . then.** The F punctuation puts a
comma after *judgement* instead of a colon. This is correct from the simple
fact that hot and dry, not cold and wet (*green*), represent the elementary
condition of judgment. She means to say that she spoke as she did then
because she was in her salad days, when her judgment was green and
her blood cold.

ACT II. SCENE I. 10. **crescent**, on the increase. **auguring**, prophesying. 21. **Salt**, wanton. **waned**, faded, withered. 23. **Tie . . .**
feasts, probably, as an animal might be staked out in a rich pasture.
25. **cloyless**, which will not satiate. 26. **prorogue**, defer the operation
of. 27. **Lethe'd**, oblivious. 31. **space**, time enough. 36. **opinion**,
of ourselves. 37. **Egypt's widow**, Cleopatra, widow of the young
king Ptolemy. 41. **His brother**, Lucius Antonius. **warr'd**, so F_2; F:
wan'd. 45. **square**, quarrel, or fight.

May cement their divisions and bind up
The petty difference, we yet not know.
Be 't as our gods will have 't! It only stands   50
Our lives upon to use our strongest hands.
Come, Menas.   [*Exeunt.*

SCENE II. *Rome. The house of Lepidus.*

Enter ENOBARBUS *and* LEPIDUS.

Lep. Good Enobarbus, 'tis a worthy deed,
And shall become you well, to entreat your captain
To soft and gentle speech.
    Eno.   I shall entreat him
To answer like himself: if Cæsar move him,
Let Antony look over Cæsar's head
And speak as loud as Mars. By Jupiter,
Were I the wearer of Antonius' beard,
I would not shave 't to-day.
    Lep.   'Tis not a time
For private stomaching.
    Eno.   Every time
Serves for the matter that is then born in 't.   10
    Lep. But small to greater matters must give way.
    Eno. Not if the small come first.
    Lep.   Your speech is passion:
But, pray you, stir no embers up. Here comes
The noble Antony.

Enter ANTONY *and* VENTIDIUS.

    Eno.   And yonder, Cæsar.

Enter CÆSAR, MECÆNAS, *and* AGRIPPA.

    Ant. If we compose well here, to Parthia:
Hark, Ventidius.
    Cæs.   I do not know,
Mecænas; ask Agrippa.
    Lep.   Noble friends,
That which combined us was most great, and let not
A leaner action rend us. What 's amiss,
May it be gently heard: when we debate   20
Our trivial difference loud, we do commit
Murder in healing wounds: then, noble partners,
The rather, for I earnestly beseech,
Touch you the sourest points with sweetest terms,
Nor curstness grow to the matter.
    Ant.   'Tis spoken well.
Were we before our armies, and to fight,
I should do thus.   [*Flourish.*
    Cæs. Welcome to Rome.
    Ant.   Thank you.
    Cæs.   Sit.
    Ant.   Sit, sir.
    Cæs.   Nay, then.
    Ant. I learn, you take things ill which are not so,
Or being, concern you not.
    Cæs.   I must be laugh'd at,   30
If, or for nothing or a little, I
Should say myself offended, and with you
Chiefly i' the world; more laugh'd at, that I should
Once name you derogately, when to sound your name

It not concern'd me.
    Ant.   My being in Egypt, Cæsar,
What was 't to you?
    Cæs. No more than my residing here at Rome
Might be to you in Egypt: yet, if you there
Did practise on my state, your being in Egypt
Might be my question.
    Ant.   How intend you, practised?   40
    Cæs. You may be pleased to catch at mine intent
By what did here befal me. Your wife and brother
Made wars upon me; and their contestation
Was theme for you, you were the word of war.
    Ant. You do mistake your business; my brother
        never
Did urge me in his act: I did inquire it;
And have my learning from some true reports,
That drew their swords with you. Did he not rather
Discredit my authority with yours;
And make the wars alike against my stomach,   50
Having alike your cause? Of this my letters
Before did satisfy you. If you'll patch a quarrel,
As matter whole you have not to make it with,
It must not be with this.
    Cæs.   You praise yourself
By laying defects of judgement to me; but
You patch'd up your excuses.
    Ant.   Not so, not so;
I know you could not lack, I am certain on 't,
Very necessity of this thought, that I,
Your partner in the cause 'gainst which he fought,
Could not with graceful eyes attend those wars   60
Which fronted mine own peace. As for my wife,
I would you had her spirit in such another:
The third o' the world is yours; which with a snaffle
You may pace easy, but not such a wife.
    Eno. Would we had all such wives, that the men
might go to wars with the women!
    Ant. So much uncurbable, her garboils, Cæsar,
Made out of her impatience, which not wanted
Shrewdness of policy too, I grieving grant
Did you too much disquiet: for that you must   70
But say, I could not help it.
    Cæs.   I wrote to you
When rioting in Alexandria; you
Did pocket up my letters, and with taunts
Did gibe my missive out of audience.
    Ant.   Sir,
He fell upon me ere admitted: then
Three kings I had newly feasted, and did want
Of what I was i' the morning: but next day
I told him of myself; which was as much
As to have ask'd him pardon. Let this fellow
Be nothing of our strife; if we contend,   80
Out of our question wipe him.
    Cæs.   You have broken
The article of your oath; which you shall never
Have tongue to charge me with.
    Lep.   Soft, Cæsar!
    Ant.   No,
Lepidus, let him speak:
The honour is sacred which he talks on now,

50-51. **It . . . upon**, it solely and vitally concerns our lives.
    SCENE II.   8. **I would not shave 't.** Since plucking the beard was a
symbolic act for starting a fight, this means that, if he were Antony,
he would not avoid a contest.   9. **stomaching**, giving way to resentment.   15. **compose**, come to an agreement. **to Parthia**, I shall go to
Parthia.   25. **curstness**, ill-humor. **grow to**, be added to (the real

business).   34. **derogately**, disparagingly.   40. **question**, business.
44. **theme for you**, had you for theme, or supplied you with a ground for
your intrigues (Cuningham).   46. **urge . . . act**, claim that he was
fighting in my behalf. **inquire**, inquire into.   51. **Having . . . cause**, I
having the same cause of resentment that you had.   52. **patch a quarrel**,
make a quarrel out of shreds and patches, since you have no real ground.

Supposing that I lack'd it. But, on, Cæsar;
The article of my oath.
    Cæs. To lend me arms and aid when I required
    them;
The which you both denied.
    Ant.   Neglected, rather;
And then when poison'd hours had bound me up   90
From mine own knowledge. As nearly as I may,
I'll play the penitent to you: but mine honesty
Shall not make poor my greatness, nor my power
Work without it. Truth is, that Fulvia,
To have me out of Egypt, made wars here;
For which myself, the ignorant motive, do
So far ask pardon as befits mine honour
To stoop in such a case.
    Lep.   'Tis noble spoken.
    Mec. If it might please you, to enforce no further
The griefs between ye: to forget them quite   100
Were to remember that the present need
Speaks to atone you.
    Lep.   Worthily spoken, Mecænas.
    Eno. Or, if you borrow one another's love for the
instant, you may, when you hear no more words of
Pompey, return it again: you shall have time to
wrangle in when you have nothing else to do.
    Ant. Thou art a soldier only: speak no more.
    Eno. That truth should be silent I had almost forgot.
    Ant. You wrong this presence; therefore speak no
    more.   111
    Eno. Go to, then; your considerate stone.
    Cæs. I do not much dislike the matter, but
The manner of his speech: for 't cannot be
We shall remain in friendship, our conditions
So differing in their acts. Yet, if I knew
What hoop should hold us stanch, from edge to edge
O' the world I would pursue it.
    Agr.   Give me leave, Cæsar,—
    Cæs. Speak, Agrippa.
    Agr. Thou hast a sister by the mother's side,   120
Admired Octavia: great Mark Antony
Is now a widower.
    Cæs.   Say not so, Agrippa:
If Cleopatra heard you, your reproof
Were well deserved of rashness.
    Ant. I am not married, Cæsar: let me hear Agrippa
further speak.
    Agr. To hold you in perpetual amity,
To make you brothers, and to knit your hearts
With an unslipping knot, take Antony
Octavia to his wife; whose beauty claims   130
No worse a husband than the best of men;
Whose virtue and whose general graces speak
That which none else can utter. By this marriage,
All little jealousies, which now seem great,
And all great fears, which now import their dangers,
Would then be nothing: truths would be tales,
Where now half tales be truths: her love to both
Would, each to other and all loves to both,
Draw after her. Pardon what I have spoke;
For 'tis a studied, not a present thought,   140
By duty ruminated.

    Ant.   Will Cæsar speak?
    Cæs. Not 'till he hears how Antony is touch'd
With what is spoke already.
    Ant.   What power is in Agrippa,
If I would say, 'Agrippa, be it so,'
To make this good?
    Cæs.   The power of Cæsar, and
His power unto Octavia.
    Ant.   May I never
To this good purpose, that so fairly shows,
Dream of impediment! Let me have thy hand:
Further this act of grace; and from this hour
The heart of brothers govern in our loves   150
And sway our great designs!
    Cæs.   There is my hand.
A sister I bequeath you, whom no brother
Did ever love so dearly: let her live
To join our kingdoms and our hearts; and never
Fly off our loves again!
    Lep.   Happily, amen!
    Ant. I did not think to draw my sword 'gainst
    Pompey;
For he hath laid strange courtesies and great
Of late upon me: I must thank him only,
Lest my remembrance suffer ill report;
At heel of that, defy him.
    Lep.   Time calls upon 's: 160
Of us must Pompey presently be sought,
Or else he seeks out us.
    Ant.   Where lies he?
    Cæs. About the mount Misenum.
    Ant. What is his strength by land?
    Cæs. Great and increasing: but by sea
He is an absolute master.
    Ant.   So is the fame.
Would we had spoke together! Haste we for it:
Yet, ere we put ourselves in arms, dispatch we
The business we have talk'd of.
    Cæs.   With most gladness;
And do invite you to my sister's view,   170
Whither straight I'll lead you.
    Ant.   Let us, Lepidus,
Not lack your company.
    Lep.   Noble Antony,
Not sickness should detain me.
        [*Flourish. Exeunt Cæsar, Antony, and Lepidus.*
    Mec. Welcome from Egypt, sir.
    Eno. Half the heart of Cæsar, worthy Mecænas! My
honourable friend, Agrippa!
    Agr. Good Enobarbus!
    Mec. We have cause to be glad that matters are so
well digested. You stayed well by 't in Egypt.   180
    Eno. Ay, sir; we did sleep day out of countenance,
and made the night light with drinking.
    Mec. Eight wild-boars roasted whole at a breakfast,
and but twelve persons there; is this true?
    Eno. This was but as a fly by an eagle: we had much
more monstrous matter of feast, which worthily deserved noting.
    Mec. She 's a most triumphant lady, if report be
square to her.   190

---

60. **graceful eyes attend,** regard favorably. 63-64. **which . . . wife,** which you may put through its paces easily with a snaffle-bit, but you cannot so control such a wife. 67. **garboils,** brawls. 74. **missive,** messenger. 93-94. **my power . . . it.** He seems to mean that he will not exert his power unless his greatness (*honour*) is recognized as intact. 112. **your . . . stone,** I shall continue to reflect, but be as silent as a stone.

121. **Octavia,** full sister, not half-sister, of Octavius. 135. **import,** carry with them. 146. **unto,** over. 155. **Fly . . . again,** desert each other again. 160. **At heel of,** immediately after. 170. **my sister's view,** to see my sister. 182. **light,** giddy and frivolous, with pun on the commoner meaning. 190. **square,** just.

Eno. When she first met Mark Antony, she pursed
up his heart, upon the river of Cydnus.

Agr. There she appeared indeed; or my reporter
devised well for her.

Eno. I will tell you.
The barge she sat in, like a burnish'd throne,
Burn'd on the water: the poop was beaten gold;
Purple the sails, and so perfumed that
The winds were love-sick with them; the oars were
   silver,
Which to the tune of flutes kept stroke, and made   200
The water which they beat to follow faster,
As amorous of their strokes. For her own person,
It beggar'd all description: she did lie
In her pavilion—cloth-of-gold of tissue—
O'er-picturing that Venus where we see
The fancy outwork nature: on each side her
Stood pretty dimpled boys, like smiling Cupids,
With divers-colour'd fans, whose wind did seem
To glow the delicate cheeks which they did cool,
And what they undid did.

   Agr.   O, rare for Antony!   210

   Eno. Her gentlewomen, like the Nereides,
So many mermaids, tended her i' the eyes,
And made their bends adornings: at the helm
A seeming mermaid steers: the silken tackle
Swell with the touches of those flower-soft hands,
That yarely frame the office. From the barge
A strange invisible perfume hits the sense
Of the adjacent wharfs. The city cast
Her people out upon her; and Antony,
Enthroned i' the market-place, did sit alone,   220
Whistling to the air; which, but for vacancy,
Had gone to gaze on Cleopatra too
And made a gap in nature.

   Agr.   Rare Egyptian!

   Eno. Upon her landing, Antony sent to her,
Invited her to supper: she replied,
It should be better he became her guest;
Which she entreated: our courteous Antony,
Whom ne'er the word of 'No' woman heard speak,
Being barber'd ten times o'er, goes to the feast,
And for his ordinary pays his heart   230
For what his eyes eat only.

   Agr.   Royal wench!
She made great Cæsar lay his sword to bed:
He plough'd her, and she cropp'd.

   Eno.   I saw her once
Hop forty paces through the public street;
And having lost her breath, she spoke, and panted,
That she did make defect perfection,
And, breathless, power breathe forth.

   Mec. Now Antony must leave her utterly.

   Eno. Never; he will not:
Age cannot wither her, nor custom stale   240
Her infinite variety: other women cloy
The appetites they feed; but she makes hungry
Where most she satisfies: for vilest things
Become themselves in her; that the holy priests
Bless her when she is riggish.

Mec. If beauty, wisdom, modesty, can settle
The heart of Antony, Octavia is
A blessed lottery to him.

   Agr.   Let us go.
Good Enobarbus, make yourself my guest
Whilst you abide here.

   Eno.   Humbly, sir, I thank you.   250
                                        [*Exeunt.*

SCENE III. *The same. Cæsar's house.*

Enter ANTONY, CÆSAR, OCTAVIA *between them, and*
  Attendants.

   Ant. The world and my great office will sometimes
Divide me from your bosom.

   Octa.   All which time
Before the gods my knee shall bow my prayers
To them for you.

   Ant.   Good night, sir. My Octavia,
Read not my blemishes in the world's report:
I have not kept my square; but that to come
Shall be all done by the rule. Good night, dear lady.
Good night, sir.

   Cæs. Good night.   [*Exeunt Cæsar and Octavia.*

   Enter Soothsayer.

   Ant. Now, sirrah; you do wish yourself in Egypt?   10

   Sooth. Would I had never come from thence, nor
   you
Thither!

   Ant. If you can, your reason?

   Sooth.   I see it in
My motion, have it not in my tongue: but yet
Hie you to Egypt again.

   Ant.   Say to me,
Whose fortunes shall rise higher, Cæsar's or mine?

   Sooth. Cæsar's.
Therefore, O Antony, stay not by his side:
Thy demon, that's thy spirit which keeps thee, is
Noble, courageous, high, unmatchable,   20
Where Cæsar's is not; but, near him, thy angel
Becomes a fear, as being o'erpower'd: therefore
Make space enough between you.

   Ant.   Speak this no more.

   Sooth. To none but thee; no more, but when to thee.
If thou dost play with him at any game,
Thou art sure to lose; and, of that natural luck,
He beats thee 'gainst the odds: thy lustre thickens,
When he shines by: I say again, thy spirit
Is all afraid to govern thee near him;
But, he away, 'tis noble.

   Ant.   Get thee gone: 30
Say to Ventidius I would speak with him:
                               [*Exit Soothsayer.*
He shall to Parthia. Be it art or hap,
He hath spoken true: the very dice obey him;
And in our sports my better cunning faints
Under his chance: if we draw lots, he speeds;
His cocks do win the battle still of mine,

---

192. **upon . . . Cydnus,** upon the banks of, or more probably, on the
river of Cydnus, by the spectacle described below.   204. **cloth-of-gold
of tissue,** cloth made of gold thread and silk woven together (Onions);
very obscure. Possibly there should be a comma after *gold.*   205. **that
Venus,** usually thought to refer to the Venus Anadyomene of Apelles.
209. **glow,** cause to glow.   212. **tended her i' the eyes,** waited in her
sight.   213. **made . . . adornings,** possibly, added to their beauty by
their obeisances; many interpretations.   216. **yarely,** nimbly, briskly.

218. **wharfs,** banks.   230. **ordinary,** meal, supper.   232. **Cæsar,** Julius
Cæsar, by whom Cleopatra had a son named Caesarion.   245. **riggish,**
wanton.   248. **lottery,** prize.
   SCENE III.   6. **kept my square,** kept within my duty. Shakespeare
means Antony to be what is called good-hearted; Antony is probably
truly repentant, but unstable.   13-14. **in My motion,** probably refers
to the motions of his spirits; might be rendered as "instinctively."
19. **demon,** guardian spirit, in accordance with the doctrine that each

When it is all to nought; and his quails ever
Beat mine, inhoop'd, at odds. I will to Egypt:
And though I make this marriage for my peace,
I' the east my pleasure lies.

Enter VENTIDIUS.

O, come, Ventidius, 40
You must to Parthia: your commission 's ready;
Follow me, and receive 't. [*Exeunt.*

SCENE IV. *The same. A street.*

Enter LEPIDUS, MECÆNAS, *and* AGRIPPA.

Lep. Trouble yourselves no further: pray you,
hasten
Your generals after.
Agr. Sir, Mark Antony
Will e'en but kiss Octavia, and we'll follow.
Lep. Till I shall see you in your soldier's dress,
Which will become you both, farewell.
Mec. We shall,
As I conceive the journey, be at the Mount
Before you, Lepidus.
Lep. Your way is shorter;
My purposes do draw me much about:
You'll win two days upon me.
Mec. }
Agr. } Sir, good success!
Lep. Farewell. [*Exeunt.* 10

SCENE V. *Alexandria. Cleopatra's palace.*

Enter CLEOPATRA, CHARMIAN, IRAS, *and* ALEXAS.

Cleo. Give me some music; music, moody food
Of us that trade in love.
Attend. The music, ho!

Enter MARDIAN *the Eunuch.*

Cleo. Let it alone; let 's to billiards: come,
Charmian.
Char. My arm is sore; best play with Mardian.
Cleo. As well a woman with an eunuch play'd
As with a woman. Come, you'll play with me, sir?
Mar. As well as I can, madam.
Cleo. And when good will is show'd, though 't come
too short,
The actor may plead pardon. I'll none now:
Give me mine angle; we'll to the river: there, 10
My music playing far off, I will betray
Tawny-finn'd fishes; my bended hook shall pierce
Their slimy jaws; and, as I draw them up,
I'll think them every one an Antony,
And say 'Ah, ha! you 're caught.'
Char. 'Twas merry when
You wager'd on your angling; when your diver
Did hang a salt-fish on his hook, which he
With fervency drew up.
Cleo. That time,—O times!—

I laugh'd him out of patience; and that night
I laugh'd him into patience: and next morn, 20
Ere the ninth hour, I drunk him to his bed;
Then put my tires and mantles on him, whilst
I wore his sword Philippan.

Enter a Messenger.

O, from Italy!
Ram thou thy fruitful tidings in mine ears,
That long time have been barren.
Mess. Madam, madam,—
Cleo. Antonius dead!—If thou say so, villain,
Thou kill'st thy mistress: but well and free,
If thou so yield him, there is gold, and here
My bluest veins to kiss; a hand that kings
Have lipp'd, and trembled kissing. 30
Mess. First, madam, he is well.
Cleo. Why, there 's more gold.
But, sirrah, mark, we use
To say the dead are well: bring it to that,
The gold I give thee will I melt and pour
Down thy ill-uttering throat.
Mess. Good madam, hear me.
Cleo. Well, go to, I will;
But there 's no goodness in thy face: if Antony
Be free and healthful,—so tart a favour
To trumpet such good tidings! If not well, 39
Thou shouldst come like a Fury crown'd with snakes,
Not like a formal man.
Mess. Will 't please you hear me?
Cleo. I have a mind to strike thee ere thou speak'st:
Yet, if thou say Antony lives, is well,
Or friends with Cæsar, or not captive to him,
I'll set thee in a shower of gold, and hail
Rich pearls upon thee.
Mess. Madam, he 's well.
Cleo. Well said.
Mess. And friends with Cæsar.
Cleo. Thou 'rt an honest man.
Mess. Cæsar and he are greater friends than ever.
Cleo. Make thee a fortune from me.
Mess. But yet, madam,—
Cleo. I do not like 'But yet,' it does allay 50
The good precedence; fie upon 'But yet'!
'But yet' is as a gaoler to bring forth
Some monstrous malefactor. Prithee, friend,
Pour out the pack of matter to mine ear,
The good and bad together: he 's friends with Cæsar;
In state of health thou say'st; and thou say'st free.
Mess. Free, madam! no; I made no such report:
He 's bound unto Octavia.
Cleo. For what good turn?
Mess. For the best turn i' the bed.
Cleo. I am pale, Charmian.
Mess. Madam, he 's married to Octavia. 60
Cleo. The most infectious pestilence upon thee!
[*Strikes him down.*
Mess. Good madam, patience.
Cleo. What say you? Hence,
[*Strikes him again.*

---

of us is attended by a special angel, or by two angels, a good and a bad.
Macbeth declares his genius is rebuked by that of Banquo as "Mark
Antony's was by Cæsar" (*Macbeth*, III, i, 54-57). This play and
Macbeth were probably written about the same time. 27. **thickens,**
grows dim. 30. **he away, 'tis,** Pope's emendation of F: *he alway 'tis.*
32. **hap,** accident, chance. 34. **cunning,** skill. 35. **chance,** luck.
38. **inhoop'd.** The birds were inclosed in hoops to make them fight.
I will to Egypt. Antony makes a gambler's decision.

SCENE IV. 6. **the Mount,** Mount Misenum.
SCENE V. 3. **billiards.** There were no billiards in those days. 10.
angle, rod and line. 17. **salt-fish . . . hook,** an incident recorded in
Plutarch; an ancient jest. 22. **tires,** probably, headdresses, though it
may be general for "attire." 23. **Philippan,** apparently named for the
victory of Philippi. 38. **tart a favour,** sour a visage. 41. **formal man,**
ordinary man, or in form of man. 51. **good precedence,** the good
news which preceded it.

Horrible villain! or I'll spurn thine eyes
Like balls before me; I'll unhair thy head:
                              [*She hales him up and down.*
Thou shalt be whipp'd with wire, and stew'd in brine,
Smarting in lingering pickle.
  Mess.   Gracious madam,
I that do bring the news made not the match.
  Cleo. Say 'tis not so, a province I will give thee,
And make thy fortunes proud: the blow thou hadst
Shall make thy peace for moving me to rage;   70
And I will boot thee with what gift beside
Thy modesty can beg.
  Mess.   He 's married, madam.
  Cleo. Rogue, thou hast lived too long. [*Draws a knife.*
  Mess.   Nay, then I'll run.
What mean you, madam? I have made no fault. [*Exit.*
  Char. Good madam, keep yourself within yourself:
The man is innocent.
  Cleo. Some innocents 'scape not the thunderbolt.
Melt Egypt into Nile! and kindly creatures
Turn all to serpents! Call the slave again:
Though I am mad, I will not bite him: call.   80
  Char. He is afeard to come.
  Cleo.   I will not hurt him.
                              [*Exit Charmian.*
These hands do lack nobility, that they strike
A meaner than myself; since I myself
Have given myself the cause.

Re-enter CHARMIAN *and* Messenger.

                  Come hither, sir.
Though it be honest, it is never good
To bring bad news: give to a gracious message
An host of tongues; but let ill tidings tell
Themselves when they be felt.
  Mess.   I have done my duty.
  Cleo. Is he married?
I cannot hate thee worser than I do,   90
If thou again say 'Yes.'
  Mess.   He 's married, madam.
  Cleo. The gods confound thee! dost thou hold there
    still?
  Mess. Should I lie, madam?
  Cleo.   O, I would thou didst,
So half my Egypt were submerged and made
A cistern for scaled snakes! Go, get thee hence:
Hadst thou Narcissus in thy face, to me
Thou wouldst appear most ugly. He is married?
  Mess. I crave your highness' pardon.
  Cleo.   He is married?
  Mess. Take no offence that I would not offend you:
To punish me for what you make me do   100
Seems much unequal: he 's married to Octavia.
  Cleo. O, that his fault should make a knave of thee,
That art not what thou 'rt sure of! Get thee hence:
The merchandise which thou hast brought from
    Rome
Are all too dear for me: lie they upon thy hand,
And be undone by 'em!   [*Exit Messenger.*
  Char.   Good your highness, patience.

  Cleo. In praising Antony, I have dispraised Cæsar.
  Char. Many times, madam.
  Cleo.   I am paid for 't now.
Lead me from hence;
I faint: O Iras, Charmian! 'tis no matter.   110
Go to the fellow, good Alexas; bid him
Report the feature of Octavia, her years,
Her inclination, let him not leave out
The colour of her hair: bring me word quickly.
                              [*Exit Alexas.*
Let him for ever go:—let him not—Charmian,
Though he be painted one way like a Gorgon,
The other way 's a Mars. Bid you Alexas [*To Mardian.*
Bring me word how tall she is. Pity me, Charmian,
But do not speak to me. Lead me to my chamber.
                              [*Exeunt.*

SCENE VI. *Near Misenum.*

Flourish. Enter POMPEY *and* MENAS *at one side, with
    drum and trumpet: at another,* CÆSAR, ANTONY,
    LEPIDUS, ENOBARBUS, MECÆNAS, *with* Soldiers
    marching.*

  Pom. Your hostages I have, so have you mine;
And we shall talk before we fight.
  Cæs.   Most meet
That first we come to words; and therefore have we
Our written purposes before us sent;
Which, if thou hast consider'd, let us know
If 'twill tie up thy discontented sword,
And carry back to Sicily much tall youth
That else must perish here.
  Pom.   To you all three,
The senators alone of this great world,
Chief factors for the gods, I do not know   10
Wherefore my father should revengers want,
Having a son and friends; since Julius Cæsar,
Who at Philippi the good Brutus ghosted,
There saw you labouring for him. What was 't
That moved pale Cassius to conspire; and what
Made the all-honour'd, honest Roman, Brutus,
With the arm'd rest, courtiers of beauteous freedom,
To drench the Capitol; but that they would
Have one man but a man? And that is it
Hath made me rig my navy; at whose burthen   20
The anger'd ocean foams; with which I meant
To scourge the ingratitude that despiteful Rome
Cast on my noble father.
  Cæs.   Take your time.
  Ant. Thou canst not fear us, Pompey, with thy sails;
We'll speak with thee at sea: at land, thou know'st
How much we do o'er-count thee.
  Pom.   At land, indeed,
Thou dost o'er-count me of my father's house:
But, since the cuckoo builds not for himself,
Remain in 't as thou mayst.
  Lep.   Be pleased to tell us—
For this is from the present—how you take   30
The offers we have sent you.

---

71. **boot thee with,** give thee into the bargain.   77. **Some . . . thunder-bolt.** The gods usually do not smite the innocent (see *King Lear,* III, ii, 49-50).   83-84. **since . . . cause,** since I myself (in striking an inferior) am the real offender who has deserved the blows.   96. **Narcissus,** a pattern of beauty.   101. **unequal,** unjust.   103. **That . . . of.** Many interpretations and conjectures; Cuningham: that art not thyself the thing of which thou art so hatefully positive; Gollancz: that art not

the evil thing of which thou art so certain. Cuningham suggests *act* for *art,* which would indicate that Cleopatra had in mind the censure of Antony, which appears again in line 107.   113. **inclination,** disposition.   116-117. **Though . . . Mars.** This alludes to a type of picture known as a perspective, which shows different objects when looked at from different points of view.
  SCENE VI.   13. **ghosted,** haunted.   27. **Thou . . . house.** Plutarch

Cæs.   There 's the point.
Ant. Which do not be entreated to, but weigh
What it is worth embraced.
Cæs.   And what may follow,
To try a larger fortune.
Pom.   You have made me offer
Of Sicily, Sardinia; and I must
Rid all the sea of pirates; then, to send
Measures of wheat to Rome; this 'greed upon,
To part with unhack'd edges, and bear back
Our targes undinted.
Cæs. Ant. Lep. That 's our offer.
Pom.   Know, then,   40
I came before you here a man prepared
To take this offer: but Mark Antony
Put me to some impatience: though I lose
The praise of it by telling, you must know,
When Cæsar and your brother were at blows,
Your mother came to Sicily and did find
Her welcome friendly.
Ant.   I have heard it, Pompey;
And am well studied for a liberal thanks
Which I do owe you.
Pom.   Let me have your hand:
I did not think, sir, to have met you here.   50
Ant. The beds i' the east are soft; and thanks to you,
That call'd me timelier than my purpose hither;
For I have gain'd by 't.
Cæs.   Since I saw you last,
There is a change upon you.
Pom.   Well, I know not
What counts harsh fortune casts upon my face;
But in my bosom shall she never come,
To make my heart her vassal.
Lep.   Well met here.
Pom. I hope so, Lepidus. Thus we are agreed:
I crave our composition may be written,
And seal'd between us.
Cæs.   That 's the next to do.   60
Pom. We'll feast each other ere we part; and let 's
Draw lots who shall begin.
Ant.   That will I, Pompey.
Pom. No, Antony, take the lot: but, first
Or last, your fine Egyptian cookery
Shall have the fame. I have heard that Julius Cæsar
Grew fat with feasting there.
Ant.   You have heard much.
Pom. I have fair meanings, sir.
Ant.   And fair words to them.
Pom. Then so much have I heard:
And I have heard, Apollodorus carried—
Eno. No more of that: he did so.
Pom.   What, I pray you?   70
Eno. A certain queen to Cæsar in a mattress.
Pom. I know thee now: how farest thou, soldier?
Eno.   Well;
And well am like to do; for, I perceive,
Four feasts are toward.
Pom.   Let me shake thy hand;
I never hated thee: I have seen thee fight,

When I have envied thy behaviour.
Eno.   Sir,
I never loved you much; but I ha' praised ye,
When you have well deserved ten times as much
As I have said you did.
Pom.   Enjoy thy plainness,   80
It nothing ill becomes thee.
Aboard my galley I invite you all:
Will you lead, lords?
Cæs. Ant. Lep. Show us the way, sir.
Pom.   Come.
          [*Exeunt all but Menas and Enobarbus.*
Men. [*Aside*] Thy father, Pompey, would ne'er have
made this treaty.—You and I have known, sir.
Eno. At sea, I think.
Men. We have, sir.
Eno. You have done well by water.
Men. And you by land.   90
Eno. I will praise any man that will praise me;
though it cannot be denied what I have done by land.
Men. Nor what I have done by water.
Eno. Yes, something you can deny for your own
safety: you have been a great thief by sea.
Men. And you by land.
Eno. There I deny my land service. But give me
your hand, Menas: if our eyes had authority, here
they might take two thieves kissing.   101
Men. All men's faces are true, whatsom-e'er their
hands are.
Eno. But there is never a fair woman has a true face.
Men. No slander; they steal hearts.
Eno. We came hither to fight with you.
Men. For my part, I am sorry it is turned to a
drinking. Pompey doth this day laugh away his
fortune.   110
Eno. If he do, sure, he cannot weep 't back again.
Men. You 've said, sir. We looked not for Mark
Antony here: pray you, is he married to Cleopatra?
Eno. Cæsar's sister is called Octavia.
Men. True, sir; she was the wife of Caius Marcellus.
Eno. But she is now the wife of Marcus Antonius.
Men. Pray ye, sir?   120
Eno. 'Tis true.
Men. Then is Cæsar and he for ever knit together.
Eno. If I were bound to divine of this unity, I would
not prophesy so.
Men. I think the policy of that purpose made more
in the marriage than the love of the parties.
Eno. I think so too. But you shall find, the band
that seems to tie their friendship together will be the
very strangler of their amity: Octavia is of a holy,
cold, and still conversation.   131
Men. Who would not have his wife so?
Eno. Not he that himself is not so; which is Mark
Antony. He will to his Egyptian dish again: then shall
the sighs of Octavia blow the fire up in Cæsar; and, as
I said before, that which is the strength of their amity
shall prove the immediate author of their variance.
Antony will use his affection where it is: he married
but his occasion here.

---

informs us that Antony bought the elder Pompey's house at auction
and later refused to pay for it; *o'er-count* has possibly the suggestion of
cheating. 30. **from the present,** away from the business. 38. **edges,**
swords. 39. **targes,** shields. 48. **well studied,** well prepared by
thinking. 52. **timelier,** earlier. 55. **What . . . face.** The figure is
from casting accounts or reckonings. 69-71. **Apollodorus . . . mattress.**
This alludes to a tale told by Plutarch according to which Cleopatra

had herself done up in a mattress and carried secretly on the shoulders
of Apollodorus into a palace to meet Julius Cæsar. 86. **known,** known
each other. 120. **Pray ye?** Are you in earnest? 124. **divine of,**
prophesy about. 129. **strangler,** destroyer. Later folios have *stranger,*
which Rowe changed to *estranger.* 140. **occasion,** according to his
personal interests.

Men. And thus it may be. Come, sir, will you aboard? I have a health for you.

Eno. I shall take it, sir: we have used our throats in Egypt.

Men. Come, let 's away. [*Exeunt.*

SCENE VII. *On board Pompey's galley, off Misenum.*

Music plays. Enter two or three Servants *with a banquet.*

First Serv. Here they'll be, man. Some o' their plants are ill-rooted already; the least wind i' the world will blow them down.

Sec. Serv. Lepidus is high-coloured.

First Serv. They have made him drink alms-drink.

Sec. Serv. As they pinch one another by the disposition, he cries out 'No more;' reconciles them to his entreaty, and himself to the drink.

First Serv. But it raises the greater war between him and his discretion. 11

Sec. Serv. Why, this it is to have a name in great men's fellowship: I had as lief have a reed that will do me no service as a partisan I could not heave.

First Serv. To be called into a huge sphere, and not to be seen to move in 't, are the holes where eyes should be, which pitifully disaster the cheeks.

A sennet sounded. Enter CÆSAR, ANTONY, LEPIDUS, POMPEY, AGRIPPA, MECÆNAS, ENOBARBUS, MENAS, *with other captains.*

Ant. [*To Cæsar*] Thus do they, sir: they take the flow o' the Nile 20
By certain scales i' the pyramid; they know,
By the height, the lowness, or the mean, if dearth
Or foison follow: the higher Nilus swells,
The more it promises: as it ebbs, the seedsman
Upon the slime and ooze scatters his grain,
And shortly comes to harvest.

Lep. You 've strange serpents there.

Ant. Ay, Lepidus.

Lep. Your serpent of Egypt is bred now of your mud by the operation of your sun: so is your crocodile. 31

Ant. They are so.

Pom. Sit,—and some wine! A health to Lepidus!

Lep. I am not so well as I should be, but I'll ne'er out.

Eno. Not till you have slept; I fear me you'll be in till then.

Lep. Nay, certainly, I have heard the Ptolemies' pyramises are very goodly things; without contradiction, I have heard that. 41

Men. [*Aside to Pom.*] Pompey, a word.

Pom. [*Aside to Men.*] Say in mine ear: what is 't?

Men. [*Aside to Pom.*] Forsake thy seat, I do beseech thee, captain,
And hear me speak a word.

Pom. [*Aside to Men.*] Forbear me till anon.

This wine for Lepidus!

Lep. What manner o' thing is your crocodile?

Ant. It is shaped, sir, like itself; and it is as broad as it hath breadth: it is just so high as it is, and moves with it own organs: it lives by that which nourisheth it; and the elements once out of it, it transmigrates. 51

Lep. What colour is it of?

Ant. Of it own colour too.

Lep. 'Tis a strange serpent.

Ant. 'Tis so. And the tears of it are wet.

Cæs. Will this description satisfy him?

Ant. With the health that Pompey gives him, else he is a very epicure.

Pom. [*Aside to Men.*] Go hang, sir, hang! Tell me of that? away!
Do as I bid you. Where 's this cup I call'd for? 60

Men. [*Aside to Pom.*] If for the sake of merit thou wilt hear me,
Rise from thy stool.

Pom. [*Aside to Men.*] I think thou 'rt mad. The matter? [*Rises, and walks aside.*

Men. I have ever held my cap off to thy fortunes.

Pom. Thou hast served me with much faith. What 's else to say?
Be jolly, lords.

Ant. These quick-sands, Lepidus,
Keep off them, for you sink.

Men. Wilt thou be lord of all the world?

Pom. What say'st thou?

Men. Wilt thou be lord of the whole world? That 's twice.

Pom. How should that be?

Men. But entertain it,
And, though thou think me poor, I am the man 70
Will give thee all the world.

Pom. Hast thou drunk well?

Men. No, Pompey, I have kept me from the cup.
Thou art, if thou darest be, the earthly Jove:
Whate'er the ocean pales, or sky inclips,
Is thine, if thou wilt ha 't.

Pom. Show me which way.

Men. These three world-sharers, these competitors,
Are in thy vessel: let me cut the cable;
And, when we are put off, fall to their throats:
All there is thine.

Pom. Ah, this thou shouldst have done,
And not have spoke on 't! In me 'tis villany; 80
In thee 't had been good service. Thou must know,
'Tis not my profit that does lead mine honour;
Mine honour, it. Repent that e'er thy tongue
Hath so betray'd thine act: being done unknown,
I should have found it afterwards well done;
But must condemn it now. Desist, and drink.

Men. [*Aside*] For this,
I'll never follow thy pall'd fortunes more.
Who seeks, and will not take when once 'tis offer'd,
Shall never find it more.

SCENE VII. *Stage Direction: banquet,* a course of the feast, probably, dessert. 2. **plants,** soles of the feet, with pun on usual sense. 6. **alms-drink.** Malone thought this meant his share and the others' too; more probably, the leavings, ordinarily saved for alms-people, besides his own share; Cuningham suggests "drinks taken as a work of charity, i.e., to further the reconciliation." 7. **pinch . . . disposition,** chafe one another, fall to bickering. Lepidus stops them but has to join them in fresh bumpers of drink. 14. **partisan,** long-bladed spear having one or more cutting edges, used by infantry. 18. **disaster,** disfigure; an astrological term following *sphere,* two lines above. 23.

foison, plenty. 29. **Your,** colloquial use; not readily translatable. 36. **I'll ne'er out,** I'll never refuse a toast. 38. **in,** in for it; also in drink. 40. **pyramises,** pyramids. 49. **it own,** its own. 51. **elements . . . it,** i.e., at its dissolution; the word *elements* may, however, mean "vital elements." 55. **tears,** allusion to the ancient belief that the crocodile wept over its victim before devouring it. 63. **held my cap off,** been a faithful servant. 65. **quick-sands.** Lepidus probably collapses at this point. 74. **pales,** impales, fences in. **inclips,** embraces. 88. **pall'd,** decayed, waning. 99. **go on wheels,** go fast or easily; proverbial. 100. **increase the reels,** increase the reeling and

Pom.　　　　This health to Lepidus!　　90

Ant. Bear him ashore. I'll pledge it for him,
　Pompey.

Eno. Here 's to thee, Menas!

Men.　　　　Enobarbus, welcome!

Pom. Fill till the cup be hid.

Eno. There 's a strong fellow, Menas.
　　[Pointing to the Attendant who carries off Lepidus.

Men. Why?

Eno. A' bears the third part of the world, man; see'st
not?

Men. The third part, then, is drunk: would it were
　all,
'That it might go on wheels!

Eno. Drink thou; increase the reels.　　100

Men. Come.

Pom. This is not yet an Alexandrian feast.

Ant. It ripens towards it. Strike the vessels, ho!
Here is to Cæsar!

Cæs.　　　　I could well forbear 't.
It 's monstrous labour, when I wash my brain,
And it grows fouler.

Ant.　　　　Be a child o' the time.

Cæs. Possess it, I'll make answer:
But I had rather fast from all four days
Than drink so much in one.

Eno.　　　　Ha, my brave emperor!
　　　　　　　　　　　　[To Antony.
Shall we dance now the Egyptian Bacchanals,　　110
And celebrate our drink?

Pom.　　　　Let 's ha 't, good soldier.

Ant. Come, let 's all take hands,
Till that the conquering wine hath steep'd our sense
In soft and delicate Lethe.

Eno.　　　　All take hands.
Make battery to our ears with the loud music:
The while I'll place you: then the boy shall sing;
The holding every man shall bear as loud
As his strong sides can volley.
　　[Music plays. Enobarbus places them hand in hand.

THE SONG.

Come, thou monarch of the vine,　　120
Plumpy Bacchus with pink eyne!
In thy fats our cares be drown'd,
With thy grapes our hairs be crown'd:
Cup us, till the world go round,
Cup us, till the world go round!

Cæs. What would you more? Pompey, good night.
　Good brother,
Let me request you off: our graver business
Frowns at this levity. Gentle lords, let 's part;
You see we have burnt our cheeks: strong Enobarb
Is weaker than the wine; and mine own tongue　　130
Splits what it speaks: the wild disguise hath almost
Antick'd us all. What needs more words? Good night.
Good Antony, your hand.

Pom.　　　　I'll try you on the shore.

Ant. And shall, sir: give 's your hand.

Pom.　　　　O Antony,
You have my father's house,—But, what? we are
　friends.
Come, down into the boat.

Eno.　　　　Take heed you fall not.
　　　　[Exeunt all but Enobarbus and Menas.
Menas, I'll not on shore.

Men.　　　　No, to my cabin.
These drums! these trumpets, flutes! what!
Let Neptune hear we bid a loud farewell
To these great fellows: sound and be hang'd, sound
　out!　　　*[Sound a flourish, with drums.* 140

Eno. Ho! says a'. There 's my cap.

Men. Ho! Noble captain, come.　　　*[Exeunt.*

ACT III.

SCENE I. *A plain in Syria.*

Enter VENTIDIUS *as it were in triumph, with* SILIUS, *and
other* Romans, Officers, *and* Soldiers; *the dead body
of* PACORUS *borne before him.*

Ven. Now, darting Parthia, art thou struck; and
　now
Pleased fortune does of Marcus Crassus' death
Make me revenger. Bear the king's son's body
Before our army. Thy Pacorus, Orodes,
Pays this for Marcus Crassus.

Sil.　　　　Noble Ventidius,
Whilst yet with Parthian blood thy sword is warm,
The fugitive Parthians follow; spur through Media,
Mesopotamia, and the shelters whither
The routed fly: so thy grand captain Antony
Shall set thee on triumphant chariots and　　10
Put garlands on thy head.

Ven.　　　　O Silius, Silius,
I have done enough; a lower place, note well,
May make too great an act: for learn this, Silius;
Better to leave undone, than by our deed
Acquire too high a fame when him we serve 's away.
Cæsar and Antony have ever won
More in their officer than person: Sossius,
One of my place in Syria, his lieutenant,
For quick accumulation of renown,
Which he achieved by the minute, lost his favour.　　20
Who does i' the wars more than his captain can
Becomes his captain's captain: and ambition,
The soldier's virtue, rather makes choice of loss,
Than gain which darkens him.
I could do more to do Antonius good,
But 'twould offend him; and in his offence
Should my performance perish.

Sil.　　　　Thou hast, Ventidius, that
Without the which a soldier, and his sword,
Grants scarce distinction. Thou wilt write to Antony?

Ven. I'll humbly signify what in his name,　　30

---

whirling of drunkenness. Steevens conjectured, *And grease the wheels.*
103. **Strike the vessels**, tap the casks; also explained as "clash your
drinking vessels together." 105. **wash my brain**, drink copiously.
106. **And it grows.** F has *grow*, with which reading *And* would mean
"if." 107. **Possess it**, have your way. 114. **Lethe**, forgetfulness.
117. **holding**, refrain, burden. 121. **pink eyne**, winking, half-shut eyes.
122. **fats**, vats, vessels. 131. **disguise**, drunkenness. 132. **Antick'd**,
made like buffoons.
　ACT III. SCENE I. 1. **darting Parthia**, Orodes, king of Parthia. The
Parthians were famous for archery and for the Parthian dart which they

discharged as they fled. Pacorus was the son of Orodes. 2. **Marcus
Crassus' death.** Crassus, member of the first triumvirate with Pompey
and Julius Caesar, was overthrown and treacherously murdered by
Orodes in 53 B.C. 12. **lower place**, i.e., one of lower rank. 20. **lost his
favour.** No authority has been discovered for this somewhat improbable
charge against Antony. 24. **darkens him**, deprives him of luster or
renown. 29. **Grants scarce distinction**, can scarcely be distinguished.

That magical word of war, we have effected;
How, with his banners and his well-paid ranks,
The ne'er-yet-beaten horse of Parthia
We have jaded out o' the field.
    Sil.   Where is he now?
    Ven. He purposeth to Athens: whither, with what
        haste
The weight we must convey with 's will permit,
We shall appear before him. On, there; pass along!
                                                        [*Exeunt.*

SCENE II. *Rome. An ante-chamber in Cæsar's house.*

Enter AGRIPPA *at one door,* ENOBARBUS *at another.*

    Agr. What, are the brothers parted?
    Eno. They have dispatch'd with Pompey, he is gone;
The other three are sealing. Octavia weeps
To part from Rome; Cæsar is sad; and Lepidus,
Since Pompey's feast, as Menas says, is troubled
With the green sickness.
    Agr.   'Tis a noble Lepidus.
    Eno. A very fine one: O, how he loves Cæsar!
    Agr. Nay, but how dearly he adores Mark Antony!
    Eno. Cæsar? Why, he 's the Jupiter of men.
    Agr. What 's Antony? The god of Jupiter.   10
    Eno. Spake you of Cæsar? How! the non-pareil!
    Agr. O Antony! O thou Arabian bird!
    Eno. Would you praise Cæsar, say 'Cæsar:' go no
        further.
    Agr. Indeed, he plied them both with excellent
        praises.
    Eno. But he loves Cæsar best; yet he loves Antony:
Ho! hearts, tongues, figures, scribes, bards, poets,
        cannot
Think, speak, cast, write, sing, number, ho!
His love to Antony. But as for Cæsar,
Kneel down, kneel down, and wonder.
    Agr.   Both he loves.
    Eno. They are his shards, and he their beetle.
        [*Trumpets within.*] So;   20
This is to horse. Adieu, noble Agrippa.
    Agr. Good fortune, worthy soldier; and farewell.

Enter CÆSAR, ANTONY, LEPIDUS, *and* OCTAVIA.

    Ant. No further, sir.
    Cæs. You take from me a great part of myself;
Use me well in 't. Sister, prove such a wife
As my thoughts make thee, and as my farthest band
Shall pass on thy approof. Most noble Antony,
Let not the piece of virtue, which is set
Betwixt us as the cement of our love,
To keep it builded, be the ram to batter   30
The fortress of it; for better might we
Have loved without this mean, if on both parts
This be not cherish'd.
    Ant.   Make me not offended
In your distrust.
    Cæs.   I have said.
    Ant.   You shall not find,

Though you be therein curious, the least cause
For what you seem to fear: so, the gods keep you,
And make the hearts of Romans serve your ends!
We will here part.
    Cæs. Farewell, my dearest sister, fare thee well:
The elements be kind to thee, and make   40
Thy spirits all of comfort! fare thee well.
    Oct. My noble brother!
    Ant. The April 's in her eyes: it is love's spring,
And these the showers to bring it on. Be cheerful.
    Oct. Sir, look well to my husband's house; and—
    Cæs.   What,
Octavia?
    Oct.   I'll tell you in your ear.
    Ant. Her tongue will not obey her heart, nor can
Her heart inform her tongue,—the swan's
        down-feather,
That stands upon the swell at full of tide,
And neither way inclines.   50
    Eno.   [*Aside to Agr.*] Will Cæsar weep?
    Agr.   [*Aside to Eno.*] He has a
        cloud in 's face.
    Eno. [*Aside to Agr.*] He were the worse for that, were
        he a horse;
So is he, being a man.
    Agr.   [*Aside to Eno.*] Why, Enobarbus,
When Antony found Julius Cæsar dead,
He cried almost to roaring; and he wept
When at Philippi he found Brutus slain.
    Eno. [*Aside to Agr.*] That year, indeed, he was
        troubled with a rheum;
What willingly he did confound he wail'd,
Believe 't, till I wept too.
    Cæs.   No, sweet Octavia,
You shall hear from me still; the time shall not   60
Out-go my thinking on you.
    Ant.   Come, sir, come;
I'll wrestle with you in my strength of love:
Look, here I have you; thus I let you go,
And give you to the gods.
    Cæs.   Adieu; be happy!
    Lep. Let all the number of the stars give light
To thy fair way!
    Cæs. Farewell, farewell!   [*Kisses Octavia.*
    Ant.   Farewell! [*Trumpets sound. Exeunt.*

SCENE III. *Alexandria. Cleopatra's palace.*

Enter CLEOPATRA, CHARMIAN, IRAS, *and* ALEXAS.

    Cleo. Where is the fellow?
    Alex.   Half afeard to come.
    Cleo. Go to, go to.

Enter the Messenger *as before.*

                    Come hither, sir.
    Alex.   Good majesty,
Herod of Jewry dare not look upon you
But when you are well pleased.
    Cleo.   That Herod's head

34. **jaded,** driven, exhausted, beaten. 36. **with 's,** with us.
    SCENE II. 2. **dispatch'd,** concluded the business. 3. **sealing,** bring-
ing matters to a conclusion. 6. **green sickness,** a kind of anemia
supposed to affect young women; used ironically, Lee thinks, with
reference to the love (?) Lepidus bore to Caesar and Antony. 11. **nonpareil,** one having no equal. 12. **Arabian bird,** the fabled phoenix,
which arose fresh from its ashes and of which there was only one. 17.
cast, calculate. **number,** write verses. 20. **shards,** wings (by means

of which the dull Lepidus might rise from earth). 26-27. **as my . . .
approof,** such as my utmost bond shall be justified on what thou shalt
prove to be. 28. **piece,** masterpiece. 48. **swan's down-feather.** The
figure seems to refer to a condition of inertia due to conflicting passions;
it may have some reference to Octavia's affections divided between
husband and brother. 51. **cloud in 's face,** phrase applied to some
marking in a horse's face which was regarded as a blemish. 57. **rheum,**
running at the eyes; used of any discharge of mucus from the head.

I'll have: but how, when Antony is gone
Through whom I might command it? Come thou
    near.
    Mess. Most gracious majesty,—
    Cleo. Didst thou behold Octavia?
    Mess. Ay, dread queen.
    Cleo. Where?   10
    Mess. Madam, in Rome;
I look'd her in the face, and saw her led
Between her brother and Mark Antony.
    Cleo. Is she as tall as me?
    Mess.   She is not, madam.
    Cleo. Didst hear her speak? is she shrill-tongued or
    low?
    Mess. Madam, I heard her speak; she is low-voiced.
    Cleo. That's not so good: he cannot like her long.
    Char. Like her! O Isis! 'tis impossible.
    Cleo. I think so, Charmian: dull of tongue, and
    dwarfish!
What majesty is in her gait? Remember,   20
If e'er thou look'dst on majesty.
    Mess.   She creeps:
Her motion and her station are as one;
She shows a body rather than a life,
A statue than a breather.
    Cleo.   Is this certain?
    Mess. Or I have no observance.
    Char.   Three in Egypt
Cannot make better note.
    Cleo.   He's very knowing;
I do perceive 't: there's nothing in her yet:
The fellow has good judgement.
    Char.   Excellent.
    Cleo. Guess at her years, I prithee.
    Mess.   Madam,
She was a widow,—
    Cleo.   Widow! Charmian, hark.   30
    Mess. And I do think she's thirty.
    Cleo. Bear'st thou her face in mind? is 't long or
    round?
    Mess. Round even to faultiness.
    Cleo. For the most part, too, they are foolish that
    are so.
Her hair, what colour?
    Mess. Brown, madam: and her forehead
As low as she would wish it.
    Cleo.   There's gold for thee.
Thou must not take my former sharpness ill:
I will employ thee back again; I find thee
Most fit for business: go make thee ready;   40
Our letters are prepared.   [*Exit Messenger.*
    Char.   A proper man.
    Cleo. Indeed, he is so: I repent me much
That so I harried him. Why, methinks, by him,
This creature's no such thing.
    Char.   Nothing, madam.
    Cleo. The man hath seen some majesty, and should
    know.
    Char. Hath he seen majesty? Isis else defend,
And serving you so long!

    Cleo. I have one thing more to ask him yet, good
    Charmian:
But 'tis no matter; thou shalt bring him to me
Where I will write. All may be well enough.   50
    Char. I warrant you, madam.   [*Exeunt.*

SCENE IV. *Athens. A room in Antony's house.*

Enter ANTONY *and* OCTAVIA.

    Ant. Nay, nay, Octavia, not only that,—
That were excusable, that, and thousands more
Of semblable import,—but he hath waged
New wars 'gainst Pompey; made his will, and read it
To public ear:
Spoke scantly of me: when perforce he could not
But pay me terms of honour, cold and sickly
He vented them; most narrow measure lent me:
When the best hint was given him, he not took 't,
Or did it from his teeth.
    Oct.   O my good lord,   10
Believe not all; or, if you must believe,
Stomach not all. A more unhappy lady,
If this division chance, ne'er stood between,
Praying for both parts:
The good gods will mock me presently,
When I shall pray, 'O, bless my lord and husband!'
Undo that prayer, by crying out as loud,
'O, bless my brother!' Husband win, win brother,
Prays, and destroys the prayer; no midway
'Twixt these extremes at all.
    Ant.   Gentle Octavia,
Let your best love draw to that point, which seeks   20
Best to preserve it: if I lose mine honour,
I lose myself: better I were not yours
Than yours so branchless. But, as you requested,
Yourself shall go between 's: the mean time, lady,
I'll raise the preparation of a war
Shall stain your brother: make your soonest haste;
So your desires are yours.
    Oct.   Thanks to my lord.
The Jove of power make me most weak, most weak,
Your reconciler! Wars 'twixt you twain would be   30
As if the world should cleave, and that slain men
Should solder up the rift.
    Ant. When it appears to you where this begins,
Turn your displeasure that way; for our faults
Can never be so equal, that your love
Can equally move with them. Provide your going;
Choose your own company, and command what cost
Your heart has mind to.   [*Exeunt.*

SCENE V. *The same. Another room.*

Enter ENOBARBUS *and* EROS, *meeting.*

    Eno. How now, friend Eros!
    Eros. There's strange news come, sir.
    Eno. What, man?

58. **wail'd,** bewailed. 61. **Out-go,** outstrip; the phrase is also interpreted as "I shall think of you while life lasts."
    SCENE III. 22. **station,** manner of standing. 24. **breather,** living
being. 25. **observance,** ability to observe. 32. **face . . . round.**
Physiognomy taught that very round faces denoted silliness. 37. **As
. . . it.** Low foreheads were attributes of ugliness. **as she would wish
it,** as could be (cant phrase). 43. **harried,** maltreated. **by,** according
to. 44. **such,** very remarkable.

SCENE IV. 3. **semblable,** similar. 4-5. **made . . . ear.** Plutarch
states that Octavius read Antony's will, not his own. 6. **scantly,**
grudgingly. 10. **from his teeth,** from the teeth only, not from the
heart. 12. **Stomach,** resent. 14. **parts,** sides. Octavia is much more
admirable in Plutarch than in Shakespeare; she here fails Antony, and
becomes in some measure responsible for his desertion of her. 27.
stain, eclipse (his preparations). **soonest,** quickest.

Eros. Cæsar and Lepidus have made wars upon
　　Pompey.
　Eno. This is old: what is the success? 　　　　　　　6
　Eros. Cæsar, having made use of him in the wars
'gainst Pompey, presently denied him rivality; would
not let him partake in the glory of the action: and not
resting here, accuses him of letters he had formerly
wrote to Pompey; upon his own appeal, seizes him:
so the poor third is up, till death enlarge his confine. 13
　Eno. Then, world, thou hast a pair of chaps, no
　　more;
And throw between them all the food thou hast,
They'll grind the one the other. Where 's Antony?
　Eros. He 's walking in the garden—thus; and spurns
The rush that lies before him; cries, 'Fool Lepidus!'
And threats the throat of that his officer　　　　　　19
That murder'd Pompey.
　Eno.　　　　　　　Our great navy 's rigg'd.
　Ero. For Italy and Cæsar. More, Domitius;
My lord desires you presently: my news
I might have told hereafter.
　Eno.　　　　　　　'Twill be naught:
But let it be. Bring me to Antony.
　Eros. Come, sir. 　　　　　　　　　　　[*Exeunt.*

SCENE VI. *Rome. Cæsar's house.*

Enter CÆSAR, AGRIPPA, *and* MECÆNAS.

Cæs. Contemning Rome, he has done all this, and
　　more,
In Alexandria: here 's the manner of 't:
I' the market-place, on a tribunal silver'd,
Cleopatra and himself in chairs of gold
Were publicly enthroned: at the feet sat
Cæsarion, whom they call my father's son,
And all the unlawful issue that their lust
Since then hath made between them. Unto her
He gave the stablishment of Egypt; made her
Of lower Syria, Cyprus, Lydia, 　　　　　　　　10
Absolute queen.
　Mec.　　　　　　　This in the public eye?
　Cæs. I' the common show-place, where they
　　exercise.
His sons he there proclaim'd the kings of kings:
Great Media, Parthia, and Armenia,
He gave to Alexander; to Ptolemy he assign'd
Syria, Cilicia, and Phœnicia: she
In the habiliments of the goddess Isis
That day appear'd; and oft before gave audience,
As 'tis reported, so.
　Mec.　　　　　　　Let Rome be thus
Inform'd.
　Agr.　　　　　　Who, queasy with his insolence 20
Already, will their good thoughts call from him.
　Cæs. The people know it; and have now received
His accusations.
　Agr.　　　　　　Who does he accuse?
　Cæs. Cæsar: and that, having in Sicily

Sextus Pompeius spoil'd, we had not rated him
His part o' the isle: then does he say, he lent me
Some shipping unrestored: lastly, he frets
That Lepidus of the triumvirate
Should be deposed; and, being, that we detain
All his revenue.
　Agr.　　　　　Sir, this should be answer'd. 　30
　Cæs. 'Tis done already, and the messenger gone.
I have told him, Lepidus was grown too cruel;
That he his high authority abused,
And did deserve his change: for what I have
　　conquer'd,
I grant him part; but then, in his Armenia,
And other of his conquer'd kingdoms, I
Demand the like.
　Mec.　　　　　　He'll never yield to that.
　Cæs. Nor must not then be yielded to in this.

Enter OCTAVIA *with her train.*

　Oct. Hail, Cæsar, and my lord! hail, most dear
　　Cæsar!
　Cæs. That ever I should call thee castaway! 　　40
　Oct. You have not call'd me so, nor have you cause.
　Cæs. Why have you stol'n upon us thus? You come
　　not
Like Cæsar's sister: the wife of Antony
Should have an army for an usher, and
The neighs of horse to tell of her approach
Long ere she did appear; the trees by the way
Should have borne men; and expectation fainted,
Longing for what it had not; nay, the dust
Should have ascended to the roof of heaven,
Raised by your populous troops: but you are come 　50
A market-maid to Rome; and have prevented
The ostentation of our love, which, left unshown,
Is often left unloved: we should have met you
By sea and land; supplying every stage
With an augmented greeting.
　Oct.　　　　　　　Good my lord,
To come thus was I not constrain'd, but did it
On my free will. My lord, Mark Antony,
Hearing that you prepared for war, acquainted
My grieved ear withal; whereon, I begg'd
His pardon for return.
　Cæs.　　　　　　Which soon he granted, 　　60
Being an obstruct 'tween his lust and him.
　Oct. Do not say so, my lord.
　Cæs.　　　　　　I have eyes upon him,
And his affairs come to me on the wind.
Where is he now?
　Oct.　　　　　　My lord, in Athens.
　Cæs. No, my most wronged sister; Cleopatra
Hath nodded him to her. He hath given his empire
Up to a whore; who now are levying
The kings o' the earth for war: he hath assembled
Bocchus, the king of Libya; Archelaus,
Of Cappadocia; Philadelphos, king 　　　　　　　70
Of Paphlagonia; the Thracian king, Adallas;
King Malchus of Arabia; King of Pont;

SCENE V. 9. **rivality,** rights of a partner. 12. **his own appeal,**
Cæsar's own accusation. 13. **up,** shut up (in prison). 14. **pair of
chaps,** two jaws (destined to grind each other). **no more.** The meaning is "no more than one pair." 20. **Pompey.** Pompey met defeat in
Sicily, escaped thence to the East with designs against Antony, and was
supposed to have been murdered by Antony's orders; here Antony
blames his officer.
SCENE VI. 3. **tribunal,** seat of eminence. 9. **stablishment,** settled
possession. The first 19 lines of this scene reflect the point of view

of imperial Rome, with which Plutarch is strongly in sympathy,
namely, the impiety of the establishment of independent kingdoms on
Roman soil. 20. **queasy,** disgusted, i.e., the Roman people. 50.
populous, numerous. 52. **ostentation,** public display. 61. **obstruct,**
impediment. 69-76. **Bocchus . . . sceptres.** The list of powers is from
Plutarch and is somewhat confused, as here, in North's translation.
Libya is here correctly given; in line 10 Shakespeare followed North in
writing *Lydia.* 81. **negligent danger,** danger neglected, or danger
through negligence. 88. **make them.** This is Capell's emendation of F

Herod of Jewry; Mithridates, king
Of Comagene; Polemon and Amyntas,
The kings of Mede and Lycaonia,
With a more larger list of sceptres.
 Oct.   Ay me, most wretched,
That have my heart parted betwixt two friends
That do afflict each other!
 Cæs.   Welcome hither:
Your letters did withhold our breaking forth;
Till we perceived, both how you were wrong led,   80
And we in negligent danger. Cheer your heart:
Be you not troubled with the time, which drives
O'er your content these strong necessities;
But let determined things to destiny
Hold unbewail'd their way. Welcome to Rome;
Nothing more dear to me. You are abused
Beyond the mark of thought: and the high gods,
To do you justice, make them ministers
Of us and those that love you. Best of comfort;
And ever welcome to us.
 Agr.   Welcome, lady.   90
 Mec. Welcome, dear madam.
Each heart in Rome does love and pity you:
Only the adulterous Antony, most large
In his abominations, turns you off;
And gives his potent regiment to a trull,
That noises it against us.
 Oct.   Is it so, sir?
 Cæs. Most certain. Sister, welcome: pray you,
Be ever known to patience: my dear'st sister! [*Exeunt.*

   SCENE VII. *Near Actium. Antony's camp.*

Enter CLEOPATRA *and* ENOBARBUS.

 Cleo. I will be even with thee, doubt it not.
 Eno. But why, why, why?
 Cleo. Thou hast forspoke my being in these wars,
And say'st it is not fit.
 Eno.   Well, is it, is it?
 Cleo. If not denounced against us, why should not
  we
Be there in person?
 Eno. [*Aside*] Well, I could reply:
If we should serve with horse and mares together,
The horse were merely lost; the mares would bear
A soldier and his horse.
 Cleo.   What is 't you say?   10
 Eno. Your presence needs must puzzle Antony;
Take from his heart, take from his brain, from 's time,
What should not then be spared. He is already
Traduced for levity; and 'tis said in Rome
That Photinus, an eunuch and your maids
Manage this war.
 Cleo.   Sink Rome, and their tongues
  rot
That speak against us! A charge we bear i' the war,
And, as the president of my kingdom, will
Appear there for a man. Speak not against it;

I will not stay behind.
 Eno.   Nay, I have done.   20
Here comes the emperor.

Enter ANTONY *and* CANIDIUS.

 Ant.   Is it not strange, Canidius,
That from Tarentum and Brundusium
He could so quickly cut the Ionian sea,
And take in Toryne? You have heard on 't, sweet?
 Cleo. Celerity is never more admired
Than by the negligent.
 Ant.   A good rebuke,
Which might have well becomed the best of men,
To taunt at slackness. Canidius, we
Will fight with him by sea.
 Cleo.   By sea! what else?
 Can. Why will my lord do so?
 Ant.   For that he dares us to 't.   30
 Eno. So hath my lord dared him to single fight.
 Can. Ay, and to wage this battle at Pharsalia,
Where Cæsar fought with Pompey: but these offers,
Which serve not for his vantage, he shakes off;
And so should you.
 Eno.   Your ships are not well mann'd;
Your mariners are muleters, reapers, people
Ingross'd by swift impress; in Cæsar's fleet
Are those that often have 'gainst Pompey fought:
Their ships are yare; yours, heavy: no disgrace
Shall fall you for refusing him at sea,   40
Being prepared for land.
 Ant.   By sea, by sea.
 Eno. Most worthy sir, you therein throw away
The absolute soldiership you have by land;
Distract your army, which doth most consist
Of war-mark'd footmen; leave unexecuted
Your own renowned knowledge; quite forego
The way which promises assurance; and
Give up yourself merely to chance and hazard,
From firm security.
 Ant.   I'll fight at sea.
 Cleo. I have sixty sails, Cæsar none better.   50
 Ant. Our overplus of shipping will we burn;
And, with the rest full-mann'd, from the head of
  Actium
Beat the approaching Cæsar. But if we fail,
We then can do 't at land.

Enter a Messenger.

     Thy business?
 Mess. The news is true, my lord; he is descried;
Cæsar has taken Toryne.
 Ant. Can he be there in person? 'tis impossible;
Strange that his power should be. Canidius,
Our nineteen legions thou shalt hold by land,
And our twelve thousand horse. We'll to our ship: 60
Away, my Thetis!

Enter a Soldier.

    How now, worthy soldier!

---

makes his, which can be perfectly well construed, since *makes* may have a plural subject, and *his* may mean "its" and refer to *justice.* 89. **Best of comfort,** i.e., may you have, etc. 95. **regiment,** government, rule. **trull,** worthless woman or prostitute. 96. **noises it,** is clamorous.
 SCENE VII. 3. **forspoke,** spoken against. 5-6. **If not . . . person.** Cuningham suggests that this means "even if the war were not declared against me (which it is)," etc. This is better than the more obvious meaning, since historically the war was declared against Cleopatra and not Antony. 9. **merely,** utterly. 15. **That . . . maids.** So F,

without punctuation. Shakespeare uses *an eunuch* to describe Mardian, not Photinus. 17. **A charge . . . war.** Plutarch states that Cleopatra wished to go to the war to prevent Antony from being reconciled to Octavia; she bribed Canidius to argue for her, so that Antony consented. Plutarch says it was predestined that the government of all the world should fall into Octavius Caesar's hands. 36. **muleters,** F: *Militers;* F_2: *Muliters. Militers* may mean "soldiers." 37. **Ingross'd,** collected. **impress,** impressment. 39. **yare,** easily managed. 61. **Thetis,** sea goddess.

Sold. O noble emperor, do not fight by sea;
Trust not to rotten planks: do you misdoubt
This sword and these my wounds? Let the Egyptians
And the Phœnicians go a-ducking: we
Have used to conquer, standing on the earth,
And fighting foot to foot.
   Ant.   Well, well; away!
         [Exeunt Antony, Cleopatra, and Enobarbus.
   Sold. By Hercules, I think I am i' the right.
   Can. Soldier, thou art: but his whole action grows
Not in the power on 't: so our leader 's led,   70
And we are women's men.
   Sold.   You keep by land
The legions and the horse whole, do you not?
   Can. Marcus Octavius, Marcus Justeius,
Publicola, and Cælius, are for sea:
But we keep whole by land. This speed of Cæsar's
Carries beyond belief.
   Sold.   While he was yet in Rome,
His power went out in such distractions as
Beguiled all spies.
   Can.   Who 's his lieutenant, hear you?
   Sold. They say, one Taurus.
   Can.   Well I know the man.

Enter a Messenger.

   Mess. The emperor calls Canidius.   80
   Can. With news the time 's with labour, and throes
     forth,
Each minute, some.   *[Exeunt.*

SCENE VIII. *A plain near Actium.*

Enter CÆSAR, *and* TAURUS, *with his army, marching.*

   Cæs. Taurus!
   Taur. My lord?
   Cæs. Strike not by land; keep whole: provoke not
     battle,
Till we have done at sea. Do not exceed
The prescript of this scroll: our fortune lies
Upon this jump.   *[Exeunt.*

SCENE IX. *Another part of the plain.*

Enter ANTONY *and* ENOBARBUS.

   Ant. Set we our squadrons on yond side o' the hill,
In eye of Cæsar's battle; from which place
We may the number of the ships behold,
And so proceed accordingly.   *[Exeunt.*

SCENE X. *Another part of the plain.*

CANIDIUS *marcheth with his land army one way over the
stage; and* TAURUS, *the lieutenant of* CÆSAR, *the
other way. After their going in, is heard the noise of a
sea-fight.*

Alarum. Enter ENOBARBUS.

   Eno. Naught, naught, all naught! I can behold no
     longer:
The Antoniad, the Egyptian admiral,
With all their sixty, fly and turn the rudder:
To see 't mine eyes are blasted.

Enter SCARUS.

   Scar.   Gods and goddesses,
All the whole synod of them!
   Eno.   What 's thy passion?
   Scar. The greater cantle of the world is lost
With very ignorance; we have kiss'd away
Kingdoms and provinces.
   Eno.   How appears the fight?
   Scar. On our side like the token'd pestilence,
Where death is sure. Yon ribaudred nag of Egypt,— 10
Whom leprosy o'ertake!—i' the midst o' the fight,
When vantage like a pair of twins appear'd,
Both as the same, or rather ours the elder,
The breese upon her, like a cow in June,
Hoists sails and flies.
   Eno. That I beheld:
Mine eyes did sicken at the sight, and could not
Endure a further view.
   Scar.   She once being loof'd,
The noble ruin of her magic, Antony,
Claps on his sea-wing, and, like a doting mallard,   20
Leaving the fight in height, flies after her:
I never saw an action of such shame;
Experience, manhood, honour, ne'er before
Did violate so itself.
   Eno.   Alack, alack!

Enter CANIDIUS.

   Can. Our fortune on the sea is out of breath,
And sinks most lamentably. Had our general
Been what he knew himself, it had gone well:
O, he has given example for our flight,
Most grossly, by his own!
   Eno.   Ay, are you thereabouts?
Why, then, good night indeed.   30
   Can. Toward Peloponnesus are they fled.
   Scar. 'Tis easy to 't; and there I will attend
What further comes.
   Can.   To Cæsar will I render
My legions and my horse: six kings already
Show me the way of yielding.
   Eno.   I'll yet follow
The wounded chance of Antony, though my reason
Sits in the wind against me.   *[Exeunt.*

SCENE XI. *Alexandria. Cleopatra's palace.*

Enter ANTONY *with* Attendants.

   Ant. Hark! the land bids me tread no more upon 't;
It is ashamed to bear me! Friends, come hither.

69-70. **his . . . on 't**, usually taken to mean "his whole action proceeds not from the source of its possible power." Johnson interpreted, with some propriety, "his whole conduct becomes ungoverned by the right, or by reason." Canidius shows, like the others, a soldier's disgust with Antony's infatuation, and is less definitely a traitor than in Plutarch. 76. **Carries beyond**, surpasses (like an arrow in archery). 77. **distractions**, detachments. 81. **throes**, puts in agony. Gollancz suggests that the F reading, *throwes forth*, may mean "brings forth."
   SCENE VIII. 5. **prescript**, direction.
   SCENE X. 2. **Antoniad**, the name of Cleopatra's admiral or chief galley of her fleet. 5. **synod**, assembly of the gods. 6. **cantle**, corner;

hence, piece or part. 9. **token'd pestilence**. Certain red spots appeared on the bodies of the plague-smitten, which were, according to Steevens, called "God's tokens," i.e., of death. Shakespeare had many ways of fighting battles on the stage; all had to be more or less indirect. In this one two old soldiers on the hill give their report. 10. **ribaudred nag**, wanton jade (abusive); many conjectures. 13. **elder**, more advanced. 14. **breese**, gadfly. 18. **loof'd**, luffed, brought close to the wind. 20. **mallard**, drake. 29. **thereabouts**, of that opinion. 32. **to 't**, to get to it. 33. **render**, surrender. 36. **wounded chance**, broken fortunes. 37. **Sits . . . against**, is in opposition to.
   SCENE XI. 3. **lated**, belated, benighted. 8. **show their shoulders,**

I am so lated in the world, that I
Have lost my way forever: I have a ship
Laden with gold; take that, divide it; fly,
And make your peace with Cæsar.
   All.   Fly! not we.
   Ant. I have fled myself; and have instructed
    cowards
To run and show their shoulders. Friends, be gone;
I have myself resolved upon a course
Which has no need of you; be gone: 10
My treasure's in the harbour, take it. O,
I follow'd that I blush to look upon:
My very hairs do mutiny; for the white
Reprove the brown for rashness, and they them
For fear and doting. Friends, be gone: you shall
Have letters from me to some friends that will
Sweep your way for you. Pray you, look not sad,
Nor make replies of loathness: take the hint
Which my despair proclaims; let that be left
Which leaves itself: to the sea-side straightway: 20
I will possess you of that ship and treasure.
Leave me, I pray, a little: pray you now:
Nay, do so; for, indeed, I have lost command,
Therefore I pray you: I'll see you by and by. [*Sits down.*

   Enter CLEOPATRA *led by* CHARMIAN *and* IRAS; EROS
    following.

   Eros. Nay, gentle madam, to him, comfort him.
   Iras. Do, most dear queen.
   Char. Do! why: what else?
   Cleo. Let me sit down. O Juno!
   Ant. No, no, no, no, no.
   Eros. See you here, sir?   30
   Ant. O fie, fie, fie!
   Char. Madam!
   Iras. Madam, O good empress!
   Eros. Sir, sir,—
   Ant. Yes, my lord, yes; he at Philippi kept
His sword e'en like a dancer; while I struck
The lean and wrinkled Cassius; and 'twas I
That the mad Brutus ended: he alone
Dealt on lieutenantry, and no practice had
In the brave squares of war: yet now—No matter.   40
   Cleo. Ah, stand by.
   Eros. The queen, my lord, the queen.
   Iras. Go to him, madam, speak to him:
He is unqualited with very shame.
   Cleo. Well then, sustain me: O!
   Eros. Most noble sir, arise; the queen approaches;
Her head's declined, and death will seize her, but
Your comfort makes the rescue.
   Ant. I have offended reputation,
A most unnoble swerving.
   Eros.   Sir, the queen.   50
   Ant. O, whither hast thou led me, Egypt? See,
How I convey my shame out of thine eyes
By looking back what I have left behind
'Stroy'd in dishonour.

   Cleo.   O my lord, my lord,
Forgive my fearful sails! I little thought
You would have follow'd.
   Ant.   Egypt, thou knew'st too well
My heart was to thy rudder tied by the strings,
And thou shouldst tow me after: o'er my spirit
Thy full supremacy thou knew'st, and that
Thy beck might from the bidding of the gods   60
Command me.
   Cleo.   O, my pardon!
   Ant.   Now I must
To the young man send humble treaties, dodge
And palter in the shifts of lowness; who
With half the bulk o' the world play'd as I pleased,
Making and marring fortunes. You did know
How much you were my conqueror; and that
My sword, made weak by my affection, would
Obey it on all cause.
   Cleo.   Pardon, pardon!
   Ant. Fall not a tear, I say; one of them rates
All that is won and lost: give me a kiss;   70
Even this repays me. We sent our schoolmaster;
Is he come back? Love, I am full of lead.
Some wine, within there, and our viands! Fortune
    knows
We scorn her most when most she offers blows. [*Exeunt.*

    SCENE XII. *Egypt. Cæsar's camp.*

   Enter CÆSAR, DOLABELLA, THYREUS, *with others.*

   Cæs. Let him appear that's come from Antony.
Know you him?
   Dol.   Cæsar, 'tis his schoolmaster:
An argument that he is pluck'd, when hither
He sends so poor a pinion of his wing,
Which had superfluous kings for messengers
Not many moons gone by.

   Enter EUPHRONIUS, *ambassador from Antony.*

   Cæs.   Approach, and speak.
   Euph. Such as I am, I come from Antony:
I was of late as petty to his ends
As is the morn-dew on the myrtle-leaf
To his grand sea.
   Cæs.   Be 't so: declare thine office.   10
   Euph. Lord of his fortunes he salutes thee, and
Requires to live in Egypt: which not granted,
He lessens his requests; and to thee sues
To let him breathe between the heavens and earth,
A private man in Athens: this for him.
Next, Cleopatra does confess thy greatness;
Submits her to thy might; and of thee craves
The circle of the Ptolemies for her heirs,
Now hazarded to thy grace.
   Cæs.   For Antony,
I have no ears to his request. The queen   20

common expression for "show their backs." 18. **loathness,** unwillingness. 23. **lost command.** Johnson rightly interpreted this as "lost command of emotion"; the usual interpretation is "lost command of his
troops." 35. **my lord,** sometimes thought to be addressed to an imaginary interlocutor or, in bitterness, to Caesar; probably it is to Eros
(ironically). **he,** i.e., Octavius, to whom Plutarch attributes poor
soldiership at Philippi. 36. **sword . . . dancer,** seems to allude to swords
worn for ornament only, as by dancers. 39. **Dealt on lieutenantry,** let
his subordinates do the fighting. 40. **squares,** squadrons. 44. **unqualited,** not himself. 51-54. **See . . . dishonour,** see how I withdraw
my disgrace from your presence and reflect on the ruin of my fortunes

and honor. 57. **by the strings,** heartstrings. In judging Antony's conduct and repentance we must remember that Shakespeare viewed his act
as that of a man utterly infatuated and one whose reason was unhinged.
62. **treaties,** propositions for settlement. 63. **palter,** use trickery. 71.
schoolmaster, Euphronius, tutor to Antony's children by Cleopatra.
   SCENE XII. 8-10. **as petty . . . sea,** as insignificant compared to his
great ends as is the dewdrop on the myrtle leaf compared to the
grand sea; several interpretations. 12. **Requires,** asks. 18. **circle,**
crown.

Of audience nor desire shall fail, so she
From Egypt drive her all-disgraced friend,
Or take his life there: this if she perform,
She shall not sue unheard. So to them both.
   Euph. Fortune pursue thee!
   Cæs.   Bring him through the bands.
                         [*Exit Euphronius.*
[*To Thyreus*] To try thy eloquence, now 'tis time:
   dispatch;
From Antony win Cleopatra: promise,
And in our name, what she requires; add more,
From thine invention, offers: women are not
In their best fortunes strong; but want will perjure   30
The ne'er-touch'd vestal: try thy cunning, Thyreus;
Make thine own edict for thy pains, which we
Will answer as a law.
   Thyr.   Cæsar, I go.
   Cæs. Observe how Antony becomes his flaw,
And what thou think'st his very action speaks
In every power that moves.
   Thyr.   Cæsar, I shall.   [*Exeunt.*

SCENE XIII. *Alexandria. Cleopatra's palace.*

Enter CLEOPATRA, ENOBARBUS, CHARMIAN, *and*
   IRAS.

   Cleo. What shall we do, Enobarbus?
   Eno.   Think, and die.
   Cleo. Is Antony or we in fault for this?
   Eno. Antony only, that would make his will
Lord of his reason. What though you fled
From that great face of war, whose several ranges
Frighted each other? why should he follow?
The itch of his affection should not then
Have nick'd his captainship; at such a point,
When half to half the world opposed, he being
The meered question: 'twas a shame no less   10
Than was his loss, to course your flying flags,
And leave his navy gazing.
   Cleo.   Prithee, peace.

Enter ANTONY *with* EUPHRONIUS, *the Ambassador.*

   Ant. Is that his answer?
   Euph. Ay, my lord.
   Ant. The queen shall then have courtesy, so she
Will yield us up.
   Euph.   He says so.
   Ant.   Let her know 't.
To the boy Cæsar send this grizzled head,
And he will fill thy wishes to the brim
With principalities.
   Cleo.   That head, my lord?
   Ant. To him again: tell him he wears the rose   20
Of youth upon him; from which the world should note
Something particular: his coin, ships, legions,
May be a coward's; whose ministers would prevail
Under the service of a child as soon
As i' the command of Cæsar: I dare him therefore

To lay his gay comparisons apart,
And answer me declined, sword against sword,
Ourselves alone. I'll write it: follow me.
              [*Exeunt Antony and Euphronius.*
   Eno. [*Aside*] Yes, like enough, high-battled Cæsar
   will
Unstate his happiness, and be staged to the show,   30
Against a sworder! I see men's judgements are
A parcel of their fortunes; and things outward
Do draw the inward quality after them,
To suffer all alike. That he should dream,
Knowing all measures, the full Cæsar will
Answer his emptiness! Cæsar, thou hast subdued
His judgement too.

Enter an Attendant.

   Att.   A messenger from Cæsar.
   Cleo. What, no more ceremony? See, my women!
Against the blown rose may they stop their nose
That kneel'd unto the buds. Admit him, sir.   40
                      [*Exit Attendant.*
   Eno. [*Aside*] Mine honesty and I begin to square.
The loyalty well held to fools does make
Our faith mere folly: yet he that can endure
To follow with allegiance a fall'n lord
Does conquer him that did his master conquer,
And earns a place i' the story.

Enter THYREUS.

   Cleo.   Cæsar's will?
   Thyr. Hear it apart.
   Cleo.   None but friends: say boldly.
   Thyr. So, haply, are they friends to Antony.
   Eno. He needs as many, sir, as Cæsar has;
Or needs not us. If Cæsar please, our master   50
Will leap to be his friend: for us, you know
Whose he is we are, and that is, Cæsar's.
   Thyr.   So.
Thus then, thou most renown'd: Cæsar entreats,
Not to consider in what case thou stand'st,
Further than he is Cæsar.
   Cleo.   Go on: right royal.
   Thyr. He knows that you embrace not Antony
As you did love, but as you fear'd him.
   Cleo.   O!
   Thyr. The scars upon your honour, therefore, he
Does pity, as constrained blemishes,
Not as deserved.
   Cleo.   He is a god, and knows   60
What is most right: mine honour was not yielded,
But conquer'd merely.
   Eno.   [*Aside*] To be sure of that,
I will ask Antony. Sir, sir, thou art so leaky,
That we must leave thee to thy sinking, for
Thy dearest quit thee.   [*Exit.*
   Thyr.   Shall I say to Cæsar
What you require of him? for he partly begs
To be desired to give. It much would please him,
That of his fortunes you should make a staff

To lean upon: but it would warm his spirits,
To hear from me you had left Antony, 70
†And put yourself under his shrowd,
The universal landlord.
   Cleo.   What 's your name?
   Thyr. My name is Thyreus.
   Cleo.   Most kind messenger,
Say to great Cæsar this: in deputation
I kiss his conquering hand: tell him, I am prompt
To lay my crown at 's feet, and there to kneel:
Tell him, from his all-obeying breath I hear
The doom of Egypt.
   Thyr.   'Tis your noblest course.
Wisdom and fortune combating together,
If that the former dare but what it can, 80
No chance may shake it. Give me grace to lay
My duty on your hand.
   Cleo.   Your Cæsar's father oft,
When he hath mused of taking kingdoms in,
Bestow'd his lips on that unworthy place,
As it rain'd kisses.

        Re-enter ANTONY *and* ENOBARBUS.

   Ant.   Favours, by Jove that thunders!
What art thou, fellow?
   Thyr.   One that but performs
The bidding of the fullest man, and worthiest
To have command obey'd.
   Eno.   [*Aside*] You will be whipp'd.
   Ant. Approach, there! Ah, you kite! Now, gods and
    devils! 90
Authority melts from me: of late, when I cried 'Ho!'
Like boys unto a muss, kings would start forth,
And cry 'Your will?' Have you no ears? I am
Antony yet.

        Enter Attendants.

           Take hence this Jack, and whip him.
   Eno. [*Aside*] 'Tis better playing with a lion's whelp
Than with an old one dying.
   Ant.   Moon and stars!
Whip him. Were 't twenty of the greatest tributaries
That do acknowledge Cæsar, should I find them
So saucy with the hand of she here,—what 's her
    name,
Since she was Cleopatra? Whip him, fellows,
Till, like a boy, you see him cringe his face, 100
And whine aloud for mercy: take him hence.
   Thyr. Mark Antony!
   Ant.   Tug him away: being whipp'd,
Bring him again: this Jack of Cæsar's shall
Bear us an errand to him.
           [*Exeunt Attendants with Thyreus.*
You were half blasted ere I knew you: ha!
Have I my pillow left unpress'd in Rome,
Forborne the getting of a lawful race,
And by a gem of women, to be abused
By one that looks on feeders?
   Cleo.   Good my lord,—

   Ant. You have been a boggler ever: 110
But when we in our viciousness grow hard—
O misery on 't!—the wise gods seel our eyes;
In our own filth drop our clear judgements; make us
Adore our errors; laugh at 's, while we strut
To our confusion.
   Cleo.   O, is 't come to this?
   Ant. I found you as a morsel cold upon
Dead Cæsar's trencher; nay, you were a fragment
Of Cneius Pompey's; besides what hotter hours,
Unregister'd in vulgar fame, you have
Luxuriously pick'd out: for, I am sure, 120
Though you can guess what temperance should be,
You know not what it is.
   Cleo.   Wherefore is this?
   Ant. To let a fellow that will take rewards
And say 'God quit you!' be familiar with
My playfellow, your hand; this kingly seal
And plighter of high hearts! O, that I were
Upon the hill of Basan, to outroar
The horned herd! for I have savage cause;
And to proclaim it civilly, were like
A halter'd neck which does the hangman thank 130
For being yare about him.

      Re-enter Attendants *with* THYREUS.
           Is he whipp'd?
   First Att. Soundly, my lord.
   Ant.   Cried he? and begg'd a' pardon?
   First Att. He did ask favour.
   Ant. If that thy father live, let him repent
Thou wast not made his daughter; and be thou sorry
To follow Cæsar in his triumph, since
Thou hast been whipp'd for following him:
    henceforth
The white hand of a lady fever thee,
Shake thou to look on 't. Get thee back to Cæsar,
Tell him thy entertainment: look, thou say 140
He makes me angry with him; for he seems
Proud and disdainful, harping on what I am,
Not what he knew I was: he makes me angry;
And at this time most easy 'tis to do 't,
When my good stars, that were my former guides,
Have empty left their orbs, and shot their fires
Into the abysm of hell. If he mislike
My speech and what is done, tell him he has
Hipparchus, my enfranched bondman, whom
He may at pleasure whip, or hang, or torture, 150
As he shall like, to quit me: urge it thou:
Hence with thy stripes, begone!   [*Exit Thyreus.*
   Cleo. Have you done yet?
   Ant.   Alack, our terrene moon
Is now eclipsed; and it portends alone
The fall of Antony!
   Cleo.   I must stay his time.
   Ant. To flatter Cæsar, would you mingle eyes
With one that ties his points?
   Cleo.   Not know me yet?
   Ant. Cold-hearted toward me?

Theobald in putting a larger stop after *this;* F has a comma at the end of
the line, where we should put a colon, which gives a better sense.
deputation, by deputy. 77. **all-obeying,** obeyed by all. 87. **fullest,**
most complete in all respects. 89. **kite,** Cleopatra (?) 91. **muss,**
scramble. 93. **Jack,** contemptuous epithet. 100. **cringe,** transitive
use. 109. **feeders,** servants. 110. **boggler,** waverer; often used of
shying horses. 112. **seel,** blind; a term in falconry for closing the eyes
of wild hawks by sewing their eyelids together. 120. **Luxuriously,**
lustfully. 121. **temperance,** probably, chastity. 127. **hill of Basan,**
allusion to Psalms 68:15, and 22:12; apparently to the Prayer Book
version. 131. **yare,** ready, quick. 138. **fever,** put thee in a fever
(imperative). 146. **orbs,** spheres. 149. **Hipparchus.** According to
Plutarch the man was a deserter. **enfranched,** enfranchised. 153.
terrene, earthly, i.e., Cleopatra eclipsed like the moon. 157. **points,**
laces by which articles of clothing were secured.

Cleo.   Ah, dear, if I be so,
From my cold heart let heaven engender hail,
And poison it in the source; and the first stone   160
Drop in my neck: as it determines, so
Dissolve my life! The next Cæsarion smite!
Till by degrees the memory of my womb,
Together with my brave Egyptians all,
By the discandying of this pelleted storm,
Lie graveless, till the flies and gnats of Nile
Have buried them for prey!
    Ant.   I am satisfied.
Cæsar sits down in Alexandria; where
I will oppose his fate. Our force by land
Hath nobly held; our sever'd navy too   170
Have knit again, and fleet, threatening most sea-like.
Where hast thou been, my heart? Dost thou hear,
    lady?
If from the field I shall return once more
To kiss these lips, I will appear in blood;
I and my sword will earn our chronicle:
There 's hope in 't yet.
    Cleo. That 's my brave lord!
    Ant. I will be treble-sinew'd, hearted, breathed,
And fight maliciously: for when mine hours
Were nice and lucky, men did ransom lives   180
Of me for jests; but now I 'll set my teeth,
And send to darkness all that stop me. Come,
Let 's have one other gaudy night: call to me
All my sad captains; fill our bowls once more;
Let 's mock the midnight bell.
    Cleo.   It is my birth-day:
I had thought to have held it poor; but, since my lord
Is Antony again, I will be Cleopatra.
    Ant. We will yet do well.
    Cleo. Call all his noble captains to my lord.
    Ant. Do so, we 'll speak to them; and to-night I 'll
    force   190
The wine peep through their scars. Come on, my
    queen;
There 's sap in 't yet. The next time I do fight,
I 'll make death love me; for I will contend
Even with his pestilent scythe.
                         [*Exeunt all but Enobarbus.*
    Eno. Now he 'll outstare the lightning. To be
    furious,
Is to be frighted out of fear; and in that mood
The dove will peck the estridge; and I see still,
A diminution in our captain's brain
Restores his heart: when valour preys on reason,
It eats the sword it fights with. I will seek   200
Some way to leave him.   [*Exit.*

ACT IV.

SCENE I. *Before Alexandria. Cæsar's camp.*

Enter CÆSAR, AGRIPPA, *and* MECÆNAS, *with his
army;* CÆSAR *reading a letter.*

    Cæs. He calls me boy; and chides, as he had power

To beat me out of Egypt; my messenger
He hath whipp'd with rods; dares me to personal
    combat,
Cæsar to Antony: let the old ruffian know
I have many other ways to die; meantime
Laugh at his challenge.
    Mec.   Cæsar must think,
When one so great begins to rage, he 's hunted
Even to falling. Give him no breath, but now
Make boot of his distraction: never anger
Made good guard for itself.
    Cæs.   Let our best heads   10
Know, that to-morrow the last of many battles
We mean to fight: within our files there are,
Of those that served Mark Antony but late,
Enough to fetch him in. See it done:
And feast the army; we have store to do 't,
And they have earn'd the waste. Poor Antony! [*Exeunt.*

SCENE II. *Alexandria. Cleopatra's palace.*

Enter ANTONY, CLEOPATRA, ENOBARBUS, CHARMIAN,
IRAS, ALEXAS, *with others.*

    Ant. He will not fight with me, Domitius.
    Eno.   No.
    Ant. Why should he not?
    Eno. He thinks, being twenty times of better fortune,
He is twenty men to one.
    Ant.   To-morrow, soldier,
By sea and land I 'll fight: or I will live,
Or bathe my dying honour in the blood
Shall make it live again. Woo 't thou fight well?
    Eno. I 'll strike, and cry 'Take all.'
    Ant.   Well said; come on.
Call forth my household servants: let 's to-night
Be bounteous at our meal.

Enter three or four Servitors.

                Give me thy hand,   10
Thou hast been rightly honest;—so hast thou;—
Thou,—and thou,—and thou:—you have served me
    well,
And kings have been your fellows.
    Cleo.   [*Aside to Eno.*] What means this?
    Eno. [*Aside to Cleo.*] 'Tis one of those odd tricks
    which sorrow shoots
Out of the mind.
    Ant.   And thou art honest too.
I wish I could be made so many men,
And all of you clapp'd up together in
An Antony, that I might do you service
So good as you have done.
    All.   The gods forbid!
    Ant. Well, my good fellows, wait on me to-night: 20
Scant not my cups; and make as much of me
As when mine empire was your fellow too,
And suffer'd my command.
    Cleo.   [*Aside to Eno.*] What does he
    mean?

Eno. [*Aside to Cleo.*] To make his followers weep.
Ant.   Tend me to-night;
May be it is the period of your duty:
Haply you shall not see me more; or if,
A mangled shadow: perchance to-morrow
You'll serve another master. I look on you
As one that takes his leave. Mine honest friends,
I turn you not away; but, like a master   30
Married to your good service, stay till death:
Tend me to-night two hours, I ask no more,
And the gods yield you for 't!
Eno.   What mean you, sir,
To give them this discomfort? Look, they weep;
And I, an ass, am onion-eyed: for shame,
Transform us not to women.
Ant.   Ho, ho, ho!
Now the witch take me, if I meant it thus!
Grace grow where those drops fall! My hearty friends,
You take me in too dolorous a sense;
For I spake to you for your comfort; did desire you   40
To burn this night with torches: know, my hearts,
I hope well of to-morrow; and will lead you
Where rather I'll expect victorious life
Than death and honour. Let 's to supper, come,
And drown consideration.   [*Exeunt.*

SCENE III. *The same. Before the palace.*

Enter two Soldiers *to their guard.*

First Sold. Brother, good night: to-morrow is the
    day.
Sec. Sold. It will determine one way: fare you well.
Heard you of nothing strange about the streets?
First Sold. Nothing. What news?
Sec. Sold. Belike 'tis but a rumour. Good night to
    you.
First Sold. Well, sir, good night.

Enter two other Soldiers.

Sec. Sold. Soldiers, have careful watch.
Third Sold. And you. Good night, good night.
            [*They place themselves in every corner of the stage.*
Fourth Sold. Here we: and if to-morrow
Our navy thrive, I have an absolute hope   10
Our landmen will stand up.
Third Sold.   'Tis a brave army,
And full of purpose.
                [*Music of the hautboys as under the stage.*
Fourth Sold.   Peace! what noise?
First Sold.   List, list!
Sec. Sold. Hark!
First Sold.   Music i' the air.
Third Sold.   Under the earth.
Fourth Sold. It signs well, does it not?
Third Sold.   No.
First Sold.   Peace, I say!
What should this mean?
Sec. Sold. 'Tis the god Hercules, whom Antony
    loved,

Now leaves him.
First Sold. Walk; let 's see if other watchmen
Do hear what we do.   [*They advance to another post.*
Sec. Sold.   How now, masters.
All.   [*Speaking together*] How now!
How now! do you hear this?
First Sold.   Ay; is 't not strange?   20
Third Sold. Do you hear, masters? do you hear?
First Sold. Follow the noise so far as we have
    quarter;
Let 's see how it will give off.
All.   Content. 'Tis strange.   [*Exeunt.*

SCENE IV. *The same. A room in the palace.*

Enter ANTONY *and* CLEOPATRA, CHARMIAN, *and others
    attending.*

Ant. Eros! mine armour, Eros!
Cleo.   Sleep a little.
Ant. No, my chuck. Eros, come; mine armour,
    Eros!

Enter EROS *with armour.*

Come, good fellow, put mine iron on:
If fortune be not ours to-day, it is
Because we brave her: come.
Cleo.   Nay, I'll help too.
What 's this for?
Ant.   Ah, let be, let be! thou art
The armourer of my heart: false, false; this, this.
Cleo. Sooth, la, I'll help: thus it must be.
Ant.   Well, well;
We shall thrive now. Seest thou, my good fellow?
Go put on thy defences.
Eros.   Briefly, sir.   10
Cleo. Is not this buckled well?
Ant.   Rarely, rarely:
He that unbuckles this, till we do please
To daff 't for our repose, shall hear a storm.
Thou fumblest, Eros; and my queen 's a squire
More tight at this than thou: dispatch. O love,
That thou couldst see my wars to-day, and knew'st
The royal occupation! thou shouldst see
A workman in 't.

Enter an armed Soldier.

                    Good morrow to thee; welcome:
Thou look'st like him that knows a warlike charge:
To business that we love we rise betime,   20
And go to 't with delight.
Sold.   A thousand, sir,
Early though 't be, have on their riveted trim,
And at the port expect you.   [*Shout. Trumpets flourish.*

Enter Captains *and* Soldiers.

Capt. The morn is fair. Good morrow, general.
All. Good morrow, general.
Ant.   'Tis well blown, lads:
This morning, like the spirit of a youth

who, however, makes the music the symbol of the departure of the god
of Antony's "singular devotion," namely Bacchus. Shakespeare tells
us that it is the god Hercules, whom Antony claimed as his ancestor
and whom he imitated.   14. **signs well,** is a good sign.   23. **give off,**
cease, end.   **Content,** all right, agreed.
    SCENE IV.   2. **chuck,** term of endearment.   7. **armourer,** armor-
bearer; i.e., she provides armor to steel his heart.   **false,** wrong.   13.

daff 't, doff it, take it off.   15. **tight,** deft, skillful.   20. **betime,** betimes.
25. **well blown,** probably refers to the flourish of trumpets above,
but has been thought to refer to the blossoming or breaking forth of
the morning.

That means to be of note, begins betimes.
So, so; come, give me that: this way; well said.
Fare thee well, dame, whate'er becomes of me:
This is a soldier's kiss: rebukeable   [Kisses her. 30
And worthy shameful check it were, to stand
On more mechanic compliment; I'll leave thee
Now, like a man of steel. You that will fight,
Follow me close; I'll bring you to 't. Adieu.
          [Exeunt Antony, Eros, Captains, and Soldiers.
  Char. Please you, retire to your chamber.
  Cleo.   Lead me.
He goes forth gallantly. That he and Cæsar might
Determine this great war in single fight!
Then, Antony,—but now—Well, on.   [Exeunt.

———————

SCENE V. Alexandria. Antony's camp.

Trumpets sound. Enter ANTONY and EROS; a Soldier
  meeting them.

  Sold. The gods make this a happy day to Antony!
  Ant. Would thou and those thy scars had once
          prevail'd
To make me fight at land!
  Sold.   Hadst thou done so,
The kings that have revolted, and the soldier
That has this morning left thee, would have still
Follow'd thy heels.
  Ant.   Who's gone this morning?
  Sold.   Who!
One ever near thee: call for Enobarbus,
He shall not hear thee; or from Cæsar's camp
Say 'I am none of thine.'
  Ant.   What say'st thou?
  Sold.   Sir,
He is with Cæsar.
  Eros.   Sir, his chests and treasure   10
He has not with him.
  Ant.   Is he gone?
  Sold.   Most certain.
  Ant. Go, Eros, send his treasure after; do it;
Detain no jot, I charge thee: write to him—
I will subscribe—gentle adieus and greetings;
Say that I wish he never find more cause
To change a master. O, my fortunes have
Corrupted honest men! Dispatch.—Enobarbus!
          [Exeunt.

———————

SCENE VI. Alexandria. Cæsar's camp.

Flourish. Enter CÆSAR, AGRIPPA, with ENOBARBUS,
  and others.

  Cæs. Go forth, Agrippa, and begin the fight:
Our will is Antony be took alive;
Make it so known.
  Agr. Cæsar, I shall.   [Exit.
  Cæs. The time of universal peace is near:
Prove this a prosperous day, the three-nook'd world

Shall bear the olive freely.

Enter a Messenger.

  Mess.   Antony
Is come into the field.
  Cæs.   Go charge Agrippa
Plant those that have revolted in the van,
That Antony may seem to spend his fury   10
Upon himself.   [Exeunt all but Enobarbus.
  Eno. Alexas did revolt; and went to Jewry on
Affairs of Antony; there did persuade
Great Herod to incline himself to Cæsar,
And leave his master Antony: for this pains
Cæsar hath hang'd him. Canidius and the rest
That fell away have entertainment, but
No honourable trust. I have done ill;
Of which I do accuse myself so sorely,
That I will joy no more.

Enter a Soldier of CÆSAR'S.

  Sold.   Enobarbus, Antony   20
Hath after thee sent all thy treasure, with
His bounty overplus: the messenger
Came on my guard; and at thy tent is now
Unloading of his mules.
  Eno.   I give it you.
  Sold. Mock not, Enobarbus.
I tell you true: best you safed the bringer
Out of the host; I must attend mine office,
Or would have done 't myself. Your emperor
Continues still a Jove.   [Exit.
  Eno. I am alone the villain of the earth,   30
And feel I am so most. O Antony,
Thou mine of bounty, how wouldst thou have paid
My better service, when my turpitude
Thou dost so crown with gold! This blows my heart:
If swift thought break it not, a swifter mean
Shall outstrike thought: but thought will do 't, I
          feel.
I fight against thee! No: I will go seek
Some ditch wherein to die; the foul'st best fits
My latter part of life.   [Exit.

———————

SCENE VII. Field of battle between the camps.

Alarum. Drums and trumpets. Enter AGRIPPA and others.

  Agr. Retire, we have engaged ourselves too far:
Cæsar himself has work, and our oppression
Exceeds what we expected.   [Exeunt.

Alarums. Enter ANTONY, and SCARUS wounded.

  Scar. O my brave emperor, this is fought indeed!
Had we done so at first, we had droven them home
With clouts about their heads.
  Ant.   Thou bleed'st apace.
  Scar. I had a wound here that was like a T,
But now 'tis made an H.
  Ant.   They do retire.
  Scar. We'll beat 'em into bench-holes: I have yet

31-32. **stand On**, be particular about, insist on. 32. **mechanic**, vulgar.
SCENE V. 14. **subscribe**, sign.
  SCENE VI. 5. **The . . . near.** This is Plutarch's theme and the justification of imperial Rome; it was handed down as a political and
historical belief to the Renaissance. Shakespeare no doubt shared it.
6. **three-nook'd**, three-cornered; thought to refer to the division of
power among the triumvirs, and also to the main regions of the Roman
world, East, West, and Africa. 17. **entertainment**, employment. 26.

best you safed, it were best you safeguarded. 34. **blows,** causes his heart
to swell with passions. 35. **mean**, i.e., he will stab himself. 36.
thought, probably in the sense of sorrow. **do 't,** i.e., break his heart.
  SCENE VII. 2. **oppression,** difficulty. 6. **clouts,** bandages, or blows
and knocks. 8. **H,** i.e., the bottom of the T has been cut
across; some see in this a pun on the pronunciation of H like modern
ache. 10. **scotches,** cuts.
  SCENE VIII. 2. **gests,** deeds. 7. **shown,** shown yourselves. 10. **con-**

Room for six scotches more.   10

Enter EROS.

Eros. They are beaten, sir; and our advantage
serves
For a fair victory.
Scar.   Let us score their backs,
And snatch 'em up, as we take hares, behind:
'Tis sport to maul a runner.
Ant.   I will reward thee
Once for thy spritely comfort, and ten-fold
For thy good valour. Come thee on.
Scar.   I'll halt after.   [*Exeunt.*

SCENE VIII. *Under the walls of Alexandria.*

Alarum. Enter ANTONY, *in a march;* SCARUS, *with others.*

Ant. We have beat him to his camp: run one before,
And let the queen know of our gests. To-morrow,
Before the sun shall see 's, we'll spill the blood
That has to-day escaped. I thank you all;
For doughty-handed are you, and have fought
Not as you served the cause, but as 't had been
Each man 's like mine; you have shown all Hectors.
Enter the city, clip your wives, your friends,
Tell them your feats; whilst they with joyful tears
Wash the congealment from your wounds, and kiss   10
The honour'd gashes whole. [*To Scarus.*] Give me thy
        hand;

Enter CLEOPATRA, *attended.*

To this great fairy I'll commend thy acts,
Make her thanks bless thee. [*To Cleo.*] O thou day o'
        the world,
Chain mine arm'd neck; leap thou, attire and all,
Through proof of harness to my heart, and there
Ride on the pants triumphing!
Cleo.   Lord of lords!
O infinite virtue, comest thou smiling from
The world's great snare uncaught?
Ant.   My nightingale,
We have beat them to their beds. What, girl! though
        grey
Do something mingle with our younger brown, yet
        ha' we   20
A brain that nourishes our nerves, and can
Get goal for goal of youth. Behold this man;
Commend unto his lips thy favouring hand:
Kiss it, my warrior: he hath fought to-day
As if a god, in hate of mankind, had
Destroy'd in such a shape.
Cleo.   I'll give thee, friend,
An armour all of gold; it was a king's.
Ant. He has deserved it, were it carbuncled
Like holy Phœbus' car. Give me thy hand:
Through Alexandria make a jolly march;   30
Bear our hack'd targets like the men that owe them:
Had our great palace the capacity
To camp this host, we all would sup together,

And drink carouses to the next day's fate,
Which promises royal peril. Trumpeters,
With brazen din blast you the city's ear;
Make mingle with our rattling tabourines;
That heaven and earth may strike their sounds
        together,
Applauding our approach.   [*Exeunt.*

SCENE IX. *Cæsar's camp.*

Sentinels at their post.

First Sold. If we be not relieved within this hour,
We must return to the court of guard: the night
Is shiny; and they say we shall embattle
By the second hour i' the morn.
Sec. Sold.   This last day was
A shrewd one to 's.

Enter ENOBARBUS.

Eno.   O, bear me witness, night,—
Third Sold. What man is this?
Sec. Sold.   Stand close, and list him.
Eno. Be witness to me, O thou blessed moon,
When men revolted shall upon record
Bear hateful memory, poor Enobarbus did
Before thy face repent!
First Sold.   Enobarbus!
Third Sold.   Peace!   10
Hark further.
Eno. O sovereign mistress of true melancholy,
The poisonous damp of night disponge upon me,
That life, a very rebel to my will,
May hang no longer on me: throw my heart
Against the flint and hardness of my fault;
Which, being dried with grief, will break to powder,
And finish all foul thoughts. O Antony,
Nobler than my revolt is infamous,
Forgive me in thine own particular;   20
But let the world rank me in register
A master-leaver and a fugitive:
O Antony! O Antony!   [*Dies.*
Sec. Sold.   Let 's speak
To him.
First Sold. Let 's hear him, for the things he speaks
May concern Cæsar.
Third Sold.   Let 's do so. But he sleeps.
First Sold. Swoons rather; for so bad a prayer as his
Was never yet for sleep.
Sec. Sold.   Go we to him.
Third Sold. Awake, sir, awake; speak to us.
Sec. Sold.   Hear you, sir?
First Sold. The hand of death hath raught him.
        [*Drums afar off.*] Hark! the drums   30
Demurely wake the sleepers. Let us bear him
To the court of guard; he is of note: our hour
Is fully out.
Third Sold. Come on, then;
He may recover yet.   [*Exeunt with the body.*

---

gealment, clotted blood. 12. **fairy,** enchantress. 15. **proof of harness,**
proof-armor, tested armor. 16. **pants,** heartbeats. 21. **nerves,**
sinews, tendons, i.e., parts of the body in which strength resides, the
brain being the source of true courage. 28. **carbuncled,** set with carbuncles; apparently a vague recollection of Ovid, *Metamorphoses,* ii,
where the yoke of Phoebus' car is said to be set with chrysolites (Furness). 37. **mingle,** union, mingling. **tabourines,** drums.
SCENE IX. 2. **court of guard,** guardroom. 3. **embattle,** fall in for

the combat. 12. **mistress . . . melancholy,** the moon, so addressed because of her influence in causing lunacy. 13. **disponge,** pour down.
17. **dried with grief.** Enobarbus has passed into the condition of despair,
his spirits having descended into his bowels, leaving his heart dry.
30. **raught,** reached. 31. **Demurely,** with subdued sound (Onions).

SCENE X. *Between the two camps.*

Enter ANTONY *and* SCARUS, *with their Army.*

Ant. Their preparation is to-day by sea;
We please them not by land.
Scar.   For both, my lord.
Ant. I would they 'ld fight i' the fire or i' the air;
We 'ld fight there too. But this it is; our foot
Upon the hills adjoining to the city
Shall stay with us: order for sea is given;
†They have put forth the haven . . .
Where their appointment we may best discover,
And look on their endeavour.   *[Exeunt.*

SCENE XI. *Another part of the same.*

Enter CÆSAR, *and his Army.*

Cæs. But being charged, we will be still by land,
Which, as I take 't, we shall; for his best force
Is forth to man his galleys. To the vales,
And hold our best advantage.   *[Exeunt.*

SCENE XII. *Another part of the same.*

Enter ANTONY *and* SCARUS.

Ant. Yet they are not join'd: where yond pine does
         stand,
I shall discover all; I'll bring thee word
Straight, how 'tis like to go.   *[Exit.*
Scar.   Swallows have built
In Cleopatra's sails their nests: the augurers
Say they know not, they cannot tell; look grimly,
And dare not speak their knowledge. Antony
Is valiant, and dejected; and, by starts,
His fretted fortunes give him hope, and fear,
Of what he has, and has not.
                    [Alarum afar off, as at a sea-fight.

Re-enter ANTONY.

Ant.   All is lost;   10
This foul Egyptian hath betrayed me:
My fleet hath yielded to the foe; and yonder
They cast their caps up and carouse together
Like friends long lost. Triple-turn'd whore! 'tis thou
Hath sold me to this novice; and my heart
Makes only wars on thee. Bid them all fly;
For when I am revenged upon my charm,
I have done all. Bid them all fly; begone. *[Exit Scarus.*
O sun, thy uprise shall I see no more:
Fortune and Antony part here; even here
Do we shake hands. All come to this? The hearts   20
That spaniel'd me at heels, to whom I gave
Their wishes, do discandy, melt their sweets
On blossoming Cæsar; and this pine is bark'd,
That overtopp'd them all. Betray'd I am:
O this false soul of Egypt! this grave charm,—

(left margin) Antony
and Cleopatra
ACT IV : SC X

1100

Whose eye beck'd forth my wars, and call'd them
         home;
Whose bosom was my crownet, my chief end,—
Like a right gipsy, hath, at fast and loose,
Beguiled me to the very heart of loss.
What, Eros, Eros!

Enter CLEOPATRA.

         Ah, thou spell! Avaunt!   30
Cleo. Why is my lord enraged against his love?
Ant. Vanish, or I shall give thee thy deserving,
And blemish Cæsar's triumph. Let him take thee,
And hoist thee up to the shouting plebeians:
Follow his chariot, like the greatest spot
Of all thy sex; most monster-like, be shown
For poor'st diminutives, for doits; and let
Patient Octavia plough thy visage up
With her prepared nails.   *[Exit Cleopatra.*
         'Tis well thou 'rt gone,
If it be well to live: but better 'twere   40
Thou fell'st into my fury, for one death
Might have prevented many. Eros, ho!
The shirt of Nessus is upon me: teach me,
Alcides, thou mine ancestor, thy rage:
Let me lodge Lichas on the horns o' the moon;
And with those hands, that grasp'd the heaviest club,
Subdue my worthiest self. The witch shall die:
To the young Roman boy she hath sold me, and I fall
Under this plot; she dies for 't. Eros, ho!   *[Exit.*

SCENE XIII. *Alexandria. Cleopatra's palace.*

Enter CLEOPATRA, CHARMIAN, IRAS, *and* MARDIAN.

Cleo. Help me, my women! O, he is more mad
Than Telamon for his shield; the boar of Thessaly
Was never so emboss'd.
Char.   To the monument!
There lock yourself, and send him word you are dead.
The soul and body rive not more in parting
Than greatness going off.
Cleo.   To the monument!
Mardian, go tell him I have slain myself;
Say, that the last I spoke was 'Antony,'
And word it, prithee, piteously: hence, Mardian,
And bring me how he takes my death. To the
         monument!   *[Exeunt.* 10

SCENE XIV. *The same. Another room.*

Enter ANTONY *and* EROS.

Ant. Eros, thou yet behold'st me?
Eros.   Ay, noble lord.
Ant. Sometime we see a cloud that 's dragonish;
A vapour sometime like a bear or lion,
A tower'd citadel, a pendent rock,

SCENE X. 6-8. **order . . . Where.** Line 7 is probably incomplete;
but if *order . . . haven* is treated as parenthetical, *Where* (whither) may
be taken to refer to *hills* (l. 5) and the passage construed. 7. **forth,**
forth from.
  SCENE XI. 1. **But being,** unless we are.
  SCENE XII. 3-5. **Swallows . . . tell.** This gives a slight indication of
how Shakespeare used his source. The swallows are mentioned in
connection with Actium. Plutarch said that in that place swallows
built under the poop of Cleopatra's galley and that others came and
drove them away; it is interpreted as an evil omen. But this allusion
Shakespeare took not from the text, but from the marginal note, The

note says, "An ill signe, foreshewed by swallowes breding in Cleopatraes
shippe." 13. **Triple-turn'd,** three times faithless. 16. **charm,**
charmer. 22. **discandy,** melt. 25. **grave charm,** destructive witchcraft. 26. **beck'd,** beckoned. 27. **crownet,** coronet. 28. **right,** veritable. **gipsy,** double sense: Egyptian and gypsy (rogue). **fast and
loose,** a cheating game the name of which is still proverbial. 35. **spot,**
disgrace. 36. **shown,** exhibited. 37. **diminutives,** undersized creatures;
or, if *doits* is correct, small coins. **doits,** Thirlby's conjecture for F:
Dolts, meaning "fools." 43. **shirt of Nessus,** the famous garment dipped
in the centaur's blood, which Dejanira used as a love charm for
Hercules, thus causing his death. 44. **Alcides,** Hercules. 45. **Lichas,**

A forked mountain, or blue promontory
With trees upon 't, that nod unto the world,
And mock our eyes with air: thou hast seen these
    signs;
They are black vesper's pageants.
    Eros.   Ay, my lord.
    Ant. That which is now a horse, even with a
    thought
The rack dislimns, and makes it indistinct,   10
As water is in water.
    Eros.   It does, my lord.
    Ant. My good knave Eros, now thy captain is
Even such a body: here I am Antony;
Yet cannot hold this visible shape, my knave.
I made these wars for Egypt; and the queen,—
Whose heart I thought I had, for she had mine;
Which whilst it was mine had annex'd unto 't
A million more, now lost,—she, Eros, has
Pack'd cards with Cæsar, and false-play'd my glory
Unto an enemy's triumph.   20
Nay, weep not, gentle Eros; there is left us
Ourselves to end ourselves.

    Enter MARDIAN.
                O, thy vile lady!
She has robb'd me of my sword.
    Mar.   No, Antony;
My mistress loved thee, and her fortunes mingled
With thine entirely.
    Ant.   Hence, saucy eunuch; peace!
She hath betray'd me and shall die the death.
    Mar. Death of one person can be paid but once,
And that she has discharged: what thou wouldst do
Is done unto thy hand: the last she spake
Was 'Antony! most noble Antony!'   30
Then in the midst a tearing groan did break
The name of Antony; it was divided
Between her heart and lips: she render'd life,
Thy name so buried in her.
    Ant.   Dead, then?
    Mar.   Dead.
    Ant. Unarm, Eros; the long day's task is done,
And we must sleep. [*To Mar.*] That thou depart'st
    hence safe,
Does pay thy labour richly; go.   [*Exit Mardian.*
    Off, pluck off:
The seven-fold shield of Ajax cannot keep
The battery from my heart. O, cleave, my sides!
Heart, once be stronger than thy continent,   40
Crack thy frail case! Apace, Eros, apace.
No more a soldier: bruised pieces, go;
You have been nobly borne. From me awhile.
                    [*Exit Eros.*
I will o'ertake thee, Cleopatra, and
Weep for my pardon. So it must be, for now
All length is torture: since the torch is out,
Lie down, and stray no farther: now all labour
Mars what it does; yea, very force entangles

Itself with strength: seal then, and all is done.
Eros!—I come, my queen:—Eros!—Stay for me: 50
Where souls do couch on flowers, we'll hand in hand,
And with our sprightly port make the ghosts gaze:
Dido and her Æneas shall want troops,
And all the haunt be ours. Come, Eros, Eros!

    Re-enter EROS.
    Eros. What would my lord?
    Ant.   Since Cleopatra died,
I have lived in such dishonour, that the gods
Detest my baseness. I, that with my sword
Quarter'd the world, and o'er green Neptune's back
With ships made cities, condemn myself to lack
The courage of a woman; less noble mind   60
Than she which by her death our Cæsar tells
'I am conqueror of myself.' Thou art sworn, Eros,
That, when the exigent should come, which now
Is come indeed, when I should see behind me
The inevitable prosecution of
Disgrace and horror, that, on my command,
Thou then wouldst kill me: do 't; the time is come:
Thou strikest not me, 'tis Cæsar thou defeat'st.
Put colour in thy cheek.
    Eros.   The gods withhold me!
Shall I do that which all the Parthian darts,   70
Though enemy, lost aim, and could not?
    Ant.   Eros,
Wouldst thou be window'd in great Rome and see
Thy master thus with pleach'd arms, bending down
His corrigible neck, his face subdued
To penetrative shame, whilst the wheel'd seat
Of fortunate Cæsar, drawn before him, branded
His baseness that ensued?
    Eros.   I would not see 't.
    Ant. Come, then; for with a wound I must be cured.
Draw that thy honest sword, which thou hast worn
Most useful for thy country.
    Eros.   O, sir, pardon me!   80
    Ant. When I did make thee free, sworest thou not
    then
To do this when I bade thee? Do it at once;
Or thy precedent services are all
But accidents unpurposed. Draw, and come.
    Eros. Turn from me, then, that noble countenance,
Wherein the worship of the whole world lies.
    Ant. Lo thee!   [*Turning from him.*
    Eros. My sword is drawn.
    Ant.   Then let it do at once
The thing why thou hast drawn it.
    Eros.   My dear master,
My captain, and my emperor, let me say,   90
Before I strike this bloody stroke, farewell.
    Ant. 'Tis said, man; and farewell.
    Eros. Farewell, great chief. Shall I strike now?
    Ant.   Now, Eros.
    Eros. Why, there then: thus I do escape the sorrow
Of Antony's death.   [*Kills himself.*

servant of Hercules who was cast by his raging master into the sea.
    SCENE XIII. 2. **Telamon,** Ajax Telamon, who after the capture of
Troy went mad and slew himself when he was not awarded the shield
and armor of Achilles. **boar of Thessaly,** the boar sent by Diana to
ravage the fields of Calydon, and slain by Meleager. 3. **emboss'd,**
foaming at the mouth, or driven to extremity. 5. **rive,** split, sever.
10. **bring me,** i.e., word.
    SCENE XIV. 10. **rack,** floating vapor or cloud. **dislimns,** effaces.
12. **knave,** boy. 33. **render'd,** gave up. 38. **seven-fold shield.** The
shield of Ajax was made of brass and was reinforced with seven thick-
nesses of ox hide. 39. **battery from my heart,** ordinarily taken to mean

the swelling of his heart denoted in its beating. Cuningham thinks it
means the battery of calamity from outside. 46. **length,** length of life.
51. **couch,** lie. 53. **Dido . . . troops,** i.e., Antony and Cleopatra will be
the most distinguished lovers there; they will outshine even Dido and
Aeneas. 60. **less noble mind,** being a less noble-minded person. 63.
exigent, exigency, decisive moment. 65. **prosecution,** pursuit. 72.
window'd, placed in a window to look on. 73. **pleach'd,** folded.
74. **corrigible,** submissive to correction. 76. **branded,** rendered conspicuous as by a brand. 77. **ensued,** followed. 83. **precedent,** former.

Ant. Thrice-nobler than myself!
Thou teachest me, O valiant Eros, what
I should, and thou couldst not. My queen and Eros
Have by their brave instruction got upon me
A nobleness in record: but I will be
A bridegroom in my death, and run into 't 100
As to a lover's bed. Come, then; and, Eros,
Thy master dies thy scholar: to do thus
                                    [*Falling on his sword.*
I learn'd of thee. How! not dead? not dead?
The guard, ho! O, dispatch me!

Enter DERCETAS *and* Guard.

First Guard.   What 's the noise?
Ant. I have done my work ill, friends: O, make an
    end
Of what I have begun.
    Sec. Guard.   The star is fall'n.
    First Guard. And time is at his period.
    All.   Alas, and woe!
Ant. Let him that loves me strike me dead.
    First Guard.   Not I.
    Sec. Guard. Nor I.
    Third Guard. Nor any one.   [*Exeunt Guard.* 110
Der. Thy death and fortunes bid thy followers fly.
This sword but shown to Cæsar, with this tidings,
Shall enter me with him.

Enter DIOMEDES.

Dio. Where 's Antony?
    Der.   There, Diomed, there.
    Dio.   Lives he?
Wilt thou not answer, man?   [*Exit Dercetas.*
    Ant. Art thou there, Diomed? Draw thy sword, and
    give me
Sufficing strokes for death.
    Dio.   Most absolute lord,
My mistress Cleopatra sent me to thee.
    Ant. When did she send thee?
    Dio.   Now, my lord.
    Ant.   Where is she?
    Dio. Lock'd in her monument. She had a
    prophesying fear 120
Of what hath come to pass: for when she saw—
Which never shall be found—you did suspect
She had disposed with Cæsar, and that your rage
Would not be purged, she sent you word she was
    dead;
But, fearing since how it might work, hath sent
Me to proclaim the truth; and I am come,
I dread, too late.
    Ant. Too late, good Diomed: call my guard, I
    prithee.
    Dio. What, ho, the emperor's guard! The guard,
    what, ho!
Come, your lord calls! 130

Enter four or five of the Guard *of* ANTONY.

Ant. Bear me, good friends, where Cleopatra bides;
'Tis the last service that I shall command you.

First Guard. Woe, woe are we, sir, you may not live
    to wear
All your true followers out.
    All.   Most heavy day!
    Ant. Nay, good my fellows, do not please sharp fate
To grace it with your sorrows: bid that welcome
Which comes to punish us, and we punish it
Seeming to bear it lightly. Take me up:
I have led you oft: carry me now, good friends,
And have my thanks for all. [*Exeunt, bearing Antony.* 140

SCENE XV. *The same. A monument.*

Enter CLEOPATRA, *and her maids aloft, with* CHARMIAN
    and IRAS.

Cleo. O Charmian, I will never go from hence.
Char. Be comforted, dear madam.
Cleo.   No, I will not:
All strange and terrible events are welcome,
But comforts we despise; our size of sorrow,
Proportion'd to our cause, must be as great
As that which makes it.

Enter, below, DIOMEDES.

                How now! is he dead?
    Dio. His death 's upon him, but not dead.
Look out o' the other side your monument;
His guard have brought him thither.

Enter, below, ANTONY, *borne by the* Guard.

    Cleo.   O sun,
Burn the great sphere thou movest in! darkling stand 10
The varying shore o' the world. O Antony,
Antony, Antony! Help, Charmian, help, Iras, help;
Help, friends below; let 's draw him hither.
    Ant.   Peace!
Not Cæsar's valour hath o'erthrown Antony,
But Antony's hath triumph'd on itself.
    Cleo. So it should be, that none but Antony
Should conquer Antony; but woe 'tis so!
    Ant. I am dying, Egypt, dying; only
I here importune death awhile, until
Of many thousand kisses the poor last 20
I lay upon thy lips.
    Cleo.   I dare not, dear,—
Dear my lord, pardon,—I dare not,
Lest I be taken: not the imperious show
Of the full-fortuned Cæsar ever shall
Be brooch'd with me; if knife, drugs, serpents, have
Edge, sting, or operation, I am safe:
Your wife Octavia, with her modest eyes
And still conclusion, shall acquire no honour
Demuring upon me. But come, come, Antony,—
Help me, my women,—we must draw thee up: 30
Assist, good friends.
    Ant.   O, quick, or I am gone.
    Cleo. Here 's sport indeed! How heavy weighs my
    lord!
Our strength is all gone into heaviness,

98-99. **got . . . record,** created in me an obvious and recorded nobleness;
also interpreted as, won for themselves (upon me) a noble place in the
story (Cuningham). 113. **enter me with,** recommend me to. 123. **disposed with,** come to terms with. 136. **To grace,** by gracing or honoring.
SCENE XV. 4. **our size of sorrow,** i.e., the size of our sorrow. 10.
sphere. The sun is here thought of as fixed in a great sphere with
which it revolved around the earth. **darkling,** in darkness. 11. **vary-**

ing shore, varying between night and day. Presumably if the sun had
burned its sphere, earth's shore would no longer vary between light and
darkness. 23. **imperious,** imperial. 25. **brooch'd,** adorned (as with a
brooch). 28. **still conclusion,** composed and quiet judgment. 29.
Demuring, looking demurely, i.e., with affected modesty. 33. **heaviness,** sadness, with play on *weight.* 44. **housewife.** The proper form
is (as in F) *Huswife,* used in a bad sense meaning "hussy," "wanton,"

That makes the weight: had I great Juno's power,
The strong-wing'd Mercury should fetch thee up,
And set thee by Jove's side. Yet come a little,—
Wishers were ever fools,—O, come, come, come;

            [*They heave Antony aloft to Cleopatra.*
And welcome, welcome! die where thou hast lived:
Quicken with kissing: had my lips that power,
Thus would I wear them out.
   All.   A heavy sight!   40
   Ant. I am dying, Egypt, dying:
Give me some wine, and let me speak a little.
   Cleo. No, let me speak; and let me rail so high,
That the false housewife Fortune break her wheel,
Provoked by my offence.
   Ant.   One word, sweet queen:
Of Cæsar seek your honour, with your safety. O!
   Cleo. They do not go together.
   Ant.   Gentle, hear me:
None about Cæsar trust but Proculeius.
   Cleo. My resolution and my hands I'll trust;
None about Cæsar.   50
   Ant. The miserable change now at my end
Lament nor sorrow at; but please your thoughts
In feeding them with those my former fortunes
Wherein I lived, the greatest prince o' the world,
The noblest; and do now not basely die,
Not cowardly put off my helmet to
My countryman,—a Roman by a Roman
Valiantly vanquish'd. Now my spirit is going;
I can no more.
   Cleo.   Noblest of men, woo 't die?
Hast thou no care of me? shall I abide   60
In this dull world, which in thy absence is
No better than a sty? O, see, my women,   [*Antony dies.*
The crown o' the earth doth melt. My lord!
O, wither'd is the garland of the war,
The soldier's pole is fall'n: young boys and girls
Are level now with men; the odds is gone,
And there is nothing left remarkable
Beneath the visiting moon.   [*Faints.*
   Char.   O, quietness, lady!
   Iras. She is dead too, our sovereign.
   Char.   Lady!
   Iras.   Madam!
   Char. O madam, madam, madam!
   Iras.   Royal Egypt,   70
Empress!
   Char. Peace, peace, Iras!
   Cleo. No more, but e'en a woman, and commanded
By such poor passion as the maid that milks
And does the meanest chares. It were for me
To throw my sceptre at the injurious gods;
To tell them that this world did equal theirs
Till they had stol'n our jewel. All 's but naught;
Patience is sottish, and impatience does
Become a dog that 's mad: then is it sin   80
To rush into the secret house of death,
Ere death dare come to us? How do you, women?
What, what! good cheer! Why, how now, Charmian!
My noble girls! Ah, women, women, look,

Our lamp is spent, it 's out! Good sirs, take heart:
We'll bury him; and then, what 's brave, what 's
   noble,
Let 's do it after the high Roman fashion,
And make death proud to take us. Come, away:
This case of that huge spirit now is cold:
Ah, women, women! come; we have no friend   90
But resolution, and the briefest end.
      [*Exeunt; those above bearing off Antony's body.*

ACT V.

SCENE I. *Alexandria. Cæsar's camp.*

Enter CÆSAR, AGRIPPA, DOLABELLA, MECÆNAS,
   GALLUS, PROCULEIUS, *and others, his council of war.*

   Cæs. Go to him, Dolabella, bid him yield;
Being so frustrate, tell him he mocks
The pauses that he makes.
   Dol.   Cæsar, I shall.   [*Exit.*

Enter DERCETAS, *with the sword of* ANTONY.

   Cæs. Wherefore is that? and what art thou that
   darest
Appear thus to us?
   Der.   I am call'd Dercetas;
Mark Antony I served, who best was worthy
Best to be served: whilst he stood up and spoke,
He was my master; and I wore my life
To spend upon his haters. If thou please
To take me to thee, as I was to him   10
I'll be to Cæsar; if thou pleasest not,
I yield thee up my life.
   Cæs.   What is 't thou say'st?
   Der. I say, O Cæsar, Antony is dead.
   Cæs. The breaking of so great a thing should make
A greater crack: †the round world
Should have shook lions into civil streets,
And citizens to their dens: the death of Antony
Is not a single doom; in the name lay
A moiety of the world.
   Der.   He is dead, Cæsar;
Not by a public minister of justice,   20
Nor by a hired knife; but that self hand,
Which writ his honour in the acts it did,
Hath, with the courage which the heart did lend it,
Splitted the heart. This is his sword;
I robb'd his wound of it; behold it stain'd
With his most noble blood.
   Cæs.   Look you sad, friends?
The gods rebuke me, but it is tidings
To wash the eyes of kings.
   Agr.   And strange it is,
That nature must compel us to lament
Our most persisted deeds.
   Mer.   His taints and honours   30
Waged equal with him.
   Agr.   A rarer spirit never
Did steer humanity: but you, gods, will give us

---

57. **a Roman by a Roman.** Shakespeare follows Plutarch very closely
in his account of Antony's death, and repeats simply and admiringly
the rhetoric of his source.   65. **pole,** lodestar; also explained as "banner
or standard."   67. **remarkable,** distinguished, noteworthy.   75. **chares,**
chores, drudgery.   79. **sottish,** merely stupid.   85. **Good sirs,** addressed
to the women.
ACT V. SCENE I.   2. **frustrate,** frustrated, baffled.   2-3. **mocks . . .**

makes, makes himself ridiculous by his delays.   15-17. **the round
. . . dens,** that is, the breaking up of the world, likened to Antony's
death, ought to have produced more striking effects.   27. **but it is,**
if it be not.   30. **persisted,** persistently desired or pursued.   31. **Waged
equal,** were equal (with him), contended equally.   32. **humanity,**
human nature.

Some faults to make us men. Cæsar is touch'd.
  Mec. When such a spacious mirror 's set before
    him,
He needs must see himself.
  Cæs.   O Antony!
I have follow'd thee to this; but we do lance
Diseases in our bodies: I must perforce
Have shown to thee such a declining day,
Or look on thine; we could not stall together
In the whole world: but yet let me lament, 40
With tears as sovereign as the blood of hearts,
That thou, my brother, my competitor
In top of all design, my mate in empire,
Friend and companion in the front of war,
The arm of mine own body, and the heart
Where mine his thoughts did kindle,—that our stars,
Unreconcilable, should divide
Our equalness to this. Hear me, good friends,—
But I will tell you at some meeter season:

Enter an Egyptian.

The business of this man looks out of him; 50
We'll hear him what he says. Whence are you?
  Egyp. A poor Egyptian yet. The queen my mistress,
Confined in all she has, her monument,
Of thy intents desires instruction,
That she preparedly may frame herself
To the way she 's forced to.
  Cæs.   Bid her have good heart:
She soon shall know of us, by some of ours,
How honourable and how kindly we
Determine for her; for Cæsar cannot live
To be ungentle.
  Egyp.   So the gods preserve thee! [*Exit.*
  Cæs. Come hither, Proculeius. Go and say, 61
We purpose her no shame: give her what comforts
The quality of her passion shall require,
Lest, in her greatness, by some mortal stroke
She do defeat us; for her life in Rome
Would be eternal in our triumph: go,
And with your speediest bring us what she says,
And how you find of her.
  Pro.   Cæsar, I shall.   [*Exit.*
  Cæs. Gallus, go you along. [*Exit Gallus.*] Where 's
    Dolabella,
To second Proculeius?
  All.   Dolabella! 70
  Cæs. Let him alone, for I remember now
How he 's employ'd: he shall in time be ready.
Go with me to my tent; where you shall see
How hardly I was drawn into this war;
How calm and gentle I proceeded still
In all my writings: go with me, and see
What I can show in this.   [*Exeunt.*

———

SCENE II. *Alexandria. A room in the monument.*

Enter CLEOPATRA, CHARMIAN, *and* IRAS.

Cleo. My desolation does begin to make

A better life. 'Tis paltry to be Cæsar;
Not being Fortune, he 's but Fortune's knave,
A minister of her will: and it is great
To do that thing that ends all other deeds;
Which shackles accidents and bolts up change;
Which sleeps, and never palates more the dug,
The beggar's nurse and Cæsar's.

Enter, to the gates of the monument, PROCULEIUS,
  GALLUS, *and* Soldiers.

  Pro. Cæsar sends greeting to the Queen of Egypt;
And bids thee study on what fair demands 10
Thou mean'st to have him grant thee.
  Cleo.   What 's thy name?
  Pro. My name is Proculeius.
  Cleo.   Antony
Did tell me of you, bade me trust you; but
I do not greatly care to be deceived,
That have no use for trusting. If your master
Would have a queen his beggar, you must tell
    him,
That majesty, to keep decorum, must
No less beg than a kingdom: if he please
To give me conquer'd Egypt for my son,
He gives me so much of mine own, as I 20
Will kneel to him with thanks.
  Pro.   Be of good cheer;
You 're fall'n into a princely hand, fear nothing:
Make your full reference freely to my lord,
Who is so full of grace, that it flows over
On all that need: let me report to him
Your sweet dependency; and you shall find
A conqueror that will pray in aid for kindness,
Where he for grace is kneel'd to.
  Cleo.   Pray you, tell him
I am his fortune's vassal, and I send him
The greatness he has got. I hourly learn 30
A doctrine of obedience; and would gladly
Look him i' the face.
  Pro.   This I'll report, dear lady.
Have comfort, for I know your plight is pitied
Of him that caused it.
  Gal. You see how easily she may be surprised:
    [*Here Proculeius and two of the Guard ascend the
      monument by a ladder placed against a window, and,
      having descended, come behind Cleopatra. Some of the
      Guard unbar and open the gates.*
  [*To Proculeius and the Guard*] Guard her till Cæsar
    come.   [*Exit.*
  Iras. Royal queen!
  Char. O Cleopatra! thou art taken, queen.
  Cleo. Quick, quick, good hands.   [*Drawing a dagger.*
  Pro.   Hold, worthy lady, hold:
            [*Seizes and disarms her.*
Do not yourself such wrong, who are in this 40
Relieved, but not betray'd.
  Cleo.   What, of death too,
That rids our dogs of languish?
  Pro.   Cleopatra,
Do not abuse my master's bounty by

39. **stall,** dwell. 42. **competitor,** associate (probably with slight sense of rivalry). 43. **In . . . design,** in height of, i.e., in all-daring, enterprise. 49. **meeter,** more fitting. 55-56. **frame . . . to,** conform or mold to. 59. **Determine,** decide. 65. **life in Rome,** presence in Rome alive. 66. **eternal in our triumph,** would be eternally recorded in our triumph (Schmidt); may be merely intensive, i.e., would contribute in the highest degree to our triumph (Cuningham).
SCENE II. 1-2. **My . . . life.** Cleopatra tells what she means in the

lines which follow; she contemplates a deed which will show her contempt of fortune. 3. **knave,** servant. 6. **bolts up,** fetters or locks up. 7-8. **Which . . . Cæsar's.** To commit suicide would be to render oneself independent of accident and change, i.e., to sleep and never taste more the breast that nurses both Caesar and the beggar; Theobald: *dug;* F: *dung.* 14. **care . . . deceived,** whether I am deceived or not. 27. **pray in aid,** beg assistance; a legal term meaning "to call in the assistance of an outside person." 29-30. **I send . . . got,** I own his superiority with

*Antony
and Cleopatra*
ACT V : SC I

1104

The undoing of yourself: let the world see
His nobleness well acted, which your death
Will never let come forth.
   Cleo.   Where art thou, death?
Come hither, come! come, come, and take a queen
Worth many babes and beggars!
   Pro.   O, temperance, lady!
   Cleo. Sir, I will eat no meat, I'll not drink, sir;
If idle talk will once be necessary,   50
I'll not sleep neither: this mortal house I'll ruin,
Do Cæsar what he can. Know, sir, that I
Will not wait pinion'd at your master's court;
Nor once be chastised with the sober eye
Of dull Octavia. Shall they hoist me up
And show me to the shouting varletry
Of censuring Rome? Rather a ditch in Egypt
Be gentle grave unto me! rather on Nilus' mud
Lay me stark naked, and let the water-flies
Blow me into abhorring! rather make   60
My country's high pyramides my gibbet,
And hang me up in chains!
   Pro.   You do extend
These thoughts of horror further than you shall
Find cause in Cæsar.

   Enter DOLABELLA.

   Dol.   Proculeius,
What thou hast done thy master Cæsar knows,
And he hath sent for thee: for the queen,
I'll take her to my guard.
   Pro.   So, Dolabella,
It shall content me best: be gentle to her.
[*To Cleo.*] To Cæsar I will speak what you shall
   please,
If you'll employ me to him.
   Cleo.   Say, I would die.   70
            [*Exeunt Proculeius and Soldiers.*
   Dol. Most noble empress, you have heard of me?
   Cleo. I cannot tell.
   Dol.   Assuredly you know me.
   Cleo. No matter, sir, what I have heard or known.
You laugh when boys or women tell their dreams;
Is 't not your trick?
   Dol.   I understand not, madam.
   Cleo. I dream'd there was an Emperor Antony:
O, such another sleep, that I might see
But such another man!
   Dol.   If it might please ye,—
   Cleo. His face was as the heavens; and therein stuck
A sun and moon, which kept their course, and lighted
The little O, the earth.
   Dol.   Most sovereign creature,—   81
   Cleo. His legs bestrid the ocean: his rear'd arm
Crested the world: his voice was propertied
As all the tuned spheres, and that to friends;
But when he meant to quail and shake the orb,
He was as rattling thunder. For his bounty,
There was no winter in 't; an autumn 'twas
That grew the more by reaping: his delights
Were dolphin-like; they show'd his back above

The element they lived in: in his livery   90
Walk'd crowns and crownets; realms and islands
   were
As plates dropp'd from his pocket.
   Dol.   Cleopatra!
   Cleo. Think you there was, or might be, such a man
As this I dream'd of?
   Dol.   Gentle madam, no.
   Cleo. You lie, up to the hearing of the gods.
But, if there be, or ever were, one such,
It's past the size of dreaming: nature wants stuff
To vie strange forms with fancy; yet, to imagine
An Antony, were nature's piece 'gainst fancy,
Condemning shadows quite.
   Dol.   Hear me, good madam.   100
Your loss is as yourself, great; and you bear it
As answering to the weight: would I might never
O'ertake pursued success, but I do feel,
By the rebound of yours, a grief that smites
My very heart at root.
   Cleo.   I thank you, sir.
Know you what Cæsar means to do with me?
   Dol. I am loath to tell you what I would you knew.
   Cleo. Nay, pray you, sir,—
   Dol.   Though he be honourable,—
   Cleo. He'll lead me, then, in triumph?
   Dol. Madam, he will; I know 't.   110
      [*Flourish, and shout within*, 'Make way there:
                        Cæsar!'

   Enter CÆSAR, GALLUS, PROCULEIUS, MECÆNAS,
     SELEUCUS, *and others of his train.*

   Cæs. Which is the Queen of Egypt?
   Dol. It is the emperor, madam.   [*Cleopatra kneels.*
   Cæs. Arise, you shall not kneel:
I pray you, rise; rise, Egypt.
   Cleo.   Sir, the gods
Will have it thus; my master and my lord
I must obey.
   Cæs.   Take to you no hard thoughts:
The record of what injuries you did us,
Though written in our flesh, we shall remember
As things but done by chance.
   Cleo.   Sole sir o' the world,   120
I cannot project mine own cause so well
To make it clear; but do confess I have
Been laden with like frailties which before
Have often shamed our sex.
   Cæs.   Cleopatra, know,
We will extenuate rather than enforce:
If you apply yourself to our intents,
Which towards you are most gentle, you shall find
A benefit in this change; but if you seek
To lay on me a cruelty, by taking
Antony's course, you shall bereave yourself   130
Of my good purposes, and put your children
To that destruction which I'll guard them from,
If thereon you rely. I'll take my leave.
   Cleo. And may, through all the world: 'tis yours;
     and we,

---

complete submission (Johnson). 42. **languish,** lingering disease. 48.
temperance, moderation. 50-51. **If . . . neither.** If interpreted as
punctuated, Cleopatra would say that, if she once gives way to idle
talk, she will not sleep. If we take the clause, *If . . . necessary,* as parenthetical, it becomes a sort of giving away of her secret determination
to slay herself. 53. **pinion'd,** bound. 56. **varletry,** rabble. 60.
abhorring, abhorrence, abomination. 61. **pyramides,** possibly obelisks.
83. **Crested,** formed a crest for. 83-84. **propertied . . . friends,**

endowed with qualities which, when he spoke to friends, recalled the
music of the spheres. 85. **quail,** make quail, overawe. **orb,** world.
92. **plates,** pieces of money. 97. **past . . . dreaming,** no dream can
come up to it. 98. **To vie . . . fancy,** to equal the strange forms
produced by fancy. 99. **piece,** masterpiece. 103. **but I do,** if I do
not. 125. **enforce,** lay stress upon. 126. **If . . . intents,** if you fall
in with my plans. 130. **bereave,** deprive. 134. **And may,** may take
your leave throughout the world.

Your scutcheons and your signs of conquest, shall
Hang in what place you please. Here, my good lord.
    Cæs. You shall advise me in all for Cleopatra.
    Cleo. This is the brief of money, plate, and jewels,
I am possess'd of: 'tis exactly valued;
Not petty things admitted. Where 's Seleucus?   140
    Sel. Here, madam.
    Cleo. This is my treasurer: let him speak, my lord,
Upon his peril, that I have reserved
To myself nothing. Speak the truth, Seleucus.
    Sel. Madam,
I had rather seal my lips, than, to my peril,
Speak that which is not.
    Cleo.   What have I kept back?
    Sel. Enough to purchase what you have made
      known.
    Cæs. Nay, blush not Cleopatra; I approve
Your wisdom in the deed.
    Cleo.   See, Cæsar! O, behold,   150
How pomp is follow'd! mine will now be yours;
And, should we shift estates, yours would be mine.
The ingratitude of this Seleucus does
Even make me wild: O slave, of no more trust
Than love that 's hired! What, goest thou back? thou
    shalt
Go back, I warrant thee; but I'll catch thine eyes,
Though they had wings: slave, soulless villain, dog!
O rarely base!
    Cæs.   Good queen, let us entreat you.
    Cleo. O Cæsar, what a wounding shame is this,
That thou, vouchsafing here to visit me,   160
Doing the honour of thy lordliness
To one so meek, that mine own servant should
Parcel the sum of my disgraces by
Addition of his envy! Say, good Cæsar,
That I some lady trifles have reserved,
Immoment toys, things of such dignity
As we greet modern friends withal; and say,
Some nobler token I have kept apart
For Livia and Octavia, to induce
Their mediation; must I be unfolded   170
With one that I have bred? The gods! it smites me
Beneath the fall I have. [*To Seleucus*] Prithee, go hence;
Or I shall show the cinders of my spirits
Through the ashes of my chance: wert thou a man,
Thou wouldst have mercy on me.
    Cæs.   Forbear, Seleucus. [*Exit Seleucus.*
    Cleo. Be it known, that we, the greatest, are
      misthought
For things that others do; and, when we fall,
We answer others' merits in our name,
Are therefore to be pitied.
    Cæs.   Cleopatra,
Not what you have reserved, nor what acknowledged,
Put we i' the roll of conquest: still be 't yours,   181
Bestow it at your pleasure; and believe,
Cæsar 's no merchant, to make prize with you
Of things that merchants sold. Therefore be cheer'd;
Make not your thoughts your prisons: no, dear queen;
For we intend so to dispose you as
Yourself shall give us counsel. Feed, and sleep:

Our care and pity is so much upon you,
That we remain your friend; and so, adieu.
    Cleo. My master, and my lord!
    Cæs.   Not so. Adieu.   190
        [*Flourish. Exeunt Cæsar and his train.*
    Cleo. He words me, girls, he words me, that I should
      not
Be noble to myself: but, hark thee, Charmian.
          [*Whispers Charmian.*
    Iras. Finish, good lady; the bright day is done,
And we are for the dark.
    Cleo.   Hie thee again:
I have spoke already, and it is provided;
Go put it to the haste.
    Char.   Madam, I will.

          Re-enter DOLABELLA.

    Dol. Where is the queen?
    Char.   Behold, sir.   [*Exit.*
    Cleo.   Dolabella!
    Dol. Madam, as thereto sworn by your command,
Which my love makes religion to obey,
I tell you this: Cæsar through Syria   200
Intends his journey; and within three days
You with your children will he send before:
Make your best use of this: I have perform'd
Your pleasure and my promise.
    Cleo.   Dolabella,
I shall remain your debtor.
    Dol.   I your servant.
Adieu, good queen; I must attend on Cæsar.
    Cleo. Farewell, and thanks.   [*Exit Dolabella.*
        Now, Iras, what think'st thou?
Thou, an Egyptian puppet, shalt be shown
In Rome, as well as I: mechanic slaves
With greasy aprons, rules, and hammers, shall   210
Uplift us to the view; in their thick breaths,
Rank of gross diet, shall we be enclouded,
And forced to drink their vapour.
    Iras.   The gods forbid!
    Cleo. Nay, 'tis most certain, Iras: saucy lictors
Will catch at us, like strumpets; and scald rhymers
Ballad us out o' tune: the quick comedians,
Extemporally will stage us, and present
Our Alexandrian revels; Antony
Shall be brought drunken forth, and I shall see
Some squeaking Cleopatra boy my greatness   220
I' the posture of a whore.
    Iras.   O the good gods!
    Cleo. Nay, that 's certain.
    Iras. I'll never see 't; for, I am sure, my nails
Are stronger than mine eyes.
    Cleo.   Why, that 's the way
To fool their preparation, and to conquer
Their most absurd intents.

          Re-enter CHARMIAN.

        Now, Charmian!
Show me, my women, like a queen: go fetch
My best attires: I am again for Cydnus,
To meet Mark Antony: sirrah Iras, go.

---

135. **scutcheons**, shields showing armorial bearings.   138. **brief**, list or schedule.   140. **Not petty things admitted**, petty things omitted.   151. **mine**, my followers.   163. **Parcel**, specify or particularize.   165. **lady**, ladylike, feminine.   169. **Livia**, Cæsar's wife.   170-171. **unfolded With**, exposed by.   174. **chance**, her misfortunes, through which her resentment will show like fire through ashes.   175. **Forbear**, withdraw.   176. **misthought**, misjudged.   178. **We...name**, we are accountable in

our name for the deserts (misdeeds) of others.   191. **He words me.** Cleopatra sees through Cæsar's treachery exactly as in the source, where, however, such subtlety is not meant to detract from Cæsar's nobility.   193. **Finish**, end, die.   195. **it**, the asp.   199. **religion**, sacred duty.   208. **an Egyptian puppet**, thought to be an allusion to Elizabethan puppet shows, of which there were many.   214. **lictors**, minor officials in attendance on Roman magistrates.   215. **scald**, scurvy, mean.   220.

Now, noble Charmian, we'll dispatch indeed; 230
And, when thou hast done this chare, I'll give thee
    leave
To play till doomsday. Bring our crown and all.
Wherefore 's this noise?   [*Exit Iras. A noise within.*

   Enter a Guardsman.

   Guard.   Here is a rural fellow
That will not be denied your highness' presence:
He brings you figs.
   Cleo. Let him come in.   [*Exit Guardsman.*
           What poor an instrument
May do a noble deed! he brings me liberty.
My resolution 's placed, and I have nothing
Of woman in me: now from head to foot
I am marble-constant; now the fleeting moon 240
No planet is of mine.

   Re-enter Guardsman, *with* Clown *bringing in a
       basket.*

   Guard.   This is the man.
   Cleo. Avoid, and leave him.   [*Exit Guardsman.*
Hast thou the pretty worm of Nilus there,
That kills and pains not?
   Clown. Truly, I have him: but I would not be the
party that should desire you to touch him, for his
biting is immortal; those that do die of it do seldom or
never recover.
   Cleo. Rememberest thou any that have died on 't? 249
   Clown. Very many, men and women too. I heard of
one of them no longer than yesterday: a very honest
woman, but something given to lie; as a woman
should not do, but in the way of honesty: how she
died of the biting of it, what pain she felt: truly, she
makes a very good report o' the worm; but he that
will believe all that they say, shall never be saved by
half that they do: but this is most falliable, the worm 's
an odd worm.
   Cleo. Get thee hence; farewell.   260
   Clown. I wish you all joy of the worm.
                  [*Setting down his basket.*
   Cleo. Farewell.
   Clown. You must think this, look you, that the worm
will do his kind.
   Cleo. Ay, ay; farewell.
   Clown. Look you, the worm is not to be trusted but
in the keeping of wise people; for, indeed, there is no
goodness in the worm.
   Cleo. Take thou no care; it shall be heeded.
   Clown. Very good. Give it nothing, I pray you, for it
is not worth the feeding.   271
   Cleo. Will it eat me?
   Clown. You must not think I am so simple but I
know the devil himself will not eat a woman: I know
that a woman is a dish for the gods, if the devil dress
her not. But, truly, these same whoreson devils do the
gods great harm in their women; for in every ten that
they make, the devils mar five.
   Cleo. Well, get thee gone; farewell.   280
   Clown. Yes, forsooth: I wish you joy o' the worm.
                       [*Exit.*

   Re-enter IRAS *with a robe, crown, &c.*

   Cleo. Give me my robe, put on my crown;
    I have
Immortal longings in me: now no more
The juice of Egypt's grape shall moist this lip:
Yare, yare, good Iras; quick. Methinks I hear
Antony call; I see him rouse himself
To praise my noble act; I hear him mock
The luck of Cæsar, which the gods give men
To excuse their after wrath: husband, I come: 290
Now to that name my courage prove my title!
I am fire and air; my other elements
I give to baser life. So; have you done?
Come-then, and take the last warmth of my lips.
Farewell, kind Charmian; Iras, long farewell.
        [*Kisses them. Iras falls and dies.*
Have I the aspic in my lips? Dost fall?
If thou and nature can so gently part,
The stroke of death is as a lover's pinch,
Which hurts, and is desired. Dost thou lie still?
If thus thou vanishest, thou tell'st the world   300
It is not worth leave-taking.
   Char. Dissolve, thick cloud, and rain; that I may
    say,
The gods themselves do weep!
   Cleo.   This proves me base:
If she first meet the curled Antony,
He'll make demand of her, and spend that kiss
Which is my heaven to have. Come, thou mortal
    wretch,   [*To an asp, which she applies to her breast.*
With thy sharp teeth this knot intrinsicate
Of life at once untie: poor venomous fool,
Be angry, and dispatch. O, couldst thou speak,
That I might hear thee call great Cæsar ass   310
Unpolicied!
   Char.   O eastern star!
   Cleo.   Peace, peace!
Dost thou not see my baby at my breast,
That sucks the nurse asleep?
   Char.   O, break! O, break!
   Cleo. As sweet as balm, as soft as air, as gentle,—
O Antony!—Nay, I will take thee too:
        [*Applying another asp to her arm.*
What should I stay—   [*Dies.*
   Char. In this vile world? So, fare thee well.
Now boast thee, death, in thy possession lies
A lass unparallel'd. Downy windows, close;
And golden Phœbus never be beheld   320
Of eyes again so royal! Your crown 's awry;
I'll mend it, and then play.

   Enter the Guard, *rushing in.*

   First Guard. Where is the queen?
   Char.   Speak softly, wake her not.
   First Guard. Cæsar hath sent—
   Char.   Too slow a messenger.
                    [*Applies an asp.*
O, come apace, dispatch! I partly feel thee.
   First Guard. Approach, ho! All 's not well: Cæsar 's
    beguiled.

boy, allusion to the practice of having women's parts acted by boys on
the Elizabethan stage. 231. **chare,** task. 240. **marble-constant,** firm
as marble. 242. **Avoid,** withdraw. 243. **worm,** snake. 247. **immortal,** blunder for "mortal." 259. **falliable,** blunder for "infallible";
so F; Globe: *fallible.* 284. **Immortal longings,** longings for immortality. 286. **Yare,** quick. 296. **aspic,** asp, venomous serpent. 304.
curled. Probably she thinks of Antony as she first saw him, *barber'd ten*

times o'er (Cuningham). 305. **He'll . . . kiss,** he will inquire of her concerning me and kiss her for giving him intelligence (Johnson). 306.
wretch, creature. 307. **intrinsicate,** intricate. 311. **Unpolicied,**
devoid of policy, stupid. 316. **What,** why. 326. **beguiled,** cheated.

Sec. Guard. There 's Dolabella sent from Cæsar; call
    him.
First Guard. What work is here! Charmian, is this
    well done?
Char. It is well done, and fitting for a princess
Descended of so many royal kings.   330
Ah, soldier!   [*Dies.*

         Re-enter DOLABELLA.

Dol. How goes it here?
Sec. Guard.   All dead.
Dol.   Cæsar, thy thoughts
Touch their effects in this: thyself art coming
To see perform'd the dreaded act which thou
So sought'st to hinder.
        [*Within* 'A way there, a way for Cæsar!'

   Re-enter CÆSAR *and all his train, marching.*

Dol. O sir, you are too sure an augurer;
That you did fear is done.
Cæs.   Bravest at the last,
She levell'd at our purposes, and, being royal,
Took her own way. The manner of their deaths?   340
I do not see them bleed.
Dol.   Who was last with them?
First Guard. A simple countryman, that brought her
    figs:
This was his basket.
Cæs.   Poison'd, then.
First Guard.   O Cæsar,
This Charmian lived but now; she stood and spake:
I found her trimming up the diadem
On her dead mistress; tremblingly she stood
And on the sudden dropp'd.
Cæs.   O noble weakness!
If they had swallow'd poison, 'twould appear
By external swelling: but she looks like sleep,
As she would catch another Antony   350
In her strong toil of grace.
Dol.   Here, on her breast,
There is a vent of blood and something blown:
The like is on her arm.
First Guard. This is an aspic's trail: and these
    fig-leaves
Have slime upon them, such as the aspic leaves
Upon the caves of Nile.
Cæs.   Most probable
That so she died; for her physician tells me
She hath pursued conclusions infinite
Of easy ways to die. Take up her bed;
And bear her women from the monument: 360
She shall be buried by her Antony:
No grave upon the earth shall clip in it
A pair so famous. High events as these
Strike those that make them: and their story is
No less in pity than his glory which
Brought them to be lamented. Our army shall
In solemn show attend this funeral;
And then to Rome. Come, Dolabella, see
High order in this great solemnity.   [*Exeunt.*

333. **Touch their effects,** meet with realization. 337. **augurer,** fore-
teller of future events. 352. **something blown,** somewhat swollen.
358. **conclusions,** experiments. 363-366. **High . . . lamented,** the very
causers of events, like the present, cannot help being touch'd by them:
and the pitifulness of them will set them as high in fame as conquest
will the person that wrought them (Steevens).

Coriolanus

Coriolanus was first published in a rather difficult
text in the First Folio of 1623. The textual difficulties
are greater because of the closely packed, obscure,
late style in which the play is composed. There is
very little external evidence to assist in dating *Coriolanus*. One is rather sorry for this deficiency in contemporary comment, because one would like to
know how a play of such pronounced political import
as this impressed a Jacobean audience. Because the
play has so many features of Shakespeare's late style,
many editors have placed it in 1608-1610, but such
dating is unsure.

One might concede that *Coriolanus* is later than
Antony and Cleopatra, but would naturally believe that
it arose out of the same return to Plutarch which
produced *Antony and Cleopatra*. A renewed interest in
Roman history seems also reflected in *Appius and
Virginia*, a play written about 1608 for the queen's
players by Webster and possibly Heywood. The
dating of that play, however, is so vague that nothing
can be told about it. Sir E. K. Chambers has suggested that *Coriolanus* may have been written in 1606
or 1608.

SOURCE AND THEME

Coriolanus is a carefully wrought work, more formal
dramatically than *Antony and Cleopatra*, to which,
however, it is inferior in variety of interest and
pure poetry. *Coriolanus* has a story to tell and a
definite theme to develop, so that it is one of the
plays in which we may be quite certain of Shakespeare's meaning. It depicts the struggles between the
plebeians and the patricians of old Rome and comes
directly out of Plutarch, who had himself conceived
the character of Coriolanus in terms not greatly
different from those in which Shakespeare conceived
it.

Coriolanus is a noble patrician and a great warrior
bred from his cradle by his mother Volumnia to
fight, to be proud, and to despise the plebeians. In
him justifiable aristocratic pride is the finest virtue;
but it turns out that his strength becomes his weakness, since his enemies use it to bring about his ruin.
He saves his country and earns every honor that it can
bestow upon him. However, when he sues according
to the law for the consulship and goes through the
form of election by the plebeians, displaying reluc-
tantly his multitudinous wounds, he behaves with such
pride and bitterness that he defeats his own ends. He
has consented to seek the consulship to gratify his
mother's ambitions; but the pride that she taught him
places him at the mercy of the rabble and their

demagogues, so that he is banished from Rome with the greatest and most cruel injustice and ingratitude.

In this situation Coriolanus puts his wrongs and their vengeance above the welfare of his country and joins the enemies of Rome, so that Rome is at the mercy of his martial prowess. Then it is that his mother, conceived of as a noble Roman matron, teaches him the lesson she should have taught earlier. She induces him to renounce his private revenge, spare his country, and, consequently, give himself up to death at the hands of the Volscians, whom he has deserted. Thus a lesson of ultimate patriotism is taught, a lesson which must have been gratifying to the monarchic minds of King James' court and may have been applicable, for all we know, to the stories of men in that age.

And yet the tragedy of Coriolanus is not so simple that it may be accounted for in terms of loyalty to country. Patriotism in this play takes on a broader and deeper quality. Volumnia pleads to Coriolanus not so much his country as his blood. Man as man can know no more irresistible appeal. Before the demands of mother, wife, and child, his wrongs, his vengeance, his plighted honor, and his life suffer defeat and destruction.

PLUTARCH

Shakespeare draws the story in the most faithful detail from Plutarch. Yet it is not without significant changes. Nor is it without all of the intercalary matters which are necessary to render a historical episode visible upon the stage and comprehensible to the commonplace intelligences of an audience in a theater.

Plutarch's three uprisings of the plebeians are condensed into one. Shakespeare makes the banishment of Coriolanus not the result of his opposition to the plebeian demand for free corn, but immediately the result of the prejudice arising out of his proud behavior when he sought election to the consulship. It is thus a meaner, narrower, more ungrateful thing which he suffers in Shakespeare than in Plutarch. Shakespeare omits irrelevant incidents and the customary Roman portents which attend the banishment of Coriolanus, who is thus made more definitely and personally responsible. Shakespeare invents the by-play of the action, such as the orations and the dialogues in the streets between groups of citizens and officers.

In Plutarch it is Valeria, a Roman matron, friend of the wife of Coriolanus, who takes the lead in the salvation of her country and induces the mother, wife, and child of Coriolanus to beg him to desist; by a stroke of rare genius Shakespeare has put the whole burden upon Volumnia, the mother of Coriolanus. It is she who induces her son to sacrifice himself for the country he was about to destroy.

Finally, Shakespeare has created Menenius Agrippa. This humorous person, as one of the pleasantest of the aged patricians, is made by Plutarch to deliver a short speech to the plebeians in defense of the senate, in which he tells them the notable tale of the rebellion of the members of man's body against the belly. Shakespeare has developed Menenius into a friend of Coriolanus and the mouthpiece of common sense and reasonable compromise. Many of Plutarch's actual words are used in Shakespeare's play, transformed from noble prose to nobler verse.[1]

CORIOLANUS

According to Plutarch Coriolanus was a loud-voiced warrior and of an enraptured valor. "For he was even such another, as Cato would have a soldier and a captain to be, not only terrible and fierce to lay about him, but to make an enemy afeard with the sound of his voice, and the grimness of his countenance"; and going to battle "oft holding up his hands to heaven, he besought the gods to be gracious and favorable unto him, that he might come in time to the battle, and in a good hour to hazard his life in defense of his countrymen." Blown with battle and covered with wounds, he refused to leave the field, but "began afresh to chase those that fled, until such time as the army of the enemies was utterly overthrown, and numbers of them slain and taken prisoners." He was likewise unselfish and magnanimous, refusing special share in the spoil and asking only that his humble friend and host among the Corioli should be spared.

But one is also given to understand that his opinions were the stiff opinions of an aristocrat. He insisted that indulgence of the plebeians had encouraged them to disobedience and bred civil confusion and anarchy. When he put forward his political opinions, he did not do so dispassionately, but in a manner that was bold, rough, and unpleasant. Plutarch knew his faults:

For he was a man too full of passion and choler, and too much given over to self-will and opinion, as one of a high mind and great courage, that lacked the gravity and affability that is gotten with judgment of learning and reason, which only is to be looked for in a governor of State: and that remembered not how wilfulness is the thing of the world, which a governor of a commonwealth, for pleasing, should shun, being that which Plato called solitariness; as in the end, all men that are wilfully given to self-opinion and obstinate mind, and who will never yield to other's reasons but to their own, remain without company, and forsaken of all men. For a man that will live in the world must needs have patience, which lusty bloods make but a mock at.

And so he "spitteth out anger from the most weak and passioned part of the heart, much like the matter of an impostume." Plutarch, a Greek of the Roman empire, is not, however, a perfect judge of the character of Coriolanus, and Shakespeare in his thinking seems to have gone beyond Plutarch. Granted the validity of the ancient belief in the rule of the best,

Coriolanus

1109

[1]C. F. Tucker Brooke, *Shakespeare's Plutarch* (Oxford, 1909).

and looked at from the point of view of truth and honor, one cannot say that Coriolanus ought to have abased himself by any compromise with the tribunes. He has operated alone as a single proponent of the noblest conduct and has before him no choice except faithfulness to his principles even if tragedy lies in wait for him.

MENENIUS

Coriolanus not only wrongs himself; he is also deeply wronged. Shakespeare had this double aspect to bring out, and he invented for his purpose the shrewd, good-natured old patrician Menenius, who was both friendly to Coriolanus and well aware of the political crookedness and the personal spite of the demagogues Sicinius and Brutus (II, i, 1-106).

Menenius knew the fickleness and cowardice of the mob, the weakness of the senate, the very truth of the whole matter. Perhaps he casts away his dignity as a useless thing. His voice is often cynical, but he yields and compromises, persuades and cajoles. He regards Coriolanus as his son; he checks him, bids him be silent, reasons with him, apologizes for him, praises him, and loves him. On the whole he rises to something very like nobility; witness the bitterness of his words after the failure of his mission to Coriolanus:

> I neither care for the world nor your general: for such things as you, I can scarce think there 's any, ye 're so slight. He that hath a will to die by himself fears it not from another: let your general do his worst. For you, be that you are, long; and your misery increase with your age! I say to you, as I was said to, Away!
>
> (V, ii, 108-114)

He stands out, as a sort of Prince Hohenstiel-Schwangau, one of those who endeavor, in the midst of ignorance, selfishness, and animosity, to carry on the world's business.

VOLUMNIA

All of the subordinate characters serve in some degree to mirror forth the personality of Coriolanus, but perhaps the most triumphant depiction in the play is of the relation of mother and son. Coriolanus' noble Roman traits are completely the result of his mother's teaching (I, iii, 6-17):

> When yet he was but tender-bodied and the only son of my womb, when youth with comeliness plucked all gaze his way, when for a day of kings' entreaties a mother should not sell him an hour from her beholding, I, considering how honour would become such a person, that it was no better than picture-like to hang by the wall, if renown made it not stir, was pleased to let him seek danger where he was like to find fame. To a cruel war I sent him; from whence he returned, his brows bound with oak.

He is, as it were, groomed to run a course for fame. His own prowess and glory are paramount, and the shrewd remark of the first Citizen (I, i, 37-41) foretells the fatal error:

Though soft-conscienced men can be content to say it was for his country, he did it to please his mother, and to be partly proud; which he is, even to the altitude of his virtue.

In the third act, when Volumnia tries to teach her son to be a politician, it is too late; there is now no room in his character for compromise and servility. He promises her that he will conduct himself wisely and graciously at his trial; but he can no more save himself by policy from banishment or the Tarpeian rock in Rome than he could save himself from the swords of the Antiates by policy in the field. Volumnia by her great speeches in the fifth act has to teach him, at the cost of his life, the lesson of self-sacrifice for the sake of his native land in terms of his own flesh and blood.

AUFIDIUS

The nature of Coriolanus is again mirrored forth in the mind of his great adversary Tullus Aufidius, also a man who prized personal glory above everything, even above honor. To give him a victory over Coriolanus is like a shout of triumph in behalf of guile, so that in this matter Shakespeare has done a peculiar thing. It is Aufidius who speaks a funeral elegy over Coriolanus at the end. His case is parallel to that of the crafty Octavius, who, at the end of *Antony and Cleopatra*, is impersonal enough to give Antony his meed of praise. We have here at the end of the fourth act, in the words of the practical man Aufidius, a profound analysis of Coriolanus and his fate (IV, vii, 35-55):

> First he was
> A noble servant to them; but he could not
> Carry his honours even: whether 'twas pride,
> Which out of daily fortune ever taints
> The happy man; whether defect of judgement,
> To fail in the disposing of those chances
> Which he was lord of; or whether nature,
> Not to be other than one thing, not moving
> From the casque to the cushion, but commanding peace
> Even with the same austerity and garb
> As he controll'd the war; but one of these—
> As he hath spices of them all, not all,
> For I dare so far free him—made him fear'd,
> So hated, and so banish'd: but he has a merit,
> To choke it in the utterance. So our virtues
> Lie in the interpretation of the time:
> And power, unto itself most commendable,
> Hath not a tomb so evident as a chair
> To extol what it hath done.
> One fire drives out one fire; one nail, one nail;
> Rights by rights falter, strengths by strengths do fail.

Shakespeare seems here to tell us very plainly that virtue is a relative matter, that honor will not "live with the living," and that "to have done is to hang quite out of fashion, like a rusty mail, in monumental mockery." It may even come about in this world that, as in the case of Coriolanus, a man's chief merit may become a contributory weakness to produce his fall. This is a well-known feature of Shakespeare's tragic thought. "In almost all [of Shakespeare's tragic heroes]," says Bradley, "we observe a marked one-sidedness, a predisposition in some particular direction; a total incapacity, in certain circumstances, of resisting the force which draws in this direction. . . . . In the circumstances where we see the hero placed, his tragic trait, which is also his greatness, is fatal to him."[2]

STAGE HISTORY

The glorious stage days of Coriolanus as a theme were before England and America were democratized, when enlightened opinion still regarded the gulf between the noble and the common man as unbridgeable. Specifically, Coriolanus was a theme dear to the hearts of Restoration royalists and eighteenth-century Tories.

It cannot be said, however, that Shakespeare's treatment of the theme in his tragedy of *Coriolanus* fared very well at their hands. The adapter of *King Lear*, Nahum Tate, conscious of the applicability of the patrician-plebeian issue to the party strifes of his own day, produced (1782) a version of *Coriolanus*, which he called *The Ingratitude of a Commonwealth, or the Fall of Caius Martius Coriolanus*. For some reason, not entirely clear, Tate chooses to accumulate horrors. Virgilia commits suicide, Menenius is murdered, Aufidius is slain, and Volumnia goes insane.

John Dennis, a critic who admired Shakespeare with many reservations, rewrote *Coriolanus* as *The Invasion of his Country or the Fatal Resentment* (1719). The poet Thomson wrote on strictly classical lines a *Coriolanus* acted after his death in 1749. Thomson's tragedy was combined with Shakespeare's *Coriolanus* to form the acting version of John Philip Kemble. In it Mrs. Siddons played Volumnia.

Kemble had saved enough of Shakespeare to make himself greatly celebrated as Coriolanus, and with that part he closed his career in 1817. Edmund Kean appeared in Shakespeare's version in 1820. His realistic style was gaining ground against the rhetorical stateliness of Kemble; but *Coriolanus* is not a play which will stand realism, and Kean was a failure in it. In 1819 Macready began his career as Coriolanus. He had the voice and person for the part, and he saw in the character of Coriolanus the faults as well as the merits of the patrician. Macready and his American contemporary, Edwin Forrest, who in some respects resembled him, were the last great actors in the role of Coriolanus. A disaster in the illustrious career of Irving was the failure of his sumptuous revival of *Coriolanus* in 1901.

The naturalistic stage customs of our day are against the play. The year 1938 saw, however, a very powerful performance of *Coriolanus* at the "Old Vic" in London with John Gielgud in the title role.

²*Shakespearian Tragedy* (1905), pp. 20-21.

Coriolanus

DRAMATIS PERSONAE

CAIUS MARCIUS, afterwards CAIUS MARCIUS CORIOLANUS.
TITUS LARTIUS, COMINIUS, } generals against the Volscians.
MENENIUS AGRIPPA, friend to Coriolanus.
SICINIUS VELUTUS, JUNIUS BRUTUS, } tribunes of the people.
Young MARCIUS, son to Coriolanus.
A Roman Herald.
TULLUS AUFIDIUS, general of the Volscians.
Lieutenant to Aufidius.
Conspirators with Aufidius.
A Citizen of Antium.
Two Volscian Guards.

VOLUMNIA, mother to Coriolanus.
VIRGILIA, wife to Coriolanus.
VALERIA, friend to Virgilia.
Gentlewoman, attending on Virgilia.

Roman and Volscian Senators, Patricians, Ædiles, Lictors, Soldiers, Citizens, Messengers, Servants to Aufidius, and other Attendants.

SCENE: *Rome and the neighbourhood; Corioli and the neighbourhood; Antium.*

ACT I.

SCENE I. *Rome. A street.*

Enter a company of mutinous Citizens, *with staves, clubs, and other weapons.*

First Cit. Before we proceed any further, hear me speak.
All. Speak, speak.
First Cit. You are all resolved rather to die than to famish?
All. Resolved, resolved.
First Cit. First, you know Caius Marcius is chief enemy to the people.
All. We know 't, we know 't.
First Cit. Let us kill him, and we'll have corn at our own price. Is 't a verdict? 11
All. No more talking on 't; let it be done: away, away!
Sec. Cit. One word, good citizens.
First Cit. We are accounted poor citizens, the patricians good. What authority surfeits on would relieve us: if they would yield us but the superfluity, while it were wholesome, we might guess they relieved us humanely; but they think we are too dear: the leanness that afflicts us, the object of our misery, is as an inventory to particularize their abundance; our sufferance is a gain to them. Let us revenge this with our pikes, ere we become rakes: for the gods

know I speak this in hunger for bread, not in thirst
for revenge.   25
Sec. Cit. Would you proceed especially against
Caius Marcius?
All. Against him first: he 's a very dog to the commonalty.
Sec. Cit. Consider you what services he has done for
his country?   31
First Cit. Very well; and could be content to give
him good report for 't, but that he pays himself with
being proud.
Sec. Cit. Nay, but speak not maliciously.
First Cit. I say unto you, what he hath done famously, he did it to that end: though soft-conscienced
men can be content to say it was for his country, he
did it to please his mother, and to be partly proud;
which he is, even to the altitude of his virtue.   41
Sec. Cit. What he cannot help in his nature, you
account a vice in him. You must in no way say he is
covetous.
First Cit. If I must not, I need not be barren of
accusations; he hath faults, with surplus, to tire in
repetition. [*Shouts within.*] What shouts are these?
The other side o' the city is risen: why stay we prating
here? to the Capitol!
All. Come, come.   50
First Cit. Soft! who comes here?

Enter MENENIUS AGRIPPA.

Sec. Cit. Worthy Menenius Agrippa; one that hath
always loved the people.
First Cit. He 's one honest enough: would all the
rest were so!
Men. What work 's, my countrymen, in hand?
        where go you
With bats and clubs? The matter? speak, I pray you.
First Cit. Our business is not unknown to the senate;
they have had inkling this fortnight what we intend
to do, which now we'll show 'em in deeds. They say
poor suitors have strong breaths: they shall know we
have strong arms too.   62
Men. Why, masters, my good friends, mine honest
        neighbours,
Will you undo yourselves?
First Cit. We cannot, sir, we are undone already.
Men. I tell you, friends, most charitable care
Have the patricians of you. For your wants,
Your suffering in this dearth, you may as well
Strike at the heaven with your staves as lift them   70
Against the Roman state, whose course will on
The way it takes, cracking ten thousand curbs
Of more strong link asunder than can ever
Appear in your impediment. For the dearth,
The gods, not the patricians, make it, and
Your knees to them, not arms, must help. Alack,
You are transported by calamity
Thither where more attends you, and you slander

The helms o' the state, who care for you like fathers,
When you curse them as enemies.   80
First Cit. Care for us! True, indeed! They ne'er
cared for us yet: suffer us to famish, and their store-
houses crammed with grain; make edicts for usury, to
support usurers; repeal daily any wholesome act
established against the rich, and provide more pierc-
ing statutes daily, to chain up and restrain the poor.
If the wars eat us not up, they will; and there 's all
the love they bear us.
Men. Either you must   90
Confess yourselves wondrous malicious,
Or be accused of folly. I shall tell you
A pretty tale: it may be you have heard it;
But, since it serves my purpose, I will venture
To stale 't a little more.
First Cit. Well, I'll hear it, sir: yet you must not
think to fob off our disgrace with a tale: but, an 't
please you, deliver.
Men. There was a time when all the body's members
Rebell'd against the belly, thus accused it: 100
That only like a gulf it did remain
I' the midst o' the body, idle and unactive,
Still cupboarding the viand, never bearing
Like labour with the rest, where the other instruments
Did see and hear, devise, instruct, walk, feel,
And, mutually participate, did minister
Unto the appetite and affection common
Of the whole body. The belly answer'd—
First Cit. Well, sir, what answer made the belly?   110
Men. Sir, I shall tell you. With a kind of smile,
Which ne'er came from the lungs, but even thus—
For, look you, I may make the belly smile
As well as speak—it tauntingly replied
To the discontented members, the mutinous parts
That envied his receipt; even so most fitly
As you malign our senators for that
They are not such as you.
First Cit.   Your belly's answer? What!
The kingly-crowned head, the vigilant eye,
The counsellor heart, the arm our soldier,   120
Our steed the leg, the tongue our trumpeter,
With other muniments and petty helps
In this our fabric, if that they—
Men.   What then?
'Fore me, this fellow speaks! What then? what then?
First Cit. Should by the cormorant belly be
        restrain'd,
Who is the sink o' the body,—
Men.   Well, what then?
First Cit. The former agents, if they did complain,
What could the belly answer?
Men.   I will tell you;
If you'll bestow a small—of what you have little—
Patience awhile, you'll hear the belly's answer.   130
First Cit. Ye 're long about it.
Men.   Note me this, good friend;

Your most grave belly was deliberate,
Not rash like his accusers, and thus answer'd:
'True is it, my incorporate friends,' quoth he,
'That I receive the general food at first,
Which you do live upon; and fit it is,
Because I am the store-house and the shop
Of the whole body: but, if you do remember,
I send it through the rivers of your blood,   139
Even to the court, the heart, to the seat o' the brain;
And, through the cranks and offices of man,
The strongest nerves and small inferior veins
From me receive that natural competency
Whereby they live: and though that all at once,
You, my good friends,'—this says the belly, mark
    me,—
    First Cit. Ay, sir; well, well.
    Men.   'Though all at once cannot
See what I do deliver out to each,
Yet I can make my audit up, that all
From me do back receive the flour of all,
And leave me but the bran.' What say you to 't?   150
    First Cit. It was an answer: how apply you this?
    Men. The senators of Rome are this good belly,
And you the mutinous members; for examine
Their counsels and their cares, digest things rightly
Touching the weal o' the common, you shall find
No public benefit which you receive
But it proceeds or comes from them to you
And no way from yourselves. What do you think,
You, the great toe of this assembly?
    First Cit. I the great toe! why the great toe?   160
    Men. For that, being one o' the lowest, basest,
    poorest,
Of this most wise rebellion, thou go'st foremost:
Thou rascal, that art worst in blood to run,
Lead'st first to win some vantage.
But make you ready your stiff bats and clubs:
Rome and her rats are at the point of battle;
The one side must have bale.

    Enter CAIUS MARCIUS.

          Hail, noble Marcius!
    Mar. Thanks. What 's the matter, you dissentious
    rogues,
That, rubbing the poor itch of your opinion,
Make yourselves scabs?
    First Cit.   We have ever your good
    word.   170
    Mar. He that will give good words to thee will
    flatter
Beneath abhorring. What would you have, you curs,
That like nor peace nor war? the one affrights you,
The other makes you proud. He that trusts to you,
Where he should find you lions, finds you hares;
Where foxes, geese: you are no surer, no,
Than is the coal of fire upon the ice,
Or hailstone in the sun. Your virtue is

To make him worthy whose offence subdues him   179
And curse that justice did it. Who deserves greatness
Deserves your hate; and your affections are
A sick man's appetite, who desires most that
Which would increase his evil. He that depends
Upon your favours swims with fins of lead
And hews down oaks with rushes. Hang ye! Trust ye?
With every minute you do change a mind,
And call him noble that was now your hate,
Him vile that was your garland. What 's the matter,
That in these several places of the city
You cry against the noble senate, who,   190
Under the gods, keep you in awe, which else
Would feed on one another? What 's their seeking?
    Men. For corn at their own rates; whereof, they say,
The city is well stored.
    Mar.   Hang 'em! They say!
They'll sit by the fire, and presume to know
What 's done i' the Capitol; who 's like to rise,
Who thrives and who declines; side factions and give
    out
Conjectural marriages; making parties strong
And feebling such as stand not in their liking
Below their cobbled shoes. They say there 's grain
    enough!   200
Would the nobility lay aside their ruth,
And let me use my sword, I 'ld make a quarry
With thousands of these quarter'd slaves, as high
As I could pick my lance.
    Men. Nay, these are almost thoroughly persuaded;
For though abundantly they lack discretion,
Yet are they passing cowardly. But, I beseech you,
What says the other troop?
    Mar.   They are dissolved: hang 'em!
They said they were an-hungry; sigh'd forth proverbs,
That hunger broke stone walls, that dogs must eat,   210
That meat was made for mouths, that the gods sent
    not
Corn for the rich men only: with these shreds
They vented their complainings; which being
    answer'd,
And a petition granted them, a strange one—
To break the heart of generosity,
And make bold power look pale—they threw their
    caps
As they would hang them on the horns o' the moon,
Shouting their emulation.
    Men.   What is granted them?
    Mar. Five tribunes to defend their vulgar wisdoms,
Of their own choice: one 's Junius Brutus,   220
Sicinius Velutus, and I know not—'Sdeath!
The rabble should have first unroof'd the city,
Ere so prevail'd with me: it will in time
Win upon power and throw forth greater themes
For insurrection's arguing.
    Men.   This is strange.
    Mar. Go, get you home, you fragments!

participating. 116. **his receipt,** what he received. 122. **muniments,** furnishings, or defenses. 124. **'Fore me,** an oath. 125. **cormorant,** ravenous, rapacious. 134. **incorporate,** belonging to one body. 141. **cranks,** winding passages. **offices,** service rooms of a household; kitchen, etc. 142. **nerves,** sinews. 155. **common,** commons, people. 163. **rascal,** lean deer not worth the hunting; hence the modern meanings. **in blood,** in vigor, condition (hunting term). 165. **stiff bats,** stout cudgels. 167. **have bale,** get the worst of it, receive injury. 168. **dissentious,** rebellious. One should not fail to note the aggressive violence of Marcius. 170. **scabs,** scurvy fellows, rascals; with play on literal meaning. 179. **subdues,** i.e., subjects to punishment. 188. **garland,** object of highest honor and praise. The fickleness of the

mob is an ancient theme and is fundamental to the play. 191. **which,** who. 192. **seeking,** demand. 197. **side,** take sides with; or possibly arrange factions on sides. 201. **ruth,** tender-heartedness. 202. **quarry,** heap of slain. 203. **quarter'd,** slaughtered. 204. **pick,** pitch. 212. **shreds,** bits, scraps (of wisdom). Marcius shows the contempt which the Renaissance felt for the traditional lore of the common man. 215. **generosity,** the nobles. 218. **emulation,** envy of superiors. 221. **'Sdeath,** an oath, by God's death. 224. **Win upon,** gain advantage over. Note the premonition in the speech of Marcius.

Enter a Messenger, *hastily.*

Mess. Where 's Caius Marcius?

Mar.　　　　　　Here: what 's the matter?

Mess. The news is, sir, the Volsces are in arms.

Mar. I am glad on 't: then we shall ha' means to vent

Our musty superfluity. See, our best elders.　　　　230

Enter COMINIUS, TITUS LARTIUS, *and other* Senators; JUNIUS BRUTUS *and* SICINIUS VELUTUS.

First Sen. Marcius, 'tis true that you have lately told us;

The Volsces are in arms.

Mar.　　　　　　They have a leader,

Tullus Aufidius, that will put you to 't.

I sin in envying his nobility,

And were I any thing but what I am,

I would wish me only he.

Com.　　　　You have fought together.

Mar. Were half to half the world by the ears and he

Upon my party, I 'ld revolt, to make

Only my wars with him: he is a lion

That I am proud to hunt.

First Sen.　　　　Then, worthy Marcius,　240

Attend upon Cominius to these wars.

Com. It is your former promise.

Mar.　　　　　　Sir, it is;

And I am constant. Titus Lartius, thou

Shalt see me once more strike at Tullus' face.

What, art thou stiff? stand'st out?

Tit.　　　　　No, Caius Marcius;

I'll lean upon one crutch and fight with t' other,

Ere stay behind this business.

Men.　　　　　O, true-bred!

First Sen. Your company to the Capitol; where, I know,

Our greatest friends attend us.

Tit.　　　　　　[*To Com.*] Lead you on.

[*To Mar.*] Follow Cominius; we must follow you;　250

Right worthy you priority.

Com.　　　　　Noble Marcius!

First Sen. [*To the Citizens*] Hence to your homes; be gone!

Mar.　　　　　Nay, let them follow:

The Volsces have much corn; take these rats thither

To gnaw their garners. Worshipful mutiners,

Your valour puts well forth: pray, follow.

[*Citizens steal away. Exeunt all but Sicinius and Brutus.*

Sic. Was ever man so proud as is this Marcius?

Bru. He has no equal.

Sic. When we were chosen tribunes for the people,—

Bru. Mark'd you his lip and eyes?

Sic.　　　　　Nay, but his taunts.　259

Bru. Being moved, he will not spare to gird the gods.

Sic. Be-mock the modest moon.

Bru. The present wars devour him: he is grown

Too proud to be so valiant.

Sic.　　　　　Such a nature,

Tickled with good success, disdains the shadow

Which he treads on at noon: but I do wonder

His insolence can brook to be commanded

Under Cominius.

Bru.　　　　Fame, at the which he aims,

In whom already he 's well graced, can not

Better be held nor more attain'd than by

A place below the first: for what miscarries　　　270

Shall be the general's fault, though he perform

To the utmost of a man, and giddy censure

Will then cry out of Marcius 'O, if he

Had borne the business!'

Sic.　　　　Besides, if things go well,

Opinion that so sticks on Marcius shall

Of his demerits rob Cominius.

Bru.　　　　Come:

Half all Cominius' honours are to Marcius,

Though Marcius earn'd them not, and all his faults

To Marcius shall be honours, though indeed

In aught he merit not.

Sic.　　　　Let 's hence, and hear　　280

How the dispatch is made, and in what fashion,

More than his singularity, he goes

Upon this present action.

Bru.　　　　Let 's along.　　　[*Exeunt.*

SCENE II. *Corioli. The Senate-house.*

Enter TULLUS AUFIDIUS *and certain* Senators.

First Sen. So, your opinion is, Aufidius,

That they of Rome are enter'd in our counsels

And know how we proceed.

Auf.　　　　Is it not yours?

What ever have been thought on in this state,

That could be brought to bodily act ere Rome

Had circumvention? 'Tis not four days gone

Since I heard thence; these are the words: I think

I have the letter here; yes, here it is.

[*Reads*] 'They have press'd a power, but it is not known

Whether for east or west: the dearth is great;　　10

The people mutinous; and it is rumour'd,

Cominius, Marcius your old enemy,

Who is of Rome worse hated than of you,

And Titus Lartius, a most valiant Roman,

These three lead on this preparation

Whither 'tis bent: most likely 'tis for you:

Consider of it.'

First Sen.　　　　Our army 's in the field:

We never yet made doubt but Rome was ready

To answer us.

Auf.　　　　Nor did you think it folly

To keep your great pretences veil'd till when　　20

They needs must show themselves; which in the hatching,

It seem'd, appear'd to Rome. By the discovery

We shall be shorten'd in our aim, which was

To take in many towns ere almost Rome

Should know we were afoot.

Sec. Sen.　　　　Noble Aufidius,

Take your commission; hie you to your bands:

---

233. **put you to 't,** i.e., to the test. 237. **by the ears,** at variance. 245. **stiff,** i.e., with age. **stand'st out,** refuse to engage. 251. **Right . . . priority,** you being right worthy of priority. 254. **Worshipful mutiners,** mock politeness. 260. **gird,** gird at, scoff at. 261. **modest,** i.e., as representing Diana. 262-274. **The . . . business.** The tribunes reveal their base natures; they completely misunderstand Marcius, who is not actuated merely by thirst for glory and by selfishness. 263. **Too proud to be,** too proud of being. 268. **whom,** which. 272. **giddy**

censure, thoughtless opinion. 276. **demerits,** merits, deserts. 277. **are to,** belong to. 282. **More . . . singularity,** i.e., in addition to his special peculiarities.

SCENE II. 2. **enter'd in,** acquainted with. 6. **circumvention,** i.e., warning enabling them to circumvent. **gone,** ago. 9. **press'd a power,** an army. 20. **pretences,** intentions. 24. **take in,** capture. 28. **set down before 's,** lay siege to us. **remove,** raising of the siege.

SCENE III. 8. **all gaze,** i.e., the gaze of all. 14. **like,** likely. 16.

Let us alone to guard Corioli:
If they set down before 's, for the remove
Bring up your army; but, I think, you 'll find
They 've not prepared for us.
 Auf.   O, doubt not that;   30
I speak from certainties. Nay, more,
Some parcels of their power are forth already,
And only hitherward. I leave your honours.
If we and Caius Marcius chance to meet,
'Tis sworn between us we shall ever strike
Till one can do no more.
 All.   The gods assist you!
 Auf. And keep your honours safe!
 First Sen.   Farewell.
 Sec. Sen.   Farewell.
 All. Farewell.   [*Exeunt.*

SCENE III. *Rome. A room in Marcius' house.*

Enter VOLUMNIA *and* VIRGILIA: *they set them down on
 two low stools, and sew.*

Vol. I pray you, daughter, sing; or express yourself
in a more comfortable sort: if my son were my
husband, I should freelier rejoice in that absence
wherein he won honour than in the embracements of
his bed where he would show most love. When yet he
was but tender-bodied and the only son of my womb,
when youth with comeliness plucked all gaze his way,
when for a day of kings' entreaties a mother should
not sell him an hour from her beholding, I, considering how honour would become such a person, that it
was no better than picture-like to hang by the wall, if
renown made it not stir, was pleased to let him seek
danger where he was like to find fame. To a cruel
war I sent him; from whence he returned, his brows
bound with oak. I tell thee, daughter, I sprang not
more in joy at first hearing he was a man-child than
now in first seeing he had proved himself a man.

Vir. But had he died in the business, madam; how
then?   21

Vol. Then his good report should have been my
son; I therein would have found issue. Hear me
profess sincerely: had I a dozen sons, each in my love
alike and none less dear than thine and my good
Marcius, I had rather eleven die nobly for their
country than one voluptuously surfeit out of action.

Enter a Gentlewoman.

Gent. Madam, the Lady Valeria is come to visit you.
Vir. Beseech you, give me leave to retire myself.   30
Vol. Indeed, you shall not.
Methinks I hear hither your husband's drum,
See him pluck Aufidius down by the hair,
As children from a bear, the Volsces shunning him:
Methinks I see him stamp thus, and call thus:
'Come on, you cowards! you were got in fear,
Though you were born in Rome:' his bloody brow
With his mail'd hand then wiping, forth he goes,
Like to a harvest-man that 's task'd to mow

Or all or lose his hire.   40
 Vir. His bloody brow! O Jupiter, no blood!
 Vol. Away, you fool! it more becomes a man
Than gilt his trophy: the breasts of Hecuba,
When she did suckle Hector, look'd not lovelier
Than Hector's forehead when it spit forth blood
At Grecian sword, contemning. Tell Valeria,
We are fit to bid her welcome.   [*Exit Gent.*
 Vir. Heavens bless my lord from fell Aufidius!
 Vol. He'll beat Aufidius' head below his knee
And tread upon his neck.   50

Enter VALERIA, *with an* Usher *and* Gentlewoman.

 Val. My ladies both, good day to you.
 Vol. Sweet madam.
 Vir. I am glad to see your ladyship.
 Val. How do you both? you are manifest house-
keepers. What are you sewing here? A fine spot, in
good faith. How does your little son?
 Vir. I thank your ladyship; well, good madam.
 Vol. He had rather see the swords, and hear a drum,
than look upon his schoolmaster.   61
 Val. O' my word, the father's son: I'll swear, 'tis a
very pretty boy. O' my troth, I looked upon him o'
Wednesday half an hour together: has such a confirmed countenance. I saw him run after a gilded
butterfly; and when he caught it, he let it go again;
and after it again; and over and over he comes, and
up again; catched it again; or whether his fall en-
raged him, or how 'twas, he did so set his teeth and
tear it; O, I warrant, how he mammocked it!   71
 Vol. One on 's father's moods.
 Val. Indeed, la, 'tis a noble child.
 Vir. A crack, madam.
 Val. Come, lay aside your stitchery; I must have
you play the idle huswife with me this afternoon.
 Vir. No, good madam; I will not out of doors.
 Val. Not out of doors!
 Vol. She shall, she shall.   80
 Vir. Indeed, no, by your patience; I'll not over the
threshold till my lord return from the wars.
 Val. Fie, you confine yourself most unreasonably:
come, you must go visit the good lady that lies in.
 Vir. I will wish her speedy strength, and visit her
with my prayers; but I cannot go thither.
 Vol. Why, I pray you?
 Vir. 'Tis not to save labour, nor that I want love.   91
 Val. You would be another Penelope: yet, they say,
all the yarn she spun in Ulysses' absence did but fill
Ithaca full of moths. Come; I would your cambric
were sensible as your finger, that you might leave
pricking it for pity. Come, you shall go with us.
 Vir. No, good madam, pardon me; indeed, I will
not forth.
 Val. In truth, la, go with me; and I'll tell you
excellent news of your husband.   101
 Vir. O, good madam, there can be none yet.
 Val. Verily, I do not jest with you; there came news
from him last night.
 Vir. Indeed, madam?

---

bound with oak, i.e., as a badge to signify that he had saved the life of
a Roman citizen. The *cruel war* was that against the Latins and Tarquin
the Proud. 22. good report, reputation. As a typical Roman matron
Volumnia lifts the public cause above her private love. 32. hear
hither, i.e., penetrating hither. 39. task'd, set the task. 43. Than
gilt his trophy, i.e., than gilding sets off his monument. 46. At . . .
Tell. Capell's emendation; F: *At Grecian sword*. contemning, tell.
The emended text suggests the brow and blood of Hector as scorning

the Grecian sword. 48. fell, cruel. 54. manifest, notorious. 55.
house-keepers, stay-at-homes. sewing, embroidering. 56. spot, pattern, figure. 63. O' my troth, mild oath. 71. mammocked, tore into
fragments. 72. on 's, of his. 74. crack, boy (suggestion of pertness).
75. stitchery, needlework. 76. huswife, housewife, with play on sense
of "hussy." 92. Penelope, faithful wife of Ulysses, king of Ithaca and
hero of Homer's *Odyssey*. 95. cambric, fine white linen.

Val. In earnest, it 's true; I heard a senator speak it. Thus it is: the Volsces have an army forth; against whom Cominius the general is gone, with one part of our Roman power: your lord and Titus Lartius are set down before their city Corioli; they nothing doubt prevailing and to make it brief wars. This is true, on mine honour; and so, I pray, go with us. 113

Vir. Give me excuse, good madam; I will obey you in every thing hereafter.

Vol. Let her alone, lady: as she is now, she will but disease our better mirth.

Val. In troth, I think she would. Fare you well, then. Come, good sweet lady. Prithee, Virgilia, turn thy solemness out o' door, and go along with us. 121

Vir. No, at a word, madam; indeed, I must not. I wish you much mirth.

Val. Well, then, farewell. [*Exeunt.*

SCENE IV. *Before Corioli.*

Enter, with drum and colours, MARCIUS, TITUS LARTIUS, Captains *and* Soldiers. *To them a* Messenger.

Mar. Yonder comes news. A wager they have met.
Lart. My horse to yours, no.
Mar.   ’Tis done.
Lart.   Agreed.
Mar. Say, has our general met the enemy?
Mess. They lie in view; but have not spoke as yet.
Lart. So, the good horse is mine.
Mar.   I’ll buy him of you.
Lart. No, I’ll nor sell nor give him: lend you him
    I will
For half a hundred years. Summon the town.
Mar. How far off lie these armies?
Mess.   Within this mile and half.
Mar. Then shall we hear their ’larum, and they
    ours.
Now, Mars, I prithee, make us quick in work,   10
That we with smoking swords may march from hence,
To help our fielded friends! Come, blow thy blast.

They sound a parley. Enter two Senators *with others on
    the walls.*

Tullus Aufidius, is he within your walls?
First Sen. No, nor a man that fears you less than he,
That 's lesser than a little. [*Drums afar off.*] Hark! our
    drums
Are bringing forth our youth. We’ll break our walls,
Rather than they shall pound us up: our gates,
Which yet seem shut, we have but pinn’d with rushes;
They’ll open of themselves. [*Alarum afar off.*] Hark
    you, far off!
There is Aufidius; list, what work he makes   20
Amongst your cloven army.
Mar.   O, they are at it!
Lart. Their noise be our instruction. Ladders, ho!

Enter the army of the Volsces.

Mar. They fear us not, but issue forth their city.
Now put your shields before your hearts, and fight

With hearts more proof than shields. Advance, brave
    Titus:
They do disdain us much beyond our thoughts,
Which makes me sweat with wrath. Come on, my
    fellows:
He that retires, I’ll take him for a Volsce,
And he shall feel mine edge.

Alarum. The Romans *are beat back to their trenches.
    Re-enter* MARCIUS, *cursing.*

Mar. All the contagion of the south light on you,   30
You shames of Rome! you herd of—Boils and plagues
Plaster you o’er, that you may be abhorr’d
Further than seen and one infect another
Against the wind a mile! You souls of geese,
That bear the shapes of men, how have you run
From slaves that apes would beat! Pluto and hell!
All hurt behind; backs red, and faces pale
With flight and agued fear! Mend and charge home,
Or, by the fires of heaven, I’ll leave the foe
And make my wars on you: look to ’t: come on;   40
If you’ll stand fast, we’ll beat them to their wives,
As they us to our trenches followed.

Another alarum. The Volsces *fly, and* MARCIUS *follows
    them to the gates.*

So, now the gates are ope: now prove good seconds:
’Tis for the followers fortune widens them,
Not for the fliers: mark me, and do the like.
                                    [*Enters the gates.*
First Sol. Fool-hardiness; not I.
Sec. Sol.   Nor I.   [*Marcius is shut in.*
First Sol. See, they have shut him in.
All.   To the pot, I warrant him.
                                    [*Alarum continues.*

Re-enter TITUS LARTIUS.

Lart. What is become of Marcius?
All.   Slain, sir, doubtless.
First Sol. Following the fliers at the very heels,
With them he enters; who, upon the sudden,   50
Clapp’d to their gates: he is himself alone,
To answer all the city.
Lart.   O noble fellow!
Who sensibly outdares his senseless sword,
And, when it bows, stands up. Thou art left, Marcius:
A carbuncle entire, as big as thou art,
Were not so rich a jewel. Thou wast a soldier
Even to Cato’s wish, not fierce and terrible
Only in strokes; but, with thy grim looks and
The thunder-like percussion of thy sounds,
Thou madest thine enemies shake, as if the world   60
Were feverous and did tremble.

Re-enter MARCIUS, *bleeding, assaulted by the enemy.*

First Sol.   Look, sir.
Lart.   O, ’tis Marcius!
Let 's fetch him off, or make remain alike.
                          [*They fight, and all enter the city.*

---

117. **disease our better mirth,** trouble our mirth which would be greater without her. 120. **out o' door,** out-of-doors; with quibble.
  SCENE IV. 2. **My horse to yours,** i.e., I’ll bet my horse against yours they have not met in battle. 7. **Summon the town,** i.e., by trumpet, to parley. 9. **’larum,** call to arms. 12. **fielded,** in the field. 17. **pound,** shut up as in a pound. 21. **cloven,** explained as split in two and routed; possibly refers to the divided formation of the Roman forces. 25. **proof,** impenetrable. 29. **edge,** sword. 30. **south,** south wind as

source of contagion. 34. **Against . . . mile,** i.e., so great that it will carry a mile against the wind. 38. **agued,** i.e., operating like an ague, trembling. **Mend,** do better, or possibly reform (your ranks). 43. **seconds,** supporters. 47. **pot,** i.e., to certain destruction. 51. **himself alone,** quite alone. 53-54. **Who . . . up,** who, though endowed with sense, dares more than his insensible sword; it might bend to fear, he would not. 54. **left,** abandoned. 57. **Cato’s,** so Theobald; F: *Calues.* The reference is to Marcus Cato, celebrated in Plutarch as a staunch

SCENE V. *Corioli. A street.*

Enter certain Romans, *with spoils.*

First Rom. This will I carry to Rome.
Sec. Rom. And I this.
Third Rom. A murrain on 't! I took this for silver.
[*Alarum continues still afar off.*

Enter MARCIUS *and* TITUS LARTIUS *with a trumpet.*

Mar. See here these movers that do prize their
    hours
At a crack'd drachma! Cushions, leaden spoons,
Irons of a doit, doublets that hangmen would
Bury with those that wore them, these base slaves,
Ere yet the fight be done, pack up: down with them!
And hark, what noise the general makes! To him!   10
There is the man of my soul's hate, Aufidius,
Piercing our Romans: then, valiant Titus, take
Convenient numbers to make good the city;
Whilst I, with those that have the spirit, will haste
To help Cominius.
    Lart.   Worthy sir, thou bleed'st;
Thy exercise hath been too violent
For a second course of fight.
    Mar.   Sir, praise me not;
My work hath yet not warm'd me: fare you well:
The blood I drop is rather physical
Than dangerous to me: to Aufidius thus   20
I will appear, and fight.
    Lart.   Now the fair goddess, Fortune,
Fall deep in love with thee; and her great charms
Misguide thy opposers' swords! Bold gentleman,
Prosperity be thy page!
    Mar.   Thy friend no less
Than those she placeth highest! So, farewell.
    Lart. Thou worthiest Marcius!   [*Exit Marcius.*
Go sound thy trumpet in the market-place;
Call thither all the officers o' the town,
Where they shall know our mind: away!   [*Exeunt.*

SCENE VI. *Near the camp of Cominius.*

Enter COMINIUS, *as it were in retire, with soldiers.*

Com. Breathe you, my friends: well fought; we are
    come off
Like Romans, neither foolish in our stands,
Nor cowardly in retire: believe me, sirs,
We shall be charged again. Whiles we have struck,
By interims and conveying gusts we have heard
The charges of our friends. Ye Roman gods!
Lead their successes as we wish our own,
That both our powers, with smiling fronts
    encountering,
May give you thankful sacrifice.

Enter a Messenger.

           Thy news?
Mess. The citizens of Corioli have issued,   10
And given to Lartius and to Marcius battle:

I saw our party to their trenches driven,
And then I came away.
    Com.   Though thou speak'st truth,
Methinks thou speak'st not well. How long is 't
    since?
    Mess. Above an hour, my lord.
    Com. 'Tis not a mile; briefly we heard their drums:
How couldst thou in a mile confound an hour,
And bring thy news so late?
    Mess.   Spies of the Volsces
Held me in chase, that I was forced to wheel
Three or four miles about, else had I, sir,   20
Half an hour since brought my report.
    Com.   Who 's yonder,
That does appear as he were flay'd? O gods!
He has the stamp of Marcius; and I have
Before-time seen him thus.
    Mar.   [*Within*] Come I too late?
    Com. The shepherd knows not thunder from a tabor
More than I know the sound of Marcius' tongue
From every meaner man.

Enter MARCIUS.

    Mar.   Come I too late?
    Com. Ay, if you come not in the blood of others,
But mantled in your own.
    Mar.   O, let me clip ye
In arms as sound as when I woo'd, in heart   30
As merry as when our nuptial day was done,
And tapers burn'd to bedward!
    Com.   Flower of warriors,
How is 't with Titus Lartius?
    Mar. As with a man busied about decrees:
Condemning some to death, and some to exile;
Ransoming him, or pitying, threatening the other;
Holding Corioli in the name of Rome,
Even like a fawning greyhound in the leash,
To let him slip at will.
    Com.   Where is that slave
Which told me they had beat you to your trenches?   40
Where is he? call him hither.
    Mar.   Let him alone;
He did inform the truth: but for our gentlemen,
The common file—a plague! tribunes for them!—
The mouse ne'er shunn'd the cat as they did budge
From rascals worse than they.
    Com.   But how prevail'd you?
    Mar. Will the time serve to tell? I do not think.
Where is the enemy? are you lords o' the field?
If not, why cease you till you are so?
    Com.   Marcius,
We have at disadvantage fought and did
Retire to win our purpose.   50
    Mar. How lies their battle? know you on which side
They have placed their men of trust?
    Com.   As I guess, Marcius,
Their bands i' the vaward are the Antiates,
Of their best trust; o'er them Aufidius,
Their very heart of hope.
    Mar.   I do beseech you,

---

soldier.   62. **make remain alike,** remain to share his fate.
SCENE V.   3. **murrain,** plague.   5. **movers,** active persons; here used
ironically.   **prize their hours,** value their time.   6. **drachma,** Greek
coin.   7-8. **would . . . them,** i.e., hangmen, entitled to the clothes of
persons put to death, would not have them.   13. **make good,** hold.
17. **second course,** usually explained as bout in fighting; more probably, reference to second course in banquet.   19. **physical,** curative.
24. **Thy friend no less,** i.e., may she be no less thy friend.

SCENE VI.   1. **are come off,** have left the field of battle.   5. **By . . .
gusts,** at intervals and borne to us on the wind.   16. **briefly,** recently.
23. **stamp,** outward look.   25. **tabor,** drum.   29. **mantled,** covered.
36. **pitying,** remitting his ransom (Johnson).   53. **vaward,** vanguard.
Antiates, inhabitants of Antium.

By all the battles wherein we have fought,
By the blood we have shed together, by the vows
We have made to endure friends, that you directly
Set me against Aufidius and his Antiates;
And that you not delay the present, but,   60
Filling the air with swords advanced and darts,
We prove this very hour.
   Com.   Though I could wish
You were conducted to a gentle bath
And balms applied to you, yet dare I never
Deny your asking: take your choice of those
That best can aid your action.
   Mar.   Those are they
That most are willing. If any such be here—
As it were sin to doubt—that love this painting
Wherein you see me smear'd; if any fear
Lesser his person than an ill report;   70
If any think brave death outweighs bad life
And that his country 's dearer than himself;
Let him alone, or so many so minded,
Wave thus, to express his disposition,
And follow Marcius.
         [They all shout and wave their swords, take him up in
              their arms, and cast up their caps.
O, me alone! make you a sword of me?
If these shows be not outward, which of you
But is four Volsces? none of you but is
Able to bear against the great Aufidius
A shield as hard as his. A certain number,   80
Though thanks to all, must I select from all: the rest
Shall bear the business in some other fight,
As cause will be obey'd. Please you to march;
†And four shall quickly draw out my command,
Which men are best inclined.
   Com.   March on, my fellows:
Make good this ostentation, and you shall
Divide in all with us.   *[Exeunt.*

SCENE VII. *The gates of Corioli.*

Titus Lartius, *having set a guard upon Corioli, going
with drum and trumpet toward* Cominius *and* Caius
Marcius, *enters with a* Lieutenant, *other* Soldiers,
and a Scout.

   Lart. So, let the ports be guarded: keep your duties,
As I have set them down. If I do send, dispatch
Those centuries to our aid; the rest will serve
For a short holding: if we lose the field,
We cannot keep the town.
   Lieu.   Fear not our care, sir.
   Lart. Hence, and shut your gates upon 's.
Our guider, come; to the Roman camp conduct us.
                        [Exeunt.

SCENE VIII. *A field of battle.*

Alarum as in battle. Enter, from opposite sides, Marcius
and Aufidius.

   Mar. I'll fight with none but thee; for I do hate
     thee
Worse than a promise-breaker.
   Auf.   We hate alike:
Not Afric owns a serpent I abhor
More than thy fame and envy. Fix thy foot.
   Mar. Let the first budger die the other's slave,
And the gods doom him after!
   Auf.   If I fly, Marcius,
Holloa me like a hare.
   Mar.   Within these three hours, Tullus,
Alone I fought in your Corioli walls,
And made what work I pleased: 'tis not my blood
Wherein thou seest me mask'd; for thy revenge   10
Wrench up thy power to the highest.
   Auf.   Wert thou the Hector
That was the whip of your bragg'd progeny,
Thou shouldst not scape me here.
        [They fight, and certain Volsces come in the aid of
           Aufidius. Marcius fights till they be driven in
                            breathless.
Officious, and not valiant, you have shamed me
In your condemned seconds.   *[Exeunt.*

SCENE IX. *The Roman camp.*

*Flourish. Alarum. A retreat is sounded. Flourish. Enter,
from one side,* Cominius *with the* Romans; *from the
other side,* Marcius, *with his arm in a scarf.*

   Com. If I should tell thee o'er this thy day's work,
Thou 'ldst not believe thy deeds: but I'll report it
Where senators shall mingle tears with smiles,
Where great patricians shall attend and shrug,
I' the end admire, where ladies shall be frighted,
And, gladly quaked, hear more; where the dull
     tribunes,
That, with the fusty plebeians, hate thine honours,
Shall say against their hearts 'We thank the gods
Our Rome hath such a soldier.'
Yet camest thou to a morsel of this feast,   10
Having fully dined before.

Enter Titus Lartius, *with his power, from the pursuit.*

   Lart.   O general,
Here is the steed, we the caparison:
Hadst thou beheld—
   Mar.   Pray now, no more: my mother,
Who has a charter to extol her blood,
When she does praise me grieves me. I have done
As you have done; that 's what I can; induced
As you have been; that 's for my country:
He that has but effected his good will
Hath overta'en mine act.
   Com.   You shall not be
The grave of your deserving; Rome must know   20
The value of her own: 'twere a concealment
Worse than a theft, no less than a traducement,
To hide your doings; and to silence that,

---

58. **endure,** continue. 60. **the present,** now. 76. **O . . . me.** F has a
comma after *alone,* colon after *me.* Herford's explanation: Yes, make
me your weapon indeed! Follow me up as strenuously as the hand
the sword. Some editors place question mark after *alone.* 77. **outward,**
external, deceptive. 83. **As . . . obey'd,** as necessity shall require.
84. **four.** Capell conjectured *I;* i.e., I shall choose from the whole
force.
   Scene vii. 3. **centuries,** companies.
   Scene viii. 3. **Afric,** famous for serpents, because when drops of

blood fell from the head of the Gorgon slain by Perseus, they turned
to snakes. 11. **Hector,** the most famous of the Trojan warriors;
allusion to supposed descent of the Romans from the Trojans. 12.
whip, possibly the scourge that urged the Trojans to deeds of valor;
also explained (by Johnson) as the whip with which the Trojans
scourged the Greeks. **progeny,** ancestors. 15. **condemned seconds,**
despised efforts at assistance.
   Scene ix. 6. **gladly quaked,** glad to be frightened. 7. **fusty,** moldy,
ill-smelling. 8. **against their hearts,** unwillingly. 12. **caparison,**

Which, to the spire and top of praises vouch'd,
Would seem but modest: therefore, I beseech you—
In sign of what you are, not to reward
What you have done—before our army hear me.
 Mar. I have some wounds upon me, and they smart
To hear themselves remember'd.
 Com.   Should they not,
Well might they fester 'gainst ingratitude, 30
And tent themselves with death. Of all the horses,
Whereof we have ta'en good and good store, of all
The treasure in this field achieved and city,
We render you the tenth, to be ta'en forth,
Before the common distribution, at
Your only choice.
 Mar.   I thank you, general;
But cannot make my heart consent to take
A bribe to pay my sword: I do refuse it;
And stand upon my common part with those
That have beheld the doing. 40
   [*A long flourish. They all cry* 'Marcius! Marcius!'
   cast up their caps and lances: Cominius and Lartius
           stand bare.
 Mar. May these same instruments, which you profane,
Never sound more! when drums and trumpets shall
I' the field prove flatterers, let courts and cities be
Made all of false-faced soothing!
When steel grows soft as the parasite's silk,
Let him be made an overture for the wars!
No more, I say! For that I have not wash'd
My nose that bled, or foil'd some debile wretch,—
Which, without note, here 's many else have done,—
You shout me forth 50
In acclamations hyperbolical;
As if I loved my little should be dieted
In praises sauced with lies.
 Com.   Too modest are you;
More cruel to your good report than grateful
To us that give you truly: by your patience,
If 'gainst yourself you be incensed, we'll put you,
Like one that means his proper harm, in manacles,
Then reason safely with you. Therefore, be it known,
As to us, to all the world, that Caius Marcius
Wears this war's garland: in token of the which, 60
My noble steed, known to the camp, I give him,
With all his trim belonging; and from this time,
For what he did before Corioli, call him,
With all the applause and clamour of the host,
Caius Marcius Coriolanus! Bear
The addition nobly ever!
   [*Flourish. Trumpets sound, and drums.*
 All. Caius Marcius Coriolanus!
 Cor. I will go wash;
And when my face is fair, you shall perceive
Whether I blush or no: howbeit, I thank you. 70
I mean to stride your steed, and at all times
To undercrest your good addition
To the fairness of my power.

 Com.   So, to our tent;
Where, ere we do repose us, we will write
To Rome of our success. You, Titus Lartius,
Must to Corioli back: send us to Rome
The best, with whom we may articulate,
For their own good and ours.
 Lart.   I shall, my lord.
 Cor. The gods begin to mock me. I, that now
Refused most princely gifts, am bound to beg 80
Of my lord general.
 Com.   Take 't; 'tis yours. What is 't?
 Cor. I sometime lay here in Corioli
At a poor man's house; he used me kindly:
He cried to me; I saw him prisoner;
But then Aufidius was within my view,
And wrath o'erwhelm'd my pity: I request you
To give my poor host freedom.
 Com.   O, well begg'd!
Were he the butcher of my son, he should
Be free as is the wind. Deliver him, Titus.
 Lart. Marcius, his name?
 Cor.   By Jupiter! forgot. 90
I am weary; yea, my memory is tired.
Have we no wine here?
 Com.   Go we to our tent:
The blood upon your visage dries; 'tis time
It should be look'd to: come.   [*Exeunt.*

SCENE X. *The camp of the Volsces.*

A flourish. Cornets. Enter Tullus Aufidius, *bloody,
 with two or three* Soldiers.

 Auf. The town is ta'en!
 First Sol. 'Twill be deliver'd back on good condition.
 Auf. Condition!
I would I were a Roman; for I cannot,
Being a Volsce, be that I am. Condition!
What good condition can a treaty find
I' the part that is at mercy? Five times, Marcius,
I have fought with thee; so often hast thou beat me,
And wouldst do so, I think, should we encounter
As often as we eat. By the elements, 10
If e'er again I meet him beard to beard,
He 's mine, or I am his: mine emulation
Hath not that honour in 't it had; for where
I thought to crush him in an equal force,
True sword to sword, I'll potch at him some way
Or wrath or craft may get him.
 First Sol.   He 's the devil.
 Auf. Bolder, though not so subtle. My valour 's poison'd
With only suffering stain by him; for him
Shall fly out of itself: nor sleep nor sanctuary,
Being naked, sick, nor fane nor Capitol, 20
The prayers of priests nor times of sacrifice,
Embarquements all of fury, shall lift up
Their rotten privilege and custom 'gainst
My hate to Marcius: where I find him, were it

trappings of a steed. 14. **charter . . . blood,** right to praise her child.
18. **effected,** manifested in action. 19-20. **You . . . deserving,** you shall
not conceal your merit. 22. **traducement,** calumny, slander. 31.
tent, cleanse, cure. 32. **good and good,** excellent ones and plenty of
them. 44. **soothing,** flattery. 46. **him.** The antecedent is *parasite's.*
an overture, so F; Globe, following Steevens: *a coverture.* 47. **For
that,** because. 48. **debile,** weak. 49. **note,** notice taken. 52. **my
little,** the little I have done. 52-53. **dieted In,** fed on. 55. **give,**
report. 60. **garland,** principal glory. 62. **trim,** trappings. 72. **un-**

dercrest, wear (as a crest). 77. **best,** i.e., in blood among the Volscians.
articulate, come to terms. 80. **bound to,** about to.
 Scene X. 2. **condition,** terms; Aufidius plays on the word (ll. 3, 5)
with the additional sense of state or quality. 15. **potch,** thrust. 16.
Or . . . craft, in which either wrath or craft. 18. **stain,** tarnishment,
eclipse. 19. **fly out,** shall deviate from its own native generosity
(Johnson). 22. **Embarquements,** embargoes, restraints.

At home, upon my brother's guard, even there,
Against the hospitable canon, would I
Wash my fierce hand in 's heart. Go you to the city;
Learn how 'tis held; and what they are that must
Be hostages for Rome.
First Sol.   Will not you go?
Auf. I am attended at the cypress grove: I pray
     you—   30
'Tis south the city mills—bring me word thither
How the world goes, that to the pace of it
I may spur on my journey.
First Sol.   I shall, sir.   [*Exeunt.*

ACT II.

SCENE I. *Rome. A public place.*

Enter MENENIUS *with the two Tribunes of the people,*
SICINIUS *and* BRUTUS.

Men. The augurer tells me we shall have news to-
night.

Bru. Good or bad?

Men. Not according to the prayer of the people, for
they love not Marcius.

Sic. Nature teaches beasts to know their friends.

Men. Pray you, who does the wolf love?

Sic. The lamb.

Men. Ay, to devour him; as the hungry plebeians
would the noble Marcius.   11

Bru. He 's a lamb indeed, that baes like a bear.

Men. He 's a bear indeed, that lives like a lamb.
You two are old men: tell me one thing that I shall
ask you.

Both. Well, sir.

Men. In what enormity is Marcius poor in, that
you two have not in abundance?

Bru. He 's poor in no one fault, but stored with all. 21

Sic. Especially in pride.

Bru. And topping all others in boasting.

Men. This is strange now: do you two know how
you are censured here in the city, I mean of us o' the
right-hand file? do you?

Both. Why, how are we censured?

Men. Because you talk of pride now,—will you not
be angry?

Both. Well, well, sir, well.   30

Men. Why, 'tis no great matter; for a very little
thief of occasion will rob you of a great deal of patience: give your dispositions the reins, and be angry
at your pleasures; at the least, if you take it as a
pleasure to you in being so. You blame Marcius for
being proud?

Bru. We do it not alone, sir.

Men. I know you can do very little alone; for your
helps are many, or else your actions would grow
wondrous single: your abilities are too infant-like for

doing much alone. You talk of pride: O that you
could turn your eyes toward the napes of your necks,
and make but an interior survey of your good selves!
O that you could!

Bru. What then, sir?

Men. Why, then you should discover a brace of
unmeriting, proud, violent, testy magistrates, alias
fools, as any in Rome.

Sic. Menenius, you are known well enough too.   50

Men. I am known to be a humorous patrician, and
one that loves a cup of hot wine with not a drop of
allaying Tiber in 't; said to be something imperfect in
favouring the first complaint; hasty and tinder-like
upon too trivial motion; one that converses more with
the buttock of the night than with the forehead of the
morning: what I think I utter, and spend my malice
in my breath. Meeting two such wealsmen as you
are—I cannot call you Lycurguses—if the drink you
give me touch my palate adversely, I make a crooked
face at it. I can 't say your worships have delivered the
matter well, when I find the ass in compound with
the major part of your syllables: and though I must
be content to bear with those that say you are reverend grave men, yet they lie deadly that tell you you
have good faces. If you see this in the map of my
microcosm, follows it that I am known well enough
too? what harm can your bisson conspectuities glean
out of this character, if I be known well enough too?

Bru. Come, sir, come, we know you well enough.   72

Men. You know neither me, yourselves, nor any
thing. You are ambitious for poor knaves' caps and
legs: you wear out a good wholesome forenoon in
hearing a cause between an orange-wife and a fosset-
seller; and then rejourn the controversy of three pence
to a second day of audience. When you are hearing a
matter between party and party, if you chance to be
pinched with the colic, you make faces like mummers;
set up the bloody flag against all patience; and, in
roaring for a chamber-pot, dismiss the controversy
bleeding, the more entangled by your hearing: all the
peace you make in their cause is, calling both the
parties knaves. You are a pair of strange ones.   89

Bru. Come, come, you are well understood to be a
perfecter giber for the table than a necessary bencher
in the Capitol.

Men. Our very priests must become mockers, if
they shall encounter such ridiculous subjects as you
are. When you speak best unto the purpose, it is not
worth the wagging of your beards; and your beards
deserve not so honourable a grave as to stuff a
botcher's cushion, or to be entombed in an ass's
pack-saddle. Yet you must be saying, Marcius is
proud; who, in a cheap estimation, is worth all your
predecessors since Deucalion, though peradventure
some of the best of 'em were hereditary hangmen.
God-den to your worships: more of your conversation
would infect my brain, being the herdsmen of the

beastly plebeians: I will be bold to take my leave of you. [*Brutus and Sicinius go aside.* 106

Enter VOLUMNIA, VIRGILIA, *and* VALERIA.

How now, my as fair as noble ladies,—and the moon, were she earthly, no nobler,—whither do you follow your eyes so fast? 109

Vol. Honourable Menenius, my boy Marcius approaches; for the love of Juno, let 's go.

Men. Ha! Marcius coming home!

Vol. Ay, worthy Menenius; and with most prosperous approbation.

Men. Take my cap, Jupiter, and I thank thee. Hoo! Marcius coming home!

Vol. Vir. Nay, 'tis true.

Vol. Look, here 's a letter from him: the state hath another, his wife another; and, I think, there 's one at home for you. 120

Men. I will make my very house reel to-night: a letter for me!

Vir. Yes, certain, there 's a letter for you; I saw 't.

Men. A letter for me! it gives me an estate of seven years' health; in which time I will make a lip at the physician: the most sovereign prescription in Galen is but empiricutic, and, to this preservative, of no better report than a horse-drench. Is he not wounded? he was wont to come home wounded. 131

Vir. O, no, no, no.

Vol. O, he is wounded; I thank the gods for 't.

Men. So do I too, if it be not too much: brings a' victory in his pocket? the wounds become him.

Vol. On 's brows: Menenius, he comes the third time home with the oaken garland.

Men. Has he disciplined Aufidius soundly?

Vol. Titus Lartius writes, they fought together, but Aufidius got off. 141

Men. And 'twas time for him too, I'll warrant him that: an he had stayed by him, I would not have been so fidiused for all the chests in Corioli, and the gold that 's in them. Is the senate possessed of this?

Vol. Good ladies, let 's go. Yes, yes, yes; the senate has letters from the general, wherein he gives my son the whole name of the war: he hath in this action outdone his former deeds doubly. 151

Val. In troth, there 's wondrous things spoke of him.

Men. Wondrous! ay, I warrant you, and not without his true purchasing.

Vir. The gods grant them true!

Vol. True! pow, wow.

Men. True! I'll be sworn they are true. Where is he wounded? [*To the Tribunes*] God save your good worships! Marcius is coming home: he has more cause to be proud. Where is he wounded? 162

Vol. I' the shoulder and i' the left arm: there will be large cicatrices to show the people, when he shall stand for his place. He received in the repulse of Tarquin seven hurts i' the body.

Men. One i' the neck, and two i' the thigh,—there 's nine that I know.

Vol. He had, before this last expedition, twenty-five wounds upon him. 170

Men. Now it 's twenty-seven: every gash was an enemy's grave. [*A shout and flourish.*] Hark! the trumpets.

Vol. These are the ushers of Marcius: before him he carries noise, and behind him he leaves tears: Death, that dark spirit, in 's nervy arm doth lie; Which, being advanced, declines, and then men die.

A sennet. Trumpets sound. Enter COMINIUS *the general, and* TITUS LARTIUS; *between them,* CORIOLANUS, *crowned with an oaken garland; with* Captains *and* Soldiers, *and a* Herald.

Her. Know, Rome, that all alone Marcius did fight Within Corioli gates: where he hath won, 180 With fame, a name to Caius Marcius; these In honour follows Coriolanus. Welcome to Rome, renowned Coriolanus! [*Flourish.*

All. Welcome to Rome, renowned Coriolanus!

Cor. No more of this; it does offend my heart: Pray now, no more.

Com. Look, sir, your mother!

Cor. O, You have, I know, petition'd all the gods For my prosperity! [*Kneels.*

Vol. Nay, my good soldier, up; My gentle Marcius, worthy Caius, and By deed-achieving honour newly named,— 190 What is it?—Coriolanus must I call thee?— But, O, thy wife!

Cor. My gracious silence, hail! Wouldst thou have laugh'd had I come coffin'd home, That weep'st to see me triumph? Ah, my dear, Such eyes the widows in Corioli wear, And mothers that lack sons.

Men. Now, the gods crown thee!

Cor. And live you yet? [*To Valeria*] O my sweet lady, pardon.

Vol. I know not where to turn: O, welcome home: And welcome, general: and ye 're welcome all.

Men. A hundred thousand welcomes. I could weep 200 And I could laugh, I am light and heavy. Welcome. A curse begin at very root on 's heart, That is not glad to see thee! You are three That Rome should dote on: yet, by the faith of men, We have some old crab-trees here at home that will not Be grafted to your relish. Yet welcome, warriors: We call a nettle but a nettle and The faults of fools but folly.

Com. Ever right.

Cor. Menenius ever, ever.

. . . **Capitol,** better at after-dinner jests than at sitting in the senate as a councilor. 98. **botcher's,** of one who patches old clothes or boots. 102. **Deucalion,** the Greek Noah with whose name was connected the tradition of a flood. 103. **God-den,** good evening. 114. **prosperous approbation,** positive success. 115. **Take . . . Jupiter,** i.e., he tosses his cap in the air. 126-127. **make a lip,** make a contemptuous face. 128. **Galen,** Greek physician; he was not born until six hundred years after the time of Coriolanus. **empiricutic,** empirical, quacklike. **to,** compared to. 137. **On 's brows,** reference to the garland of oak leaves as a token of victory; see I, iii, 16. 144. **fidiused,** coined word from Aufidius. 149. **name,** credit, reputation. 157. **pow, wow,** pish. 164. **cicatrices,** scars. 165. **stand for his place,** seek the consulship. 166.

repulse of Tarquin. Plutarch tells us that Marcius fought his first battle against King Tarquin the Proud in 499 B.C. on the occasion of Tarquin's last attempt to regain the kingdom. 177. **nervy,** sinewy. 181. **to,** added to. 192. **My gracious silence.** Arden editor suggests that this form of address was suggested by Plutarch's reference to Numa's designation of one of the muses as Tacita, or "Lady Silence." 197. **And . . . pardon.** F assigns to Cominius; some editors would also include in the speech, now assigned to Coriolanus, the words *I . . . turn.* 205. **crab-trees;** i.e., sour-natured old men. 206. **grafted to your relish,** improved by grafting until they are to your taste. 209. **Menenius ever,** same old Menenius.

Herald. Give way there, and go on!
Cor.   [*To Volumnia and Virgilia*] Your
    hand, and yours: 210
Ere in our own house I do shade my head,
The good patricians must be visited;
From whom I have received not only greetings,
But with them change of honours.
Vol.   I have lived
To see inherited my very wishes
And the buildings of my fancy: only
There 's one thing wanting, which I doubt not but
Our Rome will cast upon thee.
Cor.   Know, good mother,
I had rather be their servant in my way
Than sway with them in theirs.
Com.   On, to the Capitol!   220
    [*Flourish. Cornets. Exeunt in state, as before. Brutus*
        and Sicinius come forward.
Bru. All tongues speak of him, and the bleared
    sights
Are spectacled to see him: your prattling nurse
Into a rapture lets her baby cry
While she chats him: the kitchen malkin pins
Her richest lockram 'bout her reechy neck,
Clambering the walls to eye him: stalls, bulks,
    windows,
Are smother'd up, leads fill'd, and ridges horsed
With variable complexions, all agreeing
In earnestness to see him: seld-shown flamens
Do press among the popular throngs and puff   230
To win a vulgar station: our veil'd dames
Commit the war of white and damask in
Their nicely-gawded cheeks to the wanton spoil
Of Phœbus' burning kisses: such a pother
As if that whatsoever god who leads him
Were slily crept into his human powers
And gave him graceful posture.
Sic.   On the sudden,
I warrant him consul.
Bru.   Then our office may,
During his power, go sleep.   239
Sic. He cannot temperately transport his honours
From where he should begin and end, but will
Lose those he hath won.
Bru.   In that there 's comfort.
Sic.   Doubt not
The commoners, for whom we stand, but they
Upon their ancient malice will forget
With the least cause these his new honours, which
That he will give them make I as little question
As he is proud to do 't.
Bru.   I heard him swear,
Were he to stand for consul, never would he
Appear i' the market-place nor on him put
The napless vesture of humility;   250
Nor, showing, as the manner is, his wounds
To the people, beg their stinking breaths.

Sic.   'Tis right.
Bru. It was his word: O, he would miss it rather
Than carry it but by the suit of the gentry to him
And the desire of the nobles.
Sic.   I wish no better
Than have him hold that purpose and to put it
In execution.
Bru.   'Tis most like he will.
Sic. It shall be to him then as our good wills,
A sure destruction.
Bru.   So it must fall out
To him or our authorities. For an end,   260
We must suggest the people in what hatred
He still hath held them; that to 's power he would
Have made them mules, silenced their pleaders and
Dispropertied their freedoms, holding them,
In human action and capacity,
Of no more soul nor fitness for the world
Than camels in the war, who have their provand
Only for bearing burdens, and sore blows
For sinking under them.
Sic.   This, as you say, suggested
At some time when his soaring insolence   270
Shall touch the people—which time shall not want,
If he be put upon 't; and that 's as easy
As to set dogs on sheep—will be his fire
To kindle their dry stubble; and their blaze
Shall darken him for ever.

Enter a Messenger.

Bru.   What 's the matter?
Mess. You are sent for to the Capitol. 'Tis thought
That Marcius shall be consul:
I have seen the dumb men throng to see him and
The blind to hear him speak: matrons flung gloves,
Ladies and maids their scarfs and handkerchers,   280
Upon him as he pass'd: the nobles bended,
As to Jove's statue, and the commons made
A shower and thunder with their caps and shouts:
I never saw the like.
Bru.   Let 's to the Capitol;
And carry with us ears and eyes for the time,
But hearts for the event.
Sic.   Have with you.   [*Exeunt.

———————————————

SCENE II. *The same. The Capitol.*

Enter two Officers, *to lay cushions.*

First Off. Come, come, they are almost here. How
many stand for consulships?
Sec. Off. Three, they say: but 'tis thought of every
one Coriolanus will carry it.
First Off. That 's a brave fellow; but he 's vengeance
proud, and loves not the common people.
Sec. Off. Faith, there have been many great men
that have flattered the people, who ne'er loved them;

214. **change of honours,** variety of honors. 220. **sway,** bear rule.
Stage Direction: **Brutus . . . forward.** The malicious plotting of the
tribunes is the beginning of the countermovement against Marcius.
223. **rapture,** fit. 224. **chats,** gossips about. **malkin,** untidy servant-
maid. 225. **lockram,** linen fabric. **reechy,** dirty, filthy. 226. **bulks,**
structures projecting from the front of a shop. 227. **leads,** roofs.
horsed, bestridden (as a horse). 228. **variable,** various. 229. **seld-
shown,** rarely seen. **flamens,** priests of ancient Rome. 230. **popular,**
plebeian, vulgar. 232-234. **Commit . . . kisses,** i.e., fine ladies expose
themselves to the sun's rays. 233. **nicely-gawded,** daintily adorned.
234. **pother,** hubbub. 240-241. **He . . . end,** i.e., he cannot, as a tem-

perate man could, carry his honors throughout his course. 245. **which,**
i.e., provocation, cause. 246-247. **That . . . do 't,** i.e., I have no doubt
that he will be proud to give provocation. 250. **napless,** threadbare.
254. **but,** otherwise than. 258. **as . . . wills,** as we should have it. 260.
authorities, offices. **For an end,** to cut the matter short. 261. **suggest,**
suggest to (with implication of evil). 263. **made them mules,** made
beasts of burden of them. 264. **Dispropertied,** alienated, deprived
(them) of. 267. **provand,** provisions, food. 272. **put upon 't,** urged,
incited to it. 273. **will . . . fire,** i.e., the spark that kindles his hatred.
285. **time,** present spectacle. 286. **hearts for the event,** i.e., their
deeper desires and purposes will be for what is to follow.

and there be many that they have loved, they know
not wherefore: so that, if they love they know not
why, they hate upon no better a ground: therefore,
for Coriolanus neither to care whether they love or
hate him manifests the true knowledge he has in their
disposition; and out of his noble carelessness lets
them plainly see 't.   16

First Off. If he did not care whether he had their
love or no, he waved indifferently 'twixt doing them
neither good nor harm: but he seeks their hate with
greater devotion than they can render it him; and
leaves nothing undone that may fully discover him
their opposite. Now, to seem to affect the malice and
displeasure of the people is as bad as that which he
dislikes, to flatter them for their love.   26

Sec. Off. He hath deserved worthily of his country:
and his ascent is not by such easy degrees as those
who, having been supple and courteous to the people,
bonneted, without any further deed to have them at
all into their estimation and report: but he hath so
planted his honours in their eyes, and his actions in
their hearts, that for their tongues to be silent, and
not confess so much, were a kind of ingrateful injury;
to report otherwise, were a malice, that, giving itself
the lie, would pluck reproof and rebuke from every
ear that heard it.

First Off. No more of him; he 's a worthy man: make
way, they are coming.   40

A sennet. Enter, with Lictors *before them,* Cominius *the
consul,* Menenius, Coriolanus, Senators, Sicinius
and Brutus. *The* Senators *take their places; the*
Tribunes *take their places by themselves.*
Coriolanus *stands.*

Men. Having determined of the Volsces and
To send for Titus Lartius, it remains,
As the main point of this our after-meeting,
To gratify his noble service that
Hath thus stood for his country: therefore, please you,
Most reverend and grave elders, to desire
The present consul, and last general
In our well-found successes, to report
A little of that worthy work perform'd
By Caius Marcius Coriolanus, whom   50
We met here both to thank and to remember
With honours like himself.
First Sen.   Speak, good Cominius:
Leave nothing out for length, and make us think
Rather our state 's defective for requital
Than we to stretch it out. [*To the Tribunes*] Masters
    o' the people,
We do request your kindest ears, and after,
Your loving motion toward the common body,
To yield what passes here.
Sic.   We are convented
Upon a pleasing treaty, and have hearts
Inclinable to honour and advance   60

The theme of our assembly.
Bru.   Which the rather
We shall be blest to do, if he remember
A kinder value of the people than
He hath hereto prized them at.
Men.   That 's off, that 's off;
I would you rather had been silent. Please you
To hear Cominius speak?
Bru.   Most willingly;
But yet my caution was more pertinent
Than the rebuke you give it.
Men.   He loves your people;
But tie him not to be their bedfellow.
Worthy Cominius, speak. [*Coriolanus offers to go away.*]
    Nay, keep your place.   70
First Sen. Sit, Coriolanus; never shame to hear
What you have nobly done.
Cor.   Your honours' pardon:
I had rather have my wounds to heal again
Than hear say how I got them.
Bru.   Sir, I hope
My words disbench'd you not.
Cor.   No, sir: yet oft,
When blows have made me stay, I fled from words.
You soothed not, therefore hurt not: but your people,
I love them as they weigh.
Men.   Pray now, sit down.
Cor. I had rather have one scratch my head i' the
    sun
When the alarum were struck than idly sit   80
To hear my nothings monster'd.   [*Exit.*
Men.   Masters of the people,
Your multiplying spawn how can he flatter—
That 's thousand to one good one—when you now see
He had rather venture all his limbs for honour
Than one on 's ears to hear it? Proceed, Cominius.
Com. I shall lack voice: the deeds of Coriolanus
Should not be utter'd feebly. It is held
That valour is the chiefest virtue, and
Most dignifies the haver: if it be,
The man I speak of cannot in the world   90
Be singly counterpoised. At sixteen years,
When Tarquin made a head for Rome, he fought
Beyond the mark of others: our then dictator,
Whom with all praise I point at, saw him fight,
When with his Amazonian chin he drove
The bristled lips before him: he bestrid
An o'er-press'd Roman and i' the consul's view
Slew three opposers: Tarquin's self he met,
And struck him on his knee: in that day's feats,
When he might act the woman in the scene,   100
He proved best man i' the field, and for his meed
Was brow-bound with the oak. His pupil age
Man-enter'd thus, he waxed like a sea,
And in the brunt of seventeen battles since
He lurch'd all swords of the garland. For this last,
Before and in Corioli, let me say,

Scene ii. 3. **of,** by. 4. **will carry it,** will win (the consulship).
9. **who,** i.e., the people. 15. **in,** concerning. 19. **waved indifferently,**
wavered impartially. 23. **opposite,** adversary. 30. **bonneted,** took
their hats off. 37. **giving . . . lie,** manifesting its own falsehood. 40.
Stage Direction: **Lictors,** officials attendant upon Roman magistrates.
41. **determined of,** reached a decision concerning. 44. **gratify,** reward,
requite. 48. **well-found,** fortunately met with. 51. **remember,** commemorate. 55. **stretch it out.** If *it* refers to the state, the meaning is
"straining its resources for proper reward"; if *it* refers to *requital,* the
meaning is "in our endeavors to extend reward until it match desert."
58. **passes,** is voted. **convented,** summoned, convened. 59. **treaty,**

proposal. 61. **theme,** i.e., Coriolanus. 63. **kinder value,** more favorable estimation. 64. **That 's off,** that is not the question. 75. **disbench'd,** made (you) leave your seat. 78. **as they weigh,** according to
their deserts. 80. **alarum were struck,** battle signal sounded. 81.
monster'd, pointed at as wonderful. 83. **That's . . . one,** in which there
are a thousand bad ones to one good one. 89. **haver,** possessor. 91.
singly counterpoised, equaled by a single one. 93. **mark,** ability, reach.
95. **Amazonian,** beardless (like the female warriors, the Amazons).
97. **o'er-press'd,** overthrown. 99. **on,** to. 103. **Man-enter'd,** i.e.,
entered in the fashion of a man. 105. **lurch'd,** robbed, cheated.

I cannot speak him home: he stopp'd the fliers;
And by his rare example made the coward
Turn terror into sport: as weeds before
A vessel under sail, so men obey'd 110
And fell below his stem: his sword, death's stamp,
Where it did mark, it took; from face to foot
He was a thing of blood, whose every motion
Was timed with dying cries: alone he enter'd
The mortal gate of the city, which he painted
With shunless destiny; aidless came off,
And with a sudden re-inforcement struck
Corioli like a planet: now all 's his:
When, by and by, the din of war gan pierce
His ready sense; then straight his doubled spirit 120
Re-quicken'd what in flesh was fatigate,
And to the battle came he; where he did
Run reeking o'er the lives of men, as if
'Twere a perpetual spoil: and till we call'd
Both field and city ours, he never stood
To ease his breast with panting.
   Men.   Worthy man!
   First Sen. He cannot but with measure fit the
       honours
Which we devise him.
   Com.   Our spoils he kick'd at,
And look'd upon things precious as they were
The common muck of the world: he covets less 130
Than misery itself would give; rewards
His deeds with doing them, and is content
To spend the time to end it.
   Men.   He 's right noble:
Let him be call'd for.
   First Sen.   Call Coriolanus.
   Off. He doth appear.

        Re-enter CORIOLANUS.

   Men. The senate, Coriolanus, are well pleased
To make thee consul.
   Cor.   I do owe them still
My life and services.
   Men.   It then remains
That you do speak to the people.
   Cor.   I do beseech you,
Let me o'erleap that custom, for I cannot 140
Put on the gown, stand naked and entreat them,
For my wounds' sake, to give their suffrage: please you
That I may pass this doing.
   Sic.   Sir, the people
Must have their voices; neither will they bate
One jot of ceremony.
   Men.   Put them not to 't:
Pray you, go fit you to the custom and
Take to you, as your predecessors have,
Your honour with your form.
   Cor.   It is a part
That I shall blush in acting, and might well
Be taken from the people.
   Bru.   Mark you that? 150
   Cor. To brag unto them, thus I did, and thus;
Show them the unaching scars which I should hide,

As if I had received them for the hire
Of their breath only!
   Men.   Do not stand upon 't.
We recommend to you, tribunes of the people,
Our purpose to them: and to our noble consul
Wish we all joy and honour.
   Senators. To Coriolanus come all joy and honour!
    [*Flourish of cornets. Exeunt all but Sicinius and Brutus.*
   Bru. You see how he intends to use the people.
   Sic. May they perceive 's intent! He will require
      them, 160
As if he did contemn what he requested
Should be in them to give.
   Bru.   Come, we'll inform them
Of our proceedings here: on the market-place,
I know, they do attend us.   [*Exeunt.*

SCENE III. *The same. The Forum.*

Enter seven or eight Citizens.

   First Cit. Once, if he do require our voices, we
ought not to deny him.
   Sec. Cit. We may, sir, if we will.
   Third Cit. We have power in ourselves to do it, but
it is a power that we have no power to do; for if he
show us his wounds and tell us his deeds, we are to
put our tongues into those wounds and speak for
them; so, if he tell us his noble deeds, we must also
tell him our noble acceptance of them. Ingratitude is
monstrous, and for the multitude to be ingrateful,
were to make a monster of the multitude; of the
which we being members, should bring ourselves to
be monstrous members. 13
   First Cit. And to make us no better thought of, a
little help will serve; for once we stood up about the
corn, he himself stuck not to call us the many-headed
multitude.
   Third Cit. We have been called so of many; not
that our heads are some brown, some black, some
auburn, some bald, but that our wits are so diversely
coloured: and truly I think if all our wits were to
issue out of one skull, they would fly east, west, north,
south, and their consent of one direct way should be
at once to all the points o' the compass. 26
   Sec. Cit. Think you so? Which way do you judge
my wit would fly?
   Third Cit. Nay, your wit will not so soon out as
another man's will; 'tis strongly wedged up in a
block-head, but if it were at liberty, 'twould, sure,
southward.
   Sec. Cit. Why that way?
   Third Cit. To lose itself in a fog, where being three
parts melted away with rotten dews, the fourth would
return for conscience sake, to help to get thee a wife.
   Sec. Cit. You are never without your tricks: you
may, you may. 39
   Third Cit. Are you all resolved to give your voices?
But that 's no matter, the greater part carries it. I say,

---

107. **speak him home,** praise him properly. 111. **stem,** main timber of
the prow of a ship. 112. **took,** took possession, slew. 114. **timed,** kept
time with; Johnson explains: "The cries of the slaughter'd regularly
followed his motion as music and a dancer accompany each other."
115-116. **painted . . . destiny,** stained with the blood of those who could
not escape their doom (Brooke). 118. **like a planet,** reference to the
power of striking or blasting believed to belong to the planets. 121.
fatigate, wearied. 124. **spoil,** slaughter. 127. **with measure,** becom-

ingly. 133. **end it,** i.e., kill time. 143. **pass,** neglect, disregard.
doing, action. 145. **Put . . . to 't,** do not force the issue. 146. **fit
you,** accommodate yourself. 148. **with your form,** i.e., with the
accompanying conventionalities. 154. **breath,** votes. **stand upon 't,**
make a point of it. 155. **recommend,** commit, consign. 160. **require,**
ask, request. 161. **contemn,** scorn.
   SCENE III. 1. **Once,** once for all. 24. **consent of,** agreement upon.
32. **southward,** allusion to the south wind bringing pestilence. 39. **you**

if he would incline to the people, there was never a worthier man.

Enter CORIOLANUS *in a gown of humility, with*
MENENIUS.

Here he comes, and in the gown of humility: mark his behaviour. We are not to stay all together, but to come by him where he stands, by ones, by twos, and by threes. He 's to make his requests by particulars; wherein every one of us has a single honour, in giving him our own voices with our own tongues: therefore follow me, and I'll direct you how you shall go by him. 51

All. Content, content. [*Exeunt citizens.*

Men. O sir, you are not right: have you not known
The worthiest men have done 't?

Cor. What must I say?
'I pray, sir,'—Plague upon 't! I cannot bring
My tongue to such a pace:—'Look, sir, my wounds!
I got them in my country's service, when
Some certain of your brethren roar'd and ran
From the noise of our own drums.'

Men. O me, the gods! 60
You must not speak of that: you must desire them
To think upon you.

Cor. Think upon me! hang 'em!
I would they would forget me, like the virtues
Which our divines lose by 'em.

Men. You'll mar all:
I'll leave you: pray you, speak to 'em, I pray you,
In wholesome manner. [*Exit.*

Cor. Bid them wash their faces
And keep their teeth clean. [*Re-enter two of the Citizens.*]
So, here comes a brace.

Re-enter a third Citizen.

You know the cause, sir, of my standing here.

Third Cit. We do, sir; tell us what hath brought you
to 't. 70

Cor. Mine own desert.

Sec. Cit. Your own desert!

Cor. Ay, but not mine own desire.

Third Cit. How not your own desire?

Cor. No, sir, 'twas never my desire yet to trouble the poor with begging.

Third Cit. You must think, if we give you any thing, we hope to gain by you.

Cor. Well then, I pray, your price o' the consulship?

First Cit. The price is to ask it kindly.

Cor. Kindly! Sir, I pray, let me ha 't: I have wounds to show you, which shall be yours in private. Your good voice, sir; what say you?

Sec. Cit. You shall ha 't, worthy sir.

Cor. A match, sir. There 's in all two worthy voices begged. I have your alms: adieu.

Third Cit. But this is something odd.

Sec. Cit. An 'twere to give again,—but 'tis no matter. [*Exeunt the three Citizens.* 90

Re-enter two other Citizens.

Cor. Pray you now, if it may stand with the tune of

your voices that I may be consul, I have here the customary gown.

Fourth Cit. You have deserved nobly of your country, and you have not deserved nobly.

Cor. Your enigma?

Fourth Cit. You have been a scourge to her enemies, you have been a rod to her friends; you have not indeed loved the common people. 99

Cor. You should account me the more virtuous that I have not been common in my love. I will, sir, flatter my sworn brother, the people, to earn a dearer estimation of them; 'tis a condition they account gentle: and since the wisdom of their choice is rather to have my hat than my heart, I will practise the insinuating nod and be off to them most counterfeitly; that is, sir, I will counterfeit the bewitchment of some popular man and give it bountiful to the desirers. Therefore, beseech you, I may be consul. 110

Fifth Cit. We hope to find you our friend; and therefore give you our voices heartily.

Fourth Cit. You have received many wounds for your country.

Cor. I will not seal your knowledge with showing them. I will make much of your voices, and so trouble you no further.

Both Cit. The gods give you joy, sir, heartily![*Exeunt.*

Cor. Most sweet voices!
Better it is to die, better to starve, 120
Than crave the hire which first we do deserve.
Why in this woolvish toge should I stand here,
To beg of Hob and Dick, that do appear,
Their needless vouches? Custom calls me to 't:
What custom wills, in all things should we do 't,
The dust on antique time would lie unswept,
And mountainous error be too highly heapt
For truth to o'er-peer. Rather than fool it so,
Let the high office and the honour go
To one that would do thus. I am half through; 130
The one part suffer'd, the other will I do.

Re-enter three Citizens *more.*

Here come moe voices.
Your voices: for your voices I have fought;
Watch'd for your voices; for your voices bear
Of wounds two dozen odd; battles thrice six
I have seen and heard of; for your voices have
Done many things, some less, some more: your
voices:
Indeed, I would be consul.

Sixth Cit. He has done nobly, and cannot go without any honest man's voice. 140

Seventh Cit. Therefore let him be consul: the gods give him joy, and make him good friend to the people!

All Cit. Amen, amen. God save thee, noble consul!
[*Exeunt.*

Cor. Worthy voices!

Re-enter MENENIUS, *with* BRUTUS *and* SICINIUS.

Men. You have stood your limitation; and the
tribunes

---

may, go on, say what you like. 48. **by particulars,** one by one, in detail. 49. **single,** separate, individual. 57. **to such a pace,** i.e., gentle pace. 64. **lose by 'em,** vainly seek to propagate in them by preaching (Yale). 67. **brace,** pair (contemptuous). 91. **stand with,** be consistent with. 103. **dearer estimation of them,** higher esteem on their part. 107. **be off,** doff my hat. **counterfeitly,** hypocritically. 108. **bewitchment,** sorcery, hocus-pocus. 109. **popular man,** demagogue. **bountiful,** bountifully. 115. **seal,** confirm. 122. **woolvish toge.** The

meaning seems to be wolf's toga with apparent allusion to wolf in sheep's clothing; *woolless* has also been suggested. 123. **Hob and Dick,** typical names for rustics. 124. **vouches,** confirmations. 128. **o'er-peer,** peep over (tradition). **fool it,** play the fool. 132. **moe voices,** more votes. 134. **Watch'd,** kept watches (in camp). 139-140. **He has . . . voice.** It will be noticed that Shakespeare, in spite of all that has been said about his contempt for the mob, gives them words which show both good spirit and good sense. 146. **limitation,** allotted time.

Endue you with the people's voice: remains
That, in the official marks invested, you
Anon do meet the senate.
    Cor.   Is this done?
    Sic. The custom of request you have discharged: 150
The people do admit you, and are summon'd
To meet anon, upon your approbation.
    Cor. Where? at the senate-house?
    Sic.   There, Coriolanus.
    Cor. May I change these garments?
    Sic.   You may, sir.
    Cor. That I'll straight do; and, knowing myself
    again,
Repair to the senate-house.
    Men. I'll keep you company. Will you along?
    Bru. We stay here for the people.
    Sic.   Fare you well.
            [*Exeunt Coriolanus and Menenius.*
He has it now, and by his looks methinks
'Tis warm at 's heart.   160
    Bru. With a proud heart he wore his humble weeds.
Will you dismiss the people?

Re-enter Citizens.

    Sic. How now, my masters! have you chose this
    man?
    First Cit. He has our voices, sir.
    Bru. We pray the gods he may deserve your loves.
    Sec. Cit. Amen, sir: to my poor unworthy notice,
He mock'd us when he begg'd our voices.
    Third Cit.   Certainly
He flouted us downright.
    First Cit. No, 'tis his kind of speech: he did not
    mock us.   169
    Sec. Cit. Not one amongst us, save yourself, but says
He used us scornfully: he should have show'd us
His marks of merit, wounds received for 's country.
    Sic. Why, so he did, I am sure.
    Citizens.   No, no; no man saw 'em.
    Third Cit. He said he had wounds, which he could
    show in private;
And with his hat, thus waving it in scorn,
'I would be consul,' says he: 'aged custom,
But by your voices, will not so permit me;
Your voices therefore.' When we granted that,
Here was 'I thank you for your voices: thank you:
Your most sweet voices: now you have left your
    voices,   180
I have no further with you.' Was not this mockery?
    Sic. Why either were you ignorant to see 't,
Or, seeing it, of such childish friendliness
To yield your voices?
    Bru.   Could you not have told him
As you were lesson'd, when he had no power,
But was a petty servant to the state,
He was your enemy, ever spake against
Your liberties and the charters that you bear
I' the body of the weal; and now, arriving
A place of potency and sway o' the state,   190
If he should still malignantly remain

Fast foe to the plebeii, your voices might
Be curses to yourselves? You should have said
That as his worthy deeds did claim no less
Than what he stood for, so his gracious nature
Would think upon you for your voices and
Translate his malice towards you into love,
Standing your friendly lord.
    Sic.   Thus to have said,
As you were fore-advised, had touch'd his spirit
And tried his inclination; from him pluck'd   200
Either his gracious promise, which you might,
As cause had call'd you up, have held him to;
Or else it would have gall'd his surly nature,
Which easily endures not article
Tying him to aught; so putting him to rage,
You should have ta'en the advantage of his choler
And pass'd him unelected.
    Bru.   Did you perceive
He did solicit you in free contempt
When he did need your loves, and do you think
That his contempt shall not be bruising to you,   210
When he hath power to crush? Why, had your bodies
No heart among you? or had you tongues to cry
Against the rectorship of judgement?
    Sic.   Have you
Ere now denied the asker? and now again
Of him that did not ask, but mock, bestow
Your sued-for tongues?
    Third Cit. He 's not confirm'd; we may deny him
    yet.
    Sec. Cit. And will deny him:
I'll have five hundred voices of that sound.
    First Cit. I twice five hundred and their friends to
    piece 'em.   220
    Bru. Get you hence instantly, and tell those friends,
They have chose a consul that will from them take
Their liberties; make them of no more voice
Than dogs that are as often beat for barking
As therefore kept to do so.
    Sic.   Let them assemble,
And on a safer judgement all revoke
Your ignorant election; enforce his pride,
And his old hate unto you; besides, forget not
With what contempt he wore the humble weed,
How in his suit he scorn'd you; but your loves,   230
Thinking upon his services, took from you
The apprehension of his present portance,
Which most gibingly, ungravely, he did fashion
After the inveterate hate he bears you.
    Bru.   Lay
A fault on us, your tribunes; that we labour'd,
No impediment between, but that you must
Cast your election on him.
    Sic.   Say, you chose him
More after our commandment than as guided
By your own true affections, and that your minds,
Pre-occupied with what you rather must do   240
Than what you should, made you against the grain
To voice him consul: lay the fault on us.
    Bru. Ay, spare us not. Say we read lectures to you,

How youngly he began to serve his country,
How long continued, and what stock he springs of,
The noble house o' the Marcians, from whence came
That Ancus Marcius, Numa's daughter's son,
Who, after great Hostilius, here was king;
Of the same house Publius and Quintus were,
That our best water brought by conduits hither; 250
And [Censorinus,] nobly named so,
Twice being [by the people chosen] censor,
Was his great ancestor.
   Sic.   One thus descended,
That hath beside well in his person wrought
To be set high in place, we did commend
To your remembrances: but you have found,
Scaling his present bearing with his past,
That he 's your fixed enemy, and revoke
Your sudden approbation.
   Bru.   Say, you ne'er had done 't—
Harp on that still—but by our putting on: 260
And presently, when you have drawn your number,
Repair to the Capitol.
   All.   We will so: almost all
Repent in their election.   [*Exeunt Citizens.*
   Bru.   Let them go on;
This mutiny were better put in hazard,
Than stay, past doubt, for greater:
If, as his nature is, he fall in rage
With their refusal, both observe and answer
The vantage of his anger.
   Sic.   To the Capitol, come:
We will be there before the stream o' the people;
And this shall seem, as partly 'tis, their own, 270
Which we have goaded onward.   [*Exeunt.*

ACT III.

SCENE I. *Rome. A street.*

Cornets. Enter CORIOLANUS, MENENIUS, *all the Gentry,*
COMINIUS, TITUS LARTIUS, *and other* Senators.

   Cor. Tullus Aufidius then had made new head?
   Lart. He had, my lord; and that it was which
     caused
Our swifter composition.
   Cor. So then the Volsces stand but as at first,
Ready, when time shall prompt them, to make road
Upon 's again.
   Com.   They are worn, lord consul, so,
That we shall hardly in our ages see
Their banners wave again.
   Cor.   Saw you Aufidius?
   Lart. On safe-guard he came to me; and did curse
Against the Volsces, for they had so vilely 10
Yielded the town: he is retired to Antium.
   Cor. Spoke he of me?
   Lart.   He did, my lord.
   Cor.   How? what?
   Lart. How often he had met you, sword to sword;
That of all things upon the earth he hated

Your person most, that he would pawn his fortunes
To hopeless restitution, so he might
Be call'd your vanquisher.
   Cor.   At Antium lives he?
   Lart. At Antium.
   Cor. I wish I had a cause to seek him there,
To oppose his hatred fully. Welcome home. 20

   Enter SICINIUS *and* BRUTUS.

Behold, these are the tribunes of the people,
The tongues o' the common mouth: I do despise
   them;
For they do prank them in authority,
Against all noble sufferance.
   Sic.   Pass no further.
   Cor. Ha! what is that?
   Bru. It will be dangerous to go on: no further.
   Cor. What makes this change?
   Men. The matter?
   Com. Hath he not pass'd the noble and the
   common?
   Bru. Cominius, no.
   Cor.   Have I had children's voices? 30
   First Sen. Tribunes, give way; he shall to the
   market-place.
   Bru. The people are incensed against him.
   Sic.   Stop,
Or all will fall in broil.
   Cor.   Are these your herd?
Must these have voices, that can yield them now
And straight disclaim their tongues? What are your
   offices?
You being their mouths, why rule you not their teeth?
Have you not set them on?
   Men.   Be calm, be calm.
   Cor. It is a purposed thing, and grows by plot,
To curb the will of the nobility:
Suffer 't, and live with such as cannot rule 40
Nor ever will be ruled.
   Bru.   Call 't not a plot:
The people cry you mock'd them, and of late,
When corn was given them gratis, you repined;
Scandal'd the suppliants for the people, call'd them
Time-pleasers, flatterers, foes to nobleness.
   Cor. Why, this was known before.
   Bru.   Not to them all.
   Cor. Have you inform'd them sithence?
   Bru.   How! I inform them!
   Com. You are like to do such business.
   Bru.   Not unlike,
Each way, to better yours.
   Cor. Why then should I be consul? By yond clouds, 50
Let me deserve so ill as you, and make me
Your fellow tribune.
   Sic.   You show too much of that
For which the people stir: if you will pass
To where you are bound, you must inquire your way,
Which you are out of, with a gentler spirit,
Or never be so noble as a consul,
Nor yoke with him for tribune.

---

parts of these lines have been supplied by editors from Plutarch.
Some editors follow Delius, who inserts in line 251 the words: *Censorinus
who that was so surnam'd.* 257. **Scaling,** estimating, balancing. 260.
putting on, urging. 261. **drawn,** assembled, collected. 263. **in,** of.
264. **put in hazard,** risk (infinitive). 267-268. **answer The vantage,**
make use.
   ACT III. SCENE I. 5. **road,** raid, attack. 16. **To hopeless restitution,**
beyond hope of redemption. 23. **prank them,** dress themselves up.

24. **Against . . . sufferance,** beyond the power of nobility to suffer.
30. **children's voices,** votes like those of children; i.e., to be given and
taken away lightly. 35. **tongues,** votes. 38. **purposed,** schemed, got
up for the occasion. 47. **sithence,** since. 48. **You . . . business,**
assigned by Theobald to Coriolanus. 48-49. **Not . . . yours,** not unlikely to prove, in any case, a better way than yours. 52. **that,** i.e.,
the quality of tyranny.

Men.   Let 's be calm.
Com. The people are abused; set on. This paltering
Becomes not Rome, nor has Coriolanus
Deserved this so dishonour'd rub, laid falsely   60
I' the plain way of his merit.
Cor.   Tell me of corn!
This was my speech, and I will speak 't again—
   Men. Not now, not now.
   First Sen.   Not in this heat, sir, now.
   Cor. Now, as I live, I will. My nobler friends,
I crave their pardons:
For the mutable, rank-scented many, let them
Regard me as I do not flatter, and
Therein behold themselves: I say again,
In soothing them, we nourish 'gainst our senate
The cockle of rebellion, insolence, sedition,   70
Which we ourselves have plough'd for, sow'd, and
                                        scatter'd,
By mingling them with us, the honour'd number,
Who lack not virtue, no, nor power, but that
Which they have given to beggars.
   Men.   Well, no more.
   First Sen. No more words, we beseech you.
   Cor.   How! no more!
As for my country I have shed my blood,
Not fearing outward force, so shall my lungs
Coin words till their decay against those measles,
Which we disdain should tetter us, yet sought
The very way to catch them.
   Bru.   You speak o' the people,   80
As if you were a god to punish, not
A man of their infirmity.
   Sic.   'Twere well
We let the people know 't.
   Men.   What, what? his choler?
   Cor. Choler!
Were I as patient as the midnight sleep,
By Jove, 'twould be my mind!
   Sic.   It is a mind
That shall remain a poison where it is,
Not poison any further.
   Cor.   Shall remain!
Hear you this Triton of the minnows? mark you
His absolute 'shall'?
   Com.   'Twas from the canon.
   Cor.   'Shall'!   90
O good but most unwise patricians! why,
You grave but reckless senators, have you thus
Given Hydra here to choose an officer,
That with his peremptory 'shall,' being but
The horn and noise o' the monster's, wants not spirit
To say he'll turn your current in a ditch,
And make your channel his? If he have power,
Then vail your ignorance; if none, awake
Your dangerous lenity. If you are learn'd,
Be not as common fools; if you are not,   100
Let them have cushions by you. You are plebeians,
If they be senators: and they are no less,

When, both your voices blended, the great'st taste
Most palates theirs. They choose their magistrate,
And such a one as he, who puts his 'shall,'
His popular 'shall,' against a graver bench
Than ever frown'd in Greece. By Jove himself!
It makes the consuls base: and my soul aches
To know, when two authorities are up,
Neither supreme, how soon confusion   110
May enter 'twixt the gap of both and take
The one by the other.
   Com.   Well, on to the market-place.
   Cor. Whoever gave that counsel, to give forth
The corn o' the storehouse gratis, as 'twas used
Sometime in Greece,—
   Men.   Well, well, no more of that.
   Cor. Though there the people had more absolute
                                        power,
I say, they nourish'd disobedience, fed
The ruin of the state.
   Bru.   Why, shall the people give
One that speaks thus their voice?
   Cor.   I'll give my reasons,   119
More worthier than their voices. They know the corn
Was not our recompense, resting well assured
They ne'er did service for 't: being press'd to the war,
Even when the navel of the state was touch'd,
They would not thread the gates. This kind of service
Did not deserve corn gratis. Being i' the war,
Their mutinies and revolts, wherein they show'd
Most valour, spoke not for them: the accusation
Which they have often made against the senate,
All cause unborn, could never be the motive
Of our so frank donation. Well, what then?   130
How shall this bisson multitude digest
The senate's courtesy? Let deeds express
What 's like to be their words: 'We did request it;
We are the greater poll, and in true fear
They gave us our demands.' Thus we debase
The nature of our seats and make the rabble
Call our cares fears; which will in time
Break ope the locks o' the senate and bring in
The crows to peck the eagles.
   Men.   Come, enough.
   Bru. Enough, with over-measure.
   Cor.   No, take more: 140
What may be sworn by, both divine and human,
Seal what I end withal! This double worship,
Where one part does disdain with cause, the other
Insult without all reason, where gentry, title, wisdom,
Cannot conclude but by the yea and no
Of general ignorance,—it must omit
Real necessities, and give way the while
To unstable slightness: purpose so barr'd, it follows,
Nothing is done to purpose. Therefore, beseech you,—
You that will be less fearful than discreet,   150
That love the fundamental part of state
More than you doubt the change on 't, that prefer
A noble life before a long, and wish

58. **set on,** go on, proceed. 60. **dishonour'd,** dishonoring. 66-68. **For . . . themselves,** as for the changeable, rank-scented multitude, let them learn what they are from my unflattering attitude of hostility. 66. **many.** F: *Meynie,* retained by some editors as the word *meiny,* household retinue, multitude. 70. **cockle,** a weed (darnel); thought to be the same as the scriptural tares. 78. **measles,** loathsome disease spots. 79. **tetter,** affect with tetter (skin eruption). 86. **mind,** resolved opinion. 89. **Triton of the minnows,** god of the little fishes; Triton was Neptune's son and trumpeter. 90. **from the canon,** beyond the law. 93. **Given,** permitted. **Hydra,** Lernean Hydra slain by Hercules;

here the mob. 95. **horn and noise,** noisy horn; see allusion to Triton above. 98-99. **awake . . . lenity,** arouse yourselves from your dangerous mildness. 101. **cushions,** seats. 102-104. **and . . . theirs,** and they are to all intents and purposes senators if, when their voices are mingled with yours, the resulting action savors of them rather than of you. 109. **up,** established. 111. **gap of both,** cleavage between the two. 121. **our recompense,** reward from us. 123. **navel,** vital center. 129. **unborn,** nonexistent. **motive,** so Johnson and Heath; F: *native,* sometimes retained as meaning natural source or origin. 131. **bisson multitude,** half-blind multitude; Dyce's emendation of *Bosome-multi-*

†To jump a body with a dangerous physic
That 's sure of death without it, at once pluck out
The multitudinous tongue; let them not lick
The sweet which is their poison: your dishonour
Mangles true judgement and bereaves the state
Of that integrity which should become 't,
Not having the power to do the good it would,   160
For the ill which doth control 't.
    Bru.   Has said enough.
    Sic. Has spoken like a traitor, and shall answer
As traitors do.
    Cor. Thou wretch, despite o'erwhelm thee!
What should the people do with these bald tribunes?
On whom depending, their obedience fails
To the greater bench: in a rebellion,
When what 's not meet, but what must be, was law,
Then were they chosen: in a better hour,
Let what is meet be said it must be meet,   170
And throw their power i' the dust.
    Bru. Manifest treason!
    Sic.   This a consul? no.
    Bru. The ædiles, ho!

Enter an Ædile.

                Let him be apprehended.
    Sic. Go, call the people: [*Exit Ædile*] in whose name
        myself
Attach thee as a traitorous innovator,
A foe to the public weal: obey, I charge thee,
And follow to thine answer.
    Cor.   Hence, old goat!
    Senators, &c. We'll surety him.
    Com.   Aged sir, hands off.
    Cor. Hence, rotten thing! or I shall shake thy bones
Out of thy garments.
    Sic.   Help, ye citizens!   180

Enter a rabble of Citizens (*Plebeians*), *with the Ædiles.*

    Men. On both sides more respect.
    Sic. Here 's he that would take from you all your
        power.
    Bru. Seize him, ædiles!
    Citizens. Down with him! down with him!
    Senators, &c. Weapons, weapons, weapons!
            [*They all bustle about Coriolanus, crying*
'Tribunes!' 'Patricians!' 'Citizens!' 'What, ho!'
'Sicinius!' 'Brutus!' 'Coriolanus!' 'Citizens!'
'Peace, peace, peace!' 'Stay, hold, peace!'
    Men. What is about to be? I am out of breath;
Confusion 's near; I cannot speak. You, tribunes   190
To the people! Coriolanus, patience!
Speak, good Sicinius.
    Sic.   Hear me, people; peace!
    Citizens. Let 's hear our tribune: peace! Speak,
        speak, speak.
    Sic. You are at point to lose your liberties:
Marcius would have all from you; Marcius,
Whom late you have named for consul.

    Men.   Fie, fie, fie!
This is the way to kindle, not to quench.
    First Sen. To unbuild the city and to lay all flat.
    Sic. What is the city but the people?
    Citizens.   True,
The people are the city.   200
    Bru. By the consent of all, we were establish'd
The people's magistrates.
    Citizens.   You so remain.
    Men. And so are like to do.
    Com. That is the way to lay the city flat;
To bring the roof to the foundation,
And bury all, which yet distinctly ranges,
In heaps and piles of ruin.
    Sic.   This deserves death.
    Bru. Or let us stand to our authority,
Or let us lose it. We do here pronounce,
Upon the part o' the people, in whose power   210
We were elected theirs, Marcius is worthy
Of present death.
    Sic.   Therefore lay hold of him;
Bear him to the rock Tarpeian, and from thence
Into destruction cast him.
    Bru.   Ædiles, seize him!
    Citizens. Yield, Marcius, yield!
    Men.   Hear me one word;
Beseech you, tribunes, hear me but a word.
    Æd. Peace, peace!
    Men. [*To Brutus*] Be that you seem, truly your
        country's friend,
And temperately proceed to what you would
Thus violently redress.
    Bru.   Sir, those cold ways,   220
That seem like prudent helps, are very poisonous
Where the disease is violent. Lay hands upon him,
And bear him to the rock.
    Cor.   No, I'll die here.
                            [*Drawing his sword.*
There 's some among you have beheld me fighting:
Come, try upon yourselves what you have seen me.
    Men. Down with that sword! Tribunes, withdraw
        awhile.
    Bru. Lay hands upon him.
    Men.   Help Marcius, help,
You that be noble; help him, young and old!
    Citizens. Down with him, down with him!
        [*In this mutiny, the Tribunes, the Ædiles, and the People,
                                    are beat in.*
    Men. Go, get you to your house; be gone, away!   230
All will be naught else.
    Sec. Sen.   Get you gone.
    Com.   Stand fast;
We have as many friends as enemies.
    Men. Shall it be put to that?
    First Sen.   The gods forbid!
I prithee, noble friend, home to thy house;
Leave us to cure this cause.
    Men.   For 'tis a sore upon us,

plied, frequently retained as meaning composite idea of bosom.   140.
over-measure, excess.   140-161. **No . . . control 't.** This speech, like
the foregoing speeches of Coriolanus, is expressive of the current
theories of monarchy.   141-142. **What . . . Seal**, may all divine and
human sanctities approve.   142. **double worship**, divided authority.
145. **conclude**, come to a final conclusion.   148. **slightness**, trivialities.
purpose so barr'd, reason being so obstructed.   150. **less . . . discreet**, less actuated by fear than by foresight.   151-152. **That . . . on 't**,
that love the essentials of our government more than you fear the
troubles arising when attempt is made to change it.   156. **multitudi-**

nous tongue, voting power of the multitude.   157. **sweet**, i.e., power.
161. **Has**, he has.   164. **despite**, malice.   167. **bench**, senators collectively.   168. **what 's . . . be**, unfitting but inevitable necessity.   173.
ædiles, magistrates in ancient Rome, assistants to the tribunes.   177.
answer, defense, answer to a charge.   178. **surety**, go bail for.   206.
distinctly ranges, stretches out in proper order.   213. **rock Tarpeian**,
famous precipice on the Capitoline Hill in ancient Rome from which
persons condemned for treason were thrown down.   225. **seen me**, i.e.,
seen me do.   231. **naught else**, lost or ruined otherwise.   235. **cause**,
disease.

You cannot tent yourself: be gone, beseech you.
   Com. Come, sir, along with us.
   Cor. I would they were barbarians— as they are,
Though in Rome litter'd—not Romans—as they are
   not,
Though calved i' the porch o' the Capitol—
   Men.   Be gone;   240
Put not your worthy rage into your tongue;
One time will owe another.
   Cor.   On fair ground
I could beat forty of them.
   Men.   I could myself
Take up a brace o' the best of them; yea, the two
   tribunes.
   Com. But now 'tis odds beyond arithmetic;
And manhood is call'd foolery, when it stands
Against a falling fabric. Will you hence,
Before the tag return? whose rage doth rend
Like interrupted waters and o'erbear
What they are used to bear.
   Men.   Pray you, be gone: 250
I'll try whether my old wit be in request
With those that have but little: this must be patch'd
With cloth of any colour.
   Com.   Nay, come away.
         [*Exeunt Coriolanus, Cominius, and others.*
   A Patrician. This man has marr'd his fortune.
   Men. His nature is too noble for the world:
He would not flatter Neptune for his trident,
Or Jove for 's power to thunder. His heart 's his
   mouth:
What his breast forges, that his tongue must vent;
And, being angry, does forget that ever
He heard the name of death.   [*A noise within.* 260
Here 's goodly work!
   Sec. Pat.   I would they were a-bed!
   Men. I would they were in Tiber! What the
   vengeance!
Could he not speak 'em fair?

         Re-enter BRUTUS *and* SICINIUS, *with the rabble.*

   Sic.   Where is this viper
That would depopulate the city and
Be every man himself?
   Men.   You worthy tribunes,—
   Sic. He shall be thrown down the Tarpeian rock
With rigorous hands: he hath resisted law,
And therefore law shall scorn him further trial
Than the severity of the public power
Which he so sets at nought.
   First Cit.   He shall well know   270
The noble tribunes are the people's mouths,
And we their hands.
   Citizens. He shall, sure on 't.
   Men.   Sir, sir,—
   Sic. Peace!
   Men. Do not cry havoc, where you should but hunt
With modest warrant.
   Sic.   Sir, how comes 't that you

Have holp to make this rescue?
   Men.   Hear me speak:
As I do know the consul's worthiness,
So can I name his faults,—
   Sic.   Consul! what consul?
   Men. The consul Coriolanus.
   Bru.   He consul!   280
   Citizens. No, no, no, no, no.
   Men. If, by the tribunes' leave, and yours, good
   people,
I may be heard, I would crave a word or two;
The which shall turn you to no further harm
Than so much loss of time.
   Sic.   Speak briefly then;
For we are peremptory to dispatch
This viperous traitor: to eject him hence
Were but one danger, and to keep him here
Our certain death: therefore it is decreed
He dies to-night.
   Men.   Now the good gods forbid   290
That our renowned Rome, whose gratitude
Towards her deserved children is enroll'd
In Jove's own book, like an unnatural dam
Should now eat up her own!
   Sic. He 's a disease that must be cut away.
   Men. O, he 's a limb that has but a disease;
Mortal, to cut it off; to cure it, easy.
What has he done to Rome that 's worthy death?
Killing our enemies, the blood he hath lost—
Which, I dare vouch, is more than that he hath,   300
By many an ounce—he dropp'd it for his country;
And what is left, to lose it by his country,
Were to us all, that do 't and suffer it,
A brand to the end o' the world.
   Sic.   This is clean kam.
   Bru. Merely awry: when he did love his country,
It honour'd him.
   Men.   The service of the foot
Being once gangrened, is not then respected
For what before it was.
   Bru.   We'll hear no more.
Pursue him to his house, and pluck him thence;
Lest his infection, being of catching nature,   310
Spread further.
   Men.   One word more, one word.
This tiger-footed rage, when it shall find
The harm of unscann'd swiftness, will too late
Tie leaden pounds to 's heels. Proceed by process;
Lest parties, as he is beloved, break out,
And sack great Rome with Romans.
   Bru.   If it were so,—
   Sic. What do ye talk?
Have we not had a taste of his obedience?
Our ædiles smote? ourselves resisted? Come.
   Men. Consider this: he has been bred i' the wars   320
Since he could draw a sword, and is ill school'd
In bolted language; meal and bran together
He throws without distinction. Give me leave,
I'll go to him, and undertake to bring him

Coriolanus
ACT III : SC I

1130

236. **tent,** treat, cure.   242. **One . . . another,** a balance will be struck between one time and another, i.e., a more fitting occasion for speaking will come.   244. **Take up,** cope with.   245. **arithmetic,** computation. 248. **tag,** rabble.   249. **interrupted,** obstructed.   252-253. **this . . . colour,** we cannot be particular, we must use the roughest remedies. 254-260. **This . . . death.** These speeches serve to give the common sense view of Coriolanus side by side with the idealistic view.   259. **does,** he does.   263. **viper,** used in allusion to the parent-devouring attributes of the viper.   269. **severity,** i.e., exposure to severity.

275. **cry havoc,** originally to give the order to pillage.   276. **modest warrant,** i.e., as moderation warrants.   286. **peremptory,** determined. 293. **Jove's own book,** explained by Gordon as the rolls and registers of the Capitol, which was Jupiter's temple.   304. **brand,** i.e., of infamy. **clean kam,** quite perverse.   306-308. **The . . . was.** This speech is sometimes assigned to Sicinius or to Brutus; if spoken by Menenius, it is to be understood as ironical.   313. **unscann'd,** inconsiderate. 314. **pounds,** weights.   **process,** legal method.   322. **bolted,** refined.
   SCENE II.   2. **wheel,** instrument of torture and death by which the

Where he shall answer, by a lawful form,
In peace, to his utmost peril.
   First Sen.   Noble tribunes,
It is the humane way: the other course
Will prove too bloody, and the end of it
Unknown to the beginning.
   Sic.   Noble Menenius,
Be you then as the people's officer.   330
Masters, lay down your weapons.
   Bru.   Go not home.
   Sic. Meet on the market-place. We'll attend you
     there:
Where, if you bring not Marcius, we'll proceed
In our first way.
   Men.   I'll bring him to you.
[*To the Senators*] Let me desire your company: he must
     come,
Or what is worst will follow.
   First Sen.   Pray you, let's to him. [*Exeunt.*

SCENE II. *A room in Coriolanus's house.*

Enter CORIOLANUS *with* Patricians.

   Cor. Let them pull all about mine ears, present me
Death on the wheel or at wild horses' heels,
Or pile ten hills on the Tarpeian rock,
That the precipitation might down stretch
Below the beam of sight, yet will I still
Be thus to them.
   A Patrician.   You do the nobler.
   Cor. I muse my mother
Does not approve me further, who was wont
To call them woollen vassals, things created
To buy and sell with groats, to show bare heads   10
In congregations, to yawn, be still and wonder,
When one but of my ordinance stood up
To speak of peace or war.

Enter VOLUMNIA.

            I talk of you:
Why did you wish me milder? would you have me
False to my nature? Rather say I play
The man I am.
   Vol.   O, sir, sir, sir,
I would have had you put your power well on,
Before you had worn it out.
   Cor.   Let go.
   Vol. You might have been enough the man you are,
With striving less to be so: lesser had been   20
The thwartings of your dispositions, if
You had not show'd them how ye were disposed
Ere they lack'd power to cross you.
   Cor.   Let them hang.
   A Patrician. Ay, and burn too.

Enter MENENIUS *and* Senators.

   Men. Come, come, you have been too rough,
     something too rough;

You must return and mend it.
   First Sen.   There's no remedy;
Unless, by not so doing, our good city
Cleave in the midst, and perish.
   Vol.   Pray, be counsell'd:
†I have a heart as little apt as yours,
But yet a brain that leads my use of anger   30
To better vantage.
   Men.   Well said, noble woman!
Before he should thus stoop to the herd, but that
The violent fit o' the time craves it as physic
For the whole state, I would put mine armour on,
Which I can scarcely bear.
   Cor.   What must I do?
   Men. Return to the tribunes.
   Cor.   Well, what then? what then?
   Men. Repent what you have spoke.
   Cor. For them! I cannot do it to the gods;
Must I then do 't to them?
   Vol.   You are too absolute;
Though therein you can never be too noble,   40
But when extremities speak. I have heard you say,
Honour and policy, like unsever'd friends,
I' the war do grow together: grant that, and
     tell me,
In peace what each of them by the other lose,
That they combine not there.
   Cor.   Tush, tush!
   Men.   A good demand.
   Vol. If it be honour in your wars to seem
The same you are not, which, for your best ends,
You adopt your policy, how is it less or worse,
That it shall hold companionship in peace
With honour, as in war, since that to both   50
It stands in like request?
   Cor.   Why force you this?
   Vol. Because that now it lies you on to speak
To the people; not by your own instruction,
Nor by the matter which your heart prompts you,
But with such words that are but roted in
Your tongue, though but bastards and syllables
Of no allowance to your bosom's truth.
Now, this no more dishonours you at all
Than to take in a town with gentle words,
Which else would put you to your fortune and   60
The hazard of much blood.
I would dissemble with my nature where
My fortunes and my friends at stake required
I should do so in honour: I am in this,
Your wife, your son, these senators, the nobles;
And you will rather show our general louts
How you can frown than spend a fawn upon 'em,
For the inheritance of their loves and safeguard
Of what that want might ruin.
   Men.   Noble lady!
Come, go with us; speak fair: you may salve so,   70
Not what is dangerous present, but the loss
Of what is past.
   Vol.   I prithee now, my son,

---

victim's limbs were broken. 5. **beam,** range. 9. **woollen,** coarsely clad. 11. **yawn** i.e., with amazement. 12. **ordinance,** rank. 18. **Let go,** enough. 23. **Ere . . . you,** i.e., before you stood for the consulship. 29. **apt,** easily impressed, ready to learn (Onions). 39. **absolute,** arbitrary. 41. **But . . . speak,** except when necessity requires. 42. **Honour and policy,** the search for fame and the proper consideration of stratagem and craft; these are the two cardinal points in the teaching of leaders in war as it was presented in books on the art of war. 46-51. **If . . . request.** Volumnia endeavors to carry over the principles of the art of war into the conduct of peacetime. 52. **lies you on,** is your duty. 55. **are but roted in,** have learned by rote; so Malone; F: *roated;* Johnson conjectured *rooted.* 57. **Of no allowance to,** unsanctioned by. 59. **take in,** capture. 60. **fortune,** i.e., of war. 64-65. **I . . . wife,** in this I represent your wife. 66. **general louts,** vulgar clowns. 68. **safeguard,** for the defense. 71-72. **Not . . . past,** not only the present danger but what has been lost already.

Go to them, with this bonnet in thy hand;
And thus far having stretch'd it—here be with them—
Thy knee bussing the stones—for in such business
Action is eloquence, and the eyes of the ignorant
More learned than the ears—waving thy head,
Which often, thus, correcting thy stout heart,
Now humble as the ripest mulberry
That will not hold the handling: or say to them, 80
Thou art their soldier, and being bred in broils
Hast not the soft way which, thou dost confess,
Were fit for thee to use as they to claim,
In asking their good loves, but thou wilt frame
Thyself, forsooth, hereafter theirs, so far
As thou hast power and person.
   Men.   This but done,
Even as she speaks, why, their hearts were yours;
For they have pardons, being ask'd, as free
As words to little purpose.
   Vol.   Prithee now, 89
Go, and be ruled: although I know thou hadst rather
Follow thine enemy in a fiery gulf
Than flatter him in a bower. Here is Cominius.

   Enter COMINIUS.

   Com. I have been i' the market-place; and, sir, 'tis
     fit
You make strong party, or defend yourself
By calmness or by absence: all's in anger.
   Men. Only fair speech.
   Com.   I think 'twill serve, if he
Can thereto frame his spirit.
   Vol.   He must, and will.
Prithee now, say you will, and go about it.
   Cor. Must I go show them my unbarbed sconce?
Must I with base tongue give my noble heart 100
A lie that it must bear? Well, I will do't:
Yet, were there but this single plot to lose,
This mould of Marcius, they to dust should grind it
And throw't against the wind. To the market-place!
You have put me now to such a part which never
I shall discharge to the life.
   Com.   Come, come, we'll prompt you.
   Vol. I prithee now, sweet son, as thou hast said
My praises made thee first a soldier, so,
To have my praise for this, perform a part
Thou hast not done before.
   Cor.   Well, I must do't: 110
Away, my disposition, and possess me
Some harlot's spirit! my throat of war be turn'd,
Which quired with my drum, into a pipe
Small as an eunuch, or the virgin voice
That babies lulls asleep! the smiles of knaves
Tent in my cheeks, and schoolboys' tears take up
The glasses of my sight! a beggar's tongue
Make motion through my lips, and my arm'd knees,
Who bow'd not in my stirrup, bend like his
That hath received an alms! I will not do't, 120
Lest I surcease to honour mine own truth
And by my body's action teach my mind

A most inherent baseness.
   Vol.   At thy choice, then:
To beg of thee, it is my more dishonour
Than thou of them. Come all to ruin; let
Thy mother rather feel thy pride than fear
Thy dangerous stoutness, for I mock at death
With as big heart as thou. Do as thou list.
Thy valiantness was mine, thou suck'dst it from me,
But owe thy pride thyself.
   Cor.   Pray, be content: 130
Mother, I am going to the market-place;
Chide me no more. I'll mountebank their loves,
Cog their hearts from them, and come home beloved
Of all the trades in Rome. Look, I am going:
Commend me to my wife. I'll return consul;
Or never trust to what my tongue can do
I' the way of flattery further.
   Vol.   Do your will.   [*Exit.*
   Com. Away! the tribunes do attend you: arm
     yourself
To answer mildly; for they are prepared
With accusations, as I hear, more strong 140
Than are upon you yet.
   Cor. The word is 'mildly.' Pray you, let us go:
Let them accuse me by invention, I
Will answer in mine honour.
   Men.   Ay, but mildly.
   Cor. Well, mildly be it then. Mildly!   [*Exeunt.*

SCENE III. *The same. The Forum.*

Enter SICINIUS *and* BRUTUS.

   Bru. In this point charge him home, that he affects
Tyrannical power: if he evade us there,
Enforce him with his envy to the people,
And that the spoil got on the Antiates
Was ne'er distributed.

   Enter an ÆDILE.

What, will he come?
   Æd.   He's coming.
   Bru.   How accompanied?
   Æd. With old Menenius, and those senators
That always favour'd him.
   Sic.   Have you a catalogue
Of all the voices that we have procured
Set down by the poll?
   Æd.   I have; 'tis ready. 10
   Sic. Have you collected them by tribes?
   Æd.   I have.
   Sic. Assemble presently the people hither;
And when they hear me say 'It shall be so
I' the right and strength o' the commons,' be it either
For death, for fine, or banishment, then let them,
If I say fine, cry 'Fine;' if death, cry 'Death.'
Insisting on the old prerogative
And power i' the truth o' the cause.
   Æd.   I shall inform them.

73-78. **Go . . . heart.** Volumnia seems to act out the part—designating his bonnet, showing how far to stretch his bow, bending her knee, and waving her head from side to side; it has also been suggested that *stretch'd it* means "gone thus far." 75. **bussing,** kissing. 78. **Which . . . thus,** i.e., often repeated thus. 80. **or . . . them.** We should say, "and say to them." 83. **as they,** as for them. 94. **make strong party,** get forces together. 99. **unbarbed sconce,** unhelmeted head. 102. **this single plot,** i.e., his own person. 103. **mould,** bodily form. 110. **Well, I must do 't.** It is the strength of a character like that of Coriolanus

to abide by his nature; it is his tragic weakness that here and later he fails to be himself and follows his mother's leading. 112. **harlot's,** lewd person's. 113. **quired,** harmonized. 116. **Tent,** lodge. **take up,** fill up. 117. **glasses,** eyeballs. 121. **surcease,** cease. 125. **Than . . . them,** than for thee to beg of them. 127. **stoutness,** obstinate pride. 132. **mountebank,** win over with the tricks of a mountebank. 138. **attend,** await.

SCENE III. 1. **charge him home,** call upon him to give answer thoroughly or effectively. 3. **Enforce him,** urge him (to action or despera-

Bru. And when such time they have begun to cry,
Let them not cease, but with a din confused   20
Enforce the present execution
Of what we chance to sentence.
  Æd.   Very well.
  Sic. Make them be strong and ready for this hint,
When we shall hap to give 't them.
  Bru.   Go about it.   [*Exit Ædile.*
Put him to choler straight: he hath been used
†Ever to conquer, and to have his worth
Of contradiction: being once chafed, he cannot
Be rein'd again to temperance; then he speaks
What 's in his heart; and that is there which looks
With us to break his neck.
  Sic.   Well, here he comes.   30

  Enter CORIOLANUS, MENENIUS, *and* COMINIUS, *with*
      Senators *and* Patricians.

  Men. Calmly, I do beseech you.
  Cor. Ay, as an ostler, that for the poorest piece
Will bear the knave by the volume. The honour'd
      gods
Keep Rome in safety, and the chairs of justice
Supplied with worthy men! plant love among 's!
Throng our large temples with the shows of peace,
And not our streets with war!
  First Sen.   Amen, amen.
  Men. A noble wish.

      Re-enter Ædile, with Citizens.

  Sic. Draw near, ye people.
  Æd. List to your tribunes. Audience! peace, I say! 40
  Cor. First, hear me speak.
  Both Tri.   Well, say. Peace, ho!
  Cor. Shall I be charged no further than this present?
Must all determine here?
  Sic.   I do demand,
If you submit you to the people's voices,
Allow their officers and are content
To suffer lawful censure for such faults
As shall be proved upon you?
  Cor.   I am content.
  Men. Lo, citizens, he says he is content:
The warlike service he has done, consider; think
Upon the wounds his body bears, which show   50
Like graves i' the holy churchyard.
  Cor.   Scratches with briers,
Scars to move laughter only.
  Men.   Consider further,
That when he speaks not like a citizen,
You find him like a soldier: do not take
His rougher accents for malicious sounds,
But, as I say, such as become a soldier,
Rather than envy you.
  Com.   Well, well, no more.
  Cor. What is the matter
That being pass'd for consul with full voice,
I am so dishonour'd that the very hour   60
You take it off again?

Sic.   Answer to us.
  Cor. Say, then: 'tis true, I ought so.
  Sic. We charge you, that you have contrived to take
From Rome all season'd office and to wind
Yourself into a power tyrannical;
For which you are a traitor to the people.
  Cor. How! traitor!
  Men.   Nay, temperately; your promise.
  Cor. The fires i' the lowest hell fold-in the people!
Call me their traitor! Thou injurious tribune!
Within thine eyes sat twenty thousand deaths,   70
In thy hands clutch'd as many millions, in
Thy lying tongue both numbers, I would say
'Thou liest' unto thee with a voice as free
As I do pray the gods.
  Sic.   Mark you this, people?
  Citizens. To the rock, to the rock with him!
  Sic.   Peace!
We need not put new matter to his charge:
What you have seen him do and heard him speak,
Beating your officers, cursing yourselves,
Opposing laws with strokes and here defying
Those whose great power must try him; even this,   80
So criminal and in such capital kind,
Deserves the extremest death.
  Bru.   But since he hath
Served well for Rome,—
  Cor.   What do you prate of service?
  Bru. I talk of that, that know it.
  Cor. You?
  Men. Is this the promise that you made your
      mother?
  Com. Know, I pray you,—
  Cor.   I'll know no further:
Let them pronounce the steep Tarpeian death,
Vagabond exile, flaying, pent to linger
But with a grain a day, I would not buy   90
Their mercy at the price of one fair word;
Nor check my courage for what they can give,
To have 't with saying 'Good morrow.'
  Sic.   For that he has,
As much as in him lies, from time to time
Envied against the people, seeking means
To pluck away their power, as now at last
Given hostile strokes, and that not in the presence
Of dreaded justice, but on the ministers
That do distribute it; in the name o' the people
And in the power of us the tribunes, we,   100
Even from this instant, banish him our city,
In peril of precipitation
From off the rock Tarpeian never more
To enter our Rome gates: i' the people's name,
I say it shall be so.
  Citizens. It shall be so, it shall be so; let him away:
He 's banish'd, and it shall be so.
  Com. Hear me, my masters, and my common
      friends,—
  Sic. He 's sentenced; no more hearing.
  Com.   Let me speak:

tion). 10. **Set . . . poll,** set down by individual names; to have set
them down by hundreds would have given the plebeians fewer votes,
since in that case there would have been a property qualification. 11.
tribes, alluding to the division of the Roman people into tribes, a
democratic division. 26. **worth,** full quota or portion (Malone); many
interpretations and emendations of this passage; Malone's seems best.
29. **looks,** promises, tends. 32. **piece,** coin, piece of money. 33. **bear
. . . volume,** endure being called knave by the volume (i.e., to any extent). 40. **Audience!** Listen, give heed! 42. **this present,** i.e., oc-

casion. 43. **determine,** cease, come to an end. 45. **Allow,** acknowledge. 55. **accents,** so Theobald; F: *Actions.* 57. **Rather . . . you,**
rather than such as show malice toward you. 64. **season'd,** defined as
matured and as made palatable; former more probable. 68. **fold-in,**
enclose, encircle. 69. **injurious,** abusive. 70-72. **Within . . . numbers.**
Understand "although" before each of the three clauses. 81. **capital,**
death-deserving. 89-90. **pent . . . day,** imprisoned to starve with but a
small particle of food a day. 93. **To . . . saying,** i.e., if I might have it
with saying. 95. **Envied against,** showed malice toward.

I have been consul, and can show for Rome 110
Her enemies' marks upon me. I do love
My country's good with a respect more tender,
More holy and profound, than mine own life,
My dear wife's estimate, her womb's increase,
And treasure of my loins; then if I would
Speak that,—
    Sic.   We know your drift: speak what?
    Bru. There 's no more to be said, but he is banish'd,
As enemy to the people and his country:
It shall be so.
    Citizens.   It shall be so, it shall be so.
    Cor. You common cry of curs! whose breath I hate
As reek o' the rotten fens, whose loves I prize 121
As the dead carcasses of unburied men
That do corrupt my air, I banish you;
And here remain with your uncertainty!
Let every feeble rumour shake your hearts!
Your enemies, with nodding of their plumes,
Fan you into despair! Have the power still
To banish your defenders; till at length
Your ignorance, which finds not till it feels,
Making not reservation of yourselves, 130
Still your own foes, deliver you as most
Abated captives to some nation
That won you without blows! Despising,
For you, the city, thus I turn my back:
There is a world elsewhere.
          [*Exeunt Coriolanus, Cominius, Menenius, Senators,*
                            and Patricians.
    Æd. The people's enemy is gone, is gone!
    Citizens. Our enemy is banish'd! he is gone! Hoo!
    hoo!   [*Shouting, and throwing up their caps.*
    Sic. Go, see him out at gates, and follow him,
As he hath follow'd you, with all despite;
Give him deserved vexation. Let a guard 140
Attend us through the city.
    Citizens. Come, come; let 's see him out at gates;
    come.
The gods preserve our noble tribunes! Come. [*Exeunt.*

ACT IV.

SCENE I. *Rome. Before a gate of the city.*

Enter CORIOLANUS, VOLUMNIA, VIRGILIA,
MENENIUS, COMINIUS, *with the young Nobility of
Rome.*

    Cor. Come, leave your tears: a brief farewell: the
    beast
With many heads butts me away. Nay, mother,
Where is your ancient courage? you were used
To say extremity was the trier of spirits;
That common chances common men could bear;
That when the sea was calm all boats alike
Show'd mastership in floating; fortune's blows,
When most struck home, being gentle wounded,
    craves

A noble cunning: you were used to load me
With precepts that would make invincible 10
The heart that conn'd them.
    Vir. O heavens! O heavens!
    Cor.   Nay, I prithee, woman,—
    Vol. Now the red pestilence strike all trades in
    Rome,
And occupations perish!
    Cor.   What, what, what!
I shall be loved when I am lack'd. Nay, mother,
Resume that spirit, when you were wont to say,
If you had been the wife of Hercules,
Six of his labours you 'ld have done, and saved
Your husband so much sweat. Cominius,
Droop not; adieu. Farewell, my wife, my mother: 20
I'll do well yet. Thou old and true Menenius,
Thy tears are salter than a younger man's,
And venomous to thine eyes. My sometime general,
I have seen thee stern, and thou hast oft beheld
Heart-hardening spectacles; tell these sad women
'Tis fond to wail inevitable strokes,
As 'tis to laugh at 'em. My mother, you wot well
My hazards still have been your solace: and
Believe 't not lightly—though I go alone,
Like to a lonely dragon, that his fen 30
Makes fear'd and talk'd of more than seen—your son
Will or exceed the common or be caught
With cautelous baits and practice.
    Vol.   My first son,
Whither wilt thou go? Take good Cominius
With thee awhile: determine on some course,
More than a wild expnew
That starts i' the way before thee.
    Cor.   O the gods!
    Com. I'll follow thee a month, devise with thee
Where thou shalt rest, that thou mayst hear of us
And we of thee: so if the time thrust forth 40
A cause for thy repeal, we shall not send
O'er the vast world to seek a single man,
And lose advantage, which doth ever cool
I' the absence of the needer.
    Cor.   Fare ye well:
Thou hast years upon thee; and thou art too full
Of the wars' surfeits, to go rove with one
That 's yet unbruised: bring me but out at gate.
Come, my sweet wife, my dearest mother, and
My friends of noble touch, when I am forth,
Bid me farewell, and smile. I pray you, come. 50
While I remain above the ground, you shall
Hear from me still, and never of me aught
But what is like me formerly.
    Men.   That 's worthily
As any ear can hear. Come, let 's not weep.
If I could shake off but one seven years
From these old arms and legs, by the good gods,
I 'ld with thee every foot.
    Cor.   Give me thy hand:
Come.   [*Exeunt.*

---

114. **estimate**, reputation. 120-135. **You . . . elsewhere.** This passage presents a height of rhetorical abuse; it enforces the completeness of Coriolanus' expatriation; this renunciation of country is often regarded as his tragic guilt. 120. **cry**, pack. 124. **remain**, remain you. **uncertainty**, inconstancy, fickleness. 129. **finds not**, discovers nothing. 130. **not**, so Capell; F: *but*, frequently retained, meaning "keeping only yourselves, while you banish your defenders" (Onions).
    ACT IV. SCENE I. 1-2. **beast . . . heads**, comparison of the mob to a beast with many heads is derived from Horace, *Epistolae*, Bk. I, i,

76, *Beliua multorum es capitum.* 7-9. **fortune's . . . cunning.** The sentence starts as if fortune's blows were to be the subject, but the construction breaks and *being gentle wounded* is made to serve; this type of broken structure is called anacoluthon. Johnson gives the meaning as, "When fortune strikes her hardest blows, to be wounded, and yet continue calm, requires a generous policy." 13. **red pestilence**, allusion to the red spots which presaged death to those stricken with the plague. 14. **occupations**, trades, handicrafts. 15. **lack'd**, missed. 30. **fen**, lurking place; note ellipsis: that his lonely lurking place makes him

SCENE II. *The same. A street near the gate.*

Enter SICINIUS, BRUTUS, *and an Ædile.*

Sic. Bid them all home; he 's gone, and we'll no
    further.
The nobility are vex'd, whom we see have sided
In his behalf.
Bru.   Now we have shown our power,
Let us seem humbler after it is done
Than when it was a-doing.
Sic.   Bid them home:
Say their great enemy is gone, and they
Stand in their ancient strength.
Bru.   Dismiss them home. [*Exit Ædile.*
Here comes his mother.
Sic.   Let 's not meet her.
Bru.   Why?
Sic. They say she 's mad.
Bru. They have ta'en note of us: keep on your way. 10

Enter VOLUMNIA, VIRGILIA, *and* MENENIUS.

Vol. O, ye 're well met: the hoarded plague o' the
    gods
Requite your love!
Men.   Peace, peace; be not so loud.
Vol. If that I could for weeping, you should hear,—
Nay, and you shall hear some. [*To Brutus*] Will you be
    gone?
Vir. [*To Sicinius*] You shall stay too: I would I had
    the power
To say so to my husband.
Sic.   Are you mankind?
Vol. Ay, fool; is that a shame? Note but this fool.
Was not a man my father? Hadst thou foxship
To banish him that struck more blows for Rome
Than thou hast spoken words?
Sic.   O blessed heavens!   20
Vol. More noble blows than ever thou wise words;
And for Rome's good. I'll tell thee what; yet go:
Nay, but thou shalt stay too: I would my son
Were in Arabia, and thy tribe before him,
His good sword in his hand.
Sic.   What then?
Vir.   What then!
He 'ld make an end of thy posterity.
Vol. Bastards and all.
Good man, the wounds that he does bear for Rome!
Men. Come, come, peace.
Sic. I would he had continued to his country 30
As he began, and not unknit himself
The noble knot he made.
Bru.   I would he had.
Vol. 'I would he had'! 'Twas you incensed the
    rabble:
Cats, that can judge as fitly of his worth
As I can of those mysteries which heaven
Will not have earth to know.
Bru.   Pray, let us go.
Vol. Now, pray, sir, get you gone:

You have done a brave deed. Ere you go, hear this:—
As far as doth the Capitol exceed
The meanest house in Rome, so far my son—   40
This lady's husband here, this, do you see?—
Whom you have banish'd, does exceed you all.
Bru. Well, well, we'll leave you.
Sic.   Why stay we to be baited
With one that wants her wits?
Vol.   Take my prayers with you.
                           [*Exeunt Tribunes.*
I would the gods had nothing else to do
But to confirm my curses! Could I meet 'em
But once a-day, it would unclog my heart
Of what lies heavy to 't.
Men.   You have told them home;
And, by my troth, you have cause. You'll sup with
    me?
Vol. Anger 's my meat; I sup upon myself,   50
And so shall starve with feeding. Come, let 's go:
Leave this faint puling and lament as I do,
In anger, Juno-like. Come, come, come.
Men. Fie, fie, fie!   [*Exeunt.*

SCENE III. *A highway between Rome and Antium.*

Enter a Roman *and a* Volsce, *meeting.*

Rom. I know you well, sir, and you know me: your
name, I think, is Adrian.
Vols. It is so, sir: truly, I have forgot you.
Rom. I am a Roman; and my services are, as you
are, against 'em: know you me yet?
Vols. Nicanor? no.
Rom. The same, sir.
Vols. You had more beard when I last saw you; but
your favour is well approved by your tongue. What 's
the news in Rome? I have a note from the Volscian
state, to find you out there: you have well saved me a
day's journey.   12
Rom. There hath been in Rome strange insurrec-
tions; the people against the senators, patricians, and
nobles.
Vols. Hath been! is it ended, then? Our state thinks
not so: they are in a most warlike preparation, and
hope to come upon them in the heat of their division.
Rom. The main blaze of it is past, but a small thing
would make it flame again: for the nobles receive so to
heart the banishment of that worthy Coriolanus, that
they are in a ripe aptness to take all power from the
people and to pluck from them their tribunes for ever.
This lies glowing, I can tell you, and is almost mature
for the violent breaking out.
Vols. Coriolanus banished!
Rom. Banished, sir.
Vols. You will be welcome with this intelligence,
Nicanor.   31
Rom. The day serves well for them now. I have
heard it said, the fittest time to corrupt a man's wife
is when she 's fallen out with her husband. Your noble

feared, etc. 32. **or . . . common,** either exceed the ordinary deeds
of men. 33. **cautelous,** crafty, deceitful. **first,** one and only. 36.
exposture, exposure. 46. **wars' surfeits,** evil results of military service.
47. **bring,** conduct. 49. **touch,** i.e., approval (from the use of the
touchstone with precious metals). 53. **worthily,** worthily spoken.
   SCENE II. 2. **sided,** enlisted. 9. **mad,** probably angry, furious.
14. **some,** a part. 16. **say so,** i.e., bid him stay. **mankind,** defined as
masculine, of the male sex; also as infuriated (beyond human nature).
18. **foxship,** ingratitude (Onions), or craftiness. 24. **Arabia,** type of

a desert. 32. **noble knot,** i.e., the obligation under which he had laid
his country. 43-44. **baited With,** worried or harassed by. 48. **heavy
to 't,** heavy upon it. **told them home,** told them the complete truth.
51. **starve with feeding,** i.e., she feeds only on herself, but eating only
this food, she may die. 52. **Leave . . . puling,** cease this weak complaining (addressed to Virgilia).
   SCENE III. 9. **approved,** so Steevens; F: *appear'd,* frequently retained, meaning "made to appear, manifested." 26. **glowing,** i.e.,
like a spark.

Tullus Aufidius will appear well in these wars, his great opposer, Coriolanus, being now in no request of his country.

Vols. He cannot choose. I am most fortunate, thus accidentally to encounter you: you have ended my business, and I will merrily accompany you home.   41

Rom. I shall, between this and supper, tell you most strange things from Rome; all tending to the good of their adversaries. Have you an army ready, say you?

Vols. A most royal one; the centurions and their charges, distinctly billeted, already in the entertainment, and to be on foot at an hour's warning.   50

Rom. I am joyful to hear of their readiness, and am the man, I think, that shall set them in present action. So, sir, heartily well met, and most glad of your company.

Vols. You take my part from me, sir; I have the most cause to be glad of yours.

Rom. Well, let us go together.   [*Exeunt.*

SCENE IV. *Antium. Before Aufidius's house.*

SCENE IV. *Antium. Before Aufidius's house.*

Enter CORIOLANUS *in mean apparel, disguised and muffled.*

Cor. A goodly city is this Antium. City,
'Tis I that made thy widows: many an heir
Of these fair edifices 'fore my wars
Have I heard groan and drop: then know me not,
Lest that thy wives with spits and boys with stones
In puny battle slay me.

Enter a Citizen.

Save you, sir.
Cit. And you.
Cor.   Direct me, if it be your will,
Where great Aufidius lies: is he in Antium?
Cit. He is, and feasts the nobles of the state   9
At his house this night.
Cor.   Which is his house, beseech you?
Cit. This, here before you.
Cor.   Thank you, sir: farewell. [*Exit Citizen.*
O world, thy slippery turns! Friends now fast sworn,
Whose double bosoms seem to wear one heart,
Whose hours, whose bed, whose meal, and exercise,
Are still together, who twin, as 'twere, in love
Unseparable, shall within this hour,
On a dissension of a doit, break out
To bitterest enmity: so, fellest foes,
Whose passions and whose plots have broke their sleep
To take the one the other, by some chance,   20
Some trick not worth an egg, shall grow dear friends
And interjoin their issues. So with me:
My birth-place hate I, and my love 's upon
This enemy town. I'll enter: if he slay me,
He does fair justice; if he give me way,
I'll do his country service.   [*Exit.*

SCENE V. *The same. A hall in Aufidius's house.*

Music within. Enter a Servingman.

First Serv. Wine, wine, wine! What service is here! I think our fellows are asleep.   [*Exit.*

Enter a second Servingman.

Sec. Serv. Where 's Cotus? my master calls for him. Cotus!   [*Exit.*

Enter CORIOLANUS.

Cor. A goodly house: the feast smells well; but I
Appear not like a guest.

Re-enter the first Servingman.

First Serv. What would you have, friend? whence are you? Here 's no place for you: pray, go to the door.
   [*Exit.*
Cor. I have deserved no better entertainment,   10
In being Coriolanus.

Re-enter second Servingman.

Sec. Serv. Whence are you, sir? Has the porter his eyes in his head, that he gives entrance to such companions? Pray, get you out.
Cor. Away!
Sec. Serv. Away! get you away.
Cor. Now thou 'rt troublesome.
Sec. Serv. Are you so brave? I'll have you talked with anon.

Enter a third Servingman. *The first meets him.*

Third Serv. What fellow 's this?   20
First Serv. A strange one as ever I looked on: I cannot get him out o' the house: prithee, call my master to him.   [*Retires.*
Third Serv. What have you to do here, fellow? Pray you, avoid the house.
Cor. Let me but stand; I will not hurt your hearth.
Third Serv. What are you?
Cor. A gentleman.
Third Serv. A marvellous poor one.   30
Cor. True, so I am.
Third Serv. Pray you, poor gentleman, take up some other station; here 's no place for you; pray you, avoid: come.
Cor. Follow your function, go, and batten on cold bits.   [*Pushes him away.*
Third Serv. What, you will not? Prithee, tell my master what a strange guest he has here.
Sec. Serv. And I shall.   [*Exit.*
Third Serv. Where dwellest thou?   40
Cor. Under the canopy.
Third Serv. Under the canopy!
Cor. Ay.
Third Serv. Where 's that?
Cor. I' the city of kites and crows.
Third Serv. I' the city of kites and crows! What an ass it is! Then thou dwellest with daws too?
Cor. No, I serve not thy master.   49
Third Serv. How, sir! do you meddle with my master?
Cor. Ay; 'tis an honester service than to meddle with thy mistress.
Thou pratest, and pratest; serve with thy trencher,
   hence!   [*Beats him away. Exit third Servingman.*

Coriolanus
ACT IV : SC III

1136

37. **in no request of,** unvalued by.   39. **choose,** do otherwise.   48. **distinctly billeted,** separately enrolled.   55. **my part,** the words I should say.
   SCENE IV.   3. **'fore my wars,** facing me in battle.   15. **twin,** are like twins.   17. **dissension of a doit,** paltry dispute.   18. **fellest,** fiercest.   20. **To . . . other,** i.e., plots by which the one tries to get the better

of the other.   21. **trick,** trifle.   22. **issues,** children.
   SCENE V.   34. **avoid,** get out.   35 **function,** proper duty.   **batten,** grow fat on.   41. **canopy,** i.e., of heaven.   48. **daws,** jackdaws, types of foolishness.   67 **tackle 's,** rigging is.   77. **memory,** reminder.   84. **Whoop'd,** driven with hoots.   89. **full quit of,** fully evened with.   91. **wreak,** vengeance.   92-93. **maims Of shame,** dishonoring mutilations.

Enter AUFIDIUS *with the second* Servingman.

Auf. Where is this fellow?

Sec. Serv. Here, sir: I 'ld have beaten him like a dog,
but for disturbing the lords within.   [*Retires.*

Auf. Whence comest thou? what wouldst thou? thy
     name?
Why speak'st not? speak, man: what 's thy name?

Cor. If, Tullus,   [*Unmuffling.* 60
Not yet thou knowest me, and, seeing me, dost not
Think me for the man I am, necessity
Commands me name myself.

Auf.   What is thy name?

Cor. A name unmusical to the Volscians' ears,
And harsh in sound to thine.

Auf.   Say, what 's thy name?
Thou hast a grim appearance, and thy face
Bears a command in 't; though thy tackle 's torn,
Thou show'st a noble vessel: what 's thy name?

Cor. Prepare thy brow to frown: know'st thou me
     yet?

Auf. I know thee not: thy name?   70

Cor. My name is Caius Marcius, who hath done
To thee particularly and to all the Volsces
Great hurt and mischief; thereto witness may
My surname, Coriolanus: the painful service,
The extreme dangers and the drops of blood
Shed for my thankless country are requited
But with that surname; a good memory,
And witness of the malice and displeasure
Which thou shouldst bear me: only that name
     remains;
The cruelty and envy of the people,   80
Permitted by our dastard nobles, who
Have all forsook me, hath devour'd the rest;
And suffer'd me by the voice of slaves to be
Whoop'd out of Rome. Now this extremity
Hath brought me to thy hearth; not out of hope—
Mistake me not—to save my life, for if
I had fear'd death, of all the men i' the world
I would have 'voided thee, but in mere spite,
To be full quit of those my banishers,
Stand I before thee here. Then if thou hast   90
A heart of wreak in thee, that wilt revenge
Thine own particular wrongs and stop those maims
Of shame seen through thy country, speed thee
     straight,
And make my misery serve thy turn: so use it
That my revengeful services may prove
As benefits to thee, for I will fight
Against my canker'd country with the spleen
Of all the under fiends. But if so be
Thou darest not this and that to prove more fortunes
Thou 'rt tired, then, in a word, I also am   100
Longer to live most weary, and present
My throat to thee and to thy ancient malice;
Which not to cut would show thee but a fool,
Since I have ever follow'd thee with hate,
Drawn tuns of blood out of thy country's breast,
And cannot live but to thy shame, unless
It be to do thee service.

Auf.   O Marcius, Marcius!
Each word thou hast spoke hath weeded from my
     heart
A root of ancient envy. If Jupiter
Should from yond cloud speak divine things,   110
And say ''Tis true,' I 'ld not believe them more
Than thee, all noble Marcius. Let me twine
Mine arms about that body, where against
My grained ash an hundred times hath broke,
And scarr'd the moon with splinters: here I clip
The anvil of my sword, and do contest
As hotly and as nobly with thy love
As ever in ambitious strength I did
Contend against thy valour. Know thou first,
I loved the maid I married; never man   120
Sigh'd truer breath; but that I see thee here,
Thou noble thing! more dances my rapt heart
Than when I first my wedded mistress saw
Bestride my threshold. Why, thou Mars! I tell thee,
We have a power on foot; and I had purpose
Once more to hew thy target from thy brawn,
Or lose mine arm for 't: thou hast beat me out
Twelve several times, and I have nightly since
Dreamt of encounters 'twixt thyself and me;
We have been down together in my sleep,   130
Unbuckling helms, fisting each other's throat,
And waked half dead with nothing. Worthy Marcius,
Had we no quarrel else to Rome, but that
Thou art thence banish'd, we would muster all
From twelve to seventy, and pouring war
Into the bowels of ungrateful Rome,
Like a bold flood o'er-bear. O, come, go in,
And take our friendly senators by the hands;
Who now are here, taking their leaves of me,
Who am prepared against your territories,   140
Though not for Rome itself.

Cor.   You bless me, gods!

Auf. Therefore, most absolute sir, if thou wilt have
The leading of thine own revenges, take
The one half of my commission; and set down—
As best thou art experienced, since thou know'st
Thy country's strength and weakness,—thine own
     ways;
Whether to knock against the gates of Rome,
Or rudely visit them in parts remote,
To fright them, ere destroy. But come in:
Let me commend thee first to those that shall   150
Say yea to thy desires. A thousand welcomes!
And more a friend than e'er an enemy;
Yet, Marcius, that was much. Your hand: most
     welcome!

     [*Exeunt Coriolanus and Aufidius. The two
               Servingmen come forward.*

First Serv. Here 's a strange alteration!

Sec. Serv. By my hand, I had thought to have
strucken him with a cudgel; and yet my mind gave
me his clothes made a false report of him.

First Serv. What an arm he has! he turned me about
with his finger and his thumb, as one would set up a
top.   161

Sec. Serv. Nay, I knew by his face that there was

---

93. **through,** throughout.   97. **canker'd,** infected with evils (from the
action of the cankerworm).   98. **under fiends,** fiends of the underworld,
or possibly subordinate fiends.   99. **prove more fortunes,** try your fortunes further.   105. **tuns,** large barrels.   109. **root of ancient envy,**
source of ancient malice.   114. **grained ash,** spear with ashen shaft
showing a strong grain.   116. **anvil,** i.e., Coriolanus has been as an

anvil for his sword.   125. **power on foot,** force in the field.   126.
brawn, muscle of the arm; here, arm.   131. **fisting,** clutching.   137.
o'er bear, so Rowe; F: *o're-beate,* sometimes retained as *o'erbeat,* meaning bear all before us.   142. **absolute,** perfect.   144. **set down,** determine upon.   157. **gave,** misgave or told.   161. **set up,** set going.

something in him: he had, sir, a kind of face, me-thought,—I cannot tell how to term it.

First Serv. He had so; looking as it were—would I were hanged, but I thought there was more in him than I could think.

Sec. Serv. So did I, I'll be sworn: he is simply the rarest man i' the world.

First Serv. I think he is: but a greater soldier than he, you wot one. 171

Sec. Serv. Who, my master?

First Serv. Nay, it 's no matter for that.

Sec. Serv. Worth six on him.

First Serv. Nay, not so neither: but I take him to be the greater soldier.

Sec. Serv. Faith, look you, one cannot tell how to say that: for the defence of a town, our general is excellent.

First Serv. Ay, and for an assault too. 180

Re-enter third Servingman.

Third Serv. O slaves, I can tell you news,—news, you rascals!

First and Sec. Serv. What, what, what? let's partake.

Third Serv. I would not be a Roman, of all nations; I had as lieve be a condemned man.

First and Sec. Serv. Wherefore? wherefore?

Third Serv. Why, here 's he that was wont to thwack our general, Caius Marcius.

First Serv. Why do you say 'thwack our general'? 191

Third Serv. I do not say 'thwack our general;' but he was always good enough for him.

Sec. Serv. Come, we are fellows and friends: he was ever too hard for him; I have heard him say so himself.

First Serv. He was too hard for him directly, to say the troth on 't: before Corioli he scotched him and notched him like a carbonado.

Sec. Serv. An he had been cannibally given, he might have boiled and eaten him too. 201

First Serv. But, more of thy news?

Third Serv. Why, he is so made on here within, as if he were son and heir to Mars; set at upper end o' the table; no question asked him by any of the senators, but they stand bald before him: our general himself makes a mistress of him; sanctifies himself with 's hand and turns up the white o' the eye to his dis-course. But the bottom of the news is, our general is cut i' the middle and but one half of what he was yesterday; for the other has half, by the entreaty and grant of the whole table. He'll go, he says, and sowl the porter of Rome gates by the ears: he will mow all down before him, and leave his passage polled. 215

Sec. Serv. And he 's as like to do 't as any man I can imagine.

Third Serv. Do 't! he will do 't; for, look you, sir, he has as many friends as enemies; which friends, sir, as it were, durst not, look you, sir, show themselves, as we term it, his friends whilst he 's in directitude.

First Serv. Directitude! what 's that?

Third Serv. But when they shall see, sir, his crest up

again, and the man in blood, they will out of their burrows, like conies after rain, and revel all with him.

First Serv. But when goes this forward? 228

Third Serv. To-morrow; to-day; presently; you shall have the drum struck up this afternoon: 'tis, as it were, a parcel of their feast, and to be executed ere they wipe their lips.

Sec. Serv. Why, then we shall have a stirring world again. This peace is nothing, but to rust iron, increase tailors, and breed ballad-makers.

First Serv. Let me have war, say I; it exceeds peace as far as day does night; it 's spritely, waking, audible, and full of vent. Peace is a very apoplexy, lethargy; mulled, deaf, sleepy, insensible; a getter of more bastard children than war 's a destroyer of men. 241

Sec. Serv. 'Tis so: and as war, in some sort, may be said to be a ravisher, so it cannot be denied but peace is a great maker of cuckolds.

First Serv. Ay, and it makes men hate one another.

Third Serv. Reason; because they then less need one another. The wars for my money. I hope to see Romans as cheap as Volscians. They are rising, they are rising. 250

All. In, in, in, in! [*Exeunt.*

SCENE VI. *Rome. A public place.*

Enter SICINIUS *and* BRUTUS.

Sic. We hear not of him, neither need we fear him;
His remedies are tame i' the present peace
And quietness of the people, which before
Were in wild hurry. Here do we make his friends
Blush that the world goes well, who rather had,
Though they themselves did suffer by 't, behold
Dissentious numbers pestering streets than see
Our tradesmen singing in their shops and going
About their functions friendly.

Bru. We stood to 't in good time. [*Enter Menenius.*] Is
this Menenius? 10

Sic. 'Tis he, 'tis he: O, he is grown most kind of
late.

Both Tri. Hail, sir!

Men.   Hail to you both!

Sic.   Your Coriolanus
Is not much miss'd, but with his friends:
The commonwealth doth stand, and so would do,
Were he more angry at it.

Men. All 's well; and might have been much better, if
He could have temporized.

Sic.   Where is he, hear you?

Men. Nay, I hear nothing: his mother and his wife
Hear nothing from him.

Enter three or four Citizens.

Citizens. The gods preserve you both!

Sic.   God-den, our neighbours. 20

Bru. God-den to you all, god-den to you all.

168-180. **So did . . . too.** This guarded conversation between the servants is difficult to follow. It may be understood as it stands if one conceives that First Servant is a partisan of Aufidius, and Second Servant is a partisan of Coriolanus, both being unwilling to speak plainly; cf. what follows. Instead of *one* in line 171, Dyce suggested *on;* according to this, *you wot on* would mean you know whom I mean, i.e., Aufidius. 173. **Nay . . . that,** I won't commit myself. 174, 176. **him,** i.e., Coriolanus according to Dyce; Aufidius according to the text. 178-179. **our general,** i.e., Aufidius. 183. **let 's partake,** let's share it.

197. **directly,** plainly, pointedly. 198. **scotched,** scored, gashed. 199. **carbonado,** meat scored across for broiling. 201. **boiled,** so F; Pope, followed by Globe: *broiled.* 203. **made on,** flattered, made much of. 208. **sanctifies . . . hand,** fondles his hand as if it were a relic. 208-209. **turns . . . eye,** i.e., as an expression of veneration. 212. **other,** i.e., Coriolanus. **entreaty and grant,** requesting and granting. 213. **sowl,** drag; F: *sole.* 215. **polled,** stripped (properly of branches or foliage). 222. **directitude,** blundering form; Malone conjectured *discreditude,* which suggests the meaning. 226. **conies,** rabbits. 231.

First Cit. Ourselves, our wives, and children, on our
  knees,
Are bound to pray for you both.
  Sic.   Live, and thrive!
  Bru. Farewell, kind neighbours: we wish'd
    Coriolanus
Had loved you as we did.
  Citizens.   Now the gods keep you!
  Both Tri. Farewell, farewell.   [*Exeunt Citizens.*
  Sic. This is a happier and more comely time
Than when these fellows ran about the streets,
Crying confusion.
  Bru.   Caius Marcius was
A worthy officer i' the war; but insolent,   30
O'ercome with pride, ambitious past all thinking,
Self-loving,—
  Sic.   And affecting one sole throne,
Without assistance.
  Men.   I think not so.
  Sic. We should by this, to all our lamentation,
If he had gone forth consul, found it so.
  Bru. The gods have well prevented it, and Rome
Sits safe and still without him.

Enter an Ædile.

  Æd.   Worthy tribunes,
There is a slave, whom we have put in prison,
Reports, the Volsces with two several powers
Are enter'd in the Roman territories,   40
And with the deepest malice of the war
Destroy what lies before 'em.
  Men.   'Tis Aufidius,
Who, hearing of our Marcius' banishment,
Thrusts forth his horns again into the world;
Which were inshell'd when Marcius stood for Rome,
And durst not once peep out.
  Sic.   Come, what talk you
Of Marcius?
  Bru.   Go see this rumourer whipp'd. It
    cannot be
The Voisces dare break with us.
  Men.   Cannot be!
We have record that very well it can,
And three examples of the like have been   50
Within my age. But reason with the fellow,
Before you punish him, where he heard this,
Lest you shall chance to whip your information
And beat the messenger who bids beware
Of what is to be dreaded.
  Sic.   Tell not me:
I know this cannot be.
  Bru.   Not possible.

Enter a Messenger.

  Mess. The nobles in great earnestness are going
All to the senate-house: some news is come
That turns their countenances.
  Sic.   'Tis this slave;—
Go whip him 'fore the people's eyes:—his raising;   60

Nothing but his report.
  Mess.   Yes, worthy sir,
The slave's report is seconded; and more,
More fearful, is deliver'd.
  Sic.   What more fearful?
  Mess. It is spoke freely out of many mouths—
How probable I do not know—that Marcius,
Join'd with Aufidius, leads a power 'gainst Rome,
And vows revenge as spacious as between
The young'st and oldest thing.
  Sic.   This is most likely!
  Bru. Raised only, that the weaker sort may wish
Good Marcius home again.
  Sic.   The very trick on 't.   70
  Men. This is unlikely:
He and Aufidius can no more atone
Than violentest contrariety.

Enter a second Messenger.

  Sec. Mess. You are sent for to the senate:
A fearful army, led by Caius Marcius
Associated with Aufidius, rages
Upon our territories; and have already
O'erborne their way, consumed with fire, and took
What lay before them.

Enter COMINIUS.

  Com. O, you have made good work!
  Men.   What news? what news?   80
  Com. You have holp to ravish your own daughters
    and
To melt the city leads upon your pates,
To see your wives dishonour'd to your noses,—
  Men. What 's the news? what 's the news?
  Com. Your temples burned in their cement, and
Your franchises, whereon you stood, confined
Into an auger's bore.
  Men.   Pray now, your news?
You have made fair work, I fear me.—Pray, your
    news?—
If Marcius should be join'd with Volscians,—
  Com.   If!
He is their god: he leads them like a thing   90
Made by some other deity than nature,
That shapes man better; and they follow him,
Against us brats, with no less confidence
Than boys pursuing summer butterflies,
Or butchers killing flies.
  Men.   You have made good work,
You and your apron-men; you that stood so much
Upon the voice of occupation and
The breath of garlic-eaters!
  Com.   He will shake
Your Rome about your ears.
  Men.   As Hercules
Did shake down mellow fruit. You have made fair
    work!   100
  Bru. But is this true, sir?
  Com.   Ay; and you'll look pale

parcel, part. 237. **spritely, waking,** so Pope (*sprightly*); F: *sprightly
walking.* 238. **vent,** excitement, activity. 239. **mulled,** insipid.
247. **Reason,** i.e., this is the reason. 250. **rising,** i.e., from table.
SCENE VI. 7. **pestering,** infesting. 13. **but with,** except among.
27. **comely,** gracious. 29. **Crying confusion,** starting trouble. 34.
by this, by this time. **to all our lamentation,** to the lamentation of all
of us. 35. **gone forth,** i.e., as consul. **found,** have found. 44.
Thrusts . . . again, i.e., like a snail. 45. **inshell'd,** i.e., in the shell like a
snail's horns. 46. **what,** why. 59. **turns,** changes the color of. 68.

young'st . . . thing, every living thing. 69. **Raised,** invented, stirred
up; see *raising,* line 60 above. 78. **O'erborne their way,** carried all
before them. 82. **leads,** roofs of lead (melted by fire). 83. **to,** before.
85. **cement,** material of which the temples were made; accent on
first syllable. 86. **franchises,** privileges. 93. **brats,** mere children.
96. **apron-men,** mechanics in aprons. 97. **voice of occupation,** votes of
the laboring men. 99-100. **Hercules . . . fruit,** allusion to the eleventh labor of Hercules, the stealing of the golden apples of Hesperides.

Before you find it other. All the regions
Do smilingly revolt; and who resist
Are mock'd for valiant ignorance,
And perish constant fools. Who is 't can blame him?
Your enemies and his find something in him.
   Men. We are all undone, unless
The noble man have mercy.
   Com.   Who shall ask it?
The tribunes cannot do 't for shame; the people
Deserve such pity of him as the wolf   110
Does of the shepherds: for his best friends, if they
Should say 'Be good to Rome,' they charged him
    even
As those should do that had deserved his hate,
And therein show'd like enemies.
   Men.   'Tis true:
If he were putting to my house the brand
That should consume it, I have not the face
To say 'Beseech you, cease.' You have made fair
    hands,
You and your crafts! you have crafted fair!
   Com.   You have brought
A trembling upon Rome, such as was never
So incapable of help.
   Both Tri.   Say not we brought it.   120
   Men. How! Was it we? we loved him; but, like
    beasts
And cowardly nobles, gave way unto your clusters,
Who did hoot him out o' the city.
   Com.   But I fear
They'll roar him in again. Tullus Aufidius,
The second name of men, obeys his points
As if he were his officer: desperation
Is all the policy, strength and defence,
That Rome can make against them.

Enter a troop of Citizens.

   Men.   Here come the clusters.
And is Aufidius with him? You are they
That made the air unwholesome, when you cast   130
Your stinking greasy caps in hooting at
Coriolanus' exile. Now he 's coming;
And not a hair upon a soldier's head
Which will not prove a whip: as many coxcombs
As you threw caps up will he tumble down,
And pay you for your voices. 'Tis no matter;
If he could burn us all into one coal,
We have deserved it.
   Citizens. Faith, we hear fearful news.
   First Cit.   For mine own part,
When I said, banish him, I said, 'twas pity.   140
   Sec. Cit. And so did I.
   Third Cit. And so did I; and, to say the truth, so did
very many of us: that we did, we did for the best; and
though we willingly consented to his banishment, yet
it was against our will.
   Com. Ye 're goodly things, you voices!

Men.   You have made
Good work, you and your cry! Shall 's to the Capitol?
   Com. O, ay, what else?[*Exeunt Cominius and Menenius.*
   Sic. Go, masters, get you home; be not dismay'd: 150
These are a side that would be glad to have
This true which they so seem to fear. Go home,
And show no sign of fear.
   First Cit. The gods be good to us! Come, masters,
let 's home. I ever said we were i' the wrong when we
banished him.
   Sec. Cit. So did we all. But, come, let 's home.
                       [*Exeunt Citizens.*
   Bru. I do not like this news.
   Sic. Nor I.
   Bru. Let 's to the Capitol. Would half my wealth   160
Would buy this for a lie!
   Sic.   Pray, let us go.   [*Exeunt.*

SCENE VII. *A camp, at a small distance from Rome.*

Enter AUFIDIUS *and his* Lieutenant.

   Auf. Do they still fly to the Roman?
   Lieu. I do not know what witchcraft 's in him, but
Your soldiers use him as the grace 'fore meat,
Their talk at table, and their thanks at end;
And you are darken'd in this action, sir,
Even by your own.
   Auf.   I cannot help it now,
Unless, by using means, I lame the foot
Of our design. He bears himself more proudlier,
Even to my person, than I thought he would
When first I did embrace him: yet his nature   10
In that 's no changeling; and I must excuse
What cannot be amended.
   Lieu.   Yet I wish, sir,—
I mean for your particular,—you had not
Join'd in commission with him; but either
Had borne the action of yourself, or else
To him had left it solely.
   Auf. I understand thee well; and be thou sure,
When he shall come to his account, he knows not
What I can urge against him. Although it seems,
And so he thinks, and is no less apparent   20
To the vulgar eye, that he bears all things fairly,
And shows good husbandry for the Volscian state,
Fights dragon-like, and does achieve as soon
As draw his sword; yet he hath left undone
That which shall break his neck or hazard mine,
Whene'er we come to our account.
   Lieu. Sir, I beseech you, think you he'll carry
    Rome?
   Auf. All places yield to him ere he sits down;
And the nobility of Rome are his:
The senators and patricians love him too: 30
The tribunes are no soldiers; and their people

---

102. **other,** otherwise. 103. **smilingly,** gladly, willingly. **who resist,**
F: *resists.* 112. **they charged him even,** they would be charging him
just. 117. **made . . . hands,** made a pretty mess. *NED* defines "make
a hand" as spoil, waste. 118. **crafted fair,** advanced the interests of
the crafts or occupations and showed your craft or cunning (ironical).
124. **roar . . . again,** roar with pain when he returns. 125. **second
. . . men,** second greatest name among men. **points,** instructions.
126-127. **desperation . . . defence,** policy, strength, and defense amount
only to a desperate hope. 137. **coal,** cinder or ashes. 148. **Shall 's,**
shall we go. 151. **side,** party.
   SCENE VII. 5. **you . . . action,** your glory is dimmed in this under-

taking. 6. **your own,** i.e., followers. 7. **using means,** resorting to
treachery. 11. **changeling,** inconstant person. 15. **borne . . . yourself,** taken the whole command yourself. 18-26. **When . . . account.**
Attempt has been made to explain this from Plutarch's treatment of the
first demands of the Volsces, which the Romans were given thirty days
to answer. This may be correct; there is, however, an undercurrent in
the play which shows that Aufidius was not sincere. 21. **bears . . .
fairly,** behaves honorably in all things. 28. **sits down,** besieges. 34.
osprey, fish hawk, said to have power of fascinating fishes; F: *asprey.*
37. **Carry . . . even,** bear his honors temperately. 43. **casque,** as symbol of the warrior. **cushion,** as symbol of the senator. 44. **austerity**

Will be as rash in the repeal, as hasty
To expel him thence. I think he'll be to Rome
As is the osprey to the fish, who takes it
By sovereignty of nature. First he was
A noble servant to them; but he could not
Carry his honours even: whether 'twas pride,
Which out of daily fortune ever taints
The happy man; whether defect of judgement,
To fail in the disposing of those chances　　　　40
Which he was lord of; or whether nature,
Not to be other than one thing, not moving
From the casque to the cushion, but commanding
　　peace
Even with the same austerity and garb
As he controll'd the war; but one of these—
As he hath spices of them all, not all,
For I dare so far free him—made him fear'd,
So hated, and so banish'd: but he has a merit,
To choke it in the utterance. So our virtues
Lie in the interpretation of the time:　　　　50
And power, unto itself most commendable,
†Hath not a tomb so evident as a chair
To extol what it hath done.
One fire drives out one fire; one nail, one nail;
Rights by rights falter, strengths by strengths do fail.
Come, let 's away. When, Caius, Rome is thine,
Thou art poor'st of all; then shortly art thou mine.
　　　　　　　　　　　　　　　　　　　[Exeunt.

ACT V.

SCENE I. *Rome. A public place.*

Enter MENENIUS, COMINIUS, SICINIUS, BRUTUS, *and others.*

Men. No, I'll not go: you hear what he hath said
Which was sometime his general; who loved him
In a most dear particular. He call'd me father:
But what o' that? Go, you that banish'd him;
A mile before his tent fall down, and knee
The way into his mercy: nay, if he coy'd
To hear Cominius speak, I'll keep at home.
　Com. He would not seem to know me.
　Men.　　　　　　Do you hear?
　Com. Yet one time he did call me by my name:
I urged our old acquaintance, and the drops　　10
That we have bled together. Coriolanus
He would not answer to; forbad all names;
He was a kind of nothing, titleless,
Till he had forged himself a name o' the fire
Of burning Rome.
　Men.　　　　Why, so: you have made good
　　work!
A pair of tribunes that have rack'd for Rome,
To make coals cheap,—a noble memory!
　Com. I minded him how royal 'twas to pardon

When it was less expected: he replied,
It was a bare petition of a state　　　　　　20
To one whom they had punish'd.
　Men.　　　　　Very well:
Could he say less?
　Com. I offer'd to awaken his regard
For 's private friends: his answer to me was,
He could not stay to pick them in a pile
Of noisome musty chaff: he said 'twas folly,
For one poor grain or two, to leave unburnt,
And still to nose the offence.
　Men.　　　　　For one poor grain or two!
I am one of those; his mother, wife, his child,
And this brave fellow too, we are the grains:　　30
You are the musty chaff; and you are smelt
Above the moon: we must be burnt for you.
　Sic. Nay, pray, be patient: if you refuse your aid
In this so never-needed help, yet do not
Upbraid 's with our distress. But, sure, if you
Would be your country's pleader, your good tongue,
More than the instant army we can make,
Might stop our countryman.
　Men.　　　　　No, I'll not meddle.
　Sic. Pray you, go to him.
　Men.　　　　What should I do?
　Bru. Only make trial what your love can do　　40
For Rome, towards Marcius.
　Men.　　　　　Well, and say that Marcius
Return me, as Cominius is return'd,
Unheard; what then?
But as a discontented friend, grief-shot
With his unkindness? say 't be so?
　Sic.　　　　　Yet your good will
Must have that thanks from Rome, after the measure
As you intended well.
　Men.　　　　　I'll undertake 't:
I think he'll hear me. Yet, to bite his lip
And hum at good Cominius, much unhearts me.
He was not taken well; he had not dined:　　50
The veins unfill'd, our blood is cold, and then
We pout upon the morning, are unapt
To give or to forgive; but when we have stuff'd
These pipes and these conveyances of our blood
With wine and feeding, we have supper souls
Than in our priest-like fasts: therefore I'll watch him
Till he be dieted to my request,
And then I'll set upon him.
　Bru. You know the very road into his kindness,
And cannot lose your way.
　Men.　　　　Good faith, I'll prove him,　　60
Speed how it will. I shall ere long have knowledge
Of my success.　　　　　　　　　　　[*Exit.*
　Com.　　　　He'll never hear him.
　Sic.　　　　　Not?
　Com. I tell you, he does sit in gold, his eye
Red as 'twould burn Rome; and his injury
The gaoler to his pity. I kneel'd before him;

and garb, austere behavior. 46. spices, traces. 48-49. he . . . utterance, he has a merit to counterbalance every fault you urge against
him; Johnson: He has a merit for no other purpose than to destroy it by
boasting it. 52-53. Hath . . . done. The meaning is that deeds done
have lost their value: power seated in a chair to claim reward for what
it has done is, as it were, in its tomb. There has been much discussion among Shakespeare scholars as to the correct interpretation of
lines 28-53.
　ACT V. SCENE I. 3. dear particular, private affection. 5. knee,
crawl on knee. 6. coy'd, showed reluctance, or disdained. 12. forbad
all names, prohibited the use of all names in addressing him. 16.

rack'd, striven; F: *wrack'd*; some editors: *wreck'd fair.* 20. bare,
mere, paltry. 23. offer'd, presumed. 28. nose the offence, tolerate
the nuisance. 34. In . . . help, in this strait where help is needed
as never before. 37. instant army, i.e., army we can raise at this instant; existent army (Onions). 41. towards, in relation to. 46-47.
after . . . As, in proportion that. 49. hum, i.e., as expression of
dissatisfaction. 56. watch him, observe him; also suggested that there
is an allusion to falconry, the hawk being kept awake and without food
to tame it. 62. Not? Do you think not? 63. in gold, on a golden
throne. 63-64. eye Red, betokening anger.

'Twas very faintly he said 'Rise;' dismiss'd me
Thus, with his speechless hand: what he would do,
He sent in writing after me; what he would not,
Bound with an oath to yield to his conditions:
So that all hope is vain, 70
Unless his noble mother, and his wife;
Who, as I hear, mean to solicit him
For mercy to his country. Therefore, let 's hence,
And with our fair entreaties haste them on. [Exeunt.

SCENE II. *Entrance of the Volscian camp before Rome.*
Two Sentinels *on guard.*

Enter to them, MENENIUS.

First Sen. Stay: whence are you?
Sec. Sen. Stand, and go back.
Men. You guard like men; 'tis well: but, by your
leave,
I am an officer of state, and come
To speak with Coriolanus.
First Sen. From whence?
Men. From Rome.
First Sen. You may not pass, you must return: our
general
Will no more hear from thence.
Sec. Sen. You'll see your Rome embraced with fire
before
You'll speak with Coriolanus.
Men. Good my friends,
If you have heard your general talk of Rome,
And of his friends there, it is lots to blanks, 10
My name hath touch'd your ears: it is Menenius.
First Sen. Be it so; go back: the virtue of your name
Is not here passable.
Men. I tell thee, fellow,
Thy general is my lover: I have been
The book of his good acts, whence men have read
His fame unparallel'd, haply amplified;
For I have ever †verified my friends,
Of whom he 's chief, with all the size that verity
Would without lapsing suffer: nay, sometimes,
Like to a bowl upon a subtle ground, 20
I have tumbled past the throw; and in his praise
Have almost stamp'd the leasing: therefore, fellow,
I must have leave to pass.
First Sen. Faith, sir, if you had told as many lies in
his behalf as you have uttered words in your own,
you should not pass here; no, though it were as
virtuous to lie as to live chastely. Therefore, go back.
Men. Prithee, fellow, remember my name is Mene-
nius, always factionary on the party of your general. 31
Sec. Sen. Howsoever you have been his liar, as you
say you have, I am one that, telling true under him,
must say, you cannot pass. Therefore, go back.

Men. Has he dined, canst thou tell? for I would not
speak with him till after dinner.
First Sen. You are a Roman, are you?
Men. I am, as thy general is.
First Sen. Then you should hate Rome, as he does. 39
Can you, when you have pushed out your gates the
very defender of them, and, in a violent popular
ignorance, given your enemy your shield, think to
front his revenges with the easy groans of old women,
the virginal palms of your daughters, or with the
palsied intercession of such a decayed dotant as you
seem to be? Can you think to blow out the intended
fire your city is ready to flame in, with such weak
breath as this? No, you are deceived; therefore, back
to Rome, and prepare for your execution: you are
condemned, our general has sworn you out of reprieve
and pardon. 53
Men. Sirrah, if thy captain knew I were here, he
would use me with estimation.
First Sen. Come, my captain knows you not.
Men. I mean, thy general.
First Sen. My general cares not for you. Back, I say,
go; lest I let forth your half-pint of blood; back,—
that 's the utmost of your having: back.
Men. Nay, but, fellow, fellow,—

Enter CORIOLANUS *and* AUFIDIUS.

Cor. What 's the matter? 64
Men. Now, you companion, I'll say an errand for
you: you shall know now that I am in estimation;
you shall perceive that a Jack guardant cannot office
me from my son Coriolanus: guess, but by my entertainment with him, if thou standest not i' the state of
hanging, or of some death more long in spectatorship,
and crueller in suffering; behold now presently, and
swoon for what 's to come upon thee. [*To Cor.*] The
glorious gods sit in hourly synod about thy particular
prosperity, and love thee no worse than thy old father
Menenius does! O my son, my son! thou art preparing
fire for us; look thee, here 's water to quench it. I was
hardly moved to come to thee; but being assured
none but myself could move thee, I have been blown
out of your gates with sighs; and conjure thee to
pardon Rome, and thy petitionary countrymen. The
good gods assuage thy wrath, and turn the dregs of it
upon this varlet here,—this, who, like a block, hath
denied my access to thee.
Cor. Away!
Men. How! away!
Cor. Wife, mother, child, I know not. My affairs
Are servanted to others: though I owe
My revenge properly, my remission lies 90
In Volscian breasts. That we have been familiar,
Ingrate forgetfulness shall poison, rather
Than pity note how much. Therefore, be gone.
Mine ears against your suits are stronger than

---

66. **faintly,** coldly, indifferently. 68-69. **what . . . conditions,** a
baffling crux. By *what he would not* (do) is meant such things as burning
Rome; the following paraphrase yields a sort of meaning: what he
would not do he bound up with the proviso that we should take an
oath to yield to his conditions (before we learned what they were).
71. **Unless,** unless in, except from.
SCENE II. 10. **lots to blanks,** all the world to nothing; there is a
dispute as to whether *lots* means prizes or merely all numbers in the
lottery. 13. **passable,** current. 14. **lover,** friend. 17. **verified,**
spoken the truth about (Malone); *magnified, amplified, glorified* have
been conjectured. 18. **size,** exaggeration. 19. **lapsing,** lying. 20.
subtle, deceptively smooth (Onions). 21. **throw,** distance aimed at.

22. **stamp'd,** given currency to. **leasing,** lying. 30. **factionary,** active as a partisan. 33-34. **telling . . . him,** telling the truth in his
service. 43. **violent popular ignorance,** folly of mob violence. 45.
easy groans, i.e., groans which are easily provoked. 45-46. **virginal
. . . daughters,** uplifted hands of your virgin daughters. 47. **dotant,**
dotard, doddering old man. 53. **out of,** beyond the reach of. 61-62.
utmost of your having, all you are going to get. 65. **say an errand,**
deliver a message. 67. **Jack guardant,** common fellow on guard;
guardant is a heraldic term. 68. **office,** drive by virtue of your office.
71. **spectatorship,** in presence of spectators. 85. **block,** impediment and
blockhead. 89. **servanted,** subjected. 90. **remission,** power to forgive.
91-93. **That . . . much,** that we have been friends I shall allow ingrat-

Your gates against my force. Yet, for I loved thee,
Take this along; I writ it for thy sake,   [*Gives a letter.*
And would have sent it. Another word, Menenius,
I will not hear thee speak. This man, Aufidius,
Was my beloved in Rome: yet thou behold'st!
    Auf. You keep a constant temper.   100
                          [*Exeunt Coriolanus and Aufidius.*
    First Sen. Now, sir, is your name Menenius?
    Sec. Sen. 'Tis a spell, you see, of much power: you
know the way home again.
    First Sen. Do you hear how we are shent for keeping
your greatness back?
    Sec. Sen. What cause, do you think, I have to
swoon?
    Men. I neither care for the world nor your general:
for such things as you, I can scarce think there 's any,
ye 're so slight. He that hath a will to die by himself
fears it not from another: let your general do his
worst. For you, be that you are, long; and your misery
increase with your age! I say to you, as I was said to,
Away!   [*Exit.*
    First Sen. A noble fellow, I warrant him.   115
    Sec. Sen. The worthy fellow is our general: he 's the
rock, the oak not to be wind-shaken.   [*Exeunt.*

SCENE III. *The tent of Coriolanus.*

Enter Coriolanus, Aufidius, *and others.*

    Cor. We will before the walls of Rome to-morrow
Set down our host. My partner in this action,
You must report to the Volscian lords, how plainly
I have borne this business.
    Auf.   Only their ends
You have respected; stopp'd your ears against
The general suit of Rome; never admitted
A private whisper, no, not with such friends
That thought them sure of you.
    Cor.   This last old man,
Whom with a crack'd heart I have sent to Rome,
Loved me above the measure of a father;   10
Nay, godded me, indeed. Their latest refuge
Was to send him; for whose old love I have,
Though I show'd sourly to him, once more offer'd
The first conditions, which they did refuse
And cannot now accept; to grace him only
That thought he could do more, a very little
I have yielded to: fresh embassies and suits,
Nor from the state nor private friends, hereafter
Will I lend ear to. Ha! what shout is this? [*Shout within.*
Shall I be tempted to infringe my vow   20
In the same time 'tis made? I will not.

    Enter, in mourning habits, Virgilia, Volumnia,
    leading young Marcius, Valeria, *and* Attendants.

My wife comes foremost; then the honour'd mould
Wherein this trunk was framed, and in her hand
The grandchild to her blood. But, out, affection!
All bond and privilege of nature, break!
Let it be virtuous to be obstinate.
What is that curt'sy worth? or those doves' eyes,
Which can make gods forsworn? I melt, and am not
Of stronger earth than others. My mother bows;
As if Olympus to a molehill should   30
In supplication nod: and my young boy
Hath an aspect of intercession, which
Great nature cries 'Deny not.' Let the Volsces
Plough Rome, and harrow Italy: I'll never
Be such a gosling to obey instinct, but stand,
As if a man were author of himself
And knew no other kin.
    Vir.   My lord and husband!
    Cor. These eyes are not the same I wore in
    Rome.
    Vir. The sorrow that delivers us thus changed
Makes you think so.
    Cor.   Like a dull actor now,   40
I have forgot my part, and I am out,
Even to a full disgrace. Best of my flesh,
Forgive my tyranny; but do not say
For that 'Forgive our Romans.' O, a kiss
Long as my exile, sweet as my revenge!
Now, by the jealous queen of heaven, that kiss
I carried from thee, dear; and my true lip
Hath virgin'd it e'er since. You gods! I prate,
And the most noble mother of the world
Leave unsaluted: sink, my knee, i' the earth; [*Kneels.* 50
Of thy deep duty more impression show
Than that of common sons.
    Vol.   O, stand up blest!
Whilst, with no softer cushion than the flint,
I kneel before thee; and unproperly
Show duty, as mistaken all this while
Between the child and parent.   [*Kneels.*
    Cor.   What is this?
Your knees to me? to your corrected son?
Then let the pebbles on the hungry beach
Fillip the stars; then let the mutinous winds
Strike the proud cedars 'gainst the fiery sun;   60
Murdering impossibility, to make
What cannot be, slight work.
    Vol.   Thou art my warrior;
I holp to frame thee. Do you know this lady?
    Cor. The noble sister of Publicola,
The moon of Rome, chaste as the icicle
That 's curdied by the frost from purest snow
And hangs on Dian's temple: dear Valeria!
    Vol. This is a poor epitome of yours,
Which by the interpretation of full time
May show like all yourself.
    Cor.   The god of soldiers,   70

---

itude to obliterate, or convert into hostility, rather than grow pitiful
by remembering what friends we were. 104. **shent,** blamed. 111. **die
by himself,** destroy himself. 112. **For,** as for. **that,** what. 113. **long,**
for a long time.
    Scene III. 3. **plainly,** openly. 6. **general suit,** petitions of all
Rome. 11. **godded,** deified. 18. **Nor . . . nor,** neither . . . nor. 34.
harrow, literal use, carrying strongly the meaning "distress, harass."
35. **gosling,** young goose; here, fool. 38-40. **These . . . so.** Coriolanus
says, "I see with different eyes from those I wore in Rome." Virgilia
replies, taking his words literally, "Our sorrow has changed us past
recognition." 41. **I am out,** I am at a loss. 48. **prate,** talk idly; so
Theobald; F: *pray.* 51. **more . . . show,** i.e., sink deeper into the

ground and display thy duty more plainly. 54. **unproperly,** improperly, i.e., unnaturally. 55. **as mistaken,** i.e., as if the obligation to
show reverence had been mistaken. 57. **corrected,** submissive to correction. 58. **hungry,** unfertile (Onions), hungry for shipwreck (Malone). 59. **Fillip,** flip, strike. 61. **Murdering,** removing. 62. **slight
work,** an easy task. 65. **moon of Rome,** allusion to Diana, goddess of
chastity. 66. **curdied,** congealed. 67. **Valeria.** According to Plutarch
it was this noble lady who suggested the visit of the women to the camp
of Coriolanus. 68. **poor epitome,** reference to the son of Coriolanus.
69. **by . . . time,** when time shall have fully developed his powers.

With the consent of supreme Jove, inform
Thy thoughts with nobleness; that thou mayst
   prove
To shame unvulnerable, and stick i' the wars
Like a great sea-mark, standing every flaw,
And saving those that eye thee!
   Vol.   Your knee, sirrah.
   Cor. That 's my brave boy!
   Vol. Even he, your wife, this lady, and myself,
Are suitors to you.
   Cor.   I beseech you, peace:
Or, if you 'ld ask, remember this before:
The thing I have forsworn to grant may never   80
Be held by you denials. Do not bid me
Dismiss my soldiers, or capitulate
Again with Rome's mechanics: tell me not
Wherein I seem unnatural: desire not
To allay my rages and revenges with
Your colder reasons.
   Vol.   O, no more, no more!
You have said you will not grant us any thing;
For we have nothing else to ask, but that
Which you deny already: yet we will ask;
That, if you fail in our request, the blame   90
May hang upon your hardness: therefore hear us.
   Cor. Aufidius, and you Volsces, mark; for we'll
Hear nought from Rome in private. Your request?
   Vol. Should we be silent and not speak, our
   raiment
And state of bodies would bewray what life
We have led since thy exile. Think with thyself
How more unfortunate than all living women
Are we come hither: since that thy sight, which
   should
Make our eyes flow with joy, hearts dance with
   comforts,
Constrains them weep and shake with fear and
   sorrow;   100
Making the mother, wife and child to see
The son, the husband and the father tearing
His country's bowels out. And to poor we
Thine enmity's most capital: thou barr'st us
Our prayers to the gods, which is a comfort
That all but we enjoy; for how can we,
Alas, how can we for our country pray,
Whereto we are bound, together with thy victory,
Whereto we are bound? alack, or we must lose
The country, our dear nurse, or else thy person,   110
Our comfort in the country. We must find
An evident calamity, though we had
Our wish, which side should win: for either thou
Must, as a foreign recreant, be led
With manacles thorough our streets, or else
Triumphantly tread on thy country's ruin,
And bear the palm for having bravely shed
Thy wife and children's blood. For myself, son,
I purpose not to wait on fortune till
These wars determine: if I cannot persuade thee   120
Rather to show a noble grace to both parts

Than seek the end of one, thou shalt no sooner
March to assault thy country than to tread—
Trust to 't, thou shalt not—on thy mother's womb,
That brought thee to this world.
   Vir.   Ay, and mine,
That brought you forth this boy, to keep your name
Living to time.
   Young Mar.   A' shall not tread on me;
I'll run away till I am bigger, but then I'll fight.
   Cor. Not of a woman's tenderness to be,
Requires nor child nor woman's face to see.   130
I have sat too long.   [*Rising*.
   Vol.   Nay, go not from us thus.
If it were so that our request did tend
To save the Romans, thereby to destroy
The Volsces whom you serve, you might
   condemn us,
As poisonous of your honour: no; our suit
Is, that you reconcile them: while the Volsces
May say 'This mercy we have show'd;' the
   Romans,
'This we received;' and each in either side
Give the all-hail to thee, and cry 'Be blest   139
For making up this peace!' Thou know'st, great son,
The end of war 's uncertain, but this certain,
That, if thou conquer Rome, the benefit
Which thou shalt thereby reap is such a name,
Whose repetition will be dogg'd with curses;
Whose chronicle thus writ: 'The man was noble,
But with his last attempt he wiped it out;
Destroy'd his country, and his name remains
To the ensuing age abhorr'd.' Speak to me, son:
Thou hast affected the fine strains of honour,
To imitate the graces of the gods;   150
To tear with thunder the wide cheeks o' the air,
And yet to charge thy sulphur with a bolt
That should but rive an oak. Why dost not speak?
Think'st thou it honourable for a noble man
Still to remember wrongs? Daughter, speak you:
He cares not for your weeping. Speak thou, boy:
Perhaps thy childishness will move him more
Than can our reasons. There 's no man in the
   world
More bound to 's mother; yet here he lets me prate
Like one i' the stocks. Thou hast never in thy life   160
Show'd thy dear mother any courtesy,
When she, poor hen, fond of no second brood,
Has cluck'd thee to the wars and safely home,
Loaden with honour. Say my request 's unjust,
And spurn me back: but if it be not so,
Thou art not honest; and the gods will plague thee,
That thou restrain'st from me the duty which
To a mother's part belongs. He turns away:
Down, ladies; let us shame him with our knees.
To his surname Coriolanus 'longs more pride   170
Than pity to our prayers. Down: an end;
This is the last: so we will home to Rome,
And die among our neighbours. Nay, behold 's:
This boy, that cannot tell what he would have,

73. **stick,** stand out. 80-81. **The . . . denials,** it would be unjust to regard me as refusing to grant what I have no longer the power of granting (Wright). 117. **bear the palm,** i.e., the emblem of victory. 120. **determine,** come to an end. 121. **parts,** sides. 129. **Not . . . be,** if you are not to yield to a womanly tenderness. 146. **attempt,** undertaking. **it,** i.e., the nobility. 151. **cheeks o' the air,** supposed reference to pictures of cherubs on old maps, or possibly pictures of the winds. 152. **sulphur,** supposed source of lightning. 159-160. **ᴘrate**

. . . stocks, talk uselessly like a prisoner in the stocks who has power to do nothing else. 162. **fond of,** desirous of. 163. **cluck'd,** marshaled as a hen her brood; F: *clock'd*. 171. **an end,** let us be done. 175. **fellowship,** company. 176. **reason,** argue for. 180. **dispatch,** dismissal, leave to go. 191. **convenient,** fitting, proper. 196. **sweat compassion,** weep with pity. 199. **Stand to,** stand by. 202. **former fortune,** fortune great as formerly. 204. **better witness,** i.e., formal document of peace. 205. **counter-seal'd,** sealed with an additional seal as

But kneels and holds up hands for fellowship,
Does reason our petition with more strength
Than thou hast to deny 't. Come, let us go:
This fellow had a Volscian to his mother;
His wife is in Corioli and his child
Like him by chance. Yet give us our dispatch: 180
I am hush'd until our city be afire,
And then I'll speak a little.
                    [*He holds her by the hand, silent.*
  Cor.   O mother, mother!
What have you done? Behold, the heavens do ope,
The gods look down, and this unnatural scene
They laugh at. O my mother, mother! O!
You have won a happy victory to Rome;
But, for your son,—believe it, O, believe it,
Most dangerously you have with him prevail'd,
If not most mortal to him. But, let it come.
Aufidius, though I cannot make true wars,   190
I'll frame convenient peace. Now, good Aufidius,
Were you in my stead, would you have heard
A mother less? or granted less, Aufidius?
  Auf. I was moved withal.
  Cor.   I dare be sworn you were:
And, sir, it is no little thing to make
Mine eyes to sweat compassion. But, good sir,
What peace you'll make, advise me: for my part,
I'll not to Rome, I'll back with you; and pray you,
Stand to me in this cause. O mother! wife!
  Auf. [*Aside*] I am glad thou hast set thy mercy and
        thy honour   200
At difference in thee: out of that I'll work
Myself a former fortune.
                    [*The Ladies make signs to Coriolanus.*
  Cor.   Ay, by and by;
                    [*To Volumnia, Virgilia, &c.*
But we will drink together; and you shall bear
A better witness back than words, which we,
On like conditions, will have counter-seal'd.
Come, enter with us. Ladies, you deserve
To have a temple built you: all the swords
In Italy, and her confederate arms,
Could not have made this peace.   [*Exeunt.*

SCENE IV. *Rome. A public place.*

Enter MENENIUS *and* SICINIUS.

  Men. See you yond coign o' the Capitol, yond
corner-stone?
  Sic. Why, what of that?
  Men. If it be possible for you to displace it with
your little finger, there is some hope the ladies of
Rome, especially his mother, may prevail with him.
But I say there is no hope in 't: our throats are
sentenced and stay upon execution.
  Sic. Is 't possible that so short a time can alter the
condition of a man?   10
  Men. There is differency between a grub and a

butterfly; yet your butterfly was a grub. This Marcius
is grown from man to dragon: he has wings; he 's
more than a creeping thing.
  Sic. He loved his mother dearly.
  Men. So did he me: and he no more remembers his
mother now than an eight-year-old horse. The tartness of his face sours ripe grapes: when he walks, he
moves like an engine, and the ground shrinks before
his treading: he is able to pierce a corslet with his eye;
talks like a knell, and his hum is a battery. He sits in
his state, as a thing made for Alexander. What he
bids be done is finished with his bidding. He wants
nothing of a god but eternity and a heaven to throne
in.   26
  Sic. Yes, mercy, if you report him truly.
  Men. I paint him in the character. Mark what
mercy his mother shall bring from him: there is no
more mercy in him than there is milk in a male tiger;
that shall our poor city find: and all this is long of you.
  Sic. The gods be good unto us!
  Men. No, in such a case the gods will not be good
unto us. When we banished him, we respected not
them; and, he returning to break our necks, they
respect not us.

Enter a Messenger.

  Mess. Sir, if you 'ld save your life, fly to your
        house:
The plebeians have got your fellow-tribune
And hale him up and down, all swearing, if   40
The Roman ladies bring not comfort home,
They'll give him death by inches.

Enter a second Messenger.

  Sic.   What 's the news?
  Sec. Mess. Good news, good news; the ladies have
        prevail'd,
The Volscians are dislodged, and Marcius gone:
A merrier day did never yet greet Rome,
No, not the expulsion of the Tarquins.
  Sic.   Friend,
Art thou certain this is true? is it most certain?
  Sec. Mess. As certain as I know the sun is fire:
Where have you lurk'd, that you make doubt of it?
Ne'er through an arch so hurried the blown tide,   50
As the recomforted through the gates. Why,
        hark you!
        [*Trumpets; hautboys; drums beat; all together.*
The trumpets, sackbuts, psalteries and fifes,
Tabors and cymbals and the shouting Romans,
Make the sun dance. Hark you!   [*A shout within.*
  Men.   This is good news:
I will go meet the ladies. This Volumnia
Is worth of consuls, senators, patricians,
A city full; of tribunes, such as you,
A sea and land full. You have pray'd well to-day:
This morning for ten thousand of your throats
I 'ld not have given a doit. Hark, how they joy!   60
                    [*Music still, with shouts.*

---

a further sanction.   208. **confederate arms,** weapons of the allies.
  SCENE IV. 1. **coign,** corner. 21-22. **talks . . . battery,** his voice
is a signal of death and his hum (exclamation) is as loud as a battery.
22-23. **as . . . Alexander,** as if it were the throne of Alexander the
Great (who, of course, is too late to be referred to in a play of this
period).   26. **throne,** be enthroned.   28. **in the character,** to the life.
44. **dislodged,** gone from their camp.   50. **Ne'er . . . tide.** The Yale
editor sees in this an allusion to the rush of the tide through the arches

of the old London Bridge. **blown,** swollen. 52. **sackbuts,** bass
trumpets with a slide like that of a trombone. **psalteries,** stringed
instruments played by plucking the strings. 53. **Tabors,** drums. 54.
sun dance. According to popular superstition the sun danced on Easter
Day.

Sic. First, the gods bless you for your tidings;
    next,
Accept my thankfulness.
    Sec. Mess.   Sir, we have all
Great cause to give great thanks.
    Sic.   They are near the city?
    Sec. Mess. Almost at point to enter.
    Sic.   We will meet them,
And help the joy.   [*Exeunt.*

SCENE V. *The same. A street near the gate.*

Enter two Senators *with* VOLUMNIA, VIRGILIA,
    VALERIA, &c. *passing over the stage, followed by
    Patricians, and others.*

First Sen. Behold our patroness, the life of Rome!
Call all your tribes together, praise the gods,
And make triumphant fires; strew flowers before
    them:
Unshout the noise that banish'd Marcius,
Repeal him with the welcome of his mother;
Cry 'Welcome, ladies, welcome!'
    All.   Welcome, ladies,
Welcome!   [*A flourish with drums and trumpets. Exeunt.*

SCENE VI. *Antium. A public place.*

Enter TULLUS AUFIDIUS, *with* Attendants.

Auf. Go tell the lords o' the city I am here:
Deliver them this paper: having read it,
Bid them repair to the market-place; where I,
Even in theirs and in the commons' ears,
Will vouch the truth of it. Him I accuse
The city ports by this hath enter'd and
Intends to appear before the people, hoping
To purge himself with words: dispatch.
                    [*Exeunt Attendants.*

Enter three or four Conspirators *of* AUFIDIUS' *faction.*

Most welcome!
    First Con. How is it with our general?
    Auf.   Even so   10
As with a man by his own alms empoison'd,
And with his charity slain.
    Sec. Con.   Most noble sir,
If you do hold the same intent wherein
You wish'd us parties, we'll deliver you
Of your great danger.
    Auf.   Sir, I cannot tell:
We must proceed as we do find the people.
    Third Con. The people will remain uncertain
        whilst
'Twixt you there's difference; but the fall of either
Makes the survivor heir of all.
    Auf.   I know it;

And my pretext to strike at him admits   20
A good construction. I raised him, and I pawn'd
Mine honour for his truth: who being so
        heighten'd,
He water'd his new plants with dews of flattery,
Seducing so my friends; and, to this end,
He bow'd his nature, never known before
But to be rough, unswayable and free.
    Third Con. Sir, his stoutness
When he did stand for consul, which he lost
By lack of stooping,—
    Auf.   That I would have spoke of:
Being banish'd for 't, he came unto my hearth;   30
Presented to my knife his throat: I took him;
Made him joint-servant with me; gave him way
In all his own desires; nay, let him choose
Out of my files, his projects to accomplish,
My best and freshest men; served his designments
In mine own person; holp to reap the fame
Which he did end all his; and took some pride
To do myself this wrong: till, at the last,
I seem'd his follower, not partner, and
He waged me with his countenance, as if   40
I had been mercenary.
    First Con.   So he did, my lord:
The army marvell'd at it, and, in the last,
When he had carried Rome and that we look'd
For no less spoil than glory,—
    Auf.   There was it:
For which my sinews shall be stretch'd upon him.
At a few drops of women's rheum, which are
As cheap as lies, he sold the blood and labour
Of our great action: therefore shall he die,
And I'll renew me in his fall. But, hark!   49
    [*Drums and trumpets sound, with great shouts of the
                    People.*

    First Con. Your native town you enter'd like a post,
And had no welcomes home; but he returns,
Splitting the air with noise.
    Sec. Con.   And patient fools,
Whose children he hath slain, their base throats tear
With giving him glory.
    Third Con.   Therefore, at your vantage,
Ere he express himself, or move the people
With what he would say, let him feel your sword,
Which we will second. When he lies along,
After your way his tale pronounced shall bury
His reasons with his body.
    Auf.   Say no more:
Here come the lords.   60

Enter the Lords *of the city.*

    All the Lords. You are most welcome home.
    Auf.   I have not deserved it.
But, worthy lords, have you with heed perused
What I have written to you?
    Lords.   We have.
    First Lord.   And grieve to hear 't.
What faults he made before the last, I think

Coriolanus
ACT V : SC IV

1146

SCENE V.   4. **Unshout,** recall, or cancel by more shouting.
SCENE VI.   5. **Him,** he whom.   20. **pretext,** intention.   23. **new
plants,** i.e., Volscians.   27. **stoutness,** obstinacy.   34. **files,** men in
depth from front to rear in a military formation in line; here generally
ranks, troops.   37. **Which . . . his,** which he did gather in as all his
own.   40. **waged,** remunerated.   **countenance,** patronage, favor.
43. **carried,** virtually carried, or might have carried.   45. **my . . .
stretch'd,** I shall exert all my strength.   46. **rheum,** tears.   57. **lies**

along, lies low.   58. **your . . . pronounced,** your statement of the case.
65. **fines,** penalties.   67-68. **answering . . . charge,** rewarding us with
our own expenses (Johnson).   68. **treaty,** compromise.   69. **yielding,**
i.e., complete victory for us.   72. **infected,** affected, or possibly contaminated.   75. **prosperously . . . attempted,** my warlike enterprise
has been prosperous.   96. **twist,** skein.   102. **No more,** say no more;
also explained as no more than a boy of tears.   104. **Too . . . it,**
swollen with rage so that his breast cannot contain it.   107. **notion,**

Might have found easy fines: but there to end
Where he was to begin and give away
The benefit of our levies, answering us
With our own charge, making a treaty where
There was a yielding,—this admits no excuse.
 Auf. He approaches: you shall hear him.   70

 Enter CORIOLANUS, *marching with drum and colours;*
  Commoners being with him.

 Cor. Hail, lords! I am return'd your soldier,
No more infected with my country's love
Than when I parted hence, but still subsisting
Under your great command. You are to know
That prosperously I have attempted and
With bloody passage led your wars even to
The gates of Rome. Our spoils we have brought
  home
Do more than counterpoise a full third part
The charges of the action. We have made peace
With no less honour to the Antiates   80
Than shame to the Romans: and we here deliver,
Subscribed by the consuls and patricians,
Together with the seal o' the senate, what
We have compounded on.
 Auf.   Read it not, noble lords;
But tell the traitor, in the high'st degree
He hath abused your powers.
 Cor. Traitor! how now!
 Auf.   Ay, traitor, Marcius!
 Cor.   Marcius!
 Auf. Ay, Marcius, Caius Marcius: dost thou
  think
I'll grace thee with that robbery, thy stol'n name
Coriolanus in Corioli?   90
You lords and heads o' the state, perfidiously
He has betray'd your business, and given up,
For certain drops of salt, your city Rome,
I say 'your city,' to his wife and mother;
Breaking his oath and resolution like
A twist of rotten silk, never admitting
Counsel o' the war, but at his nurse's tears
He whined and roar'd away your victory,
That pages blush'd at him and men of heart
Look'd wondering each at other.
 Cor.   Hear'st thou, Mars?   100
 Auf. Name not the god, thou boy of tears!
 Cor.   Ha!
 Auf. No more.
 Cor. Measureless liar, thou hast made my heart
Too great for what contains it. Boy! O slave!
Pardon me, lords, 'tis the first time that ever
I was forced to scold. Your judgements, my grave
  lords,
Must give this cur the lie: and his own notion—
Who wears my stripes impress'd upon him; that
Must bear my beating to his grave—shall join
To thrust the lie unto him.   110
 First Lord. Peace, both, and hear me speak.
 Cor. Cut me to pieces, Volsces; men and lads,

Stain all your edges on me. Boy! false hound!
If you have writ your annals true, 'tis there,
That, like an eagle in a dove-cote, I
Flutter'd your Volscians in Corioli:
Alone I did it. Boy!
 Auf.   Why, noble lords,
Will you be put in mind of his blind fortune,
Which was your shame, by this unholy braggart,
'Fore your own eyes and ears?
 All Consp.   Let him die for 't.   120
 All the people. 'Tear him to pieces.' 'Do it presently.'
'He killed my son.' 'My daughter.' 'He killed my
cousin Marcus.' 'He killed my father.'
 Sec. Lord. Peace, ho! no outrage: peace!
The man is noble and his fame folds-in
This orb o' the earth. His last offences to us
Shall have judicious hearing. Stand, Aufidius,
And trouble not the peace.
 Cor.   O that I had him,
With six Aufidiuses, or more, his tribe,   130
To use my lawful sword!
 Auf.   Insolent villain!
 All Consp. Kill, kill, kill, kill, kill him!
  [*The Conspirators draw, and kill Coriolanus: Aufidius
      stands on his body.*
 Lords.   Hold, hold, hold, hold!
 Auf. My noble masters, hear me speak.
 First Lord.   O Tullus,—
 Sec. Lord. Thou hast done a deed whereat valour
  will weep.
 Third Lord. Tread not upon him. Masters all, be
  quiet;
Put up your swords.
 Auf. My lords, when you shall know—as in this
  rage,
Provoked by him, you cannot—the great danger
Which this man's life did owe you, you'll rejoice
That he is thus cut off. Please it your honours   140
To call me to your senate, I'll deliver
Myself your loyal servant, or endure
Your heaviest censure.
 First Lord.   Bear from hence his body;
And mourn you for him: let him be regarded
As the most noble corse that ever herald
Did follow to his urn.
 Sec. Lord.   His own impatience
Takes from Aufidius a great part of blame.
Let 's make the best of it.
 Auf.   My rage is gone;
And I am struck with sorrow. Take him up.
Help, three o' the chiefest soldiers; I'll be one.   150
Beat thou the drum, that it speak mournfully:
Trail your steel pikes. Though in this city he
Hath widow'd and unchilded many a one,
Which to this hour bewail the injury,
Yet he shall have a noble memory.
Assist.
  [*Exeunt, bearing the body of Coriolanus. A dead
      march sounded.*

understanding, mind. 116. **Flutter'd,** so F_{3-4}; F_{1-2}: *Flatter'd,* retained
by Schmidt with the meaning fluttered or scared; Onions also retains
it. 118. **blind fortune,** luck in a reckless undertaking, or gift of
Fortune, the blind goddess. 126. **folds-in,** overspreads (Johnson).
128. **judicious,** judicial, or possibly rational, fair. 139. **Which . . .
owe you,** which while this man lived was owing to you, would sooner or
later have befallen you (Deighton). 145-146. **herald . . . urn.** In
Shakespeare's day a herald marshaled the funeral procession of noblemen deceased and proclaimed their rank and station. 150. **I'll be one.**
The play thus closes with the eulogy of Aufidius, whose admiration for
Coriolanus has been no less in evidence throughout the play than his
jealousy and implacable enmity. 152. **Trail . . . pikes.** Mournful music,
trailing pikes and banners were customary in a soldier's burial. 153.
unchilded, slain the children of.

The Period of the Romances, 1609-1616

With reference to Shakespeare's life and work from 1609 until his death in 1616 there is to be found a good deal of information and no small amount of praise. His connections with the theater no doubt grew less and less close until he abandoned the writing of plays about 1611 or 1612 and retired to Stratford. To what extent he had continued to perform as an actor no one can tell. Perhaps he had never been supremely important in that capacity. One imagines that his stays at his pleasant home in Stratford grew longer and his sojourns in London grew shorter as time went on and that finally he was able to turn over even the writing of plays to hands more fashionable than his, to Beaumont and Fletcher, Chapman, Webster, and Ben Jonson.

One could not, however, say that Shakespeare's latest work shows any noticeable diminution either in power or in spirit. He comes out of the period of gloom represented by the tragedies and the mirthless comedies (if there was such a period in his private life) and produces at least two plays which for pure and charming gayety are almost unrivaled, namely, *The Winter's Tale* and *The Tempest*. Nor can it be said that either *Cymbeline* or *Pericles* is lacking in dramatic vigor and natural charm. It has been usual to speak of the last group of plays as romances. This is an appropriate term in consideration of the fact that the plays of the period have something of the adventurous quality of the Greek romance and all, except possibly *The Tempest*, have ascertainable source connections with that widely influential form of literature.

It would, however, be better to think of the plays of the last period of Shakespeare's work, except *The Tempest*, as tragi-comedies, since this was probably the form that Shakespeare was consciously producing. Tragi-comedies are dramas having the elements of tragedy but without a fatal issue.

The Folio editors found the classification of *Cymbeline* puzzling, not knowing whether to place it among comedies or tragedies. That they chose to place it among the tragedies is an evidence of Shakespeare's success in writing tragi-comedy. That they had no doubt as to the classification of *The Winter's Tale* and *The Tempest* indicates that those two are merely romantic comedies with more than usually threatening features.

Pericles was a most popular play on the London stage, and it is a pity that we have so poor a version of it. In fact, it may be that *Pericles* is the original romance (leading up to tragi-comedy) of the group of plays produced by Shakespeare and by Beaumont and Fletcher. It is alluded to as a well-known play in a poem called *Pimlyco* in 1609, and it was probably a year or two old at that time. It stayed on the stage and was a popular success. Since it has the qualities later developed in the romances, or tragi-comedies, and since it was a popular play, one suspects that it may have been a determining influence on the drama. Shakespeare was at best responsible for only a part of it and possibly not a sufficient part to make the Folio editors regard it as his play. It may, all the same, have started him and his younger colleagues, Beaumont and Fletcher, on a new tack. The dates of *Philaster* and of *Cymbeline* are both uncertain, but there is no question of the priority of *Pericles*, which was actually in print by 1609.[1]

As for *Henry VIII* and *The Two Noble Kinsmen*, their qualities are too divergent to be associated readily with the major plays of this period.

Henry VIII was being played at the time (June 29, 1613) that the Globe Theatre was burned. A letter of Thomas Lorkin to Sir Thomas Puckering recounts the disaster as follows:

[1]See G. E. Bentley, "Shakespeare and the Blackfriars Theatre," *Shakespeare Survey* I (Cambridge, 1948), pp. 38-49; Hardin Craig, "*Pericles* and *The Painfull Adventures*," *Studies in Philology*, XLV (1948), 600-605.

No longer since than yesterday, while Burbage his company were acting at the Globe the play of Henry VIII, and there shooting off of certain chambers in way of triumph, the fire catched and fastened upon the thatch of the house, and there burned so furiously, as it consumed the whole house, and all in less than two hours, the people having enough to do to save themselves.

If the manuscripts belonging to the theater were stored at the Globe at the time of the fire, some enterprising persons must have done posterity a favor by carrying them out of harm's way. The manuscripts may, of course, have been stored at the Blackfriars Theatre. The company moved to the Blackfriars and after a time proceeded with the erection of the new Globe. Shakespeare was one of the proprietors and continued to derive an income from its operation. Otherwise he seems to have had no connection with it.

LITERARY ALLUSIONS

The story of the last, as of other periods of Shakespeare's life, presents its quota of panegyrics on the poet. John Davies of Hereford in *The Scourge of Folly* (1611?) thus apostrophizes him:

To our English Terence, Mr. Will. Shake-speare.

Some say (good Will)—which I in sport do sing—
Had'st thou not played some kingly parts in sport,
Thou hadst been a companion for a king,
And been a king among the meaner sort.
Some others rail; but, rail as they think fit,
Thou hast no railing but a reigning wit,
And honesty thou sow'st, which they do reap,
So to increase their stock which they do keep.

The following wretched sonnet is from *Run, ana a Great Cast* (1614) by Thomas Freeman:

To Master W. Shakespeare

Shakespeare, that nimble Mercury, thy brain,
   Lulls many hundred Argus-eyes asleep,
So fit for all thou fashionest thy vein.
   At the horse-foot fountain thou hast drunk full deep:
Virtue's or vice's theme to thee all one is.
   Who loves chaste life, there's Lucrece for a teacher;
Who list read lust, there's Venus and Adonis,
   True model of a most lascivious lecher.
Besides in plays thy wit winds like Meander,
   Whence needy new-composers borrow more
Than Terence doth from Plautus and Menander.
   But to praise thee aright I want thy store.
Then let thine own works thine own worth upraise,
And help t' adorn thee with deserved bays.

A truer picture of the actual contemporary view of Shakespeare can perhaps be had from the following excerpt from the Induction to Ben Jonson's *Bartholomew Fair:*

If there be never a servant-monster i' the Fair, who can help it, he [the author] says; nor a nest of antics? He is loath to make nature afraid in his plays, like those that beget *Tales, Tempests*, and such like drolleries—to mix his head with other men's heels.

From this it is apparent that Ben Jonson did not admire *The Tempest*, and if by "a nest of antics" and "such like drolleries" he refers, as Brooke suggests, to the tricks of Autolycus and the anti-mask in *The Winter's Tale* as well, it is also apparent that he does not approve of that play.

Shakespeare was out of style and the vogue was perhaps with Jonson and the younger dramatists. One wonders if Shakespeare quit writing for the stage for that reason. John Webster certainly borrowed extensively from him both in language and technique. But in the address prefixed to his *White Devil* in 1612, after he has heartily praised Ben Jonson, Chapman, and Beaumont and Fletcher, he makes a vague and patronizing reference to "the right happy and copious industry of Master Shakespeare, Master Decker, and Master Heywood."

LATEST RECORDS

Shakespeare also purchased at least one more piece of real estate, for what purpose it is impossible to guess. This was a house in Blackfriars, London, in 1613. He did not pay the full purchase price, and the mortgage deed executed for the unpaid balance furnishes one of the six absolutely unquestioned examples of his signature.

John Combe, a wealthy bachelor of Stratford and Shakespeare's friend, left him a legacy of five pounds in his will, which was put into execution in July 1614.

Shakespeare was also consulted by various persons at Stratford during the popular resistance to William Combe's attempt to enclose Welcombe Common. Shakespeare was on friendly terms with Combe and

A ship from Drayton's "Poly-Olbion," 1612. (Folger)

Will Sommers, jester to King Henry VIII. (Huntington)

than ten years. Shakespeare admits that, at the solicitation of Mountjoy's wife, he had acted as an intermediary in the arrangement of the marriage between Belott and Mountjoy's daughter. There is some apparent hesitation in his testimony, as if, though willing to do justice to the son-in-law, he had no desire to involve his former landlord.

Shakespeare's will is dated March 24, 1616, almost exactly a month before his death. Handwriting experts have decided from the imperfect character of the three signatures endorsed on each of the three pages of the will that Shakespeare was ill at the time the will was executed. They have even suggested that his hand was at the time affected with something like palsy. On the testimony of the somewhat unreliable vicar of Stratford, John Ward, one is asked to believe that Michael Drayton and Ben Jonson visited Shakespeare at New Place in the spring of 1616, and had a "merry meeting, but it seems drank too hard, for Shakespeare died of a feavour there contracted."

The will disposes of all of the property of which Shakespeare is known to have died possessed, the greater share of it going to his daughter Susanna. A fair sum went to his daughter Judith, who was married that year to Thomas Quyny. There were legacies to various relatives and friends, ten pounds to the poor of Stratford, his sword to Mr. Thomas Combe, 28s. 8d. apiece to five Stratford friends and to his fellows John Heminges, Richard Burbage, and Henry Condell to buy them mourning rings.

An interlineation contains the bequest of his "second best bed with the furniture" to his wife and is the only mention of her name in the will. It has been pointed out that her dower rights to one-third of all freehold property were not subject to bequest and that, in an age when beds were relatively much more valuable than they are now, even a second best bed might be a proper legacy. However, the will shows no great solicitude for her comfort. A good deal has been made of this in the attempt to establish the truth of a conjecture that Shakespeare was not happy with his wife. But in the will there is really no ground for the supposition. New Place was to be the home of Shakespeare's favorite daughter Susanna, wife of the distinguished physician Dr. John Hall. Mrs. Shakespeare would make her home with her daughter and with her dower rights secured by law would be quite as wealthy as she would need to be. There was, moreover, a local tradition which credited her with the wish to be buried in the grave with her husband.

The date of Shakespeare's death, April 23, 1616, is inscribed on his monument, which is an elaborate structure standing in the chancel of Trinity Church. It was built by the London sculptors Garret and Nicholas Johnson before 1623. To what extent it was tampered with at a later time is not certain. The full epitaph is as follows:

Judicio Pylium, genio Socratem, arte Maronem:
Terra tegit, populus mæret, Olympus habet.

at the same time had property interests involved, so that he was apparently consulted as an important and fair-minded citizen. Combe attempted to secure Shakespeare's support of his high-handed project by executing a contract under the terms of which Shakespeare's own interests would be protected. The matter is obscure, and one wishes that more light might be thrown upon it.[2]

One of the most interesting documents from the later period was discovered by C. W. Wallace in the Public Record Office in 1909. It consists of the records of a lawsuit entered into in 1612 by Stephen Belott against his father-in-law Christopher Mountjoy, a Huguenot wigmaker who lived in St. Olave's parish, Silver Street, London, in order to secure the payment of a dower promised at the time of the marriage. In this suit Shakespeare was summoned as a witness and made deposition on five interrogatories. It turns out that Shakespeare was a lodger in Mountjoy's house at the time of the marriage in 1604 and probably was for some time before that, since he states in his testimony that he had known Mountjoy for more

[2]Mrs. C. C. Stopes, *Shakespeare's Environment*, pp. 81 ff. and pp. 336 ff.

Stay, passenger, why goest thou by so fast?
Read, if thou canst, whom envious death hath placed
Within this monument: Shakespeare, with whom
Quick nature died; whose name doth deck this tomb
Far more than cost; sith all that he hath writ
Leaves living art but page to serve his wit.

Obiit anno domini 1616. Ætatis 53. Die 23 Apr.

These lines, which seem to indicate, as well as anything could, the high reputation in which Shakespeare was held as a poet at the time of his death, are not so well known as those inscribed over Shakespeare's grave near the north wall of the chancel. A local tradition assigns them to Shakespeare himself and implies that he wrote them "to suit the capacity of clerks and sextons," whom he wished apparently to frighten out of the idea of digging up his bones and placing them in the charnel house near which he was buried. They have been regarded both as the merest doggerel and as verse possessed of grotesque and rustic power:

Good frend, for Iesus sake forbeare
To dig the dust enclosed heare;
Bleste be ye man y^t spares thes stones,
And curst be he y^t moves my bones.

OTHER DRAMATISTS

The outstanding feature in the history of English drama during the period from 1608 to 1616, aside from the last plays of Shakespeare, is the appearance of the famous literary partners Francis Beaumont (1584?-1616) and John Fletcher (1579-1625). Both were men of good family and both were well educated. They were intimate friends, and tradition says that they lived together on the Bankside and were both "sealed of the tribe of Ben"; that is, they were of the group of young men who frequented the Mermaid Tavern and listened to the words of wisdom of the great and dominant, if not domineering, Ben Jonson. The following quotation comes from *Master Francis Beaumont's Letter to Ben Jonson*:

Methinks the little wit I had is lost
Since I saw you! For wit is like a rest
Held up at tennis, which men do best
With the best gamesters. What things have we seen
Done at the Mermaid! heard words that have been
So nimble, and so full of subtle flame,
As if that every one from whence they came
Had meant to put his whole wit in a jest,
And had resolved to live a fool the rest
Of his dull life!

Although Beaumont and Fletcher were very different from each other, the qualities that each had seem to have reinforced and balanced those of the other, each mind supplying what the other lacked. Beaumont is believed to have been superior to Fletcher in constructive power and poetic imagination. To him are attributed the pictures of innocent maidenhood which are found in the plays, the more individualized characterization, and the ability to maintain suspense. His blank verse style is less man-

nered than that of Fletcher and more like that of Webster and Shakespeare. Fletcher is noted for lyrical sweetness, rhetorical fluency, and a realistic grasp of commoner human traits. He is the master of dialogue and of comic inventiveness. His blank verse style verges on prose, because of his use of extra syllables at the caesura and at the end of the line, thus giving better the effect of conversation. One attributes to Fletcher the typical parts, such as the blunt soldier and the gay young libertine.

Both men are aristocratic to a point of infatuation with royalty, both romantic, both sentimental. Probably both of them are responsible for the most obvious quality of their work, their sensationalism, their use of surprise. Certainly Beaumont had a share in it, and certainly Fletcher was a master of the art of piling event on event until the last possibility of sensational surprise and sentimental emotion is exhausted.

Their partnership was short lived, for Beaumont died in 1616. Yet so vital was it that all of the many works of Fletcher subsequent to Beaumont's death, works done in collaboration with Massinger, Field, Daborne, Middleton, and others, were collected in 1647 and published under the names of Beaumont and Fletcher. Indeed, they are still so known.

The two authors may have been working together as early as 1606, and their partnership must have been in full swing in 1609, to which year is ordinarily assigned *Philaster*, the typical play in the new mode. *The Woman Hater* (1606?) and *The Knight of the Burning Pestle* (1607), both comedies, are regarded as

A shepherdess, from Philip Stubbes' "Anatomy of Abuses." (Folger)

The Period of the Romances, 1609–1616

1151

substantially the work of Beaumont alone; *Philaster* (1609?), tragi-comedy, *The Maid's Tragedy* (1611?), tragedy, *A King and No King* (1611), tragi-comedy, *Cupid's Revenge* (1612), tragedy, *The Scornful Lady* (1613-1616), comedy of manners, are the result of collaboration between Beaumont and Fletcher; and *The Faithful Shepherdess* (1608-1609), pastoral comedy, *Bonduca* (1609-1614), tragedy, *Monsieur Thomas* (1610-1616), comedy, and *Valentinian* (1610-1614), tragedy, are the work of Fletcher alone. These are the principal plays written by the two men jointly or severally during the period we are considering.

It is, however, only with *Philaster*, and perhaps others of the earlier plays, that we have to do in connection with the dramas of Shakespeare. It has been the habit to think of Shakespeare as having been influenced in his earlier years by Marlowe and his contemporaries, of his having influenced in some measure his own contemporaries and dominated his successors. It is perfectly obvious, however, that Jonson, and probably Chapman, were more potent influences on Shakespeare's successors than was Shakespeare himself. The really surprising idea is that Shakespeare may, so to speak, have been influenced by his successors. That is, when Beaumont and Fletcher captured the public ear with *Philaster*, Shakespeare may actually have modified his dramatic form to agree with the new fashion.

This idea was put forward by A. H. Thorndike in 1901.[3] It is not a perfectly acceptable idea but, nevertheless, has a great deal to commend it. Shakespeare introduced masques into *Cymbeline* and *The Tempest*. There is a sensational quality in the plot of *Cymbeline* like that of *Philaster*, a use of surprise in *The Winter's Tale*, and an increase in the element of adventure in all the latest plays quite in conformity with the new drama of Beaumont and Fletcher.

But it is easy to exaggerate these resemblances. There is plenty of action in most of Shakespeare's plays, no little melodrama, and a good deal of romance and adventure. He is also fond of sentiment, which is indeed one of his greatest charms. The suggestion has been made earlier that Shakespeare himself may have started, not necessarily the whole movement—it would be too much to claim that—but at least so much of that movement as he himself ever participated in, with the play of *Pericles*.

During this period Middleton was still writing comedies, such as *A Chaste Maid in Cheapside* (1611), and had not yet begun his great career in serious drama in which he was to produce with Rowley *A Fair Quarrel* (1617) and *The Changeling* (1623), and by himself *Women Beware Women* (1625-1627).

In this period Jonson further secured his fame for all time with *The Alchemist* in 1610, and produced his second stiff classical tragedy, *Catiline his Conspiracy*, in 1611 and his typical comedy of manners, *Bartholomew Fair*, in 1614.

Dekker was chiefly engaged in writing pamphlets (*The Gull's Hornbook* in 1609) and in dramatic collaboration, his best dramatic work having already been done.

John Webster wrote his second great tragic masterpiece, *The Duchess of Malfi*, in 1613 or 1614.

Massinger had so far appeared only as a collaborator with Fletcher, Field, and Daborne in the production of plays for the King's Company.

During this period Chapman did his greatest work. He had a genius for ethical thought, and when he was genuinely moved, and not merely inflated with learning and pedantry, was capable of great poetry. *Bussy D'Ambois* had been written in 1604. He followed this with *Charles, Duke of Byron* (1608), possibly his greatest play, *The Revenge of Bussy D'Ambois* (1610?), *Chabot, Admiral of France* (1613?), and in the enlightening play *Caesar and Pompay* (1613?). The mass of serious thought that went into the composition of this group of tragedies makes them a worthy contribution to English drama.

Of Shakespeare's work in this period, *Cymbeline* is dated 1609-1610; *The Winter's Tale*, 1611; *The Tempest*, 1611; *Henry VIII*, 1613. *Pericles*, 1607, must be listed here because of its kinship with other plays of the period.

DOWDEN ON THE ROMANCES

The comments of Edward Dowden in the last chapter of his book, *Shakspere, His Mind and Art*, on Shakespeare's final period—a period which Dowden himself may almost be said to have discovered—are possibly the finest ever made. "In the latest plays of Shakspere," he says, "the sympathetic reader may discern unmistakably a certain abandonment of the common joy of the world, a certain remoteness from the usual pleasures and sadnesses of life, and, at the same time, all the more, this tender bending over those who are, like children, still absorbed in their individual joys and sorrows." He goes on,

Over the beauty of youth and the love of youth, there is shed, in these plays of Shakspere's final period, a clear yet tender luminousness not elsewhere to be perceived in his writings. In his earlier plays, Shakspere writes concerning young men and maidens—their loves, their mirth, their griefs—as one who is among them; who has a lively, personal interest in their concerns; who can make merry with them, treat them familiarly, and, if need be, can mock them into good sense. There is nothing in these early plays wonderful, strangely beautiful, pathetic, about youth and its joys and sorrows. In the histories and tragedies, as was to be expected, more massive, broader, or more profound objects of interest engage the poet's imagination. But in these latest plays, the beautiful pathetic light is always present. There are the sufferers, aged, experienced, tried—Queen Katharine, Prospero, Hermione. And over against these are the children, absorbed in their happy and exquisite egoism—Perdita and Miranda, Florizel and Ferdinand, and the boys of old Belarius.[4]

---

[3]A. H. Thorndike, *The Influence of Beaumont and Fletcher on Shakespeare* (Worcester, Mass., 1901).

[4]Dowden, *op. cit.*, pp. 415-416. For references on Shakespeare's life and work, see page 79.

COMEDIES OF THE FOURTH PERIOD

Pericles

The first mention of *Pericles* is found in the Stationers' Register under the date May 20, 1608:

Edward Blount. Entred for his copie vnder thandes of Sir George Buck knight and Master Warden Seton A booke called the booke of Pericles prynce of Tyre.

No edition is known following on this entry. However, the next year a puzzling text of the play appeared in quarto published by Henry Gossen. It was reissued the same year. Reprints were subsequently published in 1611, 1619, 1630, and 1635. The play was printed in the Third Folio in 1664 with six other plays which are certainly not Shakespeare's. These were reprinted in the Fourth Folio, 1685, and included by Nicholas Rowe in his editions of 1709 and 1714. Alexander Pope excluded the seven plays from his edition in 1725, and no editor reintroduced any of them until Malone put *Pericles* back in the canon by including it in his edition of 1790. Since that time all editors have allowed *Pericles* a place among Shakespeare's plays.

DATE AND SIGNIFICANCE

A play of Pericles was written about 1607. T. S. Graves discovered data, not accepted by Chambers, which indicate that the play was acted in the public theaters in the winter of 1606-1607.[1] In the *Calendar of State Papers*, Venetian, he found a statement that a Venetian ambassador named Giustinian went with the French ambassador and his wife to a presentation of *Pericles*, which cost him twenty crowns. Giustinian was in London from January 5, 1606, to November 23, 1608. From the correspondence between Giustinian and the French ambassador, Boderie, and from records of the plague which show

when the theaters were closed, Graves arrived at the conclusion that the date of this particular performance fell within the period above named. He found also that this Venetian Giustinian was attempting during that time to get permission to export a shipment of grain to Venice. He infers that Giustinian paid the twenty crowns for a performance of this play, which pictures Pericles as a benefactor to Tarsus in that he gave the citizens grain, in order to incite the ambition of James I to be a similar benefactor to Venice.

The text of the play, as we have it, is so irregular that the stylistic tests used in dating the plays are uncertain in determining its date. Other circumstances, however, corroborate the date 1606-1607, the consideration of which involves a discussion of the sources.

SOURCE AND AUTHORSHIP

In 1607 a translation by Lawrence Twine of the romance of Apollonius of Tyre was republished. This romance is the source of the Pericles story. The translation was entered in the Stationers' Register in 1576, and was printed (perhaps the second edition) about 1594. The popularity of the play probably prompted the reappearance of the Twine version in 1607. The story is also found in Gower's *Confessio Amantis*.

Pericles follows Twine very closely as to incident. The playwright, however, made use of the *Confessio Amantis*, since Gower appears throughout the play as "Chorus." Many changes have been made in the play in the names of characters. The brothel scene is somewhat refined in the play, a detail for which Shakespeare is given the credit.

In 1608 another prose version by George Wilkins appeared with the title page:

The Painfull Aduentures of *Pericles* Prince of Tyre. Being the true History of the Play of Pericles, as it was lately presented by the worthy and ancient poet Iohn Gower. At London *Printed* by T. P. *for* Nat: Butter, 1608.

The statement here that the novel is "a true History of the Play of Pericles" seems adequate proof that the play is the earlier of the two. There can be no doubt that one is closely patterned after the other. The striking parallel in passages and the peculiarity of details can admit of no other possibility. But it was not the play of *Pericles* as we have it that Wilkins made into a novel. On the basis of similarities between the novel and the play and their correspondence in style with other known work of Wilkins, the majority of critics ascribe to Wilkins the first authorship of the play and to Shakespeare the revision of it.[2] Recently

Pericles

1153

[1]"On the Date and Significance of *Pericles*," *Modern Philology*, XIII (1916), 545-566.

[2]Fleay, *Life and Work of Shakespeare*, pp. 158-159; Delius, *Shakespeare Jahrbuch*, III, 175-204; R. Boyle, New Shakespeare Society *Transactions*, 1882, pp. 313-340. For a fresher view see Harry T. Baker, "The Relation of *Pericles* to George Wilkins' Novel," *PMLA*, XXIII (1908), 100-118, H. Dugdale Sykes in *Sidelights on Shakespeare* (Stratford, 1919), and Chambers, *William Shakespeare*, I, 518-528. For evidence against Wilkins' authorship see Sina Spiker, "George Wilkins and the Authorship of *Pericles*," *Studies in Philology*, XXX (1933), 551-570.

the play has been assigned as a whole to Thomas Heywood, with Shakespeare recognized as only a reviser.[3]

What happened was this: Wilkins based his novel on a play about Pericles which is now lost, and Shakespeare revised that same play into the form of *Pericles* as we have it. A general agreement between *Pericles* and Wilkins' *The Painfull Adventures* with many parallels has long been familiar to students of Shakespeare.[4] Wilkins amplified his narrative from Twine's *The Patterne of Painefull Adventures* and so went further in the telling of the Apollonius story than the old play went. He had no manuscript of the play before him and seems to have used notes based on a theatrical performance. He repeats, for example, the riddle with a fair degree of accuracy, but most set speeches, such as the epitaph of Marina, are faultily reproduced. He often confuses the narrative and describes gestures and actions he had presumably seen on the stage. There was one clear and significant difference between the lost play as Wilkins reports it and *Pericles* as we have it. This is in the management of the brothel scenes and in the character and motives of Lysimachus. One sees that these differences are the result of a revision of the old play after and not before Wilkins wrote his novel.

The play whose story Wilkins retells presented Lysimachus as a customer of the brothel, a thing which he acknowledged. The point of the old story is that Marina converted him; indeed, the conversion of licentious men was her special aptitude and ability. By her eloquence she saves herself from Lysimachus, from various visitors to the house of ill fame, and from a final dangerous assault by the pandar who in *Pericles* bears the name of Boult. She ruined the business of the brothel, and one may believe that this was a main interest, both comical and serious, of the old tale. This aspect of her situation is not absent from *Pericles*, but in the revision is mainly presented in a short scene, the fifth of the fourth act. There are traces in *Pericles* of Lysimachus in the older role, but his conversation with Marina shows that his part may be fairly interpreted as like that of the duke in *Measure for Measure*, an observer of the wickedness of his city and not a participant in it. He declares that he did not bring "hither a corrupted mind" and that he came "with no ill intent." He curses Boult, condemns the place, and says other things which show that the reviser meant to make of him an acceptable lover for the chaste Marina.

In the first act of *Pericles* Wilkins' report (exclusive of borrowings from Twine) is so faithful that there is

no ground for suspecting extensive revision. The second act is also, in general, very carefully reproduced. The superior style of the third act of *Pericles* has caused many critics to regard it as the work of Shakespeare. A comparison with Wilkins, however, reveals few differences in plot, but Shakespeare may have made a good many revisions in style.

The important revision of the plot begins with the first scene of the fourth act. The material of the brothel scenes is pretty much the same in both novel and play, but the arrangement and the dramatization are much more skillful in *Pericles*. The fifth act has also been completely revised. The contrivance in Wilkins by means of which Pericles comes to recognize Marina as his daughter is not bad, but the reviser rejected it. In *The Painfull Adventures* Marina reproves Pericles for his obduracy in grief, so that he grows angry and strikes her. Her face bleeds and she weeps and recounts her own pitiful sufferings, thus her identity. The matter is handled with more subtlety in *Pericles*, however, not with greater pathos.

Definite evidence of revision makes it possible to determine with some assurance the nature of the document from which the *Pericles* quarto was printed. One sees that it is not a "bad" quarto, "stolne and surreptitious," but from the points of view of adequacy and completeness appears to be a good quarto, the result of painstaking and successful revision. The badness of the text has been greatly exaggerated, since most of its errors are due to the printer and since there are no major confusions and obscurities.

What has made the text seem worse than it is, is the fact that no Shakespearean text, except possibly the 1608 version of *King Lear*, has so much verse printed as prose. This is no casual matter to be accounted for as marginal revision. One is obliged to conclude that the reviser wrote a great deal of his verse in the form of prose, a practice not without parallel in Elizabethan manuscripts and of which there are other cases in Shakespearean texts.

There are no signs of the prompter's hand in the text. This might indicate that the manuscript back of the printed quarto had never been used in the theater. The obvious inference is, therefore, that it was that manuscript on which the reviser had worked. If so, a good deal of the manuscript of *Pericles* was in Shakespeare's own hand. The supposition that we have to do with a revised copy would account for the relative correctness of the Gower prologues and of the earlier part of the play. It would also account for those apparently metrical parts of Wilkins' prose for which there are no equivalents in *Pericles*, since, if such parts existed in the old play, they were not included in the revision. It is precisely the revised parts of *Pericles* that have been universally regarded as Shakespearean.[5] As to

[3]See H. D. Gray, "Heywood's *Pericles*, Revised by Shakespeare," *PMLA*, XL (1925), 507-529; D. L. Thomas, "On the Play *Pericles*," *Englische Studien*, XXXIX (1908), 210-239.

[4]See "Mr. Collier's Introduction." *The Patterne of painefull Adventures:* Containing the most excellent, variable and pleasant Historie of the strange accidents that befell unto Prince Apollonius, the Lady Lucina his wife, and Tharsia his daughter . . . Gathered into English by Laurence Twine, Gent. (London, n.d.), *Shakespeare's Library*, ed. W. C. Hazlitt (1875), Vol. IV, 523-526 *et passim;* also Chambers, *loc. cit.*

[5]See the editor's "*Pericles* and *The Painfull Adventures*," *Studies in Philology*, LXV (1948), 600-605.

the authorship of the play of Pericles that Wilkins put into the form of a novel, there are few grounds for speculation.

Pericles AND THE ROMANCES

Pericles is thus the first of Shakespeare's romances and probably the beginning of that form of Jacobean drama. It shows striking resemblances to *Cymbeline*, *The Winter's Tale*, and *The Tempest*. The likeness between Marina in *Pericles* and Perdita in *The Winter's Tale* is obvious. The meeting between father and daughter, long separated, is suggestive of *Cymbeline*, and the reunion of Pericles and Thaisa anticipates that of Leontes and Hermione. Pericles and Cerimon, like Prospero, are wise and superior men in the Shakespearean gallery. To be sure, back of them lies Apollonius of Tyre, a great figure in the minds of many ages, whom the author of the old play re-named for the greatest Athenian of the greatest age of Athens. *Pericles*, like the romances, disregards considerations of time and place, delights in romantic improbabilities, and employs the obscure, compact style of the latest plays. *Pericles* was a popular play, and it seems possible that its use of the faraway and the long ago and other kinds of romantic mystification paved the way, not only for Shakespeare, but for Beaumont and Fletcher.[6]

STAGE HISTORY

The story of the play has been told thus at length because of its extraordinary popularity before the closing of the theaters in 1642. It is referred to again and again by writers, always with admiration and frequently with reference to its popularity. There is a record of its performance at court in 1619 and of its revival at the Globe Theatre as late as 1631. It will be seen that the play has many of the elements of Jacobean tragi-comedy and decadent romance. It abounds in sensational situations and surprises. The repulsiveness of certain parts of its theme are characteristic of the age. The early date of *Pericles*, its romantic story, and its sentimental beauty must have done much to set the style of the new drama.

Pericles has no recent stage history. Even the Restoration yawned over it, and it was not honored with an adaptation until that of George Lillo, who presented a modified version of the last two acts at Covent Garden in 1738. Samuel Phelps revived *Pericles* at Sadler's Wells Theater in London in 1854.

Since then it has rarely appeared on the stage, but it is worth noting that the production at the "Old Vic" in 1921 under the direction of Robert Atkins gave general satisfaction. This was also true of the performance of the play at the Shakespeare Memorial Theatre at Stratford in the summer of 1947.

[6]See G. E. Bentley, "Shakespeare and the Blackfriars Theatre," *Shakespeare Survey 1* (Cambridge, 1948), pp. 38-50.

Pericles

DRAMATIS PERSONAE

ANTIOCHUS, king of Antioch.
PERICLES, prince of Tyre.
HELICANUS,
ESCANES, } two lords of Tyre.
SIMONIDES, king of Pentapolis.
CLEON, governor of Tarsus.
LYSIMACHUS, governor of Mytilene.
CERIMON, a lord of Ephesus.
THALIARD, a lord of Antioch.
PHILEMON, servant to Cerimon.
LEONINE, servant to Dionyza.
Marshal.
A Pandar.
BOULT, his servant.

The Daughter of Antiochus.
DIONYZA, wife to Cleon.
THAISA, daughter to Simonides.
MARINA, daughter to Pericles and Thaisa.
LYCHORIDA, nurse to Marina.
A Bawd.

Lords, Knights, Gentlemen, Sailors, Pirates, Fishermen, and Messengers.

DIANA.

GOWER, as Chorus.

SCENE: *Dispersedly in various countries.*

ACT I.

Enter GOWER.

Before the palace of Antioch.

To sing a song that old was sung,
From ashes ancient Gower is come;
Assuming man's infirmities,
To glad your ear, and please your eyes.
It hath been sung at festivals,
On ember-eves and holy-ales;
And lords and ladies in their lives
Have read it for restoratives:
The purchase is to make men glorious;
Et bonum quo antiquius, eo melius.   10
If you, born in these latter times,
When wit 's more ripe, accept my rhymes,
And that to hear an old man sing
May to your wishes pleasure bring,
I life would wish, and that I might
Waste it for you, like taper-light.
This Antioch, then, Antiochus the Great
Built up, this city, for his chiefest seat;
The fairest in all Syria,
I tell you what mine authors say: 20
This king unto him took a fere,

Who died and left a female heir,
So buxom, blithe, and full of face,
As heaven had lent her all his grace;
With whom the father liking took,
And her to incest did provoke:
Bad child; worse father! to entice his own
To evil should be done by none:
But custom what they did begin
Was with long use account no sin.   30
The beauty of this sinful dame
Made many princes thither frame,
To seek her as a bed-fellow,
In marriage-pleasures play-fellow:
Which to prevent he made a law,
To keep her still, and men in awe,
That whoso ask'd her for his wife,
His riddle told not, lost his life:
So for her many a wight did die,
As yon grim looks do testify.   40
What now ensues, to the judgement of your eye
I give, my cause who best can justify.   [Exit.

SCENE I. *Antioch. A room in the palace.*

Enter ANTIOCHUS, PRINCE PERICLES, *and followers.*

Ant. Young prince of Tyre, you have at large
    received
The danger of the task you undertake.
    Per. I have, Antiochus, and, with a soul
Embolden'd with the glory of her praise,
Think death no hazard in this enterprise.
    Ant. Bring in our daughter, clothed like a bride,
For the embracements even of Jove himself;
At whose conception, till Lucina reign'd,
Nature this dowry gave, to glad her presence,
The senate-house of planets all did sit,   10
To knit in her their best perfections.

Music. Enter the Daughter of Antiochus.

    Per. See where she comes, apparell'd like the spring,
Graces her subjects, and her thoughts the king
Of every virtue gives renown to men!
Her face the book of praises, where is read
Nothing but curious pleasures, as from thence
Sorrow were ever razed, and testy wrath
Could never be her mild companion.
You gods that made me man, and sway in love,
That have inflamed desire in my breast   20
To taste the fruit of yon celestial tree,
Or die in the adventure, be my helps,
As I am son and servant to your will,
To compass such a boundless happiness!
    Ant. Prince Pericles,—
    Per. That would be son to great Antiochus.

Ant. Before thee stands this fair Hesperides,
With golden fruit, but dangerous to be touch'd;
For death-like dragons here affright thee hard:
Her face, like heaven, enticeth thee to view   30
Her countless glory, which desert must gain;
And which, without desert, because thine eye
Presumes to reach, all thy whole heap must die.
Yon sometimes famous princes, like thyself,
Drawn by report, adventurous by desire,
Tell thee, with speechless tongues and semblance pale,
That without covering, save yon field of stars,
Here they stand martyrs, slain in Cupid's wars;
And with dead cheeks advise thee to desist
For going on death's net, whom none resist.   40
    Per. Antiochus, I thank thee, who hath taught
My frail mortality to know itself,
And by those fearful objects to prepare
This body, like to them, to what I must;
For death remember'd should be like a mirror,
Who tells us life's but breath, to trust it error.
I'll make my will then, and, as sick men do
Who know the world, see heaven, but, feeling woe,
Gripe not at earthly joys as erst they did;
So I bequeath a happy peace to you   50
And all good men, as every prince should do;
My riches to the earth from whence they came;
But my unspotted fire of love to you.
                [*To the daughter of Antiochus.*
Thus ready for the way of life or death,
I wait the sharpest blow, Antiochus.
    Ant. Scorning advice, read the conclusion, then:
Which read and not expounded, 'tis decreed,
As these before thee thou thyself shalt bleed.
    Daugh. Of all say'd yet, mayst thou prove
    prosperous!
Of all say'd yet, I wish thee happiness!   60
    Per. Like a bold champion, I assume the lists,
Nor ask advice of any other thought
But faithfulness and courage.
                He reads the riddle.
    I am no viper, yet I feed
    On mother's flesh which did me breed.
    I sought a husband, in which labour
    I found that kindness in a father:
    He's father, son, and husband mild;
    I mother, wife, and yet his child.
    How they may be, and yet in two,   70
    As you will live, resolve it you.
Sharp physic is the last: but, O you powers
That give heaven countless eyes to view men's acts,
Why cloud they not their sights perpetually,
If this be true, which makes me pale to read it?
Fair glass of light, I loved you, and could still,
                [*Takes hold of the hand of the Princess.*
Were not this glorious casket stored with ill:

ACT I. PROLOGUE. **1. old,** of old. **2. ancient Gower,** the fourteenth-century poet, John Gower, who related the adventures of Apollonius of Tyre (of which *Pericles* is a version) in his *Confessio Amantis.* The stylistic affectations of the Gower parts are mainly due to the dramatist's attempt to reproduce the archaic language of an earlier century. **3. Assuming man's infirmities,** taking on a mortal body. **6. ember-eves,** evenings before the ember days—the periodic fast days which coincide with the four changes of the seasons. **holy-ales,** i.e., church ales or festivals. **10. Et . . . melius,** a good thing is better for being older. **11-13. If . . . that.** The construction of the clause is parallel; *if,* if that, a conjunction of common occurrence, is to be understood with *that* after *And.* **16. Waste,** spend. **21. fere,** spouse. **23. full of face,** florid (Onions); replete with every facial charm (Deighton). **29-30. But . . . sin,** custom—familiarity—bred of long use, made

what they began accounted no sin. **32. frame,** direct their steps. **36. and men,** and to keep men. **38. His riddle told not,** if his (Antiochus') riddle were not solved. **40. yon grim looks.** Gower points to the heads of unsuccessful suitors placed on the palace gate. **42. who.** The antecedent is *your eye.* **justify,** witness (Deighton).
    SCENE I. **8. Lucina,** goddess of childbirth, in her capacity as goddess of light; the line may mean, "during the period of gestation," i.e., from her conception until her birth. **9. this dowry,** may refer to something lost from the text. Deighton conjectured *rich dowry.* As it stands, the phrase may be equated with the fact that the planets conjoined favorably at her birth. **to glad,** to make gladsome. **14. gives,** which gives. **18. her mild companion,** companion of her mildness. **27. Hesperides,** correctly speaking, nymphs who guarded the golden fruit belonging to Juno. The name was frequently applied to the garden

But I must tell you, now my thoughts revolt;
For he 's no man on whom perfections wait
That, knowing sin within, will touch the gate.   80
You are a fair viol, and your sense the strings;
Who, finger'd to make man his lawful music,
Would draw heaven down, and all the gods, to
    hearken;
But being play'd upon before your time,
Hell only danceth at so harsh a chime.
Good sooth, I care not for you.
    Ant. Prince Pericles, touch not, upon thy life,
For that 's an article within our law,
As dangerous as the rest. Your time 's expired:
Either expound now, or receive your sentence.   90
    Per. Great king,
Few love to hear the sins they love to act;
'Twould braid yourself too near for me to tell it.
Who has a book of all that monarchs do,
He 's more secure to keep it shut than shown:
For vice repeated is like the wandering wind,
Blows dust in others' eyes, to spread itself;
And yet the end of all is bought thus dear,
The breath is gone, and the sore eyes see clear   99
To stop the air would hurt them. The blind mole casts
Copp'd hills towards heaven, to tell the earth is
    throng'd
By man's oppression; and the poor worm doth die for 't.
Kings are earth's gods; in vice their law 's their will;
And if Jove stray, who dares say Jove doth ill?
It is enough you know; and it is fit,
What being more known grows worse, to smother it.
All love the womb that their first being bred,
Then give my tongue like leave to love my head.
    Ant. [*Aside*] Heaven, that I had thy head! he has
    found the meaning:
But I will gloze with him.—Young prince of Tyre,   110
Though by the tenour of our strict edict,
Your exposition misinterpreting,
We might proceed to cancel of your days;
Yet hope, succeeding from so fair a tree
As your fair self, doth tune us otherwise:
Forty days longer we do respite you;
If by which time our secret be undone,
This mercy shows we'll joy in such a son:
And until then your entertain shall be
As doth befit our honour and your worth.   120
    [*Exeunt all but Pericles.*
    Per. How courtesy would seem to cover sin,
When what is done is like an hypocrite,
The which is good in nothing but in sight!
If it be true that I interpret false,
Then were it certain you were not so bad
As with foul incest to abuse your soul;
Where now you 're both a father and a son,
By your untimely claspings with your child,

Which pleasure fits an husband, not a father;
And she an eater of her mother's flesh,   130
By the defiling of her parent's bed;
And both like serpents are, who though they feed
On sweetest flowers, yet they poison breed.
Antioch, farewell! for wisdom sees, those men
Blush not in actions blacker than the night,
Will shun no course to keep them from the light.
One sin, I know, another doth provoke;
Murder 's as near to lust as flame to smoke:
Poison and treason are the hands of sin,
Ay, and the targets, to put off the shame: 140
Then, lest my life be cropp'd to keep you clear,
By flight I'll shun the danger which I fear.   [*Exit.*

            Re-enter ANTIOCHUS.

    Ant. He hath found the meaning, for which we mean
To have his head.
He must not live to trumpet forth my infamy,
Nor tell the world Antiochus doth sin
In such a loathed manner;
And therefore instantly this prince must die;
For by his fall my honour must keep high.
Who attends us there?

        Enter THALIARD.

    Thal.   Doth your highness call?   150
    Ant. Thaliard,
You are of our chamber, and our mind partakes
Her private actions to your secrecy;
And for your faithfulness we will advance you.
Thaliard, behold, here 's poison, and here 's gold;
We hate the prince of Tyre, and thou must kill him:
It fits thee not to ask the reason why,
Because we bid it. Say, is it done?
    Thal.   My lord,
'Tis done.
    Ant. Enough.   160

        Enter a Messenger.

Let your breath cool yourself, telling your haste.
    Mess. My lord, prince Pericles is fled.   [*Exit.*
    Ant.   As thou
Wilt live, fly after: and like an arrow shot
From a well-experienced archer hits the mark
His eye doth level at, so thou ne'er return
Unless thou say 'Prince Pericles is dead.'
    Thal. My lord,
If I can get him within my pistol's length,
I'll make him sure enough: so, farewell to your
    highness.
    Ant. Thaliard, adieu! [*Exit Thal.*] Till Pericles be
    dead,   170
My heart can lend no succour to my head.   [*Exit.*

where these fruits grew. Here it implies that the princess is the embodiment of all things rich; that she is without price. 29. **death-like dragons,** alludes to the dragon which guarded the garden of the Hesperides. 40. **For going on,** from entering. 44. **must,** must expect. 49. **Gripe,** clutch. 56. **conclusion,** problem, riddle. 59, 60. **say'd,** assayed, attempted. 61. **assume the lists,** undertake the combat. 64-65. **I am no viper,** etc. Seager (*Shakespeare's Natural History*, p. 331) quotes from Bartholomew, Trevisa's translation: "Viper is a manner kind of serpents that is full venomous, and hath that name for she bringeth forth brood by strength; for when her womb draweth to the time of whelping, the whelps abideth not convenable time nor kind passing, but gnaweth and fretteth the sides of their mother, and they come so into this world with strength and with the death of the mother." 79-80. **For . . . gate,** he, however perfect, is no man who, knowing sin to be

within, will touch the gate. Pericles is thinking of his own manhood and the loss of dignity he would suffer by a possible alliance with the contaminated princess. 88. **an article,** i.e., one of the conditions under which the riddle was attempted; cf. *Prologue*, 34-35. 93. **braid,** upbraid. 97. **to spread itself,** to allow itself free action. 101. **Copp'd,** peaked. **throng'd,** beset. 102. **worm,** creature; a common term of pity. 105. **you know,** i.e., that you know that I know your riddle. 110. **gloze,** talk smoothly and speciously. 112. **Your exposition misinterpreting,** since your exposition interprets wrongly. 114. **succeeding from,** resulting from. 119. **entertain,** entertainment. 121. **would seem,** speciously endeavors (Deighton); perhaps, doth seem. 128. **untimely,** ill-fitting. 134. **men,** i.e., men who. 152. **chamber,** council. **partakes,** imparts. 164. **From,** by. 171. **My . . . head,** I can have no confidence in anything which my thoughts can contrive.

SCENE II. *Tyre. A room in the palace.*

Enter PERICLES.

Per. [*To Lords without*] Let none disturb us.—Why
    should this change of thoughts,
The sad companion, dull-eyed melancholy,
Be my so used a guest as not an hour,
In the day's glorious walk, or peaceful night,
The tomb where grief should sleep, can breed me
    quiet?
Here pleasures court mine eyes, and mine eyes shun
    them,
And danger, which I fear'd, is at Antioch,
Whose arm seems far too short to hit me here:
Yet neither pleasure's art can joy my spirits,
Nor yet the other's distance comfort me. 10
Then it is thus: the passions of the mind,
That have their first conception by mis-dread,
Have after-nourishment and life by care;
And what was first but fear what might be done,
Grows elder now and cares it be not done.
And so with me: the great Antiochus,
'Gainst whom I am too little to contend,
Since he 's so great can make his will his act,
Will think me speaking, though I swear to silence;
Nor boots it me to say I honour him, 20
If he suspect I may dishonour him:
And what may make him blush in being known,
He'll stop the course by which it might be known;
With hostile forces he'll o'erspread the land,
And with the ostent of war will look so huge,
Amazement shall drive courage from the state;
Our men be vanquish'd ere they do resist,
And subjects punish'd that ne'er thought offence:
Which care of them, not pity of myself,
Who am no more but as the tops of trees, 30
Which fence the roots they grow by and defend
    them,
Makes both my body pine and soul to languish,
And punish that before that he would punish.

Enter HELICANUS, *with other* Lords.

First Lord. Joy and all comfort in your sacred breast!
Sec. Lord. And keep your mind, till you return to us,
Peaceful and comfortable!
Hel. Peace, peace, and give experience tongue.
They do abuse the king that flatter him:
For flattery is the bellows blows up sin;
The thing the which is flatter'd, but a spark, 40
To which that blast gives heat and stronger glowing;
Whereas reproof, obedient and in order,
Fits kings, as they are men, for they may err.
When Signior Sooth here does proclaim a peace,
He flatters you, makes war upon your life.
Prince, pardon me, or strike me, if you please;
I cannot be much lower than my knees.
  Per. All leave us else; but let your cares o'erlook
What shipping and what lading 's in our haven, 49

And then return to us. [*Exeunt Lords.*] Helicanus, thou
Hast moved us: what seest thou in our looks?
  Hel. An angry brow, dread lord.
  Per. If there be such a dart in princes' frowns,
How durst thy tongue move anger to our face?
  Hel. How dare the plants look up to heaven, from
    whence
They have their nourishment?
  Per.   Thou know'st I have power
To take thy life from thee.
  Hel. [*Kneeling*] I have ground the axe myself;
Do you but strike the blow.
  Per.   Rise, prithee, rise.
Sit down: thou art no flatterer: 60
I thank thee for it; and heaven forbid
That kings should let their ears hear their faults hid!
Fit counsellor and servant for a prince,
Who by thy wisdom makest a prince thy servant,
What wouldst thou have me do?
  Hel.   To bear with patience
Such griefs as you yourself do lay upon yourself.
  Per. Thou speak'st like a physician, Helicanus,
That minister'st a potion unto me
That thou wouldst tremble to receive thyself.
Attend me, then: I went to Antioch, 70
Where as thou know'st, against the face of death,
I sought the purchase of a glorious beauty,
From whence an issue I might propagate,
†Are arms to princes, and bring joys to subjects.
Her face was to mine eye beyond all wonder;
The rest—hark in thine ear—as black as incest:
Which by my knowledge found, the sinful father
Seem'd not to strike, but smooth: but thou know'st
    this,
'Tis time to fear when tyrants seem to kiss.
Which fear so grew in me, I hither fled, 80
Under the covering of a careful night,
Who seem'd my good protector; and, being here,
Bethought me what was past, what might succeed.
I knew him tyrannous; and tyrants' fears
Decrease not, but grow faster than the years:
And should he doubt it, as no doubt he doth,
That I should open to the listening air
How many worthy princes' bloods were shed,
To keep his bed of blackness unlaid ope,
To lop that doubt, he'll fill this land with arms, 90
And make pretence of wrong that I have done him;
When all, for mine, if I may call offence,
Must feel war's blow, who spares not innocence:
Which love to all, of which thyself art one,
Who now reprovest me for it,—
  Hel.   Alas, sir!
  Per. Drew sleep out of mine eyes, blood from my
    cheeks,
Musings into my mind, with thousand doubts
How I might stop this tempest ere it came;
And finding little comfort to relieve them,
I thought it princely charity to grieve for them. 100

SCENE II. 1. **change of thoughts,** usually explained as altered disposition of mind. *Change* more likely means succession; perhaps this is a figure from the change of a peal of bells. The altered disposition does not disturb Pericles' quiet so much as the recurrence of the thoughts which he recounts in the subsequent lines (cf. I, ii, 79-98, where the details are repeated). This passage both in its analysis of the passion of fear and in its recital of the substance of Pericles' fears corresponds to the sixteenth-century doctrine regarding fearful melancholy. Burton describes how persons suffering from this passion are subject to torment and perplexity of thoughts "which so much, so

continually, tortures and crucifies their souls." Cf. R. Anderson, *Elizabethan Psychology and Shakespeare's Plays*, p. 96. 15. **cares,** takes care. 18. **so great can,** so great that he can. 23. **it,** structurally redundant; the antecedent is the clause *what . . . known* (l. 22). 25. **ostent,** display. 31. **fence,** shield, shelter. 33. **he,** i.e., Antiochus. 35. **till you return to us.** Here the lords of Tyre appear to know of Pericles' departure. In the next scene we find that he left *unlicensed of their loves,* i.e., without their knowledge. The prose narratives which recount the same story state that his departure was accomplished secretly. This is one of the several inconsistencies of this rather garbled

Hel. Well, my lord, since you have given me leave to
    speak,
Freely will I speak. Antiochus you fear,
And justly too, I think, you fear the tyrant,
Who either by public war or private treason
Will take away your life.
Therefore, my lord, go travel for a while,
Till that his rage and anger be forgot,
Or till the Destinies do cut his thread of life.
Your rule direct to any; if to me,
Day serves not light more faithful than I'll be.   110
    Per. I do not doubt thy faith;
But should he wrong my liberties in my absence?
    Hel. We'll mingle our bloods together in the earth,
From whence we had our being and our birth.
    Per. Tyre, I now look from thee then, and to Tarsus
Intend my travel, where I'll hear from thee;
And by whose letters I'll dispose myself.
The care I had and have of subjects' good
On thee I lay, whose wisdom's strength can bear it.
I'll take thy word for faith, not ask thine oath: 120
Who shuns not to break one will sure crack both:
But in our orbs we'll live so round and safe,
That time of both this truth shall ne'er convince,
Thou show'dst a subject's shine, I a true prince.
                                                    [*Exeunt.*

SCENE III. *Tyre. An ante-chamber in the palace.*

Enter THALIARD.

Thal. So, this is Tyre, and this the court. Here must
I kill King Pericles; and if I do it not, I am sure to be
hanged at home: 'tis dangerous. Well, I perceive he
was a wise fellow, and had good discretion, that, being
bid to ask what he would of the king, desired he might
know none of his secrets: now do I see he had some
reason for 't; for if a king bid a man be a villain, he's
bound by the indenture of his oath to be one. Hush!
here come the lords of Tyre.   10

Enter HELICANUS *and* ESCANES, *with other* Lords *of
Tyre.*

    Hel. You shall not need, my fellow peers of Tyre,
Further to question me of your king's departure:
His seal'd commission, left in trust with me,
Doth speak sufficiently he's gone to travel.
    Thal. [*Aside*] How! the king gone!
    Hel. If further yet you will be satisfied,
Why, as it were unlicensed of your loves,
He would depart, I'll give some light unto you.
Being at Antioch——
    Thal.   [*Aside*] What from Antioch?   19
    Hel. Royal Antiochus—on what cause I know not—
Took some displeasure at him; at least he judged so:
And doubting lest that he had err'd or sinn'd,
To show his sorrow, he'ld correct himself;
So puts himself unto the shipman's toil,

With whom each minute threatens life or death.
    Thal. [*Aside*] Well, I perceive
I shall not be hang'd now, although I would;
But since he's gone, † the king's seas must please:
He 'scaped the land, to perish at the sea.
I'll present myself. Peace to the lords of Tyre!   30
    Hel. Lord Thaliard from Antiochus is welcome.
    Thal. From him I come
With message unto princely Pericles;
But since my landing I have understood
Your lord has betook himself to unknown travels,
My message must return from whence it came.
    Hel. We have no reason to desire it,
Commended to our master, not to us:
Yet, ere you shall depart, this we desire,
As friends to Antioch, we may feast in Tyre. [*Exeunt.* 40

SCENE IV. *Tarsus. A room in the Governor's house.*

Enter CLEON, *the governor of Tarsus, with* DIONYZA, *and
others.*

    Cle. My Dionyza, shall we rest us here,
And by relating tales of others' griefs,
See if 'twill teach us to forget our own?
    Dio. That were to blow at fire in hope to quench it;
For who digs hills because they do aspire
Throws down one mountain to cast up a higher.
O my distressed lord, even such our griefs are;
Here they 're but felt, and seen with mischief's eyes,
But like to groves, being topp'd, they higher rise.
    Cle. O Dionyza,   10
Who wanteth food, and will not say he wants it,
Or can conceal his hunger till he famish?
Our tongues and sorrows do sound deep
Our woes into the air; our eyes do weep,
Till tongues fetch breath that may proclaim them
    louder;
That, if heaven slumber while their creatures want,
They may awake their helps to comfort them.
I'll then discourse our woes, felt several years,
And wanting breath to speak help me with tears.
    Dio. I'll do my best, sir.   20
    Cle. This Tarsus, o'er which I have the government,
A city on whom plenty held full hand,
For riches strew'd herself even in the streets;
Whose towers bore heads so high they kiss'd the
    clouds,
And strangers ne'er beheld but wonder'd at;
Whose men and dames so jetted and adorn'd,
Like one another's glass to trim them by:
Their tables were stored full, to glad the sight,
And not so much to feed on as delight;
All poverty was scorn'd, and pride so great,   30
The name of help grew odious to repeat.
    Dio. O, 'tis too true.
    Cle. But see what heaven can do! By this our change,
These mouths, who but of late, earth, sea, and air,

text. 37. **give experience tongue,** let the experienced speak. 62.
hear . . . hid, hear words that gloss over their faults. 66. **Such griefs
. . . upon yourself,** such griefs as are only in your imagination (Deighton). 74. **Are,** which are, or such as are, the antecedent being in
the plural idea of *issue,* i.e., sons. 92. **for . . . offence,** for my offense—
if I may call it offense. 100. **grieve for,** so Q$_{1-4}$; Globe, after Malone:
grieve. 104. **treason,** treachery. 112. **he,** Antiochus. **my liberties,**
royal rights and prerogatives (Schmidt). 117. **by . . . myself,** i.e.,
I'll act upon the advices of your letters.
    SCENE III.   17. **unlicensed of your loves,** without your loving assent

(Deighton); cf. I, ii, 35, note. 24. **toil,** travail, hence dangers. 27.
would, i.e., would have been. 28. **the king's seas must please,** so
Q; several attempts to emend: *the king, seas must please* (Mason); *the
king it sure must please* (Percy, adopted by Steevens); *the king's ears
it must please* (Dyce).
    SCENE IV. 5. **digs,** removes. **aspire,** mount up. 8. **mischief's,**
calamity's. 15. **them,** i.e., *woes* (l. 14). 19. **help me,** i.e., you help
me. 23. **riches,** a singular concept, probably derived from the French
richesse, equivalent to "plenty"; Deighton explains the image as that of
the cornucopia being held aloft over the city. 26. **jetted,** strutted.

Were all too little to content and please,
Although they gave their creatures in abundance,
As houses are defiled for want of use,
They are now starved for want of exercise:
Those palates who, not yet two summers younger,
Must have inventions to delight the taste,   40
Would now be glad of bread, and beg for it:
Those mothers who, to nousle up their babes,
Thought nought too curious, are ready now
To eat those little darlings whom they loved.
So sharp are hunger's teeth, that man and wife
Draw lots who first shall die to lengthen life:
Here stands a lord, and there a lady weeping;
Here many sink, yet those which see them fall
Have scarce strength left to give them burial.
Is not this true?   50
    Dio. Our cheeks and hollow eyes do witness it.
    Cle. O, let those cities that of plenty's cup
And her prosperities so largely taste,
With their superfluous riots, hear these tears!
The misery of Tarsus may be theirs.

    Enter a Lord.

    Lord. Where 's the lord governor?
    Cle. Here.
Speak out thy sorrows which thou bring'st in haste,
For comfort is too far for us to expect.
    Lord. We have descried, upon our neighbouring
        shore,   60
A portly sail of ships make hitherward.
    Cle. I thought as much.
One sorrow never comes but brings an heir,
That may succeed as his inheritor;
And so in ours: some neighbouring nation,
Taking advantage of our misery,
Hath stuff'd these hollow vessels with their power,
To beat us down, the which are down already;
And make a conquest of unhappy me,
Whereas no glory 's got to overcome.   70
    Lord. That 's the least fear; for, by the semblance
Of their white flags display'd, they bring us peace,
And come to us as favourers, not as foes.
    Cle. Thou speak'st like him 's untutor'd to repeat:
Who makes the fairest show means most deceit.
But bring they what they will and what they can,
What need we fear?
The ground 's the lowest, and we are half way there.
Go tell their general we attend him here,
To know for what he comes, and whence he comes, 80
And what he craves.
    Lord. I go, my lord.   [*Exit.*
    Cle. Welcome is peace, if he on peace consist;
If wars, we are unable to resist.

    Enter PERICLES *with* Attendants.

    Per. Lord governor, for so we hear you are,
Let not our ships and number of our men
Be like a beacon fired to amaze your eyes.
We have heard your miseries as far as Tyre,
And seen the desolation of your streets:

Nor come we to add sorrow to your tears,   96
But to relieve them of their heavy load;
And these our ships, you happily may think
Are like the Trojan horse was stuff'd within
With bloody veins, expecting overthrow,
Are stored with corn to make your needy bread,
And give them life whom hunger starved half dead.
    All. The gods of Greece protect you!
And we'll pray for you.
    Per.   Arise, I pray you, rise:
We do not look for reverence, but for love,
And harbourage for ourself, our ships, and men.   100
    Cle. The which when any shall not gratify,
Or pay you with unthankfulness in thought,
Be it our wives, our children, or ourselves,
The curse of heaven and men succeed their evils!
Till when,—the which I hope shall ne'er be seen,—
Your grace is welcome to our town and us.
    Per. Which welcome we'll accept; feast here awhile,
Until our stars that frown lend us a smile.   [*Exeunt.*

ACT II.

Enter GOWER.

    Gow. Here have you seen a mighty king
His child, I wis, to incest bring;
A better prince and benign lord,
That will prove awful both in deed and word.
Be quiet then as men should be,
Till he hath pass'd necessity.
I'll show you those in troubles reign,
Losing a mite, a mountain gain.
The good in conversation,
To whom I give my benison,   10
Is still at Tarsus, where each man
Thinks all is writ he speken can;
And, to remember what he does,
Build his statue to make him glorious:
But tidings to the contrary
Are brought your eyes; what need speak I?

DUMB SHOW.

Enter at one door PERICLES *talking with* CLEON; *all the
train with them. Enter at another door a* Gentleman,
with a letter to PERICLES; PERICLES *shows the letter to*
CLEON; *gives the* Messenger *a reward, and knights
him. Exit* PERICLES *at one door, and* CLEON *at another.*

Good Helicane, that stay'd at home
Not to eat honey like a drone
From others' labours; for though he strive
To killen bad, keep good alive;   20
And to fulfil his prince' desire,
Sends word of all that haps in Tyre:
How Thaliard came full bent with sin
And had intent to murder him;
And that in Tarsus was not best
Longer for him to make his rest.
He, doing so, put forth to seas,

40. **inventions**, fancy dishes.   42. **nousle**, train (Onions); a corruption
of *nursle*, to cherish (Deighton).   54. **superfluous**, i.e., prodigal.
tears, sound of weeping.   61. **portly**, majestic, stately.   70. **Whereas
. . . overcome**, where there is no glory to be gained.   74. **like . . .
repeat**, like one who has never learned the common adage that one who
makes the fairest, etc. (Steevens).   83. **consist**, insist.   94. **expecting
overthrow**, may modify *you* (l. 92).   95. **your needy bread**, bread which
you need.

ACT II. PROLOGUE.   2. **I wis**, certainly.   6. **necessity**, those hardships imposed by fate.   7. **those**, i.e., those who.   10. **benison**, blessing.   12. **writ**, holy writ.   **he speken can**, which he speaks; an archaic
affectation.   13. **remember**, commemorate.   19. **for**, difficult to explain as the text stands; some emend to *forth*, others omit.   28. **been**,
are.   35. **of man, of pelf**, partitive genitives to be construed with *All*.
38. **glad**, gladness.
SCENE I. *Stage Direction:* **Pentapolis.** This fictitious name occurs in

Where when men been, there 's seldom ease;
For now the wind begins to blow;
Thunder above and deeps below   30
Make such unquiet, that the ship
Should house him safe is wreck'd and split;
And he, good prince, having all lost,
By waves from coast to coast is tost:
All perishen of man, of pelf,
Ne aught escapen but himself;
Till fortune, tired with doing bad,
Threw him ashore, to give him glad:
And here he comes. What shall be next,
Pardon old Gower,—this longs the text.   [*Exit*. 40

SCENE I. *Pentapolis. An open place by the sea-side.*

Enter PERICLES, *wet.*

Per. Yet cease your ire, you angry stars of heaven!
Wind, rain, and thunder, remember, earthly man
Is but a substance that must yield to you;
And I, as fits my nature, do obey you:
Alas, the sea hath cast me on the rocks,
Wash'd me from shore to shore, and left me breath
Nothing to think on but ensuing death:
Let it suffice the greatness of your powers
To have bereft a prince of all his fortunes;
And having thrown him from your watery grave,   10
Here to have death in peace is all he'll crave.

Enter three Fishermen.

First Fish. What, ho, Pilch!
Sec. Fish. Ha, come and bring away the nets!
First Fish. What, Patch-breech, I say!
Third Fish. What say you, master?
First Fish. Look how thou stirrest now! come away,
or I'll fetch thee with a wanion.
Third Fish. 'Faith, master, I am thinking of the poor
men that were cast away before us even now.   20
First Fish. Alas, poor souls, it grieved my heart to
hear what pitiful cries they made to us to help them,
when, well-a-day, we could scarce help ourselves.
Third Fish. Nay, master, said not I as much when I
saw the porpus how he bounced and tumbled? they
say they 're half fish, half flesh: a plague on them, they
ne'er come but I look to be washed. Master, I marvel
how the fishes live in the sea.   30
First Fish. Why, as men do a-land; the great ones
eat up the little ones: I can compare our rich misers to
nothing so fitly as to a whale; a' plays and tumbles,
driving the poor fry before him, and at last devours
them all at a mouthful: such whales have I heard on
o' the land, who never leave gaping till they 've
swallowed the whole parish, church, steeple, bells,
and all.
Per. [*Aside*] A pretty moral.
Third Fish. But, master, if I had been the sexton, I
would have been that day in the belfry.   41
Sec. Fish. Why, man?

Third Fish. Because he should have swallowed me
too: and when I had been in his belly, I would have
kept such a jangling of the bells, that he should never
have left, till he cast bells, steeple, church, and parish,
up again. But if the good King Simonides were of my
mind,—
Per. [*Aside*] Simonides!   49
Third Fish. We would purge the land of these
drones, that rob the bee of her honey.
Per. [*Aside*] How from the finny subject of the sea
These fishers tell the infirmities of men;
And from their watery empire recollect
All that may men approve or men detect!
Peace be at your labour, honest fishermen.
Sec. Fish. Honest! good fellow, what 's that? If it be a
day fits you, †search out of the calendar, and nobody
look after it.
Per. May see the sea hath cast upon your coast.   60
Sec. Fish. What a drunken knave was the sea to cast
thee in our way!
Per. A man whom both the waters and the wind,
In that vast tennis-court, have made the ball
For them to play upon, entreats you pity him;
He asks of you, that never used to beg.
First Fish. No, friend, cannot you beg? Here 's them
in our country of Greece gets more with begging than
we can do with working.
Sec. Fish. Canst thou catch any fishes, then?
Per. I never practised it.   71
Sec. Fish. Nay, then thou wilt starve, sure; for here 's
nothing to be got now-a-days, unless thou canst fish
for 't.
Per. What I have been I have forgot to know;
But what I am, want teaches me to think on:
A man throng'd up with cold: my veins are chill,
And have no more of life than may suffice
To give my tongue that heat to ask your help;
Which if you shall refuse, when I am dead,   80
For that I am a man, pray see me buried.
First Fish. Die quoth-a? Now gods forbid! I have a
gown here; come, put it on; keep thee warm. Now,
afore me, a handsome fellow! Come, thou shalt go
home, and we'll have flesh for holidays, fish for fasting-
days, and moreo'er puddings and flap-jacks, and
thou shalt be welcome.
Per. I thank you, sir.
Sec. Fish. Hark you, my friend; you said you could
not beg.   90
Per. I did but crave.
Sec. Fish. But crave! Then I'll turn craver too, and
so I shall 'scape whipping.
Per. Why, are all your beggars whipped, then?
Sec. Fish. O, not all, my friend, not all; for if all your
beggars were whipped, I would wish no better office
than to be beadle. But, master, I'll go draw up the
net.   [*Exit with Third Fisherman.*
Per. [*Aside*] How well this honest mirth becomes
their labour!   99
First Fish. Hark you, sir, do you know where ye are?
Per. Not well.

---

the earlier versions of the Apollonius story. 12, 14. **Pilch, Patch-breech,** nicknames derived from the clothes they wear; *Pilch,* a leather garment. 13. **bring away,** bring quickly. 17. **wanion,** vengeance. 23. **well-a-day,** alas. 26. **the porpus.** These actions of porpoises were recognized prognostications of stormy weather. 52. **subject,** subjects or people, used collectively, so that *the finny subject of the sea* would be the fish, i.e., residents. 54. **recollect,** gather up. 56-59. **Peace . . . after it.** Most commentators think something lost—some reference

to the *day* to occasion the fisherman's reply. Steevens attempted to reconstruct the passage, adding to Pericles' speech the line, *The day is rough and thwarts your occupation.* Deighton prefixed to the last line of Pericles' speech the exclamation *Hoy-day!* 60. **May see,** so Qq; F: *Y'may see.* 79. **that heat,** warmth enough to enable him to move his tongue, now almost cleaving to the roof of his mouth (Deighton); heat was thought of as the source of motion. 84. **afore me,** a mild oath.

First Fish. Why, I'll tell you: this is called Pentapolis, and our king the good Simonides.

Per. The good King Simonides, do you call him?

First Fish. Ay, sir; and he deserves so to be called for his peaceable reign and good government.

Per. He is a happy king, since he gains from his subjects the name of good by his government. How far is his court distant from this shore?   111

First Fish. Marry, sir, half a day's journey: and I'll tell you, he hath a fair daughter, and to-morrow is her birth-day; and there are princes and knights come from all parts of the world to just and tourney for her love.

Per. Were my fortunes equal to my desires, I could wish to make one there.

First Fish. O, sir, things must be as they may; and what a man cannot get, he may lawfully deal for—
†this wife's soul.   121

Re-enter Second *and* Third Fishermen, *drawing up a net.*

Sec. Fish. Help, master, help! here 's a fish hangs in the net, like a poor man's right in the law; 'twill hardly come out. Ha! bots on 't, 'tis come at last, and 'tis turned to a rusty armour.

Per. An armour, friends! I pray you, let me see it.
Thanks, fortune, yet, that, after all my crosses,
Thou givest me somewhat to repair myself;
And though it was mine own, part of my heritage,
Which my dead father did bequeath to me,   130
With this strict charge, even as he left his life,
'Keep it, my Pericles; it hath been a shield
'Twixt me and death;'—and pointed to this brace;—
'For that it saved me, keep it; in like necessity—
The which the gods protect thee from!—may defend thee.'
It kept where I kept, I so dearly loved it;
Till the rough seas, that spare not any man,
Took it in rage, though calm'd have given 't again:
I thank thee for 't: my shipwreck now 's no ill,
Since I have here my father's gift in 's will.   140

First Fish. What mean you, sir?

Per. To beg of you, kind friends, this coat of worth,
For it was sometime target to a king;
I know it by this mark. He loved me dearly,
And for his sake I wish the having of it;
And that you 'ld guide me to your sovereign's court,
Where with it I may appear a gentleman;
And if that ever my low fortune 's better,
I'll pay your bounties; till then rest your debtor.

First Fish. Why, wilt thou tourney for the lady?   150

Per. I'll show the virtue I have borne in arms.

First Fish. Why, do 'e take it, and the gods give thee good on 't!

Sec. Fish. Ay, but hark you, my friend; 'twas we that made up this garment through the rough seams of the waters: there are certain condolements, certain vails. I hope, sir, if you thrive, you'll remember from whence you had it.

Per. Believe 't, I will.

By your furtherance I am clothed in steel;   160
And, spite of all the rapture of the sea,
This jewel holds his building on my arm:
Unto thy value I will mount myself
Upon a courser, whose delightful steps
Shall make the gazer joy to see him tread.
Only, my friend, I yet am unprovided
Of a pair of bases.

Sec. Fish. We'll sure provide: thou shalt have my best gown to make thee a pair; and I'll bring thee to the court myself.   170

Per. Then honour be but a goal to my will,
This day I'll rise, or else add ill to ill.   [*Exeunt.*

SCENE II. *The same. A public way or platform leading to the lists. A pavilion by the side of it for the reception of the King, Princess, Lords, &c.*

Enter SIMONIDES, THAISA, Lords, *and* Attendants.

Sim. Are the knights ready to begin the triumph?

First Lord. They are, my liege;
And stay your coming to present themselves.

Sim. Return them, we are ready; and our daughter,
In honour of whose birth these triumphs are,
Sits here, like beauty's child, whom nature gat
For men to see, and seeing wonder at.   [*Exit a Lord.*

Thai. It pleaseth you, my royal father, to express
My commendations great, whose merit 's less.

Sim. It 's fit it should be so; for princes are   10
A model, which heaven makes like to itself:
As jewels lose their glory if neglected,
So princes their renowns if not respected.
'Tis now your honour, daughter, to entertain
The labour of each knight in his device.

Thai. Which, to preserve mine honour, I'll perform.

Enter a Knight; *he passes over, and his* Squire *presents his shield to the* Princess.

Sim. Who is the first that doth prefer himself?

Thai. A knight of Sparta, my renowned father;
And the device he bears upon his shield
Is a black Ethiope reaching at the sun: 20
The word, 'Lux tua vita mihi.'

Sim. He loves you well that holds his life of you.
                [*The Second Knight passes over.*
Who is the second that presents himself?

Thai. A prince of Macedon, my royal father;
And the device he bears upon his shield
Is an arm'd knight that 's conquer'd by a lady;
The motto thus, in Spanish, 'Piu por dulzura que por fuerza.'   [*The Third Knight passes over.*

Sim. And what 's the third?

Thai.   The third of Antioch;
And his device, a wreath of chivalry;
The word, 'Me pompæ provexit apex.'   30
                [*The Fourth Knight passes over.*

Sim. What is the fourth?

Thai. A burning torch that 's turned upside down;
The word, 'Quod me alit, me extinguit.'

---

116. **just,** joust, tilt in a tournament. 118. **to make one,** i.e., to take part in the tourney. 121. **his wife's soul.** Some take this as the beginning of a sentence interrupted by the entrance of the other fishermen. 124. **bots on 't,** plague take it (*bots,* disease of horses). 129. **And though,** even though (Deighton). 142. **coat,** refers to *armour,* line 126. 156-157. **condolements,** possibly confused with "dole" (Onions). 157. **vails,** perquisites, tips. 161. **rapture,** plundering. 162. **This . . . arm,** this jewel on my arm will provide a means, i.e., to buy a courser.

167. **bases,** pleated skirts of cloth, velvet or rich brocade, appended to the doublet and reaching from the waist to the knee.
SCENE II. 1. **triumph,** festive entertainment. 4. **to . . . less,** to praise me out of proportion to my desert. 14. **entertain,** review; so Qq; Globe, following Steevens: *explain.* 17. **prefer,** introduce. 21. **'Lux . . . mihi.'** Thy light is my life. 27. **'Piu . . . fuerza,'** more by gentleness than by force. 30. **'Me . . . apex.'** The highest summit of honor has led me on. 33. **'Quod . . . extinguit.'**

Sim. Which shows that beauty hath his power and
will,
Which can as well inflame as it can kill.
[*The Fifth Knight passes over.*
Thai. The fifth, an hand environed with clouds,
Holding out gold that 's by the touchstone tried;
The motto thus, 'Sic spectanda fides.'
[*The Sixth Knight, Pericles, passes over.*
Sim. And what 's
The sixth and last, the which the knight himself   40
With such a graceful courtesy deliver'd?
Thai. He seems to be a stranger; but his present is
A wither'd branch, that 's only green at top;
The motto, 'In hac spe vivo.'
Sim. A pretty moral;
From the dejected state wherein he is,
He hopes by you his fortunes yet may flourish.
First Lord. He had need mean better than his
outward show
Can any way speak in his just commend;
For by his rusty outside he appears   50
To have practised more the whipstock than the lance.
Sec. Lord. He well may be a stranger, for he comes
To an honour'd triumph strangely furnished.
Third Lord. And on set purpose let his armour rust
Until this day, to scour it in the dust.
Sim. Opinion 's but a fool, that makes us scan
The outward habit by the inward man.
But stay, the knights are coming: we will withdraw
Into the gallery.   [*Exeunt.*
[*Great shouts within, and all cry* 'The mean knight!'

SCENE III. *The same. A hall of state: a banquet prepared.*

Enter SIMONIDES, THAISA, Lords, Attendants, *and*
Knights, *from tilting.*

Sim. Knights,
To say you 're welcome were superfluous.
To place upon the volume of your deeds,
As in a title-page, your worth in arms,
Were more than you expect, or more than 's fit,
Since every worth in show commends itself.
Prepare for mirth, for mirth becomes a feast:
You are princes and my guests.
Thai. But you, my knight and guest;
To whom this wreath of victory I give,   10
And crown you king of this day's happiness.
Per. 'Tis more by fortune, lady, than by merit.
Sim. Call it by what you will, the day is yours;
And here, I hope, is none that envies it.
In framing an artist, art hath thus decreed,
To make some good, but others to exceed;
And you are her labour'd scholar. Come, queen o'
the feast,—
For, daughter, so you are,—here take your place:
Marshal the rest, as they deserve their grace.   19
Knights. We are honour'd much by good Simonides.
Sim. Your presence glads our days: honour we love;
For who hates honour hates the gods above.

Marshal. Sir, yonder is your place.
Per.   Some other is more fit.
First Knight. Contend not, sir; for we are gentlemen
That neither in our hearts nor outward eyes
Envy the great nor do the low despise.
Per. You are right courteous knights.
Sim.   Sit, sir, sit.
By Jove, I wonder, that is king of thoughts,
These cates resist me, he not thought upon.
Thai. By Juno, that is queen of marriage,   30
All viands that I eat do seem unsavoury,
Wishing him my meat. Sure, he 's a gallant
gentleman.
Sim. He 's but a country gentleman;
Has done no more than other knights have done;
Has broken a staff or so; so let it pass.
Thai. To me he seems like diamond to glass.
Per. Yon king 's to me like to my father's picture,
Which tells me in that glory once he was;
Had princes sit, like stars, about his throne,
And he the sun, for them to reverence;   40
None that beheld him, but, like lesser lights,
Did vail their crowns to his supremacy:
Where now his son 's like a glow-worm in the night,
The which hath fire in darkness, none in light:
Whereby I see that Time 's the king of men,
He 's both their parent, and he is their grave,
And gives them what he will, not what they crave.
Sim. What, are you merry, knights?
Knights. Who can be other in this royal presence?   49
Sim. Here, with a cup that 's stored unto the brim,—
As you do love, fill to your mistress' lips,—
We drink this health to you.
Knights.   We thank your grace.
Sim. Yet pause awhile:
Yon knight doth sit too melancholy,
As if the entertainment in our court
Had not a show might countervail his worth.
Note it not you, Thaisa?
Thai.   What is it
To me, my father?
Sim.   O, attend, my daughter:
Princes in this should live like gods above,
Who freely give to every one that comes   60
To honour them:
And princes not doing so are like to gnats,
Which make a sound, but kill'd are wonder'd at.
Therefore to make his entrance more sweet,
Here, say we drink this standing-bowl of wine to him.
Thai. Alas, my father, it befits not me
Unto a stranger knight to be so bold:
He may my proffer take for an offence,
Since men take women's gifts for impudence.
Sim. How!   70
Do as I bid you, or you'll move me else.
Thai. [*Aside*] Now, by the gods, he could not please
me better.
Sim. And furthermore tell him, we desire to know of
him,
Of whence he is, his name and parentage.

That which feeds my flame puts out my light. **38. 'Sic spectanda fides.'**
Thus is faith to be tried. **44. 'In . . . vivo.'** In this hope I live. **51.
whipstock,** i e., as if he were accustomed to driving work horses.
   SCENE III. **6. every . . . itself,** everything worthy manifests its
own worth. **16. To make,** to exceed. The two infinitives are not
strictly parallel. Some are to be made good, but others are to be made excellent. **17. her labour'd scholar,** the one on whom art has bestowed
the most pains. **28-29. By . . . upon.** Malone assigned the speech to
Pericles; followed by Globe. Cambridge marks speeches (ll. 28-47) as
asides. **29. These cates resist me,** these delicacies are distasteful to
me. **he,** so Qq; Globe, following Malone: *she.* **not,** so Qq; Globe, following Mason: *but.* **51. fill to,** fill and drink to. **56. countervail,**
equal. **65. standing-bowl,** bowl resting on a pedestal.

Thai. The king my father, sir, has drunk to you.
Per. I thank him.
Thai. Wishing it so much blood unto your life.
Per. I thank both him and you, and pledge him
  freely.
Thai. And further he desires to know of you,
Of whence you are, your name and parentage. 80
  Per. A gentleman of Tyre; my name, Pericles;
My education been in arts and arms;
Who, looking for adventures in the world,
Was by the rough seas reft of ships and men,
And after shipwreck driven upon this shore.
  Thai. He thanks your grace; names himself
  Pericles,
A gentleman of Tyre,
Who only by misfortune of the seas
Bereft of ships and men, cast on this shore.
  Sim. Now, by the gods, I pity his misfortune, 90
And will awake him from his melancholy.
Come, gentlemen, we sit too long on trifles,
And waste the time, which looks for other revels.
Even in your armours, as you are address'd,
Will very well become a soldier's dance.
I will not have excuse, with saying this
Loud music is too harsh for ladies' heads,
Since they love men in arms as well as beds.
  [*The Knights dance.*
So, this was well ask'd, 'twas so well perform'd.
Come, sir; 100
Here is a lady that wants breathing too:
And I have heard, you knights of Tyre
Are excellent in making ladies trip;
And that their measures are as excellent.
  Per. In those that practise them they are, my lord.
  Sim. O, that 's as much as you would be denied
Of your fair courtesy.   [*The Knights and Ladies dance.*
  Unclasp, unclasp:
Thanks, gentlemen, to all; all have done well,
[*To Per.*] But you the best. Pages and lights, to
  conduct
These knights unto their several lodgings! [*To Per.*]
  Yours, sir, 110
We have given order to be next our own.
  Per. I am at your grace's pleasure.
  Sim. Princes, it is too late to talk of love;
And that 's the mark I know you level at:
Therefore each one betake him to his rest;
To-morrow all for speeding do their best. [*Exeunt.*

SCENE IV. *Tyre. A room in the Governor's house.*

Enter HELICANUS *and* ESCANES.

  Hel. No, Escanes, know this of me,
Antiochus from incest lived not free:
For which, the most high gods not minding longer
To withhold the vengeance that they had in store,
Due to this heinous capital offence,
Even in the height and pride of all his glory,
When he was seated in a chariot
Of an inestimable value, and his daughter with him,
A fire from heaven came and shrivell'd up

Their bodies, even to loathing; for they so stunk, 10
That all those eyes adored them ere their fall
Scorn now their hand should give them burial.
  Esca. 'Twas very strange.
  Hel.   And yet but justice; for though
This king were great, his greatness was no guard
To bar heaven's shaft, but sin had his reward.
  Esca. 'Tis very true.

Enter two or three Lords.

  First Lord. See, not a man in private conference
Or council has respect with him but he.
  Sec. Lord. It shall no longer grieve without reproof.
  Third Lord. And cursed be he that will not second it.
  First Lord. Follow me, then. Lord Helicane, a
  word. 21
  Hel. With me? and welcome: happy day, my lords.
  First Lord. Know that our griefs are risen to the top,
And now at length they overflow their banks.
  Hel. Your griefs! for what? wrong not your prince
  you love.
  First Lord. Wrong not yourself, then, noble
  Helicane;
But if the prince do live, let us salute him,
Or know what ground 's made happy by his breath.
If in the world he live, we'll seek him out;
If in his grave he rest, we'll find him there; 30
And be resolved he lives to govern us,
Or dead, give 's cause to mourn his funeral,
And leave us to our free election.
  Sec. Lord. Whose death indeed 's the strongest in our
  censure:
And knowing this kingdom is without a head,—
Like goodly buildings left without a roof
Soon fall to ruin,—your noble self,
That best know how to rule and how to reign,
We thus submit unto,—our sovereign.
  All. Live, noble Helicane! 40
  Hel. For honour's cause, forbear your suffrages:
If that you love Prince Pericles, forbear.
Take I your wish, I leap into the seas,
Where 's hourly trouble for a minute's ease.
A twelvemonth longer, let me entreat you to
Forbear the absence of your king;
If in which time expired, he not return,
I shall with aged patience bear your yoke.
But if I cannot win you to this love,
Go search like nobles, like noble subjects, 50
And in your search spend your adventurous worth;
Whom if you find, and win unto return,
You shall like diamonds sit about his crown.
  First Lord. To wisdom he 's a fool that will not yield;
And since Lord Helicane enjoineth us,
We with our travels will endeavour us.
  Hel. Then you love us, we you, and we'll clasp
  hands:
When peers thus knit, a kingdom ever stands. [*Exeunt.*

SCENE V. *Pentapolis. A room in the palace.*

Enter SIMONIDES, *reading a letter, at one door: the*
Knights *meet him.*

94. **address'd,** accoutered. 95. **Will . . . become.** The subject is *you*
understood. 97. **Loud music,** noise of armor (Malone). 101. **breathing,** exercise. 106-107. **that 's . . . courtesy,** that 's the equivalent of
your denial of your accomplishment.
  SCENE IV. 3. **minding,** intending. 11. **eyes,** eyes which. 18. **he,**

Escanes. 19. **without reproof,** i.e., such grievance cannot continue
without some bad results. 34. **Whose . . . censure,** according to our
judgment it is more likely that he is dead. 41. **suffrages,** petitions,
requests. 43. **Take . . . wish,** if I should act on your wish. 49. **to
this love,** to this regard for my request.

First Knight. Good morrow to the good Simonides.
Sim. Knights, from my daughter this I let you
   know,
That for this twelvemonth she'll not undertake
A married life.
Her reason to herself is only known,
Which yet from her by no means can I get.
  Sec. Knight. May we not get access to her, my lord?
  Sim. 'Faith, by no means; she hath so strictly tied
Her to her chamber, that 'tis impossible.
One twelve moons more she'll wear Diana's livery; 10
This by the eye of Cynthia hath she vow'd,
And on her virgin honour will not break it.
  Third Knight. Loath to bid farewell, we take our
   leaves.   *[Exeunt Knights.*
  Sim. So,
They are well dispatch'd; now to my daughter's
  letter:
She tells me here, she'll wed the stranger knight,
Or never more to view nor day nor light.
'Tis well, mistress; your choice agrees with mine;
I like that well: nay, how absolute she 's in 't,
Not minding whether I dislike or no! 20
Well, I do commend her choice;
And will no longer have it be delay'd.
Soft! here he comes: I must dissemble it.

Enter PERICLES.

  Per. All fortune to the good Simonides!
  Sim. To you as much, sir! I am beholding to you
For your sweet music this last night: I do
Protest my ears were never better fed
With such delightful pleasing harmony.
  Per. It is your grace's pleasure to commend;
Not my desert.
  Sim.   Sir, you are music's master. 30
  Per. The worst of all her scholars, my good lord.
  Sim. Let me ask you one thing:
What do you think of my daughter, sir?
  Per. A most virtuous princess.
  Sim. And she is fair too, is she not?
  Per. As a fair day in summer, wondrous fair.
  Sim. Sir, my daughter thinks very well of you;
Ay, so well, that you must be her master,
And she will be your scholar: therefore look to it.
  Per. I am unworthy for her schoolmaster. 40
  Sim. She thinks not so; peruse this writing else.
  Per. [*Aside*] What 's here?
A letter, that she loves the knight of Tyre!
'Tis the king's subtilty to have my life.
O, seek not to entrap me, gracious lord,
A stranger and distressed gentleman,
That never aim'd so high to love your daughter,
But bent all offices to honour her.
  Sim. Thou hast bewitch'd my daughter, and thou
  art
A villain. 50
  Per. By the gods, I have not:
Never did thought of mine levy offence;
Nor never did my actions yet commence
A deed might gain her love or your displeasure.
  Sim. Traitor, thou liest.

  Per.   Traitor!
  Sim.   Ay, traitor.
  Per. Even in his throat—unless it be the king—
That calls me traitor, I return the lie.
  Sim. [*Aside*] Now, by the gods, I do applaud his
  courage.
  Per. My actions are as noble as my thoughts,
That never relish'd of a base descent. 60
I came unto your court for honour's cause,
And not to be a rebel to her state;
And he that otherwise accounts of me,
This sword shall prove he 's honour's enemy.
  Sim. No?
Here comes my daughter, she can witness it.

Enter THAISA.

  Per. Then, as you are as virtuous as fair,
Resolve your angry father, if my tongue
Did e'er solicit, or my hand subscribe
To any syllable that made love to you. 70
  Thai. Why, sir, say if you had,
Who takes offence at that would make me glad?
  Sim. Yea, mistress, are you so peremptory?
[*Aside*] I am glad on 't with all my heart.—
I'll tame you; I'll bring you in subjection.
Will you, not having my consent,
Bestow your love and your affections
Upon a stranger? [*Aside*] who, for aught I know,
May be, nor can I think the contrary,
As great in blood as I myself.— 80
Therefore hear you, mistress; either frame
Your will to mine,—and you, sir, hear you,
Either be ruled by me, or I will make you—
Man and wife:
Nay, come, your hands and lips must seal it too:
And being join'd, I'll thus your hopes destroy;
And for a further grief,—God give you joy!—
What, are you both pleased?
  Thai.   Yes, if you love me, sir.
  Per. Even as my life my blood that fosters it.
  Sim. What, are you both agreed? 90
  Both. Yes, if it please your majesty.
  Sim. It pleaseth me so well, that I will see you wed;
And then with what haste you can get you to bed.
                      [Exeunt.

ACT III.

Enter GOWER.

  Gow. Now sleep yslaked hath the rout;
No din but snores the house about,
Made louder by the o'er-fed breast
Of this most pompous marriage-feast.
The cat, with eyne of burning coal,
Now couches fore the mouse's hole;
And crickets sing at the oven's mouth,
E'er the blither for their drouth.
Hymen hath brought the bride to bed,
Where, by the loss of maidenhead, 10
A babe is moulded. Be attent,
And time that is so briefly spent

SCENE V. 19. **absolute,** unconditional, positive. 38-39. **her . . .
scholar.** In the prose versions of the story there is a lapse of time
between the scholar-master proposal and the marriage proposal, although Simonides' dissimulation is essentially the same in all versions.
The telescoping may be due here to the dramatist or to the person who
transmitted the text. 41. **else,** i.e., if you don't believe me.
ACT III. PROLOGUE. 1. **yslaked,** laid to rest; an archaic affectation.
3. **breast,** lungs, i.e., breathing because of the overeating at the marriage
feast. 11. **attent,** attentive.

With your fine fancies quaintly eche:
What's dumb in show I'll plain with speech.

DUMB SHOW.

Enter, PERICLES *and* SIMONIDES, *at one door, with*
Attendants; *a* Messenger *meets them, kneels, and
gives* PERICLES *a letter:* PERICLES *shows it*
SIMONIDES; *the* Lords *kneel to him. Then enter*
THAISA *with child, with* LYCHORIDA *a nurse. The*
KING *shows her the letter; she rejoices: she and*
PERICLES *take leave of her father, and depart with*
LYCHORIDA *and their* Attendants. *Then exeunt*
SIMONIDES *and the rest.*

By many a dern and painful perch
Of Pericles the careful search,
By the four opposing coigns
Which the world together joins,
Is made with all due diligence
That horse and sail and high expense   20
Can stead the quest. At last from Tyre,
Fame answering the most strange inquire,
To the court of King Simonides
Are letters brought, the tenour these:
Antiochus and his daughter dead;
The men of Tyrus on the head
Of Helicanus would set on
The crown of Tyre, but he will none:
The mutiny he there hastes t' oppress;
Says to 'em, if King Pericles   30
Come not home in twice six moons,
He, obedient to their dooms,
Will take the crown. The sum of this,
Brought hither to Pentapolis,
Y-ravished the regions round,
And every one with claps can sound,
'Our heir-apparent is a king!
Who dream'd, who thought of such a thing?'
Brief, he must hence depart to Tyre:
His queen with child makes her desire—   40
Which who shall cross?—along to go:
Omit we all their dole and woe:
Lychorida, her nurse, she takes,
And so to sea. Their vessel shakes
On Neptune's billow; half the flood
Hath their keel cut: but fortune's mood
Varies again; the grisled north
Disgorges such a tempest forth,
That, as a duck for life that dives,
So up and down the poor ship drives: 50
The lady shrieks, and well-a-near
Does fall in travail with her fear:
And what ensues in this fell storm
Shall for itself itself perform.
I nill relate, action may
Conveniently the rest convey;
Which might not what by me is told.
In your imagination hold
This stage the ship, upon whose deck
The sea-tost Pericles appears to speak.   [*Exit.* 60

SCENE I.

Enter PERICLES, *on shipboard.*

Per. Thou god of this great vast, rebuke these
        surges,
Which wash both heaven and hell; and thou, that
        hast
Upon the winds command, bind them in brass,
Having call'd them from the deep! O, still
Thy deafening, dreadful thunders; gently quench
Thy nimble, sulphurous flashes! O, how, Lychorida,
How does my queen? Thou stormest venomously;
Wilt thou spit all thyself? The seaman's whistle
Is as a whisper in the ears of death,
Unheard. Lychorida!—Lucina, O   10
Divinest patroness, and midwife gentle
To those that cry by night, convey thy deity
Aboard our dancing boat; make swift the pangs
Of my queen's travails!

Enter LYCHORIDA, *with an Infant.*

        Now, Lychorida!
Lyc. Here is a thing too young for such a place,
Who, if it had conceit, would die, as I
Am like to do: take in your arms this piece
Of your dead queen.
Per.   How, how, Lychorida!
Lyc. Patience, good sir; do not assist the storm.
Here's all that is left living of your queen,   20
A little daughter: for the sake of it,
Be manly, and take comfort.
Per.   O you gods!
Why do you make us love your goodly gifts,
And snatch them straight away? We here below
Recall not what we give, and therein may
Use honour with you.
Lyc.   Patience, good sir,
Even for this charge.
Per.   Now, mild may be thy life!
For a more blustrous birth had never babe:
Quiet and gentle thy conditions! for
Thou art the rudeliest welcome to this world   30
That ever was prince's child. Happy what follows!
Thou hast as chiding a nativity
As fire, air, water, earth, and heaven can make,
To herald thee from the womb: even at the first
Thy loss is more than can thy portage quit,
With all thou canst find here. Now, the good gods
Throw their best eyes upon 't!

Enter two Sailors.

First Sail. What courage, sir? God save you!
Per. Courage enough: I do not fear the flaw;
It hath done to me the worst. Yet, for the love   40
Of this poor infant, this fresh-new sea-farer,
I would it would be quiet.
First Sail. Slack the bolins there! Thou wilt not,
wilt thou? Blow, and split thyself.
Sec. Sail. But sea-room, an the brine and cloudy
billow kiss the moon, I care not.
First Sail. Sir, your queen must overboard: the sea

13. **eche**, eke out. 14. **plain**, make plain. 15. **dern**, dark, drear.
perch, measure of land. 17. **coigns**, compass points. 35. **Y-ravished**,
delighted. 47. **grisled**, fearful, horrible. 51. **well-a-near**, a cry of
lamentation. 55. **nill**, will not.
        SCENE I. 1. **vast**, expanse. 6. **sulphurous flashes.** Lightning was
apparently thought to be sulphurous; cf. *Measure for Measure*, II, ii,
115; *King Lear*, III, ii, 4; *The Tempest*, I, ii, 204. 10. **Lucina.** Cf.

I, i, 8, note. 16. **conceit**, understanding (of its precarious position).
26. **Use honour**, share, or are entitled to equal honor. 27. **charge**,
i.e., care of the infant. 35. **portage**, port dues. 43. **bolins**, bowlines.
63. **e'er-remaining.** Qq: *ayre-remaining*; Malone-Stevens: *aye-remaining*.
W. Bell conjectured *air-retaining lamps*, i.e., lampreys. 67. **My . . .
jewels**, i.e., my casket of jewels. 68. **satin coffer**, perhaps a satin-
lined coffer; or one containing satins and clothes of state. 72. **bi-**

works high, the wind is loud, and will not lie till the
ship be cleared of the dead.
    Per. That 's your superstition.   50
    First Sail. Pardon us, sir; with us at sea it hath been
still observed; and we are strong in custom. Therefore
briefly yield her; for she must overboard straight.
    Per. As you think meet. Most wretched queen!
    Lyc. Here she lies, sir.
    Per. A terrible childbed hast thou had, my dear;
No light, no fire: the unfriendly elements
Forgot thee utterly; nor have I time
To give thee hallow'd to thy grave, but straight   60
Must cast thee, scarcely coffin'd, in the ooze;
Where, for a monument upon thy bones,
And e'er-remaining lamps, the belching whale
And humming water must o'erwhelm thy corpse,
Lying with simple shells. O Lychorida,
Bid Nestor bring me spices, ink and paper,
My casket and my jewels; and bid Nicander
Bring me the satin coffer: lay the babe
Upon the pillow: hie thee, whiles I say
A priestly farewell to her: suddenly, woman.   70
                      [Exit Lychorida.
    Sec. Sail. Sir, we have a chest beneath the hatches,
caulked and bitumed ready.
    Per. I thank thee. Mariner, say what coast is this?
    Sec. Sail. We are near Tarsus.
    Per. Thither, gentle mariner,
Alter thy course for Tyre. When canst thou reach it?
    Sec. Sail. By break of day, if the wind cease.
    Per. O, make for Tarsus!
There will I visit Cleon, for the babe
Cannot hold out to Tyrus: there I'll leave it   80
At careful nursing. Go thy ways, good mariner:
I'll bring the body presently.   *[Exeunt.*

    Scene II. *Ephesus. A room in Cerimon's house.*

Enter Cerimon, *with a Servant, and some Persons who
    have been shipwrecked.*

    Cer. Philemon, ho!

Enter Philemon.

    Phil. Doth my lord call?
    Cer. Get fire and meat for these poor men:
'T has been a turbulent and stormy night.
    Serv. I have been in many; but such a night as this,
Till now, I ne'er endured.
    Cer. Your master will be dead ere you return;
There 's nothing can be minister'd to nature
That can recover him. *[To Philemon]* Give this to the
    'pothecary,
And tell me how it works.   *[Exeunt all but Cerimon.*

Enter two Gentlemen.

    First Gent.   Good morrow.   10
    Sec. Gent. Good morrow to your lordship.
    Cer.   Gentlemen,
Why do you stir so early?
    First Gent. Sir,

Our lodgings, standing bleak upon the sea,
Shook as the earth did quake;
The very principals did seem to rend,
And all-to topple: pure surprise and fear
Made me to quit the house.
    Sec. Gent. That is the cause we trouble you so early;
'Tis not our husbandry.
    Cer.   O, you say well.   20
    First Gent. But I much marvel that your lordship,
    having
Rich tire about you, should at these early hours
Shake off the golden slumber of repose.
'Tis most strange,
Nature should be so conversant with pain,
Being thereto not compell'd.
    Cer.   I hold it ever,
Virtue and cunning were endowments greater
Than nobleness and riches: careless heirs
May the two latter darken and expend;
But immortality attends the former,   30
Making a man a god. 'Tis known, I ever
Have studied physic, through which secret art,
By turning o'er authorities, I have,
Together with my practice, made familiar
To me and to my aid the blest infusions
That dwell in vegetives, in metals, stones;
And I can speak of the disturbances
That nature works, and of her cures; which doth give
    me
A more content in course of true delight
Than to be thirsty after tottering honour,   40
Or tie my treasure up in silken bags,
To please the fool and death.
    Sec. Gent. Your honour has through Ephesus pour'd
    forth
Your charity, and hundreds call themselves
Your creatures, who by you have been restored:
And not your knowledge, your personal pain, but
    even
Your purse, still open, hath built Lord Cerimon
Such strong renown as time shall ne'er decay.

Enter two or three Servants *with a chest.*

    First Serv. So; lift there.
    Cer.   What is that?
    First Serv.   Sir, even now
Did the sea toss upon our shore this chest: 50
'Tis of some wreck.
    Cer.   Set 't down, let 's look upon 't.
    Sec. Gent. 'Tis like a coffin, sir.
    Cer.   Whate'er it be,
'Tis wondrous heavy. Wrench it open straight:
If the sea's stomach be o'ercharged with gold,
†'Tis a good constraint of fortune it belches upon us.
    Sec. Gent. 'Tis so, my lord.
    Cer.   How close 'tis caulk'd and
    bitumed!
Did the sea cast it up?
    First Serv. I never saw so huge a billow, sir,
As toss'd it upon shore.
    Cer.   Wrench it open;

---

tumed, smeared with pitch. 76. **Alter . . . Tyre,** change your course,
which has been for Tyre.
    Scene II. 8-9. **There 's . . . him,** i.e., only supernatural minis-
trations can restore him. 16. **principals,** main timbers of houses. 17.
all-to topple, topple down completely. 25. **Nature . . . pain,** any
human being should care to have so much to do with painful matters
(Deighton). 27. **cunning,** knowledge, skill. 29. **expend,** squander.

35. **infusions,** medicinal properties. 39. **course,** pursuit. 42. **the fool
and death,** probably alludes to the frequency of these figures in the old
Dance of Death motifs. 45. **Your creatures,** people created anew because of your restoratives. 55. **constraint of fortune,** fortunate constraint upon the stomach; a physiological metaphor.

Soft! it smells most sweetly in my sense. 60
    Sec. Gent. A delicate odour.
    Cer. As ever hit my nostril. So, up with it.
O you most potent gods! what 's here? a corse!
    First Gent. Most strange!
    Cer. Shrouded in cloth of state; balm'd and
        entreasured
With full bags of spices! A passport too!
Apollo, perfect me in the characters! [*Reads from a scroll.*
        'Here I give to understand,
        If e'er this coffin drive a-land,
        I, King Pericles, have lost 70
        This queen, worth all our mundane cost.
        Who finds her, give her burying;
        She was the daughter of a king:
        Besides this treasure for a fee,
        The gods requite his charity!'
If thou livest, Pericles, thou hast a heart
That even cracks for woe! This chanced to-night.
    Sec. Gent. Most likely, sir.
    Cer.   Nay, certainly to-night;
For look how fresh she looks! They were too rough
That threw her in the sea. Make a fire within: 80
Fetch hither all my boxes in my closet. [*Exit a Servant.*
Death may usurp on nature many hours,
And yet the fire of life kindle again
The o'erpress'd spirits. †I heard of an Egyptian
That had nine hours lien dead,
Who was by good appliance recovered.

    Re-enter a Servant, *with boxes, napkins, and fire.*

Well said, well said; the fire and cloths.
The rough and woeful music that we have,
Cause it to sound, beseech you.
The viol once more: how thou stirr'st, thou block! 90
The music there!—I pray you, give her air.
Gentlemen,
This queen will live: nature awakes; a warmth
Breathes out of her: she hath not been entranced
Above five hours: see how she gins to blow
Into life's flower again!
    First Gent.   The heavens,
Through you, increase our wonder and set up
Your fame for ever.
    Cer.   She is alive; behold,
Her eyelids, cases to those heavenly jewels
Which Pericles hath lost, 100
Begin to part their fringes of bright gold;
The diamonds of a most praised water
Do appear, to make the world twice rich. Live,
And make us weep to hear your fate, fair creature,
Rare as you seem to be.   [*She moves.*
    Thai.   O dear Diana,
Where am I? Where 's my lord? What world is this?
    Sec. Gent. Is not this strange?
    First Gent.   Most rare.
    Cer.   Hush, my gentle neighbours!
Lend me your hands; to the next chamber bear her.

Get linen: now this matter must be look'd to,
For her relapse is mortal. Come, come; 110
And Æsculapius guide us!   [*Exeunt, carrying her away.*

SCENE III. *Tarsus. A room in Cleon's house.*

Enter PERICLES, CLEON, DIONYZA, *and* LYCHORIDA
    with MARINA *in her arms.*

    Per. Most honour'd Cleon, I must needs be gone;
My twelve months are expired, and Tyrus stands
In a litigious peace. You, and your lady,
Take from my heart all thankfulness! The gods
Make up the rest upon you!
    Cle. Your shafts of fortune, though they hurt you
        mortally,
Yet glance full wonderingly on us.
    Dion.   O your sweet queen!
That the strict fates had pleased you had brought her
        hither,
To have bless'd mine eyes with her!
    Per.   We cannot but obey
The powers above us. Could I rage and roar 10
As doth the sea she lies in, yet the end
Must be as 'tis. My gentle babe Marina, whom,
For she was born at sea, I have named so, here
I charge your charity withal, leaving her
The infant of your care; beseeching you
To give her princely training, that she may be
Manner'd as she is born.
    Cle.   Fear not, my lord, but think
Your grace, that fed my country with your corn,
For which the people's prayers still fall upon you,
Must in your child be thought on. If neglection 20
Should therein make me vile, the common body,
By you relieved, would force me to my duty:
But if to that my nature need a spur,
The gods revenge it upon me and mine,
To the end of generation!
    Per.   I believe you;
Your honour and your goodness teach me to 't,
Without your vows. Till she be married, madam,
By bright Diana, whom we honour, all
Unscissar'd shall this hair of mine remain,
Though I show ill in 't. So I take my leave. 30
Good madam, make me blessed in your care
In bringing up my child.
    Dion.   I have one myself,
Who shall not be more dear to my respect
Than yours, my lord.
    Per.   Madam, my thanks and prayers.
    Cle. We'll bring your grace e'en to the edge o' the
        shore,
Then give you up to the mask'd Neptune and
The gentlest winds of heaven.
    Per.   I will embrace
Your offer. Come, dearest madam. O, no tears,
Lychorida, no tears:

---

67. **perfect . . . characters,** enable me to read the writing; may refer to the possibility of their being in a foreign tongue. 71. **cost,** wealth. 79. **rough,** hasty. 88-91. **The . . . there.** According to Burton (*Anatomy,* II, ii, vi. 3) music has animating power, "because the spirits about the heart take in that trembling and dancing air into the body, are moved together, and stirred up with it." On the power of music to revive, cf. *King Lear,* IV, vii, 25, and *The Winter's Tale,* V, iii, 98. There is some dispute as to whether *viol* designates a musical instrument or a phial of medicine. Q$_{1-3}$: *violl;* Q$_{4-6}$F$_3$: *viall;* F$_4$: *vial.* Judging from the emphasis

in Burton on "the trembling and dancing air," the stringed instrument is the more likely because of the viol's peculiar vibrancy. 95. **blow,** bloom. 102. **water,** luster. 111. **Æsculapius,** god of medicine.
SCENE III. 3. **litigious,** disturbed by disputes. 7. **wonderingly,** so Q; Globe, following Steevens: *wanderingly.* 25. **of generation,** i.e., of my generation—my descendants. 36. **mask'd Neptune,** alludes to his deceitful aspect of calm.
SCENE IV. 6. **eaning time,** time of delivery.
ACT IV. PROLOGUE. 6. **fast-growing scene,** alludes to the interval

Look to your little mistress, on whose grace 40
You may depend hereafter. Come, my lord. [*Exeunt.*

SCENE IV. *Ephesus. A room in Cerimon's house.*

Enter CERIMON *and* THAISA.

Cer. Madam, this letter, and some certain jewels,
Lay with you in your coffer: which are now
At your command. Know you the character?
  Thai. It is my lord's.
That I was shipp'd at sea, I well remember,
Even on my eaning time; but whether there
Deliver'd, by the holy gods,
I cannot rightly say. But since King Pericles,
My wedded lord, I ne'er shall see again,
A vestal livery will I take me to, 10
And never more have joy.
  Cer. Madam, if this you purpose as ye speak,
Diana's temple is not distant far,
Where you may abide till your date expire.
Moreover, if you please, a niece of mine
Shall there attend you.
  Thai. My recompense is thanks, that's all;
Yet my good will is great, though the gift small. [*Exeunt.*

ACT IV.

Enter GOWER.

  Gow. Imagine Pericles arrived at Tyre,
Welcomed and settled to his own desire.
His woeful queen we leave at Ephesus,
Unto Diana there a votaress.
Now to Marina bend your mind,
Whom our fast-growing scene must find
At Tarsus, and by Cleon train'd
In music, letters; who hath gain'd
Of education all the grace,
Which makes her both the heart and place 10
Of general wonder. But, alack,
That monster envy, oft the wrack
Of earned praise, Marina's life
Seeks to take off by treason's knife.
And in this kind hath our Cleon
One daughter, and a wench full grown,
Even ripe for marriage-rite; this maid
Hight Philoten: and it is said
For certain in our story, she
Would ever with Marina be: 20
Be't when she weaved the sleided silk
With fingers long, small, white as milk;
Or when she would with sharp needle wound
The cambric, which she made more sound
By hurting it; or when to the lute
She sung, and made the night-bird mute,
That still records with moan; or when
She would with rich and constant pen

Vail to her mistress Dian; still
This Philoten contends in skill 30
With absolute Marina: so
With the dove of Paphos might the crow
Vie feathers white. Marina gets
All praises, which are paid as debts,
And not as given. This so darks
In Philoten all graceful marks,
That Cleon's wife, with envy rare,
A present murderer does prepare
For good Marina, that her daughter
Might stand peerless by this slaughter. 40
The sooner her vile thoughts to stead,
Lychorida, our nurse, is dead:
And cursed Dionyza hath
The pregnant instrument of wrath
Prest for this blow. The unborn event
I do commend to your content:
Only I carry winged time
Post on the lame feet of my rhyme;
Which never could I so convey,
Unless your thoughts went on my way. 50
Dionyza does appear,
With Leonine, a murderer. [*Exit.*

SCENE I. *Tarsus. An open place near the sea-shore.*

Enter DIONYZA *and* LEONINE.

  Dion. Thy oath remember; thou hast sworn to do't:
'Tis but a blow, which never shall be known.
Thou canst not do a thing in the world so soon,
To yield thee so much profit. Let not conscience,
Which is but cold, inflaming love i' thy bosom,
Inflame too nicely; nor let pity, which
Even women have cast off, melt thee, but be
A soldier to thy purpose.
  Leon. I will do't; but yet she is a goodly creature. 9
  Dion. The fitter, then, the gods should have her.
†Here she comes weeping for her only mistress' death.
Thou art resolved?
  Leon. I am resolved.

Enter MARINA, *with a basket of flowers.*

  Mar. No, I will rob Tellus of her weed,
To strew thy green with flowers: the yellows, blues,
The purple violets, and marigolds,
Shall as a carpet hang upon thy grave,
While summer-days do last. Ay me! poor maid,
Born in a tempest, when my mother died,
This world to me is like a lasting storm, 20
Whirring me from my friends.
  Dion. How now, Marina! why do you keep alone?
How chance my daughter is not with you? Do not
Consume your blood with sorrowing: you have
A nurse of me. Lord, how your favour's changed
With this unprofitable woe!
Come, give me your flowers, ere the sea mar it.

---

of years between acts; cf. ll. 47-50, below. **10-11. both . . . wonder,**
the focal point of the admiration of all. **14. treason's,** treachery's.
15. in this kind, similarly; i.e., like Pericles, Cleon has a daughter,
etc. **18. Hight,** is called. **21. sleided silk,** floss silk; cf. *Troilus
and Cressida*, V, i, 35. **27. records,** sings. **28. constant,** loyal. **29.
Vail,** do homage to. **32. Paphos,** city sacred to Venus. **33. Vie
feathers white,** contend with in whiteness of plumage. **38. present,**
transferred modifier; i.e., forthwith prepares. **45. Prest,** prepared.
  SCENE I. **4-6. Let . . . nicely,** Knight's emendation of Q: *in flam-*

ing, *thy loue bosome;* Deighton emended, *or flaming love thy bosom Enslave
too nicely* and commented: Dionyza mentions three possible hindrances,
conscience, love, pity, as likely to deter Leonine, and an obvious antithesis between *cold conscience* and *flaming love* seems to be intended.
6. nicely, scrupulously. **11. only mistress',** Nicholson: *only nurse's;*
Percy: *old nurse's.* **14. Tellus,** goddess of the earth. **15. green,**
grave. **24. with sorrowing,** i.e., with sighs; cf. *blood-drinking sighs,
2 Henry VI*, III, ii, 63. **27. ere . . . it,** before your tears mar your
face.

Walk with Leonine; the air is quick there,
And it pierces and sharpens the stomach. Come,
Leonine, take her by the arm, walk with her. 30
    Mar. No, I pray you;
I'll not bereave you of your servant.
    Dion. Come, come;
I love the king your father, and yourself,
With more than foreign heart. We every day
Expect him here: when he shall come and find
Our paragon to all reports thus blasted,
He will repent the breadth of his great voyage;
Blame both my lord and me, that we have taken
No care to your best courses. Go, I pray you,
Walk, and be cheerful once again; reserve 40
That excellent complexion, which did steal
The eyes of young and old. Care not for me;
I can go home alone.
    Mar.   Well, I will go;
But yet I have no desire to it.
    Dion. Come, come, I know 'tis good for you.
Walk half an hour, Leonine, at the least:
Remember what I have said.
    Leon.   I warrant you, madam.
    Dion. I'll leave you, my sweet lady, for a while:
Pray, walk softly, do not heat your blood:
What! I must have a care of you.
    Mar.   My thanks, sweet madam. 50
                        [*Exit Dionyza.*
Is this wind westerly that blows?
    Leon.   South-west.
    Mar. When I was born, the wind was north.
    Leon.   Was 't so?
    Mar. My father, as nurse said, did never fear,
But cried 'Good seamen!' to the sailors, galling
His kingly hands, haling ropes;
And, clasping to the mast, endured a sea
That almost burst the deck.
    Leon. When was this?
    Mar. When I was born: 60
Never was waves nor wind more violent;
And from the ladder-tackle washes off
A canvas-climber. 'Ha!' says one, 'wilt out?'
And with a dropping industry they skip
From stem to stern: the boatswain whistles, and
The master calls, and trebles their confusion.
    Leon. Come, say your prayers.
    Mar. What mean you?
    Leon. If you require a little space for prayer,
I grant it: pray; but be not tedious,
For the gods are quick of ear, and I am sworn 70
To do my work with haste.
    Mar.   Why will you kill me?
    Leon. To satisfy my lady.
    Mar. Why would she have me kill'd?
Now, as I can remember, by my troth,
I never did her hurt in all my life:
I never spake bad word, nor did ill turn
To any living creature: believe me, la,
I never kill'd a mouse, nor hurt a fly:
I trod upon a worm against my will,
But I wept for it. How have I offended, 80
Wherein my death might yield her any profit,

Or my life imply her any danger?
    Leon. My commission
Is not to reason of the deed, but do it.
    Mar. You will not do 't for all the world, I hope.
You are well favour'd, and your looks foreshow
You have a gentle heart. I saw you lately,
When you caught hurt in parting two that fought:
Good sooth, it show'd well in you: do so now:
Your lady seeks my life; come you between, 90
And save poor me, the weaker.
    Leon.   I am sworn,
And will dispatch.   [*He seizes her.*

Enter Pirates.
First Pirate. Hold, villain!   [*Leonine runs away.*
Sec. Pirate. A prize! a prize!
    Third Pirate. Half-part, mates, half-part.
Come, let 's have her aboard suddenly.
                [*Exeunt Pirates with Marina.*

        Re-enter LEONINE.

Leon. These roguing thieves serve the great pirate
        Valdes;
And they have seized Marina. Let her go:
There 's no hope she will return. I'll swear she 's
        dead,
And thrown into the sea. But I'll see further: 100
Perhaps they will but please themselves upon her,
Not carry her aboard. If she remain,
Whom they have ravish'd must by me be slain.   [*Exit.*

SCENE II. *Mytilene. A room in a brothel.*

Enter PANDAR, Bawd, *and* BOULT.

Pand. Boult!
Boult. Sir?
Pand. Search the market narrowly; Mytilene is full
of gallants. We lost too much money this mart by
being too wenchless.
Bawd. We were never so much out of creatures.
We have but poor three, and they can do no more
than they can do; and they with continual action are
even as good as rotten. 9
Pand. Therefore let 's have fresh ones, whate'er we
pay for them. If there be not a conscience to be used
in every trade, we shall never prosper.
Bawd. Thou sayest true: 'tis not our bringing up of
poor bastards,—as, I think, I have brought up some
eleven—
Boult. Ay, to eleven; and brought them down again.
But shall I search the market? 18
Bawd. What else, man? The stuff we have, a strong
wind will blow it to pieces, they are so pitifully sodden.
Pand. Thou sayest true; they 're too unwholesome,
o' conscience. The poor Transylvanian is dead, that
lay with the little baggage.
Boult. Ay, she quickly pooped him; she made him
roast-meat for worms. But I'll go search the market.
                [*Exit.*
Pand. Three or four thousand chequins were as
pretty a proportion to live quietly, and so give over. 30

---

34. **more . . . heart,** more than a foreigner usually does, i.e., as his
countrymen do. 36. **paragon . . . reports,** the equal in repute to
anyone. 39. **to your best courses,** to bring you up well. 40. **reserve,**
preserve. 63. **with . . . industry,** dripping wet as they labored.
88. **caught hurt,** received an injury. 95. **Half-part,** shares. 97.

Valdes. Malone thought this name was derived from that of Don
Pedro de Valdes, a Spanish admiral captured by Sir Francis Drake.
SCENE II. 5. **this mart,** at the last market time. 28. **chequins,**
zecchinos, Italian coins. 37. **keep . . . hatched,** keep the lower halfdoor
(the hatch) closed. 47. **gone through,** made a bid. 52-53. **there 's . . .**

Bawd. Why to give over, I pray you? is it a shame to get when we are old?

Pand. O, our credit comes not in like the commodity, nor the commodity wages not with the danger: therefore, if in our youths we could pick up some pretty estate, 'twere not amiss to keep our door hatched. Besides, the sore terms we stand upon with the gods will be strong with us for giving over. 39

Bawd. Come, other sorts offend as well as we.

Pand. As well as we! ay, and better too; we offend worse. Neither is our profession any trade; it 's no calling. But here comes Boult.

Re-enter BOULT, *with the* Pirates *and* MARINA.

Boult. [*To Marina*] Come your ways. My masters, you say she 's a virgin?

First Pirate. O, sir, we doubt it not.

Boult. Master, I have gone through for this piece, you see: if you like her, so; if not, I have lost my earnest.

Bawd. Boult, has she any qualities? 50

Boult. She has a good face, speaks well, and has excellent good clothes: there 's no further necessity of qualities can make her be refused.

Bawd. What 's her price, Boult?

Boult. I cannot be bated one doit of a thousand pieces.

Pand. Well, follow me, my masters, you shall have your money presently. Wife, take her in; instruct her what she has to do, that she may not be raw in her entertainment. [*Exeunt Pandar and Pirates.* 60

Bawd. Boult, take you the marks of her, the colour of her hair, complexion, height, age, with warrant of her virginity; and cry 'He that will give most shall have her first.' Such a maidenhead were no cheap thing, if men were as they have been. Get this done as I command you.

Boult. Performance shall follow. [*Exit.*

Mar. Alack that Leonine was so slack, so slow!
He should have struck, not spoke; or that these
 pirates, 69
Not enough barbarous, had not o'erboard thrown me
For to seek my mother!

Bawd. Why lament you, pretty one?

Mar. That I am pretty.

Bawd. Come, the gods have done their part in you.

Mar. I accuse them not.

Bawd. You are light into my hands, where you are like to live.

Mar. The more my fault
To scape his hands where I was like to die. 80

Bawd. Ay, and you shall live in pleasure.

Mar. No.

Bawd. Yes, indeed shall you, and taste gentlemen of all fashions: you shall fare well; you shall have the difference of all complexions. What! do you stop your ears?

Mar. Are you a woman?

Bawd. What would you have me be, an I be not a woman? 89

Mar. An honest woman, or not a woman.

Bawd. Marry, whip thee, gosling: I think I shall

have something to do with you. Come, you 're a young foolish sapling, and must be bowed as I would have you.

Mar. The gods defend me!

Bawd. If it please the gods to defend you by men, then men must comfort you, men must feed you, men must stir you up. Boult 's returned.

Re-enter BOULT.

Now, sir, hast thou cried her through the market? 99

Boult. I have cried her almost to the number of her hairs; I have drawn her picture with my voice.

Bawd. And I prithee tell me, how dost thou find the inclination of the people, especially of the younger sort?

Boult. 'Faith, they listened to me as they would have hearkened to their father's testament. There was a Spaniard's mouth so watered, that he went to bed to her very description. 109

Bawd. We shall have him here to-morrow with his best ruff on.

Boult. To-night, to-night. But, mistress, do you know the French knight that cowers i' the hams?

Bawd. Who, Monsieur Veroles?

Boult. Ay, he: he offered to cut a caper at the proclamation; but he made a groan at it, and swore he would see her to-morrow.

Bawd. Well, well; as for him, he brought his disease hither: here he does but repair it. I know he will come in our shadow, to scatter his crowns in the sun. 122

Boult. Well, if we had of every nation a traveller, we should lodge them with this sign.

Bawd. [*To Mar.*] Pray you, come hither awhile. You have fortunes coming upon you. Mark me: you must seem to do that fearfully which you commit willingly, despise profit where you have most gain. To weep that you live as ye do makes pity in your lovers: seldom but that pity begets you a good opinion, and that opinion a mere profit.

Mar. I understand you not.

Boult. O, take her home, mistress, take her home: these blushes of hers must be quenched with some present practice.

Bawd. Thou sayest true, i' faith so they must; for your bride goes to that with shame which is her way to go with warrant. 139

Boult. 'Faith, some do, and some do not. But, mistress, if I have bargained for the joint,—

Bawd. Thou mayst cut a morsel off the spit.

Boult. I may so.

Bawd. Who should deny it? Come, young one, I like the manner of your garments well.

Boult. Ay, by my faith, they shall not be changed yet. 145

Bawd. Boult, spend thou that in the town: report what a sojourner we have; you'll lose nothing by custom. When nature framed this piece, she meant thee a good turn; therefore say what a paragon she is, and thou hast the harvest out of thine own report.

Boult. I warrant you, mistress, thunder shall not so awake the beds of eels as my giving out her beauty stir

Pericles
ACT IV : SC II

1171

---

refused, i.e., there is no requirement that she cannot meet. 77.
are light, have chanced to light. 79. **fault,** misfortune. 85. **differ-ence,** variety. 120. **repair,** quibble on the meanings "return with" and "mend" in an ironic sense, hence "made worse." 128. **despise,** parallel with *do* (l. 127). 134. **take her home,** talk plainly, i.e., be direct

with her. 155. **beds of eels.** Seager (*Natural History*, p. 98) quotes *Hortus Sanitatus*: the eel "is disturbed by the sound of thunder."

up the lewdly-inclined. I'll bring home some to-night.
Bawd. Come your ways; follow me.
Mar. If fires be hot, knives sharp, or waters deep,
Untied I still my virgin knot will keep.   160
Diana, aid my purpose!
Bawd. What have we to do with Diana? Pray you,
will you go with us?   [*Exeunt*.

SCENE III. *Tarsus. A room in Cleon's house.*

Enter CLEON *and* DIONYZA.

Dion. Why, are you foolish? Can it be undone?
Cle. O Dionyza, such a piece of slaughter
The sun and moon ne'er look'd upon!
Dion.   I think
You'll turn a child again.
Cle. Were I chief lord of all this spacious world,
I 'ld give it to undo the deed. O lady,
Much less in blood than virtue, yet a princess
To equal any single crown o' the earth
I' the justice of compare! O villain Leonine!
Whom thou hast poison'd too: 10
If thou hadst drunk to him, 't had been a kindness
Becoming well thy fact: what canst thou say
When noble Pericles shall demand his child?
Dion. That she is dead. Nurses are not the fates,
To foster it, nor ever to preserve.
She died at night; I'll say so. Who can cross it?
Unless you play the pious innocent,
And for an honest attribute cry out
'She died by foul play.'
Cle.   O, go to. Well, well,
Of all the faults beneath the heavens, the gods   20
Do like this worst.
Dion.   Be one of those that think
The petty wrens of Tarsus will fly hence,
And open this to Pericles. I do shame
To think of what a noble strain you are,
And of how coward a spirit.
Cle.   To such proceeding
Who ever but his approbation added,
Though not his prime consent, he did not flow
From honourable sources.
Dion.   Be it so, then:
Yet none does know, but you, how she came dead,
Nor none can know, Leonine being gone.   30
She did distain my child, and stood between
Her and her fortunes: none would look on her,
But cast their gazes on Marina's face;
Whilst ours was blurted at and held a malkin
Not worth the time of day. It pierced me thorough;
And though you call my course unnatural,
You not your child well loving, yet I find
It greets me as an enterprise of kindness
Perform'd to your sole daughter.
Cle.   Heavens forgive it!
Dion. And as for Pericles,   40
What should he say? We wept after her hearse,
And yet we mourn: her monument
Is almost finish'd, and her epitaphs

In glittering golden characters express
A general praise to her, and care in us
At whose expense 'tis done.
Cle.   Thou art like the harpy,
Which, to betray, dost, with thine angel's face,
Seize with thine eagle's talons.
Dion. You are like one that superstitiously
Doth swear to the gods that winter kills the flies: 50
But yet I know you'll do as I advise.   [*Exeunt*.

SCENE IV.

Enter GOWER, *before the monument of* MARINA *at Tarsus.*

Gow. Thus time we waste, and longest leagues
      make short;
Sail seas in cockles, have and wish but for 't;
Making, to take your imagination,
From bourn to bourn, region to region.
By you being pardon'd, we commit no crime
To use one language in each several clime
Where our scenes seem to live. I do beseech you
To learn of me, who stand i' the gaps to teach you,
The stages of our story. Pericles
Is now again thwarting the wayward seas,   10
Attended on by many a lord and knight,
To see his daughter, all his life's delight.
Old Escanes, whom Helicanus late
Advanced in time to great and high estate,
Is left to govern. Bear you it in mind,
Old Helicanus goes along behind.
Well-sailing ships and bounteous winds have
      brought
This king to Tarsus,—think his pilot thought;
So with his steerage shall your thoughts grow on,—
To fetch his daughter home, who first is gone.   29
Like motes and shadows see them move awhile;
Your ears unto your eyes I'll reconcile.

DUMB SHOW.

Enter PERICLES, *at one door, with all his train;* CLEON
and DIONYZA, *at the other.* CLEON *shows* PERICLES
the tomb; whereat PERICLES *makes lamentation, puts
on sackcloth, and in a mighty passion departs. Then
exeunt* CLEON *and* DIONYZA.

See how belief may suffer by foul show!
This borrow'd passion stands for true old woe;
And Pericles, in sorrow all devour'd,
With sighs shot through, and biggest tears
      o'ershower'd,
Leaves Tarsus and again embarks. He swears
Never to wash his face, nor cut his hairs:
He puts on sackcloth, and to sea. He bears
A tempest, which his mortal vessel tears,   30
And yet he rides it out. Now please you wit
The epitaph is for Marina writ
By wicked Dionyza.
      [*Reads the inscription on Marina's monument.*
'The fairest, sweet'st, and best lies here,
Who wither'd in her spring of year.

SCENE III. 9. I' . . . compare, if justly compared. 11. drunk to
him, taken a drink of the poison with him. 14. Nurses . . . fates,
i.e., nurses have not the power of the fates to control life and death.
18. for . . . attribute, for the epithet "honest" to be attached to your
name. 27. prime, original. 31. distain, defile, dishonor; i.e., my
child appeared so by comparison. 34. malkin, diminutive of Moll,
contemptuous name for a woman servant. 35. time of day, greeting.

50. Doth . . . flies, you blame the death of flies on winter, thus exculpating the gods.
SCENE IV. 2. cockles, cockleshells, i.e., as supernatural creatures
do; alludes to the imaginary crossing of the seas between scenes of the
play. have . . . for 't, have something if we but wish it. and, so Q;
Globe, following Dyce: an. 8. who . . . gaps, who bridges the gaps of
time and space between scenes. 18. think . . . thought, think or imag-

She was of Tyrus the king's daughter,
On whom foul death hath made this slaughter;
Marina was she call'd; and at her birth,
Thetis, being proud, swallow'd some part o' the
    earth:
Therefore the earth, fearing to be o'erflow'd,   40
Hath Thetis' birth-child on the heavens bestow'd:
Wherefore she does, and swears she'll never stint,
Make raging battery upon shores of flint.'

No visor does become black villany
So well as soft and tender flattery.
Let Pericles believe his daughter 's dead,
And bear his courses to be ordered
By Lady Fortune; while our scene must play
His daughter's woe and heavy well-a-day
In her unholy service. Patience, then,   50
And think you now are all in Mytilene.   [*Exit.*

SCENE V. *Mytilene. A street before the brothel.*

Enter, from the brothel, two Gentlemen.

First Gent. Did you ever hear the like?
Sec. Gent. No, nor never shall do in such a place as
this, she being once gone.
First Gent. But to have divinity preached there! did
you ever dream of such a thing?
Sec. Gent. No, no. Come, I am for no more bawdy-
houses: shall 's go hear the vestals sing?
First Gent. I'll do any thing now that is virtuous;
but I am out of the road of rutting for ever. [*Exeunt.* 10

SCENE VI. *The same. A room in the brothel.*

Enter Pandar, Bawd, *and* BOULT.

Pand. Well, I had rather than twice the worth of
her she had ne'er come here.
Bawd. Fie, fie upon her! she 's able to freeze the
god Priapus, and undo a whole generation. We must
either get her ravished, or be rid of her. When she
should do for clients her fitment, and do me the
kindness of our profession, she has me her quirks, her
reasons, her master reasons, her prayers, her knees;
that she would make a puritan of the devil, if he
should cheapen a kiss of her.   10
Boult. 'Faith, I must ravish her, or she'll disfurnish
us of all our cavaliers, and make our swearers priests.
Pand. Now, the pox upon her green-sickness for me!
Bawd. 'Faith, there 's no way to be rid on 't but by
the way to the pox. Here comes the Lord Lysimachus
disguised.
Boult. We should have both lord and lown, if the
peevish baggage would but give way to customers.   21

Enter LYSIMACHUS.

Lys. How now! How a dozen of virginities?
Bawd. Now, the gods to bless your honour!
Boult. I am glad to see your honour in good health.
Lys. You may so; 'tis the better for you that your

resorters stand upon sound legs. How now! wholesome
iniquity have you that a man may deal withal, and
defy the surgeon?
Bawd. We have here one, sir, if she would—but
there never came her like in Mytilene.   31
Lys. If she 'ld do the deed of darkness, thou wouldst
say.
Bawd. Your honour knows what 'tis to say well
enough.
Lys. Well, call forth, call forth.
Boult. For flesh and blood, sir, white and red, you
shall see a rose; and she were a rose indeed, if she had
but—
Lys. What, prithee?   40
Boult. O, sir, I can be modest.
Lys. That dignifies the renown of a bawd, no less
than it gives a good report to a number to be chaste.
       [*Exit Boult.*
Bawd. Here comes that which grows to the stalk;
never plucked yet, I can assure you.

Re-enter BOULT *with* MARINA.

Is she not a fair creature?
Lys. 'Faith, she would serve after a long voyage at
sea. Well, there 's for you: leave us.
Bawd. I beseech your honour, give me leave: a
word, and I'll have done presently.   51
Lys. I beseech you, do.
Bawd. [*To Marina*] First, I would have you note,
this is an honourable man.
Mar. I desire to find him so, that I may worthily
note him.
Bawd. Next, he 's the governor of this country, and
a man whom I am bound to.
Mar. If he govern the country, you are bound to
him indeed; but how honourable he is in that, I
know not.   61
Bawd. Pray you, without any more virginal fencing,
will you use him kindly? He will line your apron with
gold.
Mar. What he will do graciously, I will thankfully
receive.
Lys. Ha' you done?
Bawd. My lord, she 's not paced yet: you must take
some pains to work her to your manage. Come, we
will leave his honour and her together. Go thy ways. 70
      [*Exeunt Bawd, Pandar, and Boult.*
Lys. Now, pretty one, how long have you been at
this trade?
Mar. What trade, sir?
Lys. Why, I cannot name 't but I shall offend.
Mar. I cannot be offended with my trade.
Please you to name it.
Lys. How long have you been of this profession?
Mar. E'er since I can remember.
Lys. Did you go to 't so young? Were you a gamester
at five or at seven?   81
Mar. Earlier too, sir, if now I be one.
Lys. Why, the house you dwell in proclaims you to
be a creature of sale.
Mar. Do you know this house to be a place of such

---

ine his voyage (instead of tracing it). 19. **his steerage,** the steering
of his ship. 30. **mortal vessel,** human body. 31. **wit,** know. 39. **Thetis,** sea nymph; alludes to Marina's being born at sea. 42-43. **Wherefore . . . flint,** on account of which she (Thetis) continuously beats
upon rocky shores. 47. **bear,** endure, allow.
   SCENE V. 7. **shall 's,** shall we; originally expressing necessity,
shall was sometimes used as an impersonal verb.

   SCENE VI. 4. **Priapus,** god of lechery. 6. **fitment,** duty. 10.
cheapen, bargain for. 19. **lown,** stupid fellow. 42-44. **dignifies . . .
chaste,** i.e., modesty gives renown to a bawd as well as attesting the
chastity of many women. 54, 56. **note,** quibble on the meanings "observe" and "set down as having a good or bad character." 68, 69.
paced, manage, terms used in training horses.

resort, and will come into 't? I hear say you are of
honourable parts, and are the governor of this place.

Lys. Why, hath your principal made known unto
you who I am? 90

Mar. Who is my principal?

Lys. Why, your herb-woman: she that sets seeds
and roots of shame and iniquity. O, you have heard
something of my power, and so stand aloof for more
serious wooing. But I protest to thee, pretty one, my
authority shall not see thee, or else look friendly upon
thee. Come, bring me to some private place: come,
come.

Mar. If you were born to honour, show it now;
If put upon you, make the judgement good 100
That thought you worthy of it.

Lys. How 's this? how 's this? Some more; be sage.

Mar. For me,
That am a maid, though most ungentle fortune
Have placed me in this sty, where, since I came,
Diseases have been sold dearer than physic,
O, that the gods
Would set me free from this unhallow'd place,
Though they did change me to the meanest bird
That flies i' the purer air!

Lys. I did not think
Thou couldst have spoke so well; ne'er dream'd thou
couldst. 110
Had I brought hither a corrupted mind,
Thy speech had alter'd it. Hold, here 's gold for thee:
Persever in that clear way thou goest,
And the gods strengthen thee!

Mar. The good gods preserve you!

Lys. For me, be you thoughten
That I came with no ill intent; for to me
The very doors and windows savour vilely.
Fare thee well. Thou art a piece of virtue, and
I doubt not but thy training hath been noble.
Hold, here 's more gold for thee. 120
A curse upon him, die he like a thief,
That robs thee of thy goodness! If thou dost
Hear from me, it shall be for thy good.

Re-enter BOULT.

Boult. I beseech your honour, one piece for me.

Lys. Avaunt, thou damned door-keeper!
Your house, but for this virgin that doth prop it,
Would sink and overwhelm you. Away! [*Exit.*

Boult. How 's this? We must take another course
with you. If your peevish chastity, which is not worth
a breakfast in the cheapest country under the cope,
shall undo a whole household, let me be gelded like a
spaniel. Come your ways. 133

Mar. Whither would you have me?

Boult. I must have your maidenhead taken off, or
the common hangman shall execute it. Come your
ways. We'll have no more gentlemen driven away.
Come your ways, I say.

Re-enter Bawd.

Bawd. How now! what 's the matter? 140

Boult. Worse and worse, mistress; she has here
spoken holy words to the Lord Lysimachus.

Bawd. O abominable!

Boult. She makes our profession as it were to stink
afore the face of the gods.

Bawd. Marry, hang her up for ever!

Boult. The nobleman would have dealt with her
like a nobleman, and she sent him away as cold as a
snowball; saying his prayers too. 149

Bawd. Boult, take her away; use her at thy pleasure:
crack the glass of her virginity, and make the rest
malleable.

Boult. An if she were a thornier piece of ground
than she is, she shall be ploughed.

Mar. Hark, hark, you gods!

Bawd. She conjures: away with her! Would she had
never come within my doors! Marry, hang you!
She 's born to undo us. Will you not go the way of
women-kind? Marry, come up, my dish of chastity
with rosemary and bays! [*Exit.* 160

Boult. Come, mistress; come your ways with me.

Mar. Whither wilt thou have me?

Boult. To take from you the jewel you hold so dear.

Mar. Prithee, tell me one thing first.

Boult. Come now, your one thing.

Mar. What canst thou wish thine enemy to be?

Boult. Why, I could wish him to be my master, or
rather, my mistress. 170

Mar. Neither of these are so bad as thou art,
Since they do better thee in their command.
Thou hold'st a place, for which the pained'st fiend
Of hell would not in reputation change:
Thou art the damned doorkeeper to every
Coistrel that comes inquiring for his Tib;
To the choleric fisting of every rogue
Thy ear is liable; thy food is such
As hath been belch'd on by infected lungs. 179

Boult. What would you have me do? go to the wars,
would you? where a man may serve seven years for
the loss of a leg, and have not money enough in the
end to buy him a wooden one?

Mar. Do any thing but this thou doest. Empty
Old receptacles, or common shores, of filth;
Serve by indenture to the common hangman:
Any of these ways are yet better than this;
For what thou professest, a baboon, could he speak,
Would own a name too dear. O, that the gods 190
Would safely deliver me from this place!
Here, here 's gold for thee.
If that thy master would gain by me,
Proclaim that I can sing, weave, sew, and dance,
With other virtues, which I'll keep from boast;
And I will undertake all these to teach.
I doubt not but this populous city will
Yield many scholars.

Boult. But can you teach all this you speak of?

Mar. Prove that I cannot, take me home again, 200
And prostitute me to the basest groom
That doth frequent your house.

Boult. Well, I will see what I can do for thee: if I
can place thee, I will.

Mar. But amongst honest women.

Boult. 'Faith, my acquaintance lies little amongst
them. But since my master and mistress have bought
you, there 's no going but by their consent: therefore
I will make them acquainted with your purpose, and

---

96. **shall not see thee,** i.e., I'll wink at your offenses, not enforce the laws
against prostitutes. 115. **be you thoughten,** let it seem to you. 132.
cope, the firmament. 160. **rosemary and bays,** customary garnishes
for certain foods. 176. **Coistrel,** knave. **Tib,** common woman. 177.
choleric fisting, angry blows. 190. **too dear,** i.e., that he could not
afford.

I doubt not but I shall find them tractable enough.
Come, I'll do for thee what I can; come your ways.
[*Exeunt.*

ACT V.

Enter GOWER.

Gow. Marina thus the brothel 'scapes, and chances
Into an honest house, our story says.
She sings like one immortal, and she dances
As goddess-like to her admired lays;
Deep clerks she dumbs; and with her neeld com-
    poses
Nature's own shape, of bud, bird, branch, or berry,
That even her art sisters the natural roses;
Her inkle, silk, twin with the rubied cherry:
That pupils lacks she none of noble race,
Who pour their bounty on her; and her gain   10
She gives the cursed bawd. Here we her place;
And to her father turn our thoughts again,
Where we left him, on the sea. We there him lost;
Whence, driven before the winds, he is arrived
Here where his daughter dwells; and on this coast
Suppose him now at anchor. The city strived
God Neptune's annual feast to keep: from whence
Lysimachus our Tyrian ship espies,
His banners sable, trimm'd with rich expense;
And to him in his barge with fervour hies.   20
In your supposing once more put your sight
Of heavy Pericles; think this his bark:
Where what is done in action, more, if might,
Shall be discover'd; please you, sit and hark. [*Exit.*

SCENE I. *On board Pericles' ship, off Mytilene. A close
pavilion on deck, with a curtain before it; Pericles within
it, reclined on a couch. A barge lying beside the Tyrian
vessel.*

Enter two Sailors, *one belonging to the Tyrian vessel, the
other to the barge; to them* HELICANUS.

Tyr. Sail. [*To the Sailor of Mytilene*] Where is lord
    Helicanus? he can resolve you.
O, here he is.
Sir, there 's a barge put off from Mytilene,
And in it is Lysimachus the governor,
Who craves to come aboard. What is your will?
    Hel. That he have his. Call up some gentlemen.
    Tyr. Sail. Ho, gentlemen! my lord calls.

Enter two or three Gentlemen.

First Gent. Doth your lordship call?
    Hel. Gentlemen, there 's some of worth would come
    aboard;
I pray ye, greet them fairly.   10
    [*The Gentlemen and the two Sailors descend, and go
        on board the barge.*

Enter, from thence, LYSIMACHUS *and* Lords; *with the
    Gentlemen and the two* Sailors.

    Tyr. Sail. Sir,
This is the man that can, in aught you would,

Resolve you.
    Lys. Hail, reverend sir! the gods preserve you!
    Hel. And you, sir, to outlive the age I am,
And die as I would do.
    Lys.   You wish me well.
Being on shore, honouring of Neptune's triumphs,
Seeing this goodly vessel ride before us,
I made to it, to know of whence you are.
    Hel. First, what is your place?   20
    Lys. I am the governor of this place you lie before.
    Hel. Sir,
Our vessel is of Tyre, in it the king;
A man who for this three months hath not spoken
To any one, nor taken sustenance
But to prorogue his grief.
    Lys. Upon what ground is his distemperature?
    Hel. 'Twould be too tedious to repeat;
But the main grief springs from the loss
Of a beloved daughter and a wife.   30
    Lys. May we not see him?
    Hel. You may;
But bootless is your sight: he will not speak
To any.
    Lys. Yet let me obtain my wish.
    Hel. Behold him. [*Pericles discovered.*] This was a
    goodly person,
Till the disaster that, one mortal night,
Drove him to this.
    Lys. Sir king, all hail! the gods preserve you!
Hail, royal sir!   40
    Hel. It is in vain; he will not speak to you.
    First Lord. Sir,
We have a maid in Mytilene, I durst wager,
Would win some words of him.
    Lys.   'Tis well bethought.
She questionless with her sweet harmony
And other chosen attractions, would allure,
And make a battery through his deafen'd parts,
Which now are midway stopp'd:
She is all happy as the fairest of all,
And, with her fellow maids, is now upon   50
The leafy shelter that abuts against
The island's side.
            [*Whispers a Lord, who goes off in the barge of
                                        Lysimachus.*
    Hel. Sure, all 's effectless; yet nothing we'll omit
That bears recovery's name. But, since your kindness
We have stretch'd thus far, let us beseech you
That for our gold we may provision have,
Wherein we are not destitute for want,
But weary for the staleness.
    Lys.   O, sir, a courtesy
Which if we should deny, the most just gods
For every graff would send a caterpillar,   60
And so afflict our province. Yet once more
Let me entreat to know at large the cause
Of your king's sorrow.
    Hel.   Sit, sir, I will recount it to you:
But, see, I am prevented.

Re-enter, from the barge, Lord, *with* MARINA, *and a
                    young* Lady.

    Lys.   O, here is

ACT V. PROLOGUE. 5. **dumbs,** silences. **neeld,** needle. 8. **inkle,**
kind of tape; also linen or yarn from which it is made. 21. **supposing,**
imagination.

SCENE I. 9. **some,** a certain one; the Old English pronoun *sum;* cf.
Abbott, 21. 26. **prorogue,** prolong. 48. **midway stopp'd,** i.e., the
spirits of hearing are stopped midway by grief. 60. **graff,** scion, shoot.

The lady that I sent for. Welcome, fair one!
Is 't not a goodly presence?
   Hel.   She 's a gallant lady.
   Lys. She 's such a one, that, were I well assured
Came of a gentle kind and noble stock,
I 'ld wish no better choice, and think me rarely wed.
Fair one, all goodness that consists in bounty   70
Expect even here, where is a kingly patient:
If that thy prosperous and artificial feat
Can draw him but to answer thee in aught,
Thy sacred physic shall receive such pay
As thy desires can wish.
   Mar.   Sir, I will use
My utmost skill in his recovery,
Provided
That none but I and my companion maid
Be suffer'd to come near him.
   Lys.   Come, let us leave her;
And the gods make her prosperous!   [*Marina sings.* 80
   Lys. Mark'd he your music?
   Mar.   No, nor look'd on us.
   Lys. See, she will speak to him.
   Mar. Hail, sir! my lord, lend ear.
   Per. Hum, ha!
   Mar. I am a maid,
My lord, that ne'er before invited eyes,
But have been gazed on like a comet: she speaks,
My lord, that, may be, hath endured a grief
Might equal yours, if both were justly weigh'd.
Though wayward fortune did malign my state,   90
My derivation was from ancestors
Who stood equivalent with mighty kings:
But time hath rooted out my parentage,
And to the world and awkward casualties
Bound me in servitude. [*Aside*] I will desist;
But there is something glows upon my cheek,
And whispers in mine ear 'Go not till he speak.'
   Per. My fortunes—parentage—good parentage—
To equal mine!—was it not thus? what say you?   99
   Mar. I said, my lord, if you did know my parentage,
You would not do me violence.
   Per. I do think so. Pray you, turn your eyes upon
    me.
You are like something that—What countrywoman?
Here of these shores?
   Mar.   No, nor of any shores:
Yet I was mortally brought forth, and am
No other than I appear.
   Per. I am great with woe, and shall deliver weeping.
My dearest wife was like this maid, and such a one
My daughter might have been: my queen's square
    brows;
Her stature to an inch; as wand-like straight;   110
As silver-voiced; her eyes as jewel-like
And cased as richly; in pace another Juno;
Who starves the ears she feeds, and makes them
    hungry,
The more she gives them speech. Where do you live?
   Mar. Where I am but a stranger: from the deck
You may discern the place.
   Per.   Where were you bred?
And how achieved you these endowments, which

You make more rich to owe?
   Mar. If I should tell my history, it would seem
Like lies disdain'd in the reporting.
   Per.   Prithee, speak: 120
Falseness cannot come from thee; for thou look'st
Modest as Justice, and thou seem'st a palace
For the crown'd Truth to dwell in: I will believe thee,
And make my senses credit thy relation
To points that seem impossible; for thou look'st
Like one I loved indeed. What were thy friends?
Didst thou not say, when I did push thee back—
Which was when I perceived thee—that thou camest
From good descending?
   Mar.   So indeed I did.
   Per. Report thy parentage. I think thou said'st   130
Thou hadst been toss'd from wrong to injury,
And that thou thought'st thy griefs might equal mine,
If both were open'd.
   Mar.   Some such thing
I said, and said no more but what my thoughts
Did warrant me was likely.
   Per.   Tell thy story;
If thine consider'd prove the thousandth part
Of my endurance, thou art a man, and I
Have suffer'd like a girl: yet thou dost look
Like Patience gazing on kings' graves, and smiling
Extremity out of act. What were thy friends?   140
How lost thou them? Thy name, my most kind virgin?
Recount, I do beseech thee: come, sit by me.
   Mar. My name is Marina.
   Per.   O, I am mock'd,
And thou by some incensed god sent hither
To make the world to laugh at me.
   Mar.   Patience, good sir,
Or here I'll cease.
   Per.   Nay, I'll be patient.
Thou little know'st how thou dost startle me,
To call thyself Marina.
   Mar. The name
Was given me by one that had some power,   150
My father, and a king.
   Per.   How! a king's daughter?
And call'd Marina?
   Mar.   You said you would believe me;
But, not to be a troubler of your peace,
I will end here.
   Per.   But are you flesh and blood?
Have you a working pulse? and are no fairy?
Motion! Well; speak on. Where were you born?
And wherefore call'd Marina?
   Mar.   Call'd Marina
For I was born at sea.
   Per.   At sea! what mother?
   Mar. My mother was the daughter of a king;
Who died the minute I was born,   160
As my good nurse Lychorida hath oft
Deliver'd weeping.
   Per.   O, stop there a little!
[*Aside*] This is the rarest dream that e'er dull sleep
Did mock sad fools withal: this cannot be:
My daughter 's buried. Well: where were you bred?
I'll hear you more, to the bottom of your story,

72. **prosperous,** producing favorable results. **artificial,** skillful. 80. *Stage Direction: Marina sings.* On the restorative effects of music, cf. III, ii, 88-91, note. 86. **ne'er . . . eyes,** never before had to ask to be looked at. 94. **awkward,** adverse. 101. **You . . . violence.** This may refer to something lost from the text. The older prose story

of Twine records that Apollonius struck his daughter, angry at her addressing him. 140. **Extremity,** rigor, hardship. **out of act,** impotent; i.e., beguiling calamity with her smile. 209-210. Many emendations; text will make sense if *The heir of kingdoms* is in apposition with the preceding phrase. K. Deighton would read *and so be another*

And never interrupt you.
 Mar. You scorn: believe me, 'twere best I did give
 o'er.
 Per. I will believe you by the syllable
Of what you shall deliver. Yet, give me leave: 170
How came you in these parts? where were you bred?
 Mar. The king my father did in Tarsus leave me;
Till cruel Cleon, with his wicked wife,
Did seek to murder me: and having woo'd
A villain to attempt it, who having drawn to do 't,
A crew of pirates came and rescued me;
Brought me to Mytilene. But, good sir,
Whither will you have me? Why do you weep? It may
 be,
You think me an impostor: no, good faith;
I am the daughter to King Pericles,   180
If good King Pericles be.
 Per. Ho, Helicanus!
 Hel. Calls my lord?
 Per. Thou art a grave and noble counsellor,
Most wise in general: tell me, if thou canst,
What this maid is, or what is like to be,
That thus hath made me weep?
 Hel.   I know not; but
Here is the regent, sir, of Mytilene
Speaks nobly of her.
 Lys.   She would never tell
Her parentage; being demanded that,   190
She would sit still and weep.
 Per. O Helicanus, strike me, honour'd sir;
Give me a gash, put me to present pain;
Lest this great sea of joys rushing upon me
O'erbear the shores of my mortality,
And drown me with their sweetness. O, come hither,
Thou that beget'st him that did thee beget;
Thou that wast born at sea, buried at Tarsus,
And found at sea again! O Helicanus,
Down on thy knees, thank the holy gods as loud   200
As thunder threatens us: this is Marina.
What was thy mother's name? tell me but that,
For truth can never be confirm'd enough,
Though doubts did ever sleep.
 Mar.   First, sir, I pray,
What is your title?
 Per. I am Pericles of Tyre: but tell me now
My drown'd queen's name, as in the rest you said
Thou hast been godlike perfect,
†The heir of kingdoms and another like
To Pericles thy father.   210
 Mar. Is it no more to be your daughter than
To say my mother's name was Thaisa?
Thaisa was my mother, who did end
The minute I began.
 Per. Now, blessing on thee! rise; thou art my child.
Give me fresh garments. Mine own, Helicanus;
She is not dead at Tarsus, as she should have been,
By savage Cleon: she shall tell thee all;
When thou shalt kneel, and justify in knowledge
She is thy very princess. Who is this?   220
 Hel. Sir, 'tis the governor of Mytilene,
Who, hearing of your melancholy state,
Did come to see you.

 Per.   I embrace you.
Give me my robes. I am wild in my beholding.
O heavens bless my girl! But, hark, what music?
Tell Helicanus, my Marina, tell him
O'er, point by point, for yet he seems to doubt,
How sure you are my daughter. But, what music?
 Hel. My lord, I hear none.
 Per. None!   230
The music of the spheres! List, my Marina.
 Lys. It is not good to cross him; give him way.
 Per. Rarest sounds! Do ye not hear?
 Lys.   My lord, I hear.   [*Music.*
 Per. Most heavenly music!
It nips me unto listening, and thick slumber
Hangs upon mine eyes: let me rest.   [*Sleeps.*
 Lys. A pillow for his head:
So, leave him all. Well, my companion friends,
If this but answer to my just belief,
I'll well remember you.   [*Exeunt all but Pericles.* 240

DIANA *appears to* PERICLES *as in a vision.*

 Dia. My temple stands in Ephesus: hie thee thither,
And do upon mine altar sacrifice.
There, when my maiden priests are met together,
Before the people all,
Reveal how thou at sea didst lose thy wife:
To mourn thy crosses, with thy daughter's, call
And give them repetition to the life.
Or perform my bidding, or thou livest in woe;
Do it, and happy; by my silver bow!
Awake, and tell thy dream.   [*Disappears.* 250
 Per. Celestial Dian, goddess argentine,
I will obey thee. Helicanus!

 Re-enter HELICANUS, LYSIMACHUS, *and* MARINA.

 Hel.   Sir?
 Per. My purpose was for Tarsus, there to strike
The inhospitable Cleon; but I am
For other service first: toward Ephesus
Turn our blown sails; eftsoons I'll tell thee why.
[*To Lysimachus*] Shall we refresh us, sir, upon your
 shore,
And give you gold for such provision
As our intents will need?
 Lys. Sir,   260
With all my heart; and, when you come ashore,
I have another suit.
 Per.   You shall prevail,
Were it to woo my daughter; for it seems
You have been noble towards her.
 Lys.   Sir, lend me your arm.
 Per. Come, my Marina.   [*Exeunt.*

SCENE II. *Enter* GOWER, *before the temple of* DIANA
 at Ephesus.

 Gow. Now our sands are almost run;
More a little, and then dumb.
This, my last boon, give me,
For such kindness must relieve me,
That you aptly will suppose

---

life, etc.   219. **justify in knowledge,** be made certain (that).   224.
wild in my beholding, wild looking; i.e., he is in sackcloth and is un-
shaven and unkempt.   231. **music . . . spheres,** a Ptolemaic notion
first conceived of by Pythagoras, Greek philosopher and mathematician.
He thought of the spheres—orbs—in which heavenly bodies moved

as separated by intervals according to the laws of musical harmony,
their motion producing sounds of exceptional beauty, rarely heard by
mortals.   235. **nips me,** arrests my attention.   251. **argentine,** silvery in
appearance, as appropriate to the moon goddess.   256. **eftsoons,** shortly.

What pageantry, what feats, what shows,
What minstrelsy, and pretty din,
The regent made in Mytilene
To greet the king. So he thrived,
That he is promised to be wived   10
To fair Marina; but in no wise
Till he had done his sacrifice,
As Dian bade: whereto being bound,
The interim, pray you, all confound.
In feather'd briefness sails are fill'd,
And wishes fall out as they 're will'd.
At Ephesus, the temple see,
Our king and all his company.
That he can hither come so soon,
Is by your fancy's thankful doom.   [*Exit.* 20

SCENE III. *The temple of Diana at Ephesus;* THAISA
*standing near the altar, as high priestess; a number of
Virgins on each side;* CERIMON *and other Inhabitants of
Ephesus attending.*

Enter PERICLES, *with his train;* LYSIMACHUS,
HELICANUS, MARINA, *and a Lady.*

Per. Hail, Dian! to perform thy just command,
I here confess myself the king of Tyre;
Who, frighted from my country, did wed
At Pentapolis the fair Thaisa.
At sea in childbed died she, but brought forth
A maid-child call'd Marina; who, O goddess,
Wears yet thy silver livery. She at Tarsus
Was nursed with Cleon; who at fourteen years
He sought to murder: but her better stars
Brought her to Mytilene; 'gainst whose shore   10
Riding, her fortunes brought the maid aboard us,
Where, by her own most clear remembrance, she
Made known herself my daughter.
    Thai.   Voice and favour!
You are, you are—O royal Pericles!   [*Faints.*
    Per. What means the nun? she dies! help,
      gentlemen!
    Cer. Noble sir,
If you have told Diana's altar true,
This is your wife.
    Per.   Reverend appearer, no;
I threw her overboard with these very arms.
    Cer. Upon this coast, I warrant you.
    Per.   'Tis most certain.   20
    Cer. Look to the lady; O, she 's but o'erjoy'd.
Early in blustering morn this lady was
Thrown upon this shore. I oped the coffin,
Found there rich jewels; recover'd her, and placed her
Here in Diana's temple.
    Per.   May we see them?
    Cer. Great sir, they shall be brought you to my
      house,
Whither I invite you. Look, Thaisa is
Recovered.
    Thai.   O, let me look!
If he be none of mine, my sanctity
Will to my sense bend no licentious ear,   30
But curb it, spite of seeing. O, my lord,
Are you not Pericles? Like him you spake,

Like him you are: did you not name a tempest,
A birth, and death?
    Per.   The voice of dead Thaisa!
    Thai. That Thaisa am I, supposed dead
And drown'd.
    Per. Immortal Dian!
    Thai.   Now I know you better.
When we with tears parted Pentapolis,
The king my father gave you such a ring. [*Shows a ring.*
    Per. This, this: no more, you gods! your present
      kindness   40
Makes my past miseries sports: you shall do well,
That on the touching of her lips I may
Melt and no more be seen. O, come, be buried
A second time within these arms.
    Mar.   My heart
Leaps to be gone into my mother's bosom.
                        [*Kneels to Thaisa.*
    Per. Look, who kneels here! Flesh of thy flesh,
      Thaisa;
Thy burden at the sea, and call'd Marina
For she was yielded there.
    Thai.   Blest, and mine own!
    Hel. Hail, madam, and my queen!
    Thai.   I know you not.
    Per. You have heard me say, when I did fly from
      Tyre,   50
I left behind an ancient substitute:
Can you remember what I call'd the man?
I have named him oft.
    Thai.   'Twas Helicanus then.
    Per. Still confirmation:
Embrace him, dear Thaisa; this is he.
Now do I long to hear how you were found;
How possibly preserved; and who to thank,
Besides the gods, for this great miracle.
    Thai. Lord Cerimon, my lord; this man,
Through whom the gods have shown their power;
      that can   60
From first to last resolve you.
    Per.   Reverend sir,
The gods can have no mortal officer
More like a god than you. Will you deliver
How this dead queen re-lives?
    Cer.   I will, my lord.
Beseech you, first go with me to my house,
Where shall be shown you all was found with her;
How she came placed here in the temple;
No needful thing omitted.
    Per. Pure Dian, bless thee for thy vision! I
Will offer night-oblations to thee. Thaisa,   70
This prince, the fair-betrothed of your daughter,
Shall marry her at Pentapolis. And now
This ornament
Makes me look dismal will I clip to form;
And what this fourteen years no razor touch'd,
To grace thy marriage-day, I'll beautify.
    Thai. Lord Cerimon hath letters of good credit, sir,
My father 's dead.
    Per. Heavens make a star of him! Yet there, my
      queen,
We'll celebrate their nuptials, and ourselves   80
Will in that kingdom spend our following days:

SCENE II.   14. **confound,** omit.   15. **feather'd,** winged.
    SCENE III.   18. **Reverend appearer,** you who appear to be reverend.
29-30. **my . . . ear,** passion will not persuade me to give over my holy
vows.   41. **sports,** jests.   42. **That,** if.   48. **yielded,** born.   62. **mortal officer,** human agent.   70. **night-oblations,** nightly sacrifices.
73. **ornament,** i.e., hair and beard.

Our son and daughter shall in Tyrus reign.
Lord Cerimon, we do our longing stay
To hear the rest untold: sir, lead 's the way. [*Exeunt.*

Enter GOWER.

Gow. In Antiochus and his daughter you have
   heard
Of monstrous lust the due and just reward:
In Pericles, his queen and daughter, seen,
Although assail'd with fortune fierce and keen,
Virtue preserved from fell destruction's blast,
Led on by heaven, and crown'd with joy at last: 90
In Helicanus may you well descry
A figure of truth, of faith, of loyalty:
In reverend Cerimon there well appears
The worth that learned charity aye wears:
For wicked Cleon and his wife, when fame
Had spread their cursed deed, and honour'd name
Of Pericles, to rage the city turn,
That him and his they in his palace burn;
The gods for murder seemed so content
To punish them; although not done, but meant.   100
So, on your patience evermore attending,
New joy wait on you! Here our play has ending.
                               [*Exit.*

83. **we . . . stay,** we will let our desires await satisfaction.

Cymbeline

There is no text of *Cymbeline* except that in the Folio of 1623, and it is not a good one. The play is so irregular in construction and so incredible in plot that many critics, with no adequate reason, have thought it a first draft. The Vision of Posthumus (V, iv) and some other parts have been regarded as the work of another hand than Shakespeare's, and hasty composition under pressure of a ruling fashion is the hypothesis pretty generally held. A better hypothesis would regard the play as Shakespeare's experiment in a new form and as his work throughout.

On one leaf of his *Diary* Dr. Simon Forman gives, under date of April 20, 1610, a summary of the plot of *Macbeth.* On the leaf preceding he gives, with no date at all, a summary of "Cimbalin, King of England." The natural inference is that he saw *Cymbeline* a short time before he saw *Macbeth.* Other entries of plays seen are, however, dated in the year 1611, and, if Forman made these notes on the plays witnessed in one particular season, he must have made a mistake in writing down the year in which he saw *Macbeth.* Even if one regards Forman's notes mistakenly as forgeries, it does not matter, since there are other reasons, partly those of style and meter, for believing that *Cymbeline* was written in 1609 or 1610.

ROMANTIC COMEDY

There has been worked out a quite definite and plausible theory to account for a change which took place in the fashion of the London stage about the year 1608 or 1609. This is connected with the work of Beaumont and Fletcher, dramatists of the new era, who replaced the simpler and more ingenuous comedy and tragedy of Shakespeare with a drama of sensationalism and surprise. *Philaster, or Love Lies a Bleeding* (1609?) is thought to have started the fashion. It has been contended that these new dramatists influenced their master and that their methods and temper appear in Shakespeare's latest plays, particularly in *Cymbeline.*

Beaumont and Fletcher went in for ingenious plots, which to the very end might turn out to be either tragic or comic, plots that placed hard sensuality and courtly vice side by side with the ideals of saintly chastity and spotless honor. They kept many features of the older drama: maidens in boys' attire, adventures by land and sea, family separations and reunions, and sentimental pastoralism. Dramatically the plays are highly finished, with few stiff soliloquies and asides and truly dramatic depiction by dialogue and action. Chiefly, Beaumont and Fletcher played on the sensational and developed the possibilities of the surprising. Their verse loses rigidity and grows conversational.

Cymbeline preserves much of Shakespeare's genuineness in thought, action, and manner. However, compared to some of his earlier comedies and tragedies it is a dramatic miscellany of the Beaumont-Fletcher school. Therefore, one places it about the same time as *Philaster* and sees in it resemblances to that play. There is, however, no evidence to tell us definitely which is the earlier, *Cymbeline* or *Philaster.* The late Edward Dowden was of the opinion that it is at least an open question.[1] He thought that Shakespeare had opened up a romantic vein in the work he did in *Pericles* and might well have continued his experiment in *Cymbeline* on an equally thoroughgoing scale. Dowden regarded it as possible that Shakespeare may himself have originated the form of tragi-comedy or romance, represented typically by *Cymbeline, The Winter's Tale,* and *The Tempest* and by six plays believed on good grounds to be the joint work of Beaumont and Fletcher.

SOURCES

The source problem of *Cymbeline* is complex and interesting, and as it reveals a good deal about the structure and nature of the play, it is worth going into. In its sources *Cymbeline* connects itself with the work Shakespeare had been doing earlier in his career. The outer shell of the play is derived from Holinshed, and from that part of Holinshed from which had come *King Lear.*

Cymbeline was, like Lear, one of the mythical kings of Britain. We learn from Holinshed that

[1]A. H. Thorndike, *The Influence of Beaumont and Fletcher on Shakespeare* (1901). *Cymbeline,* edited by Edward Dowden, Arden Shakespeare (Methuen), Introduction.

Cymbeline had been brought up in Rome and knighted by Caesar and that his sons were Guiderius and Arviragus. However, according to Holinshed, it was not Cymbeline who refused to pay the Roman tribute but his successor Guiderius. Most of the details in the first scene of the third act come also from Holinshed, and many of the names in *Cymbeline* are picked up here and there in the *Chronicles*. One incident of real importance (V, iii, 52) comes from Holinshed, namely, the prodigious exploit of Belarius, Guiderius, and Arviragus—

A narrow lane, an old man, and two boys—

which is related of a Scotsman named Haie in a battle against the Danes. *Cymbeline* has in it many references to Roman affairs, and thus connects itself also with Plutarch.

These things are, however, of small account compared to the central incident of the play, which is based on Boccaccio's version in the *Decameron* (ninth novel, second day) of a widely current story in which a man made a wager that his wife's honor would be proof against seduction. There is every reason to think that Shakespeare knew Boccaccio, with whom he could have become acquainted through the original, a French translation, or possibly an English translation now lost; but some details he seems to have adopted from other versions of the story.

These details are so widely distributed that it is impossible to tell their source with certainty. Some are paralleled in *Westward for Smelts*, a prose tale not known to have been printed before 1620. There are two early French romances which tell the tale of the wager, the *Roman de la Violette* by Gibert de Montreuil and *Del Conte de Poitiers*, and also a French miracle play. German, Scandinavian, Gaelic, and English versions have also been discovered. W. F. Thrall brought into consideration *Frederick of Jennen*, a translation of a *Historie von vier Kaufmännern*. This translation was published three times in the sixteenth century. It was derived ultimately from Boccaccio and has many features in common with *Cymbeline* not found in the *Decameron*. Thrall does not contend that *Frederick of Jennen* is the immediate source, but believes that there may have been a lost dramatic original.[2]

To join the story of the British king with the Italian novel Shakespeare needed to create Imogen, the wronged lady, the daughter of the British king, and to supply the story of the stealing away of the king's sons by Belarius and the machinery by which Imogen is united to her brothers.

Here too there trails behind Shakespeare a series of vague sources. An old play, *The Rare Triumphs of Love and Fortune* (1589), tells how one Hermione, brought up like Posthumus as the king's ward,

marries in spite of the king's opposition the princess Fidelia and, like Posthumus, is driven from the court. Hermione also has an encounter with Fidelia's brother Armenio, a coward and a bully suggestive of Cloten. Fidelia flees to the cave of a hermit, formerly a courtier banished unjustly like Belarius. The play also contains reference to a sleeping powder and to apparel stolen by a servant and used for disguise. It undoubtedly resembles *Cymbeline*.

The adventures of Imogen also find fairly close parallel in those of the heroine of the nursery tale of *Little Snow White*. There are, indeed, many suggestions of sources and parallels. The conclusion one would draw from this fact is that back of the rather faulty text of *Cymbeline* there is a carefully constructed play, and that in *Cymbeline* Shakespeare has paid the most minute attention to the dramatic effects of the situations.

INTERPRETATION

We would agree that dramatically *Cymbeline* is a very different thing from *Much Ado about Nothing* and other comedies of the earlier period in which there is likewise an element of sensationalism and intrigue. *Cymbeline* exploits situation, and in order to do this it is less consistent in characterization, less plausible in plot construction, and in general is less careful in the telling of its story. Instead of being narrated and explained as they are put on the stage, the events are acted without comment. In this respect the play no doubt marks a technical advance in the direction of the natural. The style also seems to reflect this. There are more run-on lines than ever, more light and weak endings, and all told a more conversational effect in the verse.

It is not, however, greater drama but diverse. One has to enjoy it in a different way. One goes to it, not for profound conviction, as one goes to *Lear*, but for dramatic thrills and surprises, for the appreciation of situations as distinguished from characters. In order that situations may be realized, individuality suffers. One watches the rage, the self-sacrifice, the grief, the passion of Posthumus. He rivals Othello in passion and his cue is the same, but we do not know him as we know Othello. Cloten seems to be at least two separate kinds of fool and talks at times so rationally and so prince-like that some critics have thought that the Cymbeline plot with the part of Cloten must have been written up several years before, perhaps when Shakespeare was hunting through Holinshed on the occasion of his composition of *King Lear*.

One would not sacrifice too much to this idea in the criticism of Imogen. She has been a prime favorite with the critics of Shakespeare's women. Though one admits that she plays the standardized role of love-lorn maiden and that her part is conventional, even that she is idealized beyond Shakespeare's other women, one feels that she is somehow saved from being classed with Beaumont and Fletcher's heroines

[2] "Cymbeline, Boccaccio, and the Wager Story in England," *Studies in Philology*, XXVII (1931), 639-651. See also W. W. Lawrence, *Shakespeare's Problem Comedies* (1931), 174-233.

by her whimsical humor, her faithfulness, and her spontaneity.

THE DENOUEMENT

Another way of stating the point of the newer criticism of *Cymbeline* is to say that Shakespeare here held his threads separate until the very end, making no prefiguring of the happy denouement. The last scene of the play has been praised as Shakespeare's greatest achievement in the untangling of complications. A score of issues are there met and a score of dangerous possibilities avoided happily.

This is a leading feature of Shakespeare's latest technique and of the technique of his later contemporaries. We saw him in *Hamlet* protracting over five acts a theme which might have been solved in one. Because there is so much to tell and so much time to pass away in plots and counter plots, his hero seems, even to himself, to hesitate unnaturally. When one declares that *The Tempest* observes the Aristotelian unities of time, place, and action, one means that in that play Shakespeare has covered in his dramatic representation only so much of his sequence of events as would have made a fifth act in his earlier plays. His writing up to his denouement in *Cymbeline* shows him leaning in the direction of the structural unity he was to achieve more completely in *The Tempest*.

STAGE HISTORY

Although *Cymbeline* has not in general been a popular acting drama, there are, nevertheless, glorious pages in its stage history. Sir Henry Herbert, Master of the Revels under Charles I, records (January 1, 1633) that "Cymbeline was acted at Court by the King's Players. Well liked by the King."

The play suffered much from adaptations to the stage in the seventeenth and eighteenth centuries. Indeed, it is supposed that Tom D'Urfey's *The Injured Princess, or The Fatal Wager* (1682) is the worst of vile alterations. Different stage versions, all more or less wrenched away from the original, were produced in 1720, 1755, and 1759. Garrick produced the play, with what Genest calls "some most judicious changes," in 1761, and with him in 1767 and 1770 Mrs. Barry played the part of Imogen. John Philip Kemble revived *Cymbeline* in 1785 with Mrs. Siddons as Imogen. Macready (1818), Edmund Kean (1823), and Charles Kemble (1827) appeared in the part of Posthumus. With Macready was Helen Faucit, famous in the part of Imogen. Another celebrated Imogen was the English actress Adelaide Neilson (1877).

The greatest modern revival of *Cymbeline* was that of Henry Irving and Ellen Terry in 1896, in which Irving played Iachimo and Miss Terry, Imogen. The drama is difficult for the stage because of its complexity both in plot and style, but the playing of Imogen, at least, has often been met with popular enthusiasm. *Cymbeline* appeared in the repertory of the Stratford company in the season of 1949.

Cymbeline

DRAMATIS PERSONAE

CYMBELINE, king of Britain.
CLOTEN, son to the Queen by a former husband.
POSTHUMUS LEONATUS, a gentleman, husband to Imogen.
BELARIUS, a banished lord, disguised under the name of Morgan.
GUIDERIUS, } sons to Cymbeline, disguised
ARVIRAGUS, } under the names of Polydore and
} Cadwal, supposed sons to Morgan.
PHILARIO, friend to Posthumus, } Italians.
IACHIMO, friend to Philario, }
CAIUS LUCIUS, general of the Roman forces.
PISANIO, servant to Posthumus.
CORNELIUS, a physician.
A Roman Captain.
Two British Captains.
A Frenchman, friend to Philario.
Two Lords of Cymbeline's court.
Two Gentlemen of the same.
Two Gaolers.

Queen, wife to Cymbeline.
IMOGEN, daughter to Cymbeline by a former queen.
HELEN, a lady attending on Imogen.

Lords, Ladies, Roman Senators, Tribunes, a Soothsayer, a Dutchman, a Spaniard, Musicians, Officers, Captains, Soldiers, Messengers, and other attendants.

Apparitions.

SCENE: *Britain; Rome.*

ACT I.

SCENE I. *Britain. The garden of Cymbeline's palace.*

Enter two Gentlemen.

First Gent. You do not meet a man but frowns: our bloods
No more obey the heavens than our courtiers
Still seem as does the king.
Sec. Gent.   But what's the matter?
First Gent. His daughter, and the heir of's kingdom, whom
He purposed to his wife's sole son—a widow
That late he married—hath referr'd herself
Unto a poor but worthy gentleman: she's wedded;
Her husband banish'd; she imprison'd: all
Is outward sorrow; though I think the king
Be touch'd at very heart.
Sec. Gent.   None but the king?   10
First Gent. He that hath lost her too; so is the queen,
That most desired the match; but not a courtier,
Although they wear their faces to the bent

Of the king's looks, hath a heart that is not
Glad at the thing they scowl at.
  Sec. Gent.   And why so?
  First Gent. He that hath miss'd the princess is a thing
Too bad for bad report: and he that hath her—
I mean, that married her, alack, good man!
And therefore banish'd—is a creature such
As, to seek through the regions of the earth   20
For one his like, there would be something failing
In him that should compare. I do not think
So fair an outward and such stuff within
Endows a man but he.
  Sec. Gent.   You speak him far.
  First Gent. I do extend him, sir, within himself,
Crush him together rather than unfold
His measure duly.
  Sec. Gent.   What 's his name and birth?
  First Gent. I cannot delve him to the root: his father
Was called Sicilius, who did join his honour
Against the Romans with Cassibelan,   30
But had his titles by Tenantius whom
He served with glory and admired success,
So gain'd the sur-addition Leonatus;
And had, besides this gentleman in question,
Two other sons, who in the wars o' the time
Died with their swords in hand; for which their father,
Then old and fond of issue, took such sorrow
That he quit being, and his gentle lady,
Big of this gentleman our theme, deceased
As he was born. The king he takes the babe   40
To his protection, calls him Posthumus Leonatus,
Breeds him and makes him of his bed-chamber,
Puts to him all the learnings that his time
Could make him the receiver of; which he took,
As we do air, fast as 'twas minister'd,
And in 's spring became a harvest, lived in court—
Which rare it is to do—most praised, most loved,
A sample to the youngest, to the more mature
A glass that feated them, and to the graver
A child that guided dotards; to his mistress,   50
For whom he now is banish'd, her own price
Proclaims how she esteem'd him and his virtue;
By her election may be truly read
What kind of man he is.
  Sec. Gent.   I honour him
Even out of your report. But, pray you, tell me,
Is she sole child to the king?
  First Gent.   His only child.
He had two sons: if this be worth your hearing,
Mark it: the eldest of them at three years old,
I' the swathing-clothes the other, from their nursery
Were stol'n, and to this hour no guess in knowledge 60
Which way they went.
  Sec. Gent.   How long is this ago?
  First Gent. Some twenty years.
  Sec. Gent. That a king's children should be so
    convey'd,
So slackly guarded, and the search so slow,
That could not trace them!
  First Gent.   Howso'er 'tis strange,
Or that the negligence may well be laugh'd at,

Yet is it true, sir.
  Sec. Gent.   I do well believe you.
  First Gent. We must forbear: here comes the
    gentleman,
The queen, and princess.   [*Exeunt.*

Enter the QUEEN, POSTHUMUS, *and* IMOGEN.

  Queen. No, be assured you shall not find me,
    daughter,   70
After the slander of most stepmothers,
Evil-eyed unto you: you 're my prisoner, but
Your gaoler shall deliver you the keys
That lock up your restraint. For you, Posthumus,
So soon as I can win the offended king,
I will be known your advocate: marry, yet
The fire of rage is in him, and 'twere good
You lean'd unto his sentence with what patience
Your wisdom may inform you.
  Post.   Please your highness,
I will from hence to-day.
  Queen.   You know the peril.   80
I'll fetch a turn about the garden, pitying
The pangs of barr'd affections, though the king
Hath charged you should not speak together.   [*Exit.*
  Imo.   O
Dissembling courtesy! How fine this tyrant
Can tickle where she wounds! My dearest husband,
I something fear my father's wrath; but nothing—
Always reserved my holy duty—what
His rage can do on me: you must be gone;
And I shall here abide the hourly shot
Of angry eyes, not comforted to live,   90
But that there is this jewel in the world
That I may see again.
  Post.   My queen! my mistress!
O lady, weep no more, lest I give cause
To be suspected of more tenderness
Than doth become a man. I will remain
The loyal'st husband that did e'er plight troth:
My residence in Rome at one Philario's,
Who to my father was a friend, to me
Known but by letter: thither write, my queen,
And with mine eyes I'll drink the words you send, 100
Though ink be made of gall.

Re-enter QUEEN.

  Queen.   Be brief, I pray you:
If the king come, I shall incur I know not
How much of his displeasure. [*Aside*] Yet I'll move
    him
To walk this way: I never do him wrong,
But he does buy my injuries, to be friends;
Pays dear for my offences.   [*Exit.*
  Post.   Should we be taking leave
As long a term as yet we have to live,
The loathness to depart would grow. Adieu!
  Imo. Nay, stay a little:
Were you but riding forth to air yourself,   110
Such parting were too petty. Look here, love;
This diamond was my mother's: take it, heart;
But keep it till you woo another wife,

ACT I. SCENE I. 6. **referr'd,** handed over (married). 13-14. **bent
. . . looks,** inclination of the king's mind, as indicated by his looks.
24. **speak . . . far,** go far in praising him. 25. **I . . . himself,** I magnify
his virtues within the limits of what he actually is. 29. **join his
honour,** give his honorable assistance. 30. **Cassibelan,** according to
Holinshed, Lud's younger brother and successor. 31. **Tenantius,** son
of King Lud and apparently regarded as Cymbeline's predecessor.

33. **sur-addition,** additional title. 38. **quit being,** left existence, died.
39. **Big,** great with young. 40. **king he,** pleonastic subject. 41. **Posthumus,** accent on second syllable. 43. **time,** age. 48. **sample,** example. 49. **feated them,** constrained them to propriety (Onions); made
them *feat,* that is, graceful or elegant (Dowden). Rowe conjectured
featur'd. 78. **lean'd unto,** deferred to. 105. **But . . . friends,** that he
does not reward me for the injuries I have done him in order that I may

When Imogen is dead.
 Post.   How, how: another?
You gentle gods, give me but this I have,
And sear up my embracements from a next
With bonds of death! [*Putting on the ring.*] Remain,
 remain thou here
While sense can keep it on. And, sweetest, fairest,
As I my poor self did exchange for you,
To your so infinite loss, so in our trifles   120
I still win of you: for my sake wear this;
It is a manacle of love; I'll place it
Upon this fairest prisoner.
      [*Putting a bracelet upon her arm.*
 Imo.   O the gods!
When shall we see again?

Enter CYMBELINE *and* Lords.

 Post.   Alack, the king!
 Cym. Thou basest thing, avoid! hence, from my
 sight!
If after this command thou fraught the court
With thy unworthiness, thou diest: away!
Thou 'rt poison to my blood.
 Post.   The gods protect you!
And bless the good remainders of the court!
I am gone.   [*Exit.*
 Imo.   There cannot be a pinch in death
More sharp than this is.
 Cym.   O disloyal thing,   131
That shouldst repair my youth, thou heap'st
A year's age on me.
 Imo.   I beseech you, sir,
Harm not yourself with your vexation:
I am senseless of your wrath; a touch more rare
Subdues all pangs, all fears.
 Cym.   Past grace? obedience?
 Imo. Past hope, and in despair; that way, past grace.
 Cym. That mightst have had the sole son of my
 queen!
 Imo. O blest, that I might not! I chose an eagle,
And did avoid a puttock.   140
 Cym. Thou took'st a beggar; wouldst have made my
 throne
A seat for baseness.
 Imo.   No; I rather added
A lustre to it.
 Cym.   O thou vile one!
 Imo.   Sir,
It is your fault that I have loved Posthumus:
You bred him as my playfellow, and he is
A man worth any woman, overbuys me
Almost the sum he pays.
 Cym.   What, art thou mad?
 Imo. Almost, sir: heaven restore me! Would I were
A neat-herd's daughter, and my Leonatus
Our neighbour shepherd's son!
 Cym.   Thou foolish thing! 150

Re-enter QUEEN.

They were again together: you have done
Not after our command. Away with her,

And pen her up.
 Queen.   Beseech your patience. Peace,
Dear lady daughter, peace! Sweet sovereign,
Leave us to ourselves; and make yourself some
 comfort
Out of your best advice.
 Cym.   Nay, let her languish
A drop of blood a day; and, being aged,
Die of this folly! [*Exeunt Cymbeline and Lords.*
 Queen.   Fie! you must give way.

Enter PISANIO.

Here is your servant. How now, sir! What news?
 Pis. My lord your son drew on my master.
 Queen.   Ha!   160
No harm, I trust, is done?
 Pis.   There might have been,
But that my master rather play'd than fought
And had no help of anger: they were parted
By gentlemen at hand.
 Queen.   I am very glad on 't.
 Imo. Your son 's my father's friend; he takes his
 part.
To draw upon an exile! O brave sir!
I would they were in Afric both together;
Myself by with a needle, that I might prick
The goer-back. Why came you from your master?
 Pis. On his command: he would not suffer me 170
To bring him to the haven; left these notes
Of what commands I should be subject to,
When 't pleased you to employ me.
 Queen.   This hath been
Your faithful servant: I dare lay mine honour
He will remain so.
 Pis.   I humbly thank your highness.
 Queen. Pray, walk awhile.
 Imo.   About some half-hour hence,
I pray you, speak with me: you shall at least
Go see my lord aboard: for this time leave me. [*Exeunt.*

SCENE II. *The same. A public place.*

Enter CLOTEN *and two* Lords.

First Lord. Sir, I would advise you to shift a shirt;
the violence of action hath made you reek as a sacrifice: where air comes out, air comes in: there 's none
abroad so wholesome as that you vent.
 Clo. If my shirt were bloody, then to shift it. Have
I hurt him?
 Sec. Lord. [*Aside*] No, 'faith; not so much as his
patience.   9
 First Lord. Hurt him! his body 's a passable carcass,
if he be not hurt: it is a throughfare for steel, if it be
not hurt.
 Sec. Lord. [*Aside*] His steel was in debt; it went o'
the backside the town.
 Clo. The villain would not stand me.
 Sec. Lord. [*Aside*] No; but he fled forward still,
toward your face.
 First Lord. Stand you! You have land enough of

Cymbeline
ACT I : SC II

1183

be friends with him. The statement gives an idea of the doting quality of
the king. 116. **sear up**, dry up, blight; suggestion also of *cere*, cover
with wax, as the linen of a shroud. 124. **see**, see each other (reciprocal
sense). 126. **fraught**, burden. 129. **remainders**, those who remain.
135. **touch more rare**, feeling more overpowering or exquisite. Imogen's
description of her courage holds throughout the play; love means so
much to her that she has no fear. 140. **puttock**, kite, bird of prey the

name of which was often used as a contemptuous epithet. 146-147.
overbuys . . . pays, pays more for me than I am worth by almost as
much as, in giving himself, he has given me. 149. **neat-herd's**, cow-
herd's. 153. **Beseech**, I beseech. 156. **best advice**, most mature reflection. 176. **walk**, go aside, withdraw.
 SCENE II. 10. **passable**, affording free passage. 11. **throughfare**,
thoroughfare.

your own: but he added to your having; gave you
some ground.   20

Sec. Lord. [*Aside*] As many inches as you have
oceans. Puppies!

Clo. I would they had not come between us.

Sec. Lord. [*Aside*] So would I, till you had measured
how long a fool you were upon the ground.

Clo. And that she should love this fellow and refuse
me!

Sec. Lord. [*Aside*] If it be a sin to make a true election, she is damned.   30

First Lord. Sir, as I told you always, her beauty and
her brain go not together: she 's a good sign, but I
have seen small reflection of her wit.

Sec. Lord. [*Aside*] She shines not upon fools, lest the
reflection should hurt her.

Clo. Come, I'll to my chamber. Would there had
been some hurt done!

Sec. Lord. [*Aside*] I wish not so; unless it had been
the fall of an ass, which is no great hurt.

Clo. You'll go with us?   40

First Lord. I'll attend your lordship.

Clo. Nay, come, let 's go together.

Sec. Lord. Well, my lord.   [*Exeunt.*

SCENE III. *A room in Cymbeline's palace.*

Enter IMOGEN *and* PISANIO.

Imo. I would thou grew'st unto the shores o' the
              haven,
And question'dst every sail: if he should write,
And I not have it, 'twere a paper lost,
As offer'd mercy is. What was the last
That he spake to thee?

Pis.   It was his queen, his queen!

Imo. Then waved his handkerchief?

Pis.   And kiss'd it, madam.

Imo. Senseless linen! happier therein than I!
And that was all?

Pis.   No, madam; for so long
As he could make me with this eye or ear
Distinguish him from others, he did keep   10
The deck, with glove, or hat, or handkerchief,
Still waving, as the fits and stirs of 's mind
Could best express how slow his soul sail'd on,
How swift his ship.

Imo.   Thou shouldst have made him
As little as a crow, or less, ere left
To after-eye him.

Pis.   Madam, so I did.

Imo. I would have broke mine eye-strings; crack'd
              them, but
To look upon him, till the diminution
Of space had pointed him sharp as my needle,
Nay, follow'd him, till he had melted from   20
The smallness of a gnat to air, and then
Have turn'd mine eye and wept. But, good Pisanio,
When shall we hear from him?

Pis.   Be assured, madam,

With his next vantage.

Imo. I did not take my leave of him, but had
Most pretty things to say: ere I could tell him
How I would think on him at certain hours
Such thoughts and such, or I could make him swear
The shes of Italy should not betray
Mine interest and his honour, or have charged him, 30
At the sixth hour of morn, at noon, at midnight,
To encounter me with orisons, for then
I am in heaven for him; or ere I could
Give him that parting kiss which I had set
Betwixt two charming words, comes in my father
And like the tyrannous breathing of the north
Shakes all our buds from growing.

Enter a Lady.

Lady.   The queen, madam,
Desires your highness' company.

Imo. Those things I bid you do, get them dispatch'd.
I will attend the queen.

Pis.   Madam, I shall. [*Exeunt.* 40

SCENE IV. *Rome. Philario's house.*

Enter PHILARIO, IACHIMO, *a* Frenchman, *a*
Dutchman, *and a* Spaniard.

Iach. Believe it, sir, I have seen him in Britain: he
was then of a crescent note, expected to prove so
worthy as since he hath been allowed the name of;
but I could then have looked on him without the
help of admiration, though the catalogue of his endowments had been tabled by his side and I to peruse
him by items.

Phi. You speak of him when he was less furnished
than now he is with that which makes him both
without and within.   10

French. I have seen him in France: we had very
many there could behold the sun with as firm eyes
as he.

Iach. This matter of marrying his king's daughter,
wherein he must be weighed rather by her value than
his own, words him, I doubt not, a great deal from the
matter.

French. And then his banishment.   18

Iach. Ay, and the approbation of those that weep
this lamentable divorce under her colours are wonder-
fully to extend him; be it but to fortify her judgement,
which else an easy battery might lay flat, for taking a
beggar without less quality. But how comes it he is to
sojourn with you? How creeps acquaintance?

Phi. His father and I were soldiers together; to
whom I have been often bound for no less than my
life. Here comes the Briton: let him be so entertained
amongst you as suits, with gentlemen of your knowing,
to a stranger of his quality.   30

Enter POSTHUMUS.

I beseech you all, be better known to this gentleman,
whom I commend to you as a noble friend of mine:

---

30. **election,** choice; a theological expression. 33. **sign,** semblance,
appearance.
    SCENE III. 4. **offer'd mercy,** apparently, pardon offered, but coming
too late. 15. **left,** you left off. 16. **after-eye,** look after. 29. **shes,**
women. 32. **encounter,** meet. orisons, prayers. 35. **charming,**
having magical potency. 36. **north,** north wind.
    SCENE IV. 2. **crescent note,** growing reputation of importance. 7.
tabled, set down in a list. 10. **makes . . . within,** establishes him as

regards both his fortune and his character. 16-17. **words . . . matter,**
causes him to be described as other (and better) than he is. 20-21.
under her colours, in Imogen's party, influenced by her. 21. **extend
him,** increase his reputation. 24. **without less,** with less (double negative). 29. **knowing,** knowledge, *savoir faire.* 34. **story,** give an account of. 36. **known together,** been acquainted. 39-40. **which . . .
still,** for which I shall be forever in debt and yet be paying always.
42. **atone,** set at one, reconcile. 45. **importance,** matter, occasion.

how worthy he is I will leave to appear hereafter, rather than story him in his own hearing.

French. Sir, we have known together in Orleans.

Post. Since when I have been debtor to you for courtesies, which I will be ever to pay and yet pay still. 40

French. Sir, you o'er-rate my poor kindness: I was glad I did atone my countryman and you; it had been pity you should have been put together with so mortal a purpose as then each bore, upon importance of so slight and trivial a nature.

Post. By your pardon, sir, I was then a young traveller; rather shunned to go even with what I heard than in my every action to be guided by others' experiences: but upon my mended judgement—if I offend not to say it is mended—my quarrel was not altogether slight. 51

French. 'Faith, yes, to be put to the arbitrement of swords, and by such two that would by all likelihood have confounded one the other, or have fallen both.

Iach. Can we, with manners, ask what was the difference? 56

French. Safely, I think: 'twas a contention in public, which may, without contradiction, suffer the report. It was much like an argument that fell out last night, where each of us fell in praise of our country mistresses; this gentleman at that time vouching—and upon warrant of bloody affirmation—his to be more fair, virtuous, wise, chaste, constant-qualified and less attemptable than any the rarest of our ladies in France. 66

Iach. That lady is not now living, or this gentleman's opinion by this worn out.

Post. She holds her virtue still and I my mind.

Iach. You must not so far prefer her 'fore ours of Italy. 71

Post. Being so far provoked as I was in France, I would abate her nothing, though I profess myself her adorer, not her friend.

Iach. As fair and as good—a kind of hand-in-hand comparison—had been something too fair and too good for any lady in Britain. If she went before others I have seen, as that diamond of yours outlustres many I have beheld, I could not but believe she excelled many: but I have not seen the most precious diamond that is, nor you the lady.

Post. I praised her as I rated her: so do I my stone. 84

Iach. What do you esteem it at?

Post. More than the world enjoys.

Iach. Either your unparagoned mistress is dead, or she's outprized by a trifle.

Post. You are mistaken: the one may be sold, or given, if there were wealth enough for the purchase, or merit for the gift: the other is not a thing for sale, and only the gift of the gods.

Iach. Which the gods have given you? 94

Post. Which, by their graces, I will keep.

Iach. You may wear her in title yours: but, you know, strange fowl light upon neighbouring ponds. Your ring may be stolen too: so your brace of un-

prizable estimations; the one is but frail and the other casual; a cunning thief, or a that way accomplished courtier, would hazard the winning both of first and last. 102

Post. Your Italy contains none so accomplished a courtier to convince the honour of my mistress, if, in the holding or loss of that, you term her frail. I do nothing doubt you have store of thieves; notwithstanding, I fear not my ring.

Phi. Let us leave here, gentlemen. 109

Post. Sir, with all my heart. This worthy signior, I thank him, makes no stranger of me; we are familiar at first.

Iach. With five times so much conversation, I should get ground of your fair mistress, make her go back, even to the yielding, had I admittance and opportunity to friend.

Post. No, no. 117

Iach. I dare thereupon pawn the moiety of my estate to your ring; which, in my opinion, o'ervalues it something: but I make my wager rather against your confidence than her reputation: and, to bar your offence herein too, I durst attempt it against any lady in the world.

Post. You are a great deal abused in too bold a persuasion; and I doubt not you sustain what you're worthy of by your attempt.

Iach. What's that? 127

Post. A repulse: though your attempt, as you call it, deserve more; a punishment too.

Phi. Gentlemen, enough of this: it came in too suddenly; let it die as it was born, and, I pray you, be better acquainted.

Iach. Would I had put my estate and my neighbour's on the approbation of what I have spoke! 135

Post. What lady would you choose to assail?

Iach. Yours; whom in constancy you think stands so safe. I will lay you ten thousands ducats to your ring, that, commend me to the court where your lady is, with no more advantage than the opportunity of a second conference, and I will bring from thence that honour of hers which you imagine so reserved. 143

Post. I will wage against your gold, gold to it: my ring I hold dear as my finger; 'tis part of it.

Iach. You are afraid, and therein the wiser. If you buy ladies' flesh at a million a dram, you cannot preserve it from tainting: but I see you have some religion in you, that you fear.

Post. This is but a custom in your tongue; you bear a graver purpose, I hope. 151

Iach. I am the master of my speeches, and would undergo what's spoken, I swear.

Post. Will you? I shall but lend my diamond till your return: let there be covenants drawn between's: my mistress exceeds in goodness the hugeness of your unworthy thinking: I dare you to this match: here's my ring.

Phi. I will have it no lay. 159

Iach. By the gods, it is one. If I bring you no sufficient testimony that I have enjoyed the dearest

Cymbeline
ACT I : SC IV

1185

59. **suffer the report,** be reported or told. 63. **bloody affirmation,** affirming the truth with his blood. 65. **constant-qualified,** endowed with constancy. **attemptable,** open to attempts on their virtue. 74. **friend,** lover. 99. **unprizable,** invaluable. **estimations,** things highly esteemed. 104. **to,** as to. **convince,** overcome. 105. **in . . . that,** on the question of holding or losing her honor. 109. **leave,** leave off, cease. 115. **go back,** succumb, give way. 116. **to friend,** as my friend. 124-125. **abused . . . persuasion,** deceived by too bold an opinion. 134.

approbation, attestation, confirmation. 144. **wage,** lay as a wager. 158. **I dare . . . match.** In partial extenuation of Posthumus' shameful wager, it may be pointed out that Shakespeare's was an age of gaming and that the Italian story which he follows here brought with it an atmosphere of often brutal gallantry. 159. **I . . . lay,** I will not let it be a wager.

bodily part of your mistress, my ten thousand ducats
are yours; so is your diamond too: if I come off, and
leave her in such honour as you have trust in, she
your jewel, this your jewel, and my gold are yours:
provided I have your commendation for my more
free entertainment. 167

Post. I embrace these conditions; let us have
articles betwixt us. Only, thus far you shall answer:
if you make your voyage upon her and give me
directly to understand you have prevailed, I am no
further your enemy; she is not worth our debate: if
she remain unseduced, you not making it appear
otherwise, for your ill opinion and the assault you
have made to her chastity you shall answer me with
your sword. 176

Iach. Your hand; a covenant: we will have these
things set down by lawful counsel, and straight away
for Britain, lest the bargain should catch cold and
starve: I will fetch my gold and have our two wagers
recorded.

Post. Agreed.   [*Exeunt Posthumus and Iachimo.* 182
French. Will this hold, think you?
Phil. Signior Iachimo will not from it. Pray, let us
follow 'em.   [*Exeunt.*

SCENE V. *Britain. A room in Cymbeline's palace.*

Enter QUEEN, Ladies, *and* CORNELIUS.

Queen. Whiles yet the dew 's on ground, gather those
    flowers;
Make haste: who has the note of them?
First Lady.   I, madam.
Queen. Dispatch.   [*Exeunt Ladies.*
Now, master doctor, have you brought those drugs?
Cor. Pleaseth your highness, ay: here they are,
    madam: [*Presenting a small box.*
But I beseech your grace, without offence,—
My conscience bids me ask—wherefore you have
Commanded of me these most poisonous compounds,
Which are the movers of a languishing death;
But though slow, deadly?
Queen.   I wonder, doctor,   10
Thou ask'st me such a question. Have I not been
Thy pupil long? Hast thou not learn'd me how
To make perfumes? distil? preserve? yea, so
That our great king himself doth woo me oft
For my confections? Having thus far proceeded,—
Unless thou think'st me devilish—is 't not meet
That I did amplify my judgement in
Other conclusions? I will try the forces
Of these thy compounds on such creatures as
We count not worth the hanging, but none human,   20
To try the vigour of them and apply
Allayments to their act, and by them gather
Their several virtues and effects.
Cor.   Your highness
Shall from this practice but make hard your heart:
Besides, the seeing these effects will be

Both noisome and infectious.
Queen.   O, content thee.

Enter PISANIO.

[*Aside*] Here comes a flattering rascal; upon him
Will I first work: he 's for his master,
And enemy to my son. How now, Pisanio!
Doctor, your service for this time is ended;   30
Take your own way.
Cor.   [*Aside*] I do suspect you, madam;
But you shall do no harm.
Queen.   [*To Pisanio*] Hark thee, a word.
Cor. [*Aside*] I do not like her. She doth think she has
Strange lingering poisons: I do know her spirit,
And will not trust one of her malice with
A drug of such damn'd nature. Those she has
Will stupify and dull the sense awhile;
Which first, perchance, she'll prove on cats and dogs,
Then afterward up higher: but there is
No danger in what show of death it makes,   40
More than the locking-up the spirits a time,
To be more fresh, reviving. She is fool'd
With a most false effect; and I the truer,
So to be false with her.
Queen.   No further service, doctor,
Until I send for thee.
Cor.   I humbly take my leave.   [*Exit.*
Queen. Weeps she still, say'st thou? Dost thou think
    in time
She will not quench and let instructions enter
Where folly now possesses? Do thou work:
When thou shalt bring me word she loves my son,
I'll tell thee on the instant thou art then   50
As great as is thy master, greater, for
His fortunes all lie speechless and his name
Is at last gasp: return he cannot, nor
Continue where he is: to shift his being
Is to exchange one misery with another,
And every day that comes comes to decay
A day's work in him. What shalt thou expect,
To be depender on a thing that leans,
Who cannot be new built, nor has no friends,
So much as but to prop him?   [*The Queen drops the box:*
    Pisanio takes it up.] Thou takest up   60
Thou know'st not what; but take it for thy labour:
It is a thing I made, which hath the king
Five times redeem'd from death: I do not know
What is more cordial. Nay, I prithee, take it;
It is an earnest of a further good
That I mean to thee. Tell thy mistress how
The case stands with her; do 't as from thyself.
Think what a chance thou changest on, but think
Thou hast thy mistress still, to boot, my son,
Who shall take notice of thee: I'll move the king   70
To any shape of thy preferment such
As thou 'lt desire; and then myself, I chiefly,
That set thee on to this desert, am bound
To load thy merit richly. Call my women:
Think on my words.   [*Exit Pisanio.*

---

178. **counsel**, legal adviser.
SCENE V. 2. **note**, list. 15. **confections**, compounds of drugs. 18.
conclusions, experiments. 26. **content thee**, do not trouble thyself.
33-44. **I . . . her.** This is an occurrence of the typical aside, i.e., one
which carries matter important to the plot. Although the play is a
late one, Shakespeare still retains this stage convention characteristic
of his earlier plays. 41. **locking-up the spirits.** This was the current
theory of medicine with reference to potions whose effects were temporary, such as the one employed here and that in *Romeo and Juliet.*

43. **truer**, more honest. 47. **quench**, become cool. 54. **shift his being**,
change his abode. 58. **leans**, is about to fall. 64. **cordial**, restorative.
76. **shaked**, shaken (in his loyalty). 77. **remembrancer of her**, one
who reminds her. 78. **hand-fast**, marriage contract. 79. **unpeople
her**, deprive her of the services of. 80. **liegers**, ambassadors. 81.
Except . . . humour, unless she change her mind (about not accepting
Cloten). 84. **closet**, private chamber.
SCENE VI. 5-6. **thief-stol'n . . . brothers.** This is one of the few
allusions in the earlier part of the play to the story of the stolen princes

A sly and constant knave,
Not to be shaked; the agent for his master
And the remembrancer of her to hold
The hand-fast to her lord. I have given him that
Which, if he take, shall quite unpeople her
Of liegers for her sweet, and which she after,   80
Except she bend her humour, shall be assured
To taste of too.

Re-enter PISANIO *and* Ladies.

        So, so: well done, well done:
The violets, cowslips, and the primroses,
Bear to my closet. Fare thee well, Pisanio;
Think on my words.   [*Exeunt Queen and Ladies.*
   Pis.   And shall do:
But when to my good lord I prove untrue,
I'll choke myself: there's all I'll do for you.   [*Exit.*

SCENE VI. *The same. Another room in the palace.*

Enter IMOGEN.

Imo. A father cruel, and a step-dame false;
A foolish suitor to a wedded lady,
That hath her husband banish'd;—O, that husband!
My supreme crown of grief! and those repeated
Vexations of it! Had I been thief-stol'n,
As my two brothers, happy! but most miserable
Is the desire that's glorious: blest be those,
How mean soe'er, that have their honest wills,
Which seasons comfort. Who may this be? Fie!

Enter PISANIO *and* IACHIMO.

Pis. Madam, a noble gentleman of Rome,   10
Comes from my lord with letters.
   Iach.   Change you, madam?
The worthy Leonatus is in safety
And greets your highness dearly.   [*Presents a letter.*
   Imo.   Thanks, good sir:
You're kindly welcome.
   Iach. [*Aside*] All of her that is out of door most rich!
If she be furnish'd with a mind so rare,
She is alone the Arabian bird, and I
Have lost the wager. Boldness be my friend!
Arm me, audacity, from head to foot!
Or, like the Parthian, I shall flying fight;   20
Rather, directly fly.
   Imo. [*Reads*] 'He is one of the noblest note, to whose
kindness I am most infinitely tied. Reflect upon him
accordingly, as you value your trust—   LEONATUS.'
So far I read aloud:
But even the very middle of my heart
Is warm'd by the rest, and takes it thankfully.
You are as welcome, worthy sir, as I
Have words to bid you, and shall find it so   30
In all that I can do.
   Iach.   Thanks, fairest lady.
What, are men mad? Hath nature given them eyes
To see this vaulted arch, and the rich crop

Of sea and land, which can distinguish 'twixt
The fiery orbs above and the twinn'd stones
Upon the number'd beach? and can we not
Partition make with spectacles so precious
'Twixt fair and foul?
   Imo.   What makes your admiration?
   Iach. It cannot be i' the eye, for apes and monkeys
'Twixt two such shes would chatter this way and   40
Contemn with mows the other; nor i' the judgement,
For idiots in this case of favour would
Be wisely definite; not i' the appetite;
Sluttery to such neat excellence opposed
Should make desire vomit emptiness,
Not so allured to feed.
   Imo. What is the matter, trow?
   Iach.   The cloyed will,
That satiate yet unsatisfied desire, that tub
Both fill'd and running, ravening first the lamb
Longs after for the garbage.
   Imo.   What, dear sir,   50
Thus raps you? Are you well?
   Iach. Thanks, madam; well. [*To Pisanio*] Beseech
     you, sir, desire
My man's abode where I did leave him: he
Is strange and peevish.
   Pis.   I was going, sir,
To give him welcome.   [*Exit.*
   Imo. Continues well my lord? His health, beseech
     you?
   Iach. Well, madam.
   Imo. Is he disposed to mirth? I hope he is.
   Iach. Exceeding pleasant; none a stranger there
So merry and so gamesome: he is call'd   60
The Briton reveller.
   Imo.   When he was here,
He did incline to sadness, and oft-times
Not knowing why.
   Iach.   I never saw him sad.
There is a Frenchman his companion, one
An eminent monsieur, that, it seems, much loves
A Gallian girl at home; he furnaces
The thick sighs from him, whiles the jolly Briton—
Your lord, I mean—laughs from 's free lungs, cries 'O,
Can my sides hold, to think that man, who knows
By history, report, or his own proof,   70
What woman is, yea, what she cannot choose
But must be, will his free hours languish for
Assured bondage?'
   Imo.   Will my lord say so?
   Iach. Ay, madam, with his eyes in flood with
     laughter:
It is a recreation to be by
And hear him mock the Frenchman. But, heavens
     know,
Some men are much to blame.
   Imo.   Not he, I hope.
   Iach. Not he: but yet heaven's bounty towards him
     might
Be used more thankfully. In himself, 'tis much;

with which the latter half of the play is mainly concerned; the first
allusion occurs in I, i, 57-62. 9. **seasons comfort,** gives happiness
its proper quality. 11. **Change you,** do you change color? 17.
Arabian bird, the phoenix; pattern of rarity and beauty. 20. **Parthian,**
an allusion to the Parthian shot, the Parthians being proverbial in
ancient times for discharging a flight of arrows as they fled. 33.
crop, harvest, produce. 35. **twinn'd,** exactly alike. 36. **number'd,**
abounding (in stones). 37. **spectacles,** organs of vision. 41. **mows,**
grimaces, wry faces. 42. **in . . . favour,** in presence of a face of such

beauty. 43. **definite,** resolute. 44. **Sluttery,** the condition of being
sluttish or unclean. 45-46. **Should . . . feed,** desire would refuse
to satisfy itself and turn away in disgust. 48-49. **That . . . desire,**
that tub . . . running, in apposition with *will.* 49. **ravening,** devouring
greedily. 51. **raps,** transports. 52-53. **desire . . . abode,** bid my
servant remain. 66. **Gallian,** Gallic, French. **furnaces,** gives forth
like a furnace.

In you, which I account his beyond all talents, 80
Whilst I am bound to wonder, I am bound
To pity too.
    Imo.   What do you pity, sir?
    Iach. Two creatures heartily.
    Imo.   Am I one, sir?
You look on me: what wreck discern you in me
Deserves your pity?
    Iach.   Lamentable! What,
To hide me from the radiant sun and solace
I' the dungeon by a snuff?
    Imo.   I pray you, sir,
Deliver with more openness your answers
To my demands. Why do you pity me?
    Iach. That others do— 90
I was about to say—enjoy your——But
It is an office of the gods to venge it,
Not mine to speak on 't.
    Imo.   You do seem to know
Something of me, or what concerns me: pray you,—
Since doubting things go ill often hurts more
Than to be sure they do; for certainties
Either are past remedies, or, timely knowing,
The remedy then born—discover to me
What both you spur and stop.
    Iach.   Had I this cheek
To bathe my lips upon; this hand, whose touch, 100
Whose every touch, would force the feeler's soul
To the oath of loyalty; this object, which
Takes prisoner the wild motion of mine eye,
Fixing it only here; should I, damn'd then,
Slaver with lips as common as the stairs
That mount the Capitol; join gripes with hands
Made hard with hourly falsehood—falsehood, as
With labour; then by-peeping in an eye
Base and unlustrous as the smoky light
That 's fed with stinking tallow; it were fit 110
That all the plagues of hell should at one time
Encounter such revolt.
    Imo.   My lord, I fear,
Has forgot Britain.
    Iach.   And himself. Not I,
Inclined to this intelligence, pronounce
The beggary of his change; but 'tis your graces
That from my mutest conscience to my tongue
Charms this report out.
    Imo.   Let me hear no more.
    Iach. O dearest soul! your cause doth strike my
       heart
With pity, that doth make me sick. A lady
So fair, and fasten'd to an empery, 120
Would make the great'st king double,—to be
       partner'd
With tomboys hired with that self exhibition
Which your own coffers yield! with diseased ventures
That play with all infirmities for gold
Which rottenness can lend nature! such boil'd stuff
As well might poison poison! Be revenged;
Or she that bore you was no queen, and you

Recoil from your great stock.
    Imo.   Revenged!
How should I be revenged? If this be true,—
As I have such a heart that both mine ears 130
Must not in haste abuse—if it be true,
How should I be revenged?
    Iach.   Should he make me
Live, like Diana's priest, betwixt cold sheets,
Whiles he is vaulting variable ramps,
In your despite, upon your purse? Revenge it.
I dedicate myself to your sweet pleasure,
More noble than that runagate to your bed,
And will continue fast to your affection,
Still close as sure.
    Imo.   What, ho, Pisanio!
    Iach. Let me my service tender on your lips. 140
    Imo. Away! I do condemn mine ears that have
So long attended thee. If thou wert honourable,
Thou wouldst have told this tale for virtue, not
For such an end thou seek'st,—as base as strange.
Thou wrong'st a gentleman, who is as far
From thy report as thou from honour, and
Solicit'st here a lady that disdains
Thee and the devil alike. What ho, Pisanio!
The king my father shall be made acquainted
Of thy assault: if he shall think it fit, 150
A saucy stranger in his court to mart
As in a Romish stew and to expound
His beastly mind to us, he hath a court
He little cares for and a daughter who
He not respects at all. What, ho, Pisanio!
    Iach. O happy Leonatus! I may say:
The credit that thy lady hath of thee
Deserves thy trust, and thy most perfect goodness
Her assured credit. Blessed live you long!
A lady to the worthiest sir that ever 160
Country call'd his! and you his mistress, only
For the most worthiest fit! Give me your pardon.
I have spoke this, to know if your affiance
Were deeply rooted; and shall make your lord,
That which he is, new o'er: and he is one
The truest manner'd; such a holy witch
That he enchants societies into him;
Half all men's hearts are his.
    Imo.   You make amends.
    Iach. He sits 'mongst men like a descended god:
He hath a kind of honour sets him off, 170
More than a mortal seeming. Be not angry,
Most mighty princess, that I have adventured
To try your taking of a false report; which hath
Honour'd with confirmation your great judgement
In the election of a sir so rare,
Which you know cannot err: the love I bear him
Made me to fan you thus, but the gods made you,
Unlike all others, chaffless. Pray, your pardon.
    Imo. All 's well, sir: take my power i' the court for
       yours.
    Iach. My humble thanks. I had almost forgot 180
To entreat your grace but in a small request,

80. **talents,** evil inclinations or passions, or the phrase may mean "exceeding any sum." Dowden interprets: In his own peculiar gifts heaven's bounty is much; in you—who are his—heaven's bounty to him is beyond all gifts. 86. **solace,** take delight. 87. **snuff,** burning candlewick. 98. **remedy then born,** i.e., is then born. 99. **spur and stop,** disclose and then conceal. 108. **by-peeping,** giving sidelong glances; there is a charge against the behavior of Posthumus. 112. **Encounter;** meet. **revolt,** inconstancy. 116. **mutest,** most silent. 120. **empery,** empire. 121. **double,** as having twice the power.

partner'd, put on a level, compelled to be partners with. 122. **tomboys,** wantons. **self,** same. **exhibition,** allowance. 128. **Recoil,** fall away, degenerate. 133. **priest,** priestess. 134. **ramps,** probably, wantons, prostitutes. 137. **runagate,** renegade. 142. **attended,** listened to. 151. **saucy,** insolent. **to mart,** should bargain. 160. **sir,** man. 163. **affiance,** fidelity. 165. **new o'er,** refreshed and renewed by, made over again by. 166. **witch,** charmer, fascinating person; used of men as well as women. 167. **into,** unto. 177. **fan,** test; figure from winnowing of grain. 178. **chaffless,** without chaff, perfect.

And yet of moment too, for it concerns
Your lord; myself and other noble friends
Are partners in the business.
Imo.   Pray, what is 't?
Iach. Some dozen Romans of us and your lord—
The best feather of our wing—have mingled sums
To buy a present for the emperor;
Which I, the factor for the rest, have done
In France: 'tis plate of rare device, and jewels
Of rich and exquisite form; their values great;   190
And I am something curious, being strange,
To have them in safe stowage: may it please you
To take them in protection?
Imo.   Willingly;
And pawn mine honour for their safety: since
My lord hath interest in them, I will keep them
In my bedchamber.
Iach.   They are in a trunk,
Attended by my men: I will make bold
To send them to you, only for this night;
I must aboard to-morrow.
Imo.   O, no, no.
Iach. Yes, I beseech; or I shall short my word   200
By lengthening my return. From Gallia
I cross'd the seas on purpose and on promise
To see your grace.
Imo.   I thank you for your pains:
But not away to-morrow!
Iach.   O, I must, madam:
Therefore I shall beseech you, if you please
To greet your lord with writing, do 't to-night:
I have outstood my time; which is material
To the tender of our present.
Imo.   I will write.
Send your trunk to me; it shall safe be kept,   209
And truly yielded you. You 're very welcome. [*Exeunt.*

ACT II.

SCENE I. *Britain. Before Cymbeline's palace.*

Enter CLOTEN *and two* Lords.

Clo. Was there ever man had such luck! when I
kissed the jack, upon an up-cast to be hit away! I had
a hundred pound on 't: and then a whoreson jackanapes must take me up for swearing; as if I borrowed
mine oaths of him and might not spend them at my
pleasure.
First Lord. What got he by that? You have broke
his pate with your bowl.
Sec. Lord. [*Aside*] If his wit had been like him that
broke it, it would have run all out.   10
Clo. When a gentleman is disposed to swear, it is
not for any standers-by to curtail his oaths, ha?
Sec. Lord. No, my lord; [*Aside*] nor crop the ears of
them.
Clo. Whoreson dog! I give him satisfaction? Would
he had been one of my rank!

Sec. Lord. [*Aside*] To have smelt like a fool.   18
Clo. I am not vexed more at any thing in the earth:
a pox on 't! I had rather not be so noble as I am; they
dare not fight with me, because of the queen my
mother: every Jack-slave hath his bellyful of fighting,
and I must go up and down like a cock that nobody
can match.
Sec. Lord. [*Aside*] You are cock and capon too; and
you crow, cock, with your comb on.
Clo. Sayest thou?
Sec. Lord. It is not fit your lordship should under-
take every companion that you give offence to.   30
Clo. No, I know that: but it is fit I should commit
offence to my inferiors.
Sec. Lord. Ay, it is fit for your lordship only.
Clo. Why, so I say.
First Lord. Did you hear of a stranger that 's come
to court to-night?
Clo. A stranger, and I not know on 't!
Sec. Lord. [*Aside*] He 's a strange fellow himself, and
knows it not.
First Lord. There 's an Italian come; and, 'tis
thought, one of Leonatus' friends.   41
Clo. Leonatus! a banished rascal; and he 's another,
whatsoever he be. Who told you of this stranger?
First Lord. One of your lordship's pages.
Clo. Is it fit I went to look upon him? is there no
derogation in 't?
Sec. Lord. You cannot derogate, my lord.
Clo. Not easily, I think.   49
Sec. Lord. [*Aside*] You are a fool granted; therefore
your issues, being foolish, do not derogate.
Clo. Come, I'll go see this Italian: what I have lost
to-day at bowls I'll win to-night of him. Come, go.
Sec. Lord. I'll attend your lordship.
             [*Exeunt Cloten and First Lord.*
That such a crafty devil as is his mother
Should yield the world this ass! a woman that
Bears all down with her brain; and this her son
Cannot take two from twenty, for his heart,   60
And leave eighteen. Alas, poor princess,
Thou divine Imogen, what thou endurest,
Betwixt a father by thy step-dame govern'd,
A mother hourly coining plots, a wooer
More hateful than the foul expulsion is
Of thy dear husband, than that horrid act
Of the divorce he 'ld make! The heavens hold firm
The walls of thy dear honour, keep unshaked
That temple, thy fair mind, that thou mayst stand,
To enjoy thy banish'd lord and this great land! [*Exit.* 70

SCENE II. *Imogen's bedchamber in Cymbeline's
palace: a trunk in one corner of it.*

IMOGEN *in bed, reading; a* Lady *attending.*

Imo. Who 's there? my woman Helen?
Lady.   Please you, madam.
Imo. What hour is it?

---

196. **In my bedchamber.** The strangeness of Iachimo's request and
Imogen's compliance with it may be better understood if one remembers that bedchambers were storage places for treasure, and also that
strangers lodging at inns were often in fear of robbery in Shakespeare's
day. 200. **short my word,** impair my promise. 207. **outstood,**
outstayed. 208. **tender of our present,** offering of our gift.
ACT II. SCENE I. 2. **kissed the jack,** touched and lay near the small
bowl used as target in the game of bowls. **up-cast,** throw in the game
of bowls. 4. **take me up,** take me to task. 12. **curtail,** shorten,

abridge. The word is a corruption of *curtal,* formed to suggest the bob-
bing of a dog's tail; hence, *crop the ears* (of the *oaths*) below. 17.
rank, social class; taken, in the aside which follows, to mean "rankness." 22. **Jack-slave,** lowborn fellow. 25. **capon,** perhaps used
quibblingly for "cap on," i.e., with fool's cap or coxcomb. 27. **Sayest
thou?** What dost thou say? 29. **undertake,** engage with, give satisfaction. 47. **derogation,** action unbecoming his position. 51. **issues,**
deeds, actions.

Lady.   Almost midnight, madam.

Imo. I have read three hours then: mine eyes are
    weak:
Fold down the leaf where I have left: to bed:
Take not away the taper, leave it burning;
And if thou canst awake by four o' the clock,
I prithee, call me. Sleep hath seized me wholly.
                                    [Exit Lady.

To your protection I commend me, gods.
From fairies and the tempters of the night
Guard me, beseech ye.   10
            [Sleeps. Iachimo comes from the trunk.

    Iach. The crickets sing, and man's o'er-labour'd
    sense
Repairs itself by rest. Our Tarquin thus
Did softly press the rushes, ere he waken'd
The chastity he wounded. Cytherea,
How bravely thou becomest thy bed, fresh lily,
And whiter than the sheets! That I might touch!
But kiss; one kiss! Rubies unparagon'd,
How dearly they do 't! 'Tis her breathing that
Perfumes the chamber thus: the flame o' the taper
Bows toward her, and would under-peep her lids,   20
To see the enclosed lights, now canopied
Under these windows, white and azure laced
With blue of heaven's own tinct. But my design,
To note the chamber: I will write all down:
Such and such pictures; there the window; such
The adornment of her bed; the arras; figures,
Why, such and such; and the contents o' the story.
Ah, but some natural notes about her body,
Above ten thousand meaner moveables
Would testify, to enrich mine inventory.   30
O sleep, thou ape of death, lie dull upon her!
And be her sense but as a monument,
Thus in a chapel lying! Come off, come off:
                    [Taking off her bracelet.

As slippery as the Gordian knot was hard!
'Tis mine; and this will witness outwardly,
As strongly as the conscience does within,
To the madding of her lord. On her left breast
A mole cinque-spotted, like the crimson drops
I' the bottom of a cowslip: here 's a voucher,
Stronger than ever law could make: this secret   40
Will force him think I have pick'd the lock and ta'en
The treasure of her honour. No more. To what end?
Why should I write this down, that 's riveted,
Screw'd to my memory? She hath been reading late
The tale of Tereus; here the leaf 's turn'd down
Where Philomel gave up. I have enough:
To the trunk again, and shut the spring of it.
Swift, swift, you dragons of the night, that dawning
May have the raven's eye! I lodge in fear;
Though this a heavenly angel, hell is here.   50
                         [Clock strikes.
One, two, three: time, time!
         [Goes into the trunk. The scene closes.

SCENE III. *An ante-chamber adjoining Imogen's apartments.*

Enter CLOTEN *and* Lords.

First Lord. Your lordship is the most patient man in
loss, the most coldest that ever turned up ace.
Clo. It would make any man cold to lose.
First Lord. But not every man patient after the
noble temper of your lordship. You are most hot and
furious when you win.
Clo. Winning will put any man into courage. If I
could get this foolish Imogen, I should have gold
enough. It 's almost morning, is 't not?   10
First Lord. Day, my lord.
Clo. I would this music would come: I am advised
to give her music o' mornings; they say it will penetrate.

Enter Musicians.

Come on; tune: if you can penetrate her with your
fingering, so; we'll try with tongue too: if none will
do, let her remain; but I'll never give o'er. First, a
very excellent good-conceited thing; after, a wonderful sweet air, with admirable rich words to it: and
then let her consider.   21

                SONG.
Hark, hark! the lark at heaven's gate sings,
    And Phœbus 'gins arise,
His steeds to water at those springs
    On chaliced flowers that lies;
And winking Mary-buds begin
    To ope their golden eyes:
With every thing that pretty is,
    My lady sweet, arise:
        Arise, arise.   30

Clo. So, get you gone. If this penetrate, I will consider your music the better: if it do not, it is a vice
in her ears, which horse-hairs and calves'-guts, nor
the voice of unpaved eunuch to boot, can never
amend.   *[Exeunt Musicians.*
Sec. Lord. Here comes the king.
Clo. I am glad I was up so late; for that 's the
reason I was up so early: he cannot choose but take
this service I have done fatherly.

Enter CYMBELINE *and* QUEEN.

Good morrow to your majesty and to my gracious
mother.   41
Cym. Attend you here the door of our stern daughter?
Will she not forth?
Clo. I have assailed her with music, but she vouch-
safes no notice.
Cym. The exile of her minion is too new;
She hath not yet forgot him: some more time
Must wear the print of his remembrance out,
And then she 's yours.
Queen.   You are most bound to the
    king,

SCENE II. 9. **fairies,** evil fairies. 12. **Our Tarquin,** the Roman
Sextus Tarquinius in the story of Lucrece. 13. **press the rushes.** Elizabethan floors were strewn with rushes; certainly those in the days of
Cymbeline and Tarquin were not. 14. **Cytherea,** Venus. 22. **windows,** eyelids. 23. **tinct,** color. 26. **arras,** hangings of tapestry. Mason
joins with the next word and reads *arras-figures.* 27. **story,** subject
set forth in embroidery on the tapestry. 34. **Gordian knot.** According
to prophecy whoever untied the knot binding the yoke to the pole of the
chariot of Gordius, peasant king of Phrygia, should be king of all Asia.
Alexander severed the knot with his sword. 37. **madding,** maddening,

making mad. 38. **cinque-spotted,** with five spots. 45. **Tereus,** mythical king of Thrace, who dishonored Philomela, sister of his wife, Procne.
He had Philomela's tongue cut out so that she could not tell the story,
but she wove it into a tapestry. 49. **raven's eye.** The raven was supposed to wake at early dawn. 50. **this,** this is. 51. **time, time.**
Iachimo remembers that Imogen is to be called at four.
    SCENE III. 2. **most coldest,** coolest, most deliberate. 4. **cold,**
gloomy, dispirited. 15. **penetrate,** touch. 16. **so,** it is well. 25.
lies, usually explained as the old northern plural in *s.* 26. **Mary-
buds,** buds of marigolds. 32. **consider,** reward. 33. **horse-hairs,** of

Who lets go by no vantages that may 50
Prefer you to his daughter. Frame yourself
To orderly soliciting, and be friended
With aptness of the season; make denials
Increase your services; so seem as if
You were inspired to do those duties which
You tender to her; that you in all obey her,
Save when command to your dismission tends,
And therein you are senseless.
    Clo.   Senseless! not so.

Enter a Messenger.

    Mess. So like you, sir, ambassadors from Rome;
The one is Caius Lucius.
    Cym.   A worthy fellow, 60
Albeit he comes on angry purpose now;
But that 's no fault of his: we must receive him
According to the honour of his sender;
And towards himself, his goodness forespent on us,
We must extend our notice. Our dear son,
When you have given good morning to your mistress,
Attend the queen and us; we shall have need
To employ you towards this Roman. Come, our
    queen.   [*Exeunt all but Cloten.*
    Clo. If she be up, I'll speak with her; if not, 69
Let her lie still and dream. [*Knocks*] By your leave, ho!
I know her women are about her: what
If I do line one of their hands? 'Tis gold
Which buys admittance; oft it doth; yea, and makes
Diana's rangers false themselves, yield up
Their deer to the stand o' the stealer; and 'tis gold
Which makes the true man kill'd and saves the thief;
Nay, sometime hangs both thief and true man: what
Can it not do and undo? I will make
One of her women lawyer to me, for
I yet not understand the case myself. 80
[*Knocks*] By your leave.

Enter a Lady.

    Lady. Who 's there that knocks?
    Clo.   A gentleman.
    Lady.   No more?
    Clo. Yes, and a gentlewoman's son.
    Lady.   That 's more
Than some, whose tailors are as dear as yours,
Can justly boast of. What 's your lordship's pleasure?
    Clo. Your lady's person: is she ready?
    Lady.   Ay,
To keep her chamber.
    Clo.   There is gold for you;
Sell me your good report.
    Lady. How! my good name? or to report of you
What I shall think is good?—The princess! 90

Enter IMOGEN.

    Clo. Good morrow, fairest: sister, your sweet hand.
                       [*Exit Lady.*
    Imo. Good morrow, sir. You lay out too much pains

For purchasing but trouble: the thanks I give
Is telling you that I am poor of thanks
And scarce can spare them.
    Clo.   Still, I swear I love you.
    Imo. If you but said so, 'twere as deep with me:
If you swear still, your recompense is still
That I regard it not.
    Clo.   This is no answer.
    Imo. But that you shall not say I yield being silent,
I would not speak. I pray you, spare me: 'faith, 100
I shall unfold equal discourtesy
To your best kindness: one of your great knowing
Should learn, being taught, forbearance.
    Clo. To leave you in your madness, 'twere my sin:
I will not.
    Imo. Fools are not mad folks.
    Clo.   Do you call me fool?
    Imo. As I am mad, I do:
If you'll be patient, I'll no more be mad;
That cures us both. I am much sorry, sir,
You put me to forget a lady's manners, 110
By being so verbal: and learn now, for all,
That I, which know my heart, do here pronounce,
By the very truth of it, I care not for you,
And am so near the lack of charity—
To accuse myself—I hate you; which I had rather
You felt than make 't my boast.
    Clo.   You sin against
Obedience, which you owe your father. For
The contract you pretend with that base wretch,
One bred of alms and foster'd with cold dishes,
With scraps o' the court, it is no contract, none: 120
And though it be allow'd in meaner parties—
Yet who than he more mean?—to knit their souls,
On whom there is no more dependency
But brats and beggary, in self-figured knot;
Yet you are curb'd from that enlargement by
The consequence o' the crown, and must not soil
The precious note of it with a base slave,
A hilding for a livery, a squire's cloth,
A pantler, not so eminent.
    Imo.   Profane fellow!
Wert thou the son of Jupiter and no more 130
But what thou art besides, thou wert too base
To be his groom: thou wert dignified enough,
Even to the point of envy, if 'twere made
Comparative for your virtues, to be styled
The under-hangman of his kingdom, and hated
For being preferr'd so well.
    Clo.   The south-fog rot him!
    Imo. He never can meet more mischance than come
To be but named of thee. His meanest garment,
That ever hath but clipp'd his body, is dearer
In my respect than all the hairs above thee, 140
Were they all made such men. How now, Pisanio!

Enter PISANIO.

    Clo. 'His garment!' Now the devil—

the fiddlebow. 34. **calves'-guts,** fiddlestrings. 39. **fatherly,** as a father. 51. **Prefer,** recommend. **Frame,** conform. 57. **dismission,** dismissal, rejection. 58. **senseless,** insensible (to her commands). Cloten understands the word as meaning "stupid." 64. **forespent,** previously bestowed. 72. **line,** i.e., with gold. 74. **rangers,** nymphs (vowed to chastity). **false,** verb meaning "turn false"; or, possibly, an adjective. 75. **stand,** station of huntsman waiting for game. 88. **good report,** favorable speech. The Lady understands another meaning of the expression, namely "reputation," "good name." 102. **knowing,** knowledge, discernment; ironical. 111. **By . . . verbal.** If the phrase

refers to Cloten, the meaning of *verbal* is "verbose"; if to Imogen, "plain-spoken." In either case there is a suggestion of "playing with words." 117. **For,** as for. 124. **self-figured,** self-contracted. 125. **enlargement,** liberty. 126. **consequence,** succession. 128. **hilding,** good-for-nothing fellow. **for,** fit for. **cloth,** dress, livery. 129. **pantler,** servant who has charge of the pantry. 134. **Comparative for,** proportioned to, comparing with. 136. **south-fog.** The south wind was supposed to be charged with poisonous vapors and diseases.

Imo. To Dorothy my woman hie thee presently—
Clo. 'His garment!'
Imo.   I am sprited with a fool,
Frighted, and anger'd worse: go bid my woman
Search for a jewel that too casually
Hath left mine arm: it was thy master's: 'shrew me,
If I would lose it for a revenue
Of any king's in Europe. I do think
I saw 't this morning: confident I am   150
Last night 'twas on mine arm; I kiss'd it:
I hope it be not gone to tell my lord
That I kiss aught but he.
Pis.   'Twill not be lost.
Imo. I hope so: go and search.   [*Exit Pisanio.*
Clo.   You have abused me:
'His meanest garment!'
Imo.   Ay, I said so, sir:
If you will make 't an action, call witness to 't.
Clo. I will inform your father.
Imo.   Your mother too:
She 's my good lady, and will conceive, I hope,
But the worst of me. So, I leave you, sir,
To the worst of discontent.   [*Exit.*
Clo.   I'll be revenged: 160
'His meanest garment!' Well.   [*Exit.*

SCENE IV. *Rome. Philario's house.*

Enter POSTHUMUS *and* PHILARIO.

Post. Fear it not, sir: I would I were so sure
To win the king as I am bold her honour
Will remain hers.
Phi.   What means do you make to him?
Post. Not any, but abide the change of time,
Quake in the present winter's state and wish
That warmer days would come: in these fear'd hopes,
I barely gratify your love; they failing,
I must die much your debtor.
Phi. Your very goodness and your company
O'erpays all I can do. By this, your king   10
Hath heard of great Augustus: Caius Lucius
Will do 's commission throughly: and I think
He'll grant the tribute, send the arrearages,
Or look upon our Romans, whose remembrance
Is yet fresh in their grief.
Post.   I do believe,
Statist though I am none, nor like to be,
That this will prove a war; and you shall hear
The legions now in Gallia sooner landed
In our not-fearing Britain than have tidings
Of any penny tribute paid. Our countrymen   20
Are men more order'd than when Julius Cæsar
Smiled at their lack of skill, but found their courage
Worthy his frowning at: their discipline,
Now mingled with their courages, will make known
To their approvers they are people such
That mend upon the world.

Enter IACHIMO.

Phi.   See! Iachimo!
Post. The swiftest harts have posted you by land;

And winds of all the corners kiss'd your sails,
To make your vessel nimble.
Phi.   Welcome, sir.
Post. I hope the briefness of your answer made   30
The speediness of your return.
Iach.   Your lady
Is one of the fairest that I have look'd upon.
Post. And therewithal the best; or let her beauty
Look through a casement to allure false hearts
And be false with them.
Iach.   Here are letters for you.
Post. Their tenour good, I trust.
Iach.   'Tis very like.
Phi. Was Caius Lucius in the Britain court
When you were there?
Iach.   He was expected then,
But not approach'd.
Post.   All is well yet.
Sparkles this stone as it was wont? or is 't not   40
Too dull for your good wearing?
Iach.   If I had lost it,
I should have lost the worth of it in gold.
I'll make a journey twice as far, to enjoy
A second night of such sweet shortness which
Was mine in Britain, for the ring is won.
Post. The stone 's too hard to come by.
Iach.   Not a whit,
Your lady being so easy.
Post.   Make not, sir,
Your loss your sport: I hope you know that we
Must not continue friends.
Iach.   Good sir, we must,
If you keep covenant. Had I not brought   50
The knowledge of your mistress home, I grant
We were to question further: but I now
Profess myself the winner of her honour,
Together with your ring; and not the wronger
Of her or you, having proceeded but
By both your wills.
Post.   If you can make 't apparent
That you have tasted her in bed, my hand
And ring is yours; if not, the foul opinion
You had of her pure honour gains or loses
Your sword or mine, or masterless leaves both   60
To who shall find them.
Iach.   Sir, my circumstances,
Being so near the truth as I will make them,
Must first induce you to believe: whose strength
I will confirm with oath; which, I doubt not,
You'll give me leave to spare, when you shall find
You need it not.
Post.   Proceed.
Iach.   First, her bedchamber,—
Where, I confess, I slept not, but profess
Had that was well worth watching—it was hang'd
With tapestry of silk and silver; the story
Proud Cleopatra, when she met her Roman,   70
And Cydnus swell'd above the banks, or for
The press of boats or pride: a piece of work
So bravely done, so rich, that it did strive
In workmanship and value; which I wonder'd
Could be so rarely and exactly wrought,

---

144. **sprited,** haunted.   156. **action,** action at law.   158. **my good lady,** patroness (ironical).
SCENE IV.   2. **bold,** confident.   6. **fear'd,** mixed with fear, so F; Tyrwhit: *sear'd,* meaning "withered, blighted."   13. **arrearages,** arrears, parts of the tribute due but unpaid.   14. **Or look,** before he will

look.   16. **Statist,** statesman.   21. **more order'd,** better disciplined and governed.   25. **approvers,** those who test (their courage).   52. **question,** debate; here, settle matters by a duel.   71. **Cydnus,** a river in Cilicia, the scene of the meeting of Antony and Cleopatra which is described in *Antony and Cleopatra*, II, ii, 191-231.   83-85. **the cutter . . .**

Since the true life on 't was—
  Post.   This is true;
And this you might have heard of here, by me,
Or by some other.
  Iach.   More particulars
Must justify my knowledge.
  Post.   So they must,
Or do your honour injury.
  Iach.   The chimney   80
Is south the chamber, and the chimney-piece
Chaste Dian bathing: never saw I figures
So likely to report themselves: the cutter
Was as another nature, dumb; outwent her,
Motion and breath left out.
  Post.   This is a thing
Which you might from relation likewise reap,
Being, as it is, much spoke of.
  Iach.   The roof o' the chamber
With golden cherubins is fretted: her andirons—
I had forgot them—were two winking Cupids
Of silver, each on one foot standing, nicely   90
Depending on their brands.
  Post.   This is her honour!
Let it be granted you have seen all this—and praise
Be given to your remembrance—the description
Of what is in her chamber nothing saves
The wager you have laid.
  Iach.   Then, if you can,
                            [*Showing the bracelet.*
Be pale: I beg but leave to air this jewel; see!
And now 'tis up again: it must be married
To that your diamond; I'll keep them.
  Post.   Jove!
Once more let me behold it: is it that
Which I left with her?
  Iach.   Sir—I thank her—that: 100
She stripp'd it from her arm; I see her yet;
Her pretty action did outsell her gift,
And yet enrich'd it too: she gave it me, and said
She prized it once.
  Post.   May be she pluck'd it off
To send it me.
  Iach.   She writes so to you, doth she?
  Post. O, no, no, no! 'tis true. Here, take this too;
                            [*Gives the ring.*
It is a basilisk unto mine eye,
Kills me to look on 't. Let there be no honour
Where there is beauty; truth, where semblance; love,
Where there 's another man: the vows of women   110
Of no more bondage be, to where they are made,
Than they are to their virtues; which is nothing.
O, above measure false!
  Phi.   Have patience, sir,
And take your ring again; 'tis not yet won:
It may be probable she lost it; or
Who knows if one of her women, being corrupted,
Hath stol'n it from her?
  Post.   Very true;
And so, I hope, he came by 't. Back my ring:
Render to me some corporal sign about her,
More evident than this; for this was stolen.   120
  Iach. By Jupiter, I had it from her arm.

  Post. Hark you, he swears; by Jupiter he swears.
'Tis true:—nay, keep the ring—'tis true: I am sure
She would not lose it: her attendants are
All sworn and honourable:—they induced to steal it!
And by a stranger!—No, he hath enjoy'd her:
The cognizance of her incontinency
Is this: she hath bought the name of whore thus
    dearly.
There, take thy hire; and all the fiends of hell
Divide themselves between you!
  Phi.   Sir, be patient: 130
This is not strong enough to be believed
Of one persuaded well of—
  Post.   Never talk on 't;
She hath been colted by him.
  Iach.   If you seek
For further satisfying, under her breast—
Worthy the pressing—lies a mole, right proud
Of that most delicate lodging: by my life,
I kiss'd it; and it gave me present hunger
To feed again, though full. You do remember
This stain upon her?
  Post.   Ay, and it doth confirm
Another stain, as big as hell can hold,   140
Were there no more but it.
  Iach.   Will you hear more?
  Post. Spare your arithmetic: never count the turns;
Once, and a million!
  Iach.   I'll be sworn—
  Post.   No swearing.
If you will swear you have not done 't, you lie;
And I will kill thee, if thou dost deny
Thou'st made me cuckold.
  Iach.   I'll deny nothing.
  Post. O, that I had her here, to tear her limb-meal!
I will go there and do 't, i' the court, before
Her father. I'll do something—   [*Exit.*
  Phi.   Quite besides
The government of patience! You have won: 150
Let 's follow him, and pervert the present wrath
He hath against himself.
  Iach.   With all my heart.   [*Exeunt.*

SCENE V. *Another room in Philario's house.*

Enter POSTHUMUS.

  Post. Is there no way for men to be but women
Must be half-workers? We are all bastards;
And that most venerable man which I
Did call my father, was I know not where
When I was stamp'd; some coiner with his tools
Made me a counterfeit: yet my mother seem'd
The Dian of that time: so doth my wife
The nonpareil of this. O, vengeance, vengeance!
Me of my lawful pleasure she restrain'd
And pray'd me oft forbearance; did it with   10
A pudency so rosy the sweet view on 't
Might well have warm'd old Saturn; that I thought
    her
As chaste as unsunn'd snow. O, all the devils!
This yellow Iachimo, in an hour,—was 't not?—

---

out, the sculptor, though unable to impart voice, was like nature; indeed surpassed her but for motion and breath. 86. **relation,** hearsay. 88. **fretted,** adorned with carved or embossed work in decorative patterns (Onions). 91. **Depending,** leaning. **brands,** torches, i.e., of the Cupids. 97. **up,** put up, pocketed. 102. **outsell,** exceed in value. 111.

bondage, obligation. 127. **cognizance,** mark or token by which a thing is recognized. 147. **limb-meal,** limb from limb. 149. **besides,** beyond. 151. **pervert,** turn, divert.
  SCENE V. 8. **nonpareil,** one that has no equal. 11. **pudency,** modesty.

Or less,—at first?—perchance he spoke not, but,
Like a full-acorn'd boar, a German one,
Cried 'O!' and mounted; found no opposition
But what he look'd for should oppose and she
Should from encounter guard. Could I find out
The woman's part in me! For there's no motion   20
That tends to vice in man, but I affirm
It is the woman's part: be it lying, note it,
The woman's; flattering, hers; deceiving, hers;
Lust and rank thoughts, hers, hers; revenges, hers;
Ambitions, covetings, change of prides, disdain,
Nice longing, slanders, mutability,
All faults that may be named, nay, that hell knows,
Why, hers, in part or all; but rather, all;
For even to vice
They are not constant, but are changing still   30
One vice, but of a minute old, for one
Not half so old as that. I'll write against them,
Detest them, curse them: yet 'tis greater skill
In a true hate, to pray they have their will:
The very devils cannot plague them better.   [Exit.

ACT III.

SCENE I. *Britain. A hall in Cymbeline's palace.*

Enter in state, CYMBELINE, QUEEN, CLOTEN, *and*
Lords *at one door, and at another,* CAIUS LUCIUS *and*
Attendants.

Cym. Now say, what would Augustus Cæsar with
us?

Luc. When Julius Cæsar, whose remembrance yet
Lives in men's eyes and will to ears and tongues
Be theme and hearing ever, was in this Britain
And conquer'd it, Cassibelan, thine uncle,—
Famous in Cæsar's praises, no whit less
Than in his feats deserving it—for him
And his succession granted Rome a tribute,
Yearly three thousand pounds, which by thee lately
Is left untender'd.

Queen.   And, to kill the marvel,   10
Shall be so ever.

Clo.   There be many Cæsars,
Ere such another Julius. Britain is
A world by itself; and we will nothing pay
For wearing our own noses.

Queen.   That opportunity
Which then they had to take from 's, to resume
We have again. Remember, sir, my liege,
The kings your ancestors, together with
The natural bravery of your isle, which stands
As Neptune's park, ribbed and paled in
With rocks unscaleable and roaring waters,   20
With sands that will not bear your enemies' boats,
But suck them up to the topmast. A kind of conquest
Cæsar made here; but made not here his brag
Of 'Came' and 'saw' and 'overcame:' with shame—
The first that ever touch'd him—he was carried
From off our coast, twice beaten; and his shipping—

Poor ignorant baubles!—on our terrible seas,
Like egg-shells moved upon their surges, crack'd
As easily 'gainst our rocks: for joy whereof
The famed Cassibelan, who was once at point—   30
O giglot fortune!—to master Cæsar's sword,
Made Lud's town with rejoicing fires bright
And Britons strut with courage.

Clo. Come, there's no more tribute to be paid: our
kingdom is stronger than it was at that time; and, as I
said, there is no moe such Cæsars: other of them may
have crook'd noses, but to owe such straight arms,
none.

Cym. Son, let your mother end.   39

Clo. We have yet many among us can gripe as hard
as Cassibelan: I do not say I am one; but I have a
hand. Why tribute? why should we pay tribute? If
Cæsar can hide the sun from us with a blanket, or put
the moon in his pocket, we will pay him tribute for
light; else, sir, no more tribute, pray you now.

Cym. You must know,
Till the injurious Romans did extort
This tribute from us, we were free: Cæsar's ambition,
Which swell'd so much that it did almost stretch   50
The sides o' the world, against all colour here
Did put the yoke upon 's; which to shake off
Becomes a warlike people, whom we reckon
Ourselves to be.

Clo. and Lords.   We do.

Cym.   Say, then to Cæsar,
Our ancestor was that Mulmutius which
Ordain'd our laws, whose use the sword of Cæsar
Hath too much mangled; whose repair and franchise
Shall, by the power we hold, be our good deed,
Though Rome be therefore angry: Mulmutius made
          our laws,
Who was the first of Britain which did put   60
His brows within a golden crown and call'd
Himself a king.

Luc.   I am sorry, Cymbeline,
That I am to pronounce Augustus Cæsar—
Cæsar, that hath more kings his servants than
Thyself domestic officers—thine enemy:
Receive it from me, then: war and confusion
In Cæsar's name pronounce I 'gainst thee: look
For fury not to be resisted. Thus defied,
I thank thee for myself.

Cym.   Thou art welcome, Caius.
Thy Cæsar knighted me; my youth I spent   70
Much under him; of him I gather'd honour;
Which he to seek of me again, perforce,
Behoves me keep at utterance. I am perfect
That the Pannonians and Dalmatians for
Their liberties are now in arms; a precedent
Which not to read would show the Britons cold:
So Cæsar shall not find them.

Luc.   Let proof speak.   77

Clo. His majesty bids you welcome. Make pastime
with us a day or two, or longer: if you seek us afterwards in other terms, you shall find us in our salt-
water girdle: if you beat us out of it, it is yours; if you

---

25. **change of prides,** varying vanities (in dress, etc.). 32. **write against,** denounce.

ACT III. SCENE I. 27. **ignorant,** silly, unskilled. 30. **Cassibelan.** The incident referred to is recorded of Nennius, brother of Cassibelan, in Holinshed. 31. **giglot,** lewd, wanton. 32. **Lud's town,** London. 48. **injurious,** malicious, or insolent. 51. **against all colour,** in opposition to all reason. 53. **whom,** which. 55. **Mulmutius.** Holinshed gives

an account of the beneficent reign of Mulmutius. 57. **franchise,** free exercise. 73. **at utterance,** to the last extremity. **I am perfect,** I am well aware. 78-84. **His . . . end.** It has been pointed out that this and other speeches by Cloten in this scene are on a higher level of intelligence than might be expected from his usual boorish stupidity. There may be evidence of tampering with the text or of a change of conception, although even the better speeches are characteristically

fall in the adventure, our crows shall fare the better for
you; and there 's an end.

Luc. So, sir.

Cym. I know your master's pleasure and he mine:
All the remain is 'Welcome!'   [*Exeunt.*

SCENE II. *Another room in the palace.*

Enter PISANIO, *with a letter.*

Pis. How! of adultery? Wherefore write you not
What monster 's her accuser? Leonatus!
O master! what a strange infection
Is fall'n into thy ear! What false Italian,
As poisonous-tongued as handed, hath prevail'd
On thy too ready hearing? Disloyal! No:
She 's punish'd for her truth, and undergoes,
More goddess-like than wife-like, such assaults
As would take in some virtue. O my master!
Thy mind to her is now as low as were   10
Thy fortunes. How! that I should murder her?
Upon the love and truth and vows which I
Have made to thy command? I, her? her blood?
If it be so to do good service, never
Let me be counted serviceable. How look I,
That I should seem to lack humanity
So much as this fact comes to? [*Reading*] 'Do 't: the
          letter
That I have sent her, by her own command
Shall give thee opportunity.' O damn'd paper!
Black as the ink that 's on thee! Senseless bauble, 20
Art thou a feodary for this act, and look'st
So virgin-like without? Lo, here she comes.
I am ignorant in what I am commanded.

Enter IMOGEN.

Imo. How now, Pisanio!

Pis. Madam, here is a letter from my lord.

Imo. Who? thy lord? that is my lord, Leonatus!
O, learn'd indeed were that astronomer
That knew the stars as I his characters;
He 'ld lay the future open. You good gods,
Let what is here contain'd relish of love,   30
Of my lord's health, of his content, yet not
That we two are asunder; let that grieve him:
Some griefs are med'cinable; that is one of them,
For it doth physic love: of his content,
All but in that! Good wax, thy leave. Blest be
You bees that make these locks of counsel! Lovers
And men in dangerous bonds pray not alike:
Though forfeiters you cast in prison, yet
You clasp young Cupid's tables. Good news, gods!   39
[*Reads*] 'Justice, and your father's wrath, should he
take me in his dominion, could not be so cruel to me,
as you, O the dearest of creatures, would even renew
me with your eyes. Take notice that I am in Cambria,
at Milford-Haven: what your own love will out of this
advise you, follow. So he wishes you all happiness,
that remains loyal to his vow, and your, increasing in
love,   LEONATUS POSTHUMUS.'

O, for a horse with wings! Hear'st thou, Pisanio?   50
He is at Milford-Haven: read, and tell me
How far 'tis thither. If one of mean affairs
May plod it in a week, why may not I
Glide thither in a day? Then, true Pisanio,—
Who long'st, like me, to see thy lord; who long'st,—
O, let me bate,—but not like me—yet long'st,
But in a fainter kind:—O, not like me;
For mine 's beyond beyond—say, and speak thick;
Love's counsellor should fill the bores of hearing,
To the smothering of the sense—how far it is   60
To this same blessed Milford: and by the way
Tell me how Wales was made so happy as
To inherit such a haven: but first of all,
How we may steal from hence, and for the gap
That we shall make in time, from our hence-going
And our return, to excuse: but first, how get hence:
Why should excuse be born or e'er begot?
We'll talk of that hereafter. Prithee, speak,
How many score of miles may we well ride
'Twixt hour and hour?

Pis.   One score 'twixt sun and sun, 70
Madam, 's enough for you: [*Aside*] and too much too.

Imo. Why, one that rode to 's execution, man,
Could never go so slow: I have heard of riding wagers,
Where horses have been nimbler than the sands
That run i' the clock's behalf. But this is foolery:
Go bid my woman feign a sickness; say
She'll home to her father: and provide me presently
A riding-suit, no costlier than would fit
A franklin's housewife.

Pis.   Madam, you 're best consider.

Imo. I see before me, man: nor here, nor here,   80
Nor what ensues, but have a fog in them,
That I cannot look through. Away, I prithee;
Do as I bid thee: there 's no more to say;
Accessible is none but Milford way.   [*Exeunt.*

SCENE III. *Wales: a mountainous country with a cave.*

Enter, from the cave, BELARIUS; GUIDERIUS, *and*
          ARVIRAGUS *following.*

Bel. A goodly day not to keep house, with such
Whose roof 's as low as ours! Stoop, boys; this gate
Instructs you how to adore the heavens and bows you
To a morning's holy office: the gates of monarchs
Are arch'd so high that giants may jet through
And keep their impious turbans on, without
Good morrow to the sun. Hail, thou fair heaven!
We house i' the rock, yet use thee not so hardly
As prouder livers do.

Gui.   Hail, heaven!

Arv.   Hail, heaven!

Bel. Now for our mountain sport: up to yond hill; 10
Your legs are young; I'll tread these flats. Consider,
When you above perceive me like a crow,
That it is place which lessens and sets off:
And you may then revolve what tales I have told you
Of courts, of princes, of the tricks in war:

---

impudent. 87. **remain,** remainder, rest.
     SCENE II. 9. **take in,** cause to yield, conquer. 10. **to,** compared
to. 21. **feodary,** accomplice. 38. **forfeiters,** those who forfeit their
bonds. The contrast is between the waxen seals on forfeited bonds and
on love letters. 44. **Cambria,** Wales. 58. **thick,** quickly, fast. 67.
or e'er, before. 75. **i' the clock's behalf,** i.e., doing the service of
a clock. 79. **franklin's,** yeoman's. A *franklin* was a farmer who owned

his own land but was not of noble birth. **you 're best,** you had better.
     SCENE III. The second theme of the plot begins at this point; it
proceeds with its complications, entwining itself with the major plot,
and finally is solved in the great fifth scene of the fifth act. 1. **keep
house,** stay at home. 3. **bows you,** makes you bow. 5. **jet,** walk
pompously, strut. One may recognize in the speeches of Belarius the
traditional theme of the vanity of kingly courts.

This service is not service, so being done,
But being so allow'd: to apprehend thus,
Draws us a profit from all things we see;
And often, to our comfort, shall we find
The sharded beetle in a safer hold   20
Than is the full-wing'd eagle. O, this life
Is nobler than attending for a check,
Richer than doing nothing for a bauble,
Prouder than rustling in unpaid-for silk:
Such gain the cap of him that makes 'em fine,
Yet keeps his book uncross'd: no life to ours.
   Gui. Out of your proof you speak: we, poor
     unfledged,
Have never wing'd from view o' the nest, nor know
    not
What air 's from home. Haply this life is best,
If quiet life be best; sweeter to you   30
That have a sharper known; well corresponding
With your stiff age: but unto us it is
A cell of ignorance; travelling a-bed;
A prison for a debtor, that not dares
To stride a limit.
   Arv.   What should we speak of
When we are old as you? when we shall hear
The rain and wind beat dark December, how,
In this our pinching cave, shall we discourse
The freezing hours away? We have seen nothing;
We are beastly, subtle as the fox for prey,   40
Like warlike as the wolf for what we eat;
Our valour is to chase what flies; our cage
We make a quire, as doth the prison'd bird,
And sing our bondage freely.
   Bel.   How you speak!
Did you but know the city's usuries
And felt them knowingly; the art o' the court,
As hard to leave as keep; whose top to climb
Is certain falling, or so slippery that
The fear 's as bad as falling; the toil o' the war,
A pain that only seems to seek out danger   50
I' the name of fame and honour; which dies i' the
    search,
And hath as oft a slanderous epitaph
As record of fair act; nay, many times,
Doth ill deserve by doing well; what 's worse,
Must court'sy at the censure:—O boys, this story
The world may read in me: my body 's mark'd
With Roman swords, and my report was once
First with the best of note: Cymbeline loved me,
And when a soldier was the theme, my name
Was not far off: then was I as a tree   60
Whose boughs did bend with fruit: but in one night,
A storm or robbery, call it what you will,
Shook down my mellow hangings, nay, my leaves,
And left me bare to weather.
   Gui.   Uncertain favour!
   Bel. My fault being nothing—as I have told you
    oft—
But that two villains, whose false oaths prevail'd
Before my perfect honour, swore to Cymbeline

I was confederate with the Romans: so
Follow'd my banishment, and this twenty years
This rock and these demesnes have been my world;   70
Where I have lived at honest freedom, paid
More pious debts to heaven than in all
The fore-end of my time. But up to the mountains!
This is not hunters' language: he that strikes
The venison first shall be the lord o' the feast;
To him the other two shall minister;
And we will fear no poison, which attends
In place of greater state. I'll meet you in the valleys.
          [*Exeunt Guiderius and Arviragus.*
How hard it is to hide the sparks of nature!
These boys know little they are sons to the king;   80
Nor Cymbeline dreams that they are alive.
They think they are mine; and though train'd up thus
    meanly
I' the cave wherein they bow, their thoughts do hit
The roofs of palaces, and nature prompts them
In simple and low things to prince it much
Beyond the trick of others. This Polydore,
The heir of Cymbeline and Britain, who
The king his father call'd Guiderius,—Jove!
When on my three-foot stool I sit and tell
The warlike feats I have done, his spirits fly out   90
Into my story: say 'Thus mine enemy fell,
And thus I set my foot on 's neck;' even then
The princely blood flows in his cheek, he sweats,
Strains his young nerves and puts himself in posture
That acts my words. The younger brother, Cadwal,
Once Arviragus, in as like a figure,
Strikes life into my speech and shows much more
His own conceiving.—Hark, the game is roused!—
O Cymbeline! heaven and my conscience knows
Thou didst unjustly banish me: whereon,   100
At three and two years old, I stole these babes;
Thinking to bar thee of succession, as
Thou reft'st me of my lands. Euriphile,
Thou wast their nurse; they took thee for their
    mother,
And every day do honour to her grave:
Myself, Belarius, that am Morgan call'd,
They take for natural father. The game is up.   [*Exit.*

SCENE IV. *Country near Milford-Haven.*

Enter PISANIO *and* IMOGEN.

   Imo. Thou told'st me, when we came from horse,
    the place
Was near at hand: ne'er long'd my mother so
To see me first, as I have now. Pisanio! man!
Where is Posthumus? What is in thy mind,
That makes thee stare thus? Wherefore breaks that
    sigh
From the inward of thee? One, but painted thus,
Would be interpreted a thing perplex'd
Beyond self-explication: put thyself
Into a haviour of less fear, ere wildness

---

17. **allow'd,** acknowledged. 20. **sharded,** covered with shards or the
sheaths of insects' wings. 22. **attending,** doing service (at court). 23.
bauble, so Rowe; F: *Babe;* Hanmer: *bribe.* 25-26. **Such . . . uncross'd,**
such a one finds his tailor obsequious without having to pay his bill.
27. **we, poor unfledged.** The youths of royal blood have born in them a
taste for kingly courts and noble deeds. 29. **air 's from,** air there is
away from. 35. **stride a limit,** overpass a bound. 41. **Like,** equally.
58. **note,** distinction, importance. 63. **hangings,** hanging fruit. 70.
demesnes, domains, regions. 73. **fore-end,** earlier part. 83. **bow,**

stoop in entering. 85. **prince,** play the prince. 94. **nerves,** sinews,
parts of the body in which the chief strength lies. 99-103. **O . . . lands.**
Even in this late play Shakespeare resorts to the primitive dramaturgy
of his earliest days and has a long story told in soliloquy. 103. **reft'st,**
didst deprive.
    SCENE IV. 9. **haviour,** behavior. 15. **drug-damn'd,** condemned for
its drugs and poisons. **out-crafted,** excelled in craft. 17. **take off,**
have recourse to, reveal. **extremity,** cruelty. 32. **pandar,** accomplice.
37. **worms,** serpents. 44. **charge,** lead, burden (figurative). 51. **jay,**

Vanquish my staider senses. What 's the matter? 10
Why tender'st thou that paper to me, with
A look untender? If 't be summer news,
Smile to 't before; if winterly, thou need'st
But keep that countenance still. My husband's hand!
That drug-damn'd Italy hath out-craftied him,
And he 's at some hard point. Speak, man: thy tongue
May take off some extremity, which to read
Would be even mortal to me.

Pis.   Please you, read;
And you shall find me, wretched man, a thing
The most disdain'd of fortune. 20

Imo. [*Reads*] 'Thy mistress, Pisanio, hath played the
strumpet in my bed; the testimonies whereof lie
bleeding in me. I speak not out of weak surmises,
but from proof as strong as my grief and as certain
as I expect my revenge. That part thou, Pisanio,
must act for me, if thy faith be not tainted with the
breach of hers. Let thine own hands take away her
life: I shall give thee opportunity at Milford-Haven.
She hath my letter for the purpose: where, if thou fear
to strike and to make me certain it is done, thou art
the pandar to her dishonour and equally to me disloyal.' 33

Pis. What shall I need to draw my sword? the paper
Hath cut her throat already. No, 'tis slander,
Whose edge is sharper than the sword, whose tongue
Outvenoms all the worms of Nile, whose breath
Rides on the posting winds and doth belie
All corners of the world: kings, queens and states,
Maids, matrons, nay, the secrets of the grave 40
This viperous slander enters. What cheer, madam?

Imo. False to his bed! What is it to be false?
To lie in watch there and to think on him?
To weep 'twixt clock and clock? if sleep charge
     nature,
To break it with a fearful dream of him
And cry myself awake? that 's false to 's bed, is it?

Pis. Alas, good lady!

Imo. I false! Thy conscience witness: Iachimo,
Thou didst accuse him of incontinency;
Thou then look'dst like a villain; now methinks 50
Thy favour 's good enough. Some jay of Italy
†Whose mother was her painting, hath betray'd him:
Poor I am stale, a garment out of fashion;
And, for I am richer than to hang by the walls,
I must be ripp'd:—to pieces with me!—O,
Men's vows are women's traitors! All good seeming,
By thy revolt, O husband, shall be thought
Put on for villany; not born where 't grows,
But worn a bait for ladies.

Pis.   Good madam, hear me. 59

Imo. True honest men being heard, like false Æneas,
Were in his time thought false, and Sinon's weeping
Did scandal many a holy tear, took pity
From most true wretchedness: so thou, Posthumus,
Wilt lay the leaven on all proper men;
Goodly and gallant shall be false and perjured
From thy great fail. Come, fellow, be thou honest:

Do thou thy master's bidding: when thou see'st him,
A little witness my obedience: look!
I draw the sword myself: take it, and hit
The innocent mansion of my love, my heart: 70
Fear not; 'tis empty of all things but grief:
Thy master is not there, who was indeed
The riches of it: do his bidding; strike.
Thou mayst be valiant in a better cause;
But now thou seem'st a coward.

Pis.   Hence, vile instrument!
Thou shalt not damn my hand.

Imo.   Why, I must die;
And if I do not by thy hand, thou art
No servant of thy master's. Against self-slaughter
There is a prohibition so divine 79
That cravens my weak hand. Come, here 's my heart.
Something 's afore 't. Soft, soft! we'll no defence;
Obedient as the scabbard. What is here?
The scriptures of the loyal Leonatus,
All turn'd to heresy? Away, away,
Corrupters of my faith! you shall no more
Be stomachers to my heart. Thus may poor fools
Believe false teachers: though those that are betray'd
Do feel the treason sharply, yet the traitor
Stands in worse case of woe.
And thou, Posthumus, thou that didst set up 90
My disobedience 'gainst the king my father
And make me put into contempt the suits
Of princely fellows, shalt hereafter find
It is no act of common passage, but
A strain of rareness: and I grieve myself
To think, when thou shalt be disedged by her
That now thou tirest on, how thy memory
Will then be pang'd by me. Prithee, dispatch:
The lamb entreats the butcher: where 's thy knife?
Thou art too slow to do thy master's bidding, 100
When I desire it too.

Pis.   O gracious lady,
Since I received command to do this business
I have not slept one wink.

Imo.   Do 't, and to bed then.

Pis. I'll wake mine eye-balls blind first.

Imo.   Wherefore then
Didst undertake it? Why hast thou abused
So many miles with a pretence? this place?
Mine action and thine own? our horses' labour?
The time inviting thee? the perturb'd court,
For my being absent? whereunto I never
Purpose return. Why hast thou gone so far, 110
To be unbent when thou hast ta'en thy stand,
The elected deer before thee?

Pis.   But to win time
To lose so bad employment; in the which
I have consider'd of a course. Good lady,
Hear me with patience.

Imo.   Talk thy tongue weary; speak:
I have heard I am a strumpet; and mine ear,
Therein false struck, can take no greater wound,
Nor tent to bottom that. But speak.

flashy or light woman. 52. **Whose . . . painting,** explained as "who
owed her beauty to her painted face"; i.e., a creature born and made up
of the paint pot (Dowden); also as "whose painted face was the sum of
her woman-like qualities." 60. **Æneas,** thought of as the pattern of
faithless love because of his desertion of Dido. 61. **Sinon's.** The
Greek Sinon by his guile persuaded the Trojans to introduce within the
walls of Troy the wooden horse filled with armed men. 64. **lay the
leaven on,** taint, corrupt. 66. **fail,** fault, offense. 80. **cravens,** renders
cowardly. 83. **scriptures,** writings. It suggests the ordinary meaning,

which is played on in what follows; also, the letters which she has from
Leonatus have been as Holy Writ to her. 86. **stomachers,** ornamental
coverings for the breast. 90. **set up,** incite, encourage. 94-95.
It . . . rareness, that my choice of you is no act of ordinary occurrence but a rare and high-pitched impulse (of the heart). 96. **disedged,** surfeited. 97. **tirest on,** tearest or devourest (as a bird of
prey). 98. **pang'd,** pained. 104. **blind,** so Hanmer; Johnson: *out;* F
omits. 111. **unbent,** with unbent bow. 112. **elected,** chosen. 118.
Nor . . . that, nor probe that to the bottom.

Pis.   Then, madam,
I thought you would not back again.
    Imo.   Most like;
Bringing me here to kill me.
    Pis.   Not so, neither: 120
But if I were as wise as honest, then
My purpose would prove well. It cannot be
But that my master is abused:
Some villain, ay, and singular in his art,
Hath done you both this cursed injury.
    Imo. Some Roman courtezan.
    Pis.   No, on my life.
I'll give but notice you are dead and send him
Some bloody sign of it; for 'tis commanded
I should do so: you shall be miss'd at court,
And that will well confirm it.
    Imo.   Why, good fellow,   130
What shall I do the while? where bide? how live?
Or in my life what comfort, when I am
Dead to my husband?
    Pis.   If you'll back to the court—
    Imo. No court, no father; nor no more ado
†With that harsh, noble, simple nothing,
That Cloten, whose love-suit hath been to me
As fearful as a siege.
    Pis.   If not at court,
Then not in Britain must you bide.
    Imo.   Where then?
Hath Britain all the sun that shines? Day, night,
Are they not but in Britain? I' the world's volume   140
Our Britain seems as of it, but not in 't;
In a great pool a swan's nest: prithee, think
There 's livers out of Britain.
    Pis.   I am most glad
You think of other place. The ambassador,
Lucius the Roman, comes to Milford-Haven
To-morrow: now, if you could wear a mind
Dark as your fortune is, and but disguise
That which, to appear itself, must not yet be
But by self-danger, you should tread a course
†Pretty and full of view; yea, haply, near   150
The residence of Posthumus; so nigh at least
That though his actions were not visible, yet
Report should render him hourly to your ear
As truly as he moves.
    Imo.   O, for such means!
Though peril to my modesty, not death on 't,
I would adventure.
    Pis.   Well, then, here 's the point:
You must forget to be a woman; change
Command into obedience: fear and niceness—
The handmaids of all women, or, more truly,
Woman it pretty self—into a waggish courage;   160
Ready in gibes, quick-answer'd, saucy and
As quarrelous as the weasel; nay, you must
Forget that rarest treasure of your cheek,
Exposing it—but, O, the harder heart!
Alack, no remedy!—to the greedy touch
Of common-kissing Titan, and forget
Your laboursome and dainty trims, wherein
You made great Juno angry.

    Imo.   Nay, be brief:
I see into thy end, and am almost   169
A man already.
    Pis.   First, make yourself but like one.
Fore-thinking this, I have already fit—
'Tis in my cloak-bag—doublet, hat, hose, all
That answer to them: would you in their serving,
And with what imitation you can borrow
From youth of such a season, 'fore noble Lucius
Present yourself, desire his service, tell him
Wherein you 're happy,—which you'll make him
                    know,
If that his head have ear in music,—doubtless
With joy he will embrace you, for he 's honourable
And doubling that, most holy. Your means abroad,   180
You have me, rich; and I will never fail
Beginning nor supplyment.
    Imo.   Thou art all the comfort
The gods will diet me with. Prithee, away:
There 's more to be consider'd; but we'll even
All that good time will give us: this attempt
I am soldier to, and will abide it with
A prince's courage. Away, I prithee.
    Pis. Well, madam, we must take a short farewell,
Lest, being miss'd, I be suspected of
Your carriage from the court. My noble mistress,   190
Here is a box; I had it from the queen:
What 's in 't is precious; if you are sick at sea,
Or stomach-qualm'd at land, a dram of this
Will drive away distemper. To some shade,
And fit you to your manhood. May the gods
Direct you to the best!
    Imo. Amen: I thank thee.   [*Exeunt, severally.*

SCENE V. *A room in Cymbeline's palace.*

Enter CYMBELINE, QUEEN, CLOTEN, LUCIUS, Lords,
    and Attendants.

    Cym. Thus far; and so farewell.
    Luc.   Thanks, royal sir.
My emperor hath wrote, I must from hence;
And am right sorry that I must report ye
My master's enemy.
    Cym.   Our subjects, sir,
Will not endure his yoke; and for ourself
To show less sovereignty than they, must needs
Appear unkinglike.
    Luc.   So, sir: I desire of you
A conduct over-land to Milford-Haven.
Madam, all joy befal your grace!
    Queen.   And you!
    Cym. My lords, you are appointed for that office;   10
The due of honour in no point omit.
So farewell, noble Lucius.
    Luc.   Your hand, my lord.
    Clo. Receive it friendly; but from this time forth
I wear it as your enemy.
    Luc.   Sir, the event
Is yet to name the winner: fare you well.
    Cym. Leave not the worthy Lucius, good my lords,

Till he have cross'd the Severn. Happiness!
                              [*Exeunt Lucius and Lords.*
    Queen. He goes hence frowning: but it honours us
That we have given him cause.
    Clo.   'Tis all the better;
Your valiant Britons have their wishes in it.   20
    Cym. Lucius hath wrote already to the emperor
How it goes here. It fits us therefore ripely
Our chariots and our horsemen be in readiness:
The powers that he already hath in Gallia
Will soon be drawn to head, from whence he moves
His war for Britain.
    Queen.   'Tis not sleepy business;
But must be look'd to speedily and strongly.
    Cym. Our expectation that it would be thus
Hath made us forward. But, my gentle queen,
Where is our daughter? She hath not appear'd   30
Before the Roman, nor to us hath tender'd
The duty of the day: she looks us like
A thing more made of malice than of duty:
We have noted it. Call her before us; for
We have been too slight in sufferance.
                              [*Exit an Attendant.*
    Queen.   Royal sir,
Since the exile of Posthumus, most retired
Hath her life been; the cure whereof, my lord,
'Tis time must do. Beseech your majesty,
Forbear sharp speeches to her: she 's a lady
So tender of rebukes that words are strokes   40
And strokes death to her.

Re-enter Attendant.

    Cym.   Where is she, sir? How
Can her contempt be answer'd?
    Atten.   Please you, sir,
Her chambers are all lock'd; and there 's no answer
That will be given to the loudest noise we make.
    Queen. My lord, when last I went to visit her,
She pray'd me to excuse her keeping close,
Whereto constrain'd by her infirmity,
She should that duty leave unpaid to you,
Which daily she was bound to proffer: this
She wish'd me to make known; but our great court   50
Made me to blame in memory.
    Cym.   Her doors lock'd?
Not seen of late? Grant, heavens, that which I fear
Prove false!   [*Exit.*
    Queen.   Son, I say, follow the king.
    Clo. That man of hers, Pisanio, her old servant,
I have not seen these two days.
    Queen.   Go, look after.   [*Exit Cloten.*
Pisanio, thou that stand'st so for Posthumus!
He hath a drug of mine; I pray his absence
Proceed by swallowing that, for he believes
It is a thing most precious. But for her,
Where is she gone? Haply, despair hath seized her,   60
Or, wing'd with fervour of her love, she 's flown
To her desired Posthumus: gone she is
To death or to dishonour; and my end
Can make good use of either: she being down,
I have the placing of the British crown.

Re-enter CLOTEN.

How now, my son!
    Clo.   'Tis certain she is fled.
Go in and cheer the king: he rages; none
Dare come about him.
    Queen.   [*Aside*] All the better: may
This night forestall him of the coming day!   [*Exit.*
    Clo. I love and hate her: for she 's fair and royal,   70
And that she hath all courtly parts more exquisite
Than lady, ladies, woman; from every one
The best she hath, and she, of all compounded,
Outsells them all; I love her therefore: but
Disdaining me and throwing favours on
The low Posthumus slanders so her judgement
That what 's else rare is choked; and in that point
I will conclude to hate her, nay, indeed,
To be revenged upon her. For when fools
Shall—

Enter PISANIO.

                    Who is here? What, are you packing,
    sirrah?   80
Come hither: ah, you precious pandar! Villain,
Where is thy lady? In a word; or else
Thou art straightway with the fiends.
    Pis.   O, good my lord!
    Clo. Where is thy lady? or, by Jupiter,—
I will not ask again. Close villain,
I'll have this secret from thy heart, or rip
Thy heart to find it. Is she with Posthumus?
From whose so many weights of baseness cannot
A dram of worth be drawn.
    Pis.   Alas, my lord,
How can she be with him? When was she miss'd?   90
He is in Rome.
    Clo.   Where is she, sir? Come nearer;
No further halting: satisfy me home
What is become of her.
    Pis. O, my all-worthy lord!
    Clo.   All-worthy villain!
Discover where thy mistress is at once,
At the next word: no more of 'worthy lord!'
Speak, or thy silence on the instant is
Thy condemnation and thy death.
    Pis.   Then, sir,
This paper is the history of my knowledge
Touching her flight.   [*Presenting a letter.*
    Clo.   Let 's see 't. I will pursue her   100
Even to Augustus' throne.
    Pis.   [*Aside*] Or this, or perish.
She 's far enough; and what he learns by this
May prove his travel, not her danger.
    Clo.   Hum!
    Pis. [*Aside*] I'll write to my lord she 's dead. O
    Imogen,
Safe mayst thou wander, safe return again!
    Clo. Sirrah, is this letter true?
    Pis. Sir, as I think.   107
    Clo. It is Posthumus' hand; I know 't. Sirrah, if
thou wouldst not be a villain, but do me true service,
undergo those employments wherein I should have

drive away distemper. The presentation and subsequent employment
of the potion reflects a naive attitude toward the curative powers of
drugs characteristic of the Elizabethan age.
    SCENE V. 8. **conduct,** safe-conduct, escort. 13. **Receive,** etc. In
this scene, as in Act II, Scene i, Cloten speaks with better sense than
in the earlier scenes of the play. 22. **fits,** befits. **ripely,** speedily.
52. **drawn to head,** brought together, levied. 32. **looks us,** seems to
us. 35. **slight in sufferance,** careless in permitting it. 50. **great
court,** important courtly business. 58. **by,** from. 69. **forestall,** deprive. 71. **that,** because. **parts,** endowments, graces. 74. **Outsells,**
outvalues, excels. 82. **In a word,** answer in a word. 88. **whose so
many,** so many of whose.

cause to use thee with a serious industry, that is, what villany soe'er I bid thee do, to perform it directly and truly, I would think thee an honest man: thou shouldst neither want my means for thy relief nor my voice for thy preferment.

Pis. Well, my good lord. 117

Clo. Wilt thou serve me? for since patiently and constantly thou hast stuck to the bare fortune of that beggar Posthumus, thou canst not, in the course of gratitude, but be a diligent follower of mine: wilt thou serve me?

Pis. Sir, I will. 123

Clo. Give me thy hand; here 's my purse. Hast any of thy late master's garments in thy possession?

Pis. I have, my lord, at my lodging, the same suit he wore when he took leave of my lady and mistress.

Clo. The first service thou dost me, fetch that suit hither: let it be thy first service; go. 131

Pis. I shall, my lord. [*Exit.*

Clo. Meet thee at Milford-Haven!—I forgot to ask him one thing; I'll remember 't anon:—even there, thou villain Posthumus, will I kill thee. I would these garments were come. She said upon a time—the bitterness of it I now belch from my heart—that she held the very garment of Posthumus in more respect than my noble and natural person, together with the adornment of my qualities. With that suit upon my back, will I ravish her: first kill him, and in her eyes; there shall she see my valour, which will then be a torment to her contempt. He on the ground, my speech of insultment ended on his dead body, and when my lust hath dined,—which, as I say, to vex her I will execute in the clothes that she so praised,—to the court I'll knock her back, foot her home again. She hath despised me rejoicingly, and I'll be merry in my revenge. 150

Re-enter PISANIO *with the clothes.*

Be those the garments?

Pis. Ay, my noble lord.

Clo. How long is 't since she went to Milford-Haven?

Pis. She can scarce be there yet.

Clo. Bring this apparel to my chamber; that is the second thing that I have commanded thee: the third is, that thou wilt be a voluntary mute to my design. Be but duteous, and true preferment shall tender itself to thee. My revenge is now at Milford: would I had wings to follow it! Come, and be true. [*Exit.*

Pis. Thou bid'st me to my loss: for true to thee 163 Were to prove false, which I will never be, To him that is most true. To Milford go, And find not her whom thou pursuest. Flow, flow, You heavenly blessings, on her! This fool's speed Be cross'd with slowness; labour be his meed! [*Exit.*

SCENE VI. *Wales. Before the cave of Belarius.*

Enter IMOGEN, *in boy's clothes.*

Imo. I see a man's life is a tedious one: I have tired myself, and for two nights together

Have made the ground my bed. I should be sick, But that my resolution helps me. Milford, When from the mountain-top Pisanio show'd thee, Thou wast within a ken: O Jove! I think Foundations fly the wretched; such, I mean, Where they should be relieved. Two beggars told me I could not miss my way: will poor folks lie, That have afflictions on them, knowing 'tis 10 A punishment or trial? Yes; no wonder, When rich ones scarce tell true. To lapse in fulness Is sorer than to lie for need, and falsehood Is worse in kings than beggars. My dear lord! Thou art one o' the false ones. Now I think on thee, My hunger 's gone; but even before, I was At point to sink for food. But what is this? Here is a path to 't: 'tis some savage hold: I were best not call; I dare not call: yet famine, Ere clean it o'erthrow nature, makes it valiant. 20 Plenty and peace breeds cowards: hardness ever Of hardiness is mother. Ho! who 's here? If any thing that 's civil, speak; if savage, Take or lend. Ho! No answer? Then I'll enter. Best draw my sword; and if mine enemy But fear the sword like me, he'll scarcely look on 't. Such a foe, good heavens! [*Exit, to the cave.*

Enter BELARIUS, GUIDERIUS, *and* ARVIRAGUS.

Bel. You, Polydore, have proved best woodman and Are master of the feast: Cadwal and I Will play the cook and servant; 'tis our match: 30 The sweat of industry would dry and die, But for the end it works to. Come; our stomachs Will make what 's homely savoury: weariness Can snore upon the flint, when resty sloth Finds the down pillow hard. Now peace be here, Poor house, that keep'st thyself!

Gui. I am throughly weary.

Arv. I am weak with toil, yet strong in appetite.

Gui. There is cold meat i' the cave; we'll browse on that,

Whilst what we have kill'd be cook'd.

Bel. [*Looking into the cave*] Stay; come not in. 40 But that it eats our victuals, I should think Here were a fairy.

Gui. What 's the matter, sir?

Bel. By Jupiter, an angel! or, if not, An earthly paragon! Behold divineness No elder than a boy!

Re-enter IMOGEN.

Imo. Good masters, harm me not: Before I enter'd here, I call'd; and thought To have begg'd or bought what I have took: good troth, I have stol'n nought, nor would not, though I had found 49 Gold strew'd i' the floor. Here 's money for my meat: I would have left it on the board so soon As I had made my meal, and parted With prayers for the provider.

Gui. Money, youth?

145. **insultment,** contemptuous triumph (Onions). 149. **foot,** kick. SCENE VI. 6. **within a ken,** within sight. 7. **Foundations,** quibbling use, denoting fixed places and charitable institutions (Schmidt). 13. **sorer,** worse, more wicked. 18. **hold,** stronghold, fastness. 20. **clean,** altogether. 21. **hardness,** hardship. 22. **hardiness,** hardihood, bravery. 24. **Take or lend,** take my life or give me food. Dowden explains:

"Take what I have before you lend me food." 28. **woodman,** huntsman. 30. **match,** agreement, bargain. 34. **resty,** sluggish, indolent. 64. **in,** into. 71. **I bid . . . buy,** I bid for you as one who would have you. 77. **prize,** value, i.e., she would not have been heir to the throne. 79. **wrings,** writhes. 85-86. **laying . . . multitudes,** disregarding the valueless gift of the fickle mob (as spectators). 87. **out-peer,** excel.

Arv. All gold and silver rather turn to dirt!
As 'tis no better reckon'd, but of those
Who worship dirty gods.

Imo. I see you 're angry:
Know, if you kill me for my fault, I should
Have died had I not made it.

Bel. Whither bound?

Imo. To Milford-Haven.

Bel. What 's your name? 60

Imo. Fidele, sir. I have a kinsman who
Is bound for Italy; he embark'd at Milford;
To whom being going, almost spent with hunger,
I am fall'n in this offence.

Bel. ' Prithee, fair youth,
Think us no churls, nor measure our good minds
By this rude place we live in. Well encounter'd!
'Tis almost night: you shall have better cheer
Ere you depart; and thanks to stay and eat it.
Boys, bid him welcome.

Gui. Were you a woman, youth,
I should woo hard but be your groom. In honesty, 70
I bid for you as I 'ld buy.

Arv. I'll make 't my comfort
He is a man; I'll love him as my brother:
And such a welcome as I 'ld give to him
After long absence, such is yours: most welcome!
Be sprightly, for you fall 'mongst friends.

Imo. 'Mongst friends,
If brothers. [*Aside*] Would it had been so, that they
Had been my father's sons! then had my prize
Been less, and so more equal ballasting
To thee, Posthumus.

Bel. He wrings at some distress.

Gui. Would I could free 't!

Arv. Or I, whate'er it be, 80
What pain it cost, what danger. Gods!

Bel. Hark, boys. [*Whispering.*

Imo. Great men,
That had a court no bigger than this cave,
That did attend themselves and had the virtue
Which their own conscience seal'd them—laying by
That nothing-gift of differing multitudes—
Could not out-peer these twain. Pardon me, gods!
I 'ld change my sex to be companion with them,
Since Leonatus 's false.

Bel. It shall be so.
Boys, we'll go dress our hunt. Fair youth, come in: 90
Discourse is heavy, fasting; when we have supp'd,
We'll mannerly demand thee of thy story,
So far as thou wilt speak it.

Gui. Pray, draw near.

Arv. The night to the owl and morn to the lark less
welcome.

Imo. Thanks, sir.

Arv. I pray, draw near. [*Exeunt.*

SCENE VII. *Rome. A public place.*

Enter two Senators *and* Tribunes.

First Sen. This is the tenour of the emperor's writ:
That since the common men are now in action
'Gainst the Pannonians and Dalmatians,
And that the legions now in Gallia are
Full weak to undertake our wars against
The fall'n-off Britons, that we do incite
The gentry to this business. He creates
Lucius proconsul: and to you the tribunes,
For this immediate levy, he commends
His absolute commission. Long live Cæsar! 10

First Tri. Is Lucius general of the forces?

Sec. Sen. Ay.

First Tri. Remaining now in Gallia?

First Sen. With those legions
Which I have spoke of, whereunto your levy
Must be supplyant: the words of your commission
Will tie you to the numbers and the time
Of their dispatch.

First Tri. We will discharge our duty.
[*Exeunt.*

ACT IV.

SCENE I. *Wales: near the cave of Belarius.*

Enter CLOTEN.

Clo. I am near to the place where they should meet,
if Pisanio have mapped it truly. How fit his garments
serve me! Why should his mistress, who was made by
him that made the tailor, not be fit too? the rather—
saving reverence of the word—for 'tis said a woman's
fitness comes by fits. Therein I must play the workman. I dare speak it to myself—for it is not vain-glory
for a man and his glass to confer in his own chamber—
I mean, the lines of my body are as well drawn as his;
no less young, more strong, not beneath him in
fortunes, beyond him in the advantage of the time,
above him in birth, alike conversant in general
services, and more remarkable in single oppositions:
yet this imperceiverant thing loves him in my despite.
What mortality is! Posthumus, thy head, which now
is growing upon thy shoulders, shall within this hour
be off; thy mistress enforced; thy garments cut to
pieces before thy face: and all this done, spurn her
home to her father; who may haply be a little angry
for my so rough usage; but my mother, having power
of his testiness, shall turn all into my commendations.
My horse is tied up safe: out, sword, and to a sore
purpose! Fortune, put them into my hand! This is the
very description of their meeting-place; and the
fellow dares not deceive me. [*Exit.*

SCENE II. *Before the cave of Belarius.*

Enter, from the cave, BELARIUS, GUIDERIUS, ARVIRAGUS,
and IMOGEN.

Bel. [*To Imogen*] You are not well: remain here in
the cave;
We'll come to you after hunting.

Arv. [*To Imogen*] Brother, stay here:

---

90. **hunt,** game taken in the hunt.
SCENE VII. 6. **fall'n-off,** revolted. 9. **commends,** delivers, presents.
F has *commands,* which may be retained with the meaning, "commands
to be given." 14. **supplyant,** reinforcing, auxiliary.
ACT IV. SCENE I. 6. **saving reverence,** asking pardon. 7. **fits,** sud-
den, transitory states, with pun on the fit of the tailor. 13. **advantage**

of the time, superiority in social opportunity. 14. **alike . . . services,**
equally versed in military matters. 15. **single oppositions,** single combat. Schmidt defines "when compared as to particular accomplishments." 16. **imperceiverant,** dull of perception; possibly, giddy, thoughtless; F: *imperseuerant,* which would be the correct form of a word meaning "changeable." 17. **What,** what a thing. 24. **power of,** power over.

Are we not brothers?
 Imo.   So man and man should be;
But clay and clay differs in dignity,
Whose dust is both alike. I am very sick.
 Gui. Go you to hunting; I'll abide with him.
 Imo. So sick I am not, yet I am not well;
But not so citizen a wanton as
To seem to die ere sick: so please you, leave me;
Stick to your journal course: the breach of custom 10
Is breach of all. I am ill, but your being by me
Cannot amend me; society is no comfort
To one not sociable: I am not very sick,
Since I can reason of it. Pray you, trust me here:
I'll rob none but myself; and let me die,
Stealing so poorly.
 Gui.   I love thee; I have spoke it:
How much the quantity, the weight as much,
As I do love my father.
 Bel.   What! how! how!
 Arv. If it be sin to say so, sir, I yoke me
In my good brother's fault: I know not why 20
I love this youth; and I have heard you say,
Love's reason 's without reason: the bier at door,
And a demand who is 't shall die, I 'ld say
'My father, not this youth.'
 Bel.   [*Aside*] O noble strain!
O worthiness of nature! breed of greatness!
Cowards father cowards and base things sire base:
Nature hath meal and bran, contempt and grace.
I 'm not their father; yet who this should be,
Doth miracle itself, loved before me.
'Tis the ninth hour o' the morn.
 Arv.   Brother, farewell. 30
 Imo. I wish ye sport.
 Arv.   You health. So please you, sir.
 Imo. [*Aside*] These are kind creatures. Gods, what
  lies I have heard!
Our courtiers say all 's savage but at court:
Experience, O, thou disprovest report!
The imperious seas breed monsters, for the dish
Poor tributary rivers as sweet fish.
I am sick still; heart-sick. Pisanio,
I'll now taste of thy drug.   [*Swallows some.*
 Gui.   I could not stir him:
He said he was gentle, but unfortunate;
Dishonestly afflicted, but yet honest. 40
 Arv. Thus did he answer me: yet said, hereafter
I might know more.
 Bel.   To the field, to the field!
We'll leave you for this time: go in and rest.
 Arv. We'll not be long away.
 Bel.   Pray, be not sick,
For you must be our housewife.
 Imo.   Well or ill,
I am bound to you.
 Bel.   And shalt be ever.
       [*Exit Imogen, to the cave.*
This youth, howe'er distress'd, appears he hath had
Good ancestors.
 Arv.   How angel-like he sings!
 Gui. But his neat cookery! he cut our roots
In characters,

And sauced our broths, as Juno had been sick 50
And he her dieter.
 Arv.   Nobly he yokes
A smiling with a sigh, as if the sigh
Was that it was, for not being such a smile;
The smile mocking the sigh, that it would fly
From so divine a temple, to commix
With winds that sailors rail at.
 Gui.   I do note
That grief and patience, rooted in him both,
Mingle their spurs together.
 Arv.   Grow, patience!
And let the stinking elder, grief, untwine
His perishing root with the increasing vine! 60
 Bel. It is great morning. Come, away!—Who 's
  there?

 Enter CLOTEN.

 Clo. I cannot find those runagates; that villain
Hath mock'd me. I am faint.
 Bel.   'Those runagates!'
Means he not us? I partly know him: 'tis
Cloten, the son o' the queen. I fear some ambush.
I saw him not these many years, and yet
I know 'tis he. We are held as outlaws: hence!
 Gui. He is but one: you and my brother search
What companies are near: pray you, away;
Let me alone with him. [*Exeunt Belarius and Arviragus.*
 Clo.   Soft! What are you 70
That fly me thus? some villain mountaineers?
I have heard of such. What slave art thou?
 Gui.   A thing
More slavish did I ne'er than answering
A slave without a knock.
 Clo.   Thou art a robber,
A law-breaker, a villain: yield thee, thief.
 Gui. To who? to thee? What art thou? Have not I
An arm as big as thine? a heart as big?
Thy words, I grant, are bigger, for I wear not
My dagger in my mouth. Say what thou art,
Why I should yield to thee?
 Clo.   Thou villain base, 80
Know'st me not by my clothes?
 Gui.   No, nor thy tailor, rascal,
Who is thy grandfather: he made those clothes,
Which, as it seems, make thee.
 Clo.   Thou precious varlet,
My tailor made them not.
 Gui.   Hence, then, and thank
The man that gave them thee. Thou art some fool;
I am loath to beat thee.
 Clo.   Thou injurious thief,
Hear but my name, and tremble.
 Gui.   What 's thy name?
 Clo. Cloten, thou villain.
 Gui. Cloten, thou double villain, be thy name,
I cannot tremble at it: were it Toad, or Adder,
 Spider, 90
'Twould move me sooner.
 Clo.   To thy further fear,
Nay, to thy mere confusion, thou shalt know
I am son to the queen.

Cymbeline
ACT IV : SC II

1202

SCENE II. 8. **citizen**, effeminate. **wanton**, spoiled or pampered person. 10. **journal**, daily. 17. **How much**, however much. 35. **imperious**, imperial. 36. **as sweet fish**, breed as sweet fish (for eating) as the sea. 39. **gentle**, of gentle blood. 53. **that**, what. 58. **spurs**, roots of a tree (used of projecting roots). 59. **elder**, elder tree. **untwine**, cease to twine. 61. **great morning**, broad day. 81. **Know'st . . . clothes.** Cloten is dressed as one from the court. 86. **injurious**, malicious, insulting. 106. **absolute**, positive. 107. **very Cloten**, Cloten himself. 110. **apprehension**, comprehension, conception. 111. **effect**, result. The F reading, *defect*, is retained by the Arden editors and

Gui.   I am sorry for 't; not seeming
So worthy as thy birth.
    Clo.   Art not afeard?
    Gui. Those that I reverence those I fear, the wise:
At fools I laugh, not fear them.
    Clo.   Die the death:
When I have slain thee with my proper hand,
I'll follow those that even now fled hence,
And on the gates of Lud's-town set your heads:
Yield, rustic mountaineer.   [*Exeunt, fighting.* 100

        Re-enter BELARIUS *and* ARVIRAGUS.

    Bel. No companies abroad?
    Arv. None in the world: you did mistake him, sure.
    Bel. I cannot tell: long is it since I saw him,
But time hath nothing blurr'd those lines of favour
Which then he wore; the snatches in his voice,
And burst of speaking, were as his: I am absolute
'Twas very Cloten.
    Arv.   In this place we left them:
I wish my brother make good time with him,
You say he is so fell.
    Bel.   Being scarce made up,
I mean, to man, he had not apprehension   110
Of roaring terrors; for the effect of judgement
Is oft the cause of fear. But, see, thy brother.

        Re-enter GUIDERIUS, *with* CLOTEN'S *head.*

    Gui. This Cloten was a fool, an empty purse;
There was no money in 't: not Hercules
Could have knock'd out his brains, for he had none:
Yet I not doing this, the fool had borne
My head as I do his.
    Bel.   What hast thou done?
    Gui. I am perfect what: cut off one Cloten's head,
Son to the queen, after his own report;
Who call'd me traitor, mountaineer, and swore   120
With his own single hand he 'ld take us in,
Displace our heads where—thank the gods!—they
          grow,
And set them on Lud's-town.
    Bel.   We are all undone.
    Gui. Why, worthy father, what have we to lose,
But that he swore to take, our lives? The law
Protects not us: then why should we be tender
To let an arrogant piece of flesh threat us,
Play judge and executioner all himself,
For we do fear the law? What company
Discover you abroad?
    Bel.   No single soul   130
Can we set eye on; but in all safe reason
He must have some attendants. Though his humour
Was nothing but mutation, ay, and that
From one bad thing to worse; not frenzy, not
Absolute madness could so far have raved
To bring him here alone; although perhaps
It may be heard at court that such as we
Cave here, hunt here, are outlaws, and in time
May make some stronger head; the which he
          hearing—
As it is like him—might break out, and swear   140
He 'ld fetch us in; yet is 't not probable

To come alone, either he so undertaking,
Or they so suffering: then on good ground we fear,
If we do fear this body hath a tail
More perilous than the head.
    Arv.   Let ordinance
Come as the gods foresay it: howsoe'er,
My brother hath done well.
    Bel.   I had no mind
To hunt this day: the boy Fidele's sickness
Did make my way long forth.
    Gui.   With his own sword,
Which he did wave against my throat, I have ta'en 150
His head from him: I'll throw 't into the creek
Behind our rock; and let it to the sea,
And tell the fishes he 's the queen's son, Cloten:
That 's all I reck.   [*Exit.*
    Bel.   I fear 'twill be revenged:
Would, Polydore, thou hadst not done 't! though
          valour
Becomes thee well enough.
    Arv.   Would I had done 't,
So the revenge alone pursued me! Polydore,
I love thee brotherly, but envy much
Thou hast robb'd me of this deed: I would revenges,
That possible strength might meet, would seek us
          through   160
And put us to our answer.
    Bel.   Well, 'tis done:
We'll hunt no more to-day, nor seek for danger
Where there 's no profit. I prithee, to our rock;
You and Fidele play the cooks: I'll stay
Till hasty Polydore return, and bring him
To dinner presently.
    Arv.   Poor sick Fidele!
I'll willingly to him: to gain his colour
I 'ld let a parish of such Clotens blood,
And praise myself for charity.   [*Exit.*
    Bel.   O thou goddess,
Thou divine Nature, how thyself thou blazon'st   170
In these two princely boys! They are as gentle
As zephyrs blowing below the violet,
Not wagging his sweet head; and yet as rough,
Their royal blood enchafed, as the rudest wind,
That by the top doth take the mountain pine,
And make him stoop to the vale. 'Tis wonder
That an invisible instinct should frame them
To royalty unlearn'd, honour untaught,
Civility not seen from other, valour
That wildly grows in them, but yields a crop   180
As if it had been sow'd. Yet still it 's strange
What Cloten's being here to us portends,
Or what his death will bring us.

        Re-enter GUIDERIUS.

    Gui.   Where 's my brother?
I have sent Cloten's clotpoll down the stream,
In embassy to his mother: his body 's hostage
For his return.   [*Solemn music.*
    Bel.   My ingenious instrument!
Hark, Polydore, it sounds! But what occasion
Hath Cadwal now to give it motion? Hark!
    Gui. Is he at home?

others as meaning "defectiveness in the use of judgment." 118. **I am
perfect what,** I am perfectly well aware of what I have done. 125.
that, that which. 126. **tender,** quick, keen. 138. **Cave,** live in a cave.
141. **fetch us in,** capture us. 145. **ordinance,** what is ordained. 149.
make . . . forth, make my wandering from the cave seem long. 154.

reck, care. 160. **That . . . meet,** that strength such as ours might resist.
seek us through, call us to account. 167. **gain his colour,** restore him
to health. 168. **let . . . blood,** let a parish full of such Clotens suffer
death. 170. **blazon'st,** proclaim'st. 184. **clotpoll,** head.

Bel.   He went hence even now.
Gui. What does he mean? since death of my dear'st
        mother   190
It did not speak before. All solemn things
Should answer solemn accidents. The matter?
Triumphs for nothing and lamenting toys
Is jollity for apes and grief for boys.
Is Cadwal mad?
        Bel.   Look, here he comes,
And brings the dire occasion in his arms
Of what we blame him for.

        Re-enter ARVIRAGUS, *with* IMOGEN, *as dead,*
                bearing her in his arms.

        Arv.   The bird is dead
That we have made so much on. I had rather
Have skipp'd from sixteen years of age to sixty,
To have turn'd my leaping-time into a crutch,   200
Than have seen this.
        Gui.   O sweetest, fairest lily!
My brother wears thee not the one half so well
As when thou grew'st thyself.
        Bel.   O melancholy!
Who ever yet could sound thy bottom? find
The ooze, to show what coast thy sluggish crare
Might easiliest harbour in? Thou blessed thing!
Jove knows what man thou mightst have made; but I,
Thou diedst, a most rare boy, of melancholy.
How found you him?
        Arv.   Stark, as you see:
Thus smiling, as some fly had tickled slumber,   210
Not as death's dart, being laugh'd at; his right cheek
Reposing on a cushion.
        Gui.   Where?
        Arv.   O' the floor;
His arms thus leagued: I thought he slept, and put
My clouted brogues from off my feet, whose rudeness
Answer'd my steps too loud.
        Gui.   Why, he but sleeps:
If he be gone, he'll make his grave a bed;
With female fairies will his tomb be haunted,
And worms will not come to thee.
        Arv.   With fairest flowers
Whilst summer lasts and I live here, Fidele,
I'll sweeten thy sad grave: thou shalt not lack   220
The flower that's like thy face, pale primrose, nor
The azured harebell, like thy veins, no, nor
The leaf of eglantine, whom not to slander,
Out-sweeten'd not thy breath: the ruddock would,
With charitable bill,—O bill, sore-shaming
Those rich-left heirs that let their fathers lie
Without a monument!—bring thee all this;
Yea, and furr'd moss besides, when flowers are none,
To winter-ground thy corse.
        Gui.   Prithee, have done;
And do not play in wench-like words with that   230
Which is so serious. Let us bury him,
And not protract with admiration what
Is now due debt. To the grave!
        Arv.   Say, where shall's lay him?
        Gui. By good Euriphile, our mother.

        Arv.   Be't so:
And let us, Polydore, though now our voices
Have got the mannish crack, sing him to the ground,
As once our mother; use like note and words,
Save that Euriphile must be Fidele.
        Gui. Cadwal,
I cannot sing: I'll weep, and word it with thee;   240
For notes of sorrow out of tune are worse
Than priests and fanes that lie.
        Arv.   We'll speak it, then.
        Bel. Great griefs, I see, medicine the less; for
                Cloten
Is quite forgot. He was a queen's son, boys;
And though he came our enemy, remember
He was paid for that: though mean and mighty,
                rotting
Together, have one dust, yet reverence,
That angel of the world, doth make distinction
Of place 'tween high and low. Our foe was princely;
And though you took his life, as being our foe,   250
Yet bury him as a prince.
        Gui.   Pray you, fetch him hither.
Thersites' body is as good as Ajax',
When neither are alive.
        Arv.   If you'll go fetch him,
We'll say our song the whilst. Brother, begin.
                                    [*Exit Belarius.*
        Gui. Nay, Cadwal, we must lay his head to the east;
My father hath a reason for't.
        Arv.   'Tis true.
        Gui. Come on then, and remove him.
        Arv.   So. Begin.

                        SONG.

Gui. Fear no more the heat o' the sun,
        Nor the furious winter's rages;
    Thou thy worldly task hast done,   260
        Home art gone, and ta'en thy wages:
    Golden lads and girls all must,
    As chimney-sweepers, come to dust.

Arv. Fear no more the frown o' the great;
        Thou art past the tyrant's stroke;
    Care no more to clothe and eat;
        To thee the reed is as the oak:
    The sceptre, learning, physic, must
    All follow this, and come to dust.

Gui. Fear no more the lightning-flash,   270
Arv.   Nor the all-dreaded thunder-stone;
Gui. Fear not slander, censure rash;
Arv.   Thou hast finish'd joy and moan:
Both. All lovers young, all lovers must
        Consign to thee, and come to dust.

Gui. No exorciser harm thee!
Arv. Nor no witchcraft charm thee!
Gui. Ghost unlaid forbear thee!
Arv. Nothing ill come near thee!
Both. Quiet consummation have;   280
        And renowned be thy grave!

---

198. **on,** of.   205. **crare,** skiff, small boat, so Sympson (Steevens); F:
care, which may be retained as meaning "a vessel in search of a harbor."
214. **clouted brogues,** heavy shoes studded with nails.   224. **ruddock,**
robin redbreast.   229. **winter-ground,** cover so as to protect from frost.
230. **wench-like,** womanish.   242. **fanes,** temples.   252. **Thersites' . . .
Ajax'.** Thersites was the base scoffer in the *Iliad;* Ajax, a Greek hero.

255. **lay . . . east.** Opposite to the Christian custom. Shakespeare may
wish to suggest that the play is pagan, or he may know that the Earthly
Paradise or Happy Isles were located across the Western ocean.   271.
thunder-stone, thunderbolt (the supposed solid body accompanying a
stroke of lightning).   276. **exorciser,** conjurer.   280. **consummation,**
end, death.   287. **herblets,** small herbs, flowers.   293. **'Ods pittikins,**

Re-enter BELARIUS, *with the body of* CLOTEN.

Gui. We have done our obsequies: come, lay him
    down.
Bel. Here 's a few flowers; but 'bout midnight,
    more:
The herbs that have on them cold dew o' the night
Are strewings fitt'st for graves. Upon their faces.
You were as flowers, now wither'd: even so
These herblets shall, which we upon you strew.
Come on, away: apart upon our knees.
The ground that gave them first has them again:
Their pleasures here are past, so is their pain.   290
        [*Exeunt Belarius, Guiderius, and Arviragus.*
Imo. [*Awaking*] Yes, sir, to Milford-Haven; which
    is the way?—
I thank you.—By yond bush?—Pray, how far
    thither?
'Ods pittikins! can it be six mile yet?—
I have gone all night. 'Faith, I'll lie down and sleep.
But, soft! no bedfellow!—O gods and goddesses!
              [*Seeing the body of Cloten.*
These flowers are like the pleasures of the world;
This bloody man, the care on 't. I hope I dream;
For so I thought I was a cave-keeper,
And cook to honest creatures: but 'tis not so;
'Twas but a bolt of nothing, shot at nothing,   300
Which the brain makes of fumes: our very eyes
Are sometimes like our judgements, blind. Good faith,
I tremble still with fear: but if there be
Yet left in heaven as small a drop of pity
As a wren's eye, fear'd gods, a part of it!
The dream 's here still: even when I wake, it is
Without me, as within me; not imagined, felt.
A headless man! The garments of Posthumus!
I know the shape of 's leg: this is his hand;
His foot Mercurial; his Martial thigh;   310
The brawns of Hercules: but his Jovial face—
Murder in heaven?—How!—'Tis gone. Pisanio,
All curses madded Hecuba gave the Greeks,
And mine to boot, be darted on thee! Thou,
Conspired with that irregulous devil, Cloten,
Hast here cut off my lord. To write and read
Be henceforth treacherous! Damn'd Pisanio
Hath with his forged letters,—damn'd Pisanio—
From this most bravest vessel of the world
Struck the main-top! O Posthumus! alas,   320
Where is thy head? where 's that? Ay me! where 's
    that?
Pisanio might have kill'd thee at the heart,
And left this head on. How should this be? Pisanio?
'Tis he and Cloten: malice and lucre in them
Have laid this woe here. O, 'tis pregnant, pregnant!
The drug he gave me, which he said was precious
And cordial to me, have I not found it
Murderous to the senses? That confirms it home:
This is Pisanio's deed, and Cloten's: O!
Give colour to my pale cheek with thy blood,   330
That we the horrider may seem to those
Which chance to find us: O, my lord, my lord!
                  [*Falls on the body.*

Enter LUCIUS, *a* Captain *and other* Officers, *and a*
    Soothsayer.

Cap. To them the legions garrison'd in Gallia,
After your will, have cross'd the sea, attending
You here at Milford-Haven with your ships:
They are in readiness.
Luc.   But what from Rome?
Cap. The senate hath stirr'd up the confiners
And gentlemen of Italy, most willing spirits,
That promise noble service: and they come
Under the conduct of bold Iachimo,   340
Syenna's brother.
Luc.   When expect you them?
Cap. With the next benefit o' the wind.
Luc.   This forwardness
Makes our hopes fair. Command our present numbers
Be muster'd; bid the captains look to 't. Now, sir,
What have you dream'd of late of this war's purpose?
Sooth. Last night the very gods show'd me a vision—
I fast and pray'd for their intelligence—thus:
I saw Jove's bird, the Roman eagle, wing'd
From the spongy south to this part of the west,
There vanish'd in the sunbeams: which portends— 350
Unless my sins abuse my divination—
Success to the Roman host.
Luc.   Dream often so,
And never false. Soft, ho! what trunk is here
Without his top? The ruin speaks that sometime
It was a worthy building. How! a page!
Or dead, or sleeping on him? But dead rather;
For nature doth abhor to make his bed
With the defunct, or sleep upon the dead.
Let 's see the boy's face.
Cap.   He 's alive, my lord.   359
Luc. He'll then instruct us of this body. Young one,
Inform us of thy fortunes, for it seems
They crave to be demanded. Who is this
Thou makest thy bloody pillow? Or who was he
That, otherwise than noble nature did,
Hath alter'd that good picture? What 's thy interest
In this sad wreck? How came it? Who is it?
What art thou?
Imo.   I am nothing: or if not,
Nothing to be were better. This was my master,
A very valiant Briton and a good,
That here by mountaineers lies slain. Alas!   370
There is no more such masters: I may wander
From east to occident, cry out for service,
Try many, all good, serve truly, never
Find such another master.
Luc.   'Lack, good youth!
Thou movest no less with thy complaining than
Thy master in bleeding: say his name, good friend.
Imo. Richard du Champ. [*Aside*] If I do lie and do
No harm by it, though the gods hear, I hope
They'll pardon it.—Say you, sir?
Luc.   Thy name?
Imo.   Fidele, sir.
Luc. Thou dost approve thyself the very same: 380
Thy name well fits thy faith, thy faith thy name.

God's pity (diminutive oath). **298. cave-keeper,** one who dwells in a
cave. **301. fumes,** vapors engendered of humors which, according to
current theory, rose up into the brain and, by affecting imagination in
the forechamber of the brain, caused dreams. **310. Mercurial,** nimble
and swift like the foot of Mercury. **Martial,** powerful for war like
that of Mars. **311. brawns,** muscles; here, arms. **Jovial,** Jove-like.

313. madded, maddened. **Hecuba,** wife of Priam, king of Troy. **315.
irregulous,** lawless. **333. To,** in addition to. **334. After,** according to.
337. confiners, borderers. **341. Syenna's,** of the ruler of Sienna. **347.
fast,** fasted. **360. instruct,** inform.

Wilt take thy chance with me? I will not say
Thou shalt be so well master'd, but, be sure,
No less beloved. The Roman emperor's letters,
Sent by a consul to me, should not sooner
Than thine own worth prefer thee: go with me.
    Imo. I'll follow, sir. But first, an 't please the gods,
I'll hide my master from the flies, as deep
As these poor pickaxes can dig; and when
With wild wood-leaves and weeds I ha' strew'd his
    grave,   390
And on it said a century of prayers,
Such as I can, twice o'er, I'll weep and sigh;
And leaving so his service, follow you,
So please you entertain me.
    Luc.   Ay, good youth;
And rather father thee than master thee.
My friends,
The boy hath taught us manly duties: let us
Find out the prettiest daisied plot we can,
And make him with our pikes and partisans
A grave: come, arm him. Boy, he is preferr'd   400
By thee to us, and he shall be interr'd
As soldiers can. Be cheerful; wipe thine eyes:
Some falls are means the happier to arise.   [*Exeunt.*

SCENE III. *A room in Cymbeline's palace.*

Enter CYMBELINE, Lords, PISANIO, *and* Attendants.

    Cym. Again; and bring me word how 'tis with her.
                    [*Exit an Attendant.*
A fever with the absence of her son,
A madness, of which her life 's in danger. Heavens,
How deeply you at once do touch me! Imogen,
The great part of my comfort, gone; my queen
Upon a desperate bed, and in a time
When fearful wars point at me; her son gone,
So needful for this present: it strikes me, past
The hope of comfort. But for thee, fellow,
Who needs must know of her departure and   10
Dost seem so ignorant, we'll enforce it from thee
By a sharp torture.
    Pis.   Sir, my life is yours;
I humbly set it at your will; but, for my mistress,
I nothing know where she remains, why gone,
Nor when she purposes return. Beseech your highness,
Hold me your loyal servant.
    First Lord.   Good my liege,
The day that she was missing he was here:
I dare be bound he 's true and shall perform
All parts of his subjection loyally. For Cloten,
There wants no diligence in seeking him,   20
And will, no doubt, be found.
    Cym.   The time is troublesome.
[*To Pisanio*] We'll slip you for a season; but our
    jealousy
Does yet depend.
    First Lord.   So please your majesty,
The Roman legions, all from Gallia drawn,
Are landed on your coast, with a supply
Of Roman gentlemen, by the senate sent.

    Cym. Now for the counsel of my son and queen!
I am amazed with matter.
    First Lord.   Good my liege,
Your preparation can affront no less
Than what you hear of: come more, for more you 're
    ready: 30
The want is but to put those powers in motion
That long to move.
    Cym.   I thank you. Let 's withdraw;
And meet the time as it seeks us. We fear not
What can from Italy annoy us; but
We grieve at chances here. Away!
               [*Exeunt all but Pisanio.*
    Pis. I heard no letter from my master since
I wrote him Imogen was slain: 'tis strange:
Nor hear I from my mistress, who did promise
To yield me often tidings; neither know I
What is betid to Cloten; but remain   40
Perplex'd in all. The heavens still must work.
Wherein I am false I am honest; not true, to be true.
These present wars shall find I love my country,
Even to the note o' the king, or I'll fall in them.
All other doubts, by time let them be clear'd:
Fortune brings in some boats that are not steer'd. [*Exit.*

SCENE IV. *Wales: before the cave of Belarius.*

Enter BELARIUS, GUIDERIUS, *and* ARVIRAGUS.

    Gui. The noise is round about us.
    Bel.   Let us from it.
    Arv. What pleasure, sir, find we in life, to lock it
From action and adventure?
    Gui.   Nay, what hope
Have we in hiding us? This way, the Romans
Must or for Britons slay us, or receive us
For barbarous and unnatural revolts
During their use, and slay us after.
    Bel.   Sons,
We'll higher to the mountains; there secure us.
To the king's party there 's no going: newness
Of Cloten's death—we being not known, not
    muster'd   10
Among the bands—may drive us to a render
Where we have lived, and so extort from 's that
Which we have done, whose answer would be death
Drawn on with torture.
    Gui.   This is, sir, a doubt
In such a time nothing becoming you,
Nor satisfying us.
    Arv.   It is not likely
That when they hear the Roman horses neigh,
Behold their quarter'd fires, have both their eyes
And ears so cloy'd importantly as now,
That they will waste their time upon our note,   20
To know from whence we are.
    Bel.   O, I am known
Of many in the army: many years,
Though Cloten then but young, you see, not wore him
From my remembrance. And, besides, the king
Hath not deserved my service nor your loves;

---

386. **prefer,** recommend. 391. **century,** hundred. 399. **partisans,**
long-handled weapons with pointed and sharp-edged heads; halberds.
400. **arm,** take up into the arms.
    SCENE III. 6. **desperate bed,** bed of dangerous illness. 11. **enforce,**
force, compel. 22. **slip you,** let you go. **jealousy,** suspicion. 23.
depend, impend, threaten. 28. **matter,** business, pressure of affairs.
29. **affront,** confront, meet (in combat). 34. **annoy,** injure. 40.

betid, happened. 44. **note,** knowledge, recognition.
    SCENE IV. 4. **This way,** by this course of conduct. 6. **revolts,** de-
serters, rebels. 7. **During their use,** while they are making use of us.
11. **render,** rendering of an account, relation. 13. **answer,** something
done in punishment of an act. 18. **quarter'd fires,** regularly disposed,
or simply camp fires. 20. **our note,** noting us. 26-28. **Who ... promised,** you who find in exile want of breeding and the certain results of

Who find in my exile the want of breeding,
The certainty of this hard life; aye hopeless
To have the courtesy your cradle promised,
But to be still hot summer's tanlings and
The shrinking slaves of winter.
Gui.   Than be so   30
Better to cease to be. Pray, sir, to the army:
I and my brother are not known; yourself
So out of thought, and thereto so o'ergrown,
Cannot be question'd.
Arv.   By this sun that shines,
I'll thither: what thing is it that I never
Did see man die! scarce ever look'd on blood,
But that of coward hares, hot goats, and venison!
Never bestrid a horse, save one that had
A rider like myself, who ne'er wore rowel
Nor iron on his heel! I am ashamed   40
To look upon the holy sun, to have
The benefit of his blest beams, remaining
So long a poor unknown.
Gui.   By heavens, I'll go:
If you will bless me, sir, and give me leave,
I'll take the better care, but if you will not,
The hazard therefore due fall on me by
The hands of Romans!
Arv.   So say I: amen.
Bel. No reason I, since of your lives you set
So slight a valuation, should reserve
My crack'd one to more care. Have with you, boys! 50
If in your country wars you chance to die,
That is my bed too, lads, and there I'll lie:
Lead, lead. [*Aside*] The time seems long; their blood
      thinks scorn,
Till it fly out and show them princes born.   [*Exeunt.*

ACT V.

SCENE I. *Britain. The Roman camp.*

Enter POSTHUMUS, *with a bloody handkerchief.*

Post. Yea, bloody cloth, I'll keep thee, for I wish'd
Thou shouldst be colour'd thus. You married ones,
If each of you should take this course, how many
Must murder wives much better than themselves
For wrying but a little! O Pisanio!
Every good servant does not all commands:
No bond but to do just ones. Gods! if you
Should have ta'en vengeance on my faults, I never
Had lived to put on this: so had you saved
The noble Imogen to repent, and struck   10
Me, wretch more worth your vengeance. But, alack,
You snatch some hence for little faults; that's love,
To have them fall no more: you some permit
†To second ills with ills, each elder worse,
And make them dread it, to the doers' thrift.
But Imogen is your own: do your best wills,
And make me blest to obey! I am brought hither
Among the Italian gentry, and to fight
Against my lady's kingdom: 'tis enough
That, Britain, I have kill'd thy mistress; peace!   20

I'll give no wound to thee. Therefore, good heavens,
Hear patiently my purpose: I'll disrobe me
Of these Italian weeds and suit myself
As does a Briton peasant: so I'll fight
Against the part I come with; so I'll die
For thee, O Imogen, even for whom my life
Is every breath a death; and thus, unknown,
Pitied nor hated, to the face of peril
Myself I'll dedicate. Let me make men know
More valour in me than my habits show.   30
Gods, put the strength o' the Leonati in me!
To shame the guise o' the world, I will begin
The fashion, less without and more within.   [*Exit.*

SCENE II. *Field of battle between the British and Roman camps.*

Enter, from one side, LUCIUS, IACHIMO, *and the* Roman
    Army: *from the other side, the* British Army;
    LEONATUS POSTHUMUS *following, like a poor soldier.
    They march over and go out. Then enter again, in
    skirmish,* IACHIMO *and* POSTHUMUS: *he vanquisheth
    and disarmeth* IACHIMO, *and then leaves him.*

Iach. The heaviness and guilt within my bosom
Takes off my manhood: I have belied a lady,
The princess of this country, and the air on 't
Revengingly enfeebles me; or could this carl,
A very drudge of nature's, have subdued me
In my profession? Knighthoods and honours, borne
As I wear mine, are titles but of scorn.
If that thy gentry, Britain, go before
This lout as he exceeds our lords, the odds
Is that we scarce are men and you are gods.   [*Exit.* 10

The battle continues; the Britons *fly;* CYMBELINE *is
    taken: then enter, to his rescue,* BELARIUS, GUIDERIUS,
    and ARVIRAGUS.

Bel. Stand, stand! We have the advantage of the
      ground;
The lane is guarded: nothing routs us but
The villany of our fears.
Gui. }
Arv. }   Stand, stand, and fight!

Re-enter POSTHUMUS, *and seconds the* Britons: *they rescue*
    CYMBELINE, *and exeunt. Then re-enter* LUCIUS,
    and IACHIMO, *with* IMOGEN.

Luc. Away, boy, from the troops, and save thyself;
For friends kill friends, and the disorder's such
As war were hoodwink'd.
Iach.   'Tis their fresh supplies.
Luc. It is a day turn'd strangely: or betimes
Let's re-inforce, or fly.   [*Exeunt.*

SCENE III. *Another part of the field.*

Enter POSTHUMUS *and a* British Lord.

Lord. Camest thou from where they made the stand?
Post.   I did:

---

this hard life; yes, are even hopeless of ever finding the refinement promised you by your high birth. 29. **tanlings,** those tanned by the sun. 33. **o'ergrown,** i.e., with hair and beard. 34-35. **By . . . thither.** This is the theme of the inevitable outcropping of princely blood.

ACT V. SCENE I. 5. **wrying,** swerving from the right course. 9. **put on,** incite, encourage. 12-13. **that 's . . . more,** that is an act of kindness, since it makes them sin no more. 14. **elder,** thing of later

date. 15. **dread . . . thrift.** Possibly this means that the guilty, by knowing of the further progress of evil, repent before committing more crimes. 25. **part,** party, side. 32. **guise,** practice, custom.
SCENE II. 3. **on 't,** of it. 4. **carl,** churl, peasant. 8. **go before,** excel.

Though you, it seems, come from the fliers.
    Lord.   I did.
    Post. No blame be to you, sir; for all was lost,
But that the heavens fought: the king himself
Of his wings destitute, the army broken,
And but the backs of Britons seen, all flying
Through a strait lane; the enemy full-hearted,
Lolling the tongue with slaughtering, having work
More plentiful than tools to do 't, struck down
Some mortally, some slightly touch'd, some falling   10
Merely through fear; that the strait pass was damm'd
With dead men hurt behind, and cowards living
To die with lengthen'd shame.
    Lord.   Where was this lane?
    Post. Close by the battle, ditch'd, and wall'd with
    turf;
Which gave advantage to an ancient soldier,
An honest one, I warrant; who deserved
So long a breeding as his white beard came to,
In doing this for 's country: athwart the lane,
He, with two striplings—lads more like to run
The country base than to commit such slaughter;   20
With faces fit for masks, or rather fairer
Than those for preservation cased, or shame,—
Made good the passage; cried to those that fled,
'Our Britain's harts die flying, not our men:
To darkness fleet souls that fly backwards. Stand;
Or we are Romans and will give you that
Like beasts which you shun beastly, and may save,
But to look back in frown: stand, stand.' These three,
Three thousand confident, in act as many—
For three performers are the file when all   30
The rest do nothing—with this word 'Stand, stand,'
Accommodated by the place, more charming
With their own nobleness, which could have turn'd
A distaff to a lance, gilded pale looks,
Part shame, part spirit renew'd; that some, turn'd
    coward
But by example—O, a sin in war,
Damn'd in the first beginners!—gan to look
The way that they did, and to grin like lions
Upon the pikes o' the hunters. Then began
A stop i' the chaser, a retire, anon   40
A rout, confusion thick; forthwith they fly
Chickens, the way which they stoop'd eagles; slaves,
The strides they victors made: and now our cowards,
Like fragments in hard voyages, became
The life o' the need: having found the back-door open
Of the unguarded hearts, heavens, how they wound!
Some slain before; some dying; some their friends
O'er-borne i' the former wave: ten, chased by one,
Are now each one the slaughter-man of twenty:
Those that would die or ere resist are grown   50
The mortal bugs o' the field.
    Lord.   This was strange chance:
A narrow lane, an old man, and two boys.
    Post. Nay, do not wonder at it: you are made
Rather to wonder at the things you hear
Than to work any. Will you rhyme upon 't,
And vent it for a mockery? Here is one:
'Two boys, an old man twice a boy, a lane,

Preserved the Britons, was the Romans' bane.'
    Lord. Nay, be not angry, sir.
    Post.   'Lack, to what end?
Who dares not stand his foe, I'll be his friend;   60
For if he'll do as he is made to do,
I know he'll quickly fly my friendship too.
You have put me into rhyme.
    Lord.   Farewell; you 're angry.
    Post. Still going? [*Exit Lord.*] This is a lord! O noble
    misery,
To be i' the field, and ask 'what news?' of me!
To-day how many would have given their honours
To have saved their carcases! took heel to do 't,
And yet died too! I, in mine own woe charm'd,
Could not find death where I did hear him groan,   69
Nor feel him where he struck: being an ugly monster,
'Tis strange he hides him in fresh cups, soft beds,
Sweet words; or hath more ministers than we
That draw his knives i' the war. Well, I will find him:
For being now a favourer to the Briton,
No more a Briton, I have resumed again
The part I came in: fight I will no more,
But yield me to the veriest hind that shall
Once touch my shoulder. Great the slaughter is
Here made by the Roman; great the answer be
Britons must take. For me, my ransom 's death;   80
On either side I come to spend my breath;
Which neither here I'll keep nor bear again,
But end it by some means for Imogen.

Enter two British Captains *and* Soldiers.

    First Cap. Great Jupiter be praised! Lucius is taken.
'Tis thought the old man and his sons were angels.
    Sec. Cap. There was a fourth man, in a silly habit,
That gave the affront with them.
    First Cap.   So 'tis reported:
But none of 'em can be found. Stand! who 's there?
    Post. A Roman,
Who had not now been drooping here, if seconds   90
Had answer'd him.
    Sec. Cap.   Lay hands on him; a dog!
A leg of Rome shall not return to tell
What crows have peck'd them here. He brags his
    service
As if he were of note: bring him to the king.

Enter CYMBELINE, BELARIUS, GUIDERIUS, ARVIRAGUS,
PISANIO, Soldiers, Attendants, *and* Roman
Captives. *The* Captains *present* POSTHUMUS *to*
CYMBELINE, *who delivers him over to a* Gaoler: *then
exeunt omnes.*

SCENE IV. *A British prison.*

Enter POSTHUMUS *and two* Gaolers.

    First Gaol. You shall not now be stol'n, you have
        locks upon you;
So graze as you find pasture.
    Sec. Gaol.   Ay, or a stomach.
                                    [*Exeunt Gaolers.*

SCENE III. 7. **strait,** narrow. **full-hearted,** full of courage and
confidence. 17. **breeding,** life. 20. **base,** prisoner's base, a game in
which rapid running is the means to victory. 22. **cased,** covered.
shame, modesty, shyness. 28. **But . . . frown,** by merely looking back
in defiance. 30. **file,** rank (of soldiers). 32. **charming,** bewitching.
34. **gilded,** imparted a flush or color. 37. **gan,** began. 42. **stoop'd,**
swooped over (like eagles). 42-43. **slaves . . . made,** retracing, as
slaves, the steps they took as victors. 44. **fragments,** scraps, fragments
of food. 50. **or ere,** rather than. 51. **mortal bugs,** deadly bugbears.
52. **A narrow . . . boys,** a line highly condensed and most suggestive.
59. **'Lack,** alack; exclamation expressing sorrow. 60. **stand,** withstand. 64. **noble misery,** miserable nobility. 68. **charm'd,** i.e.,
made invulnerable. 79. **answer,** retaliation. 86. **silly,** simple. 90.
seconds, supporters.

Post. Most welcome, bondage! for thou art a way,
I think, to liberty: yet am I better
Than one that's sick o' the gout; since he had
    rather
Groan so in perpetuity than be cured
By the sure physician, death, who is the key
To unbar these locks. My conscience, thou art
    fetter'd
More than my shanks and wrists: you good gods, give
    me
The penitent instrument to pick that bolt,   10
Then, free for ever! Is't enough I am sorry?
So children temporal fathers do appease;
Gods are more full of mercy. Must I repent?
I cannot do it better than in gyves,
Desired more than constrain'd: to satisfy,
If of my freedom 'tis the main part, take
No stricter render of me than my all.
I know you are more clement than vile men,
Who of their broken debtors take a third,
A sixth, a tenth, letting them thrive again   20
On their abatement: that's not my desire:
For Imogen's dear life take mine; and though
'Tis not so dear, yet 'tis a life; you coin'd it:
'Tween man and man they weigh not every stamp;
Though light, take pieces for the figure's sake:
You rather mine, being yours; and so, great powers,
If you will take this audit, take this life,
And cancel these cold bonds. O Imogen!
I'll speak to thee in silence.   [*Sleeps.*

Solemn music. Enter, as in an apparition, SICILIUS
    LEONATUS, *father to Posthumus, an old man, attired*
    like a warrior; leading in his hand an ancient matron,
    his wife, and mother to Posthumus, with music before
    them: then, after other music, follow the two young
    LEONATI, *brothers to Posthumus, with wounds as they*
    died in the wars. They circle POSTHUMUS *round, as he*
    lies sleeping.

Sici. No more, thou thunder-master, show   30
    Thy spite on mortal flies:
With Mars fall out, with Juno chide,
    That thy adulteries
        Rates and revenges.
Hath my poor boy done aught but well,
    Whose face I never saw?
I died whilst in the womb he stay'd
    Attending nature's law:
Whose father then, as men report
    Thou orphans' father art,   40
Thou shouldst have been, and shielded him
    From this earth-vexing smart.

Moth. Lucina lent not me her aid,
    But took me in my throes;
That from me was Posthumus ript,
    Came crying 'mongst his foes,
    A thing of pity!

Sici. Great nature, like his ancestry,
    Moulded the stuff so fair,

That he deserved the praise o' the world,   50
    As great Sicilius' heir.

First Bro. When once he was mature for man,
    In Britain where was he
That could stand up his parallel;
    Or fruitful object be
In eye of Imogen, that best
    Could deem his dignity?

Moth. With marriage wherefore was he mock'd,
    To be exiled, and thrown
From Leonati seat, and cast   60
    From her his dearest one,
        Sweet Imogen?

Sici. Why did you suffer Iachimo,
    Slight thing of Italy,
To taint his nobler heart and brain
    With needless jealousy;
And to become the geck and scorn
    O' th' other's villany?

Sec. Bro. For this from stiller seats we came,
    Our parents and us twain,   70
That striking in our country's cause
    Fell bravely and were slain,
Our fealty and Tenantius' right
    With honour to maintain.

First Bro. Like hardiment Posthumus hath
    To Cymbeline perform'd:
Then, Jupiter, thou king of gods,
    Why hast thou thus adjourn'd
The graces for his merits due,
    Being all to dolours turn'd?   80

Sici. Thy crystal window ope; look out;
    No longer exercise
Upon a valiant race thy harsh
    And potent injuries.

Moth. Since, Jupiter, our son is good,
    Take off his miseries.

Sici. Peep through thy marble mansion; help;
    Or we poor ghosts will cry
To the shining synod of the rest
    Against thy deity.   90

Both Bro. Help, Jupiter; or we appeal,
    And from thy justice fly.

JUPITER *descends in thunder and lightning, sitting upon an*
    eagle: he throws a thunderbolt. The Ghosts fall on their
    knees.

Jup. No more, you petty spirits of region low,
Offend our hearing; hush! How dare you ghosts
Accuse the thunderer, whose bolt, you know,
    Sky-planted batters all rebelling coasts?
Poor shadows of Elysium, hence, and rest

SCENE IV. 14. **gyves,** fetters. 15. **constrain'd,** forced upon me.
17. **stricter,** more restricted. **render,** surrender. 24. **stamp,** coin.
25. **pieces,** coins. **for . . . sake,** for the sake of the image stamped
upon it. 30-122. **No more . . . behest.** The vision, like the masque in
the fourth act of *The Tempest*, is sometimes, thought to be by some other
hand than Shakespeare's. Certainly both compositions are of poetic
quality inferior to that of the plays in which they stand; they are,

however, written in a formal style customary in that form and are
stylistically equal or superior to the masques in the court of James I.
67. **geck,** dupe. 75. **hardiment,** bold exploit. 78. **adjourn'd,** deferred. 89. **synod,** assembly of the gods.

Upon your never-withering banks of flowers:
Be not with mortal accidents opprest;
  No care of yours it is; you know 'tis ours. 100
Whom best I love I cross; to make my gift,
  The more delay'd, delighted. Be content;
Your low-laid son our godhead will uplift:
  His comforts thrive, his trials well are spent.
Our Jovial star reign'd at his birth, and in
  Our temple was he married. Rise, and fade.
He shall be lord of lady Imogen,
  And happier much by his affliction made.
This tablet lay upon his breast, wherein
  Our pleasure his full fortune doth confine: 110
And so, away: no further with your din
  Express impatience, lest you stir up mine.
  Mount, eagle, to my palace crystalline.   [Ascends.
  Sici. He came in thunder; his celestial breath
Was sulphurous to smell: the holy eagle
Stoop'd, as to foot us: his ascension is
More sweet than our blest fields: his royal bird
Prunes the immortal wing and cloys his beak,
As when his god is pleased.
  All.   Thanks, Jupiter!
  Sici. The marble pavement closes, he is enter'd 120
His radiant roof. Away! and, to be blest,
Let us with care perform his great behest.
                            [The Ghosts vanish.
  Post. [Waking] Sleep, thou hast been a grandsire,
    and begot
A father to me; and thou hast created
A mother and two brothers: but, O scorn!
Gone! they went hence so soon as they were born:
And so I am awake. Poor wretches that depend
On greatness' favour dream as I have done,
Wake and find nothing. But, alas, I swerve:
Many dream not to find, neither deserve, 130
And yet are steep'd in favours; so am I,
That have this golden chance and know not why.
What fairies haunt this ground? A book? O rare one!
Be not, as is our fangled world, a garment
Nobler than that it covers: let thy effects
So follow, to be most unlike our courtiers,
As good as promise. 137
  [Reads] 'When as a lion's whelp shall, to himself
unknown, without seeking find, and be embraced by
a piece of tender air; and when from a stately cedar
shall be lopped branches, which, being dead many
years, shall after revive, be jointed to the old stock
and freshly grow; then shall Posthumus end his
miseries, Britain be fortunate and flourish in peace
and plenty.'
'Tis still a dream, or else such stuff as madmen
Tongue and brain not; either both or nothing;
Or senseless speaking or a speaking such
As sense cannot untie. Be what it is,
The action of my life is like it, which 150
I'll keep, if but for sympathy.

            Re-enter Gaolers.

  First Gaol. Come, sir, are you ready for death?
  Post. Over-roasted rather; ready long ago.

  First Gaol. Hanging is the word, sir: if you be ready
for that, you are well cooked.
  Post. So, if I prove a good repast to the spectators,
the dish pays the shot. 158
  First Gaol. A heavy reckoning for you, sir. But the
comfort is, you shall be called to no more payments,
fear no more tavern-bills; which are often the sadness
of parting, as the procuring of mirth: you come in
faint for want of meat, depart reeling with too much
drink; sorry that you have paid too much, and sorry
that you are paid too much; purse and brain both
empty; the brain the heavier for being too light, the
purse too light, being drawn of heaviness: of this
contradiction you shall now be quit. O, the charity of
a penny cord! it sums up thousands in a trice: you
have no true debitor and creditor but it; of what 's
past, is, and to come, the discharge: your neck, sir,
is pen, book and counters; so the acquittance follows.
  Post. I am merrier to die than thou art to live.
  First Gaol. Indeed, sir, he that sleeps feels not the
tooth-ache: but a man that were to sleep your sleep,
and a hangman to help him to bed, I think he would
change places with his officer; for, look you, sir, you
know not which way you shall go. 182
  Post. Yes, indeed so I, fellow.
  First Gaol. Your death has eyes in 's head then; I
have not seen him so pictured: you must either be
directed by some that take upon them to know, or to
take upon yourself that which I am sure you do not
know, or jump the after inquiry on your own peril:
and how you shall speed in your journey's end, I think
you'll never return to tell one. 191
  Post. I tell thee, fellow, there are none want eyes to
direct them the way I am going, but such as wink and
will not use them.
  First Gaol. What an infinite mock is this, that a man
should have the best use of eyes to see the way of
blindness! I am sure hanging 's the way of winking.

            Enter a Messenger.

  Mess. Knock off his manacles; bring your prisoner
to the king. 200
  Post. Thou bring'st good news; I am called to be
made free.
  First Gaol. I'll be hang'd then.
  Post. Thou shalt be then freer than a gaoler; no
bolts for the dead.   [Exeunt all but the First Gaoler. 205
  First Gaol. Unless a man would marry a gallows and
beget young gibbets, I never saw one so prone. Yet,
on my conscience, there are verier knaves desire to
live, for all he be a Roman: and there be some of them
too that die against their wills; so should I, if I were
one. I would we were all of one mind, and one mind
good; O, there were desolation of gaolers and
gallowses! I speak against my present profit, but my
wish hath a preferment in 't.   [Exit.

_____

            SCENE V. Cymbeline's tent.

Enter CYMBELINE, BELARIUS, GUIDERIUS, ARVIRAGUS,
  PISANIO, Lords, Officers, and Attendants.

102. delighted, delighted in.   105. Jovial star, the planet Jupiter, the
happiest of all stars to be born under.   110. confine, precisely state.
116. foot, spurn.   118. Prunes, preens, arranges the feathers with the
beak. cloys, claws, strokes with the claw (Schmidt).   125. scorn,
mockery.   129. swerve, mistake, go astray.   133. book, tablet or
scroll.   134. fangled, characterized by fopperies or gaudiness.   138.

When as, when.   147. Tongue, speak of. brain, understand. 149.
Be what it is, let it be what it may.   158. shot, tavern reckoning.
168. drawn, tapped, emptied.   171. debitor and creditor, accounting
book.   173. counters, round pieces of metal used for calculating.
190. how . . . speed, how you will succeed.   208. prone, ready, eager.
214. gallowses, gallows, or possibly, hangmen.

Cym. Stand by my side, you whom the gods have
    made
Preservers of my throne. Woe is my heart
That the poor soldier that so richly fought,
Whose rags shamed gilded arms, whose naked breast
Stepp'd before targes of proof, cannot be found:
He shall be happy that can find him, if
Our grace can make him so.
    Bel.   I never saw
Such noble fury in so poor a thing;
Such precious deeds in one that promised nought
But beggary and poor looks.
    Cym.   No tidings of him?   10
    Pis. He hath been search'd among the dead and
        living,
But no trace of him.
    Cym.   To my grief, I am
The heir of his reward; [*To Belarius, Guiderius, and*
    Arviragus] which I will add
To you, the liver, heart and brain of Britain,
By whom I grant she lives. 'Tis now the time
To ask of whence you are. Report it.
    Bel.   Sir,
In Cambria are we born, and gentlemen:
Further to boast were neither true nor modest,
Unless I add, we are honest.
    Cym.   Bow your knees.
Arise my knights o' the battle: I create you   20
Companions to our person and will fit you
With dignities becoming your estates.

Enter CORNELIUS *and* Ladies.

There 's business in these faces. Why so sadly
Greet you our victory? you look like Romans,
And not o' the court of Britain.
    Cor.   Hail, great king!
To sour your happiness, I must report
The queen is dead.
    Cym.   Who worse than a physician
Would this report become? But I consider,
By medicine life may be prolong'd, yet death
Will seize the doctor too. How ended she?   30
    Cor. With horror, madly dying, like her life,
Which, being cruel to the world, concluded
Most cruel to herself. What she confess'd
I will report, so please you: these her women
Can trip me, if I err; who with wet cheeks
Were present when she finish'd.
    Cym.   Prithee, say.
    Cor. First, she confess'd she never loved you, only
Affected greatness got by you, not you:
Married your royalty, was wife to your place;
Abhorr'd your person.
    Cym.   She alone knew this;   40
And, but she spoke it dying, I would not
Believe her lips in opening it. Proceed.
    Cor. Your daughter, whom she bore in hand to
        love
With such integrity, she did confess
Was as a scorpion to her sight; whose life,
But that her flight prevented it, she had

Ta'en off by poison.
    Cym.   O most delicate fiend!
Who is 't can read a woman? Is there more?
    Cor. More, sir, and worse. She did confess she had
For you a mortal mineral; which, being took,   50
Should by the minute feed on life and lingering
By inches waste you: in which time she purposed,
By watching, weeping, tendance, kissing, to
O'ercome you with her show, and in time,
When she had fitted you with her craft, to work
Her son into the adoption of the crown:
But, failing of her end by his strange absence,
Grew shameless-desperate; open'd, in despite
Of heaven and men, her purposes; repented
The evils she hatch'd were not effected; so   60
Despairing died.
    Cym.   Heard you all this, her women?
    First Lady. We did, so please your highness.
    Cym.   Mine eyes
Were not in fault, for she was beautiful;
Mine ears, that heard her flattery; nor my heart,
That thought her like her seeming; it had been vicious
To have mistrusted her: yet, O my daughter!
That it was folly in me, thou mayst say,
And prove it in thy feeling. Heaven mend all!

    Enter LUCIUS, IACHIMO, *the* Soothsayer, *and other*
      Roman Prisoners, *guarded;* POSTHUMUS *behind, and*
      IMOGEN.

Thou comest not, Caius, now for tribute; that
The Britons have razed out, though with the loss   70
Of many a bold one; whose kinsmen have made suit
That their good souls may be appeased with slaughter
Of you their captives, which ourself have granted:
So think of your estate.
    Luc. Consider, sir, the chance of war: the day
Was yours by accident; had it gone with us,
We should not, when the blood was cool, have
    threaten'd
Our prisoners with the sword. But since the gods
Will have it thus, that nothing but our lives
May be call'd ransom, let it come: sufficeth   80
A Roman with a Roman's heart can suffer:
Augustus lives to think on 't: and so much
For my peculiar care. This one thing only
I will entreat; my boy, a Briton born,
Let him be ransom'd: never master had
A page so kind, so duteous, diligent,
So tender over his occasions, true,
So feat, so nurse-like: let his virtue join
With my request, which I'll make bold your
    highness
Cannot deny; he hath done no Briton harm,   90
Though he have served a Roman: save him, sir,
And spare no blood beside.
    Cym.   I have surely seen him:
His favour is familiar to me. Boy,
Thou hast look'd thyself into my grace,
†And art mine own. I know not why, wherefore,
To say 'live, boy:' ne'er thank thy master; live:
And ask of Cymbeline what boon thou wilt,

SCENE V. 5. **targes of proof**, shields of steel hardened to withstand
certain tests. 35. **trip**, refute, contradict. 37-40. **First . . . person.**
This is the first of the series of discoveries by which the plot is resolved.
43. **bore in hand**, pretended with false appearances. 47. **delicate**,
subtle, ingenious. 50. **mortal mineral**, deadly poison. 55. **fitted**,
prepared. 56. **adoption**, right of an adopted heir. 58. **shameless-
desperate**, shamelessly desperate. **open'd**, revealed. 70. **razed out**,
erased. 83. **peculiar**, particular, individual. 87. **occasions**, particular
wants or requirements. 88. **feat**, adroit, neat.

Fitting my bounty and thy state, I'll give it;
Yea, though thou do demand a prisoner,
The noblest ta'en.
    Imo.   I humbly thank your highness. 100
    Luc. I do not bid thee beg my life, good lad;
And yet I know thou wilt.
    Imo.   No, no: alack,
There's other work in hand: I see a thing
Bitter to me as death: your life, good master,
Must shuffle for itself.
    Luc.   The boy disdains me,
He leaves me, scorns me: briefly die their joys
That place them on the truth of girls and boys.
Why stands he so perplex'd?
    Cym.   What wouldst thou, boy?
I love thee more and more: think more and more
What's best to ask. Know'st him thou look'st on?
    speak,   110
Wilt have him live? Is he thy kin? thy friend?
    Imo. He is a Roman; no more kin to me
Than I to your highness; who, being born your vassal,
Am something nearer.
    Cym.   Wherefore eyest him so?
    Imo. I'll tell you, sir, in private, if you please
To give me hearing.
    Cym.   Ay, with all my heart,
And lend my best attention. What's thy name?
    Imo. Fidele, sir.
    Cym.   Thou 'rt my good youth, my
    page;
I'll be thy master: walk with me; speak freely.
                [Cymbeline and Imogen converse apart.
    Bel. Is not this boy revived from death?
    Arv.   One sand another   120
Not more resembles that sweet rosy lad
Who died, and was Fidele. What think you?
    Gui. The same dead thing alive.
    Bel. Peace, peace! see further; he eyes us not;
    forbear;
Creatures may be alike: were 't he, I am sure
He would have spoke to us.
    Gui.   But we saw him dead.
    Bel. Be silent; let 's see further.
    Pis.   *[Aside]* It is my mistress:
Since she is living, let the time run on
To good or bad.   *[Cymbeline and Imogen come forward.*
    Cym.   Come, stand thou by our side;
Make thy demand aloud. *[To Iachimo]* Sir, step you
    forth;   130
Give answer to this boy, and do it freely;
Or, by our greatness and the grace of it,
Which is our honour, bitter torture shall
Winnow the truth from falsehood. On, speak to him.
    Imo. My boon is, that this gentleman may render
Of whom he had this ring.
    Post.   *[Aside]* What's that to him?
    Cym. That diamond upon your finger, say
How came it yours?
    Iach. Thou 'lt torture me to leave unspoken that
Which, to be spoke, would torture thee.
    Cym.   How! me?   140
    Iach. I am glad to be constrain'd to utter that
Which torments me to conceal. By villany

I got this ring: 'twas Leonatus' jewel;
Whom thou didst banish; and—which more may
    grieve thee,
As it doth me—a nobler sir ne'er lived
'Twixt sky and ground. Wilt thou hear more, my
    lord?
    Cym. All that belongs to this.
    Iach.   That paragon, thy daughter,—
For whom my heart drops blood, and my false spirits
Quail to remember—Give me leave; I faint.
    Cym. My daughter! what of her? Renew thy
    strength: 150
I had rather thou shouldst live while nature will
Than die ere I hear more: strive, man, and speak.
    Iach. Upon a time,—unhappy was the clock
That struck the hour!—it was in Rome,—accursed
The mansion where!—'twas at a feast,—O, would
Our viands had been poison'd, or at least
Those which I heaved to head!—the good
    Posthumus—
What should I say? he was too good to be
Where ill men were; and was the best of all
Amongst the rarest of good ones,—sitting sadly,   160
Hearing us praise our loves of Italy
For beauty that made barren the swell'd boast
Of him that best could speak, for feature, laming
The shrine of Venus, or straight-pight Minerva,
Postures beyond brief nature, for condition,
A shop of all the qualities that man
Loves woman for, besides that hook of wiving,
Fairness which strikes the eye—
    Cym.   I stand on fire:
Come to the matter.
    Iach.   All too soon I shall,   169
Unless thou wouldst grieve quickly. This Posthumus,
Most like a noble lord in love and one
That had a royal lover, took his hint;
And, not dispraising whom we praised,—therein
He was as calm as virtue—he began
His mistress' picture; which by his tongue being
    made,
And then a mind put in 't, either our brags
Were crack'd of kitchen-trulls, or his description
Proved us unspeaking sots.
    Cym.   Nay, nay, to the purpose.
    Iach. Your daughter's chastity—there it begins.
He spake of her, as Dian had hot dreams,   180
And she alone were cold: whereat I, wretch,
Made scruple of his praise; and wager'd with him
Pieces of gold 'gainst this which then he wore
Upon his honour'd finger, to attain
In suit the place of 's bed and win this ring
By hers and mine adultery. He, true knight,
No lesser of her honour confident
Than I did truly find her, stakes this ring;
And would so, had it been a carbuncle
Of Phœbus' wheel, and might so safely, had it   190
Been all the worth of 's car. Away to Britain
Post I in this design: well may you, sir,
Remember me at court; where I was taught
Of your chaste daughter the wide difference
'Twixt amorous and villanous. Being thus quench'd
Of hope, not longing, mine Italian brain

---

157. **heaved to head,** raised to lips. 163. **laming,** making seem crippled.
164. **shrine,** image. **straight-pight,** erect. 165. **Postures,** forms,
attitudes. **beyond brief nature,** immortal. **condition,** temper of
mind. 166. **shop,** store. 167. **hook of wiving,** the incentive to matrimony. 177. **crack'd of,** boasted in praise of. **kitchen-trulls,** kitchen
maids. 178. **unspeaking sots,** speechless blockheads. 189. **would so,**
would have done so. 200. **simular,** simulated, or pretended. 216-217.
That . . . they. The thought is that great crimes make lesser ones look

'Gan in your duller Britain operate
Most vilely; for my vantage, excellent:
And, to be brief, my practice so prevail'd,
That I return'd with simular proof enough   200
To make the noble Leonatus mad,
By wounding his belief in her renown
With tokens thus, and thus; averring notes
Of chamber-hanging, pictures, this her bracelet,—
O cunning, how I got it!—nay, some marks
Of secret on her person, that he could not
But think her bond of chastity quite crack'd,
I having ta'en the forfeit. Whereupon—
Methinks, I see him now—
    Post.   *[Advancing]* Ay, so thou dost,
Italian fiend! Ay me, most credulous fool,   210
Egregious murderer, thief, any thing
That's due to all the villains past, in being,
To come! O, give me cord, or knife, or poison,
Some upright justicer! Thou, king, send out
For torturers ingenious: it is I
That all the abhorred things o' the earth amend
By being worse than they. I am Posthumus,
That kill'd thy daughter:—villain-like, I lie—
That caused a lesser villain than myself,
A sacrilegious thief, to do 't: the temple   220
Of virtue was she; yea, and she herself.
Spit, and throw stones, cast mire upon me, set
The dogs o' the street to bay me: every villain
Be call'd Posthumus Leonatus; and
Be villany less than 'twas! O Imogen!
My queen, my life, my wife! O Imogen,
Imogen, Imogen!
    Imo.   Peace, my lord; hear, hear—
    Post. Shall 's have a play of this? Thou scornful
        page,
There lie thy part.   *[Striking her: she falls.*
    Pis.   O, gentlemen, help!
Mine and your mistress! O, my lord Posthumus!   230
You ne'er kill'd Imogen till now. Help, help!
Mine honour'd lady!
    Cym.   Does the world go round?
    Post. How come these staggers on me?
    Pis.   Wake, my mistress!
    Cym. If this be so, the gods do mean to strike me
To death with mortal joy.
    Pis.   How fares my mistress?
    Imo. O, get thee from my sight;
Thou gavest me poison: dangerous fellow, hence!
Breathe not where princes are.
    Cym.   The tune of Imogen!
    Pis. Lady,
The gods throw stones of sulphur on me, if   240
That box I gave you was not thought by me
A precious thing: I had it from the queen.
    Cym. New matter still?
    Imo.   It poison'd me.
    Cor.   O gods!
I left out one thing which the queen confess'd,
Which must approve thee honest: 'If Pisanio
Have' said she 'given his mistress that confection
Which I gave him for cordial, she is served
As I would serve a rat.'
    Cym.   What 's this, Cornelius?

    Cor. The queen, sir, very oft importuned me
To temper poisons for her, still pretending   250
The satisfaction of her knowledge only
In killing creatures vile, as cats and dogs,
Of no esteem: I, dreading that her purpose
Was of more danger, did compound for her
A certain stuff, which, being ta'en, would cease
The present power of life, but in short time
All offices of nature should again
Do their due functions. Have you ta'en of it?
    Imo. Most like I did, for I was dead.
    Bel.   My boys,
There was our error.
    Gui.   This is, sure, Fidele.   260
    Imo. Why did you throw your wedded lady from
        you?
Think that you are upon a rock; and now
Throw me again.   *[Embracing him.*
    Post.   Hang there like fruit, my soul,
Till the tree die!
    Cym.   How now, my flesh, my child!
What, makest thou me a dullard in this act?
Wilt thou not speak to me?
    Imo.   *[Kneeling]* Your blessing, sir.
    Bel. [*To Guiderius and Arviragus*] Though you did
        love this youth, I blame ye not;
You had a motive for 't.
    Cym.   My tears that fall
Prove holy water on thee! Imogen,
Thy mother 's dead.
    Imo.   I am sorry for 't, my lord.   270
    Cym. O, she was naught; and long of her it was
That we meet here so strangely: but her son
Is gone, we know not how nor where.
    Pis.   My lord,
Now fear is from me, I'll speak troth. Lord Cloten,
Upon my lady's missing, came to me
With his sword drawn; foam'd at the mouth, and
        swore,
If I discover'd not which way she was gone,
It was my instant death. By accident,
I had a feigned letter of my master's
Then in my pocket; which directed him   280
To seek her on the mountains near to Milford;
Where, in a frenzy, in my master's garments,
Which he enforced from me, away he posts
With unchaste purpose and with oath to violate
My lady's honour: what became of him
I further know not.
    Gui.   Let me end the story:
I slew him there.
    Cym.   Marry, the gods forfend!
I would not thy good deeds should from my lips
Pluck a hard sentence: prithee, valiant youth,
Deny 't again.
    Gui.   I have spoke it, and I did it.   290
    Cym. He was a prince.
    Gui. A most incivil one: the wrongs he did me
Were nothing prince-like; for he did provoke me
With language that would make me spurn the sea,
If it could so roar to me: I cut off 's head;
And am right glad he is not standing here
To tell this tale of mine.

---

better by comparison. 229. **There lie thy part.** Shakespeare perhaps
reaches his most sensational height in this episode, when Posthumus
strikes down his unknown love. It is in the vein of Beaumont and
Fletcher. 233. **staggers,** dizziness, bewilderment. 238. **tune,** sound

of voice. 246. **confection,** composition of drugs. 262. **rock,** cliff,
rocky eminence. Dowden conjectures: *upon a lock,* a wrestling embrace.
263. *Stage Direction:* **Embracing him,** added by Hanmer and making
clear a passage regarded as obscure. 274. **troth,** truth.

Cym. I am sorry for thee:
By thine own tongue thou art condemn'd, and must
Endure our law: thou 'rt dead.
  Imo. That headless man
I thought had been my lord.
  Cym. Bind the offender, 300
And take him from our presence.
  Bel. Stay, sir king:
This man is better than the man he slew,
As well descended as thyself; and hath
More of thee merited than a band of Clotens
Had ever scar for. [*To the Guard*] Let his arms alone;
They were not born for bondage.
  Cym. Why, old soldier,
Wilt thou undo the worth thou art unpaid for,
By tasting of our wrath? How of descent
As good as we?
  Arv. In that he spake too far.
  Cym. And thou shalt die for 't.
  Bel. We will die all three: 310
But I will prove that two on 's are as good
As I have given out him. My sons, I must,
For mine own part, unfold a dangerous speech,
Though, haply, well for you.
  Arv. Your danger 's ours.
  Gui. And our good his.
  Bel. Have at it then, by leave.
Thou hadst, great king, a subject who
Was call'd Belarius.
  Cym. What of him? he is
A banish'd traitor.
  Bel. He it is that hath
Assumed this age; indeed a banish'd man;
I know not how a traitor.
  Cym. Take him hence: 320
The whole world shall not save him.
  Bel. Not too hot:
First pay me for the nursing of thy sons;
And let it be confiscate all, so soon
As I have received it.
  Cym. Nursing of my sons!
  Bel. I am too blunt and saucy: here 's my knee:
Ere I arise, I will prefer my sons;
Then spare not the old father. Mighty sir,
These two young gentlemen, that call me father
And think they are my sons, are none of mine;
They are the issue of your loins, my liege, 330
And blood of your begetting.
  Cym. How! my issue!
  Bel. So sure as you your father's. I, old Morgan,
Am that Belarius whom you sometime banish'd:
Your pleasure was my mere offence, my punishment
Itself, and all my treason; that I suffer'd
Was all the harm I did. These gentle princes—
For such and so they are—these twenty years
Have I train'd up: those arts they have as I
Could put into them; my breeding was, sir, as
Your highness knows. Their nurse, Euriphile, 340
Whom for the theft I wedded, stole these children
Upon my banishment: I moved her to 't,
Having received the punishment before,
For that which I did then: beaten for loyalty

Excited me to treason: their dear loss,
The more of you 'twas felt, the more it shaped
Unto my end of stealing them. But, gracious sir,
Here are your sons again; and I must lose
Two of the sweet'st companions in the world.
The benediction of these covering heavens 350
Fall on their heads like dew! for they are worthy
To inlay heaven with stars.
  Cym. Thou weep'st, and speak'st.
The service that you three have done is more
Unlike than this thou tell'st. I lost my children:
If these be they, I know not how to wish
A pair of worthier sons.
  Bel. Be pleased awhile.
This gentleman, whom I call Polydore,
Most worthy prince, as yours, is true Guiderius:
This gentleman, my Cadwal, Arviragus,
Your younger princely son; he, sir, was lapp'd 360
In a most curious mantle, wrought by the hand
Of his queen mother, which for more probation
I can with ease produce.
  Cym. Guiderius had
Upon his neck a mole, a sanguine star;
It was a mark of wonder.
  Bel. This is he;
Who hath upon him still that natural stamp:
It was wise nature's end in the donation,
To be his evidence now.
  Cym. O, what, am I
A mother to the birth of three? Ne'er mother
Rejoiced deliverance more. Blest pray you be, 370
That, after this strange starting from your orbs,
You may reign in them now! O Imogen,
Thou hast lost by this a kingdom.
  Imo. No, my lord;
I have got two worlds by 't. O my gentle brothers,
Have we thus met? O, never say hereafter
But I am truest speaker: you call'd me brother,
When I was but your sister; I you brothers,
When ye were so indeed.
  Cym. Did you e'er meet?
  Arv. Ay, my good lord.
  Gui. And at first meeting loved;
Continued so, until we thought he died. 380
  Cor. By the queen's dram she swallow'd.
  Cym. O rare instinct!
When shall I hear all through? This fierce abridgement
Hath to it circumstantial branches, which
Distinction should be rich in. Where? how lived you?
And when came you to serve our Roman captive?
How parted with your brothers? how first met them?
Why fled you from the court? and whither? These,
And your three motives to the battle, with
I know not how much more, should be demanded;
And all the other by-dependencies, 390
From chance to chance: but nor the time nor place
Will serve our long inter'gatories. See,
Posthumus anchors upon Imogen,
And she, like harmless lightning, throws her eye
On him, her brothers, me, her master, hitting
Each object with a joy: the counterchange

Cymbeline
ACT V : SC V

1214

312. **given out,** reported. 315. **by leave,** with your permission. 319. **Assumed,** reached, attained. 326. **prefer,** promote. 360. **lapp'd,** enfolded. 371. **orbs,** orbits. 383-384. **circumstantial . . . in,** separate narratives which ought to be followed out in all their rich details (Herford). 388. **your three motives,** the motives of you three. 390.

by-dependencies, attendant circumstances. 391. **chance to chance,** event to event. 396-397. **the counterchange . . . all,** the exchange is in all and severally in each. 405. **forlorn,** lost, not to be found. 409. **beseeming,** appearance. **fitment,** equipment. 412. **made you finish,** put an end to you. 413. **sinks,** causes to sink. 420. **doom'd,** pro-

Is severally in all. Let 's quit this ground,
And smoke the temple with our sacrifices.
[*To Belarius*] Thou art my brother; so we'll hold thee
          ever.
   Imo. You are my father too, and did relieve me,   400
To see this gracious season.
   Cym.   All o'erjoy'd,
Save these in bonds: let them be joyful too,
For they shall taste our comfort.
   Imo.   My good master,
I will yet do you service.
   Luc.   Happy be you!
   Cym. The forlorn soldier, that so nobly fought,
He would have well becomed this place, and graced
The thankings of a king.
   Post.   I am, sir,
The soldier that did company these three
In poor beseeming; 'twas a fitment for
The purpose I then follow'd. That I was he,   410
Speak, Iachimo: I had you down and might
Have made you finish.
   Iach.   [*Kneeling*] I am down again:
But now my heavy conscience sinks my knee,
As then your force did. Take that life, beseech you,
Which I so often owe: but your ring first;
And here the bracelet of the truest princess
That ever swore her faith.
   Post.   Kneel not to me:
The power that I have on you is to spare you;
The malice towards you to forgive you: live,
And deal with others better.
   Cym.   Nobly doom'd!   420
We'll learn our freeness of a son-in-law;
Pardon 's the word to all.
   Arv.   You holp us, sir,
As you did mean indeed to be our brother;
Joy'd are we that you are.
   Post. Your servant, princes. Good my lord of Rome,
Call forth your soothsayer: as I slept, methought
Great Jupiter, upon his eagle back'd,
Appear'd to me, with other spritely shows
Of mine own kindred: when I waked, I found
This label on my bosom; whose containing   430
Is so from sense in hardness, that I can
Make no collection of it: let him show
His skill in the construction.
   Luc.   Philarmonus!
   Sooth. Here, my good lord.
   Luc.   Read, and declare the meaning.
   Sooth. [*Reads*] 'When as a lion's whelp shall, to him-
self unknown, without seeking find, and be embraced
by a piece of tender air; and when from a stately
cedar shall be lopped branches, which, being dead
many years, shall after revive, be jointed to the old
stock, and freshly grow; then shall Posthumus end his
miseries, Britain be fortunate and flourish in peace
and plenty.'   442
Thou, Leonatus, art the lion's whelp;
The fit and apt construction of thy name,
Being Leo-natus, doth import so much.
[*To Cymbeline*] The piece of tender air, thy virtuous
          daughter,

.....ounced judgment, decreed. **421. freeness,** liberality, generosity.
428. spritely, ghostly, in the form of spirits. **shows,** appearances.
430. label, tablet. **430-431. whose . . . hardness,** whose meaning is so
remote from sense in its difficulty. **432. collection of,** inference or
deduction from. **445. Leo-natus,** one born of the lion.

Which we call 'mollis aer;' and 'mollis aer'
We term it 'mulier:' which 'mulier' I divine
Is this most constant wife; who, even now,
Answering the letter of the oracle,   450
Unknown to you, unsought, were clipp'd about
With this most tender air.
   Cym.   This hath some seeming.
   Sooth. The lofty cedar, royal Cymbeline,
Personates thee: and thy lopp'd branches point
Thy two sons forth; who, by Belarius stol'n,
For many years thought dead, are now revived,
To the majestic cedar join'd, whose issue
Promises Britain peace and plenty.
   Cym.   Well;
My peace we will begin. And, Caius Lucius,
Although the victor, we submit to Cæsar,   460
And to the Roman empire; promising
To pay our wonted tribute, from the which
We were dissuaded by our wicked queen;
Whom heavens, in justice, both on her and hers,
Have laid most heavy hand.
   Sooth. The fingers of the powers above do tune
The harmony of this peace. The vision
Which I made known to Lucius, ere the stroke
Of this yet scarce-cold battle, at this instant
Is full accomplish'd; for the Roman eagle,   470
From south to west on wing soaring aloft,
Lessen'd herself, and in the beams o' the sun
So vanish'd: which foreshow'd our princely eagle,
The imperial Cæsar, should again unite
His favour with the radiant Cymbeline,
Which shines here in the west.
   Cym.   Laud we the gods;
And let our crooked smokes climb to their nostrils
From our blest altars. Publish we this peace
To all our subjects. Set we forward: let
A Roman and a British ensign wave   480
Friendly together: so through Lud's-town march:
And in the temple of great Jupiter
Our peace we'll ratify; seal it with feasts.
Set on there! Never was a war did cease,
Ere bloody hands were wash'd, with such a peace.
                           [*Exeunt.*

---

447. 'mollis aer,' tender air; a fanciful derivation of Latin *mulier*,
woman. **452. This . . . seeming,** this seems well founded (Gollancz).
476. Laud, praise. **484. Set on there!** Forward march!

THE

Winter's Tale

There is no edition of *The Winter's Tale* before that of
the First Folio of 1623. The late and complicated
style in which the play is written would make the
reproduction of the play difficult. However, the
version of the Folio is a good one and there are relatively few difficulties in the text. *The Winter's Tale* is
one of the latest of Shakespeare's plays, and it so
happens that it can be very accurately dated. The
same diary of Simon Forman, the London doctor,

which gives an account of *Macbeth* shows also that Forman saw Shakespeare's *The Winter's Tale* at the Globe on May 15, 1611, and recorded a fairly accurate summary of the plot in his "Booke of Plaies."[1] Sir Henry Herbert, Master of the Revels, allowed on August 19, 1623, to the king's players a play called "Winters Tale, formerly allowed by Sir George Buc," who had been appointed Master of the Revels in August 1610. This would place the play between August 1610, and the date on which Forman saw it acted.

A. H. Thorndike, in the work before cited, has drawn the limits still more narrowly by arguing that the dance of twelve satyrs (IV, iv) before Polixenes is imitated from Jonson's *Masque of Oberon*, which was performed at court on January 1, 1611. Every feature of the play agrees with this date (namely, between January 1, 1611, and May 15 of that year): its elliptical style, its large number of light and weak endings, and its community of spirit with the romantic comedy of those particular years.

SOURCES

Ever since the beginning of the eighteenth century it has been known that Shakespeare went to a novel called *Pandosto, the Triumph of Time* by Robert Greene for the subject of this play. It was Greene who nineteen years before had written his famous reproach against Shakespeare contained in *A Groatsworth of Wit*.

Many names are changed; in fact, only the name Mopsa is left from *Pandosto* and that is reapplied. There are also striking and not always necessary changes in plot. No intermediary drama has been found, and, because of the inaccurate way in which the story is told, one is tempted to believe that Shakespeare worked from memory rather than from the text. The relation between *The Winter's Tale* and *Pandosto* is very different, for example, from that which exists between *Coriolanus* and its source. The euphuism of Lyly and the elaborate and courtly pastoralism of Sidney, both of which Greene imitated, do not manifest themselves in *The Winter's Tale*. The eveı ıs which take place in *Pandosto* in Sicily are transferred to Bohemia, and vice versa. But in few cases has Shakespeare more completely made over a source, and nothing is more completely transformed than the pastoralism of Greene's novel. Shakespeare's shepherds are real people, and Greene's are the puppets of the traditional pastoral. The one thing that Shakespeare has retained from his source is the wild and romantic improbability which, as we have seen, characterized *Cymbeline*. It is at least possible that Shakespeare knew the version of the story appearing in Francis Sabie's poems, *The Fisherman's Tale* (1595) and its sequel *Flora's Fortune* (1595), in which some of the more striking differences from Greene that Shakespeare adopted are to be found.

[1] See footnote, p. 1043 above.

The Winter's Tale is much like *Cymbeline* in the looseness of its plot and in its disregard of probability. Perhaps nothing in *Cymbeline* forms so powerful a binding force for the whole play as does the use of the Greek oracle in *The Winter's Tale*. In fact it may be said that through the whole play there is an atmosphere of Greek piety, which serves to explain the seclusion of Hermione, and which gives color and pathos to the abasement of Leontes. Like *Cymbeline* and *The Tempest*, *The Winter's Tale* shows a determination that all shall end well. Leontes and Othello are affected by the same passion; it may even be said that the action of Leontes is quite as violent as Othello's, though much less excusable. Shakespeare seems, however, to tell us that by repentance and by obeying a god, we may escape at least a part of the consequences of the most tragic sin. The secondary title of *Pandosto* is "The Triumph of Time," which means that time and the generations may restore much that the passion of the moment has destroyed. Since it is in the power of time

> To o'erthrow law and in one self-born hour
> To plant and o'erwhelm custom,

there is in *The Winter's Tale* not only a unity of tone and of intention, but also in its own fashion a unity of plot.

This is but another illustration of Shakespeare's ability to find unity in a wide diversity. Nowhere, for example, is there greater variety and vigor in characterization of individuals. Hermione is one of Shakespeare's most steadfast characters, standing out as an example of noble and independent womanhood. Autolycus is his most famous rogue, bringing with him the ethics and the lingo of the fraternity of rogues and vagabonds. Florizel and Perdita are a pair of lovers as charming, as simple, and as youthful as Romeo and Juliet. In Mamillius Shakespeare is sometimes said to have achieved his greatest triumph in the depiction of childhood. Most of his children are pathetic figures. Camillo and Paulina are the perfection of faithful, loyal servants, and their union is perhaps not wholly the gratuitous matchmaking with which comedies are wont to close. *The Winter's Tale* is also distinguished by the beauty of its verse.

THE STATUE OF HERMIONE

The use of the device of the living statue in the denouement of *The Winter's Tale* was sufficiently common to occasion no surprise. The story of Pygmalion from Greek mythology was of course well known, and Marston's *Metamorphosis of Pygmalion's Image* (1598), an amatory poem, was popular. A statue is brought to life in Lyly's *Woman in the Moon* (1597), and the hero of the anonymous play *The Trial of Chivalry* (1600?) impersonates his own statue in order to overhear the words of his ladylove.

The device of the living statue appears elsewhere in Renaissance literature.[2] The puzzling thing is not that Shakespeare employs it, even so cleverly, but that the whole thing comes as a complete surprise. The audience has been left in ignorance of the fact that Hermione is still alive until toward the end of the play. This is not the dramatic habit of Shakespeare, who practically always takes his audience into his confidence. If one considers also the fact that Hermione's prototype in *Pandosto* actually dies, one is led to suspect that the happy restoration of Hermione may be an afterthought on Shakespeare's part, an improvement possibly introduced into the plot as a revision while the play was being written. Certain bibliographical peculiarities in the parts of the text concerned lend some color to this supposition.

STAGE HISTORY

The Winter's Tale seems to have been popular in its own day. It was played at court in 1611 (?), 1613, 1624, and 1634. After this, it is not heard of for a long time, for the story of *The Winter's Tale* was too rambling and the play did too great violence to the three unities to be endurable to the taste of the Restoration. In 1741 *The Winter's Tale* was revived at the theater in Goodman's Fields. Soon after this (1756) it underwent drastic alterations by Garrick and appeared as *Florizel and Perdita* (made up mainly from the last two acts), in which form it continued to be acted during the rest of the eighteenth century.

John Philip Kemble played Leontes to Mrs. Siddons' Hermione in a version not greatly different from the original (1802). The indefatigable reviver of Shakespeare, Samuel Phelps, put *The Winter's Tale* on at Sadler's Wells in 1845-1846, and in 1856 Charles Kean selected it for production on the grandest possible scale. Those were the days when historical accuracy was sought at all costs, and *The Winter's Tale* was, somewhat inappropriately, given a presentation perfectly Greek to the last detail. Nothing could be further from Aeschylus than Shakespeare's version of Robert Greene's imitation of the romances of the Romanized Greeks of the third and fourth centuries A.D. Ellen Terry was Mamillius in those performances. In 1906 she played Hermione in Beerbohm Tree's revival. In 1887 the American actress, Mary Anderson, played the double role of Hermione and Perdita and won great admiration by her performance. In that production Sir Johnston Forbes-Robertson was Leontes. The Ben Greet company gave a successful performance of *The Winter's Tale* in the Elizabethan manner about 1910 in which Miss Matthison acted the part of Hermione.

The Winter's Tale has appeared frequently in the repertories of English companies during the last twenty-five years and is now sufficiently familiar to theatergoers to be universally regarded as a charming play on the stage.

[2]Chambers, *William Shakespeare*, I, 488-490; H. Carrington Lancaster, "Hermione's Statue," *Studies in Philology*, XXXIX (1932), 233-238.

THE

Winter's Tale

DRAMATIS PERSONAE

LEONTES, king of Sicilia.
MAMILLIUS, young prince of Sicilia.
CAMILLO,
ANTIGONUS,
CLEOMENES, } Four Lords of Sicilia.
DION,
POLIXENES, king of Bohemia.
FLORIZEL, prince of Bohemia.
ARCHIDAMUS, a Lord of Bohemia.
Old Shepherd, reputed father of Perdita.
Clown, his son.
AUTOLYCUS, a rogue.
A Mariner.
A Gaoler.

HERMIONE, queen to Leontes.
PERDITA, daughter to Leontes and Hermione.
PAULINA, wife to Antigonus.
EMILIA, a lady attending on Hermione.

MOPSA,
DORCAS, } Shepherdesses.

Other Lords and Gentlemen, Ladies, Officers, and Servants, Shepherds, and Shepherdesses.

Time, as Chorus.

SCENE: *Sicilia, and Bohemia.*

ACT I.

SCENE I. *Antechamber in* LEONTES' *palace.*

Enter CAMILLO *and* ARCHIDAMUS.

Arch. If you shall chance, Camillo, to visit Bohemia, on the like occasion whereon my services are now on foot, you shall see, as I have said, great difference betwixt our Bohemia and your Sicilia.

Cam. I think, this coming summer, the King of Sicilia means to pay Bohemia the visitation which he justly owes him.

Arch. Wherein our entertainment shall shame us we will be justified in our loves; for indeed—   10

Cam. Beseech you,—

Arch. Verily, I speak it in the freedom of my knowledge: we cannot with such magnificence—in so rare—I know not what to say. We will give you sleepy drinks, that your senses, unintelligent of our insufficience, may, though they cannot praise us, as little accuse us.

Cam. You pay a great deal too dear for what's given freely.   19

Arch. Believe me, I speak as my understanding instructs me and as mine honesty puts it to utterance.

Cam. Sicilia cannot show himself over-kind to Bohemia. They were trained together in their childhoods; and there rooted betwixt them then such an affection, which cannot choose but branch now. Since their more mature dignities and royal necessities made separation of their society, their encounters, though not personal, have been royally attorneyed with interchange of gifts, letters, loving embassies; that they have seemed to be together, though absent, shook hands, as over a vast, and embraced, as it were, from the ends of opposed winds. The heavens continue their loves! 35

Arch. I think there is not in the world either malice or matter to alter it. You have an unspeakable comfort of your young prince Mamillius: it is a gentleman of the greatest promise that ever came into my note. 40

Cam. I very well agree with you in the hopes of him: it is a gallant child; one that indeed physics the subject, makes old hearts fresh: they that went on crutches ere he was born desire yet their life to see him a man.

Arch. Would they else be content to die?

Cam. Yes; if there were no other excuse why they should desire to live.

Arch. If the king had no son, they would desire to live on crutches till he had one. [*Exeunt.* 50

SCENE II. *A room of state in the same.*

Enter LEONTES, HERMIONE, MAMILLIUS, POLIXENES, CAMILLO, *and* Attendants.

Pol. Nine changes of the watery star hath been
The shepherd's note since we have left our throne
Without a burthen: time as long again
Would be fill'd up, my brother, with our thanks;
And yet we should, for perpetuity,
Go hence in debt: and therefore, like a cipher,
Yet standing in rich place, I multiply
With one 'We thank you' many thousands moe
That go before it.
Leon.   Stay your thanks a while;
And pay them when you part.
Pol.   Sir, that's to-morrow. 10
I am question'd by my fears, of what may chance
Or breed upon our absence; that may blow
No sneaping winds at home, to make us say
'This is put forth too truly:' besides, I have stay'd
To tire your royalty.
Leon.   We are tougher, brother,
Than you can put us to 't.
Pol.   No longer stay.
Leon. One seven-night longer.
Pol.   Very sooth, to-morrow.
Leon. We'll part the time between 's then; and in that
I'll no gainsaying.
Pol.   Press me not, beseech you, so.

There is no tongue that moves, none, none i' the
   world, 20
So soon as yours could win me: so it should now,
Were there necessity in your request, although
'Twere needful I denied it. My affairs
Do even drag me homeward: which to hinder
Were in your love a whip to me; my stay
To you a charge and trouble: to save both,
Farewell, our brother.
Leon.   Tongue-tied our queen? speak you.
Her. I had thought, sir, to have held my peace until
You had drawn oaths from him not to stay. You, sir,
Charge him too coldly. Tell him, you are sure 30
All in Bohemia's well; this satisfaction
The by-gone day proclaim'd: say this to him,
He's beat from his best ward.
Leon.   Well said, Hermione.
Her. To tell, he longs to see his son, were strong:
But let him say so then, and let him go;
But let him swear so, and he shall not stay,
We'll thwack him hence with distaffs.
Yet of your royal presence I'll adventure
The borrow of a week. When at Bohemia
You take my lord, I'll give him my commission 40
To let him there a month behind the gest
Prefix'd for 's parting: yet, good deed, Leontes,
I love thee not a jar o' the clock behind
What lady-she her lord. You'll stay?
Pol.   No, madam.
Her. Nay, but you will?
Pol.   I may not, verily.
Her. Verily!
You put me off with limber vows; but I,
Though you would seek to unsphere the stars with
   oaths,
Should yet say 'Sir, no going.' Verily,
You shall not go: a lady's 'Verily''s 50
As potent as a lord's. Will you go yet?
Force me to keep you as a prisoner,
Not like a guest; so you shall pay your fees
When you depart, and save your thanks. How say
   you?
My prisoner? or my guest? by your dread 'Verily,'
One of them you shall be.
Pol.   Your guest, then, madam:
To be your prisoner should import offending;
Which is for me less easy to commit
Than you to punish.
Her.   Not your gaoler, then,
But your kind hostess. Come, I'll question you 60
Of my lord's tricks and yours when you were boys:
You were pretty lordings then?
Pol.   We were, fair queen,
Two lads that thought there was no more behind
But such a day to-morrow as to-day,
And to be boy eternal.
Her.   Was not my lord

ACT I. SCENE I. The conversation between the two noblemen serves to bring out the unruffled friendship between Leontes and Polixenes; it is, of course, full of dramatic irony. 30. **attorneyed,** carried out by deputy. 33. **vast,** boundless, desolate sea. 37. **of,** in the person of. 40. **note,** observation. 43. **physics the subject,** acts as a cordial to the people.
SCENE II. 1. **watery star,** moon. 13. **sneaping,** pinching with cold. 16. **Than . . . to 't,** than anything you can do to try us. 17. **seven-night,** common expression for "week." 19. **I'll no gainsaying,** I will

have no refusal. 25. **your love a whip,** to make your love a punishment. 39. **borrow,** borrowing. 41. **gest,** time allotted for a halt. 42. **good deed,** a mild oath. 43. **jar,** tick. 47. **limber,** pliant. 53. **fees.** Persons leaving prison were obliged to pay for their lodging whether guilty or not. 57. **import,** imply. 74-75. **imposition . . . ours,** original sin, although imposed upon us by heredity, was swept clean away (Furness). 80. **Grace to boot,** a mild oath, "favor of God be our help!" 85. **fault,** offense. 96. **heat,** traverse (as a horse driven by the spur). 104. **clap,** clasp hands, plight troth. 110. **tremor cordis,** fluttering

The verier wag o' the two?

Pol. We were as twinn'd lambs that did frisk i' the
    sun,
And bleat the one at the other: what we changed
Was innocence for innocence; we knew not
The doctrine of ill-doing, nor dream'd   70
That any did. Had we pursued that life,
And our weak spirits ne'er been higher rear'd
With stronger blood, we should have answer'd
    heaven
Boldly 'not guilty;' the imposition clear'd
Hereditary ours.

Her.   By this we gather
You have tripp'd since.

Pol.   O my most sacred lady!
Temptations have since then been born to 's; for
In those unfledged days was my wife a girl;
Your precious self had then not cross'd the eyes
Of my young play-fellow.

Her.   Grace to boot!   80
Of this make no conclusion, lest you say
Your queen and I are devils: yet go on;
The offences we have made you do we'll answer,
If you first sinn'd with us and that with us
You did continue fault and that you slipp'd not
With any but with us.

Leon.   Is he won yet?

Her. He'll stay, my lord.

Leon.   At my request he would not.
Hermione, my dearest, thou never spokest
To better purpose.

Her.   Never?

Leon.   Never, but once.

Her. What! have I twice said well? when was 't
    before?   90
I prithee tell me; cram 's with praise, and make 's
As fat as tame things: one good deed dying tongueless
Slaughters a thousand waiting upon that.
Our praises are our wages: you may ride 's
With one soft kiss a thousand furlongs ere
With spur we heat an acre. But to the goal:
My last good deed was to entreat his stay:
What was my first? it has an elder sister,
Or I mistake you: O, would her name were Grace!
But once before I spoke to the purpose: when?   100
Nay, let me have 't; I long.

Leon.   Why, that was when
Three crabbed months had sour'd themselves to
    death,
Ere I could make thee open thy white hand
And clap thyself my love: then didst thou utter
'I am yours for ever.'

Her.   'Tis grace indeed.
Why, lo you now, I have spoke to the purpose twice:
The one for ever earn'd a royal husband;
The other for some while a friend.

Leon.   [*Aside*] Too hot, too hot!
To mingle friendship far is mingling bloods.
I have tremor cordis on me: my heart dances;   110

But not for joy; not joy. This entertainment
May a free face put on, derive a liberty
From heartiness, from bounty, fertile bosom,
And well become the agent; 't may, I grant;
But to be paddling palms and pinching fingers,
As now they are, and making practised smiles,
As in a looking-glass, and then to sigh, as 'twere
The mort o' the deer; O, that is entertainment
My bosom likes not, nor my brows! Mamillius,
Art thou my boy?

Mam.   Ay, my good lord.

Leon.   I' fecks!   120
Why, that 's my bawcock. What, hast smutch'd thy
    nose?
They say it is a copy out of mine. Come, captain,
We must be neat; not neat, but cleanly, captain:
And yet the steer, the heifer and the calf
Are all call'd neat.—Still virginalling
Upon his palm!—How now, you wanton calf!
Art thou my calf?

Mam.   Yes, if you will, my lord.

Leon. Thou want'st a rough pash and the shoots
    that I have,
To be full like me: yet they say we are
Almost as like as eggs; women say so,   130
That will say any thing: but were they false
As o'er-dyed blacks, as wind, as waters, false
As dice are to be wish'd by one that fixes
No bourn 'twixt his and mine, yet were it true
To say this boy were like me. Come, sir page,
Look on me with your welkin eye: sweet villain!
Most dear'st! my collop! Can thy dam?—may 't be?—
Affection! thy intention stabs the centre:
Thou dost make possible things not so held,
Communicatest with dreams;—how can this be?— 140
With what 's unreal thou coactive art,
And fellow'st nothing: then 'tis very credent
Thou mayst co-join with something; and thou dost,
And that beyond commission, and I find it,
And that to the infection of my brains
And hardening of my brows.

Pol.   What means Sicilia?

Her. He something seems unsettled.

Pol.   How, my lord!
What cheer? how is 't with you, best brother?

Her.   You look
As if you held a brow of much distraction:
Are you moved, my lord?

Leon.   No, in good earnest.   150
How sometimes nature will betray its folly,
Its tenderness, and make itself a pastime
To harder bosoms! Looking on the lines
Of my boy's face, methoughts I did recoil
Twenty-three years, and saw myself unbreech'd,
In my green velvet coat, my dagger muzzled,
Lest it should bite its master, and so prove,
As ornaments oft do, too dangerous:
How like, methought, I then was to this kernel,
This squash, this gentleman. Mine honest friend,   160

---

of the heart.   **118. mort,** note sounded on a horn at the death of a deer.
120. I' fecks, in faith.   **121. bawcock,** French, *beau coq*, fine fellow.
123. not . . . cleanly. Leontes changes the word because *neat* reminds
him of the cuckold's horns.   **125. virginalling,** playing on the virginals,
a keyed instrument of the piano class; here, touching hands.   **128.
pash,** head.   **shoots,** horns; an allusion to the cuckold's horns.   **132.
o'er-dyed blacks,** probably, black garments whose fabric is destroyed by
dye.   **134. bourn,** boundary.   **137. collop,** piece of meat; here, a term
of endearment.   **138. Affection . . . centre,** amorous affection by power

goes straight to the center; a puzzling line.   **139-146. Thou . . .
brows.** Affection, in the sense of amorous affection, is able to pursue
its course by dreams, unrealities, mere nothings. It is then credible
that when it has realities to work upon, it will have yet more power.
142. credent, credible.   **144. commission,** what is lawful.   **154. recoil,**
go back in memory.   **160. squash,** unripe peascod.

Will you take eggs for money?
    Mam. No, my lord, I'll fight.
    Leon. You will! why, happy man be 's dole! My
      brother,
Are you so fond of your young prince as we
Do seem to be of ours?
    Pol.   If at home, sir,
He 's all my exercise, my mirth, my matter,
Now my sworn friend and then mine enemy,
My parasite, my soldier, statesman, all:
He makes a July's day short as December,
And with his varying childness cures in me   170
Thoughts that would thick my blood.
    Leon.   So stands this squire
Officed with me: we two will walk, my lord,
And leave you to your graver steps. Hermione,
How thou lovest us, show in our brother's welcome;
Let what is dear in Sicily be cheap:
Next to thyself and my young rover, he 's
Apparent to my heart.
    Her.   If you would seek us,
We are yours i' the garden: shall 's attend you there?
    Leon. To your own bents dispose you: you'll be
      found,
Be you beneath the sky. [*Aside*] I am angling now,   180
Though you perceive me not how I give line.
Go to, go to!
How she holds up the neb, the bill to him!
And arms her with the boldness of a wife
To her allowing husband!
         [*Exeunt Polixenes, Hermione, and Attendants.*
         Gone already!
Inch-thick, knee-deep, o'er head and ears a fork'd
    one!
Go, play, boy, play: thy mother plays, and I
Play too, but so disgraced a part, whose issue
Will hiss me to my grave: contempt and clamour
Will be my knell. Go, play, boy, play. There have
    been,   190
Or I am much deceived, cuckolds ere now;
And many a man there is, even at this present,
Now while I speak this, holds his wife by the arm,
That little thinks she has been sluiced in 's absence
And his pond fish'd by his next neighbour, by
Sir Smile, his neighbour: nay, there 's comfort in 't
Whiles other men have gates and those gates open'd,
As mine, against their will. Should all despair
That have revolted wives, the tenth of mankind
Would hang themselves. Physic for 't there is none; 200
It is a bawdy planet, that will strike
Where 'tis predominant; and 'tis powerful, think it,
From east, west, north and south: be it concluded,
No barricado for a belly; know 't;
It will let in and out the enemy
With bag and baggage: many thousand on 's
Have the disease, and feel 't not. How now, boy!
    Mam. I am like you, they say.
    Leon.   Why, that 's some comfort.
What, Camillo there?
    Cam. Ay, my good lord.   210

    Leon. Go play, Mamillius; thou 'rt an honest man.
                       [*Exit Mamillius.*
Camillo, this great sir will yet stay longer.
    Cam. You had much ado to make his anchor hold:
When you cast out, it still came home.
    Leon.   Didst note it?
    Cam. He would not stay at your petitions; made
His business more material.
    Leon.   Didst perceive it?
[*Aside*] They 're here with me already, whispering,
    rounding
'Sicilia is a so-forth:' 'tis far gone,
When I shall gust it last. How came 't, Camillo,
That he did stay?
    Cam.   At the good queen's entreaty. 220
    Leon. At the queen's be 't: 'good' should be
      pertinent;
But, so it is, it is not. Was this taken
By any understanding pate but thine?
For thy conceit is soaking, will draw in
More than the common blocks: not noted, is 't,
But of the finer natures? by some severals
Of head-piece extraordinary? lower messes
Perchance are to this business purblind? say.
    Cam. Business, my lord! I think most understand
Bohemia stays here longer.
    Leon.   Ha!
    Cam.   Stays here longer.   230
    Leon. Ay, but why?
    Cam. To satisfy your highness and the entreaties
Of our most gracious mistress.
    Leon.   Satisfy!
The entreaties of your mistress! satisfy!
Let that suffice. I have trusted thee, Camillo,
With all the nearest things to my heart, as well
My chamber-councils, wherein, priest-like, thou
Hast cleansed my bosom, I from thee departed
Thy penitent reform'd: but we have been
Deceived in thy integrity, deceived   240
In that which seems so.
    Cam.   Be it forbid, my lord!
    Leon. To bide upon 't, thou art not honest, or,
If thou inclinest that way, thou art a coward,
Which hoxes honesty behind, restraining
From course required; or else thou must be counted
A servant grafted in my serious trust
And therein negligent; or else a fool
That seest a game play'd home, the rich stake drawn,
And takest it all for jest.
    Cam.   My gracious lord,
I may be negligent, foolish and fearful;   250
In every one of these no man is free,
But that his negligence, his folly, fear,
Among the infinite doings of the world,
Sometime puts forth. In your affairs, my lord,
If ever I were wilful-negligent,
It was my folly; if industriously
I play'd the fool, it was my negligence,
Not weighing well the end; if ever fearful
To do a thing, where I the issue doubted,

---

161. **take eggs for money,** proverbial for "be imposed upon." 163. **happy . . . dole,** proverbial, "may good fortune be his lot." 170. **childness,** childishness. 171. **thick my blood.** Melancholy thoughts would thicken the blood. 172. **Officed,** placed in particular function. 178. **shall 's,** shall we. 179. **To . . . you,** do with yourselves according to the inclinations of your minds. 183. **neb,** beak; here, nose. 184. **arms her with,** assumes. 188. **issue,** outcome. 201. **strike,** blast,

destroy by a malign influence. 202. **predominant,** in the ascendant (used of a planet). 216. **material,** important. 217-219. **They 're . . . last.** Staunton pointed out that these words refer to the king's fear of public disgrace and shame. Note *contempt and clamour,* line 189. 217. **rounding,** whispering. 219. **gust,** taste; here, hear of. 221. **pertinent,** i.e., appropriately applied. 222. **so,** as. **taken,** perceived. 224. **soaking,** very receptive. 225. **blocks,** blockheads. 227. **lower messes,**

Whereof the execution did cry out 260
Against the non-performance, 'twas a fear
Which oft infects the wisest: these, my lord,
Are such allow'd infirmities that honesty
Is never free of. But, beseech your grace,
Be plainer with me; let me know my trespass
By its own visage: if I then deny it,
'Tis none of mine.
    Leon.   Ha' not you seen, Camillo,—
But that 's past doubt, you have, or your eye-glass
Is thicker than a cuckold's horn,—or heard,—
For to a vision so apparent rumor 270
Cannot be mute,—or thought,—for cogitation
Resides not in that man that does not think,—
My wife is slippery? If thou wilt confess,
Or else be impudently negative,
To have nor eyes nor ears nor thought, then say
My wife 's a hobby-horse, deserves a name
As rank as any flax-wench that puts to
Before her troth-plight: say 't and justify 't.
    Cam. I would not be a stander-by to hear
My sovereign mistress clouded so, without 280
My present vengeance taken: 'shrew my heart,
You never spoke what did become you less
Than this; which to reiterate were sin
As deep as that, though true.
    Leon.   Is whispering nothing?
Is leaning cheek to cheek? is meeting noses?
Kissing with inside lip? stopping the career
Of laughter with a sigh?—a note infallible
Of breaking honesty—horsing foot on foot?
Skulking in corners? wishing clocks more swift?
Hours, minutes? noon, midnight? and all eyes 290
Blind with the pin and web but theirs, theirs only,
That would unseen be wicked? is this nothing?
Why, then the world and all that 's in 't is nothing;
The covering sky is nothing; Bohemia nothing;
My wife is nothing; nor nothing have these nothings,
If this be nothing.
    Cam.   Good my lord, be cured
Of this diseased opinion, and betimes;
For 'tis most dangerous.
    Leon.   Say it be, 'tis true.
    Cam. No, no, my lord.
    Leon.   It is; you lie, you lie:
I say thou liest, Camillo, and I hate thee, 300
Pronounce thee a gross lout, a mindless slave,
Or else a hovering temporizer, that
Canst with thine eyes at once see good and evil,
Inclining to them both: were my wife's liver
Infected as her life, she would not live
The running of one glass.
    Cam.   Who does infect her?
    Leon. Why, he that wears her like her medal,
         hanging
About his neck, Bohemia: who, if I
Had servants true about me, that bare eyes
To see alike mine honour as their profits, 310
Their own particular thrifts, they would do that
Which should undo more doing: ay, and thou,

His cupbearer,—whom I from meaner form
Have bench'd and rear'd to worship, who mayst see
Plainly as heaven sees earth and earth sees heaven,
How I am galled,—mightst bespice a cup,
To give mine enemy a lasting wink;
Which draught to me were cordial.
    Cam.   Sir, my lord,
I could do this, and that with no rash potion,
But with a lingering dram that should not work 320
Maliciously like poison: but I cannot
Believe this crack to be in my dread mistress,
So sovereignly being honourable.
I have loved thee,—
    Leon.   †Make that thy question, and
         go rot!
Dost think I am so muddy, so unsettled,
To appoint myself in this vexation, sully
The purity and whiteness of my sheets,
Which to preserve is sleep, which being spotted
Is goads, thorns, nettles, tails of wasps,
Give scandal to the blood o' the prince my son, 330
Who I do think is mine and love as mine,
Without ripe moving to 't? Would I do this?
Could man so blench?
    Cam.   I must believe you, sir:
I do; and will fetch off Bohemia for 't;
Provided that, when he 's removed, your highness
Will take again your queen as yours at first,
Even for your son's sake; and thereby for sealing
The injury of tongues in courts and kingdoms
Known and allied to yours.
    Leon.   Thou dost advise me
Even so as I mine own course have set down: 340
I 'll give no blemish to her honour, none.
    Cam. My lord,
Go then; and with a countenance as clear
As friendship wears at feasts, keep with Bohemia
And with your queen. I am his cupbearer:
If from me he have wholesome beverage,
Account me not your servant.
    Leon.   This is all:
Do 't and thou hast the one half of my heart;
Do 't not, thou split'st thine own.
    Cam.   I 'll do 't, my lord. 349
    Leon. I will seem friendly, as thou hast advised me.
                                  [*Exit.*

    Cam. O miserable lady! But, for me,
What case stand I in? I must be the poisoner
Of good Polixenes; and my ground to do 't
Is the obedience to a master, one
Who in rebellion with himself will have
All that are his so too. To do this deed,
Promotion follows. If I could find example
Of thousands that had struck anointed kings
And flourish'd after, I 'ld not do 't; but since
Nor brass nor stone nor parchment bears not one, 360
Let villany itself forswear 't. I must
Forsake the court: to do 't, or no, is certain
To me a break-neck. Happy star reign now!
Here comes Bohemia.

The
Winter's Tale
ACT I : SC II

1221

---

persons of a lower rank.   228. **purblind,** blind.   237. **chamber-coun-cils,** private affairs.   242. **bide,** insist.   244. **hoxes,** hocks, cuts the hamstrings of.   254. **puts forth,** appears.   256. **industriously,** of set purpose.   268. **eye-glass,** crystalline lens.   270. **vision,** thing visible. 277. **flax-wench,** female flax-worker.   286. **career,** full course.   288. **honesty,** chastity.   **horsing,** setting.   291. **pin and web,** cataract of the eye.   302. **hovering,** wavering.   306. **glass,** hourglass.   311. **thrifts,**

gains.   314. **bench'd,** raised to authority.   317. **lasting wink,** death. 323. **So . . . honourable,** being so supremely honorable.   324. **that,** i.e., the dishonesty of Hermione.   326. **appoint,** equip, array.   332. **ripe,** urgent.   334. **fetch off,** make way with.   337. **for sealing,** anonymous conjecture: *foresealing.*   352. **case,** position.   357-361. **If . . . forswear't.** This is a well-recognized principle of Renaissance morality.   363. **break-neck.** destruction, ruin.

Poi.   This is strange: methinks
My favour here begins to warp. Not speak?
Good day, Camillo.
     Cam.   Hail, most royal sir!
     Pol. What is the news i' the court?
     Cam.   None rare, my lord.
     Pol. The king hath on him such a countenance
As he had lost some province and a region
Loved as he loves himself: even now I met him   370
With customary compliment; when he,
Wafting his eyes to the contrary and falling
A lip of much contempt, speeds from me and
So leaves me to consider what is breeding
That changeth thus his manners.
     Cam. I dare not know, my lord.
     Pol. How! dare not! do not. Do you know, and dare
not?
Be intelligent to me: 'tis thereabouts;
For, to yourself, what you do know, you must,
And cannot say, you dare not. Good Camillo,   380
Your changed complexions are to me a mirror
Which shows me mine changed too; for I must be
A party in this alteration, finding
Myself thus alter'd with 't.
     Cam.   There is a sickness
Which puts some of us in distemper, but
I cannot name the disease; and it is caught
Of you that yet are well.
     Pol.   How! caught of me!
Make me not sighted like the basilisk:
I have look'd on thousands, who have sped the better
By my regard, but kill'd none so. Camillo,—   390
As you are certainly a gentleman, thereto
Clerk-like experienced, which no less adorns
Our gentry than our parents' noble names,
In whose success we are gentle,—I beseech you,
If you know aught which does behove my knowledge
Thereof to be inform'd, imprison 't not
In ignorant concealment.
     Cam.   I may not answer.
     Pol. A sickness caught of me, and yet I well!
I must be answer'd. Dost thou hear, Camillo?
I conjure thee, by all the parts of man   400
Which honour does acknowledge, whereof the least
Is not this suit of mine, that thou declare
What incidency thou dost guess of harm
Is creeping toward me; how far off, how near;
Which way to be prevented, if to be;
If not, how best to bear it.
     Cam.   Sir, I will tell you;
Since I am charged in honour and by him
That I think honourable: therefore mark my counsel,
Which must be even as swiftly follow'd as
I mean to utter it, or both yourself and me   410
Cry lost, and so good night!
     Pol.   On, good Camillo.
     Cam. I am appointed him to murder you.
     Pol. By whom, Camillo?

     Cam.   By the king.
     Pol.   For what?
     Cam. He thinks, nay, with all confidence he swears,
As he had seen 't or been an instrument
To vice you to 't, that you have touch'd his queen
Forbiddenly.
     Pol.   O, then my best blood turn
To an infected jelly and my name
Be yoked with his that did betray the Best!
Turn then my freshest reputation to   42
A savour that may strike the dullest nostril
Where I arrive, and my approach be shunn'd,
Nay, hated too, worse than the great'st infection
That e'er was heard or read!
     Cam.   Swear his thought over
By each particular star in heaven and
By all their influences, you may as well
Forbid the sea for to obey the moon
As or by oath remove or counsel shake
The fabric of his folly, whose foundation
Is piled upon his faith and will continue   430
The standing of his body.
     Pol.   How should this grow?
     Cam. I know not: but I am sure 'tis safer to
Avoid what 's grown than question how 'tis born.
If therefore you dare trust my honesty,
That lies enclosed in this trunk which you
Shall bear along impawn'd, away to-night!
Your followers I will whisper to the business,
And will by twos and threes at several posterns
Clear them o' the city. For myself, I'll put
My fortunes to your service, which are here   440
By this discovery lost. Be not uncertain;
For, by the honour of my parents, I
Have utter'd truth: which if you seek to prove,
I dare not stand by; nor shall you be safer
Than one condemn'd by the king's own mouth,
          thereon
His execution sworn.
     Pol.   I do believe thee:
I saw his heart in 's face. Give me thy hand:
Be pilot to me and thy places shall
Still neighbour mine. My ships are ready and
My people did expect my hence departure   450
Two days ago. This jealousy
Is for a precious creature: as she 's rare,
Must it be great, and as his person 's mighty,
Must it be violent, and as he does conceive
He is dishonour'd by a man which ever
Profess'd to him, why, his revenges must
In that be made more bitter. Fear o'ershades me:
Good expedition be my friend, and comfort
†The gracious queen, part of his theme, but nothing
Of his ill-ta'en suspicion! Come, Camillo;   460
I will respect thee as a father if
Thou bear'st my life off hence: let us avoid.
     Cam. It is in mine authority to command
The keys of all the posterns: please your highness
To take the urgent hour. Come, sir, away.   [*Exeunt.*

---

365. **warp,** change, grow askew. 372. **Wafting . . . contrary,** turning in an opposite direction. 378. **Be . . . thereabouts,** be intelligible—it must be something of this nature: that you know and dare not tell (Furness). 381. **changed,** grown pale. 394. **whose success,** succession from whom. 416. **vice,** impel. 419. **his . . . Best,** a reference to Judas. 424. **Swear . . . over,** overcome his thought by swearing. 431. **standing,** life, existence. **How . . . grow?** How could this suspicion have arisen? 435. **trunk,** body. 436. **impawn'd,** i.e., as a pledge of good faith. 441. **discovery,** revelation, disclosure. 444. **stand by,** stay to see the result. 456. **Profess'd,** openly professed friendship. 458-460. **Good . . . suspicion.** May my hasty departure prove my best course, and bring what comfort it may to the gracious queen, whose name cannot but be linked with mine in the king's thoughts, but who is not yet the fatal object of his ill-founded suspicion (Furness). 462.

ACT II.

SCENE I. *A room in* LEONTES' *palace.*

Enter HERMIONE, MAMILLIUS, *and* Ladies.

Her. Take the boy to you: he so troubles me,
'Tis past enduring.
    First Lady.   Come, my gracious lord,
Shall I be your playfellow?
    Mam.   No, I'll none of you.
    First Lady. Why, my sweet lord?
    Mam. You'll kiss me hard and speak to me as if
I were a baby still. I love you better.
    Sec. Lady. And why so, my lord?
    Mam.   Not for because
Your brows are blacker; yet black brows, they say,
Become some women best, so that there be not
Too much hair there, but in a semicircle,   10
Or a half-moon made with a pen.
    Sec. Lady.   Who taught you this?
    Mam. I learnt it out of women's faces. Pray now
What colour are your eyebrows?
    First Lady.   Blue, my lord.
    Mam. Nay, that's a mock: I have seen a lady's
        nose
That has been blue, but not her eyebrows.
    First Lady.   Hark ye;
The queen your mother rounds apace: we shall
Present our services to a fine new prince
One of these days; and then you 'ld wanton with us,
If we would have you.
    Sec. Lady.   She is spread of late
Into a goodly bulk: good time encounter her!   20
    Her. What wisdom stirs amongst you? Come, sir,
        now
I am for you again: pray you, sit by us,
And tell 's a tale.
    Mam.   Merry or sad shall 't be?
    Her. As merry as you will.
    Mam. A sad tale 's best for winter: I have one
Of sprites and goblins.
    Her.   Let 's have that, good sir.
Come on, sit down: come on, and do your best
To fright me with your sprites; you 're powerful at it.
    Mam. There was a man—
    Her.   Nay, come, sit down; then on.
    Mam. Dwelt by a churchyard: I will tell it softly;   30
Yond crickets shall not hear it.
    Her.   Come on, then,
And give 't me in mine ear.

Enter LEONTES, *with* ANTIGONUS, Lords, *and* others.

    Leon. Was he met there? his train? Camillo with
        him?
    First Lord. Behind the tuft of pines I met them;
        never
Saw I men scour so on their way: I eyed them
Even to their ships.
    Leon.   How blest am I
In my just censure, in my true opinion!

Alack, for lesser knowledge! how accursed
In being so blest! There may be in the cup
A spider steep'd, and one may drink, depart,   40
And yet partake no venom, for his knowledge
Is not infected: but if one present
The abhorr'd ingredient to his eye, make known
How he hath drunk, he cracks his gorge, his sides,
With violent hefts. I have drunk, and seen the spider.
Camillo was his help in this, his pandar:
There is a plot against my life, my crown;
All 's true that is mistrusted: that false villain
Whom I employ'd was pre-employ'd by him:
He has discover'd my design, and I   50
Remain a pinch'd thing; yea, a very trick
For them to play at will. How came the posterns
So easily open?
    First Lord.   By his great authority;
Which often hath no less prevail'd than so
On your command.
    Leon.   I know 't too well.
Give me the boy: I am glad you did not nurse him:
Though he does bear some signs of me, yet you
Have too much blood in him.
    Her.   What is this? sport?
    Leon. Bear the boy hence; he shall not come about
        her;
Away with him! and let her sport herself   60
With that she 's big with; for 'tis Polixenes
Has made thee swell thus.
    Her.   But I 'ld say he had not,
And I'll be sworn you would believe my saying,
Howe'er you lean to the nayward.
    Leon.   You, my lords,
Look on her, mark her well; be but about
To say 'she is a goodly lady,' and
The justice of your hearts will thereto add
''Tis pity she 's not honest, honourable:'
Praise her but for this her without-door form,   69
Which on my faith deserves high speech, and straight
The shrug, the hum or ha, these petty brands
That calumny doth use—O, I am out—
That mercy does, for calumny will sear
Virtue itself: these shrugs, these hums and ha's,
When you have said 'she 's goodly,' come between
Ere you can say 'she 's honest:' but be 't known,
From him that has most cause to grieve it should be,
She 's an adulteress.
    Her.   Should a villain say so,
The most replenish'd villain in the world,
He were as much more villain: you, my lord,   80
Do but mistake.
    Leon.   You have mistook, my lady,
Polixenes for Leontes: O thou thing!
Which I'll not call a creature of thy place,
Lest barbarism, making me the precedent,
Should a like language use to all degrees
And mannerly distinguishment leave out
Betwixt the prince and beggar: I have said
She 's an adulteress; I have said with whom:
More, she 's a traitor and Camillo is

---

avoid, depart.
    ACT II. SCENE I.   **11. you this,** F: *'this,* indicating that *you* was elided.
18. wanton, sport, play.   **25. A sad tale 's best for winter.** This may
have some connection with the title, *The Winter's Tale.*   **31. crickets,**
meaning court ladies "with their tittering and chirping laughter"
(Furnivall). Mamillius is one of Shakespeare's most successful children,
having about him some actual childishness. Shakespeare's children

are hardly more in their language and ideas than diminutive grown
people, and yet in spite of this they create an impression of childhood.
38. Alack, for lesser knowledge, would that my knowledge were
less.   **45. hefts,** heavings, retchings.   **51. pinch'd,** powerless, ridiculous.
62. I 'ld, I need only.   **64. nayward,** disbelief.   **69. without-door,**
outward.   **72. out,** wrong.   **73. does,** uses.   **83. place,** position.
86. mannerly distinguishment, polite distinctions.

A federary with her, and one that knows 90
What she should shame to know herself
But with her most vile principal, that she 's
A bed-swerver, even as bad as those
That vulgars give bold'st titles, ay, and privy
To this their late escape.
    Her.   No, by my life,
Privy to none of this. How will this grieve you,
When you shall come to clearer knowledge, that
You thus have publish'd me! Gentle my lord,
You scarce can right me throughly then to say
You did mistake.
    Leon.   No; if I mistake 100
In those foundations which I build upon,
The centre is not big enough to bear
A school-boy's top. Away with her! to prison!
He who shall speak for her is afar off guilty
But that he speaks.
    Her.   There 's some ill planet reigns:
I must be patient till the heavens look
With an aspect more favourable. Good my lords,
I am not prone to weeping, as our sex
Commonly are; the want of which vain dew
Perchance shall dry your pities: but I have 110
That honourable grief lodged here which burns
Worse than tears drown: beseech you all, my lords,
With thoughts so qualified as your charities
Shall best instruct you, measure me; and so
The king's will be perform'd!
    Leon.   Shall I be heard?
    Her. Who is 't that goes with me? Beseech your
        highness,
My women may be with me; for you see
My plight requires it. Do not weep, good fools;
There is no cause: when you shall know your mistress
Has deserved prison, then abound in tears 120
As I come out: this action I now go on
Is for my better grace. Adieu, my lord:
I never wish'd to see you sorry; now
I trust I shall. My women, come; you have leave.
    Leon. Go, do our bidding; hence!
                    [*Exit Queen, guarded; with Ladies.*
    First Lord. Beseech your highness, call the queen
        again.
    Ant. Be certain what you do, sir, lest your justice
Prove violence; in the which three great ones suffer,
Yourself, your queen, your son.
    First Lord.   For her, my lord,
I dare my life lay down and will do 't, sir, 130
Please you to accept it, that the queen is spotless
I' the eyes of heaven and to you; I mean,
In this which you accuse her.
    Ant.   If it prove
†She 's otherwise, I'll keep my stables where
I lodge my wife; I'll go in couples with her;
Than when I feel and see her no farther trust her;
For every inch of woman in the world,
Ay, every dram of woman's flesh is false,
If she be.
    Leon.   Hold your peaces.
    First Lord.   Good my lord,—
    Ant. It is for you we speak, not for ourselves: 140

You are abused and by some putter-on
That will be damn'd for 't; would I knew the villain,
†I would land-damn him. Be she honour-flaw'd,
I have three daughters; the eldest is eleven;
The second and the third, nine, and some five;
If this prove true, they'll pay for 't: by mine honour,
I'll geld 'em all; fourteen they shall not see,
To bring false generations: they are co-heirs;
And I had rather glib myself than they
Should not produce fair issue.
    Leon.   Cease; no more. 150
You smell this business with a sense as cold
As is a dead man's nose: but I do see 't and feel 't,
As you feel doing thus; and see withal
The instruments that feel.
    Ant.   If it be so,
We need no grave to bury honesty:
There 's not a grain of it the face to sweeten
Of the whole dungy earth.
    Leon.   What! lack I credit?
    First Lord. I had rather you did lack than I, my
        lord,
Upon this ground; and more it would content me
To have her honour true than your suspicion, 160
Be blamed for 't how you might.
    Leon.   Why, what need we
Commune with you of this, but rather follow
Our forceful instigation? Our prerogative
Calls not your counsels, but our natural goodness
Imparts this; which if you, or stupified
Or seeming so in skill, cannot or will not
Relish a truth like us, inform yourselves
We need no more of your advice: the matter,
The loss, the gain, the ordering on 't, is all
Properly ours.
    Ant.   And I wish, my liege, 170
You had only in your silent judgment tried it,
Without more overture.
    Leon.   How could that be?
Either thou art most ignorant by age,
Or thou wert born a fool. Camillo's flight,
Added to their familiarity,
Which was as gross as ever touch'd conjecture,
That lack'd sight only, nought for approbation
But only seeing, all other circumstances
Made up to the deed, doth push on this proceeding:
Yet, for a greater confirmation, 180
For in an act of this importance 'twere
Most piteous to be wild, I have dispatch'd in post
To sacred Delphos, to Apollo's temple,
Cleomenes and Dion, whom you know
Of stuff'd sufficiency: now from the oracle
They will bring all; whose spiritual counsel had,
Shall stop or spur me. Have I done well?
    First Lord. Well done, my lord.
    Leon. Though I am satisfied and need no more
Than what I know, yet shall the oracle 190
Give rest to the minds of others, such as he
Whose ignorant credulity will not
Come up to the truth. So have we thought it good
From our free person she should be confined,
Lest that the treachery of the two fled hence

90. **federary,** confederate, accomplice. 94. **vulgars,** common people.
102. **centre,** center of the earth. 104. **afar off,** to some degree. 115.
heard, obeyed. 121. **action,** indictment. 134. **stables,** usually regarded as equivalent to *kennels*; but Moorman suggests "station"—
stabilis statio—interpreting the passage, "I'll keep my station in the

same place where my wife is lodged." 135. **couples,** i.e., like hounds.
141. **putter-on,** instigator. 143. **land-damn him,** possibly, make a hell
on earth for him or abuse with rancor; many conjectures. 145. **some,**
about. 148. **false generations,** illegitimate children. 149. **glib,** geld.
153. **As . . . thus,** possibly expressed by a gesture. 159. **Upon this**

Be left her to perform. Come, follow us;
We are to speak in public; for this business
Will raise us all.
    Ant.   [*Aside*] To laughter, as I take it,
If the good truth were known.   [*Exeunt.*

SCENE II. *A prison.*

Enter PAULINA, *a* Gentleman, *and* Attendants.

Paul. The keeper of the prison, call to him;
Let him have knowledge who I am.   [*Exit Gent.*
              Good lady,
No court in Europe is too good for thee;
What dost thou then in prison?

Re-enter Gentleman, *with the* Gaoler.
              Now, good sir,
You know me, do you not?
    Gaol.   For a worthy lady
And one whom much I honour.
    Paul.   Pray you then,
Conduct me to the queen.
    Gaol.   I may not, madam:
To the contrary I have express commandment.
    Paul. Here's ado,
To lock up honesty and honour from   10
The access of gentle visitors! Is't lawful, pray you,
To see her women? any of them? Emilia?
    Gaol. So please you, madam,
To put apart these your attendants, I
Shall bring Emilia forth.
    Paul.   I pray now, call her.
Withdraw yourselves. [*Exeunt Gentleman and Attendants.*
    Gaol.   And, madam,
I must be present at your conference.
    Paul. Well, be't so, prithee.   [*Exit Gaoler.*
Here's such ado to make no stain a stain
As passes colouring.

Re-enter Gaoler, *with* EMILIA.
              Dear gentlewoman,   20
How fares our gracious lady?
    Emil. As well as one so great and so forlorn
May hold together: on her frights and griefs,
Which never tender lady hath borne greater,
She is something before her time deliver'd.
    Paul. A boy?
    Emil.   A daughter, and a goodly babe,
Lusty and like to live: the queen receives
Much comfort in't; says 'My poor prisoner,
I am innocent as you.'
    Paul.   I dare be sworn:
These dangerous unsafe lunes i' the king, beshrew
    them!   30
He must be told on't, and he shall: the office
Becomes a woman best; I'll take't upon me:
If I prove honey-mouth'd, let my tongue blister
And never to my red-look'd anger be
The trumpet any more. Pray you, Emilia,
Commend my best obedience to the queen:
If she dares trust me with her little babe,

I'll show't the king and undertake to be
Her advocate to the loud'st. We do not know
How he may soften at the sight o' the child: 40
The silence often of pure innocence
Persuades when speaking fails.
    Emil.   Most worthy madam,
Your honour and your goodness is so evident
That your free undertaking cannot miss
A thriving issue: there is no lady living
So meet for this great errand. Please your ladyship
To visit the next room, I'll presently
Acquaint the queen of your most noble offer;
Who but to-day hammer'd of this design,
But durst not tempt a minister of honour,   50
Lest she should be denied.
    Paul.   Tell her, Emilia,
I'll use that tongue I have: if wit flow from't
As boldness from my bosom, let't not be doubted
I shall do good.
    Emil.   Now be you blest for it!
I'll to the queen: please you, come something nearer.
    Gaol. Madam, if't please the queen to send the
    babe,
I know not what I shall incur to pass it,
Having no warrant.
    Paul.   You need not fear it, sir:
This child was prisoner to the womb and is
By law and process of great nature thence   60
Freed and enfranchised, not a party to
The anger of the king nor guilty of,
If any be, the trespass of the queen.
    Gaol. I do believe it.
    Paul. Do not you fear: upon mine honour, I
Will stand betwixt you and danger.   [*Exeunt.*

SCENE III. *A room in* LEONTES' *palace.*

Enter LEONTES, ANTIGONUS, Lords, *and* Servants.

Leon. Nor night nor day no rest: it is but weakness
To bear the matter thus; mere weakness. If
The cause were not in being,—part o' the cause,
She the adulteress; for the harlot king
Is quite beyond mine arm, out of the blank
And level of my brain, plot-proof; but she
I can hook to me: say that she were gone,
Given to the fire, a moiety of my rest
Might come to me again. Who's there?
    First Serv.   My lord?
    Leon. How does the boy?
    First Serv.   He took good rest to-night;
'Tis hoped his sickness is discharged.   11
    Leon. To see his nobleness!
Conceiving the dishonour of his mother,
He straight declined, droop'd, took it deeply,
Fasten'd and fix'd the shame on't in himself,
Threw off his spirit, his appetite, his sleep,
And downright languish'd. Leave me solely: go,
See how he fares. [*Exit Serv.*] Fie, fie! no thought of
    him:
The very thought of my revenges that way
Recoil upon me: in himself too mighty,   20

---

ground, in this matter. 164. **Calls,** calls for. 172. **overture,** disclosure. 176. **conjecture,** evil surmise. 177. **approbation,** proof. 185. **stuff'd sufficiency,** abundant capabilities. 186. **had,** having been obtained. 191. **he,** probably, any person. 198. **raise,** rouse.
    SCENE II. 23. **on,** in consequence of. 30. **lunes,** fits of lunacy.

49. **hammer'd of,** insisted on. 57. **pass it,** let it pass. 63. **If any be,** if there be any guilt.
    SCENE III. 4. **harlot,** lewd. 5. **blank,** white spot in the center of a target.

And in his parties, his alliance; let him be
Until a time may serve: for present vengeance,
Take it on her. Camillo and Polixenes
Laugh at me, make their pastime at my sorrow:
They should not laugh if I could reach them, nor
Shall she within my power.

    Enter PAULINA, *with a child.*

    First Lord.   You must not enter.
    Paul. Nay, rather, good my lords, be second to me:
Fear you his tyrannous passion more, alas,
Than the queen's life? a gracious innocent soul,
More free than he is jealous.
    Ant.   That 's enough.   30
    Sec. Serv. Madam, he hath not slept to-night; commanded
None should come at him.
    Paul.   Not so hot, good sir:
I come to bring him sleep. 'Tis such as you,
That creep like shadows by him and do sigh
At each his needless heavings, such as you
Nourish the cause of his awaking: I
Do come with words as medicinal as true,
Honest as either, to purge him of that humour
That presses him from sleep.
    Leon.   What noise there, ho?
    Paul. No noise, my lord; but needful conference   40
About some gossips for your highness.
    Leon.   How!
Away with that audacious lady! Antigonus,
I charged thee that she should not come about me:
I knew she would.
    Ant.   I told her so, my lord,
On your displeasure's peril and on mine,
She should not visit you.
    Leon.   What, canst not rule her?
    Paul. From all dishonesty he can: in this,
Unless he take the course that you have done,
Commit me for committing honour, trust it,
He shall not rule me.
    Ant.   La you now, you hear: 50
When she will take the rein I let her run;
But she'll not stumble.
    Paul.   Good my liege, I come;
And, I beseech you, hear me, who profess
Myself your loyal servant, your physician,
Your most obedient counsellor, yet that dare
Less appear so in comforting your evils,
Than such as most seem yours: I say, I come
From your good queen.
    Leon.   Good queen!
    Paul.   Good queen, my lord,
Good queen; I say good queen;
And would by combat make her good, so were I   60
A man, the worst about you.
    Leon.   Force her hence.
    Paul. Let him that makes but trifles of his eyes
First hand me: on mine own accord I'll off;
But first I'll do my errand. The good queen,
For she is good, hath brought you forth a daughter;
Here 'tis; commends it to your blessing.
                    [*Laying down the child.*

    Leon.   Out!
A mankind witch! Hence with her, out o' door:
A most intelligencing bawd!
    Paul.   Not so:
I am as ignorant in that as you
In so entitling me, and no less honest   70
Than you are mad; which is enough, I'll warrant,
As this world goes, to pass for honest.
    Leon.   Traitors!
Will you not push her out? Give her the bastard.
Thou dotard! thou art woman-tired, unroosted
By thy dame Partlet here. Take up the bastard;
Take 't up, I say; give 't to thy crone.
    Paul.   For ever
Unvenerable be thy hands, if thou
Takest up the princess by that forced baseness
Which he has put upon 't!
    Leon.   He dreads his wife.
    Paul. So I would you did; then 'twere past all doubt   80
You 'ld call your children yours.
    Leon.   A nest of traitors!
    Ant. I am none, by this good light.
    Paul.   Nor I, nor any
But one that 's here, and that 's himself, for he
The sacred honour of himself, his queen's,
His hopeful son's, his babe's, betrays to slander,
Whose sting is sharper than the sword's; and will not—
For, as the case now stands, it is a curse
He cannot be compell'd to 't—once remove
The root of his opinion, which is rotten
As ever oak or stone was sound.
    Leon.   A callet   90
Of boundless tongue, who late hath beat her husband
And now baits me! This brat is none of mine;
It is the issue of Polixenes:
Hence with it, and together with the dam
Commit them to the fire!
    Paul.   It is yours;
And, might we lay the old proverb to your charge,
So like you, 'tis the worse. Behold, my lords,
Although the print be little, the whole matter
And copy of the father, eye, nose, lip,
The trick of 's frown, his forehead, nay, the valley,   100
The pretty dimples of his chin and cheek,
His smiles,
The very mould and frame of hand, nail, finger:
And thou, good goddess Nature, which hast made it
So like to him that got it, if thou hast
The ordering of the mind too, 'mongst all colours
No yellow in 't, lest she suspect, as he does,
Her children not her husband's!
    Leon.   A gross hag!
And, lozel, thou art worthy to be hang'd,
That wilt not stay her tongue.
    Ant.   Hang all the husbands   110
That cannot do that feat, you'll leave yourself
Hardly one subject.
    Leon.   Once more, take her hence.
    Paul. A most unworthy and unnatural lord
Can do no more.

---

23. **Take it,** let it be taken. 27. **be second to,** aid, second. 41. **gossips,** godfathers and godmothers. 49. **Commit,** i.e., to prison. 56-57. **comforting . . . yours,** encouraging your evil courses, than those flatterers who seem to be your most loyal servants. 67. **mankind,** masculine, violent; here used as an adjective. 68. **intelligencing,** conveying secret intelligence. 74. **woman-tired,** henpecked, from "tire" in falconry, meaning "tear." **unroosted,** driven from perch. 75. **Partlet,** name of the hen in *Reynard the Fox*, who appears as *Pertelote* in the *Nun's Priest's Tale* of Chaucer. 78. **forced baseness,** false attribution of illegitimacy. 79. **He . . . wife,** he (Antigonus) is afraid of his wife

Leon.   I'll ha' thee burnt.
Paul.   I care not:
It is an heretic that makes the fire,
Not she which burns in 't. I'll not call you tyrant;
But this most cruel usage of your queen,
Not able to produce more accusation
Than your own weak-hinged fancy, something
    savours
Of tyranny and will ignoble make you,   120
Yea, scandalous to the world.
   Leon.   On your allegiance,
Out of the chamber with her! Were I a tyrant,
Where were her life? she durst not call me so,
If she did know me one. Away with her!
   Paul. I pray you, do not push me; I'll be gone.
Look to your babe, my lord; 'tis yours: Jove send her
A better guiding spirit! What needs these hands?
You, that are thus so tender o'er his follies,
Will never do him good, not one of you.
So, so: farewell; we are gone.   [*Exit.* 130
   Leon. Thou, traitor, hast set on thy wife to this.
My child? away with 't! Even thou, that hast
A heart so tender o'er it, take it hence
And see it instantly consumed with fire;
Even thou and none but thou. Take it up straight:
Within this hour bring me word 'tis done,
And by good testimony, or I'll seize thy life,
With what thou else call'st thine. If thou refuse
And wilt encounter with my wrath, say so;
The bastard brains with these my proper hands   140
Shall I dash out. Go, take it to the fire;
For thou set'st on thy wife.
   Ant.   I did not, sir:
These lords, my noble fellows, if they please,
Can clear me in 't.
   Lords.   We can: my royal liege,
He is not guilty of her coming hither.
   Leon. You 're liars all.
   First Lord. Beseech your highness, give us better
    credit:
We have always truly served you, and beseech you
So to esteem of us, and on our knees we beg,
As recompense of our dear services   150
Past and to come, that you do change this purpose,
Which being so horrible, so bloody, must
Lead on to some foul issue: we all kneel.
   Leon. I am a feather for each wind that blows:
Shall I live on to see this bastard kneel
And call me father? better burn it now
Than curse it then. But be it; let it live.
It shall not neither. You, sir, come you hither;
You that have been so tenderly officious
With Lady Margery, your midwife there,   160
To save this bastard's life,—for 'tis a bastard,
So sure as this beard 's grey,—what will you
    adventure
To save this brat's life?
   Ant.   Any thing, my lord,
That my ability may undergo
And nobleness impose: at least thus much:
I'll pawn the little blood which I have left
To save the innocent: any thing possible.

Leon. It shall be possible. Swear by this sword
Thou wilt perform my bidding.
   Ant.   I will, my lord.
   Leon. Mark and perform it, see'st thou? for the fail 170
Of any point in 't shall not only be
Death to thyself but to thy lewd-tongued wife,
Whom for this time we pardon. We enjoin thee,
As thou art liege-man to us, that thou carry
This female bastard hence and that thou bear it
To some remote and desert place quite out
Of our dominions, and that there thou leave it,
Without more mercy, to it own protection
And favour of the climate. As by strange fortune
It came to us, I do in justice charge thee,   180
On thy soul's peril and thy body's torture,
That thou commend it strangely to some place
Where chance may nurse or end it. Take it up.
   Ant. I swear to do this, though a present death
Had been more merciful. Come on, poor babe:
Some powerful spirit instruct the kites and ravens
To be thy nurses! Wolves and bears, they say,
Casting their savageness aside have done
Like offices of pity. Sir, be prosperous
In more than this deed does require! And blessing   190
Against this cruelty fight on thy side,
Poor thing, condemn'd to loss!   [*Exit with the child.*
   Leon.   No, I'll not rear
Another's issue.

   Enter a Servant.
   Serv.   Please your highness, posts
From those you sent to the oracle are come
An hour since: Cleomenes and Dion,
Being well arrived from Delphos, are both landed,
Hasting to the court.
   First Lord.   So please you, sir, their
    speed
Hath been beyond account.
   Leon.   Twenty three days
They have been absent: 'tis good speed: foretells
The great Apollo suddenly will have   200
The truth of this appear. Prepare you, lords;
Summon a session, that we may arraign
Our most disloyal lady, for, as she hath
Been publicly accused, so shall she have
A just and open trial. While she lives
My heart will be a burthen to me. Leave me,
And think upon my bidding.   [*Exeunt.*

ACT III.

SCENE I. *A sea-port in Sicilia.*

Enter CLEOMENES *and* DION.

   Cleo. The climate 's delicate, the air most sweet,
Fertile the isle, the temple much surpassing
The common praise it bears.
   Dion.   I shall report,
For most it caught me, the celestial habits,
Methinks I so should term them, and the reverence
Of the grave wearers. O, the sacrifice!

(Paulina). 90. **callet,** lewd woman. 96. **old proverb.** The sense of the proverb is given by Overbury ("Character of a Sergeant"): "The devil calls him his white son; he's so like him, that he is the worse for it." 107. **yellow,** suggestive of jealousy. 109. **lozel,** worthless person, scoundrel. 127. **What . . . hands.** She is being pushed from the room. 170. **fail,** failure. 178. **it,** its. 182. **commend,** deliver, commit. **strangely,** as a foreigner. 192. **loss,** perdition.
ACT III. SCENE I. 2. **isle,** Shakespeare follows Greene's *Pandosto* in erroneously placing Delphi on an island.

How ceremonious, solemn and unearthly
It was i' the offering!
   Cleo.   But of all, the burst
And the ear-deafening voice o' the oracle,
Kin to Jove's thunder, so surprised my sense,   10
That I was nothing.
   Dion.   If the event o' the journey
Prove as successful to the queen,—O be 't so!—
As it hath been to us rare, pleasant, speedy,
The time is worth the use on 't.
   Cleo.   Great Apollo
Turn all to the best! These proclamations,
So forcing faults upon Hermione,
I little like.
   Dion.   The violent carriage of it
Will clear or end the business: when the oracle,
Thus by Apollo's great divine seal'd up,
Shall the contents discover, something rare   20
Even then will rush to knowledge. Go: fresh horses!
And gracious be the issue!   [*Exeunt.*

SCENE II. *A court of Justice.*

Enter LEONTES, Lords, *and* Officers.

Leon. This sessions, to our great grief we pronounce,
Even pushes 'gainst our heart: the party tried
The daughter of a king, our wife, and one
Of us too much beloved. Let us be clear'd
Of being tyrannous, since we so openly
Proceed in justice, which shall have due course,
Even to the guilt or the purgation.
Produce the prisoner.
   Off. It is his highness' pleasure that the queen
Appear in person here in court. Silence!   10

Enter HERMIONE *guarded;* PAULINA *and* Ladies
    attending.

   Leon. Read the indictment.
   Off. [*Reads*] Hermione, queen to the worthy
Leontes, king of Sicilia, thou art here accused and
arraigned of high treason, in committing adultery
with Polixenes, king of Bohemia, and conspiring with
Camillo to take away the life of our sovereign lord
the king, thy royal husband: the pretence whereof
being by circumstances partly laid open, thou, Hermione, contrary to the faith and allegiance of a true
subject, didst counsel and aid them, for their better
safety, to fly away by night.   22

   Her. Since what I am to say must be but that
Which contradicts my accusation and
The testimony on my part no other
But what comes from m self, it shall scarce boot me
To say 'not guilty:' mine integrity
Being counted falsehood, shall, as I express it,
Be so received. But thus: if powers divine
Behold our human actions, as they do,   30
I doubt not then but innocence shall make
False accusation blush and tyranny
Tremble at patience. You, my lord, best know,

Who least will seem to do so, my past life
Hath been as continent, as chaste, as true,
As I am now unhappy; which is more
Than history can pattern, though devised
And play'd to take spectators. For behold me
A fellow of the royal bed, which owe
A moiety of the throne, a great king's daughter,   40
The mother to a hopeful prince, here standing
To prate and talk for life and honour 'fore
Who please to come and hear. For life, I prize it
As I weigh grief, which I would spare: for honour,
'Tis a derivative from me to mine,
And only that I stand for. I appeal
To your own conscience, sir, before Polixenes
Came to your court, how I was in your grace,
How merited to be so; since he came,
With what encounter so uncurrent I   50
Have strain'd to appear thus: if one jot beyond
The bond of honour, or in act or will
That way inclining, harden'd be the hearts
Of all that hear me, and my near'st of kin
Cry fie upon my grave!
   Leon.   I ne'er heard yet
That any of these bolder vices wanted
Less impudence to gainsay what they did
Than to perform it first.
   Her.   That 's true enough;
Though 'tis a saying, sir, not due to me.
   Leon. You will not own it.
   Her.   †More than mistress of   60
Which comes to me in name of fault, I must not
At all acknowledge. For Polixenes,
With whom I am accused, I do confess
I loved him as in honour he required,
With such a kind of love as might become
A lady like me, with a love even such,
So and no other, as yourself commanded:
Which not to have done I think had been in me
Both disobedience and ingratitude
To you and toward your friend, whose love had
    spoke,   70
Even since it could speak, from an infant, freely
That it was yours. Now, for conspiracy,
I know not how it tastes; though it be dish'd
For me to try how: all I know of it
Is that Camillo was an honest man;
And why he left your court, the gods themselves,
Wotting no more than I, are ignorant.
   Leon. You knew of his departure, as you know
What you have underta'en to do in 's absence.
   Her. Sir,   80
You speak a language that I understand not:
My life stands in the level of your dreams,
Which I'll lay down.
   Leon.   Your actions are my dreams;
You had a bastard by Polixenes,
And I but dream'd it. As you were past all shame,—
Those of your fact are so—so past all truth:
Which to deny concerns more than avails; for as
Thy brat hath been cast out, like to itself,

---

8. **burst,** utterance. 14. **worth . . . on 't,** well employed. 17. **carriage,**
execution, management. 19. **divine,** here applied to a priest of the
heathen religion. 21. **fresh horses.** This indicates that the scene is
laid at some point on the return journey.
   SCENE II. 1. **sessions,** sitting of a court of justice. **pronounce,**
declare. 7. **purgation,** clearing from the accusation. 18. **pretence,**
purpose, design. 43-46. **For . . . for.** As for life, it is only grief to
me, and I would willingly dismiss it; as for honor, it is transmitted

by descent from me to mine, and that only I maintain. 50-51.
With . . . thus, (I ask) by what behavior so improper I have exceeded
bounds so that I appear thus (in disgrace). 59. **due,** applicable. 60-
62. **More . . . acknowledge,** I will not acknowledge that I am answerable
for more than what may be called faults; i.e., she is not guilty of the
bolder vices of line 56. 82. **in . . . dreams,** at the mercy of your hal-
lucinations. 87. **Which . . . avails,** to deny this is more trouble than
it is worth. 88. **like to itself,** as it ought to be (Furness); *left* has

No father owning it,—which is, indeed,
More criminal in thee than it,—so thou 90
Shalt feel our justice, in whose easiest passage
Look for no less than death.
  Her.   Sir, spare your threats:
The bug which you would fright me with I seek.
To me can life be no commodity:
The crown and comfort of my life, your favour,
I do give lost; for I do feel it gone,
But know not how it went. My second joy
And first-fruits of my body, from his presence
I am barr'd, like one infectious. My third comfort,
Starr'd most unluckily, is from my breast, 100
The innocent milk in it most innocent mouth,
Haled out to murder: myself on every post
Proclaim'd a strumpet: with immodest hatred
The child-bed privilege denied, which 'longs
To women of all fashion; lastly, hurried
Here to this place, i' the open air, before
I have got strength of limit. Now, my liege,
Tell me what blessings I have here alive,
That I should fear to die? Therefore proceed.
But yet hear this; mistake me not; no life, 110
I prize it not a straw, but for mine honour,
Which I would free, if I shall be condemn'd
Upon surmises, all proofs sleeping else
But what your jealousies awake, I tell you
'Tis rigour and not law. Your honours all,
I do refer me to the oracle:
Apollo be my judge!
  First Lord.   This your request
Is altogether just: therefore bring forth,
And in Apollo's name, his oracle. [*Exeunt certain Officers.*
  Her. The Emperor of Russia was my father: 120
O that he were alive, and here beholding
His daughter's trial! that he did but see
The flatness of my misery, yet with eyes
Of pity, not revenge!

      Re-enter Officers, *with* CLEOMENES *and* DION.

  Off. You here shall swear upon this sword of
    justice,
That you, Cleomenes and Dion, have
Been both at Delphos, and from thence have brought
This seal'd-up oracle, by the hand deliver'd
Of great Apollo's priest and that since then
You have not dared to break the holy seal 130
Nor read the secrets in 't.
  Cleo. Dion.   All this we swear.
  Leon. Break up the seals and read.
  Off. [*Reads*] Hermione is chaste; Polixenes blame-
less; Camillo a true subject; Leontes a jealous tyrant;
his innocent babe truly begotten; and the king shall
live without an heir, if that which is lost be not found.
  Lords. Now blessed be the great Apollo!
  Her.   Praised!
  Leon. Hast thou read truth?
  Off.   Ay, my lord; even so
As it is here set down. 140
  Leon. There is no truth at all i' the oracle:

The sessions shall proceed: this is mere falsehood.

  Enter Servant.

  Serv. My lord the king, the king!
  Leon.   What is the business?
  Serv. O sir, I shall be hated to report it!
The prince your son, with mere conceit and fear
Of the queen's speed, is gone.
  Leon.   How! gone!
  Serv.   Is dead.
  Leon. Apollo 's angry; and the heavens themselves
Do strike at my injustice. [*Hermione swoons.*] How now
    there!
  Paul. This news is mortal to the queen: look down
And see what death is doing.
  Leon.   Take her hence: 150
Her heart is but o'ercharged; she will recover:
I have too much believed mine own suspicion:
Beseech you, tenderly apply to her
Some remedies for life.
      [*Exeunt Paulina and Ladies, with Hermione.*
        Apollo, pardon
My great profaneness 'gainst thine oracle!
I'll reconcile me to Polixenes,
New woo my queen, recall the good Camillo,
Whom I proclaim a man of truth, of mercy;
For, being transported by my jealousies
To bloody thoughts and to revenge, I chose 160
Camillo for the minister to poison
My friend Polixenes: which had been done,
But that the good mind of Camillo tardied
My swift command, though I with death and with
Reward did threaten and encourage him,
Not doing 't and being done: he, most humane
And fill'd with honour, to my kingly guest
Unclasp'd my practice, quit his fortunes here,
Which you knew great, and to the hazard
Of all incertainties himself commended, 170
No richer than his honour: how he glisters
Thorough my rust! and how his piety
Does my deeds make the blacker!

       Re-enter PAULINA.

  Paul.   Woe the while!
O, cut my lace, lest my heart, cracking it,
Break too!
  First Lord.   What fit is this, good lady?
  Paul. What studied torments, tyrant, hast for me?
What wheels? racks? fires? what flaying? boiling?
In leads or oils? what old or newer torture
Must I receive, whose every word deserves
To taste of thy most worst? Thy tyranny 180
Together working with thy jealousies,
Fancies too weak for boys, too green and idle
For girls of nine, O, think what they have done
And then run mad indeed, stark mad! for all
Thy by-gone fooleries were but spices of it.
That thou betray'dst Polixenes, 'twas nothing;
That did but show thee, of a fool, inconstant
And damnable ingrateful: nor was 't much,

been suggested as an emendation of *like.* 93. **bug,** bogey, imaginary
object of terror. 94. **commodity,** convenience. 100. **Starr'd,** fated.
101. **it,** its. 103. **immodest,** immoderate. 105. **fashion,** kinds, sorts.
107. **strength of limit,** limited strength. 110. **no life,** i.e., I do not
ask for life. 115. **rigour,** tyranny, injustice. 120. **Emperor of
Russia.** In *Pandosto* it is the wife of Egistus (Polixenes) who is daughter
of the emperor of Russia. 123. **flatness,** absoluteness. 154. **Apollo,
pardon.** The suddenness of Leontes' conversion is characteristic

of Shakespeare's treatment of conscience, and connects itself with
the current psychological theory of the sudden predominance of one
emotion. 163. **tardied,** delayed in executing. 166. **Not . . . done,** i.e.,
reward if he did it, and death if he did not. 168. **Unclasp'd my practice,** disclosed my conspiracy. 171. **No richer than,** with no riches
except. 185. **spices,** foretastes, samples. 187. **of,** for.

That wouldst have poison'd good Camillo's honour,
To have him kill a king; poor trespasses, 190
More monstrous standing by: whereof I reckon
The casting forth to crows thy baby-daughter
To be or none or little; though a devil
Would have shed water out of fire ere done 't:
Nor is 't directly laid to thee, the death
Of the young prince, whose honourable thoughts,
Thoughts high for one so tender, cleft the heart
That could conceive a gross and foolish sire
Blemish'd his gracious dam: this is not, no,
Laid to thy answer: but the last,—O lords, 200
When I have said, cry 'woe!'—the queen, the queen,
The sweet'st, dear'st creature 's dead, and vengeance
   for 't
Not dropp'd down yet.
   First Lord.   The higher powers forbid!
   Paul. I say she 's dead; I'll swear 't. If word nor
   oath
Prevail not, go and see: if you can bring
Tincture or lustre in her lip, her eye,
Heat outwardly or breath within, I'll serve you
As I would do the gods. But, O thou tyrant!
Do not repent these things, for they are heavier
Than all thy woes can stir: therefore betake thee 210
To nothing but despair. A thousand knees
Ten thousand years together, naked, fasting,
Upon a barren mountain, and still winter
In storm perpetual, could not move the gods
To look that way thou wert.
   Leon.   Go on, go on:
Thou canst not speak too much; I have deserved
All tongues to talk their bitterest.
   First Lord.   Say no more:
Howe'er the business goes, you have made fault
I' the boldness of your speech.
   Paul.   I am sorry for 't:
All faults I make, when I shall come to know them, 220
I do repent. Alas! I have show'd too much
The rashness of a woman: he is touch'd
To the noble heart. What 's gone and what 's past
   help
Should be past grief: do not receive affliction
At my petition; I beseech you, rather
Let me be punish'd, that have minded you
Of what you should forget. Now, good my liege,
Sir, royal sir, forgive a foolish woman:
The love I bore your queen—lo, fool again!—
I'll speak of her no more, nor of your children; 230
I'll not remember you of my own lord,
Who is lost too: take your patience to you,
And I'll say nothing.
   Leon.   Thou didst speak but well
When most the truth; which I receive much better
Than to be pitied of thee. Prithee, bring me
To the dead bodies of my queen and son:
One grave shall be for both: upon them shall
The causes of their death appear, unto
Our shame perpetual. Once a day I'll visit
The chapel where they lie, and tears shed there 240

Shall be my recreation: so long as nature
Will bear up with this exercise, so long
I daily vow to use it. Come and lead me
Unto these sorrows.   [*Exeunt.*

SCENE III. *Bohemia. A desert country near the sea.*

Enter ANTIGONUS *with a Child, and a* MARINER.

   Ant. Thou art perfect then, our ship hath touch'd
   upon
The deserts of Bohemia?
   Mar.   Ay, my lord; and fear
We have landed in ill time: the skies look grimly
And threaten present blusters. In my conscience,
The heavens with that we have in hand are angry
And frown upon 's.
   Ant. Their sacred wills be done! Go, get aboard;
Look to thy bark: I'll not be long before
I call upon thee.
   Mar. Make your best haste, and go not 10
Too far i' the land: 'tis like to be loud weather;
Besides, this place is famous for the creatures
Of prey that keep upon 't.
   Ant.   Go thou away:
I'll follow instantly.
   Mar.   I am glad at heart
To be so rid o' the business.   [*Exit.*
   Ant.   Come, poor babe:
I have heard, but not believed, the spirits o' the dead
May walk again: if such thing be, thy mother
Appear'd to me last night, for ne'er was dream
So like a waking. To me comes a creature,
Sometimes her head on one side, some another; 20
I never saw a vessel of like sorrow,
So fill'd and so becoming: in pure white robes,
Like very sanctity, she did approach
My cabin where I lay; thrice bow'd before me,
And gasping to begin some speech, her eyes
Became two spouts: the fury spent, anon
Did this break from her: 'Good Antigonus,
Since fate, against thy better disposition,
Hath made thy person for the thrower-out
Of my poor babe, according to thine oath, 30
Places remote enough are in Bohemia,
There weep and leave it crying; and, for the babe
Is counted lost for ever, Perdita,
I prithee, call 't. For this ungentle business,
Put on thee by my lord, thou ne'er shalt see
Thy wife Paulina more.' And so, with shrieks,
She melted into air. Affrighted much,
I did in time collect myself and thought
This was so and no slumber. Dreams are toys:
Yet for this once, yea, superstitiously, 40
I will be squared by this. I do believe
Hermione hath suffer'd death, and that
Apollo would, this being indeed the issue
Of King Polixenes, it should here be laid,
Either for life or death, upon the earth
Of its right father. Blossom, speed thee well!

There lie, and there thy character: there these;
Which may, if fortune please, both breed thee, pretty,
And still rest thine. The storm begins: poor wretch,
That for thy mother's fault art thus exposed   50
To loss and what may follow! Weep I cannot,
But my heart bleeds; and most accursed am I
To be by oath enjoin'd to this. Farewell!
The day frowns more and more: thou 'rt like to have
A lullaby too rough: I never saw
The heavens so dim by day. A savage clamour!   56
Well may I get aboard! This is the chase:
I am gone for ever.   [*Exit, pursued by a bear.*

Enter a Shepherd.

Shep. I would there were no age between sixteen
and three-and-twenty, or that youth would sleep out
the rest; for there is nothing in the between but getting
wenches with child, wronging the ancientry, stealing,
fighting—Hark you now! Would any but these boiled
brains of nineteen and two-and-twenty hunt this
weather? They have scared away two of my best
sheep, which I fear the wolf will sooner find than the
master: if any where I have them, 'tis by the seaside,
browsing of ivy. Good luck, an 't be thy will! what
have we here? Mercy on 's, a barne; a very pretty
barne! A boy or a child, I wonder? A pretty one; a
very pretty one: sure, some 'scape: though I am not
bookish, yet I can read waiting-gentlewoman in the
'scape. This has been some stair-work, some trunk-
work, some behind-door-work: they were warmer
that got this than the poor thing is here. I'll take it
up for pity: yet I'll tarry till my son come; he hal-
looed but even now. Whoa, ho, hoa!

Enter Clown.

Clo. Hilloa, loa!   80
Shep. What, art so near? If thou 'lt see a thing to
talk on when thou art dead and rotten, come hither.
What ailest thou, man?
Clo. I have seen two such sights, by sea and by
land! but I am not to say it is a sea, for it is now the
sky: betwixt the firmament and it you cannot thrust
a bodkin's point.
Shep. Why, boy, how is it?   88
Clo. I would you did but see how it chafes, how it
rages, how it takes up the shore! but that 's not to the
point. O, the most piteous cry of the poor souls! sometimes to see 'em, and not to see 'em; now the ship
boring the moon with her main-mast, and anon swallowed with yest and froth, as you 'ld thrust a cork
into a hogshead. And then for the land-service, to
see how the bear tore out his shoulder-bone; how he
cried to me for help and said his name was Antigonus,
a nobleman. But to make an end of the ship, to see
how the sea flap-dragoned it: but, first, how the poor
souls roared, and the sea mocked them; and how the
poor gentleman roared and the bear mocked him,
both roaring louder than the sea or weather.   104
Shep. Name of mercy, when was this, boy?
Clo. Now, now: I have not winked since I saw these

sights: the men are not yet cold under water, nor the
bear half dined on the gentleman: he 's at it now.
Shep. Would I had been by, to have helped the old
man!   111
Clo. I would you had been by the ship side, to have
helped her: there your charity would have lacked
footing.
Shep. Heavy matters! heavy matters! but look thee
here, boy. Now bless thyself: thou mettest with things
dying, I with things new-born. Here 's a sight for
thee; look thee, a bearing-cloth for a squire's child!
look thee here; take up, take up, boy; open 't. So,
let 's see: it was told me I should be rich by the fairies.
This is some changeling: open 't. What 's within,
boy?   122
Clo. You 're a made old man: if the sins of your
youth are forgiven you, you 're well to live. Gold! all
gold!
Shep. This is fairy gold, boy, and 'twill prove so: up
with 't, keep it close: home, home, the next way. We
are lucky, boy; and to be so still requires nothing but
secrecy. Let my sheep go: come, good boy, the next
way home.   131
Clo. Go you the next way with your findings. I'll
go see if the bear be gone from the gentleman and
how much he hath eaten: they are never curst but
when they are hungry: if there be any of him left, I'll
bury it.
Shep. That 's a good deed. If thou mayest discern
by that which is left of him what he is, fetch me to the
sight of him.
Clo. Marry, will I; and you shall help to put him i'
the ground.   141
Shep. 'Tis a lucky day, boy, and we'll do good deeds
on 't.   [*Exeunt.*

ACT IV.

SCENE I.

Enter TIME, *the* Chorus.

Time. I, that please some, try all, both joy and
          terror
Of good and bad, that makes and unfolds error,
Now take upon me, in the name of Time,
To use my wings. Impute it not a crime
To me or my swift passage, that I slide
O'er sixteen years and leave the growth untried
Of that wide gap, since it is in my power
To o'erthrow law and in one self-born hour
To plant and o'erwhelm custom. Let me pass
The same I am, ere ancient'st order was   10
Or what is now received: I witness to
The times that brought them in; so shall I do
To the freshest things now reigning and make stale
The glistering of this present, as my tale
Now seems to it. Your patience this allowing,
I turn my glass and give my scene such growing
As you had slept between: Leontes leaving,

has this detail, stating that the shepherd sought his sheep browsing
on sea ivy. 70. **barne,** child. 71. **child,** female infant. 73. **'scape,**
escapade, especially a transgression of the laws of chastity. 90.
takes up, swallows. 95. **yest,** foam. 97. **land-service,** military
service; here, doings on land; used blunderingly. 100. **flap-dragoned,**
swallowed as one would a flapdragon, i.e., a raisin or the like snatched
up out of burning brandy in the game of snapdragon. 119. **bearing-**
cloth, child's christening robe. 125. **well to live,** well to do.
ACT IV. SCENE I. *Stage Direction:* Time, **the Chorus.** Herford suggests
that this device is borrowed from the title, *Pandosto, or the Triumph
of Time.* It may be said, however, that the triumph of time is an
expression of the unifying principle of the whole comedy. 2. **makes**
and unfolds, make and unfold. 6. **growth untried,** progress unknown.
8. **self-born,** selfsame. 14. **glistering,** glistening freshness.

The effects of his fond jealousies so grieving
That he shuts up himself, imagine me,
Gentle spectators, that I now may be   20
In fair Bohemia; and remember well,
I mentioned a son o' the king's, which Florizel
I now name to you; and with speed so pace
To speak of Perdita, now grown in grace
Equal with wondering: what of her ensues
I list not prophesy; but let Time's news
Be known when 'tis brought forth. A shepherd's
    daughter,
And what to her adheres, which follows after,
Is the argument of Time. Of this allow,
If ever you have spent time worse ere now;   30
If never, yet that Time himself doth say
He wishes earnestly you never may.   [*Exit.*

SCENE II. *Bohemia. The palace of* POLIXENES.

Enter POLIXENES *and* CAMILLO.

Pol. I pray thee, good Camillo, be no more importunate: 'tis a sickness denying thee any thing; a
death to grant this.

Cam. It is fifteen years since I saw my country:
though I have for the most part been aired abroad, I
desire to lay my bones there. Besides, the penitent
king, my master, hath sent for me; to whose feeling
sorrows I might be some allay, or I o'erween to think
so, which is another spur to my departure.   10

Pol. As thou lovest me, Camillo, wipe not out the
rest of thy services by leaving me now: the need I
have of thee thine own goodness hath made; better
not to have had thee than thus to want thee: thou,
having made me businesses which none without thee
can sufficiently manage, must either stay to execute
them thyself or take away with thee the very services
thou hast done; which if I have not enough considered, as too much I cannot, to be more thankful to
thee shall be my study, and my profit therein the
heaping friendships. Of that fatal country, Sicilia,
prithee speak no more; whose very naming punishes
me with the remembrance of that penitent, as thou
callest him, and reconciled king, my brother; whose
loss of his most precious queen and children are even
now to be afresh lamented. Say to me, when sawest
thou the Prince Florizel, my son? Kings are no less
unhappy, their issue not being gracious, than they
are in losing them when they have approved their
virtues.   32

Cam. Sir, it is three days since I saw the prince.
What his happier affairs may be, are to me unknown: but I have missingly noted, he is of late much
retired from court and is less frequent to his princely
exercises than formerly he hath appeared.   38

Pol. I have considered so much, Camillo, and with
some care; so far that I have eyes under my service
which look upon his removedness; from whom I have
this intelligence, that he is seldom from the house of a
most homely shepherd; a man, they say, that from

very nothing, and beyond the imagination of his
neighbours, is grown into an unspeakable estate.

Cam. I have heard, sir, of such a man, who hath a
daughter of most rare note: the report of her is extended more than can be thought to begin from such
a cottage.   50

Pol. That's likewise part of my intelligence; but, I
fear, the angle that plucks our son thither. Thou shalt
accompany us to the place; where we will, not appearing what we are, have some question with the
shepherd; from whose simplicity I think it not uneasy
to get the cause of my son's resort thither. Prithee, be
my present partner in this business, and lay aside the
thoughts of Sicilia.

Cam. I willingly obey your command.   60

Pol. My best Camillo! We must disguise ourselves.
          [*Exeunt.*

SCENE III. *A road near the* Shepherd's *cottage.*

Enter AUTOLYCUS, *singing.*

When daffodils begin to peer,
    With heigh! the doxy over the dale,
Why, then comes in the sweet o' the year;
    For the red blood reigns in the winter's pale.

The white sheet bleaching on the hedge,
    With heigh! the sweet birds, O, how they sing!
Doth set my pugging tooth on edge;
    For a quart of ale is a dish for a king.

The lark, that tirra-lyra chants,
    With heigh! with heigh! the thrush and the jay,   10
Are summer songs for me and my aunts,
    While we lie tumbling in the hay.

I have served Prince Florizel and in my time wore
three-pile; but now I am out of service:

But shall I go mourn for that, my dear?
    The pale moon shines by night:
And when I wander here and there,
    I then do most go right.

If tinkers may have leave to live,
    And bear the sow-skin budget,
Then my account I well may give,   20
    And in the stocks avouch it.

My traffic is sheets; when the kite builds, look to
lesser linen. My father named me Autolycus; who
being, as I am, littered under Mercury, was likewise
a snapper-up of unconsidered trifles. With die and
drab I purchased this caparison, and my revenue is
the silly cheat. Gallows and knock are too powerful on
the highway: beating and hanging are terrors to me:
for the life to come, I sleep out the thought of it. A
prize! a prize!   32

Enter Clown.

Clo. Let me see: every 'leven wether tods; every tod yields pound and odd shilling; fifteen hundred shorn, what comes the wool to?

Aut. [*Aside*] If the springe hold, the cock 's mine. 37

Clo. I cannot do 't without counters. Let me see; what am I to buy for our sheep-shearing feast? Three pound of sugar, five pound of currants, rice,—what will this sister of mine do with rice? But my father hath made her mistress of the feast, and she lays it on. She hath made me four and twenty nosegays for the shearers, three-man-song-men all, and very good ones; but they are most of them means and bases; but one puritan amongst them, and he sings psalms to hornpipes. I must have saffron to colour the warden pies; mace; dates?—none, that 's out of my note; nutmegs, seven; a race or two of ginger, but that I may beg; four pound of prunes, and as many of raisins o' the sun. 52

Aut. O that ever I was born! [*Grovelling on the ground.*

Clo. I' the name of me—

Aut. O, help me, help me! pluck but off these rags; and then, death, death!

Clo. Alack, poor soul! thou hast need of more rags to lay on thee, rather than have these off.

Aut. O sir, the loathsomeness of them offends me more than the stripes I have received, which are mighty ones and millions. 61

Clo. Alas, poor man! a million of beating may come to a great matter.

Aut. I am robbed, sir, and beaten; my money and apparel ta'en from me, and these detestable things put upon me.

Clo. What, by a horseman, or a footman?

Aut. A footman, sweet sir, a footman. 68

Clo. Indeed, he should be a footman by the garments he has left with thee: if this be a horseman's coat, it hath seen very hot service. Lend me thy hand, I'll help thee: come, lend me thy hand.

Aut. O, good sir, tenderly, O!

Clo. Alas, poor soul!

Aut. O, good sir, softly, good sir! I fear, sir, my shoulder-blade is out.

Clo. How now! canst stand?

Aut. [*Picking his pocket*] Softly, dear sir; good sir, softly. You ha' done me a charitable office. 81

Clo. Dost lack any money? I have a little money for thee.

Aut. No, good sweet sir; no, I beseech you, sir: I have a kinsman not past three quarters of a mile hence, unto whom I was going; I shall there have money, or any thing I want: offer me no money, I pray you; that kills my heart.

Clo. What manner of fellow was he that robbed you? 90

Aut. A fellow, sir, that I have known to go about with troll-my-dames: I knew him once a servant of the prince: I cannot tell, good sir, for which of his virtues it was, but he was certainly whipped out of the court.

Clo. His vices, you would say; there 's no virtue whipped out of the court: they cherish it to make it stay there; and yet it will no more but abide. 99

Aut. Vices, I would say, sir. I know this man well: he hath been since an ape-bearer; then a process-server, a bailiff; then he compassed a motion of the Prodigal Son, and married a tinker's wife within a mile where my land and living lies; and, having flown over many knavish professions, he settled only in rogue: some call him Autolycus.

Clo. Out upon him! prig, for my life, prig: he haunts wakes, fairs and bear-baitings.

Aut. Very true, sir; he, sir, he; that 's the rogue that put me into this apparel. 111

Clo. Not a more cowardly rogue in all Bohemia: if you had but looked big and spit at him, he 'ld have run.

Aut. I must confess to you, sir, I am no fighter: I am false of heart that way; and that he knew, I warrant him.

Clo. How do you now?

Aut. Sweet sir, much better than I was; I can stand and walk: I will even take my leave of you, and pace softly towards my kinsman's.

Clo. Shall I bring thee on the way? 122

Aut. No, good-faced sir; no, sweet sir.

Clo. Then fare thee well: I must go buy spices for our sheep-shearing.

Aut. Prosper you, sweet sir! [*Exit Clown.*] Your purse is not hot enough to purchase your spice. I'll be with you at your sheep-shearing too: if I make not this cheat bring out another and the shearers prove sheep, let me be unrolled and my name put in the book of virtue! 131

[*Sings*] Jog on, jog on, the foot-path way,
　　And merrily hent the stile-a:
A merry heart goes all the day,
　　Your sad tires in a mile-a. [*Exit.*

SCENE IV. *The* Shepherd's *cottage.*

Enter FLORIZEL *and* PERDITA.

Flo. These your unusual weeds to each part of you
Do give a life: no shepherdess, but Flora
Peering in April's front. This your sheep-shearing
Is as a meeting of the petty gods,
And you the queen on 't.

Per. 　　　　　　　Sir, my gracious lord,
To chide at your extremes it not becomes me:
O, pardon, that I name them! Your high self,
The gracious mark o' the land, you have obscured
With a swain's wearing, and me, poor lowly maid,
Most goddess-like prank'd up: but that our feasts 10
In every mess have folly and the feeders
Digest it with a custom, I should blush
To see you so attired, sworn, I think,
To show myself a glass.

Flo. 　　　　　　　I bless the time
When my good falcon made her flight across
Thy father's ground.

---

stupid. 38. **counters,** token coins used in reckoning. 44. **three-man-song-men,** singers of catches or rounds. 47. **psalms to hornpipes,** psalms to merry tunes. 49. **warden,** made of the warden pear. 50. **note,** apparently, list; yet if the clown could not read, it would mean "observation" or "memory." **race,** root. 52. **o' the sun,** dried in the sun. 54. **me—,** possibly the beginning of *mercy.* 92. **troll-my-dames,** a game in which the object was to "troll" balls through arches set on a board. 99. **abide,** probably, make a temporary stay. 101. **ape-bearer,** one who carries a monkey about for exhibition. 102-103. **compassed a motion,** got possession of a puppet-show. 108. **prig,** thief. 128. **cheat,** swindle, fraud. 130. **unrolled,** taken off the roll (of rogues and vagabonds). 132. **Jog on.** Written to a popular tune of the day. 133. **hent,** take.

SCENE IV. 6. **extremes,** extravagant statements. 8. **mark,** example, pattern. 12. **with a custom,** from habit. 13. **sworn,** as though you were sworn. 14. **To . . . glass,** to show me myself as in a mirror.

Per.   Now Jove afford you cause!
To me the difference forges dread; your greatness
Hath not been used to fear. Even now I tremble
To think your father, by some accident,
Should pass this way as you did: O, the Fates!   20
How would he look, to see his work so noble
Vilely bound up? What would he say? Or how
Should I, in these my borrow'd flaunts, behold
The sternness of his presence?
     Flo.   Apprehend
Nothing but jollity. The gods themselves,
Humbling their deities to love, have taken
The shapes of beasts upon them: Jupiter
Became a bull, and bellow'd; the green Neptune
A ram, and bleated; and the fire-robed god,
Golden Apollo, a poor humble swain,   30
As I seem now. Their transformations
Were never for a piece of beauty rarer,
Nor in a way so chaste, since my desires
Run not before mine honour, nor my lusts
Burn hotter than my faith.
     Per.   O, but, sir,
Your resolution cannot hold, when 'tis
Opposed, as it must be, by the power of the king:
One of these two must be necessities,
Which then will speak, that you must change this
          purpose,
Or I my life.
     Flo.   Thou dearest Perdita,   40
With these forced thoughts, I prithee, darken not
The mirth o' the feast. Or I'll be thine, my fair,
Or not my father's. For I cannot be
Mine own, not any thing to any, if
I be not thine. To this I am most constant,
Though destiny say no. Be merry, gentle;
Strangle such thoughts as these with any thing
That you behold the while. Your guests are coming:
Lift up your countenance, as it were the day
Of celebration of that nuptial which   50
We two have sworn shall come.
     Per.   O lady Fortune,
Stand you auspicious!
     Flo.   See, your guests approach:
Address yourself to entertain them sprightly,
And let 's be red with mirth.

Enter Shepherd, Clown, MOPSA, DORCAS, *and others,*
     with POLIXENES *and* CAMILLO *disguised.*

Shep. Fie, daughter! when my old wife lived, upon
This day she was both pantler, butler, cook,
Both dame and servant; welcomed all, served all;
Would sing her song and dance her turn; now here,
At upper end o' the table, now i' the middle;
On his shoulder, and his; her face o' fire   60
With labour and the thing she took to quench it,
She would to each one sip. You are retired,
As if you were a feasted one and not
The hostess of the meeting: pray you, bid
These unknown friends to 's welcome; for it is
A way to make us better friends, more known.
Come, quench your blushes and present yourself

That which you are, mistress o' the feast: come on,
And bid us welcome to your sheep-shearing,
As your good flock shall prosper.
     Per.   [*To Pol.*] Sir, welcome: 70
It is my father's will I should take on me
The hostess-ship o' the day. [*To Cam.*] You 're
          welcome, sir.
Give me those flowers there, Dorcas. Reverend sirs,
For you there 's rosemary and rue; these keep
Seeming and savour all the winter long:
Grace and remembrance be to you both,
And welcome to our shearing!
     Pol.   Shepherdess,—
A fair one are you—well you fit our ages
With flowers of winter.
     Per.   Sir, the year growing ancient,
Not yet on summer's death, nor on the birth   80
Of trembling winter, the fairest flowers o' the season
Are our carnations and streak'd gillyvors,
Which some call nature's bastards: of that kind
Our rustic garden 's barren; and I care not
To get the slips of them.
     Pol.   Wherefore, gentle maiden,
Do you neglect them?
     Per.   For I have heard it said
There is an art which in their piedness shares
With great creating nature.
     Pol.   Say there be;
Yet nature is made better by no mean
But nature makes that mean: so, over that art   90
Which you say adds to nature, is an art
That nature makes. You see, sweet maid, we marry
A gentler scion to the wildest stock,
And make conceive a bark of baser kind
By bud of nobler race: this is an art
Which does mend nature, change it rather, but
The art itself is nature.
     Per.   So it is.
     Pol. Then make your garden rich in gillyvors,
And do not call them bastards.
     Per.   I'll not put
The dibble in earth to set one slip of them;   100
No more than were I painted I would wish
This youth should say 'twere well and only therefore
Desire to breed by me. Here 's flowers for you;
Hot lavender, mints, savory, marjoram;
The marigold, that goes to bed wi' the sun
And with him rises weeping: these are flowers
Of middle summer, and I think they are given
To men of middle age. You 're very welcome.
     Cam. I should leave grazing, were I of your flock,
And only live by gazing.
     Per.   Out, alas!   110
You 'ld be so lean, that blasts of January
Would blow you through and through. Now, my
          fair'st friend,
I would I had some flowers o' the spring that might
Become your time of day; and yours, and yours,
That wear upon your virgin branches yet
Your maidenheads growing: O Proserpina,
For the flowers now, that frighted thou let'st fall

17. **difference,** of rank. 22. **bound up,** like a book. 23. **flaunts,** finery.
41. **forced,** far-fetched, unnatural. 56. **pantler,** servant in charge of
the pantry. 65. **to 's,** of ours. 75. **Seeming,** outward form. 82.
gillyvors, gillyflower—a kind of carnation. 83. **nature's bastards.** As
indicated in lines 86-88, they are a result of artificial breeding. 92-
97. **You . . . nature,** ironical allusion to the union of the prince with
the shepherdess. 104. **Hot,** eager, ardent; here, aromatic. 116.

Proserpina, stolen away by Pluto when, according to Ovid, she was
gathering flowers in her garden. 118. **Dis's waggon,** Pluto's chariot.
122. **Cytherea's,** Venus'. 123. **unmarried,** allusion not understood. Cf.
Milton's *Lycidas:* "The rathe primrose that forsaken dies." 126. **crown
imperial,** handsome fritillary, a flower from the Levant, cultivated in
English gardens. 127. **flower-de-luce,** *fleur-de-lis.* 134. **Whitsun pastorals,** thought to allude to English morris dances often performed

From Dis's waggon! daffodils,
That come before the swallow dares, and take
The winds of March with beauty; violets dim,   120
But sweeter than the lids of Juno's eyes
Or Cytherea's breath; pale primroses,
That die unmarried, ere they can behold
Bright Phœbus in his strength—a malady
Most incident to maids; bold oxlips and
The crown imperial; lilies of all kinds,
The flower-de-luce being one! O, these I lack,
To make you garlands of, and my sweet friend,
To strew him o'er and o'er!
   Flo.   What, like a corse?
   Per. No, like a bank for love to lie and play on;   130
Not like a corse; or if, not to be buried,
But quick and in mine arms. Come, take your
    flowers:
Methinks I play as I have seen them do
In Whitsun pastorals: sure this robe of mine
Does change my disposition.
   Flo.   What you do
Still betters what is done. When you speak, sweet,
I 'ld have you do it ever: when you sing,
I 'ld have you buy and sell so, so give alms,
Pray so; and, for the ordering your affairs,
To sing them too: when you do dance, I wish you   140
A wave o' the sea, that you might ever do
Nothing but that; move still, still so,
And own no other function: each your doing,
So singular in each particular,
Crowns what you are doing in the present deed,
That all your acts are queens.
   Per.   O Doricles,
Your praises are too large: but that your youth,
And the true blood which peepeth fairly through 't,
Do plainly give you out an unstain'd shepherd,
With wisdom I might fear, my Doricles,   150
You woo'd me the false way.
   Flo.   I think you have
As little skill to fear as I have purpose
To put you to 't. But come; our dance, I pray:
Your hand, my Perdita: so turtles pair,
That never mean to part.
   Per.   I'll swear for 'em.
   Pol. This is the prettiest low-born lass that ever
Ran on the green-sward: nothing she does or seems
But smacks of something greater than herself,
Too noble for this place.
   Cam.   He tells her something
That makes her blood look out: good sooth, she is   160
The queen of curds and cream.
   Clo.   Come on, strike up!
   Dor. Mopsa must be your mistress: marry, garlic,
To mend her kissing with!
   Mop.   Now, in good time!
   Clo. Not a word, a word; we stand upon our
    manners.
Come, strike up!
   [*Music. Here a dance of Shepherds and Shepherdesses.*
   Pol. Pray, good shepherd, what fair swain is this
Which dances with your daughter?

Shep. They call him Doricles; and boasts himself
To have a worthy feeding: but I have it
Upon his own report and I believe it;   170
He looks like sooth. He says he loves my daughter:
I think so too; for never gazed the moon
Upon the water as he'll stand and read
As 'twere my daughter's eyes: and, to be plain,
I think there is not half a kiss to choose
Who loves another best.
   Pol.   She dances featly.
   Shep. So she does any thing; though I report it,
That should be silent: if young Doricles
Do light upon her, she shall bring him that
Which he not dreams of.   180

Enter Servant.

   Serv. O master, if you did but hear the pedlar at the
door, you would never dance again after a tabor and
pipe; no, the bagpipe could not move you: he sings
several tunes faster than you'll tell money; he utters
them as he had eaten ballads and all men's ears grew
to his tunes.   186
   Clo. He could never come better; he shall come in.
I love a ballad but even too well, if it be doleful matter
merrily set down, or a very pleasant thing indeed and
sung lamentably.   190
   Ser. He hath songs for man or woman, of all sizes;
no milliner can so fit his customers with gloves: he
has the prettiest love-songs for maids; so without
bawdry, which is strange; with such delicate burthens
of dildos and fadings, 'jump her and thump her;' and
where some stretch-mouthed rascal would, as it were,
mean mischief and break a foul gap into the matter,
he makes the maid to answer 'Whoop, do me no
harm, good man;' puts him off, slights him, with
'Whoop, do me no harm, good man.'   201
   Pol. This is a brave fellow.
   Clo. Believe me, thou talkest of an admirable conceited fellow. Has he any unbraided wares?   204
   Serv. He hath ribbons of all the colours i' the rainbow; points more than all the lawyers in Bohemia can
learnedly handle, though they come to him by the
gross: inkles, caddisses, cambrics, lawns: why, he
sings 'em over as they were gods or goddesses; you
would think a smock were a she-angel, he so chants
to the sleeve-hand and the work about the square
on 't.   212
   Clo. Prithee bring him in; and let him approach
singing.
   Per. Forewarn him that he use no scurrilous words
in 's tunes.   [*Exit Servant.*
   Clo. You have of these pedlars, that have more in
them than you 'ld think, sister.
   Per. Ay, good brother, or go about to think.

Enter AUTOLYCUS, *singing.*

Lawn as white as driven snow;   220
Cyprus black as e'er was crow;
Gloves as sweet as damask roses;
Masks for faces and for noses;
Bugle bracelet, necklace amber,

---

at Whitsuntide, as also were the mystery plays. 143. **each your doing,**
each thing you do. 145. **what . . . deed,** what you are at present doing.
152. **skill,** reason, cause. 154. **turtles,** turtledoves, as symbols of
faithful love. 169. **feeding,** pasturage. 171. **sooth,** truth. 176.
featly, gracefully. 187. **better,** at a better time. 192. **milliner,**
dealer in goods from Milan; here, a dealer in women's wear. 195.
burthens, under-songs; here, the bass of refrains. **dildos and fadings,**

words used as part of the refrains of ballads. 198. **gap,** a gross paren-
thesis (Staunton). 204. **unbraided,** unfaded. 206. **points,** laces for
fastening clothes; also, headings in an argument. 208. **inkles,** kind of
tape. **caddisses,** worsted tapes used for garters. 212. **sleeve-hand,**
wristband. **square,** the embroidered bosom of a garment. 217. **of
these pedlars,** a sort of partitive genitive case after *have.* 221. **Cyprus,**
crepe. 224. **Bugle bracelet,** bracelet of black gloss beads.

Perfume for a lady's chamber;
Golden quoifs and stomachers,
For my lads to give their dears:
Pins and poking-sticks of steel,
What maids lack from head to heel:
Come buy of me, come; come buy, come buy;   230
Buy, lads, or else you lasses cry:
Come buy.

Clo. If I were not in love with Mopsa, thou shouldst take no money of me; but being enthralled as I am, it will also be the bondage of certain ribbons and gloves.

Mop. I was promised them against the feast; but they come not too late now.

Dor. He hath promised you more than that, or there be liars.   240

Mop. He hath paid you all he promised you: may be, he has paid you more, which will shame you to give him again.

Clo. Is there no manners left among maids? will they wear their plackets where they should bear their faces? Is there not milking-time, when you are going to bed, or kiln-hole, to whistle off these secrets, but you must be tittle-tattling before all our guests? 'tis well they are whispering: clamour your tongues, and not a word more.   251

Mop. I have done. Come, you promised me a tawdry-lace and a pair of sweet gloves.

Clo. Have I not told thee how I was cozened by the way and lost all my money?

Aut. And indeed, sir, there are cozeners abroad; therefore it behoves men to be wary.

Clo. Fear not thou, man, thou shalt lose nothing here.

Aut. I hope so, sir; for I have about me many parcels of charge.   261

Clo. What hast here? ballads?

Mop. Pray now, buy some: I love a ballad in print o' life, for then we are sure they are true.

Aut. Here 's one to a very doleful tune, how a usurer's wife was brought to bed of twenty money-bags at a burthen and how she longed to eat adders' heads and toads carbonadoed.

Mop. Is it true, think you?

Aut. Very true, and but a month old.   270

Dor. Bless me from marrying a usurer!

Aut. Here 's the midwife's name to 't, one Mistress Tale-porter, and five or six honest wives that were present. Why should I carry lies abroad?

Mop. Pray you now, buy it.

Clo. Come on, lay it by: and let 's first see moe ballads; we'll buy the other things anon.   278

Aut. Here 's another ballad of a fish, that appeared upon the coast on Wednesday the fourscore of April, forty thousand fathom above water, and sung this ballad against the hard hearts of maids: it was thought she was a woman and was turned into a cold fish for she would not exchange flesh with one that loved her: the ballad is very pitiful and as true.

Dor. Is it true too, think you?

Aut. Five justices' hands at it, and witnesses more than my pack will hold.

Clo. Lay it by too: another.   290

Aut. This is a merry ballad, but a very pretty one.

Mop. Let 's have some merry ones.

Aut. Why, this is a passing merry one and goes to the tune of 'Two maids wooing a man:' there 's scarce a maid westward but she sings it; 'tis in request, I can tell you.

Mop. We can both sing it: if thou 'lt bear a part, thou shalt hear; 'tis in three parts.   299

Dor. We had the tune on 't a month ago.

Aut. I can bear my part; you must know 'tis my occupation; have at it with you.

Song.
A. Get you hence, for I must go
    Where it fits not you to know.
    D. Whither? *M.* O, whither? *D.* Whither?
    M. It becomes thy oath full well,
        Thou to me thy secrets tell.
        D. Me too, let me go thither.
    M. Or thou goest to the grange or mill.
    D. If to either, thou dost ill.   310
A. Neither. *D.* What, neither? *A.* Neither.
    D. Thou hast sworn my love to be.
    M. Thou hast sworn it more to me:
        Then whither goest? say, whither?

Clo. We'll have this song out anon by ourselves: my father and the gentlemen are in sad talk, and we'll not trouble them. Come, bring away thy pack after me. Wenches, I'll buy for you both. Pedlar, let 's have the first choice. Follow me, girls.   320
    [*Exit with Dorcas and Mopsa.*

Aut. And you shall pay well for 'em. [*Follows singing.*
    Will you buy any tape,
    Or lace for your cape,
    My dainty duck, my dear-a?
    Any silk, any thread,
    And toys for your head,
    Of the new'st and finest, finest wear-a?
    Come to the pedlar;
    Money 's a medler,
    That doth utter all men's ware-a.   [*Exit.* 330

Re-enter Servant.

Serv. Master, there is three carters, three shepherds, three neat-herds, three swine-herds, that have made themselves all men of hair, they call themselves Saltiers, and they have a dance which the wenches say is a gallimaufry of gambols, because they are not in 't; but they themselves are o' the mind, if it be not too rough for some that know little but bowling, it will please plentifully.

Shep. Away! we'll none on 't: here has been too much homely foolery already. I know, sir, we weary you.   342

Pol. You weary those that refresh us: pray, let 's see these four threes of herdsmen.

Serv. One three of them, by their own report, sir, hath danced before the king; and not the worst of the three but jumps twelve foot and a half by the squier.

---

226. **quoifs,** close-fitting caps.   228. **poking-sticks,** rods used for stiffening the plaits of ruffs.   248. **kiln-hole,** fire hole in a kiln used in making malt; evidently a customary gossiping place.   250. **clamour,** silence. 253. **tawdry-lace,** cheap and showy lace, or neckerchief, much worn by women in Shakespeare's time; so called from St. Audrey's Fair or because St. Audrey suffered a tumor in the throat from wearing rich necklaces.   **sweet,** with perfume.   261. **parcels of charge,** valuable parcels.   268. **carbonadoed,** scored across and grilled.   279. **ballad of a fish.** Such a ballad was actually entered in the Stationers' Register in 1604.   330. **utter,** put on the market.   333. **men of hair,** dressed in skins.   334. **Saltiers,** for "satyrs."   336. **gallimaufry,** medley, jumble. 339. **bowling,** a game played mainly by the aristocracy, who might

Shep. Leave your prating: since these good men are
pleased, let them come in; but quickly now.   351
  Serv. Why, they stay at door, sir.   [*Exit.*

Here a dance of twelve Satyrs.

  Pol. O, father, you'll know more of that hereafter.
[*To Cam.*] Is it not too far gone? 'Tis time to part
  them.
He 's simple and tells much. [*To Flor.*] How now, fair
  shepherd!
Your heart is full of something that does take
Your mind from feasting. Sooth, when I was young
And handed love as you do, I was wont
To load my she with knacks: I would have ransack'd
The pedlar's silken treasury and have pour'd it   360
To her acceptance; you have let him go
And nothing marted with him. If your lass
Interpretation should abuse and call this
Your lack of love or bounty, you were straited
For a reply, at least if you make a care
Of happy holding her.
  Flo.   Old sir, I know
She prizes not such trifles as these are:
The gifts she looks from me are pack'd and lock'd
Up in my heart; which I have given already,
But not deliver'd. O, hear me breathe my life   370
Before this ancient sir, who, it should seem,
Hath sometime loved! I take thy hand, this hand,
As soft as dove's down and as white as it,
Or Ethiopian's tooth, or the fann'd snow that 's
  bolted
By the northern blasts twice o'er.
  Pol.   What follows this?
How prettily the young swain seems to wash
The hand was fair before! I have put you out:
But to your protestation; let me hear
What you profess.
  Flo.   Do, and be witness to 't.
  Pol. And this my neighbour too?
  Flo.   And he, and more   380
Than he, and men, the earth, the heavens, and all:
That, were I crown'd the most imperial monarch,
Thereof most worthy, were I the fairest youth
That ever made eye swerve, had force and knowledge
More than was ever man's, I would not prize them
Without her love; for her employ them all;
Commend them and condemn them to her service
Or to their own perdition.
  Pol.   Fairly offer'd.
  Cam. This shows a sound affection.
  Shep.   But, my daughter,
Say you the like to him?
  Per.   I cannot speak   390
So well, nothing so well; no, nor mean better:
By the pattern of mine own thoughts I cut out
The purity of his.
  Shep.   Take hands, a bargain!
And, friends unknown, you shall bear witness to 't:
I give my daughter to him, and will make
Her portion equal his.
  Flo.   O, that must be

I' the virtue of your daughter: one being dead,
I shall have more than you can dream of yet;
Enough then for your wonder. But, come on,
Contract us 'fore these witnesses.
  Shep.   Come, your hand;   400
And, daughter, yours.
  Pol.   Soft, swain, awhile, beseech you;
Have you a father?
  Flo.   I have: but what of him?
  Pol. Knows he of this?
  Flo.   He neither does nor shall.
  Pol. Methinks a father
Is at the nuptial of his son a guest
That best becomes the table. Pray you once more,
Is not your father grown incapable
Of reasonable affairs? is he not stupid
With age and altering rheums? can he speak? hear?
Know man from man? dispute his own estate?   410
Lies he not bed-rid? and again does nothing
But what he did being childish?
  Flo.   No, good sir;
He has his health and ampler strength indeed
Than most have of his age.
  Pol.   By my white beard,
You offer him, if this be so, a wrong
Something unfilial: reason my son
Should choose himself a wife, but as good reason
The father, all whose joy is nothing else
But fair posterity, should hold some counsel
In such a business.
  Flo.   I yield all this;   420
But for some other reasons, my grave sir,
Which 'tis not fit you know, I not acquaint
My father of this business.
  Pol.   Let him know 't.
  Flo. He shall not.
  Pol.   Prithee, let him.
  Flo.   No, he must not.
  Shep. Let him, my son: he shall not need to grieve
At knowing of thy choice.
  Flo.   Come, come, he must not.
Mark our contract.
  Pol.   Mark your divorce, young sir,
                [*Discovering himself.*
Whom son I dare not call; thou art too base
To be acknowledged: thou a sceptre's heir,
That thus affect'st a sheep-hook! Thou old traitor,   430
I am sorry that by hanging thee I can
But shorten thy life one week. And thou, fresh piece
Of excellent witchcraft, who of force must know
The royal fool thou copest with,—
  Shep.   O, my heart!
  Pol. I'll have thy beauty scratch'd with briers, and
  made
More homely than thy state. For thee, fond boy,
If I may ever know thou dost but sigh
That thou no more shalt see this knack, as never
I mean thou shalt, we'll bar thee from succession;
Not hold thee of our blood, no, not our kin,   440
Far than Deucalion off: mark thou my words:
Follow us to the court. Thou churl, for this time,

---

find the satyr dance too rough. **346. danced before the king.** Thorndike (*Influence of Beaumont and Fletcher on Shakespeare*, pp. 32-34) argues
that this masque of satyrs was borrowed from Jonson's *Masque of Oberon*,
acted at Court, January 1, 1611. This play would, then, be dated after
that event. 348. **squier,** foot rule. 358. **handed,** handled. 359.
knacks, knickknacks. 362. **marted,** trafficked. 363. **Interpretation**

should abuse, should interpret wrongly. 364. **straited,** embarrassed.
374. **bolted,** sifted. 409. **altering rheums,** weakening colds. 416.
reason, it is reasonable. 438. **knack,** knickknack, referring to Perdita.
441. **Far,** F: *farre,* meaning "farther." **Deucalion,** the Noah of classical
mythology.

Though full of our displeasure, yet we free thee
From the dead blow of it. And you, enchantment,—
Worthy enough a herdsman; yea, him too,
That makes himself, but for our honour therein,
Unworthy thee,—if ever henceforth thou
These rural latches to his entrance open,
Or hoop his body more with thy embraces,
I will devise a death as cruel for thee   450
As thou art tender to 't.   [*Exit.*
    Per.   Even here undone!
I was not much afeard; for once or twice
I was about to speak and tell him plainly,
The selfsame sun that shines upon his court
Hides not his visage from our cottage but
Looks on alike. Will 't please you, sir, be gone?
I told you what would come of this: beseech you,
Of your own state take care: this dream of mine,—
Being now awake, I'll queen it no inch farther,
But milk my ewes and weep.
    Cam.   Why, how now, father!   460
Speak ere thou diest.
    Shep.   I cannot speak, nor think,
Nor dare to know that which I know. O sir!
You have undone a man of fourscore three,
That thought to fill his grave in quiet, yea,
To die upon the bed my father died,
To lie close by his honest bones: but now
Some hangman must put on my shroud and lay me
Where no priest shovels in dust. O cursed wretch,
That knew'st this was the prince, and wouldst
    adventure
To mingle faith with him! Undone! undone!   470
If I might die within this hour, I have lived
To die when I desire.   [*Exit.*
    Flo.   Why look you so upon me?
I am but sorry, not afeard; delay'd,
But nothing alter'd: what I was, I am;
More straining on for plucking back, not following
My leash unwillingly.
    Cam.   Gracious my lord,
You know your father's temper: at this time
He will allow no speech, which I do guess
You do not purpose to him; and as hardly
Will he endure your sight as yet, I fear: 480
Then, till the fury of his highness settle,
Come not before him.
    Flo.   I not purpose it.
I think, Camillo?
    Cam.   Even he, my lord.
    Per. How often have I told you 'twould be thus!
How often said, my dignity would last
But till 'twere known!
    Flo.   It cannot fail but by
The violation of my faith; and then
Let nature crush the sides o' the earth together
And mar the seeds within! Lift up thy looks:
From my succession wipe me, father; I   490
Am heir to my affection.
    Cam.   Be advised.
    Flo. I am, and by my fancy: if my reason
Will thereto be obedient, I have reason;

If not, my senses, better pleased with madness,
Do bid it welcome.
    Cam.   This is desperate, sir.
    Flo. So call it: but it does fulfil my vow;
I needs must think it honesty. Camillo,
Not for Bohemia, nor the pomp that may
Be thereat glean'd, for all the sun sees or
The close earth wombs or the profound seas hide   500
In unknown fathoms, will I break my oath
To this my fair beloved: therefore, I pray you,
As you have ever been my father's honour'd friend,
When he shall miss me,—as, in faith, I mean not
To see him any more,—cast your good counsels
Upon his passion: let myself and fortune
Tug for the time to come. This you may know
And so deliver, I am put to sea
With her whom here I cannot hold on shore;
And most opportune to our need I have   510
A vessel rides fast by, but not prepared
For this design. What course I mean to hold
Shall nothing benefit your knowledge, nor
Concern me the reporting.
    Cam.   O my lord!
I would your spirit were easier for advice,
Or stronger for your need.
    Flo.   Hark, Perdita. [*Drawing her aside.*
I'll hear you by and by.
    Cam.   He's irremoveable,
Resolved for flight. Now were I happy, if
His going I could frame to serve my turn,
Save him from danger, do him love and honour,   520
Purchase the sight again of dear Sicilia
And that unhappy king, my master, whom
I so much thirst to see.
    Flo.   Now, good Camillo;
I am so fraught with curious business that
I leave out ceremony.
    Cam.   Sir, I think
You have heard of my poor services, i' the love
That I have borne your father?
    Flo.   Very nobly
Have you deserved: it is my father's music
To speak your deeds, not little of his care
To have them recompensed as thought on.
    Cam.   Well, my lord,   530
If you may please to think I love the king
And through him what is nearest to him, which is
Your gracious self, embrace but my direction:
If your more ponderous and settled project
May suffer alteration, on mine honour,
I'll point you where you shall have such receiving
As shall become your highness; where you may
Enjoy your mistress, for the whom, I see,
There 's no disjunction to be made, but by—
As heavens forfend!—your ruin; marry her,   540
And, with my best endeavours in your absence,
Your discontenting father strive to qualify
And bring him up to liking.
    Flo.   How, Camillo,
May this, almost a miracle, be done?
That I may call thee something more than man

---

444. **enchantment,** referring to Perdita. 445. **yea, him,** i.e., worthy of him. 456. **alike,** possibly, indifferently. 465. **died,** i.e., died on. 468. **Where . . . dust.** It was the duty of the priest in the burial service to cast earth on the body while saying, "Earth to earth." The shepherd's meaning is that he will be deprived of the rite of Christian burial. 475. **straining on,** i.e., like a hound on the leash; a figure from coursing.

489. **mar the seeds,** a frequent figure in Shakespeare for the destruction of life. 513. **Shall . . . knowledge,** shall not profit you to know. 542. **discontenting,** discontented, displeased. **qualify,** appease, pacify. 543. **bring . . . to,** raise him to the pitch of. 548. **unthought-on,** unexpected. 561. **divides him,** probably, is divided in his speech. 571. **point you forth,** indicate to you. 586. **subdue the cheek,** i.e.,

And after that trust to thee.
Cam. Have you thought on
A place whereto you'll go?
Flo. Not any yet:
But as the unthought-on accident is guilty
To what we wildly do, so we profess
Ourselves to be the slaves of chance and flies 550
Of every wind that blows.
Cam. Then list to me:
This follows, if you will not change your purpose
But undergo this flight, make for Sicilia,
And there present yourself and your fair princess,
For so I see she must be, 'fore Leontes:
She shall be habited as it becomes
The partner of your bed. Methinks I see
Leontes opening his free arms and weeping
His welcomes forth; asks thee the son forgiveness,
As 'twere i' the father's person; kisses the hands 560
Of your fresh princess; o'er and o'er divides him
'Twixt his unkindness and his kindness; the one
He chides to hell and bids the other grow
Faster than thought or time.
Flo. Worthy Camillo,
What colour for my visitation shall I
Hold up before him?
Cam. Sent by the king your father
To greet him and to give him comforts. Sir,
The manner of your bearing towards him, with
What you as from your father shall deliver, 569
Things known betwixt us three, I'll write you down:
The which shall point you forth at every sitting
What you must say; that he shall not perceive
But that you have your father's bosom there
And speak his very heart.
Flo. I am bound to you:
There is some sap in this.
Cam. A course more promising
Than a wild dedication of yourselves
To unpath'd waters, undream'd shores, most certain
To miseries enough; no hope to help you,
But as you shake off one to take another;
Nothing so certain as your anchors, who 580
Do their best office, if they can but stay you
Where you'll be loath to be: besides you know
Prosperity 's the very bond of love,
Whose fresh complexion and whose heart together
Affliction alters.
Per. One of these is true:
I think affliction may subdue the cheek,
But not take in the mind.
Cam. Yea, say you so?
There shall not at your father's house these seven
years
Be born another such.
Flo. My good Camillo,
She is as forward of her breeding as 590
†She is i' the rear o' our birth.
Cam. I cannot say 'tis pity
She lacks instructions, for she seems a mistress
To most that teach.
Per. Your pardon, sir; for this

I'll blush you thanks.
Flo. My prettiest Perdita!
But O, the thorns we stand upon! Camillo,
Preserver of my father, now of me,
The medicine of our house, how shall we do?
We are not furnish'd like Bohemia's son,
Nor shall appear in Sicilia.
Cam. My lord,
Fear none of this: I think you know my fortunes 600
Do all lie there: it shall be so my care
To have you royally appointed as if
The scene you play were mine. For instance, sir,
That you may know you shall not want, one word.
[*They talk aside.*

Re-enter AUTOLYCUS.

Aut. Ha, ha! what a fool Honesty is! and Trust, his
sworn brother, a very simple gentleman! I have sold
all my trumpery; not a counterfeit stone, not a ribbon,
glass, pomander, brooch, table-book, ballad, knife,
tape, glove, shoe-tie, bracelet, horn-ring, to keep my
pack from fasting: they throng who should buy first,
as if my trinkets had been hallowed and brought a
benediction to the buyer: by which means I saw
whose purse was best in picture; and what I saw, to
my good use I remembered. My clown, who wants but
something to be a reasonable man, grew so in love
with the wenches' song, that he would not stir his
pettitoes till he had both tune and words; which so
drew the rest of the herd to me that all their other
senses stuck in ears: you might have pinched a placket,
it was senseless; 'twas nothing to geld a codpiece of a
purse; I could have filed keys off that hung in chains:
no hearing, no feeling, but my sir's song, and admiring the nothing of it. So that in this time of lethargy
I picked and cut most of their festival purses; and had
not the old man come in with whoo-bub against his
daughter and the king's son and scared my choughs
from the chaff, I had not left a purse alive in the
whole army. [*Camillo, Florizel, and Perdita come forward.*
Cam. Nay, but my letters, by this means being
there
So soon as you arrive, shall clear that doubt. 632
Flo. And those that you'll procure from King
Leontes—
Cam. Shall satisfy your father.
Per. Happy be you!
All that you speak shows fair.
Cam. Who have we here?
[*Seeing Autolycus.*
We'll make an instrument of this, omit
Nothing may give us aid.
Aut. If they have overheard me now, why, hanging.
Cam. How now, good fellow! why shakest thou so?
Fear not, man; here 's no harm intended to thee. 642
Aut. I am a poor fellow, sir.
Cam. Why, be so still; here 's nobody will steal that
from thee: yet for the outside of thy poverty we must
make an exchange; therefore disease thee instantly,—
thou must think there 's a necessity in 't,—and change
garments with this gentleman: though the penny-

with tears. 587. **take in,** overcome. 591. **o' our,** so Neilson; Rowe; *o' her;* Globe, following F, omits *o'.* 597. **medicine,** physician. 599. **appear,** i.e., as such. 609. **pomander,** ball composed of perfume. **table-book,** notebook. 615. **best in picture,** i.e., to look at. 619. **pettitoes,** pig's feet; here, feet. 621. **stuck in ears,** were occupied with their ears. 622. **pinched a placket,** stolen a petticoat. 623.

geld a codpiece, remove from a pocket. 626. **my sir's,** the Clown's. 629. **whoo-bub,** hubbub. 630. **choughs . . . chaff,** jackdaws from the chaff; here, the Clown's from his allurements. 636. **this,** i.e., Autolycus. 646. **disease,** undress.

worth on his side be the worst, yet hold thee, there 's
some boot. 650

Aut. I am a poor fellow, sir. [*Aside*] I know ye well
enough.

Cam. Nay, prithee, dispatch: the gentleman is half
flayed already.

Aut. Are you in earnest, sir? [*Aside*] I smell the trick
on 't.

Flo. Dispatch, I prithee.

Aut. Indeed, I have had earnest; but I cannot with
conscience take it.

Cam. Unbuckle, unbuckle. 660

            [*Florizel and Autolycus exchange garments.*

Fortunate mistress,—let my prophecy
Come home to ye!—you must retire yourself
Into some covert: take your sweetheart's hat
And pluck it o'er your brows, muffle your face,
Dismantle you, and, as you can, disliken
The truth of your own seeming; that you may—
For I do fear eyes over—to shipboard
Get undescried.

Per.   I see the play so lies
That I must bear a part.

Cam.   No remedy.
Have you done there?

Flo.   Should I now meet my father, 670
He would not call me son.

Cam.   Nay, you shall have no hat.

                    [*Giving it to Perdita.*

Come, lady, come. Farewell, my friend.

Aut.   Adieu, sir.

Flo. O Perdita, what have we twain forgot!
Pray you, a word.

Cam. [*Aside*] What I do next, shall be to tell the
    king
Of this escape and whither they are bound;
Wherein my hope is I shall so prevail
To force him after: in whose company
I shall review Sicilia, for whose sight
I have a woman's longing.

Flo.   Fortune speed us! 680
Thus we set on, Camillo, to the sea-side.

Cam. The swifter speed the better.

        [*Exeunt Florizel, Perdita, and Camillo.*

Aut. I understand the business, I hear it: to have an
open ear, a quick eye, and a nimble hand, is necessary
for a cut-purse; a good nose is requisite also, to smell
out work for the other senses. I see this is the time that
the unjust man doth thrive. What an exchange had
this been without boot! What a boot is here with this
exchange! Sure the gods do this year connive at us,
and we may do any thing extempore. The prince
himself is about a piece of iniquity, stealing away from
his father with his clog at his heels: if I thought it were
a piece of honesty to acquaint the king withal, I
would not do 't: I hold it the more knavery to conceal
it; and therein am I constant to my profession. 698

Re-enter Clown *and* Shepherd.

Aside, aside; here is more matter for a hot brain:
every lane's end, every shop, church, session, hanging, yields a careful man work.

Clo. See, see; what a man you are now! There is no
other way but to tell the king she 's a changeling and
none of your flesh and blood.

Shep. Nay, but hear me.

Clo. Nay, but hear me.

Shep. Go to, then. 708

Clo. She being none of your flesh and blood, your
flesh and blood has not offended the king; and so your
flesh and blood is not to be punished by him. Show
those things you found about her, those secret things,
all but what she has with her: this being done, let the
law go whistle: I warrant you.

Shep. I will tell the king all, every word, yea, and
his son's pranks too; who, I may say, is no honest man,
neither to his father nor to me, to go about to make me
the king's brother-in-law. 720

Clo. Indeed, brother-in-law was the farthest off you
could have been to him and then your blood had been
the dearer by I know how much an ounce.

Aut. [*Aside*] Very wisely, puppies!

Shep. Well, let us to the king: there is that in this
fardel will make him scratch his beard.

Aut. [*Aside*] I know not what impediment this complaint may be to the flight of my master.

Clo. Pray heartily he be at palace. 730

Aut. [*Aside*] Though I am not naturally honest, I
am so sometimes by chance: let me pocket up my
pedlar's excrement. [*Takes off his false beard.*] How now,
rustics! whither are you bound?

Shep. To the palace, an it like your worship.

Aut. Your affairs there, what, with whom, the condition of that fardel, the place of your dwelling, your
names, your ages, of what having, breeding, and any
thing that is fitting to be known, discover. 741

Clo. We are but plain fellows, sir.

Aut. A lie; you are rough and hairy. Let me have no
lying: it becomes none but tradesmen, and they often
give us soldiers the lie: but we pay them for it with
stamped coin, not stabbing steel; therefore they do not
give us the lie.

Clo. Your worship had like to have given us one, if
you had not taken yourself with the manner. 751

Shep. Are you a courtier, an 't like you, sir?

Aut. Whether it like me or no, I am a courtier. Seest
thou not the air of the court in these enfoldings? hath
not my gait in it the measure of the court? receives not
thy nose court-odour from me? reflect I not on thy
baseness court-contempt? Thinkest thou, for that I
insinuate, or †toaze from thee thy business, I am
therefore no courtier? I am courtier cap-a-pe; and
one that will either push on or pluck back thy business there: whereupon I command thee to open thy
affair.

Shep. My business, sir, is to the king.

Aut. What advocate hast thou to him?

Shep. I know not, an 't like you. 766

Clo. Advocate 's the court-word for a pheasant: say
you have none.

Shep. None, sir; I have no pheasant, cock nor hen.

Aut. How blessed are we that are not simple men!
Yet nature might have made me as these are,
Therefore I will not disdain.

650. **boot,** something to boot (giving him money). 654. **flayed,** skinned;
here, undressed. 663. **covert,** secret place. 665-666. **disliken . . .
seeming,** disguise your outward appearance. 667. **eyes over,** over-
seeing eyes. 694. **clog,** encumbrance, referring to Perdita. 699. **hot,**
active, ardent. 704. **changeling,** child left by the fairies. 719. **go**

about, make it his object. 727. **fardel,** bundle, burden. 733. **excrement,** hair, beard. 745. **they . . . lie,** i.e., they sell it to us (Johnson).
750-751. **taken . . . manner,** taken with the thing stolen in your possession (a legal phrase); hence, caught yourself in the act. 759. **toaze,**
tear (used figuratively). 761. **cap-a-pe,** head to foot. 768. **pheasant,**

Clo. This cannot be but a great courtier.

Shep. His garments are rich, but he wears them not handsomely. 776

Clo. He seems to be the more noble in being fantastical: a great man, I'll warrant; I know by the picking on 's teeth.

Aut. The fardel there? what 's i' the fardel? Wherefore that box? 781

Shep. Sir, there lies such secrets in this fardel and box, which none must know but the king; and which he shall know within this hour, if I may come to the speech of him.

Aut. Age, thou hast lost thy labour.

Shep. Why, sir?

Aut. The king is not at the palace; he is gone aboard a new ship to purge melancholy and air himself: for, if thou beest capable of things serious, thou must know the king is full of grief. 791

Shep. So 'tis said, sir; about his son, that should have married a shepherd's daughter.

Aut. If that shepherd be not in hand-fast, let him fly: the curses he shall have, the tortures he shall feel, will break the back of man, the heart of monster.

Clo. Think you so, sir? 798

Aut. Not he alone shall suffer what wit can make heavy and vengeance bitter; but those that are germane to him, though removed fifty times, shall all come under the hangman: which though it be great pity, yet it is necessary. An old sheep-whistling rogue, a ram-tender, to offer to have his daughter come into grace! Some say he shall be stoned; but that death is too soft for him, say I: draw our throne into a sheep-cote! all deaths are too few, the sharpest too easy.

Clo. Has the old man e'er a son, sir, do you hear, an 't like you, sir? 810

Aut. He has a son, who shall be flayed alive; then 'nointed over with honey, set on the head of a wasp's nest; then stand till he be three quarters and a dram dead; then recovered again with aqua-vitæ or some other hot infusion; then, raw as he is, and in the hottest day prognostication proclaims, shall he be set against a brick-wall, the sun looking with a southward eye upon him, where he is to behold him with flies blown to death. But what talk we of these traitorly rascals, whose miseries are to be smiled at, their offences being so capital? Tell me, for you seem to be honest plain men, what you have to the king: being something gently considered, I'll bring you where he is aboard, tender your persons to his presence, whisper him in your behalfs; and if it be in man besides the king to effect your suits, here is man shall do it. 828

Clo. He seems to be of great authority: close with him, give him gold; and though authority be a stubborn bear, yet he is oft led by the nose with gold: show the inside of your purse to the outside of his hand, and no more ado. Remember 'stoned,' and 'flayed alive.'

Shep. An 't please you, sir, to undertake the business for us, here is that gold I have: I'll make it as much more and leave this young man in pawn till I bring it you.

Aut. After I have done what I promised?

Shep. Ay, sir. 840

Aut. Well, give me the moiety. Are you a party in this business?

Clo. In some sort, sir: but though my case be a pitiful one, I hope I shall not be flayed out of it. 844

Aut. O, that 's the case of the shepherd's son: hang him, he'll be made an example.

Clo. Comfort, good comfort! We must to the king and show our strange sights: he must know 'tis none of your daughter nor my sister; we are gone else. Sir, I will give you as much as this old man does when the business is performed, and remain, as he says, your pawn till it be brought you. 853

Aut. I will trust you. Walk before toward the sea-side; go on the right hand: I will but look upon the hedge and follow you.

Clo. We are blest in this man, as I may say, even blest.

Shep. Let 's before as he bids us: he was provided to do us good. [*Exeunt Shepherd and Clown.* 860

Aut. If I had a mind to be honest, I see Fortune would not suffer me: she drops booties in my mouth. I am courted now with a double occasion, gold and a means to do the prince my master good; which who knows how that may turn back to my advancement? I will bring these two moles, these blind ones, aboard him: if he think it fit to shore them again and that the complaint they have to the king concerns him nothing, let him call me rogue for being so far officious; for I am proof against that title and what shame else belongs to 't. To him will I present them: there may be matter in it. [*Exit.* 874

ACT V.

SCENE I. *A room in* LEONTES' *palace.*

Enter LEONTES, CLEOMENES, DION, PAULINA, *and Servants.*

Cleo. Sir, you have done enough, and have perform'd
A saint-like sorrow: no fault could you make,
Which you have not redeem'd; indeed, paid down
More penitence than done trespass: at the last,
Do as the heavens have done, forget your evil;
With them forgive yourself.

Leon.   Whilst I remember
Her and her virtues, I cannot forget
My blemishes in them, and so still think of
The wrong I did myself; which was so much,
That heirless it hath made my kingdom and   10
Destroy'd the sweet'st companion that e'er man
Bred his hopes out of.

Paul.   True, too true, my lord:
If, one by one, you wedded all the world,
Or from the all that are took something good,
To make a perfect woman, she you kill'd
Would be unparallel'd.

Leon.   I think so. Kill'd!
She I kill'd! I did so: but thou strikest me
Sorely, to say I did; it is as bitter
Upon thy tongue as in my thought: now, good now,

F: *Pheazant*; Kenricks' emendation, *present*, is frequently adopted; it presupposes a blunder in words by the shepherd. 779. **picking on 's teeth**, a stylish thing to do in Shakespeare's time. 794. **hand-fast**, firm hold. 807. **our throne**, indicative of Autolycus' assumed position of courtier. 824. **being . . . considered**, if I receive a gentlemanly con- sideration, i.e., a bribe. 825. **tender . . . persons**, introduce you. 830. **close with him**, accept his offer. 845. **case**, condition, and skin.

Say so but seldom.

Cleo. Not at all, good lady: 20
You might have spoken a thousand things that
        would
Have done the time more benefit and graced
Your kindness better.

Paul. You are one of those
Would have him wed again.

Dion. If you would not so,
You pity not the state, nor the remembrance
Of his most sovereign name; consider little
What dangers, by his highness' fail of issue,
May drop upon his kingdom and devour
Incertain lookers on. What were more holy
Than to rejoice the former queen is well? 30
What holier than, for royalty's repair,
For present comfort and for future good,
To bless the bed of majesty again
With a sweet fellow to 't?

Paul. There is none worthy,
Respecting her that 's gone. Besides, the gods
Will have fulfill'd their secret purposes;
For has not the divine Apollo said,
Is 't not the tenour of his oracle,
That King Leontes shall not have an heir
Till his lost child be found? which that it shall, 40
Is all as monstrous to our human reason
As my Antigonus to break his grave
And come again to me; who, on my life,
Did perish with the infant. 'Tis your counsel
My lord should to the heavens be contrary,
Oppose against their wills. [*To Leontes.*] Care not for
        issue;
The crown will find an heir: great Alexander
Left his to the worthiest; so his successor
Was like to be the best.

Leon. Good Paulina,
Who hast the memory of Hermione, 50
I know, in honour, O, that ever I
Had squared me to thy counsel! then, even now,
I might have look'd upon my queen's full eyes,
Have taken treasure from her lips—

Paul. And left them
More rich for what they yielded.

Leon. Thou speak'st truth.
No more such wives; therefore, no wife: one worse,
And better used, would make her sainted spirit
Again possess her corpse, and on this stage,
Where we 're offenders now, appear soul-vex'd,
†And begin, 'Why to me?'

Paul. Had she such power, 60
She had just cause.

Leon. She had; and would incense me
To murder her I married.

Paul. I should so.
Were I the ghost that walk'd, I 'ld bid you mark
Her eye, and tell me for what dull part in 't
You chose her; then I 'ld shriek, that even your ears
Should rift to hear me; and the words that follow'd
Should be 'Remember mine.'

Leon. Stars, stars,
And all eyes else dead coals! Fear thou no wife;

I'll have no wife, Paulina.

Paul. Will you swear
Never to marry but by my free leave? 70

Leon. Never, Paulina; so be blest my spirit!

Paul. Then, good my lords, bear witness to his oath.

Cleo. You tempt him over-much.

Paul. Unless another,
As like Hermione as is her picture,
Affront his eye.

Cleo. Good madam,—

Paul. I have done.
Yet, if my lord will marry,—if you will, sir,
No remedy, but you will,—give me the office
To choose you a queen: she shall not be so young
As was your former; but she shall be such
As, walk'd your first queen's ghost, it should take joy 80
To see her in your arms.

Leon. My true Paulina,
We shall not marry till thou bid'st us.

Paul. That
Shall be when your first queen 's again in breath;
Never till then.

Enter a Gentleman.

Gent. One that gives out himself Prince Florizel,
Son of Polixenes, with his princess, she
The fairest I have yet beheld, desires access
To your high presence.

Leon. What with him? he comes not
Like to his father's greatness: his approach,
So out of circumstance and sudden, tells us 90
'Tis not a visitation framed, but forced
By need and accident. What train?

Gent. But few,
And those but mean.

Leon. His princess, say you, with him?

Gent. Ay, the most peerless piece of earth, I think,
That e'er the sun shone bright on.

Paul. O Hermione,
As every present time doth boast itself
Above a better gone, so must thy grave
Give way to what 's seen now! Sir, you yourself
Have said and writ so, but your writing now
Is colder than that theme, 'She had not been, 100
Nor was not to be equall'd;'—thus your verse
Flow'd with her beauty once: 'tis shrewdly ebb'd,
To say you have seen a better.

Gent. Pardon, madam:
The one I have almost forgot,—your pardon,—
The other, when she has obtain'd your eye,
Will have your tongue too. This is a creature,
Would she begin a sect, might quench the zeal
Of all professors else, make proselytes
Of who she but bid follow.

Paul. How! not women?

Gent. Women will love her, that she is a woman 110
More worth than any man; men, that she is
The rarest of all women.

Leon. Go, Cleomenes;
Yourself, assisted with your honour'd friends,
Bring them to our embracement. Still, 'tis strange
        [*Exeunt Cleomenes and others.*

ACT V. SCENE I. 27. **fail**, failure. 29. **Incertain**, not knowing
what to think or do (Schmidt). 30. **well**, happy, at rest. 35. **Respecting**, in comparison with. 45. **should . . . contrary.** This is the religious theme of the play; it explains the action of Hermione in hiding
herself away and permitting Leontes to expiate his sin. 52. **squared
me**, adjusted or regulated myself. 60. **'Why to me?'** i.e., why this
offense to me? 66. **rift**, split. 75. **Affront**, confront. 113. **assisted
with**, accompanied by. 123. **Unfurnish**, deprive, divest. 127. **hit,**

He thus should steal upon us.
      Paul.   Had our prince,
jewel of children, seen this hour, he had pair'd
Well with this lord: there was not full a month
Between their births.
      Leon. Prithee, no more; cease; thou know'st
He dies to me again when talk'd of: sure,   120
When I shall see this gentleman, thy speeches
Will bring me to consider that which may
Unfurnish me of reason. They are come.

      Re-enter CLEOMENES *and others, with* FLORIZEL *and*
                    PERDITA.

Your mother was most true to wedlock, prince;
For she did print your royal father off,
Conceiving you: were I but twenty one,
Your father's image is so hit in you,
His very air, that I should call you brother,
As I did him, and speak of something wildly
By us perform'd before. Most dearly welcome!   130
And your fair princess,—goddess!—O, alas!
I lost a couple, that 'twixt heaven and earth
Might thus have stood begetting wonder as
You, gracious couple, do: and then I lost—
All mine own folly—the society,
Amity too, of your brave father, whom,
Though bearing misery, I desire my life
Once more to look on him.
      Flo.   By his command
Have I here touch'd Sicilia and from him
Give you all greetings that a king, at friend,   140
Can send his brother: and, but infirmity
Which waits upon worn times hath something seized
His wish'd ability, he had himself
The lands and waters 'twixt your throne and his
Measured to look upon you; whom he loves—
He bade me say so—more than all the sceptres
And those that bear them living.
      Leon.   O my brother,
Good gentleman! the wrongs I have done thee stir
Afresh within me, and these thy offices,
So rarely kind, are as interpreters   150
Of my behind-hand slackness. Welcome hither,
As is the spring to the earth. And hath he too
Exposed this paragon to the fearful usage,
At least ungentle, of the dreadful Neptune,
To greet a man not worth her pains, much less
The adventure of her person?
      Flo.   Good my lord,
She came from Libya.
      Leon.   Where the warlike Smalus,
That noble honour'd lord, is fear'd and loved?
      Flo. Most royal sir, from thence; from him, whose
                    daughter
His tears proclaim'd his, parting with her: thence,   160
A prosperous south-wind friendly, we have cross'd,
To execute the charge my father gave me
For visiting your highness: my best train
I have from your Sicilian shores dismiss'd;
Who for Bohemia bend, to signify
Not only my success in Libya, sir,
But my arrival and my wife's in safety

Here where we are.
      Leon.   The blessed gods
Purge all infection from our air whilst you
Do climate here! You have a holy father,   170
A graceful gentleman; against whose person,
So sacred as it is, I have done sin:
For which the heavens, taking angry note,
Have left me issueless; and your father's blest,
As he from heaven merits it, with you
Worthy his goodness. What might I have been,
Might I a son and daughter now have look'd on,
Such goodly things as you!

      Enter a Lord.

      Lord.   Most noble sir,
That which I shall report will bear no credit,
Were not the proof so nigh. Please you, great sir,   180
Bohemia greets you from himself by me;
Desires you to attach his son, who has—
His dignity and duty both cast off—
Fled from his father, from his hopes, and with
A shepherd's daughter.
      Leon.   Where 's Bohemia? speak.
      Lord. Here in your city; I now came from him:
I speak amazedly; and it becomes
My marvel and my message. To your court
Whiles he was hastening, in the chase, it seems,
Of this fair couple, meets he on the way   190
The father of this seeming lady and
Her brother, having both their country quitted
With this young prince.
      Flo.   Camillo has betray'd me;
Whose honour and whose honesty till now
Endured all weathers.
      Lord.   Lay 't so to his charge:
He 's with the king your father.
      Leon.   Who? Camillo?
      Lord. Camillo, sir; I spake with him; who now
Has these poor men in question. Never saw I
Wretches so quake: they kneel, they kiss the earth;
Forswear themselves as often as they speak: 200
Bohemia stops his ears, and threatens them
With divers deaths in death.
      Per.   O my poor father!
The heaven sets spies upon us, will not have
Our contract celebrated.
      Leon.   You are married?
      Flo. We are not, sir, nor are we like to be;
The stars, I see, will kiss the valleys first:
The odds for high and low 's alike.
      Leon.   My lord,
Is this the daughter of a king?
      Flo.   She is,
When once she is my wife.
      Leon. That 'once,' I see by your good father's
                    speed,   210
Will come on very slowly. I am sorry,
Most sorry, you have broken from his liking
Where you were tied in duty, and as sorry
Your choice is not so rich in worth as beauty,
That you might well enjoy her.
      Flo.   Dear, look up:

exactly reproduced. 137. **my life,** while I live. 140. **at friend,**
friendly. 142. **worn times,** old age. 149. **offices,** messages of good will.
156. **adventure,** hazard. 170. **climate,** dwell, reside (in this clime).
171. **graceful,** full of grace, gracious. 187. **amazedly,** perplexedly.

it, i.e., my manner of speaking. 188. **marvel,** astonishment, wonder.
207. **The . . . alike.** Fortune is the same for the high and low. 214.
worth, merit.

Though Fortune, visible an enemy,
Should chase us with my father, power no jot
Hath she to change our loves. Beseech you, sir,
Remember since you owed no more to time
Than I do now: with thought of such affections,   220
Step forth mine advocate; at your request
My father will grant precious things as trifles.
    Leon. Would he do so, I 'ld beg your precious
      mistress,
Which he counts but a trifle.
    Paul.   Sir, my liege,
Your eye hath too much youth in 't: not a month
'Fore your queen died, she was more worth such
    gazes
Than what you look on now.
    Leon.   I thought of her,
Even in these looks I made. [*To Florizel.*] But your
    petition
Is yet unanswer'd. I will to your father:
Your honour not o'erthrown by your desires,   230
I am friend to them and you: upon which errand
I now go toward him; therefore follow me
And mark what way I make: come, good my lord.
                            [*Exeunt.*

SCENE II. *Before* LEONTES' *palace.*

Enter AUTOLYCUS *and a* Gentleman.

Aut. Beseech you, sir, were you present at this
relation?
First Gent. I was by at the opening of the fardel,
heard the old shepherd deliver the manner how he
found it: whereupon, after a little amazedness, we
were all commanded out of the chamber; only this
methought I heard the shepherd say, he found the
child.
Aut. I would most gladly know the issue of it.   9
First Gent. I make a broken delivery of the business;
but the changes I perceived in the king and Camillo
were very notes of admiration: they seemed almost,
with staring on one another, to tear the cases of their
eyes; there was speech in their dumbness, language in
their very gesture; they looked as they had heard of a
world ransomed, or one destroyed: a notable passion
of wonder appeared in them; but the wisest beholder,
that knew no more but seeing, could not say if the
importance were joy or sorrow; but in the extremity
of the one, it must needs be.   20

Enter another Gentleman.

Here comes a gentleman that haply knows more. The
news, Rogero?
Sec. Gent. Nothing but bonfires: the oracle is fulfilled; the king's daughter is found: such a deal of
wonder is broken out within this hour that ballad-
makers cannot be able to express it.

Enter a third Gentleman.

Here comes the Lady Paulina's steward: he can deliver you more. How goes it now, sir? this news which
is called true is so like an old tale, that the verity of it
is in strong suspicion: has the king found his heir?   32

Third Gent. Most true, if ever truth were pregnant
by circumstance: that which you hear you'll swear
you see, there is such unity in the proofs. The mantle
of Queen Hermione's, her jewel about the neck of it,
the letters of Antigonus found with it which they know
to be his character, the majesty of the creature in
resemblance of the mother, the affection of nobleness
which nature shows above her breeding, and many
other evidences proclaim her with all certainty to be
the king's daughter. Did you see the meeting of the
two kings?
Sec. Gent. No.   45
Third Gent. Then have you lost a sight, which was
to be seen, cannot be spoken of. There might you
have beheld one joy crown another, so and in such
manner that it seemed sorrow wept to take leave of
them, for their joy waded in tears. There was casting
up of eyes, holding up of hands, with countenance of
such distraction that they were to be known by garment, not by favour. Our king, being ready to leap
out of himself for joy of his found daughter, as if that
joy were now become a loss, cries 'O, thy mother, thy
mother!' then asks Bohemia forgiveness; then embraces his son-in-law; then again worries he his
daughter with clipping her; now he thanks the old
shepherd, which stands by like a weather-bitten conduit of many kings' reigns. I never heard of such
another encounter, which lames report to follow it
and undoes description to do it.   63
Sec. Gent. What, pray you, became of Antigonus,
that carried hence the child?
Third Gent. Like an old tale still, which will have
matter to rehearse, though credit be asleep and not an
ear open. He was torn to pieces with a bear: this
avouches the shepherd's son; who has not only his
innocence, which seems much, to justify him, but a
handkerchief and rings of his that Paulina knows.
First Gent. What became of his bark and his followers?   73
Third Gent. Wrecked the same instant of their master's death and in the view of the shepherd: so that all
the instruments which aided to expose the child were
even then lost when it was found. But O, the noble
combat that 'twixt joy and sorrow was fought in
Paulina! She had one eye declined for the loss of her
husband, another elevated that the oracle was fulfilled: she lifted the princess from the earth, and so
locks her in embracing, as if she would pin her to her
heart that she might no more be in danger of losing.
First Gent. The dignity of this act was worth the
audience of kings and princes; for by such was it
acted.   88
Third Gent. One of the prettiest touches of all and
that which angled for mine eyes, caught the water
though not the fish, was when, at the relation of the
queen's death, with the manner how she came to 't
bravely confessed and lamented by the king, how
attentiveness wounded his daughter; till, from one
sign of dolour to another, she did, with an 'Alas,' I
would fain say, bleed tears, for I am sure my heart
wept blood. Who was most marble there changed
colour; some swooned, all sorrowed: if all the world

---

219. **since,** when. 230. **Your . . . desires,** i.e., if your honor, etc.
    SCENE II. 2. **relation,** narrative, account. Shakespeare has chosen
to solve the plot of the young lovers by reporting the solution in conversation. 12-13. **notes of admiration,** exclamations of wonder.

14-15. **cases of their eyes,** eyelids. 19. **no . . . seeing,** nothing except
what he could see. 20. **importance,** import, meaning. 27. **ballad-
makers,** reference to the Elizabethan practice of writing ballads on
notable current events. 34. **pregnant by circumstance,** made cogent by

could have seen 't, the woe had been universal. 100

First Gent. Are they returned to the court?

Third Gent. No: the princess hearing of her mother's statue, which is in the keeping of Paulina,—a piece many years in doing and now newly performed by that rare Italian master, Julio Romano, who, had he himself eternity and could put breath into his work, would beguile Nature of her custom, so perfectly he is her ape: he so near to Hermione hath done Hermione that they say one would speak to her and stand in hope of answer: thither with all greediness of affection are they gone, and there they intend to sup.

Sec. Gent. I thought she had some great matter there in hand; for she hath privately twice or thrice a day, ever since the death of Hermione, visited that removed house. Shall we thither and with our company piece the rejoicing? 117

First Gent. Who would be thence that has the benefit of access? every wink of an eye some new grace will be born: our absence makes us unthrifty to our knowledge. Let 's along. [*Exeunt Gentlemen.*

Aut. Now, had I not the dash of my former life in me, would preferment drop on my head. I brought the old man and his son aboard the prince; told him I heard them talk of a fardel and I know not what: but he at that time, over-fond of the shepherd's daughter, so he then took her to be, who began to be much sea-sick, and himself little better, extremity of weather continuing, this mystery remained undiscovered. But 'tis all one to me; for had I been the finder out of this secret, it would not have relished among my other discredits. 133

Enter Shepherd *and* Clown.

Here come those I have done good to against my will, and already appearing in the blossoms of their fortune.

Shep. Come, boy; I am past moe children, but thy sons and daughters will be all gentlemen born.

Clo. You are well met, sir. You denied to fight with me this other day, because I was no gentleman born. See you these clothes? say you see them not and think me still no gentleman born: you were best say these robes are not gentlemen born: give me the lie, do, and try whether I am not now a gentleman born.

Aut. I know you are now, sir, a gentleman born.

Clo. Ay, and have been so any time these four hours.

Shep. And so have I, boy. 149

Clo. So you have: but I was a gentleman born before my father; for the king's son took me by the hand, and called me brother; and then the two kings called my father brother; and then the prince my brother and the princess my sister called my father father; and so we wept, and there was the first gentleman-like tears that ever we shed.

Shep. We may live, son, to shed many more.

Clo. Ay; or else 'twere hard luck, being in so preposterous estate as we are. 159

Aut. I humbly beseech you, sir, to pardon me all the faults I have committed to your worship and to give me your good report to the prince my master.

Shep. Prithee, son, do; for we must be gentle, now we are gentlemen.

Clo. Thou wilt amend thy life?

Aut. Ay, an it like your good worship.

Clo. Give me thy hand: I will swear to the prince thou art as honest a true fellow as any is in Bohemia.170

Shep. You may say it, but not swear it.

Clo. Not swear it, now I am a gentleman? Let boors and franklins say it, I'll swear it.

Shep. How if it be false, son?

Clo. If it be ne'er so false, a true gentleman may swear it in the behalf of his friend: and I'll swear to the prince thou art a tall fellow of thy hands and that thou wilt not be drunk; but I know thou art no tall fellow of thy hands and that thou wilt be drunk: but I'll swear it, and I would thou wouldst be a tall fellow of thy hands. 181

Aut. I will prove so, sir, to my power.

Clo. Ay, by any means prove a tall fellow: if I do not wonder how thou darest venture to be drunk, not being a tall fellow, trust me not. Hark! the kings and the princes, our kindred, are going to see the queen's picture. Come, follow us: we'll be thy good masters.
[*Exeunt.*

SCENE III. *A chapel in* PAULINA's *house.*

Enter LEONTES, POLIXENES, FLORIZEL, PERDITA, CAMILLO, PAULINA, Lords, *and* Attendants.

Leon. O grave and good Paulina, the great comfort
That I have had of thee!

Paul.   What, sovereign sir,
I did not well I meant well. All my services
You have paid home: but that you have vouchsafed,
With your crown'd brother and these your contracted
Heirs of your kingdoms, my poor house to visit,
It is a surplus of your grace, which never
My life may last to answer.

Leon.   O Paulina,
We honour you with trouble: but we came
To see the statue of our queen: your gallery   10
Have we pass'd through, not without much content
In many singularities; but we saw not
That which my daughter came to look upon,
The statue of her mother.

Paul.   As she lived peerless,
So her dead likeness, I do well believe,
Excels whatever yet you look'd upon
Or hand of man hath done; therefore I keep it
Lonely, apart. But here it is: prepare
To see the life as lively mock'd as ever
Still sleep mock'd death: behold, and say 'tis well. 20
[*Paulina draws a curtain, and discovers Hermione standing like a statue.*
I like your silence, it the more shows off
Your wonder: but yet speak; first, you, my liege.
Comes it not something near?

Leon.   Her natural posture!
Chide me, dear stone, that I may say indeed
Thou art Hermione; or rather, thou art she
In thy not chiding, for she was as tender
As infancy and grace. But yet, Paulina,
Hermione was not so much wrinkled, nothing

---

circumstantial evidence (Moorman). 40. **affection of,** natural disposition to. 52. **countenance,** bearing, demeanor. 98. **marble,** hardhearted. 106. **Julio Romano,** Italian painter and sculptor of the sixteenth century; an anachronism in this play. 108. **custom,** trade.

117. **piece,** add to, augment. 121. **unthrifty to,** not likely to increase. 132. **relished,** found acceptance. 159. **preposterous,** probably blunder for "prosperous." 173. **franklins,** farmers who owned their own land. SCENE III. 12. **singularities,** rarities, curiosities.

So aged as this seems.
　　Pol.　　　　　　　O, not by much.
　　Paul. So much the more our carver's excellence; 30
Which lets go by some sixteen years and makes her
As she lived now.
　　Leon.　　　　　　As now she might have done,
So much to my good comfort, as it is
Now piercing to my soul. O, thus she stood,
Even with such life of majesty, warm life,
As now it coldly stands, when first I woo'd her!
I am ashamed: does not the stone rebuke me
For being more stone than it? O royal piece,
There's magic in thy majesty, which has
My evils conjured to remembrance and　　　　40
From thy admiring daughter took the spirits,
Standing like stone with thee.
　　Per.　　　　　　And give me leave,
And do not say 'tis superstition, that
I kneel and then implore her blessing. Lady,
Dear queen, that ended when I but began,
Give me that hand of yours to kiss.
　　Paul.　　　　　　O, patience!
The statue is but newly fix'd, the colour's
Not dry.
　　Cam. My lord, your sorrow was too sore laid on,
Which sixteen winters cannot blow away,　　　50
So many summers dry: scarce any joy
Did ever so long live; no sorrow
But kill'd itself much sooner.
　　Pol.　　　　　　Dear my brother,
Let him that was the cause of this have power
To take off so much grief from you as he
Will piece up in himself.
　　Paul.　　　　　　Indeed, my lord,
If I had thought the sight of my poor image
Would thus have wrought you,—for the stone is
　　　mine—
I 'ld not have show'd it.
　　Leon.　　　　　Do not draw the curtain.　59
　　Paul. No longer shall you gaze on 't, lest your fancy
May think anon it moves.
　　Leon.　　　　　　Let be, let be.
Would I were dead, but that, methinks, already—
What was he that did make it? See, my lord,
Would you not deem it breathed? and that those
　　　veins
Did verily bear blood?
　　Pol.　　　　　　Masterly done:
The very life seems warm upon her lip.
　　Leon. The fixture of her eye has motion in 't,
As we are mock'd with art.
　　Paul.　　　　　　I'll draw the curtain:
My lord 's almost so far transported that
He'll think anon it lives.
　　Leon.　　　　　　O sweet Paulina,　70
Make me to think so twenty years together!
No settled senses of the world can match
The pleasure of that madness. Let 't alone.
　　Paul. I am sorry, sir, I have thus far stirr'd you: but
I could afflict you farther.
　　Leon.　　　　　Do, Paulina;
For this affliction has a taste as sweet
As any cordial comfort. Still, methinks,
There is an air comes from her: what fine chisel

Could ever yet cut breath? Let no man mock me,
For I will kiss her.
　　Paul.　　　　　Good my lord, forbear:　80
The ruddiness upon her lip is wet;
You'll mar it if you kiss it, stain your own
With oily painting. Shall I draw the curtain?
　　Leon. No, not these twenty years.
　　Per.　　　　　So long could I
Stand by, a looker on.
　　Paul.　　　　　Either forbear,
Quit presently the chapel, or resolve you
For more amazement. If you can behold it,
I'll make the statue move indeed, descend
And take you by the hand: but then you'll think—
Which I protest against—I am assisted　　　90
By wicked powers.
　　Leon.　　　　　What you can make her do,
I am content to look on: what to speak,
I am content to hear; for 'tis as easy
To make her speak as move.
　　Paul.　　　　　It is required
You do awake your faith. Then all stand still;
On: those that think it is unlawful business
I am about, let them depart.
　　Leon.　　　　　Proceed:
No foot shall stir.
　　Paul.　　　　　Music, awake her; strike! [*Music.*
'Tis time; descend; be stone no more; approach;
Strike all that look upon with marvel. Come,　100
I'll fill your grave up: stir, nay, come away,
Bequeath to death your numbness, for from him
Dear life redeems you. You perceive she stirs:
　　　　　　　　　　　[*Hermione comes down.*
Start not; her actions shall be holy as
You hear my spell is lawful: do not shun her
Until you see her die again; for then
You kill her double. Nay, present your hand:
When she was young you woo'd her; now in age
Is she become the suitor?
　　Leon.　　　　　O, she 's warm!
If this be magic, let it be an art　　　　　110
Lawful as eating.
　　Pol.　　　　　She embraces him.
　　Cam. She hangs about his neck:
If she pertain to life let her speak too.
　　Pol. Ay, and make 't manifest where she has lived,
Or how stolen from the dead.
　　Paul.　　　　　That she is living,
Were it but told you, should be hooted at
Like an old tale: but it appears she lives,
Though yet she speak not. Mark a little while.
Please you to interpose, fair madam: kneel
And pray your mother's blessing. Turn, good lady; 120
Our Perdita is found.
　　Her.　　　　　You gods, look down
And from your sacred vials pour your graces
Upon my daughter's head! Tell me, mine own,
Where hast thou been preserved? where lived? how
　　　found
Thy father's court? for thou shalt hear that I,
Knowing by Paulina that the oracle
Gave hope thou wast in being, have preserved
Myself to see the issue.
　　Paul.　　　　　There 's time enough for that;

67. **fixture,** fixedness, stability.　96. **On,** let us proceed.　107. **double,**
twice over.

Lest they desire upon this push to trouble
Your joys with like relation. Go together,   130
You precious winners all; your exultation
Partake to every one. I, an old turtle,
Will wing me to some wither'd bough and there
My mate, that's never to be found again,
Lament till I am lost.
    Leon.   O, peace, Paulina!
Thou shouldst a husband take by my consent,
As I by thine a wife: this is a match,
And made between 's by vows. Thou hast found
    mine;
But how, is to be question'd; for I saw her,
As I thought, dead, and have in vain said many   140
A prayer upon her grave. I'll not seek far—
For him, I partly know his mind—to find thee
An honourable husband. Come, Camillo,
And take her by the hand, whose worth and honesty
Is richly noted and here justified
By us, a pair of kings. Let 's from this place.
What! look upon my brother: both your pardons,
That e'er I put between your holy looks
My ill suspicion. This is your son-in-law
And son unto the king, who, heavens directing,   150
Is troth-plight to your daughter. Good Paulina,
Lead us from hence, where we may leisurely
Each one demand and answer to his part
Perform'd in this wide gap of time since first
We were dissever'd: hastily lead away.   [*Exeunt.*

129. **push,** emergency. 130. **like relation,** similar narrative. 132. **Partake to,** share with, communicate. 145. **noted,** reputed. 147. **What . . . brother,** addressed to Hermione.

THE

Tempest

The *Tempest*, which was first published in the folio edition of 1623, is dated with a good deal of certainty in the year 1610 or 1611. The play was acted at court in 1611 and 1613. In the composition of it Shakespeare reveals a knowledge of certain pamphlets published in 1610.

On July 28, 1609, the *Sea Venture*, a ship bearing Sir Thomas Gates, Sir George Somers, and Captain Newport and carrying supplies and settlers to the new colonies in Virginia, was cast away on the Bermudas. The fleet, of which the *Sea Venture* was the flagship, had been dispersed by a storm a few days before. The shipwrecked party spent several months in Bermuda, built two small vessels from the timbers of their wrecked ship, and proceeded to Virginia. Accounts of the adventure were subsequently published in London, where there had been much uneasiness as to the fate of the shipwrecked persons. Silvester Jourdan's account, *A Discovery of the Barmudas, otherwise called the Isle of Divels*, was published in 1610; and another by William Strachey is dated

July 15, 1610, although it does not seem to have been published until 1625. The chances are that Shakespeare saw it in manuscript. It is called *A true Reportory of the Wracke and Redemption of Sir Thomas Gates Knight; upon, and from the Ilands of the Bermudas.* Evidences of Shakespeare's use of these works will be found in the notes.

SOURCES

No direct source for the main story of Shakespeare's play has been discovered. For minor passages, however, there are an unusual number of parallels, not only to Jourdan and Strachey, but to others. Gonzalo's description of the ideal commonwealth (II, i, 147-168) offers the closest resemblance yet discovered between the works of Shakespeare and the *Essays* of Montaigne. Prospero's famous speech about "this insubstantial pageant" (IV, i, 148-158) is closely paralleled in *The Tragedie of Darius* by Sir William Alexander (1603); and another speech of Prospero's (V, i, 33-50) is borrowed from Ovid's *Metamorphoses.*

No less than three suggestions have been made as to Shakespeare's source for the main story of *The Tempest*, and in each case obvious resemblances exist; but the resemblances are in fundamentals of plot and not in such detail as to enable one to say that we have a source rather than a parallel version of the same original. There is a Spanish collection of stories called *Winter Nights* by Antonio de Eslava, the fourth of which tells of the adventures of King Dardano of Bulgaria and his daughter Serafina.[1] These stories were published in 1609 and 1610. There is also a play known as *The Fair Sidea* by the German playwright Jacob Ayrer, which must have been written before 1605 as that is when Ayrer died. Finally, there are facts from Italian history late in the fifteenth and early in the sixteenth century which in names and events offer rather striking parallels to *The Tempest*. These had been recounted by William Thomas in *The Historie of Italy* in 1549. The Spanish story and the German play have the magician prince, banished with his only daughter, who subsequently gets his enemies into his power, regains his inheritance, and effects a union between his daughter and the son of his enemy.

We seem to draw nearest of all to the dramatic substance of *The Tempest*, though no nearer to Shakespeare's immediate source, in a group of plots or scenarios of the Italian *commedie dell'arte*, printed by Sgr. Neri in 1913. Four of these offer resemblances, sometimes quite close, to the adventures of the shipwrecked crew on the enchanted island.[2]

A recent investigation by Henri Grégoire[3] throws

[1]Gustav Becker, "Zur Quellenfrage von Shakespeares *Tempest*," *Shakespeare Jahrbuch*, XLIII (1907), 155-168.
[2]F. Neri, *Scenari delle Maschere in Arcadia*, Città di Castello, 1913; Chambers, *William Shakespeare*, I, 493-494.
[3]Henri Grégoire, "The Bulgarian Origins of Shakespeare's *The Tempest*," *Studies in Philology*, XXXVII (1940), 236-256.

a good deal of light on the subject. According to him the common source of Eslava, Ayrer, and Shakespeare was a romance presumably written in Italian and now lost. This romance dealt with events, mainly of the tenth century, in the history of Serbia, Byzantium, and particularly Bulgaria.

THE STORY AS SHAKESPEARE TELLS IT

It has been suggested by J. Dover Wilson that the play may once have presented, not the closely unified scene and action that it now presents, but a rambling plot like the other romances, covering much time and happening in several places. He finds, in the repetitions in Prospero's narrative to Miranda in the second scene of the first act, evidence that the matters there recounted were once acted out in full. The cutting down, he thinks, was done in order to make room for the elaborate masque which appears in the fourth act.[4] The play is, after all, so well constructed and so intelligible in all its parts that it is hard successfully to question its integrity, nor does this critic intend to do so; it is merely the question of a possible revision.

Many critics have been of the opinion that *The Tempest* is Shakespeare's farewell to the stage, and that in Prospero's laying aside his mantle we have Shakespeare leaving his art and the mighty magic of his pen. When, however, one reads the large significance of the play as the delineation of ideal power and justice in the world, one is disposed to think that that of itself is a sufficient motive for its composition. Applications may be made to Shakespeare and to others, but an intention on Shakespeare's part to symbolize his own career is harder to believe in.

PROSPERO

Whatever views we may adopt with reference to the personal significance of *The Tempest* to its author must not blind us to the actual greatness of the conception of Prospero. We may trust the expression of it, in honest admiration, to the pen of the late Edward Dowden,[5] although in so doing, we do not subscribe to the identification of Prospero with Shakespeare:

It is not chiefly because Prospero is a great enchanter, now about to break his magic staff, to drown his book deeper than ever plummet sounded, to dismiss his airy spirits, and to return to the practical service of his Dukedom, that we identify Prospero in some measure with Shakspere himself. It is rather because the temper of Prospero, the grave harmony of his character, his self-mastery, his calm validity of will, his sensitiveness to wrong, his unfaltering justice, and, with these, a certain abandonment, a remoteness from the common joys and sorrows of the world, are characteristic of Shakspere as

discovered to us in all his latest plays. Prospero is an harmonious and fully developed *will*. In the earlier play of fairy enchantments, *A Midsummer-Night's Dream*, the "human mortals" wander to and fro in a maze of error, misled by the mischievous frolic of Puck, the jester and clown of Fairyland. But here the spirits of the elements, and Caliban, the gross genius of brute-matter—needful for the service of life—are brought under subjection to the human will of Prospero.

What is more, Prospero has entered into complete possession of himself. Shakspere has shown us his quick sense of injury, his intellectual impatience, his occasional moment of keen irritability in order that we may be more deeply aware of his abiding strength and self-possession, and that we may perceive how these have been grafted upon a temperament not impassive or unexcitable. And Prospero has reached not only the higher levels of moral attainment; he has also reached an altitude of thought from which he can survey the whole of human life, and see how small and yet how great it is. His heart is sensitive; he is profoundly touched by the joy of the children with whom in the egoism of their love he passes for a thing of secondary interest; he is deeply moved by the perfidy of his brother. His brain is readily set a-work, and can with difficulty be checked from eager and excessive energizing; he is subject to the access of sudden and agitating thought. But Prospero masters his own sensitiveness, emotional and intellectual:

> "We are such stuff
> As dreams are made on, and our little life
> Is rounded with a sleep. Sir, I am vex'd;
> Bear with my weakness; my old brain is troubled:
> Be not disturb'd with my infirmity:
> If you be pleased, retire into my cell
> And there repose: a turn or two I'll walk,
> To still my beating mind."

"Such stuff as dreams are made on." Nevertheless, in this little life, in this dream, Prospero will maintain his dream rights and fulfil his dream duties. In the dream, he, a Duke, will accomplish Duke's work. Having idealized everything, Shakspere has left everything real.

It is not, however, merely a matter of Prospero's looking down with a large and placid vision on the endless struggles and conspiracies of the world. His experience has taught him something efficacious. He has acquired a self-mastery that secures the future as the present and is able to forego the power of vengeance over his enemies. One might put it in the words of Posthumus Leonatus (*Cymbeline*, V, v, 418-420):

> The power I have on you is to spare you;
> The malice towards you to forgive you: live,
> And deal with others better.

HISTORY OF THE PLAY

The spectacular quality of *The Tempest* together with its subtle suggestiveness in the field of primitive life as contrasted with civilized life has made it one of the most popular of Shakespeare's plays. It has always been a favorite with poets and lovers of Shakespeare.

[4]*The Tempest*, edited by Sir Arthur Quiller-Couch and J. Dover Wilson (Cambridge, 1921), "Copy for *The Tempest*"; Sir Edmund K. Chambers, "The Integrity of *The Tempest*," *Review of English Studies*, I (1925), 129-150.
[5]Edward Dowden, *Shakspere* (1875), pp. 417-419.

Dryden and D'Avenant rewrote it in 1667 as *The Tempest, or the Enchanted Island*. This version pleased Samuel Pepys and suited the taste of the age, but it does frightful violence to practically everything we think worth while in Shakespeare. Since the discontinuance of Dryden and D'Avenant's modified version, *The Tempest* has not often been seen upon the stage, and when it has been produced, there has been a tendency, as in Sir Herbert Tree's presentation in 1904, to accompany it with a wealth of scenic magnificence.

The exploitations of the operatic possibilities of *The Tempest* have tended to displace the original play. The Dryden-D'Avenant version, with its Hippolito, "one that never saw woman," and its Dorinda, "one that never saw man," and its operatic ending, had its effect on the performances of Garrick (1756), John Philip Kemble (1767, 1789), and even the performances of Macready (1821).

Samuel Phelps, as Prospero, played Shakespeare's play at Sadler's Wells in 1847, and Charles Kean, appearing in the same part, directed an elaborate revival in 1857.

The play, so marvelously attractive as literature, is possibly deficient in genuine dramatic quality. If so, one can understand the universal resort to the assistance of spectacular devices by those who have staged it. Prospero's part, which has been played by the greatest of English actors, is too easy and uniform. The role of Miranda for some reason does not reward the efforts of the great actresses. Strangely enough it is the part of Caliban which has attracted the attention of some of the greater actors of recent years. Sir F. R. Benson, Sir Herbert Tree, and Sir Philip Ben Greet have taken the part and displayed great ingenuity in their attempts to delineate Shakespeare's "savage and deformed slave."

The New York performance of 1945 under the direction of Margaret Webster was brilliant but, like most performances of *The Tempest*, was possibly faulty in emphasis. Dramatic interest demands some element of struggle, and Prospero as ordinarily played has everything his own way. A Prospero who can do everything is as unprofitable dramatically as is a Timon who will do nothing. Perhaps this defect is to some extent inherent in *The Tempest*, and yet it arises in part at least from overemphasis on Prospero the magician and a disposition to subordinate his story as a man. It was no small matter in the minds of Elizabethans to lose and regain a dukedom. After all, the love story of Ferdinand and Miranda is charming, and the magic which supplies us with Ariel and Caliban has a human as well as a spectacular interest. The low comedy is good, the main action is lively, and the style of the play is poetical, witty, and delightful. One would like to see a performance of *The Tempest* which presented the play as Shakespeare seems to have designed it and not as an overglorification of Prospero in the midst of supernatural display.

THE

Tempest

DRAMATIS PERSONAE

ALONSO, King of Naples.
SEBASTIAN, his brother.
PROSPERO, the right Duke of Milan.
ANTONIO, his brother, the usurping Duke of Milan.
FERDINAND, son to the King of Naples.
GONZALO, an honest old Counsellor.
ADRIAN,
FRANCISCO, } Lords.
CALIBAN, a savage and deformed Slave.
TRINCULO, a Jester.
STEPHANO, a drunken Butler.
Master of a Ship.
Boatswain.
Mariners.

MIRANDA, daughter to Prospero.

ARIEL, an airy Spirit.
IRIS,
CERES,
JUNO, } presented by Spirits.
Nymphs,
Reapers,

Other Spirits attending on Prospero.

SCENE—*A ship at Sea: an island.*

ACT I.

SCENE I. *On a ship at sea: a tempestuous noise of thunder and lightning heard.*

Enter a Ship-Master *and* a Boatswain.

Mast. Boatswain!
Boats. Here, master: what cheer?
Mast. Good, speak to the mariners: fall to 't, yarely, or we run ourselves aground: bestir, bestir. [*Exit.*

Enter Mariners.

Boats. Heigh, my hearts! cheerly, cheerly, my hearts! yare, yare! Take in the topsail. Tend to the master's whistle. Blow, till thou burst thy wind, if room enough!

Enter ALONSO, SEBASTIAN, ANTONIO, FERDINAND, GONZALO, *and others.*

Alon. Good boatswain, have care. Where 's the master? Play the men.   11
Boats. I pray now, keep below.
Ant. Where is the master, boatswain?
Boats. Do you not hear him? You mar our labour: keep your cabins: you do assist the storm.
Gon. Nay, good, be patient.

Boats. When the sea is. Hence! What cares these roarers for the name of king? To cabin: silence! trouble us not.

Gon. Good, yet remember whom thou hast aboard.

Boats. None that I more love than myself. You are a counsellor; if you can command these elements to silence, and work the peace of the present, we will not hand a rope more; use your authority: if you cannot, give thanks you have lived so long, and make yourself ready in your cabin for the mischance of the hour, if it so hap. Cheerly, good hearts! Out of our way, I say.   [*Exit.* 29

Gon. I have great comfort from this fellow: methinks he hath no drowning mark upon him; his complexion is perfect gallows. Stand fast, good Fate, to his hanging: make the rope of his destiny our cable, for our own doth little advantage. If he be not born to be hanged, our case is miserable.   [*Exeunt.* 36

Re-enter Boatswain.

Boats. Down with the topmast! yare! lower, lower! Bring her to try with main-course. [*A cry within.*] A plague upon this howling! they are louder than the weather or our office.   40

Re-enter SEBASTIAN, ANTONIO, *and* GONZALO.

Yet again! what do you here? Shall we give o'er and drown? Have you a mind to sink?

Seb. A pox o' your throat, you bawling, blasphemous, incharitable dog!

Boats. Work you then.

Ant. Hang, cur! hang, you whoreson, insolent noisemaker! We are less afraid to be drowned than thou art.

Gon. I'll warrant him for drowning; though the ship were no stronger than a nutshell and as leaky as an unstanched wench.   51

Boats. Lay her a-hold, a-hold! set her two courses off to sea again; lay her off.

Enter Mariners *wet.*

Mariners. All lost! to prayers, to prayers! all lost!

Boats. What, must our mouths be cold?

Gon. The king and prince at prayers! let 's assist them,
For our case is as theirs.

Seb.   I 'm out of patience.

Ant. We are merely cheated of our lives by drunkards:
This wide-chapp'd rascal—would thou mightst lie drowning   60
The washing of ten tides!

Gon.   He'll be hang'd yet,
Though every drop of water swear against it
And gape at widest to glut him.
[*A confused noise within:* 'Mercy on us!'—

The Tempest
ACT I : SC I

1250

'We split, we split!'—'Farewell my wife and children!'—
'Farewell, brother!'—'We split, we split, we split!']

Ant. Let 's all sink with the king.

Seb. Let 's take leave of him.   [*Exeunt Ant. and Seb.*

Gon. Now would I give a thousand furlongs of sea for an acre of barren ground, long heath, brown furze, any thing. The wills above be done! but I would fain die a dry death.   [*Exeunt.*

SCENE II. *The island. Before* PROSPERO'S *cell.*

Enter PROSPERO *and* MIRANDA.

Mir. If by your art, my dearest father, you have
Put the wild waters in this roar, allay them.
The sky, it seems, would pour down stinking pitch,
But that the sea, mounting to the welkin's cheek,
Dashes the fire out. O, I have suffer'd
With those that I saw suffer: a brave vessel,
Who had, no doubt, some noble creature in her,
Dash'd all to pieces. O, the cry did knock
Against my very heart. Poor souls, they perish'd.
Had I been any god of power, I would   10
Have sunk the sea within the earth or ere
It should the good ship so have swallow'd and
The fraughting souls within her.

Pros.   Be collected:
No more amazement: tell your piteous heart
There 's no harm done.

Mir.   O, woe the day!

Pros.   No harm.
I have done nothing but in care of thee,
Of thee, my dear one, thee, my daughter, who
Art ignorant of what thou art, nought knowing
Of whence I am, nor that I am more better
Than Prospero, master of a full poor cell,   20
And thy no greater father.

Mir.   More to know
Did never meddle with my thoughts.

Pros.   'Tis time
I should inform thee farther. Lend thy hand,
And pluck my magic garment from me. So:
[*Lays down his mantle.*
Lie there, my art. Wipe thou thine eyes; have comfort.
The direful spectacle of the wreck, which touch'd
The very virtue of compassion in thee,
I have with such provision in mine art
So safely ordered that there is no soul—
No, not so much perdition as an hair   30
Betid to any creature in the vessel
Which thou heard'st cry, which thou saw'st sink. Sit down;
For thou must now know farther.

Mir.   You have often
Begun to tell me what I am, but stopp'd

ACT I. SCENE I. 1. **Boatswain,** under-officer in a ship, having to do with sails and rigging and the supervision of the crew at work. 3. **Good,** probably, good friend. 3-4. **fall . . . yarely,** set to work nimbly. 8. **Tend,** attend. 11. **Play the men.** New Cambridge editors define as "pipe all hands." 19. **cares,** described as a singular verb used with a plural subject on account of haste; also as an old northern plural of the verb in *s.* **roarers,** waves or winds, or both; allusion to *roarer* meaning "bully," "blusterer." 24-25. **work . . . present,** calm the storm. 25. **hand,** handle. 32. **complexion . . . gallows,** appearance shows he was born to be hanged. 35. **doth little advantage,** is of little benefit. 38. **Bring . . . course,** sail her close to the wind by means of the mainsail. 40. **they . . . office,** the passengers make more noise than the winds or than we do at work. 49. **warrant him for drown-**

ing, guarantee that he will never be drowned. 52. **a-hold,** close to the wind. 53. **courses,** probably, sails; i.e., they would set her foresail as well as her mainsail. 56. **must . . . cold,** let us heat up our mouths with liquor. 59. **merely,** absolutely, entirely. 60. **wide-chapp'd,** with mouth wide open. 60-61. **lie . . . tides.** Pirates were hanged on the shore and left until three tides had come in. 63. **glut,** swallow. 64. **split,** i.e., on the rocks. 69. **long heath,** defined as "open barren ground"; also as "heather." 70. **furze,** broom, or gorse (a prickly shrub); F: *firs,* taken to mean "firs" (New Cambridge).
SCENE II. 3. **stinking pitch,** suggestion of heat. 4. **But that,** were it not that. 13. **fraughting,** forming the cargo. 14. **amazement,** astonishment, bewilderment. **piteous,** pitiful. 20. **full,** very, exceedingly. 22. **meddle,** mingle. 24. **So,** used with a gesture, meaning

And left me to a bootless inquisition,
Concluding 'Stay: not yet.'
    Pros.   The hour 's now come;
The very minute bids thee ope thine ear;
Obey and be attentive. Canst thou remember
A time before we came unto this cell?
I do not think thou canst, for then thou wast not   40
Out three years old.
    Mir.   Certainly, sir, I can.
    Pros. By what? by any other house or person?
Of any thing the image tell me that
Hath kept with thy remembrance.
    Mir.   'Tis far off
And rather like a dream than an assurance
That my remembrance warrants. Had I not
Four or five women once that tended me?
    Pros. Thou hadst, and more, Miranda. But how is it
That this lives in thy mind? What seest thou else
In the dark backward and abysm of time?   50
If thou remember'st aught ere thou camest here,
How thou camest here thou mayst.
    Mir.   But that I do not.
    Pros. Twelve year since, Miranda, twelve year since,
Thy father was the Duke of Milan and
A prince of power.
    Mir.   Sir, are not you my father?
    Pros. Thy mother was a piece of virtue, and
She said thou wast my daughter; and thy father
Was Duke of Milan; and thou his only heir
And princess no worse issued.
    Mir.   O the heavens!
What foul play had we, that we came from thence?   60
Or blessed was 't we did?
    Pros.   Both, both, my girl:
By foul play, as thou say'st, were we heaved thence,
But blessedly holp hither.
    Mir.   O, my heart bleeds
To think o' the teen that I have turn'd you to,
Which is from my remembrance! Please you, farther.
    Pros. My brother and thy uncle, call'd Antonio—
I pray thee, mark me—that a brother should
Be so perfidious!—he whom next thyself
Of all the world I loved and to him put
The manage of my state; as at that time   70
Through all the signories it was the first
And Prospero the prime duke, being so reputed
In dignity, and for the liberal arts
Without a parallel; those being all my study,
The government I cast upon my brother
And to my state grew stranger, being transported
And rapt in secret studies. Thy false uncle—
Dost thou attend me? ·
    Mir.   Sir, most heedfully.
    Pros. Being once perfected how to grant suits,
How to deny them, who to advance and who   80
To trash for over-topping, new created

The creatures that were mine, I say, or changed 'em,
Or else new form'd 'em; having both the key
Of officer and office, set all hearts i' the state
To what tune pleased his ear; that now he was
The ivy which had hid my princely trunk,
And suck'd my verdure out on 't. Thou attend'st not.
    Mir. O, good sir, I do.
    Pros.   I pray thee, mark me.
I, thus neglecting worldly ends, all dedicated
To closeness and the bettering of my mind   90
With that which, but by being so retired,
O'er-prized all popular rate, in my false brother
Awaked an evil nature; and my trust,
Like a good parent, did beget of him
A falsehood in its contrary as great
As my trust was; which had indeed no limit,
A confidence sans bound. He being thus lorded,
Not only with what my revenue yielded,
But what my power might else exact, like one
†Who having into truth, by telling of it,   100
Made such a sinner of his memory,
To credit his own lie, he did believe
He was indeed the duke; out o' the substitution,
And executing the outward face of royalty,
With all prerogative: hence his ambition growing—
Dost thou hear?
    Mir.   Your tale, sir, would cure
    deafness.
    Pros. To have no screen between this part he play'd
And him he play'd it for, he needs will be
Absolute Milan. Me, poor man, my library

Was dukedom large enough: of temporal royalties   110
He thinks me now incapable; confederates—
So dry he was for sway—wi' the King of Naples
To give him annual tribute, do him homage,
Subject his coronet to his crown and bend
The dukedom yet unbow'd—alas, poor Milan!—
To most ignoble stooping.
    Mir.   O the heavens!
    Pros. Mark his condition and the event; then tell me
If this might be a brother.
    Mir.   I should sin
To think but nobly of my grandmother:
Good wombs have borne bad sons.
    Pros.   Now the condition.   120
This King of Naples, being an enemy
To me inveterate, hearkens my brother's suit;
Which was, that he, in lieu o' the premises
Of homage and I know not how much tribute,
Should presently extirpate me and mine
Out of the dukedom and confer fair Milan
With all the honours on my brother: whereon,
A treacherous army levied, one midnight
Fated to the purpose did Antonio open
The gates of Milan, and, i' the dead of darkness,   130
The ministers for the purpose hurried thence

"good," "very well." 28. **provision,** foresight. 29. **no soul,** i.e., lost; many emendations. 30. **perdition,** loss. 35. **bootless inquisition,** profitless inquiry. 45-46. **assurance . . . warrants,** certainty that my memory guarantees. 56. **piece,** masterpiece. 59. **issued,** born. 64. **teen . . . to,** trouble I have brought you into. 65. **from,** i.e., has no place in. 71. **signories,** states of northern Italy. 73. **liberal arts,** allusion to the learned studies of the Middle Ages. 76. **state,** position as ruler. 77. **secret studies,** magic, the occult. 79. **perfected,** informed completely. 81. **trash,** check a hound by tying a weight to its neck. **over-topping,** running too far ahead of the pack. 83. **key,** tool for tuning stringed instruments, with suggestion of the usual meaning. 90. **closeness,** retirement, seclusion. 91-92. **but . . . rate,** except that it was done in retirement, (would have) surpassed in value all popular estimate.

93. **Awaked.** *I* in line 89 is the subject. 95. **in its contrary,** of an opposite kind. 97. **lorded,** raised to lordship. 100-102. **Who . . . lie,** a difficult passage; the meaning is: He had lied so long that he believed his own lies. New Cambridge editors read *minted* for *into*, interpreting the passage as a figure from coining of baser metals, so that *telling* means "counting," *substitution* means "the substituting of baser metals for gold," and *executing . . . royalty* means "stamping the coins." 109. **Absolute Milan,** actual duke of Milan. 110. **royalties,** prerogatives and rights of a sovereign. 111. **confederates,** conspires. 112. **dry,** thirsty. 123. **in . . . premises,** in return for the stipulations.

Me and thy crying self.
 Mir.   Alack, for pity!
I, not remembering how I cried out then,
Will cry it o'er again: it is a hint
That wrings mine eyes to 't.
 Pros.   Hear a little further
And then I'll bring thee to the present business
Which now 's upon 's; without the which this story
Were most impertinent.
 Mir.   Wherefore did they not
That hour destroy us?
 Pros.   Well demanded, wench: 139
My tale provokes that question. Dear, they durst not,
So dear the love my people bore me, nor set
A mark so bloody on the business, but
With colours fairer painted their foul ends.
In few, they hurried us aboard a bark,
Bore us some leagues to sea; where they prepared
A rotten carcass of a boat, not rigg'd,
Nor tackle, sail, nor mast; the very rats
Instinctively have quit it: there they hoist us,
To cry to the sea that roar'd to us, to sigh
To the winds whose pity, sighing back again, 150
Did us but loving wrong.
 Mir.   Alack, what trouble
Was I then to you!
 Pros.   O, a cherubin
Thou wast that did preserve me. Thou didst smile,
Infused with a fortitude from heaven,
When I have deck'd the sea with drops full salt,
Under my burthen groan'd; which raised in me
An undergoing stomach, to bear up
Against what should ensue.
 Mir.   How came we ashore?
 Pros. By Providence divine.
Some food we had and some fresh water that 160
A noble Neapolitan, Gonzalo,
Out of his charity, who being then appointed
Master of this design, did give us, with
Rich garments, linens, stuffs and necessaries,
Which since have steaded much; so, of his gentleness,
Knowing I loved my books, he furnish'd me
From mine own library with volumes that
I prize above my dukedom.
 Mir.   Would I might
But ever see that man!
 Pros.   Now I arise: [*Resumes his mantle.*
Sit still, and hear the last of our sea-sorrow. 170
Here in this island we arrived; and here
Have I, thy schoolmaster, made thee more profit
Than other princesses can that have more time
For vainer hours and tutors not so careful.
 Mir. Heavens thank you for 't! And now, I pray
you, sir,
For still 'tis beating in my mind, your reason
For raising this sea-storm?
 Pros.   Know thus far forth.
By accident most strange, bountiful Fortune,
Now my dear lady, hath mine enemies
Brought to this shore; and by my prescience 180

I find my zenith doth depend upon
A most auspicious star, whose influence
If now I court not but omit, my fortunes
Will ever after droop. Here cease more questions:
Thou art inclined to sleep; 'tis a good dulness,
And give it way: I know thou canst not choose.
         [*Miranda sleeps.*
Come away, servant, come. I am ready now.
Approach, my Ariel, come.

 Enter ARIEL.

 Ari. All hail, great master! grave sir, hail! I come
To answer thy best pleasure; be 't to fly, 190
To swim, to dive into the fire, to ride
On the curl'd clouds, to thy strong bidding task
Ariel and all his quality.
 Pros.   Hast thou, spirit,
Perform'd to point the tempest that I bade thee?
 Ari. To every article.
I boarded the king's ship; now on the beak,
Now in the waist, the deck, in every cabin,
I flamed amazement: sometime I 'ld divide,
And burn in many places; on the topmast,
The yards and bowsprit, would I flame distinctly, 200
Then meet and join. Jove's lightnings, the precursors
O' the dreadful thunder-claps, more momentary
And sight-outrunning were not; the fire and cracks
Of sulphurous roaring the most mighty Neptune
Seem to besiege and make his bold waves tremble,
Yea, his dread trident shake.
 Pros.   My brave spirit!
Who was so firm, so constant, that this coil
Would not infect his reason?
 Ari.   Not a soul
But felt a fever of the mad and play'd
Some tricks of desperation. All but mariners 210
Plunged in the foaming brine and quit the vessel,
Then all afire with me: the king's son, Ferdinand,
With hair up-staring,—then like reeds, not hair,—
Was the first man that leap'd; cried, 'Hell is empty,
And all the devils are here.'
 Pros.   Why, that 's my spirit!
But was not this nigh shore?
 Ari.   Close by, my master.
 Pros. But are they, Ariel, safe?
 Ari.   Not a hair perish'd;
On their sustaining garments not a blemish,
But fresher than before: and, as thou badest me,
In troops I have dispersed them 'bout the isle. 220
The king's son have I landed by himself;
Whom I left cooling of the air with sighs
In an odd angle of the isle and sitting,
His arms in this sad knot.
 Pros.   Of the king's ship
The mariners say how thou hast disposed
And all the rest o' the fleet.
 Ari.   Safely in harbour
Is the king's ship; in the deep nook, where once
Thou call'dst me up at midnight to fetch dew
From the still-vex'd Bermoothes, there she 's hid:

The mariners all under hatches stow'd;   230
Who, with a charm join'd to their suffer'd labour,
I have left asleep: and for the rest o' the fleet
Which I dispersed, they all have met again
And are upon the Mediterranean flote,
Bound sadly home for Naples,
Supposing that they saw the king's ship wreck'd
And his great person perish.
    Pros.   Ariel, thy charge
Exactly is perform'd: but there 's more work.
What is the time o' the day?
    Ari.   Past the mid season.
    Pros. At least two glasses. The time 'twixt six and
    now   240
Must by us both be spent most preciously.
    Ari. Is there more toil? Since thou dost give me
    pains,
Let me remember thee what thou hast promised,
Which is not yet perform'd me.
    Pros.   How now? moody?
What is 't thou canst demand?
    Ari.   My liberty.
    Pros. Before the time be out? no more!
    Ari.   I prithee,
Remember I have done thee worthy service;
Told thee no lies, made thee no mistakings, served
Without or grudge or grumblings: thou didst promise
To bate me a full year.
    Pros.   Dost thou forget   250
From what a torment I did free thee?
    Ari.   No.
    Pros. Thou dost, and think'st it much to tread the
    ooze
Of the salt deep,
To run upon the sharp wind of the north,
To do me business in the veins o' the earth
When it is baked with frost.
    Ari.   I do not, sir.
    Pros. Thou liest, malignant thing! Hast thou forgot
The foul witch Sycorax, who with age and envy
Was grown into a hoop? hast thou forgot her?
    Ari. No, sir.
    Pros.   Thou hast. Where was she born?
    speak; tell me.   260
    Ari. Sir, in Argier.
    Pros.   O, was she so? I must
Once in a month recount what thou hast been,
Which thou forget'st. This damn'd witch Sycorax,
For mischiefs manifold and sorceries terrible
To enter human hearing, from Argier,
Thou know'st, was banish'd: for one thing she did
They would not take her life. Is not this true?
    Ari. Ay, sir.
    Pros. This blue-eyed hag was hither brought with
    child
And here was left by the sailors. Thou, my slave,   270
As thou report'st thyself, wast then her servant;
And, for thou wast a spirit too delicate
To act her earthy and abhorr'd commands,
Refusing her grand hests, she did confine thee,

By help of her more potent ministers
And in her most unmitigable rage,
Into a cloven pine; within which rift
Imprison'd thou didst painfully remain
A dozen years; within which space she died   279
And left thee there; where thou did'st vent thy groans
As fast as mill-wheels strike. Then was this island—
Save for the son that she did litter here,
A freckled whelp hag-born—not honour'd with
A human shape.
    Ari.   Yes, Caliban her son.
    Pros. Dull thing, I say so; he, that Caliban
Whom now I keep in service. Thou best know'st
What torment I did find thee in; thy groans
Did make wolves howl and penetrate the breasts
Of ever angry bears: it was a torment
To lay upon the damn'd, which Sycorax   290
Could not again undo: it was mine art,
When I arrived and heard thee, that made gape
The pine and let thee out.
    Ari.   I thank thee, master.
    Pros. If thou more murmur'st, I will rend an oak
And peg thee in his knotty entrails till
Thou hast howl'd away twelve winters.
    Ari.   Pardon, master;
I will be correspondent to command
And do my spiriting gently.
    Pros.   Do so, and after two days
I will discharge thee.
    Ari.   That 's my noble master!
What shall I do? say what; what shall I do?   300
    Pros. Go make thyself like a nymph o' the sea: be
    subject
To no sight but thine and mine, invisible
To every eyeball else. Go take this shape
And hither come in 't: go, hence with diligence!
                          [*Exit Ariel.*
Awake, dear heart, awake! thou hast slept well;
Awake!
    Mir.   The strangeness of your story
    put
Heaviness in me.
    Pros.   Shake it off. Come on;
We'll visit Caliban my slave, who never
Yields us kind answer.
    Mir.   'Tis a villain, sir,
I do not love to look on.
    Pros.   But, as 'tis,   310
We cannot miss him: he does make our fire,
Fetch in our wood and serves in offices
That profit us. What, ho! slave! Caliban!
Thou earth, thou! speak.
    Cal.   [*Within*] There 's wood enough
    within.
    Pros. Come forth, I say! there 's other business for
    thee:
Come, thou tortoise! when?

        Re-enter ARIEL *like a water-nymph.*

Fine apparition! My quaint Ariel,

sustained them in the sea. 223. **angle,** corner. 227. **nook,** bay. 228.
fetch dew, for some incantation. 229. **Bermoothes,** Bermudas; a possible reference to *A Discovery of the Bermudas* (1609), one of the sources
of the play. 234. **flote,** sea, or possibly, flotilla, i.e., making for the
Mediterranean flotilla (New Cambridge). 240. **glasses,** i.e., hourglasses. 243. **remember,** remind. 248. **mistakings,** errors. 250. **bate
. . . year,** remit me a year of service. Ariel, as a spirit, longs for freedom;
as a spirit, he is also incapable of affection or gratitude as entertained by
human beings. 261. **Argier,** Algiers. 266. **one thing she did,** allusion
not explained; taken by New Cambridge editors as evidence of a cut
in the play. Lamb suggested that Shakespeare was thinking of the witch
who saved Algiers from Charles v in 1541 by raising a storm that dispersed his fleet. 269. **blue-eyed,** usually interpreted as referring to
dark circles under the eyes. Staunton suggested *blear-eyed.* 274.
hests, commands. 283. **freckled,** spotted. 297. **correspondent,** responsive, submissive. 311. **miss,** do without.

Hark in thine ear.

Ari.   My lord, it shall be done.   [*Exit.*
Pros. Thou poisonous slave, got by the devil himself
Upon thy wicked dam, come forth!   320

Enter CALIBAN.

Cal. As wicked dew as e'er my mother brush'd
With raven's feather from unwholesome fen
Drop on you both! a south-west blow on ye
And blister you all o'er!
    Pros. For this, be sure, to-night thou shalt have
        cramps,
Side-stitches that shall pen thy breath up; urchins
Shall, for that vast of night that they may work,
All exercise on thee; thou shalt be pinch'd
As thick as honeycomb, each pinch more stinging
Than bees that made 'em.
    Cal.   I must eat my dinner.   330
This island 's mine, by Sycorax my mother,
Which thou takest from me. When thou camest first,
Thou strokedst me and madest much of me, wouldst
        give me
Water with berries in 't, and teach me how
To name the bigger light, and how the less,
That burn by day and night: and then I loved thee
And show'd thee all the qualities o' the isle,
The fresh springs, brine-pits, barren place and fertile:
Cursed be I that did so! All the charms
Of Sycorax, toads, beetles, bats, light on you!   340
For I am all the subjects that you have,
Which first was mine own king: and here you sty me
In this hard rock, whiles you do keep from me
The rest o' the island.
    Pros.   Thou most lying slave,
Whom stripes may move, not kindness! I have used
        thee,
Filth as thou art, with human care, and lodged thee
In mine own cell, till thou didst seek to violate
The honour of my child.
    Cal. O ho, O ho! would 't had been done!
Thou didst prevent me; I had peopled else   350
This isle with Calibans.
    Pros.   Abhorred slave,
Which any print of goodness wilt not take,
Being capable of all ill! I pitied thee,
Took pains to make thee speak, taught thee each hour
One thing or other: when thou didst not, savage,
Know thine own meaning, but wouldst gabble like
A thing most brutish, I endow'd thy purposes
With words that made them known. But thy vile race,
Though thou didst learn, had that in 't which good
        natures
Could not abide to be with; therefore wast thou   360
Deservedly confined into this rock,
Who hadst deserved more than a prison.
    Cal. You taught me language; and my profit on 't
Is, I know how to curse. The red plague rid you
For learning me your language!
    Pros.   Hag-seed, hence!
Fetch us in fuel; and be quick, thou 'rt best,

To answer other business. Shrug'st thou, malice?
If thou neglect'st or dost unwillingly
What I command, I'll rack thee with old cramps,
Fill all thy bones with aches, make thee roar   370
That beasts shall tremble at thy din.
    Cal.   No, pray thee.
[*Aside*] I must obey: his art is of such power,
It would control my dam's god, Setebos,
And make a vassal of him.
    Pros.   So, slave; hence!   [*Exit Caliban.*

Re-enter ARIEL, *invisible, playing and singing;*
    FERDINAND *following.*

ARIEL'S *song.*
    Come unto these yellow sands,
        And then take hands:
    Courtsied when you have and kiss'd
        The wild waves whist,
    Foot it featly here and there;   380
    And, sweet sprites, the burthen bear.
Burthen [*dispersedly*]. Hark, hark!
                    Bow-wow.
        The watch-dogs bark:
                    Bow-wow.
Ari. Hark, hark! I hear
        The strain of strutting chanticleer
        Cry, Cock-a-diddle-dow.
Fer. Where should this music be? i' the air or the
        earth?
It sounds no more: and, sure, it waits upon
Some god o' the island. Sitting on a bank,
Weeping again the king my father's wreck,   390
This music crept by me upon the waters,
Allaying both their fury and my passion
With its sweet air: thence I have follow'd it,
Or it hath drawn me rather. But 'tis gone.
No, it begins again.

        ARIEL *sings.*
    Full fathom five thy father lies;
        Of his bones are coral made;
    Those are pearls that were his eyes:
        Nothing of him that doth fade
    But doth suffer a sea-change   400
    Into something rich and strange.
    Sea-nymphs hourly ring his knell:
                    Burthen. Ding-dong.
Ari. Hark! now I hear them,—Ding-dong, bell.
Fer. The ditty does remember my drown'd father.
This is no mortal business, nor no sound
That the earth owes. I hear it now above me.
    Pros. The fringed curtains of thine eye advance
And say what thou seest yond.
    Mir.   What is 't? a spirit?
Lord, how it looks about! Believe me, sir,   410
It carries a brave form. But 'tis a spirit.
    Pros. No, wench; it eats and sleeps and hath such
        senses
As we have, such. This gallant which thou seest
Was in the wreck; and, but he 's something stain'd

321. **wicked,** mischievous, harmful.   323. **south-west,** i.e., wind (bringing disease).   326. **urchins,** hedgehogs; here, suggesting goblins.   327. **vast,** long hours.   328. **exercise,** practice, work.   334. **berries.** Strachey's *Repertory,* one of the sources, says that the Bermudas were full of thickets of "goodly Cedar . . . the Berries whereof, our men seething, straining, and letting stand some three or foure daies, made a kind of pleasant drinke."   338. **brine-pits,** salt springs.   342. **sty,** put in sty. 346. **human,** humane.   351-362. **Abhorred . . . prison.** F assigns

this speech to Miranda. This may be correct, since Prospero seems to break in suddenly in line 365.   357-358. **endow'd . . . known,** enabled you to make known what was going on in your mind.   358. **race,** natural disposition.   364. **red plague,** bubonic plague.   **rid,** destroy, with play on *red.*   365. **Hag-seed,** hag's offspring.   370. **aches,** pronounced "aitches."   373. **Setebos,** mentioned in Eden's *History of Travel* (1577) as a deity, or devil, of the Patagonians.   376-378. **Come . . . kiss'd,** three motions before the dance—take hands, curtsy, kiss

With grief that 's beauty's canker, thou mightst call
    him
A goodly person: he hath lost his fellows
And strays about to find 'em.
    Mir.   I might call him
A thing divine, for nothing natural
I ever saw so noble.
    Pros.   [*Aside*] It goes on, I see,   419
As my soul prompts it. Spirit, fine spirit! I'll free thee
Within two days for this.
    Fer.   Most sure, the goddess
On whom these airs attend! Vouchsafe my prayer
May know if you remain upon this island;
And that you will some good instruction give
How I may bear me here: my prime request,
Which I do last pronounce, is, O you wonder!
If you be maid or no?
    Mir.   No wonder, sir;
But certainly a maid.
    Fer.   My language! heavens!
I am the best of them that speak this speech,
Were I but where 'tis spoken.
    Pros.   How? the best?   430
What wert thou, if the King of Naples heard thee?
    Fer. A single thing, as I am now, that wonders
To hear thee speak of Naples. He does hear me;
And that he does I weep: myself am Naples,
Who with mine eyes, never since at ebb, beheld
The king my father wreck'd.
    Mir.   Alack, for mercy!
    Fer. Yes, faith, and all his lords; the Duke of Milan
And his brave son being twain.
    Pros.   [*Aside*] The Duke of Milan
And his more braver daughter could control thee,
If now 'twere fit to do 't. At the first sight   440
They have changed eyes. Delicate Ariel,
I'll set thee free for this. [*To Fer.*] A word, good sir;
I fear you have done yourself some wrong: a word.
    Mir. Why speaks my father so ungently? This
Is the third man that e'er I saw, the first
That e'er I sigh'd for: pity move my father
To be inclined my way!
    Fer.   O, if a virgin,
And your affection not gone forth, I'll make you
The queen of Naples.
    Pros.   Soft, sir! one word more.
[*Aside*] They are both in either's powers; but this
    swift business   450
I must uneasy make, lest too light winning
Make the prize light. [*To Fer.*] One word more; I
    charge thee
That thou attend me: thou dost here usurp
The name thou owest not; and hast put thyself
Upon this island as a spy, to win it
From me, the lord on 't.
    Fer.   No, as I am a man.
    Mir. There 's nothing ill can dwell in such a temple:
If the ill spirit have so fair a house,
Good things will strive to dwell with 't.
    Pros.   Follow me.

Speak not you for him; he 's a traitor. Come;   460
I'll manacle thy neck and feet together:
Sea-water shalt thou drink; thy food shall be
The fresh-brook mussels, wither'd roots and husks
Wherein the acorn cradled. Follow.
    Fer.   No;
I will resist such entertainment till
Mine enemy has more power.
              [*Draws, and is charmed from moving.*
    Mir.   O dear father,
Make not too rash a trial of him, for
He 's gentle and not fearful.
    Pros.   What? I say,
My foot my tutor? Put thy sword up, traitor;
Who makest a show but darest not strike, thy
    conscience   470
Is so possess'd with guilt: come from thy ward,
For I can here disarm thee with this stick
And make thy weapon drop.
    Mir.   Beseech you, father.
    Pros. Hence! hang not on my garments.
    Mir.   Sir, have pity;
I'll be his surety.
    Pros.   Silence! one word more
Shall make me chide thee, if not hate thee. What!
An advocate for an impostor! hush!
Thou think'st there is no more such shapes as he,
Having seen but him and Caliban: foolish wench!
To the most of men this is a Caliban   480
And they to him are angels.
    Mir.   My affections
Are then most humble; I have no ambition
To see a goodlier man.
    Pros.   Come on; obey:
Thy nerves are in their infancy again
And have no vigour in them.
    Fer.   So they are;
My spirits, as in a dream, are all bound up.
My father's loss, the weakness which I feel,
The wreck of all my friends, nor this man's threats,
To whom I am subdued, are but light to me,
Might I but through my prison once a day   490
Behold this maid: all corners else o' the earth
Let liberty make use of; space enough
Have I in such a prison.
    Pros.   [*Aside*] It works. [*To Fer.*] Come
    on.
Thou hast done well, fine Ariel! [*To Fer.*] Follow me.
[*To Ari.*] Hark what thou else shalt do me.
    Mir.   Be of comfort;
My father 's of a better nature, sir,
Than he appears by speech: this is unwonted
Which now came from him.
    Pros.   Thou shalt be as free
As mountain winds: but then exactly do
All points of my command.
    Ari.   To the syllable.   500
    Pros. Come, follow. Speak not for him.   [*Exeunt.*

(New Cambridge). 379. **whist**, silent. 380. **featly**, neatly. 381.
burthen, refrain. 405. **remember**, commemorate. 415. **canker**,
cankerworm (feeding on buds and leaves). 419. **It goes on**, my charm
works. 423. **remain**, dwell. 429. **best**, i.e., in birth. 432. **single**,
solitary, with a suggestion of feebleness. 439. **control**, confute. 441.
changed eyes, exchanged amorous glances, with suggestion of the eye
as the origin of the passion of love. 443. **done . . . wrong**, are mistaken.
451. **uneasy**, difficult. 451, 452. **light, light**, easy, cheap. 465. **entertainment**, treatment. 468. **gentle**, well-born, high-spirited. **not
fearful**, not dangerous (because incapable of treachery). 469. **foot**,
subordinate. Miranda (the foot) presumes to instruct Prospero (the
head). 471. **come . . . ward**. New Cambridge editors read comma
after *come*, with the meaning, "Come, off thy guard." 484. **nerves**,
sinews. 491-492. **all . . . of**, those who are free may have all the
rest of the world.

ACT II.

SCENE I. *Another part of the island.*

Enter ALONSO, SEBASTIAN, ANTONIO, GONZALO, ADRIAN, FRANCISCO, *and others*.

Gon. Beseech you, sir, be merry; you have cause,
So have we all, of joy; for our escape
Is much beyond our loss. Our hint of woe
Is common; every day some sailor's wife,
The masters of some merchant and the merchant
Have just our theme of woe; but for the miracle,
I mean our preservation, few in millions
Can speak like us: then wisely, good sir, weigh
Our sorrow with our comfort.
    Alon.   Prithee, peace.
    Seb. He receives comfort like cold porridge.   10
    Ant. The visitor will not give him o'er so.
    Seb. Look, he 's winding up the watch of his wit; by and by it will strike.
    Gon. Sir,—
    Seb. One: tell.
    Gon. When every grief is entertain'd that 's offer'd, Comes to the entertainer—
    Seb. A dollar.
    Gon. Dolour comes to him, indeed: you have spoken truer than you purposed.   20
    Seb. You have taken it wiselier than I meant you should.
    Gon. Therefore, my lord,—
    Ant. Fie, what a spendthrift is he of his tongue!
    Alon. I prithee, spare.
    Gon. Well, I have done: but yet,—
    Seb. He will be talking.
    Ant. Which, of he or Adrian, for a good wager, first begins to crow?
    Seb. The old cock.   30
    Ant. The cockerel.
    Seb. Done. The wager?
    Ant. A laughter.
    Seb. A match!
    Adr. Though this island seem to be desert,—
    Seb. Ha, ha, ha! So, you 're paid.
    Adr. Uninhabitable and almost inaccessible,—
    Seb. Yet,—
    Adr. Yet,—
    Ant. He could not miss 't.   40
    Adr. It must needs be of subtle, tender and delicate temperance.
    Ant. Temperance was a delicate wench.
    Seb. Ay, and a subtle; as he most learnedly delivered.
    Adr. The air breathes upon us here most sweetly.
    Seb. As if it had lungs and rotten ones.
    Ant. Or as 'twere perfumed by a fen.
    Gon. Here is every thing advantageous to life.
    Ant. True; save means to live.   50

    Seb. Of that there 's none, or little.
    Gon. How lush and lusty the grass looks! how green!
    Ant. The ground indeed is tawny.
    Seb. With an eye of green in 't.
    Ant. He misses not much.
    Seb. No; he doth but mistake the truth totally.
    Gon. But the rarity of it is,—which is indeed almost beyond credit,—
    Seb. As many vouched rarities are.   60
    Gon. That our garments, being, as they were, drenched in the sea, hold notwithstanding their freshness and glosses, being rather new-dyed than stained with salt water.
    Ant. If but one of his pockets could speak, would it not say he lies?
    Seb. Ay, or very falsely pocket up his report.
    Gon. Methinks our garments are now as fresh as when we put them on first in Afric, at the marriage of the king's fair daughter Claribel to the King of Tunis.   71
    Seb. 'Twas a sweet marriage, and we prosper well in our return.
    Adr. Tunis was never graced before with such a paragon to their queen.
    Gon. Not since widow Dido's time.
    Ant. Widow! a pox o' that! How came that widow in? widow Dido!
    Seb. What if he had said 'widower Æneas' too? Good Lord, how you take it!   80
    Adr. 'Widow Dido' said you? you make me study of that: she was of Carthage, not of Tunis.
    Gon. This Tunis, sir, was Carthage.
    Adr. Carthage?
    Gon. I assure you, Carthage.   85
    Seb. His word is more than the miraculous harp; he hath raised the wall and houses too.
    Ant. What impossible matter will he make easy next?
    Seb. I think he will carry this island home in his pocket and give it his son for an apple.   91
    Ant. And, sowing the kernels of it in the sea, bring forth more islands.
    Gon. Ay.
    Ant. Why, in good time.
    Gon. Sir, we were talking that our garments seem now as fresh as when we were at Tunis at the marriage of your daughter, who is now queen.
    Ant. And the rarest that e'er came there.
    Seb. Bate, I beseech you, widow Dido.   100
    Ant. O, widow Dido! ay, widow Dido.
    Gon. Is not, sir, my doublet as fresh as the first day I wore it? I mean, in a sort.
    Ant. That sort was well fished for.
    Gon. When I wore it at your daughter's marriage?
    Alon. You cram these words into mine ears against
The stomach of my sense. Would I had never
Married my daughter there! for, coming thence,

ACT II. SCENE I.   **5. merchant, merchant,** merchant vessel, merchant. **11. visitor,** one taking nourishment to the sick. **18. dollar,** widely circulated coin, the German *Thaler* and the Spanish *piece of eight.* **33. laughter,** sitting of eggs. When Adrian (the *cockerel*) begins to speak (l. 35), Sebastian loses the bet and pays with a *laugh* (*Ha, ha, ha!* 36) for a *laughter*. **34. A match,** a bargain; agreed. **40. He . . . miss 't,** i.e., even if it is uninhabitable and inaccessible, he could not refrain from talking about it. **42. temperance,** temperature. **43. Temperance,** a Puritan name for women, thought also to refer to Temperance, a character in Chapman's *May Day* (1611). **54. tawny,** dull brown. **55. eye,** tinge. **63. glosses,** New Cambridge: *gloss.* **65.**

pockets. Some editors suppose that reference is made to mud in the pockets. There is, at any rate, some peculiarity in Gonzalo's appearance; cf. line 30. **76. widow Dido,** queen of Carthage deserted by Aeneas; possible topical reference to Chapman's *Widow's Tears,* or some other play. **86. miraculous harp,** allusion to Amphion's harp with which he raised the walls of Thebes. **95. in good time,** vague expression of agreement or approbation. **104. sort,** lucky catch after much angling; probable suggestion of the age of the garment, with a play on *sort* in line 103. **113-122. Sir . . . land,** Francisco's only speech. New Cambridge editors think the speech belongs to Gonzalo, and see in its assignment to Francisco a relic of an older version. **120. basis,** foot, base. **125.**

My son is lost and, in my rate, she too,
Who is so far from Italy removed 110
I ne'er again shall see her. O thou mine heir
Of Naples and of Milan, what strange fish
Hath made his meal on thee?
   Fran.   Sir, he may live:
I saw him beat the surges under him,
And ride upon their backs; he trod the water,
Whose enmity he flung aside, and breasted
The surge most swoln that met him; his bold head
'Bove the contentious waves he kept, and oar'd
Himself with his good arms in lusty stroke
To the shore, that o'er his wave-worn basis bow'd, 120
As stooping to relieve him: I not doubt
He came alive to land.
   Alon.   No, no, he 's gone.
   Seb. Sir, you may thank yourself for this great loss,
That would not bless our Europe with your daughter,
But rather loose her to an African;
Where she at least is banish'd from your eye,
Who hath cause to wet the grief on 't.
   Alon.   Prithee, peace.
   Seb. You were kneel'd to and importuned otherwise
By all of us, and the fair soul herself
Weigh'd between loathness and obedience, at 130
Which end o' the beam should bow. We have lost
     your son,
I fear, for ever: Milan and Naples have
Moe widows in them of this business' making
Than we bring men to comfort them:
The fault 's your own.
   Alon.   So is the dear'st o' the loss.
   Gon. My lord Sebastian,
The truth you speak doth lack some gentleness
And time to speak it in: you rub the sore,
When you should bring the plaster.
   Seb.   Very well.
   Ant. And most chirurgeonly. 140
   Gon. It is foul weather in us all, good sir,
When you are cloudy.
   Seb.   Foul weather?
   Ant.   Very foul.
   Gon. Had I plantation of this isle, my lord,—
   Ant. He 'ld sow 't with nettle-seed.
   Seb.   Or docks, or mallows.
   Gon. And were the king on 't, what would I do?
   Seb. 'Scape being drunk for want of wine.
   Gon. I' the commonwealth I would by contraries
Execute all things; for no kind of traffic
Would I admit; no name of magistrate;
Letters should not be known; riches, poverty, 150
And use of service, none; contract, succession,
Bourn, bound of land, tilth, vineyard, none;
No use of metal, corn, or wine, or oil;
No occupation; all men idle, all;
And women too, but innocent and pure;
No sovereignty;—

   Seb.   Yet he would be king on 't.
   Ant. The latter end of his commonwealth forgets the
beginning.
   Gon. All things in common nature should produce
Without sweat or endeavour: treason, felony, 160
Sword, pike, knife, gun, or need of any engine,
Would I not have; but nature should bring forth,
Of it own kind, all foison, all abundance,
To feed my innocent people.
   Seb. No marrying 'mong his subjects?
   Ant. None, man; all idle: whores and knaves.
   Gon. I would with such perfection govern, sir,
To excel the golden age.
   Seb.   God save his majesty!
   Ant. Long live Gonzalo!
   Gon.   And,—do you mark me, sir?
   Alon. Prithee, no more: thou dost talk nothing to
me. 171
   Gon. I do well believe your highness; and did it to
minister occasion to these gentlemen, who are of such
sensible and nimble lungs that they always use to
laugh at nothing.
   Ant. 'Twas you we laughed at.
   Gon. Who in this kind of merry fooling am nothing
to you: so you may continue and laugh at nothing
still.
   Ant. What a blow was there given! 180
   Seb. An it had not fallen flat-long.
   Gon. You are gentlemen of brave mettle; you would
lift the moon out of her sphere, if she would continue
in it five weeks without changing.

Enter ARIEL, *invisible, playing solemn music.*

   Seb. We would so, and then go a bat-fowling.
   Ant. Nay, good my lord, be not angry.
   Gon. No, I warrant you; I will not adventure my
discretion so weakly. Will you laugh me asleep, for I
am very heavy?
   Ant. Go sleep, and hear us. 190
                      [All sleep except Alon., Seb., and Ant.
   Alon. What, all so soon asleep! I wish mine eyes
Would, with themselves, shut up my thoughts: I find
They are inclined to do so.
   Seb.   Please you, sir,
Do not omit the heavy offer of it:
It seldom visits sorrow; when it doth,
It is a comforter.
   Ant.   We two, my lord,
Will guard your person while you take your rest,
And watch your safety.
   Alon.   Thank you. Wondrous heavy.
                      [Alonso sleeps. Exit Ariel.
   Seb. What a strange drowsiness possesses them!
   Ant. It is the quality o' the climate.
   Seb.   Why 200
Doth it not then our eyelids sink? I find not
Myself disposed to sleep.

---

loose, so F; Globe: *lose.* 127. **Who,** which (eye). 129-131. **the fair . . .**
. . . bow, the fair soul herself was poised uncertain between unwillingness and obedience as to which end of the scale should sink. 140.
chirurgeonly, like a skilled surgeon. 143. **plantation,** colonization;
subsequent play on the literal meaning. 147-156. **I' the . . . sover-**
eignty. This passage on man in his primitive state is based on Montaigne, *Essays,* I, xxx, and derived from Florio's translation (1603).
150. **Letters,** learning. 151. **use of service,** custom of employing servants. **succession,** holding of property by right of inheritance. 152.
Bourn, boundaries. **bound of land,** landmarks. **tilth,** tillage of soil.
161. **engine,** instrument of warfare. 163. **it,** its. **foison,** plenty. 168.

God. Omitted in F in deference to the statute forbidding profanity on the
stage. 174. **nimble,** easily excited. 181. **flat-long,** with the flat of the
sword. 182. **mettle,** temper, nature. 183. **lift . . . sphere.** As a planet
in the old astronomy, the moon had a crystal sphere in which she
moved. Gonzalo means that they would lift the moon out of her sphere
if she remained steady in it. 185. **bat-fowling,** hunting birds at night
with lantern and stick; also, gulling a simpleton. Gonzalo is the simpleton (or fowl), and Sebastian will use the moon as his lantern. 187.
adventure, risk. 190. **Go . . . us,** let our laughing send you to sleep, or,
go to sleep and hear us laugh at you. 194. **omit,** neglect. **heavy,**
drowsy.

Ant.   Nor I; my spirits are nimble.
They fell together all, as by consent;
They dropp'd, as by a thunder-stroke. What might,
Worthy Sebastian? O, what might?—No more:—
And yet methinks I see it in thy face,
What thou shouldst be: the occasion speaks thee, and
My strong imagination sees a crown
Dropping upon thy head.
    Seb.   What, art thou waking?
    Ant. Do you not hear me speak?
    Seb.   I do; and surely   210
It is a sleepy language and thou speak'st
Out of thy sleep. What is it thou didst say?
This is a strange repose, to be asleep
With eyes wide open; standing, speaking, moving,
And yet so fast asleep.
    Ant.   Noble Sebastian,
Thou let'st thy fortune sleep—die, rather; wink'st
Whiles thou art waking.
    Seb.   Thou dost snore distinctly;
There 's meaning in thy snores.
    Ant. I am more serious than my custom: you
Must be so too, if heed me; which to do   220
Trebles thee o'er.
    Seb.   Well, I am standing water.
    Ant. I'll teach you how to flow.
    Seb.   Do so: to ebb
Hereditary sloth instructs me.
    Ant.   O,
If you but knew how you the purpose cherish
Whiles thus you mock it! how, in stripping it,
You more invest it! Ebbing men, indeed,
Most often do so near the bottom run
By their own fear or sloth.
    Seb.   Prithee, say on:
The setting of thine eye and cheek proclaim
A matter from thee, and a birth indeed   230
Which throes thee much to yield.
    Ant.   Thus, sir:
Although this lord of weak remembrance, this,
Who shall be of as little memory
When he is earth'd, hath here almost persuaded,—
For he 's a spirit of persuasion, only
Professes to persuade,—the king his son 's alive,
'Tis as impossible that he 's undrown'd
As he that sleeps here swims.
    Seb.   I have no hope
That he 's undrown'd.
    Ant.   O, out of that 'no hope'
What great hope have you! no hope that way is   240
Another way so high a hope that even
Ambition cannot pierce a wink beyond,
But doubt discovery there. Will you grant with me
That Ferdinand is drown'd?
    Seb.   He 's gone.
    Ant.   Then, tell me,
Who 's the next heir of Naples?
    Seb.   Claribel.
    Ant. She that is queen of Tunis; she that dwells

Ten leagues beyond man's life; she that from Naples
Can have no note, unless the sun were post—
The man i' the moon 's too slow—till new-born chins
Be rough and razorable; she that—from whom?   250
We all were sea-swallow'd, though some cast again,
And by that destiny to perform an act
Whereof what 's past is prologue, what to come
In yours and my discharge.
    Seb.   What stuff is this! how say you?
'Tis true, my brother's daughter 's queen of Tunis;
So is she heir of Naples; 'twixt which regions
There is some space.
    Ant.   A space whose every cubit
Seems to cry out, 'How shall that Claribel
Measure us back to Naples? Keep in Tunis,
And let Sebastian wake.' Say, this were death   260
That now hath seized them; why, they were no
       worse
Than now they are. There be that can rule Naples
As well as he that sleeps; lords that can prate
As amply and unnecessarily
As this Gonzalo; I myself could make
A chough of as deep chat. O, that you bore
The mind that I do! what a sleep were this
For your advancement! Do you understand me?
    Seb. Methinks I do.
    Ant.   And how does your content
Tender your own good fortune?
    Seb.   I remember   270
You did supplant your brother Prospero.
    Ant.   True:
And look how well my garments sit upon me;
Much feater than before: my brother's servants
Were then my fellows; now they are my men.
    Seb. But, for your conscience?
    Ant. Ay, sir; where lies that? if 'twere a kibe,
'Twould put me to my slipper: but I feel not
This deity in my bosom: twenty consciences,
That stand 'twixt me and Milan, candied be they
And melt ere they molest! Here lies your brother,   280
No better than the earth he lies upon,
If he were that which now he 's like, that 's dead;
Whom I, with this obedient steel, three inches of it,
Can lay to bed for ever; whiles you, doing thus,
To the perpetual wink for aye might put
This ancient morsel, this Sir Prudence, who
Should not upbraid our course. For all the rest,
They'll take suggestion as a cat laps milk;
They'll tell the clock to any business that
We say befits the hour.
    Seb.   Thy case, dear friend,   290
Shall be my precedent; as thou got'st Milan,
I'll come by Naples. Draw thy sword: one stroke
Shall free thee from the tribute which thou payest;
And I the king shall love thee.
    Ant.   Draw together;
And when I rear my hand, do you the like,
To fall it on Gonzalo.
    Seb.   O, but one word. [*They talk apart.*

---

203. **consent,** agreement as to a course of action. 207. **speaks,** calls upon, proclaims (thee) king. 217. **distinctly,** with separate and individual sounds. 221. **Trebles.** New Cambridge editors read *Troubles* in view of *standing water.* Onions defines as "makes thee three times as great." **standing water,** water which neither flows nor ebbs. 224. **purpose,** i.e., of being king. 225. **stripping it,** stripping off all pretense, revealing it. 226. **Ebbing men,** men whose fortunes ebb, leaving them stranded. 229. **setting,** set expression. 230. **matter,** matter of importance. 231. **throes,** pains. 232. **this lord,** Gonzalo.

remembrance, power of remembering. 234. **earth'd,** buried. 236. **Professes to persuade,** he was a privy councilor. 240. **that way,** i.e., in regard to Ferdinand's being saved. 242-243. **Ambition . . . there,** ambition itself cannot see any further than that hope (of the crown) without doubting the reality of the objects it sees. Furness, following Nicholson's conjecture of *dout* (extinguish) for *doubt*, interprets, "when ambition pierces to its furthest wink where discovery ceases, and the crown is found." 247. **Ten . . . life,** it would take more than a lifetime to get there. 248. **note,** intimation. 250. **she . . . whom,** broken and

Re-enter ARIEL, *invisible.*

Ari. My master through his art foresees the danger
That you, his friend, are in; and sends me forth—
For else his project dies—to keep them living.
                                        [*Sings in Gonzalo's ear.*

        While you here do snoring lie,   300
        Open-eyed conspiracy
            His time doth take.
        If of life you keep a care,
        Shake off slumber, and beware:
            Awake, awake!

Ant. Then let us both be sudden.
Gon.   Now, good angels
Preserve the king.   [*They wake.*
Alon. Why, how now? ho, awake! Why are you
    drawn?
Wherefore this ghastly looking?
Gon.   What 's the matter?
Seb. Whiles we stood here securing your repose,   310
Even now, we heard a hollow burst of bellowing
Like bulls, or rather lions: did 't not wake you?
It struck mine ear most terribly.
Alon.   I heard nothing.
Ant. O, 'twas a din to fright a monster's ear,
To make an earthquake! sure, it was the roar
Of a whole herd of lions.
Alon.   Heard you this, Gonzalo?
Gon. Upon mine honour, sir, I heard a humming,
And that a strange one too, which did awake me:
I shaked you, sir, and cried: as mine eyes open'd,
I saw their weapons drawn: there was a noise,   320
That 's verily. 'Tis best we stand upon our guard,
Or that we quit this place: let 's draw our weapons.
Alon. Lead off this ground; and let 's make further
    search
For my poor son.
Gon. Heavens keep him from these beasts!
For he is, sure, i' the island.
Alon.   Lead away.
Ari. Prospero my lord shall know what I have done:
So, king, go safely on to seek thy son.   [*Exeunt.*

SCENE II. *Another part of the island.*

Enter CALIBAN *with a burden of wood. A noise of*
    thunder heard.

Cal. All the infections that the sun sucks up
From bogs, fens, flats, on Prosper fall and make him
By inch-meal a disease! His spirits hear me
And yet I needs must curse. But they'll nor pinch,
Fright me with urchin-shows, pitch me i' the mire,
Nor lead me, like a firebrand, in the dark
Out of my way, unless he bid 'em; but
For every trifle are they set upon me;
Sometime like apes that mow and chatter at me
And after bite me, then like hedgehogs which   10

Lie tumbling in my barefoot way and mount
Their pricks at my footfall; sometime am I
All wound with adders who with cloven tongues
Do hiss me into madness.

Enter TRINCULO.
                            Lo, now, lo!
Here comes a spirit of his, and to torment me
For bringing wood in slowly. I'll fall flat;
Perchance he will not mind me.   17
Trin. Here 's neither bush nor shrub, to bear off
any weather at all, and another storm brewing; I
hear it sing i' the wind: yond same black cloud, yond
huge one, looks like a foul bombard that would shed
his liquor. If it should thunder as it did before, I know
not where to hide my head: yond same cloud cannot
choose but fall by pailfuls. What have we here? a man
or a fish? dead or alive? A fish: he smells like a fish; a
very ancient and fish-like smell; a kind of not of the
newest Poor-John. A strange fish! Were I in England
now, as once I was, and had but this fish painted, not
a holiday fool there but would give a piece of silver:
there would this monster make a man; any strange
beast there makes a man: when they will not give a
doit to relieve a lame beggar, they will lay out ten to
see a dead Indian. Legged like a man! and his fins
like arms! Warm o' my troth! I do now let loose my
opinion; hold it no longer: this is no fish, but an
islander, that hath lately suffered by a thunderbolt.
[*Thunder.*] Alas, the storm is come again! my best way
is to creep under his gaberdine; there is no other
shelter hereabout: misery acquaints a man with
strange bed-fellows. I will here shroud till the dregs of
the storm be past.   43

Enter STEPHANO, *singing: a bottle in his hand.*

Ste. I shall no more to sea, to sea,
        Here shall I die ashore—
This is a very scurvy tune to sing at a man's funeral:
well, here 's my comfort.   [*Drinks.*
[*Sings.*]
        The master, the swabber, the boatswain and I,
            The gunner and his mate
        Loved Mall, Meg and Marian and Margery,   50
            But none of us cared for Kate;
            For she had a tongue with a tang,
            Would cry to a sailor, Go hang!
        She loved not the savour of tar nor of pitch,
        Yet a tailor might scratch her where'er she did itch:
            Then to sea, boys, and let her go hang!

This is a scurvy tune too: but here 's my comfort.
                                        [*Drinks.*
Cal. Do not torment me: Oh!   58
Ste. What 's the matter? Have we devils here? Do
you put tricks upon 's with savages and men of Ind,
ha? I have not 'scaped drowning to be afeard now of
your four legs; for it hath been said, As proper a man
as ever went on four legs cannot make him give

---

difficult construction. **from whom?** Probably, from whom will she learn?
251. **cast,** were disgorged, with pun on *casting* (of parts for a play). 254.
discharge, performance, i.e., to get done. 259. **Measure us,** find (her)
way. 259-260. **Keep . . . wake,** let her stay in Tunis, and let Sebastian
wake (to his good fortune). 265-266. **I . . . chat,** I could teach a
jackdaw to talk as wisely. 269. **content,** desire, contentment. 270.
Tender, provide for. 273. **feater,** more becomingly. 276. **kibe,** sore
on the heel. 279. **candied,** frozen, congealed. 302. **time,** opportunity.
306. **sudden,** swift in action. 317. **humming,** i.e., Ariel's song.

SCENE II. 3. **inch-meal,** little by little. 9. **mow,** make faces. 19.
bear off, keep off. 22. **foul bombard,** dirty leathern bottle. 29.
Poor-John, salted hake, type of poor fare. **fish.** Malone cites a license
issued by the Master of the Revels (1632) "to shew a strange fish for
half a yeare." 33. **make a man,** i.e., make his fortune. 40. **gaberdine,**
cloak, loose upper garment. 43. **shroud,** take shelter. **dregs,** last
remains. 61. **Ind,** India, or vaguely, the East.

ground; and it shall be said so again while Stephano breathes at nostrils.

Cal. The spirit torments me; Oh! 66

Ste. This is some monster of the isle with four legs, who hath got, as I take it, an ague. Where the devil should he learn our language? I will give him some relief, if it be but for that. If I can recover him and keep him tame and get to Naples with him, he 's a present for any emperor that ever trod on neat's-leather. 73

Cal. Do not torment me, prithee; I'll bring my wood home faster.

Ste. He 's in his fit now and does not talk after the wisest. He shall taste of my bottle: if he have never drunk wine afore, it will go near to remove his fit. If I can recover him and keep him tame, I will not take too much for him; he shall pay for him that hath him, and that soundly.

Cal. Thou dost me yet but little hurt; thou wilt anon, I know it by thy trembling: now Prosper works upon thee. 84

Ste. Come on your ways; open your mouth; here is that which will give language to you, cat: open your mouth; this will shake your shaking, I can tell you, and that soundly: you cannot tell who 's your friend: open your chaps again. 89

Trin. I should know that voice: it should be—but he is drowned; and these are devils: O defend me!

Ste. Four legs and two voices: a most delicate monster! His forward voice now is to speak well of his friend; his backward voice is to utter foul speeches and to detract. If all the wine in my bottle will recover him, I will help his ague. Come. Amen! I will pour some in thy other mouth.

Trin. Stephano! 100

Ste. Doth thy other mouth call me? Mercy, mercy! This is a devil, and no monster: I will leave him; I have no long spoon.

Trin. Stephano! If thou beest Stephano, touch me and speak to me; for I am Trinculo—be not afeard—thy good friend Trinculo.

Ste. If thou beest Trinculo, come forth: I'll pull thee by the lesser legs: if any be Trinculo's legs, these are they. Thou art very Trinculo indeed! How camest thou to be the siege of this moon-calf? can he vent Trinculos? 111

Trin. I took him to be killed with a thunder-stroke. But art thou not drowned, Stephano? I hope now thou art not drowned. Is the storm overblown? I hid me under the dead moon-calf's gaberdine for fear of the storm. And art thou living, Stephano? O Stephano, two Neapolitans 'scaped!

Ste. Prithee, do not turn me about; my stomach is not constant.

Cal. [*Aside*] These be fine things, an if they be not sprites. 121

That 's a brave god and bears celestial liquor.
I will kneel to him.

Ste. How didst thou 'scape? How camest thou hither? swear by this bottle how thou camest hither. I escaped upon a butt of sack which the sailors

heaved o'erboard, by this bottle! which I made of the bark of a tree with mine own hands since I was cast ashore.

Cal. I'll swear upon that bottle to be thy true subject; for the liquor is not earthly. 130

Ste. Here; swear then how thou escapedst.

Trin. Swum ashore, man, like a duck: I can swim like a duck, I'll be sworn.

Ste. Here, kiss the book. Though thou canst swim like a duck, thou art made like a goose.

Trin. O Stephano, hast any more of this?

Ste. The whole butt, man: my cellar is in a rock by the sea-side where my wine is hid. How now, moon-calf! how does thine ague? 139

Cal. Hast thou not dropp'd from heaven?

Ste. Out o' the moon, I do assure thee: I was the man i' the moon when time was.

Cal. I have seen thee in her and I do adore thee:
My mistress show'd me thee and thy dog and thy
    bush.

Ste. Come, swear to that; kiss the book: I will furnish it anon with new contents: swear.

Trin. By this good light, this is a very shallow monster! I afeard of him! A very weak monster! The man i' the moon! A most poor credulous monster! Well drawn, monster, in good sooth! 151

Cal. I'll show thee every fertile inch o' th' island;
And I will kiss thy foot: I prithee, be my god.

Trin. By this light, a most perfidious and drunken monster! when 's god 's asleep, he'll rob his bottle.

Cal. I'll kiss thy foot; I'll swear myself thy subject.

Ste. Come on then; down, and swear.

Trin. I shall laugh myself to death at this puppy-headed monster. A most scurvy monster! I could find in my heart to beat him,—

Ste. Come, kiss. 161

Trin. But that the poor monster 's in drink: an abominable monster!

Cal. I'll show thee the best springs; I'll pluck thee
    berries;
I'll fish for thee and get thee wood enough.
A plague upon the tyrant that I serve!
I'll bear him no more sticks, but follow thee,
Thou wondrous man.

Trin. A most ridiculous monster, to make a wonder of a poor drunkard! 170

Cal. I prithee, let me bring thee where crabs grow;
And I with my long nails will dig thee pig-nuts;
Show thee a jay's nest and instruct thee how
To snare the nimble marmoset; I'll bring thee
To clustering filberts and sometimes I'll get thee
Young scamels from the rock. Wilt thou go with me?

Ste. I prithee now, lead the way without any more talking. Trinculo, the king and all our company else being drowned, we will inherit here: here; bear my bottle: fellow Trinculo, we'll fill him by and by again.

Cal. [*Sings drunkenly*]
    Farewell, master; farewell, farewell! 182

Trin. A howling monster; a drunken monster!

Cal. No more dams I'll make for fish;
    Nor fetch in firing

71. **recover,** restore.   73. **neat's-leather,** leather from the skin of an animal of the ox kind.   80. **take too much,** ironical, meaning: He will take as much as he can get.   83. **trembling,** suggestion of demonic possession.   87. **cat . . . mouth,** allusion to the proverb, "Good liquor will make a cat speak."   103. **long spoon,** allusion to the proverb, "He that sups with the devil has need of a long spoon."   111. **moon-**calf, monster, abortion (supposed to be caused by the influence of the moon).   120. **not constant,** unsteady.   126. **butt of sack,** barrel of Canary wine.   134. **kiss the book.** He gives him the bottle instead of the Bible on which to make his oath.   142. **when time was,** once upon a time.   144. **dog . . . bush.** See *A Midsummer-Night's Dream,* V, i, 136.   150. **Well drawn.** Caliban takes a good draft of the wine.   172. **pig-**

At requiring;
Nor scrape trencher, nor wash dish:
'Ban, 'Ban, Cacaliban
Has a new master: get a new man.
Freedom, hey-day! hey-day, freedom! freedom, hey-
day, freedom!   191
   Ste. O brave monster! Lead the way.   *[Exeunt.*

ACT III.

SCENE I. *Before* PROSPERO'S *cell.*

Enter FERDINAND, *bearing a log.*

   Fer. There be some sports are painful, and their
     labour
Delight in them sets off: some kinds of baseness
Are nobly undergone and most poor matters
Point to rich ends. This my mean task
Would be as heavy to me as odious, but
The mistress which I serve quickens what's dead
And makes my labours pleasures: O, she is
Ten times more gentle than her father's crabbed,
And he's composed of harshness. I must remove
Some thousands of these logs and pile them up,   10
Upon a sore injunction: my sweet mistress
Weeps when she sees me work, and says, such
     baseness
Had never like executor. I forget:
But these sweet thoughts do even refresh my labours,
†Most busy lest, when I do it.

   Enter MIRANDA; *and* PROSPERO *at a distance, unseen.*

   Mir.   Alas, now, pray you,
Work not so hard: I would the lightning had
Burnt up those logs that you are enjoin'd to pile!
Pray, set it down and rest you: when this burns,
'Twill weep for having wearied you. My father
Is hard at study; pray now, rest yourself;   20
He's safe for these three hours.
   Fer.   O most dear mistress,
The sun will set before I shall discharge
What I must strive to do.
   Mir.   If you'll sit down,
I'll bear your logs the while: pray, give me that;
I'll carry it to the pile.
   Fer.   No, precious creature;
I had rather crack my sinews, break my back,
Than you should such dishonour undergo,
While I sit lazy by.
   Mir.   It would become me
As well as it does you: and I should do it
With much more ease; for my good will is to it,   30
And yours it is against.
   Pros.   Poor worm, thou art infected!
This visitation shows it.
   Mir.   You look wearily.
   Fer. No, noble mistress; 'tis fresh morning with me
When you are by at night. I do beseech you—
Chiefly that I might set it in my prayers—
What is your name?

   Mir.   Miranda.—O my father,
I have broke your hest to say so!
   Fer.   Admired Miranda!
Indeed the top of admiration! worth
What 's dearest to the world! Full many a lady
I have eyed with best regard and many a time   40
The harmony of their tongues hath into bondage
Brought my too diligent ear: for several virtues
Have I liked several women; never any
With so full soul, but some defect in her
Did quarrel with the noblest grace she owed
And put it to the foil: but you, O you,
So perfect and so peerless, are created
Of every creature's best!
   Mir.   I do not know
One of my sex; no woman's face remember,
Save, from my glass, mine own; nor have I seen   50
More that I may call men than you, good friend,
And my dear father: how features are abroad,
I am skilless of; but, by my modesty,
The jewel in my dower, I would not wish
Any companion in the world but you,
Nor can imagination form a shape,
Besides yourself, to like of. But I prattle
Something too wildly and my father's precepts
I therein do forget.
   Fer.   I am in my condition
A prince, Miranda; I do think, a king;   60
I would, not so!—and would no more endure
This wooden slavery than to suffer
The flesh-fly blow my mouth. Hear my soul speak:
The very instant that I saw you, did
My heart fly to your service; there resides,
To make me slave to it; and for your sake
Am I this patient log-man.
   Mir.   Do you love me?
   Fer. O heaven, O earth, bear witness to this sound
And crown what I profess with kind event
If I speak true! if hollowly, invert   70
What best is boded me to mischief! I
Beyond all limit of what else i' the world
Do love, prize, honour you.
   Mir.   I am a fool
To weep at what I am glad of.
   Pros.   Fair encounter
Of two most rare affections! Heavens rain grace
On that which breeds between 'em!
   Fer.   Wherefore weep you?
   Mir. At mine unworthiness that dare not offer
What I desire to give, and much less take
What I shall die to want. But this is trifling;
And all the more it seeks to hide itself,   80
The bigger bulk it shows. Hence, bashful cunning!
And prompt me, plain and holy innocence!
I am your wife, if you will marry me;
If not, I'll die your maid: to be your fellow
You may deny me; but I'll be your servant,
Whether you will or no.
   Fer.   My mistress, dearest;
And I thus humble ever.
   Mir.   My husband, then?

---

nuts, roundish tubers of *bunium flexuosum;* earth-chestnuts. 174. **mar-moset,** small monkey. 176. **scamels,** not explained. Keightley con-jectured *seamels* (seagulls), Theobald: *stannels* (kestrels); New Cambridge editors call attention to the fact that "seamews" occurs in Strachey's letter. 179. **inherit,** take possession. 187. **trencher,** trenchers, col-lectively (Onions).

ACT III. SCENE I. 11. **sore,** grievous, severe. 15. **Most . . . lest,** unexplained; Spedding suggests *Most busiest when idlest;* New Cambridge editors suggest *busy-idlest,* employed in trifles. 46. **put . . . foil,** disgraced it; a wrestling phrase. 53. **skilless,** ignorant. 70. **hol-lowly,** insincerely, falsely.

Fer. Ay, with a heart as willing
As bondage e'er of freedom: here 's my hand.
    Mir. And mine, with my heart in 't: and now
      farewell   90
Till half an hour hence.
    Fer.   A thousand thousand!
                [*Exeunt Fer. and Mir. severally.*
    Pros. So glad of this as they I cannot be,
Who are surprised withal; but my rejoicing
At nothing can be more. I'll to my book,
For yet ere supper-time must I perform
Much business appertaining.   [*Exit.*

SCENE II. *Another part of the island.*

Enter CALIBAN, STEPHANO, *and* TRINCULO.

    Ste. Tell not me; when the butt is out, we will drink
water; not a drop before: therefore bear up, and
board 'em. Servant-monster, drink to me.
    Trin. Servant-monster! the folly of this island! They
say there 's but five upon this isle: we are three of
them; if th' other two be brained like us, the state
totters.
    Ste. Drink, servant-monster, when I bid thee: thy
eyes are almost set in thy head.   10
    Trin. Where should they be set else? he were a
brave monster indeed, if they were set in his tail.
    Ste. My man-monster hath drown'd his tongue in
sack: for my part, the sea cannot drown me; I swam,
ere I could recover the shore, five and thirty leagues
off and on. By this light, thou shalt be my lieutenant,
monster, or my standard.   19
    Trin. Your lieutenant, if you list; he 's no standard.
    Ste. We'll not run, Monsieur Monster.
    Trin. Nor go neither; but you'll lie like dogs and
yet say nothing neither.
    Ste. Moon-calf, speak once in thy life, if thou beest
a good moon-calf.
    Cal. How does thy honour? Let me lick thy shoe.
I'll not serve him; he is not valiant.   27
    Trin. Thou liest, most ignorant monster: I am in
case to justle a constable. Why, thou deboshed fish,
thou, was there ever man a coward that hath drunk
so much sack as I to-day? Wilt thou tell a monstrous
lie, being but half a fish and half a monster?
    Cal. Lo, how he mocks me! wilt thou let him, my
lord?
    Trin. 'Lord' quoth he. That a monster should be
such a natural!   37
    Cal. Lo, lo, again! bite him to death, I prithee.
    Ste. Trinculo, keep a good tongue in your head: if
you prove a mutineer,—the next tree! The poor
monster 's my subject and he shall not suffer indignity.
    Cal. I thank my noble lord. Wilt thou be pleased to
hearken once again to the suit I made to thee?
    Ste. Marry, will I: kneel and repeat it; I will stand,
and so shall Trinculo.

Enter ARIEL, *invisible.*

    Cal. As I told thee before, I am subject to a tyrant,
a sorcerer, that by his cunning hath cheated me of the
island.   50
    Ari. Thou liest.
    Cal. Thou liest, thou jesting monkey, thou: I would
my valiant master would destroy thee! I do not lie.
    Ste. Trinculo, if you trouble him any more in 's tale,
by this hand, I will supplant some of your teeth.
    Trin. Why, I said nothing.
    Ste. Mum, then, and no more. Proceed.
    Cal. I say, by sorcery he got this isle;   60
From me he got it. If thy greatness will
Revenge it on him,—for I know thou darest,
But this thing dare not,—
    Ste. That 's most certain.
    Cal. Thou shalt be lord of it and I'll serve thee.
    Ste. How now shall this be compassed?
Canst thou bring me to the party?
    Cal. Yea, yea, my lord: I'll yield him thee asleep,
Where thou mayst knock a nail into his head.
    Ari. Thou liest; thou canst not.   70
    Cal. What a pied ninny 's this! Thou scurvy patch!
I do beseech thy greatness, give him blows
And take his bottle from him: when that 's gone
He shall drink nought but brine; for I'll not show him
Where the quick freshes are.   75
    Ste. Trinculo, run into no further danger: interrupt
the monster one word further, and, by this hand,
I'll turn my mercy out o' doors and make a stock-fish
of thee.
    Trin. Why, what did I? I did nothing. I'll go
farther off.   81
    Ste. Didst thou not say he lied?
    Ari. Thou liest.
    Ste. Do I so? take thou that. [*Beats Trin.*] As you
like this, give me the lie another time.
    Trin. I did not give the lie. Out o' your wits and
hearing too? A pox o' your bottle! this can sack and
drinking do. A murrain on your monster, and the
devil take your fingers!
    Cal. Ha, ha, ha!   90
    Ste. Now, forward with your tale. Prithee, stand
farther off.
    Cal. Beat him enough: after a little time
I'll beat him too.
    Ste.   Stand farther. Come, proceed.
    Cal. Why, as I told thee, 'tis a custom with him,
I' th' afternoon to sleep: there thou mayst brain him,
Having first seized his books, or with a log
Batter his skull, or paunch him with a stake,
Or cut his wezand with thy knife. Remember
First to possess his books; for without them   100
He 's but a sot, as I am, nor hath not
One spirit to command: they all do hate him
As rootedly as I. Burn but his books.
He has brave utensils,—for so he calls them,—
Which, when he has a house, he'll deck withal.
And that most deeply to consider is
The beauty of his daughter; he himself
Calls her a nonpareil: I never saw a woman,
But only Sycorax my dam and she;
But she as far surpasseth Sycorax   110
As great'st does least.

SCENE II. 3. **bear up,** put the helm up so as to bring the ship into
the wind. **board 'em,** climb aboard; both phrases refer to drinking.
10. **thy eyes . . . head,** current description of drunkenness meaning that
the eyes are fixed in a stare, or dimmed by drink. 19. **standard,**
standard-bearer. 20. **standard,** something that stands up. 29. **case,**

condition. 30. **deboshed,** debauched. 37. **natural,** idiot. 71. **pied
ninny,** fool in motley. **patch,** common word for *fool.* 75. **quick
freshes,** running springs. 79. **stock-fish,** dried cod beaten before boiling. 88. **murrain,** plague. 99. **wezand,** windpipe. 101. **sot,** fool.
108. **nonpareil,** one having no equal. 126. **troll the catch,** sing the

Ste.   Is it so brave a lass?

Cal. Ay, lord; she will become thy bed, I warrant.
And bring thee forth brave brood.

Ste. Monster, I will kill this man: his daughter and
I will be king and queen,—save our graces!—and
Trinculo and thyself shall be viceroys. Dost thou like
the plot, Trinculo?

Trin. Excellent.

Ste. Give me thy hand: I am sorry I beat thee; but,
while thou livest, keep a good tongue in thy head.   121

Cal. Within this half hour will he be asleep:
Wilt thou destroy him then?

Ste.   Ay, on mine honour.

Ari. This will I tell my master.

Cal. Thou makest me merry; I am full of pleasure:
Let us be jocund: will you troll the catch
You taught me but while-ere?

Ste. At thy request, monster, I will do reason, any
reason. Come on, Trinculo, let us sing.   [*Sings.*

        Flout 'em and scout 'em   130
        And scout 'em and flout 'em;
            Thought is free.

Cal. That 's not the tune.

            [*Ariel plays the tune on a tabor and pipe.*

Ste. What is this same?

Trin. This is the tune of our catch, played by the
picture of Nobody.

Ste. If thou beest a man, show thyself in thy likeness:
if thou beest a devil, take 't as thou list.

Trin. O, forgive me my sins!

Ste. He that dies pays all debts: I defy thee. Mercy
upon us!   141

Cal. Art thou afeard?

Ste. No, monster, not I.

Cal. Be not afeard; the isle is full of noises,
Sounds and sweet airs, that give delight and hurt not.
Sometimes a thousand twangling instruments
Will hum about mine ears, and sometime voices
That, if I then had waked after long sleep,
Will make me sleep again: and then, in dreaming,
The clouds methought would open and show riches 150
Ready to drop upon me, that, when I waked,
I cried to dream again.

Ste. This will prove a brave kingdom to me, where
I shall have my music for nothing.

Cal. When Prospero is destroyed.

Ste. That shall be by and by: I remember the story.

Trin. The sound is going away; let 's follow it, and
after do our work.

Ste. Lead, monster; we'll follow. I would I could
see this taborer; he lays it on.   160

Trin. Wilt come? I'll follow, Stephano.   [*Exeunt.*

SCENE III. *Another part of the island.*

Enter ALONSO, SEBASTIAN, ANTONIO, GONZALO,
    ADRIAN, FRANCISCO, *and others.*

Gon. By 'r lakin, I can go no further, sir;
My old bones ache: here 's a maze trod indeed
Through forth-rights and meanders! By your
        patience,

I needs must rest me.

Alon.   Old lord, I cannot blame thee,
Who am myself attach'd with weariness,
To the dulling of my spirits: sit down, and rest.
Even here I will put off my hope and keep it
No longer for my flatterer: he is drown'd
Whom thus we stray to find, and the sea mocks
Our frustrate search on land. Well, let him go.   10

Ant. [*Aside to Seb.*] I am right glad that he 's so out
        of hope.
Do not, for one repulse, forego the purpose
That you resolved to effect.

Seb.   [*Aside to Ant.*] The next advantage
Will we take throughly.

Ant.   [*Aside to Seb.*] Let it be to-night;
For, now they are oppress'd with travel, they
Will not, nor cannot, use such vigilance
As when they are fresh.

Seb.   [*Aside to Ant.*] I say, to-night: no more.

            [*Solemn and strange music.*

Alon. What harmony is this? My good friends, hark!

Gon. Marvellous sweet music!

Enter PROSPERO *above, invisible. Enter several strange
    Shapes, bringing in a banquet; they dance about it with
    gentle actions of salutation; and, inviting the King, &c.
    to eat, they depart.*

Alon. Give us kind keepers, heavens! What were
        these?   20

Seb. A living drollery. Now I will believe
That there are unicorns, that in Arabia
There is one tree, the phœnix' throne, one phœnix
At this hour reigning there.

Ant.   I'll believe both;
And what does else want credit, come to me,
And I'll be sworn 'tis true: travellers ne'er did lie,
Though fools at home condemn 'em.

Gon.   If in Naples
I should report this now, would they believe me?
If I should say, I saw such islanders—
For, certes, these are people of the island—   30
Who, though they are of monstrous shape, yet, note,
Their manners are more gentle-kind than of
Our human generation you shall find
Many, nay, almost any.

Pros.   [*Aside*] Honest lord,
Thou hast said well; for some of you there present
Are worse than devils.

Alon.   I cannot too much muse
Such shapes, such gesture and such sound, expressing,
Although they want the use of tongue, a kind
Of excellent dumb discourse.

Pros.   [*Aside*] Praise in departing.

Fran. They vanish'd strangely.

Seb.   No matter, since   40
They have left their viands behind; for we have
        stomachs.
Will 't please you taste of what is here?

Alon.   Not I.

Gon. Faith, sir, you need not fear. When we were
        boys,
Who would believe that there were mountaineers

The Tempest
ACT III : SC III

1263

song. 127. **while-ere,** a while since. 130. **scout,** deride (Onions).
New Cambridge editors emend, *cout* (befool). 133. *Stage Direction:*
tabor, small drum. 136. **picture of Nobody,** an unexplained topical
allusion. New Cambridge editors suggest a reference to the sign of
"Nobody" used by John Trundle, bookseller and printer.

SCENE III. 1. **By 'r lakin,** by our Lady. 3. **forth-rights and mean-**
ders, paths straight and crooked. 20. **keepers,** guardian angels. 21.
drollery, puppet show. 30. **certes,** certainly. 39. **Praise in departing,**
proverbial expression meaning, "Praise comes at the end." Yale editor
interprets as "Save your praise until the end of the performance."

Dew-lapp'd like bulls, whose throats had hanging at
        'em
Wallets of flesh? or that there were such men
Whose heads stood in their breasts? which now we
        find
Each putter-out of five for one will bring us
Good warrant of.
    Alon.   I will stand to and feed,
Although my last: no matter, since I feel   50
The best is past. Brother, my lord the duke,
Stand to and do as we.

> *Thunder and lightning. Enter* ARIEL, *like a harpy; claps
> his wings upon the table; and, with a quaint device, the
> banquet vanishes.*

    Ari. You are three men of sin, whom Destiny,
That hath to instrument this lower world
And what is in 't, the never-surfeited sea
Hath caused to belch up you; and on this island
Where man doth not inhabit; you 'mongst men
Being most unfit to live. I have made you mad;
And even with such-like valour men hang and drown
Their proper selves.   [*Alon., Seb. &c. draw their swords.*
                You fools! I and my fellows   60
Are ministers of Fate: the elements,
Of whom your swords are temper'd, may as well
Wound the loud winds, or with bemock'd-at stabs
Kill the still-closing waters, as diminish
One dowle that 's in my plume: my fellow-ministers
Are like invulnerable. If you could hurt,
Your swords are now too massy for your strengths
And will not be uplifted. But remember—
For that 's my business to you—that you three
From Milan did supplant good Prospero;   70
Exposed unto the sea, which hath requit it,
Him and his innocent child: for which foul deed
The powers, delaying, not forgetting, have
Incensed the seas and shores, yea, all the creatures,
Against your peace. Thee of thy son, Alonso,
They have bereft; and do pronounce by me
Lingering perdition, worse than any death
Can be at once, shall step by step attend
You and your ways; whose wraths to guard you
        from—
Which here, in this most desolate isle, else falls   80
Upon your heads—is nothing but heart-sorrow
And a clear life ensuing.

> *He vanishes in thunder; then, to soft music, enter the Shapes
> again, and dance, with mocks and mows, and carrying
> out the table.*

    Pros. Bravely the figure of this harpy hast thou
Perform'd, my Ariel; a grace it had, devouring:
Of my instruction hast thou nothing bated
In what thou hadst to say: so, with good life
And observation strange, my meaner ministers
Their several kinds have done. My high charms work
And these mine enemies are all knit up

In their distractions; they now are in my power;   90
And in these fits I leave them, while I visit
Young Ferdinand, whom they suppose is drown'd,
And his and mine loved darling.   [*Exit above.*
    Gon. I' the name of something holy, sir, why stand
        you
In this strange stare?
    Alon.   O, it is monstrous, monstrous!
Methought the billows spoke and told me of it;
The winds did sing it to me, and the thunder,
That deep and dreadful organ-pipe, pronounced
The name of Prosper: it did bass my trespass.
Therefore my son i' the ooze is bedded, and   100
I'll seek him deeper than e'er plummet sounded
And with him there lie mudded.   [*Exit.*
    Seb.   But one fiend at a time,
I'll fight their legions o'er.
    Ant.   I'll be thy second.
                        [*Exeunt Seb. and Ant.*
    Gon. All three of them are desperate: their great
        guilt,
Like poison given to work a great time after,
Now 'gins to bite the spirits. I do beseech you
That are of suppler joints, follow them swiftly
And hinder them from what this ecstasy
May now provoke them to.
    Adr.   Follow, I pray you.   [*Exeunt.*

ACT IV.

SCENE I. *Before* PROSPERO'S *cell.*

Enter PROSPERO, FERDINAND, *and* MIRANDA.

    Pros. If I have too austerely punish'd you,
Your compensation makes amends, for I
Have given you here a thrid of mine own life,
Or that for which I live; who once again
I tender to thy hand: all thy vexations
Were but my trials of thy love, and thou
Hast strangely stood the test: here, afore Heaven,
I ratify this my rich gift. O Ferdinand,
Do not smile at me that I boast her off,
For thou shalt find she will outstrip all praise   10
And make it halt behind her.
    Fer.   I do believe it
Against an oracle.
    Pros. Then, as my gift and thine own acquisition
Worthily purchased, take my daughter: but
If thou dost break her virgin-knot before
All sanctimonious ceremonies may
With full and holy rite be minister'd,
No sweet aspersion shall the heavens let fall
To make this contract grow; but barren hate,
Sour-eyed disdain and discord shall bestrew   20
The union of your bed with weeds so loathly
That you shall hate it both: therefore take heed,
As Hymen's lamps shall light you.

---

45. **Dew-lapp'd,** having a dewlap, or fold of skin hanging from the neck, as cattle; often supposed to refer to people afflicted with goiter. 48. **putter-out . . . one,** one who invests money, or gambles on the risks of travel on the condition that, if he returns safely, he is to receive five times the amount deposited. 52. *Stage Direction:* **harpy,** a fabulous monster with a woman's face and vulture's body supposed to be a minister of divine vengeance. **quaint device,** ingenious stage contrivance; perhaps harpies seemed to swallow the food. 54. **to,** as. 65. **dowle,** soft, fine feather. **plume,** plumage (?) (Onions). 66. **like,** likewise, similarly. 71. **requit,** requited, avenged. 82. **clear,** un-

spotted, innocent. 84. **devouring.** New Cambridge editors conjecture *devoiring* (serving, waiting at table). 86. **so . . . life,** with faithful reproduction. 87. **observation strange,** rare attention to detail. 99. **bass my trespass,** proclaimed my trespass like a bass note in music. 106. **bite the spirits,** i.e., conscience troubles them.
ACT IV. SCENE I. 3. **thrid,** defined as "thread," "narrative"; F: *third,* which is correct—the other thirds were Prospero himself and his wife. 7. **strangely,** extraordinarily. 16. **sanctimonious,** sacred. 18. **aspersion,** dew, shower. 23. **Hymen's.** Hymen was the Greek and Roman god of marriage. 27. **genius,** evil genius, or evil attendant

Fer.   As I hope
For quiet days, fair issue and long life,
With such love as 'tis now, the murkiest den,
The most opportune place, the strong'st suggestion
Our worser genius can, shall never melt
Mine honour into lust, to take away
The edge of that day's celebration   29
When I shall think, or Phœbus' steeds are founder'd,
Or Night kept chain'd below.
Pros.   Fairly spoke.
Sit then and talk with her; she is thine own.
What, Ariel! my industrious servant, Ariel!

Enter ARIEL.

Ari. What would my potent master? here I am.
Pros. Thou and thy meaner fellows your last service
Did worthily perform; and I must use you
In such another trick. Go bring the rabble,
O'er whom I give thee power, here to this place:
Incite them to quick motion; for I must
Bestow upon the eyes of this young couple   40
Some vanity of mine art: it is my promise,
And they expect it from me.
Ari.   Presently?
Pros. Ay, with a twink.
Ari. Before you can say 'come' and 'go,'
          And breathe twice and cry 'so, so,'
          Each one, tripping on his toe,
          Will be here with mop and mow.
          Do you love me, master? no?
Pros. Dearly, my delicate Ariel. Do not approach
Till thou dost hear me call.
Ari.   Well, I conceive.   [*Exit.* 50
Pros. Look thou be true; do not give dalliance
Too much the rein: the strongest oaths are straw
To the fire i' the blood: be more abstemious,
Or else, good night your vow!
Fer.   I warrant you, sir;
The white cold virgin snow upon my heart
Abates the ardour of my liver.
Pros.   Well.
Now come, my Ariel! bring a corollary,
Rather than want a spirit: appear, and pertly!
No tongue! all eyes! be silent.   [*Soft music.*

Enter IRIS.

Iris. Ceres, most bounteous lady, thy rich leas   60
Of wheat, rye, barley, vetches, oats and pease;
Thy turfy mountains, where live nibbling sheep,
And flat meads thatch'd with stover, them to keep;
Thy banks with pioned and twilled brims,
Which spongy April at thy hest betrims,
To make cold nymphs chaste crowns; and thy broom-
          groves,
Whose shadow the dismissed bachelor loves,
Being lass-lorn; thy pole-clipt vineyard;
And thy sea-marge, sterile and rocky-hard,
Where thou thyself dost air;—the queen o' the sky,   70

Whose watery arch and messenger am I,
Bids thee leave these, and with her sovereign grace,
Here on this grass-plot, in this very place,
To come and sport: her peacocks fly amain:
Approach, rich Ceres, her to entertain.

Enter CERES.

Cer. Hail, many-colour'd messenger, that ne'er
Dost disobey the wife of Jupiter;
Who with thy saffron wings upon my flowers
Diffusest honey-drops, refreshing showers,
And with each end of thy blue bow dost crown   80
My bosky acres and my unshrubb'd down,
Rich scarf to my proud earth; why hath thy queen
Summon'd me hither, to this short-grass'd green?
Iris. A contract of true love to celebrate;
And some donation freely to estate
On the blest lovers.
Cer.   Tell me, heavenly bow,
If Venus or her son, as thou dost know,
Do now attend the queen? Since they did plot
The means that dusky Dis my daughter got,
Her and her blind boy's scandal'd company   90
I have forsworn.
Iris.   Of her society
Be not afraid: I met her deity
Cutting the clouds towards Paphos and her son
Dove-drawn with her. Here thought they to have
          done
Some wanton charm upon this man and maid,
Whose vows are, that no bed-right shall be paid
Till Hymen's torch be lighted: but in vain;
Mars's hot minion is return'd again;
Her waspish-headed son has broke his arrows,   99
Swears he will shoot no more but play with sparrows
And be a boy right out.
Cer.   High'st queen of state,
Great Juno, comes; I know her by her gait.

Enter JUNO.

Juno. How does my bounteous sister? Go with me
To bless this twain, that they may prosperous be
And honour'd in their issue.   [*They sing:*

Juno.   Honour, riches, marriage-blessing,
          Long continuance, and increasing,
          Hourly joys be still upon you!
          Juno sings her blessings on you.

Cer.   Earth's increase, foison plenty,   110
          Barns and garners never empty,
          Vines with clustering bunches growing,
          Plants with goodly burthen bowing;

          Spring come to you at the farthest
          In the very end of harvest!
          Scarcity and want shall shun you;
          Ceres' blessing so is on you.

spirit.   **30. founder'd,** broken down, made lame.   **37. rabble,** band,
i.e., the *meaner fellows* of line 35.   **41. vanity,** illusion.   **47. mop and
mow,** grimace and make faces.   **56. liver,** as the seat of the passions.
57. corollary, supernumerary.   **58. pertly,** briskly.   **60-138. Ceres . . .
footing.** This is the most perfect example of the masque in Shakespeare.
His authorship of it has, however, sometimes been called in question.
It is a masque in honor of betrothal. For another example see the end
of *A Midsummer-Night's Dream.*   **63. stover,** fodder for cattle.   **64.
pioned and twilled,** unexplained; excavated(?) or trenched(?) (Onions),
ridged (New Cambridge), grown over with peonies and lilies (Hanmer).

66. broom-groves, groves of broom (?)   **68. pole-clipt,** hedged in with
poles.   **71. watery arch,** rainbow.   **74. amain,** with full force or speed.
81. bosky, covered with shrubs.   **unshrubb'd down,** shrubless upland.
89. Dis . . . got. Pluto, god of the infernal regions, carried off Per-
sephone, daughter of Ceres, to be his bride in Hades.   **90. scandal'd,**
brought into disrepute; New Cambridge editors suggest *sandal'd.*   **93.
Paphos,** a town in the island of Cyprus, sacred to Venus.   **98. Mars's
. . . minion,** Venus, the beloved of Mars.   **99. waspish-headed,** fiery,
hot-headed (?).   **110. foison plenty,** plentiful harvest.

Fer. This is a most majestic vision, and
Harmonious charmingly. May I be bold
To think these spirits?
    Pros.   Spirits, which by mine art   120
I have from their confines call'd to enact
My present fancies.
    Fer.   Let me live here ever;
So rare a wonder'd father and a wife
Makes this place Paradise.
         [Juno and Ceres whisper, and send Iris on employment.
    Pros.   Sweet, now, silence!
Juno and Ceres whisper seriously;
There's something else to do: hush, and be mute,
Or else our spell is marr'd.
    Iris. You nymphs, call'd Naiads, of the windring
    brooks,
With your sedged crowns and ever-harmless looks,
Leave your crisp channels and on this green land   130
Answer your summons; Juno does command:
Come, temperate nymphs, and help to celebrate
A contract of true love; be not too late.

    Enter certain Nymphs.

You sunburnt sicklemen, of August weary,
Come hither from the furrow and be merry:
Make holiday; your rye-straw hats put on
And these fresh nymphs encounter every one
In country footing.

    Enter certain Reapers, properly habited: they join with the
    Nymphs in a graceful dance; towards the end whereof
    PROSPERO *starts suddenly, and speaks; after which, to a*
    strange, hollow, and confused noise, they heavily vanish.

    Pros. [*Aside*] I had forgot that foul conspiracy
Of the beast Caliban and his confederates   140
Against my life: the minute of their plot
Is almost come. [*To the Spirits*.] Well done! avoid; no
    more!
    Fer. This is strange: your father's in some passion
That works him strongly.
    Mir.   Never till this day
Saw I him touch'd with anger so distemper'd.
    Pros. You do look, my son, in a moved sort,
As if you were dismay'd: be cheerful, sir.
Our revels now are ended. These our actors,
As I foretold you, were all spirits and
Are melted into air, into thin air: 150
And, like the baseless fabric of this vision,
The cloud-capp'd towers, the gorgeous palaces,
The solemn temples, the great globe itself,
Yea, all which it inherit, shall dissolve
And, like this insubstantial pageant faded,
Leave not a rack behind. We are such stuff
As dreams are made on, and our little life
Is rounded with a sleep. Sir, I am vex'd;
Bear with my weakness; my old brain is troubled:
Be not disturb'd with my infirmity: 160
If you be pleased, retire into my cell
And there repose: a turn or two I'll walk,

To still my beating mind.
    Fer. Mir.   We wish your peace. [*Exeunt.*
    Pros. Come with a thought. I thank thee, Ariel:
come.

    Enter ARIEL.

    Ari. Thy thoughts I cleave to. What's thy pleasure?
    Pros.   Spirit,
We must prepare to meet with Caliban.
    Ari. Ay, my commander: when I presented Ceres,
I thought to have told thee of it, but I fear'd
Lest I might anger thee.
    Pros. Say again, where didst thou leave these
    varlets?   170
    Ari. I told you, sir, they were red-hot with
    drinking;
So full of valour that they smote the air
For breathing in their faces; beat the ground
For kissing of their feet; yet always bending
Towards their project. Then I beat my tabor;
At which, like unback'd colts, they prick'd their ears,
Advanced their eyelids, lifted up their noses
As they smelt music: so I charm'd their ears
That calf-like they my lowing follow'd through   179
Tooth'd briers, sharp furzes, pricking goss and thorns,
Which enter'd their frail shins: at last I left them
I' the filthy-mantled pool beyond your cell,
There dancing up to the chins, that the foul lake
O'erstunk their feet.
    Pros.   This was well done, my bird.
Thy shape invisible retain thou still:
The trumpery in my house, go bring it hither,
For stale to catch these thieves.
    Ari.   I go, I go.   [*Exit.*
    Pros. A devil, a born devil, on whose nature
Nurture can never stick; on whom my pains,
Humanely taken, all, all lost, quite lost;   190
And as with age his body uglier grows,
So his mind cankers. I will plague them all,
Even to roaring.

    Re-enter ARIEL, *loaden with glistering apparel, &c.*
          Come, hang them on this line.

    PROSPERO *and* ARIEL *remain, invisible. Enter* CALIBAN,
    STEPHANO, *and* TRINCULO, *all wet.*

    Cal. Pray you, tread softly, that the blind mole may
    not
Hear a foot fall: we now are near his cell.
    Ste. Monster, your fairy, which you say is a harmless
fairy, has done little better than played the Jack with
us.
    Trin. Monster, I do smell all horse-piss; at which
my nose is in great indignation.   200
    Ste. So is mine. Do you hear, monster? If I should
take a displeasure against you, look you,—
    Trin. Thou wert but a lost monster.
    Cal. Good my lord, give me thy favour still.
Be patient, for the prize I'll bring thee to

Shall hoodwink this mischance: therefore speak softly.
All 's hush'd as midnight yet.

Trin. Ay, but to lose our bottles in the pool,— 208

Ste. There is not only disgrace and dishonour in that, monster, but an infinite loss.

Trin. That 's more to me than my wetting: yet this is your harmless fairy, monster.

Ste. I will fetch off my bottle, though I be o'er ears for my labour.

Cal. Prithee, my king, be quiet. See'st thou here,
This is the mouth o' the cell: no noise, and enter.
Do that good mischief which may make this island
Thine own for ever, and I, thy Caliban,
For aye thy foot-licker.

Ste. Give me thy hand. I do begin to have bloody thoughts. 220

Trin. O king Stephano! O peer! O worthy Stephano! look what a wardrobe here is for thee!

Cal. Let it alone, thou fool; it is but trash.

Trin. O, ho, monster! we know what belongs to a frippery. O king Stephano!

Ste. Put off that gown, Trinculo; by this hand, I'll have that gown.

Trin. Thy grace shall have it.

Cal. The dropsy drown this fool! what do you mean
To dote thus on such luggage? Let 's alone 231
And do the murder first: if he awake,
From toe to crown he'll fill our skins with pinches,
Make us strange stuff.

Ste. Be you quiet, monster. Mistress line, is not this my jerkin? Now is the jerkin under the line: now, jerkin, you are like to lose your hair and prove a bald jerkin.

Trin. Do, do: we steal by line and level, an 't like your grace. 240

Ste. I thank thee for that jest; here 's a garment for 't: wit shall not go unrewarded while I am king of this country. 'Steal by line and level' is an excellent pass of pate; there 's another garment for 't.

Trin. Monster, come, put some lime upon your fingers, and away with the rest.

Cal. I will have none on 't: we shall lose our time,
And all be turn'd to barnacles, or to apes
With foreheads villanous low. 250

Ste. Monster, lay to your fingers: help to bear this away where my hogshead of wine is, or I'll turn you out of my kingdom: go to, carry this.

Trin. And this.

Ste. Ay, and this.

A noise of hunters heard. Enter divers Spirits, in shape of dogs and hounds, and hunt them about, PROSPERO *and* ARIEL *setting them on.*

Pros. Hey, Mountain, hey!

Ari. Silver! there it goes, Silver!

Pros. Fury, Fury! there, Tyrant, there! hark! hark!
[*Cal., Ste., and Trin. are driven out.*
Go charge my goblins that they grind their joints
With dry convulsions, shorten up their sinews 260

With aged cramps, and more pinch-spotted make them
Than pard or cat o' mountain.

Ari. Hark, they roar!

Pros. Let them be hunted soundly. At this hour
Lie at my mercy all mine enemies:
Shortly shall all my labours end, and thou
Shalt have the air at freedom: for a little
Follow, and do me service. [*Exeunt.*

ACT V.

SCENE I. *Before* PROSPERO'S *cell.*

Enter PROSPERO *in his magic robes, and* ARIEL:

Pros. Now does my project gather to a head:
My charms crack not; my spirits obey; and time
Goes upright with his carriage. How 's the day?

Ari. On the sixth hour; at which time, my lord,
You said our work should cease.

Pros. I did say so,
When first I raised the tempest. Say, my spirit,
How fares the king and 's followers?

Ari. Confined together
In the same fashion as you gave in charge,
Just as you left them; all prisoners, sir,
In the line-grove which weather-fends your cell; 10
They cannot budge till your release. The king,
His brother and yours, abide all three distracted
And the remainder mourning over them,
Brimful of sorrow and dismay; but chiefly
Him that you term'd, sir, 'The good old lord, Gonzalo;'
His tears run down his beard, like winter's drops
From eaves of reeds. Your charm so strongly works 'em
That if you now beheld them, your affections
Would become tender.

Pros. Dost thou think so, spirit?

Ari. Mine would, sir, were I human.

Pros. And mine shall. 20
Hast thou, which art but air, a touch, a feeling
Of their afflictions, and shall not myself,
One of their kind, that relish all as sharply,
Passion as they, be kindlier moved than thou art?
Though with their high wrongs I am struck to the quick,
Yet with my nobler reason 'gainst my fury
Do I take part: the rarer action is
In virtue than in vengeance: they being penitent,
The sole drift of my purpose doth extend
Not a frown further. Go release them, Ariel: 30
My charms I'll break, their senses I'll restore,
And they shall be themselves.

Ari. I'll fetch them, sir. [*Exit.*

Pros. Ye elves of hills, brooks, standing lakes and groves,
And ye that on the sands with printless foot
Do chase the ebbing Neptune and do fly him

---

level, i.e., by means of instruments, or, methodically, like dishonest carpenters and masons. **244. pass of pate,** folly of wit. **246. lime,** birdlime. **249. barnacles,** barnacle geese, formerly supposed to be hatched from seashells attached to trees and to fall thence into the water; possibly, the ordinary meaning is intended. **260. convulsions,** cramps. **262. pard,** panther or leopard. **cat o' mountain,** wildcat.

ACT V. SCENE I. **2. crack,** figure not entirely clear; possibly, since his project gathers "to a head," the reference is to an ulcer; "the breaking of magic bands" has been suggested. He may merely mean

that his charms do not fail. **3. carriage,** burden. **How 's the day?** What time is it? **10. line-grove,** grove of lime trees. **weather-fends,** protects from the weather. **17. eaves of reeds,** thatch. **23. all,** quite. **27. rarer,** nobler. **33-57. Ye . . . book.** This famous passage is an embellished paraphrase of Golding's translation of Ovid's *Metamorphoses,* vii, 197-219. Critics have often seen in Prospero's farewell to magic an analogue to Shakespeare's farewell to the stage. *The Tempest* is probably his last complete play. After writing it he retired to Stratford.

When he comes back; you demi-puppets that
By moonshine do the green sour ringlets make,
Whereof the ewe not bites, and you whose pastime
Is to make midnight mushrooms, that rejoice
To hear the solemn curfew; by whose aid,   40
Weak masters though ye be, I have bedimm'd
The noontide sun, call'd forth the mutinous winds,
And 'twixt the green sea and the azured vault
Set roaring war: to the dread rattling thunder
Have I given fire and rifted Jove's stout oak
With his own bolt; the strong-based promontory
Have I made shake and by the spurs pluck'd up
The pine and cedar: graves at my command
Have waked their sleepers, oped, and let 'em forth
By my so potent art. But this rough magic   50
I here abjure, and, when I have required
Some heavenly music, which even now I do,
To work mine end upon their senses that
This airy charm is for, I'll break my staff,
Bury it certain fathoms in the earth,
And deeper than did ever plummet sound
I'll drown my book.   [Solemn music.

Re-enter ARIEL *before: then* ALONSO, *with a frantic
gesture, attended by* GONZALO; SEBASTIAN *and* ANTONIO
in like manner, attended by ADRIAN *and* FRANCISCO: *they
all enter the circle which* PROSPERO *had made, and there
stand charmed; which* PROSPERO *observing, speaks*:

A solemn air and the best comforter
To an unsettled fancy cure thy brains,
Now useless, boil'd within thy skull! There stand,   60
For you are spell-stopp'd.
Holy Gonzalo, honourable man,
Mine eyes, even sociable to the show of thine,
Fall fellowly drops. The charm dissolves apace,
And as the morning steals upon the night,
Melting the darkness, so their rising senses
Begin to chase the ignorant fumes that mantle
Their clearer reason. O good Gonzalo,
My true preserver, and a loyal sir
To him thou follow'st! I will pay thy graces   70
Home both in word and deed. Most cruelly
Didst thou, Alonso, use me and my daughter:
Thy brother was a furtherer in the act.
Thou art pinch'd for 't now, Sebastian. Flesh and
    blood,
You, brother mine, that entertain'd ambition,
Expell'd remorse and nature; who, with Sebastian,
Whose inward pinches therefore are most strong,
Would here have kill'd your king; I do forgive thee,
Unnatural though thou art. Their understanding
Begins to swell, and the approaching tide   80
Will shortly fill the reasonable shore
That now lies foul and muddy. Not one of them
That yet looks on me, or would know me: Ariel,
Fetch me the hat and rapier in my cell:
I will discase me, and myself present
As I was sometime Milan: quickly, spirit;
Thou shalt ere long be free.

    ARIEL *sings and helps to attire him.*

    Where the bee sucks, there suck I:
    In a cowslip's bell I lie;

    There I couch when owls do cry.   90
    On the bat's back I do fly
    After summer merrily.
Merrily, merrily shall I live now
Under the blossom that hangs on the bough.

    Pros. Why, that's my dainty Ariel! I shall miss thee;
But yet thou shalt have freedom: so, so, so.
To the king's ship, invisible as thou art:
There shalt thou find the mariners asleep
Under the hatches; the master and the boatswain
Being awake, enforce them to this place,   100
And presently, I prithee.
    Ari. I drink the air before me, and return
Or ere your pulse twice beat.   [*Exit.*
    Gon. All torment, trouble, wonder and amazement
Inhabits here: some heavenly power guide us
Out of this fearful country!
    Pros.   Behold, sir king,
The wronged Duke of Milan, Prospero:
For more assurance that a living prince
Does now speak to thee, I embrace thy body;
And to thee and thy company I bid   110
A hearty welcome.
    Alon.   Whether thou be'st he or no,
Or some enchanted trifle to abuse me,
As late I have been, I not know: thy pulse
Beats as of flesh and blood; and, since I saw thee,
The affliction of my mind amends, with which,
I fear, a madness held me: this must crave,
An if this be at all, a most strange story.
Thy dukedom I resign and do entreat
Thou pardon me my wrongs. But how should
        Prospero
Be living and be here?
    Pros.   First, noble friend,   120
Let me embrace thine age, whose honour cannot
Be measured or confined.
    Gon.   Whether this be
Or be not, I'll not swear.
    Pros.   You do yet taste
Some subtilties o' the isle, that will not let you
Believe things certain. Welcome, my friends all!
[*Aside to Seb. and Ant.*] But you, my brace of lords,
    were I so minded,
I here could pluck his highness' frown upon you
And justify you traitors: at this time
I will tell no tales.
    Seb.   [*Aside*] The devil speaks in him.
    Pros.   No.
For you, most wicked sir, whom to call brother   130
Would even infect my mouth, I do forgive
Thy rankest fault; all of them; and require
My dukedom of thee, which perforce, I know,
Thou must restore.
    Alon.   If thou be'st Prospero,
Give us particulars of thy preservation;
How thou hast met us here, who three hours since
Were wreck'd upon this shore; where I have lost—
How sharp the point of this remembrance is!—
My dear son Ferdinand.
    Pros.   I am woe for 't, sir.
    Alon. Irreparable is the loss, and patience   140

36. **demi-puppets,** elves and fairies; literally, puppets of half-size.
37. **green sour ringlets,** fairy rings, circles of grass produced by fungus
within the soil. 44-45. **to . . . fire,** the dread rattling thunderbolt
I have discharged. 60. **boil'd,** made hot with humors. 63. **sociable,**
sympathetic. **show,** appearance. 67. **ignorant fumes.** The fumes
which rose up into the brain to produce sleep brought with them un-
consciousness. 85. **discase,** undress. 90. **couch,** to lie down as on a
couch, or, more probably, lie hidden. 96. **so, so, so,** that will do very

Says it is past her cure.
   Pros.   I rather think
You have not sought her help, of whose soft grace
For the like loss I have her sovereign aid
And rest myself content.
   Alon.   You the like loss!
   Pros. As great to me as late; and, supportable
To make the dear loss, have I means much weaker
Than you may call to comfort you, for I
Have lost my daughter.
   Alon.   A daughter?
O heavens, that they were living both in Naples,
The king and queen there! that they were, I wish   150
Myself were mudded in that oozy bed
Where my son lies. When did you lose your daughter?
   Pros. In this last tempest. I perceive, these lords
At this encounter do so much admire
That they devour their reason and scarce think
Their eyes do offices of truth, their words
Are natural breath: but, howsoe'er you have
Been justled from your senses, know for certain
That I am Prospero and that very duke   159
Which was thrust forth of Milan, who most strangely
Upon this shore, where you were wreck'd, was
     landed,
To be the lord on 't. No more yet of this;
For 'tis a chronicle of day by day,
Not a relation for a breakfast nor
Befitting this first meeting. Welcome, sir;
This cell 's my court: here have I few attendants
And subjects none abroad: pray you, look in.
My dukedom since you have given me again,
I will requite you with as good a thing;
At least bring forth a wonder, to content ye   170
As much as me my dukedom.

   Here PROSPERO *discovers* FERDINAND *and* MIRANDA,
     playing at chess.

   Mir. Sweet lord, you play me false.
   Fer.   No, my dear'st love,
I would not for the world.
   Mir. Yes, for a score of kingdoms you should
     wrangle,
And I would call it fair play.
   Alon.   If this prove
A vision of the Island, one dear son
Shall I twice lose.
   Seb.   A most high miracle!
   Fer. Though the seas threaten, they are merciful;
I have cursed them without cause.   [*Kneels.*
   Alon.   Now all the blessings
Of a glad father compass thee about!   180
Arise, and say how thou camest here.
   Mir.   O, wonder!
How many goodly creatures are there here!
How beauteous mankind is! O brave new world,
That has such people in 't!
   Pros.   'Tis new to thee.
   Alon. What is this maid with whom thou wast at
     play?
Your eld'st acquaintance cannot be three hours:
Is she the goddess that hath sever'd us,
And brought us thus together?

   Fer.   Sir, she is mortal;
But by immortal Providence she 's mine:
I chose her when I could not ask my father   190
For his advice, nor thought I had one. She
Is daughter to this famous Duke of Milan,
Of whom so often I have heard renown,
But never saw before; of whom I have
Received a second life; and second father
This lady makes him to me.
   Alon.   I am hers:
But, O, how oddly will it sound that I
Must ask my child forgiveness!
   Pros.   There, sir, stop:
Let us not burthen our remembrance with
A heaviness that 's gone.
   Gon.   I have inly wept   200
Or should have spoke ere this. Look down, you gods,
And on this couple drop a blessed crown!
For it is you that have chalk'd forth the way
Which brought us hither.
   Alon.   I say, Amen, Gonzalo!
   Gon. Was Milan thrust from Milan, that his issue
Should become kings of Naples? O, rejoice
Beyond a common joy, and set it down
With gold on lasting pillars: In one voyage
Did Claribel her husband find at Tunis
And Ferdinand, her brother, found a wife   210
Where he himself was lost, Prospero his dukedom
In a poor isle and all of us ourselves
When no man was his own.
   Alon.   [*To Fer. and Mir.*] Give me your
     hands:
Let grief and sorrow still embrace his heart
That doth not wish you joy!
   Gon.   Be it so! Amen!

   Re-enter ARIEL, *with the* Master *and* Boatswain *amazedly*
     following.

O, look, sir, look, sir! here is more of us:
I prophesied, if a gallows were on land,
This fellow could not drown. Now, blasphemy,
That swear'st grace o'erboard, not an oath on shore?
Hast thou no mouth by land? What is the news?   220
   Boats. The best news is, that we have safely found
Our king and company; the next, our ship—
Which, but three glasses since, we gave out split—
Is tight and yare and bravely rigg'd as when
We first put out to sea.
   Ari.   [*Aside to Pros.*] Sir, all this service
Have I done since I went.
   Pros.   [*Aside to Ari.*] My tricksy spirit!
   Alon. These are not natural events; they strengthen
From strange to stranger. Say, how came you hither?
   Boats. If I did think, sir, I were well awake,
I 'ld strive to tell you. We were dead of sleep,   230
And—how we know not—all clapp'd under hatches;
Where but even now with strange and several noises
Of roaring, shrieking, howling, jingling chains,
And moe diversity of sounds, all horrible,
We were awaked; straightway, at liberty;
Where we, in all her trim, freshly beheld
Our royal, good and gallant ship, our master
Capering to eye her: on a trice, so please you,

Even in a dream, were we divided from them 239
And were brought moping hither.
   Ari.   [*Aside to Pros.*] Was 't well done?
   Pros. [*Aside to Ari.*] Bravely, my diligence. Thou
   shalt be free.
   Alon. This is as strange a maze as e'er men trod;
And there is in this business more than nature
Was ever conduct of: some oracle
Must rectify our knowledge.
   Pros.   Sir, my liege,
Do not infest your mind with beating on
The strangeness of this business; at pick'd leisure
Which shall be shortly, single I'll resolve you,
Which to you shall seem probable, of every
These happen'd accidents; till when, be cheerful 250
And think of each thing well. [*Aside to Ari.*] Come
   hither, spirit:
Set Caliban and his companions free;
Untie the spell. [*Exit Ariel.*] How fares my gracious
   sir?
There are yet missing of your company
Some few odd lads that you remember not.

   Re-enter ARIEL, *driving in* CALIBAN, STEPHANO *and*
     TRINCULO, *in their stolen apparel.*

   Ste. Every man shift for all the rest, and let no man
take care for himself; for all is but fortune. Coragio,
bully-monster, coragio!
   Trin. If these be true spies which I wear in my
head, here 's a goodly sight. 260
   Cal. O Setebos, these be brave spirits indeed!
How fine my master is! I am afraid
He will chastise me.
   Seb.   Ha, ha!
What things are these, my lord Antonio?
Will money buy 'em?
   Ant.   Very like; one of them
Is a plain fish, and, no doubt, marketable.
   Pros. Mark but the badges of these men, my lords,
Then say if they be true. This mis-shapen knave,
His mother was a witch, and one so strong
That could control the moon, make flows and ebbs, 270
And deal in her command without her power.
These three have robb'd me; and this demi-devil—
For he 's a bastard one—had plotted with them
To take my life. Two of these fellows you
Must know and own; this thing of darkness I
Acknowledge mine.
   Cal.   I shall be pinch'd to death.
   Alon. Is not this Stephano, my drunken butler?
   Seb. He is drunk now: where had he wine?
   Alon. And Trinculo is reeling ripe: where should
   they
Find this grand liquor that hath gilded 'em? 280
How camest thou in this pickle?
   Trin. I have been in such a pickle since I saw you
last that, I fear me, will never out of my bones: I shall
not fear fly-blowing.
   Seb. Why, how now, Stephano!
   Ste. O, touch me not; I am not Stephano, but a
   cramp.
   Pros. You 'ld be king o' the isle, sirrah?

   Ste. I should have been a sore one then.
   Alon. This is a strange thing as e'er I look'd on.
                      [*Pointing to Caliban.*
   Pros. He is as disproportion'd in his manners 290
As in his shape. Go, sirrah, to my cell;
Take with you your companions; as you look
To have my pardon, trim it handsomely.
   Cal. Ay, that I will; and I'll be wise hereafter
And seek for grace. What a thrice-double ass
Was I, to take this drunkard for a god
And worship this dull fool!
   Pros.   Go to; away!
   Alon. Hence, and bestow your luggage where you
   found it.
   Seb. Or stole it, rather.   [*Exeunt Cal., Ste., and Trin.*
   Pros. Sir, I invite your highness and your train 300
To my poor cell, where you shall take your rest
For this one night; which, part of it, I'll waste
With such discourse as, I not doubt, shall make it
Go quick away; the story of my life
And the particular accidents gone by
Since I came to this isle: and in the morn
I'll bring you to your ship and so to Naples,
Where I have hope to see the nuptial
Of these our dear-beloved solemnized;
And thence retire me to my Milan, where 310
Every third thought shall be my grave.
   Alon.   I long
To hear the story of your life, which must
Take the ear strangely.
   Pros.   I'll deliver all;
And promise you calm seas, auspicious gales
And sail so expeditious that shall catch
Your royal fleet far off. [*Aside to Ari.*] My Ariel, chick,
That is thy charge: then to the elements
Be free, and fare thou well! Please you, draw near.
                           [*Exeunt.*

EPILOGUE.

SPOKEN BY PROSPERO.

   Now my charms are all o'erthrown,
   And what strength I have 's mine own,
   Which is most faint: now, 'tis true,
   I must be here confined by you,
   Or sent to Naples. Let me not,
   Since I have my dukedom got
   And pardon'd the deceiver, dwell
   In this bare island by your spell;
   But release me from my bands
   With the help of your good hands: 10
   Gentle breath of yours my sails
   Must fill, or else my project fails,
   Which was to please. Now I want
   Spirits to enforce, art to enchant,
   And my ending is despair,
   Unless I be relieved by prayer,
   Which pierces so that it assaults
   Mercy itself and frees all faults.
   As you from crimes would pardon'd be,
   Let your indulgence set me free. 20

---

244. **conduct,** guide, leader. 246. **infest,** harass, disturb. 247.
pick'd, chosen. 248. **single,** i.e., when we are alone together. F has
no comma after *shortly,* in which reading *single* means "unbroken,"
"absolute." 258. **Coragio,** courage. **bully-monster,** gallant monster.
267. **badges,** emblems of cloth or silver worn on the arms of retainers.

271. **deal . . . power,** wield the moon's power, either without her
authority, or beyond her influence. The line is ambiguous. 280.
gilded, flushed, made drunk. 305. **accidents,** occurrences, events.
313. **Take,** take effect upon. **deliver,** declare, relate.
EPILOGUE. 10. **hands,** applause.

A HISTORY PLAY OF THE FOURTH PERIOD

THE FAMOUS HISTORY OF THE LIFE OF
King Henry the Eighth

The last of the chronicle plays appeared in print for the first time in the First Folio (1623) and there bears the title *The Famous History of the Life of King Henry the Eight*. Since the "Histories" are arranged in historical sequence according to the reigns of the monarchs for whom they are named, *Henry VIII* follows *Richard III* and is last in the group.

A play on the subject of Henry VIII, which it seems overcautious to regard as other than Shakespeare's *Henry VIII*, was being acted at the Globe playhouse on June 29, 1613, when the theater was burned to the ground. The fire made so great a sensation that a number of accounts of it have been preserved. The following is from Sir Henry Wotton's letter to his nephew Sir Edmund Bacon, July 2, 1613:

Now, to let matters of state sleep, I will entertain you at the present with what has happened this week at the Bank's side. The King's players had a new play, called *All is True*, representing some principal pieces of the reign of Henry VIII, which was set forth with many extraordinary circumstances of pomp and majesty, even to the matting of the stage; the Knights of the Order with their Georges and garters, the Guards with their embroidered coats, and the like: sufficient in truth within a while to make greatness very familiar, if not ridiculous. Now, King Henry making a masque at the Cardinal Wolsey's house, and certain chambers being shot off at his entry, some of the paper, or other stuff, wherewith one of them was stopped, did light on the thatch, where being thought at first but an idle smoke, and their eyes more attentive to the show, it kindled inwardly, and ran round like a train, consuming within less than an hour the whole house to the very grounds. This was the fatal period of that virtuous fabric, wherein yet nothing did perish but wood and straw, and a few forsaken cloaks; only one man had his breeches set on fire, that would perhaps have broiled him, if he had not by the benefit of a provident wit put it out with bottle ale.

The play is referred to as "new"; and, although it is called *All is True*, Wotton says significantly "representing some principal pieces of the reign of Henry VIII," which is exactly what *Henry VIII* does. That *All is True* was a secondary title for the play is sufficiently indicated by the Prologue (ll. 9, 18, 21), which reiterates the words "true" and "truth." These words were, moreover, in a certain way symbolic of Henry VIII, whose willfulness and selfishness the popular mind commuted into rugged honesty. A stage direction (I, iv, 49) seems corroborative, since it reads, "chambers discharged." A set of verses preserved in manuscript, reprinted by Halliwell-Phillipps (*Outlines*, I, 310), refers to the king and Wolsey and to the actors Burbage, Condell, and Heminges. Indeed, the play conforms completely to our expectation, is in no way inconsistent with the records of the fire, and was chosen as Shakespeare's by Heminges and Condell themselves for inclusion in the First Folio. We may, therefore, conclude that the play dates from a short time before the fire.

SOURCE

The first four acts follow with surprising fidelity Holinshed's *Chronicles of England, Scotland, and Ireland*, not only in text, which often seems a paraphrase of prose in verse, but in event and in conception of characters. Holinshed himself followed two sources and is inconsistent in conception of characters and in chronology. For the earlier part of his account of the reign, Holinshed is based on Polydore Vergil, who hated Wolsey. In the later part, Holinshed substitutes a brilliant and sympathetic biography of Wolsey by George Cavendish, Gentleman Usher to the cardinal, an adherent so faithful that he followed Wolsey into disgrace and served him until his death. There are thus two conflicting conceptions of Wolsey in Holinshed, both of which reappear in the play.

King Henry appears in the play in the static and conventional, albeit kingly, figure of Holinshed, that is, as "Oberon," "bluff King Hal," the exponent of truth at any cost, scholarly, and conscientious. Katharine, as reflected by Holinshed from Polydore Vergil, is deeply wronged and pathetic.

Holinshed's account of the reign of Henry VIII is one of the most vivid and most unreliable of his stories of English kings. The play puts Holinshed on the stage as a set of dramatic scenes fundamentally inconsistent with each other and often unrelated. It treats them with the spirit and technique of a historical pageant: first, the fall of Buckingham, with an unfavorable view of Wolsey; secondly, the rejection of Katharine of Aragon; thirdly, the fall of Wolsey, sympathetically presented; fourthly, the rise of Cranmer and the marriage with Anne Bullen; lastly, the christening of the infant Elizabeth, with a prophetic view of her future greatness. This part (the fifth act) comes from Foxe's *Acts and Monuments*. The play has little structural unity.

AUTHORSHIP

On purely external evidence *Henry VIII* has as good a claim to be regarded as the work of Shakespeare as many unquestioned plays in the canon. Indeed, there is one piece of testimony which connects the play with Shakespeare's name. At the time of the revival of the play after the Restoration John Downes, prompter to the duke of York's men, records a tradition in *Roscius Anglicanus* (1708) that D'Avenant was able to instruct Betterton in the acting of Henry VIII, for "he had it from Old *Mr. Lowen*, that had his Instructions from *Mr. Shakespear* himself." John Lowin was long a member of Shakespeare's company.

John Fletcher wrote blank verse with a strong mannerism. His lines are prevailingly end-stopped, and nearly half of them have double or "feminine" endings. The poet Tennyson, who was excellent in the determination of meter, told his friend James Spedding that the meter of much of *Henry VIII* was like that of Fletcher. As a result of this conversation Spedding made his study *Who wrote Shakespeare's Henry VIII?*[1] His results, based on his count of feminine endings and checked by his feeling for style, gave Shakespeare only Act I, scenes i and ii; Act II, scenes iii and iv (Katharine's trial); Act III, scene ii (to the King's exit); Act V, scene i. This determination, which was later confirmed by the metrical studies of Fleay and Furnivall, still stands. It will be noted that Spedding's division gives to Fletcher the most famous passage of the play, Wolsey's farewell to Cromwell (III, ii, 204-459).

Nowhere else did Fletcher write so well, and the difficulty with the hypothesis is not that there are not mechanical resemblances in the style of large parts of *Henry VIII* to Fletcher's well-known style, but that they are mechanical only. The play is not like Fletcher. The only plausible solution of the difficulty is that of Peter Alexander,[2] who gives reasons for thinking that the entire play is by Shakespeare. It is a well-known fact that Shakespeare's later style, with its superabundance of feminine endings, became formally more and more like that of Fletcher, and Alexander argues that Shakespeare wrote parts of *Henry VIII* in his very latest style. The feature of the run-on line is present abundantly in the parts assigned to Fletcher, and it might be added that there is in the play much variation in style to suit character (e.g., II, iii) and that, however positive critics may be about the hypothetical partition of the play, they do not agree among themselves; and no wonder, for it seems impossible to draw a clear line between the parts. Buckingham's speeches are usually,

as also often Queen Katharine's defense, assigned to Shakespeare, and yet neither speech is free from "Fletcherian" qualities.

Sir E. K. Chambers, although he has nowhere presented the matter in detail, seems to be of the opinion that back of *Henry VIII* lies a lost play called *Buckingham*, written, so he supposes, by Shakespeare for the earl of Sussex's men in the winter of 1592-1593 and brought by Shakespeare to the Lord Chamberlain's company in 1594. His idea evidently is that, when in 1613 Shakespeare for some reason came out of his retirement at Stratford to the assistance of his fellows in London, he and Fletcher collaborated in the rewriting of this old play. F. E. Schelling calls attention to the great crop of chronicle histories dealing with the immediate past which appeared at the end of the queen's reign, such as two nonextant plays on the

Henry VIII playing the harp. At right: Will Sommers, his jester. Illustration from a Psalter written for Henry by John Mallard.

fall of Wolsey (1600, 1601), Rowley's vigorous *When You See Me You Know Me* (1604), and Heywood's *If You Know Not Me You Know Nobody* (1604-1605), and suggests that at this time Shakespeare may have begun a play later finished by Fletcher as *Henry VIII*.

Spedding, Fleay, Furnivall, and Thorndike argue for an actual division of the material to be treated and a definite collaboration. The main ground of this opinion is the obvious lateness of the Shakespearean parts.[3] But there is no need for the assumption of the hand of Fletcher.

STORY OF THE PLAY

In *Henry VIII* we see first the rivalry of Buckingham and Wolsey ending in Buckingham's condemnation for treason. He goes to his death complaining that his servants have played him false and betrayed him to

[1] Published in *The Gentleman's Magazine*, August 1850, and subsequently republished in the *Transactions* of the New Shakespeare Society, 1874.
[2] Peter Alexander, "Conjectural History of Shakespeare's *Henry VIII*," *Essays and Studies by Members of the English Association*, XVI (Oxford, 1931), 85-120.

[3] Robert Boyle, *Henry VIII*, New Shakespeare Society *Transactions*, 1880, 1886; Chambers, *The Elizabethan Stage*, II, 95, 130, 202, 217, 219, and *William Shakespeare*, I, 495-498; F. E. Schelling, *Elizabethan Drama*, I, 287, II, 383; Lee, *Life of William Shakespeare*, pp. 268-272.

the king. Meantime, the king has fallen in love with Anne Bullen, upon whom he has bestowed great gifts and whom he has created Marchioness of Pembroke.

Henry next raises the famous issue as to the validity of his marriage with Katharine, who before he married her had been married to his dead brother Arthur. His hypocrisy, though patent to posterity, is not exposed in the play. Katharine is tried; Wolsey opposes the divorce, which is nevertheless granted. Again, though Katharine is treated by Shakespeare with matchless sympathy, there is no open reflection on the king as the cause of her suffering.

Henry gets an inventory of Wolsey's vast wealth and seizes it as his own. Cranmer rises into Wolsey's place. The king weds Anne Bullen, who is crowned in great state. Cranmer is accused of disloyalty but escapes condemnation. Then follows the glory of the birth of Elizabeth, reported seriously and prophetically by the nobles and retold in very good comic style by the Porter and his Man. The play ends with the christening of Elizabeth. In no play are there fuller stage directions and a more obvious intention to have it staged as a historical pageant.

STAGE HISTORY

There seems no very close correlation in Shakespeare's plays between literary excellence and stage success. Indeed, *Henry VIII*, comparatively speaking, is not a great play. Most readers agree with Dr. Johnson's sharp criticism to the effect that "the genius of Shakespeare comes in and goes out with Katharine." *Henry VIII* has, nevertheless, a rather illustrious stage history. It has lent itself to spectacular production, and the greatest Shakespearean actors and actresses have played it. During the Restoration Betterton played the King, and Mrs. Betterton, Katharine. Pepys liked the play so well that he saw it a second time.

It was revived a dozen times or more in the eighteenth century, conspicuously with Barton Booth as Henry, in 1727, the year of the coronation of George II. In 1788 John Philip Kemble played the King, and Mrs. Siddons was magnificent as Katharine.

In a later revival (1806) Kemble played Wolsey and Mrs. Siddons again Queen Katharine. Edmund Kean and Macready also presented the play, and Charles Kean, in the role of Wolsey, revived it sumptuously in 1855. Irving also played Wolsey in his great production at the Lyceum Theater in 1892; Ellen Terry played Katharine, and Forbes-Robertson, Buckingham. Beerbohm Tree brought the play to New York in 1916 in honor of the tercentenary of Shakespeare's death. Sybil Thorndike won distinction as Queen Katharine in 1926. Charles Laughton played King Henry VIII and Flora Robson played Queen Katharine at the "Old Vic" in London during the season of 1933-1934 in what was a very popular performance. More recently *Henry VIII* was staged with much magnificence at the Shakespeare Memorial Theatre at Stratford in the season of 1949.

THE FAMOUS HISTORY OF THE LIFE OF
King Henry the Eighth

DRAMATIS PERSONAE

KING HENRY the Eighth.
CARDINAL WOLSEY.
CARDINAL CAMPEIUS.
CAPUCIUS, Ambassador from the Emperor Charles V.
CRANMER, Archbishop of Canterbury.
DUKE OF NORFOLK.
DUKE OF BUCKINGHAM.
DUKE OF SUFFOLK.
EARL OF SURREY.
Lord Chamberlain.
Lord Chancellor.
GARDINER, Bishop of Winchester.
Bishop of Lincoln.
LORD ABERGAVENNY.
LORD SANDS.
SIR HENRY GUILDFORD.
SIR THOMAS LOVELL.
SIR ANTHONY DENNY.
SIR NICHOLAS VAUX.
Secretaries to Wolsey.
CROMWELL, Servant to Wolsey.
GRIFFITH, Gentleman-usher to Queen Katharine.
Three Gentlemen.
DOCTOR BUTTS, Physician to the King.
Garter King-at-Arms.
Surveyor to the Duke of Buckingham.
BRANDON, and a Sergeant-at-Arms.
Door-keeper of the Council-chamber. Porter, and his Man.
Page to Gardiner. A Crier.

QUEEN KATHARINE, wife to King Henry, afterwards divorced.
ANNE BULLEN, her Maid of Honour, afterwards Queen.
An old Lady, friend to Anne Bullen.
PATIENCE, woman to Queen Katharine.

Several Lords and Ladies in the Dumb Shows; Women attending upon the Queen; Scribes, Officers, Guards, and other Attendants. Spirits.

SCENE: *London; Westminster; Kimbolton.*

King Henry the Eighth
PROLOGUE

1273

THE PROLOGUE.

I COME no more to make you laugh: things now,
That bear a weighty and a serious brow,
Sad, high, and working, full of state and woe,
Such noble scenes as draw the eye to flow,
We now present. Those that can pity, here
May, if they think it well, let fall a tear;

The subject will deserve it. Such as give
Their money out of hope they may believe,
May here find truth too. Those that come to see
Only a show or two, and so agree   10
The play may pass, if they be still and willing,
I'll undertake may see away their shilling
Richly in two short hours. Only they
That come to hear a merry bawdy play,
A noise of targets, or to see a fellow
In a long motley coat guarded with yellow,
Will be deceived; for, gentle hearers, know
To rank our chosen truth with such a show
As fool and fight is, beside forfeiting
Our own brains, and the opinion that we bring,   20
To make that only true we now intend,
Will leave us never an understanding friend.
Therefore, for goodness' sake, and as you are known
The first and happiest hearers of the town,
Be sad, as we would make ye: think ye see
The very persons of our noble story
As they were living; think you see them great,
And follow'd with the general throng and sweat
Of thousand friends; then in a moment, see
How soon this mightiness meets misery: 30
And, if you can be merry then, I'll say
A man may weep upon his wedding-day.

ACT I.

SCENE I. *London. An ante-chamber in the palace.*

Enter the DUKE OF NORFOLK *at one door; at the other,
the* DUKE OF BUCKINGHAM *and the* LORD
ABERGAVENNY.

Buck. Good morrow, and well met. How have ye
          done
Since last we saw in France?
    Nor.   I thank your grace,
Healthful; and ever since a fresh admirer
Of what I saw there.
    Buck.   An untimely ague
Stay'd me a prisoner in my chamber when
Those suns of glory, those two lights of men,
Met in the vale of Andren.
    Nor.   'Twixt Guynes and Arde:
I was then present, saw them salute on horseback;
Beheld them, when they lighted, how they clung
In their embracement, as they grew together;   10
Which had they, what four throned ones could have
          weigh'd
Such a compounded one?
    Buck.   All the whole time
I was my chamber's prisoner.
    Nor.   Then you lost
The view of earthly glory: men might say,
Till this time pomp was single, but now married

To one above itself. Each following day
Became the next day's master, till the last
Made former wonders its. To-day the French,
All clinquant, all in gold, like heathen gods,
Shone down the English; and, to-morrow, they   20
Made Britain India: every man that stood
Show'd like a mine. Their dwarfish pages were
As cherubins, all gilt: the madams too,
Not used to toil, did almost sweat to bear
The pride upon them, that their very labour
Was to them as a painting: now this masque
Was cried incomparable; and the ensuing night
Made it a fool and beggar. The two kings,
Equal in lustre, were now best, now worst,
As presence did present them; him in eye,   30
Still him in praise: and, being present both,
'Twas said they saw but one; and no discerner
Durst wag his tongue in censure. When these suns—
For so they phrase 'em—by their heralds challenged
The noble spirits to arms, they did perform
Beyond thought's compass; that former fabulous
          story,
Being now seen possible enough, got credit,
That Bevis was believed.
    Buck.   O, you go far.
    Nor. As I belong to worship and affect
In honour honesty, the tract of every thing   40
Would by a good discourser lose some life,
Which action's self was tongue to. All was royal;
To the disposing of it nought rebell'd,
Order gave each thing view; the office did
Distinctly his full function.
    Buck.   Who did guide,
I mean, who set the body and the limbs
Of this great sport together, as you guess?
    Nor. One, certes, that promises no element
In such a business.
    Buck.   I pray you, who, my lord?
    Nor. All this was order'd by the good discretion 50
Of the right reverend Cardinal of York.
    Buck. The devil speed him! no man's pie is freed
From his ambitious finger. What had he
To do in these fierce vanities? I wonder
That such a keech can with his very bulk
Take up the rays o' the beneficial sun
And keep it from the earth.
    Nor.   Surely, sir,
There 's in him stuff that puts him to these ends;
For, being not propp'd by ancestry, whose grace
Chalks successors their way, nor call'd upon   60
For high feats done to the crown; neither allied
To eminent assistants; but, spider-like,
Out of his self-drawing web, he gives us note,
The force of his own merit makes his way;
A gift that heaven gives for him, which buys
A place next to the king.
    Aber.   I cannot tell

PROLOGUE. 3. **working,** exciting the emotions, full of pathos. 17.
deceived, disappointed.

ACT I. SCENE I. 2. **saw,** i.e., saw each other. 4. **what I saw there.**
Norfolk's description is of the famous meeting of Henry VIII and Francis I
of France. It was near Calais, at the Field of the Cloth of Gold, so called
because of the magnificence of the display. Holinshed gives a more
prosaic account: "The two kings meeting in the field, either saluted
each other in most louing wise, first on horssebacke, and after alighting
on foot eftsoones imbraced with courteous words, to the great reioising
of the beholders: and, after they had thus saluted each other, they
went both togither into a rich tent of cloath of gold, there set vp for

the purpose, in the which they passed the time in pleasant talke, ban-
ketting, and louing devises, till it drew toward the evening, and then
departed for that night, the one to Guisnes, the other to Ard." The
dramatist deviates from the source in making Buckingham absent and
having Norfolk describe the interview, since Norfolk remained in England and Buckingham grudgingly attended the royal party to France.
The enmity depicted here between Buckingham and the cardinal is from
Holinshed although it is not verified by the facts of history. 7. **vale of
Andren.** The name, more properly Ardre, appears as Andren in Holinshed. 19. **clinquant,** glittering. 21. **India,** notorious for display of
gold and jewels. 30. **As . . . them,** i.e., when they appeared. 30-31.

What heaven hath given him,—let some graver eye
Pierce into that; but I can see his pride
Peep through each part of him: whence has he that,
If not from hell? the devil is a niggard,   70
Or has given all before, and he begins
A new hell in himself.
    Buck.   Why the devil,
Upon this French going out, took he upon him,
Without the privity o' the king, to appoint
Who should attend on him? He makes up the file
Of all the gentry; for the most part such
To whom as great a charge as little honour
He meant to lay upon: and his own letter,
The honourable board of council out,
Must fetch him in the papers.
    Aber.   I do know   80
Kinsmen of mine, three at the least, that have
By this so sicken'd their estates, that never
They shall abound as formerly.
    Buck.   O, many
Have broke their backs with laying manors on 'em
For this great journey. What did this vanity
But minister communication of
A most poor issue?
    Nor.   Grievingly I think,
The peace between the French and us not values
The cost that did conclude it.
    Buck.   Every man,
After the hideous storm that follow'd, was   90
A thing inspired; and, not consulting, broke
Into a general prophecy: That this tempest,
Dashing the garment of this peace, aboded
The sudden breach on 't.
    Nor.   Which is budded out;
For France hath flaw'd the league, and hath attach'd
Our merchants' goods at Bourdeaux.
    Aber.   Is it therefore
The ambassador is silenced?
    Nor.   Marry, is 't.
    Aber. A proper title of a peace; and purchased
At a superfluous rate!
    Buck.   Why, all this business
Our reverend cardinal carried.
    Nor.   Like it your grace,   100
The state takes notice of the private difference
Betwixt you and the cardinal. I advise you—
And take it from a heart that wishes towards you
Honour and plenteous safety—that you read
The cardinal's malice and his potency
Together; to consider further that
What his high hatred would effect wants not
A minister in his power. You know his nature,
That he 's revengeful, and I know his sword
Hath a sharp edge: it 's long and, 't may be said,   110
It reaches far, and where 'twill not extend,
Thither he darts it. Bosom up my counsel,
You'll find it wholesome. Lo, where comes that rock

That I advise your shunning.

> *Enter* CARDINAL WOLSEY, *the purse borne before him,*
> *certain of the* Guard, *and two* Secretaries *with*
> *papers. The* CARDINAL *in his passage fixeth his eye*
> *on* BUCKINGHAM, *and* BUCKINGHAM *on him, both full*
> *of disdain.*

    Wol. The Duke of Buckingham's surveyor, ha?
Where 's his examination?
    First Secr.   Here, so please you.
    Wol. Is he in person ready?
    First Secr.   Ay, please your grace.
    Wol. Well, we shall then know more; and
    Buckingham
Shall lessen this big look. [*Exeunt Wolsey and his Train.*
    Buck. This butcher's cur is venom-mouth'd, and I
Have not the power to muzzle him; therefore best   121
Not wake him in his slumber. A beggar's book
Outworths a noble's blood.
    Nor.   What, are you chafed?
Ask God for temperance; that 's the appliance only
Which your disease requires.
    Buck.   I read in 's looks
Matter against me; and his eye reviled
Me, as his abject object: at this instant
He bores me with some trick: he 's gone to the king;
I'll follow and outstare him.
    Nor.   Stay, my lord,
And let your reason with your choler question   130
What 'tis you go about: to climb steep hills
Requires slow pace at first: anger is like
A full-hot horse, who being allow'd his way,
Self-mettle tires him. Not a man in England
Can advise me like you: be to yourself
As you would to your friend.
    Buck.   I'll to the king;
And from a mouth of honour quite cry down
This Ipswich fellow's insolence; or proclaim
There 's difference in no persons.
    Nor.   Be advised;
Heat not a furnace for your foe so hot   140
That it do singe yourself: we may outrun,
By violent swiftness, that which we run at,
And lose by over-running. Know you not,
The fire that mounts the liquor till 't run o'er,
In seeming to augment it wastes it? Be advised:
I say again, there is no English soul
More stronger to direct you than yourself,
If with the sap of reason you would quench,
Or but allay, the fire of passion.
    Buck.   Sir,
I am thankful to you; and I'll go along   150
By your prescription: but this top-proud fellow,
Whom from the flow of gall I name not but
From sincere motions, by intelligence,
And proofs as clear as founts in July when
We see each grain of gravel, I do know

King Henry
the Eighth

ACT I : SC I

1275

<hr>

him . . . praise, i.e., the one in view at the moment received the praise.
38. Bevis, hero of the fourteenth-century romance, *Bevis of Hampton.*
The splendor depicted in the poem is the point to the allusion here.
39. belong to worship, am of noble rank.   40. tract, course (of events).
48-49. One . . . business, i.e., one whose mean origin would indicate
that he lacked the *savoir faire* required for managing business of such
a regal nature.   55. keech, fat of a slaughtered animal rolled into a
lump: applied to Wolsey as a butcher's son.   58. There 's . . . stuff,
etc., a description of Wolsey's ambition, a quality which was held in
contempt during the Renaissance.   63. gives us note, lets us know.   73.
going out, expedition, display.   74. privity, being privy to something.

77-78. To . . . upon, i.e., the cardinal imposed charges for defraying
the expenses of the costly interview on those noblemen to whom he gave
places of little honor.   78-80. and . . . papers, his own mandate made
him the orderer of all things.   100. Like it, may it please.   112. Bosom
up, take to heart and shut up in your bosom.   115. surveyor, overseer
of a household or estate.   119. big, haughty.   120. This butcher's cur.
Wolsey's father was a dealer in groceries and meat in the town of Ipswich.   128. bores, undermines.   138. fellow, usually refers to the servant class; hence here contemptuously glances at Wolsey's low origin.

To be corrupt and treasonous.
  Nor.   Say not 'treasonous.'
  Buck. To the king I'll say 't; and make my vouch as
    strong
As shore of rock. Attend. This holy fox,
Or wolf, or both,—for he is equal ravenous
As he is subtle, and as prone to mischief   160
As able to perform 't; his mind and place
Infecting one another, yea, reciprocally—
Only to show his pomp as well in France
As here at home, suggests the king our master
To this last costly treaty, the interview,
That swallow'd so much treasure, and like a glass
Did break i' the rinsing.
  Nor.   Faith, and so it did.
  Buck. Pray, give me favour, sir. This cunning
    cardinal
The articles o' the combination drew
As himself pleased; and they were ratified   170
As he cried 'Thus let be': to as much end
As give a crutch to the dead: but our count-cardinal
Has done this, and 'tis well; for worthy Wolsey,
Who cannot err, he did it. Now this follows,—
Which, as I take it, is a kind of puppy
To the old dam, treason,—Charles the emperor,
Under pretence to see the queen his aunt,—
For 'twas indeed his colour, but he came
To whisper Wolsey,—here makes visitation:
His fears were, that the interview betwixt   180
England and France might, through their amity,
Breed him some prejudice; for from this league
Peep'd harms that menaced him: he privily
Deals with our cardinal; and, as I trow,—
Which I do well; for I am sure the emperor
Paid ere he promised; whereby his suit was granted
Ere it was ask'd; but when the way was made,
And paved with gold, the emperor thus desired,
That he would please to alter the king's course,
And break the foresaid peace. Let the king know,   190
As soon he shall by me, that thus the cardinal
Does buy and sell his honour as he pleases,
And for his own advantage.
  Nor.   I am sorry
To hear this of him; and could wish he were
Something mistaken in 't.
  Buck.   No, not a syllable:
I do pronounce him in that very shape
He shall appear in proof.

Enter BRANDON, *a Sergeant-at-arms before him, and
    two or three of the* Guard.

  Bran. Your office, sergeant; execute it.
  Serg.   Sir,
My lord the Duke of Buckingham, and Earl
Of Hereford, Stafford, and Northampton, I   200
Arrest thee of high treason, in the name
Of our most sovereign king.
  Buck.   Lo, you, my lord,

The net has fall'n upon me! I shall perish
Under device and practice.
  Bran.   I am sorry
To see you ta'en from liberty, to look on
The business present: 'tis his highness' pleasure
You shall to the Tower.
  Buck.   It will help me nothing
To plead mine innocence; for that dye is on me
Which makes my whitest part black. The will of
    heaven
Be done in this and all things! I obey.   210
O my Lord Abergavenny, fare you well!
  Bran. Nay, he must bear you company. The king
                          [*To Abergavenny.*
Is pleased you shall to the Tower, till you know
How he determines further.
  Aber.   As the duke said,
The will of heaven be done, and the king's pleasure
By me obey'd!
  Bran.   Here is a warrant from
The king to attach Lord Montacute; and the bodies
Of the duke's confessor, John de la Car,
One Gilbert Peck, his chancellor,—
  Buck.   So, so;
These are the limbs o' the plot: no more, I hope.   220
  Bran. A monk o' the Chartreux.
  Buck.   O, Nicholas Hopkins?
  Bran.   He.
  Buck. My surveyor is false; the o'er-great cardinal
Hath show'd him gold; my life is spann'd already:
I am the shadow of poor Buckingham,
Whose figure even this instant cloud puts on,
By darkening my clear sun. My lord, farewell. [*Exeunt.*

SCENE II. *The same. The council-chamber.*

Cornets. Enter the KING, *leaning on the* CARDINAL'S
    shoulder, the Nobles, *and* SIR THOMAS LOVELL; *the*
    CARDINAL *places himself under the* KING'S *feet on his
    right side.*

  King. My life itself, and the best heart of it,
Thanks you for this great care: I stood i' the level
Of a full-charged confederacy, and give thanks
To you that choked it. Let be call'd before us
That gentleman of Buckingham's; in person
I'll hear him his confessions justify;
And point by point the treasons of his master
He shall again relate.

A noise within, crying 'Room for the Queen!' *Enter*
    QUEEN KATHARINE, *ushered by the* DUKE OF
    NORFOLK, *and the* DUKE OF SUFFOLK: *she kneels.
    The* KING *riseth from his state, takes her up, kisses and
    placeth her by him.*

  Q. Kath. Nay, we must longer kneel: I am a suitor.
  King. Arise, and take place by us: half your suit   10
Never name to us; you have half our power:

---

169. **articles o' the combination,** terms of the peace treaty. 197. **He
. . . proof,** experience shall prove him. 218, 219. **John de la Car,
Gilbert Peck.** The names are from Holinshed's account: "Maister Iohn
de la Car *alias* de la Court, the dukes confessor, and sir Gilbert Perke,
priest, the duke's chancellor." Pooler thinks *Peck* and *Perke* are errors
for *clerk* (i.e., clergyman). The official papers connected with the
trial of the duke give the names *John Delacourt* and *Robert Gilbert,
clerk.*
  SCENE II. 2. **level,** i.e., was the target of a conspiracy. 3. **full-
charged,** well-aimed. 5. **That . . . Buckingham's.** Cf. I, i, 222, *my*

surveyor is false. 6. **justify,** prove, confirm. 8. *Stage Direction:* **state,**
chair of state, a raised seat with a canopy. 21. **flaw'd,** damaged.
33. **The spinsters,** etc. This passage has a parallel in Holinshed's
account of the duke of Suffolk's meeting with the clothiers of his
shire: "The duke of Suffolke, sitting in commission about this sub-
sidie in Suffolke, persuaded by courteous meanes the rich clothiers to
assent thereto: but, when they came home and went about to discharge
and put from them their spinners, carders, fillers, weauers, and other
artificers (which they kept in worke afore time,) the people began to
assemble in companies." 37. **danger serves,** is attendant among them.

The other moiety, ere you ask, is given;
Repeat your will and take it.
   Q. Kath.   Thank your majesty.
That you would love yourself, and in that love
Not unconsider'd leave your honour, nor
The dignity of your office, is the point
Of my petition.
   King.   Lady mine, proceed.
   Q. Kath. I am solicited, not by a few,
And those of true condition, that your subjects
Are in great grievance: there have been commissions
Sent down among 'em, which hath flaw'd the heart 21
Of all their loyalties: wherein, although,
My good lord cardinal, they vent reproaches
Most bitterly on you, as putter on
Of these exactions, yet the king our master—
Whose honour heaven shield from soil!—even he
     escapes not
Language unmannerly, yea, such which breaks
The sides of loyalty, and almost appears
In loud rebellion.
   Nor.   Not almost appears,
It doth appear; for, upon these taxations,   30
The clothiers all, not able to maintain
The many to them 'longing, have put off
The spinsters, carders, fullers, weavers, who,
Unfit for other life, compell'd by hunger
And lack of other means, in desperate manner
Daring the event to the teeth, are all in uproar,
And danger serves among them.
   King.   Taxation!
Wherein? and what taxation? My lord cardinal,
You that are blamed for it alike with us,
Know you of this taxation?
   Wol.   Please you, sir,   40
I know but of a single part, in aught
Pertains to the state; and front but in that file
Where others tell steps with me.
   Q. Kath.   No, my lord,
You know no more than others; but you frame
Things that are known alike; which are not
     wholesome
To those which would not know them, and yet must
Perforce be their acquaintance. These exactions,
Whereof my sovereign would have note, they are
Most pestilent to the hearing; and, to bear 'em,
The back is sacrifice to the load. They say   50
They are devised by you; or else you suffer
Too hard an exclamation.
   King.   Still exaction!
The nature of it? in what kind, let 's know,
Is this exaction?
   Q. Kath.   I am much too venturous
In tempting of your patience; but am bolden'd
Under your promised pardon. The subjects' grief
Comes through commissions, which compel from each
The sixth part of his substance, to be levied
Without delay; and the pretence for this

Is named, your wars in France: this makes bold
     mouths: 60
Tongues spit their duties out, and cold hearts freeze
Allegiance in them; their curses now
Live where their prayers did: and it 's come to pass,
This tractable obedience is a slave
To each incensed will. I would your highness
Would give it quick consideration, for
There is no primer business.
   King.   By my life,
This is against our pleasure.
   Wol.   And for me,
I have no further gone in this than by
A single voice; and that not pass'd me but   70
By learned approbation of the judges. If I am
Traduced by ignorant tongues, which neither know
My faculties nor person, yet will be
The chronicles of my doing, let me say
'Tis but the fate of place, and the rough brake
That virtue must go through. We must not stint
Our necessary actions, in the fear
To cope malicious censurers; which ever,
As ravenous fishes, do a vessel follow
That is new-trimm'd, but benefit no further   80
Than vainly longing. What we oft do best,
By sick interpreters, once weak ones, is
Not ours, or not allow'd; what worst, as oft,
Hitting a grosser quality, is cried up
For our best act. If we shall stand still,
In fear our motion will be mock'd or carp'd at,
We should take root here where we sit, or sit
State-statues only.
   King.   Things done well,
And with a care, exempt themselves from fear;
Things done without example, in their issue   90
Are to be fear'd. Have you a precedent
Of this commission? I believe, not any.
We must not rend our subjects from our laws,
And stick them in our will. Sixth part of each?
A trembling contribution! Why, we take
From every tree lop, bark, and part o' the timber;
And, though we leave it with a root, thus hack'd,
The air will drink the sap. To every county
Where this is question'd send our letters, with
Free pardon to each man that has denied   100
The force of this commission: pray, look to 't;
I put it to your care.
   Wol.   A word with you.
                        [*To the Secretary.*
Let there be letters writ to every shire,
Of the king's grace and pardon. The grieved commons
Hardly conceive of me; let it be noised
That through our intercession this revokement
And pardon comes: I shall anon advise you
Further in the proceeding.   [*Exit Secretary.*

Enter Surveyor.

   Q. Kath. I am sorry that the Duke of Buckingham

Is run in your displeasure.

King.　　　　　　　It grieves many: 　110
The gentleman is learn'd, and a most rare speaker;
To nature none more bound; his training such,
That he may furnish and instruct great teachers,
And never seek for aid out of himself. Yet see,
When these so noble benefits shall prove
Not well disposed, the mind growing once corrupt,
They turn to vicious forms, ten times more ugly
Than ever they were fair. This man so complete,
Who was enroll'd 'mongst wonders, and when we,
Almost with ravish'd listening, could not find 　120
His hour of speech a minute; he, my lady,
Hath into monstrous habits put the graces
That once were his, and is become as black
As if besmear'd in hell. Sit by us; you shall hear—
This was his gentleman in trust—of him
Things to strike honour sad. Bid him recount
The fore-recited practices; whereof
We cannot feel too little, hear too much.

Wol. Stand forth, and with bold spirit relate what
　　you,
Most like a careful subject, have collected 　130
Out of the Duke of Buckingham.

King.　　　　　　　Speak freely.

Surv. First, it was usual with him, every day
It would infect his speech, that if the king
Should without issue die, he'll carry it so
To make the sceptre his: these very words
I've heard him utter to his son-in-law,
Lord Abergavenny; to whom by oath he menaced
Revenge upon the cardinal.

Wol.　　　　　　Please your highness, note
This dangerous conception in this point.
Not friended by his wish, to your high person 　140
His will is most malignant; and it stretches
Beyond you, to your friends.

Q. Kath.　　　　　My learn'd lord cardinal,
Deliver all with charity.

King.　　　　　Speak on:
How grounded he his title to the crown,
Upon our fail? to this point hast thou heard him
At any time speak aught?

Surv.　　　　　He was brought to this
By a vain prophecy of Nicholas Henton.

King. What was that Henton?

Surv.　　　　　Sir, a Chartreux friar,
His confessor; who fed him every minute
With words of sovereignty.

King.　　　　　　How know'st thou this? 　150

Surv. Not long before your highness sped to France,
The duke being at the Rose, within the parish
Saint Lawrence Poultney, did of me demand
What was the speech among the Londoners
Concerning the French journey: I replied,
Men fear'd the French would prove perfidious,

To the king's danger. Presently the duke
Said, 'twas the fear, indeed; and that he doubted
'Twould prove the verity of certain words
Spoke by a holy monk; 'that oft,' says he, 　160
'Hath sent to me, wishing me to permit
John de la Car, my chaplain, a choice hour
To hear from him a matter of some moment:
Whom after under the confession's seal
He solemnly had sworn, that what he spoke
My chaplain to no creature living, but
To me, should utter, with demure confidence
This pausingly ensued: Neither the king nor's heirs,
Tell you the duke, shall prosper: bid him strive
To gain the love o' the commonalty: the duke 　170
Shall govern England.'

Q. Kath.　　　　　If I know you well,
You were the duke's surveyor, and lost your office
On the complaint o' the tenants: take good heed
You charge not in your spleen a noble person
And spoil your nobler soul: I say, take heed;
Yes, heartily beseech you.

King.　　　　　Let him on.
Go forward.

Surv.　　　　　On my soul, I'll speak but truth.
I told my lord the duke, by the devil's illusions
The monk might be deceived; and that 'twas
　　dangerous for him
To ruminate on this so far, until 　180
It forged him some design, which, being believed,
It was much like to do: he answer'd, 'Tush,
It can do me no damage;' adding further,
That, had the king in his last sickness fail'd,
The cardinal's and Sir Thomas Lovell's heads
Should have gone off.

King.　　　　　Ha! what, so rank? Ah ha!
There's mischief in this man: canst thou say further?

Surv. I can, my liege.

King.　　　　　Proceed.

Surv.　　　　　　Being at Greenwich,
After your highness had reproved the duke
About Sir William Blomer,—

King.　　　　　I remember 　190
Of such a time: being my sworn servant,
The duke retain'd him his. But on; what hence?

Surv. 'If,' quoth he, 'I for this had been committed,
As, to the Tower, I thought, I would have play'd
The part my father meant to act upon
The usurper Richard; who, being at Salisbury,
Made suit to come in's presence; which if granted,
As he made semblance of his duty, would
Have put his knife into him.'

King.　　　　　A giant traitor!

Wol. Now, madam, may his highness live in
　　freedom, 　200
And this man out of prison?

Q. Kath.　　　　　God mend all!

---

110. **Is run in,** has incurred.　112. **To . . . bound,** none more indebted to nature for talents.　114. **out of himself,** beyond the treasures of his own mind (Johnson).　120-121. **could . . . minute,** when he spoke, an hour seemed but a minute.　130. **collected,** learned by spying.　132-138. **First . . . cardinal.** The substance of this speech is directly from Holinshed: "This Kneuet, being had in examination before the cardinall, disclosed all the dukes life. And first he vttered, that the duke was accustomed, by waie of talke, to saie how he meant so to vse the matter, that he would attaine to the crowne, *if king Henrie* chanced to *die without issue:* & that he had talke and conference of that matter on a time with George Neuill, lord of Aburgauennie, vnto whome he had giuen his daughter in marriage; and also that he threatned to punish the cardinall for his manifold misdooings, being without cause his mortall

enemie."　132-135. **First . . . his.** Perhaps this inconsecutiveness in syntax is dramatically intentional to make it apparent that the surveyor is fabricating his story.　133. **infect,** appear as a corrupt element.　140. **Not . . . wish,** i.e., his wish not being gratified.　145. **fail,** i.e., if we should die without an heir.　147, 148. **Henton,** so F; Globe, following Pope: *Hopkins.* Holinshed calls the monk "one Nicholas Hopkins, a monke of an house of the Chartreus order beside Bristow, called *Henton."*　151-171. **Not . . . England.** This passage parallels Holinshed often in phrasing as well as in substance.　181. **forged,** caused him to frame; *which* refers vaguely to what the monk has told him.　198. **semblance,** pretense.　209. **period,** goal, end.

SCENE III.　1. **spells of France.** Holinshed mentions the offense taken at the "French vices and brags" of some of Henry's courtiers who

King. There 's something more would out of thee;
   what say'st?
Surv. After 'the duke his father,' with 'the knife,'
He stretch'd him, and, with one hand on his dagger,
Another spread on 's breast, mounting his eyes,
He did discharge a horrible oath; whose tenour
Was,—were he evil used, he would outgo
His father by as much as a performance
Does an irresolute purpose.
   King.   There 's his period,
To sheathe his knife in us. He is attach'd;   210
Call him to present trial: if he may
Find mercy in the law, 'tis his; if none,
Let him not seek 't of us: by day and night,
He 's traitor to the height.   [*Exeunt.*

SCENE III. *An ante-chamber in the palace.*

Enter the LORD CHAMBERLAIN *and* LORD SANDS.

Cham. Is 't possible the spells of France should
   juggle
Men into such strange mysteries?
   Sands.   New customs,
Though they be never so ridiculous,
Nay, let 'em be unmanly, yet are follow'd.
   Cham. As far as I see, all the good our English
Have got by the late voyage is but merely
A fit or two o' the face; but they are shrewd ones;
For when they hold 'em, you would swear directly
Their very noses had been counsellors
To Pepin or Clotharius, they keep state so.   10
   Sands. They have all new legs, and lame ones: one
   would take it,
That never saw 'em pace before, the spavin
Or springhalt reign'd among 'em.
   Cham.   Death! my lord,
Their clothes are after such a pagan cut too,
That, sure, they 've worn out Christendom.

Enter SIR THOMAS LOVELL.
           How now!
What news, Sir Thomas Lovell?
   Lov.   Faith, my lord,
I hear of none, but the new proclamation
That 's clapp'd upon the court-gate.
   Cham.   What is 't for?
   Lov. The reformation of our travell'd gallants,
That fill the court with quarrels, talk, and tailors.   20
   Cham. I 'm glad 'tis there: now I would pray our
   monsieurs
To think an English courtier may be wise,
And never see the Louvre.
   Lov.   They must either,
For so run the conditions, leave those remnants
Of fool and feather that they got in France,

With all their honourable points of ignorance
Pertaining thereunto, as fights and fireworks,
Abusing better men than they can be,
Out of a foreign wisdom, renouncing clean
The faith they have in tennis, and tall stockings,   30
Short blister'd breeches, and those types of travel,
And understand again like honest men;
Or pack to their old playfellows: there, I take it,
They may, 'cum privilegio,' wear away
The lag end of their lewdness and be laugh'd at.
   Sands. 'Tis time to give 'em physic, their diseases
Are grown so catching.
   Cham.   What a loss our ladies
Will have of these trim vanities!
   Lov.   Ay, marry,
There will be woe indeed, lords: the sly whoresons
Have got a speeding trick to lay down ladies;   40
A French song and a fiddle has no fellow.
   Sands. The devil fiddle 'em! I am glad they are
   going,
For, sure, there 's no converting of 'em: now
An honest country lord, as I am, beaten
A long time out of play, may bring his plain-song
And have an hour of hearing; and, by 'r lady,
Held current music too.
   Cham.   Well said, Lord Sands;
Your colt's tooth is not cast yet.
   Sands.   No, my lord;
Nor shall not, while I have a stump.
   Cham.   Sir Thomas,
Whither were you a-going?
   Lov.   To the cardinal's: 50
Your lordship is a guest too.
   Cham.   O, 'tis true:
This night he makes a supper, and a great one,
To many lords and ladies; there will be
The beauty of this kingdom, I'll assure you.
   Lov. That churchman bears a bounteous mind
   indeed,
A hand as fruitful as the land that feeds us;
His dews fall every where.
   Cham.   No doubt he 's noble;
He had a black mouth that said other of him.
   Sands. He may, my lord; has wherewithal: in him
Sparing would show a worse sin than ill doctrine;   60
Men of his way should be most liberal;
They are set here for examples.
   Cham.   True, they are so;
But few now give so great ones. My barge stays;
Your lordship shall along. Come, good Sir Thomas,
We shall be late else; which I would not be,
For I was spoke to, with Sir Henry Guildford
This night to be comptrollers.
   Sands.   I am your lordship's.   [*Exeunt.*

---

returned from the continent "all French in eating, drinking, and apparell." 2. **mysteries,** mummeries; artificial fashions (Douce). 7. **A . . . face,** artificial cast of countenance (Johnson). 10. **Pepin, Clotharius,** kings of ancient France in the seventh and eighth centuries. **keep state,** maintain a position of dignified demeanor. 11. **new legs,** new forms of saluting and new legs to salute with (Pooler); *leg* frequently means an obeisance made by drawing back one leg and bending the other. 12. **spavin,** disease of horses causing swelling of joints and lameness. 13. **springhalt,** lameness in a horse. 15. **they 've . . . Christendom,** they have exhausted the repertory of Christian fashions. 23. **Louvre,** ancient palace of the kings of France in Paris, now famous as an art museum. 25. **fool and feather,** probably alludes to the extravagant feather trimming worn in men's hats. 31. **blister'd,** puffed.

34. **'cum privilegio,'** with exclusive right. 35. **lag . . . lewdness,** the last days of their worthless lives. 38. **trim vanities,** fashionable and vain courtiers. 40. **lay down,** seduce; bring to bed of a child (Onions). 45. **plain-song,** simple chant or air without harmony or tempo. 47. **Held current music,** regarded as in the height of fashion. 48. **colt's tooth,** lecherousness of youth. 63. **My barge stays.** The barge was a large river boat used for purposes of state or pageantry. Palaces built near the Thames, like York Place (now Whitehall) and Bridewell (the king's palace), were accessible by steps leading to the river, and courtiers made use of the Thames waterway in paying visits of state. 67. **comptrollers,** officers in a great household to act as managers in general; here, something like masters of ceremonies.

SCENE IV. *A Hall in York Place.*

Hautboys. A small table under a state for the CARDINAL,
a longer table for the guests. Then enter ANNE BULLEN
and divers other Ladies *and* Gentlemen *as guests,
at one door; at another door, enter* SIR HENRY
GUILDFORD.

Guild. Ladies, a general welcome from his grace
Salutes ye all; this night he dedicates
To fair content and you: none here, he hopes,
In all this noble bevy, has brought with her
One care abroad; he would have all as merry
As, first, good company, good wine, good welcome,
Can make good people. O, my lord, you 're tardy:

Enter LORD CHAMBERLAIN, LORD SANDS, *and* SIR
THOMAS LOVELL.

The very thought of this fair company
Clapp'd wings to me.
   Cham.   You are young, Sir Harry
     Guildford.
   Sands. Sir Thomas Lovell, had the cardinal   10
But half my lay thoughts in him, some of these
Should find a running banquet ere they rested,
I think would better please 'em: by my life,
They are a sweet society of fair ones.
   Lov. O, that your lordship were but now confessor
To one or two of these!
   Sands.   I would I were;
They should find easy penance.
   Lov.   Faith, how easy?
   Sands. As easy as a down-bed would afford it.
   Cham. Sweet ladies, will it please you sit? Sir
     Harry,
Place you that side; I'll take the charge of this: 20
His grace is entering. Nay, you must not freeze;
Two women placed together makes cold weather:
My Lord Sands, you are one will keep 'em waking;
Pray, sit between these ladies.
   Sands.   By my faith,
And thank your lordship. By your leave, sweet ladies:
If I chance to talk a little wild, forgive me;
I had it from my father.
   Anne.   Was he mad, sir?
   Sands. O, very mad, exceeding mad, in love too:
But he would bite none; just as I do now,
He would kiss you twenty with a breath.   [*Kisses her.*
   Cham.   Well said, my lord.   30
So, now you 're fairly seated. Gentlemen,
The penance lies on you, if these fair ladies
Pass away frowning.
   Sands.   For my little cure,
Let me alone.

Hautboys. Enter CARDINAL WOLSEY, *and takes his state.*

   Wol. You 're welcome, my fair guests: that noble
     lady,
Or gentleman, that is not freely merry,
Is not my friend: this, to confirm my welcome;
And to you all, good health.   [*Drinks.*
   Sands.   Your grace is noble:

Let me have such a bowl may hold my thanks,
And save me so much talking.
   Wol.   My Lord Sands,   40
I am beholding to you: cheer your neighbours.
Ladies, you are not merry: gentlemen,
Whose fault is this?
   Sands.   The red wine first must rise
In their fair cheeks, my lord; then we shall have 'em
Talk us to silence.
   Anne.   You are a merry gamester,
My Lord Sands.
   Sands.   Yes, if I make my play.
Here 's to your ladyship: and pledge it, madam,
For 'tis to such a thing,—
   Anne.   You cannot show me.
   Sands. I told your grace they would talk anon.
     [*Drum and trumpet, chambers discharged.*
   Wol.   What 's that?
   Cham. Look out there, some of ye.   [*Exit Servant.*
   Wol.   What warlike voice,   50
And to what end, is this? Nay, ladies, fear not;
By all the laws of war you 're privileged.

Re-enter Servant.

   Cham. How now! what is 't?
   Serv.   A noble troop of strangers;
For so they seem: they 've left their barge and landed;
And hither make, as great ambassadors
From foreign princes.
   Wol.   Good lord chamberlain,
Go, give 'em welcome; you can speak the French
     tongue;
And, pray, receive 'em nobly, and conduct 'em
Into our presence, where this heaven of beauty
Shall shine at full upon them. Some attend him.   60
   [*Exit Chamberlain, attended. All rise, and tables removed.*
You have now a broken banquet; but we'll mend it.
A good digestion to you all: and once more
I shower a welcome on ye; welcome all.

Hautboys. Enter the KING *and others, as masquers,
habited like shepherds, ushered by the* LORD
CHAMBERLAIN. *They pass directly before the*
CARDINAL, *and gracefully salute him.*

A noble company! what are their pleasures?
   Cham. Because they speak no English, thus they
     pray'd
To tell your grace, that, having heard by fame
Of this so noble and so fair assembly
This night to meet here, they could do no less,
Out of the great respect they bear to beauty,
But leave their flocks; and, under your fair conduct, 70
Crave leave to view these ladies and entreat
An hour of revels with 'em.
   Wol.   Say, lord chamberlain,
They have done my poor house grace; for which I
     pay 'em
A thousand thanks, and pray 'em take their pleasures.
   [*They choose Ladies for the dance. The King chooses
     Anne Bullen.*

King. The fairest hand I ever touch'd! O beauty,
Till now I never knew thee! [*Music. Dance.*
 Wol. My lord!
 Cham. Your grace?
 Wol. Pray, tell 'em thus much
  from me:
There should be one amongst 'em, by his person,
More worthy this place than myself; to whom,
If I but knew him, with my love and duty 80
I would surrender it.
 Cham. I will, my lord.
 [*Whispers the Masquers.*
 Wol. What say they?
 Cham. Such a one, they all confess,
There is indeed; which they would have your grace
Find out, and he will take it.
 Wol. Let me see, then.
By all your good leaves, gentlemen; here I'll make
My royal choice.
 King. Ye have found him, cardinal:
 [*Unmasking.*
You hold a fair assembly; you do well, lord:
You are a churchman, or, I'll tell you, cardinal,
I should judge now unhappily.
 Wol. I am glad
Your grace is grown so pleasant.
 King. My lord chamberlain, 90
Prithee, come hither: what fair lady 's that?
 Cham. An't please your grace, Sir Thomas Bullen's
  daughter,—
The Viscount Rochford,—one of her highness'
  women.
 King. By heaven, she is a dainty one. Sweetheart,
I were unmannerly, to take you out,
And not to kiss you. A health, gentlemen!
Let it go round.
 Wol. Sir Thomas Lovell, is the banquet ready
I' the privy chamber?
 Lov. Yes, my lord.
 Wol. Your grace,
I fear, with dancing is a little heated. 100
 King. I fear, too much.
 Wol. There 's fresher air, my lord,
In the next chamber.
 King. Lead in your ladies, every one: sweet partner,
I must not yet forsake you: let 's be merry,
Good my lord cardinal: I have half a dozen healths
To drink to these fair ladies, and a measure
To lead 'em once again; and then let 's dream
Who 's best in favour. Let the music knock it.
 [*Exeunt with trumpets.*

ACT II.

SCENE I. *Westminster. A street.*

Enter two Gentlemen, *meeting.*

First Gent. Whither away so fast?
Sec. Gent. O, God save ye!

Even to the hall, to hear what shall become
Of the great Duke of Buckingham.
 First Gent. I'll save you
That labour, sir. All 's now done, but the ceremony
Of bringing back the prisoner.
 Sec. Gent. Were you there?
 First Gent. Yes, indeed, was I.
 Sec. Gent. Pray, speak what has
  happen'd.
 First Gent. You may guess quickly what.
 Sec. Gent. Is he found guilty?
 First Gent. Yes, truly is he, and condemn'd upon 't.
 Sec. Gent. I am sorry for 't.
 First Gent. So are a number more.
 Sec. Gent. But, pray, how pass'd it? 10
 First Gent. I'll tell you in a little. The great duke
Came to the bar; where to his accusations
He pleaded still not guilty and alleged
Many sharp reasons to defeat the law.
The king's attorney on the contrary
Urged on the examinations, proofs, confessions
Of divers witnesses; which the duke desired
To have brought vivâ voce to his face:
At which appear'd against him his surveyor;
Sir Gilbert Peck his chancellor; and John Car, 20
Confessor to him; with that devil-monk,
Hopkins, that made this mischief.
 Sec. Gent. That was he
That fed him with his prophecies?
 First Gent. The same.
All these accused him strongly; which he fain
Would have flung from him, but, indeed, he could
  not:
And so his peers, upon this evidence,
Have found him guilty of high treason. Much
He spoke, and learnedly, for life; but all
Was either pitied in him or forgotten.
 Sec. Gent. After all this, how did he bear himself? 30
 First Gent. When he was brought again to the bar,
  to hear
His knell rung out, his judgement, he was stirr'd
With such an agony, he sweat extremely,
And something spoke in choler, ill, and hasty:
But he fell to himself again, and sweetly
In all the rest show'd a most noble patience.
 Sec. Gent. I do not think he fears death.
 First Gent. Sure, he does not:
He never was so womanish; the cause
He may a little grieve at.
 Sec. Gent. Certainly
The cardinal is the end of this.
 First Gent. 'Tis likely, 40
By all conjectures: first, Kildare's attainder,
Then deputy of Ireland; who removed,
Earl Surrey was sent thither, and in haste too,
Lest he should help his father.
 Sec. Gent. That trick of state
Was a deep envious one.
 First Gent. At his return
No doubt he will requite it. This is noted,

---

32. **judgement,** sentence.   36. **In all the rest,** for the remaining time.
41-44. **first . . . father.** The incident is in Holinshed: "Bicause [Wolsey]
doubted [Buckingham's] freends, kinnesmen, and alies, and cheeflie
the earle of Surrie, lord admerall, (which had married the dukes
daughter,) he thought good first to send him some whither out of the
waie, least he might cast a trumpe in his waie. . . . At length there was
occasion offered him to compasse his purpose, by occasion of the earle of
Kildare his comming out of Ireland. . . . Such accusations were framed

against [Kildare] . . . that he was committed to prison, and then by
the cardinall's good preferment, the earle of Surrie was sent into Ireland as the King's deputy, in lieu of the said earle of Kildare; there
to remaine rather as an exile than as lieutenant to the king, euen at
the cardinall's pleasure, as he himselfe well perceived."

And generally, whoever the king favours,
The cardinal instantly will find employment,
And far enough from court too.
   Sec. Gent. All the commons
Hate him perniciously, and, o' my conscience, 50
Wish him ten fathom deep: this duke as much
They love and dote on; call him bounteous
    Buckingham,
The mirror of all courtesy;—
   First Gent. Stay there, sir,
And see the noble ruin'd man you speak of.

   Enter BUCKINGHAM *from his arraignment; tipstaves*
   before him; the axe with the edge towards him; halberds
   on each side: accompanied with SIR THOMAS LOVELL,
   SIR NICHOLAS VAUX, SIR WILLIAM SANDS, *and*
   common people.

   Sec. Gent. Let 's stand close, and behold him.
   Buck. All good people,
You that thus far have come to pity me,
Hear what I say, and then go home and lose me.
I have this day received a traitor's judgement,
And by that name must die: yet, heaven bear witness,
And if I have a conscience, let it sink me, 60
Even as the axe falls, if I be not faithful!
The law I bear no malice for my death;
'T has done, upon the premises, but justice:
But those that sought it I could wish more Christians:
Be what they will, I heartily forgive 'em:
Yet let 'em look they glory not in mischief,
Nor build their evils on the graves of great men;
For then my guiltless blood must cry against 'em.
For further life in this world I ne'er hope,
Nor will I sue, although the king have mercies 70
More than I dare make faults. You few that loved me,
And dare be bold to weep for Buckingham,
His noble friends and fellows, whom to leave
Is only bitter to him, only dying,
Go with me, like good angels, to my end;
And, as the long divorce of steel falls on me,
Make of your prayers one sweet sacrifice,
And lift my soul to heaven. Lead on, o' God's name.
   Lov. I do beseech your grace, for charity,
If ever any malice in your heart 80
Were hid against me, now to forgive me frankly.
   Buck. Sir Thomas Lovell, I as free forgive you
As I would be forgiven: I forgive all;
There cannot be those numberless offences
'Gainst me, that I cannot take peace with: no black
    envy
Shall mark my grave. Commend me to his grace;
And, if he speak of Buckingham, pray, tell him
You met him half in heaven: my vows and prayers
Yet are the king's; and, till my soul forsake,
Shall cry for blessings on him: may he live 90
Longer than I have time to tell his years!
Ever beloved and loving may his rule be!
And when old time shall lead him to his end,
Goodness and he fill up one monument!
   Lov. To the water side I must conduct your grace;
Then give my charge up to Sir Nicholas Vaux,

Who undertakes you to your end.
   Vaux. Prepare there,
The duke is coming: see the barge be ready;
And fit it with such furniture as suits
The greatness of his person.
   Buck. Nay, Sir Nicholas, 100
Let alone; my state now will but mock me.
When I came hither, I was lord high constable
And Duke of Buckingham; now, poor Edward
    Bohun:
Yet I am richer than my base accusers,
That never knew what truth meant: I now seal it;
And with that blood will make 'em one day groan
    for 't.
My noble father, Henry of Buckingham,
Who first raised head against usurping Richard,
Flying for succour to his servant Banister,
Being distress'd, was by that wretch betray'd, 110
And without trial fell; God's peace be with him!
Henry the Seventh succeeding, truly pitying
My father's loss, like a most royal prince,
Restored me to my honours, and, out of ruins,
Made my name once more noble. Now his son,
Henry the Eighth, life, honour, name and all
That made me happy at one stroke has taken
For ever from the world. I had my trial,
And, must needs say, a noble one; which makes me
A little happier than my wretched father: 120
Yet thus far we are one in fortunes: both
Fell by our servants, by those men we loved most;
A most unnatural and faithless service!
Heaven has an end in all: yet, you that hear me,
This from a dying man receive as certain:
Where you are liberal of your loves and counsels
Be sure you be not loose; for those you make friends
And give your hearts to, when they once perceive
The least rub in your fortunes, fall away
Like water from ye, never found again 130
But where they mean to sink ye. All good people,
Pray for me! I must now forsake ye: the last hour
Of my long weary life is come upon me.
Farewell:
And when you would say something that is sad,
Speak how I fell. I have done; and God forgive me!
             [Exeunt Duke and Train.
   First Gent. O, this is full of pity! Sir, it calls,
I fear, too many curses on their heads
That were the authors.
   Sec. Gent. If the duke be guiltless,
'Tis full of woe: yet I can give you inkling 140
Of an ensuing evil, if it fall,
Greater than this.
   First Gent. Good angels keep it from
    us!
What may it be? You do not doubt my faith, sir?
   Sec. Gent. This secret is so weighty, 'twill require
A strong faith to conceal it.
   First Gent. Let me have it;
I do not talk much.
   Sec. Gent. I am confident;
You shall, sir: did you not of late days hear

50. **perniciously,** i.e., with deadly hatred. 53. **mirror of all courtesy.**
The phrase is from Holinshed, who says also that the duke was "no
less fauoured and beloued of the people of this realme than the cardinall
himselfe was hated and enuied." 57. **lose,** forget. 63. **premises,**
evidence. 76. **divorce,** that which causes separation. 84-85. **There
. . . with,** i.e., I can make peace with any number of those who have
offended me. 89. **forsake,** leave my body. 119. **a noble one,** i.e., trial

by his peers. Buckingham's father had been murdered by Richard III.
127. **loose,** wanting in restraint. 158. **scruple.** Katharine had been betrothed to Henry's older brother, Prince Arthur, which according to
the laws of the precontract would make illegal her marriage with any
close relative after Arthur's death. Henry's marriage to Katharine was
made possible by a papal dispensation. 160. **Cardinal Campeius,**
Cardinal Lorenzo Campeggio, sent from Rome to confer on the legality

A buzzing of a separation
Between the king and Katharine?
   First Gent.   Yes, but it held not:
For when the king once heard it, out of anger   150
He sent command to the lord mayor straight
To stop the rumour, and allay those tongues
That durst disperse it.
   Sec. Gent.   But that slander, sir,
Is found a truth now: for it grows again
Fresher than e'er it was; and held for certain
The king will venture at it. Either the cardinal,
Or some about him near, have, out of malice
To the good queen, possess'd him with a scruple
That will undo her: to confirm this too,
Cardinal Campeius is arrived, and lately;   160
As all think, for this business.
   First Gent.   'Tis the cardinal;
And merely to revenge him on the emperor
For not bestowing on him, at his asking,
The archbishopric of Toledo, this is purposed.
   Sec. Gent. I think you have hit the mark: but is 't
     not cruel
That she should feel the smart of this? The cardinal
Will have his will, and she must fall.
   First Gent.   'Tis woful.
We are too open here to argue this;
Let 's think in private more.   *[Exeunt.*

SCENE II. *An ante-chamber in the palace.*

Enter the LORD CHAMBERLAIN, *reading a letter.*

Cham. 'My lord, the horses your lordship sent for,
with all the care I had, I saw well chosen, ridden, and
furnished. They were young and handsome, and of
the best breed in the north. When they were ready
to set out for London, a man of my lord cardinal's, by
commission and main power, took 'em from me; with
this reason: His master would be served before a
subject, if not before the king; which stopped our
mouths, sir.'   10
I fear he will indeed: well, let him have them:
He will have all, I think.

   Enter, to the LORD CHAMBERLAIN, *the* DUKES OF
     NORFOLK *and* SUFFOLK.

   Nor. Well met, my lord chamberlain.
   Cham. Good day to both your graces.
   Suf. How is the king employ'd?
   Cham.   I left him private,
Full of sad thoughts and troubles.
   Nor.   What 's the cause?
   Cham. It seems the marriage with his brother's wife
Has crept too near his conscience.
   Suf.   No, his conscience
Has crept too near another lady.
   Nor.   'Tis so:
This is the cardinal's doing, the king-cardinal: 20
That blind priest, like the eldest son of fortune,
Turns what he list. The king will know him one day.
   Suf. Pray God he do! he'll never know himself else.

Nor. How holily he works in all his business!
And with what zeal! for, now he has crack'd the
   league
Between us and the emperor, the queen's great
   nephew,
He dives into the king's soul, and there scatters
Dangers, doubts, wringing of the conscience,
Fears, and despairs; and all these for his marriage:
And out of all these to restore the king,   30
He counsels a divorce; a loss of her
That, like a jewel, has hung twenty years
About his neck, yet never lost her lustre;
Of her that loves him with that excellence
That angels love good men with; even of her
That, when the greatest stroke of fortune falls,
Will bless the king: and is not this course pious?
   Cham. Heaven keep me from such counsel! 'Tis
     most true
These news are every where; every tongue speaks 'em,
And every true heart weeps for 't: all that dare   40
Look into these affairs see this main end,
The French king's sister. Heaven will one day open
The king's eyes, that so long have slept upon
This bold bad man.
   Suf.   And free us from his slavery.
   Nor. We had need pray,
And heartily, for our deliverance;
Or this imperious man will work us all
From princes into pages: all men's honours
Lie like one lump before him, to be fashion'd
Into what pitch he please.
   Suf.   For me, my lords,   50
I love him not, nor fear him; there 's my creed:
As I am made without him, so I'll stand,
If the king please; his curses and his blessings
Touch me alike, they 're breath I not believe in.
I knew him, and I know him; so I leave him
To him that made him proud, the pope.
   Nor.   Let 's in;
And with some other business put the king
From these sad thoughts, that work too much upon
   him:
My lord, you'll bear us company?
   Cham.   Excuse me;
The king has sent me otherwhere: besides,   60
You'll find a most unfit time to disturb him:
Health to your lordships.
   Nor.   Thanks, my good lord
     chamberlain.
       [Exit Lord Chamberlain; and the King draws the
                 curtain, and sits reading pensively.
   Suf. How sad he looks! sure, he is much afflicted.
   King. Who 's there, ha?
   Nor.   Pray God he be not angry.
   King. Who 's there, I say? How dare you thrust
     yourselves
Into my private meditations?
Who am I? ha?
   Nor. A gracious king that pardons all offences
Malice ne'er meant: our breach of duty this way
Is business of estate; in which we come   70

*King Henry
the Eighth*
ACT II : SC II

1283

---

of the king's marriage. 162. **to . . . emperor.** The queen was the
emperor's aunt.
   SCENE II. 3. **ridden,** broken in, trained. 6. **commission,** warrant.
7. **main,** mighty; i.e., by force. 21. **That . . . fortune,** a glance at
blind Fortune as an undiscriminating goddess; also to the special privileges of eldest sons (Hart). 29. **for,** on account of. 32-33. **like . . .
neck,** refers to the custom among gentlemen of wearing a jewel on

a chain or ribbon around the neck. 50. **pitch,** degree of dignity; i.e.,
the cardinal reduces all men of rank to one lump which he will re-
fashion into creatures of whatever stature he pleases. 52. **As . . . him,**
refers to his rank conferred by the king. The speaker was elevated to
the dukedom on his marriage with the king's sister, dowager queen of
France. 70. **estate,** public weal.

To know your royal pleasure.

King.   Ye are too bold:
Go to; I'll make ye know your times of business:
Is this an hour for temporal affairs, ha?

    Enter WOLSEY *and* CAMPEIUS, *with a commission.*

Who's there? my good lord cardinal? O my Wolsey,
The quiet of my wounded conscience;
Thou art a cure fit for a king. [*To Camp.*] You're
    welcome,
Most learned reverend sir, into our kingdom:
Use us and it. [*To Wol.*] My good lord, have great
    care
I be not found a talker.

    Wol.   Sir, you cannot.
I would your grace would give us but an hour   80
Of private conference.

    King.   [*To Nor. and Suf.*] We are busy;
    go.

    Nor. [*Aside to Suf.*] This priest has no pride in him?

    Suf.   [*Aside to Nor.*] Not to speak of:
I would not be so sick though for his place:
But this cannot continue.

    Nor.   [*Aside to Suf.*] If it do,
I'll venture one have-at-him.

    Suf.   [*Aside to Nor.*] I another.
                   [*Exeunt Nor. and Suf.*

    Wol. Your grace has given a precedent of wisdom
Above all princes, in committing freely
Your scruple to the voice of Christendom:
Who can be angry now? what envy reach you?
The Spaniard, tied by blood and favour to her,   90
Must now confess, if they have any goodness,
The trial just and noble. All the clerks,
I mean the learned ones, in Christian kingdoms
Have their free voices: Rome, the nurse of judgement,
Invited by your noble self, hath sent
One general tongue unto us, this good man,
This just and learned priest, Cardinal Campeius;
Whom once more I present unto your highness.

    King. And once more in mine arms I bid him
    welcome,
And thank the holy conclave for their loves: 100
They have sent me such a man I would have wish'd
    for.

    Cam. Your grace must needs deserve all strangers'
    loves,
You are so noble. To your highness' hand
I tender my commission; by whose virtue,
The court of Rome commanding, you, my lord
Cardinal of York, are join'd with me their servant
In the unpartial judging of this business.

    King. Two equal men. The queen shall be
    acquainted
Forthwith for what you come. Where's Gardiner?

    Wol. I know your majesty has always loved her   110
So dear in heart, not to deny her that
A woman of less place might ask by law:
Scholars allow'd freely to argue for her.

    King. Ay, and the best she shall have; and my
    favour

To him that does best: God forbid else. Cardinal,
Prithee, call Gardiner to me, my new secretary:
I find him a fit fellow.   [*Exit Wolsey.*

    Re-enter WOLSEY, *with* GARDINER.

    Wol. [*Aside to Gard.*] Give me your hand: much joy
    and favour to you;
You are the king's now.

    Gard.   [*Aside to Wol.*] But to be
    commanded
For ever by your grace, whose hand has raised me.   120

    King. Come hither, Gardiner.   [*Walks and whispers.*

    Cam. My Lord of York, was not one Doctor Pace
In this man's place before him?

    Wol.   Yes, he was.

    Cam. Was he not held a learned man?

    Wol.   Yes, surely.

    Cam. Believe me, there's an ill opinion spread then
Even of yourself, lord cardinal.

    Wol.   How! of me?

    Cam. They will not stick to say you envied him,
And fearing he would rise, he was so virtuous,
Kept him a foreign man still; which so grieved him,
That he ran mad and died.

    Wol.   Heaven's peace be with him!
That's Christian care enough: for living murmurers
There's places of rebuke. He was a fool;   132
For he would needs be virtuous: that good fellow,
If I command him, follows my appointment:
I will have none so near else. Learn this, brother,
We live not to be griped by meaner persons.

    King. Deliver this with modesty to the queen.
                   [*Exit Gardiner.*
The most convenient place that I can think of
For such receipt of learning is Black-Friars;
There ye shall meet about this weighty business.   140
My Wolsey, see it furnish'd. O, my lord,
Would it not grieve an able man to leave
So sweet a bedfellow? But, conscience, conscience!
O, 'tis a tender place; and I must leave her.   [*Exeunt.*

SCENE III. *An ante-chamber of the* Queen's *apartments.*

    Enter ANNE BULLEN *and an* OLD LADY.

    Anne. Not for that neither: here's the pang that
    pinches:
His highness having lived so long with her, and she
So good a lady that no tongue could ever
Pronounce dishonour of her; by my life,
She never knew harm-doing: O, now, after
So many courses of the sun enthroned,
Still growing in a majesty and pomp, the which
To leave a thousand-fold more bitter than
'Tis sweet at first to acquire,—after this process,
To give her the avaunt! it is a pity   10
Would move a monster.

    Old L.   Hearts of most hard temper
Melt and lament for her.

    Anne.   O, God's will! much better
She ne'er had known pomp: though 't be temporal,

---

83. **sick,** i.e., sick with pride.   88. **voice of Christendom,** i.e., the pope, through his representative Campeius.   100. **conclave,** college of cardinals.   109. **Gardiner,** Stephen Gardiner, Wolsey's secretary; he later became one of the most influential members of the king's council.   111. **that,** that which.   122. **Doctor Pace,** a brilliant foreign diplomat of Henry's reign. His abilities are said to have provoked Wolsey's envy

to the extent that the latter kept him away from court on foreign errands (cf. ll. 128-129). There is no evidence that the mental malady here referred to was due to Wolsey's ill usage. The representation here is unhistorical in that Wolsey's death occurred five years before Pace's. 127. **stick,** hesitate.   139. **Black-Friars,** convent buildings in London surrendered to the crown in Henry VIII's time.

Yet, if that quarrel, fortune, do divorce
It from the bearer, 'tis a sufferance panging
As soul and body's severing.
    Old L.   Alas, poor lady!
She 's a stranger now again.
    Anne.   So much the more
Must pity drop upon her. Verily,
I swear, 'tis better to be lowly born,
And range with humble livers in content,   20
Than to be perk'd up in a glistering grief,
And wear a golden sorrow.
    Old L.   Our content
Is our best having.
    Anne.   By my troth and maidenhead,
I would not be a queen.
    Old L.   Beshrew me, I would,
And venture maidenhead for 't; and so would you,
For all this spice of your hypocrisy:
You, that have so fair parts of woman on you,
Have too a woman's heart; which ever yet
Affected eminence, wealth, sovereignty;
Which, to say sooth, are blessings; and which gifts, 30
Saving your mincing, the capacity
Of your soft cheveril conscience would receive,
If you might please to stretch it.
    Anne.   Nay, good troth.
    Old L. Yes, troth, and troth; you would not be a
    queen?
    Anne. No, not for all the riches under heaven.
    Old L. 'Tis strange: a three-pence bow'd would hire
    me,
Old as I am, to queen it: but, I pray you,
What think you of a duchess? have you limbs
To bear that load of title?
    Anne.   No, in truth.   39
    Old L. Then you are weakly made: pluck off a little;
I would not be a young count in your way,
For more than blushing comes to: if your back
Cannot vouchsafe this burthen, 'tis too weak
Ever to get a boy.
    Anne.   How you do talk!
I swear again, I would not be a queen
For all the world.
    Old L.   In faith, for little England
You 'ld venture an emballing: I myself
Would for Carnarvonshire, although there 'long'd
No more to the crown but that. Lo, who comes here?

Enter the LORD CHAMBERLAIN.

    Cham. Good morrow, ladies. What were 't worth to
    know   50
The secret of your conference?
    Anne.   My good Lord,
Not your demand; it values not your asking:
Our mistress' sorrows we were pitying.
    Cham. It was a gentle business, and becoming
The action of good women: there is hope
All will be well.
    Anne.   Now, I pray God, amen!
    Cham. You bear a gentle mind, and heavenly
    blessings

Follow such creatures. That you may, fair lady,
Perceive I speak sincerely, and high note 's
Ta'en of your many virtues, the king's majesty   60
Commends his good opinion of you, and
Does purpose honour to you no less flowing
Than Marchioness of Pembroke; to which title
A thousand pound a year, annual support,
Out of his grace he adds.
    Anne.   I do not know
What kind of my obedience I should tender;
More than my all is nothing: nor my prayers
Are not words duly hallow'd, nor my wishes
More worth than empty vanities; yet prayers and
    wishes
Are all I can return. Beseech your lordship,   70
Vouchsafe to speak my thanks and my obedience,
As from a blushing handmaid, to his highness;
Whose health and royalty I pray for.
    Cham.   Lady,
I shall not fail to approve the fair conceit
The king hath of you. [*Aside*] I have perused her
    well;
Beauty and honour in her are so mingled
That they have caught the king: and who knows yet
But from this lady may proceed a gem
To lighten all this isle? I'll to the king,
And say I spoke with you.   [*Exit Lord Chamberlain.*
    Anne.   My honour'd lord.   80
    Old L. Why, this it is; see, see!
I have been begging sixteen years in court,
Am yet a courtier beggarly, nor could
Come pat betwixt too early and too late
For any suit of pounds; and you, O fate!
A very fresh fish here—fie, fie, fie upon
This compell'd fortune!—have your mouth fill'd up
Before you open it.
    Anne.   This is strange to me.
    Old L. How tastes it? is it bitter? forty pence, no.
There was a lady once, 'tis an old story,   90
That would not be a queen, that would she not,
For all the mud in Egypt: have you heard it?
    Anne. Come, you are pleasant.
    Old L.   With your theme, I could
O'ermount the lark. The Marchioness of Pembroke!
A thousand pounds a year for pure respect!
No other obligation! By my life,
That promises moe thousands: honour's train
Is longer than his foreskirt. By this time
I know your back will bear a duchess: say,
Are you not stronger than you were?
    Anne.   Good lady,   100
Make yourself mirth with your particular fancy,
And leave me out on 't. Would I had no being,
If this salute my blood a jot: it faints me,
To think what follows.
The queen is comfortless, and we forgetful
In our long absence: pray, do not deliver
What here you 've heard to her.
    Old L.   What do you think me? [*Exeunt.*

SCENE III. 14. **quarrel**, quarreler; the abstract for the concrete
(Johnson). 21. **perk'd up**, trimmed out. 31. **Saving**, without offense
to. **mincing**, affectation, coyness. 32. **cheveril**, kid leather; used as
a type of flexibility. 36. **bow'd**, crooked. 47. **emballing**, investing
with the ball as emblem of royalty. 62. **flowing**, abundant. 75-79. **I
. . . isle.** This passage, like the one with which the play closes, is

a record of Shakespeare's retrospective pride in the glory of the Elizabethan age. 83. **courtier beggarly**, a poor courtier, and in a beggarly
posture; used quibblingly. 85. **suit of pounds**, request for money. 87.
compell'd, unsought. 92. **mud in Egypt**, the wealth of Egypt, referring
to the overflowing of the Nile as the source of Egypt's productivity.
103. **salute**, act upon.

SCENE IV. *A hall in Black-Friars.*

Trumpets, sennet, and cornets. Enter two Vergers, *with short silver wands; next them, two* Scribes, *in the habit of doctors; after them, the* Archbishop of Canterbury *alone; after him, the* Bishops of Lincoln, Ely, Rochester, *and* Saint Asaph; *next them, with some small distance, follows a* Gentleman *bearing the purse, with the great seal, and a cardinal's hat; then two* Priests, *bearing each a silver cross; then a* Gentleman-usher *bare-headed, accompanied with a* Sergeant-at-arms *bearing a silver mace; then two* Gentlemen *bearing two great silver pillars; after them, side by side, the two* Cardinals; *two* Noblemen *with the sword and mace. The* King *takes place under the cloth of state; the two* Cardinals *sit under him as judges. The* Queen *takes place some distance from the* King. *The* Bishops *place themselves on each side the court, in manner of a consistory; below them, the* Scribes. *The* Lords *sit next the* Bishops. *The rest of the* Attendants *stand in convenient order about the stage.*

Wol. Whilst our commission from Rome is read,
Let silence be commanded.
 King.   What's the need?
It hath already publicly been read,
And on all sides the authority allow'd;
You may, then, spare that time.
 Wol.   Be 't so. Proceed.
 Scribe. Say, Henry King of England, come into the court.
 Crier. Henry King of England, &c.
 King. Here.
 Scribe. Say, Katharine Queen of England, come into the court. 11
 Crier. Katharine Queen of England, &c.
   [*The Queen makes no answer, rises out of her chair, goes about the court, comes to the King, and kneels at his feet; then speaks.*
 Q. Kath. Sir, I desire you do me right and justice;
And to bestow your pity on me: for
I am a most poor woman, and a stranger,
Born out of your dominions; having here
No judge indifferent, nor no more assurance
Of equal friendship and proceeding. Alas, sir,
In what have I offended you? what cause
Hath my behaviour given to your displeasure, 20
That thus you should proceed to put me off,
And take your good grace from me? Heaven witness,
I have been to you a true and humble wife,
At all times to your will conformable;
Ever in fear to kindle your dislike,
Yea, subject to your countenance, glad or sorry
As I saw it inclined: when was the hour
I ever contradicted your desire,
Or made it not mine too? Or which of your friends
Have I not strove to love, although I knew 30
He were mine enemy? what friend of mine
That had to him derived your anger, did I
Continue in my liking? nay, gave notice
He was from thence discharged? Sir, call to mind
That I have been your wife, in this obedience,
Upward of twenty years, and have been blest

With many children by you: if, in the course
And process of this time, you can report,
And prove it too, against mine honour aught,
My bond to wedlock, or my love and duty, 40
Against your sacred person, in God's name,
Turn me away; and let the foul'st contempt
Shut door upon me, and so give me up
To the sharp'st kind of justice. Please you, sir,
The king, your father, was reputed for
A prince most prudent, of an excellent
And unmatch'd wit and judgement: Ferdinand,
My father, king of Spain, was reckon'd one
The wisest prince that there had reign'd by many
A year before: it is not to be question'd 50
That they had gather'd a wise council to them
Of every realm, that did debate this business,
Who deem'd our marriage lawful: wherefore I
  humbly
Beseech you, sir, to spare me, till I may
Be by my friends in Spain advised; whose counsel
I will implore: if not, i' the name of God,
Your pleasure be fulfill'd!
 Wol.   You have here, lady,
And of your choice, these reverend fathers; men
Of singular integrity and learning,
Yea, the elect o' the land, who are assembled 60
To plead your cause: it shall be therefore bootless
That longer you desire the court; as well
For your own quiet, as to rectify
What is unsettled in the king.
 Cam.   His grace
Hath spoken well and justly: therefore, madam,
It 's fit this royal session do proceed;
And that, without delay, their arguments
Be now produced and heard.
 Q. Kath.   Lord cardinal,
To you I speak.
 Wol.   Your pleasure, madam?
 Q. Kath.   Sir,
I am about to weep; but, thinking that 70
We are a queen, or long have dream'd so, certain
The daughter of a king, my drops of tears
I'll turn to sparks of fire.
 Wol.   Be patient yet.
 Q. Kath. I will, when you are humble; nay, before,
Or God will punish me. I do believe,
Induced by potent circumstances, that
You are mine enemy, and make my challenge
You shall not be my judge: for it is you
Have blown this coal betwixt my lord and me;
Which God's dew quench! Therefore I say again, 80
I utterly abhor, yea, from my soul
Refuse you for my judge; whom, yet once more,
I hold my most malicious foe, and think not
At all a friend to truth.
 Wol.   I do profess
You speak not like yourself; who ever yet
Have stood to charity, and display'd the effects
Of disposition gentle, and of wisdom
O'ertopping woman's power. Madam, you do me
  wrong:
I have no spleen against you; nor injustice

Scene IV. *Stage Direction:* (1) **Vergers,** those who carry the verge or emblem of office; particularly attendants on a church dignitary. (13) *cloth of state,* canopy. (17) *consistory,* college of cardinals presided over by the pope. 37. **many children.** The queen gave birth to five children, only one of whom (later Queen Mary) survived infancy. 62. **That . . . court,** that you wish the court inquiry to be prolonged. 71. **certain,** certainly. 77. **make my challenge,** i.e., I request that, etc. 96. **wound,** show up; i.e., demonstrate me a falsifier. 99. re-

For you or any: how far I have proceeded, 90
Or how far further shall, is warranted
By a commission from the consistory,
Yea, the whole consistory of Rome. You charge me
That I have blown this coal: I do deny it:
The king is present: if it be known to him
That I gainsay my deed, how may he wound,
And worthily, my falsehood! yea, as much
As you have done my truth. If he know
That I am free of your report, he knows
I am not of your wrong. Therefore in him 100
It lies to cure me: and the cure is, to
Remove these thoughts from you: the which before
His highness shall speak in, I do beseech
You, gracious madam, to unthink your speaking
And to say so no more.
 Q. Kath.   My lord, my lord,
I am a simple woman, much too weak
To oppose your cunning. You 're meek and humble-
 mouth'd;
You sign your place and calling, in full seeming,
With meekness and humility; but your heart
Is cramm'd with arrogancy, spleen, and pride. 110
You have, by fortune and his highness' favours,
Gone slightly o'er low steps and now are mounted
Where powers are your retainers, and your words,
Domestics to you, serve your will as 't please
Yourself pronounce their office. I must tell you,
You tender more your person's honour than
Your high profession spiritual: that again
I do refuse you for my judge; and here,
Before you all, appeal unto the pope,
To bring my whole cause 'fore his holiness, 120
And to be judged by him.
     [*She curtsies to the King, and offers to depart.*
 Cam.   The queen is obstinate,
Stubborn to justice, apt to accuse it, and
Disdainful to be tried by 't: 'tis not well.
She 's going away.
 King. Call her again.
 Crier. Katharine Queen of England, come into the
 court.
 Grif. Madam, you are call'd back.
 Q. Kath. What need you note it? pray you, keep
 your way:
When you are call'd, return. Now, the Lord help,
They vex me past my patience! Pray you, pass on: 130
I will not tarry; no, nor ever more
Upon this business my appearance make
In any of their courts. [*Exeunt Queen, and her Attendants.*
 King.   Go thy ways, Kate:
That man i' the world who shall report he has
A better wife, let him in nought be trusted,
For speaking false in that: thou art, alone,
If thy rare qualities, sweet gentleness,
Thy meekness saint-like, wife-like government,
Obeying in commanding, and thy parts
Sovereign and pious else, could speak thee out, 140
The queen of earthly queens: she 's noble born;
And, like her true nobility, she has
Carried herself towards me.
 Wol.   Most gracious sir,

In humblest manner I require your highness,
That it shall please you to declare, in hearing
Of all these ears,—for where I am robb'd and bound,
There must I be unloosed, although not there
At once and fully satisfied,—whether ever I
Did broach this business to your highness; or
Laid any scruple in your way, which might 150
Induce you to the question on 't? or ever
Have to you, but with thanks to God for such
A royal lady, spake one the least word that might
Be to the prejudice of her present state,
Or touch of her good person?
 King.   My lord cardinal,
I do excuse you; yea, upon mine honour,
I free you from 't. You are not to be taught
That you have many enemies, that know not
Why they are so, but, like to village-curs,
Bark when their fellows do: by some of these 160
The queen is put in anger. You 're excused:
But will you be more justified? you ever
Have wish'd the sleeping of this business; never
 desired
It to be stirr'd; but oft have hinder'd, oft,
The passages made toward it: on my honour,
I speak my good lord cardinal to this point,
And thus far clear him. Now, what moved me to 't,
I will be bold with time and your attention:
Then mark the inducement. Thus it came; give heed
 to 't:
My conscience first received a tenderness, 170
Scruple, and prick, on certain speeches utter'd
By the Bishop of Bayonne, then French ambassador;
Who had been hither sent on the debating
A marriage 'twixt the Duke of Orleans and
Our daughter Mary: i' the progress of this business,
Ere a determinate resolution, he,
I mean the bishop, did require a respite;
Wherein he might the king his lord advertise
Whether our daughter were legitimate,
Respecting this our marriage with the dowager, 180
Sometimes our brother's wife. This respite shook
The bosom of my conscience, enter'd me,
Yea, with a splitting power, and made to tremble
The region of my breast; which forced such way,
That many mazed considerings did throng
And press'd in with this caution. First, methought
I stood not in the smile of heaven; who had
Commanded nature, that my lady's womb,
If it conceived a male child by me, should
Do no more offices of life to 't than 190
The grave does to the dead; for her male issue
Or died where they were made, or shortly after
This world had air'd them: hence I took a thought,
This was a judgement on me; that my kingdom,
Well worthy the best heir o' the world, should not
Be gladded in 't by me: then follows, that
I weigh'd the danger which my realms stood in
By this my issue's fail; and that gave to me
Many a groaning throe. Thus hulling in
The wild sea of my conscience, I did steer 200
Toward this remedy, whereupon we are
Now present here together; that 's to say,

---

port, adverse report. 103. **in,** regarding. 112. **slightly,** easily. 113.
powers . . . retainers, you command the service of people of rank. 116.
tender, are concerned for. 138. **government,** behavior. 140. **speak
thee out,** declare you as you are. 166. **speak,** describe. 178. **adver-**
tise, inform, instruct. 180. **dowager.** Cf. II, ii, 52, note. 182. **bosom,**
depths. 185. **mazed considerings,** conflicting and confused thoughts.
198. **By . . . fail,** by my lacking a son. 199. **hulling,** drifting with
sails furled.

I meant to rectify my conscience,—which
I then did feel full sick, and yet not well,—
By all the reverend fathers of the land
And doctors learn'd: first I began in private
With you, my Lord of Lincoln; you remember
How under my oppression I did reek,
When I first moved you.
    Lin.   Very well, my liege.   209
    King. I have spoke long: be pleased yourself to say
How far you satisfied me.
    Lin.   So please your highness,
The question did at first so stagger me,
Bearing a state of mighty moment in 't
And consequence of dread, that I committed
The daring'st counsel which I had to doubt;
And did entreat your highness to this course
Which you are running here.
    King.   I then moved you,
My Lord of Canterbury; and got your leave
To make this present summons: unsolicited
I left no reverend person in this court;   220
But by particular consent proceeded
Under your hands and seals: therefore, go on;
For no dislike i' the world against the person
Of the good queen, but the sharp thorny points
Of my alleged reasons, drive this forward:
Prove but our marriage lawful, by my life
And kingly dignity, we are contented
To wear our mortal state to come with her,
Katharine our queen, before the primest creature
That 's paragon'd o' the world.
    Cam.   So please your highness,   230
The queen being absent, 'tis a needful fitness
That we adjourn this court till further day:
Meanwhile must be an earnest motion
Made to the queen, to call back her appeal
She intends unto his holiness.
    King.   *[Aside]* I may perceive
These cardinals trifle with me: I abhor
This dilatory sloth and tricks of Rome.
My learn'd and well-beloved servant, Cranmer,
Prithee, return: with thy approach, I know,
My comfort comes along. Break up the court: 240
I say, set on.   *[Exeunt in manner as they entered.*

ACT III.

SCENE I. *London. The* QUEEN's *apartments.*

The QUEEN *and her Women, as at work.*

    Q. Kath. Take thy lute, wench: my soul grows sad
    with troubles;
Sing, and disperse 'em, if thou canst: leave working.

SONG.
    Orpheus with his lute made trees,
    And the mountain tops that freeze,

        Bow themselves when he did sing:
    To his music plants and flowers
    Ever sprung; as sun and showers
        There had made a lasting spring.

    Every thing that heard him play,
    Even the billows of the sea,   10
        Hung their heads, and then lay by.
    In sweet music is such art,
    Killing care and grief of heart
        Fall asleep, or hearing, die.

Enter a Gentleman.
    Q. Kath. How now!
    Gent. An 't please your grace, the two great
    cardinals
Wait in the presence.
    Q. Kath.   Would they speak with me?
    Gent. They will'd me say so, madam.
    Q. Kath.   Pray their graces
To come near. *[Exit Gent.]* What can be their business
With me, a poor weak woman, fall'n from favour?   20
I do not like their coming. Now I think on 't,
They should be good men; their affairs as righteous:
But all hoods make not monks.

Enter the two Cardinals, WOLSEY *and* CAMPEIUS.
    Wol.   Peace to your highness!
    Q. Kath. Your graces find me here part of a
    housewife.
I would be all, against the worst may happen.
What are your pleasures with me, reverend lords?
    Wol. May it please you, noble madam, to withdraw
Into your private chamber, we shall give you
The full cause of our coming.
    Q. Kath.   Speak it here;
There 's nothing I have done yet, o' my conscience,   30
Deserves a corner: would all other women
Could speak this with as free a soul as I do!
My lords, I care not, so much I am happy
Above a number, if my actions
Were tried by every tongue, every eye saw 'em,
Envy and base opinion set against 'em,
I know my life so even. If your business
Seek me out, and that way I am wife in,
Out with it boldly: truth loves open dealing.
    Wol. Tanta est erga te mentis integritas, regina
serenissima,—   41
    Q. Kath. O, good my lord, no Latin;
I am not such a truant since my coming,
As not to know the language I have lived in:
A strange tongue makes my cause more strange,
    suspicious;
Pray, speak in English: here are some will thank you,
If you speak truth, for their poor mistress' sake;
Believe me, she has had much wrong: lord cardinal,
The willing'st sin I ever yet committed
May be absolved in English.

*King Henry
the Eighth*
ACT II : SC IV

I288

---

208. **reek,** sweat. 214-215. **I . . . doubt,** with misgivings I gave counsel which I should normally have given confidently. 229. **primest,** most excellent. 230. **paragon'd,** set forth as a perfect model. 238. **Cranmer.** Thomas Cranmer, a University fellow, first attracted the king's notice with the advice that the marriage question should be resolved by the universities, not the pope. He became a useful and pliant churchman in fulfilling the king's wishes and was made archbishop of Canterbury at the death of Warham.
    ACT III. SCENE I. 3. **Orpheus with his lute,** alludes to the myth of Orpheus, who played on his lyre so beautifully that wild beasts, rocks, and trees listened to him. 11. **lay by,** subsided. 17. **presence,** pres-

ence chamber. 18-22. **Pray . . . righteous.** Pooler finds that Katharine's character changes from the strong, independent woman of II, iv, to one "full of words and weak impulses." He ascribes the change to Fletcher's authorship rather than to the effects on her of her fall from favor. But is she so weak and pliant? There is some clever equivocation in her speeches with the cardinals. Her attitude at the close of the scene (ll. 175-184) is one of resignation to the inevitable; her speech is less an apology than a plea. 22. **their affairs,** the business they come on. 23. **hoods . . . monks,** an old proverb, usually in Latin; cf. *Measure for Measure*, V, i, 263. 24-25. **part of . . . all.** *Part of a housewife* refers to her being engaged in embroidery; *I would be all,*

Wol.   Noble lady,   50
I am sorry my integrity should breed,
And service to his majesty and you,
So deep suspicion, where all faith was meant.
We come not by the way of accusation,
To taint that honour every good tongue blesses,
Nor to betray you any way to sorrow,
You have too much, good lady; but to know
How you stand minded in the weighty difference
Between the king and you; and to deliver,
Like free and honest men, our just opinions   60
And comforts to your cause.
Cam.   Most honour'd madam,
My Lord of York, out of his noble nature,
Zeal and obedience he still bore your grace,
Forgetting, like a good man, your late censure
Both of his truth and him, which was too far,
Offers, as I do, in a sign of peace,
His service and his counsel.
Q. Kath.   [*Aside*] To betray me.—
My lords, I thank you both for your good wills;
Ye speak like honest men; pray God, ye prove so!
But how to make ye suddenly an answer,   70
In such a point of weight, so near mine honour,—
More near my life, I fear,—with my weak wit,
And to such men of gravity and learning,
In truth, I know not. I was set at work
Among my maids: full little, God knows, looking
Either for such men or such business.
For her sake that I have been,—for I feel
The last fit of my greatness,—good your graces,
Let me have time and counsel for my cause:
Alas, I am a woman, friendless, hopeless!   80
Wol. Madam, you wrong the king's love with these
     fears:
Your hopes and friends are infinite.
Q. Kath.   In England
But little for my profit: can you think, lords,
That any Englishman dare give me counsel?
Or be a known friend, 'gainst his highness' pleasure,
Though he be grown so desperate to be honest,
And live a subject? Nay, forsooth, my friends,
They that must weigh out my afflictions,
They that my trust must grow to, live not here:
They are, as all my other comforts, far hence   90
In mine own country, lords.
Cam.   I would your grace
Would leave your griefs, and take my counsel.
Q. Kath.   How, sir?
Cam. Put your main cause into the king's
     protection;
He's loving and most gracious: 'twill be much
Both for your honour better and your cause;
For if the trial of the law o'ertake ye,
You'll part away disgraced.
Wol.   He tells you rightly.
Q. Kath. Ye tell me what ye wish for both,—my
     ruin:

Is this your Christian counsel? out upon ye!
Heaven is above all yet; there sits a judge   100
That no king can corrupt.
Cam.   Your rage mistakes us.
Q. Kath. The more shame for ye: holy men I
     thought ye,
Upon my soul, two reverend cardinal virtues;
But cardinal sins and hollow hearts I fear ye:
Mend 'em, for shame, my lords. Is this your comfort?
The cordial that ye bring a wretched lady,
A woman lost among ye, laugh'd at, scorn'd?
I will not wish ye half my miseries;
I have more charity: but say, I warn'd ye;
Take heed, for heaven's sake, take heed, lest at once 110
The burthen of my sorrows fall upon ye.
Wol. Madam, this is a mere distraction;
You turn the good we offer into envy.
Q. Kath. Ye turn me into nothing: woe upon ye
And all such false professors! would you have me—
If you have any justice, any pity;
If ye be any thing but churchmen's habits—
Put my sick cause into his hands that hates me?
Alas, has banish'd me his bed already,
His love, too long ago! I am old, my lords,   120
And all the fellowship I hold now with him
Is only my obedience. What can happen
To me above this wretchedness? all your studies
Make me a curse like this.
Cam.   Your fears are worse.
Q. Kath. Have I lived thus long—let me speak
     myself,
Since virtue finds no friends—a wife, a true one?
A woman, I dare say without vain-glory,
Never yet branded with suspicion?
Have I with all my full affections
Still met the king? loved him next heaven? obey'd
     him?   130
Been, out of fondness, superstitious to him?
Almost forgot my prayers to content him?
And am I thus rewarded? 'tis not well, lords.
Bring me a constant woman to her husband,
One that ne'er dream'd a joy beyond his pleasure;
And to that woman, when she has done most,
Yet will I add an honour, a great patience.
Wol. Madam, you wander from the good we aim at.
Q. Kath. My lord, I dare not make myself so guilty,
To give up willingly that noble title   140
Your master wed me to: nothing but death
Shall e'er divorce my dignities.
Wol.   Pray, hear me.
Q. Kath. Would I had never trod this English earth,
Or felt the flatteries that grow upon it!
Ye have angels' faces, but heaven knows your hearts.
What will become of me now, wretched lady!
I am the most unhappy woman living.
Alas, poor wenches, where are now your fortunes!
Shipwreck'd upon a kingdom, where no pity,
No friends, no hope; no kindred weep for me;   150

i.e., a complete housewife, in case I am divorced and obliged to earn my own living—a jesting exaggeration of the dangers before her (Pooler). 38. **Seek me out**, concerns me. **that . . . in**, my conduct as a wife. 40-41. **Tanta est erga**, etc. There is toward you such whole-heartedness, most serene queen. Holinshed relates that the cardinals spoke to her in Latin and were requested to speak English, but there is no Latin dialogue in the Chronicle. It is the dramatist's invention. 52. **And . . . you.** Edwards conjectured that this and the line following should be interchanged; *faith* and *service* would then be parallel. The parallelism is more likely in *integrity* and *service.* 78. **fit**, brief space, short spell; Pooler suggests a possible play on the meaning "canto," part of a poem. 88. **weigh out**, compensate for. 103. **two . . . virtues,** i.e., the embodiment of all good, playing on the Aristotelian virtues, called the cardinal virtues—justice, temperance, fortitude, and prudence—sometimes catalogued as twelve. 104. **cardinal sins,** i.e., the seven deadly sins. 110. **at once,** presently. 117. **If . . . habits,** alludes to the proverb quoted in line 23 above. 123-124. **all . . . curse,** i.e., No more advice! All your studies amount to a curse to me. 125. **speak,** describe. 131. **superstitious to him,** devoted to him to the point of idolatry.

Almost no grave allow'd me: like the lily,
That once was mistress of the field and flourish'd,
I'll hang my head and perish.
  Wol.   If your grace
Could but be brought to know our ends are honest,
You 'ld feel more comfort: why should we, good lady,
Upon what cause, wrong you? alas, our places,
The way of our profession is against it:
We are to cure such sorrows, not to sow 'em.
For goodness' sake, consider what you do;
How you may hurt yourself, ay, utterly   160
Grow from the king's acquaintance, by this carriage.
The hearts of princes kiss obedience,
So much they love it; but to stubborn spirits
They swell, and grow as terrible as storms.
I know you have a gentle, noble temper,
A soul as even as a calm: pray, think us
Those we profess, peace-makers, friends, and servants.
  Cam. Madam, you'll find it so. You wrong your
    virtues
With these weak women's fears: a noble spirit,
As yours was put into you, ever casts   170
Such doubts, as false coin, from it. The king loves you;
Beware you lose it not: for us, if you please
To trust us in your business, we are ready
To use our utmost studies in your service.
  Q. Kath. Do what ye will, my lords: and, pray,
    forgive me,
If I have used myself unmannerly;
You know I am a woman, lacking wit
To make a seemly answer to such persons.
Pray, do my service to his majesty:
He has my heart yet; and shall have my prayers 180
While I shall have my life. Come, reverend fathers,
Bestow your counsels on me: she now begs,
That little thought, when she set footing here,
She should have bought her dignities so dear. [*Exeunt.*

   SCENE II. *Ante-chamber to the* KING'S *apartment.*

 Enter the DUKE OF NORFOLK, *the* DUKE OF SUFFOLK,
  the EARL OF SURREY, *and the* LORD CHAMBERLAIN.

  Nor. If you will now unite in your complaints,
And force them with a constancy, the cardinal
Cannot stand under them: if you omit
The offer of this time, I cannot promise
But that you shall sustain moe new disgraces,
With these you bear already.
  Sur.   I am joyful
To meet the least occasion that may give me
Remembrance of my father-in-law, the duke,
To be revenged on him.
  Suf.   Which of the peers
Have uncontemn'd gone by him, or at least   10
Strangely neglected? when did he regard
The stamp of nobleness in any person
Out of himself?
  Cham.   My lords, you speak your
    pleasures:
What he deserves of you and me I know;
What we can do to him, though now the time

Gives way to us, I much fear. If you cannot
Bar his access to the king, never attempt
Any thing on him; for he hath a witchcraft
Over the king in 's tongue.
  Nor.   O, fear him not;
His spell in that is out: the king hath found   20
Matter against him that for ever mars
The honey of his language. No, he 's settled,
Not to come off, in his displeasure.
  Sur.   Sir,
I should be glad to hear such news as this
Once every hour.
  Nor.   Believe it, this is true:
In the divorce his contrary proceedings
Are all unfolded; wherein he appears
As I would wish mine enemy.
  Sur.   How came
His practices to light?
  Suf.   Most strangely.
  Sur.   O, how, how?
  Suf. The cardinal's letters to the pope miscarried, 30
And came to the eye o' the king: wherein was read,
How that the cardinal did entreat his holiness
To stay the judgement o' the divorce; for if
It did take place, 'I do,' quoth he, 'perceive
My king is tangled in affection to
A creature of the queen's, Lady Anne Bullen.'
  Sur. Has the king this?
  Suf.   Believe it.
  Sur.   Will this work?
  Cham. The king in this perceives him, how he coasts
And hedges his own way. But in this point
All his tricks founder, and he brings his physic   40
After his patient's death: the king already
Hath married the fair lady.
  Sur.   Would he had!
  Suf. May you be happy in your wish, my lord!
For, I profess, you have it.
  Sur.   Now, all my joy
Trace the conjunction!
  Suf.   My amen to 't!
  Nor.   All men's!
  Suf. There 's order given for her coronation:
Marry, this is yet but young, and may be left
To some ears unrecounted. But, my lords,
She is a gallant creature, and complete
In mind and feature: I persuade me, from her   50
Will fall some blessing to this land, which shall
In it be memorized.
  Sur.   But, will the king
Digest this letter of the cardinal's?
The Lord forbid!
  Nor.   Marry, amen!
  Suf.   No, no;
There be moe wasps that buzz about his nose
Will make this sting the sooner. Cardinal Campeius
Is stol'n away to Rome; hath ta'en no leave;
Has left the cause o' the king unhandled; and
Is posted, as the agent of our cardinal,
To second all his plot. I do assure you   60
The king cried Ha! at this.
  Cham.   Now, God incense him,

---

161. **carriage,** conduct.
 SCENE II. 3-4. **if . . . time,** if you let this opportunity pass. 8.
my father-in-law. Cf. II, i, 41-44, note. 13. **Out of,** excepting. 23.
come off, escape. **his,** the king's. 26. **his contrary proceedings,** pri-

vate practices opposed to public procedure (Johnson). 38. **coasts,** goes
a roundabout way. 45. **Trace,** follow. 50-52. **I . . . memorized.** Cf.
II, iii, 75-79, note. 52. **memorized,** caused to be remembered; cf.
Macbeth, I, ii, 40. 64. **in his opinions,** with unchanged opinions (Stee-

And let him cry Ha! louder!
  Nor.   But, my lord,
When returns Cranmer?
  Suf. He is return'd in his opinions; which
Have satisfied the king for his divorce,
Together with all famous colleges
Almost in Christendom: shortly, I believe,
His second marriage shall be publish'd, and
Her coronation. Katharine no more
Shall be call'd queen, but princess dowager   70
And widow to Prince Arthur.
  Nor.   This same Cranmer's
A worthy fellow, and hath ta'en much pain
In the king's business.
  Suf.   He has; and we shall see him
For it an archbishop.
  Nor.   So I hear.
  Suf.   'Tis so.
The cardinal!

Enter WOLSEY *and* CROMWELL.

  Nor.   Observe, observe, he's moody.
  Wol. The packet, Cromwell,
Gave 't you the king?
  Crom.   To his own hand, in's
    bedchamber.
  Wol. Look'd he o' the inside of the paper?
  Crom.   Presently
He did unseal them: and the first he view'd,
He did it with a serious mind; a heed   80
Was in his countenance. You he bade
Attend him here this morning.
  Wol.   Is he ready
To come abroad?
  Crom.   I think, by this he is.
  Wol. Leave me awhile.   [*Exit Cromwell.*
[*Aside*] It shall be to the Duchess of Alençon,
The French king's sister: he shall marry her.
Anne Bullen! No; I'll no Anne Bullens for him:
There's more in 't than fair visage. Bullen!
No, we'll no Bullens. Speedily I wish   89
To hear from Rome. The Marchioness of Pembroke!
  Nor. He's discontented.
  Suf.   May be, he hears the king
Does whet his anger to him.
  Sur.   Sharp enough,
Lord, for thy justice!
  Wol. [*Aside*] The late queen's gentlewoman, a
    knight's daughter,
To be her mistress' mistress! the queen's queen!
This candle burns not clear: 'tis I must snuff it;
Then out it goes. What though I know her virtuous
And well deserving? yet I know her for
A spleeny Lutheran; and not wholesome to
Our cause, that she should lie i' the bosom of 100
Our hard-ruled king. Again, there is sprung up
An heretic, an arch one, Cranmer; one
Hath crawl'd into the favour of the king,
And is his oracle.
  Nor.   He is vex'd at something.
  Sur. I would 'twere something that would fret the
    string,

The master-cord on 's heart!

Enter the KING, *reading of a schedule, and* LOVELL.

  Suf.   The king, the king!
  King. What piles of wealth hath he accumulated
To his own portion! and what expense by the hour
Seems to flow from him! How, i' the name of thrift,
Does he rake this together! Now, my lords,   110
Saw you the cardinal?
  Nor.   My lord, we have
Stood here observing him: some strange commotion
Is in his brain: he bites his lip, and starts;
Stops on a sudden, looks upon the ground,
Then lays his finger on his temple; straight
Springs out into fast gait; then stops again,
Strikes his breast hard, and anon he casts
His eye against the moon: in most strange postures
We have seen him set himself.
  King.   It may well be;
There is a mutiny in 's mind. This morning   120
Papers of state he sent me to peruse,
As I required: and wot you what I found
There,—on my conscience, put unwittingly?
Forsooth, an inventory, thus importing;
The several parcels of his plate, his treasure,
Rich stuffs, and ornaments of household; which
I find at such proud rate, that it out-speaks
Possession of a subject.
  Nor.   It's heaven's will:
Some spirit put this paper in the packet,
To bless your eye withal.
  King.   If we did think   130
His contemplation were above the earth,
And fix'd on spiritual object, he should still
Dwell in his musings: but I am afraid
His thinkings are below the moon, not worth
His serious considering.
        [*King takes his seat; whispers Lovell, who goes to the*
                                  Cardinal.
  Wol.   Heaven forgive me!
Ever God bless your highness!
  King.   Good my lord,
You are full of heavenly stuff, and bear the inventory
Of your best graces in your mind; the which
You were now running o'er: you have scarce time
To steal from spiritual leisure a brief span   140
To keep your earthly audit: sure, in that
I deem you an ill husband, and am glad
To have you therein my companion.
  Wol.   Sir,
For holy offices I have a time; a time
To think upon the part of business which
I bear i' the state; and nature does require
Her times of preservation, which perforce
I, her frail son, amongst my brethren mortal,
Must give my tendance to.
  King.   You have said well.
  Wol. And ever may your highness yoke together, 150
As I will lend you cause, my doing well
With my well saying!
  King.   'Tis well said again;
And 'tis a kind of good deed to say well:

---

vens). **66. colleges,** i.e., the opinions of the colleges. **99. A spleeny Lutheran,** probably a statement of the Elizabethan opinion, made current by Foxe, that Anne was a staunch Protestant. **106. on 's,** of his. **125. parcels,** items. **127-128. out-speaks . . . subject,** describes posses-sions exceeding what a subject should have. **142. ill husband,** unthrifty person. **148. amongst my brethren mortal,** i.e., in my human capacity, as contrasted with my divinity.

And yet words are no deeds. My father loved you:
He said he did; and with his deed did crown
His word upon you. Since I had my office,
I have kept you next my heart; have not alone
Employ'd you where high profits might come home,
But pared my present havings, to bestow
My bounties upon you.
    Wol.   [*Aside*] What should this mean?
    Sur. [*Aside*] The Lord increase this business!
    King.   Have I not made you   161
The prime man of the state? I pray you, tell me,
If what I now pronounce you have found true:
And, if you may confess it, say withal,
If you are bound to us or no. What say you?
    Wol. My sovereign, I confess your royal graces,
Shower'd on me daily, have been more than could
My studied purposes requite; which went
Beyond all man's endeavours: my endeavours
Have ever come too short of my desires,   170
Yet filed with my abilities: mine own ends
Have been mine so that evermore they pointed
To the good of your most sacred person and
The profit of the state. For your great graces
Heap'd upon me, poor undeserver, I
Can nothing render but allegiant thanks,
My prayers to heaven for you, my loyalty,
Which ever has and ever shall be growing,
Till death, that winter, kill it.
    King.   Fairly answer'd;
A loyal and obedient subject is   180
Therein illustrated: the honour of it
Does pay the act of it; as, i' the contrary,
The foulness is the punishment. I presume
That, as my hand has open'd bounty to you,
My heart dropp'd love, my power rain'd honour,
    more
On you than any; so your hand and heart,
Your brain, and every function of your power,
Should, notwithstanding that your bond of duty,
As 'twere in love's particular, be more
To me, your friend, than any.
    Wol.   I do profess   190
That for your highness' good I ever labour'd
More than mine own; †that am, have, and will be—
Though all the world should crack their duty to you,
And throw it from their soul; though perils did
Abound, as thick as thought could make 'em, and
Appear in forms more horrid,—yet my duty,
As doth a rock against the chiding flood,
Should the approach of this wild river break,
And stand unshaken yours.
    King.   'Tis nobly spoken:
Take notice, lords, he has a loyal breast,   200
For you have seen him open 't. Read o'er this;
                    [*Giving him papers.*
And after, this: and then to breakfast with
What appetite you have.
    [*Exit King, frowning upon Cardinal Wolsey: the Nobles*
        throng after him, smiling and whispering.
    Wol.   What should this mean?
What sudden anger 's this? how have I reap'd it?

He parted frowning from me, as if ruin
Leap'd from his eyes: so looks the chafed lion
Upon the daring huntsman that has gall'd him;
Then makes him nothing. I must read this paper;
I fear, the story of his anger. 'Tis so;
This paper has undone me: 'tis the account   210
Of all that world of wealth I have drawn together
For mine own ends; indeed, to gain the popedom,
And fee my friends in Rome. O negligence!
Fit for a fool to fall by: what cross devil
Made me put this main secret in the packet
I sent the king? Is there no way to cure this?
No new device to beat this from his brains?
I know 'twill stir him strongly; yet I know
A way, if it take right, in spite of fortune   219
Will bring me off again. What 's this? 'To the Pope!'
The letter, as I live, with all the business
I writ to 's holiness. Nay then, farewell!
I have touch'd the highest point of all my greatness;
And, from that full meridian of my glory,
I haste now to my setting: I shall fall
Like a bright exhalation in the evening,
And no man see me more.

    Re-enter to WOLSEY, *the* DUKES OF NORFOLK *and*
      SUFFOLK, *the* EARL OF SURREY, *and the* LORD
                CHAMBERLAIN.

    Nor. Hear the king 's pleasure, cardinal: who
      commands you
To render up the great seal presently
Into our hands; and to confine yourself   230
To Asher House, my Lord of Winchester's,
Till you hear further from his highness.
    Wol.   Stay:
Where 's your commission, lords? words cannot carry
Authority so weighty.
    Suf.   Who dare cross 'em,
Bearing the king's will from his mouth expressly?
    Wol. Till I find more than will or words to do it,
I mean your malice, know, officious lords,
I dare and must deny it. Now I feel
Of what coarse metal ye are moulded, envy:
How eagerly ye follow my disgraces,   240
As if it fed ye! and how sleek and wanton
Ye appear in every thing may bring my ruin!
Follow your envious courses, men of malice;
You have Christian warrant for 'em, and, no doubt,
In time will find their fit rewards. That seal,
You ask with such a violence, the king,
Mine and your master, with his own hand gave me;
Bade me enjoy it, with the place and honours,
During my life; and, to confirm his goodness,
Tied it by letters-patents: now, who'll take it?   250
    Sur. The king, that gave it.
    Wol.   It must be himself, then.
    Sur. Thou art a proud traitor, priest.
    Wol.   Proud lord, thou liest:
Within these forty hours Surrey durst better
Have burnt that tongue than said so.
    Sur.   Thy ambition,
Thou scarlet sin, robb'd this bewailing land

159. **pared . . . havings,** reduced my own wealth. 167-168. **more . . .
requite,** more than I could devise means to repay. 171. **filed,** kept
pace with. 181. **illustrated,** made evident. 181-182. **the . . . it,**
analogous to "Virtue is its own reward." 188-189. **notwithstanding
. . . particular,** over and above your duty as a subject, as in the case of
friends. 192. **that am, have, and will be,** auxiliary verbs and completed by *unshaken* (l. 199). 215. **main,** weighty. 226. **exhalation,**
any astronomical phenomenon, such as a meteor or a falling star. **in
the evening.** This may imply "while it is still light"; hence the exhalation goes down unobserved, in an unspectacular way. 255. **Thou
scarlet sin,** refers to his cardinal's cassock, described as scarlet; cf. III,
i, 103-104. 274. **mate,** rival, vie with. 282. **dare . . . larks,** dazzle us

Of noble Buckingham, my father-in-law:
The heads of all thy brother cardinals,
With thee and all thy best parts bound together,
Weigh'd not a hair of his. Plague of your policy!
You sent me deputy for Ireland;   260
Far from his succour, from the king, from all
That might have mercy on the fault thou gavest him;
Whilst your great goodness, out of holy pity,
Absolved him with an axe.
    Wol.   This, and all else
This talking lord can lay upon my credit,
I answer is most false. The duke by law
Found his deserts: how innocent I was
From any private malice in his end,
His noble jury and foul cause can witness.
If I loved many words, lord, I should tell you   270
You have as little honesty as honour,
That in the way of loyalty and truth
Toward the king, my ever royal master,
Dare mate a sounder man than Surrey can be,
And all that love his follies.
    Sur.   By my soul,
Your long coat, priest, protects you; thou shouldst
        feel
My sword i' the life-blood of thee else. My lords,
Can ye endure to hear this arrogance?
And from this fellow? If we live thus tamely,
To be thus jaded by a piece of scarlet,   280
Farewell nobility; let his grace go forward,
And dare us with his cap like larks.
    Wol.   All goodness
Is poison to thy stomach.
    Sur.   Yes, that goodness
Of gleaning all the land's wealth into one,
Into your own hands, cardinal, by extortion;
The goodness of your intercepted packets
You writ to the pope against the king: your goodness,
Since you provoke me, shall be most notorious.
My Lord of Norfolk, as you are truly noble,
As you respect the common good, the state   290
Of our despised nobility, our issues,
Who, if he live, will scarce be gentlemen,
Produce the grand sum of his sins, the articles
Collected from his life. I'll startle you
Worse than the sacring bell, when the brown wench
Lay kissing in your arms, lord cardinal.
    Wol. How much, methinks, I could despise this
        man,
But that I am bound in charity against it!
    Nor. Those articles, my lord, are in the king's hand:
But, thus much, they are foul ones.
    Wol.   So much fairer   300
And spotless shall mine innocence arise,
When the king knows my truth.
    Sur.   This cannot save you:
I thank my memory, I yet remember
Some of these articles; and out they shall.
Now, if you can blush and cry 'guilty,' cardinal,
You'll show a little honesty.
    Wol.   Speak on, sir;
I dare your worst objections: if I blush,

It is to see a nobleman want manners.
    Sur. I had rather want those than my head. Have at
        you!
First, that, without the king's assent or knowledge, 310
You wrought to be a legate; by which power
You maim'd the jurisdiction of all bishops.
    Nor. Then, that in all you writ to Rome, or else
To foreign princes, 'Ego et Rex meus'
Was still inscribed; in which you brought the king
To be your servant.
    Suf.   Then that, without the
        knowledge
Either of king or council, when you went
Ambassador to the emperor, you made bold
To carry into Flanders the great seal.
    Sur. Item, you sent a large commission   320
To Gregory de Cassado, to conclude,
Without the king's will or the state's allowance,
A league between his highness and Ferrara.
    Suf. That, out of mere ambition, you have caused
Your holy hat to be stamp'd on the king's coin.
    Sur. Then that you have sent innumerable
        substance—
By what means got, I leave to your own conscience—
To furnish Rome, and to prepare the ways
You have for dignities; to the mere undoing
Of all the kingdom. Many more there are;   330
Which, since they are of you, and odious,
I will not taint my mouth with.
    Cham.   O my lord,
Press not a falling man too far! 'tis virtue:
His faults lie open to the laws; let them,
Not you, correct him. My heart weeps to see him
So little of his great self.
    Sur.   I forgive him.
    Suf. Lord cardinal, the king's further pleasure is,
Because all those things you have done of late,
By your power legatine, within this kingdom,
Fall into the compass of a præmunire,   340
That therefore such a writ be sued against you;
To forfeit all your goods, lands, tenements,
Chattels, and whatsoever, and to be
Out of the king's protection. This is my charge.
    Nor. And so we'll leave you to your meditations
How to live better. For your stubborn answer
About the giving back the great seal to us,
The king shall know it, and, no doubt, shall thank
        you.
So fare you well, my little good lord cardinal.
                    [*Exeunt all but Wolsey.*
    Wol. So farewell to the little good you bear me. 350
Farewell! a long farewell, to all my greatness!
This is the state of man: to-day he puts forth
The tender leaves of hopes; to-morrow blossoms,
And bears his blushing honours thick upon him;
The third day comes a frost, a killing frost,
And, when he thinks, good easy man, full surely
His greatness is a-ripening, nips his root,
And then he falls, as I do. I have ventured,
Like little wanton boys that swim on bladders,
This many summers in a sea of glory,   360

with his cardinal's hat as birds with a mirror or a piece of scarlet cloth.
295. **sacring bell,** bell rung at the most solemn portions of the mass.
311-332. **You wrought,** etc. This and the following items are transcribed
from Holinshed.   314. **'Ego et Rex meus,'** I and my king. Pooler
remarks that in Latin the first person always came before any nouns
parallel with it and that Wolsey's offense consisted in mentioning

himself at all.   328. **To furnish Rome,** implying that Wolsey made gifts
to Rome as bribes to obtain his own advancement.   340. **præmunire,**
a form of writ for prosecuting certain offenses punishable by forfeiture
and imprisonment; also, the offense or penalty.   341. **sued,** moved.

But far beyond my depth: my high-blown pride
At length broke under me and now has left me,
Weary and old with service, to the mercy
Of a rude stream, that must for ever hide me.
Vain pomp and glory of this world, I hate ye:
I feel my heart new open'd. O, how wretched
Is that poor man that hangs on princes' favours!
There is, betwixt that smile we would aspire to,
That sweet aspect of princes, and their ruin,
More pangs and fears than wars or women have: 370
And when he falls, he falls like Lucifer,
Never to hope again.

   Enter CROMWELL, *and stands amazed.*
      Why, how now, Cromwell!
 Crom. I have no power to speak, sir.
 Wol.   What, amazed
At my misfortunes? can thy spirit wonder
A great man should decline? Nay, an you weep,
I am fall'n indeed.
 Crom.   How does your grace?
 Wol.   Why, well;
Never so truly happy, my good Cromwell.
I know myself now; and I feel within me
A peace above all earthly dignities,
A still and quiet conscience. The king has cured me, 380
I humbly thank his grace; and from these shoulders,
These ruin'd pillars, out of pity, taken
A load would sink a navy, too much honour:
O, 'tis a burden, Cromwell, 'tis a burden
Too heavy for a man that hopes for heaven!
 Crom. I am glad your grace has made that right
  use of it.
 Wol. I hope I have: I am able now, methinks,
Out of a fortitude of soul I feel,
To endure more miseries and greater far
Than my weak-hearted enemies dare offer.   390
What news abroad?
 Crom.   The heaviest and the worst
Is your displeasure with the king.
 Wol.   God bless him!
 Crom. The next is, that Sir Thomas More is chosen
Lord chancellor in your place.
 Wol.   That 's somewhat sudden:
But he 's a learned man. May he continue
Long in his highness' favour, and do justice
For truth's sake and his conscience; that his bones,
When he has run his course and sleeps in blessings,
May have a tomb of orphans' tears wept on 'em!
What more?
 Crom.   That Cranmer is return'd with
  welcome,   400
Install'd lord archbishop of Canterbury.
 Wol. That 's news indeed.
 Crom.   Last, that the Lady Anne,
Whom the king hath in secrecy long married,
This day was view'd in open as his queen,
Going to chapel; and the voice is now
Only about her coronation.
 Wol. There was the weight that pull'd me down. O
  Cromwell,
The king has gone beyond me: all my glories
In that one woman I have lost for ever:

No sun shall ever usher forth mine honours,   410
Or gild again the noble troops that waited
Upon my smiles. Go, get thee from me, Cromwell;
I am a poor fall'n man, unworthy now
To be thy lord and master: seek the king;
That sun, I pray, may never set! I have told him
What and how true thou art: he will advance thee;
Some little memory of me will stir him—
I know his noble nature—not to let
Thy hopeful service perish too: good Cromwell,
Neglect him not; make use now, and provide   420
For thine own future safety.
 Crom.   O my lord,
Must I, then, leave you? must I needs forgo
So good, so noble and so true a master?
Bear witness, all that have not hearts of iron,
With what a sorrow Cromwell leaves his lord.
The king shall have my service; but my prayers
For ever and for ever shall be yours.
 Wol. Cromwell, I did not think to shed a tear
In all my miseries; but thou hast forced me,
Out of thy honest truth, to play the woman.   430
Let 's dry our eyes: and thus far hear me, Cromwell;
And, when I am forgotten, as I shall be,
And sleep in dull cold marble, where no mention
Of me more must be heard of, say, I taught thee,
Say, Wolsey, that once trod the ways of glory,
And sounded all the depths and shoals of honour,
Found thee a way, out of his wreck, to rise in;
A sure and safe one, though thy master miss'd it.
Mark but my fall, and that that ruin'd me.
Cromwell, I charge thee, fling away ambition: 440
By that sin fell the angels; how can man, then,
The image of his Maker, hope to win by it?
Love thyself last: cherish those hearts that hate thee;
Corruption wins not more than honesty.
Still in thy right hand carry gentle peace,
To silence envious tongues. Be just, and fear not:
Let all the ends thou aim'st at be thy country's,
Thy God's, and truth's; then if thou fall'st, O
  Cromwell,
Thou fall'st a blessed martyr! Serve the king;
And,—prithee, lead me in: 450
There take an inventory of all I have,
To the last penny; 'tis the king's: my robe,
And my integrity to heaven, is all
I dare now call mine own. O Cromwell, Cromwell!
Had I but served my God with half the zeal
I served my king, he would not in mine age
Have left me naked to mine enemies.
 Crom. Good sir, have patience.
 Wol.   So I have. Farewell
The hopes of court! my hopes in heaven do dwell.
            [*Exeunt.*

ACT IV.

SCENE I. *A street in Westminster.*

Enter two Gentlemen, *meeting one another.*

First Gent. You 're well met once again.
Sec. Gent.   So are you.

395-399. **May . . . 'em.** The lines reflect the sixteenth-century sentiment
about More as a competent and fearless statesman. 452. **my robe,**
i.e., his churchman's habit; there may be a subtle glance here at the
proverb recited III, i, 23.

ACT IV. SCENE I. 8. **royal,** noble. 9. **let . . . rights,** to give them
due credit (Pooler). **forward,** i.e., eager to do. 12. **better taken,**
more enjoyed. 16. **By custom,** i.e., of having certain offices in the
coronation performed by members of families, as a hereditary right.

First Gent. You come to take your stand here, and
behold
The Lady Anne pass from her coronation?
Sec. Gent. 'Tis all my business. At our last encounter,
The Duke of Buckingham came from his trial.
First Gent. 'Tis very true: but that time offer'd
sorrow;
This, general joy.
Sec. Gent.   'Tis well: the citizens,
I am sure, have shown at full their royal minds—
As, let 'em have their rights, they are ever forward—
In celebration of this day with shows,   10
Pageants and sights of honour.
First Gent.   Never greater,
Nor, I'll assure you, better taken, sir.
Sec. Gent. May I be bold to ask what that contains,
That paper in your hand?
First Gent.   Yes; 'tis the list
Of those that claim their offices this day
By custom of the coronation.
The Duke of Suffolk is the first, and claims
To be high-steward; next, the Duke of Norfolk,
He to be earl marshal: you may read the rest.
Sec. Gent. I thank you, sir: had I not known those
customs,   20
I should have been beholding to your paper.
But, I beseech you, what 's become of Katharine,
The princess dowager? how goes her business?
First Gent. That I can tell you too. The Archbishop
Of Canterbury, accompanied with other
Learned and reverend fathers of his order,
Held a late court at Dunstable, six miles off
From Ampthill where the princess lay; to which
She was often cited by them, but appear'd not:
And, to be short, for not appearance and   30
The king's late scruple, by the main assent
Of all these learned men she was divorced,
And the late marriage made of none effect:
Since which she was removed to Kimbolton,
Where she remains now sick.
Sec. Gent.   Alas, good lady! [*Trumpets.*
The trumpets sound: stand close, the queen is coming.
                          [*Hautboys.*

THE ORDER OF THE CORONATION.

1. *A lively flourish of Trumpets.*
2. Then, two Judges.
3. Lord Chancellor, *with the purse and mace before him.*
4. Choristers, *singing.*   [*Music.*
5. Mayor of London, *bearing the mace. Then* Garter, *in
his coat of arms, and on his head a gilt copper crown.*
6. Marquess DORSET, *bearing a sceptre of gold, on his
head a demi-coronal of gold. With him, the* Earl of
SURREY, *bearing the rod of silver with the dove,
crowned with an earl's coronet. Collars of SS.*
7. Duke of SUFFOLK, *in his robe of estate, his coronet on
his head, bearing a long white wand, as high-steward.
With him, the* Duke of NORFOLK, *with the rod of
marshalship, a coronet on his head. Collars of SS.*
8. *A canopy borne by four of the* Cinqueports; *under it,
the* Queen *in her robe; in her hair richly adorned with
pearl, crowned. On each side her, the* Bishops of
London *and* Winchester.

9. *The old* Duchess of NORFOLK, *in a coronal of gold,
wrought with flowers, bearing the* Queen's *train.*
10. *Certain* Ladies *or* Countesses, *with plain circlets of
gold without flowers.*

They pass over the stage in order and state.

Sec. Gent. A royal train, believe me. These I know:
Who 's that that bears the sceptre?
First Gent.   Marquess Dorset:
And that the Earl of Surrey, with the rod.
Sec. Gent. A bold brave gentleman. That should be 40
The Duke of Suffolk?
First Gent.   'Tis the same: high-steward.
Sec. Gent. And that my Lord of Norfolk?
First Gent.   Yes.
Sec. Gent.   Heaven bless thee!
                     [*Looking on the Queen.*
Thou hast the sweetest face I ever look'd on.
Sir, as I have a soul, she is an angel;
Our king has all the Indies in his arms,
And more and richer, when he strains that lady:
I cannot blame his conscience.
First Gent.   They that bear
The cloth of honour over her, are four barons
Of the Cinque-ports.
Sec. Gent. Those men are happy; and so are all are
near her.   50
I take it, she that carries up the train
Is that old noble lady, Duchess of Norfolk.
First Gent. It is; and all the rest are countesses.
Sec. Gent. Their coronets say so. These are stars
indeed;
And sometimes falling ones.
First Gent.   No more of that.
      [*Exit procession, and then a great flourish of trumpets.*

Enter a third Gentleman.

First Gent. God save you, sir! where have you been
broiling?
Third Gent. Among the crowd i' the Abbey; where a
finger
Could not be wedged in more: I am stifled
With the mere rankness of their joy.
Sec. Gent.   You saw
The ceremony?
Third Gent.   That I did.
First Gent.   How was it?   60
Third Gent. Well worth the seeing.
Sec. Gent.   Good sir, speak it to us.
Third Gent. As well as I am able. The rich stream
Of lords and ladies, having brought the queen
To a prepared place in the choir, fell off
A distance from her; while her grace sat down
To rest awhile, some half an hour or so,
In a rich chair of state, opposing freely
The beauty of her person to the people.
Believe me, sir, she is the goodliest woman
That ever lay by man: which when the people   70
Had the full view of, such a noise arose
As the shrouds make at sea in a stiff tempest,
As loud, and to as many tunes: hats, cloaks,—
Doublets, I think,—flew up; and had their faces
Been loose, this day they had been lost. Such joy

*King Henry
the Eighth*
ACT IV : SC I

1295

36. *Stage Direction:* (5) **Garter,** i.e., Garter King of Arms.   (14) **Collars of SS,** golden chains of office made of flat, broad, S-shaped links,
ornately decorated; their significance is uncertain.   (15) **Cinqueports,**
i.e., barons of the Cinque-ports, a group of seaport towns (originally
five) situated on the southeast coast of England, in ancient times fur-
nishing the chief part of the English navy, in return for which they
had many privileges and franchises. 46. **strains,** embraces. 56. **broiling,** suffering great heat. 67. **opposing,** present in full view.

I never saw before. Great-bellied women,
That had not half a week to go, like rams
In the old time of war, would shake the press,
And make 'em reel before 'em. No man living
Could say 'This is my wife' there; all were woven   80
So strangely in one piece.
  Sec. Gent.   But, what follow'd?
  Third Gent. At length her grace rose, and with
      modest paces
Came to the altar; where she kneel'd, and saint-like
Cast her fair eyes to heaven and pray'd devoutly.
Then rose again and bow'd her to the people:
When by the Archbishop of Canterbury
She had all the royal makings of a queen;
As holy oil, Edward Confessor's crown,
The rod, and bird of peace, and all such emblems
Laid nobly on her: which perform'd, the choir,   90
With all the choicest music of the kingdom,
Together sung 'Te Deum.' So she parted,
And with the same full state paced back again
To York-place, where the feast is held.
  First Gent.   Sir,
You must no more call it York-place, that's past;
For, since the cardinal fell, that title's lost:
'Tis now the king's, and call'd Whitehall.
  Third Gent.   I know it;
But 'tis so lately alter'd, that the old name
Is fresh about me.
  Sec. Gent.   What two reverend bishops
Were those that went on each side of the queen?   100
  Third Gent. Stokesly and Gardiner; the one of
      Winchester,
Newly preferr'd from the king's secretary,
The other, London.
  Sec. Gent.   He of Winchester
Is held no great good lover of the archbishop's,
The virtuous Cranmer.
  Third Gent.   All the land knows that:
However, yet there is no great breach; when it comes,
Cranmer will find a friend will not shrink from him.
  Sec. Gent. Who may that be, I pray you?
  Third Gent.   Thomas Cromwell;
A man in much esteem with the king, and truly
A worthy friend. The king has made him master   110
O' the jewel house,
And one, already, of the privy council.
  Sec. Gent. He will deserve more.
  Third Gent.   Yes, without all doubt.
Come, gentlemen, ye shall go my way, which
Is to the court, and there ye shall be my guests:
Something I can command. As I walk thither,
I'll tell ye more.
  Both.   You may command us, sir.
                                        [*Exeunt.*

<hr>

SCENE II. *Kimbolton.*

Enter KATHARINE, *Dowager, sick; led between*
  GRIFFITH, *her gentleman usher, and* PATIENCE, *her*
  woman.

Grif. How does your grace?

  Kath.   O Griffith, sick to death!
My legs, like loaden branches, bow to the earth,
Willing to leave their burthen. Reach a chair:
So; now, methinks, I feel a little ease.
Didst thou not tell me, Griffith, as thou led'st me,
That the great child of honour, Cardinal Wolsey,
Was dead?
  Grif.   Yes, madam; but I think your
      grace,
Out of the pain you suffer'd, gave no ear to 't.
  Kath. Prithee, good Griffith, tell me how he died:
If well, he stepp'd before me, happily   10
For my example.
  Grif.   Well, the voice goes, madam:
For after the stout Earl Northumberland
Arrested him at York, and brought him forward,
As a man sorely tainted, to his answer,
He fell sick suddenly, and grew so ill
He could not sit his mule.
  Kath.   Alas, poor man!
  Grif. At last, with easy roads, he came to Leicester,
Lodged in the abbey; where the reverend abbot,
With all his covent, honourably received him;
To whom he gave these words, 'O, father abbot,   20
An old man, broken with the storms of state,
Is come to lay his weary bones among ye;
Give him a little earth for charity!'
So went to bed; where eagerly his sickness
Pursued him still: and, three nights after this,
About the hour of eight, which he himself
Foretold should be his last, full of repentance,
Continual meditations, tears, and sorrows,
He gave his honours to the world again,
His blessed part to heaven, and slept in peace.   30
  Kath. So may he rest; his faults lie gently on him!
Yet thus far, Griffith, give me leave to speak him,
And yet with charity. He was a man
Of an unbounded stomach, ever ranking
Himself with princes; one that, by suggestion,
Tied all the kingdom: simony was fair-play;
His own opinion was his law: i' the presence
He would say untruths; and be ever double
Both in his words and meaning: he was never,
But where he meant to ruin, pitiful: 40
His promises were, as he then was, mighty;
But his performance, as he is now, nothing:
Of his own body he was ill, and gave
The clergy ill example.
  Grif.   Noble madam,
Men's evil manners live in brass; their virtues
We write in water. May it please your highness
To hear me speak his good now?
  Kath.   Yes, good Griffith;
I were malicious else.
  Grif.   This cardinal,
Though from an humble stock, undoubtedly
Was fashion'd to much honour from his cradle.   50
He was a scholar, and a ripe and good one;
Exceeding wise, fair-spoken, and persuading:
Lofty and sour to them that loved him not;
But to those men that sought him sweet as summer.
And though he were unsatisfied in getting,

<hr>

77. **rams,** battering rams.   78. **press,** crowd.   91. **music,** i.e., musicians.
101-102. **Gardiner . . . secretary.** Gardiner, secretary to the king,
was made bishop of Winchester at the fall of Wolsey; he continued to
act as secretary for several years.   116. **Something . . . command,** I

can provide refreshment.
  SCENE II.   11. **the voice goes,** i.e., people say.   24. **eagerly,** sharply.
33-44. **He was a man,** etc. This characterization of Wolsey and that
recited by Griffith below are closely parallelled in Holinshed both in

Which was a sin, yet in bestowing, madam,
He was most princely: ever witness for him
Those twins of learning that he raised in you,
Ipswich and Oxford! one of which fell with him,
Unwilling to outlive the good that did it;   60
The other, though unfinish'd, yet so famous,
So excellent in art, and still so rising,
That Christendom shall ever speak his virtue.
His overthrow heap'd happiness upon him;
For then, and not till then, he felt himself,
And found the blessedness of being little:
And, to add greater honours to his age
Than man could give him, he died fearing God.
   Kath. After my death I wish no other herald,
No other speaker of my living actions,   70
To keep mine honour from corruption,
But such an honest chronicler as Griffith.
Whom I most hated living, thou hast made me,
With thy religious truth and modesty,
Now in his ashes honour: peace be with him!
Patience, be near me still; and set me lower:
I have not long to trouble thee. Good Griffith,
Cause the musicians play me that sad note
I named my knell, whilst I sit meditating   79
On that celestial harmony I go to. [*Sad and solemn music.*
   Grif. She is asleep: good wench, let 's sit down quiet,
For fear we wake her: softly, gentle Patience.

   *The vision. Enter, solemnly tripping one after another, six
   personages, clad in white robes, wearing on their heads
   garlands of bays, and golden vizards on their faces;
   branches of bays or palm in their hands. They first congee
   unto her, then dance; and, at certain changes, the first
   two hold a spare garland over her head; at which the
   other four make reverent curtsies; then the two that held
   the garland deliver the same to the other next two, who
   observe the same order in their changes, and holding the
   garland over her head: which done, they deliver the same
   garland to the last two, who likewise observe the same
   order: at which, as it were by inspiration, she makes in
   her sleep signs of rejoicing, and holdeth up her hands to
   heaven: and so in their dancing vanish, carrying the
   garland with them. The music continues.*

   Kath. Spirits of peace, where are ye? are ye all gone,
And leave me here in wretchedness behind ye?
   Grif. Madam, we are here.
   Kath.   It is not you I call for:
Saw ye none enter since I slept?
   Grif.   None, madam.
   Kath. No? Saw you not, even now, a blessed troop
Invite me to a banquet; whose bright faces
Cast thousand beams upon me, like the sun?
They promised me eternal happiness;   90
And brought me garlands, Griffith, which I feel
I am not worthy yet to wear: I shall, assuredly.
   Grif. I am most joyful, madam, such good dreams
Possess your fancy.
   Kath.   Bid the music leave,
They are harsh and heavy to me.   [*Music ceases.*
   Pat.   Do you note
How much her grace is alter'd on the sudden?
How long her face is drawn? how pale she looks,

And of an earthy cold? Mark her eyes!
   Grif. She is going, wench: pray, pray.
   Pat.   Heaven comfort her!

   Enter a Messenger.

   Mess. An 't like your grace,—
   Kath.   You are a saucy fellow: 100
Deserve we no more reverence?
   Grif.   You are to blame,
Knowing she will not lose her wonted greatness,
To use so rude behaviour; go to, kneel.
   Mess. I humbly do entreat your highness' pardon;
My haste made me unmannerly. There is staying
A gentleman, sent from the king, to see you.
   Kath. Admit him entrance, Griffith: but this fellow
Let me ne'er see again.   [*Exeunt Griffith and Messenger.*

   Re-enter GRIFFITH, *with* CAPUCIUS.
                If my sight fail not,
You should be lord ambassador from the emperor,
My royal nephew, and your name Capucius.   110
   Cap. Madam, the same; your servant.
   Kath.   O, my lord,
The times and titles now are alter'd strangely
With me since first you knew me. But, I pray you,
What is your pleasure with me?
   Cap.   Noble lady,
First, mine own service to your grace; the next,
The king's request that I would visit you;
Who grieves much for your weakness, and by me
Sends you his princely commendations,
And heartily entreats you take good comfort.   119
   Kath. O my good lord, that comfort comes too late;
'Tis like a pardon after execution:
That gentle physic, given in time, had cured me;
But now I am past all comforts here, but prayers.
How does his highness?
   Cap.   Madam, in good health.
   Kath. So may he ever do! and ever flourish,
When I shall dwell with worms, and my poor name
Banish'd the kingdom! Patience, is that letter,
I caused you write, yet sent away?
   Pat.   No, madam.[*Giving it to Katharine.*
   Kath. Sir, I most humbly pray you to deliver
This to my lord the king.
   Cap.   Most willing, madam.   130
   Kath. In which I have commended to his goodness
The model of our chaste loves, his young daughter:
The dews of heaven fall thick in blessings on her!
Beseeching him to give her virtuous breeding,—
She is young, and of a noble modest nature,
I hope she will deserve well,—and a little
To love her for her mother's sake, that loved him,
Heaven knows how dearly. My next poor petition
Is, that his noble grace would have some pity
Upon my wretched women, that so long   140
Have follow'd both my fortunes faithfully:
Of which there is not one, I dare avow,
And now I should not lie, but will deserve,
For virtue and true beauty of the soul,
For honesty and decent carriage,
A right good husband, let him be a noble:

And, sure, those men are happy that shall have 'em.
The last is, for my men; they are the poorest,
But poverty could never draw 'em from me;
That they may have their wages duly paid 'em,   150
And something over to remember me by:
If heaven had pleased to have given me longer life
And able means, we had not parted thus.
These are the whole contents: and, good my lord,
By that you love the dearest in this world,
As you wish Christian peace to souls departed,
Stand these poor people's friend, and urge the king
To do me this last right.
　　Cap.　　　　　　　By heaven, I will,
Or let me lose the fashion of a man!
　　Kath. I thank you, honest lord. Remember me   160
In all humility unto his highness:
Say his long trouble now is passing
Out of this world; tell him, in death I bless'd him,
For so I will. Mine eyes grow dim. Farewell,
My lord. Griffith, farewell. Nay, Patience,
You must not leave me yet: I must to bed;
Call in more women. When I am dead, good wench,
Let me be used with honour: strew me over
With maiden flowers, that all the world may know
I was a chaste wife to my grave: embalm me,   170
Then lay me forth: although unqueen'd, yet like
A queen, and daughter to a king, inter me.
I can no more.　　　　　*[Exeunt, leading Katharine.*

ACT V.

SCENE I. *London. A gallery in the palace.*

Enter GARDINER, Bishop of Winchester, *a Page with
a torch before him, met by* SIR THOMAS LOVELL.

　　Gar. It's one o'clock, boy, is't not?
　　Boy.　　　　　　　It hath struck.
　　Gar. These should be hours for necessities,
Not for delights; times to repair our nature
With comforting repose, and not for us
To waste these times. Good hour of night, Sir
　　Thomas!
Whither so late?
　　Lov.　　　　　　Came you from the king, my
　　lord?
　　Gar. I did, Sir Thomas; and left him at primero
With the Duke of Suffolk.
　　Lov.　　　　　　I must to him too,
Before he go to bed. I'll take my leave.
　　Gar. Not yet, Sir Thomas Lovell. What's the
　　matter?   10
It seems you are in haste: an if there be
No great offence belongs to't, give your friend
Some touch of your late business: affairs, that walk,
As they say spirits do, at midnight, have
In them a wilder nature than the business
That seeks dispatch by day.
　　Lov.　　　　　　My lord, I love you;
And durst commend a secret to your ear
Much weightier than this work. The queen's in
　　labour,

They say, in great extremity; and fear'd
She'll with the labour end.
　　Gar.　　　　　　The fruit she goes with   20
I pray for heartily, that it may find
Good time, and live: but for the stock, Sir Thomas,
I wish it grubb'd up now.
　　Lov.　　　　　　Methinks I could
Cry the amen; and yet my conscience says
She's a good creature, and, sweet lady, does
Deserve our better wishes.
　　Gar.　　　　　　But, sir, sir,
Hear me, Sir Thomas: you're a gentleman
Of mine own way; I know you wise, religious;
And, let me tell you, it will ne'er be well,
'Twill not, Sir Thomas Lovell, take't of me,   30
Till Cranmer, Cromwell, her two hands, and she,
Sleep in their graves.
　　Lov.　　　　　　Now, sir, you speak of two
The most remark'd i' the kingdom. As for Cromwell,
Beside that of the jewel house, is made master
O' the rolls, and the king's secretary; further, sir,
Stands in the gap and trade of moe preferments,
With which the time will load him. The archbishop
Is the king's hand and tongue; and who dare speak
One syllable against him?
　　Gar.　　　　　　Yes, yes, Sir Thomas,
There are that dare; and I myself have ventured   40
To speak my mind of him: and indeed this day,
Sir, I may tell it you, I think I have
Incensed the lords o' the council, that he is,
For so I know he is, they know he is,
A most arch heretic, a pestilence
That does infect the land: with which they moved
Have broken with the king; who hath so far
Given ear to our complaint, of his great grace
And princely care foreseeing those fell mischiefs
Our reasons laid before him, hath commanded   50
To-morrow morning to the council-board
He be convented. He's a rank weed, Sir Thomas,
And we must root him out. From your affairs
I hinder you too long: good night, Sir Thomas.
　　Lov. Many good nights, my lord: I rest your
　　servant.　　　　　*[Exeunt Gardiner and Page.*

Enter the KING *and* SUFFOLK.

　　King. Charles, I will play no more to-night;
My mind's not on't; you are too hard for me.
　　Suf. Sir, I did never win of you before.
　　King. But little, Charles;
Nor shall not, when my fancy's on my play.   60
Now, Lovell, from the queen what is the news?
　　Lov. I could not personally deliver to her
What you commanded me, but by her woman
I sent your message; who return'd her thanks
In the great'st humbleness, and desired your
　　highness
Most heartily to pray for her.
　　King.　　　　　　What say'st thou, ha?
To pray for her? what, is she crying out?
　　Lov. So said her woman; and that her sufferance
　　made
Almost each pang a death.

ACT V. SCENE I.　7. **primero,** gambling card game.　33. **remark'd,**
under the public eye.　36. **trade,** beaten path.　37. **the time,** tendencies
of the age (Pooler).　43. **Incensed,** instigated; Onions conjectures *in-
sensed,* i.e., made to understand.　46-47. **with . . . king,** they, moved

with this idea, have disclosed it to the king.　47. **who,** an English
adaptation of the Latin construction of the relative equivalent to *and
he who;* it is the subject of both verbs *hath . . . Given* and *hath com-*

King.   Alas, good lady!
Suf. God safely quit her of her burthen, and   70
With gentle travail, to the gladding of
Your highness with an heir!
    King.   'Tis midnight, Charles;
Prithee, to bed; and in thy prayers remember
The estate of my poor queen. Leave me alone;
For I must think of that which company
Would not be friendly to.
    Suf.   I wish your highness
A quiet night; and my good mistress will
Remember in my prayers.
    King.   Charles, good night.[*Exit Suffolk.*

Enter SIR ANTHONY DENNY.

Well, sir, what follows?
    Den. Sir, I have brought my lord the archbishop,   80
As you commanded me.
    King.   Ha! Canterbury?
    Den. Ay, my good lord.
    King.   'Tis true: where is he, Denny?
    Den. He attends your highness' pleasure.
    King.   Bring him to us.   [*Exit Denny.*
    Lov. [*Aside*] This is about that which the bishop
        spake:
I am happily come hither.

Re-enter DENNY, *with* CRANMER.

    King.   Avoid the gallery. [*Lovell seems*
to stay.] Ha! I have said. Be gone.
What!   [*Exeunt Lovell and Denny.*
    Cran. [*Aside*] I am fearful: wherefore frowns he
        thus?
'Tis his aspect of terror. All 's not well.
    King. How now, my lord! you do desire to know
Wherefore I sent for you.
    Cran.   [*Kneeling*] It is my duty   90
To attend your highness' pleasure.
    King.   Pray you, arise,
My good and gracious Lord of Canterbury.
Come, you and I must walk a turn together;
I have news to tell you: come, come, give me your
        hand.
Ah, my good lord, I grieve at what I speak,
And am right sorry to repeat what follows:
I have, and most unwillingly, of late
Heard many grievous, I do say, my lord,
Grievous complaints of you; which, being consider'd,
Have moved us and our council, that you shall   100
This morning come before us; where, I know,
You cannot with such freedom purge yourself,
But that, till further trial in those charges
Which will require your answer, you must take
Your patience to you, and be well contented
To make your house our Tower: you a brother of us,
It fits we thus proceed, or else no witness
Would come against you.
    Cran.   [*Kneeling*] I humbly thank your
        highness;
And am right glad to catch this good occasion
Most throughly to be winnow'd, where my chaff   110
And corn shall fly asunder: for, I know,

There 's none stands under more calumnious
        tongues
Than I myself, poor man.
    King.   Stand up, good Canterbury:
Thy truth and thy integrity is rooted
In us, thy friend: give me thy hand, stand up:
Prithee, let 's walk. Now, by my holidame,
What manner of man are you? My lord, I look'd
You would have given me your petition, that
I should have ta'en some pains to bring together
Yourself and your accusers; and to have heard you, 120
Without indurance, further.
    Cran.   Most dread liege,
The good I stand on is my truth and honesty:
If they shall fail, I, with mine enemies,
Will triumph o'er my person; which I weigh not,
Being of those virtues vacant. I fear nothing
What can be said against me.
    King.   Know you not
How your state stands i' the world, with the whole
        world?
Your enemies are many, and not small; their practices
Must bear the same proportion; and not ever
The justice and the truth o' the question carries   130
The due o' the verdict with it: at what ease
Might corrupt minds procure knaves as corrupt
To swear against you? such things have been done.
You are potently opposed; and with a malice
Of as great size. Ween you of better luck,
I mean, in perjured witness, than your master,
Whose minister you are, whiles here he lived
Upon this naughty earth? Go to, go to;
You take a precipice for no leap of danger,
And woo your own destruction.
    Cran.   God and your majesty   140
Protect mine innocence, or I fall into
The trap is laid for me!
    King.   Be of good cheer;
They shall no more prevail than we give way to.
Keep comfort to you; and this morning see
You do appear before them: if they shall chance,
In charging you with matters, to commit you,
The best persuasions to the contrary
Fail not to use, and with what vehemency
The occasion shall instruct you: if entreaties
Will render you no remedy, this ring   150
Deliver them, and your appeal to us
There make before them. Look, the good man weeps!
He 's honest, on mine honour. God's blest mother!
I swear he is true-hearted; and a soul
None better in my kingdom. Get you gone,
And do as I have bid you. [*Exit Cranmer.*] He has
        strangled
His language in his tears.

Enter Old Lady, LOVELL *following.*

    Gent.   [*Within*] Come back: what mean
        you?
    Old L. I'll not come back; the tidings that I bring
Will make my boldness manners. Now, good angels
Fly o'er thy royal head, and shade thy person   160
Under their blessed wings!

manded (l. 50).   52. **convented,** summoned.   84. **the bishop,** i.e., Gardiner.   85. **Avoid,** vacate.   106. **brother,** fellow member of the council.
121. **indurance,** imprisonment.   124-125. **which . . . vacant,** I don't

value my person if it is void of those virtues (*truth* and *honesty*).   129-
131. **and . . . it,** the innocence of a person does not always insure his
acquittal (Pooler).   135. **Ween you of,** do you expect.

King.   Now, by thy looks
I guess thy message. Is the queen deliver'd?
Say, ay; and of a boy.
    Old L.   Ay, ay, my liege;
And of a lovely boy: the God of heaven
Both now and ever bless her! 'tis a girl,
Promises boys hereafter. Sir, your queen
Desires your visitation, and to be
Acquainted with this stranger: 'tis as like you
As cherry is to cherry.
    King.   Lovell!
    Lov.   Sir?
    King. Give her an hundred marks. I'll to the queen.
                                                                    [*Exit*

    Old L. An hundred marks! By this light, I'll ha'
          more.   171
An ordinary groom is for such payment.
I will have more, or scold it out of him.
Said I for this, the girl was like to him?
I will have more, or else unsay 't; and now,
While it is hot, I'll put it to the issue.   [*Exeunt.*

———————

SCENE II. *Before the council-chamber.*

Pursuivants, Pages, &c. attending.

Enter CRANMER, *Archbishop of Canterbury.*

Cran. I hope I am not too late; and yet the
          gentleman,
That was sent to me from the council, pray'd me
To make great haste. All fast? what means this? Ho!
Who waits there? Sure, you know me?

Enter Keeper.

Keep.   Yes, my lord;
But yet I cannot help you.
    Cran. Why?

Enter DOCTOR BUTTS.

Keep. Your grace must wait till you be call'd for.
    Cran.   So.
    Butts. [*Aside*] This is a piece of malice. I am glad
I came this way so happily: the king
Shall understand it presently.   [*Exit.*
    Cran.   [*Aside*] 'Tis Butts,   10
The king's physician: as he pass'd along,
How earnestly he cast his eyes upon me!
Pray heaven, he sound not my disgrace! For certain,
This is of purpose laid by some that hate me—
God turn their hearts! I never sought their malice—
To quench mine honour: they would shame to make
          me
Wait else at door, a fellow-counsellor,
'Mong boys, grooms, and lackeys. But their pleasures
Must be fulfill'd, and I attend with patience.

Enter the KING *and* BUTTS *at a window above.*

Butts. I'll show your grace the strangest sight—
    King.   What 's that, Butts?   20
    Butts. I think your highness saw this many a day.
    King. Body o' me, where is it?

Butts.   There, my lord:
The high promotion of his grace of Canterbury;
Who holds his state at door, 'mongst pursuivants,
Pages, and footboys.
    King.   Ha! 'tis he, indeed:
Is this the honour they do one another?
'Tis well there 's one above 'em yet. I had thought
They had parted so much honesty among 'em,
At least, good manners, as not thus to suffer
A man of his place, and so near our favour,   30
To dance attendance on their lordships' pleasures,
And at the door too, like a post with packets.
By holy Mary, Butts, there 's knavery:
Let 'em alone, and draw the curtain close:
We shall hear more anon.   [*Exeunt.*

———————

SCENE III. *The Council-Chamber.*

Enter LORD CHANCELLOR; *places himself at the upper
    end of the table on the left hand; a seat being left void
    above him, as for* CANTERBURY's *seat.* DUKE OF
    SUFFOLK, DUKE OF NORFOLK, SURREY, LORD
    CHAMBERLAIN, GARDINER, *seat themselves in order
    on each side.* CROMWELL *at lower end, as secretary.*
    Keeper at the door.

Chan. Speak to the business, master secretary:
Why are we met in council?
    Crom.   Please your honours,
The chief cause concerns his grace of Canterbury.
    Gar. Has he had knowledge of it?
    Crom.   Yes.
    Nor.   Who waits there?
    Keep. Without, my noble lords?
    Gar.   Yes.
    Keep.   My lord archbishop:
And has done half an hour, to know your pleasures.
    Chan. Let him come in.
    Keep.   Your grace may enter now.
          [*Cranmer enters and approaches the council-table.*
    Chan. My good lord archbishop, I 'm very sorry
To sit here at this present, and behold
That chair stand empty: but we all are men,   10
In our own natures frail, and capable
Of our flesh; few are angels: out of which frailty
And want of wisdom, you, that best should teach us,
Have misdemean'd yourself, and not a little,
Toward the king first, then his laws, in filling
The whole realm, by your teaching and your
          chaplains,
For so we are inform'd, with new opinions,
Divers and dangerous; which are heresies,
And, not reform'd, may prove pernicious.
    Gar. Which reformation must be sudden too,   20
My noble lords; for those that tame wild horses
Pace 'em not in their hands to make 'em gentle,
But stop their mouths with stubborn bits, and spur
          'em,
Till they obey the manage. If we suffer,
Out of our easiness and childish pity
To one man's honour, this contagious sickness,
Farewell all physic: and what follows then?

SCENE II. The source for this and the following scene is Foxe's
Acts and Monuments. Holinshed does not relate these events. 13. **sound**,
proclaim (Pooler); possibly, ascertain, as with a sounding line. 19.
*Stage Direction: **at a window above**.* According to Steevens, this was
a peephole through which the council could be spied upon. The Folio
text makes no scene division between this and the following scene, so
that the council would assemble under the view and in the hearing of
the king. 28. **parted**, shared.
    SCENE III. *Stage Direction:* **Enter Lord Chancellor.** The identity of
the Lord Chancellor is not easy to determine, since the chronology of

Commotions, uproars, with a general taint
Of the whole state: as, of late days, our neighbours,
The upper Germany, can dearly witness, 30
Yet freshly pitied in our memories.
    Cran. My good lords, hitherto, in all the progress
Both of my life and office, I have labour'd,
And with no little study, that my teaching
And the strong course of my authority
Might go one way, and safely; and the end
Was ever, to do well: nor is there living,
I speak it with a single heart, my lords,
A man that more detests, more stirs against,
Both in his private conscience and his place, 40
Defacers of a public peace, than I do.
Pray heaven, the king may never find a heart
With less allegiance in it! Men that make
Envy and crooked malice nourishment
Dare bite the best. I do beseech your lordships,
That, in this case of justice, my accusers,
Be what they will, may stand forth face to face,
And freely urge against me.
    Suf.   Nay, my lord,
That cannot be: you are a counsellor,
And, by that virtue, no man dare accuse you. 50
    Gar. My lord, because we have business of more
        moment,
We will be short with you. 'Tis his highness' pleasure,
And our consent, for better trial of you,
From hence you be committed to the Tower;
Where, being but a private man again,
You shall know many dare accuse you boldly,
More than, I fear, you are provided for.
    Cran. Ah, my good Lord of Winchester, I thank
        you;
You are always my good friend; if your will pass,
I shall both find your lordship judge and juror, 60
You are so merciful: I see your end;
'Tis my undoing: love and meekness, lord,
Become a churchman better than ambition:
Win straying souls with modesty again,
Cast none away. That I shall clear myself,
Lay all the weight ye can upon my patience,
I make as little doubt, as you do conscience
In doing daily wrongs. I could say more,
But reverence to your calling makes me modest.
    Gar. My lord, my lord, you are a sectary, 70
That's the plain truth: your painted gloss discovers,
To men that understand you, words and weakness.
    Crom. My Lord of Winchester, you are a little,
By your good favour, too sharp; men so noble,
However faulty, yet should find respect
For what they have been: 'tis a cruelty
To load a falling man.
    Gar.   Good master secretary,
I cry your honour mercy; you may, worst
Of all this table, say so.
    Crom.   Why, my lord?
    Gar. Do not I know you for a favourer 80
Of this new sect? ye are not sound.
    Crom.   Not sound?
    Gar. Not sound, I say.
    Crom.   Would you were half so honest!

Men's prayers then would seek you, not their fears.
    Gar. I shall remember this bold language.
    Crom.   Do.
Remember your bold life too.
    Chan.   This is too much;
Forbear, for shame, my lords.
    Gar.   I have done.
    Crom.   And I.
    Chan. Then thus for you, my lord: it stands agreed,
I take it, by all voices, that forthwith
You be convey'd to the Tower a prisoner;
There to remain till the king's further pleasure 90
Be known unto us: are you all agreed, lords?
    All. We are.
    Cran.   Is there no other way of mercy,
But I must needs to the Tower, my lords?
    Gar.   What other
Would you expect? you are strangely troublesome.
Let some o' the guard be ready there.

        Enter Guard.

    Cran.   For me?
Must I go like a traitor thither?
    Gar.   Receive him,
And see him safe i' the Tower.
    Cran.   Stay, good my lords,
I have a little yet to say. Look there, my lords;
By virtue of that ring, I take my cause
Out of the gripes of cruel men, and give it 100
To a most noble judge, the king my master.
    Cham. This is the king's ring.
    Sur.   'Tis no counterfeit.
    Suf. 'Tis the right ring, by heaven: I told ye all,
When we first put this dangerous stone a-rolling,
'Twould fall upon ourselves.
    Nor.   Do you think, my lords,
The king will suffer but the little finger
Of this man to be vex'd?
    Chan.   'Tis now too certain:
How much more is his life in value with him?
Would I were fairly out on 't!
    Crom.   My mind gave me,
In seeking tales and informations 110
Against this man, whose honesty the devil
And his disciples only envy at,
Ye blew the fire that burns ye: now have at ye!

        Enter KING, *frowning on them; takes his seat.*

    Gar. Dread sovereign, how much are we bound to
        heaven
In daily thanks, that gave us such a prince;
Not only good and wise, but most religious:
One that, in all obedience, makes the church
The chief aim of his honour; and, to strengthen
That holy duty, out of dear respect,
His royal self in judgement comes to hear 120
The cause betwixt her and this great offender.
    King. You were ever good at sudden
        commendations,
Bishop of Winchester. But know, I come not
To hear such flattery now, and in my presence;
They are too thin and bare to hide offences.

the play so deviates from the actual order of historical events. Elizabeth's birth and christening took place in September 1533, at which
time the chancellorship was vacant. **11-12. capable . . . flesh,** susceptible to the weaknesses of the flesh. **22. Pace . . . hands,** i.e.,
don't lead them. **29-30. our . . . Germany,** refers to the Peasants'
Wars, 1524; possibly to the massacre of the Anabaptists in 1535. **38.
single,** honest; not given to double-dealing. **109. My mind gave me,**
i.e., I thought.

To me you cannot reach, you play the spaniel,
And think with wagging of your tongue to win me;
But, whatsoe'er thou takest me for, I 'm sure
Thou hast a cruel nature and a bloody.
[To Cranmer] Good man, sit down. Now let me see the
    proudest   130
He, that dares most, but wag his finger at thee:
By all that 's holy, he had better starve
Than but once think this place becomes thee not.
    Sur. May it please your grace,—
    King.   No, sir, it does not please me.
I had thought I had had men of some understanding
And wisdom of my council; but I find none.
Was it discretion, lords, to let this man,
This good man,—few of you deserve that title,—
This honest man, wait like a lousy footboy
At chamber-door? and one as great as you are?   140
Why, what a shame was this! Did my commission
Bid ye so far forget yourselves? I gave ye
Power as he was a counsellor to try him,
Not as a groom: there 's some of ye, I see,
More out of malice than integrity,
Would try him to the utmost, had ye mean;
Which ye shall never have while I live.
    Chan.   Thus far,
My most dread sovereign, may it like your grace
To let my tongue excuse all. What was purposed
Concerning his imprisonment, was rather,   150
If there be faith in men, meant for his trial,
And fair purgation to the world, than malice,
I 'm sure, in me.
    King. Well, well, my lords, respect him;
Take him, and use him well, he 's worthy of it.
I will say thus much for him, if a prince
May be beholding to a subject, I
Am, for his love and service, so to him.
Make me no more ado, but all embrace him:
Be friends, for shame, my lords! My Lord of
    Canterbury,   160
I have a suit which you must not deny me;
That is, a fair young maid that yet wants baptism,
You must be godfather, and answer for her.
    Cran. The greatest monarch now alive may glory
In such an honour: how may I deserve it,
That am a poor and humble subject to you?
    King. Come, come, my lord, you 'ld spare your
spoons: you shall have two noble partners with you;
the old Duchess of Norfolk, and Lady Marquess
Dorset: will these please you?   170
Once more, my Lord of Winchester, I charge you,
Embrace and love this man.
    Gar.   With a true heart
And brother-love I do it.
    Cran.   And let heaven
Witness, how dear I hold this confirmation.
    King. Good man, those joyful tears show thy true
    heart:
The common voice, I see, is verified
Of thee, which says thus, 'Do my Lord of Canterbury
A shrewd turn, and he is your friend for ever.'

Come, lords, we trifle time away; I long
To have this young one made a Christian.   180
As I have made ye one, lords, one remain;
So I grow stronger, you more honour gain.   [*Exeunt.*

SCENE IV. *The palace yard.*

Noise and tumult within. Enter Porter *and his* Man.

    Port. You 'll leave your noise anon, ye rascals: do
you take the court for Paris-garden? ye rude slaves,
leave your gaping.
    [*Within*] Good master porter, I belong to the larder.
    Port. Belong to the gallows, and be hanged, ye
rogue! is this a place to roar in? Fetch me a dozen
crab-tree staves, and strong ones: these are but
switches to 'em. I 'll scratch your heads: you must be
seeing christenings? do you look for ale and cakes here,
you rude rascals?   11
    Man. Pray, sir, be patient: 'tis as much impossible—
Unless we sweep 'em from the door with cannons—
To scatter 'em, as 'tis to make 'em sleep
On May-day morning; which will never be:
We may as well push against Powle's, as stir 'em.
    Port. How got they in, and be hang'd?
    Man. Alas, I know not; how gets the tide in?
As much as one sound cudgel of four foot—
You see the poor remainder—could distribute,   20
I made no spare, sir.
    Port.   You did nothing, sir.
    Man. I am not Samson, nor Sir Guy, nor Colbrand,
To mow 'em down before me: but if I spared any
That had a head to hit, either young or old,
He or she, cuckold or cuckold-maker,
Let me ne'er hope to see a chine again;
And that I would not for a cow, God save her!
    [*Within*] Do you hear, master porter?
    Port. I shall be with you presently, good master
puppy. Keep the door close, sirrah.   30
    Man. What would you have me do?
    Port. What should you do, but knock 'em down by
the dozens? Is this Moorfields to muster in? or have
we some strange Indian with the great tool come to
court, the women so besiege us? Bless me, what a fry
of fornication is at door! On my Christian conscience,
this one christening will beget a thousand; here will
be father, godfather, and all together.   39
    Man. The spoons will be the bigger, sir. There is a
fellow somewhat near the door, he should be a brazier
by his face, for, o' my conscience, twenty of the dog-
days now reign in 's nose; all that stand about him
are under the line, they need no other penance:
that fire-drake did I hit three times on the head, and
three times was his nose discharged against me; he
stands there, like a mortar-piece, to blow us. There
was a haberdasher's wife of small wit near him, that
railed upon me till her pinked porringer fell off her
head, for kindling such a combustion in the state. I
missed the meteor once, and hit that woman; who
cried out 'Clubs!' when I might see from far some

167-168. **you 'ld . . . spoons,** said jestingly; spoons were a common
christening gift. 176. **common voice,** etc. According to Foxe, this
proverb had its origin in Cranmer's reputation for generous gratitude.
    SCENE IV. 2. **Paris-garden,** a bear garden on the Bankside. 3. **gap-
ing,** shouting. 5. **larder,** pantry, i.e., he was a servant of the palace
household. 11. **ale and cakes,** refreshments appropriate to a fair festival. 15. **May-day morning,** allusion to the custom of rising before

dawn on May day for early morning festivities. 16. **Powle's,** St. Paul's
Cathedral. 22. **Samson,** Biblical character of great strength. **Sir Guy,
Colbrand.** Cf. *King John,* I, i, 225, note. 26. **chine,** backbone; hence
a joint of beef or other meat. 33. **Moorfields,** training ground for the
militia. 34. **some strange Indian,** allusion to the Elizabethan excitement over exhibited Indians; cf. *The Tempest,* II, ii, 29-35. 42. **brazier,** a worker in brass. 45. **fire-drake,** fiery dragon. 48. **mortar-**

forty truncheoners draw to her succour, which were
the hope o' the Strand, where she was quartered.
They fell on; I made good my place: at length they
came to the broom-staff to me; I defied 'em still:
when suddenly a file of boys behind 'em, loose shot,
delivered such a shower of pebbles, that I was fain to
draw mine honour in, and let 'em win the work: the
devil was amongst 'em, I think, surely.   61

Port. These are the youths that thunder at a playhouse, and fight for bitten apples; that no audience,
but the tribulation of Tower-hill, or the limbs of Limehouse, their dear brothers, are able to endure. I have
some of 'em in Limbo Patrum, and there they are
like to dance these three days; besides the running
banquet of two beadles that is to come.   70

Enter LORD CHAMBERLAIN.

Cham. Mercy o' me, what a multitude are here!
They grow still too; from all parts they are coming,
As if we kept a fair here! Where are these porters,
These lazy knaves? Ye have made a fine hand, fellows:
There 's a trim rabble let in: are all these
Your faithful friends o' the suburbs? We shall have
Great store of room, no doubt, left for the ladies,
When they pass back from the christening.
Port.   An 't please your honour,
We are but men; and what so many may do,
Not being torn a-pieces, we have done: 80
An army cannot rule 'em.
Cham.   As I live,
If the king blame me for 't, I'll lay ye all
By the heels, and suddenly; and on your heads
Clap round fines for neglect: ye are lazy knaves;
And here ye lie baiting of bombards, when
Ye should do service. Hark! the trumpets sound;
They 're come already from the christening:
Go, break among the press, and find a way out
To let the troop pass fairly; or I'll find
A Marshalsea shall hold ye play these two months.   90
Port. Make way there for the princess.
Man.   You great fellow,
Stand close up, or I'll make your head ache.
Port. You i' the camlet, get up o' the rail;
I'll peck you o'er the pales else.   *[Exeunt.*

SCENE V. *The palace.*

Enter trumpets, sounding; then two Aldermen, LORD
MAYOR, GARTER, CRANMER, DUKE OF NORFOLK
with his marshal's staff, DUKE OF SUFFOLK, *two*
Noblemen *bearing great standing-bowls for the
christening-gifts; then four* Noblemen *bearing a
canopy, under which the* DUCHESS OF NORFOLK,
*godmother, bearing the child richly habited in a mantle,
&c., train borne by a* Lady; *then follows the*
MARCHIONESS DORSET, *the other godmother, and*
Ladies. *The troop pass once about the stage, and*
GARTER *speaks.*

Gart. Heaven, from thy endless goodness, send

prosperous life, long, and ever happy, to the high
and mighty princess of England, Elizabeth!

Flourish. Enter KING *and Guard.*

Cran. [*Kneeling*] And to your royal grace, and the
good queen,
My noble partners, and myself, thus pray:
All comfort, joy, in this most gracious lady,
Heaven ever laid up to make parents happy,
May hourly fall upon ye!
King.   Thank you, good lord
archbishop:
What is her name?
Cran.   Elizabeth.
King.   Stand up, lord.   10
            [*The King kisses the child.*
With this kiss take my blessing: God protect thee!
Into whose hand I give thy life.
Cran.   Amen.
King. My noble gossips, ye have been too prodigal:
I thank ye heartily; so shall this lady,
When she has so much English.
Cran.   Let me speak, sir,
For heaven now bids me; and the words I utter
Let none think flattery, for they'll find 'em truth.
This royal infant—heaven still move about her!—
Though in her cradle, yet now promises
Upon this land a thousand thousand blessings,   20
Which time shall bring to ripeness: she shall be—
But few now living can behold that goodness—
A pattern to all princes living with her,
And all that shall succeed: Saba was never
More covetous of wisdom and fair virtue
Than this pure soul shall be: all princely graces,
That mould up such a mighty piece as this is,
With all the virtues that attend the good,
Shall still be doubled on her: truth shall nurse her,
Holy and heavenly thoughts still counsel her: 30
She shall be loved and fear'd: her own shall bless her;
Her foes shake like a field of beaten corn,
And hang their heads with sorrow: good grows with
her:
In her days every man shall eat in safety,
Under his own vine, what he plants; and sing
The merry songs of peace to all his neighbours:
God shall be truly known; and those about her
From her shall read the perfect ways of honour,
And by those claim their greatness, not by blood.
Nor shall this peace sleep with her: but as when   40
The bird of wonder dies, the maiden phœnix,
Her ashes new create another heir,
As great in admiration as herself;
So shall she leave her blessedness to one,
When heaven shall call her from this cloud of
darkness,
Who from the sacred ashes of her honour
Shall star-like rise, as great in fame as she was,
And so stand fix'd: peace, plenty, love, truth, terror,
That were the servants to this chosen infant,
Shall then be his, and like a vine grow to him: 50

---

piece, short piece of cannon. 50. **pinked porringer,** small close-fitting cap ornamented with perforations. 54. **truncheoners,** men armed
with cudgels. 65-66. **tribulation . . . Limehouse,** probably places in
London known for their boisterousness. 67. **Limbo Patrum,** prison;
resting place of the pre-Christian patriarchs who had to remain there
until the coming of Christ. 69. **running banquet,** whipping following
imprisonment, taking *banquet* as the dessert after a meal. 90. **Marshal-**

sea, prison in Southwark at that time under the immediate direction of
the royal household.
  SCENE V. 13. **gossips,** kinfolk in God; sponsors for a child at his
christening. 18-63. **This royal infant,** etc. Cf. II, iii, 75-79, note.
24. **Saba,** Queen of Sheba.

Wherever the bright sun of heaven shall shine,
His honour and the greatness of his name
Shall be, and make new nations: he shall flourish,
And, like a mountain cedar, reach his branches
To all the plains about him: our children's children
Shall see this, and bless heaven.
  King.   Thou speakest wonders.
  Cran. She shall be, to the happiness of England,
An aged princess; many days shall see her,
And yet no day without a deed to crown it.
Would I had known no more! but she must die, 60
She must, the saints must have her; yet a virgin,
A most unspotted lily shall she pass
To the ground, and all the world shall mourn her.
  King. O lord archbishop,
Thou hast made me now a man! never, before
This happy child, did I get any thing:
This oracle of comfort has so pleased me,
That when I am in heaven I shall desire
To see what this child does, and praise my Maker.
I thank ye all. To you, my good lord mayor, 70
And your good brethren, I am much beholding;
I have received much honour by your presence,

And ye shall find me thankful. Lead the way, lords:
Ye must all see the queen, and she must thank ye,
She will be sick else. This day, no man think
Has business at his house; for all shall stay:
This little one shall make it holiday. [*Exeunt.*

EPILOGUE.

'Tis ten to one this play can never please
All that are here: some come to take their ease,
And sleep an act or two; but those, we fear,
We have frighted with our trumpets; so, 'tis clear,
They'll say 'tis naught: others, to hear the city
Abused extremely, and to cry 'That's witty!'
Which we have not done neither: that, I fear,
All the expected good we 're like to hear
For this play at this time, is only in
The merciful construction of good women; 10
For such a one we show'd 'em: if they smile,
And say 'twill do, I know, within a while
All the best men are ours; for 'tis ill hap,
If they hold when their ladies bid 'em clap.

GLOSSARY

Shakespearean Words and Meanings of Frequent Occurrence

A

A': he (unaccented form).

Abate: lessen, diminish; blunt, reduce; deprive; bar, leave out of account, except; depreciate; humble.

Abuse (N): insult, error, misdeed, offense, crime; imposture, deception; also the modern sense.

Abuse (v): deceive, misapply, put to a bad use; maltreat; frequently the modern sense.

Addition: something added to one's name to denote his rank; mark of distinction; title.

Admiration: wonder; object of wonder.

Admire: wonder at.

Advantage (N): profit, convenience, benefit; opportunity, favorable opportunity; pecuniary profit; often shades toward the modern sense.

Advantage (v): profit, be of benefit to, benefit; augment.

Advice: reflection, consideration, deliberation, consultation.

Affect: aim at, aspire to, incline toward; be fond of, be inclined; love; act upon contagiously (as a disease). (PAST PART.) *Affected:* disposed, inclined, in love, loved.

Affection: passion, love; emotion, feeling, mental tendency, disposition; wish, inclination; affectation.

An: if; but; *an if:* if, though, even if.

Anon: at once, soon; presently, by and by.

Answer: return, requite; atone for; render an account of, account for; obey, agree with; also the modern sense.

Apparent: evident, plain; seeming.

Argument: subject, theme, reason, cause; story; excuse.

As: according as; as far as; namely; as if; in the capacity of; that; so that; that is, that they.

Assay: try, attempt; accost, address; challenge.

Atone: reconcile; set at one.

Attach: arrest, seize.

Awful: commanding reverential fear or respect; profoundly respectful or reverential.

B

Band: bond, fetters, manacle (leash for a dog). *Band* and *bond* are etymologically the same word; *band* was formerly used in both senses.

Basilisk: fabulous reptile said to kill by its look. The basilisk of popular superstition was a creature with legs, wings, a serpentine and winding tail, and a crest or comb somewhat like a cock (Sir Thomas Browne). It was the offspring of a cock's egg hatched under a toad or serpent.

Bate: blunt, abate, reduce; deduct, except.

Battle: army; division of an army.

Beshrew: curse, blame; used as a mild curse, "Bad or ill luck to."

Bias: tendency, bent, inclination, swaying influence; term in bowling applied to the form of the bowl, the oblique line in which it runs, and the kind of impetus given to cause it to run obliquely.

Blood: nature, vigor; supposed source of emotion; passion; spirit, animation; one of the four humours (see *humour*).

Boot (N): advantage, profit; something given in addition to the bargain; booty, plunder.

Boot (v): profit, avail.

Brave (ADJ.): fine, gallant; splendid, finely arrayed, showy; ostentatiously defiant.

Brave (v): challenge, defy; make splendid.

Brook: tolerate, endure.

C

Can: can do; know; be skilled; sometimes used for "did."

Capable: comprehensive; sensible, impressible, susceptible; capable of; gifted, intelligent.

Careful: anxious, full of care; provident; attentive.

Carry: manage, execute; be successful, win; conquer; sustain; endure.

Censure (N): judgment, opinion; critical opinion, unfavorable opinion.

Censure (v): judge, estimate; pass sentence or judgment.

Character (N): writing, printing, record; handwriting; cipher; face, features (bespeaking inward qualities).

Character (v): write, engrave, inscribe.

Check (N): reproof; restraint.

Check (v): reprove, restrain, keep from; control.

Circumstance: condition, state of affairs, particulars; adjunct details; detailed narration, argument, or discourse; formality, ceremony.

Clip: embrace; surround.

Close: secret, private; concealed; uncommunicative; enclosed.

Cog: cheat.

Coil: noise, disturbance, turmoil; fuss, to-do, bustle.

Colour: appearance; pretext, pretense; excuse.

Companion: fellow (used contemptuously).

Complete: accomplished, fully endowed; perfect, perfect in quality; also frequently the modern sense.

Complexion: external appearance; temperament, disposition; the four complexions—sanguine, choleric, phlegmatic, and melancholy—correspond to the four humours (see *humour*); also the modern sense.

Composition: compact, agreement, constitution.

Compound: settle, agree.

Conceit: conception, idea, thought; mental faculty, wit; fancy, imagination; opinion, estimate; device, invention, design.

Condition: temperament, disposition; characteristic, property, quality; social or official position, rank or status; covenant, treaty, contract.

Confound: waste, spend, invalidate, destroy; undo, ruin; mingle indistinguishably, mix, blend.

Confusion: destruction, overthrow, ruin; mental agitation.

Continent: that which contains or encloses; earth, globe; sum, summary.

Contrive: plot; plan; spend or pass (time).

Conversation: conduct, deportment; social intercourse, association.

Converse: hold intercourse; associate with, have to do with.

Cope: encounter, meet; have to do with.

Copy: model, pattern; example; minutes or memoranda.

Cousin: any relative not belonging to one's immediate family.

Cry you mercy: beg your pardon.

Cuckold: husband whose wife is unfaithful.

Curious: careful, fastidious; anxious, concerned; made with care, skillfully, intricately or daintily wrought; particular.

Cursed, curst: shrewish, perverse, spiteful.

D

Dainty: minute; scrupulous, particular; particular about (with *of*); refined, elegant; also the modern sense.

Date: duration, termination, term of existence; limit or end of a term or period, term.

Dear: precious; best; costly; important; affectionate; hearty; grievous, dire; also the modern sense.

Debate: discuss; fight.

Decay (N): downfall, ruin; cause of ruin.

Decay (v): perish, be destroyed; destroy.

Defeat (N): destruction, ruin.

Defeat (v): destroy, disfigure, ruin.

Defy: challenge, challenge to a fight; reject; despise.

Demand (N): inquiry; request.

Demand (v): inquire, question; request.

Deny: refuse (to do something); refuse permission; refuse to accept; refuse admittance; disown.

Depart (N): departure.

Depart (v): part; go away from, leave, quit; take leave (of one another); *depart with, withal:* part with, give up.

Derive: gain, obtain; draw upon, direct (to); descend; pass by descent, be descended or inherited; trace the origin of (refl.).

Difference: diversity of opinion, disagreement, dissension, dispute; characteristic or distinguishing feature; alteration or addition to a coat of arms to distinguish a younger or lateral branch of a family.

Digest: arrange, perfect; assimilate, amalgamate; disperse, dissipate; comprehend, understand; put up with (fig. from the physical sense of digesting food).

Discourse (N): reasoning, reflection; talk, act of conversing, conversation; faculty of conversing; familiar intercourse; relating (as by speech).

Discourse (v): speak, talk, converse; pass (the time) in talk; say, utter, tell, give forth; narrate, relate.

Discover: uncover, expose to view; divulge, reveal, make known; spy out, reconnoiter; betray; distinguish, discern; also the modern sense.

Dispose (N): disposal; temperament, bent of mind, disposition; external manner.

Dispose (v): distribute, manage, make use of; deposit, put or stow away; regulate, order, direct; come to terms. (PAST PART.) *Disposed:* in a good frame of mind; inclined to be merry.

Dispute: discuss, reason; strive against, resist.

Distemper: disturb; disorder, ill humor; illness.

Doit: old Dutch coin, one-half an English farthing.

Doubt (N): suspicion, apprehension; fear, danger, risk; also the modern sense.

Doubt (v): suspect, apprehend; fear; also the modern sense.

Doubtful: inclined to suspect, suspicious, apprehensive; not to be relied on; almost certain.

Duty: reverence, respect, expression of respect; submission to authority, obedience; due.

E

Earnest: money paid as an instalment to secure a bargain; partial payment; often used with quibble in the modern sense.

Ease: comfort, assistance, leisure; idleness, sloth, inactivity; also the modern sense.

Ecstasy: frenzy, madness, state of being beside oneself, excitement, bewilderment; swoon; rapture.

Element: used to refer to the simple substances of which all material bodies were thought to be composed; specifically earth, air, fire, and water, corresponding to the four humors (see *humour*); atmosphere, sky; atmospheric agencies or powers; that one of the four elements which is the natural abode of a creature; hence, natural surroundings, sphere.

Engage: pledge, pawn, mortgage; bind by a promise, swear to; entangle, involve; enlist; embark on an enterprise (refl.).

Engine: mechanical contrivance; artifice, device, plot.

Enlarge: give free scope to; set at liberty, release.

Entertain: keep up, maintain, accept; take into one's service; treat; engage (someone's) attention or thoughts; occupy, while or pass away pleasurably; engage (as an enemy); receive.

Envious: malicious, spiteful, malignant.

Envy: ill-will, malice; hate; also the modern sense.

Even: uniform; direct, straightforward; exact, precise; equable, smooth, comfortable; equal, equally balanced.

Event: outcome; affair, business; also frequently the modern sense.

Exclaim: protest, rail; accuse, blame (with *on*), reproach.

Excursion: stage battle or skirmish (in stage directions).

Excuse: seek to extenuate (a fault); maintain the innocence of; clear oneself, justify or vindicate oneself; decline (refl.).

F

Fact: deed, act; crime.

Faction: party, class, group, set (of persons); party strife, dissension; factious quarrel, intrigue.

Fail: die, die out; err, be at fault; omit, leave undone.

Fair (N): fair thing; one of the fair sex; someone beloved; beauty (the abstract concept).

Fair (ADJ.): just; clear, distinct; beautiful.

Fair (ADV.): fairly (q.v.).

Fairly: beautifully, handsomely; courteously, civilly; properly, honorably, honestly; becomingly, appropriately; favorably, fortunately; softly, gently, kindly.

Fall: let fall, drop; happen, come to pass; befall; shades frequently toward the modern senses.

Falsely: wrongly; treacherously; improperly.

Fame: report; rumor; reputation.

Familiar (N): intimate friend; familiar or attendant spirit, demon associated with and obedient to a person.

Familiar (ADJ.): intimate, friendly; belonging to

household or family, domestic; well-known; habitual, ordinary, trivial; plain, easily understood.

Fancy: fantasticalness; imaginative conception, flight of imagination; amorous inclination or passion, love; liking, taste.

Fantasy: fancy, imagination; caprice, whim.

Favour: countenance, face; complexion; aspect, appearance; leave, permission, pardon; attraction, charm, good will; *in favour,* benevolently.

Fear (N): dread, apprehension; dreadfulness; object of dread or fear.

Fear (V): be apprehensive or concerned about, mistrust, doubt; frighten, make afraid.

Fearful: exciting or inspiring fear, terrible, dreadful; timorous, apprehensive, full of fear.

Feature: shape or form of body, figure; shapeliness, comeliness.

Fellow: companion; partaker, sharer (of); equal, match; customary form of address to a servant or an inferior (sometimes used contemptuously or condescendingly).

Fine (N): end, conclusion; *in fine:* finally.

Fine (ADJ.): highly accomplished or skillful; exquisitely fashioned, delicate; refined, subtle; frequently the modern sense.

Flaw: fragment; crack, fissure; tempest, squall, gust of wind; outburst of passion.

Flesh: reward a hawk or hound with a piece of flesh of the game killed to excite its eagerness of the chase (Onions); hence to inflame by a foretaste of success; initiate or inure to bloodshed (used for a first time in battle); harden, train.

Flourish: fanfare of trumpets (in stage directions).

Fond: foolish, doting; *fond of:* eager for; also the modern sense.

Fool: term of endearment and pity; frequently the modern sense.

For that, for why: because.

Forfend: forbid, avert.

Free: generous, magnanimous; candid, open; guiltless, innocent.

Front: forehead, face; foremost line of battle; beginning.

Furnish: equip, fit out (furnish forth); endow; dress, decorate, embellish.

G

Gear: apparel, dress; stuff, substance, thing, article; discourse, talk; matter, business, affair.

Get: beget.

Gloss: specious fair appearance; lustrous surface.

Go to: expression of remonstrance, impatience, disapprobation, or derision.

Grace (N): kindness, favor, charm, divine favor; fortune, luck; beneficent virtue; sense of duty or propriety; mercy, pardon; embellish; *do grace:* reflect credit on, do honor to, do a favor for.

Grace (V): gratify, delight; honor, favor.

Groat: coin equal to four pence.

H

Habit: dress, garb, costume; bearing, demeanor, manner; occasionally in the modern sense.

Happily: haply, perchance, perhaps.

Hardly: with difficulty.

Have at: I shall come at (you)(i.e., listen to me), I shall attack (a person or thing); let me at.

Have with: I shall go along with; let me go along with; come along.

Having: possession, property, wealth, estate; endowments, accomplishments.

Head: armed force.

Hind: servant, slave; rustic, boor, clown.

His: its. *His* was historically the possessive form of both the masculine and neuter pronouns. *Its,* although not common in Shakespeare's time, occurs in the plays occasionally.

Holp: helped (archaic past tense).

Home: fully, satisfactorily, thoroughly, plainly, effectually; to the quick.

Honest: holding an honorable position, honorable, respectable; decent, kind, seemly, befitting, proper; chaste; genuine; loosely used as an epithet of approbation.

Humour: mood, temper, cast of mind, temperament, disposition; vagary, fancy, whim; moisture (the literal sense); a physiological, and by transference, a psychological term applied to the four chief fluids of the human body—phlegm, blood, choler, and melancholy (the last also called black choler). A person's disposition and his temporary state of mind were determined according to the relative proportions of these fluids in his body; consequently a person was said to be phlegmatic, sanguine, choleric, or melancholy.

I

Image: likeness; visible form; representation; embodiment, type; mental picture, creation of the imagination.

Influence: supposed flowing from the stars or heavens of an ethereal fluid, acting upon the characters and destinies of men (used metaphorically).

Inform: take shape, give form to, imbue, inspire; instruct, teach; charge (against).

Instance: evidence, proof, sign, confirmation; motive, cause.

Invention: power of mental creation, the creative faculty; work of the imagination, artistic creation, premeditated design; device, plan, scheme.

J

Jar (N): discord in music; quarrel, discord.

Jar (V): be out of tune; be discordant, quarrel.

Jump: agree, tally, coincide, fit exactly; risk, hazard.

K

Keep: continue, carry on; dwell, lodge, guard, defend, care for, employ, be with; restrain, control (refl.); confine in prison.

Kind (N): nature, established order of things; manner, fashion, respect; race, class, kindred, family; *by kind:* naturally.

Kind (ADJ.): natural; favorable; affectionate.

Kindly (ADJ.): natural, appropriate; agreeable; innate; benign.

Kindly (ADV.): naturally; gently, courteously.

L

Large: liberal, bounteous, lavish; free, unrestrained; *at large*, at length, in full; in full detail, as a whole, in general.

Late: lately.

Learn: teach; inform (someone of something); also the modern sense.

Let: hinder.

Level: aim; also shades toward the modern sense.

Liberal: possessed of the characteristics and qualities of gentlemen, genteel, becoming in a gentleman, refined; free in speech; unrestrained by prudence or decorum; licentious.

Lie: be in bed; be still; be confined, be kept in prison; dwell, sojourn, reside, lodge.

Like: please, feel affection; liken, compare.

List (N): strip of cloth, selvedge; limit, boundary; desire.

List (v): choose, desire, please; listen to.

'Long of: owing to, on account of.

Look: power to see; take care, see to it; expect; seek, search for.

M

Make: do; have to do (with); consider; go; be effective, make up, complete; also the modern sense.

Manage: management, conduct, administration; action and paces to which a horse is trained; short gallop at full speed.

Marry: mild interjection equivalent to "Indeed!" Originally an oath by the Virgin Mary.

May: can; also frequently the modern sense to denote probability; *might* has corresponding meanings and uses.

Mean (N): instrument, agency, method (also frequent in the plural); effort; opportunity (for doing something); something interposed or intervening; middle position, medium; tenor or alto parts in singing; money, wealth (usually plural form).

Mean (ADJ.): average, moderate, middle; of low degree, station, or position; undignified, base.

Measure (N): grave or stately dance, graceful motion; tune, melody, musical accompaniment; treatment meted out; moderation, proportion; limit; distance, reach.

Measure (v): judge, estimate; traverse.

Mere: absolute, sheer; pure, unmixed; downright, sincere.

Mew (*up*): coop up (as used of a hawk), shut up, imprison, confine.

Mind (N): thoughts, judgment, opinion, message; purpose, intention, desire; disposition; also the modern sense of the mental faculty.

Mind (v): remind; perceive, notice, attend; intend.

Minion: saucy woman, hussy; follower; favorite, favored person, darling (often used contemptuously).

Misdoubt (N): suspicion.

Misdoubt (v): mistrust, suspect.

Model: pattern, replica, likeness.

Modern: ordinary, commonplace, everyday.

Modest: moderate, marked by moderation, becoming; characterized by decency and propriety; chaste.

Moe: more.

Moiety: half; share; small part, lesser share; portion, part of.

Mortal: fatal; deadly, of or for death; belonging to mankind; human, pertaining to human affairs.

Motion: power of movement; suggestion, proposal; movement of the soul; impulse, prompting; also the modern sense.

Move: make angry; urge, incite, instigate, arouse, prompt; propose, make a proposal to, apply to, appeal to, suggest; also the modern sense.

Muse: wonder, marvel; grumble, complain.

N

Napkin: handkerchief.

Natural: related by blood; having natural or kindly feeling; also the modern sense.

Naught: useless, worthless; wicked, naughty.

Naughty: wicked; good for nothing, worthless.

Nice: delicate; fastidious, dainty, particular, scrupulous; minute, subtle; shy, coy; reluctant, unwilling; unimportant, insignificant, trivial; accurate, precise; wanton, lascivious.

Nothing: not at all.

O

Of: from, away from; during; on; by; as regards; instead of; *out of*, compelled by; made from.

Offer: make an attack; menace; venture, dare, presume.

Opinion: censure; reputation or credit; favorable estimate of oneself; self-conceit, arrogance; self-confidence; public opinion, reputation; also the modern sense.

Or: before; also used conjunctively where no alternative is implied; *or . . . or:* either . . . or; whether . . . or.

Out (ADV.): without, outside; abroad; fully, quite; at an end, finished; at variance, aligned the wrong way.

Out (INTERJ.): an expression of reproach, impatience, indignation, or anger.

Owe: own; also the modern sense.

P

Pack: load; depart, begone; conspire.

Pageant: show, spectacle, spectacular entertainment; device on a moving carriage.

Pain: punishment, penalty; labor, trouble, effort; also frequently the modern sense.

Painted: specious, unreal, counterfeit.

Parle: parley, conference, talk; bugle call for parley.

Part: depart, part from; divide.

Particular: detail; personal interest or concern; details of a private nature; single person.

Party: faction, side, part, cause; partner, ally.

Pass: pass through, traverse; exceed; surpass; pledge.

Passing (ADJ. and ADV.): surpassing, surpassingly, exceedingly.

Passion (N): powerful or violent feeling, violent sorrow or grief; painful affection or disorder of the body; sorrow; feelings or desires of love; passionate speech or outburst.

Passion (v): sorrow, grieve.

Peevish: silly, senseless, childish; perverse, obstinate, stubborn; sullen.

Perforce: by violence or compulsion; forcibly; necessarily.

Physic: medical faculty; healing art, medical treatment; remedy, medicine, healing property.

Pitch: height; specifically, the height to which a falcon soars before stooping on its prey (often used figuratively).

Policy: conduct of affairs (especially public affairs); prudent management; stratagem, trick; contrivance; craft, cunning.

Port: bearing, demeanor; state, style of living, social station; gate.

Possess: have or give possession or command (of something); inform, acquaint; also the modern sense.

Post (N): courier, messenger; post-horse; haste.

Post (v): convey swiftly; hasten, ignore through haste (with *over* or *off*).

Practice: execution; exercise (especially for instruction); stratagem, intrigue; conspiracy, plot, treachery.

Practise: perform, take part in; use stratagem, craft, or artifice; scheme, plot; play a joke on.

Pregnant: resourceful; disposed, inclined; clear, obvious.

Present (ADJ.): ready, immediate, prompt, instant.

Present (v): represent.

Presently: immediately, at once.

Prevent: forestall, anticipate, foresee; also the modern sense.

Process: drift, tenor, gist; narrative, story; formal command, mandate.

Proof: test, trial, experiment; experience; issue, result; proved or tested strength of armor or arms; also the modern sense.

Proper: (one's or its) own; peculiar, exclusive; excellent; honest, respectable; handsome, elegant, fine, good-looking.

Proportion: symmetry; size; form, carriage, appearance, shape; portion, allotment; rhythm.

Prove: make trial of; put to test; show or find out by experience.

Purchase (N): acquisition; spoil, booty.

Purchase (v): acquire, gain, obtain; strive, exert oneself; redeem, exempt.

Q

Quaint: skilled, clever; pretty, fine, dainty; handsome, elegant; carefully or ingeniously wrought or elaborated.

Quality: that which constitutes (something); essential being; good natural gifts; accomplishment, attainment, property; art, skill; rank, position; profession, occupation, business; party, side; manner, style; cause, occasion.

Quick: living (used substantively to mean "living flesh"); alive; lively, sharp, piercing; hasty, impatient; with child.

Quillets: verbal niceties, subtle distinctions.

Quit: requite, reward; set at liberty; acquit, remit; pay for, clear off.

R

Rack (v): stretch or strain beyond normal extent or capacity to endure; strain oneself; distort.

Rage (N): madness, insanity; vehement pain; angry disposition; violent passion or appetite; poetic enthusiasm; warlike ardor or fury.

Rage (v): behave wantonly or riotously; act with fury or violence; enrage; pursue furiously.

Range: extend or lie in the same plane (with); occupy a position; rove, roam; be inconstant; traverse.

Rank: coarsely luxuriant; puffed up, swollen, fat, abundant; full, copious; rancid; lustful; corrupt, foul.

Rate (N): estimate; value or worth; estimation, consideration; standard, style.

Rate (v): allot; calculate, estimate, compute; reckon, consider; be of equal value (with); chide, scold, berate; drive away by chiding or scolding.

Recreant: traitor, coward, cowardly wretch.

Remorse: pity, compassion; also the modern sense.

Remove: removal, absence; period of absence; change.

Resolve: dissolve, melt, dissipate; answer; free from doubt or uncertainty, convince; inform; decide; also the modern sense.

Respect (N): consideration, reflection, act of seeing, view; attention, notice; decency, modest deportment; also the modern sense.

Respect (v): esteem, value, prize; regard, consider; heed, pay attention to; also the modern sense.

Round: spherical; plain, direct, brusque; fair; honest.

Roundly: plainly, unceremoniously.

Rub: obstacle (a term in the game of bowls); unevenness; inequality.

S

Sack: generic term for Spanish and Canary wines; sweet white wine.

Sad: grave, serious; also the modern sense.

Sadness: seriousness; also the modern sense.

Sans: without (French preposition).

Scope: object, aim, limit; freedom, license; free play.

Seal: bring to completion or conclusion, conclude, confirm, ratify, stamp; also the modern sense.

Sennet: a series of notes sounded on a trumpet to herald the approach or departure of a procession (used in stage directions).

Sense: mental faculty, mind; mental perception, import, rational meaning; physical perception; sensual nature; *common sense:* ordinary or untutored perception, observation or knowledge.

Sensible: capable of physical feeling or perception, sensitive; capable of or exhibiting emotion; rational; capable of being perceived.

Serve: be sufficient; be favorable; succeed; satisfy the need for; serve a turn; answer the purpose.

Several: separate, distinct, different; particular, private; various.

Shadow: shade, shelter; reflection; likeness, image; ghost; representation, picture of the imagination, phantom; also the modern sense.

Shift: change; stratagem, strategy, trick, contrivance, device to serve a purpose; *make shift*, manage.

Shrewd: malicious, mischievous, ill-natured; shrewish; bad, of evil import, grievous; severe.

Sirrah: ordinary or customary form of address to inferiors or servants; disrespectful form of address.

Sith: since.

Smock: woman's undergarment; used typically for "a woman."

Something: somewhat.

Sometime: sometimes, from time to time; once, formerly; at times, at one time.

Speed (N): fortune, success; protecting and assisting power; also the modern sense.

Speed (V): fare (well or ill); succeed; be successful; assist, guard, favor.

Spleen: the seat of emotions and passions; violent passion; fiery temper; malice; anger, rage; impulse, fit of passion; caprice; impetuosity.

Spoil: destruction, ruin; plunder; slaughter, massacre.

Starve: die of cold or hunger; be benumbed with cold; paralyze, disable; allow or cause to die.

State: degree, rank; social position, station; pomp, splendor, outward display, clothes; court, household of a great person; shades into the modern sense.

Stay: wait, wait for; sustain; stand; withhold, withstand; stop.

Stead: assist; be of use to, benefit, help.

Still: always, ever, continuously or continually, constant or constantly; silent, mute; also modern senses.

Stomach: appetite, inclination, disposition; resentment; angry temper, resentful feeling; proud spirit, courage.

Straight: immediately.

Strange: belonging to another country or person, foreign, unfriendly; new, fresh; ignorant; estranged.

Success: issue, outcome (good or bad); sequel, succession, descent (as from father to son).

Suggest: tempt; prompt; seduce.

Suggestion: temptation.

T

Table: memorandum, tablet; surface on which something is written or drawn.

Take: strike; bewitch; charm; infect; destroy; repair to for refuge; modern senses.

Tall: goodly, fine; strong in fight, valiant.

Target: shield.

Tax: censure, blame, accuse.

Tell: count; relate.

Thorough: through.

Throughly: thoroughly.

Toward: in preparation; forthcoming, about to take place.

Toy: trifle, idle fancy; folly.

Train: lure, entice, allure, attract.

Trencher: wooden dish or plate.

Trow: think, suppose, believe; know.

U

Undergo: undertake, perform; modern sense.

Undo: ruin.

Unfold: disclose, tell, make known, reveal; communicate.

Unhappy: evil, mischievous; fatal, ill-fated; miserable.

Unjust: untrue, dishonest; unjustified, groundless; faithless, false.

Unkind: unnatural, cruel, faulty; cf. *kind.*

Use (N): custom, habit; interest paid.

Use (V): make practice of; be accustomed; put out at interest.

V

Vail: lower, let fall.

Vantage: advantage; opportunity; benefit, profit; superiority.

Virtue: general excellence; valor, bravery; merit, goodness, honor; good accomplishment, excellence in culture; power; essence, essential part.

W

Want: lack; be in need of; be without.

Watch: be awake, lie awake, sit up at night, lose sleep; keep from sleep (trans.).

Weed: garment, clothes.

Welkin: sky, heavens.

Wink: close the eyes; close the eyes in sleep; have the eyes closed; seem not to see.

Withal: with; with it, this, or these; together with this; at the same time.

Wot: know.

LIST OF EDITORS, EDITIONS, TEXTUAL CRITICS, AND COMMENTATORS

REFERRED TO IN THE FOOTNOTES TO THE TEXT BUT NOT ENTERED IN THE INDEX:

R. M. Alden (1873-1924)
Arden Edition (Methuen, London)
Arden Edition (Heath, New York)
H. C. Beeching (1859-1919)
Sir William Blackstone (1723-1780)
F. S. Boas
R. W. Bond (1857-1943)
James Boswell (1778-1822)
Sir Denys Bray
W. O. Brigstock
C. F. Tucker Brooke (1883-1946)
Carleton Brown (1869-1941)
Thomas Caldecott (1744-1833)
Cambridge Edition
Edward Capell (1713-1781)
R. H. Case (1857-1944)
Clarendon Press Edition
Charlotte Clark
William George Clark (1821-1878)
Charles Cowden Clarke (1789-1877)
John Payne Collier (1789-1883)
J. Churton Collins (1848-1908)
R. P. Cowl
W. J. Craig (1843-1906)
W. L. Cross (1862-1948)
Henry Cuningham
P. A. Daniel (*fl.* 1870-1877)
Kenneth Deighton
Nikolaus Delius (1813-1888)
Edward Dowden (1843-1913)
W. H. Durham
Alexander Dyce (1798-1869)
Friedrich Karl Elze (1821-1889)
A. H. R. Fairchild
Richard Farmer (1735-1779)
A. Feuillerat
H. H. Furness (1833-1912)
F. J. Furnivall (1825-1910)
Allison Gaw
Globe Edition
Sir Israel Gollancz (1849-1930)
G. S. Gordon
Zachery Grey (1688-1766)
J. W. Hales (1836-1914)
J. O. Halliwell (-Phillipps) (1820-1889)
Sir Thomas Hanmer (1677-1746)
H. C. Hart
Benjamin Heath (1704-1766)
W. E. Henley (1849-1903)
C. H. Herford (1853-1931)
H. N. Hudson (1814-1886)
William Hughes
Joseph Hunter (1783-1861)
C. M. Ingleby (1823-1886)
Alfred Jackson
Charles Jennens (1700-1773)
I. B. John
Dr. Samuel Johnson (1709-1784)
Thomas Keightley (1789-1872)

William Kenrick (1725?-1779)
F. W. Kilbourne
G. Kinnaer
G. L. Kittredge (1860-1941)
Charles Knight (1791-1873)
Richard Koppel (*fl.* 1877-1919)
Ida Langton
W. W. Lawrence
Sir Sidney Lee (1859-1926)
W. N. Lettsom (1796-1865)
Harold Littledale (1853-1930)
W. W. Lloyd (1813-1899)
Morton Luce (1849-1943)
Edmund Malone (1741-1812)
F. A. Marshall (1840-1889)
John Monck Mason (1726-1809)
John Mitford (1781-1859)
G. C. Moore-Smith (1858-1940)
F. W. Moorman
Robert Nares (1753-1829)
W. A. Neilson (1869-1946)
New Cambridge Edition
A. G. Newcomer (1864-1913)
Brinsley Nicholson (1824-1892)
C. T. Onions (*Shakespeare Glossary*)
N. B. Paradise
T. M. Parrott
Bishop Thomas Percy (1729-1811)
C. Knox Pooler
Alexander Pope (1688-1744)
William Ridgeway (1853-1926)
W. J. Rolfe (1827-1910)
Hyder E. Rollins
Nicholas Rowe (1674-1718)
Alexander Schmidt (*Shakespeare Lexicon*)
George Sewell (*fl.* 1725)
S. W. Singer (1783-1858)
J. C. Smith (b. 1867)
James Spedding (1808-1881)
Howard Staunton (1810-1874)
George Steevens (1736-1800)
Mrs. C. C. Stopes
Lewis Theobald (1688-1744)
Styan Thirlby (1686?-1753)
T. G. Tucker
Tudor Edition
Thomas Tyler (1826-1902)
Thomas Tyrwhit (1730-1785)
John Upton (1707-1760)
H. H. Vaughan
A. W. Verity (1863-1927)
Sidney Walker (1795-1846)
Bishop William Warburton (1698-1779)
Richard Grant White (1822-1885)
John Dover Wilson
W. A. Wright (1836?-1914)
George Wyndham (1863-1913)
Yale Edition

1311

INDEX

The letter n *following a reference indicates a footnote*

A

Aaron, a Moor, beloved of Tamora (*Tit. And.*), 368, 374 n., 376 n., 377 n., 380 n.

Abbott, E. A. (1808–1882), grammarian, 61, 104 n., 169 n., 212 n., 218 n., 221 n., 229 n., 247 n., 255 n., 347 n., 349 n., 362 n., 477 n., 478 n., 481 n., 482 n., 483 n., 808 n., 839 n., 865 n., 1175 n.

A B C book, 73

Abercrombie, L. (1881–1938), poet and critic, 41 n.

Abergavenny, Lord (*Hen. VIII*), 1278 n.

Abhorson, an executioner (*Meas. Meas.*), 852 n.

Accius (b. 170 B.C.), Roman tragic poet, 48

Acheron, 197 n., 386 n., 1060 n.

Acheson, Arthur, 101 n.

Achilles, Grecian prince (*T. and C.*), 226 n., 266 n., 625 n., 864, 869 n., 871 n., 873 n., 876 n., 883 n., 884 n., 890 n.

Achilles Tatius (4th c. A.D.), Greek romance writer, 23

Actaeon, 376 n., 567 n., 619 n.

Actium, 1100 n.

Actors, companies of, 30; *see also under various companies and* Theaters and theatrical practices

Adam, servant to Orlando (*A.Y.L.*), 71, 588–589

Adams, Joseph Quincy (1881–1946), Shakespeare scholar, author *Life of Shakespeare*, 32–33, 51 and n., 72, 74, 101, 206 and n., 367 and n., 463 n., 737 n., 899 n., 980 n., 1043 n.

Admiral's Servants, The Lord, 28, 31, 34, 65, 77, 155 n., 368, 499, 587, 674

Adriana, wife to Antipholus of Ephesus (*Com. Er.*), 81–82, 89 n., 97 n.

Ægeon, a merchant of Syracuse (*Com. Er.*), 81–82, 99 n.

Æmilia, wife to Ægeon, abbess at Ephesus (*Com. Er.*), 81–82, 97 n.

Æneas, Trojan commander (*T. and C.*), 885 n.

Aeneas and Dido, story of, 187 n., 255 n., 918 n., 1101 n., 1197 n., 1256 n.

Aeschylus (525–456 B.C.), Greek tragic dramatist, 48, 1045, 1217

Aesculapius, god of medicine, 570 n., 1168 n.

Aesop (*fl.* 6th c. B.C.), Greek fabulist, 297 n., 900, 1120 n.

Africa, 1098 n., 1118 n.

Agamemnon, lost play, 862

Agamemnon, the Grecian general (*T. and C.*), 717 n., 863–864, 869 n.

Agincourt, Battle of, 737, 760 n.

Ainley, Henry, actor, 772

Ajax, Grecian prince (*T. and C.*), 115 n., 266 n., 373 n., 863, 873 n., 875 n., 883 n., 884 n., 889 n., 994 n., 1101 n., 1204 n.

Alabaster, William (1567–1640), English Latin poet, author *Roxana*, 28

Alarbus, son to Tamora (*Tit. And.*), 368

Albany, Duke of (*Lear*), 982, 992 n., 1006 n.

Albright, Evelyn M. (b. 1880), scholar, 737 n.

Albumazar, 1038

Alciatus, Andrea (1492–1550), Italian emblem writer, 1050 n.

Alcibiades, an Athenian captain (*Timon*), 1017–1018, 1027 n., 1031 n.

Aldridge, Ira (1805?–1867), actor, 369

Aleppo, 979 n., 1047 n.

Alexander, Peter, 33 n., 154 n., 208 n., 1272 and n.

Alexander, Sir William (1567–1640), poet and dramatist, *Julius Caesar*, 771; *The Tragedie of Darius*, 1247

Alexander the Great, 126 n., 740 n., 762 n., 770 n., 1145 n., 1190 n.

Alice, lady attending on Princess Katharine (*Hen. V*), 750 n. ff.

Alleyn, Edward (1566–1626), actor, 28, 31–32

All Saints' Day or Hallowmas, 563 n., 669 n., 679 n., 840 n.

All Souls' Day, 334 n.

All's Well that Ends Well, 39, 53, 154–155, 213 n., 283 n., 472 n., 482 n., 802–805, **805–833,** 862; date and publication, 803–804, 833–834; interpretation, 804–805; source, 803–804.

Althaea, 241 n., 713 n.

Amamon, a demon, 688 n.

Ambassador, English (*Ham.*), 901

Amiens, lord attending on the banished Duke (*A.Y.L.*), 586, 588

Amiens, Treaty of, 218 n.

Amyot, Jacques (1513–1593), translator of Plutarch's *Lives* into French, 770

Anderson, Judith, actress, 1046

Anderson, Mary Antoinette (1859–1940), actress, 57, 589, 1217

Andrew Aguecheek, Sir (*12th Night*), 617, 620 n., 621 n., 626 n., 628 n.

Angelo, the Duke's deputy (*Meas. Meas.*), 833–834, 837 n., 839 n., 844 n., 845 n., 850 n., 851 n., 856 n., 857 n.

Anglin, Margaret, actress, 156

Anne, Lady, widow of Edward Prince of Wales, son to Henry VI, afterwards married to Richard III (*Rich. III*), 302, 304 n.

Anne Bullen, maid of honor to Queen Katharine, afterwards Queen (*Hen. VIII*), 1271, 1273, 1291 n.

Anne of Bohemia, first queen to Richard II, 644

Anne Page, daughter to Mistress Page (*Mer. Wives*), 559–560

Antichrist, 18

Antigonus, a Lord of Sicilia (*W.T.*), 1226 n., 1230 n.

Antiochus, King of Antioch (*Per.*), 1158 n., 1159 n.

Antipholus of Ephesus, twin brother to Antipholus of Syracuse, son to Ægeon and Æmilia (*Com. Er.*), 80, 82, 89 n.

Antipholus of Syracuse, twin brother to Antipholus of Ephesus, son to Ægeon and Æmilia (*Com. Er.*), 80, 82, 88 n.

Anti-Semitism, 502–504, 526 n.

Antonio, a merchant of Venice (*Mer. Ven.*), 6, 45, 502–505, 510 n., 526 n.

Antonio, brother to Leonato (*Much Ado*), 532, 555 n.

Antonio, Don, pretender to the Portuguese crown, 502

Antonius, Marcus, a triumvir after the death of Julius Caesar (*J.C., Ant. and Cleo.*), 45, 56, 770–772, 773 n., 785 n., 786 n., 788 n., 796 n., 1071–1073, 1074 n., 1077 n., 1078 n., 1079 n., 1081 n., 1082 n., 1083 n., 1085 n., 1087 n., 1088 n., 1089 n., 1090 n., 1091 n., 1092 n., 1093 n., 1094 n., 1096 n., 1097 n., 1102 n., 1105 n., 1107 n.

Chambers, R. W. (1874–1942), author *The Jacobean Shakespeare and Measure for Measure* (1938), 834 n.

Chancellor, Lord (*Hen. VIII*), 1300 n.

Chapel Royal, Children of the, 18, 22, 30–31, 797, 901, 918 n.

Chapman, George (1559?–1634), dramatist and poet, 5, 31, 73, 101, 107 n., 425, 477 n., 486 n., 497, 556 n., 797, 799, 981, 1017, 1148–1149, 1152; *All Fools*, 800; *The Blind Beggar of Alexandria*, 500; *Bussy D'Ambois*, 1152; *Caesar and Pompey*, 1152; *Charles Duke of Biron*, 1152; *An Humourous Day's Mirth*, 500; *Iliad*, 863 and n., 864; *May Day*, 1256 n.; *Revenge of Bussy D'Ambois*, 1152; *Shadow of Night*, 101, 486 n.; *Widow's Tears*, 1256 n.

Chappell, William (1809–1888), musical antiquary, author *Popular Music of the Olden Time*, 113 n., 613 n.

Charlemagne, 741 n.

Charles, wrestler to Frederick (*A.Y.L.*), 587, 592 n.

Charles I, king of Great Britain (reigned 1625–1649), 1181

Charles II, king of Great Britain (reigned 1660–1685), 66

Charlton, H. B., 505 n.

Charmian, attendant on Cleopatra (*Ant. and Cleo.*), 1073, 1074 n.

Charon, 310 n., 880 n.

Charron, Pierre (1541–1603), theologian and philosopher, author *Of Wisdom*, 277 n., 807 n., 844 n.

Chatham, Clerk of (*2 Hen. VI*), 209

Chaucer, Geoffrey (1345?–1400), poet, 6, 12, 42, 45, 47, 498, 587; *Clerk's Tale*, 167 n.; *Hous of Fame*, 375 n.; *The Knight's Tale*, 65, 183; *Legend of Good Women*, 439; *Nun's Priest's Tale*, 6, 1226 n.; *Tale of the Wife of Bath*, 162 n.; *Troilus and Creseyde*, 527 n., 863–864

Chester, religious drama at, 16

Chester, Robert (1566?–1640?), poet, author *Love's Martyr*, 458

Chettle, Henry (1560?–1607), dramatist, 31, 425, 500, 587, 644; *Hoffman*, 800; *Kind-Hart's Dream*, 76–77, 425

Chief Justice of the King's Bench, Lord (*2 Hen. IV*), 709 n., 732 n., 734 n.

Child, Francis J. (1825–1896), scholar, author *English and Scottish Popular Ballads*, 626 n.

Children of Paul's, The, 18, 22, 31, 44, 65, 78, 797, 900

Chorus (*Hen. V*), 736, 738, 739 n., 743 n., 756 n., 764 n.

Churchill, G. B. (1866–1925), American scholar, 300 n., 326 n., 616 n.

"Churlish" Priest (*Ham.*), 899

Cibber, Colley (1671–1757), actor and dramatist, 210, 301, 772, 834, 903; *Richard III*, 40; *Papal Tyranny in the Reign of King John*, 341

Cibber, Susannah Maria (1714–1766), actress, 57, 395

Cibber, Theophilus (1703–1758), actor and supposed author *The Lives of the Poets*, 70

Cicero, Marcus Tullius (106–43 B.C.), Roman statesman, orator, and philosopher (*J.C.*), 11, 73, 260 n., 770, 779 n., 981; *De divinatione*, 245 n.; *De officiis*, 259 n.; *De oratore*, 383 n., 738

Cinqueports, 1295 n.

Circe, 98 n., 234 n.

Citizen, First (*Cor.*), 1110

Clark, Charlotte, editor of Shakespeare (with Helen Porter), 54

Claudio, a young gentleman (*Meas. Meas.*), 833–834, 837 n., 841 n., 846 n.

Claudio, a young lord of Florence (*Much Ado*), 531–532, 545 n., 549 n., 551 n., 555 n.

Claudius, king of Denmark (*Ham.*), 901, 920 n., 927 n.

Clemens, S. L. [Mark Twain] (1835–1910), humorist and man of letters, 73

Cleon, governor of Tarsus (*Per.*), 1169 n.

Cleopatra, queen of Egypt (*Ant. and Cleo.*), 56, 770, 863, 1071–1073, 1074 n., 1076 n., 1077 n., 1078 n., 1079 n., 1082 n., 1084 n., 1085 n., 1091 n., 1092 n., 1095 n., 1096 n., 1100 n., 1104 n., 1105 n., 1106 n., 1107 n.

Clifford, Lord (*2 and 3 Hen. VI*), 208, 270 n.

Clifford, Young, son to Lord Clifford (*2 Hen. VI*), 270 n.

Clive, Kitty (1711–1785), actress, 57

Clopton, Sir Hugh (d. 1496), lord mayor of London, 71

Cloten, son to the Queen by a former husband (*Cymb.*), 1180. 1186 n., 1191 n., 1194 n., 1199 n., 1202 n., 1203 n.

Clown, A (*Ant. and Cleo.*), 1073

Clown, servant to Countess of Roussillon (*All's Well*), 805

Clowns and jesters, 98 n., 132, 194 n., 351 n., 588, 598 n., 617, 621 n., 630 n., 676, 744 n., 805, 922 n., 936 n., 1054 n., 1107 n.

Cobham, Henry Brooke, eighth lord (d. 1619), 425, 674, 736 n.

Cockpit, The, playhouse, 739 n., 946

Coghlan, Charles, actor, 1073

Coghlan, Rose (1853–1932), actress, 589

Cohen, Gustave, 29 n.

Cohn, A. (1827–1905), author *Shakespeare in Germany*, 56 n.

Coins and coining, *see* Money

Colbrand the giant, 344 n., 1302 n.

Coleridge, Samuel Taylor (1772–1834), poet and critic, author *Lectures upon Shakespeare and other Dramatists* and *Notes and Lectures upon Shakespeare*, 41–42, 426, 532 and n., 646, 649 n., 651 n., 654 n., 656 n., 660 n., 803, 902, 926 n., 946, 953 n., 979 n.

Coligny, Gaspard de (1519–1572), French admiral, 981

Collatinus (*Lucrece*), 440, 443 n., 497

Collier, Constance, actress, 1073

Collier, John Payne (1787–1883), Shakespeare editor, 54, 901, 1154

Colossus of Rhodes, 774 n., 894 n., 896 n.

Colyngborne, William, executed by Richard III, 308 n.

Combe, John (*fl.* 1602–1614), Stratford citizen, 798, 1149

Combe, Thomas (*fl.* 1616), Stratford citizen, 1150

Combe, William (*fl.* 1602–1614), Stratford citizen, 798, 1149

Comedy, 25, 81–82, 99 n., 102 and n., 131, 501, 558–559, 612 n., 615–616, 618, 686 n., 763 n., 863

Comedy of Errors, The, 22, 34, 37, 39, 44, 53, 74, 77–78, 80–82, **82-100**, 83 n., 84 n., 85 n., 89 n., 615, 798, 800; date and publication, 80, 91 n.; interpretation, 81–82; sources, 80–82; stage history, 82 (*'Tis All a Mistake*), 82 (*The Boys from Syracuse*); style, 80

Cominius, general against the Volscians (*Cor.*), 1121 n.

Condell, Henry, *see* Heminges, John and Henry Condell.

Conklin, Paul S., 899 n.

De la Mothe, French ambassador to Queen Elizabeth, 101
Del Conte de Poitiers, 1180
Delius, Nikolaus (1813–1888), German Shakespeare scholar, 54, 56
Della Porta, Giambattista (1535–1615), dramatist, *Gli Duoi Fratelli Rivali*, 531, 540 n.
Delphi, 1227 n.
Demetrius, matched with Helena (*Mids. Dr.*), 183–184
Demonology, *see* Magic
Demosthenes (384?–322 B.C.), Athenian orator and statesman, 770
Dennis, John (1657–1734), critic, author *The Invasion of his Country*, 1111
Denny, C. F., 206 and n.
De Quincey, Thomas (1785–1859), critic and miscellaneous writer, 41
Derby, William Stanley, sixth earl of (1561–1642), 71, 101, 182
Derby's Servants, The Earl of, 31, 33
Desdemona, daughter of Brabantio and wife of Othello (*Oth.*), 64, 944–946, 949 n., 973 n., 975 n., 976 n.
Deucalion, 1121 n., 1237 n.
Devonshire, Charles Blount, eighth Lord Mountjoy, earl of (1563–1606), 71
Devrient, Gustav Emil (1803–1872), German actor, 58
Devrient, Ludwig (1784–1832), German actor, 58
De Witt, Johannes (*fl.* 1596), Dutch traveler, 28
Diana, 114 n., 167 n., 187 n., 294 n., 372 n., 376 n., 414 n., 529 n., 549 n., 600 n., 605 n., 608 n., 898 n., 984 n., 1043, 1101 n., 1156 n., 1166 n.
Dicey, C., printer, 367
Digges, Leonard (1588–1635), poet and translator, 47, 530, 618
Dighton, John, murderer of the little princes, 327 n.
Diomedes, Grecian prince (*T. and C.*), 864, 885 n., 894 n.
Dion Cassius (155–230?), historian of Rome, 787 n.
Dionyza, wife to Cleon (*Per.*), 1169 n.
Doctor Caius, a French physician (*Mer. Wives*), 559–560
Dogberry, a constable (*Much Ado*), 51, 56, 104 n., 532, 552 n., 797
Donalbain, son to Duncan (*Macb.*), 1053 n.
Don John, bastard brother of Don Pedro (*Much Ado*), 532, 536 n., 540 n., 549 n.
Don Pedro, Prince of Arragon (*Much Ado*), 542 n., 553 n., 554 n.
Donwald, Scottish nobleman, 1044
Doran, Madeleine, 206 n., 208 n., 980 n.
Dorset, Marquis of, son to the Queen (*Rich. III*), 331 n.
Douce, Francis (1757–1834), antiquary, *Illustrations of Shakespeare* (1807), 90 n., 661 n., 931 n.
Douglas, Archibald, Earl of (*1 Hen. IV*), 705 n.
Dowdall, John (*fl.* 1693), traveler, 75
Dowden, Edward (1843–1913), Shakespeare critic and editor, 39, 41, 802, 863, 1072, 1152 and n., 1179 and n., 1248 and n.
Dowland, John (1563–1626?), lutanist and composer, 460 n.
Downes, John (*fl.* 1662–1710), writer on the stage, author *Roscius Anglicanus*, 1272
Drake, Nathan (1766–1836), author *Shakespeare and his Times*, 469
Drama: choruses, 737, 739 n., 924 n., 1231 n.;

chronicle, or history play, 33, 339, 738; *commedia dell'arte*, 1247; continental influences, 17–18, 55–56; construction or form, 20, 30, 604 n.; conventions: (acting), 41–42, 45–46, 954 n.; (asides), 621 n., 1186 n.; (battles), 760 n., 793 n.; (calumniator believed), 970 n.; (*deux ex machina*), 834; (marriage), 1216; (mixtures of comic and tragic), 763 n.; (plays within plays), 918 n.; (traitors self-convicted), 745 n.; (women's parts played by boys), 42, 1106 n.; court, 8, 21, 798, 1237 n.; Elizabethan, 13, 17–19, 27, 54, 77–79, 82, 500–501, 800–801, 1155, 1179; epic quality, 24, 868 n., 1244 n.; Germany, English drama in, 55–56, 900–901; humors, comedy of 500, 588–589, 617; indifference to dramatic reputation, 497–498; length of plays, 396 n.; masques, 8, 1023 n., 1209 n., 1265 n.; morality plays and interludes, 16–18, 29, 317 n., 638 n., 687 n., 723 n., 761 n., 921 n., 927 n., 993 n.; mystery and miracle plays, 14–17, 921 n., 1054 n., 1074 n., 1180; opposition, religious and moral, 26–28; patronage, 31, 425, 1017; pirate actor, 899; popular plays, 184, 688 n., 716 n., 734 n., 1155, 1217; printing of plays, 51–54; prologues and epilogues, 615 n., 865 n., 1231 n., 1270 n., 1271; prompt copy or stage version, 49–50, 393, 420 n., 736, 943; puppet plays and folk drama, 137 n., 849 n., 1106 n., 1120 n., 1233 n.; Senecan, or neo-classical, 18–21, 23, 300, 367, 771, 900–901, 919 n., 1073; soliloquies, 45–46, 621 n., 679 n., 1196 n.; stenography, 51, 979, 980 and n.; suspense, 20–21; texts of plays, 49–51; time and place, 20, 42, 45, 553 n., 850 n.; tragi-comedy, 1148, 1155; traveling players, 55, 154, 921 n., 922 n.; vaudeville element, 46, 401 n., 421 n., 680 n., 700 n., 701 n., 718 n., 719 n., 726 n., 727 n., 731 n., 921 n.; War of the Theatres, 31, 797, 862, 916 n.
Dramata Sacra (1547), 18
Draper, John W., 182 n.
Drayton, Michael (1563–1631), poet, 31, 34, 45, 65, 73, 497, 644, 653 n., 799, 1150; *Endimion and Phoebe*, 426, 674; *Merry Devil of Edmonton* (attributed authorship), 500–501
Dreams, *see* Popular beliefs
Dress, fashions in, 5, 42, 188 n., 407 n., 508 n., 526 n., 535 n., 538 n., 546 n., 547 n., 552 n., 554 n., 572 n., 574 n., 595 n., 596 n., 598 n., 621 n., 627 n., 629 n., 630 n., 686 n., 695 n., 735 n., 754 n., 773 n., 781 n., 906 n., 913 n., 918 n., 923 n., 924 n., 931 n., 1046, 1283 n., 1294 n., 1295 n.
Dromio of Ephesus, twin brother of Dromio of Syracuse, servant of Antipholus of Ephesus (*Com. Er.*), 81–82, 89 n., 100 n.
Dromio of Syracuse, twin brother of Dromio of Ephesus, servant to Antipholus of Syracuse (*Com. Er.*), 81–82, 84 n., 88 n., 95 n., 100 n.
Drury Lane Theatre, 57, 369, 618, 738, 946, 1018, 1073
Dryden, John (1631–1700), poet, dramatist, and critic, 40, 63, 74, 801, 1252 n.; *All for Love*, 40, 1073; *Of Dramatick Poesie*, 40; *The Tempest*, 1249; *Troilus and Cressida; or, Truth Found too Late*, 864
Duchess of Gloucester (*Rich. II*), 649 n., 657 n.
Duchess of York (*Rich. II*), 670 n.
Duchess of York, mother to Edward IV (*Rich. III*), 324 n., 325 n., 329 n., 330 n.
Dueling, fencing, and combat, 5, 396 n., 397 n., 406 n., 410 n., 554 n., 605 n., 611 n., 614 n., 635 n., 640 n., 649 n., 650 n., 652 n., 687 n., 694 n., 912 n., 934 n., 935 n., 940 n., 941 n., 942 n.,

Famous Victories of Henry V, The, anonymous drama, 44, 675, 679 n., 709 n., 732 n., 737

Farrand, Margaret L., 184 n.

Fastolfe, Sir John (*1 Hen. VI*), 207, 212 n., 674, 720 n.

Fate, *see* Cosmology

Fates, The, 204 n., 717 n., 765 n.

Faucit, Helen [Lady Martin] (1817–1898), actress, 57, 589, 1046, 1181

Faulconbridge, Philip, bastard son to Richard Coeur-de-Lion (*K. John*), 339–341, 343 n., 360 n.

Faulconbridge, Robert, son to Sir Robert Faulconbridge (*K. John*), 342 n.

Faust-Book (1587), 847 n.

Faversham, William (1868–1940), actor, 772, 946

Felix and Philiomena, lost play, 132

Fenner, Dudley (1558?–1587), Puritan divine, 12

Fenton, a gentleman (*Mer. Wives*), 559–560

Ferdinand, king of Navarre (*L.L.L.*), 101–102, 108 n.

Ferdinand, son to the king of Naples (*Temp.*), 1152

Feste, a clown (*12th Night*), 51, 56, 617, 621 n., 622 n., 625 n., 627 n., 637 n., 638 n., 639 n., 797

Fiction, 21–23, 25, 44–45, 394, 501–503, 531, 538 n., 556–557, 586–588, 803–804, 833, 901, 943–944, 982–983, 1153–1154, 1179–1180, 1216–1217; French, 101, 530–531, 618–619, 901; Greek, 22–23, 45, 394, 504, 640 n., 1148, 1153–1154, 1216; Italian, 45, 394, 501, 503, 530–531, 618–619, 803, 833, 1180

Field, Nathan (1587–1619?), actor and dramatist, 946, 1017, 1151–1152

Field, Richard (*fl.* 1590–1600), printer, 76, 425, 439

Fielding, Henry (1707–1754), novelist and playwright, author *Tom Jones*, 903

Finsbury, archery ground outside Moorgate, 693 n.

Fischer, Rudolf, 300 n.

Fitton, Mary (*fl.* 1600), maid of honor to Queen Elizabeth, 470

Flavius, a tribune (*J.C.*), 771

Flavius, steward to Timon (*Timon*), 1018, 1027 n.

Fleance, son to Banquo (*Macb.*), 1043, 1059 n., 1062 n.

Fleay, F. G. (1831–1909), Shakespeare scholar, 39, 477 n., 862, 900 and n., 1153 n., 1272

Fletcher, John, *see* Beaumont and Fletcher

Fletcher, Laurence (*fl.* 1595–1608), actor, 798

Florence, 810 n., 947 n., 960 n.

Florio, John (1553?–1625), translator of Montaigne, 802, 1257 n.

Florizel, Prince of Bohemia (*W.T.*), 1152, 1216, 1234 n.

Flowers, 191 n., 199 n., 420 n., 932 n., 933 n., 1169 n., 1190 n., 1233 n., 1234 n.

Fluellen (*Hen. V*), 737, 750 n., 753 n.

Folger Shakespeare Library, 55

Folklore, *see* Popular beliefs

Fontanne, Lynn, actress, 156

Fool (*K. Lear*), 56, 797, 982, 991 n., 1003 n.

Fools, *see* Clowns and jesters

Forbes-Robertson, Sir Johnston (1853–1937), actor, 57, 532, 903, 942 n., 946, 1217, 1273

Ford, a gentleman dwelling at Windsor (*Mer. Wives*), 558, 560

Ford, John (1586?–1639?), dramatist, 10

Ford, Mistress (*Mer. Wives*), 559–560

Fordun, John (d. 1385?), Latin chronicler of Scotland, 1044

Forman, Simon (1552–1611), astrologer, quack-

doctor, and diarist, 644, 1043 and n., 1179, 1215–1216

Forrest, Edwin (1806–1872), actor, 57, 301, 946, 982, 1111

Forrest, Miles, murderer of the princes (*Rich. III*), 327 n.

Fort, J. A., 469–470, 471 n., 488 n.

Fortinbras, prince of Norway (*Ham.*), 301, 901, 1017

Fortune, *see* Cosmology

Fortune, The, playhouse, 28

Foxe, John (1516–1587), martyrologist, *Acts and Monuments*, 44, 1272, 1291 n., 1300 n., 1302 n.

France, 2, 5–6, 12, 20, 29, 56, 58, 63, 69, 101, 339–340, 406 n., 508 n., 565 n., 572 n., 616, 620 n., 631 n., 655 n., 748 n., 749 n., 759 n., 760 n., 761 n., 767 n., 768 n., 769 n., 770, 863, 901, 944, 981, 1043, 1046, 1071, 1187, 1278 n., 1279 n.

France, King of (*All's Well*), 803–805, 808 n., 811 n., 812 n.

Francis I, king of France (reigned 1515–1547), 1274 n.

Francisco, a lord (*Temp.*), 1256 n.

Fraunce, Abraham (*fl.* 1587–1633), poet and miscellaneous writer, 12

Frederick of Jennen, 1180

Freeman, Thomas (*fl.* 1614), epigrammatist, author *Run, and a Great Cast*, 1149

French, *see* France

Friar Francis (*Much Ado*), 532, 834

Friar Laurence, Franciscan (*R. and J.*), 405 n., 532, 834

Friendship, *see* Love *and* Ethics

Froissart, Jean (1333?–1400?), chronicler, 650 n., 654 n., 673 n.

Frysar, Ingram (*fl.* 1593), slayer of Christopher Marlowe, 604 n.

Fuller, H. De W., 368 and n., 394 n.

Fuller, Thomas (1608–1661), historian and divine, *The Worthies of England*, 70

Fulman, William (1632–1688), antiquary and divine, 70, 75

Fulvia, wife of Antony (*Ant. and Cleo.*), 1074 n., 1075 n.

Furness, H. H. (1833–1912), editor of Shakespeare, 55

Furness, H. H., Jr. (1865–1930), editor of Shakespeare, 55

Furnivall, F. J. (1825–1910), scholar, 39, 41, 54–55, 72–73, 1272

G

Gadshill, 678 n.

Gadshill (*1 Hen. IV*), 682 n., 766 n.

Galen (130?–201), Greek physician, 570 n., 708 n., 814 n., 1121 n.

Galileo (1564–1642), Italian philosopher and scientist, 1

Gambling, *see* Games

Gamelyn, The Coke's Tale of, 587

Games, 75, 94 n., 189 n., 204 n., 318 n., 400 n., 407 n., 419 n., 430 n., 510 n., 512 n., 533 n., 554 n., 564 n., 592 n., 609 n., 614 n., 634 n., 696 n., 720 n., 743 n., 747 n., 814 n., 816 n., 825 n., 912 n., 927 n., 937 n., 940 n., 988 n., 1096 n., 1185 n., 1189 n., 1208 n., 1264 n., 1298 n.

Gardener, William (*fl.* 1596), justice of the peace, 500

Gardiner, Bishop of Winchester (*Hen. VIII*), 1284 n., 1296 n., 1299 n.

Gardiner, S. R. (1829–1902), historian, 650 n.

Garnet, Henry (1555–1606), Jesuit martyr, 1043, 1054 n.

Index

Humors, 12, 84 n., 87 n., 405 n., 500, 507 n., 539 n., 540 n., 544 n., 588, 617, 628 n., 648 n., 691 n., 716 n., 737, 744 n., 749 n., 750 n., 778 n., 909 n., 1205 n., 1220 n., 1250 n.; *see also* Psychology, Elizabethan

Hunsdon's Servants, Lord, 394

Hunter, Mark, 616

Hunting and falconry, 93 n., 200 n., 375 n., 404 n., 411 n., 533 n., 609 n., 629 n., 658 n., 754 n., 881 n., 934 n., 963 n., 1036 n., 1055 n.

Huntington Library, Henry E., 55

Hybla, a mountain in Sicily, 678 n., 793 n.

Hydra, 703 n., 725 n., 740 n., 959 n., 1128 n.

Hymen, 614 n., 923 n., 1264 n.

Hyperion, 390 n., 758 n., 878 n., 907 n., 927 n.

Hyrcania, 275 n., 1059 n.

Hystorie of Hamblet, The, 901

I

Iachimo, friend to Philario (*Cymb.*), 1181, 1189 n., 1190 n.

Iago, Othello's ancient (*Oth.*), 24, 45, 56, 381 n., 944–946, 947 n., 952 n., 953 n., 954 n., 960 n., 961 n., 968 n., 969 n., 974 n., 978 n.

Ibsen, Henrik (1828–1906), Norwegian dramatist, 58

Iden, Alexander (*2 Hen. VI*), 209

Imogen, daughter to Cymbeline (*Cymb.*), 132, 1180, 1183 n., 1184 n., 1189 n., 1190 n., 1191 n., 1197 n., 1198 n.

Industry, *see* Politics, economics, and industry

Inns of Court: Gray's Inn, 80; Temple, 18, 220 n.; Clement's Inn, 720 n.

Iras, attendant on Cleopatra (*Ant. and Cleo.*), 1106 n.

Ireland, 2, 55, 209, 602 n., 612 n., 652 n., 654 n., 721, 737, 750 n., 765 n., 1043 n., 1069 n.

Irving, Sir Henry (1838–1905), actor, 57, 341, 505, 532, 617–618, 903, 911 n., 946, 982, 1046, 1111, 1181

Isabella, sister to Claudio (*Meas. Meas.*), 833–834, 852 n., 856 n., 857 n., 858 n.

Isis, 1075 n.

Italy, 5–6, 12, 18, 21, 29, 45, 56, 58, 63, 155, 394, 502–503, 522 n., 523 n., 558, 615–617, 653 n., 771, 800, 804, 863, 900, 944, 1046, 1180, 1185 n., 1245 n., 1247, 1251 n.

J

Jackson, Sir Barry, actor and producer, 58

Jack Straw, The Life and Death of, 644

Jacob, Edward (*fl.* 1770), printer, 66

Jacob and Esau, interlude, 18

Jaggard, William (*fl.* 1599–1623), publisher, 52–53, 458, 468, 500, 503, 736, 980

James I, king of Great Britain and Ireland, 7, 10–11, 13, 48, 82, 102, 508 n., 798, 813 n., 833, 836 n., 909 n., 966 n., 979, 981, 989 n., 993 n., 1043–1045, 1062 n., 1065 n., 1108–1109, 1153, 1209 n.; *Demonologie,* 1045

Jameson, Anna (1794–1860), writer on Shakespeare's women, 589

Jamy (*Hen. V*), 737, 750 n.

Janus, 506 n.

Japan, 56

Jaques, lord attending on banished Duke (*A.Y.L.*), 102, 501, 586, 588–589, 611 n.

Jaques de Boys, son of Sir Rowland de Boys (*A.Y.L.*), 614 n.

Jason and Medea, story of, 268 n., 507 n., 527 n.

Jerusalem (Chamber), 730 n.; (Siege of), 348 n.

Jessica, daughter to Shylock (*Mer. Ven.*), 502, 505, 514 n., 526 n.

Joan of Arc, La Pucelle (*1 Hen. VI*), 207–208, 214 n., 219 n., 234 n.

Jodelle, Étienne (1532–1573), French dramatist, author *Cléopâtre captive,* 1071

John, King of England (*K. John*), 18, 339–341, 345 n., 346 n., 361 n.

John of Gaunt, Duke of Lancaster, uncle to Richard II (*Rich. II*), 271 n.

Johnson, Arthur (*fl.* 1600), publisher, 50, 53, 66

Johnson, Charles (1679–1748), dramatist, author *Love in a Forest,* 589

Johnson, Dr. Samuel (1709–1784), editor of Shakespeare, 40, 54, 70, 1273

Jones, Inigo (1573?–1652?), 8

Jones, William (*fl.* 1602), publisher, 65

Jonson, Ben (1573–1637), dramatist and poet, 5, 8, 31, 47–48, 70, 73–74, 206, 425, 477 n., 799–800, 862, 900, 981, 1148, 1150, 1152; *The Alchemist,* 800, 1152; *Bartholomew Fair,* 369, 801, 1149, 1152; *The Case is Altered,* 500; *Catiline,* 1152; *Conversations with Drummond,* 797; *Discoveries,* 783 n.; *Every Man in his Humour,* 500, 586, 588, 770, 801; *Every Man out of his Humour,* 500, 736 n., 797; *Masque of Blackness,* 845 n.; *Masque of Oberon,* 1216, 1237 n.; *Poetaster,* 862; *Sejanus,* 801; *Volpone,* 800

Jordan, Dorothea (1762–1816), actress, 532, 589, 618

Jourdan, Silvester (d. 1650), voyager, author *A Discovery of the Barmudas,* 1247, 1253 n.

Julia, beloved of Proteus (*Two Gent.*), 131–132, 152 n.

Juliet, beloved of Claudio (*Meas. Meas.*), 833–834

Juliet, daughter to Capulet (*R. and J.*), 34, 56, 400 n., 416 n., 532, 1216

Julio und Hypolita, 55

Julius Cæsar, 9, 24–25, 35, 44, 53, 62, 67, 211 n., 269 n., 352 n., 356 n., 440 n., 507 n., 738, 769–772, **772–796,** 944, 1017, 1042 n., 1069 n.; date and publication, 769–770; interpretation, 771–772; sources, 770–771; stage history, 772

Jupiter (Jove), 161 n., 386 n., 537 n., 557 n., 583 n., 714 n., 874 n., 892 n., 997 n., 1121 n., 1130 n., 1205 n.

Juvenal (60?–140), Roman satirist, 105 n., 915 n.

K

Kalender of Shepherdes, 1028 n.

Kant, Immanuel (1724–1804), German metaphysician and philosopher, 41

Katharina, daughter to Baptista (*Tam. Shrew*), 155–156, 173 n., 178 n., 532

Katharine, daughter to Charles VI of France (*Hen. V*), 737, 750 n. ff., 767 n., 768 n.

Katharine, Queen, wife to King Henry (*Hen. VIII*), 1152, 1271–1273, 1282 n., 1286 n., 1287 n., 1288 n.

Kean, Charles (1811?–1868), actor, 341, 560, 646, 738, 772, 946, 1217, 1249, 1273

Kean, Edmund (1787–1833), tragic actor, 57, 210, 301, 341, 505, 646, 738, 903, 946, 982, 1046, 1111, 1181, 1273

Kean, Ellen Tree (1805–1880), actress, wife of Charles Kean, 738

Leontes, King of Sicilia (*W.T.*), 1155, 1216–1217, 1218 n., 1219 n., 1220 n., 1229 n.

Lepidus, triumvir (*J.C.* and *Ant. and Cleo.*), 1072, 1074 n., 1078 n., 1086 n., 1088 n.

Lessing, Gotthold Ephraim (1729–1781), German critic and dramatist, author *Hamburgische Dramaturgie*, 56

Lethe, 331 n., 637 n., 913 n.

Lewis, Dauphin of France (*K. John*), 340, 362 n.

Lewis XI, King of France (*3 Hen. VI*), 270

Lewis, C. M. (1899–1923), educator and critic, 41 n.

Ligarius, conspirator against Caesar (*J.C.*), 771

Lillo, George (1693–1739), dramatist, 1153

Lilly, William (1468?–1522), author *Latin Grammar*, 73, 624 n.

Lincoln, Abraham (1809–1865), sixteenth president of U.S., 73

Lincoln's Inn Fields, theater, 903, 1045

Ling, Nicholas (*fl.* 1596–1602), publisher, 898–899

Lion (*Mids. Dr.*), 184

Lionel, duke of Clarence, progenitor of the Yorkist Kings, 220 n.

Little Snow White, fairy tale, 1180

Livia, wife of Octavius Caesar, 1106 n.

Livy (59 B.C.–17 A.D.), *Roman History*, 439

Locke, John (1632–1704), philosopher, 41

Locke, Matthew (1630?–1677), musical composer, 1045

Locrine, anonymous tragedy, 53, 65–66, 369

Lodge, Thomas (1558?–1625), poet and dramatist, 21, 45, 586, 588; *Glaucus and Scilla*, 425; *A Looking Glass for London*, 77; *Rosalynde*, 586, 594 n.; *Wits Miserie*, 902.

London, 1–3, 6, 28–30, 70, 73, 116 n., 262 n., 306 n., 647 n., 695 n., 712 n., 722 n., 735 n., 736 n., 747 n., 826 n., 1150, 1247, 1279 n., 1302 n., 1303 n.

London Bridge, 223 n., 319 n., 1145 n.

London Prodigal, The, anonymous play, 53, 65

Longaville, lord attending on the King (*L.L.L.*), 101–102

Lopez, Roderigo (d. 1594), Portuguese Jewish physician, 502

Lorenzo, in love with Jessica (*Mer. Ven.*), 505, 526 n.

Love, 101–102, 142 n., 402 n., 426, 504–505, 519 n., 520 n., 604 n., 607 n., 608 n., 617, 619 n., 624 n., 627 n., 628 n., 774 n., 809 n., 1183 n., 1218 n.; *see also* Courtship and marriage

Lover's Complaint, A, 458, **464–467**

Love's Labour's Lost, 8, 22–23, 33–34, 39, 49, 60, 63, 73–74, 77–78, 101–102, **102–129**, 281 n., 299, 343 n., 352 n., 382 n., 393, 458, 459 n., 461 n., 475 n., 492 n., 493 n., 500, 532, 567 n., 572 n., 671 n., 828 n., 867 n., 884 n., 923 n; date and publication, 101; interpretation, 101–102; stage history, 102

Love's Labour's Won, 34, 77, 154, 497, 802–803

Low Countries, 3, 6, 63, 310 n.

Lowin, John (*fl.* 1603–1669?), actor, 560, 1272

Lucas, F. L., 300 n.

Luce, servant to Adriana (*Com. Er.*), 81–82, 88 n., 89 n.

Lucentio, son to Vincentio (*Tam. Shrew*), 155–156

Lucetta, waiting-woman to Julia (*Two Gent.*) 133

Lucian (120?–190?), Greek satirist, author *Dialogues*, 22, 1017

Luciana, sister to Adriana (*Com. Er.*), 81–82

Lucina, *see* Diana

Lucio, a fantastic (*Meas. Meas.*), 836 n., 838 n., 852 n., 858 n.

Lucius, son to Titus Andronicus (*Tit. And.*), 368, 391 n.

Lucius, Young, a boy, son to Lucius (*Tit. And.*), 368

Lucius Pella, Roman praetor in Sardis, 790 n.

Lucretia (*Lucrece*), 167 n., 382 n., 439 n., 440, 451 n., 497, 602 n., 629 n.

Lucy, Lady Elizabeth, betrothed to Edward IV, 322 n., 324 n.

Lucy, Sir Thomas (1532–1600), owner of Charlecote Hall, 75, 561 n., 723 n.

Ludlow, 315 n., 319 n.

Ludus Coventriae or *Hegge Plays*, 16

Luna, *see* Diana

Lunacy, 95 n., 99 n., 604 n., 633 n., 747 n., 910 n., 913 n., 917 n., 921 n., 927 n., 928 n., 931 n., 935 n., 992 n., 999 n., 1000 n., 1001 n., 1003 n., 1012 n., 1040 n., 1053 n., 1063 n., 1099 n.; *see also* Humors, Medicine, *and* Psychology, Elizabethan

Lunt, Alfred, actor, 156

Lupercal, feast of, 773 n.

Lupton, J. H. (1836–1905), scholar, 72–73

Lyceum Theatre, 532, 946, 1273

Lycurgus (9th C. B.C.), Spartan lawgiver, 1120 n.

Lydgate, John (1370?–1451?), poet, author *Troy Book*, 863

Lyly, John (1554?–1606), dramatist and author, 18, 21–22, 25, 30, 35, 45, 48, 78, 102, 586, 653 n., 1216; *Cupid and my Campaspe Played*, 494 n.; *Endymion*, 22, 183; *Euphues*, 18, 21–22, 25, 30, 35, 45, 48, 102, 586, 671 n., 689 n.; *Euphues and his England*, 463 n.; *Gallathea*, 22; *Love's Metamorphosis*, 22; *Midas*, 22; *Mother Bombie*, 22; *Sapho and Phao*, 22; *The Woman in the Moon*, 22

Lymoges, Duke of Austria (*K. John*), 344 n., 345 n., 351 n.

Lysander, matched with Hermia (*Mids. Dr.*), 183–184

Lysimachus, governor of Mytilene (*Per.*) 1154, 1174 n.

Lytton, Edward G. E. Bulwer-Lytton, first baron (1803–1873), author *The Last of the Barons*, 209

M

Mabbe, James (1572–1642?), poet, 47

Macbeth, 34, 43, 53, 61–63, 210, 229 n., 298 n., 301, 327 n., 487 n., 800, 802, 887 n., 930 n., 1017, 1036 n., 1043–1046, **1046-1070,** 1048 n., 1058 n., 1071, 1083 n., 1179; authorship and date, 1042–1044, 1048 n., 1054 n., 1060 n., 1061 n., 1290 n.; interpretation, 1045, 1216; sources, 1044–1045; stage history, 1045–1046

Macbeth, general of Duncan's army, later king (*Macb.*), 43, 56, 210, 1044–1046, 1047 n., 1049 n., 1050 n., 1051 n., 1055 n., 1056 n., 1058 n., 1060 n., 1062 n., 1063 n., 1068 n., 1069 n., 1070 n., 1083 n.

McCullough, John Edward (1837–1885), actor, 57, 982

Macduff, nobleman of Scotland (*Macb.*), 298 n., 1044, 1060 n., 1062 n., 1064 n.

Machiavelli, Nicolò (1469–1527), Italian statesman and historian, author *The Prince*, 9, 210, 236 n., 276 n., 284 n., 286 n., 301 and n., 303 n., 380 n., 572 n., 738, 946 and n.

McKeithan, D. M., 981 n.

McKerrow, R. B. (1872–1940), scholar, 52 n., 902 n.

Macklin, Charles (1697?–1797), actor, 57, 341, 505, 618, 1046

Macmorris (*Hen. V*), 737, 750 n.

Peele, George (1558?–1597), dramatist and poet, 18, 22, 25, 76, 78, 206, 208, 367 n.; *The Arraignment of Paris*, 22, 30; *Battle of Alcazar*, 77, 716 n.; *Edward I*, 77; *Turkish Mahomet and the Fair Greek*, 716 n.

Pegasus, 176 n., 870 n.

Pelion, 938 n.

Pembroke, Lady Mary Sidney, countess of (1561–1621), author *Antonius*, 1071

Pembroke, Jasper Tudor, Earl of (*3 Hen. VI*), 334 n.

Pembroke, William Herbert, third earl of (1580–1630), 470

Pembroke's Servants, The Earl of, 32, 101, 155 n., 206, 208

Pendragon, Uther, 225 n.

Penker, Friar, Richard III's henchman, 322 n.

Penthesilea, queen of the Amazons, 627 n.

Pepin, French king of ninth century, 113 n., 1278 n.

Pepys, Samuel (1633–1703), diarist, 946, 1045, 1249, 1273

Percy, Henry, surnamed Hotspur, son to Earl of Northumberland (*Rich. II* and *1 Hen. IV*), 222 n., 643, 658 n., 668 n., 670 n., 674–675, 680 n., 681 n., 682 n., 685 n., 691 n., 701 n.

Percy, Lady, wife to Hotspur (*1* and *2 Hen. IV*), 685 n.

Percy, Sir Charles (d. 1628), son of 8th earl of Northumberland, 799

Perdita, daughter to Leontes and Hermione (*W.T.*), 1152, 1155, 1216–1217, 1230 n., 1234 n., 1238 n.

Pericles, 34, 47, 49–50, 52, 54–55, 64–65, 801, 1071, 1148, 1152–1155, **1155–1179**, 1158 n., 1179; authorship and source, 1153–1155; date and publication, 1153; interpretation, 1155; stage history, 1155

Pericles, Prince of Tyre (*Per.*), 1155, 1157 n., 1158 n., 1161 n., 1176 n.

Perigenia (Perigouna), 189 n.

Perrett, Wilfred (b. 1873), author *The Story of King Lear*, 980 and n.

Peter, Horner's man (*2 Hen. VI*), 244 n.

Peto (*1 Hen. IV*), 679 n., 766 n.

Petrarch (1304–1374), Italian humanist and poet, 131–132, 167 n., 406 n.

Petruchio, suitor to Katharina (*Tam. Shrew*), 155–156, 162 n., 163 n., 171 n., 532

Phaethon, 144 n., 274 n., 282 n., 411 n., 663 n.

Pharaoh, 546 n.

Pharsalia, Battle of, 773 n., 794 n.

Phebe, a shepherdess (*A.Y.L.*), 36, 586, 588, 607 n., 609 n., 614 n.

Phelps, Samuel (1804–1878), actor, 57, 82, 102, 132, 156, 184, 560, 738, 772, 903, 982, 1018, 1046, 1073, 1155, 1217, 1249

Philip, King of France (*K. John*), 344 n.

Philip II, king of Spain (reigned 1556–1598), 3, 502

Philippi, 1075 n., 1083 n., 1093 n.

Philips, Ambrose (1676–1709), poet, author *Humphrey Duke of Gloucester*, 210

Phillips, Augustine (d. 1605), actor, 31, 797–798

Philomela, story of, 191 n., 376 n., 379 n., 390 n., 463 n., 488 n., 1190 n.

Philosophy, *see* Learning of the Renaissance *and* Cosmology

Philostrate, master of revels to Theseus (*Mids. Dr.*), 202 n.

Phoebe, *see* Diana

Phoebus, *see* Apollo

Phœnix and the Turtle, The, 458, **463–464**

Physiology, *see* Psychology, Elizabethan

Pierce of Exton, Sir (*Rich. II*), 643–644, 673 n., 674 n.

Pimlyco, anonymous poem (1609), 1148

Pinch, a schoolmaster (*Com. Er.*), 81–82, 95 n., 99 n.

Pindarus, servant to Cassius (*J.C.*), 795 n.

Pistol (*2 Hen. IV, Mer. Wives*, and *Hen. V*), 562 n., 674, 716 n., 734 n., 737, 744 n., 745 n., 753 n., 760 n., 761 n., 765 n., 766 n.

Plantagenet, 220 n., 328 n.

Plantagenet, Margaret, young daughter of Clarence (*Rich. III*), 328 n.

Plato (427–347 B.C.), Greek philosopher, 103 n., 302 n., 480 n., 617, 883 n.; *Dialogues*, 883 n.; *Republic*, 738

Platter, Thomas (*fl.* 1599), German traveler, 770 and n.

Plautus (254?–184 B.C.), Latin comedy writer, 17, 19, 22, 34, 73, 78, 80, 82, 84 n., 497, 917 n.; *Amphitruo*, 44, 80; *Menaechmi*, 44, 80–81, 84 n., 615

Player, A (*Ham.*), 899, 921 n.

Pleiades, group of French poets headed by Ronsard, 22, 428 n.

Pliny (23–79), the Elder, author *Historia Naturalis*, 21, 277 n., 463 n., 595 n., 951 n., 965 n., 976 n.

Plume, Thomas (*fl.* 1660), divine, 72

Plutarch (46?–120?), Greek biographer and moralist, *Lives of the noble Grecians and Romans*, 127 n., 183, 189 n., 202 n., 214 n., 369 (*Life of Scipio Africanus*), 770–771, 779 n., 780 n., 781 n., 785 n., 786 n., 790 n., 791 n., 793 n., 794 n., 795 n., 796 n., 1017, 1023 n., 1069 n., 1071–1073, 1075 n., 1078 n., 1083 n., 1084 n., 1089 n., 1090 n., 1091 n., 1092 n., 1093 n., 1095 n., 1096 n., 1098 n., 1100 n., 1102 n., 1108–1110, 1112 n., 1116 n., 1121 n., 1126 n., 1127 n., 1140 n., 1143 n., 1180

Pluto, 386 n., 1234 n., 1265 n.

Plutus, god of riches, 830 n.

Poe, Edgar Allan (1809–1849), poet, critic, and story-writer, 981

Poel, William (1852–1934), actor and critic, 505

Poet (*Timon*), 1017–1018, 1039 n.

Poetry and poetics, 1, 20, 24–25, 35–39, 80, 134 n., 184, 186 n., 187 n., 394, 402 n., 422 n., 428 n., 439, 468, 476 n., 479 n., 483 n., 487 n., 494 n., 643, 737–738, 836 n., 1019 n.

Poins (*1* and *2 Hen. IV*), 559, 572 n., 713 n., 714 n., 717 n., 766 n.

Politics, economics, and industry, 2–9, 41, 202 n., 308 n., 322 n., 324 n., 328 n., 501–502, 514 n., 632 n., 644–645, 647 n., 649 n., 652 n., 654 n., 655 n., 658 n., 659 n., 660 n., 662 n., 672 n., 693 n., 723 n., 725 n., 730 n., 737–738, 740 n., 741 n., 742 n., 748 n., 757 n., 769–770, 784 n., 785 n., 790 n., 930 n., 981–982, 989 n., 1009 n., 1010 n., 1017, 1044, 1054 n., 1071–1072, 1108–1110, 1112 n., 1122 n., 1123 n., 1125 n., 1129 n., 1133 n., 1195 n.

Polixenes, King of Bohemia (*W. T.*), 1218 n., 1229 n.

Pollard, A. W. (1859–1944), bibliographer, 49 and n., 50–52 and n., 67 n., 129 n., 182 and n., 208 n., 559 n., 643 n., 737 n., 901 n., 979 and n.

Polonius, lord chamberlain (*Ham.*), 30, 56, 900–901, 905 n., 912 n., 913 n., 917 n., 921 n.

Polyxena, daughter of Priam, 884 n.

Pomfret, 669 n., 674 n., 707 n.

Pompeius, Cneius (106–48 B.C.), Roman consul, 260 n., 771–772, 773 n., 787 n., 841 n., 1076 n., 1085 n., 1087 n.

revisions, 35, 531, 539 n., 552 n., 559, 598 n., 856 n., 858 n., 899, 1248; rhyme, use of, 36; sources and plots, 18, 20, 43–45, 394, 531–532, 558–559, 616–617, 1071–1072, 1100 n., 1185 n., 1179; stage history, 56–58 (*see also* introductions to all plays); style, 36, 101–102, 531, 614 n., 623 n., 682 n., 786 n., 787 n., 865 n., 866 n., 952 n., 994 n., 1003 n., 1009 n., 1010 n., 1108 n., 1156 n., 1198 n., 1208 n., 1272

Shakespeareana, collections of, 55

Shakespeare Association (London), 55

Shakespeare family, 72

Shakespeare Festival (1890), 132

Shakespeare-Jahrbuch, 56

Shakespeare Memorial Theatre at Stratford, 102, 132, 210, 341, 560, 834, 864, 982, 1046, 1155, 1181, 1273

Shakespeare's England, 211 n., 213 n., 262 n., 568 n., 813 n., 854 n., 1039 n.

Shakespeare's Life and Work: Early Period, 69–70; Period of the Comedies, 497–501; Period of the Tragedies, 797–802; Period of the Romances, 1148–1152

Shakespeare Society, 55

Shallow, country justice (*2 Hen. IV* and *Mer. Wives*), 16, 75, 500, 558–559, 675, 719 n., 722 n., 734 n., 799

Shapiro, I. A., 28

Shaw, Dr. (*Rich. III*), 322 n.

Shaw, G. B. (1856–1950), dramatist and critic, 41 n.

Shearmen and Taylors Pageant, 15

Sheffield, John (1648–1721), first duke of Buckingham and Normandy, author *Julius Caesar* and *Marcus Brutus*, 772

Sheridan, Richard Brinsley (1751–1816), dramatist, 82

Shore, Jane (1445?–1527), mistress of Edward IV, 303 n., 318 n.

Shrewd and Curst Wife lapped in Morelles Skin, A Merry Geste of a, 154

Shrewsbury, Battle of, 674, 705

Shrove-tide, day before Ash Wednesday, 733 n.

Shylock, a rich Jew (*Mer. Ven.*), 6, 45, 57, 501, 503–505, 509 n., 514 n., 517 n., 518 n., 523 n., 524 n., 525 n., 526 n.

Sibyls, 163 n., 213 n., 384 n., 508 n.

Sicily, 1216, 1230 n.

Sicinius Velutus, tribune of people (*Cor.*), 1110, 1114 n., 1122 n., 1130 n.

Siddons, Sarah (1755–1831), tragic actress, 57, 341, 532, 589, 834, 946, 1046, 1111, 1181, 1217, 1273

Sidney, Algernon (1622–1683), republican leader, 41

Sidney, Sir Philip (1554–1586), poet, 1, 12, 20, 34, 45, 497, 799, 1216; *Arcadia*, 45, 132, 458, 587, 854 n., 980–981; *Astrophel and Stella*, 471; *Defence of Poesie*, 20

Sigismund, emperor of Germany, 765 n.

Silence, country justice (*2 Hen. IV*), 675, 799

Silvia, beloved of Valentine (*Two Gent.*), 131–132, 152 n.

Silvius, a shepherd (*A.Y.L.*), 588

Simcox, an impostor (*2 Hen. VI*), 247 n.

Simonides, king of Pentapolis (*Per.*), 1165 n.

Simpson, Richard (1820–1876), Shakespeare scholar, 67

Sims, Valentine (*fl.* 1599–1605), printer, 530, 643, 674

Sir John Oldcastle, The History of the Life of, play by Drayton and others, 52–53, 65, 674, 799

Sir Thomas More, play by Anthony Munday with possible additions by Shakespeare, 64, 67

Siward, Earl of Northumberland, general of the English forces (*Macb.*), 1044

Sixtus V (1521–1590), pope, 471, 491 n.

Skelton, John (1460?–1529), poet, author *Magnificence*, 18; *Phylip Sparrow*, 344 n.

Skogan, John (*fl.* 1480), jester, 720 n.

Slender, cousin to Shallow (*Mer. Wives*), 500, 558–560, 561 n.

Sly, Christopher, tinker (*Tam. Shrew*), 155, 159 n.

Sly, John (*fl.* 1600), actor, 798

Smethwick, John (*fl.* 1607–1623), publisher, 53, 899

Solinus, Duke of Ephesus (*Com. Er.*), 81–82, 97 n.

Solon (638?–559? B.C.), Athenian lawgiver, 371 n.

Solyman, Turkish sultan, 510 n.

Somers, Sir George (1554–1610), colonizer, 1247

Somerset, John Beaufort, Duke of (*1, 2,* and *3 Hen. VI*), 207–208, 251 n., 271 n., 295 n.

Son of Clarence, a young (*Rich. III*), 328 n., 329 n.

Songs and ballads, 19, 45, 106 n., 112 n., 113 n., 130 and n., 135 n., 154, 403 n., 407 n., 414 n., 420 n., 502, 547 n., 556 n., 562 n., 566 n., 571 n., 574 n., 586–587, 605 n., 624 n., 625 n., 626 n., 627 n., 633 n., 638 n., 671 n., 726 n., 734 n., 917 n., 923 n., 924 n., 933 n., 957 n., 973 n., 989 n., 1002 n., 1028 n., 1233 n., 1235 n., 1236 n., 1244 n., 1266 n.; *see also* Poetry

Sonnets, 33–34, 67, 393, 425, 429 n., 439, 458, 460 n., 468–471, **472–496,** 477 n., 478 n., 479 n., 483 n., 485 n., 494 n., 496 n., 497, 500, 1019 n.; Hotson's theory of the dating, 470–471; person addressed, 469–470; problems, 468; publication, 468; the "Rival Poet," 101 n., 470; story, 468–469

Soothsayer, A (*Ant. and Cleo.*), 1074 n., 1075 n.

Sophocles (496?–405 B.C.), Greek tragic poet, 30, 48

Sothern, E. H. (1859–1933), actor, 57, 156, 903, 1046, 1073

Southampton, Henry Wriothesley, third earl of (1573–1624), 8, 71, 101, 425, 427 and n., 439–440, 469–470, 477 n., 485 n., 488 n., 489 n., 799, 802

Spain, 2, 18, 63, 80, 616, 798

Spedding, James (1808–1881), editor of Bacon, 67, 1272 and n.

Speed, clownish servant to Valentine (*Two Gent.*), 132

Speght, Thomas (*fl.* 1598), editor of Chaucer, 439

Spencer, Hazelton (1893–1944), American scholar, 40 n., 772 n.

Spenser, Edmund (1552?–1599), poet, 1, 10, 34, 45, 47, 202 n., 217 n., 257 n., 439, 483 n., 497–498, 799; *Colin Clout's Come Home Again*, 497; *Faerie Queene*, 45, 217 n., 257 n., 448 n., 980; *Mother Hubbard's Tale*, 278 n.; *Shepheardes Calender*, 22, 44, 296 n., 541 n., 587; *Tears of the Muses*, 202 n.

Spiker, Sina K., 1153 n.

Stafford, Lord (*3 Hen. VI*), 270 n.

Staging, 20, 28–29, 41–42, 57–58, 83 n., 86 n., 88 n., 92 n., 524 n., 609 n., 704 n., 705 n., 736 n., 756 n., 810 n., 811 n., 820 n., 858 n., 871 n., 942 n., 949 n., 976 n., 1008 n., 1026 n., 1070 n., 1072, 1092 n.

Staines, town on the road from London to Southampton, 746

Stanley, Sir John (*2 Hen. VI*), 248 n.

Stanley, Sir William (*3 Hen. VI* and *Rich. III*), 334 n.

Staunton, Howard (1810–1874), editor of Shakespeare, 54

Steevens, George (1736–1800), editor of Shakespeare, 54

Stephano, a drunken butler (*Temp.*), 1266 n.

Stevenson, William (*fl.* 1553–1560), author *Gammer Gurton's Needle*, 18–19

Stoicism, 103 n., 771, 790 n.

Stoll, E. E., 41 n., 676 n., 899 and n., 944 and n.

Stow, John (1525?–1605), chronicler, author *Annals*, 44, 608 n., 666 n.

Strachey, William (*fl.* 1609–1618), colonist, author *A True Reportory of the Wracke and Redemption of Sir Thomas Gates, Knight*, 1247, 1254 n., 1261 n.

Strange's Servants, Lord, 31–33, 66, 77, 367, 499, 558

Stubbes, Philip (*fl.* 1581–1593), pamphleteer, author *The Anatomie of Abuses*, 27, 1023 n.

Stunz, A. N., 1044 n.

Suckling, Sir John (1609–1642), poet, 928 n.

Suffolk, Duke of (*Hen. viii*), 1276 n., 1283 n.

Suffolk, Earl of (*1 and 2 Hen. vi*), 78, 207–208, 211, 220 n., 239, 251 n., 258 n., 259 n., 261 n.

Sulla (138–78 B.C.), Roman dictator, 259 n., 771–772

Summers, Montague, 40 n.

Surrey, Earl of (*Hen. viii*), 63, 1281 n., 1292 n.

Surrey, Earl of, son to Norfolk (*Rich. iii*), 665 n.

Sussex's Servants, Earl of, 31, 33, 368

Sutton Co'fil' (Coldfield), Warwickshire town, 697 n.

Swan, The, playhouse, 27–28

Swinburne, A. C. (1837–1909), poet and critic, 41

Swinstead, abbey where King John died, 340

Sykes, H. Dugdale (1874?–1932), 155 n., 367 n., 1153 n.

Sylvain, Alexander van den Busche (1535?–1585?), epigrammatist, author *The Orator*, 502–503

T

Tailor (*Tam. Shrew*), 156

Talbot, Lord (*1 Hen. vi*), 206–208, 218 n., 219 n., 232 n.

Talbot, Sir Gilbert, rebel against Richard iii, 334 n.

Taming of a Shrew, The, 18, 32–33, 44, 50, 77, 154

Taming of the Shrew, The, 18, 44, 50, 61, 77, 154–156, **156-181,** 348 n., 459 n., 803, 849 n.; authorship, 155 and n.; date, 154–155; interpretation, 155–156, 157 n.; sources, 154–155, 179 n.; stage history, 156

Tamora, queen of the Goths (*Tit. And.*), 368

Tannenbaum, S. A. (1874–1948), physician and bibliographer, 67 n., 882 n., 943 n., 1043 n.

Tantalus, story of, 432 n.

Tarleton, Richard (d. 1588), comedian, 937 n.

Tarquinius Sextus (*Lucrece*), 439, 497, 1190 n.

Tarquinius Superbus, 1115 n., 1121 n.

Tartarus, 93 n., 195 n., 375 n., 378 n., 630 n., 746 n.

Tate, Nahum (1652–1715), poet and dramatist, *The Ingratitude of a Commonwealth*, 1111; *King Lear*, 40, 982, 1016 n.; *The Sicilian Usurper*, 646

Tatlock, J. S. P. (1876–1948), American scholar, 863 n.

Taurus, 195 n., 621 n.

Taylor, G. C., 802 n.

Taylor, Joseph (1586?–1652), actor, 56, 903, 946

Taylor, Rupert, 101 n.

Tearle, Godfrey, actor, 1046, 1073

Tellus, earth-goddess, 1169 n.

Tempest, The, 33, 36–37, 39, 53, 55, 61, 65, 134 n., 463 n., 884 n., 1148–1149, 1152, 1155, 1166 n., 1179, 1181, 1209 n., 1247–1249, **1249-1270,** 1267 n., 1302 n.; date, 1247; history of the play, 1249; interpretation, 1248–1249; sources, 1247–1248

Tenantius, king of ancient Britain, 1182 n.

ten Brink, Bernard (1841–1892), philologist and literary historian, 56, 154

Tennyson, Alfred, first baron (1809–1892), poet, 1272

Terence (190?–159 B.C.), Latin comedy writer, 17, 19, 22, 45, 73; *Eunuchus*, 611 n.

Termagant, pagan god, 16, 921 n.

Terry, Dame Ellen (1848–1928), actress, 57, 341, 532, 560, 618, 903, 946, 1046, 1181, 1217, 1273

Tewkesbury, Battle of, 209, 269, 328 n.

Thaisa, daughter to Simonides (*Per.*), 1155

Thaler, Alwin, 617 n., 1043 n.

Thasos, island off the coast of Thrace, 795 n.

Theaters and theatrical practices, 26–33, 50–51, 56, 74–78, 184, 188 n., 205 n., 403 n., 499, 563 n., 612 n., 617 n., 739 n., 797–798, 821 n., 833, 899–900, 916 n., 917 n., 918 n., 924 n.

Theatre, The, playhouse, 27–28, 499

Theobald, Lewis (1688–1744), editor of Shakespeare, 54, 86 n., 89 n., 90 n., 646; *The Double Falsehood*, 67

Theocritus (b. 300? B.C.), Sicilian pastoral poet, 587–588

Thersites, a deformed and scurrilous Grecian (*T. and C.*), 863, 870 n., 891 n., 892 n., 894 n., 1204 n.

Theseus, Duke of Athens (*Mids. Dr.*), 42, 78, 150 n., 183–184, 189 n., 202 n., 770

Thomas, D. L. (*fl.* 1900–1920), American scholar, 1154 n.

Thomas, William (d. 1554), author *Historie of Italy*, 1247

Thomas Lord Cromwell, history play of unknown authorship, 65

Thompson, Sir E. Maunde (1840–1929), paleographer, 67 and n., 837 n.

Thomson, James (1700–1748), poet, author *Coriolanus*, 1111

Thoreau, Henry David (1817–1862), naturalist and philosopher, 71

Thorndike, A. H. (1871–1933), editor of Shakespeare (with W. A. Neilson), 55, 1152 and n., 1179 n., 1216, 1237 n., 1272

Thorndike, Dame Sibyl, actress, 1273

Thorpe, Thomas (*fl.* 1609), publisher, *Sonnets*, 458, 468, 470–471

Thrall, W. F. (1880–1941), American scholar, 1180 and n.

Tieck, Johann Ludwig (1773–1853), German translator of Shakespeare, 56

Tilney, Edmund (d. 1610), Master of the Revels, 8, 67

Timon, of Athens (*Timon*), 117 n., 1017–1018, 1019 n., 1021 n., 1022 n., 1027 n., 1029 n., 1030 n., 1032 n., 1033 n., 1034 n., 1036 n., 1039 n., 1040 n., 1041 n., 1042 n., 1249

Timon of Athens, 53, 117 n., 482 n., 802, 1017–1018, **1019-1043;** authorship, 1017; interpretation, 1017–1018; sources, 1017; stage history, 1018

Titania, queen of the fairies (*Mids. Dr.*), 78, 184

Tito Andronico, 368

Titus Andronicus, 32–33, 39, 44, 49, 55, 74, 77–78, 306 n., 366–369, **369-393,** 430 n., 497, 567 n.; authorship, 366–367; date and text, 367–368, 392 n., 393 n.; interpretation, 368–369; sources, 367–368; stage history, 369

Titus Andronicus, Roman general against the Goths (*Tit. And.*), 368–369, 369 n., 370 n., 380 n., 382 n., 383 n., 386 n., 391 n.

Toby Belch, Sir, uncle to Olivia (*12th Night*), 617, 619 n., 620 n., 622 n., 624 n., 626 n., 629 n., 641 n.

Tofte, Robert (1561?–1620), poet, author *Alba*, 101

Tolman, A. H. (1856–1928), American scholar, 155 n.

Tomyris, Scythian queen, 219 n.

8 9 10 11 12 13 14 15 16 17 18 19 20 21 22 23 24 25   75 74 73 72 71 70 69 68 67 66